Chambers's
Twentieth Century
DICTIONARY

New Mid-century Version

Edited by

WILLIAM GEDDIE, M.A., B.Sc.

W. & R. CHAMBERS LTD.

11 THISTLE STREET, EDINBURGH   6 DEAN STREET, LONDON, W.1

Original edition 1952
(Superseding the former *Twentieth Century Dictionary*,
first published in 1901)
Latest Reprint 1955

Printed in Great Britain
by The Villafield Press, Bishopbriggs, Glasgow
and T. and A. Constable, Ltd., Edinburgh

CONTENTS

iii

PREFACE

THE Twentieth Century and the *Twentieth Century Dictionary* began together, and they ran together through half the century's course. The work of the editor, Mr. Thomas Davidson, was continued by various members of the editorial staff until it was found that ordinary revision no longer sufficed. A dictionary with a bulky supplement is a waste of time and a trier of temper. A thorough overhaul was therefore made. Every word already admitted, every definition and etymology, was subjected to scrutiny. New words and phrases— some never before given in a general dictionary, some not until now appearing in a dictionary at all—were collected from many sources. These were very numerous, owing to developments of science, social changes, new habits of life and recreation, and new habits of language resulting from these—notably furthered by the virtual drying up of the Atlantic as a speech barrier. A very few words have been discarded altogether. These belong chiefly to two classes—ghost words, which come by copying or reading amiss, and dictionary words that somebody with a Greek or Latin Dictionary has concocted but nobody so far as can be discovered has ever used.

As before, the aim has been to include all words in general use in literary and conversational English, and all words used in Shakespeare and the Authorised Version of the Bible, in the poems (and many of those in the prose writings) of Spenser and Milton, and in the novels of Walter Scott. It should be understood that to label a word *Milt.* does not mean that nobody but Milton has used it. This is not a dictionary of Scots, but many words of Burns, Ramsay, Fergusson, Galt, and Barrie will be found in it, with many that are still in familiar colloquial use in Scotland. These are marked *Scot.*, but in most cases they are current on both sides of the Border. Likewise we hope no Canadian will take it as a slight when he finds his words marked *U.S.* Indeed such has been the diffusion that many in Britain may object to such labelling ; but let them take it as historically true. Dialect words that have made good their footing in literature have been included, with such slang words as seem likely to maintain themselves as well as some dead slang that may puzzle readers, say, of Dickens.

The original edition acknowledged special indebtedness to two American Dictionaries, the *Century* and the *Standard*. The revised *Webster* has further strengthened our American side. The *Oxford Dictionary*, which of course must be the foundation of all English

iv

dictionaries, had been used as far as it went, as had Wright's *Dialect Dictionary*. The *Oxford* was completed in 1933, Wright in 1905. Two great Scottish dictionaries now in progress have been much used and would have been more used had their publication kept pace with the work—Sir William Craigie's *Dictionary of the Older Scottish Tongue* and the *Scottish National Dictionary* of Mr. Grant and his successors. For Latin etymologies we have been guided chiefly by Ernout and Meillet's *Dictionnaire étymologique de la langue latine*, for Greek by Boisacq's *Dictionnaire étymologique de la langue grecque* and the new Liddell and Scott. For old French we have Godefroy's *Dictionnaire de l'ancienne langue française*. Some definitions have been adopted or adapted from our own *Technical Dictionary*.

A great part of the construction of this dictionary has been in the hands of Miss A. M. Macdonald. The whole owes much to the vigilance of Mr. J. Liddell Geddie who read a large part of the proofs, and several other members of the staff have made useful contributions. Dr. Angus Macdonald has helped with the etymologies. Finally, scores of users of the dictionary have sent in single words and lists of words. We have not accepted all their suggestions. One was disappointed not to find *myristicivorous*, feeding upon nutmegs, a word to which we grant this place on the doorstep but still deny admission to the dictionary. To these correspondents we owe much, and we tender our thanks, especially to those who first make sure that their words are not already in.

WILLIAM GEDDIE.

NOTE TO THE USER OF THE DICTIONARY

The Arrangement of Words.—Every word is given in its alphabetical order, except in cases where, to save space, derivatives are given under a head-word. The participles and past indicative of uncompounded verbs (and other parts where desirable), and the plural of nouns, are given under the head-word when any doubt is possible. When a derivative stands under a head-word with no meaning given, its meaning can at once be got by combining that of the head-word with that of the suffix. Thus the meanings of *darkness* are obtained by adding the meaning of *-ness* to those of *dark*. Where there has been a shift of meaning or a specialised meaning has developed, derivatives are defined in full.

Key to the Pronunciation.—The pronunciation is given immediately after each head-word by spelling the word anew. Below is a summary of the only points that require comment :—

dh	is used for the initial sound of *then*
zh	is used for the sound of *s* in *pleasure*
gz	is used for the sound of *x* in *example*
hw	is used for the sound of *wh* in *when*
	(some will disagree, but they may interpret it in their own way)
hh	is used for any open guttural (Scots or German) as in *loch*
ngg	is used for the sound of *ng* in *linger*
ngk	is used for the sound of *nk* in *monkey*

The key to the long vowels and diphthongs (appearing at every opening of the dictionary) is :—

fāte, fär, âsk; mē, hər (her); *mīne; mōte; mūte; mōon*

(*â* means that the vowel may be pronounced either long or short)

Nasalised vowels are represented by a following *n^g*, as *ān^g-kōr* (encore). Neutral vowels in unaccented syllables are shown by means of a turned *e* or schwa—

el'ə-mənt, in'fənt, ran'dəm

Where the sound of a letter in a derivative differs from that in the head-word the pronunciation of at least part of the word has been added in parentheses. Sometimes several variations occur under one

vi

head-word : in such cases the position of the stress accent will serve as guide to the particular model among the derivatives to be followed.

Spelling.—Letters in brackets may be inserted or omitted. The suffix *-ise* has been given in that form. There is much to be said for *-ize*, which seems to be gaining ground. It would have taken up too much space to give both (along with *-ization*, *-izer*, etc.). Let it be understood that in all cases choice is free. This of course does not apply to such words as *surprise*, *revise*, where *ise* is not a suffix.

The Meanings.—The meanings have been arranged on two different principles according to convenience or usefulness. Sometimes the current or most important is given first ; sometimes the original or at least an early meaning, with others branching out and diverging from it. In the latter case the reader should be warned not to be turned aside by the label *obs.* (obsolete) preceding the first meaning given : it refers to that meaning, not to the word as a whole.

The Etymology.—The etymology is given in square brackets at the end of each article. The sign — is to be read ' derived from '. Whatever follows after a semicolon is not the source of the word but a word from the same ultimate source. Thus, when a word is traced back to Old English, an Old Norse, say, or a Greek word from the same root may follow, but the Old English word is not in such a case derived from Old Norse or from Greek. Within an article the partial etymologies of derivatives are often inserted in round brackets. Each long vowel in Old English and Old Norse is marked with an acute accent, in Greek and Latin with a macron. Any vowel unmarked is to be taken as short. Because we are using no accents, we have had to give Greek words in uncontracted form. Greek words with a subscript iota are also given at full length, as in inscriptions.

DETAILED CHART OF PRONUNCIATION

Respelling is a rough method of showing pronunciation compared with the use of phonetic symbols, but the following table will be useful for reference in cases of doubt.

Vowels and Diphthongs in Accented Syllables

	SOUND		EXAMPLES	PRONUNCIATION
ā	as in (1)	fate	name, aid, rein	nām, ād, rān
	(2)	bare	tare, wear, hair, heir	tār, wār, hār, ār
ä	,,	far	harm, heart, palm, toilette	härm, härt, päm, twä-let
â	,,	castle (long or short)	ask, bath	âsk, bâth
a	,,	sat	bad, have	bad, hav
ē	,, (1)	me	lean, keel, dene, chief, seize	lēn, kēl, dēn, chēf, sēz
	(2)	fear	gear, sheer, here, bier	gēr, shēr, hēr, bēr
e	,,	pet	red, thread, said, bury	red, thred, sed, ber'i
ə	,,	her	herd, heard, thirst	hərd, hərd, thərst
ī	,, (1)	mine	side, shy, dye, height	sīd, shī, dī, hīt
	(2)	sire	hire, byre	hīr, bīr
i	,,	bid	pin, busy, hymn	pin, biz'i, him
ō	,, (1)	mote	bone, road, foe, low, dough	bōn, rōd, fō, lō, dō
	(2)	more	fore, soar, floor	fōr, sōr, flōr
o	,, (1)	got	shot, shone	shot, shon
	(2)	sort	form	form
aw	,, { (a) pause;	haul, lawn, fall, bought;	hawl, lawn, fawl, bawt
	{ (b) swarthy	swarm	swawrm
oo	,, (1)	moon	fool, sou	fōōl, sōō
	(2)	poor	boor, tour	bōōr, tōōr
oo	,,	foot	good, full, would	good, fool, wood
ū	,, (1)	mute	tune, due, newt, view	tūn, dū, nūt, vū
	(2)	pure	endure	en-dūr'
u	,, (1)	bud	run, love	run, luv
	(2)	absurd	turn, word	turn, wurd
(y) oo	,, (1)	super (ū or oo)	supreme	s(y)ōō-prēm'
	(2)	lure	lurid	l(y)ōō'rid
ow	,, (1)	house	mount, frown	mownt, frown
	(2)	hour	sour	sowr -
oi	,,	boy	toy, buoy, soil	toi, boi, soil

Vowels in Unaccented Syllables

	SOUND		EXAMPLES	PRONUNCIATION
ə	as in (a)	silver	beggar, adviser, sailor, power	beg'ər, ad-vīz'ər, sāl'ər, pow'ər (or pow'r)
	(b)	absent	element, presence	el'ə-mənt, prez'əns
	(c)	infant	tenant	ten'ənt
	(d)	bearable	arable, amiable	ar'ə-bl, ām'i-ə-bl
	(e)	away	abeam, accuse	ə-bēm', ə-kūz'
	(f)	squadron	cauldron, telephonist	kawl'drən, ti-lef'ə-nist
	(g)	tomorrow	tobacco	tə-bak'ō
	(h)	autumn	quantum	kwon'təm

Vowels in Unaccented Syllables

SOUND		EXAMPLES	PRONUNCIATION
ə as in (i)	faithful	grateful	*grāt′fəl*
(j)	adventure	tenure, figure	*ten′yər, fig′ər*
(k)	nation	mention, station	*men′shən, stā′shən*
(l)	anxious	precious	*pre′shəs*
(m)	bargain	curtain, villain	*kur′tən, vil′ən*
(n)	menace	solace	*sol′əs (or sol′is)*
i ,, (a)	civil	anvil, evil	*an′vil, ē′vil (or ē′vl)*
(b)	blessed *(adj.)*	beloved *(adj.)*	*bi-luv′id*
(c)	packet	basket	*bas′kit*
(d)	terrace	solace	*sol′is (or sol′əs)*
(e)	desolate	delicate	*del′i-kit*
(f)	cottage	manage, marriage	*man′ij, mar′ij*
(g)	petty	silly, pretty	*sil′i, prit′i*
(h)	catastrophe	apostrophe	*ə-pos′trə-fi*
(i)	become	bequest, depart, pedestrian, regard, seclude	*bi-kwest′, di-pärt′, pi-des′tri-ən, ri-gärd′, si-klōōd′*
No vowel (a)	medal	penal, devil, evil	*pē′nl, dev′l, ē′vl (or ē′vil)*
(b)	burden	arson	*är′sn*
(c)	special	initial	*in-ish′l*
(d)	flower	power	*pow′r (or pow′ər)*
Apostrophe (a)	Used to mark such pronunciations as *t′h* (where the sound is two separate consonants)		
(b)	Used in French words such as timbre *(tanᵉ-br′)*		

Consonants

SOUND		EXAMPLES	PRONUNCIATION
ch as in	church	much, match, lunch	*much, mach, lunch* (or *lunsh*)
d ,,	dog	ado, dew	*ə-dōō′, dū*
dh ,,	then	father	*fä′dhər*
f ,,	fade	faint, phase, rough	*fānt, fāz, ruf*
g ,,	game	gold, guard, ghastly	*gold, gärd, gâst′li*
gz ,,	example	exact	*igz-akt′*
h ,,	home	happy	*hap′i*
hh ,,	loch	coronach, leprechaun	*kor′ə-nähh, lep′rə-hhawn*
j ,.	judge	jack, gentle, ledge, region	*jak, jen′tl, lej, rē′jən*
k ,,	king	keep, cat, chorus	*kēp, kat, kōr′əs*
ks ,,	exclaim	expand, lax	*eks-pand′, laks*
kw ,,	queen	quite, coiffeur	*kwīt, kwä-fər*
ng ,,	sing	fling, single	*fling, sing′gl*
ngk ,,	monkey	precinct, adjunct	*prē′singkt, aj′ungkt*
n′ ,,	avant (Fr.)	monseigneur	*monᵉ-sen-yər*
s ,,	sad	salt, city, circuit, scene, mass	*sawlt, sit′i, sər′kit, sēn, mas*
sh ,	ship	shine, machine, sure, lunch, Asiatic	*shīn, mə-shēn′, shōōr, lunsh* (or *lunch*), *āsh-i-at′ik (or ā-zhi-at′ik)*
th ,,	thin	three	*thrē*
y ,,	yes	young, bastion, question	*yung, bast′yən, kwest′yən*
z ,,	zebra	zoo, was, roads	*zōō, woz, rōdz*
zh ,,	pleasure	azure, measure, congé, Asiatic	*azh′ər (or ā′zhūr), mezh′ər, konᵉ-zhā, ā-zhi-at′ik (or āsh-i-at′ik)*

LIST OF ABBREVIATIONS USED IN THIS DICTIONARY

abbrev.. ......abbreviation
abl. ....ablative
acc.........according
accus ......accusative
adj(s).......adjective(s)
adv(s).......adverb(s)
aero. ......aeronautics
agri ....agriculture
alg. ....algebra
anat.......anatomy
alch.. ....alchemy
anc ......ancient(ly)
ant. ......antiquities
anthrop ....anthropology
aor.......aorist
app........apparently
approx......approximately
arch. ......archaic
archaeol ....archaeology
archit.......architecture
arith.......arithmetic
astrol. ......astrology
astron.......astronomy
at. numb......atomic number
attrib.......attributive(ly)
augm. ......augmentative

B. ....Bible
biol. ....biology
book-k. ....book-keeping
bot. ....botany

c ....about
cent. ......century
cf. ......compare
chem. ......chemistry
cog. ....cognate
coll. ......colloquial(ly)
collec. ......collective(ly)
comp.......comparative,
                composition
conj(s) ......conjunction(s)
conn. ......connected,
                connexion
contr. ......contracted,
                contraction
cook.......cookery
corr. ......corruption
crystal......crystallography

dat. ....dative
demons. ......demonstrative
der.........derived,
                derivation
dial........dialect(al)
Dict. ......Dictionary
dim........diminutive
dub ....doubtful

econ. ......economics
e.g. ......for example
elect.......electricity
entom. ......entomology
erron. ......erroneous(ly)
esp. ....especially
ety. ....etymology

facet. ....facetiously
fam........familiar,
                family
fem. ....feminine
fig.........figurative(ly)
fl.........floruit
fol. ....followed,
                following
fort........fortification
freq........frequentative
fut. ....future

gen. ....genitive
gener. ......generally
geog. ....geography
geol........geology
geom. ......geometry
ger. ....gerundive
gram.......grammar

her.........heraldry
hist ....history
hort. ......horticulture
hyperb. ......hyperbolically

i.e. ....that is
illit. ......illiterate
imit. ......imitative
imper.......imperative
impers......impersonal(ly)
incl. ......including
indic.......indicative
infin. ......infinitive
inten(s). ......intensive
interj(s). ......interjection(s)
interrog......interrogative(ly)
intrans......intransitive
irreg. ......irregular(ly)

lit. ....literal(ly)
log. ....logic

mach. ......machinery
masc. ......masculine
math.......mathematics
mech.......mechanics
med. ......medicine
metaph......metaphysics
meteor......meteorology
mil.........military
Milt. ......Milton
min. ......mineralogy
mod........modern
mus........music
myth.......mythology

n(s) ....noun(s)
nat. hist......natural history
naut........nautical
neg. ......negative
neut........neuter
nom........nominative
n.pl........noun plural
n.sing........noun singular
N.T........New Testament
North ......Northern

obs. ....obsolete
opp........opposed,
                opposite
opt.........optics
org........organic
orig........original(ly)
O.S........Old Style
O.T........Old Testament

p., part. ....participle
p.adj........participial
                adjective
paint ......painting
palaeog......palaeography
pa.p........past participle
pass........passive
pa.t........past tense
path........pathology
perf. ......perfect
perh........perhaps
pers........person(al)
petr........petrology
pfx........prefix
phil(os)......philosophy
philol........philology
phon........phonetics
phot........photography
phys........physics
physiol......physiology
pl. ....plural
poet........poetical
pol. econ......political
                economy
pop........popular(ly)
poss........possessive,
                possibly
Pr. Bk. ....Book of Com-
                mon Prayer
pr.p........present parti-
                ciple
prep(s)......preposition(s)
pres........present
pret........preterite
print........printing
priv........privative
prob........probably
pron(s)......pronoun(s)
pron........pronounced,
                pronunciation
prop........properly
pros........prosody
prov........provincial
psych........psychology

q.v. ......which see

R.C........Roman Catholic
redup........reduplication
refl(ex)......reflexive
rel........related, relative
rhet........rhetoric
R.V........Revised Version

sculp........sculpture
Shak........Shakespeare
sig.........signifying

x

sing . . . . singular	*term* . . . . termination	*usu.* . . . . usually
specif. . . . . . . specifically	*theat.* . . . . theatre,	
Spens . . . . . Spenser	theatricals	*vb(s)* . . . . . . verb(s)
subj . . . . subjunctive	*theol.* . . . . theology	*v.i.* . . . . verb intransitive
suff . . . . suffix	*trans.* . . . . transitive,	*voc.* . . . . vocative
superl. . . . . . . superlative	translation	*v.t.* . . . . verb transitive
surg. . . . . . . surgery	*trig.* . . . . trigonometry	*vulg.* . . . . vulgar
teleg. . . . . telegraphy	*ult.* . . . . ultimately	*zool.* . . . . zoology

A.F. . . . . Anglo-French	*Hung.* . . . . . . Hungarian	*O.Ir.* . . . . Old Irish
Amer. . . . . . . American		*O.N.* . . . . Old Norse
Angl. . . . . Anglian	*Icel.* . . . . Icelandic	*O.N.Fr.* . . . . Old Northern
Ar. . . . . Arabic	(Modern)	French
Austr. . . . . . . Australian	*Ind* . . . . Indian	*O. Sax* . . . . . Old Saxon
	Ir. . . . . Irish	
Bav. . . . . Bavarian	*It.* . . . . Italian	*Pers.* . . . . Persian
Beng. . . . . . . Bengali		*Peruv* . . . . . . Peruvian
Bohem. . . . . . Bohemian	*Jap* . . . . Japanese	*Pol* . . . . Polish
Braz. . . . . Brazilian	*Jav* . . . . Javanese	*Port.* . . . . Portuguese
Bret. . . . . Breton		*Prov.* . . . . Provençal
	L. . . . . Latin	
Carib. . . . . . . Caribbean	*L.G., L.Ger.* Low German	*Rom.* . . . . Roman
Celt. . . . . Celtic	*Li'h.* . . . . Lithuanian	*Russ..* . . . . . . Russian
Chin. . . . . Chinese	*L.L.* . . . . Low or Late	
	Latin	*Sans.* . . . . . . Sanskrit
Dan. . . . . Danish		*S.Afr* . . . . . . South African
Du. . . . . Dutch	*M.E.* . . . . Middle English	*Scand.* . . . . . . Scandinavian
	M.Du. . . . . . . Middle Dutch	*Scot.* . . . . Scottish (usu.
Egypt. . . . . . . Egyptian	*Mex.* . . . . Mexican	includes North
Eng. . . . . English	*M.Flem.* . . . . Middle Flemish	of England)
	M.Fr. . . . . . . Middle French	*Sinh.* . . . . Sinhalese
Finn. . . . . Finnish	*M.H.G.* . . . . Middle High	*Slav.* . . . . Slavonic
Flem. . . . . Flemish	German	*Sp.* . . . . Spanish
Fr. . . . . French	*M.L.G.* . . . . Middle Low	*Sw.* . . . . Swedish
Fris. . . . . Frisian	German	
		Turk. . . . . . . Turkish
Gael. . . . . Gaelic	*Norm* . . . . . . Norman	
Ger. . . . . German	*Norw.* . . . . . . Norwegian	*U.S.* . . . . United States
Gmc. . . . . Germanic		(often includes
Goth. . . . . Gothic	*O.E.* . . . . Old English	Canadian)
Gr. . . . . Greek	*O.Fr.* . . . . . . Old French	
	O.Fris. . . . . . Old Frisian	*W.* . . . . Welsh
Heb. . . . . Hebrew	*O.H.G.* . . . . Old High Ger-	*W.S.* . . . . West Saxon
Hind. . . . . . . Hindustani	man	

For *List of Abbreviations used in the Dictionary*, see page x

Key to Pronunciation, see page vi

(detailed chart of pronunciation, page viii)

A

A, a, *ā, n.* the first letter in our alphabet, as in the Roman, etc. (see **aleph, alpha**): in music, the major sixth of the scale of C.—**A1** (*ā wun*), the symbol for a first-class vessel in Lloyd's Register: hence (*vulg.*) first-rate.

a, *ə,* also (emphatic) *ā, adj.* the indefinite article, a broken down form of **an** used before a consonant sound. [O.E. *ān,* one.]

A, *ä, ə, pron.* (*dial.*) a monophthongised form of **I.**

a, *ä, ə, pron.* (*dial.*) he : she : it : they. [O.E. *hé,* he, *héo,* she, *híe,* they.]

a', *aw,* Scots and Northern form of **all.**—*pron.* **a'body** (*aw'*), everybody.—*adv.* **a''gate,** every way. — *pron.* **a''thing,** everything. — *adv.* **a''where,** everywhere.

a, *ə,* a reduced form of the O.E. prep. *an, on,* on, in, at, chiefly used in composition, as *abroad, asleep.*

à, *ə,* a form of the Latin prep. *ab,* from, of, as in Thomas à Kempis (Thomas from Kempen)

aardvark, *ärd'värk, n.* the ant-bear, a South African edentate. [Du. *aarde,* earth, *vark* (now *varken*), pig.]

aardwolf, *ärd'woolf, n.* the earth-wolf, a hyaena-like South African carnivore. [Du. *aarde,* earth, *wolf,* wolf.]

Aaronic, -al, *ā-ron'ik, -l, adj.* pertaining to Aaron, the Jewish high-priest: pontifical.—**Aaron's beard,** a saxifrage, grown dangling from pots : the great St. John's wort : ivy-leaved toadflax, or other plant; **Aaron's rod,** mullein, golden-rod, or other plant with tall straight flowering stem.

aasvogel, *äs'fō-gəl, n.* a South African vulture. [Du. *aas,* carrion, *vogel,* bird.]

Ab, *äb, n.* the eleventh civil, fifth ecclesiastical, month of the Jewish Calendar (parts of July and August). [Syriac.]

aba, abba, *a'bä,* or **abaya,** *ä-bä'yä, n.* a Syrian cloth, of goat's or camel's hair, usually striped : an outer garment made of it. [Ar. *'abā, 'abāya.*]

abaca, *ä-bä-kä', n.* a plantain much grown in the Philippine Islands : its fibre called Manila hemp [Tagálog.]

aback, *ə-bak', adv.* backwards : (*naut.*) said of sails pressed backward against the mast by the wind—hence (*fig.*) **taken aback,** taken by surprise. [O.E. *on bæc,* on back.]

abacot. See **bycocket.**

abactinal, *ab-ak-tī'nəl, ab-ak'ti-nəl, adj.* (*zool.*) remote from the actinal area : without rays.—*adv.* **abactinally.**

abactor, *ab-ak'tər, n.* cattle thief. [L.L.]

abacus, *ab'ə-kəs, n.* a counting-frame : (*archit.*) a level tablet on the capital of a column, supporting the entablature :—*pl.* **ab'aci** (*-sī*). [L. *abacus*—Gr. *abax, -akos.*]

Abaddon, *ə-bad'ən, n.* Apollyon : (*Milt.*) hell. [Heb. *ăbaddon,* from *ābad,* to be lost.]

abaft, *ə-bäft', adv. and prep.* (*naut.*) behind. [Prep. **a** and O.E. *bæftan,* after—pfx. *be-, æftan.* See **aft.**]

abalone, *ab-a-lō'nä, n.* the sea-ear, especially a richly coloured kind found on the Pacific coast of North America. [Uncertain origin.]

abandon, *ə-ban'dən, v.t.* to give up : to desert : to yield (oneself) without restraint : to give up all claims to : (*Shak.*) to banish.—*n.* (sometimes as Fr. *ä-bän-dong*) condition of letting oneself go : careless freedom of action.—*v.t.* **aband',** (Spens.) to abandon.—*adj.* **aban'doned,** completely deserted : given up, as to a vice : profligate: very wicked.—*adv.* **aban'donedly.**—*ns.* **abandonee'** (*law*), an insurer to whom a wreck has been abandoned; **aban'donment.** [O.Fr. *abandoner,* to put

at one's disposal or in one's control (*à bandon*), or to the ban; see **ban.**]

abase, *ə-bās', v.t.* to lower : to cast down : to humble : to degrade.—*adj.* **abased',** lowered.—*n.* **abase'ment.** [O.Fr. *abaissier,* to bring low—L. *ad,* to, L.L. *bassus,* low.]

abash, *ə-bash', v.t.* to strike with shame : to put out of countenance : to astound : to confound.—*adj.* **abash'less,** shameless : unabashed.—*n.* **abash'ment.** [O.Fr. *esbahir*—pfx. *es-* (L. *ex,* out), *bahir,* to astound—interj. *bah.*]

abask, *ə-bäsk', adv.* in genial warmth. [**bask.**]

abate, *ə-bāt', v.t.* (*obs.*) to demolish : (*law*) to put an end to : (*law*) to nullify, to bring down : to lessen : to deduct (with *of*); to mitigate : to blunt : (*Shak.*) to curtail : (*Shak.*) to except.—*v.i.* to grow less : to subside : (*law*) to be abated.—*adjs.* **abāt'able; abāt'ed,** blunted : diminished : lowered : subdued : beaten down or cut away, as the background of relief.—*n.* **abate'ment,** the act or process of abating : the sum or quantity abated : state of being abated : (*law*) the abandonment of an action, or the reduction of a legacy: (*her.*) a supposed mark of dishonour on a coat of arms—apparently never actually used. [O.Fr. *abatre,* to beat down—L. *ab,* from, and L.L. *batēre,* for L. *batuĕre,* to beat.]

abate, *ə-bāt', v.i. and v.t.* (*refl.*) to intrude on a freehold and take possession before the heir.—*ns.* **abate'ment; abāt'or.** [O.Fr. *enbatre,* to thrust in.]

abatis, abattis, *ab'ə-tis, ə-bat'ē, -is, n.* (*fort.*) a rampart of felled trees, branches outward :—*pl.* **abat(t)is** (*-ēz*). [Fr.; see **abate** (1).]

abattoir, *ä-bä-twär', n.* a public slaughterhouse. [Fr.; see **abate** (1).]

abature, *ab'ə-tyər, n.* the trail of a stag through underwood. [Fr., beating down; cf. **abate** (1).]

abaya. See **aba.**

abaxial, *ab-ak'si-əl, adj.* (*bot.*) away from the axis. [Pfx. *ab-* and **axis.**]

abb, *ab, n.* properly woof- or weft-yarn, but sometimes warp-yarn. [O.E. *āb, āweb*—pfx. *ā-,* out, *webb,* web.]

abba, *ab'ä, n.* (*N.T.*) father (applied to God): a Syriac or Coptic bishop. [Aramaic word *abbā* retained in the Greek N.T. and its translations.)

abba. See **aba.**

abbacy, *ab'ə-si, n.* the office or jurisdiction of abbot : the time during which one is abbot : an abbey.—*adj.* **abbatial** (*ab-ā'shl*), pertaining to an abbey, abbot or abbess. [App. orig. Scot.: L.L. *abbātia,* abbey.]

Abbasid(e), *a-bas'id, -īd, ab'ə-sid, -sīd, n.* any member of the later (750-1543) of the two great dynasties of caliphs, descendants of *Abbas,* uncle of Mohammed.

abbé, *ab'ā, n.* a courtesy title for a priest, an ecclesiastic in minor orders, or for a tutor or holder of a benefice, even if a layman. [Fr., orig. abbot.]

abbess, *ab'es, n.* a woman who is head of an abbey. [L.L. *abbātissa,* fem. of *abbās,* abbot.]

abbey, *ab'i, n.* a convent under an abbot or abbess, or (*loosely*) a prior or prioress: the church now or formerly attached to it : a name often retained by an abbatial building that has become a private house:—*pl.* **abb'eys.**—*ns.* **abb'ey-counter,-piece,** a pilgrim's token, evidence of a visit to an abbey; **abb'ey-laird,** (*hist.*) a debtor in sanctuary in the precincts of Holyrood Abbey; **abb'ey-lubber, a** lazy monk—a term much used by the reformers. [O.Fr. *abaïe* (Fr. *abbaye*)—L.L. *abbātia.* See **abba** (1), **abbacy.**]

abbot, *ab'ət, n.* a male head of an abbey :—*fem.* **abb'ess.**—*n.* **abb'otship.**—**abbot of unreason,** a lord of misrule or mock abbot in mediaeval revels. [L.L. *abbās*, *abbātis*—Aramaic *abbā*; see **abba**.]

abbreviate, *ə-brē'vi-āt*, *v.t.* to shorten: to contract: to abridge.—*adj.* shortened.—*ns.* **abbrēviā'tion**, an act of shortening: a shortened form: part of a word written or printed for the whole; **abbrē'viātor**. —*adj.* **abbrē'viatory** (*-ə-tor-i*).—*n.* **abbrē'viāture** (*obs.*), an abbreviation: an abridgment. [L. *abbreviāre*, *-ātum—ab*, intens., *brevis*, short.]

ABC, *ā-bē-sē'*, also (*obs.*) **abcee**, **absey**, *ab'si*, *n.* the alphabet, from its first letters : a first reading-book : hence first rudiments: anything arranged alphabetically, as an acrostic, a railway guide.—**absey book**, (*Shak.*) a primer or hornbook.

Abderian, *ab-dē'ri-ən*, *adj.* of *Abdera*, a town in Thrace, the Gotham of the ancients, and birthplace of Democritus, 'the laughing philosopher.'— Also *n.*—*n.* **Abderite** (*ab'dər-īt*), a native or citizen of Abdera; a simpleton, Gothamite.

abdicate, *ab'di-kāt*, *v.t.* and *v.i.* formally to renounce or give up (office or dignity).—*adjs.* **ab'dicable**; **ab'dicant.**—*n.* **abdicā'tion.** [L. *ab*, from or off, *dicāre*, *-ātum*, to proclaim.]

abdomen, *ab-dō'mən*, also *ab'*, *n.* the belly: in mammals, the part between diaphragm and pelvis : in arthropods, the hind-body.—*adj.* **abdominal** (*-dom'*).—*adv.* **abdom'inally.**—*adj.* **abdom'inous**, pot-bellied. [L. *abdōmen*, *-inis*.]

abduce, *ab-dūs'*, *v.t.* an earlier form of **abduct.** *adj.* **abdūc'ent**, drawing back: separating.— *v.t.* **abduct** (*-dukt'*), to take away by fraud or violence: to kidnap (esp. a woman, a child, or a voter).—*ns.* **abduction** (*-duk'shən*), the carrying away, esp. of a person by fraud or force: (*surg.*) separation of parts of the body after a wound or fracture : muscular action drawing one part away from another: (*log.*) a syllogism whose minor premiss is only probable; **abduc'tor**, one who abducts : a muscle that draws away. [L. *abducĕre— ab*, from, *ducĕre*, *ductum*, to draw, lead.]

abeam, *ə-bēm'* *adv.* (*naut.*) on the beam, or in a line at right angles to a vessel's length, hence abreast. [Prep. **a**, and **beam**.]

abear, *ə-bār'*, *v.t.* to bear, comport, behave : (now *prov.*) to endure or tolerate. [O.E. *āberan*.]

abecedarian, *ā-bi-sē-dā'ri-ən*, *adj.* pertaining to the ABC: rudimentary: arranged in the manner of an acrostic.—*n.* (*esp. U.S.*) a learner of the ABC, a beginner : a teacher of the ABC: an Anabaptist of a sect that rejected all learning. [ABC.]

abed, *ə-bed'*, *adv.* in bed. [Prep. **a**, and **bed.**]

abeigh, *ə-bēhh'*, *adv.* (*Scot.*) aloof. [Origin obscure.]

abele, *ə-bēl'*, *ā'bl*, *n.* the white poplar-tree. [Du. *abeel* —O.Fr. *abel*, *aubel*—L.L. *albellus*—L. *albus*, white.]

Aberdeen, *ab-ər-dēn'*, sometimes *ab'*, *adj.* of or originating in *Aberdeen* or Aberdeenshire.—*n.* (in full **Aberdeen terrier**) a coarse-haired kind of Scottish terrier.—*adj.* **Aberdō'nian**, of Aberdeen. —Also *n.*—**Aberdeen Angus** (*ang'gəs*), a breed of polled cattle descended from Aberdeenshire humlies and Angus doddies.

aberdevine, *ab-ər-di-vīn'*, *n.* a bird-fancier's name for the siskin. [Ety. uncertain.]

Abernethy biscuit, *ab-ər-neth'i*, *-nēth'i*, or *ab'*, a hard biscuit, apparently originally with caraway-seeds. [Poss. after Dr. John *Abernethy* (1764-1831), who was interested in diet.]

aberrate, *ab'ər-āt*, *v.i.* to wander or deviate from the right way.—*ns.* **aberrance** (*-er'*), **aberr'ancy.** —*adj.* **aberr'ant** wandering : (*bot.*, *zool.*) having characteristics not strictly in accordance with type. —*n.* **aberrā'tion** (*-ər-*), deviation from the usual, normal, or right : wandering of the intellect, mental lapse : non-convergence of rays, owing to difference in refrangibility of different colours (*chromatic aberration*) or to difference of focus of the marginal and central parts of a lens or mirror (*spherical aberration*) : an apparent displacement of a star, owing to the finite ratio of the velocity of light to that of the earth (*aberration of light*). [L. *aberrāre*, *-ātum—ab*, from, *errāre*, to wander.]

abet, *ə-bet'*, *v.t.* to incite by encouragement or aid (used chiefly in a bad sense): (*Spens.*) to back up :

to make good. (*pr.p.* **abett'ing**; *pa.p.* **abett'ed.**)— *n.* (*Spens.*) abetting.—*ns.* **abet'ment**; **abett'or.** [O.Fr. *abeter—à* (L. *ad*, to), and *beter*, to bait; see **bait.**]

abeyance, *ə-bā'əns*, *n.* suspension; temporary inactivity.—Also **abey'ancy.** [O.Fr. *abeance—à* (L. *ad*, to), and *beer*, *baer*, to gape, open wide; origin uncertain.]

abhominable, an obs. mistaken form of **abominable.**

abhor, *ab-hor'*, *v.t.* to shrink from with horror : to detest : to loathe : (*Shak.*) to protest against, to reject : (*Shak.*) to fill with horror :—*pr.p.* **abhorr'-ing**; *pa.t.* and *pa.p.* **abhorred'.**—*ns.* **abhor'ence**, extreme hatred : a thing abhorred; **abhorr'ency** (*obs.*).—*adj.* **abhorr'ent**, detesting : repugnant : strongly opposed : out of keeping : detestable : detested.—*adv.* **abhorr'ently.**—*ns.* **abhorr'er**, one who abhors : **Abhorrer** (*hist.*) a member of the court party in England in 1679, who abhorred the *Petitioners*, a tory; **abhorr'ing**, repugnance : an object of abhorrence. [L. *abhorrēre—ab*, from, and *horrēre*, to bristle, shudder.]

Abib, *ā'bib*, *n.* the seventh civil, first ecclesiastical, month of the Jewish calendar (March-April)— later called Nisan. [Heb. *ābīb*, lit. an ear of corn.]

abide, *ə-bīd'*, *v.t.* to bide or wait for; to meet, face, sustain : to endure : to tolerate.—*v.i.* to remain : to dwell or stay : to conform, adhere (with *by*).— (*pa.t.* **abōde'**, also **abīd'ed**, *Spens.* **abīd'**; *pa.p.* **abōde'**, **abīd'ed**, also **abīdd'en.**)—*n.* **abīd'ance.** —*adj.* **abīd'ing**, continual, permanent.—*n.* an enduring.—*adv.* **abīd'ingly.** [O.E. *ābīdan*—pfx. *ā-*, and *bīdan*, to wait.]

abide, *ə-bīd'*, *v.t.* (*Shak.*; *Milt.*) to aby. [**aby**, confounded with **abide** (1).]

Abies, *āb'i-ēz*, *n.* the genus of the true firs. [L.]

abigail, *ab'i-gāl*, *n.* a lady's-maid. [From *Abigail*, in Beaumont and Fletcher's *Scornful Lady*, or I Sam. XXV.]

ability, *ə-bil'i-ti*, *n.* quality or fact of being able: power (physical and mental): strength : skill. [O.Fr. *ableté* (Fr. *habileté*), remodelled on its source, L. *habilitās*, *-ātis—habēre*, to have, hold; see **able**.]

abiogenesis, *ab-i-ō-jen'is-is*, or *ā-bī-*, *n.* the origination of living by not-living matter, spontaneous generation.—*adj.* **abiogenetic** (*-ji-net'ik*).—*adv.* **abiogenet'ically.**—*n.* **abiogenist** (*-oj'ə-nist*), a believer in abiogenesis. [Coined by Huxley in 1870; Gr. *a-*, neg., *bios*, life, *genesis*, birth.]

abiturient, *ab-it-ū'ri-ənt*, *n.* in Germany, a pupil leaving school for a university. [Mod. L. *abituriēns*, *-entis*, pr.p. of *abiturīre*, desiderative of L. *abīre*, to go away—*ab*, from, *īre*, to go.]

abject, *ab-jekt'*, *v.t.* (*obs.*) to throw or cast down or away.—*adj.* **ab'ject**, cast away : mean : worthless : grovelling : base.—*ns.* **ab'ject**, an outcast; a base slave : one in more servile subjection than a subject; **abjec'tion**, abjectness : casting forth : (*bot.*) forcible expulsion of spores.—*adv.* **ab'jectly.** —*n.* **ab'jectness.** [L. *abjicĕre*, *abjectum—ab*, from, *jacĕre*, to throw.]

abjoint, *ab-joint'*, *v.t.* (*bot.*) to cut off by forming a septum.—*n.* **abjunction** (*-jungk'shən*). [L. *ab*, from, **joint**, **junction**.]

abjure, *ab-jōōr'*, *v.t.* to renounce on oath or solemnly : to recant : to repudiate.—*ns.* **abjurā'tion**; **abjur'er.** [L. *ab*, from, *jurāre*, *-ātum*, to swear.]

ablactation, *ab-lak-tā'shən*, *n.* a weaning : grafting by inarching. [L. *ab*, from, *lactāre*, to suckle—*lac*, *lactis*, milk.]

ablation, *ab-lā'shən*, *n.* removal.—*adjs.* **ablatitious** (*-lə-tish'əs*); **ab'lative** (*-lə-tiv*), pertaining to ablation : (*gram.*) in or belonging to a case which in Indo-Germanic languages originally expressed *direction from*, or *time when*, later extended to other functions.—*n.* the ablative case : a word in the ablative.—*adj.* **ablatī'val.** [L. *ab*, from, *lātum*, used as supine of *ferre*, to take.]

ablaut, *äp'lowt*, *ab'lowt*, *n.* (*philol.*) a variation in root vowel as in sing, sang, song, sung, explained by former accentuation—also called gradation. [Ger. *ab*, off, *laut*, sound.]

ablaze, *ə-blāz′,* *adv.* and *adj.* in a blaze, on fire: gleaming brightly. [Prep. **a,** and **blaze.**]

able, *ā′bl,* *adj.* having enough strength, power, or means (to do a thing): skilful.—*v.t.* (*obs.*) to enable: (*Shak.*) to warrant.—*adj.* **a′ble-bod′ied,** of a strong body: free from disability, etc.: robust.—*advs.* **a′bly**; **a(i)blins** (*ā′blinz*) or **yibbles** (*yib′lz*), (*Scot.*) perhaps.—**able seaman, able-bodied seaman** (abbrev. **A.B.**), one able to perform all the duties of seamanship and having a higher rating than the ordinary sailor. [See **ability.**]

ablet, *ab′lit,* *n.* the bleak. [Fr. *ablette*—L.L. *a(l)bula,* dim. of *alba,* white.]

abloom, *ə-blōōm′,* *adv.* and *adj.* in a blooming state. [Prep. **a,** on, and **bloom.**]

ablow, *ə-blō′,* *adv.* and *adj.* in a blowing state. [Prep. **a,** and **blow.**]

ablush, *ə-blush′,* *adv.* and *adj.* in a blushing state. [Prep. **a,** and **blush.**]

ablution, *ə-bl(y)ōō′shən,* *n.* (often in *pl.*) act of washing, esp. the body: ceremonial washing: (*sing.*) the wine and water used to rinse the chalice, drunk by the officiating priest.—*adj.* **ablu′tionary** [L. *ablūtiō,* *-ōnis*—*ab,* away, *luĕre,* to wash.]

abnegate, *ab′ni-gāt,* *v.t.* to deny: to renounce.—*ns.* **abnega′tion**; **ab′negator.** [L. *ab,* away, *negāre,* to deny.]

abnormal, *ab-nor′ml,* *adj.* not normal.—*ns.* **abnor′malism**; **abnormality** (*-mal′i-ti*).—*adv.* **abnor′mally.**—*n.* **abnor′mity** (*rare*)—*adj.* **abnor′mous** (*rare*). [Fr. *anormal*—L.L. *anormalus*—Gr. *anōmalos* (see **anomaly**); influenced by L. *norma,* rule, and *ab,* from.]

aboard, *ə-bōrd′,* *adv.* or *prep.* on board: in or into a ship, railway train, etc.: alongside. [Prep. **a,** on, and **board.**]

abode, *ə-bōd′,* *n.* a dwelling-place: stay.—*v.t.* and *v.i., pa.t.* and *pa.p.* of **abide.**

abode, *ə-bōd′,* *n.* a presage.—*v.t.* (*Shak.*) to presage.—*n.* **abode′ment,** (*obs.*) a foreboding: an omen. [O.E. *ābodian,* to proclaim; cf. **bode, forebode.**]

aboideau, aboiteau, *ā-bwä-dō′, -tō′,* *n.* a tide-gate. [Canadian Fr.]

aboil, *ə-boil′,* *adv.* and *adj.* in a boiling state. [Prep. **a,** on, and **boil.**]

abolish, *ə-bol′ish,* *v.t.* to put an end to.—*adj.* **abol′ishable.**—*ns.* **abol′ishment** (*rare*); **aboli′tion.**—*adjs.* **aboli′tional, aboli′tionary.**—*ns.* **aboli′tionism**; **aboli′tionist,** one who seeks to abolish anything, esp. slavery. [L. *abolēre, -itum,* partly through Fr. *abolir.*]

abolla, *ab-ol′ä,* *n.* a Roman military cloak. [L.]

abomasum, *ab-ō-mā′səm,* *n.* the fourth or true stomach of ruminants, lying close to the omasum.—Also **aboma′sus.** [L. *ab,* away from, *omāsum,* tripe, paunch (a Gallic word).]

abominate, *ə-bom′in-āt,* *v.t.* to abhor: to detest extremely.—*adj.* **abom′inable,** hateful: detestable.—An old spelling is **abhom′inable,** to agree with a fancied derivation from Lat. *ab homine.*—*n.* **abom′inableness.**—*adv.* **abom′inably.**—*ns.* **abominā′tion,** extreme aversion: an object of detestation; **abom′inātor.** [L. *abōmināri, -ātus,* to turn from as of bad omen; see **omen.**]

aboral, *ab-ō′rəl,* *adj.* (*zool.*) away from the mouth. [L. *ab,* from, and **oral.**]

abord, *ə-bōrd′,* *v.t.* (*arch.*) to accost.—*n.* approach. [Fr. *aborder—à bord,* to the side.]

abord, *ə-bōrd′,* *adv.* (*Spens.*) astray. [Perh. for **abroad.**]

aborigines, *ab-ə-rij′in-ēz,* *n.pl.* the original or native inhabitants of a country. A *sing.* formed by dropping *s* is used by some, esp. in Australia :— **aborigine** (*ab-ə-rij′i-nē*)—also **abor′igin** (*-bor′*), **-ine, -en.**—*adj.* **aborig′inal,** earliest, primitive, indigenous.—*n.* one of the aborigines.—*ns.* **aborig′inalism,** due recognition of native peoples; **aboriginality** (*-al′iti*), fact of being aboriginal.—*adv.* **aborig′inally.** [L. *aborigines—ab,* from, *orīgō, -inis,* beginning.]

abort, *ə-bort′,* *v.i.* to miscarry in birth: to be arrested in development at an early stage: to come to nothing.—*v.t.* to cause to abort; to check at an early stage.—*adj.* **abortifacient** (*-i-fā′shənt, -shi-ənt*), causing abortion.—*n.* means of causing

abortion.—*ns.* **abor′tion,** premature delivery, or the procuring of it, esp. (*med.*) in the first three months of pregnancy: arrest of development: the product of such arrest: anything that fails in course of coming into being: a misshapen being or monster; **abor′tionist,** one who procures abortion.—*adjs.* **abor′tive,** born untimely: unsuccessful: brought forth in an imperfect condition: checked in development.—*adv.* **abort′ively.**—*n.* **abort′iveness.**—**contagious abortion,** contagious infections of cattle and of horses due to different bacteria. [L. *aborīrī, abortus*—pfx. *ab-,* reversing the meaning, *orīrī,* to rise.]

abought, *ə-bawt′, pa.t.* and *pa.p.* of **aby.**

aboulia, abulia, *a-bōō′li-ä, -bow′, -bū′,* *n.* loss of will-power. [Gr. *a-,* priv., *boulē,* will.]

abound, *ə-bownd,* *v.i.* to be in great plenty: to be rich (with *in*): to be filled (with *with*).—*adj.* **abound′ing.** [O.Fr. *abunder*—L. *abundāre,* to overflow—*ab,* from, *unda,* a wave.]

about, *ə-bowt′, prep.* round on the outside: around: here and there in: near in place, time, size, etc.: on the person of: connected with: concerning: engaged in.—*adv.* around: halfway round, in the opposite direction: nearly: here and there: on the opposite tack: in motion or activity: on the point or in contemplation or preparation (with infinitive)—*prep.* **abouts′** (*Spens.*), about.—*v.t.* and *v.i.* **about′-ship,** to put (the ship) on the opposite tack.—*n.* **about′-sledge,** a heavy blacksmith's hammer.—**be about,** to be astir: to be on the point (of doing something); with infin.); **bring about,** to cause to take place; **come about,** to happen in the course of time; **go about,** to prepare to do; **put about** (see **put**); **turn about,** alternately: in rotation. [O.E. *onbutan—on,* in, *bútan,* without —*be,* by, *útan,* orig. a locative—*út,* out.]

above, *ə-buv′, prep.* over: in or to a position higher than that of: beyond in degree, amount, number, importance, etc.: too magnanimous or proud for:— *adv.* overhead: in a higher position, order, or power: in an earlier passage: in heaven.—*adj.* mentioned, stated, or given in an earlier passage.— *adjs.* **above′-board,** honourably open; **above′-ground,** alive: not buried; **above′-men′tioned**; **above′-named.** [Late O.E. *ābufan—*O.E. *ā-,* on, *bufan, above—be,* by, *ufan,* above, orig. a locative (Ger. *oben*).]

abracadabra, *ab-rə-kə-dab′rä, n.* a magic word, written in amulets: a spell or conjuring word: gibberish. [Found in a 2nd-cent. poem by Q. Serenus Sammonicus.]

abrade, *ə-brād′, v.t.* to wear down or off.—*adj.* and *n.* **abrā′dant,** abrasive. [L. *ab,* from, *rādĕre, rāsum,* to scrape.]

Abraham-man, *ā′brə-həm-man′,* **Abram-man,** *ā′brəm-man′, n.* originally a Bedlam inmate let out to beg: (*arch.*) a sturdy beggar, esp. one shamming insanity.—**to sham Abraham,** to feign sickness. [Said to be from an Abraham Ward in old Bedlam, London.]

abraid, abrade, *ə-brād′,* or (*Spens.*) **abray,** *ə-brā′, obs. v.t.* to awake, rouse.—*v.i.* to start: to awake. [O.E. *ābregdan—*intens. pfx. *ā-,* and *bregdan;* see **braid** (1).]

abram, *ā′brəm, adj.* (*Shak.*) an obs. form of **auburn.**

abranchiate, *ə-brang′ki-āt, adj.* without gills. [Gr. *a-,* priv., *branchia,* gills.]

abrasion, *ə-brā′zhən, n.* wearing away: a worndown or grazed place.—*adj.* and *n.* **abra′sive** (*-ziv, -siv*), tending to abrade.—*n.* an abrading agent. [See **abrade.**]

abraxas, *a-braks′as, n.* a mystic word, or a gem engraved therewith, often bearing a mystical figure of combined human and animal form, used as a charm: **Abraxas,** the genus of the gooseberry or magpie moth. [Said to have been coined by the 2nd-cent. Egyptian Gnostic Basilides to express 365 by addition of the numerical values of the Greek letters.]

abray. See **abraid.**

abreaction, *ab-rē-ak′shən, n.* (*psych.*) resolution of a neurosis by reviving forgotten or repressed ideas of the event first causing it. [L. *ab,* from, and **reaction.**]

Neutral vowels in unaccented syllables : *el′ə-mənt, in′fənt, ran′dəm*

abreast, *ə-brest'*, *adv.* with fronts in line : side by side. [Prep. **a**, on, and **breast**.]

abricock, *ab'ri-kok*, an obs. form of **apricot**.

abridge, *ə-brij'*, *v.t.* to shorten : to epitomise : to curtail.—*ns.* **abridg'er** ; **abridg'ment** (sometimes **abridge'ment**), contraction : shortening ; a compendium of a larger work : an epitome or synopsis : (*Shak.* ; *prob.*) a pastime. [O.Fr. *abregier* (Fr. *abréger*)—L. *abbreviāre*.]

abrim, *ə-brim'*, *adv.* and *adj.* in a brimming state, up to the brim. [Prep. **a, brim**.]

abroach, *ə-brōch'*, *adv.* and *adj.* in a condition to let the liquor run out : in a state to be diffused, afloat, astir. [Prep. **a**, and **broach**.]

abroad, *ə-brawd'*, *adv.* over a wide area : in full breadth : out of doors : at large : in the field : current : in or to another country : wide of the mark : astray. [Prep. **a**, and **broad**.]

abrogate, *ab'rō-gāt*, *v.t.* to annul.—*n.* **abroga'tion**. —*adj.* **ab'rogative**.—*n.* **ab'rogātor**. [L. *ab*, away, *rogāre*, *-ātum*, to ask or propose a law.]

Abroma, *a-brō'mä*, *n.* an East Indian sterculiaceous fibre-yielding tree. [Gr. *a-*, priv., *brōma*, food.]

abrooke, *ə-brook'*, *v.t.* (*Shak.*) to brook, bear, or endure. [Pfx. *a-*, intens., and **brook** (5).]

abrupt, *ə-brupt'*, *adj.* truncated : as if broken off : sudden : unexpected : precipitous : passing with sudden transitions : (of manners) short, rude.—*n.* (*Milt.*) an abyss.—*n.* **abrup'tion** (*-shən*), a breaking off.—*adv.* **abrupt'ly**.—*n.* **abrupt'ness**. [L. *abruptus—ab*, from, *rumpĕre*, *ruptum*, to break.]

Abrus, *ā'brəs*, *n.* a tropical genus akin to the bean, to which crab's-eyes belong.—*n.* **ā'brin**, a poisonous protein in its seeds. [Gr. *habros*, graceful.]

abscess, *ab'ses*, *-sis*, *n.* a collection of pus in a cavity. [L. *abscessus—abs*, from, *cēdĕre*, *cessum*, to go, retreat.]

abscind, *ab-sind'*, *v.t.* to cut off.—*n.* **abscissa** (*-sis'ä*), also **absciss**, **abscisse** (*ab'sis*) the intercept between a fixed point and the foot of an ordinate: the *x*-co-ordinate in analytical geometry:— *pl.* **abscissae** (*ab-sis'ē*), **absciss'as**, **ab'scisses**.— *n.* **abscission** (*-sizh'ən*), act of cutting off, or state of being cut off: (*rhet.*) a figure of speech in which the words demanded by the sense are left unsaid, the speaker stopping short suddenly: (*bot.*) organised shedding of a part by means of an absciss layer : liberation of a fungal spore by breakdown of part of its stalk.—**absciss layer** (*bot.*), a layer of parenchymatous cells through which a leaf, branch, or bark scale separates off. [L. *abscindĕre*, *abscissum*, to cut off—*ab*, from, *scindĕre*, to cut.]

abscond, *ab-skond'*, *v.i.* to hide, or get out of the way, esp. to escape a legal process.—*ns.* **abscond'ence** ; **abscond'er**. [L. *abscondĕre—abs*, from or away, *condĕre*, to hide.]

absent, *ab'sənt*, *adj.* being away : not present : in-attentive.—*v.t.* (*ab-sent'*) to keep (oneself) away.— *ns.* **ab'sence**, the state of being away or not present : want : non-existence : abstraction, in-attention; **absentee'**, one who is absent on any occasion : one who makes a habit of living away from his estate or his office; **absentee'ism**, the practice of absenting oneself from duty, station, or esp. estate.—*adv.* **ab'sently**.—*adj.* **ab'sent-mind'ed**, inattentive to surroundings : pre-occupied.—*adv.* **ab'sent-mind'edly**.—*n.* **ab'sent-mind'edness**. [L. *absēns, -sentis*, pr.p. of *abesse—ab*, away from, *esse*, to be.]

absey-book. See ABC.

absinth(e), *ab'sinth*, *n.* wormwood or other species of Artemisia : a liqueur containing (orig. at all events) extract of wormwood.—*adj.* **absinth'iated**, impregnated with absinth. [Fr. *absinthe*—L. *absinthium*—Gr. *apsinthion*, wormwood.]

absolute, *ab'səl-(y)ōōt*, *adj.* free from limits, restrictions, or conditions : certain, positive : complete : unlimited : free from mixture : independent of relation to other things : peremptory : unrestricted by constitutional checks : (*gram*) out of ordinary syntactic relation : (*philos.*) existing in and by itself without necessary relation to anything else : capable of being conceived independently of anything else.—*n.* (with **the** ; often **Absolute**) that which is absolute, self-existent, uncaused.—*adv.*

ab'solutely, separately, by itself : unconditionally : positively : completely—in vogue as a colourless but emphatic affirmative (*-loot'li*).—*ns.* **ab'soluteness** ; **absolu'tion**, release from punishment : acquittal : remission of sins, declared officially by a priest, or the formula by which it is expressed; **ab'solutism**, government, or theory of government, by a ruler without restriction : adherence to the doctrine of the Absolute; **ab'solutist**, a supporter of absolute government, or of a philosophy of the Absolute.—Also *adj.—adj.* **absolutory** (*ab-sol'ū-tər-i*), of, or giving, absolution.—**absolute alcohol**, water-free alcohol; **absolute magnitude**, the magnitude that a star would have at a standard distance of 10 parsecs; **absolute music**, music which does not attempt to illustrate or describe— opp. to *programme music*; **absolute pitch**, the actual pitch of a sound without reference to any arbitrary standard : a sense of or memory for absolute pitch; **absolute temperature**, tempera-ture expressed in accordance with the principles of thermodynamics alone, unaffected by the properties of the thermometric substance : also, temperature measured in degrees centigrade from absolute zero instead of from the freezing-point of water; **absolute zero**, the zero of the absolute scale of temperature (approx. —273°C.). [L. *absolūtus*, pa.p. of *absolvĕre*; see **absolve**.]

absolve, *əb-zolv'*, *-solv'*, *v.t.* to loose or set free : to pardon : to give absolution to or for : to acquit : to discharge (with *from*).—*ns.* **absolv'er**; **ab-solv'itor** (L. *3rd pers. imper. passive*, let him be absolved; *Scots law*), a decision favourable to a defender. [L. *absolvĕre—ab*, from, *solvĕre*, to loose.]

absonant, *ab'sən-ənt*, *adj.* discordant : abhorrent : unnatural : contrary to reason (with *to* or *from*)— opp. to *consonant*. [L. *ab*, from, *sonāns, -āntis*, pr.p. of *sonāre*, to sound.]

absorb, *ab-sorb'*, *-zorb'*, *v.t.* to suck in : to swallow up : to imbibe : to take in : to incorporate : to take up and transform (energy) instead of transmitting or reflecting : to engage wholly.—*n.* **absorbabil'ity**. —*adj.* **absorb'able**.—*adj.* **absorbed'**, swallowed up : entirely occupied.—*adv.* **absorb'edly**.—*n.* **absorb'ency**.—*adj.* **absorb'ent**, absorbing : able to absorb.—*n.* that which absorbs.—*n.* **absorb'er**. —*adj.* **absorb'ing**, engrossing the attention.— *adv.* **absorbingly**.—*ns.* **absorptiometer** (*-sorp-shi-om'i-tər*), an apparatus for determining the solubility of gases in liquids; **absorp'tion**, the act of absorbing : entire occupation of mind.—*adj.* **absorp'tive**, having power to absorb.—*ns.* **ab-sorp'tiveness**, **absorptiv'ity**.—**absorption bands, lines**, dark bands, lines, interrupting a spectrum, due to absorption of light in the medium traversed; **absorption spectrum**, a system of such lines and bands. [L. *ab*, from, *sorbēre*, *sorptum*, to suck in.]

absquatulate, *ab-skwot'ū-lāt*, *v.i.* (*facet.* ; *U.S.*) to decamp : to squat.

abstain, *ab-stān'*, *v.i.* to hold or refrain (from).— *ns.* **abstain'er**, one who abstains, esp. one who does not take alcoholic drinks; **absten'tion**. [Fr. *abstenir*—L. *abs*, from, *tenēre*, to hold.]

abstemious, *ab-stē'mi-əs*, *adj.* temperate : sparing in food, drink, or enjoyments.—*adv.* **abste'mious-ly**.—*n.* **abste'miousness**. [L. *abstēmius—abs*, from, *tēmētum*, strong wine.]

absterge, *ab-stərj'*, *v.t.* to wipe : to cleanse : to purge.—*adj.* **absterg'ent**, serving to cleanse.— *n.* a cleansing agent.—*n.* **abster'sion**.—*adj.* **ab-ster'sive**, having the quality of cleansing : purg-ative.—Also *n.* [L. *abstergĕre*, *-tersum*, to wipe away—*abs*, from, *tergĕre*, to wipe.]

abstinent, *ab'stin-ənt*, *adj.* abstaining : temperate.— *ns.* **ab'stinence**, an abstaining or refraining, especially from some indulgence (with *from*); **ab'stinency**, the quality of being abstinent.—*adv.* **ab'stinently**. [L. *abstinēns, -ēntis*, pr.p. of *abstinēre*; see **abstain**.]

abstract, *ab-strakt'*, *v.t.* to draw away : to separate : to remove quietly : to purloin : to summarise : to separate by the operation of the mind, as in forming a general concept from consideration of particular instances.—*n.* (*ab'strakt*) a summary, abridgment :

in *Shak. Ant. and Cleo.* III. vi., explained by some as an abridgment of time of separation—others conjecture *obstruct*: that which represents the essence: an abstraction.—*adj.* (*ab′strakt*) abstracted: apart from actual material instances, existing only as a mental concept—opp. to *concrete*: away from practice, theoretical: (of terms) denoting a quality of a thing apart from the thing, as 'redness': (*paint.* and *sculp.*) representing ideas (in geometric and other designs), not the forms of nature.—*adj.* abstract′ed, drawn off (with *from*): removed: absent in mind.—*adv.* abstract′edly.-*ns.* abstract′edness; abstrac′ter, abstrac′tor, one who makes abstracts (with -or for a grade of Civil Service clerks); abstrac′tion, act of abstracting: state of being abstracted: abstract quality or character: withdrawal from worldly things: absence of mind: a purloining: the process of abstracting by the mind: a thing existing only in idea: a theory, visionary notion: an abstract term: (*paint.* and *sculp.*) an abstract composition.—*adj.* abstrac′tional.—*n.* abstrac′tionist, one dealing in abstractions or unrealities.—*adj.* abstrac′tive, able or tending to abstract: formed by or pertaining to abstraction.—*n.* anything abstractive: an abstract.—*adv.* ab′stractly.—*n.* ab′stractness.—in the abstract, as an abstraction: in theory; abstract of title, summary of facts concerning ownership. [L. *abs*, away from, *trahĕre, tractum*, to draw.]

abstrict, *ab-strikt′*, *v.t.* (*biol.*) to set free (of spores, etc.), esp. by constriction of the stalk.—*n.* abstric′-tion. [L. *ab*, from, *stringĕre, strictum*, to tie.]

abstruse, *ab-strōōs′*, *adj.* (*arch.*) hidden: remote from apprehension: difficult to understand.—*adv.* abstruse′ly.—*n.* abstruse′ness. [L. *abstrūsus*, thrust away—*abs*, away, *trūdĕre, trūsum*, to thrust.]

absurd, *ab-surd′*, *adj.* opposed to reason: ridiculous. —*ns.* absurd′ity, absurd′ness.—*adv.* absurd′ly. [L. *absurdus*—*ab*, from, *surdus*, deaf, inaudible, indistinct, harsh, out of fashion, not to the purpose.]

abthane, *ab′thăn*, *n.* a monastic territory of the Columban church. [L.L. *abthania*—Gael. *ab-dhaine*, abbacy.]

abuna, *ä-bōō′nä*, *n.* an Ethiopian patriarch. [Ethiopian,—Ar., our father.]

abundance, *a-bund′ans*, *n.* ample sufficiency: great plenty: (*solo whist*) a call of nine tricks.—*n.* abund′ancy.—*adj.* abund′ant.—*adv.* abund′-antly. [See abound.]

abune, *a-būn′*, a Scots form of above.

aburst, *a-burst′*, *adv.* and *adj.* in a bursting condition. [Prep. a, and burst.]

abuse, *a-būz′*, *v.t.* to make a bad use of : to take undue advantage of : to betray (as confidence) : to misrepresent : to deceive : to revile : to maltreat : to violate.—*ns.* abuse (*a-būs′*), wrong use : evil or corrupt practice : deceit : hurt : undue advantage : betrayal (of confidence) : ill usage : violation : reviling ; abuser (*a-bū′zar*), abū′sion (-*zhan*), *Spens.* also -*zi-an*; now rare) misuse : deception : wrong : outrage : reviling.—*adj.* abū′sive (-*ziv*) wrong : containing, giving, of the nature of, abuse : coarsely reviling : (*arch.*) catachrestical.— *adv.* abū′sively.—*n.* abū′siveness. [L. *ab*, *ūtī*, *ūsus*, to use.]

abut, *a-but′*, *v.i.* to end or lean (*on, upon, against*) : to border :—*pr.p.* abutt′ing ; *pa.t.* and *pa.p.* abutt′ed.—*ns.* abut′ment, endwise meeting or junction : (*archit.*) that which a limb of an arch ends or rests against : place of abutting ; abutt′al, abutment : (in *pl.*) boundaries ; abutt′er, one whose property abuts.—*adj.* abutt′ing, confronting. [O.Fr. *abouter*, to touch by an end, and O.Fr. *abuter*, to touch at the end ; cf. also Fr. *aboutir*, to end at—*à*, to, *bout, but*, end ; see butt (4).]

Abutilon, *a-bū′ti-lon*, *n.* a showy-flowered genus of the mallow family, some species yielding fibres. [Ar. *aubūtilūn*.]

abuzz, *a-buz′*, *adv.* and *adj.* in a buzz. [Prep. a, buzz.]

aby, abye, *a-bī′*, *v.t.* (*arch.*) to pay the penalty for : to pay as a penalty.—*v.i.* to atone : to endure, continue :—*pa.t.* and *pa.p.* abought (*a-bawt′*). [Pfx.

a-, back, and O.E. *bycgan*, to buy ; merging and confused with abide.]

abysm, *a-bizm′*, *n.* (*arch.* and *poet.*) abyss.—*adj.* abys′mal, bottomless : unfathomable : very deep : abyssal.—*adv.* abys′mally. [O.Fr. *abisme*, from a L.L. superl. of *abyssus* ; see abyss.]

abyss, *a-bis′*, *n.* a bottomless gulf : primal chaos : the supposed water-filled cavity under the earth : hell : anything very deep : the depths of the sea : a measureless or apparently measureless chasm.— *adj.* abyss′al, abysmal—esp. of ocean depths. [Gr. *abyssos*, bottomless—*a-*, priv., *byssos*, depth, bottom.]

acacia, *a-kā′sh(y)a*, *n.* a wattle, any plant of the genus *Acacia*, akin to the sensitive plants : also applied to the *false acacia* (of the genus Robinia). [L.—Gr. *akakiā*.]

academy, *a-kad′a-mi*, *n.* (*orig.*) Plato's school of philosophy : a higher, would-be higher, or specialised school, or a university : a riding-school : a society for the promotion of science or art : the annual exhibition of the Royal Academy or of the Royal Scottish Academy.—*n.* (*poet.*) academe (*ak-a-dēm′*), an academy.—*adj.* academic (-*dem′*), of the philosophical school of Plato : of an academy or university : sceptical : scholarly : formal : theoretical only.—*n.* a Platonic philosopher : a member of a university : (*pl.*) purely theoretical arguments. —*adj.* academ′ical, academic.—*n.* (in *pl.*) university garb.—*n.* academ′icalism, close adherence to formal academic teaching.—*adv.* academ′-ically.—*ns.* academician (*a-kad-a-mish′an*) a member of an academy, esp. of the French Academy or the R.A. or R.S.A. ; academ′icism, academ′icalism ; acad′emist, (*obs.*) an academic : an academician. [Gr. *Akadēmeiā*, the garden near Athens where Plato taught.]

Acadian, *a-kā′di-an*, *adj.* and *n.* Nova Scotian. [Fr. *Acadie*, Nova Scotia—Micmac Ind. *ākāde*, abundance.]

acajou, *ak′a-zhōō, -zhōō′*, *n.* the cashew tree or its fruit or gum : a kind of mahogany. [See cashew.]

acaleph(e), *ak′a-lef, -lēf*, acalepha, -*lē′fā*, *ns.* old names for a jelly-fish—applied to a group of varying extension of coelenterates.—*n.* and *adj.* acalē′phan. [Gr. *akalēphē*, a nettle, sea-anemone.]

acanaceous, *ak-a-nā′shas*, *adj.* (*bot.*) prickly. [L. *acanos*, a kind of thistle—Gr. *akanos*—*akē*, a point.]

acanth, *a-kanth′*, *n.* acanthus.—*n.* acanth′a, a thorn, prickle : a spinous process.—*n.pl.* Acanthā′ceae (*ak-*), the acanthus family, akin to the figworts.— *adj.* acanthā′ceous, prickly : of the Acanthaceae. —*n.* acanth′in, strontium sulphate in skeletons of Radiolaria.—*adj.* acanth′ine, of, like, ornamented with, acanthus.—*n.pl.* acanthoceph′ala, a division of parasitic worms with spiny proboscis and no mouth or alimentary canal (Gr. *kephalē*, head).— *adjs.* acanthoid, like acanthus ; acanthopterygian (*ak-an-thop-tar-ij′yan*) spiny-finned (Gr. *pteryx, -ygos*, wing, fin) ; acanth′ous, spiny.—*n.* acanth′-us, any plant of the prickly-leaved genus *Acanthus*, esp. *A. spinosus* or *A. mollis* : a conventionalised representation of an acanthus leaf, as in Corinthian capitals. [Gr. *akantha*, prickle, *akanthos*, acanthus —*akē*, point.]

a cappella, *ä käp-pel′lä*, (*mus.*) " in church style," *i.e.* sung, as in the earlier church, without accompaniment or with accompaniment merely doubling the voice parts : (as a time indication) alla breve.— Also al′la cappel′la. [It.]

acapnia, *a-kap′ni-ä*, *n.* deficiency of carbon dioxide. [Gr. *a-*, priv., *kapnos*, smoke.]

acarus, *ak′a-ras*, *n.* a mite:—*pl.* ac′arī.—*adj.* acā′rian.—*ns.* acari′asis, disease due to mites ; ac′arid, one of the Acarida.—*n.pl.* Acar′ida (-*kar′*), the order of Arachnida to which mites and ticks belong.—*adj.* acar′idan.—*n.* acarid′ian. —*n.pl.* Acari′na, Acarida.—*adj.* ac′arine.—*n.* acarodomatium, acaridomatium(-*dō-mā′shyam*), a dwelling for mites provided by certain plants that benefit from their presence.—*pl.* acarodomā′tia. —*adj.* ac′aroid, mite-like.—*ns.* acarol′ogist ; acarol′ogy ; acaroph′ily, symbiotic association of plants with mites.—**acarine disease**, a disease

Neutral vowels in unaccented syllables : *el′a-mant, in′fant, ran′dam*

of bees due to mites in the spiracles. [Gr. *akari*, a mite—*akarēs*, too short to cut—*a-*, priv., *keirein*, to cut.]

acatalectic, *a-kat-ǝ-lek'tik*, *adj.* (*pros.*) having the full number of syllables.—*n.* an acatalectic verse. [Gr. *akatalēktos*—*a-*, priv.; see **catalectic**.]

acatalepsy, *a-kat-ǝ-lep'si*, *n.* (*Sceptic philos.*) the unknowableness to a certainty of all things.—*adj.* and *n.* **acatalep'tic**. [Gr. *akatalēpsiā*—*a-*, priv., *kata*, thoroughly, *lēpsis*, a seizing.]

acates, *ǝ-kāts'*, *n.pl.* (*obs.*) bought provisions.—*n.* **acāt'er,acāt'our**, an officer who bought provisions, a caterer. [O.Fr. *acat*—L.L. *accaptāre*, to acquire— L. *ad*, to, *captāre*, to seize; see **cate, cater**.]

acaulescent, *a-aw-les'ǝnt*, having a very short stem. [Gr. *a-*, priv., L. *caulis*, stem, and suff. *-escent*.]

accede, *ak-sēd'*, *v.i.* to come forward : to arrive (with *to*): to come to office or dignity : to join up, become a party, hence agree or assent (with *to*).—*ns.* **accēd'ence** ; **accēd'er**. [L. *accēdĕre*, *accēssum*, to go near—*ad*, to, *cēdĕre*, to go; see **cede**.]

accelerando, *ak-sel-ǝr-an'dō*, It. *ät-chel-er-än'dō*, *adj.* and *adv.* with increasing speed. [It.]

accelerate, *ak-sel'ǝr-āt*, *v.t.* to increase the speed of : to hasten the progress or occurrence of.—*v.i.* to become faster.—*ns.* **accel'erant**, an accelerating agent (also *adj.*) ; **accelera'tion**, increase of speed : rate of change of velocity : a cumulative advance ahead of the normal or theoretical : the power or means of accelerating :—*adj.* **accel'erative**, quickening.—*n.* **accel'erātor**, any person or thing that accelerates, esp. a substance that accelerates chemical action, a nerve or muscle that increases rate of action, an apparatus for changing the speed of a machine, or one for imparting high energies to atomic particles.—*adj.* **accel'eratory**. [L. *accelerāre*, *-ātum*—*ad*, to, *celer*, swift.]

accend, *ak-send'*, *v.i.* (*obs.*) to kindle.—*n.* **accen'sion**. [L. *accendĕre*, *accēnsum*, to kindle.]

accent, *ak'sǝnt*, *n.* modulation of the voice: tone of voice : stress on a syllable, word, or note : a mark used to direct this stress : a mark over a letter to indicate differences of stress, pitch, length, or quality of sound, or for other purpose : intensity : any mode of utterance characteristic of a region, a class, or an individual : a distinguishing mark : distinctive mode of expression, as of an artist : (*poet.*) a significant word, or words generally : (in art) a touch bringing out some particular effect : (*pl.*) speech, language.—*v.t.* (*ak-sent'*), to express or mark the accent of : to utter : (*esp. U.S.*) to accentuate.—*adj* **accent'ual**, according to, characterised by, accent.—*n.* **accentual'ity**.—*adv.* **accent'ually**.—*v.t* **accent'uate**, to mark, play, or pronounce with accent : to make prominent, emphasise.—*n.* **accentuā'tion**. [L. *accentus*—*ad*, to, *cantus*, song.]

Accentor, *ak-sent'or*, *-ǝr*, *n.* the hedge-sparrow genus. [L., one who sings with another—*ad*, to, *cantor*, singer.]

accept, *ak-sept'*, *v.t.* (old-fashioned or formal, *v.i.* with *of*) to take (something offered) : to receive (with approbation, favour, consent, resignation, or passivity) : to reply to, engaging more or less to comply : (of a bill of exchange—never with *of*) to promise to pay : to understand, take, in respect of meaning.—*adj.* **accept'able** (or *ak'*), worth accepting : welcome.—*n.* **accept'ableness** (or *ak'*). —*adv.* **accept'ably** (or *ak'*).—*ns.* **acceptabil'ity** ; **accept'ance**, accepting : favourable reception : favour : acceptableness : an agreeing to terms : an accepted bill : acceptation ; **accept'ancy** ; **accept'ant**, one who accepts.—*adj.* ready to receive.—*ns.* **accepta'tion**, a kind reception: sense in which a word, etc., is understood; **accept'er**.—*adj.* **accept'ive**, ready to receive.—*ns.* **acceptiv'ity** ; **accept'or**, one who accepts, esp. a bill of exchange. [L. *acceptāre*—*accipĕre*, *acceptum*—*ad*, to, *capĕre*, to take.]

acceptilation, *ak-sept-il-ā'shǝn*, *n.* (*Roman* and *Scots law*) the remission of a debt by fictitious payment : (*theol.*) Christ's atonement on the theory that only God's acceptance made his sacrifice

sufficient. [L. *acceptī lātiō*, accounting of (a thing as) received.]

access, *ak'sis*, still sometimes *-ses'*, *n.* approach : admittance : way, or opportunity, of approach or entrance : addition, accession : onset or attack of illness : a fit (of illness or passion).—*n.* and *adj.* **ac'cessary** (or *-ses'*), accessory (*esp.* in legal senses).—*n.* **accessibil'ity**.—*adj.* **access'ible**, within reach : approachable.—*adv.* **access'ibly**.— *n.* **accession** (*ak-sesh'ǝn*), act or event of acceding : a coming, esp. to office or dignity, or as an addition or new member : that which is added : (*law*) addition by nature or industry to existing property : acquisition of such addition by the owner of the existing property : assent : (*obs.*) an access, fit.— *v.t.* (*esp. U.S.*) to enter in a book as an accession to a library.—*adj.* **ac'cessory** (or *-ses'*), additional : subsidiary : adventitious : contributing : aiding, (*law*) participating in a crime, but not as a principal. —*n.* anything, esp. an item of equipment, that is secondary, additional, or non-essential : one who aids or gives countenance to a crime.—*adj.* **accessōr'ial**.—*adv.* **ac'cessorily** (or *-ses'*).— **accessory minerals**, those whose presence or absence is not regarded in naming a rock; **deed of accession** (*Scots law*), one by which a bankrupt's creditors accede to a settlement privately, *i.e.* by trust-deed. [See **accede**.]

acciaccatura, *ät-chäk-ä-tōō'rä*, *n.* (*mus.*) a short appoggiatura. [It.,—*acciaccare*, to crush.]

accidence, *ak'sid-ǝns*, *n.* the part of grammar treating of the ' accidents,' *i.e.* inflexions of words. —*n.* **ac'cident**, that which happens : an unforeseen or unexpected event : a chance : a mishap : an unessential quality or property : unevenness of surface.—*adj.* **accidental** (*-dent'*) happening by chance : not essential : (*mus.*) a sharp, flat, or natural not in the key-signature : (*paint.* ; in *pl.*) strong chance effects of light.—*ns.* **accident'alism**, the state or quality of being accidental : chance manner : (*med.*) a system based on symptoms rather than on causes : (*paint.*) use of accidentals : (*philos.*) the theory that events happen without a cause; **accidental'ity**.—*adv.* **accident'ally**.—*adj.* **accident'ed**, uneven : varied.—**the** (now commonly a) **chapter of accidents**, the unforeseen course of events : a series of accidents. [L. *accidēns*, *-entis*, pr.p. of *accidĕre*, to happen—*ad*, to, *cadĕre*, to fall.]

accidie, *ak'si-di*, *n.* acedia. [O.Fr. *accide*—L.L. *acēdia*; see **acedia**.]

accinge, *ak-sinj'*, *v.t.* to gird (*fig.*). [L. *ad*, to, *cingĕre*, to gird.]

accipitrine, *ak-sip'i-trīn*, *-trin*, *adj.* pertaining to hawks. [L. *accipiter*, a hawk.]

accite, *ak-sīt'*, *v.t.* to cite : to summon : (*Shak.*) to excite. [L.L. *accitāre*—*ad*, to, *citāre*, to cite, call.]

acclamation, *ak-lǝ-mā'shǝn*, *n.* a shout of applause or assent.—*v.t.* **acclaim** (*ǝ-klām'*), to hail or declare by acclamation.—*n.* acclamation.—*adj.* **acclamatory** (*ǝ-klam'ǝ-tǝr-i*). [L. *acclāmāre*— *ad*, to, *clāmāre*, *-ātum*, to shout; see **claim**.]

acclimatise, *ǝ-klī'mǝ-tīz*, *v.t.* to inure to a new climate.—Also **acclī'mate** (or *ak'li-*, *li-*).—*n.* **acclīmatīsā'tion**.—Also **acclīmatā'tion**, **acclimā'tion** (*ak-lī-*, *-li-*). [Fr. *acclimater*—*à*, to, *climat*, climate.]

acclivity, *ǝ-kliv'i-ti*, *n.* an upward slope.—*adjs.* **accliv'itous**, **accliv'ous**. [L. *ad*, to, *clīvus*, a slope.]

accloy, *ǝ-kloi'*, *v.t.* (*obs.*) to prick or lame with a horse-shoe nail : (*Spens.*) to clog, choke or encumber : to sate, cloy. [See **cloy**.]

accoast, *ǝ-kōst'*, an older form of **accost**.

accoil, *ǝ-koil'*, *n.* (*rare*) reception.—*v.i.*, *p.a.t.* (*Spens.*) **accoyld'**, assembled. [O.Fr. *acoil* (Fr. *accueil*).]

accolade, *ak-ol-ād'*, *-ād'*, *n.* an embrace : the action used in conferring knighthood, formerly an embrace, a kiss, now a tap on each shoulder with the flat of a sword : (*mus.*) a brace or other line connecting staves : a bracelike ornament. [Fr.,— L. *ad*, to, *collum*, neck.]

āte, fär, ásk; mē, hǝr (her); *mine; mōte; mūte; mōōn; dhen* (then)

accommodate, *ə-kom'ə-dāt*, *v.t.* to adapt: to make suitable: to adjust: to harmonise or force into consistency: to furnish or supply (*with*): to find or afford room, lodging, entertainment, for: to provide with a loan: to oblige.—*v.i.* to come to terms.—*adj.* **accomm'odable.**—*adj.* **accomm'odating**, ready to make adjustment: obliging: pliable: easily corrupted.—*n.* **accommoda'tion**, adaptation: adjustment, esp. of the eye to change of distance: wresting of language to a sense not intended: obligingness: settlement or compromise: supplying of wants (esp. housing or refreshment): a help towards satisfaction of a want: a convenience: lodgings, quarters (sometimes *pl.*): space for what is required: (*theol.*) adaptation of revelation by way of compromise with human ignorance or weakness: a loan of money.—*adj.* **accomm'odative.**—*ns.* **accomm'odativeness**; **accomm'odator**; **accommodation bill**, a bill drawn, accepted, or endorsed by one or more persons as security for a sum advanced to another by a third party, as a banker; **accommodation ladder**, a stairway outside of a ship for entering and leaving boats; **accommodation train**, (*U.S.*) one stopping at all or most stations on the way. [L. *accommodāre, -ātum—ad*, to, *commodus*, fitting.]

accompany, *ə-kum'pə-ni*, *v.t.* to go or be in company with: to attend: to go along with: to perform an accompaniment to or for: to associate, join, or couple.—*ns.* **accom'panier**; **accom'paniment**, that which accompanies: (*mus.*) a subsidiary part or parts supporting a solo; **accom'panist** (also **accom'panyist**), a player of accompaniments. [Fr. *accompagner*; see **company**.]

accomplice, *ə-kom'plis*, or *-kum'*, *n.* an associate in crime (*of* or *with* a person, *in* or *of* the crime): (*Shak.*) an associate. [L. *complex, -icis*, joined; pfx. unexplained.]

accomplish, *ə-kum'plish*, or *-kom'*, *v.t.* to complete: to fulfil: to achieve: to equip: to finish off, complete, in culture and acquirements.—*adjs.* **accom'plishable**; **accom'plished**, complete, finished, or highly skilled in acquirements, esp. graceful acquirements: polished.—*ns.* **accom'plisher**; **accom'plishment**, completion: achievement: rendering accomplished: a skilled acquirement in matters of culture or social grace, sometimes superficial or merely ornamental. [O.Fr. *acomplir* —L. *ad*, to, *complēre*, to fill up; see **complete**.]

accompt, accomptable, accomptant, obsolescent spellings of **account, accountable, accountant**, with the same pronunciation.

accorage. See **accourage.**

accord, *ə-kord'*, *v.i.* to agree: to be in correspondence (*with*).—*v.t.* to cause to agree: to reconcile: to grant (to a person).—*n.* agreement: harmony: the set of notes to which an instrument is tuned: grant: assent.—*adj.* **accord'able.**—*ns.* **accord'ance, accord'ancy**, agreement: conformity: a granting.—*adj.* **accord'ant**, agreeing: corresponding.—*adv.* **accord'antly.**—*n.* **accord'er.**—*adj.* **accord'ing**, in accordance: agreeing: harmonious.—*adv.* **accord'ingly**, (*obs.*) agreeably: suitably: in agreement (with what precedes): therefore.—**according as**, in proportion as: depending on whether; **according to**, in accordance with, or agreeably to: as asserted by; as **accords**, as may be appropriate; **of one's own accord**, of one's own spontaneous motion; **with one accord**, with spontaneous unanimity. [O.Fr. *acorder*—L. *ad*, to, *cor, cordis*, the heart.]

accordion, *ə-kor'di-ən*, *n.* a musical instrument consisting of folding bellows, keyboard, and free metal reeds.—*n.* **accord'ionist.**—**accordion-pleating**, *n.* pleating with very narrow folds like the bellows of an accordion. [**accord**.]

accost, *ə-kost'*, earlier **accoast**, *-kōst'*, *v.i.* (*Spens.*) to lie alongside, border: (*Spens.*) to fly along near the ground.—*v.t.* to approach and address: to speak first to: to solicit as a prostitute.—*n.* address: greeting.—*adj.* **accost'able.** [O.Fr. *acoster*— L.L. *accostāre*, to be side by side—L. *ad*, to, *costa*, a rib, a side.]

accouchement, *ä-kōōsh-män'*, *n.* delivery in childbed.—*ns.* **accoucheur** (*-shər'*), a man who assists women in child-birth; **accoucheuse** (*-shəz'*), a midwife. [Fr.]

account, *ə-kownt'*, *v.t.* to reckon: to judge, value: (*obs.*) to recount.—*v.i.* to count: to reckon: to keep accounts: to give a reason or explanation: to give a statement of money dealings: to answer as one responsible: to have the responsibility or credit (of killing or otherwise disposing of anything or anybody; with *for*).—*n.* counting: reckoning: a reckoning of money or other responsibilities: a statement of money owing: advantage: value: estimation: consideration: sake: a descriptive report: a statement: a narrative.—*n.* **accountabil'ity.**—*adj.* **account'able**, liable to account, responsible: explicable.—*n.* **account'ableness.**—*adv.* **account'ably.**—*ns.* **account'ancy**, the office or work of an accountant; **account'ant**, one who keeps, or is skilled in, accounts; **account'antship**; **account'-book**, a book for keeping accounts in.—*n.* and *adj.* **account'ing.**—**bring, call, to account**, to demand an explanation or clearing up of responsibilities of: to reprimand; **find one's account**, to derive advantage; **for account of**, on behalf of; **for the account**, for settlement on the regular settling-day; **go to one's (long) account**, go to the last judgment, die; **hold to account**, hold responsible; **in account with**, in business relations requiring the keeping of an account with; **make account of**, to set value upon; **on or to account**, as an instalment or interim payment; **on account of**, because of: **on no account**, not for any reason or consideration; **take into account**, to take into consideration; **take no account of**, to overlook; **turn to (good) account**, to turn to advantage. [O.Fr. *aconter*—L. *ad*, to, *computāre*, to reckon; see **compute, count**.]

accourage, *a-kur'ij*, **accorage**, *ak-or-āj'*, *v.t.* (*Spens.*) to encourage. [O.Fr. *acorager—à*, to, and *corage*, courage.]

accourt, *ə-kōrt'*, *v.t.* to entertain. [An invention of Spenser's—**court.**]

accoutre, *ə-kōō'tər*, *v.t.* to dress or equip (esp. a warrior):—*pr.p.* **accou'tring** (*ə-kōō'tər-ing*); *pa.p.* **accou'tred** (*-tərd*).—*n.* **accou'trement** (*-tər-* or *-trə-*), also obs. **accustrement, accoustrement**, equipping: (usu. in *pl.*) dress: military equipments. [Fr. *accoutrer*, earlier *accoustrer*; origin doubtful.]

accoy, *ə-koi'*, *v.t.* (*Spens.*) to still: to soothe: to subdue:—*pa.p.* **accoied', accoyed'.** [O.Fr. *acoyer—à*, to, and *coi*, quiet—L. *quiētus*; see **coy.**]

accoyld. See **accoil.**

accredit, *ə-kred'it*, *v.t.* to bring into credit: to furnish or send with credentials: to certify as meeting official requirements: to ascribe to (*with* the thing attributed): to attribute.—*adj.* **accred'ited.** [Fr. *accréditer—à*, to, *crédit*, credit.]

accrescent, *ak-res'ənt*, *adj.* growing: ever-increasing: (*bot.*) enlarged and persistent.—*n.* **accresc'ence.**—*v.i.* **accrēte'**, to grow together: to become attached.—*v.t.* to unite: to form or gather round itself.—*n.* **accrē'tion**, continued growth: the growing together of parts externally, or continuous coherence: that which has grown in such a way: an extraneous addition.—*adj.* **accrē'tive.** [L. *accrēscĕre, accrētum—ad*, to, *crēscĕre*, to grow.]

accrue (*Spens.* **accrew**), *ə-krōō'*, *v.i.* to come as an accession, increment, or product: to fall (to one) by way of advantage: to fall due: (*Spens.*) to increase.—*v.t.* (*Spens.*) to accumulate.—*n.* **accc⸱s al.** [O.Fr. *acrewe*, what grows up to the profit of the owner—*acreistre*—L. *accrēscĕre.*]

accubation, *ak-ū-bā'shən*, *n.* a lying or reclining on a couch. [L. *ad*, to, and *cubāre*, to lie down.]

accumbent, *ə-kumb'ənt*, *adj.* lying down or reclining on a couch: (*bot.*) having the radicle lying along the edges of the cotyledons. [L. *ad*, to, *cumbĕre*, to lie.]

accumulate, *ə-kūm'ūl-āt*, *v.t.* to heap or pile up: to amass.—*v.i.* to increase greatly: to go on increasing: to take degrees by accumulation, to take a higher degree at the same time with a lower, or at a shorter interval than usual (also *v.t.*).—*adj.* heaped up: amassed.—*n.* **accūmūlā'tion**, heaping up : a heap or mass.—*adj.* **accūm′ūlātive**, heaping up or growing by progressive addition : cumulative.—*n.* **accūm′ūlātor**, a thing or person that accumulates : a means of storing energy, esp. an electric battery that can be recharged by sending a reverse current through it. [L. *ad*, to, *cumulus*, a heap.]

accurate, *ak′ū-rit*, *adj.* exact.—*n.* **acc′ūracy** (*-ə-si*), correctness : exactness.—*adv.* **acc′ūrately**. *n.* **acc′ūrateness**. [L. *accūrātus*, performed with *care*—*ad*, to, *cūra*, care.]

accurse, *ə-kurs′*, *v.t.* to curse : to devote to misery or destruction.—*adj.* **accurs′ed** (or *-kurst′*), subjected to a curse : doomed : worthy of a curse. [O.E. pfx. *ā-*, and *cursian*, to curse.]

accuse, *ə-kūz′*, *v.t.* to bring a charge against (with *of*).—*n.* (*Shak.*) accusation.—*adj.* **accūs′able**. *ns.* **accūs′al**, accusation; **accūsā′tion**, the act of accusing : a charge brought.—*adj.* **accūs′ative**, accusing : (*gram.*) in or belonging to a case which expresses the direct object of transitive verbs— primarily expressing destination or the goal of motion.—*n.* the accusative case : a word in the accusative.—*adjs.* **accūsati′val**; **accūsatō′rial**, of an accuser; **accūs′atory**, containing accusation. —*adj.* **accused′**.—*n. sing.* or *pl.*, the person or persons accused.—*ns.* **accuse′ment** (*Spens.*) a charge; **accus′er**. [L. *accūsāre, -ātum*—*ad*, to, *causa*, cause, partly through O.Fr. *accuser*. Accusative case (L. *casus accūsātīvus*) is a mis-translation of Gr. *ptōsis aitiātikē*, the case indicating what is caused or effected—*aitiā*, cause (also accusation).]

accustom, *ə-kus′təm*, *v.t.* to make familiar by custom : to habituate.—*adj.* **accus′tomary**.— *adj.* **accus′tomed**, usual : frequent : habituated : in the habit.—*n.* **accus′tomedness**. [O.Fr. *acostumer* (Fr. *accoutumer*)—*à*, to, *costume, coustume*; see **custom**.]

ace, *ās*, *n.* a unit : the one in dice, cards, dominoes, etc. : a single point : (*tennis, golf*) a point or hole won at one stroke : a jot : a hairsbreadth : (*Burns*) one who surpasses : (*coll.*) an airman or other of distinguished achievement. [Fr. *as*—L. *as*, unity— *as*, Tarentine Doric form of Gr. *heis*, one.]

acedia, *ə-sē′di-ä*, *n.* listlessness : torpor : sloth. [Gr. *akēdiā, akēdeia*—*a-*, priv., *kēdos*, care. See **accidie**.]

acephalous, *a-sef′ə-las*, *adj.* headless. [Gr. *akeph-alos*—*a-*, priv., *kephalē*, head.]

Acer, *ā′sər*, *n.* the maple genus, giving name to the family **Acerā′ceae** (*as-*), *adj.* **acerā′ceous**. [L. *acer*, maple.]

acerb, *a-sərb′*, *adj.* bitter and sour.—*v.t.* **acerbate** (*as′ər-bāt*) to embitter : to irritate.—*n.* **acerb′ity**. [L. *acerbus*.]

acerose, *as′ər-ōs*, *adj.* (*prop.*) chaffy : (*bot.*) needle-pointed. [L. *acerōsus*—*acus, -eris*, chaff, confused with *acus, -ūs*, needle, or *acer*, sharp.]

acerous, *a-sē′rəs*, *adj.* without horns, antennae, tentacles. [Gr. *a-*, priv., *keras*, horn.]

acervate, *a-sər′vāt*, *adj.* heaped.—*n.* **acervā′tion**. [L. *acervāre, -ātum*, to heap.]

acescence, *as-es′əns*, **acescency**, *-i*, *ns.* souring : turning (of milk).—*adj.* **acesc′ent**. [L. *acēscere*, to sour—*acēre*, to be sour.]

acet-, aceto-, *as′it-(ō-)*, *a-*, *ə-set′-(ō-)*, *a-sēt′-(ō-)*, in composition, vinegar.—*ns.* **ac′etal**, a liquid formed by oxidation of alcohol, etc. : any of a class of compounds of which this is the type; **acetal′dehyde**, a liquid of characteristic smell, acetic aldehyde; **acet′amide**, the amide of acetic acid; **ac′etate**, a salt of acetic acid (**acetate silk**, an artificial silk made from cellulose acetate).—*adj.* **acetic** (*-sēt′, -set′*), of, of the nature of, producing, vinegar (**acetic acid**, the sour principle in vinegar, CH_3COOH).—*n.* **acetificā′tion** (*-set-*).—*v.t.* and *v.i.* **acet′ify**, to turn into vinegar.—*ns.* **ac′etone**, the simplest of the ketones : any ketone.—*adjs.* **acetose**, acetous; **acē′tous**, like, or producing, vinegar : sour.—*ns.* **ac′etyl**, the radical (CH_3CO) of acetic acid (**ac′etyl-salicyl′ic acid**, a substance got by heating salicylic acid with acetyl chloride— aspirin); **acetylene** (*a-set′i-lēn*), a powerful illu-

minant gas (C_2H_2), produced from calcium carbide and water. [L. *acētum*, vinegar.]

acetabulum, *as-et-ab′ū-ləm*, *n.* the hollow that receives the head of the thigh-bone : one of the cotyledons of the placenta of ruminants : the cavity that receives a leg in the body of insects : in various animals, a sucker :—*pl.* **acetab′ula**.—*adj.* **acetab′ular**. [L. *acētābulum*, a vinegar cup— *acētum*, vinegar.]

Achaean, *a-kē′ən*, **Achaian**, *-kī′, -kā′, adj.* belonging to *Achāiā*, in the Peloponnese, or to Greece generally.—Also *n.*

achates, *a-chāts′*, (*Spens.*). Same as **acates**.

Achates, *a-kā′tēz*, *n.* an intimate and trusty comrade, from Aeneas's friend the 'fidus Achates' of the Aeneid.

ache, *āk* (formerly *äch, āch*), *n.* a continued pain.— *v.i.* (*āk*) to be in continued pain.—*ns.* **ach′age** (*Tennyson*); **ach′ing**.—*adj.* **ach′y**. [The verb was properly *ake*, the noun *ache*, as in *speak, speech*.— O.E. *acan* (*vb.*), *æce* (*n.*).]

ache, *āch*. Same as **aitch**.

achene, *a-kēn′*, **achaenium**, **achenium**, *a-kē′ni-əm*, *n.* a dry, indehiscent, one-seeded fruit, formed of one carpel, the seed separate from the fruit wall, as in the buttercup.—*adj.* **achē′nial**.—*n.* **achae′-nocarp**, any dry, indehiscent fruit, esp. an achene. [From Gr. *a-*, priv., and *chainein*, to gape.]

Achernar, *ā′kər-när*, *n.* a first-magnitude star in the constellation Eridanus. [Ar. *ākhir al nahr*, end of the river (Eridanus).]

Acheron, *ak′ər-on*, *n.* (*Gr. myth.*) one of the rivers of the infernal regions.—*adj.* **Acheron′tic**. [Gr. *Acherōn*.]

Acheulean, Acheulian, *a-shə′li-ən*, *a-shōō′li-ən*; *adj.* belonging to an early Palaeolithic culture above the Chellean and below the Mousterian. [Saint *Acheul*, near Amiens, where implements of this period are found in river deposits.]

achieve (*obs.* **atchieve**), *ə-chēv′*, *v.t.* to bring to a successful issue : (*obs.*) to end : to perform : to accomplish : to win.—*adj.* **achiev′able**.—*n.* **achieve′ment**, achieving : an exploit : an escutcheon or armorial shield granted in memory of some achievement : escutcheon, armour, etc., hung over a tomb : a hatchment. [Fr. *achever*, from *à chief* (*venir*)—L.L. *ad caput*, to a head; see **chief, hatchment**.]

Achillean, *ak-il-ē′ən*, *adj.* like *Achilles*, the great Greek hero in the Trojan war, brave, swift of foot, unrelenting in wrath, invulnerable except in the heel, by which his mother held him when she dipped him in the Styx.—**Achilles′ tendon**, the attachment of the soleus and gastrocnemius muscles of the calf of the leg to the heel-bone.

Achitophel, Ahithophel, *ə-kit′*, or *-hit′ō-fel*, *n.* (*Shak.*) a cautious person : (after Dryden's application to Shaftesbury) an able but unprincipled counsellor. [From David's counsellor who abetted the rebellion of Absalom.]

achlamydeous, *ak-lə-mid′i-əs*, *adj.* (*bot.*) without perianth. [Gr. *a-*, priv., *chlamys, -ydos*, a mantle.]

achondroplasia, *ak-on-drō-plā′zhi-ä*, *n.* defective formation of cartilage, resulting in dwarfism.— *adj.* **achondroplastic** (*-plas′tik*). [Gr. *a-*, priv., *chondros*, cartilage, *plassein*, to make.]

achromatic, *ak-rō-mat′ik*, *adj.* transmitting light without much chromatic aberration.—*adv.* **achro-mat′ically**.—*ns.* **achrō′matin**, the part of a cell nucleus that does not stain with basic dyes; **achrō′matism**, the state of being achromatic.— *v.t.* **achrō′matise**, to render achromatic. [Gr. *a-*, priv., *chrōma, -atos*, colour.]

acicular, *as-ik′ū-lər*, *adj.* needle-shaped; slender and sharp-pointed.—*adj.* **acic′ulate**, marked as if with needle-scratches. [L. *acicula*, dim. of *acus*, a needle.]

acid, *as′id*, *adj.* sharp : sour : (*chem.*) pertaining to, of the nature of, having the properties of, an acid : (*geol.*) containing a large proportion of silica.—*n.* a sour substance : (*chem.*) one of a class of substances, many of them sour, containing hydrogen replaceable by a metal to form a salt.—*vs.t.* **acid′ify**, to make acid : to convert into an acid :—

pr.p. acid'ifying ; *pa.t.* and *pa.p.* acid'ified ; acid'-ūlate, to make slightly acid.—*adjs.* acid'ic ; acidifi'able ; acid'ūlous, slightly sour : subacid : containing carbonic acid, as mineral waters : (*fig.*) caustic, sharp.—*ns.* acidifica'tion ; acid'ity, the quality of being acid or sour : the extent to which a solution is acid ; acidim'etry, measurement of the concentration of acids by titration with a standard solution of alkali ; acidim'eter, apparatus for performing this ; acidō'sis (*med.*), presence of acids in the blood beyond normal limits.—acid drop, a sweet flavoured with tartaric acid ; acid dye, a dye-stuff with acid properties ; acid salt, a salt in which only part of the replaceable hydrogen is replaced by a metal ; acid test, a test for gold by acid : (*fig.*) a searching test. [L. *acidus*, sour—*acēre*, to be sour.]

acierate, *as'i-ər-āt*, *v.t.*, to turn into steel.—*n.* ac'ierage, the covering of a metal plate with a film of iron. [Fr. *aciérer—acier*, steel.—L.L. *aciārium* (*ferrum*), lit. edging (iron)—L. *aciēs*, edge.]

acinaciform, *as-in-as'i-form*, *adj.* (*bot.*) scimitar-shaped. [Gr. *akīnakēs*, a short sword (a Persian word), and L. *forma*, shape.]

acinus, *as'i-nəs*, *n.* one of the small fruits that compose an aggregate fruit, as in the raspberry : an aggregate fruit : a pip : a racemose gland :—*pl.* ac'ini.—*adjs.* acinā'ceous, full of pips : berry-like : like a cluster of grapes ; acin'iform, berry-like. [L. *acinus*, berry, pip.]

ack-ack, *ak-ak*, *adj.* anti-aircraft.—*adv.* ack-emm'a, ante meridiem. [Formerly signallers' names for the letters AA, AM.]

acknow, *ak-nō'*, *v.t.* (*obs.*) to recognise : to acknowledge.—*adj.* acknowne' (*Shak.*), confessedly cognisant. [O.E. *on*, in, on, *cnāwan*, to know.]

acknowledge, *ak-nol'ij*, *v.t.* to own a knowledge of : to own as true, or genuine, or valid, or one's own : to confess : to own with gratitude or thanks : to admit or intimate the receipt of.—*adj.* acknowl'edgeable.—*adv.* acknowl'edgeably.—*n.* acknowl'edgment (sometimes acknowl'edgement), recognition : admission : confession : thanks : an intimation of receipt. [From acknow, with suffix -*ledge*.]

aclinic, *ak-lin'ik*, *adj.* without inclination, or magnetic dip. [Gr. *aklīnēs*, horizontal—*a-*, priv., *klīnein*, to tilt.]

acme, *ak'mi*, *n.* the top or highest point : the culmination or perfection in the career of anything : (*arch.*) crisis, as of a disease.—*n.* ac'mite, a soda pyroxene whose crystals often show a steep pyramid. [Gr. *akmē—akē*, a point.]

acne, *ak'ni*, *n.* inflammation of the sebaceous follicles, as on the nose. [Perh. Gr. *akmē*, a point.]

acock, *ə-kok'*, *adv.* in a cocked manner : defiantly.—acock-bill, (*naut.*) having the end pointing upward, as an anchor ready for dropping, or yards topped up (a sign of mourning). [Prep. a, and cock.]

acoemeti, *a-sem'i-tī*, *n.pl.* an Eastern order of monks (5th-6th cent.), who by alternating choirs kept divine service going on day and night. [Latinised pl. of Gr. *akoimētos*, sleepless—*a-*, priv., and *koimaein*, to put to sleep.]

acold, *ə-kōld'*, *adj.* (*Shak.*) chilled. [Prob. O.E. *ācōlod*, *pa.p.* of *ācōlian*—pfx. *ā-*, intens., and *cōlian*, to cool.]

acolouthos, *ak-o-lōō'thos*, *n.* (*hist.*) the head of the Varangian guard of the Byzantine emperors.—*ns.* (*obs.*) acolou'thite, an acolyte ; acolyte (*ak'ə-līt*), acolyth (-*lith*), (*R.C. Church*) one in minor orders, next below sub-deacon : an inferior church officer : an attendant or assistant. [Gr. *akolouthos*, an attendant—*akoloutheein*, to follow.]

aconite, *ak'ə-nīt*, *n.* wolf's-bane or monk's-hood (*Aconitum*) : poison got from it, or (*poet.*) deadly poison in general (often aconi'tum).—*adj.* aconit'ic.—*n.* aconitine (-*kon'*), a poisonous alkaloid from aconite.—winter aconite, an early-flowering ranunculaceous plant (*Eranthis hyemalis*). [L. *aconītum*—Gr. *akoniton*.]

acorn, *ā'korn*, *n.* the fruit of the oak.—*n.* ā'corn-cup', the woody cup-shaped involucre of an acorn.

—*adj.* ā'corned.—*n.* ā'corn-shell, a cirripede of the genus Balanus (L., acorn). [O.E. *æcern*; form influenced by confusion with corn and perh. oak (Northern *aik*, O.E. *āc*).]

Acorus, *ak'ə-rəs*, *n.* the sweet-flag genus of the arum family. [Latinised from Gr. *akoros*.]

acosmism, *a-koz'mizm*, *n.* disbelief in the existence of an eternal world, or of a world distinct from God.—*n.* acos'mist. [Gr. *a-*, priv., and *kosmos*, the world.]

acotyledon, *a-kot-i-lē'dən*, *n.* a cryptogam.—*adj.* acotylē'donous. [Gr. *a-*, priv., and cotyledon.]

acouchy, *ə-kōō'shē*, a kind of agouti. [Tupi *acuchy*.]

acoustic, -al, *ə-kōōs'tik*, *-əl*, or *-kows'*, *adjs.* pertaining to the sense of hearing or to the theory of sounds : used in hearing, auditory : operated by sound vibrations, as an *acoustic mine*.—*adv.* acous'tically.—*n.* acoust'ics, (*pl.* in form, treated as *sing.*) the science of sound : (as *pl.*) acoustic properties. [Gr. *akoustikos—akouein*, to hear.]

acquaint, *ə-kwānt'*, *v.t.* to let or make to know : to inform.—*adj.* (*Scot.* and *Northern*) acquainted. —*ns.* acquaint'ance, knowledge, esp. falling short of intimacy : a person (sometimes persons) known slightly ; acquaint'anceship, slight knowledge.—*adj.* acquaint'ed, personally known : having personal knowledge of (usu. with *with*). [O.Fr. *acointer*—L.L. *accognitāre*—L. *ad*, to, *cognitus*, known.]

acquest, *ə-kwest'*, *n.* acquisition : a thing acquired. [O.Fr.; see acquist.]

acquiesce, *ak-wi-es'*, *v.i.* to rest satisfied or without making opposition : to assent (with *in*).—*n.* acquiesc'ence, quiet assent or submission.—*adj.* acquiesc'ent, acquiescing.—*n.* one who acquiesces.—*advs.* acquiesc'ently, acquiesc'ingly. [L. *acquiēscĕre—ad*, to, *quiēs*, rest.]

acquire, *ə-kwīr'*, *v.t.* to gain : to attain to.—*n.* acquirabil'ity.—*adjs.* acquir'able, that may be acquired ; acquired'.—*ns.* acquire'ment, acquisition : something learned or got by effort, not a gift of nature ; acquisition (*ak-wi-zish'ən*), the act of acquiring : that which is acquired.—*adj.* acquis'itive (*ə-kwiz'*) able or ready to acquire—*n.* acquis'-itiveness, propensity to acquire ; acquist (*ə-kwist'* ; *Milt.*), acquisition.—acquired character, a character originating in the actual life of an organism, not inherited ; acquired taste, a liking that comes after some experience : a thing so liked (often ironically). [L. *acquīrĕre*, *-quisītum—ad*, to, *quaerĕre*, to seek.]

acquit, *ə-kwit'*, (*obs.*) acquite, acquight, *ə-kwīt'*, *v.t.* to free : to release : to discharge, as a debt : to discharge (oneself of a duty) : hence to behave, conduct (oneself) : to prove (oneself) : to release from an accusation :—*pr.p.* acquitt'ing ; *pa.t.* and *pa.p.* acquitt'ed, *obs.* acquit'.—*ns.* acquit'ment (*obs.*) ; acquitt'al, a judicial discharge from an accusation ; acquitt'ance, a discharge from an obligation or debt : a receipt in evidence of such a discharge.—*v.t.* (*Shak.*) to acquit, clear. [O.Fr. *aquiter*—L. *ad*, to, *quiētāre*, to quiet, settle ; see quit.]

acrawl, *ə-krawl'*, *adv.* crawling (*with*). [Prep. a, and crawl.]

acre, *ā'kər*, *n.* a measure of 4840 sq. yards : (Scottish acre) 6150.4 sq. yards, (Irish) 7840 sq. yards—both obsolete : (*pl.*) lands, estates.—*n.* acreage (*ā'kər-ij*), area in acres.—*adj.* acred (*ā'kərd*), landed.—*n.* a'cre('s)-breadth, 22 yards. [O.E. *æcer*; Ger. *acker*, L. *ager*, Gr. *agros*, Sans. *ajras*, a plain.]

acrid, *ak'rid*, *adj.* biting : pungent.—*n.* acrid'ity. [L. *ācer*, *ācris*, sharp, keen ; suffix perh. in imitation of acid.]

acridin(e) *ak'ri-dēn*, -*din*, *n.* a compound found in coal-tar, a parent substance of dyes and anti-bacterial drugs.—*n.* acriflavin(e) (-*flā'vēn*, -*vin*), a powerful antiseptic. [acrid, suff. -*ine*, flavin(e).]

acrimony, *ak'ri-mən-i*, *n.* bitterness of feeling or language.—*adj.* acrimō'nious.—*adv.* acrimō'niously. [L. *ācrimōnia—ācer*, sharp.]

Neutral vowels in unaccented syllables : *el'ə-mənt*, *in'fənt*, *ran'dəm*

acro-, in composition, tip, point, summit. [Gr. *akron*, tip, end, *akros*, highest, outermost.]

acroamatic, -al, *ak-rō-ə-mat'ik, -əl*, *adjs.* oral (not published): esoteric. [Gr. *akroāmatikos—akroāma*, anything to be listened to—*akroaesthai*, to listen.]

acrobat, *ak'rō-bat*, *n.* a rope-dancer: a tumbler: a performer of gymnastic feats.—*adj.* **acrobat'ic**. —*n.pl.* **acrobat'ics**, acrobatic performances (esp. *fig.*); **ac'robatism**, the art of the acrobat. [Gr. *akrobatēs*, acrobat, *akrobatos*, walking on tiptoe— *akron*, point, and the root of *bainein*, to go.]

acrogen, *ak'rō-jen*, *n.* a cryptogam with growing-point at the tip—a fern or moss.—*adj.* **acrogenous** (*a-kroj'i-nəs*). [Gr. *akron*, *-genēs*, born.]

acrolein, *a-krō'li-in*, *n.* (*chem.*) the aldehyde of allyl alcohol, a pungent-smelling colourless liquid. [L. *ācer*, *ācris*, sharp, *olēre*, to smell.]

acrolith, *ak'rō-lith*, *n.* a wooden statue with stone extremities. [Gr. *akrolithos—akron*, point, *lithos*, stone.]

acromegaly, *ak-rō-meg'ə-li*, *n.* a disease character-ised by overgrowth, esp. of the face and extremities. [Gr. *akron*, point, *megas*, *megalos*, great.]

acromion, *a-krō'mi-on*, *n.* a process of the spine of the scapula (also **acromion process**).—*adj.* **acro'mial**. [Gr. *akros*, outermost, *ōmos*, shoulder.]

acronychal, *a-kron'ik-əl*, *adj.* at nightfall (of the rising or setting of stars).—*adv.* **acron'ychally**. [Gr. *akronychos*, at nightfall—*akron*, point, *nychos*, *-eos*, night.]

acronym, *ak'rō-nim*, *n.* a word formed from the initial letters of other words, as *radar*. [**acro-**, and Gr. *onoma*, name.]

acropetal, *ə-krop'i-tl*, *adj.* in the direction of the apex.—*adv.* **acrop'etally**. [Gr. *akron*, L. *petěre*, to seek.]

acrophony, *a-krof'ən-i*, *n.* the use of a symbol (derived from an ideogram) to represent the initial sound only of the name of the object for which the ideogram stood.—*adjs.* **acrophonet'ic**, **acrophon'ic** (*-fon'*). [**acro-**, Gr. *phōnē*, sound.]

acropolis, *a-krop'ol-is*, *ə-krop'ə-lis*, *n.* a citadel, esp. that of Athens. [Gr. *akropolis—akros*, highest, *polis*, a city.]

acrospire, *ak'rō-spīr*, *n.* (*bot.*) the first leaf that sprouts from a germinating seed. [Gr. *akros*, *speira*, anything twisted round.]

across, *ə-kros'*, *adv.* and *prep.* from side to side (of): on or to the other side (of): crosswise.— **come across**, to alight upon, meet: (*slang*) to hand over information, confession, money, etc. in answer to demand or inducement; **get** or **come across**, to take effect (on the audience across the footlights, and so generally); **put** or **get it across**, to make acceptable, to bring to a successful issue. [Prep. **a**, **cross**.]

acrostic, *ə-kros'tik*, *n.* a poem or puzzle in which the first (or last) letters of each line spell a word or sentence. [Gr. *akros*, extreme, *stichos*, a line.]

acroterion, *ak-rō-tē'ri-on*, *n.* (*archit.*) a pedestal or ornament at the top or side angle of a pedi-ment:—*pl.* **acrotē'ria**.—Also **acroterium**, **acrō'-ter** (or *ak'*).—*adj.* **acrotē'rial**. [Gr. *akrōtērion*, ex-tremity—*akros*.]

acrotism, *ak'rot-izm*, *n.* (*med.*) absence of pulsation. [Gr. *a-*, priv., *krotos*, sound (made by striking).]

acrylic acid, *a-kril'ik as'id*, a very reactive acid belonging to the series of oleic acids, obtainable from acrolein by oxidation.—**acrylic resins**, thermoplastic resins formed by the polymerisation of esters, amides, etc. derived from acrylic acid. [*acrolein*, Gr. *hylē*, matter.]

act, *akt*, *v.i.* to exert force or influence: to produce an effect: to behave oneself: to perform, as on the stage: to feign: to be suitable for performance.— *v.t.* to perform: to imitate or play the part of.—*n.* something done or doing: an exploit: the very process (of doing something): a decree: a legisla-tive enactment: a written instrument in verifica-tion: (*theol.*) something done once for all: (*R.C. church*) a short prayer: a distinct main section of a play: in universities, a public disputation or lecture maintained by a candidate for a degree.—*ns.* **actabil'ity**; **act'ing**, action: act or art of per-forming an assumed or a dramatic part: feigning:

—*adj.* performing some duty temporarily, or for another.—*ns.* **act'or**, one who acts: a stage-player:—*fem.* **act'ress**; **act'ure** (*Shak.*, *Lover's Compl.*) action, performance.—**act of God**, a result of natural forces, unexpected and not preventable by human foresight; **act of grace**, a favour, esp. a pardon granted by a sovereign; **act on**, to exert an influence on: to act in accord-ance with; **act up to**, to come in practice up to the standard of: to fulfil. [L. *āctus*, *-ūs*, an action, doing, *āctum*, a thing done, *āctor*, a doer, actor; *agěre*, *āctum*, to do, drive.]

Actaeon, *ak-tē'ən*, *n.* a hunter transformed into a stag by Artemis: hence one with horns implanted upon him, a cuckold.—*v.t.* to cuckold. [L. *Actaeōn*—Gr. *Aktaiōn*.]

actin(o)-, *ak'tin-(o-)*, in composition, ray.—*adj.* **actinal** (*ak-tī'nəl*, or *ak'ti-nəl*), belonging to the radiating bands on the body of an echinoderm where the tube-like feet are, or to the region of the mouth and tentacles in Anthozoa.—*ns.* **actinia** (*-tin'*), a sea-anemone (properly a particular genus).—*n.* and *adj.* **actin'ian**.—*adj.* **actin'ic**, of or showing actinism (**actinic rays**, those rays that have a marked chemical action, esp. the ultra-violet).—*ns.* **ac'tinism**, the chemical action of radiant energy; **actin'ium**, a radioactive metal (atomic number 89) found in pitchblende; **actin'-olite**, a green amphibole (Gr. *lithos*, a stone); **actinom'eter**, an instrument for measuring the heat-intensity or the actinic effect of light-rays.— *adj.* **actinomor'phic**, (*biol.*) radially symmetrical (Gr. *morphē*, form).—*ns.* **Actinomyces** (*-mī'sēz*; Gr. *mykēs*, fungus) the ray-fungus, a genus of minute fungi or filamentous bacteria with radiating mycelium; **actinomycosis** (*-kō'sis*), lumpy-jaw in cattle, etc., or other disease caused by Actinomyces; **ac'tinon**, actinium emanation, an isotope of radon; **actinother'apy**, the treatment of disease by exposure to rays, esp. ultra-violet rays.—*n.pl.* **Actinozo'a**, the Anthozoa. [Gr. *aktīs*, *aktīnos*, ray.]

action, *ak'shən*, *n.* acting: activity: behaviour: a deed: operation: gesture: fighting: a battle: a lawsuit, or proceedings in a court: mode of moving the legs: the movement of events in a drama, novel, etc.: mechanism, esp. of a keyboard instru-ment.—*adjs.* **ac'tionable**, giving ground for a lawsuit; **ac'tion-taking** (*Shak.*), resorting to law instead of fighting.—**action committee**, a Communist committee whose function is to liquid-ate non-Communists; **action radius**, the distance a ship or aircraft can go without running out of fuel before reaching its base or starting-point again; **action station**, a post to be manned during a battle. [Fr.,—L. *āctiō*, *-ōnis*.]

active, *ak'tiv*, *adj.* acting: in actual operation: given to action: brisk: busy: nimble: practical, as opp. to speculative: effective: (*gram.*) of that voice in which the subject of the verb represents the doer of the action.—*v.t.* **ac'tivate**, to make active: to increase the energy of: to increase the capacity for absorption in (charcoal): to increase the biological activity of (sewage, etc.) by aeration: to stimulate.—*ns.* **activā'tion**; **ac'tivātor**.—*adv.* **ac'tively**.—*ns.* **ac'tivism**, a philosophy of creative will, esp. the ethical idealism of Rudolf Eucken (1846-1926): a policy of vigorous action; **ac'tivist**; **activ'ity**, quality, state, or fact of being active: (esp. in *pl.*) doings; **ac'tiveness**.—**active life**, (*theol.*) life devoted to good works as opposed to contemplation; **active list**, a list of full-pay officers engaged in or available for service; **active service**, service in the battle area, or (*orig. U.S.*) in army, navy or air force even in time of peace. [L. *āctivus*.]

acton, *ak'tən*, **ha(c)queton**, *hak'(i-)tən*, *n.* a stuffed jacket worn under a coat of mail. [O.Fr. *auqueton*, through Sp. from Ar. *al qūtun*, the cotton.]

actor, actress. See under **act**.

actual, *ak'tū-əl*, *adj.* (*Shak.*) of the nature of an action: real: existing in fact: at the time being —*v.t.* **ac'tualise**, to make actual: to realise in action.—*ns.* **ac'tualist**, one who looks to actual facts; **actuality** (*-al'i-ti*), fact or state of being

actual : realism : something that really **is**.—*adv.*
ac'tually, as a matter of fact : truly, however
little one might expect it. [Fr. *actuel*—L.L.
āctuālis.]

actuary, *akt'ū-ər-i, n.* a registrar or clerk (still in
the Convocation of Canterbury) : one who makes
the calculations connected with insurance.—*adj.*
actuarial (*-ā'ri-əl*). [L. *āctuārius* (*scriba*), an
amanuensis, a clerk.]

actuate, *akt'ū-āt, v.t.* to put into, or incite to,
action.—*v.i.* to act.—*n.* actua'tion. [L. *āctus*,
action ; see **act**.]

acuity, *ə-kū'i-ti, n.* sharpness. [L.L. *acuitās*,
-*ātis*—L. *acus*, needle.]

aculeate(d), *ə-kū'li-āt(-id), adjs.* pointed : prickly :
having a sting : stinging. [L. *aculeātus*—*aculeus*,
a sting, goad, dim. of *acus*, needle.]

acumen, *ə-kū'men, n.* sharpness : quickness of
perception : penetration.—*v.t.* acu'minate, to
sharpen : to give point to.—*v.i.* (*rare*) to taper.—
adj. (*bot.*) tapering in long hollow curves to a
point (also acū'minated).—*n.* acuminā'tion.
[L. *acūmen*, -*inis*, a point.]

acupressure, *ak-ū-presh'ər, n.* arrest of haemorrhage
by a needle pressing across the artery.—*n.* acu-
punc'ture, puncturing with needles to relieve
pain. [L. *acus*, needle, **pressure, puncture**.]

acute, *ə-kūt', adj.* sharp : sharp-pointed : (*bot.*)
ending in an acute angle : keen : mentally penetrating : piercing : finely discriminating : keenly
perceptive : shrewd : urgently pressing.—*n.* an acute
accent.—*adv.* acute'ly.—*n.* acute'ness.—acute
accent, a mark (´) originally indicating a rising
pitch, now used for various purposes ; acute
angle, one less than a right angle ; acute **disease**,
one that comes to a crisis. [L. *acūtus*, pa.p. of
acuēre, to sharpen, from root *ak*, sharp.]

acyclic, *ə-sī'klik, adj.* not periodic : (*bot.*) not
whorled : (*chem.*) with open-chain structure, aliphatic. [Gr. *a-*, priv., *kyklos*, a wheel.]

ad, *ad, n.* (*coll.*) for **advertisement**.

adage, *ad'ij, n.* an old saying : a proverb. [Fr.,—L.
adagium—*ad*, to, and root of *āiō*, I say.]

adagio, *ä-dä'j(y)ō, adv.* (*mus.*) slowly.—*adj.* slow.—
n. a slow movement : a piece in adagio time :—*pl.*
ada'gios. [It. *ad agio*, at ease, leisure.]

Adam, *ad'əm, n.* the first man according to Genesis :
unregenerate human nature : (*Shak.*) a gaoler
(perh. as wearing buff).—*adjs.* Adamic, al
(*ə-dam'ik, -əl*), of or like Adam : naked.—*n.* Ad'-
amite, a descendant of Adam : one who goes
naked, esp. of a 2nd century sect in North Africa.—
adjs. Adamit'ic, -al.—*n.* Ad'amitism.—Adam's
ale or **wine**, water ; Adam's **apple**, the projection
of the thyroid cartilage in front of the throat,
fabled to be part of the forbidden fruit stuck in
Adam's throat : forbidden fruit (see **forbid**);
Adam's **flannel**, mullein ; Adam's **needle**,
yucca. [Heb. *Ādām*.]

adamant, *ad'ə-mənt, n.* a vaguely imagined very
hard substance : (*obs.*) the diamond : (*obs.*) lodestone.—*adjs.* adamantē'an (*Milt.*), hard as adamant ; adamantine (*-man'tin*), made of or like
adamant : unbreakable : impregnable : impenetrable : (*obs.*) magnetically attractive.—adamantine
lustre (*min.*) a lustre approaching the metallic but
without opacity. [Gr. *adamas*, -*antos*, prob. orig.
steel, also diamond—*a-*, priv., and *damaein*, to
tame, overcome.]

Adansonia, *ad-an-sō'ni-ä, n.* the baobab genus.
[After Michel *Adanson*, French botanist (1727-
1806).]

adapt, *ə-dapt', v.t.* to make fit or suitable.—*n.*
adaptabil'ity.—*adj.* adapt'able.—*n.* adaptation
(*ad-əp-tā'shən*), the fact, act, process, or result of
adapting : a character by which anything is adapted
to conditions : adjustment.—*adjs.* adapt'ative ;
adapt'ed, modified to suit : suitable.—*n.*
adapt'er, **-or**, one who, or that which, adapts :
an attachment or accessory enabling a piece of
apparatus to be used for a purpose, or in conditions,
other than that, or those, for which it was orig.
intended.—*adj.* adapt'ive.—*adv.* adapt'ively.—
n. adapt'iveness. [Fr. *adapter*—L. *adaptāre*—
ad, to, and *aptāre*, to fit.]

Adar, *ä'där*, or *ā'där, n.* the twelfth month of the
Jewish ecclesiastical, the sixth of the civil, year
(part of February and March). [Heb. *adār*.]

adaw, *ə-daw', v.t.* (*Spens.*) to daunt : to subdue :
to abate.—*v.i.* to subside. [App. a 16th cent.
misunderstanding of the M.E. adv. *adaw*, out of
life—O.E. of *dagum*, from days (dat. pl.).]

adaxial, *ad-aks'i-əl, adj.* next or towards the axis.
[L. *ad*, to.]

adays, *ə-dāz', adv.* (*obs.*) by day : (*Spens.*) daily.
[O.E. *dæges*, gen. of *dæg*, day, with prep. *a* added
later.]

add, *ad, v.t.* to put, join, or annex (to something
else) : to sum up, compute the sum of : to say
further.—*v.i.* to make an addition : (with *up*) to
amount on adding (*lit.* and *fig.*).—*ns.* add'er, one
who adds : a machine for adding ; additamentit
(*ə-dit'ə-mənt*, or *ad'*) something added ; addi'tion,
the act of adding : a thing added : the part of
arithmetic or algebra that deals with adding :
(*Shak.*) title, designation.—*adj.* addi'tional,
added.—*adv.* addi'tionally.—*adjs.* additi'tious,
increasing ; add'itive, of the nature of an addition :
characterised by addition : to be added.—*adv.*
add'itively.—**addition compound, product**,
(*chem.*) one formed by the direct union of two or
more substances. [L. *addĕre, additum*—*ad*, to, *dăre*,
to put.]

addax, *ad'aks, n.* a large African antelope with
long twisted horns. [L., from an African word.]

addeem, *ə-dēm', v.t.* (*obs.*) to adjudge : to award.
[Pfx. *ad-*, and **deem**.]

addendum, *a-den'dəm, n.* a thing to be added :—
pl. adden'da. [L. gerundive of *addĕre*; see **add**.]

adder, *ad'ər, n.* a viper.—*ns.* add'erstone, a prehistoric spindle-whorl or bead, popularly attributed
to the agency of adders ; ad'der's-tongue, a genus
(*Ophioglossum*) of ferns whose spores grow on a
spike resembling a snake's tongue ; ad'der's-wort,
add'erwort, the bistort, or snakeweed, supposed
to cure snake-bite. [O.E. *nædre* (*an adder* for
a nadder; cf. obs. Ger. *atter* for *natter*).]

addict, *ə-dikt', v.t.* to give up, devote, apply
habitually.—*adj.* (*obs.*) addicted.—*n.* (*ad'ikt*) a
slave to a habit or vice, esp. drugs.—*adj.* addict'-
ed, inclined or given up (with *to*).—*ns.* addict'-
edness, addic'tion. [L. *addicĕre, addictum*—*ad*,
to, *dicĕre*, to declare.]

Addison's disease, *ad'i-sanz diz-ēz', a disease
in which there is progressive destruction of the
suprarenal cortex, accompanied by wasting, weakness, low blood-pressure, and pigmentation of the
skin (bronzed skin). [Dr. Thomas *Addison*
(1793-1860), who investigated it.]

addle, *ad'l, n.* (now *dial.*) liquid filth.—*adj.* putrid :
bad (as an egg) : barren, empty : muddled.—*v.t.*
and *v.i.* to make or become addle.—*adjs.* add'led ;
add'le-brained : **-headed, -pated,** muddle-
headed.—*n.* add'lement. [O.E. *adela*, mud.]

addoom, *ə-dōōm', v.t.* (*Spens.*) to adjudge, award.
[Pfx. *ad-*, and **doom**.]

addorsed, *ə-dorst', adj.* (*her.*) turned back to
back. [L. *ad*, to, *dorsum*, back.]

address, *ə-dres' v.t.* (*obs.*) to arrange : (*obs.*) to
prepare : (*obs.*) to dress : (*arch.*) to don : to apply
or devote with direction of attention, skill, energies :
to apply oneself to : to direct : to aim : to direct one's
words to, speak directly to : to send : to put a
written or printed direction or indication of
destination upon.—*v.i.* to direct one's words : to
present a formal address.—*n.* act or mode of
addressing : deportment : adroitness : (*Milt.*) preparation, a move, incipient act : a formal communication in writing : a speech : direction, as of
a letter : place to which letters may be directed :
place where one may be found : (in *pl.*) attentions
of the nature of courtship.—*adj.* addressed',
addrest', (*Spens.*) set up : (*Shak.*) ready, prepared : arrayed : equipped : aimed : directed.—
ns. addressee', the person to whom a missive or
communication is addressed ; address'er, **-or**.
[Fr. *adresser*—L.L. *addirectiāre*—L. *ad*, to, *direc-
tum*, straight ; see **dress, direct**.]

adduce, *ə-dūs', v.t.* to bring forward in discussion,
to cite or quote.—*adj.* addūc'ent, drawing inward

---

or together, as a muscle.—*n.* **addūc'er.**—*adj.* **addūc'ible.**—*v.t.* **adduct** (*ə-dukt'*), to draw inward or together.—*n.* **adduc'tion**, the act of adducing or of adducting.—*adj.* **adduc'tive**, tending to bring forward.—*n.* **adduc'tor, an** adducent muscle. [L. *addūcĕre, adductum*—*ad,* to, and *dūcĕre,* to bring.]

adeem, *ə-dēm'*, *v.t.* (*law*; of a bequest) to cancel, by destruction or sale of the thing bequeathed, or otherwise.—*n.* **ademption** (-*dem'shən*). [L. *ad,* to, and *emĕre, emptum,* to take.]

adelantado, *ä-de-län-tä'dō,* *n.* a grandee: a provincial governor. [Sp.]

aden-, in composition, gland.—*n.* **adenitis** (*adən-ī'tis*) inflammation of glands.—*adj.* **ad'enoid,** gland-like: glandular.—*n.* an enlargement of glandular tissue at the back of the nose.—*n.* **adenō'ma,** a glandlike tumour:—*pl.* **adenō'mata,** or **-mas.**—*adj.* **adenō'matous.** [Gr. *adēn,* gland.]

adept, *ə-dept'*, *a-dept'*, *adj.* completely skilled.—*n.* (*ad'ept, ə-dept'*, *a-dept'*) a proficient: one who has attained the great secret (of the philosopher's stone, or what not). [L. *adeptus* (*artem*), having attained (an art), pa.p. of *adipiscī,* to attain—*ad,* to, and *apiscī,* to reach.]

adequate, *ad'i-kwāt, -kwit,* *adj.* sufficient: competent.—*adv.* **ad'equately.**—*ns.* **ad'equateness, ad'equacy** (-*kwə-si*).—*adj.* **ad'equative.** [L. *adaequātus,* made equal—*ad,* to, and *aequus,* equal.]

adermin, *a-dər'min,* *n.* (*chem.*) pyridoxin. [Gr. *a-* privative, *derma,* skin, because deprivation of this vitamin causes dermatitis in rats.]

Ades, *n.* (*Milt.*) variant of **Hades.**

adhere, *əd-, ad-hēr',* *v.i.* to stick: to remain fixed or attached: to cleave (as to a party, a leader, a doctrine): (*Shak.*) to be consistent: to agree: (*Scots law*) to affirm a judgment.—*n.* **adhēr'ence,** state of adhering: (*bot.*) concrescence of unlike parts.—*adj.* **adhēr'ent,** sticking: concrescent and unlike.—*n.* one who adheres: a follower: a partisan: one who is loosely associated with a body without being a member.—*n.* **adhēr'er.** [L. *ad,* to, *haerēre, haesum,* to stick.]

adhesion, *ad-, əd-hē'zhən,* *n.* the act of adhering or sticking: steady attachment: (*bot.*) concrescence of unlike parts: (*surg.*) reunion of separated surfaces: (*path.*) abnormal union of parts that have been inflamed: a band of fibrous tissue joining such parts.—*adj.* **adhē'sive** (-*ziv*), sticky: apt to adhere.—*n.* a substance used for sticking things together.—*adv.* **adhē'sively.**—*n.* **adhē'siveness.** [See **adhere.**]

adhibit, *ad-hib'it,* *v.t.* to apply: to attach: to admit: to administer.—*n.* **adhibi'tion.** [L. *adhibēre, -itum—ad,* to, *habēre,* to hold.]

adiabatic, *ad-i-ə-bat'ik,* *adj.* without transference of heat.—*adv.* **adiabiat'ically.** [Gr. *a-,* priv., *dia,* through, *batos,* passable.]

Adiantum, *ad-i-an'təm,* *n.* the maidenhair genus of ferns. [Gr. *adiantos—a-,* priv., and *diantos,* capable of being wetted.]

adiaphoron, *ad-i-af'ə-ron,* *n.* in theology and ethics, a thing indifferent—any tenet or usage considered non-essential:—*pl.* **adiaph'ora.**—*ns.* **adiaph'orism,** tolerance or indifference in regard to non-essential points in theology: latitudinarianism; **adiaph'orist.**—*adj.* **adiaph'orous.** [Gr., from *a-,* priv., *diaphoros,* differing—*dia,* apart, *pherein,* to carry.]

adiathermic, *ad-i-ə-thər'mik,* *adj.* impervious to radiant heat. [Gr. *a-,* priv., *dia,* through, *thermē,* heat.]

adieu, *ə-dū',* *interj.* (I commend you) to God: farewell.—*n.* a farewell:—*pl.* **adieus** or **adieux** (*ə-dūz'*). [Fr. *à Dieu,* to God.]

adipic, *ə-dip'ik—adj.* of fat (**adipic acid,** C₆H₁₀O₄, an acid got by treating fat with nitric acid).—*adj.* **adipose** (*ad'i-pōs*), fatty.—*n.* **adiposity** (-*pos'i-ti*)—**adipose tissue,** the vesicular structure in the animal body which contains the fat. [L. *adeps, adipis,* soft fat.]

adipocere, *ad'i-pō-sēr,* or *-sēr',* *n.* a fatty, waxy substance resulting from the decomposition of animal bodies in moist places or under water,

but not exposed to air. [L. *adeps, adipis,* soft fat, and *cēra,* wax.]

adit, *ad'it,* *n.* an opening or passage, esp. into a mine. [L. *adītus—ad,* to, *īre, itum,* to go.]

adjacent, *ə-jā'sənt, adj.* lying near.—*n.* **adja'cency.** —*adv.* **adja'cently.** [L. *ad,* to, *jacēns, -ĕntis,* pr.p. of *jacēre,* to lie.]

adjective, *aj'ik-tiv, adj.* added: dependent: subsidiary: (of dyes) requiring a mordant.—*n.* a word added to a noun to qualify it, or limit its denotation by reference to quality, number, or position.—*adj.* **adjectival** (-*tīv'l*).—*advs.* **adjecti'vally;** **ad'jectively.** [L. *adjectivum (nōmen),* added (word)—*adjicĕre, -jectum,* to add—*ad,* to, *jacĕre,* to throw.]

adjoin, *ə-join', v.t.* to join on: to lie next to.—*v.i.* to be in contact:—*adj.* **adjoin'ing.**—*n.* **adj'oint,** a civil officer who assists a French maire: an assistant professor in a French college. [Through Fr. *adjoign—,* prp. stem, and *adjoint,* pa.p., of *adjoindre—*L. *adjungĕre—ad,* to, *jungĕre,* to join.]

adjourn, *ə-jərn', v.t.* to put off to another day: to postpone: to discontinue (a meeting) in order to reconstitute it at another time or place.—*v.i.* to suspend proceedings and disperse for any time specified, or (*sine diē*) without such time being specified.—*ns.* **adjourn'al** (*obs.*); **adjourn'ment.** [O.Fr. *ajorner—*L.L. *adiurnāre—*L. *ad,* to, L.L. *jurnus,* L. *diurnus,* daily; cf. **journal.**]

adjudge, *ə-juj', v.t.* to decide: to assign: to award. —*n.* **adjudg'ment** (sometimes **adjudge'ment**), the act of adjudging: sentence. [O.Fr. *ajuger—*L. *adjūdicāre;* cf. **judge.**]

adjudicate, *ə-jōō'di-kāt, v.t.* to determine judicially: to pronounce: to award.—*v.i.* to pronounce judgment: to act as judge in a competition between amateurs in one of the arts, *e.g.* music.—*ns.* **adjudicā'tion** (*Eng. law*), an order of the Bankruptcy Court, adjudging a debtor to be a bankrupt, and transferring his property to a trustee; **adju'dicator.** [L. *adjūdicāre, -ātum.*]

adjunct, *aj'ung(k)t, adj.* joined or added.—*n.* a thing joined or added, but subordinate or not essentially a part: a person (usually subordinate) joined to another in office or service: (*gram.*) any word or clause enlarging the subject or predicate: (*logic*) any accompanying quality or non-essential attribute.—*n.* **adjunction** (*ə-jungk'shən*).—*adj.* **adjunct'ive,** forming an adjunct.—*adv.* **adjunct'ively.** [L. *adjunctus* pa.p. of *adjungĕre—ad,* to, *jungĕre,* to join.]

adjure, *ə-jōōr', v.t.* (*obs.*) to cause to swear: to charge on oath or solemnly.—*n.* **adjurā'tion** (*aj-*).—*adj.* **adjur'atory.**—*adj.* **adjur'ing.** [L. *adjūrāre—ad,* to, *jūrāre, -ātum,* to swear.]

adjust, *ə-just', v.t.* to put in due relation: to regulate: to settle.—*adj.* **adjust'able.**—*ns.* **adjust'er;** **adjust'ment;** **adjust'or,** an organ or faculty that determines behaviour in response to stimuli. [Obs. Fr. *adjuster—*L.L. *adjuxtāre,* to put side by side—L. *juxtā,* near; confused by association with *jūstus,* right.]

adjutage, ajutage, *aj'oo-tij,* *n.* a nozzle as for a fountain. [Fr. *ajutage;* cf. **adjust.**]

adjutant, *aj'oo-tənt,* *n.* an officer specially appointed to assist a commanding officer: a large Indian stork or crane (from its stalking gait).—*ns.* **adj'utancy,** the office of an adjutant: assistance; **adj'utant-gen'eral,** head of a department of the general staff: the executive officer of a general. [L. *adjūtāns, -āntis,* pr. p. of *adjūtāre,* freq. of *adjŭvāre—ad,* to, *jŭvāre,* to assist.]

adjuvant, *aj'oo-vənt, adj.* helping.—*n.* a help: (*med.*) an ingredient to help the main ingredient.— *n.* **ad'juvancy.** [Fr.,—L. *ad,* to, *jŭvāre.* to help.]

admeasure, *ad-mezh'ər, v.t.* to measure: to apportion.—*n.* **admeas'urement.** [O.Fr. *amesurer—*L.L. *admēnsūrāre—*L. *ad,* to, *mēnsūra,* measure.]

adminicle, *ad-min'i-kl,* *n.* anything that aids or supports: an auxiliary: (*law*) any corroboratory evidence.—*adj.* **adminic'ular.**—*v.t.* and *v.i.* **adminic'ulate.** [L. *adminiculum,* a support—*ad,* to, *manus,* hand.]

administer, *əd-*, *ad-min'is-tər*, *v.t.* to govern : to manage as a steward, substitute, or executor : to dispense (as justice, rites) : to tender (as an oath, medicine).—*v.i.* to minister.—*adj.* **admin'istrable**.—*adj.* and *n.* **admin'istrant**.—*n.* **administrā'tion**, the act of administering : management : dispensation of sacraments : the government.—*v.t.* (*rare* except *U.S.*) **admin'istrate**, to administer.—*adj.* **admin'istrative**, concerned with administration.—*n.* **admin'istrātor**, one who manages or directs : the person to whom is committed, under a commission entitled **letters of administration**, the administration or distribution of the personal estate of a deceased person, in default of an executor : (*Scots law*) one empowered to act for a person legally incapable of acting for himself :—*fem.* **admin'istrātrix**.—*n.* **admin'istratorship**. [L. *administrāre*, *-ātum*—*ad*, to, *ministrāre*, to minister.]

admiral, *ad'mir-əl*, *n.* the chief commander of a navy : a naval officer ranking with a general in the army (**admiral of the fleet** with field-marshal) : an admiral's flag-ship : the chief ship in a fleet of merchantmen or fishing boats : a cone-shell : a butterfly of certain kinds (see **red, white**).—*ns.* **ad'miralship**, the office or art of an admiral; **Ad'miralty**, the board of commissioners for the administration of naval affairs : the building where they transact business.—**Lord High Admiral**, an office now in abeyance, the functions falling to the Lords Commissioners of the Admiralty, and the High Court of Admiralty. [O.Fr. *a(d)miral*—Ar. *amīr-al-bahr*, a lord of the sea, confused with L. *admirābilis* (see next word).]

admire, *əd-mīr'*, *v.t.* to have a high opinion of : (*arch.*) to wonder at : (*U.S.*) to like (to do something).—*v.i.* (*obs.*) to wonder.—*adj.* **admirable** (*ad'mir-ə-bl*, *-mər-*), worthy of being admired.—*n.* **ad'mirableness**.—*adv.* **ad'mirably**.—*ns.* **admīr'a(u)nce** (*Spens.*), admiration; **admirā'tion**, the act of admiring : wonder, together with esteem, love, or veneration : (*B.*, *Shak.*, and *Milt.*) astonishment : (*Shak.*) admirableness : (*Shak.*) an object of admiration : a wonder.—*adj.* **admīrātive**.—*n.* **admīr'er**, one who admires : a lover.—*adv.* **admīr'ingly**.—**Admirable Crichton** (*krī'tən*), one who excels in many things, from James Crichton (1560-82), Scottish athlete, Latin poet, polymath. [Fr. *admirer*—L. *ad*, at, *mīrārī*, to wonder.]

admit, *əd-mit'*, *v.t.* to allow to enter : to let in : to concede : to acknowledge : to be capable of (also *v.i.* with *of*) :—*pr.p.* **admitt'ing**; *pa.p.* **admitt'ed**.—*n.* **admissibil'ity**.—*adj.* **admiss'ible**, that may be admitted or allowed (generally, or specially as legal proof).—*n.* **admission** (*-mish'ən*), the act of admitting : anything admitted or conceded : leave to enter.—*adjs.* **admiss'ive**; **admitt'able**, that may be admitted.—*n.* **admitt'ance**, admission : (*Shak.*) acceptability, acceptance.—*adj.* **admitt'ed**.—*adv.* **admitt'edly**. [Partly through Fr.,—L. *admittĕre*, *-missum*—*ad*, to, *mittĕre*, to send.]

admix, *əd-*, *ad-miks'*, *v.t.* to mix with something else.—*n.* **admix'ture**, the action of mixing : what is added to the chief ingredient of a mixture. [L. *ad*, to, and **mix**.]

admonish, *əd-*, *ad-mon'ish*, *v.t.* to warn : to reprove mildly.—*n.* **admon'ishment**, admonition. [O.Fr. *amonester*—L.L. *admonestāre*—L. *admonēre*—*ad*, to, *monēre*, to warn.]

admonition, *ad-mon-ish'ən*, or *-mən-*, *n.* reproof : counsel : advice : ecclesiastical censure.—*adjs.* **admonitive** (*-mon'*), **admon'itory**, containing admonition.—*n.* **admon'itor**. [L. *admonitiō*, *-ōnis*; cf. **admonish**.]

adnascent, *ad-nas'ənt*, *adj.* growing to or upon something else. [L. *adnāscēns*, *-entis*, pr.p. of *adnāsci*—*ad*, to, *nāsci*, to be born.]

adnate, *ad'nāt*, *ad-nāt'*, *adj.* (*bot.*) attached (esp. by the whole length) to another organ.—*n.* **adnation** (*-nā'shən*). [L. *adnātus*, usu. *agnātus*—*ad*, to, (*g*)*nātus*, born.]

ado, *ə-dōō'*, *n.* a to-do : bustle : trouble : difficulty : stir or fuss. [at do, Northern English infin. with **at** instead of **to**, borrowed from Scand.]

adobe, *ä-dō'bi*, *n.* a sun-dried brick : a house made of such bricks : (also **adobe clay**) a name for any kind of mud which, when mixed with straw, can be sun-dried into bricks.—Also *adj.* [Sp.,—*adobar*, to plaster.]

adolescent, *ad-ō-les'ənt*, *adj.* passing from childhood to maturity.—Also *n.*—*n.* **adolesc'ence**, the state or time of being adolescent. [L. *adolēscēns*, *-entis*, pr.p. of *adolēscĕre*, to grow up.]

Adonai, *ə-dōn'ī*, *ə-don-ā'ī*, *n.* a name of the Deity in the O.T., usu. translated by Lord. See also *Jehovah*. [Heb. *adōnāi*, my lord.]

Adonis, *ə-dō'nis*, *n.* a youth beloved by Aphrodite : a beautiful youth : a beau or dandy : the ranunculaceous pheasant's-eye genus.—*n.pl.* **Adō'nia**, the festival of mourning for Adonis.—*n* **Adonic** (*ə-don'ik*) a verse of a dactyl and a spondee, said to have been used in the Adonia.—Also *adj.*—*v.t.* and *v.i.* **ad'onise**, to adorn (oneself). [Gr. *Adōnis*—Phoenician *adōn*, lord.]

adoors, *ə-dōrz'*, *adv.* (*obs.*) at doors : at the door. [Prep. **a**, at, and **door**.]

adopt, *ə-dopt'*, *v.t.* to take voluntarily as one's own child, with the rights of a child : to take into any relationship : to take as one's own : to take up : to take over.—*adj.* **adopt'ed**, taken by adoption.—*ns.* **Adop'tianism**, **Adoptionism** (*ə-dop'shən-izm*; often **adoptianism**), the doctrine that Christ, as man, is the adopted son of God; **adop'tianist**, **adop'tionist**; **adop'tion**.—*adjs.* **adop'tious** (*-shəs*), (*Shak.*) adopted; **adopt'ive**, that adopts or is adopted. [L. *adoptāre*—*ad*, to, *optāre*, to choose.]

adore, *ə-dōr'*, *v.t.* to worship : to love or reverence intensely : (*Spens.*) to adorn.—*adj.* **ador'able**.—*n.* **ador'ableness**.—*adv.* **ador'ably**.—*ns.* **adorā'tion** (*ad-ō-rā'shən*); **ador'er**.—*adv.* **ador'ingly**. [L. *ad*, to, *ōrāre*, to pray.]

adorn, *ə-dorn'*, *v.t.* to deck or dress : to embellish.—*n.* (*Spens.*) adornment.—*adj.* (*Milt.*) adorned, ornate.—*n.* **adorn'ment**, ornament : decoration. [O.Fr. *āorner*, *adorner*—L. *adōrnāre*—*ad*, to, *ōrnāre*, to furnish.]

adown, *ə-down'*, *adv.* and *prep.* (*poet.*) an older form of **down**.

adpress, *ad-pres'*, *v.t.* to press together.—*adj.* **adpressed'**, (*bot.*) closely pressed together but not united.—Also **appress'**. [L. *ad*, to, *premĕre*, *pressum*, to press.]

adrad, *ə-drad'*, **adred**, *ə-dred'*, *adj.* (*Spens.*) afraid. [O.E. *ofdrǣd*—pfx. *of-*, *drǣdan*, to dread.]

adread, *ə-dred'*, *v.t.* (*obs.*) to fear.—*pa.t.* (*Spens.*) **adrad'**. [O.E. *ondrǣdan*—pfx. *on-*, *and-*, and *drǣdan*, to dread.]

adrenal, *ad-rēn'əl*, *adj.* beside the kidneys.—*n.* an adrenal gland.—*n.* **adrenalin** (*-rēn'*, *-ren'*), a hormone secreted by the adrenal glands, used to cause constriction of the small arteries.—**adrenal glands**, the suprarenal capsules, two small ductless glands over the kidneys. [L. *ad*, to, *rēnēs*, kidneys.]

adrift, *ə-drift'*, *adj.* or *adv.* in a drifting condition : loose from moorings : to one's own resources or no resources : cut loose. [Prep. **a**, and **drift**.]

adroit, *ə-droit'*, *adj.* dexterous : showing address.—*adv.* **adroit'ly**.—*n.* **adroit'ness**. [Fr. *à droit*, according to right—L. *directus*, straight; see **direct**.]

adry, *ə-drī'*, *adj.* and *adv.* in a state of thirst or dryness. [After **athirst**, **acold**, etc.]

adscititious, *ad-sit-ish'əs*, *adj.* added or assumed : additional. [L. *adscīscĕre*, *-scītum*, to take or assume—*ad*, to, *scīscĕre*, to inquire—*scīre*, to know.]

adscript, *ad'skript*, *adj.* attached to the soil.—*n.* a feudal serf so attached.—*n.* **adscrip'tion**. [L. *adscrīptus*—*ad*, to, *scrībĕre*, to write.]

adsorb, *ad-sorb'*, *v.t.* of a solid, to take up a vapour on its surface (cf. **absorb**).—*ns.* **adsorb'ate**, the vapour adsorbed; **adsorb'ent**, a solid (as charcoal) that adsorbs a vapour in contact with it; **adsorp'tion**. [L. *ad*, to, *sorbēre*, to suck in.]

adularia, *ad-ū-lā'ri-ä*, *n.* a transparent orthoclase felspar. [From the *Adula* group in the Alps.]

adulate, *ad'ū-lāt*, *v.t.* to fawn upon, to flatter.—

ns. ad′ūlātor ; adūlā′tion.—*adj.* ad′ūlatory. [L. *adūlāri, adūlātus,* to fawn upon.]

Adullamite, *ə-dul′əm-īt, n.* John Bright's name for a Whig seceder from the Liberal party (1866). [From the cave of *Adullam,* 1 Sam. xxii, 1, 2.]

adult, *ad′ult, ə-dult′, adj.* grown up : mature : of or for adults.—*n.* a grown-up person.—*n.* adult′hood. [L. *adultus,* pa.p. of *adolēscĕre,* to grow up ; see **adolescent.**]

adulterate, *ə-dult′ər-āt, v.t.* to debase, falsify, by mixing with something inferior or spurious : (*obs.*) to commit adultery with.—*v.i.* (*Shak.*) to commit adultery.—*adj.* defiled by adultery : spurious : corrupted by base elements.—*ns.* adult′erant, that with which anything is adulterated ; **adulterā′tion,** the act of adulterating : the state of being adulterated ; **adult′erator,** one who adulterates a commodity ; **adult′erer,** one guilty of adultery :—*fem.* adult′eress.—*adj.* adult′erine, resulting from adultery : spurious : (*hist.*) illegal.— *n.* the offspring of adultery.—*v.i.* adult′erise, (*arch.*) to commit adultery.—*adj.* adult′erous, pertaining to, of the nature of, guilty of, adultery.— *adv.* adult′erously.—*n.* adult′ery, violation of the marriage-bed, whether one's own or another's : (*B.*) unchastity generally : applied opprobriously, esp. by theologians, to marriages disapproved of : image-worship : (*obs.*) adulteration, falsification. [L. *adulterāre, -ātum,* prob. from *ad,* to, and *alter,* another. Some forms come from Fr., remodelled later on Latin.]

adumbrate, *ad′um-brāt,* or *-um′, v.t.* to give a faint shadow of : to shadow forth : to foreshadow : to overshadow.—*n.* adumbrā′tion. [L. *adumbrāre, -ātus—ad,* to, *umbra,* a shadow.]

adunc, *ə-dungk′, adj.* hooked.—Also adunc′ate, -d, adunc′ous.—*n.* aduncity (*ə-dun′si-ti*). [L. *aduncus, aduncātus—ad,* to, *uncus,* a hook.]

adust, *ə-dust′, v.t.* (*Milt.*) to scorch.—*adj.* burnt up or scorched : browned with the sun : sallow and atrabilious (from the old notions of dryness of body). [L. *adūstus,* pa.p. of *adūrĕre,* to burn up.]

advance, *əd-väns′, v.t.* to put forward : to promote : to further : (*Shak.*) to raise : to extol : to raise in price : to supply beforehand : to pay before due time : to lend, esp. on security.—*v.i.* to move or go forward : to make progress : to rise in rank or in value.—*n.* a forward move : progress : a rise in price, value, wages : payment beforehand : a loan : an approach, overture, move towards agreement, favour, etc.—*adj.* advanced′, at, appropriate to, a far-on stage (of education, thought, emancipation, life, etc.).—*n.* advance′ment, promotion : furthering : payment in advance.—**advance copy, proof,** one sent in advance of publication ; **advance(d) guard,** a guard or party in front of the main body ; **advance note,** an order for (generally) a month's wage given to a sailor on engaging ; **in advance,** beforehand : in front. [O.Fr. *avancer*— L.L. *abante* (Fr. *avant*)—L. *ab ante,* from before : the prefix refashioned later as if from *ad.*]

advantage, *əd-vänt′ij, n.* superiority over another : a favouring condition or circumstance : gain or benefit : (tennis, lawn-tennis) vantage.—*v.t.* and *v.i.* to benefit or profit.—*adjs.* advan′tageable (*rare*), profitable : convenient ; **advantageous** (*ad-vən-tā′jəs*), of advantage : useful (with *to* and *for*). —*adv.* advantā′geously.—*n.* advantā′geousness.—**have the advantage of,** to recognise without being recognised ; **take advantage of,** to avail oneself of : to make undue use of an advantage over ; **take at advantage,** to use favourable conditions against : to take by surprise. [Fr. *avantage—avant,* before ; see **advance.**]

advene, *ad-vēn′, v.i.* to be superadded.—*n.* **advent** (*ad′vənt*), a coming or arrival : **Advent,** the first or the second coming of Christ : the period immediately before the festival of the Nativity, including four Sundays.—*n.* **Ad′ventist,** one who expects a second coming of Christ : a millenarian. —*adj.* **adventitious** (*ad-vənt-ish′əs*), accidental : additional : foreign : appearing casually : developed out of the usual order or place.—*adv.* **adventi′tiously.**—*adj.* **adventive** (*-vent′*), adventitious :

(*bot.*) not permanently established.—*n.* a thing or person coming from without.—*n.* advent′ure, a chance : a remarkable incident : an enterprise : trial of the issue : risk : a commercial speculation : an exciting experience : the spirit of enterprise.— *v.t.* to risk : to dare : to venture : to put forward as a venture : to venture to say or utter.—*v.i.* to risk oneself : to take a risk.—*n.* advent′urer, one who engages in hazardous enterprises : a soldier of fortune, or speculator : one who pushes his fortune, esp. by unscrupulous means :—*fem.* advent′uress (chiefly in bad sense).—*adjs.* advent′urous, advent′uresome, enterprising : ready to incur risk.— *adv.* advent′urously.—*n.* advent′urousness. [L. *advenīre, adventum* (*ad,* to, *venīre,* to come), fut.p. *adventūrus ; adventus,* coming ; *adventīcius,* extraneous ; partly through Fr]

adverb, *ad′vərb, n.* a word added to a verb, adjective, or other adverb to express some modification of the meaning or an accompanying circumstance.—*adj.* adverb′ial (*əd-*)—*v.t.* adverb′ialise, to give the character of an adverb to.—*adv.* adverb′ially.— [L. *adverbium—ad,* to, *verbum,* a word (a trans. of Gr. *epirrēma,* lit. that which is said afterwards).]

adversaria, *ad-vər-sā′ri-ä, n.pl.* miscellaneous notes : a commonplace-book. [L. *adversāria.*]

adversary, *ad′vər-sər-i, n.* an opponent : the Adversary, Satan.—*adjs.* advers′ative (*əd-*), denoting opposition, contrariety, or variety ; ad′verse (also -*vərs′*), contrary (with *to*) : opposed : unfavourable : (*bot.*) facing the main axis.—*adv.* adversely.— —*ns.* adverseness ; advers′ity, adverse circumstances : misfortune : (*Shak.,* as a nickname) perversity. [L. *adversus—ad,* to, and *vertĕre, versum,* to turn.]

advert, *ad-vərt′, v.i.* to turn one's attention to : to refer.—*ns.* advert′ence, advert′ency, attention : heedfulness : regard.—*adj.* advert′ent, attentive : heedful.—*adv.* advert′ently. [L. *advertĕre—ad,* to, *vertĕre,* to turn.]

advert. See **advertise.**

advertise, *ad-vərt-īz′,* or *ad′-,* formerly (as *Shak.*) *-vərt′iz, v.t.* (*arch.*) to inform, give notice to : to give notice of : to give public information or announcement : to commend.—*v.i.* to issue advertisements : to draw attention to oneself.— *ns.* **advertisement** (*əd-vərt′iz-mənt*), the act of advertising : a public notice (*slang* abbrev. **ad,** ad′vert) : any device for obtaining public favour or notoriety : (*obs.*) news ; advertiser (*ad′,* or *-tiz′*), one who advertises : often part of a newspaper's title ; advertis′ing.—*adj.* (*Shak.*) attentive. [Fr. *avertir, avertiss*—L. *advertĕre* ; see **advert.**]

advew, *ad-vū′, v.t.* (*Spens.*) to view. [L. *ad,* to, and **view.**]

advice, *əd-vīs′, n.* counsel : intelligence (usu. in *pl.*) : formal official intelligence about anything : specially skilled opinion, as of a physician or lawyer.—*n.* advice′-boat (*obs.*), a swift vessel employed in conveying despatches.—*adjs.* advice′ful (*Spens.*), avize′full), watchful : attentive : skilled in advising. [O.Fr. *advis* (Fr. *avis*)—L. *ad vīsum,* according to what is seen or seems best.]

advise, *əd-vīz′, v.t.* (*obs.*) to view : (*obs.*) to take thought of, consider : to take to avizandum : to bethink : to counsel : to recommend : to inform : to announce.—*v.i.* (*obs.*) to reflect, deliberate : to consult.—*n.* advīsabil′ity.—*adj.* advīs′able, to be recommended : expedient : open to advice.— *n.* advīs′ableness.—*adv.* advīs′ably.—*adjs.* advīs′atory (*rare*), advisory ; advīsed′, having duly considered : considered : deliberate : apprised : amenable to advice.—*adv.* advīs′edly.—*ns.* advīs′edness, deliberate consideration : prudent procedure ; advise′ment (*obs.* or *arch.*), counsel, deliberation ; advīs′er, one who advises ; advīs′ership ; advīs′ing (*Shak.*), counsel, advice.—*adj.* advīs′ory, having the attribute or function of advising. [O.Fr. *aviser,* and L.L. *advisāre ;* cf. **advice.**]

advocaat, *ad′vō-kät, n.* a liqueur containing eggs and flavourings : a medicinal drink of eggs, rum, and lemon-juice. [Du. *advokaaten-,* advocate's dram, as a clearer of the throat.]

fāte, fär, àsk ; mē, hər (her) *; mīne ; mōte ; mūte ; mōŏn ; dhen* (then)

advocate, *ad'vō-kāt, -və-kit, n.* an intercessor or defender : one who pleads the cause of another : one who is qualified to plead before the higher courts of law—the ordinary name in Scotland corresponding to barrister in England.—*v.t.* to plead in favour of : to recommend.—*ns.* **ad'vocacy** (*-kə-si*), the function of an advocate : a pleading for : defence; **advocā'tion; ad'vocātor.**—*adj.* **ad'vocātory.**—**advocate in Aberdeen,** a solicitor (in Aberdeen); **Lord Advocate,** the first law-officer of the crown and public prosecutor of crimes for Scotland. [O.Fr. *avocat* and L. *advocātus—advocāre, -ātum,* to call in—*ad,* to, *vocāre,* to call.]

advoutrer, *ad-vow'trər,* **advou'try,** forms inter-mediate between **avoutrer** and **adulterer,** etc.

advowson, *əd-vow'zən, n.* the right of presentation to a church benefice. [O.Fr. *avoeson*—L.L. *advocātiō, -ōnis*—L. *advocātus.*]

adward (*Spens.*). Same as **award.**

adynamia, *a-di-nā'mi-ä, n.* helplessness, want of power accompanying a disease.—*adj.* **adynamic,** (*-am'*), without strength : (*phys.*) characterised by the absence of force. [Gr. *a-,* priv., and *dynamis,* strength.]

adytum, *ad'i-təm, n.* the most sacred part of a temple : the chancel of a church:—*pl.* **ad'yta.** [Latinised from Gr. *adyton—a-,* priv., *dyein,* to enter.]

adze, *adz, n.* a carpenter's tool with an arched blade with its edge at right angles to the handle. [O.E. *adesa.*]

ae, *ā, yā, ye, adi.* Scottish form of O.E. *ān,* one, used attributively.

aecidium, *ē-sid'i-əm, n.* a cup-shaped fructification in rust fungi:—*pl.* **aecid'ia.**—*n.* **aecid'iospore,** a spore produced in it. [Gr. *aikiā,* injury.]

aedile, *ē'dīl, n.* a magistrate in ancient Rome who had the charge of public buildings, games, markets, police, etc.—*n.* **ae'dileship.** [L. *aedilis—aedēs, -is,* a building.]

aegirine, *ē'jir-ēn,* **ae'girite,** *-īt, ns.* a green pleochroic pyroxene. [Ægir, Norse sea-god or giant.]

aegis, *ē'jis, n.* (*orig.*) a shield belonging to Zeus, or to Pallas : protection : patronage. [Gr. *aigis.*]

aeglogue, *ēg'log, n.* (*arch.*) for **eclogue.** [From the mistaken belief that the word meant goat-herd discourse—Gr. *aix, aigos,* goat, *logos,* discourse.]

aegrotat, *ē-grō'tat,* or *ē', n.* in universities, a medical certificate of illness, or a degree granted on it. [L. *aegrōtat,* is sick, 3rd pers. sing. pres. indic. of *aegrōtāre—aeger,* sick.]

aemule, *ē'mūl, v.t.* (*Spens.*) to emulate. [L. *aemulārī.*]

Aeneid, *ē'nē-id, n.* an epic poem written by Virgil, the hero of which is Aeneas. [L. *Aenēis, -idos.*]

Aeneolithic, *ā-ē-ni-ō-lith'ik, adj.* belonging to a transitional stage at the end of the Neolithic age, when copper was already in use. [L. *aēneus,* brazen, and Gr. *lithos,* stone.]

Aeolian, *ē-ō'li-ən, adj.* pertaining to, acted on by, or due to the agency of the wind : aerial.— **Aeolian harp,** a sound-box with strings tuned in unison, sounding harmonics in a current of air; **Aeolian rocks** (*geol.*), those deposited by wind, as desert sands. [L. *Aeolus*—Gr. *Aiolos,* god of the winds.]

Aeolian, *ē-ō'li-ən, adj.* of Aeolis or Aeolia, in north-west Asia Minor, or its Greek colonists.—*n.* an Aeolian Greek.—*adj.* **Aeolic** (*-ol'ik*), the Greek dialect of the Aeolians.—**Aeolian mode,** in ancient Greek music, the same as the Hypodorian or Hyperphrygian : in old church music, the authentic mode with A for its final. [L. *Aeolius, Aeolicus*—Gr. *Aiolios, Aiolikos.*]

aeolipile, aeolipyle, *ē'əl-i-pīl,* or *ē-ol'i-pīl, n.* a hollow ball turned by tangential escape of steam. [L. *Aeolus,* and *pila,* balı; or Gr. *Aiolou pylai,* Gates of Aeolus.]

aeolotropy, *ē-əl-ot'rə-pi, n.* variation in physical properties according to direction.—*adj.* **aeolotrop'-ic.** [Gr. *aiolos,* changeful, *tropē,* a turn.]

aeon, eon, *ē'on, n.* a vast age : eternity; **Aeon,** the personification of an age, a power emanating from the supreme deity, with its share in the creation and government of the universe.—*adj.* **aeō'nian,** eternal. [L. *aeōn*—Gr. *aiōn.*]

Aepyornis, *ē-pi-or'nis, n.* a gigantic Recent fossil wingless bird of Madagascar. [Gr. *aipys,* tall, *ornis,* bird.]

aerate, *ā'ər-āt, v.t.* to put air into : to charge with air or with carbon dioxide or other gas (as **aerated waters**).—*ns.* **ā'erātor,** an apparatus for the pur-pose; **āerā'tion,** exposure to the action of air : mixing or saturating with air or other gas : oxygena-tion of the blood by respiration.—**aerating root,** a root that rises erect into the air, a breathing organ in mud plants. [L. *āēr,* air.]

aerenchyma, *ā-ər-eng'ki-mä, n.* (*bot.*) respiratory tissue.—*adj.* **aerenchym'atous.** [Gr. *āēr,* air, *en,* in, *chyma,* that which is poured.]

aerial, *ā-ē'ri-əl,* also *-er',* often *ā'(ə-)ri-əl, adj.* of, in, belonging to, the air : atmospheric : airy : unreal : lofty : elevated : connected with aircraft.— *n.* a wire exposed to receive or emit electromagnetic waves : an antenna.—*n.* **aeriality** (*-al'i-ti*).—*adv.* **aer'ially.**—**aerial railway, ropeway,** one for overhead conveyance. [L. *āērius—āēr,* air.]

aerie, aery, ayrie, eyrie (now common), **eyry,** *ā'ri,* also *ē'ri, ī'ri, n.* the nest of a bird of prey, esp. an eagle : a house or stronghold perched on some high or steep place : (*Shak.*) the brood in the nest, or a stock of children. [O.Fr. *aire;* origin unknown.]

aeriform, *ā'ər-i-form, adj.* gaseous : unreal. [L. *āēr,* air, and *forma,* form.]

aero-, *ā'ər-ō-,* in combination, air.—*n.* **ā'ero** (*coll.*), an aircraft.—*adj.* connected with aircraft.— *n.* **āerobat'ics** (*pl.* in form, but treated as *sing.*; Gr. *batein,* to tread), the art of stunting in the air : aerial acrobatics.—*n.* **ā'erobe** (Gr. *bios,* life), an organism that requires free oxygen for respiration. —Also **aerō'biont.**—*adjs.* **āerobic** (*-ob'*), **āerobī-otic** (*-ot'ik*), requiring free oxygen for respiration : effected by aerobes, as a biochemical change : involving the activity of aerobes.—*advs.* **aerob'-ically, aerobiot'ically.**—*ns.* **āerobiō'sis,** life in presence of oxygen.—*ns.* **ā'erobomb,** a bomb for dropping from aircraft; **ā'erobus,** a large aircraft; **ā'erodart,** an arrow-headed missile of steel dropped from aircraft in warfare; **ā'ero-drome,** an aviation station or course : an early form of flying-machine (Gr. *dromos,* running). —*adjs.* **āerodynam'ic, -al.**—*ns.* **āerodynam'ics** (*pl.* in form but treated as *sing.*), the dynamics of gases; **ā'erofoil,** an air-resisting surface of an aeroplane; **ā'erogram,** a message by wireless telegraphy : a message sent by telegram (or tele-phone) and aeroplane; **āerohy'droplane,** a winged hydroplane or flying-boat; **ā'erolite, āerolith,** a meteoric stone or meteorite (Gr. *lithos,* a stone); **āerolithol'ogy,** the science of aerolites.—*adjs.* **āerolit'ic;** **āerolog'ical.**—*ns.* **āerol'ogist; āerol'ogy,** the branch of science that treats of the atmosphere; **ā'eromancy,** divination by atmos-pheric phenomena : weather forecasting (Gr. *manteiā,* divination); **āerom'eter,** an instrument for measuring the weight or density of air and gases; **āerom'etry,** pneumatics.—*adj.* **āeromet'-ric.**—*ns.* **ā'eromotor,** an engine for aircraft; **ā'eronaut** (Gr. *nautēs,* a sailor), a balloonist or airman.—*adjs.* **āeronaut'ic, -al.**—*ns.* **aeronaut'-ics** (*pl.* in form but treated as *sing.*), the science or art of aerial navigation; **āerophō'bia,** morbid fear of draughts (Gr. *phobos,* fear).—*adj.* **āerophōb'ic.** —*ns.* **ā'erophyte,** an epiphyte (Gr. *phyton,* a plant); **ā'eroplane,** any heavier-than-air power-driven flying-machine, with fixed wings : a small plane for aerostatic experiments (see **plane**); **āerosid'erite,** (Gr. *sidēros,* iron) an iron meteorite; **ā'erosol,** a colloidal system, such as a mist or a fog, in which the dispersion medium is a gas; **ā'erostat,** a balloon or other aircraft lighter than air : a balloon-ist : (*zool.*) an air-sac (Gr. *statos,* standing).—*adj.* **āerostat'ic.**—*ns.* **āerostat'ics** (*pl.* in form, but treated as *sing.*), the science of the equilibrium and pressure of air and other gases : the science or art of ballooning; **āerostation** (*-stā'shən*), ballooning.—*adj.* **āerotac'tic,** pertaining to or showing aerotaxis.—*n.* **āerotax'is** (*biol.*), movement towards or from oxygen (Gr. *taxis*, arrangement; adj. *taktikos*).—*adj.* **äerotrop'ic** (Gr. *tropĕ*, turning).—*n.* **äerot'ropism** (*bot.*), curvature in response to concentration of oxygen. [Gr. *āēr*, air.]

aeruginous, *ē-rōō'ji-nəs, adj.* pertaining to or like copper-rust or verdigris. [L. *aerūginōsus—aerūgō,* rust of copper—*aes, aeris,* brass, copper.]

aery, aerie, *ā'(ə-)ri, adj.* (*poet.*) aerial: incorporeal: spiritual: visionary.—**aerie light** (*Milt.*), light as air. [L. *āĕrius;* see **aerial.**]

aery. See **aerie.**

æsc, *ash, n.* the rune (F̄) for *a,* used in O.E. for *æ:* the ligature *æ* used in O.E. for the same sound (that of *a* in Mod. Eng. *cat*). [O.E. *æsc,* ash-tree, the name of the rune.]

Aesculapian, *ēs-kū-lā'pi-ən,* or *es-, adj.* pertaining to Aesculapius, and so to the art of healing.—Also **Esculapian.** [L. *Aesculāpius,* Gr. *Asklēpios,* god of healing.]

Aesculus, *ēs'kū-ləs, n.* the horse-chestnut genus of Hippocastanaceae.—*n.* **aes'culin,** a glucoside in horse-chestnut bark. [L. *aesculus,* a species of oak.]

aesir. See **as** (2).

aesthetic, *ēs-thet'ik,* or *es-,* sometimes *-thĕt', adj.* (*orig.*) relating to perception by the senses: (generally) relating to, possessing, or pretending to, a sense of beauty: (*coll.*) artistic, or affecting to be artistic.—*n.* **aes'thete** (*thēt*), a professed disciple of aestheticism: one who affects an extravagant love of art.—*adj.* **aesthet'ical,** pertaining to aesthetics.—*adv.* **aesthet'ically.**—*n.* **aesthetician** (*-tish'ən*), one devoted to or versed in aesthetics.—*v.t.* **aesthet'icise** (*-sīz*), to render aesthetic.—*ns.* **aesthet'icism,** the principles of aesthetics: the cult of the beautiful, applied esp. to a late 19th-century movement to bring art into life, which developed into craze and affectation; **aesthet'icist; aesthet'ics** (*pl.* in form, but treated as *sing.*), the principles of taste and art: the philosophy of the fine arts. [Gr. *aisthētikos,* perceptive—*aisthanesthai,* to feel or perceive.]

aestival, *ēs-tī'vəl,* or *es-, adj.* of summer.—*v.i.* **aes'tivate** (*-ti-vāt*), to pass the summer.—*n.* **aestivā'tion,** a spending of the summer: (*bot.*) manner of folding in the flower-bud: by others used of the arrangement of foliage leaves relatively to one another in the bud: (*zool.* and *bot.*) dormancy during the dry season. [L. *aestivus, aestivālis,* relating to summer, *aestivāre,* to pass the summer —*aestās,* summer.]

aether, *ē'thər, n.* Same as **ether** (but not generally used in the chemical sense).

aethrioscope, *ē'thri-ō-skōp, n.* an instrument for measuring the minute variations of temperature due to the condition of the sky. [Gr. *aithriā,* the open sky, *skopeein,* to look at.]

aetiology, *ē-ti-ol'o-ji, n.* the science or philosophy of causation: an inquiry into the origin or causes of anything, esp. a disease.—*adj.* **aetiolog'ical.** [Gr. *aitiologiā—aitiā,* cause, *logos,* discourse.]

Aetnean. Same as **Etnean.**

afar, *ə-fär', adv.* from a far distance (usually *from afar*): at or to a distance (usually *afar off*). [*of* and *on,* far.]

afear, affear(e), *ə-fēr', v.t.* (*Spens.*) to frighten.— *adj.* **afeard', affeard'** (*Shak.*), afraid. [Pfx. *a-,* intens., O.E. *fǣran,* to frighten.]

affable, *af'ə-bl, adj.* easy to be spoken to: courteous, esp. towards inferiors.—*n.* **affabil'ity.**—*adv.* **aff'ably.** [Fr.,—L. *affābilis—affārī,* to speak to— *ad,* to, and *fārī,* to speak.]

affair, *ə-fār', n.* that which is to be done: business: any small matter: a minor battle: a matter of intimate personal concern, as a duel (*affair of honour*), or intrigue: (*coll.*) a thing: (*pl.*) transactions in general: public concerns. [O.Fr. *afaire* (Fr. *affaire*)—*à* and *faire*—L. *ad,* to, *facĕre,* to do; cf. **ado.**]

affeard, affeared. See **afeard, affeered.**

affect, *ə-fekt', v.t.* to act upon: to infect or attack as disease: to influence: to move the feelings of: (in *pass.* only) to assign, allot.—*n.* (*obs.*) disposition of body or mind: (*obs.*) affection, love: (*psych.,*

pron. *af'ekt*) the emotion that lies behind action: pleasantness or unpleasantness of an emotional state.—*adj.* **affect'ed,** touched with a feeling.— *adj.* **affect'ing,** having power to move the emotions: pathetic.—*adv.* **affect'ingly.**—*adj.* **affect'ive,** pertaining to emotion.—*adv.* **affect'ively.**— *n.* **affectivity** (*af-ek-tiv'i-ti*). [L. *afficĕre, affectum —ad,* to, *facĕre,* to do.]

affect, *ə-fekt', v.t.* (*obs.*) to aim at, aspire to: (*arch.*) to have a liking for: to make a show of preferring: to do, wear, inhabit, by preference: to assume: to assume the character of: to make a show or pretence of.—*v.i.* to incline, tend.—*n.* **affectā'tion** (*af-ik-*), assumption of or striving after an appearance of what is not natural or real: pretence.— *adjs.* **affect'ed,** full of affectation: feigned.—*adv.* **affect'edly.**—*ns.* **affect'edness; affect'er.** [L. *affectāre, -ātum,* freq. of *afficĕre:* see **affect** above.]

affection, *ə-fek'shən, n.* the act of influencing: emotion: disposition: inclination: love: attachment: (*Shak.*) affectation: an attribute or property: a disease.—*v.t.* (*rare*) to love.—*adjs.* **affec'tional; affec'tionate,** full of affection: loving: (*obs.*) eager, passionate, well inclined.—*adv.* **affec'tionately.**—*n.* **affec'tionateness.**—*adj.* **affec'tioned** (*B.*) disposed: (*Shak.*) full of affectation. [L. *affectiō, -ōnis.*]

affeer, *ə-fēr', v.t.* to assess: to reduce to a certain fixed sum.—*adj.* **affeered'** (*Shak.* **affear'd'**), confirmed.—*n.* **affeer'ment.** [O.Fr. *affeurer*—L.L. *afforāre*—L. *ad,* to, *forum,* a market.]

afferent, *af'ər-ənt, adj.* bringing inwards, as the nerves that convey impulses to the central nervous system. [L. *afferēns, -entis—ad,* to, and *ferre,* to carry.]

affettuoso, *äf-fet-too-ō'sō, adj.* (*mus.*) tender.—*adv.* tenderly.—Also *n.* [It.]

affiance, *ə-fī'əns, n.* faith pledged: contract of marriage: trust: (*obs.*) affinity.—*v.t.* to betroth.— *adj.* **affi'anced,** betrothed. [O.Fr. *afiance;* see **affy.**]

affidavit, *af-i-dā'vit, n.* a written declaration on oath. [L.L. *affīdāvit,* 3rd pers. sing. perf. of *affīdāre,* to pledge one's faith; see **affy.**]

affied, affies. See **affy.**

affiliate, *ə-fil'i-āt, v.t.* to adopt or attach as a member or branch: to impute paternity of, to father: to assign the origin of.—*v.i.* to become closely connected, to associate: (*U.S.*) to fraternise. —*adj.* **affil'iable.**—*n.* **affiliā'tion.** [L. *affiliātus,* adopted—*ad,* to, *filius,* a son.]

affine, *ə-fīn', n.* (*obs.*) a relation, esp. by marriage. —*adjs.* **affine', affined',** related: bound by some tie. [O.Fr. *affin*—L. *affinis,* neighbouring—*ad,* to, at, *finis,* a boundary.]

affinity, *ə-fin'i-ti, n.* (*obs.*) nearness: relationship by marriage: relation of sponsor and godchild: natural or fundamental relationship, esp. common origin: attraction, esp. chemical attraction: a spiritual attraction between two persons: a person whose attraction for another is supposed to be of this kind.—*adj.* **affin'itive.** [Fr. *affinité*—L. *affinitās, -ātis—affinis;* see **affine.**]

affirm, *ə-fərm', v.t.* to assert confidently or positively: to ratify (a judgment): to confirm or stand by (one's own statement): (*log.*) to state in the affirmative: (*law*) to declare formally, without an oath.—*v.i.* to make an affirmation.—*adj.* **affirm'able.**—*n.* **affirm'ance,** affirmation: assertion: confirmation.—*adj.* and *n.* **affirm'ant.**—*n.* **affirmation** (*af-ər-mā'shən*), assertion: that which is affirmed: a positive judgment or proposition: a solemn declaration in lieu of an oath.—*adj.* **affirm'ative,** affirming or asserting: positive, not negative: dogmatic.—*n.* the affirmative mode: an affirmative word, proposition or utterance.—*adv.* **affirm'atively.**—*adj.* **affirm'atory.**—*n.* **affirm'-er.**—*adv.* **affirm'ingly.** [O.Fr. *afermer*—L. *affirmāre—ad,* to, *firmus,* firm.]

affix, *ə-fiks', v.t.* to fix to: to append: to add (to something).—*n.* (*af'iks*) an addition to a root, stem, or word, to modify its meaning or use, whether *prefix* or *suffix*: any appendage or addition. [L. *affigere*, *-fixum—ad*, to, *figĕre*, to fix.]

afflated, *ə-flā′tid*, *adj.* inspired.—*ns.* **afflā′tion**, **afflā′tus**, inspiration. [L. *afflāre*, *-flātum* (vb.), *afflātus*, *-ūs* (n.)—*ad*, to, *flāre*, to breathe.]

afflict, *ə-flikt′*, *v.t.* (B.) to humble: to distress grievously: to harass: to vex.—*adj.* **afflict′ed** (*Milt.*), overthrown: (*Spens.*) humble: harassed by disease of body or mind: suffering.—*n.* and *adj.* **afflict′ing**, distressing.—*n.* **afflic′tion**, state or cause of grievous distress.—*adj.* **afflict′ive**, causing distress. [L. *afflīgĕre*, *-flīctum*, to overthrow, cast down—*ad*, to, *flīgĕre*, to dash to the ground.]

affluent, *af′loo-ənt*, *adj.* inflowing: abounding: wealthy.—*n.* an inflowing stream.—**aff′luence**, inflow: abundance: wealth.—*adv.* **aff′luently.**—*ns.* **aff′luentness**; **aff′lux**; **affluxion** (*ə-fluk′shən*), an inflow, an accession. [L. *affluĕre*—*ad*, to, *fluĕre*, *fluxum*, to flow.]

afforce, *ə-fōrs′*, *v.t.* (*law*) to strengthen (*e.g.* a jury by addition of skilled persons).—*n.* **afforce′ment.** [O.Fr. *aforcer*—L.L. *exfortiāre*—L. *ex*, out, *fortis*, strong.]

afford, *ə-fōrd′*, *v.t.* to yield or produce: to bear the expense, concession, or disadvantage of: (*Spens.* **affoord**) to concede, grant, consent. [M.E. *aforthen*—O.E. *geforthian*, to further or cause to come forth.]

afforest, *a-*, *ə-for′ist*, *v.t.* to convert into hunting-ground: to cover with forest.—*adj.* **affor′estable.**—*n.* **afforestā′tion.** [L.L. *afforestāre*—L. *ad*, to, and L.L. *forēsta*, forest.]

affranchise, *a-*, *ə-fran′(t)shīz*, *v.t.* to free from slavery, or from some obligation.—*n.* **affran′chisement** (*-shiz-*, *-chiz-*). [O.Fr. *afranchir*, *afranchiss-*—*à*, to, *franchir*, to free, *franc*, free.]

affrap, *a-frap′*, *v.t.* and *v.i.* (*Spens.*) to strike. [It. *affrappare*—pfx. *af-* (L. *ad*, to), and *frappare*, to strike; or directly from **frap.**]

affray, *ə-frā′*, *n.* a disturbance, breach of the peace: a brawl, fight, fray: (*Spens.*) fear.—*v.t.* to disturb, startle: to frighten: to scare away.—*adj.* **affrayed′**, alarmed (now **afraid**). [O.Fr. *afrayer*, *esfreer* (Fr. *effrayer*)—L.L. *exfridāre*, to break the king's peace—L. *ex*, out of, O.H.G. *fridu* (Ger. *friede*), peace.]

affreightment, *ə-frāt′mənt*, *n.* the hiring of a vessel. [Fr. *affrétement* (*affrètement*), remodelled upon *freight*.]

affrended, *a-frend′id*, *adj.* (*Spens.*) reconciled. [**friend.**]

affret, *a-fret′*, *n.* (*Spens.*) a furious onset. [Prob. from It. *affrettare*, to hasten.]

affricate, *af′ri-kāt*, *n.* (*phon.*) a consonant sound beginning as a plosive and passing into the corresponding fricative.—*adjs.* **affric′ative**; **aff′ricated.**—*n.* **affricā′tion.** [L. *affricāre*, *-ātum*, to rub against—*ad*, to, *fricāre*, to rub.]

affright, *ə-frīt′*, *v.t.* to frighten.—*n.* sudden terror.—*adj.* **affright′ed.**—*adv.* **affright′edly.**—*v.t.* **affright′en.**—*adj.* **affright′ened.**—*adj.* **affright′ful** (*arch.*), frightful.—*n.* **affright′ment**, sudden fear. [O.E. *āfyrhtan*—ā-, intens., *fyrhten*, to frighten.]

affront, *ə-frunt′*, *v.t.* to meet face to face: to face: to confront: (*Shak.*) to throw oneself in the way of: to insult to one's face.—*n.* a contemptuous treatment: an open insult: indignity.—*adj.* **affronté**, **affrontée**, **affrontee** (*ā-fron′tā*, *ə-frun′tē*), (*her.*) facing each other; also looking frontwise, or towards the beholder.—*adj.* **affront′ed.**—*n.* and *adj.* **affront′ing.**—*adv.* **affront′ingly.**—*adj.* **affront′ive.** [O.Fr. *afronter*, to slap on the forehead—L.L. *affrontāre*—L. *ad*, to, *frōns*, *frontis*, forehead.]

affusion, *ə-fū′zhən*, *n.* pouring on (esp. in baptism). [L. *affūsiō*, *-ōnis*—*affundĕre*—*ad*, to, *fundĕre*, *fūsum*, to pour.]

affy, *ə-fī′*, *v.t.* (*obs.*) to trust: (*obs.*) to assure on one's faith: to betroth: (*obs.*) to repose or put (trust).—*v.i.* to trust or confide:—*pr.p.* **affy′ing**; *pa.t.* and *pa.p.* **affied** (*Spens.* **affyde′**). [O.Fr. *afier*—L.L. *affīdāre*—L. *ad*, to, *fidēs*, faith; cf. **affiance.**]

afield, *ə-fēld′*, *adv.* to, in, or on the field: to or at a distance. [**on**, **field.**]

afire, *ə-fīr′*, *adj.* and *adv.* on fire: in a state of inflammation. [**on**, **fire.**]

aflame, *ə-flām′*, *adj.* and *adv.* in a flaming or glowing state. [**on**, **flame.**]

afloat, *ə-flōt′*, *adv.* and *adj.* in a floating state: at sea: unfixed: in circulation. [**on**, **float.**]

afoot, *ə-foot′*, *adv.* and *adj.* on foot: astir: actively in being. [**on**, **foot.**]

afore, *ə-fōr′*, *prep.* in front of, before.—*adv.* beforehand, previously.—*adv.* **afore′hand**, beforehand: before the regular time for accomplishment: in advance.—*adjs.* **afore′mentioned**, previously mentioned, aforesaid; **afore′said**, said or named before; **afore′thought**, thought of or meditated before: premeditated.—*n.* premeditation.—*adv.* **aforetime**, in former or past times. [O.E. *onforan—on*, *foran*; see **before.**]

afoul, *ə-fowl′*, *adj.* or *adv.* in entanglement: in collision (with *of*). [**on**, **foul.**]

afraid, *ə-frād′*, *adj.* struck with fear: timid: reluctantly inclined to think (with *that*). [Pa.p. of **affray.**]

afreet. See **afrit.**

afresh, *ə-fresh′*, *adv.* anew. [Pfx. **a-**, **fresh.**]

African, *af′rik-ən*, *adj.* of Africa.—*n.* a native of Africa: a negro of African race.—*n.* **Af′ric** (*poet.*), Africa.—*adj.* African.—*ns.* **African′(d)er**, or **Afrikan′(d)er**, one born in South Africa of white parents (esp. of Dutch descent); **African′derdom** or **Afrikan′derdom**; **African′derism**, a South African word or idiom introduced into English; **Af′ricanism**, an African characteristic; **Af′ricanist**, one learned in matters relating to Africa—*adj.* **Af′ricanoid**, of African type.—*v.i.* **Af′ricanise**, to affect or adopt African characteristics.—*v.t.* to make African: to hand over to Africans.—*n.* **Afrikaans** (*af-ri-käns′*), South African Dutch—the Taal; **Afrikander Bond**, a South African nationalist league (1881–1911). [L. *Āfricānus.*]

afrit, **afreet**, *ä-frēt′*, *af′rēt*, *n.* an evil demon in Arabian mythology. [Ar. *'ifrīt*, a demon.]

afront, *ə-frunt′*, *adv.* (*obs.*) in front: (*Shak.*) abreast. [**on**, **front.**]

aft, *äft*, *adj.* or *adv.* behind: near or towards the stern of a vessel. [O.E. *æftan.*]

after, *äft′ər*, *prep.* and *adv.* behind in place: later in time (than): following in search of: in imitation of: in proportion to, or in agreement with: concerning: subsequent to, or subsequently: afterwards: in the manner of, or in imitation of: according to: in honour of.—*adj.* behind in place: later in time: more towards the stern (in this sense as if the *comp.* of **aft**).—*conj.* later than the time when.—*ns.* **aft′erbirth**, the placenta and membranes expelled from the uterus after a birth: a posthumous birth; **aft′er-care**, care subsequent to a period of treatment; **aft′er-clap**, an unexpected sequel, after an affair is supposed to be at an end; **aft′er-crop**, a second crop from the same land in the same year; **aft′er-damp**, choke-damp, arising in coal-mines after an explosion of fire-damp; **after-dinn′er**, the time following dinner.—*adj.* belonging to that time, esp. before leaving the table.—*n.* **aft′er-effect**, an effect that comes after an interval.—*v.t.* **aftereye′** (*Shak.*), to gaze after.—*ns.* **aft′ergame**, a second game played in the hope of reversing the issue of the first: means employed after the first turn of affairs; **aft′erglow**, a glow in the sky after sunset; **aft′ergrass**, the grass that springs after mowing or reaping; **aft′er-guard**, the men on the quarter-deck and poop who work the after sails, many of them unskilled: hence a drudge or person in a mean capacity: a merchant ship's officers; **aft′er-image**, an image that persists for a time after looking at an object.—*n.pl.* **aft′erings**, the last milk drawn in milking.—*ns.* **aft′er-life**, a future life: later life; **aft′ermath**, a second mowing of grass in the same season: (*fig.*) later consequences, esp. if bad; **afternoon′**, the time between noon and evening.—Also *adj.* **aft′ernoon.**—*n.pl.* **aft′erpains**, the pains after childbirth.—*ns.* **aft′erpiece**, a farce or other minor piece performed after a play; **aft′ershaft**, a second shaft arising from the quill of a feather; **aft'ersupper** (*Shak.*), prob. a dessert at the end of a supper: poss. a rere-supper.—*adj.* in the time after supper.—*ns.* aft'ertaste, a taste that remains or comes after eating or drinking; **aft'erthought**, a thought or thing thought of after the occasion: a later thought or reflection or modification; **aft'ertime**, later time.—*advs.* aft'erward (*rare* except *U.S.*), **afterwards**, in after-time: later: subsequently.—*n.* aft'erword, an epilogue.—**after** a fashion (see fashion). [O.E. *æfter*, in origin a comparative from *af* (*æf*), off, of which **aft** is orig. a superlative, but itself compared *æfter*, *æfterra*, *æftemest*, and tending to be regarded as comparative of aft; see of, off.]

aftermost, *âf'tɔr-mōst, -mɔst*, **aftmost**, *âft'*, *adjs.* superl. of aft, nearest the stern: hindmost. [O.E. *æftemest* a double superlative.]

aga, agha, *ä-gä', ä'gä*, *n.* a Turkish commander or chief officer.—**Aga Khan**, *kän*, the head of the Ismaili Mohammedans. [Turk. *aga, aghā*.]

again, *ɔ-gen'*, also *ɔ-gän'*, *adv* once more: in return: in response or consequence: back: further: on the other hand: to the same amount in addition: (*dial.*) at some future time.—*prep.* (*dial.*) against. [O.E. *ongéan, ongegn*; Ger. *entgegen*.]

against, *ɔ-genst'*, also *ɔ-gänst'*, *prep.* opposite to: in opposition or resistance to: in protection from: in or into contact or collision with or pressure upon: (*obs.*) towards the time of: in anticipation of: in contrast or comparison with: in exchange for: instead of.—*conj.* in readiness for the time that. [again, with gen. ending -*es*, and -*t* as in whilst, betwixt, amongst.]

agalactia, *ag-ɔ-lak'shi-ä*, *n.* failure to secrete milk. [Gr. *a-*, priv., *gala, galaktos*, milk.]

agalloch, *ɔ-gal'ɔk*, *n.* eaglewood. [Gr. *agallochon*, a word of Eastern origin; see eaglewood.]

agalmatolite, *ag-al-mat'ɔ-lit*, *n.* material of various kinds (steatite, pyrophyllite, etc.) from which the Chinese cut figures. [Gr. *agalma, -atos*, a statue (of a god), *lithos*, stone.]

Agama, *ag'ɔ-mä*, *n.* an Old-World genus of thick-tongued lizards giving name to the family **Agamidae** (*a-gam'i-dē*).—*adj.* and *n.* **ag'amoid**. [Carib name of another lizard.]

agami, *ag'ɔ-mi*, *n.* the golden-breasted trumpeter, a crane-like bird of South America. [Carib name.]

agamic, *a-gam'ik*, **agamous**, *ag'ɔ-mɔs*, *adjs.* a-sexual: parthenogenetic: (*obs.*) cryptogamous.—*n.* **agamogenesis** (*-jen'*), reproduction without sex, as in lower animals and in plants. [Gr. *a-*, priv., *gamos*, marriage.]

Aganippe, *ag-ɔ-nip'ē*, *n.* a fountain on Mt. Helicon, sacred to the Muses: poetic inspiration. [Gr *Aganippē*.]

agape, *ag'ɔ-pē*, *n.* a love-feast, held by the early Christians at communion time, when contributions were made for the poor:—*pl.* **ag'apae** (*-pē*).—*n.* **Agapemone** (*-pēm'* or *-pem'ɔ-nē*) a religious community of men and women whose 'spiritual marriages' were in some cases not strictly spiritual, founded in 1849 at Spaxton, near Bridgwater: any similar community, esp. with reference to its delinquencies. [Gr. *agapē*, love, *monē*, tarrying, abode.]

agape, *ɔ-gāp'*, *adj.* or *adv.* with gaping mouth. [Prep. a, gape.]

agar-agar, *ä'gär-ä'gär, ä'gär-ä'gär*, *n.* a jelly prepared from sea-weeds of various kinds used in bacteria-culture, medicine, glue-making, silk-dressing, and cooking: any of the seaweeds concerned.—Also **a'gar**. [Malay.]

agaric, *ag'ɔr-ik*, or *ɔg-ar'ik*, *n.* a fungus, properly one of the mushroom family, but loosely applied. —*adj.* **agar'ic**. [Gr. *agarikon*.]

agate, *ag'āt, -it*, *n.* a banded variegated chalcedony: (*Shak.*) a dwarfish person (as if a figure cut in agate): (*U.S.*) ruby type. [Fr.,—Gr. *achātēs*, said to be so called because first found near the river *Achates* in Sicily.]

agate, *ɔ-gāt'*, *adv.* agoing, on the way: astir: afoot: astray. [Prep. a, and gate; a Northern word.]

Agave, *a-gä'vē*, *n.* an aloe-like American genus of amaryllids, in Mexico usually flowering about the seventh year, in hothouse conditions requiring 40-60 (popularly a hundred) years.—also called American aloe, maguey, century-plant. [L. *Agāvē*, Gr. *Agauē*, daughter of Cadmus, fem. of *agauos*, illustrious.]

agaze, *ɔ-gāz'*, *adj.* and *adv.* at gaze, gazing. [Prep. a, gaze.]

agazed, *ɔ-gāzd'*, *adj.* (*Shak.*) struck with amazement. [Prob. a variant of aghast.]

age, *āj'*, *n.* duration of life: the time during which a person or thing has lived or existed: time of life reached: mature years: legal maturity (21 years): the time of being old: equivalence in development to the average of an actual age: a period of time: any great division of world, human, or individual history: a generation: a century: (*coll.*) a long time, however short (often *pl.*).—*v.i.* to grow old: to develop the characteristics of old age.—*v.t.* to make to seem old or to be like the old: to mature:—*pr.p.* **aging** or **ageing** (*āj'ing*); *pa.t.* and *pa.p.* **aged** (*ājd*).—*adj.* **aged** (*āj'id*), advanced in age: (*ā d*) of the age of.—*n.pl.* (*āj'id*), old people.—*ns.* **agedness** (*āj'idnis*), condition of being aged; **ag(e)'ing**, process of growing old or developing qualities of the old: maturing: change in properties that occurs in certain metals at atmospheric temperature after heat treatment or cold working;—*adjs.* **age'less**, never growing old, perpetually young: timeless; **age'long**, lasting an age.—**of age**, old enough to be legally deemed mature (with respect to voting, crime, contracts, marriage, etc.—21 years); **over age**, too old; **under age**, too young: not yet of age. [O.Fr. *aäge* (Fr. *âge*)—L. *aetās, -ātis*, for *aevitās*—L. *aevum*, age.]

agee. See ajee.

agen (*Milt. and other poets*). Same as again.

agene, *ä'jēn*, *n.* nitrogen trichloride, a heavy explosive liquid, the vapour of which whitens flour.—*v.t.* **a'genise**, to treat with agene. [ageing.]

agenda, *ɔ-* or *a-jen'dä*, *n.pl.* things to be done—programme of business for a meeting (sometimes treated as a *sing.*). [L. neuter pl. of *agendus*, to be done, gerundive of *agĕre*, to do.]

agent, *ā'jɔnt*, *n.* a person or thing that acts or exerts power: any natural force acting on matter: one authorised or delegated to transact business for another: a bank manager: formerly the representative of the government in a group of Indian states.—*adj.* acting: of an agent.—*n.* **agency** (*ā'jɔn-si*), the office or business, operation or action, of an agent; instrumentality: a group of Indian states assigned to an agent.—**law agent** (*Scot.*), a solicitor—any qualified legal practitioner other than an advocate. [L. *agēns, -entis*, pr.p. of *agĕre*, to do.]

agger, *aj'ɔr*, *n.* (*Rom. hist.*) a mound, esp. one of wood or earth for protection or other military purpose: any elevation, esp. artificial. [L.]

agglomerate, *ɔ-glom'ɔr-āt*, *v.t.* to make into a ball: to collect into a mass.—*v.i.* to grow into a mass.—*adj.* agglomerated: clustered: (*bot.*) gathered in a head.—*n.* a volcanic rock consisting of irregular fragments.—*n.* **agglomerā'tion**.—*adjs.* **agglom'erative**; **agglom'erated**. [L. *agglomerāre, -ātum*—ad, to, L. *glomus, glomeris*, a ball.]

agglutinate, *ɔ-glōōt'in-āt*, *v.t.* to glue together: to cause to cohere or clump.—*v.i.* to cohere as if glued: to clump.—*adj.* agglutinated.—*adjs.* **agglut'inable**; **agglut'inant**.—*n.* an agglutinating agent.—*ns.* **agglutinā'tion**, the act of agglutinating: an agglutinated mass: (*biol.*) the clumping of bacteria, blood corpuscles, protozoa, etc.; **agglut'-inin**, an antibody causing agglutination of bacteria, blood-corpuscles, etc.—*adj.* **agglut'inative**, tending, or having power, to agglutinate.—*n.* **agglut'inogen**, the substance in bacteria or in blood cells that stimulates the formation of, and unites with, agglutinin.—**agglutinative languages**, languages in which elements are combined without so losing their independence as to be mere inflexions. [L. *agglūtināre*—ad, to, *glūten, -inis*, glue.]

aggrace, *ə-grās'*, *v.t.* (*Spens.*) to grace: to favour:— (*pa.t.* **aggraced'**, *Spens.* **agraste'**).—*n.* (*Spens.*) kindness: favour. [**grace**, after It. *aggratiare* (now *aggraziare*).]

aggrandise, *ag'rən-dīz* or *-ran-*, *v.t.* to make greater.—*n.* **aggrandisement** (*əg-ran'diz-mənt*). [Fr. *agrandir*, *agrandiss-* —L. *ad*, to, and *grandis*, large.]

aggrate, *ə-grāt'*, *v.t.* (*obs.*) to gratify or please: to thank. [It. *aggratare*—L. *ad*, to, *grātus*, pleasing.]

aggravate, *ag'rə-vāt*, *v.t.* to make more grievous or worse: (*vulg.*) to irritate.—*adj.* **agg'ravating**.—*adv.* **agg'ravatingly**.—*n.* **aggrava'tion**. [L. *aggravāre*, *-ātus*—*ad*, to, *gravis*, heavy.]

aggregate, *ag'ri-gāt*, *v.t.* to collect into a mass or whole: to assemble: to add as a member to a society: (*coll.*) to amount to.—*v.i.* to accumulate. —*adj.* formed of parts that combine to make a whole: gathered in a mass or whole: united in a colonial organism: (*bot.*) formed from an apocarpous gynaeceum.—*n.* an assemblage: a mass: a total: any material mixed with cement to form concrete.—*adv.* **agg'regately**.—*n.* **aggrega'tion**.—*adj.* **agg'regative**. [L. *aggregāre*, *-ātum*, to bring together, as a flock—*ad*, to, *grex, gregis*, a flock.]

aggress, *ə-gres'*, *v.i.* to make a first attack: to begin a quarrel: to intrude.—*n.* **aggression** (*-gresh'ən*), a first act of hostility or injury.—*adj.* **aggress'ive**, making the first attack, or prone to do so: offensive as opposed to defensive.—*adv.* **aggress'ively**.—*ns.* **aggress'iveness**; **aggress'or**, one who attacks first. [L. *aggredī*, *-gressus*—*ad*, to, *gradī*, to step.]

aggri, aggry, *ag'ri*, *adj.* applied to ancient West African variegated glass beads. [Origin unknown.]

aggrieve, *ə-grēv'*, *v.t.* to press heavily upon: to pain or injure.—*adj.* **aggrieved'**, injured: having a grievance. [O.Fr. *agrever*—L. *ad*, to, and *gravis*, heavy.]

aghast, *ə-gäst'*, earlier (as *Milt.*) **agast**, *adj.* stupefied with horror. [Pa.p. of obs. *agast*—O.E. *intens.* pfx. *ā-*, and *gæstan*, to terrify.]

agila, *ag'i-lä*, *n.* eaglewood. [Port. *águila*, eaglewood, or Sp. *águila*, eagle; see **eaglewood**.]

agile, *aj'īl*, *adj.* nimble.—*adv.* **ag'ilely**.—*n.* **agility** (*ə-jil'i-ti*), nimbleness. [Fr.,—L. *agilis*—*agěre*, to do or act.]

agin, *ə-gin'*, *prep.* (*dial.*, esp. *Ir.*) against. [**again**.]

agio, *aj'(i-)ō*, *āj'*, *n.* the sum payable for the convenience of exchanging one kind of money for another, as silver for gold, paper for metal: the difference in exchange between worn or debased coinage and coinage of full value: the amount of deviation from the fixed par of exchange between the currencies of two countries: the discount on a foreign bill of exchange: money-changing.—*n.* **agiotage** (*aj'ə-tij*), agio: money-changing: stock-jobbing: speculative manoeuvres in stocks. [The word used in It. is *aggio*, a variant of *agio*, convenience.]

agist, *ə-jist'*, *v.t.* to take in to graze for payment: to charge with a public burden.—*ns.* **agist'ment**, the action of agisting: the price paid for cattle pasturing on the land: a burden or tax; **agist'or**, **agist'er**, an officer in charge of cattle agisted. [O.Fr. *agister*—à (L. *ad*) to, *giste*, resting-place—*gésir*, from a freq. of *jacêre*, to lie.]

agitate, *aj'i-tāt*, *v.t.* to keep moving: to stir violently: to disturb: to perturb: to excite: to discuss, or keep up the discussion of.—*v.i.* to stir up public feeling.—*adj.* **ag'itated**.—*adv.* **ag'itatedly**.—*n.* **agita'tion**.—*adj.* **ag'itative**.—*n.* **ag'itātor** (*hist.*), an agent, esp. for the private soldiers in the Parliamentary army: one who excites or keeps up a social or political agitation: apparatus for stirring. [L. *agitāre*, freq. of *agěre*, to put in motion.]

agitato, *äj-it-ä'tō*, *adj.* (*mus.*) agitated.—*adv.* agitatedly. [It.,—L. *agitāre*, to agitate.]

Aglaia, *ä-glī'ä*, *n.* one of the Graces. [Gr. *aglaiā*, splendour, triumph.]

aglet, aiglet, aiguillette, *ag'lit, āg'lit, ä-gwi-let'*, *n.* the metal tag of a lace or string: an ornamental tag or other metal appendage: anything dangling: (*usu.* **aiguillette**) a tagged point of braid hanging

from the shoulder in some uniforms.—**aglet babie** (*Shak.*), prob. a small figure forming the tag of a lace. [Fr. *aiguillette*, dim. of *aiguille*, a needle—from L. *acūcula*, dim. of *acus*, a needle.]

agley, aglee, *ə-glē'*, *ə-glī'*, *adv.* (*Scot.*) askew: awry. [Prep. **a**, and Scot. *gley*, squint.]

aglimmer, *ə-glim'ər*, *adj.* and *adv.* in a glimmering state. [Prep. **a**, **glimmer**.]

aglitter, *ə-glit'ər*, *adj.* and *adv.* in a glitter. [Prep. **a**, **glitter**.]

aglow, *ə-glō'*, *adj.* and *adv.* in a glow. [Prep. **a**, **glow**.]

agnail, *ag'nāl*, *n.* a hangnail or torn shred of skin beside the nail. [O.E. *angnægl*, corn—*ange, enge*, compressed, painful, *nægl*, nail (for driving in), confused with *hang, anger*, and (finger-) *nail*.]

agname, *ag'nām*, *n.* a name over and above the ordinary name and surname.—*adj.* **ag'named**. [**name**; after L.L. *agnōmen*.]

agnate, *ag'nāt*, *adj.* related on the father's side or (*Roman law*) through males only: allied.—*n.* a person so related.—*adjs.* **agnatic** (*-nat'*), **-al**. *adv.* **agnat'ically**.—*n.* **agnā'tion**. [L. *agnātus—ad*, to, (*g*)*nāscī*, to be born. See **cognate**.]

agnise, *ag-nīz'*, *v.t.* (*arch.*) to acknowledge, to confess. [L. *agnōscěre—ad*, to, (*g*)*nōscěre*, to know; on the model of **cognise**, etc.]

agnomen, *ag-nō'mən*, *n.* a name added to the family name, generally on account of some great exploit, as *Africanus* to Publius Cornelius Scipio. [L.,—*ad*, to, and (*g*)*nōmen*, a name.]

agnostic, *ag-nos'tik*, *n.* one who holds that we know nothing of things beyond material phenomena—that a First Cause and an unseen world are things unknown and (some would add) apparently unknowable.—*n.* **agnos'ticism**. [Coined by Huxley in 1869 from Gr. *a-*, priv. and *gnōstikos*, good at knowing; see **gnostic**.]

agnus castus, *ag'nəs kas'təs*, a species of *Vitex*, a verbenaceous tree. [Gr. *agnos*, the name of the tree, and L. *castus*, a translation of Gr. *hagnos*, chaste, with which *agnos* was confused.]

agnus dei, *ag'nəs dē'i*, *äg'noos dā'ē*, a part of the mass beginning with these words: music for it: a figure of a lamb emblematic of Christ, bearing the banner of the cross: a cake of wax stamped with such a figure, and blessed by the Pope. [L. *agnus Dēi*, lamb of God.]

ago, *ə-gō'*, **agone**, *ə-gon'*, *adv.* gone: past: since. [O.E. *āgān*, pa. p. of *āgān*, to pass away—*intens.* pfx. *ā-*, and *gān*, to go.]

agog, *ə-gog'*, *adj.* and *adv.* in excited eagerness. [Perh. connected with O.Fr. *en gogues*, frolicsome, of unknown origin.]

agoge, *a-gō'jē*, *n.* in ancient Greek music, tempo: sequence in melody.—*adj.* **agogic** (*a-goj'ik*), giving the effect of accent by slightly dwelling on a note.— *n.pl.* **agog'ics**. [Gr. *agōgē*, leading.]

agoing, *ə-gō'ing*, *adj.* and *adv.* in motion. [Prep. **a**, **going**.]

agone. See **ago**.

agonic, *ə-gon'ik*, *adj.* making no angle.—**agonic line**, the line of no magnetic variation, along which the magnetic needle points directly north and south. [Gr. *agōnos—a-*, priv., *gōniā*, angle.]

agony, *ag'ə-ni*, *n.* conflict in games: a violent struggle: extreme suffering: the death struggle: Christ's anguish in Gethsemane.—*v.i.* **ag'onise**, to struggle, contend: to suffer agony.—*v.t.* to subject to agony.—*adj.* **ag'onised**, suffering or expressing anguish.—*adv.* **ag'onisedly** (*-īz-id-li*). —*adj.* **ag'onising**, causing agony.—*adv.* **ag'onisingly**.—*n.* **ag'onist**, a competitor in public games.—*adjs.* **agonist'ic**, **-al**, relating to athletic contests: combative.—*adv.* **agonist'ically**.—*n.* (*pl.* in form, treated as *sing.*) **agonist'ics**, the art and theory of games and prize-fighting.—**agony column**, the part of a newspaper containing special advertisements, as for missing friends and the like. [Gr. *agōniā*, contest, agony, *agōnistēs*, competitor—*agōn*, meeting, contest.]

agood, *ə-good'*, *adv.* (*Shak.*) in good earnest, heartily. [Prep. **a**, and **good**.]

agora, *ag'ə-rä*, *n.* an assembly, place of assembly, market-place.—*n.* **agorapho'bia**, morbid fear of

---

Neutral vowels in unaccented syllables: *el'ə-mənt*, *in'fənt*, *ran'dəm*

(crossing) open places. [Gr. *agorā*, assembly, market-place, *phobos*, fear.]

agouta, *ə-gōō′tä*, *n.* a rat-like insectivore (*Solenodon*) of Haiti. [Taino *aguta*.]

agouti, aguti, *ə-gōō′tē*, *n.* a small South American rodent allied to the guinea-pig. [Fr.,—Sp. *aguti*—Guaraní *acuti*.]

agraffe, *ə-graf′*, *n.* a hooked clasp. [Fr. *agrafe*—*à*, to, *grappe*—L.L. *grappa*—O.H.G. *chrapfo* (Ger. *krappen*), hook.]

agraphia, *ə-graf′i-ä*, *n.* loss of power of writing, from brain disease or injury.—*adj.* **agraph′ic**. [Gr. *a-*, priv. *graphein*, to write.]

agrarian, *ag-rā′ri-ən*, *adj.* relating to land, or its management or distribution.—*n.* **agrā′rianism**, equitable division of lands : a political movement in favour of change in conditions of property in land. [L. *agrārius*—*ager*, a field.]

agree, *ə-grē′*, *v.i.* to be, or come to be, of one mind : (*obs.* or *dial.*) to make friends again : to suit, do well (with) : to concur : to accede : to assent : to be consistent : to harmonise : to get on together : to be in grammatical concord, take the same gender, number, case, or person.—*v.t.* to determine, to settle : to concede : to consent : (*obs.*) to compose : (*obs.*) to arrange :—*pa.p.* **agreed′**.—*n.* **agreeabil′ity**.—*adj.* **agree′able**, suitable : pleasant : in harmony : conformable : (*coll.*) willing, consenting.—*adv.* in accordance.—*n.* **agree′ableness**.—*adv.* **agree′ably**.—*n.* **agree′ment**, concord : conformity : harmony : a compact, contract, treaty : (*obs.*) an embellishment. [O.Fr. *agréer*, to accept kindly—L. *ad*, to, and *grātus*, pleasing.]

agrestic, *ə-gres′tik*, *adj.* of the fields : rural : unpolished. [L. *agrestis*—*ager*, a field.]

agriculture, *ag′ri-kult-yər*, *n.* the art or practice of cultivating the land.—*adj.* **agricult′ural**.—*n.* **agricult′urist**, one skilled in agriculture : a farmer—also **agricult′uralist**. [L. *agricultūra*—*ager*, a field, *cultūra*, cultivation.]

agrimony, *ag′ri-mən-i*, *n.* a genus (*Agrimonia*) of the rose family, with small yellow flowers and bitter taste : extended to other plants, especially **hemp agrimony** (*Eupatorium cannabinum*), a composite. [L. *agrimōnia* (a blunder or misreading)—Gr. *argemōnē*, long prickly-headed poppy.]

agrin, *ə-grin′*, *adv.* on the grin. [Prep. **a, grin**.]

agrise, agrize, agryze, *a-grīz′*, *v.t.* (*Spens.*) to terrify : to horrify : to disfigure.—*adj.* **agrised′**. [O.E. *āgrīsan*, to dread.]

agronomy, *ə-gron′ə-mi*, *n.* rural economy.—*adjs.* **agronomial**, (*-ō′miəl*); **agronomic** (*-om′ik*).—*n.* **agron′omist**. [Gr. *agros*, field, *nemein*, to dispense, manage.]

agrostology, *ag-ros-tol′ə-ji*, *n.* the study of grasses.—*adj.* **agrostological** (*-ta-loj′i-kl*).—*n.* **agrostol′ogist**. [Gr. *agrōstis*, dog's-tooth grass.]

aground, *ə-grownd′*, *adv.* in or to a stranded condition : on the ground. [Prep. **a, ground**.]

aguacate, *ä-gwä-kä′tä*, *n.* the avocado pear. [Sp.,—Nahuatl *ahuacatl*.]

aguardiente, *ä-gwär-dyen′tä*, *n.* a brandy made in Spain and Portugal : any spirituous liquor. [Sp., from *agua ardiente*, burning water—L. *aqua*, water, *ardēns, -ēntis*—*ardēre*, to burn.]

ague, *ā′gū*, *n.* (*B.*) a burning fever : a fever with hot and cold fits : malaria : a shivering fit.—*adjs.* **agued** (*ā′gūd*), struck with ague : shivering : cold ; **ā′guish**.—*adv.* **ā′guishly**.—*n.* **ā′gue-fit′**.—*adj.* **ā′gue-proof**. [O.Fr. (*fièvre*) *ague*—L. (*febris*) *acūta*, sharp (fever).]

aguise, aguize, *a-gīz′*, *v.t.* (*Spens.*) to dress : to array : to equip : to adorn : to frame, fashion. [Pfx. *a-*, and **guise**.]

ah, *ä*, *interj.* expressing surprise, joy, pity, complaint, objection, etc. [Perh. O.Fr. *ah*.]

aha, *ə-hä′*, *interj.* of exultation, pleasure, surprise, or contempt. [**ah, ha**.]

ahead, *ə-hed′*, *adv.* further on : in advance : forward : headlong. [Prep. **a, head**.]

aheap, *ə-hēp′*, *adv.* in a heap. [Prep. **a, heap**.]

aheight, *ə-hīt′*, *adv.* (*arch.*) on high, aloft. [Prep. **a, height**.]

ahem, *ə-h(e)m′*, *interj.* a lengthened form of **hem**.

Ahithophel. See **Achitophel**.

ahigh, *ə-hī′*, *adv.* on high. [Prep. **a, high**.]

ahint, *ə-hint′*, **ahind**, *ə-hin(d)′*, *adv.* and *prep.* (*Scot.* etc.) behind. [O.E. *æthindan*.]

ahold, *ə-hōld′*, *adv.* at or to grips, or a condition of holding : (*obs. naut.*; *Shak.*) near the wind (*i.e.* so as to hold there). [Prep. **a, hold**.]

ahorseback, *ə-hors′bak*, *adv.* on horseback. [Prep. **a**.]

ahoy, *ə-hoi′*, *interj.* (*naut.*) used in hailing. [**ah, hoy**.]

Ahriman, *ä′ri-män*, *n.* the evil spirit, opposed to Ormuzd. [Pers. *Ahrīman*, Zend *anro mainyus*, dark spirit.]

ahull, *ə-hul′*, *adv.* (*naut.*) with sails furled, and helm lashed to the lee-side. [Prep. **a** and **hull**.]

ahungered, *ə-hung′gərd*, **ahungry**, *-gri*, *adjs.* (*arch.*) oppressed with hunger.—Also, from confusion of prefixes, **anhung′(e)red, an-hung′ry**. [Prob. O.E. *of-hyngred*.]

Ahuramazda, *ä′hoor-ä-maz-dä*. Same as **Ormuzd**.

ai, *ä′ē*, *n.* the three-toed sloth. [Tupí *ai*, representing the animal's cry.]

aiblins. See **able**.

aid, *ād*, *v.t.* to help.—*n.* help : succour : assistance, as in defending an action : that which helps : an auxiliary : a feudal tax for certain purposes— paying the lord's ransom, the expense of knighting his son, his daughter's marriage : subsidy or money grant to the king.—*n.* **aid′ance**, aid, help, support. —*adj.* **aid′ant**, (*arch.*) aiding, helping.—*adj.* **aid′ed**.—*n.* **aid′er**.—*adjs.* **aid′ful** ; **aid′ing** ; **aid′less**. [O.Fr. *aider*—L. *adjūtāre*, freq. of *adjuvāre*—*juvāre, jūtum*, to help.]

aide-de-camp, *ed-*, *ād′də-kän*ᵍ, *n.* an officer who carries the orders of a general and acts as secretary : an officer attending a king, governor, etc. :—*pl.* **aides′-de-camp** (*ed-, ād-*). [Fr., assistant on the field.]

aiery, a variant of **aerie**.

aiglet. Same as **aglet**.

aigrette, *ā′gret, ā-gret′*, *n.* an egret : an egret plume : a plume : a tuft : a pappus : a spray of jewels. [Fr.]

aiguille, *ā-gwēl′*, *n.* a sharp, needle-like peak of rock : a slender boring-tool.—*n.* **aiguillette′** (see **aglet**). [Fr.]

ail, *āl*, *v.t.* (*impers.*) to trouble, afflict, be the matter with : to have the matter with one.—*v.i.* to be sickly, indisposed.—*n.* trouble : indisposition.— *adj.* **ail′ing**, unwell ; in poor health.—*n.* **ail′ment**, pain : indisposition : disease, esp. if not very serious.—**what ails him at ?** (*Scot.*) what is his objection to ? [O.E. *eglan*, to trouble.]

ailanto, *ā-lan′tō*, *n.* the tree of heaven (genus *Ailantus*; family *Simarubaceae*), a lofty and beautiful Asiatic tree.—Also **ailan′thus**. [Amboyna (Moluccas) name *aylanto*, tree of the gods.]

aileron, *āl′, el′ə-ron*ᵍ, *-ron*, *n.* a flap on an aeroplane wing-tip for lateral balancing : a half-gable, as on a penthouse.—*n.* **ailette** (*ā-let′*), a plate of armour for the shoulder. [Fr. dims. of *aile*—L. *āla*, a wing.]

aim, *ām*, *v.t.* (*obs.*) to estimate, guess : to place : to point, level, direct, with (or as if with) a view to hitting : to purpose, seek : to have as one's object.— *v.i.* (*obs.*) to conjecture : to direct a course : to level a weapon : to direct a blow or missile : to direct an utterance with personal or special application : to direct one's intention and endeavours with a view to attainment.—*n.* (*Shak.*) a guess or estimate : an act or manner of aiming : (*Shak.*) a shot : an object or purpose aimed at : design : intention.— *adj.* **aim′less**, without fixed aim.—*adv.* **aim′lessly**.—*n.* **aim′lessness**.—**cry aim** (*arch.*), to encourage by calling out 'aim', hence, to applaud ; **give aim** (*arch.*), to guide by reporting result of previous shots ; **take aim**, to aim deliberately. [Prob. partly O.Fr. *esmer* (Picardian *amer*)—L. *aestimāre*, partly O.Fr. *aesmer*—L. *adaestimāre*; cf. **esteem, estimate**.]

ain, *ān*, *adj.* (*Scot.*) own. [O.N. *eiginn* or O.E. *ǣgen*, a variant of *āgen*.]

ain't, *ānt*, (*coll.*) contracted form of *are not*, used also for *am* or *is not* : also of *have not*.

air, *ār, n.* the gaseous mixture (chiefly nitrogen and oxygen) of which the atmosphere is composed : (*obs.*) any gas : a light breeze : breath : effluvium : the aura or atmosphere that invests anything : bearing, outward appearance, manner, look : an assumed or affected manner : (in *pl.*) affectation of superiority : exposure, noising abroad : melody, tune : the chief, usually upper, part or tune.—*v.t.* to expose to the air : to ventilate : to warm and dry : to give an airing to : to wear openly, display : to publish abroad.—*v.i.* to take an airing : to become aired.—*ns.* **air′-arm,** the branch of the fighting services that uses aircraft; **air′-base,** a base of operations for aircraft; **air′-bath,** exposure of the body to air : apparatus for therapeutic application of compressed or rarefied air, or for drying substances in air; **air′-bed,** an inflated mattress; **air′-bell,** an air-bubble; **air′-bladder,** a sac containing gas, as those that buoy up certain seaweeds : a fish's swim-bladder, serving to regulate buoyancy and in some cases acting as a lung.—*adj.* **air′borne,** carried by air : borne up in the air.—*ns.* **air′-brake,** a brake worked by compressed air : a means of checking the speed of an aircraft; **air′-brick,** a block for ventilation; **air′brush,** a device for spraying paint by compressed air; **air′-bubble,** a bubble of air, *spec.* one causing a spot on a photograph.—*adj.* **air′-built,** built in air : having no solid foundation.—*ns.* **air′-bump,** a mass of dense air into which aircraft bump : a jolt caused thereby; **air′-cavity, air′-cell** (*bot.*), an intercellular space containing air; **air′-chief-mar′shal,** an air-force officer ranking with an admiral or general; **air′-comm′odore,** an air-force officer ranking with a commodore or brigadier; **air′-condi′tioning,** the bringing of air to the desired state of purity, temperature, and humidity.—*adj.* **air′-cooled.**—*ns.* **air′-cooling,** cooling by means of air ; **air′craft,** *sing.* and *pl.,* any structure or machine for navigating the air; **air′craft-carrier,** a vessel from which aircraft can take off and on which they may alight; **air′craftman,** an air-force member of lowest rank.—Also **air′craftsman ; air′-cushion,** a cushion that can be inflated; **air′-drain,** a cavity in the external walls of a building to prevent damp from getting through to the interior.—*adj.* **air′-drawn,** drawn in air : visionary : (*Shak.*) imaginary.—*ns.* **air′-engine,** an engine driven by heated or compressed air; **air′er,** one who airs : a frame on which clothes are dried; **air′field,** an open expanse where aircraft may land and take off; **air′-force,** a force organised for warfare in the air; **air′-gap,** a gap in the magnetic circuit of a piece of electrical apparatus, *e.g.* the gap between the rotor and stator of an electric machine; **air′-gas,** illuminating gas made by charging atmospheric air with vapour of petroleum or other hydrocarbon; **air′-graph** (*trade-name*), a letter photographically reduced for sending by air; **air′-grating,** a grating admitting air for ventilation; **air′gun,** a gun that discharges missiles by compressed air; **air′hole,** a hole for the passage of air : a hole in ice where animals come up to breathe : an air-pocket.—*adv.* **air′ily,** in an airy manner.—*ns.* **air′iness ; air′ing,** exposure to air or heat or to general notice : a short excursion in the open air; **air′-jacket,** a casing containing air to reduce loss or gain of heat : a garment with airtight cavities to buoy up in water.—*adj.* **air′less,** without air : without free communication with the outer air : without wind : stuffy.—*ns.* **air′-lift,** organised carriage by air across a barrier; **air′-line,** a route or system of traffic by aircraft : (*U.S.*) a bee-line; **air′-liner,** a large passenger aircraft : an aircraft plying in an air-line; **air′-lock,** a small chamber in which pressure of air can be raised or lowered, through which communication is made between a caisson where the air is compressed and the outer air : a bubble in a pipe obstructing flow of liquid; **air′-mail,** mail conveyed by air; **air′man,** an aviator :—*fem.* **air′woman ; air′manship,** the art of handling aircraft; **air′-mar′shal,** an air-force officer ranking with a vice-admiral or a lieutenant-general; **air′-mechan′ic,** one who tends and repairs aircraft.—*adj.* **air′-minded,** having thought habitually and favourably directed towards flying.—*ns.* **air′-officer,** an air-force officer of general rank, corresponding to flag-officer or general officer **air′plane** (*U.S.*) an aeroplane; **air′plant,** an epiphyte; **air′-pocket, a** region of rarefied or down-flowing air, in which aircraft drop; **air′port,** an opening for the passage of air : a station where aircraft receive and discharge passengers and cargo; **air′-power,** military power in point of aircraft; **air′pump,** an instrument for pumping air out or in; **air′-raid,** an attack on a place by aircraft; **air′-sac,** an outgrowth of the lung in birds, helping respiration or lightening the body : in insects a dilatation of the trachea; **air′-screw,** the propeller of an aircraft; **air′-shaft,** a passage for air into a mine; **air′ship,** a mechanically driven dirigible aircraft, lighter than air; **air′-sickness,** nausea affecting travellers by air.—*adj.* **air′sick.**—*ns.* **air′-space,** cubic contents available for respirable air : an air-cell.—*adj.* **air′tight,** impermeable to air : (*fig.*) impenetrable, such that an opponent can find no weak place.—*ns.* **air′-trap,** a device to prevent escape of foul air; **air′-vice-mar′shal,** an air-force officer ranking with a rear-admiral or major-general.—*adv.* **air′ward, air′wards,** up in the air.—*n.* **air′way,** a passage for air : an organised route for air travel : used in *pl.* to form names of air-line companies; **air′worthiness.**—*adjs.* **air′worthy,** in fit condition for safe flying; **air′y,** consisting of or relating to air : open to the air : like air : unsubstantial : sprightly : light-hearted : offhand.—**in the air,** prevalent in an indefinite form : unformed; **on the air,** broadcast by wireless : in the act of broadcasting; **take air,** to get wind, become known; **take the air,** to have an airing. [O.Fr. (and Fr.) *air*—L. *āēr, āēris*—Gr. *āēr, āeros,* air.]

Airedale, *ār′dāl, n.* (in full **Airedale terrier**) a large terrier of a breed from *Airedale* in Yorkshire.

airn, *ārn,* a Scots form of **iron.**

airt, *ārt, n.* (*Scot.*) direction, quarter.—*v.t.* to direct. [Origin obscure; cf. Gael. *aird, àrd,* Ir. *ard.*]

aisle, *īl, n.* a side division of the nave or other part of a church or similar building, generally separated off by pillars : (*loosely*) any division of a church, or a small building attached : (*loosely*) a passage between rows of seats : (*U.S.*) a passage-way : (*U.S.*) the corridor of a railway train.—*adj.* **aisled** (*īld*), having aisles. [O.Fr. *ele* (Fr. *aile*)—L. *āla,* a wing; confused with **isle** and **alley.**]

ait, eyot, *āt, n.* a small island. [Cf. O.E. *ēgath, īgeoth,* app. conn. with *ieg,* island; the phonology is obscured.]

ait, *āt,* Scots form of **oat.**

aitch, *āch, n.* the eighth letter of the alphabet (H). [O.Fr. *ache,* from which L.L. *ahha* is inferred.]

aitch-bone, *āch′bōn, n.* the bone of the rump : the cut of beef over it. [An *aitchbone* is for *a nache-bone*—O.Fr. *nache*—L. *natis,* buttock; and **bone.**]

aizle. See **easle.**

Aizoon, *ā-ī-zō′on, n.* an African genus of plants giving name to the family **Aizo′aceae,** akin to the goosefoots. [App. Gr. *āei,* ever, *zōos,* living.]

ajar, *ə-jär′, adv.* and *adj.* partly open. [O.E. *on,* on, *cerr,* a turn.]

ajee, agee, *ə-jē′, adv. (Scot.* and *prov.*) off the straight : ajar. [Prep. **a,** and **gee,** to move to one side; **jee,** a call to a horse to move to one side.]

ajowan, *aj′ō-wən,* or **ajwan,** *aj′wən, n.* a plant of the caraway genus yielding ajowan oil and thymol. [Origin uncertain.]

ajutage. See **adjutage.**

ake, *āk,* old spelling of the verb **ache.**

akee, *a-kē′, n.* a small African sapindaceous tree, now common in the West Indies : its edible fruit. [Kru *ā-kee.*]

akene, *a-ken′, n.* Same as **achene.**

akimbo, *ə-kim′bō, adv.* and *adj.* with hand on hip and elbow out. [M.E. *in kenebow ;* poss. in a keen (sharp) bow or bend; other suggestions are *can-*

Neutral vowels in unaccented syllables : *el′ə-mənt, in′fənt, ran′dəm*

bow (i.e. can-handle), and O.N. *kengboginn*, bent into a crook—*kengr*, kink, *boginn*, bowed.]

akin, *ə-kin'*, *adv.* by kin : of nature.—*adj.* related by blood : of like nature. [Prep. **a**, **kin**.]

akolouthos. Same as **acolouthos**.

ala, *ā'lä*, *n.* (*bot.*) a membranous outgrowth on a fruit : a side petal in the pea family : a large side sepal in the milkworts : a leafy expansion running down the stem from a leaf: (*zool.*) any flat winglike process, esp. of bone:—*pl.* **alae** (*ā'lē*).—*adjs.* **ā'lar**, **ā'lary**, pertaining to a wing; **ā'late**, **-d**, winged, having an ala. [L. *āla*, wing.]

alabamine, *al-ə-bām'ēn*, *n.* a name proposed for element No. 85. See **astatine**. [*Alabama*, where its discovery in nature was claimed.]

alabandine. See **almandine**.—*n.* **alaband'ite**, a cubic mineral, manganese sulphide.

alabaster, *al'ə-bäs-tər*, or *bäs'*, (*Spens.*, *Shak.*, *Milt.*, etc. **alablaster**) *n.* a semi-transparent massive gypsum.—*adj.* of or like alabaster.— **oriental alabaster**, stalactitic calcite. [Gr. *alabastros*, said to be from *Alabastron*, a town in Egypt.]

alack, *ə-lak'*, *interj.* denoting regret.—*interj.* **alack'-a-day**, alack the day : woe worth the day. [Prob. **ah**, **lack**.]

alacrity, *ə-lak'ri-ti*, *n.* briskness : cheerful readiness : promptitude. [L. *alacritās*, *-ātis*—*alacer*, *alacris*, brisk.]

alalia, *a-lā'li-ä*, *n.* loss of speech. [Gr. *a-*, priv., and *laleein*, to talk.]

alameda, *ä-lä-mä'dä*, *n.* a public walk or promenade, esp. between rows of poplars. [Sp., *álamo*, poplar.]

alamode, *ä-lä-mōd'*, *adv.* and *adj.* according to the fashion.—*n.* a light glossy silk.—**alamode beef**, beef larded and stewed with vegetables. [Fr. *à la mode.*]

alamort, *ä-lä-mort'*, *adj.* half-dead : in a depressed condition : dejected. [Fr. *à la mort*, to the death; see also **amort**.]

aland, *ə-land'*, *adv.* ashore. [Prep. **a**, **land**.]

alang, *ä'läng*, or **a'lang-a'lang.** Same as **lalang**.

alar, **alary.** See **ala**.

alarm, *ə-lärm'*, *n.* a call to arms : notice of danger : a mechanical contrivance for arousing, warning, or giving notice : the noise made by it : (*obs.*) a din : a fear-stricken state : apprehension of evil.—*v.t.* to call to arms : to give notice of danger : to arouse : to strike with dread.—*ns.* **alarm'-bell**; **alarm'-clock'**, a clock that can be set to ring an alarm at a chosen time.—*adj.* **alarmed'**.—*adv.* **alarm'-edly**.—*adj.* **alarm'ing**.—*adv.* **alarm'ingly**.—*n.* **alarm'ist**, a scaremonger.—Also *adj.*—*n.* and *v.t.* **alarum** (*ə-lä'rəm*, or *-lä'*), alarm (now *arch.* except of a warning mechanism or sound).—*ns.* **alar'um-bell'**, **-clock'**.—**alar(u)ms and excursions**, a stage direction for a sketchy conventionalised representation of skirmishing or the outskirts of a battle : hence, vague hostilities. [O.Fr. (Fr.) *alarme*—It. *all'arme*, to (the) arms.]

alas, *ə-läs'*, *interj.* expressive of grief.—**alas the day**, **alas the while**, ah! unhappy day, time. [O.Fr. *ha las*, *a las* (mod. Fr. *hélas*); *ha*, ah, and *las*, *lasse*, wretched, weary—L. *lassus*, wearied.]

alastrim, *ə-läs'trim*, *n.* a mild form of smallpox or a similar disease. [Port.]

alate, *ə-lāt'*, *adv.* (*arch.*) lately. [**of**, **late**.]

alate. See **ala**.

alay, **alaiment**, old spellings of **allay**, **allayment**.

alb, *alb*, *n.* a long white tight-sleeved vestment. [O.E. *albe*—L.L. *alba*—L. *albus*, white.]

albacore, *al'bə-kōr*, *n.* a large tunny : (*S. Afr.*) a species of mackerel.—Also **al'bicore.** [Port. *albacor*—Ar. *al*, the, *bukr*, young camel.]

Alban, *al'bən*, **Albany**, *-i*, **Albion**, *-i-ən*, *ns.* ancient names for the island of Great Britain, now used poetically for Britain, England, or esp. Scotland.—**Alban**, the ancient kingdom of the Picts and (Celtic) Scots, which the addition of Lothian and Strathclyde transformed into Scotland; **Albany**, a Scottish dukedom first conferred in 1398.—**Albany herald**, one of the Scottish heralds. [Celtic.]

albata, *al-bā'tä*, *n.* a variety of German silver. [L. *albāta* (*fem.*), whitened—*albus*, white.]

albatross, *al'bə-tros*, *n.* a large, long-winged sea-bird of remarkable powers of flight. [See **alcatras**; perh. influenced by L. *albus*, white.]

albe, **albee**, **all-be**, *awl-bē'*, *awl'bē*, *conj.* (*arch.*) albeit. [**all**, **be**.]

albedo, *al-bē'dō*, *n.* whiteness : the proportion of incident light reflected, as by a planet. [L. *albēdō*, whiteness—*albus*, white.]

albeit, *awl-bē'it*, *conj.* although it be : notwithstanding : even if, although. [**all be it** (that)= all though it be that.]

albert, *al'bərt*, *n.* a short kind of watch-chain. [After Queen Victoria's husband.]

albescent, *al-bes'ənt*, *adj.* becoming white : whitish. —*n.* **albesc'ence.** [L. *albēscēns*, *-entis*, pr.p. of *albēscēre*, to grow white—*albus*, white.]

albespyne, **albespine**, *al'bə-spīn*, *n.* (*arch.*) hawthorn. [O.Fr. *albespine* (Fr. *aubépine*)—L. *alba spīna*, white thorn.]

Albigensian, *al-bi-jen'si-ən*, *adj.* of the town of *Albi* or its district (the Albigeois), in the S. of France : of a Catharist or Manichaean sect or of the 13th century crusade (beginning in the Albigeois) by which, with the Inquisition, the Catholic Church stamped it out in blood.— Also *n.*—*n.pl.* **Albigen'ses.**—*n.* **Albigen'sianism.** [L.L. *Albigēnsēs*.]

albino, *al-bē'nō*, (*U.S. -bī'*), *n.* a person or other animal with abnormally white skin and hair and pink pupil : a plant lacking in pigment :—*pl.* **albi'nos:**—*fem.* **albiness** (*al'bin-es*).—*ns.* **al'binism** (*-bin-*), **albinoism** (*-bē'*).—*adj.* **albinotic** (*al-bin-ot'ik*). [Port. *albino*, white negro or albino—L. *albus*, white.]

albite, *al'bīt*, *n.* a white plagioclase felspar, sodium and aluminium silicate.—*v.t.* **al'bitise**, to turn into albite. [L. *albus*, white.]

albugo, *al-bū'gō*, *n.* leucoma.—*adj.* **albugineous**, (*-jin'i-əs*), like the white of an egg or of the eye. [L. *albūgō*, *-inis*, whiteness—*albus*, white.]

album, *al'bəm*, *n.* among the Romans, a white tablet or register on which the praetor's edicts and such public notices were recorded : a blank book for the insertion of photographs, autographs, poetical extracts, scraps, postage-stamps, or the like : a printed book of selections, esp. of music : (*U.S.*) a visitors' book:—*pl.* **al'bums.**—*n.* **al'bum-leaf** (trans. of Ger. *albumblatt*), a short musical composition. [L. neut. of *albus*, white.]

albumen, *al-bū'mən*, *-min*, or *al'*, *n.* white of egg : (*zool.*) the nutritive material surrounding the yolk in the eggs of higher animals, a mixture of proteins : (*bot.*) any tissue within the seed-coat other than the embryo itself—endosperm and perisperm, a store of food for the young plant, no matter what its chemical nature: (*obs.*) an albumin.—*v.t.* **albū'menise**, **albū'minise** (*phot.*) to cover or impregnate with albumen or an albuminous solution.—*ns.* **albū'min** (or *al'*), a protein of various kinds soluble in pure water, the solution coagulable by heat; **albū'minate**, an alkali compound of an albumin.—*adj.* **albū'minoid**, like albumen.—*n.* an old name for a protein in general : any one of a class of substances including keratin and chondrin.—*adj.* **albū'minous**, like or containing albumen or albumin : insipid.—*n.* **albū-minūr'ia**, presence of albumin in the urine. [L. *albūmen*, *-inis*—*albus*, white.]

alburnum, *al-burn'əm*, *n.* sapwood, the soft wood between inner bark and heart-wood.—*adj.* **alburn'ous.** [L., —*albus*, white.]

alcahest. See **alkahest**.

Alcaic, *al-kā'ik*, *adj.* of or pertaining to the Greek lyric poet *Alcaeus* (*Alkaios*, fl. 600 B.C.), or of the kind of verse invented by him.—*n.* (esp. in *pl.*) Alcaic verses.—**Alcaic strophe**, a form much used by Horace, consisting of two eleven-syllable Alcaics : ∖− ‿ ∪ − − / − ∪ ∪ − ∪ ∖' : a nine-syllable : ∖' − ‿ − ∪ − ‿ ∪ − ∪, and a ten-syllable : − ‿ ∪ ∪ − ∪ ∪ − ∪ ∪; imitated by Tennyson in 'O mighty-mouth'd inventor of harmonies'.

alcaide, alcayde, *al-kād', āl-kī'dhā, -dā, n.* (*Sp.*) governor of a fortress : a gaoler. [Sp. *alcaide*—Ar. *al-qā'id—al,* the, *qā''id,* leader—*qāda,* to lead.]
alcaide, *āl-kāl'dā, n.* (*Sp.*) a judge. [Sp.,—Ar. *al-qādī—qada,* to judge.]
alcatras, *al'kə-tras, n.* a name applied to several large water birds, as the pelican, gannet, frigate-bird albatross. [Sp. *alcatraz,* pelican.]
alchemy, alchymy, *al'ki-mi, n.* the infant stage of chemistry, its chief pursuits the transmutation of other metals into gold, and the elixir of life : (*fig.*) transmuting potency : a gold-like substance (*e.g.* brass) : a trumpet made of it.—*adjs.* **alchemic** (*-kem'ik*), **-al.**—*n.* **al'chemist.** [Ar. *al-kimīā—al,* the, and *kimīā*—late Gr. *chēmeiā, chȳmeiā,* variously explained as the Egyptian art (*Khēmiā,* 'black-land', Egypt, from the Egyptian name), the art of *Chȳmēs* (its supposed inventor), or the art of pouring (*chȳma,* fluid; cf. *cheein,* to pour).]
alcohol, *al'kə-hol, n.* (*obs.*) a fine powder, esp. a sublimate : hence (*obs.*) an essence, a distillate : a liquid generated by the fermentation of sugar or other saccharine matter, and forming the intoxicating element of fermented liquors : a general term for a class of hydrocarbon compounds analogous to common (or ethyl) alcohol, in which a hydroxyl group is substituted for an atom of hydrogen.—*adj.* **alcohol'ic,** of, like, containing, or due to alcohol.—*n.* one addicted to excessive drinking of alcohol.—*n.* **alcoholisā'tion.**—*v.t.* **al'coholise,** to convert into or saturate with alcohol : to rectify.—*ns.* **al'coholism,** alcoholic poisoning ; **al'coholist,** one who favours the use of alcohol, or who drinks it in excess ; **alcoholom'eter,** an instrument for measuring the proportion of alcohol in solutions ; **alcoholom'etry.** [Ar. *al-koh'l—al,* the, *koh'l,* antimony powder used in the East to stain the eyelids.]
Alcoran, *al-ko-rän' n.* (*arch.*) the Koran. [Fr.,—Arab. *al,* the, **Koran.**]
alcove, *al'kōv,* or *al-kōv', n.* a recess in a room : any recess : a shady retreat. [Sp. *alcoba,* a place in a room railed off to hold a bed—Ar. *al,* the, *qobbah,* a vault.)
Alcyonium, *al-si-ō'ni-əm, n.* a genus of Anthozoa growing in masses of polyps called dead men's fingers.—*n.pl.* **Alcyonā'ria,** the order to which belong Alcyonium, sea-pens, red coral and organ-pipe coral.—*n.* and *adj.* **alcyonā'rian.** [Gr. *alkyoneion,* an organism said to resemble a halcyon's nest—*alkyōn,* halcyon, kingfisher.]
Aldebaran, *al-deb'ə-ran, n.* a first-magnitude red star of the Hyades. [Ar. *al-dabarān,* the follower (of the Pleiades).]
aldehyde, *al'di-hīd, n.* a volatile fluid with a suffocating smell, obtained by the oxidation of alcohol : a compound differing from an alcohol in having two atoms less of hydrogen. [Contr. for *alcohol dēhydrogenātum,* alcohol deprived of hydrogen.]
alder, *awl'dər, n.* any tree of the genus *Alnus,* related to the birches, usually growing in moist ground : extended to various other trees or shrubs : an artificial fishing-fly.—*n.* **al'der-buck'thorn,** a species of buckthorn (*Rhamnus Frangula*) ; **al'der-fly,** a river-side neuropterous insect.—*adjs.* **al'der-leaved** ; **al'dern,** made of alder. [O.E. *alor;* Ger. *erle;* L. *alnus.*]
alder-liefest, *awl-dər-lēf'ist, adj.* (*Shak.*) most beloved of all. [O.E. *alra* (W.S. *ealra*), gen. pl. of *al* (*eal*), all, and superl. of **lief.**]
alderman, *awl'dər-mən, n.* (*hist.*) in O.E. times a nobleman of highest rank, a governor of a shire or district, a high official : later, head of a guild : in English boroughs, a civic dignitary next in rank to the mayor, elected by fellow councillors : a superior member of an English county council : (*U.S.*) a member of the governing body of a borough or of its upper house, elected by popular vote :—*pl.* **al'dermen.**—*adj.* **aldermanic** (*-man'-ik*).—*n.* **alderman'ity.**—*adjs.* **al'dermanlike, al'dermanly,** pompous and portly.—*ns.* **al'der-manry ; al'dermanship.** [O.E. *aldorman* (W.S. *ealdorman*)—*aldor* (*ealdor*), a chief—*ald* (*eald*) old, and noun-forming suffix *-or.*]

Alderney, *awl'dər-ni, n.* a small dairy-cow, formerly of a breed kept in *Alderney,* now loosely including Jersey and Guernsey.
Aldine, *awl'dīn, adj.* from the press, or named in honour, of *Aldus* Manutius of Venice and his family (15th-16th cent.).
ale, *āl, n.* a beverage made from an infusion of malt by fermentation—beer, esp. where the quantity of hops is small and that of undecomposed sugar great : (*arch.*) a festival, from the liquor drunk.—*ns.* **ale'bench,** a bench in or before an alehouse : **ale'-berry,** a beverage made from ale and bread sops with flavouring : **ale'-bush, ale'-pole, ale'-stake,** a bush, pole, or stake used as an alehouse sign ; **ale'-conner, ale'-taster,** a civic officer appointed to test the quality of ale brewed; **ale'-cost,** costmary (used in flavouring ale); **ale'-draper** (*obs.*), a tavern-keeper; **ale'hoof,** ground-ivy (O.E. *hófe*) ; **ale'-house,** a house in which ale is sold.—*adj.* **ale'washed** (*Shak.*).—*n.* **ale'wife,** a woman who sells ale : a fish akin to the herring, common off the N.E. of America (perhaps from its corpulent shape, but perhaps a different word) :—*pl.* **ale'wives.** [O.E. (Anglian) *alu* (W.S. *ealu*); O.N. *öl.*]
aleatory, *ā'li-ə-tər-i, adj.* depending on contingencies. [L. *āleātōrius—āleātor,* a dicer—*ālea,* a die.]
Alecto, *a-lek'tō, n.* one of the Furies. [Gr. *Alēktō,* lit. unceasing.]
alee, *ə-lē', adv.* on or toward the lee-side. [O.N. *á,* on, *hlé,* lee.]
aleft, *ə-left', adv.* on or to the left hand. [Prep. **a,** left.]
alegar, *al'* or *āl'i-gər, n.* sour ale, or vinegar made from it. [**ale,** with term. as **vinegar.**]
alegge, *a-lej', v.t.* (*Spens.*) to allay.—*n.* **alegg'-eaunce** (*Spens.*), allay, alleviation. [Same as **allege**=alleviate, confused with **allay.**]
Alemannic, *al-i-man'ik, adj.* of the Alemannen (L. *Alamanni, Alemanni*), an ancient people of S.W. Germany, or their dialect.—*n.* the High German dialect of Switzerland, Alsace, etc.
alembic, *a-lem'bik, n.* old distilling apparatus.—*adj.* **alem'bicated,** over-refined. [Ar. *al,* the, *anbīq*—Gr. *ambix,* cap of a still.]
alembroth, *ə-lem'broth.* See **sal alembroth.**
alength, *ə-length', adv.* at full length. [Prep. **a,** length.]
aleph, *ä'lef, ä'lef, n.* the first letter of the Phoenician and Hebrew alphabets, resembling an ox's head, representing a glottal stop, but adopted by the Greeks for a vowel sound. See **a, alpha.** [Heb. *āleph,* ox.]
alepine, *al'i-pēn, n.* a mixed fabric of wool and silk or mohair and cotton. [Perh. *Aleppo.*]
alerce, *ə-lərs', ā-ler'thā, n.* the wood of the sandarac-tree : the Chilean arbor vitae. [Sp., larch—L. *larix, -icis,* larch, perhaps confused with Ar. *al'arza,* the cedar.]
alerion, allerion, *a-lē'ri-ən, n.* (*her.*) an eagle displayed, without feet or beak. [Fr.]
alert, *ə-lərt', adj.* watchful : wide-awake : brisk.—*n.* a sudden attack or surprise : a danger warning : preparedness.—*adv.* **alert'ly.**—*n.* **alert'ness.**—**on, upon the alert,** upon the watch : wakefully attentive. [Fr. *alerte*—It. *all'erta,* on the erect—*erto*—L. *ērēctus,* erect.]
Aleurites, *al-ū-rī'tēz, n.* a genus of plants of the spurge family, yielding tung oil and candlenut. [Gr. *aleuron,* flour.]
aleurone, *a-lū'rōn, n.* a protein found in some seeds. [Gr. *aleuron,* flour.]
alevin, *al'i-vin, n.* a young fish, esp. a salmonid. [Fr.,—O.Fr. *alever,* to rear—L. *ad,* to, *levāre,* to raise.]
alew, *ə-l(y)ōō', n.* (*Spens.*), same as **halloo.**
alexanders, *al-ig-zān'dərz, n.* an umbelliferous plant (genus *Smyrnium*) formerly used like celery. [O.E. *alexandre,* connected in some way with Alexander the Great or with Alexandria.]
Alexandrian, *al-ig-zān'dri-ən, adj.* relating to *Alexandria* in Egypt, its school of philosophy, its poetry, or the general character of its culture and taste, erudite and critical rather than original in

inspiration—sometimes with a suggestion of decadence: relating to *Alexander* the Great or other of the name.—Also *n.*—*n.* and *adj.* **Alexan'drine**, Alexandrian.—*n.* **alexan'drine**, a verse of six iambs (as in English), or in French of 12 and 13 syllables in alternate couplets (perhaps from a poem on *Alexander* the Great by *Alexandre* Paris).— Also *adj.*—*n.* **alexan'drite**, a dark green chrysoberyl discovered on the day of majority of the Cesarevich later *Alexander* II.

alexia, *a-lek'si-ā*, *n.* loss of power to read: word-blindness. [Gr. *a-*, priv., *legein*, to speak, confused with L. *legĕre*, to read.]

alexin, *a-lek'sin*, *n.* a body present in the blood serum, which uniting with an anti-serum gives protection against disease.—*adj.* **alexipharmic** (-*si-fär'mik*), acting against poison.—*n.* an antidote to poison. [Gr. *alexein*, to ward off, *alexipharmakos* —*pharmakon*, poison.]

alfa, *al'fä*. See halfa.

alfalfa, *al-fal'fä*, *n.* (esp. *U.S.*) a kind of lucerne. [Sp. *alfalfa*—Ar. *alfaçfaçah*.]

alfresco, *äl-fresk'ō*, *adv.* and *adj.* on fresh or moist plaster: in the fresh or cool air. [It.; see **fresco**, **fresh**.]

alga, *al'gä*, *n.* a seaweed: any member of the Algae :—*pl.* **algae** (*al'jē*), **Algae** (*bot.*) a great group of Thallophytes, the seaweeds and allied forms.— *adj.* **al'gal** (-*gal*).—*ns.* **al'gin** (-*jin*), sodium alginate, a gummy nitrogenous organic compound got from seaweeds; **al'ginate**, a salt of alginic acid. —*adjs.* **algin'ic** (as **alginic acid**, an acid obtained from certain seaweeds, used in plastics, medicine, etc.); **al'goid** (-*goid*); **algolog'ical**.—*ns.* **algol'ogist**; **algol'ogy**, phycology. [L. *alga*, seaweed.]

algarroba, *al-ga-rō'bä*, *n.* the carob : the mesquite : the fruit of either.—Also **algaro'ba**, **algarro'bo**. [Sp. *algarroba*, -*o.*—Ar. *al kharrūbah* ; cf. **carob.**]

algate, -s, *awl'gāt(s)*, *adv.* (*obs.*) always, at all events, nevertheless : (*Spens.*) altogether. [**all** and **gate** ; orig. *dat.*, with -*s* on analogy of *always*, etc.]

algebra, *al'ji-brə*, *n.* a method of calculating by symbols—by means of letters employed to represent quantities, and signs to represent their relations, thus forming a kind of generalised arithmetic.— *adjs.* **algebraic** (-*brā'ik*), **-al**.—*n.* **algebra'ist**, one skilled in algebra. [It. and Sp.,—Ar. *al-jebr*, the resetting (of anything broken), hence combination —*jabara*, to reunite.]

Algerine, *al'ji-rēn*, *adj.* of Algeria or Algiers.—*n.* a native of Algeria : a pirate.—Also **Algē'rian**.

algid, *al'jid*, *adj.* cold, chill—especially applied to a cold fit in disease.—*n.* **algid'ity**, coldness, esp. marking failure of vitality. [L. *algidus*, cold.]

Algol, *al'gol*, *n.* a variable star in the constellation Perseus. [Ar. *al ghūl*, the ghoul.]

Algonkin, **Algonquin**, *al-gong'kin*, **Algonkian**, **Algonquian**, -*ki-ən*, *n.* a member of a leading group of Indian tribes in the valley of the Ottawa and around the northern tributaries of the St. Lawrence: their language.—Also *adj.* [Micmac Indian *algoomaking*, at the place of spearing fish.]

algorism, *al'go-rizm*, *n.* the Arabic system of numeration: arithmetic.—Also **al'gorithm.** [L.L. *algorismus*—Ar. *al-Khwārazmi*, the native of Khwārazm (Khiva), i.e. the 9th cent. mathematician Abu Ja'far Mohammed ben Musa.]

alguacil, *äl-gwä-thēl'*, **alguazil**, *al-gwa-zil'*, *n.* in Spain, an officer who makes arrests, etc. [Sp. (now) *alguacil*—Ar. *al-wazīr*. See **vizier.**]

algum, *al'gəm*, *n.* (*B.*) a wood imported into ancient Palestine, prob. red sandalwood.—Also **al'mug.** [Heb. *algūm*.]

Alhagi, *al-hä'ji*, -*hä'jē*, *n.* a papilionaceous manna-yielding genus of desert shrubs. [Ar. *al-hāj*]

Alhambra, *al-ham'-brä*, *n.* the palace of the Moorish kings of Granada in Spain.—*adj.* **Alhambresque** (-*bresk*). [Ar. *al-hamrā'*, the red (house).]

alias, *ā'li-äs*, L. *ā'li-äs*, *adv.* otherwise.—*n.* an assumed name :—*pl.* **a'liases.** [L. *aliās*, at another time, otherwise—*alius*, other.]

alibi, *al'i-bī*, L. *äl'i-bē*, *n.* the plea in a criminal charge of having been elsewhere at the material time: the fact of being elsewhere : (esp. *U.S.*,

sport) an excuse for failure. [L. *alibī*, elsewhere, orig. locative—*alius*, other.]

alicant, *al-i-kant'*, *n.* a wine made near *Alicante*, in Spain.

alidad, *al'i-dad*, or -*dad'*, **alidade**, -*dād*, *n.* a revolving index for reading the graduations of an astrolabe, quadrant, or similar instrument, or for taking the direction of objects. [Ar. *al 'idādah*, the revolving radius—'*adid*, humerus.]

alien, *ā'li-ən*, -*lyən*, *adj.* belonging to something else: extraneous: repugnant: inconsistent: incompatible: estranged.—*n.* a foreigner: a resident neither native-born nor naturalised: an outsider: a plant introduced by man but maintaining itself.— *v.t.* to alienate: to transfer: to estrange.—*n.* **alienabil'ity**.—*adj.* **a'lienable**, capable of being transferred to another.—*n.* **a'lienage**, state of being an alien.—*v.t.* **a'lienate**, to transfer: to estrange.—*adj.* withdrawn: estranged.—*ns.* **aliena'tion**; **a'lienātor**.—*adj.* **al'iened**, made alien: estranged.—*ns.* **al'ienism**, the position of being a foreigner: study and treatment of mental diseases; **a'lienist**, one who specially studies or treats mental diseases; **a'lienor**, one who transfers property. [L. *aliēnus*—*alius*, other.]

alight, *ə-līt'*, *v.i.* to dismount, descend: to perch, settle: to land: to come to rest: to come by chance (upon something): to fall, strike :—*pa.t.* and *pa.p.* **alight'ed** (or **alit'**). [O.E. *ālihtan.* See **light** (3).]

alight, *ə-līt'*, *adj.* on fire: lighted up. [Prep. **a**, **light** (1).]

align, **aline**, *ə-līn'*, *v.t.* to regulate by a line: to arrange in line.—*n.* **align'ment**, **aline'ment**, a laying out by a line: setting in a line or lines: the ground-plan of a railway or road: a row, as of standing-stones. [Fr. *aligner*—L. *ad*, to, *līneāre*, to line.]

alike, *ə-līk'*, *adj.* the same in appearance or character.—*adv.* equally. [O.E. *gelic*, combined with O.N. *ālīkr*, O.E. *onlíc*; see **like.**]

aliment, *al'i-mənt*, *n.* nourishment: food: provision for maintenance, alimony.—*v.t.* to support, sustain: to provide aliment for.—*adjs.* **alimental** (-*ment'l*), supplying food; **aliment'ary**, pertaining to aliment: nutritive.—*n.* **alimentā'tion.**—*adj.* **aliment'ative.**—*n.* **aliment'iveness**, a phrenologist's word for the instinct to seek food or drink.— **alimentary canal**, the passage from mouth to anus. [L. *alimentum*—*alĕre*, to nourish.]

alimony, *al'i-mən-i*, *n.* an allowance for support made to a wife when legally separated or divorced from her husband, or temporarily while the process is pending. [L. *alimōnia*—*alĕre*, to nourish.]

aline, **alinement.** See **align.**

alineation. See **allineation.**

aliphatic, *al-i-fat'-ik*, *adj.* (*chem.*) fatty: belonging to the open-chain class of organic compounds, or methane derivatives—opp. to *aromatic*. [Gr. *aleiphar*, *aleiphatos*, oil.]

aliquant, *al'i-kwənt*, *adj.* such as will not divide a number without a remainder, thus 5 is an aliquant part of 12. [L. *aliquantum*, somewhat—*alius*, another, and *quantus*, how great.]

aliquot, *al'i-kwot*, *adj.* such as will divide a number without a remainder. [L. *aliquot*, some, several— *alius*, other, *quot*, how many.]

Alisma, *a-liz'mä*, *n.* the water-plantain genus of monocotyledons, giving name to the family **Alismā'ceae.**—*adj.* **alismā'ceous.** [Gr. *alisma*, water-plantain.]

alit. See **alight** (1).

alive, *ə-līv'*, *adj.* in life: in vigour: in being: lively: sensitive, cognisant (with *to*).—**alive with**, swarming with; **look alive**, be brisk: hurry up. [O.E. *on life* (dat. of *līf*, life), in life.]

alizari, *al-i-zä'rē*, *n.* levantine madder.—*n.* **alizarin** (*a-liz'ə-rēn*), the colouring matter of madder root ($C_{14}H_8O_4$), now made synthetically. [Sp. and Fr., prob.—Ar. *al*, the, '*açārah*, juice pressed out.]

alkahest, **alcahest**, *al'kə-hest*, *n.* the universal solvent of the alchemists. [App. a sham Ar. coinage of Paracelsus.]

alkali, *al'kə-li*, or -*lī*, *n.* (*chem.*) a substance which in aqueous solution has more hydroxyl ions than

fāte, fär, ȧsk; mē, hər (her); mīne; mōte, mūte; mōōn; dhen (then) hydrogen ions, and has strong basic properties:—*pl.* **al'kali(e)s.**—*adj.* of, pertaining to, containing, forming, an alkali.—*ns.* **alkalesc'ence, alkalesc'ency.**—*adj.* **alkalesc'ent,** tending to become alkaline: slightly alkaline.—*v.t.* and *v.i.* **al'kalify.**—*ns.* **alkalim'eter,** an instrument for measuring the concentration of alkalies; **alkalim'etry.**—*adj.* **alkaline** (*-lin, -lin*), having the properties of an alkali: containing much alkali.—*n.* **alkalinity** (*-lin'i-ti*), the quality of being alkaline: the extent to which a solution is alkaline.—*v.t.* **al'kalise,** to render alkaline.—*n.* **al'kaloid,** any of various nitrogenous organic bases found in plants, often important in medicine owing to their physiological action.—*adj.* pertaining to or resembling alkali.—**alkali metals,** the univalent metals of the first group of the periodic system, lithium, sodium, potassium, rubidium, caesium, francium, forming strong basic hydroxides; **alkaline earth metals,** the bivalent metals of the second group, calcium, strontium, barium, radium. [Ar. *al-qaliy*, the calcined ashes.]

alkanet, *al'kə-net, n.* a Mediterranean boraginaceous plant (genus *Alkanna*): a red dye got from its root: extended to various kindred plants (*Anchusa*, etc.). [Sp. *alcaneta*, dim.—Ar. *al-hennā*, the henna.]

Alkoran, *n.* Same as **Alcoran.**

all, *awl, adj.* (preceding the article, following a personal pronoun) whole: as much as there is: as many as there are: to the whole extent or number: without exception: the greatest possible: every (see a').—*n.* the whole: everybody: everything: the totality of things—the universe: one's whole possessions (formerly often in *pl.*).—*adv.* wholly: entirely: quite: without limit, infinitely: on all sides: on each side, apiece: even, just (passing into a mere intensive, as in *all on a summer's day*, or almost into a conjunction by omission of *if* or *though*).—In composition, infinite, infinitely: universal: completely: wholly: by all: having all for object.—Possible compounds are without limit: only a selection can be given.—*adj.* **all-building** (*Shak.*), possibly, on which all is built, but prob. a misprint.—*n.* **all-chang'ing-word,** a spell that transforms everything.—*adjs.* **all-cheer'ing,** giving cheerfulness to all; **all'-day,** lasting all day; **all-dread'ed,** dreaded by all; **all-end'ing.**—*n.* **All'-father,** Woden : Zeus : God.—*adj.* **all'-fired** (*slang, orig. U.S.*) infernal (perh. for hell-fired).—*adv.* **all'-firedly.**—*ns.* **all-fives',** a game of dominoes in which it is sought to make the end pips sum a multiple of five; **all-fours',** a card game in which there are four chances that score a point (see also **four**); **all-giv'er** (*Milt.*) the giver of all—God; **all'-good,** the plant Good-King-Henry.—*adj.* **all-good',** infinitely good.—*interj.* **all-hail',** a greeting, *lit.* all health.—*n.* a salutation of 'All hail'.—*v.t.* to greet with 'All hail'.—*adj.* (*orig. gen. pl. of n.; obs.*) **all'-hall'own, -hall'owen, -holl'own, -hall'ond** (*Shak.* **al-hollown summer,** a spell of fine weather about All Hallows).—*ns.* **all-hall'owmass,** the feast of All Saints; **all-hall'-ows,** All Saints' Day; **all-hall'owtide,** the season of All-Hallows; **all'heal** (*obs.*) a panacea: the great valerian or other plant; **all-hid',** hide-and-seek.—*adjs.* **all'-night,** lasting all night; **all-obey'ing** (*Shak.*), obeyed by all; **all-o'verish,** having an indefinite sense of indisposition, discomfort, or malaise.—*n.* **all-o'verishness.**—*adjs.* **all-pow'erful,** supremely powerful: omnipotent; **all'-red',** exclusively on British territory (from the conventional colouring of maps); **all'-round',** including, applying to, all: adequate, complete, or competent on all sides; **all-rul'ing.**—*n.* **all'seed,** a weed (genus *Radiola*) of the flax family, or other many-seeded plant.—*adj.* **all-see'ing.**—*ns.* **all-sē'er** (*Shak.*), one who sees all—God; **all'spice,** pimento or Jamaica pepper, supposed to combine the flavours of cinnamon, nutmeg, and cloves (see also **Calycanthus**).—*adjs.* **all'-star',** having a cast or team all of whom are stars; **all-tell'ing** (*Shak.*).—*adv.* **all'thing** (*Shak.*), every way.—*n., adj.* **all'-up',** (of loaded aircraft) total (weight).—*adj.* **all'-wool',** made entirely of wool.—*n.* **all'-work,** all kinds of work (esp. domestic).—**after

all, when everything has been considered : in spite of all that : nevertheless; **all along,** everywhere along : all the time; **all and some** (*obs.*) one and all; **all at once,** suddenly; **all but,** everything short of, almost; **All Fools' Day,** the day of making April Fools, 1st April; **All Hallows' Day,** All Saints' Day; **all in,** exhausted : everything included; **all in all,** all things in all respects, all or everything together : that which one is wholly wrapped up in; **all out,** at full power or speed : completely exhausted; **all over,** everywhere : over the whole of : (*coll.*) covered with : thoroughly, entirely : very characteristically; **all over with,** finished, done with, completely at an end with; **all right,** a colloquial phrase expressing assent or approbation; **All Saints' Day,** 1st November, a festival in honour of the saints collectively; **all's one,** it is just the same; **All Souls' Day,** 2nd November, a R.C. day of prayer for souls in Purgatory; **all there,** completely sane : alert; **all to one** (*obs.*) altogether; **all the same** (see **same**); **all up with,** at an end with : beyond any hope for; **and all,** as well as the rest; **and all that,** and all the rest of it, *et cetera*; **at all,** in the least degree or to the least extent; **for all,** notwithstanding; **for good and all,** finally; **in all,** all told : in total; **once for all,** once and once only, finally; **when all is said and done,** after all : all things considered. [O.E. (Anglian) *all*, (W.S. *eall*) ; Ger. *all*.]

alla breve, *äl'lä brä'vä, (mus.*) in quick common time. [It., according to the breve, there being orig. a breve to the bar.]

alla cappella, *äl'lä käp-pel'lä.* See **a cappella.**

Allah, *al'ä, n.* among Mohammedans, God. [Ar. *allāh—al ilāh,* the God.]

Allamanic. Same as **Allemanic.**

allantois, *a-lan'tō-is, n.* a membranous sac-like appendage for effecting oxygenation in the embryos of mammals, birds, and reptiles.—*adjs.* **allanto'ic;** **allan'toid** (*-toid*), sausage-shaped: pertaining to the allantois.—*n.* the allantois. [Irregularly formed from Gr. *allās, -āntos,* a sausage, *eidos,* form.]

allay, earlier **aleye, alay,** etc. *ə-lā', v.t.* to put down: to quell : to calm : to alleviate : to abate : to reduce : to alloy.—*v.i.* to abate.—*ns.* **allay'er;** **allay'ing; allay'ment.** [O.E. *ālecgan*—pfx. *ā-*, intens., *lecgan*, to lay. This vb. in M.E. became indistinguishable in form in some of its parts from allay (2) or alloy, and from *allege* (1), and as the meanings overlapped became completely merged.]

allay, *ə-lā', v.t.* to alloy : to mix with something inferior : to dilute: to debase : to abate or detract from the goodness of.—*n.* alloy : alloying : dilution : abatement : impairment. [See **alloy** and the etymological note to **allay** (1).]

all-be. See **albe.**

alledge. Old spelling of **allege.**

allege (*Spens.* **allegge, alegge),** *ə-lej', v.t.* to alleviate : to allay.—*n.* **allege'ance** (*ə-lej'əns; Spens.* **aleggeaunce,** *a-lej'i-ans*), alleviation. [O.Fr. *aleger*—L. *alleviāre* (see **alleviate**) fused with O.E. *ālecgan* (see **allay** (1).]

allege, *ə-lej', v.t.* (*obs.*) to declare in court upon oath : to assert with a view to subsequent proof, hence without proof : to bring forward in argument or plea : to adduce : (*arch.*) to cite.—*n.* **allegation** (*al-i-gā'shən*), the act of alleging : that which is alleged : an unproved or unaccepted assertion : citation.—*adj.* **alleged** (*ə-lejd'*).—*adv.* **alleg'edly.** [O.Fr. *esligier,* to clear at law—L. *ex,* from, *litigāre,* to sue.]

allegiance, *ə-lē'jəns, n.* the relation or obligation of liegeman to liegelord or of subject to sovereign.—*adj.* **alle'giant** (*Shak.*). [L. *ad,* to, and **liege**.]

allegory, *al'i-gər-i, n.* a narrative to be understood symbolically : symbolical narration.—*adjs.* **allegoric** (*-gor'ik*), **-al.**—*adv.* **allegor'ically.**—*v.t.* **all'egorise,** to put in form of an allegory : to treat as allegory.—*v.i.* to use allegory.—*ns.* **allegorisā'tion; all'egoriser; all'egorist.** [Gr. *allēgoriā— allos,* other, *agoreuein,* to speak.]

allegro, *a-lā'grō* (It. *äl-lā'grō*), *adv. adj., (mus.*) with brisk movement.—*n.* an allegro piece or movement.—*adv.* and *adj.* **allegret'to,** somewhat brisk. [It.,—L. *alacer,* brisk.]

Neutral vowels in unaccented syllables : *el'ə-mənt, in'fənt, ran'dəm*

allelomorph, *al-ēl'ō-morf*, *n.* either of a pair of alternative characters inherited according to Mendelian law.—Also **allele** (*-ēl'*).—*adj.* **allelomor'phic**. [Gr. *allēlōn*, of one another, *morphē*, form.]

alleluia, alleluiah, *al-i-lōō'yă.* Same as **hallelujah**.

allemande, *al'(i-)mänd, al-män²d, n.* a smooth-running suite movement of moderate tempo, in common time, coming after the prelude (of German origin): a Swabian dance in triple time: a German dance in 2-4 time: a movement affecting change of order in a dance. [Fr. *allemande (fem.)*, German.]

allenarly, *al-en'ar-li, adv. (obs. except in Scots law)* solely, only. [**all, anerly.**]

allergy, *al'ar-ji, n.* an altered or acquired state of sensitivity: abnormal reaction of the body to substances normally harmless: hypersensitivity to certain antigens or other exciting substances: (wrongly) antipathy.—*n.* **all'ergen,** any substance that induces an allergic reaction.—*adj.* **allergic** (*ə-lər'jik*). [Gr. *allos*, other, *ergon*, work.]

allerion. See **alerion.**

alleviate, *ə-lēv'i-āt, v.t.* to make light: to mitigate.—*ns.* **allēviā'tion; allēv'iator.** [L.L. *allevāre*, *-ātum*—L. *ad* to, *levis*, light.]

alley, *al'i, n.* a walk in a garden or shrubbery: a passage: a narrow lane: (*U.S.*) a back-lane: a long narrow enclosure for bowls or skittles :—*pl.* **all'eys.**—*adj.* **alleyed** (*al'id*) having alleys or the form of an alley.—*n.* **all'eyway,** a narrow passage : a corridor. [O.Fr. *alee* (Fr. *allée*), a passage, from *aller*, to go.]

alley, ally, *al'i, n.* a choice taw or large marble.—*n.* **all'(e)y-taw', -tor'.** [Prob. originally made of **alabaster.**]

alliaceous, *al-i-ā'shəs, adj.* garlic-like. [L. *allium*, garlic.]

alliance. See **ally.**

allice, allis, *al'is, n.* a species of shad.—Also **allis shad.** [L. *alōsa, alausa,* shad.]

allicholy, allycholly, *al'i-kol-i, n.* and *adj.* (*Shak.*) jocularly, for melancholy.

alligate, *al'i-gāt, v.t.* to conjoin: to perform alligation.—*n.* **alligation** (*-gā'shən*), binding together: conjunction: (*arith.*) calculation of values or properties of a mixture. [L. *alligāre, -ātum—ad,* to, and *ligāre,* to bind.]

alligator, *al'i-gā-tər,* earlier **al(l)igarta, -gär'tā,** *n.* a reptile of a mainly American family differing from crocodiles in the broader snout and other characters.—**alligator apple,** a fruit and tree of the custard-apple genus; **alligator pear** (see **avocado**). [Sp. *el,* the (L. *ille*), *lagarto,* lizard (L. *lacertus*).]

allineation, alineation, *a-lin-i-ā'shən, n.* position in a straight line: alignment. [L. *ad,* to, *lineāre, -ātum,* to draw a line—*linea,* line.]

alliteration, *ə-* or *a-lit-ər-ā'shən, n.* the recurrence of the same initial sound (not necessarily letter) in words in close succession, as ' Sing a Song of Sixpence ': head-rhyme—the characteristic structure of versification of O.E. and other old Gmc. languages, each line having three accented syllables (two in the first half) with the same initial consonant, or with different initial vowels.—*v.i.* **allit'erate,** to begin with the same sound: to constitute alliteration: to practise alliteration.—*adj.* **allit'erative.** [L. *ad,* to, and *litera, littera,* a letter.]

allo-, in composition, other. [Gr. *allos,* other.]

allocarpy, *al'ō-kär-pi, n.* (*bot.*) fruiting after cross-fertilisation. [Gr. *karpos,* fruit.]

allocate, *al'ō-kāt, al'ə-kāt, v.t.* to place: to locate: to apportion.—*n.* **alloca'tion,** act of allocating: a share allocated: allotment: apportionment: an allowance made upon an account. [L. *allocāre—ad,* to, *locāre, -ātum,* to place—*locus,* a place.]

allocution, *al-ō-kū'shən, n.* an exhortation, esp. (*Roman hist.*) of a general to his troops: a formal address, esp. of the Pope to the cardinals. [L. *allocūtiō, -ōnis—ad,* to, and *loquī, locūtus,* to speak.]

al(l)odium, *a-lō'di-əm, n.* an estate not subject to a feudal superior.—Also **a(l)lod** (*al'od*).—*adj.*

al(l)ō'dial—opp. to *feudal.* [L.L. *allōdium,* from a Gmc. word meaning complete ownership; cf. *all* and O.E. *ēad,* wealth, prosperity.]

allogamy, *al-og'ə-mi, n.* (*bot.*) cross-fertilisation.—*adj.* **allog'amous.** [Gr. *allos,* other, *gamos,* marriage.]

allograph, *al'ō-gräf, n.* a writing made by one person on behalf of another. [Gr. *graphē,* writing.]

allonge, *al-on²zh', n.* piece of paper attached to bill of exchange for further endorsements. [Fr.]

allopathy, *al-op'ə-thi, n.* the current or orthodox medical practice, distinguished from *homoeopathy.*—*n.* **all'ōpath.**—*adj.* **allopathic** (*al-ō-path'ik*).—*n.* **allōp'athist.** [Ger. *allopathie,* coined by Hahnemann (1755-1843)—Gr.*allos,* other, *pathos,* suffering.]

allot, *ə-lot', v.t.* to divide as by lot: to distribute in portions : to parcel out : to assign :—*pr.p.* **allott'ing ;** *pa.t.* and *pa.p.* **allott'ed.**—*ns.* **allot'ment,** act of allotting: part or share allotted : a portion of a field assigned to a cottager to labour for himself : a piece of ground let out for spare-time cultivation under a public scheme; **allott'ery** (*Shak.*), a share allotted. [O.Fr. *aloter—à* to, and the Gmc. root of **lot.**]

allotriomorphic, *a-lot-ri-ō-mor'fik adj.* crystalline in internal structure but not in outward form. [Gr. *allotrios,* alien, *morphē,* form.]

allotropy, *al-ot'rə-pi, n.* the property (esp. in chemical elements, as carbon) of existing in more than one form.—*n.* **allotrope** (*al'ə-trōp*) an allotropic form.—*adj.* **allotrop'ic.**—*n.* **allot'ropism.**—*adj.* **allot'ropous,** (*bot.*) having nectar accessible to all kinds of insects : of insects, short-tongued, as visiting allotropous flowers. [Gr. *allos,* other, and *tropos,* turn, habit.]

allow, *ə-low' v.t. (obs.)* to praise: (*arch.*) to pass, sanction, accept : to concede : (*U.S.*) to conclude, hence to assert : to permit : (*Shak.*) to indulge: to accord as due : to assign : to grant or give, esp. periodically : to abate : to assume as an element in calculation or as something to be taken into account.—*v.i.* to admit (with *of*): to make allowance (with *for*).—*adj.* **allow'able,** that may be allowed : permissible : excusable.—*n.* **allow'ableness.**—*adv.* **allow'ably.**—*n.* **allow'ance,** that which is allowed: (*arch.*) approbation: (*Shak.*) admission, acknowledgment, permission : a limited portion or amount allowed, allotted, granted : a ration or stint : money allowed to meet expenses or in consideration of special conditions : abatement : a sum periodically granted : a taking into account in calculation or excuse.—*v.t.* to put upon an allowance : to supply in limited quantities.—*adj.* **allowed',** permitted : licensed : acknowledged.—*adv.* **allow'edly.** [O.Fr. *alouer,* to praise, bestow, of double origin: (1) L. *allaudāre—ad,* to, *laudāre,* to praise; (2) L. *ad, locāre,* to place.]

alloy, *al'oi, ə-loi', n.* a mixture of metals: extended to a mixture of metal with non-metal: the baser ingredient in such a mixture (esp. in gold or silver): any admixture that impairs or debases: fineness, standard, of gold or silver.—*v.t.* to mix (metal) to mix with a less valuable metal: to impair or debase by being present: to temper, qualify.—*v.i.* to become alloyed. [Fr. *aloi* (n.), *aloyer* (vb.)—O.Fr. *alei, aleier*—L. *alligāre—ad,* to, *ligāre,* to bind; **allay** (2) is from the corresponding Norm. Fr. *alai,* confused with *allay* (1).]

allspice. See under **all.**

all-to, alto, also **all to,** *awl'too,* a spurious *adv.* and *pfx.* arising from the wrong division of **all** and a word with the pfx. *to-,* asunder, as **allto brake, all to brake** for **all tobrake:** hence, altogether, as **altoruffled** (*Milt.* all to ruffl'd).

allude, *ə-l(y)ōōd', v.i.* to convey an indirect reference in passing: to refer without explicit mention, or with suggestion of further associations: (*vulg.*) to refer.—*n.* **allu'sion** (*-zhən*), indirect reference.—*adj.* **allu'sive** (*-siv*), alluding : hinting : referring indirectly: (*her.*) canting.—*adv.* **allu'sively.**—*n.* **allu'siveness.** [L. *allūdēre—ad,* at, *lūdēre, lūsum,* to play.]

allure, *ə-l(y)ōōr', v.t.* to draw on as by a lure or bait: to entice.—*ns.* **allure'; allure'ment.**—*adj.* **allur'ing.**—*adv.* **allur'ingly.** [O.Fr. *alurer—à,* to, *lurer,* to **lure.**]

alluvion, ə-l(y)ōō′vi-ən, n. land gradually gained from a river or the sea by the washing up of sand and earth : a flood : alluvium. [L. *alluviō, -ōnis*. See **alluvium**.]

alluvium, ə-l(y)ōō′vi-əm, n. matter transported in suspension and deposited by rivers or floods :—*pl.* **allu′via**.—*adj.* **allu′vial**. [L. neut. of *alluvius*, washed up—*ad*, to, *luĕre*, to wash.]

ally, a-lī′, v.t. to join in relation of marriage, friendship, treaty, co-operation, or assimilation :—*pr.p.* **ally′ing**; *pa.t.* and *pa.p.* **allied′**.—*n.* **a′lly** (formerly, and still by some, a-lī′) a member of or party to an alliance : a state or sovereign joined in league for co-operation in a common purpose : anything that co-operates or helps : (*Shak.*) a kinsman : anything near to another in classification or nature :—*pl.* **a′llies** (or *-līz′*).—*n.* **alli′ance**, state of being allied : union, or combination by marriage, treaty, etc. : kinship : a group of allies or kindred : (*bot.*) a subclass or group of families.—*adj.* **a′llied** (or *-līd′*). [O.Fr. *alier*—L. *alligāre*; see **alligate**.]

ally, **ally-taw**. See **alley** (2).

allyl, al′il, n. (*chem.*) an organic radical (C_3H_5) whose sulphide is found in oil of garlic. [L. *allium*, garlic, and Gr. *hȳlē*, matter.]

alma, **almah**, al′mä, n. an Egyptian dancing-girl. —Also **al′me**, **al′meh** (*-me*). [Ar. *'almah*, learned (in dancing and music)—*'alama*, to know.]

almacantar, **almucantar**, al-mə-kan′tər, *-mū-*, n. a circle of altitude, parallel to the horizon : an instrument for determining a star's passage across an almacantar. [Ar. *almuqantarāt*, the sundials—*al*, the, *qantarah*, bridge.]

Almagest, al′mə-jest, n. a great treatise by the Alexandrian astronomer Ptolemy (*c.* 150 A.D.) : extended to other great works. [Ar. *al-majistē*—*al*, the, Gr. *megistē* (*syntaxis*), greatest (systematic treatise).]

Almain, al′mān, n. and adj. (*obs.*) German.—*ns.* **al′main** (*obs.*) the allemande (suite movement, or leaping dance); **Al′maine**, **Al′many**, **Al′emaine**, Germany. [Fr. *allemand*, German, *Allemagne*, Germany—L. *Alamanni*, a S.W. German people.]

almanac, awl′mə-nak, n. a register of the days, weeks, and months of the year, with astronomical events, anniversaries, etc. [App. from an Ar. word *al-manākh*.]

almandine, al′man-dīn, -dēn, earlier **alaban′dine**. —*n.* precious (red iron-alumina) garnet. [L.L. *alabandīna*—*Alabanda*, a town in Caria, where it was found.]

almery. See **ambry**.

almighty, awl-mīt′i, adj. omnipotent : irresistible : invincible : (*slang*) mighty; also adv.—**the Almighty**, God : **the almighty dollar**, money, ' that great object of universal devotion throughout our land ' (Washington Irving) : also money as all-powerful. [O.E. *ælmihtig*; see **all**, **mighty**.]

almond, ä′mənd, n. the fruit, and esp. the kernel, of a tree akin to the peach, with a dry husk instead of flesh : anything of the shape of an almond (an ellipse pointed at one end), as a tonsil, a rock-crystal ornament.—*adj.* **al′mond-eyed**, with apparently almond-shaped eyes.—*ns.* **al′mond-bloss′om**; **al′mond-oil**; **al′mond-tree**. [O.Fr. *almande* (Fr. *amande*)—L. *amygdala*—Gr. *amygdalē*.]

almoner, al′mən-ər, ä′mən-ər, n. a distributor or giver of alms : one who apportions payments to be made by hospital patients.—*n.* **al′monry**, a place of distribution of alms. [O.Fr. *aumoner*, *aumonier* (Fr. *aumônier*)—L.L. *eleēmosynārius* (*adj.*). See **alms**.]

almost, awl′mōst, -məst, adv. very nearly. [**all**, **most** (in sense of nearly).]

almous. Same as **awmous**.

alms, ämz, n. sing. and pl. relief given out of pity to the poor : (*obs.*) a good or charitable deed.—*ns.* **alms′-deed**, a charitable deed; **alms′-dish**, a dish for receiving alms; **alms′-drink** (*Shak.*), leavings of drink; **alms′-fee**, Peter's pence; **alms′-folk**, people supported by alms; **alms′-house**, a house endowed for the support and lodging of the poor; **alms′-man**, a man who lives

by alms; **alms′-woman**. [O.E. *ælmysse*, through L.L. from Gr. *eleēmosynē—eleos*, compassion; see also **awmous**.]

almucantar. See **almacantar**.

almug, al′mug, n. (*B.*) algum. [Heb. *almūg*, prob. for *algūm*.]

alnage, awl′nij, n. measurement by the ell : inspection of cloth.—*n.* **al′nager**, an official inspector of cloth. [O.Fr. *aulnage—aulne*, ell.]

alod, **alodial**, **alodium**. Same as **allod**, etc.

Aloe, al′ō-ē, n. a liliaceous genus, mainly South African, mostly trees and shrubs.—*n.* **aloe** (al′ō), any member of the genus : extended to the so-called **American aloe** (see **agave**), also (often *pl.*) to aloes-wood or its resin : (usu. in *pl.* form but treated as *sing.*) a bitter purgative drug, the inspissated juice of the leaves of various species of Aloe.—*adj.* **aloed** (al′ōd), planted, shaded, mixed, flavoured, with aloes.—*n.* **al′oes-wood**, the heart-wood of eaglewood.—*adj.* **aloet′ic**.—*n.* a medicine containing a great proportion of aloes. [Directly and through O.E. *aluvan*, *alewan* (*pl.*)—L. *aloē*—Gr. *aloē*; the application to eagle-wood comes from the Septuagint translation of Heb. *ahālīm*, *ahālōth*, agalloch.]

aloft, ə-loft′, adv. on high : overhead : above : on the top : high up : up the mast : in or to heaven.—*prep.* (*Shak.*) on the top of. [O.N. *á lopt* (pron. *loft*), of motion; *á lopti*, of position—*á*, on, in, to, *lopt* (see **loft**).]

alogical, a-loj′i-kl, or ā-, adj. outside the domain of logic. [Gr. *a-*, priv., and **logical**.]

alone, ə-lōn′, adj. single : solitary : unaccompanied : without any other : by oneself : unique.—*adv.* singly.—*adv.* **alone′ly** (*obs.* or *arch.*).—*n.* **alone′ness**. [**all** and **one**.]

along, ə-long′, adv. by or through the length : lengthwise : at full length : throughout : onward : together, in company or conjunction.—*prep.* lengthwise by, through, or over : by the side of.—*adj.* **alongshore** (see **longshore**).—*n.* **alongshore′-man**.—*prep.* and adv. **along′side**, beside : side by side (with) : close to the side (of). [O.E. *andlang*—pfx. *and-*, against, and *lang*, long.]

along, ə-long′, adj. (*arch.* and *dial.*) on account. [O.E. *gelang*; see **long** (1).]

alongst, ə-longst′, adv. and prep. (*obs.* and *dial.*) along : by the length (of). [O.E. *andlanges*—*andlang*, along, with adv. gen. ending *-es* and *-t* as in **amidst**, **betwixt**, etc.]

aloof, ə-lōōf′, adv. (*obs.*) to windward : clear : some way off : apart : with avoidance or detachment : without participation : with reserve suggesting consciousness of superiority.—*adj.* distant, withdrawn.—*prep.* (*Milt.*) aloof from.—*adv.* **aloof′ly**.—*n.* **aloof′ness**. [Prep. a, **loof** (luff).]

alopecia, al-ō-pē′si-ä, -sh(y)ä, n. baldness.—*adj.* **alopecoid** (al-ō-pē′koid, al-op′i-koid), fox-like. [Gr. *alōpekiā*, fox-mange, a bald spot, *alōpekoeidēs*, fox-like—*alōpēx*, fox.]

aloud, ə-lowd′, adv. loudly : audibly. [Prep. a, **loud**.]

alow, ə-lō′, adv. below : down. [Prep. a, **low**.]

alow(e), ə-low′, adv. (*Scot.*) ablaze. [Prep. a, and **low** (flame).]

alp, alp, n. a high mountain : a mountain pasture :—*pl.* **Alps**, specially applied to the lofty ranges of Switzerland and neighbouring countries.—*ns.* **alp′-enhorn**, **alp′horn**, a long powerful horn, of wood and bark, used chiefly by Alpine cowherds; **alp′enstock**, a mountain traveller's long spiked staff.—*adj.* **Alp′ine**, **alp′ine** (*-īn*), of the Alps or other mountains : growing on mountain tops.—*n.* an alpine plant : a member of the Alpine race.—*ns.* **alp′inism** (*-in-*), the art or practice of mountain climbing; **alp′inist**.—**Alpine race**, one of the principal races of white men, characterised by broad head, sallow skin, moderate stature. [L. *Alpēs*, the Alps; perh. Celtic.]

alpaca, al-pak′ä, n. a domesticated animal akin to the llama : cloth made of its long silken wool. [Sp., prob. from Quichua.]

alpargata, äl-pär-gä′tä, n. a light sandal with rope or hemp sole. [Sp.]

alpeen, al′pēn, n. (*Anglo-Ir.*) a cudgel. [Ir. *ailpín*.]

alpha, *al'fä, n.* the first letter of the Greek alphabet (A, α) : the first or brightest star of a constellation : the beginning : as an ancient Greek numeral α' = 1, ͺα = 1,000.—**alpha and omega,** beginning and end; **alpha particle,** a helium nucleus given off by radioactive substances; **alpha rays,** streams of alpha particles. [Gr. *alpha*—Heb. *āleph*. See **aleph, A.**]

alphabet, *al'fə-bet, n.* a system of letters, esp. arranged in conventional order : first elements : (*obs.*) an index.—*v.t.* (*U.S.*) to arrange alphabetically.—*n.* **alphabetā′rian,** one learning his alphabet, a beginner : a student of alphabets.— *adjs.* **alphabet′ic, -al,** relating to or in the order of an alphabet; **alphabet′iform,** shaped like letters.—*adv.* **alphabet′ically.**—*v.t.* **al′phabetise,** to arrange alphabetically. [Gr. *alphabētos*—*alpha*, *bēta*, the first two Greek letters.]

Alphonsine, *al-fon′sīn, -zin adj.* of Alphonso X. (the Wise), king of Castile, or his planetary tables, completed in 1252.

Alpini, *äl-pē′nē, n.pl.* Italian troops for mountain warfare—*sing.* **Alpi′no.** [It., Alpine.]

already, *awl-red′i, adv.* previously, or by the time in question. [**all, ready.**]

alright, an unaccepted spelling of **all right.**

als, *äls. avls,* an old form of **also, as.**

Alsatia, *al-sā′sh(y)ä, n.* a district long disputed by Germany and France—Alsace or Elsass : cant name for the sanctuary (till 1697) for debtors and criminals at Whitefriars, London.—*adj.* **Alsa′tian,** of Alsatia in either sense : applied capriciously to a German sheep-dog, a wolf-like breed.—Also *n.*

alsike, *al′sik, n.* a white or pink-flowered clover. [From *Alsike*, near Uppsala, a habitat.]

also, *awl′sō, adv.* likewise : further.—*n.* **al′so-ran,** a horse that *also ran* in a race but did not get a 'place' : a person of like degree of importance. [O.E. *all* (W.S. *eall*) *swā,* all so.]

alsoon(e), *al-sōōn′, adv.* (*Spens.*) as soon. [**as, soon.**]

alt, *alt, n.* a high tone, in voice or instrument.— **in alt,** in the octave above the treble stave beginning with G : (*fig.*) in an exalted and high-flown mood. [L. *altus,* high.]

alt, *alt, n.* (*Milt.*) halt, rest. [Fr. *alte* or Sp. *alto*— Ger. *halt.*]

Altair, *äl-tä′ir, n.* a first-magnitude star in the constellation Aquila. [Ar. *al ta'ir,* the bird.]

altaltissimo, *ält-äl-tis′i-mō, n.* the very highest summit. [Reduplicated compound of It. *alto,* high, and *altissimo,* highest.]

altar, *awlt′ər, n.* block or table for making sacrifices on : table used for mass or the eucharist (by those who regard it as a sacrifice) : sometimes, without such implication, the communion table : (*fig.*) a scene of worship or marriage ceremony : a ledge on a dry-dock wall.—*ns.* **alt′arage,** offerings made upon the altar during the offertory, provided for the maintenance of the priest; **alt′ar-cloth,** the covering of the altar, often used as including the frontal and the superfrontal; **al′tarpiece,** a work of art placed above and behind an altar :—*n.pl.* **alt′ar-rails,** rails separating the sacrarium from the rest of the chancel.—*ns.* **alt′ar-stone,** a stone serving as an altar : a consecrated slab forming, or inserted in, the top of an altar; **al′tar-tomb,** a monumental memorial, in form like an altar, often with a canopy.—*adv.* **alt′arwise,** in the position of an altar—north and south, at the upper end of the chancel.—**family altar,** the symbol or place of family worship; **high altar,** the principal altar; **lead to the altar,** to marry (a woman—often where there is no altar). [L. *altāre*—*altus,* high.]

altazimuth, *alt-az′i-muth, n.* an instrument devised by Airy for determining *alt*itude and *azi*muth.

alter, *awl′tər, v.t.* to make different : to modify : (*U.S., Austr.*) to castrate.—*v.i.* to become different. —*n.* **alterabil′ity.**—*adjs.* **al′terable; al′terant,** altering : having the power of producing changes. —*n.* an alterative.—*n.* **alterā′tion.**—*adj.* **al′terative,** having power to alter.—*n.* a medicine that makes a change in the vital functions.—*n.* **alterity** (*awl-, al-ter′i-ti*), otherness. [L. *alter,* one of

two, the other of two, from the root of *alius,* other, and the old comp. suff. *-ter.*]

altercate, *awl′tər-kāt, v.i.* to bandy works, wrangle. —*n.* **alterca′tion.**—*adj.* **al′tercative.** [L. *alter-cārī, -ātus*—*alter,* other.]

altern, *awl-, al-tərn′, adj.* alternate.—*adv.* alternately. [L. *alternus.*]

alternate, *awl′tər-nāt,* also *al′,* formerly (as *Milt.*) *-tər′, v.t.* to cause to follow by turns or one after the other (prop. of two things).—*v.i.* to follow or interchange with each other (prop. of two things) : to happen by turns, change by turns.—*adj.* **alter′nate,** arranged or coming one after the other by turns : every other or second : of leaves, placed singly with change of side at each node : of floral whorls, each occupying, in ground plan, the spaces of the next.—*adv.* **alter′nately.**—*ns.* **alterná′tion,** the act of alternating : alternate succession : interchange : reading or singing antiphonally; **alter′-native** (*-na-tiv*), a pair (loosely a set) of possibilities (esp. of choice) excluding all others : a choice between them : one of them, esp. other than the one in question.—*adj.* possible as an alternative : disjunctive : (*obs.*) alternate.—*adv.* **alter′natively,** with an alternative : by way of alternative.—*n.* **alt′ernātor,** a generator of alternating current.— **alternating current,** an electric current that periodically reverses its direction; **alternation of generations** (*biol.*), the occurrence in a life-cycle of two or more different forms in successive generations, the offspring being unlike the parents, and commonly reproducing by a different method; **alternative vote,** a system of voting whereby, if an elector's favourite candidate is out of the running, his vote is transferred to the candidate he has marked next in order of preference. [L. *alternāre, -ātum*—*alter,* one or other of two.]

Althaea, *al-thē′ä n.* the marsh-mallow and hollyhock genus. [Gr. *althaiā,* marsh-mallow.]

Althing, *awl′thing, n.* the Icelandic parliament. [O.N. and Icel.]

althorn, *alt′horn, n.* a tenor saxhorn. [alt (1), horn.]

although, *awl-dhō′, conj.* though (esp., but not necessarily, in stating matter of fact). [**all, though.**]

altimeter, *al-tim′i-tər, n.* a barometer for measuring heights. [L. *altus,* high, and **meter.**]

altisonant, *al-tis′ən-ənt, adj.* high-sounding. [L. *altus,* high, *sonāns, -āntis,* pr.p. of *sonāre,* to sound.]

altissimo, *âl-tis′(s)i-mō adj.* (*mus.*) very high. —**in altissimo,** in the second octave above the treble stave beginning with G (fourth line above). [It., superl. of *alto,* high.]

altitonant, *al-tit′ən-ənt, adj.* thundering on high or loudly. [L. *altus,* high, *tonāns, -āntis,* pr.p. of *tonāre,* to thunder.]

altitude, *al′ti-tūd, n.* height : angle of elevation above the horizon : perpendicular from vertex upon base : high rank or eminence : a high point or position : (in *pl.*) exalted mood, passion, or manner.—*adj.* **altitūd′inal.**—*n.* **altitūdinā′rian,** one given to loftiness or flightiness.—Also *adj.*— *adj.* **altitūd′inous,** high. [L. *altitūdō, -inis,*—*altus,* high.]

alto, *āl′tō, n.* (*mus.*) prop. counter-tenor, the highest male voice : extended to contralto, the lowest female voice : the part sung by counter-tenor or contralto : the possessor of a counter-tenor or contralto voice : a viola :—*pl.* **al′tos.**—Also *adj.* [It.,—L. *altus,* high.]

altogether, *awl-too-gedh′ər,* or *-tə-, adv.* (*obs.* or by confusion) all together : wholly : completely : without exception : in total : all things considered. —**for altogether,** for all time, for good and all; **the altogether,** the nude. [**all, together.**]

alto-rilievo, *äl′tō-rēl-yā′vō, n.* high relief : figures projected by at least half their thickness from the background on which they are sculptured.—Partly anglicised as **al′to-relie′vo** (*al-tō-ri-lē′vō*). [It. See **relief.**]

altrices, *al-trī′sēz, n.pl.* birds whose young are hatched very immature and have to be fed in the nest by the parents.—*adj.* **altricial** (*-trish′l*). [L. *altrīcēs* (pl. of *altrīx*), feeders, nurses.]

fāte, fär, ȧsk; mē, hər (her)*; mīne; mōte; mōōn; dhen* (then)

altruism, *al'troo-izm, n.* the principle of living and acting for the interest of others.—*n.* **al'truist.**—*adj.* **altruist'ic.**—*adv.* **altruist'ically.** [Fr. *altruisme,* formed by Comte from It. *altrui,* someone else—L. *alterī huīc,* to this other.]

aludel, *al'(y)oo-dəl, n.* a pear-shaped pot used in sublimation. [Sp.,—Ar. *al-uthāl.*]

alula, *al'ū-lä, n.* the bastard-wing. [L. dim. of *āla,* wing.]

alum, *al'əm, n.* double sulphate of aluminium and potassium, with 24 molecules of water, crystallising in transparent octahedra : any like compound of a trivalent metal (especially aluminium) and a univalent metal or radical.—*ns.* **alumina** (*ə-lū'* or *ə-lōō'mi-nä*), oxide of aluminium; **alu'minate,** a salt whose acid is aluminium hydroxide.—*adj.* **aluminif'erous,** alum-bearing.—*n.* **alumin'ium** (*al-ū-* or *al-oo-*), a remarkably light silvery metal (at. numb. 13), first named (though not yet isolated) by Sir Humphry Davy **alu'mium,**then (as still *U.S.*) **alum'inum.**—*adjs.* **alu'minous,** of the nature of, or containing, alum or alumina; **al'umish,** having the character or taste of alum.—*ns.* **al'um-root,** an American plant of the saxifrage family with astringent root; **al'um-shale, -slate,** a slate consisting mainly of clay, iron pyrites, and coaly matter, from which alum is obtained; **al'um-stone,** alunite.—**aluminium bronze,** an alloy of aluminium and copper, of lighter weight than gold, but like it in colour. [L. *alūmen, -in's,* alum.]

alumnus, *al-um'nəs, n.* a former pupil or student :—*pl.* **alum'ni** :—*fem.* (*U.S.*) **alum'na** (*pl.* **alum'nae, -nē**). [L., foster-son, pupil—*alĕre,* to nourish.]

alunite, *al'(y)oo-nīt, n.* alum-stone, a hydrous sulphate of aluminium and potassium. [Fr. *alun,* alum.]

alure, *al'yər, n.* a walk behind battlements : a gallery : a passage. [O.Fr. *aleure—aller,* to go.]

alveary, *al'vi-ər-i, n.* a beehive : a hive of industry, hence a dictionary : (*anat.*) the hollow of the external ear, where wax collects. [L. *alveārium,* beehive—*alveus,* a hollow.]

alveolus, *al-vē'ə-ləs, al'vi-, n.* a pit or small depression : a tooth-socket : a cell, as in the lungs :—*pl.* **alveoli.**—*adjs.* **alvē'olar** (or *al'vi-*), of an alveolus : (*phon.*) produced with tongue against the roots of the teeth : pitted, honeycombed; **alvē'olate** (or *al'vi-*), pitted : inserted in an alveolus.—*n.* **al'veole,** an alveolus.—**alveolar arch,** part of the jaw in which the teeth are inserted. [L. *alveolus,* dim. of *alveus,* a hollow.]

alvine, *al'vīn, adj.* of the belly. [L. *alvīnus—alvus,* belly.]

alway, *awl'wā, adv.* (*arch.*), through all time: always.—*adv.* **al'ways,** every time: ever: continually: in any case : (*Scot.*) still. [**all** and **way.**—O.E. *ealne weg* (accus.) and M.E. *alles weis* (gen.).]

Alyssum, *a-lis'əm, n.* a genus of cruciferous plants with white or yellow flowers, grown in rock-gardens. [Gr. *alysson,* a plant reputed to cure madness—*a-,* priv., and *lyssa,* madness.]

am, *am,* used as 1st person sing. of the verb *to be.* [O.E. (Anglian) *am, eam* (W.S. *eom*), a relic of the verbs in *-mi,* from the root *es-;* cf. Gr. *eimi* (for *esmi*), L. *sum,* Sans. *asmi.*]

amadavat *am-ə-də-vat', n.* an Indian songbird akin to the weaver-birds.—Also **avadavat'.** [From *Ahmadabad,* whence they were sent to Europe.]

amadou, *am'ə-dōō, n.* tinder made from fungi (genus *Polyporus*) growing on trees, used also as a styptic. [Fr., of doubtful origin.]

amain, *ə-mān', adv.* with main force or strength: violently : at full speed: exceedingly. [Prep. **a,** **main.**]

amalgam, *ə-mal'gəm, n.* a mixture of mercury with other metal : any soft mixture : an intimate mixture : an ingredient.—*v.t.* **amal'gamate,** to mix with mercury: to merge.—*v.i.* to unite in an amalgam : to come together as one : to blend.—*n.* **amalgamā'tion,** bonding or merging : a homogeneous union of diverse elements.—*adj.* **amal'gamātive.** [L.L. *amalgama,* perh.—Gr. *malagma,* an emollient.]

amandine, *am-an'din, -dīn, -dēn,* or *am', n.* a protein in sweet almonds : a candle or a cosmetic prepared from them. [Fr. *amande,* almond.]

Amanita, *am-an-ī'tä, n.* a genus of toadstools, near akin to the mushroom, including the fly agaric and other deadly kinds. [Gr. *amānītai* (pl.), a kind of fungus.]

amanuensis, *ə-man-ū-en'sis, n.* one who writes to dictation : a copying secretary :—*pl.* **amanuen'sēs.** [L. *āmanuēnsis—ā,* from, *manus,* hand.]

amaracus, *a-mar'ə-kəs, n.* marjoram. [L. *amāracus* —Gr. *amārakos.*]

amarant(h), *am'ər-ant(h), n.* a fabled never-fading flower, emblem of immortality : any species of **Amarant(h)'us,** the love-lies-bleeding genus, with richly coloured spikes, long in withering, giving name to the family **Amarant(h)ā'ceae,** akin to the goosefoots.—*adjs.* **amarant(h)ā'ceous; amarant(h)'ine** (*-īn*), **amarant'in** (*Milt.*), of or like amaranth : fadeless : immortal : purple. [Gr. *amarantos—a-,* priv., *marainein,* to wither; the *th* forms from confusion with *anthos,* flower.]

Amaryllis, *am-a-ril'is, n.* the belladonna lily genus, giving name to the narcissus and snowdrop family **Amaryllidā'ceae,** differing from lilies in the inferior ovary.—*adj.* **amaryll'id,** any member of the family.—*adj.* **amaryllidā'ceous.** [*Amaryllis,* a girl's name in the Gr. and L. poets, and others.]

amass, *ə-mas', v.t.* and *v.i.* to gather in great quantity: to accumulate.—*adj.* **amass'able.**—*n.* **amass'ment.** [Fr. *amasser*—L. *ad,* to, and *massa,* a mass.]

amate, *ə-māt', v.t.* (*Spens.*) to match. [Pfx. **a-,** intens., and **mate.**]

amate, *ə-māt', v.t.* (*arch.*) to daunt : to dismay. [O.Fr. *amatir,* to subdue; cf. **checkmate, mat** (2), **mate** (2).]

amateur, *am'ə-tər, -tūr,* or *tər', n.* one who cultivates a particular study or art for the love of it, and not professionally, often with the suggestion that he is superficial, trifling, dilettantish, or inexpert : one who engages in sport purely for pleasure—opp. to *professional.*—Also *adj.*—*adj.* **amateur'ish,** imperfect and defective, as the work of an amateur rather than a professional hand.—*adv.* **amateur'ishly.**—*ns.* **amateur'ishness ; am'-ateurism, am'ateurship.** [Fr.,—L. *amātor, -ōris,* a lover—*amāre,* to love.]

amative, *am'ə-tiv, adj.* inclined towards love.—*n.* **am'ativeness,** propensity to love or to sexuality. [L. *amāre, -ātum,* to love.]

amatol, *am'ə-tol, n.* a high explosive composed of ammonium nitrate and trinitrotoluene.

amatory, *am'ə-tər-i, adj.* relating to or causing love : amorous.—*adjs.* **amatō'rial, amatō'rian, amatō'-rious.**—*adv.* **amatō'rially.** [L. *amātōrius.*]

amaurosis, *am-aw-rō'sis, n.* blindness without outward change in the eye.—*adj.* **amaurotic** (*-rot'ik*). [Gr. *amaurōsis—amauros,* dark.]

amaze, *ə-māz', v.t.* (*obs.*) to daze : (*obs.*) to bewilder : (*obs.*) to stun : (*obs.*) to strike with fear : to confound with astonishment or wonder.—*n.* (*obs.*) bewilderment : (*obs.*) panic: extreme astonishment.—*adv.* **amaz'edly.**—*ns.* **amaz'edness** (*rare*), **amaze'-ment,** (*obs.*) stupefaction : (*obs.*) bewilderment : (*obs.*) panic, terror : astonishment mingled with wonder.—*adj.* **amaz'ing.**—*adv.* **amaz'ingly** (often hyperbolically). [O.E. *āmasian* (found in the pa.p. *āmasod*).]

Amazon, *am'ə-zon, -zən,* formerly *a-mā'zon, n.* in Greek story, one of a nation of women warriors, located in Asia or Scythia : the great river of South America (Port. *Amazonas,* Amazons, perh. based on a misunderstood Tupí-Guaraní word *amassona, amaçunu,* tidal bore, connected with records of Amazons living on its banks): an Indian of the Amazons; **Amazon** or **amazon,** a female soldier : a warlike, manlike, strong, or vigorous woman : a tropical American green parrot : an amazon-ant.—Also *adj.*—*n.* **am'azon-ant',** a European and American ant (genus *Polyergus*) helpless in everything except slave-raiding.—*adj.* **Amazonian, amazonian** (*-zō'ni-ən*).—*adj.* and *adv.* **Am'azon-like.**—*n.* **am'azon-stone,** a green microcline, said to be given by the Brazilian Amazons to the men who visited them. [Gr. *Amāzōn, -onos*, in folk-etymology referred to *a-*, priv., *māzos*, breast, with the explanation that Amazons cut off the right breast lest it should get in the way of the bow-string.]

ambages, *am-bā′jēz*, *n.pl.* windings : roundabout ways : delays.—Also *n.sing.* **ambage** (*am′bij*) with *pl.* **am′bages**.—*adjs.* **ambagious** (*-bā′jəs*), tortuous : circumlocutory ; **ambagitory** (*-baj′i-tər-i ; Scott*). [L. *ambāgēs* (pl.)—*ambi-*, about, *agēre*, to drive, lead.]

amban, *am′ban*, *n.* a Chinese resident official in a dependency. [Manchu, minister.]

Ambarvalia, *amb-är-vā′li-ä*, *n.pl.* an ancient Roman festival with processions round the cornfields. [L. *Ambarvālia—ambi-*, around, *arvum*, field.]

ambassador, *am-bas′ə-dər*, *n.* a diplomatic minister of the highest order : a messenger or agent :—*fem.* **ambass′adress**.—*adj.* **ambassadorial** (*-dō′ri-əl*). —*ns.* **ambass′adorship** ; **am′bassage** (*-bəs-ij*), **am′bassy**, forms of **embassage**, **embassy**. **ambass′ador extraordinary**, an ambassador sent on a special occasion, as distinguished from the ordinary or resident ambassador. [Fr. *ambassadeur* —L. *ambactus*, a slave, gener. thought to be of Celtic origin.]

ambatch, *am′bach*, *n.* a tropical African leguminous marsh tree with light pithlike wood. [Apparently native name.]

amber, *am′bər*, *n.* (*obs.*) ambergris : a yellowish fossil resin.—*adj.* made of amber : amber-hued— clear brownish yellow.—*adj.* **am′bered**, (*obs.*) embedded in amber : flavoured with ambergris.— *ns.* **am′ber-fish**, a fish (genus *Seriola*) of or near the horse-mackerels ; **am′berite**, an amberlike smokeless powder.—*adjs.* **am′berous** ; **am′bery**. —*n.* **am′broid** or **am′beroid**, pressed amber. [Fr. *ambre*—Ar. *'anbar*, ambergris.]

ambergris, *am′bər-grēs*, *n.* an ash-grey strongly scented substance, found floating or cast up, and in the intestines of the spermaceti whale. [Fr. *ambre gris*, grey amber.]

ambidexter, *am-bi-deks′tər*, *adj.* able to use both hands alike : on both sides : double-dealing.—*n.* one who is ambidexter.—*n.* **ambidexterity** (*-ter′i-ti*).—*adj.* **ambidex′t(e)rous**. [L. *ambi-*, on both sides, *dexter*, right.]

ambient, *am′bi-ənt*, *adj.* going round : surrounding : investing.—*n.* that which encompasses : the air or sky. [L. *ambiēns, -entis*, pr.p. of *ambīre*—pfx. *ambi-*, about, *īre*, to go.]

ambiguous, *am-big′ū-əs*, *adj.* doubtful : undetermined : of intermediate or doubtful nature : indistinct : wavering : admitting of more than one meaning : equivocal.—*n.* **ambigū′ity**, doubtful or double meaning : an equivocal expression.—*adv.* **ambig′uously**.—*n.* **ambig′uousness**. [L. *ambiguus—ambigēre*, to go about, waver—pfx. *ambi-*, both ways, *agēre*, to drive.]

ambit, *am′bit*, *n.* circuit : scope : compass : precincts : confines. [L. *ambitus*, a going round— pfx. *ambi-*, round, *itus*, going—*īre*, *itum*, to go.]

ambition, *am-bish′ən*, *n.* aspiration after success or advancement : the object of aspiration.—*adjs.* **ambi′tionless** ; **ambitious** (*am-bish′əs*), full of ambition (with *of*, formerly *for*) : strongly desirous of anything—esp. power : aspiring : indicating ambition : pretentious.—*adv.* **ambi′tiously**.—*n.* **ambi′tiousness**. [L. *ambitiō, -ōnis*, canvassing— pfx. *ambi-*, about, and *īre*, *itum*, to go.]

ambitty, *am-bit′i*, *adj.* devitrified. [Fr. *ambité*, of obscure origin.]

ambivalence, *am-biv′ə-ləns*, **ambivalency**, *-i*, *ns.* coexistence in one person of opposing emotional attitudes towards the same object.—*adj.* **ambiv′-alent**. [L. pfx. *ambi-*, on both sides, *valēns, -ēntis*, pr.p. of *valēre*, to be strong.]

amble, *am′bl*, *v.i.* to move, as a horse, by lifting together both legs on one side alternately with those on the other side : to move at an easy pace : to go like an ambling horse : to ride an ambling animal.—*n.* an ambling pace.—*n.* **am′bler**.—*n.* and *adj.* **am′bling**. [Fr. *ambler*—L. *ambulāre*, to walk about.]

amblyopia, *am-bli-ō′pi-ä*, *n.* dullness of sight. [Gr. *amblyōpiā—amblys*, dull, *ōps*, eye.]

Amblyopsis, *am-bli-op′sis*, *n.* the blindfish of the Mammoth Cave in Kentucky. [Gr. *amblys*, dull, *opsis*, sight.]

Amblystoma, *am-blis′to-mä*, *n.* a genus of tailed amphibians in the gill-less or salamandroid sub-order, in the larval stage called axolotl. [Gr. *amblys*, blunt, *stoma*, mouth.]

ambo, *am′bō*, *n.* an early Christian raised reading-desk or pulpit :—*pl.* **am′bos**, **ambō′nes** (*-nēz*). [L.L. *ambō*—Gr. *ambōn, -ōnos*, crest of a hill, pulpit.]

Amboyna-wood, *am-boi′nä-wood*, *n.* the finely coloured knotty wood of *Pterocarpus indicus*, a papilionaceous tree. [Island of *Amboyna*.]

ambrosia, *am-brō′z(h)i-ä*, *-z(h)yä*, *n.* the food (later, the drink) of the Greek gods, which conferred everlasting youth and beauty : the anointing oil of the gods : any finely flavoured beverage : something sweet and pleasing : bee-bread : fungi cultivated for food by certain bark-beetles (**ambrosia beetles**) of the Scolytidae : Ambrosia, a genus of Compositae called in America rag-weeds. —*adj.* **ambrō′sial**, fragrant : delicious : immortal : heavenly.—*adv.* **ambrō′sially**.—*adj.* **ambrō′sian**. [Gr. *ambrosiä—ambrotos*, immortal—*a-*, priv., and *brotos*, for *mrotos*, mortal ; cf. Sans. *mrita*, dead— *mri* (L. *mori*), to die.]

Ambrosian, *am-brō′z(h)i-ən*, *-z(h)yən*, *adj.* pertaining to St. *Ambrose*, 4th-cent. bishop of Milan, to his liturgy, to the form of plain-song introduced by him, to various religious orders and to the public library at Milan (founded 1602-9 by Cardinal Federigo Borromeo) named in his honour.—*n.* a member of any of these orders.

ambry, **aumbry**, **almery**, Scot. **awmry**, **awmrie**, *âm′*, *awm′(b)ri*, *n.* a recess for church vessels : a cupboard : a pantry : a dresser : a safe. [O.Fr. *almerie*—L. *armārium*, a chest, safe—*arma*, arms, tools.]

ambs-ace, **ames-ace**, *āmz′ās*, *amz′ās*, *n.* double ace, the lowest possible throw at dice : ill-luck : worthlessness. [O.Fr. *ambes as*—L. *ambōs assēs*, both aces.]

ambulacrum, *am-bū-lā′krəm*, *n.* a radial band in the shell of an echinoderm, bearing rows of pores through which protrude the tube-feet :—*pl.* **ambulā′cra**.—*adj.* **ambulā′cral**. [L. *ambulācrum*, a walk—*ambulāre*, to walk.]

ambulance, *am′bū-ləns*, *n.* a vehicle for the sick or injured : a unit of succour for wounded in the field : a movable field hospital.—*n.* **am′bulance-chaser** (*U.S.*), a lawyer on the look-out for accidents in order to instigate actions for damages.—*adj.* **am′bulant**, walking : moving from place to place : (*rare*) unfixed : allowing or calling for walking.— *n.* (*med.*) a walking case.—*v.i.* **am′bulate**, to walk.— *ns.* **ambulā′tion** ; **am′bulātor**, a walker : a wheel for road-measuring.—*adj.* **am′bulatory** (*-ə-tər-i*), of or for walking : moving from place to place, not stationary : mutable.—*n.* a covered walk, as an aisle, cloister, portico, corridor. [L. *ambulāre*, *-ātum*, to walk about.]

ambuscade, *am-bəs-kād′*, *n.* an ambush.—*v.t.* and *v.i.* to ambush.—*n.* **ambuscā′do** (esp. 16th-17th cent. ; would-be Sp.), an ambuscade :—*pl.* **ambuscā′do(e)s**. [Fr. *embuscade* or Sp. *emboscada* ; see **ambush**.]

ambush, *am′boosh*, *n.* a lying, or laying, in wait to attack by surprise : a place of lying in wait : a body (or person) lying in wait.—*v.t.* to lay in wait : to waylay.—*v.i.* to lie in wait.—*n.* **am′bushment**, ambush. [O.Fr. *embusche* (Fr. *embûche*)—*em-buscher*—L.L. *imboscāre—im*, in, *boscus* (see **bush**).]

amearst (*Spens.*) for **amerced**.

ameer. See **amir**.

Amelanchier, *am-ə-lang′ki-ər*, *n.* the shadbush genus of the rose family. [Fr. *amélanchier*.]

amelcorn, *âm′əl-korn*, *n.* emmer. [Ger. and Du. *amelkorn* ; cf. **amylum**, **corn**.]

ameliorate, *ə-mē′lyə-rāt*, *v.t.* to make better : to improve.—*v.i.* to grow better.—*n.* **ameliorā′tion**. —*adj.* **amē′liorātive**. [Fr. *améliorer*—L. *ad*, to, *melior*, better.]

amen, *ä-men'*, or *ā-men'*, *interj.* so let it be.—*n.* an expression of assent, as by saying 'amen': the last word.—*v.t.* to say amen to: to ratify solemnly: to conclude. [Heb. *āmēn*, true, truly, retained in Gr. and English translations.]

amenable, *ə-mēn'ə-bl*, *adj.* ready to be led or won over: liable or subject.—*ns.* **amenabil'ity, amen'-ableness.**—*adv.* **amen'ably.** [Fr. *amener*, to lead—*à*—L. *ad*, to, and *mener*, to lead—L.L. *mināre*, to lead, to drive (as cattle)—L. *minārī*, to threaten.]

amenage, *am'e-nāj*, *v.t.* (*Spens.*) to tame. [O.Fr. *ame(s)nager*—*à*, to, *mesnage*, household.]

amenaunce, *am'e-nawns*, *n.* (*Spens.*) bearing. [O.Fr. *amenance*; see **amenable**.]

amend, *ə-mend'*, *v.t.* to free from fault or error: to correct: to improve: to alter in detail, with a view to improvement, as a bill before parliament: to rectify: to cure: to mend.—*v.i.* to grow or become better: to reform: to recover.—*adjs.* **amend'able; amend'atory**, corrective.—*ns.* **amend'er; amend'ment**, correction: improvement: an alteration proposed on a bill under consideration: a counter-proposal put before a meeting: a counter-motion.—*n.pl.* (in form; usu. treated as *sing.*) **amends'**, supply of a loss: compensation: reparation. [Fr. *amender*—L. *ēmendāre*—*ē*, out of, and *mendum*, a fault.]

amene, *ə-mēn'*, *adj.* (now *rare*) pleasant.—*n.* **amenity** (*-mēn'*, *-men'*), pleasantness, as in situation, climate, manners, disposition: a pleasing feature, object, characteristic: civility. [L. *amoenus*, pleasant.]

amenorrhoea, *a-men-ō-rē'ä*, *n.* failure of menstruation. [Gr. *a-*, priv., *mēn*, month, *rhoiä*, a flowing.]

ament, *ā'mənt*, *a-ment'*, *n.* one who is mentally defective by failure to develop: a sufferer from amentia.—*n.* **amentia** (*a-*, *ā-men'shi-ä*), mental deficiency. [L. *āmēns, -entis*—*ā*, from, *mēns, mentis*, mind.]

amentum, *a-men'tum*, *n.* a catkin:—*pl.* **amen'ta.**—*adjs.* **amentā'ceous, amen'tal; amentif'erous,** catkin-bearing. [L. *āmentum*, thong.]

amerce, *ə-mərs'*, *v.t.* to fine (esp. at discretion): to deprive: to punish.—*ns.* **amerce'ment, amerc'-iament**, infliction of a fine: a fine.—*adj.* **amerc'-iable.** [A.Fr. *amercier*—*à merci*, at mercy.]

American, *ə-mer'i-kən*, *adj.* pertaining to America, esp. to the United States.—*n.* a native or citizen of America: the English language as spoken in America.—*v.t.* **Amer'icanise,** to render American.—*ns.* **Amer'icanism**, a custom, characteristic, word, phrase, or idiom characteristic of Americans: condition of being an American citizen: devotion to American institutions; **Amer'icanist**, a student of American biology, archaeology, and the like.—**American aloe**, agave; **American blight**, a cottony plant-louse pest of apple-trees; **American bowls**, a variety of skittles: **American cloth**, cloth with a glazed coating; **American Indian**, a member of the native race of America, thought on discovery to be Indian; **American organ**, an instrument resembling the harmonium, in which air is sucked inwards to the reeds. [From *America*, prob. so called from Richard *Ameryk*, Sheriff of Bristol, who financed John Cabot's voyage; also said to be from Amerigo (L. *Americus*) Vespucci.]

americium, *am-ər-ish'i-əm*, *n.* the chemical element of atomic number 95, obtained artificially in *America*.

Amerind, *am'ər-ind*, *n.* and *adj.* American *Ind*ian.

ames-ace. See **ambs-ace.**

Ametabola, *am-et-ab'ə-lä*, *n.pl.* in some classifications the lowest insects, with little or no metamorphosis.—*n.* **ametab'olism.**—*adjs.* **ametabol'ic** (*-ə-bol'ik*), **ametab'olous.** [Gr. *a-*, priv., *meta-bolē*, change.]

amethyst, *am'e-thist*, *n.* a bluish violet quartz anciently supposed to prevent drunkenness: its colour.—*adj.* of, or coloured like, amethyst.—*adj.* **amethyst'ine** (*-īn*).—**oriental amethyst**, a purple corundum. [Gr. *amethystos*—*a-*, priv., *methyein*, to be drunken—*methy*, wine; cf. **mead** (1), Sans. *madhu*, sweet.]

Amharic, *am-har'ik*, *n.* an Ethiopic language prevailing in Abyssinia.—Also *adj.* [*Amhara* district.]

amiable, *ām'i-ə-bl*, *adj.* (*Shak.*) friendly: (*Shak.*) love-inspiring: lovable: of sweet and friendly disposition.—*ns.* **āmiabil'ity, ām'iableness.**—*adv.* **ām'iably.** [O.Fr. *amiable*, friendly—L. *amīcābilis*—*amīcus*, friend; confused in meaning with O.Fr. *amable* (Fr. *aimable*)—L. *amābilis*—*amāre*, to love.]

amianthus, *am-i-anth'əs*, more correctly **amiantus** (*-ant'əs*), *n.* the finest fibrous asbestos, which can be made into cloth readily cleansed by fire. [Gr. *amiantos* (*lithos*), undefiled (stone)—*a-*, priv., and *miainein*, to soil.]

amicable, *am'ik-ə-bl*, *adj.* in friendly spirit.—*ns.* **amicabil'ity, am'icableness.**—*adv.* **am'icably.** [L. *amīcābilis*—*amīcus*, a friend—*amāre*, to love.]

amice, *am'is*, *n.* a strip of fine linen, worn formerly on the head, now on the shoulders, by a priest at mass: a cloak, wrap. [O.Fr. *amit*—L. *amictus*, cloak—*amb-*, about, and *jacĕre*, to throw.]

amice, *am'is*, *n.* a furred hood with long ends hanging down in front, originally a cap or covering for the head, afterwards a hood, or cape with a hood, later a mere college hood. [O.Fr. *aumuce*, of doubtful origin.]

amid, *ə-mid'*, *prep.* in the midst of: among.—*adv.* (*arch.*) in the midst.—*adv.* and *prep.* **amid'most**, in the very middle (of).—*adv.* **amid'ships**, in, near, towards, the middle of a ship lengthwise (from gen. of **ship**).—*adv.* and *prep.* **amidst'**, amid. [O.E. *on middan* (dat. of adj.), in middle; the *s* is a later adverbial genitive ending, the *t* as in **amongst, betwixt**, etc.]

amide, *am'īd*, *n.* a derivative of ammonia in which an acid radical takes the place of one or more of the three hydrogen atoms.—*n.* **amido-group** (*a-mē'dō*), the group NH_2 in such combination. [From **ammonia.**]

amildar, *am'il-där*, *n.* a factor or manager in India: a collector of revenue amongst the Mahrattas. [Hind. *'amaldār*—Ar. *'amal*, work, Pers. *där*, holder.]

amine, *am'īn*, *-ēn*, *n.* an ammonia derivative in which alcohol or other positive radical or a metal takes the place of one or more of the three hydrogen atoms.—*ns.* **amino-a'cid** (*a-mē'nō-*), a fatty acid (e.g. **ami'no-acet'ic acid**, glycine) in which the amino-group takes the place of a hydrogen atom of the hydrocarbon radical; **ami'no-group'**, the group NH_2 in such combination. [From **ammonia.**]

amir, ameer, *ā-mēr'*, *ə-mēr'*, *n.* the title borne by certain Mohammedan princes. [Ar. *amīr*; see **admiral, emir.**]

amis (*Spens.*). Same as **amice** (1).

amiss, *ə-mis'*, *adv.* astray: wrongly: improperly: faultily.—*adj.* out of order: wrong: unsuitable: to be objected to.—*n.* an evil: a misdeed.—**come amiss**, to be unwelcome, untoward; **take amiss**, to take offence at (strictly, by misinterpretation). [Prep. **a**, **miss**.]

amissible, *ə-mis'i-bl*, *adj.* liable to be lost.—*n.* **amissibil'ity.** [L. *āmittĕre*, *āmissum*, to lose—*ā*, from, *mittĕre*, to send.]

amissing, *ə-mis'ing*, *adj.* (*Scot.*) wanting: lost. [Prep. **a**, and **missing.**]

amitosis, *am-i-tō'sis*, (*biol.*) cell-division without mitosis.—*adj.* **amitotic** (*-tot'ik*).—*adv.* **amitot'-ically.** [Gr. *a-*, priv., and *mitos*, thread.]

amity, *am'i-ti*, *n.* friendship: good-will: friendly relations. [Fr. *amitié*—L. *amīcus*, a friend.]

amman. See **amtman.**

ammeter, *am'i-tər*, *n.* an instrument for measuring electric current. [From **ampere**, and Gr. *metron*, measure.]

ammiral, an old form (*Milt.*) of **admiral.**

Ammon, *am'on*, *n.* the ancient Egyptian ram-headed god *Amūn, Amen*, identified by the Greeks with Zeus, famous for his temple and oracle in the Libyan oasis of Siwa: **ammon**, the argali (from its gigantic horns).—*n.* **ammonia** (*a-*, *ə-mō'ni-ä*), a pungent compound of nitrogen and hydrogen (NH_3) first obtained in gaseous form from *sal-ammoniac*: its solution in water, strictly ammonium hydroxide (*liquid ammonia*, long known as

---

Neutral vowels in unaccented syllables: *el'ə-mənt, in'fənt, ran'dəm*

spirits of hartshorn).—*adj.* ammō′niac, of the region of the temple of Ammon (applied only to gum-ammoniac, and to sal-ammoniac, which is said to have been first made in that district from camel-dung): ammoniacal.—*n.* gum-ammoniac (see gum).—Also ammoni′acum (*am-ə-nī′ə-kəm*). —*adjs.* ammoni′acal, of ammonia; ammō′-niated, combined, impregnated, with ammonia.— *ns.* amm′onite, a fossil cephalopod of many kinds, with coiled chambered shell like Ammon's horn; ammō′nium, a univalent radical, NH₄, resembling the alkali metals in chemical behaviour. [Gr. *Ammōn, -ōnos.*]

ammonal, *am′ən-al*, *n.* a high explosive made from *ammonium* nitrate and aluminium.

ammonia, ammonite.   See under Ammon.

ammophilous, *am-of′i-ləs*, *adj.* sand-loving. [Gr. *ammos*, sand, *phileein*, to love.]

ammunition, *am-ū-nish′ən*, *n.* orig. military stores generally : now things used for charging fire-arms—missiles, propellants, cartridges.—*adj.* for ammunition : supplied from army stores.—*v.t.* to supply with ammunition. [Obs.Fr. *amunition*, app. from *l'amunition* for *la munition*; see munition.]

amnesia, *am-nē′zi-ä*, *-zyä*, *n.* loss of memory. [Gr. *amnēsiā*.]

amnesty, *am′nest-i*, *n.* a general pardon : an act of oblivion.—*v.t.* to give amnesty to. [Gr. *amnēstiā*, forgetfulness.]

amnion, *am′ni-ən*, *n.* the innermost membrane enveloping the embryo of reptiles, birds, and mammals :—*pl.* am′nia.—*adj.* amniot′ic. [Gr.]

amoeba, *ə-mē′bä*, *n.* a protozoon of ever-changing shape :—*pl.* amoebae (*-bē*).—*adjs.* amoe′bic; amoe′biform; amoe′boid. [Gr. *amoibē*, change.]

amoebaean, *ə-mē-bē′ən*, *adj.* answering alternately, responsive, as often in pastoral poetry. [L. *amoebaeus*—Gr. *amoibaios*—*amoibē*, alternation.]

amok, *ə-mok′*, amuck, *ə-muk′*, *adj.* and *adv.*, in a frenzy, esp. in phrase to run amok, to run forth murderously assailing all who come in the way. [Malay *amoq*, frenzied.]

Amomum, *a-mō′məm*, *n.* a genus of the ginger family including cardamoms and grains of paradise. [Latinised from Gr. *amōmon*, prob. cardamom.]

among, *ə-mung′*, amongst, *ə-mungst′*, *preps.* of the number of : amidst.—*adv.* among (*arch.*), meanwhile : all the time : betweenwhiles : here and there. [O.E. *on-gemang*, lit. in mixture, crowd—*gemengan*, to mingle : for *-st* see against.]

amontillado, *ä-mon-til-*(*y*)*ä′dō*, *n.* a dry or slightly sweet sherry of light colour and body, orig. from *Montilla*. [Sp.]

amoove (*Spens.*).   Same as amove (1).

amoral, *a-mor′əl*, also *ā-*, *adj.* non-moral, outside the domain of morality.—*ns.* amor′alism, refusal to recognise the validity of any system of morality; amor′alist. [Gr. *a-*, priv., and moral.]

amorce, *ə-mors′*, *n.* a percussion cap for a toy pistol. [Fr., priming.]

amoret, *am′or-et*, *n.* (*obs.*) a sweetheart : a love-glance : a love-knot : a love-sonnet or song.—*ns.* amoret′to, a lover : a cupid :—*pl.* amoret′ti (*-tē*); amorino (*-ē′nō*), a cupid :—*pl.* amori′ni (*-nē*). [O.Fr. *amorete* and It. *amoretto*, *amorino*, dims. from L. *amor*, love.]

amorist, *am′ər-ist*, *n.* a lover : a gallant : one who writes of love : a seeker of sexual adventures or experiences.—*n.* am′orism. [L. *amor*, love.]

amornings, *ə-morn′ingz*, *adv.* (*obs.*) of a morning. [Prep. a, and morning, with gen. ending added.]

amoroso, *am-or-ō′sō*, *adj.* (*mus.*) tender.—Also *adv.* —*n.* a lover : a gallant :—*fem.* amoro′sa. [It.]

amorous, *am′ər-əs*, *adj.* inclined to love : in love : fond : amatory : relating to love.—*n.* amorosity (*-os′iti ; rare*).—*adv.* am′orously.—*n.* am′orousness. [O.Fr. *amorous* (Fr. *amoureux*)—L.L. *amōrōsus—amor*, love.]

amorphous, *ə-mor′fəs*, *adj.* without definite shape or structure : shapeless : without crystalline structure.—*n.* amor′phism. [Gr. *amorphos*, shapeless—*a-*, priv., *morphē*, form.]

amort, *ə-mort′*, *adj.* (*obs.* or *arch.*) spiritless, dejected. [Fr. *à*, to, *mort*, death; but partly from alamort wrongly understood as *all amort*.]

amortise, *ə-mor′tīz*, *-tiz*, *v.t.* to alienate in mortmain or convey to a corporation : to wipe out esp. through a sinking-fund.—*n.* amortisā′tion. [L.L. *a(d)mortizāre*—Fr. *à*, to, *mort*, death.]

amount, *ə-mownt′*, *v.i.* (*Spens.*) to go up : to come in total : to come in meaning or substance (with *to*).—*n.* the whole sum : principal and interest together : quantity : value, import, equivalence. [O.Fr. *amonter*, to ascend—L. *ad*, to, *mōns, montis*, a mountain.]

amour, *ə-mōōr′*, *n.* love (commonly in *pl.*) : a love affair (now usu. discreditable).—*n.* amourette (*ä-moo-ret′*), a petty amour : an amorette. [Fr.,—L. *amor, amōris*, love.]

amove, *ə-mōōv′*, *v.t.* (*Spens.*) to stir up : to affect : to rouse. [O.Fr. *amover*—L. *admovēre—ad*, to, *movēre*, to move.]

amove, *ə-mōōv′*, *v.t.* (*law*) to remove. [L. *āmovēre* —*ā*, from, *movēre*, to move.]

amp, *amp*, *n.* short for ampere.

ampelopsis, *am-pi-lop′sis*, *n.* Virginia creeper. [Gr. *ampelos*, vine, *opsis*, appearance.]

ampere, ampère, *am′per*, *-pēr′*, *än²-per*, *n.* (*elect.*) unit of current, the current one volt can send through one ohm : commonly (international ampere) the current which, when passed through a solution of silver nitrate in water, will deposit silver at the rate of 0.001118 grams per sec.—*n.* amper′age, current in amperes. [From A.M. *Ampère*, French physicist (1775-1836).]

ampersand, *am′pərs-and*, *n.* the character (& ; originally ligatured *E* and *T*, for L. *et*) representing *and.*—Also am′perzand, am′pussy-and, am′-passy (*amp′ə-si*). [*and per se and*—that is, &, by itself, 'and'; cf. a-per-se.]

amphibious, *am-fib′i-əs*, *adj.* leading two lives : living, or adapted to life, or use, on land and in or on water : (of military operations) in which troops are conveyed across the sea or other water in landing barges, assault-craft, etc., and land on enemy-held territory : of double, doubtful, or ambiguous nature.—*n.pl.* Amphib′ia, a class of vertebrates typically gill-breathing in the larval state and lung-breathing or skin-breathing as adults—frogs, toads, newts, salamanders, caecilians. —*adj.* amphib′ian, amphibious : of the Amphibia. —*n.* a member of the Amphibia : an aeroplane designed to alight on land or water : a vehicle for use on land or water. [Gr. *amphibios—amphi*, on both sides, *bios*, life.]

amphibole, *am′fi-bōl*, *n.* any mineral of a group differing from the pyroxenes in cleavage angle (about 56° instead of about 87°), silicates of calcium, magnesium, and other metals, including hornblende, actinolite, tremolite, etc.—*n.* amphib′olite, a rock composed essentially of amphibole. [Gr. *amphibolos*, ambiguous, on account of the resemblance between hornblende and tourmaline.]

amphibology, *am-fi-bol′ə-ji*, *n.* a phrase or sentence ambiguous not in its individual words but in its construction : the use of such ambiguities.—*adjs.* amphibol′ic, amphibological (*-bō-loj′*), am′-phib′olous (*-ə-ləs*).—*n.* amphib′oly, amphibology. [Gr. *amphibolos*—*amphi*, on both sides, *ballein*, to throw.]

amphibrach, *am′fi-brak*, *n.* in prosody, a foot of three syllables, a long between two short, or three stressed between two unstressed.—*adj.* amphibrach′ic. [Gr. *amphi*, on each side, *brachys*, short.]

Amphictyon, *am-fik′ti-on*, *n.* (*Gr. hist.*) a delegate to an (or the) Amphictyonic council.—*adj.* Am-phictyon′ic.—*n.* Amphic′tyony, a league of neighbouring communities connected with a temple and cult, esp. of Delphi. [Gr. *Amphiktyones*, app. for *amphiktiones*, dwellers around—*amphi, ktizein*, to dwell.]

amphigastrium, *am-fi-gas′tri-əm*, *n.* a scale-like leaf on the ventral side of some liverworts :—*pl.* amphigas′tria. [Gr. *amphi*, about, *gastēr*, belly.]

amphigory, *am′fi-gə-ri*, *n.* nonsense-verse. [Fr. *amphigouri* : origin unknown.]

amphimacer, *am-fim′ə-sər, n.* in prosody, a foot of three syllables, short between two long. [Gr. *amphimakros*—*amphi,* on both sides, *makros,* long.]

amphimixis, *am-fi-mik′sis, n.* fusion of gametes : sexual reproduction : combination of characters from both parents. [Gr. *amphi,* on both sides, *mixis,* intercourse, mixing.]

Amphineura, *am-fi-nū′rä, n.pl.* a class of molluscs with two ventral and two lateral nerve-cords, including Chiton. [Gr. *amphi,* on both sides, *neuron,* nerve.]

Amphioxus, *am-fi-oks′əs, n.* the lancelet, one of the lowest backboned animals. [Gr. *amphi,* at both ends, and *oxys,* sharp.]

amphipod, *am′fi-pod, n.* one of the **Amphip′oda,** an order of small sessile-eyed crustaceans with swimming feet and jumping feet—sand-hoppers, etc.—*adj.* **amphip′odous.** [Gr. *amphi,* both ways, *pous, podos,* a foot.]

amphisbaena, *am-fis-bē′nä, n.* a fabulous two-headed snake : **Amphisbaena,** a genus of snake-like lizards, chiefly tropical American, whose rounded tails give the appearance of a head at each end.—*adj.* **amphisbae′nic.** [Gr. *amphisbaina*—*amphis,* both ways, *bainein,* to go.]

amphiscian, *am-fish′i-ən, n.* an inhabitant of the torrid zone, whose shadow is thrown both ways—that is, to the north one part of the year, and to the south the other part.—Also *adj.* [Gr. *amphiskios*—*amphi,* both ways, *skiā,* a shadow.]

amphistomous, *am-fis′tə-məs, adj.* having a sucker at either end, as some worms. [Gr. *amphi,* on both sides, *stoma,* mouth.]

amphitheatre, *am-fi-thē′ə-tər, n.* a building with rows of seats one above another, around an open space : a similar configuration of hill-slopes : one of the galleries in a theatre.—*adjs.* **amphithe′atral, amphitheatrical** *(-at′ri-kəl).*—*adv.* **amphitheat′-rically.** [Gr. *amphitheātron*—*amphi, theātron,* theatre.]

amphitropous, *am-fit′rə-pəs, adj.* (of an ovule) placed T-wise on the funicle. [Gr. *amphi,* on both sides, *tropos,* a turning.]

Amphitryon, *am-fit′ri-on, n.* (*Gr. myth.*) husband of Alcmene, on whom Zeus in Amphitryon's semblance begot Herakles : a hospitable entertainer, esp. of doubtful identity (in allusion to the line in Molière's play, 'Le véritable Amphitryon est l'Amphitryon où l'on dine'). [Gr. *Amphitryōn.*]

ampholyte, *am′fō-līt, n.* an amphoteric electrolyte.

amphora, *am′fə-rä, n.* a two-handled jar used by the Greeks and Romans for holding liquids :—*pl.* **am′phorae** *(-rē).*—*adj.* **amphor′ic** *(-for′ ; med.)* like the sound produced by speaking into a bottle. [L. *amphora*—Gr. *amphoreus, amphiphoreus*—*amphi,* on both sides, and *phoreus,* a bearer.]

amphoteric, *am-fō-ter′ik, adj.* of both kinds : acting both ways, e.g. as acid and base, electropositive and electronegative. [Gr. *amphoteros,* both.]

ample, *am′pl, adj.* spacious : wide : large enough : abundant : liberal : copious : full or somewhat bulky in form.—*ns.* **am′pleness; ampliā′tion,** enlarging : an enlargement.—*adj.* **am′pliative** *(rare).*—*ns.* **amplificā′tion,** enlargement; **am′-plifier,** one who amplifies : a lens that enlarges the field of vision : a device for giving greater loudness. —*v.t.* **am′plify** *(-fī),* to make more copious in expression : to add to :—*pr.p.* **am′plifying;** *pa.p.* and *pa.t.* **am′plified.**—*n.* **am′plitude,** largeness : abundance : width : range : extent of vibratory movement (from extreme to extreme, or from mean to extreme) : the angular distance from the east point of the horizon at which a heavenly body rises, or from the west point at which it sets.—*adv.* **am′ply** *(-pli).* [Fr. *ample, amplifier, amplitude*— L. *amplus, amplificāre, amplitūdō.*]

amplexicaul, *am-pleks′i-kawl, adj.* (*bot.*) clasping the stem by a dilated base. [L. *amplexus, -ūs,* embrace, *caulis,* stem.]

ampulla, *am-pool′ä, n.* a small two-handled flask : a pilgrim's bottle : a vessel for holy oil, as at coronations : a cruet for the wine and water used at the altar : a small glass container for a hypodermic dose, etc. : (*biol.*) any small membranous

vesicle : the dilated end of a semicircular canal in the ear :—*pl.* **ampull′ae** *(-ē).*—Also **am′poule** (or *-pōōl′* ; Fr.), **am′pul.**—*n.* **ampollos′ity** (*Browning*), turgidity, bombast. [L. irregular dim. of *amphora,* a flagon; partly directly from L., partly through O.E. *ampulle,* O.Fr. *ampo(u)le,* and It. *ampolla.*]

amputate, *am′pūt-āt, v.t.* to cut off, as a limb of an animal.—*ns.* **amputā′tion; am′putātor.** [L. *amputāre, -ātum*—*amb-,* round about, *putāre,* to lop.]

amrita, *am-rē′tä, n.* the drink of the Hindu gods. [Sans. *amrta,* immortal; cf. Gr. *ambrotos.*]

amtman, *ämt′män,* **amman,** *am′an, n.* in Germany, Switzerland, the Netherlands, Scandinavia, a district magistrate. [Ger. *amtmann, amman,* Dan. and Norw. *amtmand*—*amt,* office, administration (from the root of **ambassador**) and Ger. *mann,* Dan. *mand,* man.]

amuck, *ə-muk′.* See **amok.**

amulet, *am′ū-let, -lit, n.* a charm carried about the person : a medicine supposed to have occult operation.—*adj.* **amulet′ic.** [L. *amulētum.*]

amuse, *ə-mūz′, v.t.* (*obs.*) to put in a muse : to beguile with expectation : to occupy the attention of : (*arch.*) to beguile : to occupy pleasantly : to entertain, divert : to excite mirth in.—*adj.* **amus′-able.**—*adv.* **amus′edly.**—*ns.* **amuse′ment,** distraction of attention : beguiling : trifling : a pleasant feeling of the ludicrous : that which amuses : recreation : pastime; **amus′er; amusette** *(am-ū-zet′),* a light field-gun invented by Marshal Saxe.— *adj.* **amus′ing,** affording amusement : entertaining.—*adv.* **amus′ingly.**—*adj.* **amus′ive** *(obs.),* deceptive : *(obs.)* recreational : interesting : entertaining : amusing.—*n.* **amus′iveness.** [Fr. *amuser* —*à,* to, *muser,* to stare; see **muse,** vb.]

amygdal, *ə-mig′dal, n.* (*obs.*) an almond.—*n.* **amyg′dala** (*zool.*) a lobe of the cerebellum : one of the palatal tonsils.—*adj.* **amygdalā′ceous,** akin to the almond.—*ns.* **amyg′dale** *(-dāl),* an amygdule; **amyg′dalin,** a glucoside found in cherry kernels, bitter almonds, etc.—*adjs.* **amyg′-daloid,** almond-shaped : having amygdules.—*n.* an igneous rock in which almond-shaped steam-cavities have been filled with minerals.—*adj.* **amygdaloid′al,** having amygdules.—*ns.* **amyg′-dule,** a mineral-filled steam-cavity in a lava.— **Amyg′dalus,** the almond genus, or section of Prunus. [L. *amygdala*—Gr. *amygdalē,* almond.]

amyl, *am′il, n.* an alcohol radical of composition C₅H₁₁.—*n.* **am′ylene,** a hydrocarbon of composition C₅H₁₀.—*adj.* **am′yl nitrite,** a fruity-smelling, amber-coloured liquid, inhaled medicinally. [From the first syllable of Gr. *amylon,* starch, fine meal, and *hylē,* matter, from having been first got from fusel oil made from starch.]

amylum, *am′il-əm, n.* (*chem.*) starch.—*adjs.* **amylā′-ceous, am′yloid, amyloid′al.** [Gr. *amylon,* the finest flour, starch; lit. unmilled—*a-,* priv., *mylē,* a mill.]

an, *an, ən, adj.* one : the indefinite article, used before a vowel sound, and by some before an unstressed syllable beginning with a sounded *h.* [O.E. *ān;* see **one.**]

an, *an, ən, conj.* (*arch.*) if : **an′,** and. [A form of **and.**]

an, *an, ən, prep.* (*obs.*) a form of **on.**

ana, *ä′nä, ä′nä, n.pl.* or *collective sing.* (with *pl.* **ana′s, anas**) a collection of someone's table-talk or of gossip, literary anecdotes, and the like. [The suffix **-ana.**]

anabaptist, *an-ə-bap′tist, n.* a name given by opponents to one holding that baptism should be of adults only and therefore that those baptised in infancy must be baptised again : **Anabaptist,** one of a Protestant sect of German origin (1521) rejecting infant baptism and seeking establishment of a Christian communism.—*v.t.* **anabaptise′,** to baptise anew : to rename.—*n.* **anabapt′ism.**—*adj.* **anabaptist′ic.** [Gr. *ana-,* again, *baptizein,* to dip.]

Anabas, *an′a-bas, n.* the genus to which belongs the climbing perch, an East Indian fish that often leaves the water. [Gr. *anabas,* aor. part. of *ana-bainein,* to climb—*ana,* up, *bainein,* to go.]

anabasis, *an-ab'ə-sis, n.* a going up : a military advance up-country, such as that of Cyrus the younger (B.C. 401) related (with the subsequent Katabasis or retreat of the 10,000) by Xenophon in his *Anabasis.—adj.* anabatic (*-bat'ik*), upward-moving. [Gr.,—*ana,* up, *basis,* going.]

Anableps, *an'ə-bleps, n.* a genus of bony fishes with open air-bladders, and projecting eyes divided in two for vision in air and water. [Gr. *ana,* up, *blepein,* to look.]

anabolism, *an-ab'əl-izm, n.* chemical upbuilding of complex substances by protoplasm—opp. to *kata-bolism.—adj.* anabolic (*an-ə-bol'ik*). [Gr. *anabolē,* a heaping up—*ana,* up, *bolē,* a throw.]

anabranch, *an'ə-bränsh, n.* (*Australia*) a stream that leaves a river and re-enters lower. [For *anastomosing branch.*]

Anacardium, *an-ə-kär'di-əm, n.* the cashew-nut genus, giving name to a family **Anacardia'ceae** akin to the hollies and maples.—*adj.* anacardia'ceous. [Gr. *ana,* according to, *kardiā,* heart (from the shape of the fruit).]

anacatharsis, *an-ə-ka-thär'sis, n.* vomiting.—*n.* and *adj.* anacathar'tic. [Gr. *anakatharsis,* clearing up—*ana,* up, throughout, *katharsis* (see **catharsis**).]

Anacharis, *an-ak'ə-ris, n.* the Canadian water-weed (*Helodea* or *Elodea canadensis*), a North American weed found in Britain in 1842, soon clogging canals and rivers by vegetative growth. [Gr. *ana,* up, and *charis,* grace.]

anachronism, *a-nak'rə-nizm, n.* an error assigning a thing to an earlier or (less strictly) to a later age than it belongs to : anything out of keeping with chronology.—*adjs.* anachronist'ic, anach'-ronous.—*advs.* anachronist'ically, anach'-ronously. [Gr. *ana-,* backwards, *chronos,* time.]

anaclastic, *an-ə-klâs'tik, adj.* refractive. [Gr. *anaklastos,* bent back—*ana-,* back, *klaein,* break.]

anacoluthia, *an-ə-ko-l(y)ōō'thi-ä, n.* want of syntactical sequence, when the latter part of a sentence does not grammatically fit the earlier.—*n.* anacolu'-thon, an instance of anacoluthia : anacoluthia :—*pl.* anacolu'tha. [Gr. *anakolouthiā, anakolouthon —ana-,* priv., *akolouthos,* following.]

anaconda, *an-ə-kon'da, n.* a gigantic South American water-boa, *Eunectes murinus.* [Perhaps from a Singhalese name for another snake in Ceylon.]

Anacreontic, *an-ak-ri-ont'ik, adj.* after the manner of the Greek poet Anacreon (*Anakreōn;* 6th cent. B.C.)—free, convivial, erotic.—*n.* a poem in this vein.—*adv.* anacreont'ically.

anacrusis, *an-ə-krōō'sis, n.* (*pros.*) one or more short syllables introductory to the normal rhythm of a line :—*pl.* anacru'ses (*-sēz*).—*adj.* anacrustic (*-krus'tik*). [Gr. *anakrousis,* a pushing back, striking up a tune—*ana,* up, back, *krouein,* to strike.]

anadem, *an'ə-dem, n.* a fillet, chaplet, or wreath. [Gr. *anadēma—ana,* up, and *deein,* to bind.]

anadromous, *an-ad'rə-məs, adj.* ascending rivers to spawn. [Gr. *anadromos,* running up—*ana,* up, *dromos,* a run.]

anaemia, *an-ēm'i-ä, n.* bloodlessness : lack of red blood corpuscles or of haemoglobin—a condition marked by paleness and languor.—*adj.* anaem'ic, suffering from anaemia : (*fig.*) sickly, spiritless, washed-out, lacking in body.—Also **anemia, anemic.—pernicious anaemia,** a disease characterised by anaemia, abnormalities in the red blood corpuscles, and changes in the nervous system. [Gr. *anaimiā—an-,* priv., *haima,* blood.]

anaerobe, *an'ā-ər-ōb, n.* an organism that lives in absence of free oxygen.—Also **anaero'biont.—***adjs.* anaerobic (*-ob'ik,-ōb'ik*), anaerobiotic (*-ō-bī-ot'ik*), living in the absence of free oxygen : effected by anaerobes, as a biochemical change : involving the activity of anaerobes.—*advs.* anaerob'ically, anaerobiot'ically.—*n.* anaerobio'sis, life in the absence of oxygen. [Gr. *an-,* priv., *āēr,* air, *bios,* life.]

anaesthesia, *an-ēs-thē'zi-ä, -zyä,* or *-is-,* anaes-thesis, *-sis, n.* loss of feeling : insensibility, general or local.—*adj.* anaesthetic (*-thet'ik, -thē'tik*), producing or connected with insensibil-

ity.—*n.* an anaesthetic agent.—*adv.* anaesthet'ic-ally.—*v.t.* anaes'thetise.—*n.* anaesthetist (*-ēs'thə-tist,* or *-es'*), one who administers anaesthetics.—Also **anesthesia,** etc. [Gr. *anaisthēsiā,* insensibility, *anaisthētos,* insensible—*an-,* priv.,*aisthanesthai,* to perceive.]

anaglyph, *an'ə-glif, n.* an ornament in low relief : a picture composed of two prints, in complementary colours, seen stereoscopically through spectacles of these colours.—*adjs.* anaglyph'ic ; ana-glyptic (*-glip'tik*). [Gr. *anaglyphos, anaglyptos,* in low relief—*ana,* up, back, *glyphein,* to engrave.]

anagnorisis, *an-ag-nō'ri-sis, n.* recognition leading to dénouement. [Gr. *anagnōrisis.*]

anagoge, *an-ə-gō'jē, n.* mystical interpretation.—Also **an'agogy.—***adjs.* **anagogic** (*-goj'ik*); **anagog'ical.—***adv.* anagog'ically. [Gr. *anagōgē,* leading up, elevation—*ana,* up, *agein,* to lead.]

anagram, *an'ə-gram, n.* a word or phrase formed by the letters of another in different order.—*v.t.* and *v.i.* to anagrammatise.—*adjs.* anagrammat'ic, anagrammat'ical.—*adv.* anagrammat'ically.—*v.t.* and *v.i.* anagramm'atise, to transpose so as to form an anagram.—*ns.* anagramm'atism, the practice of making anagrams ; anagramm'atist, a maker of anagrams. [Gr. *ana-,* back, *gramma,* letter.]

anal. See **anus.**

analcime, *an-al'sim,* analcite, *an-al'sīt, ns.* a cubic zeolite, a hydrated sodium aluminium silicate. [Gr. *an-,* priv., *alkimos, alkis,* strong, because weakly electrified by friction.]

analects, *an'ə-lekts,* analecta, *-lek'tä, ns.pl.* collected literary fragments.—*adj.* analec'tic. [Gr. (*pl.*) *analekta—ana,* up, *legein,* to gather.]

analeptic, *an-ə-lep'tik, adj.* restorative : comforting. [Gr. *analēptikos,* restorative—*ana,* up, and the root *lab* of *lambanein,* to take.]

analgesia, *an-al-jē'zi-ä, n.* painlessness : insensibility to pain.—*n.* analgesic (*-jē'sik*), an anodyne.—*adj.* producing analgesia. [Gr. *analgēsiā—an-,* priv., and *algeein,* to feel pain.]

analogy, *an-al'ə-ji, n.* an agreement or correspondence in certain respects between things otherwise different : a resemblance of relations : parallelism : relation in general : a likeness : (*math.*) proportion, or the equality of ratios : (*biol.*) agreement in function, as distinguished from **homology** or agreement in origin : (*philol.*) a resemblance by virtue of which a word may be altered on the model of another class of words, as *strove, striven,* remodelled upon *drove, driven, throve, thriven,* etc.—*adjs.* analogic (*an-ə-loj'ik; rare*); analog'i-cal.—*adv.* analog'ically.—*v.t.* anal'ogise, to explain or consider by analogy.—*ns.* anal'ogist, one who sees, follows, or uses analogies ; anal'ogon (*-gon;* Gr.), analogue.—*adj.* anal'ogous (*-gəs*), having analogy : bearing some correspondence or resemblance : similar in certain circumstances or relations (with *to*) : positively electrified by heating. —*adv.* anal'ogously.—*ns.* anal'ogousness ; an'-alogue (*-log*) that which is analogous to something else : (*biol.*) that which is of like function (distinguished from a *homologue*). [Gr. *analogiā—ana,* according to, and *logos,* ratio.]

analphabet(e), *an-al'fə-bet, -bēt, adj.* ignorant of the alphabet.—Also *n.—adj.* analphabet'ic, totally illiterate : not alphabetic. [Gr. *analphabētos —an-,* priv.; see **alphabet.**]

analysis, *ən-al'is-is, n.* a resolving or separating of a thing into its elements or component parts : ascertainment of those parts : a table or statement of the results of this : the tracing of things to their source, and so discovering the general principles underlying individual phenomena : (*gram.*) resolution of a sentence into its syntactic elements : (*math.*) formerly, proof by assuming the result and reasoning back to principles : use of algebraical methods :—*pl.* anal'yses (*-sēz*).—Converse **synthesis.—***adj.* analysable (*an-ə-līz'ə-bl*).—*v.t.* an'alyse (*-līz ;* a better spelling than *analyze*), to subject to analysis.—*ns.* analys'er, one who analyses : in a polariscope the nicol (or substitute) through which the polarised light passes ; an'alyst (*-list ;* an ill-formed word), one skilled in or practising analysis, esp. chemical.—*adjs.* **analytic** (-*lit'ik*), pertaining to, performing, or inclined to analysis : resolving into first principles.—*n.* (often *pl.* in form) analytical logic : analytical geometry.— *adj.* **analyt'ical.**—*adv.* **analyt'ically.**—**analysis situs** (*sīt'əs*), (*geom.*) topology ; **analytical chemistry** (also **analysis**) chemistry concerned with determination of the constituents of chemical compounds, or mixtures of compounds ; **analytical geometry,** co-ordinate geometry ; **analytical languages,** those that use separate words instead of inflexions. [Gr. *analȳsis*—*analȳein*, to unloose, from *ana*, up, *lȳein*, to loose.]

anamnesis, *an-am-nēs'is, n.* the recalling to memory of things past : the recollection of the Platonic pre-existence : a patient's remembrance of the early stages of his illness. [Gr. *anamnēsis*—*ana*, up, back, *mimnēskein*, to remind, recall to memory.]

anamorphosis, *an-ə-mor'fə-sis,* or -*fō', n.* a deformed figure appearing in proportion when rightly viewed, *e.g.* in a curved mirror, or in a particular direction.—*adj.* **anamor'phous.** [Gr. *anamorphōsis*, a forming anew—*ana*, back, anew, *morphōsis*, a shaping—*morphē*, shape.]

anan, *ə-nan', interj.* (*obs.* or *dial.*) expressing failure to understand. [**anon.**]

ananas, *ə-nä'nas, n.* the pineapple (*Ananas sativus*): the pinguin (*Bromelia Pinguin*), or its fruit.—Also **an'ana.** [From an American Indian language.]

Ananias, *an-ə-nī'əs, n.* a liar. [*Acts of the Apostles,* V. 1-5.]

anapaest, *an'ə-pēst, n.* (*pros.*) a foot of two short (or unstressed) syllables followed by a long (or stressed)—a dactyl reversed.—*adjs.* **anapaes'tic, -al.** [Gr. *anapaistos,* struck back—*ana*, back, *paiein,* to strike.]

anaphase, *an'ə-fāz, n.* the stage of mitosis at which the daughter-chromosomes move towards the poles of the spindle. [Gr. *ana,* up, back, and **phase.**]

anaphora, *an-af'ə-rä, n.* the rhetorical device of beginning successive sentences, lines, etc., with the same word or phrase. [Gr. *anaphorā,* a carrying back, reference—*ana,* back, *pherein,* to bear.]

anaphrodisiac, *an-af-rə-diz'i-ak, adj.* tending to diminish sexual desire.—*n.* an anaphrodisiac agent. [Gr. *an-,* priv., *aphrodīsiakos,* sexual.]

anaphylaxis, *an-ə-fil-aks'is, n.* an increased susceptibility to injected foreign material, protein or non-protein, brought about by a previous introduction of it.—Also **anaphylax'y.**—*adj.* **anaphylac'tic.** [Gr. *ana,* back, *phylaxis,* protection.]

anaplasty, *an'ə-plås-ti, n.* the reparation of superficial lesions by the use of adjacent healthy tissue, as by transplanting a portion of skin.—*adj.* **anaplas'tic.** [Gr. *ana,* again, *plassein,* to form.]

anaplerosis, *an-ə-plē-rō'sis, n.* the filling up of a deficiency.—*adj.* **anaplerotic** (-*rot'ik*). [Gr. *anaplērōsis*—*ana*, up, and *plēroein,* to fill.]

anaptyxis, *an-əp-tik'sis, n.* (*phon.*) development of a vowel between consonants.—*adj.* **anaptyc'tic.** [Gr. *anaptyxis,* gape—*ana,* back, *ptyssein,* to fold.]

anarchy, *an'ər-ki, n.* complete absence of law or government : a harmonious condition of society in which law is abolished as unnecessary : utter lawlessness : chaos : complete disorder.—*n.* **anarch** (*an'ärk*), an author, promoter, or personification of lawlessness.—*adjs.* **anarchal** (*an-ärk'əl ; rare*); **anarch'ial** (*rare*); **anarch'ic, anarch'ical.**—*adv.* **anarch'ically.**—*v.t.* **an'archise** (*an'ər-kīz*), to render anarchic.—*ns.* **an'archism,** the teaching of the anarchists; **an'archist,** one whose ideal of society is one without government of any kind : one who seeks to advance such a condition by terrorism.—Also *adj.*—*adj.* **anarchist'ic.** [Gr. *anarchiā,* leaderlessness, lawlessness—*an-,* priv., *archē,* government.]

anarthrous, *an-är'thrəs, adj.* used without the article (of Greek nouns) : without distinct joints.— *adv.* **anar'thrously.** [Gr. *an-,* priv, *arthron,* a joint, article.]

anasarca, *an-ə-sär'kä, n.* diffused dropsy in the skin and subcutaneous tissue. [Gr. phrase *ana sarka,* throughout the flesh.]

anastasis, *an-as'tə-sis, n.* in Byzantine art, the Harrowing of Hell : convalescence.—*adj.* **anastatic** (*an-ə-stat'ik*), of anastasis : with characters raised in relief. [Gr. *anastasis,* rising or raising up, or again—*ana,* up, again, *stasis,* a setting, standing.]

anastigmat, *an-as'tig-mat,* or -*stig', n.* an anastigmatic lens.—*adj.* **anastigmat'ic** (*an-ə-*), not astigmatic.—*n.* **anastig'matism.** [Gr. *an-,* priv., and **astigmatic.**]

anastomosis, *an-as-tə-mō'sis, n.* communication by cross-connexions to form a network :—*pl.* **anastomo'ses** (-*sēz*).—*v.i.* **anas'tomose,** to intercommunicate in such a way.—*adj.* **anastomotic** (-*mot'ik*). [Gr. *anastomōsis,* outlet—*ana,* back, *stoma,* mouth.]

anastrophe, *an-as'trə-fē, n.* (*rhet.*) inversion. [Gr. *anastrophē*—*ana,* back, and *strephein,* to turn.]

anatase, *an'ə-tās, n.* a mineral consisting of titanium oxide. [Gr. *anatasis,* a stretching, from its long crystals.]

anathema, *a-* or *ə-nath'i-mä, n.* a solemn ecclesiastical curse or denunciation involving excommunication : a curse, execration : a person or thing cursed ecclesiastically or generally : an object of abhorrence :—*pl.* **anath'emas.**—*adj.* **anathematical** (-*mat'i-kl*).—*n.* **anathematisation** (-*mə-tī-zā'shən*).—*v.t.* and *v.i.* **anath'ematise.**— **anathema ma anatha** (*mar-ə-nä'thä ;* Syriac *māran athā,* the Lord cometh, or Lord come), words happening to occur together in I. Cor. xvi, 22, wrongly understood as an intensified curse. [Gr. *anathēma,* a thing dedicated or accursed, for *anathēma,* a votive offering—*ana,* up, and the root of *tithenai,* to place.]

anatomy, *ə-nat'ə-mi, n.* the art of dissecting any organised body : the science of the structure of the body learned by dissection : (*obs.*) a subject for dissection : (*arch.*) a skeleton, shrivelled and shrunken body, alive or dead, or mummy : bodily frame or structure : dissection : analysis.—*adjs.* **anatomic** (*an-ə-tom'ik*), **-al.**—*adv.* **anatom'ically.**—*v.t.* **anat'omise,** to dissect : (*fig.*) to lay open minutely.—*n.* **anat'omist,** one skilled in anatomy. [Gr. *anatomē,* dissection—*ana,* up, *tomē,* a cutting.]

anatropous, *a-* or *ə-nat'rə-pəs, adj.* (*bot.*) of an ovule, turned back and attached at the side of the funicle, which thus becomes a ridge on the ovule. [Gr. *ana,* back, up, *tropē,* a turning.]

anatta. See **annatto.**

anbury, *an'bər-i, n.* a soft bloody wart on horses, etc. : a disease in turnips, cabbages, etc., due to a slime-fungus causing a scabbed and broken skin and swellings on the roots. [Perh. for *angberry*— O.E. *ange,* narrow, painful, and **berry.**]

ancestor, *an'sis-tər, n.* one from whom a person is descended : a forefather :—*fem.* **an'cestress.**— *adjs.* **ancestral** (-*ses'*); **ancestorial** (-*sis-tō'ri-əl*). —*ns.* **an'cestor-wor'ship; an'cestry,** a line of ancestors : lineage. [O.Fr. *ancestre*—L. *antecēssor* —*ante,* before, *cēdēre, cēssum,* to go.]

anchor, *ang'kər, n.* an implement for retaining a ship by chaining it to the bottom, or for holding a balloon to the ground, or the like : (*fig.*) anything that gives stability or security.—*v.t.* to fix by an anchor : to fasten.—*v.i.* to cast anchor : to stop, or rest.—*ns.* **anch'orage,** the act of anchoring : a place of or for anchoring : (*Shak.*) a set of anchors : (*fig.*) rest or support to the mind : duty imposed for anchoring; **anch'or-hold,** the hold of an anchor upon the ground : (*fig.*) security; **anch'orice',** ground-ice.—*adj.* **anch'orless.**—*n.* **anch'orring,** a solid generated by the revolution of a circle about an axis in its plane but no¹ cutting it or not passing through its centre; **anch'or-stock,** the cross-bar of an anchor, which causes one or other of the flukes to turn to the bottom.—**anchor escapement,** or recoil escapement, a clock escapement in which the pallets push the escape-wheel slightly backwards at the end of each swing, causing a recoil of the pendulum; **at anchor,** anchored; **cast anchor,** to let down the anchor; **weigh anchor,** to take up the anchor. [O.E. *ancor*—L. *ancora*; cf. Gr. *ankȳra*—*ankos,* a bend; conn. with **angle.**]

anchor, *ang′kər* (*Shak.*), **anchoret, -et, anchorite, -it,** *ns.* a man or woman who has withdrawn from the world, especially for religious reasons : a recluse. —*ns.* **anch′orage,** a recluse's cell; **anch′oress, anc′ress,** a female anchorite.—*adjs.* **anchoret′ic, -al.** [Gr. *anachōrētēs—ana,* apart, *chōreein,* to withdraw.]

anchovy, *an-chō′vi, an′chō-vi, n.* a small Mediterranean fish (*Engraulis encrasicholus*) of the herring family, used for pickling, and making sauce, paste, etc.—*n.* **anchō′vy-pear,** the fruit of a W. Indian lecythidaceous tree (*Grias cauliflora*), often pickled. [Sp. and Port. *anchova;* of doubtful etymology.]

anchylosis, the same as **ankylosis.**

ancient, *ān′shənt, adj.* very old : of former times : of long standing : belonging or relating to times long past, esp. before the downfall of the Western Roman Empire (476 A.D.).—*n.* an aged man : an elder or senior : one who lived in ancient times— usu. in *pl.* and applied esp. to the Greeks and Romans.—*adv.* **an′ciently.**—*ns.* **an′cientness ; an′cientry,** antiquity : seniority : ancestry : dignity of birth : (*Shak.*) old people.—**ancient lights,** the legal right to receive in perpetuity, by certain windows, a reasonable amount of daylight; **the Ancient of days** (*B.*), the Almighty. [Fr. *ancien*— L.L. *antiānus,* former, old—L. *ante,* before.]

ancient, *ān′shənt, n.* (*obs.*) a flag : a standard-bearer : an ensign. [See **ensign.**]

ancillary, *an-sil′ər-i, an′sil-ər-ı, adj.* subserving : ministering : auxiliary. [L. *ancilla,* a maid-servant.]

ancipitous, *an-sip′i-təs, adj.* (*bot.*) two-edged and flattened. [L. *anceps, -itis,* two-edged, double— *ambi-,* on both sides, *caput, capitis,* head.]

ancle, an obsolete spelling of **ankle.**

ancome, *an′kəm, n.* (*obs.* or *dial.*) a sudden inflammation : a whitlow. [Cf. **oncome, income.**]

ancon, *ang′kon, n.* the elbow : a console to support a door cornice : a breed of sheep with very short legs :—*pl.* **ancones** (*-kō′nēz*). [Latinised from Gr. *ankōn,* a bend, elbow.]

Ancona, *ang-kō′nä, n.* a speckled variety of laying poultry of Mediterranean family. [*Ancona* in Italy.]

ancora, *ang-kō′rä, adv.* encore. [It.; see **encore.**]

and, *and, ənd, ən, ′n, conj.* indicating addition : also : also of another kind : used to introduce a consequence or aim : to introduce a question expressive of surprise, realisation, wonder, incredulity, etc. : sometimes app. meaningless ('When that I was and a little tiny boy') : **as a conditional conjunction** (from M.E. times only; often in *Shak.*; now *arch.*—also **an, an if**) if : even if, although : as if.—**and all,** not without; **and how** (*U.S.*) I should think so indeed; **but and** (*obs.*) and also. [O.E. *and, ond;* cf. Ger. *und,* and L. *ante,* before, Gr. *anti,* against.]

and, *and, n.* the sign ampersand : a use of the word 'and' (if).

and, *ən, conj.* (*dial.* and *Shak.*) than. [Perh. O.N. *an, en, enn,* than.]

Andalusian, *an-də-l(y)ōō′z(h)yən, -s(h)yən, n.* a native of *Andalusia* (Sp. *Andalucía*), in Spain : a blue variety of laying poultry, of Andalusian family.—Also *adj.*—*n.* **andalu′site** (*-sīt*), a silicate of aluminium, first found in Andalusia.

andante, *ân-dän′tä, adv., adj.* and *n.* (*mus.*) moving with moderately slow, even expression : a movement or piece composed in andante time.—*adj., adv.* and *n.* **andantino** (*ân-dän-tē′nō*), (a movement, etc.) somewhat slower than andante : sometimes intended for somewhat quicker. [It., pr.p. of *andare,* to go.]

Andean, *an-dē′ən,* **Andine,** *an′dīn, adjs.* of, or like, the Andes Mountains.—*ns.* **andesine** (*an′diz-ēn, -in*), a felspar intermediate between albite and anorthite; **an′desite,** a volcanic rock with plagioclase and some ferromagnesian mineral as phenocrysts in a microlithic ground-mass (both found in the Andes).—*adj.* **andesitic** (*-it′ik*).

andiron, *and′ī-ərn, n.* an iron bar to support the end of a log in a fire : a fire-dog. [O.Fr. *andier* (Fr. *landier = l′andier*); origin unknown; early confused with **iron.**]

Andrew, *an′drōō, n.* one of the twelve Apostles, patron saint of Scotland.—**St. Andrew's cross,** a saltire, or cross of equal shafts crossed diagonally : the saltire of Scotland, white on a blue ground.

Andrew Ferrara, *an′drōō fi-rä′rä, n.* a make of sword-blade highly esteemed in Scotland from c. 1600.—Also **An′dro,** or **Andrea** (*-drä′ä,* or *an′*), **Ferrara.** [According to some from *Andrea dei Ferrari* of Belluno, to others *Andrew Ferrars* or *Ferrier* of Arbroath, poss. as a native of Ferrara, or—L. *ferrārius,* smith.]

andro-, andr-, in composition, man : male.—*adjs.* **androcephalous** (*an-drō-sef′ə-ləs*), man-headed (Gr. *kephalē,* head); **androdioecious** (*-dī-ē′shəs*), having hermaphrodite and male flowers on separate plants.—*ns* **androdioe′cism** (see **dioecious**); **androecium** (*an-drē′shi-əm,* or *-si-əm*), stamens collectively (Gr. *o′kion,* house).—*adj.* **androgynous** (*an-droj′i-nəs,* or *-drog′*), having the characteristics of both male and female in one individual : hermaphrodite : (*bot.*) having an inflorescence of both male and female flowers.—*n.* **androg′yny,** hermaphroditism (Gr. *gynē,* woman).—*adj.* **andromonoecious** (*an-drō-mon-ē′shəs*), having hermaphrodite and male flowers on the same plant.— *ns.* **andromonoe′cism** (see **monoecious**); **an′drophore** (*-fōr*), a prolongation of the receptacle carrying the stamens (Gr. *phoros,* a bearing). [Gr. *anēr, andros,* man, male.]

Andromeda, *an-drom′i-dä, n.* a genus of shrubs of the heath family : a northern constellation. [*Andromeda,* in Greek myth, a maiden delivered by Perseus from a sea-monster.]

andvile (*Spens.*). Same as **anvil.**

ane, *yin, ān* (*Scot.* and *obs.*), *adj., n.,* and *pron.* one : an, a. [O.E. *ān.*]

anear, *ə-nēr′, adv.* nearly : near.—*prep.* near.—*v.t.* to approach, to come near to. [Pfx. *a-,* and **near.**]

aneath, *ə-nēth′,* (*Scot. ə-neth′, ə-nāth′*), *adv.* and *prep.* (chiefly Scot.) beneath. [Prep. **a,** and the root of **beneath.**]

anecdote, *an′ik-dōt, n.* a short narrative of an incident of private life.—*n.* **an′ecdotage,** anecdotes collectively : garrulous old age (with pun on *dotage*); **an′ecdotist.**—*adjs.* **anecdot′al, anecdotical** (*-dot′*). [Gr. *an-,* priv., *ekdotos,* published—*ek,* out, *didonai,* to give.]

anelace. See **anlace.**

anele, *ə-nēl′, v.t.* (*arch.*) to anoint : to administer extreme unction to. [O.E. *an,* on, *ele,* oil; used in reminiscence of Shakespeare; see **unaneled.**]

anemia, anemic, etc. Same as **anaemia,** etc.

anemo-, in composition, wind.—*ns.* **anemogram** (*ə-nem′ō-gram*), an anemographic record; **anem′-ograph** (*-gräf*), an instrument for measuring and recording the pressure and velocity of the wind.— *adj.* **anemographic** (*-graf′ik*).—*ns.* **anemology** (*an-i-mol′ə-ji*), the science of the winds; **anemometer** (*-mom′i-tər*), a wind-gauge.—*adj.* **anemometric** (*-mō-met′rik*).—*ns.* **anemom′etry ; anemone** (*ə-nem′ə-ni*), wind-flower—any member of the genus **Anemō′nē** of the crowfoot family : a sea-anemone (Gr. *anemōnē*).—*adj.* **anemoph′ilous,** wind-pollinated.—*n.* **anemoph′ily.** [Gr. *anemos,* wind; cf. L. *animus, anima.*]

an-end, *ən-end′, adv.* (*Shak.*) to the end, continuously : (*Shak.*) upright : lengthwise.—**most an end,** almost always. [Prep. **an** and **end.**]

anent, *ə-nent′, prep.* (mainly *Scot.*) in a line with : against : towards : in regard to, concerning, about. [O.E. *on efen,* on even.]

anerly, *an′ər-li, adv.* (*arch. Scot.*) only. [**ane** ; *r* perh. on analogy of some other word.]

aneroid, *an′ə-roid, adj.* dispensing with the use of liquid.—*n.* an aneroid barometer. [Fr. *anéroïde* —Gr. *a-,* priv., *nēros,* wet, *eidos,* form.]

aneurin, *an′ū-rin, ə-nū′rin, n.* vitamin B₁, deficiency of which affects the nervous system.—Also called thiamine. [Gr. *a-,* priv., *neuron,* nerve.]

aneurysm, *an′ūr-izm, n.* (*path.*) dilatation of an artery : any abnormal enlargement.—*adj.* **aneurys′mal.**—Also **aneurism.** [Gr. *aneurysma—ana,* up, *eurys,* wide.]

anew, *ə-nū′, adv.* afresh : again. [**of** and **new.**]

anfractuous, *an-frakt′ū-əs, adj.* winding, involved, circuitous.—*n.* **anfractuosity** (*-os′i-ti*). [L. *anfractuōsus—ambi-,* about, *frangĕre,* to break.]

Angaraland, *ang-gä-rä′land, n.* (*geol.*) the primitive nucleus of N.E. Asia. [*Angara River.*]

angary, *ang′gər-i, n.* a belligerent's right to seize and use neutral or other property (subject to compensation). [Gr. *angareiā,* forced service— *angaros,* a courier; a Persian word—Assyrian *agarru.*]

angekkok, *ang′gi-kok, n.* an Eskimo conjurer. [Eskimo.]

angel, *ān′jl, n.* a divine messenger: a ministering spirit: an attendant or guardian spirit: a person possessing the qualities attributed to these— gentleness, purity, etc.: one supposed to have a special commission, as the head of the Church in Rev. ii and iii: in the Catholic Apostolic Church, one who corresponds in a limited sense to a bishop: (*poet.*) a messenger generally: an old Eng. coin (**6s. 8d.** to 10s.), bearing the figure of an angel.— *ns.* **ān′gel-cake, ān′gel-food** (*U.S.*), a cake made of flour, sugar, and white of egg; **ān′gel-fish,** a kind of shark (*Squatina,* or *Rhina*), with large wing-like pectoral fins: a tropical American river-fish (*Pterophyllum*) of the family Cichlidae, much compressed, almost circular in body but crescent-shaped owing to the long fin filaments, the whole banded with changing black vertical stripes: applied also to *Pomacanthus* and several other fishes of the Chaetodontidae; **ān′gelhood.**—*adjs.* **angelic** (*an-jel′ik*), **-al.**—*n.* Angel′ica, a genus of umbelliferous plants with large leaves and double-winged fruit, once highly reputed as a defence against poison and pestilence: (angelica) a garden plant by some included in the genus as *A. Archangelica,* by others called *Archangelica officinalis:* its candied leaf-stalks and midribs.—*adv.* angel′ically.—*ns.* angel′ica-tree′, an American Aralia; **angelol′atry** (*ān-*), angel-worship; **āngelol′ogy,** doctrine regarding angels; **āngeloph′any,** the manifestation of an angel to a man; **āng′els-on-horse′back,** oysters and bacon on toast; **ān′gel-water,** a perfumed liquid, at first made largely from angelica, then from ambergris, rose-water, orange-flower water, etc. [Gr. *angelos,* a messenger.]

angelus, *an′ji-ləs, n.* the 'Hail, Mary,' or prayer to the Virgin, including the angelic salutation (Luke i. 28): the bell rung in Roman Catholic countries at morning, noon, and sunset, to invite the faithful to recite it. [From the introductory words, '*Angelus* domini nuntiavit Mariae.']

anger, *ang′gər, n.* hot displeasure, often involving a desire for retaliation: wrath: (now *dial.*) in-flammation.—*v.t.* to make angry: to irritate.—*adj.* **an′gerless.**—*advs.* **an′gerly** (*arch.*), **ang′rily.**— *n.* **ang′riness.**—*adj.* **ang′ry,** excited with anger: inflamed: of threatening or lowering aspect. [O.N. *angr;* cf. agnail, anbury, angina, anguish.)

Angevin, *an′ji-vin, adj.* of *Anjou:* relating to the Plantagenet house that reigned in England from 1154 to 1485, descended from Geoffrey V., Count of Anjou.—*n.* a native of Anjou: a member of the house of Anjou—by some reckoned only down to loss of Anjou (1204), by others, till the deposition of Richard II. in 1399.

angico, *an′ji-kō, n.* a S. American mimosaceous tree (*Piptadenia*): its gum. [Port.—Tupí.]

angina, *an-ji′nä,* better *an′ji-nä, n.* any inflam-matory affection of the throat, as quinsy, croup, etc.—*adj.* anginal (*an-ji′nl, an′ji-nl*).—**angina pec′toris,** a disease of the heart marked by paroxysms of intense pain, radiating from the breastbone mainly towards the left shoulder and arm. [L. *angina.* See anguish.]

angiocarpous, *an-ji-ō-kär′pəs, adj.* having the fruit, or in fungi the hymenium, within a special covering. [Gr. *angeion,* a case, *karpos,* fruit.]

angiosperm, *an′ji-ō-spərm, n.* a plant of the **Angiosperm′ae,** one of the main divisions of flowering plants, in which the seeds are in a closed ovary, not naked as in gymnosperms.—*adjs.* **angiosperm′al, angiosperm′ous.** [Gr. *angeion,* case, *sperma,* seed.]

angioma, *an-ji-ō′-mä, n.* a tumour composed of blood or lymph vessels:—*pl.* **angiō′mata.** [Gr. *angeion,* vessel.]

angiostomous, *an-ji-os′təm-əs,* **angiostomatous,** *an-ji-ō-sto′mə-təs, adjs.* narrow-mouthed: with a mouth that is not distensible. [Gr. *angeion,* a vessel, case, confused with L. *angĕre,* to compress; Gr. *stŏma, stomatos,* mouth.]

angle, *ang′gl, n.* a corner: the point from which lines or surfaces diverge: (*geom.*) the inclination of two straight lines, or of two curves measured by that of their tangents, or of two planes measured by that of perpendiculars to their intersection: the spread of a cone, a number of meeting planes or the like, measured by the area on the surface of a sphere subtending it at the centre: an outlying corner or nook: a point of view: (*snooker,* etc.; see frame).—*v.t.* to put in a corner: to corner: to put in the jaws of a billiard pocket: to move, drive, direct, turn, adjust, present, at an angle.—*v.i.* to proceed at an angle or by an angular course.— *adj.* **ang′led,** having angles.—*adv.* **ang′lewise.**— *adj.* **ang′ular** (*ang′gū-lər*), having an angle or corner: measured by an angle: (*fig.*) stiff in manner, the opposite of easy or graceful: bony and lean in figure.—*n.* angularity (*-lar′i-ti*).—*adj.* **ang′ulated,** formed with angles.—**angle iron,** an L-shaped iron used in structural work. [Fr.—L. *angulus:* cog. with Gr. *ankylos;* both from root *ank,* to bend, seen also in **anchor, ankle.**]

angle, *ang′gl, n.* a fish-hook: fishing-tackle: an act of angling.—*v.i.* to fish with an angle.—*v.t.* to entice: to try to gain by some artifice.—*ns.* **ang′ler,** one who fishes with an angle esp. one who fishes with rod and line for sport: the devil-fish or fishing-frog, a wide-mouthed voracious fish (*Lophius piscatorius*) that attracts its prey by waving filaments like a fisher's angle: extended to related kinds, some of them remarkable for the dwarf males parasitic on the female; **ang′le-worm,** any worm used as bait by anglers; **ang′ling.** [O.E. *angul,* hook.]

Angle, *ang′gl, n.* a member or descendant of the German tribe (O.E. *Engle*) from Sleswick that settled in Northumbria, Mercia, and East Anglia.— *adj.* **Ang′lian,** of the Angles.—*n.* an Angle: the English dialect of the Angles.—*adj.* **Ang′lican,** of or characteristic of, the Church of England and churches in communion with it: (esp. *U.S.*) English.—Also *n.*—*n.* **Ang′licanism,** the princi-ples of the Church of England: attachment to English institutions, esp. the English Church.— *adv.* anglice (*ang′gli-sē;* L. *äng′gli-kä*), in English. —*v.t.* **ang′licise** (*-sīz*), to make English.—*v.i.* to assume or conform to English ways.—*n.* **ang′licism** (*-sizm*), an English idiom or peculiarity: English principles.—*v.t.* **ang′lify,** to make English. —*ns.* **ang′list,** one who has a scholarly knowledge of the English language, literature, and culture; **anglist′ic,** the study of these subjects.—*pfx.* **Anglo-** (*ang′glō-*), English: esp. conjointly English and something else.—*adj.* **Ang′lo-Amer′ican,** English in origin or birth, American by settlement or citizenship.—Also *n.*—*n.* **Anglo-Cath′olic,** one who regards himself as a Catholic of Anglican pattern: a High-Churchman.—Also *adj.*—*n.* **Anglo-Cathol′icism.**—*adj.* **Anglo-French′,** of England and France.—*n.* the form of the French language formerly spoken in England.—*adj.* **Anglo-In′dian,** of England and India: of English as spoken in India: Eurasian.—*n.* an Englishman long resident in India: a Eurasian.—*n.* **Anglo-I′rish,** the English language as spoken in Ireland: Irish people of English descent: people of mixed English and Irish descent.—*adj.* of England and Ireland: of the Anglo-Irish people or speech.—*n.* **Anglo-Is′raelite,** one who believes that the English are descendants of the Jewish 'lost tribes' carried off by the Assyrians B.C.721.—Also *adj.*—*ns.* **anglo-mā′nia,** a craze, or indiscriminate admiration, for what is English; **anglomā′niac; Anglo-Nor′-man,** the French dialect of the Normans in England.—Also *adj.*—*n.* **ang′lophil,** also **-phile** (*-fīl*), a friend and admirer of England and things English (Gr. *philos,* friend).—Also *adj.*—*n.* **ang′lo-**

phobe, one who fears or dislikes England and things English (Gr. *phobos*, fear).—Also *adj.—n.* **anglophō'bia.**—*adjs.* **anglophō'biac, -phobic** (*-fōb', -fob').*—*n.* **Anglo-Sax'on,** Old English : one of the Germanic settlers in England and Scotland, including Angles, Saxons, and Jutes, or of their descendants : a Saxon of England, distinguished from the Old Saxons of the Continent : anybody of English speech.—Also *adj.—n.* **Anglo-Sax'ondom.** [*L. Anglus.*]

anglesite, *ang'gli-sīt, n.* orthorhombic lead sulphate, first found in *Anglesey.*

Angora, *ang-gō'rä, adj.* of *Ang'ōra* (Gr. *Ankȳra,* now *Angora* or *Ankara*) a town of ancient Galatia, now capital of Turkey.—*n.* angora, an Anatolian goat : its long silky wool (the true mohair) : cloth made from it : a silky-haired cat or rabbit.—Wrongly **Ango'la.**

Angostura, *ang-gos-t(y)ōō'rä, n.* a town (now Ciudad Bolivar) on the narrows (Sp. *angostura*) of the Orinoco in Venezuela, giving name to an aromatic bitter febrifuge and tonic bark (Cusparia; fam. Rutaceae).—**angostura bitters,** an essence (not invariably) containing angostura.

angry. See anger.

Ångström, angstrom (unit), *awng'* or *ōng'strəm, ang'strəm (ū'nit), n.* a unit (10^{-8} centimetres) used in expressing wavelengths of light, ultra-violet rays, X-rays. [Anders J. *Ångström* (1814-74), Swedish physicist.]

Anguis, *ang'gwis, n.* generic name not of a snake but of the blindworm.—*n.* **ang'uifauna,** fauna of snakes.—*adj.* **ang'uiform,** snake-shaped.—*n.* **Anguill'a,** the common eel genus.—*adj.* **anguill'iform,** eel-like.—*n.* **Anguill'ūla,** the paste-eel genus of nematode worms.—*adjs.* **anguine** (*ang'-gwin*) of or like a snake; **ang'uiped(e)** (*-ped, -ped*) having feet or legs in the form of snakes. [L. *anguis,* snake; adj. *anguīnus;* dim. *anguilla,* eel.]

anguish, *ang'gwish, n.* excessive pain of body or mind : agony.—*v.t.* to afflict with anguish.—*v.i.* to suffer anguish. [O.Fr. *angoisse,* choking—L. *angustia,* tightness, narrowness.]

angular. See under angle.

angusti-, *ang-gus'ti-,* in composition, narrow.—*adjs.* **angustifo'liate,** narrow-leaved; **angustiros'trate,** narrow-beaked. [L. *angustus,* narrow.]

anharmonic, *an-här-mon'ik, adj.* not harmonic.—**anharmonic ratio,** cross-ratio (harmonic when= -1). [Gr. *an-,* priv., *harmonikos,* harmonic.]

an-heires (*Shak.*), an obscure word in *Merry Wives* II. i. 227, variously conjectured to be an error for **on here,** for **mynheers,** or for **ameers.**

anhelation, *an-hi-lā'shən, n.* shortness of breath. [L. *anhēlātiō, -ōnis—anhēlāre,* to gasp.]

anhungered. See **ahungered.**

anhydride, *an-hī'drīd, n.* a compound representing in its composition an acid *minus* water.—*n.* **anhy'drite,** a mineral, anhydrous calcium sulphate.—*adj.* **anhy'drous,** free from water. [Gr. *an-,* priv., *hydōr,* water.]

aniconic, *an-ī-kon'ik, adj.* symbolising without aiming at resemblance : pertaining to aniconism.—*ns.* **ani'conism** (*-kən-izm*), worship or veneration of an object that represents a god without being an image of him; **ani'conist.** [Gr. *an-,* priv., *eikōn,* image.]

anicut, annicut, *an'i-kut, n.* a dam. [Tamil *anai kattu.*]

anigh, *ə-nī', prep.* and *adv.,* nigh. [Pfx. *a-,* and **nigh;** a modern formation.]

anight, *ə-nīt', adv.* (*Shak.*) of nights, at night. [of and **night.**]

anil, *an'il, n.* indigo, plant or dye. [Port. *anil;* Ar. *an-nīl,* the indigo plant.]

anile, *an'īl, ān'īl, adj.* old-womanish : imbecile.—*n.* **anility** (*a-* or *ə-nil'i-ti*), old-womanishness : imbecile dotage. [L. *ānus, -ūs,* an old woman.]

aniline, *an'il-ēn, -in,* or *-īn, n.* a product of coal-tar extensively used in dyeing and other industrial arts, first obtained from *anil.*—Also *adj.*

animadvert, *an-im-əd-vərt', v.i.* to take cognisance : to comment critically : to censure.—*v.t.* to consider : to remark.—*ns.* **animadver'sion;**

animadvert'er. [L. *animus,* the mind, *ad,* to, and *vertĕre,* to turn.]

animal, *an'i-ml, n.* an organised being having life, sensation. and voluntary motion—typically distinguished from a plant, which is organised and has life, but apparently not sensation or voluntary motion : often, a lower animal—one below man : (*old-fashioned*) a mammal : a stupid or sensual man.—*adj.* of, of the nature of, derived from, or belonging to an animal or animals : sensual.—*n.* **animalisā'tion.**—*v.t.* an'**imalise,** to represent or conceive in animal form : to endow with animal life or the properties of animal matter : to convert into animal matter : to brutalise, sensualise.—*ns.* an'**imalism,** the exercise or enjoyment of animal life, as distinct from intellectual : the state of being actuated by mere animal appetites : brutishness : sensuality : (*rare*) a mere animal being; an'**imalist,** one who practises or believes in animalism : one who paints, carves, or writes stories about, animals; **animality** (*-al'i-ti*), animal nature or life : status of an animal or of a lower animal.—*adv.* an'**imally,** physically merely. — *ns.* an'**imal-worship;** -**worshipper.**—**animal spirits** (originally *spirit*), formerly, a supposed principle formed in the brain out of vital spirits and conveyed to all parts of the body through the nerves : nervous force : exuberance of health and life : cheerful buoyancy of temper : (*Milton*) the spirit or principle of volition and sensation. [L. *animal—anima,* air, breath, life, soul.]

animalcule, *an-im-al'kūl, n.* a small animal : (now) one that cannot be seen by the naked eye :— *pl.* **animal'cules, animal'cula.**—*adj.* **animal'cular.**—*n.* **animal'culist,** one who believes that the spermatozoon contains all future generations in germ. [L. *animalculum,* dim. of *animal.*]

animate, *an'im-āt, v.t.* to give life to : to enliven : to inspirit : to actuate.—*adj.* (*-mit*) living : having animal life.—*adj.* an'**imated,** lively : full of spirit : endowed with life : moving as if alive.—*adv.* an'**imatedly.** — *adj.* an'**imating.** — *adv.* an'**imatingly.**—*ns.* anima'**tion,** act of animating : state of being alive : liveliness : vigour; an'**imator.** [L. *animāre, -ātum—anima,* air, breath, life.]

animé, anime, *an'i-mā, -mē, n.* the resin of the W. Indian locust-tree : extended to other gums and resins. [Said to be Fr. *animé,* living, from the number of insects in it; but perhaps a native name.]

animism, *an'im-izm, n.* the attribution of a soul to natural objects and phenomena : G. E. Stahl's theory that the soul is the vital principle.—*n.* an'**imist.**—*adj.* **anmis'tic.** [L. *anima,* the soul.]

animosity, *an-im-os'i-ti, n.* strong dislike : enmity. [L. *animōsitās,* fullness of spirit.]

animus, *an'im-əs, n.* intention : actuating spirit : hostility. [L. *animus,* spirit, soul.]

anion, *an'ī-on, n.* an ion that seeks the anode : an electro-negative ion.—*adj.* **anion'ic.** [Gr. *ana,* up, *iōn,* going, pr.p. neut. of *ienai,* to go.]

anise, *an'is, n.* an umbelliferous plant (*Pimpinella*) whose aromatic seeds are used in making cordials : in Matt. xxiii. 23 (Gr. *anēthon*) believed to be dill.—*ns.* an'**iseed,** the seed of anise : anisette; **anisette** (*an-i-zet'*), a cordial or liqueur prepared from anise seed.—**star anise** (see star). [Gr. *anīson,* anise.]

aniso-, *an-ī'sō-,* or *-so',* in composition, unequal.—*adjs.* **anisocercal** (*-sər'kl*), with unequal tail-lobes; **anisodac'tylous** (of birds) with three toes turned forward, one backward; **anisom'erous,** with unequal numbers of parts in the floral whorls; **anisophyll'ous,** with differently formed leaves on different sides of the shoot; **anisotrop'ic,** not isotropic, showing differences of property or of effect in different directions.—*n.* **anisot'ropy.** [Gr. *anisos,* unequal—*an-,* priv., *isos,* equal.]

anker, *angk'ər, n.* a liquid measure used in Northern Europe, formerly in England, varying considerably —that of Rotterdam $8\frac{1}{4}$ imperial gallons. [Du.]

ankerite, *ang'kər-īt, n.* a rhombohedral carbonate of calcium, iron, magnesium, and manganese. [After Professor M. J. Anker (1772-1843), Styrian mineralogist.]

ankh, *angk, n.* an ansate cross—T-shaped with a

loop above the horizontal bar—symbol of life. [Egypt., life.]

ankle, or (*arch.*) **ancle,** *angk'l, n.* the joint connecting the foot and leg.—*adj.* **ank'led,** having ankles.—*n.* **ank'let** (-*lit*), a ring for the ankle.— **ankle sock,** a sock reaching to and covering the ankle. [O.E. *ancléow* or kindred form; cf. Ger. *enkel,* and **angle.**]

ankus, *ang'kəs, n.* an elephant goad. [Hind.]

ankylosis, anchylosis, *ang-ki-lō'sis, n.* fusion of bones or skeletal parts: fixation of a joint by fibrous bands or union of bones.—*v.t.* and *v.i.* **ank'ylose, anch'ylose,** to stiffen or fuse, as a joint or bones.—*adj.* **ank'ylosed, anch'ylosed.** [Gr. *ankylōsis,* stiffening of a joint—*ankyloein,* to crook.]

ankylostomiasis, anchylostomiasis, *ang-ki-lō-sto-mī'ə-sis, n.* hookworm disease or miner's anaemia, caused by a parasitic nematode (*Ankylostomum duodenale* or other). [Gr. *ankylos,* crooked, *stoma,* mouth.]

anlace, anelace, *an'las, -ləs, n.* a short two-edged tapering dagger. [Ety. unknown.]

anlage, *än'lä-gə, n.* (*biol.*) the primordium or first rudiment of an organ. [Ger.]

ann, *an, n.* (*Scot.*) annat.

anna, *an'ä, n.* an Indian coin, the sixteenth part of a rupee. [Hind. *ānā.*]

annabergite, *an'ə-bərg-īt, n.* an apple-green mineral, hydrous nickel arsenate. [*Annaberg* in Saxony.]

annal, *an'əl, n.* a year's entry in a chronicle: in *pl.* records of events under the years in which they happened: historical records generally: yearbooks.—*v.t.* **ann'alise,** to record.—*n.* **ann'alist,** a writer of annals.—*adj.* **annalist'ic.** [L. *annālis,* yearly—*annus,* a year.]

annat, *an'ət, n.* **annates,** *an'āts, n.pl.* the firstfruits, or one year's income of a benefice, paid to the Pope (in England from 1535 to the crown, from 1703 to Queen Anne's bounty; extinguished or made redeemable 1926): annat or **ann** (*Scots law*) the half year's stipend after a parish minister's death, payable to his next of kin from 1672 to 1925. [L.L. *annāta*—L. *annus,* a year.]

an(n)atto, *a-* or *ə-nat'ō,* **an(n)atta,** *-ä, arnotto, är-not'ō, n.* a bright orange colouring matter got from the fruit pulp of a tropical American tree, *Bixa Orellana* (fam. *Bixaceae*). [Supposed to be of Carib origin.]

anneal, *ə-nēl', v.t.* and *v.i.* to temper (glass or metals) by strong heating and gradual cooling: to heat in order to fix colours on, as glass.—*ns.* **anneal'er; anneal'ing.** [Pfx. *an-,* and O.E. *ǽlan,* to burn.]

annelid, *an'ə-lid, n.* member of the **Annelida** (*ə-nel'i-dä*), a class comprising the red-blooded worms, having a long body composed of numerous rings. [L. *annellus, ānellus,* dim. of *ānulus,* a ring.]

annex, *ə-neks', v.t.* to add to the end: to join or attach: to take permanent possession of: (*coll.*) to purloin, appropriate: to affix: append.—*n.* (*an'eks*) something added: a supplementary building—sometimes (as Fr.) **annexe** (*a-neks', an'eks*).—*n.* **annexa'tion** (*an-*).—*n.* and *adj.* **annexa'tionist.**—*ns.* **annexion** (*ə-nek'shən*), **annex'ment** (*Shak.*), addition: the thing annexed. [L. *annectěre, annexum—ad,* to, *nectěre,* to tie.]

annihilate, *ə-nī'(h)il-āt, v.t.* to reduce to nothing: to put out of existence: (*fig.*) to crush or wither by look or word.—*ns.* **annihila'tion,** reduction to nothing: (*theol.*) the destruction of soul as well as body; **annihila'tionism,** the belief that the soul (esp. of the unrepentant wicked) dies with the body. —*adj.* **anni'hilative.**—*n.* **anni'hilator.** [L. *annihilāre, -ātum—ad,* to, *nihil,* nothing.]

anniversary, *an-i-vərs'ə-ri, adj.* returning, happening or commemorated about the same date every year: pertaining to annual recurrence or celebration.—*n.* the day of the year on which an event happened or is celebrated as having happened in a previous year: the celebration proper to recurrence, esp. a mass or religious service. [L. *anniversārius—annus,* a year, and *vertěre, versum,* to turn.]

annotate, *an'ō-tāt, v.t.* to make notes upon.—*v.t.* to append notes.—*ns.* **annotā'tion,** the making of notes: a note of explanation: comment; **an'-notātor.** [L. *annotāre—ad,* to, *notāre, -ātum,* to mark.]

announce, *ə-nowns', v.t.* to declare: to give public notice of: to make known.—*ns.* **announce'ment; announc'er,** one who announces: in wireless broadcasting an official who reads the news and announces other items in the programme. [O.Fr. *anoncer*—L. *annuntiāre—ad,* to, *nuntiāre,* to report.]

annoy, *ə-noi', v.t.* and *v.i.* to trouble: to vex: to tease: to harm, esp. in mil:tary sense —*ns.* **annoy'** (now poetic), **annoy'ance,** that which annoys: act of annoying: state of being annoyed.—*adv.* **annoy'ingly.** [O.Fr. *anoier* (It. *annoiare*); noun *anoi* (mod. *ennui*), acc. to Diez from L. phrase, *in odiō,* as in 'est mihi *in odiō*'=it is to me hateful.]

annual, *an'ū-əl, adj.* yearly: coming every year: lasting or living for a year: requiring to be renewed every year: performed in a year.—*n.* a plant that lives but one year: a publication appearing yearly, esp. applied to the sumptuous books, usually illustrated with good engravings, much in demand in the first half of the 19th century for Christmas, New Year, and birthday presents.—*adv.* **ann'ually.—annual rings,** rings, as seen in crosssection, in a branch or trunk, representing generally a year's growth of wood. [L.L. *annuālis—annus,* a year.]

annuity, *ə-nū'i-ti, n.* a payment (generally of uniform amount) falling due in each year during a given term, such as a period of years or the life of an individual, the capital sum not being returnable.—*n.* **annū'itant,** one who receives an annuity. —**annuity due,** one whose first payment is due in advance; **certain annuity,** one for a fixed term of years, subject to no contingency whatever; **contingent annuity,** one that depends on the continuance of some status, as the life of a person; **complete annuity,** one of which a proportion is payable up to the day of death; **curtate annuity,** one payable only at the end of each year survived; **deferred** or **reversionary annuity,** one whose first payment is not to be made until the expiry of a certain number of years. [Fr. *annuité*—L.L. *annuitās, -ātis*—L. *annus,* year.]

annul, *ə-nul', v.t.* to make null, to reduce to nothing: to abolish:'—*pr.p.* **annull'ing;** *pa.t.* and *pa.p.* **annulled'.**—*n.* **annul'ment.** [Fr. *annuler*—L.L. *annullāre*—L. *ad,* to, *nullus,* none.]

annular, *an'ū-lər, adj.* ring-shaped: cutting in a ring: ring-bearing.—*n.* the ring-finger.—*n.* **an-nūlarity** (-*lar'i-ti*).—*n.pl.* **Annūlā'ta** (*obs.*), the Annelida.—*n.* **ann'ūlate** (*obs.*), an annelid.—*adjs.* **ann'ūlate, -d,** ringed.—*ns.* **annūlā'tion,** a ring or belt: a circular formation; **ann'ūlet,** a little ring (*archit.*) a small flat fillet encircling a column, etc.: (*her.*) a little circle borne as a charge.—*adj.* **ann'ūlose,** ringed.—*n.* **ann'ūlus** (*biol.*), any ringshaped structure, esp. a ring of cells that brings about dehiscence of a moss sporogonium or a fern capsule:—*pl.* **ann'ūli.—annular eclipse,** one in which a ring-shaped part of the sun remains visible. [L. *annulāris,* for *ānulāris—ānulus,* a ring—dim. of *ānus,* a rounding or ring.]

annunciate, annunciate, *ə-nun's(h)i-āt, v.t.* to proclaim.—*ns.* **annuncia'tion** (*-si-*), proclamation: esp. (**Annunciation**) that of the angel to the Virgin Mary, or its anniversary, 25th March (**Annuncia'tion-day,** Lady-day); **Annunciation-lily,** the white lily (*Lilium candidum*), often seen in pictures of the Annunciation.—*adj.* **annun'ciative.**—*n.* **annun'ciator,** a device for indicating who has rung a bell. [L. *annuntiāre, -ātum—ad,* to, *nuntiāre—nuntius,* a messenger; *c* from mediaeval spelling of Latin; cf. **announce.**]

anoa, *a-nō'ä, n.* the sapi-utan, or wild ox of Celebes, like a small buffalo. [Native name.]

anode, *an'ōd, n.* a positive pole, or the electrode by which an electric current enters an electrolyte or vacuum tube, opp. to *cathode.*—*adjs.* **anō'dal** (or *an'od-əl*), **anodic** (*an-od'ik*), of an anode: (*bot.*) upwards on the genetic spiral. [Gr. *anodos,* way up—*ana,* up, *hodos,* way.]

anodyne, *an'ō-dīn*, *n.* a medicine that allays pain. [Gr. *anōdȳnos*—*an-*, priv., and *ŏdȳnē*, pain.]

anoint, *ə-noint'*, *v.t.* to smear with ointment or oil : to consecrate with oil : (ironically) to drub.—*n.* **anoint'ment**.—the **Anointed**, the Messiah; **the Lord's anointed**, in royalist theory, king by divine right. [Fr. *enoint*, pa.p. of *enoindre*—L. *inungĕre*, *inunctum*—*in*, on, *ung*(*u*)*ĕre*, to smear.]

anomaly, *a-nom'ə-li*, *n.* irregularity : deviation from rule : (*astron.*) the angle measured at the sun between a planet in any point of its orbit and the last perihelion.—*adjs.* **anomalist'ic**, **-al**, anomalous : departing from established rules : irregular; **anom'alous**, irregular : deviating from rule : of vision, relatively insensitive to one or more colours.—**anomalistic month, year**, (see **month, year**.) [Gr. *anōmalos*—*an-*, priv., and *homalos*, even—*homos*, same.]

anon, *ə-non'*, *adv.* in one (instant) : immediately : **soon** : at another time : coming (in reply to a call).—*interj.* expressing failure to hear or understand. [O.E. *on*, in, *án*, one.]

Anona, *ä-nō'nä*, *n.* a tropical genus of dicotyledons, including custard-apple, sweet-sop, and other edible fruits, giving name to the family **Anonā'ceae**, akin to the magnolias.—*adj.* **anonā'ceous**. [Latinised from Sp. *anón*, from Taino.]

anonymous, *ə-non'i-məs*, *adj.* wanting a name : without name of author, real or feigned.—*ns.* **anonym** (*an'*), a person whose name is not given : **a** pseudonym; **anonym'ity**—*adv.* **anon'y-mously**. [Gr. *anōnymos*—*an-*, priv., and *onyma*= *onoma*, name.]

Anopheles, *an-of'el-ēz*, *n.* a genus of germ-carrying mosquitoes.—*adj.* **anoph'eline**, relating to Anopheles : useless, hurtful.—*n.* a mosquito of this genus. [Gr. *anōphelēs*, hurtful—*an-*, *ophelos*, help.]

anorexia, *an-or-ek'si-ä*, anorexy, *an'or-ek-si* (or *-ek'*), *n.* want of appetite. [Gr. *an-*, priv., *orexis*, longing—*oregein*, to reach out.]

anorthic, *an-or'thik*, *adj.* (*crystal.*) triclinic, referable to three unequal oblique axes.—*n.* **anor'thite**, a plagioclase felspar, calcium aluminium silicate (from the oblique angles between the prism faces). [Gr. *an-*, priv., *orthos*, right.]

another, *ə-nudh'ər*, *adj.* and *pron.* a different or distinct (thing or person) : one more : a second : one more of the same kind : any other.—*adj.* **anoth'erguess** (see othergates).—**one another**, now used as a compound reciprocal pronoun (of two or more); **one with another**, taken all together, taken on an average. [Orig. **an other**.]

anough (*Milt.*). Same as **enough** (*sing.*).

anourous. Same as **anurous**.

anow (*Milt.*). Same as **enow, enough** (*pl.*).

anoxia, *an-ok'si-ä*, *n.* deficient supply of oxygen to the tissues.—*adj.* **anox'ic**. [Gr. *an-*, priv., *oxygen*, *-ia*.]

ansate, **-d**, *an'sāt*, *-id*, *adjs.* having a handle.— **ansate cross** (see **ankh**). [L. *ansātus*—*ansa*, handle.]

anserine, *an'sər-īn*, *adj.* of the goose or the goose family : stupid. [L. *anserīnus*—*anser*, goose.]

answer, *än'sər*, *n.* that which is said, written, or done in meeting a charge, combating an argument, objection, or attack : that which is called for by a question or questioning state of mind : the solution of a problem : an acknowledgment : a return in kind : anything given, sent or said in return : an immediate result or outcome in definite relation to the act it follows : a repetition or echo of a sound : (*mus.*) restatement of a theme by another voice or instrument.—*v.t.* to speak, write, or act in answer to or against : to say or write as an answer : to give, send, afford, or be an answer to : to behave in due accordance with : to be in proportion to or in balance with : to give a conclusive or satisfactory answer to : to serve the purpose of : to fulfil : to recompense satisfactorily : to be punished for.— *v.i.* to give an answer : to behave in answer : to be responsible : to suffer the consequences : to be in conformity : to serve the purpose : to succeed : to react.—*adj.* **an'swerable**, able to be answered : accountable : suitable : equivalent : in due proportion.—*adv.* **an'swerably**.—*n.* **an'swerer**.—

adj. **an'swerless**.—**answer back** (*coll.*), to answer one who expects silent submission : to answer pertly; **answer to** (the name of), to show sign of accepting as one's name : (*coll.*) to have as one's name. [O.E. *andsvaru* (n.), *andswarian* (vb.)— *and-*, against, *swerian*, to swear.]

ant, *ant*, *n.* a small hymenopterous insect (of the Formicidae), of proverbial industry, the emmet or pismire : loosely, a termite (*white ant*).—*ns.* **ant'-bear**, the great ant-eater, the largest species of ant-eaters, found in swampy regions in S. America : the aardvark of S. Africa; **ant'-bird**, a S. American ant-thrush; **ant'-cow**, an aphis kept and tended by ants for its honey-dew; **ant'-eater**, any one of a S. American family of edentates, feeding chiefly on ants : a pangolin : an aardvark : an echidna.— *n.pl.* **ant'-eggs**, larvae of ants.—*ns.* **ant'-hill**, the hillock raised as nest by ants or by termites : (*fig.*) the earth; **ant'-lion**, a neuropterous insect (*Myrmeleon*) whose larva traps ants in a funnel-shaped sand-hole; **ant'-thrush**, any bird of the northern S. American family Formicariidae which feed on insects disturbed by travelling ants, or of the long-legged thrushlike Oriental and Australian family *Pittidae*. [O.E. *ǽmete*; cf. **emmet**.]

an't, *änt*, a contr. of **are not, am not, has not,** (*ant*) on it, and **it**=if it.

anta, *an'tä*, *n.* a square pilaster at either side of a doorway or the corner of a flank wall :—*pl.* **an'tae** (*-tē*). [L.]

antacid, *ant-as'id*, *adj.* counteracting acidity of the stomach.—*n.* a medicine that counteracts acidity. [Gr. *anti*, against, and **acid**.]

antagonist, *an-tag'ə-nist*, *n.* one who contends or struggles with another : an opponent : a muscle that opposes the action of another.—Also *adj.*—*n.* **antag'onism**, opposition : hostility.—*n.* **antag-onisā'tion**.—*v.t.* **antag'onise**, to struggle violently against : to counteract the action of : to arouse opposition in.—*adj.* **antagonist'ic**.—*adv.* **antag-onis'tically**. [Gr. *antagōnistēs*—*anti*, against, *agōn*, contest. See **agony**.]

antaphrodisiac, *ant-af-rō-diz'i-ak*, *adj.* counteracting sexual desire.—*n.* an antaphrodisiac agent. [Gr. *anti*, against, and **aphrodisiac**.]

antar, *an'tər*, *n.* (*Shak.*) a cave. [Fr. *antre*—L. *antrum*—Gr. *antron*.]

Antarctic, *ant-ärk'tik*, *adj.* opposite the Arctic : of, near, or relating to the south pole.—*n.* the south polar regions.—**Antarctic Circle**, a parallel of latitude about $23\frac{1}{2}°$ from the south pole. [Gr. *antarktikos*—*anti*, opposite, and *arktikos*; see **Arctic**.]

Antares, *an-tā'rēs*, or *-tä'*, *n.* a first-magnitude red star in the Scorpion. [Gr. *Antarēs*—pfx. *anti-*, like, *Arēs*, Mars.]

antarthritic, *ant-är-thrit'ik*, *adj.* counteracting gout. [Gr. *anti*, against, and **arthritic**.]

antasthmatic, *ant-as*(*th*)*-mat'ik*, *adj.* counteracting asthma. [Gr. *anti*, against, and **asthmatic**.]

ante, *an'ti*, *n.* the stake put down by a poker player after looking at his cards but before (*ante*) drawing. —*v.t.* (*slang*) to stake : to pay. [L., before.]

ante-bellum, *an'ti-bel'əm*, before the war (whichever is in mind). [L. phrase.]

antecedent, *an-ti-sē'dənt*, *adj.* going before in time : prior.—*n.* that which precedes in time : (*gram.*) the noun or its equivalent to which a relative pronoun refers : (*logic*) the conditional part of a hypothetical proposition : (*math.*) the numerator term of a ratio : (in *pl.*) previous principles, conduct, history, etc.— *n.* **antece'dence**.—*adv.* **antece'dently**. [L. *antecēdēns*, *-entis*—*ante*, before, *cēdĕre*, to go.]

antecessor, *an'ti-ses-ər*, or *-ses'*, *n.* (*rare*) a predecessor : (*obs.*) an ancestor. [L. *antecēssor*; cf. preceding word and **ancestor**.]

antechamber, *an'ti-chām-bər*, *n.* a chamber or room leading to a chief apartment. [Fr. *anti-chambre*—L. *ante*, before, *camera*, a vault.]

antechapel, *an'ti-chap-l*, *n.* the outer part of the west end of a college chapel. [L. *ante*, before, and **chapel**.]

antedate, *an'ti-dāt*, *n.* a date assigned which is earlier than the actual date.—*v.t.* to date before the true time : to assign to an earlier date : to bring about at an earlier date : to be of previous date to : to accelerate : to anticipate. [L. *ante*, before, and date.]

antediluvian, *an-ti-di-l(y)ōō'vi-ən, adj.* existing or happening before Noah's Flood : resembling the state of things before the Flood : very old-fashioned, primitive.—*n.* one who lived before the Flood : one who lives to be very old.—*adj.* **antedilu'vial.**—*adv.* **antedilu'vially.** [L. *ante*, before, *dīlūvium*, flood.]

antefix, *an'ti-fiks, n.* (usually in *pl.*) an ornament concealing the ends of roofing tiles :—*pl.* **an'tefixes**, **antefix'a** (L.).—*adj.* **antefix'al.** [L. *ante*, before, in front, and *fīgĕre*, *fīxum*, to fix.]

antelope, *an'ti-lōp, n.* (*Spens.*) a fabulous fierce horned beast : since the 17th cent., any one of a group of hollow-horned ruminants near akin to goats. [O.Fr. *antelop*—L. *antalopus*—Late Gr. *antholops*, of unknown origin.]

antelucan, *an-ti-l(y)ōō'kən, adj.* before dawn or daylight. [L. *antelūcānus*—*ante*, before, *lūx*, light.]

antemeridian, *an-ti-mə-rid'i-ən, adj.* before midday. [L. *antemerīdiānus*—*ante* merīdiem, before noon.]

antemundane, *an-ti-mun'dān, adj.* before the existence of the world. [L. *ante*, before, *mundānus*—*mundus*, world.]

antenatal, *an-ti-nā'tl, adj.* before birth.—*n.* **antenā'ti** (L. -*nä'tē*), those born before a certain time, as opposed to *post-nati*, born after it—of Scotsmen born before 1603, and Americans before the Declaration of Independence (1776). [L. *ante*, before, *nātālis*, natal, *nātus*, born.]

ante-nicene, *an-ti-nī'sēn, adj.* before the first council of *Nicaea* in Bithynia, 325 A.D.

antenna, *an-ten'ä, n.* a feeler or horn in insects, crustaceans, and myriopods : in wireless communication, a structure for sending out or receiving electric waves : an aerial :—*pl.* **antenn'ae**, (-*ē*)—*adjs.* **antenn'al**, **antenn'ary** ; **antenn'iform**, **antennif'erous**.—*n.* **antenn'ule**, one of the first or smaller pair of antennae in crustaceans. [L. *antenna*, *antenna*, a yard (of a mast).]

antenuptial, *an-ti-nup'shl, adj.* before marriage. [L. *ante*, before, and **nuptial**.]

anteorbital, *an-ti-or'bit-l, adj.* situated in front of the eyes. [L. *ante*, before, and **orbit**.]

antepast, *an'ti-pāst, n.* (*obs.*) something to whet the appetite : a foretaste. [L. *ante*, before, and *pāscĕre*, *pāstum*, to feed.]

antependium, *an-ti-pend'i-əm, n.* a frontlet, or forecloth, for an altar : a frontal. [L. *ante*, before, and *pendĕre*, to hang.]

antepenult, *an-ti-pen-ult', n.* the last syllable but two.—*adj.* **antepenult'imate**, last but two. [L. *ante*, before, and **penult**.]

anteprandial, *an-ti-prand'i-əl, adj.* before dinner. [L. *ante*, before, and *prandium*, dinner.]

anterior, *an-tē'ri-ər, adj.* before, in time or place : in front of : (*bot.*) towards the bract or away from the axis.—*n.* **antēriority** (-*or'i-ti*).—*adv.* **antē'riorly.** [L. *antērior* (comp.)—*ante*, before.]

anteroom, *an'ti-rōōm, n.* a room leading into another larger room : a waiting-room : an officers' mess sitting-room. [L. *ante*, before, and **room**.]

anthelion, *an-thē'li-ən, -lyən, n.* a luminous coloured ring seen on a cloud or fog-bank over against the sun :—*pl.* **anthe'lia**. [Gr. *ant(h)ēlios, -on,—anti*, opposite, *hēlios*, the sun.]

anthelix. See **antihelix.**

anthelminthic, **anthelmintic**, *an-thel-min'thik, -tik, adj.* destroying or expelling worms.—*n.* a drug used for that purpose. [Gr. *anti*, against, and *helmins*, *helminthos*, a worm.]

anthem, *an'thəm, n.* (*obs.*) an antiphon : a composition for a church choir, commonly with solo passages, usually set to a passage from the Bible : any song of praise or gladness : loosely applied to an officially recognised national hymn or song (*national anthem*).—*v.t.* to praise in an anthem.—*adv.* **an'themwise.** [O.E. *antefn*—Gr. *antiphōna* (*pl.*) sounding in answer—*anti*, in return, *phōnē*, voice. See **antiphon.**]

anthemion, *an-thē'mi-ən, n.* the so-called honeysuckle ornament in ancient art, a conventionalised plant-form more like a palmetto :—*pl.* **anthē'mia.** [Gr. *anthēmion*, dim. of *anthos*, a flower.]

anther, *an'thər, n.* that part of a stamen that contains the pollen.—*ns.* **antherid'ium**, (*bot.*) the gametangium in which male gametes are produced:—*pl.* **antherid'ia** ; **antherozo'oid**, **antherozo'id**, a motile male gamete produced in an antheridium (Gr. *zōoeidēs*, like an animal—*zōion*, animal, and *eidos*, shape). [Gr. *anthēra*, a medicine made from flowers, esp. their inner parts—*anthos*, flower.]

anthesis, *an-thē'sis, n.* the opening of a flower-bud : the lifetime of a flower from opening to setting of seed. [Gr. *anthēsis*, flowering—*anthos*, flower.]

Anthesteria, *an-thes-tē'ri-ä, n.pl.* the Athenian spring festival of Dionysos, held in the month of *Anthestē'rion* (February—March). [Gr. *ta Anthestēria* (Feast of Flowers), *Anthestēriōn* (the month)—*anthos*, flower.]

antho-, in composition, flower.—*n.* **anthocarp** (*an'thō-kärp ;* Gr. *karpos*, fruit), a fruit resulting from many flowers, as the pineapple : a fruit of which the perianth or the torus forms part.—*adj.* **anthocarp'ous.**—*ns.* **an'thochlore** (-*klōr ;* Gr. *chlōros*, green, yellow), a yellow pigment in flowers ; **anthocyan** (-*sī'ən*), **-cy'anin** (Gr. *kyanos*, blue), a glucoside plant pigment, violet in neutral, red in acid, blue in alkaline cell-sap.—*adj.* **an'thoid** (Gr. *eidos*, shape), flower-like.—*v.t.* and *v.i.* **anthologise** (*an-thol'ə-jīz*).—*ns.* **anthol'ogist ; anthol'ogy**, (*lit.*) a flower-gathering : a choice collection of poems (orig. of Greek epigrams); **anthomā'nia** (Gr. *maniā*, madness), a craze for flowers; **anthomā'niac** ; **Anthonomus** (*an-thon'ə-məs ;* Gr. *nomos*, herbage, food), the genus of the cotton-boll weevil. —*adj.* **anthophilous** (*an-thof'i-ləs*), loving, frequenting, or feeding on flowers.—*ns.* **an'thophore** (-*thō-fōr*), an elongation of the receptacle between calyx and corolla; **anthophyllite** (*an-thō-fil'īt ;* Mod.L. *anthophyllum*, clove—Gr. *phyllon*, leaf), an orthorhombic amphibole, usually clove-brown; **anthoxan'thin** (Gr. *xanthos*, yellow), a yellow pigment in plants.—*n.pl.* **Anthozō'a** (Gr. *zōia*, animals), the Actinozoa, a class of coelenterates including sea-anemones, corals, etc. [Gr. *anthos*, flower.]

Anthony, *an'tən-i*, **tantony**, *tan'*, **St. Anthony pig**, **tantony pig'**, the smallest pig in a litter : an obsequious follower.—**St. Anthony's cross**, a tau-cross ; **St. Anthony's fire**, (*pop.*) erysipelas; **tantony bell**, a small bell. [From St. *Anthony* (4th century) who has a pig and a bell among his symbols and who was believed to have stayed an epidemic (perhaps rhaphania, but commonly supposed to be erysipelas) in 1089.]

anthrax, *an'thraks, n.* a carbuncle, malignant boil : malignant pustule, woolsorter's disease, a deadly disease due to a bacillus, most common in sheep and cattle but communicable to men.—*n.* **anthracene** (*an'thra-sēn*), a product of coal-tar distillation ($C_{14}H_{10}$), a source of dye-stuffs.—*adj.* **anthracic** (*an-thras'ik*), of anthrax.—*n.* **an'thracite** (*an'thra-sīt*), stone-coal, a coal that burns nearly without flame or smoke, consisting almost entirely of carbon.—*adjs.* **anthracitic** (-*sit'ik*), of, of the nature of, anthracite; **anthracoid** (*an'thrə-koid*), like anthrax.—*n.* **anthracosis** (-*kō'sis*), a diseased state of the lung due to breathing coal-dust. [Gr. *anthrax, -akos*, charcoal, coal, carbuncle (stone or boil).]

anthrop-, **anthropo-** in composition, man, human. —*adjs.* **anthropic** (*an-throp'ik*), **-al**, human; **anthropocentric** (*an-thrō-pō-sent'rik ;* Gr. *kentron*, centre), centring the universe in man.—*ns.* **anthropogenesis** (-*jen'*) ; **anthropogeny** (-*poj'ən-i ;* Gr. *genos*, race, birth), the study of man's origin; **anthrōpogeog'raphy**, the geography of the races of man ; **anthropogony** (-*pog'ə-ni ;* Gr. *gonē*, *gonos*, birth, begetting), the study, or an account, of the origin of man ; **anthropography** (-*pog'rə-fi*), study of the geographical distribution of human races.— *adj.* **an'thropoid** (or -*thrōp'*), manlike : applied esp. to the highest apes—gorilla, chimpanzee, orang-utan, gibbon, but also to the higher Primates generally—man, apes, monkeys, but not lemurs.— *n.* an anthropoid ape.—*adj.* **anthropoid'al.**—*n.*

anthropol'atry (Gr. *latreiā*, worship), man-worship, the giving of divine honours to a human being.—*adj.* **anthrōpological** (-*loj'*).—*adv.* **anthrōpolog'ically**.—*ns.* **anthropol'ogist; anthropol'ogy**, the science of man in its widest sense.— *adj.* **anthropomet'ric**.—*ns.* **anthropometry** (-*pom'i-tri;* Gr. *metreein*, to measure), measurement of the human body; **anthrō'pomorph** (Gr. *morphē*, shape), a representation, esp. conventionalised, of the human form in art.—*adj.* **anthropomorph'ic**.—*v.t.* **anthropomorph'ise**, to regard as or render anthropomorphic.—*n.* **anthropomorph'ism**, conception or representation of a god as having the form, personality, or attributes of man: ascription of human characteristics to what is not human; **anthropomorph'ist; anthropomorph'ite**.—*adj.* **anthropomorphit'ic**. —*ns.* **anthropomorph'itism; anthropomorphō'sis** (or -*morf'a-sis*), transformation into human shape.— *adjs.* **anthropomorph'ous**, formed like or resembling man; **anthropopathic** (-*path'ik*).—*adv.* **anthropopath'ically**. — *ns.* **anthropopathism** (-*op'a-thizm*), **anthropop'athy** (Gr. *pathos*, suffering, passion), ascription of human passions and affections (to God, nature, etc.).—*n.pl.* **anthrōpophagi** (-*pof'a-jī*, -*gē;* Gr. *phagein*, to eat), man-eaters, cannibals.—*ns.* **anthropophaginian** (-*jin'i-an; Shak.*), a cannibal; **anthropoph'agite** (-*a-jīt*). —*adj.* **anthropoph'agous** (-*a-gas*).—*ns.* **anthrōpoph'agy** (-*a-ji*), cannibalism; **anthropoph'ūism** (Gr. *phyē*, nature), the ascription of a human nature to the gods; **Anthropopithē'cus**, the chimpanzee (Gr. *pithekos*, ape); **anthropos'ophist; anthropos'ophy** (Gr. *sophiā*, wisdom), the knowledge of the nature of men: human wisdom: esp. the spiritualistic doctrine of Rudolf Steiner (1861-1925).—*adj.* **anthrōpopsy'chic** (-*sī'kik*, -*psī'kik*) —*adv.* **anthropopsy'chically**.—*ns.* **anthropopsy'chism** (Gr. *psychē*, soul), ascription to nature or God of a soul or mind like man's; **anthropot'omy** (Gr. *tomē*, a cut), human anatomy. [Gr. *anthrōpos*, man (in general sense).]

anti-, ant'i-, *pfx.* against, in opposition to, rivalling, simulating.—*n.* and *adj.* (one who is) opposed to anything. [Gr. *anti*, against, instead of, etc.]

antiaditis, *an-ti-a-dī'tis, n.* tonsillitis. [Gr. *antias, -ados,* tonsil.]

anti-aircraft, *an-ti-ār'krăft, adj.* intended for use against hostile aircraft.

antiar, *an'chär, an'ti-är, n.* the upas-tree: its poisonous latex. [Jav. *antjar*.]

antibilious, *an'ti-bil'yas, adj.* of use against biliousness.

antibiosis, *an-ti-bī-ō'sis, n.* antagonistic relation between associated organisms : inhibition of growth by a substance produced by another organism.— *adj.* **antibiotic** (-*ot'ik*), inimical to life : inhibiting the growth of another organism : pertaining to antibiosis.—*n.* an antibiotic substance. [Gr. *anti*, against, *biōsis*, way of life; adj. *biōtikos—bios*, life.]

antibody, *an'ti-bod-i, n.* a defensive substance produced in an organism in response to the action of a foreign body such as the toxin of a parasite. [Gr. *anti*, against, and **body**.]

Antiburgher, *an-ti-burg'ar, n.* a member of that section of the Scottish Secession Church which parted from the main body (the *Burghers*) in 1747, interpreting the reference in the oath administered to burgesses in Edinburgh, Glasgow and Perth, to 'the true religion presently professed within this realm' to mean the Established Church.—Also *adj.*

antic, *ant'ik, adj.* grotesque.—*n.* a fantastic figure or ornament : (*Shak.*) a grotesque pageant : (*arch.*) a buffoon, clown, mountebank : (usu. in *pl.*) a fantastic action or trick : a caper.—*v.t.* (*Shak.*) to make grotesque.—*v.i.* to cut capers.—Formerly **ant'icke**, sometimes **ant'ique**.—*v.i.* **anticize** (*ant'i-sīz; Browning*), to play antics.—See also **antique**. [It. *antico*, ancient—L. *antiquus;* orig. used of the fantastic decorations found in the remains of ancient Rome.]

anticathode, *an-ti-kath'ōd, n.* the target of an X-ray tube, on which the cathode rays are focused and from which X-rays are emitted.

anticatholic, *an-ti-kath'a-lik, adj.* opposed to the Catholic or the Roman Catholic Church, to Catholics, or to what is catholic.

antichlor, *an'ti-klör, n.* any substance used in paper-making to free the pulp from the last traces of free chlorine. [**chlorine**.]

Antichrist, *an'ti-krīst, n.* an opponent of Christ : the great opposer of Christ and Christianity expected by the early Church, applied by some to the Pope and others.—*adj.* **antichristian** (-*krīst'*-), relating to Antichrist : opposed to Christianity.— *n.* **antichrist'ianism**.—*adv.* **antichrist'ianly**. [Gr. *Chrīstos*, Christ.]

Antichthon, *an-tik'thŏn, n.* second earth placed by Pythagoreans on the other side of the sun : the southern hemisphere.—*n.pl.* **antich'thones** (-*thon-ēz*), the antipodeans. [Gr. *chthōn*, earth.]

anticipate, *an-tis'ip-āt, v.t.* to be beforehand with (another person or thing) : to forestall : to preoccupy : to use, spend, deal with in advance or before the due time : to realise beforehand : to foresee or count upon as certain : to expect : to precede : to advance to an earlier time, bring on sooner.—*v.i.* to be before the normal time : to do anything before the appropriate time.—*adj.* and *n.* **antic'ipant**, anticipating, anticipative.—*n.* **anticipā'tion**, act of anticipating : assignment to too early a time : (*mus.*) introduction of a tone or tones of a chord before the whole chord : intuition : foretaste : previous notion : presentiment : prejudice : imagining beforehand : expectation.—*adjs.* **anti'cipative, anti'cipatory**.—*advs.* **anti'cipatively, anti'cipatorily**.—*n.* **antic'ipātor**. [L. *anticipāre, -ātum—ante*, before, *capĕre*, to take.]

anticivic, *an-ti-siv'ik, adj.* opposed to citizenship, esp. the conception of it engendered by the French Revolution.—*n.* **anticiv'ism**.

antick, anticke, obsolete forms of **antic, antique**.

anticlerical, *an-ti-kler'i-kl, adj.* opposed to the clergy or their power.—*n.* a member of an anticlerical party.—*n.* **anticler'icalism**.

anticlimax, *an-ti-klī'maks, n.* the opposite of climax : a ludicrous drop in impressiveness after a progressive rise.—*adj.* **anticlīmac'tic**.—*adv.* **anticlīmac'tically**.

anticline, *an'ti-klīn, n.* (*geol.*) an arch-like fold dipping outwards from the fold-axis.—*adj.* **anticlīn'al**, sloping in opposite directions : (*bot.*) perpendicular to the surface near the growing-point.—*n.* an anticline.—*n.* **anticlīnō'rium** (-*klīn-* or -*klīn-*), a series of folds which as a whole is anticlinal. [Gr. *anti*, against, *klīnein*, to lean; *oros*, a mountain.]

anticous, *an-tī'kas, adj.* (*bot.*) on the anterior side, or away from the axis. [L. *antīcus*, in front—*ante*, before.]

anticyclone, *an-ti-sī'klōn, n.* a rotatory outflow of air from an area of high pressure.—*adj.* **anticyclonic** (-*klon'ik*).

antidote, *an'ti-dōt, n.* that which counteracts poison : (*fig.*) anything that prevents an evil (with *against, for,* to).—*adj.* **antido'tal**. [Gr. *antidotos—didonai*, to give.]

antient, an obsolete spelling of **ancient**.

anti-federal, *an-ti-fed'ar-l, adj.* opposed to federalism : applied to the U.S. party afterwards called Democratic.—*ns.* **anti-fed'eralism ; anti-fed'eralist**.

antifouling, *an-ti-fowl'ing, adj.* intended to prevent fouling of ships' bottoms.

antifriction, *an-ti-frik'shan, adj.* intended to reduce friction.

anti-Gallican, *an-ti-gal'ik-an, adj.* opposed to what is French, or to Gallicanism.—Also *n.*—*n.* **anti-Gall'icanism**.

antigen, *an'ti-jen, n.* any substance that stimulates the production of an antibody. [Gr. *anti*, against, *gennaein*, to engender.]

antigropelo(e)s, *an-ti-grop'a-lōz, n.pl.* waterproof leggings. [Said to be from Gr. *anti*, against, *hygros*, wet, and *pēlos*, mud.]

antihelix, *an-ti-hē'liks, antehelix, an'thi-liks, an-thē'liks, n.* the inner curved ridge of the external ear : —*pls.* **antihelices**, (-*li-sēz*), **anthel'ices**. [Gr. *anthēlix—hēlix*, a coil.]

antihistamine, *an-ti-his′tə-mēn, n.* any of a group of drugs that prevent the action of histamines in allergic conditions.

anti-Jacobin, antijacobin, *an-ti-jak′ə-bin, adj.* opposed to the Jacobins and to the French Revolution or to democratic principles.—*n.* one opposed to the Jacobins; **(Anti-Jacobin)** a weekly paper started in England in 1797 by Canning and others to refute the principles of the French Revolution.—*n.* **anti-Jac′obinism.**

antiknock, *an-ti-nok′, n.* a substance that prevents knock or detonation in internal-combustion engines. [G. *anti,* against, and knock.]

antilegomena, *an-ti-leg-om′i-nä, n.pl.* those books of the New Testament not at first universally accepted but ultimately admitted into the Canon—2 Peter, James, Jude, Hebrews, 2 and 3 John, and the Apocalypse—opp. to *homologoumena.* [Gr., spoken against.]

antilogarithm, *an-ti-log′ə-ridhm, -ritʰm, n.* a number of which a particular number is the logarithm :—*contr.* **an′tilog.**

antilogy, *an-til′ə-ji, n.* a contradiction.—*adj.* **antil′-ogous** (-*gəs*), of the contrary kind: negatively electrified by heating. [Gr. *antilogiā,* contradiction.]

Antilope, *an-til′ō-pē, n.* the Indian antelope genus. *adj.* **antil′opine,** of antelopes. [See antelope.]

antimacassar, *an-ti-mək-as′ər, n.* a covering for chair-backs, etc., to protect them from Macassar oil or other grease in the hair, or for ornament.

antimalarial, *an-ti-mə-lā′ri-əl, adj.* used against malaria.

antimask, antimasque, *an′ti-mȧsk, n.* a farcical interlude dividing the parts of, or preceding, the more serious mask. [Gr. *anti,* against, and mask.]

antimetabole, *an-ti-me-tab′ol-ē, n.* (rhet.) a figure in which the same words or ideas are repeated in inverse order, as Quarles's 'Be wisely worldly, but not worldly wise.' [Gr.]

antimetathesis, *an-ti-me-tatʰ′ə-sis, n.* inversion of the members of an antithesis, as in Crabbe's 'A poem is a speaking picture; a picture, a mute poem.' [Gr.]

antimnemonic, *an-ti-ni-mon′ik, adj.* tending to weaken the memory.—Also *n.* [Pfx. **anti-** and **mnemonic.**]

antimonarchical, *an-ti-mon-ärk′i-kl, adj.* opposed to monarchy and monarchical principles.—*n.* **antimon′archist** (-*ər-kist*).

antimony, *an′ti-mən-i, n.* a brittle, bluish-white element (at. numb. 51; symbol Sb, for stibium) of metallic appearance : (*printers′ slang*) type.—*adj.* **antimonial** (-mō′ni-əl), pertaining to, or containing, antimony.—*n.* a drug containing antimony.—*adjs.* **antimonic** (-mon′ik), containing pentavalent antimony; **antimō′nious,** containing trivalent antimony.—*ns.* **an′timonate** (-mən-), **antimō′-niate,** a salt of any antimonic acid : **an′timonite,** a salt of antimonious acid : the mineral stibnite (not chemically an antimonite). [L.L. *antimōnium,* of unknown origin, prob. from some Arabic word.]

anti-national, *an-ti-nash′ə-nl, adj.* hostile to one's nation or to nationalism.

antinephritic, *an-ti-ne-frit′ik, adj.* acting against diseases of the kidney.

antinode, *an′ti-nōd, n.* (physics) a point of maximum disturbance midway between nodes.—*adj.* **antinōd′al.**

antinomian, *an-ti-nō′mi-ən, n.* one who denies the obligatoriness of moral law : one who believes that Christians are emancipated by the gospel from the obligation to keep the moral law, faith alone being necessary.—Also *adj.*—*n.* **antino′mianism.**—*adj.* **antinomic** (-nom′ik), -al, pertaining to, of the nature of, or involving, antinomy.—*n.* **antinomy** (an-tin′ə-mi), a contradiction in a law : a conflict of authority : conclusions discrepant though apparently logical. [Gr. *nomos,* law.]

Antiochian, *an-ti-ō′ki-ən,* **Antiochene,** *an-ti′ō-kēn, adjs.* of the city of *Antioch* : of the eclectic philosophy of *Antiochus* of Ascalon : of any of the Seleucid kings of the name.—*n.* **Antio′chianism,** a school of theology in the 4th and 5th centuries in revolt against Alexandrian allegorising.

antiodontalgic, *an-ti-o-dont-alj′ik, adj.* of use against toothache.—Also *n.* [Gr. *anti,* against, *odous, odontos,* tooth, and *algeein,* to suffer pain.]

antipapal. See antipope.

antiparallel, *an-ti-par′ə-ləl, adj.* making with a transverse line an internal angle equal to the external angle made by another line.—Also *n.*

antipathy, *an-tip′ath-i, n.* opposition in feeling : aversion : repugnance : incompatibility : mutual opposition : an object of antipathy.—*adjs.* **antipathet′ic, -al ; antipathic** (an-ti-patʰ′ik), belonging to antipathy : opposite : contrary.—*n.* **antip′-athist,** one possessed by an antipathy. [Gr. *pathos,* feeling.]

antiperiodic, *an-ti-pē-ri-od′ik, adj.* destroying the periodicity of diseases.—*n.* a drug with such an effect.

antiperistaltic, *an-ti-per-i-stal′tik, adj.* contrary to peristaltic motion.

antiperistasis, *an-ti-pər-ist′ə-sis, n.* opposition of circumstances : resistance or reaction. [Gr., surrounding, interchange—*anti,* against, *peristasis,* a circumstance—*peri,* around, *stasis,* a setting, stand.]

anti-personnel, *an-ti-per-sən-el′, adj.* intended to destroy military personnel and other persons.

antipetalous, *an-ti-pet′ə-ləs, adj.* opposite a petal.

antiphlogistic, *an-ti-floj-ist′ik, adj.* acting against heat, or inflammation.—*n.* a medicine to allay inflammation.

antiphon, *an′ti-fon, n.* alternate chanting or singing : a species of church music sung by two parties each responding to the other : also antiph′ony (-*ən-i*).—*adj.* **antiph′onal.**—*n.* a book of antiphons or of anthems.—Also **antiph′onary** and **antiph′oner.**—*adjs.* **antiphonic** (-fon′), **-al,** mutually responsive.—*adv.* **antiphon′ically.** [Gr. *anti,* in return, and *phōnē,* voice ; a doublet of **anthem.**]

antiphrasis, *an-tif′rə-sis, n.* (rhet.) the use of words in a sense opposite to the literal one.—*adjs.* **antiphrastic** (an-ti-fras′tik), **-al,** involving antiphrasis : ironical.—*adv.* **antiphras′tically.** [Gr.,—*anti,* against, *phrasis,* speech.]

antipodes, *an-tip′o-dēz, n.pl.* (also *sing.*) those who live on the other side of the globe, or on opposite sides, standing feet to feet : a point or place diametrically opposite to another on the surface of the earth or of any globular body or sphere : a pair of points or places so related to each other : the exact opposite of a person or a thing :—*sing.* (*rare*) **antipode** (an′ti-pōd).—*adjs.* **antip′odal,** **antipōde′an.**—**antipodal cells** (*bot.*) in flowering plants, three cells in the embryo-sac at the end remote from the micropyle, representing the prothallus. [Gr. *antipŏdēs,* pl. of *antipous,* with feet opposite—*pous, podos,* a foot.]

antipole, *an′ti-pōl, n.* the opposite pole : direct opposite.

antipope, *an′ti-pōp, n.* a pontiff set up in opposition to one canonically chosen, as those who resided at Avignon in the 13th and 14th centuries.—*adj.* **antipā′pal,** opposed to the pope or the papal system.

antipyretic, *an-ti-pī-ret′ik, adj.* counteracting fever.—*n.* an antipyretic agent.—*n.* **antipy′rin, -ine,** trade-name for a white crystalline febrifuge $(C_{11}H_{12}ON_2)$ got from coal-tar products. [Gr. *pyretos,* fever—*pȳr,* fire.]

antiquary, *an′ti-kwər-i, n.* one who studies, collects, or deals in relics of the past, but not usually very ancient things—curiosities rather than objects of serious archaeological interest.—*adj.* (*Shak.*) ancient.—*adj.* **antiquarian** (-kwā′ri-ən), connected with the study of antiquities.—*n.* an antiquary : a size of drawing-paper, 53×31 inches.—*n.* **antiquā′rianism.** [L. *antīquārius—antīquus,* old.]

antique, *an-tēk′,* formerly *an′tik* (and sometimes written **antick**), *adj.* ancient : of a good old age, olden (now generally rhetorical in a good sense) : old-fashioned : savouring of bygone times : after the manner of the ancients.—*n.* anything very old : an old relic : a piece of old furniture or other object sought by collectors : a type of thick and bold face with lines of equal thickness.—*v.t.* **antiquate** (an′ti-kwāt), to make antique, old, or obsolete : to put out of use.—*adj.* an'tiquated.—*n.* antiquā'-tion.—*adv.* antique'ly.—*n.* antique'ness.—*ns.* antiquitarian (*an-tik-wi-tā'ri-ən*), one attached to old ways or beliefs; antiq'uity, ancient times, esp. the times of the ancient Greeks and Romans : great age : (*Shak.*) old age, seniority : ancient style : the people of old time : a relic of the past : (*pl.*) manners, customs, etc., of ancient times.—the antique, ancient work in art : the style of ancient art.—See also antic. [L. *antīquus*, old, ancient—*ante*, before; influenced by Fr. *antique*.]

antirachitic, *an-ti-ra-kit'ik, adj.* tending to prevent or cure rickets.—Also *n.* [rachitis.]

Antirrhinum, *an-ti-rī'nəm, n.* the snapdragon genus. [Latinised from Gr. *antirrīnon,* snapdragon—*anti,* like, mimicking, *rhis, rhīnos,* nose.]

antiscian, *an-tish'i-ən, n.* a dweller on the same meridian on the other side of the equator, whose shadow at noon falls in the opposite direction.—Also *adj.* [Gr. *skiā,* shadow.]

antiscorbutic, *an-ti-skor-būt'ik, adj.* acting against scurvy.—*n.* a remedy or preventive for scurvy.

antiscriptural, *an-ti-skrip'tyər-əl, adj.* opposed to the authority of the Bible.

anti-Semite (*an-ti-sem'īt, -sēm'it*), *n.* a hater of Semites, esp. Jews, or of their influence.—*adj.* anti-Semitic (*-sim-it'*).—*n.* anti-Semitism (*-sem', -sēm'*). [Semite.]

antisepalous, *an-ti-sep'ə-ləs, adj.* opposite a sepal.

antisepsis, *an-ti-sep'sis, n.* destruction, or inhibition of growth, of bacteria.—*adj.* antisep'tic.—*n.* an antiseptic agent.—*n.* antisep'ticism (*-sizm*), antiseptic treatment.—*adv.* antisep'ically.—*v.t.* antisep'ticise (*-sīz*). [Gr. *sēpsis,* putrefaction.]

antisocial, *an-ti-sō'shl, adj.* opposed to the good of society, or the principles of society : disinclined to mix in society : without social instincts.—*ns.* antiso'cialism ; antiso'cialist, (formerly) an unsociable person : (now) an opponent of socialism; antisociality (*-shi-al'i-ti*), unsociableness : opposition to the principles of society.

antispasmodic, *an-ti-spaz-mod'ik, adj.* opposing spasms or convulsions.—*n.* a remedy for spasms.

antispast, *an'ti-spast, n.* a foot composed of an iambus and a trochee.—*adj.* antispast'ic. [Gr. *antispastos*—*antispaein,* to draw back—*spaein,* to draw.]

antistrophe, *an-tis'trə-fē, n.* the returning dance in Greek choruses, reversing the movement of the strophe : the stanza answering the strophe in the same metre : repetition in inverse order : retortion of an argument : an inverse relation.—*adj.* antistrophic (*an-ti-strof'ik*).—*adv.* antistroph'ically. —*n.* antis'trophon, an argument retorted on an opponent. [Gr. *antistrophē*—*strophē,* a turning.]

antithalian, *an-ti-thə-lī'ən, adj.* opposed to mirth. [Gr. *Thaleia,* the comic muse.]

antitheism, *an-ti-thē'izm, n.* doctrine antagonistic to theism : denial of the existence of a God : opposition to God.—*n.* antithē'ist.—*adj.* antithēist'ic. [Gr. *theos,* a god.]

antithesis, *an-tith'i-sis, n.* a figure in which thoughts or words are balanced in contrast : a thesis or proposition opposing another : opposition : the direct opposite :—*pl.* antith'eses (*-sēz*)—*n.* an'tithet (*-thet ; rare*), an instance of antithesis.—*adjs.* antithet'ic, *-al.*—*adv.* antithet'ically. [Gr. *antithesis*—*thesis,* placing.]

antithrombin, *an-ti-throm'bin, n.* a substance produced by the liver which prevents clotting of the blood in the veins. [Gr. *thrombos,* a clot.]

antitoxin, *an-ti-tok'sin, n.* a substance that neutralises toxin formed in the body.—*adj.* antitox'ic.

antitrade, *an'ti-trād, n.* a wind that blows in the opposite direction to the trade-wind—that is, in the northern hemisphere from south-west, and in the southern hemisphere from north-west.

antitragus, *an-ti-trā'gəs, n.* a prominence of the external ear, opposite the tragus.

antitrinitarian, *an-ti-trin-i-tā'ri-ən, adj.* opposed to the doctrine of the Trinity.—Also *n.*—*n.* antitrinitā'rianism.

antitype, *an'ti-tīp, n.* that which corresponds to the type : that which is prefigured by the type.—*adjs.* antityp'al, -typic (*-tip'ik*), -al.

antivaccinationist, *an-ti-vak-si-nā'shən-ist, n.* an opponent of vaccination.—*n.* antivaccinā'tionism.

anti-vitamin, *an-ti-vīt'ə-min, n.* a substance with a chemical structure very similar to a vitamin which prevents that vitamin from having its effect.

anti-vivisection, *an-ti-viv-i-sek'shən, n.* opposition to vivisection.—*ns.* anti-vivisec'tionism ; anti-vivisec'tionist.

antler, *ant'lər, n.* a bony outgrowth from the frontal bone of a deer : (originally) the lowest branch of a stag's horn, then any branch, then the whole.—*adj.* ant'lered.—*n.* ant'ler-moth, a noctuid moth (*Charaeas graminis*), with antler-like markings on the wings, its larvae very destructive to pastures. [O.Fr. *antoillier*—assumed L.L. *ant(e)oculāris* (*rāmus,* branch) in front of the eyes.]

antlia, *ant'li-ä, n.* the suctorial proboscis of lepidoptera (*pl.* ant'liae, *-ē*).—*adj.* ant'liate. [L. *antlia,* a pump—Gr. *antliā,* bilge-water.]

ant-lion. See under ant.

antonomasia, *ant-on-ə-mā'zi-ä, n.* use of an epithet, or the name of an office or attributive, for a person's proper name, e.g. his lordship for an earl ; and conversely, e.g. a Napoleon for a great conqueror. [Gr. *antonomasiā*—*onomazein,* to name, *onoma,* a name.]

antonym, *ant'ō-nim, n.* a word which is the opposite in meaning of another. [Gr. *onyma*=*onoma,* a name.]

antre, *an'tər, n.* a cave.—(*Shak.*) an'tar. [Fr. ; L. *antrum*—Gr. *antron,* a cave.]

Antrycide, *an'tri-sīd, n.* a drug useful for cure and prevention of trypanosome diseases. [Trademark name.]

antrorse, *an-trors', adj.* turned up or forward. [From *anterus,* hypothetical positive of L. *anterior,* front, and L. *versus,* turned.]

Anubis, *a-nū'bis, n.* the ancient Egyptian jackal-headed god of the dead. [L.,—Gr. *Anoubis*—Egypt. *Anup.*]

anuria, *an-ū'ri-ä, n.* failure in secretion of urine. [Gr. *an-,* priv., *ouron,* urine.]

anurous, *an-ū'rəs, adj.* anourous, *an-ōō'rəs, adj.* tailless. —*n.pl.* Anu'ra, Anou'ra, the Salientia or tailless amphibians, frogs and toads. [Gr. *an-,* priv., *ourā,* tail.]

anus, *ā'nəs, n.* the opening of the alimentary canal by which undigested residues are voided.—*adj.* ā'nal. [L. *ānus,* -*ī,* a ring.]

anvil, *an'vil, n.* an iron block on which smiths hammer metal into shape : the incus of the ear.—on or upon the anvil, in preparation, under discussion. [O.E. *anfilte.*]

anxious, *ang(k)'shəs, adj.* uneasy with fear and desire regarding something doubtful : solicitous.—*n.* anxiety (*ang(g)-zī'i-ti*), state of being anxious.—*adv.* an'xiously.—*n.* an'xiousness. [L. *anxius*—*angēre,* to press tightly. See anger, anguish.]

any, *en'i, adj.* and *pron.* one indefinitely : some : whichever, no matter which.—*adv.* at all, to an appreciable extent.—*n.* and *pron.* an'ybody, any single person : a person of any account.—*adv.* an'yhow, in any way whatever ; in any case, at least.—*ns.* and *prons.* an'yone (or any one), anybody at all : anybody whatever ; an'ything, a thing indefinitely, as opposed to nothing.—*adv.* any whit, to any extent.—*ns.* anything'rian, one with no beliefs in particular; anythingā'rianism. —*advs.* an'yway, an'yways, in any manner : anyhow : in any case; an'ywhen (*rare*) ; an'ywhere, in or to any place; an'ywhither (*rare*); an'ywise, in any manner to any degree.—at any rate, whatever may happen : at all events. [O.E. *ænig—ān,* one.]

Anzac, *an'zak, n.* an Australasian expeditionary soldier (1914 *et seq.*).—Also *adj.* [Coined from initials of Australian-New-Zealand Army Corps.]

Aonian, *ā-ō'ni-ən, adj.* pertaining to *Aonia* in Greece, and to the Muses supposed to dwell there. —Aonian fount, the fountain Aganippe, on a slope of Mount Helicon—the Aonian mount.

fāte, fär, ȧsk ; mē, her (her) ; *mīne, mōte, mūte, mōōn ; dhen* (then)

aorist, *ā'ər-ist, n.* a tense, esp. in Greek, expressing simple past time, with no implications of continuance, repetition, or the like.—*adj.* **aorist'ic.** [Gr. *aoristos,* indefinite—*a-,* priv., and *horistos,* limited.]

aorta, *ā-or'tä, n.* the great arterial trunk that carries blood from the heart.—*adjs.* **aor'tal, aor'tic.**—*n.* **aortī'tis,** inflammation of the aorta. [Gr. *aortē—aeirein,* to raise up.]

aoudad, *ä'oo-dad, n.* a North African wild sheep. [Native name in French spelling.]

apace, *ə-pās', adv.* at a quick pace : swiftly. [Prep. **a,** and **pace.**]

Apache, *ä-pä'chä, n.* a Red Indian of a group of tribes in Arizona, New Mexico, etc. : (**apache,** *ä-päsh'*) a lawless ruffian or hooligan in Paris or elsewhere. [Perh. Zuñi *ápachu,* enemy.]

apagoge, *ap-ə-gō'jē, n.* reduction to absurdity, indirect proof by showing the falsehood of the opposite.—*adjs.* **apagogic** (-*goj'ik*), **-al.**—*adv.* **apagog'ical y.** [Gr. *apagōgē,* leading away, *apagein,* to lead off.]

apaid. See **apay.**

apanage. See **appanage.**

apart, *ə-pärt', adv.* separately : aside : asunder, parted : separate : out of consideration.—*n.* **apart'ness.—to set apart,** to separate : to devote. [Fr. *à part*—L. *ad partem,* to the side.]

apartheid, *a-pärt'hād, n.* segregation (of races). [Afrikaans.]

apartment, *ə-pärt'mənt, n.* a separate room in a house occupied by a particular person or party : (*arch.* and *U.S.*) a suite or set of such rooms—now in this sense in the *pl.* : (*obs.*) a compartment.—*adj.* **apartmental** (-*ment'əl*). [Fr. *appartement,* a suite of rooms forming a complete dwelling—L. *ad,* to, *partire, partirī,* to divide—*pars,* part.]

apatheton, *ə-path'i-tən, n.* (*Shak.*) for **epitheton.**

apathy, *ap'əth-i, n.* want of feeling, passion, or interest : indifference.—*adjs.* **apathet'ic, -al.**—*adv.* **apathet'ically.** [Gr. *apatheia—a-,* priv., *pathos,* feeling.]

apatite, *ap'ə-tīt, n.* a mineral consisting of calcium phosphate and fluoride (or chloride). [Gr. *apatē,* deceit, from its having been confused with other minerals.]

apay, appay, *ə-pā', v.t.* (*arch.*) to satisfy, content : (*obs.*) to repay :—*pa.p.* and *pa.t.* **apaid'** (**apayd'**). [O Fr. *apayer,* from L. *ad,* and *pācāre—päx,* peace.]

ape, *āp, n.* a monkey : a large monkey without a tail or with a very short one : one who plays the ape : a mimic : an imitator.—*v.t.* to mimic : to imitate.—*ns.* **ape'dom ; ape'hood ; ap'ery,** conduct of one who apes : any ape-like action : a colony of apes.—*adj.* **ap'ish,** like an ape : imitative : foppish.—*adv.* **ap'ishly.—*ns.* **ap'ishness, ap'ism** (*Carlyle*).— **God's ape,** a born fool; **lead apes in hell,** feigned to be the lot of old maids in after life; **make one his ape, to put an ape in one's hood** (*obs.*), to make a fool of. [O.E. *apa;* Ger. *affe.*]

apeak, apeek, *ə-pēk', adv.* (*naut.*) vertical. [Prep. **a,** peak.]

apepsy, apepsia, *a-pep'si, a-pep'si-ä, n.* weakness of digestion. [Gr. *apepsiä,* indigestion; *a-,* priv., *peptein,* to digest.]

aperçu, *ä-per-sü, n.* a summary exposition : a brief outline. [Fr. pa.p. of *apercevoir.*]

aperient, *ə-pē'ri-ənt, n.* and *adj.* laxative.—*adj.* **aperitive** (*a-per'i-tiv*), laxative.—*n.* (usu. as Fr. **apéritif,** *ä-pā-rē-tēf'*) a (liquid) appetiser.—*adj.* **apert** (*ə-pərt' ; arch.*) open, public.—*n.* **apert'ness.** [L. *aperīre, apertum,* to open.]

aperiodic, *ā-pē-ri-od'ik, adj.* not periodic : coming to rest without oscillation.—*n.* **aperiodicity** (-*ə-dis'i-ti*). [Gr. *a-,* priv., and **periodic.**]

a-per-se, *ā-pər-sē', n.* (*arch.*) the letter a spelling a word by itself : (*fig.*) anything unique in excellence. [L. *a per sē,* a by itself; cf. **ampersand.**]

aperture, *ap'ər-tyər, n.* an opening : a hole : diameter of the opening through which light passes in an optical instrument. [L. *apertūra—aperīre,* to open.]

apetalous, *a-pet'əl-əs, adj.* (*bot.*) without petals.—*n.* **apet'aly.** [Gr. *a-,* priv., and *petalon,* a leaf.]

apex, *ā'peks, n.* summit, tip, or point : (*geom.*) a vertex : the culminating point, climax of anything :

—*pl.* **ā'pexes, apices** (*āp',* or *ap'i-sēz*). [L. *āpex, āpĭcis,* a tip.]

aphaeresis, *a-fē'ri-sis, n.* (*gram.*) the taking away of a sound or syllable at the beginning of a word. [Gr. *aphairesis,* a taking away, *apo,* away, and *haireein,* to take.]

Aphaniptera, *af-an-ip'tər-ä, n.pl.* the flea order (or suborder) of insects.—*adj.* **aphanip'terous.** [Gr. *aphanēs,* invisible, *pteron,* wing.]

aphasia, *a-fā'z(h)i-ä, n.* inability to express thought in words by reason of some brain disease : loss of the faculty of interchanging thought, without any affection of the intellect or will.—*n.* and *adj.* **aphā'siac.**—*adj.* **aphasic** (*a-fā'-zik, a-faz'ik*). [Gr. *a-,* priv., *phasis,* speech—*phanai,* to speak.]

aphelion, *a-fē'li-ən, n.* a planet's furthest point in its orbit from the sun :—*pl.* **aphē'lia.** [Gr. *apo,* from, *hēlios,* sun.]

apheliotropic, *a-fē-li-ō-trop'ik, adj.* turning away from the sun.—*n.* **apheliotropism** (-*ot'rə-pizm*). [Gr. *apo,* from, *hēlios,* sun, and *tropikos,* belonging to turning—*trepein,* to turn.]

apheresis. Same as **aphaeresis.**

aphesis, *af'i-sis, n.* the gradual and unintentional loss of an unaccented vowel at the beginning of a word, as in *squire* from *esquire*—a special form of aphaeresis.—*adj.* **aphetic** (*ə-fet'ik*).—*v.t.* **aph'etise.** [Gr. *aphesis,* letting go—*apo,* from, *hienai,* to send]

aphis, *af'is, āf'is,* **aphid,** *af'id, ns.* a plant-louse or greenfly, a small homopterous insect that sucks plant juices :—*pl.* **aph'ides** (-*i-dēz*), **aph'ids.**— *adj.* and *n.* **aphid'ian.** [Ety. unknown.]

aphonia, *a-fō'ni-ä,* **aphony,** *af'ə-ni, n.* loss of voice from hysteria, disease of the larynx or vocal cords, etc.—*adjs.* **aphonic** (-*fon'*), **aphonous** (*af'ə-nəs*), voiceless. [Gr. *a-,* priv., *phōnē,* voice.]

aphorism, *af'ər-izm, n.* a concise statement of a principle in any science : a brief, pithy saying : an adage.—*v.i.* **aph'orise.**—*n.* **aph'oriser ; aph'orist.**—*adj.* **aphoris'tic.**—*adv.* **aphorist'ically.** [Gr. *aphorizein,* to mark off by boundaries—*apo,* from, and *horos,* a limit.]

aphrodisiac, *af-ro-diz'i-ak, adj.* exciting sexually.— *n.* that which so excites.—*adj.* **Aphrodis'ian,** belonging to Aphrodite. [Gr. *aphrodisiakos—Aphrodītē,* the goddess of love.]

aphtha, *af'thä, n.* the disease thrush : a small whitish ulcer on the surface of a mucous membrane :—*pl.* **aph'thae** (-*thē*).—*adj.* **aph'thous.** [Gr. *aphtha,* mostly in pl. *aphthai.*]

aphyllous, *a-fil'əs, adj.* (*bot.*) without foliage leaves. —*n.* **aphyll'y.** [Gr. *a-,* priv., *phyllon,* a leaf.]

apian, *ā'pi-ən, adj.* relating to bees.—*adj.* **āpiarian** (-*ā'ri-ən*), relating to bee-hives or bee-keeping.— *ns.* **ā'piarist,** a bee-keeper; **ā'piary** (-*ər-i*), a place where bees are kept; **ā'piculture,** bee-keeping; **āpicul'turist.**—*adj.* **āpiv'orous,** feeding on bees. [L. *āpis,* a bee, *āpiārium,* a bee-house.]

apical, *ap',* or *āp'ik-l, adj.* of or at the apex.—*adv.* **ap'ically.**—*n.pl.* **ap'ices** (see **apex**).—*adj.* **apic-ūlate** (*ap-ik' ; bot.*) with a short sharp point on an otherwise blunt end. [See **apex.**]

Apician, *ə-pish'(y)ən, adj.* relating to *Apīcius,* the Roman epicure in the time of Tiberius : luxurious and expensive in diet.

apiece, *ə-pēs', adv.* for each piece, thing, or person : to each individually. [**a,** piece.]

aplacental, *ap-lə-sen'tl, adj.* without placenta. [Gr. *a-,* priv., and **placental.**]

aplanatic, *ap-lə-nat'ik, adj.* free from spherical aberration.—*ns.* **aplanatism** (*ə-plan'ə-tizm*); **ap-lan'ogamete, aplan'ospore,** a non-motile gamete, spore. [Gr. *a-,* priv., and *planaein,* to wander.]

aplomb, *a-plonˈ, n.* perpendicularity : self-possession, coolness. [Fr. *aplomb—à plomb,* according to plummet.]

aplustre, *a-plus'tər, n.* the stern ornament of an ancient ship, often a sheaf of volutes. [L. *āplustre, āplustre*—Gr. *aphlaston.*]

apnoea, *ap-nē'ä, n.* a cessation of breathing. [Gr. *apnoia—a-,* priv., *pno(i)ē,* breath.]

Apocalypse, *a-pok'əl-ips, n.* the last book of the New Testament, otherwise the Revelation of St. John: **apocalypse,** any book purporting to reveal the future or last things : a revelation or disclosure.—*adjs.* apocalyp'tic, -al.—*adv.* apocalypt'ically.—apocalyptic number, the number of the Beast, the mystical number 666, spoken of in the Apocalypse (xiii. 18), supposed to be the sum of the numerical values of the Greek and Hebrew letters of a name, for which many solutions have been offered. [Gr. *apokalypsis*, an uncovering—*apo*, from, *kalyptein*, to cover.]

apocarpous, *ap-ō-kär'pəs*, *adj.* (*bot.*) having the carpels separate. [Gr. *apo*, from, *karpos*, fruit.]

apocatastasis, *ap'ō-ka-tast'ə-sis*, *n.* (*theol.*) the final restitution of all things at the appearance of the Messiah—an idea extended by Origen to the final conversion and salvation of all created beings, the devil and his angels not excepted. [Gr. *apokatastasis*—*apo*-, again, back, *katastasis*, establishment ; cf. catastasis.]

apochromatic, *ap-ō-krō-mat'ik*, *adj.* relatively free from chromatic and spherical aberration.—*ns.* ap'ochromat, an apochromatic lens or instrument ; apochro'matism. [Gr. *apo*, from, *chrōma*, -*atos*, colour.]

apocope, *ə-pok'ō-pē*, *n.* the cutting off of the last sound or syllable of a word.—*v.t.* apoc'opate.—*n.* apocopā'tion. [Gr. *apokopē*—*apo*, off, *koptein*, to cut.]

apocrypha, *ə-pok'rif-ä*, *n.pl.* hidden or secret things : applied specially to certain books or parts of books included in the Septuagint and Vulgate translations of the Old Testament but not accepted as canonical by Jews or Protestants, and to later books (Apocrypha of the New Testament) never accepted as canonical or authoritative by any considerable part of the Christian Church :—*sing.* apoc'ryphon.—*adj.* apoc'ryphal, of the Apocrypha : of doubtful authority : spurious : fabulous. [Gr., things hidden—*apo*, from *kryptein*, to hide.]

Apocynum, *a-pos'i-nəm*, *n.* the dog-bane genus, giving name to the periwinkle family Apocynā'ceae, close akin to the asclepiads.—*adj.* apocynā'ceous. [Gr. *apokȳnon*, an asclepiad poisonous to dogs—*apo*, off, *kyōn*, *kynos*, a dog.]

apod, *ap'od*, apode, *ap'ōd*, *n.* an animal without feet or ventral fins.—*adjs.* ap'od, ap'odal, ap'ode, ap'odous. [Gr. *a*-, priv., *pous*, *podos*, a foot.]

apodeictic, *ap-ō-dīk'tik*, *adj.* necessarily true : demonstrative without demonstration : beyond contradiction.—apodeic'tical.—*adv.* apodeic'tically.—Also apodic'tic (or -*dik'*), etc. [Gr. *apodeiktikos*—*apodeiknynai* (*apo* and *deiknynai*), to demonstrate.]

apodosis, *ə-pod'ə-sis*, *n.* (*gram.*) the consequent clause in a conditional sentence : opp. *protasis.* [Gr. *apodosis*—*apo*, back, *didonai*, to give.]

apodyterium, *ap-ō-di-tēr'i-əm*, *n.* an undressing-room at an ancient bath. [Gr. *apodytērion*—*apodyein*, to undress—*apo*, from, *dyein*, to get into, put on.]

apogamy, *ə-pog'ə-mi*, *n.* (*bot.*) omission of the sexual process in the life-history—the sporophyte developing either from an unfertilised egg-cell or some other cell.—*adj.* apog'amous.—*adv.* apog'amously. [Gr. *apo*, from, *gamos*, marriage.]

apogee, *ap'ō-jē*, *n.* a heavenly body's point of greatest distance from the earth : (*obs.*) the sun's greatest meridional altitude : (*fig.*) culmination :—opp. *perigee.*—*adjs.* apogaeic (*jē'ik*), apogē'al, apogē'an ; apogeotrop'ic (*biol*), turning against the direction of gravity.—*adv.* apogeotrop'ically.—*n.* apogeotropism (-*ot'*). [Gr. *apogaion*—*apo*, from, *gaia*, or *gē*, the earth.]

apograph, *ap'ō-gräf*, *n.* an exact copy. [Gr. *apographon*, copy—*apo*, from, *graphein*, to write.]

apolaustic, *ə-ō-law'stik*, *adj.* devoted to the search of enjoyment.—*n.* the philosophy of the pleasurable. [Gr. *apolaustikos*—*apolauein*, to enjoy.]

Apollo, *ə-pol'ō*, *n.* the Greek sun-god, patron of poetry and music, medicine, archery, etc.—*adj.* Apollinarian (*-i-nā'ri-ən*), sacred to Apollo : of Apollinaris, (d. c. 390 A.D.) Bishop of Laodicea in Syria or his doctrine that in Christ the Logos took the place of a soul : of any other Apollinaris.—*n.a* follower of Apollinaris.—*ns.* Apollinā'rianism ;

Apollina'ris (water), a mineral water rich in sodium bicarbonate and carbon dioxide, from the Apollinaris spring in the Ahr valley.—*adj.* apoll'ine (-*in*), of Apollo.—*adjs.* Apollōnian (*ap-o-lō'ni-ən*), of Apollo : having the characteristics of Apollo (often opposed to *Dionysian*) : of the mathematician Apollonius of Perga (third century B.C.), or other Apollonius.—*n.* apollonicon (-*on'i-kən*), a gigantic organ, partly automatic. [Gr. *Apollōn, -ōnos*, L. *Apollō, -inis*.]

Apollyon, *a-pol'yən*, *n.* the destroyer or devil (Rev. ix. 11). [Gr. *apollyōn*, pres. p. of *apollyein*, to destroy utterly—*apo*-, indicating completeness, *ollyein*, or *ollynai*, to destroy.]

apologetic, *ə-pol-ə-jet'ik*, *adj.* (primarily) vindicatory, defensive : (now usu.) regretfully acknowledging fault.—*n.* a defence, vindication.—*adj.* apologet'ical.—*adv.* apologet'ically.—*n.* (*pl.* in form) apologet'ics, the defensive argument or method, esp. the defence of Christianity.—*n.* apologia (*ap-o-lō'ji-ä*), a written defence or vindication.—*v.i.* apologise (*ə-pol'ə-jīz*), to put forward a defence : (now usu.) to express regret for a fault.—*ns.* apol'ogist (-*jist*), a defender by argument ; apologue (*ap'ə-log*), a fable : esp. a beast-fable ; apology (*ə-pol'ə-ji*), a defence, justification, apologia : an explanation with expression of regret : a regretful acknowledgment of a fault : a poor specimen hardly worthy of its name : (*obs.*) an apologue. [Gr. *apologiā*, defence, *apologos*, a tale—*apo*, off, *logos*, speaking.]

apomixis, *ap-ō-miks'is*, *n.* omission of sexual fusion in reproduction : apogamy. [Gr. *apo*, from, *mixis* mingling, intercourse.]

apomorphine, *ap-ō-mor'fēn*, apomorphia, -*fi-ä*, *ns.* an alkaloid prepared by dehydrating morphine (morphia)—a rapid and powerful emetic. [Gr. *apo*, from, and morphine, morphia.]

aponeurosis, *ap-ō-nū-rō'sis*, *n.* a flat thin tendon.—*adj.* aponeurotic (-*rot'ik*). [Gr. *aponeurōsis*—*apo*, off, *neuron*, tendon.]

apoop, *ə-pōōp'*, *adv.* on the poop, astern.

apophlegmatic, *ap-ō-fleg-mat'ik*, *adj.* promoting the discharge of mucus.—*n.* an apophlegmatic agent. [Gr. *apophlegmatikos*—*apo*, off ; see phlegm.]

apophthegm, apothegm, *ap'ō-them*, *n.* a pithy saying, more short, pointed, and practical than the aphorism need be.—*adjs.* apophthegmat'ic, -al (-*theg*-). — *adv.* apophthegmat'ically. — *v.i.* apophtheg'matise, to speak in apophthegms.—*n.* apophtheg'matist. [Gr. *apophthegma*—*apo*, forth, and *phthengesthai*, to utter.]

apophyge, *a-pof'i-jē*, *n.* the curve where a column merges in its base or capital. [Gr. *apophygē*, escape.]

apophyllite, *a-pof'i-līt*, *ap-ō-fil'īt*, *n.* a mineral, hydrated calcium potassium silicate, that exfoliates on heating. [Gr. *apo*, off, *phyllon*, leaf.]

apophysis, *a-pof'i-sis*, -*zis*, *n.* (*biol*.) an outgrowth or protuberance, esp. on a bone, on the end of a pine-cone scale, on a moss stalk below the capsule : (*geol.*) a branch from a mass of igneous rock :—*pl.* apoph'ysēs. [Gr., offshoot—*apo*, off, *phyein*, to grow.]

apoplexy, *ap'ō-pleks-i*, *n.* sudden loss of sensation and motion, generally the result of haemorrhage in the brain or thrombosis.—*adjs.* apoplec'tic, -al.—*adv.* apoplec'tically.—*n.* ap'oplex (*arch.*), apoplexy.—*v.t.* (*Shak.*), to affect with apoplexy. [Gr. *apoplēxiā* — *apo*-, expressing completeness, *plēssein*, to strike.]

a-port, *ə-pōrt'*, *adv.* on or towards the port side.

aposematic, *ap-ō-sē-mat'ik*, *adj.* (of animal coloration) warning. [Gr. *apo*, away from, *sēma, sēmatos*, sign.]

aposiopesis, *ə-pos-i-ō-pē'sis*, *ap-ō-sī-ō-pē'sis*, *n.* a sudden breaking off in the midst of a sentence, e.g. Virgil, *Aeneid*, i. 135, 'Quos ego—' [Gr. *aposiōpēsis*—*apo*, off, and *siōpē*, silence.]

apositia, *ap-ō-sish'i-ä*, *n.* an aversion to food. [Gr. *apo*, away from, *sitos*, bread, food.]

apospory, *ə-pos'po-ri*, *n.* (*bot.*) omission of spore-formation in the life-history—the gametophyte,

developing vegetatively from the sporophyte.—*adj.*
apos'porous. [Gr. *apo*, away from, and **spore**.]

apostasy, *ə-post'ə-si*, *n*. abandonment of one's
religion, principles, or party: a revolt from
ecclesiastical obedience, from a religious profession, or from holy orders: defection.—*n.*
apost'ate (-*āt*, -*it*), one who has apostatised: a
renegade.—Also *adj.*—*adjs.* **apostatic** (*ap-ō-stat'-
ik*), -**al**.—*v.i.* **apostatise** (*ə-pos'ta-tīz*). [Gr. *apostasiā*,
a standing away—*apo*, from, *stasis*, a standing.]

a posteriori, *ā pos-tē-ri-ō'rī*, or -*te'* (L. *ā pos-ter-i-
ō-rē*) *adj.* applied to reasoning from experience,
from effect to cause: inductive: empirical: gained
from experience:—opp. to *a priori*.—Also *adv.*
[L. *ā*, from, *posteriōrī*, abl. of *posterior*, coming
after.]

apostil, **-ille**, *ə-pos'til*, *n*. a marginal note. [Fr.
apostille. See **postil**; origin of *a-* doubtful.]

apostle, *ə-pos'l*, *n*. one sent to preach the gospel:
esp. one of Christ's twelve: a first introducer of
Christianity in a country, e.g. Augustine, the
apostle of the English: a principal champion or
supporter of a new system, or of a cause: the
highest in the fourfold ministry of the Catholic
Apostolic Church: one of the twelve officials
forming a presiding high council in the Mormon
Church.—*ns.* **apos'tleship**; **apost'olate** (*ə-post'ə-
lāt*), the office of an apostle: leadership in a
propaganda.—*adjs.* **apostolic** (*ap-əs-tol'ik*), -**al**.—
ns. **apostol'icism** (-*i-sizm*), **apostolicity** (*ə-post-ə-
lis'i-ti*), the quality of being apostolic.—**Apostles'
Creed**, the oldest form of Christian creed that
exists, early ascribed to the apostles; **apostle
spoons**, silver spoons with handles ending in
figures of the apostles, once a common baptismal
present; **apostolical succession**, the derivation
of holy orders by unbroken chain of transmission
from the apostles through bishops—the theory of
the Catholic Church: the assumed succession of a
ministry so ordained to apostolic powers and
privileges; **apostolic fathers**, the immediate
disciples and fellow-labourers of the apostles,
more especially those who have left writings
(Barnabas, Clement of Rome, Ignatius, Hermas,
Polycarp); **apostolic see**, the see of Rome;
apostolic vicar, the cardinal representing the
Pope in extraordinary missions. [Gr. *apostolos*,
one sent away, *apo*, away, *stellein*, to send.]

apostrophe, *ə-pos'trə-fi*, *n*. (*rhet.*) a sudden turning
away from the ordinary course of a speech to
address some person or object present or absent,
explained by Quintilian as addressed to a person
present, but extended by modern use to the absent
or inanimate: (*bot.*) the ranging of chloroplasts
along the side walls of the cell in intense light.—
adj. **apostrophic** (*ap-ō-strof'ik*).—*v.t.* **apos'tro-
phise**, to address by apostrophe. [Gr. *apo*, from,
and *strophē*, a turning.]

apostrophe, *ə-pos'trə-fi*, *n*. a mark (') showing
(among other uses), the omission of a letter or
letters in a word: a sign of the modern Eng.
genitive or possessive case—orig. marking the
dropping of *e*. [Gr. *apostrophos*, turning away,
elision; confused with foregoing.]

apothecary, *ə-poth'i-kər-i*, *n*. (*arch.*) a druggist or
pharmacist—still a legal description for licentiates
of the Apothecaries' Society of London, or of the
Apothecaries' Hall of Ireland: (*obs.*) a medical
practitioner or an inferior branch, who often kept
a shop for drugs—**apothecaries' weight**, a
system for dispensing drugs based on the troy
ounce. [L.L. *apothēcarius*—Gr. *apothēkē*, a storehouse—*apo*, away, and *tithenai*, to place.]

apothecium, *ap-ō-thē's(h)i-əm*, *n*. an open fructification in Discomycetes and lichens:—*pl.* **apothe'-
cia**.—*adj.* **apothe'cial**. [Latinised dim. of Gr.
apothēkē, a storehouse.]

apothegm. See **apophthegm**.

apotheosis, *ə-po-thi-ō'sis*, *n*. a deification: glorification:—*pl.* **apotheo'ses** (-*sēz*).—*v.i.* **apoth'eosise**.
(or *ap-ō-thē'ō-sīz*). [Gr. *apotheōsis—apo-*, expressing completion, *theos*, a god.]

apotropaic, *ə-pot-rō-pā'ik*, or *ap'ō-trō-*, *adj.* turning
aside (or intended to turn aside) evil.—*adj.*

apot'ropous (*bot.*), anatropous with veneral raphe.
[Gr. *apo*, from, *tropē*, turning.]

apozem, *ap'ō-zem*, *n*. a decoction. [Gr. *apozema—
apo*, off, and *zeein*, to boil.]

appair, *ə-pār'*, an obs. form of **impair**.

appal, *ə-pawl'*, *v.i.* (*obs.*) to wax pale, flat, or
flavourless: (*Spens.*) to wax faint.—*v.t.* (*Spens.*) to
abate: to horrify, dismay:—*pr.p.* **appall'ing**;
pa.t. and *pa.p.* **appalled'**.—*adj.* **appall'ing**.—
adv. **appall'ingly**. [Perh. from O.Fr. *apalir,
apallir*, to wax pale, make pale. See **pall** and
pale.]

appanage, **apanage**, *ap'ən-ij*, *n*. a provision for
maintenance, esp. of a king's younger child:
dependent territory: a perquisite: an adjunct or
attribute.—*adj.* **ap(p)'anaged**, endowed with an
appanage. [Fr. *apanage*—L. *ad*, and *panis*, bread.]

apparatus, *ap-ə-rā'təs*, *n*. things prepared or
provided, material: set of instruments, tools,
natural organs, etc.; materials (as various readings)
for the critical study of a document (*apparatus
criticus*):—*pl.* **appara'tuses** or **appara'tus** (L.
appārātūs). [L. *appārātus*, -*ūs*—*ad*, to, *pārāre*,
-*ātum*, to prepare.]

apparel, *ə-par'l*, *v.t.* (*obs.*) to equip : to dress, clothe :
to adorn : (*pr.p.* **appar'elling**; *pa.t.* and *pa.p.*
appar'elled).—*n.* (*obs.*) equipment : (*arch.*) rigging :
attire, dress : (*arch.*) ecclesiastical embroidery.—
n. **appar'elment**. [O.Fr. *apareiller*. L *ad*, to,
par, equal.]

apparent, *ə-pār'ənt*, or -*par'*, *adj.* that may be seen :
obvious : conspicuous : seeming : obtained by
observation without correction, distinguished from
true or from *mean*.—*n.* (*Shak.*) heir-apparent.—*n.*
appar'ency, apparentness : position of being heir-
apparent.—*adv.* **appar'ently**.—*ns.* **appar'entness**.
[L. *appārēns*, -*ēntis*, pr.p. of *appārēre*; see **appear**.]

apparition, *ap-ə-rish'ən*, *n*. an appearing : an
appearance : reappearance after occultation : that
which appears : a phantom : a ghost.—*adj.*
appari'tional. [See **appear**.]

apparitor, *ə-par'i-tər*, *n*. (*obs.*) an officer in attendance on a court, to execute orders : still, such an
officer of an ecclesiastical court : a university
beadle : (*rare*) one who appears. [L. *appāritor*.
See **appear**.]

appay. Same as **apay**.

appeach, *ə-pēch'*, *v.t.* (*Shak.*) to accuse, censure, or
impeach.—*n.* **appeach'ment**. [O.Fr. *empechier ;*
see **impeach**.]

appeal, *ə-pēl'*, *v.i.* to call (upon), have recourse
(with *to*): to refer (to a witness or superior
authority): to make supplication or earnest request
(to a person for a thing): to resort for verification
or proof (to some principle or person): to make a
demand on the feelings that comes home: to
demand another judgment by a higher court: to
remove to another court.—*v.t.* (*arch.* except in
U.S.) to remove to a higher court: (*Spens.*, *Shak.*)
to accuse: (*Spens.*) to offer up (prayers).—*n.* (*Shak.*)
an impeachment: (*obs.*) a challenge: recourse: an
act of appealing: a supplication: removal of a
cause to a higher tribunal: an evocation of
sympathetic feeling.—*adjs.* **appeal'able**; **appeal'-
ing**, making an appeal: imploring: calling forth
sympathy.—*adv.* **appeal'ingly**.—*n.* **appeal'ingness**.—**appeal to the country**, to seek approval
by a general election; **Court of Appeal**, a section
of the English High Court of Justice; **Court of
Criminal Appeal**, an English Court created in
1907 for appeal in criminal cases. [O.Fr. *apeler*—
L. *appellāre*, -*ātum*, to address, call by name;
also to appeal to, impeach.]

appear, *ə-pēr'*, *v.i.* to become visible: to present
oneself formally before an authority or tribunal,
hence to act as the representative or counsel for
another: to come into view, to come before the
public, be published: to be manifest: to seem.—
ns. **appear'ance**, the act of appearing, *e.g.* in
court to prosecute or answer a charge: the publication of a book: the effect of appearing conspicu-
ously, show, parade: the condition of that which
appears, form, aspect: outward look or show: a
natural phenomenon: an apparition; **appear'er**.—
keep up appearances, to keep up an outward

show, often with intent to conceal absence of the inward reality; **put in an appearance**, to appear in person; **to all appearance(s)**, so far as appears to any one. [O.Fr. *apareir*—L. *appārēre*—*ad*, to, *pārēre*, *pāritum*, to come forth.]

appease, *ə-pēz'*, *v.t.* to pacify : to propitiate by concessions : to satisfy : to quiet : to allay.—*adj.* **appeas'able**.—*n.* **appease'ment**, the action of appeasing : the state of being appeased.—*adv.* **appeas'ingly**. [O.Fr. *apeser*, to bring to peace— L. *ad*. to, *pāx*, *pācis*, peace.]

appellant, *ə-pel'ənt*, *n.* one who appeals : one who impeaches : (*obs.*) a challenger to single combat : one who in the Jansenist controversy appealed against the bull Unigenitus (1713) to a pope 'better informed', or to a general council.—*adj.* **appell'ate**, relating to appeals.—*n.* **appellation** (*ap-ə-lā'shən*) that by which anything is called : name, esp. one attached to a particular person.— *adj.* **appellā'tional**.—*n.* **appell'ative** (*ə-pel'ə-tiv*), a common as distinguished from a proper name : a designation.—*adj.* common (as distinguished from proper) : of or pertaining to the giving of names.—*adv.* **appell'atively**. [L. *appellāre*, *-ātum*, to call.]

append, *ə-pend'*, *v.t.* to hang on (to something) : to add.—*n.* **append'age**, something appended : esp. one of the paired jointed structures of arthropods— antennae, jaws, legs.—*adj.* **append'ant**, attached, annexed, consequent.—*n.* an adjunct, quality.—*ns.* **appendicec'tomy** (*-dis-*), removal of the vermiform appendix (Gr. *ektomē*, cutting out); **appendici'tis**, inflammation of the vermiform appendix.—*adj.* **appendicular** (*ap-en-dik'ū-lər*), of the nature of, or belonging to, an appendix.—*n.* **Appendiculā'ria**, a genus of Ascidians that retains the larval vertebrate characters which are lost in the more or less degenerate sea-squirts.— *adj.* **appendic'ulate**, furnished with appendages.— *n.* **appendix** (*ə-pen'diks*), something appended or added : a supplement : an addition to a book or document, containing matter explanatory, but not essential to its completeness : (*anat.*) a process, prolongation, or projection : esp. the vermiform appendix :—*pl.* **append'ixes**, **append'ices** (*-sēz* *-siz*).—**appendix vermiformis**, or **vermiform appendix**, a blind process terminating the caecum. [L. *ad*, to, *pendēre*, to hang.]

apperception, *ap-ər-sep'shən*, *n.* the mind's perception of itself as a conscious agent : an act of voluntary consciousness, accompanied with self-consciousness : the assimilation of a new sense-experience to a mass already in the mind.—*adjs.* **appercep'tive**; **appercipient** (*-sip'i-ənt*).—*v.t.* **apperceive** (*-sēv'*). [L. *ad*, to, and **perception**, perceive.]

apperil(l), *ə-per'il*, *n.* (*Shak.*) peril. [L. *ad*, and **peril**.]

appertain, *ap-ər-tān'*, *v.i.* to belong, as a possession, a right, or attribute.—*n.* **appertain'ance**, appurtenance.—*adj.* **appertain'ing**, proper, appropriate (with *to*).—*n.* **appertain'ment** (*Shak.*), appurtenance.—*adj.* **apper'tinent**, appertaining.— *n.* (*Shak.*) appurtenance. [O.Fr. *apartenir*, *apertenir*—L. *ad*, to, *pertinēre*, to belong.]

appetent, *ap'i-tənt*, *adj.* eagerly desirous : craving : longing.—*ns.* **app'etence**, **app'etency**. [L. *appetēns*, *-entis*, pr.p. of *appetĕre*—*ad*, to, *petĕre*, to seek.]

appetite, *ap'i-tīt*, *n.* physical craving, accompanied with uneasy sensation (hunger, thirst, sex) : natural desire : inclination : desire for food : hunger (with *for*).—*adjs.* **app'etible**, attractive, desirable.—*v.t.* **app'etise**, to create or whet appetite in.—*ns.* **appetise'ment** (*Scott* **appeteeze'ment**); **app'etiser**, something to whet the appetite.—*adj.* **appetis'ing**.—*adv.* **appetis'ingly**.—*n.* **appetition**, (*-tish'ən*), direction of desire.—*adj.* **app'etitive** (or *a-pet'i-tiv*), having or giving an appetite. [O.Fr. *apetit*—L. *appetitus*—*appetĕre*; see foregoing.]

applaud, *ə-plawd'*, *v.t.* to express approbation of by clapping the hands or otherwise : to extol : to commend.—*v.i.* to clap the hands or otherwise express approval.—*n.* **applaud'er**.—*adj.* **applaud'ing**.—*adv.* **applaud'ingly**.—*n.* **applause**

(*-plawz'*), clapping of hands or other sign of approval : general approbation : loud praise : acclamation.—*adj.* **applausive** (*ə-plaws'iv*)—*adv.* **applaus'ively**. [L. *applaudĕre*, *-plausum*—*ad*, to, *plaudĕre*, to clap; cf. **explode**.]

apple, *ap'l*, *n.* the fruit of the apple-tree : extended to other fruits (as pineapple, custard-apple) or even galls (oak-apple) : the fruit of the forbidden tree in the Garden of Eden.—*ns.* **ap'ple-blight**, American blight, a woolly plant-louse that infests apple-trees; **app'le-blossom**; **app'le-cart**; **app'le-John** (*Shak.*), a variety of apple considered to be in perfection when shrivelled and withered—also **John app'le**; **app'le-pie**, a pie made with apples; **app'le-squire**, a prostitute's attendant : a man kept by a woman as concubine; **app'le-tree**, a tree (*Pyrus Malus*) of the rose family, close akin to the pear-tree; **app'le-wife**, **app'le-woman**, a woman who sells apples at a stall.—**apple of discord**, any cause of envy and contention, from the golden apple inscribed 'for the fairest', thrown among the gods by Eris, goddess of discord, and claimed by Aphrodite, Pallas, and Hera; **apple of Sodom** or **Dead Sea apple**, a fruit described by the ancients as fair to look upon but turning when touched to ashes, variously thought to be a gall, or the fruit of an asclepiad *Calotropis procera* : by botanists applied to the poisonous green-pulped fruit of *Solanum sodomaeum* : any fair but disappointing thing; **apple of the eye**, the pupil of the eye : something especially dear; **apple-pie bed**, a bed with sheets doubled and otherwise playfully made unavailable; **apple-pie order**, perfect order; **upset the apple-cart**, to throw all plans into confusion. [O.E. *æppel*, cf. Ger. *apfel* : O.N. *epli*; Ir. *abhal*; W. *afal*.]

appleringie, *ap'l-ring'i*, *n.* (*Scot.*) southernwood. (*Artemisia Abrotanum*.) [Anglo-Fr. *averoine*—L. *abrotanum*—Gr. *abrotanon*.]

Appleton layer, *ap'l-tən lā'ər*, an ionised region in the atmosphere, about 150 miles up, that acts as a reflector of radio waves. [From the physicist Sir Edward *Appleton*.]

appliqué, *a-plē'kā*, *-kā'*, Fr. *ä-plē-kä*, *n.* work applied to, or laid on, another material, either of metal-work or of lace or the like.—Also *adj.* [Pa.p. of Fr. *appliquer*, to apply.]

apply, *ə-plī'*, *v.t.* to lay or put in contact : to administer : to bring to bear : to put to use : to show the reference or relevance of : to assign : (*obs.*) to ascribe : to wield or ply : to direct : to devote (to a pursuit) : (*obs.*) to adapt : to lay on as appliqué : to cover with appliqué.—*v.i.* to suit or agree : to have recourse : to offer oneself as a candidate : to make or lodge a request : to be relevant : to hold good : to give close attention : (*obs.*) to betake oneself :—*pr.p.* **apply'ing**; *pa.t.* and *pa.p.* **applied'**.—*adj.* **appli'able**, applicable : (*obs.*) compliant.—*ns.* **appli'ance**, (*Shak.*) compliance : application : apparatus; **applicability** (*ap-li-ka-bil'i-ti*).—*adj.* **app'licable**, that may be applied : suitable.—*adv.* **app'licably**.—*n.* **appl'icant**, one who applies : a petitioner : a candidate for a post.—*adj.* **appl'icate**, put to practical use, applied.—*n.* **applicā'tion**, the act of applying, administering, or using : a thing applied : formal request, appeal, or petition : diligence : close thought or attention : employment, use of anything in special regard to something else : a bringing to bear : the lesson or moral of a fable : employment of a word with assignment of meaning : a kind of needlework, appliqué : (*obs.*) compliance.—*adj.* **app'licative**, put into actual use in regard to anything : practical.—*adj.* **app'licatory** (*-kə-tər-i*), having the property of applying.— *adj.* **applied** (*ə-plīd'*), placed with a flat surface against or close to something : turned to use.— **applied mathematics**, mathematics applied to observed facts of nature, or to practical life; **applied science**, science put to use for a purpose, generally utilitarian, other than its own end (opposed to *pure*). [O.Fr. *aplier*, and its source, L. *applicāre*, *-ātum*—*ad*, to, *plicāre*, to fold.]

appoggiatura, *äp-pod-jä-tōō'rä*, *n.* a leaning note— a grace-note written in smaller size taking its time

fāte, fär, ȧsk; mē, hėr (her); mīne; mōte; mūte; mōōn; dhen (then)

at the expense of the following note : a similar note with a stroke through the tail, played very quickly—an acciaccatura. [It.,—*appoggiare*, to lean upon. See **appui**.]

appoint, *ə-point'*, *v.t.* to fix : to settle : to assign, grant : to fix the time of : to engage to meet : to name to an office : to ordain : to prescribe : to destine, devote : to equip (*obs.* except in *pa.p.*) : (*Milt.*) to blame, arraign.—*adj.* **appoint'ed**, fixed : furnished.—*adj.* **appoint'ive** (*U.S.*), filled by appointment.—*n.* **appoint'ment**, engagement, esp. for a meeting : direction : nomination : an office to which one is or may be nominated : equipment : article of equipment : (*obs.*) allowance paid to a public officer : (*pl.*) equipments. [O.Fr. *apointer*—*à point*, to (the) point.]

apport, *ā-por'*, *ə-pōrt'*, *n.* (*psychical research*) the (supposed) transport of material objects without material agency : an object brought on the scene at a spiritualistic séance by no visible agency. [Fr.,—L. *apportāre*, to bring.]

apportion, *ə-pōr'shən*, *v.t.* to portion out : to divide in just shares : to adjust in due proportion.—*n.* **appor'tionment**. [L. *ad*, to, and **portion**.]

appose, *ə-pōz'*, *v.t.* to apply, e.g. a seal to a document : to place side by side. [Fr. *apposer*—L. *ad*, to, *pausāre*, to cease, rest ; confused and blended in meaning with words from *pōnĕre*, *pŏsĭtum*, to put.]

appose, *ə-pōz'*, *v.t.* to confront : (*Spens.*) to examine, question.—*ns.* **appos'er** ; **apposition** (*ap-ō-zish'-ən*), a public examination, a disputation, as on Speech Day at St. Paul's School, London. [Variant of **oppose**.]

apposite, *ap'ō-zit*, *adj.* apt : -o the purpose.—*adv.* **app'ositely**.—*ns.* **app'ositeness** ; **apposition** (*-zish'ən*), application : juxtaposition : (*gram.*) the position of a word parallel to another in syntactic relation : (*bot.*) growth by deposition on the surface. —*adjs.* **apposi'tional** ; **appositive** (*ə-poz'*), placed in apposition. [L. *appŏsĭtus*, pa.p. of *appōnĕre*, to put to—*ad*, to *pōnĕre*, to put.]

appraise, *ə-prāz'*, *v.t.* to set a price on : to value with a view to sale or (*U.S.*) payment of customs duty : to estimate the worth of.—*adj.* **apprais'able**. —*ns.* **apprais'al**, appraisement ; **appraise'ment**, a valuation : estimation of quality ; **apprais'er**, one who values property : one who estimates quality. [O.Fr. *apreiser*—L.L. *appretiāre*; see next word.]

appreciate, *ə-prē'shi-āt*, *v.t.* to estimate justly : to be fully sensible of all the good qualities in : to estimate highly : to perceive : to raise in value, to advance the quotation or price of, as opposed to *depreciate*.—*v.i.* to rise in value.—*adj.* **apprē'ciable**, capable of being estimated : perceptible.—*adv.* **apprē'ciably**.—*n.* **apprēcia'tion**, the act of setting a value, especially on a work of literature or art : just—and also favourable—estimation : a sympathetic critical essay : increase in value.—*adj.* **apprē'ciative**, characterised by, implying appreciation.—*n.* **apprē'ciātor**, one who appreciates, or estimates justly.—*adj.* **apprē'ciatory** (*-shyə-tər-i*). [L.L. *appretiāre*, *-ātum*—*ad*, to, and *pretium*, price.]

apprehend, *ap-ri-hend'*, *v.t.* to lay hold of : to arrest : to be conscious of by the senses : to lay hold of by the intellect : to catch the meaning of : to understand : to recognise : to consider : to look forward to, esp. with fear.—*n.* **apprehensibil'ity**. —*adj.* **apprehens'ible**.—*n.* **apprehen'sion**, act of apprehending or seizing : arrest : conscious perception : conception : ability to understand : fear.—*adj.* **apprehens'ive**, pertaining to the laying hold of sensuous and mental impressions : intelligent, clever : having an apprehension or notion : fearful : anticipative of something adverse.—*n.* **apprehens'iveness**. [L. *appraehendĕre*—*ad* to, *prae-hendĕre*, *-hēnsum*, to lay hold of.]

apprentice, *ə-prent'is*, *n.* one bound to another to learn a craft : a mere novice.—Also *adj.*—*v.t.* to bind as an apprentice.—*ns.* **apprent'icehood** (*Shak.*) apprenticeship ; **apprent'icement** ; **apprent'iceship**, the state of an apprentice : a term of practical training : hence, seven years.—**to serve apprenticeship**, to undergo the training of

an apprentice. [O.Fr. *aprentis*—*aprendre*, to learn—L. *appraehendĕre*. See **apprehend**.]

appress. See **adress**.

apprise, *ə-prīz'*, *v.t.* to give notice to : to inform. [Fr. *apprendre*, pa.p. *appris*. See **apprehend**.]

apprize, **-ise**, *ə-prīz'*, *v.t.* (*Scots law*) to put a selling price on : to value, appreciate : to have sold for payment of debt.—*n.* **appriz'er**, a creditor for whom an appraisal is made. [O.Fr. *appriser*, *aprisier*—*à*, to, and *prisier*, to price, prize. See **appraise**.]

approach, *ə-prōch'*, *v.t.* to bring near : to come near to in any sense : to come into personal relations or seek communication with : to resemble.—*v.i.* to come near.—*n.* a drawing near : in golf, play on drawing near the putting-green (also **approach-stroke, -shot**, etc.) : access : an avenue or means of access : approximation : (usually *pl.*) advances towards personal relations : (*pl.*) trenches, etc., by which besiegers strive to reach a fortress.—*n.* **approachabil'ity**.—*adj.* **approach'able**. [O.Fr. *aprochier*, L.L. *adpropiāre*—L. *ad*, to, *prope*, near.]

approbation, *ap-rō-bā'shən*, *n.* a formal sanction : approval : (*Shak.*) confirmation : (*Shak.*) probation. —*v.t.* **app'robate**, to approve authoritatively (*obs.* except in U.S.) : (*Scots law*) to accept as valid.—*adjs.* **app'robātive**, **approbatory** (*ap'rŏ-bə-tər-i*, or *ə-prō'*).—**approbate and reprobate** at once to accept and reject the same deed or instrument—forbidden by Scots law ; **on approbation** (*coll.* **appro**, *ap'rō*), subject to approbation : without obligation to buy. [L. *approbāre*, *-ātum*; see **approve**.]

approof, *ə-prōōf'*, *n.* trial, proof : sanction, approval. [O.Fr. *approve*; see **approve**.]

appropinque, *ap-rō-pingk'*, **appropinquate**, *-wāt*, *vs.t.* and *i.* (*arch.*) to approach.—*ns.* **appropinquā'-tion**, approach ; **appropinq'uity**, nearness. [L. *appropinquāre*, to approach—*ad*, to, *propinquus*—*prope*, near.]

appropriate, *ə-prō'pri-āt*, *v.t.* to make to be the private property of any one : to take to oneself as one's own : to filch : to set apart for a purpose, assign : to suit (with *to*).—*adj.* set apart for a purpose : peculiar : suitable.—*adv.* **approʼpriately**. —*ns.* **approʼpriateness** ; **approʼpriāʼtion**, the act of appropriating : the making over of a benefice to a monastery or other corporation : the assigning of supplies granted by parliament to particular specified objects : sometimes used loosely for *impropriation*.—*adj.* **approʼpriative**.—*ns.* **approʼpriativeness** ; **approʼpriātor**.—**appropriation bill**, a bill stating in some detail how the revenue is to be spent. [L. *appropriāre*, *-ātum*—*ad*, to, *proprius*, one's own; see **proper**.]

approve, *ə-prōōv'*, *v.t.* to show, demonstrate (esp. *refl.*) : to confirm : to sanction or ratify : to think well of, to be pleased with : to commend : (*Shak.*) to test : (*Shak.*) to convict.—*v.i.* to judge favourably, to be pleased (with *of*).—*adj.* **approv'able**, deserving approval.—*ns.* **approv'al**, **approv'ance** (*rare*), approbation ; **approv'er**, one who approves : (*law*) an accomplice in crime admitted to give evidence against a prisoner : an informer.—*adv.* **approv'ingly**.—**on approval**, **on approbation**. [O.Fr. *aprover*—L. *approbāre*—*ad*, to, and *probāre*, to test or try—*probus*, good.]

approve, *ə-prōōv'*, *v.t.* (*law*) to turn to one's profit, increase the value of. [O.Fr. *aproer*, *approuer*—*à*, to (L. *ad*), and *pro*, *prou*, advantage; see **prowess**; confused with **approve** (1).]

approximate, *ə-proks'im-āt*, *adj.* close together : nearest or next : approaching correctness (**very approximate**, very nearly exact; but by some used to mean very rough).—*v.t.* to bring near : to come or be near to.—*v.i.* to come near : to approach.—*adv.* **approx'imately**.—*n.* **approxima'tion**, an approach : a result in mathematics not rigorously exact, but so near the truth as to be sufficient for a given purpose.—*adj.* **approx'imative** (*-mā-tiv*, *mə-tiv*), approaching closely. [L. *approximāre*, *-ātum*—*ad*, to, *proximus*, nearest, superl. adj.—*prope*, near.]

appui, *ā-pwē*, *n.* support : the reciprocal action between horse's mouth and rider's hand.—*v.t.*

appui, appuy, to support : to place beside a *point d'appui:—pr.p.* **appuy'ing ;** *pa.t.* and *pa.p.* **appuied', appuyed'—point d'appui** (*pwan'-dā̆-pwē*), a position of strength or support in a line of defences : **a** prop : a fulcrum. [Fr.,—O.Fr. *apuyer*—L.L. *appodiāre*—L. *ad,* to, *pod̆um,* support.]

appulse, *ə-puls',* n. a striking against something : (*astron.; obs.*) a coming to conjunction or to the meridian. [L. *appulsus, -ūs—appellĕre—ad,* towards, *pellĕre,* to drive.]

appurtenance, *ə-pur'tən-əns,* n. that which appertains : an appendage or accessory : (*law*) a right belonging to a property.—*adj.* and n. **appur'tenant.** [O.Fr. *apurtenance.* See **appertain.**]

apricate, *ap'ri-kāt, v.i.* to bask in the sun.—*v.t.* to expose to sunlight.—n. **aprica'tion.** [L. *aprīcārī,* to bask in the sun, *aprīcus,* open to the sun.]

apricot, *ā'pri-kot, -kət,* or *a',* formerly **apricock, -kok,** n. a fruit of the plum genus, roundish, pubescent, orange-coloured, of a rich aromatic flavour : its colour : the tree that bears it. [Port. *albricoque*—Ar. *al-birqūq—al,* the, Late Gr. *praikokion*—L. *praecoquum* or *praecox,* early ripe ; the form is perh. due to a fancied connection with L. *aprīcus,* sunny ; assimilated to Fr. *abricot;* see **precocious.**]

April, *ā'pril, -prəl,* n. the fourth month of the year. —*ns.* **A'pril-fish,** an April-fool's errand or hoax (Fr. *poisson* d'Avril); **A'pril-fool,** one sent upon a bootless errand on the first of April (in Scotland a *gowk*).—*adjs.* **April'ian, A'prilish.** [L. *Aprīlis.*]

a priori, *ā prī-ō'rī.* L. *ā prē-or'ē,* a term applied to reasoning from what is prior, logically or chronologically, *e.g.* reasoning from cause to effect; from a general principle to its consequences; even from observed fact to another fact or principle not observed, or to arguing from pre-existing knowledge, or even cherished prejudices; (*Kant*) from the forms of cognition independent of experience.— *ns.* **apriō'rism, aprioriry** (*-or'i-ti*); **apriō'rist,** one who believes in Kant's view of a priori cognition. [L. *ā,* from, *priōrī* (abl.), preceding.]

apron, *ā'prən,* n. a cloth or piece of leather or the like worn in front : an English bishop's short cassock : anything resembling an apron in shape or use, as a leg-covering in an open vehicle : a timber behind the stem of a ship : that part of the stage in front of the proscenium arch or curtain, originally projecting (also **a'pron-stage**): the ground-surface at the entrance to a hangar, a lock, etc.—*v.t.* to cover, as with an apron.—*adj.* **a'proned.**—*ns.* **a'pron-man** (*Shak.*), a man who wears an apron, a mechanic; **a'pron-string,** a string by which an apron is tied.—**tied to a woman's apron-strings,** bound as a child to its mother. [M.E. *napron*—O.Fr. *naperon—nappe,* cloth, table-cloth—L. *mappa,* a napkin (*an apron* from a *napron;* cf. **adder**).]

apropos, *ā-prō-pō', -prə-,* adv. to the purpose : appropriately : in reference (with *of*).—*adj.* to the purpose. [Fr. *à propos.* See **propose, purpose.**]

apse, *aps,* n. a semicircular or polygonal recess, esp. at the east end of a church choir—where, in the Roman basilica, stood the praetor's chair : an apsis. —*adj.* **ap'sidal,** of an apse or apsis.—*ns.* **apsid'iole,** a subsidiary apse; **aps'is,** in an orbit, the point of greatest or least distance from the central body : an apse :—*pl.* **aps'ides** (L. *apsīdēs*).—*adj.* **ap'sidal.** [L. *apsis, -īdis*—Gr. *hapsis* (*apsis*), *-ĭdos,* a felloe, wheel, arch, loop.—*haptein,* to fit, connect. See **apt.**]

apt, *apt, adj.* fitting: fit: suitable: apposite: tending : liable : ready or prone : open to impressions, ready to learn (often with *at*): (*U.S.*) likely.—*v.t.* (*obs.*) to fit.—n. **ap'titude,** fitness: tendency : natural ability, readiness to learn (with *for*).—*adv.* **apt'ly.**—n. **apt'ness.** [L. *aptus,* fit, suitable.]

apterous, *ap'tər-əs, adj.* wingless.—*adj.* **ap'teral,** wingless : without side columns.—n. **apterium** (*ap-tē'ri-əm*) a bare patch on a bird's skin :—*pl.* **apte'ria.** [Gr. *a-,* priv., *pteron,* feather, wing, side-wall.]

Apteryx, *ap'tər-iks,* n. the kiwi, a genus of birds found in New Zealand, wingless and tailless, reddish-brown, about the size of a large hen.— *n.pl.* **Apterygota** (*ap-ter-i-gō'tä*), a class of primitive insects, wingless, without metamorphosis (bristle-tails, spring-tails). [Gr. *a-,* priv., *pteryx, -ygos,* wing.]

aptote, *ap'tōt,* n. an indeclinable noun.—*adj.* **aptotic** (*-tot'ik*), uninflected. [Gr. *aptōtos—a-,* priv., *ptōsis,* case.]

apyrexia, *ap-i-reks'i-ā,* n. intermission of fever.— *adj.* **apyret'ik.** [Gr. *apyrexiā—a-,* priv., *pyressein,* to be feverish.]

aqua, *ak'wə,* n. (L.) water.—*ns.* **aqua-for'tis,** nitric acid : etching with nitric acid (L. *fortis,* strong); **aquafort'ist,** an etcher or engraver who uses aqua-fortis; **a'qua-mirab'ilis,** a preparation distilled from cloves, nutmeg, ginger, and spirit of wine (L. *mīrābilis,* wonderful); **a'qua-regia** (*rē'jyā,* L. *rā'gi-ā*), a mixture of nitric and hydrochloric acids, which dissolves the royal (L. *rēgius, -a, -um*) metal, gold; **a'qua Tofana** (*tō-fä'nā*), a secret poison (probably arsenical) made by a 17th-cent. Sicilian woman Tofana; **a'qua-vi'tae** (*vī'tē*; L. *vē'tī*), alcohol : brandy, whisky, etc. (L. *vītae,* of life). [L. *aqua,* water.]

aquamarine, *ak-wə-mə-rēn', n.* a pale green beryl. —*adj.* bluish-green. [L. *aqua marīna,* sea water— *mare,* the sea.]

aquarelle, *ak-wə-rel' n.* water-colour painting : a painting in water-colours.—n. **aquarell'ist.** [Fr., —It. *acquerella, acquarella—acqua*—L. *aqua.*]

aquarium, *ə-kwā'ri-əm,* n. a tank or (a building containing) a series of tanks for keeping aquatic animals or plants :—*pl.* **aqua'riums, aquā'ria.**— *adj.* **aquā'rian.**—n. one who keeps an aquarium.— *ns.* **aquā'riist, aquā'rist,** an aquarian.—n. **Aquā'rius,** the Water-bearer, a sign of the zodiac, and a constellation once coincident with it. [L. *aquārius, -a, -um,* adj.—*aqua,* water.]

aquatic, *ə-kwat'ik, adj.* living, growing, practising sports, taking place, in or on water.—n. an aquatic plant, animal, or sportsman : (in *pl.*) water sports. [L. *aquaticus—aqua,* water.]

aquatint, *ak'wə-tint,* n. a mode of etching on copper with resin and nitric acid.—Also **aquatint'a.**—*v.t.* and *v.i.* **a'quatint,** to engrave in aquatint. [It. *acqua tinta,* dyed water—L. *aqua,* water, and *tingĕre, tinctum,* to dye.]

aqueduct, *ak'wi-dukt,* n. an artificial channel or pipe for conveying water, most commonly understood to mean a bridge across a valley : a bridge carrying a canal : a small passage in an animal body. [L. *aqua,* water, *ducĕre, ductum,* to lead.]

aqueous, *ā'kwi-əs, adj.* of water : watery : deposited by water.—**aqueous humour,** the watery fluid between the cornea and the lens in the eye. [L. *aqua,* water.]

Aquifoliaceae, *ak-wi-fō-li-ā'si-ē, n.pl.* the holly family.—*adj.* **aquifoliā'ceous** (*-shəs*). [L. *aquifolium,* holly—*acus, -ūs,* needle, *folium,* leaf.]

Aquila, *ak'wi-lä,* n. the golden eagle genus : the Eagle, a constellation north of Sagittarius.—*adj.* **aq'uiline** (*-līn*), of the eagle : hooked like an eagle's bill. [L. *aquila,* eagle.]

Aquilegia, *ak-wi-lē'j(y)ā,* n. the columbine genus. [Prob. L. *aquila,* eagle.]

Aquilon, *ak'wi-lon,* n. (*Shak.*) the north wind. [L. *aquilō, -ōnis.*]

ar, *är,* n. the eighteenth letter of the alphabet (**r**).

Arab, *ar'əb,* n. one of the Semitic people inhabiting Arabia and neighbouring countries : an Arabian horse : a neglected or homeless boy or girl (usually **street** or **city arab**).—*adj.* **Arabian.**—*adj.* **Arabian** (*ə-rā'bi-ən, -byən*), of or belonging to Arabia or the Arabs.—n. a native of Arabia.—*adj.* **Arabic** (*ar'əb-ik*), relating to Arabia, or to its language.— n. the language of the Arabs : (see also **gum**).—*ns.* **Ar'abism,** an Arabic idiom; **Ar'abist,** one skilled in the Arabic language or literature; **Araby,** a poetical form of *Arabia.*—**Arabian,** or **Arabic numerals,** the numerals in ordinary use in arithmetic, transmitted from India to Europe by the Arabs. [L. *Arabs, Arabis*—Gr. *Araps, Arabos.*]

araba, *är-ä′bä*, *n.* a heavy screened wagon used by the Tatars and others.—Also **ar′ba, arō′ba**. [Ar. and Pers. *'arābah*.]

arabesque, *ar-ə-besk′*, *adj.* after the manner of Arabian designs.—*n.* a fantastic painted or sculptured ornament among the Spanish Moors, consisting of foliage and other forms curiously intertwined : a musical composition with analogous continuity : a posture in ballet dancing in which one leg is stretched out backwards parallel with the ground and the body is bent forward from the hips. —*adj.* **arabesqued′**, ornamented with arabesques. [Fr.,—It. *arabesco; -esco* corresponding to Eng. *-ish*.]

arabin, *ar′əb-in*, *n.* the essential principle of gum-arabic (see **gum**).—**ar′abinose** (or *-ab′*) a sugar got from arabin. (See **Arab**.)

Arabis, *ar′ə-bis*, *n.* the rock-cress genus of Cruciferae. [L.L. *Arabis*, Arabian, perhaps from its dry habitats.]

arable, *ar′ə-bl*, *adj.* fit for ploughing or tillage. [L. *arābilis—arāre*, cog. with Gr. *aroein*, to plough, O.E. *erian*, Eng. **ear** (v.t.), Ir. *araim*.]

Araceae, araceous. See **Arum**.

Arachis, *ar′ə-kis*, *n.* a Brazilian genus of the pea family, including the monkey-nut, ground-nut, or pea-nut, which ripens its pods underground. [Gr. *arachos* and *arakis*, names of leguminous plants.]

Arachnida, *a-rak′ni-dä*, *n.pl.* a class of Arthropoda, embracing spiders, scorpions, mites, etc.—*n.* **arach′nid**, any member of the class.—*n.* and *adj.* **arach′nidan**.—*adj.* **arach′noid**, like a cobweb.—*n.* the arachnoid membrane.—*adjs.* **arachnoi′dal, arachnolog′ical**.—*ns.* **arachnol′ogist**, one who studies the Arachnida; **arachnol′ogy**.—**arachnoid membrane**, one of the three coverings of the brain and spinal cord, between the dura-mater and the pia-mater, non-vascular, transparent, thin. [Gr. *arachnē*, spider.]

araeometer, areometer, *ar-i-om′i-tər*, *n.* an instrument for determining specific gravity, a hydrometer.—*n.* **araeom′etry**, the measuring of specific gravity.—*adjs.* **araeometric, -al** (*-met′*). [Gr. *araios*, thin, *metron*, measure.]

araeostyle, *a-rē′ō-stīl*, *adj.* having columns four diameters or more apart.—*n.* a building or colonnade so built.—*adj.* **araeosystyle** (*-sis′tīl*), alternately araeostyle and systyle.—Also *n.* [Gr. *araios*, thin, sparse, *stŷlos*, column.]

aragonite, *ar′ə-gə-nīt, ə-rag′ə-nīt*, *n.* an ortho-rhombic mineral composed of calcium carbonate. [*Aragon*, in Spain.]

araise, arayse, *ə-rāz′*, *v.t.* (*Shak.*) to raise from the dead. [Pfx. *a-*, and **raise**.]

Aralia, *ə-rā′li-ä*, *n.* a genus of the ivy family, Araliä′ceae, much grown as decorative plants.— *adj.* **araliä′ceous**. [Perh. American Indian origin.]

Aramaic, *ar-ə-mā′ik*, *adj.* relating to Aramaea, the country to the north-east of Palestine, or to its language—also **Aramaean** (*-mē′ən*).—*n.* **Aramā′ism**, an Aramaic idiom. [Gr. *Aramaios*.]

Aranea, *a-rā′ni-ä*, *n.* the garden-spider genus (otherwise *Epeira*):—*ns.pl.* **Arā′neae** (*-ē*), **Araneida** (*ar-ə-nē′i-dä*), **-idae** (*-dē*), spiders as a class or order.—*n.* **arā′neid** (*-ni-id*), a spider.—*adj.* **arā′neous**, cobwebby. [L. *arānea*, spider.]

arapaima, *ar-ə-pī′mä*, *n.* the pirarucú (*Arapaima*, or *Sudis, gigas;* fam. Osteoglossidae), a gigantic South American river-fish, chief food-fish of the Amazon, reaching sometimes 4 cwt. [Tupí origin.]

arapunga, *ar-ə-pung′gä*, *n.* the campanero or South American bell-bird. [Tupi *araponga*.]

arar, *är′är*, *n.* the sandarac tree. [Moroccan name.]

araroba, *ä-rä-rō′bä*, *n.* Goa powder, got from cavities in a papilionaceous Brazilian tree (*Andira Araroba*), cultivated in Goa, yielding chrysarobin. [Prob. Tupí.]

Araucaria, *ar-aw-kā′ri-ä*, *n.* the monkey-puzzle genus, coniferous trees of S. America and Australasia. [*Arauco*, in S. Chile.]

arba. See **araba**.

arbalest, *är′bəl-est*, *n.* a crossbow : a cross-staff.— Also **ar′balist, ar′blast, ar′cubalist**.—*ns.* **ar′-balester, ar′balister, ar′blaster**, a crossbowman.

[L. *arcuballista—arcus*, bow, *ballista* (see **ballista**); partly through O.E. *arblast*—O.Fr. *arbaleste*.]

arbiter, *är′bi-tər*, *n.* a judge : an umpire : one chosen by parties to decide between them : one who has absolute control :—*fem.* **ar′bitress**.— *adj.* **ar′bitrable**.—*n.* **ar′bitrage** (*-trij*), arbitration : traffic in bills of exchange or stocks to profit by different prices in different markets.—*adj.* **ar′bitral** (*Scots law*).—*n.* **arbit′rament** (now less usu. **arbit′rement**), the decision of an arbiter : determination : power of decision.—*v.i.* and *v.t.* **ar′bitrate**, to decide, determine : to refer to arbitration : to judge as arbiter.—*ns.* **arbitrā′tion**, (submission to) the decision of an arbiter; **ar′bitrātor**, arbiter : —*fem.* **ar′bitrātrix**. [L. *arbiter*.]

arbitrary, *är′bi-trər-i*, *adj.* not bound by rules : despotic, absolute : capricious : arising from accident rather than from rule.—*adv.* **ar′bitrarily**.— *n.* **ar′bitrariness**. [L. *arbitrārius—arbiter*.]

arblast. See **arbalest**.

arbor, *är′bər*, *n.* (L.) a tree : a shaft or beam : a spindle or axis.—*adjs.* **arborā′ceous**, tree-like : wooded; **arboreal** (*är-bō′ri-əl*), of, of the nature of, trees : tree-dwelling; **arbō′reous**, of or belonging to trees : tree-like : in the form of a tree : wooded.— *ns.* **arboresc′ence, arborīsā′tion**, tree-like growth.—*adj.* **arboresc′ent**, growing, formed, branched, like a tree : approaching the character of a tree.—*ns.* **ar′boret** (*obs.*) shrubbery : arboretum : (*Milt.*) a little tree, shrub; **arborē′tum** (L. *är-bor-ā′toom*), a botanic garden of trees :—*pl.* **arborē′ta**.—*adj.* **arboricul′tural**.—*ns.* **ar′boriculture**, forestry, the culture of trees, esp. timber-trees; **arboricul′turist; ar′borist**, one who studies trees.—*adj.* **ar′borous**, of, or formed by, trees.— **Arbor Day**, in some countries a day yearly set apart for the general planting of trees; **arbor vitae** (L., tree of life), a coniferous genus (*Thuja*) akin to cypress : a tree-like appearance seen when the human cerebellum is cut vertically. [L. *arbor*, tree.]

arbour, *är′bər*, *n.* (*obs.*) a grass-plot, garden, herb-garden, or orchard : (*obs.*) a grassy seat : hence, a retreat or bower of trees or climbing plants : (*Milt.*) a shaded walk.—*adj.* **ar′boured**. [A.F. *herber*—L. *herbārium—herba*, grass, herb; meaning changed through confusion with L. *arbor*, tree.]

Arbutus, *ar′bū-təs* (also *-bū′*), *n.* the strawberry-tree genus.—*n.* **ar′bute**, the strawberry-tree or other Arbutus. [L. *arbūtus*.]

arc, *ärk*, *n.* a part of the circumference of a circle or other curve : (*Milt.*) an arch : a luminous discharge of electricity through an ionised gas.—*ns.* **arc-lamp, arc-light**, a lamp whose source of light is an electric arc between carbon electrodes. [L. *arcus*, a bow.]

arcade, *ärk-ād′*, *n.* a row of arches, open or closed, on columns or pilasters : a walk arched over : a long arched gallery lined with shops.—*adj.* **arcād′ed**.—*n.* **arcād′ing**. [Fr.,—L.L. *arcāta*, arched; see **arch**.]

Arcadian, *ärk-ād′i-ən*, *adj.* of *Arcadia* (*poet.* **Arcady**, *ärk′ə-di*), a district in Greece whose people were primitive in manners and given to music and dancing : pastoral : simple, innocent.— Also *n.*—*n.* **Arcād′ianism**.

arcanum, *ärk-ān′əm*, *n.* a secret : a mystery : a secret remedy or elixir :—*pl.* **arcan′a**.—*adj.* **arcane′** (*rare*). [L., neut. of *arcānus—arca*, a chest.]

arch, *ärch*, *n.* a structure of wedge-shaped stones or other pieces supporting each other by mutual pressure and able to sustain a superincumbent weight : anything of like form : an archway.—*v.t.* to cover or furnish with an arch.—*v.t.* and *v.i.* to bend in the form of an arch.—*adj.* **arched**, having the form of an arch : covered with an arch.— *ns.* **arch′let**, a little arch; **arch′way**, an arched or vaulted passage.—*adv.* **arch′wise**, in the manner of an arch.—(**Court of**) **Arches**, the ecclesiastical court of appeal for the province of Canterbury, formerly held at the church of St. Mary-le-Bow (or 'of the Arches', from the arches that support its steeple). [O.Fr. *arche*—L. *arcus*, bow (as if *arca*).]

arch, *ärch, adj.* (*Shak.*) chief, principal : (*Bunyan*) finished, accomplished, pre-eminent, esp. in evil : cunning : waggish : roguish : shrewd.—*n.* (*Shak.*) chief.—*adv.* **arch'ly.**—*n.* **arch'ness.** [From the prefix *arch-*, in words like *arch*-rogue, etc.]

arch-, *ärch- (ärk-* in direct borrowings from Greek), *pfx.* first or chief : often an intensive in an odious sense.—*ns.* **arch'-druid,** a chief or presiding druid ; **arch'-en'emy,** a chief enemy : Satan—also **arch'-fel'on, arch'-fiend', arch'-foe' ; arch'-flā'men,** a chief flamen or priest ; **arch'-her'etic,** a leader of heresy ; **arch'-mock'** (*Shak.*), the height of mockery ; **arch'-pī'rate,** a chief pirate : **arch'-pō'et,** a chief poet : (*obs.*) a poet-laureate ; **arch'-prel'ate,** a chief prelate ; **arch'-priest',** a chief priest : in early times, a kind of vicar to the bishop—later, a rural dean : a superior appointed by the Pope to govern the secular priests sent into England from the foreign seminaries during the period 1598-1621 ; **arch'-trait'or,** a chief traitor, greatest of traitors, sometimes applied esp. to the devil, or to Judas ; **arch'-vill'ain,** one supremely villainous. [O.E. *arce-, ærce-*, through L. from Gr. *archi- —archos*, chief.]

Archaean, *är-kē'ən, adj.* and *n.* (*geol.*) Pre-Cambrian. [Gr. *archaios*, ancient—*archē*, beginning.]

archaeology, *ärk-i-ol'ə-ji, n.* the scientific study of human antiquities.—*adj.* **archaeological** (*-əloj'i-kl*).—*adv.* **archaeolog'ically.**—*n.* **archaeol'ogist.** [Gr. *archaios*, ancient—*archē*, beginning, *logos*, discourse.]

Archaeopteryx, *är-ki-op'tər-iks, n.* a Jurassic fossil bird, with a long bony tail. [Gr. *archaios*, ancient, *pteryx*, wing.]

Archaeornithes, *är-ki-or-nī'thēz, n.pl.* the Saururae, or primitive reptile-like birds, the Archaeopteryx and its kin. [Gr. *archaios*, ancient, *ornīthes*, pl. of *ornīs, ornis*, bird.]

archaic, *är-kā'ik, adj.* ancient : savouring of the past : not absolutely obsolete but no longer in general use : old-fashioned.—*adv.* **archā'ically.**—*n.* **archā'icism.**—*v.i.* **ar'chāise,** to imitate the archaic.—*ns.* **ar'chāiser ; ar'chāism,** inclination to archaise : an archaic word or phrase; **ar'chāist.** —*adj.* **archāis'tic,** affectedly or imitatively archaic. [Gr. *archaikos*—*archaios*, ancient—*archē*, beginning.]

archangel, *ärk'ān-jl,* or *-ān', n.* an angel of the highest order : garden angelica : dead-nettle : a kind of pigeon.—*adj.* **archangelic** (*-an-jel'*). [Gr. *archangelos*—*archos*, chief, *angelos*, messenger.]

archbishop, *ärch-bish'əp,* or *ärch', n.* a metropolitan bishop who superintends the bishops in his province, and also exercises episcopal authority in his own diocese.—*n.* **archbish'opric.** [O.E. *ærcebiscop ;* see **arch-**, and **bishop.**]

arch-chimic, *ärch-kim'ik, adj.* (*Milt.*) supreme in alchemy. [See **arch-, chemic.**]

archdeacon, *ärch-dē'kn,* or *ärch', n.* a chief deacon : the ecclesiastical dignitary having the chief supervision of a diocese or part of it, next under the bishop—the 'bishop's eye'.—*ns.* **archdeac'onry,** the office, jurisdiction, or residence of an archdeacon; **archdeac'onship,** the office of an archdeacon. [O.E. *ærcediacon ;* see **arch-, deacon.**]

archdiocese, *arch-dī'ə-sēs, n.* an archbishop's diocese. [**arch-**, chief, and **diocese.**]

archduke, *ärch'dūk, ärch'dūk', n.* (*hist.*) the title of certain early reigning dukes of importance, and of princes of the imperial house of Austria :—*fem.* **archduchess** (*ärch'duch'is*).—*adj.* **arch'dū'cal.**— *ns.* **arch'duch'y, arch'duke'dom.** [**arch-**, chief, and **duke.**]

archegonium, *ärk-i-gō'ni-əm, n.* the flask-shaped female reproductive organ of mosses and ferns, and (in a reduced form) of flowering plants :—*pl.* **archego'nia.**—*adjs.* **archego'nial ; archego'niate,** having archegonia :—*n.pl.* **Archegoniā'tae,** a main division of the vegetable kingdom, bryophytes and pteridophytes. [Gr. *archegonos*, founder of a race.]

archenteron, *ärk-en'tər-on, n.* in the embryo, the primitive gut. [Gr. pfx. *arch-, enteron*, gut.]

archer, *ärch'ər, n.* one who shoots with a bow and arrows :—*fem.* **arch'eress.**—*ns.* **arch'er-fish,** an acanthopterygious fish of India that catches insects by shooting water at them from its mouth; **arch'ery,** the art or sport of shooting with the bow : a company of archers. [O.Fr. *archier—L. arcārius—arcus*, a bow.]

archetype, *ärk'i-tīp, n.* the original pattern or model, prototype.—*adj.* **archetyp'al.** [Gr. *archetypon, arche-, archi-*, and *typos*, a model.]

archgenethliac, *ärch'je-neth'li-ak, n.* (*Browning*) in derogatory sense) greatest of genethliacs or astrologers.

Archibald, *är'chi-bəld,* **Archie,** *är'chi, ns.* (*mil. slang*) an anti-aircraft gun.

Archichlamydeae, *är-ki-klə-mid'i-ē, n.pl.* (*bot.*) one of the main divisions of the Dicotyledons, in which the petals, if present, are in general not united. [Gr. pfx. *archi-* denoting primitiveness, *chlamys, -dos*, mantle.]

archidiaconal, *är-ki-dī-ak'ə-nl, adj.* of an archdeacon. [Gr. *archidiākonos ;* see **deacon.**]

archiepiscopal, *är-ki-i-pis'kə-pl, adj.* of an archbishop.—*ns.* **archiepis'copacy, archiepis'copate,** dignity or province of an archbishop— **archiepiscipal cross,** a patriarchal cross. [Gr. *archiepiskopos*, archbishop.]

archil, *är'chil, -kil, n.* a red or violet dye made from various lichens : a lichen yielding it, esp. species of Roccella.—Also **orchel** (*or'chəl*), **orchella** (*-chel'ä*), or **orchil, orchill'a.**—*n.* **orchill'a-weed,** an archil lichen. [O.Fr. *orchel, orseil* (Fr. *orseille*)—It. *orcello*, origin undetermined.]

Archilochian, *är-ki-lō'ki-ən, adj.* of *Archilōchus* (Gr. *Archilōchos*) of Paros (*c.* 714-676 B.C.), Greek lyric poet and lampooner, reputed originator of iambic metre, proverbially bitter.—*n.* an Archilochian verse—dactylic tetrameter catalectic, dactylic trimeter catalectic (*lesser Archilochian*), or dactylic tetrameter combined with trochaic tripody (*greater Archilochian*).

archilowe, *är'hhi-lō, n.* (*obs. Scot.*) a treat in return. [Origin unknown.]

archimage, *är'ki-māj, n.* a chief magician or enchanter. [Gr. *archi-*, chief, *magos*, a magician; older than Spenser's Archimago.]

archimandrite, *är-ki-man'drīt, n.* in the Greek Church, an abbot. [Late Gr. *archimandrītēs*— pfx. *archi-*, first, and *mandrā*, an enclosure, a monastery.]

Archimedean, *ärk-i-mē-dē'ən,* or *-mē'di-ən, adj.* pertaining to *Archimedes*, a celebrated Greek mathematician of Syracuse (*c.* 287-212 B.C.).— **Archimedean screw,** a machine for raising water, in its simplest form a tube bent spirally turning on its axis ; **Archimedean spiral,** the curve described by a point moving uniformly along a uniformly revolving radius vector, its polar equation being $r = a\theta$; **principle of Archimedes,** that a body immersed in a fluid weighs less than it does *in vacuo* by the weight of the fluid it displaces.

Archipelago, *ärk-i-pel'ə-gō, n.* the Aegean Sea : **archipelago,** a sea abounding in islands, hence a group of islands :—*pl.* **archipel'ago(e)s.**—*adj.* **archipelagic** (*-pi-laj'ik*). [An Italian compound *arcipelago* from Gr. *archi-*, chief, *pelagos*, sea, with pfx. restored to Gr. form.]

architect, *ärk'i-tekt, n.* a designer of buildings : a designer of ships (*naval architect*) : a maker : a contriver.—*adjs.* **architecton'ic,** pertaining to architecture : constructive : controlling, directing : pertaining to the arrangement of knowledge.— *n.* (often in *pl.* form) the science of architecture : the systematic arrangement of knowledge.—*adj.* **architecton'ical.**—*adv.* **architecton'ically.**— *adj.* **architect'ural** (*-yər-əl*).—*n.* **architect'ure,** the art or science of building : structure : in specific sense, one of the fine arts, the art of designing buildings : style of building. [Gr. *architektōn*, master-builder—*archi-*, chief, and *tektōn*, a builder.]

architrave, *ärk'i-trāv, n.* (*archit.*) the lowest division of the entablature resting immediately on the abacus of the column : collective name for the various parts, jambs, lintels, etc., that surround a

door or window: moulding round an arch.—
adj. **arch′itraved**. [It. *architrave*—Gr. *archi*-,
chief, and L. *trabs*, *trabis*, a beam.]
archive, *ärk′iv, n.* (in *pl.*) a repository of public
records or of records and monuments generally:
public records : (rare in *sing.*) a document, monument.—*adj.* **archiv′al** (or *ärk′i-vəl*).—*n.* **archivist**
(*ärk′i-vist*), a keeper of archives or records. [Fr.,—
L.L. *archi*(*v*)*um*—Gr. *archeion*, magisterial residence—*archē*, government.]
archivolt, *är′ki-vōlt, n.* the under curve of an arch:
moulding on it. [It. *archivolto*—*arco* (L. *arcus*,
an arch) and *volta*, vault.]
archlute, *ärch′l*(*y*)*ōōt, n.* a large double-necked
bass lute. [Pfx. **arch-** and **lute.**]
archology, *ärk-ol′ə-ji, n.* (*rare*) doctrine of the
origin of things : the science of government. [Gr.
archē, beginning, rule, *logos*, discourse.]
archon, *ärk-on, -ən, n.* one of nine chief magistrates
of ancient Athens.—*ns.* **arch′onship,** the office
of an archon; **arch′ontate,** the archon's tenure of
office.—*adj.* **archontic** (*-ont′ik*). [Gr. *archōn*,
-ontos, pr.p. of *archein*, to be first, to rule.]
Arctic, arctic, *ärk′tik, adj.* relating to the Great
Bear, or to the north: extremely cold.—*n.* (*U.S.*)
a waterproof overshoe :—*n.pl.* **Arctiidae** (*-ti′i-dē*),
the tiger-moth family, whose caterpillars are
called woolly-bears.—*ad′.* **arc′toid,** bear-like.—
Arctic Circle, a small circle about 23½ degrees
from the North Pole. [Gr. *arktos*, a bear.]
Arctogaea, *ärk-tō-jē′ä, n.* a zoological region including all lands outside of Notogaea and Neogaea.
—*adjs.* **Arctogae′an, Arctogae′ic.** [Gr. *arktos*,
bear (see preceding), *gaia*, earth.]
Arcturus, *ärk-tū′rəs, n.* the Bear-ward, a yellow
star in Bootes, fourth in order of brightness in
the entire heavens. [Gr. *Arktouros*—*arktos*, bear,
and *ouros*, guard.]
arcuate, *är′kū-āt,* **arcuated,** *-id, adjs.* arched.—
n. **arcua′tion.** [L. *arcuātus*, pa.p. of *arcuāre*, to
bend like a bow—*arcus*, a bow.]
arcubalist, *är′kū-bə-list.* See **arbalest.**
Ardea, *är′di-ä, n.* the heron and bittern genus.
[L. *ardea*, heron.]
ardeb, *är′deb, n.* an Egyptian dry measure of 5½
bushels. [Ar. *irdab*.]
ardent, *ärd′ənt, adj.* burning: fiery: fervid: combustible, inflammable (*obs.* exc. in **ardent spirits,**
distilled alcoholic liquors, whisky, brandy, etc.).—
n. **ard′ency.**—*adv.* **ard′ently.**—*n* **ard′our,**
warmth of passion or feeling: eagerness: enthusiasm (with *for*). [L. *ardēns, -ēntis,* pr.p. of
ardēre, to burn.]
Ardil, *är′dil, n.* a wool-substitute made from
monkey-nuts, etc., invented at *Ardeer* (Ayrshire).
[Registered trade-mark.]
ard-ri(gh), ardri(gh), *ord′rē,* or *-rē′, n.* a head
king. [Ir. *ārd,* noble, *rī,* king.]
arduous, *ärd′ū-əs, adj.* steep, difficult to climb :
difficult to accomplish : laborious.—*adv.* **ard′uous-
ly.**—*n.* **ard′uousness.** [L. *arduus,* steep, high.]
are, *är, n.* the unit of the metric land measure, 100
sq. metres, about 119·6 English sq. yards. [Fr.,
—L. *ārea,* a site, space, court.]
are, *är,* used as plural of the present indicative of
the verb *to be.* [Old Northumbrian *aron,* which
ousted the usual O.E. *sind, sindon*; both from the
root *es-*.]
area, *ā′ri-ä, n.* a space or piece of ground : a portion
of surface : a tract : the floor of a theatre, etc. : a
sunken space alongside the basement of a building :
superficial extent.—*adj.* **ā′real.**—*n.* **ā′rea-sneak′,**
a thief who sneaks in by area doors. [L. *ārea,* a
space of ground.]
areach, *a-rēch′, v.t.* (*obs.*) to reach, get at : to seize.
—*pa.t.* (*Spens.*) **arraught** (*a-rawt′*). [O.E. *ārǣcan
-d-,* intens., *rǣcan,* to reach.]
aread, arede, arreede, *a-rēd′, v.t.* (*Spens.*) to
declare : to utter : to guess : to interpret, explain :
to adjudge : to decide : (*Milt.*) to counsel :—*pa.t.*
and *pa.p.* **ared**(d)′. [O.E. *ārǣdan* : see **read.**]
arear, arere, Spenserian spellings of **arrear**
(*adv.*).
Areca, *ar′i-kä, n.* the betel-nut genus of palms.—
n. **ar′eca-nut,** betel-nut, the nut of *Areca*

catechu, chewed by the Malays with lime in a
betel-pepper leaf. [Port.,—Malayálam *adekka.*]
arefaction, *ar-i-fak′shən, n.* (*obs.*) drying.—*v.t.* and
v.i. **ar′efy,** to dry up, wither. [L. *ārefacĕre,* to
make dry—*ārēre,* to dry, *facĕre,* to make.]
arena, *ə-rē′nä, n.* part of the ancient amphitheatre
strewed with sand for combats : any place of public
contest : any sphere of action.—*adj.* **arenaceous**
(*ar-i-nā′shas*), sandy : composed of sand or quartz
grains : with shell of agglutinated sand-grains :
sand-growing.—*ns.* **Arena′ria,** the sandwort genus,
akin to chickweed; **arena′tion,** remedial application of sand.—*adj.* **arenic′olous,** sand-dwelling.
[L. *arēna,* sand.]
areography, *ar-i-og′rə-fi, n.* description of the
physical features of the planet Mars. [Gr. *Arēs,*
Mars, *graphein,* to write.]
areola, *a-rē′ō-lä, n.* a small area : (*biol.*) a small
space marked off by lines, or a slightly sunken
spot : (*physiol.*) an interstice in a tissue : any circular
spot such as that around the nipple : part of the
iris of the eye bordering on the pupil :—*pl.*
arē′olae (*-lē*).—*adjs.* **arē′olar; arē′olate, arē′o-
lated,** divided into small areas.—*ns.* **arēolā′tion,**
division into areolae; **areole** (*ar′i-ōl*), an areola :
a spiny or hairy spot on a cactus. [L. *āreola,*
dim. of *ārea.*]
areometer. See **araeometer.**
Areopagus, *ar-i-op′ag-əs, n.* the Hill of Arēs, on
which the supreme court of ancient Athens was
held : the court itself : any important tribunal.—*n.*
Areop′agite (*-gīt, -jīt*), a member of the Areopagus.
—*adj.* **Areopagitic** (*-git′,* or *-jit′*), pertaining to
the Areopagus. [Latinised from Gr. *Areios pagos,*
hill of Arēs (identified with Roman Mars).]
aret, arett, *a-ret′, v.t.* (*Spens.*) to entrust, commit :
to assign, allot : to adjudge, award. [O.Fr. *areter,*
a-, to, *reter*—L. *reputāre,* to reckon.]
arête, *ä-ret′, n.* a sharp ridge : esp. in French
Switzerland, a rocky edge on a mountain. [Fr.,—
L. *arista,* an ear of corn, fish-bone, spine.]
Aretinian, *ar-i-tin′i-ən, adj.* pertaining to Guido of
Arezzo (d. 1050).—**Aretinian syllables,** the
initial syllables of the half-lines of a hymn to
John the Baptist, which, falling on successive notes
of the diatonic scale, were used (apparently by
Guido) as names for the notes :—*Ut* queant laxis
*re*sonare fibris *Mi*ra gestorum *fa*muli tuorum,
*Sol*ve polluti *la*bii reatum, Sancte Ioannes. Thus
C in the bass is *C fa ut,* being the fourth note (fa)
of the first hexachord (on G) and the first note (ut)
of the second hexachord (on C). See **gamut.**
[L. *Arētīnus, Arrētīnus,* of Arrētium or Arezzo.]
arew, *a-rōō′, adv.* (*Spens.*) arow, in a row.
arfvedsonite, *är′ved-sən-īt, n.* a soda amphibole.
[After J. A. *Arfvedson* (1792-1841), Swedish
mineralogist.]
argal, *är′gl, adv.* Shakespeare's gravedigger's attempt at L. *ergō,* therefore.
argala, *är′gə-lä, n.* the adjutant stork. [Hind.
hargīla.]
argali, *är′gə-li, n.* the great wild sheep (*Ovis
ammon*) of Asia. [Mongol.]
argan, *är′gan, n.* a Moroccan timber-tree of the
family Sapotaceae : its oil-bearing seed. [N.
African pron. of Ar. *arjān.*]
argand, *är′gand, n.* a burner admitting air within a
cylindrical flame.—Also *adj.* [Invented by Aimé
Argand (1755-1803).]
Argathelian, *är-gə-thē′li-ən, adj.* of the party in
Scotland in the 18th century that approved of the
political influence of the house of Argyle. [L.L.
Argathelia, Argyle.]
argemone, *är-jem-ō′nē, n.* the prickly poppy.
[Gr. *argemonē,* a kind of poppy.]
argent, *ärj′ənt, adj.* and *n.* silver : silvery-white :
(*her.*) white.—*adj.* **argentif′erous,** silver-bearing;
ar′gentine (*-īn*), of or like silver : sounding like
silver : **Ar′gentine,** of, or belonging to, Argentina
or its people.—*n.* white metal coated with silver :
spongy tin : a small smelt with silvery sides :
Argentine, a native or citizen of Argentina (also
Argentino, *-tē′nō,* Sp. *är-hhen-tē′nō*).—*n.* **ar′gen-
tite,** silver-glance, native sulphide of silver. [Fr.,

—L. *argentum*, silver; the republic is named from the Rio de la Plata (silver river).]

Argestes, *är-jes'tēz*, *n.* (*Milt.*) the north-west wind personified. [Gr. *Argestēs*.]

arghan, *är'gan*, *n.* pita fibre, or the plant yielding it. [Origin unknown.]

argil, *är'jil*, *n.* potter's clay : pure clay or alumina.—*adj.* **argillā'ceous**, clayey.—*n.* **ar'gillite**, an indurated clay rock. [L. *argilla*, Gr. *argillos*, white clay—*argēs*, white.]

Argive, *är'gīv*, *-jīv*, *n.* and *adj.* belonging to *Argos*: Greek.

argle-bargle, **argie-bargie**. See under **argue**.

argol, *är'gol*, *n.* a hard crust formed on the sides of wine-vessels, from which cream of tartar and tartaric acid are obtained—generally reddish. [Prob. conn. with Gr. *argos*, white.]

argon, *är'gon*, *n.* an inert gas (at. numb. 18) discovered in the atmosphere in 1894 by Rayleigh and Ramsay. [Gr. *ărgon* (neut.) inactive—*a-*, priv., *ergon*, work.]

Argonaut, *är'gō-nawt*, *n.* one of those who sailed in the ship *Argo* in search of the golden fleece : **argonaut**, the paper nautilus (*Argonauta*).—*adj.* **argonaut'ic**. [Gr. *Argō*, and *nautēs*, a sailor.]

argosy, *är'gō-si*, *n.* a great merchant ship, esp. of Ragusa or Venice. [It. *Ragusea*, Ragusan (ship).]

argot, *är-gō*, *n.* slang, originally that of thieves and vagabonds : cant. [Fr.; of unknown origin.]

argue, *ärg'ū*, *v.t.* to prove or evince : to give reason to believe : to seek to show by reasoning : to discuss with reasoning : to persuade or bring by reasoning {into or out of a course of action) : (*obs.*) to accuse.—*v.i.* to offer reasons : to contend with reasoning.—*adj.* **arg'ūable**, capable of being maintained : capable of being disputed.—*adv.* **ar'gūably.**—*n.* **arg'ūer.**—*v.i.* **ar'gūfy** (*illit.*) to bandy arguments : to wrangle.—*v.t.* to beset with wrangling.—*ns.* **ar'gūment**, proof : evidence : a reason or series of reasons offered or possible towards proof or inducement : exchange of such reasons : debate : matter of debate or contention : a summary of subject-matter : hence (*Shak.*) contents : (*math.*) a quantity upon which another depends, or under which it is to be sought in a table : the angle between a vector and its axis of reference; **argūmentā'tion**, reasoning : sequence or exchange of arguments.—*adj.* **argūment'ative**, controversial : addicted to arguing.—*adv.* **argūment'atively.**—*n.* **argūment'ativeness**; **argūment'um** (see Foreign Words).—*v.i.* **ar'gy-bar'gy**, **ar'gie-bar'gie**, **ar'gle-bar'gle** (*orig. Scot.*) to argue tediously or vexatiously.—*n.* a bandying of argument. [Fr. *arguer*—L. *argūtāre*, freq. of *argūĕre*, to show, accuse; *argūmentum*, proof, accusation, summary of contents.]

Argus, *är'gas*, *n.* in Greek mythology, Io's guardian, whose hundred eyes Hera transferred to the peacock's tail : a vigilant watcher : an East Indian genus of pheasants (*Argus pheasant*) : a butterfly with many eye-spots on the wings (as some *Lycaenidae* and *Satyridae*) : an ophiuroid with much-divided coiling arms.—*adj.* **Ar'gus-eyed'**. [Gr. *Argos*, lit., bright.]

argute, *är-gūt'*, *adj.* shrill : keen : shrewd.—*adv.* **argute'ly.**—*n.* **argute'ness**. [L. *argūtus*.]

argyria, *är-jir'i-ā*, *n.* skin-pigmentation caused by taking preparations of silver.—*n.* **ar'gyrodite**, a mineral composed of silver, germanium, and sulphur. [Gr. *argyros*, silver.]

aria, *ä'ri-ā*, *n.* an air or melody, esp. an accompanied vocal solo in a cantata, oratorio, or opera : a regular strain of melody followed by another in contrast and complement, and then repeated *da capo*. [It., from root of **air**.]

Arian, *ä'ri-an*, *adj.* pertaining to, or following, *Arius* of Alexandria (d. 336).—*n.* one who adheres to the doctrines of Arius : a Unitarian.—*v.t.* and *v.i.* **A'rianise**.—*n.* **A'rianism**.

Arician, *a-rish'an*, *adj.* of or belonging to *Aricia* in Latium or its Diana cult.

arid, *ar'id*, *adj.* dry : parched : barren : jejune.—*ns.* **arid'ity**, **ar'idness**.—*adv.* **ar'idly**. [L. *aridus*.]

Ariel, *ä'ri-al*, *n.* a man's name in the Old Testament : in later demonology, a water-spirit : an

angel : a spirit of the air (as Shakespeare's Ariel, a sylph in Pope) : **ariel**, species of swallow, petrel, and toucan. [Heb. *Ariĕl*, with meaning influenced by **air**.]

ariel, *ä'ri-al*, *n.* a kind of gazelle. [Ar. *aryil*.]

Aries, *ä'ri-ēz*, *n.* the Ram, a constellation giving name to, and formerly coinciding with, a sign of the zodiac.—**first point of Aries**, the intersection of equator and ecliptic passed by the sun in (the northern) spring, now actually in Pisces. [L. *ariēs*, *-etis*, ram.]

arietta, *är-i-et'tä*, *n.* a little aria or air.—Also (Fr.) **ariette** (*-et'*). [It. *arietta*, dim. of *aria*.]

aright, *a-rīt'*, *adv.* in a right way : rightly : on or to the right.—**a rights** (*Spens.*), rightly. [Prep. **a**, **right**.]

aril, *ar'il*, *n.* a covering or appendage of some seeds, an outgrowth of the funicle : sometimes, a caruncle (*false aril*).—Also **arill'us** :—*pl.* **arill'ī**.—*adjs.* **ar'illary**, **ar'illate**, **ar'illated**, having an aril.—*n.* **ar'illode**, a caruncle or false aril, from near the micropyle. [L.L. *arillus*, raisin.]

Arimaspian, *ar-i-mas'pi-an*, *adj.* pertaining to the *Arimaspi*, described by Herodotus as a one-eyed people of the extreme north, warring perpetually with griffins for gold hoards.—Also *n.*—Also **Ar'imasp**, *adj.* and *n.*

arioso, *ä-ri-ō'sō*, *adj.* and *adv.* in the melodious manner of an aria, or between aria and recitative.—Also *n.* [It. *aria*.]

ariot, *a-rī'ot*, *adv.* in riot, riotously.

aripple, *a-rip'l*, *adv.* in a ripple.

arise, *a-rīz'*, *v.i.* to rise up : to get up : to take rise, originate : to come into being, view, or activity :—*pa.t.* **arose** (*a-rōz'*); *pa.p.* **arisen** (*a-riz'n*). [Pfx. *a-*, up, out, and **rise**.]

arish. See **arrish**.

arista, *a-ris'tä*, *n.* an awn.—*adj.* **aris'tate** (or *ar'*), awned. [L. *arista*, an awn.]

Aristarch, *ar'is-tärk*, *n.* a severe critic. [*Aristarchus*, Alexandrian grammarian (c. 160 B.C.).]

aristocracy, *ar-is-tok'ra-si*, *n.* government by, or political power of, a privileged order : a state so governed : a nobility or privileged class : an analogous class in respect of any quality.—*n.* **aristocrat** (*ar'is-tō-krat*, or *a-ris'*), a member of an aristocracy : one who has the characteristics of or attributed to an aristocracy : a haughty person : one of the, or the, best of its kind.—*adjs.* **aristocrat'ic**, **-al**, belonging to aristocracy : having the character that belongs to, or is thought to befit, aristocracy.—*adv.* **aristocrat'ically.**—*n.* **aristocratism** (*-tok'ra-tizm*), the spirit of, or belief in, aristocracy. [Gr. *aristokratiā*—*aristos*, best, and *kratos*, power.]

Aristolochia, *ar-is-tō-lō'ki-ā*, *n.* the birthwort genus, herbs and climbers, specially abundant in tropical South America, giving name to the family **Aristolochiā'ceae**. [Gr. *aristolocheia*—*aristos*, best, *locheiā*, child-birth, from the former repute of birthwort.]

aristology, *ar-is-tol'ō-ji*, *n.* the science or art of dining. [Gr. *ariston*, breakfast, luncheon, *logos*, discourse.]

Aristophanic, *ar-is-tō-fan'ik*, *adj.* relating to or characteristic of the Greek comic dramatist *Aristophanes*.

Aristotelian, *ar-is-to-tē'li-an*, **Aristotelean**, *ar-is-tot-i-lē'an*, *adj.* relating to Aristotle (Gr. *Aristotelēs*) or to his philosophy.—*n.* a follower of Aristotle.—*ns.* **Aristotē'lianism**, **Aristot'elism**.—**Aristotle's lantern**, a chewing apparatus in sea-urchins, compared by Aristotle to a ship's lantern.

arithmetic, *a-rith'ma-tik*, *n.* the science of numbers : the art of reckoning by figures : a treatise on reckoning.—*adjs.* **arithmetic** (*ar-ith-met'ik*), **-al**.—*adv.* **arithmet'ically.**—*n.* **arithmetician** (*-ma-tish'n*, or *ar'*), one skilled in arithmetic.—**arithmetical progression**, a series increasing or diminishing by a common difference, as 7, 10, 13, 16, 19, 22; or 12, 10½, 9, 7½, 6. [Gr. *arithmētikē* (*technē*, art) of numbers—*arithmos*, number.]

arithmometer, *ar-ith-mom'i-tar*, *n.* a calculating machine. [Gr. *arithmos*, number, *metron*, measure.]

ark, *ärk*, *n.* a chest or coffer : in Jewish history, the wooden coffer in which the Tables of the Law were kept: a large floating vessel, like Noah's in the Deluge (Gen. vi-viii): a toy representing Noah's ark.—*v.t.* to put in an ark.—*adj.* and *n.* **ark'ite.**—*n.* **ark'-shell,** a boxlike bivalve shell (*Arca.*). [O.E. *arc* (*earc*)—L. *arca,* a chest—*arcēre,* to guard.]

arkose, *är-kōs',* *n.* a sandstone rich in felspar grains, formed from granite, etc.

arles, *ärlz* (also *ärlz*), *n.pl.* earnest, esp. in confirmation of a bargain, or an engagement of a servant.—*ns.* **arle'-penny, arles'-penny.** [Scot. and Northern; M.E. *erles*—app. through O.Fr. from a dim. of L. *arrha.*]

arm, *ärm,* *n.* the fore-limb from shoulder to hand, esp. when used for purposes other than locomotion : a tentacle : a narrow projecting part : an inlet : a branch : a rail or support for the arm as on a chair : (*fig.*) power.—*v.t.* to take in the arms : to conduct arm-in-arm.—*n.s.* **arm'band,** a band of cloth worn round the sleeve; **arm'chair',** a chair with arms.—*adjs.* **arm'chair,** amateur : stay-at-home : doctrinaire; **armed,** having an arm or arms, as *one-armed.*—*ns.* **arm'ful; arm'hole,** the hole in a garment through which the arm is put.—*adv.* **arm'-in-arm',** with arms interlinked.—*adj.* **arm'less.**—*ns.* **arm'let,** a little arm : a ring or band round the arm; **arm'pit,** the hollow under the shoulder.—**at arm's length,** away from any friendliness or familiarity (or literally); **in arms,** carried as a child : young enough for this; **right arm,** the main support or assistant; **secular arm,** the civil authority, opp. to the spiritual or ecclesiastical; **with open arms,** with hearty welcome. [O.E. *arm* (*earm*); cog. with L. *armus,* the shoulder-joint, Gr. *harmos,* a joint.]

arm, *ärm,* *n.* a weapon : a branch of the fighting forces :—*pl.* **arms,** weapons of offence and defence : hostilities : fighting : soldiering : heraldic devices.—*v.t.* **arm,** to furnish with weapons, means of protection, armature, or equipment : to strengthen with a plate or otherwise.—*v.i.* to take arms.—*ns.* **ar'mament,** a force equipped for war : total means of making war : munitions, esp. for warships : act of arming or equipping for war: defensive equipment; **ar'mature,** armour : any apparatus for defence : a piece of iron set across the poles of a magnet : a moving part in a magnetic circuit to indicate the presence of electric current: that part of a direct-current machine in which, in the case of a generator, the electromotive force is produced, or, in the case of a motor, the torque is produced.—*adj.* **armed,** furnished with arms : provided with means of defence : thorny : (*her.*) with beak, claws, etc., of such and such a tincture.—**armed eye,** the aided eye (opp. to naked eye); **arms race,** competition among nations in building up armaments; **bear arms,** to serve as a soldier : (also **give arms**) to show armorial bearings; **in arms,** armed : (*her.*) quartered; **lay down one's arms,** to surrender, submit; **of all arms,** of every kind of troops; **take (up) arms,** to resort to fighting; **under arms,** armed; **up in arms,** in readiness to resist. [Fr. *armes,* from L. *arma* (*pl.*); L. *armāmenta,* tackle, equipment; *armātūra,* armour.]

armada, *är-mä'dä,* (sometimes -*mā'*), *n.* a fleet of armed ships, esp. that sent by Philip II of Spain against England in 1588. [Sp., fem. pa.p of *armar*—L. *armāre,* to arm.]

armadillo, *ärm-ə-dil'ō,* *n.* an American edentate armed with bands of bony plates :—*pl.* **armadill'os.** [Sp., dim. of *armado,* armed; see foregoing.]

Armageddon, *är-mə-ged'n,* *n.* the great symbolical battlefield of the Apocalypse, scene of the final struggle between the powers of good and evil: a great war or battle of nations. [*Harmagedōn* or *Armageddōn* given as Heb. name in *Rev.* xvi, 16; perh. suggested by the famous battlefield of *Megiddo,* in the plain of Esdraelon.]

armament, armature. See under **arm** (2).

Armenian, *är-mē'nyən,* *adj.* belonging to *Armenia,* in Western Asia, or its people or language, or their branch of the Christian Church.—*n.* a native of Armenia : one of the Armenian people : the language of the Armenians.—*adj.* **Armē'noid,** of the eastern branch of the Alpine race.—Also *n.*

armet, *är'mit,* *n.* a helmet introduced about 1450 in place of the basinet, consisting of an iron cap, spreading over the back of the neck, having in front the visor, beaver, and gorget. [Fr.]

armgaunt, *ärm'gawnt,* *adj.* (*Shak., Ant. and Cleop.,* I.v.48), perh. with gaunt limbs, or perh. worn with armour, but probably an error.

armiger, *är'mi-jər,* *n.* one entitled to a coat-of-arms : an esquire.—Also **armi'gero** (Slender's blunder in *Merry Wives*).—*adjs.* **armi'geral, armi'gerous.** [L., an armour-bearer—*arma,* arms, *gerēre,* to bear.]

armilla, *är-mil'ä,* *n.* (*archaeol;* also **ar'mil**) bracelet: (*bot.*) frill on a mushroom stalk.—*adj.* **armill'ary** (or *är'*).—**armillary sphere,** a skeleton sphere made up of hoops to show the motions of the heavenly bodies. [L. *armilla,* an armlet, dim. of *armus,* the upper arm and shoulder.]

Arminian, *är-min'i-ən,* *n.* a follower of *Arminius* (1560-1609), a Dutch divine, who denied the Calvinistic doctrine of absolute predestination, as well as irresistible grace.—Also *adj.*—*n.* **Armin'-ianism.**

armipotent, *är-mip'ə-tənt,* *adj.* powerful in arms. [L. *arma,* arms, *potēns, -entis,* powerful.]

armistice, *är'mi-stis,* *n.* a suspension of hostilities : a truce. [Fr.,—L.L. *armistitium,* from L. *arma,* arms, *sistēre,* to stop.]

armoire, *är-mwär',* *n.* an ambry or cupboard. [Fr.]

Armoric, *är-mor'ik,* *adj.* of *Armorica,* or Brittany.—*n.* the Breton language.—*n.* and *adj.* **Armor'ican.** [L. *Armoricus*—Gallic *are-morici,* dwellers by the sea.]

armour (*U.S.* **armor**), *är'mər,* *n.* defensive dress : protective covering : heraldic insignia.—*adj.* **ar'morial** (*-mō'ri-əl*), of heraldic arms.—*n.* a book of coats of arms.—*ns.* **ar'morist,** one skilled in heraldry; **ar'mory,** heraldry : (*U.S.*) armoury; **ar'mour-bearer,** one who carries the armour of another, a squire.—*adj.* **ar'mour-clad',** clad in armour.—*n.* **ar'mour-clad,** an armoured ship.—*adj.* **ar'moured,** protected by armour.—*ns.* **ar'moured-car, -crui'ser, -train'; ar'mourer,** a maker, repairer, or custodian of arms and armour.—*adj.* **ar'mourless.**—*n.* **ar'mour-plate,** a defensive plate for a ship, tank, etc.—*adj.* **ar'mour-plat'ed.**—*n.* **ar'moury,** a collection of arms and armour : a place where arms are kept: armour collectively.—**armorial bearings,** the design in a coat of arms. [O.Fr. *armure*—L. *armātūra*—*arma,* arms.]

armozeen, armozine, *är-mō-zēn',* *n.* a kind of taffeta or plain silk, usually black, used for clerical gowns. [Fr. *armoisin.*]

army, *ärm'i,* *n.* a large body of men armed for war and under military command : a body of men banded together in a special cause, whether mimicking military methods as the 'Salvation Army', or not, as the 'Blue Ribbon Army': a host : a great number.—*ns.* **arm'y-corps** (*-kōr*), a miniature army comprising all arms of the service; **arm'y-list,** a list of all commissioned officers : **arm'y-worm,** the larva of a small fly (*Sciara*) that collects in vast armies : the larva of an American moth (*Leucania*) with the same habit. [Fr. *armee,* pa.p. fem. of *armer*—L. *armāre, -ātum,* to arm.]

Arnaut, Arnaout, *är-nowt',* *n.* an Albanian, esp. one in the Turkish army. [Turk.]

arnica, *är'ni-kä,* *n.* a tincture of the flowers of a composite plant, *Arnica montana,* or mountain tobacco, applied to wounds and bruises. [Origin unknown.]

arnotto, *är-not'ō.* See **annatto.**

arnut, *är'nət.* Same as **earth-nut.**

aroba, *är-ob'ä.* See **araba.**

aroid, *är'oid.* See **Arum.**

aroint, aroynt, *ə-roint',* apparently *v.t.,* used twice by Shakespeare in the phrase, '*Aroint* thee, witch', meaning away, begone : (*arch.; Browning*) to bid begone : to drive or frighten away. [Origin unknown.]

arolla, *ä-rol'ä,* *n.* the Swiss stone-pine or Siberian cedar (*Pinus Cembra*). [Fr. *arolle.*]

Neutral vowels in unaccented syllables : *el'ə-mənt, in'fənt, ran'dəm*

aroma, *ā-rō'mä, n.* a spicy fragrance : (*fig.*) flavour or peculiar charm.—*adj.* **aromatic** (*ar-ō-mat'ik*), fragrant : spicy : (*chem.*) belonging to the closed-chain class of organic compounds, or benzene derivatives—opp. to *fatty* or *aliphatic.*—Also *n.*—*v.t.* arō'matise, to render aromatic : to perfume. [L., from Gr. *arōma, -atos,* spice.]

arose. See **arise.**

around, *ə-rownd', prep.* on all sides of : round, round about : somewhere near.—*adv.* on every side : in a circle : round, all about, astir. [Prep. **a,** round.]

arouse, *ə-rowz', v.t.* and *v.i.* to rouse.—*n.* an arousing, alarm.—*ns.* **arous'al** (*rare*); **arous'er.** [Prep. **a,** rouse.]

arow, *ə-rō', adv.* in a row : one following the other. [Prep. **a,** and **row.**]

aroynt. Same as **aroint.**

arpeggio, *är-ped-j(y)ō, n.* (*mus.*) a chord of which the notes are performed, not simultaneously, but in rapid (normally upward) succession.—*v.t.* **arpegg'iate** (*-ji-āt*), to play in this manner. [It. *arpeggiare,* to play the harp—*arpa,* harp.]

arpent, *är'pənt, är-pän*, *n.* an old French measure for land still used in Quebec and Louisiana varying from 1¼ acres to ⅝ of an acre. [Fr.,—L. *arepennis,* said to be a Gallic word.]

arquebus(e), harquebus, (*h*)*är'kwi-bus, n.* an old-fashioned handgun.—*ns.* **arquebusade',** a lotion for shot-wounds; **arquebusier** (*-ēr'*), a soldier armed with an arquebus. [Fr. *arquebuse* —Du. *haakbus*—*haak,* hook, and *bus,* box, barrel of a gun; Ger. *hakenbüchse.*]

arracacha, *ar-a-käch'ä, n.* an umbelliferous plant (*Arracacia*) of northern South America, with edible tubers. [Quechua *aracacha.*]

arrack, *ar'ak, n.* an ardent spirit used in the East, procured from toddy, or the fermented juice of the coco and other palms, as well as from rice and jaggery sugar. [Ar. *'araq,* juice.]

arragonite, another spelling of **aragonite.**

arrah, *ar'ə, interj.* Anglo-Irish expression of emotion, wonder, mild expostulation, etc.

arraign, *ə-rān', v.t.* to call to account : to put upon trial : to accuse publicly.—*ns.* **arraign'er ; arraign'ing ; arraign'ment.** [O.Fr. *aresnier*—L.L. *arrationāre*—L. *ad,* to, *ratiō, -ōnis,* reason.]

arrange, *ə-rānj', v.t.* to set in a rank or row : to put in order : to settle : (*mus.*) to adapt for other instruments or voices.—*n.* **arrange'ment.** [O.Fr. *arangier*—*à* (L. *ad,* to), and *rangier, rengier.* See **range.**]

arrant, *ar'ənt, adj.* downright, unmitigated, out-and-out : notorious : rascally. [A variant of **errant.**]

arras, *ar'əs, n.* tapestry (made at *Arras* in France) : a hanging screen of tapestry for a wall.—*adj.* **arr'ased,** covered with arras.—*n.* **arr'asene,** an embroidery material, of wool and silk.

arraught. See **areach.**

array, *ə-rā', n.* order : dress : equipage.—*v.t.* to put in order : to arrange : to dress, adorn, or equip. —*n.* **array'ment,** act of arraying : (*obs.*) clothing. [A.Fr. *arai,* O.Fr. *arei,* array, equipage—L. *ad,* and the Gmc. root found in Eng. **ready,** Ger. *bereit.*]

arrear, *ə-rēr', n.* that which is in the rear or behind : (*usu.* in *pl.*) that which remains unpaid or undone : (in *sing.* or *pl.*) condition of being behindhand.— *adv.* (*obs.*) aback, backward, behind.—*n.* **arrear'-age,** arrear, arrears. [O.Fr. *arere, ariere* (Fr. *arrière*)—L. *ad,* to, *retrō,* back, behind.]

arrect, *a-rekt', adj.* upright : pricked up : on the alert. [L. *arrēctus.*]

arreede. See **aread.**

arrest, *ə-rest', v.t.* to bring to a standstill, check : to seize : to catch, fix (as the attention) : to apprehend by legal authority : to seize by warrant : (*Shak.*) to take in security.—*n.* stoppage : seizure by warrant.—*adj.* **arrest'able.**—*ns.* **arrestation** (*ar-es-tā'shən*), the act of arresting : arrest ; **arrestee',** a person prevented by arrestment from making payment or delivery to another until the arrester's claim upon that other is secured or satisfied ; **arrest'er,** one who, or that which, arrests :

a lightning-arrester : one who makes an arrestment (also **arrest'or**).—*adj.* **arrest'ive,** tending to arrest.—*n.* **arrest'ment,** a checking : (*law*), detention of a person arrested till liberated on bail, or by security : (*Scots law*) the process which prohibits a debtor from making payment to his creditor until a debt due by that creditor to the arrester is paid. [O.Fr. *arester*—L. *ad,* to, *restāre,* to stand still.]

arrêt, *a-ret', ä'-re', ä-rā', n.* decision : judgment of a tribunal. [Fr. See **arrest.**]

arrhenotoky, *ar-ən-ot'ə-ki, n.* parthenogenetic production of males alone. [Gr. *arrēn,* male, *tokos,* offspring.]

arriage, *ar'ij, n.* a former feudal service in Scotland, said to have been done with the tenants' beasts of burden, later indefinite. [See **average** and **aver** (2).]

arride, *ə-rīd', v.t.* (*Lamb*) to please, gratify. [L. *arrīdēre.*]

arrière-ban, *ar'ē-er-ban', -bän, n.* a feudal sovereign's summons to all freemen to take the field : the army thus collected. [O.Fr. *ariereban*—O.H.G. *hari,* army, and *ban,* public proclamation; confused with Fr. *arrière.*]

arriero, *ar-i-ā'rō, n.* a muleteer. [Sp.]

arris, *ar'is, n.* a sharp edge on stone or metal at the meeting of two surfaces. [See **arête.**]

arrish, arish, *ar'ish, n.* (*dial.*) a stubble field. [O.E. *ersc* (in compounds).]

arrive, *ə-rīv', v.i.* (*obs.*) to reach shore or port : to reach any place : to attain to any object (with *at*) : to achieve success or recognition : to happen.— *v.t.* (*obs.*) to reach.—*ns.* **arriv'al,** the act of arriving : persons or things that arrive; **arriv'ance, -ancy** (*Shak.*), company arriving. [O.Fr. *ariver*— L.L. *adrīpāre*—L. *ad,* to, *rīpa,* shore.]

arriviste, *ä'rē-vēst, n.* a person 'on the make' : a parvenu in process : a self-seeker. [Fr.]

arroba, *ä-rō'bä, n.* a weight of 25 pounds or more, used in Spanish and Portuguese regions. [Sp. and Port.,—Ar. *ar-rub',* the quarter.]

arrogate, *ar'ō-gāt, -ə-gāt, v.t.* to claim as one's own : to claim proudly or unduly.—*ns.* **arr'ogance ; arr'ogancy,** undue assumption of importance.— *adj.* **arr'ogant,** claiming too much : overbearing.— *adv.* **arr'ogantly.**—*n.* **arroga'tion,** act of arrogating : undue assumption. [L. *arrogāre*—*ad,* to, *rogāre, -ātum,* to ask, to claim.]

arrondissement, *ä-ron-dēs'män, n.* a sub-division of a French department. [Fr.,—*arrondir,* to make round.]

arrow, *ar'ō, n.* a straight, pointed missile, made to be shot from a bow or blowpipe : any arrow-shaped mark or object : the chief shoot of a plant, esp. the flowering stem of the sugar-cane.—*ns.* **arr'ow-grass,** a genus of marsh plants (*Triglochin*) whose burst capsule is like an arrow-head; **arr'ow-head,** the head or pointed part of an arrow : an aquatic plant (*Sagittaria sagittifolia*) of the Alismaceae, with arrow-shaped leaves.—*adj.* **arr'ow-headed,** shaped like the head of an arrow.—*ns.* **arr'ow-poi'son,** poison smeared on arrow-heads; **arr'ow-root,** a West Indian plant, *Maranta arundinacea* or other species : its rhizome, esteemed in S. America as an antidote to arrow-poison : a nutritious starch from the rhizome : extended to other plants and their starch (see **Portland**); **arr'ow-shot,** the range of an arrow.—*adj.* **arr'owy,** of or like arrows. [O.E. *arwe;* prob. cog. with L. *arcus,* bow.]

arrow, *ar'ō.* See **ary.**

arroyo, *är-ō'yō, n.* a rocky ravine : a dry water-course. [Sp.]

'Arry, *ar'i, n.* a jovial vulgar cockney :—*fem.* **'Arr'iet.**—*adj.* **'Arr'yish.** [Cockney pronunciation of *Harry, Harriet.*]

arse, *ärs, n.* (now *vulg.*) the posteriors of an animal. —*adv.* and *adj.* **ars'y-vers'y,** backside foremost, contrary. [O.E. *ærs* (*ears*); Ger. *arsch,* Sw. *ars;* cog. with Gr. *orros* (for *orsos*).]

arsenal, *ärs'(i-)nl, n.* a dockyard : a public magazine or manufactory of naval and military stores. [It. *arzenale, arsenale* (Sp., Fr. *arsenal*—Ar. *där* *açcinā'ah*, workshop—(*dār*, house), *al*, the, *çinā'ah*, art.]

arsenic, *ärs'(ə-)nik*, *n.* the chemical element of atomic number 33 : a poison, the trioxide of the element (As₂O₃ ; **white arsenic**).—*ns.* **arseniate** (-*sē'ni-āt*), a salt of arsenic acid.—*adjs.* **arsenic** (-*sen'ik*), **-al, arsē'nious**, composed of or containing arsenic.—In chemistry **arsen'ic** is applied to compounds in which arsenic is penta-valent, **arsē'nious** to those in which it is trivalent. —*ns.* **ar'senide**, a compound of arsenic with a metal ; **ar'senite**, a salt of arsenious acid ; **arseno-pyrī'tēs**, mispickel, a mineral composed of iron, arsenic and sulphur ; **arsine**, *är'sēn, -sin, -sĭn*, hydride of arsenic (As H₃) : a compound in which one or more hydrogen atoms of As H₃ are replaced by an alkyl radical, etc. [Gr. *arsenikon*, yellow orpiment, fancifully associated with Gr. *arsēn*, male, and the alchemists' notion that metals have sex.]

arshin, arshine, arsheen, *är-shēn'*, *n.* an old measure of length, about 28 inches in Russia, about 30 inches (legally a metre) in Turkey. [Turkish.]

arsis, *är'sis*, *n.* (*Gr. pros.* and *mus.*) lit. a lift, an up-beat : hence the weak position in a bar or foot : understood by the Romans as the strong position : used in English in both senses : elevation of the voice to higher pitch :—*pl.* (L.) **ar'sēs**:—opp. to *thesis.* [L.—Gr. *arsis*—*airein*, to lift.]

arsmetrick, *ärz-met'rik*, *n.* an obs. form of **arithmetic**, founded on the false etymology L. *ars metrica*, art of measuring.

arson, *är'sn*, *n.* the crime of feloniously burning houses, haystacks, ships, forests, or similar property.—*ns.* **ar'sonist, ar'sonite** (*rare*). [O.Fr. *arson*—L. *arsiō, -ōnis*—*ardēre*, *arsum*, to burn.]

arson, *är'sn*, *n.* (*obs.*) a saddlebow. [O.Fr. *arçun*—L. *arcus*, a bow.]

art, *ärt* (*arch.* and *poet.*) used as 2nd pers. sing. pres. indic. of the verb *to be.* [O.E. (W.S.) *eart*, (Mercian) *earth*, (Northumbrian) *arth ;* from the root *es-* seen in **is, are.**]

art, *ärt*, *n.* practical skill, or its application, guided by principles : human skill and agency (opp. to *nature*) : application of skill to production of beauty (esp. visible beauty) and works of creative imagina-tion (as the *fine arts*) : a branch of learning, esp. one of the *liberal* arts (see **trivium, quadrivium**), as in *faculty of arts, master of arts* : skill or knowledge in a particular department : a skilled profession or trade, craft, or branch of activity : magic or occult knowledge or influence : a method of doing a thing : a knack : contrivance : address : cunning : artifice : crafty conduct : a wile.—*adj.* **art'ful** (*arch.*), dexterous, clever : cunning : produced by art.—*adv.* **art'fully.**—*n.* **art'fulness.**—*adj.* **art'less**, simple : (*rare*) inartistic : guileless, unaffected.—*adv.* **art'lessly.**—*ns.* **art'lessness ; arts'man**, one who cultivates some practical knowledge : (*arch.*) a man skilled in arts or in learning ; **art'-song**, a song whose words and music are the product of conscious art, the music reflecting every turn of meaning—distinguished from a *folk-song* ; **art'-u'nion**, an association aiming at the promotion of an interest in the fine arts, esp. by raffling pictures.— *adj.* **art'y** (*coll.*), pretentiously claiming to be artistic.—**art and part**, originally (*law*) concerned in either by art or part—*i.e.* either by *art* in contriving or by *part* in actual execution ; now loosely used in the sense of participating, sharing ; **arts student**, a student in the faculty of arts ; **art student**, a student of painting, sculpture, etc. ; **be a fine art**, to be an operation or practice requiring nicety of craftsmanship ; **term of art**, a technical word ; **useful, or applied, arts** (as opposed to fine arts), those in which the hands and body are more concerned than the mind. [Fr.,—L. *ars, artis.*]

artefact, ar'tifact, *är'ti-fakt*, *n.* (esp. *archaeol.*) a thing made by human workmanship. [L. *arte*, by art (abl. of *ars*), *factum*, made.]

artel, *är-tel'*, *n.* a Russian workers' guild. [Russ.]

Artemisia, *är-te-miz'i-ä*, *n.* a genus of composites including wormwood, southernwood, mugwort, sagebrush, etc. [Gr. *artemisiā*.]

artery, *är'tər-i*, *n.* a tube or vessel that conveys blood from the heart : (*fig.*) any main channel of communication.—*adj.* **arterial** (-*tē'ri-əl*).—*v.t.* **artē'rialise**, to make arterial.—*ns.* **artē'riole**, a very small artery ; **artēriosclerō'sis** (Gr. *sklērōsis*, hardening), hardening of the arteries ; **artēri-ot'omy** (Gr. *tomē*, a cut), the cutting or opening of an artery, to let blood ; **arterī'tis**, inflammation of an artery. [L. *artēria*—Gr. *artēriā*, windpipe, artery.]

Artesian, *är-tē'zyən, -zh(y)ən*, *adj.* of Artois (L.L. *Artesium*), in the north of France, or a type of well in early use there, in which water rises in a borehole by hydrostatic pressure from a basin whose outcrop is at a higher level.

arthritis, *är-thrī'tis*, *n.* inflammation of a joint : gout.—*adj.* **arthritic** (-*thrit'ik*), of or near a joint : of, of the nature of, arthritis.—*n.* a gouty person. [Gr. *arthrītis, arthrītikos*—*arthron*, a joint.]

arthromere, *är'thrō-mēr*, *n.* a body segment of an articulated animal—a somite. [Gr. *arthron*, a joint, *meros*, part.]

arthropod, *är'thrō-pod*, *n.* any member of the **Arthropoda** (*är-throp'od-ä*), a great division of the animal kingdom, with segmented bodies and jointed appendages—crustacea, arachnids, peri-patus, millipedes, centipedes, insects, tardigrades, etc.—*adj.* **arthrop'odal.** [Gr. *arthron*, joint, and *pous, podos*, a foot.]

arthrosis, *är-thrō'sis*, *n.* connexion by a joint, articulation. [Gr. *arthrōsis*—*arthron*, a joint.]

arthrospore, *är'thrō-spōr*, *n.* a conidium : (in-appropriately) a vegetative cell that has passed into a resting state. [Gr. *arthron*, joint, *sporā*, seed.]

Arthurian, *är-th(y)ōō'ri-ən*, *adj.* relating to King *Arthur.*

artichoke, *är'ti-chōk*, *n.* a thistle-like perennial plant (*Cynara Scolymus*) with large scaly heads and edible receptacles.—**Jerusalem artichoke**, a totally different plant, a species of sunflower with edible tubers like potatoes, Jerusalem being a corr. of It. *girasole* (turn-sun), sunflower. [North It. *articiocco* (It. *carciofo*)—Old Sp. *alcarchofa*—Ar. *al-kharshōfa, al-kharshūf.*]

article, *är'ti-kl*, *n.* a joint, segment : a juncture, critical moment, nick of time : a separate element, member, or part of anything : a particular object or commodity : an item : a single clause or term : a distinct point in an agreement, or (*pl.*) an agree-ment looked at as so made up, as in *articles of apprenticeship*, etc. : (*pl.*) rules or conditions generally : a section, paragraph, or head : a literary composition in a newspaper, periodical, encyclo-paedia, etc., treating of a subject distinctly and independently : a matter : concern : a detail : a particular : (*gram.*) the adjective the (*definite article*), *a* or *an* (*indefinite article*) or the equivalent in another language.—*v.t.* to draw up or bind by articles : to indict, charge specifically : to set forth as a charge : to stipulate.—*adj.* **ar'ticled**, bound as apprentice.—*adjs.* **artic'ulable**, that can be articulated ; **artic'ular**, belonging to the joints : at or near a joint.—*n.pl.* **Articulā'ta**, in Cuvier's classification, the arthropods and higher worms.— *adj.* **artic'ulate**, jointed : composed of distinct parts : composed of recognisably distinct sounds, as human speech : clear : capable of clear expression. —*v.t.* to joint : to connect as by joint, or joint by joint : to form into distinct sounds, syllables, or words.—*v.i.* (*Shak.*) to come to terms : to speak distinctly.—*adj.* **artic'ulated.**—*adv.* **artic'u-lately.**—*ns.* **artic'ulateness ; articulā'tion**, joint-ing : a joint : a segment : distinctness, or distinct utterance : a consonant ; **artic'ulātor**, one who articulates or speaks : one who articulates bones and mounts skeletons.—*adj.* **artic'ulatory**— **articles of association**, regulations for the business of a joint-stock company registered under the Companies Acts ; **articles of faith**, binding statement of points held by a particular Church ; **articles of war**, code of regulations for the government and discipline of the army and navy ; **in the article of death** (L. *in articulō mortis*), at the point of death ; **Lords of the Articles**, a standing committee of the Scottish parliament who drafted the measures to be submitted; **of great article** (*Shak.*), of great importance; **Thirty-nine Articles**, the articles of religious belief finally agreed upon by the bishops and clergy of the Church of England in 1562. [L. *articulus*, a little joint, *articulāre*, *-ātum*, to furnish with joints, to utter distinctly—*artus*, joint.]

artifact. See **artefact**.

artifice, *är'ti-fis*, *n.* (*Milt.*) handicraft: workmanship: constructive skill: contrivance: a crafty trick or expedient.—*n.* **artif'icer**, a workman: a mechanic: a constructor: a contriver, inventor: a creator: (*obs.*) a trickster.—*adj.* **artificial** (*-fish'l*, or *är'*), contrived (opp. to *spontaneous*): made by man: synthetic (opp. to *natural*): fictitious, factitious, feigned, made in imitation (opp. to *real*): affected in manners: (*obs.*) ingenious: (*Shak.*) perh. creative, playing the artificer, or perh. merely skilful: (*obs.*) technical.—*v.t.* **artific'ialise**, to render artificial.—*n.* **artificiality** (*-fish-i-al'i-ti*).—*adv.* **artific'ially.**—*n.* **artific'ialness.**—**artificial silk** (see **silk**); **artificial porcelain**, soft-paste porcelain; **artificial sunlight**, light from lamps rich in ultraviolet rays. [L. *artificium—artifex*, *-ficis*, an artificer—*ars*, *artis*, and *facĕre*, to make.]

artillery, *är-til'ǝr-i*, *n.* offensive weapons of war, formerly in general, now the heavier kinds—ancient ballistas, catapults, modern cannon, etc.: a branch of the military service using these: (*obs.*) missiles: gunnery.—*ns.* **artill'erist**, one skilled in artillery: a gunner; **artill'ery-man**, a soldier of the artillery; **artill'ery-plant**, a tropical American plant (*Pilea*) of the nettle family that ejects its pollen in puffs. [O.Fr. *artillerie—artiller*, to arm, of doubtful origin.]

artiodactyl, *är-ti-ō-dak'til*, *adj.* even-toed.—*n.* a member of the **Artiodac'tyla** or even-toed ungulates, in which the third and fourth digit form a symmetrical pair and the hind-foot bears an even number of digits—as distinguished from the *Perissodactyla*. [Gr. *artios*, even in number, *daktylos*, finger, toe.]

artisan, artizan, *ärt-i-zan'*, or *ärt'*, *n.* a handicraftsman or mechanic. [Fr. *artisan*—It. *artigiano*, ult. from L. *artitus*, skilled—*ars*, *artis*, art.]

artist, *ärt'ist*, *n.* one who practises or is skilled in an art, now esp. a fine art: one who has the qualities of imagination and taste required in art: a painter or draughtsman: (*obs.*) a learned man: (*obs.*) one who professes magic, astrology, alchemy, etc., or chemistry: a performer, esp. in music.—*adjs.* **artist'ic**, *-al.*—*adv.* **artist'ically.**—*n.* **art'istry**, artistic pursuits: artistic workmanship, quality, or ability. [Fr. *artiste*—It. *artista*—L. *ars*, *artis*, art.]

artiste, *är-tēst'*, *n.* a public performer: an adept in a manual art. [Fr.]

Artocarpus, *är-tō-kär'pǝs*, *n.* a genus of the mulberry family including breadfruit and jack. [Gr. *artos*, bread, *karpos*, fruit.]

Arum, *ā'rǝm*, *n.* the cuckoo-pint or wakerobin genus: **arum**, loosely any kindred plant.—*n.pl.* **Arā'ceae** (*a-*), the family of spadicifloral monocotyledons to which it belongs.—*adjs.* **araceous** (*a-rā'shǝs*), **aroid** (*ā'roid*), of the Araceae: like an arum.—*n.* any plant of the family.—**arum lily**, Richardia or Zantedeschia. [L. *arum*—Gr. *aron*.]

arundinaceous, *ǝ-run-di-nā'shǝs*, *adj.* of or like a reed. [L. *arundināceus—arundō*, *-inis*, a reed.]

arval, *är'vǝl*, *adj.* pertaining to ploughed land.—**Arval Brethren**, in ancient Rome, a college of priests who sacrificed to the field deities. [L. *arvālis—arāre*, to plough.]

Arvicola, *är-vik'ō-lä*, *n.* the water-rat genus of voles.—*adj.* **arvic'oline.** [L. *arvum*, a field, *colĕre*, to inhabit.]

ary, *ā'ri*, *e'ri*, arrow, *ar'ō*, *adj.* (*prov.*) any. [From **e'er a**, **ever a**; cf. **nary**.]

Aryan, *är'yǝn*, *ä'ri-en*, *adj.* Indo-Germanic or Indo-European: now generally of the Indian, or Indian and Iranian, branch of the Indo-European languages: speaking one of these languages: in Nazi politics, not Jewish.—*n.* the parent Indo-European language: a speaker of an Aryan language.—*v.t.* **Ar'yanise.** [Sans. *arya*, noble.]

Arya Samaj, *är'yä sä-mäj'*, *n.* a reformed Hindu religious body or school, founded by Dayananda Saraswati (1824-83), based on the Vedas, opposing idolatry, caste, child-marriage, and other evils. [Hind. *ārya samāj*, noble association.]

aryballos, *ar-i-bal'os*, *n.* a globular oil-flask with a neck.—*adj.* **aryball'oid.** [Gr.]

aryl, *ar'il*, *n.* a general name for a univalent hydrocarbon radical. [**aromatic**, and Gr. *hȳlē*, matter.]

arytaenoid, arytenoid, *ar-i-tē'noid*, *adj.* pitchershaped.—*n.* a cartilage or a muscle of the larynx. [Gr. *arytainoeidēs—arytaina*, a cup, *eidos*, form.]

as, *az*, *ǝz*, *adv.* in whatever degree, proportion, manner: to whatever extent: with what truth: in that degree: to that extent: with that truth: so far: however: specifically: (*dial.*) how (exclamatory): passing into *conj.* or almost *prep.*, for instance: in the manner, character, part, aspect, of: insofar as: whereas.—*conj.* because, since: while, when: as if: (*Milt.*) that (consequence): (*illiterate* or *dial.*) than.—*pron.* who, which, that (after *such*, *so*, *same*, or where a statement is treated as antecedent; in *Shak.* after a demons. pron.; otherwise *dial.* or *illiterate*).—**as also**, likewise; **as concerning**, **as for**, **as regards**, **as to**, for the matter of; **as how** (*illit.* or *dial.*) that (with noun clause): (*obs.*) introducing a question (similarly **as why**); **as if**, **as though**, as it would be if; **as it were**, so to speak: in some sort; **as many as**, all who; **as much**, the same: just that; **as now**, **as then**, just at this, that, time; **as well**, also: in addition: equally; **as yet**, up to the moment; **so as to**, with the purpose or consequence; **when as** (*arch.*) at what time. [O.E. *all-swā* (*eall-swā*), all so, wholly so.]

as, *äs*, *n.* a Norse god, inhabitant of Asgard :—*pl.* **aesir** (*es'ir*). [O.N. *áss*, a god (pl. *æsir*); cf. O.E. *ōs*, seen in such proper names as *Oswald*, *Osric*.]

as, *as*, *n.* a Roman unit of weight, a pound of 12 ounces: a copper coin, originally a pound in weight, ultimately half an ounce :—*pl.* **ass'es**. [L. *ās*, *assis*, a unit.]

ås, *ōs*, *n.* (*geol.*) a kame or esker :—*pl.* **åsar** (*ōs'är*). [Sw.]

asafoetida, *as-ǝ-fet'i-dä*, or *-fēt'*, *n.* an ill-smelling medicinal gum-resin, got from the root latex of species of *Ferula*—also **asafetida**, **assafoetida**, **assafetida**. [Pers. *azā*, mastic, and L. *fētida* (*fem.*) stinking.]

åsar. See **ås**.

asarabacca, *a-sä-rä-bak'ä*, *n.* hazelwort (*As'arum europaeum*), of the birthwort family formerly used in medicine. [L. *asarum* (—Gr. *asaron*), *bacca*, a berry.]

asbestos, *az-best'os*, *n.* a fine fibrous amphibole capable of being woven into incombustible cloth: (commercially) chrysotile, a fibrous serpentine.—*adjs.* **asbest'ic**, **asbest'iform**, **asbes'tine**, **asbes'tous**, of or like asbestos. [Gr., (*lit.*) unquenchable—*a-*, priv., *sbestos*, extinguished.]

ascarid, *as'ka-rid*, any nematode worm of the parasitic genus **As'caris** (family **Ascar'idae**), infesting the small intestines. [Gr. *askaris*, pl. *askarides*.]

ascaunt. See **askance**.

ascend, *ǝ-send'*, *a-send'*, *as'end*, *v.i.* to go up, mount, rise: to go back in time or ancestry.—*v.t.* to go up, mount, climb: (*Shak.*) to go up to.—*ns.* **ascend'-ance**, **-ence** (both *rare*), **ascend'ancy**, **-ency**, dominating influence; **ascend'ant**, less commonly **ascend'ent**, (*astrol.*) the part of the ecliptic just risen or about to rise, in which a planet was supposed to influence a person born at the time: hence (from the phrase **in the ascendant**) ascendency, pre-eminence: an ancestor or relative in the ascending line: one who rises or mounts: a rise, up-slope.—*adj.* rising: just risen above the horizon: predominant.—*n.* **ascend'er**, one who ascends: a letter that reaches the top of the typebody.—**ascend'ible** (also **-able**), scalable.—*adj.* **ascend'ing**, rising: (*bot.*) curving up from a prostrate to an erect position.—*n.* **ascension** (*-sen'shǝn*), ascent (a Gallicism when used of a mountain ascent): an ascent to heaven, esp. Christ's.—*adj.* **ascen'tional.**—*ns.* **Ascen'sionday** (or **Ascension Day**), Holy Thursday, ten days before Whitsunday, commemorating Christ's Ascension; **Ascen'siontide,** Ascension-day to Whitsunday.—*adj.* **ascen'sive,** moving or tending upwards.—*n.* **ascent',** a going up: advancement: a going back in time or ancestry: a way up: an up-slope.—**right ascension** (*astron.*), a coordinate of the position of a heavenly body measured (usually in terms of time) eastwards along the celestial equator from the First Point of Aries, the other coordinate being the declination. [L. *ascendĕre, ascēnsum—ad,* to, *scandĕre,* to climb.]

ascertain, *as-ər-tān',* *v.t.* (*obs.*) to apprise: to assure: to make certain: to prove: to find out for certain: to insure, prove.—*adj.* **ascertain'able.**—*n.* **ascertain'ment.** [O.Fr. *acertener—à,* to, *certain,* certain.]

ascesis, *a-sē'sis,* *n.* the practice of disciplining oneself: asceticism. [Gr. *askēsis,* exercise, training.]

ascetic, *a-* or *ə-set'ik,* *n.* one who rigidly denies himself ordinary bodily gratifications for conscience' sake: one who aims to compass holiness through mortification of the flesh: a strict hermit: one who lives a life of austerity.—*adjs.* **ascet'ic, -al,** rigorous in mortifying the flesh: of asceticism: recluse.—*adv.* **ascet'ically.**—*n.* **ascet'icism** (*-sizm*). [Gr. *askētikos—askētēs,* one who is in training—*askeein,* to work, exercise, train.]

asci, *pl.* of **ascus.**

ascian, *ash'i-ən, n.* an inhabitant of the torrid zone, shadowless when the sun is right overhead. [Gr. *askios,* shadowless—*a-,* priv., *skiā,* a shadow.]

ascidium, *a-sid'i-əm, n.* a pitcher-shaped leaf or part of a leaf, as the pitcher of the pitcher-plants, the bladder of the bladderwort:—*pl.* **ascid'ia.**—*n.* **ascid'ian,** a sea-squirt, or tunicate, a degenerate survivor of the ancestors of the vertebrates, shaped like a double-mouthed flask. [Gr. *askidion,* dim. of *askos,* a leathern bag, wine-skin.]

ascites, *a-sī'tēz, n.* dropsy of the abdomen.—*adjs.* **ascit'ic** (*-sit'ik*), **ascit'ical.** Gr. *askītēs—askos,* belly.]

ascititious. Same as **adscititious.**

Asclepius, *as-klē'pi-əs, n.* Asklēpios, the Greek god of healing (Aesculapius).—*n.* **ascle'piad,** any plant of the genus Asclepias: **Asclepiad,** a son of Asclepius, a physician: a verse used by the Greek poet *Asclepiades* (*Asklēpiadēs;* 3rd cent. B.C.)—a spondee, two (in the *Greater Asclepiad* three) choriambi, and an iambus (— —/— —/— ⌣⌣/— ⌣⌣/ ⌣—).—*n.pl.* **Asclepiadā'ceae,** the milkweed and swallowwort family, close akin to the periwinkle family.—*adj.* **asclepiadā'ceous** (*bot.*).—*ns.* and *adjs.* **Asclepiadē'an, Asclepiad'ic** (*pros.*).—*n.* **Ascle'pias,** a chiefly American genus of the swallowwort family, milkweed. [Gr. *Asklēpios,* the god, *Asklēpiadēs,* the poet, *asklēpias, -ados,* swallowwort.]

asconce, *obs.* form of **askance** (in *Shak.* **a sconce**).

ascorbic, *a-skor'bik, adj.* antiscorbutic—only in **ascorbic acid,** vitamin C ($C_6H_8O_6$). [Gr. *a-,* priv., and **scorbutic.**]

ascribe, *ə-* or *a-skrīb', v.t.* to attribute, impute, or assign.—*adj.* **ascrib'able.**—*n.* **ascription** (*-skrip'shən*), act, expression, formula of ascribing or imputing, *e.g.* that ascribing glory to God at the end of a sermon. [L. *ascrībĕre—ad,* to, *scrībĕre,* to write.]

ascus, *as'kəs, n.* (*bot.*) an enlarged cell, commonly elongated, in which usually eight spores are formed:—*pl.* **asci** (*as'ī*).—*n.* **as'comycete** (*as'kō-mī-sēt*), any one of the **Ascomycetes** (*-sē'tēz*), one of the main divisions of the fungi, characterised by formation of asci; **as'cospore,** a spore formed in an ascus. [Gr. *askos,* bag.]

Asdic, *as'dik, n.* an apparatus for detecting and locating submarines by means of ultrasonic waves echoed back from the submarines. [Allied Submarine Detection Investigation Committee.]

aseity, *a-* or *ā-sē'i-ti, n.* self-origination. [L. *ā,* from, *sē* (*abl.*), oneself.]

asepalous, *a-sep'ə-ləs, adj.* without sepals. [Gr. *a-,* priv., and **sepal.**]

aseptate, *a-sep'tāt, adj.* not partitioned by septa. [Gr. *a-,* priv., and **septum.**]

aseptic, *a-, ā-,* or *ə-sep'tik, adj.* not liable to, or preventing, decay or putrefaction: involving or accompanied by measures to exclude micro-organisms.—*n.* an aseptic substance.—*ns.* **asep'ticism** (*-sizm*), aseptic treatment; **asep'sis,** freedom from sepsis or blood-poisoning: rendering or being aseptic: exclusion of micro-organisms.—*v.t.* **asep'ticise** (*-ti-sīz*), to make aseptic: to treat with antiseptics. [Gr. *asēptos—a-,* priv., *sēpein,* to cause to decay.]

asexual, *a-, ā-,* or *ə-seks'ū-əl, adj.* without sex; not involving sexual activity: vegetative.—*n.* **asexūality** (*-al'i-ti*).—*adv.* **asex'ūally.** [Gr. *a-,* priv., and **sexual.**]

Asgard, *äs'gärd, n.* the heaven of Norse mythology, abode of the twelve gods and twenty-six goddesses, and of heroes slain in battle. [O.N. *Āsgarthr, āss,* a god, *garthr,* an enclosure.]

ash, *ash, n.* a well-known timber tree (*Fraxinus excelsior,* or other species) of the olive family: its wood, white, tough, and hard: an ashen spear-shaft or spear.—*adj.* **ash'en.**—*ns.* **ash'-key,** the winged fruit of the ash; **ash'-plant,** an ash sapling. —**mountain ash,** the rowan-tree; **prickly ash,** the toothache tree (Xanthoxylum); **quaking ash,** the aspen. [O.E. *æsc;* Ger. *esche,* O.N. *askr.*]

ash, *ash, n.* (often in *pl.*) the dust or remains of anything burnt: volcanic dust, or a rock composed of it: (*pl.*) the remains of the human body when burnt: (*fig.*) a dead body.—*n.* **ash'-bin, -buck'et,** a receptacle for household refuse.—*adjs.* **ash'en; ash'en-grey,** of the colour of wood ashes.—*ns.* **ash'ery,** a place where potash or pearl-ash is made; **ash'-heap,** a heap of ashes and household refuse; **ash'-hole, ash'-pit,** a hollow under a fireplace to receive ashes; **ash'-leach,** a tub in which alkaline salts are dissolved from wood-ashes; **ash'-pan,** a tray fitted underneath a grate to receive the ashes; **ash'-stand, ash'-tray,** a small tray or saucer for tobacco ashes; **Ash'-Wednes'day,** the first day of Lent, from the custom of sprinkling ashes on the head.—*adjs.* **ash'y, ash'y-grey.**—**the ashes,** a term applied by the *Sporting Times* (in a mock 'In Memoriam' notice) to the loss of prestige in English cricket after the Australians' successful visit in 1882, after which English teams strove to 'bring back the ashes', or mortal remains. [O.E. *asce:* O.N. *aska.*]

ashake, *ə-shāk', adv.* in a shaking state. [Prep. **a, shake.**]

ashamed, *ə-shāmd', adj.* affected with shame (with *of* for the cause of shame; *for,* the person).—*v.i.* **ashame'** (*obs.*), to feel shame.—*v.t.* to put to shame.—*adv.* **ashamed'ly** (or *-id-li*).—*n.* **ashamed'ness** (or *-id-nes*).—*adj.* **asham'ing.** [Pfx. *a-* and O.E. *sc*(*e*)*amian,* to shame.]

ashet, *ash'it, n.* (now only *Scot.*) a large meat-plate. [Fr. *assiette.*]

ashine, *ə-shīn', adv.* or predicative *adj.* in a shining state.

ashiver, *ə-shiv'ər, adv.* or predicative *adj.* in a shivering or quivering state.

Ashkenazim, *äsh-kə-näz'im, n.pl.* the Polish and German Jews, as distinguished from the *Sephardim,* the Spanish and Portuguese Jews. [Heb. *Ashkenaz,* a northern people (Gen. x.) by later Jews identified with Germany.]

ashlar, ashler, *ash'lər, n.* a squared stone used in building or facing a wall: masonry of such stones.— Also *adj.*—*v.t.* to face with ashlar.—*ns.* **ash'laring,** ashlar masonry or facing: a vertical timber between floor-joist and rafter; **ash'larwork,** ashlar masonry. [O.Fr. *aiseler*—L. *axillāris* —*axilla,* dim. of *axis,* axle, plank.]

ashore, *ə-shōr', adv.* on shore. [Prep. **a,** and **shore.**]

Ashtaroth, Ashtoreth. See **Astarte.**

Asian, *āzh'yən,* or *āsh'i-ən,* **Asiatic,** *-i-at'ik, adjs.* belonging to *Asia* (esp. Asia Minor): in literature or art, florid.—*n.* a native of Asia.—*adj.* **Asianic** (*-an'ik*), Asian, esp. of a group of non-Indo-Germanic languages of Asia and Europe.—*n.*

Asiat'icism (-*i-sizm*), imitation of Asiatic or Eastern manners.

aside, *ə-sīd'*, *adv.* on or to one side : privately : apart.—*n.* words spoken in an undertone, so as not to be heard by some person present, words spoken by an actor which the other persons on the stage are supposed not to hear : an indirect effort of any kind.—*adj.* (*U.S.*) private, apart.—*prep.* (now only *Scot.*) beside.—**aside from** (*U.S.*), apart from; **to set aside**, to quash (a judgment). [Prep. **a, side**.]

asinico, *as-i-nē'kō*, *n.* (*Shak.*) a stupid fellow. [Sp. *asnico*—dim. of *asno*—L. *asinus*, ass.]

asinine, *as'in-īn*, *adj.* of or like an ass.—*n.* **asininity** (-*in'i-ti*). [L. *asinīnus*—*asinus*, ass.]

ask, *ȧsk*, *v.t.* to seek : to beg, request : to make a request of : to inquire : to inquire of : to invite : to proclaim.—*v.i.* to make request or inquiry.—*n.* ask'er.—**to ask for it** (*coll.*), to behave in a way likely to bring trouble on oneself [O.E. *āscian, ácsian;* Ger. *heischen,* O.N. *æskja*.]

ask, *ȧsk*, *n.* (*dial.*) a newt.—Also **ask'er**. [Apparently O.E. *áthexe;* cf. Ger. *eidechse,* lizard.]

askance, *ə-skȧns'*, **askant**, *ə-skant'*, *adv.* sideways : awry : obliquely.—*v.t.* (*Shak.*) to turn aside.—*prep.* (*Shak.*) **ascaunt'** (folio reading **aslant**), with a slant over.—**to eye, look or view askance,** to look (at) with disdain, disapprobation, envy, or (now usually) suspicion. [Ety. very obscure.]

askari, *ȧs'kä-rē*, *ȧs-kä'rē*, *n.* an East African soldier. [Arab. *'askarī,* soldier.]

askew, *ə-skū'*, *adv.* obliquely : aside : awry. [App. prep. **a** and **skew**.]

aslake, *ə-slāk'*, *v.t.* (*arch.*) to slake : to mitigate : to appease. [O.E. *áslacian;* see **slake**.]

aslant, *ə-slȧnt'*, *adv.* (or *adj.*) on the slant.—Also **asklent'** (*Scot.*).

asleep, *ə-slēp'*, *adv.* (or *adj.*) in or to a sleeping state : dead : (of limbs) in a numbed condition, sometimes with tingling or prickly feeling. [Prep. **a, and sleep**.]

aslope, *ə-slōp'*, *adv.* or *adj.* on the slope. [O.E. *áslopen,* pa.p. of *áslúpan,* to slip away.]

asmear, *ə-smēr'*, *adj.* smeared over.

asmoulder, *ə-smōl'dər*, *adv.* in a smouldering state.

asp, *asp*, *n.* an aspen.

asp, *ȧsp*, **aspic**(k), *asp'ik*, *n.* a venomous snake of various kinds—*Vipera aspis* of Southern Europe, Cleopatra's asp (probably the horned viper), the biblical asp (probably the Egyptian juggler's snake, *Naja Haje*), the cobra da capello. [L.—Gr. *aspis*.]

Asparagus, *as-par'ə-gəs*, *n.* a genus of Liliaceae, with leaves reduced to scales, cultivated as ornamental plants. and one species (*A. officinalis*) for its young shoots as a table delicacy.—*ns.* **aspar'agine** (-*jin,* -*jēn*), an amide found in asparagus and other vegetables; **aspar'agus-stone,** a pale yellowish green apatite. [L.,—Gr. *asp(h)aragos.*]

aspect, *as'pekt* (in *Spens., Shak., Milt.,* etc., *as-pekt'*), *n.* a look, a glance : a view : direction of facing : appearance presented : way of viewing : face : the situation of one planet with respect to another, as seen from the earth : (*gram.*) in some languages, a verbal form expressing simple action, repetition, beginning, duration, etc.—*v.t.* **aspect** (*obs.*), to look at or for.—*adj.* **as'pectable,** visible : worth looking at. [L. *aspectus.*]

aspen, *ȧsp'ən,* -*in* (*Spens.* **aspine**), *n.* the trembling poplar.—*adj.* made of, or like, the aspen : tremulous : timorous.—*adj.* **as'pen-like.** [O.E. *æspe;* Ger. *espe.*]

asper, *as'pər,* *n.* a small (obsolete) silver Turkish coin. [Gr. *aspron,* rough, later white.]

asper, *as'pər, adj.* (*obs.*) rough, harsh.—*n.* the Greek rough breathing (*spíritus asper*).—*v.t.* **as'perate,** to roughen.—*n.* **asperity** (-*per'*), roughness : harshness : bitter coldness.—*adj.* **as'perous,** rough with short hairs. [L. *asper.*]

asperge, *as-pərj', v.t.* to sprinkle.—*n.* an aspergillum for holy water.—*ns.* **aspergation** (-*gā'*); **asper'ger** (-*jər*); **asper'ges,** a short service introductory to the mass, so called from the words *Asperges me, Domine, hyssopo et mundabor* (Ps. li.); **aspergill, -um** (*as'pər-jil,* -*jil'əm*), a holy-water sprinkler;

Aspergillum, a genus of boring Lamellibranchs in which the shell forms an elongated cone, ending in a disk pierced with numerous small tubular holes ; **Aspergill'us,** a genus of minute moulds occurring on decaying substances. [L. *aspergēre*—*ad,* to, *spargēre,* to sprinkle.]

asperse, *as-pərs', v.t.* to slander or calumniate : to bespatter.—*n.* **asper'sion,** calumny : slander : (*Shak.*) a shower or spray—*adjs.* **aspers'ive, aspers'ory,** tending to asperse : defamatory.—*n.* an aspergillum : an aspersorium.—*ns.* **aspersoir** (*äs-per-swär';* Fr.), an aspergillum; **aspersō'rium** (L.), a holy-water vessel. [L. *aspergēre, aspersum—ad,* to, *spargēre,* to sprinkle.]

asphalt, *as'falt,* **asphaltum,** *as-falt'əm, ns.* a black or dark-brown, hard, bituminous substance, found native, and got as a residue in petroleum distillation, etc., anciently used as a cement : a mixture of this with rock chips or other material, used for paving, roofing, etc.—*v.t.* to lay, cover, or impregnate with asphalt.—*adj.* **asphalt'ic.** [Gr. *asphaltos,* from an Eastern word.]

aspheterism, *as-fet'ər-izm, n.* (*Southey*) denial of the right of private property.—*v.i.* **asphet'erise.** [Gr. *a-,* priv., and *spheteros,* one's own.]

asphodel, *as'fo-del, n.* a plant of the lily family— in Greek mythology, the peculiar plant of the dead : applied to other plants, esp. **bog asphodel.** [Gr. *asphodelos;* cf. **daffodil**.]

asphyxia, *as-fik'si-ä, n.* (*lit.*) stoppage of the pulse : suspended animation owing to any cause interfering with respiration.—Also **asphyx'y.**—*n.* and *adj.* **asphyx'iant,** (a chemical substance) producing asphyxia.—*v.t.* **asphyx'iate,** to produce asphyxia in.—*adj.* **asphyx'iāted.**—*ns.* **asphyxiā'tion,** action of asphyxiating or condition of being asphyxiated; **asphyx'iātor.** [Gr. *asphyxiā* —*a-,* priv., *sphyxis,* pulse.]

aspic, aspick. See **asp**.

aspic, *as'pik, n.* a savoury meat-jelly containing fish, game, hard-boiled eggs, etc. [Perh. from *aspic,* asp, because it is 'cold as an aspic' (French proverb).]

aspic, *as'pik, n.* the broad-leaved lavender. [Fr.,—L. *spīca,* spike.]

Aspidistra, *as-pid-ist'rä, n.* a genus of plants of the asparagus group of *Liliaceae*—often grown in rooms. [Perh. Gr. *aspis,* a shield.]

Aspidium, *as-pid'i-əm, n.* the shield-fern genus (by some broken up) of ferns—from the shield-shaped or kidney-shaped indusium.—*adj.* **aspid'ioid.** [Gr. *aspidion,* dim. of *aspis,* shield.]

aspire, *əs-* or *as-pīr', v.i.* (with *to, after,* or an infinitive) to desire eagerly : to aim at or strive for high things : to tower up.—*n.* **aspīr'ant** (or *as'pir-*), one who aspires (with *after, for*) : a candidate.—*adj.* ambitious : mounting up (*rare* in both senses).—*v.t.* **aspirate** (*as'pir-āt*), to pronounce with a full breathing, as *h* in *house.*—*n.* the sound represented by the letter *h* : a consonant sound consisting of a stop followed by an audible breath, as that of *bh* in Sanskrit : sometimes extended to a fricative or spirant : a mark of aspiration, the rough breathing (ʿ) in Greek : a letter representing an aspirate sound.—Also *adj.*—In French '*h* aspirate', no longer sounded, still affects the junction with the preceding word.—*ns.* **aspirā'tion,** eager desire : lofty hopes or aims : (*obs.*) breathing : pronunciation of a sound with a full breathing : an aspirated sound (like Gr. *ch, th,* etc.) : drawing a gas or liquid in, out, or through; **as'pirator,** an apparatus for drawing air or other gases through bottles or other vessels : (*med.*) an instrument for removing fluids from cavities of the body.—*adjs.* **aspir'atory** (-*ə-tə-ri* or *as'pir-*), relating to breathing; **aspir'ing.**—*adv.* **aspir'ingly.**—*n.* **aspir'ingness.**—**to drop one's aspirates,** to omit to pronounce the sound of *h.* [L. *aspīrāre,* -*ātum—ad,* to, *spīrāre,* to breathe.]

aspirin, *as'pir-in, n.* a drug (acetyl-salicylic acid) used for relieving rheumatic pains and neuralgia.

Asplenium, *as-plē'ni-əm, n.* spleenwort, a genus of ferns, mostly tropical, with long or linear sori, with indusium arising from a vein—including wall-rue. [Gr. *asplēnon*, lit. spleenless—*a*-, priv., and *splēn*, spleen : reputed a cure for spleen.]

asport, *as-pōrt'*, *v.t.* (*rare*) to carry away, esp. wrongfully.—*n.* **asportā'tion.** [L. *asportāre*—*abs*, away, and *portāre*, to carry.]

aspout, *ə-spowt'*, *adv.* spoutingly.

asprawl, *ə-sprawl'*, *adv.* in a sprawl.

aspread, *ə-spred'*, *adv.* in or into a spreading state.

asprout, *ə-sprowt'*, *adv.* in a sprouting state.

asquat, *ə-skwot'*, *adv.* squattingly.

asquint, *ə-skwint'*, *adv.* and *adj.* towards the corner of the eye : obliquely. [App. prep. **a** and some such word as Du. *schuinte*, slant.]

ass, *âs*, *n.* a small, usually grey, long-eared animal of the horse genus : (*fig.*) a dull, stupid fellow.—**asses' bridge**, the *pons asinorum*, or fifth proposition in the first book of Euclid, for some an impassable barrier to further progress. [O.E. *assa*—L. *asinus*; cf. Gr. *onos*, ass ; perh. Semitic.]

assafetida. Same as **asafoetida.**

assagai. Same as **assegai.**

assai, *äs-sä'ē*, *adv.* (*mus.*) very. [It.,—L. *ad*, to, *satis*, enough.]

assai, *ä-sä'ē*, *n.* a S. American palm (*Euterpe edulis*) : its fruit : a drink made from its fruit. [Tupi.]

assail, *ə-sāl'*, *v.t.* to attack.—*adj.* **assail'able.**—*ns.* **assail'ant**, one who attacks ; **assail'ment.** [O.Fr. *asaillir*—L. *assilīre*—*ad*, upon, and *salīre*, to leap.]

assart, *as-ärt'*, *v.t.* (*hist.*) to reclaim for agriculture by grubbing.—*n.* a forest clearing : assarted land : grubbing up of trees and bushes. [A.Fr. *assarter*—L.L. *exsartāre*—L. *ex*, out, *sar(r)īre*, to hoe, weed.]

assassin, *ə-* or *a-sas'in*, *n.* (*hist.*) a follower of the Old Man of the Mountains, a member of his military and religious order in Persia and Syria (11th-13th cent.), notorious for secret murders : one who, usually for a reward, or for political reasons, kills by surprise or secretly.—*v.t.* **assass'-inate**, to murder by surprise or secret assault : (*Milt.*) to maltreat : (*fig.*) to destroy by treacherous means, as a reputation.—*n.* (*obs.*) one who assassinates. — *ns.* **assassinā'tion** ; **assass'inator.** [Through Fr. or It. from Ar. *hashshāshīn*, hashish-eaters.]

assault, *ə-sawlt'*, *n.* a sudden attack : a storming, as of a town : (*Eng. law*) unlawful attempt to apply force to the person of another—when force is actually applied, the act amounts to *battery* : an attack of any sort by arguments, appeals, etc.—*v.t.* to make an assault or attack upon.—*n.* **assault'er.** —**assault at** or **of arms**, a display of attack and defence in fencing. [O.Fr. *asaut*—L. *ad*, upon, *saltus*, a leap, *salīre*, to leap. See **assail.**]

assay, *a-* or *ə-sā'*, *v.t.* to put to the proof : to make trial of : to test : to determine the proportion of metals in : to give as result : (*obs.*) to test the fatness of (a killed stag) by a trial cut : (*obs.*) to taste before presenting (as a precaution or guarantee against poison) : to put to proof in action : (*Spens.*) to afflict : (*obs.*) to tempt : (*Spens.*) to affect : (*Shak.*) to experience : to endeavour (now usu. **essay**) : (*Spens.*, *Shak.*) to assail : (*Shak.*) to challenge : (*Shak.*) to accost.—*v.i.* to adventure, make an attempt : to practise assaying (of ores, etc.)—*n.* (by some *as'ā*) a test, trial : a determination of proportion of metal : a specimen used for the purpose : (*obs.*) determination of the fatness of a stag : experiment : experience : endeavour, attempt, tentative effort (usu. **essay**) : (*Spens.*, *Shak.*) assault : (*Spens.*, *Shak.*) proof, temper, quality, standard, such as might be found by assaying.—*adj.* **assay'-able.**—*ns.* **assay'er**, one who assays metals ; **assay'ing** ; **assay'-master**, an officer who determines the amount of gold or silver in coin or bullion ; **assay'-piece**, a sample chosen for assay : an example of excellence.—**cup of assay**, a small cup for trial tasting before offering. [O.Fr. *assayer*, *n.* *assai*. See **essay.**]

assegai, **assagai**, *as'ə-gī*, *n.* a slender spear of hard wood tipped with iron, some for hurling, some for thrusting with—used by Zulus and other South Africans.—*v.t.* to kill or wound with an assegai.

[Through Fr. or Port. from Ar. *azzaghāyah*—*az = al*, the, *zaghāyah*, a Berber word.]

assemble, *ə-sem'bl*, *v.t.* to call or bring together : to collect : to put together the parts of.—*v.i.* to meet together.—*ns.* **assem'blage**, a collection of persons or things ; **assem'bla(u)nce** (*Spens.*), an assembling : (*Shak.*) semblance : representation ; **assem'bler** ; **assem'bly**, the act of assembling : the putting together of parts : a company assembled : a formal ball or meeting for dancing and social intercourse : a reception or at-home : (*arch.*) a meeting for religious worship : a deliberative or legislative body, esp. in some legislatures a lower house : (*mil.*) a drum-beat, esp. a signal for striking tents ; **assem'bly-man**, a member of assembly or lower house ; **assem'bly-room**, a public ball-room.—**General Assembly**, in Scotland, Ireland and the United States, the highest court of the Presbyterian Church ; **Legislative Assembly, House of Assembly**, the lower or only house of some legislatures ; **National Assembly** (also **Constituent Assembly**), the first of the revolutionary assemblies in France (1789-91) : a body set up in 1920 'to deliberate on all matters concerning the Church of England and to make provision in respect thereof', consisting of houses of Bishops, Clergy (these two composed of members of the two Convocations), and Laity (elected by lay members of Diocesan conferences)—also **Church Assembly.** [Fr. *assembler*—L.L. *assimulāre*, to bring together—*ad*, to, *similis*, like. See **assimilate.**]

assent, *a-* or *ə-sent'*, *v.i.* to express agreement or acquiescence (with *to*).—*n.* an agreeing or acquiescence : compliance.—*adj.* **assentaneous** (*as-ən-tā'ni-əs*), ready to agree.—*ns.* **assentā'tion**, obsequious assent, adulation ; **ass'entātor** (*obs.*) ; **assent'er.**—*adjs.* **assentient** (*ə-sen'shənt*), **assent'ive.**—*adv.* **assent'ingly.**—*ns.* **assent'ive-ness** ; **assent'or**, one who subscribes a candidate's nomination-paper in addition to proposer and seconder.—**royal assent**, the sovereign's formal acquiescence in a measure which has passed the Houses of Parliament. [L. *assentārī*, to flatter, freq. of *assentīrī*, to assent, agree.]

assert, *ə-sərt'*, *v.t.* to vindicate or defend by arguments or measures (now used only with *cause* as object, or reflexively) : to declare strongly : to lay claim to : to insist upon : to affirm : (*rare*) to bear evidence of.—*adj.* **assert'able.**—*ns.* **assert'er**, **assert'or**, a champion : one who makes a positive statement ; **asser'tion** (*-shən*), affirmation : the act of claiming one's rights : averment.—*adj.* **assert'-ive**, asserting or confirming confidently : positive : dogmatic.—*adv.* **assert'ively.**—*n.* **assert'iveness.** —*adj.* **assert'ory**, affirmative.—**assert oneself**, to defend one's rights or opinions, sometimes with unnecessary zeal : to thrust oneself forward. [L. *asserĕre*, *assertum*, to lay hands on, claim—*ad*, to, and *serĕre*, to join.]

assess, *ə-ses'*, *v.t.* to fix the amount of, as a tax : to tax or fine : to fix the value or profits of, for taxation (with *at*) : to estimate.—*adj.* **assess'able.** —*ns.* **assess'ment**, act of assessing : a valuation for the purpose of taxation : a tax ; **assess'or**, a legal adviser who sits beside a magistrate : one appointed as an associate in office with another : one who assesses taxes, or value of property, income, etc., for taxation : one who shares another's dignity.—*adj.* **assessō'rial** (*as-*).—*n.* **assess'or-ship.** [L. *assidēre*, *assessum*, to sit by, esp. of judges in a court, from *ad*, to, at, *sedēre*, to sit.]

assets, *as'ets*, *n.pl.* (*orig. sing.*) the property of a deceased or insolvent person, considered as chargeable for all debts, etc. : the entire property of all sorts belonging to a merchant or to a trading association.—*false sing.* **ass'et**, an item of property : (*coll.*) something advantageous or well worth having. [From the Anglo-Fr. law phrase *aver assetz*, to have enough, O.Fr. *asez*, enough—L. *ad*, to, *satis*, enough.]

asseverate, *ə-*, *a-sev'ər-āt*, *v.t.* to declare solemnly —earlier **assev'er.**—*adj.* **assev'erating.**—*adv.* **assev'eratingly.**—*n.* **asseverā'tion.** [L. *assevĕrāre*, *-ātum*—*ad*, to, *sevērus*, serious ; see **severe.**]

Neutral vowels in unaccented syllables : *el'ə-mənt*, *in'fənt*, *ran'dəm*

assibilate, *a-* or *a-sib'i-lāt, v.t.* to sound as a sibilant.—*n.* **assibilā'tion.** [L. *ad,* to, *sibilāre,* to hiss.]

assiduity, *as-id-ū'i-ti, n.* persistent application or diligence : (*pl.*) constant attentions.—*adj.* **assiduous** (*a-sid'ū-as*), constant or unwearied in application.—*adv.* **assid'uously.**—*n.* **assid'ūousness.** [L. *assiduus*—*ad,* to, at, *sedēre,* to sit.]

assiege, *a-sēj', v.t.* (*Spens.*) to besiege. [See **siege.**]

assiento, *as-ē-en'tō, n.* (*hist.*) a treaty (esp. that with Britain, 1713) for the supply of African slaves for Spanish American possessions. [Sp. (now *asiento*), seat, seat in a court, treaty.]

assign, *a-sīn', v.t.* to allot : to designate, appoint : to put forward, adduce : to make over, transfer : to ascribe, refer : to specify : to fix, determine.—*n.* one to whom any property or right is made over : (in *pl., Shak.*) appendages.—*adj.* **assign'able,** that may be assigned.—*ns.* **assignation** (*as-ig-nā'shan*), an appointment to meet, used chiefly of love trysts, and mostly in a bad sense : (*Scots law*) the making over of any right to another; **assignee** (*as-in-ē'*), one to whom any right or property is assigned : a trustee of a sequestrated estate; **assignment** (*-sīn'*), act of assigning : anything assigned : the writing by which a transfer is made : (orig. *U.S.*) a task allotted : (*Spens.* altered in 1596 to **dessignment**) design, enterprise; **assignor** (*as-i-nor'*; law), one who makes over. [Fr. *assigner*—L. *assignāre,* to mark out—*ad,* to, *signum,* a mark or sign.]

assignat, *as'ig-nat, ä-sēn-yä', n.* one of the notes first issued in 1790 by the French government as bonds on the security of the appropriated church lands. [Fr.]

assimilate, *a-sim'il-āt, v.t.* to make similar or like (with *to, with*) : to convert into a like substance, as food in the body.—*v.i.* to become like : to be incorporated in.—*adj.* **assim'ilable**—*n.* **assimilā'tion.**—*adj.* **assim'ilātive,** having the power or tendency to assimilate. [L. *assimilāre, -ātum*—*ad,* to, *similis,* like.]

assist, *a-sist', v.t.* to help : (*Shak.*) to accompany.—*v.i.* to help : (now a *Gallicism*) to be present.—*n.* **assis'tance,** help : relief.—*adj.* **assist'ant,** helping.—*n.* one who assists : a helper. [Fr. *assister*—L. *assistĕre,* to stand by—*ad,* to, *sistĕre,* to set, take one's stand.]

assize, *a-sīz', v.t.* (*obs.*) to assess : to set or fix the quantity or price of.—*n.* (*hist.*) a statute settling the weight, measure, or price of anything : (*Scot.*) a trial by jury : (*Scot.*) a jury : judgment, sentence : (in *pl.*) periodical sittings of judges on circuit through the English counties, with a jury.—*n.* **assiz'er,** an officer with oversight of weights and measures. [O.Fr. *assise,* assembly of judges, set rate—*asseoir*—L. *assidēre*—*ad,* to, *sedēre,* to sit.]

associate, *a-sō'shi-āt, v.t.* to join, connect, link : to connect in one's mind : to make a colleague or partner : (*Shak.*) to accompany.—*v.i.* to consort, keep company (with *with*) : to combine or unite.—*adj.* associated : connected : confederate : joined as colleague or (*U.S.*) junior colleague.—*n.* one joined or connected with another : a colleague, companion, friend, partner, or ally : a person admitted to a society without full membership.—*n.* **associabil'ity.**—*adj.* **asso'ciable** (*-shi-a-bl,* or *-sha-bl*), capable of being associated.—*ns.* **asso'ciateship;** **associā'tion** (*-si-,* or *-shi-*), act of associating : union or combination : a society of persons joined to promote some object : (*biol.*) a set of species of plants or animals characteristic of a certain habitat : (*chem.*) loose aggregation of molecules : (*football*; also **association football,** *coll.* **soccer**) the game as formulated by the Football Association (formed 1863), with eleven players a side, opp. to *Rugby.*—*adj.* **asso'ciātive,** tending to association.—**association copy,** a copy of a book deriving additional interest from some association, e.g., a copy inscribed as given to or by some person of note; **association of ideas,** mental linkage that facilitates recollection—by similarity, contiguity, repetition. [L. *associāre, -ātum*—*ad,* to, *socius,* a companion.]

assoil, *a-soil', v.t.* (*arch.*) to absolve : to acquit : to discharge : to release : to solve : to dispel : to determine.—*n.* **assoil'ment.**—*v.t.* **assoilzie** (*a-soil'i, -yi; Scot.*), to absolve : (*Scots law*) to free (defender or accused) of a claim or charge. [A.Fr. *assoilier*—L. *ab,* from, *solvĕre,* to loose.]

assoil, *a-soil', v.t.* to soil, sully, dirty. [L. *ad,* and **soil** (2).]

assonance, *as'an-ans, n.* a correspondence in sound : in Spanish, Portuguese, etc., vowel-rhyme, coincidence of vowels without regard to consonants, as in *mate* and *shape, feel* and *need* : extended to correspondence of consonants with different vowels.—*adjs.* **ass'onant; assonantal** (*-ant'al*).—*v.i.* **ass'onate,** to correspond in vowel sound : to practise assonance. [L. *assonāre, -ātum*—*ad,* to, *sonāre,* to sound.]

assort, *a-sort', v.t.* to distribute in classes, classify : to class.—*v.i.* to agree or be in accordance : to suit well : (*arch.*) to keep company.—*adj.* **assort'ed,** classified, arranged in sorts : made up of various sorts.—*ns.* **assort'edness; assort'ment,** act of assorting : a quantity or number of things assorted : variety. [Fr. *assortir*—L. *ad,* to, *sors, sortis,* a lot.]

assot, *a-sot', v.t.* (*Spens.*), to befool, to besot.—*p.adj.* **assott',** or **assott'ed** (*Spens.*), infatuated. [O.Fr. *asoter*—*à,* to, *sot,* fool; see **sot.**]

assuage, *a-swāj', v.t.* to soften, mitigate, or allay.—*v.i.* to abate or subside : to diminish.—*n.* **assuage'ment.**—*n.* and *adj.* **assuag'ing.**—*adj.* **assuā'sive** (*-siv*), soothing : mitigating. [O.Fr. *assouager*—L. *ad,* to, *suāvis,* mild.]

assubjugate, *a-sub'joo-gāt, v.t.* (*Shak.*) to reduce to subjection. [Pref. *a-,* **subjugate.**]

assuefaction, *as-wi-fak'shan, n.* habituation. [L. *assuēfacĕre*—*assuētus,* accustomed, and *facĕre,* to make.]

assuetude, *as'wi-tūd, n.* accustomedness : habit. [L. *assuētus.*]

assume, *a-sūm', -sŏŏm', v.t.* to adopt, take in : to take up, to take upon oneself : to take for granted : to arrogate : to pretend to possess.—*v.i.* to make undue claims : to be arrogant.—*adj.* **assum'able.**—*adv.* **assum'ably.**—*adj.* **assumed',** appropriated, usurped : pretended : taken as the basis of argument.—*adv.* **assum'edly.**—*adj.* **assum'ing,** haughty : arrogant.—*n.* assumption : arrogance : presumption.—*adv.* **assum'ingly.**—*ns.* **assump'sit** (*a-sump'sit*), an action at law, wherein the plaintiff asserts that the defendant undertook (L. *assūmpsit*) to do a certain act and failed to fulfil his promise; **assumption** (*-sum', -sump'*), an act of assuming : reception : taking upon oneself : arrogance : taking for granted : supposition : that which is taken for granted or supposed : (*logic*) the minor premise in a syllogism : a taking up bodily into heaven, especially the **Assumption of the Virgin,** celebrated on the 15th of August (declared a dogma of the Roman Catholic Church on the 1st of November, 1950).—*n.* **Assump'tionist,** a member of the Roman Catholic congregation (*Augustinians of the Assumption*) founded at Nîmes in 1843.—Also *adj.*—*adj.* **assump'tive,** of the nature of an assumption : gratuitously assumed : apt, or too apt, to assume.—**deed of assumption** (*Scots law*), a deed executed by trustees under a trust-deed assuming a new trustee or settlement. [L. *assūmĕre, assūmptum*—*ad,* to, *sūmĕre,* to take.]

assure, *a-shŏŏr', v.t.* to make sure or secure : to give confidence : (*obs.*) to betroth : to tell positively : to insure.—*adj.* **assur'able.**—*n.* **assur'ance,** confidence : feeling of certainty : (*theol.*) subjective certainty of one's salvation : self-confidence : unabashedness : audacity : positive declaration : insurance, now esp. life-insurance : security : the securing of a title to property : a promise : a surety, warrant : (*obs.*) a betrothal.—*adj.* **assured',** secured : pledged : (*obs.*) betrothed : certain : confident : beyond doubt : insured : self-confident : overbold : brazen-faced.—*adv.* **assur'edly.**—*ns.* **assur'edness; assur'er,** one who gives assurance : an insurer or underwriter : one who insures his life. [O.Fr. *aseürer* (Fr. *assurer*)—L.L. *adsēcūrāre* —*ad*, to, *sēcūrus*, safe; see **sure**.]

assurgent, *ə-sur′jənt*, *adj.* rising, ascending : (*bot.*) rising in a curve to an erect position : (*her.*) depicted as rising from the sea.—*n.* assur′gency, the tendency to rise. [L. *ad*, to, *surgĕre*, to rise.]

asswage, an old spelling of **assuage**.

Assyrian, *a-* or *ə-sir′i-ən*, *adj.* of Assyria.—*n.* an inhabitant or native of Assyria : the Semitic language of ancient Assyria.—*ns.* **Assyriol′ogist**; **Assyriol′ogy**, the science of Assyrian antiquities. [Gr. *Assyrios*—*Assyriā*.]

assythment, *ə-sīth′mənt*, *n.* (*Scot. law*) indemnification. [O.Fr. *aset*; see **assets**.]

astarboard, *ə-stär′bōrd*, *adv.* on or towards the starboard. [Prep. **a**, and **starboard**.]

astare, *ə-stār′*, *adv.* in a state of staring. [Prep. **a**, and **stare**.]

astart, *ə-stärt′*, *v.i.* (*Spens.*) to start up : to befall.—*adv.* with a start, suddenly. [Pfx. **a-**, up, and prep. **a**, on, and **start**.]

Astarte, *as-tär′ti*, *n.* the Greek and Roman form of the name of a Semitic goddess whose attributes symbolise the notion of productive power.—Also **Ashtaroth** (*ash′tar-oth*), **Ash′toreth** (*B.*).

astatic, *a-stat′ik*, *adj.* having no tendency to stand in a fixed position : without polarity, as a pair of magnetic needles set in opposite directions.—*n.* **astatine** (*as′tə-tēn*), the chemical element of atomic number 85 (symb. At). [Gr. *astatos*, unstable—*a-*, priv., *statos*, verb. adj. of *histanai*, to make to stand.]

astatki, *as-tat′kē*, *n.* the residue of petroleum-distillation, used as fuel. [Russ. *ostatok*, residue.]

asteism, *as′tē-izm*, *n.* refined irony. [Gr. *asty*, *-eōs*, town.]

astely, *a-stē′li*, *n.* (*bot.*) absence of a central cylinder or stele.—*adj.* **astē′lic**. [Gr. *a-*, priv., *stēlē*, column.]

aster, *as′tər*, *n.* (*obs.*) a star : a starlike figure, as in mitotic cell-division : **Aster**, a genus of Compositae, with showy radiated heads, white to lilac-blue or purple, flowering in late summer and autumn, hence often called China aster (*Callistephus hortensis*) brought from China to France by a missionary in the 18th century.—*ns.* **asteria** (*as-tē′ri-ä*), a precious stone that shows asterism when cut *en cabochon*—star-sapphire, star-ruby; **Astē′rias**, the common crossfish or five-fingers genus of sea-urchins.—*adj.* **astē′riated** (*-ā-*), showing asterism.—*ns.* **as′terid**, a starfish; **as′terisk**, a star-shaped mark (*) used as a reference to a note, as a mark of omission, as a mark of a word or root inferred to have existed but not recorded, and for other purposes; **as′terism**, a group of stars : three asterisks placed to direct attention to a passage : in some minerals the property of showing by reflected or transmitted light a star-shaped luminous figure due to inclusions or tubular cavities; **as′teroid**, a minor planet : a starfish.—*adj.* resembling a star, starfish, or aster.—*adj.* **asteroid′al**.—*n.pl.* **Asteroid′ea**, a class of echinoderms, the starfishes. [Gr. *astēr*, star.]

astern, *ə-stərn′*, *adv.* in or towards the stern : behind. [Prep. **a**, and **stern**.]

astert, *ə-stərt′*, *v.i.* Same as **astart**.

asthenia, *as-thi-nī′ä*, often *as-thē′ni-ä*, *n.* debility.—*adj.* **asthenic** (*-then′ik*), of, relating to, asthenia : lacking strength : (*anthrop.*) of a slender type, narrow-chested, with slight muscular development.—*n.* a man of asthenic type. [Gr. *astheneia*—*a-*, priv., *sthenos*, strength.]

asthma, *as′mä*, also *asth′*, *ast′*, and (*U.S.*) *az′*, *n.* a chronic disorder of the organs of respiration, characterised by difficulty of breathing, wheezing, and a tightness in the chest.—*adjs.* **asthmatic** (*-mat′*), **-al**.—*adv.* **asthmat′ically**. [Gr. *asthma*, *-atos*—*aazein*, to breathe with open mouth.]

astichous, *as′ti-kəs*, *n.* (*bot.*) not in rows. [Gr. *a-*, priv., *stichos*, a row.]

astigmatism, *a-stig′mə-tizm*, *n.* a defect in an eye, lens, or mirror, by which rays from one point are not focused at one point.—*adj.* **astigmatic** (*-mat′*). [Gr. *a-*, priv., and *stigma*, *-atos*, a point.]

astir, *ə-stər′*, *adv.* on the move : out of bed : in motion or excitement. [Prep. **a**, and **stir**.]

astomatous, *a-stom′ə-təs*, or *-stōm′*, *adj.* mouthless. —Also **astomous** (*as′tə-məs*). [Gr. *a-*, priv., *stoma*, *-atos*, mouth.]

astonish, *əs-ton′ish*, *v.t.* to impress with sudden surprise or wonder : to amaze : (*Shak.*) to daze, to stun—earlier forms **astone** (*ə-stun′*), **astun′**, **astony** (*-ston′i*).—*adjs.* **aston′ied** (*obs.*); **aston′ished**, amazed : (*obs.*) dazed, stunned.—*adj.* **aston′ishing**, very wonderful, amazing.—*adv.* **aston′ishingly**.—*n.* **aston′ishment**, amazement : wonder : a cause for astonishment. [O.Fr. *estoner*—L. *ex*, out, *tonāre*, to thunder.]

astoop, *ə-stōōp′*, *adv.* in a stooping position. [Prep. **a**, and **stoop**.]

astound, *əs-townd′*, *v.t.* to amaze, to strike dumb with astonishment.—*adjs.* **astound′** (*arch.*), **astound′ed**, stunned : dazed : amazed; **astound′ing**. —*adv.* **astound′ingly**.—*n.* **astound′ment**. [From the pa.p. **astoned**; see foregoing.]

astraddle, *ə-strad′l*, *adv.* with legs wide apart. [Prep. **a**, on, and **straddle**.]

astragal, *as′trə-gəl*, *n.* (*archit.*) a small semicircular moulding around a column or elsewhere : a round moulding near the mouth of a cannon : one of the bars that hold the panes of a window : (in *pl.*) dice. —*n.* **astragalus** (*as-trag′al-əs*), the ankle-bone; **Astragalus**, the tragacanth and milk-vetch genus. [Gr. *astragalos*, a vertebra, ankle-bone, moulding, milk-vetch, in *pl.* dice.]

astrakhan, *as-trə-kan′*, *n.* lamb-skin with a curled wool from the Middle East; a rough fabric made in imitation of it. [*Astrakhan* on the Caspian Sea.]

astral, *as′trəl*, *adj.* belonging to the stars : starry : belonging to a mitotic aster : in theosophy, of a supersensible substance supposed to pervade all space and enter into all bodies.—**astral body**, as astral counterpart of the physical body : a ghost or wraith; **astral spirits**, spirits supposed to animate the heavenly bodies, forming, as it were, their souls. [L. *astrālis*—*astrum*, a star.]

astrand, *ə-strand′*, *adv.* on the strand. [Prep. **a**, on, and **strand**.]

Astrantia, *as-tran′shi-ä*, *n.* a genus of umbelliferous plants with showy petal-like bracts. [Gr. *astron*, star.]

astray, *ə-strā′*, *adv.* out of the right way : out of one's reckoning : in a lost state. [Prep. **a**, on, and **stray**.]

astrict, *ə-strikt′*, *v.t.* to bind, to compress : to constipate : to restrict.—*n.* **astric′tion** (*-shən*).—*adj.* **astrict′ive**, astringent.—*v.t.* **astringe** (*-strinj′*, *-strinzh′*), to bind : to draw together : to draw tight : to compress : to constipate.—*n.* **astrin′gency** (*-jən-si*).—*adj.* **astrin′gent** (*ə-strin′jənt*), binding : contracting : drawing together : having power to contract organic tissues : styptic : austere.—*n.* an astringent agent.—*adv.* **astrin′gently**. [L. *astringĕre*, *astrictum*—*ad*, to, *stringĕre*, to draw tight.]

astride, *ə-strīd′*, *adv.* in a striding position : with a leg on each side.—*prep.* astride of : on either side of. [Prep. **a**, on, **stride**.]

astringency, etc. See under **astrict**.

astringer, a Shakespearian form of **austringer**.

astro-, *as′trō-*, *-tro′*, in composition, star.—*ns.* **as′trodome**, a small transparent observation dome on the top of the fuselage of an aeroplane; **as′trolabe** (*-lāb*), an old instrument for taking altitudes (from *lab-*, root of Gr. *lambanein*, to take); **astrol′atry**, star-worship (Gr. *latreiā*, worship); **astrol′oger**.—*adjs.* **astrolog′ic**, **-al**.—*adv.* **astrolog′ically**.—*ns.* **astrol′ogy**, orig. practical astronomy : now almost confined to the once-supposed art or science of the influence of the stars on human and terrestrial affairs (*judicial astrology*; Gr. *logos*, discourse); **astron′omer**.—*adjs.* **astronom′ic**, **-al**, relating to astronomy : prodigiously great, like the distance of the stars—(**astronomical unit**, the earth's mean distance from the sun, about 92·9 million miles, used as a measure of distance within the solar system).—*v.i.* **astron′omise**, to study astronomy.—*n.* **astron′omy**, the science of the heavenly bodies (Gr. *nomos*, law).—*adj.* **astrophys'ical.**—*ns.* **astrophys'icist; astrophys'ics** (*pl.* in form, treated as *sing.*), the science of the chemical and physical condition of the heavenly bodies. [Gr. *astron*, star.]

astrophel, astrofell, *as'trō-fel, n.* an unidentified bitter starlike plant into which Spenser feigns Astrophel and Stella (Sir Philip Sidney and Penelope Devereux) to have been transformed— the seaside aster has been suggested. [Poss. Gr. *astron*, star, *phyllon*, leaf.]

astrut, *ə-strut', adv.* protrudingly: distendedly.— *adj.* protruding: distended. [Prep. **a**, **strut.**]

astute, *as-, əs-tūt', adj.* shrewd: sagacious: wily.— Also **astucious** (*-tū'shəs*).—*adv.* **astu'ciously.**— *n.* **astucity** (*-tū'si-ti*).—*adv.* **astute'ly.**—*n.* **astute'-ness.** [L. *astūtus*—*astus* (found in abl. *astū*), craft.]

astylar, *a-stī'lər, adj.* without columns. [Gr. *a-*, priv., *stȳlos*, a column.]

asudden, *ə-sud'ən, adv.* of a sudden.—*advs.* **asun'der,** apart : into parts : separately ; **aswarm',** in swarms; **asway',** swayingly : in a sway; **aswim',** afloat; **aswing',** swingingly : in a swing; **aswirl',** in a swirl. [Prep. **a**, and **sudden, sunder,** etc.]

aswoon, *ə-swoon', adv.* in a swoon. [Poss. for *on* or *in swoon;* or orig. a pa.p., M.E. *iswowen*—O.E. *geswógen*, swooned (not known in other parts).]

asylum, *ə-sī'ləm, n.* a place of refuge for debtors and for those accused of crime : an institution for the care or relief of the unfortunate, as the blind or insane : any place of refuge or protection :—*pl.* **asy'lums.** [L. *asȳlum*—Gr. *asȳlon* (neut.) inviolate—*a-*, priv., *sȳlon, sȳlē*, right of seizure.]

asymmetry, *a-sim'ə-tri, n.* want of symmetry.— *adjs.* **asymmetric** (*-et'rik*), **-al.**—*adv.* **asymmet'rically.** [Gr. *asymmetriā*—*a-*, priv., *symmetriā*, symmetry.]

asymptote, *a'sim-tōt, n.* (*math.*) a line that continually approaches a curve but never meets it.—*adjs.* **asymptotic** (*-tot'ik*), **-al.**—*adv.* **asymptot'ically.** [Gr. *asymptōtos*—*a-*, priv., *syn*, together, *ptōtos*, apt to fall, *piptein*, to fall.]

asynartete, *a-sin'är-tēt, adj.* and *n.* not connected, consisting of two members having different rhythms : a verse of such a kind.—Also **asynartetic** (*-tet'ik*). [Gr. *asynartētos*—*a-*, priv., *syn*, together, *artaein*, to knit.]

asynchronism, *a-sing'kro-nizm, n.* want of synchronism or correspondence in time.—*adj.* **asyn'-chronous.** [Gr. *a-*, priv., *syn*, together, *chronos*, time.]

asyndeton, *a-sin'də-ton, n.* (*rhet.*) a figure in which the conjunctions are omitted.—*adj.* **asyndet'ic.** [Gr. *asyndeton*—*a-*, priv., *syndetos*, bound together, *syn*, together, *deein*, to bind.]

asynergia, *as-in-ər'ji-ā, n.* lack of coordination in action, as of muscles. [Gr. *a-*, priv., *syn*, together, *ergon*, work.]

asyntactic, *as-in-tak'tik, adj.* loosely put together, irregular, ungrammatical. [Gr. *asyntaktikos*—*a-*, priv., *syntaktos*—*syntassein*, to put in order together.]

asystole, *a-sis'to-lē, n.* (*med.*) inability of the heart to empty itself.—Also **asys'tolism.** [Gr. *a-*, priv., *systolē*, contraction.]

at, *at, ət, prep.* denoting precise position in space or time, or some kindred relation, as occupation, aim, aggressive activity. [O.E. *æt;* cf. Goth. and O.N. *at*, L. *ad*, Sans. *adhi.*]

atabal, *at'ə-bal, ä-tä-bäl', n.* a Moorish kettledrum. [Sp.,—Ar. *at-tabl*, the drum.]

atabeg, atabek, *ät-ä-beg', -bek', n.* a ruler or high official. [Turk. *atabeg*—*ata*, father, *beg*, prince.]

atabrin, atebrin, *at'ə-brin, n.* mepacrine.

atacamite, *a-tak'ə-mīt, n.* a mineral, a basic chloride of copper. [Atacama, in Chile.]

atactic. See **ataxia.**

ataghan. Same as **yataghan.**

ataman, *at'ə-man, n.* a Cossack headman or general—a hetman :—*pl.* **atamans.** [Russ.,— Ger. *hauptmann*—*haupt*, head, *mann*, man.]

atap, attap, *at'ap, n.* the nipa palm : its leaves used for thatching. [Malay.]

ataraxia, *at-ə-rak'si-ä,* **ataraxy,** *at'ə-rak-si, n.* calmness, the indifference aimed at by the Stoics. [Gr. *ataraxiā*—*a-*, priv., *tarassein*, to disturb.]

atavism, *at'av-izm, n.* appearance of ancestral, but not parental, characteristics : reversion to an ancestral type.—*adj.* **atavist'ic.** [L. *atavus*, a great-great-great-grandfather, an ancestor—*avus*, a grandfather.]

ataxia, *a-tak'si-ä,* **ataxy,** *a-tak'si, at'aks-i, n.* (*med.*) inability to co-ordinate voluntary movements (see **locomotor**).—*adjs.* **atact'ic, atax'ic.** [Gr. *ataxiā*, disorder—*a-*, priv., *taxis*, order.]

ate, *et,* or *āt, pa.t.* of **eat.**

Ate, *ä'tē, ä'tē, ä'tā, n.* the Greek goddess of mischief and of all rash actions and their results. [Gr. *Ātē.*]

atebrin. See **atabrin.**

ateleiosis, *a-tel-ī-ō'sis, n.* dwarfism without disproportion. [Gr. *ateleiōtos*, insufficient—*a-*, priv., *telos*, an end.]

atelier, *at'əl-yā, n.* a workshop, esp, an artist's studio. [Fr.]

Athanasian, *ath-ə-nā'sh(y)ən, -z(h)yən, adj.* relating to *Athanasius* (c. 296-373), or to the creed erroneously attributed to him.

athanasy, *a-than'ə-si, n.* deathlessness. [Gr. *athanasiā*—*a-*, priv., *thanatos*, death.]

athanor, *ath'ə-nor, n.* an alchemist's self-feeding digesting furnace. [Ar. *at-tannūr*—*al*, the, *tannūr*, furnace—*nūr*, fire.]

Atharvaveda, *ä-tär'vä-vä'dä, n.* one of the Vedas. [Sans. *atharvan*, fire-priest, *veda*, knowledge.]

atheism, *ā'thi-izm, n.* disbelief in the existence of a god.—*v.i.* and *v.t.* **a'theise,** to talk or write as an atheist.—*n.* **a'theist.**—*adjs.* **atheist'ic, -al.**— *adv.* **atheist'ically.**—*adj.* **a'theous** (*Milt.*), atheistic : godless. [Gr. *atheos*—*a-*, priv., and *theos*, god.]

atheling, *ath'əl-ing, n.* (*hist.*) a member of a noble family : later, a prince of the blood royal, or the heir-apparent. [O.E. *ætheling*—*æthele*, noble; cf. Ger. *adel.*]

athematic, *ath-i-mat'ik, adj.* without a thematic vowel.—*adv.* **athemat'ically.** [Gr. *a-*, priv., and **thematic.**]

Athene, *a-thē'nē,* **Athena,** *-nä, n.* Greek goddess of wisdom, born from the head of Zeus, tutelary goddess of Athens, identified by the Romans with Minerva.—*n.* **Athenaeum** (*ath-ə-nē'əm*), a temple of Athene : an ancient institution of learning, or literary university : a name sometimes taken for a literary institution, library, or periodical.—*adj.* **Athenian** (*a-thē'ni-ən*), of Athens.—*n.* a native or citizen of Athens or Attica.

atheology, *ā-thi-ol'ə-ji, n.* opposition to theology.— *adj.* **atheological** (*-ə-loj'i-kl*). [Gr. *a-*, priv., and **theology.**]

atherine, *ath'ər-īn, n.* a genus (Atheri'na) of small fishes of a family (Atherinidae) : *-in'i-dē*), akin to the grey mullets, sometimes sold as smelt. [Gr. *atherīnē*, atherine.]

athermancy, *ath-ər'mən-si, n.* impermeability to radiant heat.—*adj.* **ather'manous.** [Gr. *a-*, priv., *thermainein*, to heat.]

atheroma, *ath'ər-ō-mä, n.* a cyst with porridge-like contents : a thickening of the inner coat of arteries. —*adj.* **atherōm'atous.** [Gr. *athērōma*—*athērē* or *athärē*, porridge.]

athetesis, *ath-i-tē'sis, n.* rejection as spurious.— *v.t.* **ath'etise,** to reject.—*n.* **atheto'sis,** involuntary movement of fingers and toes due to a lesion of the brain.—*adj.* **ath'etoid.**—*n.* a spastic who has involuntary movements. [Gr. *athetos*, without position, set aside, *athetēsis*, rejection—*a-*, priv., and the root of *tithenai*, to set.]

athirst, *ə-thərst', adj.* thirsty : eager. [O.E. *ofthyrst.* See **thirst.**]

athlete, *ath'lēt, n.* a contender for victory in feats of strength, speed, endurance, or agility : one vigorous in body or mind.—Also (*obs.*) **athlē'ta.**— *adj.* **athletic** (*-let'ik*), (*anthrop.*) of a long-limbed, large-chested, muscular type of body : relating to athletics : strong, vigorous.—*adv.* **athlet'ically.**— *n.* **athlet'icism** (*-i-sizm*), practice of, training in, or devotion to, athletics.—*n.pl.* (in form) **athlet'ics,** athletic sports. [Gr. *athlētēs*—*athlos*, contest.]

at-home. See **home.**

athrill, *ə-thril', adv.* in a thrill.—*adj.* and *adv.* **athrob',** with throbs, throbbing.—*prep.* **athwart',**

across.—*adv.* sidewise: transversely: awry: wrongly: perplexingly.—*adv.* **atilt'**, on tilt: as a tilter. [Prep. **a**, on, and **thrill**, etc.]

atimy, *at'i-mi*, *n.* loss of honour: in ancient Athens, loss of civil rights, public disgrace. [Gr. *atimiā*—*a-*, priv., *timē*, honour.]

atingle, *ə-ting'gl*, *adj.* and *adv.* in a tingle. [Prep. **a, tingle.**]

Atkins. See **Tommy Atkins.**

Atlas, *at'las*, *n.* the Titan who bore the heavens on his shoulders, and whose figure used to appear on title-pages of atlases: the African mountain range into which he was transformed: (pl. **Atlantes**, *at-lan'tēz*), a figure of a man serving as a column in a building: **atlas** (*pl.* **at'lases**), the vertebra that supports the skull: a book of maps, plates, or the like: a size of drawing-paper, 26 by 34 inches.—*adjs.* **Atlantē'an**, of Atlas: gigantic: of Atlantis; **Atlan'tic**, of Atlas: of the Atlantic Ocean.—*n.* the Atlantic Ocean, separating Europe and Africa from America.—*n.* **Atlan'tis**, a traditional vanished island in the Atlantic Ocean; **Atlantosaurus** (*-ō-saw'rəs*; Gr. *sauros*, lizard), a gigantic Jurassic dinosaur of Colorado and Wyoming. [Gr. *Atlas, Atlantos.*]

atlas, *at'las*, *n.* a silk-satin manufactured in the East. [Ar.]

atmology, *at-mol'ə-ji*, *n.* the science of the phenomena of aqueous vapour.—*n.* **atmol'ogist.** [Gr. *atmos*, vapour, and *logos*, discourse.]

atmolysis,. *at-mol'i-sis*, *n.* a method of separating mixed gases by their different rates of passage through a porous septum.—*v.t.* **at'molyse** (*-līz*). [Gr. *atmos*, vapour, *lysis*, loosing—*lyein*, to loose.]

atmometer, *at-mom'i-tər*, *n.* an instrument for measuring the rate of evaporation from a moist surface. [Gr. *atmos*, vapour, *metron*, measure.]

atmosphere, *at'mas-fēr*, *n.* the gaseous envelope that surrounds the earth or any of the heavenly bodies: any gaseous medium: a unit of atmospheric pressure—760 millimetres, or 30 inches, of mercury at freezing-point: a feeling of space and distance in a picture: (*fig.*) any surrounding influence or pervading feeling.—*adjs.* **atmospher'ic** (*-fer'ik*), **-al**, of or depending on the atmosphere.—*adv.* **atmospher'ically.**—*n.pl.* **atmospher'ics**, noises interfering with wireless reception, due to electric disturbances in the ether.—**atmospheric engine**, a variety of steam-engine in which the steam is admitted only to the under side of the piston; **atmospheric hammer**, a hammer driven by compressed air. [Gr. *atmos*, vapour, *sphaira*, a sphere.]

atocia, *a-tō-shi-ā*, *n.* sterility in a female.—*n.* **atoke** (*at'ōk*), the sexless part in certain polychaete worms.—*adjs.* **atokous** (*at'ək-əs*), **at'okal**, without offspring. [Gr. *atokiā*—*a-*, priv., *tokos*, birth, offspring.]

atok, atoc, *a-tok'*, *n.* a species of skunk. [Peruvian.]

atoll, *at'ol*, or *a-tol'*, *n.* a coral island consisting of a circular belt of coral enclosing a central lagoon. [Name in Maldive Islands.]

atom, *at'əm*, *n.* a particle of matter so small that, so far as the older chemistry goes, it cannot be cut or divided: anything very small.—*adjs.* **atomic** (*ə-tom'ik*), **-al**, pertaining to atoms.—*ns.* **atomicity** (*at-əm-is'i-ti*), state or fact of being composed of atoms: number of atoms in a molecule: valency; **atomisā'tion** (*med.*), the reduction of liquids to the form of spray; **atomi'ser**, an instrument for discharging liquids in a fine spray; **at'omism**, the doctrine that atoms arranged themselves into the universe: the atomic theory; **at'omist**, one who believes in atomism.—*adj.* **atomis'tic.**—*adv.* **atomist'ically.**—*n.* **at'omy**, an atom, or mote: (*Shak.*) a pygmy.—**atom(ic) bomb**, a bomb in which the nuclei of uranium or plutonium atoms bombarded by neutrons split with explosive transformation of part of their mass into energy; **atomic energy**, nuclear energy; **atomic number**, the number of units of charge of positive electricity on the nucleus of an atom of an element: **atomic philosophy**, a system of philosophy enunciated by Democritus, which taught that the ultimate constituents of all things are indivisible particles, differing in form and in their relations to each other; **atomic pile**, a device for the controlled release of nuclear energy, e.g. a lattice of small rods of natural uranium embedded in a mass of pure graphite which serves to slow down neutrons; **atomic theory**, the hypothesis that all atoms of the same element are alike and that a compound is formed by union of atoms of different elements in some simple ratio; **atomic warfare**, warfare using atomic bombs; **atomic weight**, the inferred weight of an atom of an element relatively to that of hydrogen as 1 or, now more usually, oxygen as 16. [Gr. *atomos*—*a-*, priv. and *tomos*, verbal adj. of *temnein*, to cut.]

atomy, *at'əm-i*, *n.* (*Shak.*) a skeleton, walking skeleton. [Formerly also *atamy* and *natomy*, for **anatomy**, mistakingly divided *an atomy.*]

atone (*Spens.* accent), *ə-tōn'*, *adv.* at one, at once, together.—*v.i.* originally to make *at one*, to reconcile; to give satisfaction or make reparation (with *for*): to make up for deficiencies: (*Shak.*) to agree, be in accordance.—*v.t.* to appease, to expiate: (*arch.*) to harmonise, or reconcile.—*ns.* **atone'ment**, the act of atoning; reconciliation: expiation: reparations: esp. (*Christian theol.*) the reconciliation of God and man by means of the incarnation and death of Christ; **aton'er.**—*advs.* **aton'ingly**; **attonce** (*ə-tons'*), **attones** (*ə-tōnz'*; both *Spens.*), at once: together.

atony, *at'ən-i*, *n.* want of tone or energy or of stress: debility: relaxation.—*adj.* **atonal** (*a-tō'nl*; *mus.*), not referred to any scale or tonic.—*ns.* **atonality** (*at-ə-nal'i-ti*); **atō'nalism.**—*adj.* **atonic** (*a-ton'ik*; *pros.*), without tone: unaccented. [Gr. *atoniā*—*a-*, priv., *tonos*, tone, strength.]

atop, *ə-top'*, *adv.* on or at the top. [Prep. **a**, and **top**.]

atrabilious, *at-rə-bil'yəs*, *adj.* of a melancholy temperament: hypochondriac: splenetic, acrimonious. [L. *āter*, *ātra*, black, *bīlis*, gall, bile.]

atramental, *at-rə-men'təl*, *adj.* inky, black. [From L. *ātrāmentum*, ink—*āter*, black.]

atremble, *ə-trem'bl*, *adv.* in a tremble.—*adv.* **atrip'** (of an anchor when it is just drawn out of the ground), in a perpendicular position: (of a sail) when it is hoisted from the cap, sheeted home and ready for trimming. [Prep. **a**, on, **tremble, trip.**]

atrium, *ā'tri-əm* (L. *āt'ri-oom*), *n.* the entrance-hall or chief apartment of a Roman house: (*zool.*) a cavity or entrance:—*pl.* **a'tria.**—*adj.* **a'trial.** [L. *ātrium.*]

atrocious, *ə-trō'shəs*, *adj.* extremely cruel or wicked: heinous: very grievous: execrable.—*adv.* **atrō'ciously.**—*ns.* **atrō'ciousness**; **atrocity** (*ə-tros'i-ti*), atrociousness: an atrocious act. [L. *ātrōx, ātrōx, -ōcis*, cruel.]

atrophy, *at'rəf-i*, *n.* wasting away: degeneration: diminution of size and functional activity by disuse: emaciation.—*v.t.* and *v.i.* to cause or suffer atrophy, to starve, to waste away.—*adj.* **at'rophied.** [Gr. *a-*, priv., and *trophē*, nourishment.]

Atropos, *at'rō-pos*, *n.* the Fate that cuts the thread of life.—*ns.* **At'ropa**, the deadly nightshade genus of the potato family; **at'ropin, atropine** (*-pēn*, *-pin*, *-pīn*), a poisonous alkaloid in deadly nightshade (**atropia**, *ə-trō'pi-ä*); **at'ropism, atropin** poisoning. [Gr. *Atropos.*]

atropous, *at'rō-pos*, *adj.* (*bot.*) of an ovule, orthotropous. [Gr. *a-*, priv., *tropos*, turning.]

Ats, *ats*, *n.pl.* women of the Auxiliary Territorial Service. [From the initials; see *Abbreviations.*]

attach, *ə-tach'*, *v.t.* to bind or fasten: to seize: to gain over: to connect, associate: to join in action, function, or affection: to arrest.—*v.i.* to adhere, to be fastened: to be attributable, incident (*to*): (*rare*) to come into effect.—*adj.* **attach'able.**—*adj.* **attached'.**—*n.* **attach'ment**, act or means of fastening: a bond of fidelity or affection: seizure of goods or person by virtue of a legal process. [O.Fr. *atachier*, from *à* (—L. *ad*), and perhaps the root of **tack**.]

attaché, *a-tash'ā*, *n.* a junior member of an ambassador's suite.—*n.* **atta'ché-case**, a small rectangular leather hand-bag for documents, etc. [Fr., attached.]

attack, *ə-tak'*, *v.t.* to fall upon violently : to assault : to assail : to begin to affect or act destructively upon.—*v.t.* and *v.i.* (*mus.*) to begin (a phrase or piece).—*n.* an assault or onset : the offensive part in any contest : the beginning of active operations on anything, even dinner : severe criticism or calumny : an access of illness : (*mus.*) an executant's approach to a piece, or mode of beginning with respect to crispness, verve, and precision : (*lacrosse*) certain positions between centre and the opponents' goal.—*adj.* **attack'able**. [Fr. *attaquer*; a doublet of **attach**.]

attain, *ə-tān'*, *v.t.* to reach or gain by effort: to arrive at.—*v.i.* to come or arrive.—*adj.* **attain'able**, that may be reached.—*ns.* **attain'ableness**, **attainabil'ity**; **attain'ment**, act of attaining : the thing attained : acquisition : (*pl.*) acquirements in learning. [O.Fr. *ataindre*—L. *attingĕre*—*ad*, to, *tangĕre*, to touch.]

attainder, *ə-tān'dər*, *n.* act of attainting : (*law*) loss of civil rights through conviction for high treason. —*v.t.* **attaint'**, to convict : to deprive of rights by conviction for treason : to accuse: to disgrace, stain (from a fancied connexion with *taint*).—*n.* (*arch.*) the act of touching, a hit (in tilting) : (*Shak.*) infection : attainder : a stain, disgrace.—Older *pa.p.* **attaint'** (*Shak.*), corrupted, tainted.—*ns.* **attaint'-ment**, **attaint'ure**. [O.Fr. *ataindre*—L. *attingĕre*. See **attain**.]

attar, *at'är*, *n.* a very fragrant essential oil made in Bulgaria and elsewhere, chiefly from the damask rose.—Also **ott'o**, **ott'ar**. [Pers. *atar*.]

attask, *ə-täsk'*, *v.t.* to take to task (only in the *pa.p.* **attaskt'**, a doubtful reading in Shak. *King Lear*). [Pfx. *a-*, and **task**.]

attemper, *ə-tem'pər*, *v.t.* to mix in due proportion : to modify or moderate: to adapt.—*adj.* **at-tem'pered**. [L. *attemperāre*—*ad*, to, *temperāre*, to regulate.]

attempt, *ə-temt'*, *v.t.* to try, endeavour : to try to obtain : to tempt, entice : to make an effort or attack upon.—*v.i.* to make an attempt or trial.— *n.* an effort : a personal assault : (*Milt.*) temptation : (*law*) any act that can fairly be described as one of a series which, if uninterrupted and successful, would constitute a crime.—*n.* **attemptabil'ity**.— *adj.* **attempt'able**, that may be attempted.—*n.* **attempt'er** (*Milt.*), a tempter. [O.Fr. *atempter*— L. *attentāre*—*ad*, and *temptāre*, *tentāre*, to try—*tendĕre*, to stretch.]

attend, *ə-tend'*, *v.t.* to wait on : to accompany : to be present at : to wait for : to give attention to.—*v.i.* to yield attention : to act as an attendant : to wait, be consequent (with *to*, *on*, *upon*).—*ns.* **attend'-ance**, act of attending : (*B.*) attention, careful regard : presence : gathering of persons attending; **attend'ancy** (*obs.*) attendance, a retinue : (*obs.*) relative position.—*adj.* **attend'ant**, giving attend-ance : accompanying.—*n.* one who attends or accompanies : a servant : what accompanies or follows : (*law*) one who owes a duty or service to another.—*ns.* **attend'er**, one who gives heed : a companion; **attend'ment** (*rare*), accompaniments : (*Spens.* **atten'dement**), intention.—*adj.* **attent'** (*Spens.*, *Shak.*), giving attention.—*n.* (*Spens.*) attention.—*n.* **atten'tion** (*-shən*), act of attending : steady application of the mind : heed : civility, courtesy : (in *pl.*) courtship: position of standing rigidly erect with hands by the sides and heels together.—*interj.* (*mil.*) a cautionary word calling for an attitude of readiness to execute a command. —*adj.* **attent'ive**, full of attention : courteous, mindful.—*adv.* **attent'ively**.—*n.* **attent'iveness**. [L. *attendĕre*, *attentum* ; *attentiō*, *-ōnis*.]

attenuate, *ə-ten'ū-āt*, *v.t.* to make thin or lean : to break down into finer parts : to reduce in density : to reduce in strength or value.—*v.i.* to become thin or fine : to grow less.—*n.* **atten'uant**, anything that attenuates.—*adjs.* **atten'uate**, **atten'uated**, thin : thinned : dilute, rarefied : tapering.—*n.* **attenua'tion**, process of making slender : reduction of intensity, density, force, or (of bacteria) virul-ence : in homoeopathy, the reduction of the active principles of medicines to minute doses. [L. *attenuāre*, *-ātum*—*ad*, to, *tenuis*, thin.]

attercop, *at'ər-kop*, *n.* (*obs.* or *dial.*) a spider : an ill-natured person. [O.E. *attorcoppa*—*attor*, *ātor*, poison, and perh. *cop*, head, or *copp*, cup.]

attest, *ə-test'*, *v.t.* to testify or bear witness to : to affirm by signature or oath : to give proof of, to manifest : (*obs.*) to call to witness.—*v.t.* and *v.i.* to enrol for military service.—*v.i.* to bear witness.— *n.* (*Shak.*) witness, testimony.—*adjs.* **attest'able**, **attest'ative**.—*ns.* **attestā'tion** (*at-*), act of attesting : administration of an oath : attest'or, attest'er. [L. *attestārī*—*ad*, to, *testis*, a witness.]

Attic, *at'ik*, *adj.* of Attica or Athens : chaste, refined, classical, in taste, language, etc., like the Athenians.—*v.t.* **Atticise** (*at'i-sīz*), to make con-formable to the language or idiom of Attica.—*v.i.* to use the idioms of the Athenians : to side with the Athenians : to affect Attic or Greek style or manners.—*n.* **Att'icism** (*-sizm*).—**Attic salt**, wit of a dry, delicate, and refined quality. [Gr. *Attikos*—*Attikē*, Attica.]

attic, *at'ik*, *n.* (*archit.*) a low story or structure above the cornice of the main part of an elevation, usually of the so-called **Attic order**, i.e. with square columns or pilasters instead of pillars : a skylighted room in the roof of a house. [The structure was supposed to be in the Athenian manner. See foregoing.]

attire, *ə-tīr'*, *v.t.* to dress, array or adorn : to prepare.—*n.* dress : any kind of covering.—*ns.* **attire'ment**, **attir'ing**. [O.Fr. *atirer*, put in order—*à tire*, in a row—*à* (L. *ad*), to, and *tire*, *tiere*, order, dress. See **tier**.]

attitude, *at'i-tūd*, *n.* posture, or position : a studied or affected posture : (of aircraft) position relative to the normal line of flight, ground or wind : any condition of things or relation of persons viewed as expressing some thought, feeling, etc.—*adj.* **atti-tud'inal**.—*n.* **attitudinā'rian**, one who studies attitudes.—*v.i.* **attitud'inise**, to assume affected attitudes.—*n.* **attitudini'ser**.—**to strike an atti-tude**, to assume a position or figure to indicate a feeling or emotion not really felt. [Fr. *attitude* or It. *attitudine*—L. *aptitūdō*, *-inis*—*aptus*, fit.]

attollent, *ə-tol'ənt*, *adj.* lifting up, raising.—*n.* a muscle that raises. [L. *attollēns*, *-entis*, pr.p of *attollĕre*, to lift up—*ad*, to, *tollĕre*, to lift.]

attorn, *ə-turn'*, *v.t.* to transfer to another.—*v.i.* to accept tenancy under a new landlord.—*n.* **at-torn'ey** (*pl.* **attor'neys**; O.Fr. pa.p. *atorné*), one legally authorised to act for another : one legally qualified to manage cases in a court of law : a solicitor.—*v.t.* (*Shak.*) to perform by proxy : to employ as a proxy.—*ns.* **Attor'ney-Gen'eral**, the chief law-officer for England, Eire, a dominion, colony, etc. : the king's attorney in the duchies of Lancaster and Cornwall, and the county palatine of Durham : in the United States, one of the seven officials who constitute the president's cabinet, the head of the Department of Justice: also the legal adviser of a State governor; **attor'neydom**; **attor'neyism**; **attor'neyship**; **attorn'ment**, acknowledgment of a new landlord.—**attorney at law**, or **public attorney**, a professional and duly qualified legal agent; **attorney in fact**, or **private attorney**, one duly appointed by power of attorney to act for another in matters of contract, money payments, and the like; **letter**, **warrant**, or **power of attorney**, a formal instrument by which one person authorises another to perform certain acts for him. [L.L. *attornāre*, to assign; see **turn**.]

attract, *ə-trakt'*, *v.t.* to draw or cause to approach otherwise than by material bonds : to allure : to entice.—*adj.* **attract'able**, that may be attracted.— *adv.* **attract'ingly**.—*n.* **attrac'tion**, act of attract-ing : an attracting force : that which attracts.—*adj.* **attract'ive**, having the power of attracting : alluring.—*adv.* **attract'ively**.—*ns.* **attract'ive-ness**; **attract'or**. [L. *attrahĕre*, *attractum*—*ad*, to, *trahĕre*, to draw.]

attrahent, *at'rə-hənt*, *adj.* attracting or drawing.— *n.* that which attracts. [L. *attrahēns*, *-entis*, pr.p. of *attrahĕre*. See **attract**.]

attrap, *ə-trap'*, *v.t.* (*Spens.*) to adorn with trappings : to dress or array. [L. *ad*, to, and **trap**.]

attribute, *ə-trib'ūt*, *v.t.* to ascribe, assign, or consider as belonging.—*n.* (*at'ri-būt*) that which is attributed: that which is inherent in, or inseparable from, anything: that which can be predicated of anything: a quality or property: an accessory: a conventional symbol: (*gram.*) a word added to another to denote an attribute.—*adj.* **attrib'utable.**—*n.* **attribution** (*at-ri-bū'shən*), act of attributing: that which is attributed.—*adj.* **attrib'utive,** expressing an attribute.—*n.* (*gram.*) a word added to another to denote an attribute.—*adv.* **attrib'utively.** [L. *attribuĕre, -tribūtum—ad*, to, *tribuĕre*, to give.]

attrist, *ə-trist'*, *v.t.* (*obs.*) to sadden. [Fr. *attrister* —L. *ad*, to, *tristis*, sad.]

attrite, *ə-trīt'*, *adj.* worn by rubbing or friction: (*theol.*) repentant through fear of punishment, not yet from the love of God.—*n.* **attrition** (*a-* or *ə-trish'ən*), rubbing together: wearing down: (*theol.*) a defective or imperfect sorrow for sin: (*fig.*) the wearing down of an adversary, resistance, resources, etc. [L. *attrītus—atterĕre—ad*, to, and *terĕre, trītum*, to rub.]

attuition, *at-ū-ish'ən*, *n.* a mental operation intermediate between sensation and perception.—*adjs.* **attui'tional;** **att'uent,** performing the function of attuition.—*v.t.* **att'uite** (*-īt*), to be conscious of by attuition.—*adj.* **attu'itive.**—*adv.* **attu'itively.** [L. *ad*, to, *tuērī*, to attend to.]

attune, *ə-tūn'*, *v.t.* to put in tune: to make to accord: to arrange fitly: to make musical.—*n.* **attune'ment.** [L. *ad*, to, and **tune.**]

atwain, *ə-twān'*, *adv.* (*arch.*) in twain: asunder. [Prep. **a, twain.**]

atweel, *ə-twēl'*, *adv.* or *interj.* (*Scot.*) well: indeed. [**wat weel,** i.e. wot well.]

atween, *ə-twēn'*, *adv.* (*Spens.*) betweenwhiles.— *prep.* between.—*adv.* and *prep.* **atwixt'** (*Spens.*), betwixt.

atypical, *a-tip'i-kl*, *adj.* not typical. [Gr. *a-*, priv., **type.**]

aubade, *ō-bäd'*, *n.* a musical announcement of dawn: a sunrise song. [Fr.,—*aube*, dawn—Prov. *alba*, dawn.]

auberge, *ō-berzh'*, *n.* an inn.—*n.* **aubergiste** (*ō-ber-zhēst'*), an inn-keeper. [Fr., of Gmc. origin. See **harbour.**]

aubergine, *ō'ber-jēn, -zhēn, n.* the fruit of the egg-plant, the brinjal: its purple colour. [Fr. dim. of *auberge*, a kind of peach—Sp. *albérchigo*—Ar. *al*, the, Sp. *pérsigo*—L. *persicum*, a peach.]

Aubrietia, *aw-bri-ē'sh(y)ä, n.* a purple-flowered Mediterranean genus of trailing cruciferous plants, much grown in rock-gardens, etc. [After Claude *Aubriet* (c. 1665–1742), naturalist-painter.]

auburn, *aw'burn, adj.* orig. light yellow: reddish brown. [L.L. *alburnus*, whitish—L. *albus*, white.]

auction, *awk'shən, n.* a public sale in which the bidder offers an increase on the price offered by another, and the articles go to him who bids highest: auction bridge.—*v.t.* to sell by auction.— *adj.* **auc'tionary.**—*n.* **auctioneer',** one who sells or is licensed to sell by auction.—*v.t.* to sell by auction.—**auction bridge,** a development of the game of bridge in which the players bid for the privilege of choosing trump suit or no-trumps; **Dutch auction,** a kind of mock auction at which the salesman starts at a high price, and comes down till he meets a bidder. [L. *auctiō, -ōnis*, an increasing—*augēre, auctum*, to increase.]

auctorial, *awk-tō'ri-əl, adj.* of an author or his trade. [L. *auctor, -ōris*, author.]

Aucuba, *aw'kū-bä, n.* the Japan laurel genus. [Jap.]

audacious, *aw-dā'shəs, adj.* daring: bold: impudent.—*adv.* **audā'ciously.**—*ns.* **audā'ciousness,** **audacity** (*aw-das'i-ti*). [Fr. *audacieux*—L. *audāx* —*audēre*, to dare.]

audible, *awd'i-bl, adj.* able to be heard.—*ns.* **audibil'ity,** the act of hearing: a judicial hearing: *adv.* **aud'ibly.**—*n.*
aud'ience, the act of hearing: a judicial hearing: admittance to a hearing: a ceremonial interview: an assembly of hearers: a court of government or justice in Spanish America: the territory administered by it (Sp. *audiencia*).—*adj.* **aud'ient,**

listening: paying attention.—*n.* a hearer.—*adj.* **aud'ile,** pertaining to hearing.—*n.* one inclined to think in terms of sound.—*ns.* **audio-frequency** (*aw'di-ō-frē'kwən-si*), a frequency of oscillation which, when the oscillatory power is converted into a sound pressure, is perceptible by the **ear** (also *adj.*); **audiom'eter,** an instrument for measuring differences in hearing: one for measuring the minimum intensities of sounds which, for specified frequencies, are perceivable by the ear.—*adj.* **audiomet'ric.**—*ns.* **aud'iphone,** an instrument which pressed against the teeth, communicates sounds through the bones to the ears; **aud'it,** an examination of accounts by an authorised person or persons: a calling to account generally: a statement of account: (*obs.*) a periodical settlement of accounts: (*obs.*) audience, hearing.—*v.t.* to examine and verify by reference to vouchers, etc.—*ns.* **audi'tion** (*aw-dish'ən*), the sense of hearing: an act of hearing: a trial hearing of a performer: mode of hearing: (*rare*) something heard: **aud'itor,** a hearer: one who audits accounts:—*fem.* **aud'itress; auditōr'ium,** in a theatre, or the like, the space allotted to the hearers: the reception-room of a monastery: (*U.S.*) the hall of a hotel; **aud'itorship.**—*adj.* **aud'itory,** relating to the sense of hearing.—*n.* an audience: a place where lectures, etc., are heard.— **audit ale,** an ale of special quality brewed for some Oxford and Cambridge colleges—orig. for use on the day of audit. [L. *audīre*, to hear.]

auf, *awf, n.* an elf's child, an oaf. [O.N. *álfr*, elf.]

Augean, *aw-jē'ən, adj.* filthy: difficult. [From *Augeas*, king of Elis into whose uncleansed oxstalls Herakles turned the river Alpheus.]

auger, *aw'gər, n.* a carpenter's boring tool.—*ns.* **au'ger-bit,** an auger that fits into a carpenter's brace; **au'ger-hole; au'ger-shell,** Terebra; **au'ger-worm,** the goat-moth larva, which bores trees. [From *nauger* (*an auger* for *a nauger*)— O.E. *nafugár—nafu*, a nave of a wheel, *gár*, a piercer. See **nave, gore,** 2.]

aught, *awt, n.* a whit: ought: anything: a part. [O.E. *á-wiht* contr. to *áht* (whence **ought**), and shortened to *aht* (whence **aught**); *a'-wiht* is from *á, ó*, ever, and *wiht*, creature, whit, wight.]

augite, *aw'jīt, -gīt, n.* one of the pyroxene group of minerals, closely allied to hornblende, usually greenish, an essential component of many igneous rocks.—*adj.* **augitic** (*-jit'*, *-git'*). [Gr. *augē*, brightness.]

augment, *awg-ment', v.t.* to increase: to make larger.—*v.i.* to grow larger.—*n.* **aug'ment** (*-mənt*), increase: (*gram.*) the prefixed vowel or initial vowel-lengthening in some past tenses of the verb in Sanskrit and Greek: sometimes applied also to such inflectional prefixes as the *ge-* of the German perfect participle.—*adjs.* **augment'able;** **augment'ative,** having the quality of power of augmenting.—*n.* (*gram.*) a word formed from another to express increase of its meaning.—*ns.* **augmentā'tion,** increase: addition: (*her.*) an additional charge in a coat-of-arms bestowed as a mark of honour: (*mus.*) the repetition of a melody in notes of greater length than the original: (*Scots law*) an increase of stipend obtained by a parish minister by an action raised in the Court of Teinds against the titular and heritors.—*adj.* **augmented.**—*ns.* **augment'er; augment'or,** a nerve that increases the rate of activity of an organ. —**augmented interval,** one increased by a semitone. [L. *augmentum*, increase—*augēre*, to increase.]

augur, *aw'gər, n.* among the Romans, one who sought knowledge of secret or future things by observing the flight and the cries of birds: a diviner: a soothsayer: (*Shak., app.*) an augury or portent.—*v.t.* to foretell from signs.—*v.i.* to guess or conjecture: to forebode.—*adj.* **au'gural** (*-ū-rəl*, *-yər-əl*).—*n.* **au'gurer** (*Shak.*), an augur; **au'gurship; au'gūry,** the art or practice of auguring: an omen. [L.; prob. from *avis*, bird.]

august, *aw-gust', adj.* venerable: imposing: sublime: majestic.—*adv.* **august'ly.**—*n.* **august'ness.** [L. *augustus—augēre*, to increase, honour.]

Neutral vowels in unaccented syllables: *el'ə-mənt, in'fənt, ran'dəm*

August, *aw'gəst, n.* the eighth month of the year. [After the Roman emperor *Augustus.*]

Augustan, *aw-gust'ən, adj.* pertaining to the Emperor Augustus, or to the time in which he reigned (31 B.C.—14 A.D.)—the most brilliant age in Roman literature : hence any similar age, as the reign of Anne in English, and that of Louis XIV. in French literature : classic : refined.

Augustine, *aw'gust-in, aw-gust'in,* **Augustinian,** *-tin'i-ən, n.* one of any order of monks or nuns whose rule is based on the writings of St. Augustine ; (*theol.*) one who holds the opinions of St. Augustine, esp. on predestination and irresistible grace.—*adj.* **Augustin'ian,** of or relating to St. Augustine.—*n.* **Augustin'ianism.—Augustinian canons,** or **Austin canons** (see **canon**); **Augustinian** or **Austin friars,** or **hermits,** the fourth order of mendicant friars, wearing a black habit, but not to be confused with the Black Friars or Dominicans.

auk, *awk, n.* a short-winged bird of the family Alcidae.—*n.* **auk'let,** one of the smaller birds of the family.—**great auk,** garefowl, extinct *c.* 1844; **little auk,** rotche. [O.N. *ālka.*]

aula, *aw'lä, n.* a hall.—*adj.* **aulā'rian,** relating to a hall.—*n.* at Oxford, a member of a hall, as distinguished from a collegian.—*adj.* **au'lic.—Aula Regis,** or *Curia Regis,* (*hist.*) a feudal assembly of tenants-in-chief : the Privy Council : the Court of King's Bench ; **Aulic Council** (Ger. *Reichshofrat*), a court or personal council of the Holy Roman Empire, established in 1501 by Maximilian I., and co-ordinate with the Imperial Chamber (*Reichskammergericht*). [L. *aula,* Gr. *aulē,* court, courtyard, hall.]

auld, *awld, adj.* (*Scot.*) old.—*adjs.* **auld'-farr'ant** (i.e. old-favouring), old-fashioned : precocious; **auld'-warld,** old-world, ancient.—**the Auld Kirk,** the Church of Scotland : whisky; **auld langsyne,** lit. old long since, long ago; **Auld Reekie,** old smoky, i.e. Edinburgh. [O.E. *ald.*]

aumail, *aw-māl', v.t.* to enamel : (*Spens.*) to figure or variegate. [See **enamel.**]

aumbry, *awm'bri, n.* Same as **ambry.**

aumil, *aw'mil, ä'mil, n.* an amildar.

aunt, *änt, n.* a father's or a mother's sister : an uncle's wife : (*obs.*) an old woman : a gossip : a procuress.—*dim.* **aunt'ie, aunt'y.—Aunt Sally,** a pastime at English fairs, in which sticks are thrown to smash a pipe in the mouth of a wooden figure. [O.Fr. *ante*—L. *amita,* a father's sister.]

aunter, *awn'tər, n.* an old form of **adventure.** [O.Fr. *aventure.*]

aura, *aw'rä, n.* a supposed subtle emanation, esp. that essence which is claimed to emanate from all living things and to afford an atmosphere for occult phenomena : (*fig.*) air, distinctive character : (*path.*) peculiar sensations that precede an attack in epilepsy, hysteria, and certain other ailments :—*pl.* **aur'ae** (-*ē*), **aur'as.**—*adj.* **aur'al,** pertaining to the air, or to a subtle vapour or exhalation arising from a body. [L. *aura,* a breeze.]

aural, *aw'rəl, adj.* pertaining to the ear.—*adv.* **aur'ally.** [L. *auris,* ear.]

aurate, *aw'rāt, n.* a salt of auric acid.—*adjs.* **au'rated,** gold-coloured : compounded with auric acid; **au'reate,** gilded : golden : floridly rhetorical. —*ns.* **aurē'ity,** the peculiar properties of gold; **Aurē'lia,** a common genus of jellyfishes : formerly, a chrysalis, from its golden colour.—*adj.* **aurē'lian,** golden : of an aurelia.—Also *n.* (*obs.*) a lepidopterist. —*ns.* **aurē'ola, aureole** (*aw'ri-ōl ; theol.*), a crown, or an increment to the ordinary blessedness of heaven, gained by virgins, martyrs, and doctors : the gold or coloured disk or ring round the head in a picture, symbolising glory : (*fig.*) a glorifying halo : (*meteor.*) a halo or corona around the sun or moon, or the clear space within it : the coloured rings around the spectre of the Brocken : (apparently erroneously) a halo surrounding the whole figure (e.g. a *vesica piscis*) : any halo-like appearance. —*adj.* **au'reoled,** encircled with an aureole.— *n.* **au'reus,** a gold coin of the Roman empire.— *adj.* **au'ric,** pertaining to gold : (*chem.*) containing trivalent gold.—**auric acid,** a hypothetic acid of composition HAuO₂—usually applied to auric

hydroxide, $Au(OH)_3$, or auric oxide, Au_2O_3. [L. *aurum,* gold.]

auricle, *awr'i-kl, n.* the external ear : either of the two upper cavities of the heart into which the blood comes from the veins : an earlike lobe of a leaf, etc. —*adj.* **aur'icled,** having appendages like ears.— *n.* **auric'ula,** a species of primula (bear's ear, or dusty-miller) : **Auricula,** a genus of gasteropod molluscs.—*adj.* **auric'ular,** pertaining to the ear : known by hearing, or by report : told in the ear.— *adv.* **auric'ularly.**—*adjs.* **auric'ulate, auric'ulated,** ear-shaped. [L. *auricula,* dim. of *auris,* the ear.]

auriferous, *awr-if'ər-əs, adj.* bearing or yielding gold.—*v.t.* and *v.i.* **aur'ify,** to turn into gold. [L. *aurifer—aurum,* gold, *ferre,* to bear; *facēre,* to make.]

auriform, *awr'i-form, adj.* ear-shaped. [L. *auris,* ear, and **form.**]

Aurignacian, *aw-rig-nā'sh(y)ən, adj.* belonging to an upper Palaeolithic culture that succeeded the Mousterian and preceded the Solutrean. [*Aurignac,* in Haute-Garonne, where objects of this culture have been found.]

aurist, *awr'ist, n.* one skilled in diseases of the ear. [L. *auris,* ear.]

aurochs, *owr'* or *awr'oks, n.* the extinct urus or wild ox : (erroneously), the European bison. [O.H.G. *ūr-ohso—ūr* (adopted into L. as *ūrus* into Gr. as *ouros*), and *ohso,* ox.]

Aurora, *aw-rō'rä, n.* the dawn : the goddess of dawn : **aurora,** a rich orange colour : a luminous meteoric phenomenon of electrical character seen in and towards the Polar regions, with a tremulous motion, and streamers of light :—*pl.* **auro'ras, -rae.** —*adjs.* **aurō'ral, aurō'rean,** pertaining to the dawn or the aurora : rosy : fresh and beautiful.— *adv.* **aurō'rally.—aurora borealis** (*bō-ri-ā'lis*), or **septentrionalis** (*sep-ten-tri-on-ā'lis*), the northern aurora or northern lights; **aurora australis** (*aws-trā'lis*), the southern lights, a similar phenomenon in the southern hemisphere. [L. *Aurōra.*]

aurous, *awr'əs, adj.* containing univalent gold. [L. *aurum,* gold.]

auscultation, *aws-kult-ā'shən, n.* the art of discovering the condition of the lungs and heart by applying the ear or the stethoscope.—*v.t.* and *v.i.* **aus'cultate,** to examine by auscultation.—*n.* **aus'cultator,** one who practises auscultation : an instrument for the purpose : in Germany, formerly one who had passed his first public examination in law, and who was merely retained, not yet employed or paid by government.—*adj.* **auscult'atory.** [L. *auscultāre,* to listen.]

Ausonian, *aw-sō'ni-ən, adj.* Italian. [L. *Ausonia,* a poetical name for Italy.]

auspice, *aws'pis, n.* an omen drawn from observing birds : augury : prognostic : (in *pl.*) patronage.— *v.t.* **auspicate** (*aws'pi-kāt*), to foreshow : to initiate or inaugurate with hopes of good luck.— *adj.* **auspicious** (-*pish'əs*), having good auspices or omens of success : favourable : fortunate : propitious.—*adv.* **auspi'ciously.**—*n.* **auspi'ciousness.** [Fr.,—L. *auspicium—auspex, auspicis,* a bird-seer, from *avis,* bird, *specēre,* to observe.]

Aussie, *aws'i, n.* and *adj.* (*slang*) Australian.

Auster, *aws'tər, n.* the south wind. [L.]

austere, *aws-tēr', adj.* sour and astringent : harsh : severe : stern : grave : severe in self-discipline : severely simple, without luxury.—*adv.* **austere'ly.** —*ns.* **austere'ness, austerity** (-*ter'*), quality of being austere : severity of manners or life : harshness : asceticism : severe simplicity of style, dress, or habits.—*adj.* evincing or adopted in austerity. [L. *austērus*—Gr. *austēros—auein,* to dry.]

Austin. See **Augustine.**

austral, *aws'trəl, adj.* southern.—*adj.* **Australasian** (-ā'zhən), pertaining to Australasia, or the lands that lie south-east of Asia.—*n.* a native or colonist of one of these.—*adj.* **Austrā'lian,** of or pertaining to Australia.—*n.* an aboriginal native of Australia proper, later also a native or resident white. [L. *austrālis—Auster,* the south wind.]

Austrian, *aws'tri-ən, adj.* of or pertaining to Austria.—*n.* a native or citizen of Austria.

Austric, *aws'trik*, *adj.* belonging to a family of languages divided into **Austroāsiat'ic** (in eastern India and Indo-China, including the Munda or Kolarian, Mon-Khmer and Khásí groups, and the languages of the Semang and Sakai) and **Austrone͞'sian** (including the Indonesian or Malay, Polynesian, and Melanesian groups). [L. *Auster*, south wind, **Asiatic**, and Gr. *nēsos*, island.]

austringer, *aw'strin-jər*, *n.* a keeper of goshawks. Also **a'stringer**, **ostreger** (*os'tri-jər; Shak.*). [O.Fr. *ostruchier*.]

autacoid, *aw'tə-koid*, *n.* an internal secretion that excites or inhibits action in various tissues : a hormone or chalone. [Gr. *autos*, self, *akos*, drug.]

autarchy, *awt'är-ki*, *n.* absolute power. [Gr. *autos*, self, and *archein*, to rule.]

autarky, *awt'är-ki*, *n.* self-sufficiency. [Gr. *autarkeiā—autos*, self, *arkeein*, to suffice.]

authentic, **-al**, *aw-thent'ik, -əl*, *adj.* genuine : authoritative : true, entitled to acceptance, of established credibility : (of writing) trustworthy, as setting forth real facts : (*Milt.*) own, proper : (*mus.*) applied to ecclesiastical modes having their sounds within the octave above the final—opp. to *plagal* : (existentialism) used to describe the way of living of one who takes full cognisance of the meaninglessness of the world yet deliberately follows a consistent course of action.—*adv.* authent'ically.—*v.t.* authen'ticate, to make authentic : to prove genuine : to give legal validity to : to certify the authorship of.—*ns.* authentica'-tion; authenticity (*aw-thən-tis'i-ti*), quality of being authentic : state of being true or in accordance with fact : genuineness. [Gr. *authentikos*, warranted —*autos*, self.]

author, *awth'ər*, *n.* one who brings anything into being : a beginner of any action or state of things : the original writer of a book : elliptically, an author's writings : (*arch.*) one's authority for something :— *fem.* auth'oress. — *n.* auth'or-craft. — *adjs.* authorial (*-thō'ri-əl*), auth'orish; authoris'able. —*n.* authorisā'tion.—*v.t.* auth'orise, to give authority to : to sanction : to justify : to establish by authority.—*adj.* auth'orless, anonymous.—*ns.* auth'oring; auth'orism, state or quality of being an author; auth'orling, a petty author; auth'orship.—**Authorised Version**, the English translation of the Bible completed in 1611. [Through Fr. from L. *auctor—augēre*, *auctum*, to increase, to produce.]

authority, *awth-or'it-i*, *n.* legal power or right : power derived from office or character or prestige : weight of testimony : permission : a person or body holding power : an expert : a passage or book referred to in witness of a statement : (*biol.*) the original bestower of a name.—*adj.* authoritā'rian, setting authority above liberty.—Also *n.*—*n.* authoritā'rianism.—*adj.* author'itative, having the sanction or weight of authority : dictatorial.— *adv.* author'itatively.—*n.* author'itativeness. [L. *auctōritas, -ātis—auctor*.]

auto-, *aw'tō-*, *aw-to'-*, in composition, self.—*ns.* au'to (chiefly *U.S.*), short for automobile; au'tobus, au'to-car, au'to-cycle, a motor bus, car, or cycle. [Gr. *autos*, self.]

autobiography, *aw-tō-bī-og'rə-fi*, *n.* a person's life written by himself.—*n.* autobiog'rapher.—*adjs.* autobiographic (*-ō-graf'ik*), **-al.** [Gr. *bios*, life, *graphein*, to write.]

autocarp, *aw'tō-kärp*, *n.* a fruit produced by self-fertilisation. [Gr. *karpos*, fruit.]

autocatalysis, *aw-tō-kə-tal'is-is*, *n.* (*chem.*) the catalysis of a reaction by a product of that reaction : (*zool.*) reaction or disintegration of a cell or tissue due to the influence of one of its own products.— *v.t.* autocatalyse (*-kat'ə-līz*).—*adj.* autocatalytic (*-lit'ik*).

autocephalous, *aw-tō-sef'ə-ləs*, *adj.* having its own head : independent.—*n.* autoceph'aly, condition of being autocephalous. [Gr. *kephalē*, head.]

autochthon, *aw-tok'thon*, *n.* one of the primitive inhabitants of a country : an aboriginal :—*pl.* autoch'thons, and autoch'thonēs.—*adj.* autoch'-thonous.—*ns.* autoch'thonism, autoch'thony,

the condition of being autochthonous. [Gr. *autochthōn*, sprung from the soil—*chthōn, chthonos*, soil; the Athenians claiming to have actually sprung from the soil.]

autoclave, *aw'tō-klāv*, *n.* a strong vessel for carrying out chemical reactions under pressure and at high temperatures, or one in which superheated steam under pressure is used for sterilising or cooking. [Gr. *autos*, self, perhaps L. *clāvis*, key.]

autocrat, *aw'tō-krat*, *n.* one who rules by his own power : an absolute sovereign.—*n.* autocracy (*-tok'rə-si*), an absolute government by one man : despotism.—*adj.* autocrat'ic.—*adv.* autocrat'ically. [Gr. *autokratēs—kratos*, power.]

auto-da-fé, *ow'tō-dä-fā'*, *n.* the public declaration of the judgment passed on heretics in Spain and Portugal by the Inquisition : the infliction of the punishment that immediately followed thereupon, esp. the public burning of the victims :—*pl.* autos-da-fé. [Port. *auto da fé* (Sp. *auto de fe*); *auto—*L. *actum*, act; *da*, of the—L. *de*, of; and *fé—*L. *fidēs*, faith.]

autodidact, *aw'tō-di-dakt*, *n.* a self-taught person. —*adj.* autodidact'ic. [Gr. *didaktos*, taught.]

autoerotic, *aw-tō-e-rot'ik*, *adj.* seeking sensual gratification from one's own person.—*n.* autoer'otism. [Gr. *erōtikos*, amorous—*erōtaein*, to love.]

autogamy, *aw-tog'ə-mi*, *n.* self-fertilisation.—*adjs.* autog'amous, autogamic (*aw-tō-gam'ik*). [Gr. *gamos*, marriage.]

autogenous, *aw-toj'ə-nəs*, *adj.* self-generated : independent.—*n.* autog'eny, spontaneous generation. [Gr. *autogenēs—genos*, offspring.]

Autogiro, Autogyro, *aw-tō-jī'rō*, *n.* a flying-machine invented by Sr. de la Cierva, partly supported by the action of the air upon freely revolving planes. [Trade-mark; Sp.,—Gr. *gyros*, circle.]

autograph, *aw'tō-gräf*, *n.* one's own handwriting : a signature : an original manuscript.—*v.t.* to write with one's hand.—*adj.* autographic (*-graf'*).— *adv.* autograph'ically.—*n.* autography (*aw-tog'-rə-fi*), act of writing with one's own hand : reproduction of the outline of a writing or drawing by facsimile. [Gr. *graphē*, writing.]

autogravure, *aw-tō-grav-ūr'*, or *aw'*, *n.* a process of photo-engraving akin to autotype. [Gr. *autos*, self; Fr. *gravure*, engraving.]

auto-intoxication, *aw'tō-in-toks-i-kā'shən*, *n.* poisoning by substances produced within the body.—*n.* and *adj.* au'to-intox'icant. [Gr. *autos*, self, and intoxication.]

autolatry, *aw-tol'ə-tri*, *n.* worship of oneself. [Gr. *latreiā*, worship.]

autology, *aw-tol'ə-ji*, *n.* scientific study of oneself. [Gr. *autos*, self, *logos*, discourse.]

Autolycus, *aw-tol'i-kəs*, *n.* a thief : a plagiarist : a snapper up of unconsidered trifles. [From the character in Shakespeare's *Winter's Tale*, or in Greek mythology.]

automaton, *aw-tom'ə-tən*, *n.* a self-moving machine, or one that moves by concealed machinery : a living being regarded as without consciousness : one who acts by routine, without intelligence :— *pl.* autom'atons, autom'ata.—*adjs.* automatic (*-tə-mat'ik*), **-al.**—*adv.* automat'ically.—*ns.* autom'atism, automatic or involuntary action : power of self-moving : power of initiating vital processes from within the cell, organ, or organism, independently of any direct or immediate stimulus from without : the self-acting power of the muscular and nervous systems, by which movement is effected without intelligent determination : action without conscious volition : the doctrine that animals are automata, their motions, etc., being the result of mechanical laws : autom'atist, one who holds the doctrine of automatism : one who acts automatically.—**automatic writing**, writing performed without the volition of the writer. [Gr. *automatos*, self-moving—*autos*, self.]

automobile, *aw-tō-mō-bēl'*, or *aw'*, or *-mō'*, *adj.* self-moving.—*n.* a motor-car.—*ns.* automō'bilism, automō'bilist. [Gr. *autos*, self; L. *mōbilis*, mobile.]

Neutral vowels in unaccented syllables : *el'ə-mənt, in'fənt, ran'dəm*

automorphism, *aw-tō-mor'fizm, n.* ascription to others of one's own characteristics.—*adj.* **automor'phic,** marked by automorphism: idiomorphic.—*adv.* **automor'phically.** [Gr. *morphē,* form.]

autonomy, *aw-ton'əm-i, n.* the power or right of self-government, esp. partial self-government: (Kant's *philos.*) the doctrine that the human will carries its guiding principle within itself.—*adjs.* **autonomic** *(aw-tō-nom'ik),* **-al.**—*n.* **auton'omist.** —*adj.* **auton'omous.** [Gr. *autonomos*—*nomos,* law.]

autonym, *aw'ton-im,* or *-tən-,* a writing published under the author's real name. [Gr. *onyma* (*onoma*), name.]

autophagous, *aw-tof'ə-gəs, adj.* self-devouring: of a bird, capable of feeding itself from the moment of hatching.—*n.* **autophagy** *(-ə-ji),* sustenance by self-absorption of the tissues of the body: eating or biting of part of one's own body. [Gr. *phagein,* to eat.]

autophanous, *aw-tof'ə-nəs, adj.* self-luminous. [Gr. *phanos,* bright.]

autophoby, *aw-tof'ob-i, n.* a shrinking from making any reference to oneself. [Gr. *phobos,* fear.]

autophony, *aw-tof'ən-i, n.* observation of the resonance of one's own voice by speaking with the ear on the patient's chest. [Gr. *phōnē,* sound.]

autoplasty, *aw'tō-plas-ti, n.* grafting of healthy tissue from another part of the same body.—*adj.* **autoplas'tic.** [Gr. *plastos,* formed.]

autopsy, *aw'top-si,* or *-top',* **autop'sia,** *n.* personal inspection: post-mortem examination.—*v.t.* **autopsy.**—*adjs.* **autopt'ic,** **-al.**—*adv.* **autopt'ically.** [Gr. *opsis,* sight.]

autoschediasm, *aw-tō-sked'i-azm,* or *-skēd',* *n.* anything extemporised.—*v.t.* **autosched'iaze** *(-āz).*—*adj.* **autoschedias'tic.** [Gr. *autoschedon,* on the spot—*autos,* self, *schedios,* off-hand.]

autosome, *aw'tō-sōm, n.* a chromosome other than a sex-chromosome. [Gr. *sōma,* body.]

auto-suggestion, *aw'tō-su-jest'yən, n.* a mental process similar to suggestion, but originating in a belief in the subject's own mind. [Gr. *autos,* self, and **suggestion.**]

autotheism, *aw-tō-thē'izm, n.* assumption of divine powers: the doctrine of the self-subsistence of God, esp. of the second person in the Trinity.—*n.* **autothe'ist.** [Gr. *autos,* self, *theos,* a god.]

autotomy, *aw-tot'ə-mi, n.* reflex separation of part of the body. [Gr. *tomē,* cut.]

autotrophic, *aw-tō-trof'ik, adj.* capable of building up food materials from inorganic matter.—*n.* **au'totroph,** an autotrophic organism. [Gr. *trophē,* food.]

autotype, *aw'tō-tīp, n.* a true impress or copy of the original: a process of printing from a photographic negative in a permanent pigment.—*v.t.* to reproduce by such a process.—*n.* **autotypog'raphy,** a process by which drawings made on gelatine are transferred to a plate from which impressions may be taken. [Gr. *typos,* a stamp.]

autumn, *aw'təm, n.* the third season of the year, when fruits are gathered in, generally (in the northern hemisphere) from August or September to October or November: astronomically, from the autumnal equinox to the winter solstice: a period of harvest or of maturity.—*adj.* **autum'nal** *(awtum'nl),* pertaining to autumn: blooming in autumn: beyond the prime: withering or withered.—*adv.* **autum'nally.**—**autumn crocus,** a species of *Colchicum,* meadow-saffron. [L. *autumnus.*]

autunite, *aw'tun-īt, n.* a mineral composed of a hydrous phosphate of uranium and calcium. [*Autun* in France, one of its localities.]

auxanometer, *awks-ən-om'it-ər, n.* an instrument for measuring plant-growth. [Gr. *auxanein,* to grow, *metron,* measure.]

auxesis, *awk-sē'sis, n.* increase in size: hyperbole. [Gr. *auxēsis,* increase.]

auxiliar, *awg-zil'yər,* **auxiliary** *-i, adjs.* helping: subsidiary.—*ns.* **auxil'iar,** an auxiliary; **auxil'iary,** a helper: *(gram.)* a verb that helps to form the moods, tenses or voices of other verbs: (esp. in

pl.) a soldier serving with another nation. [L. *auxiliāris*—*auxilium,* help—*augēre,* to increase.]

auxin, *awks'in, n.* any of a number of growth-promoting substances present in minute quantities in plants. [Gr. *auxein,* to increase.]

auxometer, *awks-om'it-ər, n. (opt.)* an instrument for measuring magnifying power. [Gr. *auxein,* to increase, *metron* measure.]

ava, *ə-vaw', adv. (Scot.)* at all. [For **of all.**]

ava, *ä'vä, n.* a species of pepper: an intoxicating drink, also called *kava,* made from its root-stock: any similar drink. [Hawaiian.]

avadavat. Same as **amadavat.**

avail, *ə-vāl', v.t.* to be of value or service to: to benefit (used reflexively with *of* in the sense of make use, take advantage): *(U.S.)* to inform, assure.—*v.i.* to be of use: to answer the purpose: (*Shak.*) to draw advantage, be the better.—*n.* effectual advantage: (in *pl.,* now *U.S.*) profit, proceeds.—*n.* **availabil'ity,** quality of being available: power of effecting or promoting an end: validity.—*adj.* **avail'able,** that one may avail oneself of: accessible: within reach: obtainable: to be had or drawn upon: profitable.—*n.* **avail'ableness.**—*adv.* **avail'ably.**—*adjs.* **avail'ful** *(obs.),* of avail: serviceable; **avail'ing.**—*adv.* **avail'ingly.** [L. *ad,* to, *valēre,* to be worth, to be strong; app. modelled on **vail.**]

avail, availe. Same as **avale.**

aval, *āv'əl, adj.* pertaining to a grandparent. [L. *avus,* grandfather.]

avalanche, *av'ə-länsh, n.* a hurtling mass of snow, with ice and rock, descending a mountain side: a snow-slip, as from a roof: an overwhelming influx.—*v.t.* and *v.i.* to carry or come down as or like an avalanche. [Fr. dial.—*avaler;* see next word.]

avale, avail, availe, *v.t. (Spens.)* to lower: to doff.—*v.i. (Spens.)* to come down: to alight. [Fr. *avaler,* to descend—*à* (L. *ad*), to, *val* (L. *vallis*), valley.]

avant-, *av'än-, -änə-, pref.,* before.—*n.* **avantcourier** *(av'än-kōōr'i-ər,* or as Fr. *av-änə̃-kōō-ryä;* for Fr. *avant-coureur*), one sent before: (in *pl.*) skirmishers or advance-guard; **avant-garde',** vanguard. [Fr. *avant,* before—L. *ab,* from, *ante,* before.]

avanturine. See **aventurine.**

avarice, *av'ər-is, n.* eager desire for wealth: covetousness.—*adj.* **avaricious** *(-ish'əs),* extremely covetous: greedy.—*adv.* **avari'ciously.**—*n.* **avari'ciousness.** [Fr.,—L. *avāritia*—*avārus,* greedy—*avēre,* to pant after.]

avast, *ə-väst', interj. (naut.)* hold fast: stop. [Prob. Dut. *houd vast,* hold fast.]

avatar, *ä-və-tär', n.* the descent of a Hindu deity in a visible form: incarnation: *(fig.)* supreme glorification of any principle. [Sans.,—*ava,* away, down, and root *tar-,* to pass over.]

avaunt, *ə-vawnt', interj.* move on: begone.—*n.* (*Shak.*) dismissal.—*v.i. (Spens.)* to advance: *(obs.)* to depart. [Fr. *avant,* forward—L. *ab,* from, *ante,* before.]

avaunt, *ə-vawnt', v.t.* and *v.i. (Spens.)* to boast.— *n.* a boast. [O.Fr. *avanter*—L.L. *vānitāre,* to boast—L. *vānus,* vain.]

ave, *ä'vä, ä'vi,* or *ä'vē, interj.* be well and happy: hail.—*n.* an address or prayer to the Virgin Mary, in full, **ave Maria** *(ä'vä mä-rē'ä, ä'vē ma-rī'ä),* or **ave Mary,** the Hail Mary, or angelic salutation (Luke, i.28). [Imper. of L. *avēre,* to be well. See **angelus.**]

Avena, *a-vē'nä, n.* the oat genus of grasses.—*adj.* **avenaceous** *(av-i-nā'shəs),* of the nature of oats. [L. *avēna,* oats.]

avenge, *ə-venj', -venzh', v.t.* to vindicate: take vengeance on someone on account of.—*n. (Spens.)* revenge.—*adj.* **avenge'ful;**—*ns.* **avenge'ment;** **aveng'er:**—*fem.* **aveng'eress.** [O.Fr. *avengier*— L. *ad,* to, *vindicāre,* to claim. See **vengeance.**]

avens, *av'ənz, n.* any plant of the rosaceous genus *Geum* (water avens, *Geum rivale;* wood avens, herb-bennet): also the related sub-alpine **mountain avens** (*Dryas octopetala*). [O.Fr. *avence.*]

aventail, aventaile, av'ən-tāl, n. the flap or movable part of a helmet in front, for admitting air. [O.Fr. *esventail*, air-hole—L. *ex*, out, *ventus*, wind.]

aventre, a-ven'tr, v.t. (*Spens.*) apparently, to thrust, direct. [Origin unknown.]

aventure, a-vent'ūr, obsolete form of adventure.

aventurine, a-ven'tū-rin, avanturine, -van', n. a brown, spangled kind of Venetian glass : a kind of quartz enclosing spangles of mica or haematite.—*adj.* shimmering or spangled, as kinds of felspar or sealing-wax. [It. *avventura*, chance—because of the accidental discovery of the glass.]

avenue, av'ən-ū, n. the principal approach to a country-house, usually bordered by trees : a double row of trees, with or wi*t*hout a road : a wide and handsome street, with or without trees, esp. in America : any passage or entrance into a place : (*fig.*) means of access or attainment. [Fr.,—L. *ad*, to, *venīre*, to come.]

aver, ə-vər', v.t. to declare to be true : to affirm or declare positively : (*law*) to prove or justify :—*pr.p.* averr'ing ; *pa.p.* averred'.—*n.* aver'ment, positive assertion : (*law*) a formal offer to prove a plea : the proof offered. [Fr. *avérer*—L. *ad*, and *vērus*, true.]

aver, ā'vər, n. (*obs.*) possessions : (*obs.*) cattle : (*Scot.*) a draught animal, esp. an old or worthless cart-horse. [O.Fr. *aveir*, *aver* (Fr. *avoir*), possessions, stock—L. *habēre*, to have.]

average, av'ər-ij, n. orig. a customs duty or similar charge : any expense other than freight payable by the owner of shipped goods : expense or loss by damage of ship or cargo : equitable distribution of expense or loss : arithmetical mean value of any quantities : estimation of such a mean : loosely, ordinary or prevailing value, common run.—*adj.* mean : prevailing, ordinary.—*v.t.* to obtain the average of : to amount to on an average : to do on an average.—*v.t.* and *v.i.* to even out to an average. [Cf. Fr. *avarie*, It. *avaria*, duty on goods ; poss. conn. with foregoing.]

Averr(h)oism, av-er-ō'izm, n. the doctrine of the Arab philosopher *Averrhoes* (1126-98), that the soul is perishable, the only immortal soul being the world-soul from which individual souls went forth, and to which they return.—*n.* Averr(h)ō'ist.

averruncate, av'ər-ung-kāt, v.t. (*rare*) to ward off : (wrongly) to uproot.—*ns.* averrunca'tion ; av'erruncātor, an instrument for cutting off branches of trees. [L. *āverruncāre*, to avert, perh. confused with *ēruncāre*, to weed out.]

averse, ə-vərs', adj. disinclined (with *to ;* but some prefer *from*) : reluctant : turned away or backward.—*adv.* averse'ly.—*ns.* averse'ness ; aver'sion, turning aside : dislike : hatred : the object of dislike.—*v.t.* avert', turn aside : to prevent : ward off.—*adj.* avert'ed.—*adv.* avert'edly.—*adj.* avert'ible, capable of being averted. [L. *āvertĕre*, *āversus*—*ab*, from, *vertĕre*, to turn.]

avertiment, for advertisement (*Milt.*).

Aves, ā'vēz, L. ā'vās, n.pl. birds as a class of vertebrates.—*adj.* ā'vian, of birds.—*ns.* ā'viarist, one who keeps an aviary ; ā'viary, a large cage or the like for keeping birds.—*v.i.* ā'viate, to fly mechanically, navigate the air.—*ns.* āviā'tion, mechanical flying ; ā'viātor, an airman, flying man ; Avicula (av-ik'ū-lä; from the winglike shape), a genus of pearl oysters, giving name to the family Avicū'lidae (-dē) ; Avicūlā'ria, the bird-catching spider genus, giving name to the family Avicūlariidae (-lar'i-i-dē) ; ā'viculture, bird-rearing : birdfancying ; aviette (av-yet', ā-vi-et'), an aeroplane driven by man-power ; āvifau'na, the assemblage of birds found in a region.—*adjs.* ā'viform, birdlike in form or structure ; avine (ā'vīn), of birds.—*n.* avion (äv'yonⁿ; Fr.), aeroplane. [L. *avis*, bird, *avicula*, little bird, *avicularius*, bird-keeper.]

Avesta, ə-ves'tä, n. the Zoroastrian holy Scriptures.—*adj.* Aves'tan, of the Avesta or its East Iranian language.—*n.* the language of the Avesta, also called Zend. [Pahlavi *Avīstāk*, lore.]

aviation. See Aves.

avid, av'id, adj. greedy : eagerly desirous.—*n.* avid'ity.—*adv.* av'idly. [L. *avidus.*]

avise, avize, avyse, a-vīz', obs. forms (*Spens.* etc.) of advise.—*n.* avise'ment.—*adj.* avize'full (*Spens.*), watchful.—*n.* avi'so, a notification : an advice-boat.

avised. See black-a-vised.

avital, ə-vī'tl, av'i-tl, adj. of a grandfather : ancestral. [L. *avītus*—*avus*, a grandfather.]

avizandum, av-iz-an'dəm, n. (*Scots. law*) private consideration of a case by a judge before giving judgment.—Also avisan'dum. [Gerund of L.L. *avizāre*, *avisāre*, to advise.]

avocado, a-vō-kä-dō, n. the alligator-pear, fruit of a tropical American lauraceous tree. [Sp. *aguacate* —Aztec *ahuacatl.*]

avocation, av-ō-kā'shən, n. properly, a diversion or distraction from one's regular employment : improperly used for vocation, business which calls for one's time and attention : (*arch.*) diversion of the thoughts from any employment : the calling of a case to a higher court. [L. *āvocātiō*, *-ōnis*, a calling away—*ab*, from, *vocāre*, to call.]

avocet, avoset, av'ō-set, n. a wading bird (genus *Recurvirostra*) with webbed feet and long, slender, curved, elastic bill. [Fr. *avocette*, It. *avosetta.*]

avoid, ə-void', v.t. to evade : to shun : (*obs.*) to empty : (*law*) to invalidate : (*Shak.*) to leave, to quit : to dismount from.—*v.i.* to take oneself off.—*adj.* avoid'able.—*n.* avoid'ance, the act of avoiding or shunning : act of annulling : (*anthrop.*) the shunning of certain relatives among primitive peoples. [A.Fr. *avoider*, O.Fr. *esvuidier*—L. *ex*, out, and root of void.]

avoirdupois, av-ər-də-poiz', or av', n. a system of weights in which the lb. equals 16 oz.—*adj.* of that system. [O.Fr. *aveir de pes*, to have weight— L. *habēre*, to have, *dē*, from, *pēnsum*, that which is weighted.]

avoset. See avocet.

avouch, ə-vowch', v.t. to avow : to acknowledge : to vouch for : to assert positively : to maintain : to guarantee : to own to : to appeal to.—*v.i.* to give assurance.—*n.* (*Shak.*) evidence.—*adj.* avouch'able.—*n.* avouch'ment. [O.Fr. *avochier*—L. *advocāre*, to call to one's aid. See vouch, advocate.]

avoure, a-vowr', n. (*Spens.*) avowal. [See avow.]

avouterer, a-vōōt'-ər-ər, avoutry, -ri, old forms of adulterer, adultery.

avow, ə-vow', v.t. to declare : to acknowledge : to maintain.—*v.i.* (*law*) to justify an act done.—*n.* a solemn promise : a vow.—*adj.* avow'able.—*ns.* avow'ableness ; avow'al, a positive declaration : an acknowledgment : a frank confession.—*adj.* avowed'.—*adv.* avow'edly.—*n.* avow'ry (*law*), the act of avowing and justifying in one's own right the distraining of goods : (*obs.*) advocacy considered as personified in a patron saint. [O.Fr. *avouer*, orig. to swear fealty to—L. *ad*, to, and L.L. *votāre*—L. *votum*, a vow : with sense affected by L. *advocāre.* See vow, avouch.]

avulse, a-vuls', v.t. to pluck or tear away.—*n.* avul'sion, forcible separation : sudden removal of land by change of a river's course, whereby it remains the property of the original owner (opp. to alluvion). [L. *āvellēre*, *āvulsum.*]

avuncular, ə-vung'kū-lər, adj. of an uncle. [L. *avunculus*, an uncle.]

await, ə-wāt', v.t. to wait or look for : to be in store for : to attend : (*obs.*) to lie in wait for, to watch.—*n.* (*Spens.*) ambush, watch. [O.N.Fr. Fr. *awaitier*—à, to ; see wait.]

awake, ə-wāk', v.t. to rouse from sleep : to rouse from inaction.—*v.i.* to cease sleeping : to rouse oneself from sleep or indifference : (*pa.t.* awoke', awaked', *pa.p.* awaked' or awoke', sometimes awōk'en)—*adj.* not asleep : vigilant : aware, cognisant (with *to*).—*v.t.* awak'en, to awake : to rouse into interest or attention : (*theol.*) to call to a sense of sin.—*v.i.* to awake : to spring into being.—*adj.* awak'ening, becoming awake : rousing : revivifying, reanimating.—*n.* a becoming awake, aware, active : a throwing off of indifference or ignorance : a rousing.—*n.* and *adj.* awak'ing.—to be awake to, to be fully aware of. [O.E. *āwæc*-

Neutral vowels in unaccented syllables : el'ə-mənt, in'fənt, ran'dəm

nan (pa.t. *áwóc*, pa.p. *áwacen*), confused with *áwacian* (pa.t. *áwacode*). See **wake, watch.**]

awanting, *ə-wont'ing, adj.* (chiefly *Scot.*) wanting : missing. [Prep. **a**, and the gerund of **want.**]

award, *ə-wawrd', v.t.* to adjudge : to determine : to grant.—*n.* judgment : final decision, esp. of arbitrators : that which is awarded : a prize. [O.Fr. *ewarder, eswarder*—L. *ex*, in sense of thoroughly, and the root of **ward, guard.**]

aware, *ə-wār', adj.* wary : informed, conscious (with *of*).—*n.* **aware'ness,** state of being aware : consciousness, esp. a dim form. [O.E. *gewær*—*wær*, cautious. See **ware.**]

awarn, *a-wawrn', v.t.* (*Spens.*) to warn. [Pfx. *a-*, and **warn.**]

awash, *ə-wosh', adv.* on a level with the surface of the water : afloat at the mercy of the waves.—*advs.* **awatch'**, on the watch ; **awave'**, in a wave : in waves. [Prep. **a**, and **wash,** etc.]

away, *ə-wā', adv.* onward : continuously : without hesitation, stop, or delay : forthwith : out of the place in question : not at home : (*sport*) on the opponents' ground : at or to a distance : off : in or into an averted direction : out of existence, life, or consciousness : with effect of removal or elimination : (*U.S.*) far : (with *here, there, where ;* now *dial.*) about : with omission of verb=go or (with *with*) take away (usu. *imper.*) : to endure (with *with*).—*interj.* begone : get out.—*adv.* **aways'** (*obs. ; Spens.* **awayes'**), away.—**do away with,** to abolish ; **explain away,** to explain so as to make the thing explained seem not to exist ; **fall away,** to dwindle : to waste away : to lose zeal and drop off, as followers ; **fire away,** go on, proceed now without further delay ; **make away with,** to destroy : to murder ; **once and away** (now usu. **once in a way**), on occasion. [O.E. *aweg, onwegon,* on, *on, weg,* way.]

awe, *aw, n.* reverential wonder or fear : dread : (*arch.*) power to inspire awe.—*v.t.* to strike with or influence by awe or fear.—*adj.* **awed** (*awd*), awe-stricken : expressive of awe ; **awe'-inspir'ing ; awe'less,** without awe : fearless : (*Shak.*) regarded without awe.—*n.* **awe'lessness.**—*adjs.* **awe'some, aw'some,** awed : (*Scot.*) awe-inspiring : dreadful.—*adv.* **awe'somely.**—*n.* **awe'someness.** —*adj.* **awe'-stricken, -struck,** struck with awe.— *v.t.* **awe'strike.**—*adj.* **aw'ful,** inspiring awe : filled with awe : (*slang*) very bad or ugly, atrocious. —*adv.* (*vulg.*) very.—*adv.* **aw'fully,** in an awe-inspiring or awe-stricken manner : with awe : (*slang*) very.—*n.* **aw'fulness.** [O.N. *agi ;* cf. O.E. *ege,* fear ; Gr. *achos,* distress.]

aweary, *ə-wē'ri, adj.* weary.—*adj.* **awea'ried,** weary. [Pfx. *a-*, and **weary.**]

a-weather, *ə-wedh'er, adv.* (*naut.*) towards the weather or windward side—opp. to *alee.*—*adv.* **a-week',** in the week. [Prep. **a**, and **weather, week.**]

aweel, *ə-wēl', interj.* (*Scot.*) well : well then. (ah well.)

a-weigh, *ə-wā', adv.* in the act of being weighed, as an anchor just raised from the bottom. [Prep. **a**, and **weigh.**]

aweto, *ä-wā'tō, n.* the so-called vegetable caterpillar, the body of a caterpillar filled with a parasitic fungus. [Maori *ahweto.*]

awhape, *ə-hwāp', v.t.* (*Spens.*) to confound, amaze. [Cf. Goth. *af-hwapjan,* to choke.]

awheel, *ə-hwēl'* (*obs.* **awheels**), *adv.* on wheels, esp. on a bicycle. [Prep. **a**, and **wheel.**]

awhile, *ə-hwīl', adv.* for some time : for a short time. [O.E. *áne hwíle,* a while (dat.) : combined as early as 13th century.]

a-wing, *ə-wing', adv.* on the wing. [Prep. **a**, and **wing.**]

awkward, *awk'wərd, adj.* (*obs.*) oblique, inverted, back-handed : clumsy : ungraceful : embarrassed : difficult to deal with : (*Shak.*) adverse : embarrassing : (*obs.*) froward.—*adj.* **awk'wardish.**—*adv.* **awk'wardly**—*n.* **awk'wardness.** [Prob. O.N. *afug,* turned wrong way, and suff. *-ward.*]

awl, *awl, n.* a pointed instrument for boring small holes. [O.E. *æl ;* O.N. *alr,* Ger. *ahle.*]

awmous, *aw'məs, n.* (*Scot.*) alms. [O.N. *almusa ;* cf. O.E. *ælmysse,* alms.]

awn, *awn, n.* the beard of barley, or similar bristly process.—*adjs.* **awned** ; **awn'less** ; **awn'y.** [O.N. *ögn* or a lost O.E. cognate ; Ger. *ahne.*]

awning, *awn'ing, n.* a covering to shelter from the sun or weather.—*v.t.* **awn,** to shelter with an awning. [Origin unknown ; Fr. *auvent,* window-shade, may be connected.]

awoke, *ə-wōk', pa.t.* of **awake.**

awork, *ə-wərk', adv.* at work.—*advs.* **awrack',** in a state of wreck ; **awrong',** wrongly.—*adj.* **awry** (*ə-rī*), twisted to one side : distorted, crooked : wrong : perverse.—*adv.* askew : unevenly : perversely : erroneously.—**to look awry,** to look askance at anything ; **to walk awry,** to go wrong. [Prep. **a**, on, and **work, wrack,** etc.]

axe, ax, *aks, n.* a tool for hewing or chopping, with edge and handle in the same plane : a stone-dressing hammer : (*fig.*) ruthless cutting down of expenditure :—*pl.* **ax'es** (see also **axis**).—*v.t.* to hew or strike with an axe.—*n.* **axe'-stone,** a kind of jade used for making axes.—**axe to grind,** a private purpose to serve. [O.E. *æx ;* cf. Gr. *axinē.*]

axerophthol, *aks-ər-of'thol, n.* vitamin A₁, a pale yellow crystalline substance, defect of which causes xerophthalmia. [Gr. *a-,* priv., and *xerophthalmia.*]

axial, axile. See under **axis.**

axilla, *ak-sil'ä, n.* (*anat.*) the armpit : (*bot.*) axil :— *pl.* **axillae** (*-ē*).—*n.* **ax'il,** the angle between leaf and stem.—*adjs.* **ax'illar, ax'illary.** [L. *axilla,* the armpit.]

axinite, *aks'in-īt, n.* a brilliant brown mineral with axe-shaped crystals, containing calcium, aluminium, boron, silicon, etc.—*n.* **axin'omancy,** divination from the motions of an axe poised upon a stake, or of an agate placed upon a red-hot axe. [Gr. *axinē,* an axe, *manteiā,* divination.]

axiology, *aks-i-ol'ə-ji, n.* the science of the ultimate nature, reality, and significance of values. [Gr. *axios,* worthy, *logos,* discourse.]

axiom, *aks'i-əm, n.* a self-evident truth : a universally received principle.—*adjs.* **axiomat'ic, axiomat'-ical.**—*adv.* **axiomat'ically.** [Gr. *axiōma, -atos*— *axioe'n,* to think worth, to take for granted—*axios,* worthy.]

axis, *aks'is, n.* (*obs.*) an axle : a line about which a body rotates, or about which a figure is conceived to revolve : a straight line about which the parts of a figure, body or system are symmetrically or systematically arranged : a fixed line adopted for reference in co-ordinate geometry, curve-plotting, crystallography, etc. : (*zool.*) the second vertebra of the neck : (*bot.*) the main stem or root, or a branch in relation to its own branches and append-ages : an alliance of powers, as if forming together an axis of rotation—esp. of Germany and Italy (1936) :—*pl.* **axes** (*aks'ēz*).—*adj.* **ax'ial,** relating to, or of the nature of, an axis.—*adv.* **ax'ially.**— *adj.* **ax'ile,** coinciding with an axis.—*ns.* **ax'oid,** a curve generated by the revolution of a point round an advancing axis ; **ax'on,** the impulse-carrying process of a typical nerve-cell.—**axis cylinder,** the excitable core of a medullated nerve-fibre ; **axis of incidence,** the line passing through the point of incidence of a ray perpendicularly to the refracting surface ; **axis of refraction,** the continuation of the same line through the refracting medium ; **axis of the equator,** the polar diameter of the earth which is also the axis of rotation. [L. *axis ;* cf. Gr. *axōn,* Sans. *aksha,* O.E. *eax.*]

axis, *aks'is, n.* a white-spotted deer of India. [L. *axis,* Pliny's name for an Indian animal.]

axle, *aks'l,* **axle-tree,** *aks'l-trē, n.* the pin or rod in the nave of a wheel on which the wheel turns : a pivot or support of any kind ; (*arch.*) an axis.— **ax'le-box,** the box in which the axle end turns.— *adj.* **axled** (*aks'ld*).—*n.* **ax'le-guard,** a pedestal or pillow-block. [More prob. O.N. *öxull* than a dim. from O.E. *eax.*]

Axminster, *aks'min-stər, adj.* of a variety of cut-pile carpet. [*Axminster* in Devon, where it used to be made.]

axolotl, *aks'o-lot-l, n.* the larval form of Amblystoma, commonly retaining its larval character for life, though capable of breeding. [Aztec.]

ay, *ā, interj.* ah : oh : alas : esp. in *ay me.* [M.E. *ey, ei,* perh. from Fr. *ahi, ai* ; cf. Sp. *ay de mi.*]

ay, aye, *ī, adv.* yea : yes : indeed.—*n.* **aye** (*ī*), a vote in the affirmative: one who votes in the affirmative. [Perh. a dial. form of **aye,** ever ; perh. a variant of **yea.**]

ayah, *ī'ä, n.* an Indian waiting-maid or nurse-maid. [Hind. *āya;* from Port. *aia,* nurse.]

aye, ay, *ā, adv.* ever : always : for ever.—**for aye,** for ever and aye, for ever, to all eternity.—In combination, with sense of ever, as in Shakespeare's **aye'-remain'ing,** etc. [O.N. *ei,* ever ; O.E. *ā;* conn. with **age, ever.**]

aye-aye, *ī'ī, n.* an aberrant squirrel-like lemur of Madagascar. [Malagasy *aiay.*]

ayelp, *ə-yelp', adv.* in a state of yelping. [Prep. **a,** yelp.]

ayenbite, *ä-yen'bīt, n.* (*obs.*) remorse, as in the book-title *Ayenbite of Inwyt* (remorse of conscience). [M.E. *ayen,* again, and **bite.**]

aygre, *ā'gər,* (*Shak.*). Same as **eager.**

Aylesbury, *ālz'bər-i, n.* a breed of ducks much valued for the table. [*Aylesbury* in Bucks.]

ayont, *ə-yont', adv.* and *prep.* (*Scot.*) beyond. [Pfx. *a-,* and **yond.**]

ayry. See **eyry.**

ayword, *ā'wurd, n.* (*Shak.*) a byword, proverbial reproach. [Origin obscure; Rowe proposed to read **nayword.**]

Azalea, *a-zā'li-ä, n.* a genus close akin to, or sub-genus of, *Rhododendron,* shrubby plants, with five stamens and annual leaves. [Gr. *azaleos,* dry, probably from the soil that suits it.]

Azilian, *a-zil'i-ən, adj.* belonging to a transition between Palaeolithic and Neolithic. [Mas d'*Azil,* Ariège, where objects of this culture have been found in a cave.]

azimuth, *az'im-əth, n.* the arc of the horizon between the meridian of a place and a vertical circle passing through any celestial body.—*adj.* **az'imu-** thal (or *-mūdh', -mūth'*), pertaining to the azimuth. [Ar. *as-sumūt, as = al,* the, *sumūt,* pl. of *samt,* direction. See **zenith.**]

azo-, *az'ō-,* in combination, nitrogen.—*ns.* **az'o-com'pound,** a compound in which two nitrogen atoms are each attached to (usually) a carbon group, as **az'oben'zene,** $C_6H_5N:NC_6H_5$; **az'o-dye',** a dye of such composition. [**azote.**]

azoic, *a-zō'ik, adj.* without life : before the existence of animal life : formed when there was no animal life on the globe, as rocks. [Gr. *a-,* priv., and *zōē,* life.]

azonic, *a-zon'ik, adj.* not limited to a zone, not local. [Gr. *a-,* priv., *zōnē,* a belt.]

azote, *a-zōt', n.* an old name for nitrogen, so called because it does not sustain animal life.—*adjs.* **azot'ic** (*a-zot'ik*), nitric; **azō'tous,** nitrous.—*v.t.* **az'otise,** to combine with nitrogen.—*n.* **Azōto-bac'ter,** a genus of nitrogen-fixing bacteria. [Gr. *a-,* priv., *zaein,* to live.]

azoth, *äz'oth, n.* the alchemist's name for mercury : Paracelsus's universal remedy. [From Ar. *az-zāüg —al,* the, *zāūg,* from Pers. *zhiwah,* quicksilver.]

Azrael, *az'rā-el, n.* in Mohammedan mythology, the angel of death.

Aztec, *az'tek, n.* one of a people dominant in Mexico before the Spanish conquest.—Also *adj.*

azure, *azh'ər, āzh'ər,* or *ā'zhūr, adj.* of a faint blue : sky-coloured : (*her.*) blue (represented in engraving, etc., by horizontal lines).—*n.* a delicate blue colour : the sky.—*adjs.* **azurē'an, az'urine** (*-in*), azure.—*ns.* **az'urine,** a blue-black aniline dye: a fresh-water fish, the blue roach; **az'urite,** blue basic carbonate of copper, chessylite.—*adjs.* **az'urn** (*Milt.*), azure; **az'ury,** bluish. [O.Fr. *azur*—L.L. *azura*—Ar. (*al*) *lazward,* Per. *lājward,* lapis lazuli, blue colour.]

azygous, *az'i-gəs, adj.* not yoked or joined with another : (*anat.*) unpaired.—*n.* **azygy** (*az'i-ji*). [Gr. *azygos*—*a-,* priv., and *zygon,* a yoke.]

azymous, *az'i-məs, adj.* unfermented : unleavened. —*ns.* **az'ym, az'yme,** unleavened bread; **az'y-mite,** a member of any church using unleaved bread in the Eucharist. [Gr. *azȳmos*—*a-,* priv., *zȳmē,* leaven.]

Neutral vowels in unaccented syllables : *el'ə-mənt, in'fənt, ran'dəm*

B

B, b, *bē, n.* the second letter of our alphabet, called by the Phoenicians *beth,* the house, corresponding to Greek β, beta.—B in music is the seventh note of the scale of C major (H in German notation, B being used for B flat); in old music **B quadratum, quadrate B,** square B, is B natural, **B rotundum, round B,** is B flat; **B or B flat,** a facetious euphemism for the domestic bug; **the three B's,** Bach, Beethoven, Brahms.

ba', *baw, n.* Scots form of ball.—*ns.* **ba''ing, ba''-spiel** (see **ball**).

baa, *bä, n.* the cry of a sheep.—*v.i.* to bleat.—*n.* **baa'ing.** [Imit.]

Baal, *bā'al, n.* a god of the Phoenicians, originally probably a fusion of many local gods : a false god generally :—*pl.* **Bā'alim.**—*ns.* **Bā'alism ; Bā'alite.** [Heb.]

baas, *bäs, n.* (*S. Africa*), master, overseer, sir. [Du.]

babassu, *bab-ə-sōō', n.* a Brazilian palm (Attalea) or its oil-yielding nut. [Prob. Tupí.]

babbitt, *bab'it, v.t.* to fit with **Babbitt('s) metal,** a soft anti-friction metal (tin, with copper, antimony, and usu. lead). [Isaac *Babbitt* (1799-1862), the Massachusetts inventor.]

babble, *bab'l, v.i.* to speak like a baby : to make a continuous murmuring sound like a brook, etc. : to talk incessantly : to tell secrets : to prate.—*v.t.* to utter confusedly or by rote : to divulge by foolish talk.—*adj.* **babb'lative.**—*ns.* **babb'le,** idle senseless talk : prattle : confused murmur, as of a stream; **babb'lement ; babb'ler,** one who babbles : a bird of an ill-defined family somewhat akin to the thrushes (also **babbling thrush**).—*n. and adj.* **babb'ling.**—*adj.* **babb'ly.** [Prob. imit., from the repeated syllable *ba* ; cf. Du. *babbelen,* Ger. *pappelen,* Fr. *babiller,* perh. influenced by *Babel.*]

babe, *bäb,* **baby,** *bā'bi, ns.* an infant, young child : (*obs.*) a doll : (*obs.*) the reflection of oneself in the pupil of another's eye : a young animal : a babyish person : a thing small of its kind, as varieties of grand-piano, aeroplane, etc. : (*U.S. slang*) a girl.—Also *adj.*—Also *adj.*—*ns.* **bā'by-farm'er,** one who takes in infants to nurse for pay; **bā'byhood.**—*adj.* **bā'byish.**—*ns.* **bā'by-jump'er,** a seat suspended by elastic straps, to enable a baby to disport itself : **bā'by-ribb'on,** a very narrow ribbon; **bā'by-sitter,** one who mounts guard over a baby to relieve the usual attendant; **bā'by-sitting.**—**to hold the baby,** to be left in the lurch with a responsibility. [Prob. imitative. See **babble**.]

Babel, *bā'bl, n.* a foolishly conceived lofty structure : a confused sound of voices : a scene of confusion.—*ns.* **bā'beldom, bā'belism.**—*adj.* **bā'belish.** [Heb. *Bābel,* prob. Assyr. *bāb-ili,* gate of God, associated in Gen. xi. 9, with confusion.]

Babi, Babee, *bä'bē, n.* a member of a Persian sect, followers of *Bāb*-ed-Din (Mirza Ali Mohammed, 1821-50), who sought to combine the best in all religions.—Also **Ba'bist.**—*n.* **Ba'bism, Ba'biism, Ba'beeism.**

babingtonite, *bab'ing-tən-īt, n.* a pyroxene, ferrous silicate with admixtures, sometimes worked as an iron ore. [After William *Babington,* mineralogist (1756-1833).]

babiroussa, -russa, *bä-bi-rōō'sä, n.* a wild hog found in Celebes, etc., with great up-turned tusks in the male, hence called the horned or deer hog. [Malay *bābi,* hog, and *rûsa,* deer.]

bablah, *bab'la,* **babul,** *bä'bōol, n.* a species of acacia (*A. arabica*) : the pods of that and other species, used for tanning. [Hind. and Pers. *babūl.*]

Baboo, Babu, *bä'bōo, n.* orig. a title in Bengal corresponding to our Mr. : an Indian clerk : an Indian with a superficial English education, using **Baboo English,** which is more copious than correct, with long and learned words often most ingeniously misapplied.—*adjs.* **bab'oo, bab'u.**—*ns.* **ba'boodom, ba'booism.** [Hind. *bābū.*]

baboon, *bə-bōōn', n.* a large monkey of various species, with long face, dog-like tusks, large lips, a tail, and buttock-callosities.—*n.* **baboon'ery.**—*adj.* **baboon'ish.** [Fr. *babouin,* remoter origin unknown.]

babouche, babuche, baboosh, *bə-bōōsh', n.* an Oriental heelless slipper. [Fr.,—Arab. *bābūsh*—Pers. *pā,* foot, *pūsh,* covering.]

Babylonian, *bab-i-lōn'i-ən, adj.* of Babylon : hence huge, gigantic : (*obs.*) Romish, popish (from the identification with Rome of the scarlet woman of Rev. xvii.): Babel-like, confused in language.— Also **Babylon'ish.—Babylonian or Babylonish captivity,** the exile of the Jews deported to Babylon in 597 and in 586 B.C., lasting till c. 538 : the exile of the popes at Avignon, 1309-77.

bacca, *bak'ä, n.* (*bot.*) a berry.—*adjs.* **bacc'ate,** having berries : berry-like : pulpy; **bacciferous** (*bak-sif'ər-us*), bearing berries; **bac'ciform,** of the shape of a berry; **bacciv'orous,** living on berries. [L. *bacca,* a berry.]

baccalaureate, *bak-ə-law'ri-āt, n.* the university degree of bachelor.—*adj.* **baccalau'rean.** [L.L. *baccalaureus,* altered from *baccalārius,* in fanciful reference to *bacca laurī,* the laurel berry. See **bachelor**.]

baccarat, baccara, *bak'-ə-rä, n.* a French card game played by betters and a banker. [Fr.]

bacchanal, *bak'ə-nl, n.* a worshipper, priest or priestess, of Bacchus : a drunken reveller : a dance, song, or revel in honour of Bacchus.—*adj.* relating to drinking or drunken revels.—Also **bacchanalian** (*-nā'li-ən*):—*ns.pl.* **bacchanā'lia, bacch'anals,** originally feasts in honour of Bacchus : hence, drunken revels.—*n.* **bacchanā'lianism.**—*n. and adj.* **bacchant** (*bak ant*), a priest or votary of Bacchus, the god of wine : a reveller : a drunkard. —*n.* **bacchante** (*bak-ănt', bak'ant,* or after Italian *baccante, ba-kant'i*), a priestess of Bacchus : a female bacchanal.—*adjs.* **bacchiac** (*bak-i'ək*), relating to the bacchius; **Bacch'ian, Bacchic** (*bak'ik*), relating to Bacchus : jovial : drunken.—*n.* **bacchi'us** (Gr. and Lat. *pros.*) a foot of two long syllables preceded or followed by one short :—*pl.* **bacchi'ī.** [L. *Bacchus,* Gr. *Bakchos,* the wine god.]

baccy, bacco, *bak'i,* abbreviations of **tobacco.**

bacharach, *bähk'ə-rähh, bak'ər-ak, n.* an excellent wine named from *Bacharach,* on the Rhine.

bachelor, *bach'əl-ər, n.* a young knight following the banner of another, as too young to display his own : an unmarried man : one who has taken his or her first degree at a university : a young unmated bull-seal or other male animal.—*n.* (*U.S. slang*) **bach,** a bachelor.—*v.i.* to live as a bachelor : to do for oneself.—Also *v.t.* with **it.**—*ns.* **bach'elor-girl',** a single woman of independent habits : a maid with a latch-key : a young unmarried woman living alone : **bach'elordom ; bach'elorhood ; bach'elorism,** habit or condition of a bachelor; **bach'elor's-butt'ons,** a double-flowered yellow or white buttercup : also applied to double feverfew, species of Centaurea, and many other plants; **bach'elorship,** the degree of bachelor.— **bachelor's wife,** a woman with none of the shortcomings of married men's wives; **knight-bachelor** (see **knight**). [O.Fr. *bacheler*—L.L. *baccalārius,* a farmer; of doubtful origin.]

bacillus, *bə-sil'əs, n.* properly a genus of Schizomycetes : popularly any bacterium :—*pl.* **bacill'i** (*-ī*).—*adjs.* **bacill'ar, bacill'ary** (or *bas'*), of the

shape or nature of a bacillus, rodlike.—*n.* **bacill'icide**, that which destroys bacilli.—*adj.* **bacill'iform**. [L.L. *bacillus*, dim. of *baculus*, a rod.]

back, *bak*, *n.* the hinder part of the body in man, and the upper part in beasts, extending from the neck and shoulders to the extremity of the backbone: put for the whole body in speaking of clothes: the hinder part, or the side remote from that presented or that habitually seen or contemplated (opposite to the front): the under side of a leaf or of a violin: part of the upper surface of the tongue opposite the soft palate; the convex side of a book, opposite to the opening of the leaves: the thick edge of a knife or the like: the upright hind part of a chair, bench, etc.: something added to the hinder side: the surface of the sea, or of a river: the keel and keelson of a ship: (*football*, etc.) one of the players behind the forwards—*full back* (who guards the goal), *half* and *three-quarter backs*: (*mining*) that side of an inclined mineral lode which is nearest the surface of the ground—the *back* of a level is the ground between it and the level above.—*adj.* rearward: remote: reversed: (*phon.*) made by raising the back of the tongue: belonging to the past.—*adv.* to or towards the back: to or towards the place from which one came: to a former state or condition: behind: behind in time: in return: again.—*v.t.* to mount or ride: to help or support, as if standing at one's back: to support one's opinion by a wager or bet on: to countersign or endorse: to write or print at the back of, as a parliamentary bill, or the like: to furnish with a back: to lie at the back of: to form the back of: to cause to move backward, as a horse: to put or propel backward, or in the opposite direction, by reversing the action, as an engine or a boat.—*v.i.* to move or go back or backwards: (of the wind) to change counter-clockwise.—*ns.* **back'-ache**, a pain in the back; **back'band**, a rope, strap, or chain passing over a cart saddle and holding up the shafts of a vehicle (also **back'-chain**, **back'-rope**); **back'-bench'er**, an occupant of a back bench, as in parliament.—*v.t.* **back'bite**, to speak evil of in absence.—*ns.* **back'biter**; **back'biting**.—*adj.* **back'-block**, of the back-blocks.—*n.* **back'-blocker**.—*n.pl.* **back'-blocks** (*Austr.*), the interior parts of a station, far from the river-front.—*ns.* **back'-board**, a board at the back of a cart, boat, etc.: a board fastened across the back to straighten the body; **back'bond** (*Scots law*), a deed attaching a qualification or condition to the terms of a conveyance or other instrument; **back'-bone'**, the spine or vertebral column: a main support or axis: mainstay: firmness.—*adj.* **back-bone'less**.—*ns.* **back'-chat**, answering back, retort, impertinence; **back'-cloth**, **back'-drop**, the painted cloth at the back of the stage; **back'-country**, districts not yet thickly populated; **back'-door**, a door in the back part of a building.—*adj.* unworthily secret: clandestine.—*n.* **back'-draught'**, a backward current.—*adj.* **backed**, having a back.—*ns.* **back'-end'**, the rear end: the later part of a season: the late autumn; **back'er**, one who backs or supports another in a contest: one who bets on a horse or the like; **back'-fall** (*mus.*), an obsolete ornament like an appoggiatura: a fall on the back as in wrestling (often *fig.*): a lever in the coupler of an organ; **back'fire**, ignition of gas in an internal-combustion engine's cylinder at wrong time, or within a bunsen-burner or the like instead of at the outlet.—*v.i.* (*bak-fīr'*) to have a backfire.—*ns.* **back'-forma'tion** (*philol.*), the making of a word from one that is, in error or jocularity, taken to be a derivative, as the verb *sidle* from the adverb *sidling* treated as if it were a participle; **back'friend** (*obs.*), a pretended friend: a backer, a friend who stands at one's back.—*adj.* **back'-ganging** (*Scot.*), in arrears.—*ns.* **back'-gar'den**, **back'-green**, a garden, green, at the back of a house; **back'ground**, ground at the back: a place of obscurity: the space behind the principal figures of a picture: (*fig.*) that against which anything is, or ought to be, seen; **back'-hair**, the hair at the back of the head; **back'-hand**, the hand turned backwards in making a stroke: handwriting with the letters sloping backwards: (*tennis*) in the part of the court to the left of a right-handed player, or the right of a left-handed: a stroke on the back-hand.—Also *adj.*—*adj.* **back'-hand'ed**, with the hand turned backwards (as of a blow): indirect, dubious, sarcastic, insincere.—*ns.* **back'-hand'er**, a blow with the back of the hand: (*coll.*) a bribe: an extra glass of wine out of turn, the bottle being passed back; **back'ing**, support at the back: mounting of a horse: the action of putting or going back: a body of helpers: anything used to form a back or line the back: counter-clockwise change of wind; **back'ing-down**, shirking; **back'-lash**, the jarring or play of ill-fitting machinery in recoil; **back'-lill** (*Scott*), the left-hand thumb-hole at the back of a bagpipe chanter (*erron.* **-lilt**); **back'-log**, a log at the back of a fire: (*coll.*) a reserve or accumulation of business, stock, etc., that will keep one going for some time.—*adj.* **back'most**, farthest to the back.—*n.* **back'-numb'er** a copy or issue of a newspaper or magazine of a bygone date: (*fig.*) a person or thing out of date or past the useful stage.—*v.i.* **back'ped'al**, to press the pedals back, as in slowing a fixed-wheel bicycle.—*ns.* **back'-ped'alling**; **back'-piece**, **back'-plate**, a piece or plate of armour for the back; **back'-room**.—*adj.* (*coll.*; of persons) doing important work behind the scenes, esp. in secret.—*ns.* **back'-saw**, a saw stiffened by a thickened back; **back'-scratcher**, a clawed instrument for scratching the back; **back'-set**, a setting back, reverse: an eddy or counter-current; **back'sey'** (*-sī*; *Scot.*) sirloin; **back'side**, the back or hinder side or part of anything: the hinder part of an animal: (*Scot.*) the premises at the rear of a house; **back'-sight**, in surveying, a sight taken backwards: the sight of a rifle nearer the stock; **back'-slang**, slang in which every word is pronounced as if spelt backwards.—*v.i.* **back'slide**, to slide or fall back in faith or morals.—*ns.* **back'slid'er**; **back'slid'ing**; **back'-spaul'd** (*Scot.*), the back of the shoulder: the hind-leg.—*v.t.* and *v.i.* **backspeir'**, **-speer'**, (*Scot.*) to cross-question.—*n.pl.* **back'stairs**, servants' or private stairs of a house.—*adj.* secret or underhand.—*n.* **back'-stall**, a garrotter's confederate on the look-out behind.—*v.i.* (*pr.p.*; *Spens.*) **backstart'ing**, starting back.—*n.pl.* **back'-stays**, ropes or stays extending from the topmast-heads to the sides of a ship, and slanting a little backward: any stay or support at the back.—*ns.* **back'-stitch**, a method of sewing in which, for every new stitch, the needle enters behind, and comes out in front of, the end of the previous one; **back'sword**, a sword with a back or with only one edge: a stick with a basket-handle; **backsword'man** (*Shak.*); **back'veld** (*-felt*) (*S. Africa*), country remote from towns.—*adj.* remote, rustic, primitive.—*ns.* **backvel'der** (*-dər*); **back'wash**, a receding wave: a backward current: a reaction.—*v.t.* to affect with back-wash: to clean the oil from (wool) after combing.—*n.* **back'water**, water held back by a dam: a pool or belt of water connected with a river but not in the line of its present course or current: water thrown back by the turning of a water-wheel: (*fig.*) a place unaffected by the movements of the day: a backward current of water: the swell of the sea caused by a passing ship.—*n.pl.* **back'-woods**, the forest beyond the cleared country.—*n.* **backwoods'man**, a dweller in the backwoods: (*fig.*) a peer who rarely attends the House of Lords.—*adj.* **back'-wound'ing** (*Shak.*), backbiting.—*n.* **back'-yard**, a yard behind a house.—**back down**, to abandon one's opinion or position; **back of** (*U.S.*), behind; **back out**, to move out backwards: to evade an obligation or undertaking; **back up**, to give support to; **back water**, to ply the oars or turn the paddle-wheels backward; **break the back of**, to overburden: to accomplish the hardest part of; **give** or **make a back**, to take up position for leap-frog; **on the back of**, close behind: (*Scot.*) just after; **put one's back into**, to do with might and main; **set** or **put one's back up**, to show or to arouse resentment; **take a back seat**, to sink into obscurity or subordination; **talk through the back of one's neck,** to talk utter nonsense; **to the backbone,** through and through. [O.E. *bæc;* Sw. *bak,* Dan. *bag.*]

back, *bak, n.* a trough for carrying fuel: a tub.—*n.* **back′et** (*Scot.*), a shallow wooden trough for carrying ashes, coals, etc. [Fr. *bac,* trough, dim. *baquet,* perh. partly through Du. *bak.*]

backare, baccare, *bak′ār,* or *bak-ā′ri, interj.* (*Shak.*), back : stand back. [Perh. for *back there;* or sham Latin.]

backfisch, *bäk′fish, n.* a young girl: a flapper. [Ger., lit. fish for frying, perhaps in allusion to immaturity.]

backgammon, *bak-gam′ən,* or *bak′, n.* a game played by two persons on a board with dice and fifteen men or pieces each : a triple game scored by bearing all one's men before the other has brought all to his own table.—*v.t.* to defeat in such a way. [**back,** because the pieces are sometimes taken up and obliged to go *back*—that is, re-enter at the table, and M.E. *gamen,* play.]

backsheesh, backshish. See baksheesh.

backward, *bak′wərd, adv.* and *adj.* towards the back: on the back: towards the past: from a better to a worse state: in a direction opposite to the normal.—*adj.* **back′ward,** keeping back: shy, bashful: unwilling: slow in development: late: dull or stupid.—*n.* the past portion of time.—*n.* **backwarda′tion,** percentage paid by a seller of stock for keeping back its delivery till the following account.—*adv.* **back′wardly.**—*n.* **back′wardness.**—*adv.* **back′wards; backward and forward,** to and fro.—**to ring bells backward,** to begin with the bass bell, in order to give tidings of dismay. [**back,** suff. **-ward, -wards.**]

bacon, *bā′kn, n.* swine's flesh (now the back and sides) salted or pickled and dried : (*Shak.*) a rustic, a chaw-bacon.—**save one's bacon,** to come off scatheless with difficulty. [O.Fr. *bacon,* of Gmc. origin; cf. O.H.G. *bahho, bacho/* Ger. *bache.*]

Baconian, *bā-kō′ni-ən, adj.* pertaining to Francis Bacon (1561-1626), or to his inductive philosophy, or to Roger *Bacon* (d. c. 1292) or his teaching, or to the theory that Francis Bacon wrote Shakespeare's plays.—Also *n.*—*n.* **Baco′nianism.**

bacteria, *bak-tē′ri-ä, n.pl.* the Schizomycetes, a class of microscopic unicellular or filamentous plants, without chlorophyll or well-defined nucleus, mostly saprophytic, but often parasitic and the cause of many diseases :—*sing.* **bactē′rium,** any member of the class, esp. a rod-shaped schizomycete.—*adjs.* **bactē′rial, bactē′rian, bacteric** (-*ter′ik*).—*n.* **bactē′ricide,** a substance that destroys bacteria.—*adj.* **bacterici′dal.**—*ns.* **bactē′rioid, bac′tēroid,** a swollen bacterium living symbiotically in the root-nodules of beans and other plants.—*adj.* **bactēriolog′ical.**—*ns.* **bactēriol′ogist; bactēriol′ogy,** the scientific study of bacteria; **bactēriolý′sin** (or -*ol′i-*), an antibody that destroys bacteria; **bactēriol′ysis,** destruction of bacteria by an antibody (Gr. *lysis,* dissolution).—*adj.* **bactēriolýt′ic.**—*ns.* **bacteriophage** (*bak-tē′ri-ō-fāj*), any of a large number of virus-like agents, present in the atmosphere, soil, water, living things, etc., whose function is to destroy bacteria (Gr. *phagein,* to eat); **bactēriō′sis,** any bacterial plant-disease; **bactē′rios′tasis,** inhibition of the growth of bacteria (Gr. *stasis,* standing); **bactē′riostat,** an agent that inhibits their growth.—*adj.* **bactēriostat′ic.**—*v.t.* **bac′tērise,** to treat with bacteria. [Gr. *baktērion,* dim. of *baktron,* a stick.]

Bactrian, *bak′tri-ən, adj.* belonging to *Bactria* (Central Asia), esp. applied to a two-humped camel. —*n.* a two-humped camel.

baculine, *bak′ū-līn, adj.* pertaining to the stick or cane—in flogging. [L. *baculum.*]

baculite, *bak′ū-līt, n.* a genus (*Baculi′tes*) of fossils, allied to the ammonites, with a straight, tapering shell. [L. *baculum,* a stick.]

bad, *bad, adj.* ill or evil : wicked : incorrect, faulty : poor : unskilful : worthless : unfavourable : painful : unwell : spurious :—*comp.* **worse;** *superl.* **worst.**—*adj.* **badd′ish,** somewhat bad: not very good.—*adv.* **bad′ly.**—*n.* **bad′ness.—bad blood,**

angry feeling; **bad debt,** a debt that cannot be recovered; **bad lands,** wastes of much eroded soft strata in South Dakota and elsewhere; **bad man** (*U.S.*) a ruffian; **bad shot,** a wrong guess; **go bad,** to decay; **go to the bad,** to go to moral ruin; **to the bad,** in a bad condition : in deficit; **with a bad grace,** ungraciously. [Ety. very obscure. The M.E. *badde* is referred by Zupitza to O.E. *bæddel,* a hermaphrodite, *bædling,* an effeminate fellow.]

badderlock, *bad′ər-lok, n.* (*Scot.*) an edible seaweed (Alaria) resembling tangle. [Poss. for **Balder's locks.**]

bade, *bad,* (*poet. bād*), *p.t.* of bid (both verbs).

badge, *baj. n.* a distinguishing mark or emblem. [M.E. *bage.* Origin obscure.]

badger, *baj′ər, n.* a burrowing, nocturnal, hibernating animal of the otter and weasel family: extended to other animals—hyrax, wombat, ratel : a painting, or other, brush made of badger's hair. —*v.t.* to pursue with eagerness, as dogs hunt the badger: to pester or worry.—*ns.* **badg′er-bait′ing, -drawing,** the sport of setting dogs to draw out a badger from a barrel; **badg′er-dog,** the dachshund, a long-bodied and short-legged dog used in drawing the badger.—*adjs.* **badg′er-legged,** having legs of unequal length, as the badger was vulgarly supposed to have; **badg′erly,** like a badger: greyish-haired, elderly. [Prob. from **badge** and suffix **-ard,** in reference to the white mark borne like a badge on its forehead.]

badinage, *bad′in-äzh, n.* light playful talk : banter. [Fr. *badinage—badin,* playful or bantering.]

badious, *bā′di-əs, adj.* (*bot.*) chestnut-coloured. [L. *badius.*]

badmash, budmash, *bud′mäsh, n.* (*India*) an evil-doer. [Pers.]

badminton, *bad′min-tən, n.* a cooling summer drink compounded of claret, sugar, and soda-water : a game played with shuttlecocks. [*Badminton* in Gloucester, a seat of the Dukes of Beaufort.]

bael, bel, bhel, *bel, n.* a thorny Indian rutaceous tree (*Aegle Marmelos*) : its edible fruit, the Bengal quince. [Hind.]

baetyl, *bē′til, n.* a magical or holy meteoric stone. [Gr. *baitylos.*]

baff, *bäf, v.t.* to strike the ground with the sole of a golf-club in playing, and so to send the ball up in the air.—*n.* **baffy,** *baf′i,* a club like a brassy, but with a shorter shaft and a more sloping face.

baffle, *baf′l, v.t.* to frustrate, confound, impede perplexingly : (*obs.*) to cheat, hoodwink, bewilder, bring to nought : (*obs.*) to disgrace publicly, as by hanging by the heels.—*n.* (*obs.*) confusion, check : a plate or like device for regulating or diverting the flow of liquid, gas, sound-waves, etc. (also **baffle-plate, baff′ler**).—*n.* **baff′ler,** a bewilderer, confounder.—*adj.* **baff′ling.**—*adv.* **baff′lingly.** [Prob. Scottish and connected with *bauchle;* but cf. Fr. *beffler,* from O.Fr. *befe,* mockery. Paul Meyer suggests a derivation from Prov. *baf,* interj. of disdain.]

baft, *bäft, n.* a coarse fabric, orig. Oriental, now made in and shipped from England. [Pers. *baft,* woven.]

baft, *bäft, adv.* and *prep.* behind : (*naut.*) abaft, astern. [O.E. *beæftan—be,* by, and *æftan,* behind.]

bag, *bag, n.* a sack, pouch : specially the silken pouch to contain the back-hair of the wig : a bagful : measure of quantity for produce : a game-bag, hence the quantity of fish or game secured, however great : an udder : (*coll.* in *pl.*) trousers.— *v.i.* to bulge, swell out : (*naut.*) to drop away from the right course.—*v.t.* to cram full: to put into a bag, specially of game : hence to kill (game) : to seize, secure or steal :—*pr.p.* **bagg′ing;** *pa.p.* **bagged.**—*ns.* **bag′ful,** as much as a bag will hold :—*pl.* **bag′fuls.**—*adj.* **bagged** (*bagd*), in a bag : bulged slackly.—*adv.* **bagg′ily.**—*n.* **bagg′ing,** cloth or material for bags.—**bagg′it** (Scots form of **bagged**), bagged : full of spawn, etc.—*n.* a ripe female salmon that has failed to shed her eggs.—*adj.* **bagg′y,** loose like a bag: bulged.— *ns.* **bag′man,** an old-fashioned name for a commercial traveller; **bag'-wig,** an 18th-cent. wig with back-hair enclosed in an ornamental bag.—**bag and baggage,** originally a military expression, as in the phrase, 'to march out with bag and baggage', i.e. with all belongings saved: to make an honourable retreat: now used in the sense of to clear out completely; **bag of bones,** an emaciated living being; **let the cat out of the bag,** to disclose the secret. [M.E. *bagge,* perh. Scand.; not Celtic, as Diez suggests.]

bagasse, *ba-gas',* n. refuse in sugar-making. [Fr.; Sp. *bagazo,* husks of grapes or olives after pressing.]

bagatelle, *bag-a-tel',* n. a trifle : a piece of music in a light style : a game played on a board with nine balls and a cue, the object being to put the balls down into holes at the end. [Fr.,—It. *bagatella,* a conjuror's trick, a trifle.]

baggage, *bag'ij,* n. the tents, provisions, and other necessaries of an army: (esp. *U.S.*) traveller's luggage: a worthless woman: a saucy woman.—*ns.* **bagg'age-animal; bagg'age-car** (*U.S.*), a railway luggage-van; **bagg'age-train,** a train of baggage-animals, wagons, etc. [O.Fr. *bagage—baguer,* to bind up, from which we may infer all the meanings, without reference to Fr. *bagasse,* It. *bagascia,* a strumpet.]

bagnio, *ban'yō,* n. a bathing-house, esp. one with hot baths : an Oriental prison : a stew or brothel. [It. *bagno*—L. *balneum,* a bath.]

bagpipe, *bag'pīp,* n. a wind-instrument consisting of a *bag* fitted with *pipes* (often in *pl.*).—*ns.* **bag'-piper, bag'piping.**

baguette, *bag-et',* n. a small moulding like an astragal. [Fr., rod, dim.—L. *baculum.*]

bah, *bä,* *interj.* expressing disgust or contempt. [Fr.]

Bahadur, *bu-hä'door,* or *haw',* n. (*India*) a title of respect often added to the names of officers and officials. [Hind. *bahādur,* hero.]

Bahai, *bä-hä'ē,* n. an adherent of a Persian religion, a development of Babism.—Also *adj.*—*ns.* **Baha'ist; Baha'ism; Baha'ite.** [From *Baha*-Ullah and Abdul *Baha,* successors of the Bab.]

baignoire, *ben-wär,* n. a theatre box on a level with the stalls. [Fr., bath.]

bail, *bāl,* n. one who procures the release of an accused person by becoming security for his appearing in court: the security given : (*Spens.*) jurisdiction, custody.—*v.t.* to set a person free by giving security for him: to release on the security of another : to deliver (goods) in trust upon a contract.—*adj.* **bail'able.**—*ns.* **bail'-bond,** a bond given by a prisoner and his surety upon being bailed; **bail'-dock, bale'-dock,** a room at the Old Bailey, London, in which prisoners were kept during the trials; **bailee',** one to whom goods are bailed; **bail'er,** one who bails goods; **bail'ment,** a delivery of goods in trust: the action of bailing a prisoner; **bails'man,** one who gives bail for another.—**to accept, admit to, allow bail,** are all said of the magistrate; the prisoner **offers, surrenders to his bail;** the one who provides it **goes, gives,** or **stands bail,** or **bails out** a prisoner; **give leg bail,** to be beholden to one's legs for escape. [O.Fr. *bail,* custody, handing over, *baillier,* to control, guard, hand over.—L. *bājulāre,* to bear a burden, carry, carry on.]

bail, bayle, *bāl,* n. a barrier : a pole separating horses in an open stable : (*Australia*) a frame for holding a cow's head during milking.—*v.t.* **bail** (*Shak.* **bale** : *rare*), to confine.—**bail up** (*Australia*), to secure in a bail : to stop and disarm in order to rob : to put one's hands up in surrender. [O.Fr. *baile,* perh. from *baillier,* to enclose; or L. *baculum,* a stick.]

bail, *bāl,* n. one of the cross pieces on the top of the wicket in cricket.—*ns.* **bail'-ball, bail'er,** a bowled ball that hits or removes a bail without disturbing the stumps. [Prob. conn. with foregoing.]

bail (also **bale**), *bāl,* n. a bucket or other vessel for ladling out water from a boat.—*v.t.* to clear of water with bails : to ladle (often with *out*).—*n.* **bail'er.**—**to bale (bail) out,** to escape from an

aeroplane by parachute. [Fr. *baille,* bucket, perh. from L.L. *bacula,* dim. of *baca,* a basin.]

bail, *bāl,* n. a hoop: a hoop-handle, as in a kettle. [Prob. O.N. *beygla,* hoop, from the Gmc. root *bug-,* to bend.]

bailey, *bāl'i,* n. the outer wall of a feudal castle: hence the outer court, or any court within the walls.—**the Old Bailey** in London was in the ancient bailey between Ludgate and Newgate. [Fr. *baille,* palisade, enclosure, from L.L. *ballium.*]

Bailey bridge, *bā'li brij,* n. a prefabricated bridge. [Inventor's name.]

bailie, *bāl'i,* n. a municipal officer in Scotland corresponding to an English alderman : (*obs.*) a sheriff's officer (but cf. **water-bailie**) : (*obs.*) the chief magistrate of a Scottish barony or part of a county, with functions like a sheriff's.—*n.* **bail'ieship.**—Also **baill'ie, baill'ieship.** [O.Fr. *bailli.* land-steward, officer of justice. See **bailiff.**]

bailiff, *bāl'if,* n. formerly any king's officer, e.g. sheriff, mayor, etc., esp. the chief officer of a hundred, surviving in certain cases as a formal title : the first civil officer in Jersey and in Guernsey : a foreign magistrate : a sheriff's officer : an agent or land-steward.—*n.* **bail'iwick,** the jurisdiction of a bailiff : jurisdiction in general. [O.Fr. *baillif*—L.L. *bājulivus*—*bājulus,* carrier, administrator. See **bail.**]

Bairam, *bī'räm, bī-räm',* n. the name of two Mohammedan festivals—the *Lesser* Bairam lasting three days, after the feast of Ramadan, and the *Greater,* seventy days later, lasting four days. [Pers.]

bairn, *bārn,* n. (*Scot.*) a child.—*adj.* **bairn'like, bairn'ly.**—*ns.* **bairn's'-part,** legitim; **bairn'team, bairn'time,** brood of children. [O.E. *bearn—beran,* to bear.]

baisemain, *bāz'manª,* n. (*obs.*) mostly in pl., compliment paid by kissing the hand. [Fr. *baiser,* to kiss, *main,* hand.]

bait, *bāt,* n. food put on a hook to allure fish or make them bite : any allurement or temptation : a refreshment, esp. taken on a journey : a stop for that purpose: (*slang*) a rage.—*v.t.* to set with food as a lure : to tempt : to give refreshment to, esp. on a journey : to set dogs on (a bear, bull, etc.) : to worry, persecute, harass.—*v.i.* to take, or stop for, refreshment on a journey.—*ns.* **bait'-fish,** fish used as bait : fish that may be caught with bait; **bait'ing.** [M.E. *beyten*—O.N. *beita,* to cause to bite—*bita,* to bite.]

baize, *bāz,* n. a coarse woollen cloth with a long nap, used mainly for coverings, linings, etc.: a table cover.—*v.t.* to cover or line with baize. [Fr. *baies,* pl. (fem.) of *bai*—L. *badius,* bay-coloured.]

bajan, *bā'jan* (*Aberdeen*), **bejant,** *bē'jant* (*St. Andrews*), n. a freshman (so formerly at several Continental universities). [Fr. *béjaune,* novice—*bec jaune,* yellow bill, unfledged bird.]

Bajocian, *ba-jō'si-an, adj.* (*geol.*) of a division of the Middle Jurassic. [L. *Bajocassēs,* a people living about Bayeux.]

bake, *bāk,* v.t. to dry, harden, or cook by the heat of the sun or of fire : to make or cook in an oven : (*Spens., Shak.*) to harden by cold : (*Shak.*) to cake.—*v.i.* to work as a baker : to become firm through heat.—*pa.p.* **baked** (*bākt*), (*arch.*) **bāk'en;** *pr.p.* **bāk'ing.**—*n.* (*Scot.*) a kind of biscuit.—*ns.* **bake'board** (*Scot.*), a board for kneading dough on; **bake'house,** a house or place used for baking in; **bake'meat** (*B.*), pastry, pies; **bak'er,** one who bakes bread, etc.—(*obs.*) **bax'ter; bak'ery,** a bakehouse: (*U.S.*) a baker's shop; **bake'stone,** a flat stone or plate of iron on which cakes are baked in the oven; **bak'ing,** the process by which bread is baked : the quantity baked at one time; **bak'ing-pow'der,** a mixture (e.g. tartaric acid and sodium bicarbonate) giving off carbon dioxide, used as a substitute for yeast in baking; **bak'ing-so'da,** sodium bicarbonate.—**baker's dozen** (see **dozen**). [O.E. *bacan;* cog. with Ger. *backen,* to bake, Gr. *phōgein,* to roast.]

Bakelite, *bā'kəl-īt,* n. a synthetic resin made by condensation of cresol or phenol with formaldehyde. [From its inventor, L. H. *Baekeland* (1863-1944).]

baksheesh, bakhshish, backsheesh, backshish, *bak′* or *buk′shĕsh, n.* a gift or present of money in the East, a gratuity or tip. [Pers. *bakhshīsh.*]

Balaam, *bā′ləm, n.* a prophet who strives to mislead, like Balaam in Numb. xxii-xxiv : unimportant paragraphs kept in readiness to fill up a newspaper. —*ns.* **Bā′laam-box,** or **-bas′ket,** a place in which such paragraphs are kept in readiness; **Bā′laamite.** —*adj.* **Bālaamit′ical.**

Balaclava cap, helmet, *bal-ə-klä′vä, n.* a warm woollen head-gear covering ears and back of head, suitable for severe weather. [*Balaklava* in Crimea.]

balalaika, *bä-lä-lī′kä, n.* a Russian musical instrument, like a guitar, with triangular body and ordinarily three strings. [Russ.]

balance, *bal′əns, n.* an instrument for weighing, usually formed of two dishes or scales hanging from a beam supported in the middle : act of weighing two things : equilibrium : harmony among the parts of anything : equality or just proportion of weight or power, as the balance of power : the sum required to make the two sides of an account equal, hence the surplus, or the sum due on the account : what is needed to produce equilibrium, a counterpoise : a contrivance that regulates the speed of a clock or watch : (*coll.*) remainder.— *v.t.* to weigh in a balance : to poise : to set or keep in equilibrium : to counterpoise : to compare : to settle, as an account : (*book-keeping*) to examine and test so as to make the debtor or creditor sides of an account agree.—*v.i.* to have equal weight or power, etc. : to be or come to be in equilibrium : to hesitate or fluctuate.—*adj.* **bal′anced,** poised so as to preserve equilibrium : well arranged, stable.—*ns.* **bal′ancer,** one who, or that which, balances : a fly's rudimentary hindwing : an acrobat : **bal′ance-sheet,** a summary and balance of accounts; **bal′ance-wheel,** a wheel in a watch or chronometer which regulates the beat or rate. [Fr.,—L. *bilanx,* having two scales—*bis,* double, *lanx, lancis,* a dish or scale.]

Balanus, *bal′ə-nəs, n.* the acorn-shell genus.—*n.* **Balanogloss′us,** a genus of worm-like animals of the Hemichordata. [Gr. *balanos,* acorn, gland, *glōssa,* tongue.]

balas, *bal′as, n.* a rose-red spinel (usu. **balas ruby**). [O.Fr. *balais* (It. *balascio*)—L.L. *balascus*—Pers. *Badakhshān,* a place near Samarkand where they are found.]

balata, *bal′ə-tä, n.* the gum of the bullet or bully tree of South America, used as a substitute for rubber and gutta-percha. [Prob. Tupí.]

balboa, *bäl-bō′ä, n.* the monetary unit of Panama. [Vasco Nuñez de *Balboa,* c. 1475-1517.]

Balbriggan, *bal-brig′ən, n.* a knit cotton fabric like that made at *Balbriggan,* Ireland : underclothing made of it.

balbutient, *bal-bū′sh(y)ənt, adj.* stammering. [L. *balbūtiēns, -entis*—*balbūtīre,* to stutter.]

balcony, *balk′ə-ni* (18th c., *bal-kō′ni*), *n.* a stage or platform projecting from the wall of a building within or without, supported by pillars or consoles, and surrounded with a balustrade or railing : in theatres, usually the gallery immediately above the dress circle (*U.S.* the dress circle itself).—*n.* **balconet(te)′,** a miniature balcony.—*adj.* **bal′conied.** [It. *balcōne*—*balco,* of Gmc. origin; O.H.G. *balcho* (Ger. *balken*), Eng. **balk.**]

bald, *bawld, adj.* without hair, feathers, etc., on the head (or on other parts of the body) : bare, unadorned : lacking in literary grace : paltry, trivial : undisguised.—*ns.* **bald′-coot, bald′icoot,** the coot, from its pure white wide frontal plate : a monk; **bald′-ea′gle,** a common but inaccurate name for the American white-headed eagle, used as the national emblem.—*adj.* **bald′-faced,** having white on the face, as a horse.—*n.* **bald′head,** a person bald on the head.—*adj.* **bald′-headed,** having a bald head.—*adj.* and *adv.* (*slang*) **bald′-head′ed,** without restraint : out and out.—*adj.* **bald′ish,** somewhat bald.—*adv.* **bald′ly.**—*ns.* **bald′ness; bald′pate,** one destitute of hair : a

kind of wild duck.—*adjs.* **bald′pate, -d.** [Perh. **balled,** rounded; perh. W. *bâl,* white.]

baldachin, baldaquin, *ba(w)l′də-kin, n.* silk brocade : a canopy over a throne, pulpit, altar, etc. : in R.C. processions, a canopy borne over the priest who carries the host. [It. *baldacchino,* Fr. *baldaquin,* a canopy, from It. *Baldacco,* Baghdad, whence was brought the stuff of which they were made.]

balderdash, *bawl′dər-dash, n.* (*obs.*) mixed liquid : idle senseless talk : anything jumbled together without judgment : (*dial.*) obscene language or writing. [Origin unknown.]

baldmoney, *bawld′mun-i, n.* spignel (*Meum athamanticum*), a subalpine umbelliferous plant : gentian of various kinds. [Ety. unknown.]

baldric, also **baldrick,** *bawld′rik, n.* a warrior's belt or shoulder sash : (*Spens.* **baudricke**) the zodiac. [Cf. M.H.G. *balderich,* girdle.]

Baldwin, *bawld′win, n.* an American variety of apple. [Personal name.]

bale, *bāl, n.* a bundle, or package of goods : (*obs.*) the set of dice for any special game.—*v.t.* to make into bales.—*n.* **bal′er.** [M.E. *bale,* perh. from O.Fr. *bale*—O.H.G. *balla, palla,* ball. See **ball.**]

bale. See **bail.**

bale, *bāl, n.* evil, injury, mischief : misery : woe.— *adj.* **bale′ful,** malignant : painful : hurtful : sorrowful.—*adv.* **bale′fully.**—*n.* **bale′fulness.** [O.E. *bealu;* O.H.G. *balo;* O.N. *böl.*]

bale, *bāl, n.* (*arch.*) a fire, esp. a funeral pyre : (*Scot.*) a beacon-fire : a bonfire.—*n.* **bale′-fire.** [O.E. *bǽl;* cf. O.N. *bál,* bale, Gr. *phalos,* bright, white.]

balection. Same as **bolection.**

baleen, *bə-, ba-lēn′, n.* horny plates growing from the palate of certain whales, the whalebone of commerce.—Also *adj.* [O.Fr. *baleine*—L. *balaena,* whale.]

balista. See **ballista.**

balk, baulk, *bawk, n.* an unploughed ridge : (*obs.*) a place overlooked, an omission : a ridge : part of a billiard table marked off by the balk-line : a forbidden action of the pitcher in baseball : a squared timber : a tie-beam of a house, stretching from wall to wall, esp. when laid so as to form a loft (the balks) : (*obs.*) the beam of a balance : a rope to connect fishing-nets : a check, frustration : a disappointment : failure to take a jump or the like.— *v.t.* to ignore, pass over : to shirk : to decline : to avoid : to let slip : to put a balk in the way of : to thwart : to frustrate : to foil : to check : (*Shak.*) to chop (logic).—*v.i.* to pull up or stop short at a difficulty : to jib : to refuse a jump, etc. : to refrain : to desist : (*Spens.*) to lie out of the way : to bandy words.—*adj.* **balk′d** (*Shak.*), prob., heaped in balks.—*n.* **balk′er.**—*n.* and *adj.* **balk′ing.**—*adv.* **balk′ingly.**—*n.* **balk-line,** a line drawn across a billiard table : a boundary line for the preliminary run in a jumping competition or the like.—*adj.* **balk′y,** apt to balk. [O.E. *balca,* ridge; O.H.G. *balcho,* beam.]

Balkanise, *bawl′kən-īz, v.t.* to reduce to the condition of the *Balkan* countries, where hostile nationalities are or were mixed together.

ball, *bawl, n.* anything spherical or nearly so : the orb of sovereignty : a globular body to play with : any rounded protuberant part of the body : a bullet, or solid missile thrown from an engine of war : a throw or delivery of the ball at cricket, etc. : a game played with a ball, esp. (*U.S.*) baseball : a spherical clew of yarn, string, etc. : the eyeball : (*obs.*) a spherical cake of soap : a bolus for a horse.—*v.t.* to form into a ball : to clog : to entangle.—*v.i.* to gather into a ball : to clog : to cluster, as swarming bees round the queen :—*n.pl.* **ball′-bear′ings,** a device for lessening friction by making a revolving part turn on loose steel balls.—*n.* **ball′-cock,** the stopcock of a cistern, turned by a floating ball that rises and falls with the water.—*adj.* **balled,** formed into a ball.—*ns.* **ball′-flower,** an ornament of Decorated Gothic architecture, resembling a ball within a globular flower; **ball′-game,** any game played with a ball; **ball′ing,** forming into a ball : snow-balling :

fāte, fär, ȧsk; mē, hėr (her); *mīne; mōte; mūte; mōōn; dhen* (then)

(*Scot.* **ba"ing**) a periodical game of football played by the population of a town in the streets (and sometimes the river)—also **ba'spiel.**—*adjs.* **ball'-pointed,** having a swollen tip, as a pen; **ball'-proof,** proof against balls discharged from fire-arms.—**ball and socket,** a joint formed of a ball partly enclosed in a cup; **no ball** (*cricket*), a delivery adjudged contrary to rule; **keep the ball rolling,** to keep things going; **the ball at one's feet,** success in one's grasp; **three balls,** the sign of a pawnbroker; **wide ball,** one out of the batsman's reach. [M.E. *bal*—O.N. *böllr;* O.H.G. *ballo, pallo.*]

ball, *bawl, n.* an assembly for dancing.—*ns.* **ball'-dress; ball'-room.**—Also *adj.*—**open the ball,** to begin operations. [O.Fr. *bal—baller,* to dance—L.L. *ballāre,* perh.—Gr. *ballizein,* to dance.]

ballad, *bal'ǝd* (*Scot.* **ballant,** *bǎl'ǝnt,* **ballat,** -*ǝt*), *n.* orig. a song accompanying a dance : a simple, straightforward narrative poem in short stanzas (usu. of four lines, of eight and six syllables alternately) : a drawing-room song, usually of a paltry and sentimental nature, in several verses sung to the same melody : any popular song, often scurrilous.—*v.t.* (*Shak.*) to make ballads about.—*ns.* **ball'adist,** a writer or singer of ballads; **ball'ad-monger,** a dealer in or composer of ballads; **ball'adry,** ballads collectively : ballad-making.—**ballad concert,** a concert of drawing-room ballads; **ballad opera,** opera with spoken dialogue, and songs set to existing popular tunes. [O.Fr. *ballade*—L.L. *ballāre,* to dance; see foregoing word.]

ballade, *bǎ-lǎd', n.* a poem of one or more terns or triplets of stanzas, each of seven, eight, or ten lines, including refrain, followed by an envoy, the whole on three (or four) rhymes : sometimes loosely, any poem in stanzas of equal length : an ill-defined form of instrumental music, often in six-eight or six-four time.—**ballade royal,** rhyme royal (James VI and I's *ballat royal* has an additional line and rhymes *ababbcbc*). [An earlier spelling of **ballad,** with old pronunciation restored.]

ballan, *bal'ǝn, n.* a species of wrasse.—Also **ball'an-wrasse'.** [Perh. Irish *ball,* spot.]

ballant, *bal'ǝnt,* a Scots form of **ballad.**

ballast, *bal'ǝst, n.* heavy material used to weigh down and steady a ship or balloon : broken stone or other material used as the bed of a road or railway : that which renders anything steady.—*v.t.* to load with ballast : to make or keep steady : (*Shak.*) to load.—*pa.p.* **ball'asted** (*Shak.* **ball'ast**).—*n.* **ball'ast-heav'er.**—**in ballast,** carrying ballast only. [Prob. Old Sw. *barlast—bar,* bare, and *last,* load.]

ballat. See **ballad, ballade.**

ballerina, *bäl-le-rē'nä,* *bal-ǝ-rē'nä, n.* a female ballet-dancer :—*pl.* **balleri'ne** (-*nä*), **balleri'nas.** [It.]

ballet, *bal'ā, n.* a theatrical exhibition of dancing, posturing, and pantomimic action : music for it : the troupe that performs it : (*obs.*) a dance : (*bal'ǝt*), a form of madrigal : (*Scot.;* also **ballat**) a ballad.—*ns.* **ball'et-dancer; ball'et-girl; ball'et-master, -mistress,** the director of a ballet; **ballet'omane** (-*ō-mān*), an enthusiast for ballet; **balletomā'nia.** [Fr.; dim. of *bal,* a dance.]

ballista, balista, *ba-lis'tä, n.* a Roman military engine in the form of a crossbow for heavy missiles.—*adj.* **ballis'tic,** projectile : relating to projectiles.—*ns.* **ballis'tics** (treated as *sing.*), the science of projectiles; **ballis'tite,** a smokeless powder composed of gun-cotton and nitroglycerine.—**ballistic pendulum,** a suspended block for finding the velocity of projectiles. [L.,—Gr. *ballein,* to throw.]

ballium, *bal'i-ǝm, n.* the L.L. form of **bailey.**

balloon, *bǝ-lōōn', n.* an apparatus for travel in the air, or for carrying recording instruments, consisting of a gas-bag and a car : a toy of similar form : anything inflated, empty : a high kick or hit at a ball : (*obs.;* also **ballon,** *bä'lonₐ,* **ba-lōn'**) a game played with a large inflated ball :—*v.t.* to inflate : to send high in the air.—*v.i.* to ascend or travel in, or as if in, a balloon : to puff out like a

balloon.—*ns.* **ballonet** (*bal-o-net'*), in a balloon or dirigible, a small bag from which air is allowed to escape, and into which air is forced, to compensate for changes of pressure in the gas-bag : a division of the air-reservoir of a dirigible : a small auxiliary gas-bag; **balloon'ing; balloon'ist; balloon'-vine',** heartseed, a tropical American climber with bladdery pods.—**balloon barrage,** a system of captive balloons as a protection against hostile aircraft. [It. *ballone,* augmentative of *balla,* ball.]

ballot, *bal'ǝt, n.* a little ball or ticket or paper used in voting : a secret vote or method of voting by putting a ball or ticket or paper into an urn or box : in *U.S.* extended to open voting.—*v.i.* to vote by ballot : to draw lots :—*pr.p.* **ball'oting;** *pa.t.* and *pa.p.* **ball'oted.**—*ns.* **ball'ot-box,** a box to receive ballots; **ball'ot-paper,** a paper on which a ballot vote is recorded. [It. *ballotta,* dim of *balla,* ball. See **ball.**]

ballow, *bal'ō, n.* (*Shak.*) a cudgel.—Other readings are **bat, battero.** [Perh. a misprint for **baton.**]

bally, *bal'i, adj.* (*slang*), a euphemism for **bloody,** but almost meaningless.

ballyhoo, *bal-i-hōō', n.* (*U.S. slang*), noisy propaganda.

ballyrag, *bal'i-rag, v.t.* to bullyrag (q.v.).

balm, *bäm, n.* an aromatic substance : a fragrant and healing ointment : aromatic fragrance : anything that heals or soothes pain : a tree yielding balm : an aromatic labiate plant of the genus *Melissa* : extended to *Melittis* (*bastard balm*) and other garden herbs.—*v.t.* (*arch.*) to embalm : (*Shak.*) to anoint with fragrant oil : (*arch.*) to soothe.—*n.* **balm'iness.**—*adj.* **balm'y,** fragrant : mild and soothing : bearing balm : (*slang;* also **barmy**) mentally unsound.—**balm, or balsam, of Gilead,** the resinous exudation of trees of the genus *Commiphora* or *Bālsamodendron,* from the belief that it is the substance mentioned in the Bible as found in Gilead : the balsam fir. [O.Fr. *basme*—L. *balsamum.* See **balsam.**]

balm-cricket, *bäm'-krik'it, n.* (*Tennyson*) a cicada. [Ger. *baum,* tree, and **cricket.**]

balmoral, *bal-mor'ǝl, n.* a flat Scottish bonnet : a figured woollen petticoat : a kind of boot lacing in front.—*n.* **balmorality** (*bal-mǝr-al'i-ti; jocular*), the Victorian type of morality. [**Balmoral,** Queen Victoria's castle in Aberdeenshire.]

balneal, *bal'ni-ǝl, adj.* of baths or bathing.—*n.* **bal'neary,** a bath : a bathing-place : a medicinal spring.—*adj.* of or for bathing.—*ns.* **balneā'tion,** bathing; **balneol'ogist; balneol'ogy,** the scientific study of bathing and of mineral springs; **balneother'apy,** treatment of disease by baths. [L. *balneum*—Gr. *balaneion,* bath.]

baloney, boloney, *ba-, bǝ-lō'ni, n.* (*slang*) deceptive talk : nonsense.

baloo, balu, *bä'lōō, n.* (*India*) a bear. [Hind. *bhālū.*]

balsa, *bäl'sä, bawl'sä, n.* a raft or float : corkwood, a tropical American tree (*Ochroma Lagopus*) of the silk-cotton family, with very light wood. [Sp., raft.]

balsam, *bawl'sǝm, n.* a plant of the genus *Impatiens* (family Balsaminaceae) : a liquid resin or resinous oily substance, esp. balm of Gilead : (*fig.*) any healing agent.—*v.t.* to heal : (*rare*) embalm.—*adjs.* **balsamic** (*-sam'ik*); **balsamif'erous,** producing balsam.—*n.* **Balsami'na,** a discarded synonym of Impatiens, giving name to the balsam family Balsaminaceae (*-in-ā'si-ē*), close akin to the geraniums.—*adj.* **bal'samy,** fragrant.—**balsam fir,** an American fir (*Abies balsamea*) : balsam poplar, an American species of poplar; **balsam of Peru, of Tolu,** see **Peru, Tolu;** **Canada balsam,** a turpentine from the balsam fir. [L. *balsamum*—Gr. *balsamon;* prob. of Semitic origin.]

Balt, *bawlt, n.* a member of the former land-owning class (of German origin) in the Baltic provinces or states.—*adj.* **Balt'ic,** of the sea separating Scandinavia from Germany and Russia : of the western division of the Baltoslavs.—*n.* **Balt'oslav'.**—*adjs.* **Balt'oslav', -ic, -on'ic,** of a family of Indo-Germanic languages including the Slavonic languages with Lettish, Lithuanian, and (extinct)

Old Prussian. [From the *Baltic* Sea—L. *Baltia*, Scandinavia.]

Baltimore, *bawl'tim-ōr*, *n.* a common orange and black North American bird of the hang-nest family, called also *Baltimore oriole*, *fire-bird*, etc. [From Lord *Baltimore*, whose livery was orange and black.]

Baluchitherium, *ba-lōō-chi-thē'ri-əm*, *n.* a gigantic Tertiary fossil rhinoceros. [*Baluchistan*, where it was found, and Gr. *thērion*, a beast.]

baluster, *bal'əs-tər*, *n.* a small pillar supporting a stair rail or a parapet coping.—*adj.* **bal'ustered.**—*n.* **bal'ustrade**, a row of balusters joined by a rail or coping. [Fr. *balustre*—L.L. *balaustium*—Gr. *balaustion*, pomegranate flower; from its form.]

bam, *bam*, *n.* (*slang*) a hoax: a false tale.—*v.t.* to cheat or hoax. [See **bamboozle**.]

bambino, *bäm-bē'nō*, *n.* a child: a picture or image of the child Jesus. [It.]

bamboo, *bam-bōō'*, *n.* a gigantic tropical and subtropical grass with hollow-jointed woody stem. [Perh. Malay *bambu*.]

bamboozle, *bam-bōō'zl*, *v.t.* to deceive: to confound or mystify.—*n.* **bamboo'zlement.** [Origin unknown; first appears about 1700.]

ban, *ban*, *n.* a proclamation: sentence of banishment: outlawry: anathematisation: a denunciation: a curse: a prohibition: a vague condemnation.—*v.t.* (*arch.*) to curse: (*prov.*) to chide or rail upon: to anathematise: to proscribe: to forbid or prohibit. [O.E. *gebann*, proclamation, *bannan*, to summon; cf. **banns**.]

Ban, *ban*, *n.* (*hist.*) the governor of a **Ban'at** (**Ban'ate**, **Bann'at**), or military division on the boundaries of the Hungarian kingdom. [Pers. *bān*, lord.]

banal, *bän'əl*, *ban'əl*, *bən-al'*, *adj.* commonplace, trivial, flat.—*n.* **banal'ity**, triviality. [Fr.]

banana, *bə-*, *ba-nä'nä*, *n.* a gigantic tree-like herbaceous plant (*Musa sapientum*) or its nutritious fruit. [Sp. or Port., from the native name in Guinea.]

banausic, *ban-aw'sik*, *adj.* mechanic: befitting or savouring of an artisan: vulgar.—Also **banau'sian.** [Gr. *banausikos*—*banausos*, a handicraftsman.]

Banbury cake, *ban'bər-i kāk*, *n.* a kind of mince-pie made in *Banbury*, Oxfordshire.

banco, *bang'kō*, *n.* standard money in which a bank keeps its accounts, as distinguished from the current money of the place. [It. See **bank**.]

band, *band*, *n.* that by which loose things are held together: (*fig.*) a moral bond of restraint or of obligation: a tie or connecting piece: (*pl.*) shackles, bonds, fetters: (*arch.*) an agreement or promise given: (*arch.*) security given: (*Spens.*) a pledge.—*ns.* **band'ster**, one who binds the sheaves after the reapers; **band'-stone**, a stone set transversely in a wall to bind the structure. [M.E. *band*, *bond*—O.N. *band*. O.E. has *bend*. See **band**, below, **bind**, **bond**.]

band, *band*, *n.* a flat strip (of cloth, rubber, metal, etc.) to bind round anything, as a hat-band, waistband, rubber-band, etc.: a stripe crossing a surface distinguished by its colour or appearance: a flat strip between mouldings, or dividing a wall surface: the neck-band or collar of a shirt, also the collar or ruff worn in the 17th century (termed a *falling-band* when turned down): a belt for driving machinery: (*pl.*) the pair of linen strips hanging down in front from the collar, worn by some Protestant clergymen and by barristers and advocates, formerly by others.—*n.* **band'age**, (esp. *surg.*) a strip of cloth for winding round part of the body: a piece of cloth used to blindfold the eyes.—*v.t.* to bind with a bandage.—*ns.* **band'box** (or *ban'boks*), a light kind of box for holding (originally bands) caps, millinery, etc.; **band'-brake**, a brake in the form of a flexible band that can be tightened about a wheel or drum:—*adj.* **band'ed**, fastened as with a band: striped with bands.—*ns.* **band'fish**, a bright red Mediterranean fish (*Cepola*), or other ribbon-shaped fish; **band'-saw**, an endless saw, a toothed steel belt; **band'-string**, an ornamental string for fastening bands or collar; **band'-wheel**, a wheel on which a strap or band runs. [M.E. *bande*—O.Fr. *bande*, of

Gmc. origin; cf. O.E. *bindan*; Ger. *binde*, a band, Eng. **band**, above, **bind**.]

band, *band*, *n.* a number of persons bound together for any common purpose: a troop of conspirators, confederates, etc.: a body of musicians, esp. performers on wind and percussion instruments, often attached to a regiment: (*U.S.*) a herd or flock.—*v.t.* to bind together.—*v.i.* to associate, assemble, confederate.—*ns.* **band'master**, the conductor of a band; **bands'man**, a member of a band of musicians; **band'stand**, a structure for accommodating a band of musicians; **band'-wagon**, *n.* (*U.S.*) the car that carries the band in a circus procession: a prominent position: a place among the crowd or the winning side.—**Band of Hope**, an association of young persons pledged to lifelong abstinence from alcoholic drinks—first instituted about 1847. [Fr. *bande*, of Gmc. origin, with changed sense; cf. **band**, **bend**, **bind**.]

band, *band*, *v.t.* (*Spens.*) to ban or banish.

band, an obsolete *pa.t.* of **bind**.

bandana, **bandanna**, *ban-dän'ä*, *n.* a silk or cotton coloured handkerchief, with spots or diamond prints, originally from India. [Hind. *bāndhnū*, a mode of dyeing.]

bandalore, *ban'-də-lōr*, *n.* a toy also called a quiz, and later a yoyo.

bandar, *bun'där*, *n.* a rhesus monkey. [Hind.]

bandeau, *ban-dō'*, *n.* a fillet or band to bind the hair: a band within a hat: a bandage for the eyes:—*pl.* **bandeaux** (*ban-dōz'*). [Fr.]

bandelet, *band'ə-let*, *n.* (*archit.*) a small flat moulding or fillet surrounding a column. [Fr. *bandelette*.]

bandelier, *ban-də-lēr'*, *n.* a form of **bandoleer**.

banderilla, *bän-dä-rēl'yä*, *n.* a dart with a streamer, stuck by bull-fighters in the bull's neck.—*n.* **banderillero** (*bän-dä-rēl-yā'rō*), a bull-fighter who uses banderillas.

banderol, **banderole**, *ban'də-rōl*, **bannerol**, *ban'ə-rōl* (*Spens.*) **bannerall**, *-awl*), *n.* a small banner or streamer, as that borne on the shaft of a lance: (*archit.*) a flat band with an inscription, common in Renaissance buildings. [Fr.]

bandersnatch, *ban'dər-snach*, *n.* a monster invented by Lewis Carroll.

bandicoot, *ban'di-kōōt*, *n.* the largest species of rat, found in India and Ceylon, called also *Malabar rat* and *pig-rat*: a genus (*Perameles*) of small marsupials. [Telugu *pandikokku*, pig-rat.]

bandit, *ban'dit*, *n.* an outlaw: a brigand:—*pl.* **ban'dits**, **banditti** (*ban-dit'ē*; also loosely used as *sing.*, a body of bandits).—*n.* **ban'ditry**. [It. *bandito*, pl. *banditi*—L.L. *bannire*, *bandīre*, to proclaim. See **ban**.]

bandog, *ban'dog*, *n.* a dog tied up as a watch-dog, or because of its ferocity. [**band**, fastening, and **dog**.]

bandobast, **bundobust**, *bun'dō-bust*, *n.* (*Ind.*) an arrangement, settlement. [Hind. and Pers. *band-o-bast*, tying and binding.]

bandoleer, **bandolier**, *ban-dō-lēr'*, *n.* a shoulder belt, esp. for ammunition. [O.Fr. *bandouillere*—It. *bandoliera*—*banda*, a band.]

bandolero, *ban-dō-lā'rō*, *n.* a highwayman. [Sp.]

bandoline, *ban'dō-lēn*, *n.* a gummy substance used for stiffening the hair. [Prob. from **band**.]

bandore, *ban-dōr'*, *n.* an Elizabethan wire-stringed instrument like a cittern, invented by John Rose. [Sp. *bandurria*, Fr. *mandore*; L. *pandura*, Gr. *pandourā*, a three-stringed lute.]

bandrol, *band'rōl*, *n.* Same as **banderol**.

bandy, *ban'di*, *n.* a club bent at the end for striking a ball: a game at ball with such a club: a game played on ice.—*n.* **ban'dy-ball**, hockey. [Origin obscure.]

bandy, *ban'di*, *v.t.* to beat to and fro: to toss from one to another (as words with any one): to pass from mouth to mouth: to give and take (blows or reproaches): (*Shak.*) to fight, strive:—*pr.p.* **ban'dying**; *pa.t.* and *pa.p.* **ban'died.**—*n.* **ban'dying**. [Origin obscure.]

bandy, *ban'di*, *adj.* bent wide apart at the knee: having bandy or crooked legs.—*adj.* **ban'dy-legged'.**

bandy, *ban'di, n.* (*Ind.*) a carriage or (bullock) cart.—*n.* ban'dyman. [Telugu *bandi.*]

bane, *bān, n.* destruction: death: mischief: poison: source or cause of evil.—*v.t.* (*arch.*) to harm: (*Shak.*) to poison.—*n.* bane'berry, a black poisonous berry, the fruit of the ranunculaceous *Actaea spicata* : the plant itself, Herb-Christopher. —*adj.* bane'ful, destructive: pernicious: poisonous.—*adv.* bane'fully.—*n.* bane'fulness. [O.E. *bana,* a murderer; O.N. *bani,* death.]

bang, *bang, n.* a heavy blow : a sudden loud noise: an explosion.—*v.t.* to beat : to strike violently: to slam, as a door : to beat or surpass.—*v.i.* to make a loud noise : to slam (*dial.*) to bounce.—*adv.* with a bang : abruptly (esp. *bang off*):—*adj.* bang'ing, dealing blows : (*coll.*) overwhelming, 'whopping'.— *n.* bang'ster (*prov.*) a violent person : a braggart: a victor.—*adj.* bang'-up (*slang*), in the height of excellence or fashion. [O.N. *banga,* to hammer; cf. Ger. *bengel,* a cudgel.]

bang, *bang, n.* hair cut square across the brow.— *v.t.* to cut square across.—*adj.* banged, wearing the hair in such a way.—*n.* bang'-tail, a tail with the end tuft squared : a beast whose tail hair is banged. [An Americanism, prob. from the phrase *bang off.*]

bang. Same as bhang.

bangle, *bang'gl, n.* a ring for arm or leg.—*adj.* ban'gled, wearing bangles. [Hind. *bangri.*]

bangsring. Same as banxring.

banian, banyan, *ban'yən, -yan, n.* an Indian fig-tree with vast rooting branches : a Hindu trader, esp. from Gujarat : loosely, out of India, any Hindu : an Indian broker or financier : a loose jacket, gown, or under-garment worn in India.— banian days (*obs.*), days on which no meat was served out, hence days of short commons generally, from the abstinence from flesh of the Banian merchants. [Port. *banian,* perh. through Ar, *banyān,* from Hind. *banya*—Sans. *vanij,* a merchant.]

banish, *ban'ish, v.t.* to condemn to exile : to drive away : to expel.—*n.* ban'ishment, exile. [Fr. *bannir, baniss*—L.L. *bannīre,* to proclaim; see ban.]

banister, *ban'is-tər, n.* a stair-rail with its supports (often in *pl.*). [baluster.]

banjo, *ban'jō, n.* a musical instrument of the guitar kind—played with the fingers or with a plectrum— having a long neck, a body of stretched parchment like a drum, and usually five strings of catgut and wire.—*n.* ban'joist (-*ist*). [Negro pronunciation of bandore.]

banjolele, *ban-jō-lā'li, n.* a small banjo with gut strings. [banjo and ukulele.]

bank, *bangk, n.* a mound or ridge : an acclivity : the margin of a river, lake, etc.: the raised border of a road, railway cutting, etc.: the surface at a pit-mouth: the coal-face in a mine : a shoal or shallow : a bed of shellfish : a mass of cloud or mist : the tilt of an aeroplane.—*v.t.* to enclose with a bank : to deposit or pile up : to cover (a fire) so as to lessen the rate of combustion.—*v.t* and *v.i.* (of aircraft) to tilt in turning.—*n.* bank'er (*Austr.*), a river full to the top of its banks.—*adv.* bank'-high, up to the top of the bank.—*n.* banks'man, an overseer at a pit-mouth.—from bank to bank, from the time the collier begins to descend for his spell of work till he reaches the top again. [M.E. *banke,* prob. Scand.; cog. with bank (2, 3), bench.]

bank, *bangk, n.* a bench in a galley : a tier or rank of oars : the bench on which judges sat : a range of apparatus or equipment : a working table in various crafts : a pottery.—*ns.* bank'er, a mason's bench; bank'er-mark, a mason's mark on a stone. [O.Fr. *banc,* of Gmc. origin; cog. with bank (1 and 3).]

bank, *bangk, n.* a bench, office, or institution for the keeping, lending, and exchanging, etc., of money : a money-box for savings : a stock of money, fund, or capital : in games of hazard, the money the proprietor or other, who plays against all, has before him : a pool to draw cards from.—*v.t.* to deposit in a bank.—*v.i.* to have a bank account : (*coll.*) to count, rely.—*ns.* bank'-ā'gent, formerly in Scotland, the head of a branch-bank (now bank'-man'ager); bank'-bill (formerly) a bank-note : a bill drawn by one bank upon another; bank'-book, a book in which record is kept of money deposited in or withdrawn from a bank; bank'-cheque', an order to pay issued upon a bank; bank'er, one who keeps a bank : one employed in banking business : a betting card game; bank'-hol'iday, a day on which banks are legally closed, bills falling due on these being payable the following day—in England observed as a general holiday; bank'ing, the business of the banker.—*adj.* pertaining to a bank.—*ns.* bank'-note, a note issued by a bank, which passes as money, being payable to bearer on demand; bank'-pap'er, bank-notes in circulation; bank'-rate, the rate at which the Bank of England is prepared to discount bills; bank'-stock, a share or shares in the capital stock of a bank.—bank of issue, one that issues its own notes, or promises to pay; break the bank, in gambling, to win from the management the sum fixed upon as the limit it is willing to lose on any one day; joint-stock bank, one whose capital is subscribed by a large number of shareholders; private bank, one carried on by less than ten persons. [Fr. *banque*—It. *banca;* of Gmc. origin, cog. with two foregoing words.]

banket, *bang-ket', n.* (*S. Africa*) an auriferous pebbly conglomerate. [Du. *banketje,* almond-rock.]

bankrupt, *bangk'rupt, n.* one who breaks or fails in business : an insolvent person.—*adj.* insolvent : destitute (with *of*).—*v.t.* to make bankrupt.— *n.* bank'ruptcy (-*si*), the state of being or act of becoming bankrupt. [Fr. *banque-route,* It. *banca rotta*—*banca,* bank, and *rotto,* -*a*—L. *ruptus,* broken.]

Banksia, *bangk'si-ä, n.* a genus of Australian Proteaceae. [After Sir Joseph *Banks* (1744-1820).]

banner, *ban'ər, n.* strictly, a square flag charged with a coat of arms : a military standard : a flag bearing some device, often carried on two poles, or hanging from a cross-piece, used in processions, etc. : (*hist.*) those who serve under a banner, esp. in the Manchu army.—*adj.* bann'ered, furnished with banners. [O.Fr. *banere*—L.L. *bandum, bannum;* cog. with band and bind.]

banneret, *ban'ər-et, n.* (*hist.*) a knight of higher grade, orig. one bringing his vassals under his own banner, later, one dubbed on the field of battle (often confused with baronet). [O.Fr. *baneret,* lit. bannered.]

bannerol, bannerall. See banderol.

bannock, *ban'ək, n.* a flat home-made cake of oatmeal, barley, or pease-meal. [O.E. *bannuc.*]

banns, *banz, n.pl.* a proclamation of intended marriage.—to forbid the banns, to make formal objection to a projected marriage. [ban.]

banquet, *bangk'wit, n.* a feast : a course of sweetmeats, fruit, and wine, separate, or after a meal— still used in the Scottish phrase, 'a cake and wine banquet'.—*v.t.* to give a feast to.—*v.i.* to fare sumptuously :—*pr.p.* banq'ueting ; *pa.t.* and *pa.p.* banq'ueted.—*ns.* banq'ueter, banqueteer'; banq'ueting ; banq'ueting-hall, -house. [Fr.,— *banc,* bench.]

banquette, *bang-ket', n.* a raised way inside a parapet : the long seat behind the driver in a French diligence. [Fr.; It. *banchetta,* dim. of *banca,* seat.]

banshee, *ban'shē, n.* a female fairy in Ireland and elsewhere who wails and shrieks before a death in the family to which she is attached. [Ir. *bean sidhe,* Old Ir. *ben síde,* woman of the fairies.]

bant. See banting.

bantam, *ban'təm, n.* a small variety of the common domestic fowl : a small man, esp. a soldier.—*adj.* of bantam breed : little and combative.—*n.* bantam-weight, a boxer not heavier than 8 stone 6 pounds. [Prob. *Bantam* in Java.]

banteng, banting, *ban'teng, -ting, n.* an East Indian wild ox. [Malay.]

banter, *ban'tər, v.t.* to assail with good-humoured raillery : to joke or jest at : (*arch.*) to impose upon, trick.—*n.* humorous raillery : jesting.—*n.* bant'erer.

—*n.* and *adj.* **bant'ering.**—*adv.* **bant'eringly.**—[Ety. quite unknown.]

banting, *bant'ing, n.* a system of diet for reducing superfluous fat.—*v.i.* **bant** (back-formation).—*n.* **bant'ingism.** [From W. *Banting* (1797-1878), a London cabinetmaker, who recommended it to the public in 1863.]

bantling, *bant'ling, n.* a child. [Prob. Ger. *bänkling, bastard—bank,* bench.]

Bantu, *ban'tŏō, n.* a native name for a large group of African languages and the peoples speaking them in South and Central Africa.—Also *adj.*

banxring, bangsring, *bangks'ring, n.* a tree-shrew. [Jav. *bangsring.*]

banyan. See **banian.**

banzai, *bän'zä-ē, interj.* a Japanese battle-cry and salute to the emperor. [Jap., forever.]

baobab, *bā'ō-bab, n.* a gigantic tropical Western African tree, the monkey-bread tree (*Adansonia digitata;* family Bombacaceae). [Prob. African.]

bap, *bap, n.* (*Scot.*) a large elliptical breakfast roll. [Ety. uncertain.]

Baphomet, *baf'ō-met, n.* a mysterious idol the Templars were accused of worshipping.—*adj.* **baphomet'ic.** [For *Mahomet.*]

baptise, *bapt-īz', v.t.* to administer baptism to : to christen, give a name to : to name at launching and break a bottle of wine on the stern of.—*n.* **bapt'ism** (*-izm*), immersion in or sprinkling with water as a religious ceremony.—*adj.* **baptis'mal.**—*adv.* **baptis'mally.**—*ns.* **bapt'ist,** one who baptises : **Baptist,** one of a body who approve only of baptising by immersion, and that only to persons who profess their faith in Christ; **bap'tistery, bap'tistry,** a place for administration of baptism, whether a separate building or part of a church.—**baptismal name,** one given at baptism, a Christian name; **baptismal regeneration,** the doctrine of the remission of sin original and actual, and of the new birth into the life of sanctifying grace, in and through the sacrament of baptism; **baptism by desire,** the grace held to be given to a believer who ardently desires baptism, but dies before he can receive it; **baptism for the dead,** the vicarious baptism of a living for an unbaptised dead Christian; **baptism of blood,** martyrdom of the unbaptised Christian; **baptism of fire,** the gift of the Holy Spirit : martyrdom by fire regarded as an equivalent to baptism : (*fig.*) any trying ordeal, as a first experience of being under fire; **clinical baptism,** baptism administered to the sick; **conditional (or hypothetical) baptism,** baptism administered conditionally when it is doubtful whether the person was previously baptised validly or at all; **private baptism,** baptism elsewhere than in church. [Gr. *baptizein—baptein,* to dip.]

bar, *bär, n.* a comparatively long and generally massive rod or strip of any solid substance, as metal, soap, wood : a strong rod or long piece used as a lever, door fastening, barrier, part of a gate or grate, etc. : a bolt : a barrier : an obstruction or impediment : that which completely puts an end to an action or claim : a bank or shoal as at the mouth of a river or harbour : a counter across which liquor or food is served : a public-house : a rail or the like marking off a space, as in a house of parliament, or that at which prisoners are arraigned in court : barristers or advocates collectively : an addition to a medal, a strip of metal below the clasp : a ridge : a stripe, esp. transverse : (*her.*) a horizontal band across a shield : (*mus.*) a vertical line across the staff marking off a measure (**double bar,** two heavy lines at the end of a section) : the measure itself : (in *pl.*) the game of (prisoner's) base (but see **base** 1).—*v.t.* to fasten, secure, shut (out, in), furnish or mark with a bar or bars : to hinder : to obstruct : to exclude the possibility or validity of : to preclude : to divide into bars : (*pr.p.* **barr'ing;** *pa.t.* and *pa.p.* **barred**).—*prep.* except, but for.—*n.* **bar'-bell,** a bar weighted at the ends for gymnastic exercises.—*adj.* **bar'ful** (*Shak.*). **barrefull**), full of obstructions.—*ns.* **bar'-iron,** iron in malleable bars; **bar'-keeper,** keeper of a refreshment bar or toll-bar; **bar'-magnet,** a permanent magnet in the form of a straight bar;

bar'maid, bar'man, a woman, man, who serves at a public-house bar; **bar'-par'lour,** a small room adjoining a bar in a public-house; **barr'ing.**—*prep.* except.—*ns.* **barr'ing-out',** the shutting out of a schoolmaster from school by the pupils, to enforce demands; **bar'-room,** a room in which there is a bar, taproom; **bar'-tend'er** (*U.S.*), a barman; **bar'wood,** a red dye-wood imported in bars from Africa.—**at the bar,** in court : in practice as a barrister or advocate; **called to the bar,** admitted as barrister or advocate; **called within the bar,** made king's (or queen's) counsel. [O.Fr. *barre*—L.L. *barra.*]

bar, *bär, baur, bawr, n.* (*Scot.*) a jest : an amusing incident or story.

bar, *bär, n.* a fish, the maigre. [Fr.]

bar, *bär, n.* (*meteor.*) a unit of atmospheric pressure, equal to 1,000,000 dynes per square centimetre, or the pressure of 760·1 millimetres of mercury at 0°C. in latitude 45° : (*chem.*) a pressure of 1 dyne per square centimetre. [Gr. *baros,* weight.]

baracan. Same as **barracan.**

baragouin, *bä-rä-gwan², -gwin', n.* any jargon or unintelligible language. [Fr.; from Bret. *bara,* bread, and *gwenn,* white, said to have originated in the Breton soldiers' astonishment at white bread.]

barb, *bärb, n.* the beard-like jag near the point of an arrow, fish-hook, etc. : one of the thread-like structures forming a feather's web.—*v.t.* to arm with barbs : to shave, trim, mow : to pierce, as with a barb.—*adjs.* **barb'ate,** bearing a hairy tuft; **barb'ated,** barbed : bearded.—*n.* **barbe,** a Waldensian teacher.—*adjs.* **barbed,** furnished with a barb or barbs (e.g. **barbed-wire,** used for fences) : (by confusion) barded.—*n.* **barb'el,** a fresh-water fish of the carp family with beard-like appendages at its mouth : such an appendage.—*adj.* **barb'ellate** (*bot.*), having barbed or bearded bristles.—*ns.* **barb'et,** a tropical bird with bristly beak : a kind of poodle : **barb'ule,** a small barb : a fish's barbel : a process on the barb of a feather. [L. *barba,* a beard.]

barb, *bärb, n.* a swift kind of horse : a dark-coloured fancy pigeon. [From *Barbary,* whence the breeds came.]

Barbados, also **Barbadoes,** *bär-bā'dōz, adj.* of the West Indian island of Barbados.—*n.* and *adj.* **Barba'dian.**—**Barbados cherry,** the cherry-like fruit of West Indian trees of the genus Malpighia; **Barbados earth,** a diatomaceous marl found in Barbados; **Barbados gooseberry,** the edible fruit of a West Indian climbing cactus, *Pereskia aculeata;* **Barbados leg,** elephantiasis; **Barbados pride,** a West Indian shrub, peacock-flower (*Caesalpinia,* or *Poinciana, pulcherrima*) : an Asiatic mimosaceous tree (*Adenanthera pavonina*) naturalised in the West Indies, called red sandalwood.

barbarous, *bär'bar-as, adj.* falling short of the standard of correctness, classical purity, and good taste : unscholarly : corrupt or ungrammatical or unidiomatic : uncultured : uncivilised : brutal : harsh.—*n.* **barbār'ian** (*hist.*), one who was not a Greek, later neither a Greek nor a Roman : a foreigner : one without taste or refinement : a somewhat uncivilised man (but usu. not a savage).—Also *adj.*—*adj.* **barbar'ic** (*-bar'ik*), foreign : uncivilised : characteristic of barbarians : rude : tastelessly ornate and ostentatious : wild and harsh.—*n.* **barbarisa'tion** (*-bar-ī-zā'shan*).—*bar'-* **barise,** to make barbarous : to corrupt, as a language.—*ns.* **bar'barism,** savage life : rudeness of manners : a form of speech offensive to scholarly taste; **barbar'ity** (*-bar'i-ti*), savageness : cruelty.—*adv.* **bar'barously.**—*n.* **bar'barousness.** [Gr. *barbaros,* foreign, lit. stammering, from the unfamiliar sound of foreign tongues.]

Barbary, *bär'bar-i, n.* the country of the *Berbers,* in North Africa.—*adj.* **barbaresque** (*-esk'*).—**Barbary ape,** the magot; **Barbary sheep,** a North African wild sheep. [See **Berber.**]

barbastel(le), *bär-bas-tel',* or *bär', n.* a hairy-lipped bat. [Fr. *barbastelle.*]

barbecue, *bärb'i-kū, v.t.* to roast whole : to cure on a barbecue.—*n.* a framework for drying and smoking meat : an animal roasted whole : an open floor on which coffee-beans and the like are spread out to dry : (*Amer.*) a large social or political entertainment, where the hospitalities are on a lavish scale. [Sp. *barbacoa*—Haitian *barbacòa*, a framework of sticks set upon posts.]

barbel. See **barb** (1).

barber, *bärb'ər, n.* one who shaves beards and dresses hair.—*v.t.* to shave or cut the hair of.—*ns.* **barb'ermon'ger** (*Shak.*), a man decked out by his barber, a fop ; **barb'er-sur'geon**, one who let blood and drew teeth as well as shaved.—**barber's block**, a round block on which wigs are made ; **barber's pole**, the barber's sign, a pole striped spirally, generally red and white, having often a brass basin hung at the end. [O.Fr. *barbour*—L. *barba*, a beard.]

barberry, *bär'bər-i, n.* a thorny shrub (*Berberis*) with yellow flowers and red berries, common in hedges. [L.L. *berberis* ; the Ar. *barbārīs* is borrowed ; not connected with **berry**.]

barbet. See **barb** (1).

barbette, *bär-bet', n.* an earthen terrace inside the parapet of a rampart, serving as a platform for heavy guns : an armoured turret in a warship. [Fr.]

barbican, *bär'bi-kən, n.* a projecting watch-tower over the gate of a castle or fortified town : esp. the outwork intended to defend the drawbridge. [O.Fr. *barbacane* ; origin unknown.]

barbituric, *bärb-it-ū'rik, adj.* (*chem.*) applied to an acid got from malonic acid and urea.—*ns.* **barbitu'rate**, a salt or ester of barbituric acid ; **barb'itone** (also **barb'ital**), veronal, a derivative of barbituric acid. [From the lichen Usnea *barbata* and *uric* acid.]

barcarol(l)e, *bär'kə-rōl, -rōl', -rol', n.* a gondolier's song : a musical composition of a similar character. [It. *barcarola*, a boat-song—*barca*, a boat.]

bard, *bärd, n.* a Celtic poet and singer : a strolling minstrel : a poet.—*n.* **bard'-craft.**—*adj.* **bard'ic.**—*ns.* **bard'ling**, a poetaster ; **bardol'atry**, Shakepeare-worship (Gr. *latreiā*, worship) ; **bard'ship.**—*adj.* **bard'y** (*Scot.*), insolent : impudent. [Gael. and Ir. *bàrd.*]

bard, *bärd, n.* (*obs.*) the protective covering of a war-horse or a man-at-arms.—*adj.* **bard'ed**, caparisoned. [Fr. *barde*—Sp. *albarda*, pack-saddle, perh. from Ar. *al-barda'ah*—*al*, the, and *barda'ah*, mule's pack-saddle.]

bard, an old spelling of **barred** ; also for **barded**.

bare, *bär, adj.* uncovered : naked : open to view : uncovered, bare-headed : unsheathed : unarmed : disfurnished : napless, threadbare, worn : unprovided or scantily provided : poor : scanty : mere : unadorned : (*Shak.*) paltry : (*Shak.*, *Milt.*) laid waste : empty : (*Spens.*) plain, without luxury.—*v.t.* to strip or uncover.—*adj.* and *adv.* **bare'back**, without saddle.—*adjs.* **bare'backed**, with bare back : unsaddled ; **bare'-breached** (*Scott*), trouserless.—*n.* **bare'bone** (*Shak.*), a very lean person.—*adj.* **bare'faced**, with the face uncovered : beardless : (*Shak.*) avowed : impudent.—*adv.* **bare'facedly** (-*fāst'li*, -*fās'id-li*).—*n.* **bare'facedness.**—*adv.* **bare'foot.**—*adjs.* **bare'foot, -ed**, having the feet bare : discalced ; **bare'gnawn** (*Shak.*), gnawed bare ; **bare'-headed** ; **bare'legged.**—*adv.* **bare'ly**, nakedly : plainly : explicitly : openly : hardly, scarcely : just and no more : not quite.—*n.* **bare'ness.**—*adj.* **bar'ish**, somewhat bare. [O.E. *bær* ; Ger. *baar, bar* ; O.N. *berr.*]

bare, *bär, old pa.t.* of **bear.**

barege, *bä-rezh', n.* a light, mixed dress-stuff.—*n.* **baregine**, *bar'i-jēn,* a gelatinous mass of bacteria and sulphur deposited in thermal waters. [*Barèges* in Hautes-Pyrénées.]

baresark, erroneous form of **berserk.**

bargain, *bär'gən, n.* (*obs.*) strife : a contract or agreement : a favourable transaction : an advantageous purchase : (*Shak.*) chaffering.—*v.i.* (*obs.Scot.*) to strive : to make a contract or agreement : to chaffer : to count (*on*), make allowance (*for* a possibility).—*v.t.* to lose by bad bargaining (with *away*).—*ns.* **bar'gain-basement, -counter**, places in a shop

where bargains are promised ; **bar'gainer** ; **bar'gain-hunter**, one who goes shopping in quest of bargains.—**bargain and sale**, in law, a mode of conveyance whereby property may be assigned or transferred for valuable consideration ; **into the bargain**, over and above ; **sell one a bargain** (*Shak.*), to befool him, esp. to trap him into saying something ridiculous or unseemly ; **strike a bargain**, to come to terms. [O.Fr. *bargaine.*]

barge, *bärj, n.* (*obs.*) a small sailing vessel : a flat-bottomed freight boat, with or without sails, used on rivers and canals : a lighter : the second boat of a man-of-war : a large pleasure or state boat.—*v.i.* to move clumsily : to bump (*into*) like a barge.—*ns.* **barg'ee**, a bargeman ; **barge'man**, the manager of a barge ; **barge'-master**, the proprietor of a barge ; **barge'-pole**, a pole for propelling a barge. [O.Fr. *barge*—L.L. *barga* ; cf. **bark.**]

barge-board, *bärj'-bōrd, n.* a board extending along the edge of the gable of a house to cover the rafters and keep out the rain.—**barge'-coup'le**, *n.* gable'rafters.—*n.pl.* **barge'-stones**, the stones that make up the sloping edge of a gable. [Perh. L.L. *bargus*, a gallows.]

barghest, barghest, bargaist, *bär'gest, -gäst, n.* a dog-like goblin portending death. [Perh. conn. with Ger. *berg-geist*, mountain-spirit.]

baric. See **barium.**

barilla, *bar-il'ä, n.* an impure sodium carbonate got by burning certain seaside plants. [Sp.]

barite. See **barytes.**

baritone, *bar'i-tōn.* See **barytone.**

barium, *bā'ri-əm, n.* a metallic element (at. numb. 56) present in baryta.—*adj.* **bā'ric.**—*n.* **bā'rite** (*rare*), barytes. [See **baryta.**]

bark, *bärk, n.* the abrupt cry uttered by a dog, wolf, etc. : report of a gun.—*v.i.* to utter a bark : to clamour : to keep watch for lack of a dog.—*v.t.* (*Spens.*) to utter with a bark : to utter abruptly and peremptorily : to make by barking.—*n.* **bark'er**, a dog : a barking dog : a tout : (*slang.*) a pistol or cannon : one who keeps watch.—**barking deer**, the muntjac ; **bark up the wrong tree**, to follow a false scent ; **his bark is worse than his bite**, his angry words are worse than his actual deeds. [O.E. *beorcan.*]

bark, barque, *bärk, n.* formerly, any small sailing ship : a ship of small size, square-sterned, without head-rails : technically, a three-masted vessel whose mizzen-mast is fore-and-aft-rigged (instead of being square-rigged like the fore and main masts) : (*poet.*) any boat or sailing ship.—*ns.* **bark'entine, barqu'entine** (-*ən-tēn*), a three-masted vessel, with the fore-mast square-rigged, and the main-mast and mizzen-mast fore-and-aft-rigged. [Fr. *barque*—L.L. *barca* ; poss. from Gr. *bāris*, a Nile barge.]

bark, *bärk, n.* the rind or covering of the trunk and branches of a tree : that used in tanning or dyeing : that used in medicine (cinchona) : an outer covering or skin.—*v.t.* to strip or peel bark or skin from : to encrust.—*v.i.* to form a bark.—*ns.* **bark'-bed**, a hotbed of spent bark ; **bark'-beet'le**, any beetle of the family Scolytidae, tunnellers in and under bark.—*adj.* **bark'-bound**, compressed by failure to shed the bark.—*v.t.* and *v.i.* **bark'en**, to dry up into a barky crust.—*adjs.* **bark'less** ; **bark'y.** [O.N. *börkr* ; Dan. *bark.*]

Barker's mill, *bärk'ərz-mil, n.* a water-wheel invented by a Dr. *Barker.*

barley, *bär'li, n.* a hardy grass (*Hordeum vulgare* and other species) : its grain used for food, and for making malt liquors and spirits.—*ns.* **bar'ley-bree, -broo, -broth**, strong ale : whisky ; **bar'ley-corn** (personified as *John Barleycorn*), the grain from which malt is made : a single grain of barley : a measure of length = ⅓ of an inch ; **bar'ley-su'gar**, sugar candied by melting and cooling (formerly by boiling with a decoction of barley) ; **bar'ley-wa'ter**, a decoction of pearl-barley ; **pearl'-bar'ley**, the grain stripped of husk and pellicle, and completely rounded by grinding ; **pot'-bar'ley**, the grain deprived by milling of its outer husk, used in making broth, etc. [O.E.

Neutral vowels in unaccented syllables : *el'ə-mənt, in'fənt, ran'dəm*

bærlic, from root of **bear** (3), and suffix -*lic*.]

barley, *bär'li*, *interj.* (*Scot.*) a word used in games in demand of a truce.—*n.* a truce: a breathing-space. [Perh. **parley**.]

barley-brake, *bär'li-brāk*, *n.* an old country game, originally played by three couples, of which one, left in a middle den called hell, had to catch the others, who could break or separate when about to be overtaken. [Perh. because often played in a *barley*-field; or perh. from the word preceding.]

barm, *bärm*, *n.* froth of fermenting liquor.—*adjs.* **barm'y**, frothy: fermenting: (*slang*) mentally unsound (for **balmy**); **barm'y-brained**. [O.E. *beorma*, Dan. *bärme*, Ger. *bärme*.]

barmbrack, *bärm'brak*, *n.* a currant-bun. [Ir. *bairigen breac*, speckled cake.]

barm-cloth, *bärm'-kloth*, *n.* (*arch.*), an apron. [O.E. *barm* (W.S. *bearm*) bosom, and **cloth**.]

Barmecide, *bär'mi-sīd*, *n.* one who offers an imaginary or pretended banquet or other benefit.—*adjs.* **Bar'mecide**, **Barmeci'dal**. [From an imaginary feast given to a beggar in the *Arabian Nights*, by one of the *Barmecide* family.]

barmkin, *bärm'kin*, *n.* a battlement, or a turret, on the outer wall of a castle: the wall itself. [Orig. obscure.]

barn, *bärn*, *n.* a building in which grain, hay, etc., are stored.—*v.t.* to store in a barn.—*ns.* **barn'-dance**, an American dance like a schottische; **barn'-door**, the door of a barn: in cricket, a player who blocks every ball: humorously, any broad target; **barn'-owl**, a species of owl, generally buff-coloured above and white below; **barn'-stormer**, a strolling player (as type of ranting actor).—*v.i.* **barn'-storm**.—*n.* **barn'yard**—also *adj.* as in **barnyard fowl**. [O.E. *bere-ern*, contracted *bern*, from *bere*, barley, *ern*, a house.]

Barnaby, *bärn'ə-bi*, *n.* a form of *Barnabas*.—*n.* **Bar'nabite**, a member of the Congregation of Regular Clerics of St. Paul, founded at Milan in 1530, so called from their church of St. Barnabas there.—**Barnaby Day**, **Barnaby Bright** or **Long Barnaby**, St. Barnabas' Day, 11th June, in Old Style reckoned the longest day.

barnacle, *bär'nə-kl*, *n.* a barnacle-goose: a cirripede crustacean that adheres to rocks and ship bottoms: a companion not easily shaken off.—*n.* **bar'nacle-goose**, **ber'nicle-goose**, a species of wild goose once believed to develop from a barnacle that grew on a tree. [O.Fr. *bernaque*—L.L. *bernaca*.]

barnacle, *bär'nə-kl*, *n.* an instrument put on a restless horse's nose to keep him quiet: (in *pl.*; *coll.*) spectacles.—*adj.* **barnacled**. [O.Fr. *bernac*.]

barney, *bär'ni*, *n.* (*slang*) humbug: a prize-fight.

barock, another spelling of **baroque**.

barograph, *bar'ō-gräf*, *n.* a recording barometer. [Gr. *baros*, weight, *graphein*, to write.]

barometer, *bə-rom'i-tər*, *n.* an instrument for measuring atmospheric pressure: a weather-glass: (*fig.*) an indicator of change (e.g. in public opinion).—*adj.* **barometric** (*bar-ō-met'rik*).—*adv.* **barometrically**.—*n.* **barometry** (-*rom'*). [Gr. *baros*, weight, *metron*, measure.]

barometz, *bar'ō-mets*, *n.* the Scythian lamb, at one time supposed to be at once plant and animal, to grow on a stalk, and to eat grass like a lamb, near the Caspian Sea: a fern, *Cibotium* or *Dicksonia Barometz*, of the East Indies and Pacific islands, whose woolly rootstock and leaf bases could easily be shaped into a lamb. [Erroneous form of Russ. *baranets*, club-moss, dim. of *baran*, ram.]

baron, *bar'ən*, *n.* a title of rank, the lowest in the peerage: a foreign noble of similar grade, as a German freiherr: (*Scot. hist.*) the owner of a freehold estate, whether titled or not: (*her.* and *Eng. law*) a husband (opposed to *feme*, wife): an industrial magnate (as a *press baron*): formerly a title of the judges of the Court of Exchequer: in feudal times a tenant-in-chief of the crown: later a peer or great lord of the realm generally: till 1832, the name for the parliamentary representatives of the Cinque Ports.—*ns.* **bar'onage**, the whole body of barons: a list or book of barons; **bar'on-bail'ie** (*hist.*), a magistrate appointed by the lord-superior in a burgh of barony; **bar'oness**,

a baron's wife, or a lady holding a baronial title in her own right.—*adj.* **baronial** (*bə-rō'ni-əl*), pertaining to a baron or barony: applied to a turreted style of architecture favoured by the Scottish land-holding class.—*ns.* **bar'on-off'icer**, (*Scott*) an estate official; **bar'ony**, the territory of a baron: in Ireland, a division of a county: in Scotland, a large freehold estate, or manor, even though not carrying with it a baron's title and rank: the rank of baron.—**baron of beef**, a joint consisting of two sirloins left uncut at the backbone. [O.Fr. *barun*, -*on*—L.L. *barō*, -*ōnis*, man.]

baronet, *bar'ən-et*, *n.* (*obs.*) a lesser baron (confused with *banneret*): (*obs.*) a baron's substitute: now the lowest British hereditary title (of England, now of Great Britain, since 1611; of Scotland, or of Nova Scotia, since 1625; of Ireland, since 1619).—*ns.* **bar'onetage**, the whole body of baronets: a list or book of baronets; **bar'onetcy**, the rank of baronet.—*adj.* **baronet'ical**. [Dim. of **baron**.]

baroque, **barock**, *bə-rok'*, -*rōk'*, **barocco**, -*rok'ō*, *n.* originally a jeweller's term applied to a rough pearl: a bold, vigorous, exuberant style in architecture, decoration, and art generally, that arose with the Counter-Reformation and prevailed in Louis XIV's time, degenerating into tasteless extravagance in ornament.—*adj.* in baroque style: whimsical: odd: sometimes rococo. [Fr. *baroque*, perh. from L. *verrūca*, wart, but referred by some to Ar. *burāq*, hard earth mixed with stones.]

baroscope, *bar'ō-skōp*, *n.* an instrument for indicating changes in the density of the air. [Gr. *baros*, weight, *skopeein*, to look at.]

barouche, *ba-* or *bə-roosh'*, *n.* a double-seated four-wheeled carriage with a falling top. [Ger. *barutsche* —It. *baroccio*—L. *bis*, twice, *rota*, a wheel.]

barque. Same as **bark** (2).

barquentine. Same as **barkentine**.

barracan, **baracan**, *bar'ə-kan*, *n.* (*obs.*) a thick, strong stuff resembling camlet. [Fr. *barracan*— Ar. *barrakān*, camlet, Pers. *barak*, a stuff made of camel's hair.]

barrace, *bar'as*, *n.* (*obs.*) the lists in a tournament. [O.Fr. *barras*—*barre*, bar.]

barrack, *bar'ək*, *n.* a building for soldiers, esp. in garrison (generally in *pl.*): a huge plain building, esp. for housing many persons—*v.t.* and *v.i.* to lodge in barracks. [Fr. *baraque*—It. *baracca*, or Sp. *barraca*, tent.]

barrack, *bar'ək*, *v.t.* and *v.i.* to make a hostile demonstration (against), especially by cheering ironically, at a cricket-match, etc.—*n.* and *adj.* **barr'acking**.—*n.* **barr'acker**. [Aboriginal Australian *borak*.]

barracoon, *bar-ə-kōōn'*, *n.* a depot for slaves. [Sp. *barracón*, augmen. of *barraca*, tent.]

barracouta, *bar-ə-kōō'tä*, *n.* a southern food-fish (Thersites) of the hairtail family, called snoek in South Africa and elsewhere: (also **barracoo'ta**, **-cuda**, -*dä*) a voracious West Indian fish (Sphyraena) akin to the grey mullets. [Sp. *baracuta*.]

barrage, *bär'ij*, or (*mil.*) *bär-äzh'*, *bar'-äzh*, *n.* an artificial bar across a river: the forming of such a bar; a barrier formed by continuous shower of projectiles along a fixed or a moving line (curtain-fire), or by captive balloons, or mines, or otherwise.—*ns.* **barr'age-balloon**; **barr'age-fire**, curtain-fire. [Fr. *barrage*—*barre*, bar.]

barramunda, *bar-ə-mun'dä*, *n.* an Australian river-fish of the Osteoglossidae (Scleropages): the Australian lung-fish. [Native name.]

barranca, *bar-ang'kä*, *n.* (*U.S.*) a deep gorge.—Also **barran'co**. [Sp. *barranco*.]

barrat, *bar'ət*, *n.* (*obs.*) deceit, strife or trouble.—*n.* **barr'ator**, one who vexatiously stirs up lawsuits, quarrels, etc.—*adj.* **barr'atrous**.—*adv.* **barr'atrously**.—*n.* **barr'atry**, fraudulent practices on the part of the master or mariners of a ship to the prejudice of the owners: vexatious litigation: stirring up of suits and quarrels, forbidden under penalties to lawyers: traffic in offices of church or state. [O.Fr. *barat*, deceit; traced by some to Gr. *prattein*, to do, by others to a Celt. or a Scand. origin.]

barrefull (*Shak.*). See **barful** under **bar** (1).

barrel, bar´əl, n. a wooden vessel made of curved staves bound with hoops: its contents or its capacity (36 imperial gallons of ale and beer; various weights or quantities of other goods): a revolving drum: a cylinder: a tube as of a gun: a button on a braided coat: the trunk of a horse, etc.: (U.S.) political funds.—v.t. to put in barrels. —ns. **barr´elage;** **barr´el-bulk,** a measurement of five cubic feet; **barr´elful** (pl. **barr´elfuls**), as much as a barrel will hold.—adj. **barr´elled,** having a barrel or barrels: put in barrels.—ns. **barr´el-or´gan,** a mechanical instrument for playing tunes by means of a revolving drum set with pins; **barr´el-vault,** a vault with a simple hemicylindrical roof.—adj. **barr´el-vault´ed.** [Fr. baril; perh. conn. with **bar.**]

barren, bar´ən, adj. incapable of bearing offspring: not producing fruit, seed, crops, vegetation, etc.: infertile: unproductive: unfruitful: arid: jejune: (Shak.) dull, stupid.—n.pl. **Barrens,** in North America, plateaus with small trees but no timber.— ns. **barr´enness;** **barr´enwort,** a herb (Epimedium) of the barberry family.—**barren strawberry,** a plant (Potentilla Fragariastrum) very like the wild strawberry, but with inedible fruit. [O.Fr. barain, brahain, brehaing.]

barret, bar´it, n. a flat cap: a biretta.—n. **barr´et-cap.** [Fr. barette; cf. **beret, biretta.**]

barricade, bar´ik-ād, n. a temporary fortification raised to block a street: a barrier.—v.t. to block: to close or enclose with a barricade.—n. and v.t. (earlier form) **barricā´do.** [Fr. barricade or Sp. barricada, perh.—Fr. barrique or Sp. barrica, cask, the first street barricades being of casks filled with stones, etc.; or from L.L. barra, bar.]

barrico, bar-ē´kō, n. a small cask. [Sp. barrica.]

barrier, bar´i-ər, n. a defensive stockade or palisade: a fence or other structure to bar passage or prevent access: (in pl.) lists: (in pl.) a martial exercise of the 15th and 16th centuries in which the combatants were on opposite sides of a fence: a separating or restraining obstacle.—v.t. to shut by means of a barrier.—n. **barr´ier-reef´,** a coral-reef fringing a coast with a navigable channel inside.—**Barrier Act,** an act of the General Assembly of the Church of Scotland (1697) decreeing that changes in the law of the Church, even when approved by the Assembly, should not become law till approved by a majority of presbyteries. [O.Fr. barrière—L.L. barrāria—barra.]

barrister, bar´is-tər, n. one who is qualified to plead at the bar in a law-court (in Scotland called advocate).—adj. **barristerial** (-tē´ri-al).—n. **barr´istership.—revising barrister,** a barrister formerly appointed to revise the voters' lists. [From L.L. barra, bar (i.e. orig. of the Inns of Court).]

barrow, bar´ō, n. a small hand or wheeled carriage used to convey a load.—n. **barr´ow-tram,** the shaft of a barrow. [O.E. bearwe—beran, to bear.]

barrow, bar´ō, n. (obs. except in place names) a hill or hillock: an ancient grave-mound, tumulus. [O.E. beorg; cf. Ger. berg.]

barrow, bar´ō, n. a long, sleeveless flannel garment for infants. [Perh. O.E. beorgan, to protect.]

barter, bär´tər, v.t. to give in exchange (with for, away).—v.i. to traffic by exchange of commodities. —n. trade or traffic by direct exchange of goods. —n. **bar´terer.** [Prob. O.Fr. barat; see **barrat.**]

Bartholomew, bär-thol´ə-mū, or (obs.) **Bartholmew, Bartlemew,** -t(h)l-mū, **Bartlemy,** -tl-mi, adj. relating to the Apostle Bartholomew, his day (24th August), or the fair held about that time at West Smithfield, London (1133-1855): sold at Bartholomew Fair.—n. **Barthol´omew-tide,** the time about St. Bartholomew's Day.—**Black Bartholomew,** 24th August 1662, on which the Act of Uniformity came into force in England.

bartisan, bartizan, bär´ti-zan, -zan´, n. a parapet or battlement: a projecting gallery on a wall-face: (erroneously) a corbelled corner turret.— adj. **bar´tisaned** (or -zand´). [Apparently first used by Scott, who found a reading bertisene, for **bratticing;** see **brattice.**]

barton, bar´tən, n. a farm-yard. [O.E. bere-tún, yard, bere, barley, and tún, enclosure.]

barycentric, bar-i-sen´trik, adj. pertaining to the centre of gravity. [Gr. barys, heavy, kentron, centre.]

baryta, bə-rī´tä, n. barium monoxide.—n. **bary´tes** (-tēz), heavy-spar, barium sulphate (also **barite,** bā´rīt): (loosely) baryta.—adj. **barytic** (ba-rit´ik), of or containing baryta or barium. [Gr. barys, heavy.]

barytone, bar´i-tōn, n. a deep-toned male voice between bass and tenor: a singer with such a voice (in these senses now usually **baritone**): an obsolete musical instrument like the viola da gamba with sympathetic strings added: a kind of saxhorn.—adj. of the pitch and compass of a baritone or barytone: in Greek, not having an acute accent on the last syllable. [Gr. barytonos, deep-sounding, not accented—barys, heavy, deep, and tonos, a tone.]

basal. See under **base.**

basalt, bas´awlt, bas-awlt´, n. an igneous rock composed essentially of plagioclase and pyroxene, and commonly olivine and magnetite or titaniferous iron: esp. a compact rock of this kind.— adj. **basalt´ic.** [L. basaltēs, an African word.]

basanite, bas´ən-īt, n. black jasper that serves as a touchstone: a variety of basalt containing nepheline, leucite, or analcime. [Gr. basanos, touchstone.]

basbleu, bä-blə´, n. a bluestocking. [Fr.]

bascule, bas´kūl, n. an apparatus of which one end rises as the other sinks.—**bascule bridge,** a bridge that rises when a counter poise sinks in a pit. [Fr. bascule, see-saw.]

base, bās, n. that on which a thing rests: foot: bottom: foundation: support: the part next the place of attachment: (archit.) the foot or lower member of a pillar, on which the shaft rests: the side or face on which a geometrical figure is regarded as standing: (her.) the lower part of a shield: (in pl.; Spens.) a skirt worn by knights on horseback: (Milt.) a horse's housing: a number on which a system of numeration or of logarithms is founded: the chief ingredient: an ingredient of a mixture that plays a subsidiary but important part, such e.g. as giving bulk: a starting-point: a base-line: a fixed station in games such as base-ball: an old game of which prisoner's-base and rounders are forms, and baseball a development (possibly a different word: see **bar**): a place from which operations are conducted or on which they depend: home, or headquarters, of a fleet, with equipment for its safe-keeping, repairs and other needs: (chem.) a substance that reacts with an acid to form a salt, or dissolves in water forming hydroxyl ions.—v.t. to found or place on a base.— pr.p. **bas´ing;** pa.p. **based** (bāst).—adj. **bās´al,** pertaining to or situated at the base: at the lowest level: (loosely) fundamental.—ns. **base´ball,** the American national game, a development of rounders, played nine a-side with bat and ball, the players on the batting side making a circuit of four bases: a ball for the game; **base´baller.**—adj. **base´less,** without a base or foundation.—ns. **base´lessness;** **base´-line,** an accurately measured line used as a base for triangulation: (lawn tennis) a line at the end of the court: (baseball) a line joining bases; **base´man** (baseball), a fielder stationed near a base; **base´ment,** an underlying support: lowest story of a building, beneath the principal one, esp. one below ground level; **base´-plate,** the foundation plate of a piece of heavy machinery; **base´-runner,** a baseball player in course of performing his circuit of bases.—adj. **bās´ic,** belonging to or of the nature of a base: containing excess of a base: (geol.) poor in silica—opp. to acid: (loosely) fundamental.—n. **basicity** (bās- or bas-is´i-ti).— adj. **basilar** (bas´i-lər), basal.—**basal anaesthesia,** anaesthesia acting as a basis for further and deeper anaesthesia; **basal plane** (crystallography), a crystal face or form parallel to the horizontal axes; **basic English,** a reduced English vocabulary for foreigners; **basic process,** a steel-making process with a furnace lined with material rich in metallic oxides; **basic salt,** a salt having one or more hydroxyl groups in place of an acid radical or radicals; **basic slag**, a by-product of the basic process rich in lime, used as manure. [Fr. *base*—L. *basis*—Gr. *basis*—root of *bainein*, to go.]

base, *bās, adj.* low in place, value, estimation, or principle: mean: vile: worthless: debased: counterfeit: (*law*) servile, as opposed to *free*: humble: (*B.* and *Shak.*) lowly: (*obs.*) bass.—*adj.* **base′-born**, low-born: illegitimate.—*adv.* **base′ly.** —*adj.* **base′-mind′ed**, of a low mind or spirit: mean.—*n.* **base′ness.**—*adj.* **base′-spir′ited**, mean-spirited.—**base coin**, spurious coin; **base metal**, any metal other than the precious metals: a metal that alters on exposure to air—opp. to *noble metal.* [Fr. *bas*—L.L. *bassus*, thick, squat.]

base, *bās, v.t.* a form of **abase.**

baseball. See base (1), and **bar** (1): also **prison-er′s-base.**

basecourt, *bās′kōrt, n.* the outer court of a castle or mansion: an inferior court of justice. [Fr. *basse-court* (now *basse-cour*).]

baselard, *bas′ə-lärd, n.* (*obs.*) a dagger or hanger. [A. Fr.]

bash, *bash, v.t.* to beat: to smash in.—*n.* a heavy blow: a dint.—*n.* **bash′er** (*slang*), a straw-hat.— **on the bash** (*slang*), on the spree. [Prob. Scand.]

bashaw, *ba-shaw′, n.* (*arch.*) a pasha: a haughty man.—*ns.* **bashaw′ism, bashaw′ship.** [Turk. *bāshā;* cf. **pasha.**]

bashful, *bash′fəl, adj.* easily confused: modest: shy, wanting confidence.—*v.i.* **bash** (*Spens.*), to be abashed.—*adv.* **bash′fully.**—*n.* **bash′fulness.** —*adj.* **bash′less**, unashamed. [See **abash.**]

bashi-bazouk, *bash-i-bə-zōōk′, n.* a Turkish ir-regular soldier.—*n.* **ba′shi-bazouk′ery.** [Turk. *bashi-bozuq*, wild head.]

bashlyk, *bash′lik, n.* a hood with long ends worn in Russia. [Russ. *bashluikŭ*, a Caucasian hood.]

basidium, *bas-id′i-əm, n.* a fungal fructification from which spores (usually four) are abstricted :— *pl.* **basid′ia.**—*adj.* **basid′ial.**—*n.pl.* **Basidiomy-cetes** (-*ō-mī-sē′tēz*), one of the main groups of fungi, characterised by the possession of basidia, including the familiar toadstools as well as rusts and smuts.—*n.* **basid′iospore**, a spore produced by a basidium. [Gr. *basis*, basis, and dim. ending *-idion.*]

basifixed, *bā′si-fikst, adj.* attached by the base. [**base** and **fixed.**]

basifugal, *bās-, or bas-if′ū-gl, adj.* developing in a direction away from the base. [**base**, and L. *fugēre*, to flee.]

basil, *baz′il, n.* an aromatic labiate plant (*Ocimum*): extended to calamint and other labiates. [O.Fr. *basile*—L. *basilisca*, representing Gr. *basilikon*, lit. royal, perh. with reference to *basiliskos*, basilisk, cobra, as a reputed cure for snakebite.]

basil, *baz′il, n.* a sheepskin roughly tanned and un-dressed. [Ar. *bitanah*, lining.]

basil. See **bezel.**

Basilian, *ba-, bə-zil′i-ən, or -sil′, adj.* of St. *Basil* (c. 329-379).—*n.* a monk or nun following his rule.

basilica, *ba-sil′i-kä, n.* orig. a royal palace: a large oblong hall, with double colonnades and commonly a semicircular apse, used for judicial and com-mercial purposes : a magnificent church formed out of such a hall, or built after its plan : a Roman Catholic church with honorific privileges.—*adjs.* **basil′ical**, royal; **basil′ican**, of a basilica.—*n.* **basil′icon**, an ointment of various kinds, as of sovereign virtue. [Gr. *basilikos, -ē, -on*, royal— *basileus*, king.]

basilisk, *bas′, baz′il-isk, n.* a fabulous creature, about a foot long, with fiery death-dealing eyes and breath, so named according to Pliny, from its crown-like crest : a harmless crested lizard of tropical America : an ancient brass cannon throwing a shot of about 200 lb. [Gr. *basiliskos*, dim. of *basileus*, a king.]

basin, *bā′sn* (*arch.* **bason**), *n.* a wide open vessel or dish : a basinful : any hollow place containing water, as a dock : the area drained by a river and its tributaries : (*geol.*) a region of synclinal structure. —*n.* **ba′sinful**, as much as will fill a basin :—*pl.* **ba′sinfuls.**—*adj.* **ba′sin-wide**(*Spens.* **basen** wide),

wide as a basin. [O.Fr. *bacin*—L.L. *bachinus*, perh. from *bacca*, a vessel.]

basinet, *bas′i-net*, **basnet**, *bas′net, n.* a light globular headpiece worn alone with a visor, or with the great helm over it. [Dim. of **basin.**]

basipetal, *bās- or bas-ip′i-tl, adj.* proceeding or developing in the direction of the base. [**base**, and L. *petēre*, to seek.]

basis, *bās′is, n.* the foundation, or that on which a thing rests : a pedestal : the ground-work or first principle : the fundamental ingredient :—*pl.* **bas′es** (*bās′ēz*). [See **base** (1).]

bask, *bāsk, v.i.* to lie in the warmth or sunshine (often *fig.*).—**basking shark**, a large but harmless shark that shows its great dorsal fin as it basks. [O.N. *bathask*, to bathe.]

basket, *bäs′kit, n.* a receptacle of plaited twigs, rushes or other flexible materials : a basketful : a net used as goal at basket-ball : the back part of a stage-coach outside : a basket-hilt.—*ns.* **bas′ket-ball**, an adaptation of lacrosse in which goals are scored by throwing a ball into a raised net (origin-ally a basket); **bas′ket-chair′**, a wicker chair; **bas′ketful**, as much as fills a basket :—*pl.* **bas′ket-fuls ; bas′ket-hilt′**, a sword hilt with a protective covering wrought like basket-work; **bas′ket-maker ; bas′ket-mak′ing ; bas′ketry**, basket-making : basket-work; **bas′ket-work**, any structure of interlaced twigs or the like. [Origin obscure.]

bason. See **basin.**

Basque, *bāsk, n.* a member of a people (in their own tongue *Euscara, Eskuara*) inhabiting the western Pyrenees, in Spain and France : their agglutinative language : **basque**, a short-skirted jacket : continuation of a bodice a little below the waist.—*adj.* **Basque**, of the Basques or their language or country.—*adj.* **basqued** (*bäskt*), fur-nished with a basque.—*n.* **basquine** (-*kēn′*), an outer petticoat worn by Basque and Spanish women. [Fr. *Basque*—L. *Vasconēs*, a people of Gascony.]

bas-relief, *bas′-ri-lēf′*, or (*Ital.*) **basso-rilievo**, *bäs′sō rēl-yā′vō*, popularly **-relievo**, *bas′ō ri-lē′vō*, *n.* sculpture in which the figures do not stand far out from the ground on which they are formed. [Fr. and It. See **base**, low, and **relief.**]

bass, *bäs, n.* the low or grave part in music : a bass-singer—often in Italian form **basso** (*bäs′sō*).— *adj.* low, deep, grave.—*v.t.* to sound in a deep tone.—*ns.* **bass′-bar**, a strip of wood on the belly of a violin, etc., under the bass foot of the bridge, to distribute the vibrations; **bass′-clef**, the F clef on the fourth line of the stave; **bass′-drum**, the large drum of an orchestra or band; **bass′-horn**, an old wind-instrument, a modification of the serpent; **bass′-tu′ba**, the lowest instrument of the saxhorn class—the bombardon; **bass′-vi′ol**, a musical instrument with four strings, used for playing the bass in concerted music, the viola da gamba or the violoncello. [See **base**, low.]

bass. Same as **bast.**

bass, basse, *bas, n.* a European sea-fish of the sea-perch family (*Labrax lupus* or *Morone labrax*): extended to other sea and freshwater fishes. [O.E. *bærs*; cf. Ger. *bars*, the perch.]

basset, *bas′it, n.* a hound (**bass′et-hound**) like a badger-dog, but bigger : an old Venetian game at cards, resembling faro, widely popular in the 18th century: (*geol.*) outcrop.—*v.i.* to crop out.—*n.* **bass′et-horn** (It. *corno di bassetto*), the richest and softest of all wind-instruments, similar to a clarinet in tone and fingering, but with a twice-bent wooden tube. [Fr.,—*bas*, low.]

bassinet, *bas′i-net, n.* a kind of basket with a hood used as a cradle : a similarly shaped perambulator. [Fr. dim. of *bassin*, a basin.]

basso. See **bass** (1).

bassoon, *bə-sōōn′, -zōōn′, n.* (It. *fagotto*) a wood-wind instrument filling an important place in the modern orchestra, its compass from B flat below the bass stave to C or F in the treble.—The **double bassoon** (It. *contrafagotto*), sounds an octave lower.—*n.* **bassoon′ist.** [It. *bassone*, aug-mentative of *basso*, low, from root of **base, bass.**]

bast, *bȧst, n.* phloem : inner bark, esp. of lime : fibre : matting.—Also **bass** (*bȧs*).—*n.* **bass'wood**, lime-tree or its wood. [O.E. *bæst*; Ger. *bast*.]

basta, *bȧs'tä, interj.* (*Shak.*) enough. [It. and Sp.]

bastaard, *bȧs'tärd, n.* (*S. Africa*) a person of mixed white and coloured parentage, whether legitimately born or not. [Du., bastard.]

bastard, *bȧs'tȧrd, n.* a child born of parents not married : (*Shak.*) a sweet Spanish wine.—*adj.* born out of wedlock : not genuine : resembling, but not identical with, the species bearing the name : of abnormal shape or size : false.—*n.* **bas'tard-bar**, a popular but inaccurate name for the baton-sinister in heraldry.—*v.t.* **bas'tardise**, to pronounce or prove to be a bastard.—*v.i.* (*Shak.*) to beget bastards : to degenerate.—*n.* **bast'ardism**, bastardy.—*adj.* **bas'tardly** (*obs.*).—*ns.* **bas'tard-wing**, three, four, or five feathers on the first digit (homologue of the thumb) of a bird's wing; **bas'tardy**, the state of being a bastard.—**bastard title**, an abbreviated title of a book on an otherwise blank page preceding the full title-page; **bastard types**, types cast with an extra deep bevel to obviate the use of leads, as longprimer face on pica body. [O.F. *bastard* (Fr. *bâtard*); child of the pack-saddle (O.Fr. *bast*).]

baste, *bȧst, v.i.* to beat with a stick.—*n.* **bast'ing**. [Prob. conn. with O.N. *beysta*, Dan. *böste*, to beat.]

baste, *bȧst, v.t.* to drop fat or butter over, as in roasting. [Ety. unknown.]

baste, *bȧst, v.t.* to sew slightly or with long stitches. [O.Fr. *bastir*—O.H.G. *bestan*, to sew.]

bastille, *bȧs-tēl', n.* (*hist.*) a tower for the defence of a fortress : a movable tower used by besiegers : the Bastille, an old fortress and state prison in Paris, demolished in the Revolution (July, 1789) : hence any prison, esp. as a symbol of tyranny.—*n.* **bastel-house** (*bȧs'tl; Scot.*), a fortified house, usu. with vaulted ground-floor. [Fr.,—O.Fr., *bastir* (Fr. *bâtir*), to build.]

bastinade, bastinade, *bast-in-ȧd'(ō), v.t.* to beat with a baton or stick, esp. on the soles of the feet (an Eastern punishment) :—*pr.p.* **bastinȧd'oing** or **bastinȧd'ing**; *pa.p.* **bastinȧd'oed** or **bastinȧd'ed**.—*ns.* **bastinade', bastinȧd'o**. [Sp. *bastonada*, Fr. *bastonnade*—*baston, bâton*; cf. **baton, batten**.]

bastion, *bast'yon, n.* a kind of tower at the angle of a fortification : (*fig.*) a defence.—*adj.* **bast'ioned**. [Fr.,—It. *bastione*—*bastire*, to build.]

basto, *bȧs'tō, n.* in quadrille, the ace of clubs. [Sp., club.]

bat, *bat, n.* a heavy stick : a flattish club for striking the ball in cricket : a club for base-ball : a batsman : the clown's or harlequin's lath : a piece of brick : (*slang*) rate of speed, style.—*v.i.* to use the bat in cricket :—*pr.p.* **batt'ing**; *pa.t.* and *pa.p.* **batt'ed**.—*ns.* **bat'fowling**, catching birds at night by showing a light and beating the bushes; **bats'man**, one who wields the bat at cricket, etc.; **bats'manship**; **batt'er**; **batt'ing**, the management of a bat in playing games : cotton fibre prepared in sheets.—**to carry (out) one's bat** (*cricket*), to be not-out at the end of an innings, esp. when one has gone in first and when all ten wickets have fallen; **off one's own bat**, by one's own activity (as a cricketer from his own hits); **take out one's bat**, to be not out at the end of an innings, esp. when one has gone in later than first and when all ten wickets have fallen. [Perh. from O.E. *bat* (a doubtful form), prob. Celt. *bat*, staff.]

bat, *bat, n.* a flying mammal with wings attached mainly to its arms and hands, but extending along its sides to the hind-feet and tail.—**bats'wing**, a gas-burner that gives a flame shaped like a bat's wing.—*adj.* **batt'y**, batlike : bat-infested : (*slang*) crazy.—**bats in the belfry**, crazy notions. [M.E. *bakke*, apparently from Scand.; cf. Dan. *aftenbakke*, evening-bat.]

batable, *bāt'ȧ-bl, adj.* debatable, disputable. [A contr. of **debatable**.]

batata, *bȧ-tä'tä, n.* the sweet-potato. [Sp. from Haitian.]

Batavian, *bȧ-tā'vi-ȧn, adj.* pertaining to the ancient

Batāvī in the Low Countries, or to the modern Dutch, or to Batavia (Jakarta).—Also *n.*

batch, *bach, n.* the quantity of bread baked, or of anything made or got ready, at one time : a set.—*v.t.* to collect into, or treat in, batches. [From the root of **bake**.]

bate, *bāt, v.t.* and *v.i.* to abate : to lessen, diminish : to blunt.—*adj.* **bate'less** (*Shak.*), not to be blunted : not bated.—*n.* **bate'ment**, reduction.—**bated breath**, restrained breathing; **batement light**, a window whose sill is not horizontal. [Aphetic form of **abate** (1).]

bate, *bāt, n.* (*Spens.*) strife, contention.—*adj.* **bate'-breed'ing** (*Shak.*). [Aphetic form of **debate**.]

bate, *bāt, v.i.* (*Shak.*) to beat the wings impatiently : (*obs.*) to be impatient. [O.Fr. *batre*—L.L. *batĕre*.]

bateau, *bȧ-tō, n.* a light river-boat, esp. on Canadian rivers :—*pl.* **bateaux** (*-tōz'*). [Fr.]

bateleur, *bat'l-ȧr, n.* a short-tailed African eagle. [Fr., mountebank, app. from its characteristic movements.]

bath, *bȧth, n.* water for immersing the body : an act of bathing : a receptacle or a house for bathing : a place for undergoing medical treatment by means of bathing : the act of exposing the body to vapour, mud, sunlight, etc. : (*chem.*) a liquid or other material (as sand), or a receptacle, in which anything is immersed for heating, washing, or steeping : —*pl.* **baths** (*bȧdhz*, also *bȧths*).—*v.t.* to subject to a bath.—*ns.* **bath'house**; **bath'man**; **bath'room**; **bath'woman**.—**Order of the Bath**, an English order of knighthood, so named from the bath before installation. [O.E. *bæth*; Ger. *bad*.]

Bath, *bȧth*, a famous city in Somerset, with Roman baths.—*ns.* **Bath'-bun**, a rich sweet bun; **Bath'-chair'**, a large wheeled chair for invalids, long in general use in Bath; **Bath' Ol'iver**, a biscuit invented by Dr. W. Oliver of Bath; **Bathō'nian** (*geol.*), a division of the Middle Jurassic (also *adj.*); **Bath'-stone'**, a building-stone quarried at Bath.

bath, *bȧth, n.* the largest Jewish liquid measure, containing about six gallons. [Heb.]

bath-brick, *bȧth'brik, n.* a preparation of siliceous silt, manufactured at Bridgwater in the form of bricks and used in cleaning knives. [Traditionally named after the first maker, one *Bath*, or from its resemblance to *Bath*-stone.]

bathe, *bȧdh, v.t.* to wash as in a bath : to wash or moisten, with any liquid : to moisten, suffuse, encompass.—*v.i.* to take a dip or swim : to bask.—*n.* the act of bathing : a swim or dip.—*ns.* **bȧth'er**; **bȧth'ing-box**, a box for bathers to undress and dress in; **bȧth'ing-cost'ume, -dress, -suit**, a garb for bathing in; **bȧth'ing-machine'**, a small carriage in which a bather may be carried out into water conveniently deep. [O.E. *bathian*.]

bathmism, *bȧth'mizm, n.* a supposed directive force in evolution, or inherent tendency to develop along divergent lines.—*adj.* **bath'mic**. [Gr. *bathmos*, step.]

batholite, *bath'ō-līt, n.* a mass of igneous rock that has risen from a great depth.—Also **bath'olith**, **bath'ylite, bath'ylith**.—*adj.* **batholit(h)ic, bathylit(h)ic** (*-lit', -lith'*). [Gr. *bathos*, depth, *bathys*, deep, *lithos*, a stone.]

bathometer, *bath-om'it-ȧr, n.* a bathymeter. [Gr. *bathos*, depth, *metron*, measure.]

bathorse, *bä', bat', or baw'hors, n.* a pack-horse carrying an officer's baggage. [Fr. *bât*, a pack-saddle.]

bathos, *bä'thos, n.* a ludicrous descent from the elevated to the mean in writing or speech.—*adj.* **bathetic** (*bȧ-thet'ik*; irregularly formed on the analogy of *pathos, pathetic*). [Gr. *bȧthos*, depth.]

bathy-, *bath'i-, -i', in composition, deep.—*n.* **bathyb'ius**, (Gr. *bios*, life), a once supposed low form of life on the sea bottom.—*adj.* **bathygraph'-ical** (Gr. *graphein*, to write), of maps, indicating depth of water.—*n.* **bathymeter** (*-im'*; Gr. *metron*, measure), a sounding instrument.—*adjs.* **bathy-met'ric, -al.**—*n.* **bathym'etry**, the science of sounding seas and lakes.—*adjs.* **bathyorograph'-ical** (Gr. *oros*, mountain), representing height and depth—applied to maps that show height of land and depth of water; **bathypelagic** (-*aj'ik*; Gr. *pelagos*, sea) found in the depths of the sea.—*n.* **bath'ysphere** (Gr. *sphaira*, sphere), a submersible observation chamber (**bath'yscaphe, -scope,** later types). [Gr. *bathys*, deep.]

batik, *bat'ik, n.* an East Indian method of producing designs on cloth by covering with wax, for each successive dipping, those parts that are to be protected from the dye. [Malay.]

bating, *bāt'ing, prep.* abating, excepting. [bate, 1.]

batiste , *bä-tēst', n.* a fine fabric of linen, cotton, or wool. [Fr., cambric—*Baptiste*, the original maker; or from its use in wiping the heads of children after baptism.]

batler, *bat'lər, n.* (*Shak.*) a beetle for clothes.— Altered by some editors to **bat'let.** [bat.]

batman, *bat'mən*, formerly *bä'* or *baw', n.* one who has charge of a bathorse: an officer's attendant.— *n.* **batwoman** (*bat'*). [Fr. *bât*, pack-saddle.]

batology, *ba-tol'ə-ji, n.* the study of brambles.— *adj.* **batological** (*-loj'*).—*n.* **batol'ogist.** [Gr. *batos*, bramble.]

baton, *bat'n,* (*arch.*) **batoon,** *bə-tōōn', n.* a staff or truncheon, esp. of policeman, conductor, or marshal.—*v.t.* to strike with a baton.—*n.* **bat'on-sin'ister,** a well-known heraldic indication of illegitimacy, improperly called *bar-sinister,* a diminutive of a bend-sinister, not extending to the sides of the shield, so as to resemble a marshal's baton laid diagonally over the family arms from sinister to dexter. [Fr. *bâton.*]

Batrachia, *bə-trā'ki-ä, n.pl.* the Amphibia: the Salientia, tailless amphibia, or frogs and toads.— *adj.* and *n.* **batra'chian.** [Gr. *batrachos,* a frog.]

batsman. See **bat** (1).

batswing. See **bat** (2).

batta, *bat'ä, n.* an allowance in addition to ordinary pay: subsistence money. [Prob. Kanarese *bhatta,* rice.]

battailous, *bat'-ä-ləs, adj.* (*Spens.*) war-like. [O.Fr. *bataillos*; see **battle**.]

battalia, *bat-āl'yä, n.* order of battle: the main body of an army in array. [It. *battaglia*; see **battle.**]

battalia pie, *bat-āl-yä'pī, n.* articles like pin-cushions, embroidered by nuns in convents with scenes from the Bible: titbits in a pie. [Fr. *béatilles,* dim. from L. *beātus.*]

battalion, *bə-tal'yən, n.* a body of soldiers consisting of several companies: a body of men drawn up in battle-array. [Fr. *bataillon*—It. *battaglione;* see **battle.**]

batteilant, *bat'ä-lant, adj.* (*Spens.*) combatant. [Fr. *bataillant.*]

battels, *bat'lz, n.pl.* (*Oxford*) accounts for provisions received from college kitchens and butteries: sums charged in college accounts generally. —*v.i.* **batt'el, batt'ill** (*Spens.*), to have such an account.—*n.* **batt'eler,** one who battels: (*obs.*) a student of rank below a commoner. [Poss. conn. with **battle** (2).]

batten, *bat'n, v.i.* to thrive: to grow fat: to feed abundantly.—*v.t.* (*obs.*) to fatten. [O.N. *batna,* to grow better—*bati,* advantage; cf. Du. *baten,* to avail.]

batten, *bat'n, n.* a piece of sawn timber used for flooring, support of laths, etc.: a strip of wood fastened across parallel boards, or used to fasten down hatches aboard ship, etc.: a row of electric lamps or a strip of wood carrying them.—*v.t.* to fasten or furnish with battens.—*n.* **batt'ening,** battens forming a structure. [baton.]

batter, *bat'ər, v.t.* to beat with successive blows: to wear with beating or by use: to attack with artillery.—*n.* ingredients beaten along with some liquid into a paste: paste for sticking.—*n.* **batt'ering-ram,** a large beam with a metal head like a ram's used for battering down walls. [O.Fr. *batre* (Fr. *battre*)—L.L. *battĕre* (L. *ba*(*t*)*tuĕre*) to beat.]

batter, *bat'ər, n.* inward inclination from the perpendicular.—*v.i.* to slope inward. [Origin doubtful.]

batter, batting. See **bat** (1).

battery, *bat'ər-1, n.* the act of battering: (*Shak.*) a wound: a number of cannon with their equipment: the place on which cannon are mounted: a unit of artillery or its personnel: a combination of cells, Leyden jars, lenses, or other apparatus: (*law*) an assault by beating or wounding: apparatus for preparing or serving meals: (*baseball*) pitcher and catcher.—**cross batteries,** two batteries commanding the same spot from different directions; **masked battery,** a battery out of the enemy's view.

battill, Spenser's spelling of **battle** (2).

battle, *bat'l, n.* a contest between opposing armies: a fight or encounter: (*arch.*) a battalion.—*v.i.* to fight: to struggle: to contend (with *against, with*). —*v.t.* (*rare*) to dispose in battalions: to contest.— *ns.* **batt'le-axe, -ax,** a kind of axe once used in battle; **batt'le-cruiser,** *n.* a large cruiser with battleship qualities; **batt'le-cry,** a war-cry, slogan; **batt'le-dress,** a simplified military uniform, close-fitting at the waist, allowing freedom of movement; **batt'le-field,** the place on which a battle is or was fought; **batt'le-piece,** a picture or description of a battle; **batt'le-plane,** *n.* a large fighting aeroplane.—*adj.* **batt'le-scarred,** scarred in battle.—*n.* **batt'leship,** a warship of the first class.—**battle royal,** a general melée; **half the battle,** anything that brings one well on the way to success. [Fr. *bataille*—L. *battuālia,* fighting.]

battle, *bat'l, adj.* (*dial.*) nourishing: fertile.—*v.t.* and *v.i.* to feed: to fatten: to make or become fertile. [Perh. conn. with O.N. *bati,* improvement; see **batten.**]

battle, *bat'l, v.t.* to furnish with battlements (esp. in *pa.p.*).—*n.* **batt'lement,** a wall or parapet with embrasures.—*adj.* **batt'lemented.** [O.Fr. *batailler,* movable defences.]

battledore, battledoor, *bat'l-dōr, n.* a wooden bat used for washing, etc.: a light ba+ for striking a ball or shuttlecock: (*obs.*) a hornbook.—**not to know a B from a battledore,** to be thoroughly ignorant. [Perhaps Sp. *batidor,* a beater, a washing beetle.]

battology, *bat-ol'ə-ji, n.* futile repetition in speech or writing.—*adj.* **battolog'ical.** [Gr. *battologiā,* stuttering, said to be from *Battos,* who consulted the Delphic oracle about his defect of speech (Herodotus iv. 155), and *legein,* to speak.]

batts. See **bot.**

battue, *bä-tōō', ba-tū', bä-tü', n.* a hunt in which animals are driven into some place for the convenience of the shooters: indiscriminate slaughter. [Fr.,—*battre,* to beat.]

bauble, *baw'bl, n.* a trifling piece of finery: a child's plaything: a jester's sceptre, a stick surmounted by a head with ass's ears: a piece of childish foolery: (*Shak.*) a foolish person.—*adj.* **bau'bling** (*Shak.*), trifling. [O.Fr. *babel, baubel,* toy, trinket.]

bauchle, *bawhh'l, n.* (*Scot.*) a loose, down-at-heel, or badly worn, shoe: any person or thing worn out or awkward. [Origin obscure.]

baudekin, *bawd'i-kin,* **bawdkin,** *bawd'kin.* Same as **baldachin.**

baudric, baudrick, *bawd'rik.* Same as **baldric**(k).

Baudrons, *bawd'rəns, n.* Scottish quasi-proper name for the cat: also for the hare. [Origin obscure.]

bauk, baulk. Same as **balk.**

bausond, *baws'ənd, adj.* having white spots, esp. on the forehead, or a white stripe down the face.— *adj.* **baus'on-faced.** [O.Fr. *bausant,* black and white spotted.]

bauxite, *bawk'sīt, -zīt, bō'zīt, n.* a clay found at Les *Baux,* near Arles, a source of aluminium.— Also **beau'xite.**

bavardage, *bäv-är-däzh, n.* chattering, prattle. [Fr. *bavard,* garrulous—*bave,* drivel.]

bavin, *bav'in, n.* a fagot of brushwood.—**bavin wits** (*Shak.*), wits that blaze and die like bavins. [Origin unknown.]

bawbee, *baw-bē', n.* (*Scot.*) a halfpenny: originally a silver coin worth three Scots pennies. [Prob. from a Scottish mint-master (1538), Alexander Orrok of Sillebawbe.]

bawble. Same as **bauble**.

bawcock, *baw′kok, n.* (*Shak.*) a fine fellow. [From Fr. *beau,* fine, and *coq,* a cock.]

bawd, *bawd, n.* a procuress (or till about 1700 procurer) of women for lewd purposes.—*adj.* **bawd′-born** (*Shak.*), born of a bawd.—*ns.* **bawd′iness; bawd′ry,** procuring: unchastity: bawdy talk.—*adj.* **bawd′y,** lewd.—*n.* bawdy talk.—*n.* **bawd′y-house,** a brothel. [Prob. M.E. *bawdstrot,* pander—O.Fr. *baldestrot,* prob.—*bald,* bold, gay, and the root of **strut**.]

bawd, *bawd, n.* (*Shak.* **baud**) a hare. [Perh. **Baudrons**.]

bawl, *bawl, v.t.* and *v.i.* to shout or cry out very loudly.—*n.* a loud cry or shout.—*ns.* **bawl′er; bawl′ing.—to bawl out** (*U.S.*) to reprimand bullyingly. [Perh. L.L. *baulāre,* to bark, but cf. Icel. *baula,* to low like a cow, O.N. *baula,* a cow.]

bawley, *baw′li, n.* (*Essex* and *Kent*) a small fishing-smack. [Origin obscure.]

bawn, *bawn, n.* a fortification round a house: an enclosure for cattle. [Ir. *bábhun,* enclosure.]

baxter. See **bake**.

bay, *bā, adj.* reddish brown inclining to chestnut.—*n.* a bay horse. [Fr. *bai*—L. *badius,* chestnut-coloured.]

bay, *bā, n.* an inlet of the sea with a wider opening than a gulf: an inward bend of the shore.—*n.* **bay′-salt,** coarse-grained salt, orig. from sea-water.—**the Bay State,** Massachusetts. [Fr. *baie*—L.L. *baia,* a harbour.]

bay, *bā, n.* the space between two columns, timbers, walls, etc.: (*Shak.*) the space under one house gable: any recess or stall: a passing-place in a military trench: a side-line in a railway station (also **bay′-line**).—*n.* **bay′-win′dow,** any window forming a recess.—*adj.* **bay′-win′dowed.** [O.Fr. *baée*—*baer,* to gape, be open; prob. conn. **bay,** 2.]

bay, *bā, n.* the laurel-tree; extended to other trees and shrubs, species of *Magnolia, Myrica,* etc.: (in *pl.*) an honorary garland or crown of victory, originally of laurel: hence, literary renown.—*ns.* **bay′-berry,** the berry of the bay-tree, or of candleberry: a tree (*Pimenta acris*) akin to allspice; **bay′-rum,** an aromatic liquid prepared from the leaves of *Pimenta acris.* [O.Fr. *baie,* a berry—L. *bāca.*]

bay, *bā, n.* barking, baying (esp. of a dog in pursuit): the combined cry of hounds in conflict with a hunted animal: the last stand of a hunted animal when it faces the hounds at close quarters.—*v.i.* to bark (esp. of large dogs).—*v.t.* to bark at: to utter by baying: to follow with barking: to bring to bay.—**to hold, keep at bay,** said of a hunted animal; **to stand, be, at bay,** to face the dogs at close quarters. [Partly O.Fr. *abai,* barking, *bayer,* to bark, partly O.Fr. *bay,* open-mouthed suspense—L.L. *badāre,* to open the mouth.]

bay, *bā, bez, bā, bāz, n.* (in full **bay′-antler, -tine**), the second tine of a deer's horn. [O.Fr. *besantlier*—*bes-,* secondary (—L. *bis,* twice), *antlier,* antler.]

bay, bayee, *bā, v.t.* (*Spens.*) to bathe.

bayadère, *bā-yā-der′, n.* a Hindu dancing-girl. [Fr.,—Port. *bailadeira.*]

Bayard, *bā′är(d),* Fr. *bā-yār, n.* a type of the knight 'without fear and without reproach'. [From the French knight *Bayard* (1476-1524).]

Bayard, *bā′ärd, -ərd, n.* in romance, Rinaldo's horse: **bayard,** a bay horse or horse generally: a type of blind recklessness or bold ignorance.

bayonet, *bā′ə-nit, n.* a stabbing instrument of steel fixed to the muzzle of a fire-arm: military force: a soldier armed with a bayonet.—*v.t.* to stab with a bayonet: to force at the point of the bayonet.—*adj.* **bay′oneted,** armed with a bayonet. [Fr. *baïonnette,* perh. from *Bayonne,* in France; or from O.Fr. *bayon,* arrow.]

bayou, *bi′ōō, n.* (*U.S.*) the marshy offshoot of a lake or river. [Perh. Fr. *boyau,* gut, or Choctaw *báyuk,* little river.]

bay-salt, *bā′-sawlt, n.* salt obtained by slow evaporation, originally from sea-water. [Prob. from **bay,** an inlet, and **salt**.]

bayt, a Spenserian spelling of **bate** (1); also of **bait**.

bazaar, bazar, *bə-zär′, n.* an Eastern market-place or exchange: a fancy fair in imitation of an Eastern bazaar: sometimes, a big shop. [Pers. *bāzār,* a market.]

bazooka, *bə-zōō′kä, n.* a slide wind-instrument used for humorous purposes: a gun for rocket-driven projectiles.

bdellium, *del′i-əm, n.* a gum got from *Commiphora* trees: used to translate, but prob. unconnected with, Heb. *b′dōlakh* (Gen. II, 12; meaning unknown.) [L.,—Gr. *bdellion.*]

be, *bē, v.i.* (*infin.*) to live: to exist: to have the state or quality mentioned:—*pr.p.* **bē′ing;** *pa.p.* **been;** *pr.subj.* **be;** *arch.* and *dial. pr.indic.* **be** (see **am, art, is, are** for ordinary forms); for *pa.t.* see **was, wast, were, wert.**—*n.* **be′-all** (*Shak.*), the whole being. [O.E. *béon;* Ger. *bin* (1st pers.); Gael. *bi,* to exist; W. *byw,* to live; Gr. *phyein,* to produce, grow; L. *fuī,* I was, *fīō,* I become; Sans. *bhu,* to be; orig. meaning to grow.]

beach, *bēch, n.* the shore of the sea or of a lake, esp. when sandy or pebbly: a marginal terrace formed by waves: the strand.—*v.t.* to drive or haul up on a beach.—*ns.* **beach′comber** (-*kōm-*), a long rolling wave: a loafer about the wharfs in Pacific seaports: a settler on a Pacific island who maintains himself by pearl-fishery, or often by less reputable means; **beach′combing.**—*adj.* **beached,** having a beach: driven on a beach.—*ns.* **beach′head,** an area held on an enemy's shore for purpose of landing; **beach′-master,** an officer in charge of disembarking troops.—*adj.* **beach′y,** pebbly. [Orig. a dial. word for shingle.]

beach-la-mar, *bēch-lä-mär′, n.* a South Sea jargon used in the bêche-de-mer trade. [Port. *bicho do mar,* sea-slug, bêche-de-mer.]

beacon, *bē′kn, n.* a fire on an eminence used as a sign of danger: a hill on which it could be lighted: an erection with or without a light marking a rock or shoal in navigable waters: a light to guide air-men: a sign marking a street crossing—e.g. a Belisha (*bə-lē′shä*) beacon, named after the Minister of Transport 1934: a wireless transmitter in which the radiation is concentrated in one or more narrow beams, so as to act as a guide to shipping or aircraft: anything that warns of danger.—*v.t.* to act as a beacon to: to light up: to mark by beacons.—*n.* **float′ing-bea′con,** a lightship. [O.E. *béacn,* a beacon, a sign.]

bead, *bēd,* (*obs.*) a prayer: a little ball strung with others in a rosary, for counting prayers: a similar ball or the like pierced for stringing to form a necklace, etc.: a bead-like drop: the front-sight of a gun: a narrow moulding of semi-circular section, sometimes broken into bead-like parts: the flange of a tire.—*v.t.* to furnish with beads or beading.—*v.i.* to form a bead or beads.—*adj.* **bead′ed,** having beads or a bead: in beadlike form.—*ns.* **bead′-house,** orig. a chapel: an almshouse whose inmates were required to pray for the founder's soul; **bead′ing,** bead moulding: work in beads.—*adj.* **bead′-proof,** of such proof or strength as to carry beads or bubbles after shaking, as alcoholic liquors.—*ns.* **bead′-roll,** orig. a list of the dead to be prayed for, hence a list of names, a long series: a rosary; **beads′man, bedes′man,** one bound or endowed to pray for others: (*Scot.*) a licensed beggar:—*fem.* **beads′woman.**—*adj.* **bead′y,** bead-like, small and bright (as eyes): covered with beads or bubbles—**draw a bead on** (*U.S.*) to take aim at; **tell one's beads,** to say one's prayers. [O.E. *gebed,* prayer; see **bid**.]

beadle, *bēd′l, n.* a mace-bearer, esp. (Oxford and Cambridge **bedel**(**l**), -*del′,* or *bēd′*) a vice-chancellor's: a petty officer of a church, college, etc.: a parish officer with the power of punishing petty offenders: in Scotland, the church-officer attending on the minister: (*obs.*) a messenger or crier of a court.—*ns.* **bead′ledom, bead′lehood,** stupid officiousness; **bead′leship, bedel**(**l**)′**ship,** the office of beadle or bedel. [O.E. *bydel—béodan,* to proclaim, to bid; affected by O.Fr. form *bedel.*]

beadman, bedeman, old forms of **beadsman.** [See under **bead.**]

Neutral vowels in unaccented syllables: *el′ə-mənt, in′fənt, ran′dəm*

beagle, *bē′gl*, *n.* a small hound tracking by scent, formerly much used in hunting hares : sometimes, a harrier : a spy : a bailiff : a small kind of shark.—*v.i.* to hunt with beagles.—*ns.* **bea′gler**; **bea′gling**, hunting with beagles. [Ety. unknown; poss. O.Fr. *beegueule*, clamourer—*béer*, to gape, *gueule*, throat.]

beak, *bēk*, *n.* a bird's bill : a hard or sharp snout : a nose : a pointed process or projection : in the ancient galley, a pointed iron fastened to the prow for piercing the enemy's vessel : (*slang*.) a magistrate, schoolmaster, or schoolmistress.—*adj.* **beaked** (*bēkt*). [O.Fr. *bec*—L. *beccus* (recorded by Suetonius), a cock's bill.]

beaker, *bēk′ər*, *n.* a large drinking-bowl or cup, or its contents : a deep glass or other vessel used by chemists.—**Beaker Folk**, a round-headed, heavy-browed, square-jawed people that appeared in Britain at the dawn of the Bronze Age, makers of round barrows in which bell-shaped beakers are often found. [O.N. *bikarr*, prob.—L.L. *bicārium*, or *bicārium*, app.—Gr. *bīkos*, a drinking bowl.]

beam, *bēm*, *n.* a tree (*obs.* except in *hornbeam*, *whitebeam*, etc.): a large and straight piece of timber or iron forming one of the main structural members of a building, etc. : (*fig.*) a great fault (from the figure of the mote and the beam—Matt. vii. 3): any of the transverse pieces of framing extending across a ship's hull : the greatest width of a ship or boat : breadth : the part of a balance from which the scales hang : the pole of a carriage : the stem, or main part of a deerhorn, an anchor, a plough : a cylinder of wood in a loom : a shaft or ray of light or other radiations : a gleam.—*v.t.* to send forth : to place on a beam : to transmit by beam system.—*v.i.* to shine : to smile radiantly.—*n.pl.* **beam′-ends′**, the ends of the transverse beams of a ship.—*ns.* **beam′-en′gine**, a steam-engine with a beam connecting the piston-rod and the crank of the wheel-shaft; **beam′er**, a workman or machine that puts yarn on the beam of a loom.—*adv.* **beam′ily**, radiantly.—*n.* **beam′iness**, radiance : breadth.—*n.* and *adj.* **beam′ing**.—*adv.* **beam′ingly**.—*adjs.* **beam′ish**, radiant; **beam′less**, without beams : emitting no rays.—*ns.* **beam′-trawl**, a trawling net kept open by a beam along its upper lip, resting on runners; **beam′-trawling**; **beam′-tree**, a pleonastic name for the whitebeam.— *adj.* **beam′y**, shining : radiant : massive like a weaver's beam : broad.—*abaft*, *before*, *the beam*, behind, before, the direction at right angles to a ship's course; **beam sea**, one rolling against the ship's side; **beam system**, a system whereby, with the aid of reflectors, short wireless waves are projected (like a lighthouse beam) in a particular direction, not radiated in all directions; **lee**, **weather**, **beam**, the side away from, or towards, the wind; **on her beam-ends**, of a ship, so much inclined to one side that the beams become nearly vertical; **on one's beam-ends**, in acute distress, destitute; **on the beam**, in the direction of a ship's beams, at right angles to her course : by help of a direction-finding signal; **on the port, starboard, beam**, applied to any distant point out at sea, at right angles to the keel, and on the left, or right, side. [O.E. *béam*, tree, stock of a tree, ray of light; Ger. *baum*, tree; perh. akin to Gr. *phȳma*, a growth—*phyein*, to grow.]

bean, *bēn*, *n.* the name of several kinds of leguminous plants and their seeds, esp. the common or broad bean (*Vicia Faba*) and the French, kidney, or haricot bean (*Phaseolus vulgaris*): applied also to the seeds of some other plants, from their bean-like form, as coffee.—*ns.* **bean′-ca′per**, a genus (*Zygophyllum*) of Old-World steppe and desert shrubs whose flower-buds are used as capers; **bean′feast**, an annual dinner given by employers to their hands at which beans used to be prominent : a jollification; **bean′-king**, the king of the festivities on Twelfth Night, finder of a bean hidden in the Twelfth Cake; **bean′o** (*slang*), a beanfeast, a disturbance, a jollification; **bean′tree**, a name given to several trees, as Moreton Bay chestnut, coral tree, and Catalpa.—**full of beans**, in high spirits; **give one beans**, to treat one severely;

old bean, a familiar disrespectful form of address. [O.E. *béan*; Ger. *bohne*.]

bear, *bār*, *v.t.* to carry : to have : to convey : (*backgammon*) to remove from the board in the final stage of the game : to sustain or support : to thrust or drive : to endure : to admit of : to purport : to be entitled to (heraldically) : to afford : to behave or conduct (oneself) : to bring forth.—*v.i.* to suffer : to be patient : to have reference (with *on* or *upon*) : to press (with *on* or *upon*) : to lie in, or take, a direction : to be capable of sustaining weight : to be productive :—*pr.p.* **bear′ing**; *pa.t.* **bōre** (*arch.* **bare**); *pa.p.* **bōrne** (but **born** when referring adjectively to something brought forth).—*n.* (*Spens.* **beare**, *bēr*) a burden : also (*Spens.*) a bier (see **bier**).—*adj.* **bear′able**, that may be borne or endured.—*n.* **bear′ableness**.—*adv.* **bear′ably**.—*ns.* **bear′er**, one who or that which bears : the actual holder of a cheque or the like : one who helps to carry a body to the grave : a carrier or messenger : in India, a body-servant; **bear′ing**, demeanour : direction : a supporting surface : relation : that which is borne upon an escutcheon : (*mach.*) the part of a machine that bears friction, esp. a journal and its support (often in *pl.* : see **ball-bearings**).—Also *adj.*—*ns.* **bear′ing-cloth**, the mantle or cloth in which a child was carried to the font; **bear′ing-rein**, a fixed rein between the bit and the saddle, by which a horse's head is held up and its neck made to arch.—**bear a hand**, to give assistance; **bear away**, to sail away; **bear down** (with *upon* or *towards*), to sail with the wind; **bear hard** (*Shak.*), to press or urge; **bear in hand** (*arch.*), to make out, maintain : (*Shak.*) to keep in expectation, to flatter one's hopes; **bear out**, to corroborate; **bear up**, to keep up one's spirits; **bear up for** (*a place*), to sail towards; **bear with**, to make allowance for; **borne in upon**, forcibly impressed upon; **bring to bear**, to bring into operation (with *against*, *upon*); **lose one's bearings**, to become uncertain of one's position or orientation. [O.E. *beran*; Goth. *bairan*, L. *ferre*, Gr. *pherein*, Sans. *bhri*.]

bear, *bār*, *n.* a heavy carnivorous animal with long shaggy hair and hooked claws : any rude, rough or ill-bred fellow : one who sells stocks for delivery at a future date, anticipating a fall in price—opp. to *bull* (the old phrase *a bearskin jobber* suggests an origin in the proverbial phrase, to sell the bearskin before one has caught the bear) : (*astron.*) the name of two constellations, the Great and Little Bear (Ursus major and minor).—*v.i.* to speculate for a fall.—*ns.* **bear′-animal′cule**, a tardigrade—one of a group of degenerate arthropods; **bear′baiting**, the sport of setting dogs to worry a bear; **bear′berry**, a trailing plant (*Arctostaphylos*) of the heath family : extended to various plants; **bear′bine**, a bindweed; **bear′-cat**, a panda; **bear′-garden**, an enclosure for bear-baiting : a turbulent assembly.—*adj.* **bear′ish**, like a bear in manners.—*ns.* **bear′ishness**; **bear′-leader**, one who leads about a performing bear : the tutor of a youth on travel; **bear's′-breech**, acanthus; **bear's′-ear**, auricula; **bear's′-foot**, black hellebore; **bear′skin**, the skin of a bear : a shaggy woollen cloth for overcoats : the high fur cap worn by the Guards in England : **bear′-ward**, a warden or keeper of bears. [O.E. *bera*; Ger. *bar*; Du. *beer*; apparently from an Indo-Germ. root *bhero-*, brown.]

bear, **bere**, *bēr*, *n.* barley : in Scotland now the little grown four-rowed (really six-rowed) variety. [O.E. *bere*.]

bear, **beer**, *bēr*. See **bere**.

beard, *bērd*, *n.* the hair that grows on the chin and adjacent parts of a grown man's face : the tuft on the lower jaw of a goat, seal, etc. : a fish's barbel : (*bot.*) an awn or threadlike spike as on the ears of barley : a tuft of hairs : a barb of a hook, an arrow, etc. : the gills of an oyster, etc.—*v.t.* to take by the beard : to oppose to the face.—*adj.* **beard′ed**, having a beard : prickly : awned : barbed.—*n.* **beard′-grass**, a kind of bearded grass (*Polypogon*).—*adj.* **beard′less**. [O.E. *beard*; Ger. *bart*, Russ. *boroda*.]

beast, *bēst, n.* an irrational animal, as opposed to man : a four-footed animal : a brutal person : (*coll.*) anything beastly : the **Beast,** Antichrist in *Revelation :—dim.* **beast′ie.—***ns.* **beast′-fa′ble,** a story in which animals play human parts; **beast′hood,** state or nature of a beast.—*adv.* **beast′ily** (*Shelley*), bestially.—*n.* **beast′liness.—***adjs.* **beast′like** (also *adv*); **beast′ly,** like a beast in actions or behaviour : bestial : foul : sensual : (*coll.*) vile, disagreeable.—*adv.* brutishly : (*coll.*) abominably.—*n.* **beast′lyhead** (*Spens.*), personality or self of a beast.—**mark of the Beast** (see **mark**); **number of the beast,** the apocalyptic number. [O.Fr. *beste* (Fr. *bête*)—L. *bestia.*]

beastings. Same as **beestings.**

beat, *bēt, v.t.* to strike repeatedly : (B.) to break or bruise : to pound : to batter : to whip up or switch : to flap : to strike (as bushes) in order to rouse game : to thrash : to defeat : to be too difficult for : to spread flat and thin by beating with a tool (as gold) : to mark (time) with a baton, etc.—*v.i.* to give strokes repeatedly : to pulsate : to impinge : to mark time in music : (*pr.p.* **beat′ing;** *pa.t.* **beat;** *pa.p.* **beat′en,** now rarely **beat).—***n.* a recurrent stroke, its sound, or its moment, as of a watch or the pulse, or a conductor's baton : accent : pulsation, esp. that heard when two notes nearly in tune are sounded together : a round or course, as a policeman's : a place of resort.—*adj.* weary : fatigued : affected with bursitis (as *beat elbow, knee*).—*adj.* **beat′en,** made smooth or hard by beating or treading : trite : worn by use.—*ns.* **beat′er,** one that beats or strikes : one who rouses or beats up game : a crushing instrument; **beat′ing,** the act of striking : thrashing : pulsation or throbbing : rousing of game : exercising the brain.—**beat about the bush,** to approach a subject in an indirect way; **beat a retreat,** to retreat, originally to beat the drum as a signal for retreat; **beat down,** of a buyer, to try to reduce the price of goods; **beat it,** (*slang*) to make off hastily or furtively; **beat off,** to drive back; **beat the air,** to fight to no purpose, or against an imaginary enemy; **beat the bounds,** to trace out boundaries in a perambulation, certain objects in the line of journey being formally struck, and sometimes also boys whipped to make them remember; **beat one's brains,** to puzzle one's brains about something; **beat out,** to flatten or reduce in thickness by beating; **beat up,** to pound or whip into froth, paste, a mixture, etc. : to put up as by beating the bushes : to alarm by a sudden attack : (*slang*) to thrash, to subject to a violent and brutal attack : to disturb : to pay an untimely visit to : to go about in quest of anything : to make way against wind or tide. [O.E. *béatan,* pa.t. *béot.*]

beath, *bēdh, v.t.* (*Spens.*) to bathe, heat. [O.E. *bethian,* to foment.]

beatify, *bi-at′i-fī, v.t.* to make blessed or happy : to declare to be in the enjoyment of eternal happiness in heaven.—*adjs.* **beatific** (*bē-ə-tif′ik*), **-al,** making supremely happy.—*adv.* **beatif′ically.—***n.* **beatifica′tion,** act of beatifying : (*R.C.*) a declaration by the Pope that a person is blessed in heaven, authorising a certain definite form of public reverence payable to him—the first step to canonisation.—**beatific vision,** a glimpse of the glory of heaven. [L. *beātus,* blessed, and *facĕre,* to make.]

beatitude, *bi-at′i-tūd, n.* heavenly happiness : happiness of the highest kind : a title given to patriarchs in the Orthodox Churches : (in *pl.*) sayings of Christ in Matt. v, declaring certain classes of persons to be blessed. [L. *beātitūdo—beātus,* blessed.]

beau, *bō, n.* a man attentive to dress or fashion : a fop or dandy : a lover :—*pl.* **beaux** (*bōz*) :—*fem.* **belle.—***n.* **beau′-idē′al,** ideal beauty : (blunderingly) a type or embodiment of the highest excellence.—*adj.* **beau′ish.—***ns.* **beau′-monde** (*bō-mon*ᵈ), the gay or fashionable world; **beau-pere** (*bū-pēr′; obs.;* Fr. *père,* father), a term of courtesy for father, esp. of ecclesiastical persons : (*Spens.;* O.Fr. *per,* equal, peer) a companion. [Fr. *beau. bel*—L. *bellus,* fine, gay.]

beaufet, beauffet, *buf-et′, n.* obs. forms of **buffet,** sideboard, cupboard.

beaufin, a sophisticated spelling of **biffin.**

Beaufort, *bū′fərt, adj.* devised by Sir Francis Beaufort (1774-1857), English admiral and hydrographer.—**Beaufort scale,** a scale of wind velocity, with o for calm, 12 for hurricane.

Beaujolais, *bō-zho-lā, n.* a red wine of Southeastern France. [From *Beaujolais,* a subdivision of Lyonnais.]

beaumontag(u)e, *bō-mon-tāg′, n.* a composition for hiding cracks and holes in wood or iron, of varying composition. [Said to be from Élie de Beaumont (1798-1874), the French geologist.]

Beaune, *bōn, n.* a wine of Burgundy. [From the town of *Beaune.*]

beauty, *bū′ti, n.* the quality that gives pleasure to the sight, or aesthetic pleasure generally : a particular grace or excellence : a beautiful person (often *ironical*), esp. a woman; also applied collectively : a very fine specimen of its kind : (in *pl.*) beautiful passages or extracts.—*v.t.* (*Shak.*) to make beautiful.—*adj.* **beau′teous** (*-ti-əs*), a bookish word for beautiful.—*adv.* **beau′teously.—***ns.* **beau′teousness; beautifica′tion; beau′tifier,** one who or that which beautifies or makes beautiful.—*adj.* **beau′tiful,** fair : with qualities that give delight to the senses, esp. the eye and ear, or which awaken admiration in the mind.—*adv.* **beau′tifully.—***v.t.* **beau′tify,** to make beautiful : to grace : to adorn.—*v.i.* (*rare*) to become beautiful, or more beautiful.—**beauty parlour,** a shop for operations that give a more fashionable if not more beautiful look to ladies; **beauty sleep,** the sleep before midnight, considered the most refreshing; **beauty spot,** a patch placed on the face to heighten beauty : a birthmark resembling such a patch : a foil : a scene of outstanding beauty. [O.Fr. *biaute* (Fr. *beauté*)—L.L. *bellitās, -ātis*—L. *bellus.*]

beauxite. See **bauxite.**

beaver, *bēv′ər, n.* an amphibious rodent (Castor): its valuable fur : a hat of beaver fur or a substitute : a glove of beaver fur : a heavy woollen cloth.—*ns.* **beav′er-board,** a building board of wood-fibre; **beav′er-rat,** the coypu : the musquash : Hydromys; **bea′ver-tree, -wood,** a species of magnolia whose bark beavers eat; **beav′ery,** a place where beavers are kept.—**mountain beaver,** the sewellel. [O.E. *befer, beofor;* Du. *bever,* Ger. *biber,* Gael. *beaghar,* L. *fiber.*]

beaver, *bēv′ər, n.* in mediaeval armour, the covering for the lower part of the face, the visor being that for the upper part—later the movable beaver was confounded with the visor : (*slang*) a beard or bearded man.—*adj.* **beav′ered.** [O.Fr. *bavière,* child's bib—*bave,* slaver.]

bebeeru, *bi-bē′rōō, n.* the greenheart tree of Guiana. —*n.* **bebee′rine** (*-rin, -rēn*), an alkaloid yielded by its bark, a substitute for quinine. [Native name.]

beblubbered, *bi-blub′ərd, adj.* disfigured by weeping. [Pfx. *be-,* and **blubber.**]

becall, *bi-kawl′, v.t.* to call names. [Pfx. *be-,* and **call.**]

becalm, *bi-käm′, v.t.* to make calm, still, or quiet. —*adj.* **becalmed′,** motionless from want of wind. [Pfx. *be-,* and **calm.**]

became, *bi-kām′, pa.t.* of **become.**

because, *bi-koz′, bi-kawz′, adv.* and *conj.* for the reason that : on account (of). [**by, cause.**]

beccafico, *bek-a-fē′kō, n.* a garden warbler or kindred bird, considered a delicacy by the Italians : —*pl.* **beccafi′cos.** [It., from *beccare,* to peck, and *fico,* a fig.]

bechance, *bi-chäns′, v.i.* (with *dat.*) to happen by chance : to befall.—*adv.* by chance : accidentally. [O.E. *be-,* and **chance.**]

becharm, *bi-chärm′, v.t.* to charm : to enchant.

bêche-de-mer, *besh′-də-mer, n.* the trepang or seaslug, a species of Holothuria, much esteemed in China as a food delicacy : South Sea English, or beach-la-mar. [Fr.,—Port. *bicho do mar,* sea-slug.]

beck, *bek, n.* a brook. [O.N. *bekkr;* Ger. *bach.*]

beck, *bek, n.* a sign with the finger or head : a nod : (*Scot.*) a gesture of salutation.—*v.i.* to make such a sign.—*v.t.* to call by a nod.—**at one's beck**

(and call), subject to one's will. [A contr. of **beckon**.]

becke, *bek*, *n*. (*Spens.*). Same as **beak**.

becket, *bek'it*, *n*. (*naut.*) a loop of rope having a knot at one end and an eye at the other : a large hook, or a wooden bracket used to keep loose tackle or spars in a convenient place. [Perh. Du. *bogt*, *bocht*, a bend of rope.]

beckon, *bek'n*, *v.t.* and *v.i.* to nod or make a summoning sign (to). [O.E. *biecnan—béacn*, a sign. See **beacon**.]

becloud, *bi-klowd'*, *v.t.* to obscure by clouds : to dim.

become, *bi-kum'*, *v.i.* to come to be : (*obs.*) to arrive, have got (to a place) : to be the fate (followed by *of*).—*v.t.* to suit or befit : to grace : to adorn fittingly : to look well in.—*pa.t.* **became'** ; *pa.p.* **become'**.—*adj.* **becom'ingly**.—*n.* **becom'ingness**. [O.E. *becuman*; see **come**.]

becurl, *bi-kurl'*, *v.t.* to curl. [Pfx. *be-* and **curl**.]

bed, *bed*, *n*. a couch or place to sleep on : a mattress : a bedstead : a garden plot : a layer of oysters, etc. : a place in which anything rests, in carpentry, architecture, etc. : conjugal union, the marriage-bed, matrimonial rights and duties, or a marriage as a source of offspring : the channel of a river : sea or lake bottom : a layer or stratum.—*v.t.* to put to bed : to provide, or make, a bed for : to plant in a bed : to lay in layers or on a surface : to embed.—*v.i.* to go to bed : to cohabit :—*pr.p.* **bedd'ing** ; *pa.p.* **bedd'ed**.—*ns.* **bed'bug**, the common bug (*Cimex lectularius*) ; **bed'chamber**, a bedroom ; **bed'-closet**, a closet serving as a bedroom.—*n.pl.* **bed'clothes**, sheets, blankets, etc., for a bed.—*ns.* **bed'cover**, an upper covering for a bed ; **bedd'er**, a plant suitable for a flower bed ; **bedd'ing**, mattress, bedclothes, etc. : litter for cattle : stratification (**false bedding**, irregular or diagonal bedding due to action of currents).—*adj.* **bed'fast**, confined to bed.—*ns.* **bed'fellow**, a sharer of a bed ; **bed'-key**, a tool for tightening a bedstead ; **bed'maker**, one who makes the beds and sweeps college rooms at Oxford, etc. ; **bed'-of-hon'our**, the grave of a soldier who has fallen in battle ; **bed'-of-just'ice** (Fr. *lit de justice*), the king's throne in the Parlement of Paris : a sitting at which the king was present, chiefly for the registration of his own decrees ; **bed'-pan**, a chamber utensil for use in sick-bed : a warming-pan ; **bed'-plate** (*mech.*), the foundation plate of a machine ; **bed'post**, a corner support of a bedstead ; **bed'presser** (*Shak.*), a heavy, lazy fellow.—*adjs.* **bed'rid(den)**, confined to bed by age or sickness : worn out.—*ns.* **bed'right**, **-rite** (*Shak.*), the privilege or due of the marriage-bed ; **bed'rock'**, the solid rock underneath superficial formations : (*fig.*) fundamental principles : the lowest state.—*adj.* **bottom**, lowest.—*ns.* **bed'room**, a room with a bed : a sleeping apartment : room in bed, sleeping space ; **bed'-sitt'ing-room**, a combined bedroom and sitting-room (abbrev. **bed'-sitt'er**) ; **bed'side**, position by a bed.—Also *adj.* as **bedside book**, one suitable for sleepless nights ; *bedside manner*, a doctor's way in the presence of the patient.—*ns.* **bed'sore**, an ulcer arising from long confinement to bed, esp. over the bony prominences ; **bed'spread**, a coverlet put over a bed by day ; **bed'-staff**, a staff or stick formerly used for making or fixing a bed, a handy weapon ; **bed'stead**, a frame for supporting a bed ; **bed'straw**, any plant of the genus *Galium*, esp. (Our) Lady's Bedstraw (*Galium verum*) ; **bed'-swerver** (*Shak.*), one who is false to his marriage vow ; **bed'-table**, a table for use by a person in bed ; **bed'tick**, the case in which stuffing is put for a bed ; **bed'time**, the hour for going to bed.—*adv.* **bed'ward(s)**, in the direction of bed : towards bedtime.—*n.* **bed'work** (*Shak.*), work easily performed, as if done in bed.—**bed and board**, food and lodging : full connubial relations ; **bed of down**, or **roses**, any easy or comfortable place ; **brought to bed**, confined in childbirth (with *of*) ; **keep one's bed**, to remain in bed ; **lie in the bed one has made**, to have to accept the consequences of one's own acts ; **Lords, Ladies, of the Bedchamber**,

officers in the royal household who wait in turn upon a king or queen ; **make a bed**, to put a bed in order. [O.E. *bed*(*d*) ; Ger. *bett*, O.N. *bethr* ; prob. akin to L. *fodĕre*, to dig (as orig. a hole).]

bed, *bed* (*Spens.*). Same as **bid** (order, pray).

bedabble, *bi-dab'l*, *v.t.* to dabble or wet. [Pfx. *be-*, and **dabble**.]

bedad, *bi-dad'*, *interj.* an Irish minced oath, from *begad* = by God.

bedaggle, *bi-dag'l*, *v.t.* to soil by dragging along the wet ground.

bedarken, *bi-därk'n*, *v.t.* to cover with darkness.

bedash, *bi-dash'*, *v.t.* to bespatter with water.

bedaub, *bi-dawb'*, *v.t.* to daub over or smear.

bedawin. Same as **bedouin**.

bedaze, *bi-dāz'*, **bedazzle**, *bi-daz'l*, *vs.t.* to dazzle or overpower by any strong light.—*pa.ps.* **bedazz'led**, **bedazed**, stupefied, besotted.—*n.* **bedazz'lement**.

bede. Same as **bead**, a prayer.

bedeafen, *bi-def'n*, *v.t.* to make deaf : to stun.

bedeck, *bi-dek'*, *v.t.* to deck or ornament.

bedeguar, *bed'i-gär*, *n.* a soft spongy gall found on the branches of sweet-brier and other roses, called also the sweet-brier sponge. [Fr. *bédeguar*—Pers. and Ar. *bādā-war*, lit. wind-brought.]

bedel, **bedell**, old spellings of **beadle**, still used at Oxford and Cambridge.

bedel, *bē'dl*, *n.* (*Bridges*) app. for **bevel**, i.e. *bevel-wheel*.

bedesman. Same as **beadsman**.

bedevil, *bi-dev-l*, *v.t.* to throw into confusion : to play the devil with : to torment : to treat with devilish malignity : to possess as a devil, to be devil-rid.—*pr.p.* **bedev'illing** ; *pa.t.* and *pa.p.* **bedev'illed**.—*n.* **bedev'ilment**.

bedew, *bi-dū'*, *v.t.* to moisten gently, as with dew.

bedide, *bi-dīd'*, (*Spens.*). Same as **bedyed**.

bedight, *bi-dīt'*, *v.t.* (*arch.* or *poet.*) to equip, array, furnish, adorn.—*pa.t.* and *pa.p.* **bedight'**. [Pfx. *be-*, and **dight**.]

bedim, *bi-dim'*, *v.t.* to make dim or dark :—*pr.p.* **bedimm'ing** ; *pa.t.* and *pa.p.* **bedimmed'**.—*n.* and *adj.* **bedimm'ing**.

bedizen, *bi-dīz'n*, **bi-diz'n**, *v.t.* to dress gaudily.—*adj.* **bediz'ened**.—*n.* **bediz'enment**.

bedlam, *bed'lam*, *n.* an asylum for lunatics : a madhouse : a place of uproar : (*obs.*) a madman.—*adj.* fit for a madhouse.—*ns.* **bed'lamism**, anything characteristic of madness ; **bed'lamite**, a madman. [From the priory St. Mary of *Bethlehem*, in London, afterwards a madhouse (Bethlehem Royal Hospital).]

Bedlington (terrier), *bed'ling-tən*, *n.* a long-bodied, lightly-built terrier, swiftest of its kind. [*Bedlington*, near Morpeth, where it was first bred.]

bedouin, **bedawin**, *bed'ōō-in*, *-ēn*, *bed'ä-win*, *-wēn*, *bed'win*, *n.* a tent-dwelling nomad Arab (properly *pl.*). [Fr. *bédouin*—Ar. *badäwin*, dwellers in the desert.]

bedraggle, *bi-drag'l*, *v.t.* to soil by dragging in the wet or dirt.—*adj.* **bedragg'led**. [See **draggle**.]

bedral, **bederal**, *bed'(ə-)rəl*, *n.* (*Scot.*) a beadle, church-officer, or minister's man : also a grave-digger. [**beadle**.]

bedrench, *bi-drensh'*, *v.t.* to drench or wet thoroughly.

bedrop, *bi-drop'*, *v.t.* to drop upon.—*adj.* **bedropped'**, **bedropt'**, sprinkled as with drops : strewn.

beduck, *bi-duk'*, *v.t.* to duck or plunge under water.

beduin, a form of **bedouin**.

bedung, *bi-dung'*, *v.t.* to manure : to befoul with dung.

bedust, *bi-dust'*, *v.t.* to cover with dust.

bedwarf, *bi-dwawrf'*, *v.t.* to make dwarfish.

bedye, *bi-dī'*, *v.t.* to dye or stain :—*pa.t.* and *pa.p.* **bedyed'** (*Spens.* **bedide'**, **bedyde'**).

bee, *bē*, *n.* a four-winged insect that makes honey : (chiefly *U.S.*) a gathering of persons to unite their labour for the benefit of one individual or family, or for some joint amusement, exercise or competition (as *quilting bee*, *husking bee*, *spelling bee* ; from the bee's habit of combined labour).—*ns.* **bee'-bread**, the pollen of flowers collected by bees as food for their young; **bee'-eat'er,** any bird of a brightly-plumaged family (Meropidae) nearly allied to the kingfishers, which feed on bees; **bee'-flower,** a flower pollinated by bees; **bee'-glue,** propolis; **bee'hive,** a case or box in which bees are kept, of straw-work, wood, etc. (**beehive house, tomb,** an ancient domed house, tomb, like an old-fashioned beehive); **bee'house; bee'keeper; bee'keeping; bee'-kite,** the honey-buzzard; **bee'-line,** the most direct road, like the honey-laden bee's way home; **bee'-master,** a beekeeper; **bee'-moth,** a moth whose larvae are very destructive to young bees; **bee'-or'chis,** an orchid whose flower resembles a bee; **bee'-skep,** a bee hive, properly of straw; **bees'wax,** the wax secreted by bees and used by them in constructing their cells.—*v.t.* to polish with beeswax.—**bees'-wing,** a filmy crust of tartar formed in port and some other wines after long keeping.—*adj.* **bees'-winged,** so old as to show beeswing.—**a bee in one's bonnet,** a whimsical or crazy fancy on some point. [O.E. *béo;* Ger. *biene.*]

bee, *bē, n.* the second letter of the alphabet (B).

beech, *bēch, n.* a common forest tree of the genus *Fagus* with smooth silvery bark: extended to the kindred genus *Nothofagus* and to many trees not related.—*n.* **beech'-drops,** cancer-root, an American orobanchaceous plant parasitic on beech roots. —*adj.* **beech'en.**—*ns.* **beech-fern,** a fern of the polypody family (a mistranslation of Phegopteris; from Gr. *phēgos,* a kind of oak); **beech'-mar'ten,** the stone-marten; **beech'-mast,** the mast or nuts of the beech-tree, which yield a valuable oil; **beech'-oil.** [O.E. *boece, béce;* Ger. *buche,* L. *fāgus,* Gr. *phēgos* (oak).]

beef, *bēf, n.* the flesh of the ox as food: extended to that of some other animals, as the horse: muscle: vigorous muscular force: (*arch.*) an ox, esp. one fattened for the butcher (*pl.* in this sense **beefs, beeves,** *bēvz*).—*adj.* of beef.—*adj.* **beef'-brained,** stupid.—*ns.* **beef'-brew'is; beef'eater,** an ox-bird: a consumer of beef: a yeoman of the guard: a warder of the Tower of London (the form *buffetier* supposed to connect with *buffet* is not known); **beef'-ham; beef'steak,** a thick slice of beef for broiling or frying; **beef'tea,** stimulating rather than nutritious food for invalids, juice of beef strained off, after simmering in water.—*adj.* **beef'-witt'ed,** dull or heavy in wits: stupid.— *n.* **beef'-wood,** the wood of Casuarina and other trees.—*adj.* **beef'y,** like beef: fleshy, muscular: stolid. [O.Fr. *boef* (Fr. *bœuf*)—L. *bōs, bovis;* cf. Gr. *bous,* Gael. *bò,* Sans. *go,* O.E. *cú.*]

beegah. Same as **bigha.**

Beelzebub, *bi-el'zi-bub, n.* a form of Baal worshipped by the Philistines at Ekron: the prince of the evil spirits. [Heb. *ba'al z'būb,* fly-lord.]

been, *bēn,* sometimes *bin, pa.p.* of **be:** (*arch.*) *pres. infin.* and *pl. pres. indic.* of **be.**

beenah, *bē'nä, n.* a form of marriage (in Ceylon, etc.) in which the man goes to live with his wife's relatives and the children belong to her group. [Ar. *bīnah,* separate.]

beer, *bēr, n.* an alcoholic beverage made by fermentation from malted barley flavoured with hops: the generic name of malt liquor, including ale and porter.—*ns.* **beer'-barrel; beer'-bottle; beer'-engine, beer'-pump,** a machine for drawing beer up from the casks to the bar; **beer'-gar'den,** a garden with tables where beer and other refreshments may be had; **beer'-house,** a house where beer or malt liquors are sold; **beer'-iness; beer'-mon'ey,** money given to soldiers in lieu of beer and spirits.—*adj.* **beer'y,** of, or affected by, beer.—**beer and skittles,** idle enjoyment; **bitter beer,** pale ale, a highly hopped beer made from the very finest selected malt and hops (**mild** or **sweet** ale being of greater gravity or strength, and comparatively lightly hopped); **black beer,** a kind of beer made at Danzig, black and syrupy; **small beer,** weak beer: hence trifling things, as in the familiar phrase, *to think no small beer of oneself.* [O.E. *béor;* Ger. and Du. *bier,* O.N. *bjorr.*]

beer, bear, *bēr.* See **bere.**

beesome, *bē'sǝm, adj.* (*Shak.*) supposed to be for **bisson.**

beestings, *bēst'ingz, n.* the first milk drawn from a cow after calving. [O.E. *býsting, béost;* Ger. and Du. *biest.*]

beet, *bēt, n.* a plant (*Beta*) of the goosefoot family, with a carrot-shaped succulent root, used as food and as a source of sugar.—*ns.* **beet'-fly,** a fly whose larvae are injurious to beet and mangel-wurzel; **beet'root,** the root of the beet plant; **beet'-sugar.** [O.E. *béte*—L. *bēta.*]

beet, bete, *bēt, v.t.* (*obs.* except *dial.*) to improve: to mend (esp. a fire): to relieve, assuage.—*n.* **beet'mister** (*Scott,* -master), a help in need. [O.E. *bétan;* cf. *bót,* **boot,** 2.]

beetle, *bē'tl, n.* any insect of the Coleoptera, an order in which the fore-wings are reduced to hard and horny covers for the hind-wings.—*v.i.* (first found in *Shak.*) to jut: to overhang.—*adj.* (always applied to brows) overhanging, scowling.— *adj.* **beet'le-browed,** with overhanging or prominent brows.—*n.* **beet'le-crusher** (*slang*), a big heavy foot or boot: a policeman: an infantryman.— *adjs.* **beet'le-eyed,** blind; **beet'ling,** jutting: prominent: overhanging.—**black beetle,** the cockroach, not a beetle. [M.E. *bityl*—O.E. *bitula, bitela—bītan,* to bite; the connexion of beetle brows with the insect is not accepted by all.]

beetle, *bē'tl, n.* a heavy wooden mallet used for driving wedges, crushing or beating down paving-stones, or the like: a wooden pestle-shaped utensil for mashing potatoes, beating linen, etc.—*n.* **bee'tlehead,** a heavy, stupid fellow.—*adj.* **bee'tle-headed.** [O.E. *bietl—béatan,* to beat.]

beeves, *bēvz, n.pl.* cattle, oxen. [See **beef.**]

befall, *bi-fawl', v.t.* (or *v.i.* with *dat.*) to fall or happen to: to occur to.—*v.i.* to happen or come to pass: (*Spens.*) to befit: to fall in one's way:—*pr.p.* **befall'ing;** *pa.t.* **befell';** *pa.p.* **befall'en** (*Spens.* **befeld').** [O.E. *bef(e)allan;* see **fall.**]

befana, beffana, *be-fä'nä, n.* an Epiphany gift. [It. *La Befana,* a toy-bringing old woman, a personification of Epiphany, Gr. *epiphaneia.*]

befit, *bi-fit', v.t.* to be fitting, or suitable to: to beseem.—*v.i.* to be right:—*pr.p.* **befitt'ing;** *pa.p.* **befitt'ed.**—*adj.* **befitt'ing.**—*adv.* **befitt'ingly.** [Pfx. *be-,* and **fit.**]

beflower, *bi-flow'ǝr, v.t.* to cover or besprinkle with flowers.

beflum, *bi-flum', v.t.* (*Scott*) to befool, cajole. [Cf. **flummery.**]

befoam, *bi-fōm', v.t.* to bespatter or cover with foam.

befog, *bi-fog', v.t.* to envelop in fog: to obscure.

befool, *bi-fool', v.t.* to make a fool of, or deceive: to treat as a fool.

before, *bi-fōr', prep.* in front of: ahead of: in presence or sight of: under the consideration or cognisance of: previous to: previous to the expiration of: in preference to: superior to.—*adv.* in front: sooner: earlier: in the past: formerly.— *conj.* previous to the time when (sometimes with *that*).—*adj.* (*Shak.*) previous.—*adv.* **before'hand,** before the time: in advance or anticipation: by way of preparation: in advance of one's needs. —*adj.* **before'-men'tioned.**—*adv.* **before'time,** in former time.—**be beforehand with,** to forestall (a person); **before Christ** (*abbrev.* **B.C.**), before the date formerly assigned to the birth of Christ (corresponding to the year 753 in Roman reckoning);**beforehand with the world,** comfortably provided for; **before the wind,** in the direction in which the wind is blowing, and hence helped along by it. [O.E. *beforan.* See **fore.**]

befortune, *bi-for'tūn, v.t.* (*Shak.*) to happen to, to befall.

befoul, *bi-fowl', v.t.* to make foul: to soil.

befriend, *bi-frend', v.t.* to act as a friend to: to favour.

befringe, *bi-frinj', v.t.* to adorn with fringes.

befuddle, *bi-fud'l, v.t.* to reduce to a fuddled condition.

beg. Same as **bey.**

Neutral vowels in unaccented syllables : el'ǝ-mǝnt, in'fǝnt, ran'dǝm

beg, *beg*, *v.t.* to ask alms or charity, esp. habitually : to sit up on the hind quarters, as a dog for a reward.—*v.t.* to ask earnestly : to beseech : to pray : to take unwarrantedly for granted (esp. *to beg the question*—to fall into the fallacy of *petitio principii*, assuming what is to be proved as part of the would-be proof) :—*pr.p.* **begg'ing**; *pa.t.* and *pa.p.* **begged** (*begd*).—*n.* **beggar** (*beg'ər*), one who begs : one who lives by begging : (hyperbolically) one who is indigent : a mean fellow : a poor fellow : often used playfully and even affectionately.—*v.t.* to reduce to beggary : to exhaust or impoverish : (*fig.*) to go beyond the resources of, as of description.—*ns.* **begg'ardom**, the fraternity of beggars; **begg'arliness.**—*adj.* **begg'arly**, poor : mean : worthless.—*adv.* meanly.—*ns.* **begg'ar-man**; **begg'ar-my-neigh'bour**, a game that goes on till one has gained all the others' cards; **begg'ary**, extreme poverty.—*n.* and *adj.* **begg'ing.**—*n.* **begg'ing-lett'er**, a letter soliciting alms or subscriptions.—*adv.* **begg'ingly.**—**beg off**, to obtain another's release through entreaty : to seek remission of some penalty or liability; **beg for a fool** (*obs.*), to sue for the guardianship of, and administration of the estate of, on grounds of mental deficiency; **go a-begging**, to be in want of a purchaser, occupant, etc. [Perh. from **beghard** (q.v.), the verb being a back-formation.]

begad, *bi-gad'*, **begar**, *bi-gär'* (*Shak.*), *interjs.* minced oaths for **by God.**

began, *bi-gan'*, *pa.t.* of **begin.**

begem, *bi-jem'*, *v.t.* to adorn, as with gems.

beget, *bi-get'*, *v.t.* to produce or cause : to generate (commonly of the father) : to produce as an effect, to cause :—*pr.p.* **begett'ing**; *pa.t.* **begot'** (*arch.* **begat'**); *pa.p.* **begott'en** (or **begot'**).—*n.* **begett'er**, one who begets : a father : the agent that occasions or originates anything. [O.E. *begitan*, to acquire; see **get.**]

beghard, *beg'ärd*, *n.* in Flanders or elsewhere from the 13th century, a man living a monastic life without vows and with power to return to the world. [Flem. *beggaert;* origin doubtful; cf. **béguine.**]

begift, *bi-gift'*, *v.t.* to present with gifts.

begild, *bi-gild'*, *v.t.* to gild : to cover or overlay with gold-leaf.

begin, *bi-gin'*, *v.i.* to come into being : to take rise : to perform the first act : to open : to have an opening.—*v.t.* to perform the first act of : to enter on : to start :—*pr.p.* **beginn'ing**; *pa.t.* **began'** (now rarely **begun'**); *pa.p.* **begun'**.—*ns.* **beginne'r** (*Spens.*), beginning; **beginn'er**, one who begins : one who is in the early stages of learning or doing anything; **beginn'ing**, origin : a start : an entering upon action : an opening or first part : a rudiment.—*adj.* **beginn'ingless.** [O.E. *beginnan* (less usual than *onginnan*), from pfx. *be-*, and *ginnan*, to begin.]

begird, *bi-gərd'*, *v.t.* to gird or bind with a girdle : to surround or encompass :—*pa.t.* and *pa.p.* **begirt'** (or **begird'ed**). [O.E. *begyrdan.* See **gird.**]

beglerbeg, *beg'lər-beg*, *n.* formerly, the governor of a Turkish province, in rank next to the grand vizier. [Turk., lit. bey of beys.]

begloom, *bi-glōōm'*, *v.t.* to render gloomy.

begnaw, *bi-naw'*, *v.t.* to gnaw or bite, to eat away.

bego, *bi-gō'*, *v.t.* to beset (obs. except in compound **woe-begone**). [O.E. *begán*, to beset, surround.]

begone, *bi-gon'*, *interj.* be gone : be off: get away. [**be gone.**]

Begonia, *bi-gō'ni-ä*, *n.* a genus (giving name to a family **Begoniä'ceae**) of tropical, especially American, plants cultivated in greenhouses for their pink flowers and their remarkable unequal-sided and often coloured leaves—elephant's ears, angel's wings. [Named from Michel Bégon (1638-1710), patron of botany.]

begored, *bi-gōrd'*, *adj.* (*Spens.*) besmeared with gore.

begorra, **begorrah**, *bi-gor'ä*, *interj.* an Anglo-Irish modification of **by God.**

begot, *bi-got'*, **begotten**, *bi-got'n.* See **beget.**

begrime, *bi-grīm'*, *v.t.* to soil with grime.

begrudge, *bi-gruj'*, *v.t.* to grudge : to envy the possession of.

beguile, *be-gīl'*, *v.t.* to cheat or deceive : to pass with diversion of attention from anything tedious or painful : to wile into some course.—*ns.* **beguile'ment**; **beguil'er.**—*adv.* **beguil'ingly.** [See **guile.**]

béguine, **beguine** *bāg'ēn*, *beg'in*, *n.* a member of a sisterhood living as nuns but without vows, and with power to return to the world :—*masc.* **béguin**, **beguin** (*bāg-an²*, *beg'in*), a beghard.—*n.* **béguinage** (*bāg'ēn-äzh*, *beg'in-ij*), an establishment for béguines. [Fr. *béguine;* see **beghard.**]

begum, *bē'gum*, *n.* a Moslem princess or lady of rank. [Urdu *begam;* cf. **beg, bey.**]

begun, *bi-gun'*, *pa.p.* (sometimes *pa.t.*) of **begin.**

begunk, *bi-gungk'*, *v.t.* (*Scot.*) to trick : to befool : to jape : to jilt.—*n.* a trick : a befooling.

behalf, *bi-häf'*, *n.* favour or benefit : cause : sake, account : part. [M.E. *behalve*—O.E. *be healfe*, by the side. See **half.**]

behappen, *bi-hap'n*, *v.t.* (*Spens.*) to happen to.

behave, *bi-hāv'*, *v.t.* to bear or carry : to wield, manage, conduct (commonly with *self*).—*v.i.* to conduct oneself, also to conduct oneself well : to act :—*pa.t.* and *pa.p.* **behaved'.**—*n.* **behaviour** (*bi-hāv'yər*), conduct : manners or deportment, esp. good manners : general course of life : treatment of others : mode of action : (*physiol.*) response to stimulus.—*ns.* **behav'iourism**, a psychological method which substitutes for the subjective element of consciousness, the objective one of observation of conduct in other beings under certain stimuli; **behav'iourist**, an upholder of behaviourism.—**upon one's best behaviour**, so placed that watchfulness over one's conduct is called for. [Pfx. **be-**, and **have**; O.E. had *behabban*, to detain, restrain.]

behead, *bi-hed'*, *v.t.* to cut off the head of.—*ns.* **behead'al** (*rare*); **behead'ing.**

beheld, *bi-held'*, *pa.t.* and *pa.p.* of **behold.**

behemoth, *bē'i-moth*, *bi-hē'moth*, *n.* an animal described in the book of Job, usually taken to be the hippopotamus : a great beast. [Heb. *b'hēmōth*, *pl.* of *b'hēmāh*, beast, or a Hebraistic form of the Egyptian *p-ehe-mout*, water-ox.]

behest, *bi-hest'*, *n.* (*obs.*) promise : command : charge. [O.E. *behǣs*, a promise. See **hest.**]

behight, *bi-hīt'*, **behote**, *bi-hōt'*, *v.t.* (*obs.*) to vow : to promise : (*Spens.*) to speak to, to ordain, to adjudge, to name :—*pa.t.* and *pa.p.* **behight** or **behote.** [O.E. *behátan*, to vow—*be-* and *hátan*, to be called, to call, to command. For the confusion of tenses and voices and for reduplication, see **hight.**]

behind, *bi-hīnd'*, *prep.* at the back of (in place, or as support) : in the place or state left by : at the far side of : after (in time, rank, order) : in inferiority to, or less far advanced than.—*adv.* at the back, in the rear : backward : past.—*n.* the hinder part : (*vulg.*) the rear, rump.—*adj.* and *adv.* **behind'-hand**, being behind : tardy : ill-provided : in arrears.—*adj.* **behind'-door'**, surreptitious, clandestine. [O.E. *behindan;* Ger. *hinten;* see **hind** (3).]

behold, *bi-hōld'*, *v.t.* to look upon : to contemplate : to view, see : (*Spens.*) perhaps, to restrain.—*v.i.* to look :—*pa.t.* and *pa.p.* **beheld'.**—*imper.* or *interj.* see : lo : observe.—*adj.* **behold'en**, bound in gratitude : under an obligation.—*n.* **behold'er**, one who beholds : an onlooker.—*adj.* **behold'ing** (*Shak.*), beholden.—*n.* (*Shak.*) sight, contemplation. [O.E. *behaldan* (W.S. *behealdan*), to hold, observe—pfx. *be-*, and *h(e)aldan*, to hold.]

behoof, *bi-hōōf'*, *n.* benefit : convenience. [O.E. *behóf.*]

behote, **behot.** See **behight.**

behove, **behoove**, *bi-hōōv'* (unhistorically *bi-hōv'*), *v.t.* and *v.i.* to be fit, right, or necessary—now only used impersonally with *it*.—*adjs.* **behove'ful**, **behove'ly**, useful : profitable. [O.E. *behófian*, to be fit, to stand in need of.]

behowl, *bi-howl'*, *v.t.* to howl at (Warburton's emendation for 'beholds' in *Midsummer Night's Dream*, V. ii. 2).

---

fāte, fär, ȧsk; mē, hər (her); *mīne; mōte; mūte; mōōn; dhen* (then)

beige, *bāzh, n.* a woollen fabric of undyed wool.—*adj.* greyish: (*recently*) buff with a slight suffusion of pink. [Fr.]

bein, *bēn, adj.* and *adv.* (*Scot.*) comfortable: well off: well found: (*slang*) good.—*n.* bein′ness. [M.E. *bene,* of dubious origin; O.N. *beinn,* L. *bene,* Fr. *bien,* all offer difficulties.]

being, *bē′ing, n.* existence: substance: essence: any person or thing existing.—*adj.* existing, present.—*adj.* bē′ingless.—*n.* bē′ingness. [Verbal noun and *pr.p.* of **be.**]

beinked, *bē-ingkt′, adj.* smeared with ink.

bejade, *bi-jād′, v.t.* (*obs.*) to tire out.

bejant. See **bajan.**

bejesuit, *bi-jez′ū-it, v.t.* to initiate or seduce into Jesuitism.

bejewel, *bi-jōō′əl, v.t.* to deck with jewels.

bekah, *bē′kä, n.* (*B.*) a half-shekel (4.39 drams avoirdupois). [Heb.]

bekiss, *bi-kis′, v.t.* to cover with kisses.

beknave, *bi-nāv′, v.t.* to call or treat as a knave.

beknown, *bi-nōn′, adj.* (*arch.* or *dial.*) known.

bel, *bel, n.* a measure for comparing intensity of noises, electric currents, etc., the number of bels being the logarithm to the base 10 of the ratio of one to the other. [From Graham *Bell* (1847-1922), telephone inventor.]

belabour, *bi-lā′bər, v.t.* to beat soundly.

bel-accoyle, *bel-a-koil′, n.* (*Spens.*) favourable or kind reception. [O.Fr. *bel acoil,* fair welcome. See **accoil.**]

belace, *bi-lās′, v.t.* to adorn with lace.

belamoure, bellamoure, *bel-a-mowr′, n.* (*Spens.*) a beloved one: (*Spens.*) some kind of flower. [Fr. *bel amour,* fair love.]

belamy, *bel′a-mē, n.* (*Spens.*) a good or intimate friend. [Fr. *bel ami,* fair friend.]

belate, *bi-lāt′, v.t.* to make late: to retard.—*adj.* **belāt′ed,** coming too late: out of date: benighted. —*n.* belāt′edness.

belaud, *bi-lawd′, v.t.* to praise up.

belay, *bi-lā′, v.t.* to set, overlay, with ornament: to beset: to besiege: to waylay: to make fast: to secure by a turn about a cleat, belaying-pin, point of rock, etc.—*interj.* avast: hold.—*n.* a turn of a rope in belaying.—*n.* **belay′ing-pin,** a pin for belaying ropes about. [O.E. *belecgan;* Ger. *belegen,* Du. *beleggen.* See **lay.**]

belch, *belch, belsh, v.t.* and *v.i.* to void (wind) from the stomach by the mouth: to eject violently: to cast up, as of the smoke from a volcano or a cannon. —*n.* eructation. [O.E. *bealcian;* Du. *balken.*]

belcher, *bel′chər, n.* a dark-blue neckerchief with blue-centred white spots. [From Jim *Belcher,* a famous English boxer.]

beldam, beldame, *bel′dəm, n.* (*obs.*) a grandmother or remoter ancestress: an old woman (formerly a term of address): a hag: a furious woman. [Formed from **dam,** mother, and *bel-,* used like *grand-*—Fr. *bel, belle,* but not a French use.]

beleaguer, *bi-lēg′ər, v.t.* to lay siege to.—*n.* **be-, leag′uerment.** [Du. *belegeren,* to besiege—*be-,* and *leger,* camp. See **leaguer.**]

belee, *bi-lē′, v.t.* (*Shak.*) to place on the lee-side of something.

belemnite, *bel′əm-nīt, n.* a fossil pointed like a dart, being the internal shell of cephalopod, formerly known as *thunder-bolt, thunder-stone, elf-bolt.* [Gr. *belemnītēs—belemnon,* a dart.]

belfry, *bel′fri, n.* the part of a steeple or tower in which bells are hung: a bell-tower, sometimes standing apart: a movable wooden tower, used in the Middle Ages in attacking a fortification.—*adj.* **bel′fried,** having a belfry. [Orig. and properly a watch-tower, from O.Fr. *berfroi*—M.H.G. *berchfrit, bergan,* to protect—*frid, frit,* a tower.]

belga, *bel′gä, n.* the currency unit of Belgium (from 1926), value five paper francs. [L. *Belga,* a Belgian.]

belgard, *bel-gärd′, n.* (*Spens.*) a fair or kind look. [It. *bel guardo,* lovely look.]

Belgian, *bel′jən, adj.* of Belgium, a country of Europe.—*n.* a native or citizen of Belgium.—*adj.* **Belgic,** of the *Belgae,* who anciently possessed

Belgium, or of Belgium.—**Belgian hare,** a harelike breed of domestic rabbit. [L. *Belga, Belgicus.*]

Belgravian, *bel-grā′vi-ən, adj.* belonging to *Belgravia* (a fashionable part of London), or to fashionable life: aristocratic.

Belial, *bēl′yəl, n.* the devil: in Milton, one of the fallen angels. Not a proper name in O.T. [Heb. *b′li-ya′al,—b′li,* not, *ya′al,* use.]

belie, *bi-lī′, v.t.* to give the lie to: to speak falsely of: to present in a false character: to counterfeit: to be false to: falsify: (*Shak.*) to fill with lies: to fail to fulfil or justify:—*pr.p.* bely′ing; *pa.t.* and *pa.p.* **belied′.** [O.E. *be-,* and **lie.**]

believe, *bi-lēv′, v.t.* to regard as true: to accept as true what is said by.—*v.i.* to be firmly persuaded: to have faith (with *in, on*): to judge.—*n.* **belief′,** persuasion of the truth of anything: faith: the opinion or doctrine believed: intuition, natural judgment (as used by some philosophers).—*adjs.* **belief′less; believ′able.**—*n.* **believ′er,** one who believes: a professor of Christianity, Mohammedanism, or whatever religion is relevant.—*adj.* **believ′ing,** trustful: having belief.—*adv.* **believ′ingly.—the belief** (*arch.*), the Apostles' Creed; **make believe** (see **make**). [M.E. *bileven* —*bi-, be,* and *leven,* superseding O.E. *gelēfan.*]

belike, *bi-līk′, adv.* (*arch.*) probably: perhaps. [O.E. pfx. *be-,* and **like.**]

belittle, *bi-lit′l, v.t.* to make small: to cause to appear small, to depreciate or disparage.—*n.* **belitt′lement.**—*adj.* **belitt′ling.** [Pfx. *be-,* and **little.**]

belive, *bi-līv′, adv.* (*arch.* and *Scot.*) with speed: promptly. [M.E. *bi life*—*be, bi,* by, *life,* dat. of *lif,* **life.**]

bell, *bel, n.* an instrument for giving a ringing sound, typically a hollow vessel of metal with flared mouth struck by a tongue or clapper, but taking many other forms, as a hollow sphere containing a loose ball, a shallow cup, a tube, or a coiled spring struck by a hammer: a corolla shaped like an ordinary bell: the body of a Corinthian or Composite capital, without the surrounding foliage: anything bell-shaped, as in diving-bell, bell-glass, the outward-turned orifice of a wind-instrument, etc.: the sound of a bell: a signal or intimation by bell: (*naut.*) a stroke or double stroke of a bell to indicate the number of half-hours of the watch that have elapsed—'two bells', 'three bells', etc., meaning that there are two, three, etc. half-hours past—the watch of four hours is eight bells.— *v.i.* to ring.—*v.t.* to furnish with a bell, esp. in **to bell the cat,** to take the leading part in any hazardous movement, from the ancient fable of the mice who proposed to hang a warning bell round the cat's neck.—*n.* **bell-bird,** the campanero: (*Australia*) a honey-eater (Manorina) with a tinkling note: also a thickhead (Oreoica) with a clear bell-like call: elsewhere, other birds with bell-like notes.—*adj.* **bell′-bottomed,** widening towards the ankle.—*ns.* **bell′-boy** (*U.S.*), a hotel attendant; **bell′-buoy,** a buoy carrying a bell, rung by the waves; **bell′cote** (*archit.*), an ornamental structure made to contain one or two bells, and often crowned by a small spire; **bell′-crank,** a lever having two arms, usu. at right angles, with a common fulcrum at their junction; **bell′-flower,** a campanula; **bell′-founder,** one who casts bells; **bell′-glass,** a bell-shaped glass for sheltering flowers, etc.; **bell′-heather,** heath; **bell′hanger,** one who hangs and repairs bells; **bell′man,** one who rings a bell, esp. on the streets, before making public announcements: a town-crier; **bell′-metal,** the metal of which bells are made—an alloy of copper and tin; **bell′-pull,** a cord or handle used in ringing a bell; **bell′-punch,** a ticket-punch containing a signal-bell; **bell′push,** a button used in ringing an electric or spring bell; **bell′-ringer,** one who rings a bell on stated occasions: a performer with musical hand-bells; **bell′-ringing**; **bell′-rope,** the rope by which a bell is rung.— *adj.* **bell′-shaped.**—*ns.* **bell′-tent,** a bell-shaped tent; **bell′-tower,** a tower built to contain one or more bells, a campanile; **bell′-turret,** a turret containing a chamber for a bell, usually crowned with a spire; **bell'-wether,** the leading sheep of a flock, on whose neck a bell is hung : (*fig.*) any loud, turbulent fellow, a ringleader; **bell'wort,** any plant of the *Campanulaceae* : (*U.S.*) the liliaceous genus *Uvularia.*—**bear, or carry off, the bell,** to have or gain the first place; **bell, book, and candle,** a phrase popularly used in reference to a form of excommunication ending, 'Do to (shut) the book, quench the candle, ring the bell'. [O.E. *belle*; *cog.* with Du. *bel.*]

bell, *bel,* n. a bubble formed in a liquid. [Ety. dub.; cf. Du. *bel,* a bubble in water, perh. from L. *bulla,* bubble in water.]

bell, *bel, v.i.* to bellow, roar : to utter loudly.—*n.* the cry of a stag at rutting-time. [O.E. *bellan,* to roar; cf. Ger. *bellen.*]

belladonna, *bel'ä-don'ä, n.* the deadly nightshade or dwale (*Atropa Belladonna*), all parts of which are narcotic and poisonous from the presence of atropine : the drug prepared from it.—**belladonna lily,** a pink-flowered South African Amaryllis. [It. *bella donna,* fair lady; one property of belladonna is to enlarge the pupil of the eye.]

bellarmine, *bel'är-mēn,* a greybeard, or large jug with a big belly, decorated with a bearded face, said to represent Cardinal *Bellarmine,* made in mockery by Dutch Protestants.

Bellatrix, *bel-ā'triks* (L. -*ā'treks*), *n.* a second-magnitude star, eastmost in Orion's belt. [L. *bellātrix,* female warrior.]

belle, *bel, n.* a handsome woman : the chief beauty of a place : a fair lady generally.—*n.* **belle-de-nuit** (-*da-nwē*; Fr.; night beauty), the marvel of Peru. [Fr. *belle* (*fem.*)—L. *bellus, -a, -um.*]

belles-lettres, *bel-let'r', n.pl.* polite or elegant literature, including poetry, fiction, criticism, aesthetics, etc.—*n.* **bellet(t)'rist.**—*adjs.* **belletris'tic, -al.** [Fr., lit. fine letters.]

belleter, *bel'a-tar, n.* a bell-founder. [For *bell-yetter*—bell, and O.E. *géotan,* to pour.]

bellibone, *bel'i-bōn, n.* (*Spens.*) a beautiful and good woman. [Apparently Fr. *belle* (*et*) *bonne.*]

bellicose, *bel'i-kōs, adj.* contentious, war-like.—*adv.* **bell'icosely.**—*n.* **bellicosity** (-*kos'i-ti*). [L. *bellicōsus.*]

bellied, *bel'lid, adj.* with a belly, esp. a big belly, pot-bellied : bulging : puffed out. [See **belly.**]

belligerent, *bel-ij'ar-ant, adj.* waging war : recognised legally as waging war.—*n.* a party or person waging war : one recognised as so doing.—*n.* **bellig'erency.** [L. *belligerāre,* to wage war—*bellum,* war, *gerēre,* to wage.]

Bellona, *bel-ō'nä, n.* the Roman goddess of war—hence (*fig.*) a woman of great spirit and vigour.

bellow, *bel'ō, v.i.* to roar like a bull : to make any violent outcry.—*v.t.* to roar out.—*n.* the roar of a bull : any deep sound or cry.—*n.* **bell'ower.** [M.E. *belwen*; O.E. *bylgian,* to roar; cf. bell (3).]

bellows, *bel'ōz,* or (old-fashioned) *bel'us, n.pl.* (often treated as *sing.*) an instrument for producing a current of air to blow up a fire, or sound an organ, accordion, etc. : a contrivance for expanding a photographic camera or the like : (*fig.*) that which fans the fire of hatred, jealousy, etc. : the lungs.—*n.* **bell'ows-fish,** the trumpet-fish. [Same as belly; the sing. did not survive the 15th century.]

belly, *bel'i, n.* the part of the body between the breast and the thighs, containing the bowels : the stomach, as the receptacle of the food : the bowels proper : the womb or uterus : the interior of anything : the bulging part of anything, as a bottle, or any concave or hollow surface, as of a sail : the front or under surface, as opposed to the *back* : in a violin or a leaf the upper surface : a sound-board.—*adj.* ventral, abdominal : (*theol.*) belonging to the flesh, carnal.—*v.i.* to swell or bulge out.—*ns.* **bell'y-ache'; bell'y-band,** a saddle-girth : a band fastened to the shafts of a vehicle, and passing under the belly of the horse drawing it; **bell'yful,** a sufficiency; **bell'y-god,** one who makes a god of his belly, a glutton.—*n.* and *adj.* **bell'ying.** —*n.* **bell'y-timber,** (*arch.*) provisions. [M.E. *bali, bely*—O.E. *bælig, belig, bælg, belg,* bag.]

belomancy, *bel'ō-man-si, n.* divination by means of arrows. [Gr. *belos,* a dart, *manteiä,* divination.]

belong, *bi-long', v.i.* to go along (with) : to pertain (to) : to be the property (of) : to be part or appendage (of), or in any way connected (with) : to be specially the business (of) : to be a native or inhabitant, or member (of)—in all senses usually with *to.*—*n.pl.* **belong'ings,** matters connected with any person : possessions : persons connected, relatives : accessories. [M.E. *bi-, be-longen,* intens. of *longen,* with pfx. *be-.* See long (2).]

belove, *bi-luv', v.t.* (*obs.* except in *pa.p.,* **beloved,** *bi-luvd'*), to love.—*adj.* **beloved** (*bi-luv'id*) much loved, very dear—often compounded with *well-, best-,* etc.—*n.* (*bi-luv'id*) one who is much loved.—*adj.* **belov'ing** (*Shak.*), loving. [Pfx. *be-* and love.]

below, *bi-lō', prep.* beneath in place, rank or quality : underneath : not worthy of.—*adv.* in a lower place : downstairs : (*fig.*) on earth, or in hell.—*adj.* and *adv.* **below'stairs.** [Pfx. *be-,* and adj. **low.**]

belt, *belt, n.* a girdle, zone, or band : a band of flexible material used to transmit motion in machinery, or otherwise : a broad stripe of anything, different in colour or material : that which confines or restrains : (*geog.*) a zone of country, a district : a strait.—*v.t.* to surround with a belt, or to invest formally with one, as in conferring knighthood: to encircle : to thrash with a belt.—*adj.* **belt'ed,** wearing a belt, of a knight : marked with a belt.—*n.* **belt'ing—**hit, etc., **below the belt,** to hit, etc., an opponent's body lower than the waist (forbidden in some sports) : hence (*fig.*) to deliver a mean blow, attack unfairly; **hold the belt,** to hold the championship in wrestling, boxing, or the like. [O.E. *belt*—L. *balteus.*]

Beltane, *bel'tān, n.* an ancient Celtic festival, held in the beginning of May, when bonfires were lighted on the hills : the first day of May (O.S.)—one of the four old quarter-days of Scotland, the others being Lammas, Hallowmas, and Candlemas.—Also *adj.* [Gael. *bealltainn, beilteine,* apparently bright fire. It has nothing to do with Baal.]

beluga, *bi-lōō'gä, n.* the white whale, one of the dolphin family, closely allied to the narwhal, found in Arctic seas : a great Russian sturgeon—*Acipenser huso.* [Russ. *belyi,* white.]

belvedere, *bel'vi-dēr, n.* a pavilion or raised turret or lantern on the top of a house, open for the view, or to admit the breeze : a summer-house on an eminence. [It. *belvedere*—*bel,* beautiful, *vedere,* to see.]

bema, *bē'mä, n.* the tribune or rostrum from which Athenian orators made their speeches; hence the apse or chancel of a basilica. [Gr. *bēma,* a step.]

bemad, *bi-mad', v.t.* to madden.

bemaul, *bi-mawl', v.t.* to maul thoroughly.

bemazed, *bi-māzd', adj.* stupefied, bewildered.

Bembex, *bem'beks, n.* a genus of sand-wasps, noted for their loud buzz. [Gr. *bembix,* a buzzing insect.]

bemean, *bi-mēn', v.t.* to make mean, to lower or debase.

bemean, *bi-mēn', v.i.* (*obs.*) to signify.

bemire, *bi-mīr', v.t.* to soil with mire.—*adj.* **bemired.**

bemoan, *bi-mōn', v.t.* to lament, bewail : to pity.—*v.i.* to grieve.—*ns.* **bemoan'er; bemoan'ing.**

bemock, *bi-mok', v.t.* to mock at, to deride.

bemoil, *bi-moil', v.t.* (*Shak.*) to bemire, to bedraggle.

bemonster, *bi-mon'star, v.t.* to make monstrous : to regard or treat as a monster.

bemouth, *bi-mowdh', v.t.* to mouth about.

bemud, *bi-mud', v.t.* to bespatter with mud : to confuse.

bemuddle, *bi-mud'l, v.t.* to confuse or muddle completely.

bemuffle, *bi-muf'l, v.t.* to wrap or muffle up completely.

bemuse, *bi-mūz', v.t.* to put in confusion : stupefy.

ben, *ben, n.* a mountain peak. [Gael. *beinn,* oblique case of *beann.*]

ben, *ben, prep.* and *adv.* (*Scot.*) in or toward the inner or better, or vaguely another, apartment (of).—*n.* the inner or better apartment of a house, as opposed to the *but* or kitchen through which formerly one had generally to pass first.—**a but and a ben,** a two-roomed house; **but and ben,** out and in; **far ben,** on terms of great intimacy or favour; **live but and ben,** to live respectively in these rooms, in close neighbourhood with anyone. [M.E. *binne*—O.E. *binnan,* within.]

ben, *ben, n.* the winged seed of the horse-radish tree, *Moringa pterygosperma.*—*ns.* **ben′-nut; ben′-oil.** [Ar. *bān,* the ben-tree.]

bename, *bi-nām′, v.t.* to name, mention: to vow:—*pa.t.* and *pa.p.* **benamed′** (*arch.* **benempt′**). [O.E. *benemnan*—pfx. *be-* and *nemnan,* to name.]

bench, *bensh, bench, n.* a long seat or form with or without a back: a seat in a boat: a work-table or working-place: a judge's seat: the body or assembly of judges: a tribunal: an official seat: a level ledge or set-back in the slope of masonry or earthwork: (*Amer.*) a level tract between a river and neighbouring hills: a terrace.—*v.t.* to place on or furnish with benches.—*ns.* **bench′er,** a senior member of an inn of court; **bench′ership; bench′-hole,** (*Shak.*) a latrine; **bench′-mark,** a surveyor's mark cut on a rock, stone, or the like indicating a point of reference in levelling (from its horizontal line forming a bench for a levelling instrument); **bench′-warr′ant,** one issued by a judge rather than a justice or magistrate; **on the bench,** holding the office of a judge or bishop: officiating as judge; **raise to the bench,** to make a judge or bishop. [O.E. *benc; cog.* with Ger. and Du. *bank.*]

bend, *bend, v.t.* to constrain: to subject to tension: to brace: to string: to nerve: to tie: to force into (or out of) a curved or angled form: to curve: to bow, turn downwards: to dispose, incline: to aim: to direct: to deflect: to subdue: (*Scot.*) to drink hard at.—*v.i.* to curve: to stoop: to bow: to give way, yield: to turn: to incline: (*Scot.*) to drink hard (perh. from the phrase *bend the bicker,* turn up the cup, drink cup-out): (*pa.t.* and *pa.p.* **bent;** also **bend′ed).**—*n.* (*Spens.*) a strengthening band: a knot by which a line is tied to another, or to itself after passing through a ring, etc.: a band, strip: (*her.*) an ordinary bounded by two parallel lines crossing the shield from dexter chief to sinister base (**bend′-sin′ister** from sinister chief to dexter base), occupying a fifth of the shield, or a third if charged: half a butt of leather cut lengthwise: an act of bending: state of being bent: a bent thing: a place of bending: a bow or stoop: (*Shak.*) a directing of the eye: (*Scot.*) a pull of liquor, or a drinking bout: (in *pl.*) caisson disease.—*adj.* **bend′ed.**—*n.* **bend′er,** one who, or that which, bends: (*slang.*) a sixpence.—*n.* and *adj.* **bend′ing.**—*adv.* **bend′ingly.**—*n.* **bend′let** (*her.*), a half-width bend.—*adv.* **bend′wise** (*her.*), diagonally.—*adj.* **bend′y** (*her.*), divided into bends. —*n.* and *adj.* **bent** (see **bent).**—*n.* **bent′wood,** wood artificially curved for chair-making, etc.— Also *adj.* [O.E. *bendan,* to constrain, bind, fetter, string (as a bow), *bend,* bond, fetter.]

bend, *bend, n.* (*Spens.*). Same as **band** (2).

bene, *bēn, n.* (*arch.; Wordsworth*) a prayer: a boon. [O.E. *bēn.*]

bene, an old spelling of **been.**

beneath, *bi-nēth′, adv.* and *prep.* below: in a lower position so as to have overhead, or nearly so, or to be covered: inside, behind, at the back (of): at a lower level relatively to.—*prep.* in a manner unworthy the dignity of, unbecoming to.—*adj.* (*Shak.*) lower. [O.E. *beneothan.*]

benedicite, *ben-i-dis′i-ti* (L. *ben-e-dēk-i-te*), *interj.* bless you (an old form of greeting).—*n.* a blessing: a grace at table: the canticle beginning *Benedicite omnia opera* (All ye works of the Lord, bless ye) from *The Song of the Three Holy Children.* [L. *benedicite,* plur. imper. of *benedicere,* to bless— *bene,* well, *dicere,* to say, speak.]

Benedick, *ben′i-dik,* or (blunderingly) **Benedict,** -*dikt, n.* a common name for a newly married man, esp. one who has long held out against marriage— from *Benedick* in Shakespeare's *Much Ado about Nothing.*

benedict, *ben′i-dikt, adj.* blessed: benign.—*n.* **benedic′tion** (*-shn*), a blessing: a solemn invocation of the divine blessing on men or things: one pronounced at the end of a religious service: a brief and popular service in the Roman Catholic Church: grace before or after a meal: blessedness.—*adjs.* **benedic′tional; benedict′ive; benedict′ory.**— *n.* **Benedict′us,** the canticle of Zacharias (Luke, i. 68-79), used in the Roman and Anglican services. —*adj.* **benedight** (*-dit′; Longfellow*), blessed.— **apostolic benediction,** that at the end of 2 Cor. [L. *benedicere, -dictum*—*bene,* well, *dicere,* to say, speak.]

Benedictine, *ben′i-dik′tin, adj.* pertaining to St. *Benedict* of Nursia (480-543), or his monastic rule. —*n.* a monk or nun of the order founded by him at Monte Cassino: (*-tēn*) a cordial or liqueur resembling Chartreuse, distilled at Fécamp in Normandy—once distilled by Benedictine monks.

benefaction, *ben-i-fak′shon, n.* the act of doing good: a good deed done or benefit conferred: a grant or endowment.—*v.t.* **ben′efact,** to confer a benefit on.—*n.* **benefac′tor,** one who confers a benefit: one who leaves a legacy to an institution, a patron:—*fem.* **benefac′tress.**—*adj.* **benefac′tory.** [L. *benefactio, -ōnis; cf.* following words.]

benefic, *bi-nef′ik, adj.* kindly: benign: beneficent: (*astrol.*) favourable.—*n.* **benefice** (*ben′i-fis*), a church living, esp. with cure of souls: (*hist.*) a fief.—*adj.* **ben′eficed,** possessed of a benefice.—*n.* **beneficence** (*bi-nef′i-sons*), active goodness: kindness: charity: a beneficent gift.—*adjs.* **benef′icent; beneficential** (*-sen′shl*).—*adv.* **benef′icently.**— *adj.* **beneficial** (*ben-i-fish′l*), useful: advantageous: (*law*) enjoying the usufruct of property.—*n.* (*Spens.*) app., a letter of presentation to a benefice. —*adv.* **benefic′ially.**—*ns.* **benefic′ialness; beneficiary,** a holder of a benefice or a fief: one who receives a gift or advantage: one who enjoys or has the prospect of enjoying, any interest or estate held in trust by others. [L. *beneficus,* kindly, beneficent, *beneficium,* a service, benefit— *bene,* well, *facere,* to do.]

benefit, *ben′i-fit, n.* a kindness: a favour: any advantage, natural or other: a performance whose proceeds go to one of the company or other particular person or object: a right in the form of money or services enjoyed under insurance schemes. —*v.t.* to do good to.—*v.i.* to gain advantage (with *from,* or *by*):—*pr.p.* **ben′efiting;** *pa.t.* and *pa.p.* **ben′efited.**—**benefit of clergy** (see clergy); **benefit of inventory** (*Scots law*), an heir's privilege of securing himself against unlimited liability for his ancestor, by giving up within a year an inventory of his heritage or real estate, to the extent of which alone was he liable; **benefit of the doubt,** favourable judgment when culpability is uncertain; **benefit society,** a friendly society. [M.E. *benfet*—A.Fr. *benfet*—L. *benefactum.*]

Benelux, *ben′o-luks, n.* a name for *Be*lgium, the *Ne*therlands and *Lux*emburg.

benempt. See **bename.**

benet, *bi-net′, v.t.* to catch in a net, to ensnare.

benet, *ben′it, n.* an exorcist, the third of the four lesser orders in the Roman Catholic church. [O.Fr. *beneit*—L. *benedictus,* blessed.]

benevolence, *bi-nev′o-lans, n.* disposition to do good: an act of kindness: generosity: a gift of money, esp. for support of the poor: (*Eng. hist.*) a kind of forced loan or contribution, levied by kings without legal authority, first so called under Edward IV in 1473.—*adj.* **benev′olent,** charitable, generous, well disposed.—*adv.* **benev′olently.** [O.Fr. *benivolence* and L. *benevolentia.*]

Bengali, *ben-gaw′lē, adj.* of or belonging to *Bengal.* —*n.* a native of Bengal: the language of Bengal.— *n.* **Ben′gal-light,** a brilliant light, black sulphide of antimony, used as a shipwreck signal and to illuminate country at night.

benight, *bi-nīt′, v.t.* to involve in darkness: to cloud with disappointment.—*adj.* **benight′ed,** overtaken by night: involved in darkness, intellectual or moral: ignorant.—*v.t.* **benight′en,** to benight.—*ns.* **benight′ening; benight′er; be-**

night'ing (also *adj.*); **benight'ment.** [Pfx. *be-* and **night.**]

benign, *bi-nīn',* adj. favourable, esp. in astrology, as opposed to *malign* : gracious : kindly : (*med.*) of a mild type, as opposed to *malignant* : salubrious.— *n.* **benignancy** (*bi-nig'nən-si*), benignant quality.— *adj.* **benig'nant,** kind : gracious : beneficial—*adv.* **benig'nantly.**—*n.* **benig'nity,** goodness of disposition : kindness : graciousness : favourable circumstances—of climate, weather, disease, planets. —*adv.* **benign'ly.** [O.Fr. *benigne*—L. *benīgnus,* prob.—*bene,* well, and root of *genus,* birth, kind.]

benison, *ben'i-zn, -sn,* n. a benediction, blessing, esp. blessing of God. [O.Fr. *beneiçun*—L. *benedictiō, -ōnis.*]

bénitier, *bā-nē'tyā,* n. a holy-water font, or stoup. [Fr.,—L.L. *benedictārium*—L. *benedictus.*]

benj, *benj,* n. bhang. [Ar.]

Benjamin, *ben'jə-min,* n. a youngest son : a favourite child. [As in Genesis xlii.]

benjamin, *ben'jə-min,* n. an old kind of overcoat. [Perh. alluding to **Joseph** (q.v.); or a tailor's name.]

benjamin, *ben'jə-min,* n. gum benzoin (also **gum benjamin**).—*n.* **ben'jamin-tree,** Styrax : the American spice-bush : a kind of fig-tree. [**benzoin.**]

bennet, *ben'it.* See **herb-bennet** (at **herb**). [O.Fr. *herbe beneite*—L. *herba benedicta,* being a charm against the devil.]

bennet, *ben'it,* n. (*S. England*) a dry grass stalk. [**bent.**]

bent, *bent,* pa.t. and pa.p. of **bend.**—adj. curved : having a bend : intent, set (upon doing something), determined : (*Spens.*) obedient, governed.—*n.* curvature : curved part : tendency : trend : inclination : direction : leaning or bias : natural inclination of the mind : the extent to which a bow may be bent : degree of tension : capacity of endurance.— **to the top of one's bent,** to the full measure of one's inclination. [**bend.**]

bent, *bent,* n. any stiff or wiry grass : the old dried stalks of grasses : a genus (*Agrostis*) of grasses, slender and delicate in appearance, some useful as pasture-grasses and for hay : a place covered with bents, a heath : a hillside.—Also **bent'-grass.**— *adj.* **bent'y.**—**take (to) the bent** (*Scot.*), to take flight. [O.E. *beonet,* found in place-names, as *Beonetléah,* Bentley.]

Benthamism, *ben'thəm-izm,* n. the social and political teaching of Jeremy *Bentham* (1748-1832), whose leading principle is the doctrine of utility, that happiness is identical with pleasure, summed up in Hutcheson's phrase, 'the greatest happiness of the greatest number'.—*n.* **Ben'thamite.**

benthos, *ben'thos,* n. the flora and fauna of the sea-bottom—opp. to *plankton* and *nekton.*—adj. **ben'thic.** [Gr. *benthos,* depth.]

benumb, *bi-num',* v.t. to make insensible or powerless : to stupefy (now chiefly of *cold*) : to deaden the feelings of : to paralyse generally.—adj. **benumbed'.**—*ns.* **benumbed'ness, benumb'ment.** [Pfx. *be-* and **numb.**]

Benzedrine, *ben'zi-drēn,* n. amphetamine, a synthetic drug used to relieve nasal congestion or taken internally to stimulate the central nervous system. [Trade-mark name.]

benzene, *ben'zēn,* n. simplest of the aromatic series of hydrocarbons, discovered by Faraday in 1825, now mostly prepared by destructive distillation of coal-tar, its molecule consisting of a ring or closed chain of six carbon atoms each with a hydrogen atom attached—formerly called benzine, benzol, names now used differently (see below).— *ns.* **ben'zal** or **benzyl'idine,** a radical whose oxide is **benzal'dehyde** or oil of bitter almonds; **benz'idine,** a base used in preparing azo-dyes; **benzil,** a double benzoyl radical; **ben'zine** (*ben'zēn*), a mixture of hydrocarbons got by destructive distillation of petroleum, used as a solvent, motor fuel, etc.: improperly, benzene; **ben'zoate** (*-zō-āt*), a salt of benzoic acid.—adj. **benzo'ic,** pertaining to benzoin (see next article), as **benzoic acid,** an acid, $C_6H_5 \cdot COOH$, found in benzoin and other gums.—*ns.* **ben'zol(e),** crude benzene, used as a motor-spirit: improperly, benzene,

ben'zoline, benzine: impure benzene; **benzoyl** (*ben'zō-il*), the radical C_6H_5 : CO; **ben'zyl** (*-zil*), the radical $C_6H_5CH_2$. [From **benzoin.**]

benzoin, *ben'zō-in,* or *-zoin,* n. gum benjamin, the aromatic and resinous juice of *Styrax Benzoin,* a tree of Java and Sumatra, used in perfumery, in pastilles, for incense and court-plaster, and friar's balsam.—adj. **benzo'ic.** [In the 16th century, **benjoin,** most prob. through It. from Ar. *lubān jāwī,* frankincense of Jawa (i.e. Sumatra).]

bepaint, *bi-pānt',* v.t. to paint over : to colour.

bepat, *bi-pat',* v.t. to pat frequently, to beat.

bepatched, *bi-pacht',* adj. mended with patches : wearing patches on the face by way of adornment.

bepearl *bi-pərl',* v.t. to cover over with pearls.

bepelt, *bi-pəlt',* v.t. to pelt vigorously.

bepepper, *bi-pep'ər,* v.t. to pelt with a rain of shot or of blows.

bepester, *bi-pest'ər,* v.t. to vex or pester greatly.

bepity, *bi-pit'i,* v.t. to pity greatly.

beplaster, *bi-plås'tər,* v.t. to plaster thickly : to daub.

beplumed, *bi-plōōmd',* adj. adorned with feathers.

bepommel, *bi-pum'l,* v.t. to pommel soundly.

bepowder, *bi-pow'dər,* v.t. to powder over.

bepraise, *bi-prāz',* v.t. to lavish praise on.

beprose, *bi-prōz',* v.t. to reduce to prose: to discuss in prose, and tediously.

bepuff, *bi-puf',* v.t. to puff out: to praise beyond measure.

bequeath, *bi-kwēdh,* v.t. to leave by will to another (strictly of personal property): to transmit to posterity, to leave behind: to commit or entrust to any one.—adj. **bequeath'able.**—*ns.* **bequeath'al; bequeath'ment.** [O.E. *becwethan*—pfx. *bi-, be-,* and *cwethan,* to say; see **quoth.**]

bequest, *bi-kwest',* n. act of bequeathing: that which is bequeathed, a legacy. [M.E. *biqueste*—O.E. pfx. *bi-, be-, cwethan,* to say; see **quoth.**]

berate, *bi-rāt',* v.t. to scold or chide vigorously.

beray, *bi-rā',* v.t. to befoul.—Also (erroneously) **bewray.** [Pfx. *be-* and **ray.**]

Berber, *bər'bər,* n. a member of one of the Hamitic peoples of Barbary: the language of the Berbers.— Also *adj.* [Ar. *barbar;* connexion with Gr. *barbaros,* doubtful.]

Berberis, *bər'bər-is,* n. the barberry genus, giving name to the family **Berberidā'ceae,** akin to the buttercup family.—*adj.* **berberidā'ceous.**—*n.* **ber'berine,** an alkaloid got from barberry roots. [Latinised from Ar.; see **barberry.**]

berceuse, *ber-səz',* n. a cradle song: a musical composition in similar rhythm. [Fr.]

bere, another spelling of **bear,** barley.

bere, beer, bear, *bēr,* n. a pillow-case (usu. **pill'ow-bere**). [Origin obscure; cf. Ger. *bühre.*]

Berean, *be-rē'ən,* n. one of an extinct Scottish sect of the 18th century.—Also *adj.* [*Beroea,* Gr. *Beroia,* in Macedonia, where the people searched the scriptures daily (Acts, xvii. 11).]

bereave, *bi-rēv',* v.t. to rob of anything valued: to deprive: to widow, orphan, or deprive by death of some dear relative or friend: to snatch away :—pa.t. and pa.p. **bereaved'** (usu. by death), **bereft'** (usu. in general sense); arch. pa.p. **bereav'en.**—adj. **bereaved'.**—*n.* **bereave'ment,** loss of a relative or friend. [O.E. *beréafian,* to plunder; see **reave.**]

beret, *ber'i,* **berret,** *ber'et,* n. a flat, round, woollen cap worn by Basques and others. [Fr. *béret.*]

berg, *bərg* (*S. Afr. berhh*), a hill or mountain: short for **iceberg.**—*ns.* **berg'-add'er,** a venomous South African viper, living on hill-sides; **berg'ce'dar,** a rare conifer (*Widdringtonia juniperoides*) of the Cedarbergen in South Africa; **bergfall,** (*berhh'fäl, bərg'fawl;* Ger.), fall of mountain-rock; **berghaan** (*berhh'hän;* S. Afr.), the bateleur eagle (Du., mountain cock); **berg-mehl** (*berhh'māl,* or *bərg*), a powdery deposit of diatom frustules (Ger., mountain flour); **bergschrund** (*berhh'shroont*), a crevasse formed where a glacier or snowfield starts away from a mountain wall (Ger., mountain cleft). [Ger., Du., Sw. *berg,* hill; cogn. with **barrow** (O.E. *beorg*).]

bergamask, *bər′gə-mȧsk*, *n.* a native of *Bergamo*, in Italy: a rustic dance attributed to them.—Also **ber′gomask.**

bergamot, *bər′gə-mot*, *n.* a kind of citron or orange, whose aromatic rind yields oil of bergamot, used in perfumery: the essence so extracted: a mint of similar smell. [Said to be from *Bergamo* in Italy; or *Bergama* (Pergamum) in Asia Minor; or as next word.]

bergamot, *bər′gə-mot*, *n.* a fine pear. [Fr.,—It.,— Turk. *begarmudi*, prince of pears.]

bergander, *bərg-an′dər*, *n.* the sheldrake. [Perh. equal to **burrow-gander.**]

Bergsonian, *berg-sō′ni-ən*, *adj.* pertaining to Henri *Bergson* (1859-1941) and his philosophy of creative evolution.—*n.* a follower of Bergson.—*n.* **Berg′-sonism** (*-sən-izm*).

bergylt, *bər′gilt*, *n.* a red northern sea-fish of the Scorpaenidae. [Norw. *berggylta*, rock-pig.]

beriberi, *ber′i-ber-i*, *n.* an Eastern disease due to lack of vitamin B. [Sinh. *beri*, weakness.]

Berkeleian, *bärk-lē′ən, bärk′li-ən*, pertaining to Bishop *Berkeley* (1685-1753), who maintained that the world we see and touch is not an abstract independent substance, of which conscious mind may be an effect, but is the very world which is presented to our senses, and which depends for its actuality on being perceived.—*n.* a follower of Berkeley.—*n.* **Berkelei′anism** (or *bärk′*).

berkelium, *bərk′li-əm*, *n.* an element (Bk; at. number 97), prepared in a cyclotron at *Berkeley*, California.

berlin, *bər′lin, bər-lēn′, -lin′*, *n.* an old-fashioned four-wheeled covered carriage, with a seat behind covered with a hood—also **ber′line:** a closed motor-car with the driver's seat partitioned off.— **Berlin blue**, Prussian blue; **Berlin wool**, a fine dyed wool for worsted-work, knitting, etc. [From the city of *Berlin*.]

berm, *bərm*, *n.* a ledge. [Fr. *berme;* Ger. *berme*.]

Bernardine, *bər′nər-din, -dēn, adj.* Cistercian. [From *Bernard* of Clairvaux, founder of the order.]

bernicle-goose. Same as **barnacle-goose.**

berob, *bi-rob′*, *v.t.* (*Spens.*) to rob or plunder.

berry, *ber′i*, *n.* any small succulent fruit: (*bot.*) a simple fruit with pericarp succulent throughout (thus excluding strawberry, raspberry, blackberry): a coffee-bean: a cereal grain: a lobster's or crayfish's egg: a knob on a swan's bill: (*pl.* **berr′ies**).— *v.i.* to come into berry, to swell: to gather berries.— *adj.* **berr′ied**, bearing berries.—*n.* **berr′ying.** [O.E. *berie*.]

berry, *ber′i*, *n.* a pottage or sop (as in **ale-berry, bread-berry**). [O.E. *briw*, pottage, porridge.]

bersaglieri, *ber-säl-yā′rē*, *n.pl.* the riflemen or sharpshooters of the Italian army, first organised in the Sardinian army in 1836. [It.; pl. of *bersagliere—bersaglio*, a mark.]

berserk, -er, *bər′sərk, -ər*, *n.* a Norse warrior whom the sight of the field of battle would fill with a frenzied and resistless fury.—Also *adj.* [O.N. *berserkr*, probably bear-sark.]

berth, *bərth*, *n.* sea-room: a ship's station at anchor or at a wharf: a room or sleeping-place in a ship, sleeping-carriage, etc.: any allotted or assigned place: a situation or place of employment, usually a comfortable one.—*v.t.* to moor: to furnish with a berth.—**to give a wide berth to**, to keep well away from generally. [Ety. obscure.]

bertha, *ber′thä*, **berthe**, *bərth, n.* a woman's falling collar: *Bertha* (*slang*), a big German gun (from Frau *Berta* Krupp). [Woman's name.]

Bertholletia, *berth-ō-lē′sh(y)ä*, *n.* the brazil-nut genus of Lecythidaceae. [Named in honour of the chemist C. L. *Berthollet*.]

Berthon-boat, *bər′thon*, *n.* a type of collapsible boat. [Edward L. *Berthon* (1813-99), its inventor.]

bertillonage, *ber-tē-yon-äzh′*, *n.* a system of criminal identification by measurement, worked out by Alphonse *Bertillon*.

beryl, *ber′il*, *n.* a precious stone of which emerald and aquamarine are varieties, a silicate of beryllium and aluminium crystallising in the hexagonal system, green, colourless, yellow or blue, once esteemed as a magic crystal.—*adj.* pale greenish.— *ns.* **beryll′ium**, a metallic element (Be; atomic number 4), also called glucinum; **beryll′ia**, glucina, its oxide. [O.Fr. *beryl*—L. *bēryllus*—Gr. *bēryllos*.]

bes. See **bay** (6).

besaint, *bi-sānt′*, *v.t.* to make a saint of.—*pa.p.* **besaint′ed**, canonised: haunted with saints.

bescatter, *bi-skat′ər*, *v.t.* to scatter over.

bescrawl, *bi-skrawl′*, *v.t.* to scrawl or scribble over.

bescreen, *bi-skrēn′*, *v.t.* to screen: to overshadow.

bescribble, *bi-skrib′l*, *v.t.* to write in a scribbling hand: to scribble about, over, or upon.

besee, *bi-sē′*, *v.t.* (*obs.; Spens.*) to look to: to provide for: to treat: to provide, furnish, apparel, adorn:—*pa.p.* **beseen′**—*adj.* **beseen′**, of good appearance, comely: furnished. [O.E. *beséon— be-*, pfx., *séon*, to see.]

beseech, *bi-sēch′* (*Spens.* **beseeke**, *bi-sēk′*), *v.t.* to entreat, to implore: to ask or pray earnestly: to solicit:—*pa.t.* and *pa.p.* **besought** (*bi-sawt′*), also **beseeched**.—*n.* (*Shak.*) entreaty.—*n.* **beseech′er.**—*n.* and *adj.* **beseech′ing.**—*adv.* **beseech′ingly.**—*n.* **beseech′ingness.** [Pfx. *be-*, and M.E. *sechen;* see **seek**.]

beseem, *bi-sēm′*, *v.i.* (*obs.*) to seem: to be fitting or becoming.—*v.t.* to be seemly for: to become: to be fit for or worthy of.—*n.* and *adj.* **beseem′ing.** —*n.* **beseem′ingness.**—*adv.* **beseem′ingly.**— *adj.* **beseem′ly** (*rare*).

beseen. See **besee.**

beset, *bi-set′*, *v.t.* to surround or set round with anything (now only in *pa.p.*): to surround with hostile intentions, to besiege: to occupy so as to allow none to go out or in: to assail, perplex, endanger, as by temptations, obstacles, etc.: —*pr.p.* **besett′ing;** *pa.t.* and *pa.p.* **beset′.**—*ns.* **beset′ment;** **besett′er.**—*adj.* **besett′ing.** [O.E. *besettan—settan*, to set.]

beshadow, *bi-shad′ō*, *v.t.* to cast a shadow over.

beshame, *bi-shām′*, *v.t.* to put to shame.

beshine, *bi-shīn′*, *v.i.* to light up.—*adj.* **beshone** (*-shon′*).

beshrew, *bi-shrōō′*, *v.t.* to invoke evil upon, to curse—now only in imprecations. [Pfx. *be-*, and **shrew**.]

beside, *bi-sīd′*, *prep.* by the side of, near: (*rare*) over and above, besides: outside of: away from: distinct from: apart from, not falling within, as of a question, resolution, etc.—*adv.* near by: besides: apart: to the side.—*adv.* **besides′**, in addition: moreover: otherwise, else.—*prep.* over and above: else than: (*obs.*) beside: (*obs.*) away from, apart from.—**beside oneself**, having lost self-possession; **beside the mark**, irrelevant. [O.E. *be sídan*, by the side (dat.); the *s* is of the adverbial gen.]

besiege, *bi-sēj′*, *v.t.* to lay siege to: to beset with armed forces: to throng round: to importune: to pester.—*ns.* **besiege′ment; besieg′er.**—*n.* and *adj.* **besieg′ing.**—*adv.* **besieg′ingly** (*rare*), urgently.

besigh, *bi-sī′*, *v.t.* to sigh over.

besing, *bi-sing′*, *v.t.* to celebrate in song.—*adj.* **besung′.**

besit, *bi-sit′*, *v.t.* (*obs.*) to besiege: to sit well on, as clothes, to become.—*adj.* **besitt′ing** (*Spens.*), becoming.

beslave, *bi-slāv′*, *v.t.* to make a slave of: to call slave.

beslaver, *bi-slav′ər*, *v.t.* to slaver or slobber upon: to cover with fulsome flattery.

beslobber, *bi-slob′ər*, *v.t.* to besmear with the spittle running from one's mouth: to cover with drivelling kisses: to flatter fulsomely.

beslubber, *bi-slub′ər*, *v.t.* to bedaub or besmear.

besmear, *bi-smēr′*, *v.t.* to smear over: to bedaub: to pollute.

besmirch, *bi-smərch′*, *v.t.* to soil, as with smoke or soot: to sully.

besmutch, *bi-smuch′*, *v.t.* to besmirch.

besmut, *bi-smut′*, *v.t.* to blacken with soot.—*adj.* **besmutt′ed.**

besognio, *bi-zōn′yō*, *n.* a beggar. [See **bezonian.**]

besom, *bē′zəm, bez′əm*, *n.* a bunch of twigs for sweeping: (Scot., pron. *biz′əm, buz′əm*) a broom:

Neutral vowels in unaccented syllables: *el′ə-mənt, in′fənt, ran′dəm*

(*fig.*) any cleansing or purifying agent.—*ns.* **be'-somhead**, a blockhead : **be'som-rid'er**, a witch.—**to jump the besom** (see **broom**). [O.E. *besema;* Ger. *besen*, Du. *bezem*.]

besom, *biz'əm, bē'zəm, n.* (*Scot.* and *dial.*) a term of reproach for a woman, implying generally slatternliness, laziness, impudence, or unscrupulous energy. [Perh. the same word as the preceding; perh. connected with O.E. *bysn, bisn,* example, or O.N. *bysn,* wonder.]

besort, *bi-sort', v.t.* (*Shak.*) to match, befit, become. —*n.* (*Shak.*) suitable company.

besot, *bi-sot', v.t.* to make sottish, dull, or stupid : to make a sot of : to cause to dote : to infatuate :—*pr.p.* **besott'ing;** *pa.p.* **besott'ed.**—*adj.* **besott'ed,** infatuated.—*adv.* **besott'edly.**—*n.* **be'sott'edness.**

besought, *bi-sawt', pa.t.* and *pa.p.* of **beseech.**

besouled, *bi-sōld', adj.* endowed with a soul.

bespangle, *bi-spang'gl, v.t.* to adorn with spangles, or with anything sparkling or shining.

bespatter, *bi-spat'ər, v.t.* to spatter or sprinkle with dirt or anything moist : to defame.

bespeak, *bi-spēk', v.t.* to speak for or engage beforehand, to order or apply for : to stipulate or ask for : to betoken : (*obs. dial.*) to bewitch.—*v.i.* (*obs.*) to speak : (*pa.t.* **bespoke**, *arch.* **bespake'**; *pa.p.* **bespōk'en**, also **bespoke'**).—*n.* an actor's benefit, so called because his friends and patrons choose the piece to be performed : an application in advance.

bespeckle, *bi-spek'l, v.t.* to mark with speckles or spots.

bespectacled, *bi-spek'tə-kld, adj.* having spectacles on.

bespeed, *bi-spēd', v.t.* to help on.—*pa.t.* and *pa.p.* **besped'.**

bespice, *bi-spīs', v.t.* (*Shak.*) to season with spice.

bespit, *bi-spit', v.t.* to spit upon, defile with spittle : —*pa.t.* and *pa.p.* **bespit', bespat'**; *pa.p.* (*Browning*) **bespate'.**

bespoke, *bi-spōk',* **bespoken,** *be-spōk'n, pa.p.* of **bespeak,** ordered to be made, as clothes.

besport, *bi-sport', v.t.* to disport.

bespot, *bi-spot', v.t.* to cover with spots.—*adj.* **bespott'ed.**—*n.* **bespott'edness.**

bespout, *bi-spowt', v.t.* to spout over : to declaim pompously.

bespread, *bi-spred', v.t.* to spread over : to cover :—*pr.p.* **bespread'ing;** *pa.t.* and *pa.p.* **bespread'.**

besprent, *bi-sprent', pa.p.* sprinkled over : scattered. [O.E. *besprengan;* see **sprinkle.**]

besprinkle, *bi-spring'kl, v.t.* to sprinkle over.

Bessemer, *bes'əm-ər, adj.* pertaining to the steel-making process invented by Sir Henry *Bessemer.*—**Bessemer iron, pig,** pig-iron suitable for making Bessemer steel.

best, *best, adj.* (serving as *superl.* of **good**) good in the highest degree : first : highest : most excellent. —*n.* one's utmost endeavour : the highest perfection : the best share, part, success, or lot (as the *best of the bargain, the best of three*—tosses, games, etc.).—*adv.* (as *superl.* of **well**) in the highest degree : in the best manner.—*v.t.* (*coll.*) to get the better of.—*n.* **best'-sell'er,** a book that has had one of the biggest sales of the season : the writer of such a book.—**at best,** on the most favourable supposition; **best boy, girl,** (*coll.*) a favourite associate of the opposite sex; **best man** and **best maid,** the groomsman and bridesmaid at a wedding; **for the best,** with the best intentions or outcome; **give one best,** to concede the victory; **have the best of it,** to gain the advantage in a contest; **I had best, I were best** (for earlier *me were best*), it were best for me; **to make the best of one's way,** to go as well as one can; **put one's best foot foremost** (see **foot**). [O.E. *betst, betest;* see **better.**]

bestain, *bi-stān', v.t.* to stain all over.

bestar, *bi-stär', v.t.* to cover with stars.

bestead, *bi-sted', v.t.* to help, relieve : to be of use to, to avail.—*v.i.* to profit, be advantageous :—*pa.t.* **bestead'ed**; *pa.p.* **bestead', bested'.** [Pfx. *be-* and **stead.**]

bestead, bested, *bi-sted'* (*Spens.* **bestad, bestadde,** *bi-stad'*), *adj.* set about (*with*) : beset (with *by*, of foes; *with*, of dangers, etc.) : situated—usually with *ill, hard,* etc. [Pfx. *be-* and **stead,** placed.]

bestial, *best'i-əl, adj.* like a beast : rude : brutally sensual.—*n.* (*Scot.*) a collective name for cattle.—*v.t.* **best'ialise,** to make like a beast.—*ns.* **best'-ialism,** irrationality; **bestiality** (*-al'i-ti*), beastliness : disgusting vice. [L. *bestiālis*—*bestia,* beast.]

bestiary, *best'i-ər-i, n.* a book of a class popular in the Middle Ages, describing animals, a mixture of natural and unnatural history allegorised for edification. [L.L. *bestiārium,* a menagerie—*bestia,* a beast.]

bestick, *bi-stik', v.t.* to stick over, as with sharp points : to transfix : to stick about, adorn :—*pa.t.* and *pa.p.* **bestuck'.**

bestill, *bi-stil', v.t.* to make quiet, to hush.

bestir, *bi-stər', v.t.* to put into lively action : arouse into activity.

bestorm, *bi-storm', v.t.* to assail with storms or tumult.

bestow, *bi-stō', v.t.* to stow, place, or put by : to give or confer : to accommodate with quarters : to apply (with *on* and *upon*) : (*refl., Shak.*) to acquit (oneself).—*ns.* **bestow'al,** act of bestowing : disposal; **bestow'er; bestow'ment.**

bestraddle, *bi-strad'l, v.t.* to bestride.

bestraught, *bi-strawt', adj.* (*obs.*) distraught : distracted : mad. [distraught, with change of pfx.]

bestreak, *bi-strēk', v.t.* to overspread with streaks.

bestrew, *bi-strōō', v.t.* to cover loosely with something strewn or scattered over :—*pa.p.* **bestrewed'**, **bestrown'** (*-strōn'*), **bestrewn'** (with).

bestride, *bi-strīd', v.t.* to stride over : to sit or stand across : to defend, protect, from the sense of standing over a fallen man to defend him :—*pa.t.* **bestrid', bestrode'**; *pa.p.* **bestrid', bestridd'en.**—*adj.* **bestrid'able.**

bestuck, *pa.t.* and *pa.p.* of **bestick.**

bestud, *bi-stud', v.t.* to adorn as with studs, as the sky with stars.

bet, *bet, n.* a wager : something staked to be lost or won on the result of a doubtful issue.—*v.t.* and *v.i.* to lay or stake, as a bet :—*pr.p.* **bett'ing**; *pa.t.* and *pa.p.* **bet** or **bett'ed.**—*ns.* **bett'er,** one who bets—also **bett'or**; **bett'ing.—an even bet,** an equal chance; **you bet** (*slang*, esp. *U.S.*), certainly. [Possibly shortened from the noun **abet.**]

beta, *bē'tä, n.* the second letter (B, β) of the Greek alphabet : as a numeral β' = 2, ,β = 2,000.—*n.* **be'tacism** (*-sizm*), pronunciation of the sound of b as that of v.—*n.pl.* **be'ta-rays',** streams of **be'ta-particles,** or electrons, given off by radium and other radio-active substances.—*n.* **be'tatron** (Gr. *-tron,* agent suffix), an apparatus for obtaining particles of high energy by keeping a beam of accelerated electrons moving in a stable orbit. [Gr. *bēta;* see **B, beth.**]

betake, *bi-tāk', v.t.* to take (oneself) to, to go (with *self*) : to apply or have recourse :—*pa.t.* **betook'**; *pa.p.* **betāk'en.**

beteem, beteeme, *bi-tēm', v.t.* (*Spens., Shak.*) to grant, vouchsafe, allow (also with the under-meaning of teem upon). [Perh. from a lost O.E. word answering to Du. *betamen,* to beseem.]

betel, *bē'tl, n.* the leaf of the **be'tel-pepp'er** (*Piper Betle*), which is chewed in the East along with the areca-nut and lime.—*n.* **be'tel-nut,** the areca-nut. [Through Port. from Malayalam *vettila.*]

Betelgeuse, Betelgeuze, *bet'əl-jōōz, n.* a reddish first-magnitude star in Orion's shoulder. [Fr.,—Ar. *bayt-al-jawzā',* Orion.]

beth, *beth, bāth, n.* the second letter of the Hebrew and Phoenician alphabets, resembling a house. [Heb. *bēth,* house; see **B, beta.**]

bethankit, *bi-thangk'it, interj.* (*Scot.*) God be thanked.—*n.* a grace.

bethel, *beth'əl, n.* a Methodist or Baptist church : an old ship fitted as a place of worship for sailors. [Heb. *Bēth-ēl,* house of God.]

bethink, *bi-thingk', v.t.* to think on or call to mind : to recollect (generally followed by a reflexive pronoun and *of*) : to propose to oneself.—*v.i.* to con-

fāte, fär, ȧsk; mē, hėr (her); *mīne; mōte; mūte; mōōn; dhen* (then)

sider :—*pa.t.* and *pa.p.* **bethought** (bi-thawt′). [O.E. *bithencan;* cf. Ger. *bedenken.* See **think**.]

bethrall, bi-thrawl′, *v.t.* (Spens.) to enslave.

bethumb, bi-thum′, *v.t.* to mark with the thumbs :—*pa.p.* **bethumbed′**.

bethump, bi-thump′, *v.t.* to thump or beat soundly.

bethwack, bi-thwak′, *v.t.* to thrash soundly.

betide, bi-tīd′, *v.i.* (with *dat.*) to happen (to), to befall.—*v.t.* (*erroneous and rare*) to betoken :—*pa.t.* **betid′ed**, **betid** (-tid′); *pa.p.* **betid′** (Spens.)

betight, bi-tīt′). [See **tide**.]

betime, bi-tīm′, *v.i.* (Shak.) to betide.

betimes, bi-tīmz′, *adv.* in good time : early : seasonably : speedily. [Pfx. *be-*, and **time**, with adverbial gen. *-s.*]

betitle, bi-tī′tl, *v.t.* to give a name to.

betoil, bi-toil′, *v.t.* to weary with toil.

betoken, bi-tō′kn, *v.t.* to show by a sign : to foreshow : (*arch.*) to mean : to symbolise. [See **token**.]

béton, bā′ton², *n.* lime concrete : concrete. [Fr.]

betony, bet′ɔn-i, *n.* a common labiate plant (*Stachys*, or *Betonica, officinalis*) growing in woods, of great repute in ancient and mediaeval medicine : extended to various labiate and scrophulariaceous plants. [Fr. *bétoine*—L. *betonica, vettonica*.]

betook, bi-took′, *pa.t.* of **betake**.

betoss, bi-tos′, *v.t.* (Shak.) to agitate.

betray, bi-trā′, *v.t.* to give up treacherously : to disclose in breach of trust : to let go basely or weakly : to deceive (the innocent and trustful), to seduce : to discover or show : to show signs of.—*ns.* **betray′al**, act of betraying ; **betray′er**, a traitor : the seducer of a trustful girl. [Pfx. *be-*, and O.Fr. *traïr* (Fr. *trahir*)—L. *tradĕre*, to deliver up.]

betread, bi-tred′, *v.t.* to tread over or walk upon :—*pa.t.* **betrod′** ; *pa.p.* **betrodd′en**.

betrim, bi-trim′, *v.t.* to trim or set in order, to deck, to dress.

betroth, bi-trōdh′, or -trōth′, *v.t.* to contract or promise in order to marriage : to affiance : (*obs.*) to pledge oneself to.—*ns.* **betroth′al**, **betroth′ment**, an engagement to marry : ceremonious declaration of such an engagement.—*adj.* and *n.* **betroth′ed**. [Pfx. *be-*, and **troth** or **truth**.]

better, bet′ɔr, *adj.* (serves as *comp.* of **good**) good in a greater degree : preferable : improved : more suitable : larger : kinder : stronger in health : (Scot.) completely recovered, quite well again (partial recovery being expressed by *some better*).—*adv.* (*comp.* of **well**) well in a greater degree : more fully or completely : over or more : with greater advantage.—*n.* superior (esp. in *pl.*).—*v.t.* to make better : to surpass.—*v.i.* to grow better.—*adjs.* **bett′ered** ; **bett′ering**.—*ns.* **bett′ering**, amelioration : improvement ; **bett′erment**, improvement, esp. in standard of life or value of property.—*adj.* **bett′ermost**, best.—*n.* **bett′erness**.—**better half**, a jocose term for a wife, once applied seriously to wife or husband, intimate friend, and even the soul as opposed to the body ; **be better than one's word**, to do more than one had promised ; **better off**, in superior circumstances : more fortunate : richer ; **get the better of**, to gain the advantage over, overcome ; **had better** (see **have**) **think better of**, to revise one's decision about, esp. to decide not to do so : to have the better opinion of. [O.E. *bet* (adv.), *betera* (adj.), better ; Goth. *batiza*, Ger. *besser* ; prob. cog. with **boot**.]

betty, bet′i, *n.* a man who troubles himself with the women's work in a household : (*old slang*) name for a burglar's jemmy.—**Bett′y Mar′tin** (*obs.*), an expression inviting incredulity (usu. *all my eye and Betty Martin*). [Dim. of *Elizabeth*.]

Betula, bet′ū-lä, *n.* the birch genus, giving name to the family **Betulä′ceae**, which includes hazel and hornbeam. [L. *betula*.]

betumbled, bi-tum′bld, *adj.* (Shak.) tumbled or disordered.

between, bi-twēn′, *prep.* in, to, through, or across the space that separates : intermediate to : on the part of in reciprocal relation : by combined action or influence of : from one to another of : in joint possession of (generally of two).—*adv.* in or to an intermediate place : at intervals.—*n.* (Shak.) an interval : an intermediate variety of needle.—*ns.* **between′-decks**, the space between any two decks of a ship (also *adv.*); **between′ity** (*playful*), **between′ness**, state of being between ; **between′-maid**, a servant subsidiary to two others (esp. cook and tablemaid)—a tweeny—*advs.* **between′-time**, **between′whiles**, at intervals.—**between ourselves**, **between you and me** (*slang* **and the cat**, **or post**, **or bedpost**, etc.), in confidence ; **between the devil and the deep sea**, in a desperate dilemma ; **go between**, to act as a mediator. [O.E. *betwéonum*, and *betwéon*—be, by, and *twégen, twá*, twain, two.]

betwixt, bi-twikst′, *prep.* and *adv.* between.—**betwixt and between**, in a middling position. [O.E. *betweox*—*twá*, two, and the suffix *-ix*, *-ish*, with added *-t*, as in *against*, and *amidst*.]

bevel, bev′l, *n.* a slant or inclination of a surface : an instrument opening like a pair of compasses, and adjustable for measuring angles.—*adj.* having the form of a bevel : slanting.—*v.t.* to form with a bevel or slant :—*pr.p.* **bev′elling** ; *pa.t.* and *pa.p.* **bev′elled**.—*ns.* **bev′el-gear**, **bev′el-wheels** (*mech.*), wheels working on each other in different planes, the cogs of the wheels being bevelled or at oblique angles to the shafts.—*adj.* **bev′elled**, cut to an oblique angle, sloped off.—*ns.* **bev′eller**, **bev′elling** ; **bev′elment**. [From the older form of Fr. *beveau*, bevel (instrument).]

bever, an obsolete form of **beaver**.

beverage, bev′ɔr-ij, *n.* a liquor for drinking : a mixture of cider and water : a drink or drinkmoney to celebrate an occasion.—*n.* **bever** (*bēv′ɔr*), a small repast between meals : (*obs.*) a time for drinking. [O.Fr. *bevrage* (Fr. *breuvage*), *beivre*—L. *bibĕre*, to drink.]

bevue, bā-vü′, *n.* a blunder. [Fr. *bévue*.]

bevy, bev′i, *n.* a company or flock of larks, quails, roes, or ladies. [Origin obscure.]

bewail, bi-wāl′, *v.t.* to lament : to mourn loudly over (esp. the dead).—*v.i.* to utter lamentations.—*adj.* **bewailed′**.—*n.* and *adj.* **bewail′ing**. [See **wail**.]

beware, bi-wār′, *v.i.* (usu. with *of* or a clause) to be on one's guard : (*obs.*) to take heed.—*v.t.* to be on one's guard against : (*obs.*) to see to it.— Used normally only in infinitive and imperative: old writers have *was ware*, etc. [**be**, **ware**.]

beweep, bi-wēp′, *v.t.* to weep over, to lament : wet or disfigure by weeping :—*pa.t.* and *pa.p.* **bewept′**.

beweltered, bi-wel′tɔrd, *adj.* besmeared by weltering in blood. [Pfx. *be-*, and **welter**.]

bewet, bi-wet′ *v.t.* (Shak.) to wet or moisten.—*pa.t.* and *pa.p.* **bewett′ed**, **bewet′**.

bewhore, bi-hōr′, *v.t.* (Shak.) to call a whore : to make a whore of.

bewig, bi-wig′, to cover with a wig.—*adj.* **bewigged′**.

bewilder, bi-wil′dɔr, *v.t.* to perplex or lead astray.—*adjs.* **bewil′dered**, lost, confused in mind : confused, trackless ; **bewil′dering**.—*adv.* **bewil′deringly**.—*n.* **bewil′derment**, confusion, mental confusion : perplexity. [Pfx. *be-*, and obs. Eng. *wildern*—O.E. *wilddéoren*, wilderness—*wild*, wild, *déor*, beast.]

bewitch, bi-wich′, *v.t.* to affect by witchcraft (mostly malignantly) : to fascinate or charm.—*n.* **bewitch′ery**.—*adj.* **bewitch′ing**, charming, enchanting.—*adv.* **bewitch′ingly**.—*n.* **bewitch′ment**.

bewray, bi-rā′, *v.t.* to reveal : to divulge : to show up : to reveal the existence, presence, or whereabouts of.—Sometimes confused with **beray**. [M.E. *bewreien*—be-, and O.E. *wrégan*, to accuse.]

bey, bā, *n.* a Turkish governor. [Turk. *bey*.]

beyond, bi-yond′, *prep.* on the farther side of : farther onward in comparison with : out of reach of : above, superior to : apart from.—*adv.* farther away.—*n.* the unknown : the hereafter.—**beyond measure**, excessively ; **beyond one**, past one's comprehension ; **beyond seas**, abroad ; **go beyond**, to surpass : to circumvent : (B., Shak.) to overreach ; **the back of beyond**, a place of extreme remoteness. [O.E. *begeondan*—pfx. *be-*, and *geond*, across, beyond; see **yon**.]

bez, bez-antler, -tine. See **bay** (6).

bezant, *bez′ənt,* or *biz-ant′, n.* a gold coin first struck at Byzantium or Constantinople : (*her.*) a small circle or (i.e. yellow), like a gold coin.

bezel, *bez′l, n.* the part of the setting of a precious stone which encloses it : the oblique side or face of a cut gem : the grooved rim in which a watch-glass is set : a sloped cutting edge (usually **basil,** *baz′l*). [From an O.Fr. word represented by mod. Fr. *biseau;* ult. origin uncertain.]

bezique, *bi-zēk′, n.* a game at cards for two, three, or four, played with two to four packs, from which cards below the seven have been removed : the combination of the knave of diamonds and queen of spades. [Fr. *besigue,* of obscure origin.]

bezoar, *bē′zōr, n.* a stony concretion found in the stomachs of goats, antelopes, llamas, chamois, etc., formerly esteemed an antidote to all poisons.— *adj.* **bezoardic** (*bez-ō-ärd′ik*). [Through Sp. *bezoar* and Ar. *bāzahr*—Pers. *pādzahr,* antidote— *zahr,* poison.]

bezonian, *bi-zō′nyən, n.* (*Shak.*) a beggar. [It. *bisogno,* need.]

bezzle, *bez′l, v.i.* (*obs.*) to drink hard.—*v.t.* to squander : to despoil : to consume. [O.Fr. *besiler.* See **embezzle.**]

bhang, *bang, n.* a narcotic and intoxicant, leaves and shoots of hemp. [Hind. *bhāng;* Pers. *bang;* Sans. *bhangā.*]

bharal, *bur′əl, n.* the blue sheep of the Himalaya, connecting the true wild sheep with the goats.— Also **burrel, burrell, burrhel, burhel.** [Hind.]

bhisti, bheesty, bheestie, bhistee, *bēs′tē,* an Indian water carrier. [Urdu. *bhīstī*—Pers. *behistī*— *bihisht,* paradise.]

biannual, *bī-an′ū-əl, adj.* two-yearly : also half-yearly. [L. *bi-,* twice, *annus,* year.]

bias, *bī′əs, n.* an obliquity : an oblique line : a bulge or greater weight on one side of a bowl (in the game of bowling), making it turn to one side : a turning to one side : a one-sided inclination of the mind : a prejudice : any special influence that sways the mind.—*adj.* biased : cut slantwise.—*adv.* slant-wise.—*v.t.* to cause to turn to one side : to prejudice, or prepossess : to cut obliquely :—*pr.p.* **bī′asing** (by some **bī′assing**); *pa.t.* and *pa.p.* **bī′ased (bī′assed)**.—*ns.* **bī′as-draw′ing** (*Shak.*), a turn awry; **bī′asing,** a bias or inclination to one side. [Fr. *biais,* slant; of unknown origin.]

biaxial, *bi-aks′i-əl, adj.* having two (optic, etc.) axes.—Also **biax′al.** [L. *bi-,* and **axial.**]

bib, *bib, n.* a cloth put under a child's chin : a similar article of dress for adults : the pout, a fish of the cod and haddock genus with a large chin barbel.—*v.t.* and *v.i.* to drink, to tipple.— *adj.* **bibā′cious.**—*ns.* **bibā′tion,** tippling; **bibb′er,** a tippler : chiefly used in composition as (*B.*) wine-bibber; **bib′cock,** a tap with down-turned nozzle. [Prob. from L. *bibere,* to drink; perh. partly imit.]

bibble-babble, *bib′l-bab′l, n.* (*Shak.*) idle talk. [Reduplication of **babble.**]

bibelot, *bēb′lō, n.* a knick-knack. [Fr.]

Bible, *bī′bl, n.* the sacred writings of the Christian Church, consisting of the Old and New Testaments : (also **bible**) a big or authoritative book : the third stomach of a ruminant, with many folds like the leaves of a book.—*adj.* **biblical** (*bib′li-kl*), of or relating to the Bible.—*adv.* **bib′lically.**—*ns.* **bib′licism** (*-sizm*), biblical doctrine, learning, or literature : literal acceptance of the Bible; **bib′licist, bib′list,** one versed in biblical learning : one who makes the Bible the sole rule of faith : one who adheres to its letter. [Fr.,—L.L. *biblia,* fem. sing., earlier neut. pl., from Gr. *biblia,* books, esp. the canonical books (sing. *biblion,* a book, dim. of *biblos,* papyrus, paper).]

bibli-, *bib′li-,* in composition, book.—*n.* **bibliographer** (*-og′rə-fər*), one versed in bibliography : the compiler of a bibliography.—*adjs.* **bibliographic** (*-ō-graf′ik*), **-al.**—*ns.* **bibliog′raphy,** study, description or knowledge of books, in regard to their outward form, authors, subjects, editions, and history : a descriptive list of books : a book containing such a list; **bibliolater** (*-ol′ə-tər*), one given to bibliolatry.—*adj.* **bibliol′atrous.**—*n.* **bibliol′atry** (Gr. *latreiā,* worship), a superstitious reverence for a book, esp. the Bible.—*adj.* **bibliological** (*-ō-loj′i-kl*).—*ns.* **bibliologist** (*-ol′ə-jist*); **bibliol′ogy,** bibliography : book-lore; **bib′liomancy** (*-man-si;* Gr. *manteiā,* divination), divination by opening the Bible or other book at hazard; **bibliomā′nia** (Gr. *maniā,* madness), a mania for collecting or possessing books : book-fancying; **bibliomā′niac.**—*adjs.* **bibliomaniacal** (*-mə-nī′ə-kl*); **bibliopegic** (*-pej′ik;* Gr. *pēgnynai,* to fix).—*ns.* **bibliopegist** (*-op′i-jist*), a bookbinder : a fancier of bindings; **bibliop′egy,** the fine art of bookbinding; **bibliophagist** (*-of′ə-jist;* Gr. *phagein,* to eat), a devourer of books; **bib′liophil, -phile** (*-fil;* Gr. *philos,* friend), a lover or collector of books.—Also *adj.*—*ns.* **bibliophilism;** **bibliophilist; bibliophily; bibliophō′bia** (Gr. *phobeein,* to fear), hatred of books; **bib′liopole** (Gr. *pōlēs,* seller), a bookseller.— *adjs.* **bibliopolic** (*-pol′ik*), **-al.**—*ns.* **bibliop′olist; bibliop′oly,** bookselling; **bibliothē′ca** (Gr. *bibliothēkē—thēkē,* repository), a library : a bibliography : a series of books; **biblioth′ecary,** a librarian. [Gr. *biblion,* book; cf. **Bible.**]

bibulous, *bib′ū-ləs, adj.* drinking or sucking in : spongy. [L. *bibulus—bibere,* to drink.]

bicameral, *bī-kam′ər-əl, adj.* having two chambers. [L. *bi-,* twice, and *camera,* chamber.]

bicarbonate, *bī-kär′bən-āt, n.* an acid salt of carbonic acid. [L. *bi-,* twice, and **carbonate.**]

bice, *bīs, n.* a pale blue or green paint. [Fr. *bis.*]

bicentenary, *bi-sen′tin-ər-i,* or *-tēn′,* or *-ten′, adj.* pertaining to two hundred (years).—*n.* a bicentennial. [L. *bi-,* twice, *centēnārius,* pertaining to a hundred—*centum,* a hundred.]

bicentennial, *bi-sen-ten′yəl, adj.* pertaining to two hundred years.—*n.* a two hundredth anniversary. [L. *bi-,* twice, *centum,* a hundred, *annus,* a year.]

biceps, *bī′seps, n.* a two-headed muscle : esp. one in front of the upper arm or one on the back of the thigh.—*adj.* **bicip′ital,** two-headed. [L. *biceps,* two-headed—*bis,* twice, and *caput,* head.]

bichromate, *bi-krō′māt, n.* a dichromate, or salt of dichromic acid. [L. *bi-,* twice, and **chromate.**]

bicker, *bik′ər, v.i.* to contend in a petty way : to quiver : to brawl, as running water : to patter.— *n.* a fight, a quarrel, esp. (*Scot.*) a street or school encounter : a clattering noise : (*Scot.*) a strife. [Poss. a freq. conn. with **beak.**]

bicker, *bik′ər, n.* a bowl, esp. of wood, for holding liquor : a vessel of wooden staves for porridge. [Scot. form of **beaker.**]

biconcave, *bī-kon′kāv, adj.* concave on both sides. [L. *bi-,* twice, and **concave.**]

biconvex, *bi-kon′veks, adj.* convex on both sides. [L. *bi-,* twice, and **convex.**]

bicorporate, *bī-kor′pər-āt, adj.* (*her.*) double-bodied, as the head of a lion to which two bodies are attached. [L. *bi-,* twice, and **corporate.**]

bicuspid, *bī-kus′pid, adj.* having two cusps.—*n.* a premolar tooth.—*adj.* **bicusp′idate.** [L. *bi-,* twice, and **cusp.**]

bicycle, *bī′si-kl, n.* a vehicle with two wheels, one before the other, driven by pedals or a motor.— *v.i.* to ride a bicycle.—*n.* **bī′cyclist.** [L. *bi-,* twice, Gr. *kyklos,* a circle, wheel.]

bid, *bid, v.t.* to offer : to propose : to proclaim, as the banns of marriage : to command : (*arch.*) to invite : to offer to pay at an auction : to call (in card games).—*v.i.* to make an offer or venture.— *pr.p.* **bidd′ing;** *pa.t.* **bade** (*bad;* also, as in the poets, *bād*), **bid;** *pa.p.* **bidd′en, bid.**—*n.* an offer of a price : a venturesome attempt or proposal : a call (at cards).—*adj.* **bidd′able,** tractable.—*ns.* **bidd′er,** one who bids or offers a price; **bidd′ing,** offer : command : calling.—**to bid fair,** to seem likely. [O.E. *béodan;* Goth. *biudan,* Ger. *bieten,* to offer.]

bid, *bid, v.t.* to ask for : to invite : to command : (nearly *obs.*) to pray : hence to salute with, say as a greeting :—Tenses are as in the preceding verb, with which it has been confused.—*n.* **bidd′-ing-pray′er,** originally the praying, or saying, of a prayer, then by confusion with the foregoing word taken to mean enjoining or inviting of prayer. [O.E. *biddan;* Goth. *bidjan;* Ger. *bitten.* See bead.]

biddy, *bid'i, n. (dial.)* a fowl: in *Shak.* applied to Malvolio.—**red-biddy** (see **red**). [Poss. the woman's name Biddy for Bridget.]

bide, *bīd, v.i.* to wait: to dwell: to remain fixed or persistently.—*v.t.* to await: to face unshrinkingly: to endure:—*pa.t.* **bīd'ed, bōde,** (*Shak.*) **bid,** (*Scot.*) **bade** (*bād*); *pa.p.* **bīd'ed,** (*obs.* and *Scot.*) **bidd'en.**—*n.* **bīd'ing** (*Shak.*), residence, habitation. [O.E. *bīdan;* but sometimes for **abide.**]

bident, *bī'dant, n.* a two-pronged tool: a two-year-old sheep.—*adj.* **bidental** (*bī-dent'l*), two-pronged: two-toothed.—*n.* a place struck by lightning (possibly consecrated by the Romans by sacrifice of a sheep).—*adjs.* **bident'ate, -d,** two-toothed. [L. *bi-,* twice, *dēns, dentis,* a tooth.]

bidet, *bē-dā, bi-det', n.* a nag: a bestridable bath and stand. [Fr., pony.]

bield, *bēld, n.* (*Scot.; Wordsworth*) shelter: protection.—*adj.* **bield'y.** [Northern; O.E. *beldo* (W.S. *bieldo*), courage; cf. **bold.**]

bien, another spelling of **bein.**

biennial, *bī-en'yəl, adj.* lasting two years: happening or appearing once in two years.—*n.* a plant that flowers and fructifies only in its second year, then dies.—*adv.* **bienn'ially.** [L. *biennium,* two years—*bi-,* twice, and *annus,* a year.]

bier, *bēr, n.* a carriage or frame of wood for bearing the dead to the grave. [O.E. *bǣr;* Ger. *bahre,* L. *feretrum.* From root of verb **bear.**]

biestings. Same as **beestings.**

bifacial, *bī-fā'shl, adj.* two-faced: having two unlike sides. [L. *bi-,* twice, and **facial.**]

bifarious, *bī-fā'ri-əs, adj.* double: in two rows. [L. *bifārius,* double.]

biff, *bif, n.* (*coll.*) a blow.—*v.t.* to strike hard.

biffin, *bif'in, n.* a variety of apple: such an apple slowly dried and flattened into a cake. [For *beefing,* from its colour of raw beef.]

bifid, *bif'id, bī'fid, adj.* (*bot.*) cleft in two. [L. *bifidus—bi-,* twice, and *findere,* to cleave or split.]

bifilar, *bī-fī'lər, adj.* having two threads. [L. *bi-,* twice, *fīlum,* thread.]

bifocal, *bī-fō'kəl, adj.* composed of parts of different focal lengths.—*n.pl.* **bifo'cals,** spectacles with bifocal lenses, for far and for near vision. [L. *bi-,* twice, and **focal.**]

bifold, *bī'fōld, adj.* twofold: (*Shak.*) of two kinds. [L. *bi-,* twice, and **fold.**]

bifoliate, *bī-fō'li-āt, adj.* having two leaves or leaflets.—*adj.* **bifo'liolate,** having two leaflets. [L. *bi-,* twice, *folium,* leaf.]

biform, *bī-'form, adj.* having two forms. [L. *biformis—bi-,* twice, and *forma,* form.]

bifurcate, *bī'fur-kāt,* or *-fur', adj.* two-forked: having two prongs or branches.—*v.i.* to divide into two branches.—*n.* **bifurca'tion,** a forking or division into two branches.—*adj.* **bifurcated.** [L. *bifurcus—bi-, bis,* twice, *furca,* a fork.]

big, *big, adj. (compar.* **bigg'er;** *superl.* **bigg'est)** large or great: pregnant: grown up: magnanimous: great in air, mien, or spirit: loud: pompous.— Also *adv.* (as in *talk big*).—*adj.* **beg-bell'ied,** having a big belly: pregnant (*with*).—*n.* **big'-bud',** a swelling of currant buds owing to a gall-mite.— *adj.* **bigg'ish.**—*ns.* **big'horn,** the Rocky Mountain goat or sheep; **big'ness,** bulk, size; **big'wig** (*colloq.*), a leading man, a person of some importance.—**big business,** large business enterprises and organisations, esp. collectively; **big end,** in an internal-combustion engine, the larger end of the connecting rod. [M.E. *big;* origin obscure.]

big, *big, v.t.* (*Scot.*) to build, to pile up.—*n.* **bigg'in,** anything built, a house. [O.N. *byggja,* O.E. *būian.*]

bigamy, *big'ə-mi, n.* the custom, crime, or fact of having two legal or supposed wives or husbands at once: (*eccl. law*) a second marriage.—*n.* **big'amist,** one who has committed bigamy.—*adj.* **big'amous.**—*adv.* **big'amously.** [L. *bi-,* twice; Gr. *gamos,* marriage.]

bigener, *bī'jin-ər, n.* a hybrid between different genera.—*adj.* **bigeneric** (*-er'ik*). [L. *bīgener,* a hybrid.]

bigg, big, *n.* six-rowed barley: sometimes bear. [O.N. *bygg.*]

biggin, *big'in, n.* a child's cap or hood: a nightcap: a serjeant's coif. [Fr. *béguin,* from béguine's cap.]

bigha, *bē'gä, n.* a land measure in India, ⅓ to ⅔ of an acre. [Hindi.]

bight, *bīt, n.* a wide bay: a bend or coil. [O.E. *byht;* cf. Dan. and Sw. *bugt,* Du. *bocht.*]

Bignonia, *big-nō'ni-ä, n.* a genus of tropical plants with trumpet-shaped flowers, giving name to the family **Bignoniä'ceae.** [Named after the Abbé Bignon, Louis XIV's librarian.]

bigot, *big'ət, n.* one blindly and obstinately devoted to a particular creed or party.—*adj.* **big'oted,** having the qualities of a bigot.—*n.* **big'otry,** blind or excessive zeal, esp. in religious matters. [O.Fr.; origin unknown.]

bijou, *bē'zhōō, n.* a trinket: a jewel: a little box:— *pl.* **bijoux** (*bē'zhōōz*).—*adj.* small and elegant. [Fr.]

bijwoner. Same as **bywoner.**

bike, *bīke, bīk, n.* (*Scot.*) a nest of wasps, wild bees, etc.: a swarm of people.—*v.i.* to swarm. [Origin unknown.]

bike, *bīk, n.* and *v.i.* (*coll.*) for **bicycle.**

bilabial, *bī-lā'bi-əl, adj.* two-lipped: (*phon.*) produced by contact or approximation of the two lips, as the sound of b, w.—*n.* a bilabial consonant. —*adj.* **bilä'biate,** two-lipped, as some corollas. [L. *bi-,* twice, and *labium,* a lip.]

bilander, *bī'land-ər, n.* a two-masted hoy, having her mainsail bent to the whole length of her yard, hanging fore and aft, and inclined to the horizontal at an angle of about 45°.—Also **by'lander.** [Du. *bijlander.*]

bilateral, *bī-lat'ər-əl, adj.* having or involving two sides: affecting two parties or participants reciprocally.—*n.* **bilat'eralism,** two-sidedness: equality in value of trade between two countries.— *adv.* **bilat'erally.** [L. *bi-,* twice, *latus, -eris,* side.]

bilberry, *bil'bər-i, n.* a whortleberry or blaeberry shrub: its dark blue berry. [Cf. Dan. *böllebær.*]

bilbo, *bil'bō, n.* a rapier or sword. [From *Bilbao,* in Spain.]

bilboes, *bil'bōz, n.pl.* a bar with sliding shackles. [Perh. connected with the foregoing.]

bile, *bīl, n.* a thick bitter fluid secreted by the liver— yellow in man and carnivorous animals, green in vegetable feeders: derangement of its secretion: (*fig.*) ill-humour.—*n.* **bile'-duct,** the duct that conveys the bile to the small intestine.—*adjs.* **biliary** (*bil'yər-i*), belonging to or conveying bile; **bilious** (*bil'yəs*), pertaining to or affected by bile.—*adv.* **bil'iously.**—*n.* **bil'iousness.** [Fr.,— L. *bilis.*]

bilge, *bilj, n.* the bulging part of a cask: the broadest part of a ship's bottom: filth such as collects there: (*slang*) piffle.—*v.i.* to spring a leak by a fracture in the bilge, as a ship.—*ns.* **bilge'-keel,** a ridge along the turn of the bilge of a ship to check rolling; **bilge'-pump; bilge'-wat'er.**—*adj.* **bilg'y,** having the appearance and disagreeable smell of bilge-water. [Perh. **bulge.**]

Bilharzia, *bil-här'zi-ä, n.* a genus of trematode worms parasite in human and other blood.—*n.* **bilharzi'asis, bilharziö'sis,** a disease caused by it, common in Egypt. [From the helminthologist, Theodor *Bilharz.*]

bilian, *bil'i-an, n.* a heavy ant-proof lauraceous timber tree of Borneo. [Malay.]

bilimbi, *bil-im'bi, n.* an East Indian tree of the woodsorrel family: its acid fruit.—Also **bilim'bing, blim'bing.** [Dravidian and Malay.]

bilingual, *bī-ling'gwəl, adj.* expressed in two languages: speaking two languages, esp. native or habitual languages.—*ns.* **biling'ualism; biling'-uist.** [L. *bilinguis—bi-,* twice, *lingua,* tongue.]

bilirubin, *bil-i-rōō'bin, n.* a reddish pigment in bile.—*n.* **biliver'din,** a green pigment in bile. [L. *bilis,* bile, *ruber,* red, Fr. *verd,* green.]

biliteral, *bī-lit'ər-əl, adj.* of or involving two letters: written in two scripts. [L. *bi-,* twice, *lītera, littera,* a letter.]

bilk, *bilk, v.t.* to elude: to cheat.—*n.* **bilk'er.** [Perh. a form of **balk;** at first a term in cribbage.]

bill, *bil, n.* a concave battle-axe with a long wooden handle : a kind of hatchet with a long blade and wooden handle in the same line with it, often with a hooked point, used in cutting thorn hedges or in pruning.—*ns.* **bill'-hook,** a bill or hatchet with curved point; **bill'-man,** a soldier armed with a bill. [O.E. *bil ;* Ger. *bille.*]

bill, *bil, n.* the beak of a bird, or anything like it : a sharp promontory : the point of an anchor fluke.—*v.i.* to join bills as doves : to caress fondly.—*n.* **bill'-board,** a board used to protect the planking from injury by the bill when the anchor is weighed.—*adj.* **billed,** having a bill.—*n.* and *adj.* **bill'ing.** [O.E. *bile,* most prob. same word as preceding.]

bill, *bil, n.* an account of money : a draft of a proposed law : a written engagement to pay a sum of money at a fixed date : (*U.S.*) a bank-note : a placard : a slip of paper serving as an advertisement : any written statement of particulars : (*Eng. criminal law*) a written accusation of serious crime.—*v.t.* to announce or advertise by bill.—*ns.* **bill'-board,** a board on which placards are posted; **bill'-book,** a book used in commerce in which an entry is made of all bills accepted and received; **bill'-broker,** one who deals in bills of exchange and promissory notes; **bill'-chamber,** a department of the Scottish Court of Session dealing with summary business—so called because formerly both summonses and diligence or execution were usually commenced by a writ called a bill; **bill'-discounter,** one who discounts or advances the amount of bills of exchange and notes which have some time to run; **bill'-head,** a form used for business accounts, with name and address printed at the top; **bill'-sticker, -poster,** one who sticks or posts up bills or placards.—**bill of adventure,** a writing by a merchant stating that goods shipped by him, and in his name, are the property of another, whose adventure or chance the transaction is; **bill of costs,** an account of a solicitor's charges and disbursements in the conduct of his client's business; **bill of exceptions,** a statement of objections, by way of appeal against the ruling of a judge who is trying a case with a jury in the Court of Session; **bill of exchange,** a document purporting to be an instrument of pecuniary obligation for value received, employed for the purpose of settling a debt in a manner convenient to the parties concerned; **bill of fare,** a list of dishes or articles of food; **bill of health,** an official certificate of the state of health on board ship before sailing; **bill of indictment,** a statement of a charge made against a person; **bill of lading,** a paper signed by the master of a ship, by which he makes himself responsible for the safe delivery of the goods specified therein; **bill of mortality,** (*hist.*) an official return of births and deaths—hence **within the bills of mortality,** within the London district for which such returns were made; **bill of sale,** in English law, a formal deed assigning personal property; **bill of sight,** an entry of imported goods of which the merchant does not know the quantity or the quality; **bill of store,** a licence from the customs authorities to reimport British goods formerly exported : **bill of victualling,** a list of necessary stores shipped from the bonded warehouse, or for drawback on board vessels proceeding on oversea voyages. [L.L. *billa*—L. *bulla,* a knob, a seal, hence a document bearing a seal, etc.; cf. **bull.**]

billabong, *bil'ə-bong, n.* (*Austr.*) a cut-off loop of a river, replenished only by floods : an effluent from a river (strictly one that does not rejoin). [Native words *billa,* river, *bung,* dead.]

billet, *bil'it, n.* a little note or paper : a ticket assigning quarters to soldiers or others : quarters requisitioned : a destined resting-place : (*coll.*) a post or occupation.—*v.t.* to quarter or lodge, as soldiers.—*pr.p.* **bill'eting;** *pa.t.* and *pa.p.* **bill'eted.** [O.Fr. *billette,* dim. of *bille ;* see **bill.**]

billet, *bil'it, n.* a small log of wood used as fuel : a piece of timber sawn on three sides and rounded on the fourth : a bar of metal : (*archit.*) an ornament in Norman architecture in the form of short cylinders with spaces between : (*her.*) a bearing

in the form of an upright rectangle.—*n.* **bill'et-head,** a piece of wood round which a harpoon-line is turned. [Fr. *billette*—*bille,* the young stock of a tree; orig. unknown.]

billet-doux, *bil-i-dōō', n.* a love-letter :—*pl.* **billets-doux'** (same pron. as *sing.*). [Fr. *billet,* letter, *doux,* sweet.]

billiards, *bil'yərdz, n.* a game played with a cue and balls on a table with pockets at the sides and corners.—*adj.* **bill'iard.**—*ns.* **bill'iard-ball ; bill'iard-cloth,** a green cloth for covering a billiard table; **bill'iard-marker,** a person who marks the points made by the players; **bill'iard-table.** [Fr. *billard*—*bille,* a stick, also a ball.]

billingsgate, *bil'ingz-gāt, n.* foul and abusive language like that once familiar to the ear at *Billingsgate* (the London fish-market).

billion, *bil'yən, n.* a million millions (1,000,000,-000,000) : in U.S.A. and France, one thousand millions (1,000,000,000) or milliard.—*n.* **bill'ion-aire.**—*adj.* and *n.* **bill'ionth.** [L. *bi-,* twice, and **million.**]

billon, *bil'ən, n.* base metal : esp. an alloy of silver with copper, tin, or the like. [Fr., from same root as **billet** (2).]

billow, *bil'ō, n.* a great wave : (*poet.*) a wave, the sea.—*v.i.* to roll or swell in great waves : to bulge flowingly.—*adjs.* **bill'owed, bill'owing, bill'owy.** [App. O.N. *bylgja ;* Sw. *bölja,* Dan. *bölge,* wave.]

billy, billie, *bil'i, n.* (*Scot.*) a brother : a comrade, a companion-in-arms : an Australian bushman's (or other's) boiling-pan or tea-pot (also **billy-can ;** poss. for *bouilli can*) :—*pl.* **bill'ies.**—*n.* **bill'y-goat,** a he-goat. [Prob. from *Bill,* a familiar abbrev. of William.]

billyboy, *bil'i-boi, n.* a bluff-bowed one-masted trading-vessel. [Prob. conn. with **bilander.**]

billycock, *bil'i-kok, n.* a bowler hat. [From *bully-cocked, i.e.* cocked like the bullies.]

bilobar, *bī-lō'bər,* **bilobed,** *bī'lōbd, adjs.* having two lobes.—*adj.* **bilobular,** *bī-lob'ū-lər,* having two lobules. [L. *bi-,* twice, and **lobe, lobule.**]

bilocation, *bī-lō-kā'shən, n.* the power of being in two places at the same time. [Coined from *bi-,* twice, and **location.**]

bilocular, *bī-lok'ū-lər, adj.* divided into two cells. [L. *bi-,* twice, *loculus,* dim. of *locus,* place.]

biltong, *bil'tong, n.* (*S. Africa*) sun-dried lean meat. [Du. *bil,* buttock, *tong,* tongue.]

Bimana, *bim'ə-nä,* *bī-mā'nä, n.pl.* two-handed animals, an obsolete name for mankind.—*adjs.* **bim'anal, bim'anous.** [L. *bi-,* twice, *manus,* hand.]

bimbashi, *bim-bä'shē, n.* a military officer (in Turkey or Egypt). [Turk. *bin,* thousand, *bash,* head.]

bimestrial, *bī-mes'tri-əl, adj.* of two months' duration. [L. *bimestris*—*bi-,* and *mēnsis,* a month.]

bimetallism, *bī-met'əl-izm, n.* a monetary system in which gold and silver are on precisely the same footing as regards mintage and legal tender.—*adj.* **bimetallic** (*bī-mi-tal'ik*).—*n.* and *adj.* **bimet'allist.** [L. *bi-,* twice, and **metal.**]

bimonthly, *bī-munth'li, adj.* once in two months : also twice a month. [L. *bi-,* two, and **month.**]

bin, *bin, n.* a receptacle for corn, wine, dust, etc. [O.E. *binn,* a manger.]

bin, *bin* (*Shak.*) used for **be** and **been.**

binary, *bī'nər-i, adj.* composed of two : twofold.—*n.* a double star : two stars revolving about their centre of gravity (also **binary star, binary system**).—*adj.* **bi'nate,** growing in pairs : double : consisting of two leaflets; **binary form** (*mus.*), a form of movement founded on two themes; **binary scale,** the scale of notation whose radix or base is 2 (instead of 10). [L. *bīnārius*—*bīni,* two by two, *bis,* twice.]

binaural, *bin-aw'rl, adj.* having, employing, or relating to two ears. [L. *bīnī,* two by two, *auris,* ear.]

bind, *bīnd, v.t.* to tie or fasten together with a band : to encircle round : to restrain : to fix : to make fast : to sew a border on : to tie up or bandage : to fasten together and put a cover on (a book) : to impose an obligation upon : to oblige by oath :

or promise: to indenture: to hold or cement firmly: to render hard: to constipate.—*v.i.* to become bound: (*pa.t.* and *pa.p.* **bound**, *bownd*).— *n.* a stalk of hop or other twiner: the indurated clay of coal-mines: (*mus.*) the tie for indicating that a note is to be held on, not repeated (of the same form as the slur or legato mark): (*Scot.*) capacity, measure.—*ns.* **bind′er**, one who binds, as books or sheaves: anything that binds, as a rope, a bandage, a cementing agent, a tie-beam, a header in masonry, a case for binding loose papers: an attachment to a reaping-machine for tying the bundles of grain cut and thrown off: a reaping-machine provided with one; **bind′ery** (esp. U.S.), a bookbinder's establishment.—*adj.* **bind′- ing**, restraining: obligatory.—*n.* the act of one who binds: anything that binds: the covering of a book.—*ns.* **bind′weed**, convolvulus: also (**black bindweed**) a species of *Polygonum*; **bine**, the slender stem of a climbing plant.—**be bound up in**, to be wholly devoted to; **bind over**, to subject to legal obligation; **I dare** or **will be bound, I** will be responsible for the statement. [O.E. *bindan*; Ger. *binden*, Sans. *bandh*.]

binervate, *bī-nėrv′āt*, *adj.* with two ribs or nerves. [L. *bi-*, twice, and **nerve**.]

bing, *bing*, *n.* a heap or pile: a bin. [O.N. *bingr*.]

bing, *bing*, *v.i.* (*obs. slang*; *Scott*) to go.

binge, *binj*, *binzh*, *v.t.* and *v.i.* (*dial.*) to soak: to drink deep.—*n.* (*slang*) a spree.

bingo, *bing′gō*, *n.* a familiar name for brandy. [Prob. B, for **brandy**, and **stingo**.]

bink, *bingk*, *n.* (*Scot.*), a bench, a bank, a shelf: a plate-rack: a wasp's or bee's nest: a small heap of mortar. [Northern form of **bench**.]

binnacle, *bin′a-kl*, *n.* (*naut.*) the box in which a ship's compass is kept. [Formerly *bittacle*— Port. *bitácola*—L. *habitáculum*, a dwelling-place— *habitāre*, to dwell.]

binocle, *bin′o-kl*, *-ō-kl*, *n.* a telescope for use with both eyes at once.—*adj.* **binocular** (*bī-*, *bi-nok′ū-lėr*), with two eyes: suitable for use with two eyes: stereoscopic.—*n.* a binocular telescope (usually in *pl.*) or microscope.—*adv.* **binoc′ularly.** [L. *bīnī*, two by two, *oculus*, an eye.]

binomial, *bī-nōm′i-ǝl*, *adj.* (*alg.*) consisting of two terms, as *a+b*.—*n.* a binomial expression.—*adj.* **binominal** (*bī-nom′in-ǝl*), making use of two names, as the Linnaean nomenclature which names every species by giving first the generic and then the trivial name.—**binomial theorem**, Newton's theorem giving any power of a binomial. [L. *bi-*, twice, and *nōmen*, a name, a term.]

binturong, *bin′tū-rong*, *n.* an East Indian prehensile-tailed carnivore, akin to the civet. [Malay.]

bio-, *bī′ō-*, *bi-o′-*, in composition, life.—*adj.* **bio-bibliograph′ical**, dealing with the life and writings of any one.—*n.* **bi′oblast** (Gr. *blastos*, germ), a hypothetical unit of living matter: a minute granule in protoplasm.—*adj.* **biochem′ical.** —*ns.* **biochem′ist**; **biochem′istry**, the chemistry of living things, physiological chemistry; **bio-coenosis** (*bī-ō-sē-nō′sis*; Gr. *koinos*, common), an association of organisms ecologically interdepend-ent.—*adj.* **biocoenotic** (*-not′ik*), ecological.—*ns.* **bi′ogen** (*-jen*; Gr. *genos*, race, offspring), a hypo-thetical unit of protoplasm; **biogen′esis** (Gr. *genesis*, production), the derivation of living things from living things only: biogeny.—*adjs.* **bio-genet′ic**, relating to biogens or to biogeny, or to biogenesis; **biogenous** (*-oj′*), parasitic.—*ns.* **biog′-eny**, the course of organic evolution or develop-ment of the individual or the race; **biogeog′-rapher.**—*adj.* **biogeograph′ical.**—*ns.* **biogeog′-raphy**, the geography of living things: geographical distribution of plants and animals; **bi′ograph** (Gr. *graphein*, to write), a biography: a bioscope; **biog′rapher**, one who writes biography.—*adjs.* **biograph′ic, -al.**—*adv.* **biograph′ically.**—*n.* **biog′raphy**, a written account or history of the life of an individual: the art of writing such ac-counts.—*adj.* **biological** (*-loj′*), of, pertaining to, biology: physiological: produced by physiological means: effected by living organisms.—*adv.* **bio-log′ically.**—*ns.* **biol′ogist**; **biol′ogy**, the science

of living things: sometimes restricted to ecology.— *adj.* **biomet′ric** (Gr. *metron*, measure).—*ns.* **bio-metrician** (*-trish′ǝn*); **biomet′rics**, **biom′etry**, the statistical or quantitative study of biology; **bi′omorph** (Gr. *morphē*, form), a representation of a living thing in decoration.—*adjs.* **biomorph′ic**; **bionom′ic.**—*ns.* **bionom′ics** (Gr. *nomos*, law), the study of the relations between the organism and its environment: ecology; **biophys′ics**, a form of biology dealing with biological structures and processes in terms of physics; **biophor(e)** (*bī′ō-for*, *-fōr*; Gr. *phoros*, carrying), Weismann's hypothetical unit of living matter; **bi′oplasm** (Gr. *plasma*, form, *plastos*, moulded), protoplasm; **bi′oplast**, a minute portion of protoplasm; **bi′oscope** (Gr. *skopeein*, to look at), a cinemato-graphic apparatus or theatre.—*adj.* **biotic** (*bī-ot′ik*), pertaining to life.—**biogenetic law**, the law of recapitulation of the history of the race in that of the individual; **biological warfare**, methods of fighting involving the use of disease bacteria. [Gr. *bios*, life.]

biotin, *bi′ō-tin*, *n.* one of the members of the vitamin B₂ complex (also known as vitamin H).

biotite, *bi′ō-tīt*, *n.* a black or dark ferro-magnesian mica. [Named after J. B. *Biot* (1774-1862).]

biparous, *bip′ǝr-ǝs*, *adj.* bearing two at a birth: dichasial. [L. *bis*, twice, *parĕre*, to bring forth.]

bipartite, *bī-pärt′īt*, *adj.* divided into two parts: having two corresponding parts, as a document: affecting two parties, as an agreement.—*adj.* **bipart′isan** (*-i-zan*), pertaining to, supported by, or consisting of members of, two parties.—*n.* **bi-partition** (*-tish′ǝn*), division into two parts. [L. *bi-*, *bis*, twice, *partītus*, divided—*partĭre*, *-īrī*, to divide.]

biped, *bī′ped*, *n.* an animal with two feet.—*adjs.* **bī′ped**, **bī′pedal**, having two feet. [L. *bipēs*, *-pedis*—*bi-*, twice, *pēs*, *pedis*, foot.]

bipetalous, *bī-pet′ǝl-ǝs*, *adj.* having two petals. [L. *bi-*, twice, and **petal**.]

bipinnaria, *bī-pin-ā′ri-ä*, *n.* a starfish larva with two ciliated bands. [L. *bi-*, twice, *pinna*, a feather.]

bipinnate, *bī-pin′āt*, *adj.* pinnate with each pinna itself pinnate. [L. *bi-*, twice, and **pinnate**.]

biplane, *bī′plān*, *n.* an aeroplane or glider with two sets of wings, one above the other. [L. *bi-*, twice, and **plane**.]

bipod, *bī′pod*, *n.* a two-legged stand. [L. *bi-*, twice, Gr. *pous*, *podos*, a foot.]

bipyramid, *bī-pir′ǝ-mid*, *n.* a form of two pyramids base to base, or with a pyramid at each end.

biquadratic, *bī-kwod-rat′ik*, *n.* a quantity twice squared, or raised to the fourth power.—**biquad-ratic equation**, an equation involving the fourth, and no higher, power of the unknown quantity; **biquadratic root**, the square root of the square root. [L. *bi-*, twice, and *quadrātus*, squared.]

biquintile, *bī-kwin′til*, *n.* (*astron.*) the aspect of planets when they are twice the fifth part of a great circle (i.e. 144 degrees) from each other. [L. *bi-*, twice, *quīntus*, the fifth.]

birch, *bėrch*, *n.* a hardy forest-tree (*Betula*), with smooth white bark and very durable wood: a rod for punishment, consisting of a birch twig or twigs.—*v.t.* to flog.—*adjs.* **birch**, **birch′en**, made of birch.—*n.* **birch′-rod′**, a birch for punishment. [O.E. *berc*, *bierce*; O.N. *björk*, Sans. *bhūrja*.]

bird, *bėrd*, *n.* a general name for a feathered animal (orig. applied to the young): (*slang*) a person: (*slang*) an object of admiration: (*arch.* and *dial.*) a girl or woman (confused with **bride** or **burd 1** or 2.—*v.i.* to shoot at, seek to catch or snare birds. —*n.*, *adj.*, *adv.* **bird-alane** (see **burd**, 2).—*ns.* **bird′bath**, a basin set up for birds to bathe in; **bird′-batting**, bat-fowling; **bird′-bolt** (*Shak.*), a short thick blunted bolt or arrow for killing birds without piercing; **bird′-cage**, a cage of wire or wicker for holding birds; **bird′call**, a bird-catcher's instrument for imitating birds' notes; **bird′-catcher**, a professional catcher of birds.—*n.* and *adj.* **bird′-catching** (**bird-catching spider**, see **bird-spider**).—*n.* **bird′-cherry**, a small wild cherry tree (*Prunus Padus*): its astringent fruit.—*adj.* **bird′-eyed**, quick-sighted.—*ns.* **bird′-**

fancier, one who has a fancy for rearing birds : one who keeps birds for sale; **bird′ie** (*dim.*), a little bird : (orig. *U.S.*) the achievement of a hole in golf in one stroke less than par; **bird′ing,** the hunting, shooting, snaring, or catching of birds; **bird′ing-piece,** a fowling-piece; **bird′-louse,** a louse-like insect of the Mallophaga, parasitical on birds and mammals (*pl.* **bird′-lice**); **bird′-lime,** a sticky substance for catching birds; **bird′-of-par′adise** (see **paradise**; **bird-of-paradise flower,** Strelitzia); **bird′-pepper,** a species of capsicum; **bird′-seed,** seed (hemp, etc.) for cage-birds; **bird′s′-eye,** a kind of primrose, of speedwell, or of tobacco.—*adj.* such as might be seen by a flying bird : having markings like birds' eyes.—*ns.* **bird′s′-foot,** a papilionaceous genus (*Ornithopus*) with clawlike pods; **bird′s′-nest,** the nest in which a bird lays and hatches her eggs : a name given to several plants from their appearance, esp. Monotropa and Neottia (bird's nest orchis); **bird′s′-nesting, bird′-nesting,** seeking and robbing birds' nests; **bird′-spī′der,** a large spider (Mygale) that preys on small birds, found in Brazil : extended to others of the Aviculariidae; **bird′-table,** a table, inaccessible to cats, for wild birds to feed on.—*adj.* **bird′-witt′ed,** flighty : incapable of sustained attention.—**a bird in the hand is worth two in the bush,** a certainty is not to be thrown away for a poor chance of something better; **a little bird told me,** I heard in a way I will not reveal; **bird′s-eye view,** a general view from above : a general view of a subject; **bird′s-foot trefoil,** a papilionaceous genus (Lotus) with clustered pods like birds' feet; **get the bird** (i.e. the goose) in stage slang, to be hissed, hence dismissed; **like a bird,** with alacrity. [O.E. *brid*, the young of a bird, a bird.]

birefringent, *bī-rə-frin′jənt, adj.* doubly refracting, like Iceland spar.—*n.* **birefrin′gence.** [L. *bi-*, twice, and **refringent.**]

bireme, *bī′rēm, n.* an ancient vessel with two banks of oars. [L. *birēmis*—*bi-*, twice, and *rēmus,* an oar.]

biretta, *bir-et′ä, n.* a square cap worn by clergy—by priests, black; bishops, purple; cardinals, red. [It. *berretta*—L.L. *birrettum,* cap.]

birk, *birk, bork, n.* Scots and prov. for **birch.**—*adj.* **birk′en** (*Scot.*), birchen.

birkie, *birk′i, n.* (*Scot.*) a strutting or swaggering fellow : a fellow generally.—*adj.* active. [Perh. conn. with O.N. *berkja,* O.E. *beorcan,* to bark.]

birl, *birl, v.t.* and *v.i.* (*Scot.*) to spin round : to toss (a coin) : to spend (esp. on liquor). [Apparently onomatopoeic.]

birl, birle, *birl, v.t.* and *v.i.* (*Scot.*) to pour out : to ply with drink : to carouse.—*ns.* **birl′er** (*Cumberland*); **birl′ing,** the act of drawing liquor. [O.E. *byrelian—byrele,* a cup-bearer, *beran,* to bear.]

birlieman, *bir′li-mən, n.* (*Scott*). Same as **byrlaw-man.**

birlinn, *bir′lin, n.* a chief's barge in the Western Isles. [Gael. *birlinn*—O.N. *byrthingr—byrthr,* burden.]

Birminghamise, *bər′ming-əm-īz, v.t.* to make up artificially. [See **Brummagem.**]

birostrate, *bī-ros′trāt, adj.* double-beaked. [L. *bi-,* twice, *rōstrātus,* beaked—*rōstrum,* a beak.]

birr, *bir, n.* (*Scot.*) impetuosity : a violent push : stress in pronunciation : any sharp whirring sound. [O.N. *byrr,* a favouring wind.]

birse, *birs, n.* (*Scot.*) bristle.—*adj.* **bir′sy.**—**lick the birse,** to draw a hog's bristle through the mouth—as in admission as a burgess in Selkirk; **set up one's birse,** to rouse the wrath of, from the bristling up of enraged animals. [O.E. *byrst.*]

birsle, *birs′l, v.t.* (*Scot.*) to scorch, to toast. [Origin unknown.]

birth, *bərth, n.* a ship's station at anchor. [Same as **berth.**]

birth, *bərth, n.* the act of bearing or bringing forth : coming into the world : the offspring born : dignity of family : origin.—*ns.* **birth′-control,** the control of reproduction by contraceptives; **birth′day,** the day on which one is born, or (usually) its anniversary, or a day officially held

instead.—*adj.* relating to the day of one's birth.—*ns.* **birth′day-book,** a book for autograph records of friends' birthdays; **birth′day-suit,** the naked skin; **birth′dom** (*Shak.*), birthright; **birth′-mark,** a peculiar mark on one's body at birth; **birth′night,** the night on which one is born, or the anniversary of that night : (*obs.*) the evening of the king's (or queen's) birthday; **birth′place,** the place of one's birth; **birth′-rate,** proportion of births to population; **birth′right,** the right or privilege to which one is entitled by birth : native rights.—*adj.* **birth′-strangled** (*Shak.*), strangled at birth.—*n.* **birth′wort,** a plant (*Aristolochia Clematitis*) formerly reputed to help parturition.—**birthday honours,** titles, etc., conferred on the king's (or queen regnant's) official birthday. [Prob. O.N. *byrthr.*]

bis, *bis, adv.* twice : (*mus.*) a direction for repetition. [L.]

biscacha. Same as **viscacha.**

Biscayan, *bis′kā-ən,* or *kā′, adj.* and *n.* of or pertaining to *Biscay* in Spain, or its people : Basque generally : a long heavy musket, or its bullet.

biscuit, *bis′kit, n.* hard dry bread in small cakes : (*U.S.*) a soft round cake : pottery that has been fired but not yet glazed : (*mil. slang.*) a square mattress.—*adj.* pale brown in colour.—*n.* **biscuit-root,** camass. [O.Fr. *bescoit* (mod. *biscuit*)—L. *bis,* twice, *coquĕre, coctum,* to cook or bake.]

bise, *bēz, n.* a cold north or north-east wind prevalent at certain seasons in and near Switzerland. [Fr.]

bisect, *bī-sekt′, v.t.* and *v.i.* to divide into two (usu. equal) parts.—*ns.* **bisec′tion; bisec′tor,** a line that divides an angle, etc., into two equal parts. [L. *bi-,* twice, and *secāre, sectum,* to cut.]

biserial, *bī-sē′ri-əl, adj.* arranged in two series or rows. [L. *bi-,* twice, and **series.**]

biserrate, *bī-ser′āt, adj.* doubly serrate. [L. *bi-,* twice, and **serrate.**]

bisexual, *bī-seks′ū-əl, adj.* hermaphrodite. [L. *bi-,* twice, and **sexual.**]

bishop, *bish′əp, n.* in the Western and Eastern Churches, and in the Anglican communion, a clergyman consecrated for the spiritual direction of a diocese, usu. under an archbishop, and over the priests or presbyters and deacons : a spiritual overseer in the early Christian Church, whether of a local church or of a number of churches : a chessman whose move is in a diagonal line, its upper part carved into the shape of a bishop's mitre (formerly the *archer*) : a wholesome hot drink compounded of red wine (claret, Burgundy, etc.) poured warm or cold upon ripe bitter oranges, sugared and spiced to taste : any of several kinds of weaver-bird (**bish′op-bird**).—*v.t.* (*jocularly*) to play the bishop, to confirm : to supply with bishops : to let (milk or the like) burn while cooking.—*ns.* **bish′opess,** a bishop's wife : (*joc.*) a she-bishop; **bish′opric,** the office and jurisdiction of a bishop : sometimes a diocese — also **bish′opdom; bish′opweed,** goutweed or goatweed.—**bishop's cap,** a genus (Mitella) of the saxifrage family, with one-sided inflorescences; **the bishop has put his foot in it,** it has burnt while cooking. [O.E. *biscop*—L. *episcopus*—Gr. *episkopos,* an overseer—*epi,* upon, *skopeein,* to view.]

bishop, *bish′əp, v.t.* to fill, or otherwise tamper with, the teeth of (to make a horse seem younger). [From a person of the name.]

bisk. See **bisque** (1).

bismar, *bis′, biz′mər, n.* (*Orkney* and *Shetland*) a kind of steelyard. [O.N. *bismari.*]

bismillah, *bis-mil′ä, interj.* in the name of Allah. [Ar.]

bismuth, *bis′* or *biz′məth, n.* a brittle reddish-white element, of atomic number 83. [Ger. *bismuth, wissmuth* (now *wismut*), origin unknown.]

bison, *bī′sn, -zn, n.* a large wild ox with shaggy hair and a fatty hump—the European bison, extinct except in parks, and the American, commonly called buffalo in America. [From L. *bisōn, -ontis.* prob. of Gmc. origin; cf. O.H.G. *wisunt,* O.E. *wesend.*]

bisque, bisk, *bisk, n.* a rich soup, esp. crayfish soup. [Fr.]

bisque, bisk, *n.* a kind of unglazed white porcelain : pottery that has undergone the first firing before being glazed. [See **biscuit.**]

bisque, bisk, *n.* a term at tennis, golf, etc., for the handicap whereby a player allows a weaker opponent (at latter's choice of time) to score a point in a set, or deduct a stroke at a hole, etc. [Fr.]

bissextile, *bis-ekst'il, adj.* having an intercalary day.—*n.* leap-year. [L. *bisextilis*—*bis,* twice, *sextus,* sixth, the sixth day before the kalends of March (24th February) being doubled.]

bisson, *bis'ən, adj.* (*Shak.* beesome), blind, purblind : (*Shak.* bisson) perh. blinding. [O.E. *bisene,* blind.]

bistort, *bis'tort, n.* adderwort or snakeweed, a plant (*Polygonum Bistorta*) of the dock family, with twisted rootstock. [L. *bistorta*—*bis,* twice, *tortus,* -*a,* -*um,* twisted.]

bistoury, *bis'tər-i, n.* a narrow surgical knife for making incisions. [Fr. *bistouri.*]

bistre, bister, *bis'tər, n.* a pigment of a warm brown colour made from the soot of wood, esp. beechwood.—*adj.* bis'tred. [Fr. *bistre;* origin unknown.]

bistro, *bē-strō', n.* (Fr. *slang*) a small tavern.

bisulcate, *bī-sul'kāt, adj.* (*zool.*) cleft in two: cloven-footed : with two furrows. [L. *bi-,* twice, *sulcus,* a furrow.]

bisulphate, *bī-sul'fāt, n.* an acid sulphate.—*n.* **bisulph'ide,** a disulphide.

bit, *bit, n.* a bite, a morsel : a small piece : a coin : the smallest degree : a brief space of time : a small boring tool (see **brace**): the boring part of a drilling machine : the part of the bridle that the horse holds in his mouth : somewhat (as *a bit of a fool*) : (*Scot.*) used in the sense of a bit of, sometimes with the effect of a diminutive (as *a bit laddie, pl. bits o' laddies*).—*v.t.* to put the bit in the mouth of : to curb or restrain.—*pr.p.* **bitt'ing;** *pa.p.* **bitt'ed.**—*n.* **bitt'ock** (*Scot.*), a little bit.— **bit and sup,** something to eat and drink; **bit by bit,** piecemeal : gradually; **do one's bit,** do one's due share; **take the bit in one's teeth,** to throw off control. [From **bite.**]

bitch, *bich, n.* the female of the dog, wolf, and fox : (abusively) a woman, very rarely a man. [O.E. *bicce;* O.N. *bikkja.*]

bite, *bit, v.t.* and *v.i.* to seize or tear with the teeth : to puncture with the mouth-parts, as an insect : to cut or penetrate : to eat into chemically : to take effect : to grip : to wound by reproach : to deceive, to take in (now only in passive) : (*pa.t.* **bit;** *pa.p.* bit or bitt'en).—*n.* a grasp by the teeth : a puncture by an insect : the wound or sore caused thereby : a nibble at the bait : something bitten off : a mouthful : biting quality : grip : pungency : corroding action : (*old slang*) a playful imposition or befooling.—*v.t.* **bite-in'** (*etching*), to eat out the lines of with acid : to repress.—*n.* **bit'er,** one who bites : an animal with a habit of biting : a fish apt to take the bait : a cheat.—*n.* and *adj.* **bit'ing.**—*n.* **bit'ing-louse,** a bird-louse ; **bite the dust,** to fall, to die; **bite the thumb,** to express defiance by knocking the thumb-nail against the teeth. [O.E. *bitan;* Goth. *beitan,* O.N. *bita,* Ger. *beissen.*]

bito, *bē'tō, n.* a tree (*Balanites aegyptiaca;* family Zygophyllaceae) of dry tropical Africa and Asia : its oil-yielding fruit.

bitt, *bit, n.* (*naut.*) a post for fastening cables (usu. in *pl.*).—*v.t.* to fasten round the bitts.—*n.* **bitt'er,** the turn of cable round the bitts, hence perhaps **the bitter end,** the end of the rope that remains aboard, and so the last extremity (but perhaps from **bitter** *adj.*). [Perh. O.N. *biti,* a cross-beam.]

bittacle. Same as **binnacle.**

bitter, *bit'ər, adj.* having a taste like that of quinine or hops : sharp : painful : acrimonious.—*n.* any substance having a bitter taste, esp. a type of ale.— *ns.* **bitter-apple,** colocynth; **bitter-cress,** Cardamine; **bitter-earth,** magnesia.—*adj.* **bitt'erish.**— *n.* **bitter-king,** an intensely bitter shrub of the quassia family, growing in the Eastern Archipelago.—*adv.* **bitt'erly.**—*ns.* **bitt'erness; bitterpit,** a disease of apples, etc., characterised by brown

spots and depressions; **bitter-root,** an American xerophytic plant of the purslane family :—*n.pl.* **bitt'ers,** a liquid prepared from bitter herbs or roots, and used as a stomachic.—*ns.* **bitter-spar,** dolomite; **bitter-sweet,** the woody nightshade (*Solanum Dulcamara*), whose stems when chewed taste first bitter, then sweet : (*Shak.*) an apple that has a compound taste of sweet and bitter : a mixture of sweet and bitter; **bitt'erwood,** various trees, esp. of the Simarubaceae. [O.E. *biter*— *bitan,* to bite.]

bittern, *bit'ərn, n.* a marsh bird of the heron family. [M.E. *bittour, botor*—O.Fr. *butor.*]

bittern, *bit'ərn, n.* an oily liquid remaining in saltworks after crystallisation of the salt. [**bitter.**]

bittor, bittour, bittur, *bit'ər, n.* (*Spens., Dryden*) the bittern.

bitumen, *bi-tū'mən,* or *bit', n.* a name applied to various inflammable mineral substances, as naphtha, petroleum, asphalt.—*v.t.* **bitū'minate,** to mix with or make into bitumen—also **bitū'minise.**— *adjs.* **bitū'minous, bitūmed'** (or *bit'; Shak.*), impregnated with bitumen; **bituminous coal,** coal that flames in burning, from richness in volatile hydrocarbons. [L. *bitūmen,* -*inis.*]

bivalent, *biv'ə-lənt,* or *bī-vā'lənt, adj.* (*chem.*) having a valency of two.—*ns.* **bivalence, bivalency.** [Pfx. *bis-* and **valent.**]

bivalve, *bī'valv, n.* an animal having a shell in two valves or parts, like the oyster—esp. a lamellibranch ; a seed-vessel of like kind.—*adj.* having two valves.—*adj.* **bivalv'ular.** [L. *bi-,* twice, *valva,* a door-leaf.]

bivious, *biv'i-əs, adj.* leading two, or different, ways.—*n.* **biv'ium,** in echinoderms the two rays enclosing the madreporite. [L. *bivius*—*bi-,* twice, *via,* a way.]

bivouac, *biv'ŏŏ-ak, n.* the resting at night of soldiers in the open air, instead of under cover in camp.— *v.i.* to pass the night in the open air :—*pr.p.* **biv'ouacking;** *pa.p.* **biv'ouacked.** [Fr.,—Ger. *beiwacht,* additional watch.]

bi-weekly, *bī'-wēk'li, adj.* occurring or appearing once in two weeks or twice a week.—*adv.* fortnightly : twice a week.—*n.* a periodical issued twice a week.

Bixa, *bik'sä, n.* a tropical American genus of plants yielding anatta, giving name to the **Bixā'ceae,** a family of parietal Archichlamydeae. [Sp. *bixa* (*bija*)—Taino *bixa.*]

bizarre, *bi-zär', adj.* odd : fantastic : extravagant.— *n.* **bizarr'erie.** [Fr.,—Sp. *bizarro,* gallant, brave, poss.—Basque *bizarra,* beard.]

bizcacha. See **viscacha.**

bizone, *bī'zōn, n.* a unit formed of the British and U.S. occupation zones in Germany after 1945.

blab, *blab, v.i.* to talk much : to tell tales.—*v.t.* to let out (a secret) : (*pr.p.* **blabb'ing;** *pa.p.* **blabbed).** —*n.* (*Milt.*) one who lets out secrets : a tattler : tattling.—*n.* **blabb'er.**—*n.* and *adj.* (*Shak.*) **blabb'ing.** [M.E. *blabbe,* cf. O.N. *blabbra,* Ger. *plappern.*]

blab, *blab, n.* (*obs.*) a blister.—*v.t.* to swell.—*adj.* **blabb'er,** swollen. [bleb.]

black, *blak, adj.* of the darkest colour : reflecting no light : obscure : dismal : sullen : horrible : dusky : foul, dirty : malignant : dark-haired : wearing dark armour or clothes.—*n.* black colour or absence of colour : a negro or other dark-skinned person : a black pigment : a smut : smut fungus : black clothes (formerly, still in Scotland, in *pl.*).— *v.t.* to make black : to soil or stain : to draw in black.—*n.* **black'amoor,** a black Moor : a negro.— *adj.* **black'-and-tan',** having black hair on the back, and tan or yellowish-brown elsewhere, esp. of a terrier.—*n.* an auxiliary policeman in Ireland, about 1920 (from his khaki uniform with black cap and armlet).—*adjs.* **black'-and-white',** partly black, partly white : drawing or drawn in black on a white ground; **black-a-vised** (*blak'-ə-vist, -vizd;* perh. Fr. *à vis,* in the face) swarthy.—*v.t.* **black'-ball',** to vote against by putting a black ball into a ballot-box.—*ns.* **black'ball'ing,** the act of so rejecting a candidate; **black'-band,** iron ore containing enough of coal to calcine it; **black'-**

bass′, a North American freshwater fish (*Microp-terus*); black′-bee′tle, a cockroach; black′berry, the fruit of the bramble : in some districts the black currant or the crowberry; black′bird, a black species of thrush : (*U.S.*) a grackle or other bird of the *Icteridae* : a negro or Polynesian recruited or kidnapped for labour; black′birder; black′-birding ; black′board, a board painted black, for writing on.—*adj*. black′-bod′ing, of evil omen.—*n*. black′boy, the Australian grass-tree.—*adj*. black′-browed, having black eye-brows : sullen.—*ns*. black′buck, the common Indian antelope; black′-bull′y, sapodilla; black′cap, a warbler with a black crown : an apple roasted until it is black : a black American raspberry : the cap put on by English judges to pronounce sentence of death; black′-cat, the pecan or fisher; black′-cattle, (*arch*.) bovine animals of any colour : (*orig*.) Welsh and Scottish cattle; black′-chalk, bluish-black clay-slate, used for drawing, and for making black paint.—*adj*. black′-coated, wearing a black coat : of the professional class.—*ns*. black′cock, the male of the black′grouse or black′game, a species of grouse, common in the north of England and in Scotland :—*fem*. grey′-hen; black′-curr′ant, the small black berry of a garden shrub of the gooseberry genus, used in making jam.—*adj*. black′-currant.—*ns*. black′-damp, air in which the oxygen has been displaced by carbon dioxide; black′-death′, a deadly epidemic of bubonic plague that swept over Asia and Europe, reaching England in 1348 (from the black spots that appeared on the skin); black′-di′amond, the Brazilian mineral carbonado, used for drilling very hard substances : (*pl. coll.*) coal; black′-draught, (*coll.*) a purgative medicine, chiefly senna and Epsom salts; black -drop′, a liquid preparation of opium, vinegar, and sugar; black′-earth, a fertile deposit covering wide regions in S. Russia and in Central India.—*v.t*. black′en, to make black : to defame.—*v.i*. to become black.—*adj*. black′-faced.—*ns*. black′fellow, an Australian aboriginal; black′-fish, a name given to several kinds of fish, e.g. the black ruff, a kind of perch : the ca′ing whale : a salmon after spawning; black′-fisher, poacher of fish by night; black′-fishing ; black′-flag, the flag of a pirate : that hoisted at the execution of a criminal; black′-fox′, the pekan; black′-fri′ar, a Dominican, from his black mantle (over a white woollen habit); blackguard (*blag′-ärd*), originally applied to the lowest menials about a court, who took charge of the pots, kettles, etc. : a low, ill-conducted fellow.—*adj*. low : scurrilous.—*v.t*. to vituperate.—*v.i*. to play the blackguard.—*n*. black′guardism.—*adj*. black′guardly.—*ns*. black′head, a bird of various kinds, as the black-headed gull : a comedo.—*adj*. black′headed, having a black head.—*n*. black′heart, a dark kind of cherry.—*adj*. black-heart′ed, of an evil dis-position.—*ns*. black′-hole, a punishment cell, esp. that at Fort William barracks, Calcutta, in which the English prisoners of 1756 were confined; black′ing, a substance used for blacking leather, etc.—*adj*. black ish.—*ns*. black′jack, a large jug for holding drink, originally made of leather : a pirate flag : zinc blende : black′-lead, a black mineral (plumbago, not lead) used in making pen-cils, blacking grates, etc.; black′leg, black-quarter : a low, gambling fellow : a turf-swindler : a man willing to work during a strike (also black′-neb); black′-letter, the Old English (also called Gothic) letter (𝔅𝔩𝔞𝔠𝔨-𝔩𝔢𝔱𝔱𝔢𝔯); black′-list, a list of defaulters or persons against whom a warning is necessary; black′mail, rent or tribute formerly paid to robbers for protection : hush-money extorted under threat of exposure, often on a baseless charge.—*v.t*. to extort money from (a per-son) by this expedient.—*ns*. blackmail′er ; black′-ness; black′out, total extinction or concealment of lights : sudden loss of consciousness, or failure of the mind to work.—*adj*. for blacking out with.—*ns*. black′-pudd′ing, a blood-pudding (q.v.); black′-quart′er, an apoplectic disease of cattle; black′smith, a smith who works in iron; black′-thorn, a dark-coloured thorn bearing sloes : a

stick made from its stem.—*adj*. black′-vis′aged, having a black visage or appearance.—*ns*. black′-wash, a lotion of calomel and lime-water : any-thing that blackens; black′water, a cattle disease (see red-water).—black and blue, with the livid colour of a bruise; black art, magic (perh. a translation of L. *nigromantia*, erroneously used for Gr. *nekromanteiā*, see necromancy); black body, one that absorbs all incident radiation, re-flecting none; black book, an important book bound in black : a book recording the names of persons deserving punishment; black bread, rye-bread; black eye, an eye of which the iris is dark : a discoloration around the eye due to a blow or fall; black frost, frost without rime or snow; black hand, a secret society or under-ground influence, often imaginary; black in the face, purple through strangulation, passion, or effort; black Maria, a prison van : (*mil. slang*) a shell that emits dense black smoke or a gun dis-charging it; black market, surreptitious trade in rationed goods; black mass, a travesty of the mass in diabolism or devil-worship; black Monday, Easter Monday : the day of return to school; black monk, a Benedictine; black out, to obliterate with black : to extinguish or cover all lights; black rat, the smaller of the two British rats (usually brown) now comparatively rare; Black Rod, the usher of the chapter of the Garter and of the House of Lords; black sheep, a dis-reputable member of a family or group; black snake (*U.S.*), a large agile non-poisonous snake (*Bascanium constrictor*) : (*Australia*) a very venom-ous snake (*Pseudechis porphyriacus*), nearly allied to the cobra : a long whip; black swan, a swan with black plumage and red beak, found in Australia : (*fig.*) something rare or non-existent; Black Watch (see watch); black-water fever, a fever in which the urine is dark-coloured; black widow, a very venomous American spider, the female with a black body and the habit of eating her mate; in black and white, in writing or in print : in art, in no colours but black and white; in one′s black books, having incurred one′s displeasure.   [O.E. *blæc*, black.]

bladder, blad′ər, *n*. a thin distended or distensible bag : any such bag in the animal body, esp. the receptacle for urine.—*adjs*. bladd′ered, bladd′-ery.—*ns*. bladd′er-camp′ion, a species of Silene with inflated calyx; bladd′er-cherry, the winter-cherry or strawberry-tomato; bladd′er-nut, a genus (*Staphylea*) of shrubs with inflated capsule; bladd′er-worm, the asexual stage of a tapeworm or cestode; bladd′erwort, a genus (*Utricularia*) of floating plants with bladders that catch small animals; bladd′er-wrack, a common brown sea-weed with bladders.   [O.E. *blædre—blāvan*, to blow; O.H.G. *blā(h)en*, *blājen*, to blow; Ger. *blatter—blāhen*; cf. L. *flātus*, breath.]

blade, blād, *n*. the flat or expanded part of a leaf or petal, esp. a leaf of grass or corn : the cutting part of a knife, sword, etc. : the flat part of an oar : the paddle-like part of a propeller : the free outer part of the tongue : a dashing fellow.—*n*. blade′-bone, the flat bone at the back of the shoulder, the scapula.—*adj*. blad′ed.   [O.E. *blæd*; O.N. *blath*; Ger. *blatt*.]

blae, blā, *adj*. (*Scot*.) blackish or dark bluish : livid : bleak.—*n*. (in *pl*.) hardened clay or somewhat carbonaceous shale, often blae in colour.—*n*. blae′berry, the whortleberry or bilberry.   [O.N. *blār*, livid.]

blague, blåg, *n*. humbug : bounce.—*n*. blagueur (*blā-gər*), one given to blague.   [Fr.]

blah, blä, *n*. (*U.S. slang*) bunkum.

blain, blān, *n*. a boil or blister.   [O.E. *blegen*.]

blain, blān, *n*. a fish (*Gadus luscus*), the bib or pout.

blame, blām, *v.t*. to find fault with : to censure : to impute fault to : to charge with being cause : (*Spens.* ; *B.*) to bring discredit upon.—*n*. imputation of a fault : culpability : responsibility for what is amiss : (*Spens.*) injury.—*adj*. (*U.S.*) confounded (also *adv*.).—*adj*. blăm′able.—*n*. blăm′ableness. —*adv*. blăm′ably.—*adjs*. blamed (*U.S. slang*), damned, confounded (also *adv*.); blame′ful, meriting blame.—*adv.* **blame′fully.**—*n.* **blame′-fulness.**—*adj.* **blame′less,** without blame : guiltless : innocent.—*adv.* **blame′lessly.**—*ns.* **blame′worthy,** worthy of blame : culpable.—*n.* **blame,** blameworthy as being the cause. [Fr. *blâmer,* O.Fr. *blasmer*—Gr. *blasphēmeein,* to speak ill ; see **blasphemie.**]

blanch, *blänsh, v.t.* to whiten.—*v.i.* to grow white.—*adj.* and *adv.* (see **blench**). [Fr. *blanchir*—*blanc,* white ; see **blank.**]

blanc-mange, *blə-mänᵃzh′,* -*monzh′, n.* a jelly prepared with milk : orig. fowl or other flesh with cream, etc. : a shaped milk pudding. [Fr. *blanc-manger*—*blanc,* white, *manger,* food.]

bland, *bland, adj.* smooth : gentle : mild : polite, suave : ironical.—*adv.* **bland′ly.**—*n.* **bland′ness.** [L. *blandus.*]

bland, *bland, n.* in Orkney and Shetland, buttermilk and water. [O.N. *blanda.*]

blandish, *bland′ish, v.t.* to flatter and coax, to cajole. —*n.* **bland′ishment,** act of expressing fondness : flattery : winning expressions or actions. [Fr. *blandir, blandiss-,* from L. *blandīrī.*]

blank, *blangk, adj.* without writing or marks, as white paper : empty : featureless : expressionless : nonplussed : sheer : unrhymed.—*n.* a paper without writing : a lottery-ticket that brings no prize : an empty space, a void or vacancy : (*archery*) the white mark in the centre of a target : (*arch.* except U.S.) a form of document having blank spaces to be filled up : blank verse : a roughly shaped piece to be fashioned into a manufactured article.—*v.t.* to make blank : to make pale : (*Milton*) to disconcert : mincingly used for damn, from the once usual form of printing d——.—*adv.* **blank′ly.**—*ns.* **blank′ness**—**blank cartridge,** one without a bullet ; **blank cheque,** a signed cheque in which the sum is not filled in ; **blank door, window,** a recess imitating a doorway or window ; **blank verse,** unrhymed verse of five feet ; **in blank,** with blank spaces to be filled in. [Fr. *blanc,* from root of Ger. *blinken,* to glitter—O.H.G. *blichen* ; cf. Gr. *phlegein,* to shine.]

blanket, *blangk′it, n.* originally a white woollen fabric : a covering, generally woollen, for a bed, or used as a garment by American Indians, etc. : a covering generally.—*v.t.* to cover, obstruct, or extinguish with, or as with, a blanket (as a ship by taking the wind out of her sails, gun-fire by getting in the way) : to toss in a blanket.—*n.* **blank′eting,** cloth for blankets : tossing in a blanket.—**blanket Indian, Kaffir,** one who wears a blanket, not European clothes ; **blanket stitch,** a stitch used for the edge of a blanket ; **blanket vote,** the Kaffir vote ; **on the wrong side of the blanket,** illegitimately ; **wet blanket,** a damper of spirits : a kill-joy. [O.Fr. *blankete,* dim. of *blanc,* white.]

blare, *blār, v.i.* to roar : to sound loudly, usu. harshly, as a trumpet.—*n.* roar : noise. [M.E. *blaren.*]

blarney, *blär′ni, n.* flattery or cajoling talk.—*v.t.* to cajole.—*n.* **blar′ney-land,** Ireland. [*Blarney* Castle, near Cork, where a stone difficult to reach confers the gift on those who kiss it.]

blasé, *blä′zā, adj.* dulled to pleasures : used up : surfeited. [Fr. *pa.p.* of *blaser,* to cloy.]

blash, *blash, n.* (*Scot.*) a dash or splash of liquid or semi-liquid : battering rain : watery stuff.— *adj.* **blash′y.**

blaspheme, *blas-fēm′, v.t.* to speak impiously of.—*v.i.* to speak profanely or impiously : to curse and swear.—*n.* **blasphēm′er.**—*adj.* **blasphemous** (*blās′fi-məs ; Spens.* -*fē′*).—*adv.* **blas′phemously** (*Spens.* -*fē′*).—*n.* **blas′phemy** (*Spens.* also -*fē′*), impious or profane speaking : contempt or indignity offered to God. [Gr. *blasphēmiā* ; see **blame.**]

blast, *blåst, n.* a blowing or gust of wind : a forcible stream of air : a sound of a wind-instrument : an explosion or detonation : a golf stroke of explosive effect : any scorching, withering or pernicious influence : a blight.—*v.i.* to emit blasts, blow : to use explosives : (*dial.*) to swell : (*obs.*) to wither : to curse.—*v.t.* to blow up : to rend asunder with an explosive : to blow into : (*dial.*) to inflate : to

strike with a blast : to blight, wither, scorch : to strike with a curse.—*adj.* **blast′ed,** blighted : cursed, damned.—*ns.* **blast′er,** one who blasts : a kind of niblick ; **blast′-furnace,** a smelting furnace into which hot air is blown ; **blast′-hole,** a hole in the bottom of a pump through which water enters. —*n.* and *adj.* **blast′ing.**—*ns.* **blast′ment** (*Shak.*), blight ; **blast′-pipe,** a pipe in a steam-engine, to convey the waste steam up the chimney.—**in, at, full blast,** in a state of maximum activity. [O.E. *blǣst ;* cf. O.N. *blāsa ;* Ger. *blasen.*]

blastema, *blås-tē′mä, n.* primordial material : the primordium of an organ : the protoplasmic part of an ovum, distinguished from the yolk : the axial part of a plant embryo. [Gr. *blastēma,* sprout.]

blasto-, *blas′tō-,* in composition, sprout, bud, germ.—*ns.* **blas′toderm** (Gr. *derma,* skin ; *embryology*), the layer or layers of cells arising from the germinal disk, or the portion of a partially segmenting egg which undergoes division ; **blastogen′esis** (-*jen′*), transmission of hereditary characters by the germ-plasm : reproduction by budding.—*adj.* **blastogen′ic,** pertaining to the germ-plasm.—*adj.* and *n.* **blast′oid.**—*n.pl.* **Blastoid′ea** (Gr. *eidos,* form), a group of bud-like calcareous fossil echinoderms.—*ns.* **blas′tomere** (Gr. *meros,* part), a cell formed in an early stage of the cleavage of a fertilised ovum ; **blastopore** (Gr. *poros,* a passage), the orifice of a gastrula ; **blas′tosphere** (Gr. *sphaira,* a sphere) a blastula ; **blas′tūla,** a hollow sphere of cells, one cell thick, formed in the cleavage of a fertilised ovum.—*adj.* **blast′ūlar.**—*n.* **blas-tulā′tion.** [Gr. *blastos,* a sprout.]

blatant, *blāt′ant* (*Spens.* also **blattant,** prob. *blat′ənt*)*, adj.* clamorous : calumniously clamorous : egregiously vulgar.—*adv.* **blat′antly.** [Prob. a coinage of Spenser : for the *blatant* or *blattant beast,* see *Faerie Queene,* V. xii. 37 onward.]

blate, *blāt, adj.* (*Scot.*) bashful, timidly awkward. [Perh. O.E. *blāt,* pale.]

blather, blatherskite. See **blether.**

blatter, *blat′ər, n.* a clattering rainy blast : (*Scott*) a clatter or torrent of words.—*v.i.* to beat with clattering, like rain on a window.—*v.t.* to utter volubly. [L. *blaterāre,* to prate, with sense probably modified by sound.]

blaud, *blawd, n.* (*Scot.*) a fragment : a broken-off slab : a screed or selection of verse.—*v.t.* (*Scot.*) to strike : to disfigure. [Perh. conn. with O.E. *blāwan,* to blow.]

blauwbok, *blow′bok, n.* a small South African antelope : also a large extinct species. [D. *blaauw,* blue, *bok,* goat.]

blawort, *blä′, blä′wərt, n.* the harebell : the corn bluebottle.—Also **blewart** (*bloo′ərt*). [Scot. **blae,** and O.E. *wyrt,* herb.]

blay, bley, *blä, n.* the bleak (fish). [O.E. *blǣge.*]

blaze, *blāz, n.* a rush of light or of flame : a bursting out or active display.—*v.i.* to burn with a strong flame : to throw out a brilliant light.—*n.* **blaz′er,** a light sporting jacket, originally bright-coloured.— *n.pl.* **blazes,** the fires of hell, in imprecations **like to blazes ;** also **like blazes,** with fury. [O.E. *blǣse,* torch.]

blaze, *blāz, n.* a white mark on a beast's face : a mark on a tree made by chipping the bark or otherwise.—*v.t.* to mark (a tree or a track) with a blaze. —**blaze the trail,** to show the way as a pioneer. [Perh. Du. *bles* or O.N. *blesi ;* or **blaze** (1).]

blaze, *blāz, v.t.* to proclaim, to spread abroad.— *n.* **blaz′er** (*Spens.*), one who spreads abroad or proclaims. [Connected with O.N. *blāsa,* to blow ; confused with **blazon.**]

blazon, *blā′zn, v.t.* to make public : to display : (*her.*) to depict or to explain in heraldic terms.— *n.* a coat-of-arms, heraldic bearings (also *fig.*) : the science or rules of coats-of-arms.—*ns.* **blaz′oner,** one who blazons : a herald : a slanderer ; **blaz′onry,** the art of drawing or of deciphering coats-of-arms : heraldry. [Fr. *blason,* a shield, confused with **blaze** (3).]

bleach, *blēch, v.t.* to make pale or white : to whiten, as textile fabrics.—*v.i.* to grow white.—*n.* a process or act of bleaching : a bleaching agent.—*ns.*

Neutral vowels in unaccented syllables : *el′ə-mənt, in′fənt, ran′dəm*

bleach′er; bleach′ery, a place for bleaching; **bleach′-field,** a place for bleaching cloth: a bleacher's office or works.—*n.* and *adj.* **bleach′ing; bleach′ing-green,** a green for bleaching clothes on; **bleach′ing-powder,** a compound of calcium, chlorine, and oxygen (CaClOCl). [O.E. *blǽcan.*]

bleak, *blēk, adj.* colourless : dull and cheerless : cold, unsheltered.—*adv.* **bleak′ly.**—*n.* **bleak′ness.** —*adj.* **bleak′y,** bleak. [Apparently O.N. *bleikr,* answering to O.E. *blǽc, blác,* pale, shining, black; cf. **bleach.**]

bleak, *blēk, n.* a small white river-fish. [O.N. *bleikja,* or a lost equivalent O.E. word.]

blear, *blēr, adj.* dim, watery : blurred as with inflammation.—*v.t.* to dim : to blur : to dim the sight of : to hoodwink.—*adjs.* **bleared; blear′-eyed.** —*n.* **blear′iness.**—*adj.* **blear′y.** [Cf. Ger. *blerr,* soreness of the eyes.]

bleat, *blēt, v.i.* to cry like a sheep.—*n.* a sheep's cry or similar quavering sound.—*n.* and *adj.* **bleat′ing.** [O.E. *blǽtan; imit.; cf. L. bālāre,* to bleat; Gr. *blēchē,* a bleating.]

bleb, *bleb, n.* a transparent blister of the cuticle : a bubble, as in water. [Prob. imit.]

bled, *bled, pa.t.* and *pa.p.* of **bleed.**

blee, *blē, n.* (*arch.*) complexion, colour. [O.E. *bléo.*]

bleed, *blēd, v.i.* to lose blood or sap : to die by slaughter : to issue forth or drop as blood : to have money, etc., extorted from one : (*fig.*) to feel great pity.—*v.t.* to draw blood from, esp. surgically : to draw sap from : to extort from : (in bookbinding) to trim so as to encroach on letterpress or illustrations :—*pa.t.* and *pa.p.* **bled.**—*ns.* **bleed′er,** one who bleeds : an extortioner : one who suffers from haemophilia; **bleed′ing,** a discharge of blood or sap : the operation of letting blood : diffusion or running of colouring matter.—*adj.* full of compassion : emitting sap : terribly weakened by war : (*Shak.*) bloody.—**bleeding heart,** a name given to various plants of the genera *Dicentra, Colocasia,* etc. [O.E. *blédan.* See **blood.**]

blemish, *blem′ish, n.* a stain or defect : reproach.— *v.t.* to mark with any deformity : to tarnish : to defame.—*n.* **blem′ishment** (*Spens.*). [O.Fr. *blesmir, blemir,* pr.p. *blemissant,* to stain, of dubious origin.]

blench, *blensh, blench, v.i.* to shrink or start back : to flinch : (*Shak.*) to start aside, fly off : (*Shak.*) to be inconstant.—*n.* (*Shak.*) a starting aside. [O.E. *blencan.*]

blench, *blensh, blench, adj.* or *adv.* on the basis of payment of a nominal yearly duty.—Also **blanch.** [See **blank.**]

blend, *blend, v.t.* to mix together, esp. intimately or harmoniously : (*Spens.*) to pollute, vitiate.—*v.i.* to be mingled : to harmonise : to shade off : (*pa.t.* and *pa.p.* usu. **blend′ed,** also, esp. *poet.,* **blent).**— *n.* a mixture.—*ns.* **blend′er; blend′ing.** [M.E. *blenden;* cf. O.E. *blandan,* O.N. *blanda.*]

blend, *blend, v.t.* (*Spens.*) to blind : to dazzle : to obscure :—*pa.p.* (y)**blent′.** [O.E. *blendan.*]

blende, *blend, n.* a mineral, zinc sulphide. [Ger. *blende—blenden,* to deceive, from its resemblance to galena.]

Blenheim, *blen′əm, n.* a kind of spaniel named from the Duke of Marlborough's seat.

blennorrhoea, *blen-ō-rē′ä, n.* a discharge of mucus. [Gr. *blennos,* mucus, *rhoiā,* flow.]

blenny, *blen′i, n.* a genus (Blennius) of acanthopterygian fishes, usually slimy. [Gr. *blennos,* mucus.]

blent, *blent, pa.t.* and *pa.p.* of **blend** (1) and (2).

blepharism, *blef′ər-izm, n.* spasm of the eyelid.— *n.* **blephari′tis,** inflammation of the eyelid. [Gr. *blepharon,* eyelid.]

blesbok, *bles′bok, n.* a South African antelope with a blazed forehead. [Du. *bles,* blaze, *bok,* goat.]

bless, *bles, v.t.* to consecrate : to make the sign of the cross over : to extol as holy, to pronounce holy or happy : to invoke divine favour upon : to wish happiness to : to make joyous, happy, or prosperous : to glorify :—*pa.p.* **blessed** (*blest*), or **blest.**—*adj.* **bless′ed, blest,** happy : prosperous : in heaven : beatified : (euphemistically) accursed,

confounded.—*adv.* **bless′edly.**—*ns.* **bless′edness; bless′ing,** a wish or prayer for happiness or success : any means or cause of happiness : (*B.*) a gift or present : a form of invoking the favour of God at a meal.—**single blessedness,** the unmarried state. [O.E. *blédsian, blétsian, bletsian,* to bless, prob. from *blód,* blood.]

bless, *bles, v.t.* (*Spens.*) to brandish : to brandish around :—*pa.t.* **blest, blist.** [Perh. from **bless** (1) as if to make the sign of the cross; or from **bless** (3); or poss. conn. with **blaze.**]

blest, *blest, pa.p.* of **bless.**—Also *adj.*

blet, *blet, n.* incipient internal decay in fruit, sleepiness (without external sign) : a part so affected.— *v.i.* to become soft or sleepy :—*pr.p.* **blett′ing;** *pa.t.* and *pa.p.* **blett′ed.** [Fr.]

blether (*Scot.*), **bledh′ər, blather** (*U.S.,* etc.), *bladh′ər, v.i.* to talk garrulous nonsense.—*n.* one who blethers : (often in *pl.*) fluent, garrulous nonsense.—*n.* **blethera′tion.**—*n.* and *adj.* **bleth′ering.** —*ns.* **bleth′erskate, bleth′eranskate** (*Scot.*), **blath′erskite** (*U.S.*), a loquacious talker of nonsense. [M.E. *blather*—O.N. *blathra,* to talk foolishly, *blathr,* nonsense; prob. **skate** (the fish).]

blew, *blōō, pa.t.* of **blow.**

blew, an old spelling (*Spens., Milt.*) of **blue.**

blewits, *blū′its, n.* a kind of edible mushroom, bluish in part. [Perh. from **blue.**]

bley, *blā, n.* same as **blay.**

blight, *blīt, n.* a disease in plants which blasts or withers them : a fungus, insect, or other cause of blight : anything that injures, destroys, depresses, or frustrates : a damp, depression, decay, set-back, check.—*v.t.* to affect with blight : to blast : to frustrate.—*n.* **blight′er,** a cause of blighting : (*slang*) a term of (usually playful) abuse, scamp, beggar, wretch.—*n.* and *adj.* **blight′ing.**—*adv.* **blight′ingly.** [17th cent.; origin obscure; poss. conn. with **bleach, bleak.**]

blighty, *blī′ti, n.* (*mil. slang*) home : the home country : a wound necessitating return home. [Hind. *bilāyatī,* foreign, European—Ar. *wilāyat,* province, country. Cf. **vilayet.**]

blimbing. Same as **bilimbi.**

blimey, blimy, *blī′mi, interj.* a Cockney vulgarism for *God blind me.*

blimp, blimp, *n.* a small type of air-ship for scouting, etc.

blin, *blin, v.t.* (*Spens.*) to cease.—*n.* cessation : stoppage. [O.E. *blinnan,* to cease, pfx. *be-,* and *linnan,* to cease.]

blind, *blīnd, adj.* without sight : dark : obscure : invisible : concealed : not directed, or affording no possibility of direction, by sight or by foresight : ignorant or undiscerning : unobserving : voluntarily overlooking : without an opening : failing to flower or fruit.—*n.* something intended to blind one to the facts : a window-screen : a shade : (*poker*) a stake put up without seeing one's cards.— *v.t.* to make blind : to darken, obscure, or deceive : to dazzle.—*ns.* **blind′age** (*mil.*), a temporary wooden screen faced with earth as a protection against splinters of shell and the like; **blind′-all′ey,** a cul-de-sac.—*adj.* (of a juvenile employment) leading to no settled occupation in adult life.—*ns.* **blind′-coal,** anthracite (as burning without flame) : coal partly carbonised by an igneous intrusion. —*adjs.* **blind′-drunk,** so drunk as to be like a blind man; **blind′ed,** deprived of sight : without intellectual discernment.—*ns.* **blind′er,** one who or that which blinds : a horse's blinker; **blind′fish,** an eyeless fish (Amblyopsis) of the Kentucky Mammoth Cave.—*adj.* **blind′fold** (earlier **blind-felled,** struck blind), having the eyes bandaged so as not to see : thoughtless : performed without seeing : reckless.—Also *adv.*—*v.t.* to cover the eyes of : to mislead.—*n.* **blind′-gut,** the caecum.— *n.* and *adj.* **blind′ing.**—*adj.* **blind′less.**—*adv.* **blind′ly.**—*ns.* **blind′man's-buff** (i.e. buffet), a game in which a blindfold player tries to catch the others; **blind′ness,** want of sight : ignorance : folly; **blind′-side,** the side on which a person is blind to danger : weak point; **blind′-story,** a triforium; **blind′worm**, a slow-worm, a legless lizard with eyes so small as to be supposed blind.— **blind road**, a grassy track invisible to those that are on it; **blind spot**, the spot on the retina where the optic nerve joins and where there are no visual cells : (*radio*) a point within the normal range of a transmitter at which the field strength is abnormally small : a point just outside the range of one's vision : a region of understanding in which one's intuition and judgment always fail; **blind tooling**, impression without gilding. [O.E. *blind*; O.N. *blindr*.]

blink, *blingk*, *v.i.* to glance, twinkle, or wink : to see obscurely : to look with the eyes half-closed : to shine unsteadily.—*v.t.* to shut out of sight : to ignore or evade.—*n.* a glimpse, glance, or wink : a gleam, esp. momentary.—*n.* **blink′ard**, one who blinks or has bad eyes.—*adj.* **blinked**, affected with blinking.—*n.* **blink′er**, a leather flap to prevent a horse from seeing sidewise.—*adj.* **blink′ing** (*slang*), a meaningless substitute for bloody.—*n.* **blinks**, a mud or water weed (*Montia*) of the purslane family, with minute flowers. [Cf. **blench**.]

bliss, *blis*, *n.* the highest happiness : the special happiness of heaven.—*adj.* **bliss′ful**.—*adv.* **bliss′-fully**.—*n.* **bliss′fulness**.—*adj.* **bliss′less**. [O.E. *blīths*—*blīthe*, blithe.]

blist, *blist*, (*Spens.*) *pa.t.* and *pa.p.* of **bless** (1 and 2).

blister, *blis′tər*, *n.* a thin bubble or bladder on the skin, often containing watery matter : a similar spot elsewhere, as on a leaf, metal, paint : (*naut.*) the protective bulging outer hull of a double-hulled ship, to lessen risk of sinking : a plaster applied to raise a blister.—*v.t.* to raise a blister or blisters on : (*fig.*) to burn with scathing words : (*Shak.*) to ornament with puffs.—*v.i.* to develop blisters.—*ns.* **blis′ter-bee′tle**, **blis′ter-fly**, an insect used for blistering, esp. Spanish fly (Cantharis); **blis′ter-plas′ter**, a plaster made of Spanish flies used to raise a blister; **blis′ter-steel**, **blis′tered-steel**, steel made from wrought-iron with blistered surface.—*adj.* **blis′tery**. [M.E.; most prob. O.Fr. *blestre*, conn. with O.N. *blástr*, *blása*, to blow; Ger. *blase*.]

blite, *blīt*, *n.* a name for several plants of the goose-foot family. [Gr. *bliton*.]

blithe, *blīdh*, *adj.* jocund : cheerful : gay : sprightly. —*adv.* **blithe′ly**.—*n.* **blithe′ness**.—*adj.* **blithe′-some**, joyous.—*adv.* **blithe′somely**.—*n.* **blithe′-someness**. [O.E. *blīthe*, joyful. See **bliss**.]

blither, *blidh′ər*, *v.i.* another form of **blather**, **blether**.—*adj.* **blith′ering**, as an expression of contempt.

blitz, *blits*, *n.* an attack or bombing from the air.— *v.t.* to attack or damage by air-raid.—**blitzed area**, a district extensively damaged by aerial warfare. [Ger. *blitzkrieg*, lightning war, the German method in 1939—*blitz*, lightning, *krieg*, war.]

blive, *bliv*, *adv.* (*Spens.*). Same as **belive**.

blizzard, *bliz′ərd*, *n.* a blinding storm of wind and snow, a snow-squall.—*adjs.* **blizz′ardly**, **blizz′-ardous**. [A modern coinage, most prob. onomatopoeic, on the analogy of *blow*, *blast*, etc.]

bloat, *blōt*, *v.t.* to swell or puff out : to dry partially by smoke (applied to fish).—*v.i.* to swell or dilate : to grow turgid.—*n.* hoove (also **bloating**) : bloatedness : (*U.S.*) a drunkard.—*adj.* **bloat′ed**.—*n.* **bloat′er**, a herring partially dried in smoke, esp. at Yarmouth. [Cf. O.N. *blautr*, soft.]

blob, *blob*, *n.* a drop or globule : anything soft and round, as a gooseberry : a round spot : zero. [Imit.]

bloc, *blok*, *n.* a combination of parties, nations, or other units to achieve a common purpose. [Fr.]

block, *blok*, *n.* a mass of wood or stone, etc., usu. flat-sided : a piece of wood or other material used as a support (as for chopping, beheading), or as a mould (as for hats), or for printing from (as wood-engravings, process-blocks), or as a toy (for building) : a pulley with its framework or the framework alone : a connected group of houses, seats, sheets of paper, shares, etc.: a section of territory : (*U.S.*) a building lot bounded by streets : an obstruction : a blockhead : an impassive person : (*cricket*) the place where a batsman rests his bat.— *v.t.* to enclose or shut up : to restrict : to obstruct :

to make inactive : to shape as on a block, or to sketch out roughly (often with *in* or *out*) : to stop (a ball) with bat resting upright on the ground.—*n.* **blockade′**, the blocking up of a place by surrounding it with troops or by ships.—*v.t.* to block up by troops or ships.—*ns.* **blockade′-runner**, a person or ship that passes through a blockading force; **block′-book**, a book printed from engraved blocks, not movable types; **block′-chain′**, an endless chain of blocks and links; **block′-coal**, coal that breaks into cuboidal blocks.—*adj.* **blocked**, meanings as *pa.p.* of verb : subject to restriction in use.— *ns.* **block′head**, a wooden head : a dolt; **block′-house**, a small temporary fort.—*adj.* **block′ish**, like a block : stupid : dull.—*ns.* **block′-ship**, a war-ship too old for action, but useful in port defence : **block′-system**, a system in which no train is allowed on to a section of railway so long as any other is on it; **block′-tin**, tin in the form of blocks or ingots.—**block capital**, **block letter**, a capital letter written in imitation of type : block type; **block type**, a heavy-letter type, without serifs; **blocking motion**, notice of intention to bring up a certain matter at a future date, and thus prevent (or block) raising the subject on a motion for adjournment. [Fr. *bloc*, probably Gmc.]

bloke, *blōk*, *n.* (*slang*) a man : (*naut.*) the commander.

bloncket, *blongk′et*, *adj.* (*Spens.*) grey. [Fr. *blanquet*, *blanchet*, whitish, dim. of *blanc*, white.]

blond (*fem.* **blonde**), *blond*, *n.* a person of fair complexion and light-coloured hair—opp. to *brunet*(te). —*adj.* (of hair) between golden and light chestnut in colour : of a fair complexion : fair.—*n.* **blond(e)′-lace**, lace made of silk, originally raw silk. [Fr.]

blood, *blud*, *n.* the oxygenating fluid (red in the higher animals) circulating in the body : descent, good birth : relationship : kindred : (elliptically) a blood-horse, one of good pedigree : a swaggering dandy about town : temperament : bloodshed or murder : the juice of anything, esp. if red : the supposed seat of passion—hence temper, anger (as *his blood is up*), etc. : the sensual nature of man : (*slang*) a sensational or melodramatic tale, a penny-dreadful. —*v.t.* to bleed : to smear with blood : to initiate into blood sports or to war.—*adj.* **blood-and-thun′der**, sensational, melodramatic.—*n.* **blood′-bath**, a bath in warm blood : a massacre.—*adj.* **blood′-bespott′-ed**, spotted, sprinkled with blood.—*n.* **blood′-bird**, an Australian honey-eater with scarlet plumage in the cock-bird.—*adjs.* **blood′-bol′tered**, clotted or matted with blood; **blood′-bought** (*Shak.*), bought at the expense of blood or life.— *n.* **blood′-broth′er**, a brother by blood : among primitive peoples, one who has entered a close and binding friendship with another by ceremonies involving the mixing of blood.—*adjs.* **blood′-consuming** (*Shak.*), **blood′-curdling**, exciting horror with a physical feeling as if the blood had curdled; **blood′ed**, having blood : of pure blood—pedigreed : initiated.—*ns.* **blood′-dust**, haemoconia; **blood′-feud**, a family feud arising out of an act of bloodshed : a vendetta; **blood′-flower**, *Haemanthus* : a species of *Asclepias*.—*adj.* **blood′-froz′en** (*Spens.*), having the blood frozen or chilled.—*ns.* **blood′-group**, any one of the four groups distinguished by different kinds of blood which may or may not prove incompatible on transfusion; **blood′-guilt′iness**, the guilt of shedding blood, as in murder.—*adj.* **blood′-guilty**.— *ns.* **blood′heat**, the temperature of human blood (about 98° Fahr.); **blood′-horse**, a horse of the purest and most highly prized blood, origin, or stock.—*adj.* **blood′-hot**, as hot or warm as blood.— *n.* **blood′hound**, a large, keen-scented (sleuth) hound, noted for its powers of tracing : (*fig.*) a detective.—*adv.* **blood′ily**.—*adj.* **blood′less**, without blood : dead : anaemic : without the shedding of blood : (*Shak.*) without spirit or activity.—*ns.* **blood′lessness**; **blood′letter**; **blood′letting**, bleeding by opening a vein; **blood′-money**, money earned by laying or supporting a capital charge against anyone, esp. if the charge be false or made by an accomplice : money paid to a hired assassin : compensation formerly paid to the next of kin of a

Neutral vowels in unaccented syllables : *el′ə-mənt*, *in′fənt*, *ran′dəm*

victim slain; **blood'-plate,** a platelet; **blood'-pois'oning,** a name popularly, but loosely, used of pyaemia and allied diseases; **blood'-pudding,** a pudding made with blood and other materials; **blood'-rain,** rain coloured by red dust from the desert.—*adj.* **blood'-red',** of the colour of blood.—*ns.* **blood'-relation,** one related by common ancestry; **blood'root,** a plant (*Sanguinaria canadensis*) of the poppy family with red rootstock and sap; **blood-roy'al,** royal descent; **blood'-sac'rifice** (*Shak.*), a sacrifice made with bloodshed; **blood'-shed,** the shedding of blood: slaughter.—*adjs.* **blood'shot** (of the eye), red or inflamed with blood; **blood'-sized,** sized or smeared with blood.—*ns.* **blood'-spav'in,** a disease of horses consisting of the swelling of a vein on the inside of the hock, from a checking of the blood.—*adj.* **blood'sprent,** sprinkled with blood.—*n.* **blood'stain.**—*adj.* **blood'stained,** stained with blood: guilty of murder.—*ns.* **blood'stone,** a green chalcedony with blood-like spots of red jasper: haematite; **blood'sucker,** an animal that sucks blood, esp. a leech: an extortioner: one who sponges upon another.—*adj.* **blood'sucking** (*Shak.*), that sucks or draws blood.—*ns.* **blood'-tax,** conscription or universal military service, as drawing from the nation a number of lives or recruits annually; **blood'thirstiness,** eager desire to shed blood.—*adj.* **blood'thirsty.**—*ns.* **blood'-transfusion,** transfer of blood from the veins of one person to those of another; **blood'-vessel,** a vein or artery; **blood'-wite, -wit** (*hist.*), a fine for shedding blood: the right to levy it; **blood'wood,** a name for various trees with red wood or juice, or their timber, as a lythraceous tree of the East Indies (Lagerstroemia), eucalyptus of different kinds, logwood; **blood'-worm,** a red aquatic midge larva (*Chironomus*).—*adj.* **blood'y,** of the nature of blood: stained with blood: murderous, cruel: vulgarly, as an *adj.* emphasising anger or the like, or almost meaningless: as an *adv.* employed as a mere intensive—most prob. from the habits of the late 17th century bloods (Etheredge, '*bloody*-drunk').—*v.t.* to make bloody.—*n.* **blood'y-bones'** (see **rawhead**).—*adjs.* **blood'y-eyed; blood'y-faced.**—*ns.* **blood'y-flux,** dysentery, in which the discharges from the bowels are mixed with blood; **blood'y-hand** (see **hand**).—*adj.* **blood'y-mind'ed.**—*ns.* **blood'y-mind'edness; blood'y-sweat,** a sweat accompanied with the discharge of blood.—**avenger of blood,** the next-of-kin to a murdered man whose duty it was thought to avenge his death; **blood agar,** agar-agar for growing bacteria to which blood has been added before the jelly set; **blood bank,** a supply of blood plasma, or the place where it is kept; **blood orange,** a variety of orange with red or red-streaked pulp; **blood pressure,** the pressure of the blood on the walls of the blood-vessels, varying with age and physical condition; **blood sports,** those involving the killing of animals—fox-hunting and the like; **blood test,** an examination (chemical, microscopical, bacteriological) of a small specimen of blood usually drawn from a blood-vessel; **in blood,** in full vigour; **in hot or cold blood,** under or free from excitement or sudden passion. [O.E. *blôd;* O.Fris. *blôd;* Ger. *blut.*]

bloom, *blōōm, n.* a blossom or flower (also collectively): the state of being in flower: the prime or highest perfection of anything: the first freshness of beauty of anything: rosy colour: the glow on the cheek: a powdery, waxy, or cloudy surface or appearance: an efflorescence.—*v.i.* to put forth blossoms: to flower: to be in a state of beauty or vigour: to flourish.—*v.t.* to give a bloom to.—*n.* **bloom'er,** a plant that blooms: a floriated initial letter: (*slang*) an absurd and embarrassing blunder.—*adj.* **bloom'ing,** flowering: flourishing: fresh and youthful: bright: (*slang*) euphemistically for bloody.—*adjs.* **bloom'less,** without bloom; **bloom'y,** flowery: flourishing: covered with bloom. [O.N. *blóm;* cf. Goth. *blôma,* Ger. *blume.*]

bloom, *blōōm, n.* a mass or bar of iron or steel in an intermediate stage of manufacture, esp. one thicker than a *billet.*—**bloom'ery,** a furnace for making iron ore or iron into blooms. [O.E. *blóma.*]

bloomer, *blōōm'ər, n.* and *adj.* a dress for women, devised by Mrs. *Bloomer* of New York about 1849, consisting of a jacket with close sleeves, a skirt falling a little below the knee, and Turkish trousers: (in *pl.*) bloomer trousers, or similar garment.

bloosme, *blōōm, n.* and *v.i.* Spenser's form of **blossom,** modified by **bloom.**

blore, *blōr, n.* a violent gust of wind. [Prob. related to **blare** and **blow.**]

blossom, *blos'əm, n.* a flower or bloom, esp. one that precedes edible fruit: the state of being in flower, literally or figuratively.—*v.i.* to put forth blossoms or flowers: to flourish and prosper.—*n.* **bloss'oming.**—*adj.* **bloss'omy,** covered with flowers, flowery. [O.E. *blóstm, blóstma,* from the same root as **bloom,** and L. *flôs.*]

blot, *blot, n.* a spot, as of a drop of ink: an obliteration: a stain in reputation: a blemish.—*v.t.* to obliterate: to spot or smudge: to disgrace: to blemish: to dry with blotting-paper:—*pr.p.* **blott'ing;** *pa.t.* and *pa.p.* **blott'ed.**—*n.* **blott'er,** one who blots: a bad author: a sheet, pad, or book of blotting-paper.—*n.* **blottesque** (*-esk'*), a painting executed with heavy blot-like touches: a daub: (*fig.*) a vigorous descriptive sketch.—Also *adj.*—*ns.* **blott'ing,** spotting as with ink: obliterating: smudging: drying with blotting-paper: blotting-paper; **blott'ing-pad,** a pad of blotting-paper; **blott'ing-paper,** unsized paper, used for absorbing ink.—*adjs.* **blott'o** (*slang*), helplessly drunk; **blott'y,** blotted: smudged.—**blot one's copybook,** to blemish one's record, esp. by an indiscretion. [Origin obscure.]

blot, *blot, n.* a piece liable to be taken at backgammon: exposure of a piece: a weak place in anything. [Cf. Dan. *blot,* Du. *bloot,* naked, exposed.]

blot, *blot, n.* (*Spens.*) spawn. [Perh. conn. with **blow** (3).]

blotch, *bloch, n.* an irregular discoloration: a pustule: any plant disease characterised by blotching.—*v.t.* to mark or cover with blotches.—*adj.* **blotched.**—*n.* **blotch'iness.**—*n.* and *adj.* **blotch'ing.**—*adj.* **blotch'y.** [Prob. formed on **blot.**]

blouse, *blowz, n.* a loose sack-like, belted outer garment, like the smock-frock: a loose-fitting bodice for women, tucked in at the waist. [Fr.]

blow, *blō, n.* a stroke or knock: a sudden misfortune or calamity.—**at a blow,** by a single action, suddenly. [Found from the 15th century; perh. from **blow** (3), or conn. with Ger. *bläuen,* to beat, beetle.]

blow, *blō, v.i.* to bloom or blossom:—*pr.p.* **blow'ing;** *pa.t.* **blew** (*blōō*); *pa.p.* **blown** (*blōn*).—*n.* blossom, bloom: display of blossom. [O.E. *blôwan;* Ger. *blühen;* cf. **bloom, blossom.**]

blow, *blō, v.i.* to produce a current of air: to move, as air or wind (often *impers.*): to breathe hard or with difficulty: to spout, as whales: to boast: (*slang*) to tell tales, peach, inform: (of insects) to deposit eggs.—*v.t.* to drive air upon or into: to drive by a current of air: to sound, as a wind-instrument: to spread by report: to inform upon: to fan or kindle: (of insects) to deposit eggs on: to curse: (*slang*) to squander: (*pa.t.* **blew,** *blōō;* *pa.p.* **blown,** *blōn,* in imprecations **blowed,** *blōd*).—*n.* a blast: an insect egg.—*ns.* **blow'ball,** the downy head of a dandelion in seed; **blow'er,** one who blows: a metal plate on the upper part of a fireplace, to increase the draught: a machine for driving a blast of air; **blow'fly,** a flesh-fly (*Sarcophaga*): a blue-bottle (*Calliphora*); **blow-gun,** a blowpipe (weapon); **blow'-hole,** a whale's nostril: a hole in ice to which seals, etc., come to breathe: a hole for escape of gas: a bubble in metal; **blow'lamp,** a portable lamp producing heat by a blast.—*adj.* **blown,** out of breath, tired: swelled: stale, worthless.—*ns.* **blow-out'** (*slang*), a feast; **blow'pipe,** a pipe through which air is blown on a flame, to increase its heat, used in *blowpipe analysis,* etc.: a long straight tube from which an arrow, pellet, etc., is blown by the breath: a glass-blower's tube: **blow'-valve,** a snifting valve.—*adj.* **blow'y,** windy: gusty.— **blow hot and cold,** to be favourable and unfavourable by turns, to be irresolute: **blow in,** to turn up casually; **blow off** (steam, etc.), to allow to escape, to escape forcibly; **blow one's own trumpet,** to sound one's own praises; **blow over,** to pass away, as a danger or a scandal; **blow up,** to shatter or destroy by explosion: to inflate: to scold; **blow upon,** to take the bloom, freshness, or the interest off: to bring into discredit: to inform upon. [O.E. *bláwan;* Ger. *blähen, blasen;* L. *fláre.*]

blowze, *blowz, n.* a ruddy, fat-faced wench.—*adjs.* **blowzed, blowz'y,** fat and ruddy, or flushed with exercise: dishevelled. [Perh. related to **blush** or **blow,** or of cant origin.]

blubber, *blub'er, n.* a jellyfish: the fat of whales and other sea animals: excessive fat: a weeping.—*v.i.* to weep effusively (shortened to **blub**).—*adj.* **blubb'ered,** of a face, swollen with weeping. [M.E. *blober, bluber;* prob. imit.]

blucher, properly *blühh'ər,* often *blōōk'ər,* or *blōōch'er, n.* a strong leather half-boot or high -shoe. [Marshal *Blücher,* the Prussian general at Waterloo.]

blude, *blüd, n.* a Scots form of **blood.**—*adj.* **blud'y blud'ie.**

bludgeon, *bluj'n, n.* a short stick with a heavy striking end.—*v.t.* to beat with a bludgeon: to assail heavily. [First in 18th century; origin very obscure.]

blue, *blōō, adj.* of the colour of the unclouded sky, or that of wood-smoke, skim-milk, lead: livid: greyish: dismal: learned, pedantic: indecent or obscene: dressed in blue: symbolised by blue.— *n.* one of the colours of the rainbow: the sky: the sea: a blue pigment: a blue powder or liquid (indigo, Prussian blue, etc.) used in laundries: a member of a party whose colour is blue (as the opponents of the Greens in ancient Constantinople, *hist.* the Presbyterians, and later often the Conservatives): a present or past representative of Oxford or Harrow (dark), Cambridge or Eton (light blue) in sports: a similar representative of any university: the badge awarded to him, or the honour of wearing it: blue clothes: a blue-stocking: a butterfly of the family *Lycaenidae:* a former squadron of the British fleet: (in *pl.*) the blue devils: (in *pl.*) a very slow and dismal American negro dance or dance-tune.—*v.t.* to make blue: to treat with blue.—*v.i.* to turn blue.—*ns.* **blue'- back,** the sockeye, the principal salmon of the North Pacific; **blue'bell,** in S. England the wood or wild hyacinth: (*blōō'bel'*), in Scotland and N. England the harebell; **blue'berry,** the fruit of *Vaccinium vacillans* and other American species; **blue'bird,** a small American bird (*Sialia sialis*) akin to the warblers.—*n.* and *adj.* **blue'-black,** black with a tinge of blue: blue changing in time to black.—*ns.* **blue-bonn'et,** a round flat blue woollen cap: hence a Scottish peasant, a Scotsman; **blue'book,** a report or other paper printed by parliament (from its blue paper wrapper); **blue'bottle,** the blue cornflower: a large fly (*Calliphora*) with metallic blue abdomen: (*slang*) a policeman or beadle; **blue'-buck,** the blauwbok; **blue'cap,** a salmon of one year, with blue-spotted head: the blue titmouse: (*Shak.*) a Scotsman; **blue'-chip,** term applied to the most reliable industrial shares; **blue'coat** (*arch.*), a serving-man, almsman, or other wearing a blue coat: a pupil of Christ's Hospital or other *Bluecoat school,* whose garb is a blue coat.—Also *adj.*—*ns.* **blue'eye,** a blue-cheeked Australian honey-eater; **blue'fish,** a large voracious fish (*Pomatomus saltatrix*) of the Serranidae, on the U.S. Atlantic coast; **blue'-fox,** an arctic fox; **blue'gown,** one of a former class of licensed beggars in Scotland, a King's Bedesman; **blue'grass,** a slightly glaucous permanent grass (*Poa pratensis,* etc.) of Europe and North America, esp. Kentucky.—*adjs.* **bluegreen, blue-grey,** between blue and green or grey (blue-green algae, the *Cyanophyceae*).—*ns.* **blue'-ground,** a greyish-blue decomposed agglomerate in which diamonds are got; **blue'-gum,**

species of Eucalyptus, esp. *E. globulus;* **blue'- hare',** the mountain hare; **blue'ing, blu'ing,** the process of imparting a blue colour, esp. to metal, or of neutralising yellow; blue-rot in wood: (*U.S.*) laundress's blue; **blue'jacket,** a seaman in the navy; **blue'-jay,** an American jay (*Cyanocitta cristata*); **blue'-mould,** a fungus that turns bread, cheese, etc., blue; **blue'ness;** **blue'nose,** a nickname for a Nova Scotian; **blue-pen'cil,** to correct, edit, or censor, as if with a blue pencil; **blue'-pill,** a mercurial pill; **blue'print,** a photographic print, white upon blue, on paper sensitised with a ferric salt and potassium ferricyanide from a photographic negative or a drawing on transparent paper—also called cyanotype, ferroprussiate print: a preliminary sketch or plan of work to be done. —Also *v.t.*—*ns.* **blue'-rot',** a blue discoloration in coniferous wood, caused by a fungus, *Cera-tostomella;* **blue'stocking,** a learned lady, esp. one inclining to pedantry (said to be from Benjamin Stillingfleet, a member of Mrs. Montagu's coterie, who preferred worsted to black silk); **blue'stone,** or **blue vitriol,** hydrated copper sulphate; **blue'- throat,** or **blue'breast,** a bird akin to the nightingale; **blue'-water,** open sea; **blue'weed,** viper's bugloss (also **blue thistle**); **blue'wing,** an American teal.—*adj.* **bluey** (*blōō'i*), inclined towards blue (esp. in compounds, as **blu'ey-green'**). —*n.* (*Austr.*) a bushman's bundle, often in a blue cloth.—*adj.* **blu'ish.**—**blue baby,** a baby with congenital cyanosis; **Blue Blanket,** the banner of the Edinburgh craftsmen; **blue blood,** aristocratic blood (Sp. *sangre azul,* from the blue veins of descendants of the Visigoths); **blue devil,** an evil demon: (in *pl.*) the apparitions seen in delirium tremens, hence deep despondency; **Blue Ensign,** a blue flag with the Union Jack in canton, till 1864 flag of the Blue squadron, now flown by the Naval Reserve and certain yachts and merchant vessels; **blue funk** (*slang*), great terror; **blue John,** ornamental fluorspar; **blue laws,** sumptuary laws; **Blue Mantle,** one of the pursuivants of the English Heralds' College; **blue moon,** a very long but quite indeterminate time; **blue murder,** extreme activity or commotion; **Blue Peter,** a blue flag with a white rectangle hoisted when a ship is about to sail: a call for trumps in whist; **blue ribbon, riband,** the ribbon of the Order of the Garter: any very high distinction or prize: the badge of the teetotal Blue Ribbon Army, founded in America in 1878; **blue ruin** (*slang*), gin; **blue sheep,** the bharal; **blue sky laws** (*U.S.*), laws to prevent fraud in the sale of stocks (against capitalising of the blue skies); **blue whale,** Sibbald's rorqual, the biggest living animal; **burn blue,** to burn with a blue flame, as in the presence of sulphur, terrestrial or infernal; **out of the blue,** from the cloudless sky: hence, entirely unexpectedly; **the Blues,** the Royal Horse Guards; **true blue,** faithful to blue principles (see above). [M.E. *blew*—O.Fr. *bleu,* of Gmc. origin; O.N. *blá* gave M.E. *bla, blo,* and **blae.**]

blue, *blōō, v.t.* to squander. [Prob. for **blow.**]

bluff, *bluf, adj.* steep or upright in front: blustering: rough and hearty: outspoken.—*n.* a high steep bank: a horse's blinker: a bluffing act or behaviour. —*v.t.* and *v.i.* to deceive or seek to deceive by concealment of weakness or show of self-confidence or threats.—*adv.* **bluff'ly.**—*n.* **bluff'ness.** [Origin unknown; perh. different words.]

bluggy, *blug'i, adj.* jocularly for **bloody.**

bluid, *blüd, n.* a Scots form of **blood.**—*adj.* **bluid'y.**

blunder, *blun'dər, v.i.* to make a gross mistake: to flounder about.—*v.t.* to utter thoughtlessly: to mismanage, bungle: to achieve, put, render, by blundering.—*n.* a gross mistake.—*n.* **blun'derer.** —*n.* and *adj.* **blun'dering.**—*adv.* **blun'deringly.** [M.E. *blondren;* prob. conn. with **bland,** to mix.]

blunderbuss, *blun'dər-bus, n.* a short hand-gun with a wide bore. [Du. *donderbus—donder,* thunder, *bus,* a box, gun-barrel, gun; Ger. *donner-büchse.*]

blunk, *blungk, v.t.* (*Scot.*) to spoil: to bungle.—*n.* **blunk'er,** (*Scott*) a bungler, or according to Jamieson, one who prints cloth.

blunt, *blunt, adj.* having a dull edge or point : rough : outspoken : dull : (*Spens.*) barren.—*v.t.* to dull.—*v.i.* to become dull.—*n.* (*slang*) money.—*adj.* blunt′ish.—*adv.* blunt′ly.—*n.* blunt′ness.—*adj.* blunt′-witt′ed (*Shak.*), dull, stupid. [Origin unknown.]

blur, *blur, n.* an ill-defined spot or smear : a confused impression.—*v.t.* to blot : to render indistinct in outline : to blemish.—*v.i.* to make blurs : —*pr.p.* blurr′ing ; *pa.t.* and *pa.p.* blurred. [Perh. a variety of **blear**.]

blurb, *blurb, n.* a publisher's puff or commendatory description of a book, commonly printed on the jacket. [Attributed to Gelett Burgess, American author.]

blurt, *blurt, v.t.* to utter suddenly or unadvisedly (with *out*).—*v.i.* (*Shak.*) to snort or puff in scorn.—*n.* an abrupt outburst.—*adv.* with a blurt.—*n.* and *adj.* blurt′ing. [Prob. imit.]

blush, *blush, n.* a red glow on the skin caused by shame, modesty, etc. : any reddish colour or suffusion.—*adj.* pinkish.—*v.i.* to show shame or confusion by growing red : to grow red.—*ns.* blush′er (*Ben Jonson*), a blushing girl. —*adj.* blush′et (*Ben Jonson*), a blushing girl. —*adj.* blush′ful.—*n.* and *adj.* blush′ing.—*adv.* blush′ingly.—*adj.* blush′less.—*adv.* blush′lessly.—*n.* blush′-rose′, a pink variety of rose. —**at the first blush**, at the first glance or sight : offhand ; **put to the blush**, to cause to blush. [Cf. O.E. *blyscan*, to shine.]

bluster, *blus′tər, v.i.* to blow boisterously : to storm, rage : to bully or swagger.—*v.t.* to utter stormily : to drive by storming.—*n.* a blast or roaring as of the wind : bullying or boasting language : a storm of anger.—*n.* and *adj.* blus′tering.—*adv.* blus′teringly.—*adjs.* blus′terous (*Shak.* blus′trous), noisy : boastful ; blus′tery, stormy : swaggering. [Cf. E. Frisian *blüstern*, to bluster.]

bo, boh, *bō, interj.* a word used to drive geese or to frighten children.—**cannot say bo to a goose**, is inarticulate from extreme meekness.

bo, *bō, n.* (*U.S. slang*) man (as a term of address.)

Boa, *bō′ä, n.* a genus, mainly South American, of large snakes that kill their prey by pressure : **boa**, popularly any large constricting snake : long, serpent-like coil of fur, feathers, or the like, worn round the neck by ladies.—**boa constric′tor**, properly the name of one species ; popularly any boa, python, or similar snake. [L. *bõa*, a kind of snake.]

Boanerges, *bō-ən-ər′jēz, n.* a noisy preacher or shouting orator (*sing.* and *pl.*). [Sons of thunder—Mark, iii. 17.]

boar, *bōr, n.* the male swine, or its flesh.—*ns.* boar′fish, a fish (*Capros*) of the horse-mackerel family with hoglike snout ; boar′hound, a powerful dog used for hunting the wild boar, esp. the great Dane or German mastiff.—*adj.* boar′ish, swinish : brutal.—*n.* boar′-spear, a spear used in boar-hunting. [O.E. *bár* ; Du. *beer*.]

board (*Spens.*, etc., **bord, boord, boorde**), *bōrd, n.* a broad and thin strip of timber : a table : supply of food : provision of meals (with or without lodging) : a council-table : a council or authorised body : a slab prepared for playing a game (as a chess-board) or other special purpose (as a notice-board, blackboard, knife-board) : side (*obs.* except seaboard, and the side of a ship) : (in *pl.*) the stage : a kind of thick stiff paper or sheets of paper pasted together, as in pasteboard, Bristol-board, esp. that used in the binding of books : a rectangular piece forming the side of a book-binding : (*Spens.*) conversation : (*Spens.*) coast.—*v.t.* to cover with boards : to supply with food (and bed) at fixed terms : to enter (a ship, or, orig. U.S., a train, bus, etc.) : (*Shak.*) to accost : to attack.—*v.i.* to receive food (and lodging) : (*Spens.*) to border.—*ns.* board′er, one who receives board : one who boards a ship : board′-foot, a unit of board′-measure, for timber, a piece one inch thick by 12 inches square ; board′ing, the act of covering with boards : a structure or collection of boards : act of boarding a ship ; board′ing-house, a house where boarders are kept ; board′ing-pike, a pike used in boarding a ship, or in defending it when attacked ; board′ing-

school, a school in which board and lodging are provided for pupils ; board′-school, a school under control of a school-board.—*n.pl.* board′-wa′ges, payment to a servant in lieu of food.—**above board**, openly ; **Board of Trade** unit (*elect.*), a kilowatt-hour (contracted B.T.U.) ; **board out**, to have board elsewhere than where one lives : to place in a house for board ; **by the board**, over the board or side of a ship ; **on board**, aboard ; **sweep the board**, to take all the cards : to win everything. [O.E. *bord*, board, the side of a ship ; O.N. *borth*, conn. either with **bear** or with **broad**.]

boart. See **bort**.

boast, *bōst, v.i.* to talk vaingloriously : to brag (with *of*).—*v.t.* to brag of : to speak proudly or confidently of, esp. justifiably : to possess with pride.—*n.* an expression of pride : a brag : the cause of boasting.—*n.* boast′er.—*adj.* boast′ful, given to bragging.—*adv.* boast′fully.—*ns.* boast′fulness, boast′ing.—*adj.* boast′less, without boasting ; simple, unostentatious. [M.E. *bōst* ; origin unknown ; apparently W. *bostio*, Gael. *bòsd*, a bragging, are borrowed from English.]

boat, *bōt, n.* a small open craft usually moved by oars : a ship : a boat-shaped utensil (as *sauce-boat*). —*v.i.* to sail about in a boat.—*v.t.* to put or convey in a boat : to ship (as oars) : (with *it*) to go in a boat. —*ns.* boat′bill, a bird of the heron family (from the shape of its bill) ; boat′-builder, one who constructs boats ; boat′-deck, a ship's top deck, on which the small boats are carried ; boat′er, one who boats : a straw hat ; boat′-fly, a water-bug (*Notonecta*), with boat-shaped body, that swims on its back ; boat′-hook, a hook fixed to a pole used for pulling or pushing off a boat ; boat′house, a house or shed for a boat ; boat′ing, the art, sport, or practice of sailing in boats ; boat′-load ; boat′man, a man who has charge of a boat : a rower ; boat′race, a race of rowing-boats ; boat′-racing ; boat′-song, a song sung by a boatman ; boat′tail, a grakle ; boat′-train, a train run in connexion with a ship.—**have an oar in another's boat**, to meddle with his affairs ; **in the same boat**, in the same circumstances. [O.E. *bát* ; cf. Du. *boot* ; Fr. *bateau*.]

boatswain (also often spelt **bosun**, or **bo's'n, bos'n**), *bō′sn, n.* the foreman of a crew (warrant-officer in the navy) who looks after a ship's boats, rigging, flags, etc. : a skua (prob. from its aggressiveness) : transferred (apparently) to the tropic-bird (**boat′swain-bird**).—**boatswain's mate**, the boat-swain's assistant. [**boat, swain**.]

bob, *bob, v.i.* to move quickly up and down : to curtsey : to ride a bobsled : to fish with a bob.—*v.t.* to move in a short jerking manner : to execute with a bob : to cut (hair) square across : to dock, to bobtail : (*pr.p.* bob′bing ; *pa.t.* and *pa.p.* bobbed).—*n.* a short jerking motion : a curtsey : (*Scot.*) a dance : a slight blow : a jibe : anything that moves with a bob or swing : the weight of a pendulum, plumb-line, or the like : a pendant : a knot of hair : bobbed or docked hair : a bunch or cluster (as of cherries) : a bunch of lobworms, used in catching eels : any small roundish body : the refrain or burden of a song : a short line at or near the end of a stanza : a term in bell-ringing for certain changes—a **bob minor** is rung upon six bells ; a **bob major** on eight ; a **bob royal** on ten ; a **bob maximus** on twelve.—*adj.* bobb′ish, in good spirits.—*ns.* bobb′le, the movement of water in commotion : a woolly ball for trimming dresses ; bob′-cat, a kind of lynx ; bob′-cherry, the pastime of catching a swinging cherry with the teeth ; bob′sled, bob′sleigh, a short sledge or a sleigh made up of two smaller sledges coupled together ; bob′tail, a short or cut tail : an animal with a bobbed tail (also *adj.*) : a word applied in contempt to the rabble, as in *tag-rag and bobtail*.—Also *v.t.*—*adj.* bob′tailed, with tail cut short.—*ns.* bob′wheel, in verse, the bob with the lines following it ; bob′-wig, one with the ends turned up into short curls. [Poss. Gael. *baban, babag*.]

bob, *bob, v.t.* to befool : (*Shak.*) to take by cheating : (*Shak.*) to cheat (out of). [O.F. *bober*.]

bob, *bob*, *n*. (*slang*) a shilling :—*pl*. **bob**. [Prob. not O.Fr. *bobe* = 1½d.]

bobak, bobac, *bō'bak*, *n*. a species of marmot. [Pol. *bobak*.]

Bobadil, *bob'ə-dil*, *n*. a swaggering boaster, from the soldier in Ben Jonson's *Every Man in his Humour*.

bobbery, *bob'ər-i*, *n*. a noisy row. [Perh. Hind. *bāp re*, O father.]

bobbin, *bob'in*, *n*. a reel or spool for winding yarn, wire, etc.—*ns*. **bobb'in-lace'**, lace made on a pillow with bobbins; **bobb'in-net'** or **bobb'inet**, a fine machine-made netted lace. [Fr. *bobine*.]

bobby, *bob'i*, *n*. (*slang*) a policeman. [Familiar form of *Robert*, from Sir Robert Peel, Home Secretary at the passing of the Metropolitan Police Act, 1828; cf. **peeler**.]

bobbysock, *bob'i-sok*, *n*. (*slang*) an ankle-sock.—*n*. **bobbysox'er**, an adolescent girl, a teenager.

bobolink, *bob'ō-lingk*, *n*. a North American singing bird. [At first *Bob Lincoln*, from its note.]

bobstays, *bob'stāz*, *n.pl*. (*naut*.) ropes or stays used to confine the bowsprit downward to the stem or cutwater, and counteract the strain of the foremast-stays.

bob-white, *bob'hwīt*, *n*. an American quail. [From its note.]

bocage. See **boscage**.

boche, bosche, *bosh*, *n*. abusive French slang for a German.

bode, *bōd*, *v.t*. to portend : to foreshow : to augur : to have a presentiment of.—*v.i*. to augur.—*n*. (*Scot*.) a bid, offer.—*adj*. **bode'ful**, **boding**, ominous.—*n*. **bode'ment**, an omen, presentiment.—*adj*. **bod'ing**, presaging.—*n*. an omen or portent. [O.E. *bodian*, to announce—(*ge*)*bod*, a message; allied to **bid**.]

bode, *bōd*. See **bide**.

bodega, *bo-dē'gä*, *n*. a wine-shop. [Sp.]

bodge, *boj*. Same as **botch** : (*Shak*.) prob. same as **budge**.—*n*. **bodg'er**.

bodice, *bod'is*, *n*. (*arch*.) a stiffened inner garment (orig. *pl*. of *body*) : a woman's outer garment covering the waist and bust : the close-fitting waist or body of a woman's gown.

bodikin, *bo'i-kin*, *n*. dim. of *body*, in *'Od's bodikins*, God's little body.

bodkin, *bod'kin*, *n*. a small dagger : a small instrument for pricking holes, for dressing the hair, for correcting type, etc. : a large blunt needle.—**to sit**, or **ride, bodkin**, to be wedged in tight between two others. [Poss. conn. with W. *bidog*, dagger.]

bodle, also **boddle**, *bod'l, bōd'l*, *n*. a 17th century Scots copper coin, worth about one-sixth of an English penny, the smallest coin. [Origin unknown.]

bodrag, *bod'rag*, *n*. (*Spens*.) a hostile attack, a raid. —Also **bord'raging**. [Perh. Ir. *buaidhreadh*, a disturbance.]

body, *bod'i*, *n*. the whole frame of a man or lower animal : the main part of an animal, as distinguished from the limbs : the main or middle part of anything : a garment or part of a garment covering the trunk : a bodice : a corpse : matter, as opposed to spirit : substance or substantial quality : fulness, solidity : opacity of a paint or pigment : a mass : (*coll*.) a person : a number of persons united by some common tie : size of type :—*pl*. **bod'ies**.—*v.t*. to give form to : to embody :—*pr.p*. **bod'ying**; *pa.t*. and *pa.p*. **bod'ied**.—*adj*. **bod'iless**, without a body : incorporeal.—*adj*. **bod'ily**, of the body, esp. as opposed to the mind : (*Shak*.) actual, real.—*adv*. in the flesh : as a whole.—*ns*. **bod'y-cav'ity**, the coelom, or cavity in which the viscera of the higher animals lie; **bod'y-colour**, degree of consistence, substance, and tingeing power of a paint : water-colour mixed with zinc or other white to give it body; **bod'y-cur'er** (*Shak*.), a doctor; **bod'yguard**, a guard to protect the person, esp. of a sovereign; **bod'y-pol'itic**, the collective body of the people in its political capacity; **bod'y-servant**, a personal attendant; **bod'y-snatcher**, one who secretly disinters the bodies of the dead for the purposes of dissection.—**bod'y-line bowl-**ing, in cricket, fast bowling delivered at the batsman's body. [O.E. *bodig*.]

Boeotian, *bi-ō'sh(y)ən, adj*. of *Boeotia* in Greece, proverbial for the dullness of its inhabitants : hence, stupid, dull.—Also *n*.

boer, *bōōr*, *n*. a S. African of Dutch descent, esp. one engaged in farming.—Also *adj*. [Du.; see **boor, bower**.]

boffin, *bof'in*, *n*. (*service slang*) a scientist.

bog, *bog*, *n*. spongy, usu. peaty, ground : a marsh or quagmire.—*v.t*. to sink or to entangle.—*ns*. **bog'-as'phodel**, a yellow-flowered liliaceous bog-plant (*Narthecium ossifragum*); **bog'bean**, buck-bean; **bog'-butt'er**, a fatty hydrocarbon found in the peat-bogs of Ireland; **bogg'iness**.—*adj*. **bog'gy**. —*ns*. **bog'land**; **bog'-Lat'in**, Shelta; **bog'-moss'**, the sphagnum genus; **bog'-myr'tle**, sweet-gale (*Myrica Gale*), a bog plant; **bog'-oak'**, trunks of oak embedded in bogs and preserved from decay— of a deep black colour, often used for making ornaments; **bog'-ore, bog'-iron**, an iron ore found in boggy land, limonite; **bog'-spav'in**, distension of the capsule of the hock-joint of the horse; **bog'trotter**, one who lives in a boggy country, hence an Irishman.—*n*. and *adj*. **bog'trotting**. [Ir. and Gael, *bogach; bog*, soft.]

bogey, *bō'gi*, *n*. in golf, the score, for a given hole or for the whole course, of an imaginary good player, Colonel *Bogey*, fixed as a standard—the bogey score for a course is higher than par. [Perh. **bogy**.]

boggard, *bog'ərd*, **boggart**, *-ərt*, **boggle**, *bog'l*. See **bogle**.

boggle, *bog'l*, *v.i*. to stop or hesitate as if at a bogle : to start with fright : to make difficulties about a thing : to equivocate.—*n*. a scruple, objection : a bungle.—*n*. **bogg'ler**, one who boggles : a doubter : (*Shak*.) one who hesitates or swerves. [See **bogle**.]

bogie, bogey, *bō'gi*, *n*. a low heavy truck, a trolley : a pivoted undercarriage, as in a locomotive engine. [Ety. unknown: perh. conn. with **bogy**, goblin.]

bogle, *bō'gl*, *n*. a spectre or goblin : a scarecrow (**tatt'ie-bo'gle**) : a bugbear, or source of terror.— **bogg'le, bogg'ard, bogg'art**, are North of England forms.—**bogle about the bush, stacks**, a kind of hide-and-seek. [Scot.; possibly connected with **bug** (1).]

bogong. See **bugong**.

bogus, *bō'gəs, adj*. counterfeit, spurious. [An American cant word, of very doubtful origin—it may possibly be ult. related to **bogy**.]

bogy, bogey, *bō'gi*, *n*. a goblin : a bugbear or special object of dread : the devil :—*pl*. **bo'gies, bo'geys**.—*ns*. **bog'(e)yism** ; **bo'g(e)y-man'**. [Perhaps a form of **bogle** and **boggard**.]

bohea, *bō-hē'*, *n*. the lowest quality of black tea : black tea generally. [From the *Wu-i* hills, in China.]

Bohemian, *bō-hē'mi-ən*, *n*. a native or inhabitant of Bohemia : a Czech : a gypsy : a person of loose or irregular habits : an artist or man of letters, or indeed anyone, who sets social conventionalities aside : the Czech language.—Also *adj*.—*n*. **Bohē'mianism**.—**Bohemian ruby**, rose quartz; **Bohemian topaz**, citrine. [Fr. *bohémien*, a gypsy, from the belief that these wanderers came from *Bohemia*.]

boil, *boil*, *v.i*. to pass rapidly from liquid into vapour with violent evolution of bubbles : to bubble up as if from the action of heat : to be heated in boiling liquid : to be hot : to be excited or agitated.—*v.t*. to heat to a boiling state : to cook, dress, clean or otherwise treat by boiling.— *n*. act or condition of boiling.—*ns*. **boil'er**, one who boils : that in which anything is boiled : a vessel in which steam is generated : a vessel for heating water for baths, etc. : an electric apparatus for boiling a kettle or the like; **boil'ery**, a place for boiling, esp. for obtaining salt; **boil'ing**, the act of causing to boil : the condition of being boiled or at boiling-point : a quantity boiled at once : (*coll*.) collection, set.—*adj*. at boiling-point : very hot : bubbling : swelling with heat or passion.—*n*.

boil'ing-point, the temperature at which a liquid, esp. water, boils, esp. at atmospheric pressure.—**boil'ed shirt,** (*U.S.*) a dress shirt; **boil down,** to reduce in bulk by boiling : to extract the substance of : to epitomise; **boil over,** to bubble over the sides of the containing vessel : to break out into unrestrained indignation. [O.Fr *boillir*—L. *bullīre*—*bulla*, a bubble.]

boil, *boil*, *n.* an inflamed swelling. [O.E. *bȳl*; Ger. *beule*.]

boisterous, *bois'tər-əs*, *adj.* wild : noisy : turbulent : stormy.—*adv.* **bois'terously.**—*n.* **bois'terousness.** [M.E. *boistous*.]

bok, *bok*, *n.* (*S. Africa*) a goat : an antelope—used alike of male and female. [Du. *bok*, goat.]

boko, *bō'kō*, *n.* (*slang*) the nose. [Origin unknown.]

bolas, *bō'läs*, *n.* (properly *pl.*) a South American missile, consisting of two or more balls or stones strung together, swung round the head and hurled so as to entangle an animal. [Sp., balls.]

bold, *bōld*, *adj.* daring : actively courageous : forward or impudent : presumptuous : executed with spirit : striking to the sense, standing out clearly, well marked : steep or abrupt.—*v.t.* **bold'en** (*obs.*), to make bold.—*adj.* **bold'-faced,** impudent : of type, having a heavy face.—*adv.* **bold'ly.**—*n.* **bold'ness.** —**to make bold,** to take the liberty, to make free. [O.E. *bald;* O.H.G. *bald,* O.N. *ballr*.]

bold-beating, *bōld'bēt'ing*, *adj.* (*Shak.*) poss. for bowl-beating, pot-thumping.

bole, *bōl*, *n.* the trunk of a tree. [O.N. *bolr;* Ger. *bohle,* a plank.]

bole, *bōl*, *n.* ə friable earthy clay, usually red. [Gr. *bōlos,* a clod.]

bole, *bōl*, *n.* (*Scot.*) a recess in a wall : an opening to admit light and air. [Origin unknown.]

bolection, balection, *bō-*, *bə-lek'shən*, *n.* a moulding around a panel projecting beyond the surface of the framing. [Origin unknown.]

bolero, *bo-lā'rō*, or *bo-lē'rō*, *n.* Spanish national dance : a tune to which it may be danced : a jacket-like bodice, coming barely to the waist. [Sp.]

Boletus, *bol-ē'təs*, *n.* a genus of fungi, edible and poisonous, with a pore-like surface instead of gills. [L. *bōlētus*—Gr. *bōlītēs,* mushroom.]

bolide, *bō'līd*, *n.* a large meteor, esp. one that bursts : a fireball. [Fr.,—L. *bolis, -idis*—Gr. *bolis, -idos,* a missile.]

bolivar, *bol-ē'vär*, *n.* the standard monetary unit of Venezuela. [From Simón *Bolívar*.]

boliviano, *bol-ē-vi-ä'nō*, *n.* a Bolivian dollar (100 centavos).

boll, *bōl*, *n.* a swelling : a knob : a round capsule, as in cotton, flax, poppy, etc.—*v.i.* to swell, to form bolls.—*adjs.* **bolled** (*bōld*), swollen, podded; **bollen** (*bōln*), swollen (*Shak.*).—*ns.* **boll'-weevil,** a weevil (*Anthonomus grandis*) whose larvae infest cotton-bolls; **boll'-worm,** a moth caterpillar that destroys cotton-bolls, maize, tomatoes, etc.—in U.S. *Chloridea obsoleta,* in Egypt and India *Earias insulana* and *E. fabia.* [A form of bowl—O.E. *bolla*.]

boll, *bōl*, *n.* a measure of capacity for grain, etc., used in Scotland and the north of England—in Scotland usually = 6 imperial bushels; in England varying from 2 to 6 bushels : also a measure of weight, containing, for flour, 140 lb. [Prob. O.N. *bolli*.]

Bollandist, *bol'ən-dist*, *n.* any of the Jesuit writers who continued the *Acta Sanctorum* by John *Bolland* (1596-1665).

bollard, *bol'ərd*, *n.* a short post on a wharf or ship round which ropes are secured. [Prob. bole.]

bolletrie, *bol'ə-trē.* Same as **bully-tree.**

Bologna, *bol-ōn'yä*, *adj.* of the town of *Bologna* in Italy.—**Bologna phial,** an unannealed bottle that shatters on scratching; **Bologna phosphorus,** barium sulphide; **Bologna sausage; Bologna stone,** fibrous barytes.—*adj.* and *n.* **Bologn'ese** (or *-ēz'*). [L. *Bonōnia*.]

bolometer, *bō-lom'i-tər*, *n.* an instrument for measuring radiant energy. [Gr. *bolē,* stroke, ray (*ballein,* to throw), *metron,* a measure.]

boloney. See **baloney.**

Bolshevik (or **bol-**), *bol'shə-vik, -vik'*, *n.* a member of the Russian Majority (or Extreme) Socialist party (opp. to *Menshevik*) : a violent revolutionary Marxian communist.—Also *adj.*—coll. contracted **bol'-shie, bol'shy.**—*v.t.* **bol'shevise.**—*ns.* **bol'she-vism; bol'shevist,** a Bolshevik : an extreme revolutionary communist (of any country)—loosely used by opponents.—Also *adj.* [Russ.—*bolshe,* greater, from its more thorough-going programme, or from its being in a majority (i.e. at the Russian Social Democratic Congress in 1903).]

bolster, *bōl'stər*, *n.* a long round pillow or cushion : a pad : anything resembling it in form or use, esp. any piece of mechanism affording a support against pressure.—*v.t.* to support as with a bolster : to hold up.—*adj.* **bol'stered,** supported : swelled out.—*n.* and *adj.* **bol'stering,** propping up or supporting. [O.E. *bolster*.]

bolt, *bōlt*, *n.* a bar used to fasten ə door, etc. : a stout pin with a head : an arrow, esp. for a cross-bow : a thunderbolt : a roll of a definite measure (of cloth, etc.) : the uncut edge of a sheet folded for a book.—*v.t.* to fasten with a bolt : to shackle or fetter : to throw or ulter precipitately : to expel suddenly : to discharge, as a bolt : to swallow hastily : (*U.S.*) to break away from, withhold support from.—*v.i.* to spring, dart : to rush away : to take flight : to run away : to start up : (*U.S.*) to withhold support from one's party, or its policy or nominee.—*adv.* like a bolt.—*ns.* **bolt'er,** one who bolts : a horse given to running away; **bolt'-head,** the head of a bolt; **bolt'hole,** a hole to receive a bolt : a secret passage or way of escape : a refuge from danger : (*arch.*) a distilling receiver; **bolt'-rope,** a rope sewed all round the edge of a sail to prevent it from tearing.—*adv.* **bolt'-up'right, -upright',** upright and straight as a bolt or arrow : (*obs.*) supine.—*n.* **bolt'up'rightness** (or *-rit'*).—**a fool's bolt is soon shot,** a fool soon gives away the initiative and leaves himself unprotected. [O.E. *bolt;* O.H.G. *bolz*.]

bolt. See **boult.**

bolus, *bō'ləs*, *n.* a rounded mass : a large pill. [L. *bōlus*—Gr. *bōlos,* a lump.]

boma, *bō'mä*, *n.* a fenced enclosure. [Swahili.]

boma, *bō'mä*, *n.* a boa or anaconda. [Congo; thence carried by Portuguese to Brazil.]

bomb, *bom* (old-fashioned *bum*), *n.* a hollow case containing explosive, incendiary, smoke-producing, poisonous, or other offensive material, deposited, thrown, dropped, or shot from a mortar : a rounded mass of lava thrown out by a volcano.—*v.i.* to throw, discharge, or drop bombs.—*v.t.* to attack, injure, or destroy with bombs.—*n.* **bombard** (*bom'bärd*), an early cannon, throwing stones, etc. : (*Shak.*) a large liquor-jug, a black-jack : an old form of bassoon.—*v.t.* **bombard',** to attack with artillery : to batter or pelt : to subject to a succession of blows or impingements : (*fig.*) to assail (as with questions).—*ns.* **bombardier** (*bom-, bum-bər-dēr'*), the lowest non-commissioned officer in the British artillery, formerly a man employed about a bombard; **bombardment** (*bom-bärd'mənt*); **bombar'don** (or *bom'*), the bass tuba.—*n.* **bomber** (*bom'ər*), one who bombs : a bombing aeroplane.—Also *adj.*—*n.* **bomb'-calorim'eter,** an apparatus for determining the calorific value of fuels by ignition in a thick-walled steel vessel.—*adj.* **bomb'proof,** proof or secure against the force of bombs.—*n.* a bomb-proof structure.—*ns.* **bomb'shell,** a bomb : now only *fig.,* a sudden and surprising piece of news : **bomb'-vessel, bomb'-ketch,** a vessel for carrying the mortars used in bombarding from the sea.—**bombardier beetle,** a name given to beetles (*Brachinus,* etc.) that discharge an acrid volatile fluid with explosive force from the abdomen. [Fr. *bombe*—Sp. *bomba*—L. *bombus*—Gr. *bombos,* a humming sound; imit.]

bombasine, bombazine, *bom'-, bum'bə-zēn, or -zēn',* *n.* a twilled or corded fabric of silk and worsted, or of cotton and worsted. [Fr. *bombasin*—L.L. *bombȳcinus*—Gr. *bombȳkinos, bombȳx,* silkworm.]

bombast, *bom'-, bum'bast,* *n.* cottonwool : padding : stuffing : inflated or high-sounding language, fustian.—*adj.* (*Shak.*) inflated.—*v.t.* (-*bast'*, also *bom'*, *bum'*) to pad, stuff : to inflate, render grandiose.—*adj.* **bombas'tic**, high-sounding : inflated.—*adv.* **bombas'tically**.—*n.* **Bom'bax**, a genus of tropical, chiefly S. American trees, giving name to the silk-cotton family, **Bombacā'ceae**. [L.L. *bombax*, cotton—Gr. *bombȳx*, silk.]

Bombay duck, *bom'bā duk*, *n.* a fish, the bummalo.

Bombyx, *bom'biks*, *n.* the silkworm genus, giving name to the family **Bombycidae** (-*bis'i-dē*).—*n.* **bom'bycid**, an insect of the family.—Also *adj.* [Gr. *bombȳx*.]

bonanza, *bon-an'zä*, *n.* (*U.S.*) a rich mass of gold : any mine of wealth or stroke of luck.—*adj.* very prosperous. [Sp., good weather.]

Bonapartean, *bō-nə-pärt'i-ən*, *adj.* of Napoleon *Bonaparte* or his family.—*n.* **Bo'napartism**, attachment to his dynasty or policy.—*n.* and *adj.* **Bo'napartist**.

bona-roba, *bō'nä-rō'bä*, *n.* (*Shak.*) a showy wanton, a courtesan. [It. *buona roba*, lit. good stuff (or dress).]

bonas(s)us, *bon-as'əs*, *n.* a bison. [L.,—Gr. *bonasos*, *bonassos*.]

bonbon, *bon'bon*, *n.* a sweetmeat : a cracker (for pulling).—*n.* **bonbonniere** (*bonɡ-bon-yer'*), a fancy box for holding sweets. [Fr., redup. of *bon*, good.]

bond, *bond*, *n.* that which binds, a band : link of connexion or union : a writing of obligation to pay a sum or to perform a contract : a debenture : (Scots *law*) a mortgage : any constraining or cementing force : in building, the overlapping connexion of one stone or brick with another, as in **English bond**, **Flemish bond**, etc. : (in *pl.*) imprisonment, captivity : the condition of goods retained in a warehouse, called a **bonded warehouse** or **bonded store**, until duties are paid.—*v.t.* to connect, secure, or bind with a bond : to put in a bonded warehouse : to put in a condition of bond.—*adj.* **bond'ed**, secured by bond.—*ns.* **bond'er**, a bondstone or header; **bond'holder**, one who holds bonds of a private person or public company; **bond'ing**; **bonds'man**, a surety; **bond'stone**, a stone that reaches a considerable distance into or entirely through a wall for the purpose of binding it together; **bond'timber**, timber built into a wall as it is carried up for the purpose of binding it together in a longitudinal direction.—**bonded debt**, the debt of a corporation represented by the bonds it has issued, as contrasted with its floating debt; **bond paper**, a superior kind of paper, originally intended for bonds. [A variant of **band**—O.E. *bindan*, to bind.]

bond, *bond*, *adj.* in a state of servitude.—*ns.* **bond'age**, captivity : slavery; **bond'ager**, a female outworker in the Borders and North of England, whom the *hind* or married cottar was bound to provide for the farm-work; **bond'maid**, **bond'woman**, **bonds'woman**, a woman-slave; **bond'man**, **bonds'man**, a man-slave; **bond'manship**; **bond'serv'ant**, a slave; **bond'-service**, the condition of a bond-servant: slavery; **bond'-slave**, a slave. [O.E. *bonda*, a boor, a householder, from O.N. *bóndi*, *búandi*, a tiller, a husbandman, *búa*, to till, cog. with O.E. *búan*, meaning affected by association with **bond** (1).]

bonduc, *bon'duk*, *n.* the nicker seed. [Ar. *bonduq*, a kind of nut.]

bone, *bōn*, *n.* a hard substance forming the skeleton of the higher animals : a separate piece of the skeleton : a piece of whalebone : a bobbin for lace-making : (in *pl.*) the skeleton or anything analogous : (in *pl.*) mortal remains : (in *pl.*) pieces of bone or the like held between the fingers of the hand and rattled together to keep time to music : (in *pl.*) dice. —*v.t.* to take the bones out of, as meat : to furnish with bones : (*slang*) to seize, to steal.—*ns.* **bone'-ache**, pain in the bones; **bone'-ash**, **bone'-earth**, the remains of bones burned in an open furnace; **bone'-bed**, a deposit of fossil bones; **bone'-brecc'ia**, rock formed of broken fossil bones; **bone'-black**, the carbonaceous remains of bones heated in a close vessel; **bone'-cave'**, a cave containing deposits of fossil bones of animals that lived in it or their prey.—*adjs.* **bone'-dry**, as dry

as bone : having complete prohibition of the liquor trade; **boned**, having bones : having the bones removed.—*ns.* **bone'-dust**, ground or pulverised bones, used in agriculture; **bone'head** (*U.S.*), a blockhead.—*adj.* **bone'-idle**, utterly idle, idle to the bone.—*n.* **bone'-lace**, lace woven with bobbins, which were often made of bone.—*adj.* **bone'less**, wanting bones : (*fig.*) spineless.—*ns.* **bone'-meal'**, coarse-ground bones; **bone'-mill**, a mill where bones are ground; **bone'-oil'**, a liquid got in dry distillation of bones; **bone'set**, an American species of hemp agrimony; **bone'-setter**, one who treats broken bones without being a duly qualified surgeon; **bone'shaker**, a familiar name for earlier forms of bicycle: any crazy vehicle; **bone'-spavin**, a bony excrescence or hard swelling on the inside of the hock of a horse; **bone'-tur'quoise**, blue fossil bone or tooth, used as turquoise; **bōn'iness**.—*adj.* **bōn'y**, full of, or consisting of, or like bones : thin.—**a bone of contention**, something that causes strife; **a bone to pick**, something to occupy one, a difference to be cleared up with somebody; **bony fishes**, the Teleostei, an order of fishes including most of the living forms; **bony pike**, the American (and fossil) garfish; **make no bones of, about,** to have no scruples about; **to the bone**, to the inmost part. [O.E. *bán*; Ger. *bein*, leg.]

bonfire, *bon'fīr*, *n.* a large fire in the open air on occasions of public rejoicing, for consuming garden refuse, etc.—perhaps originally a fire in which bones were burnt. [**bone**, and **fire**.]

bongrace, *bon'grās*, *n.* a shade from the sun once worn by women on the front of the bonnet : a broad-brimmed hat or bonnet. [Fr. *bonne* (*fem.*) good, *grâce*, grace.]

bongo, *bong'gō*, *n.* an African bushbuck. [Native name.]

bonhom(m)ie, *bon'-o-mē*, *n.* easy good-nature. [Fr.]

bonie. See **bonny**.

boniface, *bon'i-fās*, *n.* an inn-keeper—from the hearty *Boniface* of Farquhar's *Beaux' Stratagem*, or the *Bonifazio* of Ariosto's *La Scolastica*.

boning, *bōn'ing*, *n.* estimation of straightness by looking along a row of poles, as in **boning-rod** or **-telescope**.

bonito, *bo-nē'tō*, *n.* a tunny of various kinds. [Sp.]

bonne, *bon*, *n.* a French maid or nursemaid. [Fr.; fem. of *bon*, good.]

bonne-bouche, *bon-boosh*, *n.* a delicious morsel. [Fr., pleasant taste; *bonne* (fem.), good, *bouche*, mouth.]

bonnet, *bon'it*, *n.* a woman's head-covering, tied on by strings : a soft cap : the velvet cap within a coronet : (*fort.*) a small work before the salient or flanked angle of the ravelin : (*naut.*) an additional part laced to the foot of jibs, or other fore-and-aft sails, to gather more wind : a wire-cowl over a chimney-top : the cover of a motor-car engine, or of various parts of machinery, etc. : the second stomach of a ruminant : a decoy or pretended player or bidder at a gaming-table or an auction, the accomplice of a thimble-rigger or other petty swindler.—*v.t.* to put a bonnet on : to crush his hat over the eyes of.—*adj.* **bonn'eted**.—*ns.* **bonn'et-monkey**, an Indian macaque (from the appearance of the head); **bonn'et-piece**, a gold coin of James V of Scotland, on which the king wears a bonnet instead of a crown; **bonn'et-rouge** (Fr. : *bon-ā-rōozh*), the red cap of liberty of the French Revolution, in the form of a Phrygian cap.—**bonnet laird** (*Scot.*), a small landowner who wore a bonnet, not the hat of the gentry. [O.Fr.,—L.L. *bonnetum*, orig. the name of a stuff.]

bon(n)ibell, *bon-i-bel'*, *n.* (*Spens.*) a good and fair maid. [Fr. *bonne et belle*, good and fair : or for **bonny belle**.]

bon(n)ilasse, *bon'i-läs*, *n.* (*Spens.*) for **bonny lass**.

bonny, **bonnie**, *bon'i* (*Scot.* also *bō'ni*; *Burns* bonie), *adj.* comely : pretty : gay : plump : pleasant-looking : as a general term expressing appreciation, considerable, etc., often ironically : cheerful : (*Shak.*) stout, strong.—Also *adv.*—*adv.* **bonn'ily**, beautifully : gaily.—*n.* **bonn'iness,** handsomeness : gaiety. [Origin obscure.]

bonny-clabber, *bon'i-klab'ər, n.* milk naturally clotted on souring. [Ir. *bainne,* milk, *claba,* thick.]

bonspiel, *bon'spēl, n.* a great match, now only a curling match. [App. from some Du. compound of *spel,* play; cf. **ba'spiel.**]

bontebok, *bon'tə-bok, n.* a South African antelope. [Du. *bont,* particoloured, *bok,* goat.]

bonus, *bōn'əs, n.* a premium beyond the usual interest for a loan : an extra dividend to shareholders : a policy-holder's share of profits : an extra payment to workmen or others : a douceur or bribe. [L. *bonus,* good.]

bonxie, *bongks'i, n.* (*Shetland*) the great skua. [O.N. *bunki,* heap.]

bonze, *bonz, n.* a Buddhist priest. [Jap. *bonzô* or *bonzi,* a priest.]

bonzer, *bon'zər, adj.* (*slang; Austr.*) very good.

boo, booh, *bōō, interj.* expressive of disapprobation or contempt.—*v.t.* and *v.i.* to hoot.—*v.t.* **boo'-hoo',** to weep noisily.

boobook, *bōō'bŏŏk, n.* an Australian owl (*Ninox boobook*). [From its cuckoo-like cry.]

booby, *bōō'bi, n.* a lubberly lout : a stupid fellow (*U.S.* **boob**) : a boy at the bottom of the class : a sea-bird of the gannet tribe, remarkable for its apparent stupidity in allowing itself to be knocked down with a stick.—*adjs.* **boo'by, boo'byish,** like a booby : stupid.—*ns.* **boo'byism ; boo'by-prize,** a prize for the worst score; **boo'by-trap,** a rude form of practical joke, by which something is made to fall upon one entering a door, or the like. [Perh. Sp. *bobo,* a dolt.]

boodle, *bōō'dl, n.* a collection of sheets of paper, etc., bound together or made into a roll, either printed, written on, or blank : a large-scale literary composition : a division of a volume or composition : the Bible : a betting-book, or record of bets made with different people : (*fig.*) any source of instruction : a libretto : the first six tricks gained by a side in whist : a structure resembling a book : (*pl.*) formal accounts of transactions, as minutes of meetings, records kept of his business by a merchant.— *v.t.* to write or enter in a book : to engage in advance.—*v.i.* to take a ticket.—*ns.* **book'-account,** an account of debt or credit in a book : **book'-binder,** one who binds books; **book'binding,** the cover of a book : the art or practice of binding or putting the boards on books; **book'-can'vasser,** one who goes around soliciting orders for a book; **book'case,** a case with shelves for books; **book'-club,** a society that buys, circulates on loan, or prints books for its members; **book'-debt,** a sum owing to a seller as shown in his business-books; **book'-end,** a prop for the end of a row of books.— *adj.* **book'ful,** full of information gathered from books.—*ns.* **book'-hold'er,** one who holds the book of the play and prompts the actor in the theatre; **book'-hunt'er,** one who hunts for rare books; **book'ie** (*coll.*), a bookmaker; **book'ing-clerk,** one who sells tickets; **book'ing-hall; book'ing-off'ice,** an office where names are booked or tickets sold.—*adj.* **book'ish,** fond of books : acquainted only with books : savouring of books.—*ns.* **book'ishness; book'keeper; book'keep'ing,** the art of keeping accounts in a regular and systematic manner; **book'-land** (O.E. *bócland*), land taken from the *folcland* or common land, and granted by *bóc* or written charter to a private owner; **book'-learn'ing,** learning got from books, as opposed to practical knowledge.—*adj.* **book'less,** without books : unlearned.—*ns.* **book'let,** a small book; **book'lore** (*Scot.* **book-, buik-lear,** *-lär*), booklearning : bibliographical lore; **book'louse,** a wingless insect of the Corrodentia, found among books and papers :—*pl.* **book'lice ; book'mak'er,** one who makes up books from the writings of

others, a compiler : one who makes a living by betting at race-courses; **book'making; book'-man,** a scholar, student; **book'-mark,** something placed or to be placed in a book to mark one's place; **book'-mate** (*Shak.*), a companion in study : a schoolfellow; **book'-mind'edness,** habitual direction of the mind towards books; **book'-mus'lin,** muslin used in book-binding; **book'-oath** (*Shak.*), an oath made on the Book or Bible; **book'-plate,** a label usually pasted inside the cover of a book, bearing the owner's name, crest, coat-of-arms, or peculiar device; **book'-post,** the arrangement in the Post-office for the transmission of books; **book'-scor'pion,** a scorpion-like arachnid found in libraries, probably feeding on booklice; **book'-seller,** one who sells books : formerly a publisher; **book'selling; book'shelf,** a shelf for books; **book'shop,** a shop where books are sold; **book'-stall,** a stall or stand, generally in the open air, where books are sold; **book'-stand,** a book-stall : a stand or support for holding up a book in reading; **book'-tally, -token,** a paper to be exchanged for books of a stated price, sent as a gift; **book'-trade,** the trade of dealing in books; **book'worm,** a grub that eats holes in books, esp. a beetle larva (*Anobium*) : a hard reader.—**be upon the books,** to have one's name in an official list; **bring to book,** to bring to account; **take a leaf out of another's book,** to profit by his example; **talk like a book,** to talk pedantically, or with precision and readiness; **without book,** from memory : unauthorisedly. [O.E. *bóc,* book, beech; Ger. *buche,* beech, *buch,* book, supposed to be from early Germanic use of beechen boards.]

boom, *bōōm, n.* a pole by which a sail is stretched : a chain or bar stretched across a harbour : a barrier of floating logs : a long beam : (*S. Africa*) a tree (in combination, as Kaffir-boom, etc.).—*ns.* **boom'-iron,** a ring in which a spar slides; **boom'-slang,** a venomous S. African tree-snake. [Du. *boom,* beam, tree.]

boom, *bōōm, v.i.* to make a hollow sound or roar.— *n.* a hollow roar, as of the sea, the cry of the bittern, etc. [From a L.G. root found in O.E. *byme,* a trumpet, Du. *bommen,* to drum; like **bomb,** of imit. origin.]

boom, *bōōm, v.i.* to go on with a rush : to become suddenly prosperous.—*v.t.* to push into sudden prominence.—*n.* a sudden increase of activity in business, or the like—often specially worked up.— *n.* and *adj.* **boom'ing.** [Prob. from **boom** (2).]

boomer, *bōōm'ər, n.* the sewellel : the chickaree.

boomerang, *bōōm'a-rang, n.* a bent missile used by the natives of Australia, sometimes so balanced that it returns towards the thrower : (*fig.*) an act that recoils upon the agent. [Australian.]

boon, *bōōn, n.* a petition : a gift, favour. [O.N. *tón,* prayer : O.E. *bén.*]

boon, *bōōn, adj.* gay, merry, or kind. [Fr. *bon*— L. *bonus,* good.]

boor, *bōōr, n.* a countryman, a peasant : a Dutch colonist in South Africa : a coarse or awkward person.—*adj.* **boor'ish,** like a boor : awkward or rude.—*adv.* **boor'ishly.**—*n.* **boor'ishness.** [Du. *boer;* perh. partly O.E. *búr, gebúr,* farmer.]

boord, boorde, *bōrd,* old spellings of **board** (*Spens.,* etc.).

boose. See **bouse.**

boost, *bōōst, v.t.* (*orig. U.S. slang*) to help forward : to push : to advertise or promote fervently, to boom : (*elect.*) to supplement the voltage of (a battery).—*n.* a help forward : a push. [Origin unknown.]

boot, *bōōt, n.* a covering for the foot and lower part of the leg, generally made of leather : an instrument of torture for the leg : a box or receptacle in a coach.—*v.t.* to put boots on : to kick : to turn out, dismiss.—*ns.* **boot'black,** a shoeblack; **boot'-catcher,** an inn servant who helped to pull off guests' boots; **boot'-closer,** one who closes the upper leathers of boots.—*adj.* **boot'ed,** having boots on, equipped for riding.—*ns.* **bootee',** a lady's short boot : an infant's woollen boot; **boot'-hook,** an instrument for pulling on long boots; **boot'hose** (*Shak.*), a stocking used instead of a jack-boot:—*pl.* **boot'hose**; **boot'ikin**, the boot for torture: a boot or mitten for the gouty; **boot'-jack**, an instrument for taking off boots; **boot'-lace**, a lace for fastening boots; **boot'-last**, **boot'-tree**, the last or foot-like mould on which boots or shoes are made or stretched to keep their shape; **boot'leg**, the leg of a high boot.—*v.t.* to smuggle (liquor).—*ns.* **boot'legger**, one who smuggles alcoholic liquor in a bootleg or elsewhere: an illicit dealer; **boot'legging**.—*adj.* **boot'less**, without boots.—*ns.* **boot'licker**, a toady (*U.S.* **boot'lick**; also *v.t.*); **boot'licking**; **boot'maker**; **boot'making**; **boots**, an inn servant who cleans boots, runs messages, etc.: also used in combination, as *lazyboots, slyboots*.—**boot and saddle** (a corr. of Fr. *boute-selle*, place saddle), the signal for mounting; **like old boots** (*slang*), vigorously; **the boot is on the other leg**, the tables are turned: the responsibility is (now) the other way: the reverse is the truth; **die in one's boots**, to die a sudden death, not in bed; **get the boot** (*slang*), to be dismissed; **have one's heart in one's boots**, to have lost courage. [O.Fr. *bote* (mod. *botte*)— L.L. *botta*, boot, of doubtful origin.]

boot, *bōōt, v.t.* to profit or advantage.—*n.* advantage: profit: in old law, any reparation or compensation paid: (*Shak.*) booty.—*adj.* **boot'less**, without boot or profit: useless.—*adv.* **boot'lessly**.—*n.* **boot'lessness**.—**to boot**, in addition. [O.E. *bót*, compensation, amends, whence *bétan*, to amend.]

Bootes, *bō-ō'tēz, n.* a northern constellation beside the Great Bear, containing the bright star Arcturus. [Gr. *Boötēs*, lit. an ox-driver.]

booth, *bōōdh, bōōth, n.* a hut or temporary erection formed of slight materials: a small shop of simple construction: a covered stall at a fair or market: a polling place. [O.N. *búth*, or a cognate word; cf. Ger. *bude*.]

booty, *bōōt'i, n.* spoil taken in war or by force: plunder, a prize.—**play booty**, to join with others in orde to cheat one player, to play a game with intention to lose. [O.N. *býti*, share—*býta*, to divide.]

booze. See **bouse**.

bo-peep, *bō-pēp', n.* a simple play among children in which one peeps from behind something and cries 'Bo'.

bor, *baw(r), n.* neighbour, an East Anglian form of address to man or woman. [O.E. *búr*, usu. *gebúr*, farmer; cf. **neighbour**.]

bora, *bō'rä, n.* a strong north-east wind in the upper Adriatic. [Venetian variant of It. *borea*—L. *boreas*; or Slav.; cf. Serbian *bura*.]

bora, *bō'rä, n.* an Australian initiation rite. [Native word.]

borachio, *bor-ach'(i-)ō, n.* a Spanish wine-skin: a drunken fellow. [Sp. *borracha, borracho*.]

borage, *bur'ij, n.* a blue-flowered bristly plant of the genus Borago, giving name to the family **Boragina'ceae**, tubiflorous dicotyledons with cincinnate inflorescence and four nutlets. [L.L. *borrāgō*.]

borax, *bō'raks, n.* a mineral, hydrated sodium tetraborate, found on alkaline lake shores.—*adjs.* **bo'ric**, **boracic** (*bō-ras'ik*), of or relating to borax or boron.—*ns.* **bo'racite** (*-rə-sīt*), a mineral composed of magnesium borate and chloride; **bo'rate**, a salt of boric acid.—**boric** or **boracic** or **orthoborac'ic acid**, an acid (H₃BO₃) obtained by dissolving borax, and also found native in mineral springs in Italy, changing successively by loss of water on heating to metaboric acid, tetraboric or pyroboric acid, and boric anhydride. [Fr. and L.L. *borax*—Ar. *búraq*.]

bord, **borde**, obs. spellings of **board**.

bordar, *bord'ər, n.* a villein who held his hut at his lord's pleasure. [L.L. *bordārius*; of Gmc. origin. See **board**.]

Bordeaux, *bor-dō', n.* claret, wine of *Bordeaux*.—**Bordeaux mixture**, a mixture of lime and copper sulphate, used to kill fungus and insect parasites on plants.

bordel, *bor'dəl, n.* (*arch.*) a house for prostitution.— Also **bordello** (*-del'ō*; It.). [O.Fr. *bordel*, a cabin— L.L. *borda*.]

border, *bord'ər, n.* the edge or margin of anything: the march or boundary of a country, esp. that between England and Scotland (also in *pl.*): a flower-bed in a garden: a piece of ornamental edging or trimming.—*adj.* of or on the border.—*v.t.* to come near or to be adjacent (with *on, upon, with*).—*v.t.* to furnish with a border: to bound.—*adj.* **bord'ered**.—*ns.* **bord'erer**, one who dwells or was born on the border of a country: **bord'erland**, a border region.—*adj.* belonging to the undefined margin between two things, e.g. sanity and insanity.—*adj.* **bord'erless**.—*n.* **bord'er-line**.

bordered pit (*bot.*), a thin area in the wall between two vessels or tracheides, surrounded by overhanging rims of wall-thickening. [O.Fr. *bordure*; from root of **board**.]

bordraging, *bord'rag-ing, n.* See **bodrag**.

bordure, *bor'dūr, n.* (*her.*) a border surrounding a shield, generally said to occupy one-fifth of the field. [See **border**.]

bore, *bōr, v.t.* to pierce so as to form a hole: to thrust against (as one racehorse against another): to weary or annoy with tediousness (perh. a different word—not known before mid-18th century). —*n.* a hole made by boring: the size of the cavity of a tube: a person or thing that wearies.—*ns.* **bore'dom**, tedium; **bore'hole**, a bore in the earth's crust for investigation or for water, oil, etc.; **bor'er**, the person or thing that bores: a name common to many animals that pierce wood, rocks, etc.; **bor'ing**, the act of making a hole in anything: a hole made by boring: (in *pl.*) the chips produced by boring. [O.E. *borian*, to bore; cf. Ger. *bohren*; allied to L. *forāre*, to bore, Gr. *pharynx*, the gullet.]

bore, *bōr, pa.t.* of **bear**.

bore, *bōr, n.* a tidal flood that rushes with great violence up the estuaries of certain rivers, also called eagre. [O.N. *bára*, a wave or swell.]

Boreas, *bor'i-as, n.* the north wind personified.— *adj.* **bo'real** (*bō'ri-əl*). [L. and Gr. *Boréas*.]

borecole, *bōr'kōl, n.* kale. [Du. *boerenkool*, lit. peasant's cabbage.]

boric. Same as **boracic**. [See **borax**.]

born, *born.* (See **bear**, 2.)—**born again**, having received new spiritual life; **born fool**, one whose folly is from his birth; **in one's born days**, in one's whole lifetime.

borne, *bōrn, pa.p.* of **bear**, to carry.

borné, *bor'nā, adj.* limited, narrow-minded. [Fr. *pa.p.* of *borner*, to limit.]

bornite, *born'īt, n.* a copper ore, sulphide of copper and iron. [Ignaz von *Born*, mineralogist (1742-91).]

boron, *bō'ron, n.* a non-metallic element (symbol B), of atomic number 5, present in borax and boric acid, obtained as an amorphous powder or impure in diamond-like crystals. [See **borax**.]

borough, *bur'ə, n.* a town with a corporation and special privileges granted by royal charter; a town that sends representatives to parliament.— *ns.* **bor'ough-English**, a custom in some ancient English boroughs (till 1925), by which estates descended to the youngest son; **bor'oughmonger**, a buyer or seller of the patronage of boroughs; **bor'ough-reeve**, the chief municipal official in some unincorporated English towns prior to 1835. —**close** or **pocket borough**, a borough whose representation was in the nomination of some person—common before 1832; **county borough**, a borough (of above 50,000 inhabitants by Act of 1888, of 75,000 or more by Act of 1926) with some of the characters of a county; **rotten borough**, one which still returned members to parliament although the constituency had disappeared—all abolished in 1832.—The Scottish terms are grouped under **burgh**. [O.E. *burg, burh*, a city, from *beorgan;* Ger. *bergen*, to protect.]

borrel, **borrell**, **borel**, *bor'əl, adj.* (*arch.*) rustic, clownish. [O.Fr. *burel*, coarse cloth worn by peasantry.]

borrow, *bor'ō, n.*(*arch.*) a pledge or surety: (*Shak.*) a borrowing.—*v.t.* to obtain on loan or trust: to adopt from a foreign source: to derive from another (with *from, of*).—*adj.* **borr'owed**, taken on loan: counterfeit: assumed.—*n.* **borr'ower.**—*n.* and *adj.* **borr'owing.**—**borrowing days,** the last three days of March (O.S.), supposed in Scottish folklore to have been borrowed by March from April, and to be especially stormy; **to borrow,** for a pledge or surety. [O.E. *borgian—borg, borh,* a pledge, security.]

borstal, borstall, *bor'stal, n.* a way up a hill, still used in the district of the Downs.—**Borstal system,** a system of detaining juvenile-adult delinquents, named from the first reformatory of the kind at Borstal, a suburb of Rochester. [O.E. *beorh,* a hill, and *stígel,* a stile, or *borg,* security, *steall,* place.]

bort, boart, *bort, n.* diamond fragments or dust: a coarse diamond or semicrystallic form of carbon. [Fr.]

borzoi, *bor'zoi, n.* a dog like a huge greyhound, but with a soft coat about the length of a deerhound's. [Russ., swift.]

boscage, *bosk'ij, n.* thick foliage: woodland. [Fr. *boscage, bocage*—L.L. *boscus,* conn. with Ger. *busch,* Eng. **bush.**]

bosch, *bos, bosh.* See **bush.**

bosche. See **boche.**

bosh, *bosh, n.* nonsense: foolish talk.—Also *interj.* [Turk. *bosh,* worthless, frequent in Morier's novel *Ayesha* (1834).]

bosk, *bosk, n.* a thicket: a little wood.—*ns.* **bosk'et,** a thicket: a plantation; **bosk'iness.**—*adj.* **bosk'y,** woody or bushy: shady: (*coll.*) somewhat tipsy. [Cf. **bush, boscage.**]

bosker, *bos'kər, adj.* (*slang; Austr.*) very good.

bo's'n, bos'n. See **boatswain.**

bosom, *booz'əm, n.* the breast of a human being: the part of the dress that covers it: the imagined seat of the passions and feelings: the heart: (*Shak.*) desire: embrace, enclosure: any close or secret receptacle.—in composition, confidential: intimate.—*v.t.* to enclose in the bosom.—*adj.* **bos'omed,** having a bosom: enclosed.—**Abraham's bosom,** the abode of the blessed dead. [O.E. *bósm;* Ger. *busen.*]

boss, *bos, n.* a knob or stud: a raised ornament.—*v.t.* to ornament with bosses.—*adjs.* **bossed,** embossed; **boss'y,** having bosses. [O.Fr. *boce* (Fr. *bosse*), from O.H.G. *bōzan,* to beat.]

boss, *bos, n.* a chief or leader: a master, manager, or foreman: the person who pulls the wires in political intrigues.—*adj.* chief, excellent.—*v.t.* to manage or control: to domineer over.—*adj.* **boss'y.** [New York Dutch *baas,* master.]

boss, *bos, adj.* (*Scot.*) hollow: empty. [Origin obscure.]

bostangi, *bos-tan'ji, n.* a Turkish palace guard. [Turk. *bostanji.*]

boston, *bost'ən, n.* a game at cards, somewhat similar to whist: a kind of waltz. [From *Boston,* U.S.A.]

bostryx, *bos'triks, n.* (*bot.*) a cymose inflorescence in which each lateral axis arises on the same side (cyclically) of its parent axis. [Gr., curl.]

bosun. See **boatswain.**

Boswellian, *boz-wel'li-ən, adj.* after the manner of James Boswell, the famous biographer of Samuel Johnson.—*v.i.* **Bos'wellise** (*-wəl-īz*), to write after the manner of Boswell—full of an absolute admiration for one's hero and interest in him descending to the smallest particulars.—*n.* **Bos'wellism.**

bot, bott, *bot, n.* the maggot of a botfly, parasitic in the intestines of the horse and other animals: (in *pl.*) the diseased condition thereby caused: (*Scot.* batts) colic.—*n.* **bot'fly,** a name for various flies of the family Oestridae that lay their eggs on horses, etc.; **bot'hole,** a hole in a hide due to boring by a bot. [Origin unknown.]

botany, *bot'ən-i, n.* the science of plants: fine wool, orig. from Botany Bay.—*adjs.* **botanic** (*-an'ik*), **-al.**—*adv.* **botan'ically.**—*v.i.* **bot'anise,** to seek for and collect plants for study.—*ns.* **bot'anist,** one skilled in botany; **bot'anomancy,** divination by means of plants, esp. the leaves of sage and fig.—**Botany Bay,** a famous convict settlement in New South Wales, near to what is now Sydney: con-

vict settlements generally. [Gr. *botanē,* grass, fodder.]

botargo, *bot-är'gō, n.* a relish made of mullet or tunny roe. [It.,—Ar. *butarkhah.*]

botch, *boch, n.* a swelling on the skin: (*Milt.*) a boil, pimple, or sore: a blemish: a clumsy patch: ill-finished work.—*v.t.* to patch or mend clumsily: to put together unsuitably or unskilfully: to bungle.—*v.i.* to do repairs: to bungle.—*ns.* **botch'er,** a repairer: a bungler; **botch'ery.**—*n.* and *adj.* **botch'ing.**—*adj.* **botch'y,** marked with or full of botches. [Partly O.N.Fr. *boche* (O.Fr. *boce*), ulcer; partly perh. some other root.]

botfly. See **bot.**

both, *bōth, adj.* and *pron.* the two: the one and the other.—*adv.* or *conj.* as well (sometimes of more than two). [O.N. *báthar* (superseding O.E. *bégen, bá*); Ger. *beide;* cf. L. *ambō,* Gr. *amphō,* Sans. *ubha,* orig. *ambha.*]

bother, *bodh'ər, v.t.* to perplex or tease: to fluster.—*n.* petty trouble, difficulty, or perplexity.—*interj.* expressing irritation.—*n.* **bothera'tion** (*coll.*).—*adj.* **both'ersome.** [First found in 18th-cent. Irish-born writers; poss. Anglo-Irish for **pother.**]

bothy, bothie, *both'i, n.* a humble cottage or hut: a one-roomed hut or temporary dwelling: a barely furnished dwelling for farm-servants in the north-east of Scotland.—*n.* **both'y-man.** [Cf. **booth.**]

botoné, bottony, *bot'ən-i, adj.* (*her.*) having buds or knobs at the extremity, applied to a cross having each arm terminated in three buds, like trefoil. [O.Fr.; see **button.**]

bo-tree, *bō'trē, n.* in Ceylon, the pipal (*Ficus religiosa*), holy tree of the Buddhists, planted close by every temple. [Sinh. *bo,* from Pali *bodhi,* perfect knowledge.]

botryoid, -al, *bot'ri-oid, -oid'əl, adjs.* like a bunch of grapes.—*adj.* **bot'ryose,** botryoidal: (*bot.*) racemose. [Gr. *botrys,* a bunch of grapes, *eidos,* form.]

bottine, *bot-ēn', n.* a high boot: a half-boot: a lady's boot: a small boot. [Fr., dim. of *botte,* boot.]

bottle, *bot'l, n.* a bundle (of hay). [O.Fr. *botel.*]

bottle, *bot'l, n.* a narrow-necked hollow vessel for holding liquids: the contents of such a vessel: liquor or drinking.—*v.t.* to enclose in bottles.—*ns.* **bott'le-brush,** a brush for cleaning bottles, with bristles standing out from a central axis: a name given to various plants of like appearance, as horsetail, mare's-tail, *Banksia,* and *Callistemon;* **bott'le-chart,** a chart showing currents from evidence of bottles thrown into the sea; **bott'le-coaster,** a bottle-slider.—*adj.* **bott'led,** enclosed in bottles: shaped or protuberant like a bottle: kept in restraint: (*slang*) drunk.—*ns.* **bott'le-fish,** a fish, *Saccopharynx ampullaceus,* that can blow its body out like a bottle; **bott'le-glass,** a coarse green glass used in the making of bottles; **bott'le-gourd,** or *false calabash,* a climbing, muskyscented Indian cucurbitaceous annual, whose fruit is shaped like a bottle, an urn, or a club.—*adj.* and *n.* **bott'le-green,** dark green, like bottle-glass.—*ns.* **bott'le-head,** a bottle-nosed whale; **bott'le-holder,** a boxer's attendant: a backer or supporter generally; **bott'le-imp,** an imp confined in a bottle; **bott'le-neck,** a narrow place in a road where traffic is apt to be congested (often *fig.*); **bott'le-nose,** a large swollen nose: a bottle-nosed toothed whale (Hyperoodon).—*adjs.* **bott'le-nosed; bott'-le-shouldered,** with sloping shoulders like a champagne bottle.—*ns.* **bott'le-slider,** a tray for passing a decanter round the table; **bott'le-tree,** an Australian sterculiaceous tree with swollen trunk; **bott'le-washer,** one whose business it is to wash out bottles: a factotum generally.—**bottle off,** to draw from the cask and put into bottles; **bottle up,** to enclose as in a bottle: to hold back.—**bring up on the bottle,** to rear artificially rather than by the breast; **pass the bottle of smoke,** to acquiesce in some falsehood: to make pretence; **three-bottle man,** one who could drink three bottles of wine without losing his decorum. [O.Fr.

bouteille, dim. of *botte*, a vessel for liquids—L.L. *butis*, a vessel.]

bottom, *bot'əm*, *n.* the lowest part or surface of anything: that on which anything rests or is founded: the sitting part of the body: the bed of the sea, a river, etc.: the part that supports the contents of a vessel: the seat of a chair: the less dignified end: the foot of a page, hill, etc.: low land, as by a river: the lower part of a ship, hence the ship itself: groundwork: fundamental character or ingredient: staying power: financial resources: the portion of a wig hanging down over the shoulder: (*Shak.*) a ball of thread.—*adj.* undermost.—*v.t.* to ground or base: (*Shak.*) to wind.—*v.i.* to find bottom: to found, rest.—*adj.* **bott'omed.**—*ns.* **bott'om-fish**, a fish that feeds on the bottom (also collectively); **bott'om-glade** (*Milt.*), a glade or open space in a bottom or valley; **bott'om-grass** (*Shak.*), grass growing on low grounds; **bott'oming**, foundation; **bott'om-land** (*U.S.*), alluvial deposits.—*adj.* **bott'omless.**—*ns.* **bott'omry**, a contract by which money is borrowed on the security of a ship or bottom; **bott'om-sawyer**, the sawyer who works at the bottom of the saw-pit.—**at bottom**, fundamentally; **at the bottom of**, the real origin of; **bet one's bottom dollar**, to bet all one has; **bottom drawer**, a supposed receptacle for possessions hoarded by a young woman against marriage; **bottomless pit**, hell; **from the bottom of the heart**, with heartfelt sincerity; **get to the bottom of**, to investigate exhaustively; **stand on one's own bottom**, to be independent; **touch bottom**, to reach the lowest point. [O.E. *botm;* Ger. *boden;* conn. with L. *fundus*, bottom, Gael. *bonn*, the sole.]

bottony. See **botoné.**

botulism, *bot'ū-lizm*, *n.* sausage-poisoning, or poisoning by tinned or other food infected with *Bacillus botulinus* (or *Clostridium botulinum*). [L. *botulus*, sausage.]

boudoir, *bōōd'wär*, *n.* a lady's private room. [Fr.,—*bouder*, to pout, to be sulky.]

bouffe. See **opera-bouffe.**

Bougainvillaea, *bōōg-ān-vil-ē'ä*, or *-vil'*, *n.* a Neotropical genus of Nyctaginaceae, frequently trained over trellises, its triplets of flowers almost concealed by rosy or purple bracts.—Also **Bougainvil'ia.** [From the first French circumnavigator of of globe, Louis Antoine de *Bougainville* (1729-1811).]

bouge. A Shakespearian form of **budge** (vb.).

bouget. A Spenserian form of **budget.**

bough, *bow*, *n.* a branch of a tree: the gallows.—*n.* **bough'pot**, **bow'pot** (*arch.*), a pot for boughs as an ornament: a flower-pot: a bunch of flowers. [O.E. *bóg*, *bóh*, an arm, the shoulder; Ger. *bug*, shoulder, the bow of a ship—O.E. *búgan*, to bend.]

bought, *bawt*, *pa.t.* and *pa.p.* of **buy.**—*arch. pa.p.* **bought'en.**

bought, *bowt*, *n.* a bight or bend: (*Spens.*) a twist or coil: the bend of a sling. [See **bight.**]

bougie, *bōō'zhē*, *n.* a wax candle: an instrument (orig. of waxed linen) for distending contracted mucous canals. [Fr.,—*Bougie* in Algeria.]

bouillabaisse, *bōō-yä-bes'*, *n.* a Provençal kind of fish chowder, familiar through Thackeray's appreciative ballad. [Fr.]

bouilli, *bōō-yē*, *n.* boiled or stewed meat.—*n.* **bouillon** (*bōō-yon⁹*), a strong broth. [Fr.; see **boil.**]

bouk, *bōōk*, *n.* (*Scot.*) body: bulk. [O.E. *búc*, belly, O.N. *búkr*, coalescing with **bulk.**]

boulder, *bōld'ər*, *n.* a large stone rounded by the action of water: (*geol.*) a mass of rock transported by natural agencies from its native bed.—*adj.* containing boulders.—*n.* **bould'er-clay**, a stiff stony mass of finely ground rock, usually containing boulders and pebbles, formed as a ground-moraine under land-ice. [Origin obscure; Swed. dial. *bullersten*, large stone in a stream, has been compared.]

boule. Same as **buhl.**

boule, *bōō'lē*, *n.* in ancient Greece, a council or senate. [Gr. *boulē.*]

boulevard, *bōōl'(ə-)vär*, *n.* a broad road, walk, or promenade bordered with trees, originally applied to those formed upon the demolished fortifications of a town: (esp. *U.S.*) a broad main road.—**boulevardier** (*bōōl-vär-dyä*), a frequenter of boulevards. [Fr.,—Ger. *bollwerk;* see **bulwark.**]

bouleversement, *bōōl-vers-män⁹*, *n.* an overturning, overthrow, ruin. [Fr.]

boult, **bolt**, *bōlt*, *v.t.* to sift through coarse cloth: to examine by sifting.—*ns.* **bo(u)lt'er**, a sieve: a machine for separating bran from flour; **bo(u)lt'ing**; **bo(u)lt'ing-hutch**, a hutch or large box into which flour falls when it is bolted. [O.Fr. *bulter—buleter*, app. from *bure*—L.L. *burra*, a coarse reddish-brown cloth—Gr. *pyrrhos*, reddish.]

boun, **bowne**, *bōōn*, *bown*, *v.t.* and *v.i.* (used *refl.*) to prepare: to get ready: to dress: to set out.—*adj.* ready. [See **bound** (4); revived by Scott.]

bounce, *bowns*, *v.i.* to jump or spring suddenly: to bound like a ball, to throw oneself about: to burst (into or out of a room, etc.): to boast, to exaggerate.—*v.t.* (*obs.*) to beat: to cause to rebound: (*U.S.*) to turn out, eject, dismiss.—*n.* a thud: a leap or spring: a boast: (*U.S.*) dismissal: a bold lie.—*adv.* and *interj.* expressing sudden movement or the noise of a gun.—*n.* **bounc'er**, one who bounces: something big: a bully: a liar: (*U.S.*) a chucker-out.—*adj.* **bounc'ing**, large and heavy: lusty: swaggering. [Du. *bonzen*, to strike, from *bons*, a blow.]

bounce, *bowns*, *n.* the lesser spotted dogfish.

bound, *bownd*, *pa.t.* and *pa.p.* of **bind.**—*n.* **bound'-bail'iff**, a sheriff's officer, so called from his bond given to the sheriff for the discharge of his duty.—**bound to**, obliged to: certain to (perhaps partly from **bound**, 4).

bound, *bownd*, *n.* a limit: (in *pl.*) the limit of that which is reasonable or permitted: (in *pl.*) a borderland, land generally within certain understood limits, the district.—*v.t.* to set bounds to: to limit, restrain, or surround.—*ns.* **bound'ary**, limit: border: termination: (*cricket*) a hit to the limit of the ground: a score for such a hit; **bound'ary-rider** (*Austr.*), one who rides around a station and repairs fences.—*adjs.* **bound'ed**, restricted, cramped; **bound'less**, having no limit: vast.—*n.* **bound'lessness.** [O.Fr. *bonne*—L.L. *bodina;* cf. Bret. *bonn*, a boundary.]

bound, *bownd*, *v.i.* to spring or leap.—*n.* a spring or leap.—*n.* **bound'er**, one who bounds: an obtrusively ill-bred man: one whose moral conduct is objectionable.—*adj.* **bound'ing**, moving forward with a bound: leaping.—**by leaps and bounds**, by startlingly rapid stages. [Fr. *bondir*, to spring, in O.Fr. to resound—L. *bombitāre.*]

bound, *bownd*, *adj.* ready to go, going: on the way. [O.N. *búinn*, *pa.p.* of *búa*, to prepare; cf. **boun.**]

bounden, *bownd'n*, *adj.* obligatory. [Archaic *pa.p.* of **bind.**]

bountree, *bōōn'tri.* See **bourtree.**

bounty, *bown'ti*, *n.* liberality in bestowing gifts: the gift bestowed: money offered as an inducement to enter the army, or as a premium to encourage any branch of industry, or (king's, or queen's bounty) to a mother who has three or more children at a birth.—*adjs.* **boun'teous**, **boun'tiful**, liberal in giving: generous.—*advs.* **boun'teously**, **boun'tifully.**—*ns.* **boun'teousness**, **boun'tifulness; boun'tihood; boun'tyhed** (*Spens.*).—**Lady Bountiful**, a character in Farquhar's *Beaux' Stratagem*: now used for the charitable great lady of a district. [O.Fr. *bontet* (*bonté*), goodness—L. *bonitās*, *-ātis—bonus*, good.]

bouquet, *bōōk'ā*, or *-ā'*, *n.* a bunch of flowers: a nosegay: the perfume exhaled by wine. [Fr. *bouquet*, dim. of *bois*, a wood; cf. It. *bosco;* see **boscage**, bush.]

bourasque, *bōō-råsk'*, *n.* a tempest. [Fr. *bourrasque;* It. *borasco*, a storm.]

Bourbon, *bōōr'-bon*, *n.* (*U.S.*) a reactionary: a race of roses: maize whisky (orig. made in Bourbon County, Kentucky).—*ns.* **Bour'bonism; Bour'bonist**, an adherent of the Bourbons. [From the *Bourbon* family, which long reigned in France and Spain.]

Neutral vowels in unaccented syllables : *el'ə-mənt, in'fənt, ran'dəm*

bourd, *boŏrd*, *n.* (*Spens.*) a jest, sport.—*n.* **bourd'er** (*obs.*), a jester. [O.Fr. *bourde*, origin unknown.]

bourdon, *boŏr'dən*, *n.* the refrain of a song : a drone bass : a bass stop in an organ or harmonium. [See **burden**.]

bourdon, *boŏr'dən*, *n.* (*obs.*) a pilgrim's staff : a club. [Fr.,—L.L. *burdō*, *-ōnis*, a mule.]

bourg, *burg*, *n.* Same as **burgh**, **borough**.

bourgeois, *bur-jois'*, *n.* a type larger than brevier and smaller than longprimer. [Fr.; perh. from the name of the type-founder.]

bourgeois, *boŏrzh'wä*, *n.* a citizen : a member of the middle class : a merchant or shopkeeper.— *adj.* middle class : conventional : humdrum : conservative.—*n.* **bourgeoisie** (*boŏrzh'wä-zē̄*, *-zē̄'*), the middle class of citizens. [Fr. *bourgeois*, a citizen.]

bourgeon, *bur'jən*, *v.i.* to put forth sprouts or buds : to grow. [Fr. *bourgeon*, a bud, shoot.]

Bourignian, *boŏr-in'yən*, *adj.* of or pertaining to Antoinette *Bourignon* (1616-80), a religious visionary who made religion consist in inward emotion, not in knowledge or practice.

bourlaw. See **byrlaw.**

bourn, bourne, *bōrn*, or *boŏrn*, *n.* a boundary, a limit, or goal : (*Keats*) domain. [Fr. *borne*, a limit.]

bourn, bourne. See **burn** (1).

bourrée, *boŏr-ā'*, *n.* a brisk dance in duple time, originating in Auvergne or in the Basque provinces : a musical composition in the same rhythm, often introduced in old suites. [Fr.]

bourse, *boors*, *n.* an exchange where merchants meet for business. [Fr. *bourse*. See **purse.**]

bourtree, *boŏr'tri*, *n.* (*Scot.*) the elder-tree.—Also **boun'tree** (*boŏn'tri*).—*n.* **bour'tree-gun**, a popgun made of an elder twig. [Ety. unknown.]

bouse, booze, boose, *boŏz, bowz, v.i.* to drink deeply.—*n.* intoxicating liquor : a drinking bout.— *adj.* **bous'ing,** etc., drinking : for drinking (*Spens.* **bouzing can**).—*n.* **bous'ingken** (*obs. thieves' slang*), a low drinking-shop.—*adj.* **bous'y,** etc., inclined to bouse : drunken. [Apparently Middle Du. *būsen*, to drink deeply—*buis*, a tube or flask; allied to **box.**]

bouse, bowse, *bowz, v.t.* and *v.i.* to haul with tackle. [Orig. unknown.]

boustrophedon, *boŏ-* or *bow-strof-ē'don*, *adj.* and *adv.* (of ancient writing) ploughwise, alternately from right to left and from left to right. [Gr. *boustrophēdon*—*bous*, ox, *strophē*, a turning.]

bout, *bowt*, *n.* a turn, round : a spell : a trial : a fit. [**bought** (2).]

boutade, *boŏ-tād'*, *n.* a sudden outburst : a caprice. [Fr.,—*bouter*, to thrust.]

bouts-rimés, *boŏ-rē-mā'*, *n.pl.* rhyming words given out by some one as the line-endings of a stanza, for others to fill up the lines. [Fr., rhymed ends.]

bovate, *bō'vāt*, *n.* (*hist.*) an oxgang. [L.L. *bovāta*— *bōs* *bovis,* an ox.]

bovine, *bō'vīn*, *adj.* pertaining to cattle. [L. *bōs,* *bovis,* an ox or cow.]

Bovril, *bov'ril*, *n.* a registered trade-mark applied to a special meat extract.—*v.t.* **bov'rilise.** [Coined from L. *bōs, bovis,* an ox, and *vril,* the electric fluid represented as the one common origin of the forces in matter in Lytton's novel *The Coming Race,* 1871.]

bow, *bow, v.i.* to bend : to bend the neck or body in saluting, acknowledging a compliment, etc. : to submit.—*v.t.* to bend or incline downwards, to crush down : to usher with a bow : to express by a bow.—*n.* a bending of the neck or body in salutation.—*adj.* **bowed** (*bowd*), bent forward, esp. in the back.—**a bowing acquaintance,** a slight acquaintance ; **make one's bow,** to retire ceremoniously : to leave the stage. [O.E. *būgan,* to bend; akin to L. *fugĕre,* to flee, to yield.]

bow, *bō,* *n.* a piece of elastic wood or other material for shooting arrows, bent by means of a string stretched between its ends : anything of a bent or curved shape, as the rainbow : (*Shak.*) a yoke : the instrument by which the strings of a violin etc. are sounded : a ring of metal forming a handle : a knot with one or two loops : a looped knot of

ribbons : a necktie or the like, so tied : a single movement (up or down) or stroke of the bow in playing an instrument.—*v.i.* to handle the bow in playing.—*v.t.* to play with a bow : to distribute between up-bows and down-bows : to mark such distribution.—*adjs.* **bow'-backed,** with bent back : **bow'bent** (*Milton*), bent like a bow.—*n.* **bow'-boy,** a boy archer : (*Shak.*) Cupid :—*n.pl.* **bow'-compasses,** a small pair of compasses, often with a bow-shaped spring instead of a hinge.—*ns.* **bow'fin,** a North American fresh-water fish (*Amia*) of the Holostei ; **bow'-hand,** the hand in which the bow is held—normally in archery, the left, in violinplaying the right ; **bow'-leg,** a bandy leg like a bow.—*adj.* **bow'-legged.**—*ns.* **bow'man,** an archer ; **bow'-saw,** a saw with a narrow blade stretched like a bowstring in a strong frame ; **bow'shot,** the distance to which an arrow can be shot from a bow ; **bow'string,** the string by which a bow is drawn : a string with which the Turks strangled offenders : a horizontal tie on a bridge or girder.— *v.t.* to strangle with a bowstring (*pa.t.* and *pa.p.* **bow'stringed,** sometimes **bow'strung**).—*adj.* of, for, having, a bowstring.—*ns.* **bow'string-hemp,** the genus Sansevieria or its fibre ; **bow'-win'dow,** a window projecting in a curve : (*slang*) a potbelly.—*adj.* **bow'-win'dowed.**—*n.* **bow'yer,** a bowman : a maker of bows.—**draw the long bow,** to make extravagant statements ; **on the bow hand,** wide of the mark ; **two strings to one's bow,** an alternative in reserve. [O.E. *boga*; cog. with Ger. *bogen*.]

bow, *bow, n.* the forepart of a ship—often used in *pl.,* the ship being considered to have starboard and port bows, meeting at the stem.—*ns.* **bow'er,** **bow'er-anch'or,** an anchor at the bow or forepart of a ship (*best-bower* and *small-bower*); **bow'-oar,** the oar nearest the bow.—**bold,** or **bluff, bow,** a broad bow; **lean bow,** a narrow one; **on the bow,** within 45° of the point right ahead. [From a L.G., Du. or Scand. word for shoulder; see **bough.**]

bowat, bowet, buat, *boŏ'ət, n.* (*Scot.*) a lantern.— **MacFarlane's buat** (*Scott*), the moon. [L.L. *boeta,* box.]

bowdlerise, *bowd'lər-īz, v.t.* to expurgate a book or writing, by removing whatever might raise a blush, esp. to do so unnecessarily.—*ns.* **bowdlerisā'tion; bowd'leriser; bowd'lerism.** [From Dr. T. *Bowdler* (1754-1825), who published an expurgated Shakespeare in ten volumes in 1818.]

bowel, *bow'əl, n.* an interior part of the body : (in *pl.*) the entrails, intestines : the interior part of anything : (*fig.*) the heart, pity, tenderness (the emotions being supposed to be seated in the bowels—*B.* and *Shak.*).—*v.t.* **bow'el,** to take out the bowels (*pr.p.* **bow'elling;** *pa.p.* and *pa.t.* **bow'elled**). [O.Fr. *boel*—L. *botellus,* a sausage, an intestine.]

bower, *bow'ər, n.* a shady enclosure or recess in a garden, an arbour : an inner apartment : a lady's private room, boudoir : (*poet.*) a dwelling.—*v.t.* to enclose : (*Shak.*) to embower.—*v.i.* (*Spens.*) to lodge.—*n.* **bow'er-bird,** an Australian bird that makes a bower ornamented with gay feathers, shells, etc.—*adj.* **bow'ery,** containing bowers : shady. [O.E. *būr,* a chamber; root of *būan,* to dwell.]

bower, *bow'ər, n.* the name in euchre for the two highest cards, the knave of trumps, and the other knave of the same colour, the *right* and *left* bower respectively. [Ger. *bauer,* peasant.]

bowery, *bow'ə-ri, n.* (*U.S.*) a farm.—**the Bowery,** a street in New York. [Du. *bouwerij.*]

bowes. A Miltonic spelling of **boughs.**

bowet. Same as **bowat.**

bowget. A variant of **budget.**

bowie-knife, *bō'i-nīf, n.* a dagger-knife with a blade about twelve inches long. [From Colonel *Bowie,* its inventor.]

bowl, *bōl, n.* (*obs.*) a ball : a heavy wooden ball with a bias : (in *pl.*) a game played by rolling such balls on a green towards a jack : (*dial.,* in *pl.*) skittles : (*Scot. bōōl*) a marble : (in *pl.*) the game of marbles.— *v.i.* to play at bowls : to roll or trundle : to travel swiftly and smoothly in a wheeled vehicle : to deliver a ball in cricket : to be bowler.—*v.t.* to roll or trundle : (*cricket*) to deliver legitimately : to put out by hitting the wicket with a bowled ball : to put or render by bowling.—*ns.* **bowl'er**, one who plays at bowls : one who bowls in cricket; **bowl'ing ; bowl'ing-all'ey**, a long narrow covered place for skittles ; **bowl'ing-crease** (see **crease**); **bowl'ing-green**, a smooth grassy plot for bowls. —to **bowl over**, to knock down : to overwhelm. [Fr. *boule*—L. *bulla*.]

bowl, *bōl*, *n.* a nearly hemispherical basin for domestic use : a large vessel for brewing punch : a round drinking-cup, rather wide than deep—hence a synonym for conviviality : the round hollow part of anything : the pocket of a pound-net. [O.E. *bolla*. See **bole**.]

bowlder, *bōld'ər*, *n.* Same as **boulder**.

bowler, *bō'lər*, *n.* a round felt hat.—Also **bow'ler-hat'**. [Prob. **bowl** (2), but perh. **bowl** (1) or possibly the name of a hatter.]

bowline, *bō'lin*, *n.* a rope from the weather side of the square sails (to which it is fastened by *bridles*) to the larboard or starboard bow, to keep the sail close to the wind.—**bowline knot**, a simple but secure knot used in fastening the bowline bridles to the cringles. [Origin obscure.]

bow-pot. Same as **bough-pot**.

bowr, *bowr*, *n.* (*Spens.*) muscle. [**bow**, to bend.]

bowse. Same as **bouse**.

bowsprit, *bō'sprit*, *n.* a strong spar projecting over the bows of a ship. [Apparently Du. *boegspriet*.]

bowwow, *bow'wow'*, *n.* a dog's bark : (*Scott*) a full-mouthed literary style : (*childish* or *facet.*) a dog. [Imit.]

box, *boks*, *n.* an evergreen shrub or small tree (*Buxus sempervirens*) with hard smooth yellowish wood, often used to border garden-walks and flower-beds (also **box'-tree**, **box'wood**) : its wood : extended to various other plants : a case or receptacle for holding anything : the contents of a box : a fund : a (Christmas) present : a compartment : a ruled off space : (*baseball*) a pitcher's standing-place : a small house or lodge, as a *shooting-box*, etc. : in a theatre, a small enclosure with several seats : an old square pew or similar enclosure, as a *sentry-box*, *signal-box*, *bathing-box*, *witness-box*, etc. : the driver's seat on a carriage : the case of a ship's compass : a predicament.—*v.t.* to put into or furnish with boxes : to enclose : (*Scot.*) to panel, wainscot : (*slang*) to overturn (a watchman) in his box : (*Austr.*) to mix, as flocks of sheep.—*ns.* **box'-bed**, a kind of bed long common in Scottish cottages, having its ends, sides and roof of wood, and capable of being closed in front by two sliding panels; **box'-car**, (*U.S.*) a box-wagon; **box'-cloth**, a heavy cloth for riding garments; **box'-coat**, a heavy overcoat for coaching; **box'-day**, one of the Court of Session vacation days when papers ordered to be deposited in court must be lodged.—*adj.* **box'en**, made of or like boxwood.—*n.* **box'ful**, as much as a box will hold :— *pl.* **box'fuls**.—*v.t.* **box'haul**, to veer (a ship) sharp round on her heel, by putting the helm a-lee, bracing the head-yards flat aback, and hauling to windward the head-sheets.—*ns.* **Box'ing-day**, the day after Christmas, when boxes or presents are given; **box'-iron**, a hollow smoothing-iron heated by a heater put into it; **box'-keeper**, an attendant who opens the doors of boxes at theatres, etc.; **box'-kite**, a kite composed of open-ended boxes; **box'-lobb'y**, the lobby leading to the boxes in a theatre; **box'-office**, in a theatre, etc., the office at which seats may be booked; **box'-pleat**, a double fold of cloth turned opposite ways; **box'-room**, a room in which boxes are stored; **box'seat**, a driver's seat; **box'-wag'on**, a closed railway wagon; **box'wood**, wood of the box-tree : the plant itself.—**box the compass**, to name the 32 points in their order and then backwards : hence to make a complete roundabout in any opinion; **in the wrong box**, in a false position, in a scrape. [O.E. *box*—L. *buxus*—Gr. *pyxos*, the tree, *pyxis*, a box.]

box, *boks*, *n.* a blow on the head or ear with the hand.—*v.t.* to strike with the hand or fist.—*v.i.* to fight with the fists.—*v.t.* and *v.i.* (*Scot.*) to butt.—*ns.* **box'er**, one who boxes or is skilled in boxing; **Boxer**, a member of a Chinese society hostile to foreigners; **box'ing**, the act or art of fighting with the fists : a combat with the fists; **box'ing-glove**, a padded glove used in boxing. [Possibly connected with Gr. *pyx*, with the fist.]

box-calf, *boks'käf*, *n.* a chrome-tanned calfskin with rectangular markings made by rolling. [Said to be named after one Joseph *Box*, shoemaker.]

boy, *boi*, *n.* a male child : a lad : a young man generally : (Ireland and elsewhere) a man : (*Shak.*) a camp-follower : (*obs.*) knave : in some countries a native servant or labourer : a slave.—*v.t.* (*Shak.*) to play (a female part) as a boy.—*n.* **boy'hood**.— *adj.* **boy'ish**.—*adv.* **boy'ishly**.—*n.* **boy'ishness**. —**boy bishop**, a mock bishop formerly elected by choirboys or schoolboys, in office from St. Nicholas' to Holy Innocents' Day (6th–28th December); **boy friend**, a girl's favourite boy for the time being; **Boys' Brigade**, an organisation of boys for the promotion of habits of obedience, reverence, discipline, and self-respect; **Boy Scout**, a member of an organisation of boys formed to develop mental and physical alertness and strong character; **boy's love**, southernwood; **boy's play**, trifling. [M.E. *boi*, *boy*; Fris. *boi*; Du. *boef*, Ger. *bube*.]

boyar, *bo-yär'*, *boi'är*, *n.* a member of the old Russian aristocracy next in rank to the ruling princes, before the reforms of Peter the Great. [Russ. *boyarin*.]

boyau, *bwo'yō*, *bwä'yō*, *boi'ō*, *n.* a long narrow lane : a communication trench :—*pl.* **bo'yaux**. [Fr. *boyau*, bowel.]

boycott, *boi'kot*, *v.t.* to shut out from all social and commercial intercourse.—*n.* an act of boycotting, a kind of secular excommunication. [From Captain *Boycott* of County Mayo, who was so treated by his neighbours in Dec., 1880.]

brabble, *brab'l*, *v.i.* to babble or clamour : to brawl or wrangle.—*n.* (*Shak.*) a clamorous contest, a brawl : a quibble.—*n.* **brabb'lement**. [Du. *brabbelen*, to stammer, to jabber.]

braccate, *brak'āt*, *adj.* having feathered legs or feet. [L. *brācātus*, wearing breeches.]

braccio, *brät'chō*, *n.* an Italian measure of length, varying from half a yard to a yard :—*pl.* **braccia** (*brät'chä*). [It., lit. arm.]

brace, *brās*, *n.* (*Shak.*) armour for the arm : anything that draws together and holds tightly : a bandage : an instrument of wood or iron used by carpenters and metal-workers for turning boring tools : a mark $\left(\}\right)$ connecting words, lines, staves of music, indicating that they are taken together, and also used as a bracket in algebra : a pair or couple (esp. of game shot) : (in *pl.*) a combination of straps for supporting the trousers : (in *pl.*) ropes for squaring or traversing horizontally the yards of a ship.—*v.t.* to tighten or strengthen, to give firmness to : to tone up : (*Spens.*) to embrace, encompass.—*n.* **brac'er**.—*adj.* **brac'ing**, giving strength or tone. [O.Fr. *brace* (Fr. *bras*), the arm, power—L. *brāchium*, *brācchium*, Gr. *brāchiōn*.]

bracelet, *brās'lit*, *n.* an ornament for the wrist : (*coll.*) a handcuff. [Fr. dim.,—L. *brāchiāle*—*brāchium*; see **brace**.]

brach, *brach*, *n.* a dog for the chase, a bitch hound. —*n.* **brach'et**, **bratch'et**, a brach : a whelp : a brat. [O.Fr. *brachet*, *pl.* *brachès*, dim. of *brac*— L.L. *braccō*, of Gmc. origin.]

brachial, *brāk'* or *brak'i-əl*, *adj.* of the arm.— **brachial artery**, the great arterial trunk supplying the upper extremity between the armpit and the elbow, direct continuation of the axillary artery. [See **brace**.]

brachiopod, *brak'i-ō-pod*, *n.* a member of a class **Brachiopoda** (*-op'o-dä*) of shelled animals allied to worms and Polyzoa, having usually two long arm-like processes serving to waft food particles to the mouth. [Gr. *brāchiōn*, an arm, and *pous*, *podos*, a foot.]

brachistochrone, *bra-kis'tō-krōn, n.* the curve along which a particle acted on by a force (e.g. gravity) will pass in shortest time from one given point to another. [Gr. *brachistos,* superl. of *brachys,* short, *chronos,* time.]

brachy-, *brak'i-, -i'-,* in composition, short.—*ns.* **brachy-ax'is** (*crystall.*), the shorter lateral axis; **brachycephal** (*sef'l;* Gr. *kephalē,* head), a short-headed person.—*adjs.* **brachycephalic** (*-si-fal'ik*), **brachycephalous** (*-sef'ə-ləs*), short-headed, having a skull whose breadth is 80 (or 78) per cent. or more of its length.—*n.* **brachyceph'aly,** short-headedness—opp. to *dolichocephaly.*—*adjs.* **brachydac'tyl, brachydactyl'ic, brachydac'tylous** (Gr. *daktylos,* finger, toe).—*ns.* **brachydac'tyly,** abnormal shortness of fingers and toes; **brachydiag'onal** (*crystall.*), the shorter lateral axis; **brach'ydome,** a dome parallel to the brachydiagonal; **brachyg'raphy,** abbreviated writing; **brachyl'ogy,** condensed expression; **brachypin'akoid, brach'yprism,** a pinakoid, prism, parallel to the brachydiagonal.—*adjs.* **brachyp'-terous** (Gr. *pteron,* wing), short-winged: short-finned.—*n.pl.* **Brachyura** (*-ū'rä;* Gr. *ourā,* tail), a group of decapod crustaceans having the abdomen reduced and bent forward under the thorax, the crabs.—*adjs.* **brachyu'ral, brachyu'rous.** [Gr. *brachys,* short.]

brack, *brak, n.* a flaw in cloth. [See **break** (1).]

bracken, *brak'ən, n.* a fern, esp. *Pteris aquilina,* the commonest British fern, abundant on hillsides, etc. [Ety. obscure.]

bracket, *brak'it, n.* a projecting support: a small shelf fastened to a wall: a gas-pipe projecting from a wall: in printing, one of the marks used to enclose words or mathematical symbols: one of the side pieces of a gun-carriage, supporting the trunnions: (*artillery*) the space intervening between over-estimated and underestimated shots at a target in straddling: a bracketed group.—*v.t.* to support by brackets: to enclose by brackets: to group, as in an honour list, implying equality: (*artillery*) to straddle. [Fr. *braguette*—Sp. *bragueta*—L. *brāca,* sing. of *brācae,* breeches.]

brackish, *brak'ish, adj.* saltish, rather salt.—*n.* **brack'ishness.** [Du. *brak,* brackish; prob. the same as *brack,* refuse.]

bract, *brakt, n.* a leaf (often modified) that bears a flower in its axil.—*adjs.* **bract'eal.**—*n.* **bract'eate** (*archaeology*), a thin-beaten plate of gold or silver.—*adj.* of metal beaten thin: having bracts.—*adj.* **bract'eolate,** having bracteoles.—*n.* **bract'eole,** a small leaf on the axis of a flower.—*adj.* **bract'-less.**—*n.* **bract'let,** a bracteole. [L. *bractea,* a thin plate of metal, gold-leaf.]

brad, *brad, n.* a small nail with a side projection instead of a head.—*n.* **brad'awl,** a small boring tool. [O.N. *broddr,* spike.]

Bradshaw, *brad'shaw, n.* a noted railway-guide, first issued in 1839 by George *Bradshaw* (1801-53).

brady-, *brad'i-,* in composition, slow.—*n.* **bradycard'ia** (Gr. *kardia,* heart), slowness of heart-beat.—*adj.* **bradypept'ic** (Gr. *peptikos,* digesting), slow of digestion.—Also *n.*—*n.* **brad'yseism** (*-sīzm;* Gr. *seismos,* a shake), a slow up and down movement of the earth's crust. [Gr. *bradys,* slow.]

brae, *brā, n.* (*Scot.*) the slope bounding a riverside plain: a hill-slope. [O.N. *brá,* eyelid; cf. **brow.**]

brag, *brag, v.i.* and *v.t.* to boast or bluster: (*pr.p.* **bragg'ing;** *pa.t.* and *pa.p.* **bragged**).—*n.* a boast or boasting: a thing one boasts of or is proud of: a card game like poker.—*adj.* or *adv.* (*Spens.*) proud, proudly.—*advs.* **bragg'ingly, brag'ly** (*Spens.*). [Origin doubtful.]

bragadisme. See under **braggart.**

Braggadocio, *brag-ə-dō'(t)shi-ō, n.* a braggart or boaster: empty boasting. [From *Braggadochio* (prob. *-dok'yō*) in Spenser's *Faerie Queene.*]

braggart, *brag'ərt, adj.* boastful.—*n.* a vain boaster.—*n.* **bragg'artism** (*Shak.* **bragadisme**), boastfulness. [Fr. *bragard,* vain, bragging.]

Brahma, *brä'mä, n.* a fowl of Chinese breed, modified in Europe and America. [*Brahmaputra,* whence it is said to have been brought.]

Brahma, *brä'mä* (*brä-mä'*), *n.* the supreme post-Vedic Hindu deity.—*n.* **Brah'man** (*-mən*), **Brah'-min,** a person of the highest or priestly caste among the Hindus.—*adjs.* **Brahmanic** (*-man'*), **-al, Brahmin'ic, -al, Brah'minee,** appropriated to the Brahmans.—*ns.* **Brah'manism, Brah'minism,** one of the religions of India, the worship of Brahma; **Brahmi** (*brä'mē*), an ancient Indian alphabet.— **Brahma Samaj** (*sum-äj'*) or **Brah'mo Somaj,** a reformed Hindu theistic society or church, founded in 1830; **brahmin bull, cow, ox,** the zebu.

braid, *brād, v.t.* (*obs.*) to jerk. whip out: to plait, intertwine: to arrange in plaits: to thread, wind about through: to trim, bind, or outline with braid.—*v.i.* (*obs.*) to start: (*obs.*) to change colour or appearance.—*n.* (*obs.*) a sudden movement, start: a plait, especially of hair: a band for the hair: a fabric woven in a narrow band: an inter-weaving, plaiting: embroidery.—*adj.* **braid'ed,** plaited: entwined: trimmed with braid: (*obs.*) tarnished, faded.—*n.* **braid'ing,** plaiting: manu-facture of braid: work in braid: embroidery: braids collectively. [O.E. *bregdan,* to move quickly, flash, change colour, plait, weave; O.N. *bregtha.*]

braid, *brād, v.t.* (*Shak.*) to upbraid. to reproach. [Prob. from **upbraid**; or **braid** (1).]

braid, *brād, adj.* Scots form of **broad.**

braide, *brād, adj.* (*Shak.*) dissembling, deceitful. [O.E. *brǣgd,* falsehood—*bregdan,* to weave.]

Braidism, *brād'izm, n.* (*arch.*) hypnotism. [From Dr. James *Braid,* who practised it c. 1842.]

brail, *brāl, n.* a piece of leather to bind up a hawk's wing: (*pl.*) the feathers about a hawk's rump: (*naut.*) one of the ropes used to truss up a sail.— *v.t.* to haul in, as a sail, by pulling upon the brails. [O.Fr. *brail*—L. *brācāle,* a waist-belt—*brācae,* breeches.]

Braille, *brāl, n.* a kind of type in relief for the blind, having arbitrary signs consisting of varying combinations of six points arranged thus (∷), there being sixty-three distinguishable combinations—also *adj.* [From Louis *Braille,* the inventor (1809-52).]

brain, *brān, n.* (often in *pl.*) in vertebrates, that part of the central nervous system that is contained within the skull: in invertebrates, the nervous ganglia near the head end of the body: the seat of the intellect and of sensation: the intellect (often used in *pl.*).—*v.t.* to dash out the brains of: (*Shak.*) to conceive of.—*n.* **brain'-cor'al,** a coral with brain-like convolutions.—*adj.* **brained,** having brains.—*ns.* **brain'-fag,** a tired condition of the nerves or brain; **brain'-fe'ver,** a loose popular term which includes congestion of the brain and its membranes, delirium tremens, and inflammation of the brain substance itself.—*adjs.* **brain'ish** (*Shak.*), brain-sick, hot-headed, furious; **brain'-less,** without brains or understanding: silly.—*n.* **brain'-pan,** the skull.—*adj.* **brain'-sick,** diseased in the understanding, deranged.—*adv.* **brain'-sick'ly** (*Shak.*).—*ns.* **brain'-sickness; brain'-storm,** a sudden and severe disturbance of the mind; **brain'-wave,** a sudden bright idea: an access of cleverness.—*adj.* **brain'y,** well endowed with brains: intellectual.—**brain'-fe'ver bird,** an Indian cuckoo that sings scales in the night.— **brains trust,** a committee of experts: a number of reputedly well-informed persons chosen to answer questions of general interest in public and without preparation. [O.E. *brægen;* Du. *brein,* prov. Ger. *bregen.*]

braird, *brārd,* **breer,** *brēr, n.* (orig. *Scot.*) the first shoots of corn or other crop.—*v.i.* to appear above ground. [O.E. *brerd,* edge.]

braise, *brāz, v.t.* to stew in a closed vessel. [Fr. *braiser.*]

braise, braize, *brāz, n.* a sea-bream or porgy. [Perh. conn. with **bream,** or with **bass(e).**]

brake, *brāk,* obsolete *pa.t.* of **break.**

brake, *brāk, n.* a fern: a bracken. [Perh. **bracken.**]

brake, *brāk, n.* a thicket.—*adj.* **brak'y.** [Ety. obscure.]

brake, *brāk, n.* an instrument for breaking flax or hemp: a harrow: a contrivance for retarding by friction : a kind of vehicle (see **break**).—*n.* **brake'-block,** a block pressed against a wheel as brake.— *adj.* **brake'less,** without a brake.—*ns.* **brakes'man,** the man whose business it is to manage the brake of a railway train; **brake'-shoe,** the rubbing part of a brake; **brake'-van,** the carriage wherein the brake is worked; **brake'-wheel,** the wheel to which a brake is applied. [From root of **break,** cf. Du. *braak,* a flax-brake.]

brake, *brāk, n.* a handle, as of a pump : a lever for working a machine. [Prob. through O.Fr. *brac,* from L. *brāchium,* an arm.]

brake, *brāk, n.* (*Shak.*) an obscure word in *Measure for Measure,* II. i. 39 (not made clearer by emendation of *ice* to *vice*).

Bramah-press, *brăm'ā-pres, n.* a hydraulic press invented by Joseph *Bramah* (c. 1748-1814), inventor also of the **Bramah-lock,** etc.

bramble, *bram'bl, n.* the blackberry bush, a wild prickly shrub of the raspberry genus (*Rubus*) : any rough prickly shrub : (*Scot.*) a blackberry.— *ns.* **bram'ble-berry; bram'ble-bush,** blackberry bush or thicket; **bram'ble-finch, bram'bling,** a bird nearly allied to the chaffinch.—*adj.* **bram'bly.** [O.E. *brémel;* Du. *braam,* Ger. *brombeere.*]

brame, *brām, n.* (*Spens.*) sharp passion, longing. [Prob. It. *brama.*]

bran, *bran, n.* the refuse of grain : the inner husks of corn sifted from the flour; the coarser part of anything. — *ns.* **bran'fulness; bran'-mash'; bran'-pie', bran'-tub,** a tub of bran from which Christmas presents, etc., are drawn.—*adj.* **brann'y.** [O.Fr. *bran,* bran, perh. Celt.]

brancard, *brangk'ärd, -ərd, n.* a horse litter. [Fr.]

branch, *bränsh, n.* a shoot or arm-like limb of a tree : anything like a limb of a tree : any off-shoot from a main trunk : a sub-division, a section or department of a subject : any subordinate division of a business, subsidiary shop, office, etc. : (*U.S.*) a tributary or brook.—*v.t.* to divide into branches : (*Spens.,* etc.) to adorn with figures of branches, by embroidery or otherwise.—*v.i.* to spread out as a branch (with *out, off, from*), or in branches.— *adj.* **branched.**—*ns.* **branch'er,** a young hawk or other bird when it leaves the nest and begins to take to the branches; **branch'ery,** branches collectively (*lit.* and *fig.*).—*n.* and *adj.* **branch'ing.**— *adj.* **branch'less,** without branches.—*ns.* **branch'let,** a little branch; **branch'-pi'lot,** one who holds the Trinity House certificate; **branch'-work,** ornamental figured patterns.—*adj.* **branch'y.**— **root and branch,** thorough : thoroughly. [Fr. *branche*—L.L. *branca,* a beast's paw.]

branchia, *brangk'i-ā, n.* a gill;—*pl.* **branchiae** (*-ē*).—*adjs.* **branch'ial; branch'iate,** furnished with branchiae. [L. *branchia*—Gr. *branchion* (pl. *-a*).]

Branchiopoda, *brangk-i-op'o-dä, n.pl.* a class or subclass of Crustacea with numerous flattened, leaf-shaped, lobed swimming-feet that serve also as breathing organs.—*n.* and *adj.* **branch'iopod.** [Gr. *branchia,* gills, *pous, podos,* foot.]

brand, *brand, n.* a piece of wood burning or partly burned : an instrument for branding : a mark burned into anything with a hot iron : a trademark, made by burning or otherwise, as on casks : a particular class of goods (as if distinguished by a trade-mark) : a sword, from its glitter : a mark of infamy : a general name for the fungoid diseases or blights of grain crops (*bunt, mildew, rust,* and *smut*).—*v.t.* to burn or mark with a hot iron, or otherwise : to fix a mark of infamy upon.—*adj.* **brand'ed.**—*n.* **brand'er** (*Scot.*) a gridiron.—*v.t.* to cook on the gridiron.—*adjs.* **brand'ered, brand'ering.**—*ns.* **brand'ing-i'ron; brand'-i'ron,** a gridiron : an iron to brand with : a trivet or tripod to set a pot or kettle upon : (*Spens.*) **brond-yron,** etc.) a sword; **brandise** (*brand'is;* O.E. *isen,* iron), a trivet; **brand'ling,** a salmon-parr : an earthworm banded in red and yellow, found in dunghills, used by anglers.—*adj.* **bran(d)'-new,** quite new (as if newly from the fire).—*n.* **brand'-reth** (O.N. *brandreith*—*reith,* carriage), a stand of wood for a cask or barrel : a rail round a well.— **a brand from the burning,** one snatched out of

a pressing danger—from Amos, IV. 11. [O.E. *brand, brond,* O.N. *brandr,* from root of **burn.**]

brandish, *brand'ish, v.t.* to wave or flourish as a brand or weapon.—*n.* a waving or flourish. [Fr. *brandir, brandiss-* from root of **brand.**]

brandy, *brand'i, n.* an ardent spirit distilled from wine.—*adj.* **bran'died,** heartened or strengthened with brandy.—*ns.* **brand'y-ball,** a kind of sweet; **brand'y-paw'nee** (Hind. *pānī,* water), brandy and water; **brand'y-snap,** a thin gingerbread biscuit flavoured with brandy. [Formerly *brand-wine*—Du. *brandewijn*—*branden,* to burn, to distil, and *wijn,* wine; cf. Ger. *branntwein.*]

brangle, *brang'gl, v.i.* (*arch.*) to wrangle.—*n.* (*obs.*) a brawl.—*n.* **brang'ling,** disputing. [Fr. *branler.*]

brank, *brangk, n.* buckwheat. [Pliny says *brance* (doubtful reading, perh. *brace*) is the Gallic name of a kind of corn.]

brank, *brangk, v.i.* to prance, toss the head : to strut or swagger.—*adj.* **brank'y** (*Scot.*), showy. [Prob. a variant of **prank.**]

branks, *brangks, n.pl.,* rarely in *sing.* (*Scot.*) a bridle : a scold's bridle, having a hinged iron framework to enclose the head and a bit or gag. [Ety. very obscure; O.Fr. *bernac* (see **barnacle** 2); Ger. *pranger,* pillory, Du. *prang,* fetter, have been compared.]

brankursine, *brangk'ər-sin,* or *-ur', n.* acanthus, or bear's-breech. [L.L. *branca ursīna,* a bear's paw.]

bran-new. See **brand.**

bran(s)le, *brawl.* See **brawl** (2).

brant-goose. See **brent-goose.**

brantle, *bran'tl.* See **brawl** (2).

brasero, *brä-sā'rō, n.* a brazier : a place for burning criminals or heretics. [Sp.,—*brasa,* a live coal.]

brash, *brash, n.* angular fragments of rock, which occasionally form the basement bed of alluvial deposits : fragments of crushed ice : clippings of hedges or trees.—*adj.* **brash'y.** [Prob. Fr. *brèche.*]

brash, *brash, n.* an eructation or belching of acid water from the stomach—water-brash : a sudden burst of rain : (*Scot.*) a slight attack of illness : (*obs.*) an attack or bout.—*v.t.* to disturb. [Prob. onomatopoeic.]

brash, *brash, adj.* (*U.S.*) impetuous : forward.

brasier. Same as **brazier.**

brass, *brăs, n.* an alloy of copper and zinc : (*obs.*) bronze : (*fig.*) effrontery : (*slang*) money : an article or fixture of brass : a monumental plate of brass, commonly with effigy : (*collectively* and in *pl.*) the brass wind-instruments or their players in an orchestra or band.—*adj.* of brass.—*ns.* **brass'-bounder,** a midshipman : a privileged apprentice on a ship for whom a premium is paid (from his gold braid); **brass'founder,** one who casts objects in brass; **brass'founding; brass'-hat** (*mil. slang*), a staff officer (with gold braid on his hat).—*adv.* **brass'ily.**—*ns.* **brass'iness; brass'y,** a brass-soled wooden golf-club (also **brassie**); a bronze-coloured fish, the bib or pout.—*adj.* like brass in appearance, hardness, sound, or otherwise : brazen-faced.—**brass band,** a band of players of (mainly) brass wind instruments : a small military band; **brass farthing,** a whit; **brass tacks,** details of practical business. [O.E. *bræs.*]

brassard, *bras'ärd, n.* a piece of armour for the arm (also **brassart,** *bras'ərt,* **brass'et**) : an armband or armlet : a symbolic band for the arm. [Fr.—*bras,* arm.]

brasserie, *brăs'(ə-)rē, n.* a beer garden or restaurant. [Fr., brewery.]

Brassica, *bras'i-kä, n.* the turnip and cabbage genus of Cruciferae. [L., cabbage.]

brassière, *bras'-i-er, -er', n.* a woman's undergarment supporting the breasts. [Fr.]

brast, *obs.* and *Northern* for **burst** (*pr.t., pa.t.,* and *pa.p.*).

brat, *brat, n.* a contemptuous name for a child : an annoying child : any over-garment of coarse cloth : a child's pinafore : an apron.—*n.* **brat'ling,** a little brat. [O.E. *bratt,* prob. Old Ir. *brat,* plaid, Gael. *brat,* apron.]

bratchet, *brach'it, n.* See **brach.**

brattice, *brat'is*, **brattish**, *brat'ish*, **brettice**, *bret'is*, *n.* in mediaeval siege operations, a fixed tower of wood : a covered gallery on a castle wall, commanding the wall-face below (in these senses also **bretesse**, *bri-tes'*, **bretasche**, *bri-tash'*) : a wooden partition : a wooden lining : a partition to control ventilation in a mine.—*v.t.* to furnish with a brattice.—*ns.* **bratt'ice-cloth**, strong tarred cloth used for mine brattices ; **bratt'icing, bratt'ish-ing**, work in the form of brattices (*archit.*) crest-ing, or ornamental work along a ridge, cornice or coping. [O.Fr. *breteshe*—L.L. *bretachia;* cf. **bartisan**.]

brattle, *brat'l*, *n.* a clattering noise : a quarrel : tumult.—*v.i.* to make a clattering noise.—*n.* and *adj.* **bratt'ling**. [Imit.]

braunch. An old spelling of **branch**.

bravado, *brav-ä'dō*, *n.* a display of bravery : a boast-ful threat : a swaggerer :—*pl.* **brava'do(e)s**.—*v.i.* to display bravado. [Sp. *bravada;* see **brave**.]

brave, *brāv*, *adj.* daring, courageous : noble : making a fine appearance : finely dressed, showy, handsome (*Scot.* braw) : a general word for ex-cellent.—*v.t.* to meet boldly : to defy : to face (out). —*n.* (*obs.*) a bully : (*arch.*) a bravo : a hired assassin : a brave soldier, esp. among the North American Indians : (*arch.*) bravado.—*adv.* (*poet.*) bravely.—*interj.* excellent.—*adv.* **brave'ly**.—*n.* **brav'ery**, (*obs.*) bravado : courage : heroism : finery, showy dress. [Fr. *brave;* It. and Sp. *bravo;* origin un-known.]

bravo, *brä'vō*, *n.* a daring villain : a hired assassin :— *pl.* **bravo(e)s**.—*interj.* well done : excellent (also **bra'va** when addressed to a woman, **bravi**, *-vē*, to a number of persons). [Sp. and It.]

bravura, *brä-vōō'rä*, *n.* (*mus.*) spirit and dash in execution : a florid air with difficult and rapid passages.—Also *adj.* [It.]

braw, *braw*, *adj.* fine : attired in finery.—*adj.* **braw'ly**.—*n.pl.* **braws**, fine clothes. [Scots form of **brave**.]

brawl, *brawl*, *n.* a noisy quarrel.—*v.i.* to quarrel noisily : to make a disturbance : to murmur or gurgle.—*n.* **brawl'er**.—*n.* and *adj.* **brawl'ing**. [M.E. *bralle*, of doubtful origin ; perh. conn. with Du. *brallen*, Ger. *prahlen*, to boast.]

brawl, *brawl*, *n.* an old French dance or dance-tune. —Also **branle**, **bransle**, **brantle**. [Fr. *branle*.]

brawn, *brawn*, *n.* muscle, esp. of the arm or calf of the leg : thick flesh : muscular strength : a boar : a preparation of meat made from pig's head and ox-feet, cut up, boiled, and pickled.—*adj.* **brawned**. —*n.* **brawn'iness**, quality of being brawny : muscularity.—*adj.* **brawn'y**, fleshy : muscular : strong. [O.Fr. *braon*, flesh (for roasting) ; of Gmc. origin, cf. Ger. *braten*, to roast.]

braxy, *brak'si*, *n.* (*Scot.*) a bacterial disease of sheep : applied loosely to various diseases of sheep : a sheep so infected : its flesh.—Also *adj.* **braxy mutton**, the flesh of a braxy sheep or generally of a sheep that has died of disease or accident. [Prob. originally plural of *brack*, a variant of **break**.]

bray, *brā*, *v.t.* to break, pound, or grind small, as in a mortar.—*n.* **bray'er**, an instrument for grinding or spreading ink in printing. [O.Fr. *breier* (Fr. *broyer*).]

bray, *brā*, *n* the cry of the ass : any harsh grating sound.—*v.i.* to cry like an ass : to give forth harsh sounds, esp. of the trumpet.—*n.* **bray'er**. [O.Fr. *brai, brait;* *braire*—L.L. *bragīre*, perh. of Celt. origin.]

braze, *brāz*, *v.t.* to cover with, or make like, brass.— *adj.* **bra'zen**, of or belonging to brass : impudent. —*v.t.* to face (out) with impudence.—*n.* **bra'zen-face**, one remarkable for effrontery.—*adj.* **bra'zen-faced**.—*adv.* **bra'zenly**.—*ns.* **bra'zenness**, **brā'-zenry**, effrontery ; **bra'zier** (*brāz'yər, brāzh'(y)ər*), a worker in brass. [**brass**.]

braze, *brāz*, *v.t.* to join with hard solder.—*adj.* **braze'less**, without soldering.—*n.* **brazier** (*brāz'-yər, brāzh'(y)ər*), a vessel or tray for hot coals. [O.Fr. *braser*, to burn ; perh. influenced by **brass**. Cf. **braise**, **brasero**.]

brazil, *brə-zil'*, *n.* usually **brazil'-wood**, the hard reddish wood of the East Indian sappan tree or other species of *Caesalpinia*, used in dyeing : also that of *Guaiacum*.—*n.* **Brazil'ian**, a native or citizen of Brazil, in South America.—*adj.* of Brazil. —*ns.* **Brazil'ian-wax**, carnauba ; **Brazil'-nut**, the edible seed of a large lecythidaceous Brazilian tree (*Bertholletia*). [O.Fr. *bresil* (Sp. *brasil*, It. *brasile*)— L.L. *brasilium*, a red dye-wood brought from the East, itself prob. a corr. of some Oriental word. When a similar wood was discovered in South America the country became known as *terra de brasil*, land of red dye-wood.]

breach, *brēch*, *n.* a break : an act of breaking : an opening, or discontinuity : a breaking of law, contract, covenant, promise, etc. : a rupture : a broken condition or part of anything : a gap made in a fortification : surf.—*v.t.* to make a breach or opening in.—**breach of promise**, often used simply for breach of promise of marriage ; **breach of the peace**, a violation of the public peace by riot or the like. [O.E. *bryce, brice*, related to **break**.]

bread, *bred*, *n.* food made of flour or meal baked : food : livelihood.—*n.* **bread-and-butt'er**, bread sliced and buttered : livelihood.—*adj.* connected with making a living or with the consumption of bread-and-butter : materialistic : youthfully insipid. —*ns.* **bread'-basket**, a basket for holding bread : (*slang*) the stomach ; **bread'berry**, a sop of bread in hot milk ; **bread'-chipper** (*Shak.*), one who chips bread, an under-butler ; **bread'-corn**, corn of which bread is made ; **bread'-crumb**, the inner parts of a loaf : bread crumbled down as for dressing food (also in *pl.*).—*v.t.* to cover with bread-crumbs. —*ns.* **bread'fruit**, the fruit of a moraceous tree (*Artocarpus incisa*) of the South Sea Islands, which when roasted forms a good substitute for bread ; **bread'nut**, the fruit of a tropical American tree (*Brosimum alicastrum*) akin to the breadfruit tree, used as bread when boiled or roasted ; **bread'-room**, an apartment in a ship's hold where the bread is kept ; **bread'root**, the prairie-turnip, a North American papilionaceous plant (*Psoralea esculenta*) with an edible root : also the yam ; **bread'-stud'y**, any branch of study taken up as a means of gaining a living ; **bread'-stuff**, bread in any form : any material of which bread is made ; **bread'-tree**, a name for various trees whose seeds or pith yield a substitute for bread, e.g. *Kaffir-bread;* **bread'winner**, one who earns a living for a family.—**bread-and-butter letter**, a letter of thanks for hospitality ; **bread buttered on both sides**, very fortunate circumstances ; **know which side one's bread is buttered on**, to know how to act from self-interest ; **take the bread out of one's mouth**, to deprive of the means of living. [O.E. *brēad*, prob. from a Gmc. root meaning a fragment ; cf. Scots use of **piece**.]

breaded See **brede**.

breadth, *bredth*, *n.* extent from side to side : width : liberality of mind : in art, subordination of details to the harmony of the whole.—*adv.* **breadth'ways**, **-wise**, in the direction of breadth : broadside on. [O.E. *brǣdu;* Ger. *briete;* see **broad**.]

break, *brāk*, *v.t.* to divide, part, or sever, wholly or partially, by applying a strain : to rupture : to shatter : to crush : to make by breaking : to destroy the continuity or integrity of : to interrupt (a fall, journey, etc.) : to bruise or penetrate the surface of : to break a bone in, or separate the bones of : to subject, overcome, or wear out : to tame or habitu-ate to obedience (also with *in*) : to crush the spirit of : to cure (of a habit) : to violate (as a law, promise, bounds, prison) : to set aside (as a will) : to cut up (an animal's body) : to unfurl : to impart (esp. with delicacy) : to make bankrupt : to degrade or cashier : to arpeggiate : to cause to change from a simple vowel to a diphthong.—*v.i.* to separate, come apart, or go to pieces, esp. with suddenness : to give way : to start away : to burst forth : to force a passage : to pass suddenly into a condition or action (as into laughter, revolt, sweat, spots) : to become variegated or striped : to open or come into view (as day, hope, a scene) : (*coll.*) (of news) sudden-ly to become generally known : to become bankrupt :

to crack (as the voice) : to collapse : to burst into foam : to sever a connexion : to fall out (with a friend) : to change direction (as a cricket-ball on pitching) : to change from a simple vowel to a diphthong under influence of a neighbouring sound : (*pa.t.* brōke, *arch.* brāke ; *pa.p.* brŏk′en, less usu. brōke).—*n.* an act of breaking : the state of being broken : an opening : a discontinuity : a pause, interval, or interruption : (*billiards, croquet*) a consecutive series of successful strokes : the number of points so scored at billiards : a continuous run of anything : (*cricket*) the deviation of a ball on striking the pitch : the dawn (*break of day*) : onset (of the monsoon) : (*U.S.*) a social blunder : (*U.S.*) a chance (as in *an even break,* a fair or equal chance).—*adj.* break′able.—Also *n.,* in *pl.*—*ns.* break′ableness ; break′age, an act of breaking or its consequences : a broken place ; break′away, a revolt or secession : (*Austr.*) a stampede, a stampeding animal.—*adj.* break′back, crushing.—*ns.* break′down′, a stoppage by accident : collapse : disintegration : a vigorous and noisy negro dance or the like ; break′er, a person or machine that breaks : a wave broken on rocks or shore.—*n. and adj.* break′ing.—*adjs.* break′-jaw, very difficult to pronounce accurately ; break′-neck, headlong : threatening to break the neck.—*ns.* break′-prom′ise, break′-vow (both *Shak.*), one who habitually breaks promises or vows ; break′-through, a forcible passage through a barrier ; break′-up′, dissolution ; break′water, a barrier against force of waves.—break a jest, to utter a jest ; break a lance with, to enter into a contest with ; break away, to go away, escape, abruptly : (*fig.*) to sever connexion forcibly or abruptly : to be scattered, as clouds after a storm ; break-bone fever, dengue ; break bulk, to open the hold and take out a portion of the cargo : to begin to use goods supplied in bulk ; break cover, to burst forth from concealment, as a fox ; break down, to crush down or level : to collapse : to fail completely ; break′-down gang, a squad of men who clear away wreckage after an accident ; break forth, to burst out, issue ; break ground, to begin digging or ploughing untouched ground : to lead the way in new work ; break in, in upon, or into, to enter violently : to interpose abruptly ; break loose, to extricate oneself forcibly : to break through all restraint ; break no squares, to make no difference, do no harm, matter little ; break off, to detach by breaking : to put an abrupt end to : to leave off abruptly ; break one's mind, to communicate one's thoughts to somebody ; break out, to appear suddenly : to break through all restraint : to come into sudden activity : to become covered with (with *in*) ; break sheer (said of a ship riding at anchor), to be forced by wind or tide out of a position clear of the anchor ; break the balls (or simply break ; *billiards*), to open the game by striking the red ball or giving a miss, or to continue the game thus when a similar position occurs ; break the heart, to crush with grief ; break the ice (*fig.*), to get through first difficulties, esp. restraint on first meeting ; break through, to force a passage through (a barrier) ; break up, to break open : to break in pieces : to go to pieces : to put an end to : to disperse : to dig or plough up : to decay in health or faculties ; break upon the wheel, to punish by stretching on a wheel and breaking the bones ; break wind, to void wind. [O.E. *brecan* ; Ger. *brechen*.]

break, brake, brāk, *n.* a long wagonette : a carriage frame all wheels and no body, used in breaking in horses. [break, *v.t.*]

breaker, brāk′ər, *n.* a small water-cask, used on shipboard. [Prob. Sp. *bareca,* barrel.]

breakfast, brek′fəst, *n.* a break or breaking of fast : the first meal of the day.—*v.i.* to take breakfast.—*v.t.* to furnish with breakfast.—*n.* break′-fast-set, the china or other ware used at breakfast ; break fast-table.

bream, brēm, *n.* a fresh-water fish of the carp family, with high-arched back : a fish of the family Sparidae (sea-bream) : a fish (Ray's bream, *Brama raii*) akin to the mackerel : extended to other fishes. [O.Fr. *bresme* (Fr. *brême*)—O.H.G. *brahsema* (mod. Ger. *brassen*).]

bream, brēm, *v.t.* to clean, as a ship's bottom, by burning off seaweed, shells, etc. [Prob. conn. with broom, Du. brem.]

breare, brēr, *n.* (*Spens.*). Same as brier.

breast, brest, *n.* the forepart of the human body between the neck and the belly : one of the two mammary glands in women (or rudimentary in men), forming soft protuberances on the chest : the corresponding part of any animal : a swelling slope : (*fig.*) conscience, disposition, affections : (*obs.*) voice.—*v.t.* to oppose the breast to : to oppose manfully : to mount.—*n.* breast′-bone, the sternum, the bone running down the middle of the breast, to which the first seven ribs are attached.—*adv.* breast′-deep, deep, as up to the breast.—*adj.* breast′ed, having a breast.—*n.* breast′-girdle, the pectoral girdle.—*adv.* breast′-high, high as the breast : breast-deep.—*ns.* breast′-knot, a knot of ribbons worn on the breast ; breast′-pin, an ornamental pin for the breast ; breast′plate, a plate or piece of armour for the breast : (*B.*) an embroidered square of linen with precious stones worn on the breast of the Jewish high-priest ; breast′-plough, a kind of spade for cutting turf, with a cross-bar against which the breast is pressed ; breast′rail, the upper rail of a breastwork ; breast′-stroke, a stroke made in swimming on the breast ; breastsummer, bressummer (bres′ə-mər) a summer or beam supporting the whole, or a great part, of the front of a building in the manner of a lintel ; breast′-wall, a retaining wall ; breast′-wheel, a water-wheel turned by water delivered upon it at about half its height ; breast′work, a hastily constructed earthwork.—make a clean breast, to make a full confession. [O.E. *brēost* ; Ger. *brust,* Du. *borst.*]

breath, breth, *n.* the air drawn into and then expelled from the lungs : power of breathing : life : a single act of breathing : (*phon.*) breathing without vibrating the vocal cords : a sound so produced : the time occupied by one breathing : a very slight breeze.—*adj.* produced by breath without voice.—*adjs.* breathed (bretht), having a breath (esp. in compounds, as long-breathed ; see also under breathe) ; breath′ful (*Spens.*), full of breath or air, also full of scent or odour ; breath′less, out of breath : excessively eager, as if holding one's breath from excitement : dead.—*adv.* breath′lessly.—*n.* breath′lessness.—above one's breath, aloud ; below, under, one's breath, in a low voice ; catch the breath, to stop breathing for an instant ; out of breath, having difficulty in breathing ; spend one's breath, as in profitless talk ; take breath, to recover freedom of breathing : to stop for breath, rest, or refreshment ; with bated breath, with breath restrained from reverence or fear. [O.E. *brǣth* ; Ger. *brodem,* steam, breath.]

breathe, brēdh, *v.i.* to draw in or expel breath or air to or from the lungs or other respiratory organs : to respire : to take breath, to rest or pause : to live.—*v.t.* to draw into or expel from the lungs : to infuse : to give out as breath : to utter by breath : to utter softly, whisper : to express : to keep in breath, to exercise : to tire by some brisk exercise.—*adj.* breathed (brēdhd), pronounced without voice (see also under breath).—*ns.* breath′er, one who breathes or lives : a spell of exercise : a rest to recover breath ; breath′ing, the act of breathing : aspiration, secret prayer : respite : one or other of two signs used in Greek to signify presence (' rough breathing) or absence (' smooth breathing) of the aspirate.—*adj.* life-like.—*ns.* breath′ing-space, breath′ing-time, time to breathe or rest : a brief respite ; breath′ing-while, time sufficient for drawing breath : any very short period.—breathe again, to be relieved from an anxiety ; breathe freely, to be at ease ; breathe upon, to tarnish the name of. [From breath.]

breccia, brech′yä, *n.* a rock composed of angular

fragments.—*adj.* **brecciated** (brech′i-ā-tid) reduced to or composed of breccia. [It.]

brecham, brehh′əm, *n.* (Scot.) a horse-collar. [O.E. beorgan, to protect, hama, covering.]

bred, bred, *pa.t.* and *pa.p.* of **breed.**

brede, brēd, *n.* and *v.t.* an archaic form of **braid.** —*pa.t.* and *adj.* (Spens.) **bread′ed.**

bree, brē, *n.* (still in Scot.) the eyebrow. [O.E. brǽw, bréaw; cf. Ger. (augen) braue; and **brae.**]

bree, brē, *n.* the liquor in which anything has been boiled. [O.E. briw; cf. **berry** (2), Ger. brei.]

breech, brēch, *n.* (almost always in *pl.*, **breeches,** brich′iz), a garment worn by men on the lower parts of the body—strictly, as distinguished from trousers, coming just below the knee, but often used generally for trousers : (arch.) the lower part of the body behind : the hinder part of anything, esp. of a gun : *pl.* in these senses pron. brēch′iz.— *v.t.* (brich, brēch) to put into breeches : to flog.— *adj.* **breeched.**—*n.* **breeching** (brich′ing), a part of a horse's harness attached to the saddle, coming round the breech and hooked to the shafts : a strong rope attached to the breech of a gun to secure it to a ship's side.—*adj.* (Shak.) subject to whipping.— *n.* **breech′es-buoy,** a life-saving apparatus enclosing the person like a pair of breeches.—*adj.* **breech′less,** trouserless.—*n.* **breech′-loader,** a firearm loaded by introducing the charge at the breech instead of the muzzle.—*adj.* **breech′- loading.—Breeches Bible,** the Geneva Bible produced by the English Protestant exiles in 1560, so named from the rendering 'breeches' in Gen. iii. 7; **breeches part** (*theat.*), a part in which a girl wears men's clothes; **wear the breeches** (said of a wife), to be master. [O.E. bréc, plur. of bróc; cf. Ger. bruch, Du. broek.]

breed, brēd, *v.t.* to generate or bring forth : to cause or promote the generation of, or the production of breeds of : to train or bring up : to cause or occasion.—*v.i.* to be with young : to produce offspring : to be produced or brought forth : (Scot.) to be in training : (*pa.t.* and *pa.p.* **bred**).—*n.* that which is bred, progeny or offspring : a strain, variety or race : a kind.—*ns.* **breed′-bate** (Shak.), one who foments debate or strife; **breed′er;** **breed′ing,** act of producing : education or manners.—**breeding in-and-in,** in-breeding, breeding from near kin. [O.E. brédan, to cherish, keep warm; Ger. brüten, to hatch.]

breeks, brēks, *n.pl.* Scots form of **breeches,** trousers.

breer. See **braird.**

breeze, brēz, *n.* a gentle gale : a wind : a disturbance or quarrel : a whispered rumour.—*n.* to blow as a breeze : (*slang*) to go briskly.—*adjs.* **breeze′less;** **breez′y,** fanned with or subject to breezes : bright, lively, exhilarating.—**to breeze up,** to freshen into a breeze. [Old Sp. briza, north-east wind.]

breeze, breese, brize, brēz, *n.* a gadfly, botfly, or other dipterous pest of horses and cattle. [O.E. briosa.]

breeze, brēz, *n.* furnace refuse used by brickmakers. [Perh. O.Fr. brese.]

bregma, breg′mä, *n.* the part of the skull where the frontal and the two parietal bones join—sometimes divided into the right and left bregmata :—*pl.* **breg′mata.**—*adj.* **bregmat′ic.** [Gr.]

brehon, brē′hon, *n.* an ancient Irish judge.—**Brehon Law(s),** the system of jurisprudence in use among the Irish until near the middle of the 17th century. [Ir. breitheamh, pl. breitheamhuin.]

breloque, brə-lok′, *n.* an ornament attached to a watch-chain. [Fr.]

breme, breem, brēm, *adj.* (Spens.) fierce, keen. [Perh. related to O.E. bréman, to rage.]

bren, brenne, bren, *v.t.* and *v.i.* (Spens.) to burn : (*pa.t.* and *pa.p.* **brent**).—*adj.* **brent.** [See **burn** (2).]

bren-gun, bren′gun, *n.* a light machine-gun fired from the shoulder. [Brno, Brünn, in Moravia, and Enfield, in Middlesex.]

brent, brent, *adj.* (Scot.) lofty : steep : smooth, unwrinkled. [O.E. brant, steep; O.N. brattr.]

brent-goose, brent′-gōōs, *n.* a small wild goose, having the head, neck, long wing feathers, and

tail black, the belly white, the rest slaty-grey, often confounded with the barnacle goose.—Also **brant′-goose,** or **brent barnacle.** [Prob. branded, brindled.]

brer, brər, *n.* a negro pronunciation of **brother.**

brere, brēr, *n.* (Spens.) a form of **brier.**

bressummer. Same as **breastsummer.**

bretasche, bretesse. See **brattice.**

brethren, bredh′ran, *pl.* of **brother.**

Breton, bret′ən, *n.* a native of Brittany (Bretagne), France : the Celtic tongue of Brittany—i.e. Brezonek.—*adj.* of Brittany : Armoric.

brettice. See **brattice.**

Bretwalda, bret-wawl′dä, *n.* a title of certain kings of old English kingdoms, whose superiority over the others was more or less acknowledged. [Prob. Lord of the Britons, or of Britain.—O.E. walda, ruler.]

breve, brēv, *n.* a pope's letter : the mark (˘) of a short vowel, opp. to macron : (mus.) an obsolescent note, ‖ ◯ ‖, twice as long as the longest now used (the semibreve), but half (or in 'perfect' time one-third) as long as the obsolete long. [L. brevis, short.]

brevet, brev′it, *n.* a military commission entitling an officer to take rank above that for which he receives pay.—*v.t.* to confer such rank on :—*pr.p.* **brev′eting;** *pa.t.* and *pa.p.* **brev′eted** (those who pronounce bri-vet′ write **brevett′ing, brevett′ed**). [Fr.,—L. brevis, short.]

breviary, brēv′i-ər-i, *n.* a book containing the daily service of the R.C. Church. [L. brēviārium—brevis, short.]

breviate, brē′vi-āt, *n.* a short compendium : a lawyer's brief. [L. brēviātus—brēviāre, to shorten.]

brevier, brə-vēr′, *n.* a type (8-point) between bourgeois and minion, said (doubtfully) to have been used for breviaries.

brevity, brev′it-i, *n.* shortness : conciseness. [L. brevitās, -ātis—brevis, short.]

brew, brōō, *v.t.* to prepare by infusion, boiling and fermentation, as beer from malt and other materials, or by infusion, mixing, or boiling, without fermentation, as tea, punch : to contrive or plot.— *v.i.* to perform the operation of brewing ale or beer : to be gathering or forming.—*n.* a brewing : a brewage : a variety or making of a brewed beverage : a variety.—*ns.* **brew′age,** something brewed : mixed liquor; **brew′er,** one who brews; **brew′ery, brew′-house,** a place for brewing; **brew′ing,** the act of making liquor from malt : the quantity brewed at once; **brew′ster** (now mainly Scot.; orig. fem.), a brewer. [O.E. bréowan; cf. Ger. brauen.]

brewis, brōō′is, *n.* (arch. and dial.) broth, esp. beef broth : bread soaked in broth, fat, gravy, or the like. [O.Fr. broez, influenced by O.E. briw, bree.]

Brezonek, brez′ə-nek, *n.* See **Breton.**

briar. See **brier** (1 and 2).

Briarean, brī-ā′ri-ən, *adj.* relating to Briareus (Gr. Briārēōs), a hundred-handed giant : hence many-handed. [Gr. briāros—strong.]

bribe, brīb, *n.* (obs.) spoil : something offered to influence the judgment unduly or corrupt the conduct.—*v.t.* (obs.) to steal : to influence by a bribe : to gain over.—*v.i.* to practise bribery.—*ns.* **brib′er,** one who bribes; **brib′ery,** the act of giving or taking bribes : **brib′ery-oath,** an oath taken by an elector that he has not been bribed. [O.Fr. bribe, a lump of bread; origin dub.]

bric-à-brac, bricabrac, brik′ə-brak, *n.* old curiosities, knick-knacks, or other treasured odds and ends. [Fr.]

brick, brik, *n.* baked or 'burned' clay : a shaped block of burned clay, generally rectangular (the standard dimensions being 9 × 4½ × 3 inches) : a brick-shaped block of other material, often compressed : a child's building block of wood, etc. : a loaf or a bun more or less in the shape of a brick : (*slang*) a spirited good fellow.—*v.t.* to build (in, up, etc.) with brick : to cover with brick or an appearance of brick.—*ns.* **brick′bat,** a piece of brick, esp. as a missile; **brick′-clay,** a clay containing sand and a good deal of iron : any clay, loam, or earth used for brick-making; **brick'-dust**, powdered brick : the colour of powdered red brick; **brick'-earth'**, a clayey silt or loam used for brick-making.—*adj.* **brick'en**, made of brick.—*ns.* **brick'field**, a place where bricks are made; **brick'fielder** (*Austr.*) a hot dry wind (orig. one bringing dust from the brickfields of Sydney suburbs); **brick'ing**, brickwork : imitation brickwork; **brick'kiln**, a kiln in which bricks are made; **brick'layer**, one who builds with bricks; **brick'-laying**; **brick'maker**; **brick'-nog, -nogging** (see nogging).—*adjs.* **brick'-red**, of the colour of an ordinary red brick; **brick'shaped**, of the shape of a standard brick.—*ns.* **brick'-tea'**, tea pressed into cakes; **brick'work**, work constructed in brick : bricklaying : a factory for bricks.—*adj.* **brick'y**, like or of brick.—*n.* **brick'yard**, a brickfield.—**drop a brick**, to make an undisguisable and horrifying blunder; **like a ton of bricks**, heavily and promptly. [Fr. *brique*, from the root of **break**.]

brickle, *brik'l*, *adj.* (*Spens.* and *Scot.*) apt to break : weak : troublesome. [Cf. **bruckle**.]

brickwall, *brik'wawl*, a corruption of **bricole**.

bricole, *brik'əl*, or *-ōl*, or *brik-ōl'*, *n.* an ancient engine for throwing stones : the rebound of a ball from the wall of a tennis-court : an indirect stroke : a similar stroke in billiards. [Fr.,—L.L. *briccola*.]

bridal, *brīd'əl*, *n.* a marriage feast : a wedding.—*adj.* belonging to a bride or a wedding : nuptial. [O.E. *brȳdealo*, lit. bride-ale; see **bride** and **ale** (feast).]

bride, *brīd*, *n.* a woman about to be married or newly married.—*v.i.* and *v.t.* (with *it; Shak.*) to act the bride.—*ns.* **bride'-ale** (*arch.;* see **bridal**), the ale-drinking at a marriage feast; **bride'-bed**, the marriage bed; **bride'cake**, **bride's'-cake**, a cake distributed at a wedding; **bride'-chamber**, a nuptial apartment : the room in which a wedding is performed; **bride'groom**, a man about to be married or newly married; **bride'maid(en)**, **brides'-maid**, **brides'maid**, **bride'man**, **bride's'-man**, **brides'man**, young unmarried people who attend the bride and bridegroom at a wedding. [O.E. *brȳd;* O.N. *brúthr*, Ger. *braut*.]

bridewell, *brīd'wəl*, *n.* a house of correction : a gaol. [From a palace near *St. Bride's Well* in London.]

bridge, *brij*, *n.* a structure spanning a river, road, etc., giving communication across it : the narrow raised platform whence the captain of a ship gives directions : a thin upright piece of wood supporting the strings in a violin or similar instrument : the bony part of the nose : a support for a billiard cue : a bridge-like structure by which false teeth are borne by natural teeth or roots : in the theatre, a platform that rises above the stage : anything that connects across a gap.—*v.t.* to be or to build a bridge over : (*fig.*) to connect the extremities of a gap).—*ns.* **bridge'board**, a notch-board; **bridge'-head**, a fortification covering the end of a bridge nearest to the enemy's position : a place suitable for such fortification : any advanced position seized in enemy territory; **bridge'-house**, a house at the end of a bridge.—*adj.* **bridge'less**.—*n.* **bridge'-of-boats'**, a bridge resting on boats moored abreast across a piece of water.—*n.* and *adj.* **bridg'ing**. [O.E. *brycg;* Ger. *brücke*, O.N. *bryggja*.]

bridge, *brij*, *n.* a modification of whist in which the dealer or his partner chooses the trump-suit, or no-trumps, and the dealer plays his partner's hand as a dummy, with peculiarities in scoring—superseded by *auction bridge* and *contract bridge*.—*n.* **bridge'-drive** a tournament of bridge-playing. [Earlier known as *bridge whist*, *biritch;* etymology unknown.]

bridle, *brī'dl*, *n.* the apparatus on a horse's head by which it is controlled : any curb or restraint : a movement expressing resentment, scorn, or vanity—a throwing back of the head with a forward tilt, like a horse pulled up by the bridle.—*v.t.* to put a bridle on : to manage by a bridle : to check or restrain.—*v.i.* to make the movement described (often with *up; at* the thing taken amiss).—*ns.* **brī'dle-hand**, the hand that holds the bridle in riding—the left hand; **brī'dle-path, -road, a** path or way for horsemen; **brī'dler**, one who governs or restrains as by a bridle; **brī'dle-rein**, the strap of a bridle. [O.E. *bridel;* O.H.G. *brittel*.]

bridoon, *brid-ōōn'*, *n.* the light snaffle usual in a military bridle in addition to the ordinary bit, controlled by a separate rein. [Fr. *bridon—bride*, a bridle.]

brief, *brēf*, *n.* a short account of a client's case for the instruction of counsel : a writ : a short statement of any kind.—*adj.* short : concise.—*v.t.* to issue instructions to.—*n.* **brief'-bag**, a case for carrying briefs.—*adj.* **brief'less**.—*adv.* **brief'ly**.—*n.* **brief'ness**.—**hold a brief** to be retained as counsel : to assume the attitude of advocate rather than judge; **in brief**, in few words; **king's briefs**, royal mandates ordering collections to be made in chapels for building churches, etc.; **papal brief**, a papal document issued without some of the solemnities proper to bulls; **take a brief**, to undertake a case; **the brief and the long** (*Shak.*), the short and the long; **to be brief**, to speak in a few words. [Fr. *bref*—L. *brevis*, short.]

brier, briar, *brīr*, *brī'ər*, *n.* a prickly shrub : a wild rose bush.—Also (*Spens.*, etc.) **brere** (*brēr*).—*adjs.* **briered, briared**, caught in, covered with, briers; **brier'y**, thorny : abounding in, beset with, briers.—**sweet brier**, eglantine, a wild rose (*Rosa rubiginosa*) with scented leaves. [O.E. (Anglian) *brēr* (W.S. *brǣr*).]

brier, briar, *brī'ər*, *n.* the white heath, a shrub grown in Algeria : a tobacco-pipe made of its root.—*ns.* and *adjs.* **bri'er-root, -wood**. [Fr. *bruyère*, heath.]

brig, *brig*, *n.* a two-masted, square-rigged vessel. [Shortened from **brigantine**.]

brig, *brig*, *n.* Scots form of **bridge** (1).

brigade, *brig-ād'*, *n.* a body of troops consisting of a group of regiments, battalions, or batteries commanded by a general officer : a band of people more or less organised.—*v.t.* to form into brigades : to organise, esp. oppressively.—*ns.* **brigade'-ma'jor**, a staff-officer attached to a brigade; **brigadier** (*brig-ə-dēr'*), formerly **brigadier'-gen'eral**, a general officer of the lowest grade, who has command of a brigade : (*brē-gä-dyā*), in the French army, a lance-corporal. [Fr. *brigade*—It. *brigata*—L.L. *briga*, strife.]

brigand, *brig'ənd*, *n.* a bandit or freebooter.—*ns.* **brig'andage**, freebooting : plundering : **brigandine, brigantine** (*brig'ən-dēn, -tēn*), a coat-of-mail of steel rings or plates sewed upon linen or leather. [Fr.,—It. *brigante—briga*, strife.]

brigantine, *brig'ən-tēn*, *n.* a two-masted vessel, with the main mast of a schooner and the foremast of a brig. [Fr. *brigantin*—It. *brigantino*, pirate ship.]

bright, *brīt*, *adj.* shining : full of light : vivid : clear : (*arch.*) beautiful : cheerful : vivacious : clever : illustrious.—*adv.* brightly : clearly.—*v.t.* and *v.i.* **bright'en**, to make or grow bright or brighter : to clear up.—*adv.* **bright'ly**.—*n.* **bright'ness**.—*adj.* **bright'some**, bright : brilliant. [O.E. *byrht, beorht;* cog. with Goth. *bairhts*, clear, L. *flagrāre*, to flame.]

Bright's disease, *brīts'-diz-ēz'*, *n.* a generic name for diseases of the kidneys with albumen in the urine. [From Dr. Richard *Bright* (1789-1858).]

brigue, *brēg*, *v.i.* to intrigue.—*n.* strife : intrigue.—*n.* **briguing** (*brēg'ing*), canvassing. [Fr. *brigue*.]

brill, *bril*, *n.* a fish akin to the turbot, spotted with white. [Ety. unknown.]

brilliant, *bril'yənt*, *adj.* sparkling : glittering : splendid : superlatively bright, having a dazzling hard lustre : of out-standing or conspicuous ability : showily, strikingly, or superficially clever : performing or performed in a hard or showy manner or with great display of technical skill : brilliant-cut.—*n.* a diamond or other gem cut in a many-faceted form resembling two truncated cones base to base : a very small type (about 4-point).—*ns.* **brill'iance, brill'iancy; brill'iantine**, a dressing for making the hair glossy.—*adv.* **brill'iantly**.—*n.* **brill'iantness**. [Fr. *brillant*, pr.p. of *briller*, to shine, which, like Ger. *brille*, eyeglass, is from L.L. *beryllus*, a beryl.]

brim, *brim*, *n.* the margin or brink of a river or lake: the upper edge of a vessel: the rim of a hat.— *v.t.* to fill to the brim.—*v.i.* to be full to the brim: (*pr.p.* **brimm'ing**; *pa.t.* and *pa.p.* **brimmed**).— *adj.* **brim'ful, brim'-full**, full to the brim: brimming with tears. — *n.* **brim'ful(l')ness.** — *adjs.* **brim'less**, without a brim; **brimmed**, brim-full: having a brim (used also in composition).—*n.* **brimm'er**, a bowl full to the brim.—*adj.* **brimm'ing.** [M.E. *brymme*.]

brimstone, *brim'stən*, *n.* sulphur: (*fig.*) a virago: (in full, **brimstone butterfly**) a common yellow pierid butterfly (*Gonepteryx rhamni*).—*adj.* **brim'-stony.** [Lit. burning stone; from O.E. *brȳne*, a burning—*byrnan*, to burn, and **stone**; cf. Ger. *bernstein*.]

brinded, *brin'did*, **brindled**, *brin'dld*, **brindle**, *brin'dl*, *adjs.* marked with spots or streaks.—*n.* **brin'dle**, state of being brindled. [See **brand**.]

brine, *brīn*, *n.* very salt water: the sea.—*ns.* **brine'-pan, -pit**, a pan or pit in which brine is evaporated to obtain salt: a salt spring: **brine'-shrimp**, a small phyllopod crustacean of salt-lakes and brine-pools.—*adjs.* **brīn'ish**, like brine; somewhat salt; **brin'y**, pertaining to brine or to the sea: salt.— **the briny** (*vul.*), the sea. [O.E. *brȳne*, a burning.]

bring, *bring*, *v.t.* to fetch: to cause to come: to persuade: to adduce or institute (as an argument, charge, action):—*pa.t.* and *pa.p.* **brought** (*brawt*). —*ns.* **bring'er**; **bring'ing** (*Shak.* **bringings forth**, the fruits of his own actions; **bringing up**, upbringing, rearing, training).—**bring about**, to bring to pass, effect: to turn round; **bring down**, to humble: to shoot: to overthrow: to lower; **bring down the house**, to call forth a general burst of applause; **bring forth**, to give birth to, produce; **bring forward**, to advance: in book-keeping (used in *pa.p.*) to transfer (a partial sum) to the head of the next column; **bring home**, to prove: to impress; **bring in**, to introduce: to yield: to pronounce (a verdict); **bring off**, to bring away, as by a boat from a ship, to rescue: to achieve; **bring on**, to induce: to cause to advance; **bring out**, to make clear, or prominent: to put before the public, as a book, a play, a singer: to introduce (a young woman) formally into so-called society; **bring over**, to convert; **bring round**, to restore from illness or unconsciousness: to win over; **bring to**, to restore to consciousness: (*naut.*) to bring to a standstill; **bring under**, to subdue; **bring up**, to rear or educate: to introduce to notice: to make prominent: to vomit; **bring up the rear**, to come last. [O.E. *bringan*, to carry, to bring; allied perh. to **bear**.]

brinjal, *brin'jawl*, *n.* the egg-plant, or its fruit.— Corrupted **brown jolly**. [Sans. *vātingana*, through Pers., Ar. and Port.]

brinjarry, *brin-jär'i*, *n.* a travelling dealer in grain and salt, in Southern India. [Urdu *bānjāra*.]

brink, *bringk*, *n.* the edge or border of a steep place or of a river: often *fig.* [Prob. Dan. *brink*, declivity.]

brio, *brē'ō*, *n.* liveliness, vivacity, spirit. [It.]

brioche, *brē-osh'*, *n.* a sponge cake or roll. [Fr.]

briony. Same as **bryony**.

briquette, *bri-ket'*, *n.* a brick-shaped block made of coal-dust: a small brick-shaped slab. [Fr. *briquette*, dim. of *brique*, **brick**.]

brisk, *brisk*, *adj.* (*obs.*) spruce: (*obs.*) pert: full of life and spirit: lively: promptly active: sharp: effervescing.—*v.t.* and *v.i.* to make or become brisk: to move briskly.—*v.t.* and *v.i.* **brisk'en**, to make or become brisk.—*adjs.* **brisk'ish**, **brisk'y** (*Shak.*).—*adv.* **brisk'ly.**—*n.* **brisk'ness.** [First found in Shakespeare's time; poss. Welsh *brysg*, brisk of foot; perh. Fr. *brusque*.]

brisket, *bris'kit* (*Scott*), **breaskit**, *bres'kit*, *n.* the breast: the part of the breast next to the ribs [Perh. conn. with Fr. *brechet*, *brichet*.]

brisling, *bris'ling*, *n.* a Norwegian sprat. [Norw., sprat.]

brissel-cock, *bris'l-kok*, *n.* (*obs. Scot.*) a fowl conjectured to be the turkey. [Origin unknown.]

bristle, *bris'l*, *n.* a short stiff hair.—*v.i.* to stand erect, as bristles: to be set as with bristles: to have or set bristles erect: (*fig.*) to show rage or resistance.—*v.t.* to cover, as with bristles: to make bristly: to erect (as bristles):—*pr.p.* **brist'ling**; *pa.t.* and *pa.p.* **brist'led.**—*adj.* **brist'led**, furnished with bristles.—*ns.* **brist'le-fern'**, a filmy fern (*Trichomanes radicans*) with a bristle on the receptacle; **brist'le-tail**, any insect of the Thysanura, **brist'le-worm**, a chaetopod; **brist'li-ness.**—*adj.* **brist'ly**, set with bristles: rough.—**to set up one's bristles**, to show resistance. [Conn. with O.E. *byrst;* Scot. *birse;* cog. with Ger. *borste,* O.N. *burst.*]

Bristol, *bris'tl*, *n.* a city of Gloucestershire.—*ns.* **Bris'tol-board'**, a smooth pasteboard; **Bris'tol-brick'**, an earthy material for scouring cutlery, like bath-brick; **Bris'tol-di'amond**, a kind of quartz crystal found near Bristol; **Bris'tol-milk'**, sherry.—**Bristol fashion**, in good order.

brisure, *brizh'yər*, *brē-zür'*, *n.* (*fort.*) any part of a rampart or parapet which breaks off at an angle from the general direction; (*her.*) a variation of a coat-of-arms showing the relation of a younger to the main line. [Fr.—*briser*, to break.]

brit, *brit*, *n.* a young herring, sprat, or other fish.

Britannic, *brit-an'ik*, *adj.* pertaining to Britannia or Britain (*arch.*, surviving officially in *Britannic majesty*).—**Britannia metal**, an alloy of tin with antimony and a little copper, sometimes zinc. [L. *Britannia, Brittan(n)ia*, Great Britain or the British Islands.]

British, *brit'ish*, *adj.* pertaining to Britain, to its former or present inhabitants or citizens, or to the empire or commonwealth of nations of which it is the nucleus.—*n.* the language of the ancient Britons: Welsh.—*v.t.* and *v.i.* **Brit'icise**, to make or become British or like the British: to assimilate to the British.—*ns.* **Brit'ishism, Brit'icism** (-*sizm*), an expression characteristic of the English spoken in Britain; **Brit'isher** (orig. *U.S.*) a native or citizen of Britain.—**British gum**, dextrin; **British plate**, a kind of German silver; **British thermal unit**, the heat required to raise 1 pound of water from 60° to 61° F. [O.E. *Brettisc*—*Bret*, a Briton, Welshman.]

Briton, *brit'ən*, *n.* one of the Brythonic inhabitants of Britain before the coming of the English, or of their present representatives: the Welsh: a native or citizen of Great Britain or of any of the associated states: (*rare*) a Breton:—*fem.* (*Spens.*) **Brit'oness.** [L. *Brittō, -ōnis,* or *-ōnis;* see **Brythonic**.]

brittle, *brit'l*, *adj.* apt to break: easily broken: frail.—*ns.* **britt'leness**; **britt'le-star**, an ophiuroid or sand-star. [O.E. *bréotan*, to break.]

britzka, **britzska**, **britska**, *brits'kä*, **britschka**, *brich'kä*, *n.* an open four-wheeled carriage with one seat. [Polish *bryczka*.]

brize. See **breeze** (2).

broach, *brōch*, *n.* a tapering, pointed instrument, used chiefly for boring or rounding holes: a spit: a church spire, now restricted to one without parapets, consisting of a tall octagonal and a low square pyramid interpenetrating each other: a visible corner of the square pyramid in such a spire.—*v.t.* to pierce as a cask, to tap; to open up or begin: to utter.—*n.* **broach'er**, a broach or spit: one who broaches or utters.—**broach the admiral**, to steal some liquor from a cask in transit or in store; **broach to** (*naut.*), to turn to windward. [Fr. *broche;* cf. **brooch**.]

broad, *bravd*, *adj.* wide: large, free or open: outspoken: coarse, indelicate: liberal minded: widely diffused: giving prominence to main elements, or harmony of the whole, without insisting on detail: slow and full-toned: strongly marked in pronunciation or dialect.—*n.* the broad part: (in East Anglia) a lake-like expansion of a river.—*advs.* **broad'ly.**—*ns.* **broad'-arr'ow**, a mark (↑) en government property; **broad'-bean'**, the common bean (*Vicia Faba*); **broad'-brim**, a hat with a broad brim, such as those once worn by Quakers: (*coll.*) a Quaker.—*adj.* **broad'cast**, scattered or sown over the general surface: dispersed widely:

communicated generally, by word of mouth, pamphlets, wireless, or any other means: by means of broadcast.—*adv.* in all directions.—*n.* sowing by broadcasting: general dissemination: the sending forth by wireless apparatus of messages, news, discourses, music, etc., for reception by the public.—*v.t.* and *v.i.* to scatter broadcast or freely: to disseminate by any means, esp. wireless telephony: (*pa.t.* and *pa.p.* **broad'cast**, by some **broad'casted**).—*ns.* **broad'caster**; **broad'casting**; **broad'cloth**, a fine woollen fulled cloth, used for men's garments.—*v.t.* and *v.i.* **broad'en**, to make or grow broad or broader.—*adjs.* **broad'-gauge** (see **gauge**); **broad'ish**; **broad'-leaf**, having broad leaves, not needles.—*ns.* **broad'ness**; **broad'piece** (or **broad**), a 17th century 20-shilling coin; **broad'side**, the side of a ship: all the guns on one side of a ship of war: their simultaneous discharge: (also **broad'sheet**) a sheet of paper printed on one side, containing a proclamation, a ballad, or other popular matter; **broad'sword**, a cutting sword with a broad blade: a man armed with such a sword; **broad'way**, a broad road, often the name of the chief thoroughfare of a town or district.—*adv.* **broad'ways, -wise**, breadthwise.— **as broad as it is long**, six of one and half-a-dozen of the other; **Broad Church**, a party within the Church of England favouring a broad and liberal interpretation of dogmatic definitions and creed subscription—the name was used in 1853 by W. J. Conybeare; **broad day(light)**, fully diffused daylight; **broad Scots** or **Scotch**, Scottish dialect. [O.E. *brád*, Goth. *braiths.*]

Brobdingnagian, *brob-ding-nag'i-ən, n.* an inhabitant of the fabulous region of *Brobdingnag* in *Gulliver's Travels*, where everything was gigantic.— *adj.* gigantic.—*adj.* **Brob'dingnag**, immense (often erroneously *Brobdignag*).

brocade, *brōk-ād', n.* a silk stuff on which figures are wrought.—*adj.* **brocād'ed**, woven or worked in the manner of brocade: dressed in brocade. [It. *broccato*, Fr. *brocart*, from It. *broccare*, Fr. *brocher*, to prick, stitch; from root of **broach**.]

brocage. See **brokage** (under **broker**).

brocard, *brŏk'ärd, n.* an elementary law or principle: a canon: (Fr.) a gibe. [Fr. *brocard*, L.L. *brocarda*, from *Brocard* or Burchard, Bishop of Worms, who published a book of ecclesiastical rules.]

broccoli, *brŏk'ə-li, n.* a hardy variety of cauliflower. [It.; pl. of *broccolo*, a sprout, dim. of *brocco*, a skewer, a shoot.]

broch, *brohh, n.* an ancient dry-built circular castle with galleries in the thickness of the wall, common in the north of Scotland, very rare in the south.—Also **brogh** and **brough**. [Scots,—O.N. *borg*; O.E. *burh*.]

broch, *brŏch*, obsolete spelling of **broach**, **brooch**.

brochure, *bro-shōōr', n.* a pamphlet. [Fr.,— *brocher*, to stitch—*broche*, a needle. See **broach**.]

brock, *brok, n.* a badger—hence, from the smell, a dirty, stinking fellow.—*adj.* **brocked**, **brock'it**, (*Scot.*), variegated, esp. in black and white. [O.E. *brocc* from Celtic (as Gael. *broc*, badger; *breac*, speckled).]

brocket, *brok'it, n.* a stag in its second year, with its first horns, dagger-shaped. [Fr. *brocard—broque*, a spike.]

brockram, *hrok'rəm, n.* (*N. England*) breccia.

brod, *brod*, a Scots form of **board**: esp. a church collection plate or box.

brod, *brod, n.* (*Scot.*) a goad: a spike: a kind of nail: a prick.—*v.t.* to prick: to prod. [O.E. *brord;* O.N. *broddr.*]

brodekin, **brodkin**, *brŏd'kin, n.* a buskin. [Fr. *brodequin.*]

brog, *brog, n.* (*Scot.*) an awl.—*v.t.* to prick. [Origin obscure.]

brogue, *brōg, n.* a stout shoe (also **brō'gan**): an accent, esp. Irish (perh. a different word). [Ir. *bróg*, dim. *brógan* and Gael. *bròg*, a shoe.]

broider, *broid'ər, v.t.* and *v.i.* to embroider.—*ns.* **broid'erer**; **broid'ering**; **broid'ery**. [O.Fr. *brouder*, *broder*; see **embroider**.]

broil, *broil, n.* a noisy quarrel: a confused disturbance—(*Scot.*) **brulyie, brulzie** (*brool'i*).—*n.* **broil'er**, one who stirs up broils. [Fr. *brouiller*, to trouble.]

broil, *broil, v.t.* to cook over hot coals: to grill.— *v.i.* to be greatly heated. [Ety. dub.]

broke, *brōk, pa.t.* and old *pa.p.* of **break**, surviving as *pa.p.* chiefly in the sense of hard up.—*pa.p.* **brōk'en**.—*adj.* **brok'en**, rent: infirm: humbled or crushed: thrown into disorder: dispersed, routed: altered in direction: shattered in health, spirit, estate or position: bankrupt: (*obs.*) outlawed: trained to the saddle or bridle: infringed: variegated: with surface interrupted: incomplete, fragmentary: interrupted: uncertain: of a language, ill spoken, as by a foreigner.—*adjs.* **brok'en-backed**, having the back dislocated: of a ship, so loosened in her frame as to droop at both ends; **brok'en-down**, disintegrated: decayed: ruined in character or strength; **brok'en-heart'ed**, crushed with grief: greatly depressed in spirit.—*adv.* **brok'enly**.—*n.* **brok'enness**.—*adj.* **brok'en-wind'ed**, having short breath or disordered respiration, as a horse.—**broken man** (*hist.*), one under outlawry, esp. in the Highlands and Border country; **broken meats**, the leavings of a banquet; **broken music** (*Shak.*), concerted music.

broker, *brōk'ər, n.* one employed to buy and sell for others: a second-hand dealer: a go-between, pander, or intermediary: (*obs.*) a petty or disreputable trafficker.—*v.i.* **broke**, to bargain, negotiate: (*Shak.*) to act as broker.—*ns.* **brok'erage**, **brok'age**, the business of a broker: commission for transacting business for others: procuring; **brok'ery**, the business of a broker: broker's wares. [M.E. *brocour*—A.Fr. *brocour*. The original meaning seems to be tapster; cf. **broach**.]

brolly, *brol'i, n.* (*slang*; a clipped form), **umbrella**.

brome-grass, *brōm'-gräs, n.* a grass (Bromus) strongly resembling oats. [Gr. *bromos*, a kind of oats.]

Bromelia, *brə-mēl'yä, n.* a genus of plants giving name to the pineapple family, **Bromelia'ceae**, a tropical American family of monocotyledons, mainly epiphytic and xerophytic, with stiff leaves in rosettes.—*adj.* **bromēliā'ceous**.—*n.* **bromēl'iad**, any plant of the family. [Named in honour of the Swedish botanist Olaus *Bromel* (1639-1705).]

bromine, *brō'mēn, -min, -min, n.* a non-metallic chemical element (at. numb. 35), a red liquid giving off an irritating, poisonous brown vapour.— *n.* **brō'mate**, a salt of bromic acid.—*adj.* **brō'mic**.— *n.* **brō'mide**, a salt of hydrobromic acid: a person who does not fail to make the expected conventional remark (from the use of bromides as sedatives): an utterance worthy of such a person, as 'How small the world is after all'.—*adj.* **brō'mid'ic**, conventionally commonplace.—*n.* **brō'moform**, a bromine compound analogous to chloroform.—**bromic acid**, a compound of hydrogen, bromine and oxygen, HBrO₃; **bromide paper**, in photography, a paper with a sensitive surface containing bromide of silver, used in printing from a negative. [Gr. *brōmos*, stink.]

bronco, broncho, *brong'kō, n.* (*U.S.*) a half-tamed horse.—*n.* **bronc'o-bust'er**, one who breaks in broncos: a cowboy. [Sp. *bronco*, rough, sturdy.]

bronchus, *brongk'əs, n.* either of the main forks of the windpipe:—*pl.* **bronch'i** (*-ī*).—*n.pl.* **bronch'ia** (erroneously *bronchiae*), the ramifications of the bronchi.—*adjs.* **bronch'ial**, pertaining to the bronchi, or the bronchia; **bronchitic** (*-it'ik*), pertaining to bronchitis.—*n.* **bronchitis** (*-ī'tis*), inflammation of the lining of the bronchial tubes. [Gr. *bronchos*, windpipe; *bronchia*, bronchia.]

brond. See **brand**.

Brontosaurus, *bron-tō-sawr'əs, n.* a genus of dinosaurs found fossil in Wyoming and Colorado. [Gr. *brontē*, thunder, *sauros*, lizard.]

bronze, *bronz, n.* an alloy of copper and tin used in various ways since prehistoric times: anything cast in bronze: the colour of bronze: (*fig.*) impudence.—*adj.* made of bronze: coloured like bronze.—*v.t.* and *v.i.* to make or become bronze-like : (*fig.*) to harden.—*adjs.* **bronzed**, coated with bronze : bronze-coloured, sunburned : hardened ; **bronz'en**.—*ns.* **bronze'-wing, bronze'-pi'geon,** an Australian pigeon of various species with lustrous bronze markings on the wings.—*v.t.* **bronz'ify,** to make into bronze.—*ns.* **bronz'ing,** the process of giving or assuming the appearance of bronze ; **bronz'ite,** an enstatite with bronzy lustre.—*adj.* **bronz'y,** having the appearance of bronze.— **Bronze Age,** a prehistoric condition or stage of culture marked by the use of bronze as the material for tools and weapons—coming between the Stone Age and the Iron Age ; **bronzed skin,** Addison's disease. [Fr.,—It. *bronzo, bronzino*—L. (*aes*) *Brundusīnum,* (brass) from Brindisi.]

broo, *broō, brɔ, brā, n.* (*Scot.*) liquor that comes off from anything or in which anything has been boiled. [Prob. O.Fr. *bro, breu,* broth.]

broo, brow, *broō, n.* (*Scot.*) brow in any sense : (perh. a different word) liking (with *of*). [**brow.**]

brooch, *brōch, n.* an ornamental clasp with a jointed pin fitting into a hook.—*v.t.* (*Shak.*) to adorn as with a brooch. [Fr. *broche,* a spit. See **broach.**]

brood, *broōd, n.* something bred : offspring, children, or family : a race, kind : parentage, extraction : the number hatched, produced, or cherished at once : condition of breeding or brooding.—*adj.* for breeding (as in **brood-**mare, etc.).—*v.t.* to sit upon or cover in order to breed or hatch : to hatch : to cover, as with wings : to mature or foster with care : to meditate moodily upon.—*v.i.* to sit as a hen on eggs : to hang envelopingly : to think anxiously for some time : to meditate silently (with *on, over*).—*adv.* **brood'ingly.**—*n.* **brood'-pouch,** a body-cavity in which eggs or embryos are put to develop.—*adj.* **brood'y,** inclined to sit or incubate : apt to brood or to breed. [O.E. *brōd ;* Du. *broed ;* cf. **breed.**]

brook, *brook, n.* a small stream.—*ns.* **brook'let,** a little brook ; **brook'weed,** water pimpernel (Samolus), a water-plant of the primrose family superficially like a crucifer. [O.E. *brōc,* water breaking forth : Du. *broek.* Ger. *bruch.*]

brook, *brook, v.t.* to enjoy : to bear or endure. [O.E. *brúcan,* to use, enjoy ; Ger. *brauchen,* L. *fruī, fructus.*]

brookite, *brook'īt, n.* a mineral, titanium oxide. [After Henry James *Brooke* (1771-1857), English mineralogist.]

brooklime, *brook'līm, n.* a speedwell that grows in brooks and ditches. [**brook,** and O.E. *hleomoc,* brooklime.]

brool, *broōl, n.* a deep murmur. [Ger. *brüll,* a roar.]

broom, *broōm, n.* a papilionaceous shrub, *Cytisus scoparius,* or kindred kind : a besom made of its twigs or of anything else : a long-handled domestic sweeping brush.—*v.t.* to sweep with a broom.— *ns.* **broom'-corn,** a kind of millet of which brooms are made ; **broom'rape** (L. *rapum,* a knob), a genus (*Orobanche*) of plants parasitic on broom and other roots ; **broom'staff, broom'stick,** the handle of a broom.—*adj.* **broom'y,** abounding in or consisting of broom.—**marry over the broomstick or jump the besom,** to go through an irregular form of marriage in which both jump over a broomstick ; **new brooms sweep clean,** people newly appointed to a position work very conscientiously, or try to sweep away abuses. [O.E. *brōm.*]

broose (*Scott,* **brouze**), *broōz, brɔz, brāz, n.* (*Scot.*) a race at a wedding. [Derivation unknown.]

brose, *brōz, n.* a food made by pouring boiling water or milk on oatmeal or peasemeal, seasoned with salt and butter.—**Athole brose,** a mixture of whisky and honey. [Scot. ; perh. conn. with **brewis, broo.**]

broth, *broth, n.* an infusion or decoction of vegetable and animal substances in water, used as soup or as a medium for culture of bacteria.—**a broth of a boy** (*Irish*), the quintessence of a good fellow. [O.E. *broth—bréowan,* to brew. See **brew.**]

brothel, *broth'l, brodh'l, n.* a house of prostitution. [M.E. *brothel,* worthless person—O.E. *brothen,*

ruined, *bréothan,* to go to ruin ; influenced in meaning by **bordel.**]

brother, *brudh'ər, n.* a male born of the same parents : any one closely united with or resembling another, associated in common interests, occupation, etc. : a fellow-member of a religious order, a guild, etc. : a fellow-creature : a fellow-citizen : a co-religionist : (*B.*) a kinsman : *pl.* **broth'ers** and **breth'ren,** the latter esp. used in the sense of fellow-members and in the names of certain bodies, as Christian Brethren, Moravian Brethren, Plymouth Brethren, etc.—*adj.* associated in any relation (also in composition as **brother-man**).— *ns.* **broth'er-ger'man,** a full-brother, one having both parents in common, in contradistinction to a *half-brother :* **broth'erhood,** the state of being a brother : an association of men for any purpose ; **broth'er-in-law,** the brother of a husband or wife : a sister's husband.—*adj.* **broth'er-like.**—*n.* **broth'erliness.**—*adj.* **broth'erly,** like a brother : kind : affectionate. [O.E. *bróthor,* pl. *bréther ;* cog. with Ger. *bruder,* Gael. *brathair,* L. *frāter,* Sans. *bhrátar ;* Gr. *phrátēr,* fellow-clansman.]

brougham, *broō'əm, brō'əm,* or *broōm, n.* a one-horse close carriage, named after Lord *Brougham* (1778-1868) : a motor-car with uncovered driver's seat.

brought, *brawt, pa.t.* and *pa.p.* of **bring.**

brouze. See **broose.**

brow, *brow, n.* the eyebrow : the ridge over the eyes : the forehead : the edge of a hill : a gallery in a coal-mine running across the face of the coal : a pit-head ; (*fig.*) aspect, appearance.—*n.* **brow'-antler, -tine,** the first tine of a deer's horn.— *v.t.* **brow'beat,** to bear down with stern looks or speech : to bully.—*adjs.* **brow'-bound,** crowned : **brow'less,** without eyebrows : without shame. [O.E. *brú.*]

brown, *brown, adj.* of a dark or dusky colour, inclining to red or yellow : dark-complexioned : sunburnt : formerly conventionally applied to a sword, perh. burnished, perh. rusty, perh. blood-stained. —*n.* a dark-reddish colour : (*slang*) a copper.—*v.t.* to give a brown colour to : to roast brown.—*v.i.* to become brown.—*n.* **brown'ing,** the process of making or becoming brown : a preparation for the purpose.—*adj.* **brown'ish.**—*ns.* **brown'ness ;** **brown'spar,** a brownish variety of dolomite.— *adj.* **brown'y** (*Shak.*), of a brownish colour.— **brown algae, brown seaweeds,** the Phaeophyceae, one of the main divisions of the algae ; **brown bear,** the common bear of Europe and Asia ; **brown Bess,** the old British flint-lock musket—from the brown walnut stock ; **brown bill,** a foot-soldier's or watchman's halberd, painted brown ; **brown bread,** any dark coloured bread, esp. that made of unbolted flour ; **brown coal,** lignite ; **browned off** (*slang*), fed up : bored : dejected ; **brown George,** a hard biscuit : a brown earthen vessel ; **brown owl,** the tawny owl : a woman who has charge of a group of Brownies ; **brown paper,** coarse and strong paper used chiefly for wrapping ; **brown rat,** the larger and commoner of the two British rats (often black) ; **brown stone** (*U.S.*), a dark brown sandstone, regarded as the favourite building material of the prosperous classes ; **brown stout,** a kind of porter ; **brown study,** reverie : absent-mindedness ; **brown sugar,** unrefined or partially refined sugar ; **do brown** (*slang*), to do thoroughly, to deceive or take in completely. [O.E. *brún ;* Du. *bruin,* Ger. *braun.*]

Brownian, *brown'i-ən, adj.* pertaining to Robert *Brown* (1773-1858), who drew attention to **Brownian movement,** an agitation of particles in a colloid solution caused by impact of molecules in the surrounding medium.

brownie, *brown'i, n.* (*Scottish folklore*) a drudging domestic goblin : a member of the junior section of the Girl Guides, in brown garb. [**brown.**]

Brownist, *brown'ist, n.* one holding the church principles of Robert *Browne* (c. 1550-c. 1633), which may be said to have given birth to the Independents or Congregationalists of England.

brown jolly, *brown jol'i,* a corruption of **brinjal.**

browse, *browz*, *v.i.* to feed on rough shoots of plants : to read desultorily.—*v.t.* to browse on.— *ns.* **browse**, a twig : a browsing ; **brows'ing**, the shoots and leaves of plants : fodder : the action of the verb browse. [O.Fr. *brouster* (Fr. *brouter*)— *broust*, a sprout.]

browst, *browst*, *n.* (*Scot.*) a brewing. [brew.]

brucine, *brōōs'ēn*, *n.* an alkaloid got from nux vomica, wrongly thought to come from the simaru-baceous genus *Brucea*, named after James *Bruce* (1730–94), Scottish African traveller.

brucite, *brōōs'īt*, *n.* a mineral, magnesium hydroxide. [Named after A. *Bruce*, American mineralogist.]

bruckle, *bruk'l*, *adj.* (*Scot.*) liable to break, brittle and unstable. [O.E. *brucol—brecan*, to **break**.]

Bruin, *brōō'in*, *n.* the name of the bear in the beast-epic *Reynard the Fox;* hence in general use. [Du., brown.]

bruise, *brōōz*, *v.t.* to crush by beating or pounding without breaking the surface : to pound : to pulverise by pounding : to mark and discolour part of the surface of.—*v.i.* to box : to ride recklessly.—*n.* an injury with discoloration of the skin made by anything blunt and heavy : a spot slightly injured in this manner.—*n.* **bruis'er**, one who bruises : a prize-fighter.—*n.* and *adj.* **bruis'ing**. [O.E. *brȳsan*, to crush, combined with O.Fr. *brisier, bruiser, bruser*, to break.]

bruit, *brōōt*, *n.* noise : something noised abroad : a rumour or report : a murmur heard in ausculta-tion.—*v.t.* to noise abroad : to report : to make famous. [Fr. *bruit*—Fr. *bruire;* cf. L.L. *brugītus;* prob. imit.]

brulzie, bruilzie, *brool'(y)i, brŭl'yi*, *n.* Scottish and northern form of **broil**.

Brumaire, *brü-mer'*, *n.* the second month in the French revolutionary calendar, about Oct. 22 to Nov. 20. [Fr. *brume*, fog—L. *brūma*, winter.]

brumby, *brum'bi*, *n.* (*Austr.*) a wild horse. [Origin unknown.]

brume, *brōōm*, *n.* fog.—*adjs.* **brum'al**, relating to winter ; **brum'ous**, foggy, wintry. [L. *brūma*, winter, contr. from *brevima*, the shortest day.]

Brummagem, *brum'a-jǝm*, *n.* a local form of *Birmingham* (the town) : a thing made in Birming-ham.—*adj.* showy and worthless, sham, counter-feit. [*Brūnō*, -*ōnis*, Latinisation of Brown.]

brummer, *brōōm'ǝr*, *n.* (*S. Africa*) a large fly, resembling the common house-fly, its larva des-tructive of locusts. [Onomatopoeic.]

brunch, *brunsh*, *n.* a compromise between *br*eakfast and *lunch* [Portmanteau word.]

brunette, *broon-et'*, *n.* a woman with brown or dark hair and complexion.—Also (esp. *anthrop.*) in *masc.* **brunet'**. [Fr. dim. of *brun*, brown.]

Brunonian, *brōō-nō'ni-ǝn*, *adj.* relating to the system of medicine founded by Dr. John *Brown* of Edin-burgh (c. 1736–88)—all diseases *sthenic* or *asthenic*, depending on excess or deficiency of excitement.

brunt, *brunt*, *n.* the shock of an onset or contest : the force of a blow : the chief stress or crisis of anything.—*v.t.* to bear the brunt of.—**at the in-stant brunt**, at the outset, at once. [Origin obscure.]

brush, *brush*, *n.* an instrument set with bristles or the like for cleansing or for applying friction or a coating of some material : a painter's hair pencil : a manner of painting : a painter : a tuft : a bushy tail : a bundle of wires, strips, or the like, making electrical contact between surfaces in relative motion : a brushlike discharge of electricity or any brushlike appearance : an application of a brush : a grazing contact : a skirmish : lopped or broken twigs : an assemblage of shrubs and small trees : an area covered with thickets : (*Australia*) a forest : the backwoods : (*U.S.*) a brisk run or race. —*v.t.* to pass a brush over : to touch or rub as if with a brush : to remove by a sweeping motion (with *off*, or *away*).—*v.i.* to use a brush : to pass with light contact : to make off.—*ns.* **brush'er**, one who brushes : a small wallaby ; **brush'ing**, the act or process of brushing.—*adj.* in a lively manner : brisk.—*ns.* **brush'wheel**, a revolving brush : a friction wheel with bristles on the rubbing sur-face ; **brush'wood**, loppings and broken branches : underwood or stunted wood ; **brush'work**, work done with a brush : a painter's manner of using the brush.—*adj.* **brush'y**, like a brush : covered with brush.—**brush kangaroo**, a wallaby ; **brush turkey**, an eastern Australian mound-bird ; **brush up**, to brighten : to revive. [O.Fr. *brosse*, brush-wood ; prob. connected with **bristle**.]

brusque, *broŏsk, brusk, adj.* blunt and abrupt in manner.—*adv.* **brusque'ly**.—*ns.* **brusque'ness, brusquerie** (*broos'kǝ-rē*). [Fr.]

Brussels, *brus'ǝlz*, *n.* the capital of Belgium : (in full **Brussels carpet**), a kind of carpet in which the worsted threads are arranged in the warp, and are interwoven into a network of linen, the bulk of the carpet consisting of wool.—**Brussels lace**, a fine lace with sprigs applied on a net ground ; **Brussels sprouts**, a variety of the common cabbage with sprouts like miniature cabbages.

brust, *brust* (*Spens.*). Same as **burst**.

brute, *brōōt*, *adj.* belonging to the lower animals : irrational : stupid : rude : crude.—*n.* one of the lower animals, esp. the larger mammals : a brutal man.—*adj.* **brut'al** like a brute : unfeeling : in-human : stupidly cruel or sensual.—*v.t.* **brut'al-ise**, to make like a brute, to degrade.—*v.i.* to live like a brute.—*n.* **brutal'ity**.—*adv.* **brut'ally**.—*n.* **brute'ness**, brutelike state : brutality : (*Spens.*) stupidity.—*v.t.* **brut'ify**, to make brutal, stupid or uncivilised :—*pr.p.* **brut'ifying** ; *pa.p.* **brut'ified**. —*adj.* **brut'ish**, brutal : (*B.*) unwise.—*adv.* **brut'-ishly**.—*n.* **brut'ishness**. [Fr. *brut*—L. *brūtus*, dull, irrational.]

Brutus, *brōō'tas*, *n.* a kind of wig : a way of wearing the hair brushed back from the forehead, popular at the time of the French Revolution, when it was an affectation to admire the old Romans, as *Brutus*.

bryology, *brī-ol'a-ji*, *n.* the study of mosses.—*adj.* **bryological** (-*a-loj'i-kl*).—*ns.* **bryol'ogist**. [Gr. *bryon*, moss, liverwort, and *logos*, discourse.]

bryony, *brī'a-ni*, *n.* a wild climbing plant (*Bryonia dioica*, **white bryony**) of the gourd family, com-mon in English hedgerows : **black bryony**, a climbing plant (*Tamus communis*) of the yam family, similar to bryony in habit and disposition. [L. *bryōnia*—Late Gr. *bryōniā*.]

bryophyte, *brī'ō-fīt*, *n.* a member of the **Bryoph'yta** (-*of'i-tä*), one of the main groups of the vegetable kingdom, mosses and liverworts. [Gr. *bryon*, a moss, a liverwort, *phyton*, plant.]

Bryozoa, *brī-ō-zō'ä*, *n.pl.* an old name for the Polyzoa, from their resemblance to mosses. [Gr. *bryon*, moss, *zōia*, living things.]

Brython, *brith'on*, *n.* a Celt of the group to which Welsh, Cornish, and Bretons belong—distinguished from Goidel.—*adj.* **Brython'ic**. [Welsh *Brython*, Briton—introduced in philological use by Sir John Rhŷs.]

buat. Same as **bowat**.

buaze, bwazi, *bwä'zi, bū'āz*, *n.* an African fibre-yielding polygalaceous shrub (*Securidaca*). [Native name.]

bub, *bub*, **bubby**, *bub'i*, *n.* (*U.S.*) boy (in addressing). [Cf. Ger. *bube*, boy.]

bub, *bub*, *n.* (*slang*) strong drink. [Origin unknown.]

Bubalis, *bū'bal-is*, *n.* the hartebeest genus of an-telopes, not to be confused with Bubalus, the buffalo.—*adj.* **bub'aline**. [Gr. *boubalis.*]

bubble, *bub'l*, *n.* a bladder of liquid or solidified liquid blown out with gas : anything empty : an unsound or fraudulent scheme.—*adj.* unsub-stantial : deceptive : fleeting, transient.—*v.i.* to rise in bubbles : to give off bubbles : to make sounds as of rising and bursting bubbles : (*Scot.*) to blubber.—*v.t.* to cheat with bubble schemes.—*n.* **bubb'le-shell**, a gasteropod (*Bulla*) with thin globose shell.—*adj.* **bubb'ly**.—*n.* **bubb'ly-jock** (*Scot.*), a turkey-cock.—**bubble and squeak**, meat and cabbage fried together ; **bubble over**, as of a pot boiling, with anger, mirth, etc. ; **bubbly** (**water**), (*slang*) champagne. [Cf. Sw. *bubbla*, Du. *bobbel.*]

bubo, *bū'bō*, *n.* an inflammatory swelling of the glands, esp. in the groin or armpit.—*adj.* **bubonic**

(-*bon'*). accompanied by buboes.—*n.* **būb'ukle**, a ridiculous word of Fluellen's for a red pimple, compounded of *bubo* and *carbuncle*. [L. *būbō*—Gr. *boubōn*, the groin, a bubo.]

buccal, *buk'əl, adj.* pertaining to the cheek. [L. *bucca*, cheek.]

buccaneer, buccanier, *buk-ən-ēr', n.* one of the piratical adventurers in the West Indies during the 17th century, who plundered the Spaniards chiefly.—*v.i.* to act as a buccaneer.—*n.* **buccaneer'ing.**—*adj.* **buccaneer'ish.** [Fr. *boucanier*—*boucan*, a Carib wooden gridiron (used by French settlers in the West Indies).]

buccina, *buk'sin-ā*, a Roman curved trumpet.—*n.* **buc'cinātor**, a flat cheek muscle used in chewing and blowing.—*adj.* **buc'cinatory.**—*n.* **buc'cinum**, the whelk genus of molluscs, with trumpet-like shell. [L. *būcīna*, trumpet, *būcīnātor*, trumpeter.]

Bucentaur, *bū-sen'tawr, n.* the state barge used formerly on Ascension Day in the ceremony of the marriage of Venice with the Adriatic. [It. *bucentoro, bucintoro;* ety. uncertain; usually explained as from Gr. *bous*, an ox, *kentauros*, a centaur—perhaps from the figurehead.]

bucellas, *b(y)ōō-sel'əs, n.* a white wine from *Bucellas* near Lisbon.

Bucephalus, *bū-sef'ə-ləs, n.* the famous war-horse of Alexander the Great : a familiar name for a riding-horse. [Gr. *Boukephalos*—*bous*, ox, *kephalē*, head.]

buchu, bucku, *bōō'hhōō, -chōo, -kōo, n.* (*S. Africa*) a rutaceous genus (*Barosma*) with leaves of medicinal value for wounds, etc. [Zulu.]

buck, *buk, n.* the body of a cart.—*ns.* **buck'board**, a board or rail projecting over cart-wheels : (*Amer.*) a plank on four wheels, with a light seat to hold two persons : **buck'-cart**, a buck-board : a cart with boards projecting over the wheels; **buck'-wag'on** (*S. Africa*), a large canvas-covered trek wagon. [O.E. *būc*, body.]

buck, *buk, n.* the male of the deer, goat, hare, and rabbit (cf. *doe*) : (*spec.*) a male fallow-deer : (*S. Africa*) a goat or antelope (of either sex) : a dashing fellow : a male negro or American Indian : (*cards*) a counter : (*U.S.*) a dollar : an act of bucking.—*v.i.* (of a horse or mule) to attempt to throw by rapid jumps into the air, coming down with the back arched, head down, and forelegs stiff.—*v.t.* to throw by bucking : (*U.S.*) to resist : (*slang*) to cheer, invigorate, tone up.—*ns.* **buckeen'**, a poor Irish gentleman, without means to support his gentility; **buck'er**, an animal that bucks; **buck'-eye**, the American horse-chestnut (genus *Aesculus*); **buck'horn, buck's'-horn**, the material of a buck's horn (**buck's-horn plantain**, a British plantain with pinnatifid leaves); **buck'hound**, a small kind of staghound used for hunting bucks. —*adj.* **buck'ish**, lively, frisky : dandified : goatish. —*ns.* **buck'-jumper**, an animal that bucks; **buck'-rabb'it**, a male rabbit : a Welsh rabbit with poached egg; **buck'-saw**, a large frame-saw used with a saw-buck; **buck'-shot**, a large kind of shot, used in shooting deer; **buck'skin**, a soft leather made of deerskin or sheepskin : a strong twilled woollen cloth, cropped of nap : a horse of buckskin (greyish-yellow) colour : an American : (*pl.*) breeches or suit of buckskin.—*adj.* made of or like the skin of a buck.—*ns.* **buck'thorn**, a genus (*Rhamnus*) of shrubs whose berry supplies the sap-green used by painters : (see also **sea-buckthorn**) ; **buck'-tooth**, a projecting tooth.—**buck up** (*slang*), to bestir oneself : to cheer up : to improve : to stimulate : (*prov.*) to dress up ; **pass the buck**, (*slang; orig. U.S.*) to shift the responsibility to someone else (as one passes a marker to the next dealer in forms of poker). [O.E. *buc, bucca;* Du. *bok*, Ger. *bock*, a he-goat.]

buck, *buk, v.t.* to soak or steep in lye, a process in bleaching.—*n.* lye in which clothes are bleached. —*ns.* **buck'-basket**, a basket in which clothes are carried to be bucked; **buck'ing; buck'-wash, -ing**. [Ety. obscure : M.E. *bouken;* cog. words are Ger. *bäuchen, beuchen.*]

buckaroo, *buk'ə-rōō*, or *-rōō', n.* (*U.S.*) a cowboy. [Sp. *vaquero.*]

buckbean, *buk'bēn, n.* a trifoliate marsh plant (*Menyanthes trifoliata*) of the gentian family.— Also **bogbean**. [Flem. *bocks boonen*, goat's beans.]

bucket, *buk'it, n.* a vessel for drawing or holding water, etc. : one of the compartments on the circumference of a water-wheel : one of the scoops of a dredging-machine : a leather socket for holding a whip, carbine or lance : the pitcher in some orchids : a bucketful.—*v.t.* to lift in a bucket : to ride very hard : to push forward mercilessly : to swindle.—Also *v.i.*—*ns.* **buck'etful**, as much as a bucket will hold :—*pl.* **buck'etfuls ; buck'eting** (*U.S.*), jerky rowing; **buck'et-shop**, the office of an outside broker—a mere agent for bets on the rise or fall of prices ot stock, etc.; **buck'et-wheel**, a contrivance for raising water by means of buckets attached to the circumference of a wheel.—**give the bucket**, to dismiss; **kick the bucket** (*slang*), to die. [Prob. conn. with O.E. *būc*, a pitcher : or O.Fr. *buket*, a pail. Not Gael. *bucaid*, a bucket.]

buckie, *buk'i, n.* (*Scot.*) a shellfish such as the whelk : a refractory person. [Prob. related somehow to L. *buccinum*, a shellfish.]

buckle, *buk'l, n.* fastening for a strap or band, consisting of a rim and a tongue : a crisped, curled, or warped condition.—*v.t.* and *v.i.* to connect with a buckle : to prepare for action : to join closely as in fight or marriage : to bend or warp.—*v.i.* to apply oneself zealously (with *to*).—*ns.* **buck'le-beggar**, a hedge-parson; **buck'ler**, a small shield used for parrying. [Fr. *boucle*, the boss of a shield, a ring—L.L. *buccula*, dim. of *bucca*, a cheek.]

buckra, *buk'rä, n.* a word used by West Indian and American negroes for a white man—said to mean 'demon' in a dialect of the Calabar coast.

buckram, *buk'rəm, n.* a coarse open-woven fabric of jute, cotton, or linen made very stiff with size : stiffness in manners and appearance.—*adj.* made of buckram : stiff : precise.—*v.t.* to give the quality of buckram. [O.Fr. *boquerant.*]

buckshish. Same as **backsheesh**.—*n.* **buck'shee** (*mil. slang*) spoil, a windfall.—*adj.* free, gratuitous. [See **backsheesh, bukshi.**]

bucksom, a Miltonic spelling of **buxom.**

buckwheat, *buk'hwēt, n.* a *Polygonum* or *Fagopyrum* used in Europe for feeding horses, cattle and poultry, in America made into cakes for the breakfast table. [Prob. Du. *boekweit*, or Ger. *buchweizen*, beech-wheat, from the shape of the seeds.]

bucolic, -al, *bū-kol'ik, -əl, adjs.* pertaining to the tending of cattle : pastoral : rustic, countrified.— *n.* **bucol'ic**, a pastoral poem or poet : a rustic. [L. *būcolicus*—Gr. *boukolikos*—*boukolos*, a herdsman.]

bud, *bud, n.* a rudimentary shoot of a plant : (*biol.*) a protuberance that develops asexually into a new individual : a young person (as a term of endearment) : (*U.S.*) a débutante.—*v.t.* to put forth as buds : to graft by inserting a bud under the bark of another tree.—*v.i.* to put forth buds : to come as a bud : to be in or issue from the bud : (*pr.p.* **budd'ing** ; *pa.p.* **budd'ed**).—*n.* and *adj.* **budd'ing.**—*n.* **bud'-scale**, a leaf specialised as a scale protecting a bud.—*adjs.* **budd'y ; bud'less**. —**nip in the bud**, to destroy at its very beginning. [M.E. *budde;* perh. related to Du. *bot*, a bud.]

bud, *bud*, **buddy**, *bud'i, n.* (*U.S.*) brother : pal, most constant companion. [Childish or negro for **brother.**]

Buddha, *bōōd'ä, n.* a title applied to Sakyamuni or Gautama, the founder of the Buddhist religion : a general name for any one of a series of teachers of whom he is one.—*ns.* **Budd'hism**, the religion founded by the Buddha; **Budd'hist**, a believer in Buddhism.—*adjs.* **Budd'hist, Buddhist'ic.**—**Buddhist cross** the swastika. [Sans. *buddha*, wise, from *budh*, to know.]

buddle, *bud'l, n.* an inclined hutch for washing ore.—*v.t.* to wash with a buddle. [Origin obscure.]

Buddleia, *bud'li-ä, bud-lē'ä, n.* a genus of plants of the Loganiaceae, shrubs and trees with opposite leaves and showy clusters of purple or orange flowers. [Named in honour of Adam *Buddle* (d. 1715), botanist.]

buddy. See **bud** (2).

budge, *buj, v.i.* and *v.t.* to move or stir.—*n.* **budg′er,** one who stirs. [Fr. *bouger*—It. *bulicare,* to boil, to bubble—L. *bullīre.*]

budge, *buj, n.* lambskin fur.—*adj.* pompous : stiff. [Origin obscure.]

budgeree, *buj′ər-ē, adj.* (*Austr.*) good. [Native word, *budgeri.*]

budgerigar, *buj-ər-i-gär′, n.* a favourite cage and aviary bird, an Australian parrakeet. [Australian native *budgeri,* good, *gar,* cockatoo.]

budget, *buj′it, n.* a sack or its contents : a compact collection of things : news : a socket in which the end of a cavalry carbine rests : a financial statement and programme put before parliament by the Chancellor of the Exchequer : a plan of domestic expenditure or the like.—*v.i.* to prepare a budget.—*v.t.* to provide for in a budget : (*pr.p.* **budg′eting ;** *pa.t.* and *pa.p.* **budg′eted).** [Fr. *bougette,* dim. of *bouge,* a pouch—L. *bulga.*]

budmash. See **badmash.**

buff, *buf, n.* originally buffalo-hide : now white leather from which the grain surface has been removed, used for army accoutrements : a military coat : the colour of buff, a light yellow : the bare skin : a buff-stick or buff-wheel : (in *pl.*) certain regiments in the British army, from their former buff-coloured facings—e.g. East Kent Regiment, Ross-shire Buffs : a member of a party whose colour is buff.—Also *adj.*—*v.t.* to polish with a buff. —*ns.* **buff′-coat, buff′-jer′kin,** a strong, military coat : a soldier ; **buff′er,** one who buffs or polishes ; **buff′-leath′er ; buff′-stick, buff′-wheel,** a stick or wheel covered with buff-leather or the like, and charged with an abrasive for polishing.—**in buff,** naked. [Fr. *buffle,* a buffalo.]

buff, *buf, n.* (*obs.*) a buffet, blow, or stroke : a dull blow or its sound.—*v.t.* to strike, esp. with a dull sound : to burst out.—*ns.* **buff′er,** a mechanical apparatus for deadening the force of a concussion, as in railway carriages : a fellow, especially a dull or ineffectual fellow (as in *old buffer*) ; **buff′er-state′,** a neutral country lying between two others, whose relations are or may become strained. (O.Fr. *buffe,* a blow.]

buffalo, *buf′ə-lō, n.* a name for certain large animals of the ox kind, esp. the tame, often domesticated Asiatic buffalo, and the entirely wild and fierce Cape buffalo : (*U.S.*) the American bison : a bison : —*pl.* **buff′aloes.**—*v.t.* to bewilder : to overawe.— *ns.* **buff′alo-berry,** a North American shrub of the Elaeagnaceae, or its edible fruit ; **buff′alo-bird,** an ox-pecker ; **buff′alo-grass,** a low creeping grass (*Buchloe dactyloides*) growing on the western prairies of the U.S. : any of several other prairie grasses ; **buff′alo-nut,** a North American shrub of the sandalwood family : its oil-yielding nut ; **buff′alo-robe,** a bison-hide rug or cloak. [It. *buffalo,* through L. from Gr. *boubalos.*]

buffet, *buf′it, n.* a blow with the fist : a slap : a stroke, esp. heavy and repeated, as of the wind, fortune, etc.—*v.t.* to strike with the hand or fist : to struggle against, beat back.—*v.i.* to deal heavy blows.—*n.* **buff′eting,** a striking with the hand, boxing : contention : repeated blows. [O.Fr. *buffet—buffe,* a blow, esp. on the cheek.]

buffet, *buf′it, n.* a sideboard : a low (esp. rectangular) stool : a refreshment-bar (in this sense usu. *büf′ā*). [Fr. *buffet ;* origin unknown.]

bufflehead, *buf′l-hed, n.* a N. American diving duck resembling the golden-eye. [From *buffalo* and **head.**]

buffo, *boof′fō, adj.* comic.—*n.* the comic actor in an opera :—*pl.* **buf′fi** (*fē*) ; *fem.* **buf′fa ;** *pl.* **buf′fe** (*fā*). [It.]

buffoon, *buf-ōōn′, n.* one who sets himself to amuse by jests, grimaces, etc. : a low, vulgar, or indecent jester, one without self-respect.—*n.* **buffoon′ery,** the practices of a buffoon : low or vulgar jesting. [Fr. *bouffon*—It. *buffone ; buffare,* to jest.]

bufo, *bū′fō, n.* (*Ben Jonson*) a black tincture in alchemy. [L. *būfō,* toad.]

bug, *bug, n.* an object of terror.—*ns.* **bug′aboo,** a bogy, or object of terror ; **bug′bear,** an object of terror, generally imaginary.—*adj.* causing fright.—

n. **bug′-word,** (*arch.*) a terrifying or threatening word. [M.E. *bugge,* prob. W. *bwg,* a hobgoblin.]

bug, *bug, n.* a name applied loosely to certain insects, esp. of the Hemiptera (Heteroptera), and specifically to one (*Cimex lectularius*) that infests houses and beds : in America applied to any insect, small animal, or even disease-germ ; (*U.S.*) a craze : a crazy person : an important person (**big bug).**—*adj.* crazy.—*ns.* **bug′bane, bug′wort,** a ranunculaceous plant (*Cimifuga foetida*) akin to banebery, reputed to drive away insects.—*adj.* **bug′house,** mad.—*n.* **bug′-hunter,** a collecting entomologist. [Ety. unknown.]

bug, *bug, v.i.* (*U.S.*) to start or bulge :—*pr.p.* **bugg′ing ;** *pa.t.* and *pa.p.* **bugged.**

bugger, *bug′ər, n.* orig. a Bulgarian heretic, believed capable of any crime : one guilty of bestiality and unnatural vice : a low term of abuse, often quite colourless or even kindly.—*n.* **bugg′ery** (*law*), bestiality, unnatural vice. [Fr. *bougre*—L. *Bulgarus,* a Bulgarian.]

buggy, *bug′i, n.* a light carriage or gig of several kinds—in America, a one-horse, four-wheeled vehicle with one seat : in England, two-wheeled ; in India, hooded. [By some conn. with **bogie ;** ety. really quite unknown.]

bugle, *bū′gl, n.* orig. a buffalo or wild ox : hence (also **bū′gle-horn**) a horn used as a drinking vessel or hunting-horn : a treble instrument with or without keys, usually made of copper, like the trumpet, but having the bell less expanded and the tube shorter and more conical, used more for signalling than music.—*v.i.* to sound a bugle.— *ns.* **bū′gle-band ; bū′gle-call ; bū′gler,** one who sounds the bugle ; **bū′glet,** a small bugle. [O.Fr. *bugle ;*—L. *būculus,* dim. of *bōs,* an ox.]

bugle, *bū′gl, n.* a slender elongated bead, usually black.—*adj.* (*Shak.*) like bugles. [Poss. conn. with L.L. *bugulus,* hair-pad, or with Du. *beugel,* ring.]

bugle, *bū′gl, n.* a genus (*Ajuga*) of labiate plants without upper lip. [Fr., It. *bugola*—L.L. *bugula,* *būgillō.*]

bugloss, *bū′glos, n.* a name for several plants of the borage family, esp. *Lycopsis arvensis,* a common cornfield weed, and **viper's bugloss** (q.v.). [Fr. *buglosse*—L. *būglōssa*—Gr. *bouglōssos*—*bous,* ox, *glōssa,* tongue.]

bugong, *boo′gong, n.* a noctuid moth eaten by Australian blacks. [Native name.]

buhl, *bool, n.* a complicated form of inlay, gold, silver, or brass and pewter, ivory and mother-of-pearl in tortoiseshell, etc., forming panels for furniture decoration : furniture thus decorated.— Also **boulle, boule.** [From André Charles *Boulle* (1642–1732), a cabinet-maker in the service of Louis XIV.]

buhrstone, *bur′stōn, n.* a variety of quartz, containing many small empty cells, which give it a peculiar roughness of surface particularly adapted for millstones.—Also **burr′stone.** [Perh. conn. with **burr,** from its roughness.]

buik, *bak, n.* a Scots form of **book:** a variant of Scots **bouk.**

build, *bild, v.t.* to erect, as a house or bridge : to form or construct, as a railway, etc.—*v.i.* to depend (with *on, upon*) : (*pa.t.* and *pa.p.* **built,** *arch.* **build′ed).**—*n.* form : make.—*ns.* **build′er,** one who builds, or controls the work of building ; **build′ing,** the art of erecting houses, etc. : anything built : a house ; **build′ing-board,** an artificial material made in slabs for lining walls.— *adj.* **built,** formed or shaped.—*n.* **build′-up,** (*coll.*) the act of building up, esp. a reputation (particularly if it is not merited).—**build in,** to enclose or fix by building ; **building society,** a society that advances money to its members towards providing them with dwelling-houses, against periodical subscriptions ; **build up,** to close up by building, as a door : to cover with buildings : to erect (any structure, as a reputation) : to put together from parts already made : to edify spiritually. [O.E. *gebyld,* pa.p. of an assumed *byldan,* to build—*bold,* a dwelling.]

Neutral vowels in unaccented syllables : *el′ə-mənt, in′fənt, ran′dəm*

buirdly, *bərd′li*, *adj*. (*Scot.*) stalwart, large and well made. [Poss. a variant of **burly**.]

buist, *büst*, *n*. (*Scot.*) a box: a tar-box: an owner's mark on sheep or cattle.—*v.t.* to mark thus. [O.Fr. *boiste* (Fr. *boîte*), box.]

buke, *bŏk*, *n*. a Scots form of **book**: a variant of Scots **bouk**.

bukshi, bukshee, *buk′shē*, *n*. a paymaster. [Pers. *bakhshī*.]

bulb, *bulb*, *n*. a subterranean bud with swollen leaf-bases in which reserve materials are stored: a protuberance or swelling: a dilatation or expansion of a glass tube: the glass of an electric light.—*v.i.* to form bulbs: to bulge out or swell.—*adjs.* **bulb′ar, bulbed, bulbif′erous.**—*n.* **bulb′il**, a small bud that may grow into an independent plant.—*adj.* **bulb′ous.**—**bulb of percussion**, a raised cone on a worked flint, marking where a blow was struck. [L. *bulbus*—Gr. *bolbos*, an onion.]

bulbul, *bool′bool*, *n*. properly, a Persian nightingale: in India, extended to a genus (*Pycnonotus*) of birds akin to the babblers: a sweet singer. [Arab.]

Bulgarian, *bul-gā′ri-ən*, *adj*. of *Bulgaria* or its language.—*n.* a native or citizen of Bulgaria: the Bulgarian language (Slavonic).—*n.* **Bul′gar** (-*gär*), a member of an ancient Finnic or Ugrian tribe that moved from the Volga towards Bulgaria.—*adj.* **Bulgaric** (-*gar′ik*).—*n.* the ancient language of the Bulgars.

bulge, *bulj*, *n*. a protuberance, swelling.—*v.i.* to swell out.—*ns.* **bul′ger**, a wooden golf-club with a convex face; **bul′giness.**—*adj.* **bul′gy.**—**to get the bulge on one** (*slang*), to get a decided advantage over a person. [O.Fr. *boulge*, prob. L. *bulga*, a leather knapsack: a Gallic word; cf. **bilge**.]

bulimy, *būl′i-mi*, *n*. morbid voracity.—Also **bulī′mia.** [Gr. *boulīmiā*—*bous*, ox, *līmos*, hunger.]

bulk, *bulk*, *n*. a stall or framework built in front of a shop.—*n.* **bulk′er**, a street thief or strumpet. [Ety. dub.; cf. O.N. *bálkr*, beam, O.E. *bolca*, gangway of a ship.]

bulk, *bulk*, *n*. a heap (now only of tobacco): a cargo: the belly, trunk, or body: a hull or hold: volume or size: great size: the greater part: any huge body or structure: mass.—*v.i.* to be in bulk: to be of weight or importance.—*v.t.* to put or hold in bulk.—*n.* **bulk′iness.**—*adj.* **bulk′y**, having bulk: filling much space: unwieldy.—**break bulk**, see **break** (1); **load in bulk**, to put cargo in loose; **sell in bulk**, to sell cargo as it is in the hold: to sell in large quantities. [Prob. (hypothetical) O.N. *bulki*, heap or cargo, confused with O.E. *buc*, belly; see **bouk**.]

bulkhead, *bulk′hed*, *n*. a partition separating one part of a ship's interior from another, either transverse or longitudinal, and usually watertight: a protecting barrier or structure: the roof of a bulk: the bulk itself.—**collision bulkhead**, that nearest the bow. [**bulk** (1) and **bulk** (2).]

bull, *bool*, *n*. an uncastrated male of the ox kind: a male whale, walrus, elephant, moose, etc.: the sign or the constellation *Taurus*: one who seeks to raise the price of stocks, and speculates on a rise (cf. **bear**): a bull's-eye.—*adj.* male: massive: favourable to the bulls, rising.—*v.t.* to try to raise the price of: to copulate with (a cow).—*v.i.* to be in heat, of a cow.—*ns.* **bull′-bait′ing**, the sport of baiting or exciting bulls with dogs; **bull′-bat** (*U.S.*), the night-hawk or goat-sucker; **bull′-beef**, the beef or flesh of bulls, coarse beef: (*Shak.* in *pl.*) **bull′-beeves; bull′-begg′ar**, a hobgoblin, etc.; **bull′-calf**, a male calf: a stupid fellow, a lout; **bull′-dance**, a dance of men only; **bull′dog**, a breed of dogs of great courage, formerly used for baiting bulls: hence a person of obstinate courage: a short-barrelled revolver of large calibre: a proctor's attendant at Oxford or Cambridge.—*v.t.* to assail like a bulldog: (*U.S.*) to wrestle with and throw (a steer, etc.).—*ns.* **bull′fight**, a popular spectacle in Spain, in which a bull is goaded to fury by mounted *picadores* armed with lances,

and despatched by a specially skilful *espada* or swordsman; **bull′fight′er; bull′fight′ing; bull′finch**, a plump red-breasted finch: (perh. for *bull-fence*) a kind of high, thick hedge hard to jump; **bull′frog**, a large frog.—*adj.* **bull′-fronted**, having a forehead like a bull.—*n.* **bull′head**, the miller's thumb, a small river fish with large, flat head: extended to various similar fishes, as the pogge (*armed bullhead*).—*adj.* **bull′-head′ed**, impetuous and obstinate.—*ns.* **bull′-head′edness; bull′-hoof**, a West Indian passion-flower (from the shape of its leaf).—*adjs.* **bull′ish; bull′-necked′**, thick-necked.—*ns.* **bull′ock**, an ox or castrated bull; **bull′ock's-heart′**, the custard-apple; **bull′-pen**, a pen for a bull: (*U.S.*) a similar enclosure for prisoners; **bull′-of-the-bog** (*Scot.*), the bittern; **bull′-pup**, a young bulldog; **bull′-ring**, the enclosure for bull-fighting or bull-baiting: a ring: a ring for a bull's nose; **bull′-roar′er**, a boy's plaything, made of an oblong slip of wood, whirled at the end of a string to give a loud whirring noise—the native Australian *turndun*, the *rhombos* of the Greek mysteries; **bull's′-eye**, the central boss formed in making a sheet of blown glass: a thick lens, or round piece of glass, as in a lantern: a policeman's lantern: a round opening or window: the centre of a target: a shot that hits it: a big round hard peppermint sweet; **bull′-terr′ier**, a cross between bulldog and terrier; **bull′-trout**, a variety of sea-trout (*Salmo trutta eriox*): a large trout with a big head: a salmon that has re-entered fresh water after spawning; **bull′-whack**, a heavy whip.—*v.t.* to lash with a bull-whack.—**a bull in a china shop**, one who lacks the delicacy that the situation calls for; **bull into**, to plunge hastily into; **take the bull by the horns**, to grapple boldly with a danger or difficulty. [M.E. *bole*, prob. O.N. *bole*, *boli*; most prob. related to **bellow**.]

bull, *bool*, *n*. an edict of the pope with his seal affixed.—*n.* **bull′ary**, a collection of papal bulls. [L. *bulla*, a knob, a leaden seal.]

bull, *bool*, *n*. a ludicrous inconsistency in speech, often said to be an especial prerogative of Irishmen—'I was a fine child, but they changed me'. [Prob. O.Fr. *boul*, cheat.]

bull, *bool*, *n*. drink made by pouring water into a cask that had held liquor. [Origin unknown.]

bull, *bool*, *n*. a deck game in which pads are thrown at an inclined board, the **bull′-board**. [Origin unknown.]

bulla, *bool′ä*, *n*. a round metal ornament worn by ancient Roman children: a seal attached to a document: a blister: anything rounded or globular: **Bulla**, the bubble-shell genus.—*adj.* **bull′ate**, blistered or puckered: bubble-like: knobbed: inflated. [L. *bulla*.]

bullace, *bool′is*, *n*. a shrub closely allied to the sloe. [Cf. O.Fr. *beloce*.]

bulldoze, *bool′dōz*, *v.t.* (*U.S.*) to intimidate: to bully.—*n.* **bull′dozer**, one who bulldozes: a pistol or other means of compulsion: a tractor machine for levelling land and clearing away obstacles. [Origin obscure.]

buller, *bool′ər*, *n*. (*Scot.*) turbulence in water: a bubbling: a bellow.—*v.i.* to seethe: to gurgle: to bellow. [Cf. Dan. *bulder*, Swed. *buller*, rumble, noise, roar; prob. partly from or influenced by O.Fr. *bullir*, Icel. *bulla*, to boil.]

bullet, *bool′it*, *n*. (*obs.*) a little ball: a projectile, now esp. one (round or conical) discharged from any kind of small-arm: a plumb or sinker in fishing.—*n.* **bull′et-head**, a round head: (*U.S.*) an obstinate fellow.—*adjs.* **bull′et-head′ed; bull′et-proof**, proof against bullets. [Fr. *boulette*, dim. of *boule*, a ball—L. *bulla*.]

bulletin, *bool′e-tin*, *n*. an official report of public news, or of a patient's progress. [Fr.,—It. *bullettino*.]

bullet-tree, bulletrie. Same as **bully-tree.**

bullion, *bool′yən*, *n*. gold and silver in the mass and uncoined: occasionally, precious metal, coined and uncoined: a heavy twisted cord fringe, often covered with gold or silver wire.—*n.* **bull′ionist**, one in favour of metallic currency. [Perh. conn. with L.L. *bullīo*, *-ōnis*, a boiling.]

bullock. See **bull** (1).

bully, *bool'i*, *n.* a cruel oppressor of the weak: a blustering, noisy, overbearing fellow: a ruffian hired to beat or intimidate anyone: one who lives upon the gains of a prostitute: (*obs.*) a term of genial familiarity, esp. to a man.—*adj.* blustering: brisk: (*U.S.*) excellent.—*v.i.* to bluster. —*v.t.* to oppress cruelly: to threaten in a noisy way: (*pr.p.* **bull'ying**; *pa.p.* **bull'ied**.)—*interj.* good.—*ns.* **bull'yism**; **bull'y-rook**, a bully: a comrade. [Perh. Du. *boel*, a lover; cf. Ger. *buhle*.]

bully, *bool'i*, *n.* a miner's hammer.

bully, *bool'i*, *n.* (*football*) a scrimmage: (*hockey*) the opening (or reopening) of the game—two opposing players each striking the ground on his own side of the ball and his opponent's stick alternately, three times, and then trying to strike the ball—also **bully-off'**.—*v.t.* and *v.i.* **bull'y** (-off).

bully, *bool'i*, **bully-beef**, *bool'i-bēf*, *ns.* canned or pickled beef. [Prob. Fr. *bouilli*, boiled beef, influenced by **bull**.]

bullyrag, *bool'i-rag*, **ballyrag**, *bal'i-rag*, *v.t.* (*coll.*) to assail with abusive language or horse-play: to badger. [Origin unknown; perh. from **rag**, 2.]

bully-tree, *bool'i-trē*, *n.* a name for several West Indian sapotaceous trees yielding good timber, edible fruits, and balata, esp. *Minusops Balata*.— Also **bull'et-tree**, **bull'etrie**, **boll'etrie**. [Perh. from **bullace**; perh. from **balata**.]

bulrush, *bool'rush*, *n.* a name given to two distinct tall marsh or water plants—the reed-mace or cat's-tail, and clubrush, a plant of the sedge family (*Scirpus lacustris*).—*adj.* **bul'rushy.**—**bulrush millet**, pearl millet. [Perh. **bole** (1) or **bull** (1) in sense of great or coarse, and **rush** (2).]

bulse, *buls*, *n.* a bag for or of diamonds, etc. [Port. *bolsa*—L.L. *bursa*, a purse. See **purse**.]

bulwark, *bool'wǝrk*, *n.* a fortification or rampart: a breakwater or sea-wall: the side of a ship projecting above the deck: any means of defence or security.—*v.t.* to defend: to fortify. [Cf. Ger. *bollwerk*.]

bum, *bum*, *n.* (*Shak.*) the buttocks.—*n.* **bum'bai'liff** (*Shak.* **bum'-bay'lie**), a bailiff who comes behind to make arrests: a sheriff's officer. [Cf. **bump** in sense of swelling.]

bum, *bum*, *v.i.* to hum or make a murmuring sound, as a bee.—*v.t.* (*Scot.*) to toss, hurl: (*pr.p.* **bum'-ming**; *pa.p.* **bummed**).—*n.* a humming sound.— *ns.* **bum'-bee** (*Scot.*), a bumble-bee; **bum'-clock** (*Scot.*), a drone-beetle; **bumm'er**, a person or thing that bums.—**head'-bumm'er** (*Scot.*) a manager or person in authority. [Imit.]

bum, *bum*, *n.* (*U.S. slang*) a spree: a dissolute fellow: a sponger.—*adj.* worthless: despicable.— *v.i.* to loaf: to sponge: to live dissolutely.—*n.* **bumm'er**, a plundering straggler or camp-follower (during the American Civil War): a dissolute fellow: a loafer: a sponger.

bumbaze, *bum-bāz'*, *v.t.* to confound, bamboozle. [Origin obscure.]

bumble, **bummle**, *bum'(b)l*, *v.i.* (*prov.*) to bungle: to utter indistinctly: to bustle about blunderingly. —*n.* confusion: indistinct utterance: a bungler: an idler.—*ns.* **bum'ble-bee**, a large wild loud-humming bee, a humble bee; **bum'ble-foot**, cellulitis in a fowl's foot, due to pus-forming organisms: club-foot; **bum'ble-puppy**, the old game of nine-holes: unscientific whist: a racket game in which a string is wound round a post by hitting a slung ball or bag. [Freq. of **bum** (2).]

Bumble, *bum'bl*, *n.* a beadle: a self-important minor official.—*n.* **Bum'bledom**. [From Mr. *Bumble* in Dickens's *Oliver Twist*.]

bumbo, *bum'bō*, *n.* a mixture or rum or gin, water, sugar, and nutmeg, or similar drink. [Perh. It. *bombo*, a child's word for drink.]

bum-boat, *bum'bōt*, *n.* orig. a Thames scavenger's boat: a boat bringing vegetables, etc., for sale to ships. [Origin doubtful.]

bumkin, **bumpkin**, *bum'kin*, *n.* a short beam of timber projecting from each bow of a ship, for the purpose of extending the lower corner of the foresail to windward: a small outrigger over the stern of a boat, usually serving to extend the mizzen. [From **boom**, and dim. termination *-kin*.]

bummalo, **bumalo**, *bum'ǝ-lō*, *n.* the Bombay duck, a small Indian fish of a family (*Scopelidae*) akin to the salmon, dried and eaten as a relish.—Also **bummalō'ti**. [Marathi *bombīl*.]

bummaree, *bum-ǝr-ē'*, *n.* a middleman in the Billingsgate fish-market. [Ety. unknown.]

bummer. See **bum** (2 and 3).

bummle. See **bumble** (1).

bummock, *bum'ǝk*, *n.* (*Orkney*) a brewing of ale for a feast. [Ety. unknown.]

bump, *bump*, *v.i.* to make a heavy or loud noise: to knock dully: to jolt: to move joltingly: (of a cricket-ball) to bound high on striking the pitch.— *v.t.* to strike with a dull sound: to strike against: (*boat-racing*) to overtake and impinge upon—the bumper consequently taking the place of the bumped in rank: to spread out in printing so as to fill any desired number of pages.—*n.* a dull heavy blow: a thump: an irregular condition of air causing an aeroplane to jolt: a high rebound of a cricket-ball: a jolt: a lump or swelling: a protuberance on the head confidently associated by phrenologists with qualities or propensities of mind: hence (*coll.*) faculty.—*n.* **bump'er**, anything or person that bumps: a bar on a motor-car to lessen the shock of collision: (*U.S.*) a railway buffer: a bumping race: a cup or glass filled to the brim for drinking a toast: anything large or generous in measure: a crowded house at a theatre or concert.—*adj.* full to overflowing.—*v.i.* to drink bumpers.—*ns.* **bump'iness**; **bumpol'ogy** (*jocose*), phrenology.—*adj.* **bump'y.**—**bumping race**, a boat-race in which the competitors seek to bump, not to pass; **bump off** (*slang*), to kill, murder. [Imit.]

bump, *bump*, *n.* the booming cry of the bittern.— *v.i.* to utter that cry. [Imit.]

bumpkin, *bump'kin*, *n.* an awkward, clumsy rustic: a clown.—*adj.* **bump'kinish.** [Prob. Du. *boomken*, a log; cf. **bumkin**.]

bumptious, *bump'shǝs*, *adj.* offensively self-important.—*adv.* **bump'tiously.**—*n.* **bump'tiousness.** [Prob. formed from **bump** (1).]

bun, *bun*, *n.* a kind of sweet cake: a rounded mass of hair. [Perh. from O.Fr. *bugne*, a swelling.]

bun, *bun*, *n.* a dry stalk: a hare's scut. [Possibly Gael. *bun*, a root, a stump.]

bun, *bun*, *n.* a playful name for a rabbit or a squirrel. [Origin unknown.]

Buna, *bōō'na*, *n.* an artificial rubber made by the polymerisation of butadiene.

bunch, *bunsh*, *bunch*, *n.* a lump: a lumpish gathering: a number of things aggregated or fastened together: a definite quantity fastened together, as of linen yarn (180,000 yards), etc.: a cluster: a handful as of flowers: something in the form of a tuft or knot.—*v.i.* to swell out in a bunch: to cluster. —*v.t.* to make a bunch of: to concentrate.—*adjs.* **bunch'-backed** (*Shak.*), hump-backed; **bunched**, humped, protuberant: lumpy.—*ns.* **bunch'-grass**, a clumped Western American grass of several kinds; **bunch'iness**.—*adj.* **bunch'y**, growing in bunches or like a bunch: bulging.—**bunch of fives**, the fist with fingers clenched. [Origin unknown.]

buncombe. See **bunkum.**

bund, *boont*, *n.* a league or confederacy.—*n* **bundesrat(h)** (*boon'dǝs-rät*), federal council. [Ger.]

bund, *bund*, *n.* (India, etc.) an embankment or dam. [Hind. *band*, from Pers.]

bundle, *bun'dl*, *n.* a number of things loosely bound together: a bunch: a loose parcel, esp one contained in a cloth: (*biol.*) a strand of conducting vessels, fibres, etc.: a definite measure or quantity, as two reams of paper, twenty hanks of linen yarn, etc.—*v.t.* to make into bundles: to put hastily or unceremoniously: to hustle.—*v.i.* to pack up one's things for a journey: to go hurriedly or in confusion (with *away*, *off*, *out*): to lie in bed together fully clad (an old custom in Wales and New

Neutral vowels in unaccented syllables : *el'ǝ-mǝnt*, *in'fǝnt*, *ran'dǝm*

England for sweethearts and others). [Conn. with bind and bond.]

bundobust. Same as bandobast.

bundook, *bun′dōōk, n.* (*mil. slang*) a rifle. [Hind. *bandūq.*]

bung, *bung, n.* the stopper of the hole in a barrel : a large cork.—*v.t.* to stop up or enclose with a bung (also *fig.*).—*ns.* **bung′-hole,** a hole for a bung ; **bung′-vent,** a small hole in a bung to let gases escape, etc. [Ety. dubious.]

bung, *bung, n.* (*obs. ; thieves' cant*) a purse : (*Shak.*) a cutpurse.—**nip a bung,** to cut a purse. [Cf. O.E. *pung,* purse.]

bung, *bung, v.t.* (*slang*) to toss.

bungalow, *bung′ga-lō, n.* a lightly-built house, properly with a veranda and one story : now loosely, a one-story house.—*adj.* and *n.* **bung′aloid.**—**dâk-bungalow,** a house for travellers in India. [Hind. *banglā,* Bengalese.]

bungle, *bung′gl, n.* anything clumsily done : a gross mismanagement.—*v.i.* to act in a clumsy manner.—*v.t.* to make or mend clumsily : to mismanage grossly : to make a failure of by want of skill.—*n.* **bung′ler.**—*adj.* **bung′ling,** clumsy, awkward : unskilfully or ill done.—Also *n.*—*adv.* **bung′lingly.** [Ety. dub. ; prob. onomatopoeic ; cf. Sw. dial. *bangla,* to work ineffectually ; Hindes Groome suggests Gypsy *bongo,* left, awkward.]

bunion, *bun′yon, n.* a lump or inflamed swelling on the first joint of the great toe. [Ety. unknown ; poss. It. *bugnone,* a botch.]

bunk, *bungk, n.* a box or recess in a ship's cabin, a sleeping-berth anywhere.—*v.i.* to occupy a bunk.—*n.* **bunk′er,** (*Scot.*) a window-seat and chest : (*Scot.*) a turf seat : (*Scot.*) a large bin or chest, esp. one used for stowing coals : (*Scot.*) a slab beside a sink : a compartment for fuel on shipboard : a sand-pit or sandy gap in turf, esp. one forming a hazard in a golf course : a bomb-proof shelter or fort.—*v.t.* to fuel : to play into a bunker.—*v.i.* to fuel.—*adj.* **bunk′ered,** in a bunker : in difficulties. [Cf. O.N. *bunki,* Swed., Norw., Dan. *bunke,* heap.]

bunk, *bungk, n.* (*slang*) flight (esp. in phrase **to do a bunk**).—*v.i.* to flee.

bunko, bunco, *bung′kō, n.* (*U.S.*) a form of confidence-trick by which a simple fellow is swindled or taken somewhere and robbed.—*v.t.* to rob or swindle in such a way.—*n.* **bunk′o-steer′er,** that one of the swindling confederates who allures the victim.

bunkum, *bung′kəm, n.* bombastic speechmaking intended for the newspapers rather than to persuade the audience : humbug ; claptrap.—Also **bun′combe, bunk.** [From *Buncombe,* a county in North Carolina, whose member is said to have gone on talking in Congress, explaining apologetically to the few hearers that remained that he was 'only talking for Buncombe'.]

bunny, *bun′i, n.* a pet name for a rabbit.—*n.* **bunn′y-hug,** a 20th-century American dance—also *v.i.* [Ety. unknown ; cf. **bun.**]

bunodont, *bū′nō-dont, adj.* having tuberculate molars—opp. to *lophodont.* [Gr. *bounos,* a rounded hill, *odous, odontos,* a tooth.]

bunsen, *boon′sən,* or *bun′sən, adj.* invented by the great chemist, R. W. *Bunsen* of Heidelberg.—*n.* **bun′sen-burn′er,** a gas-burner in which a plentiful supply of air is caused to mingle with the gas before ignition, so that a smokeless flame of low luminosity but great heating power is the result.

bunt, *bunt, n.* stink-brand, a disease of wheat : the fungus (*Tilletia*) that causes it.—*adj.* **bunt′ed, bunt′y.** [Ety. unknown.]

bunt, *bunt, n.* the bagging part of a fishing-net, a sail, etc.—*v.i.* to belly, as a sail.—*n.* **bunt′line,** a rope passing from the foot-rope of a square sail to prevent bellying in furling. [Ety. unknown.]

bunt, *bunt, v.i.* to push with the horns, butt : to spring, rear.—*n.* a push.—*n.* **bunt′ing,** pushing : a boy's game, played with sticks and a small piece of wood : a strong timber, a stout prop.

bunter, *bunt′ər, n.* a rag-picker : a low woman.

Bunter, *boon′tər, n.* (*geol.*) the lowest division of the Trias. [Ger., mottled.]

bunting, *bunt′ing, n.* a thin worsted stuff for ships' colours : flags, cloth decorations. [Ety. dub.]

bunting, *bunt′ing, n.* any finch of a group (*Emberiza,* etc.) nearly allied to the crossbills.

bunting. See bunt.

bunya, *bun′yä,* **bun′ya-bun′ya,** *n.* an Australian monkey-puzzle with large edible seeds. [Native word.]

bunyip, *bun′yip, n.* an Australian swamp monster, invisible to whites : an impostor. [Native word.]

buoy, *boi, n.* a floating secured mark, serving (by its shape, colour, light, sound, etc.) as a guide or as a warning.—*v.t.* to furnish or mark with buoys or marks : to keep afloat, bear up, or sustain : to raise, lift.—*v.t.* to rise.—*ns.* **buoy′age,** a series of buoys or floating beacons to mark the course for vessels : the providing of buoys ; **buoy′ance** (*rare*), **buoy′ancy,** capacity for floating lightly on water or in the air : loss of weight owing to immersion in a fluid : (*fig.*) lightness of spirit, cheerfulness.—*adj.* **buoy′ant,** tending to float or to buoy up : light, cheerful, and elastic.—*n.* **buoy′antness.** [Du. *boei,* buoy, fetter, through Romance forms (Norman *boie*), from L.L. *boia,* a collar of leather.]

Buphaga, *bū′fa-gä, n.* a small genus of African birds, nearly related to the starlings, feeding on the larvae of gadflies and the like, which they find on the backs of cattle, camels, etc.—Also *beef-eater* and *ox-pecker.* [Gr. *bous,* an ox, *phagein,* to eat.]

buplever, *bū-plev′ər, n.* hare's-ear (Bupleurum). [Fr. *buplèvre*—L. *būpleurum*—Gr. *bous,* ox, *pleuron,* rib.]

Buprestis, *bū-pres′tis, n.* a genus of beetles, typical of a large family, **Bupres′tidae,** those occurring in warmer countries having lively colour and metallic sheen—some known as golden beetles. [Gr. *bouprēstis,* a kind of poisonous beetle—*bous,* ox, *prēthein,* to swell.]

bur, burr, *bur, n.* the prickly seed-case or head of certain plants, which sticks to clothes or animals : any impediment or inconvenient adherent : any lump, ridge, etc., more or less sharp, an excrescence on a tree, or markings representing it in wood : a knot in thread : a knob at the base of a deer's horn : the rough edge to a line made by an engraving tool, which, when the plate is inked, gives a further quality to the line : waste raw silk : the sweetbread or pancreas : (*Scot.*) club-moss : the name for various tools and appliances, as the triangular chisel for clearing the corners of mortises, etc. : the blank driven out of a piece of sheet-metal by a punch : a partly vitrified brick.—*ns.* **bur′dock,** a composite plant (*Arctium Lappa*) with hooked involucral bracts and docklike leaves : any species of *Xanthium* ; **bur′-mar′igold,** any plant of the composite genus *Bidens,* with barbed pappus : a species of Xanthium ; **bur′-reed,** a reedlike genus (*Sparganium*) of water-plants with globular flower-heads.—*adj.* **burr′y.**—*ns.* **bur′thistle,** spear-thistle ; **bur′weed,** various burry plants, as burdock, bur-reed, clotbur (*Xanthium*), etc.—**bur in the throat,** something seeming to stick in the throat, producing a choking sensation. [Cog. with Dan. *borre,* a bur.]

bur, burr, *bur, n.* the rough sound of *r* pronounced in the throat, as by many Northumberland people.—*v.i.* to whisper hoarsely, to murmur. [Usually associated with **bur,** I, but perh. from the sound.]

burble, *burb′l, n.* a tangle.—*v.t.* to confuse. [Scot. ; prob. conn. wth O.Fr. *barbouiller,* to confound.]

burble, *burb′l, n.* a murmur.—*v.t.* and *v.i.* to murmur : to gurgle : (*coll.*) to talk excitedly and rather incoherently. [Prob. onomatopoeic.]

burbot, *bur′bot, n.* a fresh-water fish, like the ling, with a longish barbel on its lower jaw. [Fr. *bourbotte, barbotte.*—L.L. *borba,* mud, or L. *barba,* a beard.]

burd, *burd, n.* (*obs.*) a maiden : a lady. [O.E. *byrde,* well-born (or perh. *bryd,* bride), prob. combined or confused with O.N. *byrthr,* O.E. *byrd,* birth, offspring.]

burd, *burd* (*Scot.*) *n.* a bird : a young bird : a young animal of any kind : offspring, progeny : a term of endearment.—*n.* **burd′-alane′, bird′-alane′,** the last remaining of a family.—*adj.* and *adv.* (*Morris* bird'-alone) quite alone.—*n.* burd'ie (*dim.*).

burdash, *burd'-ash, n.* a fringed sash worn by fine gentlemen in the time of Anne and George I. [Origin unknown.]

burden, *bur'dn* (*arch.* **burthen,** *-dhən*), *n.* a load : weight : cargo : a ship's carrying capacity (still often **burthen**) : that which is grievous, oppressive, or difficult to bear : an obligation : (*Scots law*) any restriction, limitation, or encumbrance affecting person or property : (*obs.*) a child in the womb : a birth : (in *pl.*) a boat's floor-boards.—*v.t.* to load : to oppress : to encumber.—*adjs.* bur'denous, bur'densome, heavy : oppressive.—**burden of proof,** the obligation to prove one's contention. [O.E. *byrthen—beran,* to bear.]

burden, *bur'dn,* (*arch.* **burthen,** *-dhən*), *n.* bourdon or bass : part of a song repeated at the end of every stanza, refrain : the leading idea of anything. [Fr. *bourdon,* a humming tone in music—L.L. *burdō,* a drone bee; confused with **burden** (1).]

burden, *bur'dn, n.* a pilgrim's staff. [See **bourdon**.]

burdock. See **bur** (1).

bureau, *bū-rō' bü-rō', bū'rō, n.* a writing-table combined with chest of drawers : a room or office where such a table is used : a department or office for the transacting of business, such as collecting and supplying information : a government department :—*pl.* bureaux, bureaus (*-ōz*). [Fr. *bureau* —O.Fr. *burel,* russet cloth—L. *burrus,* red.]

bureaucracy, *bū-rok'rə-si,* or *-rōk', n.* a system of government by officials, responsible only to their departmental chiefs.—*ns.* bur'eaucrat, bureau'cratist, one who practises or favours bureaucracy. —*adv.* bureaucrat'ically. [bureau, and Gr. *kratos,* power.]

burette, *bū-ret', n.* a graduated glass tube with a tap, for measuring liquids run off : an altar-cruet. [Fr.]

burg, *boorg, burg, n.* (*hist.*) a fortress : a walled town : (*U.S. coll.,* pron. *burg*) a town. [West Gmc. *burg ;* O.E. *burh.*]

burgage, *bur'gij, n.* a tenure in socage for a yearly rent : a tenure in Scotland in royal burghs under nominal service of watching. [L.L. *burgāgium,* from the root of **borough, burgh.**]

burganet, burgonet, *bur'gə-net, n.* a light 16th-century helmet with cheek-pieces. [Fr. *bourguignotte,* lit. Burgundian.]

burgee, *bur'jē, n.* a swallow-tailed flag or pennant : a kind of small coal for furnaces. [Origin unknown.]

burgeon, *bur'jən, n.* and *v.i.* Same as **bourgeon.**

burgess, *bur'jis, n.* a freeman or citizen of a borough : a member of a privileged class in a town : (*hist.*) a member of parliament for a borough : (*hist.*) a borough magistrate or town councillor. [O.Fr. *burgeis.*]

burgh, *bur'ə,* another spelling for **borough,** used for Scottish burghs, otherwise archaic.—*adj.* burghal (*burg'l*).—*n.* burgher (*burg'ər*), a freeman or citizen of a borough (burgh) : a townsman : (*Scot. eccles.*) a Seceder who felt himself free to take the burgess oath (see **antiburgher**) : (*hist.*) a citizen of one of the South African Boer republics : in Ceylon, a Eurasian, or a person of European race assimilated to the native population.—**burgh of barony,** a corporation under a feudal superior or baron, who sometimes nominated the magistrates; **burgh of regality,** a burgh of barony enfranchised by crown charter, with regal or exclusive criminal jurisdiction within its territory; **parliamentary burgh,** one whose boundaries, as first fixed in 1832 for parliamentary representation, were adopted later for municipal purposes : a burgh which by itself or in combination elects a member of parliament : often applied to one that has ceased to do so; **police burgh,** a burgh constituted by the sheriff for purposes of improvement and police; **royal burgh,** a corporate body deriving its existence, constitution, and rights from a royal charter, actual or presumed to have existed. [See **borough.**]

burglar, *burg'lər, n.* one who breaks into a house by night to commit a felony, esp. to steal.—*v.t.* to rob or take as a burglar.—*v.i.* to commit burglary.

—*adj.* burglarious (*-lā'ri-əs*).—*adv.* burglār'-iously.—*v.t.* burg'larise, burg'le (a facetious back-formation).—*n.* burg'lary. [Ety. dub.]

burgomaster, *bur'gō-mäs-tər, n.* the chief magistrate of a Dutch, Flemish or German town. [Du. *burgemeester ;* Ger. *bürgermeister,* lit. borough-master.]

burgonet. See **burganet.**

burgoo, *bur-goo', bur'goo, n.* a sailors' dish of boiled oatmeal with salt, butter, and sugar : a stew or thick soup for American picnics. [Derivation unknown.]

burgrave, *bur'grāv, n.* the governor or hereditary ruler of a town or castle. [Ger. *burg-graf.*]

burgundy, *bur'gən-di, n.* a generous French wine (generally red), made in *Burgundy* : a similar wine made elsewhere.—**Burgundy mixture,** a fungicide composed of copper sulphate, sodium carbonate, and water; **Burgundy pitch,** a resin prepared by melting and straining the exudation from Norway spruce (now got mainly elsewhere).

burhel. Same as **bharal.**

burial, *ber'i-əl, n.* the act of burying : (*arch.*) a tomb.—*ns.* bur'ial-ground, a ground set apart for burials; bur'ial-place, a burial-ground : the place where anyone is buried.—**burial society,** an insurance society for providing the expenses of burial. [O.E. *byrgels,* a tomb; see **bury.**]

burin, *bur'in, n.* a kind of chisel of tempered steel, used in copper engraving : the distinctive style of an engraver.—*n.* bur'inist, an engraver. [Fr.; from root of **bore.**]

buriti, *boo-ri-tē', n.* the miriti palm. [Tupí.]

burke, *burk, v.t.* to murder, esp. by stifling : hence (*fig.*) to put an end to quietly. [From *Burke,* an Edinburgh Irishman (hanged 1829), who committed the crime in order to sell the bodies of his victims for dissection.]

burl, *burl, n.* a small knot in thread : a knot in wood. —*v.t.* to pick knots, etc., from, in finishing cloth.— *ns.* bur'ler ; bur'ling-i'ron ; bur'ling-machine'. —*adj.* bur'ly, knotty.

burlap, *bur'lap, n.* a coarse canvas for wrappings, wall-coverings, etc.—usually in *pl.* [Origin unknown.]

burlesque, *bur-lesk', n.* ludicrous imitation : a piece of literature, of acting, or other performance that mocks its original by grotesque exaggeration or by combining the dignified with the low or the familiar : (*mus.*) a playful or jocular composition.— *adj.* of the nature of burlesque : practising burlesque.—*v.t.* to mock by burlesque : to make a burlesque of. [It. *burlesco ;* prob. from L.L. *burra,* a flock of wool, a trifle.]

burletta, *bur-let'ä, n.* a musical farce : comic opera [It. ; dim. of *burla,* a jest.]

burly, *bur'li, adj.* big and sturdy.—*n.* bur'liness. [M.E. *borlich ;* perh. the same as O.H.G. *burlih,* high—*bōr,* a height.]

Burmese, *bur'mēz, -mēz', adj.* relating to *Burma* or its people or language.—*n.* a native of Burma : the language of Burma.—Also **Bur'man.**

burn, *burn, n.* (now chiefly *Scot.*) a small stream or brook.—*n.* burn'side, the ground beside a burn. [O.E. *burna,* brook, spring; cf. Du. and Ger. *born.*]

burn, *burn, v.t.* to consume or injure by fire or great heat : to produce an effect of heat upon (as to bake pottery, calcine lime, scorch food, wither grass) : to oxidise : to use (up), e.g. uranium, in a nuclear reactor; to corrode : to make by fire or analogous means.—*v.i.* to be burnt : to be on fire : to give out heat or light : to glow : to feel excess of heat : to be inflamed with passion : (*pa.t.* and *pa.p.* burnt or burned).—*n.* a hurt or mark due to burning.—*ns.* burn'er, one who burns : a fixture or part of a lamp or gas-jet from which a flame comes; burn'ing, act of consuming by fire : conflagration : inflammation : a quantity burned at one time.— *adj.* very hot : scorching : ardent : excessive.— Also *adv.*—*ns.* burn'ing-glass, a convex lens concentrating the sun's rays at its focus; burn'ing-house, a kiln; burn'ing-mirr'or, a concave mirror for producing heat by concentrating the sun's rays; burn'ing-point, the temperature at which a volatile oil in an open vessel will take fire

Neutral vowels in unaccented syllables : *el'ə-mənt, in'fənt, ran'dəm*

from a match held close to its surface; **burnt'-almonds** (*pl.*) almonds in burnt sugar; **burnt'-cork'**, charred cork used for blacking the face.—Also *v.t.*—*ns.* **burnt'-ear**, a smut in oats, wheat, etc.; **burnt'-off'ering**, something offered and burned upon an altar as a sacrifice; **burnt'-sienn'a** (see **sienna**); **burn'-the-wind** (*Scot.*), a blacksmith.—**burn a hole in one's pocket**, said of money when one is eager to spend it; **burn blue** (see **blue**); **burn daylight** (*Shak.*), to waste time; **burn down**, to burn to the ground; **burn in**, to fix and render durable by intense heat, to imprint indelibly: **burning bush**, the emblem of the Church of Scotland and other Presbyterian churches with the motto, 'Nec tamen consumebatur,' adopted from Exodus iii, 2, in memory of the unconquerable courage of the Covenanters under the cruel persecutions of the 17th century: applied to various plants, as dittany, whose volatile oil may catch fire in the air, some American species of spindle-tree with bright red fruits, artillery plant, etc.; **burning mountain**, a volcano; **burning question**, one keenly discussed; **burn one's boats**, to cut oneself off from all chance of retreat, to stake everything on success; **burn one's fingers**, to suffer from interfering, from embarking in speculations, etc.; **burn out**; to destroy or drive out by burning: to burn till the fire dies down from want of fuel; **burn the candle at both ends** (see **candle**); **burn the midnight oil**, to study late into the night; **burn the water**, to spear salmon by torchlight; **burn up**, to consume completely by fire: to be burned completely: to increase in activity of burning; **(money) to burn**, in great abundance. [O.E. the transitive weak verb *bærnan, bærnde, bærned*, has been confused with the intransitive strong verb *beornan, byrnan, barn, bornen*; cf. Ger. *brennen*, to burn.]

burnet, *bur'nit*, *adj.* (*obs.*) dark brown.—*n.* a fine dark woollen cloth of the Middle Ages: the name of two closely related rosaceous plants, the great burnet (*Sanguisorba officinalis* or *Poterium officinale*), a meadow-plant, and common or salad burnet (*P. Sanguisorba*) found on the chalk and sometimes used in salads, cool-tankard, etc., both with close aggregates of brownish-purple flowers.—**burnet moth** (or **burnet**). a moth of the Zygaenidae, esp. of the genus *Arthrocera*, with red-spotted or red-streaked fore-wings; **burnet (-leaved) rose**, a wild rose (*Rosa spinosissima*) with leaves like burnet, the Scotch rose; **burnet saxifrage**, a plant (*Pimpinella Saxifraga*) neither burnet-coloured nor a saxifrage but a green umbellifer akin to anise, with burnet-like leaves. [O.Fr. *burnete, brunette*; see **brunette**.]

burnettise, *bur'nit-īz*, *v.t.* to treat with Burnett's fluid, a solution of zinc chloride, a preservative for timber, etc., against dry-rot and insects, introduced by Sir William *Burnett* (1779-1861.).

burnish, *burn'ish*, *v.t.* to polish: to make bright by rubbing.—*n.* polish: lustre.—*ns.* **burn'isher**, an instrument employed in burnishing: one who burnishes; **burn'ishing**; **burn'ishment**. [Fr. *burnir, burniss-*, to burnish—*brun*, brown.]

burnous, *bur-nōōs'*, *n.* a mantle with a hood much worn by the Arabs. [Fr.,—Ar. *burnus.*]

Burnsian, *burnz'i-ən*, *adj.* pertaining to Robert *Burns* (1759-1796), the Scottish poet.—*n.* a student or admirer of Burns.—*n.* Burns'ite, a devotee of Burns.

burnt, *pa.t.* and *pa.p.* of **burn**.—Also *adj.*

burr. Same as **bur**.—**burrstone**, see **buhrstone**.

burramundi, *bur-ə-mun'di*, a variant of **barramunda**.

burrel, *bur'l*, *n.* a coarse russet cloth of mediaeval times. [See **bureau**.]

burrel, burrell. See **bharal**.

burro, *boor'ō*, *n.* a donkey. [Sp.]

burrow, *bur'ō*, *n.* a hole in the ground dug esp. by certain animals for shelter or defence: a passage, hole, or gallery dug or eaten through wood, stone, etc.: a refuge.—*v.i.* to make holes underground as rabbits: to work one's way through earth, etc.: to dwell in a concealed place.—*v.t.* to make a burrow in: to make by burrowing.—*ns* **burr'ow-**

duck, the sheldrake or bergander; **burr'owing-owl**, a small long-legged diurnal American owl nesting in burrows. [Prob. a variant of **borough**—O.E. *beorgan*, to protect.]

burrowstown, *bur'əs-toon*, *n.* (*Scot.*) a town that is a burgh. [**burgh**.]

bursa, *bur'sä*, *n.* (*zool.*) a pouch or sac, esp. one containing viscid lubricating fluid at points of friction.—*pl.* **bur'sae** (*-sē*).—*adj.* **bur'sal**, relating to a bursa: fiscal.—*n.* **bur'sar**, one who keeps the purse, a treasurer: in Scotland, a student or pupil maintained at a university or school by funds derived from endowment.—*adj.* **bursarial** (*-sā'ri-əl*).—*ns.* **bur'sarship**, the office of a bursar; **bur'sary**, in Scotland, an endowment for a pupil or student; **burse**, a purse: an obsolete form of **bourse**.—*adjs.* **bursic'ulate**, resembling a small pouch; **burs'iform**, pouch-shaped.—*n.* **bursi'tis**, inflammation of a bursa. [L.L. *bursa*, a purse—Gr. *byrsa*, skin or leather.]

bursch, *boorsh*, *n.* a German student:—*pl.* **bursch'en**.—*ns.* **bursch'enism**; **bursch'enschaft** (*-shäft*), a student's association. [Ger. *bursch*, a companion, student.]

Bursera, *bur'sər-ä*, *n.* a tropical American genus of trees yielding elemi and timber, giving name to the family **Burserā'ceae**, akin to the rue family.—*adj.* **bursērā'ceous**. [Named after Joachim *Burser* (1593-1689), German botanist.]

burst, *burst*, *v.t.* to break into pieces: to break open or cause to give way suddenly or by violence: to make by bursting.—*v.i.* to fly open or in pieces, esp. owing to a force from within: to give way suddenly: to break forth or away: to force a way: to break suddenly into being, or into some condition, activity, or expression of feeling: (*pa.t.* and *pa.p.* **burst**, *arch.*, *dial.*, and *U.S.* **burst'ed, bust'ed**; *pa.p.* **burst'en**).—*n.* an act, occasion, or result of bursting: a sudden outbreak: a hard gallop: a spurt: a drunken bout.—*ns.* **burst'er** (see also **buster**); **burst'-up**, a complete break: disruption: commotion: collapse: failure. [O.E. *berstan*; Ger. *bersten*.]

burthen, *bur'dhn*, *n.* and *v.t.* See **burden**, (1 and 2).

burton, *bur'tn*, *n.* a tackle of two or three blocks.

bury, *ber'i*, *v.t.* to hide in the ground: to cover: to consign to the grave, the sea, etc., as a dead body: to hide or blot out of remembrance:—*pr.p.* **bur'ying**; *pa.t.*, *pa.p.* **bur'ied**.—*ns.* **bur'ying-beetle**, a beetle (*Necrophorus* or kindred genus) that buries small animals as food for its larvae; **bur'ying-ground**, ground set apart for burying the dead: a graveyard; **bur'ying-place**; **bury the hatchet**, to renounce enmity. [O.E. *byrgan*, to bury; Ger. *bergen*, to hide.]

bus, 'bus, (*obs.* **buss**), **bus**, *n.* an omnibus: (*slang*) a heavy aeroplane:—*pl.* **bus'es**.—*ns.* **bus'-bar**, an electric conductor connecting with a number of circuits: **bus'boy, bus'girl** (*U.S.*), an assistant waiter or waitress; **bus'-fare**; **bus'man**, the driver or conductor of a bus.—**busman's holiday**, a holiday spent in activities similar to one's work; **miss the bus**, to lose an opportunity. [Short for **omnibus**.]

busby, *buz'bi*, *n.* a fur hat with a bag hanging on its right side, worn esp. by hussars. [Prob. Hung.]

bush, *boosh*, *n.* a woody plant in size between a tree and an undershrub: a shrub thick with branches: anything of bushy tuft-like shape: forest: wild uncultivated country (even though treeless): country covered with bushes: the wild: a bunch of ivy hung up as a tavern sign: a tavern.—*v.i.* to grow thick or bushy.—*v.t.* to use bushes about: to support with bushes: to cover (seeds) by means of the bush-harrow.—*ns.* **bush'-ba'by**, a small South African lemur (*Galago maholi*) also called night-ape; **bush'-buck**, a small S. African antelope, or any other of the same genus (Tragelaphus).—Also (Du.) **bosch-bok** (*bos'-bok*); **bush'-cat**, the serval; **bush'craft**, practical knowledge of the bush and skill in its ways.—*adj.* **bushed**, lost in the bush.—*ns.* **bush'-fruit**, a fruit growing on a bush, as gooseberry, raspberry; **bush'-harr'ow**, a light harrow for covering grass-seeds, formed of a barred frame interwoven with bushes or branches; **bush′iness**; **bush′man**, a settler in uncleared land: a woodsman: **Bushman**, one of a now almost extinct nomadic, stunted, yellowish-brown, aboriginal race of huntsmen in S. Africa—Cape Du. *Bos(jes)man.*—Also *adj.*—*ns.* **bush′manship**, bushcraft; **bush′master**, a venomous South American snake (*Lachesis muta*); **bush′ranger**, in Australia, a lawless person, often an escaped criminal, who takes to the bush and lives by robbery; **bush′-rope**, a liana; **bush′-shrike**, any bird of a sub-family of Formicariidae (ant-thrushes); **bush′-tit**, a small long-tailed titmouse of West America, building a large hanging-nest; **bush′veld, bosch′veld** (*bos′*), veld made up largely of woodland.—*v.i.* **bush′whack**, to range through the bush: to fight in guerilla warfare.—*ns.* **bush′whacker**, a guerilla fighter: a country lout: a short heavy scythe for cutting bushes; **bush′whack′ing**, the habits or practice of bush-whackers: the process of forcing a way for a boat by pulling at the bushes overhanging a stream.—*adj.* **bush′y**, full of or like bushes: thick and spreading.—**beat about the bush**, to go round about anything, to evade coming to the point. [M.E. *busk, busch*—O.N. *buskr*, from a Gmc. root found in Ger. *busch*, L.L. *boscus*, Fr. *bois.* Some uses are from the corresponding Du. *bosch.*]

bush, *boosh, n.* the metal box or lining of any cylinder in which an axle works.—*v.t.* to furnish with a bush.—*n.* **bush′-met′al**, hard brass, gun-metal, a composition of copper and tin, used for journals, bearings, etc. [Du. *bus*—L. *buxus*, box-tree.]

bushel, *boosh′l, n.* a dry measure of 8 gallons, for measuring grain, fruit, etc.: a container for this quantity. [O.Fr. *boissiel*, from the root of **box**.]

bushel, *boosh′l, v.t.* and *v.i.* (U.S.) to mend or alter, as men's clothes.—*ns.* **bush′eller**; **bush′elling**; **bush′el-man, -woman**. [Cf. Ger. *bosseln*.]

bushido, *boō′shi-dō, n.* a Japanese code of chivalry. [Jap.]

business, *biz′nis, n.* employment: trade, profession, or occupation: a task or errand incumbent or undertaken: matter requiring attention: dealings, commercial activity: a commercial or industrial concern: one's concerns or affairs: a matter or affair: (*theat.*) action as distinguished from dialogue: (*coll.*) a thing, used quite indefinitely: (*biz′i-nis*, also written **busyness**) state of being busy.—Also *adj.* (*biz′nis*).—*adj.* **bus′iness-like**, methodical, systematic, practical.—*n.* **bus′iness-man′**, one engaged in commercial transactions.—**do the business for**, to settle, make an end of: to ruin; **genteel business** (*theat.*), such parts as require good dressing; **make it one's business**, to undertake to accomplish something or see it done; **man of business**, a law agent who conducts one's affairs, **mean business**, to be in earnest; **mind one's own business**, to confine oneself to one's own affairs; **place of business**, the ordinary place for the practice of one's vocation; **send about one's business**, to dismiss promptly. [**busy**.]

busk, *busk, v.t.* or *v.i.* to prepare: to dress. [O.N. *búa*, to prepare, and *-sk*, contr. of *sik*, the refl. pron. self.]

busk, *busk, n.* the piece of bone, wood, or steel in the front of a woman's stays: a corset.—*adj.* **busked**. [Fr. *busc*.]

busk, *busk, v.i.* (*naut.*) to cruise along a shore, to beat about: to seek. [Prob. Sp. *buscar*, to seek.]

busket, *busk′et, n.* (*Spens.*) a little bush. [See **bush**.]

buskin, *busk′in, n.* a high thick-soled boot worn in ancient times by actors in tragedy.—*adj.* **busk′ined**, wearing buskins: tragic. [Ety. uncertain; cf. O.Fr. *brousequin*; Du. *brooseken*; Sp. *borcegui*.]

busky, *busk′i, adj.* (*Shak.*). Same as **bosky**.

buss, *bus, n.* a rude or playful kiss, a smack.—*v.t.* to kiss, esp. in a rude or playful manner. [Cf. Ger. dial. *buss*, W. and Gael. *bus*, L. *bāsium*.]

buss, *bus, n.* a small two-masted Dutch vessel, used in the herring and mackerel fisheries. [O.Fr. *busse*, L.L. *bussa*; cf. Ger. *büse*.]

bussu, *boos′oō, n.* a tropical American palm (*Manicaria*) with gigantic leaves and netted spathe that serves as cloth. [Port. from Tupi *bussú*.]

bust, *bust, n.* a sculpture representing the head and breast of a person: the upper front part of the human body, esp. a woman's.—*adj.* **bust′ed**, breasted: adorned with busts. [Fr *buste*; It. and Sp. *busto*.]

bust, *bust, n.* and *v.* a vulgar form of burst:—*pa.t.* and *pa.p.* **bust′ed**.—*ns.* **bust′er**, something large: a frolic: (*slang*) a roisterer: (*U.S.*) a horse-breaker: (*Austr.*) a stormy south wind: **bust′-up**, a burst-up.

bustard, *bust′ard, n.* any bird of the genus *Otis*, sometimes made the type of a large family, usually ranked with cranes. [Fr. *bistard*—L. *avis tarda*, slow bird (a misnomer).]

bustle, *bus′l, v.i.* to busy oneself noisily or fussily.—*n.* hurried activity: stir: tumult.—*n.* **bust′ler**. [M.E. *bustelen*, of doubtful relations.]

bustle, *bus′l, n.* a contrivance for causing a skirt to hang back from the hips. [Origin doubtful.]

busy, *biz′i, adj.* fully employed: active: diligent: meddling: fussily active.—*v.t.* to make busy: to occupy :—*pr.p.* **bus′ying**; *pa.t.* and *pa.p.* **bus′ied.**—*adv.* **bus′ily.**—*ns.* **bus′ybody**, one busy about others' affairs, a meddling person; **bus′yness**, state of being busy (some'imes used to distinguish from disyllabic **business**). [O.E. *bysig*.]

but, *but, prep.* (*obs.*) without: except: (*Scot.*) in or toward the outer room of.—*conj.* on the other hand: in contrast: nevertheless: unless, if not: otherwise than (that): except that (merging in *prep.*): that not (developing into a negative *rel. pron.*): (*arch.*) than, sooner than.—*adv.* only: (*Scot.*) in or to the outer room, outwards.—*n.* an objection (as in Mrs. Centlivre's 'But me no buts'): (*Scot.*) an outer room.—Also *adj.*—*v.t.* to put forward as an objection—**but and** (*obs.*), and also; **but and ben** (see **ben**); **but for, but that**, were it not for, or that; **but if** (*obs.*) unless: sometimes equivalent to but alone in various senses. [O.E. *be-útan, bútan*, without—*be*, by, and *útan*, out—near, and yet outside.]

but, *but, n.* Same as **butt**.

butadiene, *bū-tə-dī′ēn, n.* (L. *dis*, twice) a hydrocarbon, C_4H_6, used in making synthetic rubber.—*n.* **bu′tane**, a hydrocarbon of the methane series, C_4H_{10}. [**butyl**.]

butcher, *booch′ər, n.* one whose business is to slaughter cattle for food, or who deals in their flesh: one who delights in bloody deeds: (*U.S.*) a sweet-seller on a railway train.—*v.t.* to slaughter for food: to put to a bloody death, to kill cruelly: (*fig.*) to spoil, as a bad actor or the like.—*ns.* **butch′er-bird**, a shrike; **butch′ering, butch′ing** (back-formation), the act of killing for food, or cruelly.—*adv.* **butch′erly**, butcher-like, cruel, murderous.—*ns.* **butch′er('s) meat**, the flesh of animals slaughtered by butchers, as distinguished from fish, fowls and game; **butch′er's-broom**, an evergreen shrub (*Ruscus aculeatus*) of the lily family, with phyllodes, formerly used by butchers for sweeping their blocks; **butch′ery**, great or cruel slaughter: a slaughter-house or shambles. [O.Fr. *bochier, bouchier*, one who kills he-goats—*boc*, a he-goat; allied to Eng. **buck**.]

Butea, *būt′i-ä, n.* the dhak genus of papilionaceous trees, yielding Bengal kino. [Named after Lord *Bute*, prime minister and botanist.]

but-end. Same as **butt-end**.

butene, *bū′tēn, n.* butylene.

butler, *but′lər, n.* a servant who has charge of liquors, plate, etc.: an officer in a royal household.—*v.i.* to act as butler.—*ns.* **but′lerage**, (*obs.*) a duty on imported wine once paid to the king's butler: (*obs.*) the office of butler: a butler's department; **but′lership**; **but′lery**, the butler's pantry. [Norm. Fr. *butuiller*—L.L. *buticulārius.* See **bottle**.]

butment. Same as **abutment**.

butt, *but, v.i.* and *v.t.* to strike with the head, as a goat, etc.—*n.* a push or blow with the head.—*n.* **butt′er**, an animal that butts.—**butt in**, to interpose: thrust oneself in. [O.Fr. *boter*, to push, strike.]

butt, *but*, *n.* a large cask : a wine butt = 126 gallons, a beer and sherry butt = 108 gallons. [Cf. Fr. *botte*, Sp. *bota*, L.L. *butta*.]

butt, *but*, *n.* a mark or mound for archery practice : a mound behind targets : one who is made an object of ridicule : a hiding place for grouse-shooters.—*n.* **butt'-shaft** (*Shak.*), a shaft for shooting at butts with. [Fr. *but*, goal.]

butt, *but*, *n.* the thick and heavy end : the stump : a tree trunk : hinder part of a hide : thick leather : the fag-end of a cigar or cigarette : remnant : to square end of a plank meeting another.—*v.i.* to abut : to meet end to end.—*ns.* **butt'(ed)-joint**, a joint formed between the squared ends of the two jointing pieces, which come together but do not overlap; **butt'-end**. [Ety. dub.; prob. connected with **butt** (3) and **abut**.]

butt, *but*, *n.* a flat-fish of various kinds. [Cf. Sw. *butta*, turbot, Du. *bot.* flounder; and **halibut**, **turbot**.]

butte, *būt*, *n.* a conspicuous and isolated hill, cliff-sided, often flat-topped, in the western United States. [Fr.]

butter, *but'ər*, *n.* an oily substance obtained from cream by churning : extended to various substances resembling or containing it : an old chemical name for certain oily chlorides (butter of *antimony*, of *tin*, etc.) : flattery.—*v.t.* to spread over with butter, mortar, or other soft substance : to flatter : to fail to catch, let slip.—*ns.* **butt'er-bake** (*Scot.*), **-bis'cuit**, a cake like a biscuit but softer; **butt'er-bean**, an American bean akin to the French-bean; **butt'er-bird**, in Jamaica, the bobolink; **butt'er-boat**, a table vessel for melted butter; **butt'er-box**, a box for butter : an old nickname for a Dutchman; **butt'erbur**, **butt'er-dock**, a plant akin to coltsfoot with knobbed masses of flower heads and great rhubarb-like leaves; **butt'er-cloth**, **-mus'lin**, a loose-woven cloth suitable for wrapping butter; **butt'er-cool'er**, a dish for keeping butter in water at table; **butt'ercup**, a crowfoot (*Ranunculus*), esp. of one of those species that have golden-yellow cup-shaped flowers; **butt'er-dish**, **-plate**, a dish or plate for holding butter at table; **butt'er-fat'**, the fat contained in butter, chiefly glycerides of palmitic and oleic acids.—*adj.* **butt'er-fingered**, prone to let things slip.—*ns.* **butt'er-fingers**, (*sing.*) one who lets a ball, etc., he ought to catch slip through his fingers; **butt'er-fish**, a name for various slimy fishes, notably the gunnel; **butt'erfly**, a general name for any of the daylight Lepidoptera, roughly distinguished from moths by their clubbed antennae : (*fig.*) a gay, flighty person.—*pl.* **butt'er-flies.**—*adj.* light, flighty, like a butterfly.—*ns.* **butt'erfly-bow'**, a bow whose loops and ends are spread like butterfly's wings; **butt'erfly-fish'**, a blenny with an eye-spot on the dorsal fin : any fish of the family Chaetodontidae; **butt'erfly-flow'er**, one adapted for pollination by butterflies; **butt'er-fly-or'chis**, an orchid (of various kinds) with flowers resembling a butterfly; **butt'erfly-screw'**, **-nut'**, a screw or nut, turned by winged finger-grips; **butt'erfly-weed'**, pleurisy-root; **butt'er-ine** (*-ēn*), a margarine partly made from milk; **butt'er-knife**, a blunt knife for taking butter from a butter-dish; **butt'er-milk**, the milk that remains after the butter has been separated from the cream by churning; **butt'ernut**, the oily nut of the North American white walnut : the tree itself : its light-coloured close-grained wood : the souari-nut of Guiana; **butt'er-paper**, a translucent paper suitable for wrapping butter; **butt'er-pat'**, a pat of butter : a wooden instrument for working butter into shape; **butt'er-print'**, a stamp for shaping butter : (old *slang*) a child; **butt'er-scotch**, a kind of toffee containing much butter; **butt'er-tree**, a name for many trees that yield a buttery substance, notably of the genera *Bassia*, *Butyrospermum*, *Caryocar*, *Pentadesma*; **butt'er-wife**, **butt'er-wom'an**, a woman who makes and sells butter; **butt'erwort**, any species of Pinguicula, a genus of insectivorous bog-plants (family Lentibulariaceae) with glistening leaves.—*adj.* **butt'-ery**, like butter : smeared with butter or the like.—

buttered eggs, (*arch.*) scrambled eggs. [O.E. *butere*; Ger. *butter*; both from L. *būtȳrum*—Gr. *boutȳron* app.—*bous*, ox, *tȳros*, cheese.]

butter. See **butt** (1).

butter-bump, *but'ər-bump*, *n.* the bittern. [See **bittern**, and **bump** (2).]

buttery, *but'əri*, *n.* a domestic storeroom for provisions, esp. liquors.—*ns.* **butt'ery-bar'**, the ledge for holding tankards in the buttery; **butt'ery-hatch'**, a half-door over which provisions are handed from the buttery. [Fr. *bouteillerie*, lit. place for bottles; **butler**, **bottle**.]

buttock, *but'ək*, *n.* the rump or protuberant part of the body behind : in wrestling, a throw by use of the buttock.—*v.t.* to throw in this way.—*n.* **butt'ock-mail** (*Scot.*), the fine formerly exacted by the church in commutation of sitting on the stool of repentance. [Dim. of **butt**, end.]

button, *but'n*, *n.* a knob or disk, used as a fastening, ornament, or badge : a knob, e.g. that at the end of a foil, that for winding a watch, that to which a violin tailpiece is looped : a bud : the head of an unexpanded mushroom : a pimple : the knob of an electric bell, etc. : anything of small value : a person who acts as a decoy; (in *pl.*) sheep's dung : (*pl.* in form, treated as *sing.*) a page of livery (also **boy in buttons**).—*v.t.* to fasten by means of buttons : to close up tightly.—*v.i.* to admit of fastening with buttons.—*ns.* **butt'on-bush**, a North American shrub (*Cephalanthus*) of the madder family, having globular flower-heads; **butt'on-hole**, the slit through which a button is passed : a flower or flowers therein.—*v.t.* to make button-holes in : to work with a stitch suitable for defence of edges (*button-hole stitch*) : to detain in talk (orig. **butt'onhold**).—*ns.* **butt'on-hook**, a hook for pulling buttons through button-holes; **butt'on-wood**, a small tropical Atlantic coast evergreen tree (*Conocarpus erecta*) of the myrobalan family : (*U.S.*) a plane-tree—also **butt'on-ball**.—*adj.* **butt'ony**, set with buttons : like a button.—**button scurvy**, yaws; **in his buttons**, a conjectural reading in *Merry Wives* where the quarto has *betmes*, prob. a misprint for *talons*. [Fr. *bouton*, any small projection, from *bouter*, to push.]

buttress, *but'ris*, *n.* a projecting support built on to the outside of a wall : any support or prop.—*v.t.* to prop or support, as by a buttress.—*n.* **butt'ress-root**, a root, often adventitious, that helps to keep a plant upright. [App. O.Fr. *bouterez*—*bouter*, to push, bear against.]

butty, *but'i*, *n.* (*prov.*) a chum, comrade, workfellow, partner, esp. in a coal-mine : one who takes a contract for work in a coal-mine : a barge towed by another.—*ns.* **butt'y-coll'ier**; **butt'y-gang.** [App. dim. of prov. *butt*, a companion.]

butyric, *bū-tir'ik*, *adj.* pertaining to or derived from butter.—*ns.* **bū'tyl** (*-til*; Gr. *hȳlē*, matter) an alcohol radical, C_4H_9; **bū'tylene**, (also **bū'tene**), an olefine hydrocarbon (C_4H_8) in three isomers.—*adj.* **būtyrā'ceous**, buttery, containing butter.—*n.* **bū'tyrate**, a salt of butyric acid.—**butyric acid**, a volatile fatty acid ($C_3H_7 \cdot$ COOH), smelling like rancid butter. [See **butter**.]

buxom, *buks'əm*, *adj.* yielding, elastic : gay, lively, jolly : plump and comely.—*n.* **bux'omness.** [M.E. *buhsum*, pliable, obedient—O.E. *būgan*, to bow, yield, suff. *-some*.]

buy, *bī*, *v.t.* to purchase for money : to bribe : to obtain in exchange for something :—*pr.p.* **buy'ing**; *pa.t.* and *pa.p.* **bought** (*bawt*).—*adj.* **buy'able.**—*n.* **buy'er**, one who buys : one employed to buy goods.—**a good buy** (*coll.*), a wise purchase, a bargain; **buy and sell** (*Shak.*), to traffic in; **buy in**, to collect a stock of by buying : to buy back for the owner at an auction; **buy off**, to buy exemption or release for : to get rid of by paying; **buy out**, to dispossess entirely by payment : to buy off; **buy over**, to win over by payment; **buy up**, to purchase the whole stock of. [O.E. *bycgan*, *bohte*, *boht*; Goth. *bugjan*.]

buzz, *buz*, *v.i.* to make a noise like that of insects' wings : to murmur : (*slang*) to move quickly.—*v.t.* to utter with a buzzing sound : to whisper or spread secretly : to transmit by Morse over a

telephone wire by means of a key: (*slang*) to throw.
—*n.* the noise of bees and flies: a humming sound:
a voiced hiss: a whispered report.—*n.* **buzz′er**,
one who buzzes: (*Shak.*), a whisperer or tell-tale:
an apparatus that makes a buzzing sound, as a
hooter, a circular saw, or an electrical device for
signalling, etc.—*n.* and *adj.* **buzz′ing**.—*adv.* **buzz′-
ingly**.—*ns.* **buzz′-saw** (*U.S.*) a circular saw;
buzz′-wig, a great bushy wig.—*adj.* **buzz′y**.
[From the sound.]

buzz, *buz*, *v.t.* to drain to the last drop of wine.

buzzard, *buz′ərd*, *n.* a large bird of prey of the
genus *Buteo*, despised by falconers: extended to
some others, as the *honey-buzzard, turkey-buzzard*:
a blockhead, coward or sluggard. [Fr. *busard*.]

buzzard, *buz′ərd*, *n.* a blundering insect, as a cockchafer or night-flying moth: an ignorant blunderer
(often *blind buzzard*).—*n.* **buzz′ard-clock** (*dial.*)
a cockchafer. [**buzz**.]

bwana, *bwä′nä*, *n.* master: sir. [Swahili.]

by, *bī*, *prep.* at the side of: near to: along a route
passing through, via: past: in oaths, in the
presence of, or with the witness of: through (denoting the agent, cause, means, etc.): to the extent
of: in quantity measurable in terms of: in accordance with: in respect of: of time, not after: multiplied into, or combined with another dimension
of: in succession to (*Scot.*) besides: (*Scot.*) in
comparison with.—*conj.* (*arch.* and *Scot.*) by the
time that: (*Scot.*) than.—*adv.* near: aside: away:
past: in reserve.—*n.* and *adj.* see **bye**.—*adv.*
by′-and-by, at some future time: before long:
(*Spens.*) successively.—*ns.* **by′-blow**, a side blow:
an illegitimate child; **by′-cor′ner**, an out-of-the-
way place; **by′-drink′ing** (*Shak.*), drinking between meals; **by′-elec′tion**, a parliamentary election for a seat during the sitting of parliament:
by′-end, a subsidiary aim; **by′-form**, a subsidiary form: a form varying from the usual one;
by′-going, the action of passing by (esp. in **in
the by-going**, in passing).—*adj.* **by′gone** (*-gon*).—
n.pl. **by′gones**, past happenings or grievances.—*ns.*
by′-lane, a side lane or passage out of the common
road; **by′-mō′tive**, an unavowed motive; **by′-
name**, a nickname.—*adj.* **by′-ordinar** (*Scot.*)
extraordinary.—*n.* **by′-pass**, a side track for carrying traffic, fluids, electricity, etc., round an
obstruction or congested place.—*v.t.* to supply
with, conduct by, or pass by, a by-pass: to circumvent.—*n.* **by′-passage**, a side passage.—*adj.*
by′-past (*Shak.*), past: gone by.—*ns.* **by′path**, a
secluded or indirect path; **by′-place**, a retired
place; **by′play**, action subordinate to and apart
from the main action of a play; **by′-plot**, a subsidiary plot; **by′-product**, a product formed in the
process of making something else; **by′road**, a
retired side road, **by′-room** (*Shak.*), a side or
private room; **by′-speech**, a casual speech, **by′-
stander**, one who stands by or near one: a looker-
on; **by′-street**, an obscure street; **by′-thing**, a
thing of minor importance; **by′-time**, leisure time;
by′way, a private, secluded, or obscure way;
by′word, a common saying: a proverb: a term of
reproach: an object of common derision; **by′work**,
work for leisure hours.—**by and large** (*naut.*),
whether close-hauled or before the wind: (*U.S.*;
not a nautical use) speaking generally: on the
whole; **by the by(e)**, **by the way**, in passing:
incidentally; **let bygones be bygones**, let the
past be ignored. [O.E. *bī, bi, big*; Ger. *bei*, L.
ambi-.]

bycoket, *bī′kok-it*, *n.* a turned-up peaked cap
worn by noble persons in the 15th century—sometimes erroneously *abacot*. [O.Fr. *bicoquet*, prob.
bi- (L. *bis*), double, *coque*, a shell.]

bye, **by**, *bī*, *n.* anything of minor importance, a side
issue, a thing not directly aimed at: in games, the
state of one who has not drawn an opponent, and
passes without contest to the next round: in cock-
fighting, a battle not forming part of a main: in
golf, the holes remaining after the match is decided, played as a subsidiary game: in cricket, a
run made from a ball bowled but not struck or
touched by the batsman.—*adj.* subsidiary: apart:
indirect. See also by.

byke. Same as **bike** (1).

bylander. Same as **bilander**.

bylaw, bye-law, *bī′-law*, *n.* the law of a local
authority or private corporation: a supplementary
law or an inferred regulation. [The same as
byrlaw, from O.N. *bȳjar-lög*; Dan. *by-lov*, town-
law; from O.N. *búa*, to dwell. See **bower**.]

bylive (*Spens.*). Same as **belive**.

bynempt. See **bename**.

byre, *bīr*, *n.* (mainly *Scot.*) a cow-house.—*ns.*
byre′man, **byre′woman**, a farm-servant with
care of cows. [O.E. *bȳre*.]

byrlady, *bər-lā′di*, **byrlakin**, *bər-lā′kin*, (*arch.*) contractions for *By Our Lady, Ladykin*.

byrlaw, *bir′law*, *n.* a sort of popular jurisprudence
long surviving in Scotland in villages and among
husbandmen, concerning local matters in dispute.
—*n.* **byr′law-man** (*Scott* **bir′lieman**), an arbiter,
oddsman, or umpire in such matters. [See **bylaw**.]

byrnie, *bir′ni*, *n.* (*hist.*) a mail-coat: a breast-plate.
[A Scots form—O.N. *brynja*; O.E. *byrne*.]

byroad, bystander, byway, etc. See **by**.

Byronic, *bī-ron′ik*, *adj.* possessing the characteristics of Lord Byron (1788–1824), or of his poetry,
overstrained in sentiment or passion, cynical and
libertine.—*adv.* **Byron′ically**.—*n.* **By′ronism**
(*-rən-izm*).

byssus, *bis′əs*, *n.* a fine yellowish flax: linen made
from it (the 'fine linen' of the Bible): the bundle
of filaments by which some shellfish attach themselves.—*adjs.* **byssā′ceous**, composed of a mass
of fine threads: delicately filamentous; **byss′al**,
pertaining to a mollusc's byssus; **byss′ine**, made
of fine linen.—*n.* **byssinos′is**, an allergic lung
disease of cotton workers.—*adj.* **byss′oid**, byss-
aceous. [L.,—Gr. *byssos*, a fine flaxen substance.]

bytownite, *bī′town-īt*, *n.* a plagioclase intermediate
between anorthite and labradorite. [*Bytown*, now
Ottawa, where it occurs.]

bywoner, *bī′won-ər*, *bī′vōn-ər*, *n.* an authorised
squatter on another's farm: a poor white parasite.
[Du. *bijwonen*, to be present.]

byzant, *biz′ənt*, or *biz-ant′*. Same as **bezant**.

Byzantine, *biz-an′tīn*, or *bīz-an′tīn*, or *-tin*, or
biz ən-, *adj.* relating to *Byzantium* or Constantinople.—*n.* an inhabitant thereof.—*n.* **Byzan′tinism**,
manifestation of Byzantine characteristics.—**Byzantine architecture**, the style prevalent in the
Eastern Empire down to 1453, marked by the round
arch springing from columns or piers, the dome
supported upon pendentives, capitals elaborately
sculptured, mosaic or other incrustations, etc.;
Byzantine Church, the Eastern or Greek Church;
Byzantine Empire, the Eastern or Greek Empire
from 395 A.D. to 1453; **Byzantine historians**,
the series of Greek chroniclers of the affairs of the
Byzantine Empire down to its fall in 1453.

C

C, c, *sē*, *n.* the third letter of our alphabet, a rounded form of the Greek *gamma* (see **G**), which the Romans used instead of *k*, and in some languages came to have the sound of *s* or one like it : (*mus.*) name of one of the notes of the gamut, the sound on which the system is founded—the keynote of the natural scale, C major, having neither flats nor sharps : as a time-signature indicating common time : as a Roman numeral, C = 100.

ca', *kaw*, (*Scot.*) *v.t.* and *v.i.*, to call : to drive : to propel : to knock (with *down, off, over,* etc.).—*n.* **ca'ing-** or **caa'ing-whale,** a species of dolphin (*Globiocephalus melas*) often taken by ca'ing or driving ashore.—**ca' canny,** to go easy : deliberately to restrict output or effort. [**call.**]

caatinga, *kä-ä-ting'gä*, *n.* in Brazil, open, comparatively low forest, on white sandy soil derived from granite. [Tupí, white forest.]

cab, *kab*, *n.* a public carriage of various sizes and shapes, with two or four wheels, horse-drawn or motor-driven : the driver's shelter on a locomotive, motor-lorry, etc.—*ns.* **cabb'y,** familiar dim. of **cab'man,** one who drives a horse cab; **cab'-rank, cab'stand,** a place where cabs stand for hire; **cab'-runner, cab'tout,** one whose business it is to call cabs. [Shortened from **cabriolet.**]

cab, *kab*, *n.* a Hebrew dry measure nearly three pints. [Heb. *qab.*]

cabal, *kə-bal'*, *n.* a small party united for some secret design : the plot itself : a name in English history esp. given to five unpopular ministers of Charles II (1672), whose initials happened to make up the word.—*v.i.* to form a party for a secret purpose : to intrigue : (*pr.p.* **caball'ing**; *pa.t.* and *pa.p.* **caballed'**).—*n.* **caball'er.** [Fr. *cabale;* from Heb. *qabbalah;* see **cabbala.**]

caballero, *kä-bä-lyä'rō*, *n.* a Spanish gentleman. [Sp.,—L. *caballārius,* horseman—*caballus,* horse.]

caballine, *kab'ə-lin*, *adj.* pertaining to, or suited to, a horse. [L. *caballīnus*—*caballus,* a horse.]

cabaret, *kab'a-rā*, *n.* a restaurant with variety turns : the kind of entertainment there given. [Fr., tavern; prob. for *cabanaret*—*cabane,* a hut.]

cabas, caba, *kab'ä*, *n.* (*U.S.*) a woman's workbasket, reticule, or hand-bag. [Fr., flat basket.]

cabbage, *kab'ij*, *n.* a vegetable (*Brassica oleracea*) of the Cruciferae : the edible terminal bud of various palms.—*ns.* **cabb'age-butt'erfly, cabb'age-white,** a large white butterfly (*Pieris*) whose larvae injure the leaves of cabbage and kindred plants; **cabb'age-fly,** a fly (*Anthomyia brassicae*), whose maggots injure cabbage roots; **cabb'age-lett'uce,** a lettuce with cabbage-like head; **cabb'age-moth,** a moth (*Mamestra brassicae*) whose larva feeds on the cabbage; **cabb'age-palm, cabb'age-tree,** *Oreodoxa oleracea* or other palm with an edible cabbage; **cabb'age-rose,** a rose of bunchy cabbage-like form; **cabb'age-worm,** the larva of the cabbage-butterfly or of the cabbage-moth.—*adj.* **cabb'agy.**—**Kerguelen cabbage,** a wind-pollinated plant of the cabbage family growing on Kerguelen island. [Fr. *caboche,* head; cf. It. *capocchia,* augmentative—*capo,* head —L. *caput.*]

cabbage, *kab'ij* *v.t.* and *v.i.* to purloin, orig. of tailors who took portions of a customer's cloth as a perquisite.—*n.* cloth so appropriated.

cabbala, cabala, *kab'ə-lä*, *n.* a secret traditional lore, theological, metaphysical, and magical, of Jewish rabbis, who read hidden meanings into the Bible.—*ns.* **cabb'alism,** the science of the cabbala; **cabb'alist,** one versed in the cabbala.—*adjs.* **cabbalist'ic, -al,** relating to the cabbala : having

a hidden meaning. [Heb. *qabbālāh,* tradition, *qibbēl,* to receive.]

caber, *kāb'ər, kåb'ər*, *n.* a pole, generally the stem of a young tree, which is poised and tossed or hurled by Highland athletes. [Gael. *cabar.*]

cabin, *kab'in*, *n.* a hut or cottage : a small room, esp. in a ship, for officers or passengers.—*v.t.* shut up in a cabin.—*v.i.* to dwell in a cabin.—*n.* **cab'in-boy,** a boy who waits on the officers or cabin-passengers of a ship; **cab'in-pass'enger,** one entitled to superior accommodation; **cab'in-ship',** a ship carrying only one class of passengers. [Fr. *cabane*—L.L. *capanna.*]

cabinet, *kab'(i-)nit*, *n.* (*obs.*) a little cabin or hut : (*Shak.*) the bed or nest of a beast or bird : a small room, closet, or private apartment : a case for storing or displaying articles of value : a private room for consultation, esp. a king's : hence a select inner group of the ministers who govern a country.—*ns.* **cab'inet-coun'cil,** a council or consultation of the members of the Cabinet; **cab'inet-edi'tion,** one less in size and price than a library edition, but still elegant in format; **cab'inet-maker,** a maker of cabinets and other fine furniture; **cab'inet-making,** the occupation or art of the cabinet-maker : the getting together of a new set of cabinet-ministers; **cab'inet-min'ister,** a member of a cabinet; **cab'inet-pho'tograph,** one of the size larger than a carte-de-visite; **cab'inet-pudd'ing,** a cake-like pudding. [Dim. of **cabin**; cf. Fr. *cabinet.*]

Cabiri, *ka-bī'rī* (L. *kä-bē'rē*), *n.pl.* ancient mystic divinities whose cult spread from Lemnos, Samothrace, and Imbros—also **Cabei'ri.**—*adjs.* **Cabir'-ian, Cabir'ic.** [Latinised from Gr. *Kabeiroi.*]

cable, *kā'bl*, *n.* a strong rope or chain for hauling or tying anything, esp. a ship's anchor : a cable-laid rope : a cable-length : a line of submarine telegraph wires embedded in gutta-percha and encased in coiled strands of iron wire : a bundle of insulated wires laid underground : a cabled message. —Also *adj.*—*v.t.* and *v.i.* to provide with a cable, to tie up : to telegraph by cable.—*n.* **ca'blegram,** a telegram sent by cable.—*adj.* **ca'ble-laid,** composed of hawsers with a right-handed twist, twisted together to the left hand; **ca'ble-length, cable's-length,** a tenth of a nautical mile, approximately 200 yards.—*ns.* **ca'ble-mould'ing,** a bead or moulding carved in imitation of a thick rope; **ca'ble-tramway, -rail'way,** one along which cars or carriages are drawn by an endless cable; **ca'ble-way,** a structure for transport of material in cars suspended from a cable; **ca'bling,** a bead or moulding like a thick rope : the filling of flutes on a column with a moulding like a cable. [Fr.— L.L. *caplum,* a halter—L. *capēre,* to hold.]

cabob, *kə-bob'*, *n.* an Oriental dish of pieces of meat roasted with herbs : roast meat generally in India. [Ar. *kabāb.*]

caboceer, *kab-ō-sēr'*, *n.* a West African head-man. [Port. *cabeceira*—*cabo*—L. *caput,* head.]

caboched, caboshed, *kə-bosht'*, *adj.* (*her.*) in full face with no neck showing. [Fr. *caboché*—L. *caput,* head.]

cabochon, *ka-bō-shonᵉ*, *n.* a precious stone polished but uncut, or cut en (*änᵉ*) cabochon, i.e. rounded on top and flat on back, without facets—also *adj.* [Fr.,—*caboche*—L. *caput,* head.]

caboodle, *kə-bōō'dl*, *n.* (*slang*) crowd, collection. [Origin unknown.]

caboose, *kə-bōōs'*, *n.* a ship's kitchen : an open-air cooking stove : (*U.S.*) the brakeman's car on a goods train : a hut. [Du. *kombuis;* cf. Ger. *kabuse.*]

fāte, fär, åsk; mē, hər (her); *mïne; mōte; mūte; mōōn; dhen* (then)

cabrie, *kab'rē*, *n.* a prong-horn.—Also **cab'rit**. [Sp. *cabrito*, kid.]

cabré, *kä'brä*, *adj.* (*her.*) rearing : of an aeroplane, flying tail-down. [Fr.—*cabrer*, to caper.]

cabriole, *kab'ri-ōl*, *n.* a capriole—*adj.* (of furniture legs) curved, often like an animal's paw.—*n.* **cabriolet** (*-lā'*), a light carriage with two wheels : (after 1830) a cab : a type of motor-car like a coupé, with folding top : a small armchair of curved design (18th century). [Fr.—L. *capra*, a goat.]

cacafogo, *kak-ə-fō'gō*, **cacafuego**, *-fū'gō* (Sp. *kä-kä-fwä'gō*), *n.* (*obs.*) a spitfire, blusterer. [Sp. *cagar*, to void excrement, Port. *fogo*, Sp. *fuego*, fire.]

cacao, *kä-kä'ō*, *kä-kā'ō*, *n.* the tropical American tree *Theobroma Cacao* (family *Sterculiaceae*) or its seeds from which cocoa and chocolate are made. [Mex. *cacauatl*, cacao tree.]

cachaemia, *ka-kē'mi-ä*, *n.* a morbid state of the blood.—*adj.* **cachae'mic**. [Gr. *kakos*, bad, *haima*, blood.]

cachalot, *kash'ə-lot*, or *-lō*, *n.* the sperm-whale. [Fr.]

cache, *kash*, *n.* a hiding-place for treasure, provisions, ammunition, etc. : stores so hidden.—*v.t.* to hide.—*n.* **cache-pot** (*käsh'pō*, *-pot*), an ornamental flower-pot enclosing a common one. [Fr. *cacher*, to hide.]

cachet, *käsh'ā*, *n.* a seal : any distinctive stamp : a capsule enclosing a medicine.—**lettre de cachet** (*hist.*), a letter under the private seal of the king of France, by which his pleasure was made known to individuals, and the administration of justice often interfered with. [Fr.]

cachexy, cachexia, *ka-kek'si*, *-ä*, *n.* a bad state of body : a depraved habit of mind.—*adjs.* **cachec'-tic, -al.** [L.—Gr. *kachexiā—kakos*, bad, *hexis*, condition, from the root of *echein*, to have.]

cachinnate, *kak'in-āt*, *v.i.* to laugh loudly.—*n.* **cachinna'tion.**—*adj.* **cachinn'atory** (or *kak'*). [L. *cachinnāre*, to laugh loudly.]

cacholong, *kach'o-long*, *n.* a variety of quartz or of opal, generally of a milky colour. [Fr. from Kalmuk.]

cacholot. Same as **cachalot**.

cachou, *kä-shōō'*, *n.* a pill or lozenge of extract of liquorice, cashew-nut, or the like, used by some smokers in the hope of sweetening the breath. [Fr.]

cachucha, *kä-chōō'chä*, *n.* a lively Spanish dance in 3-4 time, like the bolero. [Sp.]

cacique, *kä-sēk'*, *n.* a West Indian chief : a political boss. [Haitian.]

cackle, *kak'l*, *n.* the sound made by a hen or goose : talk or laughter of similar sound or value.—*v.i.* to make such a sound.—*n.* **cack'ler**, a fowl or person that cackles. [M.E. *cakelen*; cog. with Du. *kakelen*.]

cacodaemon, cacodemon, *kak-ō-dē'mən*, *n.* an evil spirit : (*Shak.*) a nightmare. [Gr *kakos*, bad, *daimōn*, spirit.]

cacodoxy, *kak'ō-dok-si*, *n.* bad doctrine, wrong opinion, heterodoxy. [Gr. *kakos*, bad, *doxa*, an opinion.]

cacodyl, *kak'ō-dil*, *n.* a colourless stinking liquid, composed of arsenic, carbon, and hydrogen. [Gr. *kakōdēs*, stinking, *hȳlē*, matter.]

cacoethes, *kak-ō-ē'thēz*, *n.* a bad habit or itch. [Gr. *kakoēthēs, -ēs*, ill-disposed—*kakos*, bad, *ēthos*, habit.]

cacogastric, *kak-ō-gas'trik*, *adj.* pertaining to a disordered stomach, dyspeptic. [Gr. *kakos*, bad, *gastēr*, the belly.]

cacography, *kak-og'rə-fi*, *n.* bad hand-writing or spelling.—*adj.* **cacographic** (*-ō-graf'ik*). [Gr. *kakos*, bad, and *graphē*, writing.]

cacolet, *kāk'ō-lā*, *n.* a military mule-litter. [Fr., prob. from Basque.]

cacology, *ka-kol'ə-ji*, *n.* faulty vocabulary or pronunciation. [Gr. *kakos*, bad, *logos*, speech.]

cacoon, *ka-kōōn'*, *n.* the large seed of a tropical climber (*Entada scandens*) of the mimosa family, used for making scent-bottles, snuff-boxes, etc. : the purgative and emetic seed of a tropical Ameri-

can climber (*Fevillea cordifolia*) of the gourd family. [Origin doubtful.]

cacophony, *ka-kof'ə-ni*, *n.* a disagreeable sound : discord of sounds.—*adjs.* **cacoph'onous, cacophonic** (*-ō-fon'ik*), **-al, cacophonious** (*-fō'ni-əs*), harsh-sounding. [Gr. *kakos*, bad, *phōnē*, sound.]

cacotrophy. *ka-kot'rə-fi*, *n.* bad nourishment. [Gr. *kakos*, bad, *trophē*, nourishment.]

cactus, *kak'tus*, *-təs*, *n.* a name given to any plant of the American family Cactaceae (now divided into several genera), fleshy xerophytes whose stems store water and do the work of leaves, which are generally reduced to spines.—*pl.* **cac'tī** or **cac'tuses.**—*adjs.* **cactā ceous, cac'tiform.** [L.,— Gr. *kaktos*, a prickly plant found in Sicily.]

cacumen, *ka-kū'men*, *n.* a top or point.—*adjs.* **cacū'minal**, pertaining to the top : (*phon.*) produced by turning the tip of the tongue up and back; **cacū'minous**, with pointed or pyramidal top. [L. *cacūmen, -inis*.]

cad, *kad*, *n.* (*obs.*) an inferior assistant : (*obs.*) a hanger-on, tavern-yard loafer, or errand-runner : (*obs.*) a bus-conductor : (*obs.*) a passenger taken by a conductor for his own profit : a townsman (at Oxford) : a low vulgarian : one who lacks the instincts of a gentleman.—*adj.* **cadd'ish.**—*n.* **cadd'ishness.** [Short for **cadet**.]

cadastral, *ka-das'trəl*, *adj.* pertaining to a **cadas'tre** or public register of the lands of a country for fiscal purposes : applied also to a survey on a large scale. [Fr.—L.L. *capitastrum*, register for a poll-tax— L. *caput*, the head.]

cadaverous, *kə-dav'ə-rəs*, *adj.* corpse-like : sickly-looking : gaunt, haggard.—*n.* **cadāv'er** (*surg.* and *anat.*), a corpse.—*adj.* **cadāv'eric.**—*n.* **cadāv'er-ousness.** [L. *cadāver*, a dead body—*cadēre*, to fall (dead).]

caddie, caddy, *kad'i*, *n.* one who attends a golfer at play, carrying the clubs : (18th cent.) a messenger or errand porter in Edinburgh.—*v.i.* to carry clubs. [See **cadet**.]

caddis, *kad'is*, *n.* (*Shak.* **caddyss**) worsted ribbon. [O.Fr. *cadaz, cadas*, tow.]

caddis, caddice, *kad'is*, *n.* the larva of the **cadd'is**-**fly** (*Phryganea*) or other insect of the Trichoptera, which lives in water in a **cadd'is-case**, a silken sheath covered with fragments of wood, stone, shell, leaves, etc., open at both ends.—Also **cadd'is**-**worm**. [Origin obscure.]

caddy, *kad'i*, *n.* a small box for holding tea. [Malay *kati*, the weight of a small packet of tea.]

cade, *kād*, *n.* a barrel or cask. [Fr.—L. *cadus*, a cask.]

cade, *kād*, *n.* and *adj.* a lamb or colt brought up by hand, a pet lamb. [Ety. unknown.]

cadence, *kā'dəns*, *n.* (*Milton*) falling, sinking : the fall of the voice : rise and fall of sound, modulation : rhythm : a succession of chords closing a musical period (**perfect cadence**, chord on the tonic preceded by dominant or sub-dominant; **imperfect cadence**, finishing on dominant chord).—*adj.* **cā'denced**, rhythmical.— *n.* **cā'dency**, rhythm : (*her.*) the relative status of younger sons.—*adj.* **cā'dent** (*Shak.*), falling.—*n.* **caden'za** (*kā-dent'sä, kə-den'zä*), a flourish given by a solo voice or instrument towards the end or at some important stage of a movement. [Fr. *cadence*, It. *cadenza*—L. *cadēre*, to fall.]

cadet, *kə-*, *ka-det'*, *n.* a younger son : a member of the younger branch of a family : one studying or qualifying for a commission in the army, navy, or other service, or (formerly) in the East India Company's service : a boy undergoing training for one of the armed forces : in New Zealand, a newcomer gaining experience.—*n.* **cadet'ship.**— **cadet corps**, an organised body of boys undergoing military training. [Fr. *cadet*, formerly *capdet*—dim. of L. *caput*, the head.]

cadge, *kaj*, *v.t.* and *v.i.* to beg or go about begging : to sponge.—*n.* **cadg'er**, a carrier who collects country produce for disposal : a hawker : a fellow who picks up his living about the streets. [Prob. conn. with **catch**.]

cadge, *kaj*, *n.* a padded wooden frame on which a number of hawks may be carried. [Prob. **cage**; perh. **cadge** (1).]

cadgy, *kaj'i*, *adj.* (*prov.*) cheerful and friendly: folicsome : wanton. [Cf. Dan. *kaad*, wanton, O.N. *kátr*, merry.]

cadi, *kä'di*, *kā'di*, *n.* a magistrate in Mohammedan countries. [Ar. *qādī*, a judge.]

Cadmean, *kad-mē'ən*, *adj.* relating to *Cadmus* (Gr. *Kadmos*), who introduced the original Greek alphabet.

cadmium, *kad'mi-um*, *n.* the element of atomic number 48, a white metal, occurring in zinc ores. [Gr. *kadmiā*, *kadmeiā* (*gē*), Cadmean (earth), calamine.]

cadrans, *kad'rənz*, *n.* an instrument by which a gem is adjusted while being cut. [Fr. *cadran*, a quadrant.]

cadre, *kad'r'*, *kä'dər*, *n.* a nucleus, framework, esp. the permanent skeleton of a military unit, the commissioned and non-commissioned officers, etc., around whom the rank and file may be quickly grouped. [Fr.]

caduac, *kad'ū-ak*, *n.* a casualty or windfall. [Scot. —L. *cadūcum*.]

caduceus, *ka-dū'si-us*, *n.* (*myth.*) the rod of Hermes, messenger of the gods—a wand surmounted with two wings and entwined by two serpents :—*pl.* **cadū'cei.**—*adj.* **cadū'cean.** [L. *cādūceus*, akin to Gr. *kērȳkeion*, a herald's wand—*kēryx*, -*ykos*, a herald.]

caducibranchiate, *ka-dū-si-brang'ki-āt*, *adj.* losing the gills on attaining maturity. [L. *cadūcus*, caducous, *branchiae*, gills.]

caducous, *ka-dū'kəs*, *adj.* falling early, as leaves or flowers : (*Rom. law*) lapsing.—*n.* **caducity** (*ka-dū'si-ti*), transitoriness, senility : lapse. [L. *cadūcus—cadēre*, to fall.]

Caecilia, *sē-sil'i-ä*, *n.* a genus of legless burrowing Amphibia with hidden eyes.—*adj.* **caecil'ian.**—*n.* any member of the class to which Caecilia belongs. [L. *caecus*, blind.]

caecum, *sē'kum*, *n.* a blind sac : a sac or bag having only one opening, connected with the intestine of an animal :—*pl.* **cae'ca.**—*adj.* **cae'cal.** [L., neut. of *caecus*, blind.]

caen-stone, *kä'ən-stōn*, *n.* a cream-coloured limestone brought from Caen (*kän'*) in France.

caerulean. Same as **cerulean.**

Caesalpinia, *ses-*, *sēz-al-pin'i-ä*, *n.* a genus, including brazil-wood and divi-divi, giving name to a family **Caesalpinia'ceae** of leguminous plants. [Named after Andrea *Cesalpino* (1519-1603), botanist.]

Caesar, *sē'zər*, *n.* an absolute monarch, an autocrat, from the Roman dictator Gaius Julius *Caesar* (100-44 B.C.).—*adj.* **Caesarean, -ian** (-*ā'ri-ən*), relating to Julius Caesar.—*n.* an adherent of Caesar, an imperialist.—*ns.* **Cae'sarism ; Cae'sarist ; Cae'sarship.**—**Caesarean operation, section,** the delivery of a child by cutting through the walls of the abdomen, as is improbably said to have been the case with Julius Caesar or an ancestor.

caesium, *sēz'i-əm*, *n.* the element of atomic number 55, a silver-white, soft, and extensile alkaline metal, with blue lines in its spectrum, discovered by Bunsen and Kirchoff in 1860 by spectrum analysis.—*adj.* **caes'ious**, bluish or greyish green. [L. *caesius*, bluish grey.]

caespitose, *sēs'pi-tōs*, *adj.* tufted : turf-like. [L. *caespes, -itis*, turf.]

caesura, cesura, *si-zū'rä*, *n.* (*pros.*) division of a foot between two words : a pause in a line of verse (generally near the middle).—*adj.* **caesū'ral.** [L. *caesūra—caedēre, caesum*, to cut off.]

café, *kaf'ā*, *n.* a coffee-house, a restaurant. [F.]

cafeteria, *ka-fi-ti-rē'ä* (also -*tē'ri-ä*), *n.* a coffee-stall, a restaurant with a counter for self-service. [Cuban Span. *cafetería*, a tent in which coffee is sold.]

caffeine, *kaf'i-ēn*, or *kaf-ē'in* (or -*īn*), *n.* theine, an alkaloid present in coffee and tea.—*n.* **caff'e-(in)ism**, a morbid state caused by caffein.—

caff'elite, a plastic made from coffee. [Fr. *caféine;* see **coffee.**]

caffre. See **kaffir.**

caftan, *kaf-tän'*, *kaf'tən*, *n.* a long-sleeved Persian or Turkish garment. [Turk. *qaftān.*]

cage, *kāj*, *n.* a box or compartment wholly or partly of open work for captive animals : (*obs.*) a prison : a frame with a platform or platforms used in hoisting in a vertical shaft : the framework supporting a peal of bells : a wire-guard : any structure resembling a bird's cage : (*prov.*) a squirrel's nest.—*v.t.* to imprison in a cage :—*pr.p.* **cag'ing ;** *pa.t.* and *pa.p.* **caged.**—*adj.* **caged,** confined.—*ns.* **cage'bird**, a bird of a kind habitually kept in a cage ; **cage'ling**, a bird that is or has been kept in a cage ; **cage'work**, open work like the bars of a cage. [Fr.,—L. *cavea*, a hollow place.]

cagot, *käg'ō*, *n.* one of an outcast class found scattered in the western Pyrenees, supposed to be the descendants of lepers. [Fr.; origin unknown.]

cahoot, *kə-hōōt'*, *n.* (*U.S.*) company or partnership.

cailleach, *käl'yahh*, *n.* an old woman.—Also **caillach, cailliach.** [Gael. *cailleach.*]

caimac, caimacam. See **kaimakam.**

caiman. Same as **cayman.**

Cain, *kān*, *n.* Adam's son, murderer of Abel (Gen. iv), hence allusively a murderer.—*adj.* **Cain'-col'oured** (*Shak.*), of the traditional colour of Cain's beard and hair, red.—*n.* **Cain'ite**, a descendant of Cain : a member of a 2nd century set of Gnostics who revered Cain and Judas.—**raise Cain**, to make a determined or angry fuss.

cain, kain, *kān*, *n.* in old Scots law, rent paid in kind, esp. in poultry, etc. : tribute.—*n.* **cain'-hen**, a hen given up as cain.—**pay the cain**, to pay the penalty. [Ir. and Gael. *cáin*, rent, tax.]

ca'ing-whale. See **ca'.**

Cainozoic, *kī-nō-zō'ik*, *adj.* and *n.* (*geol.*) Tertiary. [Gr. *kainos*, new, *zōē*, life.]

caique, *kä-ēk'*, *n.* a light skiff used on the Bosporus : the skiff of a galley. [Fr.,—Turk. *kaik*, a boat.]

caird, *kārd*, *n.* a tramping tinker, a gypsy, a vagrant. [Gael. and Ir. *ceard.*]

cairn, *kārn*, *n.* a heap of stones, esp. one raised over a grave, or as a landmark on a mountain-top or path : a small variety of Scottish terrier (in full **cairn terrier**) suitable for driving foxes from their earths among cairns.—*n.* **cairngorm' (-stone),** brown or yellow quartz found among the Cairngorm Mountains. [Gael. *càrn.*]

caisson, *kā'sən*, *kə-sōōn'*, *n.* a tumbril or ammunition wagon : a chest of explosive materials : a strong case for keeping out the water while the foundations of a bridge are being built : an apparatus for lifting a vessel out of the water for repairs or inspection : the pontoon or floating gate used to close a dry-dock.—**caisson disease,** bends, a disease affecting divers, caisson-workers, etc., who are too suddenly subjected to atmospheric pressure ; it is due to formation of nitrogen bubbles in the tissues while under reduced air-pressure. [Fr., from *caisse*, a case or chest. [See **case.**]

caitiff, *kā'tif*, *n.* a mean despicable fellow.—*adj.* mean, base.—*n.* **cai'tive** (*Spens.*), captive, subject. [O.Fr. *caitif* (Fr. *chétif*)—L. *captīvus*, a captive—*capēre*, to take.]

cajole, *kə-jōl'*, *v.t.* to coax : to cheat by flattery.—*ns.* **cajole'ment**, coaxing for the purpose of deluding : wheedling language : flattery ; **cajol'er ;** **cajol'ery.** [Fr. *cajoler*, to chatter; ety. dub.]

cajuput, *kaj'ə-put*, *n.* a pungent, volatile, aromatic oil, distilled from the leaves of an Indo-Malayan and Australian myrtaceous tree *Melaleuca Leucodendron.*—Also **caj'eput.** [Malay.]

cake, *kāk*, *n.* a piece of dough that is baked : a small loaf of fine bread : any flattened mass baked, as **oat-cake** (whence Scotland has been called the 'Land of Cakes'), or formed by pressure or drying, as of soap, clay, snow, blood : a breadlike composition enriched with additions such as sugar, spices, currants, peel, etc. : a separately made mass of such composition : (*slang*) a madcap or fool.—*v.t.* and *v.i.* to form into a cake or hard mass.—*n.* and *adj.* **cāk'ing.**—*n.* **cake'-walk**, a prancing movement performed by American negroes in competition for a *cake*: a dance developed therefrom: music for the dance.—*v.i.* to perform a cake-walk or execute similar movements.—*adj.* **cak'y.**—**cakes and ale**, vaguely, all the good things of life; **caking coal**, a bituminous coal that fuses into a mass in burning; **eat one's cake and have it**, to have the advantage of both alternatives; **his cake is dough**, his hope has failed; **take the cake** (*slang*), to carry off the honours, rank first (ironically). [O.N. *kaka*, cog. with Ger. *kuche*(*n*), Du. *koek*.]

Calabar-bean, *kal-ə-bär'-bən*, or *kal'*, *n.* the seed of the tropical African *Physostigma venenosum* (*Papilionaceae*), used in emulsion in witchcraft ordeal, the accused being acquitted if he can vomit the poison.

calabash, *kal'ə-bash*, *n.* a gourd, or its shell used as a vessel, tobacco-pipe, etc.: the fruit of the calabash tree or its shell similarly used.—**calabash nutmeg**, the fruit of a tropical anonaceous tree *Monodora myristica*, whose seeds are used as nutmegs; **calabash tree**, a bignoniaceous tree of tropical America (*Crescentia Cujete*) with large melon-like fruit. [Fr. *calebassse*—Sp. *calabaza*—Pers. *kharbuz*, melon.]

calaboose, *kal'ə-bōōs*, *bōōs'*, *n.* (*U.S.*) a prison. [Sp. *calabozo*.]

Caladium, *kal-ā'di-um*, *n.* an American genus of plants of the arum family, with edible starchy root-stocks. [Latinised from Malay *kélády*, a kindred plant.]

calamanco, *kal-ə-mangk'ō*, *n.* a satin-twilled woollen stuff, checkered or brocaded in the warp. [Du. *kalamink*, Ger. *kalmank*, Fr. *calmande*; origin unknown.]

calamander, *kal-ə-man'der*, *n.* a hard and valuable cabinet-wood of the ebony genus, brownish with black stripes, brought from India and Ceylon. [Prob. Sinh.]

calamary, *kal'ə-mər-i*, *n.* a squid. [L. *calamārius*—*calamus*—Gr. *kalamos*, pen, from its internal shell.]

calamine, *kal'ə-mīn*, *-min*, *n.* a mineral, zinc carbonate (smithsonite): in *U.S.*, hydrous zinc silicate (hemimorphite, or electric calamine). [Fr.—L.L. *calamīna*, prob.—L. *cadmia*; see **cadmium**.]

calamint, *kal'ə-mint*, *n.* a genus (*Calamintha*) of labiate plants allied to mint and thyme. [Fr.—Gr. *kalaminthē*, some related plant.]

calamite, *kal'ə-mīt*, *n.* a general name for a family of fossil plants abundant in the Coal-Measures, gigantic trees related to horse-tails. [L. *calamus*, a reed.]

calamity, *kə-lam'i-ti*, *n.* a great misfortune: affliction.—*adj.* **calam'itous**, making wretched, disastrous.—*adv.* **calam'itously.**—*n.* **calam'itousness.** [Fr. *calamité*—L. *calamitās*, *-ātis*.]

calamus, *kal'ə-mus*, *n.* the traditional name of the sweet-flag: the reed pen used by the ancients in writing: (*zool.*) a quill: **Calamus**, a genus of palms whose stems make canes or rattans :—*pl.* **cal'ami**. [L.—Gr. *kalamos*, reed, cane, pen.]

calando, *kä-län'dō*, *adj.* and *adv.* (*mus.*) gradually slower with diminishing volume of tone. [It., falling off.]

calash, *kə-lash'*, *n.* a light low-wheeled carriage with a folding top: a hood with hoops formerly worn by ladies over the cap. [Fr. *calèche*; of Slav. origin.]

calavance, *kal'ə-vans*, *n.* a name for certain varieties of pulse.—Also **car'avance**. [Sp. *garbanzo*, chick-pea, said to be Basque *garbantzu*.]

calcaneum, *kal-kā'ni-əm*, *n.* the heel-bone.—*adjs.* **calcā'neal**, **calcā'nean**. [L. *calcāneum*, the heel—*calx*, the heel.]

calcar, *kal'kär*, *n.* (*biol.*) a spur or spur-like projection, esp. from the base of a petal: a bird's spur: the prehallux: the hippocampus minor or **calcar ā'vis** (bird's spur) in the brain.—*adjs.* **cal'carate** ; **calcar'iform** ; **cal'carine**. [L., a spur—*calx*, the heel.]

calcar, *kal'kär*, *n.* a fritting furnace, an oven or furnace for calcining the materials of frit before melting: an arch or oven for annealing. [L. *calcāria*, a lime-kiln.]

calcareous, *kal-kā'ri-əs*, *adj.* chalky : limy. [L. *calcārius*, from *calx*, lime.]

calceamentum, *kal-si-ə-men'tum*, *n.* a red silk embroidered sandal forming part of the insignia of the Holy Roman Empire. [L. *calceāmentum*, a shoe.]

calced, *kalst*, *adj.* shod, wearing shoes—opp. to *discalced*—of Carmelites.—*v.t.* **cal'ceate**, to shoe.—*adjs.* **cal'ceate**, **-d**, shod; **cal'ceiform**, **cal'ceolate**, slipper-shaped. [L.L. *calceus*, a shoe—*calx*, the heel.]

calcedony. See **chalcedony**.

Calceolaria, *kal-si-ō-lā'ri-ä*, *n.* a South American genus of Scrophulariaceae, largely cultivated for the beauty of the slipper-like flowers. [L. *calceolus*, dim. of *calceus*, a shoe.]

calcium, *kal'si-əm*, *n.* the metal present in lime, chalk, gypsum, etc.—*adjs.* **cal'cic**, containing calcium; **cal'cicole**, **calcic'olous**, growing on limestone or limy soils.—*n.* **calcif'erol**, vitamin D₂ (*calciferous* and *ergosterol*).—*adjs.* **calcif'erous**, containing lime; **cal'cific**, calcifying or calcified.—*n.* **calcificā'tion**, the process of calcifying, a changing into lime.—*adjs.* **cal'cifuge** (*-fūj*), **calcif'ugous** (*-ū-gəs*), avoiding limestone.—*v.t.* and *v.i.* **cal'cify**, to make or become limy, by secretion, deposition, or substitution.—*adjs.* **calcig'erous** (*-sij'ə-rəs*), containing lime; **cal'cinable**.—*n.* **calcinā'tion.**—*v.t.* **cal'cine** (or *-sīn'*), to reduce to a calx by the action of heat : to subject to prolonged heating, esp. so as to oxidise, or so as to drive off water and carbon dioxide.—*v.i.* to become calx or powder by heat.—*ns.* **cal'cite**, **calcspar** (*kalk'spär*), a mineral, calcium carbonate crystallised in the hexagonal system; **calc'sinter**, **calc'-tuff**, travertine, a porous deposit from springs charged with calcium carbonate.—**Calciferous Sandstone**, the lowermost group of Carboniferous rocks in Scotland, answering to part of the English Carboniferous Limestone. [L. *calx*, *calcis*, lime, limestone.]

calculate, *kal'kū-lāt*, *v.t.* to count or reckon : to think out, esp. mathematically : (*U.S.*) to think, purpose, suppose.—*v.i.* to make a calculation : to estimate.—*adj.* **cal'culable**—*p.adjs.* **cal'culāted**, thought out : reckoned : computed : (now *rare*) fitted, likely, of such a nature as probably; **cal'culating**, given to forethought : deliberately selfish and scheming.—*n.* **calculā'tion**, the art or process of calculating : estimate : forecast.—*adj.* **cal'culative**, relating to calculation.—*n.* **cal'culātor**, one who calculates : a book, table, or machine for obtaining arithmetical results.—**calculating machine**, a machine for obtaining arithmetical results without calculation. [L. *calculāre*, *-ātum*, to reckon by help of little stones—*calculus*, dim. of *calx*, a stone.]

calculus, *kal'kū-lus*, *n.* a stone-like concretion which forms in certain parts of the body (*pl.* **cal'culī**) : a system of computation used in the higher branches of mathematics (*pl.* **cal'culuses**).—*adjs.* **cal'cular**, pertaining to the mathematical calculus; **cal'culary**, **cal'culose**, **cal'culous**, pertaining to or affected with stone or with gravel.—**calculus of finite differences** is concerned with changes in functions due to finite changes in variables—it does not assume continuity; **differential calculus**, a method of treating the values of ratios of differentials or the increments of quantities continually varying; **integral calculus**, the summation of an infinite series of differentials. [L.; see foregoing.]

caldera, *käl-dā'rä*, *n.* (*geol.*) a volcanic crater of great size. [Sp., cauldron.]

caldron. Same as **cauldron**.

Caledonian, *kal-i-dō'ni-ən*, *adj.* pertaining to ancient *Caledonia*, to the Highlands of Scotland, or to Scotland generally, or (*geol.*) to a mountain-forming movement with folds and overthrusts trending generally N.E. and S.W. in Silurian and Old Red Sandstone times, well developed in Scotland.—*n.* (*facetious*) a Scot. [L. *Cālēdonia*.]

calefaction, *kal-i-fak'shən*, *adj.* act of heating : state of being heated.—*adj.* **calefacient** (*-fā'shənt*), warming.—*n.* anything that warms : a blister or superficial stimulant.—*adj.* **calefac'tive**, communicating heat.—*n.* **calefac'tor**, a small stove.—*adj.* **calefac'tory**, warming.—*n.* a room in which monks warmed themselves : a warming-pan, or pome.—*v.t.* and *v.i.* **cal'efy**, to make or grow warm. [L. *calefacĕre—calēre*, to grow hot, *facĕre*, *factum*, to make.]

calendar, *kal'ən-dər*, *n.* the mode of adjusting the natural divisions of time with respect to each other for the purposes of civil life : an almanac or table of months, days, and seasons, or of special facts, etc. : a list of documents arranged chronologically with summaries of contents : a list of canonised saints, or of prisoners awaiting trial : any list or record.—*v.t.* to place in a list : to analyse and index.—*ns.* **cal'endarer**, **cal'endarist**; **calendar-line**, the date-line. —**calendar month, year**, see under **month, year**. [O.Fr. *calendier*—L. *calendārium*, an account-book, *kalendae*, calends.]

calender, *kal'ən-dər*, *n.* a machine with bowls or rollers for finishing the surface of cloth, paper, etc., by combined moisture, heat, and pressure : a person who calenders (properly a calendrer).—*v.t.* to dress in a calender.—*ns.* **cal'endering**; **cal'endrer**; **cal'endry**, a place where calendering is done. [Fr. *calandre*—L. *cylindrus*—Gr. *kylindros*, roller.]

calender, *kal'ən-dər*, *n.* a dervish. [Pers. *qalandar*.]

calends, *kal'əndz*, *n.pl.* among the Romans, the first day of each month. [L. *kalendae—calāre*; Gr. *kaleein*, to call (because the beginning of the month was proclaimed).]

Calendula, *ka-len'dū-lä*, *n.* the marigold genus : a preparation of marigold flowers, as a vulnerary. [L. *kalendae*, calends (but the connexion is not obvious).]

calenture, *kal'ən-tyər*, *n.* a fever or delirium occurring on board ship in hot climates. [Fr.—Sp. *calentura*—L. *calēns*, *-ēntis—calēre*, to be hot.]

calescence, *kal-es'əns*, *n.* increase in heat. [L. *calēscĕre*, inchoative of *calēre*, to be hot.]

calf, *käf*, *n.* the young of the cow, elephant, whale, and certain other mammals : calf-skin leather : a stupid or loutish person : an iceberg in relation to its parent glacier :—*pl.* **calves** (*kävz*).—*adj.* **calf'-bound**, bound in calf-skin.—*ns.* **calf'-country**, **-ground**, home of one's youth : **calf'dozer**, a small bulldozer; **calf'-lick**, a cow-lick; **calf'-love**, a boy's or girl's transient amorous attachment; **calf's'-foot, calves'-foot**, the foot of the calf, used in making a jelly; **calf'skin**, the skin of the calf, making a good leather for book-binding and shoes; **calf'-time**, youth.—*v.t.* and *v.i.* **calve** (*käv*), to bring forth (as) a calf : to detach (as) an iceberg.—**divinity calf**, a dark-brown calf bookbinding with blind stamping, and without gilding—common on theological books; **golden calf**, the image set up by Aaron during the absence of Moses on Sinai, or one of those erected by Jeroboam at Bethel and Dan : wealth as an object of worship; **half-calf**, a bookbinding in which the back and corners are in calf-skin; **mottled calf**, a light coloured bookbinding, decorated by the sprinkling of acid in drops; **smooth calf**, a binding in plain or undecorated calf leather; **tree calf**, a bright brown calf bookbinding, stained by acids with a pattern resembling the trunk and branches of a tree. [O.E. (Anglian) *cælf* (W.S. *cealf*); Ger. *kalb*.]

calf, *käf*, *n.* the thick fleshy part of the leg behind.—*adj.* **calf'less**, with a thin poor calf. [O.N. *kálfi*; perh. the same word as the preceding.]

caliature-wood, *kal'i-ə-tūr-wood*, *n.* red sanders.— Also **caliatour**, **calliature**, etc.

Caliban *kal'i-ban*, *n.* a man of beastly nature, from the monster in Shakespeare's *Tempest*.

calibre, **caliber**, *kal'i-bər*, *n.* the size of the bore of a tube : diameter : (*fig.*) character, capacity.—*adj.* **cal'ibred**, **cal'ibered**.—*v.t.* **cal'ibrāte**, to determine the calibre of, or the true values answering to the graduations of.—*n.* **calibrā'tion**. [Fr. *calibre*, the bore of a gun; perh. L. *quā librā*, of what weight, or from Ar. *qālib*, a mould.]

caliche, *kä-lē'chä*, *n.* Chile saltpetre. [Sp.]

calico, *kal'i-kō*, *n.* a cotton cloth first brought from *Calicut* in India : plain white unprinted cotton cloth, bleached or unbleached : coarse printed cotton cloth :—*pl.* **cal'icos, cal'icoes.**—*adj.* made of calico : spotted.—*ns.* **cal'ico-bush, -flower, -tree**, kalmia; **cal'ico-print'er**, one employed in printing calico(e)s; **cal'ico-wood**, the snowdrop-tree.

calid, *kal'id*, *adj.* warm.—*n.* **calid'ity**. [L. *calidus*, hot.]

calif. See **caliph**.

californium, *kal-i-for'ni-əm*, *n.* element 98 (symbol Cf). [Produced at the University of *California*.]

caligo, *kal-ī'gō*, *n.* dimness of sight.—*adj.* **caliginous** (*kal-ij'i-nəs*), dim, obscure, dark.—*n.* **caliginos'ity**. [L. *cālīgō*, *-inis*, fog.]

caligraphy, a faulty spelling of **calligraphy**.

caliology, *kal-i-ol'ə-ji*, *n.* the science of birds' nests. [Gr. *kaliā*, *kaliā*, a nest, *logos*, discourse.]

calipash, *kal'i-pash*, *n.* the part of a turtle close to the upper shell, a dull greenish fatty gelatinous substance.—*n.* **cal'ipee**, the light-yellowish portion from the belly. [Prob. from West Ind. words.]

calipers. See **callipers**.

caliph, *kal'if*, or *kā'lif*, *n.* a successor of Mohammed. —Also **calif, khalif.**—**cal'iphate**, the office, rank, government or empire of a caliph. [Fr. *calife*—Ar. *khalifah*, a successor.]

Calippic, Callippic, *ka-lip'ik*, *adj.* pertaining to the Athenian astronomer *Kal(l)ippos* (c. 350 B.C.) whose cycle equalled four Metonic cycles less one day, or seventy-six years.

calisaya, *kal-i-sä'yä*, *n.* a variety of Peruvian bark.

calisthenics. See **callisthenics**.

caliver, *kal'i-vər*, *n.* (*Shak.*) a kind of light musket. [Same as **calibre**.]

calix. See **calyx**.

Calixtin, Calixtine, *kal-iks'tin*, *n.* a member of the more moderate party among the Hussites—a Utraquist.—Also *adj.* [From their demanding the cup (L. *calix*) as well as the bread for the laity.]

Calixtin, Calixtine, *kal-iks'tin*, *n.* a follower of the Syncretist Lutheran divine, George *Calixtus* (1586-1656).

calk. See **caulk**.

calk, *kawk*, *n.* a pointed piece on a horse-shoe to prevent slipping—also **calk'in, calk'er, caulk'er**.—*v.t.* to provide with a calk. [O.E. *calc*, shoe—L. *calx*, a heel.]

calk, calque, *kawk, kalk*, *v.t.* to copy by rubbing the back with colouring matter and then tracing with a blunt point. [L. *calcāre*, to tread, *calx*, the heel.]

call, *kawl*, *v.i.* to cry aloud (often with *out*) : to make a short visit (with *upon, for, at*) : to make a telephone call : (*poker*) to demand a show of hands after repeated raising of stakes.—*v.t.* and *v.i.* (*card games*) to undertake to score : to declare (trump suit, etc.).—*v.t.* to name : to summon : to rouse : to appoint or proclaim : to designate or reckon : to select for a special office, as to the bar : to read out the names in (a roll) : to demand the playing of (an exposed card) : (*coll.*) to apply bad names to.—*n.* a summons or invitation (to the witness-box, to telephone, before the curtain, etc.) : a sense of vocation : a demand : a short visit : a signal by trumpet, bell, etc. : a telephone connexion or conversation, or a request for one : (*cards*) a declaration or undertaking, or the right to make it in turn : a cry, esp. of a bird : an instrument mimicking a bird's cry : admission to the rank of barrister : an invitation to the pastorate of a congregation : (*coll.*) occasion, cause.—*ns.* **call'-at-large**, a form of pastoral call sometimes adopted by a presbytery where a congregation is not unanimous, in which the name of the person to be called is not inscribed beforehand, and the names cannot be adhibited by mandate; **call'-bird**, a bird trained to allure others into snares; **call'-box**, a public telephone-box; **call'-boy**, a boy who waits upon the prompter in a theatre, and calls the actors when wanted on the stage; **call'er**, one who calls; **call'ing**, vocation; **call'ing-crab**, the fiddler-crab, which waves its larger claw when disturbed; **call'-loan**, **call'-mon'ey**, a loan or money payable when asked for; **call'-note**, the note by which a bird or beast calls to its kind; **call-'up**, an act of calling up.—**at call**, readily available; **call attention to**, to point out; **call away**, to divert the mind; **call back**, to recall; **call cousins**, claim kindred; **call down**, to invoke: (*U.S.*) to rebuke; **call for**, to ask loudly: to claim; **call forth**, to evoke; **call for trumps**, to play a card as a signal to a partner to lead a trump; **call in**, to bring in from outside, as the notes in circulation, etc.: to call to one's help (as a doctor, the police); **call'ing card**, a visiting card; **call in question**, to challenge, throw doubt on; **call off**, to summon away: to withdraw or back out: to cancel or abandon; **call on**, or **upon**, to invoke, appeal to: to make a short visit to; **call out**, to challenge to fight a duel: to summon to service, bring into operation; **call over**, to read aloud (a list); **call to account**, to summon to render an account; **call to mind**, to recollect; **call to order**, to call upon to observe the rules of debate; **call up**, to summon from beneath, or from another world, to a tribunal, to the colours, to memory; **within call**, with calling distance.—**boatswain's call** (see **whistle**). [Found in O.E. (W.S.) as *ceallian*; O.N. *kalla*.]

call, *kawl*, *n.* (*Spens.*) a caul or cap.

Calla, *kal'ä*, *n.* a marsh plant of the arum family: erroneously (often **call'a-li'ly**) the lily of the Nile (*Richardia* or *Zantedeschia*). [Origin doubtful.]

callant, *käl'ant*, *n.* (*Scot.*) a lad. [Du. *kalant*.]

caller, *käl'ər*, *kawl'ər*, *adj.* fresh: (*Scot.*) cool. [Prob. the same as **calver**.]

callet, *kal'it*, *n.* (*Shak.*) a scold, a woman of bad character, a trull. [Origin obscure.]

callid, *kal'id*, *adj.* shrewd.—*n.* **callid'ity**, shrewdness. [L. *callidus*, expert.]

calligraphy, *kə-lig'rə-fi*, *n.* fine penmanship: characteristic style of writing.—*n.* **callig'rapher**.—*adjs.* **calligraph'ic** (*kal-i-grăf'ik*), **-al**.—*n.* **callig'raphist**. [Gr. *kallos*, beauty, *graphein*, to write.]

Calliope, *kal-ī'o-pē*, *n.* the muse of epic poetry: a set of steam-whistles played by a keyboard. [Gr. *Kalliopē*.]

callipers, **calipers**, *kal'i-pərz*, *n.pl.* compasses with legs suitable for measuring the inside or outside diameter of bodies.—Also **calliper-compasses**.—*adj.* **call'iper**.—**calliper splint**, a splint fitted to the leg, so that the patient may walk without any pressure on the foot. (**calibre**.)

callippic. Same as **calippic**.

Callistemon, *kal-i-stē'mon*, *n.* an Australian genus of the myrtle family, bottle-brush shrubs. [Gr. *kallos*, beauty, *stēmōn*, a thread (stamen).]

callisthenics, *kal-is-then'iks*, *n.pl.* exercises for cultivating gracefulness and strength.—*adj.* **callisthen'ic**.—Also **calisthenics**, **-ic**. [Gr. *kallos*, beauty, *sthenos*, strength.]

Callitriche, *kal-it'ri-kē*, *n.* the water-starwort genus, constituting the **callitrichā'ceae**, a family of uncertain affinities, placed by some beside the spurges and boxes, by others with the mare's tails. [Gr. *kallos*, beauty, *thrix*, *trichos*, hair.]

callous, *kal'əs*, *adj.* hardened: unfeeling.—*n.* **callos'ity**, a thickening of the skin.—*adv.* **call'ously**.—*n.* **call'ousness**. [L. *callōsus*—*callus*, hard skin.]

callow, *kal'ō*, *adj.* not covered with feathers: unfledged, unbearded: inexperienced. [O.E. *calu*; Ger. *kahl*, bald.]

callow, *kal'ō*, *adj.* low-lying and liable to be submerged.—*n.* an alluvial flat. [Perh. Irish *calad*, a riverside meadow.]

Calluna, *kə-l(y)ōō'nä* *n.* the heather genus. [Gr. *kallȳnein*, to beautify, to sweep—*kalos*, beautiful.]

callus, *kal'us*, *n.* a thickening of the skin: (*path.*) new material by which fractured bones are consolidated: (*bot.*) soft tissue that forms over a cut surface. [L.]

calm, *käm*, *adj.* still or quiet: serene, tranquil.—*n.* absence of wind—also in *pl.*: repose: serenity of feelings or actions.—*v.t.* and *v.i.* to make or become calm: to quiet.—*v.t.* to becalm.—*ns.* and *adjs.* (*med.*) **calmant**, **calmative** (both *kal'* or *kä'*).—*adj.* **calmed** (*kämd*).—*adv.* **calm'ly**.—*n.* **calm'ness**.—*adj.* **calm'y** (*Spens.*), characterised by

calm. [Fr. *calme* (It. *calma*), from L.L. *cauma*—Gr. *kauma*, noonday heat—*kaiein*, to burn.]

calm, **calmstane**. See **cam** (3).

calmuck. See **kalmuck**.

calomel, *kal'ō-mel*, *n.* mercurous chloride, used in medicine. [Fr. *calomel*, apparently from Gr. *kalos*, beautiful, *melas*, black, possibly because, itself a colourless crystalline substance, it gives a black product with ammonia, or is got from a black mixture.]

caloric, *ka-lor'ik*, *n.* (*arch.*) heat: the once supposed material principle or cause of heat.—*ns.* **calorescence** (*kal-ər-es'əns;* an ill-formed word, meaning the contrary of what it should mean), the transmutation of heat rays into luminous rays; **cal'orie**, the amount of heat needed to raise a gram (*small* or *gram-calorie*) or a kilogram (*great, large, kilogram-calorie*) of water 1° centigrade in temperature (the great calorie is used as a unit in reckoning the heat- or energy-producing value of food): the hundredth part of the heat required to raise a gram (*mean calorie*) or a pound (*pound-calorie*) from 0° to 100°C.—*adj.* **calorif'ic**, causing heat: heating.—*ns.* **calorifica'tion**; **calorim'eter**, an instrument for measuring heat (not temperature) or thermal constants; **calorim'etry**; **cal'orist**, one who held heat to be a subtle fluid called caloric.—**calorific value**, of a food or fuel, the number of heat units got by complete combustion of unit mass. [L. *calor*, heat.]

calotte, *kal-ot'*, *n.* a plain skull-cap or coif worn by R.C. clergy. [Fr.]

calotype, *kal'ō-tīp*, *n.* an early kind of photography (invented *c.* 1840 by W. H. Fox Talbot) by means of silver iodide and silver nitrate.—*n.* **cal'otypist**. [Gr. *kalos*, beautiful, *typos*, an image.]

caloyer, *kal-ō-yər*, *n.* a Greek monk, esp. of the order of St. Basil. [Fr.—It.—Late Gr. *kalogéros*.—Gr. *kalos*, beautiful, *gēras*, old age.]

calp, *kalp*, *n.* in Ireland, a dark shaly limestone occurring in the middle of the Carboniferous Limestone.

calpa. Same as **kalpa**.

calpac, **calpack**. See **kalpak**.

calque. See **calk** (3).

caltrop, *kal'*, *kawl'trop*, *n.* an instrument armed with four spikes, so arranged that one always stands upright, used to obstruct an enemy: a sponge spicule of like shape: a name for several plants with fruits so shaped, e.g. (esp. in *pl.*) water chestnut.—Also **cal'trap**, **cal'throp**. [O.E. *coltetræppe*, *calcatrippe*—L. *calx*, heel, and the root of **trap** (1).]

calumba, *ka-lum'bä*, *n.* the root of an East African plant (*Jateorhiza columba*, fam. Menispermaceae) used as a stomachic and tonic. [Perh. from *Colombo* in Ceylon.]

calumet, *kal'ū-met*, *n.* the peace pipe of the North American Indians, a tobacco-pipe smoked in token of peace. [Norman Fr. *calumet*, shepherd's pipe (Fr. *chalumet*)—L. *calamus*, reed.]

calumny, *kal'əm-ni*, *n.* false accusation: slander.—*v.t.* **calumniāte** (*kə-lum'ni-āt*), to accuse falsely: to slander.—*v.i.* to spread evil reports.—*ns.* **calum'niātion**; **calum'niātor**.—*adjs.* **calum'niātory**, **calum'nious**, of the nature of calumny: slanderous.—*adv.* **calum'niously**. [L. *calumnia*, prob. conn. with *calvī*, to deceive.]

Calvados, *kal-və-dōs'*, *n.* a liqueur made from cider or apple-pulp, esp. in the Calvados department of Normandy.

Calvary, *kal'və-ri*, *n.* the name of the place where Jesus was crucified: a representation of Christ's crucifixion, or a series of scenes connected with it.—**Calvary cross**, a Latin cross on three steps. [L. *calvāria*, Vulgate rendering of Gr. *krānion*, as that again of Aramaic *gogulthō* or *gogolthā* (Heb. *gulgōleth*)—Grecised as *golgotha*), all three words meaning skull.]

calve, **calves**. See **calf**.

calver, *kal'vər*, *v.t.* to prepare (salmon or other fish) when alive or freshly caught.—*p.adj.* **cal'vered**. [cf. **caller**.]

Calvinism, *kal'vin-izm*, *n.* the doctrines of the great Genevan religious reformer, John *Calvin*

(1509-1564), as these are given in his *Institutio*, esp. on particular election, predestination, the incapacity for true faith and repentance of the natural man, efficacious grace, and final perseverance.—*n.* Cal′vinist.—*adjs.* Calvinist′ic, -al.

calvities, *kal-vish′i-ēz, n.* baldness. [L. *calvities*—*calvus*, bald.]

calx, *kalks, n.* the substance of a metal or mineral that remains after strong heating:—*pl.* **calxes** (*kalk′siz*), or **calces** (*kal′sēz*). [L. *calx, calcis*, lime.]

Calycanthus, etc. See under **calyx**.

calypso, *ka-lip′sō, n.* a West-Indian folk-song made up as the singer goes, or singers go, along.

calyptra, *ka-lip′trä, n.* a Greek veil: a hood, covering, esp. that of a moss capsule, or of a root.—*adj.* **calyp′trate**, capped.—*n.* **calyp′trogen**, the group of cells giving rise to the root-cap. [Gr. *kalyptra*, a veil.]

calyx, *kal′iks*, or *kā′liks, n.* (*bot.*) the outer covering of a flower, its separate leaves termed sepals: (*zool.* by confusion with L. *calix*, cup) applied to various cup-like structures, as the cup of a coral:—*pl.* **ca′lyces** (*-sēz*), or **ca′lyxes.**—*n.pl.* **Calycanthaceae** (*kal-ik-an-thā′si-ē;* Gr. *anthos*, flower), the Carolina allspice family of plants, in which there is a transition from sepals to petals.—*ns.* **calycanthemy** (*kal-ik-an′thi-mi;* Gr. *anthemon*, flower), the condition of having the calyx like a corolla; **Calycan′thus**, a small North American genus of shrubs, Carolina allspice or strawberry shrub.—*n.pl.* **Calyciflorae** (*kal-is-i-flō′rē;* L. *flōs, flōris*, flower).—*adj.* **calyciform** (*kal-is′*), having the form of a calyx; **calyc′inal, calycine** (*kal′i-sīn*), pertaining to a calyx.—*n.* **cal′ycle, cal′ycule** (*bot.*) a whorl of bracts, epicalyx or involucre: (*zool.*) a calyx.—*adjs.* **cal′ycled**, having a calycle; **cal′ycoid, calycoi′deous**, like a calyx. [Gr. *kalyx*, a covering—*kalyptein*, to cover.]

cam, *kam, n.* (*mech.*) an eccentric projection on a revolving shaft, shaped so as to give some desired linear motion to another part.—*ns.* **cam′-shaft, -wheel**, a shaft, wheel, bearing a cam or cams. [Du. *kam*, cam, comb; cf. **comb, kame.**]

cam, *adj.* and *adv.* See **kam**.

cam, caum, calm, *käm, kawm, n.* (*Scot.*) pale blaes : a slate-pencil: pipeclay: (*obs.*) limestone.—*v.t.* to whiten with camstone.—*n.* **cam′stone, -stane**, a white argillaceous stone used for whitening hearthstones and doorsteps.—*adj.* **calm′y**, clayey. [Origin unkown.]

camaieu, *käm-ä-yə′, n.* a cameo: a painting in monochrome, or in simple colours not imitating nature: a style of printing pictures producing the effect of pencil-drawing. [Fr.; see **cameo**.]

Camaldolite, *kam-al′dō-līt, n.* a member of a religious order founded by St. Romuald at *Camaldoli* early in the 11th century.—Also *adj.*—*n.* and *adj.* **Camal′dolese**.

caman, *kam′an, n.* a shinty stick.—*n.* **camanachd** (*kam-an-ahh′*), shinty. [Gael.]

camaraderie, *kam-ə-räd′ə-rē, n.* good-fellowship : the intimacy of comradeship. [Fr.]

camarilla, *kam-ə-ril′ä, n.* a body of secret intriguers, esp. of a court party against legitimate ministers : a small room. [Sp. dim. of *cámara*, a chamber.]

camass, camas, camash, quamash, *kam′as, -ash, kwom′ash, kwam-ash′, n.* a small plant (*Camassia*) of the lily family growing in the north-western United States: its nutritious bulb.—*n.* **camass′-rat**, a small gopher rodent that devours the bulbs. [Chinook *kámass*.]

camber, *kam′bər, n.* a slight convexity upon an upper surface: the curve of a ship's plank : a small dock for timber.—*v.t.* and *v.i.* to arch slightly. [Fr. *cambre*—L. *camerāre*, to vault.]

Camberwell beauty, *kam′bər-wəl bū′ti, n.* (*Vanessa*, or *Nymphalis, antiopa*) a large and beautiful butterfly, first recorded in England in 1748 at *Camberwell*, then a rural place.

cambist, *kam′bist, n.* one skilled in the science of exchange.—*ns.* **cam′bism, cam′bistry.** [It. *cambista*—L. *cambīre*, to exchange.]

cambium, *kam′bi-əm, n.* a layer or cylinder of meristem by whose differentiation into xylem and phloem new wood and bast are formed.—*adjs.* **cam′bial, cam′biform.** [L.L.—L. *cambīre*, to change.]

camboge, obsolete form of **gamboge**.

cambrel, *kam′brəl, n.* a bent stick or rod for hanging a carcase: an animal's hock. [Perh. conn. with **camber**, or with **gambrel**.]

Cambrian, *kam′bri-ən, adj.* pertaining to *Cambria* or Wales: Welsh: (*geol.*) the system (well represented in Wales) next above the Archaean.—*n.* an inhabitant of Cambria, or Wales : the Cambrian system. [Latinised from W. *Cymry*, Welshmen, *Cymru*, Wales.]

cambric, *kām′brik, n.* a fine white linen, originally manufactured at *Kamerijk* (Cambrai) in French Flanders : a cotton imitation.

came, *kām, pa.t.* of **come**.

camel, *kam′əl, n.* an animal of Asia and Africa with one or two humps on its back, used as a beast of burden and for riding: a watertight structure for raising a vessel in shallow water : a humped type of aeroplane.—*adj.* **cam′el-backed**, humpbacked.—*ns.* **cam′eleer**, one who drives or rides a camel; **cam′eline**, camlet.—*adjs.* **cam′eline**, of the nature of a camel; **cam′elish**, like a camel, obstinate; **cam′eloid**, of the camel family—also *n.*—*ns.* **cam′elry, cam′el-corps**, troops mounted on camels.—**camel('s) hair**, the hair of the camel : the hair of the squirrel's tail used for paint-brushes; **camel's thorn**, a papilionaceous manna-yielding desert plant (*Alhagi maurorum*) which camels eat greedily. [L. *camēlus*—Gr. *kamēlos*—Phoenician or Heb. *gāmāl*.]

cameleon. See **chameleon**.

Camellia, *kə-mel′yä*, often *kə-mēl′yä, n.* a genus of evergreen shrubs close akin to tea, natives of eastern Asia, grown for the singular beauty of their flowers. [Named from Kamel, Latinised *Camellus*, a Moravian Jesuit, who collected plants in the Philippine Islands in 1639.]

camelopard, *kam-el′ō-pärd,* or *kam′əl-ō-pärd, n.* the giraffe.—Also **cameleopard** (*kam-ə-lep′ərd;* as by Shelley, by confusion with **leopard**). [L. *camēlopardus*—Gr. *kamēlopardālis;* from Gr. *kamēlos*, the camel, and *pardālis*, the panther.]

camelot, *kam′lot, n.* Same as **camlet**.

Camembert, *kam-əm-ber′, -än′-ber′, n.* a soft rich cheese made near *Camembert*, in Normandy.

cameo, *kam′i-ō* or (as It.) *kä-mā′ō, n.* a gem with figure carved in relief, esp. one in which a differently coloured lower layer serves as ground :—*pl.* **cam′eos.**—*n.* **cam′eo-shell′**, a helmet-shell.—**cameo ware**, pottery with relief figures against a different colour. [It. *cammeo*—L.L. *cammaeus*, of unknown origin.]

camera, *kam′ər-ä, n.* (*rare*) a vaulted room : a judge's private chamber : a legislative chamber : the papal treasury : a form of camera-obscura used by photographers :—*pl.* **cam′eras.**—*adj.* **cam′eral.**—*ns.* **cam′era-lu′cida** (L., light chamber), a drawing device by which the image of the object is made by reflection to appear as if projected on the paper; **cam′era-man**, a photographer, esp. for newspapers or cinematograph; **cam′era-obscu′ra** (L., dark chamber), a dark chamber in which an image of outside objects is thrown upon a screen.—*adj.* **cam′erāted**, chambered : vaulted.—*n.* **camerā′tion**. [L. *camera*; Gr. *kamarā*, vault.]

camerlengo, *kam-ər-leng′gō,* **camerlingo**, *-ling′gō, n.* a papal treasurer. [It.; cf. **chamberlain**.]

Cameronian, *kam-ə-rōn′i-ən, n.* a follower of the Covenanter Richard *Cameron*, killed at Airds Moss in 1680, a member of the Reformed Presbyterian Church, a body that refused to accept the Revolution settlement (for the most part united with the Free Church in 1876): a soldier of the Cameronian regiment (26th Foot, now the First Battalion of Scottish Rifles) formed from a body of Cameronians (1689).—Also *adj.*

camion, *kam′i-ən, n.* a heavy lorry, wagon. [Fr.]

camis, *kam′is*, **camus**, *kam′əs, n.* (*Spens.*) a loose light robe.—*ns.* **camisāde′, camisā′do** (for Sp. *camisada*), a night attack, probably because shirts were often put on over the armour; **cam′isard** (*-sär, -zär*), an insurgent Huguenot of the Cevennes, so called from the *camise* or blouse worn by the peasants; **cam′isole**, a sleeved jacket, a woman's loose morning gown or jacket: a loose under-bodice with or without sleeves:—*n.pl.* **cam′i-knick′ers**, combined camisole and knickers. [Sp. and Prov. *camisa*, shirt—L. *camisia*.]

camise, camese, *kam-ēs′, n.* the usual Arab shirt. [Ar. *qamīç*, perh. L. *camisia*.]

camlet, *kam′lit, n.* a cloth perhaps originally of camel's hair, but now chiefly of wool and goat's hair. [Fr.—L.L. *camelotum*—L. *camēlus*; or perh. Ar. *khamlat*, nap.]

camomile, chamomile, *kam′ō-mīl, n.* a name for several plants akin to chrysanthemum, or their dried flowers, used in medicine, affording a bitter stomachic and tonic—esp. *Anthemis nobilis* (common camomile) and *Matricaria Chamomilla* (wild camomile). [Fr. *camomille*—L. *chamomilla*—Gr. *chamaimēlon*, lit. earth-apple, from the apple-like smell of its blossoms—*chamai*, on the ground, *mēlon*, an apple.]

Camorra, *kam-or′ä, n.* a Neapolitan secret society.—*ns.* **Camorr′ism**; **Camorr′ist**. [It.]

camouflet, *kä-mōō-flā, n.* a mine to destroy an underground hostile gallery.—*n.* **cam′ouflage** (*-fläzh*), any device (esp. visual) for deceiving an adversary.—*v.t.* and *v.i.* to deceive, to counterfeit, to disguise. [Fr. *camouflet*, a whiff of smoke intentionally blown in the face, an affront, a camouflet.]

camp, *kamp, n.* a place on which a tent or tents or the like are pitched: a collection of temporary dwellings, or their inhabitants collectively: temporary quarters of an army, tribe, travellers, holiday-makers, or others: an old fortified site: a permanent military station: a mushroom town, as a mining camp: (*fig.*) military service or life: a party or side.—*v.i.* to encamp, or pitch tents: to lodge in a camp (often with *out*, i.e. in the open).—*ns.* **camp′-bed, -chair, -stool,** a portable folding bed, etc.; **camp′-fe′ver,** typhus, typhoid, or other fever apt to occur in camps; **camp′-fire,** the fire of an encampment: a reunion, lodge, or section, of certain organisations; **camp′-foll′ower,** a non-combatant who follows in the train of an army, as sutler, servant, etc.; **camp′-meet′ing,** a religious gathering in the open air or in a temporary encampment; **camp′-preach′er,** one who preaches at such meetings. [Fr. *camp*, camp—L. *campus*, a plain.]

camp, *kamp, n.* (*obs.*) conflict: an old form of the game of football.—*v.i.* to fight, struggle.—*v.i.* **cam′ple,** to wrangle. [O.E. *camp*, battle; cf. Ger. *kampf*.]

campaign, *kam-pān′, n.* (*arch.*) champaign or open country: the time during which an army keeps the field: the operations of that time: an excursion into the country: an organised series of operations in the advocacy of some cause or object.—*v.i.* to serve in a campaign.—*ns.* **campagna** (*käm-pän′yä*; Ital.), once equivalent to *champaign*, now used only as a proper name; **campaign′er,** one who has served in several campaigns. [Fr. *campagne*—L. *campania*—*campus*, a field.]

campanero, *kam-pa-nē′rō, n.* the South American bell-bird or arapunga, a snow-white chatterer with a note like a church bell. [Sp., bellman.]

campanile, *kam-pan-ē′lā, n.* a bell-tower, esp. a tall one detached from the church:—*pl.* **campaniles,** sometimes (*It.*) **campanili** (*-lē*). [It., from *campana*, a bell.]

campana, *kam-pā′nä, n.* a bell-shaped object, as the core of a Corinthian capital; (*Drayton*) a flower, perhaps the pasque-flower.—*n.* **campanist** (*kam′-pan-ist*), one versed in bells.—*adjs.* **campaniform** (*-pan′*), bell-shaped; **campanolog′ical.**—*ns.* **campanol′ogist**; **campanol′ogy,** the subject or science of bells or bell-ringing; **Campan′ula,** a genus (giving name to a family **Campanulā′ceae**) commonly known as bell-flowers or bells, the best-known the harebell or Scottish bluebell.—*adis.* **campanulā′ceous, campan′ular.**—*n.* **Campan-ulā′ria,** a common genus of Hydrozoa, with stems simple or branched, the nutritive polyps surrounded by transparent bell-shaped sheaths.—

adj. **campan′ulate,** bell-shaped. [It. *campana*, a bell.]

Campbellite, *kam′bəl-īt, n.* a member of the sect known as Disciples of Christ, founded by Alexander Campbell (1788–1866).

campeachy-wood, *kam-pēch′i-wood, n.* logwood, first exported from Campeachy (*Campeche*).

campeador, *kam-pi-ə-dōr′, n.* a champion, esp. the Cid. [Sp.]

campestral, *kam-pes′trəl, adj.* growing in or pertaining to fields.—Also **campes′trian.** [L. *campester*—*campus*, field.]

camphire, *kam′fīr, n.* an old name for camphor: (*Bible*) henna. [**camphor.**]

camphor, *kam′fər, n.* a solid essential oil, got from the camphor laurel (a species of cinnamon-tree) of Formosa, etc., or synthetically manufactured, having a peculiar aromatic taste and smell: any similar compound of the terpene series.—*ns.* **camphane** (*kam′fān*), a terpene hydrocarbon ($C_{10}H_{18}$), parent substance of the camphor group; **camphene** (*kam′fēn, -fēn′*), a camphor-like terpene hydrocarbon ($C_{10}H_{16}$); **camphine** (*kam′fēn, -fīn*), an old name for rectified oil of turpentine.—*adj.* **camphorā′ceous,** like camphor.—*v.t.* **cam′phorate,** to impregnate with camphor.—*adj.* **camphoric** (*-for′ik*), pertaining to camphor. [Fr. *camphre*—L.L. *camphora*—Ar. *kāfūr*.]

campion, *kam′pi-ən, n.* any plant of the genera *Lychnis* (or *Melandryum*) and *Silene*. [Origin unknown.]

Campodea, *kam-pō′di-ä, n.* a genus of bristle-tails.—*adj.* **campode′iform,** resembling a Campodea, as certain six-legged active insect grubs. [Gr. *kampē*, caterpillar, *eidos*, form.]

camp-sheathing, -shedding, -sheeting, -shot, *kamp′shē′dhing, -shed′ing, -shēt′ing, -shot, ns.* piles and boarding protecting a river bank or the like. [Origin unknown.]

Camptonite, *kamp′tən-īt, n.* an igneous rock composed essentially of plagioclase and hornblende.—*adj.* **camptonitic** (*-it′ik*). [*Campton* in New Hampshire.]

campus, *kam′pus, n.* (*U.S.*) college grounds. [L. field.]

campylotropous, *kam-pil-ot′rə-pəs, adj.* of an ovule, curved so as to bring the micropyle near the chalaza. [Gr. *kampylos*, curved, *tropē*, turning.]

camsho, *kâm′shō,* **camshoch, camsheugh,** *kâm′-shəhh, adj.* (*Scot.*) crooked. [Cf. **cam,** and O.E. *sceolh*, awry.]

camstairy, camsteerie, camsteary, *kam-stār′i, -stēr′i, adj.* (chiefly *Scot.*) perverse, unruly. [Ety. dub.]

camstone. See **cam** (3).

camus, *kam′əs, adj.* flat-nosed. [Prob. Fr. *camus.*]

camus. See **camis.**

cam-wood, *kam′-wood, n.* the wood of *Baphia nitida,* a West African papilionaceous tree, at first white, turning red on exposure to air, used as a red dye. [Perh. from African name *kambi.*]

can, *kan, v.t.* (*obs.* in *infin.* except in Scots) to be able: to have sufficient power: (*obs.*) to know: to have skill in:—*3rd pers.* **can**; *participles obs.* except **could** in Scots; *p.a.t.* **could.—can** is used for *gan* in M.E. and in Spenser. [O.E. *cunnan,* to know (how to do a thing), to be able; pres. indic. *can*; Goth. *kunnan,* Ger. *können,* to be able. See **con, ken, know**; also **cannot, can't, couth.**]

can, *kan, n.* a vessel for holding or carrying liquids, generally of tinned iron, with a handle over the top: a chimney-pot: (*esp. U.S.*) a tin, vessel of tin-plate in which meat, fruit, etc., are sealed up: a drinking-mug.—*v.t.* to put up for preservation in tins (*pr.p.* **cann′ing,** *pa.p.* and *pa.t.* **canned**).—*p.adj.* **canned,** packed in tins (or in U.S. jars): (*slang*) drunk.—*ns.* **can′ful,** as much as a can will hold:—*pl.* **can′fuls**; **cann′er**; **cann′ery,** a place where provisions are tinned. [O.E. *canne.*]

caña, *kän-yä′dä, n.* a narrow cañon. [Sp.]

Canadian, *kə-nā′di-ən, adj.* pertaining to *Canada.*—*n.* a native or citizen of Canada.—**Can′ada balsam** (see **balsam**); **Canada rice** (see **Zizania**); **Canadian water-weed** (see **Anacharis**).

Neutral vowels in unaccented syllables : *el′ə-mənt, in′fənt, ran′dəm*

canaigre, *ka-nā′gər, n.* a Texan dock whose root is used in tanning. [Mexican Sp.]

canaille, *kä-nä′ē, n.* the mob, the vulgar rabble. [Fr.,—L. *canis,* a dog.]

canakin. See **cannikin.**

canal, *ka-nal′, n.* an artificial watercourse, esp. for navigation : (*biol.*) a duct that conveys fluids : a groove.—*ns.* **canal′-boat,** a boat for canal traffic; **canal′-cell,** a cell in the neck of an archegonium.—*adjs.* **canalic′ular** (*kan-ə-lik′ū-lər*), like or pertaining to a canaliculus; **canalic′ulate, -d,** channelled, grooved.—*ns.* **canalic′ulus** (*anat.*), a small furrow or channel :—*pl.* **canalic′ulī; canalisā′tion** (*kan-əl-ī-zā′shən*), the construction of canals : formation of an artificial channel : conversion into a canal : (*lit.* and *fig.*) direction into a fixed channel.—*v.t.* **can′alise,** to make a canal through : to convert into a canal : (*lit.* and *fig.*) to direct into a fixed channel.—*n.pl.* **canal′-rays′,** (*phys.*) positive rays, a stream of positively electrified particles through a perforation in the cathode of a vacuum-tube. [L. *canālis,* a waterpipe.]

canapé, *kä-nä-pā′, n.* a piece of fried or toasted bread with caviare, or other dainty, etc. [Fr.]

canard, *kä-när(d)′ n.* a false rumour : an early duck-like type of aeroplane. [Fr., lit. duck.]

Canarese. See **Kanarese.**

canary, *kə-nā′ri, n.* a light sweet wine from the *Canary* Islands : a song-bird (finch) found in the Canary Islands, bright yellow in domestic breeds : a lively dance said to have taken origin in the Canary Islands (often in *pl.*).—*adj.* canary-coloured, bright yellow.—*v.i.* to dance the canary : to prance about.—*ns.* **canā′ry-bird,** a canary : (*slang*) a jail-bird : a mistress; **can′ary-cree′per,** a yellow-flowered Tropaeolum (popularly but ungrammatically **canarien′sis**); **canā′ry-grass,** a grass (*Phalaris canariensis*) whose seed (**canā′ry-seed**) is used to feed canaries; **canā′ry-wood,** the timber of two species of *Persea* or *Laurus* of the Canaries, Azores, and Madeira.

canasta, *kə-nas′tä, n.* a card-game of the rummy type, originating in South America. [Sp., basket.]

canaster, *kə-nas′tər, n.* a kind of tobacco, so called from the rush basket in which it was originally brought from Spanish America. [Sp. *canastra,* *canasta*—Gr. *kanastron.*]

can-can, *kan′kan, n.* a wild and indecorous dance of French origin. [Fr. *cancan,* chatter, scandal, the can-can; usually referred to L. *quamquam,* the pronunciation of which was long hotly disputed in the French schools; Littré quotes O.Fr. *caquehan,* a noisy assembly.]

cancel, *kan′sl, v.t.* to cross out : to annul or suppress : to abolish or wipe out : to counterbalance or compensate for : to remove as balancing each other, e.g. like quantities from opposite sides of an equation, like factors from numerator and denominator of a fraction (*pr.p.* **can′celling;** *pa.t* and *pa.p.* **can′celled**).—*n.* the suppression of a printed leaf or sheet : the part so cancelled, or (usually) the new one substituted.—*n.pl.* **cancelli** (*kan-sel′ī;* L. *kang-kel′ē*), cross-pieces forming a lattice-work or grating, as in the division between the choir and the body of a church : (*anat.*) reticulations.—*adjs.* **can′cellate, -d,** marked latticewise, reticulated.— *n.* **cancellā′tion,** cancelling : crosswise marking.— *adj.* **can′cellous.** [L. *cancellāre,* to cross out, *cancellī,* lattice-work, dim. of *cancer,* a lattice.]

cancelier, canceleer, *kan-si-lēr′, v.i.* (*Scott*) of a hawk, to turn on the wing before stooping.—Also *n.*

Cancer, *kan′sər, n.* the genus to which the edible crab belongs : a constellation (the Crab) between Gemini and Leo, and a sign of the zodiac (once coincident with it) whose first point marks the limit of the sun's course northward in summer : **cancer,** loosely any malignant new growth or tumour : properly a carcinoma or disorderly growth of epithelial cells which invade adjacent tissue and spread by the lymphatics and blood-vessels to other parts of the body : (*fig.*) any corroding evil.—*v.i.* **cancer′ate,** to become cancerous. —*ns.* **cancerā′tion.**—*adj.* **can′cerous,** of, like,

affected with, cancer.—*n.* **can′cer-root,** beech-drops.—*adjs.* **cancriform** (*kang′kri-form*), crab-shaped : like cancer; **can′crine** (*kang′krīn*), crab-like : palindromic (from the false notion that a crab walked backwards); **cancrizans** (*kang′kri-zanz; mus.*), of a canon, having the answer repeating the subject backwards; **cancroid** (*kang′kroid*), crab-like : cancer-like.—Also *n.* [L. *cancer;* cog. with Gr. *karkinos,* a crab.]

cancionero, *kän-thyō-nā′rō, n.* a collection of songs. [Sp.]

candela, *kan-del′ä, n.* a unit of luminance such that the brightness of a black body radiator at the temperature of solidification of platinum is 60 candela per sq. cm. [candle.]

candelabrum, *kan-di-lä′brəm,* or -*lä′, n.* a branched and ornamented candlestick or lamp-stand :—*pl.* **candela′bra**—also used as a false *sing.* with *pl.* **candela′bras.** [L. *candēlābrum*—*candēla,* candle.]

candelilla, *kän-dä-lēl′yä, n.* a Mexican wax-yielding spurge. [Sp. dim. of *candela,* candle.]

candent, *kan′dənt, adj.* glowing : white-hot. [L. *candēre,* to glow.]

candescence, *kan-des′əns, n.* a white heat.—*adj.* **candesc′ent.** [L. *candēscēre,* inceptive of *candēre,* to glow.]

candid, *kan′did, adj.* (*obs.*) white : shining, clear : frank, ingenuous : free from prejudice : fair, impartial.—*adv.* **can′didly.**—*n.* **can′didness.**—**candid camera,** a type of camera used for taking unposed photographs of people engaged in the normal occupations of their daily life : this style of photography. [L. *candidus,* white.]

candidate, *kan′di-dāt, n.* one who offers himself for any office or honour, so called because, at Rome, the applicant used to dress in white.—*ns.* **can′didā′ture, can′didateship, can′didacy** (*-də-si*). [L. *candidātus*—*candidus,* white.]

candied. See **candy.**

candle, *kan′dl, n.* a cylinder of wax, tallow, or the like surrounding a wick : a luminary : a candle-shaped object : a jet in a gas-stove : a photometric unit.—*ns.* **can′dle-berry,** wax-myrtle or bay-berry (*Myrica cerifera*) of the spurge family, or its fruit: **can′dle-bomb,** a small glass bomb filled with water, exploding in a candle-flame; **can′dle-coal** (same as **cannel-coal**); **can′dle-dipp′ing,** the method of making candles by dipping instead of moulding; **can′dle-end,** the end-piece of a burnt-out candle; **can′dle-fish,** the eulachon : another West American fish, a cheek-armoured acanthopterygian (*Anoplopoma fimbria*)—the *black candle-fish;* **can′dle-holder,** one who holds a candle to another while working—hence one who abets or connives; **can′dle-light,** the light of a candle : illumination by candles : the time when candles are lighted; **can′dle-lighter,** one whose business is to light the candles : a spill; **can′dle-nut,** the oil-yielding fruit of a species of *Aleurites* (spurge family) of the Pacific Islands; **can′dle-power,** illuminating power in terms of a standard candle—a name applied to various units of photometry; **can′dle-snuffer,** an instrument for snuffing candles : an attendant, esp. in a theatre, who snuffed the candles; **can′dlestick,** a portable stand for a candle, originally a stick or piece of wood; **can′dle-tree,** a tropical American tree (*Parmentiera cerifera*) of the Bignonia family, with candle-like pods; **can′dle-waster,** one who studies late; **can′dle-wood,** the wood of various West Indian and Mexican resinous trees.—**burn the candle at both ends,** to waste or use up in two ways at once; **not fit to hold a candle to,** not to be compared with; **sell by the candle,** to offer for sale as long as a small piece of candle burns, the bid made just before it goes out being successful; **the game is not worth the candle,** the thing is not worth the labour or expense of it. [O.E. *candel*—L. *candēla,* from *candēre,* to glow.]

Candlemas, *kan′dl-məs, n.* the R.C. festival of the purification of the Virgin Mary, on 2nd February, when candles are blessed : a quarter-day in Scotland. [candle, mass.]

candock, *kan′dok, n.* the yellow water-lily. [can (*n.*) and **dock.**]

candour, *kan'dər, n.* freedom from prejudice or disguise : sincerity : justice : openness. [L. *candor,* whiteness, from *candēre,* to shine.]

candy, *kan'di, n.* a sweetmeat of sugar boiled and crystallised (also **su'gar-can'dy**) : (*U.S.*) any form of confectionery : (*U.S. pl.* **candies**).—*v.t.* to preserve or dress with sugar : to crystallise as sugar or the like : to encrust.—*v.i.* to crystallise : to become encrusted.—*adj.* **can'died,** encrusted with candy or sugar : (*fig.*) sugared, flattering. [Fr. *candi,* from Ar. *qandah,* candy.]

candy, *kan'di, n.* a South Indian weight, generally containing 20 maunds, about 500 pounds English. —Also **can'die** and **kan'dy.** [Tamil.]

candytuft, *kan'di-tuft, n.* a cruciferous plant (*Iberis*), with flowers in tufts or corymbs, the outer petals larger than the inner. [From *Candia* or Crete, whence a species was brought, and *tuft.*]

cane, *kān, n.* the stem of one of the small palms (as calamus or rattan) or the larger grasses (as bamboo, sugar-cane), or raspberry or the like : a slender rod for beating : a walking-stick.—*v.t.* to beat with a cane.—*adj.* **cane'-bottomed,** having a seat of interwoven cane strips.—*ns.* **cane'-brake,** a thicket of canes, esp. (in Southern U.S.) of a giant reed; **cane'-chair,** chair made of rattan; **cane'fruit,** fruit borne upon canes, as raspberries, blackberries; **cane'-mill,** a mill for crushing sugar-cane; **cane'-su'gar,** sucrose, esp. that obtained from the sugar-cane; **cane'-trash,** refuse of sugar-cane used for fuel in boiling the juice; **can'ing,** a thrashing with a cane.—*adj.* **can'y,** like, made of, or abounding in cane. [Fr. *canne*—L. *canna*—Gr. *kannē,* a reed.]

caneh. Same as **kaneh.**

canella, *kan-el'ä, n.* (*obs.*) cinnamon : **Canella,** a genus of low aromatic trees of a small family **Canellä'ceae,** one of which yields white cinnamon or *canella* bark. [L.L., dim. of *canna,* reed.]

canephor, *kan'i-fŏr, n.* (*archit.*) a female figure bearing a basket on her head.—Also **canephorus** (*ka-nē'for-əs*). [Gr. *kanēphoros,* a basket bearer, as at the Panathenaic festival—*kaneon,* basket, *phoros,* bearing.]

canescent, *ka-nes'ənt, adj.* tending to white : hoary.—*n.* **canesc'ence.** [L. *cānēscēns*—*cānēre*—*cānus,* hoary.]

cangue, cang, *kang, n.* a Chinese portable pillory borne on the shoulders by petty offenders. [Fr. *cangue*—Port. *cango,* a yoke.]

canicular, *ka-nik'ū-lər, adj.* pertaining to the Dogstar (*Canic'ula*) or to the Dog-days : (*facetious*) pertaining to a dog.—**canicular year, cycle,** Sothic year, cycle. [L. *canīculāris, canīcula,* dim. of *canis,* a dog.]

canine, *kan'īn, kān'īn, kan-īn', adj.* like or pertaining to the dog.—**canine appetite,** a huge appetite : **canine letter,** R (from its growling sound); **canine tooth,** a sharp-pointed tooth between the incisors and the premolars. [L. *canīnus*—*canis,* a dog.]

canister, *kan'is-tər, n.* a box or case, for holding tea, shot, etc. : (for **can'ister-shot**), case-shot. [L. *canistrum,* a wicker-basket; Gr. *kanastron*—*kannē,* a reed.]

canities, *ka-nish'i-ēz, n.* whiteness of the hair. [L.]

canker, *kang'kər, n.* an eating sore : a gangrene : a fungus disease in trees, esp. one due to Nectria : inflammation in horses' feet : eczema of dogs' ears : an abscess or ulcer in birds : anything that corrupts, consumes, irritates or decays : a cankerworm : (*Shak.*) a dog-rose.—*v.t.* to eat into, corrupt, or destroy : to infect or pollute : to make sour and ill-conditioned.—*v.i.* to grow corrupt : to decay.—*adj.* **cank'ered,** corroded : venomous, malignant : soured : crabbed.—*adv.* **cank'eredly.** —*n.* **cank'eredness.**—*adj.* **cank'erous,** corroding like a canker.—*n.* **cank'er-worm,** a larva that cankers or eats into plants.—*adj.* **cank'ery,** affected with canker : (*Scot.*) crabbed. [L. *cancer* a crab, gangrene.]

cann, *kan, v.i.* to con.

Canna, *kan'ä, n.* the Indian shot genus of plants. [L., a reed.]

canna, *kän'ä* (*Scot.*). See **cannot.**

canna, *kän'ä,* **cannach,** *kän'ahh, n.* (*Scot.*) cottongrass. [Gael. *canach.*]

cannabic, *kan'əb-ik,* or *-ab', adj.* pertaining to hemp.—*ns.* **cann'abin,** a resin obtained from the hemp plant; **Cann'abis,** the hemp genus of the nettle family. [Gr. *kannabis;* cf. O.E. *hænep.*]

cannel, *kan'l, n.* a bituminous coal that burns with a bright flame, much used for making oils and gas.— Also **cann'el-coal, can'dle-coal.** [Prob. *candle.*]

cannelure, *kan'i-l(y)ōōr, n.* a groove or a fluting : a groove round the cylindrical part of a bullet. [Fr.]

cannibal, *kan'i-bl, n.* an eater of the flesh of his own species.—*adj.* relating to or practising cannibalism.—*n.* **cann'ibalism,** the practice of eating one's own kind.—*adj.* **cannibalist'ic.**—*adv.* **cann'ibally** (*Shak.*).—*v.t.* **cann'ibalise,** (*U.S.*) to repair (a vehicle) with parts taken from other vehicles : to take (parts) for such repairs. [Sp. *Canibal, Caribal,* Carib.]

cannikin, *kan'i-kin, n.* a small can.—Also **can'akin, can'ikin.** [Dim. of **can.**]

cannon, *kan'ən, n.* a great gun (*pl.* **cann'ons** or **cann'on**) : a cannon-bone : a cannon-bit : a stroke in billiards in which the cue-ball hits both the red and the opponent's ball (perh. for **carom**) : a similar stroke in certain other games.—*v.i.* to cannonade : to make a cannon at billiards : to strike on the rebound : to collide.—*v.t.* to collide with.— *n.* **cannonade',** an attack with cannon.—*v.t.* to attack or batter with cannon.—*ns.* **cann'on-ball,** a ball to be shot from a cannon; **cann'on-ball'-tree,** a South American tree (*Couroupita guianensis*) with a large woody fruit; **cann'on-bit,** a smooth round bit; **cann'on-bone,** in mammals in which the digits are reduced in number, a bone formed by the fusion of the persisting metacarpals or metatarsals, which supports the limb from 'knee' (wrist) or hock to fetlock : in birds, the tarsometatarsus; **cannoneer', cannonier',** one who manages cannon; **cann'on-fodder,** men regarded merely as material to be consumed in war; **cann'on-game,** a form of billiards in which, the table having no pockets, the game consists in making a series of cannons; **cann'on-met'al,** gun-metal.— *adj.* **cann'on-proof,** proof against cannon-shot.— *ns.* **cann'onry,** cannonading : artillery; **cann'on-shot,** a cannon-ball : the distance to which a cannon will throw a ball. [Fr. *canon,* augmentative—L. *canna,* a reed.]

cannot, *kan'ət, v.t.* can not (contracted **can't,** *känt,* Scots **canna,** *kan'ä*). [**can** and **not.**]

cannula, *kan'ū-lä, n.* a surgical tube, esp. one enclosing a trocar or perforator, or the breathingtube inserted in the windpipe after tracheotomy.— *adj.* **cann'ulate.** [Dim. of *canna,* a reed.]

canny, *kän'i, adj.* (*Scot.* and *Northern*) knowing : skilful : shrewd : lucky : of good omen : free from taint of the supernatural or dangerous : comfortable : sparing in money matters : gentle : innocent, harmless (sometimes euphemistically) : sly or pawky.—Also *adv.*—*adv.* **cann'ily.**—*n.* **cann'iness.**—**ca' canny** (see **ca'**); **no' canny,** preternatural : dangerous. [App. conn. with **can.**]

canoe, *kə-nōō', n.* a boat made of the hollowed trunk of a tree, or of bark or skins : a skiff driven by paddling.—*v.i.* to paddle a canoe.—*ns.* **canoeing; canoe'ist.** [Sp. *canoa*—Haitian *canoa.*]

cañon, canyon, *kan'yən, n.* a deep gorge or ravine. [Sp. *cañón,* a hollow, from root of **cannon.**]

canon, *kan'ən, n.* a law or rule, esp. in ecclesiastical matters : a general rule : standard : the books of the Bible accepted as the standard or rule of faith by the Christian Church : the recognised genuine works of any author : a species of musical composition constructed according to a rule, one part following another in imitation : a list of saints canonised : (*print.*) a large kind of type.—*adjs.* **canonic** (*kə-non'ik*), **-al,** of the nature of, according to, or included in a canon : regular : ecclesiastical. —*adv.* **canon'ically.**—*n.pl.* **canon'icals,** the official dress of the clergy, regulated by the church canons.—*ns.* **canonicity** (*kan-ən-is'i-ti*), the state of belonging to the canon; **canonisā′tion.**—*v.t.* **can′onise** (*Shak. -non′*), to enrol in the canon or list of saints : to recognise as canonical.—*n.* **can′onist,** one versed in the canon law.—*adj.* **canonist′ic.** —*ns.* **can′on-law,** a digest of the formal decrees of councils, oecumenical, general, and local, of diocesan and national synods, and of patriarchal decision as to doctrine and discipline; **canon of the mass,** that part of the mass which begins after the 'Sanctus' with the prayer 'Te igitur', and ends just before the 'Paternoster'; **canonical hours,** set hours for prayer : those wherein marriage may take place in an English parish church (formerly 8 a.m. to 12 noon, extended in 1886 to 3, in 1934 to 6 p.m.). [O.E. *canon*—L. *canōn*—Gr. *kanōn,* a straight rod—*kannē,* a reed.]

canon, *kan′ən, n.* a member of a body of clergymen serving a cathedral or other church and living under a rule; a clerical dignitary belonging especially to a cathedral, enjoying special emoluments, and obliged to reside there part of the year.—*ns.* **can′oness,** a member of a community of women living under a rule : a woman holding a prebend or canonry, often living in the world; **can′onry,** the benefice of a canon.—**Canon Regular,** a member of an order (Augustinian, Austin, or Black Canons) living under a rule based on St. Augustine's teaching, or of an offshoot (Premonstratensians, White Canons), intermediate between monks and secular clergy; **canon residentiary,** a canon obliged to reside at a cathedral and take a share in the duty; **honorary canon,** one other than a canon regular; **minor canon,** one having the titular rank of canon in a cathedral, but without duties or emoluments; **minor canon,** one who conducts cathedral services but is not a member of the chapter. [O.E. *canonic*—L. *canonicus*—*canōn*; see previous article.]

canoodle, *ka-nōōd′l, v.i.* (*slang*) to fondle amorously. [Origin obscure.]

canophilist, *kə-nof′i-list, n.* a lover of dogs. [L. *canis,* a dog, Gr. *phileein,* to love.]

Canopus, *ka-nō′pus, n.* a bright star in the southern constellation *Argo navis* : an Egyptian human-headed vase for holding the entrails of the embalmed body.—*adj.* **cano′pic.** [L.,—Gr. *Kanōpos,* Menelaus's steersman who died at Canopus in Egypt, was stellified as Canopus, and identified with an Egyptian god worshipped in the form of a jar with human head.]

canopy, *kan′ə-pi, n.* a covering hung over a throne or bed : a covering of state held over the head : any overhanging covering, as the sky : a roof-like projection over a niche, tomb, statue, stall, altar, etc.—*v.t.* to cover with a canopy (*pr.p.* **can′opying**; *pa.t.* and *pa.p.* **can′opied**). [Fr. *canapé*— L. *cōnōpium, cōnōpēum*—Gr. *kōnōpion,* a couch with a mosquito curtain—*kōnōps,* a mosquito.]

canorous, *kan-ō′rəs, adj.* musical : singing : melodiously resonant.—*adv.* **cano′rously.**—*n.* **cano′rousness.** [L. *canōrus*—*canor,* melody—*canēre,* to sing.]

canstick, *kan′stik, n.* (*Shak.*) a candlestick. [Contr.]

cant, *kant, v.i.* to speak whiningly : to use language whose meaning has evaporated from continued repetition : to use the language of thieves, etc. : to talk in an affectedly solemn or hypocritical way.— *n.* a hypocritical or affected or perfunctory style of speech or thought : the language peculiar to a sect : odd or peculiar talk of any kind : slang : a common saying : affected use of religious phrases or sentiments.—Also *adj.*—*n.* **cant′er,** one who *cants,* a beggar : one who makes hypocritical professions.—*adj.* **cant′ing,** whining, pretending to piety : (*her.*) in the form of a rebus, or implying a pun on the bearer's name, allusive. [L. *cantāre,* freq. of *canēre,* to sing.]

cant, *kant, n.* an inclination from the level : a toss or jerk : a sloping or tilted position or face : one of the segments forming a side-piece in the head of a cask : a ship's timber lying obliquely to the line of the keel.—*v.t.* and *v.i.* to turn on the edge or corner : to tilt or toss suddenly.—*ns.* **cant′-board,** a sloping board; **cant′ing,** tilting; **cant′ing-coin,** a piece of wood to prevent rolling

of casks; **cant′ing-wheel,** a wheel with bevelled cogs; **cant′-rail,** a timber supporting the roof of a railway-carriage. [Prob. conn. with Du. *kant;* Ger. *kante,* corner.]

cant, *kant, n.* sale by auction.—*v.t.* to sell by auction. [O.Fr. *encant,* auction; der. uncertain, cf. L.L. *incantāre,* to put up to auction.]

cant, *kant, adj.* (*Scot.*) brisk : lively. [Cf. L.G. *kant,* and **canty.**]

can′t, *känt,* a colloquial contraction for **cannot.**

Cantab, *kan′tab,* for **Cantabrigian,** *kan-tə-brij′i-ən, adj.* of or pertaining to Cambridge (Latinised *Cantabrigia*).—Also *n.*

cantabank, *kan′tə-bangk, n.* a strolling singer. [It. *cantambanco.*]

cantabile, *kän-tä′bē-lā, adj.* easy and flowing. [It.]

cantaloup, *kan′tə-lōōp, n.* a small, ribbed muskmelon : in U.S. extended to other varieties. [Fr.,— It. *Cantalupo,* near Rome, where it was first grown in Europe.]

cantankerous, *kən-tang′kər-əs, adj.* cross-grained : perverse in temper.—*adv.* **cantan′kerously.**—*n.* **cantan′kerousness.** [M.E. *contek,* strife.]

cantar. Same as **kantar.**

cantata, *kän-tä′tä, n.* originally the name applied to a sort of musical narrative by one person, accompanied by a single instrument; subsequently an air was introduced—the modern concert-aria : now also a choral work, a short oratorio or opera intended for concert performance only.—*n.* **can-** **,tatrice** (*kän-tä-trē′chä*), a female singer. [It.,— L. *cantāre,* freq. of *canēre,* to sing.]

cantate, *kän-tä′tä, kan-tä′tē,* the 98th Psalm, from its opening words in Latin, 'Cantate Domino'.

canteen, *kan-tēn′, n.* a vessel used by soldiers for holding liquors : a box of cooking utensils or of knives, forks and spoons : a barrack-tavern, or refreshment house for soldiers : a restaurant attached to an office, works, or the like : (*S. Africa*) a public house.—**wet, dry, canteen,** one in which alcoholic liquors are, are not, sold. [Fr. *cantine*— It. *cantina,* a cellar; further der. uncertain.]

canter, *kan′tər, n.* an easy gallop.—*v.i.* to move at an easy gallop.—*v.t.* to make to canter. [Orig. *Canterbury-gallop,* from the easy pace at which the pilgrims rode to Canterbury.]

canterbury, *kan′tər-ber-i, n.* a stand with divisions in it for holding books, music, etc.—**Canterbury bells, bell,** orig. the nettle-leaved bell-flower, or throatwort: transferred to a cultivated species *Campanula Medium* with large blue, white, or pink bells, in some varieties double : loosely applied to other large-flowered bell-flowers.

cantharis, *kan′thər-is, n.* a blister-beetle or Spanish fly (*Lytta*) : in *pl.* **cantharides** (*kan-thar′i-dēz*), their dried bodies, used for blistering, etc.—*n.* **can′tharid,** a member of the genus Cantharis, otherwise Lytta.—*adjs.* **canthar′idal, cantharid′-ian, cantharid′ic.**—*n.* **canthar′idine,** the active principle of blistering-flies. [L. *cantharis*—Gr. *kantharis* (a blister-beetle), pl. *kantharidēs.*]

cantharus, *kan′thə-rus, n.* a large two-handled drinking-cup : a laver in the atrium before ancient churches :—*pl.* **can′thari.** [L.,—Gr. *kantharos.*]

canthus, *kan′thus, n.* the angle at the junction of the eyelids :—*pl.* **can′thī.** [Gr. *kanthos.*]

canticle, *kan′ti-kl, n.* a song : a non-metrical hymn, esp. one used in church service as the *Benedicite* : (*Spens.*) a canto : a short canto : (*pl.*) the Song of Solomon.—*n.* **can′ticum,** a canticle : a part-song in an ancient play. [L. *canticum,* dim. *canticulum.*]

Cantico(y). See **Kantikoy.**

cantilena, *kan-ti-lē′nä, n.* a ballad or light song : a vocal or instrumental melody : a cantus firmus or melody for church use : a singing exercise or solfeggio. [L. *cantilēna.*]

cantilever, *kan′-ti-lēv-ər,* or **-lēv′,** *n.* a large bracket for supporting cornices, balconies, and even stairs.—**cantilever bridge,** one composed of arms projecting from the piers and connected together in the middle of the span. [Perh. **cant,** angle, and **lever.**]

cantillate, *kan′ti-lāt, v.t.* and *v.i.* to chant, intone. —*n.* **cantillā′tion.**—*adj.* **can′tillatory.**

cantion, *kan'shən, n.* (*Spens.*) a song. [L. *cantiō, -ōnis.*]

cantle, *kan'tl, n.* a corner, edge or slice of anything: the raised hind part of a saddle: (*Scot.*) the crown of the head or of the causeway.—*v.t.* to cut a piece from: to divide.—*n.* cant'let, a fragment. [cant, edge.]

canto, *kan'tō, n.* a division of a long poem: (*mus.*) the part that carries the melody:—*pl.* cantos.— Also (*Shak.*) can'ton.—can'to fer'mo, plainsong, the unornamented melody used in the Western Church from the earliest times, to which later other parts in counterpoint were added. [It.,—L. *cantus—canēre,* to sing.]

canton, *kan'tən, kan-ton', n.* a corner: a division or space: a division of territory, constituting in Switzerland a separate government, in France a subdivision of an arrondissement: a pilastered or quoined corner of a building: (*her.*) an ordinary of a shield, being a square occupying generally the dexter, sometimes the sinister, chief of the field.— *v.t.* to divide into cantons: (mil. pron. *kən-tōōn'*) to allot quarters to.—*adj.* can'tonal, pertaining to or divided into cantons; can'toned (*archit.*), ornamented at the corners with projecting pilasters: (*her.*) placed in the midst of charges occupying the corners.—*n.* canton'ment (mil. pron. *kəntōōn'mənt*), the temporary quarters of troops taking part in manoeuvres or active operations: in India, a permanent military or civil town generally a few miles from an Indian town. [O.Fr. *canton;* It. *cantone,* corner, district—*canto,* a corner: cf. cant (2).]

cantor, *kan'tor, n.* the leader of the singing in a church, a precentor.—*adjs.* canto'rial (*-tō'ri-əl*); cantō'ris (gen. of L. *cantor*) of the cantor, i.e. on the north side of a choir (opposed to *decani*). [L., singer, *canēre,* to sing.]

cantred, *kan'tred,* **cantref,** *kan'trev, n.* (*hist.*) a division of the country—a hundred. [W. *cantref—cant,* hundred, and *tref,* town.]

cantrip, *kăn'trip, n.* (*Scot.*) a freak or wilful piece of trickery: a witch's spell. [Ety. unknown.]

Cantuarian, *kan-tū-ā'ri-ən, adj.* pertaining to Canterbury as the archiepiscopal see of the primate of the Church of England. [L.L. *Cantuārius, Cantuarensis—*O.E. *Cantware* (*pl.*) the people of Kent.]

cantus, *kan'tus, n.* a melody, esp. an ecclesiastical style of music:—*pl.* can'tus.—can'tus firmus, canto fermo. [L., song—*canēre,* to sing.]

canty, *kăn'ti, adj.* (*Scot.*) cheerful, lively.—*n.* can'tiness. [cant (4); cf. L.G. *kantig.*]

canuck, *kə-nuk', n.* (*U.S.*) a Canadian: (*Canada*) a French-Canadian: a small horse.

canvas, *kan'vas, n.* a coarse cloth made of hemp or other material, now esp. cotton, used for sails, tents, etc., and for painting on: the sails of a ship: a piece of stretched canvas, painted or to be painted: material for covering the ends of a racing-boat (whence a canvas-length, win by a canvas).—*v.t.* to cover with canvas.—*ns.* can'vas-back, a North American duck, very good eating, its back ashy white, crossed by broken, zigzag, dark lines; can'vas-climb'er (*Shak.*), a sailor; can'vas-stretch'er, a wooden frame on which canvas is stretched for oil-painting; can'vas-work, embroidery upon canvas, or upon cloth over which canvas has been laid to guide the stitches.—under canvas, having the sails unfurled, under sail: living in tents. [O.Fr. *canevas—*L. *cannabis—*Gr. *kannabis,* hemp.]

canvass, *kan'vas, v.t.* (*Shak.*) to toss in canvas, or in a blanket: to toss or turn about: to examine: to discuss: to solicit votes, orders, contributions, etc., from: (in American elections) to scrutinise.— *v.i.* to solicit votes, etc. (with *for*).—*n.* close examination: a seeking or solicitation: (*U.S.*) an election scrutiny.—*n.* can'vasser. [canvas.]

cany, *kăn'i, adj.* (*Milton*) made of canes.

canyon. Same as cañon.

canzone, *kănt-sō'nā, n.* a song or air resembling a madrigal but less strict: an instrumental piece of like character: a series of stanzas in Italian poetry, of various metrical arrangements :—*pl.* canzoni (*-nē*).—*ns.* (dim.) canzonet (*kan-zō-net'*), canzonetta (*kăn-tsō-net'tä*; pl. canzonette, *-tä*). [It., a song, L. *cantiō, -ōnis—canēre,* to sing.]

caoutchouc, *kow'chook, n.* india-rubber, gum-elastic: the latex of rubber trees. [Fr.,—Carib. *cahuchu.*]

cap, *kap, n.* a woman's light head-dress: brimless covering for the head: an official or symbolic head-dress or one appropriated to a special class or use, academic, athletic, etc.: membership of a team symbolised by a cap: a caplike covering of any kind: the top of a toadstool: the uppermost or terminal part of anything: a percussion-cap (see percussion): a paper disk enclosing a fulminating substance for use with toy pistols, etc.: a lifting of the cap in salutation.—*v.t.* to cover the end or top of: to touch with a cap in conferring a degree: to admit to membership of a team: to outdo or surpass by following with a better.—*v.t.* and *v.i.* to salute by raising the cap: (*pr.p.* capp'ing, *pa.p.* and *pat.t.* capped, *kapt*).—*ns.* cap'-case, (*obs.*) a small travelling-case, a chest; cap'-paper, a kind of wrapping paper: a size of writing paper; capp'ing, a covering: a graduation ceremony.— feather in one's cap, something to be proud of; black cap, that put on by the judge before pronouncing sentence of death; cap and bells, the marks of a professional jester; cap in hand, submissively: supplicatingly; cap of liberty, or Phrygian cap, the conical cap given to a Roman slave on enfranchisement, now the symbol of republicanism; cap of maintenance (see maintenance); cap verses, to quote verses in turn, according to rule; college cap, a mortar-board or trencher-cap; set one's cap at, of a woman, to set herself to captivate a man; the cap fits, the allusion is felt to apply; throw up one's cap, in token of immoderate joy. [O.E. *cæppe—*L.L. *cappa,* a cape or cope.]

cap, caup, *kăp, kawp, n.* (*Scot.*) a wooden drinking-bowl, with two handles. [O.E. *copp,* a cup; or Scand. *koppr.*]

capa, *kä'pä, n.* a Spanish cloak: fine Cuban tobacco for the outsides of cigars. [Sp.]

capable, *kāp'ə-bl, adj.* able (often with *of*): qualified.—*ns.* capab'ility, cap'ableness. [Fr.,—L.L. *capābilis—*L. *capēre,* to hold, take.]

capacity, *kə-pas'i-ti, n.* power of holding, containing, absorbing, or grasping: room: volume: ability: power of mind: character in which one does something: legal competence: maximum possible output or performance: capacitance.— *adj.* (*U.S.*) attaining the full capacity.—*adj.* capacious (*kə-pā'shəs*), including much: roomy: wide: extensive.—*adv.* capā'ciously.—*ns.* capā'ciousness; capac'itance, ratio of electric charge to potential.—*v.t.* capac'itate, to make capable: to qualify.—*n.* capac'itor, an electrical condenser; —capacity for heat, power of absorbing heat; legal capacity, the power to alter one's rights or duties by the exercise of free-will, or responsibility for one's acts; to capacity (*U.S.*) to the utmost capacity, the fullest extent possible. [Fr., *capacité* —L. *capāx, -ācis,* able to receive—*capēre,* to hold.]

cap-à-pie, *kap-ə-pē', adv.* from head to foot, referring to arming, as a knight. [O.Fr. *cap a pie* (mod. *de pied en cap*)—L. *caput,* head, *ad,* to, *pēs,* foot.]

caparison, *kə-par'i-sən, n.* the covering of a horse: a rich cloth laid over a war-horse: dress and ornaments generally.—*v.t.* to cover with a cloth, as a horse: to dress very richly.—*adj.* capar'isoned. [Fr. *caparaçon—*Sp. *caparazón,* augmentative of *capa,* a cape, cover—L.L. *cappa.*]

cape, *kāp, n.* a covering for the shoulders attached as a tippet to a coat or cloak: a sleeveless cloak. [O.F. *cape—*L.L. *cappa.*]

cape, *kāp, n.* a head or point of land running into the sea or a lake.—*v.i.* (*naut.*) to keep a course.— Cape boy, girl, a S. African half-breed; Cape cart, a two-wheeled vehicle with hood and pole; Cape doctor, a south-east wind at the Cape, so named by Anglo-Indians formerly invalided there; Cape Dutch, the Taal or Afrikaans, the Dutch spoken in S. Africa; Cape gooseberry, the strawberry-tomato (*Physalis peruviana*), a S. American solanaceous plant with bladdery calyx, naturalised in S. Africa : its edible fruit; **Cape nightingale**, a frog; **Cape pigeon**, the pintado petrel; **Cape smoke**, S. African brandy, dop.—the **Cape**, Cape of Good Hope : Cape Colony or Province. [Fr. *cap*—L. *caput*, the head.]

capelin, *kap'ə-lin*, *n.* a small fish of the smelt family, abundant off Newfoundland, much used as bait.—Also **cap'lin**. [Fr. *capelan*.]

capeline, *kap'ə-lin*, *n.* a small iron skull-cap worn by archers : a light woollen hood for evening wear : a surgical bandage for the head.—Also **cap'elline**. [Fr.,—L.L. *capella*—*capa*, a cap.]

Capella, *ka-pel'ä*, *n.* a first-magnitude star in the constellation Auriga. [L., lit. she-goat.]

capellet, *kap'ə-lit*, *n.* a wen-like swelling on a horse's elbow, or on the back part of his hock. [Fr.,—L.L. *capella*—*capa*, a cap.]

capellmeister. Same as **kapellmeister**.

caper, *kā'pər*, *n.* the pickled flower-bud of a bush (*Capparis spinosa*) grown in Sicily.—*ns.* **cā'per-bush**; **cā'per-sauce**, a sauce for boiled mutton, etc., made with capers; **cā'per-spurge**, a kind of spurge whose capsules are sometimes pickled; **cā'per-tea**, a black tea with a knotty curled leaf. [L. *capparis*—Gr. *kapparis*.]

caper, *kā'pər*, *v.i.* to leap or skip like a goat : to dance in a frolicsome manner.—*n.* a leap : a frisk.— *n.* **cā'perer.**—**to cut a caper**, to execute a frisk. [See **capriole**.]

capercailzie, -llie, -lzie, *cap-ər-kā'l(y)i*, *n.* a species of grouse almost as big as a turkey. [Gael. *capull coille*, horse of the wood.]

Capernaite, *ka-*, *kə-pər'ni-īt*, *n.* an inhabitant of *Capernaum* in Galilee : (polemically) a believer in transubstantiation (John vi, 35, 51).—*adj.* **Capernaitic** (*-it'ik*).—*adv* **Capernait'ically.**

capernoity, -ie, cappernoity, *kap-ər-noi'ti*, *n.* (*Scot.*) the head, noddle.—*adj.* peevish : crabbed : capricious.—*adj.* **capernoit'ed**, capernoity. [Origin unknown.]

capillaceous, *kap-i-lā'shəs*, *adj.* hairlike.—*ns.* **capillaire** (*-lār'*), orig. an infusion of maidenhair fern (Fr. *capillaire*) : a syrup flavoured with orangeflower water; **capillarity** (*-lar'i-ti*), capillary quality : capillary attraction.—*adj.* **capillary** (*kə-pil'ə-ri*, sometimes *kap'*), having to do with hair : hairlike : of very small bore.—*n.* a fine-bored tube : a minute vessel such as those that connect arteries with veins.—*n.* **capillitium** (*kap-i-lish'i-əm*), a mass of threads.—**capillary attraction**, the force that causes liquids to rise in capillary tubes and wicks, to spread through blotting-paper, etc. [L. *capillus*, hair.]

capital, *kap'it-l*, *adj.* relating to the head : involving the death penalty : placed at the head : main, chief, principal : (*coll.*) excellent : relating to capital.— *n.* the chief or most important thing : the chief town or seat of government : a large letter, such as is used at the beginning of a sentence, etc. : the stock of money used for carrying on any business or as a means of acquiring more : possessors of capital collectively, or their political and economic influence and interests : any advantage used as a means of gaining further advantages.—*n.* **capitalisā'tion**, the act of converting into capital : use of capital letters.—*v.t.* **cap'italise**, to convert into capital or money : to print or write with capital letters.—*ns.* **cap'italism**, condition of possessing capital : the economic system which generates and gives power to capitalists; **cap'italist**, one who derives income and power from capital.—Also *adj.*—*adj.* **capitalist'ic**.—*adv.* **cap'itally**, chiefly : principally : (*coll.*) excellently : by capital punishment.—**capital cross**, a Greek cross with terminations like Tuscan capitals; **capital goods**, producers' goods; **capital levy**, an exaction by a state, for a specific purpose, of a proportion of the capital (money value—cash, securities, mortgages, houses, machinery, goodwill, etc.) of its members; **capital ship**, a warship of the largest and strongest class.—**circulating** or **floating capital**, that which constantly changes hands, as wages paid to workmen, raw material used; **fixed capital** consists of buildings, machines,

tools, etc.; **make capital out of**, to turn to advantage. [O.Fr. *capitel*—L. *capitālis*—*caput*, the head.]

capital, *kap'it-l*, *n.* the head or top part of a column, etc. : a chapter of a book. [L. *capitellum*, dim. of *caput*, head.]

capitan, *kāp-i-tän'*, or *kap'i-tan*, *n.* (*hist.*) the chief admiral of the Turkish fleet.—*n.* **capitan'o**, a head-man. [Sp. *capitán*, and It. *capitano;* see **captain**.]

capitate, *kap'it-āt*, *adj.* having a head, knob, or capitulum.—*n.* **capitā'tion**, numbering of heads or individuals : a poll-tax.—**capitation grant**, a grant of so much a head. [L. *capitātus*, headed, *capitātiō, -ōnis*, poll-tax—*caput*, head.]

capitayn, *kap-i-tān'*, *n.* (*Spens.*) **captain.**

Capitol, *kap'it-ol, -l*, *n.* the temple of Jupiter at Rome, built on the *Capitoline* hill : (*U.S.*) the house where Congress or a state legislature meets.—*adjs.* **capitō'lian**, **capit'oline**. [L. *Capitōlium*—*caput*, the head.]

capitular, *kə-pit'ūl-ər*, *n.* a statute passed in a chapter or ecclesiastical court : a member of a chapter.—*adj.* relating or belonging to a chapter in a cathedral.—*adv.* **capit'ularly.**—*n.* **capit'ulary**, a collection of ordinances : a heading.— *adj.* of a chapter. [See **chapter.**]

capitulate, *kə-pit'ūl-āt*, *v.i.* to treat : to draw up terms of agreement : to yield or surrender on certain conditions or heads.—*ns.* **capit'ulant**, one who capitulates; **capitulā'tion**.—*adj.* **capit'ulatory**. [L.L. *capitulātus*, *pa.p.* of *capitulāre*, to arrange under heads—*capitulum*, a chapter.]

capitulum, *kə-pit'ū-lum*, *n.* (*bot.*) a close head of sessile flowers, as in Compositae : (*anat.*) the head of a bone, esp. of a rib (also **capitell'um**) :— *pl.* **capit'ula**, **capitell'a**.—*adjs.* **capit'ulate**; **capit'ular**. [L., dim. of *caput*, head.]

caple, capul, *kā'pl*, *n.* a horse. [M.E. *capel;* cf. O.N. *kapall;* Ir. *capall;* L.L. *caballus*, a horse.]

caplin. See **capelin.**

capnomancy, *kap'nō-man-si*, *n.* divination by smoke. [Gr. *kapnos*, smoke, *manteiā*, divination.]

capocchia, *kä-pok'kyä*, *n.* (*Shak.* **chipochia**) a fool. [It.]

capon, *kā'pn*, *n.* a castrated cock : (jocularly) a fish, esp. a herring : (*Shak.*) a letter.—*v.t.* **cā'ponise**. [O.E. *capun;* L. *capō, -ōnis*, Gr. *kapōn-koptein*, to cut. See **chop.**]

caponiere, *kap-ō-nēr'*, *n.* a covered passage across the ditch of a fortified place.—Also **caponier'**. [Fr. *caponnière*, Sp. *caponera*, capon-coop.]

caporal, *kap-or-āl'*, *n.* a kind of shag tobacco. [Fr.]

capot, *kə-pot'*, *n.* the winning of all the tricks at the game of piquet, and scoring forty.—*v.t.* to score capot against. [Fr.]

capote, *kə-pōt'*, *n.* a long kind of cloak or mantle. [Fr. dim. of *cape*, a cloak; see **cape**.]

capotaine. See **copataine.**

Cappagh-brown, *kap'ä-brown*, *n.* a brown bituminous earth pigment, stained with oxide of manganese and iron from *Cappagh* near Cork.—Also **Capp'ah-brown.**

Capparis, *kap'ər-is*, *n.* the caper genus, giving name to the family **Capparidā'ceae**, akin to the crucifers.—*adj.* **capparidā'ceous.** [See **caper.**]

capreolate, *kap'ri-ō-lāt*, *adj.* tendrilled. [L. *căprĕŏlus*, a tendril.]

capric, *kap'rik*, **caproic**, *kap-rō'ik*, **caprylic**, *kap-ril'ik*, *adjs.* applied to three fatty acids obtained from butter, etc., with goat-like smell.— *ns.* **cap'rate**, **cap'roate**, **cap'rylate**, salts respectively of these. [L. *caper*, a goat.]

caprice, *kə-prēs'*, *n.* a change of humour or opinion without reason : a freak : changeableness.—*ns.* **capriccio** (*kä-prēt'chō*), a sportive motion : (*mus.*) a species of free composition, not subject to rule as to form or figure; **capriccioso** (*-chō'sō*), a direction in music for a free style.—*adj.* **capricious** (*kə-prish'əs*) (*Shak.*), humorous : full of caprice : changeable.—*adv.* **capri'ciously.**—*n.* **capri'ciousness.** [Fr. *caprice* and It. *capriccio;* perh. from L. *caper*, *capra*, a goat.]

Capricorn, *kap′ri-korn, n.* a constellation and a sign of the zodiac represented as a horned goat or monster. [L. *capricornus—caper,* a goat, *cornū,* a horn.]

caprifig, *kap′ri-fig, n.* a goat-fig, wild fig.—*n.* **caprifica′tion,** a method of promoting the fertilisation and ripening of cultivated figs (which are practically dioecious) by hanging on the trees branches of caprifig (which have male flowers as well as sterile female or gall flowers) so that the gall-wasps emerging from the galls and flying to the cultivated fig to lay their eggs, carry with them some pollen.—*v.t.* **cap′rify.** [L. *capricus,* the wild fig—*caper,* a goat, and *ficus,* a fig.]

caprine, *kap′rin, adj.* goat-like.

caprifole, *kap′ri-fōl (Spens.* **caprifoil,** *-foil),* an old name for honeysuckle.—*n.pl.* **Caprifolià′ceae,** the honeysuckle family.—*adj.* **caprifolià′ceous.** [L. *caper,* goat, *folium,* leaf.]

capriform, *kap′ri-form, adj.* goatlike. [L. *caper,* goat, *forma,* form.]

capriole, *kap′ri-ōl, n.* a caper: a leap without advancing.—*v.i.* to leap: to caper. [O.Fr. *capriole*—It. *capriola*—L. *caper, capra,* a goat.]

caps, *kaps, n.pl.* (*coll.*) for **capitals,** capital letters.

Capsian, *kap′si-ən, adj.* of a Mediterranean culture answering to the Aurignacian. [L. *Capsa,* Gafsa, in Tunisia.]

Capsicum, *kap′si-kəm, n.* a tropical shrubby genus of the potato family, yielding cayenne pepper.—*n.* **cap′sicin** (*-sin*), an extract from capsicum. [Perh. L. *capsa,* a case.]

capsize, *kap-sīz′, v.t.* to upset.—*v.i.* to be upset.—*adj.* **capsiz′able.** [Origin unknown.]

capstan, *kap′stən, n.* an upright machine turned by bars or otherwise so as to wind a cable upon it. [Fr. *cabestan, capestan,* through L.L. forms from L. *capěre,* to take, hold.]

capsule, *kap′sūl, n.* (*bot.*) a dry dehiscent fruit of more than one carpel: the spore-bearing part of a moss: (*zool.*) a fibrous or membranous covering: a small dish: a small gelatine case for holding a dose of medicine.—*adjs.* **cap′sular, cap′sulary; cap′sulate.** [Fr.,—L. *capsula,* dim. of *capsa,* a case—*capěre,* to hold.]

captain, *kap′tin, n.* a head or chief officer: the commander of a troop of horse, a company of infantry, a ship, or a portion of a ship's company: in the navy, an officer ranking with a colonel: in the army, an officer ranking with a naval lieutenant: the overseer of a mine: the leader of a team or club: the head-boy of a school.—*v.t.* to lead.—*ns.* **cap′taincy,** the rank or commission of a captain; **cap′tain-gen′eral,** commander of an army; **cap′tainship** (*obs.*), rank or condition of a captain: skill in commanding.—**captain of industry,** a great industrial employer. [O.Fr. *capitaine*—L.L. *capitāneus,* chief—L. *caput,* head.]

caption, *kap′shən, n.* the act of taking: an arrest: (*Engl. law*) the formal title of an indictment or deposition which shows the authority under which it is executed or taken: in Scotland, before 1837, a formal warrant to apprehend a debtor or other defaulting obligant, given in the Bill Chamber after letters of horning had been executed: (esp. *U.S.*) a heading, legend, or accompanying wording of an article, chapter, illustration, or cinematograph picture, etc.—*adj.* **cap′tious,** ready to catch at faults or take offence: peevish.—*adv.* **cap′tiously.** —*n.* **cap′tiousness.** [L. *captiō, -ōnis—capěre,* to take.]

captive, *kap′tiv, n.* a prisoner: a person or animal kept in confinement.—*adj.* confined: kept in bondage: restrained by a line (as a balloon): (*fig.*) charmed or subdued by anything: pertaining to captivity.—*v.t.* (*kap′tiv;* also in *Spens., Milt. kap-tiv′*) to make captive or to captivate.—*v.t.* **cap′tivate,** to charm: to engage the affections of.—*adj.* **cap′tivating.**—*ns.* **cap′tiva(u)nce** (*Spens.*), captivity; **captiv′ity,** **cap′tor,** one who takes a captive or a prize; **cap′ture,** the act of taking: the thing taken: an arrest: (*geol.*) transference of a tributary to another river by more active denudation.—*v.t.* to take as a prize: to take by force. [L.

captīvus, captor, captūra—capěre, captum, to take.]

capuccio, *kə-poot′chō, n.* (*Spens.*) a hood. [It.]

capuche, *kə-pōōsh′, -pōōch′, n.* a hood, esp. that worn by the *Capuchins.*—*n.* **Capuchin** (*kap′ū-chin* or *kap-ōō-shēn′*), a friar of a branch of the Franciscan order so called from the hood he wears: a cloak like a capuchin's: a hooded pigeon: a capuchin monkey.—**capuchin cross,** a cross with each arm terminated by a ball; **capuchin monkey,** a South American monkey (*Cebus*) with hair like a cowl. [Fr., cowl—L.L. *cappa;* see **cap, cape.**]

capul. See **caple.**

caput, *kap′ut, -ət, n.* a head: a knob:—*pl.* **cap′ita.**—**caput mortuum,** the residuum after distillation: worthless residue. [L.]

capybara, *kap-i-bä′rä, n.* the largest living rodent, a native of South America, allied to the guinea-pig. [Port. from Tupí.]

car, *kär, n.* a vehicle moved on wheels, applied to very various forms—a large and splendid vehicle, as a triumphal car, a funeral car, the two-wheeled Irish jaunting-car, a motor-car: (*prov.*) a four-wheeled cab, as opposed to a hansom: a street tramway carriage: in America, applied to all vehicles for railway travelling, as a passenger-car, freight-car, etc.; in Britain, to certain forms of railway carriage, as dining-car, sleeping-car, Pullman-car: (*poet.*) a chariot: the part of a balloon or airship that carries passengers and load.—*n.* **car′man,** a man who drives a car or cart: a carter. [O.Fr. *carre*—L.L. *carra,* a Celt. word, seen in Ir. *carr,* Bret. *karr.*]

carabine. See **carbine.**

Carabus, *kar′ə-bəs, n.* a genus of beetles giving name to the ground-beetle family, **Carabidae** (*kə-rab′i-dē*). [Gr. *kārabos,* a kind of beetle.]

caracal, *kar′ə-kal, n.* the Persian lynx. [Fr., prob.—Turk. *qara-qulaq,* black ear.]

caracara, *kär-rä-kä-rä′,* or *kä-rä-kä′rä, n.* a name for several South American vulture-like hawks. [Imit.]

carack. See **carrack.**

caracol, caracole, *kar′ə-kōl, n.* a half-turn or wheel made by a horseman: a winding stair.—*v.i.* to turn half-round: to prance about. [Fr. *caracole*—It. *caracollo*—Sp. *caracol,* a spiral snail shell.]

caract, *kar′əkt, n.* (*Shak.*) mark: sign. [App. Gr. *charaktos,* marked.]

caracul. See **karakul.**

carafe, *kə-räf′, n.* a water-bottle for the table. [Fr. *carafe,* prob. from Ar. *gharafa,* to draw water.]

carambola, *ka-rəm-bō′lä, n.* a small East Indian tree (*Averrhoa Carambola*) of the wood-sorrel family: its acrid pulpy fruit used for tarts, etc. [Port.]

carambole, *kar′əm-bōl.* See **carom.**

caramel, *kar′ə-mel, n.* a dark-brown substance produced from sugar by loss of water on heating, used in colouring puddings, whisky, wines, etc.: a tenacious sweetmeat made with sugar, butter, etc.—*vs.t.* and *vs.i.* **car′amel** or **car′amelise.**—Also **car′omel.** [Fr.,—Sp. *caramelo.*]

Caranx, *kar′angks, n.* the scad genus of fishes, giving name to a family **Carangidae** (*kar-an′ji-dē*).—*adj.* **carangoid** (*kar-ang′goid*). [Origin obscure.]

caranna, *kar-an′ä,* **carauna,** *-aw′nä, n.* a resinous substance yielded by various South American burseraceous trees. [Sp. *caraña,* from Tupí.]

Carapa, *kar′a-pä, n.* a genus of tropical trees of the mahogany family yielding **car′ap** (or **crab′**)-**nuts, -oil, -wood.** [*caraipi,* the native Guiana name.]

carapace, *kar′ə-pās, n.* the shell of the crab, tortoise, etc.—*adj.* **carapa′cial** (*-shl*). [Fr.,—Sp. *carapacho.*]

carat, *kar′ət, n.* (*gems*) a weight of approximately 205 milligrams—the *metric carat* (C.M.) = 200 milligrams: (*gold*) a twenty-fourth part in stating fineness. [Fr.,—Ar. *qīrāt,* perh. from Gr. *keration,* a carob-seed used as a weight.]

carauna. See **caranna.**

caravan, *kar'ə-van*, *-van'*, *n.* a company travelling together for security, esp. in crossing the deserts : a company of people : a fleet with convoy : a covered van : a house on wheels.—*v.i.* to travel in a caravan (*pr.p.* **car'avaning** or **caravann'ing**; *pa.p.* and *pa.t.* **car'avaned, caravann'ed**).—*ns.* **caravaneer'**, the leader of a caravan; **caravanserai** (*-van'sə-ri*), a kind of unfurnished inn or extensive enclosed court where caravans stop.—Also **caravansarai, -sary.** [Pers. *kārwān*, caravan, *kārwānsarāī* (*sarāī*, inn).]

caravel, *kar'ə-vel*, *n.* a light Mediterranean sailing-ship. [Fr. *caravelle*—It. *caravella*; cf. L.L. *cārabus*, Gr. *kārabos*, a light ship.]

caraway, *kar'ə-wā*, *n.* an umbelliferous plant (*Carum Carvi*) with aromatic fruits (**caraway seeds**) used as a tonic and condiment. [Prob. Sp. *alcaravea* (and *carvi*) from Ar. *karwiyā*—Gr. *karon*.]

carbamide, *kärb-am'īd*, *kärb'əm-īd*, *n.* urea. [**carbonyl, amide.**]

carbide, *kär'bīd*, *n.* a compound of carbon with another element. [**carbon.**]

carbine, *kär'bīn*, **carabin(e)**, *kar'ə-bin*, *-bīn*, *n.* a short light musket.—*n.* **car(a)bineer'**, a soldier armed with a carbine : a light cavalryman : a soldier of the 6th Dragoon Guards. [Fr. *carabine*.]

carbocyclic, *kär-bō-sīk'lik*, *adj.* homocyclic. [**carbon, cyclic.**]

carbohydrate, *kär-bō-hī'drāt*, *n.* a compound of carbon, hydrogen, and oxygen, the last two being in the same proportion as in water : extended to include kindred compounds. [See **carbon, hydrate.**]

carbolic, *kär-bol'ik*, *n.* (in full **carbolic acid**) phenol. [L. *carbō*, coal, *oleum*, oil.]

carbon, *kär'bən*, *n.* a non-metallic element (atomic number 6), widely diffused, occurring uncombined as diamond and graphite : a piece of carbon (esp. an electrode or a lamp-filament), or of carbon paper : a carbonado diamond.—Also *adj.*—*adj.* **carbonā'ceous**, coaly : containing much carbon : like carbon.—*n.* **car'bonate**, a salt of carbonic acid.—*v.t.* to combine or impregnate with carbon dioxide : to carbonise.—*n.* **carbonā'tion.**—*adjs.* **carbonic** (*-bon'ik*), pertaining to carbon; **carbonif'erous**, producing carbon or coal : (*geol.*) **Carboniferous**, belonging to the **Carboniferous System**, one of the main divisions of the Palaeozoic rocks, overlying the Devonian or Old Red Sandstone, underlying the Permian, and including the Mountain or Carboniferous Limestone, the Millstone Grit, and the Coal Measures.—*n.* **carbonisā'tion.**—*v.t.* **car'bonise**, to reduce to carbon : to char or coke : to cover with carbon.—*v.i.* to become carbonised.—**carbon copy**, a duplicate of writing or typed matter made by interleaving sheets of **carbon paper**, a paper coated with lampblack; **carbon dioxide, carbonic anhydride**, an oxide of carbon (CO_2), popularly called *carbonic acid*, which in solution in water forms **carbonic acid** (H_2CO_3), a weak acid; **carbon disulphide**, CS_2, a solvent for rubber; **carbon process** (*phot.*), printing process using paper coated with gelatine and a pigment and sensitised with potassium bichromate; **carbon tetrachloride** ($C Cl_4$), a solvent, etc. [Fr. *carbone*—L. *carbō*, *-ōnis*, coal, charcoal.]

carbonado, *kär-bən-ā'dō*, *n.* (*obs.*) a piece of meat cut crossways for broiling on coals.—*v.t.* to cut crossways for broiling : to slash. [Sp. *carbonada*.]

carbonado, *kär-bən-ā'dō*, *n.* a variety of crystalline carbon, black, opaque, harder than diamond, used in drilling, etc., called also *black diamond, carbon*. [Port., carbonated.]

Carbonari, *kär-bon-är'ē*, *n.pl.* members of a secret society in Italy at the beginning of the 19th century, founded to help forward a republican government.—*n.* **Carbonar'ism.** [It., lit. charcoal burners.]

carbonyl, *kär-bən-il*, *n.* (*chem.*) the radical CO. [**carbon**, and Gr. *hylē*, matter.]

Carborundum, *kär-bər-un'dum*, *n.* a silicon carbide, used as a substitute for corundum. [**carbon** and **corundum**; a trade-mark in some countries.]

carboy, *kär'boi*, *n.* a large glass bottle, with basket-work or other casing, for dangerous chemicals. [Pers. *qarābah*.]

carbuncle, *kär'bung-kl*, *n.* a mythical self-luminous gem : a fiery-red precious stone (almandine or precious garnet) : an inflamed ulcer : a pimple on the nose.—*adjs.* **car'buncled**, set with the gem carbuncle; afflicted with carbuncles : having red inflamed spots; **carbun'cular**, belonging to or like a carbuncle : red : inflamed. [L. *carbunculus*, dim. of *carbō*, a coal.]

carburet, *kär'bū-ret*, or *ret'*, *n.* (*obs.*) a carbide.—*vs.t.* **carburet, car'burate, car'burise**, to combine with carbon : to charge with carbon compounds.—*ns.* **carburā'tion, carburīsā'tion.**—*p.adj.* **car'buretted** (or *ret'*).—*n.* **car'burettor, -er** (or *ret'*), an apparatus for charging a gas with carbon compounds, esp. part of an internal-combustion engine in which air is mixed with volatile fuel in the desired proportion.—**carburetted gas**, a mixed illuminant got by passing water-gas over hot hydrocarbons; **carburetted hydrogen**, marsh-gas, olefiant gas, or other compound of carbon and hydrogen. [Fr. *carbure*—L. *carbō*, coal.]

carcajou, *kär'kə-jōō*, *n.* the glutton or wolverine. [Canadian Fr., prob. from an Indian name.]

carcake, *kär'kāk*, *n.* (*Scot.*) a kind of cake for Shrove Tuesday. [O.E. *caru*, grief, and **cake.**]

carcanet, *kär'kə-net*, *n.* a collar of jewels : (*obs.*) a jewelled head-ornament. [Fr. (and obs. Engl.) *carcan*, an iron collar used for punishment—L.L. *carcannum*, from Gmc.]

carcass, carcase, *kär'kəs*, *n.* a dead body, no longer used of a human corpse : (disrespectfully) a live human body : the framework of anything : a ruin : an incendiary shell. [O.Fr. *carquois* (mod. *carcasse*), a skeleton.]

carcinogen. See **carcinoma**.

carcinology, *kär-si-nol'ə-ji*, *n.* the study of crustaceans.—*adj.* **carcinolog'ical** (*-ō-loj'i-kl*).—*n.* **carcinol'ogist.** [Gr. *karkinos*, a crab, *logos*, discourse.]

carcinoma, *kär-si-nō'mä*, *n.* a cancer :—*pl.* **carcinō'mata.**—*adj.* **carcinō'matous.**—*ns.* **carcin'ogen** (*-jen*), a substance that encourages the growth of cancer; **carcinogen'esis; carcinō'sis, carcinōmatō'sis**, spread of cancer in the body. [Gr. *karkinōma*—*karkinos*, crab.]

card, *kärd*, *n.* a small piece of pasteboard : one with figures for playing a game, with a person's name and address, with a greeting, invitation, message, programme, etc. (*playing-card, visiting-card, Christmas card, wedding card, race-card*, etc.) : a domino : the dial of a mariner's compass : a map : a perforated plate used as a guide in weaving : (*U.S.*) a personal announcement in a newspaper or elsewhere : an invitation : (*slang*) a waggish or eccentric character:—in *pl.* a game played with cards.—*ns.* **card'board**, a stiff, finely finished pasteboard : **card'-case**, a case for carrying visiting-cards : **card'-castle**, an erection of playing cards in storeys : any flimsy or precarious structure; **card-catalogue, -index**, one with entries on separate cards; **card'-sharper**, one who cheats at cards; **card'-table**, a table for playing cards on; **card'-vote**, a voting system that gives each delegate's vote a value in proportion to the number he represents.—**cards in one's hands**, everything under one's control; **cards on the table**, one's resources and moves freely laid open; **cooling card** (see **cool**); **knowing card**, one who is wide awake; **on the cards**, not improbable; **play one's cards well, badly**, to make, not to make, the best of one's chances; **show one's cards**, to expose one's secrets or designs; **speak by the card**, to speak with precision and to the point; **sure card**, a sure means to succeed; **throw up the cards**, to give in : to confess defeat. [Fr. *carte*—L. *c(h)arta*—Gr. *chartēs*, paper; cf. **carte.**]

card, *kärd*, *n.* an instrument for combing wool or flax.—*v.t.* to comb (wool, etc.).—*n.* **card'er.** [Fr. *carde*—L. *carduus*, a thistle.]

Cardamine, *kär-dam'i-nē*, *n.* a genus of cress, including the cuckoo-flower or lady's smock. [Gr. *kardaminē*—*kardamon*, cress.]

cardamom, kär′də-mom, n. the capsules of several tropical plants of the ginger family, which form an aromatic, pungent spice. [L. *cardamōmum*—Gr. *kardamōmon*.]

cardecu, **cardecue**, kär′di-kū, n. (obs.) an old French silver coin, about 1s. 6d. [Fr. *quart d'écu*, quarter of a crown.]

cardiac, kär′di-ak, adj. belonging to the heart or to the upper end of the stomach: cordial.—n. a cordial—adj. **cardiacal** (-dī′ə-kl), cardiac.—ns. **cardialgia** (-di-al′ji-ä; Gr. *algos*, pain), **car′dialgy**, an uneasy sensation or burning pain at the upper orifice of the stomach, apparently at the heart—hence called heartburn; **car′diograph**, an instrument for recording movements of the heart; **car′diogram**, a tracing so obtained.—adj. **car′dioid**, heart-shaped.—n. a heart-shaped curve traced by a point on the circumference of a circle rolling on an equal circle.—n. **cardit′is**, inflammation of the heart. [Gr. *kardiā*, heart, the upper end of the stomach.]

cardigan, kär′di-gən, n. a knitted woollen jacket, named after Lord *Cardigan* (1797-1868).

cardinal, kär′di-nl, adj. pertaining to a hinge: on which a thing hinges: fundamental: of a deep scarlet colour, like a cardinal's cassock or hat.—n. one of the seventy (or fewer) princes of the church constituting the sacred college at Rome, to whom pertains the right of electing a new pope: a short cloak, formerly worn by ladies: a cardinal-bird.—ns. **car′dinalate**, the office or dignity of a cardinal; **car′dinalship**, the office or dignity of a cardinal; **car′dinal-bird**, a large American finch, the cock bright red with a crest, a song-bird; **car′dinal-flower**, a scarlet-flowered American lobelia: extended to a blue species (blue cardinal).—adv. **car′dinally**, fundamentally.—**cardinal numbers**, numbers expressing how many (1, 2, 3, distinguished from *ordinals*); **cardinal points**, the four chief points of the compass—north, south, east, and west; **cardinal virtues**, justice, prudence, temperance, fortitude, upon which the whole of human nature was supposed to hinge. [L. *cardinālis*—*cardō*, *cardinis*, a hinge.]

cardoon, kär-dōōn′, n. a Mediterranean plant close akin to the true artichoke, its leafstalks and ribs eaten like celery. [Obs. Fr. *cardon*—L. *carduus*, a thistle.]

carduus, kär′dū-us, n (Shak.) a thistle. [L.]

cardophagus, kär-dof′ə-gəs, n. a thistle-eater, a donkey. [Latinised from Gr. *kardos*, thistle; *phagos*, eater, glutton.]

care, kār, n. affliction: anxiety: heedfulness: heed: charge, oversight: an object of anxiety or watchfulness.—v.i. to be anxious: to be inclined: to be concerned: to mind: to have liking or fondness: to provide, look after, watch over (with *for*).—adjs. **care′-crazed** (Shak.), crazed or broken with care and solicitude; **care′-free**, void of anxiety; **care′ful**, full of care: heedful: (B.) anxious: (Spens.) grievous: (Spens.) sorrowful.—adv. **care′fully**.—n. **care′fulness**.—adj. **care′less**, without care: heedless, unconcerned.—adv. **care′lessly**.—ns. **care′lessness**; **care′taker**, one put in charge of anything, esp. a building.—adj. exercising temporary supervision or control.—adj. **care′-worn**, worn or vexed with care.—**care of**, to be delivered to the custody of, or at the address of; **take care**, to be careful or cautious; **take care of**, to look after with care: (coll.) to make the necessary arrangements regarding. [O.E. *caru*; Goth. *kara*, sorrow; O.N. *kæra*, to lament.]

careen, kə-rēn′, v.t. and v.i. to turn over on the side, esp. for repairing or cleaning.—n. a heeling position.—n. **careen′age**, a place where ships are careened: the cost of careening. [L. *carina*, keel.]

career, kə-rēr′ (obs. **cariere**; Spens. kar′), n. (obs.) a racecourse or lists, a course passed over: a rush: progress through life, esp. advancement in profession.—v.i. to gallop: to move or run rapidly.—n. **career′ist**, one intent on his own advancement. [Fr. *carrière*, a racecourse—L.L. *carrāria*, carriage-road—*carrus*, wagon.]

caress, kə-res′, v.t. to touch endearingly: to fondle.—n. an endearing touch.—n. and adj. **caress′ing**.

—adv. **caress′ingly**. [Fr. *caresser*—It. *carezza*, an endearment—L. *cārus*, dear.]

caret, kar′et, n. a mark, ∧, to show where to insert something omitted. [L., 'there is wanting'.]

Carex, kā′reks, n. a genus of sedges. [L. *cārex*.]

carfax, -**fox**, kär′faks, -foks, n. a place where four roads meet—now used mainly of particular examples, as at Oxford. [L. *quadrifurcus*, four-forked.]

cargo, kär′gō, n. the goods a ship carries:—pl. **car′goes**. [Sp., from root of car.]

cargoose, kär′gōōs, n. the crested grebe:—pl. **cargeese**. [O.N. *kjarr*, copsewood, and goose.]

cariacou, kar′i-ə-kōō, **carjacou**, kär′jə-kōō, n. any deer of the American genus or subgenus *Cariacus*, including the Virginian deer. [Tupí, *cariacu*.]

cariama, sä-ri-ä′mä, n. Same as **seriema**.

Carib, kar′ib, one of a race inhabiting parts of Central America and northern South America: their language.—Also adj.—ns. and adjs. **Caribbē′an**, **Caribbee′**.—**Caribbee bark**, the bark of a West Indian rubiaceous genus (*Exostema*) once esteemed a substitute for cinchona. [Cf. **cannibal**.]

caribe, kä-rē′bä, n. the piranha. [Sp., Carib, savage, piranha.]

Carica, kar′i-kä, n. the papaw genus, giving name to a family **Caricā′ceae**, akin to the passion-flowers. [L. *Carica* (*ficus*), a Carian dried fig.]

caribou, kar-i-bōō′, n. the American reindeer. [Canadian Fr.]

caricature, kar′i-kə-tūr, or tūr′, n. a likeness of anything so exaggerated or distorted as to appear ridiculous.—v.t. to turn into ridicule by distorting a likeness: to burlesque.—Formerly **caricatū′ra**.—n. **caricatur′ist**. [It. *caricatura*—*caricare*, to load, from root of **car**.]

cariere, an obs. form of **career**.

caries, kā′ri-ēz, n. decay, esp. of teeth.—adj. **ca′rious**, decayed. [L. *cariēs*.]

carillon, kə-ril′yən, kar′il-yən, n. a set of bells for playing tunes: a mechanism for playing them: a melody played on them.—n. **carill′onist** (or kar′). [Fr.,—L.L. *quadrilīō*, *-ōnis*, a quaternary, as formerly rung on four bells.]

carina, kə-rī′nä, n. a keel or keel-like ridge: the boat-shaped structure formed by the two lower petals in the pea family.—adj. **carinate** (kar′i-nāt), keeled. [L. *carina*, a keel.]

cariole, **carriole**, kar′i-ōl, n. a small open carriage: a light cart. [Fr. *carriole*—root of **car**.]

cark, kärk, n. (arch.) care, anxiety, or solicitude.—v.t. to burden, harass.—v.i. to be anxious.—adj. **cark′ing**. [Norm. Fr. *kark(e)*—L.L. *carcāre*—*carricāre*, to load. See **charge**.]

carl, kärl, n. a husbandman, a clown: a churl: (Scot.) a niggard.—ns. **carl′-hemp**, the female plant of hemp (lit. male-hemp, as stronger than fimble, the true male): **car′line** (-lin), an old woman: a witch.—adj. **carl′ish**, churlish: clownish.—n. **car′lot** (Shak.), a churl, peasant. [O.N. *karl*, a man, a male; see **churl**.]

carline, kär′lin, n. any plant of a genus (*Carlina*: **Carline thistle**) closely allied to the true thistles. [From a legend that an angel showed the root to *Carolus*, *Karl*, or Charlemagne, as a remedy for a plague.]

Carlist, kär′list, n. a supporter of the claims of the Spanish pretender Don *Carlos* de Borbón (1788-1855), second son of Charles IV., and his representatives.—Also adj.—n. **Car′lism**.

carlock, kär′lok, n. a Russian isinglass. [Russ. *karluk*.]

Carlovingian, kär-lo-vin′ji-ən, adj. relating to a dynasty of Frankish kings, so called from *Karl* the Great or Charlemagne (742-814).—Also **Carolin′gian**.

Carlylese, kär-līl-ēz′, n. the vigorous, irregular phraseology and vocabulary of Thomas *Carlyle* (1795-1881).—adjs. **Carlylesque**, **Carlyl′ean**.—n. **Car′lylism** (or līl′).

carmagnole, kär-man-yōl′, n. a popular song and dance of the French Revolution: a kind of jacket worn by revolutionists at that time, with short skirts, a broad collar and lapels, and several rows of buttons. [Prob. from *Carmagnola* in Piedmont.]

Neutral vowels in unaccented syllables: el′ə-mənt, in′fənt, ran′dəm

Carmelite, *kär'mi-līt, n.* a White Friar, or friar of the order of Our Lady of Mount *Carmel*, in Syria, founded there about 1156, made a mendicant order in 1247—the habit brown, with a white cloak and scapular: a nun of a similar order (from 1452): a variety of pear: a fine woollen stuff like beige.

carminative, *kär'min-ə-tiv*, or *-min', adj.* expelling flatulence.—*n.* a medicine with that effect. [L. *cārmināre*, to card, comb out—*cārmen*, a card for wool.]

carmine, *kär'mīn, -min, n.* the red colouring matter of the cochineal insect: its colour.—*adj.* of that colour. [Fr. *carmin* or Sp. *carmín*—Sp. *carmesí*, crimson—Ar. *qirmazī*, crimson. Same root as **crimson**.]

carnage, *kär'nij, n.* (obs.) a heap of slain: slaughter. [Fr.,—It. *carnaggio*, carnage—L. *carō, carnis,* flesh.]

carnahuba. See **carnauba**.

carnal, *kär'nl, adj.* fleshly: sensual: unspiritual: bodily: sexual: (*Shak.*) murderous, flesh-eating.—*v.i.* to act carnally.—Also **car'nalise**.—*ns.* **car'nalism**; **car'nalist**, a sensualist: a worldling: **carnal'ity** (*-nal'i-ti*), state of being carnal.—*adv.* **car'nally**.—*adjs.* **car'nal-mind'ed**, worldly-minded; **carnass'ial** (Fr. *carnassier*), adapted for flesh-eating.—*n.* a carnivore's scissor-tooth, usually long and large, used for tearing flesh.—*adjs.* **car'neous, carnose'**, fleshy: of or like flesh.—*n.* **car'nifex** (L.), an executioner.—*adj.* **carnificial** (*-fish'l*).—*n.* **carnos'ity**, a fleshy excrescence growing in and obstructing any part of the body. [L. *carō, carnis,* flesh.]

carnallite, *kär'nəl-īt, n.* a milk-white or pinkish hydrous chloride of potassium and magnesium. [Named from the mineralogist Von *Carnall* (1804-74).]

carnation, *kär-nā'shən, n.* (obs.) flesh-colour: a colour ranging from light pink to deep crimson: a florists' double-flowering variety of the clove pink. —*adj.* of the colour carnation.—*adj.* **carna'tioned**, ruddy. [L. *carnātiō, -ōnis,* fleshiness.]

carnauba, carnahuba, *kär-nä-ōō'bä,* or *-now', n.* a Brazilian palm (*Copernicia*): its yellowish wax— also *Brazilian wax.* [Braz.]

carnelian. See **cornelian**.

carnival, *kär'ni-vl, n.* a feast observed by Roman Catholics just before the fast of Lent: any season of revelry or indulgence: riotous feasting, merriment, or amusement: a fair-like entertainment. [It. *carnevale*—L.L. *carnelevārium*, apparently from L. *carnem levāre*, to put away flesh.]

Carnivora, *kär-niv'ə-rä, n.pl.* an order of flesh-eating mammals.—*n.* **car'nivore** (*-vōr*), a carnivorous animal.—*adj.* **carniv'orous**, flesh-eating.— *adv.* **carniv'orously**.—*n.* **carniv'orousness**. [L. *carō, carnis,* flesh, *vorāre*, to devour.]

carnotite, *kär'nō-tīt, n.* a mineral (hydrated vanadate of uranium and potassium) notable as a source of radium. [From Adolphe *Carnot*, French mine inspector.]

carny, carney, *kär'ni, v.t.* and *v.i.* (prov.) to coax, wheedle.—*n.* flattery. [Origin unknown.]

carob, *kar'ob, -əb, n.* the algarroba or locust-tree (*Ceratonia Siliqua*), a caesalpiniaceous Mediterranean tree. [Fr. *carobe*—Ar. *kharrūbah;* cf. **algarroba**.]

caroche, *kä'rōsh', n.* a coach or carriage. [Fr.,—It. *caroccio, carro*—L. *carrus,* car.]

carol, *kar'əl, n.* (arch.) a ring-dance of the song accompanying it: a song of joy or praise: a cheerful Christmas hymn: an enclosure for a study in a cloister, etc.—*v.i.* to dance or sing a carol: to sing or warble.—*v.t.* to praise or celebrate in song (*pr.p.* **car'olling**; *pa.p.* and *pa.t.* **car'olled**). [O.Fr. *carole;* It. *carola,* orig. a ring-dance; acc. to Diez, a dim. of L. *chorus,* Gr. *choros.*]

Carolina, *kar-ō-lī'nä, n.* two states (North and South) of the United States.—Also *adj.*—**Carolina allspice** (see **Calycanthus**); **Carolina pink**, an American species of Silene (see also **Spigelia**).

Carolingian, *kar-ə-lin'ji-ən, adj.* Same as **Carlovingian**.

Carolus, *kar'ə-ləs, n.* a gold coin of the time of Charles I.—*adj.* **Car'oline**, belonging to the time

of Charles (I. or II., or Charlemagne, or any other Charles). [L. *Carolus,* Charles.]

carom, *kar'əm, n.* and *v.* an abbreviation for **carambole** (*kar'əm-bōl*), the same as **cannon** in billiards.

carotene, *kar'ō-tēn, n.* any of a number of reddish-yellow pigments widely distributed in plants, precursors of vitamin A.—*n.* **carotenoid** (*kar-ot'in-oid*), any of a group of pigments similar to carotenes, some of which are precursors of vitamin A.—Also **car'otin, carot'inoid.**

carotid, *kə-rot'id, adj.* relating to the two great arteries of the neck. [Gr. *karōtidēs* (pl.)—*karos,* sleep, the ancients supposing that deep sleep was caused by compression of them.]

carouse, *kə-rowz', adv.* (obs.) in drinking, all out.— *n.* a drinking-bout: a noisy revel.—*v.i.* to hold a drinking-bout: to drink freely and noisily.—*ns.* **carous'al**, a carouse: a feast: **carous'er.**—*adv.* **carous'ingly.** [O.Fr. *carous,* Fr. *carrousse*—Ger. *gar aus,* quite out, that is, empty the glass.]

carousel, *kar-ōō-zel', n.* a tilting match or tournament, to which were added games, shows, and allegorical representations: (*U.S.*) a merry-go-round. [Fr. *carrousel.*]

carp, *kärp, v.i.* to catch at small faults or errors (with *at*).—*n.* **carp'er.**—*n.* and *adj.* **carp'ing,** cavilling: fault-finding.—*adv.* **carp'ingly.** [Most prob. Scand., O.N. *karpa,* to boast, modified in meaning through likeness to L. *carpĕre,* to pluck, deride.]

carp, *kärp, n.* a fresh-water fish common in ponds. [O.Fr. *carpe*—L.L. *carpa;* poss. Gmc.]

carpal. See **carpus**.

carpel, *kär'pl, n.* a modified leaf forming the whole or part of the gynaeceum of a flower.—*adj.* **car'pellary.**—*n.* **carpogō'nium,** the female organ in red seaweeds, indirectly producing **carp'ospores.**— *adj.* **carpoph'agous,** fruit-eating.—*n.* **carp'ophore,** a prolongation of a flower axis below or between the carpels. [Gr. *karpos,* fruit.]

carpenter, *kär'pent-ər, n.* a worker in timber as used in building houses, etc.—*v.i.* to do the work of a carpenter.—*ns.* **car'penter-bee,** a bee that excavates its nest in wood; **car'pentry,** the trade or work of a carpenter. [O.Fr. *carpentier*—L.L. *carpentārius*—*carpentum,* a car, from root of **car.**]

carpet, *kär'pit, n.* the woven or felted covering of floors, stairs, etc.: (*Shak.*) a table-cloth: a carpet-moth.—*v.t.* to cover with or as if with a carpet: to have up for reprimand (*pr.p.* **car'peting**; *pa.p.* and *pa.t.* **car'peted**).—*ns.* **car'pet-bag,** a travelling-bag made of carpeting: **car'pet-bagger,** one who comes to a place for political or other ends (as if he carried his whole property qualification for citizenship with him in his carpet-bag); **car'pet-beat'ing,** the removing of dust from carpets by beating; **car'pet-bedd'ing,** a system of horticulture in which plants are arranged in mosaic or geometrical designs; **car'peting,** material of which carpets are made: carpets in general; **car'pet-knight',** one dubbed a knight by mere court favour, not on account of his military exploits—hence an effeminate person; **car'pet-monger** (*Shak.*), an effeminate person; **car'pet-moth',** any of the larger moths, with carpet-like markings, of the geometrid family Larentidae; **car'pet-rod,** one of the rods used to keep a stair carpet in its place; **car'pet-slipper,** a slipper made of carpeting; **car'pet-snake,** a variegated python of Australia; **car'pet-sweeper,** an apparatus with a revolving brush and a dust-pan, for sweeping carpets.—**on the carpet,** under discussion (a jocular translation of Fr. *sur le tapis*). [O.Fr. *carpite* (Fr. *carpette*)—L.L. *carpeta, carpita,* a coarse fabric made from rags pulled to pieces— L. *carpĕre,* to pluck.]

carphology *kär-fol'ə-ji, n.* floccillation, fitful plucking movements as in delirium. [Gr. *karphos,* straw, *logeiā,* gathering.]

carpus, *kär'pus, n.* the wrist, or corresponding part of the fore-limb.—*adj.* **car'pal,** pertaining to the carpus.—*n.* a bone of the carpus.—*n.* **carpometa-car'pus,** in birds, a bone of the wing formed by fusion of some of the carpals with the metacarpals. [Latinised from Gr. *karpos,* wrist.]

carr, *kär, n.* (a copse in) boggy ground. [O.N. *kjarr*.]

carrack, *kar'ək, n.* (*hist.*) a large ship of burden, which was also fitted for fighting.—Also **car'ack**, **carr'act**, **carr'ect**.[O.Fr. *carraque*—L.L. *carraca*; ety.dub.]

carrag(h)een, *kar-ə-gēn', n.* a purplish-red North Atlantic seaweed (*Chondrus crispus*) and a related species (*Gigartina mamillosa*), used for making a highly digestible soup and a kind of blanc-mange, as well as size—also called *Irish moss.* [From *Carragheen*, near Waterford, where it abounds.]

carrat, carraway. Same as **carat, caraway.**

carriage, *kar'ij, n.* act or cost of carrying : a vehicle for carrying, esp. a luxurious road vehicle, or a railway passenger-car : a wheeled support of a gun : the structures on which an aeroplane lands : a carrying part of a machine : (*Shak.*) the loop of a sword-belt : behaviour : bearing : (*Shak.*) burden : (*B.*) baggage.—*adj.* **carr'iageable**, that may be conveyed in carriages.—*ns.* **carr'iage-com'pany**, or **-peo'ple**, people who keep their carriages; **carr'iage-clock**, a small portable clock, usu. with a case; **carr'iage-dog'**, a coach-dog; **carr'iage-drive**, a road for carriages through parks, etc.— *advs.* **carr'iage-free'**, without charge for transport; **carr'iage-for'ward**, without prepayment of carriage.—*n.* **carr'iage-horse**, a horse that draws a carriage.—*adv.* **carriage-paid'**, with prepayment of carriage.—*n.* **carr'iage-way**, a road, or part of a road, used by vehicles.—**carriage and pair**, a turn-out of a carriage and two horses. [See **carry.**]

carrick-bend, *kar'ik-bend', n.* (*naut.*), a kind of knot, formed on a bight by putting the end of a rope over its standing part, and then passing it. [Perh. conn. with **carrack**, and the root of **bind.**]

carriole. See **cariole.**

carrion, *kar'i-ən, n.* the dead and putrid body or flesh of any animal : anything vile.—*adj.* relating to, or feeding on, putrid flesh.—*ns.* **carr'ion-crow**, the common crow : (*U.S.*) the black vulture; **carr'ion-flower**, a S. African asclepiad (*Stapelia*) with fleshy stem and stinking flowers. [Fr. *carogne*—L.L. *carōnia*—L. *carō, carnis*, flesh.]

carritch, *kär'ich, n.* (*Scot.*) a catechism. [Fr. *catéchèse*, taken to be a plural.]

carriwitchet, *kar-i-wich'it, n.* a quip : a quibble. [Origin unknown.]

Carron, *kar'ən, n.* a town in Stirlingshire with iron works.—*ns.* **carronade'**, a short cannon of large bore, first made there; **carr'on-oil'**, a liniment of linseed-oil and lime-water, used for burns at the iron works.

carrot, *kar'ət, n.* a plant of the *Umbelliferæ*, having a tapering root of a reddish or yellowish colour : the root itself, which is edible and sweet.—*adj.* **carr'oty**, carrot-coloured, applied to the hair. [Fr. *carotte*—L. *carōta*.]

carry, *kar'i, v.t.* to convey : to bear : to lead or transport : to take by force : (*mil.*) to hold in saluting position : to effect : to gain : to behave or demean : (of money) to be sufficient for : to pass, by a majority : (*arith.*) to add to another column ; (of a newspaper) to publish e.g. an item of news, or to publish as a regular feature.—*v.i.* (of a voice, a gun, etc.) to reach, indicating its range (*pr.p.* **carr'ying**; *pa.p.* and *pa.t.* **carr'ied**).—*n.* the distance a golf-ball goes when struck till it touches the ground : range : an act of carrying : the portage of a boat : land across which a boat has to be carried between one navigable stream or stretch and another : the position of 'carry arms' : (*prov.*) the sky, cloud-drift.—*ns.* **carr'ier**, one who carries, esp. for hire : anything that carries : an instrument for carrying : a basket, framework, or the like, for carrying luggage, as on a bicycle : one who transmits disease (without suffering from it) by harbouring germs, virus, etc. : (*wireless*) the independent component of a modulated wave, frequency, etc. : a carrier-pigeon; **carr'ier-pig'eon**, a pigeon with homing instinct, used for carrying messages : a pigeon of a fancy breed no longer so used; **carr'y-tale** (*Shak.*), a tale-bearer.—**carry all before one**, to bear down all obstacles; **carry away**, to carry

off : deprive of self-control by exciting the feelings : to transport; **carry it**, to behave, demean oneself : to gain the advantage, carry the day (also **carry it away**) : **carry off**, to cause the death of : to gain, to win, as a prize : to cause to pass muster, to make to pass by assurance or dissimulation; **carry on.** to promote : to manage : to behave incorrectly : to misbehave : (*mil.*) to continue : to proceed; **carry one's bat** (see **bat**) ; **carry one's point**, to overrule objections to one's plan or view; **carry out**, to accomplish : to carry out for burial; **carry over**, to bring into the other party : to take to a new page, as an account, etc. : to postpone to next occasion ; **carry the day**, to be successful : to win the day; **carry through**, to support through difficulties : to succeed in putting into effect, to accomplish; **carry too far**, to continue beyond reasonable limits; **carry up**, to continue a building upward : to trace back; **carry weight**, to possess authority : to have force.   [O.Fr. *carier*—L.L. *carricāre*, to cart—L. *carrus*, a car.]

carry-all, *kar'i-awl, n.* (*U.S.*) a light four-wheeled one-horse carriage.   [**cariole**, changed by folk-etymology.]

carse, *kärs, n.* (*Scot.*) an alluvial river-side plain. [Perh. **carr.**]

cart, *kärt, n.* a two-wheeled vehicle without springs, used for farm purposes, or for conveying heavy loads : a light two-wheeled vehicle with springs.— *v.t.* to convey in a cart : to carry publicly in a cart as a punishment—formerly done to bawds.—*ns.* **cart'age**, the act or cost of carting; **cart'er**, one who drives a cart; **cart'-horse**, a horse suitable for drawing a cart; **cart'-house**, a shed for keeping carts; **cart'-load**, as much as a cart can carry; **cart'-road**, **cart'way**, a road or way by which carts may pass; **cart's-tail**, the hind part of a cart, formerly a place of punishment; **cart'-wheel'**, the wheel of a cart : a sideways somersault, or Catherine-wheel; **cart'wright**, a carpenter who makes carts; see also **dog-cart**, **mail-cart**, **tax-cart**, etc.—in the cart (*slang*), in the lurch : in a fix; **put the cart before the horse**, to reverse the natural order of things; **village cart**, an uncovered two-wheeled carriage for one horse, with a low body and one seat; **whitechapel cart**, or **chapel cart**, a light two-wheeled spring-cart much used by butchers in delivering goods to their customers.   [Ety. dub.; O.E. *cræt*, or O.N. *kartr*.]

carte, *kärt, n.* the fourth position of the wrist in fencing.   [Fr. *quarte*—It. (and L.) *quarta*, fourth.]

carte, *kärt, n.* a bill of fare : (*Scot.*) a playing-card : a *carte-de-visite.*—*ns.* **carte'-blanche** (*-blän^(g)sh*), a blank paper, duly signed, to be filled up at the recipient's pleasure : freedom of action; **carte-de-visite** (*-də-vē-zēt'*), a small photographic portrait pasted on a card; **cart'el**, a challenge : an agreement for exchange of prisoners : a card with writing on it : a political condition or bloc : (also *kär-tel'*), a combination of firms for certain purposes, esp. to keep up prices and kill competition.—*v.t.* and *v.i.* **cartelise'.**   [Fr.,—L. *c(h)arta ;* see **card.**]

Cartesian, *kär-tē'zi-ən*, or *-zhyən, adj.* relating to the French philosopher René *Descartes* (1596-1650), or his philosophy, or his system or coordinates.— **Cartesian devil, diver,** or **bottle-imp**, a scientific toy named after Descartes, a bottle with a floating figure that sinks when the cover is pressed.

carthamine, *kär'thə-min, n.* a dye got from safflower. [L.L. *carthamus*—Ar. *qartum*, saffron.]

Carthusian, *kär-thū'zi-ən*, or *-thōō', n.* a monk or (since 1229) a nun of an order founded by St. Bruno in 1086, noted for its strictness : a scholar of the Charterhouse School, founded on the site of a Carthusian monastery in London, now in Godalming. —*adj.* of or pertaining to the order or the school. [L. *Cartusiānus—Catorissium*, Chatrousse, a village in Dauphiné, near which their first monastery, La Grande Chartreuse, was founded.]

cartilage, *kär'ti-lij, n.* gristle, a firm pearly white substance, often converted later into bone.—*adj.* **cartilaginous** (*-laj'*).—**cartilaginous fishes**, fishes with a cartilaginous skeleton—sharks, rays, chimaeras.   [Fr.,—L. *cartilāgō, -inis ;* cog. with *crātis*, wickerwork, Gr. *kartallos*, a basket.]

cartography, *kär-tog'rə-fi*, *n.* map-making.—*n.* **cartog'rapher.**—*adjs.* **cartographic** (*-tō-graf'ik*), **-al.** [L. *c*(*h*)*arta*—Gr. *chartēs*, a sheet of paper, and Gr. *graphein*, to write.]

cartomancy, *kär'tō-man-si*, *n.* divination by playing-cards. [L.L. *carta*, a card, Gr. *manteiā*, divination.]

carton, *kär'tən*, *n.* a thin pasteboard : a box made from it : a small disk within the bull's-eye of the target : a shot that strikes it.—*ns.* **car'tonnage**, pasteboard : the outer covering of a mummy; **carton-pierre** (*kär-ton⁵-pyer*), a kind of papier-maché, imitating stone. [Fr. See **cartoon.**]

cartoon, *kär-tōōn'*, *n.* a preparatory drawing on strong paper to be reproduced in fresco, tapestry, etc. : any large sketch or design on paper : a comic or satirical representation of current events or politics in a paper : a cinematograph film made by photographing a succession of drawings.—*v.t.* to make a cartoon or working design of : to caricature by a cartoon.—*n.* **cartoon'ist**, one who makes cartoons. [Fr. *carton* or It. *cartone*, augm. of *carta*.]

cartouche, *kär-tōōsh'*, *n.* a case for cartridges or formerly for mortar bullets : (*archit.*) a scroll-like ornament with rolled ends : an ancient Egyptian oval figure enclosing royal or divine names.—Also **cartouch'.** [Fr.,—It. *cartoccio*—L. *c*(*h*)*arta*—Gr. *chartēs*, paper.]

cartridge, *kär'trij*, *n.* a case containing the charge for a gun (**blank'-car'tridge**, with powder only; **ball'-car'tridge**, with a bullet as well).—*ns.* **car'tridge-belt**, a belt having pockets for cartridges; **cartridge-pā'per**, a light-coloured, strong paper, originally manufactured for making cartridges. [A corr. of **cartouche**.]

cartulary, *kär'tū-lər-i*, *n.* a register-book of a monastery, etc. : one who kept the records : the place where the register is kept. [L.L. *chartulārium*—L. *chartula*, a document—*charta*, paper.]

carucate, *kar'(y)oo-kāt*, *n.* as much land as a team of oxen could plough in a season.—*n.* **car'ucage**, a tax on the carucate, first imposed by Richard I. in 1198. [L.L. *carrūcāta*, ploughland—*carrūca*, plough, from root of **car**.]

caruncle, *ka-*, *kə-rung'kl*, *n.* a small fleshy excrescence : an outgrowth on a seed near the micropyle.—*adjs.* **carun'cular**, **carun'culate**, **carun'culous.** [Fr.—L. *caruncula*.]

carvacrol, *kär'və-krol*, *n.* an isomer of and substitute for thymol, obtained from origanum, etc. [Fr. *carvi*, caraway, L. *acer* sharp, *oleum*, oil.]

carve, *kärv*, *v.t.* to cut into forms, devices, etc. : to make or shape by cutting : to cut up (meat) into slices or pieces : to apportion or distribute.—*v.i.* to exercise the art or perform the act of carving : (*Shak.*) app., to make affected gestures or amorous advances : (*infin.*, *Spens.*, **carv'en**; *pa.p.* **carved**, *arch.* **carv'en**).—*adj.* **carv'en**, carved.—*ns.* **carv'er**, one who carves : a wood-carver : a sculptor : a carving-knife : (*Spens.*) a tree used for carving; **carv'ing**, the act or art of sculpture esp. in wood or ivory : a carved device or figure : the act or art of cutting up meat at table; **carv'ing-knife**, a large knife for carving meat.—**carve out**, to hew out : to gain by one's exertions.—**cut and carve**, to refine. [O.E. *ceorfan*, to cut; Du. *kerven*; Ger. *kerben*, to notch.]

carvel, *kär'vel*, *n.* older form of **caravel**.—*adj.* **car'vel-built**, built without overlap of planks (distinguished from *clinker-built*).

carvy, *kär'vi*, *n.* (*Scot.*) caraway : a caraway seed, esp. one coated with sugar. [Fr. *carvi*; see **caraway**.]

caryatid, *kar-i-at'id*, *n.* a female figure used instead of a column to support an entablature :—*pl.* **caryat'ids**, **caryat'ides** (*-i-dēz*).—*adjs.* **caryat'ic**, **caryat'idal**, **caryatidē'an**, **caryatid'ic.** [Gr. *Karyātis*, a priestess of Artemis at *Karyai* (*Caryae*), pl. *Karyātidēs*.]

Caryocar, *kar'i-ō-kär*, *n.* the butternut genus, giving name to the family **Caryocarā'ceae.** [Gr. *karyon*, nut, *karā*, head.]

caryophyllaceous, *kar-i-ō-fi-lā'shəs*, *adj.* belonging to the pink family (**Caryophyllā'ceae**). [*Caryophyllus*, an early botanical name for the clove-pink

—Gr. *karyophyllon*, clove-tree (from similar smell).]

caryopsis, *kar-i-op'sis*, *n.* a dry indehiscent fruit in which the pericarp is united with the testa, characteristic of the grasses. [Gr. *karyon*, a nut, *opsis*, appearance.]

Casanova, *kas-ə-nō'vä*, *n.* (*coll.*) a person conspicuous for his amorous adventures, as was Giovanni Jacopo *Casanova* de Seingalt (1725-1798).

cascabel, *kas'ka-bel*, *n.* the part behind the basering of a cannon. [Sp.]

cascade, *kas-kād'*, *n.* a waterfall : a trimming of lace or other material in a loose wavy fall : connexion of apparatus in series.—*v.i.* to fall in cascades. [Fr.,—It. *cascata*—L. *cadēre*, to fall.]

cascara, *käs-kä'rä*, or (Sp.) *käs'kä-rä*, *n.* (*cáscara sagrada*), a Californian buckthorn (Rhamnus) bark used as a tonic aperient : (*cáscara amarga*), a bitter Honduras bark of the quassia family.—*n.* **cascarill'a**, the aromatic bitter bark of a West Indian Croton. [Sp. *cáscara*, bark.]

casco, *kas'kō*, *n.* a Philippine lighter. [Sp.]

case, *kās*, *n.* a covering, box, or sheath : a set : a facing for walls : the boards and back of a book : the tray in which a compositor has his types before him.—*v.t.* to enclose in a case : to skin.—*n.* **case'-bottle**, a bottle made to fit into a case with others, a bottle with a covering.—*v.t.* **case'-hard'en**, to harden on the surface, as by carbonising iron : (*fig.*) to make callous or insensitive.—*ns.* **case'-hard'ening**; **case'-knife**, a large knife kept in a sheath; **case'-maker**, one who makes covers for books; **case'man**, a compositor.—*ns.* **case'-shot**, canister-shot, an artillery projectile for use at close quarters; **case'-worm**, caddis-worm; **cas'ing**, the act of putting on a case or of skinning : an outside covering of any kind, as of boards, plaster, etc. [O.N.Fr. *casse* (mod. Fr. *châsse* and *caisse*)—L. *capsa*—*capēre*, to take.]

case, *kās*, *n.* that which falls or happens, event : state or condition : subject of question or inquiry : an instance of disease : a person under medical treatment : (*slang*) an odd character : a legal statement of facts : a law-suit : a plausible contention, something to be said for a position or action : the grammatical relation of a noun, pronoun, or (in some languages) adjective to another word in the sentence, or its variation in form to express that relation—the nominative being imagined as a vertical line, and the oblique cases in various stages of falling or *declension*.—*n.* **case'-book**, a book in which a doctor records the history of his cases; **case'-law**, law as decided in previous cases.—**case history**, record of ancestry, environment, personal history, etc., for use in diagnosis and treatment, or for other purpose; **in any case**, at all events : at any rate; **in case**, in the event that : lest; **in case to**, in fit condition for; **make out one's case**, to give good reasons for one's statements or position; **put (the) case**, to suppose an instance : to take for example; **the case**, the fact, the reality. [O.Fr. *cas*—L. *cāsus*—*cadēre*, to fall.]

casemate, *kās'māt*, *n.* any bomb-proof vaulted chamber, even when merely used as quarters for a garrison : (*orig.*) a loopholed gallery, from which the garrison of a fort could fire upon an enemy who had obtained possession of the ditch.—*adj.* **case'-mated.** [Fr.; der. uncertain.]

casement, *kās'mənt*, *n.* the case or frame of a window : a window that opens on vertical hinges : a hollow moulding.—*ns.* **case'ment-cloth**, a plain cotton fabric, suitable for casement-curtains; **case'ment-cur'tain**, a curtain hung from a window-sash.—*adj.* **case'mented**, having casements.—*n.* **case'ment-window.** [For encasement (Fr. *enchassement*), or L.L. *casamentum*, house-frame, or directly from case (1).]

caseous, *kā'si-əs*, *adj.* cheeselike.—*ns.* **caseā'tion**, becoming cheeselike; **casein** (*kā'si-in*), the principal albuminous constituent of milk, in which it is found as a calcium salt. [L. *cāseus*, cheese.]

casern(e) *kä-zern'*, *n.* a barrack. [Fr.,—Sp. *caserna*.]

cash, *kash*, *n.* coin or money : ready money.—*v.t.* to turn into or exchange for money.—*ns.* **cash'-**

account', an account to which nothing is carried but cash : a form of account with a bank, by which a person is entitled to draw out sums as required by way of loan to a stipulated amount—also called **cash'-cred'it**; **cash'-book**, a book in wh'ch an account is kept of the receipts and disbursements of money; **cashier** (*-ēr'*), **cash'-keeper**, one who has charge of the receiving and paying of money; **cash'-pay'ment**, payment in ready money; **cash'-rail'way**, a mechanical device for interchange of cash between counter and cash-desk in a shop; **cash'-reg'ister**, a till that automatically and visibly records the amount put in.—**cash in (one's checks)** to exchange counters for money on leaving the gaming-table : to die; **hard cash**, spot cash, ready money; **out of cash, in cash**, without, or with, money : out of, or in, pocket. [A doublet of **case**, a box—O.Fr. *casse*, a box.]

cash, *kash*, *n.* a small Eastern coin. [Port. *caixa*—Sinh, *kāsi*, coin.]

cashaw, *ka-shaw'*, *n.* (*U.S.*) a kind of pumpkin : a W. Indian mesquite. [Algonkin.]

cashew, *kă-shōō'*, *kash'ōō*, *n.* a spreading tropical American tree (*Anacardium occidentale*) with kidney-shaped nuts (**cash'ew-nuts**) whose kernels and fleshy stalks (**cash'ew-app'les**) are used as food. [Tupi *caju*; cf. **acajou**.]

cashier, *kash-ēr'*, *v.t.* to dismiss from a post in disgrace : to discard or put away : to annul.—*ns.* **cashier'er**; **cashier'ing**, a punishment for army and naval officers, severer than dismissal, in that it disqualifies from entering the public service in any capacity; **cashier'ment**, dismissal. [Du. *casseren* (*kasseren*), to cashier—Fr. *casser*—L. *cassāre* —*cassus*, void, empty.]

cashmere, *kash'mēr*, *n.* (a shawl or fabric made from) fine soft *Kashmir* goats' hair : any similar product.

casino, *ka-sē'nō*, *n.* a room for public dancing : a building with public dance halls, gaming tables, etc. : a card-game. [It. : from L. *casa*, a cottage.]

cask, *kâsk*, *n.* a hollow round vessel for holding liquor, made of staves bound with hoops : a measure of capacity : (*obs.*) a casque.—*v.t.* to put in a cask. [Fr. *casque*—Sp. *casco*, skull, helmet, cask.]

casket, *kask'it*, *n.* a little cask or case : a small case for holding jewels, etc. : (*U.S.*) a coffin. [Ety. uncertain; hardly a dim. of **cask**.]

casque (*obs.* **cask**), *kâsk*, *n.* a cover for the head : a helmet. [A doublet of **cask**.]

Cassandra, *cas-an'drä*, *n.* a daughter of Priam, king of Troy, beloved by Apollo, who gave her the gift of prophecy, but not of being believed—hence any one who expresses gloomy views of the political or social future and is not listened to.

cassareep, cassaripe, *kas'ə-rēp*, *n.* the juice of the bitter cassava, a potent antiseptic, used in sauces, and in the West Indian pepper-pot. [From Tupi.]

cassation, *ka-sā'shon*, *n.* annulment : (*French law*) the quashing of a decision of a court—hence **court of cassation**, the supreme tribunal. [L.L. *cassātiō*, *-ōnis*—*cassāre*, to bring to nought.]

cassava, *kə-sä'vä*, *n.* manioc : tapioca. [From a Taino name.]

casserole, *kas'ə-rōl*, *n.* a stew-pan : a vessel in which food is both cooked and served : the outer part of several dressed dishes.—**casserole cookery**, cooking in the dish in which the food is to be served. [Fr.]

cassia, *kas(h)'yä*, *n.* a coarser kind of cinnamon (**cass'ia-bark'**): the tree that yields it; **Cassia**, a genus of shrubs of the Caesalpinia family, yielding senna, and the drug cassia fistula or purging cassia. [L. *cassia*—Gr. *kasiā* (also *kassiā*)—Heb. *qetsī'āh*.]

cassimere, *kas'i-mēr*, *n.* a twilled cloth of the finest wools.—Also **kerseymere'**. [Corr. of **cashmere**.]

cassino, *ka-sē'nō*, *n.* a game at cards. [See **casino**.]

Cassiopeia, *kas-i-ō-pē'(y)ä*, *n.* a northern constellation named after the mother of Andromeda.—*n.* **cassiope'ium**, the element of atomic number 71.

cassiterite, *ka-sit'ə-rīt*, *n.* a brown native tin dioxide. [Gr. *kassiteros*, tin.]

cassock, *kas'ək*, *n.* a long loose robe or outer coat, formerly in common wear, but now worn only by

clergy and choristers : a shorter garment, usually of black silk, worn under the Geneva gown by Scottish ministers.—*adj.* **cass'ocked**. [Fr. *casaque*—It. *casacca*.]

cassolette, *kas'ō-let*, *n.* a censer : a perfume-box with perforated lid. [Fr.,—Sp. *cazoleta*—*cazo*, a saucepan.]

cassonade, *kas-o-nād'*, *n.* unrefined sugar. [Fr.]

cassowary, *kas'ə-twr-i*, *n.* a genus (*Casuarius*) of birds, found esp. in New Guinea, nearly related to the emu. [Malay *kasuārī* or *kasavārī*.]

cassumunar, *kas-ōō-mū'nər*, *n.* an East Indian ginger. [Origin unknown.]

cast, *kâst*, *v.t.* to throw or fling : to throw off, shed, drop : to drop prematurely : to throw down : to throw up : to reckon : to add : to project : (*arch.*) to reject, condemn, decide against : to mould or shape : (*arch.*) to purpose, devise, consider : to appoint as actor (*for* a part) : to assign as his part (*to* an actor) : (*Scot.*) to cut and throw up to dry (peat).—*v.i.* to warp (*pa.t.* and *pa.p.* **cast**).—*n.* act of casting : a throw of anything, as the sounding-lead, a fishing-line : the thing thrown, esp. in angling : the distance thrown : a motion, turn, or squint, as of the eye : a turn or sample performance : (*Scot.*) a good turn, as a lift or conveyance in a vehicle : matter ejected by a bird, earthworm, etc. : a throw or turn of fortune, a chance : a mould : form, manner, stamp, or quality : a shade of colour, a degree of guilt, etc. : the assignment of the various parts of a play to the several actors : the company of actors playing rôles : a couple of hawks.—*adj.* **moulded** : rejected, cast off : defeated at law.—*n.* **cast'away**, one shipwrecked in a desolate place : an outcast.—*adj.* worthless, rejected.—*adj.* **cast'ed** (*Shak.*), cast off.—*ns.* **cast'ing**, act of casting or moulding : that which is cast : a mould; **cast'ing-net**, a species of net for fishing; **cast'ing-vote**, a chairman's deciding vote in case of equality; **cast'ing-weight**, the weight that makes the balance cast or turn when exactly poised; **cast'-iron**, an iron-carbon alloy distinguished from steel by its containing substantial amounts of cementite or graphite, which make it unsuitable for working.—*adj.* hard, rigid, unadaptable.—*adj.* **cast'-off**, laid aside or rejected.—*n.* anything thrown aside. *n.* **cast'-steel**, steel that has been cast, not shaped by mechanical working.—**cast about**, to contrive, to look about, to search for, as game : (*B.*) to turn, to go round; **cast a horoscope nativity**, to make an astrological calculation; **cast anchor**, to anchor a ship; **cast an eye, a glance**, to look; **cast a spell upon**, to put under an enchantment; **cast a vote**, to record or make a vote; **cast away**, to wreck : to waste; **cast back**, to revert; **cast down**, to deject or depress in mind : to turn downward; **cast in one's teeth**, to bring up as a reproach against some one : to calculate; **cast loose**, to set loose or adrift; **cast lots** (see **lot**); **cast off**, to reject : to loose (hawks, hounds) : to unmoor : to eliminate stitches : to estimate amount of printed matter that copy will make; **cast on**, to make stitches; **cast out** (*Scot.*), to quarrel; **cast up**, to throw up : to bring up as a reproach : (*Scot.*) to turn up, appear, emerge; **cast water** (*arch.*), to inspect urine in diagnosis; **the last cast**, extremities. [O.N. *kasta*, to throw.]

Castalian, *kas-tā'li-ən*, *adj.* pertaining to *Castalia*, a fountain on Parnassus, sacred to Apollo and the Muses.

castanets, *kas'tə-nets*, *-nets'*, *n.pl.* two hollow shells of ivory or hard wood, bound by a band on the thumb, and struck by the finger to produce a clicking sound—much used in Spain as an accompaniment to dances and guitars. [Sp. *castañeta*—L. *castanea*, a chestnut.]

Castanospermum, *kas-tan-ō-sper'məm*, *n.* an Australian papilionaceous tree, the Moreton Bay chestnut, so called from the taste of its nuts. [Gr. *kastanon*, chestnut, *sperma*, seed.]

caste, *kâst*, *n.* a social class in India : an exclusive social class : a type of individual in some polymorphic social insects.—*n.* **caste'-mark**, an indication of caste on the forehead.—**lose caste**, to

descend in social rank. [Port. *casta*, breed, race—
L. *castus*, pure, unmixed.]
castellan, castellated. See **castle.**
caster. Same as **castor** (2).
castigate, *kas'tig-āt, v.t.* to chastise; to criticise
severely: to emend.—*ns.* **castigā'tion**; **cas'ti-
gātor.**—*adj.* **cas'tigatory** (*-ə-tər-i*). [L. *casti-
gāre, -ātum,* from *castus,* pure.]
Castilian, *kas-til'yən, adj.* of Castile.—*n.* a native of
Castile: the language thereof, standard Spanish.—
Castile soap, a hard soap made with olive-oil and
soda. [Sp. *Castellano.*]
castle, *kås'l, n.* a fortified house or fortress: the
residence of a prince or nobleman, or a large
country mansion generally: a rook in chess: a
defensive tower borne on an elephant's back: a
large ship, esp. of war.—*v.t.* to enclose or fortify
with a castle.—*v.i.* (*chess*) to bring the castle or
rook up to the square next the king, and move the
king to the other side of the castle.—*n.* **castellan,**
(*kas'təl-an*), governor or captain of a castle.—*adj.*
cas'tellated (*kas'tel-āt-id*), having turrets and
battlements like a castle.—*n.* **cas'tle-build'ing,**
the act of building castles in the air or forming
visionary projects.—*adj.* **cas'tled,** furnished with
castles.—*n.* **cas'tle-guard,** the guard for the
defence of a castle.—**castles in the air, or in
Spain,** groundless or visionary projects. [O.E.
castel—L. *castellum,* dim. of *castrum,* a fortified
place.]
castock, *kås'tək,* **custock,** *kus', n.* (*Scot.*) a cabbage
stock. [**kale, stock.**]
Castor, *kås'tor, -tər, n.* one of the Dioscuri, twin-
brother of Pollux, son of Leda, famous for his skill
in horse-taming: a bright star in the constellation
Gemini (the Twins). [L.,—Gr. *Kastōr.*]
castor, caster, *kåst'ər, n.* a small solid swivelled
wheel on a leg of furniture: a vessel with perforated
top for sprinkling.—**castor sugar, caster sugar,**
white powdered sugar. [**cast.**]
castor, *kås'tər, n.* the beaver (genus Castor):
castoreum: a hat of beaver-fur or substitute.—*ns.*
castoreum (*kas-tō'ri-əm*), the perineal sacs of the
beaver, or a brown unctuous strong-smelling
substance got from them, once used in medicine
and perfumery; **cas'tory** (*Spens.*), a red or pink
colour got from castoreum. [L. *castōr, -ŏris*—Gr.
kastōr, -oros, beaver; cf. Sans. *kastūrī,* murk.]
castor-oil, *kås'tər-oil', n.* a medicinal and lubricating oil obtained from the seeds of a tropical
African euphorbiaceous plant, *Ricinus communis.*
[Perh. from use as substitute for **castor(eum).**]
castral, *kas'trol, adj.* belonging to the camp. [L.
castra.]
castrametation, *kas-tra-me-tā'shən, n.* the art of
designing a camp. [L. *castra,* a camp, *mētārī,
-ātus,* to measure off—*mēta,* a boundary.]
castrate, *kas'trāt, v.t.* to deprive of the power of
generation: to remove the testicles from, geld,
emasculate: to take from or render imperfect.—
adj. **cas'trated,** gelded: expurgated.—*ns.* **castrā'-
tion**; **castrato** (*kås-trä'tō;* Ital.), a male singer
castrated in boyhood so as to preserve a soprano
or alto voice:—*pl.* **castra'ti** (*-tē*). [L. *castrāre,
-ātum.*]
casual, *kaz(h)'ū-əl, adj.* accidental: unforeseen:
occasional: off-hand: negligent: unceremonious.—
n. a chance or occasional visitor, labourer, pauper,
etc.: a weed not naturalised.—*n.* **cas'ualism,** the
belief that chance governs all things.—*adv.*
cas'ually.—*ns.* **cas'ualness**; **cas'ualty,** that which
falls out: an accident: a misfortune: (*mil.*) loss
by wounds, death, desertion, etc.: an incidental
charge or payment.—**casual labourer,** a worker
without fixed employment; **casualties of superiority,** in the feudal law of Scotland, payments to
the superior in certain contingencies (e.g. death)—
ultimately redeemed or extinguished by Act of
1914; **casualty ward,** a hospital ward in which
accidents are treated; **casual ward,** a workhouse
department for casuals. [L. *cāsuālis—cāsus.* See
case.]
Casuarina, *kas-ū-ə-rī'nä, n.* the she-oak or beefwood genus of trees, mainly Australian, constituting
a family **Casuarinā'ceae,** perhaps akin to birch

but superficially like horsetails. [Named from its
resemblance to *Cassowary* plumage.]
casuist, *kaz'ū-ist, n.* one who studies and resolves
cases of conscience: often, one who argues
sophistically in such cases.—*adjs.* **casuist'ic, -al,**
—*n.* **cas'uistry,** the science or doctrine of cases of
conscience: the reasoning which enables a man to
decide in a particular case between apparently
conflicting duties—often with a suggestion of
sophistry. [Fr. *casuiste*—L. *cāsus;* see **case.**]
cat, *kat, n.* a carnivore of genus *Felis,* esp. the
domesticated kind or any of the smaller wild
species: a spiteful woman: a movable penthouse
to protect besiegers: a double tripod with six legs:
a piece of wood tapering at each end, struck with
the **cat'-stick** in the game of *tip-cat:* the game
itself: short for the **cat-o'-nine-tails,** a whip with
nine knotted tails or lashes, once used in the army
and navy.—*v.t.* to raise the anchor to the cathead.—
ns. **cat'amount,** the European wild cat: (*U.S.*)
the puma, the lynx, or other beast of the cat
family; **catamoun'tain,** or **cat o' mountain,** a
leopard, panther, or ocelot: a wild mountaineer.—
adj. ferocious, savage.—*adj.* **cat'-and-dog',** constantly quarrelling.—*ns.* **cat'-bird,** an American
bird of the thrush family with a mewing note: an
Australian bower-bird; **cat'-bur'glar,** a burglar
who performs nimble climbing feats; **cat'-call,** a
squeaking instrument used in theatres to express
disapprobation: a shrill whistle or cry.—*v.i.* to
sound a cat-call.—*v.t.* to assail with one.—*adj.*
cat'-eyed, having eyes like a cat: able to see in the
dark.—*ns.* **cat'-fish,** a fish with cat-like features, in
Britain usually the wolf-fish, in America a salt or
fresh-water fish of the family Siluridae; **cat'gut,** a
kind of cord made from the intestines of sheep and
other animals used for violin strings, surgical
ligatures, etc.: the violin or other stringed instrument: a coarse corded cloth.—*adj.* **cat'-hammed,**
with thin hams like a cat's.—*ns.* **cat'head,** one of
two strong beams of timber projecting from the
bow of a ship, on each side of the bowsprit,
through which the ropes pass by which the anchor
is raised; **cat'-hole,** one of two holes in the after
part of a ship, through which hawsers may pass for
steadying the ship or for heaving astern; **cat'hood,**
state of being a cat or having the nature of a cat;
cat'kin, a crowded spike or tuft of small unisexual
flowers with reduced scale-like bracts, as in the
willow, hazel, etc.; **cat'-lap,** any thin or despised
drink.—*adj.* **cat'-like,** noiseless, stealthy.—*ns.* **cat'-
ling,** a little cat, a kitten: (*Shak.*) a catgut string;
cat'mint, cat'nep, cat'nip, a mint-like labiate
plant (*Nepeta Cataria*) of which cats are fond;
cat's'-cradle, a pastime in which a string looped
about the fingers and passed from player to player
is transformed from one symmetrical figure to
another; **cat's'-ear,** *n.* a name given to two genera
of British compositous plants—Hypochoeris, of
the ligulate-flowered group, and Antennaria, or
mountain-everlasting; **cat's-eye,** a name for
various chatoyant minerals, esp. a variety of
chrysoberyl, also a fibrous quartz, and a quartz
pseudomorph after crocidolite: a reflector set in a
frame fixed in a road surface.—*ns.* **cat's'-foot,**
the mountain-everlasting: ground-ivy; **cat'-sil'ver,**
a variety of silvery mica; **cat'skin**; **cat's-
meat,** horse's flesh, or the like, sold for cat's;
cat's'-paw (*naut.*), a light breeze: a hitch in a
rope providing two loops for a hook: one who is
made the tool of another—from the fable of the
monkey who used the paws of the cat to draw
chestnuts out of the fire; **cat's-tail,** a catkin:
Timothy grass: the reed-mace or bulrush; **cat's'-
whisk'er** (*wireless*), a delicate wire brought in
contact with a crystal to rectify the current in
some forms of crystal detector and produce
audibility.—*adjs.* **catt'ish, catt'y,** like a cat:
spiteful: back-biting.—*n.* **cat'-walk,** a narrow footway, as on a bridge.—*adj.* **cat'-witted,** small-
minded, conceited, and spiteful.—**bell the cat** (see
bell); **catted and fished** (of an anchor), raised to
the cathead and secured to the ship's side; **care
killed the** (or a) **cat,** even with his proverbial
nine lives; **Cheshire cat,** proverbially notable for

grinning; **enough to make a cat laugh**, i.e. even the least inclined; **Kilkenny cats** proverbially fight till each destroys the other; **rain cats and dogs**, to pour down heavily; **room to swing a cat**, a minimum of space; **see which way the cat jumps**, to watch how things are going to turn before committing oneself; **turn (the) cat in (the) pan**, to change sides with dexterity; **whip the cat** (see **whip**). [O.E. *cat;* found also in Celt., Slav., Ar., Finn., etc.]

cat, *kat*, *n.* an old name for a coal and timber vessel on the north-east coast of England.—*n.* **cat′boat**, a cat-rigged boat.—*adj.* **cat′-rigged**, having one great fore-and-aft main-sail spread by a gaff at the head and a boom at the foot, for smooth water only. [Obscurely connected with **cat** (1).]

catabolism. See **katabolism.**

catacaustic, *kat-ə-kaws′tik*, *adj.* (*geom.*) belonging to caustic curves formed by reflection. [Gr. *kata*, against, and **caustic.**]

catachresis, *kat-ə-krē′sis*, *n.* (*rhet.*) misapplication of a word.—*adjs.* **catachrestic** (*-kres′tik*, or *-krēs′tik*), **-al.**—*adv.* **catachres′tically.** [Gr. *katachrēsis*, misuse—*chrēsis* use.]

cataclasm, *kat′ə-klazm*, *n.* a disruption, breaking down.—*adjs.* **cataclas′mic**, pertaining to or of the nature of a cataclasm; **cataclas′tic** (*geol.*), mylonitic, or granular in consequence of crushing. [Gr. *kataklasma*—*kata*, down, *klaein*, to break.]

cataclysm, *kat′ə-klizm*, *n.* a flood of water: a debacle: a great revolution.—*adj.* **cataclys′mic.** [Gr. *kataklysmos*—*kata*, downward, *klyzein*, to wash.]

catacomb, *kat′ə-kōm*, *n.* a subterranean excavation used as a burial-place, esp. near Rome, where many of the early Christian victims of persecution were buried: any place built with crypt-like recesses for storing books, wine, etc.—*adj.* **catacumbal** (*-kum′bl*). [It. *catacomba*—L.L. *Catacumbas*, perh. in some way—Gr. *kata*, down, and *kymbē*, a cup.]

catacoustics, *kat-ə-kōōs′tiks*, or *-kows′*, *n.* the part of acoustics that treats of echoes or sounds reflected. [Gr. *kata*, back, and **acoustics.**]

catadioptric, **-al**, *kat-ə-di-op′trik*, *-əl*, *adjs.* pertaining to both reflection and refraction. [See **catoptric, dioptric.**]

catadromous, *kat-ad′rom-əs*, *adj.* of fishes, descending periodically for spawning to the lower parts of a river or to the sea. [Gr. *kata*, down, *dromos*, a run.]

catafalque, *kat′ə-falk*, *n.* a temporary tomb-like structure used in funeral ceremonies: a funeral car.—Also **catafal′co.** [Fr.,—It. *catafalco.*]

Cataian, Catayan, *kə-tā′ən*, *n.* (*Shak.*) a Cathayan, Chinese—a vague term of reproach. [*Cathay*, poetical name for China.]

Catalan, *kat′ə-lan*, *adj.* of or belonging to Catalonia or its language, a dialect of Provençal.—*n.* a native of Catalonia: the language thereof.

catalectic, *kat-ə-lek′tik*, *adj.* incomplete: (*pros.*) wanting one syllable in the last foot.—*n.* **catalex′is.** [Gr. *katalēktikos*, incomplete—*katalēgein*, to stop.]

catalepsy, *kat′ə-lep-si*, *n.* a state of more or less complete insensibility, with bodily rigidity: cataplexy in animals.—*adj.* **catalep′tic.** [Gr. *katalēpsis*, seizure, catalepsy—*kata*, down, *lēpsis*, taking, seizure.]

catallactic, *kat-ə-lak′tik*, *adj.* pertaining to exchange.—*adv.* **catallac′tically.**—*n.* **catallac′tics**, political economy. [Gr. *katallaktēs*, a moneychanger.]

catalogue, *kat′ə-log*, *n.* a systematic list of names, books, pictures, etc.—*v.t.* to put in a catalogue: to make a catalogue of.—*n.* **cat′aloguer.**—*v.t.* **cat′aloguise.**—*n.* **cat′alog** (*U.S.*), a university calendar. [Gr. *katalogos*, from *kata*, in order, *legein*, to reckon.]

Catalpa, *kat-al′pä*, *n.* an American and Japanese genus of low bignoniaceous trees with profuse blossoms and long cigar-like pendent pods. [American Indian (Creek) *kutuhlpa*.]

catalysis, *ka-tal′i-sis*, *n.* the chemical influence of a substance not itself permanently changed.—*n.* **cat′alase**, an enzyme that reduces hydrogen peroxide.—*v.t.* **cat′alyse** (*-līz*), to subject to

catalysis.—*ns.* **cataly′ser, cat′alyst** (*-list*), a catalysing agent.—*adjs.* **catalytic** (*-lit′ik*), **-al.** [Gr. *katalysis*—*kata*, down, *lyein*, to loosen.]

catamaran, *kat′ə-mə-ran′*, or *kat-am′ə-ran*, *n.* a raft of logs lashed together: a double boat: an old kind of fire-ship, long superseded: an ill-natured woman. [Tamil *katta-maram*, tied wood.]

catamenia, *kat-ə-mē′ni-ä*, *n. pl.* the menstrual discharge.—*adj.* **catamē′nial.** [Neut. pl. of Gr. *katamēnios*, monthly—*kata*, against, *mēn*, a month.]

catamite, *kat′ə-mīt*, *n.* a boy kept for unnatural purposes. [Corruption of **Ganymede.**]

catamount. See **cat.**

catapan, *kat′ə-pan*, *n.* the governor of Calabria and Apulia for the Byzantine emperor. [Acc. to Littré, from Gr. *katepanō tōn axiōmatōn*, one placed over the dignities.]

cataphonics, *kat-ə-fon′iks*, *n.* catacoustics.—*adj.* **cataphon′ic.** [Gr. *kata*, back, *phōnē*, sound.]

cataphract, *kat′ə-frakt*, *n.* a suit of mail: (*Milton*) a soldier in full armour.—*adj.* **cataphrac′tic.** [Gr. *kataphraktēs*, a coat-of-mail—*kata*, inten., and *phrassein*, to enclose, protect.]

cataphyll, *kat′ə-fil*, *n.* a rudimentary or simplified leaf.—*adj.* **cataphyll′ary.** [Gr. *kata*, down, *phyllon*, leaf.]

cataphysical, *kat-ə-fiz′i-kl*, *adj.* (*rare*) unnatural. [Gr. *kata*, down, against, *physis*, nature.]

cataplasm, *kat′ə-plazm*, *n.* a plaster or poultice. [Gr. *kataplasma.*]

cataplexy, *kat′ə-plek-si*, *n.* a condition of immobility induced by emotion: in animals the state called shamming death.—*adj.* **cataplec′tic.** [Gr. *kataplēxis*, amazement—*kata*, down, *plēssein*, to strike.]

catapult, *kat′ə-pult*, *n.* anciently, an engine of war (properly one resembling the ballista) for throwing stones, arrows, etc.: a small forked stick having an elastic string fixed to the two prongs, used by boys for throwing small stones: any similar device, as for launching aeroplanes.—*v.t.* and *v.i.* to shoot out from, or as if from, a catapult.—*adj.* **catapul′tic.**—*n.* **catapultier′.**—**catapult fruit**, one that shoots out its seeds. [L. *catapulta*—Gr. *katapeltēs.*]

cataract, *kat′ə-rakt*, *n.* (*rare*) a portcullis: a waterspout, etc.: a waterfall: (*Milton*) a floodgate: an opaque condition of the lens of the eye, painless, unaccompanied by inflammation. [L. *caracta*—Gr. *kataraktēs*, portcullis, waterfall.]

catarrh, *kat-är′*, *n.* a discharge of fluid from the inflammation of a mucous membrane, esp. of the nose, caused by cold in the head: the cold itself.—*adjs.* **catarrh′al, catarrh′ous.** [L. *catarrhus*—Gr. *katarroos*—*kata*, down, *rheein*, to flow.]

catarrhine, catarhine, *kat′ə-rīn*, *adj.* pertaining to that one of the two divisions of Primates, including all the Old-World monkeys, having a narrow partition between the nostrils. [Gr. *katarris*, with hanging nose—*kata*, down, *rhis*, *rhinos*, nose.]

catasta, *kat-as′tä*, *n.* a block on which slaves were exposed for sale: a stage or place for torture. [L.]

catastasis, *kat-as ta-sis*, *n.* the part of a drama in which the action has reached its height. [Gr. *katastasis*, settlement.]

catastrophe, *kat-as′trə-fi*, *n.* an overturning: a final event: the climax of the action of the plot in play or novel: an unfortunate conclusion: a sudden calamity: (*Shak.*) rear.—*adj.* **catastrophic** (*kat-ə-strof′ik*).—*ns.* **catas′trophism**, the old theory of geological change by vast catastrophes and new creations (opp. to *uniformitarianism*); **catas′trophist.** [Gr. *kata*, down, *strophē*, a turning.]

catatonia, *kat-ə-tō′ni-ä*, **catatony**, *kat-at′ə-ni*, *ns.* a type of schizophrenia characterised by periodic states of stupor.—*adj.* **catatonic** (*-ton′*). [Gr. *kata*, down, *tonos*, stretching, straining—*teinein*, to stretch.]

catawba, *ka-taw′ba*, *n.* an American grape (*Vitis Labrusca*): a red wine made from it. [*Catawba* River in Carolina.]

cat-bird; **cat-call.** See **cat.**

catch, *kach*, *v.t.* to take hold of, esp. of a thing in motion: (*cricket*) to gather (the ball) after the batsman has hit it and before it touches the ground : to dismiss (a batsman) thus : to apprehend or understand : to seize after pursuit : to trap or ensnare : to come upon : to be in time for : to strike : to take (a disease) by infection : to take (fire) : to take up by sympathy or imitation.—*v.i.* to be contagious : to be entangled or fastened (*infin.* in *Spens.* sometimes **catchen, ketch ;** *pa.t.* and *pa.p.* **caught,** *kawt,* also *obs.* and *dial.* **catched, catcht ;** *pa.t.* in *Spens.* also **keight,** *kīt*).—*n.* seizure : an act of catching, esp. the ball at cricket, etc. : a clasp, or anything that seizes or holds : that which is caught or is worth catching : a sudden advantage taken : a concealed difficulty or disadvantage : a round for three or more voices, later seeking comic effect by the interweaving of the words.—*adj.* **catch'able,** that may be caught.— *ns.* **catch'-as-catch'-can',** a style of wrestling in which any hold is allowed.—Also *adj.* and *adv.*—*ns.* **catch'-basin, -pit,** a trap for dirt in a drain; **catch'-drain,** a drain on a hillside to catch the surface-water; **catch'er; catch'fly,** a name for a species of campion (*Lychnis viscaria*) and several of bladder-campion (*Silene*) with sticky stems; **catch'ing,** the action of the verb : a nervous or spasmodic twitching.—*adj.* infectious : captivating, attractive.—*ns.* **catch'ment,** river drainage; **catch'ment-area, -basin,** the area from which a river or a reservoir is fed; **catch'penny,** any worthless thing, esp. a publication, intended merely to gain money.—Also *adj.*—*ns.* **catch'-phrase,** a phrase repeated from mouth to mouth : a slogan; **catch'-weed,** goosegrass or cleavers; **catch'word,** among actors, the last word of the preceding speaker—the cue : the word at the head of the page in a dictionary or encyclopaedia : the first word of a page given at the bottom of the preceding page : any word or phrase taken up and repeated esp. as the watchword or symbol of a party.—*adj.* **catch'y,** attractive : deceptive : readily caught up, or taking hold of the mind, as an air, etc. : fitful.—**catch at,** to snatch at; **catch fire,** to become ignited : to become inspired by passion or zeal; **catch hold of,** to seize; **catch it,** to get a scolding or the like; **catch me, him,** etc., an emphatic colloquial phrase implying that there is not the remotest possibility of my or his doing something suggested; **catch on,** to comprehend : to catch the popular fancy; **catch out,** to put out at cricket by catching the ball after it has been hit and before it touches the ground : (*fig.*) to detect in error; **catch sight of,** to get a glimpse of; **catch up,** to overtake; **catch up,** or **away,** to snatch or seize hastily. [From O.Fr. *cachier*— L.L. *captiāre* from *captāre,* inten. of *capĕre,* to take; see **chase.**]

catchpole, -poll, *kach'pōl, n.* a constable, petty officer of justice. [Through O.Fr. from L.L. *cachepolus, chassipullus,* one who chases fowls. See **chase** and **pullet.**]

catchup, catsup. See **ketchup.**

cate, *kāt, n.* (nearly always in *pl.*) a viand : a dainty. [Aphetic; see **acates**; cf. **cater.**]

catechise, *kat'i-kīz, v.t.* to instruct by question and answer : to question as to belief : to examine systematically by questioning.—*adjs.* **catechetic** (*ket'ik*), **-al,** relating to a catechism or oral instruction in the first principles, esp. of Christianity.—*adv.* **catechet'ically.**—*ns.* **catechet'ics,** the art or practice of teaching by question and answer : that part of theology which treats of catechesis (-*kē'sis*), or primary oral instruction, as that given to catechumens; **cat'echiser; cat'echising; cat'echism,** any compendious system of teaching drawn up in the form of question and answer : a set of questions : an examination by questions; **cat'echist,** one who catechises : a teacher of catechumens : a native teacher in a mission church.—*adjs.* **catechist'ic, -al, catechis'mal,** pertaining to a catechist or catechism. [L. *catēchismus,* formed from Gr. *katēchizein, katēcheein,* to din into the ears—*kata,* back, *echē,* a sound.]

catechu, *kat'i-chōō, -shōō, n.* a dark extract of

Indian plants (acacia, betel-nut, etc.) rich in tannin. [Cf. Malay *cachu.*]

catechumen, *kat-i-kū'mэn, n.* one who is being taught the rudiments of Christianity : in the early Christian Church a converted Jew or heathen undergoing instruction preparatory to baptism.— *n.* **catechu'menate.**—*adj.* **catechumen'ical.**— *adv.* **catechumen'ically.**—*ns.* **catechū'menism, catechū'menship.** [Gr. *katēchoumenos,* being taught, *pr.p.* pass. of *katēcheein,* to teach; cf. **catechise.**]

category, *kat'i-gэr-i, n.* what may be affirmed of a class : a class or order.—*adjs.* **categorematic** (-*gor-i-mat'ik*), capable of being used by itself as a term; **categorical** (-*gor'*), positive : absolute : without exception.—*adv.* **categor'ically,** absolutely : without qualification : expressly.—*n.* **categor'icalness,** the quality of being absolute and unqualified.—*n.pl.* **cat'egories** (*phil.*), the highest classes under which objects of philosophy can be systematically arranged, understood as an attempt at a comprehensive classification of all that exists : in Kant's system, the root-notions of the understanding, the specific forms of the *a priori* or formal element in rational cognition (*quantity, quality, relation, modality,* etc.).—*v.t.* **cat'egorise,** to place in a category or list : to class.—*n.* **cat'egorist,** one who categorises.—**categorical imperative,** in the ethics of Kant, the absolute unconditional command of the moral law, irrespective of every ulterior end or aim—universally authoritative, belonging to the fixed law of nature. [Gr. *katēgoriā,* assertion, predication, accusation—*katēgoros,* an accuser, *kata,* down, against, *agorā,* assembly.]

catelog, an obs. spelling of **catalogue.**

catena, *ka-tē'nä, n.* a chain or connected series, as in **catena patrum,** a chronological series of extracts from the Fathers on any doctrine of theology.—*adj.* **catenarian** (*kat-i-nā'ri-эn*), of, of the nature of, a chain or a catenary.—*n.* **catē'nary,** the curve formed by a flexible homogeneous cord, hanging freely between two points of support, and acted on by no other force than gravity.—*adj.* relating to a chain, like a chain.—*v.t.* **catenate** (*kat'i-nāt*), to connect as in or by a chain.—*adj.* linked as in a chain.—*n.* **catenā'tion.** [L. *catēna,* chain.]

cater, *kā'tэr, n.* (*obs.*) an acater : a purveyor.— *v.i.* to provide food, entertainment, etc. (with *for*). —*ns.* **cā'terer; cā'teress; cā'tering.** [See **acater.**]

cateran, *kat'э-rэn, n.* a Highland reiver or free-booter : a robber or brigand generally. [Gael. *ceathairne, ceatharn,* Ir. *ceithern,* a band of soldiers.]

cater-cousin, *kā'tэr-kuz'n, n.* (*Shak.*) vaguely, or allied by familiarity, affection, sympathy, rather than kindred. [More prob. conn. with **cater** than *quatre* or *quarter.*]

caterpillar, *kat'эr-pil-эr, n.* a butterfly or moth grub : extended to other insect larvae : an unproductive consumer : (in full **caterpillar tractor**) a tractor or other vehicle whose wheels carry endless chains forming an articulated track. [Prob. O.Fr. *chatepelose,* hairy cat; see **cat, pile.**]

caterwaul, *kat'эr-wawl, n.* the shriek or cry emitted by the cat when in heat.—*v.i.* to make such a noise : to make any discordant sound : to behave lasciviously : to quarrel like cats.—*n.* **cat'erwauling.** [cat; the second part prob. imit.]

cates. See **cate.**

catgut. See **cat.**

Cathari, *kath'ar-ī, n.pl.* a mediaeval Manichaean sect, chiefly in S. France and N. Italy, the Albigensians.—*ns.* **Cath'arism; Cath'arist.** [Gr. *katharos,* pure.]

cathartic, -al, *kath-ärt'ik, -al, adjs.* cleansing, purifying : having the power of cleansing the bowels : purgative.—*n.* **cathart'ic,** a purgative medicine.—*v.t.* **cath'arise,** to render absolutely clean.—*n.* **cathar'sis,** purification : evacuation of the bowels : purification of the emotions, as by the drama according to Aristotle : (*psych.*) the purging of the effects of a pent-up emotion, by bringing them to the surface of consciousness. [Gr. *kathartikos*, fit for cleansing, *katharos*, clean.]

Cathayan, Cathaian, *ka-thā'an, n.* and *adj.* Chinese. (See **Cataian.**)

cathead. See **cat.**

cathedral, *ka-thē'dral, n.* the principal church of a diocese, containing the bishop's throne.—*adj.* belonging to a seat of authority or a cathedral.—*n.* **cathedra** (*-thē'dra, -thed'ra*), a bishop's seat, the episcopal dignity.—*adj.* **cathedrat'ic,** promulgated *ex cathedra,* authoritative. [L. *cathēdra, cathēdra*—Gr. *kathēdra,* a seat.]

Catherine-wheel, *kath'(a-)rin-hwēl, n.* (*archit.*) a rose-window: (*her.*) a wheel set round with teeth: a rotating firework: a sidewise somersault.— **Catherine pear,** a small and early variety of pear. [From St. *Catherine* of Alexandria (4th cent.), tortured, says legend, on a wheel.]

catheter, *kath'i-tar, n.* a tube for admitting or removing gases or liquids through channels of the body, especially for removing urine from the bladder.—*ns.* **cath'eterism,** use of the catheter; **cathetom'eter,** an instrument for measuring small differences of level of different liquids in tubes; **cath'etus,** a straight line perpendicular to another straight line or surface. [Gr. *kathetos,* perpendicular, *kathetēr,* a catheter—*kathienai,* to send down—*kata,* down, *hienai,* to send.]

cathexis, *ka-thek'sis, n.* (*psych.*) a charge of mental energy attached to any particular idea or object. [Gr. *kathexis,* holding.]

cathisma, *ka-thiz'mä, n.* in Greek use, a section of the psalter: a troparion or short hymn used as a response. [Gr.—*kathīzein,* to sit down.]

cathode, *kath'ōd, n.* the electrode at which an electric current leaves an electrolyte or gas (opposed to *anode*)—*adjs.* **cath'odal; cathod'ic.**—*ns.* **cath'odograph,** a photograph by X-rays; **cathodog'rapher; cathodog'raphy.**—**cathode rays,** streams of negatively electrified particles, or electrons, proceeding from the cathode of a vacuum-tube; **cathode ray tube,** a device in which a narrow beam of electrons, which can be deflected by magnetic and/or electrostatic fields, impinges on a fluorescent screen or photographic surface—used in television, etc. [Gr. *kathodos,* a going down, *kata,* down, *hodos,* a way.]

cat-hole. See **cat.**

catholic, *kath'a-lik, adj.* universal: general, embracing the whole body of Christians: orthodox, as opposed to *heterodox* and *sectarian*: liberal, the opposite of exclusive: belonging to the Christian Church before the great schism between East and West, or to any church claiming to be in historic continuity with it, esp. after the schism the Western church, after the Reformation the Church of Rome (Roman Catholic), but applied also, e.g., to Anglicans: relating to the Roman Catholics.—*n.* an adherent of the R.C. Church.—*v.t.* and *v.i.* **cathol'icise** (*-sīz*), to make or become Catholic.—*ns.* **Cathol'icism,** the tenets of the R.C. Church: (*rare*) catholicity; **catholic'ity** (*-is'i-ti*), universality: liberality or breadth of view: (*rare*) Catholicism; **cathol'icon** (*-kon*), a panacea; **cathol'icos,** the Patriarch of Armenia.—**Catholic (and) Apostolic,** Irvingite; **catholic creditor** (*Scots law*), one whose debt is secured over two or more subjects belonging to the debtor—*e.g.* over two or more heritable estates; **Catholic emancipation,** the relief of the Roman Catholics from certain vexatious penal regulations and restrictions, granted in 1829; **catholic** or **general epistles,** certain epistles in the canon addressed to the Church universal or to a large and indefinite circle of readers; **Catholic King** (*hist.*), the king of Spain; **German Catholics,** a body that broke away from the Roman Catholic Church in Germany in 1844 on the occasion of the exhibition of the Holy Coat at Trier; **Old Catholics,** a body that broke away from the Roman Catholic church in Germany in opposition to the dogma of papal infallibility proclaimed by the Vatican Council in 1870. [Gr. *katholikos,* universal—*kata,* throughout, *holos,* the whole.]

Catiline, *kat'i-lïn, n.* the type of a daring and reckless conspirator, L. Sergius *Catilina,* whose plot to destroy Rome was foiled by Cicero, 63 B.C.—*adj.* **catilinarian** (*-li-nā'ri-an*).

cation, kation, *kat'ī-on, n.* an ion that travels towards the cathode. [Gr. *kata,* down, *iŏn,* neut.—pr.p. of *ienai,* to go.]

catkin, catling, catmint. See **cat.**

Catonian, *ka-tō'ni-an, adj.* resembling or relating to *Cato,* the Roman censor (234-149 B.C.), or Cato Uticensis (95-46 B.C.), both remarkable for gravity of manners—hence grave, severe, unbending.

catoptric, *kat-op'trik, adj.* relating to reflection.—*n.pl.* **catop'trics,** the part of optics which treats of reflected light. [Gr. *katoptron,* a mirror—*kata,* back, and the root of *opsomai,* I shall see.]

cat's-tail. See **cat.**

cattabu, *kat'a-bū, n.* a cross between common cattle and zebu. [From *Cattle* and *Zebu.*]

cattalo, *kat'a-lō, n.* a cross between the bison ('buffalo') and the domestic cow. [From *Cattle* and *Buffalo.*]

cattle, *kat'l, n.pl.* beasts of pasture, esp. oxen, bulls, and cows: sometimes also horses, sheep, etc.—*ns.* **catt'le-lift'er,** a stealer of cattle, **catt'le-lift'ing; catt'le-man,** one who tends cattle, or who rears them on a ranch; **catt'le-plague,** plague among cattle, esp. rinderpest or steppe murrain; **catt'le-show,** an exhibition of cattle or other domestic animals in competition for prizes. [O.Fr. *catel, chatel*—L.L. *captāle,* L. *capitāle*—*caput,* the head.]

catty, *kat'i, n.* the Chinese kin or pound, usually a little over 1¼ lb. avoirdupois. [Malay *katï.*]

Caucasian, *kaw-kā'z(h)i-an, adj.* pertaining to the *Caucasus* or the country around it.—*n.* and *adj.* adopted by Blumenbach for one of his main ethnological divisions of mankind, by some later anthropologists used for the white race.

caucus, *kaw'kas, n.* (*U.S.*) a meeting of members of a party to nominate candidates or delegates or to decide how to vote on any question, its decision binding on those who attend: (in Britain) party organisation. [Ety. dub.; perh. John Smith's Algonkin word *Caw-cawaassough,* an adviser; perh. a corr. of 'caulkers' meetings'.]

caudal, *kaw'dl, adj.* pertaining to the tail.—*adjs.* **cau'date, -d,** tailed. [L. *cauda,* tail.]

caudex, *kaw'deks, n.* (*bot.*) the stem of a tree, esp. of a palm or tree-fern:—*pl.* **caud'icēs** (*-i-sēz*), **caud'exes.**—*n.* **caudicle,** the stalk of the pollen-masses of certain orchids. [L.]

caudle, *kaw'dl, n.* a warm drink, sweetened and spiced, given to the sick, esp. women in childbed.—*v.t.* to give a caudle to: to mix.—**hempen caudle** (*Shak.*), the hangman's noose. [O.Fr. *chaudel*—L. *calidus,* hot.]

caudron, *kaw'dran, n.* (*Spens.*). Same as **cauldron.**

caught, *kawt,* pa.t. and pa.p. of **catch.**

cauk, cawk, *kawk, n.* chalk: barytes in platy crystals. [A form of **chalk.**]

cauker. See **caulk.**

caul, *kawl, n.* a net or covering for the head: the membrane covering the head of some infants at their birth. [O.Fr. *cale,* a little cap, prob. Celt.; cf. Ir. *calla,* a veil, hood.]

cauld, *kawld, n.* (*Scot.*) a dam in a stream, a weir. [Origin obscure.]

cauld, *kawld, adj.* and *n.* (*Scot.*) cold.—*adj.* **cauldrife** (*kawld'rif*), apt to feel chilly: chilling, lifeless, without vigour.

cauldron, caldron, *kawl'dran, n.* a large kettle for boiling or heating liquids. [O.Fr. *caudron*—L. *caldārium*—*calidus,* hot—*calēre,* to be hot.]

caulis, *kaw'lis* (L. *kow'lis*), *n.* the stem of a plant: one of the main stems at the angles of the Corinthian capital:—*pl.* **cau'lēs** (*-lēz; -lās*).—*adj.* **caulesc'ent,** having a stem rising above the ground.—*n.* **cau'licle,** a rudimentary stem.—*adjs.* **caulic'olous,** growing on a stem; **caulic'ulāte.**—*ns.* **caulic'ulus,** one of the slender stems springing from the *caules* or main stalks supporting the volutes in the Corinthian capital; **cauliflo'ry,** production of flowers on old stems from dormant buds.—*adjs.* **caul'iform,** having the form of a stem; **caulig'enous**, borne upon the stem; **caul'inary**, **cau'line**, belonging to a stem.—*n.* **cau'lōme**, a plant's stem-structure as a whole. [L. *caulis*, a stalk.]

cauliflower, *kav'li-flowr*, *n.* a variety of cabbage whose young inflorescence is eaten. [Earlier *cole-florye*, *colie-florie*—L.L. *cauliflōra*—L. *caulis*, cabbage; see **cole** and **flower**.]

caulk, **calk**, *kawk*, *v.t.* to render watertight by pressing oakum, etc. into the seams.—*v.i.* (*sailors' slang*) to snooze.—*ns.* **caulk'er**, one who caulks: a dram: a big lie—also **cauk'er**; **caulk'ing**; **caulk'ing-i'ron**, an instrument like a chisel used for pressing oakum into the seams of ships. [O.Fr. *cauquer*, to press—L. *calcāre*, to tread—*calx*, heel.]

caulker. See **calk** (1).

caum, **caumstane.** See **cam** (3).

cause, *kawz*, *n.* that which produces an effect: that by or through which anything happens: motive: inducement: a legal action between contending parties: sake, advantage: that side of a question which is taken up by an individual or party: (*Shak.*) accusation: (*Shak.*) matter, affair in general.—*v.t.* to produce: to make to exist: to bring about: (*Spens.; infin.* **caus'en**) to give excuses for.—*conj.* (*dial.*) because (usu. **'cause**).—*adj.* **caus'al**, being the cause, that causes: relating to a cause or causes. —*n.* **causal'ity**, the relation of cause and effect: the working of a cause.—*adv.* **caus'ally**.—*ns.* **causā'tion**, the act of causing: the bringing about of an effect; the relation of cause and effect: **causā'tionism**, the principle of universal causation; **causā'tionist**.—*adj.* **caus'ative**, causal: of the nature of, or expressing, causation.—*n.* a form of verb expressing causation.—*adv.* **caus'atively**. —*adj.* **cause'less**, without cause: without just cause.—*adv.* **cause'lessly**.—*ns.* **cause'lessness**; **caus'er.**—**efficient cause**, the means by which a thing took its present form; **final cause**, the end or object for which a thing is done, esp. the design of the universe; **first cause**, the original cause or creator of all; **formal cause**, the essence or idea of a thing; **hour of cause** (*Scot.*), hour or time of trial; **make common cause** (*with*), to unite for a common object; **material cause**, that out of which a thing is framed; **occasional causes** (*occasionalism*): **secondary causes**, such as are derived from a primary or first cause; **have** or **show cause**, to have to give reasons for a certain line of action; **show cause** (*Eng. law*), to argue against the confirmation of a provisional order or judgment. [Fr.,—L. *causa*.]

causerie, *kōz'ər-ē*, *n.* a talk or gossip: a paragraph of chat about literature or art: a short and informal essay on any subject in a newspaper or magazine. [Fr.]

causeway, *kawz'wā*, **causey**, *kawz'i*, *n.* a raised way through a marsh or water: a pathway raised and paved with stone: a paved or cobble-stoned road.—*v.t.* to pave.—*p.adjs.* **cause'wayed**, **caus'eyed.** [M.E. *causee*—O.Fr. *caucie*—L.L. (*via*) *calciāta*, a trodden way—L. *calx*, heel; **causeway** is for **causey-way**.]

caustic, *kaws'tik*, *adj.* burning: (*fig.*) bitter, severe, cutting.—*n.* a substance that exerts a corroding or disintegrating action on the skin and flesh: (*math.*) an envelope of rays of light proceeding from a fixed point and reflected (*catacaustic*) or refracted (*diacaustic*) by a surface or a curve.—*adv.* **caus'tically**.—*n.* **causticity** (*-tis'i-ti*), quality of being caustic.—**caustic ammonia**, ammonia as a gas, or in solution; **caustic lime**, quicklime; **caustic potash**, potassium hydroxide; **caustic soda**, sodium hydroxide; **common caustic**, potash: also silver nitrate; **lunar caustic**, silver nitrate in sticks for surgical use. [L. *causticus*— Gr. *kaustikos*—*kaiein*, fut. *kausein*, to burn.]

cautel, *kaw'tl*, *n.* (*Shak.*) craft: insidious purpose: caution: wariness: a traditionary caution or written direction about the proper manner of administering the sacraments.—*adj.* **cau'telous** (*Shak.*), cautious: insidious: artful. [Fr. *cautèle*— L. *cautēla*—*cavēre*, *cautum*, to guard against.]

cauterise, *kaw'tər-īz*, *v.t.* to burn with a caustic or a hot iron: (*fig.*) to sear.—*ns.* **cau'ter**, **cau'tery**,

a burning with caustics or a hot iron: a burning iron or caustic used for burning tissue; **cauterisā'-tion**, **cau'terism.** [Fr. *cautériser*—L.L. *cautērizāre* —Gr. *kautēr*, a hot iron—*kaiein*, to burn.]

caution, *kaw'shən*, *n.* heedfulness: warning: (*coll.*) an alarming, amusing, or astonishing person or thing: (*Scots law;* also *kā'*) security, surety, bail.— *v.t.* to warn to take care.—*adj.* **cau'tionary**, containing caution: given as a pledge.—*ns.* **cau'tioner**; one who cautions or advises: (*Scots law;* also *kā'*) a surety; **cautionry** (*Scots law;* *kā'*), the act of giving security for another.—*adj.* **cau'tious** (*-shəs*), possessing or using caution: watchful: prudent.—*adv.* **cau'tiously**.—*n.* **cau'tiousness.**—**caution money**, money paid in advance as security for good behaviour. [Fr.,—L. *cautiō*, *-ōnis*—*cavēre*, to beware.]

cavalcade, *kav-əl-kād'*, *n.* a train or procession of persons on horseback.—*v.i.* to go in a cavalcade. [Fr., through It. and L.L.—L. *caballus*, a horse.]

cavalier, *kav-əl-ēr'*, *n.* a knight: a Royalist in the great Civil War: a swaggering fellow: a gallant or gentleman in attendance upon a lady, as her escort or partner in a dance or the like: in military fortification, a raised work so situated as to command the neighbouring country.—*adj.* like a cavalier: gay: war-like: haughty, supercilious, free-and-easy, off-hand.—*v.i.* to act as cavalier.— *adjs.* **cavalier'ish**, **cavalier'ly**, like, character-istic of, a cavalier. — *n.* **cavalier'ism.** — *adv.* **cavalier'ly**, off-hand: with supercilious disregard or curtness.—*n.* **cavaliero** (*kav-əl-yā'rō;* Sp. *caballero*). [Fr.,—It. *cavallo;* see **cavalcade**.]

cavally, *kə-val'i*, *n.* an American fish of the scad family. [Sp. and Port. *cavalla*, mackerel.]

cavalry, *kav'əl-ri*, *n.* horse-soldiers: a troop of horse or horsemen. [Fr. *cavallerie*—It. *cavalleria*— L. *caballārius*, horseman—*caballus*, horse.]

cavass. See **kavass.**

cavatina, *kāv-ät-ē'nä*, *n.* a melody with no second part or da capo: loosely, a short operatic air, of a smooth and melodious character, often part of a grand scena. [It.]

cave, *kāv*, *n.* a hollow place in a rock: a small faction of seceders from a political party (from the Cave of Adullam i.Sam. 22, 1-2).—*v.t.* to hollow out.—*v.i.* to lodge in a cave.—*ns.* **cave'-bear** (*Ursus spelaeus*), a Pleistocene bear found fossil in caves; **cave'-dweller**, one who lives in a cave, esp. one of the Stone Age of pre-historic times: **cave'-earth'**, a fine deposit on cave floors; **cave'-man**, a cave-dweller: (*coll.*) a modern male of primitive ways.—*n.* **cav'ing**, yielding.—**cave in**, to slip, to fall into a hollow: to yield to outside pressure, to give way, collapse. [Fr. *cave*—L. *cavus*, hollow.]

cave, *kav'i*, *v.i.* or *interj.* (*schoolboy slang*) beware.— *n.* **caveat** (*kā'vi-at*), a notice or warning: a formal warning, entered in the books of a court or public office, that no step be taken in a particular matter without notice to the person lodging the caveat. [L. *căvē*, imperat. sing., *căveat*, 3rd. sing. pres. subj., of *căvēre*, to take care.]

cavel, *kāv'l*, *n.* (*Scot.*) a piece of wood, etc. used in casting lots: a lot. [Du. *kavel*.]

cavendish, *kav'ən-dish*, *n.* tobacco moistened and pressed into quadrangular cakes. [Possibly from the name of the original manufacturer.]

cavern, *kav'ərn*, *n.* a deep hollow place in rocks.— *v.t.* to put in a cavern: to hollow out.—*adjs.* **cav'erned**, full of caverns: dwelling in a cavern; **cav'ernous**, hollow: full of caverns.—*adv.* **cav'ernously.**—*adj.* **caver'nulous**, full of little cavities. [Fr. *caverne*—L. *caverna*—*cavus*, hollow.]

cavesson, *kav'əs-ən*, *n.* a nose-band for a horse. [Fr. *caveçon*—It. *cavezzone*—L. *capitia*, *capitium*, a head-covering.]

cavetto, *kā-vet'tō*, *n.* a hollowed moulding whose curvature is the quarter of a circle, used chiefly in cornices. [It.; dim. of *cavo*—L. *cavus*, hollow.]

caviare, **caviar**, *kāv-i-är'*, *kāv-yär'*, also *kāv-i-är'*, (*Shak.*) **caviar'ie**, (*obs.*) **cavier**, *kə-vēr'*, *n.* salted roe of the sturgeon, etc.: (*fig.*) something whose flavour is too fine for the vulgar taste. [Prob. the 16th-cent. It. *caviale;* the Turk. *khāvyär* is prob. borrowed.]

cavicorn, *kav'i-korn*, *adj.* hollow-horned, as a ruminant.—*n.* one of the Cavicor'nia, or Bovidae. [L. *cavus*, hollow, *cornu*, a horn.]

cavie, *kāv'i*, *n.* a hen-coop or cage. [Cf. Du. *kevie* Ger. *käfig*—L. *cavus*.]

cavil, *kav'il*, *v.t.* to make empty, trifling objections: to use false arguments (*pr.p.* **cav'illing**; *p.a.t.* and *pa.p.* **cav'illed**).—*n.* a frivolous objection.—*ns.* **cavillā'tion**, **cav'illing**; **cav'iller**. [O.Fr. *caviller*—L. *cavillāri*, to practise jesting.]

cavity, *kav'it-i*, *n.* a hollow: a hollow place: hollowness: an opening.—*n.* **cavitā'tion**, the formation of cavities in a structure, or of gas bubbles in a liquid, or of a vacuum.—*adj.* **cav'itied**. [L. *cavitās*—*cavus*, hollow.]

cavo-rilievo, *kä'vō-rē-lyä'vō*, *n.* a kind of relief in which the highest surface is level with the plane of the original stone, which is left round the outlines of the design. [It. *cavo*, hollow, *rilievo*, relief; see **cave and relief**.]

cavort, *ka-vort'*, *v.i.* (*U.S. slang*) to curvet, bound. [Explained as a corr. of *curvet*.]

cavy, *kāv'i*, *n.* the guinea-pig genus (*Cavia*) of rodents. [*Cabiai*, native name in French Guiana.]

caw, *kaw*, *v.i.* to cry as a crow.—*n.* the cry of a crow—also **kaw**.—*n.* **caw'ing**. [From the sound.]

cawk. See **cauk, caulk**.

cawker. Same as **calker**.

caxon, *kak'sɔn*, *n.* a kind of wig formerly worn. [Origin obscure.]

Caxton, *kaks'tɔn*, *n.* a book printed by William *Caxton* (1422-91), the first English printer: a kind of printing-type in imitation of Caxton's.

cay, *kā*, *n.* a low islet, the same as **key**. [Sp. *cayo*.]

cayenne, *kā-en'*, *n.* a very pungent red pepper (**cay'enne-pepp'er**), made from several species of Capsicum.—*adj.* **cayenned'**, seasoned with cayenne. [Usually referred to *Cayenne* in French Guiana; but prob. from Tupi.]

cayman, *kā'man*, *n.* an alligator, esp. of South American kinds:—*pl.* **caymans**. [Sp. *caimán*, most prob. Carib.]

cayuse, *kī-ūs'*, *n.* (*U.S.*) an Indian pony: a small or poor horse. [Amer. Indian.]

cazique, a form of **cacique**.

Ceanothus, *sē-ɔ-nō'thɔs*, *n.* an American genus of shrubs of the buckthorn family. [Gr. *keanōthos*, corn-thistle.]

cease, *sēs*, *v.t.* and *v.i.* to give over: to stop: to end.—*n.* end: cessation.—*n.* **cease'-fire**, an order to cease firing: an agreed cessation of active hostilities.—*adj.* **cease'less**, without ceasing: incessant.—*adv.* **cease'lessly**.—*n.* **ceas'ing**. [Fr. *cesser*—L. *cessāre*, give over—*cēdere*, yield.]

ceaze, an obs. spelling of **seize**.

cebadilla. See **sabadilla**.

Cebus, *sē'bus*, *n.* generic name of the Capuchin monkeys.—*n.pl.* **Cebidae** (*seb'i-dē*) a family including all the New-World monkeys except the marmosets. [Gr. *kēbos*, a kind of monkey.]

Cecidomyia, *ses-id-o-mī'i-ä*, *n.* a gall-midge, a genus of flies destructive to vegetation. [Gr. *kēkis, -idos*, a gall, *myia*, a fly.]

cecils, *ses'*, *ses'ilz*, *n.pl.* minced meat, bread-crumbs, onions, etc., made up into balls and fried.

cecity, *sē'si-ti*, *n.* blindness.—*n.* **cecutiency** (*si-kū'shyɔn-si*), a tendency to blindness. [L. *caecus*, blind.]

Cecropia, *si-krō'pi-ä*, *n.* a tropical American genus of trees of the mulberry family, some with hollow stems that give food and housing to a protective garrison of ants. [Named after the mythical Attic King *Cecrops* (Gr. *Kekrōps*).]

cedar, *sē'dɔr*, *n.* a large evergreen coniferous tree (*Cedrus*, including *Cedar of Lebanon*, *Atlantic cedar*, and *deodar*) remarkable for the durability and fragrance of its wood; applied also to many more or less similar trees, as the Barbados cedar, properly a juniper, and the Bastard Barbados cedar, properly a Cedrela.—*adj.* made of cedar.—*n.* **cē'dar-bird**, an American waxwing.—*adjs.* **cē'dared**, covered with cedars; **cē'darn**, of cedar —*n.* **cedar-nut**, the seed of the cembra pine.—*adj.* **cē'drine**, belonging to the cedar-tree. [L. *cedrus*— Gr. *kedros*.]

cede, *sēd*, *v.t.* to yield or give up to another.—*v.i.* to give way. [L. *cēdere, cēssum*, to yield, to give up.]

cedilla, *se-dil'ä*, *n.* a mark placed under the letter c (thus ç), originally a subscript Z, formerly used in Spanish to indicate that it had the sound of (Spanish) Z where that of K would be expected, still used esp. in French and Portuguese to indicate an S- sound as before *a, o, u.* [Sp. (Fr. *cédille*, It. *zediglia*), all dims. from *zēta*, the Greek name of *z*. See *z*.]

cedrate, *sē'drāt*, *n.* citron. [Fr. *cédrat*—L. *citrus*.]

Cedrela, *sed-rē'lä*, *n.* a tropical genus of Meliaceae, allied to mahogany.—*adj.* **cedrelā'ceous**. [Sp.— dim. of *cedro, cedra*, cedar; see **cedar**.]

cedula, *sed'ū-lä*, *n.* a South American promissory-note or mortgage-bond on lands. [Sp.; cf. **schedule**.]

cee-spring, c-spring, *sē'-spring*, *n.* a spring in the shape of a C to support the frame of a carriage.

ceil, *sēl*, *v.t.* to overlay the inner roof of: to overlay or line.—*n.* **ceil'ing**, the inner roof of a room: the limiting height of aircraft: an upper limit. [Prob. conn. with Fr. *ciel*, It. *cielo*, L.L. *caelum*, a canopy.]

celadon, *sel'ɔ-don*, *n.* a pale-green colour. [Fr. *céladon*, said to be named after a character in D'Urfé's *Astrée*.]

celandine, *sel'an-dīn*, *n.* swallow-wort (*Chelidonium majus*; **greater celandine**) a plant of the poppy family, supposed to flower when the swallows appeared, and to perish when they departed: also pile-wort (*Ranunculus Ficaria*; **lesser celandine**). [O.Fr. *celidoine*—Gr. *chelidonion*—*chelidōn*, a swallow.]

celebrate, *sel'i-brāt*, *v.t.* to make famous: to distinguish by solemn ceremonies, as a festival or an event: to perform with proper rites and ceremonies, as mass, the eucharist, marriage, etc.: to publish the praises of.—*n.* **cel'ebrant**, one who celebrates: the principal officiant at a rite.—*adj.* **cel'ebrated**, distinguished: famous.—*ns.* **celebrā'tion**, act of celebrating: any solemn ceremony: an extolling; **cel'ebrātor**; **celebrity** (*si-leb'ri-ti*), the condition of being celebrated: fame: notoriety: a person of distinction or fame. [L. *celebrāre, -ātum—celeber*, frequented.]

celerity, *si-ler'i-ti*, *n.* quickness: rapidity of motion. [Fr. *célérité*—L. *celeritās*—*celer*, quick.]

celery, *sel'ɔr-i*, *n.* an umbelliferous plant (*Apium graveolens*) whose blanched leaf-stalks are eaten cooked or uncooked.—*n.* **celeriac** (*si-ler'i-ak*), a turnip-rooted variety of celery. [Fr. *céleri*—Gr. *selīnon*, parsley.]

celesta, *si-les'tä*, *n.* a keyboard instrument in which the hammers strike steel plates over wooden resonators. [Fr. *céleste*, heavenly.]

celeste, *si-lest'*, *adj.* sky-blue.—*n.* voix céleste: a kind of soft pedal on a piano. [Fr. *céleste*.]

celestial, *si-lest'yal*, *adj.* heavenly: dwelling in heaven: in the visible heavens: (*coll.*) Chinese.— *n.* an inhabitant of heaven: a Chinese.—*adv.* **celest'ially**.—*n.* **celestine** (*sel'-is-tēn, -tīn, -tin*), a mineral, strontium sulphate, sometimes sky-blue. —**the Celestial Empire**, China. [Through French from L. *caelestis—caelum*, heaven.]

Celestine, *sel'is-tīn*, or *sil-es'tin*, *n.* a monk of an order founded 1264 by Pietro da Morrone, afterwards Pope *Celestine* V.

celiac. Same as **coeliac**.

celibacy, *sel'i-bɔs-i*, an unmarried state, esp. under a vow.—*adjs.* **celibatā'rian**, favouring celibacy; **cel'ibate**, living single.—*n.* one who is unmarried, or bound not to marry. [L. *caelebs*, single.]

cell, *sel*, *n.* a small room in a prison, monastery, etc.: a monastery or nunnery dependent on another: a hermit's one-roomed dwelling: a small cavity: a vessel with electrodes and an electrolyte, for electrolysis or for generating an electric current by chemical action: a unit-mass of living matter, whether walled or unwalled, by itself or associated with others in a higher unity: a unit group, esp. of communist propagandists.—*n.* **cell'a**, the naos or inner chamber of a temple.—*adj.* **celled**, having cells, cellular; **cell'iferous**, having or producing cells; **cell'ūlar**, consisting of, characterised by, or containing cells or compartments: composed of ordinary cells without vessels (as the lower cryptogams) : porous : of open texture; **cell'ulated.**—*n.* **cell'ule,** a little cell.—*adj.* **cellulif'erous,** having or producing little cells.—*ns.* **celluli'tis,** spreading infection of subcutaneous tissue with pyogenic bacteria; **cell'uloid,** a hard elastic substitute for ivory, made by hydraulic pressure from pyroxylin mixed with camphor, etc.—*adj.* **cell'ulose,** containing cells.—*n.* a carbohydrate forming the chief component of cell-wa¹ls of plants and of wood (cotton down, linen fibre, wood pulp being almost pure cellulose) : extended to cellulose acetate, cellulose nitrate, etc. compounds used in making artificial silk, etc. [O.Fr. *celle*—L. *cella,* conn. with *celāre,* to cover.]

cellar, *sel'ər, n.* any underground room or vault : a room for storing wine, beer, coal, etc. : a stock of wine.—*v.t.* to store in a cellar.—*ns.* **cell'arage,** cellars : charge for storing in cellars; **cell'ar-book,** a record of wines kept in a cellar; **cell'arer,** **cell'arist,** one who has charge of the cellar : an officer in a monastery who looks after the provisions; **cell'aret,** a case for holding bottles; **cell'ar-flap,** a plate covering an entrance to a cellar; **cell'arman,** one who has the care of a cellar.—*adj.* **cell'arous** (*Dickens*), belonging to a cellar : excavated : sunken. [O.Fr. *celier*—L. *cellārium*—*cella.*]

cellar. See **saltcellar.**

cello, *chel'ō,* for **violoncello**: sometimes written **'cello.**—**cellist, 'cellist,** for **violoncellist.**

celsitude, *sels'i-tūd, n.* loftiness. [L. *celsitūdō*—*celsus,* lofty.]

Celsius, *sel'si-us.* See **centigrade.**

celt, *selt, n.* a prehistoric axe-like instrument. [Founded on *celte,* perh. a misreading for *certe* (surely), in the Vulgate, Job, xix. 24, taken to be from a supposed L. word *celtes,* a chisel.]

Celt, *kelt, selt, n.* (*hist.*) a Gaul : extended to include members of other Celtic-speaking or recently Celtic-speaking peoples—also **Kelt.**—*adj.* **Celt'ic,** **Kelt'ic,** pertaining to the Celts : of a branch of the Indo-Germanic family of languages including Breton, Welsh, Cornish, Irish, Gaelic, Manx.—*ns.* **Celt'icism, Kelt'icism,** a Celtic idiom or custom; **Celtomā'nia, Keltomā'nia.**—**Celtic cross,** a type varying from a cross incised on a flat slate to an elaborate monument carved in the style common to the Celts, Scandinavians, and Northumbrian Angles, sometimes miscalled Runic cross. [L. *Celtae;* Gr. *Keltoi* or *Keltai.*]

cembalo, *chem'bä-lō, n.* a musical instrument with strings struck by hammers, a dulcimer : a similar instrument with a keyboard, as a harpsichord or pianoforte.—*n.* **cembalist** (*chem'* or *sem'*). [It.; see **cymbal.**]

cembra, *sem'brä, n.* (also **cembra pine**), the Swiss stone-pine. [Ger. dial. *zember*=*zimmer,* timber.]

cement, *si-ment'* formerly *sem'ənt, n.* anything that makes two bodies stick together : mortar : a bond of union : the bony substance forming the outer layer of the root of a tooth.—*v.t.* to unite with cement : to join firmly.—*ns.* **cementation** (*sem-ən-tā'shən*), the act of cementing : the process of impregnating the surface of one substance with another by surrounding it with powder and heating, as in steel-making, case-hardening, turning glass into porcelain : precipitation; **cement'ite,** iron carbide (Fe₃C);—*adjs.* **cement'atory, cementi'-tious,** having the quality of cementing or uniting firmly.—*ns.* **cement'-copper,** copper obtained by precipitation; **cement'-stone,** a clayey limestone, suitable for making hydraulic cement; **cement'-water,** water containing copper salts, as in copper mines. [O.Fr. *ciment*—L. *caementum,* chip of stone used to fill up in building a wall, *caedimentum* —*caedĕre,* to cut.]

cemetery, *sem'i-tri, n.* a burying-ground. [L.L. *coemētērium*—Gr. *koimētērion,* sleeping-place.]

cemitare, Spenser's spelling of **scimitar.**

cenacle, *sen'ə-kl, n.* a supper-room, esp. that in which the Last Supper was eaten by Christ and the apostles : a coterie, or its meeting-place. [Fr. *cénacle*—L. *cēnāculum*—*cēna,* supper.]

cenobite. Same as **coenobite.**

cenotaph, *sen'ō-täf, n.* a sepulchral monument without a burial. [Gr. *kenotaphion*—*kenos,* empty, and *taphos,* a tomb.]

Cenozoic, *sē-nō-zō'ik.* Same as **Cainozoic.**

cense, *sens, v.t.* to burn incense before. [**incense.**]

cense, *sens, v.t.* (*obs.*) to think : to assess.—*n.* (*obs.*) a public rate or tax : rank, condition. [L. *cēnsēre,* to estimate.]

censer, *sens'ər, n.* a pan in which incense is burned. [O.Fr. *censier, encensier* (mod. *encensoir*)—L.L. *incēnsorium*—L. *incendĕre, incēnsum,* to burn.]

censor, *sen'sor,* or *-sər, n.* a magistrate who kept account of the property of Roman citizens, imposed taxes, and watched over their morals : an official with analogous functions elsewhere : an official who examines books, papers, telegrams, plays, letters, etc. with power to delete or to forbid publication, acting, or delivery : (*psych.*) an unconscious inhibitive mechanism in the mind, that prevents what is painful to conscious aims from emerging into consciousness : one who censures or blames.—*v.t.* to subject to censorial examination or condemnation.—*adjs.* **censorial** (*-sō'ri-əl*), belonging to a censor, or to the correction of public morals; **censō'rian,** censorial; **censō'rious,** expressing censure : fault-finding.—*adv.* **censō'riously.**—*ns.* **censō'riousness; cen'sorship,** office of censor : time during which he holds office. [L. *cēnsor, -ōris.*]

censure, *sen'shər, n.* an opinion or judgment (formerly general, now unfavourable only) : blame : reproof.—*v.t.* to form or give an opinion or judgment (now unfavourable) of : to blame : to condemn as wrong : (*Shak.*) to sentence.—*adj.* **cen'surable,** deserving of censure : blamable.— *n.* **cen'surableness.**—*adv.* **cen'surably.** [L. *cēnsūra*—*cēnsēre,* to estimate.]

census, *sen'sus, n.* an official enumeration of inhabitants with statistics relating to them.—*adj.* **cen'sual,** relating to or containing a census. [L. *cēnsus, -ūs,* a register.]

cent, *sent, n.* a hundredth part, esp. of a dollar : a coin of that value.—*n.* **cent'age,** rate by the hundred : **cent'al,** a weight of 100 lb.—**per cent.,** by the hundred. [L. *centum,* a hundred.]

centaur, *sen'tawr, n.* a fabulous monster, half man, half horse.—*adj.* **centau'rian.** [Gr. *kentauros.*]

centaury, *sen'taw-ri, n.* a name applied to plants of the gentianaceous genera Erythraea and Chlora, and to the composite genus Centaurea (knapweed, etc.). [The *centaur* Chiron is said to have healed a wound with *kentaurion,* one of these plants.]

centavo, *sen-tä'vō, n.* a Portuguese and Brazilian money of account, 100 centavos making 1 escudo or cruzeiro. [Port.]

centavo, *sen-tä'vō, n.* a Spanish American coin and money of account. [Sp.]

centenary, *sen'tin-ər-i* (also *-tēn'* or *-ten'*), *n.* a hundred : a century or hundred years : a centennial. —*adj.* pertaining to a hundred.—*ns.* **centenā'rian,** one who is a hundred years old; **centenā'rianism;** **centenier** (*sen'ten-ēr*), a centurion; a police-officer in Jersey. [L. *centēnārius*—*centēni,* a hundred each—*centum.*]

centennial, *sen-ten'yəl, adj.* happening once in a hundred years.—*n.* a hundredth anniversary. [L. *centum,* a hundred, *annus,* a year.]

center, American spelling of **centre.**

center, *sen'tər, n.* (*Shak.*) **cincture,** waist-belt.

centering, centreing, *sen'tər-ing, n.* (*archit.*) the framework upon which an arch or vault of stone, brick, or iron is supported during its construction.

centesimal, *sen-tes'i-məl, adj.* hundredth : designating a centigrade thermometer.—*adv.* **centes'imally.** [L. *centēsimus*—*centum.*]

centiare, *sen'ti-är, n.* the hundredth part of an are, 1·196 sq. yards. [L. *centum,* a hundred, *area,* area.]

centigrade, *sen'ti-grād, adj.* having a hundred degrees : divided into a hundred degrees, as the centigrade thermometer constructed by Celsius (1701-44), in which freezing-point of water is zero and boiling-point is 100° (to convert degrees Celsius or centigrade to Fahrenheit multiply by g, and add 32). [L. *centum*, and *gradus*, a step, a degree.]

centigram(me), *sen'ti-gram*, *n.* the hundredth part of a gram(me) or ·15432 of a grain troy. [Fr.,—L. *centum*, a hundred, and **gram(me)**.]

centilitre, *sen'ti-lē-tər*, *n.* the hundredth part of a litre, 10 cubic centimetres, or a little more than ·6 cubic inch. [Fr.,—L. *centum*, a hundred, and **litre**.]

centillion, *sen-til'yən*, *n.* the hundredth power of a million—i.e. 1 followed by 600 ciphers : (*U.S.* and *France*) the hundredth power of a thousand—i.e. 1 followed by 300 ciphers.—*n.* **centill'ionth**. [L. *centum*, a hundred, and the ending of **million**.]

centime, *sän°'tēm*, *n.* the hundredth part of anything, esp. of a franc. [Fr.,—L. *centesimum*, a hundredth.]

centimetre, *sen'ti-mē-tər*, *n.* a lineal measure, the hundredth part of a metre, 0·3937 inches.— **centimetre-gram(me)-second** (contr. C.G.S.) **system**, the metric system, with these as units. [Fr.,—L. *centum*, a hundred, and **metre**.]

centinel(l), *obs.* spellings of **sentinel**.—**centinel** **(private)**, a private soldier.

centipede, *sen'ti-pēd*, *n.* any myriapod of the class Chilopoda, carnivorous flattened animals with many joints, most of which bear one pair of legs. [L. *centum*, and *pēs, pedis*, a foot.]

centner, *sent'nər*, *n.* a hundredweight, usually of 50 kilograms. [Ger.—L. *centēnārius*; cf. **centenary**.]

cento, *sen'tō*, *n.* a poem manufactured by putting together verses or passages of one author, or of several authors, so as to make a new meaning : a composition formed by joining scraps from other authors : a mere string of commonplace phrases and quotations :—*pl.* usually **cen'tos**.—*adj.* **cen'-tonate** (*bot.*) blotched.—*ns.* **cen'toist, cen'tonist**. [L. *centō, -ōnis*, Gr. *kentrōn*, patchwork.]

centonel(l), Spenserian spellings of **sentinel**.

centre (or, esp. *U.S.*, **center**), *sen'tər*, *n.* the middle point of anything, esp. a circle or sphere : the middle : a fixed point of reference : the point toward which all things move or are drawn : a nucleus : a resort : the chief leader of an organisation—head-centre : a player in a central position : a centre-forward : the men of moderate political opinions in the French Chamber, sitting right in front of the president : the Ultramontane party in Germany. —*v.t.* to place on or collect to a centre.—*v.i.* to be placed in the middle : to have a centre : to lie or move in relation to a centre (*pr.p.* **cen'tring**, **cen'tering**; *pa.t.* and *pa.p.* **cen'tred, cen'tered**). —*adj.* **cen'tral**, belonging to, in, or near, the centre : principal, dominant.—*ns.* **centralisa'tion**, **cen'tralism**, the tendency to administer by the sovereign or central government matters which would be otherwise under local management.— *v.t.* **cen'tralise**, to draw to or concentrate at a centre.—*n.* **centrality** (-*tral'i-ti*), central position. —*adv.* **cen'trally**.—*ns.* **cen'tre-bit**, a joiner's tool, turning on a centre, for boring circular holes—one of the chief tools of the burglar; **cen'tre-board**, a movable plate, fitted to drop below the keel of a racing yacht; **cen'tre-for'ward**, in association football and hockey, the central player among the forwards; **cen'tre-half (-back)**, the central player among the half-backs; **cen'tre-piece**, an ornament for the middle of a table, ceiling, etc.; **cen'tre-rail**, a rail between the ordinary rails.—*adjs.* **cen'tric** (*bot.*) terete : relating to, placed in, or containing the centre; **cen'trical**.—*adv.* **cen'tri-cally**.—*ns.* **cen'tricalness, centricity** (-*tris'i-ti*); **cen'tring** (see **centering**); **cen'trum**, the body of a vertebra.—**central conic**, a conic section that has a centre—ellipse or hyperbola; **central fire**, of a cartridge having the fulminate in the centre of the base; **central forces**, forces causing an acceleration towards or from a fixed point, the centre of force; **central heating**, a system of heating a building by water or steam from one boiler; **central nervous system** (*zool.*) the main ganglia of the nervous system with their associated nerve cords; **Central Powers**, in and before the war of 1914-18, the German Empire and Austria-

Hungary.—**centre of attraction**, the point to which bodies tend by the force of gravity or the like; **centre of buoyancy**, or **displacement**, the centre of gravity of the fluid displaced; **centre of gravity**, the point at which the weight of a body may be supposed to act; **centre of inertia**, or **mass**, the point through which any plane divides a body into two parts of equal mass; **centre of oscillation**, the point in a pendulum such that, if all the matter were concentrated there, the pendulum would have the same period; **centre of percussion**, the point where the direction of a blow meets the plane in which lie the centre of inertia and a possible axis of rotation such that the blow imparts a rotation without pressure on the axis; **centre of pressure**, the point on an immersed surface at which the pressure resultant may be taken to act; **centre of symmetry**, a point in a figure such that any straight line through it meets the figure in two points at equal distances on either side. [Fr.,—L. *centrum*—Gr. *kentron*, a sharp point.]

centri-, *sen-tri'*, **centro-**, *sen'tro-*, in composition, centre.—*adj.* **centrifugal** (*sen-trif'ū-gəl*; L. *fugĕre*, to flee from), tending away from a centre : efferent : (*bot.*) proceeding in development from the apex towards the base : using, or produced by centri-fugal force.—*v.t.* **centrif'ugalise**, to subject to centrifugal force.—*adv.* **centrif'ugally**.—*n.* **cen'-trifuge** (*-fūj*; also **centrifugal machine**), a machine which, by rapid rotation, separates substances of different densities—used in industry, biochemistry, etc.—*v.t.* to subject to such whirling.—*n.* **centrifugation** (*-fū-gā'shən*).— *adj.* **centrip'etal** (L. *petĕre*, to seek), tending towards a centre : afferent : proceeding from base towards apex.—*n.* **centrip'etalism**.—*adjs.* **centro-baric** (*-bar'ik*; Gr. *baros*, weight), relating to the centre of gravity; **centrocli'nal** (Gr. *klinein*, to lean; *geol.*) dipping towards a centre from all direc-tions.—*ns.* **cen'trode** (Gr. *hodos*, a path), a locus traced out by the successive positions of an instant-aneous centre of pure rotation; **cen'troid** (Gr *eidos*, form), the point where the medians of a triangle intersect; **cen'trosome** (Gr. *sōma*, a body), a small body found in the protoplasm of a cell, forming by division the two poles of the mitotic spindle.—**centrifugal force**, the resistance of a revolving body, by virtue of its inertia, to an acceleration towards the centre, equal and opposite to the constraining force. [Gr. *kentron* and L. *centrum* (from Gr.) a sharp point.]

centre (*Shak.*) for **cincture**.

centry, an obs. spelling of **sentry**.

centumvir, *sen-tum'vir*, *n.* one of the Roman judges chosen annually for civil suits, orig. 105 in number (three from each of the thirty-five tribes) :— *pl.* **centum'viri**.—*n.* **centum'virate**. [L. *centum*, a hundred, and *vir*, a man.]

centuple, *sen'tū-pl*, *adj.* hundredfold.—*v.t.* to multiply or increase a hundred times.—*n.* **centu-plica'tion**.—*adi.* **centū'plicate**, centuple.—*n.* one of a hundred like things or copies.—*v.t.* to centuple. [L. *centuplus* and *centuplex*—*centum*, *plicāre*, to fold.]

century, *sen'tū-ri*, *n.* a set or series of a hundred, as Roman soldiers, runs at cricket, or miles ridden, or consecutive years (esp. reckoned from the conventionally accepted date of Christ's birth).— *adj.* **centūr'ial**.—*ns.* **centū'riātor**, one of a company of 16th-century Reformed divines of Magdeburg who compiled a church history in 13 vols., each volume covering a century; **centū'rion**, the commander of a century : one who has scored or achieved a hundred in any way.—**century plant** (see **agave**). [L. *centuria*—*centum*.]

ceorl, *chāorl, kāorl*, *n.* before the Norman Conquest an ordinary freeman, not of noble birth. [O.E. *ceorl*; see **churl**.]

cephal-, *sef'əl-, si-fal'-*, in composition, head.—*ns.* **cephalag'ra** (Gr. *agrā*, a catching), gout in the head; **cephalalgia** (-*al'ji-ä*; Gr. *algos*, pain), headache.—*adj.* **cephalal'gic**.—*n.* **Cephalas'pis** (Gr. *aspis*, shield), an Upper Silurian and Old Red Sandstone genus of fishes or fishlike animals (ostracoderms) with a head-shield.—*adjs.* **ceph'a-late,** having a head; **cephal'ic,** of, belonging to, the head: for curing pains in the head.—*n.* a remedy for head-pains.—*n.* **cephali'tis,** inflammation of the brain.—*n.pl.* **Cephalochorda** (-ō-kor'dä; Gr. *chordē,* cord), a lowly class of chordate animals in which the persisting notochord projects beyond the nerve-cord to the end of the snout—the lancelets or amphioxus.—*n.* **ceph'alopod** (-ō-pod; Gr. *pous, podos,* foot), a member of the **Cephalopoda** (-op'od-ä), the highest class of molluscs, usu. large animals, exclusively marine, with the foot modified into arms surrounding the mouth—*cuttle-fish,* etc.—*ns.* **cephalothō'rax,** the fused head and thorax in some arthropods; **cephalotomy** (-ot'ə-mi; Gr. *tomē,* a cut), the dissection of the head.—*adj.* **ceph'alous,** having a head.—**cephalic index,** the ratio of the breadth to the length of the skull expressed as a percentage. [Gr. *kephalē,* head.]

ceramic, keramic, *se-* or *ke-ram'ik adj.* pertaining to pottery.—*n.* (treated as *sing.*) **ceram'ics, keram'ics,** the potter's art. [Gr. *keramos,* potter's earth.]

cerargyrite, *ser-är'jər-īt, n.* horn-silver—a horn-like mineral, silver chloride. [Gr. *keras,* horn, *argyros,* silver.]

cerasin, *ser'ə-sin, n.* the insoluble portion of cherry-tree gum. [L. *cerasus,* Gr. *kerasos,* the cherry-tree.]

Cerastes, *se-ras'tēz, n.* the North African horned viper, with a horny process over each eye.—*n.* **Ceras'tium,** the mouse-ear chickweed, with horn-shaped capsules. [Gr. *kerastēs—keras,* a horn.]

cerate. See **cere.**

ceratitis. See **keratitis.**

Ceratodus, *ser-at'ō-dəs, n.* the barramunda, an Australian lung-fish, now called Neoceratodus, the name Ceratodus being reserved for a fossil genus. [Gr. *keras, -atos,* horn, *odous,* tooth.]

ceratoid, *ser'ə-toid. adj.* horny. [Gr. *keratoeidēs —keras,* horn, *eidos,* form.]

Cerberus, *sər'bər-əs, n.* (*myth*) the monster that guarded the entrance to Hades, a dog with (at least) three heads.—*adj.* **cerbērian.** [L.—Gr. *Kerberos.*]

cercal. See **cercus.**

cercaria, *sər-kā'ri-ä n.* a larval stage of many trematodes.—*adj.* **cerca'rian.** [Gr. *kerkos,* a tail.]

Cercopithecus, *sər-kō-pi-thē'kus, n.* an African genus of long-tailed monkeys, including the Diana monkey, vervet, and mona. [Gr. *kerkos,* tail, *pithēkos,* monkey.]

cercus, *sər'kəs,* a tail-like appendage.—*adj.* **cer'cal,** pertaining to a tail. [Gr. *kerkos,* tail.]

cere, *sēr, v.t.* to cover with wax.—*n.* the bare waxlike patch at the base of the upper part of a bird's beak.—*adj.* **cērā'ceous,** waxy.—*ns.* **cēr'ate,** a paste or stiff ointment containing wax; **cere'-cloth, cerement** (*sēr'mənt*), a cloth dipped in melted wax to wrap a dead body in: a winding-sheet or grave-clothes generally.—*adjs.* **cēr'eous,** waxy. [L. *cēra,* wax.]

cereal. See **Ceres.**

cerebrum, *ser'i-brəm, n.* the front and larger part of the brain.—*adjs.* **cerebell'ar, cerebell'ous.—** *n.* **cerebell'um,** the hinder and lower part of the brain.—*adj.* **cer'ebral,** pertaining to the brain or the cerebrum: (*phon.*) of consonant sounds, produced by inverting the tip of the tongue on the palate.—*ns.* **cer'ebralism,** the theory that all mental operations originate in the brain; **cer'e-bralist.**—*v.i.* **cer'ebrate,** to show brain action.— *n.* **cerebrā'tion,** action of the brain, esp. unconscious.—*adjs.* **cer'ebric** (or *sər-eb'rik*), cerebral; **cerebriform** (-*eb'*), brain-shaped.—*ns.* **cerebrī'tis,** inflammation of the cerebrum.—*adj.* **cer'ebro-spin'al,** relating to the brain and spinal cord together.—**cerebral hemispheres,** the two great divisions of the cerebrum; **cerebro-spinal fever,** meningitis. [L. *cerebrum,* the brain; prob. cog. with Gr. *karā,* the head, *krānion,* the cranium.]

ceremony, *ser'i-mə-ni, n.* a rite: a formal act: the outward form, religious or other: any empty form without inwardness: pomp or state.—*adj.* **cere-monial** (-*mō'ni-əl*), relating to ceremony.—*n.* outward form: a system of ceremonies.—*n.* **ceremō'nialism,** adherence to outward form.— *adv.* **ceremō'nially.**—*adj.* **ceremō'nious,** full of ceremony: particular in observing forms: precise. —*adv.* **ceremō'niously.**—*n.* **ceremōniousness.** —**master of ceremonies,** the person who directs the form and order of the ceremonies to be observed on some public occasion; **stand on ceremony,** to be punctilious about forms. [L. *caerimōnia,* sanctity.]

Ceres, *sē'rēz, n.* the Roman name for the Greek Demeter, goddess of tillage and corn: one of the minor planets.—*adj.* **ce'real** (*sē'ri-əl*), relating to edible grain.—*n.* a grain used as food, such as wheat, barley, etc.: a food prepared from such grain, esp. a breakfast food easily got ready.—*n.* **cē'realist,** a specialist in cereals: a feeder on cereals. [L. *Cērēs, -eris,* prob. from root of *creāre,* to create.]

Cereus, *sē'ri-əs, n.* a large genus of cactuses, including some of the most imposing forms. [L. *cēreus,* waxen, wax-taper (from their stiff form).]

cerge, *sərj, n.* a large wax-candle burned before the altar.—Also **cierge, serge.** [O.Fr.,—L. *cēreus— cēra,* wax.]

Cerinthian, *sər-in'thi-ən, adj.* pertaining to *Cerinthus,* one of the earliest heretics in the Christian Church, against whose crude Gnosticism the Gospel of John was written, according to Irenaeus.

ceriph. Same as **serif.**

cerise, *ser-ēz',* also *-ēs', n.* and *adj.* light and clear red. [Fr., cherry.]

cerium, *sē'ri-əm, n.* the metallic element of atomic number 58.—*ns.* **cē'ria,** its oxide; **cē'rite,** a mineral, its hydrous silicate. [Named from the planet *Ceres,* discovered about the same time.]

cerne, *sərn* (*Shak.*), a short form of **concern.**

cernuous, *sər'nū-əs, adj.* (*bot.*) nodding, bowing down, drooping. [L. *cernuus,* inclined forwards.]

cerograph, *sē'rō-gräf, n.* a writing on wax: an encaustic painting: engraving by means of a plate spread with wax.—*adjs.* **cerographic** (-*graf'ik*), **-al**—*ns.* **cerographist** (-*rog'rə-fist*); **cerog'raphy.** [Gr. *kēros,* wax, *graphein,* to write.]

ceromancy, *sē'rō-man-si, n.* divination by dropping melted wax in water. [Gr. *kēros,* wax, *manteiā,* divination.]

ceroon. See **seroon.**

ceroplastic, *sē-rō-plas'tik, adj.* pertaining to wax-modelling.—*n.pl.* **ceroplas'tics,** the art of wax-modelling. [Gr. *kēros,* wax, *plastikos,* plastic—*plassein,* to mould.]

cerris, *ser'is, n.* the Turkey oak (*Quercus cerris*).— *adj.* **cerr'ial.** [L. *cerreus.*]

certain, *sər'tn, adj.* sure: not to be doubted: resolved: fixed: determinate: regular: inevitable: some: one.—*adv.* **cer'tainly.**—*ns.* **cer'titude; cer'tainty** (*slang* **cert,** sometimes in phrase **dead cert**).—**a certain person,** implying some degree of contempt; **a lady of a certain age, of an age** best not stated accurately—at least no longer young; **for certain,** assuredly; **in a certain condition,** newspaper euphemism for pregnant; **moral certainty** (see **moral**). [O.Fr.,—L. *certus —cernère,* to decide.]

certes, *sər'tiz, adv.* certainly: in sooth.—**my cer'tie, cer'ty** (*Scot.*) assuredly. [Fr.]

certificate, *sər-tif'i-kāt, n.* a written declaration of some fact: a testimonial of character or definite statement of qualifications.—*v.t.* to give a certificate.—*adj.* **cer'tifiable** (-*fī-ə-bl*), capable of being certified (esp. as a lunatic).—*adv.* **cer'tifiably.**— *adj.* **certif'icāted,** holding a certificate.—*ns.* **certificā'tion; certif'icatory,** a certificate—Also *adj.*—*n.* **cer'tifier,** one who certifies.—*v.t.* **cer'-tify,** to make known as certain: to inform: to declare in writing: to certify as insane: (*pr.p.* **cer'-tifying;** *pa.p.* **cer'tified).** [Fr. *certificat—*L. *certificāre, certus,* certain, and *facĕre,* to make.]

certiorari, *sər-shi-ō-rā'rī, n.* a writ by which causes are removed from inferior courts into the High Court of Justice. [L.L. *certiōrārī,* to be informed of—*certior,* comp. of *certus,* certain.]

cerulean, caerulean, *si-rōō'li-ən*, *adj.* sky-blue : dark-blue : sea-green.—*adjs.* caerule (*sēr'ūl; Spens.*) sky-blue; ceru'leous.—*n.* ceru'lein, a coal-tar colour, producing fast olive-greens. [L. *caerŭleus,* dark blue or green.]

cerumen, *si-rōō'men, n.* ear wax.—*adj.* ceru'-minous. [L. *cēra,* wax.]

ceruse, *sē'rōōs,* or *si-rōōs', n.* white-lead.—*n.* cē'rus(s)ite, native lead carbonate. [Fr.,—L. *cērussa,* conn. with *cēra,* Gr. *kēros,* wax.]

cervix, *sər'viks, n.* the neck of an organ.—*adj.* cervical (*sər'vi-kl, sər-vī'kl*). [L. *cervix, cervicis,* neck.]

cervine, *sər'vīn, adj.* relating to deer : like deer : fawn coloured. [L. *cervinus—cervus,* a stag.]

cesarean. See caesarean.

cesarevitch, -witch, cesarevna. See tsar.

cespitose. Same as caespitose.

cess, *ses, n.* a tax, a local rate.—*v.t.* to impose a tax.
—bad cess to (in Ireland), ill luck to you : out of all cesse (*Shak.*), excessively, immoderately. [Shortened from *assess.*]

cessation, *ses-ā'shən, n.* a ceasing or stopping : a rest : a pause. [L. *cessātiō, -ōnis.* See cease.]

cesse, *ses, v.i.* (*Spens.*). Same as cease.

cession, *sesh'ən, n.* a yielding up.—*n.* cess'ionary, one to whom an assignment has been legally made. —cessio (*ses'i-ō, sesh'i-ō*) bono'rum (Scots law), a debtor's surrender of his estate to his creditors in return for a judicial protection from imprisonment in respect of his debt—after 1880 a summary process in small bankruptcies, finally abolished 1913. [L. *cessiō, -ōnis; see* cede.]

cesspool, *ses'pōōl, n.* a pool or pit for collecting filthy water. [Origin obscure.]

cestode, *ses'tōd, n.* a tapeworm or bladder-worm.—*n.* ces'toid, a cestode : a ribbon-like ctenophoran (Venus's girdle).—Also *adj.*—*n.* and *adj.* ces-toid'ean. [Gr. *kestos,* a girdle, a strap, and *eidos,* form.]

Cestracion, *ses-trā'si-on, n.* an antiquated type of shark represented by the Port Jackson shark. (Perh. Gr. *kestrā,* a kind of fish, or *kestros,* sharp, *akē,* point.]

cestui, *set-ē', sest'wē, n.* that one—in such phrases as cestui que trust (*ki-trust*), a person entitled to the benefit of a trust. [O.Fr., dat. of *cest,* that.]

cestus, *ses'təs, n.* a girdle, esp. Aphrodite's. [L.,— Gr. *kestos,* girdle.]

cestus, *ses'təs, n.* an ancient boxing-glove loaded with metal. [L. *caestus.*]

cesure, *sē'zūr, n.* (*Spens.*) a break : interruption. [caesura.]

Cetacea, *si-tā'shi-ä, -shyä, n.pl.* an order of mammals of aquatic habit and fish-like form, including the toothed whales, or *Odontoceti* (sperm whales, bottle-nose, dolphins, etc.) and the baleen whales, or *Mystacoceti* (right whale, hump-backs, rorquals). —*n.* and *adj.* cetā'cean.—*adj.* cetā'ceous.—*n.* cetol'ogy, the study of whales; ceteosau'rus (Gr. *sauros,* lizard), a large Jurassic dinosaur. [Gr. *kētos,* a sea-monster.]

Ceterach, *set'ər-ak, n.* the scale-fern genus. [Ety. unknown.]

cevadilla. See sabadilla.

Ceylonese, *sē-lən-ēz', adj.* of or belonging to Ceylon.—*n.* a native of Ceylon : a Sinhalese.—*n.* cey'lonite, cey'lanite, a magnesia-iron spinel.

ch, *ch, pron.* obs. S.W. and conventional dialect for ich, I, fused with the verb, as cham, I am, chave, I have, chill, I will. [M.E. *ich*—O.E. *ic.*]

cha, *chä, n.* tea : rolled tea. [Chin. *ch'a.*]

chabazite, *kab'ə-zīt, n.* a zeolite, a hydrated calcium-aluminium silicate, in pink and glassy white crystals. [From a misreading of Gr. *chalazios,* a kind of stone—*chalaza,* hailstone.]

Chablis, *shäb'lē, n.* a celebrated white Burgundy wine made at *Chablis,* near Auxerre, in France.

chabouk, *chä'bōōk, n.* a horsewhip. [Pers. *chābuk.*]

chace. See chase (1).

chack, *chäk, n.* (*Scot.*) a snack or slight hasty meal : a snapping or pinching, as by a door or window.— *v.t.* to pinch or nip in such a way. [Imit.]

chacma, *chak'mä, n.* a large South African baboon. [From Hottentot.]

chaco. Same as shako.

chaconne, *sha', shə-kon', n.* an old dance, with slow movement : its music, a series of variations on a ground bass, mostly eight bars in length, appearing in sonatas as well as ballets. [Fr.,—Sp. *chacona*— Basque *chucun,* pretty.]

chad, *shad, n.* a kind of fish. [See shad.]

Chaetodon, *kē'tō-don, n.* a tropical genus of fishes with slender teeth, giving name to the family Chaetodont'idae. [Gr. *chaitē,* hair, *odous, odontos* tooth.]

chaetopod, *kē'tō-pod, n.* a worm (as earthworm, lobworm, sea-mouse) that crawls by the help of bristles. [Gr. *chaitē,* hair, and *pous, podos,* foot.]

chafe, *chāf, v.t.* to heat, fret, or wear by rubbing : to cause to fret or rage.—*v i.* to fret or rage (with *against, at*).—*n.* heat caused by rubbing : rage : passion.—*ns.* chaf'er (*obs.*), a chafing-dish, a saucepan; chaf'ing-dish, a vessel for heating by hot coals, etc. : (esp. *U.S.*) a dish for cooking on the table; chaf'ing-gear, mats, spun-yarn, battens, etc., put upon the rigging and spars of a ship to prevent their being chafed. [Fr. *chauffer*—L. *calefacēre—calēre,* to be hot, and *facēre,* to make.]

chafer, *chāf'ər, n.* a beetle, esp. of the Scarabaeidae. [O.E. *cefer;* Du. *kever,* Ger. *käfer.*]

chaff, *chäf, n.* the husks of corn as threshed or winnowed : cut hay and straw : refuse, or worthless matter : (*slang*) perh. a different word) light banter, badinage.—*v.t.* (*slang*) to banter.—*ns.* chaff'-cut'ter, chaff'-en'gine, a machine for cutting up straw or hay.—*n.* and *adj.* chaff'ing.— *adv.* chaff'ingly.—*adjs.* chaff'less; chaff'y. [O.E. *ceaf;* cf. Du. *kaf.*]

chaffer, *chaf'ər,*—*v.i.* to bargain : to haggle about price : (*Spens.*) to sell, exchange, or bandy.—*ns.* chaff'erer, a haggler; chaff'ery, buying and selling : (*Spens*) haggling. [M.E. *chapfare,* a bargain, from O.E. *cēap,* price, *faru,* way.]

chaffinch, *chaf'insh, n.* a little song-bird of the finch family. [Said to delight in *chaff.* See finch.]

chaffron. See chamfrain.

chaft, *chäft, n.* (*Scot.* and *Northern English*) the jaw. [O.N. *kjaptr;* cf. Sw. *kaft,* Dan. *kieft.*]

chagan, *käg-än', n.* an early form of khan.

chagrin, *shə-grēn', -grin', shag'rin, n.* that which wears or gnaws the mind : vexation : annoyance.— *v.t.* (-grēn') to vex or annoy.—*p.adj.* chagrined'. [Fr. *chagrin,* shagreen, rough skin, ill-humour.]

chai, chi, *chī,* fem. of chal.

chain, *chān, n.* a series of links or rings passing through one another : a number of things connected in series : a linked series : a mountain range : a string of islands : something that binds : a connected course or train of events : a measure of 100 links, or 66 feet (see Gunter) : a succession of cigars or cigarettes smoked without intermission : (*chem.*) a number of atoms linked in succession : (*pl.*) fetters, bonds, confinement generally.—*v.t.* to fasten : to fetter : to restrain : (*Shak.*) to embrace.— *ns.* chain'-arm'our, chain-mail; chain'-bolt, a large bolt used to secure the chain-plates to the ship's side; chain'-bridge, a bridge suspended on chains : a suspension-bridge; chain'-cable, a cable composed of iron links; chain'-drive, transmission of power by chain-gear.—*adj.* chain'-driven.—*p.adj.* chained, bound or fastened, as with a chain : fitted with a chain.—*ns.* chain'-gang, a gang of convicts chained together; chain'-gear, -gearing, gearing consisting of an endless chain and (generally) sprocket-wheels; chain'-harrow, a harrow composed of chainwork.—*adj.* chain'-less, without chains : unfettered.—*ns.* chain'let, a small chain; chain'-letter, a letter soliciting (among other things) the sending of duplicates with or without a limit; chain'-light'ning, forked or zigzag lightning : a harsh whisky; chain'-mail, armour of connected links, much used in Europe in the 12th and 13th centuries; chain'-mould'ing, moulding in the form of a chain; chain'-pier, a pier supported by chains like a chain-bridge.— *n.pl.* chain'-plates, on ship-board, iron plates bolted below the channels to serve as attachments for the dead-eyes, through which the standing rigging or shrouds and backstays are rove and secured.—*ns.* **chain'-pump**, a pump consisting of an endless chain, usually with disks; **chain'-reac'tion**, a process in which each reaction is in turn the stimulus of a similar reaction; **chain'-rule**, an arithmetical rule, so called from the terms of the problem being stated as equations, and connected, as if by a chain, so as to obtain by one operation the same result as would be obtained by a number of different operations in simple proportion : the rule for solving problems by compound proportion; **chain'-shot**, two bullets or half-bullets fastened together by a chain, used formerly to destroy ships' rigging; **chain'-smo'ker**; **chain'-stitch**, a stitch resembling the links of a chain; **chain'-store**, (*U.S.*) a multiple shop; **chain'-work**, work consisting of threads, cords, etc., wrought with open spaces like the links of a chain: network. [O.Fr. *chaeine*—L. *catēna*.]

chair, *chār*, *n.* a movable seat for one, with a back to it : a chariot : a vehicle, wheeled or carried, for one person : the seat or office of one in authority, as a judge, a bishop, or the person presiding over any meeting : the chairman : the seat from which a professor delivers his lectures : a professorship : a pulpit : (*U.S.*) a witness-box : the instrument or the punishment of electrocution : a support for a railway rail securing it to a sleeper.—*v.t.* to place in a seat of authority : to carry publicly in triumph. —*n.* **chair'-bed**, a chair capable of being turned into a bed.—*n.pl.* **chair'-days** (*Shak.*; *fig.*) the evening of life.—*ns.* **chair'man**, one who takes the chair, or presides at an assembly or meeting : one who carries a sedan or draws a Bath chair; **chair'manship**; **chair'-or'gan**, a choir-organ (perhaps because it sometimes formed the back of the organist's seat); **chair'woman**. [Fr. *chaire*—L.—Gr. *kathedrā*.]

chaise, *shāz*, *n.* a light open carriage for one or more persons : a travelling carriage (see **post-chaise**).—*n.* **chaise'-cart**, a light vehicle for going about in.—*adj.* **chaise'less**.—*n.* **chaise-longue**, (*lon²g*) a couch with back at one end and short armrest. [Fr., a form of *chaire*; see **chair**. **chay** and **shay** are vulgar singulars of imaginary *pl.* **chaise**.]

chal, *chal*, *n.* fellow: person:—*fem.* **chai**, *chī*. [Romany.]

chalaza, *ka-lā'zä*, *n.* (*zool.*) in a bird's egg, the string that holds the yolk-sac in position : (*bot.*) the base of the ovule.—*adj.* **chalazogamic** (*kal-az-ō-gam'ik*).—*n.* **chalazog'amy** (*-og'ə-mi*; *bot.*) entrance of the pollen-tube through the chalaza (opp. to *porogamy*). [Gr. *chalaza*, hail, lump.]

chalcedony, *kal-sed'ə-ni*, or *kal'*, *n.* a beautiful mineral composed of silica, usually banded, translucent, of waxy lustre, generally white or bluish-white, apparently amorphous but consisting of crystalline fibres.—*adj.* **chalcedonic** (*-si-don'ik*) —*n.* **chalced'onyx** (or *-on'*; from **onyx**), an agate of alternating white opaque and greyish translucent chalcedony. [Gr. *chalkēdōn*, possibly from *Chalcedon*, in Asia Minor.]

Chalcidian, *kal-sid'i-ən*, *adj.* pertaining to Chalcis in Euboea, or its people.—**Chalcidian alphabet**, the alphabet used by Chalcidian settlers in southern Italy and Sicily, from which the Latin alphabet developed.

chalcography, *kal-kog'rə-fi*, *n.* the art of engraving on copper or brass.—*ns.* **chalcog'rapher**, **chalcog'raphist**. [Gr. *chalkos*, copper, *graphein*, to write.]

chalcopyrite, *kal-kō-pī'rīt*, *n.* copper pyrites. [Gr. *chalkos*, copper, and **pyrite**.]

Chaldaic, *kal-dā'ik*, **Chaldee**, *kal'dē*, *adj.* relating to *Chaldaea*.—*n.* the language of the Chaldaeans : an ancient inhabitant of Chaldaea : a soothsayer : a member of the Chaldaean church.—*n.* **chal'-däism**, a Chaldaic idiom.—*adj.* **chaldae'an**, **chalde'an**, Chaldaic.—*n.* a native of Chaldaea.

chalder, *chawl'dər*, *n.* an old Scottish dry measure, containing 16 bolls. [Prob. a form of **chaldron**.]

chaldron, *chawl'drən*, *n.* an old coal-measure,

holding 36 heaped bushels (=25½ cwt.). [Fr. *chaudron*; see **cauldron**.]

chalet, *shål'ä*, *n.* a summer hut used by Swiss herdsmen in the Alps : a wooden villa : a urinal. [Fr.; *châlet* is wrong.]

chalice, *chal'is*, *n.* a cup or bowl : a communion-cup.—*adj.* **chal'iced**, cup-like. [O.Fr. *chalice*—L. *calix*, *calicis*; cf. Gr. *kylix*, a cup; **calyx** is a different word.]

chalk, *chawk*, *n.* the well-known white soft rock, a foraminiferal limestone, composed of calcium carbonate : a substitute for this used for writing (as French chalk).—*v.t.* to rub, mark, or manure with chalk : in a tavern to score with chalk.—*ns.* **chalk'iness**; **chalk'-pit**, a pit in which chalk is dug; **chalk'-stone**, a stone or piece of chalk : (*pl.*) the white concretions formed round the joints in chronic gout.—*adj.* **chalk'y.**—**by a long chalk**, by a considerable distance, referring to the habit of scoring with chalk; **chalking the door**, in Scotland, a form of warning tenants to remove from burghal tenements; **chalk out**, to trace out, as with chalk, to plan; **not to know chalk from cheese**, to know nothing about the matter, not to know a B from a bull's foot; **the Chalk** (*geol.*), the uppermost part of the Cretaceous system in England. [O.E. *cealc*—L. *calx*, limestone.]

challenge, *chal'inj*, *v.t.* to call on to settle a matter by fighting or by any kind of contest : to claim as one's own : to accuse : to object to : (*Spens.*) to track.—*n.* a summons to a contest of any kind, but esp. a duel : a calling of any one or anything in question : exception to a juror : the demand of a sentry : an accusation : a claim.—*adj.* **chall'enge-able**, that may be challenged.—*n.* **chall'enger**, one who challenges to a combat of any kind : a claimant : one who objects, calls in question.—*adj.* **chall'enging**.—*adv.* **chall'engingly**. [O.Fr. *chalenge*, a dispute, claim—L. *calumnia*, a false accusation—*calvi* or *calvēre*, to deceive.]

challis, **shalli**, *chal'is*, *shal'is*, *shal'i*, *n.* a soft glossless silk and worsted fabric, later of other materials. [Origin uncertain.]

chalone, *kal'ōn*, *n.* an internal secretion which inhibits action as a hormone excites it.—*adj.* **chalon'ic**. [Gr. *chalaein*, to relax.]

chalumeau, *shal-(y)oo-mō', shal-ü-mō'*, *n.* an early reed instrument that developed into the clarinet : the lowest register of the clarinet :—*pl.* **chalu-meaux** (*-mōz'*). [Fr.,—O.Fr. *chalemel*—L.L. *calamellus*, dim. of *calamus*, a pipe, a reed.]

Chalybean, *kal-ib-ē'ən*, or *ka-lib'i-ən*, *adj.* (*Milt.*) forged by the Chalybes : well tempered.—*adj.* **chalyb'eate**, containing iron.—*n.* a water or other liquor containing iron.—*n.* **cha'lybite**, siderite, a common iron ore, ferrous carbonate. [Gr. *chalyps*, *chalybos*, steel, or *Chalyps*, one of the *Chalybes*, a nation in Pontus famous for steel.]

cham, *kam*, *n.* an obs. form of **khan**: (*fig.*) an autocrat.

chamade, *shâ-mäd'*, *n.* a drum or trumpet call for a parley or surrender. [Fr.]

chamber, *chām'bər*, *n.* a room : the place where an assembly meets : a house of a legislature, esp. the French Chamber of Deputies : an assembly or body of men met for some purpose, as a chamber of commerce : a hall of justice : a compartment : a cavity : the back end of the bore of a gun : (*Shak.*) a small cannon : (*pl.*) a suite of rooms in a house occupied separately, esp. by lawyers : a judge's room for hearing cases not taken into court.—*v.t.* to put in a chamber : to confine.—*v.i.* to be wanton. —*ns.* **cham'ber-con'cert**, a concert of chamber-music; **cham'ber-coun'cil** (*Shak.*), a private or secret council; **cham'ber-counsel**, **-counsellor**, a counsel who gives his advice privately, but does not plead in court.—*adj.* **cham'bered**.—*ns.* **cham'berer**, a man of intrigue : (*Shak.*) a gallant; **cham'ber-fellow**, one sharing a chamber.—*n.pl.* **cham'ber-hangings** (*Shak.*), the hangings or tapestry of a chamber.—*ns.* **cham'bering** (*B.*), lewd behaviour; **cham'ber-lye** (*Shak.*), urine; **cham'ber-maid**, a female servant who has the care of bedrooms at an inn : formerly, and still in U.S., a housemaid; **cham'ber-music**, music suitable for a room, rather than a theatre or a large hall, now almost confined to music for strings with or without piano or winds; **cham'ber-organ,** a small organ suitable for a room; **cham'ber-pot,** a bedroom vessel for urine—often merely **cham'ber**; **cham'ber-prac'tice,** the business of a chamber-counsel. [Fr. *chambre*—L. *camera*—Gr. *kamarā*, a vault, a room.]

chamberlain, *chām'bər-lin, n.* an officer appointed by a king or nobleman, or by a corporation, to perform domestic and ceremonial duties or to act as factor or steward.—*n.* **cham'berlainship.**—**Lord Chamberlain,** an officer of high standing in the royal household, having control over all the officers and servants 'above stairs', except those of the bedchamber, over the establishment attached to the Chapel Royal, the physicians, surgeons, and apothecaries of the household; **Lord Great Chamberlain,** a hereditary officer who has the government of the palace of Westminster and to whom upon solemn occasions the keys of Westminster Hall and of the Court of Requests are delivered. [O.Fr. *chambrelenc*; O.H.G. *chamerling*—L. *camera,* a chamber, and affix *-ling* or *-lenc*=Eng. *-ling* in *hireling*.]

Chambertin, *shän'-ber-tan⁹, n.* a famous red Burgundy from the vineyard of that name near Dijon.

chameleon, chamaeleon, *ka-mēl'yən, n.* a small lizard famous for changing its colour: (*fig.*) an inconstant person.—*adjs.* **chameleonic** (*-i-on'ik*), **chamel'eon-like.** [L. *chamaeleōn*—Gr. *chamaileōn—chamai* (cf. L. *humī*), on the ground (i.e. dwarf) and *leōn,* a lion.]

chamelot, *cham',* or *kam'e-lot, n.* (*Spens.*) same as **camlet.**

chamfer, *cham'fər, n.* a bevel or slope made by paring off the edge of anything originally right-angled: a groove, channel, or furrow.—*v.t.* to cut or grind off bevel-wise, as a corner: to channel or make furrows upon: to flute, as a column.—*adj.* **cham'fered,** bevelled: furrowed, grooved, wrinkled. [Fr. *chanfrein*–O.Fr. *chanfraindre,* apparently from *chant fraindre*—L. *cantum frangēre,* to break the edge or side.]

chamfrain, *cham'fren, n.* a piece of leather or plate of steel to protect the face of a horse in battle.—Also **cham'fron, chaf'fron.** [Fr. *chânfrein;* origin unknown.]

chamiso, *chä-mē'sō,* **chamise,** *chä-mēz', n.* a rosaceous shrub (*Adenostoma fasciculatum*) of California.—*n.* **chamisal',** a chamiso thicket. [Sp. *chamiza,* cane.]

chamlet, *cham'* or *kam'let, n.* Same as **camlet.**

chamois, *sham'wä, n.* a goat-like antelope inhabiting high mountains in southern and central Europe: (pl. **chamois,** *sham'wä*): (*sham'i*), a soft kind of leather originally made from its skin (in this sense also **shammy,** or **shamoy**). [Fr., perh. from Swiss Romanic; cf. Ger. *gemse,* a chamois.]

chamomile. See **camomile.**

champ, *champ, v.i.* to make a snapping noise with the jaws in chewing.—*v.t.* to bite or chew: to munch: to crush: to mash.—*n.* a champing. [cf. **jam.**]

champ, *champ, n.* (*her.*) field. [Fr.]

champagne, *sham-pān', n.* a white sparkling wine, strictly from *Champagne* in France (sometimes still or coloured red): the amber-like colour of white champagne.

champaign, *cham'pān',* also *sham-pān', adj.* level, open.—*n.* an open, level country. [A doublet of **campaign,** from O.Fr. *champaigne*—L. *campānia,* a plain.]

champak, champac, *chum'puk, cham'pak, n.* an Indian tree (*Michelia Champaca*) of the magnolia family, of great beauty, with oppressively scented flowers. [Hind.]

champerty, *cham'pər-ti, n.* an illegal bargain whereby the one party is to assist the other in a suit, and is to share in the proceeds.—*n.* **cham'part,** the division of the produce of land, the right of the feudal lord. [Norm. Fr.—L. *campi pars,* part of the field.]

champignon, *cham-,* or *sham-pin'yən, n.* a mushroom or other edible fungus esp. the fairy-ring champignon (*Marasmius oreades*).

champion, *cham'pi-ən, n.* one who fights in single combat for himself or for another: one who defends a cause: a successful combatant: in sports, one who has excelled all others: a hero.—*adj.* acting or ranking as champion, first: (*slang*) excellent.—*v.t.* (*obs.*) to challenge: to defend: to support.—*ns.* **cham'pioness; cham'pionship,** the position of honour gained by being champion: the act of championing. [Fr.,—L.L. *campiō, -ōnis*—L. *campus,* a plain, a place for games.]

champlevé, *shän⁹-lə-vā', n.* enamel work done with vitreous powders in channels cut in a metal base.—Also *adj.* [Fr.]

chance, *châns, n.* that which falls out or happens fortuitously, or without assignable cause: fortune: an unexpected event: risk: opportunity: possibility of something happening: probability: (*pl.*) misfortunes.—*v.t.* to risk.—*v.i.* to happen.—*adj.* happening by chance.—*adv.* perchance.—*n.* **chance'-com'er,** one who comes by chance or unexpectedly.—*adjs.* **chance'ful,** full of risk or danger, hazardous; **chance'less,** without an opportunity; **chanc'y** (*coll.*), lucky, bringing good luck: also risky, uncertain.—**by chance,** accidentally; **even chance,** equal probability for or against; **how chance?** (*Shak.*) how does it happen that?; **stand a good chance,** to have a reasonable expectation; **take one's chance,** to accept what happens: to risk an undertaking; **the main chance,** the chief object (esp. an eye to **the main chance,** thought for self-enrichment). [O.Fr. *cheance*—L.L. *cadentia*—L. *cadēre,* to fall.]

chancel, *chän'sl, n.* the eastern part of a church, originally separated from the nave by a screen of lattice-work, so as to prevent general access thereto, though not to interrupt either sight or sound. [O.Fr.,—L. *cancellī,* lattices.]

chancellor, *chän'səl-ər, n.* (*Shak.*) secretary: a chief minister: the president, or a judge, of a court of chancery or other court: the official who keeps the registers of an order of knighthood: the titular (or in *U.S.* active) head of a university: (*Scot.*) the foreman of a jury.—*ns.* **chan'cellorship; chan'cellory, -ery.—chancellor of a cathedral,** an officer who had charge of the chapter library, custody of the common seal, superintendence of the choir practices, and headship of the cathedral schools; **chancellor of a diocese,** an ecclesiastical judge uniting the functions of vicar-general and official principal, appointed to assist the bishop in questions of ecclesiastical law, and hold his courts for him; **Chancellor of the Exchequer,** the chief minister of finance in the British government; **Lord Chancellor, Lord High Chancellor,** the Speaker of the House of Lords, presiding judge of the Chancery Division, keeper of the great seal. [Fr. *chancelier*—L.L. *cancellārius,* orig. an officer that had charge of records, and stood near the *cancelli* (L.), the cross-bars that surrounded the judgment-seat.]

chance-medley, *châns-med'li, n.* a casualty that is not pure chance but has a mixture of chance in it: esp. unintentional homicide in which the killer is not entirely without blame: action with an element of chance: (wrongly) pure chance. [O.Fr. *chance medlée,* mingled chance.]

Chancery, *chän'sər-i, n.* formerly the highest court of justice next to the House of Lords, presided over by the Lord High Chancellor—now a division of the High Court of Justice: a court of record generally: (*slang*) the position of a boxer's head under his adversary's arm: (*obs.*) the office of a chancellor or ambassador.—**Chancery Office,** in Scotland, an office in the General Register House at Edinburgh, managed by a director, in which all royal charters of novodamus, patents of dignities, gifts of offices, remissions, legitimations, presentations, commissions, and other writs appointed to pass the Great and Quarter Seals are recorded; **in chancery,** in litigation, as an estate: (*slang*) in an awkward predicament. [Fr. *chancellerie.*]

Neutral vowels in unaccented syllables : *el'ə-mənt, in'fənt, ran'dəm*

chancre, *shang'kər*, *n.* the hard swelling that constitutes the primary lesion in syphilis.—*n.* **chanc'roid**, a non-syphilitic ulceration of the genital organs due to venereally contracted infection. —*adjs.* **chanc'roid**, **chanc'rous**. [Fr.; a form of **canker**.]

chandelier, *shan-di-lēr'*, *n.* a frame with branches for holding lights.—*ns.* **chandler** (*chand'lər*), a candle-maker : a dealer in candles, oil, soap, etc. : a dealer generally (as in *corn-chandler, ship-chandler*); **chand'lering**.—*adj.* **chand'lerly**.—*ns.* **chand'lery**, goods sold by a chandler. [Fr.,—L.L. *candēlārius*, a candle-maker, *candēlāria*, a candlestick.—L. *candēla*, a candle.]

change, *chānj*, *v.t.* to alter or make different : to put or give for another : to make to pass from one state to another : to exchange.—*v.i.* to suffer change : to change one's clothes or vehicle.—*n.* the act of changing : alteration or variation of any kind : (*Shak.*) exchange : (*Shak.*) fickleness : a shift : variety : money given for money of a different kind, or in adjustment of a payment : small coin : (*coll.*) satisfaction : an exchange (now usu. **'change**) —*ns.* **changeabil'ity**, **change'ableness**, fickleness : power of being changed.—*adj.* **change'able**, subject or prone to change : fickle : inconstant : admitting possibility of change : (*Shak.*) showing change of colours, shot.—*adv.* **change'ably**.—*adj.* **change'ful**, full of change : changeable.—*adv.* **change'fully**.—*ns.* **change'fulness** ; **change'-house** (*Scot.*), a small inn or alehouse.—*adj.* **change'less**, without change : constant.—*ns.* **change'ling**, a surreptitious substitute : a child substituted for another, esp. one supposed to be left by the fairies : hence, an undersized crabbed child : a half-wit : (*arch.*) one apt to change; **change'-o'ver**, transition to a new system or condition; **chang'er**, one who changes the form of anything : one employed in changing or discounting money; **chang'ing-piece** (*Shak.*), a fickle person. —**change colour**, to blush or turn pale; **change of life**, the time of life at which menstruation is about to cease—a woman's climacteric, the menopause; **change oneself** (now *Scot.*) to change one's clothes; **change one's mind**, to form a different opinion; **change one's tune**, to change from joy to sorrow : to change one's manner of speaking; **put the change on**, to delude, trick; **ring the changes**, to go through all the possible permutations in ringing a peal of bells : to go over in every possible order : to pass counterfeit money : to bemuddle a shopman into giving too much change. [Fr. *changer*—Late L. *cambiāre*—L. *cambīre*, to barter.]

chank, *changk*, **chank-shell**, *changk'-shel*, *n.* the shell of several species of Turbinella, gasteropod molluscs of the East Indian seas, sliced into bangles for Hindu women. [Hind. *chankh*; cf. **conch**.]

channel, *chan'l*, *n.* the bed of a stream of water : a strait or narrow sea : a navigable passage : a passage for conveying a liquid : a groove or furrow : a gutter : means of passing or conveying : (*Scot.*) gravel.—*v.t.* to make a channel : to furrow : to convey :—*pr.p.* **chann'elling**; *pa.t.* and *pa.p.* **chann'elled**.—*adj.* **chann'elled**.—*n.* **chann'el-stone**, **-stane**, (*Scot.*), a curling-stone.—**the Channel**, the English Channel. [O.Fr. *chanel, canel*—L. *canālis*, a canal.]

channel, *chan'l*, *n.* a flat piece of wood or iron projecting horizontally from a ship's side to spread the shrouds and keep them clear of the bulwarks—*fore*, *main*, and *mizzen* channels. [For *chain-wale*.]

chanson, *shän'son*[2], *n.* (*Shak.*) a song.—*n.* **chansonette** (*-son-et'*), a little song, a ditty.—**chanson de geste** (*di zhest*; *see* **gest**), an old French epic poem. [Fr.]

chant, chaunt, *chänt*, *v.t.* to sing : to celebrate in song : to recite in a singing manner : to intone : to sell (a horse) fraudulently.—*n.* song : melody : a kind of church music, in which prose is sung.—*ns.* **chant'er, chaunt'er, chant'or**, a singer : a precentor : in a bagpipe, the pipe with finger-holes, on which the melody is played : one who cries up horses; **chant'ress, chaunt'ress**; **chant'ry**,

chaunt'ry, an endowment, or chapel, for the chanting of masses; **chanty** (see **shanty**, 2). [Fr. *chanter*—L. *cantāre*—*canēre*, to sing.]

chantage, *shän[2]-täzh', chänt'ij*, *n.* blackmail. [Fr.]

chanterelle, *shan-, shän[2]-tər-el'*, *n.* the highest string of a musical instrument. [Fr.,—L. *cantare*, to sing.]

chanterelle, *chân-tər-el'*, *n.* a yellowish edible fungus (*Cantharellus cibarius*). [Fr., dim. from Gr. *kantharos*, cup.]

chanticleer, *chânt'i-klēr, -klēr'*, *n.* a cock. [From the name of the cock in the old beast-epic of *Reynard the Fox*—O.Fr. *chanter*, to sing, *cler*, clear.]

chaos, *kā'os*, *n.* the shape of matter before it was reduced to order : disorder : shapeless mass.—*adj.* **chaot'ic**, confused.—*adv.* **chaot'ically**. [Gr.]

chap, *chap*, *v.i.* to crack : (*Scot.*) to strike, of a clock, etc., or to knock at a door.—*v.t.* to fissure.—*n.* a crack : an open fissure in the skin, caused by exposure to cold : a knock.—*adj.* **chap'less**.—*adj.* **chapped**, cracked, of a heavy soil in dry weather, or of the skin in cold weather : cut short.—*adj.* **chapp'y**. [M.E. *chappen;* cog. with Du. and Ger. *kappen*.]

chap, *chap*, *n.* (*obs.* or *dial.*) a customer (for **chapman**) : (*coll.*) a fellow.—*ns.* **chap'book**, a book or pamphlet of a popular type such as was hawked by chapmen; **chap'man**, one who buys or sells : an itinerant dealer : a pedlar : (*obs.*) a purchaser; **chapp'ie**, a familiar dim. of **chap**. [O.E. *céap*, trade, *céapman*, trader; cf. **cheap**; Ger. *kaufen, kaufmann*.]

chap, *chap*, *n.* a chop or jaw : a cheek.—*adjs.* **chap'-fall'en**, (see **chop-fallen**) ; **chap'less**, without a lower jaw. [Cf. **chop** (3); Northern Eng. and Scot. *chaft*, O.N. *kjaptr*, jaw.]

chaparajos, *chä-pä-rä'hhôs*, **chaparejos**, *-rä'*, *n.pl.* cowboy's leather riding leggings (abbrev. **chaps, shaps**). [Mex. Sp.]

chaparral, *chäp-ä-räl'*, *n.* dense tangled brushwood. —**chaparral cock**, a ground-cuckoo of the Californian and Mexican chaparral. [Sp.,— *chaparro*, evergreen oak, one of its constituents.]

chapbook. See **chap** (2).

chape, *chāp*, *n.* the plate of metal at the point of a scabbard : the catch or hook by which the sheath of a weapon was attached to the belt.—*adj.* **chape'-less**. [Fr.,—L.L. *capa*, a cap.]

chapeau, *shä-pō*, *n.* a hat.—**chapeau-bras** (*brä*; English French), a three-cornered hat formerly carried under the arm. [Fr.]

chapel, *chap'l*, *n.* a place of worship inferior or subordinate to a regular church, or attached to a house or institution : an oratory in a mausoleum, etc. : a cell of a church containing its own altar : a dissenters' place of worship, as of Nonconformists in England, Roman Catholics or Episcopalians in Scotland, etc. : a chapel service (*to keep one's chapels*, to make the requisite number of attendances in chapel) : a body of musicians, as a choir, an orchestra, or both, whether connected with a chapel or not : a printing office : an association of workmen therein.—*ns.* **chap'el-master** (Ger. *kapell-meister*), a music-director : a conductor; **chap'elry**, the jurisdiction of a chapel.—**chapel cart** (see **cart**); **chapel of ease**, a chapel for worshippers at some distance from the parish church; **chapel royal**, the oratory of a royal palace; **lady chapel** (see **lady**); **proprietary chapel**, one that is private property. [O.Fr. *capele*—L.L. *cappella*, dim. of *cappa*, a cloak or cope; orig. from the cloak of St. Martin.]

chaperon, *shap'ə-rōn*, *n.* a kind of hood or cap : one (esp. now an older woman) who accompanies a lady for protection, restraint, or appearance' sake.—*v.t.* to attend in such a capacity.—*n.* **chap'eronage**. [Fr., a large hood—*chape*, a hooded cloak—L.L. *cappa;* see **cape**.]

chapiter, *chap'i-tər*, *n.* the head or capital of a column. [Fr. *chapitre*—L. *caput*, the head.]

chaplain, *chap'lin*, *n.* a clergyman attached to an institution, establishment, organisation, or family. —*ns.* **chap'laincy**, **chap'lainry**, **chap'lainship**,

[O.Fr. *chapelain*—L.L. *cappellānus*—*cappella;* see **chapel**.]

chaplet, *chap'lit, n.* a garland or wreath for the head : a circlet of gold, etc. : a string of beads used in counting prayers, one-third of a rosary in length : anything in a string : a metal support of a cylindrical pipe.—*adj.* **chap'leted.** [O.Fr. *chapelet*—*chape,* a head-dress.]

chapman. See chap (2).

chaprassi, *chu-präs'i, n.* an office messenger : a household attendant : an orderly. [Hind. *chaprāsi,* badge-wearer, messenger—*chaprās,* a badge.]

chaps. See chaparajos.

chapter, *chap'tər, n.* a main division of a book, or of anything : a subject or category generally : a division of the Acts of Parliament of a session : an assembly of the canons of a cathedral or collegiate church, or the members of a religious or military order (from the custom of reading a chapter of the rule or of the Bible) : its members collectively : an organised branch of a society or fraternity : a Roman numeral on a clock or watch face : (*Spens.*) a chapiter.—*v.t.* to put into chapters : to take to task.—*n.* **chap'ter-house.**—**chapter and verse,** the exact reference to the passage of the authority of one's statements; **chapter of accidents** (see **accident**) ; **to the end of the chapter,** throughout. [O.Fr. *chapitre*—L. *capitulum,* dim. of *caput,* the head.]

chaptrel, *chap'trəl, n.* the capital of a pillar which supports an arch. [Dim. of **chapiter**.]

char, charr, *chär, n.* a small fish (*Salvellinus*) of the salmon kind, found in mountain lakes and rivers. [Prob. Celt. ; cf. Gael. *ceara,* red, blood-coloured.]

char, *chär, v.t.* to reduce to carbon.—*v.t.* and *v.i.* to scorch (*pr.p.* **charr'ing ;** *pa.t.* and *pa.p* **charred**). —*adj.* **charr'y,** pertaining to charcoal. [Origin obscure.]

char, *chär,* **chare** (*Shak.*), *chär, n.* an occasional piece of work, an odd job; (*pl.*) household work—also **chore** (*chōr*).—*v.i.* to do odd jobs of work : to do house-cleaning.—*v.t.* (*Scott*) to do, accomplish : (*pr.p.* **charr'ing, chär'ing ;** *pa.t.* and *pa.p.* **charred, chäred**).—*n.* **char'woman,** a casual domestic servant hired to do rough work. [O.E. *cerran, cierran,* to turn; see also **jar** (3), **ajar**.]

Chara, *kā'rä, n.* a genus of freshwater plants of a family and class (stoneworts, **Chara'ceae, Charoph'yta**) more or less akin to the green seaweeds, having stems encrusted with calcareous matter and whorled branches. [L. *chara,* a plant unidentified.]

char-à-banc, *shar'-ə-bang, -bän⁹, n.* a long open vehicle with rows of transverse seats, now loosely applied to a tourist coach.—*Vulg. contr.* **cha'ra**—*pl.* **char'-à-bancs** or (as in French) **chars-à-bancs.** [Fr. *char à bancs,* carriage with benches.]

Characinidae, *kar-a-sin'i-dē, n.pl.* a family of freshwater fishes to which belong the dorado and the piranha.—*adj.* **chara'cinoid.** [Gr. *charax,* a fish of some kind.]

character, *kar'ək-tər,* (*Spens., Shak.,* etc. *-ak'*) *n.* a letter, sign, figure, stamp, or distinctive mark : a mark of any kind, a symbol in writing, etc. : writing generally, handwriting : a secret cipher : any essential feature or peculiarity : a quality : nature : (*obs.*) personal appearance : the aggregate of peculiar qualities which constitutes personal or national individuality : esp. moral qualities : the reputation of possessing these : a formal statement of the qualities of a person who has been in one's service or employment : official position, rank, or status, or a person who has filled it : a person noted for eccentricity or well-marked personality : a personality as created in a play or novel (*Shak.* **char'act**) or appearing in history : a literary *genre,* consisting in a description in prose or verse of a human type, or of a place or object on that model, a dominant form of literature in the 17th century under the influence of Theophrastus and the theory of humours.—*v.t.* to engrave, imprint, write : (*arch.*) to represent, delineate, or describe. —*ns.* **char'acter-essay ; char'acter-lit'erature ; characterisā'tion.**—*v.t.* **char'acterise,** to describe by peculiar qualities : to be a distinguishing

mark or quality of.—*ns.* **char'acterism,** a characteristic : a characterisation; **characteris'tic,** that which marks or constitutes the character : the integral part of a logarithm.—*adjs.* **characteris'tic, -al.**—*adv.* **characteris'tically.**—*adj.* **char'acterless,** without character or distinctive qualities.—*ns.* **char'acterlessness ; char'actery** (in *Shak. -ak'*), writing : impression : that which is charactered.— **in character,** in harmony with the part assumed, appropriate : dressed for the part. [Fr. *caractère*— L. *charactēr*—Gr. *charaktēr,* from *charassein,* to cut, engrave.]

charade, *shə-, shä-räd', n.* a species of riddle, the subject of which is a word proposed for solution from an enigmatical description of its component syllables and of the whole : an acted riddle in which the syllables and the whole are uttered or represented in successive scenes. [Fr., perh.—Prov. *charrada,* chatter, or Sp. *charrada,* clownishness.]

Charadrius, *kar-ad'ri-əs, n.* the plover genus, giving name to the family **Charad'riidae.** [Gr. *charadrios,* a bird, prob. the thick-knee.]

charas. Same as **churrus.**

charcoal, *chär'kōl, n.* charred wood, or coal made by charring wood : the carbonaceous residue of substances that have undergone smothered combustion. [**char, coal**.]

chard, *chärd, n.* the edible leafstalk of cardoon, artichoke, or a variety (*Swiss chard*) of white beet. [L. *carduus,* thistle.]

chare. See char (3).

charet, *char'et, n.* (*Spens.*) same as **chariot.**

charge, *chärj, v.t.* to load, to put something into, to fill : to load heavily, burden : to fill completely : to cause to accumulate electricity : to lay a task upon, to enjoin, command : to deliver an official injunction, exhortation or exposition to : to bring an accusation against : (*her.*) to place a bearing upon (with *with*) : to exact or demand from, to ask as the price : to set down as a liability against : to attack at a rush.—*v.i.* to make an onset.—*n.* that which is laid on : cost or price : the load of powder, etc., for a gun : attack or onset : care, custody : the object of care : an accumulation of electricity : command : exhortation : accusation : (*her.*) a device borne on a shield : (*pl.*) expenses.—*adj.* **charge'-able,** liable to be charged, imputable : blamable : (*B.*) burdensome.—*n.* **charge'ableness.**—*adv.* **charge'ably.**—*adj.* **charge'ful** (*Spens.; Shak.*) burdensome, or expensive.—*ns.* **charge'-hand, -man,** the leader of a gang of workmen; **charge'-house** (*Shak.*), a school.—*adj.* **charge'less.**—*ns.* **charg'er,** a flat dish capable of holding a large joint, a platter : a war-horse; **charge'-sheet,** a police list of accused and the charges against them. —**give in charge,** to hand over to the police; **take charge of,** to assume the care of. [Fr. *charger*—L.L. *carricāre,* to load—L. *carrus,* a wagon; see **car, cargo**.]

chargé-d'affaires, *shär'zhä-dä-fer', n.* a diplomatic agent of lesser rank, accredited, not to the sovereign, but to the department for foreign affairs and holding his credentials from the minister : the person in charge for the time. [Fr.]

charily, chariness. See **chary.**

chariot, *char'i-ət, n.* a pleasure or state car : a god's car : a car used in ancient warfare or racing : a light four-wheeled carriage with back-seats and box.—*v.t.* to carry in a chariot.—*v.i.* to ride in a chariot.—*n.* **charioteer',** one who drives a chariot. —*v.t.* and *v.i.* to drive or to ride in such. [Fr., dim. of *char,* a **car**.]

Charis, *kar'is* (Gr. *hhär'is), n.* any one of the three **Char'ites** (*-tēz,* Gr. *-tes*), the Graces (Aglaia, Euphrosyne, Thalia), Greek goddess of whatever imparts graciousness to life.—*n.* **char'ism,** a free gift of grace.—*adj.* **charismat'ic.** [Gr. *charis, -itos,* grace.]

charity, *char'i-ti, n.* (*N.T.*) universal love : the disposition to think favourably of others, and do them good : almsgiving : a charitable foundation, institution, or cause : (*pl.*) affections.—*adj.* **char'i-table,** of or relating to, showing, inspired by charity.—*n.* **char'itableness.**—*adv.* **char'itably.** —*ns.* **char'ity-boy', -girl',** a pupil in a **char'ity-**

school', a school for the poor supported by endowments or gifts.—**charity begins at home**, usually an excuse for not allowing it to get abroad; **cold as charity**, an ironical phrase. [Fr. *charité*—L. *cāritās*, -*ātis*—*cārus*, dear.]

charivari, *shär-i-vär'i*, *n.* a cacophonous mock serenade, rough music, cats' concert. [Fr.]

chark, *chärk*, *v.t.* to burn to charcoal.—*n.* charcoal, coke. [charcoal.]

charlatan, *shär'lə-tən*, *n.* a mere talking pretender: a quack.—*adjs.* **charlatanic** (-*tan'ik*), **-al**.—*ns.* **char'latanism**, **char'latanry**. [Fr.,—It. *ciarlatano*—*ciarlare*, to chatter; imit.]

Charles's wain, *chärlz'iz wān*, *n.* the seven bright stars in the Plough. [O.E. *Carles wægn*, Carl being Charlemagne.]

Charleston, *chärls'tən*, *n.* a 20th century dance characterised by spasmodic knee action. [*Charleston* in South Carolina.]

Charley, Charlie, *chär'li*, *n.* a night-watchman: the small triangular beard familiar in the portraits of *Charles* I.: the fox.—**Char'ley-pitch'er** (*slang*), a thimble-rigger. [From the name *Charles*.]

charlock, *chär'lək*, *n.* wild mustard, a common yellow-flowered cornfield weed. [O.E. *cerlic*.]

charlotte, *shär'lət*, *n.* a dish of apple marmalade or the like, covered with crumbs of toast: a kind of tart containing fruit.—**charlotte russe** (*rüs*), a custard or cream enclosed in a kind of spongecake. [From the name *Charlotte*.]

charm, *chärm*, *n.* a spell: something thought to possess occult power, a metrical form of words; an amulet, etc.: a trinket: power of fascination: attractiveness: (*pl.*) personal attractions: that which can please irresistibly: (*Spens.*) a song.—*v.t.* to influence by a charm: to subdue by secret influence: to enchant: to delight: to allure: to tune or play.—*adj.* **charmed**, bewitched: delighted: protected as by a special charm.—*n.* **charm'er**.—*adj.* **charm'ful**, abounding in charms. —*adj.* **charm'ing**, highly pleasing: delightful: fascinating.—*adv.* **charm'ingly**.—*adj.* **charm'less**, wanting or destitute of charms.—*adv.* **charm'lessly**. [Fr. *charme*—L. *carmen*, a song.]

charm. Same as **chirm**.

charneco, *chär'ni-kō*, *n.* (*Shak.*) a kind of sweet wine. [Prob. from a village near Lisbon.]

charnel, *chär'nəl*, *n.* (*obs.*) a burial place.—*adj.* sepulchral: death-like.—*n.* **char'nel-house**, a place where the bones thrown up by grave-diggers are put. [O.Fr. *charnel*—L.L. *carnāle*—L. *carnālis* —*carō*, *carnis*, flesh.]

Charon, *kā'ron*, *n.* in Greek mythology, the ferryman who rowed the shades of the dead across the river Styx in the lower world: a ferryman. [Gr. *Charōn*.]

charpie, *shär'pē*, or -*pē'*, *n.* lint shredded down to form a soft material for dressing wounds. [O.Fr. *charpir*—L. *carpere*, to pluck.]

charpoy, *chär'poi*, *n.* the common Indian bedstead, sometimes handsomely wrought and painted. [Hind. *chārpāī*—Pers. *chahār-pāī*, four feet.]

charqui, *chär'kē*, *n.* beef cut into long strips and dried in the sun—jerked beef. [Quichua.]

charr. Same as **char** (1).

chart, *chärt*, *n.* a marine or hydrographical map, exhibiting part of a sea or other water, with the islands, contiguous coasts, soundings, currents, etc.: an outline-map, curve, or a tabular statement giving information of any kind.—*v.t.* to map.—*ns.* **chart'-house**, **chart'room**, the room in a ship where charts are kept.—*adj.* **chart'less**. [O.Fr. *charte*—L. *c(h)arta*, a paper—Gr. *chartēs*.]

charta, carta, *kär'tä*, *n.* a charter.—*adj.* **chartā'ceous**, papery. [L. *c(h)arta*—Gr. *chartēs*, a sheet of paper.]

charter, *chärt'ər*, *n.* any formal writing in evidence of a grant, contract, or other transaction, conferring or confirming titles, rights, or privileges, or the like: the formal deed by which a sovereign guarantees the rights and privileges of his subjects: a document creating a borough or other corporation: any instrument by which powers and privileges are conferred by the state on a body of persons for a special object: a patent: grant:

allowance: immunity.—*v.t.* to establish by charter: to let or hire, as a ship, on contract.—*n.* **chart'er-chest**, a box in which charters are preserved.— *adj.* **chart'ered**, granted or protected by a charter: privileged: licensed: hired by contract.— *ns.* **chart'er-hand'**, court-hand; **chart'er-may'or**, the mayor of a borough at the time of its charter; **char'ter-mem'ber**, an original member of an incorporation; **chartered accountant**, one qualified under the regulations of the Institute of Accountants; **chartered company**, a trading company acting under a charter from the crown. [O.Fr. *chartre*—L. *cartula*, *c(h)arta*—Gr. *chartēs*, a sheet of paper.]

Charterhouse, *chärt'ər-hows*, *n.* a Carthusian monastery: the famous hospital and school instituted in London in 1611, on the site of a Carthusian monastery.—*ns.* **Chartreuse** (*shär-trəz'*), a Carthusian monastery, esp. the original one, La Grande Chartreuse near Grenoble in France: a famous liqueur, green, yellow, or white, long manufactured there by the monks from aromatic herbs and brandy: a kind of enamelled pottery: a mould of rice or blancmange enclosing some other food: a pale greenish colour; **Chartreux** (*shär-trə'*), a Carthusian: the Charterhouse School. [See **Carthusian**.]

charterparty, *chärt'ər-pär-ti*, *n.* the common written form in which the contract of affreightment is expressed—viz. the hiring of the whole or part of a ship for the conveyance of goods. [Fr. *charte partie*, lit. a divided charter, as the practice was to divide it in two and give a half to each person— [L. *c(h)arta partīta*; see **charta**.]

Chartism, *chärt'izm*, *n.* a movement in Great Britain for the extension of political power to the working-classes—its programme, the People's Charter (1838), since achieved, except annual parliaments.—Also *adj.* [See **charta**.]

chartography, *kär-tog'rə-fi*. See **cartography**.

chartreuse, chartreux. See **Charterhouse**.

chartulary, *kär'tū-lər-i*. Same as **cartulary**.

charwoman. See **char**.

chary, *chā'ri*, *adj.* sparing: cautious.—*adv.* **char'ily**.—*n.* **char'iness**. [O.E. *cearig*—*cearu*, care.]

Charybdis, *kə-rib'dis*, *n.* in the Odyssey a dangerous monster that dwelt under a rock opposite to Scylla, and three times a day swallowed and threw up the waters of the sea, later a current or a whirlpool on the Sicilian side of the Straits of Messina—with Scylla providing a proverbial alternative of evil or disaster.

chase (*obs.* **chace**), *chās*, *v.t.* to pursue: to hunt: to drive away: put to flight.—*n.* pursuit: a hunting: that which is hunted: an unenclosed game preserve: (*tennis*; *Shak.*) the second impact of an unreturned ball, for which the player scored unless his opponent bettered it (and scored) by a like impact nearer the end wall.—*ns.* **chase'-port**, the porthole at bow or stern through which a gun is fired during pursuit; **chas'er**, a pursuer: a hunter: a horse for steeplechasing: an aeroplane for pursuing hostile air-craft: a woman over-assiduous in pursuit of men: a cooling drink after spirits: a chasse.—**beasts of chase**, properly the buck, doe, fox, marten, and roe: wild beasts that are hunted generally; **wild-goose chase**, a chase hither and thither: any foolish or profitless pursuit of the unattainable. [O.Fr. *chacier*, *chasser*—L. *captāre*, freq. of *capere*, to take.]

chase, *chās*, *v.t.* to enchase, to decorate by engraving.—*ns.* **chas'er**, one who practises chasing: a tool for chasing; **chas'ing**, the art of engraving on the outside of raised metal work: the art of cutting the threads of screws. [Short for **enchase**.]

chase, *chās*, *n.* a case or frame for holding types: a groove. [Fr. *châsse*, a shrine, a setting—L. *capsa*, a chest, and Fr. *chas*, a hollow (now eye of a needle)—L.L. *capsum*. See **case** (1).]

chasm, *kazm*, *n.* a yawning or gaping hollow: a gap or opening: a void space.—*adjs.* **chasmed**; **chasm'y**. [Gr. *chasma*, from *chainein*, to gape; cf. **chaos**.]

chasmogamy, *kaz-mog'ə-mi*, *n*. (*bot*.) the condition of having open, not cleistogamic, flowers, allowing cross-fertilisation.—*adj*. **chasmogamic** (*-mō-gam'ik*). [Gr. *chasma*, a gape, *gameein*, to marry.]

chasse, *shäs*, *n*. a dram or liqueur taken after coffee.—Also **chasse-café**. [Fr. *chasser*, to chase.]

chassé, *shäs'ā*, *n*. a gliding step in dancing.—*v.i*. to make such a step.—*v.t*. (*slang*) to dismiss. [Fr.]

Chassepot, *shäs'pō*, *n*. a rifle adopted by the French army in 1866. [From the inventor's name.]

chasseur, *shäs-ər'*, *n*. a hunter or huntsman : one of a select body of French light infantry or cavalry : a liveried attendant. [Fr.,—*chasser*, to hunt; see **chase**.]

chassis, *shas'ē*, *n*. the frame, wheels, and machinery of a motor-car : an aeroplane's landing-carriage : a casemate gun carriage : (*obs*.) a frame, sash :—*pl*. **chassis** (*shas'ēz*). [Fr. *chassis*, frame.]

chaste, *chāst*, *adj*. sexually virtuous : modest : refined and pure in taste and style.—*adv*. **chaste'ly**.—*v.t*. **chasten** (*chās'n*), to free from faults by punishing : hence, to punish : to purify or refine : to restrain or moderate.—*p.adj*. **chas'tened**, purified : modest : tempered.—*ns*. **chas'tener** ; **chaste'ness** ; **chas'tenment**.—*v.t*. **chastise** (*chas-tīz'*), to inflict punishment upon for the purpose of correction : to reduce to order or to obedience.—*adj*. **chastīs'able**.—*ns*. **chas'tisement** (*chas'tiz-mənt*); **chastity** (*chas'ti-ti*), sexual purity : virginity : refinement of style : moderation.—**chaste tree**, agnus castus. [O.Fr. *chaste*—L. *castus*, pure.]

chasuble, *chaz'* or *chas'ū-bl*, *n*. a sleeveless vestment worn over the alb by the priest while celebrating mass. [Fr.—L.L. *casubula*—L. *casula*. dim. of L. *casa*, a hut.]

chat, *chat*, *v.i*. to talk easily or familiarly (*pr.p*. **chatt'ing** ; *pa.t*. and *pa.p*. **chatt'ed**).—*n*. familiar, easy talk.—*n*. **chatt'iness**.—*adj*. **chatt'y**, given or inclined to chat : of the nature of chat. [From **chatter**.]

chat, *chat*, *n*. a genus (*Saxicola*) of small birds in the thrush family, including the stone-chat and the whin-chat. [From the sound of their voice.]

château, *shä'tō*, *n*. a castle : a great country-seat, esp. in France (common in names of places and associated wines) :—*pl*. **chât'eaux** (*-tōz*).—*ns*. **châtelain** (*shät'ə-lanᵍ*), a castellan; **chât'elaine** (*-len*), a female castellan : an ornamental bunch of short chains bearing keys, scissors, etc., attached to the waist-belt : a similar thing in miniature attached to the watch-chain. [Fr. *château* (O.Fr. *chastel*)—L. *castellum*, dim. of *castrum*, a fort.]

chaton, *shä-tonᵍ'*, *n*. the head of a finger-ring. [Fr.]

chatoyant, *shät-wä-yonᵍ'*, *shat-oi'ənt*, *adj*. with a changing lustre, like a cat's eye in the dark. [Fr.]

chatta, *chät'ä*, *n*. an umbrella. [Hind.]

chattel, *chat'l*, *n*. any kind of property which is not freehold, distinguished further into *chattels-real* and *chattels-personal*, the latter being mere personal movables—money, plate, cattle, and the like; the former including leasehold interests.—**goods and chattels**, all corporeal movables. [O.Fr. *chatel*—L.L. *captāle*—L. *capitāle*, etc., property, goods.]

chatter, *chat'ər*, *v.i*. to talk idly or rapidly : (of birds) to utter a succession of rapid short notes : to sound as the teeth when one shivers.—*n*. noise like that made by a magpie, or by the striking together of the teeth : idle talk.—*ns*. **chatt'erbox**, one who talks or chatters incessantly; **chatt'erer**, one that chatters : an idle talker : a name applied to two families of birds, the wax-wings and the cotingas; **chatt'ering**. [From the sound.]

chatty, *chat'i*, *n*. (*India*) an earthen water-pot. [Hind.]

Chaucerian, *chaw-sē'ri-ən*, *adj*. like or pertaining to *Chaucer*.—*n*. a student or follower of Chaucer.—*n*. **Chau'cerism**, anything characteristic of Chaucer.

chaud-mellé, *shōd-mel'ā*, *n*. (*Scots law*) a fight arising in the heat of passion : the killing of a man in such a fight. [O.Fr. *chaude-mellee*, hot fight; see **mêlée**.]

chaufe, chauff (*Spens*.), *chawf*. Forms of **chafe**.

chauffer, *chaw'fər*, *n*. a metal box for holding fire, a portable furnace or stove. [See **chafer**.]

chauffeur, *shō'fər*, *-fər'*, *n*. one employed to drive a motor-car :—fem. **chauffeuse** (*-fəz*). [Fr., stoker.]

chaulmoogra, chaulmugra, *chawl-mōō'grä*, *n*. a name for various Indian trees of the family Flacourtiaceae, yielding **chaulmoogra oil**, used in the treatment of leprosy. [Beng.]

chaunce, chaunge, old forms of **chance, change**.

chaunter. See **chanter**.

chausses, *shōs*, or *shō'siz*, *n.pl*. any closely fitting covering for the legs, hose generally : the defence-pieces for the legs in ancient armour.—*n*. **chaussure** (*-ür'*), a general name for boots and shoes. [O.Fr. *chauces*—L. *calcia*, hose.]

Chautauquan, *shɔ-taw'kwən*, *adj*. pertaining to a system of instruction for adults by home reading and study under guidance, evolved from the *Chautauqua* (New York State) Literary and Scientific Circle, organised in 1878.

Chauvinism, *shō'vin-izm*, *n*. an absurdly extravagant pride in one's country, with a corresponding contempt for foreign nations : Jingoism.—*ns*. **Chau'vin, Chau'vinist**.—*adj*. **Chauvinist'ic**. [From Nicolas *Chauvin*, an ardent veteran of Napoleon's, who figures in Cogniard's *La Cocarde tricolore*.]

chavender, *chav'ən-dər*, *n*. the chub. [Cf. **cheven**.]

chaw, *chaw*, *n*. (*Spens*.) a jaw. [See **jaw**.]

chaw, *chaw*, *v.t*. to chew (still used of tobacco and in dial.).—*n*. a quantity for chewing.—*n*. **chaw'-bä'con**, a country clown, a rustic fellow.—**chawed up** (*U.S. slang*), destroyed : defeated : crushed : reprimanded. [By-form of **chew**.]

chawdron, *chaw'drən*, *n*. (*Shak*.) the entrails of an animal. [O.Fr. *chaudun*.]

chay, a vulgar form of **chaise**.

chay, *chī*, *chā*, **chaya**, *chī'ä*, **shaya**, *shī'ä*, *n*. an Indian plant (Oldenlandia) of the madder family whose root (**chay-root**, etc.) yields a red dye. [Cf. Tamil *saya*.]

che, *chə*, *pron*. (*Shak*.) a S.W. dialect form of I. [O.E. *ic*; cf. **ch**.]

cheap, *chēp*, *n*. (*obs*.) bargain, buyer's advantage.—*adj*. (from the phrase *good cheap*) low in price : charging low prices : of a low price in relation to the value : easily obtained : of small value, or so reckoned : paltry : inferior.—Also *adv*.—*v.t*. **cheap'en**, to ask the price of a thing : to make cheap, to lower the price of : to lower the reputation of : to beat down the price of.—*n*. **cheap ener**.—*adv*. **cheap'ly**.—*n*. **cheap'ness**.—**cheap and nasty**, offensively inferior and of low value; **cheap Jack**, or **John**, a travelling hawker who professes to give great bargains; **cheap labour**, labour paid at a poor rate; **cheap of** (*Scot*.), having got off lightly with : served right; **dirt cheap**, ridiculously cheap; **feel cheap**, to have a sense of inferiority and humiliation; **on the cheap**, cheap or cheaply. [O.E. *céap*, price, a bargain, *ceapian*, O.N. *kaupa*, Ger. *kaufen*, to buy.]

cheat, *chēt*, *n*. (*obs*.) an escheat, a forfeit : (*obs*.) a piece of plunder, a stolen thing : (*thieves' cant*) a thing in general, esp. the gallows : a fraud : a deception : a card game in which deception is allowed : one who cheats.—*v.t*. to deceive, defraud, impose upon.—*v.i*. to practise deceit.—*ns*. **cheat'er**, one who cheats : (*Shak*.) an officer who collected the fines to be paid into the Exchequer; **cheat'ery** (*coll*.) cheating.—**put a cheat upon**, to deceive; **tame cheater** (*Shak*.), a decoy. [**Escheat**.]

chechacho. Same as **cheechacho**.

chéchia, *shā'shyä*, *n*. a cylindrical skull-cap, worn by Arabs and adopted by French troops in Africa. [Fr.—Berber *tashashit*, pl. *tishushai*, skull-cap.]

check, *chek*, *v.t*. to bring to a stand : to restrain or hinder : to rebuke : to control by comparison : to verify : o punch (as a ticket) : (*Scot*. also **chack**) to nip, pinch, as in a window : to deposit or receive for safe-keeping in exchange for a check : (*U.S*.) to send (baggage) on a passenger's ticket : to place in check at chess : o mark with a pattern of crossing lines.—*v.i.* (*falconry*) to forsake the quarry for some other bird (with *at*) : to come to a stop.— *n.* a position in chess when one party obliges the other either to move or guard his king : anything that checks : a sudden stop, repulse, or rebuff : restraint : control : (*B., Shak.*) a rebuke : a mark put against items in a list : an order for money (usually written **cheque**, except in U.S.) : a means of verification or testing : any counter-register used as security, a counterfoil : a token, given for example to a person leaving his seat in a theatre with the intention of returning : a restaurant bill : (*U.S.*) a counter used in games at cards (hence 'to pass in one's checks'=to die) : a mechanism that holds a piano hammer after striking : a pattern of cross lines forming small squares, as in a chess-board : any fabric woven with such a pattern.—*adj.* divided into small squares by crossing lines.—*ns.* **check'-ac'tion,** piano action with checks : **check'-clerk,** a clerk who checks accounts, etc. ; **check'er,** one who hinders, rebukes, or scrutinises ; **check'er-board,** a checked board on which checkers or draughts is played ; **check'ers** (*U.S.*) draughts : **check'-key,** a latch-key ; **check'-list,** a list for verification purposes ; **check'mate,** in chess, a check given to the adversary's king when in a position in which it can neither be protected nor moved out of check, so that the game is finished : a complete check : defeat : overthrow.—*v.t.* in chess, to put in check-mate : to defeat.—*ns.* **check'-rein,** a coupling rein, a strap hindering a horse from lowering its head : **check'-room, check'ing-room** (*U.S.*) a cloak-room or luggage-room ; **check'-string,** a string by which the occupant of a carriage may attract the driver's notice ; **check'-tak'er,** one who takes tickets ; **check'-till,** a till that records sums received ; **check'-up,** a testing scrutiny : (*U.S.*) one of a series of regular medical examinations ; **check'-weigh'er,** one who on the part of the men checks the weight of coal sent up to the pit-mouth.— **check in, out** (*U.S.*), to perform the necessary business at a hotel office on arriving or leaving ; **check up** (*U.S.*), to examine and test (often with *on*). [O.Fr. *eschec, eschac* (L.L. *scaccus, scāchus,* It. *scacco,* Sp. *jaque,* Ger. *schach*), through Ar. from Pers. *shāh,* king, **checkmate** being O.Fr. *eschec mat*—Ar. *shāh māt*(*a*), the king is dead.]

checker. See **chequer.**

checker-berry, *chek'ər-ber-i, n.* the American winter-green (*Gaultheria*).

checklaton, s(c)hecklaton, *chek-, shek-lat'ən, n.* understood and explained by Spenser as gilded leather used for making embroidered jacks. [**ciclaton,** perh. with association with **latten.**]

Cheddar, *ched'ər, n.* an excellent kind of cheese first made at *Cheddar* in Somersetshire.—**Cheddar pink,** a species of pink (*Dianthus caesius*) found on the limestone cliffs at Cheddar.

cheechako, *chē-chä'kō, n.* (*Canada* and *Alaska*) a tenderfoot.—Also **checha'ko, cheechal'ko, che-cha'quo.** [Chinook jargon, new-come.]

chee-chee, *chē'chē, n.* in India, a Eurasian : affected Eurasian English. [Perh. Hind. *chī-chī,* dirt, fie !]

cheek, *chēk, n.* the side of the face below the eye, the fleshy lateral wall of the mouth : (*coll.*) effront-ery, impudence : a side-post of a door, window, etc. : the cheek-strap of a horse's bridle : the ring at the end of a bit : anything arranged in lateral pairs.— *v.t.* to address insolently.—*ns.* **cheek'-bone,** the bone above the cheek ; **cheek'-pouch,** a dilatation of the cheek, forming a bag, as in monkeys, etc. ; **cheek'-tooth,** a molar tooth.—*adj.* **cheek'y,** saucy.—**cheek by jowl,** side by side. [O.E. *céce, céace,* cheek, jaw ; cf. Du. *kaak.*]

cheep, *chēp, v.i.* to chirp, as a young bird.—*n.* a sound of cheeping.—*n.* **cheep'er,** a young bird, esp. of game. [Imit.]

cheer, *chēr, n.* (*arch.*) face : disposition, frame of mind (with *good,* etc.) : joy : a shout of approval or welcome : kind treatment : entertainment : fare, food.—*v.t.* to comfort : to encourage : to applaud : to inspirit.—*v.i.* to take comfort : to be of good cheer.—*n.* **cheer'er.**—*adj.* **cheer'ful,** in, of,

promoting, or accompanied by good spirits.—*adv.* **cheer'fully.**—*ns.* **cheer'fulness.**—*adv.* **cheer'-ily.**—*n.* **cheer'iness.**—*interj.* **cheer'io, cheer'o,** a bright vulgar good-bye.—*ns.* **cheer'ishness** (*Milton*), cheerfulness ; **cheer'-leader,** (*U.S.*) one who directs organised cheering, as at team games.—*adj.* **cheer'less,** comfortless.—*adv.* **cheer'lessly.**—*n.* **cheer'lessness.**—*adj.* **cheer'ly,** cheerful.—*adv.* in a cheery manner : heartily.— *adj.* **cheer'y,** cheerful : promoting cheerfulness.— **cheer up,** (*coll.*) to make, or become, more cheerful. [O.Fr. *chiere,* face.—L.L. *cara,* the face.]

cheese, *chēz, n.* a wholesome article of food, made from the curd of milk coagulated by rennet, separated from the whey, and pressed into a solid mass : a compressed cake of various nature : the receptacle of a thistle-head.—*ns.* **cheese'-cake,** a cup of pastry containing formerly cheese, now some sort of curd ; **cheese'-cloth,** a loose-woven cloth suitable for pressing cheeses ; **cheese'-cutter,** a square-peaked cap ; **cheese'-hopper,** the larva of a small fly, remarkable for its leaping power, found in cheese ; **cheese'-mite,** a very small arachnid that breeds in cheese ; **cheese'-monger,** a dealer in cheese ; **cheese'-paring** (*Shak.*), paring, or rind, of cheese : a very thin man : parsimony.—*adj.* mean and parsimonious.— *ns.* **cheese'-press,** a machine in which curds for cheese are pressed ; **cheese'-renn'et,** the plant lady's bed-straw, said to have been used as rennet in curdling milk ; **cheese'-straw,** a long thin biscuit flavoured with cheese ; **cheese'-taster,** a scoop for taking a sample from the inside of a cheese ; **cheese'-vat,** a vat or wooden case in which curds are pressed ; **cheese'-wring,** a cheese-press ; **chees'iness.**—*adj.* **chees'y,** having the nature of cheese.—**green cheese,** cheese not yet dried ; **make cheeses,** to whirl round and then sink down suddenly so as to make the skirt stand out like a cheese. [O.E. *cése, cýse,* curdled milk (Ger. *käse*)—L. *cāseus.*]

cheese, *chēz, n.* (*obs. slang*) the correct thing : anything of excellent quality. [Prob. Pers. and Hind. *chīz,* thing.]

cheese, *chēz, v.t.* (*slang*), in the phrase **cheese it,** stop, have done, run off.

cheetah, *chē'tä, n.* an Eastern animal like the leopard, used in hunting. [Hind. *chītā*—Sans. *chitraka, chitrakāya,* having a speckled body.]

cheewink. Same as **chewink.**

chef, *shef, n.* a head-cook (in full **chef de cuisine,** *də kwē-zēn,* kitchen-head) : a reliquary in the shape of a head.—**chef d'œuvre** (*shā-də-vr'*), a master-piece :—*pl.* **chefs d'œuvre** (*shā-*). [Fr. ; see **chief.**]

cheiro-, *kī'rō-, kī-ro'-,* (see also **chiro-**) in compo-sition, hand.—*ns.* **cheirog'nomy, chirog'nomy** (Gr. *gnōmē,* understanding), palmistry ; **chi'ro-graph,** a written or signed document ; **ch(e)irog'-rapher** (*obs.*), an official of the Court of Common Pleas ; **ch(e)irog'raphist,** an expert in hand-writing : (*Pope*) a palmist ; **ch(e)irog'raphy,** hand-writing, penmanship ; **ch(e)irol'ogist, ch(e)irol'-ogy,** gesture-language : the study of the hand ; **ch(e)i'romancy** (*-man-si*), fortune-telling by the hand (Gr. *manteiā,* divination).—*adjs.* **ch(e)iro-mant'ic, -al.**—*n.* **ch(e)iron'omer** (Gr. *nomos,* law), a gesticulator.—*adj.* **ch(e)ironom'ic.**—*n.* **ch(e)iron'omy,** the art of gesticulation or of pantomime.—*n.pl.* **Ch(e)irop'tera** (Gr. *pteron,* wing), the order of bats.—*adj.* **ch(e)iropteroph'-ilous** (Gr. *phileein,* to love), pollinated by bats ; **ch(e)irop'terous.**—*n.* **Cheirothē'rium** (Gr. *thērion,* beast), a Triassic labyrinthodont with hand-like footprints. [Gr. *cheir,* hand.]

cheka, *chä'kä, n.* the Russian secret police of 1917-1922. [Russ. *che ka,* names of the initial letters of the words for extraordinary commission.]

chela, *kē'lä, n.* the prehensile claw of an arthropod. —*adj.* **chē'late.**—*n.* **Chē'lifer,** the book-scorpion. [Latinised from Gr. *chēlē.*]

chela, *chā'lä, n.* a novice in Buddhism.—*n.* **che'laship.** [Hind. *chēlā,* servant, disciple.]

fāte, fär, àsk ; mē, hər (her) *; mīne ; mōte ; mūte ; mōon ; dhen* (then)

chelicera, *kē-lis'ə-rä, n.* a biting appendage in Arachnida :—*pl.* **chelic'erae (-rē).** [Gr. *chēlē*, a crab's claw, *keras*, horn.]

Chellean, *shel'i-ən, adj.* belonging to an early Palaeolithic culture, older than Acheulean. [*Chelles*, near Paris, where flints of this stage are found.]

Chelonia, *ki-lō'ni-ä, n.* an order of reptiles with horny shell and horny beak, tortoises, and turtles. —*adj.* and *n.* **chelō'nian.** [Gr. *chelōnē*, a tortoise.]

chemin de fer, *shə-man²-də-fer', n.* a variety of baccarat (familiarly **chemmy**, *shem'i*). [Fr., railway.]

chemic, etc. See under **chemistry**.

chemise, *shi-mēz', n.* a woman's shirt, a smock or shift.—*n.* **chemisette'**, a kind of bodice worn by women : lace or muslin filling up the open front of a woman's dress. [Fr. *chemise*—L.L. *camisia*, a nightgown, surplice.]

chemistry, *kem'is-tri*, formerly **chymistry**, *kim'is-tri, n.* the science of the properties of substances elementary and compound, and of the laws of their combination and action one upon another.—*adjs.* **chemiat'ric**, iatrochemical; **chem'ic**, (*obs.*) alchemical : (*obs.*) iatrochemical : chemical.—*n.* (*obs.*) an alchemist or a chemist : bleaching powder.—*v.t.* to treat with bleaching powder (*pr.p.* **chem'icking**; *pa.t.* and *pa.p.* **chem'icked**).—*adj.* **chem'ical**, (*obs.*) alchemical : (*obs.*) iatrochemical : relating to chemistry : versed in or studying chemistry.—*n.* a substance obtained by chemical means or used in chemical operations.—*adv.* **chem'ically.**—*ns.* **chem'ism**, chemical action; **chem'ist**, (*obs.*) an alchemist : one skilled in chemistry : a manufacturer of or dealer in chemicals and drugs : a pharmacist; **chem'itype**, any chemical process for obtaining impressions from an engraving; **chem'itypy**; **chem'onasty**, nastic movement under diffuse chemical stimulus.—*adj.* **chemotac'tic**, pertaining to chemotaxis.—*ns.* **chemotax'is**, movement of a whole organism in a definite direction in response to chemical stimulus; **chemotherapeu'tics**; **chemother'apy**, treatment of a disease by means of a chemical compound, having a specific bactericidal or bacteriostatic effect against the micro-organism involved; **chemot'ropism** (*bot.*), orientation by differential growth in response to chemical stimulus. —*adj.* **chemotrop'ic.**—*n.* **chemurgy** (*kem'ər-ji*), a branch of applied chemistry concerned with the use of agricultural products, or other organic raw materials, for industry.—*adjs.* **chemur'gic, -al.**—**chemical affinity**, the tendency to combine with one another exhibited by many substances, or the force by which the substances constituting a compound are held together; **chemist and druggist**, one who has passed the lower, **pharmaceutical chemist**, one who has passed the higher examinations, qualifying him to practise as a pharmacist. [See **alchemy**.]

chenille, *shə-nēl', n.* a thick, velvety cord of silk or wool resembling a woolly caterpillar : a velvet-like material used for table-covers, etc. [Fr. *chenille*, caterpillar—L. *canicula*, a hairy little dog, *canis*, a dog.]

Chenopodium, *ken-ō-pō'di-əm, n.* the goosefoot genus, giving name to the family **Cheno-podiā'ceae**, akin to the pink family.—*adj.* **chenopodiā'ceous.** [Gr. *chēn*, goose, *pous*, *podos*, foot.]

cheque (*U.S.* **check**), *chek, n.* (*obs.*) a counterfoil : a money order on a banker.—*ns.* **cheque'-book**, a book of cheque forms; **cheq'uer** (*arch.*), a chess-board, also a chess-man : alternation of colours, as on a chess-board (see also **checker**).— *v.t.* to mark in squares of different colours : to variegate : to interrupt.—*adjs.* **cheq'uered**, **check'ered**, variegated, like a chess-board : varying in character : eventful, with alternations of good and bad fortune.—*adv.* **cheq'uerwise.**—*n.* **cheq'uer-work**, any pattern having alternating squares of different colours.—*adj.* **cheq'uy**, **check'y** (*her.*) chequered.—**blank cheque**, a cheque signed by the drawer without having the amount indicated : (*fig.*) concession of power without limit; **crossed cheque**, an ordinary cheque with two transverse lines drawn across it,

which have the effect of making it payable only through a bank account. [See **check**.]

cherchef't, a Miltonic spelling of **kerchiefed**.

cherimoya, **cherimoyer**, *cher-i-moi'ä, -ər, n.* a Peruvian fruit (*Anona Cherimolia*) resembling the custard-apple. [Quechua.]

cherish, *cher'ish, v.t.* to protect and treat with affection : to nurture, nurse : to entertain in the mind.—*n.* **cher'ishment.** [Fr. *chérir*, *chérissant* —*cher*, dear—L. *cārus*.]

chernozem, *chər'nō-zem, n.* a very fertile soil of subhumid steppe, consisting of a dark topsoil over a lighter calcareous layer. [Russ., black earth.]

cheroot, *shə-rōōt', n.* a cigar not pointed at either end. [Fr. *cheroute*, representing the Tamil name *shuruttu*, a roll.]

cheroot. See **shaya-root**.

cherry, *cher'i, n.* a small stone-fruit : the tree (*Cerasus*, a subgenus of *Prunus*) that bears it : extended to many fruits resembling it in some way, as **Barbados cherry** (family Malpighiaceae), **winter-cherry** (*q.v.*).—*adj.* like a cherry in colour : ruddy.—*ns.* **cherr'y-bean**, cow-pea; **cherr'y-bob'**, in children's games, two cherries joined by the stalks; **cherr'y-bounce'**, cherry-brandy : brandy and sugar; **cherr'y-brandy**, a pleasant liqueur made by steeping Morello cherries in brandy; **cherr'y-coal'**, a soft shining coal; **cherr'y-lau'rel**, a species of cherry with evergreen laurel-like leaves; **cherr'y-pepp'er**, a West Indian Capsicum; **cherr'y-pie**, a pie made of cherries : the common heliotrope; **cherr'y-pit**, a game in which cherry-stones are thrown into a small hole; **cherr'y-plum**, a plum of flavour approaching a cherry; **cherr'y-stone**, the hard endocarp of the cherry. [O.E. *ciris*—L. *cerasus*— Gr. *kerasos*, a cherry-tree. It is said to have been introduced from *Kerasous* (*Cerasus*) in Pontus, by Lucullus, but was known in Europe long before his time.]

cherry, *cher'i, v.t.* (*Spens.*) to cheer. [See **cherish**.]

chersonese, *kər'sə-nēz, -nēs, n.* a peninsula. [Gr. *chersonēsos*—*chersos*, land, dry land, *nēsos*, an island.]

chert, *chərt, n.* a compact flinty chalcedony.—*adj.* **chert'y.** [Etymology doubtful.]

cherub, *cher'əb, n.* a winged creature with human face, represented as associated with Jehovah : a celestial spirit : a chubby-faced person, esp. a child :—*pl.* **cher'ubs**, **cher'ubim** (-(*y*)*oo-bim*), **cher'ubims.**—*adjs.* **cherubic** (-ōō'bik), **-al**, **cherubim'ic**, angelic.—*adv.* **cheru'bically.**—*n.* **cheru'bin** (*Shak.*), a cherub. [Heb. *k'rub*, pl. *k'rubim*.]

cherup, *cher'up.* Same as **chirrup**.

chervil, *chər'vil, n.* an umbelliferous plant (*Anthriscus Cerefolium*) cultivated as a pot-herb : also other species of Anthriscus (**common**, **wild**, and **rough chervil**) : extended to sweet cicely (*sweet chervil*). [O.E. *cerfille*—L. *caerefolium*—Gr. *chairephyllon*.]

chesil, *chez'il, n.* gravel : shingle : bran.—Also **chis'el.** [O.E. *cisil*.]

chess, *ches, n.* a game of skill for two, played with figures or men of different kinds which are moved on a chequered board.—*ns.* **chess'-board**, the board on which chess is played : a chequered design; **chess'man.** [O.Fr. *eschès* (Fr. *échecs*) : It. *scacchi*; Ger. *schach*)—Pers. *shāh*, a king.]

chess, *ches, n.* one of the parallel planks of a pontoon-bridge—generally in *pl.*

chessel, *ches'l, n.* a cheese mould. [**cheese**.]

chessylite, *ches'i-līt, n.* basic carbonate of copper, azurite. [*Chessy*, near Lyons, where it occurs.]

chest, *chest, n.* a large strong box : the part of the body between the neck and the abdomen, the thorax : a treasury : a chestful.—*adj.* **chest'ed**, having a chest : placed in a chest.—*ns.* **chest'ful**, enough to fill a chest; **chest'-note**, in singing or speaking, a deep note; **chest'-protec'tor**, a covering to keep the chest warm; **chest'-register**, **-tone**, **-voice**, the lowest register of the voice.—*adj.* **chest'y**, of the quality of chest-voice : (*coll.*) suggestive of disease of the chest : (*slang*) self-important.—**chest of drawers**, a case in which drawers slide; **chest of viols** (*arch.*), a set of viols (two trebles, two tenors, two basses); **off one's chest,** (*coll.*) off one's mind. [O.E. *cyst*—L. *cista*—Gr. *kistē*; Scot. *kist*.]

chesterfield, *chest′ər-fēld, n.* a long overcoat: a heavily padded sofa. [Lord *Chesterfield*.]

chestnut (now rarely **chesnut**), *ches′nut, n.* a tree of genus Castanea, esp. the *Spanish* or *Sweet Chestnut* : its edible nut, encased (three together) in a prickly husk: its hard timber : the **horse-chestnut** (*Aesculus Hippocastanum*), its fruit or nut : a chestnut horse : in Australia, Castano-spermum : a horny knob on a horse's foreleg: (*slang*) a stale joke.—*adj.* of chestnut colour, reddish-brown. [O.Fr. *chastaigne*—L. *castanea*—perh. from *Castana*, in Thessaly.]

cheval-de-frise, *shə-val′-də-frēz′, n.* a spiky defensive structure used esp. to stop cavalry:—*pl.* **chevaux-de-frise** (*shə-vō′-*). [Fr. *cheval*, horse, *de*, of, *Frise*, Friesland.]

cheval-glass, *shə-vâl′gläs, n.* a large glass or mirror supported on a frame. [Fr. *cheval*, horse, stand.]

chevalier, *shev-ə-lēr′, n.* a cavalier : a knight : a gallant. [Fr.,—L.L. *caballārius*—L. *caballus*, a horse.]

chevelure, *shev′(ə-)lür, n.* a head of hair : a periwig : the nebulous part of a comet. [Fr.,—L. *capillātūra*—*capillus*, hair.]

cheven, *chev′ən, n.* the chub.—Also **chev′in.** [Fr. *chevin, chevanne.*]

cheverel, *chev′ər-əl, n.* a kid : soft, flexible kid-skin leather.—*adj.* like kid leather, pliable.—*n.* **chev-rette** (*shəv-ret′*) a thin kind of goat-skin. [Fr. *chevreau, chevrette,* a kid—*chèvre; L. capra,* a she-goat.]

chevesaile, *chev′ə-sāl, n.* an ornamental collar of a coat. [O.Fr. *chevesaile—chevece,* the neck.]

Cheviot, *chē′vi-ət* (or *chev′i-ət*), *n.* a hardy breed of short-woolled sheep reared on the *Cheviot Hills* : a cloth made from their wool.

chevisance, *chev′i-zǎns, n.* achievement: resource: gain : money dealings : (*Spens.*) performance : an unidentified flower. [Fr.,—*chevir*, to accomplish; *chef*, the head, the end.]

chevron, *shev′rən, n.* a rafter : (*her.*) the representation of two rafters of a house meeting at the top : a V-shaped band on the sleeve, a mark of non-commissioned rank or (in army and R.A.F., inverted) of long service and good conduct.—*adjs.* **chev′roned; chev′rony.** [Fr. *chevron*, rafter—L. *capreolus*, dim. of *caper*, a goat.]

chevrotain, *shev′rō-tān*, or *-tən, n.* a mouse-deer, any member of the *Tragulidae*, an Old World tropical family of small deerlike animals not very near the deer but forming a separate section of artiodactyls. [Fr., dim. of *chèvre*—L. *capra,* she-goat.]

chevy, *chev′i,* **chivy,** *chiv′i, n.* a hunting cry : a pursuit : playman's base.—*v.t.* to chase : to harass. —*v.i.* to scamper. [Perh. from *Chevy Chase,* a well-known ballad relating a Border battle.]

chew, *chōō, v.t.* to bruise and grind with the teeth : to masticate : (*fig.*) to meditate, reflect.—*n.* action of chewing : a quid of tobacco.—*n.* **chew′ing-gum,** a preparation made from chicle gum, produced by the Sapodilla plum tree, sweetened and flavoured. —**chew the cud,** to masticate a second time food that has already been swallowed and passed into the first stomach : to ruminate in thought; **chew the rag, the fat,** (*slang*) to dwell naggingly on old grievances. [O.E. *cēowan;* Ger. *kauen;* cf. **jaw.**]

chewet, *chōō′it, n.* a chough : (*Shak.*) a chatterer. [Fr. *chouette*, chough (now owl).]

chewet, *chōō′it, n.* a pie or pudding of miscellaneous chopped meats.

chewink, *chə-wingk′, n.* a large finch of eastern N. America, the red-eyed towhee. [Imit.]

chi, *kī, hhē, n.* the twenty-second letter (Χ, χ) of the Greek alphabet, representing an aspirated k sound : as a numeral χ′ = 600, χ = 600,000 : in inscriptions χ = 1,000 (*chilioi*). [Gr. *chei, chī.*]

chi, *clū.* Same as **chai.**

Chian, *kī′ən, adj.* pertaining to *Chios* in the Aegean Sea.

Chianti, *kē-än′ti, n.* a red (or white) wine of Tuscany. [*Chianti* Mountains.]

chiaroscuro, *kyär-o-skōō′rō, n.* management of light and shade in a picture.

chiasm, *kī′azm, n.* (*anat.*) a decussation or intersection, esp. that of the optic nerves—also **chias′ma.**—*n.* **chias′mus** (*rhet.*), contrast by parallelism in reverse order, as *Do not live to eat, but eat to live.*—*adj.* **chias′tic.**—*n.* **chias′tolite,** (*min.*) a variety of andalusite with black cruciform inclusions. [Gr. *chiasma,* a cross-shaped mark, *chiastos,* laid crosswise, like the Greek letter X (*chi, chei*), *lithos,* a stone.]

chiaus, *chows, n.* Same as **chouse.**

chibol, *chib′əl.* See **cibol.**

chibouk, chibouque, *chi-book′, n.* a long straight-stemmed Turkish pipe. [Turk. *chibūk.*]

chic, *shēk, n.* style, elegance : artistic skill.—*adj.* having chic : smart and fashionable. [Fr.]

chica, *chē′kä, n.* an orange-red dye-stuff, got by boiling the leaves of a South American Bignonia. [From a native name.]

chicane, *shi-kān′, v.i.* to use shifts and tricks.—*v.t.* to deceive.—*n.* a trick or artifice : a bridge hand without trumps, for which a score above the line used to be allowed.—*ns.* **chicā′ner,** one who chicanes : a quibbler; **chicā′nery,** trickery or artifice, esp. in legal proceedings: quibbling; **chicā′ning,** quibbling. [Fr. *chicane,* sharp practice at law, from Late Gr. *tzykanion,* a game at mall, *tzykanizein,* to play at mall.—Pers. *tchaugan,* a crooked mallet.]

chich, chich. Same as **chick-pea.**

chicha, *chēch′ä, n.* a South American liquor fermented from maize. [Said to be Haitian.]

chick, *chik, n.* the young of fowls, esp. of the hen : a child, as a term of endearment.—*ns.* **chick′-a-bidd′y, chick′-a-didd′le,** terms of endearment addressed to children; **chick′en,** the young of birds, esp. of the domestic fowl : the flesh of a fowl, not always very young : a prairie chicken : a youthful person : a faint-hearted person; **chick′en-feed** (*U.S.*), poultry food: (*slang*) small change; **chick′en-haz′ard,** a game at hazard for low stakes—*adj.* **chick′en-heart′ed.**—*ns.* **chick′en-pox,** a contagious febrile disease, chiefly of children, not unlike a very mild form of smallpox; **chick′-ling,** a little chicken; **chick′weed,** a species of stitchwort, one of the commonest of weeds, much relished by fowls and cage-birds (**mouse-ear chickweed,** the kindred genus Cerastium); **chick′weed-win′tergreen** (see **wintergreen,** under **winter**). [O.E. *cicen;* cf. Du. *kieken,* Ger. *küchlein.*]

chick, *chik, n.* (*Ind.*) a hanging door-screen or sun-blind of laced bamboo slips, etc. [Hind. *chik.*]

chickadee, *chik-ə-dē′, n.* an American titmouse. [From its note.]

chickaree, *chik-ə-rē′, n.* an American red squirrel. [From its cry.]

chickling, *chik′ling, n.* a species of pea (also **chickling vetch,** *Lathyrus sativus*).—*n.* **chick′-pea,** gram, a plant of the pea family (*Cicer arieti-num*): its edible seed. [Earlier *chich, chichling, chichpease*—Fr. *chiche*—L. *cicer,* chick-pea.]

chicle, *chik′l, chik′li, n.* the gum of the sapodilla tree, chewing-gum. [Sp.,—Mex.]

chicory, (also **chiccory**), *chik′ə-ri, n.* succory, a blue-flowered composite (*Cichorium Intybus*): its carrot-like root (ground to mix with coffee). [Fr. *chicorée*—L. *cichorēum*—Gr. *kichorion.*]

chide, *chīd, v.t.* to scold, rebuke, reprove by words: to be noisy about, as the sea.—*v.i.* to make a snarling, murmuring sound, as a dog or trumpet: *pr.p.* **chīd′ing;** *pa.t.* **chīd,** sometimes **chīd′ed,** *pa.p.* **chīd,** **chīdd′en.**—*ns.* **chīd′er** (*Shak.*), a quarrelsome person; **chīd′ing,** scolding. [O.E. *cidan* (a weak verb).]

chief, *chēf, adj.* head: principal, highest, first : outstanding, important (with *comp.* **chief′er,** *superl.* **chief′est**) : (*Scot.*) intimate.—*adv.* chiefly. —*n.* a head or principal person : a leader : the principal part or top of anything : the greater part : (*her.*) an ordinary, consisting of the upper part of the field cut off by a horizontal line, generally made to occupy one-third of the area of the shield.—*ns.* **chief'-bar'on**, the President of the Court of Exchequer; **chief'dom**, **chief'ship**, state of being chief: sovereignty: **chief'ery**, **chief'ry** (in *Spens.* **cheverye**), an Irish chieftaincy: the dues paid to a chief or the supreme lord: a chief's lands; **chief'ess**, a female chief; **chief'-jus'tice** (see justice).—*adj.* **chief'less**, without a chief or leader.—*n.* **chief'ling**.—*adv.* **chief'ly**, in the first place: principally: for the most part.—*ns.* **chief'- tain**, the head of a clan: a leader or commander :— *fem.* **chief'tainess**; **chief'taincy**, **chief'tainry**; **chief'tainship**.—**in chief** (*her.*) borne in the upper part of the shield: of a tenure, held directly from the sovereign: at the head, as commander-in-chief. [Fr. *chef*—L. *caput*, the head.]

chield, *chēld*, *n.* (*Scot.*) a lad, a man.—Also **chiel**. [Apparently a form of **child**.]

chiff-chaff, *chif'-chäf*, *n.* a small warbler. [Imit.]

chiffon, *shē'fon²*, *shif'on*, *n.* a thin gauzy material used as a trimming: (*pl.*) trimmings, etc.— **chiffonier** (*shif-ən-ēr'*), an ornamental cupboard or cabinet. [Fr.—*chiffe*, rag.]

chignon, *shē'nyon²*, *n.* a fold or roll of hair worn on the back of the head and neck. [Fr., meaning first the nape of the neck (jointed like a chain)— *chaînon*, link of a chain—*chaîne*, a chain.]

chigoe, *chig'ō;* **chigre**, **chigger**, *chig'ér*, *n.* a West Indian and South American flea (*Sarcopsylla penetrans*), the gravid female of which buries itself, esp. beneath the toe-nails: the larva of an American harvest-mite that burrows in the skin.— Also **jigg'er**. [West Indian name.]

chikara, *chi-kä'rä*, *n.* a four-horned Indian ante-lope: an Indian gazelle. [Hind. *chikārā.*]

chikara, *chik'ə-rä*, *n.* an Indian instrument of the violin class. [Hind. *chihārā.*]

chik(h)or. See **chukor**.

chilblain, *chil'blān*, *n.* a painful red swelling, esp. on hands and feet in cold weather. [**chill** and **blain**.]

child, *chīld*, *n.* a very young person (up to the age of sixteen for the purpose of some acts of parliament): (*Shak.*) a female infant: a son or daughter: one who stands in relation of origin or adoption: a disciple: a youth of gentle birth, esp. in ballads, etc. (sometimes **childe** and **chylde**): (*in pl.*) offspring: descendants: inhabitants:—*pl.* **children** (*chil'dren*; a double pl. from older and dial. **chil'der**).—*v.t.* and *v.i.* (*arch.*) to bring forth.— *ns.* **child'-bearing**, the act of bringing forth children; **child'bed**, the state of a woman brought to bed with child; **child'birth**, the giving birth to a child: parturition; **child'-crow'ing**, a nervous affection with spasm of the muscles closing the glottis.—*adj.* **child'ed** (*Shak.*), possessed of a child.—*n.* **child'hood**, state of being a child: the time of being a child.—*adjs.* **child'ing** (*Shak.*), fruiting, teeming; **child'ish**, of or like a child: silly: trifling.—*adv.* **child'ishly**.—*ns.* **child'ishness**, what is natural to a child: puerility.—*adj.* **child'less**, without children.—*child'-life**, the life or lives of children.—*adjs.* **child'like**, like a child: becoming a child: docile: innocent; **child'ly**, natural or becoming to a child.—*ns.* **child'ness** (*Shak.*), nature or character of a child; **child'-study**, the psychology and physiology of children; **child'-wel'fare**, health and well-being of young children as an object of systematic social work; **child'-wife**, a very young wife.— **child's play**, something very easy to do, **from** or **of** a child, since the days of childhood; **second childhood**, the childishness of old age; **with child**, pregnant. [O.E. *cild*, pl. *cild*, later *cildru*, *-ra*.]

childermas, *chil'dər-məs*, *n.* Innocents' Day, a festival (Dec. 28) to commemorate the slaying of the children by Herod. [O.E. *cildra*, gen. pl. of *cild*, child, *mæsse*, mass.]

Chile, *chil'i*, *adj.* of Chile.—*n.* and *adj.* **Chil'ean** (*obs.* **Chil'ian**).—**Chile saltpetre**, sodium nitrate.

chiliad, *kil'i-ad*, *n.* the number 1,000: 1,000 of anything (e.g. years).—*ns.* **chil'iagon**, a plane figure with 1,000 angles; **chil'iahēdron**, a solid

figure with 1,000 plane faces; **chiliarch** (*kil'i-ärk*), a leader or commander of a thousand men; **chil'iarchy**, the posicion of chiliarch; **chil'iasm**, the doctrine that Christ will reign bodily upon the earth for 1,000 years; **chil'iast**, one who holds this opinion. [Gr. *chīlias*, *-ados*—*chilioi*, 1,000.]

chill, *chil*, *n.* coldness : a cold that causes shivering : anything that damps or disheartens : a foundry mould.—*adj.* shivering with cold : slightly cold : opposite of *cordial*.—*v.i.* to grow cold.—*v.t.* to make chill or cold : to cool : to preserve by cold : to injure with cold : to discourage : to cloud or bloom the surface of (by cold air) : (*dial.*) to take the chill off :—*adj.* **chilled**, made cold : hardened by chilling, as iron : preserved by cold, as beef.— *adv.* **chill'ily**.—*n.* **chill'iness**—*n* and *adj.* **chill'- ing**.—*n.* **chill'ness**.—*adj.* **chilly**, cold : chilling : sensitive to cold.—**take the chill off**, to warm slightly : to make lukewarm. [O.E. *cele*, *ciele*, cold; see **cold**, **cool**.]

chilli, *chil'i*, *n.* the pod of the capsicum, extremely pungent and stimulant, used in sauces, pickles, etc. and dried and ground to form Cayenne pepper. [Nahuatl.]

chillum, *chil'um*, *n.* the part of a hookah containing the tobacco and charcoal balls : a hookah itself: the act of smoking it. [Hind. *chilam.*]

Chilognatha, *ki-log'nä-thä*, *n.pl.* millipedes. [Gr. *cheilos*, lip, *gnathos*, jaw.]

Chilopoda, *ki-lop'o-dä*, *n.pl.* centipedes. [Gr. *cheilos*, lip, *pous*, *podos*, foot.]

Chiltern hundreds. See **hundreds**.

chimaera, **chimera**, *ki-mē'rä*, *n.* a fabulous, fire-spouting monster, with a lion's head, a serpent's tail, and a goat's body: any idle or wild fancy : a picture of an animal having its parts made up of various animals : a genus of cartilaginous fishes, often ranked with the sharks and rays: an organism made up of two genetically distinct tissues.—*adjs.* **chimeric** (*-mer'ik*), **-al**, of the nature of a chimaera: wild: fanciful.—*adv.* **chimer'ically**. [L.,—Gr. *chimaira*, a she-goat.]

chime, *chīm*, *n.* a set of bells tuned in a scale : the ringing of such bells in succession (often in *pl.*): a definite sequence of bell-like notes sounded as by a clock : the harmonious sound of bells or other musical instruments : agreement of sound or of relation : harmony : rhyme : jingle.—*v.i.* to sound a chime or in chime : to accord or agree: to jingle : to rhyme.—*v.t.* to strike, or cause to sound in chime : to indicate by chiming : to say words over mechanically.—**chime in**, to join in, in agreement. [M.E. *chimbe*, prob. O.Fr. *cymbale*—L. *cymbalum*, a cymbal.]

chime, **chimb**, *chīm*, *n.* the rim formed by the ends of the staves of a cask : (*naut.*) a hollowed or bevelled channel in the water-way of a ship's deck. [Cog. with Du. *kim*, Ger. *kimme*, edge.]

chimer, *chim'ər*, **chimere**, *chi-mēr'*, *n.* a long sleeveless tabard : the upper robe worn by a bishop. [O.Fr. *chamarre*; cf. **cymar**; Sp. *zamarra*, *chamarra*, sheepskin.]

chimney, *chim'ni*, (*dial.* **chimley**, **chumley**, *chim'*, *chum'li*), *n.* a passage for the escape of fumes, smoke, or heated air from a fireplace or furnace : a glass tube surrounding a lamp flame : a cleft in a rock-face.—*ns.* **chim'ney-board**, a board blocking up a fireplace; **chim'ney-can**, a chimney-pot; **chim'ney-cor'ner**, **-nook** (*Scot.* **-nuik**), in old chimneys, the space between the fire and the side-wall of the fireplace: fireside, commonly spoken of as the place for the aged and infirm; **chim'ney-piece**, a shelf over the fireplace; **chim'ney-pot**, a cylindrical pipe of earthenware or other material at the top of a chimney : a top-hat (in full **chimney-pot hat**); **chim'ney-shaft**, the stalk of a chimney which rises above the building; **chim'ney-stack**, a group of chimneys carried up together; **chim'-ney-stalk**, a very tall chimney; **chim'ney-swall'ow**, the common swallow : (*U.S.*) a species of swift; **chim'ney-sweep**, **chim'ney-sweeper**, one who sweeps or cleans chimneys; **chim'ney-top**, the top of a chimney. [Fr. *cheminée*—L. *caminus*; Gr. *kaminos*, a furnace.]

Neutral vowels in unaccented syllables : *el'ə-mənt*, *in'fənt*, *ran'dəm*

chimpanzee, *chim-pən-zē'*, also *-pan'*, *n.* an African ape, the highest of the anthropoid apes. [West African.]

chin, *chin*, *n.* the jutting part of the face below the mouth.—*n.* and *v.i.* **chin'-wag** (*slang*), talk. [O.E. *cin*; Ger. *kinn*, Gr. *genys*.]

china, *chī'nä*, *n.* fine kind of earthenware, originally made in China, porcelain.—*adj.* of china: **China**, Chinese.—*ns.* **chin'a-clay**, a fine white clay used in making porcelain; **Chin'a-grass**, ramie; **Chin'a-man**, a Chinese: off-break bowled by left-handed bowler to right-handed batsman; **Chin'a-root**, the root-stock of *Smilax China*; **Chin'a-rose**, name applied to several varieties of garden roses; **chi'na-stone**, partly decomposed granite; **Chi'natown**, a Chinese quarter in a town; **chin'a-ware**, porcelain-ware.—*n.* **Chinese'**, a native or citizen of China (*pl.* **Chinese'**—hence *coll. sing.* **Chinee'**): the language of China.—Also *adj.* (in names of commodities, sometimes without capital).—**China aster** (see **aster**); **China jute**, a species of Abutilon; **Chinese lantern**, a paper lantern; **Chinese paper**, a fine soft brownish paper-like material made from bamboo bark, giving fine impressions of engravings: also the so-called rice paper; **Chinese pavilion** (see **pavilion**); **Chinese white**, a zinc oxide pigment.

china, *kī'nä, ken'ä.* See **kina**.

chinampa, *chin-am'pä*, *n.* a floating garden. [Sp.,— Nahuatl *chinamitl*.]

chinch, *chinch*, *n.* the bed-bug in America. [Sp. *chinche*—L. *cimex*.]

chincha, *chin'chä*, *n.* a small South American rodent, allied to the chinchilla. [Sp.]

chinchilla, *chin-chil'ä*, *n.* a small rodent of South America valued for its soft grey fur: the fur itself [Sp.]

chincough, *chin'kof*, *n.* whooping-cough. [For *chink-cough*; cf. Scot. *kink-hoast*, Du. *kinkhoest*; see **chink** (3) and **cough**.]

chine, *chin*, *n.* the spine or backbone: a piece of the backbone and adjoining parts for cooking: (*Spens.*) the back: a ridge crest.—*v.t.* to break the back of. [O.Fr. *eschine*, prob. from O.H.G. *scina*, pin, thorn.]

chine, *chīn*, *n.* a ravine. [O.E. *cinu*, a cleft.]

chiné, *shē-nā'*, *adj.* mottled, with the pattern printed on the warp. [Fr., dyed in a (supposedly) Chinese way.]

Chinese. See **China**.

chink, *chingk*, *n.* a cleft, a narrow opening.—*v.i.* to crack.—*v.t.* to fill up cracks.—*adj.* **chink'y**, full of chinks. [Apparently formed upon M.E. *chine*, a crack—O.E. *cinu*, a cleft.]

chink, *chingk*, *n.* the clink, as of coins: (*slang*) money (in *Shak.* **chinks**).—*v.i.* to give forth a sharp sound. [Imit.]

chink, *chingk*, (*Northern* **kink**, *kingk*), *n.* a gasp for breath.—*v.i.* to gasp. [Cf. Du. *kinken*, to cough; Ger. *keichen*, to gasp.]

Chink, *chingk*, *n.* and *adj.* (*slang*) Chinese. [**China**.]

chinkapin, chincapin, chinquapin, *ching'kə-pin*, *n.* the dwarf chestnut of the U.S. [Ind.]

Chinook, *chin-ōōk'*, a traders' jargon, consisting of words from French, English, Chinook, and other American-Indian tongues: **chinook**, a warm, dry wind blowing down the eastern side of the Rocky Mts, making winter grazing possible: also a warm moist wind from the Pacific.

chinovnik, *chin-ov'nik*, *n.* a high official in the Russian civil service: a bureaucrat. [Russ. *chin*, rank.]

chintz, *chints*, *n.* a cotton printed generally in several colours on a white or light ground. [Orig. pl.—Hind, *chīnt*, spotted cotton-cloth.]

Chionodoxa, *kī-ō-nō-dok'sä*, *n.* glory of the snow, an early-blooming blue-flowered genus of liliaceous plants. [Gr. *chiōn*, snow, *doxa*, glory.]

chip, *chip*, *v.t.* to strike with small sharp cutting blows: to strike small pieces off the surface of: to remove by chipping: to slice or pare: (of hatching chickens) to crack by pecking: to cut as with an adze: (*coll.*) to chaff, tease.—*v.i.* to become chipped: to play a chip-shot (*pr.p.* **chipp'ing**; *pa.t.* and *pa.p.* **chipped**).—*n.* an act of chipping: a piece chipped off, esp. a flattish fragment: a surface flaw: a thin slice, esp. of fried potato: a thin strip of wood, used for making boxes, baskets, etc.: a chip-basket: a counter: a sovereign: a piece of dried dung of cow or bison: (*Shak.*) a key on a musical instrument.— *ns.* **chip'-bas'ket**, a fruit basket of interwoven chips; **chip'-car'ving**, wood carving by removal of splinters; **chip'-hat**, a hat of palm-leaf strips; **chips** (*slang*) a ship's carpenter: a regimental pioneer sergeant—usually a carpenter: fried chipped potatoes: money; **chip'-shot** (*golf*), a short lofted approach.—*adj.* **chipp'y**, abounding in chips: dry as a chip: seedy from an overdose of liquor; **chip in**, to enter the game by putting chips on the table: to interpose; **chip of the old block**, one with the characteristics of his father; **chip on one's shoulder**, a defiant challenging manner, as if daring anybody to knock it off. [M.E. *chippen*, to cut in pieces; conn. with **chop**.]

chipmunk, **chipmuck**, *chip'mungk*, *-muk*, a North American squirrel. [From Indian name.]

Chippendale, *chip'ən-dāl*, *adj.* applied to a light style of drawing-room furniture, after the name of a well-known cabinet-maker of the 18th century: also applied to a style of book-plates.

chipper, *chip'ər*, *adj.* (esp. *U.S.*), brisk and cheerful. [Perh. same word as Northern dial. *kipper*, lively.]

chiquichiqui, *chē-kē-chē'kē*, *n.* a piassava palm (Leopoldinia). [Tupi.]

chiragra, *ki-rag'rä*, *n.* gout in the hand.—*adjs.* **chirag'ric, -al.** [Gr. *cheiragrā*—*cheir*, hand, *agrā*, a catching.]

chi-rho, *ki-rō*, *n.* a monogram of XP (*chī*, *rhō*, ch, r), the first letters of the Greek *Christos* (Christ).

chirimoya. See **cherimoyer**.

chirk, *chərk*, *v.i.* to chirp or squeak: (*Scot.*) to grate. [O.E. *cearcian*, to creak.]

chirl, *chirl*, *v.i.* (*Scot.*) to emit a low sound: to warble.—*n.* a kind of musical warble. [Imit.]

chirm, *chərm*, *v.i.* to cry out: to chirp.—*n.* noise, din, hum of voices: a flock of goldfinches (also **charm**). [O.E. *cirman*, to cry out; cf. Du. *kermen*.]

chiro. See **cheiro-**.

Chironomus, *kī-ron'ō-məs*, *n.* a large genus of common midges, giving name to the family **Chironomidae** (*kī-rō-nom'i-dē*).—*n.* **chiron'omid**, any member of the family. [Gr. *cheironomōn*, gesticulator.]

chiropodist, *ki-rop'o-dist*, *n.* one who treats corns, bunions, warts, etc. [App. Gr. *cheir*, hand, and *pous, podos*, foot; but *cheiropodēs* means having chapped feet.]

chiropractic, *ki-rō-prak'tik*, *n.* a method of healing which relies upon the removal of nerve interference by manual adjustment of the spinal column: a chiropractor.—*n.* **chiroprac'tor**, one who practices chiropractic. [Gr. *cheir*, hand, *praktikos*, concerned with action—*prattein*, to do.]

chirp, *chərp*, *n.* the sharp thin sound of certain birds and insects.—*v.i.* to make such a sound; to talk in a cheerful and lively strain.—*v.t.* to urge by chirping.—*n.* **chirp'er**, a little bird: a chirping-cup.—*adv.* **chirp'ily**.—*adj.* **chirp'ing**.—*n.* **chirp'ing-cup**, a cup that cheers.—*adj.* **chirp'y**, lively: merry. [Imit.]

chirr, *chər*, *v.i.* to chirp like a cricket or grasshopper. [Imit.]

chirrup, *chir'əp*, *v.i.* to chirp: to make a sound with the mouth to urge on a horse: to cheer up. [Lengthened form of **chirp**, associated with **cheer up**.]

chirt, *chərt*, *n.* a squeeze: a squirt.—*v.t.* to squeeze: to squirt. [Conn. with **chirr**.]

chirurgeon, chirurgery, chirurgical, *kīr-ur'jən. -jər-i, -ji-kl*, old forms of **surgeon, surgery, surgical**, with pronunciation readjusted to the ultimate Greek etymology.—*adv.* **chirur'geonly** (*Shak.*), in a manner becoming a surgeon. [Fr. *chirurgien*—Gr. *cheirourgos*—*cheir*, hand, *ergon*, a work.]

chisel, *chiz'l*, *n.* a tool with the end bevelled to a cutting edge: esp. the tool of the sculptor.—*v.t.* to cut, carve, etc. with a chisel: (*slang*) to cheat (*pr.p.* **chis'elling**; *pa.t.* and *pa.p.* **chis'elled**).—

adj. **chis'elled,** cut with a chisel : (*fig.*) having sharp outlines, as cut by a chisel.—*ns.* **chis'elling ; chis'el-tooth,** a rodent's chisel-shaped incisor. [O.Fr. *cisel*—L. *caedĕre,* to cut.]

chisel, *chiz'l, n.* See **chesil.**

Chisleu, *kis'lū, n.* the ninth month of the Jewish year (parts of November and December). [Heb.]

chit, *chit, n.* a short informal letter : an order or pass.—Also **chitt'y.** [Hind. *chitthi.*]

chit, *chit, n.* a child : (*slightingly*) a girl.—*adjs.* **chitt'y ; chitt'y-faced.** [Same as **kit** (3).]

chit, *chit, n.* (*prov.*) a shoot.—*v.i.* to sprout. [Perh. O.E. *cīth,* a shoot.]

chital, *chē'tāl, n.* the axis deer. [Hind.]

chitchat, *chit'chat, n.* chatting or idle talk : prattle : gossip. [A reduplication of **chat.**]

chitin, *kī'tin, n.* the substance which forms most of the hard parts of joint-footed animals.—*adj.* **chi'tinous.** [Fr. *chitine*—Gr. *chitōn,* a tunic.]

chiton, *kī'ton, n.* the ancient Greek tunic : *Chiton,* a genus of marine molluscs with shell of movable plates. [Gr. *chitōn,* a tunic.]

chittagong, *chit'ə-gong, n.* an Indian variety of domestic fowl.—*n.* **chitt'agong-wood',** a cabinet-maker's wood, usu. that of *Chickrassia tabularis* (mahogany family). [*Chittagong* in Bengal.]

chitter, *chit'ər, v.i.* (*Scot.*) to shiver : to chatter.—*n.* **chitt'ering.** [Cf. **chatter.**]

chitterling, *chit'ər-ling, n.* the smaller intestines of a pig or other edible animal (usu. *pl.*) : (*obs.*) a frill. —Also (*prov.*) **chid'lings, chit'lings.** [Ety. dub.]

chitwah, *chit'wä, n.* a panda.

chivalry, *shiv'əl-ri* (orig. *chiv'-*), *n.* the usages and qualifications of chevaliers or knights : bravery and courtesy : the system of knighthood in feudal times and its social code.—*adjs.* **chivalric** (*-al'*), **chiv'alrous,** pertaining to chivalry : bold : gallant. —*adv.* **chiv'alrously.**—*n.* **chiv'alrousness.** [Fr. *chevalerie*—*cheval*—L.L. *caballus,* a horse.]

chive, *chīv, n.* a herb like the leek and onion, with tufts of leaves (used in soup) and clustered bulbs : a small bulb.—Also **cive** (*sīv*). [Fr. *cive*—L. *cēpa,* an onion.]

chivy, *chiv'i, n.* and *v.* See **chevy.**

chlamys, *klam'is, n.* a short cloak for men : a purple cope :—*pl.* **chlam'ydes** (*-i-dēz*).—*adjs.* **chlam'y-date** (*zool.*), having a mantle ; **chlamyd'eous** (*bot.*) having a perianth.—*n.* **chlam'ydospore,** a thick-walled spore. [Gr. *chlamys,* pl. *chlamydēs.*]

chloasma, *klō-az'mä, n.* a skin-disease marked by yellowish-brown patches. [Gr. *chloasma,* greenness, yellowness—*chloē,* verdure.]

chlorine, *klō'rēn, -rin, rīn, n.* a yellowish-green gas (Cl) with a peculiar and suffocating odour, used in bleaching, disinfecting, and poison gas warfare. —*ns.* **chlor'al,** (or *-al'*) a limpid, colourless, oily liquid (C Cl₃ · C HO), of penetrating odour, formed when anhydrous alcohol is acted on by dry chlorine gas : (*loosely*) **chloral hydrate,** a white crystalline substance used as an anaesthetic and hypnotic ; **chlo'ralism,** the habit or morbid effects of using chloral ; **chlorar'gyrite** (*klō-rär'ji-rīt ;* Gr. *argyros,* silver) horn silver ; **chlo'rate,** a salt of chloric acid.—*adjs.* **chlo'ric, chlor'ous,** of or from chlorine (see below).—*ns.* **chlo'ride,** a compound of chlorine with another element or radical : bleaching powder (*chloride of lime*), not a true chloride.—*v.t.* **chlo'ridise,** to convert into a chloride : (*phot.*) to cover with chloride of silver.— Also **chlo'ridate.**—*ns.* **chlorim'eter** (same as **chlorometer**).—*adj.* **chlorimet'ric.**—*n.* **chlo-rim'etry.**—*v.t.* **chlor'inate,** to treat with chlorine (as in sterilisation of water, extraction of gold from ore).—*n.* **chlorina'tion.**—*v.t.* **chlo'rinise,** to chlorinate.—*ns.* **chlo'rite,** (*chem.*) a salt of chlorous acid : (*min.*) a general name for a group of minerals, hydrated silicates of magnesia, iron, and alumina— dark green and rather soft, like mica but not elastic ; **chlo'rite-schist',** a schistose rock com-posed of chlorite, usually with quartz, epidote, etc. ;—*adj.* **chlorit'ic,** pertaining to, of the nature of, or containing, the mineral chlorite.—*n.* **chloritisā'tion,** alteration of ferro-magnesian minerals into chlorite or similar material ; **chlo'ro-dyne,** a patent medicine—anodyne and hypnotic,

containing chloroform ; **chloroform** (*klor'ō-form* or *klō'rō-form*), a limpid, mobile, colourless, volatile liquid (C H Cl₃) with a characteristic odour and a strong sweetish taste, used to induce in-sensibility.—*v.t.* to administer chloroform to.—*ns.* **chlor'oformer, -ist ; chlōrom'eter,** an apparatus for measuring the available chlorine in bleaching powder, etc.—*adj.* **chlōromet'ric.**—*ns.* **chlo-rom'etry ; chloromy'cetin,** a drug used against scrub typhus and typhoid :—*n.pl.* **Chlorophyceae** (*-fis'i-ē ;* Gr. *phȳkos,* seaweed), the green seaweeds and their kindred, one of the main divisions of the Algae.—*ns.* **chlorophyll, -phyl** (*klor'ō-fil,* or *klō'rō-fil ;* Gr. *phyllon,* leaf), the ordinary green colouring-matter of vegetation ; **chlo'roplast** (Gr. *plastos,* moulded), a chlorophyll-bearing corpuscle ; **chlo'roquin,** a drug taken to suppress malaria ; **chlorō'sis,** properly *green-sickness,* a form of anaemia affecting young women : (*bot.*) blanching of the green parts of a plant, esp. for want of iron.— *adj.* **chlorot'ic,** pertaining to or affected by chlorosis.—**chloric acid** (H Cl O₃), a syrupy liquid, a vigorous oxidising agent ; **chlorine water,** an aqueous solution of chlorine ; **chloritic marl,** a marl at the base of the English Chalk stained green with glauconite (not chlorite) ; **chlorous acid,** a hypothetical acid (H Cl O₂), known in solution and by its salts. [Gr. *chlōros,* pale-green.]

chobdar, *chōb'där, n.* in India, an usher. [Pers.]

chock, *chok, v.t.* to fasten as with a block or wedge. —*n.* a wedge to prevent movement : a log.—*adjs.* **chock-a-block', chock'-full, choke'-full,** quite full ; **chock'-tight,** very tight. [See **choke.**]

chocolate, *chok'(ə-)lit, n.* a paste made of the ground seeds of *Theobroma cacao* (cocoa), with sugar and flour or similar material : a sweetmeat made of the paste : a beverage made by dissolving the paste in boiling water.—*adj.* chocolate-coloured, dark reddish-brown : made of or flavoured with chocolate. [Sp. *chocolate ;* from Nahuatl *chocólatl,* a mixture containing chocolate.]

chode, *chōd,* an occasional *pa.t.* of **chide.**

choice, *chois, n.* act or power of choosing : the thing chosen : alternative : preference : the prefer-able or best part.—*adj.* worthy of being chosen : select : appropriate.—*adjs.* **choice'-drawn** (*Shak.*), selected with care ; **choice'ful** (*Spens.*), making many choices, fickle.—*adv.* **choice'ly,** with dis-crimination or care.—*n.* **choice'ness,** particular value : excellence : nicety.—**for choice,** by preference ; **Hobson's choice,** the choice of a thing offered or nothing, from *Hobson,* a Cambridge horse-keeper, who lent out the horse nearest the stable door, or none at all ; **make choice of,** to select ; **take one's choice,** to take what one wishes. [Fr. *choix*—*choisir ;* cf. **choose.**]

choir, *kwīr, n.* a chorus or band of singers, esp. those belonging to a church : the part of a church appropriated to the singers : the part, the eastern end, often separated from the nave by a rail or screen.—*v.i.* (*Shak.*) to sing in chorus.—*ns.* **choir'-boy, choir'-man,** a boy, man, who sings in a choir ; **choir'-master,** the leader or director of a choir ; **choir'-organ,** a department of a large organ, probably originally called chair organ (renamed as if an organ suitable for accompanying a choir) ; **choir'-screen,** a screen of lattice-work, separating the choir from the nave.—*n.pl.* **choir'-stalls,** fixed seats in the choir of a church, generally of carved wood. [Fr. *chœur*—L. *chorus*—Gr. *choros ;* see **chorus.**]

choke, *chōk, v.t.* to stop or interfere with the breathing of (whether by compression, blocking, fumes, emotion, or otherwise) : to injure or sup-press by obstruction, overshadowing, or deprivation of air, etc. : to constrict : to block : to clog : to obstruct.—*v.i.* to be choked.—*n.* a complete or partial stoppage of breath : the sound of choking : a constriction : a device to prevent the passage of too much gas, electric current, etc., e.g. a choking coil.—**choke'-berry,** a small astringent American fruit akin to the apple ; **choke'bore,** a gun-bore narrowed at the muzzle : a shot-gun so bored ; **choke'-cherry,** an astringent American cherry ;

choke′damp, carbon dioxide or other suffocating gas in mines.—*adj.* **choke-full** (see **chock-full**).— *ns.* **choke′-pear,** an astringent pear : anything that reduces one to silence ; **chok′er,** that which, or one who chokes : a large neckcloth : a very high collar ; **chok′ing-coil,** a coil of thick wire, used to limit the supply of electric light.—*adj.* **chok′y,** tending or inclined to choke.—**choke back, down,** repress as if by a choking action ; **choke off,** get rid of ; **choke up,** fill completely ; **block′ up.** [Ety. obscure.]

choky, *chō′ki, n.* a prison : a toll-station.—*n.* **chokidar, chowkidar** (*chō′, chow′ki-där*), a watch-man. [Hind. *chaukī, chaukīdar.*]

cholaemia, *ko-lē′mi-ä, n.* a morbid accumulation of the constituents of bile in the blood.—*adj.* **cholae′mic.** [Gr. *cholē,* bile, *haima,* blood.]

cholagogue, *kol′ə-gog, n.* a purgative causing evacuations of bile.—*adj.* **cholagog′ic** (*-goj′ik, -goj′ik*). [Gr. *cholē,* bile, *agōgos,* leading.]

cholecyst, *kō′li-sist, n.* the gall-bladder.—*ns.* **cholecysti′tis,** inflammation of the gall-bladder ; **cholecystos′tomy** (Gr. *stoma,* mouth), **chole-cystot′omy** (Gr. *tomē,* a cut), surgical opening of the gall-bladder. [Gr. *cholē,* bile, *kystis,* a bladder.]

choler, *kol′ər, n.* the bile : (*Shak.*) biliousness : anger, irascibility.—*adj.* **chol′eric,** full of choler : passionate. [Gr. *cholerā—cholē,* bile, partly through Fr.]

cholera, *kol′ər-ä, n.* a highly infectious and deadly disease characterised by bilious vomiting and purging.—*adj.* **choleraic** (*kol-ər-ā′ik*).—**British cholera,** an acute catarrhal affection of the mucous membrane of the stomach and small intestines ; **chicken, fowl cholera,** a contagious septicaemia of birds ; **hog cholera,** swine fever ; **cholera belt,** a waist-band of flannel or other material worn as a precaution against disease. [Gr. *cholerā—cholē,* bile.]

cholesterol, *ko-les′tər-ol, n.* an alcohol ($C_{27}H_{45}OH$) occurring abundantly in gall-stones, nerves, etc., a white crystalline solid—formerly **choles′terin.**— *adj.* **cholester′ic.** [Gr. *cholē,* bile, *stereos,* solid.]

choliamb, *kō′li-amb, n.* a variety of iambic trimeter having a spondee for an iambus as the sixth foot.— *n.* and *adj.* **choliam′bic.** [Gr. *chōliambos— chōlos,* lame, *iambos,* iambus.]

cholic, *kol′ik, kōl′ik, adj.* pertaining to bile, as **cholic acid** ($C_{24}H_{40}O_5$) got from bile.—*n.* **chol′ine,** an alcohol ($C_5H_{15}NO_2$) discovered in bile. [Gr. *cholē,* bile.]

choltry, *chōl′tri, n.* a caravanserai : a shed used as a place of assembly.—Also **choul′try.** [From Malayalam.]

chondrus, *kon′drəs, n.* a cartilage : a chondrule : Chondrus, a genus of cartilaginous red seaweeds to which carrageen belongs :—*pl.* **chon′dri.**—*adj.* **chon′dral.**—*ns.* **chondre** (*kon′dər*), a chondrule ; **chondrifica′tion,** formation of chondrin or de-velopment of or change into cartilage.—*v.t.* and *v.i.* **chon′drify,** to change into cartilage.—*ns.* **chon′-drin,** a firm, elastic, translucent, bluish-white gelatinous substance, the ground-substance of cartilage ; **chon′driosome,** a minute body in the cytoplasm of a cell ; **chon′drite,** a meteorite containing chondrules : a fossil resembling *Chondrus.* — *adj.* **chondrit′ic.** — *ns.* **chondro-crān′ium,** a cartilaginous skull, as in embryos, fishes, etc. ; **chondrogen′esis,** chondrification.— *adj.* **chon′droid,** like cartilage.—*ns.pl.* **chon-dropterygii** (*kon-drop-tər-ij′i-ī*; Gr. *pteryx, -ygos,* fin), the selachians or elasmobranchs ; **Chon-dros′tei** (*kon-dros′ti-ī;* Gr. *osteon,* bone), an order of fishes including the sturgeon.—*n.* **chon′drule,** a rounded granule found in meteorites and in deep-sea deposits. [Gr. *chondros,* a grain, grit, cartilage.]

choose, *chōōz, v.t.* to take or pick out in preference to another thing : to select : to will or determine : to think fit.—*v.i.* to make a choice (*pa.t.* **chose,** *chōz* ; *pa.p.* **chōs′en**).—*n.* **choos′er.**—*adj.* **choos′(e)y,** (*slang*) difficult to please, fastidious.— **cannot choose,** can have no alternative ; **choosers of the slain,** the Valkyries ; **not much to choose between,** each about equally good or bad ; **pick**

and choose, to select with care or at leisure.— **the chosen people,** the Israelites (1. *Chron.* xvi. 13). [O.E. *cēosan,* Du. *kiesen.*]

chop, *chop, v.t.* to cut with a sudden blow : to cut into small pieces : to thrust or clap.—*v.i.* to hack : to come suddenly or accidentally : to thrust : to crack or fissure : to take a direction (running into **chop,** 2).—*n.* an act of chopping : chopped food : a piece cut off : a slice of mutton or pork, containing a rib : a crack.—*ns.* **chop′-house,** a house where mutton-chops and beef-steaks are served : an eating-house ; **chopp′er,** one who or that which chops : a cleaver.—*n.* and *adj.* **chopp′ing.**—*ns.* **chopp′ing-block,** a block on which material to be chopped is placed ; **chopp′ing-knife,** a knife for chopping or mincing meat.—*adj.* **chopp′y,** full of chops or cracks : running in irregular waves (also **chopp′ing**).—**chop at,** to aim a blow at ; **chop in,** to break in, interrupt ; **chop up,** to cut into small pieces. [A form of **chap,** 1.]

chop, *chop, v.t.* and *v.i.* (*Milton*) to buy and sell, barter, or exchange : to change : to change direction (running into **chop,** 1).—*n.* an exchange : a change. —*n.* **chop′-log′ic,** chopping of logic : one who chops logic.—**chop and change,** to buy and sell : to change about : vicissitude ; **chop logic,** to argue contentiously. [Connexion with **chop,** 1 and with **chap,** 2 is not clear.]

chop, *chop, n.* the chap or jaw :—(in *pl.*) a person with fat cheeks : the mouth or jaws of anything, as a cannon or a vice.—*v.t.* to eat : *v.i.* to snap.—*adj.* **chop′-fallen,** lit. having the chop or lower jaw fallen down : cast-down : dejected. [See **chap** (3).]

chop, *chop, n.* in China and India, a seal : a brand : a sealed document.—**first chop,** best quality ; **no chop,** no good. [Hind. *chhāp,* seal, impression.]

chop-chop, *chop′-chop′, adv.* promptly. [Pidgin.]

chopin, *chop′in, n.* an old French liquid measure containing nearly an English imperial pint : a Scottish measure containing about an English quart. [O.Fr. *chopine,* Old Du. *schoppe*; Scot. *chappin,* Ger. *schoppen,* a pint.]

chopin, chopine, *chop-ēn′, chop′in, n.* a high clog or patten introduced into England from Venice during the reign of Elizabeth. [Sp. *chapin.*]

chopping, *chop′ing, adj.* stout, strapping, plump. [Perh. **chop,** 1.; cf. *thumping.*]

chop-sticks, *chop′-stiks, n.pl.* two small sticks used by the Chinese instead of a fork. [**chop-chop,** and **stick.**]

chop-suey, *chop-sōō′i, n.* a miscellaneous Chinese dish, fried in sesame-oil. [Chin., mixed bits.]

choragus, choregus, *ko-rā′gəs, -rē′gəs, n.* in Athens, the organiser of a chorus : the leader of a choir.—*adj.* **choragic, choregic,** (*-raj′, rāj′, -rēj′ik*). [Gr. *chorāgos, chorēgos—choros,* chorus, and *agein,* to lead.]

choral, chorale. See **chorus.**

chord, *kord, n.* (*mus.*) the simultaneous and harmonious union of sounds of a different pitch.— **common chord,** a note with its third and perfect fifth reckoned upwards. [From **accord.**]

chord, *kord, n.* a string of a musical instrument : (*fig.*) of the emotions : (*geom.*) a straight line joining any two points on a ′curve′ : a cord (see **spinal, vocal**):—*n.pl.* **Chordā′ta,** the highest phylum of the animal kingdom, including the vertebrates, ascidians, and Hemichordata—animals possessing a notochord.—*n.* **chor′date,** a member of the Chordata—Also *adj.* [Gr. *chordē,* a string, intestine.]

chore. See **char.**

chorea, *ko-rē′ä, n.* St. Vitus's dance, a nervous disease causing irregular involuntary movements of the limbs or face. [L.,—Gr. *choreiā,* a dance.]

choree, *kō′rē, n.* a trochee.—Also **chore′us.** [Gr. *choreios.*]

choreographer, etc. See **chorus.**

chorepiscopal, *kō-ri-pis′kə-pl, adj.* pertaining to a local or suffragan bishop. [Gr. *chōrā,* place, country.]

choriamb, *kor′i-amb, n.* a foot of four syllables, the first and last long, the others short.—*adj.* and *n.*

choriam'bic. [Gr. *choriambos—choreios*, a trochee, *iambos*, iambus.]

choric. See **chorus.**

chorion, *kō'ri-on, n.* the outer foetal envelope:— *pl.* **chō'ria.**—*adjs.* **chō'rioid ; chō'roid.**—Also *ns.* —**choroid** (**coat**) the vascular tunic of the eye, between the retina and the sclerotic. [Gr. *chorion.*]

chorisis, *kō'ris-is, n.* (*bot.*) multiplication of parts by branching.—*n.pl.* **chōripet'alae,** a series of dicotyledons having the petals separate if present at all.—*ns.* **chō'rizont, -zont'ist,** one who disputes identity of authorship, as of the *Iliad* and *Odyssey.* [Gr. *chōrisis*, separation, *chōrizōn, -ontos,* separating.]

chorography, *kō-rog'rə-fi, n.* geography : topography.—*adjs.* **chorographic** (*-ro-graf'ik*), **-al ; chorolog'ical.**—*ns.* **chorol'ogist ; chorol'ogy,** the science of geographical distribution. [Gr. *chōrā*, region, country.]

chortle, *chort'l, v.i.* to chuckle : to utter a low, deep laugh. [Coined by Lewis Carroll in 1872.]

chorus, *kō'ros, n.* a band of singers and dancers : in Greek plays, a number of persons who between the episodes danced, and chanted comment and counsel : a person who performs similar functions by himself : a company of singers : that which is sung by a chorus : the combination of voices in one simultaneous utterance : a refrain, in which the company may join : an obsolete kind of bagpipe.— *v.t.* to sing or say together :—*pr.p.* **chō'rusing ;** *pa.t.* and *pa.p.* **chō'rused.**—*adj.* **chōr'al,** pertaining to a chorus or a choir.—*n.* (*kō-räl'* ; often altered to **chorale'**), a simple harmonised composition with slow rhythm : a psalm or hymn tune : in R.C. usage, any part of the service sung by the whole choir.—*adv.* **chōr'ally,** in the manner of a chorus : suitable for a choir.—*n.* **choreographer** (*kor-i-og'rə-fər*).—*adj.* **choreograph'ic** (*-graf'ik*).—*ns.* **choreog'raphy, choreg'raphy,** the art, or the notation, of dancing, esp. ballet-dancing : the art of arranging dances, esp. ballets : the arrangement of a ballet.—*adj.* **choric** (*kor'ik, kō'rik*).—*ns.* **chorist** (*kor'ist, kō'rist*), **chōr'ister, quir'ister,** a member of a choir, **chor'us-girl,** a woman employed to sing or dance in a chorus on the stage. [L.,—Gr. *choros,* dance; see also **choir.**]

chose, chosen. See **choose.**

chota-hazri, *chō'tə-häz'ri, n.* (*Anglo-Indian*) early light breakfast. [Hind. *chhotī*, little, *hazrī*, breakfast.]

chough, *chuf, n.* the red-legged crow, or any bird of the genus *Fregilus* or *Pyrrhocorax* : (*obs.*) a jackdaw. [Perh. from its cry.]

chough. See **chuff.**

choultry. See **choltry.**

chouse, *chows, n.* (*obs.*) a cheat : one easily cheated : a trick.—*v.t.* to cheat, swindle. [Prob. from Turk. *chaush,* a messenger or envoy.]

chout, *chowt, n.* one-fourth part of the revenue, extorted by the Mahrattas as blackmail : blackmail, extortion. [Hind. *chauth,* the fourth part.]

chow-chow, *chow'chow,* shortened as **chow,** *n.* food : a Chinese mixed condiment : a dog of a Chinese breed.—*adj.* mixed, miscellaneous.—*n.* **Chow,** (*slang*) a Chinese. [Pidgin English, food.]

chowder, *chow'dər, n.* a dish made of a mixture of fish and biscuits. [Fr. *chaudière,* a pot.]

chowkidar. See **choky.**

chowry, *chow'ri, n.* an instrument used for driving away flies. [Hindi, *chaunri.*]

choy-root. See **chay** (2).

chremist, *krē'mə-tist, n.* a political economist.— *adj.* **chrematist'ic,** pertaining to finance, moneymaking, or political economy.—*n.* **chrematis'tics,** the science of wealth. [Gr. *chrēmatistēs,* a moneygetter—*chrēma, -atos,* a thing, possession, money.]

chrestomathy, *kres-tom'ə-thi, n.* a book of selections esp. in a foreign language, usu. for beginners.— *adjs.* **chrestomathic** (*-tō-math'ik*), **-al.** [Gr. *chrēstos,* useful, *mathein,* (aorist) to know.]

chrism, *krizm, n.* consecrated or holy oil : unction : confirmation : chrisom.—*adj.* **chris'mal,** pertaining to chrism.—*n.* a case for containing chrism : a ДУХ : a veil used in christening.—*ns.* **chris'ma-**

tory, a vessel for containing chrism; **chris'om, chris'om-cloth,** a white cloth or robe put on a child newly anointed with chrism after its baptism : the child itself.—**chrisom child** (*Shak.*), a child still wearing the chrisom-cloth : a child that died in its first month, buried in its chrisom-cloth : an innocent child. [O.Fr. *chresme* (Fr. *chrême*)—Gr. *chrisma—chriein,* to anoint.]

Christ, *krīst, n.* the Anointed, a name given to Jesus : a Messiah.—*ns.* **criss-, Christ-cross-row** (*kris'-kros-rō*), the alphabet, from the use in hornbooks of having a cross at the beginning; **Christ's-thorn,** a prickly shrub (*Paliurus Spina-Christi*), of the buckthorn family common in the Mediterranean region, from which the crown of thorns is fancied to have been made : a kind of jujube tree (*Zizyphus Spina-Christi*) with the like legend. —*v.t.* **christen** (*kris'n*), to baptise in the name of Christ : to give a name to.—*ns.* **Chris'tendom,** that part of the world in which Christianity is the received religion : the whole body of Christians; **chris'tening,** the ceremony of baptism; **Christ'-hood,** the condition of being the Christ or Messiah; **Christian** (*krist'yən*), a believer in the religion of Christ or one so classified : a follower of Christ : one whose behaviour is considered becoming to a follower of Christ : often a vague term of approbation, a decent, respectable, kindly, charitably minded person : (*coll.*) a human being.—*adj.* relating to Christ or his religion : in the spirit of Christ.—*v.t.* **christ'ianise,** to make Christian : to convert to Christianity.—*ns.* **Christ'ianism, Christianity** (*kris-ti-an'i-ti*), the religion of Christ : the spirit of this religion.—*adjs.* **Christ'ianlike, Christ'ianly.**—*ns.* **Christ'ianness ; Christ'ianness.** *adjs.* **Christ'less ; Christ'like ; Christ'ly,** like Christ.—**Christian era,** the era counted from the date formerly assigned to the birth of Christ; **Christian name,** the name given at christening : the personal name as distinguished from the surname; **Christian Science,** a religion which includes spiritual or divine healing, founded in 1866 by Mrs. Eddy; **Christian Scientist,** a believer in Christian Science; **Christian Socialism,** a mid-nineteenth century movement for applying Christian ethics to social reform : the principles of an Austrian Roman Catholic political party. [O.E. *Críst*—Gr. *Christos—chriein,* to anoint.]

Christadelphian, *kris-tə-del'fi-ən, n.* a member of a small religious body believing in conditional immortality—sometimes called *Thomasites* from Dr. John *Thomas,* of Brooklyn (1805-71). [Gr. *Christos,* Christ, and *adelphos,* brother.]

Christmas, *kris'mas, n.* an annual festival, orig. a mass, in memory of the birth of Christ, held on the 25th of December : the season at which it occurs : evergreens, esp. holly, for Christmas decoration.—Also *adj.*—*adj.* **Christ'mas(s)y,** savouring of Christmas.—*n.* **Christ'mas-tide, -time,** the season of Christmas.—**Christmas box,** a box containing Christmas presents : a Christmas gift; **Christmas card,** a card, more or less ornamented, sent from friend to friend at Christmas; **Christmas daisy,** the aster; **Christmas eve,** Dec. 24; **Christmas rose,** or **flower,** Helleborus niger, flowering in winter; **Christmas tree,** a tree, usu. fir, set up in a room or a public place, and loaded with Christmas gifts and/or gauds. [**Christ** and **mass.**]

Christolatry, *kris-tol'ə-tri, n.* worship of Christ. [Gr. *Christos,* Christ, *latreiā,* worship.]

Christology, *kris-tol'ə-ji, n.* that branch of theology which treats of the nature and person of Christ.— *adj.* **Christological** (*-to-loj'i-kl*).—*n.* **Christol'ogist.** [Gr. *Christos,* and *logos,* discourse.]

christom, *kriz'əm.* Same as **chrisom.**

christophany, *kris-tof'ə-ni, n.* an appearance of Christ to men. [Gr. *Christos,* and *phainesthai,* to appear.]

Christy-minstrel, *krist'i-min'strəl, n.* one of a troupe of minstrels imitating negroes, with bones, banjos, etc. [Instituted by George *Christy,* in New York.]

chroma, *krō'mä*, *n*. quality of colour : a hue.—*n.* **chrō'mate**, a salt of chromic acid.—*adj.* **chrōmat'ic**, pertaining to, or consisting of, colours : coloured : (*mus.*) relating to notes in a melodic progression, which are raised or lowered by accidentals, without changing the key of the passage, and also to chords in which such notes occur.—*ns.* **chrōmat'ics** (*pl.* in form), the science of colours ; **chrō'matin**, a readily stained substance in the nucleus of a cell ; **chrōmatog'raphy**, methods of separating substances in a mixture which depend on selective adsorption, partition between non-mixing solvents, etc., and which present the substances as a **chrōmat'ogram**, such as a series of visible bands in a vertical tube.—*adj.* **chrōmatographi'c**.—*ns.* **chrōmat'ophore** (*zool.*) a pigment-cell : (*bot.*) a plastid or pigment-bearing body in protoplasm ; **chrōmatop'sia** (Gr. *opsis*, sight), coloured vision ; **chrō'matype, chrō'motype**, a photographic process that uses chromium salts : a photograph in colours : a sheet printed in colour.—*ns.* **chrome**, chromium or a chromium compound.—Also *adj.*—*ns.* **chrome'-al'um**, potassium chromium sulphate ; **chrome'-leath'er**, leather prepared by chrome-tanning ; **chrome'-plating**, electroplating with chromium ; **chrome'-spinel**, picolite ; **chrome'-steel'**, an alloy steel containing chromium ; **chrome'-tann'ing**, tanning with salts of chromium ; **chrome'-yell'ow**, a pigment of lead chromate.—*adj.* **chrō'mic**, pertaining to trivalent chromium.—*n.* **chrōmid'ium**, an algal cell in a lichen : a free fragment of chromatin :—*pl.* **chrōmid'ia**.—*ns.* **chrō'mite**, a mineral, a double oxide of chromium and iron ; **chrō'mium**, a metal (at. numb. 24) remarkable for the beautiful colour of its compounds ; **chrō'mōgram**, a combination of photographs in different colours to give an image in natural colours ; **chrō'mō-lith'ograph**, or merely **chrō'mō**, a lithograph printed in colours ; **chrō'mōlithog'raphy** ; **chrō'mōplast** (*bot.*) a chromatophore ; **chrō'mōscope**, an apparatus for combining coloured images ; **chrō'mōsome**, a rod-like portion of the chromatin of a cell-nucleus, performing an important part in mitotic cell-division, and, it is believed, in the transmission of hereditary characters ; **chrō'mōsphere**, a layer of incandescent gas surrounding the sun through which the light of the photosphere passes—also **chrō'matosphere** ; **chrō'mō-typog'raphy**, printing in colours ; **chrō'mō-xy'lograph** (Gr. *xylon*, wood), a picture printed in colours from wooden blocks ; **chrō'mō-xylog'raphy**—**chromatic scale**, a scale proceeding by semitones ; **chromic acid**, an acid of chromium (H₂Cr O₄), of an orange-red colour, much used in dyeing and bleaching. [Gr. *chrōma*, *-atos* colour.]

chron-, chrono-, *kron'*, *-ō-*, *-ə-*, *krən-*, *kron-o'*, in composition, time.—*adj.* **chron'ic**, (*obs.*) relating to time : lasting a long time : of a disease, deep seated or long continued, as opp. to *acute* : (*slang*) deplorable.—*n.* a chronic invalid : (*slang*) a student who repeatedly fails in examinations.—*adj* **chron'ical**, chronic.—*adv.* **chron'ically**.—*n.* **chron'icle**, a bare record of events in order of time : a history : a story, account ; **Chronicles**, the name of two of the O.T. books.—*v.t.* to record as in a chronicle.—*ns.* **chron'icler**, a writer of a chronicle ; **chron'ogram** (Gr. *gramma*, letter), an inscription from which a date is got by adding the values of such letters as are Roman numerals ; **chron'ograph** (Gr. *graphein*, to write), a chronogram : an instrument for taking exact measurements of time, or for recording graphically the moment or duration of an event ; **chronog'rapher**, a chronicler ; **chronog'raphy**, chronology ; **chronol'oger**.—*adjs.* **chronolog'ic, -al**.—*adv.* **chronolog'ically**.—*ns.* **chronol'ogist** ; **chronol'ogy** (Gr. *logos*, discourse), the science of computing time : a scheme of time : order of time ; **chronom'eter** (Gr. *metron*, measure), an instrument for accurate measurement of time.—*adjs.* **chronomet'ric, -al**.—*ns.* **chronom'etry**, the art of measuring time by means of instruments : measurement of time ; **chron oscope** (Gr. *skopeein*, to look), an instru-

ment used for measuring extremely short intervals of time, especially in determining the velocity of projectiles.—**chronological age**, age in years, etc.—opp. e.g. to *mental age*. [Gr. *chronos*, time ; adj. *chronikos* ; partly through A.Fr. *cronicle* (O.Fr. *cronique*).]

chrys-, kris-, chryso-, *kris'ō-*, *-ə-*, *kris-ō'*, in composition, gold.—*ns.* **chrys'alid, chrys'alis** (Gr. *chrysallis*), orig. a golden-coloured butterfly pupa : a pupa generally : a pupa case :—*pl.* **chrysalides** (*kris-al'i-dēz*), **chrys'alises, chrys'alids**.—*ns.* **Chrysan'themum** (*kris-* or *kriz-* ; Gr. *anthemon* flower), a genus of composite plants to which belong the corn marigold and ox-eye daisy ; **chrysarō'bin** (see **araroba**), a yellow crystalline mixture got from Goa powder and from rhubarb root : also one of its components, an active purgative ; **chryselephant'ine** (Gr. *elephantinos*, made of ivory—*elephas*, *-antos*, ivory), made of gold and ivory ; **chrysober'yl**, a mineral, beryllium aluminate, of various shades of greenish-yellow or gold colour ; **chrysocoll'a** (Gr. *chrȳsokolla*, gold-solder, perh. applied to this mineral—*kolla*, glue), a silicate of copper, bluish-green ; **chrysoc'racy** (Gr. *krateein*, to rule), the rule of wealth ; **chrys'olite** (Gr. *lithos*, stone), olivine, esp. yellow or green precious olivine ; **chrys'ophan** (Gr. *phainesthai*, to appear), an old name for chrysarobin.—*adj.* **chrysophan'ic** (**chrysophanic acid**, an oxidation product of chrysarobin used against skin diseases).—*ns.* **chrysoph'ilite** (Gr. *phileein*, to love), a lover of gold ; **chrys'oprase** (*-prāz* ; Gr. *prason*, a leek), a green chalcedony ; **chrys'otile** (Gr. *tilos*, a shred), a fibrous serpentine. [Gr. *chrȳsos*, gold.]

chthonian, *thō'ni-ən*, *adj.* pertaining to the earth or the underworld.—Also **chthonic** (*thon'ik*). [Gr. *chthōn*, *chthonos*, the ground.]

chub, *chub*, *n.* a small fat river-fish of the carp family.—*adjs.* **chubbed, chubb'y**, short and thick, plump ; **chub'-faced**, plump-faced.—*n.* **chubb'iness**. [Origin unknown.]

Chubb, *chub*, *n.* a lock invented by *Chubb*, a locksmith in London.—Also **chubb'-lock**. [Registered trade-mark.]

chuck, *chuk*, *n.* the call of a hen : a chicken (dim. **chuck'ie**) : a word of endearment.—*v.i.* to call, as a hen. [A variant of **cluck**.]

chuck, *chuk*, *n.* a gentle blow under the chin : (*coll.*) a toss or throw, hence dismissal : a pebble or small stone (usu. **chuck'ie, chuck'ie-stone, -stane**) : (in *pl.*) a game with such stones, often called **chuck'ies** : any game of pitch and toss.—*v.t.* to tap under the chin : to toss : to pitch : to abandon or dismiss.—*ns.* **chuck'er-out**, one who expels undesirable people ; **chuck'-far'thing**, a game in which a farthing is chucked into a hole.—**chuck it** (*coll.*), stop, give over ; **chuck up** (*coll.*), to give up : to give in : to throw up (the sponge). [Fr. *choquer*, to jolt : allied to **shock**.]

chuck, *chuk*, *n.* a lump or chunk : an instrument for holding an object so that it can be rotated, as upon the mandrel of a lathe : (*slang*) food.—**chuck'-wagon**, a wagon carrying food, cooking apparatus, etc. [Der. uncertain ; cf. It. *cioco*, a block, stump.]

chuck-full. Same as **chock-full**. [See **chock**.]

chuckle, *chuk'l*, *n.* a quiet laugh : the cry of a hen.—*v.t.* to call, as a hen does her chickens.—*v.i.* to laugh in a quiet, suppressed manner, in derision or enjoyment.—*n.* **chuck'ling**. [Cf. **chuck** (1).]

chuckle, *chuk'l*, *adj.* clumsy.—*n.* **chuck'le-head**, a loutish fellow. [Prob. **chock**, a log.]

chuddar, chuddah, *chud'ä(r)*, *n.* (*Anglo-Ind.*) a sheet worn as a shawl or cloak by the women of northern India : a cloth spread on a Mohammedan tomb. [Hind. *chadar*, a square of cloth.]

chufa, *chōō'fä*, *n.* a sedge with edible tubers. [Sp.]

chuff, *chuf*, *n.* a clown : a surly fellow.—*n.* **chuff'iness**, boorishness.—*adj.* **chuff'y**, coarse and surly. [M.E. *chuffe, choffe*, a boor (ety. dub.).]

chukker, chukka, *chuk'ər*, *-ä*, *n.* a period of play in polo. [Hind. *chakar*, a round.]

chukor, *chu-kor'*, **chukar**, *-kär'*, **chik(h)or**, *chi-kor'*, *n.* an Indian partridge. [Hind. *chakor*.]

chum, *chum*, *n.* a chamber-fellow : a friend or associate.—*v.i.* to share a room : to be or become a chum.—*v.t.* to assign as chum (with *on*) : to be or become a chum to : to accompany.—*n.* **chumm'-age**, the quartering of two or more persons in one room : a fee demanded from a new chum.— *adj.* **chumm'y**, sociable.—*n.* a chum : a compact motor-car body for a small company.—**chum up with**, to become intimate with. [Perh. a mutilation of **chamber-fellow**.]

chum, *chum*, *n.* a dog-salmon or keta.

chummy, *chum'i*, *n.* (*old slang*) a chimney sweeper's boy. (**chimney**.]

chump, *chump*, *n.* an end lump of wood, mutton, etc. : a thick lump : a blockhead : the head.—**off his chump**, out of his mind. [Perh. related to **chunk**.]

chunk, *chungk*, *n.* a thick piece of anything, as wood, bread, etc. [Perh. related to **chuck**.]

chupati, **chupattie**, **chupatty**, *chup-ät'i*, *n.* a thin cake of unleavened bread. [Hind. *chapāti.*]

chuprassy, *chup-räs'i.* Same as **chaprassi.**

church, *church*, *n.* a house set apart for public worship, esp. that of a parish, and esp. that of an established or once established form of religion : a church service : the whole body of Christians : the clergy : any particular sect or denomination of Christians : any body professing a common creed, not necessarily Christian.—*adj.* of the church : ecclesiastical.—*v.t.* to perform a service in church with (e.g. a woman after childbirth, a newly-married couple, a new town council).—*ns.* **church'-ale**, a church festival; **church'-bench** (*Shak.*), a seat in the porch of a church; **church'-court**; a court for deciding ecclesiastical causes : a kirk session : a presbytery, synod, or general assembly; **church'-goer**, one who habitually goes to church; **church'-going**, the act or habit of going to church; **churchian'ity**, religion centring in the church rather than in Christ; **church'ing**; **church'ism**, adherence to the form or principles of some church, esp. established.—*adjs.* **church'-less**, not belonging to a church : (*Tennyson*) without church approval; **church'ly**, concerned with the church : ecclesiastical; *ns.* **church'man**, a clergyman or ecclesiastic : a member or upholder of the established church; **church'-mouse**, a mouse inhabiting a church, a proverbial type of poverty; **church'-off'icer**, a church attendant or beadle; **church'-parade**, military parade for the purpose of church-going : promenade of fashionable church-goers after service; **church'-rate**, an assessment for the sustentation of the fabric, etc., of the parish church; **church'-ser'vice**, a religious service in a church : the form followed, a book containing it; **church'-text**, a thin and tall form of black-letter print.—*advs.* **church'ward**, **-s.**— *ns.* **church'-war'den**, an officer who represents the interests of a parish or church : a long clay-pipe; **church'way**, the public way or road that leads to the church.—Also *adj.* (*Shak.*).—*n.* **church'woman**, a female member or upholder of a church, esp. the Anglican Church.—*adj.* **church'y**, obtrusively devoted to the church : savouring of church.—*n.* **church'yard**, a burial-ground round a church.—**Church Army**, an organisation of the Church of England, resembling the Salvation Army; **church militant**, the church on earth in its struggle against evil; **church triumphant**, the portion of the church which has overcome and left this world. [O.E. *cirice, circe*— Gr. *kȳriakon*, belonging to the Lord—*kȳrios*, lord.]

churinga, *choo-ring'gä*, *n.* a stone amulet. [Austr.]

churl, *churl*, *n.* a rustic, labourer : an ill-bred, surly fellow.—*adj.* **churl'ish**, rude : surly : ungracious.—*adv.* **churl'ishly**.—*n.* **churl'ishness**. [O.E. *ceorl*, a countryman; O.N. *karl*, Ger. *kerl*, a man; Scot. *carl*.]

churn, *churn*, *n.* a machine used for the production of butter from cream or from whole milk : a large milk-can suggestive of an upright churn.—*v.t.* to agitate so as to obtain butter.—*v.i.* to perform the act of churning.—*ns.* **churn'-drill**, a drill worked by hand, not struck with the hammer, a jumper; **churn'ing**, the act of making butter : the quantity of butter made at once; **churn'-milk**, butter-milk; **churn'-staff**, the plunger of an upright

churn : the sun-spurge. [O.E. *cyrin*; O.N. *kirna*, a churn, Du. *karnen*, and Ger. *kernen*, to churn.]

churn-owl, *churn'-owl*, *n.* the night-jar. [App. **churr** and **owl**.]

churr, *chur*, *n.* a low sound made by certain birds and insects.—*v.i.* to make this sound.—*n.* **churr'-worm**, the fen-cricket. [Prob. imit.]

churrus, **charas**, *chur'us*, *n.* the resinous exudation of hemp, a narcotic and intoxicant. [Hind. *charas.*]

chuse, *chōōz*, an obs. spelling of **choose**.

chut, *chut*, *interj.* an expression of impatience.

chute, **shoot**, *shōōt*, *n.* a waterfall, rapid : a passage or sloping trough for sending down goods, water, logs, rubbish, etc. ; a narrow passage for controlling cattle. [Fr. *chute*, fall, combined with **shoot**.]

chutney, *chut'ni*, *n.* an East Indian condiment, of mangoes, chillies, etc. ; an imitation made with home materials, as apples. [Hind. *chatni.*]

chyle, *kīl*, *n.* a white fluid, mainly lymph mixed with fats derived from food in the body.—*n.* **chylū'ria** (Gr. *ouron*, urine), presence of chyle in the urine. [Gr. *chȳlos*, juice—*cheein*, to pour.]

chyme, *kīm*, *n.* the pulp to which the food is reduced in the stomach.—*n.* **chymifica'tion**, the act of being formed into chyme.—*v.t.* **chym'ify**, to form into chyme.—*adj.* **chym'ous**. [Gr. *chȳmos*, chyme, juice—*cheein*, to pour.]

chymical, chymistry. See **chemical, chemistry.**

chynd, *chīnd*, *p.adj.* (*Spens.*) cut into chines.

chypre, *shē'pr'*, *n.* a scent from Cyprus. [Fr., Cyprus.]

cibation, *si-bā'shən*, *n.* (*obs*) the seventh of the twelve processes employed in the search for the philosopher's stone, 'feeding the matter'; taking food, feeding. [L. *cibātiō, -ōnis*, feeding.]

cibol, *sib'əl*, **chibol**, *chib'əl*, *n.* a variety of onion. [Fr. *ciboule* (Sp. *cebolla*—L.L. *cēpola*, dim. of L. *cēpa*, an onion; see **sybo(w)**).]

ciborium, *si-bō'ri-əm*, *n.* (*R.C.*) a vessel nearly resembling a chalice, with an arched cover, in which the host is deposited : a canopy supported on four pillars over the high altar :—*pl.* **cibō'ria**. [L., a drinking-cup—Gr. *kibōrion*, the seed-vessel of the Egyptian water-lily.]

cicada, *si-kä'dä, -kä'dä*, **cicala**, *-kä'lä*, *n.* homopterous insect remarkable for its loud chirping sound. [L. *cicāda*; It. *cicala.*]

cicatrix, *sik-ā'triks*, or *sik'ə-triks*, **cicatrice**, *sik'ə-tris*, *ns.* a scar over a healed wound : scar in the bark of a tree : mark left where a leaf, etc., has been attached : (*Shak.*) mark, impression; *pl.* **cicatri'cēs**; **cic'atrixes**.—*ns.* **cicatric'ula**, the germinating point in the yolk of an egg; **cicatrīsa'-tion**, the process of healing over.—*v.t.* **cic'atrise**, to help the formation of a cicatrix on : to scar.— *v.i.* to heal. [L. *cicātrīx, -īcis*, a scar.]

cicely, *sis'ə-li*, *n.* a name for several umbelliferous plants allied to chervil, esp. *Myrrhis odorata* (**sweet cicely**). [L. and Gr. *seseli.*]

Cicero, *sis'ə-rō* (L. *kik-e-rō*), *n.* a famous Roman orator : **cicero**, a type-body between pica and English.—*n* **cicerone** (*chich-ə-rō'nä*, also *sis-ə-rō'ni*), one who shows strangers the curiosities of a place : a guide :—*pl.* **ciceroni** (*-nē*).—*v.i.* to act as cicerone.—*adjs.* **Cicero'nian** (*sis-*), **Ciceronic** (*-ron'ik*).—*n.* **Cicero'nianism**, the character of Cicero's Latin style. [L. *Cicerō, -ōnis*; It. *Cicerone.*]

cichlid, *sik'lid*, *n.* any fish of the family **cich'lidae**, to which the angel-fish of the Amazon belongs.— *adj.* **cich'loid**. [Gr. *kichlē*, a kind of wrasse.]

Cichorium, *si-kō'ri-əm*, *n.* the chicory and endive genus of Compositae.—*adj.* **cichorā'ceous**. [L. *cichōrium*—Gr. *kichorion.*]

Cicindela, *si-sin-dē'lä*, *n.* a genus of carnivorous beetles, type of the family **Cicinde'lidae**, the tiger-beetles, active in running down their insect prey. [L. *cicindēla*, glow-worm—*candēla*, a candle.]

cicinnus, *si-sin'əs*, *n.* a cincinnus. [Latinised from Gr. *kinkinnos*, a ringlet.]

cicisbeo, *chē-chēz-bā'ō*, *n.* a married woman's gallant or *cavaliere servente* in Italy :—*pl.* **cicisbe'i** (*-ē*).—*n.* **cicisbe'ism**. [It.]

ciclaton, ciclatoun, *sik'lə-tən, -tōōn, n. (obs.)* cloth of gold or other rich stuff: misunderstood by Spenser (see **checklaton**). [O.Fr. *ciclaton*, from Ar., perh. from the root of **scarlet.**]

Cicuta, *si-kū'tä, n.* a genus of poisonous umbelliferous plants—*water-hemlock* or *cowbane*. [L. *cicūta*, hemlock.]

Cid, *sid, n.* a chief, captain, hero—title of the 11th-cent. Castilian champion Rodrigo, or Ruy, Diaz. [Ar. *sayyid*, lord.]

cidaris, *sid'ə-ris, n.* a Persian tiara: **Cidaris,** a genus of sea-urchins, mostly fossil. [Gr. *kidaris.*]

cide, *sid, v.t.* a proposed emendation for Shakespeare's **side** (q.v.), as if aphetic for **decide,** adjudge.

cider (sometimes **cyder**), *si'dər, n.* a drink made from apples.—*ns.* **ci'der-and,** a mixture of cider and other spirits; **ci'der-cup,** a drink of sweetened cider, with other ingredients; **ci'derkin,** an inferior cider.—*adj.* **ci'dery.** [Fr. *cidre*—L.—Gr. *sikera*, strong drink—Heb. *shēkar.*]

ciel, a variant of **ceil.**

cierge. See **cerge.**

cigar, *si-gär', n.* a roll of tobacco-leaves with a pointed end for smoking.—*ns.* **cigarette** (*sig-ə-ret'*), finely-cut tobacco rolled in thin paper (contr. **cig**); **cigarette'-card',** a picture card given away with a packet of cigarettes, much valued by youthful collectors; **cigarette'-holder,** a mouthpiece for a cigarette; **cigarette'-lighter,** a mechanical contrivance for lighting cigarettes: **cigarette'-paper,** paper for making cigarettes; **cigar'-tree,** a species of Catalpa with long cigar-like pods. [Sp. *cigarro.*]

cilice, *sil'is, n.* haircloth: a penitential garment made of haircloth.—*adj.* **cilic'ious.** [L.,—Gr. *kilikion,* a cloth made of Cilician goat's hair.]

cilium, *sil'i-əm, n.* a hair-like lash borne by a cell: a flagellum:—*pl.* **cil'ia.**—*adj.* **cil'iary.**—*n.pl.* **Cilia'ta,** a subclass of Infusoria retaining cilia throughout life.—*adjs.* **cil'iate, -d,** bearing a cilium or cilia: fringed with hairs; **cil'iolate,** fringed with very short fine hairs.—*n.pl.* **Cilioph'ora** (Gr. *phoros,* bearing), the Infusoria. [L. *cilium,* eyelash.]

cimar. See **cymar, chimer.**

cimelia, *si-mē'li-ä, n.pl.* treasures. [Gr. *keimēlia.*]

Cimex, *si'meks, n.* the bed-bug genus of Hemiptera, giving name to the family **cimicidae** (*si-* or *si-mis'i-dē*).

cimier, *sē-myä', n.* the crest of a helmet. [Fr.]

ciminite, *sim'in-īt, n.* a rock intermediate between trachyte and andesite, containing olivine. [Monte *Cimini,* in Italy.]

Cimmerian, *sim-ē'ri-ən, adj.* relating to the Cimmerii, a tribe fabled to have lived in perpetual darkness.

cimolite, *sim'ō-līt, n.* a species of clay, or hydrous silicate of aluminium, used as fuller's earth. [Gr. *kimōliā,* prob. from *Kimōlos,* an island of the Cyclades.]

cinch, *sinch, n. (U.S.)* a saddle-girth: (coll.) a certainty, a secure hold.—*v.i.* to tighten the cinch. [Sp. *cincha*—L. *cingula.*]

Cinchona, *sing-kō'nä,* a rubiaceous genus of trees, yielding the bark from which quinine and its congeners are obtained—also called *Peruvian bark.* —*adjs.* **cinchonaceous** (*-kən-ā'shəs*), **cinchonic** (*-kon'ik*).—*n.* **cinch'onine,** an alkaloid obtained from cinchona bark.—*adj.* **cinchonin'ic.**—*n.* **cinchonīsa'tion.**—*v.t.* **cinch'onise,** to bring under the influence of cinchona or quinine.—*n.* **cinch'onism,** a morbid state due to overdoses of cinchona or quinine. [Said to be so named from the Countess of *Chinchón,* who was cured of a fever by it in 1638.]

cincinnus, *sin-sin'əs, n. (bot.)* a uniparous cymose inflorescence in which the plane of each daughter axis is at right angles, alternately to right and left, with that of its parent axis.—*adj.* **cincinn'ate.** [L., a curl.]

cincture, *singk'tyər, n.* a girdle or belt: a moulding round a column.—*v.t.* to gird, encompass.—*adjs.* **cinct,** surrounded; **cinc'tured,** having a cincture. [L. *cinctūra*—*cingĕre, cinctum,* to gird.]

cinder, *sin'dər, n.* the refuse of burned coals: an ember: anything charred by fire: a scoriaceous fragment of lava: (slang) a strong stimulant put in tea, soda-water, etc.—*ns.* **cin'der-cone,** a hill of loose volcanic materials; **Cinderell'a,** a scullery-maid: the despised and neglected one of a set; **Cinderel'la-dance,** a dancing-party ending at midnight—from the nursery tale; **cin'der-path,** **-track,** a path, racing-track, laid with cinders.—*adj.* **cin'dery.** [O.E. *sinder,* slag; cf. Gr. *sinter;* not connected with Fr. *cendre.*]

cinematograph, *sin-i-mat'ə-gräf, n.* apparatus for projecting a series of instantaneous photographs or pictures so as to give a moving representation of a scene, with or without reproduction of sound: a camera for taking such photographs (*cinematograph camera*): an exhibition of such photographs or pictures: a building in which they are shown.— Also **kinemat'ograph** (*kin', kīn'*). Shortened familiarly to **cin'ema, kin'ema** (or *kin-ē'mä, kīn'i-mä*), and in composition **cine-** (*sin'i-*); sometimes **ciné-**).—*ns.* **ciné-biology,** the study of biological phenomena by means of cinematographic records; **cin'ema-or'gan,** a theatre-organ, an organ of greater adaptability and showier effects than a church or concert organ.—*adj.* **cinemat'ic,** pertaining to, suitable for, or savouring of the cinema.—*n.* **cinematographer** (*-mə-tog'rə-fər*).—*adjs.* **cinematographic** (*-graf'ik*), **-al.** —*ns.* **cinematog'raphist; cinematog'raphy.** [Fr. *cinématographe*—Gr. *kinēma, -atos,* motion, *graphein,* to write, represent.]

cineol, -ole, *sin'i-ol, -ōl, n.* eucalyptol, a camphor-smelling disinfectant liquid ($C_{10}H_{18}O$) got from several essential oils, as eucalyptus, wormwood, cajeput. [From *Artemisia Cina,* a species of wormwood, and L. *oleum,* oil.]

Cineraria, *sin-ə-rā'ri-ä, n.* a South African genus of plants, close akin to Senecio, with ashy down on the leaves. [L. *cinerārius,* ashy—*cinis, cineris,* ash.]

cinerary, *sin'ə-rə-ri, adj.* pertaining to ashes: for containing ashes of the dead.—*ns.* **cinerā'tion;** **cinerāt'or; ciné'rea,** grey nerve matter.— **ciné'real,** ashy: cinerary; **ciné'reous,** ashy-grey: ashy; **cineri'tious,** ashy-grey: pertaining to grey nerve matter. [L. *cinereus,* ashy—*cinis, cineris,* ash.]

Cingalese. See **Sinhalese.**

cingulum, *sing'gū-ləm, n.* a girdle: a girdle-like structure. [L.—*cingĕre,* to gird.]

cinnabar, *sin'ə-bär, n.* a mineral, sulphide of mercury, called vermilion when used as a pigment. —*adj.* **vermilion-coloured.**—*adjs.* **cinnabaric** (*-bar'ik*), **cinn'abarine** (*-bə-rēn*).—**cinnabar moth,** a large red moth whose black and yellow caterpillars feed on ragwort. [Gr. *kinnabari,* from Persian.]

cinnamon, *sin'ə-mən, n.* the spicy bark of a lauraceous tree of Ceylon: the tree: a light yellowish brown.—Also *adj.*—*adjs.* **cinnamic** (*-am'ik*), **cinnamonic** (*-ə-mon'ik*), obtained from, or consisting of, cinnamon.—*ns.* **cinn'amon-bear,** a cinnamon-coloured variety of grizzly or American black bear; **cinna'mon-stone,** a yellowish grossular garnet. [Gr. *kinnamōmon,* later *kinnamon*— Heb. *qinnāmōn.*]

cinque, *singk, n.* the number five as on dice.—*ns.* **cinque-foil** (*her.*), a common bearing representing a flower with five petals borne full-faced and without a stalk: (*arch.*) a similar figure formed by cusps in a circular window or the head of a pointed arch: (*bot.*) species of the genus *Potentilla:* the five-bladed clover; **cinque'-pace** (*Shak.* also **sinke'-a-pace**), a kind of dance, the pace or movement of which is characterised by five beats. —*adj.* **cinque'-spott'ed** (*Shak*), having five spots.— **Cinque Ports,** the five ancient ports on the south of England lying opposite to France—Sandwich, Dover, Hythe, Romney, and Hastings (later associated with Winchelsea, Rye, and a number of subordinate ports). [Fr.]

cinque-cento *ching'kwe-chen-tō, n.* the 16th century —the art and architecture of the Renaissance period. [It., five hundred, *mil,* one thousand, being understood.]

cion, a spelling of **scion** still used in U.S.

cipher (sometimes **cypher**), *sī′fər*, *n.* (*arith.*) the character 0 : any of the Arabic numerals : any person or thing of little value : a nonentity : an interweaving of the initials of a name : a secret mode of writing : in an organ, continuous sounding of a note not played.—*v.i.* to work at arithmetic : of an organ, to sound a note continuously when it is not played.—*v.t.* to write in cipher : to calculate : (*Shak.*), to decipher.—*ns.* **ci′phering**; **ci′pher-key**, a key to a cipher or piece of secret writing. [O.Fr. *cyfre*, Fr. *chiffre*—Ar. *çifr*, zero, empty.]

cipollino, *chē-pol-lē′nō*, *n.* a marble with green bands in which calcite is interfoliated with mica or talc.—Also **cipolin** (*sip′ō-lin*). [It.,—*cipolla*, an onion.]

cippus, *sip′əs*, *n.* the stocks : a monumental pillar :—*pl.* **cipp′i.** [L. *cippus*, a post.]

circa, *sər′kä*, *prep.* and *adv.* about, around. [L.]

Circaean, *sər-sē′ən*, *adj.* relating to the beautiful sorceress Circe, who transformed the companions of Ulysses into swine by a magic beverage: infatuating and degrading.—Also **Circe′an.**—*n.* **Circae′a**, the enchanter's nightshade genus. [L. *Circē*—Gr. *Kirkē.*]

circar. Same as **sircar.**

Circassian, *sər-kas(h)′yən*, *adj.* belonging to *Circassia*, the country of the *Tcherkesses*, in the western Caucasus.—*n.* a Tcherkess : the language of the Tcherkesses : **circassian**, a kind of light cashmere (also **circassienne′**).

circensian, *sər-sen′shi-ən*, *adj.* relating to the Circus Maximus in Rome, where the games and contests were held.—Also **circen′sial** (*obs.*). [L. *circēnsis*—*circus.*]

circinate, *sər′sin-āt*, *adj.* ring-shaped : (*bot.*) rolled inwards. [L. *circināre*, *-ātum*, to make round.]

circle, *sər′kl*, *n.* a plane figure bounded by one line every point of which is equally distant from a fixed point called the centre : the circumference of the figure so defined : a circular object : a ring : a planet's orbit : a series ending where it began : a figure in magic : a group of things in a circle : a company surrounding or associating with the principal person : those of a certain class or group. —*v.t.* to move round : to encompass.—*v.i.* to move in a circle : to stand in a circle.—*adj.* **cir′cled,** circular : encircled.—*ns.* **cir′cler**; **cir′cle-rider,** one who rides in circles to round up cattle; **cir′cle-riding**; **cir′clet,** a little circle : a little circular band or hoop, esp. a metal headband.—*n.* and *adj.* **cir′cling**, moving in a circle.—**dress circle** (see **dress**); **fairy circle** (see **fairy**); **great, small, circle,** a circle on the surface of a sphere whose centre is, is not, the centre of the sphere; **reasoning in a circle,** assuming what is to be proved as the basis of the argument. [O.E. *circul*— L. *circulus*, dim. of *circus;* allied to O.E. *hring*, a ring.]

circs, *sərks*, *n.pl.* a slang contraction of **circumstances.**

circuit, *sər′kit*, *n.* a journey round : a way round : perimeter : a roundabout way : area enclosed : the path of an electric current : a round made in the exercise of a calling, esp. by judges : the judges making the round : a district in which such a round is made, as by Methodist preachers, commercial travellers : a group of theatres, cinemas etc., under common control, through which an entertainment circulates : (*Shak.*) diadem.—*v.t.* to go round.—*ns.* **cir′cuit-breaker,** a switch or other device for interrupting an electric circuit; **cir′cuiteer′,** a judge who goes on a circuit.—*adj.* **circuitous** (*-kū′i-təs*), round-about.—*adv.* **circū′itously.** — *ns.* **circū′itousness**; **cir′cuit-ri′der,** a preacher who goes on circuit; **circū′ity,** motion in a circle : an indirect course. [Fr.,—L. *circuitus*—*circuīre, circum*, round, *īre*, to go.]

circular, *sər′kū-lər*, *adj.* of or pertaining to a circle : in the form of a circle : round : ending in itself : recurring in a cycle : addressed to a circle of persons.—*n.* an intimation sent to a number of persons.—*v.t.* **cir′cularise**, to make circular : to send circulars to.—*n.* **circularity** (*-lar′i-ti*).—*adv.* **cir′cularly.**—**circular function,** any of the trigonometrical functions with argument in radians; **circular letter,** a letter of which copies are sent to several persons; **circular measure,** the reckoning of angles in radians; **circular note,** a letter of bank-credit for the use of a traveller,being a kind of bill personal to the bearer, who also bears a letter of indication addressed to foreign bankers. [L. *circulāris.*]

circulate, *sər′kū-lāt*, *v.t.* to make to go round as in a circle : to spread.—*v.i.* to move round : to be spread about : to repeat in definite order (of decimals).—*adj.* **cir′culable,** capable of being circulated.—*n.* and *adj.* **cir′culating.**—*ns.* **circulā′tion**, the act of moving in a circle or in a closed path (as the blood) : spreading or moving about : dissemination : the sale of a periodical : the money in use at any time in a country.—*adjs.* **cir′culātive**, **cir′culatory**, circulating.—*n.* **cir′culātor.**—**circulating library,** one from which books are circulated among subscribers. [L. *circulāre*, *-ātum.*]

circum-, *sər′kəm-*, *sər-kum′-*, *pfx.* around. [L. *circum.*]

circumambages, *sər-kəm-am-bā′jēz*, *-am′bi-jiz*, *n. sing.* and *pl.* roundabout speech.—*adj.* **circumambā′gious** (*-jəs*), roundabout in speech. [L. *ambāgēs*, a winding.]

circumambient, *sər-kəm-am′bi-ənt*, going round about, encompassing.—*ns.* **circumam′bience**, **circumam′biency.** [L. *ambīre*, to go round.]

circumambulate, *sər-kəm-am′bū-lāt*, *v.i.* to walk round about.—*n.* **circumambulā′tion.** [L. *ambulāre*, *-ātum*, to walk.]

circumbendibus, *sər-kəm-ben′di-bəs*, *n.* a roundabout way or expression. [Jocular formation from L. *circum*, round, *bend*, and L. abl. pl. ending *-ibus.*]

circumcentre, *sər′kəm-sen-tər*, *n.* the centre of the circumscribed circle or sphere.

circumcise, *sər′kəm-sīz*, *v.t.* to cut off the foreskin or the labia minora of : (*fig.*) to purify.—*ns.* **cir′cumciser**; **circumcision** (*-sizh′n*), the act of circumcising : the state of being circumcised : those who are circumcised, esp. the Jews. [L. *circumcīdĕre*, *-cīsum*—*caedĕre*, to cut.]

circumdenudation, *sər-kəm-den-ū-dā′shən*, *n.* (*geol.*) denudation or erosion of surroundings, leaving an isolated elevation.

circumduct, *sər′kəm-dukt*, *v.t.* to lead around or about, to cause to revolve round an imaginary axis so as to describe a cone.—*v.t.* **circumduce** (*-dūs′*) (*Scots law*) to declare at an end (of the term for bringing proof).—*n.* **circumduc′tion.**—*adj.* **circumduct′ory.** [L. *dūcĕre*, *ductum*, to lead.]

circumference, *sər-kum′fər-əns*, *n.* the boundary-line, esp. of a circle : compass : distance round.—*adj.* **circumferential** (*-en′shl*).—*n.* **circum′ferentor** (*-en-tər*), an instrument for measuring horizontal angles, consisting of a graduated circle, sights, and a magnetic needle : a graduated wheel for measuring the circumference of wheels. [L. *ferre*, to carry.]

circumflect, *sər-kəm-flekt′*, *v.t.* to bend round : to mark with a circumflex.—*ns.* **cir′cumflex**, an accent (∧) originally denoting a rising and falling of the voice on a vowel or syllable—also *adj.*; **circumflexion** (*-flek′shən*), a bending round. [L. *flectĕre, flexum*, to bend.]

circumfluence, *sər-kum′floo-əns*, *n.* a flowing round : the engulfing of food by surrounding it (as by protozoa, etc.).—*adjs.* **circum′fluent, circum′fluous.** [L. *fluĕre*, to flow.]

circumforaneous, *sər-kəm-fō-rā′ni-əs*, *adj.* wandering about as from market to market, vagrant.— Also **circumfora′nean.** [L. *forum*, the forum, market-place.]

circumfuse, *sər-kəm-fūz′*, *v.t.* to pour around.— *p.adj.* **circumfused′.**—*adj.* **circumfus′ile**, molten. —*n.* **circumfusion** (*-fū′zhən*). [L. *fundĕre, fūsum*, to pour.]

circumgyrate, *sər-kəm-jī′rāt*, *v.i.* to whirl round.— *n.* **circumgyrā′tion.**—*adj.* **circumgy′ratory.** [L. *gyrāre*, *-ātum*, to turn.]

circumjacent, *sər-kəm-jā′sənt*, *adj.* lying round: bordering on every side.—*n.* **circumjā′cency.** [L. *jacēns*, *-ēntis*, lying—*jacēre*, to lie.]

circumlittoral, *sər-kəm-lit'ō-rəl*, *adj.* adjacent to the shore-line. [L. *littus*, for *litus*, *-oris*, shore.]

circumlocution, *sər-kəm-lō-kū'shən*, *n.* roundabout speaking.—*v.i.* **circumlocute'**, to use circumlocution.—*n.* **circumlocū'tionist**, one who practises circumlocution.—*adj.* **circumlocutory** (*-lok'ū-tər-i*).—**Circumlocution Office**, in Dickens's *Little Dorrit*, a government department, dilatory in attending to business. [L. *loquī*, *locūtus*, to speak.]

circummure, *sər-kəm-mūr'*, *v.t.* (*Shak.*) to wall round. [L. *mūrus*, a wall.]

circumnavigate, *sər-kəm-nav'i-gāt*, *v.t.* to sail round.—*adj.* **circumnav'igable**.—*ns.* **circumnavigā'tion**; **circumnav'igator**. [**navigate**.]

circumnutation, *sər-kəm-nū-tā'shən*, *n.* rotation in a nodding position, as in the growing point of a plant.—*v.i.* **circumnū'tate**.—*adj.* **circumnū'tatory**. [L. *nūtāre*, *-ātum*, to nod.]

circumpolar, *sər-kəm-pō'lər*, *adj.* situated or ranging round the pole.—**circumpolar stars**, stars so near the pole of the heavens that (for places at the latitude in question) they never set but merely revolve round the pole. [See **polar**.]

circumpose, *sər-kəm-pōz'*, *v.t.* to place round.—*n.* **circumposi'tion**, the act of placing round. [See **position**.]

circumscissile, *sər-kəm-sis'il*, *adj.* opening by a circular rent. [L. *scissilis*, cleavable.]

circumscribe, *sər-kəm-skrīb'*, *v.t.* to draw a line round: to describe a curve or figure touching externally: to enclose within certain limits, to curtail, abridge.—*adj.* **circumscrīb'able**, able to be circumscribed.—*ns.* **circumscrīb'er**, one who circumscribes; **circumscription** (*-skrip'shən*), limitation: the line that limits: the act of circumscribing: an inscription running round: a defined district.—*adj.* **circumscrip'tive**, marking the external form or outline. [L. *scrībĕre*, *scrīptum*, to write.]

circumspect, *sər'kəm-spekt*, *adj.* looking round on all sides watchfully: cautious: prudent.—*n.* **circumspec'tion**, watchfulness: caution: examining.—*adj.* **circumspec'tive**, looking around: wary.—*adv.* **cir'cumspectly**.—*n.* **cir'cumspectness**. [L. *specĕre*, *spıcĕre*, *spectum*, to look.]

circumstance, *sər'kəm-stəns*, *n.* the logical surroundings of an action: an attendant fact: an accident or event: ceremony: detail: (*pl.*) the state of one's affairs.—*v.t.* to place in particular circumstances.—*adj.* **circumstantial** (*-stan'shl*), consisting of details: minute.—*n.* **circumstantiality** (*-stan-shi-al'i-ti*), the quality of being circumstantial: minuteness in details: a detail.—*adv.* **circumstan'tially**.—*n.pl.* **circumstan'tials**, incidentals: details.—*v.t.* **circumstan'tiate**, to prove by circumstances: to describe exactly.—**circumstantial evidence**, evidence which is not positive nor direct, but which is gathered inferentially from the circumstances in the case; in good or bad circumstances, prosperous or unprosperous; in, under, the circumstances, conditions being what they are: not a circumstance to, (*U.S.*) nothing to. [L. *stāns*, *stāntis*, standing—*stāre*, to stand.]

circumvallate, *sər-kəm-val'āt*, *v.t.* to surround with a rampart.—*n.* **circumvallā'tion**, a surrounding with a wall: a wall or fortification surrounding a town or fort: (*zool.*) engulfing of food by surrounding it (as by protozoa). [L. *vallum*, rampart.]

circumvent, *sər-kəm-vent'*, *v.t.* to go round: to encompass: to surround so as to intercept or capture: to get round, or to outwit.—*n.* **circumven'tion**.—*adj.* **circumvent'ive**, deceiving by artifices. [L. *venīre*, *ventum*, to come.]

circumvolve, *sər-kəm-volv'*, *v.t.* to roll round.—*v.i.* to revolve.—*n.* **circumvolu'tion** (*-lōō'*, *-lū'*), a turning or rolling round: anything winding or sinuous. [L. *volvĕre*, *volūtum*, to roll.]

circus, *sər'kəs*, *n.* a circular building for the exhibition of games: a place, building, or tent for the exhibition of feats of horsemanship and other performances: a show of this kind or the company of performers: a group of houses arranged in the form of a circle: an open place at a street junction:

a natural amphitheatre.—*adj.* **cir'cus(s)y**.—*n.* **cirque** (*sərk*; Fr.), a circus: a ring: a corrie. [L. *circus*—Gr. *kirkos*.]

cirl, *sərl*, *n.* a species of bunting (usu. **cirl bunting**). [It. *cirlo*.]

cirrhopod, **cirrhopoda**, older forms of **cirripede**, **cirripedia**. [As if from Gr. *kirrhos*, tawny, *pous*, *podos*, foot; so by confusion **cirrhipede**, **cirrhipedia**.]

cirrhosis, *si-rō'sis*, *n.* a wasting of the proper tissue of an organ, accompanied by abnormal growth of connective tissue. [Gr. *kirrhos*, tawny—from the colour of the liver so diseased.]

cirripede, *sir'i-pēd*, *n.* one of the **Cirripē'dia**, a degenerate class of Crustacea, the barnacles and acorn-shells.—Also **cirr'iped** (*-ped*). [L. *cirrus*, a curl, *pēs*, *pedis*, foot.]

cirrus, *sir'əs*, *n.* the highest form of clouds consisting of curling fibres: (*bot.*) a tendril: (*zool.*) any curled filament:—*pl.* **cirr'i**.—*adjs.* **cirr'ate**, **cirr'i-form**, like a cirrus; **cirr'igrade**, moving by cirri.—*n.* **cirr'o-cu'mulus**, a fleecy cloud intermediate between cirrus and cumulus.—*adj.* **cirr'ose**, with tendrils.—*n.* **cirr'o-strā'tus**, a mottled-looking cloud intermediate between cirrus and stratus.—*adj.* **cirr'ous**, having a cirrus. [L., a curl, tuft. The common spellings Cirrhus, etc. are due to confusion with Gr. *kirrhos*, tawny.]

Cisalpine, *sis-alp'in*, *-īn*, *adj.* on this (i.e. the Roman) side of the Alps.—So **Cisatlan'tic**; **Cisleithan** (*-lī't(h)ən*) on this side the Leitha (which once in part separated Austria and Hungary): Austrian; **cismon'tane**, on this side the mountains—opp. to *ultramontane*; **Cispadane** (*-pā'dān*, *sis'pa-dān*; L. *Padus*), on this (Roman) side the Po; **cispon'tine**, on this side of the bridges, viz. in London, north of the Thames. [L. *cis*, on this side.]

ciselure, *sēz'lōōr*, *n.* the art or operation of chasing: the chasing upon a piece of metal-work.—*n.* **cis'eleur** (*-lər*), a chaser. [Fr.]

cissoid, *sis'oid*, *n.* a plane curve consisting of two infinite branches symmetrically placed with reference to the diameter of a circle, so that at one of its extremities they form a cusp, while the tangent to the circle at the other extremity is an asympote. [Gr. *kissoeidēs*, ivy-like—*kissos*, ivy, *eidos*, form.]

cissy, *sis'i*, *n.* (*slang*) an effeminate person.—Also *adj.* [Partly from the name *Cecily*, partly from *sister*; cf. **sis**.]

cist, *sist*, *n.* a tomb consisting of a stone chest covered with stone slabs.—*adjs.* **cist'ed**, containing cists: **cist'ic**, like a cist. [See **chest**.]

Cistercian, *sis'tər-shən*, *n.* a member of the order of monks established in 1098 in the forest of Cîteaux, (*Cistercium*), in France—an offshoot of the Benedictines.—Also *adj.*

cistern, *sis'tərn*, *n.* any receptacle for holding water or other liquid: a reservoir: in a steam-engine, the vessel surrounding the condenser. [L. *cisterna*—*cista*, a chest.]

Cistus, *sis'tus*, *n.* the rock-rose genus of shrubby plants, giving name to the family **Cistā'ceae**, cultivated for the beauty of their flowers. [Gr. *kistos*, rock-rose.]

cistvaen. See **kistvaen**.

cit, *sit*, *n.* (*arch. slang*) a term of contempt for a townsman, not a gentleman :—*fem.* **cit'ess** (*Dryden*).—*n.pl.* **cits** (*U.S. slang*) civilian clothes. [**citizen**.]

citadel, *sit'ə-dəl*, *n.* a fortress in or near a city: the place where the guns are kept in a war-ship. [It. *cittadella*, dim. of *città*, a city; see **city**.]

cite, *sīt*, *v.t.* to call or summon: to summon to appear in court: to quote: to name: to adduce as proof.—*adj.* **cit'able**, that can be cited.—*ns.* **cit'al**, summons to appear: **citā'tion**, an official summons to appear: the document containing the summons: the act of quoting: the passage or name quoted: (*U.S.*) mention in dispatches.—*adj.* **cit'atory**, having to do with citation: addicted to citation. [L. *citāre*, *-ātum*, to call, inten. of *ciēre*, *cīre*, to make to go.]

cithara, *sith'ə-rä*, *n.* an ancient Greek musical instrument differing from the lyre in its flat shallow sound-chest.—*n.* **cith'arist**, a player on it.—*adj.*

citharist'ic.—*ns.* **cith'er, cith'ern, citt'ern,** an early modern metal-stringed musical instrument, played with a plectrum : the Tirolese zither. [L.,— Gr. *kithara*; cf. **guitar, zither.**]

citigrade, *sit'i-grād, adj.* moving quickly : applied to a tribe of spiders that run down their prey— Lycosidae or wolf-spiders. [L. *citus,* quick, *gradus,* a step.]

citizen, *sit'i-zən, n.* an inhabitant of a city : a member of a state : a townsman : a freeman : (*U.S.*) a civilian :—*fem.* **cit'izeness.**—*adj.* (*Shak.*) like a citizen.—*v.t.* **cit'izenise,** to make a citizen of.—*ns.* **cit'izenry,** the general body of citizens; **cit'izenship,** the rights of a citizen. [M.E. *citesein*—O.Fr. *citeain;* see **city.**]

citole, *sit'ōl, sit-ōl', n.* a mediaeval stringed instrument, app. of the nature of a cithara, psaltery, or rote. [O.Fr.—L. *cithara;* see **cithera.**]

citron, *sit'rən, n.* the fruit of the citron-tree, resembling a lemon : the tree that bears it (*Citrus medica*), considered to be the parent of the lemon and lime-fruit.—*ns.* **cit'range (-rənj),** a hybrid between citron and orange; **cit'rate,** a salt of citric acid.—*adjs.* **cit'reous,** citrine; **cit'ric,** derived from the citron; **cit'rine (-rin),** dark and greenish yellow, like a citron or lemon.—*n.* citrine colour : a rock-crystal of this colour.—*ns.* **citronell'a,** a Ceylon grass (**citronella-grass,** *Cymbopogon Nardus*) yielding **citronella-oil,** used in perfumery; **cit'ron-tree; cit'ron-wood, cit'rus-wood,** the most costly furniture wood of the ancient Romans (perhaps sandaracch).—**cit'rus,** a citron tree: **Citrus,** a genus of Rutaceae including the citron, lemon, orange, etc.—**citric acid,** the acid to which lemon and lime juice owe their sourness ($C_6H_8O_7$); **citrus fruits,** citrons, lemons, limes, oranges, grapefruit. [L. *citrus,* from which comes also Gr. *kitron,* a citron.]

cittern. Same as **cither.** [See under **cithara.**]

city, *sit'i, n.* a large town : an incorporated town that has or had a cathedral : a town on which the dignity has been conferred by tradition or grant : in various countries a municipality of higher rank, variously defined : the business centre or original area of a large town.—**city article,** in a newspaper, a financial or commercial article; **city company,** a London corporation representing any of the mediaeval trade guilds; **city editor,** the financial editor; **city fathers,** the magistrates : the Town or City Council; **city man,** a man engaged in commercial or financial work in a city; **city manager,** a man appointed by an elected body to manage the administrative affairs of a city; **city mission,** a mission for evangelising the poor classes in the large cities; **city of God, heavenly city,** etc., the ideal of the Church of Christ in glory; **city of refuge,** by the Jewish law a city where the perpetrator of an accidental homicide might flee for refuge; **city state,** a sovereign state consisting of a city with a small surrounding territory.—**Eternal City,** Rome; **Holy City,** Jerusalem. [Fr. *cité,* a city—L. *civitās, -ātis,* the state—*civis,* a citizen.]

cive, *siv.* See **chive.**

civet, *siv'it, n.* a perfume obtained from the **civet** or **civ'et-cat,** a small cat-like carnivore (*Viverra*) of Africa, India, etc. [Fr. *civette*—Ar. *zabād.*]

civic, *siv'ik, adj.* pertaining to a city or citizen.—*n.* **civ'ics,** the science of citizenship.—**civic centre,** a place in which the chief public buildings of a town are grouped; **civic crown,** an oak wreath awarded to a Roman soldier for saving a citizen's life in battle. [L. *civicus*—*civis,* citizen.]

civil, *siv'il, adj.* pertaining to the community : having the refinement of city-bred people : polite (in any degree short of discourtesy) : pertaining to ordinary life, not military : lay, secular, temporal, not ecclesiastical : pertaining to the individual citizen : (*law*) relating to private relations amongst citizens, and such suits as arise out of these, as opposed to *crim'nal* : (*theol.*) naturally good, as opposed to good through regeneration.—*n.* **civil'ian,** a professor or student of civil law (not canon law) : one engaged in civil as distinguished from military and naval pursuits.—Also *adj.*—*ns.*

civ'ilist, one versed in civil law; **civil'ity,** civilisation : good-breeding : politeness : polite attentions. —*adv.* **civ'illy.**—*adj.* **civ'il-suit'ed** (*Milton*), sombrely clad.—*n.* **civ'ism,** good citizenship : state of being well-affected to French Revolution principles; **civv'y** (*slang*), civilian : (in *pl.* **civvies**) civilian clothes :—Also *adj.*—**civil day, year, time,** the day, year, time, as reckoned for ordinary purposes; **civil death,** the loss of all civil and legal privileges; **civil engineer,** one who plans and builds railways, docks, etc., as opposed to a military engineer, or to a mechanical engineer, who makes machines, etc.; **civil law,** as opposed to criminal law, the law laid down by a state regarding the rights of the inhabitants, esp. that founded on Roman law; **civil list,** formerly a list of charges for civil government purposes : now the expenses of the sovereign's household only; **civil list pensions,** those granted by royal favour; **civil service,** the paid service of the state, in so far as it is not military or naval; **civil war,** a war between citizens of the same state. [L. *civilis*—*civis, civitas,* citizen.]

civilise, *siv'il-iz, v.t.* to reclaim from barbarism : to instruct in arts and refinements.—*adj.* **civilis'- able.**—*n.* **civilisa'tion,** state of being civilised : culture : cultural condition or complex.—*adj.* **civ'ilised.**—*n.* **civ'iliser.** [See **civil.**]

cizers, an old spelling (*Shak.*) of **scissors.**

clabber, *klab'ər, n.* (esp. *Ir.*) mud. [Ir. *clabar,* mud.]

clachan, *klăhh'ən, n.* (*Scot.*) a small village. [Gael. *clachan*—*clach,* stone.]

clack, *klak, v.i.* to make a noise as of a flat thing flapping : to chatter : to cackle.—*n.* a noise of this kind : an instrument making it : sound of voices : (*coll.*) the tongue.—*ns.* **clack'-box,** the box containing the clack-valve of an engine; **clack'-dish** (*Shak.*), a wooden dish carried by beggars, having a movable cover which they clacked to attract attention; **clack'er,** **clack'-valve,** a valve consisting of a hinged flap or other device that falls back with a clacking noise. [Prob. from the sound.]

clad, *klad, pa.t.* and *pa.p.,* also (*Spens.*) *pres.infin.,* of **clothe.**

cladode, *klad'ōd, n.* (*bot.*) a branch with the appearance and functions of a leaf. [Gr. *klados,* a shoot.]

claes, *klāz, n.pl.* Scots for **clothes.**

clag, *klag, v.i.* (*prov.*) to stick.—*v.t.* to bedaub.— *adj.* **clagg'y,** tenacious. [Prob. Scand.; Dan. *klag,* mud; cf. **clay.**]

claim, *klām, v.t.* to call for : to demand as a right : to maintain or assert.—*n.* a demand for something supposed due : right or ground for demanding : the thing claimed, esp. a piece of land appropriated by a miner or other : (*Spens.* **clame**) a call, shout.— *adj.* **claim'able,** that can be claimed.—*ns.* **claim'- ant,** **claim'er,** one who makes a claim; **claim'- jump'er,** one who takes possession of another's mining claim.—**lay claim to,** to assert a right to. [O.Fr. *claimer*—L. *clamāre,* to call out.]

clairaudience, *klăr-awd'i-əns, n.* the alleged power of hearing things not present to the senses.—*n.* and *adj.* **clairaud'ient.** [Fr. *clair*—L. *clārus,* clear, and **audience.**]

clair-obscure, clare obscure, *klăr-ob-skūr'.* Same as **chiaroscuro** (q.v.). [Fr. *clair*—L. *clārus,* clear, and Fr. *obscur*—L. *obscūrus,* obscure.]

clairschach, *klăr'shăhh, n.* the old Celtic harp strung with wire. [Gael. and Ir. *clairseach,* a harp.]

clairvoyance, *klăr-voi'əns, n.* the alleged power of seeing things not present to the senses.—*n.* and *adj.* **clairvoy'ant.** [Fr. *clair*—L. *clārus,* clear, and Fr. *voir*—L. *vidēre,* to see.]

clam, *klam, n.* a gripping instrument : (*coll. U.S.*) a very reticent person : a scallop or scallop-shell (Pecten) : in America an edible shellfish of various kinds, esp. the round clam or quahog (*Venus mercenaria*) and the long clam (*Mya arenaria*).— *v.i.* to take clams : (*coll.*) to be silent (*pr.p.* **clamm'- ing;** *pa.t.* and *pa.p.* **clammed**).—*ns.* **clam'- bake,** *n.* a baking of clams on hot stones, with layers of potatoes, fish, Indian corn, etc., popular at picnic parties in U.S.: such a party; **clam-chow'der**, chowder made with clams; **clam'-shell**. [O.E. *clam*, fetter; cf. Ger. *klamm;* Dan. *klamme*.]

clam, *klam, v.t.* to clog: to smear (*pr.p.* **clamm'ing** *pa.t.* and *pa.p.* **clammed**).—*n.* dampness.—*adv.* **clamm'ily.**—*n.* **clamm'iness.**—*adj.* **clamm'y**, sticky: moist and adhesive. [O.E. *clǽman*, to anoint; cf. Du., Dan. *klam*, damp.]

clam, *klam, n.* noise produced by ringing two or more bells together.—Also *v.t.* and *v.i.* [Prob. onomatopoeic.]

clamant, *klam'ənt, klām'ənt, adj.* calling aloud or earnestly.—*n.* **clam'ancy**, urgency. [L. *clāmāre*, to cry out.]

clambe, *klām,* (*Spens.*) *pa.t.* of **climb.**

clamber, *klam'bər, v.i.* to climb with difficulty, grasping with hands and feet.—*n.* the act of clambering. [From root of **climb**; cf. Ger. *klammern—klemmen*, to squeeze or hold tightly.]

clame (*Spens.*). Same as **claim.**

clamjamphrie, *klăm-jăm'fri, n.* (*Scot.*) rubbish: nonsense : rabble.—Also **clanjamfray.** [Der. uncertain.]

clamour, *klam'ər, n.* a loud continuous outcry: uproar: any loud noise: persistent expression of dissatisfaction.—*v.i.* to cry aloud in demand : to make a loud continuous outcry.—*adj.* **clam'orous**, noisy, boisterous.—*adv.* **clam'orously.**—*ns.* **clam'orousness; clam'ourer.** [L. *clāmor, -ōris.*]

clamour, *klam'ər, v.t.* (*Shak.*) to silence, check the ringing of. [Perh. conn. with **clam** (3).]

clamp, *klamp, n.* a piece of timber, iron, etc., used to fasten things together or to strengthen any framework : any instrument for holding.—*v.t.* to bind with a clamp. [From a root seen in O.E. *clam*, fetter; Du. *klamp*, a clamp; akin to **clip, climb.**]

clamp, *klamp, n.* a heavy tread.—*v.i.* to tread heavily. [Prob. from the sound.]

clamp, *klamp, n.* a stack, as of bricks for burning, peats, etc. : a heap : a covered heap of potatoes. —*v.t.* to put in clamps. [Prob. Du. *klamp,* heap.]

clamper, *klam'pər, v.t.* to botch up. [Der. unknown; prob. conn. with **clamp** (1).]

clan, *klan, n.* a tribe or collection of families subject to a single chieftain, commonly bearing the same surname, and supposed to have a common ancestor : a clique, sect : a collective name for a number of persons or things.—*adj.* **clann'ish**, closely united and holding aloof from others, like the members of a clan.—*adv.* **clann'ishly.**—*ns.* **clann'ishness;** **clan'ship**, association of families under a chieftain : feeling of loyalty to a clan; **clans'man, clans'-woman**, a member of a clan. [Gael. *clann*, off-spring, tribe—L. *planta*, a shoot.]

clandestine, *klan-des'tin, adj.* concealed or hidden : private : sly.—*adv.* **clandes'tinely.** [L. *clan-destīnus—clam*, secretly.]

clang, *klang, v.i.* to produce a loud deep ringing sound.—*v.t.* to cause to clang.—*n.* a ringing sound, like that made by striking large pieces of metal, or that of a trumpet: the sonorous cry of some birds, as cranes or geese.—*n.* and *adj.* **clang'ing.** —*adj.* **clangorous** (*klang'gər-əs*).—*adv.* **clang'or-ously.**—*n.* **clang'our**, a clang : loud ringing noise. —*v.i.* to make a clangour. [L. *clangĕre*, to sound; *clangor*, noise of birds or wind instruments.]

clang. See **klang.**

clank, *klangk, n.* a metallic sound, less prolonged than a clang, such as is made by a chain.—*v.i.* or *v.t.* to make or cause to make a clank.—*n.* **clank'-ing.**—*adj.* **clank'less**, without clank. [Prob. formed under the influence of **clink** and **clang.**]

clap, *klap, n.* a sudden blow or stroke (*lit.* or *fig.*): a slap : (*Scot.*) a pat : the noise made by the sudden striking together of two things, as the hands : a burst of sound, esp. thunder.—*v.t.* to strike together so as to make a noise : to thrust or drive together suddenly : to fasten promptly : (*Scot.*) to pat : to applaud with the hands : to bang : to put suddenly (e.g. in prison).—*v.i.* to strike the hands together : to strike or slam with noise : to applaud : (*arch.*) to come or go suddenly (*pr.p.* **clapp'ing;**

pa.t. and *pa.p.* **clapped**).—*ns.* **clap'-board** (or *klab'ərd*), wood for barrel staves, wainscot : (*U.S.*) a thin board used in covering wooden houses; **clap'-bread**, a kind of hard-baked oatmeal cake; **clap'-dish** (same as **clack-dish**); **clap'-net**, a net made to clap together suddenly by pulling a string; **clapp'er**, one who claps : that which claps, as the tongue of a bell : a contrivance for shaking a mill hopper : an instrument for making a noise, as a rattle, or (in *pl.*) the bones of negro minstrels : a glib tongue.—*v.t.* **clapp'er-claw** (*Shak.*) to claw or scratch : to scold.—*ns.* **clapp'ing**, noise of striking: applause; **clap'-sill**, a lock-sill, the bottom part of the frame on which lock-gates shut; **clap'trap** (*Shak.*), a trick to gain applause : flashy display : empty words : **claptrapp'ery.**—*adj.* **clap-trapp'ish.**—**clap eyes on**, to catch sight of; **clap hands** (*Shak.*), to make an agreement; **clap hold of**, to seize roughly; **clap up** (*Shak.*), to conclude suddenly. [O.N. *klappa*, to pat; Du. and Ger. *klappen.*]

clap, *klap, n.* gonorrhoea.—*v.t.* to infect with gonorrhoea. [Cf. Du. *klapoor.*]

clapper, *klap'ər, n.* (esp. in Devon) a rude bridge of slabs or planks laid across supports : a raised footpath : a rabbit-hole. [L.L. *claperium*, heap of stones, rabbit-hole.]

claque, *klăk, n.* an institution for securing the success of a performance, by preconcerted applause : a body of hired applauders.—*n.* **claqueur** (*klä-kər'*), a member of the claque. [Fr.,—*claquer*, to clap.]

clarabella, *klar-ə-bel'ä, n.* an organ-stop of a sweet, fluty tone. [L. *clārus*, clear, *bellus*, beautiful.]

Clare, *klār, n.* a nun of a Franciscan order founded by St. *Clare* (1212).—Also **Poor Clare.**

clarence, *klar'əns, n.* a four-wheeled carriage, seated inside for two or more persons. [Named after the Duke of *Clarence* (William IV.).]

Clarenceux, Clarencieux, *klar'ən-sū, n.* (*her.*) the second king-of-arms in England, so named from the Duke of *Clarence*, son of Edward III.

clarendon, *klar'ən-dən, n.* (*print.*) a form of type having a heavy face.

clare-obscure. Same as **chiaroscuro.**

claret, *klar'ət, n.* originally applied to wines of a light-red colour, but now used in England for the dark-red wines of Bordeaux : (*slang*) blood.—*v.i.* to drink claret.—*ns.* **clar'et-cup**, a drink made up of iced claret, brandy, sugar, etc.; **clar'et-jug**, a fancy jug for holding claret. [Fr. *clairet—clair*— L. *clārus*, clear.]

clarichord, *klar'i-kord, n.* a clavichord. [As if from L. *clārus*, clear; see **clavichord.**]

clarify, *klar'i-fī, v.t.* to make clear or pure.—*v.i.* to become clear (*pr.p.* **clar'ifying;** *pa.t.* and *pa.p.* **clar'ified**)—*ns.* **clarificā'tion;** **clar'ifier.** [L. *clārus*, clear, and *facĕre*, to make.]

clarinet, clarionet, *klar-in-et',* or *klar',* n. a wind-instrument, usually of wood, in which the sound is produced by a single thin reed, the compass being approximately that of the violin.—*n.* **clarinett'ist.** —**the bass clarinet** is pitched an octave lower than the ordinary clarinet. [Fr.—L. *clārus*, clear.]

clarion, *klar'i-ən, n.* a kind of trumpet whose note is clear and shrill : the sound of a trumpet, or a sound resembling that of a trumpet. [Fr. *clairon*— *clair*—L. *clārus*, clear.]

clarity, *klar'i-ti, n.* clearness. [M.E. *clarte*—L. *clāritās, -ātis.*]

Clarkia, *klärk'i-ä, n.* a North American genus of the evening-primrose family, a favourite border plant. [Named in honour of Captain *Clark*, of Lewis and Clark's expedition.]

clarty, *klär'ti, adj.* (*Scot.*) sticky and dirty. [Der. unknown.]

clary, *klā'ri, n.* a plant of the sage genus (*Salvia Sclarea*) with pale-blue flowers and large coloured bracts : extended to others of the genus. [L.L. *sclarea;* origin unknown.]

clash, *klash, n.* a loud noise, such as is caused by the striking together of sheets of metal: opposition: contradiction : (*Scot.*) chatter, country talk.—*v.i.* to dash noisily together : to meet in opposition : to act in a contrary direction : to disagree : of events, to coincide disturbingly : (*Scot.*) to gossip.—*v.t.* to strike noisily against : (*dial.*) to bang, slam.— *n.* **clash'ing**, a striking against : opposition, conflict, disagreement. [Imit; cf., Ger. and Sw. *klatsch.*]

clasp, *klåsp*, *n.* a fastening : a supplementary decoration in the form of a bar on the ribbon of a medal : an embrace : a grasp.—*v.t.* to fasten with a clasp : to enclose and hold in the hand or arms : to embrace.—*ns.* **clas'per**, that which clasps : the tendril of a plant : (*zool.*) a clasping organ; **clasp'-ing**; **clasp'-knife**, a knife whose blade folds into the handle. [M.E. *clapse.*]

class, *klås*, *n.* a rank or order of persons or things : high rank or social standing : a number of students or scholars who are taught together, or are (esp. in *U.S.*) in the same year of their course : a scientific division or arrangement in biological classification, a division above an order : a grade, as of merit in examination, accommodation in a ship or railway train : a section of a Methodist congregation.—*v.t.* to form into a class or classes : to arrange methodically.—*v.i.* to take rank.—*adj.* (*slang*) of high class.—*adjs.* **class'able**, **class'ible**, capable of being classed.—*n.* **class'-book**, a book used in class teaching.—*adjs.* **class'-con'scious**, clearly or acutely conscious of membership of a social class; **classed**.—*ns.* **class'-fellow**, **class'-mate**, a pupil in the same class at school or college; **classic**, (*klas'-ik*) any great writer, composer, or work, esp. in Greek and Latin literature : a student of the ancient classics : a standard work.—(*pl.*) Greek and Latin studies :— *adjs.* **class'ic, -al**, of the highest class or rank, esp. in literature and music : originally and chiefly used of the best Greek and Roman writers : (as opposed to *romantic*) like in style to the authors of Greece and Rome or the old masters in music : chaste, refined, restrained, in keeping with classical art : having literary or historical associations : traditionally accepted, long established : (*slang*) excellent, standard : (*Milt.*) Presbyterian, of a class.— *n.* **classical'ity**.—*adv.* **class'ically**.—*ns.* **class'-icalness**; **class'icism** (-*sizm*), a classical idiom : in literature, music, etc., a principle, character, or tendency such as is seen in Greek classical literature, marked by beauty of form, good taste, restraint, and clarity—opposed to *romanticism;* **class'icist**, one versed in the classics, or devoted to their being used in education : one who is for classicism rather than romanticism; **class'-lead'er**, the leader of a class in a Methodist church; **class'man**, one who has gained honours of a certain class at the Oxford examinations—opp. to *passman;* **class'-room**, a room in which a class is held; **class'-war'**, hostility or hostilities between different social ranks or classes, esp. between the proletariat and the combined middle and upper classes.—*adj.* (*slang*) **class'y**, of or characteristic of high or upper class. —**classic races**, the five chief annual horse-races —the Two Thousand Guineas, One Thousand, Derby, Oaks, and St. Leger; **class legislation**, legislation in the interests of a class; **take a class**, to take honours in an examination, as opposed to the mere pass. [L. *classis*, a division of the Roman people.]

classify, *klas'i-fī*, *v.t.* to arrange in classes (*pr.p.* **class'ifying**; *pa.p.* **class'ified**).—*adjs.* **classi-fī'able**, capable of being classified; **classif'ic**, denoting classes.—*n.* **classificā'tion**, act or system of arranging in classes.—*adj.* **classificātory**.—*n.* **class'ifīer**. [L. *classis*, and *facĕre*, to make.]

classis, *klas'is*, *n.* a group : (*obs.*) a Presbytery : (*obs.*) a bay of a library. [L.]

clastic, *klas'tik*, *adj.* composed of fragments, fragmental. [Gr. *klastos*—*klaein*, to break.]

clat. See **claut**.

clatch, *klåch*, *n.* (*Scot.*) a splashy slapping sound : a slap : anything sloppy and pasty : anything lumbering or clumsy, as an old gig : an ungainly person : a slut : a botched piece of work.—*v.i.* to dabble or work in miry matter.—*v.t.* to daub, plaster : to work up into a pasty mess : to botch. [Cf. Ger. *klatsch*, slap.]

clatter, *klat'ər*, *n.* a repeated rattling noise : a repetition of abrupt, sharp sounds : noisy talk : (*Scot.*, often in *pl.*) gossip.—*v.i.* to make rattling sounds : to chatter.—*v.t.* to cause to rattle.—*n.* **clatt'erer**.—*adv.* **clatt'eringly**. [O.E. *clatrung*, clattering (verbal noun).]

Claude Lorraine glass, *klawd lor-ān' glås*, *n.* a convex mirror, usu. coloured, employed for viewing landscape. [Named after the painter *Claude Gelée*, known as *le Lorrain* (1600-82).]

Claudian, *klaw'di-ən*, *adj.* pertaining to the Romans of the name of *Claudius*, esp. the emperors of that gens (Tiberius, Caligula, Claudius, Nero), or to their period (14-68 A.D.).

claudication, *klaw-di-kā'shon*, *n.* a limp. [L. *claudicātio̅, -ōnis*—*claudus*, lame.]

claught, claucht, *klawhht*, *v.t.* and *v.i.* (*Scot.*) to snatch : to clutch.—*n.* a hold : a snatch : a clutch. [From the pa.t. of **cleek**.]

clause, *klawz*, *n.* a sentence : part of a sentence with subject and predicate : an article or part of a contract, will, act of parliament, etc.—*adj.* **claus'ū-lar**, pertaining to, or consisting of, a clause or clauses. [Fr. *clause*—L. *claudĕre*, to shut.]

claustral, *klaws'trəl*, *adj.* cloistral, secluded : pertaining to a claustrum.—*ns.* **claustrā'tion**, the act of shutting in a cloister; **claustropho̅'bia** (Gr. *phobos*, fear), a morbid dread of confined places.— *adj.* **claustrophobic** (-*fob'ik*).—*n.* **claus'trum**, a thin layer of grey matter in the brain hemispheres : —*pl.* **claus'tra**. [L. *claustrum*, an enclosed place.]

claut, *klawt*, **clat**, *klåt*, *n.* (*Scot.*) a claw : a scratch : a blow : a grasp : a scraping hoe : something scraped together, a lump.—*v.t.* to scratch, claw : to scrape : to hoe. [Perh. conn. with **claw**.]

clavate, -d, *klā'vāt*, *klav'āt, -id, adj.* (*biol.*) club-shaped.—*n.* **clavā'tion**, articulation in a socket.— *adj.* **clav'iform**, in the form of a club.—*n.* **clav'iger** (-*i-jər*), a club-bearer.—*adj.* **clavig'-erous** (-*ij'er-əs*), club-bearing (see also under **clavis**).—*adj.* **clav'ūlate**, somewhat club-shaped. [L. *clāva*, a club.]

clave, *klāv*, *pa.t.* of **cleave** (both verbs).

clavecin, *klav'ə-sin*, *n.* a harpsichord.—*n.* **clav'e-cinist**. [Fr. *clavecin*—L. *clāvis*, a key.]

claver, *klā'vər*, *n.* (*Scot.*) idle talk, gossip.—*v.i.* to talk idly. [Der. uncertain.]

clavicembalo, *klav-i-chem'bə-lō*, *n.* a cembalo with keys—a harpsichord. [It.,—L. *clāvis*, key and cembalo.]

clavichord, *klav'i-kord*, *n.* an old keyboard stringed instrument in which the tangent which struck the string and produced the sound also determined the vibrating length. [L. *clāvis*, a key, *chorda*, a string.]

clavicle, *klav'i-kl*, *n.* the collar-bone : the merry-thought of birds—Also **clavic'ūla**.—*adj.* **clavic'-ūlar**. [Fr. *clavicule*—L. *clāvicula*, dim. of *clāvis*, a key.]

clavicorn, *klav'i-korn*, *adj.* having clavate antennae. —*n.* a member of the **Clavicorn'ia**, a group of beetles. [L. *clāva*, a club, *cornū*, a horn.]

clavier, *klā-vēr'*, *n.* the keyboard of a musical instrument : a stringed keyboard instrument, esp. clavichord or the pianoforte. [Fr.,—L. *clāvis*, a key.]

clavis, *klā'vis* (L. *klä'wis*), *n.* a key, hence a clue or aid for solving problems, interpreting a cipher, etc. :—*pl.* **clā'ves** (-*vēz;* L. *klä'wās*).—*n.* **claviger** (*klav'i-jər*), one who keeps a key, a custodian.— *adj.* **clavig'erous**, keeping keys (see also under **clavate**). [L. *clāvis*, a key.]

claw, *klaw*, *n.* the hooked nail of a beast or bird : the leg of a crab, insect, etc., or its pointed end or pincer : an instrument shaped like a claw : (*bot.*) the narrow basal part of a petal : anything like a claw.—*v.t.* to scratch : to tear : to scrape : to seize : (*fig.*) to flatter, fawn on.—*n.* **claw'back**, a toady, flatterer.—*adj.* **clawed**, having claws.—*ns.* **claw'-hammer**, a hammer with one part of the head divided into two claws, for drawing nails; **claw'-hamm'er-coat**, a facetious name for a dress-coat.—*adj.* **claw'less**.—**claw me and I'll claw thee**, favour me and I shall do you good in

Neutral vowels in unaccented syllables : *el'ə-mənt*, *in'fənt*, *ran'dəm*

return. [O.E. *clawu;* cog. with Ger. *klaue;* akin to **cleave**, to stick.]

clay, *klā, n. (agri.)* earth in very fine particles, tenacious and impervious : *(chem.* and *min.)* a tenacious ductile earthy material, hydrated aluminium silicates more or less impure : earth in general : the human body : (in full **clay-pipe**) a tobacco-pipe of baked clay.—*v.t.* to purify with clay, as sugar.—*adjs.* **clay′-bank,** *(U.S.)* brownish yellow; **clay′-brained** *(Shak.),* stupid; **clay′-cold,** cold as clay, lifeless.—*n.* **clay′-eat′er,** one addicted to chewing a fatty clay—in Brazil and elsewhere.—*adjs.* **clayed,** clay-like; **clay′ey,** made of clay : covered with clay : like clay.—*ns.* **clay′-ground,** ground consisting mainly of clay; **clay′-ir′on-stone,** a clayey chalybite.—*adj.* **clay′ish,** of the nature of clay.—*ns.* **clay′-marl,** a whitish chalky clay; **clay′-mill,** a mill for preparing clay; **clay′-pigeon,** a clay disk thrown from a trap and shot at as a substitute for a live pigeon; **clay′-slate,** hard, fissile argillaceous rock; **clay′-pit,** a pit from which clay is dug.—**wet one's clay,** to drink. [O.E. *clǽg;* cf. Dan. *klæg,* Ger. *klei.*]

claymore, *klā-mōr′, n.* a large sword formerly used by the Scottish Highlanders : the old Celtic one-handed, two-edged longsword : now applied inaccurately to the basket-hilted sword of the officers of Highland regiments. [Gael. *claidheamhmór*—Gael. and Ir. *claidheamh,* sword, *mór,* great.]

clean, *klēn, adj. (Spens.)* clear : clear-cut : sharply defined : even : neat : free from dirt, stain, or whatever defiles : pure : guiltless : complete : *(angling)* without a catch.—*adv.* quite : entirely : smoothly : without mishap.—*v.t.* to make clean, or free from dirt.—*n.* **clean′er,** one who or that which cleans.—*n.* and *adj.* **clean′ing,** the act of making clean.—*adj.* **clean′-limbed,** with shapely limbs : trim.—*n.* **cleanliness** *(klen′li-nis),* habitual cleanness or purity.—*adj.* **cleanly** *(klen′li),* clean in habits and person : pure : neat.—*adv. (klēn′li)* in a clean manner.—*n.* **cleanness** *(klēn′nis).*—*adj.* **clean′-tim′bered** *(Shak.),* well-proportioned.—*n.* **clean′-up,** an act of thorough cleaning : the stamping-out of an evil.—**clean slate,** a fresh start; **clean hands,** freedom from guilt or corruption; **come clean,** *(slang)* to confess, to divulge, everything; **show a clean pair of heels,** to escape by running. [O.E. *clǽne;* Ger. *klein,* small.]

cleanse, *klenz, v.t.* to make clean or pure.—*adj.* **cleans′able.**—*ns.* **cleans′er,** one who, or that which, cleanses; **cleans′ing,** purification. [O.E. *clǽnsian.*]

clear, *klēr, adj.* pure, bright, undimmed, unclouded, undulled : free from obstruction, difficulty, complication, contents, blame, or accusation : disengaged : plain : distinct : obvious : without blemish defect, drawback, or diminution : perspicuous : transparent.—*adv.* in a clear manner : plainly : wholly : quite.—*v.t.* to make clear : to empty : to free from obscurity, obstruction, or guilt : to free, acquit, or vindicate : to leap, or pass by or over : to make as profit : to settle, as a bill : (of wounded) to move on from a temporary movable hospital (casualty **clear′ing-sta′tion**) to a stationary hospital : to set free for sailing.—*v.i.* to become clear : to grow free, bright, transparent : to sail after satisfying all demands and obtaining permission.—*ns.* **clear′age,** a piece of land cleared; **clear′ance,** act of clearing : a general removal or emptying : eviction from lands : removal of hindrances : intervening space : play between parts, as of a machine : a certificate that a ship has been cleared at the custom-house; **clear′er.**—*adjs.* **clear′-eyed,** clear-sighted, discerning; **clear′-head′ed,** having a clear understanding.—*ns.* **clear′ing,** the act of making clear : a tract of land cleared of wood, etc., for cultivation : a method by which bankers change cheques and drafts, and arrange the differences; **clear′ing-house,** an office where such clearing business is done (**railway clear′ing-house,** an office for adjusting claims of different railways for shares of freights and through tickets);

clear′ing-nut, the seed of *Strychnos potatorum,* used in the East Indies for clearing muddy water.—*adv.* **clear′ly,** in a clear manner : distinctly.—*ns.* **clear′ness; clear′-obscure′** (see **chiaroscuro**).—*adj.* **clear′-sight′ed,** having clearness of sight : discerning.—*ns.* **clear′-sight′edness; clear′-skin** *(Australian),* an unbranded animal; **clear′-starch′er,** a laundress; **clear′-starch′ing,** the act of stiffening linen with clear starch; **clear′-story** (see **clerestory**); **clear′wing,** a transparent-winged moth.—**clear off,** to get rid of, dispose of : *(coll.)* to go away, esp. in order to avoid something; **clear out,** to get rid of : to empty : of a ship, to clear and leave port : to take oneself off; **clear the air,** simplify the situation and relieve tension; **clear the way,** to make the way open; **clear up,** to make or to become clear. [Fr. *clair*—L. *clārus,* clear.]

clearcole, *klēr′kōl, n.* a priming coat consisting of size or glue with whiting.—Also **clere′cole, claircolle** *(klār′).* [Fr. *claire colle,* clear glue.]

cleat, *klēt, n.* a wedge : a piece of wood, etc., nailed across anything to keep it in its place or give it an additional strength : a piece attached to parts of a ship for fastening ropes.—*v.t.* to strengthen with a cleat. [From a supposed O.E. *cléat;* cf. Du. *kloot;* Dan. *klode;* Ger. *kloss.*]

cleave, *klēv, v.t.* to divide, to split : to separate with violence : to go through : to pierce.—*v.i.* to part asunder : to crack *(pr.p.* **cleav′ing;** *pa.t.* **clōve** or **cleft,** *arch.* **clāve;** *pa.p.* **clōv′en** or **cleft**).—*adj.* **cleav′able,** capable of being cleft.—*ns.* **cleav′ableness; cleav′age,** a split : a tendency to split, esp. (in rocks and minerals) in certain directions : mitotic cell-division; **cleav′er,** one who or that which cleaves : a butcher's chopper.—*adj.* **cleav′ing,** splitting.—*n.* a cleft. [O.E. *cléofan,* cog. with Ger. *klieben.*]

cleave, *klēv, v.i.* to stick or adhere : to unite *(pa.t.* **cleaved** or **clave;** *pa.p.* **cleaved**).—*ns.* **cleav′ers, clivers** *(kliv′ərz),* goose-grass *(Galium Aparine)* which cleaves to fur or clothes by its hooks; **cleav′ing,** the act of adhering.—Also *adj.* [O.E. *clifian;* cog. with Ger. *kleben.*]

cleché, *klech′ā, klesh′ā, adj. (her.)* voided or hollowed throughout, showing only a narrow border. [Fr.]

cleck, *klek, v.t. (Scot.)* to hatch.—*n.* **cleck′ing,** a brood. [O.N. *klekja;* cf. Dan. *klække,* to hatch.]

cleek, *klēk, n. (Scot.)* a large hook : a narrow-faced iron-headed golf-club.—*v.t.* to seize, to hook.—*v.i. (Scot.)* to go arm in arm : to link : to marry *(pa.t.* and *pa.p.* **cleeked, cleekit, claught,** pron. *klawhht).* [Northern, perh. related to **clutch.**]

cleep. See **clepe.**

clef, *klef, n.* a character placed on the stave by which the absolute pitch of the notes is fixed. [Fr. *clef,* key—L. *clāvis;* Gr. *kleis,* a key.]

cleft, *kleft, pa.t.* and *pa.p.* of **cleave,** (1).—**cleft-palate.** See **palate.**

cleft, *kleft, n.* an opening made by cleaving or splitting : a crack, fissure, or chink.—Also **clift** *(B.).* [Cf. Ger. *kluft,* Dan. *klyft,* a hole.]

cleg, *kleg, n.* gadfly, horse-fly. [O.N. *kleggi.*]

cleistogamy, clistogamy, *klīs-tog′ə-mi, n. (bot.)* production of small flowers, often simplified and inconspicuous, which do not open, and in which self-pollination occurs.—*adjs.* **cleistogamic** *(-tə-gam′ik),* **cleistog′amous.** [Gr. *kleistos,* closed, *gamos,* marriage.]

cleithral, clithral, *klī′thrəl, adj.* completely roofed over. [Gr. *kleithron,* a bar.]

clem, *klem, v.i.* and *v.t.* to starve. [Prov. Eng. *clam;* Ger. *klemmen,* to pinch.]

Clematis, *klem′ə-tis, n.* a genus of Ranunculaceae, including *Virgin's Bower* or *Traveller's Joy.* [L., —Gr. *klēmatis,* a plant, prob. periwinkle—*klēma,* a twig.]

clement, *klem′ənt, adj.* mild : gentle : kind : merciful.—*ns.* **clem′ence** *(Spens.),* **clem′ency,** the quality of being clement : mildness : readiness to forgive.—*adv.* **clem′ently.** [Fr.,—L. *clēmēns, -entis.*]

clench, *klensh, klench, v.t.* to close tightly : to grasp : to clinch. [Same as **clinch.**]

clepe, cleep, *klēp, v.t. (arch.)* to call : to name.—
pa.p. **yclept** (*i-klept'*). [O.E. *clipian,* to call.]

clepsydra, *klep'si-drä, n.* an instrument for
measuring time by the trickling of water, a water-
clock. [L.,—Gr. *klepsydrā—kleptein,* to steal,
hydōr, water.]

clerestory, clear-story, *klēr'stō-ri, n.* an upper
story or part with its own row of windows—esp.
the story above the triforium in a church. [**clear,**
prob. in sense of lighted, and **story** (2).]

clergy, *klәr'ji, n.* the ministers of the Christian or
other religion, as holders of an allotted office, in
contra-distinction to the laity : (*arch.*) learning,
education.—*adjs.* **cler'gyable, cler'giable,** entitled to or admitting of the benefit of clergy.—*ns.*
cler'gyman, one of the clergy, a regularly ordained
minister; **cler'gy-woman,** a woman who is a
minister of religion : (jocular) a woman belonging
to a clergyman's family.—*adjs.* **cleric, -al,** (*kler'ik,
-әl*) belonging to the clergy : pertaining to a clerk
or scribe.—*ns.* **cler'ic,** a clergyman; **cler'icalism,**
undue influence of the clergy : sacerdotalism.—*n.pl.*
cler'icals, clerical garb.—*ns.* **cler'icate,** clerical
position; **clericity** (*klәr-is'i-ti*), state of being a
clergyman; **clerisy** (*kler'i-si*), the class of learned
men, scholars.—**benefit of clergy,** originally an
exemption of clergymen, in certain cases, from
criminal process before a secular judge, but later
covering the first offence of all who could read.—
black clergy, in Russia, all the regular or monastic,
as distinct from the secular or parochial, clergy;
clergyman's sore throat, chronic pharyngitis.
[Fr. *clergé*—L. *clēricus*—Gr. *klērikos,* from *klēros,*
a lot, a heritage, then the clergy.]

clerihew, *kler'i-hū, n.* a jingle in two short couplets
purporting to quintessentialise the life and character
of some notable person. [Started by E. *Clerihew*
(Bentley) in his *Biography for Beginners* (1905).]

clerk, *klärk* (*U.S.* *klәrk*), *n.* a clergyman or priest :
a scholar : one who leads the responses in the
English Church service : in common use, one
employed as a writer, assistant, copyist, account-
keeper, or correspondent in an office : (*U.S.*) a
shop-assistant.—*v.i.* to act as clerk.—*adj.* **cler'ical**
(see under **clergy**).—*ns.* **clerk'dom; clerk'ess,**
a female clerk.—*adj.* **clerk'ish,** like a clerk;
clerk'less, ignorant; **clerk'-like,** scholarly.—*n.*
clerk'ling, a young clerk.—*adj.* **clerk'ly,** scholarly.
—*adv.* in a scholar-like or learned manner.—*n.*
clerk'ship.—**Bible clerk,** a scholar who reads
the lessons in some college chapels; **clerk of the
weather,** an imaginary functionary facetiously
supposed to direct the weather; **clerk of works,**
one who superintends the erection of a building,
etc.; **Lord Clerk Register** (see **register**); **St.
Nicholas's clerks,** (*arch.*) thieves. [O.E. *clerc,*
a priest—L.L. *clēricus;* see **clergy**.]

cleromancy, *kler'o-man-si, n.* divination by lot.
[Gr. *klēros,* lot, *manteiā,* divination.]

cleruch, *kler'ōōk, -uk, n.* (*Greek hist.*) an allotment-
holder in foreign territory retaining his Athenian
citizenship.—*n.* **cler'uchy, cleruch'ia.** [Gr.
klērouchos—klēros, allotment, *echein,* to have.]

cleuch, cleugh, *klōōhh,* Scottish form of **clough.**

cleve, *klēv, n.* cliff : hillside. [Now rare. M.E.
cleof, a variant of **cliff.**]

cleveite, *klē'vīt, klä'vә-īt, n.* a pitchblende in
octahedral crystals containing helium. [P.T. *Cleve,*
Swedish chemist.]

clever, *klev'әr, adj.* able or dexterous : ingenious :
skilful : (*U.S.*) good-natured.—*ns.* **cleveral'ity**
(*Scot.*), **clev'erness.**—*adj.* **clev'erish,** somewhat
clever.—*adv.* **clev'erly.** [Ety. dub.]

clew, clue, *klōō, n.* a ball of thread, or the thread
in it : a thread that guides through a labyrinth :
anything that points to the solution of a mystery
(in this sense usually clue) : the corner of a sail.—
v.t. to coil up into a clew or ball : to truss or tie up
to the yards.—*n.* **clew'-gar'net** (*naut.*), a tackle
for clewing up the smaller square sails for furling.
—*n.pl.* **clew'-lines,** ropes on the smaller square
sails by which they are clewed up for furling.
[O.E. *cliwen;* cf. Du. *kluwen;* Ger. *knäuel*.]

cliché, *klē-shā, n.* the impression made by a die in
any soft metal : an electrotype or stereotype plate :
a stereotyped phrase, or literary tag. [Fr.,—
clicher, to stereotype.]

click, *klik, n.* a short, sharp ticking sound : anything that makes such a sound, as a small piece of
iron falling into a notched wheel : a clucking sound
produced by sudden retraction of the tongue from
the upper teeth, palate, or elsewhere; characteristic
of Hottentot and other South African languages,
represented by C (dental), Q (palatal), and X
(lateral); a latch for a gate.—*v.i.* to make a light,
sharp sound : (*slang*) to fit into place opportunely
or successfully, esp. to succeed in coming into
relations of sociability with a person of the other
sex.—*ns.* **click'-bee'tle,** any beetle of the family
Elateridae, characterised by leaping in the air with
a click when laid on their backs; **click'-clack,** a
persistent clicking noise; **click'er,** the compositor
who distributes the copy among a compositorship
of printers, makes up pages, etc. : one who cuts up
leather for the uppers and soles of boots; **click'ing,**
the action of the verb. [Dim. of **clack.**]

clicket, *klik'et, n.* a latch.—*v.i.* to make a clicking
sound. [O.Fr. (and Fr.) *cliquet.*]

client, *klī'әnt, n.* one who employs a lawyer or
professional adviser : a dependant : a customer.—
n. **cli'entage,** the whole number of one's clients :
the client's relation to the patron.—*adj.* **cli'ental**
(*-ent'l*).—*ns.* **clientele** (*klī'en-tēl*), **clientèle** (*klē-
än°-tel'*), a following : the whole connexion of a
lawyer, shop-keeper, etc.; **cli'entship.** [L. *cliēns,
-entis,* a dependent upon a *patrōnus.*]

cliff, *klif, n.* a high steep rock : the steep side of a
mountain.—*adjs.* **cliffed, cliff'y,** having cliffs :
craggy. [O.E. *clif;* Du. *clif;* O.N. *klif.*]

cliff, *klif, n.* (*mus.*). Same as **clef.**

clift. See **cleft** (2).

clift, *klift, n.* same as **cliff** (through the influence of
cleft).—*adjs.* **clift'ed, clift'y,** broken into cliffs.

climacteric, *klī-mak-ter'ik,* or *klī-mak'tәr-ik, n.* a
critical period in human life, in which some great
bodily change is supposed to take place : a critical
time.—*adj.* pertaining to such a period : critical.—
adj. **climacter'ical.**—**the grand climacteric,**
(generally) the sixty-third year, supposed to be a
critical period for men. [Gr. *klimaktēr—klīmax,*
a ladder.]

climate, *klī'māt, -mit, n.* the condition of a country
or place with regard to temperature, moisture, etc. :
(*fig.*) character of something.—*v.i.* (*Shak.*) to
remain in a certain place.—*adjs.* **cli'matal,
climatic** (*-mat'ik*), **-al.**—*v.t.* **cli'matise** (see
acclimatise).—*adj.* **climatograph'ical.**—*n.* **cli-
matog'raphy,** a description of climates.—*adj.*
climatolog'ical.—*ns.* **climatol'ogist;** **climatol'ogy,** the science of climates, or an investigation
of the causes on which the climate of a place
depends; **cli'mature** (*Shak.*), region.—**climate of
opinion,** the critical atmosphere, complex of
opinions prevalent at a particular time or in a
particular place. [Fr. *climat*—L. *clima*—Gr. *klima,
-atos,* slope—*klīnein,* to slope.]

climax, *klī'maks, n.* (*rhet.*) the arranging of discourse in order of increasing strength : (*loosely*) the
last term of the rhetorical arrangement : hence, a
culmination.—*v.i.* to ascend in a climax : to culminate.—*adjs.* (wrongly formed) **climac'tic, -al,**
pertaining to a climax.—*adv.* **climac'tically.**
[Gr. *klīmax, -akos,* a ladder—from *klīnein,* to slope.]

climb, *klīm, v.i.* or *v.t.* to ascend or mount by
clutching with the hands and feet : to ascend with
difficulty : to mount : of plants, to ascend by
clinging to other objects, by means of hooks,
tendrils, twining stems, or otherwise : extended to
similar downward movement (to *climb down*—also
fig. to abandon an excessive or overweening
demand, position, or attitude) (*pa.t.* and *pa.p.*
climbed, *arch.* **clomb,** *klōm*).—*n.* an act of
climbing : an ascent.—*adj.* **climb'able.**—*ns.*
climb'-down; climb'er, one who or that which
climbs : one who is intent upon his own social
advancement : an old-fashioned name for a bird
whose feet are mainly adapted for climbing : (*bot.*)
a climbing plant.—*n.* and *adj.* **climb'ing.** [O.E.
climban; cf. Ger. *klimmen;* **clamber, cleave** (2).]

clime, *klīm, n.* a country, region, tract. [**climate.**]

clinamen, klin-ā′mən, n. inclination. [L. clīnāmen.]

clinch, klinsh, klinch, v.t. to fasten or rivet a nail by bending and beating down the point: to clench: (fig.) to drive home (as an argument): to settle or confirm.—v.i. to grapple.—n. something set firmly: the fastening of a nail by beating it back: (boxing) a holding grapple: a pun: a punning retort.—n. clinch′er, one that clinches: a decisive argument.—adj. clinch′er-built (same as clinker-built).—n. clinch′er-work, the disposition of the side planks of a vessel, when the lower edge of one row overlaps the row next under it. [Same as clench; causal form of clink.]

cling, kling, v.i. to stick close by adhesive surface or by clasp: to adhere in interest or affection: to remain by an opinion: of wood, to shrink.—v.t. to attach: to shrivel (pa.t. and pa.p. clung).—n. adherence.—adjs. cling, cling′stone, having the pulp adhering firmly to the stone (of peaches)—opp. to freestone; cling′y, sticky. [O.E. clingan.]

clinic, -al, klin′ik, -əl, adj. pertaining to a bed: (med.) applied to practical instruction given in hospitals.—n. clin′ic, one confined to bed by sickness: the teaching of medicine or surgery at the bedside of hospital patients: a private hospital or nursing-home: an institution for treating out-patients or for diagnosis or giving advice—also clinique (klin-ēk′).—adv. clin′ically.—n. clin-ician (-ish′ən).—clinical baptism, baptism administered to persons on their sick-bed; clinical convert, one converted on his death-bed; clinical medicine, or surgery, medicine or surgery as taught by clinics; clinical lecture, one to students at the bedside of the sick; clinical thermometer, one for taking the temperature of patients. [Gr. klīnikos—klīnē, a bed.]

clink, klingk, n. a ringing sound made by striking metal, glass, etc.—v.t. to cause to make a ringing sound.—v.i to ring: to go with a clink.—n. clink′er, a hard brick (also klinker, as Dutch): a scale or globule of black iron oxide obtained from red-hot iron under the hammer: incombustible residue of fused ash raked out of furnaces: furnace slag: the cindery crust of some lava-flows.—adj. clink′er-built, made of planks which overlap those below (as distinguished from carvel-built) and fastened with clinched nails.—n. clink′-stone, phonolite (from its metallic clink when struck). [A form of click and clank.]

clink, klingk, n. (slang) prison. [Appar. orig. one in Southwark.]

clink, klingk, n. (Spens.) said to mean keyhole, or latch. [Cf. Du. klink, latch.]

clink, klingk, v.t. to clinch: to rivet.—n. clink′er, anything worthy of warm admiration in its kind.—adj. (slang) clink′ing. [Northern form of clinch.]

clino-, klī′nō-, in composition, oblique.—ns. cli′no-axis (crystall.), the clinodiagonal; clinodiag′onal, in a monoclinic crystal, that lateral axis which is not perpendicular to the vertical axis; clinometer (klīn-, klin-om′i-tər), an instrument for measuring dip of strata.—adj. clinomet′ric.—ns. clinom′-etry; clinopin′acoid, -pin′akoid, a form consisting of two faces parallel to the clinoaxis and the vertical axis; cli′noprism, a form parallel to the clinodiameter. [Gr. klīnein, to lean.]

clinochlore, klī′nō-klōr, n. a green mineral, a distinctly monoclinic variety of chlorite.

clinquant, klingk′ant, adj. (Shak.) tinselly: glittering.—n. tinsel: glitter. [Fr.,—Du. klinken, to clink.]

Clio, klī′ō, n. the muse of history. [Gr. Kleiō, proclaimer.]

Clio, klī′ō, n. a genus of shell-less pteropods, 'whales' food'. [Gr. Kleiō, a sea-nymph.]

clip, klip, v.t. to cut with shears: to cut off: to trim or cut off the hair, twigs, ends, edges, etc. of: to pare down: to reduce or curtail: to shorten in indistinct utterance.—v.i. to go at a good speed (pr.p. clipp′ing; pa.p. clipped, clipt).—n. an act of clipping: the thing removed by clipping: yield of wool: a smart blow: (U.S.) a high speed.—adj. clipped, clipt.—ns. clipp′er, one who clips: a clipping instrument: a swift mover: a sharp-built fast sailing-vessel: (slang) a dashing person, or

anything admired in its kind; clipp′ing, the act of clipping, esp. the edges of coins: a small piece clipped off, shred, paring: a newspaper cutting.—adj. superb: fast-going.—clip coin, to pare the edges of coins; clip the wings, to cut the feathers of a bird's wings to prevent it from flying: (fig.) to restrain ambition: to deprive of the means of rising. [Prob. from O.N. klippa, to cut; Dan. klippe.]

clip, klip, v.t. (Shak.) to embrace: to encircle: to hold firmly.—n. a device for gripping or clasping, or holding things together.—n. clip′-hook, a sister-hook. [O.E. clyppan, to embrace; O.N. klýpa, to pinch; Ger. kluppe, pincers.]

clique, klēk, n. an exclusive group of persons: a faction: a coterie—used generally in a bad sense.—adj. cliqu′ish, relating to a clique: exclusive.—ns. cliqu′ishness; cliqu′ism, tendency to form cliques. [Fr., orig. in sense of claque; prob. conn. with click.]

clish-clash, klish′-klash, clishmaclaver, klish′mə-kläv′ər, n. gossip. [Scot. See clash, claver.]

clistogamy. See cleistogamy.

clitellum, kli-, klī-tel′əm, n. a glandular belt on a worm, secreting a cocoon:—pl. clitell′a.—adj. clitell′ar. [L. clītellae, pack-saddle.]

clithral. Same as cleithral.

clitoris, klī′ or klī′tə-ris, n. a homologue of the penis in the female. [Gr. kleitoris.]

clitter, klit′ər, v.t. and v.i. to make, or cause to make, a shrill rattling noise.—n. clitt′er-clatt′er, idle talk, chatter. [Related to clatter.]

clivers. Same as cleavers.

cloaca, klō-ā′kä (L. -ā′kä), n. a sewer: a privy: a cavity in birds and reptiles, in which the intestinal and urinary ducts terminate: a sink of moral filth:—pl. cloacae (klō-ā′sē; L. -ā-kī).—adjs. cloā′cal, cloā′calin(e), cloacinal (klō-ə-sī′nl). [L. cloāca—cluēre, to purge.]

cloak, klōk, n. a loose outer garment: a covering: that which conceals: a disguise, pretext.—v.t. to clothe with a cloak: to cover: to conceal.—ns. cloak′-bag (obs.), a portmanteau; cloak′-room, a room for keeping coats and hats: a railway office where luggage may be left: a lavatory.—Also cloke. [O.Fr. cloke, cloque—L.L. cloca, a bell, a horseman's bell-shaped cape; see clock.]

cloam, klōm, n. and adj. earthenware, clay, or made of such. [O.E. clám, mud.]

clobber, klob′ər, n. a paste used by shoemakers to hide the cracks in leather. [Ety. dub.]

cloche, klosh, n. a glass under which plants are forced: a lady's close-fitting hat. [Fr., bell; see clock.]

clock, klok, n. a machine for measuring time, strictly one with a bell: a time-measurer in general: (Shak.) the striking of the hour.—v.t. to time by a clock or stop-watch.—v.i. to register a time by a recording clock.—n. clock′-golf, a putting game on a green marked like a clock dial, in which the player putts from each hour-figure to a hole near the centre.—adv. clock′wise, in the manner or direction of the hands of a clock.—n. clock′work, the works or machinery of a clock: machinery steady and regular like that of a clock.—adj. automatic.—clock in, out, on, off, to register time of coming or going, in, out, on, off; know what o'clock it is, to be wide awake, to know how things are; o'clock, for earlier of the clock, as reckoned or shown by the clock. [M.E. clokke, prob. through O.Fr. from L.L. cloca, clocca, a bell; mod. Fr. cloche, Du. klok; Ger. glocke, a bell.]

clock, klok, n. an ornament on the side of a stocking.—adj. clocked, ornamented with clocks. [Ety. dub.]

clock, klok, n. (Scot. and dial.) a beetle—common name in Scotland. [Origin unknown; cf. Swed. dial. klocka, beetle, earwig.]

clock, klok, v.i. (Scot.) to cluck: to brood or sit.—n. a brooding hen's cry: a cluck.—n. clock′er, a clocking hen. [O.E. cloccian; Du. klokken.]

clod, klod, n. a thick round mass or lump, that sticks together, esp. of earth or turf: a concreted mass: the ground: a bed of fireclay in a coal-mine: the body of a man, as formed of clay: a stupid fellow.—

v.t. to pelt.—*v.i.* to throw clods : (*Scot.*) to throw (*pr.p.* clodd'ing ; *pa.t.* and *pa.p.* clodd'ed).— *adjs.* clodd'ish ; clodd'y, abounding in clods : earthy.—*n.* clod'hopper, a countryman : a peasant : a dolt.—*adj.* clodhopp'ing, boorish.—*adv.* clod'ly.—*ns.* clod'pate, clod'pole, clod'poll, a stupid fellow.—*adj.* clod'pated. [A later form of clot.]

cloff, *klof, n.* a cleft. [Cf. O.N. *klof.*]

cloff, *klof, n.* an allowance on buying goods whole-sale, of 2 lb. in every 3 cwt., after tare and tret have been deducted. [Origin obscure.]

clog, *klog, n.* a block of wood : anything hindering motion : an obstruction : an impediment : a shoe with a wooden sole.—*v.t.* to fasten a piece of wood to : to choke up with an accumulation : to obstruct : to encumber : to sole with wood.—*ns.* clog'-al'manac, an early form of almanac having the indicating characters notched on wood, horn, etc.; clog'-dance, a dance performed with clogs, the clatter keeping time to the music.—*adj.* clogged, encumbered.—*ns.* clogg'er, one who make clogs; clogg'iness.—*adj.* clogg'y, lumpy, sticky. [Ety. dub.]

cloison, *klwä-zon*, *kloi'zn, n.* a partition, dividing fillet or band.—*n.* cloisonnage (*klwäz-on-äzh*), cloisonné work or process.—*adj.* cloisonné (*klwäz-on-ā, kloi-zon'ā,* or *-ā'*), decorated in enamel, in compartments formed by small fillets of metal.— *n.* work of this kind. [Fr.]

cloister, *klois'tər, n.* a covered arcade forming part of a monastic or collegiate establishment : a place of religious retirement, a monastery or nunnery : an enclosed place : monastic life.—*v.t.* to confine in a cloister : to confine within walls.—*adj.* clois'tered, dwelling in cloisters.—*ns.* clois'terer, one belonging to a cloister; clois'ter-garth, the court or yard enclosed by a cloister.—*adj.* clois'tral, claustral, pertaining or confined to a cloister : secluded.—*n.* clois'tress (*Shak.*), a nun. [O.Fr. *cloistre* (O.E. *clauster*)—L. *claustrum*— *claudĕre, clausum,* to shut.]

cloke. Same as cloak.

clomb, *klōm,* old *pa.t.* and *pa.p.* of climb.

clone, *klōn, n.* (*biol.*) the whole stock of individuals derived asexually from one sexually produced. [Gr. *klōn,* shoot.]

clonus, *klō'nəs, n.* a spasm of alternate contractions and relaxations of the muscles.—*adj.* clonic (*klon'ik*). [Latinised from Gr. *klŏnos,* tumult.]

cloop, *klōōp, n.* the sound of drawing a cork. [Imit.]

cloot, *kloot, Scot. klüt, klit, n.* a division of a cloven hoof : (*loosely*) a hoof.—*ns.* Cloot'ie, Cloots, the devil. [Scot.; ety. dub.]

clop, *klop, n.* the sound of a horse's hoof-tread.— *adv.* with a clop.—*v.i.* to make, or go with, such a sound.—Also clop-clop. [Imit.]

close, *klōs, adj.* shut up : with no opening : con-fined, unventilated : stifling : narrow : stingy : near, in time or place : intimate : compact : crowded : hidden : reserved : private : secret : (of a vowel) pronounced with slight opening, or with the tongue tense.—*adv.* in a close manner : tightly : nearly : densely : secretly.—*n.* an enclosed place : a small enclosed field : a narrow passage of a street : the precinct of a cathedral.—*adjs.* close'-band'ed, closely united; close'-barred, firmly closed; close'-bod'ied, fitting close to the body; close'-fist'ed, close'-hand'ed, penurious, covetous; close'-grained, with the particles, fibres, etc., close together, compact; close'-hauled, in trim for sailing as near as possible to the wind.—*adv.* close'ly.—*n.* close'ness.—*adj.* close'-reef'ed, having all reefs taken in.—*n.* close'-stool, a chamber utensil enclosed in a box or stool.—*adj.* close'-tongued (*Shak.*), cautious in speaking.—*n.* close'-up', a photograph or film taken near at hand and thus detailed and big in scale : a close scrutiny; close call (*U.S.*), a narrow escape; close corporation, a corporation which fills up its own vacancies, without outside interference; close season, time, a time of the year when it is illegal to kill certain game or fish : the breeding season : a prohibited period; close tennis, tennis properly so called, distinguished from lawn tennis. [Fr.

clos, shut—L. *claudĕre, clausum,* to close, shut up.]

close, *klōz, v.t.* to make close : to draw together and unite : to end.—*v.i.* to come together : to grapple : to come to an end.—*n.* the manner or time of closing : a pause or stop : a cadence : the end : junction : (*Shak.*) encounter.—*adj.* closed'-chain' (*chem.*) having a molecule in which the atoms are linked ringwise, like a chain with the ends united.— *ns.* clos'er, one who or that which concludes : any portion of a brick used to close up the bond next to the end brick of a course; clos'ing, en-closing : ending : agreement; clos'ure, the act of closing : the end : the stopping of a debate by vote of the House.—*v.t.* to apply the closure to.—close a bargain, to make an agreement; close down, to come to a standstill or stoppage of work : to give up business; closed shop, an establishment in which only members of a trade union, or of a particular trade union, will be employed : the principle or policy implied in such a regulation : an establishment boycotted by the trade unions; closed syllable, one ending in a consonant; close in upon, to surround and draw near to; close with, to accede to : to grapple with; with closed doors, in private, the public being excluded, as in special cases in court, etc. [Fr. *clore, clos*— L. *claudĕre, clausum.*]

closet, *kloz'it, n.* a small private room : a recess off a room : a privy : the private chamber of a sovereign, an apartment for private audience or council, or for private or domestic devotions.—*v.t.* to shut up in or take into a closet : to conceal :—*pr.p.* clos'-eting; *pa.t.* and *pa.p.* clos'eted.—*ns.* clos'et-play, -drama, a play to be read rather than acted; clos'et-strat'egist, a mere theorist in strategy. [O.Fr. *closet,* dim. of *clos;* see close.]

clot, *klot, n.* a mass of soft or fluid matter concreted, as blood.—*v.t.* and *v.i.* to form into clots : to coagulate (*pr.p.* clott'ing ; *pa.t.* and *pa.p.* clott'ed). —*n.* clot'poll (*Shak.*), a clodpoll, a blockhead.— *v.t.* clott'er, to coagulate.—*n.* clott'iness ; clott'-ing, coagulation.—*adj.* clott'y.—clotted (also clouted) cream, a famous Devonshire dainty, prepared by scalding milk. [O.E. *clott,* a clod of earth; cf. Du. *klos,* block; Dan. *klods;* Ger. *klotz.*]

clote, *klōt, n.* the burdock : extended to other plants of burry character.—*n.* clotbur (*klot'bur*), burdock : a species of *Xanthium.*—Also clote'-bur. [O.E. *clāte.*]

cloth, *kloth, n.* woven material from which garments or coverings are made : a piece of this material : clothing : the usual dress of a trade or profession, esp. the clerical : a table-cloth : sails : a theatre curtain :—*pl.* cloths (*kloths, klawdhz*).—*v.t.* clothe (*klōdh*), to cover with a garment : to provide with clothes : (*fig.*) to invest as with a garment : to cover : *pr.p.* clothing (*klōdh'ing*); *pa.t.* and *pa.p.* clothed (*klōdhd*), or clad.—*n.pl.* clothes (*klōdhz ; coll. klōz*), garments or articles of dress : blankets, sheets and cover for a bed.—*ns.* clothes'-basket, a large basket for holding and carrying clothes for the wash; clothes'-brush, a brush for clothes; clothes'-horse, clothes'-screen, a frame for hanging clothes on to dry; clothes'-line, a rope or wire for hanging clothes on to dry; clothes'-moth, one of various tineas whose larvae feed on woollens; clothes'-peg, -pin, a forked piece of wood or clamp to secure clothes on a line; clothes'-pole, a pole from which clothes-lines are hung; clothes'-press, a place for holding clothes : apparatus for pressing clothes; clothes'-prop, a movable notched pole for raising or supporting a clothes-line; cloth'-hall, exchange building or market for the cloth trade; clothier (*klō'dhi-ər*), one who makes or sells cloth or clothes; clothing (*klō'dhing*), clothes, garments : covering; cloth-yard, the yard by which cloth was measured, formerly 37 inches.—clothe in words, to express in words; clothe on, or upon, to invest : to cover; cloth of gold, a tissue of threads of gold and silk or wool; cloth of state, a canopy; cloth-yard shaft, an arrow a cloth-yard long.—the cloth, the clerical profession : the clergy. [O.E. *cláth,* cloth; Ger. *kleid,* a garment.]

Clotho, *klō'thō, n.* (*Gr. myth.*) the Fate that spins

the thread of life: the puff-adder genus. [Gr. *klōthō.*]

cloture, *klō-tür*, *n.* and *v.t.* closure. [Fr. *clôture*: see **closure**.]

cloud, *klowd*, *n.* a mass of fog, consisting of minute particles of water, often in a frozen state, floating in the atmosphere: (*fig.*) anything unsubstantial: a great number or multitude of anything (as cloud of witnesses): anything that obscures, as a cloud: a dullness: a dark or dull spot: (*Shak.*) a dark spot on a horse's face: a great volume of dust or smoke: anything gloomy, overhanging or bodeful.—*v.t.* to overspread with clouds: to darken: to defame: to stain with dark spots or streaks: to dull.—*v.i.* to become clouded or darkened.—*ns.* **cloud′age**; **cloud′berry**, a low plant related to the bramble, found on elevated moors in Britain, with an orange-red berry of delightful flavour.—*adj.* **cloud′-built**, made of clouds, unsubstantial.—*n.* **cloud′-burst**, a sudden flood of rain over a small area.—*adj.* **cloud′-capt** (*Shak.*), capped with or touching the clouds.—*ns.* **cloud′-castle**, **cloud′land**, **cloud′-cuck′oo-land**, or **-town**, an imaginary situation or land (the last translating Aristophanes's *Nephelokokkȳgiā*); **cloud′-chamber**, an apparatus in which the path of charged particles is made visible by means of water-drops condensed on gas ions.—*adjs.* **cloud′-compell′ing**, driving or collecting the clouds, an epithet of Zeus; **cloud′ed**, hidden by clouds: (*fig.*) darkened: indistinct: dull: variegated with spots.—*adv.* **cloud′ily.**—*ns.* **cloud′iness**; **cloud′ing**, a cloudy appearance.—*adj.* growing dim.—*adjs.* **cloud′-kiss′ing** (*Shak.*), touching the clouds; **cloud′less**, unclouded, clear.—*adv.* **cloud′lessly.**—*n.* **cloud′-let**, a little cloud.—*adj.* **cloud′-topped**, covered with or touching the clouds; **cloud′y**, darkened with, or consisting of, clouds: obscure: gloomy: stained with dark spots: (*coll.*) 'shady'.—**under a cloud**, in trouble, disgrace, or disfavour. [O.E. *clúd*, a hill (as still in Derbyshire), then a cloud, the root idea being a mass or ball; cf. **clod**, **clot**.]

clough, *kluf*, or *klow*, *n.* a ravine: a valley. [O.E. would be *clōh*; Scot. *cleuch*.]

clour, *klōōr*, *n.* (*Scot.*) a knock: a swelling caused by a knock.—*v.t.* to knock: to raise a bump. [Origin doubtful.]

clout, *klowt*, *n.* a piece of cloth, esp. used for mending: a patch: a protective plate or nail: a rag: a mark for archers to shoot at: a shot that hits: a blow or cuff.—*v.t.* to mend with a patch: to protect with a plate or with nails: to cover with a cloth: to cuff.—*adj.* **clout′ed** (*Shak.*), heavy and patched or having nails in the soles, as shoes: covered with a clout.—*adj.* **clout′erly**, clownish.—*ns.* **clout′-nail**, a large-headed nail: **clout′-shoe**, a shoe with clout-nails: a clown. [O.E. *clút*; cf. O.N. *klútr*, a kerchief; Dan. *klud*, rag.]

clouted, *klowt′id*, *adj.* clotted. [See **clot**.]

clove, *klōv*, *pa.t.* of **cleave**.—*ns.* **clove-hitch** (see **hitch**); **clove-hook**, a sister-hook.

clove, *klōv*, *n.* a division of a bulb, as in garlic. [O.E. *clufu*; cf. **cleave**.]

clove, *klōv*, *n.* an old weight (7, 8, or 10 pounds) for wool and cheese. [Fr. *clou*—L. *clāvus*, nail.]

clove, *klov*, *n.* the flower-bud of the **clove-tree** (*Eugenia caryophyllata*), a native of the Moluccas, dried as a spice, and yielding an essential oil: (*pl.*) a cordial got therefrom.—*ns.* **clove′-gill′yflower**, **clove′-pink**, a variety of pink, smelling of cloves. [Fr. *clou*, nail, from its shape—L. *clāvus*, a nail.]

cloven, *klōv′n*, *p.adj.* split: divided.—*adjs.* **clov′en-foot′ed**, **clov′en-hoofed**, having the hoof divided, as the ox or sheep.—**the cloven hoof**, applied to any indication of devilish agency or temptation, from the early representation of the devil with cloven hoofs—prob. from Pan, some of whose characteristics he shares. [*Pa.p.* of **cleave**, to divide.]

clover, *klō′vər*, *n.* a genus (Trifolium) of papilionaceous plants, with heads of small flowers and trifoliate leaves, affording rich pasturage.—*adj.* **clov′ered**, covered with clover.—*n.* **clov′er-grass**, clover.—*adj.* **clov′ery**, abounding in clover.—**live in clover**, to live luxuriously or in abundance.

[O.E. *cláfre* (usu. *clǣfre*); Du. *klaver;* Dan. *klöver;* Ger. *klee.*]

clow, *klow*, *n.* a Scots form of **clove** (4).—*n.* **clow′-gillieflower.**

clown, *klown*, *n.* a rustic or country-fellow: one with the awkward manners of a countryman: an ill-bred fellow: a fool or buffoon, esp. of the harlequinade or the circus.—*v.i.* to play the clown.—*ns.* **clown′ery**, a clown's performance; **clown′ing.**—*adj.* **clown′ish**, of or like a clown: coarse and awkward: rustic.—*adv.* **clown′ishly.**—*ns.* **clown′ishness**; **clown′ship**. [Prob. conn. with **clod** and **clot**.]

cloy, *kloi*, *v.t.* (*obs.*) to prick (a horse in shoeing): to gore: (of a cannon) to spike: to block up: to overcharge with food, to satiate, esp. with sweetness: to disgust, weary.—*v.i.* to cause distaste, become distasteful from excess.—*adjs.* **cloyed**; **cloy′ing**; **cloy′less** (*Shak.*), that cannot cloy.—*n.* **cloy′ment** (*Shak.*), satiety, surfeit.—*adj.* **cloy′some**, satiating. [Aphetised from *accloy*—O.Fr. *encloyer* (Fr. *enclouer*)—L.L. *inclāvāre*, to drive in a nail—*in*, in, *clāvus*, a nail.]

cloye, *kloi*, *v.t.* (*Shak.*) app., to claw, stroke with the claw. [Perh. **claw**.]

club, *klub*, *n.* a heavy tapering stick, knobby or massy at one end, used to strike with: a cudgel: a bat used in certain games: an instrument for playing golf, with a wooden, iron, or aluminium head, or a wooden head with brass sole: a bunch: a card of one of the four suits: a combination: a clique, set: an association of persons for social, political, athletic, or other ends: an association of persons who possess a building as a common resort for the members: a club-house, or the house occupied by a club.—*v.t.* to beat with a club: to gather into a bunch: to combine: to use as a club: (*mil.*) to throw into confusion.—*v.i.* to join together for some common end: to combine together: to share in a common expense.—*adjs.* **club′(b)able**, sociable; **clubbed**, enlarged at the end like a club.—*n.* **clubb′ing**, beating: combination: a thickening, as of finger-ends, or of cabbage-stems attacked by insect larvae.—*adj.* **clubb′ish**, given to clubs.—*ns.* **clubb′ism**, the club system; **clubb′ist**, a clubman; **club′-face**, the face of a golf-club; **club′-foot**, a deformed foot.—*adj.* **club′-foot′ed.**—*v.t.* **club′-haul** (*naut.*), to tack by dropping the lee anchor and slipping the cable.—*n.* **club′-head**, the head of a golf-club.—*adj.* **club′-head′ed**, having a thick head.—*ns.* **club′-house**, a house for the accommodation of a club; **club′-law**, government by violence; **club′-line**, a short line at the end of a paragraph; **club′-man**, one who carries a club: a member of a club: a frequenter of clubs, man about town: **club′-master**, the manager of, or purveyor for, a club; **club′-moss**, a lycopod; **club′-room**, the room in which a club meets; **club′-rush**, any sedge of the genus Scirpus; **club′-woman.**—*n.pl.* **clubs** (see **clumps**). [O.N. and Sw. *klubba*; same root as **clump**.]

cluck, *kluk*, *n.* the call of a hen to her chickens: any similar sound.—*v.i.* to make such a sound. [Imit.; cf. Du. *klokken*, Ger. *glucken*, Dan. *klukke*, and **clock**.]

clue, *klōō* (see **clew**).—*adj.* **clue′less**, without trace: trackless.

clumber, *klumb′ər*, *n.* a kind of spaniel, formerly bred at *Clumber*, in Notts.

clump, *klump*, *n.* a thick, short, shapeless piece of anything: a cluster: a clot: a thick additional sole: a blow.—*v.i.* to walk heavily: to clot: to cluster.—*v.t.* to put in a clump: to beat.—*n.* (*pl.* in form) **clumps**, a parlour game of question and answer—also **clubs.**—*adj.* **clump′y**, abounding in clumps: heavy. [Prob. Scand.; Dan. *klump*, a lump. Cf. Ger. *klump*, and **club**.]

clumsy, *klum′zi*, *adj.* shapeless: ill-made: unwieldy: awkward: ungainly.—*adv.* **clum′sily.**—*n.* **clum′siness.** [M.E. *clumsen*, to be stiff or benumbed.]

clunch, *klunsh*, *n.* a tough clay. [Prob. related to **clump.**]

clung, *klung*, *pa.t.* and *pa.p.* of **cling.**

Cluniac, *klōōn'i-ak*, *n.* a monk or nun of a branch of the Benedictine order originating at *Cluny* in France in 910.—Also *adj.*

Clupea, *klōō'pi-ä*, *n.* the herring genus.—*n.* **clu'peoid**, any fish of the herring family, Clupē'idae.—Also *adj.* [L. *clupea*, a kind of fish.]

Clusia, *klōō's(h)i-ä*, *n.* a typical American genus of (mostly) climbing plants, giving an alternative name **Clusiä'ceae** to the Guttiferae. [After the French botanist Charles de Lécluse (L. *Clusius*).]

cluster, *klus'tər*, *n.* a number of things of the same kind growing or joined together : a bunch : a mass : a crowd.—*v.i.* to grow in or gather into clusters.—*v.t.* to collect into clusters : to cover with clusters.—*n.* **clus'ter-cup**, an aecidium.—*adjs.* **clus'tered**, grouped; **clus'tering**.—*n.* **clus'ter-pine'**, the pinaster (*Pinus Pinaster*), a pine with clustered cones.—*adj.* **clus'tery**.—**clustered column**, a pier which consists of several columns or shafts clustered together. [O.E. *clyster*; L.G. *kluster*; cf. *clot*.]

clutch, *kluch*, *v.t.* to close the hand upon : to hold firmly : to seize or grasp.—*v.i.* to make a snatching movement.—*n.* a claw : a hand (often in *pl.*) : a device by which two shafts or rotating members may be connected or disconnected either while at rest or in relative motion : grasp : a snatching movement. [O.E. *clyccan*, to clench.]

clutch, *kluch*, *n.* a brood of chickens : a sitting of eggs.—*v.t.* to hatch. [Cf. **cleck**.]

clutter, *klut'ər*, *n.* a clotted or confused mass : confusion : stir : noise.—*v.i.* to crowd together : to go about in noisy confusion.—*v.t.* to litter. [From **clot**; influenced in meaning by **cluster** and **clatter**.]

cly, *klī*, *v.t.* (*slang*) to seize, steal.—*ns.* **cly'-fāk'er**, a pickpocket; **cly'-fāk'ing**, pocket-picking. [Prob. related to **claw**; referred by some to Du. *kleed*, a garment, *to fake a cly*, to take a garment.]

Clydesdale, *klīdz'dāl*, *adj.* originating in *Clydesdale* (of a breed of cart-horses).—*n.* a Clydesdale horse.

clypeus, *klip'i-əs*, *n.* the shield-like part of an insect's head.—*adjs.* **clyp'eal**, of the clypeus; **clyp'eate**, **clyp'eiform**, buckler-shaped. [L. *clipeus* (*clypeus*), a round shield.]

clyster, *klis'tər*, *n.* a liquid injected into the intestines.—*n.* **clys'ter-pipe** (*Shak.*), a pipe or syringe for injecting a clyster. [Gr. *klystēr*, a clyster-pipe—*klyzein*, to wash out.]

Cnicus, *(k)nī'kəs*, *n.* a genus of thistles. [Gr. *knēkos*.]

cnida, *(k)nī'dä*, *n.* a nematocyst :—*pl.* **cnī'dae** (*-dē*).—*n.pl.* **cnīdā'ria**, a division of the Coelenterata characterised by cnidae.—*n.* **cnī'doblast**, the mother-cell of a cnida. [Gr. *knīdē*, a nettle, a sea-anemone.]

co-, *kō-*, *pfx.* with : together. [L. *co-* for *com*, old form of *cum*, with.]

co', *kə*, Scots form of **quoth**.

co., *kō*, an abbreviation for **company**.

coacervate, *kō-as'ər-vāt* (or *-ər'*), *v.t.* to heap : to mass.—*adj.* heaped : massed.—*n.* **coacervā'tion**. [L. *coacervāre*, *-ātum*—*acervus*, heap.]

coach, *kōch*, *n.* formerly, a private carriage : a large, close, four-wheeled carriage, esp. one for state occasions or one plying for conveyance of passengers : a railway carriage : a motor vehicle for tourists and sight-seers : a ship's cabin near the stern : a private tutor : a professional trainer in athletics : a decoy animal.—*v.t.* to carry in a coach : to tutor, instruct, prepare for an examination, boat-race, etc.—*v.i.* to go by coach : to act as tutor : to study with a coach.—*ns.* **coach'-box**, the driver's seat on a coach; **coach'builder**; **coach'-building**; **coach'dog**, a spotted dog, kept chiefly as an attendant on carriages, a Dalmatian dog; **coach'ee**, **coach'y**, a coachman; **coach'er**, one who coaches : a coach-horse; **coach'-fellow**, a yoke-fellow; **coach'-hire**, money paid for the use of a hired coach; **coach'-horn**, a post-horn; **coach-horse**, a horse used for drawing a coach; **coach'-house**, a house to keep a coach in; **coach'ing**, travelling by coach : tutoring : instruction; **coach'man**, the driver of a coach : a servant employed to drive a carriage; **coach'-**

office, a stage-coach booking-office; **coach'-road**; **coach'-stand**, a place where coaches stand for hire; **coach'-way**; **coach'-wheel**; **coach'-whip**, a coachman's whip : a kind of whip-snake; **coach'whip-bird**, an Australian bird (Psophodes) that utters a sound like the crack of a whip; **coach'work**, the fine work of a motor-car body.—*adj.* **coach'y**, pertaining to a coach. [Fr. *coche*—Hung. *kocsi*, from *Kocs*, in Hungary.]

coact, *kō-akt'*, *v.i.* (*Shak.*) to act together.—*n.* **coaction** (*kō-ak'shən*), mutual relations.—*adj.* **coact'ive** (*Shak.*), acting together.—*n.* **co-activ'ity**. [Pfx. **co-** and **act**.]

coact, *kō-akt'*, *v.t.* to compel.—*n.* **coaction** (*kō-ak'shən*), compulsion.—*adj.* **coact'ive**, compulsory. [L. *cōgĕre*, *cōāctum*, to compel.]

coadjacent, *kō-ə-jās'ənt*, *adj.* contiguous.—*n.* **coadja'cency**.

coadjutant, *kō-ə-jōō'tənt*, *kō-aj'oo-tənt*, *adj.* mutually helping.—*n.* one who helps another.—*ns.* **co-adju'tor** (or *aj'*), a helper, assistant : an associate :—*fem.* **coadju'tress**, **coadju'trix**; **coadju'torship**. [L. *adjūtor*, a helper—*ad*, to, *juvāre*, to help.]

coadunate, *kō-ad'ū-nāt*, *v.t.* to unite : to combine.—*n.* **coadūnā'tion**.—*adj.* **coad'ūnative**. [L. *adūnāre*, *-ātum*, to unite—*ad*, to, *unus*, one.]

co-agent, *kō-ā'jənt*, *n.* a joint agent.—*n.* **co-ā'gency**.

coagulate, *kō-ag'ū-lāt*, *v.t.* to make to curdle, clot, or set by a chemical reaction.—*v.i.* to curdle, clot, or set irreversibly.—*adj.* (*rare*) clotted : curdled.—*n.* **coagūlabil'ity**.—*adj.* **coag'ūlable**.—*ns.* **coag'ūlant**, a substance that causes coagulation; **coagūlā'tion**.—*adjs.* **coag'ūlative**; **coag'ūlatory**.—*n.* **coag'ūlum**, what is coagulated. [L. *coāgulāre*, *-ātum*—*agĕre*, to drive.]

coaita, *kō-ī-tä'*, *n.* the red-faced spider monkey. [Tupí.]

coal, *kōl*, *n.* (*obs.*) charcoal : a piece of charcoal, esp. glowing : a firm, brittle, generally black combustible carbonaceous rock derived from vegetable matter (the usual sense now) : a piece of this rock : a cinder : an ember.—*v.i.* to take in coal.—*v.t.* to supply with coal : to char.—*ns.* **coal'ball**, a calcareous nodule found in coal; **coal'-bed**, a stratum of coal.—*adj.* **coal'-black**, black as coal, very black.—*ns.* **coal'-box**, a box for holding coal : (*mil. slang*) a shell that emits black smoke; **coal'-brass**, iron pyrites found with coal; **coal'-bunker**, a box, recess, or compartment for holding coal; **coal'-cellar**, a cellar or similar place for storing coal; **coal'-cutter**, a machine for undercutting a coal-bed; **coal'-dust**, coal in fine powder; **coal'-face**, the exposed surface of coal in a mine; **coal'field**, a district containing coal strata; **coal'-fish**, a dusky fish of the cod family, with a green back—the saith or sillock; **coal'-flap**, **coal'-plate**, a flap or plate covering the entrance from the pavement to a coal-cellar; **coal'-gas**, the mixture of gases produced by the distillation of coal, used for lighting and heating; **coal'-heaver**, one employed in carrying coal; **coal'-hole**, a small coal-cellar : (*U.S.*) a hole in the pavement for filling a coal cellar; **coal'-house**, a covered-in place for keeping coal; **coal'ite**, a smokeless fuel got by low-temperature carbonisation of coal; **coal'man**, one who has to do with coals; **coal'-master**, the owner or lessee of a coalfield; **coal'-mine**, **-pit**, a pit or mine from which coal is dug; **coal'-miner**; **coal'-mouse**, **coal'-tit**, **coal'-tit'mouse** (also **cole-**), a dark species of tit; **coal'-oil** (*U.S.*), rock-oil, shale-oil, petroleum; **coal'-own'er**, one who owns a colliery; **coal'-plant**, a fossil plant of the Carboniferous strata; **coal'-port'er**, one who carries coal; **coal'-scutt'le**, a fireside vessel for holding coal; **coal'-tar**, gas-tar, a thick, black, opaque liquid formed when coal is distilled; **coal'-trimmer**, one who stores or shifts coal on board vessels; **coal'-whipper**, one who unloads coal from vessels to barges.—*adj.* **coal'y**, of or like coal : covered with coal.—**blow the coals**, to excite passion, foment strife; **carry coals to Newcastle**, to take a thing where it is already most abundant; **coaling station**, a port at which steamships take in coal; **Coal Measures** (*geol.*), the uppermost division of the Carboniferous; **coal-scuttle bonnet,** a bonnet shaped like a coal-scuttle upside down; **haul** (or **call**) **over the coals,** to reprimand—from the discipline applied to heretics; **heap coals of fire on the head,** to excite remorse by returning good for evil (Rom. xii. 20). [O.E. *col;* cog. with O.N. *kol,* Ger. *kohle.*]

coalesce, *kō-ə-les',* *v.i.* to grow together or unite into one body.—*n.* **coalesc'ence,** growing into each other : fusion.—*adj.* **coalesc'ent.**—*v.t.* and *v.i.* **co'alise** (*kō'ə-līz*), to bring or come into coalition.—*n.* **coalition** (*-lish'ən*), combination or alliance short of union, esp. of states or political parties.—*adj.* **coali'tional.**—*n.* **coali'tioner,** **coali'tionist.**—**coalition government,** government by a coalition of parties, sometimes called a national government. [L. *coalēscĕre—alēscĕre,* to grow up.]

coamings, *kōm'ingz, n.pl.* (*naut.*) raised work about the edges of the hatches of a ship to keep water out. [Der. unknown.]

coapt, *kō-apt', v.t.* to adjust.—*n.* **coaptā'tion.** [L. *coaptāre—aptāre,* to fit.]

coarb, *kō'ärb, n.* (*hist.*) head of a family in an Irish sept : an ecclesiastical successor.—Also **comarb** (*kō'ärb*). [Ir. *comharba,* successor.]

coarctate, *kō-ärk'tāt, adj.* compressed : constricted.—*n.* **coarctā'tion.** [L. *coar(c)tāre, -ātum—ar(c)tāre,* to draw together.]

coarse, *kōrs, adj.* common, base, or inferior : rough : rude : uncivil : harsh : gross : large in grain, fibre, or mesh, etc. : without refinement : roughly approximate.—*adj.* **coarse'-grained,** large in grain : (*fig.*) coarse in nature : gross.—*adv.* **coarse'ly.**—*v.t.* and *v.i.* **coars'en,** to make or become coarse.—*n.* **coarse'ness.**—*adj.* **coars'ish,** somewhat coarse.—**coarse fish,** freshwater fish other than those of the salmon family; **coarse metal,** impure cuprous sulphide got in course of smelting. [From phrase 'in course', hence *ordinary.*]

coast, *kōst, n.* (*obs.*) side : border of land next the sea : the seashore : (*obs.*) limit or border : (*Milt.*) region : a hill suitable for coasting : an act or spell of coasting; **cost, coste** (*kōst, kost, Spens.*) coast : region : direction : footing, terms : side.—*v.i.* **coast** (*Spens.,* also **cost**), to approach : to sail along or near a coast : to travel downhill on a sledge, on a cycle without pedalling or in a motor-car out of gear : to glide.—*v.t.* to sail by or near to.—*adj.* **coast'al.**—*ns.* **coast'er,** vessel that sails along the coast: foot-rest on bicycle: container for decanter, etc. on table; **coast'-guard,** body of men organised to watch along coast for prevention of smuggling, for life-saving, defence, etc. : a member thereof; **coast'guard(s)man.**—*adj.* **coast'ing,** keeping near the coast : trading between ports in the same country.—*n.* the act of sailing, or of trading, along the coast : advances towards acquaintance, courtship : sliding downhill.—*ns.* **coast'-line,** the line or boundary of a coast : shore-line; **coast'-wait'er,** a custom-house officer for coasting shipping.—*advs.* **coast'ward, -s,** toward the coast; **coast'wise,** along the coast.—*adj.* carried on along the coast.—**the coast is clear,** there is no obstacle or danger in the way. [O.Fr. *coste* (Fr. *côte*)—L. *costa,* a rib, side.]

coat, *kōt, n.* an outer garment with sleeves : an overcoat : the hair or wool of a beast : vesture or habit : any covering : a membrane or layer, as of paint, etc. : a coat of arms (see below) : (*dial.*) a skirt or petticoat.—*v.t.* to clothe : to cover with a coat or layer.—*ns.* **coat'-arm'our,** coat of arms, or heraldically embroidered garment worn over armour : armorial devices; **coat'-card,** a card bearing the representation of a coated figure, the king, queen, or knave—now, less correctly, called *court-card;* **coatee',** a close-fitting coat with short tails; **coat'-frock,** a dress for use without coat or jacket; **coat'-hanger,** a curved piece of wood, etc., with a hook, by which a coat may be hung and kept in shape; **coat'ing,** a covering, layer : cloth for coats.—**coat of arms,** the family insignia embroidered on the surcoat worn over the hauberk, or coat of mail : the heraldic bearings of a gentle-

man; **coat of mail,** a piece of armour for the upper part of the body, made of metal scales or rings linked one with another.—**turn one's coat,** to change one's principles, or to turn from one party to another. [O.Fr. *cote* (Fr. *cotte*)—L.L. *cottus, cotta,* a tunic; the further etymology is uncertain.]

coat, coate, Shakespearian forms of **quote.**

coati, *kō-ä'ti,* or *kō'ə-ti, n.* an American plantigrade carnivorous mammal allied to the raccoons.—Also **coäti-mun'di, -mon'di.** [Tupi.]

coax, *kōks, v.t.* to persuade by fondling or flattery : to humour or soothe : to pet.—*ns.* **coax, coax'er,** one who coaxes.—*adv.* **coax'ingly.** [cokes.]

co-axial, *kō-ak'si-əl, adj.* having the same axis.—*adv.* **coax'ially.**

cob, *kob, n.* (*dial.*) a big or notable man : a short-legged strong horse : a male swan (also **cob'-swan**): a lump (esp. of coal, ore, clay) : a rounded object : a herring's head : a cobloaf : the axis of a head of maize, a corncob : a cobnut.—*adj.* **cobb'y,** like a cob : (*dial.*) stout, brisk, lively, arrogant.—*ns.* **cob'loaf,** a rounded, round-headed, or misshapen loaf : (*Shak.*) an expression of contempt; **cob'nut,** a large hazel-nut : a game played by children with nuts; **cob'-pipe,** a tobacco pipe made from a corncob. [Perh. conn. with **cop.**]

cob, *kob, n.* a kind of composition of clay and straw for building.—*n.* **cob'-wall.** [Origin unknown.]

cob, *kob, n.* a wicker basket used by sowers. [Origin unknown.]

cob, *kob, v.t.* to strike : to thump on the buttocks.

cobalt, *kō'bawlt,* or *-bawlt', n.* a metallic element, of atomic number 27 : a blue pigment prepared from it—also **cō'balt-blue'.**—*adj.* of this deep-blue colour.—*n.* **cob'alt-bloom',** erythrite.—*adjs.* **cobalt'ic ; cobaltif'erous.**—*n.* **cō'baltite,** a sulph-arsenide of cobalt (also **cobalt glance**). [Ger. *kobalt,* from *kobold,* a demon, a nickname given by the German miners, because they supposed it to be a mischievous and hurtful metal.]

cobber, *kob'ər, n.* (*Austr.; coll.*) mate, chum, buddy. [Origin unknown.]

cobble, *kob'l,* **cobble-stone,** *-stōn, ns.* a rounded stone, esp. used in paving.—*vs.t.* to pave with cobble-stones. [Ety. dub.]

cobble, *kob'l, v.t.* to patch up or mend coarsely, as shoes.—*ns.* **cobb'ler,** one who cobbles or mends shoes : a drink made up of wine, sugar, etc., and sucked through a straw; **cobbler's punch,** a warm drink made of beer, with the addition of spirit, sugar, and spice. [Der. unknown.]

co-belligerent, *kō-bi-lij'ə-rənt, adj.* co-operating in warfare.—Also *n.*

Cobdenism, *kob'dən-izm, n.* the policy of Richard *Cobden* (1804-1865), the English 'Apostle of Free Trade'.—*n.* **Cob'denite,** a supporter of Cobdenism, esp. a free-trader.

cobia, *kō'bi-ä, n.* the sergeant-fish. [Perh. of West Indian origin.]

coble, cobble, *kōb'l, n.* a small flat-bottomed boat. [Cf. W. *ceubal,* a hollow trunk, a boat.]

cobra, cobra de capello, *kō'brä, kob'rä, di ka-pel'ō, n.* a poisonous snake, found in India and Africa, which dilates its neck so as to resemble a hood.—*adjs.* **cob'ric ; cob'riform,** like or akin to the cobra. [Port., snake of the hood.]

coburg, *kō'burg, n.* a thin fabric of worsted with cotton or silk, twilled on one side. [*Coburg,* in Germany.]

cobweb, *kob'web, n.* a spider's web or net : any snare or device intended to entrap : anything flimsy or easily broken : anything that obscures.—*n.* **cobwebb'ery.**—*adj.* **cob'webby.** [Prob. *attercop-web;* see **attercop, web.**]

coca, *kō'kä, n.* a Peruvian shrub (*Erythroxylon Coca*) of a family akin to flax, whose leaves furnish an important narcotic and stimulant.—*ns.* **cocaine** (*kō'kā-in,* kō'kā-in, ko-kān'), an alkaloid obtained from coca-leaves, used as a local anaesthetic and as an intoxicant; **cocainīsā'tion.**—*v.t.* **cō'cainise.**—*ns.* **cōca'inism,** a morbid condition induced by over-use of cocaine; **coca'inist.** [Sp.—Quichua *coca.*]

Coca-Cola, *kō'kə-kō'lä, n.* a carbonated **soft** drink. [Registered trade-mark.]

fāte, fär, àsk; mē, hər (her); *mīne; mōte; mūte; mōōn; dhen* (then)

cocagne, cocaigne. Same as **cockaigne.**

coccineous, *kok-sin'i-əs, adj.* bright red. [L. *coccineus—coccum,* cochineal.]

cocco, *kok'ō,* **coco,** *kō'kō, n.* the taro or other edible araceous tuber.

coccolite, *kok'ō-līt, n.* a variety of pyroxene: a small rounded body found in deep-sea ooze (also **cocc'olith).** [Gr. *kokkos,* a berry, *lithos,* a stone.]

coccus, *kok'əs, n.* (*bot.*) a one-seeded portion of a dry fruit that breaks up: a spherical bacterium: **Coccus,** a genus of insects in the Hemiptera, type of a family **Coccidae** (*kok'si-dē*):—*pl.* **cocci** (*kok'sī*).—*adj.* **cocc'oid.**—*n.* **Cocc'ulus,** a tropical genus of climbing plants (*Menispermaceae*).— **cocculus indicus,** the dried fruit of *Anamirta Cocculus* (same family), narcotic and poisonous. [L.,—Gr. *kokkos,* a berry.]

coccyx, *kok'siks, n.* (*anat.*) the terminal triangular bone of the vertebral column:—*pl.* **coccyges** (*kok-sī'jēz*).—*adjs.* **coccygeal** (*kok-sij'i-əl*), **coc-cyg'ian.** [Gr. *kokkyx, -ȳgos,* cuckoo, coccyx (as resembling its bill).]

coch, *kōch, n.* (*Spens.*). Same as **coach.**

Cochin, *koch'in,* **Cochin-China,** *-chī'nä, n.* a large feathery-legged domestic hen, originally from Cochin-China.

cochineal, *koch'i-nēl, -nēl', n.* a scarlet dye-stuff consisting of the dried bodies of a Coccus insect gathered from a cactus in Mexico, the West Indies, etc.: the insect itself. [Sp. *cochinilla,* dim. of L. *coccinus,* scarlet—*coccum* (Gr. *kokkos*), a berry, as the similar kermes insect was formerly supposed to be the berry or seed of an oak.]

cochlea, *kok'li-ä, n.* anything spiral-shaped, esp. a snail-shell, a medick-pod, a winding stair: (*anat.*) the spiral cavity of the ear.—*adj.* **coch'lear** (*-li-ər*), pertaining to the cochlea of the ear: spoon-shaped.— *ns.* **coch'lear, cochleār'e** (L.) a spoon.—*n.pl.* **Cochleār'ia,** the scurvy-grass genus.—*adjs.* **coch-lear'iform,** spoon-shaped; **coch'leāte, coch'-leated,** twisted spirally: spoon-like. [L. *coc(h)lea,* a shell, screw, and *coc(h)lear(e),* a spoon—Gr. *kochlias,* a snail.]

cock, *kok, n.* a male bird, esp. of the domestic fowl (often compounded, as **cock'bird, cock-rob'in, cock-sparr'ow**): the time of cock-crowing: a weathercock: a plucky chap, a term of familiarity: a strutting chief or leader: anything set erect: a **tap**: part of the lock of a gun, held back by a **spring,** which, when released by the trigger, produces the discharge: an upward turn, as of a nose or a hat-brim.—*v.t.* to set erect or upright: to **set up** the brim of: to draw back, as the cock of a gun: to turn up or to one side: to tilt up knowingly, inquiringly, or scornfully.—*v.i.* to **strut:** to swagger.—*n.* **cock-a-doo'dle (-doo'),** the crow of a cock.—*v.i.* to crow.—*adj.* **cock-ahoop',** in exultant spirits.—*n.* **cockalō'rum,** a bumptious little person: a boy's jumping game.— *adj.* **cock'-and-bull',** rambling and incredible.— *ns.* **cock'-broth,** the broth made from a boiled cock; **cock'chāfer,** a large greyish brown beetle (*Melolontha vulgaris*), most destructive to vegetation; **cock'-crow, -ing,** early morning, when cocks crow.—*adj.* **cocked,** set erect: turned up or to one side.—*ns.* **cock'er,** one who follows cock-fighting: a small spaniel employed in pheasant and woodcock shooting; **cock'erel,** a young cock: a young man—also **cock'le,** whence **cock'le-brained,** foolish; **cock'-eye,** a squinting eye: the loop by which a trace is attached to the whipple-tree.—*adj.* **cock'-eyed.**—*ns.* **cock'-fight, -ing,** a fight or contest between game-cocks: a fight; **cock-horse,'** a child's imaginary or toy horse: a trace-horse for a coach: a spirited animal.—*adj.* prancing, proud.—*adv.* properly *a-cock-horse* (i.e. on cock-horse) on horseback: exultingly.—*ns.* **cockie-leek'ie, cocky-leek'y, cockaleek'ie** (*Scot.*), soup made from a fowl and leeks; **cock'-laird** (*Scot.*), a yeoman; **cock'loft,** a room just under the roof; **cock'-match,** a cock fight; **cock-of-the-rock,'** a South American bird of the cotinga family; **cock'-pad(d)'le, -paid'le** (see **paddle,** 2); **cock'pit,** a pit or enclosed space where **game-cocks** fought: a frequent battle-ground:

part of a ship-of-war's lower regions used for the wounded in action: a sheltered depression in the deck of a yacht or small ship: in air-craft a compartment in the fuselage for pilot or passenger: the driver's seat in a racing car; **cock's'-comb, cocks'comb,** the comb or crest on a cock's head: a jester's cap: (*Shak.*) a head: a crest-like crystalline mineral aggregate (as in *cockscomb pyrites*): a name for various plants, esp. a monstrous Celosia (fam. Amarantaceae) with fasciated inflorescence like a cock's comb, also yellow-rattle (Rhinanthus), and sainfoin: a coxcomb; **cock's'-foot,** a genus (Dactylis) of grasses with inflorescences like a cock's foot; **cock'shoot** (*obs.*), a glade where wood-cock were netted as they shot through; **cock'shot,** a shy at a mark; **cock'shut** (*Shak.*), twilight, probably referring to the time when poultry are shut up, or when woodcock shoot; **cock'-shy,** a throw at a thing, originally a cock, as for amusement: the object set up, or a showman's outfit for the purpose; **cocks'iness, cox'iness.**—*adjs.* **cock'sure,** quite sure, esp. offensively.—*adj.* **cock'sy, coxy** (*schoolboy slang*), bumptious.—*n.* **cock'tail,** a racing horse that is not thoroughbred: one who apes the gentleman: a concoction of spirituous or other liquors, used as an appetiser.— *adjs.* **cock'tailed,** having the tail cocked or tilted up; **cock-thropp'led, -thrapp'led,** of a horse, bending the windpipe on bridling.—*n.* **cock'-throw'ing,** the old sport of throwing sticks at a cock.—*adjs.* **cock'-up,** turned up: (*print.*), rising above the tops of the other letters, superior; **cock'y,** pert.—*n.* **cock'yolly** (*kok-i-ol'i*), a nursery or pet name for a bird.—**cock a snook,** to put the thumb to the nose; **cocked hat,** an old-fashioned three-cornered hat: a note folded into a three-cornered shape; **cock of the walk,** chief of a set; **knock into a cocked hat,** to give a profound beating. [O.E. *coc;* O.N. *kokkr.*]

cock, *kok, n.* a small pile of hay, dung, etc.—*adj.* **cocked,** heaped up in cocks. [Cf. O.N. *kökkr,* a lump.]

cock, *kok, n.* (*Shak.*) a cockboat, a ship's small boat: a small frail boat; **cockswain** (see **coxwain**). [Cf. **cog** (3).]

cock, corr. of god.—**cock and pie** (see **pie** (2)).

cock-a-bondy, *kok'ə-bon'di* (*coll. kok'i-bun'di*), *n.* a fly for angling. [Welsh *coch a bon ddu,* red, with black stem.]

cockade, *kok-ād', n.* a rosette worn on the hat as a badge. [Fr. *cocarde—coq,* cock.]

Cockaigne, Cockayne, *kok-ān', n.* an imaginary country of luxury and delight. [Ety. dub.; Fr. *cocagne,* acc. to some from L. *coquĕre,* to cook.]

cockatoo, *kok-ə-tōō', n.* a large crested parrot of the Australian region: (*Austr.;* also **cock'y**) a small farmer.—*n.* **cockatiel, cockateel** (*-tēl'*), a small crested parrot of Australia.—**cow cocky,** a dairy farmer. [Malay, *kakatua.*]

cockatrice, *kok'ə-trīs, -tris, n.* a fabulous monster like a serpent, often confounded with the basilisk: (*her.*) a cock-like monster with a dragon's tail: (*obs.*) a prostitute. [O.Fr. *cocatris.*]

cockboat. See **cock** (3).

cocker, *kok'ər, v.t.* to pamper: to fondle: to indulge. [Ety. dub.; cf. Du. *kokelen,* O.Fr. *coqueliner,* to dandle.]

Cocker, *kok'ər, n.* a standard of accuracy and orthodoxy. [From Edward *Cocker* (1631-75) reputed author of a popular arithmetic book.]

cockernony, *kok-ər-non'i, n.* (*Scot.; obs.*) the gathering of hair in a fillet: a coiffure: a pad of false hair: a starched cap. [Origin obscure.]

cocket, *kok'it, n.* (*hist.*) the custom-house seal: a custom-house certificate. [Origin doubtful.]

cockle, *kok'l, n.* a cornfield weed, esp. now the corncockle.—*n.* **cock'le-bur,** clotbur (*Xanthium*). [O.E. *coccel.*]

cockle, *kok'l, n.* a large bivalve mollusc (*Cardium edule* or other species) with thick, ribbed, heart-shaped, equal-valved shell: its shell: a bivalve shell generally.—*adj.* **cock'led,** shelled like a cockle.—*ns.* **cock'le-hat,** a hat bearing a scallop-shell, the badge of a pilgrim; **cock'le-shell,** the shell of a cockle: a frail boat.—**cockles of the**

heart, the heart itself. [Fr. *coquille*—Gr. *konchylion*—*konchē*, a cockle.]

cockle, *kok'l*, *n.* a pucker.—*v.i.* to pucker.—*v.t.* to cause to pucker. [Perh. Fr. *coquiller*, to blister—*coquille*; see **cockle** (2).]

cockle, *kok'l*, *n.* a furnace or stove. [Perh. Du. *kachel*.]

cockney, *kok'ni*, *n.* (*obs.* or *dial.*) an egg, esp. a small misshapen egg: (*obs.*) a coddled child: (*Shak.*) a milksop: one whose experience and knowledge are exclusively townish: (still in *U.S.*) a townsman: one born in London, strictly within hearing of Bow Bells: London dialect.—*ns.* **cock'neydom**, the domain of Cockneys; **cockney-fica'tion**.—*v.t.* **cock'neyfy**, to make Cockney.—*adj.* **cock'neyish**.—*n.* **cock'neyism**, a Cockney idiom or characteristic.—**the Cockney School**, an old nickname for a supposed school of writers belonging to London—Leigh Hunt, Keats, and others. [M.E. *coken-ey*, cock's egg. Others would connect with Fr. *coquin*, a rogue—L. *coquus*, a cook.]

cockroach, *kok'rōch*, *n.* an orthopterous insect, the so-called black beetle. [Sp. *cucaracha*, woodlouse, cockroach.]

cocky. See **cock**, **cockatoo**.

coco, *kō'kō*, *n.* a tropical seaside palm-tree (*Cocos nucifera*), with curving stem (also **co'co-palm**, **co'conut-palm**, **co'co-tree**), producing the coconut.—*ns.* **co'co-de-mer** (*-də-mer'*; Fr.) the double coconut; **co'conut**, (less correctly) **co'coanut**, **co'kernut**, a large edible nut, yielding **co'conut-butt'er** or **co'conut-oil'**, and **co'conut-milk'**; **co'conut-matt'ing**, matting made from the husk of the coconut; **co'conut-shy**, a cockshy with coconuts as targets or as prizes.—**double coconut**, the large two-lobed nut of the Seychelles palm, *Lodoicea Sechellarum*. [Port. and Sp. *coco*, a bugbear; applied to the nut from the three marks at the end of it, which form a grotesque face.]

cocoa, *kō'kō*, *n.* the seed of the cacao or chocolate tree: a powder made from the seeds: a drink made from the powder.—*ns.* **co'coa-beans'**, the seeds, esp. when dried and fermented; **co'coa-butt'er**, **co'coa-fat'**, a fat got from the seeds (different from *coconut* butter); **co'coa-nibs**, cocoa-beans shelled and bruised. [**cacao**.]

coconscious, *kō-kon'shəs*, *adj.* conscious in a subsidiary stream, apart from the main stream.—*n.* **cocon'sciousness**.

cocoon, *ko-kōōn'*, *n.* the silken sheath spun by many insect larvae in passing into the pupa stage and by spiders for their eggs: the capsule in which earthworms and leeches lay their eggs.—*n.* **cocoon'ery**, a place for keeping silkworms when feeding and spinning cocoons. [Fr. *cocon*, from *coque*, a shell—L. *concha*, a shell.]

cocoplum, *kō'kō-plum*, *n.* a West Indian rosaceous tree (*Chrysobalanus Icaco*): its edible fruit. [Sp. *icaco*, and **plum**.]

cocotte, *kō-kot'*, *n.* a light-o'-love: a loose woman: a small fireproof dish, usu. for an individual portion. [Fr.]

coco-wood, **cocoa-wood**, *kō'kō-wood*, *n.* the wood of a West Indian mimosaceous tree, *Inga vera*: a trade-name for kokra-wood.

coction, *kok'shən*, *n.* boiling: cooking.—*adj.* **coc'tile**, baked: hardened by fire, as a brick. [L. *coquĕre*, *coctum*, to boil, cook.]

cocus-wood, *kō'kəs-wood*, *n.* the so-called Jamaica ebony (*Brya Ebenus*; Papilionaceae): a trade-name for kokra-wood.

cod, *kod*, **codfish**, *kod'fish*, *n.* a food fish (*Gadus morrhua*) of northern seas.—*ns.* **cod'-fisher**; **cod'-fish'ery**; **cod'-fishing**; **cod'ling**, small cod.—**cod'-liver oil**, a medicinal oil extracted from the fresh liver of the common cod. [Ety. dub.]

cod, *kod*, *n.* (*obs.*) a bag: a pod: the scrotum.—*adjs.* **codd'ed**, enclosed in a cod; **codd'ing** (*Shak.*), lecherous.—*n.* **cod'-piece**, a baggy appendage once worn in front of tight hose. [O.E. *codd*, a small bag; cf. next.]

cod, *kod*, *n.* (*Scot.*) a pillow or cushion. [O.N. *koddi*, a pillow; cf. foregoing.]

cod, *kod*, *n.* (*slang*) a fellow: a codger: a Charter-

house pensioner: a jest: a hoax.—*v.t.* to hoax: to poke fun at. [Ety. dub.]

coda, *kō'dä*, *n.* (*mus.*) a passage forming the completion of a piece, rounding it off to a satisfactory conclusion. [It.,—L. *cauda*, a tail.]

coddle, *kod'l*, *v.t.* to pamper: to fondle: to parboil.—*n.* an effeminate person. [Ety. dub.]

code, *kōd*, *n.* a collection or digest of laws: a system of rules and regulations (*spec.* regarding education): established principles or standards (of art, moral conduct, etc.): a volume: a system of signals: a system of words, letters, or symbols which represent sentences or other words, to ensure economy or secrecy in transmission: a cipher.—*v.t.* to codify: to express in code.—*ns.* **codifica'tion** (*kod'*, *kōd'*); **codifier** (*kod'*, *kōd'*), **cōd'ist**, one who codifies.—*v.t.* **codify** (*kod'*, *kōd'*), to put into the form of a code: to digest: to systematise (*pr.p.* **cod'ifying**; *pa.t.* and *pa.p.* **cod'ified**). [Fr. *code*; see **codex**.]

codeine, *kō'di-ēn*, *n.* an alkaloid got from poppyjuice. [Gr. *kōdeia*, poppy-head.]

codex, *kō'deks*, *n.* a code: a manuscript volume:—*pl.* **codices** (*kōd'i-sēz*). [L. *cōdex* or *caudex*, *-icis*, the trunk of a tree, a set of tablets, a book.]

codger, *koj'ər*, *n.* a mean fellow: an old person: a chap. [Prob. a variant of **cadger**.]

codicil, *kod'i-sil*, *n.* a supplement to a will.—*adj.* **codicill'ary**. [L. *cōdicillus*, dim. of *cōdex*.]

codilla, *kō-dil'ä*, *n.* the coarsest part of hemp or flax. [Dim. of It. *coda*—L. *cauda*, a tail.]

codille, *kō-dil'*, *n.* a situation in ombre when the challenger loses. [Fr.]

codling, *kod'ling*, **codlin**, *kod'lin*, *n.* an elongated apple.—*n.* **cod'lin-moth**, the moth whose larvae cause 'worm-eaten' apples to fall prematurely. [Ety. dub.]

codling. See **cod** (1).

coeducation, *kō-ed-ū-kā'shən*, *n.* education of the sexes together.—*n.* **co'ed'** (*U.S.*), a girl or woman educated at a coeducational institution.—*adj.* **coeduca'tional**.

coefficient, *kō-ef-ish'ənt*, *n.* that which acts together with another thing: (*math.*) a numerical or literal expression for a factor of a quantity in an algebraic term: (*phys.*) a numerical constant used as a multiplier to a variable quantity, in calculating the magnitude of a physical property.

coehorn, **cohorn**, *n.* a small mortar for throwing grenades. [Baron van *Coehoorn* (1641-1704).]

coelacanth, *sē'lə-kanth*, *n.* any of a group of crossopterygian fishes of very great antiquity. [From Gr. *koilos*, hollow, *akantha*, spine.]

coelanaglyphic, *sēl-an-ə-glif'ik*, *adj.* in cavo-rilievo. [Gr. *koilos*, hollow, *ana*, up, *glyphein*, carve.]

Coelenterata, *sə-len-tər-ā'tä*, *n.pl.* a phylum of many-celled animals, radially symmetrical, with a single body-cavity, the enteron—Hydrozoa, Scyphozoa, Anthozoa, Ctenophora.—*adj.* and *n.* **coelen'terate**. [Gr. *koilos*, hollow, *enteron*, intestine.]

coeliac, *sē'li-ak*, *adj.* relating to the belly. [Gr. *koiliakos*—*koiliā*, the belly.]

coelom(e), *sē'lōm*, *-lom*, *n.* the body-cavity, or space between the intestines and the body-wall in animals above the Coelenterates.—*n.pl.* **Coelō'mata**, animals possessing a coelom.—*adj.* **coe'lomate**, having a coelom.—*n.* a coelomate animal.—*adjs.* **coelomat'ic**, **coelom'ic**. [Gr. *koilōma*, *-atos*, a cavity.]

coelostat, *sē'lō-stat*, *n.* a clock-driven mirror on an axis parallel to the earth's, so as to reflect continuously the same region of the sky. [L. *caelum* (misspelt *coelum*), sky, Gr. *statos*, fixed.]

coemption, *kō-emp'shən*, *n.* the buying up of the whole of a commodity: in Roman law, a mode of marriage under the fiction of a mutual sale. [L. *coemptiō*, *-ōnis*—*emĕre*, to buy.]

coenaesthesis, *sē-nēs-thē'sis*, *n.* the general bodily consciousness. [Gr. *koinos*, common, *aisthēsis*, perception.]

coenobite, *sēn'o-bīt*, *n.* a monk who lives in a community.—*adjs.* **coenobitic** (*-bit'ik*), **-al**.—*ns.* **coen'obitism**; **coenō'bium**, a religious community: (*biol.*) a colony of unicellular organisms:—*pl.* **-bia**. [Gr. *koinōbion*—*koinos*, common, *bios*, life.]

coenosarc, sēn'ō-särk, n. the common tissue uniting the polyps of a coral or the like. [Gr. koinos, common, sarx, flesh.]

coequal, ko-ē'kwol, adj. equal with another of the same rank or dignity.—n. one of the same rank.—n. coequality (-kwawl').—adv. coē'qually.

coerce, kō-ərs', v.t. to restrain by force: to compel.—adj. coer'cible.—adv. coer'cibly.—ns. coer'cion, restraint: government by force; coer'cionist.—adj. coer'cive, having power to coerce: compelling.—adv. coer'cively.—n. coer'civeness. [L. coercēre—arcēre, to shut in.]

co-essential, kō-es-en'shəl, adj. partaking of the same essence.—n. co-essentiality (-shi-al'i-ti).

coetaneous, kō-i-tā'ni-əs, adj. of the same age: contemporary. [L. aetās, aetātis, age.]

co-eternal, kō-i-tər'nəl, adj. alike eternal with another.—adv. co-eter'nally.—n. co-eter'nity.

coeval, kō-ē'vəl, adj. of the same age.—n. one of the same age: a contemporary. [L. coaevus—aevum, age.]

co-exist, kō-egz-ist', v.i. to exist at the same time.—n. co-exist'ence.—adj. co-exist'ent.

co-extend, kō-eks-tend', v.i. to extend equally.—n. co-exten'sion.—adj. co-exten'sive.

coff, kof, v.t. (Scot.) to buy. [A new present formed from coft, pa.t. and pa.p. originally of cope—M.Du. copen, cofte, (ghe)coft (Mod. Du. koopen, kocht, gekocht) to buy.]

coffee, kof'i, n. a drink made from the seeds of tree (Coffea arabica and other species) of the madder family : the powder made by roasting and grinding the seeds.—ns. coff'ee-bean, the seed of the coffee-plant; coff'ee-berr'y, the fruit or the seed of the coffee-tree; coff'ee-bug, a coccus destructive to the coffee-plant; coff'ee-cup, a cup for coffee; coff'ee-disease', a leaf-disease of coffee caused by a rust-fungus, Hemileia vastatrix; coff'ee-house, a house where coffee and other refreshments are sold; coff'ee-mill, a machine for grinding coffee-beans; coff'ee-pot, a pot in which coffee is prepared and served; coff'ee-room, a room in a hotel where coffee and other refreshments are served : a public room; coff'ee-stall, a movable street stall for coffee and other refreshments; coff'ee-tree. [Turk. kahveh—Ar. qahwah, orig. meaning wine.]

coffer, kof'ər, n. a chest for holding money or treasure : a deep panel in a ceiling.—v.t. to hoard up.—n. coff'er-dam, a water-tight structure allowing under-water foundations to be built dry.—adj. coff'ered.—n. coff'er-fish, a fish (Ostracion) enclosed in a box of bony scales. [O.Fr. cofre, a chest—L. cophinus, a basket—Gr. kophinos.]

coffin, kof'in, n. (obs.) a pie-crust : a chest for a dead body.—v.t. to place in a coffin.—ns. coff'in-bone, a bone enclosed in a horse's hoof; coff'in-ship, a dangerously unsound ship.—drive a nail in one's coffin, to do something tending to hasten death or ruin. [O.Fr. cofin—L. cophinus—Gr. kophinos, a basket.]

coffle, kof'l, n. a gang, esp. of slaves. [Ar. qāfilah, a caravan.]

cog, kog, v.t. to cheat or deceive : to wheedle : to manipulate (dice) so that they may fall in a given way.—n. the act of cheating : deception.—n. cogg'er. [Thieves' slang.]

cog, kog, n. a catch or tooth as on a wheel.—v.t. to furnish with cogs : to stop (a wheel) by putting a block before it (pr.p. cogg'ing; pa.t. and pa.p. cogged).—n. cog'-wheel, a toothed wheel. [M.E. cogge; ety. dub.; cf. Sw. kugge.]

cog, kog, n. formerly a large ship of burden or for war : a small boat : a cock-boat. [M.E. cogge, perh. from O.Fr. cogue, a ship, or O.N. kuggr, a merchant ship.]

cogent, kō'jənt, adj. powerful : convincing.—ns. cō'gence, cō'gency, convincing power.—adv. cō'gently. [L. cōgēns, -entis, pr.p. of cogēre, co-, agēre, to drive.]

coggie, cogie, kog'i, kōg'i, n. (Scot.) a small wooden bowl.—Also cog. [Dim. of cogue.]

coggle, kog'l, v.i. to be unsteady.—n. a cobblestone.—adv. cogg'ly (Scot.), shaky. [Origin doubtful.]

cogitate, koj'i-tāt, v.i. to turn a thing over in one's mind : to meditate : to ponder.—adj. cog'itable, capable of being thought.—n. cogita'tion, deep thought : meditation.—adj. cog'itative, having the power of thinking : given to cogitating. [L. cōgitāre, -ātum, to think deeply, co-, agitāre, to put in motion.]

Cognac, kon'yäk, n. an excellent quality of French brandy, much of which is made near Cognac, in Charente.

cognate, kog'nāt, adj. of the same family, kind, or nature : derived from the same ancestor, root, or other original : related or allied.—n. (Roman law, and generally) one related by blood, a kinsman (whether agnate or not): often, any kinsman on either side other than an agnate : (Scots law) a relative on one's mother's side.—n. cogna'tion.—cognate object, a word akin in origin or meaning to a normally intransitive verb, and used as its object. [L. cognātus—co-, (g)nāscī, (g)nātus, to be born.]

cognition, kog-nish'ən, n. knowledge : apprehension : (psychol.) knowing, in the widest sense, including sensation, perception, etc., distinguished from emotion and conation.—adj. cognisable (kog'niz-ə-bl; also kon'iz-), that may be known or understood : that may be judicially investigated.—adv. cog'nisably.—ns. cog'nisance, -zance (or kon'iz-), knowledge or notice, judicial or private : observation : jurisdiction : that by which one is known, a badge.—adj. cog'nisant (or kon'iz-), having cognisance or knowledge of.—v.t. cognise', to become conscious of.—adj. cog'nitive, capable of, or pertaining to, cognition. [L. cognitiō, -ōnis—cognōscĕre, cognitum—co-, (g)nōscĕre, to know.]

cognomen, kog-nō'men, n. a surname : a nickname : a name : the last of the three names of a Roman, indicating the house or family to which he belonged.—adj. cognominal (-nom'), like-named : relating to a cognomen.—v.t. cognom'inate, to name.—n. cognomina'tion. [L. cognōmen, -inis—co-, (g)nōmen, a name.]

cognosce, kog-nos', v.t. (Scots law) to examine : to give judgment upon : to declare to be an idiot.—adj. cognosc'ible. [L. cognōscĕre—co-, (g)nōscĕre, to know.]

cognoscente, ko-nyō-shent'ā, n. one professing a critical knowledge of works of art, and of a somewhat more pretentious character than amateurs :—pl. cognoscenti (-ē). [It.,—L. cognōscĕre.]

cognovit, kog-nō'vit, n. (law) an acknowledgment by a defendant that the plaintiff's cause is just. [L. cognōvit actiōnem, (he) has confessed the action.]

cogue, cog, kōg, kog, n. (esp. Scot.) a round wooden vessel, usu. of staves and hoops. [Ety. dub.]

cohabit, kō-hab'it, v.i. to dwell together as husband and wife, or as if husband and wife.—ns. cohab'itant, one dwelling with others; cohabita'tion. [L. cohabitāre—co-, habitāre, to dwell.]

co-heir, kō-ār', n. a joint heir :—fem. co-heir'ess.—n. coheritor (kō-her'it-ər), a co-heir.

cohere, kō-hēr', v.i. to stick together : to be consistent.—ns. cohēr'ence, a sticking together : congruity; cohēr'ency.—adj. cohēr'ent, sticking together : connected : consistent in thought or speech.—adv. cohēr'ently.—n. cohēr'er, an apparatus for detection of electric waves by reduced resistance of imperfect contact, as if by cohesion.—adj. cohēsible (-hēz'), capable of cohesion.—n. cohē'sion (-zhən), the act of sticking together : a form of attraction by which particles of bodies stick together : (bot.) concrescence of like parts : logical connexion.—adj. cohē'sive, having the power of cohering : tending to unite into a mass.—adv. cohē'sively.—n. cohē'siveness.—n. cohesibil'ity. [L. cohaerēre, cohaesum—co-, haerēre, to stick.]

cohibit, kō-hib'it, v.t. to restrain.—n. cohibition (-ish'ən).—adj. cohib'itive. [L. cohibēre—co-, habēre, to have, hold.]

coho, cohoe, kō'hō, n. a Pacific salmon, a species of Oncorhynchus.

cohog. Same as quahog.

cohort, *kō'hort, n.* a tenth part of a Roman legion : any band of men, esp. warriors : (*bot.*) a group of families. [L. *cohors, -tis,* an enclosed place, a multitude enclosed, a company of soldiers.]

cohortative, *kō-hor'tə-tiv, adj.* encouraging.—*n.* in Heb. grammar, a lengthened form of the imperfect. [L. *cohortārī, -ātus—co-,* hortārī, to exhort.]

cohune, *kō-hōōn', n.* a Central and South American palm (*Attalea cohune*) yielding **cohune** nuts and **cohune** oil.

coif, *koif, n.* a covering for the head, esp. the close-fitting cap of white lawn or silk originally worn by serjeants-at-law : a covering for the head worn by women.—*v.t.* to provide with a coif : to dress (the hair).—*ns.* **coiff'eur** (*kwäf-ər'*), a hairdresser : *fem.* **coiffeuse** (*-əz'*); **coiff'ure** (*kwäf-ür'*), style of hairdressing : a head-dress.— Also *v.t.* [Fr. *coiffe*—L.L. *cofia,* a cap.]

coign, coigne, *koin.* Same as **coin** (esp. first sense—after *Shak.*), **quoin.**

coil, *koil, v.t.* to wind in rings : to enclose in twists.—*v.i.* to wind.—*n.* a coiled object : one of the rings into which anything is coiled : a wire wound spirally to conduct electricity. [O.Fr. *coillir* (Fr. *cueillir*)—L. *colligĕre—col-,* together, *legĕre,* to gather; cf. **cull, collect.**]

coil, *koil, n.* tumult : hubbub : noise : fuss.—**mortal coil** (*Hamlet* III.i.68), the toil and trouble of human life. [Der. unknown.]

coin, *koin, n.* (*Shak.*) a corner-stone, quoin, or coign : a piece of metal legally stamped and current as money : money.—*v.t.* to convert into money : to stamp : to make, invent, fabricate : gain money by means of.—*ns.* **coin'age,** the act of coining money : the currency : the pieces of metal coined : the invention, or fabrication, of something new : what is invented ; **coin'er,** one who coins money : a maker of counterfeit coins : an inventor ; **coin'ing,** minting : invention.—**coin money,** to make money rapidly ; **coign(e) of vantage,** an advantageous salient corner : hence, a good position generally ; **pay a man in his own coin,** to give tit for tat : to give as good as one got. [Fr. *coin,* a wedge, also the die to stamp money—L. *cuneus,* a wedge.]

coincide, *kō-in-sīd', v.i.* to occupy the same place or time : agree : to correspond : to be identical.—*ns.* **coincidence** (*kō-in'si-dəns*), fact, event, or condition of coinciding : the occurrence of events simultaneously or consecutively in a striking manner but without any causal connexion between them ; **coin'cidency.**—*adjs.* **coin'cident, coincidental** (*-dent'l*).—*adv.* **coin'cidently.** [L. *co-, incidĕre—in,* in, *cadĕre,* to fall.]

co-inhere, *kō-in-hēr', v.i.* to inhere together.—*n.* **co-inher'ence.**

co-inheritor, *kō-in-her'it-ər, n.* a joint heir.—*n.* **co-inher'itance.**

co-instantaneous, *kō-in-stən-tā'ni-əs, adj.* exactly simultaneous.—*ns.* **co-instantaneity** (*-tə-nē'i-ti*), **-instantā'neousness.**—*adv.* **co-instantā'neously.**

co-insurance, *kō'in-shōō'rəns, n.* insurance jointly with another, esp. when the insurer bears part of the risk.

coir, *koir, n.* the strong fibre of coconut husk. [Malayalam, *kāyar,* cord—*kāyaru,* to be twisted.]

coistril, *kois'tril, n.* a groom : (*Shak.*) a knave. [See **custrel.**]

coition, *kō-ish'ən, n.* sexual intercourse. [L. *coitiō, -ōnis—co-, īre, ītum,* to go.]

cojoin, *kō-join', v.t.* (*Shak.*). Same as **conjoin.**

coke, *kōk, n.* a form of fuel obtained by the heating of coal in confined space whereby its more volatile constituents are driven off.—*v.t.* to make into coke. [Ety. dub. ; not before 17th century.]

cokernut, *kō'kər-nut, n.* a faulty form of **coconut.**

cokes, *kōks, n.* (*obs.*) a simpleton. [Origin unknown.]

col, *kol, n.* (*geog.*) a depression or pass in a mountain-range : (*meteor.*) a region between two anticyclones, giving a similar figure when represented in contour. [Fr.,—L. *collum,* a neck.]

col-. See **con-.**

colander, cullender, *kul'ən-dər, n.* a vessel having small holes in the bottom, used as a strainer in cookery.—*ns.* **colā'tion, col'ature,** straining.— *adj.* **cō'liform,** like a sieve. [L. *cōlāre,* to strain.]

colatitude, *kō-lat'i-tūd, n.* the complement of the latitude. [complement, latitude.]

Colbertine, *kol'bər-tin, n.* a kind of lace, so called from Jean Baptiste *Colbert* (1619-83), Minister of Finance to Louis XIV., a great patron of the arts.

colcannon, *kol-kan'ən, n.* an Irish dish, being a stew of pounded cabbage and potatoes with butter. [cole, cabbage ; *cannon* unknown.]

Colchicum, *kol'ki-kum, n.* a genus of *Liliaceae* including meadow saffron : its corm and seeds, used for gout and rheumatism and yielding **col'-chicine** (*-chi-* or *-ki-sēn*), an alkaloid used to produce polyploidy, etc. [L.,—Gr. *kolchikon,* meadow saffron, neut. of *Kolchikos,* relating to *Kolchis,* the sorceress Medea's country.]

colcothar, *kol'kō-thär, n.* a dark-red iron peroxide formed by calcining iron sulphate. [Ar. *qolqotār.*]

cold, *kōld, adj.* giving or feeling a sensation that is felt to be the opposite of hot : chilly : low in temperature : without passion or zeal : spiritless : unfriendly : indifferent : reserved : (*paint.*) suggesting cold rather than heat, as blue or grey.—*n.* a relative want of heat : the feeling or sensation caused by the absence of heat : coldness : a spell of cold weather : a disease caused by cold, a catarrhal inflammation of the mucous membrane of the respiratory organs, usually accompanied by hoarseness and coughing (**cold in the head,** coryza) : catarrh : chillness.—*adj.* **cold'-blood'ed,** having body-temperature depending upon environment, as fishes : without feeling : hard-hearted—of persons or actions.—*adv.* **cold'-blood'edly.**—*ns.* **cold'-blood'edness ; cold'-chis'el,** a strong and finely-tempered chisel for cutting cold metal, as distinguished from a blacksmith's chisel for cutting hot iron; **cold'-cream',** a creamy ointment usually of almond-oil, spermaceti, white wax, and rose-water, used as a cooling dressing for the skin.—*v.t.* (*coll.*) to apply cold-cream to.—*adj.* **cold'-drawn,** drawn through a die without heating.—*ns.* **cold'-frame', cold'house,** a plant frame, greenhouse, without artificial heat.—*adjs.* **cold'-heart'ed,** wanting feeling : indifferent ; **cold'ish,** somewhat cold.—*adv.* **cold'ly.**—*n.* **cold'ness.**—*adj.* **cold'-short,** brittle when cold : (*fig.*) of the temper.—*v.t.* **cold-shoul'der,** to give the cold shoulder to.—*n.* **cold-without',** brandy with cold water and no sugar.—**catch cold,** to contract a cold; **cold as charity,** a proverbial phrase expressing ironically great coldness or indifference; **cold feet,** discouragement : fear; **cold front** (*meteor.*), the advancing front of a mass of cold air ; **cold pack,** a wet pack prepared with cold water; **cold pig** (*coll.*), an application of cold water to rouse a sleeper; **cold snap,** a sudden spell of cold weather ; **cold steel,** cutting or stabbing weapons, opp. to bullets ; **cold storage,** storage and preservation of goods in refrigerating chambers : (*fig.*) suspense; **cold war** (see **war**); **cold water,** water at its natural temperature in ordinary conditions; **give (show) the cold shoulder,** to show studied indifference : to give a rebuff ; **in cold blood,** with deliberate intent, not under the influence of passion; **leave one cold,** to fail to impress; **leave out in the cold,** to neglect, ignore; **throw cold water on,** to discourage. [O.E. (Anglian) *cald* (W.S. *ceald*); Scot. *cauld,* Ger. *kalt;* cf. **cool,** O.N. *kala,* to freeze, L. *gelidus*—*gelū,* frost.]

cole, *kōl, n.* a general name for all sorts of cabbage. —*ns.* **cole'-garth,** a cabbage garden; **cole'-seed,** the seed of rape : rape; **cole'-wort,** cole—esp. heartless kinds. [O.E. *cawel;* Ger. *kohl,* Scot. **kail** ; all from L. *cōlis, caulis,* a stem, esp. of cabbage.]

Coleoptera, *kol-i-op'tər-ä, n.pl.* an order of insects having the fore-wings hard or horny, serving as wing-cases for the functional wings—the beetles.— *adjs.* **coleop'teral, coleop'terous.**—*n.* **coleop'-terist,** a student of beetles. [Gr. *koleos,* a sheath, and *pteron,* a wing.]

coleor(r)hiza, *kol-i-ō-rī'za, n.* a protective layer on the radicle of some plants. [Gr. *koleos*, sheath, *rhiza*, root.]

cole-slaw, *kōl'slaw*, *n.* cabbage salad. [Du. *koolsla*, for *kool salade*, cole salad.]

colibri, *kol'ib-rē*, *n.* a humming-bird. [Sp. *colibrí*, and Fr. *colibri*, said to be the Carib name.]

colic, *kol'ik*, *n.* a disease attended with severe pain and flatulent distension of the abdomen, without diarrhoea.—*adj.* (see under **colon**).—*adj.* col'icky, like, suffering or causing colic.—*n.* coli'tis (see **colon**). [colon (2).]

colin, *kol'in*, *n.* the Virginian quail. [Ety. dub.]

coliseum. See **colosseum.**

coll, *kol*, *v.t.* (*Spens.*) to embrace.—*n.* coll'ing, embracing. [Fr. *col*—L. *collum*, the neck.]

collaborate, *kol-ab'ər-āt*, *v.i.* to work in association (sometimes invidiously, with an enemy).—*ns.* collabora'tion; collab'orator, collabora'tionist (in invidious sense). [L. *collabōrāre*, *-ātum*— *labōrāre*, to work.]

collagen, *kol'ə-jen*, *n.* a protein in fibrous connective tissue, readily turned into gelatine. [Gr. *kolla*, glue, and *gen-*, the root of *gignesthai*, to become.]

collapse, *kol-aps'*, *n.* a falling away or breaking down : any sudden or complete breakdown or prostration.—*v.i.* to cave in : to close or fold up : to break down : to go to ruin : to lose heart.—*adj.* collaps'able, -ible, capable of collapsing. [L. *collāpsus—col-*, together, and *lābī*, *lāpsus*, to slide or fall.]

collar, *kol'ər*, *n.* something worn round the neck by man, horse, dog, etc. : the part of a garment at the neck : a ring : a surrounding band : the junction of root and stem in a plant.—*v.t.* to seize by the collar : to put a collar on : (*slang*) to seize.—*ns.* **coll'ar-beam,** a horizontal piece of timber connecting or bracing two opposite rafters, to prevent sagging; **coll'ar-bone,** the clavicle, a bone connecting the shoulder-blade and breast-bone.— *adj.* **coll'ared,** having, or ornamented with, a collar : rolled up and bound with a string, as a piece of meat having the bones removed : captured. —*ns.* **collarette',** a small collar; **coll'ar-stud,** a stud for fastening a collar; **coll'ar-work,** hard work against the horse-collar : drudgery. [O.Fr. *colier*—L. *collāre—collum*, the neck.]

collard, *kol'ərd*, *n.* cole-wort. [cole-wort.]

collate, *kol-āt'*, *v.t.* to bring together for comparison : to examine and compare, as books, and esp. old manuscripts : to place in or confer a benefice upon : to place in order, as the sheets of a book for binding : to examine with respect to completeness and sequence of sheets, etc. :—*adj.* collā'table.— *ns.* collā'tion, act of collating : a bringing together for examination and comparison : presentation to a benefice : a description of a book as collated : a repast between meals, from the habit of reading the *Collationes* of Johannes Cassianus during a slight meal in monasteries.—*adj.* collā'tive, having the power of conferring : of livings where the bishop and patron are one and the same person.— *n.* collā'tor, one who collates or compares : one who bestows or presents. [L. *collātum*, used as supine of *conferre—pfx. col-* and *lātum* (*ferre*, to bring).]

collateral, *kol-at'ər-l*, *adj.* side by side : running parallel or together : corresponding : descended from the same ancestor, but not in direct line.—*n.* a collateral relation : a contemporary : a rival.— *adv.* collat'erally.—**collateral security,** an additional and separate security for the performance of an obligation. [L. *col-*, *latus*, *lateris*, a side.]

colleague, *kol'ēg*, *n.* one associated with another in some employment—not a partner in business.— *n.* **coll'eagueship.** [Fr. *collègue*—L. *collēga— col-*, *legĕre*, to choose.]

colleague, *kol-ēg'*, *v.i.* to ally : to conspire :—*pr.p.* **colleaguing** (*kol-ēg'ing*); *pa.p.* **colleagued** (*kol-ēgd'*). [O.Fr. *colliguer*, to join in alliance—L. *colligāre*, to bind together.]

collect, *kəl-*, *kol-ekt'*, *v.t.* to assemble or bring together : to infer : to put (one's thoughts) in order : to receive payment of : to call for and remove.—*v.i.* to run together : to accumulate.—*n.* **collect** (*kol'*), a short prayer, peculiar to the

liturgies of the Western Church, consisting of one sentence, conveying one main petition.—*adj.* **collect'able, -ible.**—*n.pl.* **collectā'nea,** a collection of passages : a miscellany.—*adj.* **collect'ed,** gathered together : having unscattered wits : cool : firm.—*adv.* **collect'edly.**—*ns.* **collect'edness,** self-possession : coolness.—*n.* and *adj.* **collect'ing.** —*ns.* **collect'ing-box,** a field-naturalist's box for specimens : a box for receiving money contributions; **collec'tion,** act of collecting : gathering of contributions, esp. of money : the money collected : an assemblage : a book of selections : (*Shak.*) inference : composure : an examination at the end of the terms in certain colleges.—*adj.* **collect'ive,** considered as forming one mass or sum : congregated : common : (*Milt.*) inferential : (*gram.*) expressing a number or multitude.—*adv.* **collect'ively.**—*v.t.* **collect'ivise,** to give a collectivist organisation to.—*ns.* **collect'ivism,** the economic theory that industry should be carried on with a collective capital—a form of socialism : a system embodying this; **collect'ivist**—Also *adj.*—*ns.* **collect'or,** one who collects or takes up, as tickets, taxes, etc. : one who sets himself to acquire and set together examples or specimens, as of books, minerals, curiosities : in India, the chief official of a district, collecting revenue and acting as a magistrate; **collect'orate, collect'orship.**— **collective fruit** (*bot.*), a multiple fruit—one derived from several flowers, as fig, mulberry. [L. *colligĕre*, *collēctum—legĕre*, to gather.]

colleen, *kol'ēn*, *kol'ēn'*, *n.* a girl. [Irish *cailín*.]

college, *kol'ij*, *n.* an incorporation, company, or society of persons joined together generally for literary or scientific purposes, and often possessing peculiar or exclusive privileges : a body or society that is a member of a university or is coextensive with a university : a seminary of learning : a literary, political, or religious institution : the edifice appropriated to a college.—*n.* **coll'eger,** a member of a college : one of the foundationers at Eton College.—*adj.* **collegial** (*kə-lē'ji-əl*), pertaining to a college.—*ns.* **collē'gian,** a member or inhabitant of a college : (*slang*) inmate of a prison; **collē'gianer,** a member of a college, a student.—*adj.* **collē'giate,** pertaining to or resembling a college : containing a college, as a town : instituted like a college : corporate.—*n.* inmate of a prison, etc.—**College of Arms, Heralds' College,** a collegiate body incorporated in 1483, presided over by the Earl Marshal, and including Garter, principal King-of-arms, Clarenceux, and Norroy, besides six heralds and four pursuivants; **college of cardinals,** the whole body of cardinals, electors of the pope; **College of Justice,** in Scotland, a great forensic society, composed of judges, advocates, writers to the signet, and solicitors; **collegiate church, collegial church,** a church having a college or chapter, consisting of a dean or provost and canons, attached to it : in Scotland, a church occupied by two or more pastors of equal rank (also **collegiate charge**). [Fr. *collège*—L. *collēgium*, from *col-*, and *legĕre*, to gather.]

Collembola, *kol-em'bō-lä*, *n.pl.* an order of entirely wingless insects (Apterygota), whose abdomen has six segments or fewer, a forward-pointing springing fork and an adhesive apparatus—the springtails. [Gr. *kolla*, glue, *embolos*, a peg, pin.]

collenchyma, *kol-eng'ki-mä*, *n.* (*bot.*) strengthening tissue of thick-cornered cells.—*adj.* **collenchym'-atous.** [Gr. *kolla*, glue, *en* in, *chyma*, that which is poured.]

collet, *kol'it*, *n.* a ring or collar : the collar of a plant : the part of a ring which contains the stone. [Fr.,—L. *collum*.]

collide, *kə-līd'*, *v.i.* to dash together : to clash.— *ns.* **collision** (-*lizh'n*), state of being struck together : a violent impact, a crash : conflict : opposition : clashing; **colli'sion-mat,** a mat for covering a hole in a ship's side caused by a collision. [L. *collīdĕre*, *collīsum—col-*, *laedĕre*, to strike.]

collie, colly, *kol'i*, *n.* a long-haired, intelligent breed of sheep-dog, originating in Scotland. [Ety. dub.]

Neutral vowels in unaccented syllables : *el'ə-mənt*, *in'fənt*, *ran'dəm*

collier, *kol′yər, n. (obs.)* a charcoal-burner or dealer in charcoal or coal : a coal-miner : a ship that carries coal : a sailor in such a ship.—*n.* **coll′iery,** a coal-mine. [**coal.**]

collieshangie, *kol-i-shang′i, n. (Scot.)* a noisy wrangling : an uproar : a disturbance. [Origin unknown.]

colligate, *kol′i-gāt, v.t.* to bind together.—*n.* **colligā′tion,** conjunction : bringing together under a general principle or conception.—*adj.* **coll′igative** *(physical chem.)* depending on concentration, not nature of substance. [L. *colligāre, -ātum—col-, ligāre,* to bind.]

collimation, *kol-i-mā′shən, n.* the adjustment of the line of sight of a telescope.—*v.t.* **coll′imāte.**—*n.* **coll′imātor,** a subsidiary telescope used to detect errors in collimation : in a spectroscope, etc., a fine slit at the principal focus of a convex lens, throwing parallel rays on the prism or grating : the lens itself. [*collimāre,* a wrong reading for L. *collīneāre,* to bring into line with—*col-,* together, *līnea,* a line.]

collinear, *ko-lin′i-ər, adj.* in the same straight line.

Collins, *kol′inz, n.* a letter of thanks for hospitality. [From the notable example sent by Mr. *Collins* in *Pride and Prejudice.*]

colliquate, *kol′i-kwāt, v.t.* to melt.—*adjs.* **colliq′-uable, colliq′uant,** melting, wasting.—*n.* **colliquā′tion,** melting : wasting away.—*adj.* **colliq′ua-tive,** profuse in flow : wasting.—*n.* **colli-quesc′ence,** readiness to liquefy. [L. *col-,* together, *liquāre, -ātum* to make melt.]

collocate, *kol′ō-kāt, v.t.* to place together : to set : to arrange.—*n.* **collocā′tion.** [L. *collocāre, -ātum, col-, locāre,* to place.]

collocutor, collocutory. See **colloquy.**

collodion, *kol-ō′di-ən, n.* a gluey solution of nitrated cotton (or cellulose nitrates) in alcohol and ether, used in surgery and photography. [Gr. *kollōdēs*—*kolla,* glue, *eidos,* form, appearance.]

collogue, *kə-lōg′, v.i. (obs.)* to simulate belief : to conspire : to converse confidentially.—*v.t. (obs.)* to coax : *(obs.)* to flatter. [Prob. from L. *colloquī,* to speak together.]

colloid, *kol′oid, n.* a substance in a state in which, though apparently dissolved, it cannot pass through a membrane : a substance that readily assumes this state : a **colloidal system,** i.e. the dispersed substance plus the material in which it is dispersed.—*adj.* **colloid′al.** [Gr. *kolla,* glue, *eidos,* form.]

collop, *kol′əp, n. (obs.)* an egg fried with bacon : a slice of meat, fried or not : *(Shak.)* a child.—**Collop Monday,** the day before Shrove Tuesday, when collops-and-eggs were eaten : **minced collops** *(Scot.),* minced meat. [Origin obscure.]

colloquy, *kol′a-kwi, n.* a speaking together : mutual discourse : conversation.—*v.i. (rare)* to converse.—*n.* **collocutor** *(kol-ok′ū-tər).*—*adj.* **colloc′ūtory.**—*v.i.* **colloque** *(kol-ōk′),* to hold colloquy.—*adj.* **colloquial** *(kə-lō′kwi-əl),* pertaining to or used in common conversation.—*ns.* **collō′quialism,** a form of expression used in familiar talk; **collō′-quialist.**—*adv.* **collō′quially.**—*v.i.* **coll′oquise,** to converse.—*n.* **coll′oquist,** a speaker in a colloquy. [L. *colloquium—col-, loquī,* to speak.]

collotype, *kol′ō-tīp, n.* a form of gelatine process in book illustration and advertising. [Gr. *kolla,* glue, and **type.**]

colluctation, *kol-uk-tā′shən, n.* strife : opposition. [L. *colluctāri—col-, luctāri,* to wrestle.]

collude, *kol-(y)ōōd′, v.i.* to play into each other's hands : to act in concert, esp. in a fraud.—*ns.* **collud′er; collu′sion,** act of colluding : a secret agreement to deceive : deceit : in *Love's Lab. Lost,* Goodman Dull's blunder for *allusion.*—*adj.* **collu′sive,** fraudulently concerted : deceitful.—*adv.* **collu′sively.** [L. *collūdēre, collūsum,* from *col-,* and *lūdĕre,* to play.]

colluvies, *ko-l(y)ōō′vi-ēz, n.* accumulated filth : a rabble. [L. *colluviēs,* washings—*colluĕre,* to wash thoroughly.]

colly, *kol′i, v.t.* to begrime with coal-dust : *(Shak.)* to darken.—*p.adj.* **coll′ied.** [See **coal.**]

colly. See **collie.**

collyrium, *ko-lir′i-əm, n.* eye-wash. [Latinised from Gr. *kollȳrion,* eye-salve, dim. of *kollȳrā,* a roll of bread.]

collywobbles, *kol′i-wob-lz, n. (facetious)* abdominal pain. [Prob. **colic** and **wabble, wobble.**]

Colmar, *kol′mär, n.* a kind of fan fashionable in Queen Anne's time. [Perh. *Colmar* in Alsace.]

Colobus, *kol′ō-bəs, n.* an African genus of monkeys, almost thumbless. [Gr. *kolobos,* maimed.]

Colocasia, *kol-ō-kā′zi-ä, -si-ä, n. (bot.)* a genus of plants of the arum family—taro, etc. [Gr. *kolokāsiā,* water-lily root.]

colocynth, *kol′ō-sinth, n.* a kind of cucumber *(Citrullus Colocynthis)* : a cathartic drug got from it. [Gr. *kolokynthis.*]

Cologne-earth, *ko-lōn′-ərth, n.* a brown earth prepared from lignite, found originally near *Cologne.*—**Cologne water,** or **eau de Cologne** *(ō də ko-lōn′),* a perfumed spirit first made at Cologne in 1709 by Johann Farina.

colon, *kō′lon, n.* the punctuation mark (:) used especially to indicate a distinct member or clause of a sentence. [Gr. *kōlon,* a limb, member.]

colon, *kō′lən, n.* that portion of the large intestine which extends from the caecum to the rectum.—*adj.* **colic** *(kol′ik;* for noun see **colic**).—*n.* **colitis** *(kō-, ko-lī′tis),* inflammation of the colon. [Gr. *kōlon,* the large intestine.]

colon, *kō-lōn′, n.* the monetary unit of El Salvador and Costa Rica. [Named after Columbus (Sp. *Colón*).]

colonel, *kər′nəl, n.* an officer who has command of a regiment or one of equivalent rank : *(U.S.)* a state governor's aide-de-camp : *(U.S.)* by courtesy, any prominent citizen.—*ns.* **col′onelcy** *(-si),* his office or rank; **col′onelling** (or *kor-ō-nel′ing*), playing the colonel; **col′onelship,** colonelcy; quality of a colonel. [Older Fr. and Sp. **coronel;**—It *colonello,* the leader of a *colonna,* or column—L. *columna;* spelling assimilated to mod. Fr.]

colonnade, *kol-ən-ād′, n.* a range of columns placed at regular intervals : a similar row, as of trees.—*adj.* **colonnad′ed.** [Fr.,—L. *columna.*]

colony, *kol′an-i, n.* a name vaguely applied to a state's dependencies overseas or abroad (distinguished from a *dominion*) : *(Rom. hist.)* a military settlement planted in subject territory : *(Greek hist.)* a band of emigrants or their new home, connected with the mother-city by no political tie : a body of persons settled in a foreign country, or forming a separate group in any way (as by common occupation, or organised for purposes of support, labour, treatment, etc. : the settlement so formed : the place they inhabit : *(biol.)* a number of organisms, esp. of one kind, living together as a community : a coenobium.—*adj.* **colonial** *(kə-lō′ni-əl),* pertaining to or of the nature of a colony.—*n.* an inhabitant, citizen, or member of a colony, a colonist.—*ns.* **colo′nialism,** a trait of colonial life or speech : the colonial system (see below); **colonīsā′tion,** act or practice of colonising : state of being colonised.—*v.t.* **col′onise,** to plant or establish a colony in : to form into a colony : *(U.S.)* to plant fraudulent voters in.—*v.t.* to settle.—*n.* **col′onist,** an inhabitant of a colony : a voter set up for election purposes : *(bot.)* a weed of cultivated ground.—**colonial animals,** organisms consisting of numerous individuals in bodily union; **colonial experience man** *(Australia),* a jackaroo; **colonial system,** the theory that the settlements abroad should be treated as proprietary domains exploited for the benefit of the mother-country. [L. *colōnia*—*colōnus,* a husbandman—*colĕre,* to till.]

colophon, *kol′ə-fon, -fən, n.* an inscription at the end of a book or literary composition, often naming the author and scribe or printer, with place and date of execution, etc. as on a modern title-page : a publisher's imprint or device, with name, date, etc. [L. *colophōn*—Gr. *kolophōn,* summit, finishing touch.]

colophony, *kol-of′ə-ni,* or *kol′, n.* rosin : the residue of distillation of crude turpentine. [Gr. *kolophōniā* (*rhētinē*, gum) from *Kolophōn*, Colophon, in Asia Minor.]

coloquintida, kol-o-kwin'ti-dä. Same as **colocynth.**

color, American spelling of colour.

Colorado beetle, kol-*ə*r-ä'dō bē'tl, an American beetle, yellow with black stripes, a potato pest. [State of *Colorado*.]

coloratura, kol-or-ät-ōō'rä, n. (mus.) florid vocal passages.—adj. florid.—**coloratura soprano,** a high and flexible soprano voice, capable of singing coloratura passages : a singer with such a voice. [It., colouring.]

colossus, kol-os'*ə*s, n. a gigantic statue, esp. that of Apollo at (but not astride of) the entrance of the harbour of Rhodes.—adjs. **coloss'al,** like a colossus : gigantic.—ns. **colossē'um, colise'um,** a large place of entertainment, from Vespasian's amphitheatre at Rome, which was the largest in the world; **coloss'us-wise,** astride (*Shak.*). [L.,—Gr. *kolossos.*]

colostrum, ko-los'tr*ə*m, n. a mammal's first milk after parturition.—n. **colostrā'tion,** a disease of infants due to colostrum.—adjs. **colos'tric, -trous.** [L.]

colour, also, esp. in America, **color**, kul'*ə*r, n. a sensation of light induced in the eye by ether waves of a certain frequency—the particular colour being determined by the frequency : a property whereby bodies have different appearances to the eye through surface reflection or absorption of rays : hue, one of the constituents into which white light can be decomposed : appearance of blood in the face : race or race-mixture other than European : appearance : plausibility : reason : pretext : tint : shade : paint : rhetorical figure : false show : vividness : (*mus.*) timbre : variety : (*pl.*) a flag, ensign, or standard : (*pl.*) symbol of membership of a party, club, college, team, etc.—v.t. to put colour on : to stain : to paint : to set in a fair light : to exaggerate : to disguise : to misrepresent.—v.i. to take on colour : to blush.—n. **colorā'tion** (also **colouration**), colouring : mode of colouring : disposition of colours.—adj. **colorif'ic** (kol-, kul-), producing colours.—n. **colorim'eter** (kol-, kul-), an instrument for comparison of colours.—adi. **col'ourable** (kul'), having a fair appearance : designed to conceal.—adv. **col'ourably.**—adj. **col'our-blind,** unable to distinguish some colours from others, or to see them at all.—n. **col'our-blind'ness.**—adj. **col'oured,** having colour : (*Spens.*) having a specious appearance, deceitful : of the complexion, other than white : of mixed descent—partly European, partly of darker race : not of European race.—ns. **col'our-film,** a cinematograph film in colour; **col'our-filter,** a film or plate transparent for the required colours only or chiefly.—adj. **col'ourful,** full of colour : vivid.—ns. **col'our-hearing,** the association of colours with sounds heard; **col'ouring,** any substance used to give colour : the actual colours of anything, and their arrangement : manner of applying colours : appearance : tone; **col'ourist,** one who colours or paints : one who excels in colouring.—adj. **col'ourless,** without colour : transparent : pale : neutral : lacking distinctive character.—ns. **col'our-line,** social discrimination between white and other races (also **col'our-bar**) : **col'ourman,** one who prepares or sells paints : **col'our-music,** the art of displaying colours on a screen with effect analagous to music; **col'our-organ,** an instrument for doing this; **col'our-party,** a guard carrying colours; **col'our-scheme,** general conception of combination of colours in a design; **col'our-screen,** a colour-filter; **col'our-sergeant,** the sergeant who guards the colours of a regiment.—adj. **col'oury,** having much colour.—**colour a pipe,** to cause a pipe, esp. a meerschaum, to darken by smoking; **come off with flying colours,** to do something with éclat : **come out in one's true colours,** to appear in one's real character; **fear no colours,** fear no enemy; **false colours,** a false pretence; **give colour,** to give plausibility; **high colour,** ruddiness of complexion; **join the colours,** to enlist; **lose colour,**

to lose one's good looks; **nail one's colours to the mast,** to commit oneself to some party or plan of action; **off colour,** faded : indisposed : past one's best; **pair of colours** (see **pair**); **primary colours** (see **primary**). [O.Fr. *color*—L. *color, -ōris*; akin to *cēlāre,* to cover, to conceal.]

colporteur, kol-pōr-t*ə*r', or kol'pōrt-*ə*r, n. a peddler, esp. one selling religious tracts and books.—n. **col'portage** (or -täzh'), the distribution of books by colporteurs. [Fr. *colporteur,* from *col*—L. *collum,* the neck, and *porter*—L. *portāre,* to carry.]

colt, kōlt, n. a young horse : an awkward fellow : an inexperienced youth : (B.) a young camel or ass : (*naut.*) a rope's end.—v.i. (*Spens.*) to frisk like a colt.—v.t. (*Shak.*) to cheat : to give the rope's end, to beat.—adj. **colt'ish,** like a colt : frisky : wanton.—ns. **colts'foot,** a composite plant (*Tussilago Farfara*) with shaggy stalk and large soft leaves; **colt's-tooth,** one of a horse's first set of teeth : (*Shak.*) love of youthful pleasures : wantonness; **colt'wood** (*Spens.*), a plant used by Glauce in her incantations (F.Q. III ii. 49. 8)—said to be coltsfoot, which is not woody. [O.E. *colt*; Sw. *kult,* a young boar, a stout boy.]

Colt, kōlt, n. a pistol invented by Samuel *Colt* (1814-62).

colter. Same as **coulter.**

Coluber, kol'ū-b*ə*r, n. an extensive genus of nonvenomous snakes.—ns. **colūb'riad** (*Cowper*), the epic of a snake; **Colu'bridae,** the largest family of snakes—in which some include cobras and other venomous snakes.—adj. **colubriform** (-ōō, -ā'), resembling Coluber; **col'ūbrine,** snakelike : colubriform. [L. *coluber,* a snake.]

colugo, ko-lōō'gō, n. the so-called flying lemur.

Columban, k*ə*l-um'b*ə*n, adj. pertaining to St. *Columba* or his church.

Columbian, k*ə*l-um'bi-*ə*n, adj. American : (of type) in size between English and Great Primer—16-point.—n. **colum'bate,** niobate.—adj. **colum'bic,** niobic.—ns. **colum'bite,** a mineral, niobate and tantalate of iron and manganese; **colum'bium** (*U.S.*), niobium. [*Columbus,* discoverer of America.]

columbine, kol'*ə*m-bīn, adj. of or like a dove : dove-coloured.—n. any plant of the ranunculaceous genus Aquilegia, with coloured sepals and spurred petals, giving the appearance of a bunch of pigeons : **Columbine,** in pantomime, the sweetheart of Harlequin.—ns. **columbā'rium,** a dovecot : a niche for a sepulchral urn : a recess in a wall to receive the end of a rafter; **col'umbary,** a dovecot. [L. *columba,* a dove.]

column, kol'*ə*m, n. a long round body, used as support or adornment : any upright body or mass like a column : a body of troops with narrow front : a perpendicular row of figures, etc. : a perpendicular section of a page or of a table : a special section in a newspaper; a bundle of nervefibres : the central part of an orchid.—ns. **col'ūmel,** a small column; **colūmell'a,** the central axis of a spiral univalve; the auditory ossicle in lower vertebrates : the central axis of the spore-case of mosses : in the opening of fruits, what remains in the centre after the carpels have split away.—adjs. **columnal** (k*ə*-lum'nl), **colum'nar,** pertaining to columns : like a column : formed in columns.—n. **columnar'ity.**—adjs. **columnated** (kol'*ə*m-nāt-id, or k*ə*-lum'); **columned** (kol'*ə*md), **colum'niated,** having columns.—ns. **columniation** (k*ə*-lum-ni-ā'shən), use or arrangement of columns; **columnist** (kol'*ə*m-ist, -nist; vulg. or facet. kol'ūm-ist), one who conducts a column in a newspaper. [L. *columna,* akin to *celsus,* high; Gr. *kolōnē,* a hill; hill.]

colure, kō-lūr', kōl', kol'y*ə*r, n. (*astron.*) a great circle of the celestial sphere passing through the poles of the equator and either the solstitial or the equinoctial points. [Gr. *kolouros—kolos,* docked, *ourā,* tail.]

colza, kol'zä, n. cole-seed, yielding oil. [Du. *koolzaad,* cabbage-seed.]

com-. See **con-.**

coma, kō'mä, n. deep sleep : stupor.—adj. **com'-atose,** affected with coma : drowsy. [Gr. *kōma, -atos.*]

coma, *kō′mă*, *n*. (*bot*.) a tuft : the head of a tree : (*astron*.) the nebulous envelope of the head of a comet.—*adjs*. **cō′mal**, **cō′mate**, **cō′mose**, **cō′-mous**.—**Coma Berenices** (*ber-a-nī′sēz*), Berenice's Hair, a small northern constellation. [Gr. *kŏmē*, hair of head.]

comarb. See **coarb.**

comart, *kō-märt′*, *n*. (*Shak*.) an agreement. [Perh. pfx. *co-* and **mart**; or a misprint for *cou′nant*, i.e. **covenant**.]

comate, *kō′māt′*, *n*. (*Shak*.) a mate or companion.

comb, *kōm*, *n*. a toothed instrument for separating and cleaning hair, wool, flax, for graining paint, etc. : anything of similar form : the fleshy crest of some birds : the top or crest of a wave, of a roof, or of a hill : an aggregation of cells for honey.—*v.t.* to separate, to arrange, or clean by means of a comb or as if with a comb : to dress with a comb : to search thoroughly : (*Shak*.) to beat.—*v.i.* to break with a white foam, as the top of a wave.—*adj*. **combed**.—*n*. **comb′er**, one who or that which combs wool, etc. : a long foaming wave.—*n.pl.* **comb′ings**, hairs combed off.—*adj*. **comb′-less**.—*n*. **comb′-out′**, the process of searching for and removing, e.g. lice, men for military service.—*adv*. **comb′wise**.—*adj*. **comb′y**. [O.E. *camb*.]

comb, combe. See **coomb.**

combat, *kum′bat*, or *kom′bat*, *v.i.* to contend or struggle.—*v.t.* to beat against : to contest : to oppose : to debate.—*n*. a struggle : a fight.—*adjs*. **com′batable**, capable of being combated; **com′batant**, disposed to combat : taking part or liable to take part in action.—*n*. one who takes part in a combat.—*adj*. **com′bative**, inclined to quarrel.—*n*. **com′bativeness.** [Fr. *combattre*, to fight—L. pfx. *com-* and *bātuĕre*, to strike.]

comber, *kom′bar*, *n*. the gaper (a sea-perch): a species of wrasse.

combine, *kəm-bīn′*, *v.t.* to join together : to unite intimately : (*Shak*.) to bind, restrict.—*v.i.* to come into close union : to co-operate : (*chem*.) to unite and form a new compound.—*n*. (*kom′bīn*), a syndicate, a trust, an association of trading companies : a combined harvesting and threshing machine.—*adj*. **combinate** (*kom′bin-āt*), combined : (*Shak*.) betrothed.—*ns*. **combinā′tion**, the act of combining : union of individual things : a motor-cycle with sidecar : persons united for a purpose : (*math*.) a possible set of a given number of things selected from a given number, irrespective of arrangement within the set (distinguished from a *permutation*); **combinā′tion-room**, at Cambridge, a fellows' common-room.—*n.pl.* **combinā′tions**, an under-garment comprising vest and drawers.—*adjs*. **com′binative**; **combinato′rial** (*combining*) ; **combīn′ing**. [L. *combīnāre*, to join—*com-*, *bīnī*, two and two.]

Combretum, *kom-brē′təm*, *n*. a tropical and subtropical genus of trees and shrubs noted for the beauty of their flowers, giving name to the **Combretā′ceae**, a family akin to the myrtles. [L. *combrētum*, an unknown plant.]

comburgess, *kom-bur′jis*, *n*. a fellow-burgess.

combust, *kom-bust′*, *adj*. burned by the sun; in conjunction with the sun, or apparently very near it, so as to be obscured by its light, said of a planet when it is not more than 8½° from the sun.—*n*. that which is burned.—*v.t.* to burn up.—*n*. **combustibil′ity.**—*adj*. **combust′ible**, liable to take fire and burn : excitable.—*n*. anything that will take fire and burn.—*ns*. **combust′ibleness**, quality of being combustible; **combust′ion** (*-yən*), a burning : the action of fire on combustible substances : confusion, turmoil : oxidation or analogous process with evolution of heat.—*adjs*. **combust′ious** (*Shak*.), combustible, inflammable : turbulent; **combust′ive**, disposed to take fire.—**spontaneous combustion**, burning caused by heat generated in the substance itself. [L. *combūrēre*, *combūstum*, to consume—*com-*, intens., *ūrēre*, to burn.]

come, *kum*, *v.i.* to move toward the place that is the point of view (the opposite of *go*) : to draw near : to arrive at a certain state or condition : to

issue : to happen : (*Shak*.) to yield : to become : to turn out : to amount : to reach : to begin to be in some condition.—*v.t.* (*slang* or *coll*.) to perform (*pr.p.* **com′ing**; *pa.t.* **came**; *pa.p.* **come**).—*interj*. (or *imper*.) expressive of encouragement, protest, or reproof (often in phrases **come come**, **come now**).—*n*. **come′-and-go′**, passage to and fro.—*adj*. **come-at′-able**, accessible.—*ns*. **come′-back**, a return : a revival : a retort; **come′down**, a descent : a humiliating disappointment : a degradation; **come′-off**, a conclusion : an evasion of duty; **come′-o′-will**, something that comes of its own accord : an illegitimate child (also **come′-by-chance**); **com′er**, one who comes or has come : one who shows promise; **com′ing**.—*interj*. or *pr.p.*, used as a promise of attention.—*adj*. future : of future importance : ready to make or meet advances.—*n.pl.* **com′ings-in**, income.—**all comers**, anyone that likes; **come about**, to happen; **come across** (also **across**); **come and go**, to fluctuate : to have freedom of action : passage to and fro; **come at**, to reach : **come back**, to return to popularity, office, etc. : (*U.S.*) to retort; **come by**, to come near : to pass : to obtain : (*U.S.*) come in; **come down**, to descend : to be reduced; **come down upon**, to be severe with : **come down with**, to pay down; **come high, or low**, to cost much, or little; **come home**, to return to one's house : to touch one's interest or feelings closely (with *to*) : (*naut*.) to drag or slip through the ground—of an anchor; **come in**, to enter : to give in, to yield, (*fencing*) to get within the opponent's guard (*Shak*.); **come in for**, to receive as, or as if as, one's share : to receive incidentally; **come into**, to fall heir to; **come it strong** (*coll*.), to do or say much, go to great lengths, exaggerate; **come of**, to descend from : become of; **come of age**, to reach full legal age (21 years); **come off**, to come away : to turn out : to escape : (*Shak*.) to pay up : (*U.S.*) to desist from; **come on**, to advance : to thrive : to proceed : to begin : often in imper. as a challenge or invitation to attack; **come out**, to result : to be published : to become known or evident : to enter society; **come out with**, to utter : to exclaim; **come over**, (*Shak*.) to surpass : to befall : to come into the mind of : (*slang*) to overreach; **come round**, to come by a circuitous path : to happen in due course : to veer : to become favourable : to recover from a faint, etc; **come short**, to fail; **come short of**, to fail to attain; **come to**, to obtain : to amount to : to recover consciousness or sanity; **come to grief**, to meet with disaster; **come to oneself**, return to normal state of mind; **come to pass**, to happen; **come to stay**, to become permanent; **come true**, to be fulfilled; **come under**, to be included under; **come up**, to present itself; **come upon**, to attack : to affect : to hold answerable : to meet; **come up with**, to overtake; **to come**, future. [O.E. *cuman*; Ger. *kommen*.]

co-meddle, *kō-med′l*, *v.t.* to mix : (*Shak*.) to temper.

comedo, *kom′i-do*, *n*. a blackhead, a small, black-tipped white mass sometimes found in the sebaceous glands. [L. *comedō*, *-ōnis*, glutton—*comedĕre*, to eat up, from its wormlike appearance.]

comedy, *kom′i-di*, *n*. a dramatic piece of a pleasant or humorous character : a story with a happy ending : an incident suggesting comic treatment.—*ns*. **comedian** (*ka-mē′di-ən*), one who acts or writes comedies.—*fem.* (Fr.) **comédienne** (*kom-ā-di-en′*); **comediett′ā**, a short comic piece. [Fr. *comédie*—L. *cōmoedia*—Gr. *kōmōidiā*—*kōmos*, revel, or *kōmē*, village, *ōidē*, song.]

comely, *kum′li*, *adj*. pleasing : graceful : handsome.—*adv*. in a comely manner.—*n*. **come′liness**. [O.E. *cýmlíc*—*cýme*, suitable, *líc*, like.]

comestible, *kom-est′i-bl*, *adj*. eatable.—*n*. (usu. in *pl*.) food. [Fr.,—L. *comedĕre*, to eat up.]

comet, *kom′it*, *n*. a heavenly body with a very eccentric orbit, having a definite nucleus, a nebulous light surrounding the nucleus, and commonly a luminous tail turned away from the sun.—*adjs*. **com′etary**, **cometic** (*-et′ik*).—*ns*. **com′et-finder**, a telescope of low power used to

search for comets; **cometog'raphy**; **cometol'-
ogy**. [Gr. *komētēs*, long-haired—*komē*, hair.]
comether, *kəm-edh'ər, n.* (mainly *Ir.*) wheedling:
charm. [**come hither**, a call to cows, etc.]
comfit, *kum'fit, n.* a sweetmeat: a sugar-coated
seed or almond.—*n. (obs.)* **com'fiture**, conserve.
[A doublet of **confect**; Fr. *confit, confiture.*]
comfort, *kum'fərt* (Spens. *com-fort'*), *v.t.* to relieve
from pain or distress: to soothe: to cheer, revive.
—*n.* relief: encouragement: ease: quiet enjoyment: freedom from annoyance: whatever gives
ease, enjoyment, etc.: a subject of satisfaction.—
adj. **com'fortable**, imparting or enjoying comfort.
—*n. (U.S.)* a bed quilt.—*adv.* **com'fortably.**—*n.*
com'forter, one who administers comfort: *(B.)*
the Holy Ghost: a long, narrow woollen scarf: a
dummy teat: *(U.S.)* a bed quilt.—*adj.* **com'fortless.**—*n.* **com'fortlessness.**—**Job's comforter**,
one who, while seeking or pretending to comfort,
only aggravates the distress (Job xvi.2.). [O.Fr.
conforter—L. *con-*, and *fortis*, strong.]
comfrey, *kum'fri, n.* a rough boraginaceous plant
(*Symphytum*). [O.Fr. *confirie*.]
comic, *kom'ik, adj.* relating to comedy: raising
mirth: droll.—*n.* the quality or element that
arouses mirth: *(coll.)* an actor of droll parts:
(coll.) an amusing person: *(coll.)* a comic paper,
strip (now not necessarily intended to be funny).—
adj. **com'ical**, funny.—*ns.* **comical'ity**, **com'icalness.**—*adv.* **com'ically.**—*n.* **comique** (*kŏ-mēk'*),
a comic actor or singer. [See **comedy**.]
Cominform, *kom'in-form, n.* the Communist *Information* Bureau, created in 1947, taking the
place of the Comintern.
Comintern, *kom'in-tərn, n.* the Communist *International*, or Third International (q.v.).
comitadji. Same as **komitaji**.
comitatus, *kom-i-tā'təs, n.* a prince's escort: a
county or shire. [L. *comitātus, -ūs—comes, -itis*,
companion, count.]
comitia, *ko-mish'i-ā, n.pl.* the assemblies of the
Romans for electing magistrates, passing laws, etc.
[L.,—*com*, together, *īre, itum*, to go.]
comity, *kom'i-ti, n.* courteousness: civility.—
comity of nations (*comitas gentium*), the international courtesy by which effect is given (within
limits) to the laws of one state within the territory
of another. [L. *cōmitās, -ātis—cōmis*, courteous.]
comma, *kom'ā, n.* (*rhet.; Shak.*) a phrase: in
punctuation, the point (,) that marks the smallest
division of a sentence: the smallest interval, break,
discontinuity: hence perh. (*Shak.*) a connecting
link: (*mus.*) a name for various minute intervals,
esp. the difference between twelve perfect fifths
and seven octaves.—**comma bacillus**, the micro-
organism that causes cholera; **comma butterfly**,
a nymphaline butterfly (*Polygonia*) with a white
comma-shaped mark on the under side of the
hind-wing; **inverted commas**, marks of quotation
(". .", '. .'). [L.,—Gr. *komma*, a section of a
sentence, from *koptein*, to cut off.]
command, *kəm-änd', v.t.* to order: to bid: to
exercise supreme authority over: (*Shak.*) to
demand: to cause to act: (*Shak.*) to exact: to have
within sight, range, influence, or control.—*v.i.* to
have chief authority: to govern.—*n.* an order:
authority: control: power to overlook, influence
or use: the thing commanded.—*ns.* **commandant**
(*kom-ən-dant'*), an officer who has the command of
a place or of a body of troops: **commandant'-
ship.**—*v.t.* **commandeer'** (*Cape Dutch*), to compel to military service, or seize for military use:
(*coll.*) to take arbitrarily.—*ns.* **command'er**, one
who commands: an officer in the navy next in rank
under a captain: a member of a higher class in an
order of knighthood: a district administrator in
religious military orders: **command'er-in-
chief'**, the officer in supreme command of an
army, or of the entire forces of the state;
command'ership; **command'ery**, the district
under a commander, esp. in the religious military
orders.—*adj.* **command'ing**, fitted to impress or
control.—*adv.* **command'ingly.**—*ns.* **command'ment**, a command: a precept; **command'o**
(*Port.*) in South Africa, a military party: (*mil.*) a

unit of a special service brigade equivalent to a
battalion: (inaccurately) one serving in such a unit.
command paper, one laid before Parliament by
command of the crown; **command performance**, a performance by royal command; **at
command**, available for use; **commander of
the faithful**, a title of the caliphs; **on commando**,
on military service in the field; **ten commandments**, the ten Mosaic laws: (*Shak.*) the finger-
nails, esp. a woman's. [Fr. *commander*—L.L.
commandāre (L. *commendāre*)—L. *mandāre*, to
entrust.]
commeasure, *kəm-ezh'ər, v.t.* to equal in measure:
to coincide with.—*n.* **commeas'urable** (same as
commensurable.)
Commelina, *kom-ə-lī'nä, n.* a tropical genus of
monocotyledons, giving name to the fam. **Com-
melinaceae** (*-li-nā'si-ē*). [After the Dutch
botanists Johannes (1629-72) and Caspar (1667-
1731) *Commelin*.]
commemorate, *kəm-em'ə-rāt, v.t.* to call to
remembrance by a solemn or public act: to
celebrate: to preserve the memory of.—*adj.*
commem'orable.—*n.* **commemora'tion**, preserving the memory of some person or thing, esp.
by a solemn ceremony: the specification of individual saints in the prayers for the dead: the
great festival of the Oxford academic year, usually
taking place on the third Wednesday after Trinity
Sunday.—*adjs.* **commem'orative**, **commem'-
oratory**, tending or serving to commemorate.—*n.*
commem'orator. [L. *commemorāre, -ātum*, to
remember—*com-*, inten., and *memor*, mindful.]
commence, *kəm-ens', v.i.* to begin: to originate:
to take rise.—*v.t.* to begin: to originate: to enter
upon: to take a university degree (as *commence
M.A.*)—*n.* **commence'ment**, the beginning: at
certain universities the act of taking the degrees:
the ceremony when these are conferred. [O.Fr.
commencer—L. *com-*, and *initiāre*, to begin—*in*,
into, and *īre*, to go.]
commend, *kəm-end', v.t.* to commit as a charge:
to recommend as worthy: to praise: to adorn, set
off.—*n.* (*Shak.*) a greeting: (*Shak.*) praise.—*adj.*
commend'able.—*n.* **commend'ableness.**—*adv.*
commend'ably.—*ns.* **commend'am** (L.L.
accus.), an ecclesiastical benefice held, or the
tenure or grant of a benefice held, *in commendam*,
i.e. theoretically till a pastor was provided for it,
but often for life and without duties; **commendation** (*kom-ən-dā'shən*), the act of commending, esp.
of commending the dying or dead to the favour
mercy of God: praise: declaration of esteem;
comm'endator, one who holds a benefice *in
commendam*: a titular abbot, etc.: the head of a
commandery.—*adj.* **commend'atory**, commending: containing praise or commendation: presenting to favourable notice or reception: held, or
holding, *in commendam.*—**commend me to**,
remember me kindly to: give me by preference.
[L. *commendāre*—*com-*, and *mandāre*, to trust.]
commensal, *kə-men'səl, adj.* eating at the same
table: (*biol.*) living together for mutual benefit:
esp. an association of less intimate kind than that
called symbiosis.—*n.* a messmate: an organism
living in partnership (not parasitism) with another.
n. **commen'salism.**—*adv.* **commen'sally**. [L.
com-, together, *mēnsa*, a table.]
commensurable, *kəm-en'sū-rə-bl, adj.* having a
common measure: capable of being measured
exactly by the same unit: in due proportion.—*ns.*
commensurabil'ity, **commen'surableness.**—
adv. **commen'surably.**—*adj.* **commen'surāte**,
equal in measure or extent: in due proportion.—
adv. **commen'surately.**—*ns.* **commen'surāte-
ness**, **commensura'tion**. [L. *com-*, *mēnsūra*, a
measure—*mētīrī, mēnsus*, to measure.]
comment, *kom'ənt, n.* a note conveying an illustration or explanation: a remark, observation,
criticism.—*v.i.* (or *kəm-ent'*) to make critical or
explanatory notes: to annotate: (*Shak.*) to meditate.—*v.t.* to say in comment: (*Spens.*) to expound.
—*ns.* **comm'entary**, a comment: a remark: a
series or book of comments or notes; **commentā'-
tion**, annotation; **comm'entātor**, one who com-

Neutral vowels in unaccented syllables: *el'ə-mənt, in'fənt, ran'dəm*

ments ; the writer of a commentary : a broadcaster of a running commentary.—*adj.* **commenta-tō′rial**, pertaining to the making of commentaries. —*n.* **comm′enter, -or** (or *-ment′*). [L. *commentārī*, to devise, contrive—*com-* and L. *mēns, mentis*, the mind.]

commerce, *kom′ərs, n.* interchange of merchandise on a large scale between nations or individuals : extended trade or traffic : intercourse : fellowship. —*v.i.* **commerce** (*kəm-ərs′*), to trade : to have communication with.—*adj.* **commer′cial** (*-shl*), pertaining to commerce : mercantile.—*n.* a commercial traveller.—*v.t.* **commer′cialise**, to reduce to a branch of commerce : to subject to the commercial spirit.—*ns.* **commer′cialism**, the commercial spirit : an expression characteristic of commercial language ; **commer′cialist** ; **commerciality** (*-shi-al′i-ti*).—*adv.* **commer′cially.**— **commercial room**, a room in a hotel set apart for commercial travellers ; **commercial traveller**, an accredited travelling representative of a trading house. [Fr.,—L. *commercium*—*com-*, *merx, mercis*, merchandise.]

commère, *kom-er′, n.* fem. of **compère**. [Fr., godmother ; cf. **cummer**.]

commerge, *kə-mərj′, v.i.* to merge together.

comminate, *kom′in-āt, v.t.* to threaten.—*n.* **comminā′tion**, threatening, denunciation : a recital of God's threatenings made on Ash-Wednesday and at other times in the English Church.—*adjs.* **comm′inative, comm′inatory**, threatening punishment. [L. *comminārī, -ātum*—*com-*, inten., and *minārī*, to threaten.]

commingle, *kam-ing′gl, v.t.* and *v.i.* to mingle or mix together.—*adj.* **commin′gled.**

comminute, *kom′in-ūt, v.t.* to reduce to minute particles : to pulverise.—*n.* **comminū′tion.**— **comminuted fracture**, the breaking of a bone in several places : a compound fracture. [L. *comminuĕre, -ūtum*, to break into pieces—*com-*, and *minuĕre*, to make small—root of *minus*, less.]

Commiphora, *kom-if′ər-ä, n.* a genus of plants of the family Burseraceae, natives of tropical Asia and Africa, yielding myrrh, bdellium, and other resins. [Gr. *kommi*, gum, *phoreein*, to bear.]

commiserate, *kəm-iz′ər-āt, v.t.* to feel or express compassion for : to pity : to condole with.—*adj.* **commis′erable**, requiring commiseration : pitiable.—*n.* **commiserā′tion**, pity.—*adj.* **commis′erative**, feeling or expressing sympathetic sorrow. *n.* **commis′erator.** [L. *com-*, *miserārī*, to deplore —*miser*, wretched.]

commissary, *kom′is-ər-i, n.* one to whom any charge is committed : a deputy : (Scots *law*) the judge in a commissary court : a higher officer of police : (*eccles.*) an officer representing a bishop, and performing his duties in distant parts of the diocese : an officer who furnishes provisions, etc., to an army : a commissar.—*n.* **commissar′, a** commissary : in the Soviet Union, a minister or head of a government department (also **komissar′**). —*adj.* **commissā′rial**, pertaining to a commissary. —*ns.* **commissā′riat**, the department charged with the furnishing of provisions, as for an army : the supply of provisions : the office of a commissary or of a commissar : a body of commissars ; **comm′-issary-gen′eral**, the head of the department for supplying provisions, etc., to an army ; **comm′-issaryship.**—**Commissary Court**, a Scottish court with jurisdiction in matters that had belonged to the bishops' courts, abolished in 1836. [L.L. *commissārius*—*committĕre, commissum.*]

commission, *kəm-ish′ən, n.* act of committing : the state of being commissioned or committed : that which is committed : an instrument conferring authority, or the authority itself, esp. that of a military, naval, or air officer, or a justice of the peace : a percentage paid to an agent : a body of persons appointed to perform certain duties : an order for a piece of work, esp. of art : (of a warship, etc.) a state of being manned, equipped, and ready for service : (of an office) temporary or permanent delegation to a number of persons who act jointly. —*v.t.* to give a commission to or for : to empower : to appoint : to put in commission.—*v.i.* to be put

in commission.—*ns.* **commiss′ion-ag′ent, -mer′-chant**, one who transacts business for another for a commission ; **commissionaire** (*-ār′*), a messenger or doorkeeper in uniform : a member of a corps of old soldiers and sailors employed as doorkeepers, etc.—*adj.* **commiss′ioned.**—*ns.* **commiss′ioner**, one who holds a commission to perform some business : a member of a commission ; **commiss′ionership.**—**commissioned officer**, one appointed by commission ; **High Commission Court**, a court established in 1529 to investigate ecclesiastical cases, abolished as illegal in 1641 ; **Lord High Commissioner**, the representative of the crown at the General Assembly of the Church of Scotland. [See **commit.**]

commissure, *kom′is-ūr, n.* a joint : a surface of junction : a suture : a bundle of nerve-fibres connecting two nerve-centres.—*adj.* **commissū′-ral.** [L. *commissūra*, a joining ; see **commit.**]

commit, *kə-mit′, v.t.* to give in charge or trust : to consign : to become guilty of, perpetrate : to compromise or involve : to pledge (*pr.p.* **commit′ting** ; *pa.p.* **commit′ted**).—*ns.* **commit′-ment**, act of committing : an order for sending to prison : imprisonment : an obligation undertaken ; **committ′al**, commitment : a pledge, actual or implied ; **committ′ee**, a portion selected from a more numerous body (or the whole body) to which some special business is committed : (*kom-i-tē′*) a person to whom something is committed : (*law*) one charged with the care of a lunatic or imbecile ; **committ′eeship.**—**Committee of the whole House**, the House of Commons, or other legislative body, when it resolves itself into a committee with chairman, etc. ; **committee stage**, the stage in the passage of a bill through parliament, between the second and third readings, when it is discussed in detail in committee ; **commit to memory**, to learn by heart ; **go into committee**, to resolve itself into a committee ; **in committee**, during the deliberations of a committee. [L. *committĕre*—*com-*, with, *mittĕre*, to send.]

commix, *kə-miks′, v.t.* to mix together.—*v.i.* to mix.—*ns.* **commix′tion** (*-tyən*), **commix′ture**, act of mixing together : the state of being mixed : the compound formed by mixing : the rite of putting a piece of the host into the chalice, emblematic of the reunion of body and soul at the resurrection : (*obs.*) sexual intercourse.

commodious, *kə-mō′dyəs, adj.* suitable or convenient : roomy, spacious : (*Shak.*) serviceable : comfortable.—*n.* **commode′**, a small sideboard : an ornamental chest of drawers : a night-stool : a large, high head-dress formerly worn by ladies.— *adv.* **commo′diously.**—*ns.* **commo′diousness** ; **commodity** (*-mod′*), convenience : (*Shak.*) profit, expediency, advantage, privilege : (*Shak.*) parcel, portion : an article of traffic : (*pl.*) goods, produce. [L. *commodus*—*com-*, *modus*, measure.]

commodore, *kom′ə-dōr, n.* an officer intermediate between an admiral and a captain : the senior captain in a fleet of merchantmen : the president of a yacht-club : a commodore's ship. [Perh. from Du. *kommandeur.*]

common, *kom′ən, adj.* belonging equally to more than one : public : general : usual : frequent : ordinary : easy to be had : of little value : vulgar : of low degree.—*n.* (*Shak.*) the commonalty : a tract of open land, used in common by the inhabitants of a town, parish, etc.—*v.i.* (*Shak.*) to share : (*Spens.*) to converse : (*arch.*) to board.—*adj.* **comm′onable**, held in common.—*ns.* **comm′on-age**, right of pasturing on a common : the right of using anything in common : a common ; **comm′-onalty**, the general body of the people without any distinction of rank or authority : the common people (also, esp. *Scot.*, in this sense **common-al′ity**) ; **comm′oner**, one who is not a noble : a member of the House of Commons : at Oxford, a student who pays for his commons ; **comm′oney**, an ordinary playing marble.—*adv.* **comm′only**, in a common manner : meanly, vulgarly : ordinarily : usually : generally : (*Spens.*) familiarly, intimately : (*B.*) publicly.—*ns.* **comm′onness** ; **comm′on-place**, a common topic or subject : a platitude : a memorandum : a note.—*adj.* lacking distinction : hackneyed.—*v.t.* to make notes of : to put in a commonplace-book.—*v.t.* to platitudinise.—*ns.* **comm'onplace-book,** a note or memorandum book; **comm'on-riding,** the Scottish equivalent of beating the bounds; **comm'on-room,** in schools, colleges, etc., a room to which the members have common access.—*n.pl.* **comm'ons,** the common people; their representatives—i.e. the lower House of Parliament or House of Commons : common land : food at a common table : at Oxford, rations served at a fixed rate from the college buttery : food in general, rations.—*ns.* **comm'on-sense',** (*obs.*) an inner consciousness unifying the five outer senses : average understanding : good sense or practical sagacity : the opinion of a community : the universally admitted impressions of mankind; **comm'on-shore'** (see shore)—**Court of Common Bench, Common Pleas,** one of the divisions of the High Court of Justice; **common chord,** a tone with its third (major or minor) and perfect fifth; **common forms,** the ordinary clauses which are of frequent occurrence in identical terms in writs and deeds; **common gender,** the gender of a noun or pronoun having one form for male and female, as L. *bōs,* bull, cow, Eng. *student;* **common law,** in England, the ancient customary law of the land; **common measure,** (*math.*) a quantity that is a measure of several quantities : (*mus.*) common time; **common noun,** a name that can be applied to all the members of a class—opp. to *proper* noun; **Common Prayer (Book of),** the liturgy of the Church of England; **common school** (*U.S.*) a public elementary school; **common stair,** an interior stair giving access to several independent flats or dwellings; **common time** (*mus.*), four-beat or two-beat rhythm.—**in common,** together : equally with others; **make common cause with,** to cast in one's lot with : to have the same interest and aims with; **philosophy of common-sense,** that school of philosophy which takes the universally admitted impressions of mankind as corresponding to the facts of things without any further scrutiny; **short commons,** scant fare; **the common,** that which is common or usual; **the common good,** the interest of the community at large : the corporate property of a burgh in Scotland; **the common people,** the people in general. [Fr. *commun*—L. *commūnis,* prob. from *com-,* together, and *mūnis,* serving, obliging.]

commonweal, *kom'ən-wēl,* **commonwealth,** *kom'ən-welth, ns.* the common or public good : the government in a free state : the public or whole body of the people : a form of government in which the power rests with the people, esp. that in England after the overthrow of Charles I : a state or dominion, esp. applied to the Australian federation and certain states of America : a group of states united by a strong but elastic link.—*n.* **comm'onwealth'sman, comm'onwealthsman,** (*obs.*) a (good) citizen : an adherent of Cromwell's Commonwealth. [See **wealth.**]

commorant, *kom'ər-ənt, n.* and *adj.* resident (esp. at a university). [L. *commorāns, -āntis,* pr.p. of *commorārī,* to abide.]

commove, *kə-mōōv', v.t.* to put in motion : to agitate : to disturb, excite.—*n.* **commotion** (-*mō'-shən*), a violent motion or moving : excited or tumultuous action, physical or mental : agitation : tumult.—*adj.* **commō'tional.** [L. *com-,* inten., and *movēre, mōtum,* to move.]

commune, *kom'ūn, n.* a corporation : in France, etc., a small territorial division with some self-government and a mayor.—*adj.* **communal** (*kə-mū'nl* or *kom'*), pertaining to a commune or a community.—*ns.* **communalisā'tion; commū'-nalism; commū'nalist; comm'ūnard** (or -*ärd'*), an adherent of the Paris *Commune* in 1871 : a communist.—**the Commune** at Paris in 1871 was a revolt against the national government, the principle of the revolt being that each city or district should be ruled independently by its own

commune or local government. [Fr. *commune.* See **common.**]

commune, *kə-mūn', kom'ūn, v.i.* to converse or talk together : to have intercourse, esp. spiritual : to receive Holy Communion.—*n.* **comm'une,** converse.—*n.* and *adj.* **commūn'ing.** [O.Fr. *communer,* to share.]

communicate, *kə-mū'ni-kāt, v.t.* to give a share of, impart : to reveal : to bestow.—*v.i.* to have something in common with another : to have communication : to have means of passage : to have intercourse : to partake of Holy Communion.—*ns.* **commūnicabil'ity** (-*kə-bil'i-ti*), **commū'-nicableness.**—*adj.* **commū'nicable,** that may be communicated : affable.—*adv.* **commū'nic-ably.**—*ns.* **commū'nicant,** one who partakes of Holy Communion; **commūnicā'tion,** act of communicating : that which is communicated : intercourse : correspondence : a means of communicating, a connecting passage or channel.—*adj.* **commū'nicative,** inclined to communicate or give information : unreserved.—*adv.* **commū'-nicatively.**—*ns.* **commū'nicativeness; commū'nicator.**—*adj.* **commū'nicatory,** imparting knowledge.—*n.* **communiqué** (*kom-ū-nē-kā'*), an official announcement. [L. *commūnicāre, -ātum—commūnis,* common.]

communion, *kə-mūn'yən, n.* act of communing : spiritual intercourse : fellowship : common possession : interchange of transactions : union in religious service : the body of people who so unite : **(Holy Communion),** the celebration of the Lord's Supper.—*n.* **commūn'ionist,** a communicant.—**Communion of Saints,** the spiritual fellowship of all true believers, the blessed dead as well as the faithful living—in R.C. doctrine held to involve a mutual exchange of examples, prayers, merits and satisfactions. [L. *commūniō, -ōnis,* from *commūnis,* common.]

communism, *kom'ū-nizm, n.* a theory or condition of things according to which private property should be abolished, and all things held in common : Marxian socialism as understood in Russia.—*n.* **comm'ūnist,** one who holds such principles.—*adj.* **commūnist'ic,** pertaining to communism.

community, *kə-mūn'i-ti, n.* common possession or enjoyment : agreement : communion : (*Shak.*) commonness : people having common rights, etc. : the public in general : a body of persons in the same locality : a body of persons leading a common life, or under a socialistic or similar organisation : a monastic body.—*n.* **communitā'rian,** a member of a community.—**community singing,** organised singing by a gathering. [O.Fr. *communité*—L. *commūnitās, -ātis—commūnis,* common.]

commute, *kə-mūt', v.t.* to exchange : to exchange for a punishment less severe : to compound for (by a single payment, a simple or more convenient method, etc.) : to change (electric current) from alternating to direct or vice versa.—*v.i.* (*U.S.*) to use a season ticket, esp. between suburban home and town office.—*n.* **commūtabil'ity.**—*adj.* **commū'table,** that may be commuted or exchanged.—*v.t.* **commutate** (*kom'; electr.*) to commute.—*n.* **commūtā'tion,** the act of commuting : change or exchange of one thing for another : the change to a lighter penalty, simpler or easier mode of payment, etc.—*adj.* **commū'tative** (or *kom'*), relating to exchange : interchangeable.—*adv.* **commū'tatively.**—*ns.* **commū'tator,** an apparatus for reversing electric currents; **commūt'er** (*U.S.*), a season ticket-holder—**commutation ticket** (*U.S.*), a season ticket. [L. *commūtāre—com-,* with *mūtāre,* to change.]

commutual, *kə-mū'tū-əl, adj.* mutual, reciprocal.

comose, comous. See **coma.**

comp, *komp, n.* abbreviated form of **compositor.**

compact, *kəm-pakt', adj.* closely placed or fitted together : composed or framed : firm : close : brief.—*n.* **compact** (*kom'*), a compacted body or structure, a combination : a small case containing face-powder for carrying in the handbag (**powder compact**).—*v.t.* (-*pakt'*) to press closely together : to consolidate : (*Shak.*) to confirm.—*adj.* **com-**

pact'ed.—*adv.* compact'edly.—*n.* compact'edness.—*adv.* compact'ly.—*ns.* compact'ness; compac'ture (*Spens.*), close union or knitting together. [L. *compāctus*, pa.p. of *compingĕre*—*com*-, *pangĕre*, to fix.]

compact, kom'pakt, *n.* a mutual bargain or agreement: a league, treaty, or union: (*Shak.*) league, in bad sense.—*adj.* (*kom-pakt'*) united: leagued: (*Spens.*) agreed upon, arranged. [L. *compactum*—*compaciscī*, from *com*-, *paciscī*, to bargain.]

compages, kəm-pā'jēz, *n.* structure (also *obs.* compage'):—*pl.* compages.—*n.* compagination (-*paj-i-nā'shən*).—*v.t.* compag'inate, to join, connect. [L. *compāgēs*, *compāginăre*, -*ātum*, *com*- and root of *pangĕre*, to fasten.]

companion, kəm-pan'yən, *n.* one who keeps company or frequently associates with another: an associate or partner: a higher rank of servant, who, though receiving pay, stands rather in the relation of a friend: fellow, in a bad sense: a member of an order, esp. in a lower grade: one of a pair or set of things.—*v.t.* to accompany.—*adj.* of the nature of a companion: accompanying.—*adjs.* compan'iable (*obs.*), sociable; compan'ionable, fit to be a companion: agreeable.—*ns.* compan'ionableness.—*adv.* compan'ionably.—*adjs.* compan'ionate, shared in companionship; compan'ioned, having a companion.—*n.* compan'ionhood.—*adj.* compan'ionless.—*n.* compan'ionship, state of being a companion: company, fellowship: a body of companions.—companionate marriage, an easily dissolved union, with birth-control, etc. [Fr. *compagnon*, from L.L. *compānium*, a mess—L. *com*-, with, and *pānis*, bread.]

companion, kəm-pan'yən, *n.* (*naut.*) the skylight or window-frame through which light passes to a lower deck or cabin: companion-ladder.—*ns.* compan'ion-hatch, the covering of an opening in a deck; compan'ion-ladd'er, the ladder or stair leading from the deck to a cabin or to the quarter-deck; compan'ion-way, a staircase from the deck to a cabin. [Cf. Du. *kompanje*; O.F. *compagne*; It. *compagna*, store-room.]

company, kum'pə-ni, *n.* a person or persons associating with one: any assembly of persons: a number of persons associated together for trade, etc.: a society: a sub-division of a regiment: the crew of a ship: state of being a companion: presence in association: fellowship: social intercourse.—*v.t.* to accompany.—*v.i.* to associate: to cohabit (*pr.p.* com'panying, *Spens.* companing; *pa.t.* and *pa.p.* com'panied).—company promoter, one who promotes or superintends the formation of joint-stock companies; good, or bad, company, having or lacking companionable qualities; keep company, to associate with: to court; know a man by his company, to determine his character by the quality of his friends. [Fr. *compagnie*; see companion.]

compare, kəm-pār', *v.t.* to set together so as to ascertain how far things agree or disagree (often with *with*): to liken or represent as similar (with *to*): (*gram.*) to give the degrees of comparison of.—*v.i.* to make comparison: to stand in comparison: to vie.—*n.* (*obs.*) compeer: comparison.—*adj.* comparable (*kom'pər-ə-bl*).—*n.* com'parableness.—*adv.* com'parably.—*adj.* comparative (*kəm-par'ə-tiv*), pertaining to or making comparison: estimated by comparing with something else: not positive or absolute: (*gram.*) expressing more.—*adv.* compar'atively.—*n.* comparison (-*par'i-sən*), the act of comparing: capacity of being compared: a comparative estimate: a simile or figure by which two things are compared: (*gram.*) the inflection of an adjective or adverb to express different relative degrees of its quality.—beyond compare, without any rival or like. [L. *comparāre*, to match, from *com*-, *parāre*, to make or esteem equal—*par*, equal.]

compare, kəm-pār', *v.t.* (*Spens.*) to get or provide. [L. *comparāre*—*com*-, inten., *parāre*, to prepare.]

compartment, kəm-pärt'mənt, *n.* a partioned off or marked off division of an enclosed space or area: a division of a railway carriage: a division of

anything.—*v.t.* compart', to divide into parts. [Fr. *compartiment*—L. *com*-, *partīrī*, to part.]

compass, kum'pəs, *n.* a circuit or circle: space: limit: range of pitch of a voice or instrument: circumference: girth: an instrument consisting of a magnetised needle, used to find directions: (*pl.*) a pair of jointed legs, for describing circles, etc.—*v.t.* to pass or go round: to surround or enclose: to besiege: to grasp, comprehend: to bring about, accomplish, achieve, or obtain: to devise: to contrive or plot: (*Shak.*) to curve, bend.—*adj.* com'passable, capable of being compassed.—*ns.* com'pass-card, the circular card of a compass; com'passing, contrivance: design: com'pass-plane, a plane, convex on the under side, for smoothing curved timber; com'pass-plant, any plant (as species of lettuce and *Silphium*) that places its leaves north and south to avoid the midday sun; com'pass-saw, one for cutting in curves; com'pass-sig'nal, a signal denoting a point in the compass; com'pass-tim'ber, curved timber, used for shipbuilding, etc.; com'pass-win'dow, a semicircular bay-window.—*adj.* com'past (*Spens.*), rounded.—box the compass (see box); fetch a compass, to go round in a circuit. [Fr. *compas*, a circle, prob. from L.L. *compassus*—L. *com*-, *passus*, a step.]

compassion, kəm-pash'ən, *n.* fellow-feeling, or sorrow for the sufferings of another: pity.—*v.t.* to pity.—*adjs.* compass'ionable, pitiable; compass'ionate, inclined to pity or mercy: merciful.—*v.t.* to have compassion for: to have pity or mercy upon.—*adv.* compass'ionately.—*n.* compass'ionateness. [Fr.,—L.L. *compassiō*, -*ōnis*—*com*-,with, *patī*, *passus*, to suffer.]

compatible, kəm-pat'i-bl, *adj.* consistent: congruous: capable of coexistence: admissible in combination.—*ns.* compatibil'ity, compat'ibleness.—*adv.* compat'ibly. [Fr.,—L. *com*-, with, *patī*, to suffer.]

compatriot, kəm-pāt'ri-ət, or -*pat'*, *n.* a fellow-countryman.—Also *adj.*—*adj.* compatriotic (-*ot'ik*).—*n.* compa'triotism. [Fr. *compatriote*—L. *compatriōta*; see patriot.]

compear, kəm-pēr', *v.i.* (*Scots law*) to appear in court.—*ns.* compear'ance; compear'ant. [Fr. *comparoir*—L. *compārēre*—*com*-, *pārēre*, to appear.]

compeer, kəm-pēr', kom'pēr, *n.* an equal: a companion: an associate.—*v.t.* (-*pēr*; *Shak.*) to equal. [L. *compar*—*com*-, *par*, equal.]

compel, kəm-pel', *v.t.* to drive or urge on forcibly: (*Spens.*) to bring with urgency: to oblige: to force: to obtain by hard labour (*pr.p.* compell'ing; *pa.t.* and *pa.p.* compelled').—*adj.* compell'able. [L. *com*-, inten., *pellĕre*, *pulsum*, to drive.]

compellation, kom-pə-lā'shən, *n.* style of address: an appellation.—*adj.* compellative (*kəm-pel'ə-tiv*).—*n.* compellation. [L. *compellāre*, -*ātum*, to address, freq. of *compellĕre*.]

compend, kom'pend, compen'dium (*kəm*-; *pl.* -diums, -dia), *ns.* a shortening or abridgment: a book or treatise containing the substance of a larger one: an epitome: an abstract: a comprehensive, generally compressed, treatise.—*adj.* compen'dious, short: concise: comprehensive.—*adv.* compen'diously.—*n.* compen'diousness. [L. *compendium*, what is weighed together, or saved (opp. to *dispendium*, what is weighed out or spent)—*com*-, together, *pendĕre*, to weigh.]

compensate, kom'pən-sāt, or kəm-pen'sāt, *v.t.* to make amends for, or to recompense: to counter-balance.—*v.i.* to make up.—*n.* compensā'tion (*kom*-), act of compensating: amends for loss sustained: (*phys.*) the neutralisation of opposing forces: (*U.S.*) salary.—*adjs.* compensā'tional, compensative (*kom'*, or -*pen'*), compen'satory, giving compensation.—*n.* com'pensātor, one who or that which compensates.—compensation balance, pendulum, a balance-wheel or pendulum so constructed as to counteract the effect of the expansion and contraction of the metal under variation of temperature. [L. *com*-, inten., and *pēnsāre*, freq. of *pendĕre*, to weigh.]

compère, *kon'-per*, *n.* one who introduces and interlinks items of an entertainment. [Fr., godfather.]

compesce, *kəm-pes'*, *v.t.* (*arch. Scot.*) to restrain. [L. *compēscĕre*.]

compete, *kəm-pēt'*, *v.i.* to seek or strive for something in opposition to others : to contend for a prize.—*n.* **competition** (*kom-pi-tish'ən*), the act of competing : rivalry in strife for the same object : a match or trial of ability.—*adj.* **compet'itive** (*kəm-pet'i-tiv*), pertaining to or characterised by competition.—*n.* **compet'itor**, one who competes : a rival or opponent : (*Shak.*) an associate, confederate, fellow. [L. *competĕre*, to strive together —*com-*, *petĕre*, to seek, strive after.]

competent, *kom'pi-tənt*, *adj.* suitable : sufficient : fit : belonging : legally qualified : legitimate.—*ns.* **com'petence**, **com'petency**, fitness : capacity : sufficiency : enough to live on with comfort : legal power or capacity.—*adv.* **com'petently**. [L. *competĕre*, to come together, be convenient—*com-*, *petĕre*, to seek.]

compile, *kəm-pīl'*, *v.t.* to write or compose by collecting the materials from other books : to draw up or collect : to compose : (*Spens.*) to heap up, to put or bring together : (*Spens.*) to compose (in peace and rest) : (*cricket slang*) to pile up a score of.—*ns.* **compilā'tion** (*-pil-* or *-pīl-*), the act of compiling : the thing compiled, a literary work made by gathering the material from various authors; **compile'ment**, a compilation; **compil'er**, **com'pilātor**, one who compiles.—*adj.* **compil'atory**. [Fr. *compiler*, prob. from L. *compilāre*—*com-*, together, *pīlāre*, to plunder, or *pīlāre*, to pound down; influenced by **pile.**]

compital, *kom'pit-əl*, *adj.* pertaining to cross-roads, or to the intersection of leaf-veins : acutely intersecting. [L. *compita*, cross-roads.]

complacent, *kəm-plā'sent*, *adj.* showing satisfaction : self-satisfied : pleased : inclined to please.—*ns.* **complā'cence**, **complā'cency**, pleasure : satisfaction : complaisance.—*adv.* **complā'cently**. [L. *complacēre*—*com-*, inten., *placēre*, to please.]

complain, *kəm-plān'*, *v.i.* (also *refl.*) to express grief, pain, censure : to murmur or express a sense of injury : to accuse : to make a mournful sound : to show that one is ill.—*v.t.* to deplore : to utter as a complaint.—*n.* complaint.—*ns.* **complain'ant**, one who complains : (*law*) one who raises a suit, a plaintiff : **complain'er**, a murmurer : complainant. —*n.* and *adj.* **complain'ing**.—*adv.* **complain'ingly**.—*n.* **complaint'**, a complaining : an expression of grief and dissatisfaction : a poem setting forth matter of grief or dissatisfaction : a representation of pains or injuries : a finding fault : the thing complained of : a grievance : a disease : an ailment. [Fr. *complaindre*—L.L. *complangĕre*—L. *com-*, inten., *plangĕre*, bewail.]

complaisant, *kom'ple-zänt*, *kom-ple-zänt'*, *kəm-plā'-zənt*, *adj.* desirous of pleasing : obliging : facile, ready to condone.—*n.* **com'plaisance** (or *zäns'*, or *-plā'*), care or desire to please, esp. in excess : an obliging civility.—*adv.* **complaisantly**. [Fr., *complaire*—L. *complacēre*.]

complanate, *kom'plən-āt*, *adj.* flattened.—*n.* **complanā'tion**. [L. *complānāre*, *-ātum*—*com-*, and *plānus*, flat.]

complect, *kəm-plekt'*, *v.t.* to embrace : to interweave.—*adj.* **complect'ed**, interwoven. [L. *com-*, *plectī*, to embrace—*com-*, *plectĕre*, to twine.]

complected. See **complexion**.

complement, *kom'pli-mənt*, *n.* that which completes or fills up : that by which an angle or arc falls short of a right angle or quadrant : one of the parallelograms not intersected by the diagonal of a given parallelogram when it is divided into four parallelograms by straight lines through a point in the diagonal : that by which a logarithm falls short of 10 : that which is added to certain verbs to make a complete predicate : that by which an interval falls short of an octave : one of two colours which together give white : full number or quantity : (*Spens.*) consummateness, completeness : (*her.*) fulness (of the moon) : (*Spens.*; *Shak.*) politeness.—*v.t.* **complement** (*-ment'* or *kom'pli-*

mənt), to be the complement of : (*arch.*) to compliment.—*adjs.* **complement'al**, completing : (*Shak.*) complimental; **complement'ary**, completing : together making up a whole, a right angle, ten, an octave, white. [L. *complēmentum*—*com-*, and *plēre*, to fill.]

complete, *kəm-plēt'*, *adj.* free from deficiency : perfect : finished : entire : fully equipped : consummate.—*v.t.* to finish : to make perfect or entire : to accomplish.—*adjs.* **complēt'able** ; completed.—*adv.* **complete'ly**.—*ns.* **complete'ness**, the state of being complete; **complē'tion**, the act of completing : the state of being complete : fulfilment.—*adjs.* **complēt'ive**; **complēt'ory**, fulfilling : completing. [L. *complēre*, *-ētum*, to fill up—*com-*, inten., and *plēre*, to fill.]

complex, *kom'pleks*, *adj.* composed of more than one, or of many parts : not simple : intricate : difficult.—*n.* a complex whole : (*psychology*) a group of (repressed and forgotten) ideas or impressions to which are ascribed abnormal mental conditions and abnormal bodily conditions due to mental causes : loosely applied to the mental condition itself.—*v.t.* **complex'**, to complicate.—*ns.* **complex'edness**, **com'plexness**, **complex'ity**, state of being complex : complication.—*adv.* **com'plexly**.—*n.* **complex'us**, a complicated system : a large muscle of the back, passing from the spine to the head.—**complex number**, the sum of a real and an imaginary number; **complex sentence**, one consisting of a principal clause and one or more subordinate clauses. [L. *complex*—*com-*, together, and root of *plicāre*, to fold. See **complicate.**]

complexion, *kəm-plek'shən*, *n.* disposition : colour : quality : colour or look of the skin, esp. of the face : general appearance, temperament, or texture : (*Shak.*) bodily constitution.—*v.t.* to give a colour to.—*adjs.* **complex'ional**, pertaining to the complexion; **complex'ioned** (*U.S.* **complect'ed**), having a certain complexion, or temperament; **complex'ionless**, colourless : pale. [Fr.,—L. *complexiō*, *-ōnis*, a combination, physical structure of body—*com-*, and *plectĕre*, to plait.]

compliance, *kəm-plī'əns*, *n.* a yielding : agreement : complaisance : assent : submission (in bad sense).— *adj.* **compli'able**, disposed to comply.—*n.* **compli'ancy**, compliance.—*adj.* **compli'ant**, yielding : pliant : civil.—*adv.* **compli'antly**. [See **comply.**]

complicate, *kom'pli-kāt*, *v.t.* to twist or plait together : to render complex : to entangle.—*adj.* complex : involved : folded together.—*n.* **com'plicacy** (*-kə-si*), the quality or state of being complicated.—*adj.* **com'plicant**, overlapping, **com'plicated**, intricate, confused.—*n.* **complicā'tion**, an intricate blending or entanglement.— *adj.* **com'plicātive**, tending to complicate.— **complicated fracture**, a fracture where there is some other injury (e.g. a flesh wound not communicating with the fracture, a dislocation, a rupture of a large blood-vessel); **complication of diseases**, a number of diseases present at the same time. [L. *com-*, together, and *plicāre*, *-ātum*, to fold.]

complice, *kom'plis*, *n.* (*Shak.*) an associate : an accomplice.—*n.* **complic'ity**, state or condition of being an accomplice : complexity.

compliment, *kom'pli-mənt*, *n.* an expression of regard or praise : delicate flattery : an expression of formal respect of civility : a present.—*v.t.* **compliment** (*-ment'* or *kom'pli-mənt*), to pay a compliment to : to express respect for : to praise : to flatter : to congratulate : to present in compliment.—*v.i.* to make compliments.—*adjs.* **compliment'al**, expressing or implying compliment; **compliment'ary**, conveying, or expressive of, civility or praise : using compliments : bestowed in compliment, given free.—*n.* **compliment'er**, one who pays compliments.—**compliments of the season**, compliments appropriate to special times, as Christmas and birthdays; **left-handed compliment**, a saying intended to seem a compliment, but in reality the reverse; **pay**, or **present**, **one's compliments**, to give one's respects or greeting. [Fr. *compliment*—L. *complimentum*; see **comply.**]

complin, compline, *kom'plin, n.* the 7th and last service of the day, at 9 p.m., completing the canonical hours. [O.Fr. *complie* (mod. *complies*)— L. *complēta* (hōra); *n* unexplained.]

complish, *kom'plish, v.t.* (*Spens.*) to accomplish.

complot, *kom'plot, n.* a conspiracy.—*v.i.* **complot'** (*kəm-*), to plot together : to conspire.—*v.t.* to plan (*pr.p.* **complott'ing**; *pa.t.* and *pa.p.* **complott'ed**). [Fr.]

compluvium, *kom-plōō'vi-əm, n.* a quadrangular open space in the middle of a Roman house. [L.]

comply, *kəm'plī', v.i.* to yield to the wishes of another : to agree or consent to (*with*) : (*Shak.*) to use ceremony : (*pr.p.* **comply'ing**; *pa.t.* and *pa.p.* **complied'**).—*n.* **compli'er,** one who complies. —*p.adj.* **comply'ing,** compliant. [It. *complire,* to fulfil, to suit, to offer courtesies—L. *complēre,* to fulfil; see **complete.**]

compo, *kom'pō, n.* a mortar of cement : a mixture of whiting, resin, and glue for ornamenting walls and cornices : a bankrupt's composition.—**compo ration** (*milit.*), a composite "hard" ration for use in the field when no fresh food is available. [Abbrev. of **composition.**]

component, *kəm-pō'nənt, adj.* making up : forming one of the elements or parts.—*n.* one of the parts or elements of which anything is made up, or into which it may be resolved.—*n.* **compo'nency.**— *adj.* **componental** (*kom-pō-nent'l*). [L. *compō- nēre.*]

compony, componé, *kom-pō'ni, adj.* (*her.*) con- sisting of a row of squares of alternate tinctures. [Origin doubtful.]

comport, *kəm-pōrt', v.i.* to agree, suit (*with*).—*v.t.* (*refl.*) to bear : to behave.—*n.* manner of acting.— *ns.* **comport'ance** (*Spens.*); **comport'ment,** be- haviour. [L. *comportāre—com-, portāre,* to carry.]

compose, *kəm-pōz', v.t.* to form by putting to- gether or being together : to set in order or at rest : to settle or soothe : to dispose artistically : to set up for printing : to create (esp. in literature and music). —*v.i.* to write (mus.) : music : to set type.—*p.adj.* **composed',** settled : quiet : calm.—*adv.* **com- pōs'edly.**—*ns.* **compōs'edness**; **compōs'er,** a writer or author, esp. of music; **compōs'ing- stick,** a boxlike instrument for holding type before it is placed on the galley; **composure** (*kom- pōzh'(y)ər*), calmness : self-possession : tranquillity : composition : (*Shak.*) temperament, character. [Fr. *composer*—L. *com-,* and *pausāre,* to cease, rest; confused and blended in meaning with words from *pōnĕre, positum,* to place.]

composite, *kom'pəz-it,* formerly *-pōz', adj.* made up of distinct parts or elements : (*archit.*) blending Ionic and Corinthian : (*bot.*) belonging to the **Compositae** (*kəm-poz'i-tē*), a great family akin to the bell-flowers but having small flowers crowded together in heads on a common receptacle sur- rounded by bracts so as to resemble single flowers. —*n.* **com'posite,** a composite thing : a plant of the Compositae.—*ns.* **com'positeness**; **composi'- tion,** the act or art of composing : the nature or proportion of the ingredients of anything; a thing composed : a work of art, esp. in music : an exercise in writing prose or verse : disposition of parts : congruity : combination : an artificial mix- ture, esp. one used as a substitute : mental or moral make-up : a compromise : a percentage accepted by a bankrupt's creditors in lieu of full payment : the compounding of vector quantities, as velocities, forces, into a single resultant.—*adjs.* **compo- si'tional** or **compositive** (*-poz'*).—*ns.* **compos'itor,** one who sets up type; **compost** (*kom'post, -pōst*), **compost'ure** (*Shak.*), a mixture, esp. for manure. —**composite carriage,** a railway carriage with compartments of different class; **composite por- trait,** a blend of several portraits : a photograph printed from several negatives representing differ- ent persons or the same person at different times; **composition of felony,** compounding of felony. [L. *compositus, compostus—com-,* and *pōnĕre,* to place.]

compossible, *kəm-pos'i-bl, adj.* possible in co- existence with something else.—*n.* **compossi- bil'ity.**

compot, compote, *kom'pot,* or *kom'pōt, n.* fruit preserved in syrup : stewed fruit. [Fr. *compote*; cf. **composite.**]

compotation, *kom-pō-tā'shən, n.* a carouse to- gether.—*ns.* **compotā'tionship**; **com'potātor,** a bottle-companion.—*adj.* **compot'atory.** [L. *compōtātiō, -ōnis—com-, pōtāre,* to drink.]

compound, *kəm-pownd', v.t.* to make up : to com- bine : to settle or adjust by agreement : to agree for a consideration not to prosecute (a felony).—*v.i.* to agree, or come to terms : to bargain in the lump— *adj.* **compound** (*kom'*), mixed or composed of a number of parts : (*chem.*) resolvable into two or more elements, so united that the whole has properties of its own which are not necessarily those of its constituents, as in the case of a mixture : (*arith.*) not simple, dealing with numbers of various denominations of quantity, etc., as in *compound addition,* etc; or with processes more complex than the simple process, as in *compound proportion.*—*n.* a mass made up of a number of parts : a word made up of two or more words : (*chem.*) a compound substance : a compounded drug.—*n.* **compound'er.**—**compound animal** (see **colonial animal**); **compound engine,** a condensing engine in which the mechanical action of the steam is begun in one cylinder, and ended in a larger cylinder; **compound fracture,** breaking of a bone, communicating with a co-existing skin wound; **compound householder,** one who pays his rates in his rent, the landlord being im- mediately chargeable with them; **compound interest** (see **interest**); **compound leaf,** one divided into leaflets by divisions reaching the mid- rib; **compound quantity** (*alg.*), a quantity consisting of more than one term, as $a+b$; **com- pound ratio,** the product of ratios; **compound sentence** (*gram.*), one containing more than one principal clause; **compound time** (*mus.*), time in which each bar is made up of two or more simple measures. [O.Fr. *compundre* from L. *compōnĕre— com-, pōnĕre,* to place.]

compound, *kom'pownd, n.* an enclosure round a house or factory (in India), or for confining native labourers (S. Africa). [Malay *kampong,* enclosure.]

comprador(e), *kom-prä-dōr', n.* an intermediary through whom a foreign firm trades with Chinese dealers. [Port., buyer—L. *com-, parāre,* to furnish.]

comprehend, *kom-prə-hend', v.t.* to seize or take up with the mind, to understand : to comprise or include.—*ns.* **comprehensibil'ity,** compre- hen'sibleness.—*adj.* **comprehen'sible,** capable of being understood.—*adv.* **comprehen'sibly.**— *n.* **comprehen'sion,** power of the mind to under- stand : (*logic*) the intension of a term or the sum of the qualities implied in the term : the inclusion of Nonconformists within the Church of England.— *adj.* **comprehen'sive,** having the quality or power of comprehending or containing much : inclusive : compendious.—*adv.* **comprehen'sively.**—*n.* **com- prehensiveness.** [L. *comprehendĕre, -hēnsum— com-, prehendĕre,* to seize.]

compress, *kəm-pres', v.t.* to press together : to force into a narrower space : to condense or concentrate : (*arch.*) to embrace.—*n.* **compress** (*kom', surg.*), a pad used to apply pressure to any part : a folded cloth applied to the skin.—*adj.* **compressed',** pressed together : compacted : (*biol.*) laterally flattened or narrowed.—*ns.* **compressibil'ity, compress'ibleness,** the property of being reduced in volume by pressure : the ratio of the amount of compression per unit volume to the compressing force applied : (*aero.*) a shock-wave phenomenon causing increased drag, which asserts itself when an aircraft in flight approaches the speed of sound, the hypothesis of the air as an incompressible fluid being no longer valid.—*adj.* **compress'ible,** that may be compressed.—*n.* **compression** (*kəm- presh'ən*), act of compressing : state of being compressed : condensation : flattening : deforma- tion by pressure : the stroke that compresses the gases in an internal combustion engine.—*adjs.* **compress'ional**; **compress'ive,** able to com- press.—*ns.* **compress'or,** anything that compresses or raises pressure; a muscle that compresses certain parts; **compressure** (-*presh'ər*). [L. *compressāre*, *com*-, together, and *pressāre*, to press—*premĕre*, *pressum*, to press.]

comprint, *kəm-print'*, *v.t.* to share in printing—of the former privilege shared with the Stationers' Company and the King's Printer by Oxford and Cambridge universities.

comprise, *kəm-prīz'*, *v.t.* to contain, include: to comprehend: to consist of: (*Spens.*) to hold together.—*adj.* **compris'able**.—*n.* **compris'al**, the act, condition, or fact of comprising. [Fr. *compris*, *pa.p.* of *comprendre*—L. *comprehendĕre*; see **comprehend**.]

compromise, *kom'prō-mīz*, *n.* (*Shak.*) arbitration: a settlement of differences by mutual concession: partial waiving of theories or principles for the sake of settlement: anything of intermediate or mixed kind, neither one thing nor another.—*v.t.* to settle by mutual concession; to involve or bring into question: to expose to risk of injury, suspicion, censure, or scandal.—*v.i.* to make a compromise. [Fr. *compromis*—L. *comprōmittĕre*, *-missum*—*com*-, together, *prōmittĕre*, to promise.]

comprovincial, *kom-pro-vin'shəl*, *adj.* (*Spens.*) belonging to the same province.

compt, **compter**, **comptible**, *kownt*, *-ər*, *-ə-bl*, obs. forms of **count**, etc.—*n.* **Comptom'eter** (*komp-tom'*), a machine that adds, subtracts, multiplies and divides (*trade-mark*).

comptroll, **comptroller**. See under **control**.

compulse, *kəm-puls'*, *v.t.* to compel.—*adjs.* **com-pul'satory**, **compul'sative** (*Shak.*), compulsory.—*n.* **compul'sitor** (*Scots law*), a means of compelling. [L. *compulsāre*, freq. of *compellĕre*; see **compel**.]

compulsion, *kəm-pul'shən*, *n.* the act of compelling: force.—*n.* **compul'sionist**, a believer in compulsion.—*adj.* **compul'sive**, coercive: with power to compel.—*adv.* **compul'sively**; **compul'sorily**.—*adj.* **compul'sory**, compelled: obligatory: compelling. [L. *compellĕre*, *-pulsum*, to compel; see **compel**.]

compunction, *kəm-pungk'shən*, *n.* (*obs.*) pricking or uneasiness of conscience: remorse tinged with pity.—*adj.* **compunc'tious**, of the nature of compunction: feeling compunction.—*adv.* **compunc'tiously**. [O.Fr.,—L. *compunctiō*, *-ōnis*—*com*-, intens., and *pungĕre*, *punctum*, to prick.]

compurgation, *kom-pur-gā'shən*, *n.* in Old English and other Germanic law, the clearing of the accused by witnesses joining their oaths to his: evidence in favour of the accused: vindication.—*n.* **com'purgator**, one who testifies to the innocency or veracity of another.—*adjs.* **compurga-tō'rial** (*kom*-), **compur'gatory**. [L. *compūrgāre*, to purify wholly—*com*-, intens., *pūrgāre*, to purify: taken as if meaning to clear together; see **purge**.]

compursion, *kəm-pur'shən*, *n.* a pursing together (*Sterne*).

compute, *kəm-pūt'*, *v.t.* to calculate: to number: to estimate.—*adj.* **computable** (*kom'* or *-pūt'*), calculable.—*ns.* **com'putant**, **com'putator**, **com'-putist**, a calculator; **comput'er**, a calculator: a large machine carrying out calculations of several stages automatically; **computa'tion**, the act of computing: reckoning: estimate.—*adj.* **com'-putative** (or *-pūt*), given to computation. [L. *computāre*—*com*-, *putāre*, to reckon.]

comrade, *kom'rid*, *kum'rid* (*Shak.*, *Milt.*; *-rād'*), *n.* a close companion: an intimate associate: in some socialist and communist circles used as a term of address, or prefixed to a name.—*n.* **com'radeship**. [Sp. *camarada*, a roomful, a room-mate—L. *camera*, a room—Gr. *kamarā*.]

comstockery, *kum'stok-ə-ri*, or *kom'*, *n.* prudery.—*ns.* **com'stocker**; **com'stockism**. [From Anthony Comstock (1844-1915), an American denunciator of the nude in art.]

Comtism, *komt'izm*, *kont'izm*, *n.* the philosophical system of Auguste Comte, the founder of Positivism (1798-1857).—*ns.* and *adjs.* **Comt'ian**; **Comt'ist**.

Comus, *kō'məs*, *n.* (*Milt.*) a god of mirth: **comus**, a revel. [L.,—Gr. *kōmos*, a revel.]

con, **kon**, *adv.* and *n.* a contraction of L. *contrā*, against, as in **pro and con**, for and against.

con (*Spens.* **conne**, **kon**), *kon*, *v.t.* (*Spens.*) to know: (*Spens.*) to learn: to study carefully, scan, pore over: to commit to memory: (*obs.*) to acknowledge (as *to con thanks*): (*obs.*) to teach, show (*pr.p.* **conn'ing**; *pa.t.* and *pa.p.* **conned**, *Spens.* **cond**, **kond**).—*ns.* **conn'er**; **conn'ing**. [Another form of **can**, O.E. *cunnan*, to know; perh. partly *cunnian*, to seek to know, examine. (See **conner**, 2).]

con, **conn**, *kun*, *kon*, *v.t.* to direct the steering of.—*n.* the act or station of conning.—*ns.* **con'der**, **conner** (*kun'ər*, *kon'ər*), one who directs steering: a look-out on land, who signals the movements of fish to fishermen; **conn'ing**; **conn'ing-tow'er**, the pilot-house of a warship or submarine. [Older forms *cond*, *condue*, etc., apparently—Fr. *conduire*—L. *condūcĕre*; see **conduct**.]

con, *kon*, *n.* (*dial.*) a knock. [Fr. *cogner*, to knock.]

con-. See Prefixes.

conacre, *kon'ā-kər*, *n.* the custom of letting land in Ireland in small portions for a single crop, for rent in money or labour—also **corn'acre**.—*v.t.* to sublet in conacre.—*n.* **con'acreism**. [**corn**, **acre**.]

conarium, *kō-nā'ri-əm*, *n.* the pineal gland.—*adj.* **cona'rial**. [Gr. *kōnarion*, pineal gland, dim. of *kōnos*, cone.]

conatus, *kō-nā'təs*, *n.* an effort: an impulse: a tendency, nisus :—*pl.* **cona'tus**.—*n.* **cona'tion**, the active aspect of mind, including desire and volition.—*adj.* **conative** (*kon'*, *kōn'ə-tiv*). [L. *cōnātus*, *-ūs*, effort.]

concatenate, *kən-kat'ə-nāt*, *v.t.* to chain or link together: to connect in a series.—*n.* **concatena'-tion**, a series of links united: a series of things depending on each other. [L. *con*-, *catēna*, a chain.]

concause, *kon'kawz*, *n.* a co-operating cause.

concave, *kon'kāv*, *kon'kāv'*, *adj.* curved inwards (opposed to *convex*).—*n.* a hollow: an arch or vault.—*v.t.* and *v.i.* to make or become hollow.—*adv.* **con'cavely**.—*n.* **concav'ity** (*kən-kav'i-ti*), the quality of being concave: a hollow.—*adjs.* **concā'vo-con'cave**, or **doub'le-con'cave**, concave on both sides; **concā'vo-con'vex**, concave on one side, and convex on the other. [L. *concavus*, from *con*-, inten., and *cavus*, hollow. See **cave**.]

conceal, *kən-sēl'*, *v.t.* to hide completely or carefully: to keep secret: to disguise: to keep from telling.—*adj.* **conceal'able**.—*n.* **conceal'ment**, hiding: keeping secret: secrecy: disguise: hiding-place: (*Shak.*) a mystery. [O.Fr. *conceler*—L. *concēlāre*, from *con*-, inten., and *cēlāre*, to hide.]

concede, *kən-sēd'*, *v.t.* to yield or give up.—*v.i.* to make concession.—*n.* **conced'er**. [L. *concēdĕre*, *-cēssum*—*con*-, wholly, and *cēdĕre*, to yield.]

conceit, *kən-sēt'*, *n.* overweening self-esteem: fancy: thought: wit: a witty thought, esp. far-fetched, affected or over-ingenious: (*Spens.*) idea: (*Shak.*) understanding: estimate.—*v.t.* to conceive: to think.—*adj.* **conceit'ed**, (*obs.*) clever, witty, fantastical: having a high opinion of oneself: egotistical.—*adv.* **conceit'edly**.—*n.* **conceit'ed-ness**.—*adjs.* **conceit'ful** (*Spens.*) thoughtful; **conceit'less** (*Shak.*), without conceit, stupid; **conceit'y**, characterised by conceit.—**out of conceit with**, displeased with. [From **conceive**, on the analogy of **deceive**, **deceit**.]

conceive, *kən-sēv'*, *v.t.* to receive into or form in the womb: to form in the mind: to imagine or think: to understand: to grasp as a concept: to express.—*v.i.* to become pregnant: to think.—*ns.* **conceivabil'ity**, **conceiv'ableness**.—*adj.* **conceiv'able**.—*adv.* **conceiv'ably**. [O.Fr. *conceveir*—L. *concipĕre*, *conceptum*, from *con*-, and *capĕre*, to take.]

concent, *kən-sent'*, *n.* (*arch.*) a harmony or concord of sounds: concert of voices.—*v.t.* (*Spens.*) to fit, adjust duly. [L. *concentus*, *pa.p.* of *concinĕre*—*con*-, *canĕre*, to sing.]

concentrate, *kon'sən-trāt*, or *kən-sen'-*, *v.t.* to bring towards a common centre: to focus: to direct with exclusive attention upon the matter in hand: to condense, to increase the quantity in unit space.—*v.i.* to draw towards a common centre: to direct one's thoughts or efforts towards one object.—*n.* a product of concentration.—*adj.* **concen'trate**,

---

Neutral vowels in unaccented syllables : *el'ə-mənt*, *in'fənt*, *ran'dəm*

having a common centre : concentrated.—*n.* **concentra'tion**, act of concentrating : condensation : proportion of molecules or ions to unit volume : the keeping of the mind fixed on something.—*adj.* **concen'trative**, tending to concentrate.—*ns.* **concen'trativeness ; con'centrator**, apparatus for concentrating solutions or for obtaining minerals from ores by physical means.—**concentration camp**, a settlement for segregating persons who might be in the way of, or obnoxious to, the authorities. [A lengthened form of **concentre**.]

concentre, concenter, *kən-sent'ər, v.i.* to tend to or meet in a common centre : to be concentric.—*v.t.* to bring or direct to a common centre or point :—*pr.p.* **concent'ring, -cent'ering**; *pa.t.* and *pa.p.* **concent'red, concent'ered**.—*adjs.* **concen'tric, -al**, having a common centre.—*adv.* **concen'trically.**—*n.* **concentricity** (*kon-sən-tris'i-ti*). [Fr. *concentrer*—L. *con-, centrum*—Gr. *kentron*, point.]

concept, *kon'sept, n.* a thing conceived, a general notion.—*ns.* **conceptacle** (*kən-sep'ta-kl*; *obs.*) a receptacle : a reproductive cavity ; **concep'tion**, the act of conceiving : the fertilisation of an ovum : the formation, or power of forming in the mind, a concept, plan, thought, etc. : a concept : a notion : (*Shak.*) a mere fancy : a plan : a thing conceived, esp. in some seaweeds ; **Concep'tionist**, a nun of an order founded in Portugal in 1484 in honour of the Immaculate Conception.—*adjs.* **concep'tious** (*Shak.*), fruitful ; **concept'ive**, capable of conceiving ; **concep'tual**, pertaining to conception.—*ns.* **concep'tualism**, the doctrine in philosophy that universals exist in the mind ; **concep'tualist.**—*adj.* **conceptualis'tic.** [L. *concipĕre, -ceptum*, to conceive.]

concern, *kən-sərn', v.t.* to relate or belong to : to affect or interest : to involve by interest, occupation or duty : to implicate : to make uneasy : to trouble :—*n.* that which concerns or belongs to one : affair : business : interest : regard : anxiety : a business establishment.—*n.* **concern'ancy** (*Shak.*, in burlesque), bearing, relevancy.—*adj.* **concerned'**, interested : involved : troubled : (*obs.*) under the influence of liquor, drunk.—*adv.* **concern'edly.**—*n.* **concern'edness.**—*prep.* **concern'ing**, regarding : about.—*n.* **concern'ment**, concern : importance.—**as concerns**, as regards. [L. *concernĕre*, to distinguish, later to have respect to—*con-, cernĕre*, to distinguish.]

concert, *kon'sərt, n.* union or agreement in any undertaking : harmony : musical harmony : a musical entertainment.—*v.t.* **concert** (*kən-sərt'*), to frame or devise together : to arrange, adjust.—*n.* **concertante** (*kon-cher-tän'tä*), a composition for two or more solo instruments, usu. with orchestra.—*adj.* **concert'ed** (*-sərt'*), mutually planned : (*mus.*) arranged in parts.—*ns.* **con'cert-goer**, a habitual attender of concerts ; **con'cert-grand**, a grand piano suitable for concerts ; **concertina** (*kon-sər-tē'nə*), a musical instrument consisting of a pair of bellows, usually hexagonal, the sounds produced by free vibrating reeds of metal, as in the accordion.—*v.i.* to collapse or fold up like a concertina.—*ns.* **concertino** (*kon-cher-tē'nō*) a short concerto ; **concerto** (*kon-cher'tō*), a composition for solo instrument(s) and orchestra in sonata form : applied by the older composers to various combinations and forms :—*pl.* **concer'tos.** —**concert pitch**, a standard of pitch that has varied (see **international concert pitch, French pitch**): also *fig.* [It. *concertare*, sing in concert, perh.—L. *con-, certāre*, to strive.]

concession, *kən-sesh'ən, n.* the act of conceding : the thing conceded : a grant.—*adj.* **concessible** (*-ses'*).—*n.* **concessionaire**, one who has obtained a concession.—*adj.* **concess'ionary.**—*n.* **concess'ionist.**—*adj.* **concess'ive**, implying concession. [See **concede**.]

concetto, *kon-chet'tō, n.* an ingenious turn of expression : a conceit :—*pl.* **concet'ti**, (*-tē*).—*n.* **concet'tism**, the use of concetti ; **concet'tist.** [It.,—L. *conceptum*, conceit.]

conch, *kongk, n.* a name for various marine gasteropods, esp. chank and Strombus, and for their

shells : a shell used as a trumpet, as by the Tritons : a poor white or other native of the Bahamas or Florida Keys (from their feeding on conchs) : a concha.—*n.* **conch'a**, (*archit*) the semi-dome of an apse : the apse itself : the outer ear, or its cavity.—*adjs.* **conch'ate, conch'iform**, shaped like a shell, esp. one valve of a bivalve shell ; **conchif'erous**, having a shell : shelly.—*ns.* **conchi'tis**, inflammation of the concha ; **conch'oid**, a plane curve, the locus of a point making with a fixed straight line a constant intercept on a ray of a pencil through a fixed point.—*adjs.* **conchoid'al**, pertaining to a conchoid : (*min.*) shell-like, applied to a fracture like that seen in glass : **conchoïog'ical.**—*ns.* **conchol'ogist ; conchol'ogy**, the study of molluscs and their shells. [L. *concha*—Gr. *konchē*, a cockle or mussel; Sans. *cankha*, a shell; conn. with **chank, cockle**.]

conchy, conch'ie, *kon'shi, n.* (*slang*) a conscientious objector.

concierge, *konᵈ-si-erzh', n.* a warden : a janitor : a porter or a portress. [Fr.; ety. unknown.]

conciliar, *kən-sil'i-ər, adj.* pertaining to a council.— Also **concil'iary.** [L. *concilium*, council.]

conciliate, *kən-sil'i-āt, v.t.* to gain, or win over : to reconcile.—*v.i.* to make friends.—*adj.* **concil'iable** (*obs.*).—*n.* **concil'iātion**, act of conciliating. —*adj.* **concil'iative.**—*n.* **concil'iātor.**—*adj.* **concil'iatory.** [L. *conciliāre, -ātum*—*concilium*, council.]

concinnity, *kən-sin'i-ti, n.* harmony : congruity : elegance.—*adj.* **concinn'ous**, elegant : harmonious. [L. *concinnus*, well adjusted.]

concipient, *kən-sip'i-ənt, adj.* conceiving.—*n.* **concip'iency.** [L. *concipiēns, -entis*, pr.p. of *concipĕre*, to conceive.]

concise, *kən-sīs', adj.* cut short : brief.—*v.t.* (*Milt.*) to mutilate.—*adv.* **concise'ly.**—*ns.* **concise'ness**, the quality of being concise : terseness.—*n.* **concision** (*-sizh'ən*), mutilation : (*B.*) circumcision : conciseness. [L. *concīsus*, pa.p of *concīdĕre* —*con-, caedĕre*, to cut.]

conclamation, *kon-klə-mā'shən, n.* a shout of many together. [L. *conclāmātiō, -ōnis*.]

conclave, *kon'klāv, n.* (*obs.*) a private room : the room in which cardinals meet to elect a pope : the body of cardinals : any close assembly.—*n.* **con'clavist**, an attendant on a cardinal in conclave. [L. *conclāve*—*con-, clāvis*, a key.]

conclude, *kən-klōōd', v.t.* (*arch.*) to enclose : to include : to restrain or debar : to close : to end : to decide : to settle or arrange finally : to infer.—*v.i.* to end : to form a final judgment : (*Scots law*) to state the object sought.—*p.adj.* **conclud'ed**, finished : settled.—*adj.* **conclud'ing**, final, closing. —*n.* **conclu'sion** (*-zhən*), act of concluding : the end, close, or last part : inference : judgment : an experiment (*Shak.*) a problem, a riddle.—*adjs.* **conclusive** (*-klōō'siv*), **conclu'sory**, final : convincing.—*adv.* **conclus'ively.**—*n.* **conclus'iveness.**—**in conclusion**, finally.—**to try conclusions**, to experiment : to engage in a contest. [L. *conclūdĕre, conclūsum*—*con-, claudĕre*, to shut.]

concoct, *kən-kokt', v.t.* to digest : to prepare or mature : to make up or put together : to plan, devise : to fabricate.—*ns.* **concoct'er, concoct'or ; concoc'tion**, act of concocting : ripening : preparation of a medical prescription, etc. : a made-up story.—*adj.* **concoct'ive.** [L. *concoquĕre, concoctum*—*con-, together, and coquĕre*, to cook, to boil.]

concolor, *kon'kul-ər, adj.* of uniform colour.— Also **concol'orate, concol'orous.** [L.,—*con-, color*, colour.]

concomitant, *kən-kom'i-tənt, adj.* accompanying : conjoined.—*n.* he who or that which accompanies. —*ns.* **concom'itance, concom'itancy**, state of being concomitant.—*adv.* **concom'itantly.** [L. *con-, comitāns, -āntis*, pr.p. of *comitārī*, to accompany—*comes*, a companion.]

concord, *kon'kord*, or *kong'-, n.* state of being of the same heart or mind : harmony : agreement : a combination of sounds satisfying to the ear.—*v.i.* **concord'** (*kən-*), to agree : to harmonise.—*n.* **concord'ance**, agreement : an index of the words or passages of a book or author.—*adj.* **concord'ant,**

harmonious, united.—*adv.* **concord'antly.**—*n.*
concord'at, an agreement, generally between the
pope and a secular government.—*adj.* **concor'dial,**
harmonious. [Fr. *concorde*—L. *concordia*—*concors,*
of the same heart, from *con-, cor, cordis,* the heart.]
concorporate, kən-kor'pər-āt, *v.t.* to unite in one
body.—*adj.* united in the body.
concourse, kon'kōrs, or kong'-, *n.* an assembly of
persons or things running or drawn together:
(*Scots law*) concurrence of an officer who has legal
right to grant it: a large hall: an open space, esp.
at a road-junction or in a railway station. [Fr.
concours—L. *concursus*—*con-, currĕre,* to run.]
concreate, kon'krē-āt, *v.t.* to create with or at the
same time.
concremation, kon-kri-mā'shən, *n.* complete burning: cremation: burning together: suttee. [L.
concremāre, -ātum—*con-,* intens., *cremāre,* to burn.]
concrescence, kən-kres'əns, *n.* a coalescence or
growing together.—*adj.* **concresc'ent.** [L. *con-
crēscentia*—*con-, crēscĕre,* to grow.]
concrete, kon'krēt (or kən-krēt'), *adj.* formed into
one mass: the opposite of *abstract,* and denoting a
particular thing: (*kon'*) made of concrete.—*n.*
(*kon'*) a mass formed by parts growing or sticking
together: a mixture of lime, sand, pebbles, etc.,
used in building.—*v.t.* **concrēte',** to form into a
solid mass: (*kon'*) to cover with concrete.—*v.i.*
(*krēt'*) to harden.—*adv.* **concrēte'ly** (or *kon'*)—
ns. **concrēte'ness** (or *kon'*); **concrētion** (-krē'-
shən), a mass concreted: (*geol.*) a nodule or lump
formed within a rock by materials rearranging
themselves about a centre: a solid mass formed
within an animal or plant body, whether by
deposition or by accumulation of foreign matter.—
adjs. **concrē'tionary; concrēt'ive,** having power
to concrete.—**concrete steel,** reinforced concrete.
[L. *concrētus*—*con-, crēscĕre, crētum,* to grow.]
concrew, kon-krōō', *v.i.* (*Spens.*) to grow together.
[Fr. *concrû,* pa.p of *concroître*—L. *concrēscĕre.*]
concubine, kong'kū-bīn, *n.* one (esp. a woman) who
cohabits without being married.—*n.* **concubinage** (kon-kū'bin-āj), state of living together as
man and wife without being married.—*adj.*
concu'binary.—*ns.* **concu'bitancy,** a custom by
which marriage between certain persons is obligatory; **concu'bitant,** one subject to such an
obligation.—Also *adj.* [Fr.,—L. *concubīna*—*con-,
cubāre,* to lie down.]
concupiscence, kon-kū'pis-əns, *n.* a violent desire:
sexual appetite: lust.—*adjs.* **concu'piscent, con-
cū'piscible.** [L. *concupīscentia*—*concupīscĕre*—
con-, inten., *cupĕre,* to desire.]
concupy, kon(g)'kū-pi, *n.* (*Shak.*) a shortened form
of concupiscence (or perh. of concubine).
concur, kən-kur', *v.i.* to run together: to meet in
one point: to coincide: to act together: to agree:
to assent (*pr.p.* **concurr'ing** *pa.p.* **concurred'**).—
ns. **concurr'ence,** the meeting of lines in one
point: coincidence: joint action: assent: competition; **concurr'ency.**—*adj.* **concurr'ent,** meeting
in the same point: running, coming, acting, or
existing together: coinciding: accompanying.—*n.*
one that concurs: a competitor: one who accompanies a sheriff's officer as witness.—*adv.* **concurr'ently.**—*adj.* **concurr'ing,** agreeing. [L.
concurrĕre—*con-, currĕre,* to run.]
concuss, kən-kus', *v.t.* to disturb: to overawe: to
coerce.—*n.* **concussion** (-kush'), state of being
shaken: a violent shock caused by the sudden
contact of two bodies: a violent blow, esp. on the
head: the resulting condition: any undue pressure
or force exerted upon anyone.—*adj.* **concuss'ive,**
having the power or quality of concussion. [L.
concussus, pa.p. of *concutĕre*—*con-,* together, *quatĕre,*
to shake.]
concyclic, kon-sī'klik, *adj.* (*geom.*) lying on the
circumference of the same circle.—*adv.* **concy'-
clically.** [L. *con-,* together, Gr. *kyklos,* wheel.]
cond. See con (2).
condemn, kən-dem', *v.t.* to pronounce guilty: to
censure or blame: to sentence: to give up to some
fate: to pronounce unfit for use: to reject.—*adj.*
condemnable (-dem'na-bl), blamable.—*n.* **con-
demna'tion** (kon-dəm-nā'shən), state of being

condemned.—*adj.* **condem'natory,** expressing or
implying condemnation.—*p.adj.* **condemned',**
pronounced to be wrong, guilty, or useless:
belonging or relating to one who is sentenced to
punishment (e.g. *condemned cell*): declared
dangerous or unfit. [L. *condemnāre,* from *con-,*
inten., and *damnāre,* to hurt.]
condense, kən-dens', *v.t.* to reduce to smaller
compass: to render more dense or more intense:
to reduce to a denser form, as vapour to liquid:
(*chem.*) to subject to condensation.—*v.i.* to become
condensed.—*n.* **condensabil'ity.**—*adj.* **condens'-
able.**—*v.t.* and *v.i.* **condens'āte,** to condense :—
n. a product of condensation.—*ns.* **condensā'-
tion** (kon-), act of condensing: (*chem.*) the union
of two or more molecules of the same or different
compounds with the elimination of water, alcohol,
or other simple substance: loosely applied to
almost any reaction in which a product of higher
molecular weight than the reactant is obtained;
condens'er, an apparatus for reducing vapours to
a liquid form: a mirror or lens for focusing light:
an appliance for collecting or condensing electricity.
—**condensed milk,** milk reduced by evaporation,
and sugared; **condensed type,** printing type of
narrow face. [L. *condēnsāre*—*con-,* inten., and
dēnsus, dense.]
condescend, kon-də-send', *v.i.* to descend willingly
from a superior position: to act graciously to
inferiors: to deign: to stoop to what is unworthy:
to comply: to agree, consent.—*v.t.* (*obs.*) to concede
or grant: (*Scot.*) to specify.—*n.* **condescend'-
ence,** condescension: (*Scots law*) an articulate
statement annexed to a summons, setting forth the
allegations in fact upon which an action is founded.
—*adj.* **condescend'ing,** gracious to inferiors:
offensively patronising.—*adv.* **condescend'ingly.**
—*n.* **condescen'sion.**—**condescend upon,** to
specify: to mention. [L. *con-,* inten., and *dēscendĕre,* to descend—*dē,* down from, *scandĕre,* to
climb.]
condiddle, kən-did'l, *v.t.* (*Scott*) to steal. [L.
con-, and **diddle.**]
condign, kən-dīn', *adj.* well merited (usu. of
punishment): (*Spens.*) worthy, deserving.—*adv.*
condign'ly.—*n.* **condign'ness.** [L. *condignus*—
con-, inten., *dignus,* worthy.]
condiment, kon'di-mənt, *n.* a seasoning.—*v.t.* to
season. [L. *condīmentum*—*condīre,* to preserve,
to pickle.]
condisciple, kon-di-sī'pl, *n.* a fellow-disciple: a
schoolfellow: a fellow-student. [L. *con-,* and
disciple.]
condition, kən-dish'ən, *n.* state in which things
exist: a good or fit state: a particular manner of
being: quality: rank (as *a person of condition*):
prerequisite: temper: a term of a contract: (in
pl.) circumstances: (*logic*) that which must precede
the operation of a cause: (*law*) a provision upon
which an obligation depends: (*U.S.*) obligation of
passing a future examination to make up a
deficiency.—*v.i.* to make terms.—*v.t.* to agree
upon: to restrict, limit: to determine: to put into
the required state: (*U.S.*) to allow to proceed in
an education course on condition of passing a
future examination.—*adj.* **condi'tional,** depending
on conditions: expressing condition.—*n.* **conditional'ity.**—*adv.* **condi'tionally.**—*v.t.* **condi'-
tionate,** to condition: to qualify.—*adj.* **condi'-
tioned,** having a certain condition, state, or
quality: circumstanced: depending: relative—the
opposite of *absolute*: subject to condition.—
conditioned reflex, a reflex response to a
stimulus which depends upon the former experience of the individual; **conditioning house,**
an establishment in which the true weight, length,
and condition of articles of trade and commerce
are determined scientifically. [L. *condiciō* (wrongly *conditio*), *-ōnis,* a compact—*condīcĕre*—*con-,
dīcĕre,* to say.]
condole, kən-dōl', *v.i.* to grieve with another: to
express sympathy in sorrow: (*Shak.*) to grieve.—
adj. **condol'atory,** expressing condolence.—*ns.*
condole'ment, condol'ence, expression of sym-

pathy with another's sorrow.—*adj.* **condol'ent.**
[L. *con-*, with, *dolēre*, to grieve.]

condominium, *kon-dō-min'i-əm,* *n.* joint sovereignty. [L. *con-*, together, *dominium*, lordship.]

condone, *kən-dōn',* *v.t.* to forgive : to pass over without blame, overlook : to excuse, atone for.— *n.* **condonā'tion** (*kon-*), forgiveness : (*law*) such forgiveness granted by the injured party as may be urged against divorce for adultery. [L. *con-*, inten., *dōnāre*, to give. See **donation.**]

condor, *kon'dor, -dər, n.* a large South American vulture. [Sp. *cóndor*—Quichua *cuntur.*]

condottiere, *kon-dot-tyā'rā, n.* a leader of a mercenary band of military adventurers :—*pl.* **condottie'ri** (*-rē*). [It.,—*condotto*, way—L. *con-*, and *dūcĕre*, to lead.]

conduce, *kən-dūs', v.i.* to help to bring about, contribute (towards a result) : (*Shak.*) app., to go on, conduct itself, or poss. to assemble).—*n.* **conduce'ment** (*Milt.*).—*adjs.* **conduc'ible, conduc'ive,** leading or tending : having power to promote : advantageous. [L. *con-*, together, *dūcĕre*, to lead.]

conduct, *kən-dukt', v.t.* to lead or guide : to convey (water, blood, sap, etc.) : to direct : to manage : to behave : (*elect.*), to carry or transmit : (*mus.*) to beat time for and coordinate :—*n.* (*kon'*), act or method of leading or managing : guidance : escort : guide : management : behaviour.—*ns.* **conduct'-ance,** a conductor's power of conducting electricity, the reciprocal of the resistance; **conducti-bil'ity.**—*adj.* **conduct'ible,** capable of conducting heat, etc. : capable of being conducted or transmitted.—*n.* **conduc'tion,** act or property of conducting or transmitting : transmission by a conductor, as heat.—*adj.* **conduct'ive,** having the quality or power of conducting or transmitting.— *ns.* **conductiv'ity,** power of transmitting heat, electricity, stimuli : a substance's specific power of conducting electricity, conductance across a unit cube, reciprocal of the resistivity; **conduct'or,** the person or thing that conducts : a leader : a manager : a director of an orchestra, or choir; one in charge of a bus, etc. : (*U.S.*) a railway guard : that which has the property of transmitting electricity, heat, etc. :—*fem.* **conduct'ress; conduct'orship,** the office of conductor. [L. *con-ductus*—*condūcĕre.* See **conduce.**]

conduit, *kun'dit,* or *kon'-, n.* a channel or pipe conveying water or other fluid, or covering electric wires, etc. : a fountain for supplying the public with water. [Fr. *conduit*—L. *conductus*—*condūcĕre,* to lead.]

conduplicate, *kən-dūp'li-kāt, adj.* folded together lengthwise. [L. *conduplicāre, -ātus,* to double— *con-*, and *duplex,* double.]

condyle, *kon'dil, n.* a protuberance at the end of a bone serving for articulation with another bone.— *adjs.* **con'dylar, con'dyloid.**—*n.* **condylō'ma,** an overgrowth of skin about the mucous passages :— *pl.* **condylō'mata.**—*adj.* **condylō'matous.** [Gr. *kondylos,* knuckle.]

cone, *kōn, n.* an infinite solid figure generated by a straight line passing through a fixed point and intersecting some curve in space : esp. (*right circular cone*) one generated by revolution of a triangle about one of its sides : a portion of such a figure terminated at the vertex : anything shaped like a cone : a form of weather signal : a tapering part of a machine, as a race for ball-bearings : a volcanic hill : a fan of alluvium where a torrent is checked at the foot of a declivity or in a lake : the typical flower (or fruit) or inflorescence of the Coniferae, a more or less conical mass of scale-like sporophylls set closely about an axis : a similar structure in other plants, e.g. horsetails : a sensory body in the retina : an ice-cream cornet.—*adj.* **cone'-in-cone'** (*petrology*), showing a series of cones, one within another.—*ns.* **cone'-shell,** a Gasteropod mollusc of a family (Conidae) with substantial conical shells; **cone'-wheat,** a bearded variety of wheat.—*adjs.* **conic** (*kon'ik*), **-al,** having the form of or pertaining to a cone.—*n.* a conic section : (in *pl.*) the geometry of the cone and its

sections.—*adv.* **con'ically.**—*adj.* **cō'niform,** in the form of a cone.—**conic section,** a figure made by the section of a cone by a plane. [Gr. *kōnos.*]

coney. See **cony.**

confabulate, *kən-fab'ū-lāt, v.i.* to chat (*coll.* confab').—*adjs.* **confab'ular; confab'ulatory.**— *ns.* **confabulā'tion** (*coll.* confab', con'fab); **confab'ulātor.** [L. *cōnfābulārī—con-, fābulārī,* to talk.]

confarreation, *kən-far-i-ā'shn, n.* a Roman patrician mode of marriage, in which a spelt cake was offered up.—*adj.* **confarr'eate.** [L. *cōnfarreātiō —con-,* with, *fār,* spelt.]

confect, *kon'fekt, n.* fruit, etc., prepared with sugar : a sweetmeat; a comfit.—*v.t.* (*kən-fekt'*), to prepare : to preserve.—*n.* **confec'tion,** composition, compound : a composition of drugs : a sweetmeat : the French word for a ready-made article of dress for women's wear.—*v.t.* to make (into a confection).—*n.* **confec'tionary** (*B.*), a confectioner : a sweetmeat : a place where confections are made or kept.—*adj.* pertaining to or of the nature of confectionery.—*ns.* **confec'tioner,** one who makes or sells sweets; **confec'tionery** confectioners' work or art : sweetmeats in general. [L. *cōnficĕre, cōnfectum,* to make up together—*con-, facĕre,* to make.]

confederate, *kən-fed'ər-āt, adj.* leagued together : allied (esp. the seceding American states of the Civil War).—*n.* one united in a league : an ally : an accomplice.—*v.i.* and *v.t.* to league together or join in a league.—*ns.* **confed'eracy,** a league or mutual engagement : persons or states united by a league : a conspiracy; **Confederacy,** (*U.S. hist.*) the league of eleven seceding states in the Civil War; **confederā'tion,** a league : alliance, esp. of princes, states, etc.—*adj.* **confed'erative,** of or belonging to a confederation. [L. *cōnfoederāre, -ātum—con-, foedus, foedĕris,* a league.]

confer, *kən-fər', v.t.* to give or bestow : to compare : to collate—abbrev. **Cf.**—*v.i.* to talk or consult together (*pr.p.* **confer'ring;** *pa.t.* and *pa.p.* **conferred'**).—*ns.* **conferee'** (*kon-*), one conferred with; **conference** (*kon'*), the act of conferring : an appointed meeting for instruction or discussion.— *adj.* **conferential** (*kon-fər-en'shl*).—*n.* **confer'ment,** bestowal : a thing bestowed.—*adj.* **confer'able.**—*n.* **confer'rer.** [L. *cōnferre—con-,* together, *ferre,* to bring.]

Conferva, *kon-fər'vā, n.* a genus of fresh-water Algae (Heterocontae) forming slimy masses or tufts of unbranched filaments.—*adj.* **confer'void,** like conferva. [L. *cōnferva,* a kind of water-plant.]

confess, *kən-fes', v.t.* to acknowledge fully (esp. something wrong) : to own or admit : to make known, as sins to a priest : to hear a confession from, as a priest : (*poet.*) to reveal, betray, or make manifest.—*v.i.* to make confession.—*ns.* **confession** (*kən-fesh'ən*), acknowledgment of a crime or fault : avowal : the thing confessed : a statement of religious belief : acknowledgment of sin to a priest : a religious body of common belief; **confess'ional,** the seat or enclosed recess where a priest hears confessions : the institution of confession.—*adj.* pertaining to confession.—*ns.* **confess'ionalism; confess'ionalist.**—*adj.* **confess'-ionary,** of or belonging to confession.—*n.* a confessional.—*ns.* **confess'or** (or *kon'*), a priest who hears confessions and grants absolution : one who makes avowal, esp. of religious faith : one who endures persecution but not death :—*fem.* **confess'oress; confess'orship.**—*adjs.* **confessed', confest',** admitted : avowed : evident.—*advs.* **confess'edly, confest'ly.**—**confession of faith,** a formulary embodying the religious beliefs of a church or sect : a creed; **confess to,** to admit, acknowledge; **stand confessed,** to be revealed. [Fr. *confesser*—L. *cōnfitērī, cōnfessus—con-,* sig. completeness, and *fatērī,* to compress—*fārī,* to speak.]

confetti, *kon-fet'tē, kən-fet'i, n.pl.* sweetmeats or comfits : plaster or paper imitations of them flung in carnival : bits of paper flung at brides and bridegrooms. [It. (*sing. confetto*); see **comfit, confect.**]

confide, kən-fīd′, v.i. to trust wholly or have faith (with in): to impart secrets with trust: to rely.— v.t. to entrust: to impart with reliance upon secrecy.—ns. **confidant** (kon-fi-dant′), one confided in or entrusted with secrets, esp. in love affairs: a bosom friend.—fem. **confidante′**; con′fidence (kon′fi-dəns), firm trust or belief: faith: trust in secrecy: self-reliance: firmness: boldness: presumption: admission to knowledge of secrets or private affairs: a confidential communication; **con′fidency**.—adj. **con′fident**, trusting firmly: having full belief: assured: bold.—n. a confidential friend.—adj. **confiden′tial** (-den′shl), given in confidence: admitted to confidence: private.— advs. **confiden′tially**; **con′fidently**.—n. **confid′er**, one who confides.—adj. **confid′ing**, trustful.—adv. **confid′ingly**.—n. **confid′ingness**.— **confidence trick**, a swindler's trick, whereby a person is induced to hand over money as a mark of confidence in the swindler; **confident person**, in Scots law, a confidential person, partner, agent, etc. [L. cōnfīdĕre—con-, sig. completeness, and fīdĕre, to trust.]

configuration, kən-fig-ū-rā′shən, n. external figure or shape; outline: relative position or aspect, as of planets: (chem.) spatial arrangements of atoms in a molecule.—vs.t. **config′urate, config′ure**, to shape. [L. cōnfigūrāre, to form.]

confine, kon′fīn, n. border, boundary, or limit— generally in pl.: (kən-fīn′) confinement: (Shak.) a prison.—v.t. **confine′**, to border; to be adjacent to: to limit, enclose: to imprison.—adjs. **confin′able; confined′**, limited: imprisoned: narrow; **confine′less** (Shak.), without bound: unlimited. —ns. **confine′ment**, state of being shut up: restraint: imprisonment: restraint from going abroad by sickness, and esp. of women in childbirth; **confin′er**, one within the confines: (Shak.) an inhabitant.—adj. **confin′ing**, bordering: limiting.—**be confined**, to be limited: to be in child-bed. [L. cōnfīnis, bordering—con-, together fīnis, the end.]

confirm, kən-fərm′, v.t. to strengthen: to fix or establish: to ratify: to verify: to assure: to admit to full communion.—adj. **confirm′able**.—n. **confirmā′tion**, a making firm or sure: convincing proof: the rite by which persons are admitted to full communion in many churches: (Scots law) ratification by a competent court of the appointment of an executor, constituting his right to act.—adj. **confirm′ative**, tending to confirm.—n. **con′firmator**.—adjs. **confirm′atory**, giving additional strength to: confirming; **confirmed′**, settled: inveterate.—ns. **confirmee′**, one to whom a confirmation is made; **confirm′er; confirm′ing; confirm′or**. [O.Fr. confermer—L. cōnfirmāre— con-, inten., and firmāre—firmus, firm.]

confiscate, kon′fis-kāt, or kən-fis′-, v.t. to appropriate to the state, as a penalty: to take possession of by authority.—adj. forfeited.—adj. **con′fiscable** (or -fis′), **confiscatory** (kon′fis-kā-tər-i or kən-fis′ka-tər-i), of the nature of confiscation.—ns. **confiscā′tion**, the act of confiscating; **con′fiscātor**, one who confiscates. [L. cōnfiscāre, -ātum—con-, together, fiscus, a basket, purse, treasury.]

confit, kon′fit, n. (obs.). Same as **còmfit.**

confiteor, kon-fit′i-or, n. a form of prayer or confession used in the Latin Church. [L. cōnfiteor, I confess.]

confiture, kon′fit-ūr, n. (obs.). Same as **comfiture.**

confix, kən-fiks′, v.t. (Shak.) to fix firmly. [L. cōnfigĕre, -fixum—con-, inten., figĕre, to fix.]

conflagrate, kon′flə-grāt, v.t. and v.i. to burn up.— adj. **conflăg′rant** (Milt.), burning.—n. **conflăgrā′tion**, a great burning or fire. [L. cōnflagrāre—con-, inten., and flagrāre, to burn; see **flagrant.**]

conflate, kən-flāt′, v.t. to fuse: to combine (two variant readings of a text) into one.—n. **conflā′tion.** [L. cōnflāre, -ātum, to blow together—con-, and flāre, to blow.]

conflict, kon′flikt, n. violent collision: a struggle or contest: a battle: a mental struggle.—v.i. (kən-flikt′), to fight: contend: to be in opposition:

to clash.—adj. **conflict′ing**, clashing: contradictory.—n. **conflic′tion.**—adj. **conflict′ive**, tending to conflict. [L. cōnflīgĕre, -flīctum—con-, together, and flīgĕre, to strike.]

confluence, kon′floo-əns, n. a flowing together: meeting-place, as of rivers: a concourse: the act of meeting together.—adj. **con′fluent**, flowing together: running into one: uniting.—n. a stream uniting and flowing with another.—adv. **con′fluently**.—n. **con′flux** (-fluks), a flowing together. [L. cōnfluĕre, from con-, together, fluĕre, fluxum, to flow.]

conform, kən-form′, v.t. to make like or of the same form: to adapt.—v.i. to be or become of the same form: to comply: to obey.—n. **conformabil′ity**, state of being conformable.—adj. **conform′able**, corresponding in form: suitable: compliant: (geol.) in unbroken continuity of bedding.—adv. **conform′ably**.—ns. **conformā′tion**, particular form, shape, or structure: adaptation; **conform′er, conform′ist**, one who conforms, esp. to the worship of the Established Church; **conform′ity**, likeness: compliance: consistency: (geol.) conformability.—**in conformity with**, in accordance with. [L. cōnformāre—con-, formāre—forma, form.]

confound, kən-fownd′, v.t. to overthrow, defeat: to mingle so as to make the parts indistinguishable: to confuse, fail to distinguish: to throw into disorder: to defeat in argument: to perplex: to astonish: used in the imperative as a mild curse: (pa.p., Spens., **confound′**).—adj. **confound′ed**, confused: astonished: (coll.) consummate, egregious (a term of disapprobation).—advs. **confound′edly** (coll.), hatefully, shamefully: cursedly; **confound′ingly**, astonishingly.—**confound you**, a gentle execration or curse. [O.Fr. confondre— L. cōnfundĕre, -fūsum—con-, fundĕre, to pour.]

confraternity, kon-frə-tər′ni-ti, n. a brotherhood: clan: brotherly friendship. [L. con-, frāter, brother.]

confrère, konᵇ-frer, n. a colleague: a fellow-member or associate. [Fr.,—L. con-, together, frāter, a brother.]

confront, kən-frunt′, v.t. to come or be face to face with: to face in opposition: to bring face to face: to compare.—n. **confrontā′tion** (kon-), **confront′ment**, the bringing of people face to face.—adj. **confronté** (kon-frunt′ā; her.) face to face. [Fr. confronter—L. con-, together, and frōns, frontis, forehead; see **front.**]

Confucian, kon-fū′shyən, adj. of or belonging to Confucius, the Chinese philosopher (551-479 B.C.). —ns. **Confū′cianism; Confū′cianist.**

confuse, kən-fūz′, v.t. to pour or mix together so that things cannot be distinguished: to throw into disorder: to perplex: to fail to distinguish.—v.i. to be confused.—adj. **confused′**, perplexed: disordered.—adv. **confus′edly**, in a confused manner: disorderly.—ns. **confus′edness**, state of being confused: disorder; **confū′sion** (-zhən), the state of being confused: disorder: shame: overthrow: perdition: perplexity: embarrassment: turmoil. [See **confound.**]

confute, kən-fūt′, v.t. to prove to be false: to refute: to bring to naught.—adj. **confut′able**.—n. **confūtā′tion** (kon-).—adj. **confūt′ative**, tending to confute.—n. **confute′ment.** [L. cōnfūtāre—con-, intens., and perh. fūtis, a water-vessel, from fundĕre, to pour (as if to pour cold water on); see **futile.**]

congé, konᵍ′zhā, **congee**, kon′ji, n. a bow: dismissal: leave to depart.—v.i. to take leave: to bow.—**congé d′élire** (dā-lēr′; Fr.), permission to elect: the crown's formal permission to a dean and chapter to elect a certain person as bishop. [Fr. congé—L. commeātus, leave of absence—com-, together, meāre, to go.]

congeal, kən-jēl′, v.t. to change from fluid to solid by cold: to solidify, as by cold.—v.i. to pass from fluid to solid, as by cold: to stiffen: to coagulate.—adj. **congeal′able**.—ns. **congeal′ableness**, **congeal′ment**, **congelation** (kon-ji-lā′shən), act or process of congealing: anything

congealed. [L. *congelāre*, from *con*-, and *gelū*, frost.]

congee. See **congé, conjee.**

congener, *kon'ji-nər*, *n.* a person or thing of the same kind or nature : a member of the same genus.—*adj.* akin.—*adjs.* **congeneric** (*-ner'ik*), **-al**, of the same genus, origin, or nature; **congenerous** (*kən-jen'ər-əs*), of the same nature or kind; **congenet'ic** (*kon-ji-net'ik*), alike in origin. [L., *con*-, with, and *genus, generis,* kind.]

congenial, *kən-jē'ni-əl*, *adj.* of the same genius, spirit, or tastes : kindred, sympathetic : to one's taste : suitable.—*n.* **congēniality** (*-al'i-ti*).—*adv.* **congē'nially.** [L. *con*, with, and *genialis,* see **genial.**]

congenital, *kən-jen'i-təl*, *adj.* begotten or born with one—said of diseases or deformities dating from birth : innate.—*adv.* **congen'itally.** [L. *congenitus,* from *con*-, together, *gignĕre, genitum,* to beget.]

conger, *kong'gər*, *n.* a large sea-fish of the eel family—also **con'ger-eel.** [L.,—Gr. *gongros.*]

conger, *kong'gər*, *n.* (*hist.*) a company of co-operating booksellers. [Origin unknown.]

congeries, *kon-jer'i-ēz, -jēr', n.* an aggregation :—*pl.* **conger'ies :**—false *sing.* **congery** (*kon'jər-i*). [L. *congeriēs—con*-, together, *gerĕre, gestum,* to bring.]

congest, *kən-jest', v.t.* to bring together, or heap up : to accumulate : to cause congestion in.—*adjs.* **congest'ed**, affected with an unnatural accumulation of blood : overcrowded : packed closely : overcharged : clogged : incapable of supporting its population; **congest'ible.**—*n.* **congest'ion** (*-yən*), an accumulation of blood in any part of the body : fullness : an overcrowded condition.—*adj.* **congest'ive**, indicating or tending to congestion. [L. *congerĕre, congestum—con*-, together, and *gerĕre, gestum,* to bring.]

congiary, *kon'ji-ər-i,* *n.* a gift to the Roman people or soldiery, originally in corn, oil, etc., later in money. [L. *congiārium—congius,* the Roman gallon.]

conglobe, *kən-glōb', v.t.* or *v.i.* to collect together into a globe or round mass.—*adj.* **conglobate** (*kon'glō-bāt, kən-glō'bāt*) formed into a globe or ball.—*v.t.* or *v.i.* to form into a globe or ball.—*n.* **conglobā'tion.**—*v.i.* **conglobūlate** (*-glob'*), to gather into a globule or small globe. [L. *con*-, together, and *globāre, -ātum—globus,* a ball, globe.]

conglomerate, *kən-glom'ər-āt, adj.* gathered into a clew or mass : bunched : (*geol.*) composed of pebbles cemented together.—*v.t.* and *v.i.* to gather into a ball.—*n.* (*geol.*) a conglomerate rock : a miscellaneous mass or collection.—*adj.* **conglomeratic** (*-at'ik*) (*geol.*) of the nature of conglomerate.—*n.* **conglomerā'tion**, state of being conglomerated : a collection or jumble of things. [L. *conglomerāre, -ātum—con*-, together, and *glomus, glomeris,* a clew, akin to *globus.*]

conglutinate, *kən-glōō'tin-āt, v.t.* to glue together : to heal by uniting.—*v.i.* to unite or grow together.—*adj.* **conglu'tinant.**—*n.* **conglutinā'tion**, a joining by means of some sticky substance : healing.—*adj.* **conglu'tinative**, having power to conglutinate.—*n.* **conglu'tinātor.** [L. *conglūtināre, -ātum—con*-, together, and *glūten,* glue.]

congou, *kong'gōō, n.* a kind of black tea.—Also **congo.** [Chinese *kung-fu,* labour, referring to that expended in producing it.]

congratulate, *kən-grat'ū-lāt, v.t.* to express pleasure in sympathy with : to felicitate : to pronounce or deem happy (esp. *refl.*).—*adjs.* **congrat'ūlable.**—*adj.* **congrat'ūlant**, expressing congratulation.—*n.* a congratulator.—*ns.* **congratūlā'tion;** **congrat'ūlator.**—*adj.* **congrat'ūlatory.** [L. *con-grātulāri, -ātus—con*-, inten., *grātulāri—grātus,* pleasing.]

congree, *kən-grē', v.i.* (*Shak.*) to agree together : to accord. [L. *con*-, together, and Fr. *gré,* good-will—L. *grātus,* pleasing.]

congreet, *kən-grēt', v.t.* (*Shak.*) to salute mutually. [L. *con*-, together, and **greet.**]

congregate, *kong'grə-gāt. v.t.* to gather together : to assemble.—*v.i.* to flock together.—*p.adj.* (*Spens.*)

congregated.—*p.adj.* **congregated**, assembled : aggregated.—*n.* **congregā'tion**, the act of congregating : an assemblage of persons or things : (*O.T.*) a name given to the children of Israel : a body of people actually or habitually attending a particular church : the body of Protestant Reformers in Scotland in the time of Mary : a board charged with some department of administration in the Roman Catholic Church : a name given to certain religious orders without solemn vows : an academic assembly—at Cambridge, the senate, at Oxford, the resident masters, doctors, etc., or a smaller degree-conferring body.—*adj.* **congregā'tional**, pertaining to a congregation : **Congregational**, pertaining to the Independent Church.—*ns.* **Congregā'tionalism**, a form of church government in which each congregation is independent in the management of its own affairs—also called *Independency;* **Congregā'tionalist**, an Independent. [L. *congregāre, -ātum—con*-, together, and *grex, gregis,* a flock.]

congress, *kong'gres, n.* the act of meeting together : interwoven : an assembly of delegates, specialists, ambassadors, etc., for discussion or settlement of problems : **Congress**, the federal legislature of the United States and of some other American republics.—*v.i.* to meet in congress.—*adj.* **congressional** (*-gresh'*).—*n.* **Con'gressman**, a member of Congress, esp. of the House of Representatives. [L. *con*-, together, and *gradī, gressus,* to step, to go.]

Congreve, *kong'grēv, n.* a rocket for use in war.—*n.* **Con'greve-match**, a kind of friction match. [Both invented by Sir William *Congreve* (1772-1828).]

congrue, *kong-grōō', v.i.* (*Shak.*) to agree.—*ns.* **cong'ruence, cong'ruency**, quality of being congruent : agreement : suitableness.—*adj.* **cong'ruent**, agreeing : suitable : congruous : giving the same remainder on division by the same number : (*geom.*) capable of coincident superposition.—*n.* **congru'ity**, agreement, between things : consistency : fitness.—*adj.* **cong'ruous**, suitable : fit : consistent.—*adv.* **cong'ruously.**—*n.* **cong'ruousness.** [L. *congruĕre,* to run together.]

conia. See **coniine.**

conic, -al. See **cone.**

conidium, *kon-id'i-əm, n.* a spore produced by abstriction, not in a sporangium :—*pl.* **conid'ia.**—*adj.* **conid'ial.**—*ns.* **conid'iophore** (Gr. *phoros,* bearing), a hypha that produces conidia; **conid'iospore**, a conidium. [Gr. *konis,* dust.]

conifer, *kon'* or *kōn'i-fər, n.* a member of the **Conif'erae**, an order of gymnosperms, including yews, pines, firs, etc., which typically bear cones.—*adj.* **conif'erous**, cone-bearing : of the Coniferae. [L. *cōnus* (Gr. *kōnos*) a cone, *ferre,* to bear.]

conform. See **cone.**

coniine, *kō'ni-ēn, n.* a liquid, highly poisonous alkaloid ($C_8H_{17}N$) found in hemlock (*Conium*).—Also **co'nia, co'nine.** [Gr. *kōneion,* hemlock.]

conima, *kon'i-mä, n.* the fragrant resin of a tropical American burseraceous tree (*Protium*). [Carib name.]

conirostral, *kōn-i-ros'trəl, adj.* having a strong conical beak. [L. *cōnus* (Gr. *kōnos*), cone, *rōstrālis—rōstrum,* a beak.]

conject, *kən-jekt', v.i.* (*Shak.*) to conjecture.—*n.* **conject'ure**, a forecast : an opinion formed on slight or defective evidence or none : an opinion without proof : a guess : an idea.—*v.t.* to make conjectures regarding : to infer on slight evidence : to guess.—*adjs.* **conject'urable**, that may be conjectured; **conject'ural**, involving conjecture : given to conjecture.—*adv.* **conject'urally.** [L. *conjicĕre, conjectum,* to throw together *con*-, *jacĕre,* to throw.]

conjee, congee, *kon'jē, n.* water in which rice has been boiled.—*v.t.* to starch with conjee. [Tamil *kañji.*]

conjoin, *kən-join', v.t.* to join together : to combine.—*v.i.* to unite.—*adjs.* **conjoined'**, united : in conjunction; **conjoint'**, joined together : united.—*adv.* **conjoint'ly.** [Fr. *conjoindre*—L. *con*-, *jungĕre, junctum,* to join; see **join.**]

conjugal, *kon'joo-gl*, *adj.* pertaining to marriage.—*n.* **conjugality** (-*gal'i-ti*).—*adv.* **con'jugally.** [L. *conjugālis*—*conjux*, a husband or wife—*con*-, and *jugum*, a yoke.]

conjugate, *kon'joo-gāt*, *v.t.* (*gram.*) to give the various inflections or parts of (a verb): (*biochemistry*) to unite.—*v.i.* to unite.—*adj.* joined: connected: coupled: (*bot.*) occurring in pairs: reciprocally related: (*math.*) of two complex numbers, having their real parts equal and their imaginary parts equal but of opposite sign.—*n.* a word agreeing in derivation with another word: anything conjugate with another.—*n.pl.* **Conjugatae** (*-gā'tē*) a class of fresh water algae reproducing by conjugation of like gametes, including desmids, Spirogyra, etc.—*adjs.* **con'jugated**, conjugate: (*chem.*; of atoms, groups, bonds, or the compounds in which they occur) showing a special type of mutual influence, esp., characterised by an arrangement of alternate single and double bonds between carbon atoms; **conjugā'tional**, **con'jugative**, conjugate.—*n.* and *adj.* **con'jugating.**—*n.* **conjugā'tion**, the act of joining: union: (*gram.*) a connected view or statement of the inflectional forms of a verb: a class of verbs similarly inflected: (*biol.*) temporary or permanent union of two cells or individuals preparatory to the development of new individuals: esp. the union of isogametes: in *Infusoria*, an exchange of nuclear material.—**conjugate diameters**, two diameters in a conic section, such that each is parallel to the tangent at the extremity of the other; **conjugate foci** (see **focus**); **conjugate mirrors**, mirrors set so that rays from the focus of one are reflected to that of the other. [L. *conjugāre*, *-ātum*—*con*-, together, and *jugāre*—*jugum*, a yoke.]

conjunct, *kən-jungkt'*, or *kon'*, *adj.* conjoined: joint.—*n.* **conjunc'tion**, connexion, union: combination: (*gram.*) a word that connects sentences, clauses, and words: one of the aspects of the planets, when two bodies have the same celestial longitude or the same right ascension (formerly when they were in the same sign).—*adj.* **conjunc'tional**, relating to a conjunction.—*adv.* **conjunc'tionally.**—*n.* **conjunctiva** (*kon-jungkt-ī'vä*), the modified epidermis of the front of the eye, covering the cornea externally and the inner side of the eyelid.—*adjs.* **conjuncti'val**, of the conjunctiva; **conjunc'tive**, closely united: serving to unite: connective: (*gram.*) copulative: of the nature of, or introduced by, a conjunction.—*adv.* **conjunc'tively.**—*ns.* **conjunc'tiveness**; **conjunctivitis** (*-iv-ī'tis*), inflammation of the conjunctiva.—*adv.* **conjunct'ly**, conjointly: in union.—*n.* **conjunc'ture**, combination of circumstances: important occasion, crisis.—**conjunctive mood**, the subjunctive mood generally, or when used in a principal clause, or in the principal clause of a conditional sentence; **conjunct tetrachords** (*Greek music*), tetrachords in which the highest note of the lower is the lowest note of the higher. [L. *conjunctiō*, *-ōnis*—*conjungĕre*; see **conjoin**.]

conjure, *kun'jər*, *v.i.* to practise magical arts: to make an invocation: (*obs.*) to conspire.—*v.t.* (usu. *kən-jōōr'*) to call on or summon by a sacred name or in a solemn manner: to implore: to implore earnestly: (*kun'jər*) to compel (a spirit) by incantations: to put a spell upon: to call before the imagination: to render, effect, cause to be or become, by magic or jugglery.—*ns.* **conjurā'tion**, conspiracy: act of summoning by a sacred name or solemnly: enchantment; **con'jurātor**, a conspirator; **conjure'ment**, adjuration; **con'jurer**, **-or**, one who practises magic: an enchanter; **con'juror**, one bound by oath with others; **con'juring**, magic-working: the production of effects apparently miraculous by natural means; **con'jury**, magic. [Fr. *conjurer*—L. *conjūrāre*, to swear together—*con*-, and *jūrāre*, to swear.]

conk, *kongk*, *n.* (*U.S.*) the fructification of a fungal parasite on a tree: timber disease due to the parasite: (*slang*) the nose.—*ns.* **conk'er**, a strung snail-shell or horse-chestnut used in the game of **conkers**, in which each seeks to break his opponent's: a horse-chestnut; **conk'y** (*slang*) a large-nosed person.—*adj.* affected by the disease of conk. [**conch**.]

conk, *kongk*, *v.i.* (*slang*) to get out of order, fail, break down (often with *out*). [Origin unknown.]

conn. See **con** (3).

connascent, *kən-as'ənt*, *adj.* born or produced at the same time.—*ns.* **connasc'ence**, **connasc'ency** —*n.* **connā'tion** (*biol.*) union, esp. of like parts.—*adj.* **connate** (*kon'āt*), inborn: innate: allied: congenial: united in growth.—*adj.* **connatural** (*kon-at'yər-əl*), of the same nature with another.—*v.t.* **connat'uralise.**—*n.* **connatural'ity.**—*adv.* **connat'urally.**—*ns.* **connat'uralness**; **connā'ture.** [L. *con*-, *nāscī*, *nātus*, to be born.]

conne. See **con** (2).

connect, *kən-ekt'*, *v.t.* to tie or fasten together: to establish a relation between: to associate.—*adj.* **connect'able**, **-ible**, capable of being connected.—*p.adj.* **connect'ed**, joined: linked: coherent: related.—*adv.* **connect'edly**, in a connected manner.—*ns.* **connect'er**, **-or**, one who or that which connects.—*ns.* **connec'tion** (same as connexion)—*adjs.* **connect'ive**, **connex'ive** (*obs.*), binding together.—*n.* a word that connects sentences and words.—*adv.* **connect'ively.**—*n.* **connexion** (*-ek'shən*), act of connecting: that which connects: a body or society held together by a bond: coherence: intercourse: context: relation: intimacy: opportunity of change of trains, buses, etc.: a relative.—**connective tissue**, an animal tissue including a great variety —e.g. bone, cartilage, ligaments, and enswathing membranes. [L. *con*-, and *nectĕre*, *nexum*, to tie.]

conner. See **con** (2) and (3).

conner, *kun'ər*, *n.* an inspector or tester. [O.E. *cunnere—cunnian*, to learn, seek to know.]

conner, **cunner**, *kun'ər*, *n.* a kind of wrasse, the goldsinny or corkwing: an allied American fish. [Origin obscure.]

conning-tower. See **con** (3).

connive, *kən-īv'*, *v.i.* to wink (usu. *fig.*, as at a fault): to take no notice: to have a private understanding: (*biol.*) to converge.—*ns.* **conniv'ance**, **-ancy**, **conniv'ence**, **-ency**.—*adj.* **conniv'ent**.—*n.* **conniv'er**. [L. *connīvēre*, *cōnīvēre*, to wink.]

connoisseur, *kon-es-ər'*, *-is-ür'*, *n.* a well-informed judge in the arts, etc.—*n.* **connoisseur'ship**, the skill of a connoisseur. [Fr. (now *connaisseur*),— *connoître* (*connaître*)—L. *cognōscĕre*, to know.]

connote, *kon-ōt'*, *v.t.* to signify secondarily: to imply as inherent attributes: to include.—*v.t.* **connotate** (*kon'ō-tāt*), to connote.—*n.* **connotā'tion**, implication of something more than the denotation of an object: the aggregation of attributes connoted by a term.—*adjs.* **conn'otātive** (or *-nōt'*), **conno'tive.** [L. *con*-, with, *notāre*, to mark.]

connubial, *kən-ū'bi-əl*, *adj.* pertaining to marriage. —*n.* **connubiality** (*-al'i-ti*).—*adv.* **connū'bially.** [L. *con*-, *nūbĕre*, to marry.]

connumerate, *kən-ū'mə-rāt*, *v.t.* to count together. —*n.* **connumerā'tion.**

conoid, *kōn'oid*, *n.* anything like a cone in form; a solid generated by the revolution of a conic section about its axis.—*adjs.* **cōn'oid**, **cōnoid'al**, **-ic**, **-ical.** [Gr. *kōnos*, a cone, *eidos*, form.]

conquer, *kong'kər*, *v.t.* to gain by force or with an effort: to overcome or vanquish.—*v.i.* to be victor. —*adj.* **con'querable.**—*n.* **con'querableness.**—*adj.* **con'quering.**—*adv.* **con'queringly.**—*ns.* **con'queror**, one who conquers: a victor:—*fem.* **con'queress**; **conquest** (*kong'kwest*), the act of conquering: that which is conquered or acquired by physical or moral force: the act of gaining the affections of another: (*Scots law*) acquisition otherwise than by inheritance.—**the Conqueror**, William I. of England (L. *conques'tor*); **the Conquest**, the acquisition of the throne of England by William, Duke of Normandy, in 1066. [O.Fr. *conquerre*—L. *conquīrĕre*, *conquaerĕre*—*con*-, inten., *quaerĕre*, to seek.]

conquistador, *kong-kĕs-ta-dōr'*, or *kwis'*, *n.* a conqueror, applied to the conquerors of Mexico and Peru :—*pl.* -dors, -dores (*dōr'es*). [Sp.,—L. conquirère.]

consanguine, *kon-sang'gwin*, *adj.* related by blood : of the same family or descent—also **consanguin'-eous**.—*n.* **consanguin'ity**, relationship by blood : opposed to affinity or relationship by marriage. [L. *cōnsanguineus*—*con*-, with, *sanguis*, or *sanguis*, blood.]

conscience, *kon'shəns*, *n.* (*Shak.*) inmost thought, consciousness : moral sense : scrupulousness, conscientiousness : in genitive case commonly written **conscience'**.—*interj.* (*Scot.*) an expression of surprise (also **my conscience!**).—*adjs.* **con'-science-proof**, unvisited by any compunctions of conscience; **con'science-smitten**, stung by conscience; **conscien'tious** (*-shi-en'shəs*), regulated by a regard to conscience : scrupulous.—*adv.* **conscien'tiously**.—*n.* **conscien'tiousness**.—*adj.* **con'scionable** (*-shən-ə-bl*), governed or regulated by conscience.—*n.* **con'scionableness**.—*adv.* **con'scionably**.—**case of conscience**, a question in casuistry; **conscience clause**, a clause in a law to relieve persons of conscientious scruples, esp. against religious instruction; **conscience money**, money given to relieve the conscience, by discharging a claim previously evaded; **conscientious objector**, one who objects on grounds of conscience, esp. to military service; **good, or bad, conscience**, an approving or reproving conscience; **in all conscience**, certainly : (*coll.*) by all that is right and fair; **make a matter of conscience**, to have scruples about; **speak one's conscience** (*Shak.*), to speak frankly : to give one's opinion; **upon conscience, o' my conscience**, truly. [Fr.,—L. *cōnscientia*, knowledge—*cōnscīre*, to know well, in one's own mind—*con*-, *scīre*, to know.]

conscious, *kon'shəs*, *adj.* having the feeling or knowledge of something : aware : having consciousness.—*adv.* **con'sciously**.—*n.* **con'sciousness**, the waking state of the mind : the knowledge which the mind has of anything : awareness : thought. [L. *cōnscius*—*cōnscīre*, to know; see **conscience**.]

conscribe, *kən-skrib'*, *v.t.* to enlist by conscription. —*adj.* **conscript** (*kon'skript*), enrolled, registered, esp. compulsorily.—*n.* one enrolled and liable to serve compulsorily.—*v.t.* (*kən-skript'*) to enlist compulsorily.—*n.* **conscrip'tion**, a compulsory enrolment for service, in a narrower sense, of a number drawn, but now usu. employed of universal service : the obtaining of recruits by compulsion.— *adj.* **conscrip'tional**.—*n.* and *adj.* **conscrip'-tionist**—**conscript fathers** (L. *patrēs cōnscriptī*), the senators of ancient Rome. [L. *cōnscrībĕre*, to enrol—*con*-, together, *scrībĕre*, *scriptum*, to write.]

consecrate, *kon'si-krāt*, *v.t.* to set apart for a holy use : to render holy or venerable; to hallow; to devote.—*adj.* consecrated : devoted : sanctified.— *ns.* **con'secratedness**; **consecra'tion**, the act of devoting to a sacred use; **con'secrātor**.—*adj.* **consecratory** (*-krā'tər-i*), making sacred. [L. *cōnsecrāre*, *-ātum*, to make wholly sacred—*con*-, *sacrāre*, to set apart as sacred—*sacer*, sacred.]

consectaneous, *kon-sek-tā'ni-əs*, *adj.* following as a natural consequence.—*n.* **consect'ary**, a deduction, corollary. [L. *cōnsectārī*, freq. of *cōnsequī*; see next.]

consecution, *kon-si-kū'shən*, *n.* a train of consequences or deductions : a series of things that follow one another : (*mus.*) succession of similar intervals in harmony.—*adj.* **consecutive** (*kən-sek'ū-tiv*), following in regular order or one after another : (*gram.*) expressing consequence.—*adv.* **consec'utively**.—*n.* **consec'utiveness**. [L. *cōnsequī*—*con*-, *sequī*, *secūtus*, to follow.]

consenescence, *kon-sən-es'əns*, *n.* general decay.— Also **consenesc'ency**. [L. *con*-, *senēscĕre*, to grow old.]

consensus, *kən-sen'səs*, *n.* agreement of various parts : agreement in opinion : unanimity : (*loosely*) trend of opinion.—*n.* **consen'sion**, mutual consent. —*adj.* **consen'sual**, relating to consent : involving voluntary and involuntary action in correlation.— *adv.* **consen'sually**.—**consensual contract**, a contract requiring merely the consent of the

parties. [L. *cōnsēnsus*—*cōnsentīre*; see next word.]

consent, *kən-sent'*, *v.i.* to be of the same mind : to agree : to give assent : to yield : to comply.—*v.t.* to agree : (*Milt.*) to allow.—*n.* agreement : accordance with the actions or opinions of another : concurrence.—*adj.* **consentaneous** (*kon-sən-tā'ni-əs*), agreeable or accordant : consistent.—*adv.* **consentā'neously**.—*ns.* **consentā'neousness**, **consentaneity** (*kon-sen-tə-nē'i-ti*).—*n.* **consen'tience** (*kən-sen'shəns*), agreement : power of unifying impressions below the level of consciousness : imperfect consciousness.—*adj.* **consen'tient**, agreeing : having consentience.—*adv.* **consent'ingly.**—**age of consent**, the age at which a person is legally competent to give consent to certain acts, esp. marriage, sexual intercourse : **be of consent** (*Shak.*), to be accessory : **with one consent**, unanimously. [L. *cōnsentīre*—*con*-, *sentīre*, to feel, to think.]

consequence, *kon'si-kwəns*, *n.* that which follows or comes after as a result or inference : effect : the relation of an effect to its cause : importance : social standing : consequentiality : (in *pl.*) a game describing the meeting of a lady and gentleman and its consequences, each player writing a part of the story, not knowing what the others have written.— *v.i.* (*Milt.*) to draw inferences.—*adj.* **con'sequent**, following, esp. as a natural effect or deduction : (*geol.*) flowing in the direction of the original slope of the land (distinguished from *subsequent* and *obsequent*).—*n.* that which follows : the natural effect of a cause.—*adj.* **consequen'tial** (*-kwen'shl*), following as a result, esp. an indirect result : self-important.—*advs.* **consequen'tially**; **con'sequently**. [Fr.,—L. *cōnsequī*—*con*-, *sequī*, to follow.]

conserve, *kən-sərv'*, *v.t.* to keep entire : to retain : to preserve : (*obs.*) to preserve in sugar.—*n.* something preserved, as fruits in sugar.—*adj.* **conser'vable**.—*n.* **conser'vancy**, a court or board having authority to preserve the fisheries, navigation, banks, etc., of a river : the act of preserving : esp. official care of a river, forest, etc.—*p.adj.* **conser'vant**.—*n.* **conservā'tion** (*kon*-), the act of conserving : the keeping entire.—*adj.* **conservā'-tional**.—*n.* **conser'vātism**, the opinions and principles of a Conservative : dislike of innovations. —*adj.* **conser'vātive**, tending or having power to conserve : averse to change : (*loosely*) moderately estimated or understated.—*n.* **Conservative**, one of the political party which desires to preserve the institutions of the country against innovation : one averse to change.—*ns.* **conser'vativeness**; **conservatoire** (*konᵊ-ser-vä-twär'*, *kən-sər'-və-twär'*), **conservatō'rium**, a school of music; **con'-servātor** (or *kən-sər'və-tər*), one who preserves from injury or violation : a guardian, custodian :— *fem.* **conservā'trix**; **conser'vatorship**; **conser'-vatory**, a storehouse : a greenhouse or place in which exotic plants are kept : a school or music.— *adj.* preservative.—*n.* **conser'ver**.—**conservation of energy**, the principle that the total amount of energy in an isolated system is constant; **conservation of matter**, the principle of indestructibility of matter. [L. *cōnservāre*—*con*-, *servāre*, to keep.]

consider, *kən-sid'ər*, *v.t.* to look at attentively or carefully : to think or deliberate on : to take into account : to attend to : to regard as : to think, hold the opinion (that) : to reward.—*v.i.* to think seriously or carefully : to deliberate.—*adj.* **consid'erable**, worthy of being considered : of some importance : more than a little.—*n.* **consid'erable-ness**.—*adv.* **consid'erably**.—*n.* **consid'erance** (*Shak.*), consideration.—*adjs.* **consid'erāte**, **consid'erative** (*obs.*), thoughtful : serious : prudent : thoughtful for the feelings and interests of others. —*adv.* **consid'erately**.—*ns.* **consid'erateness**, thoughtfulness for others; **considerā'tion**, deliberation : importance : motive or reason : compensation, reward : the reason or basis of a compact : (*law*) the thing given or done or abstained from by agreement with another, and in view of that other giving, doing, or abstaining from something.—*n.* and *adj.* **consid'ering** (*pl.* in *Shak.*).—*prep.* in view of.—*conj.* seeing that.—*adv.* everything considered.—*adv.* **consid'eringly**, with consideration. [L. *cōnsīderāre*, supposed to have been orig. a term of augury—*con-*, and *sīdus*, *sīderis*, a star.]

consign, *kən-sīn′*, *v.t.* to sign or seal: to devote: to transfer: to entrust: to commit: to transmit.—*adj.* **consign′able**.—*ns.* **consignation** (*kon-sig-nā′shən*); **consignatory** (*kən-sig′nə-tər-i*), a cosignatory.—*adj.* **consigned′**, given in trust.—*ns.* **consignee** (*kon-sīn-ē′*), one to whom anything is consigned or entrusted; **consign′er**, **consign′or**; **consign′ment**, the act of consigning: the thing consigned: a set of things consigned together. [L. *cōnsignāre*, to attest.]

consignify, *kon-sig′ni-fī*, *v.t.* to mean when taken along with something else.—*n.* **consignifica′tion**.—*adj.* **consignif′icative**.

consilience, *kən-sil′i-əns*, *n.* concurrence: coincidence.—*adj.* **consil′ient**, agreeing. [L. *con-*, together, and *salīre*, to leap.]

consimilar, *kən-sim′i-lər*, *adj.* like each other.—*ns.* **consimilar′ity**, **consimil′itude**, **consimil′ity**. [L. *cōnsimilis*.]

consist, *kən-sist′*, *v.i.* to exist, subsist: to be composed: (*Shak.*) to insist: to co-exist: to agree: to hold together.—*ns.* **consist′ence**, degree of density: substance; **consist′ency**, consistence: agreement: self-consistency.—*adj.* **consist′ent**, fixed: not fluid: agreeing together, compatible: free from self-contradiction: true to principles.—*adv.* **consist′ently**.—*adjs.* **consistō′rial**, **consistō′rian**.—*n.* **con′sistory** (or *-sist′*), properly, a place of assembly: the place where the privy-council of the Roman emperor met: the council itself: an assembly or council: a spiritual or ecclesiastical court.—Also *adj.*—**consist in**, to inhere in: to have as essence: to be composed of; **consist of**, to be made up of. [L. *cōnsistĕre*—*con-*, together, *sistĕre*, to set, stand.]

consociate, *kon-sō′shi-āt*, *v.t.* and *v.i.* to associate together.—*p.adj.* **consō′ciated**.—*n.* **consociation** (*-si-* or *-shi-ā′shən*), companionship: association: alliance, esp. of churches: a federal council of Congregational churches. [L. *cōnsociāre*, *-ātum*—*con-*, *sociāre*, to associate—*socius*, a companion.]

console, *kən-sōl′*, *v.t.* to give solace or comfort to: to cheer in distress.—*adj.* **consōl′able**.—*v.t.* **consolate** (*kon′səl-āt*; *Shak.*), to console.—*ns.* **consolā′tion**, solace: alleviation of misery: a comforting circumstance; **consolā′tion-match**, **-prize**, **-race**, etc., a match, prize, race, etc., for the otherwise unsuccessful.—*adj.* **consolatory** (*kən-sol′ə-tər-i*, or *-sōl′*), comforting.—*n.* (*Milt.*) a message of comfort.—*ns.* **console′ment**; **consol′er**;—*fem.* **consolā′trix**. [L. *cōnsōlārī*—*con-*, *sōlārī*, to comfort.]

console, *kon′sōl*, *n.* (*archit.*) a projection resembling a bracket, frequently in the form of the letter S, used to support cornices, or for placing busts, vases, or figures on: the key-desk of an organ: a large cabinet radio set or radiogram: a cabinet for this or similar apparatus.—*n.* **con′sole-tā′ble**, a table supported against a wall by consoles or brackets. [Fr. *console*; prob. conn. with **consolidate**.]

consolidate, *kən-sol′i-dāt*, *v.t.* to make solid: to form into a compact mass: to unite into one: to merge: (*mil.*) to rearrange and strengthen.—*v.i.* to grow solid or firm: to unite.—*adj.* made firm or solid: united.—*p.adj.* **consol′idated**.—*n.* **consolidā′tion**.—*adj.* **consol′idative**, tending to consolidate: having the quality of healing.—*n.* **consol′idator**.—**consolidated annuities**, that part of the British national debt which consists of several stocks consolidated into one fund; **consolidated fund**, a fund made up by uniting the yield of various taxes, etc., from which are paid interest on national debt, grants to royal family, etc.; **consolidation acts**, acts of parliament which combine into one general statute several special enactments. [L. *cōnsolidāre*, *-ātum*—*con-*, inten., and *solidus*, solid.]

consols, *kon′solz*, or *kon-solz′*, *n.pl.* short for **consolidated annuities**.

consommé, *kon^s-som-ā*, *n.* a soup made from meat by slow boiling: a clear soup. [Fr., *pa.p.*—L. *cōnsummāre*, *-ātum*, to consummate.]

consonant, *kon′sən-ənt*, *adj.* consistent: suitable: harmonious.—*n.* an articulation which can be sounded only with a vowel: a letter of the alphabet representing such a sound.—*ns.* **con′sonance**, a state of agreement: agreement or unison of sounds: (*mus.*) a combination of notes which can sound together without the harshness produced by beats: concord; **con′sonancy**, harmony.—*adj.* **consonantal** (*-ant′l*).—*adv.* **con′sonantly**.—*adj.* **con′sonous**, harmonious. [L. *cōnsonāns*, *-āntis*, pr.p. of *cōnsonāre*, to harmonise—*con-*, *sonāre*, to sound.]

consort, *kon′sort*, *-sərt* (*Spens.*, *-sort′*), *n.* a partner: a companion: a wife or husband: an accompanying ship: (*obs.*) a number of people: partnership: company: agreement: accord: formerly (by confusion) for **concert**: a group of instruments played or musicians playing together.—*v.t.* **consort′**, to accompany: to associate.—*v.i.* to associate or keep company: to agree.—*adj.* **consort′ed**, associated.—*ns.* **consort′er**, one who consorts; **con′sortism**, symbiosis; **consortium** (*kon-sor′shi-əm*), fellowship: association: an international banking or financial combination: the association of fungus and alga in a lichen: a lichen thallus:—*pl.* **consor′tia**; **con′sortship**.—**in consort**, in company: in harmony. [L. *cōnsors*, *-sortis*—*con-*, *sors*, a lot.]

conspectus, *kən-spek′təs*, *n.* a comprehensive view or survey: a synopsis.—*n.* **conspectuity** (*kon-spek-tū′i-ti*; *Shak.*), sight. [L. *cōnspectus*—*cōnspicĕre*, to look at; see next.]

conspicuous, *kən-spik′ū-əs*, *adj.* catching the eye: prominent.—*ns.* **conspicū′ity** (*kon-*), conspic′uousness.—*adv.* **conspic′uously**. [L. *cōnspicuus*—*cōnspicĕre*—*con-*, inten., *specĕre*, to look.]

conspire, *kən-spīr′*, *v.i.* to plot or scheme together: to devise: to concur to one end.—*v.t.* to plan, devise.—*n.* **conspiracy** (*-spir′ə-si*), the act of conspiring: a banding together for a secret purpose: a plot: concurrence.—*adj.* **conspir′ant**, conspiring.—*ns.* **conspirā′tion**, conspiracy; **conspir′ātor**, one who conspires:—*fem.* **conspir′atress**.—*adj.* **conspirātō′rial**.—*n.* **conspir′er** (*Shak.*), conspirator.—*adv.* **conspir′ingly**. [L. *cōnspīrāre*—*con-*, together, *spīrāre*, to breathe.]

conspurcation, *kon-spur-kā′shən*, *n.* (*obs.*) defilement. [L. *cōnspurcāre*, *-ātum*, to defile.]

constable, *kun′stə-bl*, or *kon′*, *n.* formerly a state-officer of the highest rank: the warden of a castle: a peace-officer: a policeman.—*ns.* **con′stableship**; **con′stablewick**, the district of a constable; **constabulary** (*kən-stab′ū-lər-i*), an organised body of constables.—*adj.* of or pertaining to constables, or peace-officers.—**Constable of France**, chief of the household under the old French kings, then commander-in-chief of the army, judge in questions of chivalry, tournaments, and martial displays; **High Constable**, one of two constables formerly ordained in every hundred or franchise, to make the view of armour, and to see to the conservation of the peace; **Lord High Constable of England**, an officer of the crown, formerly a judge in the court of chivalry; **Lord High Constable of Scotland**, a similar officer (now a mere hereditary title); **outrun the constable**, to go too fast: to get into debt; **petty constable**, a parish constable who was under the High Constable; **special constable**, a person sworn in by the justices to preserve the peace, or to execute warrants on special occasions. [O.Fr. *conestable* (Fr. *connétable*)—L. *comes stabulī*, count or companion of the stable.]

constant, *kon′stənt*, *adj.* fixed: unchangeable: firm: continual: faithful.—*n.* (*math.*) a fixed quantity.—*n.* **con′stancy**, fixedness: unchangeableness: faithfulness: (*Shak.*) perseverence: (*Shak.*) certainty.—*adv.* **con′stantly**. [L. *cōnstāns*, *-stāntis*, from *cōnstāre*, to stand firm—*con-*, inten., *stāre*, to stand.]

Constantia, *kən-stan′shi-ä*, *n.* a sweet wine produced around *Constantia*, near Cape Town.

Constantinian, *kon-stən-tin′yən*, *adj.* pertaining to Constantine I. (A.D. *c.*274-337; emperor 306-337).

Constantinopolitan, *kon-stan-ti-nō-pol′it-ən*, *adj.* of or pertaining to *Constantinople*.

Neutral vowels in unaccented syllables : *el′ə-mənt*, *in′fənt*, *ran′dəm*

constate, *kon-stāt'*, *v.t.* to assert (a Gallicism). [Fr. *constater*.]

constellate, *kon'stəl-āt*, or *kon-stel'āt*, *v.t.* to cluster : to compel or affect by stellar influence.— to cluster together.—*n.* **constellā'tion**, a group of stars : an assemblage of persons distinguished in some way : (*astrol.*) a particular disposition of the planets, supposed to influence the course of human life or character.—*adj.* **constell'atory**. [L. *cōnstellātus*, studded with stars—*con-*, *stellāre*—*stella*, a star.]

conster. See **construe.**

consternate, *kon'stər-nāt*, *v.t.* to fill with dismay.— *n.* **consternā'tion**, terror that throws into confusion : dismay. [L. *cōnsternāre*, *-ātum*, from *con-*, wholly, *sternēre*, to strew.]

constipate, *kon'stip-āt*, *v.t.* to stop up : to make costive : (*obs.*) to press together.—*n.* **constipā'tion**, costiveness, an irregular and insufficient action of the bowels. [L. *cōnstīpāre*, *-ātum*, to press together —*con-*, *stīpāre*, to pack.]

constitute, *kon'stit-ūt*, *v.t.* to set up : to establish : to form or make up : to appoint : to give being to.— *n.* **constituency** (*kən-stit'ū-ən-si*), the whole body of voters, or a district, or population, represented by a member of parliament or the like.—*adj.* **constit'uent**, constituting or forming : essential : elemental : component : electing : constitution-making.—*n.* an essential or elemental part : one of those who elect a representative, esp. in parliament : an inhabitant of one's constituency.—*n.* **constitū'tion** (*kon-*), the act of constituting : the natural condition of body or mind : disposition : a system of laws and customs established by the sovereign power of a state for its own guidance : an established form of government : a particular law or usage : (*chem.*) molecular structure, taking into account not only the kinds and numbers of atoms but the way in which they are linked.—*adj.* **constitū'tional**, inherent in the natural frame : natural : agreeable to the constitution or frame of government : essential : legal : reigning subject to fixed laws : supporting the existing constitution.—*n.* a walk for the sake of one's health.—*v.t.* **constitū'tionalise**, to make constitutional.—*ns.* **constitū'tionalism**, adherence to the principles of the constitution ; **constitū'tion(al)ist**, one who favours or studies a constitution or the constitution ; **constitutional'ity**.—*adv.* **constitū'tionally**.—*adj.* **con'stitutive**, that constitutes or establishes : having power to constitute : essential : component. [L. *cōnstituĕre*, *cōnstitūtum*—*con-*, *statuĕre*, to make to stand, to place.]

constrain, *kən-strān'*, *v.t.* to urge with irresistible power : to bring about by force : to force, compel : to distress : to violate . to confine : to limit : to cause constraint to : to restrict by a condition.—*adj.* **constrain'able**.—*p.adj.* **constrained'**, forced, compelled : lacking ease and spontaneity of manner : embarrassed.—*adv.* **constrain'edly**.—*n.* **constraint'**, irresistible force : compulsion : confinement : repression of one's feelings : embarrassment : a restricting condition. [O.Fr. *constraindre*—L. *cōnstringĕre*—*con-*, *stringĕre*, to press ; see following words and **strain.**]

constrict, *kən-strikt'*, *v.t.* to press together : to contract : to cramp : to narrow locally.—*p.adj.* **constrict'ed**, narrowed : cramped : (*bot.*) narrowed in places.—*n.* **constric'tion**, a pressing together : contraction : tightness : a narrow place.—*adj.* **constrict'ive**.—*n.* **constrict'or**, that which constricts or draws together : a muscle that compresses an organ or structure : a snake that crushes its prey in its folds. [L. *cōnstringĕre*, *-strictum ;* see preceding and following.]

constringe, *kən-strinj'*, *v.t.* to draw together : to cause to contract.—*v.i.* to contract.—*n.* **constrin'gency**.—*adj.* **constrin'gent**, having the quality of contracting. [L. *cōnstringĕre ;* see preceding.]

construct, *kən-strukt'*, *v.t.* to build up : to compile : to put together the parts of : to make : to compose : to put in grammatical relation.—*adj.* **constructed**.— *n.* (*kon'strukt*), a thing constructed, esp. in the mind. —*adjs.* **construct'able, construct'ible**, able to be

constructed.—*ns.* **construct'er, construct'or ; construc'tion**, the act of constructing : anything piled together : building : a stage structure : manner of forming : (*gram.*) the syntactic relations of words in a sentence : interpretation : meaning.—*adj.* **construc'tional**, pertaining to construction : used for structures : making use of structures.—*n.* **struc'tionism**, use of structures : principle of using structures or of following structure.—*adj.* **construct'ive**, capable of, tending towards, or concerned in, constructing : embodying positive advice—opp. to *destructive* : not direct or expressed, but inferred.—*adv.* **construct'ively**.—*ns.* **construct'iveness ; construct'ivism**, constructionism ; **construct'ure**.—**bear a construction**, to allow of a particular interpretation ; **construct state**, in Semitic languages, the state of a noun depending on another noun, where in Indo-Germanic languages the other would be in the genitive case—e.g. House of God—house being in the construct state. [L. *cōnstruĕre*, *-structum*— *con-*, *struĕre*, to build.]

construe, *kən-strōō'*, *kon'strōō*, (old form **conster**, *kon'stər*), *v.t.* to exhibit in another language the grammatical structure and literal meaning of : to translate : to explain : to interpret : to construct grammatically : to infer.—*v.i.* to admit of grammatical analysis.—*n.* **con'strue**, an act of construing.—*adj.* **constru'able**.—*ns.* **construabil'ity ; construer** (*kon'*, or *-strōō'*). [L. *cōnstruĕre*, *cōnstructum*, to pile together.]

constuprate, *kon'stū-prāt*, *v.t.* (*obs.*) to ravish.—*n.* **constuprā'tion**. [L. *cōnstuprāre*—*con-*, intensive, *stuprum*, defilement, disgrace.]

consubsist, *kon-sub-sist'*, *v.i.* to subsist together.

consubstantial, *kon-sub-stan'shl*, *adj.* of the same substance, nature, or essence, esp. of the Trinity.— *ns.* **consubstan'tialism**, the doctrine of consubstantiation ; **consubstan'tialist**, one who believes in consubstantiation ; **consubstantiality** (*-shi-al'i-ti*).—*adv.* **consubstan'tially**, with sameness of substance.—*v.t.* and *v.i.* **consubstan'tiate** (*-shi-āt*), to unite in one common substance or nature.—*adj.* so united.—*n.* **consubstantiā'tion**, the Lutheran doctrine of the actual, substantial presence of the body and blood of Christ co-existing in and with the bread and wine used at the Lord's Supper ; **consubstantiā'tionist**. [L. *con-*, with, and **substantial**, etc.]

consuetude, *kon'swi-tūd*, *n.* custom : familiarity.— *adj.* **consuetū'dinary**, customary.—*n.* an unwritten law established by usage, derived by immemorial custom from antiquity : a ritual of customary devotions. [L. *cōnsuētūdō, -inis*, custom.]

consul, *kon'səl*, *n.* one of the two chief-magistrates in the Roman republic : one of the three heads of the French republic, 1799-1804 : an agent for a foreign government appointed to attend to the interests of its citizens and commerce.—*n.* **con'-sulage**, duty paid to a consul for protection of goods.—*adj.* **con'sular** (*-sū-lər*), pertaining to a consul.—*n.* a man of consular rank.—*ns.* **con'sulate** (*sūl-*, or *səl-*), the office, residence, jurisdiction, government, or time of a consul or consuls ; **con'sulship**, the office, or term of office, of a consul. [L. *cōnsul.*]

consult, *kən-sult'*, *v.t.* to ask advice of : to decide or act in favour of : to look up for information or advice : to discuss : to consider : to take measures for the advantage of.—*v.i.* to consider jointly : to take counsel.—*n.* (*kən-sult'*, or *kon'sult*) consultation : council : a meeting for conspiracy or intrigue. —*ns.* **consulta** (*kon-sōōl'tä ;* It and Sp.), a meeting of council ; **consultant** (*kən-sult'ənt*), one who seeks advice or information : one who gives professional advice or takes part in consultation ; **consultā'tion** (*kon'səl-*, *-sul-*), deliberation, or a meeting for deliberation, esp. of physicians or lawyers.—*adjs.* **consult'ative**, of or pertaining to consultation, esp. of bodies without vote on the decision ; **consult'atory**, of the nature of consultation.—*ns.* **consultee'**, the person consulted ; **consult'er**, one who consults.—*adjs.* **consult'ing**, of a physician or lawyer prepared to give advice ; **consult'ive**, consultative.—*n.* **consult'or.**—*adj.*

consult'ory, consultatory. [L. *cōnsultāre*, inten. of *cōnsulĕre*, to consult.]

consume, kən-sūm', -sōōm', *v.t.* to destroy by wasting, fire, evaporation, etc.: to use up: to devour: to waste or spend: to exhaust.—*v.i.* to waste away.—*adj.* **consum'able**.—*adv.* **consum'-edly**, exceedingly—originally a fantastic variant of *confoundedly*, and prob. influenced in meaning by *consummately*.—*ns.* **consum'er**, one who consumes: as opposed to *producer*, one who uses an article produced.—*n.* and *adj.* **consum'ing**, wasting or destroying: engrossing.—**consumer(s') goods**, goods to be used without further manufacturing process to satisfy human needs. [L. *cōnsūmĕre*, *-sūmptum*, to destroy—*con-*, sig. completeness, *sūmĕre*, to take.]

consummate, kon'sum-āt, or -səm-, *v.t.* to raise to the highest point: to perfect or finish: to make (marriage) legally complete by sexual intercourse.—*adj.* (kən-sum'āt, -it), complete, supreme, perfect of its kind.—*adv.* **consumm'ately**, perfectly.—*n.* **consummā'tion**, act of completing: perfection: conclusion of life or of the universe: the subsequent intercourse which makes a marriage legally valid.—*adj.* **consumm'ative**.—*n.* **con'summātor**.—*adj.* **consumm'atory**. [L. *cōnsummāre*, *-ātum*, to perfect—*con-*, *summus*, highest, perfect, *summa*, a sum.]

consumption, kən-sum(p)'shən, *n.* the act or process of consuming or using up: the quantity consumed: wasting of the body: pulmonary tuberculosis.—*n.* **consumpt** (kon'sum(p)t, kən-sum(p)t'), quantity consumed.—*adj.* **consump'tive**, wasting away: inclined to the disease consumption.—*adv.* **consump'tively**.—*ns.* **consump'tiveness**, **consumptiv'ity** (kon-), a tendency to consumption. [See **consume**.]

contabescent, kon-tăb-es'ənt, *adj.* wasting away, atrophied: failing to produce pollen.—*n.* **contabesc'ence**. [L. *contābēscēns*, *-entis*, *-em*—*contābēscĕre*, to waste away.]

contact, kon'takt, *n.* touch: meeting: (*math.*) meeting in a point without intersection: close approximation allowing passage of electric current or communication of disease: a place or part where electric current may be allowed to pass: association: means or occasion of communication: a person who has been exposed to contagion.—*v.t.* and *v.i.* (*slang*) also kon-takt') to bring or come into contact: to get into touch with, or establish a connexion with.—*ns.* **con'tact-lens**, a lens, usu. of plastic material, worn in contact with the eyeball, instead of spectacles, to correct defects of vision; **con'tact-metamor'phism**, alteration of rocks in the neighbourhood of igneous materials; **con'tactor**, a device for repeatedly making and breaking an electric current.—*adj.* **contact'ual**, pertaining to contact.—**contact man** (*coll.*), an intermediary in transactions, esp. shady ones. [L. *contingĕre*, *contactum*, to touch—*con-*, wholly, *tangĕre*, to touch.]

contadino, kon-tä-dē'nō, *n.* an Italian peasant:— *pl.* **contadini** (-nē):—*fem.* **contadi'na** (-nä):— *pl.* **contadi'ne** (-nä), **contadi'nas**. [It.]

contagion, kən-tā'jən, *n.* transmission of a disease by direct contact with an infected person or object: a disease or poison so transmitted: the means of transmission: a hurtful influence.—*n.* **contā'gionist**, one who believes in the contagiousness of a disease.—*adj.* **contā'gious**, communicable by contact: carrying disease or other contagion: (*obs.*) noxious.—*adv.* **contā'giously**.—*ns.* **contā'giousness**; **contā'gium**, contagion: contagious matter. [L. *contāgiō*, *-ōnis*—*con-*, *tangĕre*, to touch.]

contain, kən-tān', *v.t.* to have within, enclose: to comprise, include: to restrain: to keep fixed: to hold back (*Shak.*) to retain.—*adj.* **contain'able**.—**contain'er**, that which contains: that in which goods are enclosed for transport: a vessel for holding gas; **contain'ment**. [O.Fr. (Fr.) *contenir* —L. *continēre*—*con-*, *tenēre*, to hold.]

contaminate, kən-tam'i-nāt, *v.t.* to defile by touching or mixing with: to pollute: to corrupt: to infect: to blend.—*adj.* **contaminated**.—*adj.* **contam'inable**.—*n.* **contaminā'tion**, pollution:

blending.—*adj.* **contam'inative**. [L. *contāmināre*, *-ātum*—*contāmen* (for *contagmen*), pollution; see **contact**.]

contango, kən-tang'gō, *n.* a percentage paid by the buyer to the seller of stock for keeping back its delivery to the next settling-day, continuation— opp. to *backwardation*:—*pl.* **contang'os**.—Also *v.t.*—*n.* **contang'o-day** (see **continuation-day**). [Arbitrarily from **continue**.]

conte, kōn²t, *n.* a short story (as a literary genre). [Fr.]

conteck, kon'tek, *n.* (*Spens.*), strife. [O.Fr. *contek*, prob. conn. with *contekir*, to touch.]

contemn, kən-tem', *v.t.* to despise (*pr.p.* **contemning**, *-tem'ing*; *pa.t.* and *pa.p.* **contemned'**, *Spens.* *pa.p.* **contempt**').—*n.* **contem'ner** (-ər, -nər). [L. *contemnĕre*, *-temptum*, to value little—*con-*, inten., *temnĕre*, to slight.]

contemper, kən-temp'ər, *v.t.* to blend together, to qualify by mixture: to adapt.—*ns.* **contemperā'tion** (*obs.*), **contem'perature**. [L. *contemperāre*.]

contemplate, kon'tem-plāt, older kən-tem'plāt, *v.t.* to consider or look at attentively: to meditate on or study: to intend.—*v.i.* to think seriously: to meditate (with *on*, *upon*).—*adj.* **contemp'lable**.— *ns.* **contem'plant**; **contemplā'tion**, meditation: a meditative condition of mind: attentive viewing or consideration: matter for thought: purpose; **contemp'latist**.—*adj.* and *n.* **con'templative** (or kən-tem'plə-), given to contemplation.—*adv.* **con'templatively** (or *-tem'*).—*ns.* **con'templativeness** (or *-tem'*); **con'templātor**, one who contemplates: a student.—**contemplative life** (*theol.*) life devoted to meditation (opposed to the *active life*). [L. *contemplārī*, *-ātus*, to mark out carefully a *templum* or place for auguries—*con-*, sig. completeness, and *templum*.]

contemporaneous, kən-tem-pə-rā'nyəs, *adj.* living, happening, or being at the same time: (*geol.*) belonging approximately to the same relative place in the succession, not necessarily strictly synchronous.—*n.* and *adj.* **contemporā'nean**, contemporary.—*n.* **contemporaneity** (-ə-nē'i-ti).— *adv.* **contemporā'neously**.—*ns.* **contemporā'neousness**; **contem'porariness**.—*adj.* **contem'-porary**, belonging to the same time (*with*).—*n.* one who lives at the same time: a newspaper or magazine of the same time.—*v.t.* **contem'porise**, to make contemporary in mind. [L. *con-*, *tempus*, *-oris*, time.]

contempt, kən-tempt', *n.* scorn: disgrace: (*law*) disregard of the rule, or an offence against the dignity, of a court (with *of*, *for*).—*ns.* **contemptibil'ity**, **contempt'ibleness**.—*adj.* **contempt'ible** (*Spens.* kon') despicable.—*adv.* **contempt'ibly**.— *adj.* **contempt'ūous**, haughty, scornful.—*adv.* **contempt'uously**.—*n.* **contempt'uousness**. [See **contemn**.]

contend, kən-tend', *v.i.* to strive: to struggle in emulation or in opposition: to dispute or debate (with *against*, *for*, *with*, *about*): to urge one's course.—*v.t.* to maintain in dispute (with *that*). —*ns.* **contend'ent**, **contend'er**, one who contends.—*n.* and *adj.* **contend'ing**, striving.—*n.* **conten'tion**, a violent straining after any object: strife: debate: a position argued for.—*adj.* **conten'tious**, quarrelsome: given to dispute: in, or relating to, dispute.—*adv.* **conten'tiously**.—*n.* **conten'tiousness**. [L. *contendĕre*, *-tentum*—*con-*, *tendĕre*, to stretch.]

contenement, kon-ten'i-mənt, *n.* (*obs.*) property necessary to maintain one's station. [L. *con-*; see **tenement**.]

content, kon'tent, sometimes kən-tent', *n.* that which is contained: capacity: the substance: (in *pl.*) the things contained: (in *pl.*) the list of chapters, sections etc., in a book. [See **contain**.]

content, kən-tent', *adj.* having the desire limited by present enjoyment: satisfied: quietly happy.— *n.* satisfaction.—*interj.* I am content, agreed!—the formula of assent in the House of Lords.—*v.t.* to make content: to satisfy the mind: to quiet: to please.—*n.* **contentā'tion** (*obs.*).—*adj.* **content'ed**, content.—*adv.* **content'edly**.—*ns.* **content'edness**, **content'ment**.—*adj.* **content'less**, without

content : discontented. [Fr.,—L. *contentus*, contained, hence satisfied—*con-*, and *tenēre*, to hold.]
conterminous, kən-tər'min-əs, *adj.* adjacent, meeting along a common boundary : meeting end to end : coincident : co-extensive in range.—*adjs.* **conter'minal**, adjacent : end to end ; **conter'minant**, **conter'minate**, adjacent. [L. *conterminus*, neighbouring—*con-*, *terminus*, a boundary.]
contest, kən-test', *v.t.* to call in question or make the subject of dispute : to strive to gain.—*v.i.* to contend.—*n.* (*kon'*), a struggle for victory : competition : strife : debate.—*adj.* **contest'able**.—*ns.* **contest'ant**, one who contests ; **contesta'tion**, the act of contesting : contest, strife : emulation.—*p.adjs.* **contest'ed** ; **contest'ing**.—*adv.* **contest'ingly.**—contested election, one in which there are more candidates than are to be elected : (*U.S.*) one whose validity is disputed. [Fr. *contester*—L. *contestārī*, to call to witness—*con-*, *testārī*, to be a witness—*testis*, a witness.]
context, kon'tekst, *n.* the parts of a discourse or treatise which precede and follow a special passage and may fix its true meaning.—*adj.* **context'ual.**—**context'ually.**—*n.* **context'ure**, the process or manner of weaving together : structure : fabric. [L. *contextus*, *contexěre*—*con-*, *texěre*, *textum*, to weave.]
conticent, kon'tis-ənt, *adj.* (*Thackeray*) silent. [L. *conticēns*, *-ēntis*—*con-*, intens., *tacēre*, to be silent.]
contignation, kon-tig-nā'shən, *n.* joining together of timber : framework boarding. [L. *contignātiō*, *-ōnis*,—*contignāre*—*con-*, *tignum*, beam.]
contiguous, kən-tig'ū-əs, *adj.* touching, adjoining : near.—*ns.* **contigū'ity**, **contig'uousness**.—*adv.* **contig'uously.** [L. *contiguus*—*contingěre*, to touch on all sides—*con-*, wholly, *tangěre*, to touch.]
continent, kon'ti-nənt, *n.* that which contains : a bank or shore : sum and substance : a great extent of land not broken up by seas : one of the great divisions of the land surface of the globe : the mainland portion of one of these, esp. Europe or North America : mainland : solid earth : land : the main or whole body of anything.—*adj.* restraining within due bounds, or absolutely abstaining from, the indulgence of pleasure, esp. sexual : temperate : virtuous.—*ns.* **con'tinence**, **con'tinency**, self-restraint or abstinence, esp. sexual : chastity.—*adj.* **continental** (-ent'l), of, characteristic of, or of the nature of, a continent, esp. the European continent, the colonies of North America at the period of independence, or the main body of the United States.—*n.* a native or inhabitant of a continent : an American soldier of the War of Independence : a currency note of the Continental Congress.—**continent'alism**, anything peculiar to the usage of the Continent.—*adv.* **con'tinently.**—Continental Congress, an assembly of delegates of the revolting American colonies, before the United States constitution was in force ; **Continental System**, Napoleon's plan for shutting out England from all commercial connexion with Europe. [L. *continēns*, *-ēntis*—*continēre*, to contain—*con-*, *tenēre*, to hold.]
contingent, kən-tin'jənt, *adj.* dependent on something else : liable but not certain to happen : accidental.—*n.* an event liable but not certain to occur : a share, quota, or group, esp. of soldiers.—*ns.* **contin'gence**, contact : (*rare*) contingency ; **contin'gency**, quality or state of being contingent : contact : close connexion : uncertainty : chance : a chance happening or concurrence of 'vents : a possible future event : something dependent on such : an incidental.—*adv.* **contin'gently.** [L. *contingēns*, *-entis*—*con-*, *tangěre*, to touch.]
continue, kən-tin'ū, *v.t.* to draw out or prolong : to extend : to maintain : to go on with : to resume : to adjourn : to be a prolongation of.—*v.i.* to remain in the same place or state : to last or endure : to persevere.—*adjs.* **contin'uable** ; **contin'ual**, without interruption : unceasing : persistent.—*adv.* **contin'ually.**—*n.* **contin'uance**, duration : uninterrupted succession : stay.—*adj.* **contin'uant**, continuing : capable of continuing.—*n.* an open consonant.—*adj.* **contin'uate**, closely united :

(*Shak.*) unbroken.—*ns.* **continua'tion**, going on : persistence : constant succession : extension : resumption : a further instalment ; **continua'tion-class**, a class for continuing the education of those who have left school ; **continua'tion-day**, the same as **contango-day**, that on which contangos are fixed.—*adj.* **contin'uative**, continuing.—*n.* **contin'uātor**, one who continues : one who keeps up a series or succession.—*adj.* **contin'ued**, uninterrupted : unceasing : extended : resumed : in instalments.—*adv.* **contin'uedly.**—*ns.* **contin'uedness** ; **contin'uer**, one who continues : one who has the power of persevering ; **continū'ity**, state of being continuous : uninterrupted connexion : a complete scenario of a motion-picture : the person who writes it (in full **continū'ity-wri'ter**) ; **continuo** (*kon-tin'ū-ō* ; It. *-tēn'wō*), thorough-bass.—*adj.* **contin'uous**, joined together without interruption.—*adv.* **contin'uously.**—*ns.* **contin'uousness** ; **contin'ūum** (L.), that which is continuous : that which must be regarded as continuous and the same and which can be described only relatively :—*pl.* **contin'ua**. [L. *continuāre*—*continuus*, joined, connected, from *continēre*, to hold together.]
contline, kont'līn, *n.* the space between stowed casks : a spiral interval between the strands of a rope. [Prob. **cant**, **line**.]
conto, kon'tō, *n.* a Portuguese and Brazilian money of account, 1000 escudos or cruzeiros. [Port., million (reis)—L. *computus*, a sum.]
contorno, kon-tor'nō, *n.* contour or outline.—*n.* **contor'niate**, a coin or medal with a deep groove round the disk.—*adj.* having this. [It. *contorno*, circuit, contour.]
contort, kən-tort', *v.t.* to twist or turn violently : to writhe.—*adj.* **contort'ed**, twisted : twisted, as some flower-buds when each floral leaf overlaps its neighbour always on the same side round the circle : (*geol.*) much and irregularly plicated.—*n.* **contor'tion**, a violent twisting : deformation.—*adjs.* **contor'tional**, **contor'tionate.**—*n.* **contor'tionist**, a gymnast who practises contorted postures : one who twists words and phrases.—*adj.* **contort'ive**. [L. *con-*, inten., and *torquēre*, *tortum*, to twist.]
contour, kon'tōōr, or kon-tōōr', *n.* outline : the line that bounds the figure of any object : general character or aspect : artistic quality of outline : a contour line : a point, line, or surface, at, along, or on which some property or characteristic is constant, or its representation in a map or diagram.—*v.t.* to mark with contour lines : to follow the contour lines of.—**contour feathers**, those that determine the contours of the body ; **contour line**, a line on the ground whose points are all at the same height above sea-level, or the intersection of the ground surface by a level surface of constant elevation : representation of such a line on a map ; **contour map**, a map in which the configuration of land is shown by contour lines. [Fr. *contour* (It. *contorno*)—L. *con-*, *tornus*—Gr. *tornos*, a lathe.]
contra, kon'trä, *-trə*, *adv.* and *prep.* against.—*n.* an argument against : the other side. See also **Prefixes**. [L. *contrā*.]
contraband, kon'trə-band, *adj.* excluded by law : prohibited.—*n.* illegal traffic : smuggled or prohibited goods : in the American Civil War, a refugee slave.—*ns.* **con'trabandism**, trafficking in contraband goods ; **con'trabandist**, a smuggler.—contraband of war, commodities not to be supplied by neutral to belligerent powers. [Sp. *contrabanda*—It. *contrabbando*—L. *contrā*, L.L. *bandum*, ban.]
contrabass, kon'trə-bās, *n.* the double-bass or bass-viol, playing an octave below the 'cello.—*adj.* applied to other instruments taking a similar part.—Also **contrabasso** (-*bäs'sō*) and **coun'terbase**. [It. *contra*(b)*basso*—pfx. *contra-* indicating an octave lower, and *basso*, bass.]
contra-bassoon, kon'trə-bas-ōōn', *n.* the double bassoon.
contraception, kon-trə-sep'shən, *n.* prevention of

conception.—*n.* **contracep'tive,** a means of contraception.—Also *adj.* [**conception.**]

contract, *kən-trakt'*, *v.t.* to draw together : to lessen : to shorten : to effect by agreement : to come into, become the subject of : to incur, catch (a disease) : to bargain for : to betroth.—*v.i.* to shrink : to become less : to become shorter.—*n.* (*kon'*), an agreement on fixed terms : a bond : a betrothal : the writing containing an agreement : a season-ticket : contract bridge : a final bid in contract bridge : (*coll.*) an undertaking.—*n.* **contractabil'ity.**—*adjs.* **contract'able** (*kən-*), able to be contracted, esp. of a disease or habit; **contract'ed,** drawn together : shortened : narrow : mean : affianced.—*adv.* **contract'edly,** -*ns.* **contract'edness; contractibil'ity.**—*adjs.* **contract'ible,** capable of being contracted; **contract'ile,** tending or having power to contract or to draw in.—*ns.* **contractil'ity** (*kon-*): **contrac'tion** (*kən-*), act of contracting : a word shortened in speech or spelling : a symbol for shortening in palaeography, etc.—*adj.* **contract'ive,** tending to contract.—*n.* **contract'or,** one of the parties to a bargain or agreement : one who engages to execute work or furnish supplies at a stated rate.—*adj.* **contract'ual.**—*n.* **contract'ure,** persistent muscular contraction : shortening due to spasm or paralysis of muscles, etc. : tapering of a column.—**contract bridge,** a development of auction bridge, in which tricks beyond the number bid for count only like honours; **contract out,** to arrange that certain conditions shall not apply. [L. *contractus—con-,* together, *trahĕre, tractum,* to draw.]

contra-dance. See **country-dance.**

contradict, *kon-trə-dikt'*, *v.t.* (*obs.*) to oppose by words : to deny what is affirmed by : to assert the contrary of : to deny : to be contrary to in character. —*adj.* **contradict'able.**—*n.* **contradic'tion,** act of contradicting : a speaking against : denial : inconsistency.—*adj.* **contradic'tious,** prone to contradiction.—*advs.* **contradic'tiously; contradic'torily.**—*adj.* **contradict'ive.**—*adv.* **contradict'ively.**—*n.* **contradict'or.**—*adv.* **contradict'orily.**—*n.* **contradict'oriness,** the quality of being contradictory.—*adj.* **contradict'ory,** affirming the contrary : inconsistent. [L. *contrādīcĕre,* -*dictum.*]

contradistinction, *kon-trə-dis-tingk'shən,* *n.* distinction by contrast.—*adj.* **contradistinct'ive,** distinguishing by opposite qualities.—*v.t.* **contradistin'guish,** to contrast and mark the difference between.

contrafagotto, *kon-trə-fə-got'tō,* *n.* the double bassoon, an octave lower than the bassoon. [It. *contra-,* indicating an octave lower, and *fagotto,* bassoon.]

contrahent, *kon'trə-hənt,* *adj.* entering into a contract.—*n.* a contracting party. [L. *contrahēns,* -*entis—contrahĕre,* to contract.]

contra-indicate, *kon'trə-in'di-kāt,* *v.t.* (*med.*) to point to as unsuitable : to forbid.—*ns.* **contrain'dicant, con'tra-indicā'tion.**—*adj.* **contraindic'ative.**

contraire, *kən-trār',* an obsolete form of **contrary.**

contralto, *kən-träl'tō,* *n.* the lowest musical voice in women : the part sung by it : possessor of such a voice :—*pl.* **contralti** (*-tē*), -**tos.**—Also *adj.* [It.]

contranatant, *kon-trə-nā'tənt,* *adj.* swimming upstream. [L. *contrā, natāns,* -*āntis,* pr.p. of *natāre,* to swim.]

contraplex, *kon'trə-pleks,* *adj.* (*teleg.*) having messages passing opposite ways at once. [L. *contrā,* against, and -*plex,* as in **duplex, simplex.**]

contraposition, *kon-trə-po-zish'ən,* *n.* opposition, contrast : (*logic*) an immediate inference, which consists in denying the original subject of the contradictory of the original predicate.—*adj.* and *n.* **contrapos'itive.**

contraption, *kən-trap'shən,* *n.* (*U.S.*) a contrivance. [Perh. arbitrarily from **contrive.**]

contrapuntal. See **counterpoint.**

contrary, *kon'trə-ri;* still sometimes *kən-trā'ri, adj.* opposite : contradictory : (*coll.;* usu. *kən-trā'ri*) perverse.—*n.* an extreme opposite : (*logic*) a proposition so related to another that both cannot

be true though both may be false.—*v.t.* and *v.i.* to oppose : to contradict : to annoy.—*n.* **contrariety** (*-ri'i-ti*), opposition : inconsistency.—*adv.* **contrarily** (*kon'* or *trā'*).—*n.* **contrariness** (*kon'* or *trā'*).—*adj.* **contrarious** (*kən-trā'ri-əs*), showing contrariety : repugnant : opposite.—*advs.* **contrā'riously,** contrarily; **con'trariwise** (or *trā',* or *tra'*), in the contrary way : on the other side : on the other hand.—**contrary motion** (*mus.*), move-ment of parts in opposite directions—one up, another down; **on the contrary,** far otherwise; **to the contrary,** to the opposite effect. [L. *contrārius—contrā,* against.]

contrast, *kən-träst',* *v.i.* to stand in opposition.—*v.t.* to set in opposition to, in order to show difference.—*n.* **contrast** (*kon'*), opposition or unlikeness in things compared : exhibition of differences.—*adj.* **contrast'ive.** [Fr. *contraster*—L. *contrā,* opposite to, *stāre,* to stand.]

contrate, *kon'trāt, adj.* having cogs parallel to the axis. [L. *contrā,* opposite.]

contra-tenor. See **counter-tenor.**

contravallation, *kon-trə-val-ā'shən, n.* a fortification built by besiegers about the place invested. [L. *contrā, vallāre,* -*atum,* to fortify.]

contravene, *kon-trə-vēn', v.t.* to oppose : to infringe.—*n.* **contravēn'tion.** [L. *contrā, venīre, ventum,* to come.]

contrayerva, *kon-trə-yər'və, n.* a tropical American plant of the mulberry family, once esteemed as an antidote : a Jamaican birthwort of like reputation. [Sp. (now *contrahierba*)—L. *contrā,* against, *herba,* a herb.]

contretemps, *kon°-tr'-tän°, n.* something happening inopportunely or at the wrong time, anything embarrassing, a hitch. [Fr. *contre* (L. *contrā*) against, *temps* (L. *tempus*) time.]

contribute, *kon-trib'ūt* (*Milt. kon'*), *v.t.* to give along with others : to give for a common purpose : to add towards a common result, to a fund, etc. : to write and send for publication with others.—*v.i.* to give or bear a part : to be a contributor.—*adj.* **contrib'utable,** payable : subject to contribution.—*n.* **contribū'tion** (*kon-*), the act of contributing : a levy or charge imposed upon a number of persons : anything furnished to a common stock or done towards a common end : a written composition supplied to a periodical, etc.—*adjs.* **contrib'utive, contrib'utory, (contrib'utary,** *obs.*) giving a share : helping.—*n.* **contrib'utor.** [L. *con-, tribĕre,* -*ūtum,* to give.]

contrist, *kən-trist', v.t.* (*obs.*) to sadden.—*n.* **contristā'tion.** [Fr. *contrister*—L. *contristāre—con-,* inten., and *tristis,* sad.]

contrite, *kon'trīt, adj.* broken-hearted for sin : penitent.—*adv.* **con'tritely.**—*ns.* **con'triteness; contrition** (*kon-trish'ən*), deep sorrow for sin : remorse. [L. *contrītus—conterĕre—con-,* wholly, *terĕre,* to bruise.]

contriturate, *kən-trit'ū-rāt, v.t.* to pulverise.

contrive, *kən-trīv', v.t.* to plan : to invent : to bring about or effect : to plot : (*Spens.*) to conceive, understand.—*adj.* **contriv'able,** that may be contrived.—*ns.* **contriv'ance, contrive'ment,** act of contriving : the thing contrived : invention : design : artifice; **contriv'er,** a schemer, a manager. [O.Fr. *controver—con-, trover,* to find.]

contrive, *kən-trīv', v.t.* (*Shak.*) to spend, as time. [L. *conterĕre, contrītum,* perf. *contrīvi,* to wear out.]

control, *kən-trōl', n.* restraint : authority : command : regulation : a check : a means of controlling or testing : a station for doing so : an experiment performed to afford a standard of comparison for other experiments (also **control experiment**) : a disembodied spirit or other agency supposed to direct a spiritualistic medium : a lever ('joy-stick') or wheel to move ailerons and elevator, and so control the movements of air-craft (also **control-column,** -**lever,** -**stick**) : a plane that controls the movements of an aircraft, as rudder, elevator, stabiliser (also **control-surface**).—*adj.* pertaining to control.—*v.t.* to check : to restrain : to govern (*pr.p.* **controll'ing;** *pa.t.* and *pa.p.* **controlled'**).—*n.* Formerly **comptroll', countrol', controul'.**—*adj.* **controll'able,** capable of, or subject to, control.—

ns. **controll'er,** one who checks the accounts of others by a counter-roll (also **comptroller**): an official authorised to control some activity or department: one who controls or regulates: an apparatus for regulating—e.g. the speed of an electric car; **controll'ership; control'ment,** act or power of controlling: state of being controlled: control. [Fr. *contrôle*, from *contre-rôle*, a duplicate register—L. *contrā*, against, *rotulus*, a roll.]

controvert, *kon'trə-vərt, v.t.* to oppose: to argue against: to dispute.—*n.* **con'troverse** (*Spens.*), dispute.—*adj.* **controver'sial** (*-shl*), relating to controversy.—*n.* **controver'sialist,** one given to controversy.—*adv.* **controver'sially.**—*ns.* **con'troversy,** a debate: contention: dispute: a war of opinions, in books, pamphlets, etc.—*adj.* **controvert'ible.** — *adv.* **controvert'ibly.** — *n.* **con'trovertist** (or *vert'*). [L. *contrā*, against, and *vertĕre*, to turn.]

contumacious, *kon-tū-mā'shəs, adj.* opposing lawful authority with contempt: obstinate: stubborn.—*adv.* **contuma'ciously.**—*ns.* **contuma'ciousness; contumacity** (*-mas'i-ti*); **con'tumacy** (*-mas-i*), obstinate disobedience or resistance. [L. *contumāx, -ācis,* insolent, from *con-* and *tumēre,* to swell, or *temnēre,* to despise.]

contumely, *kon'tū-mil-i* (also *-tū'*, or *-mēl'*, or *kon'tŭm-li,* etc.), *n.* insolence.—*adj.* **contume'lious** (*-mē'*), haughtily insolent.—*adv.* **contume'liously.**—*n.* **contume'liousness.** [L. *contumēlia,* prob. from the same source as *contumāx.*]

contund, *kən-tund', v.t.* to bruise or pound.—*v.t.* **contūse** (*-tūz'*), to beat or bruise: to crush.—*n.* **contusion** (*-tū'zhən*), act of bruising: state of being bruised: a bruise.—*adj.* **contū'sive,** apt to bruise. [L. *contundĕre, contūsum—con-, tundĕre,* to bruise.]

conundrum, *kən-un'drəm, n.* a riddle turning on some odd or fanciful resemblance between things quite unlike: any puzzling question. [Ety. dub.]

conurbation, *kon-ur-bā'shən, n.* a congeries of towns. [L. *con-,* together, *urbs,* city.]

convalesce, *kon-val-es', v.i.* to regain health.—*ns.* **convalesc'ence, convalesc'ency,** gradual recovery of health and strength.—*adj.* **convalesc'ent,** gradually recovering health.—*n.* one recovering health. [L. *con-,* and *valēscĕre—valēre,* to be strong.]

Convallaria, *kon-va-lā'ri-ä, n.* the lily-of-the-valley, a genus of Liliaceae. [L. *convallis,* a sheltered valley.]

convection, *kən-vek'shən, n.* transmission, esp. that of heat or electricity through liquids or gases by means of currents.—*adjs.* **convec'tion, convec'tional, convec'tive.**—*n.* **convec'tor,** apparatus for heating by convection. [L. *convectiō, -ōnis,* bringing together—*con-,* and *vehĕre,* to carry.]

convenance, *konᵍ-və-nänᵍs, kon'vən-ǎns, n.* what is suitable or proper :—(*pl.*) the conventional usages or social proprieties. [Fr.]

convene, *kən-vēn', v.i.* to come together: to assemble.—*v.t.* to call together.—*adj.* **convēn'able.**—*n.* **convēn'er,** one who convenes a meeting: the chairman of a committee. [Fr. *convenir*—L. *convenīre—con-,* together, and *venīre,* to come.]

convenient, *kən-vēn'yənt, adj.* suitable: handy: commodious.—*adj.* **convenable** (*kon'vən-ə-bl; obs.*), fitting.—*ns.* **convēn'ience, convēn'iency,** suitableness: an advantage: any particular domestic accommodation, as a closet, etc.—*adv.* **convēn'iently.** [L. *convenīre.*]

convent, *kon'vənt, n.* an association of persons secluded from the world and devoted to a religious life: the house in which they live, a monastery or nunnery.—*adj.* **convent'ual,** belonging to a convent.—*n.* a monk or nun: a member of one of the two divisions of the Franciscans, following a mitigated rule—the other being the *Observants.* [Through Fr. from L. *conventum, convenīre,* to come together.]

convent, *kən-vent', v.t.* (*Spens., Shak.*) to convene, summon, cite.—*v.i.* (*Shak.*) to be suitable. [L. *convenīre, conventum—con-, venīre,* to come.]

conventicle, *kən-vent'i-kl* (earlier *kon'vənt-*), *n.* a

secret, illegal, or forbidden religious meeting, applied esp. to those of English dissenters and to the Scottish Presbyterian field-preachings in the persecutions under Charles II and James VII: any private, clandestine, or irregular meeting.—*v.i.* to hold such a meeting.—*n.* **conven'ticler.** [L. *conventiculum,* a secret meeting of monks, dim. of *conventus.*]

convention, *kən-ven'shən, n.* the act of convening: an assembly, esp. of representatives or delegates for some common object: any extraordinary assembly called upon any special occasion: a parliament not summoned by the sovereign: an assembly for framing or revising a constitution: (*U.S.*) a meeting of political party delegates for nominating a candidate for the presidency or other purpose: any temporary treaty: an agreement: established usage: fashion: in card games, a mode of play in accordance with a recognised code of signals, not determined by the principles of the game.—*adj.* **conven'tional,** formed or adopted by convention: bound or influenced by convention: growing out of tacit agreement or custom: customary: not spontaneous: stylised: arbitrary.—*v.t.* **conven'tionalise,** to make conventional: to delineate according to a convention rather than nature.—*ns.* **conven'tionalism,** that which is established by tacit agreement, as a mode of speech, etc.; **conven'tionalist,** one who adheres to a convention, or is swayed by conventionalism; **conventional'ity,** state of being conventional: that which is established by use or custom.—*adv.* **conven'tionally.**—*adj.* **conven'tionary,** acting under contract.—*ns.* **conven'tioner, conven'tionist.** [L. *conventiō, -ōnis;* see **convene.**]

converge, *kən-vərj', v.i.* to tend towards or meet in one point or value: to acquire like character independently.—*ns.* **conver'gence, conver'gency.**—*adjs.* **conver'gent,** converging: due to or characterised by convergence; **conver'ging,** meeting in a point: coming nearer together: (*bot.*) with gradually approaching tips. [L. *con-, vergĕre,* to bend, to incline.]

conversazione, *kon-vər-sät-si-ō'nä, n.* a meeting for conversation, particularly on learned subjects :—*pl.* **conversazio'nes,** or **conversaziō'ni** (*-nē*). [It.]

converse, *kən-vərs', v.i.* to have intercourse: to talk familiarly: to commune.—*n.* **converse** (*kon'*), familiar intercourse: conversation: communing.—*adj.* **convers'able,** disposed to converse: sociable.—*adv.* **convers'ably.**—*ns.* **con'versance, con'versancy,** state of being conversant: familiarity.—*adj.* **con'versant** (also *-vers'*), acquainted by study: familiar: concerned or occupied: associating: (*obs.*) dwelling.—*n.* **conversā'tion,** intercourse: talk: familiar discourse; (*B.*) behaviour or deportment.—*adj.* **conversā'tional.**—*ns.* **conversā'tionalist, conversā'tionist,** one who excels in conversation; **conversā'tionism,** a colloquialism.—*adj.* **conver'sative,** ready to talk. [Fr. *converser*—L. *conversārī,* to turn about, go about, associate, dwell.—*con-,* intens. and *versāre,* to keep turning—*vertĕre,* to turn.]

convert, *kən-vərt', v.t.* (*obs.*) to turn about: to change or turn from one thing, condition, opinion, party or religion to another: to change from an irreligious to a holy life: to change by a spiritual experience: to change into the converse: to alter into something else (esp. iron into steel, a try into a goal, a merchant ship into a cruiser): to apply to a particular purpose.—*n.* (*kon'*), one who is converted.—*adj.* **con'verse,** reversed in order or relation.—*n.* that which is the opposite of another : (*log.*) a proposition in which the subject and predicate have changed places : (*math.*) a proposition in which that which is given and that which is to be proved in another proportion are interchanged.—*adv.* **converse'ly**—*ns.* **conver'sion,** change from one condition, use, opinion, party, religion or spiritual state to another: appropriation to a special purpose : (*logic*) act of constructing a proposition in accordance with the rules of direct inference, in which the terms of another proposition are interchanged; **con'vertend,** the proposition to be converted;

convert'er, one who converts : a vessel in which materials are changed from one condition to another (esp. iron into steel) : apparatus for making a change in electric current (also **conver'ter**); **convertibil'ity.**—*adj.* **convert'ible,** that may be converted : of currency, that may be converted into gold (or dollars) at a fixed price : equivalent. —*n.* anything convertible : a car with folding top. —*adv.* **convert'ibly.**—*n.* **con'vertite,** a convert : a reformed woman. [L. *convertĕre, conversum*— *con-, vertĕre,* to turn.]

convex, *kon'veks,* also *kon-veks',* *adj.* rising into a round form on the outside, the reverse of concave. —*n.* a convex figure, surface, body, or part : the vault of heaven, etc.—*adj.* **convexed',** made convex.—*adv.* **convex'edly.**—*ns.* **convex'ity,** roundness of form on the outside : a convex part or figure; **con'vexness** (or *veks'-*).—*adv.* **con'vexly** (or *veks'*).—*adjs.* **convex'o-con'cave,** convex on one side, and concave on the other; **convex'o-con'vex,** convex on both sides. [L. *convexus*—*convehĕre*—*con-, vehĕre,* to carry.]

convey, *kən-vā',* *v.t.* to carry : to transmit : to impart : to steal : to communicate, as ideas : to make over in law.—*adj.* **convey'able.**—*ns.* **convey'al**; **convey'ance,** act or means of conveying : trickery : a vehicle of any kind : (*law*) the act of transferring property : the writing that transfers it; **convey'ancer,** one whose business is the preparation of deeds for the transference of property; **convey'ancing**; **convey'er, convey'or,** a person or thing that conveys in any sense : a mechanism for continuous transport of materials, packages, goods in process of manufacture, etc. [O.Fr. *conveier*—L. *con-, via,* a way.]

convicinity, *kon-vi-sin'i-ti,* *n.* neighbourhood.

convict, *kən-vikt',* *v.t.* to prove guilty : to pronounce guilty.—*n.* **convict** (*kon'*), one convicted or found guilty of crime : one who has been condemned to penal servitude.—*ns.* **convic'tion,** act of convincing : strong belief : a proving guilty : (*theol.*) the condition of being consciously convicted of sin; **con'victism,** the convict system.— *adj.* **convict'ive,** able to convince or convict.— **carry conviction,** to bear irresistibly the stamp or proof of truth. [See **convince.**]

convince, *kən-vins',* *v.t.* (Shak., Spens.) to overcome, get the better of : to subdue the mind of by evidence : to satisfy as to truth or error : (*B.*) to convict : to refute.—*n.* **convince'ment.**—*adjs.* **convinc'ible**; **convinc'ing,** producing conviction. —*adv.* **convinc'ingly.** [L. *convincĕre, con-,* sig. completeness, and *vincĕre, victum,* to conquer.]

convivial, *kən-viv'i-əl,* *adj.* feasting or drinking in company : relating to a feast : social : jovial.—*v.i.* **convive** (-*vīv',* Shak.), to feast together.—*n.* (*kon'-vēv;* obs. *kon'vīv*) a companion at table.— *ns.* **conviv'ialist,** a convivial fellow; **convivial'ity.** —*adv.* **conviv'ially.** [L.,—*convivium,* a living together, a feast—*con-, vivĕre, vivĕre,* to live.]

convoke, *kən-vōk',* *v.t.* to call together : to assemble —also **convocate** (*kon'vō-kāt*).—*n.* **convoca'tion,** act of convoking : a provincial synod of clergy, esp. those of the provinces of Canterbury and York in the Church of England : the great legislative assembly of the university at Oxford and elsewhere. —*adj.* **convoca'tional.**—*n.* **convoca'tionist.** [L. *convocāre*—*con-,* together, and *vocāre, -ātum,* to call.]

convolve, *kən-volv',* *v.t.* to roll together, or one part on another.—*adjs.* **convolute** (*kon'və-lōōt, -lūt*), **-d,** rolled together, or one part on another : (*bot.*) coiled laterally with one margin within, one without : of a flower-bud, contorted : of a gasteropod shell, having the inner whorls concealed or overlapped by the outer.—*n.* **convolution** (-*lōō', -lū'*), twisting : a fold or sinuosity, esp. of the brain surface. [L. *con-,* together, *volvĕre, -ūtum,* to roll.]

Convolvulus, *kən-vol'vū-ləs,* *n.* the bindweed genus of twining or trailing plants, giving name to the fam. **Convolvūlā'ceae,** akin to the nightshade family : **convolvulus,** a plant of the genus or of the kindred Calystegia. [L.,—*convolvĕre.*]

convoy, *kon-voi',* *v.t.* to accompany for protection. —*n.* (*kon'*), the act of convoying : protection : that which convoys or is convoyed, esp. a ship or ships of war guarding a fleet of merchant-vessels, also the ships so protected : an honourable escort : a supply of stores, etc., under escort : a train of military wagons or the like. [Fr. *convoyer;* see **convey.**]

convulse, *kən-vuls',* *v.t.* to agitate violently : to affect by spasms.—*adj.* **convul'sible,** subject to convulsion.—*n.* **convul'sion,** any involuntary contraction of the voluntary muscles of the body, esp. such seizures in which the body is thrown into violent spasmodic contractions : any violent disturbance.—*adjs.* **convul'sional, convul'sionary,** pertaining to convulsions.—*ns.* **convul'sionary,** one who has convulsions, esp. one of a fanatical sect of Jansenists who sprang up in France about 1730; **convul'sionist,** a religious convulsionary : a believer in the importance of convulsions in geological history (opposed to *uniformitarian*).— *adj.* **convuls'ive,** attended with convulsions : spasmodic.—*adv.* **convuls'ively.**—*n.* **convuls'-iveness.** [L. *con,* inten., and *vellĕre, vulsum,* to pluck, to pull.]

cony, coney, *kō'ni,* or (historically right) *kun'i, n.* a rabbit : rabbit-skin : (*B.*) a hyrax : (*obs.*) a term of endearment for a woman : (*obs.*) a dupe.—*n.* **co'ny-burr'ow,** a rabbit-warren.—*v.t.* **co'ny-catch** (Shak.), to cheat.—*ns.* **co'ny-catcher,** a cheat; **co'ny-wool,** rabbits' fur. [Prob. through O.Fr. *conil,* from L. *cunĭculus,* a rabbit.]

coo, *kōō, v.i.* to make a sound as a dove : to converse fondly.—*v.t.* to murmur softly or ingratiatingly : to effect as by cooing : (*pr.p.* **coo'ing**; *pa.t.* and *pa.p.* **cooed,** *kōōd*).—*n.* the sound emitted by doves. —*n.* and *adj.* **coo'ing.**—*adv.* **coo'ingly.** [Imit.]

coo, *kōō, interj.* (slang) expressive of gentle wonder.

cooee, cooey, *kōō'ē, n.* and *interj.,* an Australian signal-call.—*v.i.* to utter the call. [Native word.]

coof, *kœf, kif, n.* (Scot.) a lout. [Origin obscure.]

cook, *kook, v.t.* to prepare as food by heat : to manipulate for any purpose, or falsify, as accounts, etc. : to concoct : (slang) to ruin : to spoil (as a chess-problem, by finding another way out).—*v.i.* to practise cookery : to undergo cooking.—*n.* one who undertakes or is skilled in cooking : a process of heating : an unforeseen alternative that ruins a chess-problem.—*ns.* **cook'er,** a stove, special vessel, or other apparatus for cooking : a variety suitable for cooking; **cook'ery,** the art or practice of cooking; **cook'ery-book,** a book of recipes for cooking dishes (*U.S.* **cook'-book**); **cook'-gen'eral, cook'-house'maid,** a servant combining the functions of cook and general servant or housemaid; **cook'-house,** a building or room for cooking in.—*n.pl.* **cook'ing-app'les,** etc., apples, etc., specially suitable for cooking.—*ns.* **cook'ing-range,** a stove adapted for cooking several things at once; **cook'maid,** a maid who cooks or assists a cook; **cook'-room,** a room in which food is cooked; **cook'-shop,** an eating-house.—**to cook one's goose** (slang), to finish off, to kill, to ruin, to spoil one's plans. [O.E. *cóc,* a cook (cf. Ger. *koch*)—L. *coquus.*]

cook, *kook, v.i.* to make the sound of the cuckoo.

cook, *kook, kook, v.i.* (Scot.) to appear and disappear by turns : to peep. [Origin obscure.]

cookie, *kook'i, n.* a kind of sweet cake used at tea : in Scotland, a plain bun : in U.S. (usu. **cook'y**), a biscuit.—*n.* **cook'ie-shine** (facet.), a tea-party. [Du. *koekje,* a cake.]

cool, *kōōl, adj.* slightly cold : free from excitement : calm : not zealous, ardent or cordial : indifferent : impudent : colloquially of a large sum of money, as *a cool thousand.*—*v.t.* to make cool : to allay or moderate, as heat, excitement, passion, etc.—*v.i.* to grow cool.—*n.* that which is cool : coolness.— *ns.* **cool'ant,** a cooling agent; **cool'er,** anything that cools : a vessel in which something is cooled.— *adj.* **cool'-head'ed,** not easily excited : capable of acting with composure.—*n.* **cool'-house,** a greenhouse kept at a cool temperature.—*adj.* **cool'ish,** somewhat cool.—*adv.* **cool'ly,** in a cool manner : indifferently : impudently.—*ns.* **cool'ness,** moderate cold : indifference : diminution of friendship : want of zeal; **cool'-tank'ard,** a cooling drink of wine and water, with lemon-juice, spices, and borage: a local name of borage; **coolth** (*dial.*), coolness.—*adj.* **cool'y** (*Spens.*) cool.—**cooling card** (*Shak.*) anything that discourages, or dashes hopes; **cool one's heels**, to be kept waiting. [O.E. *cól*; cf. Ger. *kühl*.]

coolie, cooly, *kōōl'i, n.* an Indian or Chinese labourer who has emigrated under contract to a foreign land : a European's name for a hired native labourer in India and China. [Prob. *Koli*, a tribe of W. India; or Tamil, *kūli*, hire.]

coom, *kōōm, n.* soot : coal-dust : dust of various kinds.—*v.t.* to begrime.—*adj.* **coom'y.** [App. Northern form of **culm.**]

coom, *kōōm, n.* (*Scot.*) the wooden centering on which a bridge is built : anything arched or vaulted.—*adj.* **coom'-ceiled,** said of a garret with the inside ceiling sloping from the wall. [Origin obscure.]

coomb, comb(e), *kōōm, n.* a deep little wooded valley : a hollow in a hillside. [O.E. *cumb*, a hollow.]

coomb, comb, *kōōm, n.* a measure of capacity=4 bushels. [O.E. *cumb*, a measure.]

coon, *kōōn, n.* the raccoon : a sly fellow : a negro.— *n.* **coon'-song,** a nigger-song.—**a gone coon,** one whose case is hopeless. [U.S.; for **raccoon.**]

coon-can, *kōōn'kan, n.* a card game in which one tries to form sequences. [Sp. *con quién* with whom.]

coontie, coonty, *kōōn'ti, n.* an American cycad yielding a sort of arrowroot. [Seminole *kunti*.]

coop, *kōōp, n.* a wicker basket : a box or cage for fowls or small animals : a prison.—*v.t.* to confine in a coop or elsewhere. [Perh. from an unknown O.E. *cúpe*, collateral with *cýpe*, cask; cf. L. *cūpa*, cask.]

cooper, *kōōp'ər, n.* one who makes tubs, casks, etc. : a mixture of stout and porter.—*v.t.* to repair (tubs, etc.) : to prepare, patch up.—*ns.* **coop'erage,** the work or workshop of a cooper : the sum paid for a cooper's work; **coop'ering; coop'ery,** the business of a cooper. [Also L.G.—L.L. *cūpārius—cūpa*, cask; cf. **coop.**]

co-op, *kō-op', (coll.)* short for **cooperative society** or **store.**

cooper, *kōp'er.* See **coper.**

co-operate, *kō-op'ər-āt, v.i.* to work together.—*n.* **co-opera'tion,** joint operation : combination in co-operative societies :—*adjs.* **co-op'erative** (also *n.*); **co-op'erant,** working together.—*n.* **co-op'erator,** one who co-operates : a member of a co-operative society.—**co-operating grace** (*theol.*), the R.C., Arminian, and Socinian doctrine that the human will co-operates with the divine in the matter of saving grace; **co-operative society,** an association for supplying goods or for carrying on some branch of industry, the profits going to the members; **co-operative store,** the shop of a co-operative society. [**co-**, together, and **operate.**]

co-opt, *kō-opt', v.t.* to elect into any body by the votes of its members.—*ns.* **co-opta'tion, co-op'tion.**—*adj.* **co-op'tative.** [L. *cooptāre, -ātum— co-,* together, *optāre,* to choose.]

co-ordinate, *kō-or'di-nāt, adj.* of the same order or rank : pertaining to or involving co-ordination or co-ordinates.—*v.t.* to place or classify in the same order or rank : to adjust the relations or movements of : to combine or integrate harmoniously : to harmonise.—*n.* an element of the same order as another : each of a system of two or more magnitudes used to define the position of a point, line, or surface by reference to a fixed system of lines, points, etc.—*v.i.* **co-or'dinance,** a joint ordinance. —*adv.* **co-or'dinately.**—*ns.* **co-or'dinateness; co-ordina'tion.**—*adj.* **co-or'dinative:** co-ordinating : co-ordinated, indicating co-ordination; **co-ordinate geometry,** geometry by the use of co-ordinates, analytical geometry.

coosen, coosin, obs. spellings of **cousin, cozen.**

coost, *kast,* a Scottish form of **cast** (*pa.t.*).

coot, *kōōt, n.* a short-tailed water-fowl, with a characteristic white spot—an extension of the bill— on the forehead; hence called *bald*, as in phrase, *bald as a coot.* [M.E. *cote*; cf. Du. *koet*.]

coot. See **cuit.**

cop, *kop, n.* a top or head of anything; a conical ball of thread on a spindle.—Also **cop'in.**—*adj.* **copped,** rising to a cop or head. [O.E. *cop, copp.*]

cop, *kop, v.t.* (*slang*) to capture : to catch.—*ns.* **cop** (*slang*), a policeman : a capture; **copp'er** (*slang*), a policeman.

copaiba, copaiva, *kō-pī'bä, -vä,* or -*pä', n.* a balsam obtained from S. American caesalpiniaceous trees (*Copaifera*) much used in medicine. [Sp. and Port. from Tupí.]

copal, *kō'pal, n.* a hard resin got from many tropical trees, and also fossil. [Sp.,—Nahuatl *copalli,* resin.]

coparcener, *kō-pär'sən-ər, n.* a joint heir to an undivided property.—*n.* and *adj.* **copar'cenery, -ary.**

copartner, *kō-pärt'nər, n.* a joint partner.—*ns.* **copart'nership, copart'nery.**

copataine, *kop'ə-tān, adj.* (*Shak.*) high-crowned like a sugar-loaf. [Ety. obscure.]

copatriot, a form of **compatriot.**

cope, *kōp, n.* a covering : a cap or hood : anything spread overhead : a coping : a semicircular, sleeveless hooded vestment worn over the alb or surplice in processions, at solemn lauds and vespers.—*v.t.* to cover as with a cope.—*ns.* **cope'-stone,** **cop'ing-stone,** a stone that copes or tops a wall; **cop'ing,** the covering course of masonry of a wall : **cop'ing-saw,** (*U.S.*) a narrow saw with a handle at each end, for cutting curves. [M.E. *cape*— hypothetical O.E. *cápe*—L.L. *cāpa;* cf. **cap.**]

cope, *kōp, v t.* and *v.i.* to barter or exchange. [Cf. Du. *koopen.*]

cope, *kōp, v.i.* to contend : to have to do, esp. on equal terms or successfully.—*v.t.* (*Shak.*) to encounter, meet : to match.—*n.* **copes'-mate** (*Spens., Shak.*), a companion : an accomplice : a partner : an adversary : a paramour. [Fr. *couper*—L. *colaphus* (Gr. *kolaphos*), a buffet.]

cope, *kōp, v.t.* (*obs.*) to tie or sew up the mouth of (a ferret). [Origin obscure; cf. **uncape, uncope.**]

copeck. Same as **kopeck.**

copepod, *kō'pe-pod, n.* a member of the **Copep'oda,** a class of crustacea, minute animals with oarlike swimming feet. [Gr. *kōpē,* handle, oar, *pous, podos,* foot.]

coper, often **cooper,** *kop'ər, n.* a ship employed in surreptitiously supplying strong drink to deep-sea fishermen.—*v.i.* to supply liquor in such a way. [Du. *kooper—koopen,* to trade; cf. Ger. *kaufen,* to buy; O.E. *céapan.*]

Copernican, *ko-pər'ni-kən, adj.* relating to *Copernicus,* the famous Prussian astronomer (1473-1543), or to his system, in which the earth revolves about the sun.

copier. See **copy.**

coping. See **cope** (1).

co-pilot, *kō'pī-lət, n.* a fellow pilot.

copious, *kō'pi-əs, adj.* plentiful : overflowing : abounding : rich in words : not concise.—*adv.* **co'piously.**—*n.* **co'piousness.** [L. *cōpiōsus— cōpia,* plenty—*co-,* inten., and *ops, opis,* wealth.]

co-polymer, *kō-pol'i-mər, n.* a substance polymerised along with another, the result being a chemical compound, not a mixture.—*v.t.* **copol'ymerise.**—*n.* **co-polymerisā'tion.**

co-portion, *kō-pōr'shən, n.* (*Spens.*) share.

copper, *kop'ər, n.* a moderately hard metal (symbol Cu for L. *cuprum;* atomic number 29), of a reddish colour, perhaps the first metal used by man : money made of copper : a copper coin : a copper vessel : a boiler (*orig.* of copper) for clothes, or soap, etc.—*adj.* made of copper : coppercoloured.—*v.t.* to cover with copper.—*n.* **copp'erbeech',** a variety of the common beech with purplish, copper-coloured leaves.—*adj.* **copp'erbott'omed,** having the bottom covered with copper : sound, esp. financially.—Also *v.t.*—*n.* **copp'er-cap'tain,** one who styles himself captain without grounds.—*adjs.* **copp'er-faced,** faced with copper, as type; **copp'er-fas'tened,** fastened with copper bolts.—*ns.* **copp'er-glance',** a mineral, cuprous sulphide; **copp'erhead,** a venomous United States snake akin to the rattle-snake :

(*U.S.*) a northern sympathiser with the South in the Civil War; copp'ering, the act of sheathing with copper : a covering of copper.—*adjs.* copp'er-ish, somewhat like copper.—*ns.* copp'er-nick'el, niccolite, a copper-red mineral, arsenide of nickel; copp'er-nose, a red nose; copp'erplate, a plate of polished copper on which something has been engraved: an impression taken from the plate: faultless handwriting; copp'er-pyrī'tes, a yellow double sulphide of copper and iron; copp'er-skin, an American Indian; copp'er-smith, work in copper : a smith who works in copper; copp'er-work, a place where copper is wrought or manu-factured; copp'er-worm, the ship-worm.—*adj.* copp'ery, like copper.—Copper Age, a stage in culture in some regions leading up to the Bronze Age, characterised by the use of copper unmixed with tin; hot coppers, parched tongue and throat after a bout of drinking. [O.E. *copor*—L.L. *cuper*—L. *cuprum*, a form of *cyprium* (*aes*), Cyprian (brass), because found in *Cyprus*.]

copperas, *kop'ər-as, n.* a name formerly applied to copper and other sulphates, now only to ferrous sulphate. [Fr. *couperose* (It. *coparosa*), perh.—L. *cuprī rosa*, rose of copper, or *aqua cuprōsa*, copper water.]

coppice, *kop'is, copse, kops, ns.* a wood of small growth for periodical cutting : a wood of sprouts from cut stumps.—*v.t.* to make into coppice : to cover with coppice.—*n.* copse'wood.—*adj.* cop'sy. [O.Fr. *copeiz*, wood newly cut—L.L. *colpare*, to cut—L. *colaphus*—Gr. *kolaphos*, a buffet.]

coppin. See cop (1).

copple, *kop'l, n.* (*obs.*) a bird's crest.—*n.* copp'le-crown.—*adj.* copp'le-crowned. [App. from cop.]

copple-stone, an obsolete form of cobble-stone.

copra, *kop'rä, n.* the dried kernel of the coconut, yielding coconut oil. [Port., from Malayalam.]

co-presence, *ko-prez'əns, n.* presence together.—*adj.* co-pres'ent.

copro-, in composition, dung.—*n.* coprolite (*kop'rə-lit;* Gr. *lithos*, stone), a piece of fossil dung: loosely applied to phosphatic concretions.—*adj.* coprolitic (-*lit'ik*).—*ns.* coprol'ogy (Gr. *logos*, dicourse), the unclean in literature and art; coproph'agan (Gr. *phagein*, to eat), a dung-beetle.—*n.* coproph'agist (-*jist*), a dung-eater.—*adj.* coproph'agous.—*n.* coprophil'ia (Gr. *philiā*, love), morbid pleasure in dung or filth.—*adj.* coproph'ilous, delighting in dung or filth : growing on or in dung.—*n.* copros'terol, a compound formed from cholesterol in the intestine. [Gr. *kopros*, dung.]

copse, copsewood. See coppice.

Copt, *kopt, n.* a Christian descendant of the ancient Egyptians.—*adj.* Copt'ic.—*n.* the language of the Copts. [Gr. *Aigyptios*, Egyptian.]

copula, *kop'ū-lä, n.* that which joins together : a bond or tie : copulation : (*logic*) the word joining the subject and predicate.—*adj.* cop'ular.—*v.t.* and *v.i.* cop'ulāte, to unite in sexual intercourse.—*n.* copulā'tion.—*adj.* cop'ulātive, uniting: indi-cating combination, not alternative or adversative relation.—*n.* (*gram.*) a conjunction that does this.—*adj.* cop'ulatory. [L. *cōpula*—*co-, apère,* to join.]

copy, *kop'i, n.* (*obs.*) abundance, copiousness: an imitation : a transcript : a reproduction : an exemplar : that which is imitated or reproduced : a specimen to be imitated : matter for printing : a size of paper, 16 by 20 inches.—*v.t.* to write, paint, etc. after : to imitate closely : to transcribe : to reproduce or duplicate by copying-press or other-wise.—*v.i.* to make a copy : to follow : to look on a schoolfellow's work and filch the result (*pr.p.* cop'ying; *pa.t.* and *pa.p.* cop'ied).—*ns.* cop'ier, one who copies : an imitator; cop'y-book, a writing or drawing book of models printed for imitation : (*U.S.*) a letter-book, or collection of copies of documents; cop'y-cat (*slang*) a term applied in resentful derision to an imitator.—*v.t.* and *v.i.* to imitate.—*ns.* cop'yhold (*Eng. law*), a species of estate or right of holding land, according to the custom of a manor, by copy of the roll originally made by the steward of the lord's court;

cop'yholder, a holder of land by copyhold : an assistant who reads copy aloud to a proof-reader; cop'ying-ink', ink suitable for copying by im-pression; cop'ying(-ink)-pencil, an ink-pencil; cop'ying-press, a machine for copying manuscript letters by pressure; cop'yism, servile or plagiaristic copying; cop'yist, one whose business is to copy documents : a mere copier; copy'right, the sole right to reproduce a literary, dramatic, musical, or artistic work—also to perform, translate, film, or record such a work (in the United Kingdom, since July 1, 1912, for books the term is the author's lifetime and fifty years after his death).—*adj.* protected by copyright.—*v.t.* to secure the copy-right of.—*n.* cop'y-wri'ter, a writer of copy (esp. advertisements) for the press.—a copy of verses, a set of verses, esp. a college exercise. [Fr. *copie*, from L. *cōpia*, plenty; in L.L. a transcript.]

coquelicot, *kok'li-kō, n.* (*Jane Austen*) a brilliant red, the colour of the red poppy. [Fr., poppy.]

coquet, coquette, *ko-, kō-ket', v.i.* to flirt : to dally.—*v.t.* (*obs.*) to flirt with (*pr.p.* coquet'ting; *pa.p.* and *pa.t.* coquet'ed).—*ns.* cō'quetry (-*kit-ri*), act of coquetting : attempt to attract admiration, with-out serious affection : deceit in love : any artful prettiness; coquette', a woman (rarely a man) who seeks admiration from mere vanity : a flirt.—Also *adj.*—*adj.* coquett'ish, practising coquetry: be-fitting a coquette.—*adv.* coquett'ishly.—*n.* co-quett'ishness. [Fr. *coqueter*—*coquet,* dim. of *coq,* a cock.]

coquilla, *kō-kil'yä, n.* the nut of the piassava palm (Attalea), whose mottled, dark-brown endosperm is used by button-makers and turners. [Sp.; dim. of *coca,* shell.]

coquimbite, *kō-kim'bīt, n.* a yellowish hydrous sulphate of iron found in *Coquimbo.*

coquito, *kō-kē'tō, n.* a beautiful Chilean palm, *Jubaea spectabilis.* [Sp. dim. of *coco,* coco-palm.]

cor, *kor, n.* a Hebrew measure, the homer, 10 ephahs or baths (roughly 11 bushels). [Heb. *kōr,* round vessel.]

coracle, *kor'ə-kl, n.* a small oval rowing-boat used in Wales, made of skins or oilcloth stretch on wickerwork. [W. *corwgl*—*corwg,* anything round; Gael. *curach,* a wicker-boat.]

coracoid, *kor'ə-koid, adj.* shaped like a crow's beak.—*n.* (*anat.*) a paired ventral bone in the breast-girdle, forming along with the scapula the articula-tion for the fore-limb; in mammals, except monotremes, reduced to a coracoid process, fused to the scapula. [Gr. *korax, korakos,* a crow, and *eidos,* form.]

co-radicate, *kō-rad'i-kāt, adj.* (*philol.*) of the same root.

coraggio, *kor-ad'jō, interj.* courage! [It.]

coral, *kor'əl, n.* a hard substance of various colours growing on the bottom of the sea, skeleton, mostly calcareous, of Anthozoa and of some Hydrozoa: the animal or colony that produces it : a young child's toy of coral or other material for biting.—*adj.* made of or like coral, esp. red coral.—*ns.* cor'al-berr'y, an American shrub of the snow-berry genus, or its red berry; cor'al-fish, a tropical, spiny-finned fish of many kinds abundant about coral reefs; cor'al-is'land.—*adjs.* corallā'ceous, like, or having the qualities of, coral.—*n.* Corallian (-*al'; geol.*) a Jurassic formation over-lying the Oxfordian, including the Coral-Rag and Coralline Oolite.—*adjs.* corallif'erous, containing coral; coralliform (-*al'*), having the form of coral; corallig'enous, producing coral; cor'alline, of, like, or containing coral.—*n.* a common limy sea-weed (*Corallina*) of a delicate pinkish or purplish colour : a coral-like substance or animal.—*n.* cor'allite, the cup of a simple coral or of one polyp : a fossil coral.—*adjs.* cor'alloid, coralloid'-al, in the form of coral : resembling coral.—*ns.* corallum (-*al'*), the skeleton of a coral colony : —*pl.* corall'a; Cor'al-Rag, a coarse limestone rock formed chiefly of coral in the Corallian formation; cor'al-reef', a reef or bank formed by the growth and deposit of coral; cor'al-rock', a limestone composed of coral; cor'al-root', a species of Cardamine with knobbed rootstock : a genus of

Neutral vowels in unaccented syllables : *el'ə-mənt, in'fənt, ran'dəm*

orchids (*Corallorhiza*) with coral-like rootstock; **cor′al-snake**, an American genus, Elaps (or Micrurus), of small venomous snakes; **cor′al-tree**, a tropical genus (Erythrina) of trees and shrubs with red coral-like flowers; **cor′al-wort**, coral-root, in either sense.—**Coralline Crag** (*geol.*) a division of the English Pliocene, shelly sands and clays with fossil polyzoa; **Coralline Oolite**, a massive limestone underlying the Coral-Rag. [L. *corallum* —Gr. *korallion*.]

coranach. See **coronach**.

cor anglais, *kor än⁹-glā′*, an oboe set a fifth lower than the ordinary oboe—also called (It.) **corno inglese** (*kor′nō ing-glā′sä*). [Fr., English horn, but probably not English.]

coranto, *ko-ränt′ō*, *n*. a rapid and lively dance: the music for it, in triple time.—Also **courante** (*kōō-rän⁹t*). [Fr. *courante*, lit. running—L. *currĕre*, to run—(It. *coranta*, from Fr.).]

corban, *kor′ban*, *n*. anything devoted to God in fulfilment of a vow. [Heb. *qorbān*, an offering, sacrifice.]

corbe, *korb* (*Spens.*). See **corbel**, **courbe**.

corbeau, *kor-bō′*, *n*. a blackish green colour. [Fr., raven.]

corbeil, *kor′bel*, *-be′i*, *n*. (*fort.*) a basket filled with earth, set up as a protection: (*archit.*) a carved representation of a basket.—*n*. **corbeille′**, a basket of flowers. [Fr. *corbeille*—L. *corbicula*, dim. of *corbis*, a basket.]

corbel, *kor′bl*, *n*. (*archit.*) a projection from the face of a wall, supporting a weight.—*adj*. **cor′belled**.— *ns*. **cor′belling**; **cor′bel-tä′ble**, a row of corbels and the parapet or cornice they support. [O.Fr. *corbel*—L.L. *corvellus*, dim. of *corvus*, a raven.]

corbicula, *kor-bik′ū-lä*, *n*. the pollen basket of bees, consisting of the dilated posterior tibia with its fringe of long hairs:—*pl*. **corbic′ulae** (*-lē*).—*adj*. **corbic′ulate**. [L., dim. of *corbis*, a basket.]

corbie, *kor′bi*, *n*. a raven: a crow.—**corbie messenger** (*Scot.*), one who returns too late, or not at all; **cor′bie-steps**, crow-steps. [O.Fr. *corbin*—L. *corvus*, a crow.]

corcass, *kor′kas*, *n*. in Ireland a salt-marsh, or readily flooded land by a river. [Ir. *corcach*.]

Corchorus, *kor′ko-rəs*, *n*. the jute genus. [Gr. *korchoros*, the name of a plant.]

cord, *kord*, *n*. a small rope or thick string: something resembling a cord (as spinal cord, umbilical cord): anything that binds or restrains : a measure of cut wood (128 cubic feet), orig. determined by use of a cord or string : a raised rib on cloth : a string crossing the back of a book in binding.—*v.t.* to supply with a cord : to bind with a cord.—*n*. **cord′age**, a quantity of cords or ropes, as the rigging of a ship, etc.—*adj*. **cord′ed**, fastened with cords : (*her.*) wound about with cords: ribbed : piled in cords.—*ns*. **cord′-grass**, a genus (*Spartina*) of grasses of which one species found in muddy salt-marshes is used for making ropes; **cord′ing**, the act of binding: cordage; **cord′ite**, a cord-like smokeless explosive; **cord′-wood**, wood put up in cords. [Fr.—*corde*—L. *chorda*; see **chord**.]

Cordaites, *kor-dā-ī′tēz*, *n*. a Palaeozoic genus of fossil plants, typical of the family **Cordaitā′ceae**, gymnosperms nearer the conifers than the cycads. [Named after A. K. J. *Corda*, botanist (1809-49).]

cordate, *kor′dāt*, *adj*. heart-shaped : (*bot.*) having the base indented next the petiole.—*adj*. **cord′i-form**, heart-shaped. [L. *cordātus* (in modern sense)—L. *cor*, *cordis*, the heart.]

Cordelier, *kor-də-lēr′*, *n*. a Franciscan friar, from the knotted cord worn as a girdle: (in *pl*.) a club in the French Revolution, meeting in an old Cordelier convent. [O.Fr. *cordele*, dim. of *corde*, a rope.]

cordial, *kor′di-əl*, *adj*. hearty: with warmth of heart: sincere: affectionate: reviving the heart or spirits.—*n*. anything which revives or comforts the heart: a medicine or drink for refreshing the spirits : a beverage containing alcohol or sugar or stimulating drugs.—*v.i.* **cor′dialise**, to become cordial, to fraternise.—*ns*. **cordiality** (*-al′i-ti*), **cor′dialness**.—*adv*. **cor′dially**. [Fr.,—L. *cor*, *cordis*, the heart.]

cordierite, *kor′di-ər-īt*, *n*. the mineral iolite or dichroite. [After P. L. A. *Cordier* (1777-1861), French mineralogist.]

cordillera, *kor-dil-yā′rä*, *n*. a chain of mountains, as the Andes and Rocky Mountains. [Sp.,—Old Sp. *cordilla*—L. *chorda*, cord—Gr. *chordē*.]

cordiner, *kor′di-nər*. Same as **cordwainer**.

córdoba, *kor′dō-bä*, *n*. the monetary unit of Nicaragua. [Named after Francisco Fernández de *Córdoba* (d. about 1518).]

cordon, *kor′don*, *-dən*, *n*. a cord or ribbon bestowed as a badge of honour : (*fort.*) a row of stones along the line of a rampart : a line of men set to prevent passage : a single-stemmed fruit-tree.—*v.t.* to enclose with a cordon. [Fr.]

cordovan, *kor′do-vən*, **cordwain**, *kord′wān*, *n*. goat-skin leather, originally from Cordova (*Córdoba*) in Spain.—*ns*. **cord′wainer**, **cord′iner**, a worker in cordovan or cordwain: a shoemaker; **cord′-wainery**.

corduroy, *kor-də-roi′*, or *kor′*, *n*. a ribbed fustian, a cotton stuff made after the fashion of velvet : (in *pl*.) corduroy trousers.—*adj*. of corduroy.— **corduroy road**, a track laid transversely with tree-trunks. [Perh. Fr. *corde du roi*, king's cord.]

Cordyline, *kor-di-lī′nē*, *n*. a tropical and subtropical liliaceous genus similar to the dragon-tree. [Gr. *kordylē*, club.]

core, *kor*, *n*. the innermost part, esp. of fruit.—*v.t.* to take out the core of.—*adjs*. **cored**, having the core removed : cast by means of a core : having a core; **core′less**, without core : pithless : hollow. —*n*. **cor′er**, an instrument for removing the core. [Poss. L. *cor*, the heart, or Fr. *cor*, horn, corn (on the foot), or *corps*, body.]

core, *kōr*, *n*. a company, gang, shift. [See **corps**.]

co-regent, *kō-rē′jənt*, *n*. a joint-regent.

Coregonus, *kor-i-gō′nəs*, *n*. whitefish, a genus of herring-like fishes of the salmon family, pollan, vendace, etc.—*adj*. **corego′nine**. [Gr. *korē*, pupil of the eye, *gōniā*, angle.]

co-relation, **co-relative**. See **correlate**.

co-religionist, *kō-ra-lij′ən-ist*, *n*. one of the same religion as another.

co-respondent, *kō-ra-spond′ənt*, *n*. (*law*) a man or woman charged with adultery, and proceeded against along with the wife or husband who is the respondent.

corf, *korf*, *n*. a coal-miner's basket, now usu. a tub or trolley : a cage for fish or lobsters :—*pl*. **corves** (*korvz*).—*n*. **corf′-house** (*Scot.*), a salmon-curing house. [Du.—L. *corbis*, basket.]

corgi, *kor′gē*, *n*. a small Welsh dog. [Welsh *corr*, dwarf, *ci*, dog.]

coriander, *kor-i-an′dər*, *n*. an umbelliferous plant (*Coriandrum sativum*), whose seeds are used as spice, etc.—*n*. **corian′der-seed**. [Fr. *coriandre*— L. *coriandrum*—Gr. *koriannon*.]

Corinthian, *kor-inth′i-ən*, *adj*. of Corinth (Gr. *Korinthos*) in Greece : of an ornate style of Greek architecture, with acanthus capitals : over-brilliant in literary style : profligate.—*n*. a profligate : a man of fashion : an amateur sportsman.—*n*. **Cor′inth** (*obs.*) a brothel.—*v.i.* **corinth′ianise**, to be licentious.—**Corinthian brass**, **bronze**, an alloy made in Corinth, much valued in ancient times : assurance or effrontery.

corium, *kō′ri-um*, *n*. (*ant.*) leather armour : (*anat.*) the true skin, under the epidermis.—*adjs*. **coriā′ceous**, **co′rious**, leathery. [L. *corium*—Gr. *chorion*, skin, leather.]

co-rival, **co-rivalry**, **co-rivalship**. See **corrival**.

cork, *kork*, *n*. the outer bark of the cork-tree, an oak found in S. Europe, N. Africa, etc. : a stopper made of cork : any stopper : (*bot.*) a tissue of close-fitting, thick-walled cells, almost air-tight and water tight, forming bark or covering the surfaces of wounds : a piece of cork : a float of cork.—*adj*. made of cork.—*v.t.* to stop with a cork : to stop up. —*ns*. **cork′age**, corking or uncorking of bottles : a charge made by hotel-keepers for uncorking of bottles when the liquor has not been supplied from the house.—*ns*. **cork′-borer**, an instrument for boring holes in corks to receive glass tubes in chemical apparatus; **cork′-cam′bium**, phellogen;

cork'-car'pet, -lino'leum, -mat, a floor-covering, **mat,** made of pieces of cork with rubber and linseed oil; **cork'-cutter,** one employed in cutting corks for bottles, etc. : an instrument used for this. —*adj.* **corked,** stopped as by a cork : tainted as if by the cork, as wine : blackened by burnt cork.— *ns.* **cork'er,** a finisher : (*slang*) a conclusive argument : a person or thing that surpasses; **cork'-heel',** a shoe-heel of cork.—*adj.* **cork'-heeled',** having cork heels; wanton.—*n.* **cork'iness.**—*adj.* **cork'ing** (*slang*), surpassing.—*ns.* **cork'-jack'et,** a jacket made of or lined with cork, to aid in swimming; **cork'-leg,** an artificial leg; **cork'-oak,** a species of oak (*Quercus Suber*) which supplies the cork of commerce in Spain and Portugal; **cork'-screw,** a screw for drawing corks from bottles.— *adj.* like a cork-screw in shape.—*v.i.* to move in a spiral manner.—*v.t.* to pull out with difficulty, as a cork : to obtain information from by force or cunning.—*ns.* **cork'-sole',** an inner shoe-sole made of cork; **cork'-tree,** the cork-oak : applied to various trees with corky bark or very light wood; **cork'wing,** the goldsinny; **cork'wood,** very light wood : applied to many trees with light wood, e.g. **balsa,** alligator apple.—*adj.* **cork'y,** of or resembling cork : (*Shak.*) withered. [Perh. from Sp. *alcorque,* cork slipper, which may be from L. *quercus,* oak, with the Arabic article *al.* Sp. has also *corche, corcha, corcho,* perh. L. *cortex,* bark, rind.]

corking-pin, *kork'ing-pin, n.* a pin of the largest size. [Perh. for **calking-pin.**]

corkir, korkir, *kor'kər, n.* (*Scot.*) a lichen used for dyeing (red or purple). [Gael. *corcur*—L. *purpura,* purple.]

corm, *korm, n.* a short, bulbous, subterranean stem as in the crocus.—*n.* **corm'ophyte** (*-fīt*), a plant differentiated into leaf, stem, and root.—*adj.* **cormophyt'ic** (*-fit'*).—*n.* **corm'us,** the differentiated body of a cormophyte : the whole body of a compound animal. [Gr. *kormos,* the lopped trunk of a tree.]

cormorant, *kor'mə-rənt, n.* a genus (*Phalacrocorax*) of web-footed sea-birds, of great voracity : a glutton. [Fr. *cormoran,* from L. *corvus marīnus,* sea crow.]

corn, *korn, n.* a grain, hard particle : a kernel, small hard seed : collectively seeds of cereal plants, or the plants themselves :—esp. (in England) wheat, (in Scotland and Ireland) oats, (in North America) maize.—*adj.* of, for, pertaining to, made from, growing among, feeding upon, corn : granular.— *v.t.* to make granular : to sprinkle with grains of salt : to salt : (*Scot.*) to give corn to, as a horse : (*slang*) to intoxicate.—*v.i.* to form seed.—*ns.* **corn'-baby** (see **kirn**); **corn'-ball,** (*U.S.*) a sweetened ball of popcorn; **corn'-bin,** a bin for corn; **corn'-bor'er,** a European moth (*Pyrausta nubilalis*) whose larvae have become a maize pest in America; **corn'brake',** a maize plantation; **corn'-bran'dy,** spirits made from grain; whisky; **corn'brash,** (*geol.*) a clayey limestone of the Oolite, giving good corn soils; **corn'-bread, -cake** (*U.S.*), bread, a cake, made of maize meal; **corn'-chandler,** a retailer of grain; **corn'-chandlery;** **corn'-cob,** the woody axis of a maize ear : a corn-cob pipe; **corn'cockle,** a tall, beautiful cornfield weed (*Agrostemma Githago*) akin to the campions; **corn'-cracker** (*U.S.*) a poor white : a Kentuckian; **corn'crake,** a rail with characteristic cry, inhabiting cornfields; **corn'-dealer, -factor, -merchant,** one who buys and sells corn; **corn'-dodger** (*U.S.*), a cake, small loaf, or dumpling of maize.—*p.adj.* **corned,** granulated : salted (e.g. **corned** beef—also **corn'-beef**).—*n.* **corn'-exchange',** a mart for trade in corn.—*adj.* **corn'-fed,** fed on corn : well-fed.—*ns.* **corn'field,** a field in which corn is growing; **corn'-flag,** a gladiolus; **corn'-flour,** finely ground maize, rice, or other grain : a pudding made of it : **corn'flower,** the bluebottle, a beautiful blue-flowered cornfield weed of the Compositae (*Centaurea Cyanus*); **corn'-fly,** the gout-fly; **corn'husk** (*U.S.*), a cornshuck; **corn'husker,** a person or machine that removes cornhusks; **corn'husking;** **corn'ing-house,** a place where gunpowder is granulated;

corn'land, ground suitable for growing grain; **corn'-law,** a law regulating trade in grain, esp. (in *pl.*) laws that restricted importation to Britain by a duty, repealed 1846; **corn'loft,** a granary; **corn'-maiden** (see **kirn**); **corn'-mar'igold,** a yellow cornfield chrysanthemum; **corn'-mill,** a flour-mill; **corn'miller;** **corn'-moth,** a moth of the clothes-moth genus (*Tinea granella*) whose larvae feed on grain; **corn'pipe,** a musical instrument made of a stalk of oat or other cereal; **corn'-pit** (*U.S.*), part of an exchange where business is done in maize; **corn'-pone** (*U.S.*), maize-bread : a maize loaf; **corn'-popper,** a pan or grating for popping corn; **corn'-rent,** rent paid in corn, not money; **corn'-rig** (*Scot.*), a ridge or strip on which oats are grown; **corn'-sal'ad,** lamb's lettuce, a genus (*Valerianella*) of humble weeds of the valerian family, sometimes used as salads; **corn'-shuck** (*U.S.*), the leaves enclosing a maize ear; **corn'-shucking,** the removal of corn-shucks : an assembly for the purpose; **corn'-snow,** granulated snow; **corn'-spirit,** a vegetation god or spirit concerned in the growth of corn; **corn'stalk,** a stalk of corn : a tall thin person, esp. one born in New South Wales; **corn'starch,** maize starch or flour, for puddings; **corn'stone,** a silicious limestone, favourable for corn-growing; **corn'-thrips,** a minute insect of the Thysanura, that sucks the sap of grain; **corn'-van,** an instrument for winnowing corn; **corn'-whisky,** an American whisky made from maize; **corn'-weevil,** a small weevil (*Calandra granaria*), destructive in granaries; **corn'worm,** a corn-weevil : a corn-moth larva.— *adj.* **corn'y,** like corn : produced from corn : (*slang*) tipsy.—**corn-cob pipe,** a tobacco-pipe with the bowl made of a maize cob; **corn in Egypt,** abundance (Gen. xlii. 2.). [O.E. *corn;* Goth. *kaurn;* akin to L. *grānum.*]

corn, *korn, n.* a small hard growth chiefly on the toe or foot, resulting from an increase of thickness of cuticle, caused by pressure or friction.—*ns.* **corn'-cure,** a remedy for corns; **corn'-cutter,** one who cuts corns.—*adj.* **corn'eous,** horny.—*ns.* **corn'icle, cornic'ulum,** a little horn : a hornlike process; *esp.* one of the wax-secreting tubes of a greenfly.—*adj.* **cornic'ulate,** horned : hornshaped; **cornif'erous,** containing hornstone; **cornif'ic,** producing or forming horn or horns.— *n.* **cornifica'tion.**—*adjs.* **corn'iform,** shaped like a horn; **cornigerous** (*kor-nij'ər-əs*) horned.—*ns.* **corn'-plaster,** a remedial plaster for corns; **cor'nū** (L. *kor'noo*), a horn, hornlike part, or process :— *pl.* **cor'nūa.**—*adj.* **cor'nūal.**—*adj.* **corn'y,** of or pertaining to horns or corns; having corns : horny. —**corniferous limestone,** a coral limestone with chert nodules in the Devonian of North America; **tread on one's corns,** to hurt one's feelings. [L. *cornū,* horn.]

cornage, *korn'ij, n.* (*hist.*) a feudal service or rent fixed according to number of horned cattle— horngeld. [O.Fr.,—L. *cornū,* horn.]

cornea, *kor'ni-ä, n.* the transparent horny membrane that forms the front covering of the eye.— *adj.* **cor'neal.** [L. *cornea* (*tēla*), horny (tissue).]

cornel, *kor'nəl, n.* the so-called cornelian cherry or cornelian tree, a small tree (*Cornus mas*) of middle and southern Europe : any species of the genus **Cor'nus,** type of the family **Corna'ceae** (akin to Umbelliferae), such as **dwarf cornel,** an alpine herb with four white bracts surrounding its umbel, and dogwood.—*ns.* **cor'nel-tree, cornē'lian-tree.** [L.L. *cornolium*—L. *cornus,* cornel.]

cornelian, *kor-nē'li-ən, n.* a fine chalcedony, generally translucent red.—Also **carnē'lian** (*kär-*). [Fr. *cornaline*—L. *cornū,* a horn, or *cornum,* cornelian cherry, from its appearance : confused with *carō, carnis,* flesh.]

cornemuse, *kor'ni-mūz, n.* a French bagpipe. [Fr.]

corner, *kor'nər, n.* the point where two lines or several planes meet : an angular projection or recess : a secret or confined place : an embarrassing position, difficulty : (*obs.*) a point in a rubber at whist : a free kick given to the opposite side when a player in football kicks the ball over his own goal-line : an operation by which the whole of a

stock or commodity is bought up so that the
buyers may resell at their own price.—*v.t.*
to supply with corners : to put in a corner; to put
in a fix or difficulty : to form a corner against : to
get control of by forming a corner.—*adj.* **cor′-
nered,** having corners : put in a difficult position.—
ns. **cor′ner-man,** the man at the end of the row
in a nigger-minstrel performance; **cor′ner-stone,**
a stone that unites the two walls of a building at a
corner : the principal stone, esp. the corner of the
foundation of a building; (*fig.*) something of very
great importance.—*n.pl.* **cor′ner-teeth,** the lateral
incisors of a horse.—*adv.* **cor′nerwise,** with the
corner in front : diagonally.—**turn the corner,**
to go round the corner : to get past a difficulty or
danger; **within the four corners of,** contained
in. [O.Fr. *corniere*—L. *cornū,* horn.]

cornet, *kor′nit* (*U.S.* also -*net′*), *n.* an obsolete
woodwind instrument : an organ stop of various
kinds : a treble brass valve instrument, more
tapering than the trumpet—also **corno′pean,
cornet-à-piston(s)** (*kor-nā-ä-pēs-ton⁰*) : a cornet-
player : any funnel-shaped object, as a piece of
gold for assaying, a shopkeeper's screwed paper
bag, an ice-cream-filled wafer cone, a cream-filled
pastry.—*n.* **cor′netist** (*U.S.* **cornett′ist**), a cornet-
player. [Fr. *cornet,* dim. of *corne*—L. *cornū,* horn.]
cornet, *kor′nit, n.* an old form of ladies' head-dress,
with side lappets: its lappet : (*obs.*) a cavalry
standard : till 1871 a cavalry officer—later sub-
lieutenant : a standard-bearer at riding the marches.
—*n.* **cor′netcy,** commission or rank of cornet.
[Fr. *cornette,* ult. from L. *cornū,* horn.]
cornet. See **coronet.**
cornice, *kor′nis, n.* (*classical archit.*) the uppermost
member of the entablature, surmounting the frieze :
a projecting moulding along the top of a building,
window, etc. : a plaster moulding round a ceiling :
a support for picture-hooks : an overhanging crest
of snow.—*v.t.* to furnish with a cornice.—*adj.*
cor′niced.—ns.** **cor′nice-hook,** **-pole,** **-rail,** a
hook, pole, rail, for hanging pictures, curtains, etc.
—*n.* **cor′nice-ring,** a ring or moulding on a
cannon next below the muzzle-ring. [Fr.,—It.,
poss. Gr. *korōnis,* a curved line; cf. L. *corōna.*]
corniculate, etc. See **corn.**
corno, *kor′nō, n.* the French horn.—*n.* **corn′ist,** a
horn-player.—**corno di basset′to,** the basset-
horn : an organ-stop. [It.,—L. *cornū,* a horn.]
cornopean. See **cornet** (1).
cornu. See **corn** (2).
cornucopia, *kor-nū-kō′pi-ä, n.* the horn of plenty :
according to the fable, the horn of the goat that
suckled Jupiter, placed among the stars as an
emblem of plenty.—*adj.* **cornuco′pian.** [L.
cornū cōpiae—*cornū,* horn, *cōpia,* plenty.]
cornute, *kor-nūt′, v.t.* (*obs.*) to cuckold.—*adjs.*
cornute′, -d, horned : hornlike : (*obs.*) cuckolded.
—*n.* **cornūt′o** (or *-nōō′; It.: obs.*), a cuckold.
[L. *cornūtus,* horned—*cornū,* horn.]
corny, *kor′ni, adj.* (*U.S. slang*) old-fashioned, out-
of-date, uninteresting from frequent use, dull,
foolish.
corocore, corocoro, *kor′ō-kōr, -ō, n.* a Malay form
of boat. [Malay *kurakura.*]
corody. See **corrody.**
corolla, *kor-ol′ä, n.* the inner circle or whorl of the
floral envelopes.—*adj.* **corollā′ceous.—**n.pl.*
Corolliflorae (*-i-flō′rē;* L. *flōs, flōris,* flower), in
some classifications the Gamopetalae or Sym-
petalae.—*adjs.* **corolliflo′ral, corollflo′rous;**
coroll′iform; **coroll′ine** (or *kor′*). [L. *corolla,*
dim. of *corōna,* a crown.]
corollary, *kor′ol-ə-ri,* or *kər-ol′ə-ri, n.* an easy
inference : a consequence or result : a supplement,
surplus, or supernumerary. [L. *corollārium,* a
garland, money for a garland, a tip—*corolla.*]
corona, *ko-rō′nä, kə-, n.* (*archit.*) the large, flat,
projecting member of a cornice crowning the
entablature : (*bot.*) the trumpet of a daffodil, etc.,
composed of ligules of the perianth leaves : a
coloured ring round the sun or moon, in haze, due
to diffraction, distinguished from a halo by having
the red outermost : (*astron.*) one of the sun's
envelopes, outside the chromosphere, observable

during total eclipse : a round pendent chandelier :—
pl. **corō′nas, corō′nae.—**n.* **cor′onal** (*-ə-nl*), a
circlet, small crown or garland.—*adjs.* **corō′nal,**
cor′onary (*-ən-ə-ri*), pertaining to a crown, a
corona, or to the top of the head : like a crown :
surrounding a part (**coronary arteries,** those
that supply the muscle of the heart-wall with
blood; so **coronary circulation**) ; **cor′onāte, -d,**
crowned : applied to shells with a row of projections round the apex.—*ns.* **coronā′tion,** the act
of crowning; **corō′nium,** name given to a hypothetical element in the solar corona assumed to
explain spectral lines now known to be due to
iron and nickel atoms that have lost a large number
of electrons. [L. *corōna,* a crown.]
coronach, *kor′ə-nähh, -nahh, n.* a dirge. [Said
to be a Gaelic word, but evidence insufficient.]
coronation (*Spens.*), for **carnation.**
coroner, *kor′ə-nər, n.* originally guardian of the
pleas of the crown : now an officer who enquires
into the causes of accidental or suspicious deaths.
[O.Fr. *corouner*—L. *corōna,* crown.]
coronet, *kor′ə-nit, n.* a small crown worn by the
nobility : an ornamental head-dress : the part of a
horse's pastern just above the coffin—also **cor′net.**
—*adj.* **cor′oneted.** [O.Fr. *coronete,* dim. of
corone, crown—L. *corōna.*]
coronis, *ko-rō′nis, n.* in Greek, a sign (′) marking
a crasis, as κᾱν = καὶ ἄν. [Gr. *korōnis,* a curved
line.]
coronium. See **corona.**
coronoid, *kor′ə-noid,* or *kor-ō′noid, adj.* (*anat.*) like
a crow's bill, as the coronoid process of the lower
jaw. [Gr. *korōnē,* a crow, *eidos,* form.]
corozo, *kor-ō′sō, n.* a South American short-
stemmed palm (*Phytelephas*) whose seed (**corozo
nut**) gives vegetable ivory : also the cohune palm,
or other. [Sp. from an Indian language.]
corporal, *kor′pə-ral, n.* a non-commissioned officer
next under a sergeant; in the navy, a petty officer
under a master-at-arms; the leader of a gang of
miners, etc.—*n.* **cor′poralship.** [Fr. *caporal*—It.
caporale—*capo,* the head—L. *caput,* the head.]
corporal, *kor′pə-ral, adj.* belonging or relating to
the body : having a body : material : not spiritual.—
n. the cloth used in Catholic churches for covering
the elements of the Eucharist—also **cor′poras**
(*obs.*).—*n.* **corporality** (*-al′i-ti*).—*adv.* **cor′poral-
ly.—**adj.* **cor′porate,** legally united into a body so
as to act as an individual : belonging to a corporation : united.—*adv.* **cor′porately.—**ns.* **cor′-
porateness; corporā′tion,** a body or society
authorised by law to act as one individual : a town
council : (*U.S.*) a company : (*vulg.*) a belly, esp. a
pot-belly.—*adj.* **cor′porātive.—**n.* **cor′porātor,** a
member of a corporation.—*adj.* **corporeal** (*kor-
pō′ri-əl*) having a body or substance : material.—
v.i. and *v.t.* **corpō′realise.—**ns.* **corpō′realism,**
materialism; **corpō′realist; corporeality** (*-al′i-ti*).
—*adv.* **corpō′really.—**ns.* **corporeity** (*-pə-rē′i-ti*);
corporificā′tion, act of corporifying.—*v.t.* **cor-
por′ify,** to embody : solidify.—**aggregate corporation,** a corporation consisting of several
persons; **corporal punishment,** punishment inflicted on the body, as flogging, etc; **sole corporation,** a corporation which consists of one person
and his successors. [L. *corpus, corpŏris,* the body].
corposant, *kor′pə-zant, n.* St. Elmo's fire, an
electrical brush discharge forming a glow about a
mast-head, etc. [Port. *corpo santo*—L. *corpus
sanctum,* holy body.]
corps, *kōr, n.* a division of an army forming a
tactical unit : a branch or department of an army :
an organised body : a German students' society :
a set of people working more or less together :—*pl.*
corps (*korz*). [Fr.,—L. *corpus,* body.]
corpse, *korps,* or *kors, n.* a dead human body.—*ns.*
corpse′-can′dle, a light seen hovering over a
grave—an omen of death; **corpse′-gate,** a lichgate. [M.E. *corps,* earlier *cors*—O.Fr. *cors*—L.
corpus, the body.]
corpus, *kor′pəs, n.* a body, esp. a dead body : any
special structure in the body : a body of literature,
law, etc. :—*pl.* **cor′pora, -pə-rä.—**ns.* **cor′pulence,
cor′pulency,** fleshiness of body : excessive fatness.

—adj. **cor′pulent.—***adv.* **cor′pulently.—***n.* **cor′-puscle** (*-pus-l*; sometimes *-pus′l*), a minute particle—also **corpus′cule.—***adjs.* **corpus′cular, corpuscula′rian.—***ns.* **corpuscula′rian,** one who holds the corpuscular philosophy; **corpuscularity.—corpus Chris′ti** (*-ti, -tī*), the festival in honour of the Eucharist, held on the Thursday after the festival of the Trinity; **corpus delicti** (*de-lik′tē*), (Scots *law*) the essential facts of the crime charged, e.g. in a murder trial, that somebody is actually dead and has been murdered; **corpuscular theory of light,** Newton's theory that light consists in the emission of material particles; **corpus vile** (*vē′lā, vī′lē*), a useless thing (suitable for experiment)—see Foreign Words under **fiat.** [L. *corpus,* the body.]

corral, *kor-al′, n.* a pen for cattle: an enclosure to drive hunted animals into: a defensive ring of wagons.—*v.t.* to pen: to form into a corral. [Sp.]

correct, *kər-, kor-ekt′, v.t.* to make right or supposedly right: to remove or mark faults or supposed faults from or in: to do this and evaluate: to set (a person) right: to punish: to counterbalance: to bring into a normal state: to reduce to a standard.—*adj.* right: according to standard: free from faults.—*adjs.* **correct′able, correct′ible.** —*adv.* **correct′ly.—***n.* **correc′tion,** emendation or would-be emendation: amendment: punishment: reduction: compensation: quantity to be added to bring to a standard or balance an error: bodily chastisement.—*adj.* **correc′tional.—***ns.* **correc′tioner** (*Shak.*), one who administers correction; **correct′itude.—***adj.* **correct′ive,** of the nature of, by way of, correction: tending to correct: correcting.—*n.* that which corrects.—*ns.* **correct′ness; correct′or,** he who, or that which, corrects: a director or governor: a proof-reader.— *adj.* **correct′ory,** corrective.—**under correction,** subject to correction—often used as a formal expression of deference to a superior authority. [L. *corrigĕre, corrēctum*—*cor-,* inten., *regĕre,* to rule.]

corregidor, *ko-rehh′-i-dōr, n.* the chief magistrate of a Spanish town. [Sp., corrector.]

correlate, *kor-ep′lāt, v.i.* to be related to one another. —*v.t.* to bring into relation with each other: to establish relation or correspondence between.—*n.* either of two things so related that one implies the other or is complementary to it: (*rare*) an analogue. —*adj.* (*rare*) correlated.—*n.* **correla′tion.—***adj.* **correlative** (*-el′ə-tiv*).—*n.* a person or thing correspondingly related to another person or thing.—*adv.* **correl′atively.—***ns.* **correl′ativeness, correlativ′ity.** [L. *cor-,* with, and **relate.**]

correligionist. See **co-religionist.**

correption, *kər-ep′shən, n.* shortening in pronunciation: (*obs.*) reproof. [L. *correptiō, -ōnis—cor-,* inten. and *rapĕre,* to seize.]

correspond, *kor-i-spond′, v.i.* to answer, suit, agree (with *to, with*): to hold intercourse, esp. by letter. —*ns.* **correspond′ence, correspond′ency,** suitableness: harmony: relation of agreement, part to part, or one to one: friendly intercourse: communication by letter: a body of letters.—*adj.* **correspond′ent,** answering: agreeing: suitable.—*n.* one with whom intercourse is kept up by letters: one who contributes letters, or is employed to send special reports (e.g. *foreign correspondent, war correspondent*), to a periodical: a person or firm that regularly does business for another elsewhere.— *adv.* **correspond′ently.—***adj.* **correspond′ing,** correspondent: answering: suiting: carrying on correspondence by letters.—*adv.* **correspond′-ingly.—***adj.* **correspon′sive,** corresponding: answering—**correspondence course, school,** etc., one conducted by postal correspondence; **corresponding member,** a member living at a distance who communicates with a society without taking part in its administration; **doctrine of correspondences,** the theory of Swedenborg that there is a spiritual antitype corresponding to every natural object and that Scripture contains the key to these correspondences. [L. *cor-,* with, and *respondēre.*]

corridor, *kor′i-dor, n.* a passage-way or gallery

communicating with separate chambers in a building or compartments in a railway train: a strip of territory by which a country has access to a port, etc.—*ns.* **corr′idor-carr′iage, -train,** a carriage, train, in which one can pass along from one compartment to another. [Fr.,—It. *corridore*—It. *correre,* to run—L. *currĕre.*]

corrie, *kor′i, n.* a semicircular mountain recess or cirque. [Gael. *coire,* a cauldron.]

corrigendum, *kor-i-jen′dəm* (L. *-gen′doom*), *n.* that which requires correction:—*pl.* **corrigen′da,** esp. corrections to be made in a book. [L., gerundive of *corrigĕre,* to correct.]

corrigent, *kor′i-jənt, adj.* and *n.* corrective.—*adj.* **corr′igible,** that may be corrected: open to correction.—*n.* **corrigibil′ity.** [L. *corrigĕre,* to correct; see **correct.**]

corrival, *kor-ī′vəl, n.* a rival: a competitor: an equal.—*adj.* contending: emulous.—*v.i.* to rival.— *v.t.* to vie.—*ns.* **corri′valry; corri′valship.** [L. *con-,* with, and **rival.**]

corroborate, *kər-ob′ə-rāt, v.t.* to confirm: to make more certain.—*adj.* confirmed: (*Shak.*) used blunderingly by Ancient Pistol, perh. for *corroded* or *corrupt.*—*adjs.* **corrob′orable; corrob′orant; corrob′orative,** tending to confirm.—*n.* that which corroborates.—*ns.* **corrobora′tion,** confirmation; **corrob′orator.—***adj.* **corrob′oratory,** corroborative. [L. *cor-,* inten., and *rōborāre, -ātum,* to make strong; see **robust.**]

corroboree, *kə-rob′ə-rē, n.* a dance of Australian aborigines: a song for such a dance: a festive gathering.—*v.i.* to hold a corroboree. [Native word.]

corrode, *kər-ōd′, v.t.* to eat away by degrees, esp. chemically: to rust.—*v.i.* to be eaten away.—*adj.* **corrōd′ent,** having the power of corroding.—*n.* that which corrodes.—*n.pl.* **Corrodentia** (*-en′shyä*), the Psocoptera, or book-lice, etc.—*n.* **corrosibil′-ity** (*-rōz*).—*adj.* **corrōs′ible** (also **corrōd′ible**). —*n.* **corrosion** (*-rō′zhən*), act or process of eating or wasting away.—*adj.* **corrōs′ive,** having the quality of eating away.—*n.* that which has the power of corroding.—*adv.* **corrōs′ively.—***n.* **corrōs′iveness.—corrosive sublimate,** mercuric chloride. [L. *cor-,* inten., *rōdĕre, rōsum,* to gnaw.]

corrody, corody, *kor′ō-di, n.* an allowance: pension: originally the right of the lord to claim free lodging from the vassal. [O.Fr. *conrei, conroi.*]

corrugate, *kor′(y)oo-gāt, v.t.* to wrinkle or draw into folds.—*ns.* **corruga′tion,** the act of wrinkling or state of being wrinkled: a wrinkle; **corr′ugator** (*anat.*), a wrinkling muscle.—**corrugated iron,** sheet iron bent by ridged rollers into a wavy form for the sake of strength; **corrugated paper,** a wrinkled paper used as wrapping material. [L. *cor-,* inten., *rūgāre, -ātum,* to wrinkle—*rūga,* a wrinkle.]

corrupt, *kər-upt′, v.t.* to make putrid: to taint: to debase: to spoil: to destroy the purity of: to pervert: to bribe.—*v.i.* to rot: to lose purity.— *adj.* putrid: depraved: defiled: not genuine: much vitiated or debased in transcription: bribed: venal: of the nature of bribery.—*ns.* **corrupt′er; corruptibil′ity, corrupt′ibleness.—***adj.* **corrupt′-ible,** liable to be corrupted.—*adv.* **corrupt′ibly—** *ns.* **corrup′tion,** rottenness: putrid matter: impurity: bribery; **corrup′tionist,** one who defends or who practises corruption.—*adj.* **corrupt′ive,** having the quality of corrupting.—*adv.* **corrupt′ly.—***n.* **corrupt′ness.—corruption of blood,** the former inability of an attainted person to inherit or transmit lands, titles or dignities. [L. *cor-,* inten., and *rumpĕre, ruptum,* to break.]

corsage, *kor′sij, kor-säzh′, n.* the bodice or waist of a woman's dress: (*U.S.*) a bouquet to be worn there or elsewhere. [O.Fr.,—*cors*—L. *corpus,* the body.]

corsair, *kor′sār, n.* a privateer (esp. of Barbary): a privateering ship: a pirate. [Fr. *corsaire,* one who courses or ranges—L. *cursus,* a running—*currĕre.*]

corse, *kors, n.* a poetic form of **corpse.**

corselet. Same as **corslet.**

corset, *kor′sit, n.* a close-fitting stiff inner bodice: stays: a stiff belt coming down over the hips.—*v.t.* to furnish with a corset (*pr.p.* **corseting,** *pa.t.* and *pa.p.* cor'seted). [Dim. of O.Fr. *cors*—L. *corpus*, the body.]

corsive, *kor'siv, n.* (*Spens.*) and *adj.* Same as corrosive.

corslet, corselet, *kors'lit, n.* a cuirass, a protective body-covering of leather, or steel, etc : a modified corset, or combined belt and brassière.—*adj.* cors'leted. [Fr. *corselet,* dim. of O.Fr. *cors*—L. *corpus,* the body.]

corsned, *kors'ned, n.* the ordeal of swallowing a piece of bread or cheese, taken to prove guilt if it stuck in the throat. [O.E. *corsnæd—gecor* (cf. *coren,* pa.p. of *céosan,* to choose) and *snæd,* a piece, from *snidan,* to cut.]

cortège, *kor-tezh', n.* a train of attendants : a procession, a funeral procession. [Fr.,—It. *corte, court.*]

Cortes, *kor'tes, n.* the parliament of Spain and of Portugal. [Sp. pl. of *corte,* a court.]

cortex, *kor'teks, n.* the bark of skin of a plant, between the epidermis and the vascular bundles : a covering :—*pl.* cortices (*kor'ti-sēz*).—*adjs.* cor'tical, pertaining to the cortex : external ; cor'ticate, -d, furnished with bark. [L. *cortex, cortĭcis,* bark.]

cortile, *kor-tē'lā, n.* an enclosed courtyard within a building, generally roofless. [It.]

cortisone, *kor'ti-sōn, n.* 'compound E', a steroid isolated from the adrenal cortex, or prepared from ox bile, etc., effective against rheumatoid arthritis.

corundum, *ko-run'dəm, n.* a mineral consisting of alumina, second in hardness only to the diamond—including sapphire, ruby, emery. [Tamil *kurundam,* ruby.]

coruscate, *kor'əs-kāt, v.i.* to sparkle : to throw off flashes of light.—*adj.* corus'cant, flashing.—*n.* corusca'tion, a glittering : sudden flash of light. [L. *coruscāre, -ātum,* to vibrate, glitter.]

corvée, *kor'vā', n.* the obligation to perform gratuitous labour (such as the maintenance of roads) for the sovereign or feudal lord. [Fr.,—L.L. *corrogāta*—L. *corrogāre—cor-,* together, *rogāre,* to ask.]

corves. See corf.

corvet. Same as curvet.

corvette, *kor-vet', n.* formerly a flush-decked vessel, with one tier of guns : now an escort vessel specially designed for protecting convoys against submarine attack. [Fr.,—Sp. *corbeta*—L. *corbīta,* a slow-sailing ship, from *corbis,* a basket.]

Corvus, *kor'vəs, n.* the crow genus, typical of the family Cor'vidae and subfamily Corvi'nae : a southern constellation : corvus, a grappling-hook in ancient Roman naval warfare : a hooked ram for destroying walls.—*adj.* cor'vine (*-vīn*). [L. *corvus,* a raven.]

corybant, *kor'i-bant, n.* a priest of Cybele, whose rites were accompanied with noisy music and wild dances (Eng. *pl.* cor'ybants ; L. *pl.* corybant'es).—*adj.* coryban'tic, wildly excited.—*n.* cor'ybantism. [Gr. *korybās, korybantos.*]

Corydalis, *kor-id'ə-lis, n.* a genus akin to fumitory.—*n.* cor'ydaline, an alkaloid (C₂₂H₂₇O₄N) obtained from Corydalis root. [Gr. *korydallis,* crested lark, from a fancied resemblance of the flower.]

Corydon, *kor'i-don, n.* generic proper name for a rustic. [L.,—Gr. *Korydōn,* a shepherd's name in Theocritus and Virgil.]

Corylus, *kor'i-ləs, n.* the hazel genus. [L.]

corymb, *kor'imb, n.* (*bot.*) a flattish-topped raceme.—*adjs.* cor'ymbose (or *-imb'*).—*n.* corym'bus, a girl's top-knot. [L. *corymbus*—Gr. *korymbos,* a cluster.]

Corypha, *kor'i-fə, n.* the talipot genus of gigantic tropical Asian palms. [Gr. *koryphē,* top.]

coryphaeus, *kor-i-fē'əs, n.* the chief or leader, esp. the leader of a chorus (*pl.* coryphaei, *-fē'ī*).—*n.* coryphée (*kor-ē-fā' ;* Fr.), the principal *danseuse* in the ballet. [L.,—Gr. *koryphaios—koryphē,* the head.]

coryphene, *kor'i-fēn, n.* a fish of the genus Coryphaena, called dolphin. [Gr. *koryphaina.*]

coryza, *ko-rī'zä, n.* a cold in the head. [L.,—Gr. *koryza.*]

cos, *kos, n.* a long-leaved lettuce. [Introduced from the Aegean island of Cos (Gr. *Kōs*).]

cos, *kos,* (*math.*) for cosine.

coscinomancy, *kos'i-no-man-si, n.* an ancient mode of divination by a sieve and pair of shears. [Gr. *koskinon,* a sieve, *manteiā,* divination.]

cose, *kōz, v.i.* to make oneself cosy. [See cosy.]

cosecant, *kō-sek'ənt, -sēk', n.* the secant of the complement of an angle—*abbrev.* cosec (*kō'sek*).—*n.* cosech (*kōsh-ek'*), for hyperbolic *cosecant.*

coseismal, *kō-sīz'məl, adj.* experiencing an earthquake shock simultaneously.—Also coseis'mic. [L. *co-,* together, Gr. *seismos,* earthquake.]

co-sentient, *kō-sen'sh(y)ənt, adj.* perceiving together.

cosh, *kosh, adj.* (*Scot.*) cosy, snug.

cosh, *kosh, n.* (slang) a bludgeon, truncheon, lead-pipe, piece of flexible tubing filled with metal, or the like, used as a weapon.—Also *v.t.*

cosh, *kosh, n.* a conventional abbreviation for *hyperbolic cosine.*

cosher, *kosh'ər, v.t.* to pamper, to coddle.—*v.i.* to chat in a friendly way.

cosher. See kosher.

coshery, *kosh'ər-i, n.* the ancient right of an Irish chief to quarter himself and his retainers on his tenantry—also cosh'ering.—*v.i.* cosh'er, to live on dependants.—*n.* cosh'erer. [Ir. *coisir,* a feast.]

cosier. Same as cozier.

co-signatory, *kō-sig'nə-tə-ri, adj.* uniting with others in signing.—*n.* one who does so.—*adj.* co-signif'icative, having the same signification.

cosine, *kō'sīn, n.* the sine of the complement of an angle—*abbrev.* cos (*kos*).

cosmetic, *koz-met'ik, adj.* purporting to improve beauty, esp. that of the complexion.—*n.* a preparation for the purpose.—*adj.* cosmet'ical.—*adv.* cosmet'ically.—*v.t.* cosmet'icise (*-sīz*).—*n.* cosmet'icism. [Gr. *kosmētikos—kosmeein,* to adorn—*kosmos,* order.]

cosmos, *koz'mos, n.* the world or universe as an orderly or systematic whole—opp. to chaos : order.—*adjs.* cos'mic, relating to the cosmos : orderly ; cos'mical, cosmic : (*astron.*) happening at sunrise : rising with the sun.—*adv.* cos'mically.—*ns.* cos'mism, the notion of the cosmos as a self-existing whole ; cos'mist, a secularist ; cos'mocrat, ruler of the world.—*adjs.* cosmocrat'ic ; cosmogon'ic, -al, relating to cosmogony.—*ns.* cosmog'onist, one who speculates on the origin of the universe ; cosmog'ony (Gr. *kosmogoniā*), a theory or a myth of the origin of the universe, esp. of the stars, nebulae, etc.—Also cosmogeny (*-moj'*) ; cosmog'rapher.—*adjs.* cosmograph'ic, -al.—*n.* cosmog'raphy, a description of the world : the science of the constitution of the universe ; cosmol'atry (Gr. *latreiā,* worship), worship of the world.—*adj.* cosmolog'ical.—*ns.* cosmol'ogist ; cosmol'ogy, the science of the universe as a whole : a treatise on the structure and parts of the system of creation.—*adj.* cosmoplas'tic (Gr. *plassein,* to form), moulding the universe : world-forming.—*ns.* cosmopol'icy (Shelley) ; cosmop'olis (Gr. *polis,* city, state), an international city : a world-city ; cosmopol'itan, a citizen of the world : one free from local or national prejudices.—*adj.* belonging to all parts of the world : unprejudiced.—*n.* cosmopol'itanism.—*n.* and *adj.* cosmopolite (*koz-mop'ə-līt*).—*adjs.* cosmopol'itic, -polit'ical.—*n.* cosmopol'itics, world politics ; cosmop'olitism (or *-pol'*) ; cosmo-rama (*-rä'mä ;* Gr. *horāma,* a spectacle), a view, or a series of views, of different parts of the world, tricked out with mirrors, lenses, etc.—*adj.* cosmoramic (*-ram'*).—*n.* cos'mosphere, an apparatus for showing the position of the earth at any given time with reference to the fixed stars ; cosmothe'ism (Gr. *theos,* god), the belief that identifies God with the cosmos : pantheism.—*adjs.* cosmothet'ic, -al, assuming an external world.—cosmical constant, a number, at present of the order of 10⁷⁸, believed to be fundamental to the structure of the universe ; cosmic rays, the shortest electro-magnetic waves known, discovered in 1925 by Dr. R. A. Millikan, thought to come from inter-

stellar space. [Gr. *kosmos*, order, world, universe.]
co-sphered, *kō-sfērd'*, *adj.* being in the same sphere.

coss, *kos*, *n.* a measure of distance in India, averaging about 1¼ mile. [Hindi *kōs*—Sans. *kroça*, a call.]

Cossack, *kos'ək*, *n.* one of a people in south-eastern Russia, formerly holding by military tenure and serving as cavalry.—**Cossack boots**, Russian boots; **Cossack post**, a small group of mounted troops on outpost duty. [Turk. *quzzāq*, freebooter.]

cosset, *kos'it*, *n.* a hand-reared lamb : a pet.—*v.t.* to fondle (*pr.p.* **cosset'ing**; *pa.t.* and *pa.p.* **coss'eted**). [Perh. O.E. *cot-sǣta*, *cot-setla*, cot-dweller.]

cost, *kost*, *v.t.* or *v.i.* to be obtainable at a price (of) : to involve an expenditure (of) : to require to be laid out or suffered or lost.—*v.t.* to estimate the cost of production of.—*pa.t.* and *pa.p.* **cost**.—*n.* what is or would have to be laid out or suffered or lost to obtain anything : (in *pl.*) expenses of a law-suit.—*adj.* and *adv.* **cost'-free**, free of charge.— *n.* **cost'liness**.—*adj.* **cost'ly**, of great cost : high-priced : valuable.—**at all costs**, **cost what may**, no matter what the cost or consequences may be; **cost price**, the price the merchant pays; **prime cost**, the price of production, without regard to profit or overhead expenses. [O.Fr. *couster* (Fr. *coûter*)—L. *cōnstāre*, to stand at.]

cost, coste, *kost*, *n.* (*Spens.*). See **coast**.—*v.t.* and *v.i.* (*Shak.*, *Spens.*) to approach. [**coast**.]

costa, *kos'tä*, *n.* a rib : a rib-like structure, vein, ridge : the fore-edge of an insect's wing : the nervure next it.—*adj.* **cos'tal**, of or near the ribs, the costa, or the side of the body.—*n.* the costal nervure.—*adjs.* **cos'tāte**, **-d**, ribbed : having the appearance of ribs. [L. *costa*, a rib.]

costard, *kos'tərd*, *n.* a large kind of apple : the human head (contemptuously).—*ns.* **cos'tard-monger**, **cos'termonger**, **cos'ter**, a seller of apples and other fruit : a seller of fruit and other wares from a barrow : (*Shak.*) a term of abuse. [Perh. L. *costa*, a rib.]

costean, *kos-tēn'*, *v.i.* to dig down to bed-rock in prospecting.—*ns.* **costean'ing**; **costean'-pit**. [Said to be from Cornish *cothas*, dropped, *stean*, tin.]

costive, *kos'tiv*, *adj.* constipated.—*adv.* **cos'tively**. —*n.* **cos'tiveness**. [Fr. *constipé*; see **constipate**.]

costmary, *kost'mär-i*, *n.* alecost (*Chrysanthemum Balsamita*), a composite of southern Europe, grown in gardens for its fragrant leaves. [L. *costum*—Gr. *kostos*, costus, and *Maria*, the Virgin Mary.]

costrel, *kos'trəl*, *n.* an eared bottle, to be hung at the waist. [O.Fr. *costerel*.]

costume, *kos'tūm*, *kos-tūm'*, *n.* a manner of dressing : dress, garb : a woman's outer dress as a unit : fancy dress.—*v.t.* (*kos-tūm'*) to dress.—*adj.* **costumed'**.—*ns.* **costum'er**, **costum'ier**, one who makes or deals in costumes. [Fr.,—It. *costume*—L. *cōnsuētūdō*, *-inis*, custom.]

Costus, *kos'tas*, *n.* a genus of plants of the ginger family : **costus**, an aromatic root wrongly assigned to it, really that of a composite of Kashmir, *Saussurea hypoleuca*—also **cos'tus arabicus**, **cos'-tus-root**. [Latinised from Gr. *kostos*.]

cosy, cozy, *kō'zi*, *adj.* (orig. *Scot.*) snug : comfort-able.—*n.* a covering used for a teapot, to keep the tea warm (also **tea'-cosy**) : a similar covering for a boiled egg.—*adv.* **cō'sily**. [Ety. unknown.]

cot, *kot*, *n.* a small dwelling, a cottage.—*ns.* **cot'-folk** (*Scot.*), cottars; **cot'-house**, a house occupied by a cottar; **cot'-land**, land belonging to a cottage; **cot'-quean**, a scolding woman : (*Shak.*), a man who busies himself with women's affairs.—*adj.* **cott'ed**, lined with cots.—*n.* **cot'-town**, a group of cot-houses. [O.E. *cot*; cf. O.N. and Du. *kot*.]

cot, cott, *kot*, *n.* a small bed or crib : (*naut.*) a swinging bed of canvas (for officers, sick, etc.) : a hospital bed. [Anglo-Ind.,—Hind. *khāt*.]

cot (*Spens.* **cott**), *kot*, *n.* a small boat. [Ir.]

cotangent, *kō-tan'jənt*, *n.* the tangent of the com-plement of an angle—*abbrev.* **cot** (*kot*).—*n.* **coth** (*koth*), for hyperbolic *cotangent*.

cote, *kōt*, *n.* a place for animals, as **dove-cote** or **dove-cot**, **sheep-cote**. [O.E. *cote*; cf. **cot** (1).}

cote, *kōt*, *v.t.* (*Shak.*) to pass by : to outstrip (as one dog another). [Poss. conn. with **coast**.]

cote, a Shakespearian form of **quote**.

cote-hardie, *kōt'-här'di*, *n.* a mediaeval close-fitting tight-sleeved body garment. [O.Fr.]

coteline, *kōt-lēn'*, *n.* a kind of muslin, corded or ribbed. [Fr. *côte*, a rib—L. *costa*.]

cotemporaneous, etc. faulty forms of **con-temporaneous**, etc.

co-tenant, *kō-ten'ənt*, *n.* a joint tenant.—*n.* **co-ten'ancy**.

coterie, *kō'tə-rē*, *n.* a social, literary, or other exclusive circle. [Fr.; orig. a number of peasants holding land jointly from a lord—L.L. *cota*, a cot.]

coterminous, a faulty form of **conterminous**.

cothurnus, *kō-thur'nəs*, **cothurn**, *kō'thurn*, or *-thurn'*, *n.* the tragedian's buskin (*pl.* **cothur'nī**). [Latinised from Gr. *kothornos*.]

coticular, *kō-tik'ū-lər*, *adj.* pertaining to whet-stones. [L. *cōticula*, dim. of *cōs*, *cōtis*, whetstone.]

co-tidal, *ko-tīd'əl*, *adj.* having high tide at the same time.

cotillion, *ko-til'yən*, **cotillon**, *ko-tē'yon*s, *n.* a sort of country dance. [Fr., petticoat—*cotte*, a coat— L.L. *cotta*, a tunic; see **coat**.]

Cotinga, *kō-ting'gä*, *n.* a tropical American genus of passerine birds of bright plumage : **cotinga**, any bird of its fam., Cotingidae (*-tin'ji-dē*). [Of Tupi origin.]

cotise, cottise, *kot'is*, *n.* (*her.*) one of the diminu-tives of the bend.—*v.t.* to border with cotises, barrulets, etc. [Fr. *cotice*; origin obscure.]

Cotoneaster, *ko-tō-ni-as'tər*, *n.* a genus of shrubs or small trees akin to hawthorn. [L. *cotōnea*, quince.]

Cotswold, *kots'wōld*, *n.* a breed of sheep.—**Cots-wold lion**, a sheep. [*Cotswold* Hills.]

cott. See **cot** (2) and (3).

cotta, *kot'ä*, *n.* a surplice. [L.L. *cotta*.]

cottabus, *kot'ä-bus*, *n.* an amusement in ancient Greece among young men, consisting in throwing wine into a vessel, success at which betokened fortune in love. [L.,—Gr. *kottabos*.]

cottage, *kot'ij*, *n.* a small dwelling-house : a country residence : (*U.S.*) a summer residence : (*Austr.*) a one-storey house.—*adj.* **cott'aged**, covered with cottages.—*n.* **cott'ager**, one who dwells in a cottage, esp. of labourers.—**cottage hospital**, a small, simply organised hospital : one housed in a cottage or cottages; **cottage loaf**, a loaf consisting of a smaller lump on the top of a bigger one; **cottage piano**, a small upright piano. [L.L. *cottagium*—O.E. *cot*; see **cot** (1).]

cottar, cotter, *kot'ər*, *n.* (*Scot.*) a peasant occupying a cot or cottage for which he has to give labour. [**cot** (1).]

cottier, *kot'i-ər*, *n.* a cottar : an Irish tenant holding land as the highest bidder; **cott'ierism**, the cottier system of land tenure. [Fr. *cotier*; cf. **cot** (1).]

cotter, *kot'ər*, *n.* a pin or wedge for fastening and tightening.—*n.* **cott'er-pin**, a pin for keeping a cotter in place. [Origin obscure.]

cotton, *kot'n*, *n.* a soft substance like fine wool, the long hairs covering the seeds of the cotton-plant : the plant itself, individually or collectively : yarn or cloth made of cotton.—*adj.* made of cotton.— *v.t.* to provide with cotton.—*v.i.* to agree : to take, or become attached (the connexion of the intransi-tive meanings is unknown).—*ns.* **cottonade'**, an inferior cotton cloth; **cott'on-boll**, the pod of the cotton-plant; **cott'on-gin**, a machine for separating the seeds from the fibre of cotton; **cott'on-grass**, a genus (Eriophorum) of sedges with long, silky, or cottony hairs about the ripened ovary; **cott'on-mill**, a factory where cotton is spun or woven; **cott'on-mouth**, the venomous water mocassin snake (from the white inside of its mouth); **cottonoc'racy** (*coll.*), the cotton planting or the cotton manufacturing interest; **cott'on-plant**, one of various species of Gossypium (family Malvaceae), yielding cotton; **cott'on-press**, a press for com-pressing cotton into bales; **cott'on-seed**, the seed of the cotton-plant, yielding a valuable oil; **cott'on-spinner**, one who spins cotton, or employs those who do; **cott'on-tail**, the ordinary United States rabbit; **cott'on-thistle**, a strong thistle (*Onopordon Acanthium*) covered with a cottony down; **cott'on-tree**, the American cotton-wood: the Indian *Bombax malabaricum*: an Australian Hibiscus; **cott'on-waste**, refuse from cotton mills, used for cleaning machinery, etc.; **cott'on-weed**, cudweed, a cottony seaside composite, *Diotis maritima*: **cott'on-wood**, any one of several American species of poplar; **cott'on-wool'**, cotton in its raw or woolly state: loose cotton pressed in a sheet as an absorbent or protective agent, for stuffing, etc.; **cott'on-worm**, the caterpillar of an owlet moth (*Aletia xylina*) destructive to American cotton crops.—*adj.* **cott'ony**, like cotton: soft: downy. [Fr. *coton*—Ar. *qutun*.]

Cottus, *kot'əs*, *n.* a genus of fishes including the bullhead and father-lasher.—*n.* and *adj.* **cott'oid**. [Gr. *kottos*, a fish, perhaps the bullhead.]

cotyle, *kot'i-lē*, *n.* an ancient Greek drinking-cup: (*zool.*) a cup-like cavity:—*pl.* **cot'ylae** (*-lē*), or **cot'yles**.—*adjs.* **cotȳl'iform** (*bot.*) disk-shaped with raised rim; **cot'yloid**, cup-shaped. [Gr. *kotylē*.]

cotyledon, *kot-i-lē'dən*, *n.* (*bot.*) a seed-leaf: (*zool.*) a tuft or patch of villi on the placenta, as in most ruminants.—*adjs.* **cotyle'donary**; **cotyle'donous**, pertaining to or having cotyledons.—*n.pl.* Cotyloph'ora, the Pecora, or ruminants other than camels and chevrotains. [Gr. *kotylēdōn—kotylē*, a cup.]

coucal, *kōō'käl*, *n.* a genus (*Centropus*) of common bush-birds in Africa, India, and Australia, the lark-heeled cuckoos. [Imit.]

couch, *kowch*, *v.t.* to lay down: to lower: to cause to lie close: to spread: to level: to arrange in language, to express: to depress or remove (a cataract in the eye).—*v.i.* to lie down for the purpose of sleep, concealment, etc.: to bend or stoop.—*n.* any place for rest or sleep: a bed: a kind of sofa with half back and one raised end: the lair of a wild beast: a layer: that on which something is spread.—*adj.* **couch'ant**, couching or lying down: (*her.*) lying down with head up.—*n.* **couch'ing**, embroidery in which the surface is covered with threads and these are secured by stitches forming a pattern.—**couch a spear**, to fix it in its rest at the side of the armour. [Fr. *coucher*, to lay down—L. *collocāre*, to place—*col-*, together, *locus*, a place.]

couch, couch-grass, *kowch'*, *kōōch'* (*-grâs*), *ns.* a grass akin to wheat, a troublesome weed owing to its creeping rootstocks. [A variant of **quitch**.]

couchee, *kōō'shā*, *n.* an evening reception. [Fr. *couché*, a reception before going to bed; see **couch**.]

Couéism, *kōō'ā-izm*, *n.* psychotherapy by auto-suggestion.—*n.* Cou'éist. [Emile *Coué* (1862–1926), its expounder.]

cougar, *kōō'gär*, *-gər*, **couguar**, *-gwär*, *n.* a puma. [Fr. *couguar*, adapted from a Guarani name.]

cough, *kof*, *v.i.* to expel air with a sudden opening of the glottis and a characteristic sound.—*v.t.* to expel by coughing.—*n.* the act or the sound of coughing: an ailment of which coughing is a symptom.—**cough'-drop'**, a cough-lozenge: (*slang*) a person of spicy character; **cough'er**; **cough'ing**; **cough'-loz'enge**, a medicated lozenge to allay coughing; **cough'-mix'ture**.—**cough down**, to put to silence by coughing; **cough up**, (*slang*) to pay out, hand over, under compulsion. [M.E. *coughen*; cf. Du. *kuchen*, Ger. *keuchen*, *keichen*, to gasp.]

could, *kood*, *pa.t.* of **can**. [M.E. *coude*, *couth*—O.E. *cúthe* for *cunthe*, was able; *l* is inserted from the influence of *would* and *should*.]

coulée, *kōō-lā'*, *n.* a lava-flow: (*U.S.* and *Can.*) a ravine. [Fr.,—*couler*, to flow.]

coulisse, *kōō-lēs'*, *n.* a piece of grooved wood, as the slides in which the side-scenes of a theatre run —hence (in *pl.*) the wings. [Fr.,—*couler*, to glide, to flow—L. *cōlāre*, to strain.]

couloir, *kool-wär*, *n.* a gully. [Fr., passage.]

coulomb, *kōō-lom'*, *n.* the unit of quantity in measuring current electricity: the quantity furnished by a current of one ampere in one second. [From the French physicist, C. A. de *Coulomb* (1736–1806).]

coulter, colter, *kōl'tər* (*Scot. koot'ər*), *n.* the iron cutter in front of a ploughshare. [O.E. *culter*—L. *culter*, knife.]

coumarin, cumarin, *koo'mə-rin*, *n.* a crystalline compound ($C_9H_6O_2$) obtained in Tonka beans, woodruff, melilot, etc.—*adjs.* coumaric (*-mar'*), coumaril'ic. [Tupí *cumarú*, Tonka bean.]

council, *kown'sl*, *-sil*, *n.* an assembly called together for deliberation, advice, administration or legislation: the persons constituting such an assembly: the body directing the affairs of a town, county, parish, etc.: an assembly of ecclesiastics met to regulate doctrine or discipline: a governing body in a university: a committee that arranges the business of a society.—*ns.* **coun'cil-board**, the board or table round which a council meets for deliberation: the council itself: **coun'cil-cham'ber**, the room where a council is held; **coun'cil-house**, a house in which a council meets: a house erected by a municipal council; **coun'cil-lor**, (*U.S.*) **coun'cilor**, a member of a council; **coun'cilman** (*London* and *U.S.*) a member of a municipal council.—*adj.* **councilman'ic** (*U.S.*). —**council of war**, a conference of officers called to consult with the commander; **council school**, a school governed by a town or county council; **general council**, one called by an invitation to the church at large, also **oecumenical**, if received by the Catholic Church in general—as the first seven, 325–787; **in council**, in the council-chamber: in consultation; **legislative council**, a council to assist a governor, with power to make laws; **Council, House, of States**, upper house of Indian parliament. [Fr. *concile*—L. *concilium*.]

counsel, *kown'sl*, *n.* consultation: deliberation: advice: plan: purpose: a confidential matter: one who gives counsel, a barrister or advocate.—*v.t.* to advise: to warn (*pr.p.* **coun'selling**; *pa.t.* and *pa.p.* **coun'selled**).—*n.* **coun'sel-keep'er** (*Shak.*), one who can keep counsel or a secret.—*adjs.* **coun'sel-keep'ing** (*Shak.*); **coun'sellable**, that may be counselled.—*ns.* **coun'sellor**, one who counsels: a barrister; **coun'sellorship**.—**counsel of perfection**, a commendation of something beyond the binding minimum, something not absolutely imperative, but commended as the means of reaching greater 'perfection'; **keep counsel**, to keep a secret; **King's, Queen's Counsel** (K.C., Q.C.), a barrister or advocate appointed by letters-patent—the office is honorary, but gives the right of precedence in all the courts. [Fr. *conseil*—L. *consilium*, advice—*consulĕre*, to consult.]

count, *kownt*, *n.* (*Rom. hist.*) an imperial official: on the Continent, a noble equal in rank to an earl:—*fem.* **count'ess**, a lady of the same rank: the wife of a count or earl (fem. of *earl*).—*ns.* **count'ship**, a count's dignity or domain (also used as a title); **coun'ty** (*obs.*) a count: (*obs.*) a countship: a portion of a country separated for administrative, parliamentary or other purposes, a shire.—**Count of the Saxon Shore**, in Roman Britain, an official in charge of the S.E. coast, liable to attacks by Saxons (if not already partly peopled by them); **county borough** (see **borough**); **county council**, a council for managing the public affairs of a county; **county councillor**; **county court**, the highest court of law within a county; **county cricket**, cricket played in matches between clubs representing counties; **county family**, a family of nobility or gentry (**coun'ty-people**), with estates and a seat in the county; **county seat**, (*U.S.*) the seat of county government; **county school**, a school under a county council; **county town**, the town in which the public business of the county is transacted: sometimes the titular or historic capital of a county. [O.Fr. *conte*—L. *comes*, *comitis*, a companion, *con-*, with, *īre*, to go.]

count, *obs.* **compt**, *kownt*, *v.t.* to number, sum up: to name the numerals up to: to take into account, reckon as significant or to be recognised: to ascribe: to reckon, esteem, consider.—*v.i.* to number: to be numbered: to be of account: to be recognised in reckoning: to have a certain value: to reckon: to name the numerals in order.—*n.* act of numbering: reckoning: the number counted: a number indicating size of yarn: (*boxing*) the counting of the seconds in which a fallen man may rise and resume (also **count-out**): esteem, consideration, account: a particular charge in an indictment.—*adjs.* **count′able** (formerly **compt′-able**, **-ible**), capable of being counted: to be counted: accountable: (*Shak.*) sensitive; **count′ed**, accounted, reckoned.—*ns.* **count′er**, he who or that which counts: that which indicates a number: a disk or the like, used in reckoning or as a substitute for a coin in games: a table on which money is counted or goods laid: (*hist.*) the name of certain prisons (officially **compter**); **count′er-caster** (*Shak.*), an arithmetician, reckoner; **count′er-jumper**, **-skipp′er**, contemptuous names for a shopman; **count′ing-house**, **count′ing-room**, a room in which a merchant keeps his accounts and transacts business.—*adj.* **count′less**, that cannot be counted: innumerable.—*n.* **count′-wheel**, a wheel with notched edge controlling the stroke of a clock in sounding the hours.—**count out**, of a meeting (esp. of the House of Commons), to bring to an end by pointing that a quorum is not present: in children's games, to eliminate by counting the players by repeating a rhyme (**counting-out rhyme**): in boxing, etc., to adjudge defeated by counting seconds; **out for the count**, (*fig.*) unconscious, or completely exhausted; **under the counter**, hidden from customers' sight (*adj.* **under-the-counter**, reserved for the favoured: secret, furtive). [O.Fr. *cunter* (Fr. *compter*)—L. *computāre*.]

countenance, *kown′tən-əns*, *n.* the face: the expression of the face: appearance: demeanour shown towards a person: favour: approbation: acquiescence.—*v.t.* to favour or approve: (*Spens.*) to make a show of.—*n.* **coun′tenancer.**—**change countenance**, to change expression of the face; **in countenance**, unabashed; **out of countenance**, abashed. [O.Fr. *contenance*—L. *continentia*, restraint, demeanour—*continēre*, to contain.]

counter, *kown′tər*, *adv.* the opposite way: in opposition.—*adj.* contrary: opposing: opposite.—*n.* that which is counter or opposite: (*mus.*) the voice-part set in immediate contrast with the air: (*Spens.*) an encounter: (*fencing*) a parry in which one foil follows the other in a small circle: the part of a horse's breast between the shoulders and under the neck: (*naut.*) the part of a ship's stern from the lower moulding to the water-line.—*v.t.* to encounter: to contradict: to meet or answer by a stroke or move: (*boxing*) to strike while receiving or parrying a blow. [Partly aphetic for **encounter**, partly directly from A.Fr. *countre*, O.Fr. (Fr.) *contre*—L. *contrā*, against.]

counter. See **count** (2).

counter-, *kown′tər-*, in composition, against.—*v.t.* **counteract′**, to act counter or in opposition to: to hinder or defeat: to neutralise.—*n.* **counterac′tion.**—*adj.* **counteract′ive**, tending to counteract.—*n.* one who or that which counteracts.—*adv.* **counteract′ively.**—*ns.* **coun′ter-ag′ent**, anything which counteracts; **coun′ter-approach′**, a work thrown up outside a besieged place to command or check the approaches of the besieger; **coun′ter-attack**, an attack in reply to an attack; **coun′ter-attrac′tion**, attraction in an opposite direction: a rival show.—*adj.* **coun′ter-attract′-ive.**—*v.t.* **counterbal′ance**, to balance by weight on the opposite side: to act against with equal weight, power, or influence.—*ns.* **coun′ter-balance**, an equal weight, power, or agency working in opposition; **coun′ter-base** (see **contrabass**); **coun′ter-batt′ery** (*mil.*), a battery erected to oppose another; **coun′terblast**, a defiant pronouncement or denunciation; **coun′terblow**, a return blow; **coun′terbond**, a bond to protect from contingent loss one who has given bond for another.—*v.t.* **coun′ter-brace** (*naut.*), to brace or fasten (the head-yards and after-yards) in opposite ways.—*n.* the lee-brace of the fore-topsail-yard.—*n.* **coun′terbuff**, a stroke that stops motion or causes a recoil: reaction: return blow: rebuff.—*v.t.* to rebuff.—*ns.* **coun′ter-cast** (*Spens.*), a

contrary cast, counterplot, trick; **coun′terchange** (*Shak.*), exchange, reciprocation.—*adj.* **coun′ter-changed′**, exchanged: (*her.*) having the tinctures reversed or interchanged.—*n.* **coun′tercharge**, a charge brought forward in opposition to another charge.—*v.t.* **coun′tercharm**, to destroy or dissolve the effects of (another charm).—*n.* that which destroys the effects of another charm.—*v.t.* **countercheck′**, to check by some obstacle: to rebuke.—*ns.* **coun′tercheck**, a check in opposition to another: a rebuke; **coun′ter-claim**, (esp. *law*) a claim brought forward as a partial or complete set-off against another claim.—*adv.* **coun′ter-clock′wise**, in a direction contrary to that of the hands of a clock.—*ns.* **coun′ter-curr′ent**, a current flowing in an opposite direction; **coun′ter-drain**, a drain alongside a canal, etc., to carry off water oozing out.—*v.t.* **coun′terdraw**, to trace on oiled paper or other transparent material.—*ns.* **count′er-esp′ionage**, spying in opposition, espionage directed against the enemy's spy system; **coun′ter-ev′idence**, evidence brought forward in opposition to other evidence; **coun′terfoil**, the corresponding part of a bank cheque, postal order, ticket, etc., retained by the giver.—*adj.* **counter-fleury** (*-floo′ri*, *-flə′ri*), **-flo′ry**, **-flow′ered**, with flowers placed the contrary way.—*ns.* **coun′ter-force**, an opposing force; **coun′ter-fort**, a buttress or arch supporting a retaining wall; **coun′ter-gauge**, an adjustable scribing gauge for marking the measurements of a mortise on a piece to be tenoned; **coun′ter-guard** (*fort.*), an outwork consisting of two lines of rampart running parallel to the faces of the bastion, to guard the bastion from being breached; **coun′ter-in′fluence**, an opposing influence; **coun′ter-irr′itant**, an irritant used to relieve another irritation; **coun′ter-irritā′tion**; **coun′terlight** (*paint.*), a light opposite to any object, disturbing the effect of its light.—*v.i.* **coun′termarch**, to march back or in a direction contrary to a former one.—*n.* a marching back or in a direction different from a former one: (*mil.*) an evolution by which a body of men change front, and still retain the same men in the front rank: change of measures.—*n.* **coun′termark**, an additional mark put on a bale of goods belonging to several merchants, so that it may not be opened except in the presence of all the owners: a mark put on standard metal by the London Goldsmiths' Company in addition to the artificers: an artificial cavity made in the teeth of horses to disguise their age.—*v.t.* **countermine′**, to make a mine in opposition to: to oppose by means of a countermine: (*fig.*) to frustrate by secret working.—*n.* (**kownt′**) a mine or chamber excavated by the besiegers to counteract or destroy the mines made by the besiegers: (*fig.*) any means of counteraction.—*ns.* **coun′ter-mō′tion**, an opposite motion; **coun′ter-move**, **-move′ment**, a contrary move, movement; **coun′termure**, a wall-facing: a supplementary wall: a wall raised by besiegers against a wall.—*v.t.* (*-mūr′*) to defend with a countermure.—*ns.* **coun′ter-offen′sive**, counter-attack: attack by the defenders; **coun′ter-o′pening**, an aperture or vent on the opposite side, or in a different place; **coun′ter-pace**, a step in opposition to another, a contrary measure.—*adj.* **coun′ter-paled** (*her.*), divided equally, as an escutcheon, first palewise, then by a line fesswise, with tinctures counterchanged.—*ns.* **coun′ter-parole**, a word in addition to the password; **coun′terpart**, the part that answers to another part: that which fits into or completes another, having the qualities which another lacks, and so an opposite: a duplicate: a double.—*adj.* **coun′ter-pass′ant** (*her.*), passing each other contrary ways.—*n.* **coun′terplea**, a replication to a plea or request.—*v.t.* **counterplead′**, to plead the contrary of; **coun′ter-plot′**, to plot against in order to frustrate another plot.—*n.* a plot or stratagem opposed to another plot.—*v.t.* **coun′terpoise** (*obs.* **coun′ter-peise**, **-pēz**), to poise or weigh against or on the opposite side: to act in opposition to with equal effect.—*n.* an equally heavy weight in the other scale.—*ns.* **coun′ter-poison**, a poison used as the antidote of another; **coun′ter-pressure**, opposing pressure; **coun′ter-proof**, an inverted impression obtained from a newly printed proof of an engraving, by laying it, while the ink is still wet, upon plain paper, and passing it through the press; **Coun′ter-Reforma′tion** (*hist.*), a reform movement within the Roman Catholic Church, following and counteracting the Reformation; **coun′ter-revolū′tion**, a subsequent revolution counteracting the effect of a previous; **coun′ter-roll**, a copy of the rolls relating to appeals, inquests, etc., serving as a check on another's roll; **coun′ter-round**, a body of officers to inspect the rounds.—*adj.* **coun′ter-sā′lient** (*her.*), salient in opposite directions.—*n.* **coun′terscarp** (*fort.*), the side of the ditch nearest to the besiegers and opposite to the scarp.—*v.t.* **counterseal′** (*Shak.*), to seal along with others.— *ns.* **coun′ter-secur′ity**, security given to one who has become surety for another; **coun′ter-sense**, an interpretation contrary to the real sense.—*v.t.* **coun′tershaft**, an intermediate shaft driven by the main shaft; **countersign′**, to sign on the opposite side of a writing : to sign in addition to the signature of a superior, to attest the authenticity of a writing. —*n.* (*kownt′*), a military private sign or word, which must be given in order to pass a sentry : a counter-signature.—*ns.* **coun′ter-sig′nal**, a signal used as an answer to another; **coun′ter-sig′nature**, a name countersigned to a writing.—*v.t.* **coun′tersink**, to bevel the edge of a hole, as for the head of a screw-nail.—*ns.* **coun′ter-stand**, opposition, resistance; **coun′ter-state′ment**, a statement in opposition to another statement; **coun′terstroke** (*Spens.*), a stroke in return; **coun′ter-sub′ject** (*mus.*), part of a figure in which the first voice accompanies the answer of the second; **coun′ter-tall′y**, a tally serving as a check to another; **coun′ter-ten′or**, the highest alto male voice (so called because a contrast to tenor); **coun′ter-time**, the resistance of a horse that interrupts his cadence and the measure of his manège : resistance, opposition; **coun′terturn**, a turn in a play different from what was expected.— *v.t.* **countervail′**, to be of avail against : to act against with equal effect : to be of equal value to : to compensate.— *adj.* **countervail′able**.—*n.* **coun′ter-view**, an opposing view : a posture in which two persons face each other : opposition : contrast.—*v.t.* **counter-vote′**, to vote in opposition to; **counter-weigh′**, to weigh against, counterbalance.—*ns.* **coun′ter-weight**, a weight in an opposite scale.—*v.i.* **coun′ter-wheel**, to wheel in an opposite direction.—*n.* **coun′ter-work**, a work raised in opposition to another.—*v.t.* **counter-work′**, to work in opposition to.—*p.adj.* **coun′ter-wrought**. [A.Fr. *countre*, O.Fr. *contre*—L. *contrā*, against.]

counterfeit, *kown′tər-fit*, *-fēt*, *v.t.* to imitate : to copy without authority : to forge.—*n.* something false or copied, or that pretends to be true and original.—*adj.* (*Spens.* **coun′terfect**) pretended : made in imitation : forged : false.—*n.* **coun′ter-feiter**, one who counterfeits.—*adv.* **coun′terfeitly**, in a counterfeit manner : falsely.—*n.* **coun′ter-feisance** (*-fēz′əns; Spens.* **counterfesaunce**), act of counterfeiting : forgery. [O.Fr. *contrefet*, from *contrefaire*, to imitate—L. *contrā*, against, *facĕre*, to do.]

countermand, *kown-tər-mand′*, *v.t.* to give a command in opposition to one already given : to revoke.—*n.* a revocation to a former order.—*adj.* **countermand′able**. [O.Fr. *contremander*—L. *contrā*, against, and *mandāre*, to order.]

counterpane, *kown′tər-pān*, *n.* a coverlet for a bed. —Older form (*Shak.*) **coun′terpoint**. [O.Fr. *contrepoint*—*coultepointe*—L. *culcita puncta*, a stitched pillow; see **quilt**.]

counterpoint, *kown′tər-point*, *n.* (*mus.*) the art of combining melodies : a melody added to another : (*Spens.*) app. a trick : an opposite point.—*adj.* **contrapunt′al**.—*n.* **contrapunt′ist**. [Fr. *contrepoint* and It. *contrappunto*—L. *contrā*, against, *punctum*, a point, from the pricks, points or notes placed against those of the melody; in some senses **counter-** and **point.**]

country, *kun′tri*, *n.* a region : a state : a nation : rural districts as distinct from town : land of birth or citizenship : the district hunted by a pack of foxhounds : the rock surrounding a mineral lode (also **coun′try-rock′**).—*adj.* belonging to the country : rural : rustic : rude.—*adj.* **coun′trified**, **coun′tryfied**.—*ns.* **coun′try-box**, a small country-house; **coun′try-dance**, a dance as practised by country people : a dance in which an indefinite number of couples can take part, arranged in two lines; **coun′try-dan′cing**.—*n.pl.* **coun′try-folk**, fellow-countrymen : rural people.—*ns.* **coun′try-house**, **-seat**, the residence of a country gentleman; **coun′tryman**, one who lives in the country : a farmer : one belonging to the same country, fellow-countryman; **coun′tryside**, a district or part of the country.—*adj.* **countrywide′**, all over the country.—*n.* **coun′try-woman**, a woman who dwells in the country : a woman of the same country. —**country cousin**, a relative from the country, unaccustomed to town sights or manners; **country gentleman**, a landed proprietor who resides on his estate in the country; **country party** (*hist.*), the party opposed to the court; **country town**, a small town in a rural district; **go to the country**, to appeal to the community by a general election; **the country** (*cricket slang*), the outfield. [O.Fr. *contrée*—L.L. *contrāta*, *contrāda*, an extension of L. *contrā*, over against.]

county. See **count** (1).

coup, *kōō*, *n.* a blow, stroke, a successful hit : (*billiards*) the act of putting a ball in a pocket without having hit another ball. [Fr.,—L.L. *colpus*—L. *colaphus*—Gr. *kolaphos*, a blow.]

coup, *kowp*, *v.t.* (*Scot.*) to exchange or barter.—*n.* **coup′er**, a dealer. [O.N. *kaupa*, to buy.]

coup, **cowp**, *kowp*, *v.t.* and *v.i.* (*Scot.*) to overturn : to tip up.—*n.* an upset. [O.Fr. *colp*, blow.]

coupé, *kōō-pā*, *n.* the front part of a French stage-coach : a four-wheeled carriage seated for two inside, with a separate seat for the driver : an end compartment of a railway carriage with a seat on one side only : a covered motor-car seated for two. —*adj.* (*her.*), cut evenly off, as the head or limb of an animal.—Also **couped** (*kōōpt*).—*n.* **coupee**, (*kōō-pē′*) in dancing, a salute to a partner, while swinging one foot. [Fr.,—*pa.p.* of *couper*, to cut.]

couple, *kup′l*, *n.* that which joins two things together : two of a kind joined together, or connected : two : a pair, esp. of married or betrothed persons, dancers, golfers, hunting dogs : a rafter : (*statics*) a pair of equal forces acting on the same body in opposite and parallel directions.—*v.t.* to join together.—*v.i.* to pair sexually.—*ns.* **coup′lement**, union : a couple; **coup′ler**, one who or that which couples or unites : an organ mechanism by which stops of one manual can be played from another or from the pedals; **coup′let**, a pair, couple : a twin : two successive lines of verse that rhyme with each other; **coup′ling**, that which connects : an appliance for transmitting motion in machinery, or for connecting vehicles as in a railway train; **coup′ling-box**, the box or ring of metal connecting the contiguous ends of two lengths of shafts.— *adj.* **well′-coupled**, of a horse, well formed at the part where the back joins the rump. [O.Fr. *cople*— L. *cōpula*.]

coupon, *kōō′pon*, *-pən*, *-ponᵍ*, *-pong*, *n.* a billet, check, or other slip of paper cut off from its counterpart : a separate ticket or part of a ticket, a voucher that payments will be made, services performed, goods sold, or the like : a piece cut from an advertisement entitling one to some privilege. [Fr.,—*couper*, to cut off.]

coupure, *kōō-pūr′*, *n.* an entrenchment made by the besieged behind a breach : a passage cut to facilitate sallies. [Fr.,—*couper*, to cut.]

cour, **coure**, obsolete forms of **cover**, **cower**.

courage, *kur′ij*, *n.* the quality that enables men to meet danger without giving way to fear : bravery : spirit : (*obs.*) desire.—*interj.* take courage.—*adjs.* **cour′ageful**; **courageous** (*kə-rā′jəs*), full of courage : brave.—*adv.* **courā′geously**.—*n.* **courā′geousness.**—**Dutch courage**, a factitious courage induced by drinking; **pluck up courage**, to nerve oneself : to gather boldness; **the courage of one's convictions,** courage to act up to, or consistently with, one's opinions. [O.Fr. *corage* (Fr. *courage*), from L. *cor*, the heart.]

courant, *kōō-ránt'*, *adj.* (*her.*) in a running attitude. —*ns.* **courante'**, **courant'**, an old dance with a kind of gliding step, a coranto : music for it : a newspaper (now in titles only). [Fr., pr.p. of *courir*, to run; see **current.**]

courb, curb, *kōōrb, kurb, v.i.* (*Shak.*) to bend, stoop to supplicate.—*adj.* (*Shak.*) bent (*Spens.* **corbe**). [Fr. *courber*—L. *curvāre*, to bend.]

courbaril, *kōōr'ba-ril, n.* the West Indian locust-tree : its resin, gum anime. [Fr. from Carib.]

courbette, *kōōr-bet'*, French form of **curvet.**

courd (*Spens.*) for **covered.**

courier, *kōō'ri-ər, n.* a runner : a messenger : a state messenger : a travelling attendant : a frequent title of newspapers. [Fr.,—L. *currĕre*, to run.]

courlan, *kōōr'lən, n.* any bird of the American genus Aramus, akin to the rails. [Fr., from a South American name.]

course, *kōrs. n.* a run : the path in which anything moves : the ground over which a race is run, golf is played, or the like : a channel for water : the direction pursued : a voyage : a race : regular progress from point to point : habitual method of procedure : a prescribed series, sequence, process, or treatment, as of lectures, training, water-drinking, etc. : each of the successive divisions of a meal—soup, fish, etc. : conduct : a range of bricks or stones on the same level in building : (*naut.*) one of the sails bent to a ship's lower yards (main-sail = *main-course :* fore-sail = *fore-course :* cross-jack = *mizzen-course)* : (in *pl.*) the menses.— *v.t.* to run, chase, or hunt after.—*v.i.* to run : to move with speed, as in a race or hunt.—*ns.* **cours'er,** a runner : a swift horse (*orig.* a charger) : one who courses or hunts : a swift running bird (Cursorius) ; **cours'ing,** hunting with greyhounds; **cours'ing-joint,** a joint between two courses of masonry.—**in course,** in regular order : (*arch.* or *vulg.*) of course, of course, by natural consequence : indisputably, often a mere apology for making a statement. [Fr. *cours*—L. *cursus*, from *currĕre*, *cursum*, to run.]

court, *kōrt, n.* a space enclosed : a space surrounded by houses : a piece of ground or floor on which certain games are played : a division marked off by lines on such a place : the palace of a sovereign : the body of persons who form his suite or council : an assembly of courtiers : attention, civility, as 'to pay court' : (*law*) hall of justice; the judges and officials who preside there : any body of persons assembled to decide causes : a sitting of such a body.—*v.t.* to pay attentions to : to woo : to solicit : to seek.—*ns.* **court'-bar'on,** the assembly of free-hold tenants of a manor under a lord; **court'-card** (see **coat-card**); **court'-craft,** the courtier's art, intrigue; **court'-cup'board** (*Shak.*), a movable cupboard or sideboard on which plate was displayed; **court'-day,** a day on which a judicial court sits; **court'-dress,** the special regulation costume worn on state or ceremonious occasions; **court'-dress'er,** a flatterer; **court'-fool,** a fool or jester, formerly kept at court for amusement; **court'-guide,** a guide to, or directory of, the names and residences of the nobility in a town; **court'-hand,** a modification of the Norman hand-writing, as distinguished from the modern or Italian handwriting, in use in the English law-courts from the 16th century to the reign of George II; **court'-house,** a building where the law-courts are held; **court'ier,** one who frequents courts or palaces : one who courts or flatters; **court'ierism,** the behaviour or practices of a courtier.—*adj.* and *adv.* **court'ierlike.**—*adv.* **court'ierly.**—*ns.* **court'ing,** paying addresses, wooing ; (*Spens.*) attendance at court; **court'-leet,** a court of record held in a manor before the lord or his steward; **court'let,** a petty court.—*adj.* **court'like,** courtly : polite.—*ns.* **court'liness;** **court'ling,** a hanger-on at court.—*adj.* **court'ly,** having manners like those of, or befitting, a court : politely stately : fair and flattering.—*ns.* **court'-**

mar'tial, a court held by officers of the army, navy or air force for the trial of offences against service laws (one improvised in time of war round an upturned drum for summary judgment was a **drumhead court-martial**) :—*pl.* **courts'-mar'tial;** **court'-plas'ter,** sticking-plaster made of silk, originally applied as patches on the face by ladies at court; **court'-roll,** the record of a court of justice; **court'ship,** courtly behaviour : wooing; **court'-sword,** a light sword worn as part of court-dress; **court'yard,** a court or enclosed ground attached to a house.—**court holy water** (*obs.*), empty compliments : flattery; **court tennis,** the old game of tennis, distinguished from lawn tennis; **out of court,** without claim to be considered. [O.Fr. *cort* (Fr. *cour*)—L.L. *cortis,* a courtyard—L. *cors, cohors, -tis,* an enclosure; akin to Gr. *chortos,* an enclosed place; L. *hortus,* a garden. See **yard.**]

courteous, *kurt'yəs, kōrt'yəs, adj.* polite, considerate or respectful in manner and action : obliging.— *adv.* **court'eously.**—*ns.* **court'eousness;** **court'esy,** (*kurt'*, or *kōrt'e-si*) courteous behaviour : an act of civility or respect : a curtsy : (*law*) the life interest of the surviving husband in his wife's estate.—*v.i.* to make a curtsy (*pr.p.* **court'esying;** *pa.t.* and *pa.p.* **court'esied**).—*n.* **court'esy-ti'tle,** a title really invalid, but allowed by the usage of society—as to children of peers.—**remember your courtesy** (*obs.*), please put on your hat; **strain courtesy** (see **strain**). [O.Fr. *corteis, cortois;* see **court.**]

courtesan, -zan, *kōrt', kurt'i-zan,* or *-zan', n.* a court mistress : a whore. [Fr. *courtisane*—It. *cortigiana,* orig. a woman of the court.]

couscous, *koos'koos,* **couscousou,** *-ōō', n.* a N. African dish of granulated flour steamed over broth. [Fr.,—Ar. *kuskus—kaskasa,* to pound; see **cuscus** (2).]

cousin, *kuz'n, n.* formerly a kinsman generally : now, the son or daughter of an uncle or aunt : a term used by a sovereign in addressing another, or to one of his own nobles : something kindred or related to another.—*ns.* **cous'in-ger'man,** a first cousin : something closely related; **cous'inhood,** **cous'inship.**—*adj.* **cous'inly,** like, or having the relation of, a cousin.—*n.* **cous'inry,** cousins collectively.—**first cousins,** children of brothers and sisters, full cousins; **first cousin once removed,** the son or daughter of a cousin-german —sometimes loosely called *second cousin;* **second cousins,** the children of first cousins. [Fr.,—L. *consōbrīnus—con-,* sig. connexion, and *sobrīnus,* applied to the children of sisters from the root of *soror,* a sister.]

couter, *kōō'tər, n.* (*slang*) a sovereign. [Said to be from Gypsy *cuta,* a gold piece.]

couth, *kōōth,* obsolete *pa.t.* and *pa.p.* of **can:** could : knew : known : did. [O.E. *pa.t. cúthe,* pa.p. *cúth;* see **could.**]

couthie, *kōōth'i, adj.* (*Scot.*) friendly, kindly : comfortable : snug. [Prob. O.E. *cúth,* known.]

coutil, coutille, *kōō-til', n.* a strong cotton fabric used in mattresses, etc. [Fr. *coutil.*]

couvade, *kōō-väd', n.* a custom among savages in many parts of the world for the father to take to his bed at the birth of a child, and submit to certain restrictions of food, etc. [Erroneously attributed to the Basques; the O.Fr. *couvade,* from *couver,* to hatch, never having had this special meaning.]

covalency, *kō-vā'lən-si, n.* the union of two atoms by the sharing of a pair of electrons, one from each atom—cf. **electrovalency.**—*adj.* **cova'lent.** [L. *co-,* together, and **valency.**]

cove, *kōv, n.* a small inlet of the sea : a bay : a cavern or rocky recess : (*archit.*) a curved junction of wall and ceiling.—*v.t.* to overarch.—*adj.* **coved,** formed with an arch.—*n.* **cove'let,** a small cove. [O.E. *cofa,* a room; O.N. *kofi,* Ger. *koben.*]

cove, *kōv, n.* (*slang*) a fellow, a customer :—*dim.* **cov'ey.** [Origin obscure.]

covellite, *kō-vel'it, n.* a blue mineral, cupric sulphide. [*Covelli,* its discoverer.]

coven. See **covin.**

Neutral vowels in unaccented syllables : *el'ə-mənt, in'fənt, ran'dəm*

covenant, *kuv'ə-nənt*, *n.* a mutual agreement : the writing containing the agreement : an engagement entered into between God and a person or a people—a dispensation, testament.—*v.i.* to enter into an agreement.—*v.t.* to agree to : to stipulate.—*n.* cov'enant-break'er, one who violates a covenant.—*adj.* cov'enanted, agreed to by covenant : bound by covenant : holding a position under a covenant or contract.—*ns.* covenantee', the person to whom a covenant is made ; cov'-enanter (usually in Scotland, *kuv-ə-nant'ər*), one who signed or adhered to the *Scottish National Covenant* of 1638 (the *Solemn League and Covenant* of 1643 was in effect an international treaty between Scotland and England for securing civil and religious liberty) ; cov'enantor, that party to a covenant who subjects himself to the penalty of its breach.—**covenant of grace, redemption**, in Christian theology, that by which life is freely offered to sinners on condition of faith in Christ ; **covenant of works**, that made with Adam as federal representative of the human race on condition of obedience. [O.Fr.,—L. *con-*, together, and *venīre*, to come.]

covent, *kov'ənt*, *kuv'ənt*, *n.* (*Shak.*) a variant of **convent**.

Coventry, *kuv'*, *kov'ənt-ri*, *n.* a town of Warwickshire.—**Coventry blue**, a blue thread once made there ; **send to Coventry**, to exclude from social intercourse.

cover, *kuv'ər*, *v.t.* to put or spread something on, over or about : to come or be on, over or about : to hide : to clothe : to protect : to screen : to brood or sit on : to suffice for : to provide for or against : to comprise : to traverse : to take as field of operations : to play a higher card upon : to table upon a coin of equal value in wagering : to set as for a meal : to copulate with—esp. of a stallion : to command with a weapon : (*U.S.*) to report.—*v.i.* to lay a table for a meal : to put one's hat on.—*n.* that which covers or is intended to cover : a lid : the binding of a book : an envelope : undergrowth, thicket, concealing game, etc. : the table requisites for one person—plate, knife, fork, napkin, etc. : a pretext : a disguise : a confederate.—*ns.* cov'erage, area or (*fig.*) amount covered or included : the group or section of the community reached by an advertising medium : risks covered by an insurance : amount available to cover liabilities ; cov'er-crop, a subsidiary crop grown partly to protect the soil.—*adj.* cov'ered, having a cover : sheltered, concealed : roofed over : with a hat on.—*ns.* cov'ered-way, cov'ert-way (*fort.*), a path outside the ditch of a fort, sunk below the crest of the glacis to afford cover ; cov'er-glass, a thin glass placed over the object on a microscope slide ; cov'ering, anything that covers ; cov'er-point, in cricket, etc., the player who supports point and stands to his right : the position of such a player ; cov'er-slut, an outer garment worn to hide rags or dirty clothes.—*adj.* cov'ert, covered : concealed : secret : (*Spens.*) concealing.—*n.* a feather covering the quill-bases of wings and tail : (usu. pron. *kuv'ər*) a cover for game : a shelter.—*ns.* cov'ert-coat, a short light overcoat ; cov'ert-coat'ing, cloth for such.—*adv.* cov'ertly, in a covered or concealed manner.—*n.* cov'erture, covering, shelter : disguise : (*Spens.*) secret proceedings : (*law*) the condition of a married woman as legally deemed under the protection of her husband.—**cover girl**, a girl pictured on a magazine cover ; **covering letter**, letter to explain documents enclosed with it ; **cover into**, to transfer into ; **cover shorts**, to buy in such stocks as have been sold short, in order to meet one's engagements, etc. : **cover the buckle**, to execute a certain difficult step in dancing. [Fr. *couvrir* (It. *coprire*)— L. *co-operīre*—*co-*, and *operīre*, to cover.]

coverlet, *kuv'ər-lit*, *n.* a bedcover.—Also **cov'er-lid**. [Fr. *couvrir*, to cover, *lit*—L. *lectum*, a bed.]

covet, *kuv'it*, *v.t.* to desire or wish for eagerly : to wish for wrongfully.—*v.i.* (*Shak.*) to desire (with *for* ; *pr.p.* cov'eting : *pa.t.* and *pa.p.* cov'eted).—*adjs.* cov'etable ; cov'eted.—*adv.* cov'etingly.—*ns.* cov'etise (*obs.*), covetousness : ardent desire ; cov'etiveness (*obs.*), acquisitiveness.—*adj.* cov'et-

ous, inordinately desirous : avaricious.—*adv.* cov'etously.—*n.* cov'etousness. [O.Fr. *coveiter* (Fr. *convoiter*)—L. *cupiditās*, *-ātis*—*cupēre*, to desire.]

covey, *kuv'i*, *n.* a brood or hatch of partridges : a small flock of game birds : a party, a set. [O.Fr. *covée*—L. *cubāre*, to lie down.]

covin, covyne, coven, *kŏv'in, kuv'in, -ən*, *n.* a compact : a conspiracy : plotting : a muster of witches : a gang of thirteen witches.—*adj.* covinous (*kuv'*), fraudulent.—*n.* cov'in-tree', a tree before a Scottish mansion at which guests were met and parted from. [O.Fr. *covin*—L.L. *convenium*— *con-*, together, *venīre*, to come.]

coving, *kō'ving*, *n.* the projection of upper stories over lower : the vertical sides connecting the jambs with the breast of a fireplace. [See **cove**.]

cow, *kow*, *n.* the female of the bovine animals : the female of certain other animals, as the elk, elephant, whale, etc :—*pl.* **cows**, older **kine** (*kīn*) and (still in *Scots*) **kye** (*kī*).—*ns.* cow'-bane, the water hemlock (*Cicuta virosa*), often destructive to cattle ; cow'-bell, a bell for a cow's neck ; cow'-berry, the red whortleberry (*Vaccinium Vitis-Idaea*) ; cow'-bird, -black'bird, -bunt'ing, an American bird (*Molothrus*) of the troupial family, that accompanies cattle, and drops its eggs into other birds' nests ; cow'boy, a boy who has the care of cows : (*U.S.*) a man who has the charge of cattle on a ranch ; cow'-calf, a female calf ; cow'-catcher (*U.S.*), an apparatus on the front of a railway engine to throw off obstacles ; cow'-cher'vil, -pars'ley, -weed, wild chervil ; cow'feeder, a dairyman ; cow'-fish, a coffer-fish (with cowlike head) : a manati : any small cetacean ; cow'-grass, perennial red clover : zigzag clover ; cow'-heel, an ox-foot stewed to a jelly ; cow'herd, one who herds cows ; cow'hide, the hide of a cow : the hide of a cow made into leather : a coarse whip made of twisted strips of cowhide.—*v.t.* to whip with a cowhide.—*n.* cow'house, a building in which cows are stalled, a byre.—*adj.* cow'ish, like a cow : (*Shak.*) cowardly.—*ns.* cow'-leech, a cow-doctor ; cow'lick, a tuft of turned-up hair on the forehead ; cow'-pars'nip, an umbelliferous plant, hogweed (*Heracleum Sphondylium*) used as fodder ; cow'-pea, a leguminous plant (*Vigna sinensis*) of Asia, used like French beans ; cow'-pil'ot, a West Indian demoiselle fish, said to accompany the cow-fish ; cow'-plant, an asclepiadaceous plant of Ceylon (*Gymnema lactiferum*) with a milky juice ; cow'-pox, a disease that appears in pimples on the teats of the cow, the matter thereof used for vaccination ; cow'-puncher, a cowboy : a driver of cows ; cow'shed, a cowhouse ; cow'-tree, a South American tree (*Brosimum Galactodendron*) of the mulberry family, that produces a nourishing fluid resembling milk ; cow'-wheat, a yellow flowered scrophulariaceous plant (*Melampyrum*), with seeds somewhat like grains of wheat. [O.E. *cú*, pl. *cý* ; Ger. *kuh* ; Sans. *gáus' go-*.]

cow, *kow*, *n.* (*Scot.*) a branch, bunch of twigs, besom. [Poss. O.Fr. *coe*—L. *cauda*, tail.]

cow, *kow*, *v.t.* to subdue the spirit of : to keep under.—*adj.* cowed, abjectly depressed or intimidated. [Perh. from O.N. *kúga* ; Dan. *kue*, to subdue.]

cow, *kow*, *n.* (*Dickens*) a chimney cowl. [A variant of **cowl**.]

cowan, *kow'ən*, *n.* (*Scot.*) a dry-stone-diker : a mason who never served an apprenticeship : one who tries to enter a Freemason's lodge, or the like, surreptitiously. [Origin doubtful.]

coward, *kow'ərd*, *n.* a reprehensibly faint-hearted person : one without courage : often applied to one who, whether courageous or not, brutally takes advantage of the weak.—*v.t.* to make cowardly.—*adj.* cowardly : (*her.*) with tail between legs.—*ns.* cow'ardice (*-is*), want of courage : timidity ; cow'ardliness.—*adj.* cow'ardly, having the character of a coward : befitting a coward : characteristic of a coward.—*adv.* like a coward : with cowardice.—*ns.* cow'ardry (*Spens.* cowardree) ; cow'ardship (*Shak.*). [O.Fr. *couard* (It. *codardo*)—L. *cauda*, a tail.]

cowdie-gum ; **-pine** ; **cowrie-pine**. See **kauri**.

cower, *kow'ər, v.i.* to sink down through fear, etc. : to crouch shrinkingly.—*adv.* **cow'eringly**. [Cf. O.N. *kúra,* Dan. *kure,* to lie quiet.]

cowhage, cowage, *cowitch,* **cowich,** *kow'ij, -ich, n.* a tropical leguminous climber (Mucuna) : the stinging hairs on its pod, used as a vermifuge : its pods. [Hind. *kawānch.*]

cowheard, cowherd, Spenserian spellings of **coward.**

cowl, *kowl, n.* a cap or hood : a monk's hood : the badge of monkhood : a monk : a cover for a chimney : an engine bonnet : a cowling.—*v.t.* to make a monk of : to cover like a cowl.—*adj.* **cowled,** wearing a cowl.—*n.* **cowl'ing,** the casing of an aeroplane engine. [O.E. *cugele;* O.N. *kofl;* akin to L. *cucullus,* hood.]

cowl, *kōl, kōōl, kowl, n.* (*dial.* or *arch.*) a tub or large vessel for liquids.—*n.* **cowl'-staff** (*Shak.*), a pole on which a basket or vessel is slung. [O.E. *cúfel* or O.Fr. *cuvele,* both—L. *cūpella,* dim. of *cūpa,* a cask.]

cowrie, cowry, *kow'ri, n.* a large genus (Cypraea) of gasteropods used among primitive people as money and magical objects. [Hindi *kaurī.*]

cowslip, *kow'slip, n.* a species of primrose, with flowers in umbels, common in pastures : in U.S. the marsh-marigold.—*adj.* **cow'slip'd,** covered with cowslips. [O.E. *cúslyppe—cú,* cow, *slyppe,* slime, i.e. cow-dung.]

cox, koks, a shortened form of **coxswain.**

coxa, *koks'ā, n.* the hip : the proximal joint of an arthropod's leg.—*adj.* **cox'al.**—*n.* **coxal'gia** (*ji-ä*), pain in the hip. [L.]

coxcomb, *koks'kōm, n.* a strip of red cloth notched like a cock's comb, which professional fools used to wear : (*Shak.*) the head : a fool : a fop.—*adjs.* **coxcombic** (*-kōm', -kom'*), **-al, coxcom'ical,** foppish : vain.—*n.* **coxcombical'ity.**—*adv.* **coxcomb'ically.**—*n.* **cox'combry,** the manner of a coxcomb. [**cock's comb.**]

coxswain, cockswain, *kok'sn,* or *kok'swän, n.* one who steers a boat : a petty officer in charge of a boat and crew.—*v.t.* and *v.i.* to act as coxswain (for).—Often contr. **cox.** [**cock,** a boat, and **swain.**]

coxy. See **cock.**

coy, *koi, adj.* retiring : bashful : shy.—*v.t.* (*Shak.*) to caress : (*Shak.*) to disdain : to affect coyness (with *it*).—*adj.* **coy'ish.**—*adv.* **coy'ishly.**—*n.* **coy'ishness.**—*adv.* **coy'ly.**—*n.* **coy'ness.** [Fr. *coi*—L. *quiëtus,* quiet.]

coyote, *kō-yō'tā, kī-ōt'e, kī'ōt, kī'ət, n.* a prairie-wolf, a small wolf of N. America. [Mex. *coyotl.*]

coypu, *koi'pōō,* or *-pōō', n.* a large South American aquatic rodent (Myopotamus) yielding nutria fur. [Native name.]

coystrel, coystril. Same as **coistril.**

coz, *kuz, n.* a contraction of **cousin.**

coze, *kōz, v.i.* to chat.—Also *n.* [Fr. *causer.*]

cozen, *kuz'n. v.t.* to cheat.—*ns.* **coz'enage,** deceit; **coz'ener.** [Perh. Fr. *cousiner,* to claim kindred; see **cousin.**]

cozier, cosier, *kō'zi-ər, n.* (*Shak.*) a cobbler. [O.Fr. *cousere,* tailor—L. *cōnsuĕre,* to sew together, *—con-, suĕre,* to sew.]

crab, *krab, n.* any of the Brachyura or short-tailed decapod crustaceans : Cancer (sign of the zodiac and constellation) : a portable winch : the lowest throw at hazard—two aces.—*v.i.* to drift or fly sideways : to fish for crabs.—*n.* **crab'-eat'er,** a sergeant-fish : an antarctic seal.—*adj.* **crab'-faced,** having a peevish countenance.—*adj.* and *adv.* **crab'-like.**—**crab'-louse,** a crab-shaped louse infesting the hair of the pubis, etc.—*n.,pl.* **crab's'-eyes, crab'-stones,** prayer-beads, the scarlet and black seeds of the Indian liquorice tree (*Abrus precatorius*) : a limy concretion in the crayfish's stomach.—*v.i.* **crab'-sī'dle,** to go sideways like a crab.—*n.pl.* **crab'-yaws,** framboesia tumours on the soles and palms.—**catch a crab,** to sink the oar too deeply (or not enough) in the water and fall back in consequence. [O.E. *crabba;* Ger. *krebs.*]

crab, *krab, n.* a wild bitter apple : a sour-tempered person.—*ns.* **crab'-apple; crab'stick; crab'-tree.** [Ety. doubtful.]

crab, *krab, v.t.* (of hawks) to claw : (*coll.*) to decry : to obstruct, wreck, or frustrate.—*n.* dejection : fault-finding. [**crab** (1).]

crabbed, *krab'id, adj.* ill-natured : harsh : rough : rugged : crooked : knotted : undecipherable.—*adv.* **crabb'edly.**—*n.* **crabb'edness.** [**crab** (1), intermixed in meaning with **crab** (2).]

crab-nut, -oil, -wood. See **carapa.**

crack, *krak, v.t.* and *v.i.* to make or cause to make a sharp sudden sound : to break into chinks : to split : to break partially or suddenly : (of petroleum, etc.) to break into simpler molecules : (*obs.*) to boast.—*v.i.* (*Scot.*) to chat.—*n.* a sudden sharp splitting sound : a chink : a flaw : a blow, a smack : a moment : break (of day) : (*Scot.*) a friendly chat : (*U.S.*) a biting speech : (*slang*) housebreaking : an expert : a craze : one who has a craze : (*Shak.*) a pert boy.—*adj.* (*coll.*) excellent : expert.—*n.* **crack'-brain,** a crazy person.—*adjs.* **crack'-brained; cracked,** rent : damaged : crazy.—*ns.* **crack'ajack, crack'erjack,** a person or thing of the highest excellence; **crack'er,** one who or that which cracks : a boaster, a lie : the pin-tail duck : (*U.S.*) a thin crisp biscuit : a small firework, exploding when pulled asunder : a firework tied zigzagwise that bounces at each explosion; (*U.S.*) a poor white; **crack'er-box** (*U.S.*), a biscuit-box.—*adj.* **crack'ers,** crazy: unbalanced.—*ns.* **crack'-halt'er, crack'-hemp** (*Shak.*), **crack'-rope,** one likely or deserving to be hanged.—*adj.* **crack'-jaw,** hard to pronounce.—*ns* **crack'-shot,** an expert marksman; **cracks'man,** a burglar; **crack'-tryst,** one who breaks an engagement.—**crack a bottle,** open or drink a bottle; **crack a crib** (*thieves' slang*), to break into a building; **crack a joke,** to utter a joke with some effect; **crack credit,** to destroy one's credit; **crack up,** to praise : to fail suddenly, to go to pieces. [O.E. *cracian,* to crack; cf. Du. *kraken,* Gael. *crac.*]

crackle, *krak'l, v.i.* to give out slight but frequent cracks.—*n.* the giving out of slight cracks.—*ns.* **crack'lin,** a kind of china-ware, purposely cracked in the kiln as an ornament; **crack'ling,** the rind of roast pork : (*pl.*) skinny part of suet without tallow : four bars of velvet worn on both sleeves of students' gowns at St. John's College, Cambridge.—*adj.* **crack'ly,** brittle.—*n.* **crack'nel,** a light, brittle biscuit : (in *pl.*) pieces of fat pork fried crisp. [Freq. of **crack.**]

Cracovian, *kra-kō'vi-ən, adj.* pertaining to *Cracow.*—*ns.* **cracovienne** (*-en'*), a lively Polish dance : music for it, in 2-4 time.—Also **krako'viak;** **cracowe** (*krak'ow*), a long-toed boot fashionable under Richard II.

cradle, *krā'dl, n.* a bed or crib in which a child is rocked : (*fig.*) infancy : place of origin or nurture : a framework, esp. one for keeping bedclothes from pressing on a patient or one under a ship for launching : a rocking box for gold-washing : an engraver's knife used with a rocking motion.—*v.t.* to lay or rock in a cradle : to nurture.—*ns.* **crā'dle-scythe,** a broad scythe used in a cradle for cutting grain; **crā'dle-walk,** an avenue arched over with trees; **crā'dling.** [O.E. *cradol;* ety. obscure.]

craft, *kräft, n.* cunning : artifice : dexterity : art : skilled trade : occupation : a ship or ships (of any kind, orig. small).—*v.i.* to exercise one's craft (*Shak., Cor.,* IV. vi. 118).—*ns.* **craft'-broth'er,** a person engaged in the same trade as another; **craft'-guild,** an association of men engaged in the same trade.—*adv.* **craft'ily.**—*n.* **craft'iness.**—*adj.* **craft'less,** free from craft : unskilled in any craft.—*ns.* **crafts'man,** one engaged in a craft; **crafts'-manship, craft'manship;** **crafts'master,** one skilled in a craft.—*adj.* **craft'y** (*arch.*), having skill : cunning : wily. [O.E. *cræft;* Ger. *kraft,* power.]

crag, *krag, n.* a rough steep rock or point : (*geol.*), a shelly deposit mixed with sand, found in the Pliocene of East Anglia.—*n.* **crag'-and-tail'** (*geol.*), a hill-form with steep declivity at one end and a gentle slope at the other.—*adjs.* **crag'fast,** unable to move from a position on a crag; **cragg'ed,**

craggy.—ns. cragg'edness, cragg'iness; crags'-man, one skilled in climbing rocks.—adj. cragg'y, full of crags or broken rocks: rough: rugged. [App. conn. with Gael. creag, carraig.]

crag, krag, n. neck: throat. [Cf. Du. kraag, Ger. kragen, the neck.]

craig, krāg, n. Scots form of crag (cliff) and of crag (neck).—craig'fluke', the witch (Pleuronectes cynoglossus), a flat fish.

crake, krāk, n. (dial.) a crow, a raven: a corncrake: a croak: the cry of the corncrake.—v.i. to utter a crake.—n. crake'-berry (dial.), crowberry. [Cf. corncrake, croak.]

crake, krāk, n., v.t. and v.i. (Spens.) boast. [crack.]

cram, kram, v.t. to press close: to stuff: to fill to superfluity: to overfeed: to feed with a view to fattening: (slang) to make believe false or exaggerated tales: to teach, or get up, hastily for a certain occasion (as an examination, a lawsuit), to the extent required for the occasion.—v.i. to eat greedily: to get up by cramming (pr.p. cramm'ing: pa.t. and pa.p. crammed).—n. a crush: (slang) a lie: information that has been crammed: the system of cramming.—adjs. cram'-full'; cramm'able; crammed.—n. cramm'er, a person or machine that crams poultry: one who crams pupils or a subject: (slang) a lie. [O.E. crammian; O.N. kremja, to squeeze; Dan. kramme, to crumple.]

crambo, kram'bō, n. a game in which one gives a word to which another finds a rhyme: rhyme.—ns. cram'boclink, -jingle, rhyming. [Prob. from L. crambē repetīta, cabbage served up again.]

crame, krām, n. (Scot.) a booth for selling goods. [From Du. or Low Ger.]

cramoisy, cramesy, kram'əz-i (or -oi-zi), adj. and n. crimson. [See crimson.]

cramp, kramp, n. an involuntary and painful contraction of a voluntary muscle or group of muscles (in U.S. often in pl.): restraint: cramp-iron: a contrivance with a movable part that can be screwed tight so as to press things together.—adj. hard to make out (used of handwriting): cramped: narrow.—v.t. to affect with spasms: to confine: to hamper: to fasten with a cramp-iron.—ns. cramp'bark (U.S.), the guelder-rose, or its medicinal bark; cramp'-bone, the patella of the sheep, an old charm for cramp; cramp'et, cramp'it, a scabbard-chape: a cramp-iron: a crampon: an iron foot-board for curlers; cramp'-fish, the electric ray or torpedo; cramp'-iron, a piece of metal bent at both ends for binding things together; cramp'on, a grappling-iron: a spiked contrivance for climbing mountains or telegraph poles or walking on ice; cramp'-ring, a ring formerly blessed by the sovereign on Good-Friday against cramp and falling sickness.—adj. cramp'y, affected or diseased with cramp: producing cramp.—bather's cramp, paralysis attacking a bather; writer's cramp, or Scrivener's palsy, a common disease affecting those in the habit of constant writing, the muscles refusing to obey only on attempting to write. [O.Fr. crampe; cf. Du. kramp, Ger. krampf.]

cran, kran, n. a measure of capacity in Scotland for herrings when just taken out of the net—37½ gallons, about 750 herrings.—coup the cran (Scot.), to be upset. [Prob. from Gael. crann, a measure.]

cranberry, kran'bər-i, n. the red acid berry of a small evergreen shrub (Vaccinium Oxycoccos; Ericaceae) growing in peaty bogs and marshy grounds: the larger berry of an American species (V. macrocarpum): extended loosely to other species of the genus: the shrub itself.—n. cran'-berry-tree (U.S.), the guelder-rose. [For cranberry; a late word; origin obscure; cf. Ger. kranbeere or kranichbeere.]

cranch, craunch, krânsh, kravnsh, n. and v.t. Same as crunch.

crane, krān, n. any bird of the Gruidae, large wading birds with long legs, neck, and bill: a bent pipe for drawing liquor out of a cask: a machine for raising heavy weights—both named from their likeness to the bird.—v.t. to raise with a crane: to stretch as a crane does its neck.—v.i. to stretch out the neck: to pull up before a jump.—ns. crān'age, the use of a crane: the price paid for the use of it; crane'-fly, a fly (Tipula) with very long legs—the daddy - long - legs.—adj. crane'-necked.—n. cranes'bill, crane's'-bill, any wild species of Geranium, from the beaked fruit. [O.E. cran; Ger. kranich, W. garan.]

crane. Same as cranium.

cranium, krā'ni-əm, n. the skull: the bones enclosing the brain:—pl. crā'nia.—adj. crā'nial. —n.pl. Crāniā'ta (zool.), the main division of Chordata, having a cranium.—n. crāniog'nomy, cranial physiognomy.—adj. crāniolog'ical.—ns. crāniol'ogist; crāniol'ogy, the study of skulls: phrenology; crāniom'eter, an instrument for measuring the skull; crāniom'etry; crānios'-copist, a phrenologist; crānios'copy, phrenology; crāniot'omy (Gr. tomē, a cut; obstetrics), the act of breaking down the head of the foetus.—cranial index, the breadth of a skull as a percentage of the length. [L.L. crānium—Gr. krānion, the skull.]

crank, krangk, n. a crook or bend: a conceit in speech: a whim: a faddist: (mach.) an arm on a shaft for communicating motion to or from the shaft.—v.i. to move in a zigzag manner: to turn a crank (often with up).—v.t. to shape like a crank: to provide with a crank: to move or seek to move by turning a crank.—adj. crooked: crabbed: loose or slack.—adv. crank'ily.—n. crank'iness. —adj. crank'y, crooked: infirm: full of whims: cross. [O.E. cranc, cf. Ger. krank.]

crank, krangk, adj. brisk: merry.—Also adv. [Origin unknown.]

crank, krangk, crank-sided, krangk-sī'did, adj. (naut.) liable to be upset.—n. crank'ness, liability to be upset. [Ety. uncertain.]

crankle, krangk'l, crinkle, kringk'l, n. a turn, winding, or wrinkle, an angular protuberance.— v.t. and v.i. to bend: to twist. [Freq. of crank.]

crannog, kran'og, n. in Scotland and Ireland a fortified island (partly natural and partly artificial) in a lake: a lake-dwelling. [Gael. crann, a tree.]

cranny, kran'i, n. a rent: a chink: a secret place.— v.i. to enter crannies.—adj. crann'ied, having crannies, rents, or fissures. [Fr. cran, a notch.]

cranreuch, krän'ruhh, n. (Scot.) hoar-frost. [Origin obscure: poss. for Gaelic.]

crants, krants, n. (Shak.) the garland carried before the bier of a maiden and hung over her grave. [Ger. kranz, a wreath, a garland.]

crap, krāp, n. Scots form of crop.—v.t. to crop: to cram, stuff.—n. crappit-head, -heid (krăp'it-hēd), a haddock's head stuffed with a compound of oatmeal, suet, onions, and pepper.

crape, krāp, n. a thin silk fabric, tightly twisted, without removing the natural gum—usually dyed black, used for mournings.—adj. made of crape.— v.t. to cloth with crape: to frizzle (hair).—adj. crap'y. [O.Fr. crespe (Fr. crêpe)—L. crispus, crisp.]

craple, krap'l, n. (Spens.). Same as grapple.

crapulence, krap'ū-ləns, n. sickness caused by excessive drinking: intemperance.—adjs. crap'-ulent, crap'ulous.—n. crapulos'ity. [Fr. crapule —L. crāpula, intoxication.]

crare, crayer, krār, n. a trading vessel. [O.Fr. craier.]

crash, krash, n. a noise as of things breaking or being crushed by falling: the shock of two bodies meeting: the failure of a commercial undertaking: a fall or rush to destruction.—v.i. to fall to pieces with a loud noise: to move with such a noise: to come to grief: (of aircraft) to alight with damage. —v.t. to dash in pieces: to drive to a crash: to intrude upon uninvited.—n. crash'-dive', a sudden dive of a submarine.—adj. crash'-proof. [From the sound.]

crash, krash, n. a coarse strong linen. [Perh. from Russ.]

crasis, krā'sis, n. the mixture of different elements in the constitution of the body: temperament: (gram.) the mingling or contraction of two vowels into one long vowel, or into a diphthong:—pl. crā'sēs (-sēz). [Gr. krāsis, mixture.]

crass, *kras, adj.* gross : thick : dense : stupid.—*ns.* **crassament'um,** the thick part of coagulated blood : the clot ; **crass'itude,** coarseness : density : stupidity.—*adv.* **crass'ly.**—*n.* **crass'ness.**—*n.pl.* **Crassūlā'ceae,** a family of succulent plants including stone-crop and house-leek. [L. *crassus.*]

Crataegus, *kra-tē'gəs, n.* the hawthorn genus. [Latinised from Gr. *krataigos.*]

cratch, *krach, n.* a crib to hold hay for cattle, a manger.—*n.pl.* **cratches,** a swelling on a horse's pastern, under the fetlock. [Fr. *crèche,* manger ; from a Gmc. root, whence also **crib.**]

crate, *krāt, n.* a wicker-work case for packing crockery in, or for carrying fruit : a packing-case : an open frame-work of spars.—*v.t.* to pack in a crate. [L. *crātis,* a hurdle.]

crater, *krāt'ər, n.* (*ant.*) a large bowl for mixing wine : the mouth of a volcano : a hole in the ground made by the fall of a meteor or the explosion of a shell or a mine : a cavity formed in the carbon of an electric arc.—*n.* **Crāterell'us,** a genus of funnel-shaped fungi.—*adjs.* **crateriform** (*krat-er'i-form,* or *krāt'*) cup-shaped : **crāt'erous.** [L., —Gr. *krātēr.*]

craunch, *krawnch.* A form of **crunch.**

cravat, *krə-vat', n.* a kind of neckcloth worn chiefly by men.—*v.t.* to dress in a cravat. [Fr. *cravate*—introduced in 1636 from the *Cravates* or Croatians.]

crave, *krāv, v.t.* to beg earnestly : to beseech : to require : to long for.—*n.* a longing : (*Scots law*) a claim.—*ns.* **crav'er,** one who craves : a beggar : **crav'ing,** a longing. [O.E. *crafian,* to crave ; O.N. *krefja.*]

craven, *krāv'n, n.* a coward : a spiritless fellow.— *adj.* cowardly : spiritless.—*v.t.* (*Shak.*) to render spiritless.—*adv.* **crav'enly.**—*n.* **crav'enness.**— **to cry craven,** to surrender. [Origin obscure.]

craw, *kraw, n.* the crop, throat, or first stomach of fowls : the stomach of animals generally. [M.E. *crawe ;* not found in O.E. ; cf. Du. *kraag,* neck.]

crawfish. See **crayfish.**

crawl, *krawl, v.i.* to move slowly with the body on or close to the ground : to move on hands and knees : to creep : to move slowly or stealthily : to behave abjectly : to warp : to be covered with crawling things.—*n.* the act of crawling : a slow pace : an alternate overhand swimming stroke.—*n.* **crawl'er,** one who or that which crawls : an abject person : a sluggish person : a creeping thing : a cab moving slowly in hope of a fare : a caterpillar tractor : a baby's overall.—*n.* and *adj.* **crawl'ing.** —*adj.* **crawl'y** (*coll.*), with, or like the feeling of, something crawling over one : creepy. [Scand. ; O.N. *krafla,* to paw ; Dan. *kravle.*]

crawl, *krawl, n.* a pen for keeping fish : a kraal (q.v.).

Crax, *kraks, n.* the curassow genus of birds.

crayfish, *krā'fish,* **crawfish,** *kraw'fish, n.* a large fresh-water decapod crustacean : the Norway lobster : the small spiny lobster. [M.E. *crevice*— O.Fr. *crevice* (Fr. *écrevisse,* a crayfish.)—O.H.G. *krebiz,* a crab.]

crayon, *krā'ən, n.* a pencil made of chalk or pipeclay, variously coloured, used for drawing : a drawing done with crayons.—*v.t.* to draw with a crayon.— **in crayons,** of a picture, made by crayons. [Fr. *crayon*—*craie,* chalk, from L. *crēta,* chalk.]

craze, *krāz, v.t.* (*Milt.*) to shatter : to crack : to cover with fine cracks (as pottery) : to weaken : to impair : to derange (of the intellect).—*v.i.* to develop fine cracks : to become mad.—*n.* a crack, flaw : a finely cracked condition : insanity : fashion, fad.—*adj.* **crazed.**—*adv.* **craz'ily.**—*ns.* **craz'i-ness ; craz'ing-mill,** a mill for crushing tin-ore. —*adj.* **craz'y,** frail : cracked : insane : demented : fantastically composed of irregular pieces (as a quilt or pavement). [Scand. ; cf. Sw. *krasa,* Dan. *krase,* to crackle ; also Fr. *écraser,* to crush.]

creagh, creach, *krehh, n.* a foray : booty. [Gael. *creach.*]

creak, *krēk, v.i.* to make a sharp, grating sound, as of a hinge, etc.—*n.* a grating noise, as of an unoiled hinge.—*adv.* **creak'ily.**—*adj.* **creak'y.** [From the sound, like **crake,** and **croak.**]

cream, *krēm, n.* the oily substance that rises on milk, yielding butter when churned : that which rises to the top : the best part of anything : any cream-like substance, as *cold cream* for the skin, etc., or any dish largely made of cream, or like cream, as *chocolate-cream, ice-cream, whipped-cream,* etc.—*v.t.* to take off the cream from : to treat with cream : to make creamy.—*v.t.* to gather or form as or like cream.—*adj.* of the colour of cream : prepared with cream.—*ns.* **cream'-cake,** a kind of cake filled with creamy material, etc. ; **cream'-cheese',** cheese made with cream.— *adj.* **cream'-coloured,** of the colour of cream, light yellow.—*n.* **cream'ery,** an establishment where butter and cheese are made from the milk supplied by a number of producers : a shop for milk, butter, etc.—*adj.* **cream'-faced,** pale-faced. —*n.* **cream'iness.**—*adj.* **cream'-laid,** of a cream-colour or white with a laid water-mark.—*ns.* **cream'-nut,** the Brazil nut ; **cream'-slice,** a wooden blade for skimming cream from milk.— *adj.* **cream'-wove,** of a cream-colour or white, and wove ; **cream'y,** full of or like cream : gathering like cream.—**cream of tartar,** a white crystalline compound made by purifying argol, potassium hydrogen tartrate ; **cream of tartar tree,** the baobab : an Australian tree of the same genus. [O.Fr. *cresme, creme*—L. *chrisma*—Gr. *chrīsma,* unction.]

creance, *krē'əns, n.* the cord which secures the hawk in training. [Fr. *créance.*]

creant, *krē'ənt, adj.* creating : formative. [L. *creāns, -āntis, pr.p.* of *creāre ;* see **create.**]

crease, *krēs, n.* a mark made by folding or doubling anything : (*cricket*) a regulative line, of three kinds —*bowling-crease,* from behind or astride of which the bowler must bowl, *popping-crease,* 4 feet in front of it, at which the batsman plays and behind which is his ground, *return-crease,* marking the sideward limits of the bowler.—*v.t.* to make creases in.—*v.i.* to become creased.—*adj.* **creas'y,** full of creases. [Origin uncertain.]

crease. See **kris.**

creasote. See **creosote.**

create, *krē-āt', v.t.* to bring into being or form out of nothing : to bring into being by force of imagination : to make, produce, or form : to design : to invest with a new form, office, or character : to institute : to be the first to act (a part) : (*slang*) to make a fuss.—*adj.* (*Milt.*) created.— *adj.* **creāt'able.**—*n.* **creā'tion** (*krē-ā'shən*), the act of creating, esp. the universe : that which is created, the world, the universe : a specially designed garment.—*adj.* **creā'tional.**—*ns.* **creā'-tionism,** the theory of special creation (opp. to *evolutionism*) : the theory that God immediately creates a soul for every human being born (opp. to *traducianism*)—**creā'tianism ; creā'tionist.**—*adj.* **creā'tive,** having power to create : that creates.— *adv.* **creā'tively.**—*ns.* **creā'tiveness ; creā'tor,** one who creates : a maker.—*fem.* **creā'trix ; creā'tress ;** **creā'torship.**—*adjs.* **creatural** (*krē'tyər-əl*), **crea'turely,** pertaining to a creature or thing created.—*ns.* **creature** (*krē'tyər*), anything that has been created, animate or inanimate, esp. an animated being, an animal, a man : a term of contempt or of endearment : a dependent, instrument, or puppet : (*coll.*) alcoholic liquor ; **crea'ture-ship ; creature comforts,** material comforts, food, etc. : liquor, esp. whisky ; **the Creator,** the Supreme being, God. [L. *creāre, -ātum,* to create, *creātūra,* a thing created.]

creatine, *krē'ə-tin, -tēn, n.* a constant and character-istic constituent of the striped muscle of verte-brates ($C_1H_9N_3O_2$).—*adj.* **creatic** (*kri-at'ik*), re-lating to flesh.—*n.* **crē'atinine,** dehydrated creatine ($C_4H_7N_3O$) found in urine and muscles. [Gr. *kreas, kreatos,* flesh.]

crèche, *kresh, n.* a public nursery for children. [Fr. *crèche,* manger.]

credence, *krē'dəns, n.* belief : trust : (*obs.*) pre-cautionary tasting of food for a great man's table : (*obs.*) a sideboard : the small table beside the altar on which the bread and wine are placed before being consecrated : a shelf over a piscina.—*n.*

credendum (kri-den′dəm), a thing to be believed, an act of faith (*pl.* **creden′da**).—*adjs.* **crē′dent**, credible : credulous : believing ; **credential** (*kri-den′shl*), giving a title to belief or credit.—*n.* that which entitles to credit or confidence : (in *pl.*) esp. the letters by which one claims confidence or authority among strangers.— **credibil′ity** (*kred-*), **cred′ibleness**.—*adj.* **credible**, that may be believed.—*adv.* **cred′ibly**.—*n.* **cred′it**, belief : esteem : reputation : honour : distinction : good character : sale on trust : time allowed for payment : the side of an account on which payments received are entered : a sum placed at a person's disposal in a bank on which he may draw to its amount : in American schools and colleges certified completion of a course of study counting towards a final pass. —*v.t.* to believe : to trust : to sell or lend to on trust : to enter on the credit side of an account : to set to the credit of (with *to* or *with*).—*adj.* **cred′it-able**, trustworthy : bringing credit or honour.—*n.* **cred′itableness.** — *adv.* **cred′itably.** — *ns.* **cred′itor**, one to whom a debt is due ; **crē′dō** (L. *crēdō*, pron. *krā′dō*, I believe), the Creed, or a musical setting of it for church services ; **credulity** (*kri-dū′li-ti*), credulousness : dispositon to believe on insufficient evidence.—*adj.* **credūlous** (*kred′*), easy of belief : apt to believe without sufficient evidence : unsuspecting.—*adv.* **cred′ūlously.— cred′ūlousness.** [L. *crēdĕre*, *crēditum*, to believe.]

cree, *krē*, *v.t.* of grain, to soften by boiling or soaking. [Fr. *crever*, to burst.]

creed, *krēd*, *n.* a summary of articles of religious belief, esp. those called the Apostles', Nicene, and Athanasian : any system of belief.—*adjs.* **creed′al**, **cred′al.** [O.E. *créda*—L. *crēdō*, I believe.]

creek, *krēk*, *n.* a small inlet or bay, or the tidal estuary of a river : any turn or winding : in America and Australia, a small river or brook.—*adj.* **creek′y**, full of creeks : winding. [Prob. Scand., O.N. *kriki*, a nook ; cf. Du. *kreek*, a bay ; Fr. *crique*.]

creel, *krēl*, *n.* a basket, esp. a fish basket. [Origin obscure.]

creep, *krēp*, *v.i.* to move with the belly on or near the ground : to move or advance slowly or stealthily : to slip or encroach very gradually : to grow along the ground or on supports, as a vine : to fawn or cringe : to have the physical sensation of something creeping over or under the skin : to shudder : (*naut.*) to drag with a creeper.—*v.t.* (*Milt.*, etc.) to creep on : (*pa.t.* and *pa.p.* **crept**).—*n.* a crawl : a slow slipping or yielding to stress : crystallisation or rise of a precipitate on the side of a vessel above the surface of a liquid : a narrow passage : (in *pl.*) a horrible shrinking.—*ns.* **creep′er**, anything that creeps : a creeping plant, esp. a Virginia creeper : a small bird that runs up trees (Certhia) : a kind of grapnel : an endless chain or conveyor.—*adj.* **creep′ered**, covered with a creeper.—*ns.* **creep′-hole**, a hiding hole : a subterfuge ; **creep′ie**, a low stool : a stool of repentence.—*adj.* **creep′ing.**—*adv.* **creep′ingly.**—*adjs.* **creep′mouse**, silent and shrinking ; **creep′y**, **creep′y-crawl′y.—creeping Jesus** (*slang*), a slinking person ; **creeping Jenny**, moneywort, a creeping plant (*Lysimachia Nummularia*). [O.E. *créopan*; Du. *kruipen*.]

creese, **crease**. See **kris**.

creesh, *krēsh*, *v.t.* (*Scot.*) to grease.—*n.* grease.— *adj.* **creesh′y.** [O.Fr. *craisse*—L. *crassus*, fat.]

crémaillère, *krā-mä-yer′*, *n.* a zigzag line of fortification : a rack railway. [Fr., pot-hook.]

cremaster, *kri-mas′tər*, *n.* a muscle of the spermatic cord : the organ of attachment in lepidopterous pupae. [Gr. *kremastēr*, suspender—*kremannynai*, to hang.]

cremate, *kri-māt′*, *v.t.* to burn (esp. a dead body). —*ns.* **crema′tion ; crema′tionist**, one who advocates cremation ; **cremāt′or**, one who cremates : a furnace for cremation : an incinerator.—*adj.* **crematorial** (*krem-ə-tō′ri-əl*).—*n.* **cremato′rium**, a place for cremating dead bodies.—*adj.* **crem′atory** (*-ə-tər-i*).—*n.* a crematorium. [L. *cremāre*, *-ātum*, to burn.]

crème, *krem*, *n.* (for Fr. **crème**) cream—applied to various creamy substances.—**crème de menthe** (*də män⁹t*), a peppermint-flavoured liqueur.

cremocarp, *krem′ō-kärp*, *n.* (*bot.*) the characteristic fruit of the Umbelliferae, composed of two one-seeded halves which split apart and dangle from the top of the axis. [Gr. *kremannynai*, to hang, *karpos*, fruit.]

Cremona, *krim-ō′nä*, *n.* a superior kind of violin made at *Cremona* in Italy.

cremona, *kri-mō′nä*, *n.* an erroneous form of **cromorna.**

cremor, *krē′mor*, *n.* thick juice. [L.]

cremosin, **cremsin**, *krem′zin*, *adj.* (*Spens.*) **crimson.**

crenate, -d, *krēn′āt*, *kren′āt*, *kren-āt′*, *-id*, *adj.* (*bot.*) having rounded teeth between sharp notches.—*ns.* **crē′na**, a notch or tooth ; **crenā′tion ; cren′ature.** —*adjs.* **cren′ulate, -d**, finely notched or crenate. [From an inferred L. *crēna*, a notch.]

crenel, *kren′l*, *n.* (*archit.*) a notch in a parapet.—*v.t.* to indent with crenels.—*v.t.* **cren′ellate**, to embattle.—*adjs.* **cren′ellate, -d**, embattled : indented.—*n.* **crenellā′tion.—*adj.* **cren′elled.** These words are sometimes spelt with one *l.* [O.Fr. *crenel*—inferred L. *crēna*, a notch.]

creodont, *krē′ō-dont*, *n.* any member of a group of primitive fossil carnivores, appearing in Eocene times. [Gr. *kreas*, flesh, *odous*, *odontos*, tooth.]

creole, *krē′ōl*, *krē-ōl′*, *adj.* and *n.* strictly applied in the former Spanish, French, and Portuguese colonies of America, Africa, and the East Indies to natives of pure European blood (in opposition to immigrants born in Europe or to coloured natives) : native, but not aboriginal or indigenous (*loosely*) native, but of mixed blood : (*U.S.*) applied to the native French or Spanish stock in Louisiana : a colonial patois (French, Spanish, etc.) : a negro born in America—earlier **creō′lian**. [Fr. *créole*— Sp. *criollo*, dim. of *criado*, nursling—*criar*, lit. to create, hence to bring up, nurse—L. *creāre*.]

creophagous, *krē-of′ə-gəs*, *adj.* flesh-eating. [Gr. *kreas*, flesh, *phagein*, to eat.]

creosote, **creasote**, *krē′ə-sōt*, *n.* an oily liquid obtained by destructive distillation of wood-tar : a somewhat similar liquid got from coal-tar (**creosote oil**, or **coal-tar creosote**).—*v.t.* to treat with creosote.—*n.* **creosote-plant**, an American bush (*Larrea mexicana* ; fam. *Zygophyllaceae*) that smells of creosote and forms dense scrub. [Gr. *kreas*, flesh, *sōtēr*, saviour—*sōzein*, to save.]

crepance, *krē′pəns*, *n.* a wound on a horse's hind ankle-joint, caused by the shoe of the other hind-foot. [L. *crepāre*, to break.]

crêpe, *krāp*, *krep*, *n.* a crape-like fabric : rubber rolled in thin crinkly sheets (**crêpe rubber**).—*v.t.* to frizz, as hair.—*ns.* **crêpe-de-chine** (*də shēn*), a crape-like fabric, originally of silk ; **crep′oline**, a light crape-like dress material.—*adj.* **crêpe′-soled′**, soled with crêpe rubber.—**crêpe paper**, thin crinkled paper. [See **crape.**]

crepitate, *krep′i-tāt*, *v.i.* to crackle, snap : to rattle : (of beetles) to discharge an offensive fluid.—*adj.* **crep′itant**, crackling.—*n.* **crepita′tion**, the act of crepitating : crackle : a sound detected in the lungs by auscultation in certain diseases.—*adj.* **crep′itative.—*n.* **crep′itus.** [L. *crepitāre*, *-ātum*, freq. of *crepāre*, to crack, rattle.]

crept, *krept*, *pa.t.* and *pa.p.* of **creep.**

crepuscular, *kri-pus′kū′lər*, *adj.* of or pertaining to twilight—also **crepus′culous**.—*ns.* **crepuscle** (*krep′əs-kūl*, or *-us′*), **crepuscle** (*krep′əs-l*, or *us′*), twilight. [L. *crepusculum*—*creper*, dusky, obscure.]

crescendo, *kresh-en′dō*, *adj.* and *adv.* (*mus.*) gradually increasing in loudness—*n.* increase of loudness : a passage of increasing loudness.—Also *v.i.*—Often *cres.*, *cresc.*, or <. [It., increasing.]

crescent, *kres′ənt*, *adj.* increasing : shaped like the waxing moon.—*n.* the waxing moon : a figure like the crescent moon : the Turkish (originally Byzantine) standard or emblem : the Turkish power : the Moslem faith : a curved range of buildings (sometimes applied at random) : a crescent-shape roll or bun.—*n.* **cresc′entade**, a religious war for Islam.—*adjs.* **cresc′ented**, **crescentic** (*-ent′ik*), formed like a crescent ; **cresc′ive**

cresol   **249**   **cringe**

(*Shak.*), increasing. [L. *crēscĕre*, to grow, pr.p. *crēscens, -entis.*]

cresol, *krēs'ol, n.* a product of distillation of coal-tar resembling phenol—C₇H₈O. [From *creos*ote and alcohol.]

cress, *kres, n.* a name for many pungent-leaved cruciferous plants of Lepidium (garden cress), Nasturtium (watercress), Arabis (rock-cress) and other genera : extended to other plants of similar character, as Indian cress (Tropaeolum).—*adj.* **cress'y,** abounding in cresses. [O.E. *cresse, cerse;* cf. Du. *kers,* Ger. *kresse.*]

cresset, *kres'it, n.* an iron basket, or the like, for combustibles, placed on a beacon, lighthouse, wharf, etc. : a torch generally. [O.Fr. *cresset, crasset* (Fr. *creuset*)—Old Du. *kruysel,* a hanging lamp.]

crest, *krest, n.* the comb or tuft on the head of a cock or other bird : the summit of anything, as a roof-ridge, hill, wave : the mane of a horse, etc. : (*anat.*) a ridge along the surface of a bone : a plume of feathers or other ornament on the top of a helmet : (*her.*) an accessory figure originally surmounting the helmet, placed on a wreath, etc., also used separately as a personal cognisance on plate, etc.—*v.t.* to furnish with a crest or serve as a crest for : to surmount.—*adj.* **crest'ed,** having a crest : (*bot.*) having an elevated appendage like a crest.—*adjs.* **crest'fallen,** dejected : cast-down; **crest'less,** without a crest : not of high birth. [O.Fr. *creste* (Fr. *crête*)—L. *crista.*]

cretaceous, *kri-tā'shəs, adj.* composed of or like chalk : **Cretaceous,** belonging to the uppermost system of the Secondary or Mesozoic rocks, including in England the Wealden, the Gault and Greensand, and the Chalk.—Also *n.* [L. *crētāceus*—*crēta,* chalk.]

Cretic, *krē'tik, adj.* and *n.* Cretan, belonging to *Crete* : **cretic,** a metrical foot consisting of one short syllable between two long.—*n.* **cre'tism,** a lie. [Gr. *krētikos*—*Krētē,* Crete.]

cretin, *krēt'in, kret'in, n.* one affected with cretinism.—*n.* **cret'inism,** a state of defective mental development, with bodily deformity or arrested growth, due to failure of secretion of the thyroid gland.—*adjs.* **cret'inous,** **cret'inised,** **cret'inoid.** [Fr. *crétin*—L. *christiānus* (cf. use of **innocent**).]

cretonne, *kret-on',* or *kret'on, n.* a strong printed cotton fabric used for curtains or for covering furniture. [Fr., prob. from *Creton* in Normandy.]

creutzer. Same as **kreutzer.**

crevasse, *kriv-as', n.* a crack or split, esp. applied to a cleft in a glacier : (*U.S.*) a breach in a canal or river bank.—*v.t.* to fissure with crevasses.—*n.* **crevice** (*krev'is*), a crack or rent : a narrow opening. [O.Fr. *crevace*—L. *crepāre,* to creak, break.]

crew, *krōō, n.* a company, squad, or gang, often in a bad or contemptuous sense : a ship's company.—*n.* **crew'man,** a member of a gang of workmen. [O.Fr. *creue,* increase—*croistre,* to grow.]

crew, *krōō, pa.t.* of **crow.**

crewe, *krōō, n.* (*Spens.*) a pot. [O.Fr. *crue.*]

crewel, *krōō'əl, n.* a fine worsted yarn used for embroidery and tapestry : work in crewels.—*v.t.* to work in crewel.—*ns.* **crew'elist, crew'ellery.** [Orig. a monosyllable, *crule, crewle;* ety. dub.]

crewels, *cruel(l)s, krōō'əlz, n.pl.* (*Scot.*) the king's evil, scrofula. [Fr. *écrouelles.*]

crib, *krib, n.* a manger or fodder-receptacle : a stall for oxen : a bin : a crate : a child's bed : a cabin or hut : a confined place : (*slang*) a house : (*slang*) a job : a timber framework for a dam, a pier foundation : a mine-shaft lining, etc. : a pilfering, or the thing pilfered : a plagiarism : a key or baldly literal translation, used by schoolboys, etc. : the discarded cards at cribbage, used by the dealer in scoring.—*v.t.* to put in a crib : to confine : to pilfer : to plagiarise (*pr.p.* **cribb'ing;** *pa.t.* and *pa.p.* **cribbed**).—*ns.* **cribb'age,** a card game in which each player discards a certain number of cards for the *crib,* and scores by holding certain combinations and by bringing the sum of the values of cards played to certain numbers; **cribb'age-board,** a scoring-board for cribbage, with holes for pegs; **crib'-bit'ing,** in horses, a vicious habit of biting the manger, etc., and swallowing air; **crib'-work,** work formed of cribs. [O.E. *crib;* Ger. *krippe.*]

cribble, *krib'l, n.* a coarse screen or sieve used for sand, gravel or corn : coarse flour or meal.—*v.t.* to sift or riddle.—*n.* **cribell'um,** an accessory spinning-organ of certain spiders :—*pl.* **cribell'a.**—*adjs.* **cribell'ar; criblé** (Fr. *krē-blā*), punctured like a sieve, dotted; **crib'rate** (or *krīb'*), **crib'rose,** perforated like a sieve.—*n.* **cribrā'tion,** sifting.—*adj.* **crib'riform,** perforated. [L. *cribrum,* dim. *cribellum,* a sieve.]

Cricetus, *kri-sē'təs, n.* the hamster genus. [Mod. L.—Slav. name of hamster.]

crick, *krik, n.* a spasm or cramp of the muscles, esp. of the neck.—*v.t.* to produce a crick in. [Prob. imit.]

cricket, *krik'it, n.* a saltatory, orthopterous insect, allied to grasshoppers and locusts. [O.Fr. *criquet;* cf. Du. *krekel,* Ger. *kreckel.*]

cricket, *krik'it, n.* an outdoor game played with bats, a ball, and wickets, between two sides of eleven each : (*coll.*) that which is fair and sporting.—*v.i.* to play at cricket.—*n.* **crick'eter.**—and *adj.* **crick'eting.** [Fr. *criquet;* not O.E. *cryce,* a stock.]

cricket, *krik'it, n.* a low stool. [Ety. unknown.]

cricoid, *krī'koid, adj.* (*anat.*) ring-shaped.—*n.* a cartilage of the larynx. [Gr. *krikoeides*—*krikos,* a ring, and *eidos,* form.]

cried, crier, cries. See **cry.**

crikey, cricky, crickey, *krīk'i, krik'i, interj.* (*slang*), a mild oath or expression of surprise. [Perh. softened from *Christ.*]

crime, *krīm, n.* a violation of law, esp. if serious : an act punishable by law : such acts collectively or in the abstract : an act gravely wrong morally : sin : (*Spens.*) an accusation : (*Spens.*), a cause or motive of wrongdoing.—*v.t.* (*mil.*) to charge or convict of an infraction of law.—*adjs.* **crime'ful,** criminal; **crime'less,** without crime, innocent.—*n.* **crime'-sheet** (*mil.*), a record of offences.—*adj.* **criminal** (*krim'-*), relating to crime : guilty of crime : violating laws.—*n.* one guilty of crime.—*ns.* **crim'inalist,** one versed in criminal law; **criminal'ity,** guiltiness.—*adv.* **crim'inally.**—*v.t.* **crim'inate,** to accuse.—*n.* **criminā'tion,** act of criminating : accusation.—*adjs.* **crim'inative, crim'inatory,** involving crimination.—*ns.* **criminol'ogist; criminol'ogy,** that branch of anthropology which treats of crime and criminals.—*adj.* **crim'inous,** criminal—now chiefly in the phrase 'a criminous clerk'.—*n.* **crim'inousness.—criminal conversation,** often **crim. con.,** adultery. [Fr.,—L. *crīmen, -inis.*]

crimine, crimini, *krim'i-ni, interj.* an ejaculation of surprise or impatience. [Perh. from *Gemini;* see **crikey.**]

crimp, *krimp, adj.* made crisp or brittle.—*v.t.* to wrinkle : to plait : to make crisp : to gash : to seize or decoy.—*n.* a plait : one who presses or decoys (sailors, etc.).—*ns.* **crimp'age,** act of crimping; **crimp'er,** one who or that which crimps or corrugates; **crimp'ing-iron,** an iron instrument used for crimping hair; **crimp'ing-machine',** a machine for forming crimps or plaits on ruffles.—*v.t.* **crimp'le,** to contract or draw together : to plait : to curl. [O.E. *gecrympan,* to curl; cf. **cramp,** and Du. *krimpen,* to shrink.]

crimson, *krim'zn, n.* a deep red colour, tinged with blue : red in general.—*adj.* deep red.—*v.t.* to dye crimson.—*v.i.* to become crimson : to blush. [M.E. *crimosin*—O.Fr. *cramoisin;* from Ar. *qirmizī,* scarlet —*qirmiz,* kermes, from which it is made.]

crinal, *krī'nal, adj.* of or belonging to the hair.—*adjs.* **crin'ate, -d,** having hair; **crinicul'tural,** relating to the culture or growth of the hair; **crinig'erous,** hairy; **cri'nite,** hairy : (*bot.*) resembling a tuft of hair; **cri'nose,** hairy. [L. *crīnis,* the hair.]

crine, *krīn, v.i.* (*Scot.*) to shrink or shrivel. [Gael. *crìon,* dry.]

cringe, *krinj, v.i.* to bend or crouch with servility : to submit : to fawn : to flatter with mean servility.—*n.* a servile obeisance.—*ns.* **cringe'ling, crin'ger,** one who cringes.—*n.* and *adj.* **cring'ing.**—*adv.*

crin'gingly, in an obsequious manner. [Related to O.E. *crincan, cringan*, to shrink; cf. **crank**, weak.]

cringle, *kring'gl, n.* a small piece of rope worked into the bolt-rope of a sail, and containing a metal ring or thimble. [Gmc.; cf. Ger. *kringel.*]

crinite. See crinal, crinoid.

crinkle, *kringk'l, v.t.* to twist, wrinkle, crimp.— *v.i.* to wrinkle up, curl.—*n.* a wrinkle.—*adj.* crink'ly, wrinkly.—*n.* and *adj.* crink'um-crank'um, a word applied familiarly to things intricate or crooked.

crinoid, *krin'oid, krīn'oid, n.* a feather-star or sea-lily, an echinoderm of the class **Crinoid'ea**, with cup-shaped body and branching arms and well developed skeleton, usually attached by a jointed stalk, mouth upwards, well known in fossil forms as encrinites or stone-lilies.—Also *adj.*—*n.* crinite (*krin'* or *krīn'it*), an encrinite or fossil crinoid.— *adj.* crinoid'al.—*adj.* and *n.* crinoid'ean. [Gr. *krinoeidēs*, like a lily—*krīnon*, a lily, *eidos*, form.]

crinoline, *krin'ə-lēn, -lin, n.* originally a stiff fabric of horse-hair and flax: this or other means to distend women's attire: a hooped petticoat or skirt made to project all round by means of steel-wire: a netting round ships as a guard against torpedoes.—*n.* crinolette', a small crinoline causing the dress to project behind only.—*adj.* crin'olined. [Fr., *crin*—L. *crīnis*, hair, and *lin*—L. *līnum*, flax.]

crio-sphinx, *krī'ō-sfingks, n.* a ram-headed sphinx. [Gr. *krios*, a ram, *sphinx*, a sphinx.]

cripple, *krip'l, n.* a lame person.—*adj.* lame.—*v.t.* to make lame: to lame: to disable, impair the efficiency of.—*ns.* cripp'ledom; cripp'ling, a prop set up as a support against the side of a building. [O.E. *crypel*; conn. with **creep**.]

crisis, *krī'sis, n.* point or time for deciding anything, the decisive moment or turning-point :—*pl.* crises (*krī'sēz*). [Gr. *krisis*, from *krīnein*, to decide.]

crisp, *krisp, adj.* curling closely: having a wavy surface: so dry as to be crumbled easily: brittle, or short: fresh and bracing: firm, the opposite of limp or flabby.—*v.t.* to curl or twist: to make crisp or wavy: to ripple.—*n.* a piece of food fried or roasted to crispness.—*adjs.* cris'pate, -d, having a crisped or wavy appearance.—*ns.* crispā'-tion; crisp'ature, a curling; crisp'er, one who or that which crisps; crisp'ing-i'ron, -pin, a curling-iron.—*adv.* crisp'ly.—*n.* crisp'ness.—*adj.* crisp'y. [O.E.,—L. *crispus.*]

crispin, *kris'pin, n.* a shoemaker, from *Crispin* of Soissons, the patron saint of shoemakers, martyred 25th October 287.

criss-cross, *kris'-kros, n.* the cross at the beginning of the alphabet on a hornbook (see **criss-cross-row**, at **Christ**): a mark formed by two lines in the form of a cross, as the signature of a person unable to write his name: a network of crossing lines: repeated crossings: cross-purposes: a game of noughts and crosses.—*adj.* and *adv.* crosswise.— *v.t.* and *v.i.* to cross repeatedly. [From christ-cross.]

crista, *kris'tā, n.* a crest.—*adjs.* crist'ate, crested; cris'tiform. [L.]

criterion, *krī-tē'ri-ən, n.* a means or standard of judging: a test: a rule, standard, or canon :—*pl.* crite'ria. [Gr. *krītērion—krītēs*, a judge.]

crithomancy, *krith'ō-man-si, n.* divination by the meal strewed over the victims of sacrifice. [Gr. *krithē*, barley, and *manteiā*, divination.]

critic, *krit'ik, n.* one skilled in estimating the quality of literary or artistic work: a professional reviewer: one skilled in textual studies, various readings, and the ascertainment of the original words: a fault-finder.—*adj.* crit'ical, at or relating to a turning-point, transition or crisis: decisive: relating to criticism: rigorously discriminating: captious.—*adv.* crit'ically.—*ns.* crit'icalness, critical'ity; crit'icaster, a petty critic.—*adj.* criticisable (*-sīz'*).—*v.t.* crit'icise, to pass judgment on: to censure.—*ns.* crit'icism, the art of judging, esp. in literature or the fine arts: a critical judgment or observation; critique (*kri-tēk'*;

Fr.), a critical examination of any production: a review.—crit'ical angle, the least angle of incidence at which a ray is totally reflected; critical philosophy, that of Kant is based on a critical examination of the faculty of knowledge; critical temperature, that temperature above which a gas cannot be liquefied by pressure alone; higher or historical criticism, as distinguished from textual or verbal criticism, the inquiry into the composition, date, and authenticity of the books of the Bible, from historical and literary considerations. [Gr. *kritikos—krīnein*, to judge.]

croak, *krōk, v.i.* to utter a low hoarse sound, as a frog or raven: to grumble: to forebode evil: (*slang*) to die.—*v.t.* to utter croakingly.—*n.* the sound of a frog or raven.—*n.* croak'er.—*adv.* croak'ily.— *n.* croak'ing.—*adj.* croak'y. [Imit.]

croche, *krōch, n.* a knob at the top of a deer's horn. [Fr.]

crochet, *krō'shā, n.* looping work done with a small hook.—*v.i.* and *v.t.* to work in crochet (*pr.p.* crocheting, *krō'shā-ing*; *pa.t.* and *pa.p.* crocheted *krō'shād*). [Fr. *crochet—croche, croc*, a hook.]

crocidolite, *kro-sid'o-līt, n.* a fibrous mineral consisting mainly of silicate of iron and sodium, called *blue asbestos*: in S. Africa also a golden alteration product or pseudomorph of this mineral, largely quartz. [Gr. *krokis, -idos*, nap of cloth, and *lithos*, stone.]

crock, *krok, n.* a pot or jar: a potsherd.—*n.* crock'ery, earthenware: vessels of baked clay. [O.E. *croc*; Ger. *krug*; perh. of Celt. origin, as in W. *crochan*, a pot, Gael. *crogan*, a pitcher.]

crock, *krok, n.* dirt, smut.—*v.t.* to besmut. [Origin doubtful.]

crock, *krok, n.* an old ewe: an old horse: a broken down or decrepit person or thing.—*v.i.* to break down (often with *up*). [Cf. Norw. and Sw. *krake*, a poor beast.]

crocket, *krok'it, n.* (*archit.*) an ornament on the sloping side of a pediment, pinnacle, etc., usu. like curled leaves or flowers. [See **croquet**.]

crocodile, *krok'ə-dīl, n.* a large reptile of the Nile with bony scutes and horny scales: extended to others of the genus (**Crocodi'lus**) or order (**Crocodi'ia**, or *Loricata*, alligators, gavials, etc.): leather from crocodile skin: a double file of school pupils taking a walk.—*adj.* and *n.* crocodilian (*dil'*).—*n.* crocodil'ity, captious arguing—from a sophistical problem about a crocodile.—crocodile bird, a bird, perh. a plover, said to pick the crocodile's teeth or take leeches from its throat; crocodile tears, hypocritical grief—from the old story that crocodiles (which have large lachrymal glands) shed tears over the hard necessity of killing animals for food. [L. *crocodīlus*—Gr. *krokodeilos*, a lizard.]

crocus, *krō'kəs, n.* a bulbous iridaceous plant with brilliant yellow, purple, or white flowers: in old chemistry, various yellow or red powders (*crocus of Mars*, colcothar).—*adj.* croceous (*krō'shi-əs*), saffron-coloured.—*n.* crocoite (*krō'kō-īt*); croco-isite (*krō'*, or *kō'*), a bright red mineral, lead chromate. [L. *crocus*—Gr. *krokos*; prob. of Eastern origin; cf. Heb. *karkom*, and Ar. *kurkum*, saffron.]

crocus, *krō'kəs, n.* (*slang*) a quack.

Croesus, *krē'səs, n.* a very rich man. [*Croesus,* king of Lydia, of fabulous wealth.]

croft, *kroft, n.* a small piece of arable land esp. adjoining a dwelling: a small farm.—*ns.* croft'er; croft'ing. [O.E. *croft*; perh. cog. with Du. *kroft,* hillock.]

croissant, *krwä-sän², n.* a crescent roll. [Fr.]

Cro-Magnon, *krō-man'yon², adj.* pertaining to a type of man, long-skulled but short-faced, sur-viving from Aurignacian times to the present day. [From *Cro-Magnon*, in Dordogne, where the first skulls of this race were found.]

crome, cromb, *krōm, krōōm, n.* a hook or crook.— *v.t.* to draw with a crome. [Cf. Du. *kram.*]

cromlech, *krom'lehh, n.* a stone circle: formerly applied to a dolmen. [W. *cromlech—crom*, curved, circular, and *llech*, a stone.]

cromorna, cromorne, *krŏ-morn'(ä̆), n.* a krummhorn : a krummhorn stop. [Fr. *cromorne*—Ger. *krummhorn.*]

crone, *krōn, n.* an old woman, usually in contempt—rarely an old man : an old ewe. [Perh. O.Fr. *carogne,* carrion, hag, directly or through Du.]

cronet, *krŏ'net, n.* the hair growing over the top of a horse's hoof. [coronet.]

crony, *krōn'i, n.* an old and intimate companion. [Said to be orig. university slang—Gr. *chronios,* long-continued, perennial.]

croodle, *krŏŏd'l, v.i.* to cower down, snuggle. [Origin unknown.]

croodle, *krŏŏd'l, krood'l, v.i.* (*Scot.*) to murmur like a dove. [Imit.]

crook, *krook, n.* a bend, anything bent : a curved tube used to lower the pitch of a wind instrument : the bending of the body in reverence : a staff bent at the end, as a shepherd's or bishop's : an artifice or trick : (*Spens.*) gibbet : (*slang*) a professional swindler or thief.—*v.t.* to bend or form into a hook : to turn from the straight line or from what is right.—*v.i.* to bend or be bent.—*n.* crook'back (*Shak.*), a hunchback.—*adj.* crook'backed ; crook'ed, bent like a crook : not straight : deviating from rectitude, perverse.—*adv.* crook'edly.—*n.* crook'edness.—*adjs.* crook'-kneed ; crook'-shoul'dered.—a crook in the lot, any trial in one's experience. [Prob. O.N. *krókr ;* cf. Dan. *krog.*]

croon, *krōōn, v.i.* (*Scot. krün*) to utter a low, monotonous inarticulate sound like a bull : to murmur : to lament murmuringly : to sing or hum in an undertone.—*v.t.* and *v.i.* to sing quietly in an extravagantly sentimental manner.—Also *n.*—*ns.* croon'er ; croon'ing. [Cf. Du. *kreunen* to groan.]

crop, *krop, n.* (*arch.*) the top or end of anything, as a tree or twig : a sprout : (*archit.*) a finial : a whip-handle : a hunting whip with loop instead of lash : an end cut off : an act or mode of cutting : mode of cutting or wearing short hair : the total quantity produced, cut, or harvested : total growth or produce : a cultivated plant, collectively ; that which is produced at a time, a growth, supply : a season's yield : an entire hide : the craw, a dilatation of a bird's oesophagus : a similar structure in another animal : an outcrop.—*v.t.* to cut off the top, ends, margins, or loose parts of : to cut short : to mow, reap, or gather : to bite off in eating : to raise crops on : to cut the hair of.—*v.i.* to yield a crop : to come to the surface (with *up* or *out*) : hence, to come (up) casually, as in conversation : (*pr.p.* cropp'ing ; *pa.t.* and *pa.p.* cropped).—*adj.* crop'-bound, suffering from impaction of the crop.—*ns.* crop'comb, a semicircular comb to hold back a girl's hair ; crop'-ear, a person, horse, dog, etc. with cropped ears.—*adj.* crop'-eared, having ears cropped, or hair cropped to show the ears (a Cavalier jibe at a Puritan).—*n.* crop'ful, as much as the crop can hold (*pl.* crop'fuls).—*adj.* crop'full (*Milt.*) satiated.—*ns.* cropp'er, one who or that which crops : a plant that yields a crop : one who raises a crop for a share of it : a kind of pigeon noted for its large crop : a small platen printing machine : a fall : a failure ; cropp'ing, act of cutting off : the raising of crops : (*geol.*) an outcrop ; cropp'y, one of the Irish rebels of 1798 who cut their hair short, like the French Revolutionists.—*adj.* crop'-sick, sick of a surfeit.—come a cropper to have a fall, perhaps from phrase *neck and crop.* [O.E. *crop,* the top shoot of a plant, the crop of a bird ; Du. *crop,* a bird's crop.]

croquet, *krŏ'kā, n.* a game in which wooden balls are driven by means of long-handled mallets, through a series of arches.—*v.t.* to drive away by striking another ball in contact. [North Fr. *croquet,* a dial. form of *crochet,* dim. of *croc, croche* a crook.]

croquette, *krŏ-ket', n.* a ball or round cake, especially of minced meat or fish, seasoned and fried. [Fr.,—*croquer,* to crunch.]

crore, *krōr, n.* ten millions, or one hundred lakhs. [Hind. *krŏr.*]

crosier, crozier, *krō'z(h)yər, n.* the pastoral staff or crook of a bishop or abbot : erroneously, an archbishop's cross.—*adj.* cro'siered. [M.E. *crose* or *croce*—Late L. *crocia,* a crook.]

cross, *kros, n.* a gibbet on which the Romans exposed malefactors, typically consisting of two pieces of timber, one placed transversely to the other : the particular one on which Christ suffered : the symbol of the Christian religion, or of the crusades : the Christian doctrine of atonement : a representation of Christ's cross : any object, figure, or mark formed by two parts or lines transverse to each other, with or without elaboration : a staff surmounted by a cross : a monument not always in the form of a cross, where proclamations are made, etc. : a place in a town or village where such a monument stands or stood : a cross-shaped pendant or medal : the transverse part of an anchor, or the like : a surveyor's cross-staff : a crossing or crossway : anything that crosses or thwarts : adversity or affliction in general : mixing of breeds : a hybrid : something intermediate in character between two other things : unfairness or dishonest practices, esp. in sport where one corruptly allows himself to be beaten : a game or race lost by collusion : (*obs.*) the obverse of a coin, formerly often stamped with a cross : hence, a coin.—*adj.* lying across or crosswise : transverse : oblique : adverse : interchanged : peevish : hybrid : dishonest : balancing, neutralising.—*adv.* across (often written 'cross).—*v.t.* to mark with a cross : to make the sign of the cross over : to set something, or draw a line, across : (*Spens.*) to set in position athwart the mast : to place crosswise : to cancel by drawing cross lines : to pass from one side to the other of : to extend across : to interbreed : of a cheque, to draw two lines across, with name of a banking company or the words '& Co.' between (thereby restricting it to payment through a bank) : to obstruct : to thwart : to confront : to bestride.—*v.i.* to lie or pass across : to meet and pass : to interbreed.—*pa.t.* and *pa.p.* crossed, sometimes crost.—*ns.* cross'-ac'tion (*law*), an action brought by the defender against the pursuer ; cross'-aisle (*obs.*) a transept ; cross'-and-pile (or -or-), heads or tails : a toss-up.—*adj.* cross'-armed, having the arms crossed.—*n.* cross'band, a deal plank nailed across the hull of a ship to keep the frame in position till the knees are fastened.—*adj.* cross'-band'ed, having the grain of the veneer run across that of the rail—of a hand-rail.—*n.* cross'-bar, a transverse bar : a kind of lever.—*adj.* cross'-barred.—*ns.* cross'beam, a large beam stretching across a building and serving to hold its sides together ; cross'-bearer, one who carries a cross in a procession ; cross'-bedd'ing (*geol.*) false bedding ; cross'-bench, a bench laid crosswise : a bench on which independent members of parliament sometimes sit.—*adj.* independent : impartial.—*ns.* cross'-bencher ; cross'-bill, a bill brought by the defendant in a Chancery suit against the plaintiff ; cross'bill, a finch of the genus Loxia with mandibles crossing near the points ; cross'-birth, a birth in which the child lies transversely in the uterus.—*v.t.* cross'bite (*arch.*) to bite in return : to cheat in return : to outwit : to entrap.—*n.pl.* cross'bones, a figure of two thigh-bones laid across each other—forming with the skull a conventional emblem of death or piracy.—*ns.* cross'bow, a weapon for shooting arrows, formed of a bow placed crosswise on a stock ; cross'bower, -bow'man, one who uses a crossbow.—*adj.* cross'bred.—*ns.* cross'breed, a breed produced by crossing : the offspring of a cross ; cross'breed'ing ; cross'-bun, a bun bearing a cross, customarily eaten on Good Friday (also hot cross bun) ; cross'-butt'ock, a particular throw over the hip in wrestling ; cross'-correspon'dence, (*psychical research*) fitting together of communications separately unintelligible to give an intelligible whole.—*adj.* and *adv.* cross'-coun'try, across the fields rather than by the road.—*ns.* cross'-cross'let, a cross with its ends crossed ; cross'cut, a crosswise cutting : a short way across from one point to another.—*v.t.* (-kut')

Neutral vowels in unaccented syllables : *el'ə-mənt, in'fənt, ran'dəm*

to cut across.—*ns.* **cross′cut-saw**, a large saw worked by two men, one at each end, for cutting beams crosswise; **cross′-divi′sion**, division into groups or classes that overlap.—*adj.* **crossed**.— *n.* **cross′-examina′tion**.—*v.t.* **cross′-exam′ine**, to question minutely, or with a view to checking evidence already given: to subject to examination by the other side.—*adj.* **cross′-eyed**, squinting.— *ns.* **cross′-fertilisa′tion**, the fecundation of a plant by pollen from another; **cross′-fire** (*mil.*), the crossing of lines of fire from two or more points: (also *fig.*); **cross′fish**, the common sea-urchin *Asterias rubens*; **cross′-gar′net**, a T-shaped hinge. —*adjs.* **cross′-gar′tered** (*Shak.*), wearing the garters crossed on the leg; **cross′-grained**, having the grain or fibres crossed or intertwined: perverse: contrary: intractable.—*adv.* across the grain: perversely.—*ns.* **cross′-grained′ness**; **cross′-guard**, the bar, at right angles to the blade, forming the hilt-guard of a sword; **cross′-hatch′ing**, shading by intersecting sets of parallel lines; **cross′-head**, a beam across the head of something, esp. the bar at the end of the piston-rod of a steam-engine; **cross′ing**, the act of making the sign of the cross: act of going across: a place where a roadway, etc. may be crossed: intersection: esp. transepts and nave: act of thwarting: cross-breeding.—*adj.* **cross′ing**.—*ns.* **cross′ing-o′ver**, (*biol.*) interchange of parts of two chromosomes when they separate again after synapsis; **cross′ing-sweeper**, one who sweeps a street crossing.—*adj.* **cross′ish**.—*n.* **cross′-jack**, a mizzen course.— *adjs.* **cross′leaved**, having leaves in four rows, set crosswise; **cross′-legged**, having the legs crossed. —*ns.* **cross′let**, a small cross; **cross′light**, a light whose direction makes an angle with that of another light, and which illumines additional parts or regions.—*adj.* **cross′-lighted**.—*adv.* **cross′ly**. —*ns.* **cross′ness**; **cross′-patch**, an ill-natured person (see **patch**, 2); **cross′-piece**, a piece of material of any kind crossing another: (*naut.*) a timber over the windlass, with pins for belaying the running rigging; **cross′-pollina′tion**, convey-ance of pollen from one flower to the stigma of another; **cross′-pur′pose**, a contrary purpose: contradictory conduct or system: (in *pl.*) a game in which answers to questions are transferred to other questions: (in *pl.*) confusion in conversation or action by misunderstanding; **cross′-quar′ters**, an ornament of tracery like the four petals of a cruciform flower: a quatrefoil.—*v.t.* **cross′-ques′tion**, to cross-examine.—*ns.* **cross-ra′tio**, of four points in a range, or rays in a pencil, the quotient of the position ratios of two with respect to the other two; **cross′-ref′erence**, a reference in a book to another title or passage; **cross′-road**, a road crossing the principal road, a bypath: a road joining main roads: a place where roads cross—in *U.S.* often a hamlet (also **cross′roads**): (in *pl.*) a stage at which an important decision has to be made.—*adj.* **cross′-roads**.—*ns.* **cross′-row** (same as **christ-cross-row**); **cross′-ruff**, alter-nate ruffing by partners, each leading a suit that the other lacks; **cross′-saddle**, a saddle for riding stridelegs; **cross′-sea**, a sea that sets at an angle to the direction of the wind; **cross′-sec′tion**, a transverse section: a comprehensive representation. —*v.t.* to make a cross-section of.—*ns.* **cross′-sill**, a railway sleeper; **cross′-spring′er**, a cross-rib in a groined vault; **cross′-staff**, a surveying instru-ment consisting of a staff surmounted with a frame carrying two pairs of sights at right angles; **cross′-stitch′**, a stitch in the form of a cross; needlework of such stitches; **cross′-stone**, chiastolite: stauro-lite: harmotome; **cross′-talk′**, interference of one telephone conversation with another: backchat; **cross′-tie**, a supporting tie placed transversely: a railway sleeper; **cross′-tin′ing**, a mode of harrowing crosswise; **cross′tree**, a piece of timber or metal placed across the upper end of a ship's mast; **cross′-vault′ing**, vaulting formed by the intersection of simple vaults; **cross′-way**, a way that crosses another or links others; **cross′-wind**, an unfavourable, a side-wind.—*adv.* **cross′wise**, in the form of a cross: across.—*ns.* **cross′word**

(puzzle), a puzzle in which a square with blank spaces is to be filled with letters which, read across or down, will give words corresponding to clues given; **cross′wort**, a bedstraw with leaves set crosswise.—**cross as two sticks**, particularly perverse and disagreeable; **cross one's mind**, to flash across the mind; **cross one's palm**, put a coin in one's hand; **cross one's path**, come in one's way: thwart one; **on the cross**, diagonally. [O.E. *cros*—O.N. *kross*—L. *crux, crucis*.]

crosse, *kros*, *n.* a bent stick with a shallow net, used in playing lacrosse. [Fr.,—O.Fr. *croce*, crook.]

crossette, *kro-set′*, *n.* a small projecting part of an impost-stone at the extremity of an arch: a shoulder in an arch-stone fitting into the stone next to it. [Fr.]

Crossopterygii, *kros-op-tər-ij′i-ī*, *n.pl.* a subclass of fishes, nearly extinct, whose paired fins have an axis fringed with rays.—*adj.* and *n.* **crossopteryg′-ian**. [Gr. *krossoi*, tassels, fringe, *pteryx*, *-gos*, fin.]

crotal, *krō′tal*, *n.* a crotalum: a small spherical bell. —*n.* **Crotalaria**, *krot-*, *krōt-ə-lā′ri-ā*, the sunn-hemp genus of Papilionaceae, including the American rattle-boxes (from their inflated pods)— *n.pl.* **Crotalidae** (*-tal′*), the rattlesnake family.— *adjs.* **crotaline** (*krot′ə-līn*), like a rattlesnake.—*ns.* **crot′alism**, poisoning by crotalaria; **crotalum** (*krot′ə-ləm*), a clapper or castanet used in ancient Mysteries; **Crotalus** (*krot′*), the rattlesnake genus. [Gr. *krotalon*, a rattle, castanet.]

crotal, crottle, *krot′l*, *n.* a lichen (of various kinds) used for dyeing. [Gael. *crotal*.]

crotch, *kroch*, *n.* a fork, as of a tree: the bifurcation of the human body.—*adj.* **crotched**. [Ety. obscure.]

crotchet, *kroch′it*, *n.* a hook: a note in music, equal to half a minim,♩ : a crooked or perverse fancy: a whim, or conceit.—*adjs.* **crotch′eted**, **crotch′-ety**, having crotchets or peculiarities: whimsical. —*n.* **crotch′eteer**, a crotchety person. [Fr. *crochet*, dim. of *croche*, a hook; see **crochet**.]

Croton, *krō′tən*, *n.* a genus of tropical plants of the spurge family: extended by gardeners, etc. to a tropical hedge-plant of the same family, *Codiaeum variegatum;* **croton oil**, a powerful purgative got from the seeds of *Croton Tiglium*. [Gr. *krotōn*, a sheep-tick, which the seed resembles.]

crouch, *krowch*, *v.i.* to squat or lie close to the ground, as an animal preparing to spring: to bend low with legs doubled: to cringe: to fawn.—*v.t.* to bend.—*n.* act or position of crouching. [Possibly connected with **crook**.]

crouched-friars, crutched-friars. See **crutch**.

crouch-ware, *krowch′-wār*, *n.* an old salt-glazed stoneware made at Burslem. [Origin unknown.]

croup, *krōōp*, *n.* inflammation of the larynx and trachea in children, associated with a peculiar ringing cough, present especially in diphtheria: a burr.—*v.i.* to croak or speak hoarsely.—*n.* **croup′i-ness**.—*adjs.* **croup′ous, croup′y**. [Imit.]

croup, croupe, *krōōp*, *n.* the rump of a horse: the place behind the saddle.—*n.* **croup′on** (*obs.*), the croup; the human buttocks. [Fr. *croupe*, a protuberance; allied to **crop**.]

croupade, *kroo-pād′*, *n.* a leap in which the horse draws up his hind-legs toward the belly. [Fr.]

crouper, *krōōp′ər*, *n.* obsolete form of **crupper**.

croupier, *krōō′pi-ər*, or *-pēr′*, *n.* one who sits at the lower end of the table as assistant chairman at a public dinner: a vice-president: one who officiates at a gaming-table, collecting the stakes and paying the winners. [Fr., one who rides on the croup.]

crouse, *krōōs*, *adj.* (*Scot.*) lively, cheerfully confident. —*adv.* boldly, pertly.—*adv.* **crouse′ly**. [M.E. *crūs;* cf. L.G. *krūs*, gay, Ger. *kraus*, Du. *kroes*, crisp, cross.]

croustade, *krōōs-tâd′*, *n.* a case of fried bread or pastry for serving game, etc. [Fr.]

crout, *krowt*, *n.* See **sauer-kraut**.

croute, *krōōt*, *n.* a thick slice of fried bread for serving entrées.—*n.* **crouton** (*-ton′′*, *-ton′*), a small piece of fried bread. [Fr. *croûte*, crust.]

crow, *krō*, *n.* a moderately large black bird, of the genus *Corvus*—in England *C. Corone* (the so-called *carrion crow*), in Scotland the rook: extended to other birds: inferior coal: the defiant or triumphant cry of a cock: a child's inarticulate cry of joy: a crow-bar.—*v.i.* to croak: to utter a crow: to boast, swagger, triumph (often with *over*):—*pa.t.* **crew,** *kroo̅,* or **crowed**; *pa.p.* **crowed,** also **crown** (*krōn*).—*ns.* **crow'-bar,** a large iron bar mostly bent at the end, to be used as a lever; **crow'-berry,** a small creeping moorland shrub (Empetrum) producing small black berries; **crow'-flower** (*Shak.*), perhaps crowfoot; **crow'foot,** a buttercup, sometimes extended to other plants (*pl.* in this sense **crow-foots**): crow's-foot: a number of l'nes rove through a long wooden block, supporting the backbone of an awning horizontally; **crow'-keeper** (*Shak.*), a scarecrow; **crow'-quill,** a pen made of the quill of a crow, etc., for fine writing or etching, **crow's'-bill, crow'-bill** (*surg.*), a kind of forceps for extracting bullets, etc., from wounds; **crow's-foot,** one of the wrinkles produced by age, spreading out from the corners of the eyes: (*mil.*) a caltrop; **crow'-shrike,** a piping-crow (see pipe); **crow's'-nest** (*naut.*), an elevated shelter for a man on the lookout.—*n.pl.* **crow'-steps,** steps on a gable.—*n.* **crow'-toe** (*Milt.*), probably the same as crowfoot.—**as the crow flies,** in a straight line; **eat crow, eat boiled crow,** to be forced to do something very disagreeable, humiliate oneself; **have a crow to pluck with,** to have something to settle with someone; **Royston crow,** the hooded crow (*Corvus cornix*)—said to be common near Royston in Herts. [O.E. *cráwe,* a crow, *cráwan,* to crow.]

crowd, *krowd, n.* a number of persons or things closely pressed together, without order: the rabble: multitude: (*U.S.*) a set.—*v.t.* to gather into a lump or crowd: to fill by pressing or driving together: to compress: (*U.S.*) to thrust, put pressure on.—*v.i.* to press on: to press together in numbers: to swarm.—*adj.* **crowd'ed.—crowd sail,** to carry a press of sail for speed. [O.E. *crúdan,* to press.]

crowd, *krowd, n.* (*obs.*) the crwth.—*n.* **crowd'er** (*obs.*) a fiddler. [See **crwth.**]

crowdie, *krowd'i, n.* (*Scot.*) a mixture of meal and water: brose: a cheese-like preparation of milk. [Der. unknown; perh. in part for **crud.**]

crown, *krown, n.* a circular head ornament, esp. as a mark of honour: the diadem or state-cap of royalty: kingship: the sovereign: governing power in a monarchy: honour: the top of anything, as a head, hat, tree, arch: (*archit.*) a species of spire or lantern, formed by converging flying-buttresses: a stag's surroyals: the visible part of a tooth: the junction of root and stem: a short rootstock: a clasping metal cap for a bottle: chief ornament: completion or consummation: a coin originally stamped with a crown, esp. a 5s. piece: used to translate various coin names, as krone: the old French écu: a size of paper (15 × 20 in., in U.S. 15 × 19), originally water-marked with a crown.—*v.t.* to cover or invest with a crown: to cap: to invest with royal dignity: to fill with foaming liquor: in draughts, to convert into a king or crowned man by placing another draught on the top on reaching the crown-head: to adorn: to dignify: to complete happily.—*ns.* **crown'-ag'ent,** a solicitor in Scotland who prepares criminal prosecutions; **crown'-ant'ler,** the uppermost tine of an antler; **crown'-bark,** a kind of cinchona bark:—*adj.* **crowned.**—*ns.* **crown'er** (*Shak.*), a coroner; **crown'et,** a coronet: (*Shak.*), that which crowns or accomplishes; **crown'-gall,** a bacterial disease of plants, forming tumours; **crown'-glass,** an alkali-lime glass: a window-glass formed in circular plates or disks; **crown'-graft,** insertion of scions between bark and wood; **crown'-green,** a bowling-green with a crown or arched surface; **crown'-head,** in draughts, the back row of squares, where a man is crowned; **crown'-impe'rial,** a plant, a species of fritillary; **crown'ing;** **crown'-jew'el,** a jewel pertaining to the crown or sovereign; **crown'-land,** land belonging to the crown or sovereign; **crown'-law'yer,** the lawyer who acts for the crown in criminal cases.—*adj.* **crown'less.**—*ns.* **crown'let,** a small crown; **crown'-piece,** a five-shilling piece;

crown'-post, a king-post; **crown'-saw,** a circular saw made by cutting teeth round the edge of a disk; **crown'-wheel,** a wheel resembling a crown, with teeth or cogs set at right angles to its plane; **crown'-work** (*fort.*), an outwork composed of a bastion between two curtains, with demi-bastions at the extremes.—**crown colony,** a colony whose administration is directly under the home government; **crown Derby,** a late 18th-century porcelain made at Derby, marked with a crown; **crowned head,** a monarch; **crown living,** a church living in the gift of the crown; **crown octavo,** an octavo 5 × 7½ in.; **Crown Office,** the office for the business of the crown side of the King's Bench: the office in which the great seal is affixed; **crown of the causeway,** the middle of the street; **crown prince,** the heir apparent to the crown; **crown witness,** a witness for the crown in a criminal prosecution instituted by it. [O.Fr. *corone* (Fr. *couronne*)—L. *corōna;* cf. Gr. *koronos,* curved.]

croze, *krōz, n.* the groove in the staves of a cask in which the edge of the head is set. [Perh. O.Fr. *croz* (Fr. *creux*), groove.]

crozier. See crosier.

crucial, cruciate. See crux.

crucian, crusian, *kroo̅'shan, n.* the German carp, without barbels. [L.G. *karusse* (Ger. *karausche*)—L. *coracīnus*—Gr. *korakīnos,* a black perch-like fish—*korax,* raven.]

crucible, *kroo̅'si-bl, n.* an earthen pot for melting ores, metals, etc. [L.L. *crucibulum.*]

crucifer, *kroo̅'si-fər, n.* a cross-bearer in a procession: a member of the Cruciferae.—*n.pl.* **Crucif'erae,** a family of archichlamydeous dicotyledons, with cross-shaped flowers, including cabbage, turnip, cress, wallflower.—*adj.* **crucif'erous,** bearing or marked with a cross: with four petals placed crosswise: of the Cruciferae. [L. *crux, crucis,* a cross, *ferre,* to bear.]

cruciform, crucigerous. See crux.

crucify, *kroo̅'si-fī, v.t.* to expose or put to death on a cross: to fasten to a wheel or the like, as a military field punishment: to subdue completely: to mortify: to torment: (*pr.p.* **cru'cifying**; *pa.t.* and *pa.p.* **cru'cified**).—*ns.* **cru'cifier,** one who crucifies; **cru'cifix,** a figure or picture of Christ fixed to the cross; **crucifixion** (*-fik'shan*). [O.Fr. *crucifier*—L. *crucifīgere, crucifīxum*—*crux,* cross, and *fīgere,* to fix.]

cruck, *kruk, n.* in crude building, a curved timber supporting a roof. [Cf. **crook.**]

crud, *krud, krood, obs.* and *dial.* form of **curd.**—*v.t.* (*Spens.*) and *v.i.* **crudd'le,** curdle.—*adj.* **crudd'y** (*Spens.*) curdy.

crude, *krood, adj.* raw, unprepared: not reduced to order or form: unfinished: undigested: immature: unrefined: inartistic.—*adv.* **crude'ly.**—*ns.* **crude'ness; crud'ity,** rawness: unripeness: that which is crude.—*adj.* **crud'y** (*Shak.*), crude, raw. [L. *crūdus,* raw.]

crue, a Miltonic spelling of **crew** (*n.*).

cruel, *kroo̅'əl, adj.* disposed to inflict pain, or pleased at suffering: void of pity, merciless, savage: severe.—*adj.* **cru'el-heart'ed,** delighting in cruelty: hard-hearted: unrelenting.—*adv.* **cru'elly.**—*ns.* **cru'elness** (*obs.*); **cru'elty.** [Fr. *cruel*—L. *crūdēlis.*]

cruels, cruells. Same as **crewels.**

cruet, *kroo̅'it, n.* a small jar or phial for sauces and condiments for the table: a vessel for wine, oil, or water for religious ceremonies.—*n.* **cru'et-stand,** a stand or frame for holding cruets. [A.Fr. dim. of O.Fr. *cruye,* jar, from root of **crock.**]

cruise, *kroo̅z, v.i.* to sail to and fro: to fly at a speed economical in fuel, etc.: (*coll.;* with *about,* etc.) to wander about seeking something.—*n.* a sailing to and fro: a wandering voyage in search of an enemy or for the protection of vessels or for pleasure or health: a land journey of similar character.—*ns.* **cruis'er,** one who or that cruises: speedy warship, specially intended for cruising: a privateer: a cruising yacht; **cruis'er-weight,** a boxer between middle and heavy, a light heavyweight. [Du. *kruisen,* to cross.]

cruisie. See **crusie.**

cruive, cruve, krōōv (*Scot.* krᴧv, kriv), *n.* a pen, sty : a hovel : a wattled fish-trap.

cruller, krul′ᴧr, *n.* (*U.S.*) a friedcake. [Cf. Du. *krullen,* to curl.]

crumb, krum, *n.* a small bit or morsel of bread : a small particle of anything : the soft part of bread.—*v.t.* to break into crumbs : to put crumbs in or on : to remove crumbs from.—*v.i.* to crumble.—*ns.* **crumb′-brush,** a brush for sweeping crumbs off the table : **crumb′-cloth,** a cloth laid under a table to keep crumbs from the carpet : drugget; **crumb′-tray,** a tray for crumbs removed from the table.—*adj.* **crumb′y, crumm′y,** in crumbs : soft. [O.E. *cruma;* Du. *kruim;* Ger. *krume;* **crimp**].

crumble, krum′bl, *v.t.* to break into crumbs.—*v.i.* to fall into small pieces : to decay.—*n.* a crumb : that which crumbles easily.—*adj.* **crum′bly,** apt to crumble. [Orig. dim. of **crumb** ; Du. *kruimelen;* Ger. *krümeln.*]

crumen, krōō-mᴧn, *n* a deer's tear-pit.—*n.* **cru′menal** (*Spens.*), a purse. [L. *crumēna,* a purse.]

crummock, crummack, krum′ᴧk, *n.* a crook, stick with curved head. [Gael. *cromag,* hook, crook.]

crump, krump, *adj.* crooked : wrinkled : (*Scot.*) crisp or friable.—*ns.* **crumm′y,** a cow with a crumpled horn : **crump′et,** a kind of soft cake or muffin : (*slang*) the head.—*adj.* **crump′y** (*dial.*) crisp. [O.E. *crump*—**crumb,** crooked ; Ger. *krumm.* Cf. **cramp, crimp.**]

crumple, krump′l, *v.t.* to crush into irregular wrinkles : to wrinkle : to cause to collapse.—*v.i.* to wrinkle : to collapse.—*adj.* **crump′led.**—*n.* **crump′ling.** [**crump.**]

crunch, krunsh, *v.t.* to crush with harsh noise, with the teeth, under foot, or otherwise : to chew anything hard, and so make a noise.—*n.* the act or sound of crunching.—*n.* **crunch′iness.**—*adj.* **crunch′y.** [Cf. **craunch.**]

crunkle, krunk′l, *v i.* to crumple. [Cf. **crinkle.**]

cruor, krōō′or, *n.* coagulated blood. [L.]

crupper, krup′ᴧr, *n.* a strap of leather fastened to the saddle and passing under the horse's tail to keep the saddle in its place : the hind part of a horse. [O.Fr. *cropiere*—*crope,* the croup.]

crural, krōō′rᴧl, *adj.* belonging to or like a leg. [L. *crūrālis,* from, *crūs, crūris,* the leg.]

crusade, krōō-sād′, *n.* a military expedition under the banner of the cross to recover the Holy Land from the Turks : any daring or romantic undertaking : concerted action to further a cause.—*v.i.* to go on a crusade.—*n.* **crusad′er,** one engaged in a crusade. [Fr. *croisade*—Prov. *crozada*—*croz*—L. *crux,* a cross.]

crusado, krōō-sā′dō, *n.* a Portuguese coin, so called because marked with a cross. [Port. *cruzado.*]

cruse, krōōz, also krōōs, *n.* an earthen pot : a small cup or bottle. [Cf. O.N. *krús;* Ger. *krause.*]

cruset, krōō′sit, *n.* a goldsmith's crucible. [Cf. Fr. *creuset,* M.Du. *kruysel,* M.L.G. *krusel.*]

crush, krush, *v.t.* to break or bruise : to squeeze together : to beat down or overwhelm : to subdue : to ruin.—*v.i.* to become broken or crumpled under pressure.—*n.* a violent squeezing : a close crowd of persons or things : a drink made from fruit juice; (*slang*) a set of people : a narrowing passage for cattle : (*U.S.*) an infatuation (with *on*), or its object.—*n.* **crush′-barr′ier,** a barrier erected to restrain a crowd.—*adj.* **crushed.**—*ns.* **crush′er,** one who, or that which, crushes or subdues : (*slang*) a policeman : **crush′-hat,** an opera-hat.—*adj.* **crushing.**—*adv.* **crush′ingly.**—*n.* **crush′-room,** a room where an audience may promenade during the intervals of the entertainment.—**crush a cup,** to empty a cup : to quaff; **crushed strawberry,** of the pinky colour of strawberries that have been crushed. [O.Fr. *croissir;* perh. cog. with M.H.G. *krosen,* to crunch.]

crusie, crusy, krōō′zi, *n.* (*Scot.*) an open iron lamp used with a rush wick. [From **cruset.**]

crust, krust, *n.* the hard rind or outside coating of anything : the outer part of bread : covering of a pie, etc. : the solid exterior of the earth.—*v.t.* to cover with a crust or hard case.—*v.i.* to gather into a hard crust.—*adjs.* **crust′al,** pertaining to a crust; **crust′ate, crustāt′ed,** covered with a crust.—*n.* **crustā′tion,** an adherent crust.—*adv.* **crust′ily.**—*n.* **crusti′ness.**—*adjs.* **crust′less** ; **crust′y,** of the nature of or having a crust, as port or other wine : having a hard or harsh exterior : hard : snappy : surly. [L. *crusta,* rind.]

crusta, krus′tä, *n.* a piece prepared for inlaying : a hard coating : a cocktail served in a glass, its rim encrusted in sugar :—*pl.* **crustae** (-*tē*). [L.]

Crustacea, krus-tā′sh(y)ä, -shi-ä, *n.pl.* a large class of arthropod animals, almost all aquatic—crabs, lobsters, shrimps, sand-hoppers, wood-lice, water-fleas, barnacles, etc.—*adj.* and *n.* **crustā′cean.**—*adj.* **crustā′ceous,** crusty.

crutch, kruch, *n.* a staff with a cross-piece at the head to place under the arm of a lame person : any support of like form : a bifurcation, crotch : (*arith.*) a small figure inserted to show the number to be carried.—*v.t.* to support : to prop.—*v.i.* to go on crutches.—*adj.* **crutched,** marked by the sign of or wearing a Cross.—*n.pl.* **Crutch′ed-fri′ars,** an order of friars so called from the sign of the cross which they wore—*Crouched-* or *Crossed-friars.* [O.E. *crycc.*]

crux, kruks, *n.* a cross : (*fig.*) something that occasions difficulty or perplexity : that on which a decision turns : the essential point, as of a problem :—*pl.* **cruxes, cruces** (krōō′sēz).—*adjs.* **crucial** (krōō′shal, shyal), crosslike : of the nature of a crux : testing or decisive, as if of the nature of a finger-post at a cross-road; **cruciate** (krōō′shi-āt), cross-shaped.—*v.t.* to torment.—*adjs.* **cruciform** (krōō′si-form), cross-shaped; **crucigerous** (krōō′sij′ᴧr-ᴧs), bearing a cross. [L. *crux, crucis,* a cross.]

cruzeiro, krōō-zā′rō, *n.* the monetary unit of Brazil. [Port.,—*cruz,* cross.]

crwth, krooth, *n.* the crowd, an old Welsh stringed instrument, four of its six strings played with a bow, two plucked by the thumb. [W. *crwth,* a hollow protuberance, a fiddle; Gael., Ir. *cruit.*]

cry, krī, *v.i.* to utter a shrill loud sound, esp. one of pain or grief : to lament : to weep : to bawl.—*v.t.* to utter loudly : to exclaim : to proclaim or make public : to offer for sale by crying : (*Scot.*) to proclaim the banns of marriage of (*3rd pers. sing.* **cries:** *pr.p.* **cry′ing,** *pa.t.* and *pa.p.* **cried,** krīd).—*n.* any loud sound, esp. of grief or pain : a call or shout : a fit of weeping : a pack of hounds, hence of people : a particular sound uttered by an animal : the creak of bent tin : bawling : lamentation : prayer : clamour : report or rumour : a general utterance : a watchword, battle-cry, or slogan : a street call of wares for sale or services offered :—*pl.* **cries.**—*ns.* **cri′er,** one who cries, esp. an official maker of proclamations : **cry′-baby,** one who cries childishly; **cry′ing,** act of calling loudly : weeping.—*adj.* calling loudly : claiming notice : notorious.—**a far cry,** a great distance; **cry against,** to protest against ; **cry down,** to condemn : to decry; **cry off,** to withdraw from a bargain; **cry on,** to call upon ; **cry out** (*obs.*) to be in childbirth; **cry over spilt milk,** to waste time in bemoaning what is irreparable; **cry quits,** to declare a thing even; **cry up,** to praise; **cry you mercy** (*obs.*). I beg your pardon; **great cry and little wool,** much ado about nothing; **hue and cry** (see **hue**); **in full cry,** in full pursuit, used of dogs in hunt; **out of cry,** (*obs.*) beyond measure; beyond dispute; **within cry of,** within hearing distance. [Fr. *crier*—L. *quirītāre,* to scream.]

cryo-, krī′ō-, krī-o′-, in composition, frost, ice.—*ns.* **cryoc′onite** (Gr. *konis,* dust), dust found on the surface of polar ice; **cry′ogen** (-*jen;* Gr. root of *gignesthai,* to become), a substance used for obtaining low temperatures, a freezing mixture.—*adj.* **cryogen′ic.**—*ns.* **cryogen′ics,** the branch of physics concerned with phenomena at very low temperatures; **cryogeny** (-*of′ᴧ-ni*), refrigeration : the study of methods of producing very low temperatures; **cry′olite** (Gr. *lithos,* a stone), an ice-stone or Greenland spar, sodium aluminium fluoride, earliest source of aluminium; **cryom′eter** (Gr. *metron,* measure), a thermometer for low temperatures.—*adj.* **cryomet′ric.**—*ns.* **cryoph′orus** (Gr. *pherein,* to bear), an instrument for showing the decrease of temperature in water by evaporation; **cry'oscope** (Gr. *skopeein*, to look at), at instrument for determining freezing points.—*adj.* **cryoscop'ic.**—*ns.* **cryos'copy**, the study of the effect of dissolved substances on the freezing-points of solvents; **cry'ostat**, apparatus for achieving or demonstrating cooling by evaporation: any apparatus for maintaining a low temperature. [Gr. *kryos*, frost.]

crypt, *kript*, *n.* an underground cell or chapel: (*zool.*) a small cavity, a tubular gland.—*adjs.* **cryp'tal**, pertaining to, or of the nature of, a crypt; **cryp'tic**, **-al**, hidden: secret: unseen: mysteriously obscure: (*zool.*) protectively concealing. [L. *crypta*—Gr. *kryptē*—*kryptrin*, to hide; cf. **grot**.]

crypt-, **crypto-**, *kript-*, *-ō-*, *-o-*, in composition, hidden.—*n.* **cryptaesthesia** (*kript-ēs-thē'zyā*, *-zhā*; Gr. *aisthēsis*, perception), supranormal perception, e.g. clairvoyance.—*adj.* **cryptaes-thĕt'ic.**—*n.pl.* **cryptadia** (*krip-tā'di-ā*; Gr.), things to be kept secret.—*adj.* **cryptocryst'alline**, with crystalline structure visible only under the microscope.—*n.* **cryp'togam** (Gr. *gamos*, marriage), any member of the **Cryptogamia** (*krip'tō-gā'mi-ā*), the class of flowerless plants, so named by Linnaeus in the expectation that sexual reproduction would one day be discovered in them.—*adjs.* **cryptogā'-mian**, **cryptogamic** (*-gam'ik*), **cryptogamous** (*-tog'ə-məs*).—*ns.* **cryptog'amist**; **cryptog'amy.** —*ns.* **cryp'togram**, **cryp'tograph** (Gr. *gramma*, a letter, *graphein*, to write), anything written in cipher.—*ns.* **cryptŏg'rapher**, **-ist**,—*adj.* **cryp-tograph'ic.**—*ns.* **cryptog'raphy**; **cryptol'ogy**, secret language; **Cryptomēr'ia** (Gr. *meros*, part), the Japanese cedar; **crypton** (same as **krypton**); **cryp'tonym** (Gr. *onyma*, name), a secret name.—*adj.* **crypton'ymous.** [Gr. *kryptos*, hidden.]

crystal, *kris'tl*, *n.* (*obs.*) ice: rock-crystal, a clear quartz, like ice: a body, generally solid, whose atoms are arranged in a definite pattern, outwardly expressed by geometrical form with plane faces: a globe of rock-crystal or the like in which one may see visions: anything bright and clear: a superior glass of various kinds: cut glass: a watch-glass.—*adj.* composed of or like crystal.— *ns.* **crys'tal-gazer**; **crys'tal-gazing**, gazing in a crystal or the like to obtain visual images, whether in divination or to objectify hidden contents of the mind.—*adj.* **crys'talline** (*-īn*, *-in*; in the poets also *-tal'*) like crystal or a crystal: composed of crystal, crystals, or parts of crystals: having the structure of a crystal.—*n.* a crystalline substance: (*obs.*) aniline: a shining fabric of silk and wool; **crystalli'sable.**—*n.* **crystallisā'tion.**—*v.t.* and *v.i.* **crys'tallise**, to form into crystals: to make or become definite or concrete.—*ns.* **crys'tallite**, a small, imperfectly formed or incipient crystal: a minute body in glassy igneous rocks; **crystalli'tis**, inflammation of the crystalline lens; **crystallo-gen'esis**, origination of crystals.—*adj.* **crystal-logenet'ic.**—*n.* **crystallog'rapher.**—*adj.* **crystal-lograph'ic.**—*ns.* **crystallog'raphy**, the science of the structure, forms, and properties of crystals; **crys'talloid**, a substance in a state in which it dissolves to form a true solution which will pass through a membrane: (*bot.*) a minute crystalline particle of protein.—*adj.* like a crystal: of the nature of a crystalloid.—*n.* **crys'tallomancy** (Gr. *manteiā*, divination), divination by transparent bodies.—**crystalline heaven, sphere**, in ancient astronomy a sphere between the fixed stars and the *primum mobile*, assumed to explain precession of the equinoxes; **crystalline lens**, the transparent refractive body of the eye; **crystal set**, a simple wireless receiving apparatus in which a crystal and a cat's-whisker rectify the current. [O.Fr. *cristal* —L. *crystallum*—Gr. *krystallos*, ice—*kryos*, frost.]

csárdás, *chär'däsh*, *n.* a Hungarian dance, or its music, in 2-4 time, generally consisting of a slow movement or *lassu* and a quick *fris* or *friska*.— Also (wrongly) **czardas**. [Hung.]

ctene, *tēn*, *n.* a comb-like swimming organ in the Ctenophora.—*adjs.* **cteniform** (*tēn'*, or *ten'*), **cten'oid**, *adj.* comb-shaped.—*n.pl.* **Ctenoph'ora**, a class of Coelenterates—beautifully delicate, free-swimming marine organisms, moving by means of meridionally placed comb-like plates.— *n.*, *adj.* **ctenoph'oran**. [Gr. *kteis*, *ktenos*, comb.]

cub, *kub*, *n.* the young of certain animals, as foxes, etc.: a whelp: a young boy or girl (playful or contemptuous, esp. of the ill-conditioned, unmannerly, raw, or conceited): a wolf-cub or embryo boy scout: (*U.S.*) an apprentice or novice. —*v.t.* and *v.i.* to bring forth: to hunt (fox-cubs):— *pr.p.* **cubb'ing**; *pa.t.* and *pa.p.* **cubbed.**—*adjs.* **cubb'ish**, like a cub: awkward or ill-mannered; **cub'-drawn** (*Shak.*), drawn or sucked by cubs.— *ns.* **cub'hood**; **cub'-hunting**, **cubb'ing**, hunting young foxes.—*adj.* **cub'less**. [Ety. dub.]

cub, *kub*, *n.* a cattle-pen: a chest.—*ns.* **cubb'y**, **cubb'y-hole**, a snug enclosed place. [Prob. from L.G.]

Cuban, *kū'bən*, *adj.* pertaining to *Cuba* or its people. —*n.* a native of Cuba.—**Cuban heel**, on footwear, a high heel without curves.

cube, *kūb*, *n.* a solid body having six equal square faces, a solid square: the third power of a quantity. —*v.t.* to raise to the third power.—*ns.* **cūb'age**, **cū'bature**, the act of finding the solid or cubic content of a body: the result thus found.—*adjs.* **cū'bic**, **-al**, pertaining to a cube: of or involving the third power or degree: solid: (*crystal.*) isometric.—*adv.* **cū'bically.**—*n.* **cū'bicalness.**—*adj.* **cū'biform.**—*n.* **cū'bism**, a modern movement in painting, which seeks to represent several aspects of an object seen from different standpoints arbitrarily grouped in one composition, making use of cubes and other solid geometrical figures.— *n.* and *adj.* **cū'bist.**—*n.* **cū'boid**, a rectangular parallelepiped, esp. one whose faces are not all equal.—*adjs.* **cū'boid**, **cū'boid'al**, resembling a cube in shape.—**cube root**, the quantity of which the given quantity is the cube. [Fr.,—L. *cubus*— Gr. *kybos*, a die.]

cubeb, *kū'beb*, *n.* the dried berry of *Piper Cubeba*, a Sumatran climbing pepper shrub—used in medicine. [Fr. *cubèbe*—Ar. *kabābah*.]

cubica, *kū'bi-kā*, *n.* a fine worsted for linings. [Sp. *cúbica*.]

cubicle, *kū'bi-kl*, *n.* a bedroom: part of a dormitory partitioned off: a cell or compartment. [L. *cubiculum*—*cubāre*, to lie down.]

cubit, *kū'bit*, *n.* an old measure, the length of the arm from the elbow to the tip of the middle-finger, from 18 to 22 inches—also **cū'bitus.**—*adj.* **cū'bital**, of the length of a cubit. [L. *cubitum*, the elbow; cf. L. *cubāre*, to lie down.]

cucking-stool, *kuk'ing-stōol*, *n.* a stool in which scolds and other culprits were placed, usually before their own door, to be pelted by the mob. [Mentioned in Domesday Book as in use in Chester, and called *cathedra stercoris*. From an obs. word *cuck*, to defecate; cf. O.N. *kúka*.]

cuckold, *kuk'old*, *n.* a man whose wife has proved unfaithful.—*v.t.* to make cuckold.—*v.t.* **cuck'-oldise**, to make a cuckold.—*adj.* **cuck'oldly** (*Shak.*).—*ns.* **cuck'old-mak'er**; **cuck'oldom**, **cuck'oldry**, state of a cuckold: act of making a cuckold.—*adj.* **cuck'oldy**. [O.Fr. *cucuault*—*cucu*, cuckoo.]

cuckoo, *kook'ōō*, *n.* a bird (*Cuculus*) that cries *cuckoo*, remarkable for depositing its eggs in the nests of other birds: a silly person.—*ns.* **cuck'oo-bud** (*Shak.*), name of a plant; **cuck'oo-clock**, a clock in which the hours are told by a cuckoo-call; **cuck'oo-flower**, a species of *Cardamine*— *Lady's-smock*: ragged robin; **cuck'oo-fly**, a gold-wasp—from laying its eggs in wasps' and bees' nests; **cuck'oo-pint** (*-pint*), the Wake-robin, *Arum maculatum*; **cuck'oo-spit**, **-spitt'le**, a froth secreted by frog-hoppers on plants, surrounding the larvae and pupae. [Imit.; cf. Fr. *coucou*, Ger. *kuckuck*, L. *cuculus*, Gr. *kokkyx*, *-ȳgos*.]

cucullate, **-d**, *kū'kul-āt* or *-kul'*, *-id*, *adjs.* hooded: shaped like a hood. [L. *cucullatus*—*cucullus*.]

cucumber, *kū'kam-bər*, *n.* a creeping plant (*Cucumis sativus*) of the Cucurbitaceae, with bristly lobed leaves and tendrils: its large oblong fruit, used as a salad and pickle: (*U.S.*) a cucumber-tree.—

cū′cumber-tree, the bilimbi tree: (*U.S.*) a magnolia: also a tulip-tree.—*adj.* **cūcūm′iform.** [L. *cucumis, -eris.*]

cucurbit, *kū-kər′bit, n.* a chemical vessel used in distillation, originally shaped like a gourd.—*adjs.* **cucur′bital, cucurbitā′ceous,** pertaining to the **Cucurbitā′ceae,** a family of sympetalous dicotyledons, including gourd, melon, etc.: gourd-like. [L. *cucurbita,* a gourd.]

cud, *kud, n.* food brought back from first stomach of a ruminating animal to be chewed again. —*n.* **cud′weed,** a woolly composite plant of the genus Gnaphalium: extended to kindred plants.—**chew the cud,** to meditate. [O.E. *cwidu.*]

cudbear, *kud′bār, n.* a purple dye-stuff, a powder prepared from various lichens. [From Dr. *Cuthbert* Gordon, who made it an article of commerce.]

cuddle, *kud′l, v.t.* to hug: to embrace: to fondle.— *v.i.* to lie close and snug together.—*n.* a close embrace. [Origin unknown.]

cuddy, *kud′i, n.* a small cabin or cook-room, in the fore-part of a boat or lighter: in large vessels, the officers' cabin under the poop-deck. [Origin uncertain; cf. Fr. *cahute;* Du. *kajuit;* Ger. *kajüte.*]

cuddy, *kud′i, n.* the right of a lord to entertainment from his tenant: rent—(*Spens.*) **cuddeehih.** [Ir. *cuid oidhche—cuid,* a share, *oidhche,* night.]

cuddy, cuddie, *kud′i, n.* a donkey: (*Scot.*) a stupid person. [Perh. *Cuthbert.*]

cudgel, *kuj′l, n.* a heavy staff: a club.—*v.t.* to beat with a cudgel (*pr.p.* **cudg′elling;** *pa.t.* and *pa.p.* **cudg′elled**).—*ns.* **cudg′eller; cudg′elling; cud′gel-play.**—*adj.* **cudg′el-proof,** not to be hurt by beating.—**take up the cudgels,** to join in defence. [O.E. *cycgel.*]

cue, *kū, n.* the last words of an actor's speech serving as a hint to the next speaker: any hint: the part one has to play. [Acc. to some from Fr. *queue,* tail (see next word); in 17th cent. written Q, and derived from L. *quando,* when, i.e. when the actor was to begin.]

cue, *kū, n.* a twist of hair at the back of the head: a rod used in playing billiards.—*v.t.* of the hair, to form in a cue.—*ns* **cue′-ball,** the ball struck by the cue; **cue′ist,** a billiard-player. [Fr. *queue*—L. *cauda,* a tail.]

cuff, *kuf, n.* a stroke with the open hand.—*v.t.* to strike with the open hand: to beat. [Origin obscure; cf. Sw. *kuffa,* to knock.]

cuff, *kuf, n.* the end of the sleeve near the wrist: a covering for the wrist: a handcuff (q.v.). [Prob. cog. with **coif.**]

cuff, *kuf, n.* a Scottish form of **scuff, scruff.**— **cuff of the neck.** See **scruff.**

cuffin, *kuf′in, n.* a man.—**queer cuffin,** a justice of the peace: a churl. [Thieves' slang.]

cuffle, *kuf′l, v.i.* (*Spens.*) to scuffle.

Cufic. Same as **Kufic.**

cuif. Same as **coof.**

cuirass, *kwi-ras′* (or *kū′), n.* a defensive breastplate and backplate fastened together: a breastplate alone.—*v.t.* to furnish with a cuirass.—*n.* **cuirassier** (*-ēr′),* a horse-soldier armed with cuirass. [Fr. *cuirasse—cuir,* leather—L. *corium,* skin, leather.]

cuir-bouilli, *kwēr-bōō′yē, n.* leather boiled or soaked in hot water and moulded.—Also **cuir-bouilly.** [Fr., boiled leather.]

cuisine, *kwē-zēn′, n.* a kitchen or cooking department: cookery.—*n.* **cuisin′ier** (*-yā),* a cook. [Fr.,—L. *coquina—coquère,* to cook.]

cuisse, *kwis,* **cuish, kwish,** (*Shak.* **cush,** *kush*) *n.* thigh armour.—*n.* **cuisse-madame** (*-däm′),* a jargonelle pear. [Fr. *cuisse*—L. *coxa,* hip.]

cuit, cute, coot, *kət, küt, kit, n.* (*Scot.*) the ankle.— *n.* **cuit′ikin, cut′ikin, coot′ikin** (*Scot.*), a gaiter. [Cf. Du. *koot,* Flem. *keute.*]

cuiter *küt′ər, v.t.* (*Scot.*) to wheedle: to cocker, pamper.

cuittle, *küt′l, v.t.* (*Scot.*) to coax: to cajole: to curry (favour): (perh. by confusion with **kittle**) to tickle. [Origin obscure.]

culch, cultch, *kulch, n.* (*S. England*) rubbish: flooring of an oyster-bed: oyster-spawn. [Origin doubtful.]

Culdee, *kul′dē, n.* one of a fraternity of monks living in Scotland from the 8th century in groups of cells. [Old Ir. *céle dé,* servant or companion of God—Latinised by Boece into *Culdei* (*pl.*) as if *cultōrēs Deī.*]

cul-de-four, *kü(l)-də-fōōr* (Fr. **kü**), *n.* (*archit.*) a sort of low spherical vault, oven-like.—*ns.* **cul-de-lampe** (*län′p),* an ornamental design used in filling up blank spaces in a book; **cul-de-sac,** a street, etc., closed at one end: a blind-alley. [Fr. *cul,* bottom—L. *cūlus;* Fr. *de,* of, *four,* furnace, *lampe,* lamp, *sac,* sack.]

culet, *kū′lit, n.* the back of a brilliant-cut diamond: armour protecting the hips. [O.Fr. *culet,* dim. of *cul;* see foregoing.]

Culex, *kū′leks, n.* the typical genus of Culic′idae or gnats (*pl.* **culices,** *kū′li-sēz*).—*adjs.* **culiciform** (*-lis′);* **cu′licine.**—*n.* **cu′licid.** [L. *culex, -icis.*]

culinary, *kū′lin-ər-i, adj.* pertaining to the kitchen or to cookery: used in the kitchen. [L. *culinārius* —*culina,* a kitchen.]

cull, *kul, v.t.* to select, pick out.—*n.* an unsuitable animal eliminated from a flock or herd.—*ns.* **cull′er; cull′ing.** [Fr. *cueillir,* to gather—L. *colligĕre—col-,* together, *legĕre,* to gather.]

cull. See **cully.**

cullender. See **colander.**

cullet, *kul′it, n.* waste glass, melted up again with new material. [Fr. *collet*—L. *collum,* neck.]

cullion, *kul′yən, n.* a wretch: a rascal.—*adj.* **cull′ionly** (*Shak.*), mean, base. [Fr. *couillon,* testicle, poltroon (It. *coglione*)—L. *cŏleus,* a leather bag—Gr. *koleos,* sheath.]

cullis, *kul′is, n.* a strong broth. [O.F. *coleis*—L. *cōlāre,* to strain.]

cullis, *kul′is, n.* a roof gutter or groove. [Fr. *coulisse.*]

cully, *kul′i, n.* a mean dupe: fellow, mate, a man generally.—*v.t.* to deceive meanly (*pr.p.* **cull′ying;** *pa.t.* and *pa.p.* **cull′ied**).—*ns.* **cull,** a dupe; **cull′yism,** state of being a cully. [Prob. a contr. of **cullion.**]

culm, *kulm, n.* a grass or sedge stem.—*v.i.* to form a culm.—*adj.* **culmif′erous,** having a culm. [L. *culmus,* a stalk.]

culm, *kulm, n.* coal-dust: anthracite dust: in some parts of England, anthracite.—*adj.* **culmif′erous,** producing culm.—**Culm, Culm Measures,** a Lower Carboniferous formation of Europe and Southwest England, with grits, sandstones, shales, etc. [Origin unknown; cf. **coom.**]

culmen, *kul′men, n.* highest point: the top ridge of a bird's bill. [L.; see next.]

culminate, *kul′min-āt, v.i.* (*astron.*) to be on, or come to, the meridian, and thus the highest (or lowest) point of altitude: to reach the highest point (with *in*).—*v.t.* to bring to the highest point. —*adj.* **cul′minant,** at its highest point.—*n.* **culminā′tion,** act of culminating: the top: the highest point: (*astron.*) transit of a body across the meridian. [L.L. *culmināre, -ātum—culmen,* or *columen, -inis,* a summit.]

culpable, *kul′pə-bl, adj.* faulty: criminal.—*ns.* **culpabil′ity, cul′pableness,** liability to blame.—*adv.* **cul′pably.**—*adj.* **cul′patory,** expressive of blame. [L. *culpa,* a fault.]

culprit, *kul′prit, n.* one in fault: a criminal: (*Eng. law*) a prisoner accused but not yet tried. [From the fusion in legal phraseology of *cul.* (*culpable, culpābilis*), and *prit, prist* (O.Fr. *prest*), ready.]

cult, *kult, n.* a system of religious belief: worship: a fad.—Also **cult′us.**—*adjs.* **cult, cult′ic.** [L. *cultus—colĕre,* to worship.]

culter, *kul′tər, n.* obsolete form of **coulter.**—*adjs.* **cul′trate, -d, cul′triform,** knife-shaped. [L., knife.]

cultism, *kult′izm, n.* Gongorism.—*ns.* **cult′ist, cult′orist.** [Sp. *culto,* elegant—L. *cultus.*]

cultivate, *kul′ti-vāt, v.t.* to till or produce by tillage: to prepare for crops: to devote attention to: to civilise or refine.—*adjs.* **cul′tivable, cultivat′able,** capable of being cultivated.—*ns.* **cultivā′tion,** the art or practice of cultivating: civilisation: refinement; **cul′tivator,** one who cultivates: an agricultural implement—a grubber.

—cultivate one's friendship, to seek to gain or foster it. [L.L. *cultivāre*, -*ātum*—L. *colēre*, to till, to worship.]

culture, *kult'yǝr, n.* cultivation : the state of being cultivated : refinement the result of cultivation : a type of civilisation : a crop of experimentally grown bacteria or the like.—*v.t.* to cultivate : to improve.—*adjs.* **cul'turable : cul'tural.**—*adj.* **cul'tured,** cultivated : well educated : refined.— *adj.* **cul'tureless.** [L. *cultūra*—*colēre.*]

cultus. See **cult.**

culver, *kul'vǝr, n.* a dove, a pigeon : a wood-pigeon. —*n.* **cul'ver-key,** (often in *pl.*) the wild hyacinth : the cowslip : ash-keys.—*adj.* **cul'vertailed,** dove-tailed. [O.E. *culfre.*]

culverin, *kul'vǝr-in, n.* an early form of cannon of great length, generally an 18-pounder, weighing 50 cwt.—*ns.* **culverineer'; dem'i-cul'verin,** a 9-pounder of 30 cwt. [Fr. *coulevrine,* from *couleuvre,* snake—L. *colubrīnus,* snake-like—*coluber,* snake.]

Culver's physic, root, *kul'vǝrz,* the rhizome of speedwell *Veronica virginica,* used medicinally. [From one Dr. *Culver.*]

culvert, *kul'vǝrt, n.* an arched channel for carrying water beneath a road, railway, etc. [Perh. from Fr. *couler,* to flow—L. *colāre.*]

culvertage, *kul'vǝr-tij, n.* degradation of a vassal to the position of a serf. [O.Fr *culvert,* a serf.]

cumbent, *kum'bǝnt, adj.* lying down : reclining. [L. *cumbēns,* -*entis, pr.p.* of *cumbĕre,* to lie down.]

cumber, *kum'bǝr, v.t.* to trouble or hinder with something useless : to get in the way of : to occupy obstructively :—*n.* encumbrance : cumbering.— *adj.* **cum'bered,** hampered : obstructed.—*ns.* **cum'berer ; cum'ber-ground,** a useless thing, from Luke, xiii, 7.—*adj.* **cum'berless,** unencumbered.—*n.* **cum'berment.**—*adj.* **cum'bersome,** unwieldy.—*n.* **cum'brance,** encumbrance.—*adj.* **cum'brous,** hindering : obstructing : unwieldy.— *adv.* **cum'brously.** — *n.* **cum'brousness.** [Apparently O.Fr. *combrer,* to hinder—L.L. *cumbrus,* a heap—L. *cumulus,* a heap.]

cumin, cummin, *kum'in, n.* an umbelliferous plant (*Cuminum Cyminum*) of the Mediterranean region, with seeds like caraway, valuable as carminatives. [O.E. *cymen*—L. *cumīnum*—Gr. *kymīnon,* cog. with Heb. *kammon.*]

cummer, *kum'ǝr,* **kimmer,** *kim'ǝr, n.* (*Scot.*) a godmother (*obs.*) : a gossip : a woman : a girl. [Fr. *commère*—L. *con-,* with *māter,* mother.]

cummerbund, *kum'ǝr-bund, n.* (*India*) a waist-belt, a sash. [Pers. *kamarband,* a loin-band.]

cumquat, same as **kumquat.**

cumshaw, *kum'shaw, n.* a gift, a tip. [Pidgin-English.]

cumulate, *kūm'ū-lāt, v.t.* and *v.i.* to heap together : to accumulate.—*adjs.* **cum'ulate, -d,** heaped up. —*n.* **cumula'tion,** accumulation.—*adj.* **cum'ulative,** increasing by successive additions.—*adv.* **cum'ulatively.**—**cumulative vote,** a system by which a voter may distribute a number of votes at will among the candidates, giving more than one to a candidate if he chooses. [L. *cumulāre,* -*ātum*—*cumulus,* a heap.]

cumulus, *kū'mū-lǝs, n.* a heap : a kind of cloud consisting of rounded heaps with a darker horizontal base :—*pl.* **cū'mulī.**—*adj.* **cū'muliform ; cū'mulose.**—*n.* **cū'mulo-stra'tus,** a cloud looking like a combination of the *cumulus* and *stratus.* [L. *cumulus,* a heap.]

cunabula, *kū-nab'ū-lǝ, n.pl.* a cradle : incunabula. [L. *cūnābula.*]

cunctator, *kungk-tā'tǝr, n.* one who delays or puts off.—*n.* **cuncta'tion,** delay.—*adjs.* **cuncta'tious, cunc'tative, cunc'tatory,** inclined to delay. [L. *cunctātor*—*cunctārī,* to delay.]

cuneal, *kū'ni-ǝl,* **cuneate,** *kū'ni-āt, adj.* wedge-shaped.—*adjs.* **cuneat'ic,** cuneiform; **cuneiform** (*kū-nē'i-form,* *kū'ni-(i-)form*), wedge-shaped— specially applied to the old Hittite, Babylonian, Assyrian and Persian writing, of which the characters were impressed by the wedge-shaped facets of a stylus.—*n.* cuneiform writing. [L. *cuneus,* a wedge.]

cunette, *kū-net', n.* a cuvette. [Fr.]

cunner. See **conner** (fish.).

cunning, *kun'ing, adj.* knowing : skilful : artful : crafty : (*U.S.*) dainty or quaintly pleasing.—*n.* knowledge : skill : faculty of using stratagem to accomplish a purpose : craftiness : artifice.—*adv.* **cunn'ingly.**—*n.* **cunn'ingness,** quality of being cunning : artfulness, slyness. [O.E. *cunnan,* to know.]

cup, *kup, n.* a drinking-vessel, usu. nearly hemispherical : an ornamented vessel offered as a prize : a hollow : a cup-shaped structure : a cupful : (*U.S.*) half a pint : the liquid contained in a cup : a mixed beverage made with wine (as *claret-cup*) : that which we must receive or undergo : afflictions : blessings.—*v.t.* to form into a cup : to lodge in a cup : to extract blood from by means of cupping-glasses : (*Shak.*) to make drunk.—*v.i.* to become cup-shaped (*pr.p.* **cupp'ing;** *pa.t.* and *pa.p.* **cupped**).—*ns.* **cup'-and-ball,** a ball and socket joint : the game of catching a tethered ball in a cup on the end of a stick; **cup'-and-ring',** a prehistoric marking on rocks and stones, consisting of a cup surrounded by rings; **cup'-bear'er,** one who attends at a feast to fill out and hand the wine; **cupboard** (*kub'ǝrd*), a place for keeping victuals, dishes, etc.—*v.t.* to store.—*ns.* **cup'board-love, -faith,** love or faith with a material end; **cup'-cor'al,** a simple cup-shaped coral; **cup'ful,** as much as fills a cup :—*pl.* **cup'fuls; cup'-gall,** a cup-shaped gall in oak-leaves; **cup'head,** a hemispherical bolt-head or rivet-head; **cup'-li'chen,** or **-moss,** any lichen with cup-shaped structures; **cup'man,** a boon companion; **cup'-mark,** a cup-shaped hollow made by prehistoric man on cave walls, standing-stones, etc.; **cupp'er,** a cup-bearer : one professionally engaged in cupping; **cupp'ing,** the application of cups from which the air has been exhausted in order to draw blood; **cupp'ing-glass,** a glass used in cupping; **cup'-tie,** one of a series of games to determine the winners of a cup.—**cry cupboard,** to cry for food; **in his cups,** under the influence of liquor; **there's many a slip 'twixt the cup and the lip,** failure is possible at the last moment. [O.E. *cuppe*—L.L. *cūpa, cuppa,* a tub.]

cupel, *kū'pǝl, n.* a small vessel used by goldsmiths in assaying precious metals : the movable hearth of a reverberatory furnace for refining.—*v.t.* to assay in a cupel (*pr.p.* **cu'pelling;** *pa.t.* and *pa.p.* **cu'pelled**).—*n.* **cupella'tion** recovery of precious metal in assaying. [L. *cūpella,* dim. of *cūpa;* see **cup.**]

Cupid, *kū'pid, n.* the Roman love-god, identified with Greek Eros : (*U.S.*) a kind of jam-tart.—*adj.* **cūpid'inous,** full of desire, esp. amorous.—*n.* **cūpid'ity,** covetousness. [L. *Cūpīdo,* -*inis* — *cupĕre,* to desire.]

cupola, *kū'po-lä, n.* a spherical vault, or concave ceiling, on the top of a building : the internal part of a dome : a dome : a lantern on the top of a dome : an armoured dome or turret to protect a gun : a furnace used in iron-foundries.—*v.t.* to furnish with a cupola.—*adjs.* **cū'pola'd** (or **cū'polaed**); **cū'polar; cū'polated.** [It.,—L. *cūpula,* dim. of *cūpa,* a cask.]

cuprammonium, *kū-prä-mō'ni-ǝm, n.* a solution of cupric hydroxide in ammonia.—**cuprammonium rayon** artificial silk made by dissolving cellulose in cuprammonium. [L. *cuprum,* copper, and **ammonium.**]

cupreous, *kū'pri-ǝs, adj.* of, containing, or like copper.—*adjs.* **cū'pric,** of or containing bivalent copper; **cuprif'erous,** yielding copper.—*n.* **cū'prite,** red copper ore or ruby copper, cupric oxide (Cu₂O).—*adj.* **cū'preous,** of or containing univalent copper.—*n.* **cū'pro-nick'el,** an alloy of copper and nickel. [L. *cupreus*—*cuprum;* see **copper.**]

Cupressus, *kū-pres'ǝs, n.* the cypress genus. [L.]

cupule, *kū'pūl, n.* a small cup in a liverwort containing gemmae : a cup-shaped envelope on the fruit of some trees, e.g. oak, beech, chestnut.— *adjs.* **cū'pular, cū'pulate,** cup-like : pertaining to a cupule.—*n.pl.* **Cupulif'erae,** in some classifica-

tions a family including beech, oak, chestnut, with or without birch, hazel, and hornbeam.—*adj.*
cupulif'erous, of the Cupuliferae: bearing cupules. [L. *cūpula,* dim. of *cūpa,* tub.]
cur, *kur, n.* a worthless dog, of low breed: a contemptible scoundrel.—*adj.* **curr'ish.**—*adv.* **curr'ishly.**—*n.* **curr'ishness.** [M.E. *curre;* cf. O.N. *kurra,* to grumble.]
curaçoa, curaçao, *kū'rə-sō, koo-ra-sō', n.* a liqueur flavoured with bitter orange peel. [*Curaçao,* Dutch island in West Indies, where first made.]
curare, curari, *kū-* or *koo-rä'ri, n.* a paralysing poison extracted from wourali root (*Strychnos toxifera*), etc. by South American Indians for arrows—now a source of valuable drugs.—*Also* **cura'ra.**—*n.* **cura'rine,** a highly poisonous alkaloid therefrom, used, e.g. in surgery, as a muscle relaxant.—*v.t.* **cu'rarise.** [Port. from Tupí.]
curassow, *kū'rə-sō, kū-ras'ō, n.* a large turkey-like S. American bird. [From the island of *Curaçao.*]
curat, *kū'rat, n.* (*Spens.*) a cuirass. [See **cuirass.**]
curate, *kūr'it, n.* one who has the cure of souls: an inferior clergyman in the Church of England, assisting a rector or vicar: (*coll.*) a small poker: a cake-stand.—*ns.* **cur'acy** (*-ə-si*), **cur'ateship,** the office, employment, or benefice of a curate.— **curate's egg,** anything of which parts are excellent. [L.L. *cūrātus,* L. *cūra,* care.]
curator, *kūr-ā'tər* (in Scots law *kūr'ə-tər*), *n.* one who has the charge of anything: a superintendent, esp. of a museum: one appointed by law as guardian: a member of a board for electing university professors and the like:—*fem.* **cura'trix.** —*n.* **cura'torship.** [L. *cūrātor.*]
curb, *kurb, n.* a chain or strap attached to the bit for restraining a horse: a hearth fender: a curbstone or kerb-stone, pavement edge (also **kerb**): a curb-market: an edging or margin of various kinds: a check or restraint: a disease of horses, marked by hard swellings on the leg: the swelling itself.—*v.t.* to furnish with or guide by a curb: to restrain or check.—*adjs.* **curb'able; curb'less.** —*ns.* **curb'-mar'ket** (*U.S.*) a market in stocks outside the stock-exchange, originally on the pavement; **curb'-roof,** a roof whose upper slope is less than its lower; **curb'stone, kerb'stone,** a stone placed edgeways as an edging to a path or pavement.—See also **courb, kerb.** [Fr. *courbe*—L. *curvus,* bent.]
curch, *kurch, n.* a covering for the head, a kerchief. [See **kerchief.**]
Curculio, *kur-kū'li-ō, n.* a weevil. [L.]
Curcuma, *kur-kū'mä, n.* a genus of the ginger family yielding turmeric.—*n.* **cur'cumine,** the colouring matter of turmeric. [Ar. *kurkum,* saffron.]
curd, *kurd, n.* milk thickened or coagulated by acid: the cheese part of milk, as distinguished from the whey: any similar substance: in soapmaking the granular soap that rises in the lye upon salting: the fatty matter between the flakes of salmon flesh.—*n.* **curd'iness.**—*v.t.* and *v.i.* **curd'le,** to turn into curd: to coagulate: to thicken.—*adj.* **curd'y,** like or full of curd. [Prob. Celt.; Gael. *gruth,* Ir. *cruth.*]
cure, *kūr, n.* care of souls or spiritual charge: care of the sick: act of healing: that which heals: a remedy, or course of remedial treatment: course or method of preserving: the total quantity cured: vulcanisation.—*v.t.* to heal: to preserve as by drying, salting, etc.: to vulcanise.—*v.i.* to undergo a process or course of curing.—*adj.* **cūr'able.**—*ns.* **cūr'ableness, cūrabil'ity.**—*adjs.* **cūr'ative,** **cūr'atory,** tending to cure.—*n.* **cūre'-all,** a panacea.—*adj.* **cūre'less,** that cannot be cured.— *ns.* **cūr'er,** one who cures: a physician; **cūr'inghouse,** a house or place in which anything ıs cured, esp. a building in which sugar is drained, as in the West Indies. [O.Fr. *cure*—L. *cūra,* care; not the same as **care.**]
curé, *kū-rā', kū'rā, n.* a parish priest in France. [Fr.; see **curate.**]
curfew, *kur'fū, n.* in feudal times the ringing of a bell as a signal to put out all fires and lights: the ringing of a bell at a certain hour continued as a traditional custom: a signal for the imposition of restrictions of other kinds, e.g. from being abroad in the streets at night: the time of curfew: the bell itself.—*n.* **cur'few-bell.** [O.Fr. *covrefeu; couvrir,* to cover, *feu,* fire—L. *focus.*]
curia, *kū'ri-ä, n.* one of the ten divisions of a Roman tribe: a building in which the senate met: a provincial senate: a court, legislative or judicial: the court of the papal see.—*ns.* **cū'rialism; cū'rialist.**—*adj.* **cūrialist'ic**—**cu'ria reg'is** (see **aula**). [L. *cūria.*]
curie, *kū-rē', kū'rē, n.* orig., the quantity of radon in radioactive equilibrium with a gram of radium: now, the quantity of a radioactive substance that undergoes $3 \cdot 70 \times 10^{10}$ radioactive transformations per sec.—*ns.* **curiether'apy,** treatment of disease by radium; **curium** (*kū'*), the chemical element of atomic number 96 (symbol Cm). [After Marie and Pierre *Curie,* discoverers of radium.]
curiet, *kū'ri-et, n.* (*Spens.*) a cuirass. [See **cuirass.**]
curio, *kū'ri-ō, n.* any article of virtu or bric-à-brac, or anything considered rare and curious:—*pl.* **cū'rios.** [For **curiosity.**]
curious, *kū'ri-əs, adj.* anxious to learn: inquisitive: showing great care or nicety: (*Shak.*) solicitous: skilfully made: singular: rare: (in booksellers' catalogues) indecent: (*coll.*) odd.—*n.* **curiosity** (*-os'i-ti*), state or quality of being curious: inquisitiveness: that which is curious: anything rare or unusual.—*adv.* **cū'riously.**—*n.* **cū'riousness.** —**curious arts** (*B.*), magical practices. [Fr. *curieux*—L. *cūriōsus*—*cūra.*]
curl, *kurl, v.t.* to twist into ringlets: to coil: to cause to move in a curve: to ripple.—*v.i.* to shrink into ringlets: to move in curves: to writhe: to ripple: to eddy: to play at the game of curling.— *n.* a ringlet of hair, or what is like it: a wave, bending, or twist: an eddy: a plant disease in which leaves curl: a curled condition.—*adjs.* **curled; curled'-pate** (*Shak.*), having curled hair.—*ns.* **curl'er,** one who, or that which, curls: a player at the game of curling; **curl'icue,** a fantastic curl; **curl'iewurlie** (*Scot.*), any fantastic round ornament; **curl'iness; curl'ing,** a game, common in Scotland, consisting in sliding heavy smooth stones along a sheet of ice.—*ns.pl.* **curl'ing-i'rons, curl'ing-tongs,** an iron instrument used for curling the hair.—*ns.* **curl'ing-pond,** a pond for curling; **curl'ing-stone,** a heavy stone with a handle, used in curling; **curl'-pa'per,** a paper twisted into the hair to give it curl.—*adj.* **curl'y,** having curls: full of curls.—*n.* **curl'y-greens',** kale or borecole.—*adj.* **curl'y-head'ed.** [M.E. *crull;* Du. *krullen,* Dan. *krolle,* to curl.]
curlew, *kur'l(y)ōō, n.* a moorland bird (Numenius) of the woodcock family with long curved bill and long legs, and plaintive whistling cry—the whaup: the thick-knee (**stone-curlew**). [O.Fr. *corlieu;* prob. from its cry.]
curmudgeon, *kər-muj'ən, n.* an avaricious, ill-natured churlish fellow: a miser.—*adj.* and *adv.* **curmud'geonly.** [Origin unknown.]
curmurring, *kər-mur'ing, n.* a rumbling sound, esp. that made in the bowels by flatulence. [Imit.]
curn, *kurn, n.* (*Scot.*) a grain: a particle: a small quantity, a little.—*adj.* **curn'y, curn'ey,** granular, coarse-grained. [**corn.**]
curpel, *kur'pl, n.* a Scots form of **crupper.**
curr, *kur, v.i.* (*Wordsworth*) to make a whirring or purring sound. [Imit.]
currach, -agh, *kur'ə(hh), n.* a coracle. [Ir. *curach.*]
currant, *kur'ənt, n.* a small black raisin or dried seedless grape (imported from the Levant): extended to several species of Ribes (*black, red, white, flowering currant*), and to various other plants, and their fruits.—*ns.* **curr'ant-bread',** ordinary bread with some (grape) currants in it; **currant-bun', currant-loaf',** a dark spiced cake full of currants; **curr'ant-cake',** a cake with currants in it; **curr'ant-jell'y,** a jelly made from red or black currants; **currant-wine'.**—*adj.* **curr'anty,** full of currants. [Corinth.]
current, *kur'ənt, adj.* running or flowing: passing from person to person: generally or widely

received : now passing : present : belonging to the period of time now passing.—*n.* a running or flowing : a stream : a portion of water or air moving in a certain direction : a flow of electricity : course.—*ns.* **curr'ency**, circulation : that which circulates, as the money of a country : general estimation; **curr'ent-bedding** (*geol.*), false-bedding.—*adv.* **curr'ently.**—*n.* **curr'entness.**—currency note, paper-money, esp. that issued by the Treasury in 1914-28 as legal tender; **current account**, a bank account to meet current expenses; **pass current**, to be received as genuine. [L. *currēns, -entis—pr.p.* of *currĕre*, to run.]

curricle, kur'i-kl, *n.* a two-wheeled open chaise, drawn by two horses abreast : a chariot.—*n.* **curric'ulum**, a course, esp. the course of study at a university :—*pl.* -a. [L. *curriculum*, from *currĕre*.]

currish, currishly, etc. See **cur.**

curry, kur'i, *n.* a condiment much used in India, compounded of turmeric and mixed spices : food prepared with curry or curry powder.—*v.t.* to make a curry of.—*ns.* **curr'y-leaf**, a rutaceous Indian tree (*Murraya koenijii*) whose leaves are an ingredient in curry; **curr'y-pow'der**, ground spices and turmeric. [Tamil *kari*, sauce.]

curry, kur'i, *v.t.* to dress (leather) : to rub down and dress (a horse) : to beat : to scratch (*pr.p.* **curr'ying**; *pa.t.* and *pa.p.* **curr'ied**).—*ns.* **curr'ier**, one who curries or dresses tanned leather; **curr'y-comb**, an iron instrument or comb used for currying or cleaning horses; **curr'ying.**—**curry favour** (orig. **curry favell**, to curry the chestnut horse), to seek to ingratiate oneself. [O.Fr. *correier* (Fr. *corroyer*), *conrei*, outfit, from L. *con-*, with, and the root seen in **array.**]

curry, currie, obsolete forms of **quarry.**

curse, kurs, *v.t.* to invoke or wish evil upon : to devote to perdition : to vex or torment.—*v.i.* to utter imprecations : to swear.—*n.* invocation or wishing of evil or harm : evil invoked on another : torment : any great evil.—*adj.* **curs'ed**, under a curse : blasted by a curse : hateful.—*adv.* **curs'edly** —*ns.* **curs'edness; curs'er; curs'ing.**—*adj.* **curst,** cursed : deserving a curse : ill-tempered : shrewish : froward.—*n.* **curst'ness**, state of being curst : peevishness : frowardness.—**curse of Scotland**, the nine of diamonds (origin unknown). [O.E. *cursian—curs*, a curse; ety. doubtful; not conn. with **cross.**]

cursitor, kur'si-tər, *n.* a clerk or officer in the Court of Chancery who made out original writs *de cursu*, i.e. of ordinary course: (*obs.*) a vagrant. [L.L. *cursitor*.]

cursive, kur'siv, *adj.* written with a running hand, of handwriting : flowing.—*adv.* **cur'sively.** [L.L. *cursivus*—L. *currĕre*, to run.]

cursor, kur'sər, *n.* a sliding part of an instrument.—*adj.* **cur'sorary** (*Shak.*; other readings **cur'senary, cur'selarie**; prob. intended for **cursitory**), cursory.—*n.pl.* **cursores** (-sō'rēz), in old classifications, running birds, variously limited.—*adj.* **cursō'rial**, adapted for running.—*adv.* **cur'sorily** (-sər-).—*n.* **cur'soriness.**—*adj.* **cur'sory,** running quickly over : hasty : superficial. [L. *cursor*, pl. *cursōrēs*, a runner—*currĕre*, *cursum*, to run.]

curst. See **curse.**

cursus, kur səs, *n.* a race-course : a form of daily prayer or service : an academic curriculum.—*adj.* **cur'sal.** [L.]

curt, kurt, *adj.* short : concise : discourteously brief or summary.—*adj.* **curt'āte**, shortened or reduced; applied to the distance of a planet from the sun or earth projected on the plane of the ecliptic.—*n.* **curta'tion**.—*adv.* **curt'ly**.—*n.* **curt'ness.** [L. *curtus*, shortened.]

curtail, kər-tāl', *v.t.* to cut short : to cut off a part of : to abridge.—*ns.* **curtail'ment; cur'tail-step,** a round-ended step at the bottom of a flight. [Old spelling *curtal*, O.Fr. *courtault*—L. *curtus*.]

curtain, kur'tən, *n.* hanging drapery at a window, around a bed, etc. : the part of a rampart between two bastions : a curtain-wall : (*theat.*) a screen of cloth or metal concealing the stage, or restricting the spread of fire : the fall of the curtain, close of a scene : a protective barrier in general, as the fire of many guns directed along a certain line to prevent the passage of an enemy (also called **cur'tain-fire**).—*v.t.* to enclose or furnish with curtains.—*ns.* **cur'tain-call**, a summons from the audience to appear at the end of a scene; **cur'tain-lec'ture**, a lecture or reproof given in bed by a wife to her husband; **cur'tain-raiser**, a short play preceding the main performance; **cur'tain-speech**, a speech made before the curtain by actor, author, or manager; **cur'tain-wall**, a wall that merely fills a gap.—**behind the curtain**, away from public view; **draw the curtain**, to draw it aside, so as to show what is behind, or in front of anything so as to hide it; **iron curtain**, an impenetrable barrier to observation or communication. [O.Fr. *cortine* —L.L. *cortina*; prob. L. *cōrs, cŏrtis*, a court.]

curtal, kur'tal, *n.* a horse or other animal with a docked tail : anything docked or cut short.—*adj.* docked or shortened.—*n.* **cur'tal-fri'ar** (*Scott*), a friar with a short frock. [See **curtal.**]

curtal-ax, kur'tal-aks, **curtaxe,** kurt'aks, *n.* (*Spens.*), a short, broad sword. [A corr. of the earlier forms *coutelas, curtelas.* See **cutlass.**]

curtana, kur-tä'nä, -tä'nä, *n.* a pointless sword carried at coronations. [L. *curtus*, short.]

curtilage, kur'til-ij, *n.* a court attached to a dwelling-house. [O.Fr. *courtillage;* see **court.**]

curtsy, curtsey, kurt'si, *n.* a woman's obeisance, by bending the knees.—*v.i.* to make or 'drop' a curtsy. [See **courtesy.**]

curule, kū'r(y)ōōl, *adj.* like a camp-stool with curved legs, applied to the chair of a higher Roman magistrate. [L. *curūlis—currus*, a chariot.]

curve, kurv, *n.* anything bent : a line that is not straight : a line (including a straight line) answering to an equation : a graph : a curved surface : an arch.—*v.t.* to bend : to form into a curve.—*v.i.* to bend : to move in a curve.—*adjs.* **cur'vate**, -d, curved or bent in a regular form.—*n.* **curva'tion.** —*adj.* **cur'vative** (-*va-tiv*).—*n.* **cur'vature** (-*va-tyər*), a curving or bending : the continual bending, or the amount of bending, from a straight line : the reciprocal of the radius at any point.—*adjs.* **curved; curvicau'date**, having a crooked tail; **curvicos'tate**, having curved ribs; **curvifō'liate**, having curved leaves; **cur'viform; curvilin'eal, curvilin'ear**, bounded by curved lines.—*n.* **curvilinear'ity.**—*adjs* **cur'ving; curviros'tral**, with the bill curved downward; **cur'vital**, of or pertaining to curvature.—*n.* **cur'vity**, the state of being curved. [L. *curvus*, crooked.]

curvet, kur'vet, kur-vet', *n.* a light leap of a horse in which he raises his forelegs together, next the hind-legs with a spring before the forelegs touch the ground : a leap, frolic.—*v.i.* (*kur-vet', kur'vet*) to leap in curvets : to frisk (*pr.p.* **curvett'ing,** **cur'veting;** *pa.t.* and *pa.p.* **curvett'ed, cur'veted**). [It. *corvetta*, dim. of *corvo*—L. *curvus*.]

cus-cus, kus-kus, or *koos'-koos*, *n.* a phalanger of the Malay Archipelago. [Native name in the Moluccas.]

cuscus, kus'kus, *n.* the grain of the African millet. [Same as **couscous.**]

cuscus, kus'kus, *n.* the fragrant fibrous root of an Indian grass (*Andropogon squarrosus*), used for making fans, etc. [Pers. *khas khas.*]

cush. See **cuisse.**

cushat, kush'ət, *n.* the ringdove or wood-pigeon. [O.E. *cúscute*, perh. from its note, and *scéotan*, to shoot.]

cushion, koosh'ən, *n.* a case filled with some soft, elastic stuff, for resting on : a pillow : a pad : the pillow used in making bone-lace : an engraver's pad : the rubber of an electrical machine : a pad supporting a woman's hair : (*archit.*) the cap of a pier : the elastic lining of the inner side of a billiard-table (*coll.* **cush**) : a body of steam remaining in the cylinder of a steam-engine, acting as a buffer to the piston : anything that serves to deaden a blow.—*v.t.* to seat on or furnish with a cushion : to serve as a cushion for or against.—*adj.* **cush'ioned**, furnished with a cushion, padded : having cushion-tires.—*ns.* **cush′ionet**, a little cushion; **cush′ion-plant**, a plant of cushion-like form reducing transpiration; **cush′ion-fire, -tyre**, a cycle tire of rubber tubing, with rubber stuffing.—*adj.* **cush′iony**, like a cushion, soft. [O.Fr. *coissin*—L. *coxinum*, *coxa*, hip.]

cushy *kŏŏsh′i*, *adj.* (*slang*) easy and comfortable : not dangerous. [Perh. Hind. *khush*, pleasant, *khushī*, happiness.]

cusk, *kusk*, *n.* the torsk : the burbot.

cusp, *kusp*, *n.* a point : the point or horn of the moon, etc. : (*math.*) a tooth-like meeting of two branches of a curve, with sudden change of direction : (*archit.*) a tooth-like ornament common in Gothic tracery : a prominence on a tooth.—*adjs.* **cus′pid**; **cus′pidal**; **cus′pidate, -d** (*biol.*), having a rigid point. [L. *cuspis, -idis*, a point.]

cuspidor(e), *kus′pi-dōr*, *n.* (*U.S.*) a spittoon. [Port.,—L. *conspuĕre*, to spit upon.]

cuss, *kus*, *n.* (*slang*) a curse : a fellow.—*adj.* **cuss′ed**, cursed : obstinate.—*ns.* **cuss′edness**, contrariness; **cuss′-word.** [*curse*; prob. sometimes associated with **customer**.]

cusser, cuisser, cooser, *kŭs′ər, koos′ər, kus′ər, n.* (*Scot.*) a stallion. [**courser**.]

custard, *kus′tərd*, *n.* a composition of milk, eggs, etc., sweetened and flavoured.—*ns.* **cus′tard-apple**, the fruit of a W. Indian tree (*Anona reticulata*) with eatable pulp, like a custard; **cus′tard-coff′in** (*Shak.*), paste or crust covering a custard. [Earlier *custade*, a corr. of *crustade*, a pie with a crust; see **crust**.]

custock. Same as **castock**.

custody, *kus′ta-di*, *n.* a watching or guarding : care : security : imprisonment.—*adj.* **custō′dial.**—*ns.* **custō′dian, cus′tode, custō′dier, cus′tos**, one who has care, esp. of some public building. [L. *custōdia*, guard, *custōs, -ōdis*, a keeper.]

custom, *kus′təm, n.* what one is wont to do : what is usually done by others : usage : frequent repetition of the same act : regular trade or business : applied to various local usages, as periodical massacres in West Africa : the usages of a manor or of a district : a tax on goods : (*pl.*) duties imposed on imports and exports.—*adj.* (*U.S.*) made to order, bespoke.—*adj.* **cus′tomable**, customary : common : subject to custom duties.—*adv.* **cus′tomarily.**—*n.* **cus′-tomariness.**—*adjs.* **cus′tomary**, according to use and wont : usual : holding or held by custom : copyhold.—*n.* (also **customary**, *kus′tŭm-ər-i*,) a body or book of the customs of a manor, etc. or the ritual of a religious community; **cus′tomed**, accustomed : usual.—*ns.* **cus′tomer**, one accustomed to frequent a certain place of business : a buyer : (*Shak.*) a prostitute; (*slang*) a person; **cus′tom-house**, the place where customs or duties on exports and imports are collected.—*adj.* **cus′tom-shrunk** (*Shak.*), having fewer customers than formerly.—**customs union**, a territory treated as if one state for purposes of custom duties. [O.Fr. *custume, costume*—L. *cōnsuētūdō, -inis*—*cōnsuēscĕre*, to accustom.]

custrel, *kus′trəl, n.* an attendant on a knight : a knave. [O.Fr. *coustillier*—*coustille*, dagger; cf. **coistrel.**]

cut, *kut, v.t.* to penetrate with a sharp edge : to make an incision in : to cleave or pass through : to divide : to carve, hew, or make or fashion by cutting : to sever : to reap : to excise : to intersect : to divide (a pack of cards) by lifting the upper portion at random : to expose (a card or suit) in this way : to strike obliquely, imparting spin to : to reduce or lessen : to abridge : (of a book) to trim by guillotine : to wound or hurt : to affect deeply : to shorten : to break off acquaintance with : to pass intentionally without saluting : to renounce, give up : to stay away from : to castrate : to perform or execute (as a caper).—*v.i.* to make an incision : to intersect : to strike obliquely : to be cut : to dash, go quickly : (*slang*) to run away, to be off : to twiddle the feet rapidly in dancing : in motion picture-making, to cease photographing :—*pr.p.* **cutt′ing**; *pa.t.* and *pa.p.* **cut**.—*n.* a cleaving or dividing : an excavation for a road, railway, etc.; a cross passage : a stroke or blow : in various games, a particular stroke, generally implying obliquity and spin : in

cricket, a stroke to the off side with horizontal bat : the spin imparted to the ball : a reduction or diminution : an act of unkindness : the act, or outcome, of cutting a pack of cards : an incision or wound : an excision : a piece cut off : total quantity cut : a varying unit of length for cloth and yarn : an engraved block or the picture from it : manner of cutting, or fashion : (*Shak.*) a working horse : (*Shak.*) a general term of abuse (as in 'call me cut') : (usu. in *pl.*) a lot.—*ns.* **cut′-away**, a coat with the skirt cut away in a curve in front.—Also *adj.*—*ns.* **cut′-glass**, flint glass shaped by cutting or grinding; **cut′-in, -out′**, an act of cutting in or out.—*adj.* **cut′-leaved**, having leaves deeply cut.—*ns.* **cut′-off**, that which cuts off or shortens, a straighter road, a shorter channel cut across a bend of a river : a bend thus cut off : a device for shutting off steam, water, light, electricity, supply of cartridges in a magazine rifle, etc.; **cut′purse**, one who stole by slitting purses worn at the girdle : a pickpocket : **cutt′er**, a person or thing that cuts : a tailor who measures and cuts out the cloth : a small vessel with one mast, a mainsail, a forestay-sail, and a jib set to bowsprit-end : any sloop of narrow beam and deep draught : in quarrying, a joint parallel to the dip of the rocks; **cut′-throat**, an assassin : ruffian : a modification of bridge or other card games played by three, each for himself : an open razor; **cutt′ing**, a dividing or lopping off : an incision : a piece cut from a newspaper : a piece of a plant cut off for propagation : an open excavation for road, railway, etc.; **cut′-wa′ter**, the fore-part of a ship's prow : the angular edge of a bridge-pier; **cut′worm**, a caterpillar, esp. of the moth genus *Agrotis*, that cuts off young plants near the ground.—**a cut above**, something distinctly better; **cut a dash, or figure**, to make a conspicuous appearance; **cut and come again**, abundant supply, from the notion of cutting a slice, and returning at will for another; **cut and cover**, a method of forming a tunnel by making an open cutting, arching it over, and covering in; **cut and dry, or cut and dried**, ready made, fixed beforehand—from the state of herbs in the shop instead of the field; **cut and run**, to be off quickly; **cut back**, to prune close to the stem : to revert to a previous scene; **cut dead**, to refuse to recognise; **cut down**, to take down by cutting the rope on which one has been hanged : to bring down by cutting : to reduce, curtail; **cut in**, to interpose : to deprive one of a dancing partner : to eavesdrop by telephone : to take one's place in a line of traffic in front of an overtaken vehicle, etc. esp. when meeting others : to come into a game by cutting a card : **cut it fine**, to take risks by calculating too narrowly; **cut if out** (*coll.*), to make an end of it, leave off; **cut it too fat**, to overdo a thing; **cut off**, to sever : to destroy, put to an untimely death : to intercept : to stop : to disinherit; **cut off with a shilling**, to bequeath only a shilling; **cut one's losses**, to have done with an unprofitable matter; **cut one's stick**, to take one's departure; **cut out**, to shape : to contrive : to debar : to supplant : to separate from a herd : to pass out of a game on cutting a card : to pass out of a line of traffic in order to overtake : to capture and carry off (a ship) as from a harbour, etc., by getting between her and the shore; **cut short**, to abridge : to make short by cutting : to silence by interruption; **cut one's coat according to one's cloth**, to adapt oneself to circumstances; **cut the teeth**, to have the teeth grow through the gums, as an infant; **cut up**, to cut into pieces : criticise severely : turn out (well or ill) when divided into parts : (in *pass.*) to be deeply afflicted; **cut up rough**, to take something amiss; **short cut, or near cut**, a shorter way than the usual one. [Origin unknown.]

cutaneous. See **cutis**.

cutch, *kuch, n.* catechu. [Malay *kachu*.]

cutch, **kutch**, *kuch, n.* a set of vellum or tough paper sheets used by gold-beaters. [App.—Fr. *caucher*, cutch—L. *calcāre*, to tread.]

cutcha, *kuch′ä*, (*adj.*) of dried mud : makeshift. [Hind. *kachchā*, raw.]

cutcherry, cutchery. Same as **kachahri.**

cute, *kūt, adj.* an aphetic form of **acute:** (*U.S.*) daintily or quaintly pleasing.—*n.* cūt'ie, cūt'ey, a smart girl.

Cuthbert, *kuth'bərt, n.* the apostle of Northumbria (c. 635-687).—(St) **Cuthbert's beads,** perforated joints of encrinites found on Holy Island; (St) **Cuthbert's duck,** the eiderduck.

cutikin. Same as **cuitikin.**

cutis, *kū'tis, n.* the skin: the true skin, as distinguished from the cuticle.—*adj.* **cūtān'eous,** belonging to the skin.—*n.* cū'ticle, the outermost or thin skin: (*bot.*) a waxy or corky layer on the epidermis in plants.—*adj.* cūtic'ular.—*ns.* cū'tin, material forming plant cuticle; **cūtinisā'tion.**—*v.t.* and *v.i.* cū'tinise. [L.]

cutlass, *kut'ləs, n.* a short, broad sword, with one cutting edge, used in the navy. [Fr. *coutelas*, augmentative from L. *cultellus,* dim. of *culter,* a ploughshare, a knife.]

cutler, *kut'lər, n.* one who makes or sells knives.—*n.* cut'lery, the business of a cutler: edged or cutting instruments in general. [Fr. *coutelier*—O.Fr. *coutel*—L. *culter,* knife.]

cutlet, *kut'lit, n.* rib and the meat belonging to it or similar piece of mutton, veal, etc.: other food made up in the shape of a cutlet. [Fr. *côtelette,* dim. of *côte,* from L. *costa,* a rib.]

cuttle, *kut'l, n.* a cephalopod mollusc (Sepia) remarkable for its power of ejecting a black, inky liquid—also **cutt'lefish:** extended to other cephalopods.—*n.* cutt'le-bone, the internal shell of the cuttlefish, used for making tooth-powder, for polishing the softer metals and for cage-birds to sharpen their beaks on. [O.E. *cudele.*]

cuttle, *kut'l, n.* (*obs.*) a knife: (*Shak.*) a bully. [Perh. L. *cultellum,* knife; perh. also for **cut-throat, cutpurse,** or **cuttlefish.**]

cutto, cuttoe, *kut'o, n.* a large knife. [Fr. *couteau.*]

cutty, *kut'i, adj.* (*Scot.*) short, curtailed.—*n.* a short clay pipe: a short, dumpy girl: applied to a woman, a term of reprobation, serious or playful: a mischievous or teasing girl or woman.—*ns.* cutt'y-sark, a short shift, or its wearer; cutt'y-stool, the stool of repentance in old Scottish church discipline. [cut.]

cuvette, *küv-et', n.* a trench sunk along the middle of a dry ditch or moat, a cunette. [Fr.]

cyanogen, *sī-an'ō-jən, n.* a compound of carbon and nitrogen (CN)$_2$ forming a colourless, poisonous gas with a characteristic odour—an essential ingredient of Prussian blue.—*ns.* cyan, a greenish blue: printers' blue ink; **cyan'amide,** the amide of cyanogen, a white crystalline substance (NCNH$_2$): loosely applied to **calcium cyanamide** (NCNCa), a fertiliser; **cyanate** (*sī'an-āt*) a salt of cyanic acid.—*adj.* cyan'ic, of or belonging to cyanogen.—*n.* cy'anide, a direct compound of cyanogen with a metal.—*v.t.* to treat with a cyanide.—*ns.* **cy'aniding,** extraction of gold or silver from ore by means of potassium cyanide; **cy'anin,** a plant pigment, blue in cornflower, red in the rose.—*v.t.* **cy'anise,** to turn into cyanide.—*ns.* cy'anite (see **kyanite**); **cyanom'eter,** an instrument for measuring the blueness of the sky or ocean: **Cyanophyceae** (*sī-ən-ō-fish'i-ē*), the blue-green algae, simply organised unicellular or filamentous thallophytes growing in water and on damp earth, rocks, or bark.—*n.* cyano'sis, morbid blueness of the skin.—*adj.* cyanot'ic.—*ns.* cyan'otype, blue-print; cyan'ūret (*obs.*), a cyanide.—**cyanic acid,** an acid composed of cyanogen, oxygen and hydrogen (HCNO). [Gr. *kyanos,* blue.]

cyathus, *sī'ə-thəs, n.* an ancient Greek filling or measuring cup—about $\frac{1}{12}$ of a pint.—*n.* **Cyath'ea,** a genus of tree-ferns, often with cup-shaped indusium, giving name to the family **Cyathea'ceae.**—*adj.* cy'athiform (or *ath'*), cup-shaped.—*ns.* **cyath'ium,** the characteristic inflorescence of the spurges; **Cyathophyll'um** (Gr. *phyllon,* leaf), a fossil genus of cup-corals. [Gr. *kyathos.*]

Cybele, *sib'i-lē, n.* a flora, treatise on the plants of a region. [L. *Cybelē*—Gr. *Kybelē,* the mother goddess.]

cybernetics, *sī-bər-net'iks, n.* (*pl.* in form, treated as *sing.*) the study of communication and control mechanisms in machines and in living creatures. [Gr. *kybernētēs,* a steersman.]

cycad, *sī'kad, n.* one of an order of gymnospermous plants, more or less akin to conifers but superficially resembling ferns and palms.—*adj.* cycadā'ceous. [Formed from supposed Gr. *kykas,* a misreading of *kotkas,* accus. pl. of *kotx,* dum-palm.]

cyclamen, *sik'lə-mən, n.* a S. European genus of Primulaceae, with nodding flowers and bent-back petals. [Gr. *kyklaminos.*]

Cyclanthaceae, *sī-klan-thā'si-ē, n.pl.* a tropical S. American family of plants akin to the screwpines, with a spadix sometimes resembling a pile of disks.—*adj.* cyclanthā'ceous. [Gr. *kyklos,* wheel, *anthos,* flower.]

cycle, *sī'kl, n.* a period of time in which events happen in a certain order, and which constantly repeats itself: a recurring series of changes: an age: an imaginary circle or orbit in the heavens: a series of poems, romances, etc., centring in a figure or event (also **cy'clus**): a group of songs with related subjects: a bicycle of tricycle.—*v.i.* to move in cycles: to ride on a cycle.—*ns.* cy'cle-car, a small light motor-car; cy'cler (*U.S.*), a cyclist.—*adj.* cy'clic, -al, pertaining to or containing a cycle: recurring in cycles: arranged in a ring or rings.—*ns.* cy'clist, a bicyclist or tricyclist; cy'clograph, an instrument for describing arcs of circles without compasses; cy'cloid, a figure like a circle: a curve made by a point on a radius of a circle when the circle is rolled along a straight line.—*adj.* nearly circular: (of fish) having scales with evenly curved border.—*adj.* cycloid'al.—*ns.* cycloid'ian, a fish with cycloid scales; cyclom'eter, an instrument for measuring circular arcs: an apparatus attached to the wheel of a cycle for registering the distance traversed; cyclo'sis, circulation. [Gr. *kyklos,* a circle.]

cyclone, *sī'klōn, n.* a system of winds blowing spirally inwards towards a centre of low barometric pressure: (*loosely*) a wind-storm: a separating apparatus, a kind of centrifuge.—*adj.* cyclōn'ic. [Gr. *kyklōn,* contr. pr.p. of *kykloein,* whirl round.]

cyclopaedia, cyclopedia, *sī-klō-pē'di-ä, n.* a shortened form of **encyclopaedia.**—*adj.* cyclopae'dic, cyclope'dic.

cyclopropane, *sī-klō-prō'pān, n.* a cyclic hydrocarbon C$_3$H$_6$, a general anaesthetic. [Gr. *kyklos,* circle, and propane.]

Cyclops, *sī'klops, n.* one of a fabled race of giants who lived chiefly in Sicily, with one eye in the middle of the forehead: a one-eyed monster: a genus of minute fresh-water copepods with an eye in front:—*pl.* cyclō'pes (*-pēz*), cy'clopses.—*adjs.* cyclopē'an, cyclō'pian, cyclop'ic, relating to or like the Cyclopes: giant-like: vast: pertaining to a prehistoric style of masonry with immense stones of irregular form. [Gr. *kyklōps,* pl. *kyklōpēs*—*kyklos,* a circle, and *ōps,* an eye.]

cyclorama, *sī-klō-rä'mä, n.* a circular panorama. [Gr. *kyklos,* circle, *horāma,* view.]

cyclospermous, *sī-klō-spər'məs, adj.* (*bot.*) with embryo bent round the endosperm. [Gr. *kyklos,* circle, *sperma,* seed.]

Cyclostomata, *sī-klō-stō'mə-tä, n.pl.* a class of animals with fixed open mouth, including the lampreys.—*n.* cy'clostome, a member of the class.—*adj.* cyclostomous (*-klos'to-məs*). [Gr. *kyklos,* wheel, *stōma,* mouth.]

cyclostyle, *sī'klō-stīl, n.* an apparatus for multiplying copies of a writing by use of a pen with a small puncturing wheel. [Gr. *kyklos,* circle, and style.]

cyclothymia, *sī-klō-thī'mi-ä, n.* a temperament inclined to alternation of high and low spirits.—*adj.* cyclothy'mic. [Gr. *kyklos, thymos,* spirit.]

cyclotron, *sī'klō-tron, n.* (*phys.*) an apparatus for accelerating the circular movement of subatomic particles in a magnetic field, used for work in nuclear disintegration, artificial radioactivity, etc. [Gr. *kyklos,* circle, *-tron,* agent suffix.]

cyder. Same as **cider.**

cygnet, *sig'nit, n.* a young swan. [Dim. from L. *cygnus,* directly or through Fr. *cygne,* which seems to be a reshaping of *cisne*—L.L. *cicinus*, L. *cycnus*— Gr. *kyknos*, a swan.]

cylinder, *sil'in-dər*, *n.* a solid figure of uniform cross-section generated by a straight line remaining parallel to a fixed axis and moving round a closed curve—ordinarily in a circle perpendicular to the axis (giving a *right circular cylinder*) : a roller-shaped object : (*mech.*) a cylindrical part, solid or hollow, as a rotating part of a printing press, the tubular chamber in which a piston works.—*ns.* **cyl'inder-head**, the closed end of the cylinder of an internal-combustion engine ; **cyl'inder-block**, a casing in which the cylinders of an internal-combustion engine are contained ; **cyl'inder-seal'** (*ant.*), a stone engraved in intaglio, used in the ancient East for sealing clay tablets by rolling.—*adjs.* **cylindra'ceous**, somewhat cylindrical ; **cylin'dric, -al**—*n.* **cylindricity** (*-dris'i-ti*).—*adj.* **cylin'driform**, in the form of a cylinder.—*ns.* **cylin'drite**, a mineral of cylindrical habit, compound of tin, lead, antimony, and sulphur ; **cyl'indroid**, a body like a cylinder.—Also *adj.* [Gr. *kylindros*, roller, *kylindein*, to roll.]

cylix, *sil'* or *sil'iks*, *n.* a shallow two-handled stemmed drinking cup :—*pl.* **cyl'ices** (*-sēz*).—Also **kylix**. [Gr. *kȳlix, -ikos.*]

cyma, *sī'mä*, *n.* an ogee moulding of the cornice (*cyma rec'ta* concave in front, convex behind ; *cyma rever'sa* convex in front, concave behind).— *ns.* **cy'mograph** (improperly **cy'magraph**), an instrument for tracing the outline of mouldings (see also **kymograph**) ; **cymā'tium**, a cyma. [Gr. *kyma*, a billow.]

cymar, *si-mär'*, *n.* a loose light dress or undergarment worn by ladies : a chimer. [See **chimer**.]

cymbal, *sim'bəl*, *n.* a hollow brass plate-like musical instrument, beaten together in pairs.—*ns.* **cym'balist**, a cymbal-player ; **cym'balo**, the dulcimer. —*adj.* **cym'biform**, boat-shaped. [L. *cymbalum*— Gr. *kymbalon—kymbē*, the hollow of a vessel.]

cyme, *sīm*, *n.* a young shoot : (*bot.*) any sympodial inflorescence, the main shoot ending in a flower, the subsequent flowers growing on successive lateral branches.—*adjs.* **cym'oid, cym'ose, cym'ous**. [L. *cȳma, cīma*—Gr. *kȳma*, a sprout.]

cyme, *si'əm*, *n.* (*Shak.*) app. for **Sium**.

cymophane, *sī'mō-fān*, *n.* cat's eye, a variety of chrysoberyl with wavy opalescence.—*adj.* **cymophanous** (*-mof'ə-nəs*), opalescent. [Gr. *kȳma*, wave, *phainein*, to show.]

cymotrichous, *si-mot'ri-kəs*, *adj.* (*anthrop.*) wavy-haired.—*n.* **cymot'richy**. [Gr. *kȳma*, wave, *thrix*, gen. *trichos*, hair.]

Cymric, *kim'rik*, *adj.* Welsh.—*n.* **Cym'ry**, the Welsh. [W. *Cymru*, Wales.]

cynanche, *si-nang'kē*, *n.* disease of the throat, esp. quinsy. [Gr., *kyōn, kynos*, a dog, *anchein*, to throttle.]

cynegetic, *sin-ē-jet'ik*, *adj.* relating to hunting. [Gr. *kynēgetēs*, huntsman—*kyōn, kynos*, dog, *hēgetēs*, leader.]

cynic, -al, *sin'ik, -əl*, *adj.* dog-like : surly : snarling : disinclined to recognise goodness.—*ns.* **Cyn'ic**, one of a sect of philosophers founded by Antisthenes of Athens (born c. 444 B.C.), characterised by an ostentatious contempt for riches, arts, science, and amusements—so called from their morose manners : a morose man : a snarler ; **cynicism** (*-i-sizm*), surliness : contempt for human nature : heartlessness, misanthropy.—*adv.* **cyn'ically**.—*n.* **cyn'icalness**. [Gr. *kynikos*, dog-like—*kyōn, kynos*, a dog.]

Cynips, *sin'ips, sīn'ips*, a genus of gall-wasps, giving name to the family **Cynip'idae**. [Origin doubtful.]

Cynocephalus, *sin-* or *sīn'ō-sef-ə-ləs*, *n.* the so-called flying lemur or Galeopithecus : the dog-faced baboon : a dog-headed man. [Gr. *kyōn, kynos*, dog, *kephalē*, head.]

cynosure, *sin'- or *sīn'ō-shōōr*, *n.* the dog's tail, or Lesser Bear (*Ursa Minor*), the constellation containing the North Star : the North Star itself : hence anything that strongly attracts attention or admiration.—**Cynosur'us**, dog's-tail grass. [Gr. *kyōn, kynos*, dog, *ourä*, a tail.]

Cyperus, *sīp-, sīp-ē'rus*, *n.* a tropical genus of the sedge family, **Cyperā'ceae**, including papyrus.—

adj. **cyperaceous** (*ə-rā'shəs*), belonging to, or like, sedge plants. [From Gr. *kypeiros*, sedge.]

cypher. Same as **cipher**.

cy pres, *sē prā*, in the law of charitable trusts in England, the principle of applying the money to some object *as near as possible* to the one specified, when that is impracticable. [O.Fr., so near.]

cypress, *sī'prəs, -pris, n.* a coniferous tree(Cupressus), whose branches used to be carried at funerals : hence a symbol of death : extended to various other trees, esp. in America to the swamp-growing deciduous conifer *Taxodium distichum.*—*ns.* **cypress'-knee**, a hollow upgrowth from the root of the swamp-cypress, a breathing organ ; **cypress'-swamp**. [O.Fr. *ciprès* (Fr. *cyprès*)—L. *cupressus*— Gr. *kyparissos*.]

cypress, *sī'prəs, -pris, n.* a thin transparent black stuff like crape.—*adj.* of cypress.—Also **cyprus**. [Prob. from the island of *Cyprus*.]

Cyprian, *sip'ri-ən, adj.* of the island of Cyprus : lewd, licentious—Cyprus being the place where Aphrodite was worshipped.—*n.* a Cypriot : a lewd woman.—*n.* **Cyp'riot(e)**, a native of Cyprus.

Cyprinus, *si-prī'nəs, n.* the carp genus of fishes, giving name to the fam. **Cyprinidae** (*si-prin'i-dē*). —*adjs.* **cyprine** (*sip'rīn*), **cyp'rinoid** (*-rin-oid*). [L.—Gr. *kyprīnos*, a kind of carp.]

Cypripedium, *sip-ri-pē'di-əm, n.* a genus of orchids, lady's slipper. [Gr. *Kypris*, Aphrodite, *podion*, a little foot, modified by L. *pēs*, foot.]

Cypris, *sip'ris, n.* a genus of fresh-water ostracod crustaceans.—*n.* **cyp'rid**. [Gr. *Kypris*, Aphrodite.]

cyprus. Same as **cypress** (2).

Cyrenaic, *si-rin-ā'ik, adj.* pertaining to Cyrēnē, or to the hedonism of its philosopher Aristippus.

Cyrillic, *sir-il'ik, adj.* pertaining to the alphabet attributed to St Cyril (9th cent.), distinguished from the other Slavonic alphabet, the Glagolitic.

cyst, *sist, n.* (*biol.*) a bladder or bag-like structure, whether normal or containing morbid matter : a membrane enclosing an organism in a resting stage. —*adjs.* **cyst'ic, cyst'iform**.—*ns.* **Cysticer'cus** (Gr. *kerkos*, tail), a bladderworm ; **cyst'id, cystid'ean**, a cystoid ; **cysti'tis**, inflammation of the bladder ; **cyst'ocarp** (Gr. *karpos*, fruit), the fructification in red seaweeds ; **cys'tocele** (Gr. *kēlē*, tumour), hernia of the bladder ; **cyst'oid**, any echinoderm of the extinct class **Cystoid'ea**, globular or bladder-like animals enclosed in calcareous plates, stalked or sessile ; **cyst'olith** (Gr. *lithos*, stone), a stalked limy concretion in some plant cells ; **cyst'oscope** (Gr. *skopeein*, to view), an instrument for examining the inside of the bladder ; **cystos'copy** ; **cystot'omy** (Gr. *tomē*, a cut), the operation of cutting into the bladder. [L.L. *cystis*—Gr. *kystis*, a bladder.]

cyte, *sīt, n.* (*biol. ; rare*) a cell.—*ns.* **cyt'ase**, an enzyme that breaks down cellulose ; **cyt'ochrome**, any of a group of substances in living cells, of great importance in cell oxidation ; **cyt'ode**, a protoplasm body without nucleus ; **cytogen'esis**, cell-formation.—*adjs.* **cyt'oid**, cell-like ; **cytolog'ical**.—*ns.* **cytol'ogist** ; **cytol'ogy**, that part of biology that deals with cells ; **cytol'ysis** (Gr. *lysis*, loosening), dissolution of cells ; **cyt'on**, the body of a nerve-cell ; **cyt'oplasm** (Gr. *plasma*, form, body), the protoplasm of a cell apart from that of the nucleus. [Gr. *kȳtos*, vessel, hollow.]

Cytherean, *sith-ə-rē'ən, adj.* pertaining to Aphrodite. [L. *Cytherēa*—Gr. *Kythereia*, Cytherean (goddess), Aphrodite, worshipped in the island of *Kythēra*.]

Cytisus, *sit'i-səs, n.* the broom genus of Papilionaceae.—*n.* **cyt'isine**, a poisonous alkaloid found in laburnum. [Gr. *kytisos*, a kind of medick, laburnum.]

czar, czarina, etc. See **tsar**, etc.

czardas, a faulty spelling of **csárdás**.

Czech, *chehh, chek, n.* a member of a westerly branch of the Slavs, the Bohemians and Moravians : the language of the Czechs, Bohemian, closely allied to Polish.—*adj.*, also **Czech'ic**.—*n.* **Czech'o-slovak**, a native or citizen of *Czechoslovakia*.— a member of the Slavic people including the Czechs and the Slovaks—also *adj.* [Polish.]

D

D, d, *dē, n.* the fourth letter in our alphabet, as well as in the Phoenician, Hebrew, Greek, and Latin, from which last it was immediately derived—its sound the voiced dental stop: (*mus.*) the second note in the natural scale: as a Roman numeral, D=500.

'd, *d,* a shortened form of **had, would.**—'**dst,** hadst, wouldst.

da, dah, *dä, n.* a heavy Burmese knife. [Burmese *da.*]

dab, *dab, v.t.* to strike gently with something soft or moist: to peck; to smear (*pr.p.* **dabb′ing;** *pa.t.* and *pa.p.* **dabbed**).—*n.* a gentle blow: a small lump of anything soft or moist: a species (*Limanda limanda*) of fish of the Pleuronectidae: applied to other (esp. to small) flatfish.—*ns.* **dabb′er,** a pad for dabbing ink on blocks or plates; **dab′-chick,** the little grebe. [Cf. M. and early Mod. Du. *dabben,* to pinch; Ger. *tappe,* a pat; confused with **daub** and **tap.**]

dab, *dab, n.* an expert person.—Also *adj.*—*n.* **dab′ster** (*coll.*). [Origin unknown.]

dabble, *dab′l, v.t.* to shake about in liquid: to spatter with moisture.—*v.i.* to play in liquid with hands or feet: to do anything in a trifling or small way.—*n.* the act of dabbling.—*n.* **dabb′ler.**—*n.* and *adj.* **dabb′ling.**—*adv.* **dabb′lingly.** [Freq. of **dab.**]

dace, *dās,* **dare,** *dār,* **dart,** *dārt, n.* a small river fish (*Leuciscus vulgaris*) of the carp family and chub genus. [M.E. *darce*—O.Fr. *dars*—L.L. *dardus,* a dart or javelin—of Gmc. origin; from its quickness.]

dachshund, *däks′hoont, däks′hoond, n.* a badger-dog or teckel, of German origin, with long body and very short legs. [Ger. *dachs,* badger, *hund,* dog.]

dacite, *dās′īt, n.* a fine-grained eruptive rock composed of quartz and plagioclase, with mica, etc. [*Dacia,* where it occurs.]

dacker, *dak′ər,* **daker, daiker,** *dā′kər, v.i.* (*Scot.*) to lounge, saunter: to potter. [Origin unknown.]

dacoit, *dä-koit′, n.* one of a gang of robbers in India and Burma—also **dakoit′.**—*ns.* **dacoit′y, dakoit′i, dacoit′age,** robbery by gang-robbers, brigandage. [Hind. *dākait, dakait,* a robber.]

dactyl, *dak′til,* (*zool.*) a digit: (*classical pros.*) a foot of three syllables, one long followed by two short, like the joints of a finger: in English, etc., a foot of three syllables, the first accented.—*adjs.* **dac′-tylar, dactyl′ic.**—*ns.* **dactyliog′raphy, dactyliol′ogy,** the study or lore of finger-rings or engraved gems; **dactyl′iomancy** (Gr. *manteiā,* divination), divination by means of a finger-ring; **Dac′tylis,** the cock's-foot grass genus; **dac′tylist,** a writer of dactylic verse; **dac′tylogram,** a finger-print; **dactylog′raphy,** the study of finger-prints; dactylology; **dactylol′ogy,** the art of talking with the fingers, like the deaf and dumb. [Gr. *daktylos,* a finger, *daktylios,* a finger-ring.]

dad, *dad,* **daddy,** *dad′i, ns.* (*childish and coll.*) father.—*n.* **dadd′y-long′-legs,** the crane-fly. [History uncertain.]

dad, daud, *däd, dawd, v.t.* (*dial.*) to throw against something: to dash, thump.—*n.* a lump: a blow, thump. [Der. unknown.]

Dada, Dadaism, *dä′dä* (*-izm*), *n.* a short-lived movement in art (from 1916) which sought to abandon all form and throw off all tradition. [Fr., perh.—*dada* (childish), hobby-horse.]

daddle, *dad′l, v i.* (*dial.*) to walk in an unsteady manner, as a child or very old person: to totter. [Perh. conn. with **dawdle.**]

daddle, *dad′l, n.* (*dial.*) the hand. [Origin uncertain.]

daddock, *dad′ək, n.* (*prov.*) the heart of a rotten tree. [Perh. conn. with **dodder.**]

dado, *dä′dō, n.* (*classical archit.*) the cubic block forming the body of a pedestal: a skirting of wood along the lower part of the walls of a room, often represented merely by wall-paper, painting, etc. (*pl.* **dados, dadoes**). [It.; see **die** (2).]

daedal, daedale, *dē′dəl,* **Daedalian,** *dē-dā′li-ən,* *adj.* formed with art: displaying artistic skill: intricate, varied. [From L. *Daedalus,* Gr. *Daidalos,* the mythical artist who constructed the Cretan labyrinth.]

daemon, *dē′mən, n.* a spirit holding a middle place between gods and men, as the daemon or good genius of Socrates.—*adj.* **daemonic** (*-mon′ik*), supernatural: of power or intelligence more than human: inspired. [L. *daemōn, -ōnis*—Gr. *daimōn, -ōnos,* a spirit, a genius, and later a devil; see **demon.**]

daff, *däf, v.i.* to make sport, to play the fool.—*n.* **daff′ing,** foolery, gaiety. [Origin doubtful.]

daff, *daf, v.t.* (*Shak.*) to put off: to turn aside, dismiss, put by. [A variant of **doff.**]

daffodil, *daf′ə-dil,* familiarly, playfully, or childishly, **daff′y, daffodill′y, daffadowndilly,** *daf′ə-down-dil′i, n.* a yellow-flowered narcissus. [M.E. *affodille*—O.Fr. *asphodile*—Gr. *asphodelos,* asphodel; the *d* is unexplained.]

daffy, *daf′i, n.* an 'elixir of health' invented by one Thomas *Daffy* (d. 1680).

daft, *däft, adj.* (*Scot.*) silly: weak-minded: insane: unreasonably merry.—*n.* **daft′ie.**—*adv.* **daft′ly.**—*n.* **daft′ness.** [See **deft.**]

dag, *dag, n.* a heavy pistol of the 15th and 16th centuries. [Origin uncertain.]

dag, *dag, n.* (*obs.*) a tag, scallop, or laciniation: a dirt-clotted tuft of wool.—*v.t.* (*obs.*) to cut into dags: to bedraggle. [Origin uncertain.]

dagger, *dag′ər, n.* a knife or short sword for stabbing at close quarters; (*print.*) a mark of reference †; **double dagger,** diesis ‡.—**at daggers drawn,** in a state of hostility; **look daggers,** to look in a hostile manner. [M.E. *dagger;* cf. Fr. *dague.*]

daggle, *dag′l, v.t.* and *v.i.* to wet or grow wet by dragging or sprinkling.—*n.* **dagg′le-tail,** a draggle-tail. [Freq. of **dag.**]

dago, *dä′gō, n.* (*U.S.*) a man of Spanish, Portuguese, or Italian origin:—*pl.* **da′goes.** [Prob. Sp. *Diego*—L. *Jacōbus,* James.]

dagoba, *dä′gō-bä, n.* in Ceylon, a tope. [Sinh. *dägaba.*]

Dagon, *dā′gən, -gon, n.* the national god of the Philistines, half-man, half-fish. [Heb. *dāgōn*—*dāg,* fish.]

daguerreotype, *də-ger′ō-tīp, n.* a method of photography by mercury vapour development of silver iodide exposed on a copper plate: a photograph so taken: (*obs.*) a faithful representation.—*v.t.* to photograph by that process.—*adj.* **daguerr′-ean.**—*n.* **daguerre′otypy,** the art of daguerreotyping. [Fr., from Louis *Daguerre* (1789-1851).]

dagwood. Same as **dogwood.** See under **dog.**

dahabiyah, -iyeh, -ieh. -eeah, *dä-hä-bē′(y)ä, -ə, n.* a Nile sailing boat. [Ar. *dhahabīyah,* golden.]

Dahlia, *dāl′yä,* U.S. *däl′yä, n.* a Mexican genus of garden composites with large flowers. [From *Dahl,* a Swedish botanist.]

daidle, *dā′dl, v.i* (*Scot.*) to waddle: to stagger: to idle about: to trifle: to potter.—*adj.* **daid′ling,** feeble: dawdling. [**daddle.**]

daiker, *dā′kər, v.i.* (*Scot.*) to deck out. [Perh. Fr. *décorer.*]

daker. See **dacker.**

Dail, *doil, n.* the lower house of the legislature of Eire. [Irish, assembly.]

daily, *dā′li, adj.* and *adv.* every day.—*n.* a daily paper: a non-resident servant. [**day.**]

Neutral vowels in unaccented syllables: *el′ə-mənt, in′fənt, ran′dəm*

daimen, *dem'ən, dām'ən, adj.* (*Burns*) occasional. [Origin obscure.]

daimio, *dī'myō, n.* a Japanese territorial noble under the old feudal system. [Jap.]

daine (*Shak.*). Same as **deign**.

dainty, *dān'ti, adj.* pleasant to the palate: delicate: tasteful: fastidious: choicely or fastidiously neat: (*Spens.*) elegant.—*n.* that which is dainty, a delicacy.—*adj.* **daint**, **daynt** (*Spens.*).—*adv.* **dain'tily**.—*n.* **dain'tiness**. [M.E. *deintee*, anything worthy or costly—O.Fr. *daintié*, worthiness—L. *dignitās*, -*ātis*—*dignus*, worthy.]

dairy, *dā'ri, n.* the place where milk is kept, and butter and cheese made: an establishment for the supply of milk.—*ns.* **dai'ry-farm**; **dai'rying**; **dai'rymaid**; **dai'ryman**; **dayr''-house** (*Spens.*), a dairy. [M.E. *deye*—O.E. *dæge*, a dairymaid; orig. a kneader of dough.]

dais, *dās* (*dā'is* is only a guess from the spelling), *n.* a raised floor at the upper end of the dining-hall where the high table stood: a raised floor with a seat and canopy: the canopy over an altar, etc. [O.Fr. *deis*—L.L. *discus*, a table—L. *discus*, a quoit—Gr. *diskos*, a disk.]

daisy, *dā'zi, n.* a very common composite plant (*Bellis perennis*) growing in pastures and meadows: extended to other plants, as the *Ox-eye daisy*, which is a chrysanthemum: a general term of admiration, often ironical.—*adj.* **dai'sied**, covered with daisies. —*ns.* **dai'sy-chain**, a succession of daisies strung one upon another; **dai'sy-cutter**, a fast-going horse that does not lift its feet high: a cricket-ball skimmed along the ground. [O.E. *dæges éage*, day's eye.]

dâk, *dâk*, **dawk**, *dawk, n.* in India, the mail-post: travelling as the mail goes (orig. by relays of bearers or horses).—**dâk bungalow**, a house for travellers in India; **dâk runner**, a runner or horseman who carries mails. [Hind. *dâk*, a relay of men.]

dakoit. See **dacoit**.

dal, *dāl, n.* the pigeon-pea, a pealike plant (*Cajanus indicus*) cultivated in India and the tropics: pulse.—Also **dhal**, **dholl**. [Hind.—*dal*, to split.]

dalai lama, *dāl-ī' lām'ä*, the head of the Buddhist hierarchy in Tibet. [Mongolian, *dalai*, ocean, Tibetan, *lama*, high-priest.]

dale, *dāl, n.* the low ground between hills: the valley through which a river flows.—*n.* **dales'-man**, specifically, a man of the dales of the Lake District. [O.E. *dæl*, reinforced by O.N. *dalr*; cf. Sw. *dal*; Ger. *tal*.]

dali, *dā'li, n.* a tropical American tree akin to nutmeg yielding staves, etc. and wax seeds. [Native name.]

Dalila. See **Delilah**.

dalle, *dāl, n.* a slab or tile, esp. decorative: (*U.S.*) a rapid where a river runs over smooth slabs, esp. between steep rocks. [Fr.]

dallop. See **dollop**.

dally, *dal'i, v.i.* to lose time by idleness or trifling: to play: to exchange caresses (*pr.p.* **dall'ying**; *pa.t.* and *pa.p.* **dall'ied**).—*ns.* **dall'iance**, dallying, toying, or trifling: interchange of embraces: delay: **dall'ier**, a trifler. [O.Fr. *dalier*, to chat.]

dalmahoy, *dal'mə-hoi, -hoi', n.* (obs.) a bushy bobwig worn in the 18th cent. [Said to be named from a wearer.]

Dalmatian, *dal-mā'shən, adj.* belonging to *Dalmatia.* —**Dalmatian dog**, the spotted coach-dog, like the pointer in shape.

dalmatic, *dal-mat'ik, n.* a loose-fitting, wide-sleeved ecclesiastical vestment, worn specially by deacons in the R.C. Church, also sometimes by bishops. [L.L. *dalmatica*, a robe worn by persons of rank, on the pattern of a dress worn in *Dalmatia*.]

Dalradian, *dal-rā'di-ən, adj.* applied to a series of Pre-Cambrian rocks well represented in the Scottish Highlands.—Also *n.* [From the ancient kingdom of *Dalriada*.]

dalt, **dault**, *dawlt, n.* (*Scot.*) a foster-child. [Gael. *dalta*.]

Daltonism, *dawl'tən-izm, n.* colour-blindness: inability to distinguish red from green.—*adj.*

Daltō'nian. [From the chemist John **Dalton** (1766-1844), who described his own case.]

Daltonism, *dawl'tən-izm, n.* the Dalton plan, a school method by which each pupil pursues separately in his own way a course suited to himself, mapped out into monthly instalments. [First tried in 1920 at *Dalton*, Massachusetts.]

dam, *dam, n.* an embankment to restrain water: the water thus confined: (*Scot.*) a mill-stream.— *v.t.* to keep back by a bank (*pr.p.* **damm'ing**; *pa.t.* and *pa.p.* **dammed**). [Gmc.; Du. *dam*, Ger. *damm*, etc.]

dam, *dam, n.* a mother, usu. of beasts, or contemptuous. [A form of **dame**.]

dam, *däm, n.* an obsolete Indian copper coin, one fortieth of a rupee. [Hind. *dām*.]

dam, *dâm, n.* (obs. Scot.) a draughtsman.—*n.* **dam'-board**, **dam'brod** (*Scot.*), a draught-board. [Fr. *dame*, lady.]

damage, *dam'ij, n.* hurt, injury, loss: the value of what is lost: (*coll.*) cost:—(*pl.*) the pecuniary reparation due for loss or injury sustained by one person through the fault or negligence of another.— *v.t.* to harm.—*v.i.* to take injury.—*adj.* **dam'ageable.**—**damage feasant** (*fez'ənt*), doing damage (of beasts trespassing). [O.Fr. *damage* (Fr. *dommage*)—L. *damnum*, loss.]

daman, *dam'an, n.* the Syrian hyrax, the coney of the Bible. [Ar.]

damar. Same as **dammar**.

damask, *dam'-əsk, n.* figured stuff, originally of silk, now usually of linen, also of cotton or wool, the figure woven but not printed: Damascus steel or its surface appearance: the red colour of the damask rose.—*v.t.* to flower or variegate, as cloth: to damascene.—*adj.* red, like a damask-rose.—*n.* **Damascene** (*dam'ə-sēn*, or -*sēn'*), a native or inhabitant of Damascus: **damascene**, a Damascus or damascened sword: inlay of metal (esp. gold) or other materials on steel, etc.: the structure or surface appearance of Damascus steel: a damson.— *v.t.* to decorate (esp. steel) by inlaying or encrusting: to ornament with the watered or wavy appearance of Damascus steel, or in imitation of it.—Also **damascene**, **damaskeen**, **-kin**, **-quin** (-*kēn*).— *ns.* **damascening**, inlaying upon steel: production of watered appearance on steel; **dam'ask-plum**, the damson; **dam'ask-rose**, a pink variety of rose; **dam'ask-steel**, Damascus steel; **dam'assin**, damask with flowered patterns in gold or silver thread.—**Damascus blade**, a Damascus sword, the surface marked by wavy and variegating lines. [From *Damascus*, whence these things came; see also **damson**.]

damboard, **dambrod**. See **dam** (4).

dame, *dām, n.* the mistress of a house, a matron (now usu. jocular or patronising): a mother: (*U.S. slang*) a woman: the comic vulgar old woman of the pantomime: a noble lady: a lady of the same rank as a knight: a baronet's or knight's wife (as a formal title prefixed to the lady's first name).—*ns.* **dame'-school**, a school for young children usually kept by a woman: **dame's'-vi'olet**, a cruciferous plant (*Hesperis matronalis*) formerly cultivated in pots by ladies for its sweet scent at night. [Fr. *dame*—L. *domina*, a mistress.]

dammar, *dam'ər, n.* a copal used for making varnish, obtained from various conifers. [Malay *damar*.]

damn, *dam, v.t.* to censure or condemn: to sentence to eternal punishment: to doom: to curse or swear at.—*v.i.* to utter curses.—*n.* an oath: a curse.— *adj.* **damnable** (*dam'nə-bl*), deserving or tending to damnation: hateful: pernicious.—*n.* **dam'-nableness.**—*adv.* **dam'nably.**—*n.* **damnā'tion** (-*nā'shən*), condemnation: (*theol.*) the punishment of the impenitent in the future state: eternal punishment.—*adjs.* **dam'natory** (-*nə-tər-i*), consigning to damnation; **damned** (*damd; poet. dam'nid*), sentenced to everlasting punishment: hateful: an intensive, meaning merely thorough (formerly often written d——d, and softened into *darned*, *dashed*, etc.).—*adv.* very, exceedingly. —*n.* **damnification** (*dam'ni-fi-kā'shən*), infliction of injury or loss.—*v.t.* **dam'nify**, to cause loss to.—*adj.* **damning** (*dam'ing, -ning*), exposing to condemnation. [Fr. *damner*—L. *damnāre*, to condemn—*damnum*, loss.]

Damoclean, *dam-ō-clē'ən, adj.* like *Damoclēs*, flatterer of Dionysius of Syracuse, taught the insecurity of happiness by being made to sit through a feast with a sword suspended over his head by a single hair.

damosel, damozel, *dam'ō-zel, n.* Same as **damsel.**

damp, *damp, n.* vapour, mist : moist air : in mines, etc., any gas other than air : lowness of spirits : a gloom : discouragement.—*v.t.* to wet slightly : to discourage : to check : to make dull : to diminish the amplitude of.—*adj.* moist : foggy.—*v.t.* and *v.i.* **damp'en,** to make or become damp or moist.— *ns.* **damp'er,** one who or that which damps : a depressive influence : a door or shutter for shutting off or regulating a draught : a device for diminishing the amplitude of vibrations or cycles : (*mus.*) a mute : (*Austr.*) a kind of unfermented bread; **damp'ing-off',** a disease of seedlings caused by Pythium or other fungus in excess of moisture.— *adj.* **damp'ish.**—*n.* **damp'ishness.**—*adv.* **damp'-ly.**—*n.* **damp'ness.**—*adj.* **damp'-proof,** impervious to moisture; **damp'y** (*poet.*), damp. [M.E. *dampen;* akin to Du. *damp,* Ger. *dampf,* vapour.]

damsel, *dam'zl, n.* a young unmarried woman : a girl. [O.Fr. *dameisele* (Fr. *demoiselle*)—L.L. *domicella* dim. of L. *domina,* lady.]

damson, *dam'zn, n.* a rather small oval-fruited dark purple plum.—**damson cheese,** damsons pressed into a solid cake. [Shortened from *Damascene—Damascus.*]

Dan, *dan, n.* a title of honour equivalent to Master or Sir formerly applied esp. to monks, and now by the poets to great poets, etc. [O.Fr. *dan.* (Sp. *don;* Port. *dom*)—L. *dominus,* lord.]

dan, *dan, n.* (*prov.*) a box for carrying coal : a tub.

dance, *dâns, v.i.* to move with measured steps, esp. to music : to spring.—*v.t.* to make to dance or jump : to perform, execute, as a dance.—*n.* a movement of one or more persons with measured steps : the tune to which dancing is performed : the musical form of a dance-tune : a meeting for dancing.—*ns.* **dance'-band; dance -hall; dance' music,** music specially arranged for accompanying dancing; **danc'er; dance'-tune; danc'ing; danc'ing-girl,** a professional dancer; **danc'ing-mas'ter.**—**dance a bear** (*obs.*), to exhibit a performing bear; **dance attendance,** to wait assiduously : **dance of death,** a series of allegorical paintings symbolising the universal power of death, represented as a skeleton; **dance upon nothing,** to be hanged; **lead one a dance,** to keep him involved in a series of wearying perplexities and vexations; **merry dancers,** the aurora. [O.Fr. *danser,* from Gmc.; O.H.G. *dansôn,* to draw along.]

dancette, *dân-set', n.* (*her.*) a zigzag or indented line or figure : the chevron or zigzag moulding common in Romanesque architecture.—*adj.* **dan-cetté, -ee, -y** (*dân'set-ā, -i,* or *-set'*), deeply indented. [O.Fr. *dent, dant,* tooth, notch—L. *dēns, dentis.*]

dandelion, *dan'di-lī-ən, n.* a common yellow-flowered composite (*Taraxacum officinale*) with jagged-toothed leaves. [Fr. *dent de lion,* lion-tooth.]

dander, *dân'dər,* **daunder, dawner,** *dawn'(d)ər, v.i.* (*Scot.*) to stroll, saunter.—*n.* a stroll, saunter. [Origin unknown.]

dander, *dân'dər, n.* a form of dandruff: (*U.S.*) anger : passion.—**raise one's dander,** to put him out of temper.

dander, *dân'dər, n.* (*Scot.*) furnace cinders. [Origin unknown.]

Dandie Dinmont, *dan'di din'mənt, n.* a short-legged rough-coated terrier of Scottish Border breed, of pepper or mustard colour. [From *Dandie Dinmont* in Scott's *Guy Mannering,* whose Peppers and Mustards are represented as the origin of the breed.]

dandiprat, dandyprat, *dan'di-prat, n.* (*obs.*) a silver three-halfpenny piece : an insignificant person : a little boy. [Origin unknown.]

dandle, *dan'dl, v.t.* to play with : to fondle or toss in the arms, as a baby. [Origin unknown.]

dandriff, dandruff, *dand'rəf, n.* a scaly scurf on the skin under the hair. [Origin unknown.]

dandy, *dan'di, n.* a foppish, silly fellow : one who pays much attention to dress.—*adj.* (*coll.* esp. *U.S.*) smart, fine—a word of general commendation : a dandy-cock : a dandy-roll.—*adjs.* **dandi'acal; dand'ified,** inclined to be a dandy.—*v.t.* **dand'ify,** to dress up.—*adv.* **dan'dily.**—*ns.* **dan'dy-brush,** a hard brush of whalebone bristles; **dan'dy-cart,** a light spring-cart :—*ns.* **dan'dy-cock, -hen,** a bantam; **dan'dy-horse,** an early bicycle without pedals, driven by kicking the ground; **dan'dy-roll,** a wire-gauze cylinder that impresses the ribs and water-mark on paper.—*adj.* **dan'dyish.**—*n.* **dan'dyism.** [Origin unknown; orig. Scots; poss. one spoiled by overmuch dandling.]

dandy, *dan'di, n.* a sloop-like vessel with jigger-mast abaft.—*adj.* **dan'dy-rigged.**

dandy-fever. See **dengue.**

Dane, *dān, n.* a native or citizen of Denmark : a very large dog (great Dane) : a Dalmatian dog (lesser Dane).—*adj.* **Dān'ish,** belong to Denmark. —*n.* the language of the Danes—(*Spens.*) **Dan'isk.** [Dan. *Daner* (pl.); O.E. *Dene.*]

danegeld, *dān'geld, n.* a tax imposed in the 10th cent., to buy off the Danes or to defend the country against them. [O.E. *Dene,* Danes, *geld,* payment.]

dane-hole, *dān'hōl, n.* Same as **dene-hole.**

dang, *dang, v.t.* a minced form of **damn.**

danger, *dān'jər, n.* peril, hazard, or risk: insecurity : (*obs.*) power.—*v.t.* (*Shak.*) to endanger.— *adj.* **dan'gerous,** full of danger : (*obs.*) arrogant, stand-offish : unsafe : insecure.—Also (*Shak.*) *adv.*—*adv.* **dan'gerously.**—*ns.* **dan'gerousness; dan'ger-point.**—**danger line,** the boundary between safety and danger. [O.Fr. *dangier,* absolute power (of a feudal lord), hence power to hurt.—L.L. *dominium,* feudal authority—L. *dominus,* a lord.]

dangle, *dang'gl, v.i.* to hang loosely or with a swinging motion : to follow about.—*v.t.* to make to dangle.—*n.* **dang'ler,** one who dangles about others, esp. about women.—*n.* and *adj.* **dang'ling.** —**dangling participle,** (*U.S.*) a misrelated participle. [Cf. Dan. *dangle*—O.N. *dingla.*]

Daniel, *dan'yəl, n.* a wise judge (in phrases as *a second Daniel, a Daniel come to judgment*). [From Daniel in the *Book of Susannah.*]

Danish. See **Dane.**

Danite, *dan'īt, n.* one of a secret society amongst the early Mormons. [*Dan;* cf. Gen. xlix. 16, 17.]

dank, *dangk, adj.* moist, wet.—*n.* (*Milt.*) a wet place.—*adj.* **dank'ish.** [Origin uncertain.]

Dannebrog, *dan'e-brog, n.* the Danish national flag : the second of the Danish orders instituted by King Valdemar in 1219. [Dan.]

danseuse, *dän⁰-səz', n.* a female dancer : a ballet dancer. [Fr.]

Dansker, *dan'skər, n.* (*Shak.*) a Dane.

Dantean, *dan'tē-ən,* **Dantesque,** *dan-tesk', adjs.* like the poet *Dante:* sublime : austere.—*ns.* **Dan'tist,** a Dante scholar; **Dantoph'ilist,** a lover of Dante.

danton. See **daunton.**

dap, *dap, v.i.* to bounce : to drop bait gently into the water.—*n.* a bait so used : a bounce :—*n.* **dapp'er.** [Origin obscure.]

Daphne, *daf'nē, n.* a genus (fam. Thymelaeaceae) of shrubs, including mezereon and spurge-laurel. [Gr. *daphnē,* sweet bay.]

dapper, *dap'ər, adj.* quick : little and active : neat : spruce.—*n.* **dapp'erling,** a dapper little fellow. [Du. *dapper,* brave; cf. Ger. *tapfer,* quick, brave.]

dapple, *dap'l, adj.* marked with spots.—*v.t.* to variegate with spots.—*adjs.* **dapp'le-bay'**, of bay colour, variegated with dapples; **dapp'led; dapp'le-grey'.** [Origin unknown.]

darbies, *där'biz, n.pl.* (*slang*) handcuffs. [App. from the personal name *Darby.*]

Neutral vowels in unaccented syllables : *el'ə-mənt, in'fənt, ran'dəm*

Darbyite, *där′bi-īt, n.* one of the Plymouth Brethren, esp. of those branches that insist on excommunicating others. [From their principal founder, J. N. *Darby* (1800-82).]

dare, *dār, v.i.* and *v.t.* to be bold enough : to venture (*3rd pers. sing.* **dare**(s) ; *pa.t.* **durst,** commonly in subjunctive sense, **dared** ; *pa.p.* **dared**).—*v.t.* to challenge : to defy : to face (*3rd pers.* **dares** ; *pa.t.* and *pa.p.* **dared**).—*n.* (*Shak.*) boldness : an act of daring or (*Shak.*) a challenge to perform it.—*n.* **dare′-devil,** a rash, venturesome fellow.—*adj.* unreasonably rash and reckless.—*adjs.* **dare′ful** (*Shak.*), full of daring, adventurous : **dar′ing,** bold : courageous : fearless.—*n.* boldness.—*n.* **dar′ing-do** (see **derring-do**).—*adj.* **dar′inghard′y** (*Shak.*), fool-hardy.—*adv.* **dar′ingly.**— **I dare say,** I suppose. [O.E. *durran* (preterite-present vb.), pres.t. *dearr,* pret. *dorste;* Goth. *daursan;* akin to Gr. *tharseein.*]

dare, *dār, v.i.* (*obs.*) to lurk, crouch, shrink, be dismayed, doze, be fascinated, stare.—*v.t.* (*Spens.; Shak.*) to daze : to frighten.—*n.* a contrivance for fascinating larks with mirrors. [O.E. *darian,* to lurk, be hidden.]

dare, *dār.* Same as **dace.**

darg, *därg, n.* (*Scot.*) a day's work : a task. [Contr. from *dawerk,* day-*wark,* day-work.]

dargle, *där′gl, n.* (*Scott*) a dell. [Prob. from the *Dargle* near Bray, mistaken by Scott for a common noun.]

dari. See **durra.**

daric, *där′ik, n.* an old gold coin larger than an English sovereign, named after *Darius* I. of Persia.

dark, *därk, adj.* without light : black, or somewhat blackish : gloomy : difficult to understand : unenlightened : secret : sinister.—*n.* absence of light : obscurity : a state of ignorance.—*adv.* (*Shak.*) in a state of dark.—*v.t.* **dark′en,** to make dark or darker : to render ignorant : to sully.—*v.i.* to grow dark or darker.—*n.* **dark′-house** (*Shak.*), a mad-house.— *adj.* **dark′ish.**—*n.* **dark′-lant′ern,** a lantern whose light can be covered.—*v.i.* **dark′le,** to grow dark (a back-formation of *darkling*).—*adv.* and *adj.* **dark′ling,** dark : in the dark.—*adv.* and *adj.* **dark′lings** (*poet.*), in the dark; **dark′ly.**—*ns.* **dark′mans** (*thieves' slang*) night; **dark′ness;** **dark′-room,** a chamber free from such light as would affect photographic plates.—*adj.* **dark′some,** dark : (*poet.*) gloomy.—*ns.* **dark′y, dark′ey** (*coll.*) a negro : (*slang*) a dark-lantern.—**Dark Ages,** the period of intellectual darkness in Europe, from the 5th to the 9th or 12th (or 15th) century; **Dark Continent,** Africa; **darken one's door,** to enter one's house, visit one; **dark horse,** in racing, a horse whose capabilities are not known : also *fig.* of a person (usually implying undisclosed ability) : a candidate not brought forward till the last moment; **keep dark,** to be silent or secret; **keep it dark,** to conceal it; **prince of darkness,** Satan. [O.E. *deorc.*]

darling, *där′ling, n.* one dearly beloved : a favourite. [O.E. *déorling;* see **dear.**]

Darlingtonia, *där-ling-tō′ni-ä, n.* a Californian pitcher-plant of the Sarracenia family. [Named after William *Darlington* (1782-1863), American botanist.]

darn, *därn, v.t.* to mend by interwoven stitches : to embroider or sew with the stitches used in mending holes.—*n.* a darned place.—*ns.* **darn′er ; darn′ing; darn′ing-need′le.** [Etymology unknown.]

darn, *därn, v.i.* a minced form of **damn.**

darnel, *där′nl, n.* a species of rye-grass : perh. the tares of the Bible. [Poss. conn. with O.Fr. *darne,* stupid, from its supposed narcotic properties.]

darraign(e), darrain(e), darrayn, deraign, *dǝ-rān′, v.t.* (*obs.*) to vindicate : to justify : to prove : to claim : to challenge : to decide : (*Spens., Shak.*) to set in battle array, to do (battle). [O.Fr. *derainier, desraisnier,* to plead, vindicate.—L.L. *dē-, disrationāre*—L. *dē-* or *dis-, ratiō,* reason; cf. **arraign.**]

darre, *där* (*Spens.*). Same as **dare** (1).—**darred** (*därd*), *pa.p.* of **dare** (2).

dart, *därt, n.* a pointed weapon or toy for throwing with the hand : anything that pierces : (in *pl.*) a

game in which darts are thrown at a board : in some snails, a calcareous needle supposed to be used as a sexual stimulus : a sudden forward movement : (in full **dart′-moth**) a cutworm moth (*Agrotis*) with a dart-like mark on the forewing.—*v.t.* to hurl suddenly : to send or shoot forth.—*v.i.* to start or shoot forth rapidly—freq. **dar′tle.**—*ns.* **dart′-board,** the target used in the game of darts; **dar′ter,** one who or that which, darts : a freshwater diving bird (*Plotus*) allied to cormorants : an archer-fish : applied also to various small American fishes akin to perch.—*adv.* **dart′ingly.**—*n.* **dart′-sac,** the gland that secretes the dart in snails. [O.Fr. *dart;* cf. O.E. *daroth.*]

dart. See **dace.**

dartre, *där′tǝr, n.* herpes.—*adj.* **dar′trous.** [Fr.]

Darwinism, *där′win-izm, n.* the theory of the origin of species propounded by C. *Darwin* (1809-82).—*adj.* and *n.* **Darwin′ian.**

dash, *dash, v.t.* to throw, thrust, or drive violently : to break by throwing together : to bespatter : to blotch : to frustrate : to confound : to modify by dilution or admixture.—*v.i.* to rush with violence. —*n.* a violent striking : a rush : a violent onset : a blow : a splash : a splash of colour : a stroke of the pen or similar mark : a mark (—) at a break in a sentence or elsewhere : a euphemism for damn (sometimes represented by this sign) : a staccato mark : an acute accent used in algebra and in lettering of diagrams as a discriminating mark : a long element in the Morse code : verve : ostentation : a slight admixture : a dash-board.— *ns.* **dash′-board,** a board, screen, or partition in front of a driver, on a horse-vehicle to keep off splashes of mud, in a motor-car or aeroplane to carry instruments; **dash′er,** one who dashes : (*coll.*) one who makes a great show.—*adj.* **dash′ing,** spirited : showy : ostentatiously fashionable.—*adv.* **dash′ingly.**—*ns.* **dash′-pot,** a device for damping vibration by a piston moving in a cylinder containing liquid; **dash′-wheel,** a washing-machine in the form of a partitioned drum.—**dash off,** to throw off or produce hastily; **dash out,** to knock out by striking against something. [M.E. *daschen, dassen,* to rush, or strike with violence—cf. Dan. *daske,* to slap.]

dassie *das′i, n.* (S. Africa) the hyrax. [Du. *dasje,* dim. of *das,* badger.]

dastard, *dǎs′tǝrd, n.* a cowardly fellow : loosely, one who does a brutal act without giving his victim a chance.—*adj.* shrinking from danger : cowardly— *adj.* and *adv.* **das′tardly.**—*ns.* **das′tardness, das′tardliness** or **das′tardy.** [Prob. conn. with **dazed.**]

dasyphyllous, *das-i-fil′ǝs, adj.* having crowded, thick, or woolly leaves. [Gr. *dasys,* thick, bushy, hairy, *phyllon,* leaf.]

Dasypus, *das′i-poos, -pǝs, n.* a genus of armadillos. —*n.* **das′ypod,** any member of the genus.—*n.pl.* **Dasipod′idae** the armadillo family. [Gr. *dasypous,* a hare—*dasys,* hairy, *pous, podos,* foot.]

dasyure, *das′i-ūr, n.* any marsupial of the flesh-eating genus **Dasyu′rus** (called native cat) or the fam. **Dasyu′ridae** (Tasmanian devil, Tasmanian wolf, etc.). [Gr. *dasys,* shaggy, *ourā,* tail.]

data, *dā′tä, n.pl.* facts given, from which others may be inferred (*sing.* **dā′tum,** q.v.). [L. *dāta,* things given, *pa.p. neut. pl.* of *dāre,* to give.]

datary, *dā′tǝ-ri, n.* an officer of the papal court charged with registering and dating bulls, etc., and with duties relating to the granting of indults and graces : his office (also **data′ria**). [L.L. *datārius*— L. *dāre,* to give.]

date, *dāt, n.* a statement of time, or time and place. of writing, sending, executing, as on a letter, book, document, etc. : the time of an event : (*arch.*) duration, or end, of existence : term of life : (*Spens.*) death-day, doom (with pun on *debt*) : (*coll.* esp. *U.S.*) an appointment or engagement.—*v.t.* to affix a date to : to ascertain the date of : to suggest the date of.—*v.i.* to reckon : to take beginning : to savour of a particular time.—*adjs.* **dāt′able;** **dāt′al; date′less,** without date or fixed limit : free from engagements.—*ns.* **dāt′er; date′-line,** the line east and west of which the date differs—

the 180th meridian with deviations.—**out of date**, antiquated; **up to date**, abreast of the times: adapted or corrected to the present time: modern. [O.Fr. *date*—L. *dătum*, given.]

date, *dāt*, *n*. the fruit of the date-palm.—*ns*. **date'-palm, -tree**, a palm (*Phoenix dactylifera*) of N. Africa and S.W. Asia; **date'-plum**, a fruit of the ebony genus, persimmon; **date'-shell**, the date-shaped shell of Lithodomus, or the animal itself, of the mussel family, a borer in limestone rocks; **date'-su'gar**. [Fr. *datte*—L. *dactylus*—Gr. *daktylos*, a finger, a date.]

dative, *dāt'iv*, *adj*. given or appointed: (*gram*.) expressing an indirect object.—*n*. the dative case: a word in the dative.—*adj*. **datival** (*də-tī'vəl*). [L. *dătivus*—*dăre*, to give.]

datolite, *dat'ə-līt*, *n*. a hydrated silicate of boron and calcium. [Gr. *dateesthai* to divide, *lithos*, stone.]

datum, *dā'təm* (see **data**).—*n*. **dā'tum-line**, the horizontal base-line from which heights and depths are measured. [L. *dătum*, given—*dăre*, to give.]

Datura, *də-tū'rā*, *n*. the thorn-apple genus of the potato family, with strongly narcotic properties.—*n*. **datu'rine**, atropine, or a mixture of atropine with other alkaloids. [Hind. *dhatūrā*.]

daub, *dawb*, *v.t*. to smear: to paint coarsely.—*n*. a coarse painting.—*ns*. **daub'er**, one who daubs: a coarse painter; **daub'ery** (*Shak*. **dawb'ry**), a daubing, or crudely artful device, false pretence; **daub'ing**.—*adj*. **daub'y**, sticky. [O.Fr. *dauber*, to plaster—L. *dealbāre*, to whitewash—*dē*, down, and *albus*, white.]

daud, dawd, *dawd*, *v.t*. (*Scot*.) to knock, thump.—*n*. a lump: large piece. [dad, 2.]

daughter, *daw'tər*, *n*. a female in relation to her parent: a female descendant: woman (generally).—*adj*. (*biol*.) derived from another.—*ns*. **daugh'ter-in-law**, a son's wife: formerly a step-daughter:—*pl*. **daughters - in - law**; **daugh'terliness**; **daugh'terling**, a little daughter.—*adj*. **daugh'terly**, like or becoming a daughter. [O.E. *dohtor*; Scot. *dochter*, Ger. *tochter*, Gr. *thygatēr*.]

dault. See **dalt**.

daunder, dauner. Same as **dander**.

daunt, *dawnt*, or *dänt*, *v.t*. to frighten: to discourage: to subdue.—*adj*. **daunt'less**, not to be daunted.—*adv*. **daunt'lessly**.—*n*. **daunt'lessness**.—*v.t*. **daun'ton**, to subdue: to dare. [O.Fr. *danter* (Fr. *dompter*)—L. *domitāre—domāre*, tame.]

dauphin, *daw'fin*, *n*. the eldest son of the king of France (1349-1830).—*n*. **dau'phiness**, his wife. [O.Fr. *daulphin* (Fr. *dauphin*)—*Delphinus*, family name of the lords of the Viennois—hence dolphins in their crest and name Dauphiné for their province (ceded to the king, 1349).]

daur, *dawr*, a Scots form of **dare**.

daut, dawt, *dawt*, *v.t*. (*Scot*.) to pet.—*n*. **daut'ie, dawt'ie**, a pet. [Origin unknown.]

davenport, *dav'n-pōrt*, *n*. a small ornamental writing-desk—also **dev'onport**: (*U.S.*) a large sofa. [Prob. from the maker.]

davenport-trick, *dav'n-pōrt-trik*, *n*. an artifice by which a man can free himself from ropes wound round him and tied. [From two impostors who practised it (flor. 1845-65).]

davit, *dav'it*, *n*. one of a pair of erections on a ship for lowering or hoisting a boat. [App. from the name *David*.]

Davy, *dā'vi*, **Da'vy-lamp**, *-lamp*, *n*. the safety-lamp for coal-miners invented by Sir Humphry *Davy* (1778-1829).

Davy Jones, *dā'vi jōnz'*, *n*. a sailor's familiar name for the (malignant) spirit of the sea, the devil.—**Davy Jones's locker**, the sea, as the grave of men drowned at sea. [Origin unknown.]

daw, *daw*, *v.i*. (*obs*.) to dawn. [O.E. *dagian—dæg*, day.]

daw, *daw*, *n*. a bird of the crow kind, a jackdaw: (*arch*.) a simpleton.—**daw'cock** (*arch*.) a cock jackdaw: a noodle.—*adj*. **daw'ish**. [M.E. *dawe*.]

dawd. See **daud**.

dawdle, *daw'dl*, *v.i*. to waste time by trifling: to act or move slowly.—*n*. **daw'dler**. [Cf. **daddle**.]

dawk. See **dâk**.

dawn, *dawn*, *v.i*. to become day: to begin to grow light: to begin to appear.—*n*. daybreak: beginning.—Also **dawn'ing**.—*n*. **dawn'-man**, Eoanthropus.—**dawn on**, to begin to become evident to or be understood by. [Appears first as **dawning**, prob. from O.N.; cf. Sw. and Dan. *dagning*.]

dawner. See **dander** (1).

dawt, dawtie. See **daut**.

day, *dā*, *n*. the time of light, from sunrise to sunset, morning till night: twenty-four hours, from midnight to midnight (formerly by some reckoned from sunrise, or sunset, or—by astronomers—from noon): the time the earth takes to make a revolution on its axis—this being the *sidereal* day (between two transits of the first point of Aries, or approximately of the same star), distinguished from the *apparent solar* day (between two transits of the sun), and the *mean solar* day (between two transits of the mean, or imaginary uniformly moving, sun): the hours devoted to work (*working-day*): a day set apart for a purpose, as for receiving visitors: lifetime: time of existence, vogue, or influence: a time: daylight: space between mullions of a window: ground surface over a mine.—*ns*. **day'-bed** (*Shak*.), a couch or sofa; **day'-blind'ness**, a defect of vision in which objects are best seen by a dim light; **day'-board'er**, a pupil who feeds but does not sleep at a boarding school; **day'-book**, a book for entering the transactions of each day; **day'break**, break of day; **day'-coal**, the upper stratum of coal; **day'dream**, a dreaming or musing while awake; **day'-fly**, a May fly; **day'-lâ'bour**, labour paid by the day; **day'-lâ'bourer**; **day'-level** (*mining*), a level driven from the surface; **day'light**, the light of day: a clear space: **day'light-sav'ing**, reduction of loss of daylight, for work or play, by advancing the clock; **day'-lil'y**, a liliaceous plant (*Hemerocallis*) whose blossoms last only for a day.—*adj*. **day'long**, during the whole day.—*ns*. **day'mark**, an unlighted sea-mark.—*adj*. **day'-old**, one day old.—*ns*. **day'-peep** (*Milt*.), dawn; **day'-scholar**, a pupil who attends a boarding-school during the school-hours, but boards at home (also **day'-boy, day'-girl**); **day'-school**, a school held during the day, as opposed both to a night-school and to a boarding-school; **day'-sight**, night-blindness; **days'man**, one who appoints a day to hear a cause: an umpire; **day'spring**, dawn; **day'star**, the morning star; **day'time**, the time of daylight.—*adj*. **day'-wea'ried** (*Shak*.), wearied with the work of the day.—*n*. **day'-work**.—**call it a day**, to announce a decision to leave off; **day by day**, daily; **day in day out**, for an indefinite succession of days; **day off**, a day's holiday; **day out**, a servant's free day; **days of grace**, three days allowed for payment of bills, etc., beyond the day named; **one of these days**, some indefinite time in the near future; **see day-light**, to arrive at some comprehension, illumination, prospect of a solution; **the day**, the time spoken of or expected: (*Scot*.) to-day; **the day after the fair**, too late; **the other day**, not long ago; **the time of day**, the hour of the clock: a greeting; **win the day**, to gain the victory. [O.E. *dæg*; Ger. *tag*; not L. *diēs*.]

dayes-man, daynt, dayr'house (all *Spens*.). See **day** (**daysman**), **dainty**, **dairy**.

day-nettle, *dā'-net'l*, *n*. a dead-nettle: (in Scotland and N. England) the hemp-nettle (which often cuts harvesters' hands): a gathering on the finger.—Also **dae'-nett'le**. [Perh. for dead-nettle; but cf. O.N. (*akr*)*dai*, hemp-nettle.]

day-woman (*Shak*.). Same as **dey-woman**.

daze, *dāz*, *v.t*. to stun, to stupefy.—*n*. bewilderment: (*arch*.) mica.—*adj*. **dazed** (*dāzd*).—*adv*. **dazedly** (*dāz'-id-li*). [O.N. *dasa-sk* (refl.) to be breathless.]

dazzle, *daz'l*, *v.t*. to daze or overpower with strong light: to confound by brilliancy, beauty, or cleverness.—*v.i*. to be dazzled.—*ns*. **dazz'le, dazz'lement**, the act of dazzling: that which dazzles; **dazz'le-paint'ing**, fantastic painting for camouflage; **dazz'ler**; **dazz'ling**.—*adv*. **dazz'lingly**. [Freq. of **daze**.]

de-, *de-*, *pfx.* See Prefixes: much used in civil service jargon in coining words expressing undoing or ridding.

deacon, *dē'kn*, *n.* in Episcopal churches, a member of the order of clergy under priests: in some Presbyterian churches, an officer, distinct from the elders, who attends to the secular affairs of the church: in Congregational and some other churches, an officer who advises the pastor, distributes the elements at communion, and dispenses charity: in Scotland, the master of an incorporated company: (*U.S.*) the skin of a very young calf:—*fem.* **dea'con** (in Presbyterian churches), a woman who is a deacon; **dea'coness**, a female servant of the Christian society in the time of the apostles: in a convent a nun who has the care of the altar: one of an order of women in some Protestant churches who nurse the sick and tend the poor.—*ns.* **dea'conhood**, **dea'conry**, **dea'conship**. [L. *diāconus*—Gr. *diākonos*, a servant.]

deactivation, *dē-ak-tiv-ā'shən*, *n.* return from activation to the normal state. [Pfx. *de-* and active.]

dead, *ded*, *adj.* without life: deathlike: at rest, out of play, of a ball: of a golf-ball, within a certain putt: out of use: obsolete: inactive: cold and cheerless: dull: numb: insensitive: as good as dead: inelastic: dull: without vegetation: utter: unerring.—*v.t.* to deaden, dull: to benumb.—*v.i.* to lose vitality: to become numb.—*adv.* in a dead manner: absolutely: utterly: directly.—*n.* one who is dead: the time of greatest stillness, as *the dead* of night.—*adjs.* **dead'-alive**, **dead'-and-alive'**, dull, inactive; **dead'-beat**, quite overcome, exhausted; **dead'-born**, still-born.—*n.* **dead'-cart**, a cart for collecting the bodies of those dead of a pestilence.—*n.pl.* **dead'-clothes**, clothes to bury the dead in.—*ns.* **dead'-col'ouring**, the first broad outlines of a picture; **dead'-deal**, a board for measuring and lifting a corpse.—*adjs.* **dead'-do'ing** (*Spens.*), putting to death, destructive; **dead'-drunk'**, completely drunk.—*v.t.* **dead'en**, to make dead: to deprive partly of vigour, sensibility, or sensation: to blunt: to lessen: to make soundproof.—*ns.* **dead'-end**, a pipe, passage, etc., closed at one end: a cul-de-sac or blind alley; **dead'ener**.—*n.* and *adj.* **dead'-ening**.—*ns.* **dead'-eye**, (*naut.*), a round, flattish wooden block with a rope or iron band passing around it, and pierced with three holes for a lanyard; **dead'-fall**, a trap with a weight that falls when its support is removed; **dead'-fin'ish** (*Austr.*), a thicket or a thicket-forming shrub of the mimosa family (*Albizzia*, *Acacia*): a complete standstill or vanquishment; **dead'-fire**, an appearance of fire taken as a death-omen; **dead'-freight**, money paid for the empty space in a ship by a person who engages to freight her, but fails to make out a full cargo: **dead'-ground** (*mil.*), ground that cannot be covered by fire; **dead'-hand**, mortmain; **dead'-head**, one who enjoys privileges without paying, as in a theatre, etc.: a sprue; **dead'-heat'**, a heat or race in which two or more competitors are equal; **dead'-house**, a mortuary; **dead'-lett'er**, a letter undelivered and unclaimed at the post-office: a law or ordinance made but not enforced; **dead'-lev'el**, a stretch of land without any rising ground: sameness; **dead'-lift, -pull**, a lift, pull, made without help, leverage, etc.: hence an effort under discouraging conditions.—*n.pl.* **dead'-lights**, storm-shutters for a cabin window.—*ns.* **dead'liness**; **dead'-line**, a line drawn in a military prison, by going beyond which a prisoner makes himself liable to be shot instantly—also *fig.*: (*U.S.*) the closing date; **dead'lock**, the case when matters have become so complicated that all is at a complete standstill; **dead'-loss'**, a loss without any compensation.—*adj.* **dead'ly**, causing death: fatal: implacable.—*adv.* in a manner resembling death.—*ns.* **dead'ly-night'shade**, Belladonna; **dead'-march'**, a piece of solemn music played at funeral processions, esp. of soldiers; **dead'-meat**, the flesh of animals ready for the market.—*n.pl.* **dead'-men**, empty

bottles after a carouse.—*ns.* **dead'ness**; **dead'-nett'le**, any species of Lamium, labiate plants superficially like nettles but stingless; **dead'-pay**, continued pay dishonestly drawn for men actually dead; **dead'-point**, a position of a crank in which the force exerted on it does not help to turn it; **dead'-reck'oning**, an estimation of a ship's place simply by the log-book; **dead'-rope**, a rope not running in any block; **dead'-set**, a complete standstill, as of a setting dog: a determined and prolonged onslaught, esp. with a view to captivation; **dead'-shot**, an unerring marksman.—*adj.* **dead'-stroke**, without recoil.—*ns.* **dead'-wall**, a wall unbroken by windows or other openings; **dead'-wa'ter**, still water, the eddy water closing in behind a ship's stern as she sails; **dead'-weight**, unrelieved weight: a heavy and oppressive burden; **dead'-wind**, a calm (in the vortex of a storm): (*obs.*) a head wind; **dead'-wood**, pieces of timber laid on the upper side of the keel at either end: useless material: **dead'-work**, work, itself unprofitable, which is necessary as a preliminary, as the opening of a mine.—**dead as a door-nail**, a herring, absolutely dead; **dead language**, one no longer spoken; **deadly sin**, a mortal sin (see seven); **dead-men's bells**, the foxglove; **dead-men's fingers**, a very common actinozoan coelenterate (*Alcyonium digitatum*); **dead men's shoes**, succession to one who dies; **dead's part** (*Scots law*), the part of a man's moveable property which he may bequeath by will, and which is not due to wife and children; **Dead Sea apple, fruit**, apple of Sodom; **dead** (set) **against**, utterly opposed to; **put the dead wood on** (*U.S. slang*), to gain a great advantage over. [O.E. *déad*; Goth. *dauths*, Ger. *tot*, from root of **die**.]

deaf, *def*, *adj.* dull of hearing: unable to hear at all: not willing to hear: inattentive: hollow, with no kernel.—*v.t.* **deaf'en**, to make deaf: to stun: to render impervious to sound.—*n.* **deaf'ening**, stuffing put into floors, partition-walls, etc., to prevent sounds from passing through.—*adv.* **deaf'ly**.—*ns.* **deaf'-mute**, one who is both deaf and dumb; **deaf'-mut'ism**; **deaf'ness**. [O.E. *déaf*; Du. *doof*, Ger. *taub*.]

deal, *dēl*, *n.* a portion: an indefinite quantity: a large quantity: the act of dividing cards: a bargain.—*v.t.* to divide, to distribute: to throw about: to deliver.—*v.i.* to transact business: to act: to distribute cards.—*pa.t.* and *pa.p.* dealt (*delt*).—*ns.* **deal'er**, one who deals or whose turn it is to deal, or who has dealt the hand in play: a trader; **deal'ing**, manner of acting towards others: intercourse of trade. [O.E. *dǽlan*—*dǽl*, a part; Ger. *teilen*—*teil*, a part or division; cf. **dole**.]

deal, *dēl*, *n.* a fir or pine board of a standard size: timber.—*adj.* of deal.—*n.* **deal'fish**, a ribbon-fish (*Trachypterus*). [M.L.G. *dele*; cf. O.E. *thel*, *thille*, and mod. **thill**.]

dealbate, *dē-al'bāt*, *adj.* whitened.—*n.* **dealbā'tion**. [L. *dealbāre*, *-ātum*, to whitewash—pfx. *de-*, in sense of over a surface, *albus*, white.]

deambulatory, *dē-am'bū-lə-tər-i*, *n.* a place for walking about in: a passage or aisle round the choir and apse of a church.—[L. *deambulāre*, *-ātum*, to walk about.]

dean, **dene**, *dēn*, *n.* a small valley. [O.E. *denu*, a valley; cf. **den**.]

dean, *dēn*, *n.* a dignitary in cathedral and collegiate churches who presides over the canons: the president of a faculty in a college or of the Faculty of Advocates: a resident fellow of a college who has administrative and disciplinary functions: the senior member of a corps or body: the chief chaplain of the Chapel Royal: the chief judge of the Court of Arches: the president of a trade-guild.—*ns.* **dean'ery**, the office of a dean: a group of parishes presided over by a dean: a dean's house; **dean'ship**, the office or dignity of a dean.—**Dean of Arches**, dean of the Court of Arches (see **arch**); **Dean of Faculty**, president of the Faculty of Advocates in Scotland: **Dean of Guild**, a municipal functionary in Scotland who has authority over building and altering of houses;

rural dean, one who, under the bishop, has the special care and inspection of the clergy in certain parishes. [O.Fr. *deien* (Fr. *doyen*)—L.L. *decānus* or Gr. *dekānos*, a chief of ten—L. *decem* or Gr. *deka* ten.]

deaner, *dēn'ər, n.* (*slang*) a shilling. [Prob. L. *denārius*.]

dear, *dēr, adj.* high in price : costly : characterised by high prices : scarce : highly valued : beloved : (*Shak.*), earnest.—*n.* one who is dear or beloved.— *adv.* at a high price : dearly.—*interj.* indicating surprise, pity, or other emotion.—*adj.* **dear'- bought.**—*n.* and *adj.* **dear'ling** (*Spens.*), darling. —*adj.* **dear'ly.**—*ns.* **dear'ness**; **dear'y**, one who is dear. [O.E. *déore, dýre*; cog. with Ger. *teuer.*]

dear, deare, deere, *dēr, adj.* (*Spens.; Shak.; Milt.*) grievous.—Also *adv.* [O.E. *déor.*]

deare. See **dere.**

dearn, dearnful, dearnly. See **dern**, etc.

dearth, *dərth, n.* dearness, high price : scarcity : want : famine : barrenness. [**dear.**]

dearticulate, *dē-är-tik'ū-lāt, v.t.* to disjoint. [Pfx. *de-*, and **articulate.**]

deasil, *dēz'l, des'l, desh'l, dēsh'l, n.* (*Scot.*) sunwise motion—opp. to *withershins.*—*adv.* sunwise.— also **dea'soil, dei's(h)eal, dea'siul.** [Gael. *deiseil.*]

deaspirate, *dē-as'pir-āt, v.t.* to remove the aspirate from.—*n.* **deaspira'tion.**

death, *deth, n.* state of being dead : extinction or cessation of life : manner of dying : mortality : a deadly plague : cause of death : spiritual lifeless- ness : the killing of the animal in hunting.—*ns.* **death'-add'er**, a poisonous Australian snake (*Acanthophis antarcticus*); **death'-ag'ony**, the struggle often preceding death; **death'-bed**, the bed on which one dies : the last illness; **death'- bell**, the passing bell; **death'-blow**, a blow that causes death; **death'-cup**, a very poisonous toadstool (*Auranita phalloide.*) often mistaken for a mushroom; **death'-damp**, a cold, clammy sweat preceding death.—*adj.* **death'-dealing.**— *n.pl.* **death'-dū'ties**, duties paid on inheritance of property.—*n.* **death'-fire**, a light supposed to presage death.—*adjs.* **death'ful**, deadly, destruc- tive : mortal : deathlike; **death'less**, never dying : everlasting.—*n.* **death'lessness.**—*adj.* **death'like**, deadly : like death.—*n.* **death'liness.**—*adjs.* **death'ly**, deadly : deathlike; **death'-marked**, marked for or by death, destined to die.—*n.* **death'-mask**, a plaster-cast taken from the face after death.—*adj.* **death'-prac'tised** (*Shak.*), threatened with death by malicious arts.—*ns.* **death'-rate**, the proportion of deaths to the population; **death'-ratt'le**, a rattling in the throat that sometimes precedes death; **death'-ray**, a pretended ray that could destroy all life; **death'- roll**, a list of the dead; **death's'-head**, the skull of a human skeleton, or a figure of it : a memor- ial ring bearing such a figure; **deaths'man** (*Shak.*), an executioner; **death'-song**, a song sung before dying; **death'-stroke**, a death-blow; **death'- throe**, the dying agony; **death'-token** (*Shak.*), a sign or token of impending death, a plague-spot; **death'-trap**, an unsafe structure or place that exposes one to great danger of death.—*advs.* **death'ward, -s.**—*ns.* **death'-warrant**, an order from the authorities for the execution of a criminal; **death'-watch**, a watch by a dying person : an insect that produces a ticking noise, esp. a beetle of the genus Anobium; **death'-wound**, a wound that causes death.—*adj.* **death'y.**—**at death's door**, very near to death; **death's-head moth**, a hawk-moth with pale markings on the back of the thorax somewhat like a skull; **death on**, to be fatal to, fond of, good at; **do**, or **put**, **to death**, to kill : to cause to be killed; **gates**, or **jaws**, **of death**, the point of death; **in at the death**, in hunting, to be up on the animal before the dogs have killed it; **to death**, expressive of intensity, very much : to excess. [O.E. *déath*; Ger. *tod*; see **dead and die.**]

deave, *dēv, v.t.* (*Scot.*) to deafen. [See **deaf.**]

deaw, deawy, -ie (*Spens.*). See **dew, dewy.**

débâcle, debacle, *dā-bäk'l', di-bak'l, n.* a breaking up of ice on a river : (*geol.*) a sudden flood of water leaving its path strewed with debris : a complete break-up or collapse : a stampede. [Fr. *débâcle; dé, des*, and *bâcler*, to bar—L. *baculus*, a stick.]

debar, *di-bär', v.t.* to bar out : to exclude : to hinder (*pr.p.* **debarr'ing**; *pa.t.* and *pa.p.* **de- barred'**).—*n.* **debar'ment.** [Pfx. *de-*, and **bar.**]

debark, *di-bärk', v.t.* or *v.i.* to disembark.—*n.* **dēbarkā'tion, dēbarcā'tion.** [Fr. *débarquer— des* (—L. *dis-*), away, and Fr. *barque*, a ship.]

debarrass, *di-bar'əs, v.t.* to disembarrass, disen- tangle, free. [Fr. *débarrasser; dé-, des-* and *barre*, a bar.]

debase, *di-bās', v.t.* to lower : to make mean or of less value : to adulterate.—*adj.* **debased'**, de- graded : (*her.*) reversed.—*n.* **debase'ment**, de- gradation.—*adj.* **debas'ing.**—*adv.* **debas'ingly.** [L. *dē*, down, and **base.**]

debate, *di-bāt', n.* a contention in words or argu- ment : (*obs.*) fight, strife.—*v.t.* to contend for in argument : (*arch.*) to fight for : to argue about.—*v.i.* (*obs.*) to fight, contend : to deliberate : to join in debate.—*adjs.* **debāt'able**, liable to be disputed : open to argument : contentious.—Also **debate'- able**; **debate'ful** (*Spens.*), quarrelsome.—*ns.* **debate'ment** (*Spens.; Shak.*), controversy; **de- bāt'er.**—*adv.* **debāt'ingly.**—**Debat(e)able Land**, a tract of border land between Esk and Sark formerly claimed both by England and Scotland. [O.Fr. *debatre*—L. *dē*, and *batuěre*, to beat.]

debauch, *di-bawch', v.t.* to lead away from duty or allegiance : to corrupt with lewdness : to seduce : to vitiate.—*v.i.* to over-indulge.—*n.* a fit of in- temperance or debauchery.—*adj.* **debauched'**, corrupt : profligate.—*adv.* **debauch'edly.**—*ns.* **debauch'edness**; **debauchee** (*deb'osh-ē*), a liber- tine; **debauch'er**; **debauch'ery**, excessive in- temperance : habitual lewdness; **debauch'ment.** [O.Fr. *desbaucher* (Fr. *débaucher*), to corrupt—*des-* (L. *dis-*), and *baucher*, to hew—*bauche* or *bauc*, a beam, a course of stones.]

debel, *di-bel', v.t.* (*Milt.*) to conquer in war (*pr.p.* **debell'ing**; *pa.t.* and *pa.p.* **debelled'**). [L. *dēbellāre—dē*, down, *bellāre*, to war—*bellum*, war.]

debenture, *di-bent'yər, n.* a written acknowledg- ment of a debt : a security issued by a company for borrowed money : a certificate entitling an exporter of imported goods to a repayment of the duty paid on their importation.—*adj.* **debent'ured**, en- titled to drawback or debenture, as goods. [L. *dēbentur*, there are due, 3rd pers. pl. pass. of *dēbēre*, to owe—the first word of the receipt.]

debilitate, *di-bil'i-tāt, v.t.* to make weak : to impair the strength of.—*adi.* **debile** (*deb'il, deb'il, arch.*), weak, feeble.—*ns.* **debilitā'tion**; **debil'ity**, weakness and languor : a weak action of the animal functions. [L. *dēbilitāre, -ātum—dēbilis*, weak—*dē*, from, *habilis*, able. See **ability.**]

debit, *deb'it, n.* a debt or something due : an entry on the debtor side of an account.—*v.t.* to charge with debt : to enter on the debtor side of an account.—*n.* **deb'itor** (*Shak.*), a debtor. [L. *dēbitum*, what is due, from *dēbēre*, to owe.]

debonair, debonnaire, *deb-ə-nār', adj.* of good appearance and manners : elegant : courteous : gay.—*adv.* **debonair'ly.**—*n.* **debonair'ness.** [Fr. *de*, of, *bon*, good, and the old word *aire* (*masc.*), manner, origin; mod. Fr. *débonnaire.*]

debosh, *di-bosh'*, an old form of **debauch.**

debouch, *di-bōsh', v.i.* to issue, emerge, to march or flow out from a narrow pass or confined place.— *ns.* **débouché** (*dā-bōō-shā'*), an outlet; **debouch'- ment**, an act or place of debouching; **de- bouchure'**, the mouth of a river or strait. [Fr. *déboucher—de*, from, *bouche*, mouth—L. *bucca*, cheek.]

débris, debris, *dāb'* or *dəb'rē*, or *-rē'*, *n.* wreckage : ruins : rubbish : a mass of rocky fragments. [Fr., from *briser*, akin to **bruise.**]

debruised, *di-brōōzd', adj.* (*her.*) surmounted or partly covered by one of the ordinaries. [O.Fr. *debruisier—de-*, apart, *brusier*, to break.]

debt, *det, n.* what one owes to another : what one becomes liable to do or suffer : a state of obligation or indebtedness: a duty: (*B.*) a sin.—*adj.* **debt'ed** (*Shak.*), indebted, obliged.—*ns.* **debt'ee,** a creditor; **debt'or,** one who owes a debt.—**bad debt,** a debt of which there is no prospect of payment; **debt of honour,** a debt not recognised by law, but binding in honour—esp. a gambling or betting debt; **debt of nature,** death; **floating debt,** miscellaneous public debt, like exchequer and treasury bills, as opposed to *funded debt,* that which has been converted into perpetual annuities like consols in Britain; **in one's debt,** under a pecuniary obligation to one. [O.Fr *dette*—L. *dēbitum, dēbēre,* to owe.]

debunk, *dē-bungk′, v.t.* (*slang,* esp. *U.S.*) to clear of bunk or humbug: to remove the whitewash from (a reputation). [L. *dē,* from, and **bunk.**]

début, *dā-bū′, n.* a beginning or first attempt: a first appearance before the public, or in society.— *n.* **débutant** (*dā-bū-tān⁸, deb′ū-tänt*), one who makes his first appearance:—*fem.* **débutante** (*-tän⁸t, deb′-ū-tänt*); *U.S.* dim. **deb, debb′y**). [Fr. *début,* a first stroke—*débuter*—*de,* from, *but,* aim, mark.]

decachord, *dek′ə-kord, n.* an old ten-stringed musical instrument. [Gr. *dekachordos*—*deka,* ten, and *chordē,* a string.]

decade, decad, *dek′ad, dek′ād, -ād′, n.* a group of ten, esp. a series of ten years.—*adj.* **dec′adal.** [Gr. *dekas, -ados*—*deka,* ten.]

decadence, *dek′ə-dəns,* or *di-kā′-,* **dec′adency** (or *di-kā′-*), *n.* state of decay: applied to a school in late 19th century French literature, the symbolists, and their like.—*adj.* **dec′adent** (or *di-kā′-*), decaying: lacking in moral and physical vigour: symbolist.—*n.* one who is degenerate: a symbolist. [Fr.,—L.L. *dēcadentia,* from L. *dē,* down— *cadēre,* to fall.]

decagon, *dek′ə-gon, n.* a plane figure of ten angles and sides.—*adj.* **decagonal** (*-ag′ən-əl*). [Gr. *deka,* and *gōniā,* an angle.]

decagramme, decagram, *dek′ə-gram, n.* a weight of ten grammes, equal to 0.353 oz. avoirdupois. [Fr. *décagramme*—Gr. *deka,* ten, and **gramme.**]

Decagynia, *dek-ə-jin′i-ä, n.pl.* in the Linnaean system a class of plants with ten pistils.—*adjs.* **decagyn′ian, decagynous** (*-aj′*). [Gr. *deka,* ten, *gynē,* a woman.]

decahedron, *dek-ə-hē′drən, n.* a solid figure having ten faces.—*adj.* **decahē′dral.** [Gr. *deka,* and *hedrā,* a seat.]

decalcify, *dē-kal′si-fī, v.i.* to deprive of lime.—*n.* **decalcificā′tion.** [L. pfx. *dē,* and **calcify.**]

decalescence, *dē-kəl-es′əns, n.* the behaviour of iron or steel which in heating from red to white reaches a point where it seems to go back for a little—the opposite of *recalescence.* [L. *dē,* down, *calēscēre,* to grow hot.]

decalitre, *dek′ə-lēt-ər, n.* ten litres, about 2·2 imperial gallons. [Fr. *décalitre*—Gr. *deka,* ten, and *litrā,* a pound.]

decalogue, *dek′ə-log, n.* the ten commandments.— *n.* **decal′ogist** (*di-kal′ə-jist*) an exponent as of the decalogue. [Gr. *deka,* ten, *logos,* a discourse.]

Decameron, *de-kam′ə-ron, -rən, n.* Boccaccio's book of a hundred tales, supposed to be told in ten days.—*adj.* **decameron′ic.** [Gr. *deka,* ten, *hēmerā,* a day.]

decamerous, *dek-am′ər-əs, adj.* having the parts in tens. [Gr. *deka,* ten, *meros,* part.]

decametre, *dek′ə-mēt-ər, n.* ten metres—about 32.8 feet. [Fr. *décamètre*—Gr. *deka,* ten, *metron,* a measure. See **metre.**]

decamp, *di-kamp′, v.i.* to make off, esp. secretly.— *n.* **decamp′ment.** [Fr. *décamper.*]

decanal, *dek-ān′əl, adj.* pertaining to a dean or deanery: decani.—*adj.* **decān′ī,** dean's, i.e. south (of the side of a choir where the dean sits, opposed to *cantoris*). [L.L. *decānus, -ī*]

Decandria, *de-kan′dri-ä, n.pl.* in the Linnaean system a class of plants with ten stamens.—*adjs.* **decan′drian, decan′drous,** with ten stamens. [Gr. *deka,* ten, and *anēr, andros,* a man, male.]

decane, *dek′ān, n.* a hydrocarbon ($C_{10}H_{22}$) tenth of the methane series. [Gr. *deka,* ten.]

decant, *di-kant′, v.t.* to pour off, leaving sediment: to pour from one vessel into another.—*ns.* **decantā′tion** (*dē-*); **decant′er,** an ornamental bottle for holding decanted liquor. [Fr. *décanter* (It. *decantare*)—L. *dē,* from, *canthus,* beak of a vessel—Gr. *kanthos,* corner of the eye.]

decantate, *dē-kant′āt, v.t.* and *v.i.* to chant or say repeatedly. [L. *dēcantāre*—pfx. *dē-, cantāre,* intens. of *canĕre,* to sing.]

decapitate, *di-kap′i-tāt, v.t.* to behead.—*n.* **decapitā′tion.** [L.L. *dēcapitāre*—L. *dē,* from, and *caput, capitis,* the head.]

Decapoda, *di-kap′o-dä, n.pl.* an order of higher crustaceans with ten feet (including pincers)— crabs, lobsters, shrimps, prawns, etc.: an order of cephalopods with ten arms.—*n.* **dec′apod,** a member of either of these orders.—Also *adj.*— *adjs.* **decap′odal, decap′odan, decap′odous.** [Gr. *deka,* ten, and *pous, podos,* a foot.]

decarbonise, *dē-kär′bən-īz, v.t.* to remove carbon or carbon dioxide from (also **decar′bŭrise;** **decar′bonate**).—*ns.* **decarbonīsā′tion, decarburīsā′tion.** [Pfx. *de-* and **carbon.**]

decastere, *dek′ə-stēr, n.* ten steres. [Gr. *deka,* ten, and **stere.**]

decastich, *dek′ə-stik, n.* a poem of ten lines. [Gr. *deka,* ten, and *stichos,* a row, a verse.]

decastyle, *dek′ə-stīl, n.* a portico with ten columns in front.—Also *adj.* [Gr. *deka,* ten, *stylos,* a column.]

decasyllable, *dek-ə-sil′ə-bl, n.* a verse-line, or a word, of ten syllables.—*adj.* **decasyllabic** (*-ab′ik*). [Gr. *deka,* ten, *syllabē* a syllable; see **syllable.**]

decaudate, *dē-kaw′dāt, v.t.* to cut off the tail of. [L. *dē,* from, *cauda,* tail.]

decay, *di-kā′, v.i.* to fall away from a state of health or excellence: to waste away: to rot.—*v.t.* to cause to waste away: to impair.—*n.* a falling into a worse or less perfect state: a wearing away: rotting: loss of fortune: (*obs.*) ruin, downfall.— *adj.* **decayed′,** reduced in circumstances. [O.Fr. *decair*—L. *dē,* from *cadēre,* to fall.]

decease, *di-sēs′, n.* death.—*v.i.* to die.—*adj.* **deceased′,** dead: lately dead: (almost a *n.*) the dead person in question. [O.Fr. *deces* (Fr. *décès*) —L. *dēcessus*—*dē,* away, *cēdēre, cessum,* to go.]

decedent, *di-sē′dənt, n.* (*U.S.*) a deceased person. [L. *dēcēdēns, -tis,* pr.p. of *dēcēdēre* to depart—*dē,* away, *cēdēre,* to go.]

deceit, *di-sēt′, n.* act of deceiving: anything intended to mislead another: fraud: falseness.—*adj.* **deceit′ful,** full of deceit: disposed or tending to deceive: insincere.—*adv.* **deceit′fully.**—*n.* **deceit′fulness.** [O.Fr. *deceite*—L. *dēcipĕre, dēceptum,* to deceive.]

deceive, *di-sēv′, v.t.* to mislead or cause to err: to cheat: to disappoint.—*adj.* **deceiv′able,** that may be deceived: exposed to imposture.—*n.* **deceiv′ableness.**—*adj.* **deceiv′ably.**—*n.* **deceiv′er.** [Fr. *décevoir*—L. *dēcipĕre, deceptum*—*dē,* from *capĕre,* to take, catch.]

decelerate, *dē-sel′ər-āt, v.t.* and *v.i.* to retard.— *ns.* **decelerā′tion; decel′erator.** [L. *dē,* down, *celer,* swift.]

December, *di-sem′bər, n.* formerly the tenth, now the twelfth month of the year.—*adj.* **Decem′berish, Decem′berly,** wintry, cold.—*n.* **Decem′brist,** one of those who took part in the Russian conspiracy of December, 1825. [L. *December*— *decem,* ten.]

decemvir, *di-sem′vər, n.* a member of a body of ten men: esp. of those who drew up the Laws of the Twelve Tables at Rome (451-0 B.C.):—*pl.* **decem′virs,** or **decem′virī** (L. *dekem-vi-rē*).— *adj.* **decem′viral.**—*n.* **decem′virate,** a body of ten men in office: the term of office of decemvirs. [L. *decem,* ten, and *vir,* a man.]

decennary, *di-sen′ər-i, n.* a period of ten years— also **decen′nium.**—*adj.* **decenn′ial,** consisting of, or happening every, ten years. [L. *decem,* ten, and *annus,* a year.]

decennoval, *di-sen′ō-vəl, adj.* pertaining to the number 19. [L. *decemnovalis*—*decem,* ten, *novem,* nine.]

decent, dē'sənt, adj. becoming: seemly: proper: modest: moderate: fairly good: passable: (coll.) showing tolerant or kindly moderation.—n. **dē'cency**, becomingness: modesty: (coll.) considerateness, sense of what may be fitly expected of one.—adv. **dē'cently**. [L. decēns, -entis, pr.p. of decēre, to be becoming.]

decentralise, dē-sen'trəl-īz, v.t. to withdraw from the centre: to transform by transferring functions from the central government to local centres.—n. **decentralisā'tion**.

deception, di-sep'shən, n. act of deceiving: state of being deceived: means of deceiving: error due to being deceived.—n. **deceptibil'ity**.—adjs. **decept'ible**, capable of being deceived; **decep'tious** (Shak.), deceitful; **decep'tive**, tending to deceive: misleading.—adv. **decep'tively**.—n. **decep'tiveness**.—adj. **decep'tory**, tending to deceive. [O.Fr.,—L.L. dēceptiō, -ōnis—dēcipĕre, to deceive.]

decerebrate, dē-ser'ə-brāt, v.t. to deprive of cerebrum.—n. **decerebrā'tion**. [L. pfx. dē-, and cerebrum.]

decern, di-sərn', v.t. and v.i. (Scots law) to judge: to decree: to pass judgment. [O.Fr. decerner—L. dēcernēre—dē, and cernĕre, to distinguish.]

decession, di-sesh'ən, n. departure. [See decease.]

dechristianise, dē-krist'yən-īz, v.t. to turn from Christianity.

deciare, des'i-är, n. the tenth part of an are. [Fr., —L. deci- (in decimus), and **are**.]

decibel, des'i-bel, n. the tenth part of a bel. [L. deci-, and **bel**.]

decide, di-sīd', v.t. to determine: to end: to settle: to resolve.—v.i. to make up one's mind.—adjs. **decid'able**, capable of being decided; **decid'ed**, determined: clear, unmistakable: resolute.—adv. **decid'edly**. [O.Fr. decider—L. dēcīdĕre—dē, away, caedĕre, to cut.]

deciduous, di-sid'ū-əs, adj. liable to be shed at a certain period: transitory, not permanent: (bot.) shedding all the leaves together (opp. to evergreen): shedding wings (as some insects).—n. **decid'ua**, a membrane of the uterus discharged after parturition.—adj. **decid'uate**.—n. **decid'uousness**. [L. dēciduus—dēcīdĕre, dē, from, cadĕre, to fall.]

decigram(me), des'i-gram, n. the tenth part of a gramme.

decilitre, des'i-lē-tər, n. a tenth part of a litre.

decillion, di-sil'yən, n. a million raised to the tenth power: in French and American notation, a thousand raised to the eleventh power.

decimal, des'i-məl, adj. numbered or proceeding by tens.—n. a decimal fraction.—v.t. **dec'imalise**, to reduce to the decimal system.—ns. **dec'imalism**, use or advocacy of a decimal system; **dec'imalist**.—adv. **dec'imally**.—**decimal fraction**, a fraction expressed by continuing ordinary decimal notation into negative powers of ten, a point being placed after the unit figure—the fraction being reduced to a vulgar fraction by taking the series of figures as numerator and for denominator a power of ten, allowing a zero for every figure; **decimal notation**, a system of writing numbers based on ten and powers of ten, our ordinary system; **decimal system**, a system in which each unit is ten times the next below it, esp. the metric system of weights and measures. [L. decima (pars), a tenth (part.).]

decimate, des'i-māt, v.t. to take the tenth part of: to punish by killing every tenth man: (loosely) to reduce very heavily.—ns. **decimā'tion**, **dec'imātor**. [L. decimāre, -ātum—decimus, tenth—decem, ten.]

décime, dā-sēm, n. a French coin equal to ¹⁄₁₀ franc. [Fr.,—L. decima (pars), a tenth (part.).]

decimetre, des'i-mē-tər, n. a tenth of a metre.

decinormal, des-i-nor'ml, adj. (chem.) of one-tenth of normal concentration. [L. decimus, tenth, and normal.]

decipher, di-sī'fər, v.t. to uncipher: to read or transliterate or interpret from secret, unknown, or difficult writing: to make out: (Shak.) to detect: (Shak.) to reveal: (obs.) to show forth.—adj. **deci'pherable**.—n. **deci'pherment**. [L. pfx. dē-, and **cipher**.]

decision, di-sizh'ən, n. the act of deciding: settlement: judgment: the quality of being decided in character.—adj. **decisive** (-sīs'iv), having the power of deciding: showing decision: final: positive.—adv. **deci'sively**.—n. **deci'siveness**. —adj. **deci'sory**, decisive. [See decide.]

decistere, des'i-stēr, n. one tenth of a stere.

decitizenise, dē-sit'i-zən-īz, v.t. to deprive of citizenship.

decivilise, dē-siv'i-līz, v.t. to reduce from a civilised to a more savage state.

deck, dek, v.t. to cover: to clothe: to adorn: to furnish with a deck: to pile up on a platform.—n. a covering: a horizontal platform extending from one side of a vessel to the other, thereby joining them together, and forming both a floor and a covering: a floor, platform, or tier as in a bus, bridge, etc.: (slang) the ground: a pile of things laid flat: (Shak. and U.S.) a pack of cards: the part of a pack used in a particular game, or the undealt part.—ns. **deck'-bridge**, a bridge whose upper stringer carries the roadway; **deck'-car'go**, cargo stowed on the deck of a vessel; **deck'-chair**, a chair such as passengers sprawl on deck in, whether a long chair with leg-rest or a camp-chair; **deck'er**, the person or thing that decks: a vessel, vehicle, or other structure that has a deck or decks (used only in composition, as three-decker): one who adorns; **deck'-game**, a game played on a ship's deck; **deck'-hand**, a person employed on deck: a common sailor; **deck'-house**, a house, room, or box on deck; **deck'ing**, adornment: a platform; **deck'-load**, a deck-cargo; **deck'-passage**, a passage securing only the right of being on deck, without cabin accommodation; **deck'-pass'enger**; **deck'-quoits**, quoits as played on a ship's deck, with rope rings; **deck'-tenn'is**, lawn-tennis modified for playing on board ship. [Du. dekken, to cover; cf. **thatch**; Ger. decken; L. tegĕre.]

deckle, dek'l, n. in paper-making a contrivance for fixing width of sheet: a deckle-edge.—adj. **deckled** (dek'ld), deckle-edged.—n. **deck'le-edge**, the raw or ragged edge of handmade paper or an imitation of it.—adj. **deck'le-edged**, having a rough uncut edge. [Ger. deckel, lid.]

declaim, di-klām', v.i. to make a set or rhetorical speech: to harangue: to recite.—v.i. to utter, repeat, or recite declamatorily.—ns. **declaim'ant**, **declaim'er**.—n. and adj. **declaim'ing**.—n. **declamation** (dek-lə-mā'shən), act of declaiming: a set speech in public: display in speaking.—adv. **declamatorily** (di-klam'ə-tə-ri-li).—adj. **declamatory**, of the nature of declamation: appealing to the passions: noisy and rhetorical. [L. dēclāmāre—dē-, intens., clāmāre, to cry out.]

declare, di-klār', v.t. to make known: to announce: to assert: to make a full statement of, as of goods at a custom-house: (bezique, etc.) to expose and claim a score for: (bridge) to announce as one's choice of trump-suit or no trumps.—v.i. to make a statement: to announce one's decision or sympathies: to show cards in order to score: (cricket) to end an innings voluntarily before ten wickets have fallen.—adj. **declar'able**, capable of being declared, exhibited, or proved.—ns. **declar'ant**, one who makes a declaration; **declaration** (dek-lə-rā'shən), act of declaring: that which is declared: a written affirmation: in the criminal law of Scotland, the statement made by the prisoner before the magistrate: in common law, the pleading in which the plaintiff in an action at law sets forth his case against the defendant.—adjs. **declarative** (di-klar'ə-tiv), **declar'atory**, explanatory.—advs. **declar'atively**, **declar'atorily**.—n. **declar'ator**, a form of action in the Court of Session, with the view of having a fact judicially ascertained and declared.—adj. **declāred'**, avowed.—n. **declār'er**, one who declares.—adv. **declā'redly**, avowedly.—**declaratory act**, an act intended to explain an obscure or disputed law; **declare off**, to renounce: to withdraw. [L. dēclārāre, -ātum—pfx. dē-, wholly, clārus, clear (partly through Fr. déclarer).]

declass, dē'kläs', v.t. to remove or degrade from

one's class.—*adj.* **déclassé,** *fem.* **déclassée** (*dā-klä-sā;* Fr.) having lost caste. [Fr. *déclasser.*]

declassify, *dē'klas'-i-fī, v.t.* to take off the security list. [Pfx. *de-,* and **classify.**]

declension, *di-klen'shən, n.* a falling off : decay : descent : (*gram.*) system of cases and case-endings : a class of words similarly declined : a statement in order of the cases of a word. [See **decline.**]

decline, *di-klīn', v.i.* to bend or turn away : to deviate : to refuse : to bend or slope down : to fail or decay : to stoop or condescend : to draw to an end.—*v.t.* to bend down : to turn away from : to refuse : to avoid : (*gram.*) to give the various cases of.—*n.* a falling off : deviation : decay : a gradual sinking of the bodily faculties, consumption : a down-slope.—*adjs.* **declin'able,** having inflection for case; **decli'nal,** bending downward; **declinant** (*dek'lin-ənt ; her.*), having the tail hanging down; **dec'linate** (*bot.*), curving downwards.— *ns.* **declinā'tion** (*U.S.*), act of declining : a sloping or binding downwards : deviation : (*astron.*) angular distance from the celestial equator; **dec'linātor,** an instrument determining declination.—*adj.* **declin'atory,** containing a declination or refusal.—*ns.* **declin'ature,** act of declining or refusing; (*law*) a plea declining the jurisdiction of a judge; **declinom'eter,** an instrument for measuring the **declination of the compass**—i.e. the deviation of the magnetic needle from the true north. [L. *dēclīnāre—dē,* down, away from, *clīnāre,* to bend (partly through Fr. *décliner*).]

declivity, *di-kliv'i-ti, n.* a place that declines, or slopes downward, opposite of *acclivity* : inclination downwards.—*adjs.* **decliv'itous, decli'vous.** [Fr., —L. *dēclīvitās, -ātis—dē,* downward, *clīvus,* sloping, akin to *clīnāre.*]

declutch, *dē-kluch', v.i.* to release the clutch.

decoct, *di-kokt', v.t.* to prepare by boiling : to extract the substance of by boiling : to boil : to devise.— *adjs.* **decoc'tible, decoc'tive.**—*ns.* **decoc'tion,** an extract of anything got by boiling; **decoc'ture,** a substance prepared by decoction. [L. *dēcoquěre, dēcoctum—dē,* down, *coquěre,* to cook.]

decode, *dē-kōd', v.t.* to translate from a code.

decoherer, *dē-kō-hē'rər, n.* a device for bringing a coherer back to its former condition after it has been affected by an electric wave.

decollate, *dē-kol'āt, v.t.* to behead.—*adj.* **decoll'ated,** rounded off, as the apex of a shell.—*n.* **decollā'tion,** the act of beheading : a picture of a decapitation, esp. of the head of St. John the Baptist on a charger : the festival of the Baptist, Aug. 29. [L. *dēcollāre—dē,* from, *collum,* the neck.]

décolleté, *dā-kol-tā', adj.* with neck uncovered : of dress, low cut. [Fr., p.a.p. of *décolleter,* to bare the neck and shoulders—*collet,* collar. Cf. **decollate.**]

decolour, *dē-kul'ər, v.t.* to deprive of colour—also **decol'o(u)rise.**—*n.* **decol'orant,** a substance that bleaches or removes colour.—*v.t.* **decol'orate,** to deprive of colour.—*adj.* without colour.—*ns.* **decolorā'tion,** removal or absence of colour; **decolo(u)rīsā'tion.** [L. *dēcolōrāre—dē,* from, *color,* colour.]

decomplex, *dē'kom-pleks, adj.* repeatedly compound.

decompose, *dē-kom-pōz', v.t.* to separate the component parts of : to resolve into elements.—*v i.* to decay, rot.—*adj.* **decompos'able.** [Fr. *dé-composer*—pfx. *dé-* (—L. *dis-,* apart), and *composer* ; see **compose.**]

decomposition, *di-kom-pə-zish'ən, n.* act or state of decomposing : decay.—*v.t.* **decompound** (*dē-kəm-pownd'*), to decompose.—*adj.* **decompound'able.** [Fr. pfx. *dé-* (L. *dis-*), apart, and **composition;** accidentally associated in meaning with **decompose.**]

decomposition, *dē-komp-ə-zish'ən, n.* the compounding of things already compound—*adj.* **decomp'osite,** (or *-oz'*) doubly or further compounded.—*v.t.* **decompound** (*-kəm-pownd'*), to compound again, or further.—*adj.* (*dē'*) compounded more than once : (*bot.*) having leaflets themselves composed of separate parts. [L. pfx. *dē-,* intens., and **composition, compound.**]

decompound. See **decomposition** (1) and (2).

decompress, *dē-kəm-pres', v.t.* to release from pressure.—*ns.* **decompression** (*-presh'ən*), **decompress'or.**

deconsecrate, *dē-kon'si-krāt, v.t.* to deprive of the character given by consecration : to secularise.— *n.* **deconsecrā'tion.**

decontaminate, *dē-kən-tam'in-āt, v.t.* to free from contamination.—*n.* **decontaminā'tion.**

decontrol, *dē-kən-trōl', v.t.* to remove (esp. official) control from.—*n.* removal of control.

décor, *dā-kor, n.* scenery and stage embellishments : disposition or setting or ornament. [Fr.]

decorate, *dek'ə-rāt, v.t.* to ornament, to beautify : to honour with a badge or medal.—*adj.* **dec'orated.**—*n.* **decorā'tion,** ornament : badge of an order.—*adj.* **dec'orative** (*-rə-tiv*) ornamental.—*ns.* **dec'orativeness** or **dec'orātor,** one who decorates, esp. houses.—**Decorated style** (*archit.*), a style of Gothic architecture, elaborated and richly decorated, which prevailed till near the end of the 14th century; **Decoration Day,** May 30th, when the memory of the soldiers who fell in the American Civil War of 1861-65 is honoured by the decoration of their graves and by speeches, processions, etc. [L. *decorāre, -ātum—decus,* what is becoming —*decēre,* to be becoming.]

decorous, *de'kə-rəs,* or *-kō', adj.* becoming : suitable : proper : decent.—*adv.* **decorously.**—*ns.* **decorousness;** **deco'rum,** (*arch.*) that which is in keeping, congruous : that which is becoming in outward appearance : propriety of conduct : decency. [L. *decōrus,* becoming.]

decorticate, *dē-kor'ti-kāt, v.t.* to deprive of the bark, husk, or peel.—*n.* **decorticā'tion.** [L. *dēcorticāre, -ātum—dē,* from, and *cortex,* bark.]

decoy, *di-koi', v.t.* to allure : to entrap : to lure into a trap—*n.* anything intended to allure into a snare : an apparatus of hoops and network for trapping wild-ducks—sometimes *duck-coy.*—*n.* **decoy'-duck,** a wild-duck tamed and trained to entice others into a trap : (*fig.*) one employed to allure others into a snare. [Perh. Du. *de,* the, or L. pfx. *dē-,* down, and Du. *kooi*—L. *cavea,* a cage.]

decrassify, *dē-kras'i-fī, v.t.* to make less crass.

decrease, *di-krēs', v.i.* to become less.—*v.t.* to make less.—*n.* (*dē'krēs*) a growing less : loss.— *adv.* **decreas'ingly.** [O.Fr. *decrois,* a decrease— L. *dēcrēscěre—dē,* from, *crēscěre,* to grow.]

decree, *di-krē', n.* an order by one in authority : an edict or law : a judicial decision : (*theol.*) a predetermined purpose.—*v.t.* to decide or determine by sentence in law : to appoint.—*v.i.* to make a decree (*pr.p.* **decree'ing** ; *pa.t.* and *pa.p.* **decreed'**).—*adj.* **decree'able,** capable of being decreed.—*n.* **decreet'** (*Scots law*), a court judgment.—*adj.* **decrē'tal,** pertaining to a decree.— *n.* a decree, esp. of the pope : a book containing decrees : specif. in *pl.* the second part of the canon law, the decrees of various popes determining points of ecclesiastical law.—*n.* **decrē'tist,** in mediaeval universities, a student of the decretals, a student of law.—*adjs.* **decrē'tive** ; **decrē'tory,** pertaining to a decree, judicial : having the force of a decree; **decree nisi** (*nī'sī;* L. *nisi,* unless), a decree that becomes absolute unless cause be shown to the contrary—granted esp. in divorce cases. [O.Fr. *decret* and L. *dēcrētālis*—L. *dēcrētum—dēcernēre,* to decide.]

decrement, *dek'ri-mənt, n.* the act or state of decreasing : the quantity lost by decrease. [L. *dēcrēmentum.*]

decrepit, *di-krep'it, adj.* worn out by the infirmities of old age : in the last stage of decay.—*ns.* **decrep'-itness ; decrep'itude,** state of being decrepit or worn out with age. [L. *dēcrepitus,* noiseless, very old—*dē,* from, *crepitus,* a noise.]

decrepitate, *di-krep'i-tāt, v.i.* to crackle, as salts when heated.—*v.t.* to roast so as to cause a continual crackling, to calcine.—*n.* **decrepitā'tion.** [L. *dē-,* intens., *crepitāre,* to rattle much, freq. of *crepāre.*]

decrescent, *di-kres'ənt, adj.* becoming gradually

fāte, fär, àsk ; mē, hər (her*)*; *mīne ; mōte ; mūte ; mōōn ; dhen* (then)

less.—*n.*, *adj.* and *adv.* (*mus.*) **decrescendo** (*dā-kre-shen'dō*; It.), diminuendo. [L. *dē*, *crēscĕre*.]
decretal. See **decree.**
decrew, *di-krōō'*, *v.i.* (*Spens.*) to decrease. [O.Fr. *decru*, pa.p. of *decroistre*. See **decrease.**]
decrown, *dē-krown'*, *v.t.* to discrown.
decrustation, *dē-krus-tā'shən*, *n.* removal of a crust.
decry, *di-krī'*, *v.t.* to cry down : to condemn : to censure as worthless : to blame (*pr.p.* **decry'ing**; *pa.t.* and *pa.p.* **decried'**).—*ns.* **decrī'al**; **decrī'er.** [Fr. *dé-*, *des-* (L. *dis-*), and *crier*, to cry; see **cry.**]
decuman, *dek'ū-mən*, *adj.* principal, large—of waves, etc. : connected with the principal gate of a Roman camp (near which the 10th cohort of the legion was stationed).—*n.* a great wave, as every tenth wave was supposed to be. [L. *decumānus—decem*, ten.]
decumbent, *di-kum'bənt*, *adj.* lying down : reclining on the ground : (*bot.*) lying flat with rising tip.—*ns.* **decubitus** (*-kūb'i-təs*; *med.*), posture in bed; **decum'bence, decum'bency,** the act or posture of lying down.—*adv.* **decum'bently.**—*n.* **decum'biture,** the time when a sick person takes to bed. [L. *dēcumbēns, -entis—dē*, down, and *-cumbĕre* (in compounds only), to lie.]
decuple, *dek'ū-pl*, *adj.* tenfold.—*n.* a number ten times repeated.—*v.t.* to make tenfold. [Fr. *décuple—*L. *decuplus.*]
decurion, *di-kū'ri-ən*, *n.* in a Roman army, an officer over ten soldiers : any overseer of ten : a councillor.—*ns.* **decū'ria, decury** (*dek'ū-ri*), a company of ten (or more); **decū'rionate.** [L.]
decurrent, *di-kur'ənt*, *adj.* running or extending downward : (*bot.*) continued down the stem.—*n.* **decurr'ency.**—*adv.* **decurr'ently.**—*n.* **decur'sion,** a running down : a military manoeuvre or parade.—*adj.* **decur'sive.**—*adv.* **decur'sively.** [L. *dēcurrēns, -entis—dē*, down, *currĕre*, *cursum*, to run.]
decussate, *di-kus'āt*, *v.i.* to cross in the form of an X : to cross, as lines, etc.—*adjs.* **decuss'ate, -d,** crossed : arranged in pairs which cross each other, like some leaves.—*adv.* **decuss'ately.**—*n.* **decussā'tion** (*dek-*). [L. *decussāre*, *-ātum—decussis*, a coin of ten asses (*decem asses*) marked with X, symbol of ten.]
dedal, dedalian. See **daedal.**
dedicate, *ded'i-kāt*, *v.t.* to set apart and consecrate to some sacred purpose : to devote wholly or chiefly : to inscribe to any one : (*U.S.*) to inaugurate or open.—*adj.* devoted : (*Shak.*) dedicated.—*ns.* **ded'icant,** one who dedicates; **dedicatee** (*ded'i-kā-tē'*), one to whom a thing is dedicated; **dedicā'tion,** the act of dedicating : an address to a patron, prefixed to a book; **ded'icātor.**—*adjs.* **dedicatorial** (*-kə-tō'ri-əl*), **ded'icatory** (*-kə-* or *-kā-*). [L. *dēdicāre, -ātum—dē*, down, *dīcāre*, to declare.]
dedimus, *ded'i-məs*, *n.* a writ commissioning one not a judge to act as a judge. [From the opening, *dedimus* (*potestātem*; L.), we have given (power)—*dāre*, to give.]
deduce, *di-dūs'*, *v.t.* to derive : to infer from what precedes or from premises.—*ns.* **deduce'ment,** what is deduced; **deducibil'ity,** the quality of being deducible.—*adj.* **deduc'ible,** that may be deduced or inferred.—*v.t.* **deduct** (*-dukt'*), to take away : to separate : to subtract : (*Spens.*) to reduce, weaken : (*obs.*) to deduce.—*adj.* **deduct'ible.**—*n.* **deduc'tion,** the act of deducing : that which is deduced : the drawing of a particular truth from a general, antecedently known, as distinguished from *induction*, rising from particular truths to a general : the act of deducting : that which is deducted : abatement.—*adj.* **deduct'ive,** concerned with deduction from premises or accepted principles.—*adv.* **deduct'ively.** [L. *dēdūcĕre, dēductum—dē*, from *dūcĕre*, to lead.]
dee, *dē*, *v.i.* Scots. for **die.**
dee, *dē*, *n.* name of the fourth letter of the alphabet : anything shaped like it.—*n.*, *v.t.*, *interj.* a substitute for **damn.** [See **D.**]
deed, *dēd*, *n.* something done : an act : an exploit : a legal transaction : the written evidence of it.—*adj.* **deed'ful** (*Tenn.*), marked by deeds or exploits.

—*adv.* **deed'ily.**—*adjs.* **deed'less** (*Shak.*), not having performed deeds.—*n.* **deed'pōll,** a deed executed by one party, originally having the edge polled or cut even, not indented.—*adj.* **deed'y,** industrious, active.—**deed of saying** (*Shak.*), performance of what has been said or promised; **in deed,** in reality. [O.E. *dǣd—dón*, to do; Ger. *tat.*]
deed, *dēd*, a Scottish form of **indeed**; also for **died, dead.**
deem, *dēm*, *v.t.* or *v.i.* to judge : to think : to believe (*pa.t.* and *pa.p.* **deemed,** Spens. **dempt**).—*n.* (*Shak.*) opinion.—*ns.* **deem'ster,** a judge—now only in the Isle of Man; **dempster** (*dem'stər*), (*obs.*) a judge : formerly in Scotland an officer who repeated the sentence after the judge (also **doom'-ster**). [O.E. *dēman*, to form a judgment—*dóm*, judgment; see **doom.**]
deen, *dēn*, (*Spens.*) for **din.**
deep, *dēp*, *adj.* extending or placed far down or far from the outside : far recessed : far involved : engrossed : difficult to understand : secret : wise and penetrating : profoundly versed : cunning : very still : profound : intense : excessive : heart-felt : sunk low : low in pitch : (of a road) encumbered with mud, sand, or ruts : (*cricket*) in the out-field, not close to the wickets.—*adv.* in a deep manner.—*n.* that which is deep : the sea : a deep place : the middle, deepest, or most intense part : anything profound or incomprehensible.—*adjs.* **deep'-browed,** of high intellectual powers; **deep'-draw'ing** (of ships), requiring considerable depth to float in; **deep'-drawn; deep'-dyed,** thoroughgoing, extreme—in a bad sense.—*v.t.* **deep'en,** to make deeper in any sense : to increase.—*v.i.* to become deeper.—*adjs.* **deep'felt; deep'-fet,** (*Shak.*) fetched from a depth; **deep'-laid.**—*adv.* **deep'ly.**—*adjs.* **deep'most,** deepest; **deep'-mouthed,** with deep voice.—*n.* **deep'ness.**—*adjs.* **deep'-read,** profoundly versed; **deep'-sea,** pertaining to the deeper parts of the sea; **deep'-seat'ed,** not superficial; **deep'-sink'er** (*Austr.*), a drinking vessel of the largest size; **deep'-toned,** having a deep tone.—**deep field,** fielding position deep behind the bowler; **go in off the deep end,** to express strong feelings with abandonment; **in deep water,** in difficulties; **two deep, three deep,** etc., in two, three, etc., layers or rows. [O.E. *déop*; Ger. *tief*; cf. **dip, dive.**]
deer, *dēr*, *n.* (*obs.*) any kind of animal (as in *small deer*) : any animal of the Cervidae, a family of even-toed ungulates characterised by the possession of antlers by the males at least—including stag, reindeer, etc. :—*pl.* **deer.**—*ns.* **deer'berry,** the huckleberry (Gaylussacia) : the fruit of Gaultheria : that of *Vaccinium stamineum*, an inedible American whortleberry (Gaylussacia) : a very high fence that deer cannot jump over; **deer'-forest,** wild tract (not necessarily woodland) reserved for deer; **deer'-hair,** a small species of club-rush; **deer'(-)horn,** a deer's antler or its material : (*U.S.*) a fresh-water mussel; **deer'-hound,** a large roughcoated greyhound; **deer'let,** a chevrotain; **deer'-lick,** a spot of salt ground whither deer come to lick the earth; **deer'-mouse,** the American deerfooted mouse—so called from its agility; **deer'-neck,** a thin, ill-shaped neck—of horses; **deer'-park; deer'-skin,** skin of the deer, or leather therefrom; **deer'-stalker,** one who stalks deer : a sportsman's helmet-shaped cap; **deer'-stalking.** [O.E. *déor*; Ger. *tier*, Du. *dier*; O.N. *dýr.*]
deev, *dēv.* Same as **div.**
deface, *di-fās'*, *v.t.* to destroy or mar the face or external appearance of, to disfigure : to obliterate : (*Spens.*) to put out of countenance : (*Spens.*) to defame.—*n.* **deface'ment,** act of defacing : injury to form or appearance : that which defaces.—*adv.* **defā'cingly.** [O.Fr. *desfacer*—L. *dis-*, away, *faciēs*, face.]
defaecate. Same as **defecate.**
defalcate, *dē'* or *de'fal-kāt*, or *di-fa(w)l'kāt*, *v..* (*obs.*) to deduct a part of.—*v.i.* to embezzle money held on trust.—*ns.* **defalcā'tion,** a diminution : a misappropriation of funds entrusted to one; **def'alcātor,** a defaulter. [L.L. *dēfalcāre. -ātum*,

to cut away—L. *dē*, from *falcāre*, to cut—*falx, falcis*, a sickle.]

defame, di-fām', *v.t.* to take away or destroy the good fame or reputation of : to speak evil of : to charge falsely.—*n.* (*Spens.*) infamy.—*n.* **defamation** (*def-ə-mā'shən*), the act of defaming : calumny : slander.—*adv.* **defamatorily** (*di-fam'ə-tər-i-li*).—*adj.* **defăm'atory**, containing defamation : injurious to reputation : caluminous.—*n.* and *adj.* **defā'ming**. [O.Fr. *diffamer*—L. *diffāmāre*—*dis-*, away, *fāma*, report.]

defast(e), Spenserian spellings of **defaced** (*pa.p.*).

default, di-fawlt', *n.* a fault, failing, or failure : defect : neglect to do what duty or law requires : failure to account for money entrusted to one's charge : offence.—*v.i.* to fail through neglect of duty : to fail to appear in court when called upon.—*n.* **default'er**, one who fails to appear in court, or to account for money entrusted to his care, or to settle a debt of honour : a military offender.—**judgment by default**, judgment given against a person because he fails to plead or make an appearance in court. [O.Fr. *defaute* (noun) and *default* (3rd sing. of *defaillir*)—L. pfx. *dē-* and *fallĕre*; see **fault**.]

defeasance, di-fēz'əns, *n.* (*obs.*) undoing : defeat : (*law*) a rendering null or void : a condition whose fulfilment renders a deed void.—*adjs.* **defeas'anced**, liable to be forfeited; **defeas'ible**, that may be annulled.—*ns.* **defeasibil'ity**, **defeas'ibleness**.—**deed of defeasance** (*Eng. law*), an instrument which defeats the operation of some other deed or estate. [O.Fr. *defesance*—*desfaire*; see **defeat**.]

defeat, di-fēt', *v.t.* (*Shak.*) to undo : (*Shak.*) to frustrate : (*Shak.*) to disfigure : to ruin : to win a victory over.—*n.* a frustration of plans : ruin : overthrow, as of an army in battle : loss of a game, race, etc.—*ns.* **defeat'ism**, disposition to accept, welcome, help to bring on, defeat; **defeat'ist**.—Also *adj.*—*n.* **defeat'ure**, (*Spens.*) undoing : defeat : (*Shak.*) disfigurement : disguise. [O.Fr. *defait*—*desfaire*, to undo—L. *dis-*, neg., *facĕre*, to do.]

defecate, def'i-kāt, *v.t.* to clear from dregs or impurities : to purify from extraneous matter.—*v.i.* to void excrement.—*n.* **defecā'tion**. [L. *dēfaecāre, -ātum*, to cleanse—*dē*, from, *faex, faecis*, dregs.]

defect, di-fekt', *n.* a deficiency : a want : imperfection : blemish : fault.—*n.* **defectibil'ity**.—*adj.* **defect'ible**, liable to imperfection : deficient.—*ns.* **defec'tion**, a failure, a falling away from duty : revolt; **defec'tionist**.—*adj.* **defect'ive**, having defect : wanting in some necessary quality : imperfect : faulty : insufficient : (*gram.*) incomplete in inflexions or forms.—*n.* a person deficient in physical or mental powers.—*adv.* **defect'ively**.—*n.* **defect'iveness**.—**the defects of one's qualities**, virtues carried to excess, the faults apt to accompany or flow from good qualities. [L. *dēficĕre, dēfectum*, to fail—*dē*, down, and *facĕre*, to de.]

defence, di-fens', *n.* a defending : protection : vindication : (*law*) a defendant's plea.—*adj.* **defenced'**, fortified.—*adj.* **defence'less**.—*adv.* **defence'lessly**.—*n.* **defence'lessness**.—*v.t.* defend (di-fend'), to keep off anything hurtful from : to guard or protect : to maintain against attack : (*obs.*) to prohibit, forbid : to ward off : (*law*) to resist, as a claim : to contest.—*adj.* **defend'able**, that may be defended.—*n.* **defend'ant**, a defender : (*law*) a person accused or sued.—*adj.* **defend'ed**, guarded : protected : maintained against attack : (*Milt.*) forbidden.—*ns.* **defend'er**, one who defends : the holder of a championship, etc., who seeks to maintain his title : (*obs.*) one who accepts a challenge : (*Scots law*) a person sued or accused; **defen'sative**, a protection; **defense'** (*U.S.*), defence; **defensibil'ity**.—*adj.* **defens'ible**, that may be defended.—*adv.* **defens'ibly**.—*adj.* **defens'ive**, serving to defend : in a state or posture of defence.—*n.* that which defends : posture of defence.—*adv.* **defens'ively**.—**defender of the faith**, a title borne by the sovereigns of England since Henry VIII, on whom it was conferred in 1521 for his book against Luther; **stand on the**

defensive, to be in the attitude of self-defence. [L. *dēfendĕre, dēfēnsum*, to ward off—*dē*, off, and *fendĕre*, to strike (found in compounds).]

defenestration, dē-fen-is-trā'shən, *n.* a flinging out of window. [L. *dē*, from, *fenestra*, window.]

defer, di-fər', *v.t.* to put off to another time : to delay (*pr.p.* deferr'ing; *pa.t.* and *pa.p.* deferred').—*ns.* **defer'ment**; **deferr'er**, a procrastinator.—**deferred annuity** (see **annuity**); **deferred pay**, an allowance paid to soldiers on their discharge, or to their relations on their death : a government servant's pension; **deferred shares**, shares not entitling the holder to a full share of profits, and sometimes to none at all, until the expiration of a specified time or the occurrence of some event. [L. *differre*—*dis-*, asunder, *ferre*, to bear, carry; cf. **differ**.]

defer, di-fər', *v.i.* to yield (to the wishes or opinions of another, or to authority).—*v.t.* to submit to or lay before somebody (*pr.p.* deferr'ing; *pa.t.* and *pa.p.* deferred').—*n.* **deference** (*def'ər-əns*), a deferring or yielding in judgment or opinion : respectful compliance : submission.—*adj.* **def'erent**, bearing away, carrying off : deferential.—*n.* a deferent duct (as opposed to an *afferent* one) in the body.—*adj.* **deferential** (*-en'shl*), showing deference.—*adv.* **deferen'tially**. [L. *dēferre*—*dē*, down, and *ferre*, to bear.]

defervescence, dē-fər-ves'əns, *n.* abatement of heat : coolness : decrease of feverish symptoms.—Also **defervesc'ency**. [L. *dēfervēscĕre*, to cease boiling—*dē*, down, and *fervēscĕre*, from *fervēre*, to boil.]

defeudalise, dē-fū'dəl-īz, *v.t.* to deprive of feudal character.

deffly (*Spens.*). For **deftly**.

defiance, di-fī'əns, *n.* the act of defying : a challenge to combat : aggressiveness : contempt of opposition.—*adj.* **defi'ant**, full of defiance, insolently bold.—*adv.* **defi'antly**.—*n.* **defi'antness**.—**bid defiance to**, to defy. [defy.]

defibrinate, dē-fī'bri-nāt, *v.t.* to deprive of fibrin—also **defi'brinise**.—*n.* **defibrinā'tion**.

deficient, di-fish'ənt, *adj.* wanting.—*n.* a defective.—*n.* **defic'iency** (sometimes **defic'ience**), defect.—*adv.* **defic'iently**.—*ns.* **defic'ientness**; **deficit** (*def'i-sit*; L., *dā'fi-kit*, is wanting), deficiency, esp. of revenue, as compared with expenditure; **deficiency disease**, a disease due to lack of necessary substances (as vitamins) in dietary, such as rickets, scurvy, beri-beri, pellagra. [L. *dēficĕre*; see **defect**.]

defied, defier, etc. See **defy**.

defile, di-fīl', *v.i.* to march off in file or line, or file by file.—*n.* (*dē'fīl, di-fīl'*) a long narrow pass or way, in which troops can march only in file, or with a narrow front : a gorge.—*v.t.* **defilade** (*def-i-lād'*), to plan a fortification so as to protect it from enfilading fire.—*n.* **defile'ment**. [Fr. *défiler*—L. *dis-*, and *filum*, a thread.]

defile, di-fīl', *v.t.* to befoul : to pollute or corrupt : to violate.—*ns.* **defile'ment**, act of defiling : foulness; **defil'er**. [L. *dē*, and O.E. *fȳlan*—*fūl*, foul; confused with O.Fr. *defouler*, to trample, violate.]

defiliation, dē-fil-i-ā'shən, *n.* depriving a parent of his child. [L. *dē*, from, and *filius*, a son.]

define, di-fīn', *v.t.* (*obs.*) to bring to an end : to decide : to fix the bounds or limits of : to determine with precision : to describe accurately : to fix the meaning of.—*adj.* **defin'able**.—*adv.* **defin'ably**.—*n.* **define'ment** (*Shak.*), description.—*adj.* **definite** (*def'i-nit*), defined : having distinct limits : fixed : exact : clear : (*bot.*) sympodial or cymose.—*adv.* **def'initely**, in a definite manner : determinately : (*coll.*) yes indeed.—*ns.* **def'initeness**; **defini'tion**, a defining : a description of a thing by its properties : an explanation of the exact meaning of a word, term, or phrase : sharpness of outline.—*adj.* **definitive** (*di-fin'ə-tiv*), defining or limiting : positive : final.—*n.* (*gram.*) an adjective used to limit the extent of signification of a noun.—*adv.* **defin'itively**.—*ns.* **defin'itiveness**; **defin'itude**, definitiveness. [L. *dēfīnīre, -ītum*, to set bounds to—*dē, fīnis*, a limit.]

fāte, fär, ásk; mē, hər (her); *mīne; mōte; mūte; mōōn; dhen* (then)

deflagrate, *def'lə-grāt, v.i.* or *v.t.* to burn suddenly, generally with flame and crackling noise.—*ns.* **deflagrabil'ity; def'lagrating-spoon'**, a cup with long vertical shank for handling chemicals likely to deflagrate; **deflagrā'tion; def'lagrātor**, apparatus for deflagration. [L. *dēflagrāre—dē*, down, *flagrāre*, to burn.]

deflate, *dē-flāt', v.t.* to reduce from a state of inflation.—*v.i.* to become deflated.—*n.* **deflā'tion**, the act or process of deflating: the state of being deflated: removal of loose material by the wind.—*adj.* **deflā'tionary**.—*n.* **deflā'tionist**, one who favours deflation of currency.—Also *adj.* [L. *dē*, from, *flāre*, to blow.]

deflect, *di-flekt', v.i.* or *v.t.* to turn aside: to swerve or deviate from a right line or proper course.—*adj.* **deflect'ed** (*bot.*), bent abruptly downward.—*ns.* **deflec'tion, deflex'ion** (L. *dēflexiō*), bending: turning: deviation.—*adjs.* **deflec'tional, deflex'ional; deflec'tive**, causing deflection.—*n.* **deflec'tor**, a device for deflecting a flame, electric arc, etc.—*v.t.* **deflex'** (*zool., bot.*), to bend down.—*adj.* **deflexed'**.—*n.* **deflex'ure**, deviation. [L. *dē*, from, down, and *flectĕre, flexum*, to bend, turn.]

deflorate, *dē-flō'rāt, adj.* past flowering: of an anther, having shed its pollen.—*v.t.* to deflower.—*n.* **deflorā'tion**, the act of deflowering. [L. *dēflōrāre*; see next.]

deflower, *di-flowr', v.t.* to deprive of flowers: to deprive of grace and beauty, or of virginity: to ravish.—*n.* **deflower'er**. [O.Fr. *desflorer*—L.L. *dēflōrāre*, to strip flowers off—L. *dē*, from, *flōs flōris*, a flower.]

defluent, *def'loo-ənt, adj.* running down, decurrent.—*n.* **defluxion** (*di-fluk'shən: obs.*), a downflow: a disease supposedly due to a flow of humour: a discharge of fluid in the body. [L. *dēfluĕre—dē*, down, *fluĕre, fluxum*, to flow.]

defoliate, *di-fō'li-āt, v.t.* to deprive of leaves.—*adjs.* **defō'liate, -d**.—*ns.* **defoliā'tion**, the falling off of leaves: the time of shedding leaves; **defō'liātor**. [L.L. *dēfoliāre, -ātum—dē*, off, *folium*, a leaf.]

deforce, *di-fōrs', v.t.* (*law*) to keep out of possession by force: (*Scots law*) to resist (an officer of the law in the execution of his duty).—*ns.* **deforce'ment; deforc'iant**, one who deforces: **deforciā'tion**, a legal distress. [A.Fr. *deforcer—de-* (L. *dis-*); see **force**.]

deforest, *dē-for'ist, v.t.* to disforest: to deprive of forests.—*n.* **deforestā'tion**.

deform, *di-form', v.t.* to alter or injure the form of: to disfigure: to change the shape of without breach of continuity.—*adj.* (*Milt.*, etc.) hideous, unshapely.—*n.* **dēformā'tion**.—*adj.* **deformed'**, misshapen.—*adv.* **deform'edly**.—*ns.* **deformed'ness; deform'er; deform'ity**, state of being deformed: want of proper form: ugliness: disfigurement: anything that destroys beauty: an ugly feature or characteristic. [L. *dēformis*, ugly—*dē*, from, *fōrma*, beauty.]

defoul, *di-fowl', v.t.* to befoul, defile. [O.E. *fúl*, foul, with *de-* from confusion with O.Fr. *defouler*, to trample; cf. **defile**.]

defraud, *di-frawd', v.t.* to deprive by fraud: to cheat or deceive.—*ns.* **defraudā'tion, defraud'ment**. [L. *dēfraudāre—dē*, from, *fraus, fraudis*, fraud.]

defray, *di-frā', v.t.* to pay: (*Spens.*) to satisfy, appease (*pr.p.* **defray'ing**; *pa.t.* and *pa.p.* **defrayed'**).—*ns.* **defray'al, defray'ment**. [O.Fr. *desfrayer—de-*=L. *dis-*, and *frais*, expenses.]

deft, *deft, adj.* handy, clever.—*adv.* **deft'ly**.—*n.* **deft'ness**. [M.E. *deft, dafte*, simple, meek; O.E. *gedæfte*, meek—*dæftan, gedæftan*, prepare, make fit; the stem appears in *gedafen*, fit.]

defunct, *di-fungkt', adj.* having finished the course of life, dead.—*n.* a dead person.—*n.* **defunc'tion** (*Shak.*), death.—*adj.* **defunc'tive** (*Shak.*), pertaining to the dead. [L. *dēfungī, dēfunctus*, to finish—*dē, fungī*, to perform.]

defuse, *di-fūz', v.t.* (*Shak.*) to disorder.—*adj.* **defus'd'** (*Shak.*). [For **diffuse**.]

defy, *di-fī', v.t.* to challenge: to brave: (*obs.*) to

discard, dislike (*pr.p.* **defy'ing**; *pa.t.* and *pa.p.* **defied'**; *3rd pers. pres. ind.* **defies'**).—*n.* (*Dryden*) a defiance.—*n.* **defi'er**. [O.Fr. *defier*—L.L. *diffīdāre*, to renounce faith or allegiance—L. *dis-*, asunder, and *fīdēre*, to trust—*fīdēs*, faith.]

dégagé, *dā-gä-zhā, adj.* unembarrassed, unconstrained, easy. [Pa.p. of Fr. *dégager*, to disentangle.]

degarnish. See **disgarnish**.

degauss, *dē-gows', v.t.* to protect against magnetic mines by equipment for neutralising the earth's magnetic field. [Pfx. *de-*, **gauss**.]

degenerate, *di-jen'ər-it, adj.* having departed from the high qualities of race or kind: become base.—*n.* one who is degenerate.—*v.i.* (*-āt*) to fall from a nobler state: to be or to grow worse.—*v.t.* (*Milton*) to cause to degenerate.—*v.i.* **degen'der** (*Spens.*), to degenerate.—*ns.* **degen'eracy, degenerā'tion**, the act or process of becoming degenerate: the state of being degenerate.—*adv.* **degen'erately**.—*n.* **degen'erateness**.—*adj.* **degen'erating**.—*n.* **degenerā'tionist**, one who believes that the tendency of man is not to improve, but to degenerate.—*adj.* **degen'erative**, tending or causing to degenerate.—*adj.* **degen'erous** (*obs.*). [L. *dēgenerāre, -ātum*, to depart from its kind—*dē*, from, down, *genus, generis*, kind.]

deglutinate, *di-glōō'tin-āt, v.t.* to separate from a being glued. [L. *dēglūtināre, -ātum—dē*, from, and *glūtināre—glūten*, glue.]

deglutition, *dē-glōō-tish'ən, n.* the act or power of swallowing.—*adjs.* **deglu'titive, deglu'titory**. [L. *dē*, down, and *glūtīre*, to swallow; see **glut**.]

degrade, *di-grād', v.t.* to lower in grade or rank: to deprive of office or dignity: to lower in character, value, or position, or in complexity: to disgrace: (*geol.*) to wear down.—*n.* **degradation** (*deg-rə-dā'shən*), degrading: disgrace: degeneration: abortive structural development: a lowering in dignity.—*adjs.* **degrād'ed**, reduced in rank: base: low: (*her.*) placed on steps; **degrād'ing**, debasing: disgraceful. [O.Fr. *degrader*—L. *dē*, down, and *gradus*, a step. See **grade**.]

degras, *deg'räs, n.* a fat got from sheepskins. [Fr. *dégras—dégraisser*, to degrease.]

degrease, *dē-grēs', v.t.* to deprive of grease, to cleanse from grease.

degree, *di-grē', n.* a grade or step: a gradation on a scale, or that which it measures: a unit of temperature: one of a series of advances or steps: relative position: rank: extent: a mark of distinction conferred by universities, whether earned by examination or granted as a mark of honour: the 360th part of a revolution: 60 geographical miles: nearness of relationship: comparative amount of criminality: one of the three stages (*positive, comparative, superlative*) in the comparison of an adjective or adverb: (*alg.*) the highest sum of exponents in any term: the number of points in which a curve may be met by a straight line.—**by degrees**, by little and little, gradually; **forbidden degrees**, the degrees of consanguinity within which marriage is not allowed; **Songs of degrees**, or *Songs of ascents*, Psalms cxx.-cxxxiv., either because sung by the Jews returning from captivity, or by the Jews coming up annually to attend the feasts at Jerusalem; **third degree**, an American police method of extracting a confession by bullying or torture; **to a degree**, to a great degree, to an extreme. [Fr. *degré*—L. *dē*, down, *gradus*, a step.]

degum, *dē-gum', v.t.* to free from gum.

degust, *dē-gust', v.t.* to taste, to relish.—*v.i.* to have a relishing taste.—*v.t.* **degust'āte**, to degust.—*n.* **degustā'tion**, the act of tasting.—*adj.* **degust'atory**. [L. *dē*, down, and *gustāre*, to taste.]

dehisce, *di-his', v.i.* to gape, to open, as plants.—*n.* **dehisc'ence**.—*adj.* **dehisc'ent**. [L. *dēhiscēns*, *pr.p.* of *dēhiscĕre—dē*, intens., and *hīscĕre*, inceptive of *hiāre*, to gape.]

dehorn, *dē-horn', v.t.* to dishorn.

dehort, *di-hort', v.t.* to dissuade.—*n.* **dehortā'tion** (*dē-*), dissuasion.—*adjs.* **dehor'tative, dehor'tat-**

ory, dissuasive.—*n.* **dehort'er.** [L. *dĕhortārī*—*dē,* off, *hortārī,* to exhort.]

dehumanise, *dē-hū'man-īz, v.t.* to deprive of specifically human qualities. [L. *dē,* from, down, and **humanise.**]

dehydrate, *dē-hī'drāt, v.t.* to deprive of water, chemically: to dry.—*v.i.* to lose water.—*n.* **dēhydrā'tion.** [L. *dē,* from, Gr. *hydōr,* water.]

de-ice, *dē'-īs', v.t.* to dislodge ice from (aircraft surfaces), or to treat them so as to prevent its formation.—*n.* **dē'-īc'er,** any means of doing this, whether a fluid, a paste, or a mechanical or pneumatic device. [Pfx. *de-,* and **ice.**]

deicide, *dē'i-sīd, n.* the killing or killer of a god. [L. *deus,* a god, and *caedĕre,* to kill.]

deictic, *dīk'tik, adj.* proving directly.—*adv.* **deic'tically.** [Gr. *deiktikos*—*deiknynai,* to show.]

deid, *dēd,* Scots form of **dead, death.**—*n.* **deid'-thraw,** death-throe.

deify, *dē'i-fī, v.t.* to exalt to the rank of a god: to worship as a deity: to make god-like (*pr.p.* **dē'ifying;** *pa.t.* and *pa.p.* **dē'ified).**—*adjs.* **deif'ic, -al,** making god-like or devine.—*n.* **dēificā'tion,** the act of deifying: a deified embodiment. [Fr. *déifier*—L. *deificāre*—*deus,* a god, and *facĕre,* to make.]

deign, *dān, v.i.* to condescend.—*v.t.* to condescend to give or (*Shak.*) take. [Fr. *daigner*—L. *dīgnārī,* to think worthy—*dīgnus,* worthy.]

deil, *dēl,* Scots form of **devil.**

Deinoceras, Deinornis, deinosaur, Deinotherium. See **Dinoceras,** etc.

deiparous, *dē-ip'a-ras, adj.* bearing a god—used of the Virgin. [L. *deus,* a god, *parĕre,* to bring forth.]

deipnosophist, *dīp-nos'a-fist, n.* one who converses learnedly at dinner, a table-philosopher—from Athenaeus's work, *Deipnosophistai* (end of 2nd century). [Gr. *deipnon,* dinner, *sophos,* wise.]

deis(h)eal. Same as **deasil.**

deist, *dē'ist, n.* one who believes in the existence of God, but not in a revealed religion.—*n.* **de'ism.** —*adjs.* **deist'ic, -al.**—*adv.* **deist'ically.** [L. *deus,* a god.]

deity, *dē'i-ti, n.* godhood: divinity: godhead: a god or goddess: the Supreme Being. [Fr., *déité*—L.L. *deitās*—L. *deus,* god; Sans. *deva*—*div,* to shine.]

deject, *di-jekt', v.t.* to cast down the countenance or spirits of.—*adj.* (*Shak.*) cast down.—*adj.* **de-ject'ed,** cast down: dispirited.—*adv.* **deject'edly.** —*ns.* **deject'edness; deject'ion,** lowness of spirits: (in *pl.*) faecal discharge (also **dejec'ta).**—*adj.* **dejec'tory,** promoting evacuations. [L. *dĕjicĕre, -jectum*—*dē,* down, *jacĕre,* to cast.]

dejeune, *di-jōōn', n.* (*arch.*) a breakfast or luncheon. [See **disjune,** and **Foreign Words.**]

Dekabrist, *dek'a-brist, n.* **Decembrist.** [Russ. *Dekabri,* December.]

dekko, *dek'ō, n.* (*army slang*) look.—*v.i.* to look. [Hind. *dekho,* imp. of *dekhnā,* to see.]

delaine, *di-lān', n.* an untwilled light dress material, originally of wool. [Fr. *mousseline de laine,* wool muslin.]

delaminate, *di-lam'i-nāt, v.i.* to split into layers.— *n.* **delaminā'tion.** [L. *dēlamināre*—*dē, lāmina,* a layer.]

delapse, *di-laps', v.i.* (*obs.*) to sink down.—*n.* **delap'sion.** [L. *dē,* down, *lābī, lapsus,* to slip.]

delate, *di-lāt', v.t.* to pass on: to publish: to charge with a crime.—*ns.* **delā'tion; delāt'or.** [L. *dēlātum,* used as supine of *dēferre,* to bring a report against, to inform—*dē-,* inten., *ferre, lātum,* to bear.]

delate (*Shak.*), for **dilate.**

delay, *di-lā', v.t.* to put off to another time: to defer: to hinder or retard.—*v.i.* to pause, linger, or put off time (*pr.p.* **delay'ing;** *pa.p.* **delayed).**— *n.* a putting off or deferring: a lingering: hindrance. —*n.* **delay'er.**—*adv.* **delay'ingly.** [O.Fr. *delaier.*]

delay, *di-lā', v.t.* (*Spens.*) to temper, dilute, weaken. [Fr. *delayer,* to dilute—L. *dēliquāre,* to clarify or dis-, *ligāre,* to bind.]

del credere, *del crād'a-ri, adj.* applied to an agent who becomes surety for the solvency of persons to

whom he sells. [It. *del,* of the, *credere,* to believe, trust.]

dele, *dē'le, v.t.* delete, efface, a direction in proof-reading to remove a superfluous letter or word, usu. marked thus, δ.—*adj.* **deleble, delible** (*del'*), that can be deleted.—*n.pl.* **delen'da,** things to be deleted. [L. *dēlē,* imper. of *dēlēre,* to delete; or for *dēleātur,* subj. pass.; *dēlenda,* neut. pl. of gerundive.]

delectable, *di-lekt'a-bl,* (*Spens., Shak., del'*), *adj.* delightful: pleasing.—*n.* **delect'ableness.**—*adv.* **delect'ably.**—*n.* **delectā'tion** (*dē-*), delight. [Fr., —L. *dēlectābilis*—*dēlectāre,* to delight.]

delegate, *del'i-gāt, v.t.* to send as a legate or representative: to entrust or commit.—*n.* one who is delegated: a deputy or representative: (*U.S.*) a a person elected to represent a Territory in Congress, as distinguished from the representatives of the States.—*adj.* **delegated, deputed.**—*ns.* **del'egacy,** act or system of delegating: a delegate's appointment or authority: a body of delegates; **delegā'tion,** a delegating: (*U.S.*) a deputation: a body of delegates: (*hist.*) a body of delegates that was appointed every ten years by each of the two portions of the Dual Monarchy to negotiate a treaty between the Austrian Empire and the Kingdom of Hungary. [L. *dē,* away, and *lēgāre, -ātum,* to send as ambassador.]

delete, *di-lēt', v.t.* to blot out: to erase: to destroy. —*n.* **delē'tion.**—*adjs.* **delē'tive, delē'tory.** [L. *dēlēre, dēlētum,* to blot out.]

deleterious, *del-i-tē'ri-as, adj.* hurtful or destructive: poisonous.—*adv.* **deletē'riously.**—*n.* **deletē'riousness.** [Gr. *dēlētērios,* hurtful—*dēleesthai,* to hurt.]

delf, delft, *delf(t), n.* (in full **Delft'ware**), a kind of earthenware originally made at *Delft,* Holland.

delf, delph, *delf, n.* a drain, ditch, excavation: (*her.*) a charge representing a square sod:—*pl.* **delfs, delphs, delves.** [O.E. *delf; delfan,* to dig.]

Delian, *dē'li-an, adj.* pertaining to *Dēlos* in the Aegean Sea, birthplace of Apollo and Artemis.

delibate, *del'i-bāt, v.t.* (*obs.*) to sip.—*n.* **delibā'tion.** [L. *dēlibāre*—*dē,* from, *lībāre,* to take, taste.]

deliberate, *di-lib'ar-āt, v.t.* to weigh well in one's mind.—*v.i.* to consider the reasons for and against anything: to reflect: to consider: to take counsel: to debate.—*adj.* (*-it*) well considered: not impulsive: intentional: considering carefully: slow in determining: cautious.—*adv.* **delib'erately,** in a deliberate manner: (loosely) quietly, without fuss or haste.—*ns.* **delib'erateness; deliberā'tion,** the act of deliberating: mature reflection: calmness: coolness.—*adj.* **delib'erative,** proceeding or acting by deliberation.—*adv.* **delib'eratively.** [L. *dēlīberāre, -ātum*—*dē-,* inten., and *lībrāre,* to weigh—*lībra,* a balance.]

delicate, *del'i-kit, adj.* pleasing to the senses, esp. the taste: dainty: nicely discriminating or perceptive: fastidious: of a fine, slight texture or constitution: tender: frail, not robust: requiring nice handling: refined in manners: not immodest: gentle, polite: luxurious.—*n.* a luxurious or fastidious person: a luxury: a delicacy.—*n.* **del'icacy** (*-ka-si*), state or quality of being delicate: refinement: nicety: tenderness, weakness: luxuriousness: anything delicate or dainty, esp. to eat.—*adv.* **del'icately.**—*n.* **del'icateness.**— *n.pl.* **delicātess'en** (Ger. pl. of Fr. *délicatesse*), table delicacies. [L. *dēlicātus,* prob. conn. with *dēliciae,* allurements, luxury—*dēlicēre*—*dē-,* inten., *lacēre,* to entice.]

delicious, *di-lish'as, adj.* highly pleasing to the senses: affording exquisite pleasure.—*n.* **delice** (*di-lēs'; Spens. del'is*), delight: a delight: a delicacy.—*adv.* **deli'ciously,** in a delicious manner: (*B.*) luxuriously.—*n.* **deli'ciousness.**—flower **delice'** (*Spens.* also *del'is*), see **fleur-de-lis.** [L. *dēliciōsus*—*dēliciae,* or *dēlicium,* delight.]

delict, *di-likt', n.* a transgression, a misdemeanour. [L. *dēlictum,* an offence; see **delinquent.**]

deligation, *del-i-gā'shan, n.* a binding up, ligature. [L. *dēligāre,* to bind up—*dē-,* intens. and *ligāre,* to bind.]

delight, di-līt', v.t. to please highly.—v.i. to have or take great pleasure : to be greatly pleased.—n. a high degree of pleasure : extreme satisfaction : that which gives great pleasure.—adj. **delight'ed,** greatly pleased : (Shak.) delightful : (Shak.) capable of delight.—adjs. **delight'ful, delight'some,** full of delight.—adv. **delight'fully.**—n. **delight'fulness.**—adj. **delight'less,** affording no delight. [O.Fr. deliter—L. dēlectāre, inten. of dēlicĕre; cf. **delicate, delicious;** spelling influenced by confusion with **light.**]

Delilah, di-lī'lä, n. the Philistine woman who befooled Samson : a courtesan : a temptress : an alluring object.—Also **Dali'lah, Dalila** (Milt. dal'i-lä).

delimit, di-lim'it, v.t. to fix or mark the limit of.—n. **delimita'tion.** [L. dēlimitāre—dē-, intens., līmitāre; see **limit.**]

delineate, di-lin'i-āt, v.t. to mark out with lines : to represent by a sketch or picture : to draw : to describe.—adj. **delin'eable.**—ns. **delinea'tion,** the act of delineating : a sketch, representation, or description; **delin'eător.** [L. dēlīneāre, -ātum—dē, down, and līnea, a line.]

delinquent, di-ling'kwənt, adj. failing in duty.—n. one who fails in or leaves his duty : an offender : a person lacking in moral and social sense, without showing impairment of intellect.—n. **delin'quency,** failure in or omission of duty : a fault : a crime.—adv. **delin'quently.** [L. dēlinquēns, -entis, pr.p. of dēlinquĕre—dē-, inten., and linquĕre, lictum, to leave.]

deliquesce, del-i-kwes', v.i. to melt and become liquid by absorbing moisture, as certain salts, etc.—n. **deliquesc'ence.**—adj. **deliquesc'ent,** liquefying in the air : (bot.) lost in a mass of branches. [L. dēl'iquescĕre—dē-, inten., liquēscĕre, to become fluid—liquēre, to be fluid.]

deliquium, di-lik'wi-əm, n. (obs.) swoon : eclipse : (Carlyle) melting away. [Really two different words, partly confused : (1) L. dēliquium—dēlinquĕre, to leave; (2) L. dēliquium—dēliquāre, to melt.]

delirious, di-lir'i-əs, adj. wandering in mind : light-headed : insane.—n. **delira'tion** (del-), madness, aberration.—adj. **delirifacient** (di-lir-i-fā'-shənt), producing delirium.—n. that which produces delirium.—adv. **delir'iously.**—ns. **delir'iousness; delir'ium,** state of being delirious : strong excitement : wild enthusiasm.—**delirium tremens** (trē'menz), a delirious disorder of the brain produced by over-absorption of alcohol, often marked by convulsive or trembling symptoms. [L. dēlīrus, crazy—dēlīrāre, lit. to turn aside—dē, from, and līra, a furrow; tremēns, the pr.p. of tremĕre, to tremble.]

delitescent, del-i-tes'ənt, adj. latent.—n. **delitesc'ence.** [L. dēlitēscēns, -entis, pr.p. of dēlitēscĕre—dē, from, and latēscĕre—latēre, to lie hid.]

deliver, di-liv'ər, v.t. to liberate or set free from restraint or danger : to rescue from evil or fear : to give up or part with : to hand over : to communicate : to pronounce : to give forth, as a blow, a ball, etc. : to discharge, as water : to disburden, of a child in childbirth.—adj. nimble.—adj. **deliv'erable.**—ns. **deliv'erance,** liberation : release : parturition : the utterance of a judgment or authoritative opinion ; **deliv'erer.**—adv. **deliv'erly.**—n. **deliv'ery** the act of delivering : a giving up : the act or manner of speaking in public, of discharging a shot, or water, of throwing a cricket-ball, etc. : withdrawal of a pattern from a mould : a distribution : a round of distribution : the act of giving birth.—ns. **deliv'ery-man,** a man who goes round delivering goods; **deliv'ery-pipe, -tube,** one that delivers water, etc., at the place where it is required; **deliv'ery-van,** a tradesman's van for delivering goods at customers' houses; **deliver the goods** (slang), to carry out what is required or promised; **general delivery,** the delivery of letters at a post-office to the persons to whom they are addressed—opp. to house-to-house delivery; **gaol,** or **jail, delivery** (see **gaol**). [Fr. délivrer—L. dē, from, līberāre, to set free—līber, free.]

dell, del, n. a deep hollow or small valley, usually wooded : (Spens.) a hole. [O.E. dell; cf. **dale.**]

dell, del, n. a vagrant girl : a trull. [Rogues' slang.]

Della-Cruscan, del-ə-krus'kən, del-lä-kroos'kən, n. a member of the old Florentine Accademia della Crusca (It., academy of the bran, as sifters of the language; 1582), or of a group of sentimental English poetasters crushed by Gifford's Baviad and Maeviad (1794 and 1796).—Also adj.

Della-Robbia, del-lä-rob'byä, n. a term applied to enamelled terra-cotta, said to have been invented by Luca della Robbia.

delouse, dē-lows', v.t. to free from lice, or (fig.) from land-mines, etc. [Pfx. de-, and **louse.**]

delph. See **delf.**

Delphic, del'fik, adj. relating to Delphi, a town of ancient Greece, or to its famous oracle : oracular.—Also **Del'phian.** [Gr. Delphikos—Delphoi.]

delphin, del'fin, adj. pertaining to the dauphin (q.v.) of France, or to an edition of the Latin classics prepared for his use, 64 vols., 1674–1730.

Delphinidae, del-fin'i-dē, n.pl. a family of cetaceans, including dolphins, grampuses, etc.—adj. **del'phinoid.** [L. delphīnus—Gr. delphīs, -īnos, a dolphin.]

Delphinium, del-fin'i-əm, n. a genus of Ranunculaceae, comprising the larkspurs and stavesacre. [Latinised from Gr. delphīnion, larkspur, dim. of delphīs, dolphin, from the appearance of the flowers.]

delta, del'tä, n. the fourth letter (Δ δ) of the Greek alphabet, answering to D : an alluvial deposit at the mouth of a stream, Δ-shaped in the case of the Nile : as an ancient Greek numeral Δ'=4, ,Δ = 4,000.—n. **del'ta-wing** (aeroplane), a jet aeroplane with triangular wings.—adjs. **deltā'ic,** belonging to a delta; **del'toid,** of the form of the Greek Δ : triangular.—**deltoid muscle,** the large triangular muscle of the shoulder. [Gr.,—Heb. daleth, a tent-door.]

delubrum, de-l(y)ōō'brəm, n. a temple, shrine, sanctuary : a church having a font : a font. [L. dēlūbrum.]

deluce. See **fleur-de-lis.**

delude, di-l(y)ōōd', v.t. to play or impose upon : to deceive.—adj. **delud'able.**—n. **delud'er.** [L. dēlūdĕre, to play—dē, down, lūdĕre, lūsum, to play.]

deluge, del'ūj, n. a great overflow of water : a flood, esp. Noah's.—v.t. to inundate : to overwhelm as with water. [Fr. déluge—L. dīluvium—dīluĕre—dis-, away, luĕre, to wash.]

delundung, del'ən-dung, n. the weasel-cat of Java and Malacca, a small carnivore akin to the civet. [Javanese.]

delusion, di-l(y)ōō'zhən, n. the act of deluding : the state of being deluded : a hallucination : a false belief : error.—adj. **delu'sional,** pertaining to delusions, afflicted with such.—n. **delu'sionist.**—adjs. **delu'sive** (-siv), **delu'sory,** apt or tending to delude : deceptive.—adv. **delu'sively.**—n. **delu'siveness.** [See **delude.**]

delve, delv, v.t. and v.i. to dig with a spade : (fig.) to make deep research : to dip, slope suddenly.—n. (Spens.) a hollow, hole, depression, a cave.—n. **delv'er.** [O.E. delfan, to dig; conn. with **dale, delf, dell.**]

demagnetise, dē-mag'nit-īz, v.t. to deprive of magnetic properties.—n. **demagnetīsā'tion.**

demagogue, dem'ə-gog, n. a leader of the people : a popular and factious orator.—adjs. **demagogic, -al** (-gog' or -goj').—ns. **demagogism, demagoguism** (dem'ə-gog-ism); **dem'agoguery, dem'agogy** (-gog-; -goj-). [Gr. dēmagōgos—dēmos, people, agōgos, leading—agein, to lead.]

demain. See **demesne.**

demaine. See **demean** (1).

demand, di-mänd', v.t. to claim : to ask peremptorily or authoritatively : to call for : to question.—n. the asking for what is due : peremptory asking for something : a claim : desire shown by consumers : inquiry.—adj. **demand'able,** that may be demanded.—ns. **demand'ant,** one who demands : a plaintiff; **demand'er.**—**in great demand,** much sought after. [Fr. demander—L.L. dē-

mandāre, to demand—L. *dē-*, intens., and *mandāre*, to put into one's charge.]

demarcation, demarkation, *dē-märk-ā′shən, n.* the act of marking off or setting bounds: separation: a fixed limit.—*v.t.* dē′marcate (or *di-märk′*), to mark off or limit.—Also **demark.** [Sp. *demar-cación*—*de*, from, *marcar*, to mark. See **mark.**]

dematerialise, *dē-mə-tē′ri-əl-īz, v.t.* to deprive of material qualities or character.—*v.i.* to become immaterial.

deme, *dēm, n.* a subdivision of ancient Attica and of modern Greece, a township. [Gr. *dēmos*, people.]

demean, *di-mēn′, v.t.* to bear, behave, conduct (*refl.*): (*Spens.*) to treat: (*Spens.*; *obs. Scot*) to ill-treat.—*n.* (*Spens.* **demaine′, demayne′, de-meane′**), air, bearing: treatment.—*n.* **demeanour** (*di-mēn′ər; Spens.* **demeasnure**), behaviour: bearing towards another. [O.Fr. *demener*—*de-*, intens., and *mener*, to lead—L. *mināre*, to drive—*minārī*, to threaten.]

demean, *di-mēn′, v.t.* to make mean: to lower. [Prob. on the analogy of *debase*, from *de-*, and **mean.**]

dement, *di-ment′, v.t.* to drive crazy, render insane.—*adj.* insane, demented.—*n.* a demented person.—*v.t.* **dement′āte,** to dement.—*adj.* **dement′ed,** out of one's mind: insane: suffering from dementia.—*n.* **dementia** (*di-men′shi-ä*), general mental enfeeblement, with loss of memory, reason, feeling, and will, often the consequence of acute mania. [L. *dēmēns, dēmentis,* out of one's mind—*dē*, from, and *mēns,* the mind.]

démenti, *dā-män′-tē, n.* a contradiction, denial. [Fr. *démentir,* to give the lie to.]

demerge, *dē-mərj′ v.t.* to immerse, plunge. [L. *dē,* down, *mergēre,* to plunge.]

demerit, *dē-, di-mer′it, n.* (*obs.*) desert: ill-desert: fault. [L. *dēmerērī, dēmeritum,* to deserve fully, later understood as to deserve ill—*dē-,* fully, *merērī,* to deserve.]

demerse, *də-mərs′, v.t.* (*obs.*) to immerse.—*adjs.* **demer′sal,** subaqueous: found on or near the bottom; **demersed′** (*bot.*), growing under water.—*n.* **demer′sion.** [L. *dē,* down, *mergēre, mersum,* to plunge.]

demesne, *di-mān′, -mēn′,* **demain,** *di-mān′, n.* a manor-house with lands adjacent to it not let out to tenants: any estate in land. [Forms of **domain.**]

demi-, *dem′i, pfx.* half, half-sized.—*ns.* **dem′i-bast′ion,** a kind of half-bastion, consisting of one face and one flank; **dem′i-cann′on** (*Shak.*), an old kind of gun which threw a ball of from 30 to 36 lb.; **dem′i-cul′verin,** an old kind of cannon which threw a shot of 9 or 10 lb.—*v.t.* **dem′i-de′ify,** to treat as a demi-god: to go half-way towards deifying.—*ns.* **dem′i-dev′il,** a half-devil; **dem′i-dis′tance** (*fort.*) the distance between the outward polygons and the flank; **dem′i-di′tone** (*mus.*) a minor third; **dem′igod,** a half-god: one whose nature is partly divine, esp. a hero fabled to be the offspring of a god and a mortal—*fem.* **dem′i-godd′ess; dem′i-gorge** (*fort.*) the part of the polygon remaining after the flank is raised, going from the curtain to the angle of the polygon.

demigration, *dem-i-grā′shən, n.* change of abode. [L. *dēmigrāre, -ātum,* depart—*dē, migrāre.*]

demijohn, *dem′i-jon, n.* a glass bottle with a full body and narrow neck, enclosed in wicker-work. [Fr. *dame-jeanne,* Dame Jane, analogous to **bell-armine,** grey-beard; not from the town *Dam-aghan.*]

demi-, *cont.*—*ns.* **dem′i-lance,** a short, light spear of the 16th century; a soldier armed with such a weapon; **dem′i-lune** (*lōōn*) (*fort.*) a half-moon: an old name for *ravelin;* **demi-monde** (*dem′i-mond, dəm-ē-mon′d*), a class of women in an equivocal moral and social position; **demi-mondaine** (*-en′*), a member of the class.—*adj.* **demipique** (*dem′i-pēk*) of an 18th century war-saddle, having a lower peak than usual.—Also *n.* —*ns.* **dem′irep** (for *demi-reputable*), a person,

esp. a woman, of dubious reputation; **demirep′-dom.**

demise, *di-mīz′, n.* a transferring: death, esp. of a sovereign or a distinguished person: a transfer of the crown or of an estate to a successor.—*v.t.* to send down to a successor: to bequeath by will.—*adj.* **demi′sable.** [O.Fr. *demise,* pa.p. of *desmettre,* to lay down.—L. *dis-,* aside, *mittēre, missum,* to send.]

demi-semiquaver, *dem-i-sem′i-kwā-vər, n.* (*mus.*) a note equal in time to the half of a semiquaver. [Fr. *demi,* half, and **semiquaver.**]

demiss, *di-mis′, adj.* (*Spens.*) humble.—*n.* **de-mission** (*di-mish′ən*), lowering: degradation: de-pression: relinquishment: resignation.—*adj.* **de-miss′ive** (*obs.*), humble.—*adv.* **demiss′ly.** [L. *dēmittēre, -missum—dē,* down, *mittēre,* to send.]

demit, *di-mit′, v.t.* to send down: to lower. [See **demiss.**]

demit, *di-mit′, v.t.* to dismiss: to relinquish: to resign. [Fr. *démettre*—L. *dīmittēre—dis-,* apart, *mittēre,* to send.]

demiurge, *dem′i-ərj, n.* the maker of the world: among the Gnostics, the creator of the world and of man, subordinate to God the supreme—also **demiur′gus** (*-gəs*)—*adj.* **demiur′gic** (*-jik*). [Gr. *dēmiourgos—dēmos,* the people, and *ergon,* a work.]

demi-, *cont.*—*ns.* **dem′i-volt,** a half-turn of a horse, the forelegs being raised in the air; **dem′i-wolf,** (*Shak.*) a half-wolf, the offspring of a dog and a wolf. [Fr. *demi*—L. *dīmidium—dī-,* apart, *medius,* the middle.]

demobilise, *di-mob′il-īz, v.t.* to take out of mobil-isation: to disband: (*coll.*) to discharge from the army (abbrev. **demob′;** *pr.p.* **demobb′ing;** *pa.p.* **demobbed′).**—*n.* **demobilisā′tion.**

democracy, *di-mok′rə-si,* a form of government in which the supreme power is vested in the people collectively, and is administered by them or by officers appointed by them: the people, esp. the common people: in the United States, the Democratic party.—Also **democracy** (*-ok′; Milt.*).—*n.* **democrat** (*dem′ō-krat*), one who adheres to or promotes democracy as a principle: a member of the Democratic party in the United States, the party generally inclining to look to the rights of States against centralisation of govern-ment, and favouring a low tariff: (*U.S.*) a light four-wheeled cart with several seats (also **demo-crat wagon**).—*adjs.* **democrat′ic, -al,** relating to democracy: insisting on equal rights and privileges for all.—*adv.* **democrat′ically.**—*adj.* **democratifi′able,** capable of being made demo-cratic.—*v.t.* **democratise** (*di-mok′*), to render democratic.—*n.* **democ′ratist,** a democrat. [Fr. *démocratie*—Gr. *dēmokratiā—dēmos,* the people, *kratos,* strength.]

demoded, *dē-mod′id, adj.* (disparagingly) no longer in fashion. [Pfx. *de-,* mode.]

Demogorgon, *dē-mō-gor′gən, n.* a mysterious in-fernal deity first mentioned about 450 A.D. [Apparently Gr. *daimōn,* deity, *Gorgō,* Gorgon, *gorgos,* terrible.]

demography, *dē-mog′rə-fi, n.* the study of popula-tion.—*n.* **demog′rapher.**—*adj.* **demographic** (*-ō-graf′ik*). [Gr. *dēmos,* the people, *graphein,* to write.]

demoiselle, *dəm-wä-zel′, n.* (*arch.* or *playful*) a young lady: a graceful kind of crane (*Anthropoides virgo*): a dragonfly: a fish of the genus Pomacentrus or its family (akin to the wrasses): a tiger-shark. [Fr.; see **damsel.**]

demolish, *di-mol′ish, v.t.* to destroy, lay in ruins, to ruin.—*n.* **demoli′tion** (*dem-ō-*), act of pulling down: ruin. [Fr. *démolir*—L. *dēmōlīrī,* to throw down—*dē,* down, and *mōlīrī,* to build—*mōlēs,* a heap.]

demology, *dē-mol′ə-ji, n.* demography: the theory of the origin and nature of communities. [Gr. *dēmos,* people, *logos,* a discourse.]

demon, *dē′mən, n.* an evil spirit, a devil: sometimes like **daemon,** a friendly spirit or good genius:—*fem.* **de′moness.**—*adjs.* **demoniac** (*di-mōn′i-ək*); **demoniacal** (*dē-mə-nī′ə-kl*), pertaining to or like demons or evil spirits: influenced by demons.—

ns. **demō'niac**, one possessed by a demon or evil spirit.—*adv.* **demoni'acally.**—*n.* **dēmoni'acism** (*-ə-sizm*), state of being a demoniac.—*adj.* **demō'-nian** (*Milt.*).—*n.* **demō'nianism**, possession by a demon.—*adj.* **demon'ic** (*dē-mon'ik;* see **daemon-ic**).—*v.t.* **dē'monise**, to convert into a demon : to control or possess by a demon.—*ns.* **dē'monism**, a belief in demons; **dē'monist;** **dēmonoc'racy**, the power of demons; **dēmonol'atry**, the worship of demons; **dēmonol'ater;** **dēmonology**, an account of, or the study of, demons and their agency.—*adjs.* **dēmonolog'ic, -al.**—*ns.* **dēmon-ol'ogist;** **dēmonomā'nia**, a form of mania in which the subject believes himself possessed by devils; **dē'monry**, demoniacal influence. [L. *daemōn*—Gr. *daimōn*, a spirit, genius; in N.T. and Late Greek, a devil; see **daemon.**]

demonetise, *dē-mon'i-tīz*, or *-mun'*, *v.t.* to divest of value as money.—*n.* **demonetīsā'tion.**

demonstrate, *dem'ən-strāt* (or *di-mon'strāt*), *v.t.* to make manifest : to give proof of : to prove with certainty : to teach, expound, explain, or exhibit by practical means.—*v.i.* to exhibit one's feelings : to act as demonstrator.—*adj.* **demon'strable** (or *dem'ən-*), that may be demonstrated.—*ns.* **demon'strableness, -strabil'ity.**—*adv.* **demon'strably** (or *dem'*).—*ns.* **demonstrā'tion**, a pointing out : proof beyond doubt : expression of the feelings by outward signs : a public expression of feelings, as by a mass-meeting, a procession, etc. : show : a movement to exhibit military intention, or to deceive an enemy : a practical lesson or exhibition. —*adj.* **demon'strative**, pointing out (as a *demon-strative adjective*) : making evident : proving with certainty : of the nature of proof : given to the manifestation of one's feelings.—*adv.* **demon'-stratively.**—*ns.* **demon'strativeness; dem'on-strātor**, one who proves beyond doubt : a teacher or assistant who helps students with practical work : one who goes about exhibiting the uses and merits of a commodity : one who takes part in a public demonstration.—*adj.* **demon'stratory**, de-monstrative. [L. *dēmōnstrāre, -ātum—dē-*, inten., and *mōnstrāre*, to show.]

demoralise, *dē-mor'əl-īz*, *v.t.* to corrupt in morals : to lower the morale of—that is, to deprive of spirit and confidence : to throw into confusion.—*n.* **demoralisā'tion**, act of demoralising : corruption or subversion of morals.—*adj.* **demoralis'ing.**

demos, *dē'mos*, *n.* the people (esp. contemptuously). —*adj.* **demot'ic**, pertaining to the people: popular : (*Egypt. ant.*), of a simplified kind of writing distinguished from the hieratic, or priestly, and from hieroglyphics.—*n.* **demot'icist**, a student of demotic script. [Gr. *dēmos.*]

Demosthenic, *de-mos-then'ik, adj.* of or like *Dēmosthenēs*, the Athenian orator : eloquent.

demote, *dē-mōt'*, *v.t.* to reduce in rank.—*n.* **demō'-tion.** [On the analogy of *promote—dē*, down.]

dempster. Same as **deemster.** [See under **deem.**]

dempt, *demt* (*Spens.*), *pa.p.* and *pa.t.* of **deem.**

demulcent, *di-mul'sənt, adj.* soothing.—*n.* a medi-cine that allays irritation. [L. *dēmulcēns, -entis—dē*, down, *mulcēre*, to stroke, to soothe.]

demulsify, *dē-mul'si-fī*, *v.t.* to separate from an emulsion : to make resistent to emulsification.

demur, *di-mur'*, *-mər'*, *v.i.* to hesitate from uncer-tainty or before difficulty : to object.—*v.t.* (*Milt.*) to hesitate about (*pr.p.* **demurr'ing;** *pa.t.* and *pa.p.* **demurred'**).—*n.* a stop : pause, hesitation.—*adj.* **demurr'able**.—*n.* **demurr'age**, undue delay or detention of a vessel, railway wagon, etc. : com-pensation for such detention; **demurr'er**, one who demurs : (*law*) a plea in law that, even if the opponent's facts are as he says, they yet do not support his case. [Fr. *demeurer*—L. *dēmorārī*, to loiter, linger—*dē-*, inten., and *morārī*, to delay—*mora*, delay.]

demure, *di-mūr', adj.* sober : staid : modest : affectedly modest : making a show of gravity.— *v.i.* (*Shak.*) app., to look demurely.—*adv.* **de-mure'ly.**—*n.* **demure'ness.** [O.Fr. *meur* (Fr. *mûr*)—L. *matūrus*, ripe; pfx. unexplained.]

demy, *di-mī'*, *n.* a size of paper, 22½ by 17½ in., for printing—for writing, 20 by 15¼ in., or (*U.S.*)

21 by 16 in. : a holder of certain scholarships in Magdalen College, Oxford, orig. allowed half the commons assigned to a fellow :—*pl.* **demies'.**—*n.* **demy'ship.** [Fr. *demi*—L. *dimidium*, half—*dis-*, apart, *medius*, the middle.]

**den, *den*, *n.* the hollow lair of a wild beast : a pit, cave : a haunt of vice or misery : (*coll.*) a private retreat for work : (*prov.*) a narrow valley, a dean.—*v.i.* to retire to a den. [O.E. *denn*, a cave, lair; akin to *denu*, a valley.]

den, *den*, *n.* (*obs.*) for **good-e'en, good-even.**

denary, *dēn'ər-i, adj.* containing or depending on the number ten : ten.—*n.* the number ten : a group of ten.—*n.* **denarius** (*di-nā'ri-əs*), the chief Roman silver coin under the Republic, divided into ten asses—about 8d.; translated *penny* in the N.T.—hence the use of d for penny. [L. *dēnārius—dēnī*, ten by ten—*decem*, ten.]

denationalise, *dē-nash'ən-əl-īz*, *v.t.* to deprive of national rights or character.—*n.* **denationalisā'-tion.**

denaturalise, *dē-nat'ū-rəl-īz*, *v.t.* to make un-natural : to deprive of naturalisation.—*n.* **dē-naturalisā'tion.**

denature, *dē-nā'tyər*, *v.t.* to change the nature or properties of, as a protein by heat or other treat-ment : of alcohol, etc., to render unfit for con-sumption.—*n.* **denā'turant**, a substance used to denature another.

denay, *di-nā'*, obs. form of **deny, denial.**

dendron, *den'dron*, *n.* a branching process of a nerve-cell.—*n.* **dendrachate** (*den'drə-kāt;* Gr. *achātēs*, agate), arborescent agate.—*adj.* **den'-driform**, tree-like.—*n.* **den'drite** (Gr. *dendrītēs*, of a tree), a tree-like crystalline aggregate or skele-ton crystal : a dendron.—*adjs.* **dendrit'ic, -al**, tree-like, arborescent : marked with branching figures like plants.—*ns.* **Dendrō'bium** (Gr. *bios*, life), a genus of epiphytic orchids, chiefly of tropical Asia; **Dendrocal'amus** (Gr. *kalamos*, cane), a genus of bamboos.—*adj.* **den'droid**, tree-like.—*n.* **dendrol'atry** (Gr. *latreiā*, worship), the worship of trees.—*adj.* **dendrolog'ical.**—*ns.* **dendrol'ogist; dendrol'ogy**, a treatise on trees : the natural history of trees; **dendrom'eter**, an instrument for measuring trees; **Den'drophis** (Gr. *ophis*, snake), a genus of tree-snakes, Indian and Australian. [Gr. *dendron*, tree.]

dene, *dēn*, *n.* a small valley. [See **dean** (1).]

dene, *dēn*, *n.* a sandy tract, a dune. [Ety. doubtful.]

Deneb, *den'eb*, *n.* the brightest star in the constella-tion Cygnus.—*n.* **Deneb'ola**, a star at the tail of the constellation Leo. [Ar. *dhanab*, tail, *al-asad*, of the lion.]

denegation, *den-i-gā'shən*, *n.* a denial. [L. *dēne-gāre, -ātum*, to deny—*dē-*, inten., and *negāre*, to deny.]

dene-hole, *dēn'hōl*, *n.* a prehistoric artificial cham-ber in the chalk, in Kent, Essex, etc., perhaps a flint-mine or a storehouse. [Perh. from **dene** (1), or O.E. *Dene*, Danes, from popular association; and **hole.**]

dengue, *deng'gā*, *n.* an acute tropical epidemic fever, seldom fatal—also *breakbone fever, dandy-fever*. [Apparently Swahili *dinga*.]

denial, *di-nī'əl*, *n.* act of denying : refusal : re-jection.—*adj.* **deni'able.**—*n.* **deni'er.** [deny.]

denier, *də-nēr'*, *n.* (*Shak.*) an old small French silver coin : also later, a copper coin of the value of ¹⁄₁₂ sou—hence a very trifling sum : a unit of silk, rayon, and nylon yarn weight. [Fr.,—L. *dēnārius.*]

denigrate, *den'i-grāt*, *v.t.* to blacken (esp. of a reputation).—*adj.* **blackened.**—*ns.* **denigrā'tion; den'igrātor.** [L. *dē-*, inten., *nigrāre*, to blacken, *niger*, black.]

denim, *den'im*, *n.* coloured twilled cotton goods for overalls, etc. [Fr. *de*, of, and *Nîmes.*]

denitrate, *dē-nī'trāt*, *v.t.* to free from nitric acid or other nitrogen compounds.—*ns.* **denītrā'tion; denī'trificā'tion**, removal of nitrogen or its com-pounds; **deni'trificātor.**—*v.t.* **denī'trify.**

denizen, *den'i-zn*, *n.* an inhabitant (human or animal) : one admitted to the rights of a citizen : a wild plant, probably foreign, that keeps its foot-

Neutral vowels in unaccented syllables : *el'ə-mənt, in'fənt, ran'dəm*

ing : a naturalised foreign word, etc.—Also *adj.*—*v.t.* to make a denizen : to provide with occupants.—*v.i.* to inhabit.—*ns.* **deniza′tion**, act of making one a citizen ; **den′izenship**. [O.Fr. *deinzein*—*deinz*, *dens* (Fr. *dans*), within—L. *dē intus*, from within.]

dennet, *den′it*, *n.* a light gig. [Prob. a surname.]

denominate, *di-nom′in-āt*, *v.t.* to give a name to : to call.—*adj.* **denom′inable**.—*n.* **denomina′tion**, the act of naming : a name or title : a collection of individuals called by the same name : a sect.—*adj.* **denomina′tional**, belonging to a denomination or sect.—*n.* **denomina′tionalism**, a denominational or class spirit or policy : devotion to the interests of a sect.—*adj.* **denom′inative**, giving or having a title.—*adv.* **denom′inatively**.—*n.* **denom′inātor**, he who, or that which, gives a name : (*arith.*) the lower number in a vulgar fraction, which names the parts into which the integer is divided.—**common denominator**, number that is a multiple of each of the denominators of a set of fractions, esp. the least : something that makes comparison, communication, agreement, etc. possible. [L. *dē-*, intens., *nōmināre*, to name—*nōmen*, name.]

denote, *di-nōt′*, *v.t.* to note or mark off : to indicate by a sign : to signify or mean : (*log.*) to indicate the objects comprehended in a class.—*adj.* **denō′table**.—*v.t.* **dē′nōtate**, to denote.—*n.* **dēnōtā′tion**, (*log.*) that which a word denotes, in contradistinction to that which it *connotes*.—*adj.* **denō′tative** (or *dē′*).—*adv.* **denō′tatively** (or *dē′*).—*n.* **denōte′ment** (*Shak.*), a sign or indication. [Fr. *dénoter*—L. *dēnotāre*,-*ātum*—*dē*, inten., and *notāre*.]

dénouement, *dā-nōō′mäṅg²*, *n.* the unravelling of a plot or story : the issue, event, or outcome. [Fr. *dénouement* or *dénoûment*; *dénouer*, O.Fr. *desnoer*, to untie—L. *dis-*, *nodāre*, to tie—*nodus*, a knot.]

denounce, *di-nowns′*, *v.t.* to inform against or accuse publicly : to inveigh against : to proclaim as imminent : to notify formally termination of (treaties, etc.) : (*U.S.*) to claim mining rights of.—*ns.* **denounce′ment**, denunciation ; **denounc′er**. [Fr. *dénoncer*—L. *dēnuntiāre*—*dē-*, inten., and *nuntiāre*, to announce.]

dense, *dens*, *adj.* thick, close, compact : impenetrably stupid.—*adv.* **dense′ly**.—*ns.* **dense′ness** ; **dens′ity**, the quality of being dense : the proportion of a mass to bulk or volume : the quantity of matter per unit of bulk ; **densim′eter**, an instrument for measuring the relative density or the closeness of grain of a substance. [L. *dēnsus*, thick, dense.]

dent, *dent*, *n.* and *v.t.* Same as **dint**, **dunt**. [Confused with next.]

dent, *dent*, *n.* a notch.—*v.t.* to notch.—*adj.* **dent′al**, pertaining to or concerned with the teeth or dentistry : produced by the aid of the teeth.—*n.* a sound pronounced by applying the tongue to the teeth or (loosely) the gums.—*ns.* **Dent′alium**, a genus of scaphopod molluscs with shell like an elephant's tusk—tooth-shell or tusk-shell ; **Dentā′ria**, the cruciferous toothwort.—*adj.* **dent′ary**, belonging to dentition : bearing teeth.—*n.* a bone of the lower jaw of some vertebrates usually bearing teeth.—*adjs.* **dent′ate**, **-d**, toothed : notched : set as with teeth.—*ns.* **dentā′tion**, condition of being dentate : a toothlike projection ; **dent′el** (see **dentil**) ; **dent′ex**, a strongly toothed voracious fish akin to perch, found in the Mediterranean ; **dent′icle**, a small tooth-like structure : a dentil.—*adjs.* **dentic′ulāte**, **-d**, notched : having dentils.—*n.* **denticulā′tion**.—*adj.* **dent′iform**, having the form of a tooth or of teeth.—*n.* **dent′ifrice** (L. *fricāre*, to rub), a substance used in rubbing or cleaning the teeth—toothpaste or tooth-powder.—*adj.* **dentig′erous** (-*ij′*), bearing teeth.—*n.* **dent′il**, a denticle : one of a series of square blocks or projections as in the bed-moulding of a cornice of columns.—Also **dent′el**.—*adj.* **dentilin′gual** (L. *lingua*, tongue), formed between the teeth and the tongue, as *th* in *thin*, *this*.—*n.* a consonant so formed.—*n.* **dent′ine** (-*ēn*), the substance of which teeth are mainly composed.—*adj.* **dentiros′tral** (L. *rōstrum*, a beak), with notched bill.—*ns.* **dent′ist**, one who extracts teeth, remedies diseases of the teeth, or inserts artificial teeth ; **dent′istry**,

the art or work of a dentist ; **dent′ition**, the cutting or growing of teeth : the conformation, number, and arrangement of the teeth.—*adj.* **dent′oid** (Gr. *eidos*, form), formed or shaped like a tooth.—*n.* **dent′ure**, a set of (esp. artificial) teeth.—**dental formula**, a formula showing the number and distribution of the different kinds of teeth in an animal's jaws. [L. *dēns*, *dentis*, a tooth ; dim. *denticulus*.]

denude, *di-nūd′*, *v.t.* to make nude or naked : to lay bare.—*n.* **denudation** (*den-ū-dā′shen*), a making nude or bare : (*geol.*) the wearing away of rocks whereby the underlying rocks are laid bare. [L. *dēnūdāre*—*dē-*, inten., *nūdāre*, -*ātum*, make naked.]

denunciate, *di-nun′s(h)i-āt*, *v.t.* to denounce.—*n.* **denunciā′tion**, any formal declaration : act of denouncing : a threat ; **denun′ciātor**, one who denounces.—*adj.* **denun′ciatory**, containing a denunciation : threatening. [L. *dēnunciāre* or *dēnuntiāre*; see **denounce**.]

deny, *di-nī′*, *v.t.* to gainsay or declare not to be true : to reject : to refuse : to refuse to admit : to refuse a visitor access to : to disown (*pr.p.* **deny′ing** ; *pa.t.* and *pa.p.* **denied′**).—*adv.* **deny′ingly.**—**deny oneself**, to refuse to allow oneself gratification : to exercise self-denial. [Fr. *dénier*—L. *dēnegāre*—*dē-*, inten., and *negāre*, to say no.]

deobstruent, *dē-ob′stroo-ent*, *adj.* (*med.*) removing obstructions.—Also *n.* [L. *dē*, away ; see **obstruct**.]

deodand, *dē′ō-dand*, *n.* in old English law, a personal chattel which had been the immediate accidental cause of the death of a human being, forfeited to the crown for pious uses. [L. *deō*, to God, *dandum*, that must be given—*dăre*, to give.]

deodar, *dē′ō-där*, *n.* a cedar (*Cedrus Deodara*) of the Himalayas, much praised by Indian poets. [Sans. *deva-dāru*, divine tree.]

deodate, *dē′ō-dāt*, *n.* a gift to God : extended to mean a gift from God. [L. *deō*, to God (*ā Deō*, by God), *dătum*, given, pa.p. of *dăre*, to give.]

deodorise, *dē-ō′der-īz*, *v.t.* to take the odour or smell from.—*ns.* **deō′dorant**, **deō′doriser**, a substance that destroys or conceals unpleasant smells ; **deōdorisā′tion**.

deontology, *dē-on-tol′a-ji*, *n.* the science of duty, ethics.—*adj.* **deontolog′ical** (-*ta-loj′*).—*n.* **deontol′ogist**. [Gr. *deon*, -*ontos*, neut. pr.p. of *deein*, to be necessary, to behove, *logos*, discourse.]

deoppilate, *dē-op′i-lāt*, *v.t.* to free from obstruction.—*n.* **deoppilā′tion**.—*adj.* **deopp′ilative.**

deoxidate, *dē-oks′i-dāt*, *v.t.* to take oxygen from, or reduce.—Also **deox′idise**.—*ns.* **deoxidā′tion** ; **deoxidi′ser**, a substance that deoxidises.

deoxygenate, *dē-oks′ij-en-āt*, *v.t.* to deprive of oxygen.—Also **deox′ygenise.**

depaint, *di-pānt′*, *v.t.* (*Spens.*) to paint : depict. [Fr. *dépeindre*—L. *dēpingēre* ; see **depict**.]

depart, *di-pärt′*, *v.i.* to go away : to quit or leave : to die : (*obs.*) to separate from one another.—*v.t.* (*obs.*) to separate, divide.—*n.* (*Shak.* ; *Spens.*) departure, parting.—*ns.* **depart′er** ; **depart′ing** ; **depart′ure**, act of departing : a going away from a place : deviation : the distance in nautical miles made good by a ship due east or west : death.—**a new departure**, a change of purpose or method, a new course of procedure ; **the departed**, the deceased. [Fr. *départir*—L. *dis-*, apart, and *partīre* (*partīrī*), to part, to divide.]

department, *di-pärt′ment*, *n.* a part : a special or allotted function, sphere of activity, duty, or competence : a section of an administration, university, office or other organisation : a division of a country, esp. of France.—*adj.* **departmental** (*dē-pärt-ment′l*).—*adv.* **department′ally.**—**department store**, (orig. *U.S.*) a big shop selling a variety of goods in different departments.

depasture, *di-päs′tyer*, *v.t.* to eat bare : to put to pasture : to afford pasture for.—*v.i.* to graze.

depauperise, *di-paw′per-īz*, *v.t.* to remove from the state of pauper.—*v.t.* **depau′perate**, to impoverish.—*adj.* impoverished.

depeinct, *di-pānt′*, *v.t.* (*Spens.*) to paint. [**depaint.**]

depend, *di-pend′*, *v.i.* to hang down : to be sustained by or connected with anything : to be pending : to rely : to rest.—*adj.* **depend′able**, that may be

fāte, fär, ȧsk ; mē, hėr (her) ; mīne ; mōte ; mūte ; mōōn ; dhen (then) depended on.—*n.* **depend'ant** (also **-ent**), one who depends on another for support or otherwise: a hanger-on.—*adj.* **depend'ent** (also **-ant**), depending, relying, contingent, relative: awaiting settlement.—*ns.* **depend'ence** (rarely **-ance**), state of being dependent: reliance, trust: that on which one depends: a quarrel or duel pending; **depend'ency**, that which depends: (*Shak.*) connected consistency: a foreign territory dependent on a country, a kind of subordinate colony without self-government: (rarely) dependence (*Shak.* **depend'acie**, submissiveness).—*adj.* **depend'ing**, still undetermined.—*adv.* **depend'ingly**. [Fr. *dépendre*—L. *dēpendēre*—*dē*, from, and *pendēre*, to hang.]

depersonalise, *dē-pər'sən-əl-īz*, *v.t.* to take away the characteristics of personality of.

dephlegmate, *di-fleg'māt*, *v.t.* (*old chem.*) to free from water: to concentrate, rectify.—*ns.* **dephlegmā'tion** (*dē-*); **dephlegmā'tor**. [phlegm.]

dephlogisticate, *dē-flo-jis'ti-kāt*, *v.t.* to deprive of phlogiston.—**dephlogisticated air**, Priestley's name for oxygen.

depict, *di-pikt'*, *v.t.* to paint carefully: to make a likeness of: to describe minutely.—*ns.* **depict'er**, **-or**; **depic'tion**.—*adj.* **depict'ive**. [L. *dēpingĕre*, *dēpictum*—*dē-*, inten., *pingĕre*, to paint.]

depicture, *di-pikt'yər*, *v.t.* to picture: to paint: to represent.—*n.* depicting, representation.

depilate, *dep'i-lāt*, *v.t.* to remove the hair from.—*ns.* **depilā'tion**, removal or loss of hair; **depilatory** (*di-pil'ə-tər-i*), an application for removing superfluous hairs.—*adj.* possessing this quality. [L. *dēpilāre*, *-ātum*—*dē*, out, *pilus*, hair.]

deplete, *di-plēt'*, *v.t.* to empty, reduce, exhaust.—*n.* **deple'tion**, the act of emptying or exhausting: (*med.*) the act of relieving congestion or plethora.—*adjs.* **deple'tive**, **deple'tory**. [L. *dēplēre*, *dēplētum*, to empty, *dē-*, neg., *plēre*, to fill.]

deplore, *di-plōr'*, *v.t.* to feel or express deep grief for.—*adj.* **deplor'able**, lamentable: sad: hopelessly bad.—*n.* **deplor'ableness**.—*adv.* **deplor'ably**.—*n.* **deplorā'tion** (*dep-*, *dēp-*), lamentation.—*adv.* **deplor'ingly**. [L. *dēplōrāre*—*dē-*, inten., *plōrāre*, to weep.]

deploy, *di-ploi'*, *v.t.* to unfold: to open out or extend.—*v.i.* to open: to extend from column into line, as a body of troops.—*ns.* **deploy'**, **deploy'ment**. [Fr. *déployer*—L. *dis-*, apart, and *plicāre*, to fold.]

deplume, *di-plōōm'*, *v.t.* to take the plumes or feathers from.—*n.* **deplumā'tion** (*dē-*).

depolarise, *dē-pō'lər-īz*, *v.t.* to deprive of polarity.—*n.* **depolarisā'tion**.

depone, *di-pōn'*, *v.t.* to lay down: to deposit: to testify upon oath.—*adj.* **depo'nent**, (*gram.*) having a passive form but active signification (as if having laid aside the passive—really middle or reflexive—meaning).—*n.* a deponent verb: one who makes a deposition, esp. under oath, or whose written testimony is used as evidence in a court of justice [L. *dēpōnĕre*; pr.p. *dēpōnēns*, *-entis*—*dē*, down, *pōnĕre*, to place, lay.]

depopulate, *dē-*, *di-pop'ū-lāt*, *v.t.* (*obs.*) to overrun and lay waste: to deprive of population, to dispeople.—*v.i.* to become dispeopled.—*adj.* depopulated.—*ns.* **depopulā'tion**, act of depopulating: havoc: destruction; **depop'ulator**. [L. *dēpopulārī*, *-ātus*—*dē-*, inten., and *populārī*, to swarm over, to spread over a country, said of hostile people (L. *populus*)—hence to ravage, to destroy; later understood as to deprive of people.]

deport, *di-*, *dē-pōrt'*, *v.t.* to transport, to exile: to expel (e.g. as an undesirable alien).—*ns.* **deportā'tion**. [Fr. *déporter*—L. *dēportāre*—*dē-*, away, and *portāre*, *-ātum*, to carry.]

deport, *di-pōrt'*, *v.t.* to behave (*refl.*).—*n.* **deport'ment**, behaviour: bearing: manners. [O.Fr. *déporter*—L. *dē-*, inten., *portāre*, to carry.]

depose, *di-pōz'*, *v.t.* to remove from a high station: to degrade: to set down: to remove: to attest: (*Shak.*) to examine or put upon oath.—*v.i.* to bear witness: (*Shak.*) to swear.—*adj.* **depos'able**.—*n.* **depos'al**. [Fr. *déposer*—L. *dē*, from, *pausāre*, to pause, (late) to place.]

deposit, *di-poz'it*, *v.t.* to put or set down: to place: to lay: to lay up or past: to entrust: to lodge as a pledge: to lay down as a coating, bed, vein or the like:—*n.* that which is deposited or put down: an accumulation by sedimentation, precipitation, sublimation, or other natural means: something entrusted to another's care, esp. money put in a bank: a pledge: a bailment where one entrusts goods to another to be kept without recompense (in Scots law, **deposità'tion**): the state of being deposited.—*ns.* **depos'itary**, a person with whom anything is left for safe keeping: a guardian—sometimes **depos'itory**.—*adj.* **depos'itive**.—*ns.* **depos'itor**; **depos'itory**, a place where anything is deposited—sometimes **depos'itary**; **depos'-it-receipt'**, a receipt for money deposited in a bank, etc. [L. *dēpŏsitum*, placed—*dēpōnĕre*, *dē*, down, and *pōnĕre*, to place.]

deposition, *dēp-ə-zish'ən*, *n.* act of deposing: act of deponing: declaration, testimony taken authoritatively, to be used as a substitute for the production of the witness in open court: removal: act of depositing: what is deposited, sediment. [**deposit**; blended with root of **depose**.]

depot, **dépôt**, *dep'ō*, *di-pō'*, *dā'pō'* or *dē'pō*, *n.* a place of deposit: a storehouse: a military station where stores are kept and recruits trained: the headquarters of a regiment: the portion of a regiment left at home: (*U.S.*) a railway station: a place where buses or tram-cars are kept. [Fr. *dépôt*—L. *dēpōnĕre*, *-pŏsitum*.]

deprave, *di-prāv'*, *v.t.* (*obs.*) to represent as bad: to make bad or worse: to corrupt.—*n.* **deprava'tion** (*dep-rə-vā'shən*), act of depraving: state of being depraved: depravity.—*adj.* **deprāved'**, corrupt.—*adv.* **deprāv'edly**.—*ns.* **deprāv'edness**; **deprāve'ment**, vitiation.—*adv.* **deprāv'ingly**.—*n.* **depravity** (*di-prav'iti*), a vitiated or corrupt state of moral character: extreme wickedness: corruption: (*theol.*) the hereditary tendency of man toward sin: original sin. [L. *dēprāvāre*—*dē-*, inten., *prāvus*, bad.]

deprecate, *dep'ri-kāt*, *v.t.* to try to ward off by prayer: to desire earnestly the prevention or removal of: to invoke or beseech with a view to the averting or withholding of evil: to regret deeply: to argue or protest against.—*adj.* **dep'recable**, to be deprecated.—*n.* **deprecā'tion**, act of deprecating, earnest prayer, esp. a special petition against some evil, in litanies.—*adv.* **dep'recatingly**.—*adjs.* **dep'recative**, **dep're-catory**.—*n.* **dep'recātor**. [L. *dēprecārī*, *-ātus*—*dē*, away, and *precārī*, to pray.]

depreciate, *di-prē'shi-āt*, *v.t.* to lower the worth of: to undervalue: to disparage.—*v.i.* to fall in value.—*n.* **depreciā'tion** (*-s(h)i-ā'shən*), the falling of value: disparagement.—*adjs.* **deprē'ciative**, **deprē'ciatory**, tending to depreciate or lower.—*n.* **deprē'ciātor**. [L. *dēpretiāre*, *-ātum*—*dē*, down, and *pretium*, price.]

depredate, *dep'ri-dāt*, *v.t.* to plunder or prey upon: to rob: to lay waste: to devour.—*ns.* **depredā'tion**, act of plundering: state of being depredated; **dep'redātor**.—*adj.* **depredatory** (*dep'rəd'ət-ə-ri*). [L. *dēpraedārī*, *-ātus*—*dē-*, inten., and *praedārī*—*praeda*, plunder.]

deprehend, *dep-ri-hend'*, *v.t.* (*obs.*) to catch, seize: to apprehend: to detect. [L. *dēpraehendĕre*—*dē-*, aside, and *praehendĕre*, to take.]

depress, *di-pres'*, *v.t.* to press down: to let down: to lower: to cause to sink: to humble: to make subject: to dispirit or cast a gloom over.—*n.* **depress'ant**, that which lowers activity: a sedative: (*mining*) a chemical that causes a mineral to sink in flotation.—Also *adj.*—*adj.* **depressed'**, pressed down: lowered: flattened or slightly hollowed: humbled: dejected: dispirited.—*adj.* **depress'ing**, able or tending to depress.—*adv.* **depress'ingly**.—*ns.* **depression** (*di-presh'ən*), a falling in or sinking: a lowering: a region of low barometric pressure: a hollow: abasement: dejection: a reduced condition of trade and prosperity.—*adj.* **depress'ive**, tending to depress.—*n.* **depress'or**, an oppressor: that which lowers activity: a muscle that draws down: a surgical instrument for pressing down.—**depressed area,** a region suffering from depression of trade. [L. *dēprimĕre, -pressum—dē,* down, *premĕre,* to press.] **deprive,** *di-prīv', v.t.* to dispossess: to keep out of enjoyment: to degrade (esp. a clergyman) from office: to bereave.—*adj.* **depriv'able.**—*ns.* **depriv'al, deprivation** (*dep'ri-* or *dē'prī-*), act of depriving: state of being deprived: degradation from office: loss: bereavement: suffering from hardship.—*adj.* **depriv'ative.**—*n.* **deprive'ment.** [L.L. *dēprivāre,* to degrade—L. *dē,* from, and *privāre,* to deprive—*privus,* one's own.]

depth, *depth, n.* deepness: the measure of deepness down or inwards: a deep place: intensity: the innermost or intensest part, as depth of winter: abstruseness: extent of sagacity and penetration.— *ns.* **depth'-bomb, -charge,** a powerful bomb that explodes under water (dropped over or near submarines).—*adj.* **depth'less,** having no depth: bottomless.—**out of one's depth,** in water where one cannot touch bottom, or too deep for one's safety: beyond one's understanding; **the depths,** the lowest pitch of humiliation and misery. [Not in O.E.; possibly O.N. *dýpth;* or formed from **deep,** on analogy of **length,** etc.]

depurate, *dep'ū-rāt, di-pū'rāt, v.t.* to purify.— *adj.* and *n.* **dep'ūrant.**—*ns.* **depūrā'tion; dep'-ūrātor.**—*n.* and *adj.* **depurative** (*dep'ū-rā-tiv, di-pūr'ə-tiv*).—*adj.* **depū'ratory.** [L.L. *dēpūrāre, -ātum,* to purify—L. *dē-,* inten., and *pūrāre,* to purify—*pūrus,* pure.]

depute, *di-pūt', v.t.* to appoint or send as a substitute or agent: to send with a special commission: to make over one's powers to.—*adj.* (*dep'ūt*) in Scotland, appointed deputy (as in *sheriff-depute* —often simply *the depute*).—*n.* **deputation** (*dep-ū-tā'shon*), act of deputing: the person or persons deputed or appointed to transact business for another: a body of persons sent to state a case: the privilege of shooting game, or a document granting it, formerly given by the lord of a manor, nominally as to a gamekeeper.—*v.t.* **dep'ūtise,** to appoint as deputy.—*v.i.* to act as deputy.—*n.* **dep'ūty,** one deputed or appointed to act for another, esp. (*London*) for an alderman or (*U.S.*) for a sheriff: a delegate or representative, or substitute: a legislator, member of a chamber of deputies: one who attends to protective arrangements in a coal-mine. [L. *dēputāre,* to prune, (later) to select.]

deracialise, *dē'rāsh'(y)əl-īz, v.t.* to divest of racial character.

deracinate, *dē-ras'i-nāt, v.t.* to root up. [Fr. *déraciner*—L. *dē,* from, L.L. *rādīcīna,* dim. of L. *rādix,* a root.]

deraign. See **darraigne.**

derail, *di-rāl', v.t.* to cause to leave the rails.—*v.i.* to go off the rails.—*ns.* **derail'er; derail'ment.**

derange, *di-rānj', v.t.* to put out of place or order: to disorder.—*adj.* **deranged',** disordered: insane.—*n.* **derange'ment,** disorder: insanity. [Fr. *déranger—dé-* (L. *dis-*), asunder, and *ranger,* to rank.]

derate, *dē-rāt', v.t.* to relieve (wholly or partially) from local rates.—*n.* and *adj.* **derat'ing.**

deray, *di-rā', v.t.* (*obs.*) to derange.—*v.i.* to go wild.—*n.* tumult, disorder. [O.Fr. *desreer— des-,* neg., and *rei, roi,* order see **array.**]

Derby, *där'bi, n.* a kind of porcelain made at *Derby:* a great horse-race held annually on Epsom Downs, so called from the Derby stakes, instituted by the Earl of *Derby* in 1780: (*dər'bi; U.S.*), a bowler hat (origin unknown): a strong type of boot or shoe.—**Derby dog,** a stray dog on a race-course: (*fig.*) an intruder or an interruption; **Derby-shire neck,** a form of goitre (occurring in Derbyshire); **Derbyshire spar,** fluor-spar (found in Derbyshire).

der-doing, *dər-dōō'ing, adj.* (*Spens.*) doing daring deeds. [See **derring-do.**]

dere, deare, *dēr, v.t.* (*obs.*) to injure.—*n.* (*Spens.*) injury. [O.E. *derian.*]

derelict, *der'i-likt, adj.* forsaken: abandoned.— *n.* anything (esp. a ship) forsaken or abandoned.— *n.* **derelic'tion,** act of forsaking, unfaithfulness

or remissness: state of being abandoned: land gained from the water by a change of water-line. [L. *dērelinquĕre, -lictum—dē-,* inten., *re-,* behind, and *linquĕre,* to leave.]

dereligionise, *dē-ri-lij'ən-īz, v.t.* to make irreligious.

deride, *di-rīd', v.t.* to laugh at: to mock.—*n.* **derid'er.**—*adj.* **derid'ingly.**—*n.* **derision** (*di-rizh'ən*), act of deriding: mockery: a laughing-stock.—*adjs.* **derisive** (*di-rīs'iv,* or *-riz'*), scoffing; **deris'ory,** scoffing: ridiculous.—*adv.* **deris'ively** (or *-riz'*).—*n.* **deris'iveness** (or *-riz'*). [L. *dērīdēre, -risum—dē-,* inten., and *rīdēre,* to laugh.]

derive, *di-rīv', v.t.* to conduct, draw, take, obtain, or receive (from a source or origin): (*Shak.*) to bring down (upon oneself): to infer: to trace to an origin.—*v.i.* to descend or issue.—*adj.* **deriv'able.** —*adv.* **deriv'ably.**—*adj.* **derivate** (*der'i-vāt*), derived.—*n.* a derivative.—*n.* **deriva'tion,** act of deriving: a drawing off: the tracing of a word to its root: source: that which is derived: descent or evolution of man or animals.—*adj.* **deriva'tional.** —*n.* **deriva'tionist.**—*adj.* **derivative** (*di-riv'ə-tiv*), derived or taken from something else: not radical or original.—*n.* that which is derived: a word formed from another word.—*adv.* **deriv'atively.** [Fr. *dériver*—L. *dērīvāre—dē,* down, from, *rīvus,* a river.]

derm, *dərm, n.* the true skin—also **der'ma, der'mis.** —*adjs.* **der'mal, dermat'ic, der'mic,** pertaining to the skin: consisting of skin.—*ns.pl.* **Dermap'-tera,** an order of insects with forewings, when present, in the form of firm elytra—the earwigs; **Dermop'tera,** an order of mammals, the flying lemurs, sometimes included in Insectivora.—*ns.* **dermati'tis,** inflammation of the skin; **dermat'-ogen** (*bot.*), the layer from which epidermis is formed at the growing-point; **dermatog'raphy,** anatomical description of the skin—also **dermog'-raphy.**—*adjs.* **der'matoid,** of the form of skin: skin-like; **dermatolog'ical.**—*ns.* **dermatol'-ogist; dermatol'ogy,** the branch of science that treats of the skin; **der'matophyte,** a parasitic fungus on the skin. [Gr. *derma, -atos,* the skin— *derein,* to flay.]

dern, dearn, *dərn, adj.* (*arch.* and *dial.*) secret: hidden: (*Shak.*) dreadful.—*n.* secrecy: hiding.— *adjs.* **dern'ful, dearn'ful,** solitary: mournful.— *advs.* **dern'ly, dearn'ly,** secretly: sorrowfully: grievously. [O.E. *dyrne, derne,* secret.]

derogate, *der'o-gāt, v.i.* to lessen by taking away: to detract.—*adj.* (*Shak.*) degenerate.—*adv.* **der'o-gately** (*Shak.*), in a derogatory manner.—*n.* **deroga'tion,** a taking from: detraction: depreciation.—*adv.* **derogatorily** (*di-rog'ə-tər-i-li*).—*n.* **derog'atoriness.**—*adj.* **derog'atory,** detracting: injurious. [L. *dērogāre, -ātum,* to repeal part of a law—*dē,* down, from, and *rogāre,* to propose a law.]

derrick, *der'ik, n.* an arrangement for hoisting materials, by a boom stayed from a central post: a framework or tower over a borehole or the like. [From *Derrick,* a 17th century hangman.]

derring-do, derring do, doe, *der'ing-dōō, n.* (*false archaic*) daring action.—*adj.* **der-do'ing.**—*n.* **derr'ing doo'er.** [Spenser mistook Lydgate's *dorrynge do,* i.e. daring (to) do, misprinted *derrynge do,* for a noun.]

derringer, *der'in-jər, n.* a short American pistol. [Inventor's name.]

Derris, *der'is, n.* a tropical genus of papilionaceous plants whose roots yield an insecticide powder. [Gr. *derris,* a leather coat.]

derth, *dərth, n.* (*Spens.*). Same as **dearth.**

dervish, *dər'vish, n.* a member of one of numerous Mahommedan fraternities, professing poverty and leading an austere life. [Turkish *dervīsh*—Pers. *darvīsh,* a dervish—lit., a poor man.]

descant, *des'kant, n.* an accompaniment above and harmonising with the air: (*obs.*) counterpoint: a discourse or disquisition under several heads.— *v.i.* **descant** (*Shak. des'*), to sing a descant: to discourse at length: to comment. [O.N.Fr. *descant*—L. *dis-,* apart, and *cantus,* a song.]

descend, *di-send'*, *v.i.* to climb down : to pass from a higher to a lower place or condition : to pass from general to particulars : to make an invasion : to be derived.—*v.t.* to go down upon : to traverse downwards.—*n.* **descend'ant**, one who descends, as offspring from an ancestor.—*adjs.* **descend'ed**, derived by descent; **descend'ent**, going down : proceeding from an ancestor; **descend'ible** (also **-able**), that may descend or be descended : capable of transmission by inheritance, heritable.— *adj.* **descend'ing**.—*n.* (*Shak.*) lineage.—*n.* **descen'sion**.—*adj.* **descen'sional**.—*n.* **descent'**, act of descending : transmission by succession : motion or progress downward : slope : a raid or invasion : derivation from an ancestor : a generation, a degree in genealogy; descendants collectively.—**descent from the cross**, a picture representing Christ being taken down from the cross. [Fr. *descendre*— L. *dēscendĕre*—*dē*, down, *scandĕre*, to climb.]

describe, *di-skrīb'*, *v.t.* to trace out or delineate : to give an account of.—*adj.* **describ'able**.—*n.* **describ'er** ; **description** (*di-skrip'shən*), act of describing : an account of anything in words : (loosely) sort, class, or kind.—*adj.* **descrip'tive**, containing description.—*adv.* **descrip'tively**.—*n.* **descrip'tiveness**. [L. *dēscrībĕre*—*dē*, down, *scrībĕre*, *scrīptum*, to write.]

descrive, *di-skrīv'*, *v.t.* (*obs.*) to describe. [O.Fr. *descrivre*—L. *dēscrībĕre*.]

descry, *di-skrī'*, *v.t.* (*Spens.*) to reveal : to discover by the eye : to espy (*pr.p.* **descry'ing** ; *pa.t.* and *pa.p.* **descried'**).—*n.* discovery : (*Shak.*) a thing discovered. [App. two words : O.Fr. *descrire* for *descrivre*—L. *dēscrībĕre*, and O.Fr. *descrier*, *decryer*, proclaim, announce—*des-*, *de-*, and *crier*, to cry; cf. **describe**, **decry**.]

desecrate, *des'i-krāt*, *v.t.* to divert from a sacred purpose : to profane.—*ns.* **des'ecrater**, **-or** ; **desecrā'tion**, act of desecrating : profanation. [Coined on the analogy of **consecrate**—L. *dē*, from. L. *dēsecrāre* meant consecrate.]

desensitise, *dē-sen'sit-īz*, *v.t.* and *v.i.* to make or become less sensitive.

desert, *di-zərt'*, *n.* that which is deserved : claim to reward : merit.—*adj.* **desert'less**, without merit. [O.Fr., pa.p. of *deservir* ; see **deserve**.]

desert, *di-zərt'*, *v.t.* to leave : to forsake.—*v.i.* to run away : to quit a service, as the army, without permission.—*ns.* **desert'er**, one who deserts or quits a service without permission; **deser'tion**, act of deserting : state of being deserted : wilful abandonment of a legal or moral obligation. [L. *dēserĕre*, *dēsertum*—*dē*-, neg., and *serĕre*, to bind.]

desert, *dez'ərt*, *adj.* deserted : desolate : uninhabited : uncultivated.—*n.* a desolate or barren tract : a waste : a solitude.—**desert pea**, an Australian glory-pea (Clianthus) with purple-spotted scarlet flower. [O.Fr. *desert*—L. *dēsertum*, *dēserĕre*, to desert, unbind.]

deserve, *di-zərv'*, *v.t.* to be entitled to by merit : to merit.—*v.i.* to be worthy of reward.—*adj.* **deserved'**.—*adv.* **deserv'edly**.—*adj.* **deserv'ing**, worthy.—*adv.* **deserv'ingly**, according to desert : justly. [O.Fr. *deservir*—L. *dēservīre*—*dē*, inten., *servīre*, to serve.]

desexualise, *dē-seks'ū-əl-īz*, *v.t.* to deprive of sexual character or quality.

deshabille. Same as **dishabille**.

desiccate, *des'i-kāt*, formerly *di-sik'āt*, *v.t.* to dry up : to preserve by drying.—*v.i.* to grow dry.—*adjs.* **des'iccant**, **desiccative** (*di-sik'ə-tiv*), drying : having the power of drying.—*ns.* a drying agent.—*ns.* **desiccā'tion**, the act or process of drying up : state of being dried up; **des'iccātor**, apparatus for drying. [L. *dēsiccāre*, *-ātum*, to dry up—*dē*-, inten., *siccus*, dry.]

desiderate, *di-sid'ər-āt*, *v.t.* to long for or earnestly desire : to want or miss.—*n.* **desiderā'tion**, the act of desiderating : the thing desiderated. —*adj.* **desid'erative**, implying desire (as in *desiderative verb*).—*ns.* **desiderā'tum**, something desired or much wanted :—*pl.* **desiderā'ta** ; **desiderium** (*des-i-dē'ri-əm*), longing : grief for what is lost. [L. *dēsīderāre*, *-ātum*, to long for; *dēsīdĕrium*, longing. A doublet of **desire**.]

design, *di-zīn'*, *v.t.* (*Shaks.* ; *Spens.*) to indicate : to draw : to form a plan of : to contrive : to intend : to set apart or destine.—*n.* a drawing or sketch : a plan in outline : a plan or scheme formed in the mind : plot : intention.—*adj.* **design'able**.—*v.t.* **designate** (*dez'ig-nāt*), to mark out so as to make known : to show : to name : to be a name for : to appoint or nominate.—*adj.* nominated to but not yet in possession of an office.—*ns.* **designā'tion**, a showing or pointing out : name : title : appellation descriptive of occupation, standing, etc. : nomination to office; **des'ignātor**.—*adv.* **designedly** (*di-zīn'id-li*), by design : intentionally.—*n.* **design'er**, one who furnishes designs or patterns : a draughtsman : a plotter.—*adjs.* **design'ful**, full of design; **design'ing**, artful : scheming : working secretly for self-interest.—*n.* the art of making designs or patterns.—*adj.* **design'less**.—*n.* **design'ment**, the design or sketch of a work : (*Shak.*) intention, purpose, enterprise.—**argument from design**, the argument for the existence of God from evidence of design in creation. [Fr. *désigner* —L. *dēsignāre*, *-ātum*—*dē*-, off, and *signum*, a mark.]

desilver, *dē-sil'vər*, *v.t.* to remove silver from— also **desil'verise**.—*n.* **desilverīsā'tion**.

desine (*Spens.*). Same as **design**.

desinent, *des'in-ənt*, *adj.* terminal.—*n.* **des'inence**, ending. [L. *dēsinēns*, *-entis*, pr.p. of *dēsinĕre*, to leave off—*dē*, from, *sinĕre*, to allow.]

desipient, *di-sip'i-ənt*, *adj.* playing the fool : trifling. —*n.* **desip'ience**. [L. *dēsipiēns*, *-entis*, pr.p. of *dēsipĕre*—*dē*-, neg., *sapĕre*, to be wise.]

desire, *di-zīr'*, *v.t.* to long for : to wish for : to ask : (*B.*) to regret the loss of—*v.i.* to be in a state of desire.—*n.* an earnest longing or wish : a prayer or request : the object desired : lust.—*adj.* **desir'able**, worthy of desire : to be approved of : pleasing : agreeable.—*n.* a desirable person or thing.—*ns.* **desir'ableness**, **desirabil'ity**.—*adv.* **desir'ably**. —*adj.* **desire'less**.—*n.* **desir'er**.—*adj.* **desir'ous**, full of desire : wishful : eager : (*obs.*) desirable.— *adv.* **desir'ously**.—*n.* **desir'ousness**. [Fr. *désirer*—L. *dēsīderāre*.]

desist, *di-zist'*, *v.i.* to leave off.—*ns.* **desist'ance**, **-ence**. [L. *dēsistĕre*—*dē*-, away from, and *sistĕre*, to cause to stand.]

desk, *desk*, *n.* a sloping or flat table for writing or reading, often fitted with drawers, etc. : a shut-up writing-box : a pulpit or lectern.—*n.* **desk'-work**, work done at a desk, as by a clerk or author. [M.E. *deske*—L. *discus*—Gr. *diskos* ; see **dish**, **disk**.]

desman, *des'mən*, *n.* a Russian aquatic insectivore with long snout and musk-glands : a kindred Pyrenean species. [Sw. *desman*, musk.]

desmid, *des'mid*, *n.* one of a group of microscopic algae, unicellular or strung in chains.—*ns.* **desmine** (*des'mēn*, *-min*), the mineral stilbite occurring in bundles; **Desmod'ium**, the telegraph-plant genus.—*adj.* **des'moid**, arranged in bundles. [Gr. *desmos*, a chain, *desmē*, a bundle, *eidos*, form.]

desolate, *des'ō-lāt*, *v.t.* to make lonely or forlorn : to make joyless : to deprive of inhabitants : to lay waste.—*adj.* (*-lit*) comfortless : dreary : forlorn : lonely : destitute of inhabitants : laid waste.— *adv.* **des'olately**.—*ns.* **des'olateness** ; **de'solāter**, **-or** ; **desolā'tion**, waste : destruction : a place desolated.—*adj.* **des'olatory**. [L. *dēsōlāre*, *-ātum* —*dē*-, inten., and *sōlāre*, to make alone—*sōlus*, alone.]

desorption, *dē-sorp'shən*, *n.* release from an adsorbed state.—*v.t.* **desorb'**. [Pfx. *de-*, and **adsorption**.]

despair, *di-spār'*, *v.i.* to be without hope.—*n.* hopelessness : that which causes despair.—*adj.* **despair'ful** (*Spens.*).—*adj.* **despair'ing**, apt to despair : full of despair.—*adv.* **despair'ingly**. [O.Fr. *desperer*—L. *dēspērāre*, *-ātum*—*dē*-, neg., and *spērāre*, to hope.]

despatch. Same as **dispatch**.

desperado, *des-pər-ä'dō*, *-ā'dō*, *n.* a desperate fellow : one reckless of danger : a wild ruffian : a madman :—*pl.* **despera'do(e)s**. [Old Sp. (mod. *desesperado*),—L. *dēspērātus*.]

desperate, *des'par-it*, *adj.* in a state of despair: hopeless: beyond hope: despairingly reckless: (loosely) furious: extremely bad.—*adv.* **des'perately.**—*ns.* **des'perateness**, **despera'tion**, state of despair: despairing: disregard of danger: fury. [See **despair.**]

despicable, *des'pi-ka-bl*, *adj.* deserving to be despised: contemptible: worthless.—*ns.* **des'picability**, **des'picableness.**—*adv.* **des'picably.** [See **despise.**]

despight, *di-spīt'*, an old spelling of **despite.**

despise, *di-spīz'*, *v.t.* to look down upon with contempt.—*adj.* **despis'able.**—*ns.* **despis'al**, contempt; **despis'edness** (*Milt.*); **despis'er.** [O.Fr. *despire* (*despis-*)—L. *despicĕre—dē*, down, *specĕre*, to look.]

despite, *di-spīt'*, *n.* a looking down with contempt: violent malice or hatred.—*prep.* in spite of: not-withstanding.—*adj.* **despite'ful.**—*adv.* **despite'fully.**—*n.* **despite'fulness.**—*adj.* **despiteous** (*dis-pit'i-əs; Spens.*). [O.Fr. *despit* (mod. *dépit*)—L. *dēspectus—dēspicĕre;* see **despise.**]

despoil, *di-spoil'*, *v.t.* to plunder completely: to strip: to bereave: to rob.—*ns.* **despoil'er**; **despoil'ment.** [O.Fr. *despoiller* (mod. *dépouiller;* see next).]

despoliation, *di-spōl-i-ā'shən*, *n.* despoiling. [L. *dēspoliāre—dē-*, inten., and *spolium*, spoil.]

despond, *di-spond'*, *v.i.* to be wanting in hope.—to be dejected.—*n.* (*Bunyan*) despondency.—*ns.* **despond'ence**, **despond'ency.**—*adj.* **despond'ent.**—*adv.* **despond'ently.**—*n.* and *adj.* **despond'ing.**—*adv.* **despond'ingly.** [L. *dēspondēre*, to promise, to devote, to resign, to despond—*dē*, away, and *spondēre*, to promise.]

despot, *des'pot, -pət*, *n.* one invested with absolute power: a tyrant.—*n.* **des'potat**, a territory governed by a despot.—*adjs.* **despot'ic, -al**, pertaining to or like a despot: having absolute power: tyrannical.—*adv.* **despot'ically.**—*ns.* **despot'icalness**, **des'potism**, absolute power: tyranny; **despotoc'racy**, government by a despot. [O.Fr. *despot*—Gr. *despotēs*, a master.]

despumate, *di-spū'māt*, or *des'pū-māt*, *v.i.* to throw off in foam or scum.—*n.* **despumā'tion.** [L. *dēspūmāre, -ātum—dē-*, off, and *spūma*, foam.]

desquamate, *des'kwə-māt*, *v.i.* to scale off.—*n.* **desquamā'tion**, a scaling off: the separation of the cuticle or skin in scales.—*adjs.* **desquamative** (*di-skwam'ə-tiv*), **desquam'atory.** [L. *dēsquāmāre, -ātum—dē*, off, and *squāma*, a scale.]

desse, *des*, *n.* (*Spens.*) a desk. [**dais.**]

dessert, *diz-ərt'*, *n.* a final course of fruits, pudding, or other sweet.—*ns.* **dessert'-serv'ice**, the dishes used for dessert; **dessert'-spoon**, a spoon smaller than a table-spoon and larger than a tea-spoon; **dessert'-spoon'ful.** [O.Fr. *dessert, desservir*, to clear the table—*des-* (L. *dis-*), away, and *servir*, to serve—L. *servīre.*]

dessiatine, **dessyatine**, **desyatin**, *des'yə-tēn*, *n.* a Russian measure of land, 2·7 English acres. [Russ. *desyatīna*, a measure of land, a tenth; *desyati*, ten.]

destine, *des'tin*, *v.t.* to ordain or appoint to a certain use or state: to fix: to doom—also **des'tinate** (*obs.*).—*n.* **destinā'tion**, the purpose or end to which anything is destined or appointed: end: purpose: design: fate: place to which one is going; **des'tiny**, the purpose or end to which any person or thing is appointed: unavoidable fate: necessity. [Fr. *destiner*—L. *dēstināre—dē-*, inten., and root of *stāre*, to stand.]

destitute, *des'ti-tūt*, *adj.* left alone: forsaken: in utter want: entirely lacking.—*v.t.* (*obs.*) to forsake: to deprive.—*n.* **destitū'tion**, the state of being destitute: deprivation of office: poverty. [L. *dēstituĕre, -ūtum—dē-*, away, and *statuĕre*, to place.]

destrier, *des'tri-ər, des-trēr'*, *n.* (*arch.*) a war-horse. [Fr.,—L. *dextrārius*, led by the (squire's) right hand.]

destroy, *di-stroi'*, *v.t.* to unbuild or pull down: to overturn: to ruin: to put an end to:—*pr.p.* **destroy'ing**; *pa.t.* and *pa.p.* **destroyed'.**—*n.* **destroy'er**, a person or thing that destroys: a torpedo-boat destroyer. [O.Fr. *destruire* (Fr.

détruire)—L. *dēstruĕre, dēstructum—dē-*, down, and *struĕre*, to build.]

destruction, *di-struk'shən*, *n.* act or process of destroying: overthrow: physical or moral ruin: death: a cause of destruction.—*adj.* **destruc'tible**, liable to be destroyed.—*adj.* **destruc'tional.**—*ns.* **destructibil'ity**, **destruc'tibleness.**—*n.* **destruc'tionist**, one engaged in destruction: one who believes in the final annihilation of the damned.—*adj.* **destruc'tive**, causing or concerned with destruction: mischievous.—*n.* a destroying agent.—*adv.* **destruc'tively.**—*ns.* **destruc'tiveness**; **destruc'tivist**, a representative of destructive principles; **destructiv'ity** (*dē-*); **destruc'tor** (*di-*), a destroyer: a furnace for burning up refuse. [L. *dēstruĕre, -structum;* see **destroy.**]

desuetude, *di-sū'i-tūd, des'wi-tūd*, *n.* disuse: discontinuance. [L. *dēsuētūdō—dēsuētum, dēsuēscĕre—dē*, neg., and *suēscĕre*, to become used.]

desulphur, *dē-sul'fər*, *v.t.* to remove sulphur from—also **desul'phurāte**, **desul'phurise.**—*n.* **desulphurā'tion.**

desultory, *des'əl-tər-i*, *adj.* jumping from one thing to another: without rational or logical connexion: rambling: hasty: loose.—*adv.* **des'ultorily.**—*n.* **des'ultoriness.** [L. *dēsultōrius—dēsultor*, a vaulter, *dēsilīre, -sultum*, to leap—*dē*, from, and *salīre*, to jump.]

desyne (*Spen.*). Same as **design.**

detach, *di-tach'*, *v.t.* to unfasten: to take away or separate: to withdraw: to send off on special service.—*v.i.* to separate.—*adj.* **detach'able.**—*adj.* **detached'**, unconnected: separate: aloof: free from care, passion, ambition, and worldly bonds.—*adv.* **detach'edly.**—*ns.* **detach'edness**; **detach'ment**, state of being separated: that which is detached, as a body of troops. [Fr. *détacher*—O.Fr. pfx. *des-* (L. *dis-*), apart, and root of **attach.**]

detail, *di-tāl'*, *v.t.* to relate minutely: to enumerate: to set apart for a particular service.—*v.i.* to give details about anything.—*n.* (*di-tāl'*, or *dē'tāl*) a small part: an item: a particular account: (chiefly *mil.*) a small body set apart for special duty.—*adj.* **detailed'**, giving full particulars: exhaustive.—**in detail**, circumstantially, point by point: piecemeal. [Fr. *détailler—de-*, inten., and *tailler*, to cut.]

detain, *di-tān'*, *v.t.* to hold back: to withhold: to stop: to keep: to keep in custody.—*n.* (*Spens.*) detention.—*ns.* **detain'er**, one who detains: (*law*) the holding of what belongs to another: a warrant to a sheriff to keep in custody a person already in confinement; **detain'ment**, detention. [O.Fr. *detenir*—L. *dētinēre;* see **detent.**]

detect, *di-tekt'*, *v.t.* (*obs.*) to uncover, expose: (*Shak.*) to accuse: to discover: discern: to find out (esp. something elusive or secret).—*adjs.* **detect'able, -ible.**—*n.* **detec'tion**, discovery of something hidden or not easily observed: state of being found out.—*adj.* **detect'ive**, employed in or concerned with detection.—*n.* a policeman, usually not in uniform, or other person (*private detective*) who investigates cases of crime or watches behaviour of suspected persons.—*ns.* **detect'ivist**, a writer of detective fiction; **detect'ophone**, a secret telephone for eavesdropping; **detec'tor**, one who detects: an apparatus for detecting something, as tampering with a lock, pressure of electric currents, of electric waves.—**detective story**, one in which clues to the detection of a criminal are set forth and unravelled. [L. *dētegĕre, -tēctum—dē-*, neg., *tegĕre*, to cover.]

detent, *di-tent'*, *n.* that which checks motion: a catch, esp. for regulating the striking of a clock.—*n.* **deten'tion**, act of detaining: state of being detained: confinement, or restriction of liberty, esp. of a political prisoner, a military offender, as pupil out of school hours: delay. [L. *dētinēre, dētentum—dē*, from, *tenēre*, to hold.]

deter, *di-tər'*, *v.t.* to frighten from: to hinder or prevent (*pr.p.* **deterr'ing**; *pa.t.* and *pa.p.* **deterred'**).—*n.* **deter'ment.**—*adj.* **deterrent** (*di-ter'ənt*), serving to deter.—*n.* anything that deters. [L. *dēterrēre—dē*, from, *terrēre*, to frighten.]

fāte, fär, ȧsk; mē, hėr (her); *mīne; mōte; mūte; mōōn; dhen* (then)

deterge, *di-tərj'*, *v.t.* to wipe off: to cleanse (as a wound).—*ns.* **deterg'ence, deterg'ency**.—*adj.* **deterg'ent**, cleansing: purging.—*n.* that which cleanses: any cleansing agent, as an abrasive, or (*chem.*) a substance that combines wetting, emulsifying, and suspending properties (see **wetting agent**). [L. *dētergēre, dētersum*—*dē*, off, and *tergēre*, to wipe.]

deteriorate, *di-tē'ri-ə-rāt*, *v.t.* to make worse.—*v.i.* to grow worse.—*ns.* **detēriorā'tion**, the act of making worse: the process of growing worse; **detēriorā'tionist**, a believer in deteriorism.—*adj.* **detē'riorātive**.—*ns.* **detē'riorism**, the doctrine that the world grows worse; **detēriority** (*-or'i-ti; obs.*), worseness. [L. *dēteriōrāre, -ātum*, to make worse—*dēterior*, worse—*dē*-, down.]

determine, *dē-tər'min*, *v.t.* to put terms or bounds to: to limit: to fix or settle: to define: to decide: to resolve: to cause to resolve: to put an end to.—*v.i.* to come to a decision: to come to an end: (*Shak.*) to cease to exist: (*obs.*) to take part in a dispute, esp. in completing the degree of bachelor of arts.—*n.* **determinabil'ity**.—*adj.* **deter'minable**, capable of being determined, decided, or finished.—*n.* **deter'minableness**.—*adv.* **deter'minably**.—*n.* **deter'minacy** (*-ə-si*).—*adj.* **deter'minant**, serving to determine.—*n.* that which serves to determine: (*math.*) the sum of all the products got by taking one from each row and column of a square block of quantities, each product being reckoned positive or negative according as an even or an odd number of transpositions reduces it to the order of the rows (or of the columns)—used for the solution of equations and other purposes: a hypothetical unit in the germ-plasm determining the course of development of a cell: (*obs.*) a determining bachelor.—*adj.* **deter'mināte**, determined or limited: fixed: decisive: (*bot.*) cymose.—*v.t.* (*Shak.*) to determine.—*adv.* **deter'minately**.—*n.* **determinā'tion**, the act of determining: condition of being determined: that which is determined or resolved on: end: direction to a certain end: resolution: fixedness of purpose: decision of character.—*adj.* **deter'minātive**, that determines, limits, or defines. —*n.* in hieroglyphics an additional sign attached to a word as a guide to its meaning.—*adj.* **deter'mined**, ascertained: fixed: firm in purpose: resolute.—*adv.* **deter'minedly**.—*n.* **deter'minism**, the doctrine that all things, including the will, are determined by causes—the converse of free-will: necessitarianism.—*n.* **deter'minist**.—*adj.* **determinis'tic**. [L. *dētermināre, -ātum*—*dē*-, intens., and *terminus*, a boundary.]

deterrent. See **deter**.

detersion, *di-tər'shan*, *n.* act of cleansing.—*adj.* and *n.* **deter'sive**, detergent. [See **deterge**.]

detest, *di-test'*, *v.t.* to hate intensely.—*adj.* **detestable** (*Spens.* and *Shak.* *dē'*), worthy of being detested: extremely hateful: abominable.—*n.* **detest'ableness**.—*adv.* **detest'ably**.—*n.* **detestā'tion** (*dē-tes-tā'shon*), extreme hatred. [Fr.,—L. *dētestārī*—*dē*-, inten., and *testārī*, to call to witness, execrate—*testis*, a witness.]

dethrone, *di-thrōn'*, *v.t.* to remove from a throne.—*ns.* **dethrone'ment; dethrōn'er; dethrōn'ing**.

detinue, *det'in-ū*, *n.* (*law*) wrongful detention of property. [O.Fr. *detenue*, fem. pa.p. of *detenir*; see **detain**.]

detonate, *det'ō-nāt* or *dēt'ō-nāt*, *v.t.* and *v.i.* to explode or cause to explode rapidly ahd loudly: in an internal-combustion engine, to explode by spontaneous combustion with a hammering sound (pinking or knock).—*ns.* **detonā'tion**, an explosion with report: knock; **det'onātor**, a substance that detonates: a substance or contrivance whose explosion initiates that of another explosive. [L. *dētonāre, -ātum*—*dē*, down, and *tonāre*, to thunder.]

detort, *di-tort'*, *v.t.* to distort: to untwist: to twist the other way.—*ns.* **detor'sion, detor'tion**. [L. *dētorquēre, dētortum*; *dē*, away, also neg., and *torquēre*, to twist.]

detour, *di-tōōr'* or *dā'tōōr'*, *n.* a winding: a circuitous way. [Fr. *dé-* (L. *dis-*), asunder, and *tour*, turning.]

detract, *di-trakt'*, *v.t.* to take away, abate: to defame.—*v.i.* to take away reputation (with *from*): to reduce in degree: diminish.—*n.* **detract'or**:—*fem.* **detract'ress**.—*n.* and *adj.* **detract'ing**.—*adv.* **detract'ingly**.—*n.* **detrac'tion**, depreciation: slander.—*adjs.* **detract'ive, detract'ory**, tending to detract: derogatory. [L. *dē*, from, and *trahēre, tractum*, to draw.]

detrain, *dē-trān'*, *v.t.* to set down out of a railway train.—*v.i.* to alight from a train.—*n.* **detrain'ment**.

detriment, *det'ri-mənt*, *n.* diminution: damage: loss.—*adj.* **detrimental** (*-ment'l*).—*n.* a suitor undesirable owing to lack of means or other defect: one whose presence lessens the chances of a good match. [L. *dētrīmentum*—*dē*, off, and *terēre, trītum*, to rub.]

detritus, *di-trī'tas*, *n.* a mass of substance gradually worn off solid bodies: an aggregate of loosened fragments, esp. of rock.—*adj.* **detrī'tal**.—*n.* **detrition** (*di-trish'ən*), a wearing away. [L. *dētrītus*, worn—*dē*, off, and *terēre, trītum*, to rub.]

detrude, *di-trōōd'*, *v.t.* to thrust down.—*n.* **detru'sion**. [L. *dē*, down, and *trūdēre*, to thrust.]

detruncate, *di-trung'kāt*, *v.t.* to cut short: to lop: to mutilate.—*n.* **detruncā'tion** (*dē*-). [L. *dētruncāre, -ātum*—*dē*, off, *truncāre*, to lop.]

detumescence, *dē-tū-mes'əns*, *n.* diminution of swelling—opp. to **intumescence**.

deuce, *dūs*, *n.* a card or die with two spots: (*lawn tennis*) a situation ('forty all') in which one side must gain two successive points to win the game, or ('five all', 'games all') two successive games to win the set.—*n.* **deuce'-ace**, a throw of two dice turning up deuce and ace: bad luck. [Fr. *deux*, two—L. *duōs*, accus. of *duo*, two.]

deuce, *dūs*, *n.* the devil—in exclamatory phrases.— *adj.* **deuced** (*dū'sid*, or *dūst*), devilish: excessive.— *adv.* confoundedly.—Also **deuc'edly**. [Prob. from the **deuce** (see foregoing), the lowest throw at dice.]

deutero-, *dū'tər-ō-*, *-o'-*, *pfx.* second, secondary.— *adj.* **deuterocanon'ical** (Gr. *kanōn*, rule), pertaining to a second canon of inferior authority—the O.T. Apocrypha and the N.T. Antilegomena.— *ns.* **deuterog'amy** (Gr. *gamos*, marriage), second marriage, esp. of the clergy, after the death of the first wife; **deuterog'amist**, one who allows or practises it; **deu'teron**, the nucleus of heavy hydrogen, of mass 2, carrying unit positive charge (also **deu'ton**); **deuterium** (*-tē'ri-əm*), heavy hydrogen, an isotope of hydrogen of double mass; **Deuteronomy** (*-on'ə-mi*, or *dū'*; Gr. *nomos*, law), the fifth book of the Pentateuch, containing a repetition of the decalogue and laws given in Exodus.—*adjs.* **Deuteronom'ic, -al**.—*ns.* **Deuteron'omist**, the author of the book of Deuteronomy or part of it; **deuteros'copy** (Gr. *skopiā*, a look-out), a second view or meaning (*obs.*): second sight.—*adj.* **deuteroscop'ic**. [Gr. *deuteros*, *-ā*, *-on*, second.]

Deutzia, *dūt'si-ā*, or *doit'si-ā*, *n.* a genus of saxifragaceous plants with panicles of white flowers, introduced from China and Japan. [After Jan *Deutz*, 18th cent. Dutch naturalist.]

deva, *dā'vä*, *n.* (*Hindu myth.*) a god: a good spirit. [Sans. *dēva*, a shining one, a god.]

devall, *di-vawl'*, *v.i.* (*obs.*) to sink, decline: (*Scot.*) to cease.—*n.* a stop. [Fr. *dévaler*—L. *dē*-, down, *vallis*, a valley.]

devalue, *dē-val'ū*, *v.t.* to reduce the value of.— *vs.t.* **deval'orise, deval'uate**.—*ns.* **devalorisā'tion, devaluā'tion**.

devanagari, *dā-və-nä'-gə-ri*, *n.* the character in which Sanskrit is usually written and printed. [Sans. *dēvanāgarī*, town-script of the gods.]

devastate, *dev'as-tāt*, *v.t.* to lay waste: to plunder. —*adj.* **dev'astating** (*slang*), overpoweringly effective.—*adv.* **dev'astatingly**.—*ns.* **devastā'tion**, act of devastating: state of being devastated: havoc: waste of property by an executor; **dēvastā'vit** (L., has wasted), a writ lying against an executor for devastation: the offence of devastation. [L. *dēvastāre, -ātum*—*dē*-, inten., *vastāre*, to lay waste.]

develop, -e, *di-vel'əp*, *v.t.* to unroll: to unfold:

to lay open by degrees : to free from integuments or that which envelops : to bring out what is latent or potential in : to bring to a more advanced or more highly organised state : to work out the potentialities of : to elaborate : to cause to grow or advance : to evolve : to make more available : to exploit the natural resources of (a region) : to build on or prepare for building on (land) : (*chess*) to bring into a position useful in attack : to disclose : (*math.*) to express in expanded form : to unroll into a plane surface.—*v.i.* to open out : to evolve : to advance through successive stages to a higher, more complex, or more fully grown state (*pr.p.* devel′oping ; *pa.t.* and *pa.p.* devel′oped). —*adjs.* devel′opable ; devel′oped.—*ns.* devel′oper, one who develops : a reagent for developing photographs : an apparatus for developing muscles : devel′opment, the act or process of developing : state of being developed : a gradual unfolding or growth : evolution : (*math.*) the expression of a function in the form of a series : (*mus.*) elaboration of a theme, or that part of a movement in which this occurs : new situations that emerge.—*adj.* develop′mental, pertaining to development.—*adv.* develop′mentally. [Fr. *développer*, opposite to *envelopper*, of obscure origin.]

devest, di-vest′, *v.t.* (*Shak.*) to undress : (*law*) to alienate : to take off : to strip. [A form of divest.]

deviate, dē′vi-āt, *v.i.* to go from the way : to turn aside from a certain course : to diverge, differ, from a standard, mean value, etc. : to err.—*v.t.* to cause to diverge.—*n.* (*psych.*) one who deviates much from the normal.—*ns.* dēviā′tion ; dēviā′tionist, a communist whose doctrine deviates from the strictly orthodox ; dē′viātor.—deviation of the compass, departure of the mariner′s compass from the magnetic meridian, owing to the ship′s magnetism or other local causes ; standard deviation, the square root of the variance of a number of observations. [L. *dēviāre*, -*ātum*—*dē*, from, *via*, a way.]

device, di-vīs′, *n.* that which is devised or designed : contrivance : power of devising : (*her.*) an emblem : a motto : (*obs.*) a conceit : (*obs.*) a masque. —*adj.* device′ful (*Spens.*), full of devices. [O.Fr. *devise* ; see devise.]

Devil, dev′l, -*il*, *n.* the supreme spirit of evil, Satan : devil, any evil spirit : a very wicked person : (familiar or pitying) a fellow : one who excels or exceeds in anything : a printer′s devil : a drudge (esp. legal or literary) : a firework : a grilled or highly seasoned dish : a dust-storm : fighting spirit : a plumber′s portable furnace : a machine of various kinds, esp. for tearing : used as a mild oath, an expression of impatience, irritation, etc., or a strong negative.—*v.t.* to season highly and broil.—*v.i.* to perform another man′s drudgery (*pr.p.* dev′illing ; *pa.t.* and *pa.p.* dev′illed).—*ns.* dev′il-crab, the velvet crab ; dev′il-dodger (*slang*), a preacher, esp. of the ranting kind : one who attends churches of various kinds, to be on the safe side ; dev′ildom ; dev′iless ; dev′ilet ; dev′il-fish, the fishing-frog or angler : the giant-ray of the United States : the octopus ; devil-in-a-bush, a garden flower, love-in-a-mist ; dev′iling, dev′ling, a young devil : (*dial.*) a swift.—*adj.* dev′ilish, fiendish, malignant : very bad.—*adv.* (*coll.* ; often *dev′lish*) very : exceedingly.—*adv.* dev′ilishly.—*ns.* dev′ilism ; dev′ilkin.—*adjs.* dev′illed ; dev′il-may-care′, reckless, audacious. —*ns.* dev′ilment, frolicsome mischief ; dev′il-on-the-neck, an old instrument of torture ; dev′ilry ; dev′ilship ; dev′iltry (*U.S.*) ; dev′il-worship, the worship of the Devil, or of devils : Satanism : the Yezidi religion ; dev′il-worshipper.—between the devil and the deep sea, in a desperate dilemma ; devil a bit, one, thing, etc., not at all, not one, etc. ; devil of a mess, a very bad mess ; devil′s advocate, the Promoter of the Faith, an advocate at the papal court whose duty it is to propose objections against a canonisation ; devil′s-bit, a species of scabious (*Scabiosa succisa*) with rootstock as if bitten off ; devil′s books, playing-cards ; devil′s coach-horse, a large dark-coloured beetle (*Ocypus olens*) ; devil′s dozen,

thirteen ; devil′s dung, asafoetida ; devil′s dust, shoddy made by a machine called the devil ; devil′s own, a name given to the 88th Regiment in the Peninsular War, as also to the Inns of Court Volunteers ; devil′s snuff-box, a puff-ball ; devil′s tattoo (see tattoo) ; devil to pay, serious trouble ahead.—printer′s devil, the youngest apprentice in a printing-office : a printer′s errand-boy ; play the devil, to make havoc ; talk of the devil, here comes the person we were talking of ; the devil and all, much ado : turmoil. [O.E. *déofol*, *déoful*—L. *diabolus*—Gr. *diabolos*, from *diaballein*, to throw across, to slander, from *dia*, across, and *ballein*, to throw ; cf. Ger. *teufel*, Fr. *diable*, It. *diavolo*, Sp. *diablo*.]

devious, dē′vi-as, *adj.* remote : out of the way : round-about : winding : erring.—*adv.* dē′viously. —*n.* dē′viousness. [L. *dēvius* ; see deviate.]

devise, di-vīz′, *v.t.* to imagine : to compose : (*Spens.*) to suppose, guess : (*Spens.*) to purpose : (*obs.*) to meditate : (*obs.*) to describe : (*obs.*) to depict : to scheme : to contrive : to bequeath.— *v.i.* to consider : (*obs.*) to talk : to scheme.—*n.* act of bequeathing : a will : property bequeathed by will.—*adj.* devīs′able.—*ns.* devīs′al ; devisee (*dev-i-zē′*), one to whom real estate is bequeathed ; devīs′er, one who contrives ; devīs′or, one who bequeaths. [O.Fr. *deviser*, *devise*—L.L. *dīvīsa*, a division of goods, a mark, a device—L. *dīvidēre*, *dīvīsum*, to divide.]

devitalise, dē-vī′ta-līz, *v.t.* to deprive of vitality or life-giving qualities.—*n.* devitalisā′tion.

devitrify, dē-vit′ri-fī, *v.t.* to change from glassy to minutely crystalline.—*n.* devitrification (-*fi-kā′*).

devocalise, dē-vō′ka-līz, *v.t.* to make voiceless.

devoid, di-void′, *adj.* destitute, free : empty. [O.Fr. *desvoidier*—*des*- (L. *dis*-, away), *voidier*—L. *viduāre* —*viduus*, deprived.]

devoir, dev′wär (historically *dev′ər*), *n.* what is due, duty : service : an act of civility. [Fr.,—L. *dēbēre*, to owe.]

devolution, dev- or *dēv-ə-l*(*y*)*ōō′shən*, *n.* a passing from one person to another : a handing over of powers : a modified home rule.—*adj.* devolu′-tionary.—*n.* devolu′tionist. [See devolve.]

devolve, di-volv′, *v.t.* to roll down : to hand down : to deliver over.—*v.i.* to roll down : to fall or pass over in succession.—*n.* devolve′ment. [L. *dēvolvēre*, -*volūtum*—*dē*, down, *volvēre*, to roll.]

Devonian, di-vō′ni-ən, *adj.* belonging to Devonshire : (*geol.*) belonging to a system above the Silurian and below the Carboniferous, and esp. to the marine type, well seen in Devon—the continental type being the Old Red Sandstone.— *n.* a native of Devonshire : the Devonian system.— Devonshire cream, clotted cream.

devonport, dev′n-pōrt. Same as davenport.

devote, di-vōt′, *v.t.* to set apart or dedicate by a vow or solemn act : to doom : to give up wholly.— *adj.* (*Shak.*) devoted.—*adj.* devōt′ed, given up, as by a vow : doomed : strongly attached : zealous. —*adv.* devōt′edly.—*ns.* devōt′edness ; devotee (*dev-o-tē′*, or *dev′*), one wholly or superstitiously devoted, esp. to religion : a votary : one strongly and consistently interested in something (with *of*) ; devōte′ment (*Shak.*) ; devō′tion, the act of devoting : state of being devoted : consecration : giving up of the mind to the worship of God : piety : prayer : strong affection or attachment : ardour : faithful service : (*pl.*) prayers : (*obs.*) religious offerings : alms.—*adj.* devō′tional.—*ns.* devō′-tionalist, devō′tionist.—*adv.* devō′tionally. [L. *dēvovēre*, *dēvōtum*—*dē*, away, and *vovēre*, to vow.]

devour, di-vowr′, *v.t.* to swallow greedily : to eat up : to consume or waste with violence or wantonness : to take in eagerly by the senses or mind.—*n.* devour′er.—*adj.* devour′ing.—*adv.* devour′-ingly.—*n.* devour′ment. [O.Fr. *devorer*—L. *dēvorāre*—*dē*, inten., and *vorāre*, to swallow.]

devout, di-vowt′, *adj.* given up to religious thoughts and exercises : pious : solemn : earnest.—*adv.* devout′ly.—*n.* devout′ness. [O.Fr. *devot*—L. *dēvōtus* ; see devote.]

devvel, devel, dev′l, *n.* (*Scot.*) a hard blow.—*v.t.* to hit hard : to stun with a blow. [Ety. dub.]

dew, *dū*, *n.* moisture deposited from the air on cooling, esp. at night, in minute specks upon the surface of objects : a similar deposit or exudation of other kinds : early freshness.—*v.t.* to wet with dew : to moisten.—*ns.* **dew′-berry**, a kind of bramble or blackberry (*Rubus caesius;* in America other species) having a bluish, dew-like bloom on the fruit; **dew′-bow**, a rainbow-like appearance seen on a dewy surface; **dew′-claw**, a rudimentary inner toe, esp. of a dog's hind-foot; **dew′-drop**; **dew′fall**, the deposition, or time of deposition, of dew; **dew′iness**; **dew′point**, the temperature at which dew begins to form; **dew′-pond**, a hollow supplied with water by mist; **dew′-retting**, the process of rotting away the gummy part of hemp or flax by exposure on the grass to dew and rain; **dew′-worm**, the common earth-worm.—*adj.* **dew′y.—mountain dew** (*coll.*), whisky. [O.E. *déaw;* cf. O.N. *dögg,* Ger. *tau,* dew.]

dew, *dū*, *n.* an obsolete spelling of due.—*adj.* **dew′full** (*Spens.*), due.

dewan, *dē-wän′*, *n.* in India, a financial minister : a state prime minister : the native steward of a business house.—*ns.* **dewani, dewanny** (*dē-wä′-nē*), the office of dewan. [Pers. *diwān;* see divan.]

Dewar-flask, *dū′ər-flåsk, n.* a vacuum flask. [From Sir James *Dewar* (1842-1923), its inventor.]

dewitt, *di-wit′, v.t.* to lynch—from the fate of Jan and Cornelius *De Witt* in Holland in 1672.

dewlap, *dū′lap, n.* the pendulous skin under the throat of oxen, dogs, etc. : the fleshy wattle of the turkey.—*adjs.* **dew′lapped, dew′lapt.** [Prob. **dew** and O.E. *læppa,* a loose hanging piece.]

dexiotropic, *deks-i-ō-trop′ik, adj.* turning to the right. [Gr. *dexios,* right, *tropos,* turning.]

dexter, *deks′tər, adj.* on the right-hand side : right : (*her.*) of that side of the shield on the right-hand side of the bearer, the spectator's left : so sometimes in description of a picture, to avoid ambiguity.—*n.* **dexterity** (*-ter′i-ti*), skill of manipulation, or generally : adroitness : right-handedness.—*adjs.* **dex′terous, dex′trous,** right-handed : adroit : subtle.—*adv.* **dex′t(e)rously.—*n.* dex′t(e)rousness.—*adv.* **dex′terwise.—*adj.* **dex′tral,** right : turning to the right : of flatfish, lying right-side-up : of a spiral shell, turning in the normal manner.— *n.* **dextral′ity,** right-handedness.—*adv.* **dex′-trally.—*n.* **dex′tran,** a carbohydrate formed in sugar solutions by a bacterium, *Leuconostoc mesenteroides,* a substitute for blood plasma in transfusion; **dex′trin, dex′trine,** British gum, a gummy mixture got from starch by heating or otherwise.—*adjs.* **dextrogyrate** (*-ji′*), causing to turn to the right hand; **dextrorotatory,** rotating the plane of polarisation of light to the right (clockwise).—*ns.* **dextrorotä′tion ; dex′trose,** glucose. [L. *dexter;* Gr. *dexios,* Sans. *dakshina,* on the right, on the south.]

dexter, *deks′tər, n.* a small breed of Kerry cattle. [Prob. breeder's name.]

dextrorse, *deks-trors′,* or *deks′, adj.* (*biol.*) rising spirally and turning to the left, i.e. crossing an outside observer's field of view from left to right upwards (like a screw-nail) : formerly used in the contrary sense (sinistrorse). [L. *dextrōrsus,* towards the right—*dexter, vertĕre,* to turn.]

dey, *dā, n.* a dairy-maid.—Also **dey′-woman.** [See dairy.]

dey, *dā, n.* the pasha or governor of Algiers before the French conquest. [Turk. *dāi,* orig. a maternal uncle, a familiar title of the chief of the Janizaries.]

dhak, *dāk, n.* an Indian Butea. [Hind. *dhāk.*]

dhal, dholl. Same as dal.

dharma, *där′mä, n.* the righteousness that underlies the law : the law. [Sans.]

dhobi, *dō′bi, n.* an Indian washerman. [Hind. *dhobi.*]

dhole, *dōl, n.* the Indian wild dog. [Supposed to be from some Indian language.]

dhooly. See doo′lie.

dhoti, *dō′ti, **dhooti**, *doō′ti, n.* the Hindu loin-cloth : a cotton fabric so used. [Hind. *dhoti.*]

dhow, better **dow**, *dow, n.* an Arab lateen-sailed vessel of the Indian Ocean. [Origin unknown; cf. Ar. *dāw,* Marathi *dāw.*]

dhurra. See durra.

dhurrie. Same as **durrie.**

di-, *dī-,* in composition, two, twice, double. [Gr. *dis,* twice.]

diabase, *dī′ə-bās, n.* (formerly) diorite : an altered dolerite or basalt.—*adj.* **diabä′sic.** [Appar. originally a faulty derivative of Gr. *di-,* double, *basis,* base; confused or combined with *diabasis,* transition.]

diabetes, *dī-ə-bē′tēz, n.* a disease marked by a morbid and excessive discharge of urine—**diabetes insip′idus,** without, **diabetes melli′tus** (L., honied) with, excess of sugar in the blood and urine.—*adjs.* **diabetic** (*-bēt′* or *-bet′*), **-al.** [Gr. *diabētēs,* a siphon, *dia,* through, and *bainein,* to go.]

diablerie, diablery, *dē-äb′lə-rē, n.* magic : the black art : sorcery. [Fr.,—*diable;* see devil.]

diabolic, -al, *dī-ə-bol′ik, -əl, adjs.* devilish.—*adv.* **diabol′ically.—*v.t.* **diabolise** (*-ab′ə-līz*), to render devilish.—*ns.* **diab(ol)ol′ogy,** the doctrine of devils : devil-lore. [Gr. *diabolikos—diabolos;* see devil.]

diabolo, *di-a′bol-ō,* or *dī-, n.* a game in which a two-headed top is spun, tossed, and caught on a string attached to two sticks, held one in each hand. [Gr. *diaballō,* I throw over, toss, or *diabolos,* devil : an old name was the devil on two sticks.]

diacatholicon, *dī-ə-kə-thol′i-kon, n.* (*obs.*) a purgative electuary : a panacea. [Gr. *dia katholikōn,* of universal (ingredients).]

diacaustic, *dī-ə-kaws′tik, adj.* pertaining to curves formed by the intersections of rays of refracted light.—*n.* a curve so formed. [Formed from Gr. *dia,* through, and **caustic.**]

diachylon, *dī-ak′i-lon,* **diachylum,** *-ləm, n.* formerly a plaster of plant juices : now lead-plaster. [Gr. *dia chylōn,* through (i.e. composed of) juices or *diachylōn* (*neut.*), juicy.]

diacid, *dī-as′id, adj.* having two replaceable hydrogen atoms : capable of replacing two hydrogen atoms of an acid. [Gr. *di-,* twice, and **acid.**]

diacodion, *dī-ə-kō′di-on,* **diacodium,** (*-əm*), *n.* a syrup of poppies. [L.,—Gr. *dia kōdeiōn,* composed of poppy-heads—*dia* and gen. pl. of *kōdeia,* a poppy-head.]

diaconate, *dī-ak′ə-nāt, n.* the office of a deacon.— *adj.* **diac′onal,** pertaining to a deacon. [See **deacon.**]

diaconicon, *dī-ə-kon′i-kən, n.* a sacristy for sacred vessels, in a Greek church, on the south side of the bema or sanctuary. [Gr. *diākonikon.*]

diacoustic, *dī-ə-kōōs′tik,* or *kows′, adj.* pertaining to the refraction of sound.—*n.* **diacous′tics,** the branch of physics that deals with refracted sounds. [Gr. *dia,* through, and **acoustic.**]

diacritic, -al, *dī-ə-krit′ik, -əl, adjs.* distinguishing —used of marks or points attached to letters. [Gr. *diakritikos—dia,* between, and *kritikos;* see **critic.**]

diact, *dī′akt, adj.* two-rayed.—*adjs.* **diactinal** (*-ak′,* or *-ti′*), **diact′ine.** [Gr. *di-,* twice, *aktis, aktinos,* ray.]

diactinic, *dī-ak-tin′ik, adj.* capable of transmitting actinic rays. [Gr. *dia,* through, *aktis, aktinos,* ray.]

diadelphous, *dī-ə-del′fəs, adj.* of stamens, united by the filaments in two bundles : having stamens so joined.—*n.pl.* **Diadel′phia,** in the Linnaean classification a class with stamens so joined. [Gr. *di-,* twice, *adelphos,* brother.]

diadem, *dī′ə-dem, n.* a crown, head-band, or the like : an arch of a crown.—*adj.* **dī′ademed,** wearing a diadem.—**diadem spider,** the common garden spider (from its markings). [O.Fr. *diademe* —L. *diadēma—*Gr. *diadēma—dia,* round, and *deein,* to bind.]

diadochi, *dī-ad′o-kī, n.pl.* the generals who became monarchs of the various kingdoms (Syria, Egypt, etc.) into which the empire of Alexander the Great split after his death (323 B.C.). [Gr. *diadochos,* succeeding, a successor; *diadechesthai,* to succeed.]

diadrom, *dī′ə-drom, n.* a course or passing : a

Neutral vowels in unaccented syllables : *el′ə-mənt, in′fənt, ran′dəm*

vibration.—*adj.* (of leaf nerves) radiating fan-wise. [Gr. *dia*, across, *dromos*, a run.]

diaeresis, dieresis, *dī-ēr'i-sis, n.* a mark (¨) placed over the second of two adjacent vowel-letters to show that each is to be pronounced separately, as *naïf* :—*pl.* **diaer'eses, dier'eses** (*-ēz*). [Gr. *diairesis*, separation—*dia*, apart, *haireein*, to take.]

diageotropic, *dī-ə-jē-ō-trop'ik, adj.* (*bot.*) taking a position perpendicular to the direction of gravity.—*adv.* **diageotrop'ically.**—*n.* **diageotropism** (*-ot'*). [Gr. *dia*, across, and **geotropic.**]

diaglyph, *dī'ə-glif, n.* an intaglio. [Gr. *dia*, through, *glyphein*, to carve.]

diagnosis, *dī-əg-nō'sis, n.* the identification of a disease by means of its symptoms : a formal determining description :—*pl.* **diagnō'ses** (*-ēz*).—*v.t.* **diagnose** (*-nōz'*, *-nōs'*), to ascertain from symptoms, as a disease.—*adj.* **diagnōs'tic,** distinguishing : differentiating.—*n.* that by which anything is known : a symptom.—*n.pl.* **diagnos'tics,** diagnosis as a branch of medicine.—*n.* **diagnostic'ian** (*-nostish'-ən*), one skilled in diagnosis. [Gr., *dia*, between, *gnōsis*, knowing.]

diagometer, *dī-ə-gom'i-tər, n.* a form of electroscope for ascertaining electric conductivity. [Gr. *diagein*, to conduct, *metron*, a measure.]

diagonal, *dī-ag'ə-nəl, adj.* through the corners, or joining two vertices that are not adjacent, of a polygon : (of a plane) passing through two edges, not adjacent, of a polyhedron : slantwise.—*n.* a straight line or plane so drawn.—*adv.* **diag'onally.**—**diagonal scale,** a scale for laying down small fractions of the unit of measurement, by lengthwise parallel lines intersected by two sets of parallel lines, crosswise and oblique. [L. *diagōnālis*, from Gr. *diagōnios*—*dia*, through, and *gōniā*, a corner.]

diagram, *dī'ə-gram, n.* a figure or plan intended to explain rather than represent actual appearance : an outline figure or scheme : a curve symbolising a set of facts : a record traced by an automatic indicator.—*adj.* **diagrammatic** (*-grə-mat'ik*).—*adv.* **diagrammat'ically.**—*n.* **dī'agraph** (*-grâf*), an instrument for copying, enlarging, or projecting drawings.—*adj.* **diagraphic** (*-graf'ik*). [Gr. *diagramma*—*dia*, round, *graphein*, to write.]

diaheliotropic, *dī-ə-hē-li-ō-trop'ik, adj.* (*bot.*) turning transversely to the light.—*n.* **diaheliotropism** (*-ot'rə-pizm*). [Gr. *dia*, across, and **heliotropic.**]

dial, *dī'əl, n.* an instrument for showing the time of day by the sun's shadow (*sun-dial*) : (*obs.*) a time-piece : the face of a watch or clock : a circular plate on which a movable index shows the value of some quantity measured, or can be set to make an adjustment (as in getting a telephone connexion) : a miner's compass with sights for surveying : (*slang*) a face.—*v.t.* to measure or indicate or get into communication with by dial (*pr.p.* **di'alling** ; *pa.t.* and *pa.p.* **di'alled**).—*ns.* **di'alist,** a maker of dials : one skilled in dialling ; **di'aller,** one who surveys by dial ; **di'alling,** the art of constructing sun-dials : the science which explains the measuring of time by the sun-dial : surveying by dial ; **di'alplate,** the plate to which the pillars of a watch are fixed. [L.L. *diālis*, daily—L. *diēs*, a day.]

dialect, *dī'ə-lekt, n.* a variety or form of a language peculiar to a district or class, esp. but not necessarily other than a literary or standard form : a peculiar manner of speaking.—*adj.* **dialect'al.**—*adv.* **dialect'ally.**—*ns.* **dialect'icism** ; **dialectol'ogist** ; **dialectol'ogy.** [Through Fr. and L. from Gr. *dialektos*, speech, manner of speech, peculiarity of speech—*dia*, between, *legein*, to speak.]

dialectic, -al, *dī-ə-lek'tik, -əl, adj.* pertaining to dialect or to discourse or to dialectics : logical.—*ns.* **dialec'tic, dialec'tics,** art of discussing : that branch of logic which teaches the rules and modes of reasoning.—*adv.* **dialec'tically.**—*n.* **dialecti'cian,** one skilled in dialectics, a logician.—**dialectical materialism** (see **materialism**). [Gr. *dialektikos.*]

diallage, *dī-al'ə-jē, n.* (*rhet.*) a figure of speech by which arguments, after having been considered

from various points of view, are all brought to bear upon one point. [Gr. *diallagē ;* see next word.]

diallage, *dī'əl-āj, n.* a mineral nearly allied to augite, brown, grey, or green, with play of colour.—*adjs.* **diallagic** (*-aj'ik*), **diallagoid** (*-al'ə-goid*). [Gr. *diallagē*, change—*dia*, between, *allassein*, to change—*allos*, other.]

dialogite, *dī-al'ə-jīt, n.* a rose-red manganese carbonate. [Gr. *dialogē*, selection, doubt.]

dialogue, *dī'ə-log, n.* conversation between two or more persons, esp. of a formal or imaginary nature.—*v.i.* (*Shak.*) to converse.—*v.t.* (*Shak.*) to put into dialogue form.—*adjs.* **dialog'ic** (*-loj'*), **dialogist'ic, -al.**—*v.i.* **dialyse** (*dī'ə-līz*), to discourse in dialogue.—*n.* **dial'ogist,** a speaker in, or writer of, dialogue. [Fr.,—L. *dialogus*—Gr. *dialogos*, a conversation—*dialegesthai*, to discourse.]

dialypetalous, *dī-ə-li-pet'ə-ləs, adj.* having the petals separate, polypetalous. [Gr. *dialyein*, to separate—*dia*, asunder, *lyein*, to loose, and *petalon*, a leaf.]

dialysis, *dī-al'i-sis, n.* (*chem.*) the separation of substances by diffusion through a membranous septum or partition : diaeresis : dissolution : separation.—*pl.* **dial'yses** (*-sēz*).—*adj.* **dialysable** (*dī-ə-līz'ə-bl*).—*v.t.* **dialyse** (*dī'ə-līz*), to separate by dialysis.—*n.* **dī'alyser.**—*adj.* **dialytic** (*-lit'ik*). [Gr. *dialysis*—*dia*, asunder, *lyein*, to loose.]

diamagnetic, *dī-ə-mag-net'ik, adj.* cross-magnetic —applied to any substance, of which a rod suspended between the poles of a magnet arranges itself across the lines of force (opp. to *paramagnetic*).—*adv.* **diamagnet'ically.**—*n.* **diamag'netism,** the form of magnetic action possessed by diamagnetic bodies : the branch of magnetism which deals with diamagnetic phenomena. [Gr. *dia*, through, and **magnetic.**]

diamanté, *dē-ä-män²-tā, n.* a fabric covered with glittering particles.—Also *adj.* [Fr.,—*diamant*, diamond.]

diamantiferous, *dī-ə-man-tif'ər-əs, adj.* yielding diamonds. [Fr. *diamantifère.*]

diameter, *dī-am'i-tər, n.* the measure through or across : a straight line passing through the centre of a circle or other figure, terminated at both ends by the circumference : in the parabola a straight line parallel to the axis extending from the curve to infinity.—*adjs.* **diam'etral, diametric** (*dī-ə-met'rik*), **-al,** in the direction of a diameter : pertaining to the diameter : as of opposite ends of a diameter (as in *diametrical opposition*).—*advs.* **diam'etrally,** in a diametral manner ; **diamet'rically,** along a diameter : as at the ends of a diameter. —**tactical diameter,** the perpendicular distance between a ship's courses before and after turning 180°. [Through Fr. and L. from Gr. *diametros*—*dia*, through, *metron*, a measure.]

diamond, *dī-ə-mənd, n.* the most valuable of all gems, and the hardest of all minerals, carbon crystallised in the cubic system : a rhombus : a card of a suit distinguished by pips of that form : (*U.S.*) a baseball field, or the part between bases : one of the smallest kinds of English printing type (about 4½-point).—*adj.* resembling diamonds : made of diamonds : marked with diamonds : lozenge-shaped, rhombic.—*ns.* **diamond-bee'tle,** a beautiful sparkling S. American weevil ; **di'amond-drill,** a borer whose bit is set with bort ; **di'amond-dust, -pow'der,** the powder made by the friction of diamonds on one another in the course of polishing.—*adjs.* **di'amonded,** furnished with diamonds ; **diamondif'erous,** yielding diamonds.—*ns.* **di'amond-field,** a region that yields diamonds ; **di'amond-hitch,** a mode of fastening a rope for heavy burdens ; **di'amond-ju'bilee,** a sixtieth anniversary (of marriage, di'amond-wedd'ing) ; **di'amond-wheel,** a wheel covered with diamond-dust and oil for polishing diamonds, etc.—**black diamonds,** (*fig.*) coal ; **diamond cut diamond,** an encounter between two very sharp persons ; **rough diamond,** an uncut diamond : a person possibly of great worth, but of rude exterior and unpolished manners. [M.E. *diamaunt*—O.Fr.

fāte, fär, àsk ; mē, hər (her) ; *mīne ; mōte ; mūte ; mōōn ; ∂hen* (then)

diamyl 289 diatom

diamant.—L.L. *diamas, -antis*—Gr. *adamas, -antos;* see adamant.]

diamyl, *dī-am'il, adj.* having two amyl groups. [Gr. *di-,* twice, amyl.]

Diana, *dī-an'ä, n.* Roman goddess of light, the moon-goddess, representative of chastity and hunting—identified with the Greek Artemis : a huntress.—Also Dī'an.—Diana monkey, a large long-tailed W. African monkey (*Cercopithecus diana*) with a white crescent on the forehead; Diana of the Ephesians, a goddess of fertility worshipped at Ephesus ; Diana's tree, tree of silver (see tree). [L. *Diāna.*]

diandrous, *dī-an'drəs, adj.* having, or allowing, two husbands or male mates (at a time) : having two stamens or antheridia.—*n.pl.* Dian'dria, in Linnaeus's classification, a class of plants with two stamens.—*n.* dian'dry, the practice or condition of being diandrous. [Gr. *dis,* twice, *anēr, andros,* a man, male.]

dianodal, *dī-ə-nō'dl, adj.* (*math.*) passing through a node. [Gr. *dia,* through, and nodal.]

dianoetic, *dī-ə-nō-et'ik, adj.* capable of or relating to thought. [Gr. *dianoētikos—dia,* through, *noeein,* to think.]

Dianthus, *dī-an'thəs, n.* the genus of herbaceous flowers to which carnations and pinks belong. [Poss. Gr. *Dios anthos,* Zeus's flower; or *dianthēs,* flowering in succession.]

diapason, *dī-ə-pā'zn, -sn, n.* a whole octave : a bass part : a harmony : a full volume of various sounds in concord : the whole range or compass of tones : a standard of pitch : a foundation-stop of an organ (open or stopped diapason) extending through its whole compass.—(*Spens.*) dī'apase. [Gr. *dia pasōn chordōn symphōniā,* concord through all the notes.]

diapedesis, *dī-ə-pi-dē'sis, n.* (*physiol.*) the migration of white blood-corpuscles through the walls of the blood-vessels without apparent rupture.—*adj.* diapedetic (-*det'ik*). [Gr. *dia,* through, *pēdēsis,* leaping.]

diapente, *dī-ə-pen'ti, n.* (*mus.*) the interval of a fifth : a medicine of five ingredients. [Gr. *dia,* through, *pente,* five.]

diaper, *dī'ə-pər, n.* linen or cotton cloth with a square or diamond pattern of a counter-changing character, used chiefly for table linen : a pattern for ornamentation, woven, not coloured, in textiles : a floral or geometric pattern in low relief in architecture, often repeated over a considerable surface : paving in a chequered pattern.—*v.t.* to variegate with figures, as diaper.—*n.* dī'apering. [O.Fr. *diaspre, diapre*—L.L. *diasprus*—Byzantine Gr. *diaspros, dia,* through, *aspros,* white.]

diaphanous, *dī-af'ə-nəs, adj.* transparent : translucent : pellucid : clear.—*ns.* diaphaneity (*dī-ə-fə-nē'i-ti*); diaphanom'eter, an instrument for measuring the transparency of the air.—*adv.* diaph'anously.—*n.* diaph'anousness. [Gr. *diaphanēs—dia,* through, and *phainein,* to show, shine.]

diaphoresis, *dī-ə-for-ē'sis, n.* sweat, esp. artificially induced.—*adj.* diaphoretic (-*et'ik*), promoting sweating.—*n.* a sudorific. [Gr. *diaphorēsis,* sweating—*dia,* through, *pherein,* to carry.]

diaphototropic, *dī-ə-fō-tō-trop'ik, adj.* diaheliotropic.—*n.* diaphototropy (-*tot'rə-pi*). [Gr. *dia,* across, and phototropic.]

diaphragm, *dī'ə-fram, -frəm, n.* a thin partition or dividing membrane : the midriff, a structure separating the chest from the abdomen : a metal plate with a central hole, for cutting off side-rays in optical instruments.—*adjs.* diaphragmatic (-*fragmat'*), diaphrag'mal.—*n.* diaphragmat'tis, inflammation of the diaphragm. [Gr. *diaphragma,* partition, midriff—*dia,* across, *phragma,* a fence.]

diaphysis, *dī-af'i-sis, n.* (*bot.*) an abnormal elongation of the axis : (*anat.*) the shaft of a long bone. [Gr. *diaphysis,* a separation—*dia,* through, *phyesthai,* to grow.]

diapophysis, *dī-ə-pof'i-sis, n.* a dorsal transverse process of a vertebra :—*pl.* diapophyses (-*sēz*).—*adj.* diapophysial (*dī-ap-ō-fiz'i-əl*). [Gr. *dia,* apart, *apophysis,* offshoot.]

diapositive, *dī-ə-poz'i-tiv, n.* a transparent photographic positive. [Gr. *dia,* through, and positive.]

diapyesis, *dī-ə-pī-ē'sis, n.* suppuration.—*adj.* diapyetic (-*et'ik*), producing suppuration.—*n.* a medicine of this property. [Gr. *diapyēsis—dia,* through, *pyon,* pus.]

diarch, *dī'ärk, adj.* (*bot.*) having two xylem strands. [Gr. *di-,* twice, *archē,* origin.]

diarchy, *dī'är-ki, n.* a form of government in which two persons, states, or bodies are jointly vested with supreme power—less correctly dī'narchy, dy'archy.—*adjs.* diarch'al, diarch'ic. [Gr. *di-,* twice, *archein,* to rule.]

diarrhoea, diarrhea, *dī-ə-rē'ä, n.* a persistent purging or looseness of the bowels.—*adjs.* diarrhoe'al, diarrhoe'ic (also -rhē'al, etc.). [Gr. *diarroia—dia,* through, *rhoiā,* a flow.]

diarthrosis, *dī-är-thrō'sis, n.* articulation admitting free movement. [Gr. *diarthrōsis,* jointing—*dia,* through, *Arthron,* joint.]

diary, *dī'ə-ri, n.* a daily record : a book for making daily records, noting engagements, etc.—*adjs.* diarial (*dī-ā'ri-əl*), diā'rian.—*v.t.* or *v.i.* dī'arise.—*n.* dī'arist, one who keeps a diary. [L. *diārium —diēs,* day.]

diascordium, *dī-ə-skor'di-əm, n.* a medicine made from water-germander, etc. [Medical L.—Gr. *dia skordiōn,* composed of *skordiōn* (perhaps water-germander).]

diaskeuast, *dī-ə-skū'ast, n.* a reviser : an interpolator. [Gr. *diaskeuazein,* to make ready—*dia,* through, *skeuos,* a tool.]

diaspora, *dī-as'por-ä, n.* dispersion, used collectively for the dispersed Jews after the Babylonian captivity, and also in the apostolic age for the Jews living outside of Palestine. [Gr. *diasporā—dia,* through, *speirein,* to scatter.]

diaspore, *dī'ə-spōr, n.* a mineral, aluminium hydroxide, AlO (O H). [Gr. *diasporā,* scattering, from its decrepitation.]

diastaltic, *dī-ə-stal'tik, adj.* (Greek mus.) of intervals, extended : bold. [Gr. *diastaltikos,* expanding.]

diastase, *dī-ə-stās, n.* a ferment that converts starch into sugar, produced in germinating seeds and in pancreatic juice.—*adj.* diastatic (-*stat'ik*). [Gr. *diastasis,* division—*dia,* apart, *stasis,* setting.]

diastasis, *dī-as'tə-sis, n.* (*surg.*) separation of bones without fracture. [See foregoing.]

diastema, *dī-ə-stē'mä, n.* a natural space between two consecutive teeth, or series of teeth :—*pl.* diastē'mata.—*adj.* diastemat'ic. [Gr. *diastēma, -atos,* interval.]

diastole, *dī-as'tō-lē, n.* dilatation of the heart, auricles, and arteries—opp. to *systole,* or contraction : the lengthening of a short syllable, as before a pause.—*adj.* diastolic (*dī-ə-stol'ik*). [Gr. *diastolē—dia,* asunder, and *stellein,* to place.]

diastrophism, *dī-as'trō-fizm, n.* (*geol.*) processes of deformation of the earth's crust.—*adj.* diastrophic (*dī-ə-strof'ik*). [Gr. *diastrophē,* distortion —*dia,* aside, *strophē,* a turning.]

diastyle, *dī'ə-stīl, adj.* (*archit.*) with columns about three diameters apart.—*n.* a building or colonnade so proportioned. [Gr. *diastylos—dia,* apart, *stylos,* column.]

diatessaron, *dī-ə-tes'ə-rōn, -ron, -rən, n.* a harmony of the four gospels, esp. the earliest, that of Tatian (prob. 110-180 A.D.) : (*mus.*) the interval of a fourth : a medicine of four ingredients. [Gr. *dia tessarōn,* through, or composed of, four.]

diathermic, *dī-ə-thər'mik, adj.* permeable by radiant heat.—Also diather'mal, diather'manous, diather'mous.—*ns.* diather'macy, diather'mancy, diathermanē'ity, permeability by radiant heat; di'athermy, heating of internal parts of the body by electric currents. [Gr. *dia,* through, *thermē,* heat.]

diathesis, *dī-ath'i-sis, n.* a particular condition or habit of body, esp. one predisposing to certain diseases : a habit of mind.—*adj.* diathetic (*dī-ə-thet'ik*). [Gr. *diathesis—dia,* asunder, *tithenai,* to place.]

diatom, *dī'ə-təm, n.* one of a class of microscopic unicellular algae with flinty shells in two halves, fitting like box and lid.—*adj.* diatomā'ceous.—*n.*

Neutral vowels in unaccented syllables : *el'ə-mənt, in'fənt, ran'dəm*

diatomite (dĭ-at'ǝm-īt, or dī'ǝt-), diatomaceous earth or kieselguhr, a powdery silicious deposit of diatom frustules.—**diatom ooze**, a deep-sea deposit of diatom frustules. [Gr. *diatomos*, cut through—*dia*, through, *temnein*, to cut.]

diatomic, dī-ǝ-tom'ik, adj. consisting of two atoms : having two replaceable atoms or groups : bivalent. [Gr. *di-*, *dis*, twice, and **atom**.]

diatonic, dī-ǝ-ton'ik, adj. proceeding by the tones and intervals of the natural scale in music.—adv. **diaton'ically**. [Gr. *diatonikos*—*dia*, through, *tonos*, tone.]

diatribe, dī'ǝ-trīb, n. a continued discourse or disputation : an invective harangue.—n. **di'atribist**, a writer or utterer of such. [Gr. *diatrĭbē*, a spending of time—*dia*, through, *tribein*, to rub, wear away.]

diatropism, dī-at'rŏ-pizm, n. orientation at right angles to the direction of a stimulus.—adj. **diatropic** (dī-ǝ-trop'ik). [Gr. *dia*, across, *tropos*, turning.]

diaxon, dī-aks'on, adj. having two axes or two axis-cylinder processes.—n. a bipolar nerve-cell. [Gr. *di-*, twice, *axōn*, an axis.]

diazeuxis, dī-ǝ-zūk'sis, n. (*Greek mus.*) the separation of two tetrachords by a whole tone.—adj. **diazeuc'tic**. [Gr. *diazeuxis*, disjunction—*dia*, apart, *zeuxis*, yoking.]

diazo-, dī-az'ō-, in combination, applied to compounds containing two nitrogen atoms and a hydrocarbon radical.

dib, dib, v.i. to dip, as in angling :—pr.p. **dibb'ing**; pa.t. and pa.p. **dibbed**. [Prob. a form of **dab**.]

dib, dib, n. one of the small bones of a sheep's leg : (pl.) a children's game, played by throwing up such small bones or stones (**dib'-stones**) from the palm and catching them on the back of the hand—in Scots *chuckie-stanes*, or *chucks*: (slang) money.

dibasic, dī-bā'sik, adj. capable of reacting with two equivalents of an acid : (of acids) having two replaceable hydrogen atoms. [Gr. *di-*, twice, and **basic**.]

dibble, dib'l, n. a pointed tool used for making holes for seeds or plants—also **dibb'er**.—v.t. **dibb'le** to plant with a dibble.—v.i. to make holes : to dip, as in angling.—n. **dibb'ler**. [Prob. connected with **dab**.]

dibranchiate, dī-brang'ki-āt, adj. having two gills.—ns.pl. **Dibran'chia**, **Dibranchiā'ta**, the two-gilled sub-class of cephalopods. [Gr. *di-*, twice, *branchia*, gills.]

dibromo-, dī-brō'mō-, in composition, having two atoms of bromine, esp. replacing hydrogen.

dicacity, dī-kas'i-ti, n. raillery, pert speech.—adj. **dicacious** (dī-kā'shǝs). [L. *dicāx*, sarcastic.]

dicarpellary, dī-kär'pǝl-ǝr-i, or -pel', adj. of or with two carpels.

dicast, **dikast**, dik'ast, n. one of the 6,000 Athenians annually chosen to act as judges.—n. **dicas'tery**, their court. [Gr. *dikastēs*—*dikē*, justice.]

dice. See **die** (2).

Dicentra, dī-sen'trä, n. a genus of the fumitory family including bleeding-heart (*D. spectabilis*) with the two outer petals broadly pouched.—Also **Dielytra** (dī-el'i-trä; orig. a misprint). [Gr. *di-*, double, *kentron*, a point, spur.]

dicephalous, dī-sef'ǝ-lǝs, adj. two-headed. [Gr. *dikephalos*—*di-*, double, *kephalē*, a head.]

dich, dich, (*Shak.*, *Timon*) supposed to be for **do it**, may it do.

dichasium, dī-kā'zi-ǝm, n. a cymose inflorescence in which each axis in turn produces a pair of nearly equal branches (pl. **dicha'sia**).—adj. **dicha'sial**. [Gr. *dichāsis*, division, halving.]

dichlamydeous, dī-klǝ-mid'i-ǝs, adj. having both a calyx and a corolla. [Gr. *di-*, double, *chlamys*, *-ydos*, mantle.]

dichloro-, dī-klō'rō-, in composition, having two atoms of chlorine, esp. replacing hydrogen.—n. **dichlo'ro-diphēn'yl-trichlo'ro-eth'ane**, known as D.D.T., a white, practically odourless powder used to kill lice and thus prevent the spread of typhus; effective also against other insects.

dichogamy, dik- or dīk-og'ǝ-mi, n. an arrangement for preventing the self-fertilisation of hermaphro-

dite flowers, the stamens and stigmas ripening at different times.—adj. **dichog'amous**. [Gr. *dicha*, in two, *gamos*, marriage.]

dichord, dī'kord, n. an ancient two-stringed lute.

dichotomy, dik- or dīk-ot'ǝ-mi, n. a division into two parts.—v.t. and v.i. **dichot'omise.**—n. **dichot'omist.**—adj. **dichot'omous.**—adv. **dichot'omously.** [Gr. *dichotomiā*—*dicha*, in two, *tomē*, a cut—*temnein*, to cut.]

dichroism, dī'krō-izm, n. the property of showing different colours exhibited by doubly refracting crystals when viewed in different directions by transmitted light.—adjs. **dichrō'ic**, **dichrōit'ic.**—ns. **di'chroïte**, a strongly dichroic mineral, iolite or cordierite; **dī'chrō(o)scope**, an instrument for testing the dichroism of crystals.—adj. **dichrō(o)scop'ic**. [Gr. *dichroos*, two-coloured—*di-*, twice, *chroā*, colour.]

dichromate, dī-krō'māt, a salt of **dichro'mic acid** ($H_2Cr_2O_7$), containing two chromium atoms. —Also **bichromate**. [Gr. *di-*, double, and **chromate**.]

dichromatic, dī-krō-mat'ik, adj. having two colours, esp. in different individuals of the same species : able to see two colours and two only, as in red-green colour-blind persons who see only blue and yellow.—n. a person of dichromatic vision, a dichromat.—ns. **di'chromat(e)**, a person who can distinguish two colours only; **dichrō'matism.**—adj. **dichrō'mic**, dichroic : dichromatic.—n. **dichrō'mism**. [Gr. *di-*, twice, *chrōma*, *-atos*, colour.]

dichromic. See (1) **dichromate**; (2) **dichromatic**.

dicht, diht, v.t. (*Scot.*) to wipe.—n. a wipe. [dight.]

dick, dik, n. (slang) fine words (for **dictionary**): also for **declaration**, as *to take one's dick*, and prob. *up to dick*, excellent (up to declared value).

dickcissel, dik-sis'l, n. the black-throated bunting, an American migratory bird.

dickens, dik'ǝnz, n. the deuce, the devil, as in *what the dickens, play the dickens*. [App. *Dickon*, Richard, as a substitute for **devil**.]

Dickensian, dik-en'zi-ǝn, adj. pertaining to Charles *Dickens* (1812-1870), the novelist.—n. an admirer or student of Dickens.

dicker, dik'ǝr, n. (*Amer.*) petty trade by barter, etc.—v.i. to haggle. [Prob. the obs. *dicker*, the number ten, esp. of hides or skins.—L. *decuria*.]

dickey, **dicky**, dik'i, n. a leathern apron for a gig, etc. : the driver's seat in a carriage : a seat for servants at the back of a carriage : a folding seat at the back of a motor-car : a false shirt-front. [Perh. from *dick*, a prov. Eng. word for a leathern apron; perh. Du. *dek*, a cover.]

Dicksonia, dik-sōn'i-ä, n. a tropical and southern genus of ferns, mainly tree-ferns. [After James *Dickson* (d. 1822), botanist.]

dicky, **dickey**, dik'i, n. (*E. Anglian*) an ass.—n. **dick'y-bird** (childish), a small bird. [*Dick*, for Richard.]

dicky, **dickey**, dik'i, adj. (coll.) shaky. [Origin unknown.]

diclinous, dī'kli-nǝs, or -klī', adj. having the stamens and pistils in separate flowers, whether on the same or on different plants.—n. **di'clinism**. [Gr. *di-*, twice, double, *klīnē*, a bed.]

dicotyledon, dī-kot-i-lē'dǝn, n. a plant of the **Dicotylē'donēs** (-ēz) or **Dicot'ylae**, one of the two great divisions of Angiosperms, having embryos with two cotyledons, leaves commonly net-veined, the parts of the flowers in two, fives, or multiples of these, and the vascular bundles in the axes usually containing cambium.—adj. **dicotylē'donous**. [Gr. *di-*, twice, and **cotyledon**.]

dicrotic, dī-krot'ik, adj. of the pulse, having two beats to one beat of the heart.—Also **di'crotous.**—n. **di'crotism**. [Gr. *di-*, twice, *krotos*, beat.]

Dictaphone, dik'tǝ-fōn, n. a recording apparatus for dictating letters, etc. [Trade-mark: L. *dictāre*, to dictate, Gr. *phōnē*, sound.]

dictate, dik-tāt', formerly dik'tāt, v.t. to say or read for another to write : to lay down with authority : to command.—n. (dik'tāt) an order, rule, direction : impulse.—*n.* **dict** (*obs.*), a saying.—*v.t.* (*obs.*) to dictate.—*ns.* **dicta′tion**, act, art, or practice of dictating : speaking or reading of words for a pupil, amanuensis, etc., to write : overbearing command; **dicta′tor**, one invested with absolute authority—originally an extraordinary Roman magistrate :—*fem.* **dicta′tress, dicta′trix.**—*adj.* **dictatorial** (*dik-tə-tō′ri-əl*), like a dictator : absolute : overbearing.—*adv.* **dictā′tō′rially.**—*ns.* **dictā′torship, dicta′ture.**—*adj.* **dic′tātory.** [L. *dictāre, -ātum*, freq. of *dicĕre*, to say.]

diction, *dik′shən*, *n.* a saying or speaking : manner of speaking or expressing : choice of words : style : (*U.S.*) enunciation. [L. *dictiō, -ōnis—dicĕre, dictum*, to say.]

dictionary, *dik′shən-ə-ri*, *n.* a book containing the words of a language alphabetically arranged, with their meanings, etymology, etc. : a lexicon : a work containing information on any department of knowledge, alphabetically arranged. [L.L. *dictiōnārium*; see **diction.**]

Dictograph, *dik′tō-gråf*, *n.* a telephone for transmitting speech from room to room, with or without the speaker's knowledge. [Trade-mark : L. *dictum*, thing said, Gr. *graphein*, to write.]

dictum, *dik′təm*, *n.* something said : a saying : an authoritative saying :—*pl.* **dic′ta.** [L.]

dictyogen, *dik′ti-ō-jen*, *n.* (*obs.*) a monocotyledon with net-veined leaves. [Gr. *diktyon*, a net; *gennaein*, to produce.]

dicyclic, *dī-sik′lik*, *adj.* having two whorls or rings. [Gr. *di-*, twice, double, *kyklos*, wheel.]

dicynodont, *dī-sin′o-don′*, *n.* an extinct tusked reptile, showing affinities with mammals. [Gr. *di-*, twice, *kyōn, kynos*, dog, and *odous, odontos*, tooth.]

did, *did*, **didst**, *didst*, *pa.t.* of **do.**

didactic, -al, *di-dak′tik, -əl*, *adjs.* fitted or intended to teach : instructive : preceptive.—*adv.* **didac′tically.**—*n.* **didac′ticism** (*-sizm*).—*n.pl.* **didactics**, the art or science of teaching. [Gr. *didaktikos—didaskein*, to teach; akin to L. *docēre, discēre*.]

didactyl, *di-dak′til*, *adj.* two-fingered, two-toed, or two-clawed.—Also *n.*—*adj.* **didac′tylous.** [Gr. *di-*, twice, *daktylos*, finger, toe.]

didapper, *di′dap-ər*, *n.* the dabchick or little grebe : one who disappears and bobs up again. [**dive** and **dapper**, a variant of **dipper**; cf. O.E. *dúfedoppa*, pelican.]

didascalic, *did-as-kal′ik*, *adj.* didactic. [Gr. *didaskalikos—didaskalos*, teacher.]

didder, *did′ər*, *v.i.* (*prov.*) to shake. [See **dither.**]

diddle, *did′l*, *v.t.* to cajole, swindle.—*n.* **didd′ler.** [Origin uncertain.]

didelphic, *dī-del′fik*, *adj.* having or pertaining to a double womb.—*n.pl.* **Didel′phia**, the marsupials.—*adjs.* **didel′phian, didel′phic, didel′phine, didel′phous.**—*n.* **Didel′phys** (*-fis*), an American genus of opossums.—*n.pl.* **Didelphyidae** (*-fī′i-dē*), the opossum family. [Gr. *di-*, double, *delphys*, womb.]

dido, *dī′dō*, *n.* (*slang*) an antic, caper.—**cut up didoes**, to behave in an extravagant way. [Origin unknown.]

didrachma, *dī-drak′mä*, **didrachm**, *dī′dram*, *n.* a double drachma. [Gr. *di-*, double, and **drachma.**]

Didunculus, *di-dung′kū-lus*, *n.* a remarkable genus of birds—the tooth-billed pigeon of Samoa. [Dim. of *Didus*, zoological name of the dodo, from its similar bill.]

didymium, *di-* or *dī-dim′i-əm*, *n.* a supposed element discovered in 1841, later resolved into neodymium and praseodymium. [Gr. *didymos*, twin, from its constant association with *lanthanum*.]

didymous, *did′i-məs*, *adj.* twin : twinned : growing in pairs : composed of two parts slightly connected. [Gr. *didymos*, twin.]

Didynamia, *did-i-nä′mi-ä*, *n.pl.* a class of plants in the Linnaean system with two long stamens and two short.—*adjs.* **didynä′mian, didyn′-amous.** [Gr. *di-*, double, *dynamis*, strength.]

die, *dī*, *v.i.* (or *v.t.* with object *death*) to lose life : to perish : to wither : (hyperbolically) to languish, suffer, or long : to become insensible : to merge (*pr.p.* **dy′ing**; *pa.t.* and *pa.p.* **died**, *dīd*).—*adj.*

die′-away′, languishing.—*n.* **die′-hard**, an irreconcilable conservative.—**die away**, to disappear by degrees, become gradually inaudible; **die back**, to die by degrees from the tip backwards; **die down**, to subside : to die above ground, leaving only roots or rootstocks; **die game**, to keep up one's spirit to the last; **die hard**, to struggle hard against death, to be long in dying; **die off**, to die quickly or in large numbers ; **die out**, to become extinct, to disappear. [Prob. from a lost O.E. (Anglian) *dégan*; but commonly referred to a Scand. root seen in O.N. *deyja, dōyja*; akin to M.H.G. *touwen*, whence Ger. *tod*. The O.E. word in use was *steorfan*.]

die, *dī*, *n.* a small cube with numbered faces thrown from a box in gaming : a small cubical piece : hazard : a stamp for impressing coin, etc. : applied to various tools for shaping things by stamping or cutting : *pl.* (gaming, cookery, and the like) **dice** (*dīs*); (stamping and shaping) **dies** (*dīz*).—*v.i.* **dice**, to play with dice.—*v.t.* to cut into dice : to chequer (*pr.p.* **dic′ing**; *pa.t.* and *pa.p.* **diced**, *dīst*).—*ns.* **dice′-box**, an hour-glass-shaped box from which dice are thrown; **dice′-coal**, a coal that breaks into cubical blocks.—*adj.* **diced** (*dīst*), ornamented with a chequer pattern.—*ns.* **dice′-play**; **dice′-player, dic′er**; **dic′ing**, a chequered pattern : dice-playing; **die′-sink′er**; **die′-sink′ing**, the engraving of dies; **die′-stock**, a contrivance for holding the dies used in screw-cutting; **die′-work**, ornamentation of a metal surface by impressions with a die.—**the die is cast**, an irrevocable step has been taken : there is no turning back now. [O.Fr. *de*, pl. *dez* (Prov. *dat*, It. *dado*), from L.L. *dadus*=L. *datus*, given or cast.]

dieb, *dēb*, *n.* a jackal of northern Africa. [Ar. *dhib*.]

diegesis, *dī-ē-jē′sis*, *n.* (*rhet.*) in an oration, the narration of the facts. [Gr. *diēgēsis*.]

dielectric, *dī-i-lek′trik*, *adj.* non-conducting : transmitting electric effects without conducting.—*n.* a substance capable of supporting an electric stress. [Gr. *dia*, through, and **electric.**]

Dielytra, *dī-el′i-trä*, *n.* an erroneous name for *Dicentra*. [As if from Gr. *di-*, twice, double, *elytron*, cover.]

Diesel, *dēz′l*, *n.* the name of the inventor (1858-1913).—**diesel engine**, a compression-ignition engine in which the oil fuel is introduced into the heated compressed-air charge by a blast of air.

diesis, *dī′e-sis*, *n.* (*mus.*) the difference between a major and a minor semitone : (*print.*) the double dagger (‡) :—*pl.* **dī′eses** (*-sēz*). [Gr. *diesis*, a quarter-tone.]

diet, *dī′ət*, *n.* mode of living, now only with especial reference to food : planned or prescribed selection of food : (*obs.*) allowance of provisions.—*v.t.* to furnish with food : to prescribe a diet for, put on a diet : to keep fasting.—*v.i.* to feed : to take food according to rule.—*n.* **dietā′rian**, one who observes prescribed rules for diet.—*adj.* **dī′etary**, pertaining to diet or the rules of diet.—*n.* course of diet : allowance of food, esp. in large institutions.—*ns.* **dī′et-bread**, bread designed for persons on a diet; **dī′et-drink**, medicated liquor : **dī′eter** (*Shak.*), one who regulates diet.—*adjs.* **dietet′ic, -al**, pertaining to diet.—*adv.* **dietet′ically.**—*ns.* **dietet′ics**, rules for regulating diet; **dī′etist**; **dietitian, -cian** (*-ish′ən*), an authority on diet. [Fr. *diète*—L.L. *diaeta*—Gr. *diaita*, mode of living, diet.]

diet, *dī′ət*, *n.* a national, federal, or provincial assembly, council, or parliament : a conference : (*Scots law*) the proceedings under a criminal libel : a clerical or ecclesiastical function in Scotland, as a *diet of worship*.—*n.* **dī′etine**, a minor or local diet.—**desert the diet**, to abandon criminal proceedings under a particular libel—in Scottish usage. [O.Fr. *diete*—L.L. *diēta*—Gr. *diaita*; or acc. to Littré from L. *diēs*, a (set) day, with which usage cf. Ger. *tag*, day, *reichstag*.]

diethyl, *dī-eth′il*, *adj.* having two ethyl groups.—*n.* **diethylamine** (*-mēn′*), a liquid resembling ethylamine, answering to ammonia, with ethyl replacing two hydrogen atoms.

Neutral vowels in unaccented syllables : *el′ə-mənt, in′fənt, ran′dəm*

diffarreation, *di-far-i-ā'shən, n.* divorce from a Roman marriage by *confarreation.* [L. *dif-* (=*dis-*), asunder.]

differ, *dif'ər, v.i.* to be unlike, distinct, or various (used by itself, or followed by *from*): to disagree (with *with*, sometimes *from*): to fall out, dispute (*with*).—*n.* (*Scot.*) difference.—*ns.* **diff'erence, diff'erency** (*Shak.*), dissimilarity: the quality distinguishing one thing from another: a contention or quarrel: the point in dispute: the excess of one quantity or number over another: differentia: a distinguishing mark: (*her.*) a modification to distinguish the arms of a branch from those of the main line: discrimination.—*v.t.* to make or perceive a difference between or in.—*adj.* **diff'erent,** distinct: separate: unlike: not the same (with *from*, not now *to* or *than*): (*slang*) out of the ordinary: novel.—*n.* **differentia** (*-en'-shi-ä;* L.), in logic, that property which distinguishes a species from others :—*pl.* **differen'tiae** (*-ē*).—*adj.* **differen'tial** (*-shəl*), constituting or pertaining to a difference or differentia: discriminating: (*math.*) pertaining to infinitesimal differences.—*n.* an infinitesimal difference: a differential gear: a price or wage difference.—*adv.* **differen'tially.**—*v.t.* **differentiate** (*-en'shi-āt*), to make different: to create a difference between: to classify or distinguish as different: (*math.*) to obtain the differential coefficient of.—*v.i.* to become different by specialisation: to discriminate.—*ns.* **differentiā'tion,** the act of distinguishing: description of a thing by giving its differentia: exact definition: a change by which what was generalised or homogeneous became specialised or heterogeneous: (*math.*) the act or process of differentiating, or determining the ratio of the rates of change of two quantities one of which is a function of the other; **differen'tiator,** one who or that which differentiates.—*adv.* **diff'erently.—difference tone, differential tone,** a tone heard when two tones are sounded together, its frequency the difference of their frequencies; **differential calculus** (see **calculus**); **differential coefficient,** the ratio of the rate of change of a function to that of its independent variable; **differential gear,** a gear permitting relative rotation of two shafts driven by a third; **differential motion,** a mechanical movement in which the velocity of a driven part is equal to the difference of the velocities of two parts connected to it; **differential thermometer,** a thermometer for measuring difference of temperature. [L. *differre—dif-* (for *dis-*), apart, *ferre,* to bear.]

difficile, *di-fis'il, dif'i-sil, adj.* (*arch.* or reintroduced) difficult. [O.Fr. and Fr., *difficile;* see **difficult.**]

difficult, *dif'i-kəlt, adj.* not easy: hard to be done: requiring labour and pains: hard to please: not easily persuaded: unmanageable.—*adv.* **diff'icultly** (mainly *chem.*).—*n.* **diff'iculty,** quality or fact of being difficult: laboriousness: obstacle: objection: that which cannot be easily understood or believed: embarrassment of affairs: a quarrel. [The adj. was formed from *difficulty*—Fr. *difficulté*—L. *difficultās, -ātis—difficilis—dif-* (*dis-*), neg., and *facilis,* easy.]

diffident, *dif'i-dənt, adj.* distrusting: wanting in self-confidence.—*n.* **diff'idence.**—*adv.* **diff'idently.** [L. *diffidēns, -entis,* pr.p. of *diffidĕre,* to distrust—*dif-* (*dis-*), neg., *fidĕre,* to trust—*fidēs,* faith.]

diffluent, *dif'loo-ənt, adj.* readily flowing away: fluid: deliquescent. [L. *dis-,* apart, *fluēns, -entis,* pr.p. of *fluĕre,* to flow.]

difform, *di-form', adj.* unlike: irregular in form.—*n.* **difform'ity.** [L. *dis-,* apart, *fōrma,* form.]

diffract, *di-frakt', v.t.* to break up: to subject to diffraction.—*n.* **diffrac'tion,** the spreading of light or other rays passing through a narrow opening or by the edge of an opaque body or reflected by a grating, etc., with interference phenomena, coloured and other.—*adj.* **diffrac'tive.**—*n.* **diffrangibil'ity** (*-franj-*).—*adj.* **diffrang'ible,** capable of being diffracted. [L. *diffringĕre, diffrāctum—dis-,* asunder, *frangĕre,* to break.]

diffuse, *di-fūz', v.t.* to pour out all round: to send out in all directions: to scatter: to circulate: to publish.—*v.i.* to spread.—*adj.* **diffūsed',** spread widely: loose.—*adv.* **diffūs'edly.**—*ns.* **diffūs'edness; diffūs'er; diffūsibil'ity.**—*adj.* **diffūs'ible.** —*ns.* **diffū'sion,** a spreading or scattering abroad: extension: distribution: mixture through each other of gases or liquids in contact; **diffū'sion-tube,** an instrument for determining the rate of diffusion for different gases.—*adj.* **diffū'sive** (*-siv*), extending: spreading widely.—*adv.* **diffū'sively.** —*ns.* **diffū'siveness; diffūsiv'ity.** [L. *diffundĕre, diffūsum—dif-* (*dis-*), asunder, *fundĕre,* to pour out.]

diffuse, *di-fūs', adj.* diffused: widely spread: wordy: not concise.—*adv.* **diffuse'ly.**—*n.* **diffuse'ness.** [See above.]

dig, *dig, v.t.* to excavate: to turn up with a spade or otherwise: to get or put by digging: to poke or thrust.—*v.i.* to use a spade: to scoop out: to burrow: to mine: (*slang*) to lodge: (*U.S. slang*) to study hard (*pr.p.* **digg'ing;** *pa.t.* and *pa.p.* **dug,** (*B.*) **digged**).—*n.* an act or course of digging: an archaeological excavating expedition: a thrust, a poke: (*U.S. slang*) a hard student.—*adj.* **digg'-able.**—*ns.* **digg'er,** a person or animal that digs: a miner, esp. a gold-miner: (*slang*) an Australian or New Zealander: a machine for digging; **digg'erwasp,** a burrowing wasp of various kinds.—*n.pl.* **digg'ings,** places where mining is carried on, esp. for gold: (*slang, orig. U.S.*) lodgings, rooms (abbrev. **digs**).—**dig in,** to cover over by digging: to work hard; **dig oneself in,** to entrench oneself: to establish oneself in a position; **dig out** (*U.S. slang*), to decamp; **dig up,** to remove from the ground by digging: (*U.S. slang*) to get. [Prob. O.Fr. *diguer,* to dig; of Gmc. origin.]

digamma, *di-gam'ä, n.* vau, the obsolete sixth letter (*F, Ϝ,* later *ç*) of the Greek alphabet with the sound of our W: as a numeral *ç'*=6, *ç*=6,000. See **episemon.** [Gr. *di-,* twice, and *gamma,* from its form like one capital Γ over another.]

digamy, *dig'ə-mi, n.* a second marriage.—*n.* **dig'amist.**—*adj.* **dig'amous.** [Gr. *di-,* twice, *gamos,* marriage.]

digastric, *dī-gas'trik, adj.* double bellied, or fleshy at each end, as is one of the muscles of the lower jaw. [Gr. *di-,* double, *gastēr,* the belly.]

digest, *di-jest'* (also *dī-*), *v.t.* to dissolve in the stomach: to soften by heat and moisture: to distribute and arrange: to prepare or classify in the mind: to think over.—*v.i.* to be dissolved in the stomach: to be softened by heat and moisture.— *adv.* **digest'edly.**—*n.* **digest'er,** one who digests: a close vessel in which by heat and pressure strong extracts are made from animal and vegetable substances.—*n.* **digestibil'ity.**—*adj.* **digest'ible,** that may be digested.—*n.* **digestion** (*di-jest'yən*), the dissolving of the food in the stomach: orderly arrangement: exposing to slow heat, etc.—*adj.* **digest'ive,** pertaining to digestion: promoting digestion.—*adv.* **digest'ively.** [L. *dīgerĕre, dīgestum,* to carry asunder or dissolve—*dī-* (*dis-*), asunder, and *gerĕre,* to bear.]

digest, *dī'jest, n.* a body of laws collected and arranged, esp. the Justinian code of civil laws: a synopsis: an abstract: a periodical abstract of news or current literature. [L. *dīgesta,* neut. pl. of *dīgestus,* pa.p. of *dīgerĕre,* to carry apart, to arrange.]

dight, *dīt, v.t.* (*arch.*) to adorn: to equip.—*adj.* disposed: adorned. [O.E. *dihtan,* to arrange, prescribe, from L. *dictāre,* to dictate (whence Ger. *dichten,* to write poetry); cf. **dicht.**]

digit, *dij'it, n.* a finger or toe: a finger's breadth or ¾ inch: a figure used in arithmetic to represent a number: the twelfth part of the diameter of the sun or moon.—*adj.* **dig'ital,** pertaining to the fingers.—*n.* **finger:** a key of a piano, etc.—*ns.* **digitalin** (*dij-i-tā'lin,* or *dij'it-ə-lin*), a glucoside or mixture of glucosides got from foxglove; **Digitā'lis,** the foxglove genus: dried foxglove leaves used as a drug.—*adjs.* **dig'itate, -d,** consisting of several finger-like sections.—*adv.* **dig'itately.**—*n.* **digitā'tion,** finger-like arrangement: a finger-like division.—*adj.* **dig'itiform,** formed like fingers; **dig'itigrade,** walking on the toes.—

n. an animal that walks on its toes.—*n.* **digitō'-rium,** a pianist's dumb keyboard for finger exercises. [L. *digitus*, finger, toe.]

digladiate, *dī-glad'i-āt, v.i.* to fight with swords : to fence : to wrangle.—*ns.* **digladiā'tion ; diglad'-iātor.** [L. *digladiārī*, to contend fiercely—*dis-*, this way and that, and *gladius*, sword.]

diglot, *dī'glot, adj.* bilingual. [Gr. *diglōttos—di-,* double, *glōtta*, tongue.]

diglyph, *dī'glif, n.* (*archit.*) an ornament consisting of a double groove. [Gr. *di-*, double, *glyphē*, carving.]

dignify, *dig'ni-fī, v.t.* to invest with honour : to exalt (*pr.p.* **dig'nifying ;** *pa.t.* and *pa.p.* **dig'nified**).—*n.* **dignificā'tion.**—*adj.* **dig'nified,** marked or consistent with dignity : exalted : noble : grave : ranking as a dignitary. [L.L. *dignificāre—dignus,* worthy, *facĕre*, to make.]

dignity, *dig'ni-ti, n.* the state of being dignified : elevation of mind or character : grandeur of mien : elevation in rank, place, etc. : degree of excellence : preferment : high office : a dignitary.—*n.* **dig'-nitary,** one in a high position or rank, esp. in the church; **stand on one's dignity,** to assume a manner that asserts a claim to deference. [Fr. *dignité—*L. *dignitās, -ātis—dignus,* worthy.]

digonal, *dig'э-nl, adj.* of symmetry about an axis, such that a half-turn (180°) gives the same figure. [Gr. *di-*, twice, *gōniā*, angle.]

digoneutic, *dig-ə-nūt'ik, adj.* breeding twice a year. [Gr. *di-*, twice, *goneus*, a parent.]

digraph, *dī'grȧf, n.* two letters expressing but one sound, as *ph* in digraph. [Gr. *di-*, twice, *graphē*, a mark, a character—*graphein*, to write.]

digress, *di-gres', dī-gres', v.i.* to depart from the main subject : to introduce irrelevant matter.—*n.* **digression** (*-gresh'эn*), a going from the main point : a part of a discourse not upon the main subject.—*adjs.* **digress'ional, digress'ive,** of the nature of a digression : departing from the main subject.—*adv.* **digress'ively.** [L. *digredī, dīgressus—dī-* (*dis-*), aside, *gradī*, to step. [See **grade.**]

Digynia, *di-jin'i-ä, n.pl.* in various Linnaean classes of plants, an order with two styles or a deeply cleft style.—*adjs.* **digyn'ian ; digynous** (*dij'* or *dij'i-nəs*), digynian : with two styles or two carpels. [Gr. *di-*, twice, and *gynē*, a woman.]

dihedral, *dī-hē'drəl, adj.* bounded by two planes, or two plane faces—also **diē'dral.**—*n.* **dihē'dron,** the limiting case of a double pyramid when the vertices coincide. [Gr. *di-*, twice, *hedrā*, a seat.]

dihybrid, *dī-hī'brid, n.* a cross between parents that differ in two independently heritable characters.—Also *adj.* [Gr. *di-*, double, twice, and **hybrid.**]

dihydric, *dī-hī'drik, adj.* having two hydroxyl groups.

dijudicate, *dī-jōō'di-kāt, v.t.* and *v.i.* to judge : to decide.—*n.* **dijudicā'tion.** [L. *dī-* (*dis-*), asunder, and *jūdicāre*, judge.]

dika, *dī'kä, dē'kä, n.* a W. African simarubaceous tree, *Irvingia gabonensis*, the so-called wild-mango. —*ns.* **di'ka-bread,** a compressed mass of dika and other seeds, smelling like chocolate; **di'ka-butter, -oil,** a fat expressed from its seeds. [From a W. African name.]

dik-dik, *dik'dik, n.* a name for several very small E. African antelopes, species of *Madoqua*, etc. [Said to be a name in Abyssinia.]

dike, dyke, *dīk, n.* a trench, or the earth dug out and thrown up : a ditch : a mound raised to prevent inundation : in Scotland, a wall (**dry-stane dike,** a wall without mortar; **fail-dike,** a wall of turf), sometimes even a thorn-hedge : (*geol.*) an igneous mass injected into a fissure in rocks, sometimes weathered out into wall-like forms.—*v.t.* to provide with a dike.—*v.i.* to make a dike.—*n.* **dīk'er,** one who makes dikes. [O.E. *dīc;* Du. *dijk*, Ger. *teich*, a pond; see **dig, ditch.**]

dilacerate, *di-las'эr-āt, v.t.* to rend or tear asunder. —*n.* **dilacerā'tion.** [L. *dī-*, asunder, and **lacerate.**]

dilapidate, *di-lap'i-dāt, v.t.* to pull down, stone from stone : to waste : to suffer to go to ruin.— *adj.* **dilap'idated,** in ruins.—*ns.* **dilapidā'tion,**

the state of ruin : (*pl.*) damage done to a building during tenancy : impairing of church property during an incumbency : (*pl.*) money paid at the end of an incumbency by the incumbent or his heirs for the purpose of putting the parsonage, etc., in good repair; **dilap'idātor.** [L. *dīlapidāre—dī-,* asunder, *lapis, lapidis*, a stone.]

dilate, *di-lāt', dī-lāt', v.t.* to spread out in all directions : to enlarge : (*Shak.*) to set forth at full length.—*v.i.* to widen : to swell out : to speak at length.—*ns.* **dilātabil'ity ; dilāt'ancy ; dilatation** (*-lэ-tā'shэn*), or (irregularly formed) **dilā'tion,** expansion.—*adjs.* **dilāt'able,** that may be dilated or expanded; **dilā'tant.**—*adj.* **dilāt'ed,** expanded and flattened.—*ns.* **dī'latātor** (dilā'tor), an instrument or a muscle that expands; **dilāt'er,** one who dilates : a dilatator.—*adj.* **dilāt'ive.** [L. *dīlātus* (used as pa.p. of *differre*), from *dī-* (*dis-*), apart, and *lātus*, borne.]

dilatory, *dil'э-tər-i, adj.* slow : given to procrastination : loitering : tending to delay.—*adv.* **dil'-atorily.**—*n.* **dil'atoriness.** [L. *dīlātōrius.* See **dilate.**]

dilemma, *di-, dī-lem'ä, n.* a form of argument in which the maintainer of a certain proposition is committed to accept one of two propositions each of which contradicts his original contention : a position where each of two alternative courses (or of all the feasible courses) is eminently undesirable. The argument was called a 'horned syllogism', and the victim compared to a man certain to be impaled on one or other of the horns of an infuriated bull, hence the **horns of a dilemma.**—*adj.* **dilemmat'ic.** [L.—Gr. *dilēmma—di-*, twice, double, *lēmma*, an assumption—*lambanein*, to take.]

dilettante, *dil-et-an'ti, n.* one who loves the fine arts but in a superficial way and without serious purpose (the *amateur* usually practises them) : a dabbler in art, science, or literature :—*pl.* **dilettan'ti** (*-tē*).—*adj.* **dilettan'tish.**—*ns.* **dilettan'tism, dilettan'teism.** [It., pr.p. of *dilettare*—L. *dēlectāre*, to delight.]

diligent, *dil'i-jэnt, adj.* steady and earnest in application : industrious.—*n.* **dil'igence,** steady application : industry : (*Scots law*) a warrant to produce witnesses, books, etc., or a process by which persons or goods are attached : a French or continental stage-coach (also pronounced *dē-lē-zhän's*)—also **dill'y.**—*adv.* **dil'igently.** [Fr. *dīli-gēns, -entis*, pr.p. of L. *dīligĕre*, to choose.]

dill, *dil, n.* an umbelliferous annual akin to parsnip, the fruits or 'seeds' used as condiment and carminative.—*n.* **dill'-wa'ter,** a drink prepared from them. [O.E. *dile;* Ger. and Sw. *dill.*]

dilling, *dil'ing, n.* a darling : the youngest child : the weakling of a litter. [Origin doubtful.]

dilly-bag, *dil'i-bag, n.* an Australian native-made rush or bark-bag.—Also **dill'i, dill'y.** [Native *dilli.*]

dilly-dally, *dil'i-dal'i, v.i.* to loiter, trifle. [Re-duplication of **dally;** cf. **shilly-shally.**]

dilucidate, *di-l(y)ōō'si-dāt, v.t.* (*obs.*) to elucidate. —*n.* **dilucidā'tion.** [L. *dīlūcidāre, -ātum.*]

dilute, *di-l(y)ōōt', dī-l(y)ōōt', v.t.* to make thinner or more liquid : to diminish the concentration of, by mixing, esp. with water : of labour, to increase the proportion of unskilled to skilled in.—*v.i.* to become mixed.—*adj.* (*di-* or *dī-l(y)ōōt'*, or *dī'*) diminished in concentration by mixing.—*adj.* **diluent** (*dil'ū-эnt*), diluting.—*n.* that which dilutes. —*ns.* **dilute'ness ; dilu'tion.** [L. *dīluĕre, dīlūtum —dī-,* away, *luĕre*, to wash.]

diluvium, *dil-(y)ōō'vi-эm, n.* an inundation or flood : (*geol.; obs.*) a deposit of sand, gravel, etc., made by extraordinary currents of water.—Also **dilu'vion.**—*adjs.* **dilu'vial, dilu'vian,** pertaining to a flood, esp. Noah's : caused by a deluge : composed of diluvium.—*n.* **dilu'vialist,** one who explains geological phenomena by the flood. [L. *dīluvium—dīluĕre*, to wash away.]

dim, *dim, adj.* not bright or distinct : obscure : not seeing clearly.—*v.t.* to make dark : to obscure.— *v.i.* to become dim :—*pr.p.* **dimm'ing ;** *pa.t.* and *pa.p.* **dimmed.**—*adv.* **dim'ly.**—*n.* **dimm'er,** an arrangement for regulating the supply of light.—

Neutral vowels in unaccented syllables : *el'ə-mэnt, in'fэnt, ran'dэm*

adj. **dimm'ish**, somewhat dim.—*n.* **dim'ness**. [O.E. *dimm;* akin to O.N. *dimmr*, dark, and Ger. *dämmerung*, twilight.]

dimble, *dim'bl*, *n.* a dell, dingle.

dime, *dīm, n.* the tenth part of an American dollar, 10 cents.—**dime museum**, a cheap show; **dime novel**, a cheap novel, usually sensational. [Fr., orig. *disme*, from L. *decima* (*pars*), a tenth (part).]

dimension, *di-* or *dī-men'shən, n.* measure in length, breadth, or thickness (the three dimensions of space): extent: size: (*alg.*) the sum of the indices in a term.—*adjs.* **dimen'sional**, concerning dimension: in composition, of so many dimensions; **dimen'sioned**; **dimen'sionless**. — **dimension work**, masonry in stones of specified size; **fourth dimension**, an additional dimension attributed to space by a hypothetical speculation. [Fr.,—L. *dimēnsiō, -ōnis—dīmētīrī, dīmēnsus—dī-* (*dis-*), apart, *mētīrī*, to measure.]

dimerous, *dim'ə-rəs, adj.* consisting of two parts: (*bot.*) with two members in each whorl: (*entom.*) having two-jointed tarsi.—*adj.* **dimeric** (*dī-mer'ik*), bilaterally symmetrical: dimerous: (*chem.*) having the same empirical formula, but double the molecular weight.—*n.* **dimerism** (*dim'ər-izm*). [Gr. *di-*, double, *meros*, a part.]

dimeter, *dim'i-tər, adj.* containing two measures.— *n.* a verse of two measures. [L.,—Gr. *dimetros— di-*, twice, *metron*, a measure.]

dimethyl, *dī-meth'il, n.* ethane.—*adj.* containing two methyl radicals in combination.—*ns.* **dimeth'ylamine** (*-ə-mēn′*), a compound answering to ammonia with methyl replacing two hydrogen atoms; **dimethylan'iline**, an oily liquid, aniline heated with methyl alcohol and hydrochloric acid— from which dyes are obtained. [Gr. *di-*, twice, **methyl**.]

dimetric, *dī-met'rik, adj.* (*crystal.*) tetragonal.

dimidiate, *di-mid'i-āt, adj.* divided into halves: having a shape that appears as if halved: having only one side developed: split on one side.—*v.t.* (*her.*) to represent the half of.—*n.* **dimidiā'tion**. [L. *dīmidiāre, -ātum*, to halve—*dīmidius*, half— *dis-*, apart, *medius*, the middle.]

diminish, *di-min'ish, v.t.* to make less: to take a part from: to degrade.—*v.i.* to grow or appear less: to subside.—*adj.* **dimin'ishable**.—*adj.* **dimin'ished**, made smaller: humbled: (*mus.*) a semitone less than perfect or minor.—*n.* and *adj.* **dimin'ishing**.—*adv.* **dimin'ishingly**.—*n.* **dimin'ishment**.—**diminishing glass**, a lens or combination of lenses that makes objects appear smaller. [Coined from **minish**, with influence of L. *dīminuĕre*, to break in pieces—*dī-* (*dis-*), apart, *minuĕre*, to make less.]

diminuendo, *di-min-ū-en'dō, adj.* and *adv.* (*mus.*) letting the sound die away, marked thus >. —Also *n.* [It.,—L.L. *dīminuendus*, for L. *dēminuendus*, ger. of *dēminuĕre, dēminūtum*, to lessen.]

diminution, *dim-in-ū'shən, n.* a lessening: degradation.—*adj.* **dimin'utive**, of a diminished size: very small: contracted.—*n.* (*gram.*) a word formed from another to express a little one of the kind.— *adv.* **dimin'utively**.—*n.* **dimin'utiveness**.

dimissory, *dim'is-ə-ri, di-, dī-mis'ə-ri, adj.* sending away or giving leave to depart to another jurisdiction. [L. *dīmissōrius—dīmittĕre, dīmissum—dis-*, apart, *mittĕre*, to send.]

dimity, *dim'i-ti, n.* a stout white cotton, striped or figured in the loom by weaving with two threads. [Gr. *dimitos—di-*, twice, *mitos*, a thread.]

dimorphism, *dī-mor'fizm, n.* (*biol.*) occurrence of two forms in the same species: (*chem.*) the property of crystallising in two forms.—*adjs.* **dimor'phic, dimor'phous**. [Gr. *di-*, twice, *morphē*, form.]

dimple, *dim'pl, n.* a small hollow, esp. on the surface of the body.—*v.i.* to form dimples.—*adj.* **dim'pled**. —*n.* **dim'plement**.—*adj.* **dim'ply**. [Apparently cogn. with Ger. *tumpel*, pool.]

dimyarian, *dim-i-* or *dī-mī-ā'ri-ən, adj.* having two adductor muscles. [Gr. *di-*, twice, *mўs, myos*, muscle.]

din, *din, n.* a loud continued noise.—*v.t.* to assail (the ears) with noise: to annoy with clamour. to obtrude noisily and persistently (*pr.p.* **dinn'ing**; *pa.t.* and *pa.p.* **dinned**).—*adj.* **din'ful**. [O.E. *dynn, dyne;* cf. O.N. *dynr*, Dan. *dön*, noise.]

dinanderie, *dē-nän°-də-rē, n.* domestic decorative brassware, originally that made at *Dinant* in Belgium: extended to Indian and Levantine brassware. [Fr.]

Dinantian, *din-an'shi-ən, adj.* (*geol.*) Lower Carboniferous. [*Dinant* in Belgium.]

dinar, *dē-när', n.* an ancient Arab gold coin of 65 grains' weight: the monetary unit of Iraq: a Yugoslav franc. [L. *dēnārius.*]

dinarchy. See **diarchy**.

dindle. See **dinnle**.

dine, *dīn, v.i.* to take dinner.—*v.t.* to furnish with a dinner.—*n.* (*obs.*) dinner, dinner-time.—*ns.* **din'er**, one who dines: a dining-car; **din'er-out**, one who goes much to dinner-parties; **din'ing-car**, a railway carriage in which meals are served; **din'ing-hall**; **din'ing-room**; **din'ing-table**.— **dine out**, to dine elsewhere than at home; **dine with Duke Humphrey** (*hist.*), to go without a meal, loiter about Duke Humphrey's Walk in Old St. Paul's. [O.Fr. *disner* (Fr. *dîner*) prob.—L. *dis-*, expressing undoing, and *jējūnus*, fasting (cf. **disjune**); according to others—L. *dē-*, inten., and *cēna*, a meal.]

ding, *ding, v.t.* to dash: to beat: to thump: to knock: (*Scot.*) to surpass.—*v.i.* to beat: to dash (*pa.t.* **dang, dung; dung;** *pa.p.* **dinged, dung**). —*n.* **ding'er** (*slang*), anything superlative in its kind.—**ding doun** (*Scot.*), to knock or throw down. [M.E. *dingen, dyngen;* cf. O.N. *dengja*, Sw. *dänga*, to bang.]

ding, *ding, v.i.* to ring, keep sounding.—*v.t.* to reiterate to a wearisome degree.—*n.* **ding'-dong'**, the sound of bells ringing: monotony: sameness.— *adj.* and *adv.* like a bell ringing: hammer-and-tongs: keenly contested with rapid alternations of success.—*v.t.* and *v.i.* to ring: to nag. [Imit., but partly confounded with preceding.]

dinges, *ding'əs, n.* (*S. Africa*) an indefinite name for any person or thing whose name one cannot or will not remember.—Also **ding'us**. [Du. *dinges— ding*, thing; cf. Eng. **thingummy, thingumbob**.]

dinghy, dingy, dingey, *ding'gi, n.* a small rowing-boat or ship's tender: an airman's collapsible rubber boat. [Hind. *dīngī*, a small boat.]

dingle, *ding'gl, n.* a dell. [Origin uncertain.]

dingle-dangle, *ding'gl-dang'gl, adv.* danglingly: with swinging to and fro. [Reduplication of **dangle**.]

dingo, *ding'gō, n.* the native dog of Australia:—*pl.* **ding'oes**. [An extinct native name.]

dingy, *din'ji, adj.* of a dim or dark colour: dull: soiled.—*n.* **dinge**, dinginess.—*v.t.* to make dingy. —*n.* **din'giness**. [Origin obscure.]

dinic, *din'ik adj.* relating to vertigo or dizziness.— *n.* a remedy for dizziness. [Gr. *dīnos*, whirling.]

dinitro-, *dī-nī'trō-*, in composition, having two nitro-groups (NO_2), esp. replacing hydrogen.—*n.* **dinitroben'zene**, $C_6H_4(NO_2)_2$, answering to *benzene*, C_6H_6.

dink, *dingk, adj.* (*Scot.*) neat, trim.—*v.t.* to dress neatly.—*adj.* **dink'y** (*U.S.* and *prov.*), neat: dainty.

dinkum, *ding'kəm, adj.* (*Austr. slang*) real, genuine: square, honest.—Also *adv.*

dinmont, *din'mənt, n.* a Border name for a male sheep between the first and second shearing. [Origin obscure.]

dinner, *din'ər, n.* the chief meal of the day: a feast.—*v.i.* to dine.—*v.t.* to provide with dinner.— *ns.* **dinn'er-dance**, a dance following a dinner; **dinn'er-gown**, a less formal evening dress; **dinn'er-hour**; **dinn'er-jack'et**, a tailless dress-coat.—*adj.* **dinn'erless**.—*ns.* **dinn'er-pail'** (*U.S.*), a vessel in which a workman carries his dinner; **dinn'er-service, -set**, a complete set of plates and dishes for a company at dinner; **dinn'er-time**; **dinn'er-wagon**, orig. a shelved trolley for a dining-room: a sideboard in two tiers. [O.Fr. *disner*, prop. breakfast; see **dine**.]

dinnle, *din'l*, *v.i.* (*Scot.*) to tingle.—*n.* a thrill.— Also **din'dle**. [Prob. imitative.]

Dinoceras or **Deinoceras**, *dī-nos'ər-as*, *n.* a large Eocene fossil stump-footed ungulate of Wyoming, otherwise Uintatherium, named from three pairs of protuberances on the skull. [Gr. *deinos*, terrible, *keras*, horn.]

dinoflagellate, *dī-nō-flaj'ə-lāt*, *n.* a unicellular organism on the boundary-line of plants and animals, with two flagella. [Gr. *dīnos*, whirl, and **flagellate**.]

Dinornis, *dī-nor'nis*, *n.* a genus of moas, including the biggest. [Gr. *deinos*, terrible, and *ornis*, a bird.]

dinosaur, deinosaur, *dī'nō-sawr*, *n.* any extinct (Mesozoic) reptile of the order **Dinosaur'ia**, in length from two to eighty feet. See **dinosaurian**. [Gr. *deinos*, terrible, and *sauros*, lizard.]

Dinotherium, Deinotherium, *dī-nō-thē'ri-əm*, *n.* **a** huge extinct (Tertiary) proboscidean, with elephant-like tusks and trunk. [Gr. *deinos*, terrible, *thērion*, a beast.]

dint, *dint*, *n.* a blow or stroke : the mark of a blow (often **dent**) : force : (as in *by dint of*).—*v.t.* to make a dint in. [O.E. *dynt*, a blow; cf. **dunt**; O.N. *dyntr*.]

diocese, *dī'ə-sis*, *-sēs*, *n.* the circuit or extent of a bishop's jurisdiction.—*adj.* **diocesan** (*dī-os'i-sn*, *-zn*), pertaining to a diocese.—*n.* a bishop in relation to his diocese : one of the clergy in the diocese. [Through Fr. and L. from Gr. *dioikēsis*—*dioikeein*, to keep house—*di-*, for *dia-*, sig. completeness, *oikeein*, to keep house—*oikos*, a house.]

Diodon, *dī'ə-don*, *n.* a genus of globe-fishes with all the teeth in each jaw consolidated. [Gr. *dis-*, twice, double, *odous, odontos*, a tooth.]

dioecious, *dī-ē'shəs*, *adj.* having the sexes separate: having male or female flowers on different plants.— *n.pl.* **Dioe'cia**, a class in the Linnaean system, dioecious plants.—*n.* **dioe'cism** (*-sizm*). [Gr. *di-*, twice, *oikos*, a house.]

Diogenic *Diogenēs* (*c.* 412-323 B.C.) : cynical.

Dionaea, *dī-ə-nē'ā*, *n.* Venus's fly-trap, an American droseraceous insectivorous plant. [L.—Gr. *Dīōnaiā*, Aphrodite, from her mother *Diōnē*.]

Dionysia, *dī-ə-niz'i-ā*, or *-nis'*, *n.pl.* dramatic and orgiastic festivals in honour of *Dionysos* (Bacchus), god of wine.—*adjs.* **Dionys'iac**, Bacchic; **Dionys'-ian**, relating to *Dionysos* or to *Dionȳsios* (Dionysius—of Syracuse, the Areopagite, Exiguus, or any other of the name).

Diophantine, *dī-ə-fan'tīn*, *adj.* pertaining to the Alexandrian mathematician *Diophantos* (*c.* 275 A.D.).—**Diophantine analysis**, the part of algebra which treats of finding particular rational values for general expressions under a surd form.

diopside, *dī-op'sīd*, *n.* a strongly birefringent monoclinic calcium-magnesium pyroxene. [Gr. *di-*, double, *opsis*, a view.]

dioptase, *dī-op'tās*, *n.* an emerald-green acid copper silicate. [Gr. *di-*, through, *optazein*, to see; from its internal glitter.]

dioptric, -al, *dī-op'trik*, *-əl*, *adjs.* pertaining to dioptrics or a diopter : transparent (as a *dioptric bee-hive*).—*ns.* **diop'ter**, an ancient form of theodolite : the index-arm of a graduated circle : (also **diop'tre**) a unit of measurement of the power of a lens, the reciprocal of the focal distances in metres, negative for a divergent lens.—*adj.* **diop'trate** (*entom.*) having the compound eye divided transversely.—*n.* **diop'trics**, the part of optics that treats of refraction. [Gr. *dioptrā*, a levelling instrument, *dioptron*, a spyglass—*dia*, through, and the root of *opsesthai*, used as fut. of *horaein*, to see.]

diorama, *dī-ə-rä'mä*, *n.* an exhibition of pictures seen through an opening with lighting effects.— *adj.* **dioräm'ic**. [Gr. *dia*, through, *horäma*, a sight.]

diorism, *dī'ə-rizm*, *n.* distinction, definition.—*adjs.* **dioris'tic, -al**.—*adv.* **dioris'tically**. [Gr. *diorizein*, to divide, *dia*, through, *horos*, a boundary.]

diorite, *dī'ə-rīt*, *n.* a crystalline granular igneous rock composed of plagioclase and hornblende.—

---

adj. **diorit'ic**. [Gr. *diorizein*, to distinguish—*dia*, through, *horos*, a boundary.]

diorthosis, *dī-or-thō'sis*, *n.* (*surg.*) the reduction of a dislocation : the correction of a deformity : a critical revision of a text.—*adj.* **diorthot'ic**. [Gr. *dia*, through, *orthos*, straight.]

Dioscorea, *dī-os-kōr'i-ä*, *n.* the yam genus, of the monocotyledonous family **Dioscoreä'ceae**.—*adj.* **dioscoreä'ceous**. [From the 1st century (A.D.) Greek physician *Dioskoridēs*.]

Dioscuri, *dī-os-kū'rī*, *n.pl.* Castor and Pollux, as sons of Zeus. [Gr. *Dios*, gen. of *Zeus*, and *koros* (Ion. *kouros*), a son, a lad.]

diota, *dī-ō'tä*, *n.* a two-handled ancient vase. [Gr. *diōtos*, two-handled—*di-*, twice, *ous, ōtos*, ear.]

dioth'elism, dioth'elite. See **ditheletism**.

dioxide, *dī-oks'īd*, *n.* an oxide with two atoms of oxygen in the molecule. [Gr. *di-*, twice, and **oxide**.]

dip, *dip*, *v.t.* to immerse for a time : to lower and raise again (as a flag) : to baptise by immersion : to lift by dipping : (*Milt.*) to moisten, suffuse : (*coll.*) to involve in money difficulties : to mortgage : to pawn.—*v.i.* to plunge and emerge : to sink : to reach down into something : to enter slightly : to look cursorily : to incline downwards (*pr.p.* **dipp'-ing**; *pa.t.* and *pa.p.* **dipped**).—*n.* the act of dipping : a hollow : a sag : that which is taken by dipping : inclination downwards : a sloping : (*geol.*) the angle a stratum of rock makes with a horizontal plane : a bath : a liquid in which anything is dipped (as sheep) : a candle made by dipping a wick in tallow.—*ns.* **dip-circle** or **dipp'ing-needle**, an instrument for determining magnetic dip : **dip'-net**, a long-handled net for dipping up fish : **dipp'er** (q.v.); **dip'-pipe**, a pipe with submerged outlet, esp. in gas-works; **dip'-sec'tor**, an instrument for determining the dip of the visible horizon; **dip'-slope'** (*geol.*), a slope of ground coinciding with the dip of the rocks; **dip'stick**, a rod for measuring depth of liquid in a sump, etc.; **dip'-trap**, a bend in a pipe containing liquid to cut off gases.—**dip of the horizon**, the angle of the visible horizon below the level of the eye; **dip of the needle**, the angle a balanced magnetic needle makes with the horizontal plane. [O.E. *dyppan*, causal of *dýpan*, to plunge in—*déop*, deep; cf. Dan. *dyppe*; Ger. *taufen*, to immerse.]

dipchick, *dip'chik*. Same as **dabchick**.

dipetalous, *dī-pet'ə-ləs*, *adj.* having two petals. [Gr. *di-*, twice, and *petalon*, a leaf.]

diphenyl, *dī-fē'nil*, *n.* a hydrocarbon consisting of two phenyl groups.—*adj.* having two phenyl groups, esp. replacing hydrogen.

diphone, *dī'fōn*, *n.* a shorthand sign representing a diphthongal sound. [Gr. *di-*, twice, *phōnē*, sound.]

diphtheria, *dif-thē'ri-ä*, *n.* an infectious throat disease in which the air-passages become covered with a leathery membrane.—*adjs.* **diphtheric** (*-ther'ik*), **diphtheritic** (*-thər-it'ik*).—*n.* **diphther-i'tis**, diphtheria.—*adj.* **diph'theroid**. [Gr. *diphtherā*, leather.]

diphthong, *dif'thong*, *n.* two vowel-sounds pronounced as one syllable (as in *out*) : (loosely) a digraph : the ligature *æ* or *œ*.—*adjs.* **diphthongal** (*-thong'gəl*), **diphthon'gic** (*-gik*).—*adv.* **diph-thong'ally**.—*v.t.* **diph'thongise** (*-gīz*). [Gr. *diph-thongos*—*di-*, twice, *phthongos*, sound, vowel.]

diphycercal, *dif-i-sər'kəl*, *adj.* having the tail symmetrical about the vertebral column, which runs horizontally (of fishes, etc.). [Gr. *diphyēs*, of double nature, twofold, *kerkos*, a tail.]

diphyletic, *dī-*, *dī-fil-et'ik*, *adj.* (*biol.*) of dual origin : descended from two distinct ancestral groups. [Gr. *di-*, double, *phȳletikos*, pertaining to a tribesman—*phȳlē*, a tribe.]

diphyodont, *dif'i-ō-dont*, *adj.* having two sets of teeth (milk and permanent).—*n.* a mammal with these. [Gr. *diphyēs*, of double nature, *odous, odontos*, a tooth.]

Diphysite, *dif'i-zīt*, *-sīt*, *n.* a believer in the existence of two natures in Christ, a divine and a human —opp. to *Monophysite*.—Also **Dyoph'ysite**, less

---

Neutral vowels in unaccented syllables: *el'ə-mənt*, *in'fənt*, *ran'dəm*

correctly **Dioph'ysite.**—*n.* **Diph'ysitism** (-*it-izm*). [Gr. *di-*, double, *physis*, nature.]

dipleidoscope, *di-plī'də-skōp, n.* an instrument for ascertaining the moment of meridian passage by observing the coincidence of two images. [Gr. *diploos*, double, *eidos*, appearance, *skopeein*, to view.]

diplex, *dī'pleks, adj.* pertaining to the transmission of two simultaneous messages over one wire in the same direction. [**duplex**, with substitution of Gr. *di-*, double.]

Diplodocus, *dip-lod'ə-kəs, n.* a genus of gigantic dinosaurs, reaching about 80 feet in length, from the Jurassic rocks of the United States. [Gr. *diploos*, double, *dokos*, beam, from its appearance.]

diploe, *dip'lō-ē, n.* (*anat.*) the spongy tissue between the hard inner and outer tables of the skull. [Gr. *diploē*, doubling, fold.]

diplogen, *dip'lə-jən, n.* an alternative name for deuterium or heavy hydrogen. [Gr. *diploos*, double, and **hydrogen**.]

diplogenesis, *dip-lə-jen'i-sis, n.* doubling of parts normally single. [Gr. *diploos*, double, *genesis*, generation.]

diploid, *dip'loid, adj.* (*biol.*) having the full or un-reduced number of chromosomes characteristic of the species, as in body-cells: opp. to *haploid.*—*n.* **diploid'y.** [Gr. *diploos*, double, *eidos*, form.]

diploma, *di-plō'mä, n.* a writing conferring some honour or privilege, as a university degree, etc.—*v.t.* to furnish with a diploma.—*ns.* **diplomacy** (*di-plō'mə-si*, or -*plo'*), the art of negotiation, esp. of treaties between states: tact in management of persons concerned in any affair; **diplomat**, (*dip'lə-mat*), one employed or skilled in diplomacy; **diplomate** (*dip'lə-māt*), one who holds a diploma. —*v.t.* to confer a diploma on.—*ns.* **diplomatic** (*-mat'ik*), a minister at a foreign court: (in *pl.*) the science of deciphering ancient writings, as charters, etc.—palaeography.—*adjs.* **diplomat'ic, -al,** per-taining to diplomacy: tactful and skilful in negotia-tion.—*adv.* **diplomat'ically.**—*v.i.* and *v.t.* **diplo'-matise,** to practise, or effect by, diplomacy.—*ns.* **diplo'matist,** a diplomat; **diplomatol'ogy,** the study or science of diplomatics, charters, decrees, etc.—**diplomatic corps,** the whole body of foreign diplomatists resident in any capital. [L.,—Gr. *diplōma*, a letter folded double—*diploos*, double.]

diplon, *dip'lon, n.* an alternative name for deuter-on, the nucleus of heavy hydrogen. [Gr. *diploos*, double.]

diplopia, *dip-lō'pi-ä, n.* double vision. [Gr. *di-ploos*, double, *ōps*, eye.]

diplostemonous, *dip-lə-stē'mən-əs, adj.* (*bot.*) hav-ing two whorls of stamens, the outer alternating with the petals, the inner with the outer. [Gr. *diploos*, double, *stēmōn*, a thread.]

Diplozoon, *dip-lə-zō'on, n.* a flat worm that lives fused together in pairs parasitically upon the gills of minnows, etc. [Gr. *diploos*, double, *zōion*, an animal.]

Dipnoi, *dip'nō-ī, n.pl.* the lung fishes.—*adj.* and *n.* **dip'noan.**—*adj.* **dip'noous,** having both lungs and gills. [Gr. *di-*, double, *pnoē*, breath.]

dipody, *dip'ə-di, n.* (*pros.*) a double foot. [Gr. *di-*, double, *pous, podos*, foot.]

dipolar, *dī-pō'lər, adj.* having two poles.—*n.* **di'pole,** an object having two poles: a molecule in which the effective centres of the positive and negative charges are separated. [Gr. *di-*, double.]

dipper, *dip'ər, n.* one that dips: a ladle: a bucket or scoop of a dredge or excavator: a contrivance for directing motor-car headlights upwards or downwards: a dabbling bird (*Cinclus*), the water-ouzel: (*U.S.A.*) a dabchick: (*astron.*) the Plough: a nickname for a Baptist, esp. a Dunker. [**dip**.]

dippy, *dip'i, adj.* crazy: insane. [Origin obscure.]

diprionidian, *dī-prī-ə-nid'i-ən, adj.* serrated on both sides (of graptolites). [Gr. *di-*, twice, *prīōn*, a saw.]

diprotodont, *dī-prō'to-dont, n.* any marsupial of the **Diprotodont'ia,** the suborder including kang-aroos, wombats, etc., with one pair of incisors in the lower jaw. [Gr. *di-*, twice, *prōtos*, first, *odous, odontos*, tooth.]

Dipsacus, *dip'sə-kəs, n.* the teasel genus, giving name to the **Dipsacā'ceae,** akin to the valerian and madder families. [Gr. *dipsakos*, teasel—*dipsa*, thirst, because the leaf-axils hold water.]

dipsas, *dip'sas, n.* a snake whose bite was believed to cause intense thirst: **Dipsas,** a genus of non-venomous snakes. [Gr. *dipsas*—*dipsa*, thirst.]

dipsomania, *dip-sō-mā'ni-ä, n.* a morbid craving for alcoholic stimulants.—*n.* **dipsomā'niac.** [Gr. *dipsa*, thirst, and *maniā*, madness.]

Diptera, *dip'tər-ä, n.pl.* two-winged insects or flies. —*adj.* **dip'teral,** two-winged: with double peri-style.—*ns.* **dip'teran,** a dipterous insect; **dip'ter-ist,** a student of flies; **dip'teros,** a building with double peristyle or colonnade.—*adj.* **dip'terous,** with two wings or winglike expansions. [Gr. *dipteros*, two-winged, *di-*, twice, *pteron*, a wing.]

dipterocarp, *dip'tər-ō-kärp, n.* any tree of the genus **Dipterocar'pus** or its family **Dipterocarpā'ceae** (chiefly Indian), in which some of the sepals en-large as wings for the fruit.—*adjs.* **dipterocarpā'-ceous, dipterocarp'ous.** [Gr. *di-*, double, *pteron*, wing, *karpos*, fruit.]

diptych, *dip'tik, n.* a double-folding writing-tablet: a register of bishops, saints, etc., read aloud during the eucharist: a pair of pictures as folding-tablets. [Gr. *diptychos*—*di-*, and *ptychē*, a tablet, a fold.]

dirdum, *dir'dəm, n.* (*Scot.*) uproar: a scolding. [Origin obscure.]

dire, *dīr, adj.* dreadful: calamitous in a high degree.—*adj.* (*poet.*) **dire'ful.**—*adv.* **dire'fully.**—*n.* **dire'fulness.** [L. *dīrus.*]

direct, *di-rekt', dī'rekt, adj.* straight: straight-forward: by the shortest way: forward, not back-ward or oblique: at right angles: immediate: without intervening agency or interposed stages: (of a dye) fixing itself without a mordant: in the line of descent: outspoken: sincere: unambiguous: unsophisticated in manner.—*n.* (*mus.*) an indication of the first note or chord of next page or line.—*adv.* straight: by the shortest way: without deviation, intervening agency or interposed stages. —*v.t.* to keep or lay straight: to point or aim: to point out the proper course to: to guide: to order: to address, mark with the name and residence of a person.—*v.i.* to act as director: to direct letters, etc.—*n.* **direc'tion,** aim at a certain point: the line or course in which anything moves or on which any point lies: guidance: command: the body of persons who guide or manage a matter: the ad-dress, or written name and residence of a person.— *adj.* **direc'tional,** relating to direction in space.—*n.* **direc'tion-find'er,** a wireless receiver that deter-mines the direction of arrival of incoming waves.— *adj.* **direct'ive,** having power or tendency to direct.—*n.* a general instruction.—*n.* **directiv'ity.** —*adv.* **direct'ly,** in a direct manner: without intermediary: immediately (in time and otherwise). —*conj.* (*coll.*) as soon as.—*ns.* **direct'ness;** **direct'or,** one who directs: one who directs the shooting of a motion picture: a manager or govern-or: a member of a board conducting the affairs of a company: a counsellor: a father confessor or spiritual guide: part of a machine or instrument which guides the motion:—*fem.* **direct'ress,** **direct'rix.**—*ns.* **direct'orate,** the office of direc-tor: a body of directors: **Directorate,** the French Directory or Directoire.—*adjs.* **directō'rial; direct'ory,** containing directions: guiding.—*n.* a body of directions: a guide: a book with the names and residences of the inhabitants of a place: a body of directors: **Directory,** the *Directoire*, or French Republican government of 1795-99.—*ns.* **direc'torship; direct'rix,** a line serving to des-cribe a conic section, which is the locus of a point whose distances from focus and directrix have a constant ratio:—*pl.* **directrices** (-*trī'sēz*).—**direct-action,** coercive methods of attaining industrial ends as opposed to pacific, parliamentary, or political action; **direct current,** an electric current flowing in one direction only; **direct motion** (*mus.*), progression of parts in the same direction; **director circle,** the locus of the intersection of a pair of tangents to a conic at right angles to each other; **direct speech,** speech reported as spoken, in the very words of the speaker (L. *ōrātiō rēcta*). [L. *dīrigĕre*, *dīrēctum—dī-*, apart, *regĕre*, to rule.]

Directoire, *dē-rek-twär'*, *n.* the French Directorate of 1795-99.—*adj.* after the fashion in dress or furniture then prevailing. [Fr.; see direct.]

dirge, *dərj*, *n.* a funeral song or hymn. [Contracted from *dīrige* (imper. of L. *dīrigĕre*, to direct), the first word of an antiphon sung in the office for the dead—the words from the Vulgate, Psalm v. 8.

dirhem, *dir-hem'*, *n.* an oriental weight and silver coin, originally two-thirds of an Attic drachma.— Also **dirham'**, **derham'**. [Ar., Pers., and Turk. modifications of the Greek *drachmē*, a drachma or dram.]

dirige, *dir'i-ji*, *n.* a dirge.

dirigible, *dir'i-ji-bl*, *adj.* that can be directed.— *n.* a navigable balloon or airship.—*adj.* **dir'igent**, directing. [See direct.]

diriment, *dir'i-mənt*, *adj.* nullifying. [L. *dirimĕre*.]

dirk, *dərk*, *n.* a Highland dagger : a side-arm worn by midshipmen and naval cadets.—*v.t.* to stab with a dirk. [Ety. unknown.]

dirk, **dirke**, *dərk*, *adj.*, *adv.* and *v.t.* (*Spens.*) for **dark**, **darkly**, **darken**.

dirl, *dirl*, *v.i.* (*Scot.*) to thrill, vibrate.—*n.* vibration, a sensation of tingling as after a blow. [drill, thrill.]

dirndl, *dirn'dl*, *dərn'dl*, *n.* an Alpine peasant woman's dress : a skirt of similar form. [Ger. dim. of *dirne*, girl.]

dirt, *dərt*, *n.* any filthy substance, such as dung, mud, etc. : foreign matter adhering to anything : loose earth.—*v.t.* to make dirty.—*n.* **dirt'-bed**, a quarryman's term for a layer representing an old soil, esp. in the Purbeck group.—*adj.* **dirt'-cheap**, cheap as dirt, very cheap.—*n.* **dirt'-eating**, a practice of eating clay as among various primitive peoples : a morbid impulse to eat dirt.—*adv.* **dirt'ily.**—*ns.* **dirt'iness** ; **dirt'-pie**, mud moulded by children in play ; **dirt'-road** (*U.S.*), a soft road, unpaved and unmacadamised.—*adj.* **dirt'-rott'en** (*Shak.*), wholly decayed.—*n.* **dirt'-track**, a motor-cycling racing-track, with earthy or cindery surface.—*adj.* **dirt'y**, foul, filthy : stormy : obscene : unclean in thought or conversation : despicable : mean : treacherous.—*v.t.* to soil with dirt : to sully (*pr.p.* **dirt'ying** ; *pa.t.* and *pa.p.* **dirt'ied**).—**dirty work**, work that dirties the hands or clothes : dishonourable practices, esp. undertaken on behalf of another : foul play ; **eat dirt**, submissively to acquiesce in a humiliation ; **throw dirt**, to besmirch a reputation. [M.E. *drit*, prob. O.N. *drit*, excrement ; cf. O.E. *gedrītan*, to defecate.]

Dis, *dis*, *dēs*, *n.* a name for Pluto, hence, the infernal world. [L. *Dīs*, cog. with *deus*, *dīvus*.]

disable, *dis-ā'bl*, *v.t.* to deprive of power : to weaken : to cripple, incapacitate : to disqualify : (*Shak.*) to depreciate, disparage, undervalue.—*ns.* **disā'blement** ; **disābil'ity**, want of power : want of legal qualification : disqualification.

disabuse, *dis-ə-būz'*, *v.t.* to undeceive or set right.

disaccharide, *dī-sak'ə-rīd*, *n.* a sugar that hydrolyses into two molecules of simple sugars.

disaccommodate, *dis-ə-kom'ə-dāt*, *v.t.* to put to inconvenience.—*n.* **disaccommodā'tion.**

disaccord, *dis-ə-kord'*, *v.i.* (*Spens.*) to refuse to accord : to be at discord.—*adj.* **disaccord'ant.**

disaccustom, *dis-ə-kus'təm*, *v.t.* to make to be lost through disuse.

disacknowledge, *dis-ək-nol'ij*, *v.t.* to refuse to acknowledge, disown.

disadorn, *dis-ə-dorn'*, *v.t.* to deprive of ornaments.

disadvance, *dis-əd-vâns'*, *v.t.* to cause to retreat : (*Spens.*) to draw back, cease to put forward.

disadvantage, *dis-əd-vânt'ij*, *n.* unfavourable circumstance or condition : loss : damage.—*adjs.* **disadvan'tageable** (*obs.*); **disadvantageous** (*dis-ad-vənt-ā'jəs*), attended with disadvantage : unfavourable.—*adv.* **disadvant'geously.**—*n.* **disadvantā'geousness.**

disadventurous, *dis-əd-vent'yə-rəs*, *adj.* unfortunate.—*ns.* **disadven'ture**, **disaven'ture** (*Spens.*), a mishap.—*adj.* **disaven'trous** (*Spens.*), unfortunate.

disaffect, *dis-ə-fekt'*, *v.t.* to take away the affection of : to make discontented or unfriendly.—*pa.p.* and *adj.* **disaffect'ed**, ill-disposed : tending to break away.—*adv.* **disaffect'edly.**—*ns.* **disaffect'edness** ; **disaffec'tion**, state of being disaffected : want of affection or friendliness : alienation : ill-will.—*adj.* **disaffec'tionate.**

disaffirm, *dis-ə-fərm'*, *v.t.* to contradict : to repudiate.—*ns.* **disaffirm'ance**, **disaffirmā'tion** (*dis-a-*).

disafforest, *dis-ə-for'ist*, *v.t.* to bring out of the operation of forest laws : to clear of forest, disforest.—*ns.* **disafforestā'tion**, **disaffor'estment** (see **disforest**). [L. *dis-*, neg., and L.L. *afforestāre*, to make into a forest. See **forest**.]

disagree, *dis-ə-grē'*, *v.i.* to differ or be at variance : to disaccord : to dissent : to quarrel : to prove unsuitable or a source of annoyance, as of food disagreeing with the stomach.—*adj.* **disagree'able**, not amicable : unpleasant : offensive.—*ns.* **disagree'ableness**, **disagreeabil'ity.**—*n.pl.* **disagree'ables**, annoyances.—*adv.* **disagree'ably.**— *n.* **disagree'ment**, want of agreement : difference : unsuitableness : dispute.

disallow, *dis-ə-low'*, *v.t.* (*obs.*) to dispraise : not to allow : to refuse to sanction : to deny the authority, validity, or truth of : to reject, to forbid. —*v.i.* (*obs.*) to disapprove.—*adj.* **disallow'able.**— *n.* **disallow'ance.**

disally, *dis-ə-lī'*, *v.t.* to break the alliance of : (*Milt.*) to separate, sunder.

disanchor, *dis-angk'ər*, *v.t.* to free from the anchor. —*v.i.* to weigh anchor.

disanimate, *dis-an'i-māt*, *v.t.* to deprive of spirit or animation : (*Shak.*) to deject.

disannex, *dis-ə-neks'*, *v.t.* to disjoin.

disannul, *dis-ə-nul'*, *v.t.* to annul completely.— *ns.* **disannull'er** ; **disannul'ment**, **disannull'ing.**

disanoint, *dis-ə-noint'*, *v.t.* to undo the anointing or consecration of.

disapparel, *dis-ə-par'əl*, *v.t.* to disrobe.

disappear, *dis-ə-pēr'*, *v.i.* to vanish from sight.— *n.* **disappear'ance**, a ceasing to be in sight : removal from sight, flight, secret withdrawal.

disappoint, *dis-ə-point'*, *v.t.* (*obs.*) to deprive of what is appointed : to frustrate the hopes of : to defeat the fulfilment of.—*adjs.* **disappoint'ed**, balked : frustrated : (*Shak.*) unequipped or ill-equipped ; **disappoint'ing**, causing disappointment.—*n.* **disappoint'ment**, the defeat of one's hopes : frustration : the vexation accompanying failure. [O.Fr. *desapointer—des-* (L. *dis-*), away, and *apointer*, to appoint. See **appoint**.]

disapprobation, *dis-ap-rō-bā'shən*, *n.* disapproval. —*adjs.* **disapp'robative**, **disapp'robātory.**

disappropriate, *dis-ə-prō'pri-āt*, *v.t.* to take away from the condition of being appropriated.—*adj.* (*-it*) deprived of appropriation.

disapprove, *dis-ə-proōv'*, *v.t.* and *v.i.* to give or have an unfavourable opinion (of) : to reject.—*n.* **disapprov'al.**—*adv.* **disapprov'ingly.**

disarm, *dis-ärm'*, *v.t.* to deprive of arms : to strip of armour : to render defenceless : to deprive of the power to hurt : (*fig.*) to conciliate : to reduce to a peace footing.—*v.i.* to disband troops, reduce national armaments.—*n.* **disarm'ament.**

disarrange, *dis-ə-rānj'*, *v.t.* to undo the arrangement of : to disorder : to derange.—*n.* **disarrange'-ment.**

disarray, *dis-ə-rā'*, *v.t.* to break the array of : to throw into disorder : to strip of array or dress.— *n.* want of array or order : undress.

disarticulate, *dis-är-tik'ūl-āt*, *v.t.* to separate the joints of.—*v.i.* to separate at a joint.—*n.* **disarticulā'tion.**

disassemble, *dis-ə-sem'bl*, *v.t.* to take apart.—*n.* **disassem'bly.**

disassimilate, *dis-ə-sim'i-lāt*, *v.t.* to subject to katabolism.—*n.* **disassimilā'tion.**—*adj.* **disassim'ilative.**

disassociate, *dis-ə-sō'shi-āt*, *v.t.* to disconnect : to dissociate.—*n.* **disassociā'tion.**

disaster, *diz-âs'tər*, *n.* an adverse or unfortunate event : a great and sudden misfortune : calamity.— *adj.* **disas'trous**, calamitous, ruinous : gloomy, foreboding disaster.—*adv.* **disas'trously.** [O.Fr. *desastre, des*-(—L. *dis*-), with evil sense, *astre*, a star, destiny—L. *astrum*, Gr. *astron*, star.]

disattire, *dis-ə-tīr'*, *v.t.* (*Spens.*) to undress.

disattune, *dis-ə-tūn'*, *v.t.* to put out of harmony.

disauthorise, *dis-aw'thor-īz*, *v.t.* to deprive of authority.

disavaunce. See **disadvance.**

disaventure. See **disadventure.**

disavouch, *dis-ə-vowch'*, *v.t.* to disavow.

disavow, *dis-ə-vow'*, *v.t.* to disclaim knowledge of, or connexion with: to disown: to deny.—*n.* **disavow'al.** [O.Fr. *desavouer, des*- (L. *dis*-), away, *avouer*, to avow. See **avow.**]

disband, *dis-band'*, *v.t.* to disperse, break up, esp. of troops.—*v.i.* to break up.—*n.* **disband'ment.** [O.Fr. *desbander*, to unbind, *des*- (L. *dis*-), neg., *bander*.]

disbar, *dis-bär'*, *v.t.* to expel from the bar.

disbark, *dis-bärk'*, *v.t.* to land from a ship: to disembark. [O.Fr. *desbarquer, des*- (L. *dis*-), neg., *barque*, bark.]

disbark, *dis-bärk'*, *v.t.* to strip of bark, to bark.

disbelieve, *dis-bə-lēv'*, *v.t.* to believe to be false: to refuse belief or credit to.—*v.i.* to have no faith (with *in*).—*ns.* **disbelief'; disbeliev'er.**

disbench, *dis-bensh'*, *v.t.* (*Shak.*) to drive from a bench or seat: to deprive of the privilege of a bencher (e.g. in the Inns of Court).

disbodied, *dis-bod'id*, *adj.* disembodied.

disbosom, *dis-bōōz'əm*, *v.t.* to make known, reveal.

disbowel, *dis-bow'əl*, *v.t.* (*fig.*) to disembowel (*pr.p.* **disbow'elling**; *pa.t.* and *pa.p.* **disbow'elled**).

disbranch, *dis-bränsh'*, *v.t.* to remove branches from: to sever.

disbud, *dis-bud'*, *v.t.* to remove buds from.

disburden, *dis-bur'dn*, **disburthen,** *dis-bur'dhn*, *v.t.* to rid of a burden: to free: to unload, discharge.

disburse, *dis-burs'*, *v.t.* to pay out.—*ns.* **disburs'al, disburse'ment,** a paying out: that which is paid. [O.Fr. *desbourser*—*des*- (L. *dis*-), apart, and *bourse*, a purse.]

disc. Same as **disk.**—*adjs.* **disc'al,** pertaining to, or of the nature of, a disk; **disc'oid, discoid'al,** in the form of a disk: (*bot.*) of a capitulum, without ray-flowers.—*n.* **discog'raphy,** collection, description, etc. of gramophone records. See also **disk.**

discage, *dis-kāj'*, *v.t.* to free from a cage.

discalced, *dis-kalst'*, *adj.* without shoes, barefooted, as a branch of the Carmelite order.—*n.* and *adj.* **discal'ceate.** [L. *discalceātus*—*dis*-, neg., and *calceāre, -ātum*, to shoe, *calceus*, a shoe—*calx*, the heel.]

discandy, discandie, *dis-kan'di*, *v.i.* (*Shak.*) to dissolve or melt from a state of being candied.—*n.* **discan'dering** (*Shak.*), supposed to be for **discandying.**

discant, *dis'kant.* Same as **descant.**

discapacitate, *dis-kə-pas'i-tāt*, *v.t.* to incapacitate.

discard, *dis-kärd'*, *v.t.* and *v.i.* to throw away, as not needed or not allowed by the game, said of cards: in whist, to throw down a (useless) card of another suit when one cannot follow suit and cannot or will not trump: to cast off: to discharge: to reject.—*n.* (also *dis'*) the act of discarding: the card or cards thrown out of the hand: discharge, dismissal, abandonment: (*U.S.*) a cast-off, anything discarded.—*n.* **discard'ment.—throw into the discard** (*U.S.*), to throw on the scrap-heap. [Pfx. *dis*- and **card.**]

discase, *dis-kās'*, *v.t.* (*Shak.*) to remove a case or covering from, to undress.

discept, *di-sept'*, *v.i.* (*Browning*) to dispute, debate.—*n.* **discepta'tion.**—*adj.* **discepta'tious.**—*n.* **discepta'tor.**—*adj.* **disceptato'rial.** [L. *disceptāre, -ātum*, to contend—*dis*-, *captāre.*]

discern, *di-sərn', -zərn'*, *v.t.* to make out: to distinguish by the eye or understanding: (*obs.*, a blunder for *decern*) to judge.—*n.* **discern'er.**—*adj.* **discern'ible.**—*adv.* **discern'ibly.**—*adj.* **discern'ing,** discriminating, acute.—*n.* **discern'ment,** power or faculty of discriminating: judgment: acuteness. [L. *discernĕre*—*dis*-, thoroughly, and *cernĕre*, to sift, perceive.]

discerp, *di-sərp'*, *v.t.* to separate.—*n.* **discerpibil'ity,** capability of being disunited.—*adjs.* **discerp'ible** (*obs.*), **discerp'tible.**—*n.* **discerp'tion.**—*adj.* **discerp'tive.** [L. *discerpĕre*, to tear in pieces—*dis*-, apart, *carpĕre*, to pluck.]

discharge, *dis-chärj'*, *v.t.* to free from or relieve of a charge of any kind (burden, explosive, electricity, liability, accusation, etc.): to set free: to acquit: to dismiss: to fire (as a gun): to take the superincumbent weight from: to set down or send forth: to eject: to pour out: to emit or let out: to perform: to pay: to give account for: to distribute (as weight): (*obs.*) to forbid.—*v.i.* to unload: to become released from a charged state: to allow escape of contents: to flow away or out.—*n.* the act of discharging: release from a charge of any kind: unloading: liberation: acquittal: dismissal: outflow: rate of flow: emission: release of tension: payment: performance: that which is discharged.—*ns.* **discharg'er,** one who discharges: an apparatus for discharging, esp. electricity, e.g. a spark-gap, discharging tongs: apparatus for firing an explosive; **discharge'-tube,** a tube in which an electric discharge takes place in a vacuum.—**discharging arch,** an arch built in a wall to protect a space beneath from the weight above; **discharging tongs,** metal tongs used for discharging condensers. [O.Fr. *descharger*—*des*-, apart, and *charger*; see **charge.**]

dischurch, *dis-church'*, *v.t.* to deprive of church rank or privileges.

discide, *di-sīd'*, *v.t.* (*Spens.*) to cut asunder, to divide. [L. *dis*-, asunder, and *caedĕre*, to cut.]

discinct, *di-singkt'*, *adj.* ungirded. [L. *discingĕre, -cinctum*, to ungird.]

disciple, *dis-ī'pl*, *n.* one who professes to receive instruction from another: one who follows or believes in the doctrine of another: a follower, esp. one of the twelve apostles of Christ.—*v.t.* (*Spens.*) to teach.—*n.* **disci'pleship.—Disciples of Christ,** a sect that seeks a restoration of New Testament Christianity—by some called Campbellites. [Fr.,—L. *discipulus*, from *discĕre*, to learn: akin to *docēre*, to teach.]

discipline, *dis'i-plin*, *n.* instruction: training, or mode of life in accordance with rules: subjection to control: order: severe training: mortification: punishment: an instrument of penance or punishment.—*v.t.* to subject to discipline: to train: to educate: to bring under control: to chastise.—*adjs.* **disc'iplinable; disc'iplinal** (or *-plī'*).—*ns.* **disc'iplinant,** one who subjects himself to a discipline, esp. one of an order of Spanish flagellants; **disciplina'rian,** one who enforces strict discipline; **disciplina'rium,** a scourge for penitential flogging.—*adj.* **disc'iplinary,** of the nature of discipline.—*n.* **disc'ipliner,** one who disciplines.—**First, Second, Book of Discipline,** two documents (1560 and 1578) embodying the constitution and order of procedure of the Church of Scotland from the period of the Reformation. [L. *disciplina*, from *discipulus*.]

discission, *di-sish'ən*, *n.* an incision into a tumour or cataract. [L. *discissiō, -ōnis*—*discindĕre, -scissum* —*dī*-, apart, *scindĕre*, to cut.]

disclaim, *dis-klām'*, *v.t.* to renounce all claim to: to refuse to acknowledge or be responsible for: to repudiate: to reject: to cry out against the claim of.—*v.i.* to make a disclaimer: (*obs.*) to declaim, cry out.—*ns.* **disclaim'er,** a denial, disavowal, or renunciation; **disclamā'tion** (*-kləm-*), a disavowal. [O.Fr. *disclaimer*—L. *dis*-, apart, *clāmāre,* to cry out.]

disclose, *dis-klōz'*, *v.t.* to unclose: to open: to lay open: to bring to light: to reveal: (*Shak.*) to hatch: (*Spens.*) to transform and give vent to (*pa.p.* in *Spens.* **disclo'st**).—*n.* a disclosure: (*Shak.*) emergence from the egg.—*n.* **disclō'sure** (*-zhər*), act of disclosing: a bringing to light or revealing: that which is disclosed or revealed. [O.Fr. *desclos*—L. *dis*-, apart, *claudĕre, clausum,* to shut.]

discobolus, *dis-kob'ə-ləs*, *n.* a disk-thrower: the name of a famous lost statue ascribed to Myron, of which copies exist. [L.,—Gr. *diskobolos—diskos*, a quoit, *ballein*, to throw.]

discoid,-al, etc. See **disc.**

discolour, *dis-kul'ǝr, v.t.* to take away colour from: to change or to spoil the natural colour of: to alter the appearance of: to mark with other colours, to stain: to dirty, disfigure.—*v.i.* to become discoloured.—*n.* **discolo(u)rā'tion**, act of discolouring: state of being discoloured: stain.—*adj.* **discol'oured**, stained, etc.: (*Spens.*) many-coloured. [O.Fr. *descolorer—*L. *dis-,* apart, and *colōrāre—color,* colour.]

Discomedusae, *dis-kō-me-dū'sē, n.pl.* an order of jellyfishes with flattened umbrella.—*n.* and *adj.* **discomedū'san.** [Gr. *diskos*, disk, and *medusa.*]

discomfit, *dis-kum'fit, v.t.* to disconcert, to balk: to defeat or rout (*pr.p.* **discom'fiting**; *pa.t.* and *pa.p.* **discom'fited**).—*n.* (*Milt.*) defeat.—*n.* **discom'fiture.** [O.Fr. *desconfit*, pa.p. of *desconfire—*L. *dis-,* neg., *conficĕre*, to prepare—*con-,* inten., *facĕre,* to make.]

discomfort, *dis-kum'fǝrt, n.* want of comfort: uneasiness.—*v.t.* to deprive of comfort: to make uneasy.—*adj.* **discom'fortable**, causing discomfort: uncomfortable. [O.Fr. *desconforter—des-,* priv., *conforter,* to comfort; see **comfort.**]

discommend, *dis-kǝm-end', v.t.* to blame: to dispraise.—*adj.* **discommend'able.**—*ns.* **discommend'ableness, discommendation** (*dis-ko-mǝn-dā'shǝn*).

discommission, *dis-kǝ-mish'ǝn, v.t.* (*Milt.*) to deprive of a commission.

discommode, *dis-kǝ-mōd', v.t.* to incommode.—*adj.* **discommō'dious.**—*adv.* **discommō'diously.**—*n.* **discommŏd'ity**, inconvenience.

discommon, *dis-kom'ǝn, v.t.* to deprive of the right of common, or, at Oxford and Cambridge, of dealing with undergraduates.

discommunity, *dis-kǝ-mūn'i-ti, n.* want of community.

discompose, *dis-kǝm-pōz', v.t.* to deprive of composure: to disarrange, to disorder: to disturb: to agitate.—*n.* **discompō'sure** (*-zhǝr, -zhyǝr*).

Discomycetes, *dis-kō-mī-sē'tēz, n.pl.* a group of fungi (Ascomycetes) with open apothecia.—*n.* **dis'comycete.**—*adj.* **discomyce'tous.** [Gr. *diskos*, disk, *mykētēs,* pl. of *mykēs,* a fungus.]

disconcert, *dis-kǝn-sǝrt', v.t.* to throw into confusion: to disturb: to frustrate: to defeat: to put out of countenance.—*ns.* **disconcert** (*dis-kon'sǝrt*), disunion; **disconcer'tion**, confusion; **disconcert'ment.** [Obs.Fr. *disconcerter—des-* (L. *dis-*), apart, and *concerter,* to concert.]

disconformable, *dis-kǝn-form'ǝ-bl, adj.* not conformable.—*n.* **disconform'ity**, want of conformity: inconsistency: (*geol.*) unconformity.

disconnect, *dis-kǝn-ekt', v.t.* to separate or disjoin (with *from*).—*adj.* **disconnect'ed**, separated: loosely united, as of a discourse.—*adv.* **disconnect'edly.**—*n.* **disconnex'ion, disconnec'tion.**

disconsent, *dis-kǝn-sent', v.i.* to differ, dissent.

disconsolate, *dis-kon'sǝ-lit, adj.* without consolation or comfort.—*adv.* **discon'solately.**—*ns.* **discon'solateness, disconsolā'tion.** [L. *dis-,* neg., and *consōlāri, consōlātus,* to console.]

discontent, *dis-kǝn-tent', adj.* not content: dissatisfied.—*n.* want of contentment: dissatisfaction: (*Shak.*) a discontented person.—*v.t.* to deprive of content: to stir up to ill-will.—*adj.* **discontent'ed**, dissatisfied.—*adv.* **discontent'edly.**—*n.* **discontent'edness.**—*adj.* **discontent'ful.**—*adj.* **discontent'ing**, not contenting or satisfying: (*Shak.*) discontented.—*n.* **discontent'ment.**

discontinue, *dis-kǝn-tin'ū, v.t.* to cease to continue: to put an end to: to leave off: to stop.—*v.i.* to cease: to be separated.—*ns.* **discontin'uance, discontinuā'tion**, a breaking off or ceasing; **discontinu'ity.**—*adj.* **discontin'uous**, not continuous: broken off: separated: interrupted by intervening spaces.—*adv.* **discontin'uously.** [O.Fr. *discontinuer—*L. *dis-,* neg., and *continuāre,* to continue.]

Discophora, *dis-kof'ǝ-rä, n.pl.* the Discomedusae.—

n. and *adj.* **discoph'oran.**—*adj.* **discoph'orous.** [Gr. *diskos*, disk, *phoros,* carrying.]

discord, *dis'kord, n.* opposite of *concord*: disagreement, strife: difference or contrariety of qualities: a combination of inharmonious sounds: uproarious noise: a dissonance, esp. unprepared.—*v.i.* **discord'**, to disagree.—*ns.* **discord'ance, discord'ancy.**—*adj.* **discord'ant**, without concord or agreement: inconsistent: contradictory: harsh: jarring.—*adv.* **discord'antly.**—*adj.* **discord'ful** (*Spens.*).—**apple of discord** (see **apple**). [O.Fr. *descord—*L. *discordia—dis-,* apart, and *cor, cordis* the heart.]

discorporate, *dis-kor'pǝ-rit, adj.* disembodied.

discounsel, *dis-kown'sǝl, v.t.* (*Spens.*) to dissuade. [O.Fr. *desconseillier—des-,* apart, and *conseillier,* to counsel.]

discount, *dis'kownt, n.* a sum taken from the reckoning: a sum returned to the payer of an account: the rate or percentage of the deduction granted: a deduction made for interest in advancing money on a bill.—*v.t.* **discount'**, to allow as discount: to allow discount on: to pay (rarely to receive) beforehand the present worth of: to put a reduced value on, as in an extravagant statement or fabulous story or an event foreseen: to ignore.—*v.i.* to practise discounting.—*adj.* **discount'able.**—*ns.* **dis'count-brok'er**, one who cashes notes or bills of exchange at a discount; **discount'er.**—**at a discount**, below par: not sought after: superfluous: depreciated in value. [O.Fr. *descompter—des-* (L. *dis-*), away, *compter,* to count.]

discountenance, *dis-kown'tan-ǝns, v.t.* to put out of countenance: to abash: to refuse countenance or support to: to discourage.—*n.* cold treatment: disapprobation. [O.Fr. *descontenancer—des-,* neg., *contenance,* countenance.]

discourage, *dis-kur'ij, v.t.* to take away the courage of: dishearten: to oppose by showing disfavour.—*n.* **discour'agement**, act of discouraging: that which discourages: dejection.—*n.* and *adj.* **discour'aging**, disheartening, depressing.—*adv.* **discour'agingly.** [O.Fr. *descourager.* See **courage.**]

discoure, *dis-kowr', v.t.* (*Spens.*) to discover.

discourse, *dis-kōrs',* or *dis',* n.* speech or language generally: conversation: the reasoning faculty: a treatise: a speech: a sermon: (*Spens.*) apparently, process of combat.—*v.i.* to talk or converse: to reason: to treat formally.—*v.t.* to utter or give forth.—*n.* **discours'er** (*Shak.*).—*adj.* (*obs.*) **discours'ive.** [Fr. *discours—*L. *discursus—dis-,* away, and *currĕre,* to run.]

discourteous, *dis-kurt'yǝs* (or *-kōrt'*), *adj.* wanting in courtesy: uncivil.—Also (*Spens.*) **discour'teise.**—*adv.* **discourt'eously.**—*n.* **discourt'eousness, discourt'esy.**

discover, *dis-kuv'ǝr, v.t.* to uncover: to lay open or expose: to exhibit: to reveal: to make known: to find out: to espy.—Also (*Spens.*) **discoure', discure'.**—*adj.* **discov'erable.**—*ns.* **discov'erer**, one who makes a discovery, esp. of something never before known: (*obs.*) an informer: (*Shak.*) a scout; **discov'ery**, the act of finding out: the thing discovered: gaining knowledge of the unknown: the unravelling of a plot: exploration or reconnaissance (*obs.* except in **voyage of discovery**, voyage of exploration). [O.Fr. *descouvrir—des-* (L. *dis-*), away, *couvrir,* to cover; see **cover.**]

discovert, *dis-kuv'ǝrt, adj.* (*law*) not under the bonds of matrimony, of a spinster or widow.—*n.* **discov'erture.** [Lit. uncovered, unprotected; O.Fr. *descovert;* see **discover, cover.**]

discredit, *dis-kred'it, n.* want of credit: bad credit: ill-repute: disgrace.—*v.t.* to refuse credit to, or belief in: to deprive of credibility: to deprive of credit: to disgrace.—*adj.* **discred'itable**, not creditable: disgraceful.—*adv.* **discred'itably.**

discreet, *dis-krēt', adj.* having discernment: wary: circumspect: prudent: (*arch.*) discrete, separate, detached.—*adv.* **discreet'ly.**—*n.* **discreet'ness.** [O.Fr. *discret—*L. *discrētus—discernĕre,* to separate, to perceive; see **discern, discrete.**]

discrepancy, *dis'krip-ǝn-si,* or *dis-krep', n.* disagreement, variance of facts or sentiments.—*n.*

Neutral vowels in unaccented syllables: *el'ǝ-mǝnt, in'fǝnt, ran'dǝm*

dis'crepance (or -crep').—adj. dis'crepant (or -crep'), contrary, disagreeing. [L. discrepāns, -āntis, different—dis-, asunder, and crepāns, pr.p. of crepāre, to sound.]

discrete, dis'krēt, dis-krēt', adj. separate: discontinuous : consisting of distinct parts : referring to distinct objects : abstract—opp. to concrete.—adv. discrete'ly.—n. discrete'ness.—adj. discret'ive, separating : disjunctive.—adv. discret'ively. [L. discrētus; cf. discreet.]

discretion, dis-kresh'ən, n. quality of being discreet : prudence : liberty to act at pleasure.—adjs. discre'tional, discre'tionary, left to discretion : unrestricted.—advs. discre'tionally, discre'tionarily.—age, years, of discretion, mature years; at discretion, according to one's own judgment; be at one's discretion, to be completely under one's power or control; surrender at discretion, to surrender unconditionally, that is, to another's discretion. [O.Fr. discrecion—L. discrētiō, -ōnis, discernēre, -crētum.]

discriminate, dis-krim'i-nāt, v.t. to note the difference of or between : to distinguish : to select from others.—v.i. to make or note a difference or distinction : to distinguish.—adj. (-nit) discriminated : discriminating.—adj. discrim'inant, discriminating.—n. a special function of the roots of an equation, expressible in terms of the coefficients—zero value of the function showing that at least two of the roots are equal.—adv. discrim'inately.—adj. discrim'inating, noting distinctions : gifted with judgment and penetration.—adv. discrim'inatingly.—n. discriminā'tion.—adj. discrim'inative, that marks a difference : characteristic : observing distinctions.—adv. discrim'inatively.—n. discrim'inator. [L. discrimināre, -ātum—discrīmen, that which separates; cf. discernēre, to discern.]

discrown, dis-krown', v.t. to deprive of a crown.

disculpate, dis-kul'pāt, v.t. to free from blame.

discumber, dis-kum'bər, v.t. to disencumber.

discure, dis-kūr', v.t. (Spens.) to discover.

discursive, dis-kur'siv, adj. running from one thing to another : roving, desultory : proceeding regularly from premises to conclusion : intellectual, rational.—ns. discur'sion, desultory talk : act of reasoning; discur'sist, a disputer.—adv. discur'sively.—n. discur'siveness.—adj. discur'sory, discursive.—n. discur'sus (L.L.), discourse, reasoned treatment. [See discourse.]

discus, dis'kəs, n. a quoit, disk.—Gr. diskos.]

discuss, dis-kus', v.t. to examine in detail, or by disputation : to debate : to sift : (coll.) to consume, as a bottle of wine : (Spens.) to throw off : to dispel : (obs.) to settle, decide : (Shak.) to declare, make known.—adj. discuss'able, -ible.—n. discussion (dis-kush'ən), debate : (surg.) dispersion of a tumour.—adjs. discuss'ive, discutient (-kū'shi-ənt), able or tending to discuss or disperse tumours.—n. discū'tient, a medicine with this property. [L. discutĕre, discussum—dis-, asunder, quatĕre, to shake.]

disdain, dis-dān', or diz-, v.t. to think unworthy : to scorn.—n. a feeling of contempt, generally tinged with superiority : haughtiness.—adjs. disdained' (Shak.), disdainful; disdain'ful.—adv. disdain'fully.—n. disdain'fulness. [O.Fr. desdaigner with substitution of des- (L. dis-) for L. dē in L. dēdīgnārī—dīgnus, worthy.]

disease, diz-ēz', n. uneasiness (in this sense often written dis-ease and pron. dis'ēz') : a disorder or want of health in mind or body : ailment : cause of pain.—v.t. (Spens.) to make uneasy.—adj. diseased', affected with disease.—n. diseas'edness.—adj. disease'ful. [O.Fr. desaise—des- (L. dis-), neg., aise, ease; see ease.]

disedge, dis-ej', v.t. (Shak.) to deprive of the edge: to blunt : to dull.

disembark, dis-im-bärk', v.t. to set ashore : to take out of a ship.—v.i. to quit a ship : to land.—ns. disembarkā'tion (dis-em-, dis-im-), disembark'ment. [O.Fr. desembarquer—des- (L. dis-, neg.), embarquer. See embark.]

disembarrass, dis-im-bar'əs, v.t. to free from embarrassment or perplexity.—n. disembarr'assment.

disembellish, dis-im-bel'ish, v.t. to deprive of embellishment.

disembitter, dis-im-bit'ər, v.t. to free from bitterness.

disembody, dis-im-bod'i, v.t. to take away from or out of the body (esp. of spirits) : to discharge from military embodiment.—adj. disembod'ied.—n. disembod'iment.

disembogue, dis-im-bōg', v.t. and v.i. to discharge at the mouth, as a stream.—n. disembogue'ment. [Sp. desembocar—des- (L. dis-), asunder, embocar, to enter the mouth—en (L. in), into, boca (L. bucca), cheek, mouth.]

disembosom, dis-im-booz'əm, v.t. to separate from the bosom : to disburden.

disembowel, dis-im-bow'əl, v.t. to take out the bowels of : to tear out the inside of.—n. disembow'elment.

disembrangle, dis-im-brang'gl, v.t. to free from dispute.

disembroil, dis-im-broil', v.t. to free from broil or confusion.

disemburden, dis-im-bur'dn, v.t. to disburden.

disemploy, dis-im-ploi', v.t. remove from employment.—adj. disemployed'.

disenable, dis-in-ā'bl, v.t. to make unable : to disable : (obs.) to deprive of power.

disenchain, dis-in-chān', v.t. to free from restraint.

disenchant, dis-in-chānt', v.t. to free from enchantment, to disillusion.—ns. disenchant'er:—fem. disenchant'ress; disenchant'ment.

disenclose, dis-in-klōz', v.t. to free from the condition of being enclosed : to dispark.—Also disinclose'.

disencumber, dis-in-kum'bər, v.t. to free from encumbrance : to disburden.—n. disencum'brance.

disendow, dis-in-dow', v.t. to take away the endowments of (esp. of an established church).—adj. disendowed'.—n. disendow'ment.

disenfranchise, dis-in-fran'chīz, -shīz, v.t. (rare) to disfranchise : to deprive of suffrage.—n. disenfran'chisement (-chiz-, -shis-).

disengage, dis-in-gāj', v.t. to separate or free from being engaged : to separate : to set free : to release.—v.i. to come loose.—adj. disengaged', at leisure, without engagement.—ns. disengag'edness; disengage'ment. [O.Fr. desengager—des- (L. dis-, neg.), engager, to engage.]

disennoble, dis-i-nō'bl, v.t. to deprive of title, or of what ennobles : to degrade.

disenrol, dis-in-rōl', v.t. to remove from a roll.

disenshroud, dis-in-shrowd', v.t. to divest of a shroud, to unveil.

disenslave, dis-in-slāv', v.t. to free from bondage.

disentail, dis-in-tāl', v.t. to break the entail of (an estate) : to divest.—n. the act of disentailing.

disentangle, dis-in-tang'gl, v.t. to free from entanglement or disorder : to unravel : to disengage or set free.—n. disentang'lement.

disenthral, disenthrall, dis-in-thrawl', v.t. to free from enthralment.—n. disenthral'ment.

disenthrone, dis-in-thrōn', v.t. (Milt.) to dethrone.

disentitle, dis-in-tī'tl, v.t. to deprive of title.

disentomb, dis-in-tōōm', v.t. to take out from a tomb.

disentrail, disentrayle, dis-in'trāl, v.t. (Spens.) to let forth as if from the entrails.

disentrain, dis-in-trān', v.t. to set down from a train.—v.i. to alight from a train.

disentrance, dis-in-trāns', v.t. to awaken from a trance or entrancement : to arouse from a reverie.—n. disentrance'ment.

n. disentrance'ment.

disentwine, dis-in-twīn', v.t. to untwine.

disenvelop, dis-in-vel'əp, v.t. to free from that in which a thing is enveloped : to unfold.

disenviron, dis-in-vī'rən, v.t. to deprive of environment.

disespouse, dis-is-powz', v.t. (Milt.) to separate after espousal or betrothal.

disestablish, *dis-is-tab'lish*, *v.t.* to undo the establishment of.—*n.* **disestab'lishment.**

disesteem, *dis-is-tēm'*, *n.* want of esteem : disregard.—*v.t.* to disapprove : to dislike.—*n.* **disestimā'tion** (*-es-tim-*).

disfame, *dis-fām'*, *n.* evil reputation.

disfavour, *dis-fā'vər*, *n.* want of favour : displeasure : dislike.—*v.t.* to withhold favour from : to disapprove : to oppose.—*n.* **disfā'vourer.**

disfeature, *dis-fēt'yər*, *v.t.* to deprive of a feature : to deface.

disfellowship, *dis-fel'ō-ship*, *n.* want of, or exclusion from, fellowship.—*v.t.* to excommunicate.

disfigure, *dis-fig'ər*, *v.t.* to spoil the figure of : to change to a worse form : to spoil the beauty of : to deform.—*ns.* **disfig'urement**, **disfigūrā'tion.** [O.Fr. *desfigurer*—L. *dis-*, neg., *figūrāre*, to figure.]

disflesh, *dis-flesh'*, *v.t.* to deprive of flesh, to disembody.

disforest, *dis-for'ist*, *v.t.* to strip of trees : to disafforest.

disform, *dis-form'*, *v.t.* to alter the form of.

disfranchise, *dis-fran'chīz*, *-shīz*, *v.t.* to deprive of a franchise, or of rights and privileges, esp. that of voting for an M.P.—*n.* **disfran'chisement.**

disfrock, *dis-frok'*, *v.t.* to unfrock, deprive of clerical garb or character.

disfurnish, *dis-fur'nish*, *v.t.* (*Shak.*) to strip, render destitute.—*n.* **disfur'nishment.**

disgarnish, *dis-gär'nish*, *v.t.* to despoil.

disgarrison, *dis-gar'i-sn*, *v.t.* to deprive of a garrison.

disgavel, *dis-gav'l*, *v.t.* to relieve from the tenure of gavelkind.

disgest, *dis-jest'*, *-jēst'*, **disgest'ion** (*-yən*), *obs.* or *dial.* forms of **digest**, **-ion.**

disglorify, *dis-glō'ri-fī*, *v.t.* (*Milt.*) to deprive of glory.

disgodded, *dis-god'id*, *adj.* deprived of divinity.

disgorge, *dis-gorj'*, *v.t.* to discharge from the throat : to vomit : to throw out with violence : to give up.—*n.* **disgorge'ment.** [O.Fr. *desgorger*, *des*, away, *gorge*, throat. See **gorge.**]

disgospelling, *dis-gos'pəl-ing*, *adj.* (*Milt.*) withholding the gospel, stopping the channel of the gospel.

disgown, *dis-gown'*, *v.t.* or *v.i.* to strip of a gown : to deprive of or to renounce orders or a degree.

disgrace, *dis-grās'*, *n.* state of being out of grace or favour, or of being dishonoured : cause of shame : dishonour : disfigurement : ugliness : defect of grace.—*v.t.* to put out of favour : to bring disgrace or shame upon.—*adj.* **disgrace'ful**, bringing disgrace : causing shame : dishonourable.—*adv.* **disgrace'fully.**—*ns.* **disgrace'fulness ; disgra'cer.**—*adj.* **disgracious** (*-grā'shəs ; Shak.*), ungracious, unpleasing. [Fr. *disgrâce*—L. *dis-*, neg., and *grātia*, favour, grace.]

disgrade, *dis-grād'*, *v.t.* to deprive of rank or status.—*n.* **disgradā'tion** (*-grə-dā'shən*). [O.Fr. *desgrader*, with substitution of *des-* (L. *dis-*), for L. *dē* in L.L. *dēgradāre*—*gradus*, a step.]

disgregation, *dis-gri-gā'shən*, *n.* separation : scattering. [L. *disgregātiō*, *-ōnis*—*dis-*, apart, *grex*, *gregis*, flock.]

disgruntle, *dis-grun'tl*, *v.t.* (*prov.* and *U.S.*) to disappoint, disgust.—*adj.* **disgrun'tled**, rendered sulky. [L. pfx. *dis-* and **gruntle**, freq. of **grunt.**]

disguise, *dis-gīz'*, *v.t.* to change the guise or appearance of : to conceal the identity of by a dress intended to deceive, or by a counterfeit manner and appearance : (*arch.* and *slang*) to intoxicate (usu. *disguised in liquor*).—*n.* a dress intended to disguise the wearer : a false appearance : change of behaviour in intoxication.—*adj.* **disguised'.**—*adv.* **disguis'edly.**—*n.* **disguis'edness.**—*adj.* **disguise'less.**—*ns.* **disguise'ment ; disguis'er ; disguis'ing.** [O.Fr. *desguiser*—*des-* (L. *dis-*), neg., *guise*, manner ; see **guise.**]

disgust, *dis-gust'*, *n.* (formerly, e.g. in Milton, Johnson, Jane Austen) distaste, disfavour, displeasure : (now) loathing :extreme annoyance.—*v.t.* to excite disgust in.—*adv.* **disgust'edly.**—*adj.* **disgust'ful.**—*adv.* **disgust'fully.**—*n.* **disgust'fulness.**—*adj.* **disgust'ing.**—*adv.* **disgust'ingly.**—*ns.* **disgust'-ingness.** [O.Fr. *desgouster*—*des-* (L. *dis-*), and *gouster*—L. *gustāre*, to taste.]

dish, *dish*, *n.* a vessel, esp. one that is flat, or shallow, or not circular, or one for food at table : a dishful : the food in a dish : (*obs.*) a cup (of tea, coffee, etc.) : a particular kind of food : a hollow : concavity of form, as in a wheel, a chair-back.—*v.t.* to put in a dish, for table : to make concave : (*coll.*) to outwit, to circumvent.—*ns.* **dish'-clout**, **dish'-cloth**, a cloth for drying or wiping dishes; **dish'-cover**, a cover for a dish to keep it hot.—*adjs.* **dished**, having a concavity; **dish'-faced**, having a round, flat face, or (in animals) a concavity in the face.—*ns.* **dish'ful**, enough to fill a dish; **dish'ing**, putting in a dish : a hollow, concavity.—*adj.* hollow like a dish.—*n.* **dish'-water**, water in which dishes have been washed.—**dish up**, to serve up, esp. figuratively of old materials cooked up anew. [O.E. *disc*, a plate, a dish, a table—L. *discus*—Gr. *diskos*; cf. **disk**, **desk** ; Ger. *tisch*, table.]

dish, *dish*, *v.t.* (*print.*) to distribute (type).

dishabilitate, *dis-(h)ə-bil'i-tāt*, *v.t.* to disqualify : to attaint.—*n.* **dishabilitā'tion.**

dishabille, *dis-ə-bēl'*, *n.* a negligent toilet : undress : an undress garment.—Also **déshabillé** (*dā-zā-bē-yā*). [Fr. *déshabillé*, pa.p. of *déshabiller*, to undress —*des-* (L. *dis-*), apart, *habiller*, to dress.]

dishabit, *dis-hab'it*, *v.t.* (*Shak.*) to drive from a habitation. [O.Fr. *deshabiter*—L.L. *dis-*, neg., *habitāre*, to inhabit.]

dishable, *dis-hā'bl*, an obsolete form (*Spens.*) of **disable.**

dishallow, *dis-hal'ō*, *v.t.* to desecrate.

disharmony, *dis-här'mə-ni*, *n.* lack of harmony : discord : incongruity.—*adjs.* **disharmonic** (*-mon'*), out of harmony : discordant : incongruous : dysharmonic; **disharmonious** (*-mō'*).—*adv.* **disharmō'niously.**—*v.t.* and *v.i.* **dishar'monise**, to put out of, or be out of, harmony.

dishearten, *dis-härt'n*, *v.t.* to deprive of heart, courage, or spirits : to discourage : to depress.— *adjs.* **disheart'ened ; disheart'ening.**

dishelm, *dis-helm'*, *v.t.* to divest of a helmet.

disherit, *dis-her'it*, *v.t.* (*Spens.*) to disinherit.—*ns.* **disher'ison** (*-zən*); **disher'itor.** [O.Fr. *desheriter* —L. *dis-*, neg., L.L. *hērēditāre*, to inherit—L. *hērēs*, heir.]

dishevel, *di-shev'l*, *v.t.* to disorder, as hair : to cause to hang loose : to ruffle.—*v.i.* to spread in disorder (*pr.p.* **dishev'elling;** *pa.t.* and *pa.p.* **dishev'elled).** —*n.* **dishev'elment.** [O.Fr. *discheveler*—L.L. *discapillāre*, to tear out or disorder the hair—L. *dis-*, in different directions, *capillus*, the hair.]

dishome, *dis-hōm'*, *v.t.* to deprive of a home.

dishonest, *dis-on'ist*, *adj.* not honest : wanting integrity : disposed to cheat : insincere : (*Shak.*) unchaste.—*adv.* **dishon'estly.**—*n.* **dishon'esty.** [O.Fr. *deshoneste*—*des-* (L. *dis-*), neg., *honeste* (L. *honestus*), honest.]

dishonour, *dis-on'ər*, *n.* want of honour : disgrace : shame : reproach.—*v.t.* to deprive of honour : to disgrace : to cause shame to : to seduce : to degrade : to refuse the payment of, as a cheque.—*adjs.* **dishon'orary**, causing dishonour; **dishon'ourable**, not in accordance with a sense of honour : disgraceful.—*n.* **dishon'ourableness.**—*adv.* **dishon'ourably.**—*n.* **dishon'ourer.** [O.Fr. *deshonneur*—*des-* (L. *dis-*), neg., *honneur* (—L. *honor*), honour.]

dishorn, *dis-horn'*, *v.t.* to deprive of horns.

dishorse, *dis-hors'*, *v.t.* to unhorse.

dishouse, *dis-howz'*, *v.t.* to deprive of house or housing : to turn out of doors : to pull down of houses.

dishumour, *dis-(h)ū'mər*, *n.* ill-humour.—*v.t.* to put out of humour.

disillude, *dis-i-l(y)ood'*, *v.t.* to free from illusion.— *n.* **disillusion** (*dis-i-l(y)oo'zhən*), a freeing from illusion : state of being disillusioned.—*v.t.* to free from illusion, disenchant.—*adjs.* **disillu'sionary ; disillu'sioned**, freed from illusion : often, bereft of comfortable beliefs whether they were false or true.—*v.t.* **disillu'sionise.**—*n.* **disillu'sionment.** —*adj.* **disillu'sive** (*-siv*).

disilluminate, *dis-i-l(y)oo'mi-nāt*, *v.t.* to destroy the light of, to darken.

disimagine, *dis-i-maj'in*, *v.t.* to banish from the imagination : imagine not to be.

disimmure, *dis-i-mūr'*, *v.t.* to release from walls.

disimpassioned, *dis-im-pash'ənd*, *adj.* free from the influence of passion, tranquil.

disimprison, *dis-im-priz'n*, *v.t.* to free from prison or restraint.—*n.* **disimpris'onment.**

disimprove, *dis-im-proōv'*, *v.t.* to render worse.—*v.i.* to grow worse.

disincarcerate, *dis-in-kär'sər-āt*, *v.t.* to free from prison.—*n.* **disincarcerā'tion.**

disinclination, *dis-in-kli-nā'shən*, *n.* want of inclination : unwillingness.—*v.t.* **disincline** (*-klīn'*), to turn away inclination from : to excite the dislike or aversion of.—*adj.* **disinclined'**, not inclined : averse.

disinclose. Same as **disenclose.**

disincorporate, *dis-in-kor'pə-rāt*, *v.t.* to deprive of corporate rights.—*n.* **disincorporā'tion.**

disindividualise, *dis-in-di-vid'ū-əl-īz*, *v.t.* to deprive of individuality.

disinfect, *dis-in-fekt'*, *v.t.* to free from infection : to purify from infectious germs.—*n.* **disinfect'ant**, anything that destroys the causes of infection.—Also *adj.*—*ns.* **disinfec'tion ; disinfect'or.**

disinfest, *dis-in-fest'*, *v.t.* to free from infesting animals.—*n.* **disinfestā'tion.**

disinflation, *dis'in-flā-shən*, *n.* return to the normal condition after inflation.

disingenuous, *dis-in-jen'ū-əs*, *adj.* not ingenuous : not frank or open : crafty.—*adv.* **disingenu'ity** (*rare*).—*adv.* **disingen'uously.**—*n.* **disingen'uousness.**

disinherit, *dis-in-her'it*, *v.t.* to cut off from hereditary rights : to deprive of an inheritance.—*ns.* **disinher'ison** (*-zən*), act of disinheriting ; **disinher'itance.**

disinhume, *dis-in-hūm'*, *v.t.* to take out of the earth, to disinter.

disintegrate, *dis-in'ti-grāt*, *v.t.* and *v.i.* to separate into parts : to break up : to crumble.—*adjs.* **disin'tegrable, disin'tegrative.**—*ns.* **disintegrā'tion ; disin'tegrātor**, a machine for crushing or pulverising.

disinter, *dis-in-tər'*, *v.t.* to take out of the earth, from a grave, or from obscurity.—*n.* **disinter'ment.**

disinterest, *dis-in'tər-ist*, *n.* disadvantage : disinterestedness : lack of interest.—*v.t.* to free from interest.—*adj.* **disint'erested**, not influenced by private feelings or considerations : not deriving personal advantage : impartial : unselfish, generous : (revived from obsolescence) uninterested.—*adv.* **disin'terestedly.**—*n.* **disin'terestedness.**—*adj.* **disin'teresting** (*obs.*), uninteresting.

disinthral. Same as **disenthral.**

disintricate, *dis-in'tri-kāt*, *v.t.* to free from intricacy.

disinure, *dis-in-ūr'*, *v.t.* (*Milt.*) to render unfamiliar.

disinvest, *dis-in-vest'*, *v.t.* to divest.—*n.* **disinvest'iture**, the action of disinvesting.

disinvigorate, *dis-in-vig'ər-āt*, *v.t.* to weaken.

disinvolve, *dis-in-volv'*, *v.t.* to unfold : to disentangle.

disjaskit, *dis-jås'kit*, *adj.* (*Scot.*) jaded : worn out. [Prob. dejected.]

disject, *dis-jekt'*, *v.t.* to dismember : to scatter.—*n.* **disjec'tion.** [L. *disjicĕre*, *-jectum*—*dis-*, apart, *jacĕre*, to throw.]

disjoin, *dis-join'*, *v.t.* to separate after having been joined.—*v.t.* **disjoint'**, to put out of joint : to separate united parts of : to break the natural order or relations of : to make incoherent.—*adj.* **disjoint'ed**, incoherent, esp. of discourse : badly assorted.—*adv.* **disjoint'edly.**—*n.* **disjoint'edness.** [O.Fr. *desjoindre*—L. *disjungĕre*—*dis-*, apart. *jungĕre*, to join.]

disjunct, *dis-jungkt'*, also *dis'*, *adj.* disjoined : (*biol.*) deeply constricted: (*ancient Gr. mus.*) of tetrachords, having the highest note of the lower and the lowest of the upper a tone or semitone apart.—*n.* **disjunc'tion**, the act of disjoining : disunion : separation.—*adj.* **disjunct'ive**, disjoining : tending to separate : (*gram.*) uniting sentences but disjoining the sense, or rather marking an adverse

sense.—*n.* a word which disjoins.—*adv.* **disjunct'ively.**—*ns.* **disjunct'or**, a device for breaking an electric circuit : (*bot.*) a weak place where separation between conidia occurs ; **disjunct'ure.** [O.Fr. *desjoinct*, *desjoindre.* See above.]

disjune, *dis-joōn'*, *n.* (*Scot. ; arch.*), breakfast. [O.Fr. *desjun*—L. *dis-*, expressing undoing, *jējūnus*, fasting.]

disk, disc, *disk*, *n.* a quoit thrown by ancient Greek athletes : any flat thin circular body or structure : a circular figure, as that presented by the sun, moon, and planets : the enlarged torus of a flower : the inner part of a capitulum in composite plants.—*v.t.* and *v.i.* to work with a disk-harrow.—*ns.* **disk'-flower', -flor'et**, one of the tubular inner flowers of a capitulum—opp. to *ray-flower ;* **disk'-harr'ow, -plough,** a harrow, or plough, in which the soil is cut by inclined disks; **disk'-jockey,** (*slang*) one who gives a recital of gramophone records. See also **disc.** [Gr. *diskos.*]

disleaf, *dis-lēf'*, *v.t.* to deprive of leaves.—Also **disleave'.**

disleal, *dis-lē'əl*, *adj.* (*Spens.*) disloyal, dishonourable. [See **disloyal.**]

dislike, *dis-līk'*, *v.t.* to be displeased with : to disapprove of : to have an aversion to : (*obs.*) to displease.—*n.* (*dis-līk'*, sometimes *dis'*) disinclination : aversion : distaste : disapproval.—*adjs.* **dislike'able, dislik'able ; dislike'ful.**—*v.t.* **dislik'en** (*Shak.*), to make unlike.—*n.* **dislike'ness** (*obs.*), unlikeness. [L. *dis-*, neg., and **like** ; the genuine Eng. word in *mislike.*]

dislimb, *dis-lim'*, *v.t.* to tear the limbs from : to dismember.

dislimn, *dis-lim'*, *v.t.* (*Shak.*) to efface.

dislink, *dis-lingk'*, *v.t.* to unlink, to separate.

disload, *dis-lōd'*, *v.t.* to unload, to disburden.

dislocate, *dis'lō-kāt*, *v.t.* to displace : to put out of joint.—*adv.* **dis'locatedly.**—*n.* **dislocā'tion**, a dislocated joint : displacement : disorganisation : derangement (of traffic, plans, etc.) : (*geol.*) a fault. [L.L. *dislocāre*, *-ātum*—L. *dis*, apart, *locāre*, to place.]

dislodge, *dis-loj'*, *v.t.* to drive from a lodgment or place of rest : to drive from a place of hiding or of defence.—*v.i.* to go away.—*n.* **dislodg(e)'ment.** [O.Fr. *desloger*—*des-* (L. *dis-*), apart, *loger*, to lodge.]

disloign, *dis-loin'*, *v.t.* (*Spens.*) to put far apart or at a distance, to remove. [O.Fr. *desloignier*—*des-* (L. *dis-*), apart, *loignier*, to remove.]

disloyal, *dis-loi'əl*, *adj.* not loyal : unfaithful.—*adv.* **disloy'ally.**—*n.* **disloy'alty.** [O.Fr. *desloyal*—*des-* (L. *dis-*), neg., *loyal*, *leial*—L. *lēgālis*, legal.]

dislustre, *dis-lus'tər*, *v.t.* to deprive of lustre.—*v.i.* to lose lustre.

dismal, *diz'məl*, *adj.* gloomy : dreary : sorrowful : depressing.—*n.* (*obs.*) unlucky days : (*U.S.*) a swamp : a dismal person : (in *pl.*) the dumps : (in *pl., obs.*) mournings.—*adv.* **dis'mally.**—*ns.* **dis'malness, dismality** (*-mal'i-ti*)—**dismal day** (*Spens*), a day of ill omen; **the dismal science,** political economy. [O.Fr. *dismal*—L. *diēs malī*, evil, unlucky days.]

disman, *dis-man'*, *v.t.* to deprive of men (of a country, or ship) : to unman : to deprive of human character (of the body by death).

dismantle, *dis-man'tl*, *v.t.* to strip : to deprive of furniture, fittings, etc., so as to render useless : to raze the fortifications of : to take to bits, pull down. [O.Fr. *desmanteller*—*des-* (L. *dis-*), away, *manteler*—*mantel*, a mantle.]

dismask, *dis-måsk'*, *v.t.* to strip a mask from : to remove a disguise from : to uncover. [O.Fr. *desmasquer*—*des-* (L. *dis-*), neg., *masquer*, to mask.]

dismast, *dis-måst'*, *v.t.* to deprive of a mast or masts.—*n.* **dismast'ment.**

dismay, *dis-*, *diz-mā'*, *v.t.* to appal : to discourage : (*Spens.*) to distress.—*v.i.* (*Shak.*) to be daunted.—*n.* loss of strength and courage through fear : (*Spens.*) discouraging onslaught.—*n.* **dismay'edness.**—*adj.* **dismay'ful.**—*adv.* **dismay'fully** (*Spens.*). [App. through O.Fr.—L. *dis-*, and

O.H.G. *magan* (Ger. *mögen*; O.E. *magan*), to have might or power; see **may.**]

dismayd, *dis-mād', adj.* (*Spens.*) apparently, misshapen, deformed, mismade.

dismayl, *dis-māl', v.t.* to deprive of mail: (*Spens.*) to break mail from. [O.Fr. *desmailler*—*des-* (L. *dis-*), neg., *maille*, mail.]

disme, *dim, n.* (*Shak.*) a tenth or tithe. [O.Fr.; see **dime.**]

dismember, *dis-mem'bər, v.t.* to divide member from member: to separate a limb from: to disjoint: to tear to pieces: (*obs.*) to carve for the table (certain birds—herons, cranes).—*adj.* **dismem'bered** (*her.*) without limbs or with limbs detached.—*n.* **dismem'berment.** [O.Fr. *desmembrer*—*des-* (L. *dis-*), neg., *membre*, a member (L. *membrum*).]

dismiss, *dis-mis', v.t.* to send away: to dispatch: to discard: to remove from office or employment: (*law*) to reject, to put out of court, to discharge.—*ns.* **dismiss'al, dismission** (*-mish'ən*).—*adjs.* **dismiss'ive, dismiss'ory.** [L. *dis-*, away, *mittĕre*, *missum*, to send.]

dismoded, *dis-mōd'id, adj.* out of fashion. [L. *dis-*, neg., and **mode.**]

dismount, *dis-mownt', v.i.* to come down: to come off a horse, bicycle, etc.—*v.t.* to throw or bring down from any elevated place: to unhorse: to remove from a stand, framework, setting, carriage, or the like. [O.Fr. *desmonter*—*des-* (L. *dis-*), neg., *monter*, to mount.]

dismutation, *dis-mū-tā'shən, n.* in biochemistry, simultaneous oxidation and reduction. [Pfx. *dis-*, **mutation.**]

disnatured, *dis-nā'tyərd, adj.* unnatural, devoid of natural affection.—*v.t.* **disnaturalise** (*-nat'*), to make alien or unnatural.

disnest, *dis-nest', v.t.* to dislodge from a nest: to clear as of nestlings.

disobedient, *dis-ō-bēd'yənt, adj.* neglecting or refusing to obey.—*n.* **disobed'ience.**—*adv.* **disobed'iently.**

disobey, *dis-ō-bā', dis-ə-bā', v.t.* and *v.i.* to neglect or refuse to obey. [O.Fr. *desobeir*—*des-* (L. *dis-*), and *obeir*, to obey.]

disoblige, *dis-ō-blīj', -ə-blīj', v.t.* to relieve from an obligation: to refuse or fail to oblige or grant a favour to: to offend or injure thereby.—*n.* **disobligation** (*dis-ob-li-gā'shən*), freedom from obligation: act of disobliging.—*adj.* **disob'ligatory** (*-gə-tə-ri*), releasing from obligation.—*n.* **disobligement** (*-blīj'*).—*adj.* **disoblig'ing,** not obliging: not careful to attend to the wishes of others: unaccommodating: unkind.—*adv.* **disoblig'ingly.**—*n.* **disoblig'ingness.**

disorbed, *dis-orbd', adj.* (*Shak.*) thrown from its sphere, as a star: deprived of the orb of sovereignty.

disorder, *dis-or'dər, n.* want of order: confusion: disturbance: breach of the peace: disease.—*v.t.* to throw out of order: to disarrange: to disturb: to produce disease in.—*adj.* **disor'dered,** confused, deranged.—*n.* **disor'derliness.**—*adj.* **disor'derly,** out of order: in confusion: irregular: lawless: defying the restraints of decency.—*adv.* confusedly: in a lawless manner.—*n.* a disorderly person.—**disorderly house,** a brothel: a gaminghouse. [O.Fr. *desordre*—*des-* (L. *dis-*), neg., *ordre*, order.]

disordinate, *dis-or'din-āt, adj.* (*rare*) not in order: disorderly: (*Milt.*) inordinate.—*adv.* **disor'dinately.**

disorganise, *dis-or'gən-īz, v.t.* to destroy the organic structure of: to disorder.—*adj.* **disorganic** (*-gan'*). —*n.* **disorganisā'tion.**

disorient, *dis-ō'ri-ənt, v.t.* to turn from the east: to confuse as to direction: to throw out of one's reckoning.—Also **diso'rientate.**—*n.* **disorientā'tion.**

disown, *dis-ōn', v.t.* to refuse to own or acknowledge as belonging to oneself: to deny: to repudiate, cast off.—*n.* **disown'ment.**

dispace, *dis-pās', v.i.* (*Spens.*) to range about.— Also *v.t.* (*reflex.*). [Perh. L. *di-*, apart, *spatiārī*, to walk about; or *dis-* and **pace.**]

disparage, *dis-par'ij, v.t.* to dishonour by comparison with what is inferior: to match in marriage with an inferior: to lower in rank or estimation: to talk slightingly of: (*Spens.*) to dishearten.—*ns.* **dis'parage** (*Spens.*), an unequal match; **dispar'agement; dispar'ager.**—*adv.* **dispar'agingly.** [O.Fr. *desparager*—*des-* (L. *dis-*), neg., and *parage*; see **parage.**]

disparate, *dis'pər-āt, adj.* unequal: incapable of being compared.—*ns.* **dis'parateness.**—*n.pl.* **dis'parates,** things or characters of different species. [L. *disparātus*—*dis-*, neg., and *parāre*, make ready; influenced by *dispar*, unequal.]

disparity, *dis-par'i-ti, n.* inequality: unlikeness so great as to render comparison difficult and union unsuitable. [L. *dispar*, unequal—*dis-*, neg., *par*, equal.]

dispark, *dis-pärk', v.t.* to throw open, deprive of the character of a park: to remove from a park.

dispart, *dis-pärt', v.t.* to part asunder: to divide, to separate.—*v.i.* to separate.—*n.* the difference between the thickness of metal at the breech and the mouth of a gun.

dispassion, *dis-pash'ən, n.* freedom from passion: a calm state of mind.—*adj.* **dispass'ionate** (*-it*), free from passion: unmoved by feelings: cool: impartial.—*adv.* **dispass'ionately.**

dispatch, despatch, *dis-pach', v.t.* to send away hastily: to send out of the world: to put to death: to dispose of: to perform speedily.—*v.i.* (*Shak.*) to make haste.—*n.* a sending away in haste: dismissal: rapid performance: haste: taking of life: the sending off of the mails: that which is dispatched, as a message, esp. telegraphic: (*pl.*) state-papers (military, diplomatic, etc.).—*ns.* **dispatch'-boat,** a vessel for carrying dispatches; **dispatch'-box,** a box for holding dispatches or valuable papers; **dispatch'er.**—*adv.* **dispatch'ful** (*Milt.*), swift.—*n.* **dispatch'-ri'der,** a carrier of dispatches, on horse-back or bicycle. [It. *dispacciare* or Sp. *despachar*—L. *dis-*, apart, and some L.L. word from the root of *pangĕre*, *pactum*, to fasten; not connected with Fr. *dépêcher*.]

dispathy, a misspelling of **dyspathy.**

dispauperise, *dis-paw'-pər-īz, v.t.* to free from pauperism or from paupers.—*v.t.* **dispau'per,** to declare no longer a pauper.

dispeace, *dis-pēs', n.* lack of peace: dissension.

dispel, *dis-pel', v.t.* to drive away and scatter: to make disappear.—*v.i.* to scatter or melt away (*pr.p.* **dispell'ing;** *pa.t.* and *pa.p.* **dispelled'.** [L. *dispellĕre*—*dis-*, away, *pellĕre*, to drive.]

dispence, *dis-pens'* (*Spens.*). Same as **dispense.**

dispend, *dis-pend', v.t.* (*arch.*) to expend, pay out. [O.Fr. *despendre*—L. *dis-*, out, and *pendĕre*, to weigh.]

dispensary, *dis-pens'ər-i, n.* a place where medicines are dispensed, esp. to the poor, gratis and advice given: an out-patient department of a hospital.

dispensation, *dis-pən-sā'shən, n.* the act of dispensing or dealing out: administration: a dealing of Providence, or of God, or nature: a method or stage of God's dealing with man (*Patriarchal, Mosaic, Christian*): licence or permission to neglect a rule: ground of exemption.—*adj.* **dispens'able,** that may be dispensed, or dispensed with: (*arch.*) pardonable.—*ns.* **dispensabil'ity, dispens'ableness.**—*adv.* **dispens'ably.**—*adj.* **dispens'ative,** granting dispensation.—*adv.* **dispens'atively.**— *n.* **dis'pensātor,** a dispenser: a distributor: an administrator.—*adv.* **dispens'atorily.**—*adj.* **dispens'atory,** granting dispensation.—*n.* a book containing medical prescriptions.—*v.t.* **dispense',** to deal out: to distribute: to administer: to make up for distributing or administering.—*v.i.* (*Spens.*) to make amends: to compound.—*n.* expense: expenditure: supplies: (*Milt.*) dispensation.—*adj.* **dispensed'.**—*n.* **dispens'er.**—**dispense with,** to permit the want of: to do without. [Fr. *dispenser*— L. *dis-*, asunder, *pēnsāre*, inten. of *pendĕre*, to weigh.]

dispeople, *dis-pē'pl, v.t.* to empty of inhabitants.

disperse, *dis-pərs', v.t.* to scatter in all directions: to spread: to diffuse: to drive asunder: to cause to vanish: to put in a colloidal state.—*v.i.* to separate: to spread abroad: to vanish.—*n.* dis-pers'al, dispersion: distribution: (*biol.*) the spread of a species to new areas.—*adv.* dispers'edly.—*ns.* dispers'edness; dispers'er; dispersion (*dis-pər'shən*), a scattering, or state of being scattered: (*med.*) the removal of inflammation: (*phys.*) the spreading out of rays owing to different refrangibility: the state of a finely divided colloid: a substance in that state: the Diaspora. — *adj.* dispers'ive, tending or serving to disperse.—*n.* dispers'oid, a substance in a state of dispersion— also dispersed phase. [L. *dīspergĕre, dispersum*— *dī-*, asunder, apart, *spargĕre,* to scatter.]

dispersonate, *dis-pər'sən-āt, v.t.* to divest of personality.

dispirit, *dis-pir'it, v.t.* to dishearten: to discourage. —*adj.* dispir'ited, dejected: feeble, spiritless.— *adv.* dispir'itedly.—*n.* dispir'itedness.—*adj.* dispir'iting, disheartening.—*n.* dispir'itment.

dispiteous, *dis-pit'i-əs, adj.* (*obs.*) despiteous: pitiless.—*adv.* dispit'eously.—*n.* dispit'eousness. [See despite; influenced by piteous.]

displace, *dis-plās', v.t.* to put out of place: to disarrange: to remove from a state, office, or dignity: to supplant: to substitute something for.— *adj.* displace'able.—*n.* displace'ment, a putting or being out of place: the difference between the position of a body at a given time and that occupied at first: the quantity of water displaced by a ship afloat or an immersed body.—displaced person, one removed from his country as a prisoner or as slave labour: a refugee or stateless person. [O.Fr. *desplacer*—*des-* (L. *dis-*), neg., and *place,* place.]

displant, *dis-plänt', v.t.* to remove from a fixed position: to drive from an abode.—*n.* displantā'-tion. [O.Fr. *desplanter*—L. *dis-*, neg., and *plantāre,* to plant.]

display, *dis-plā', v.t.* to unfold or spread out: to exhibit: to set out ostentatiously: (*print.*) to make prominent by large type, wide spacing, etc.—*n.* a displaying or unfolding: exhibition: ostentatious show.—*adj.* displayed', unfolded: spread: printed in prominent letters: (*her.*) erect, with wings expanded, as a bird.—*n.* display'er. [O.Fr. *despleier*—*des-* (L. *dis-*), neg., and *plier, ploier*— L. *plicāre,* to fold; double deploy; see ply.]

disple, *dis'pl, v.t.* (*Spens.*) to discipline, chastise. [Apparently from discipline.]

displease, *dis-plēz', v.t.* to offend: to make angry in a slight degree: to be disagreeable to.—*v.i.* to raise aversion.—*n.* displeasance (*dis-plez'əns, Spens.*), displeasure.—*adj.* displeas'ant (*obs.*). — *adj.* displeased', vexed, annoyed. — *adv.* displeas'edly.—*n.* displeas'edness.—*adj.* dis-pleas'ing, causing displeasure: giving offence.— *adv.* displeas'ingly.—*ns.* displeas'ingness; displeasure (*dis-plezh'ər*), the feeling of one who is offended: anger: cause of irritation.—*v.t.* (*arch.*) to displease, offend. [O.Fr. *desplaisir*—*des-* (L. *dis-*), neg., *plaisir,* to please.]

displenish, *dis-plen'ish, v.t.* to deprive of plenishing or furniture, implements, etc.: to sell the plenishing of.—*n.* displen'ishment.

displode, *dis-plōd', v.t.* (*Milt.*) to discharge, to explode.—*v.i.* to explode.—*n.* displōsion (*-plō'-zhən*). [L. *displōdĕre*—*dis-*, asunder, *plaudĕre,* to beat.]

displume, *dis-plōōm', v.t.* to deprive of plumes or feathers.

dispondee, *dī-spon'dē, n.* a double spondee.—*adj.* dispondā'ic. [Gr. *dispondeios*—*di-*, twice, *spondeios,* spondee.]

dispone, *dis-pōn', v.t.* (*arch.*) to set in order, dispose: (*Scots law*) to make over to another: to convey legally.—*ns.* disponee', the person to whom anything is disponed; dispon'er. [L. *dispōnĕre,* to arrange.]

disponge. See dispunge.

disport, *dis-pōrt', v.t.* (usually reflex.) and *v.i.* to divert, amuse: to move in gaiety.—*n.* disport'-ment. [O.Fr. (*se*) *desporter,* to carry (oneself) away from one's work, to amuse (oneself)—*des-* (L. *dis-*), and *porter*—L. *portāre,* to carry; see sport.]

dispose, *dis-pōz', v.t.* to arrange: to distribute: to place: to apply to a particular purpose: to make over by sale, gift, etc.: to bestow: to incline.— *v.i.* to settle things: to ordain what is to be: to make a disposition: to get rid.—*n.* disposal, management: behaviour, disposition.—*adj.* dispos'able.—*n.* dispos'al, the act of disposing: order: arrangement: management: right of bestowing: availability for one's own use or control.—*adj.* disposed', inclined: of a certain disposition (with *well, ill,* etc.). —*adv.* dispos'edly, in good order: with measured steps.—*n.* dispos'er.—*n.* and *adj.* dispos'ing.— *adv.* dispos'ingly.—*n.* disposure (*-pō'zhər*), disposal, arrangement: disposition.—dispose of, to settle what is to be done with: to make an end of: to have done with: to part with: to get rid of: to sell. [Fr. *disposer*—dis- (L. *dis-*), asunder, *poser,* to place—L. *pausāre,* to pause, (late) to place.]

disposition, *dis-pə-zish'ən, n.* arrangement: distribution: plan for disposing one's property, etc.: natural tendency: temper: (*N.T.*) ministration: (*Scots law*) a giving over to another, conveyance or assignment—often *disposition and settlement,* a deed for the disposal of a man's property at his death.—*adjs.* disposi'tional; disposi'tioned; dispositive (*-poz'i-tiv*).—*adv.* dispos'itively.— *ns.* dispos'itor, a planet that disposes or controls another. [Fr.,—L., from *dis-*, apart, *pōnĕre,* *positum,* to place.]

dispossess, *dis-pə-zes', v.t.* to put out of possession. —*n.* dispossess'or.

dispost, *dis-pōst', v.t.* to displace from a post.

dispost, *dis-pōst',* (*Spens.*) for disposed.

disposure. See dispose.

dispraise, *dis-prāz', n.* expression of an unfavourable opinion: blame: reproach.—*v.t.* to blame: to censure.—*n.* disprais'er.—*adv.* disprais'ingly. [O.Fr. *despreisier*—*des-* (L. *dis-*), neg., *preisier,* to praise.]

dispread, *dis-pred', v.t.* to spread in different ways. —*v.i.* to spread out: to expand.—Spenser has the forms dispred, dispredden (*plur.*), disprad (*pa.p.*).

disprinced, *dis-prinst', adj.* (*Tenn.*) deprived of the appearance of a prince.

disprison, *dis-priz'n, v.t.* to set free.

disprivacied, *dis-priv'ə-sid, adj.* deprived of privacy.

disprivilege, *dis-priv'i-lij, v.t.* to deprive of a privilege.

disprize, *dis-prīz', v.t.* to set a low price upon: to undervalue.

disprofess, *dis-prə-fes', v.t.* to cease to profess, renounce.

disprofit, *dis-prof'it, n.* loss, damage.

disproof, *dis-prōōf', n.* a disproving: refutation.

disproove, *dis-prōōv', v.t.* (*Spens.*) to disapprove of.

disproperty, *dis-prop'ər-ti, v.t.* (*Shak.*) to deprive one of possession of.

disproportion, *dis-prə-pōr'shən, n.* want of suitable proportion.—*v.t.* to make unsuitable in form or size, etc.—*adj.* dispropor'tionable (*arch.*).—*n.* dispropor'tionableness.—*adv.* dispropor'tion-ably.—*adj.* dispropor'tional.—*adv.* dispropor'-tionally.—*adj.* dispropor'tionate.—*adv.* dispro-por'tionately.—*n.* dispropor'tionateness.

dispropriate, *dis-prō'pri-āt, v.t.* to disappropriate.

disprove, *dis-prōōv', v.t.* to prove to be false or wrong: (*arch.*) to disapprove.—*pa.p.* disproved'.— disproven (*-prōv'* : *-prōōv'*).—*n.* disprov'al. [O.Fr. *desprover;* see prove.]

disprovide, *dis-prō-vīd', v.t.* to leave or render unprovided.

dispunge, *dis-punj', v.t.* (*Shak.*) to sprinkle or discharge as if from a sponge.

dispurse, *dis-purs', v.t.* (*Shak.*) to disburse.

dispurvey, *dis-pər-vā', v.t.* (*arch.*) to deprive of provisions.—*n.* dispurvey'ance (*Spens.*).

dispute, *dis-būt', v.t.* to make a subject of argument: to contend for: to oppose by argument: to call in question.—*v.i.* to argue: to debate.—*n.* a contest with words: an argument: a debate: a quarrel.—*adj.* dis'putable (also *-pūt'*), that may be disputed: of doubtful certainty.—*n.* dis'putableness.—*adv.* **dis'putably.**—*ns.* **dis'putant, disput'er; disputā'tion,** a contest in argument: an exercise in debate.—*adjs.* **disputā'tious, disput'ative,** inclined to dispute, cavil, or controvert. —*adv.* **disputā'tiously.**—*n.* **disputā'tiousness.**— beyond, or without, **dispute,** indubitably, certainly. [O.Fr. *desputer*—L. *disputāre*—*dis-*, apart, and *putāre*, to think.]

disqualify, *dis-kwol'i-fī, v.t.* to deprive of the qualities or qualifications necessary for any purpose: to make unfit: to disable: to debar: to declare to be disqualified.—*n.* **disqualifica'tion,** state of being disqualified: anything that disqualifies or incapacitates.

disquiet, *dis-kwī'ət, adj.* (*obs.*) unquiet, uneasy, restless.—*n.* want of quiet: uneasiness, restlessness: anxiety.—*v.t.* to render unquiet: to make uneasy: to disturb.—Also **disquī'eten.**—*adjs.* **disquī'etful; disquī'etive, disquī'eting.**—*adv.* **disquī'etly** (*Shak.*).—*ns.* **disquī'etness, disquī'etude.**—*adj.* **disquī'etous.**

disquisition, *dis-kwi-zish'ən, n.* a careful inquiry into any matter by arguments, etc.: an essay.— *adjs.* **disquisi'tional, disquisi'tionary, disquis'itory, disquis'itive,** pertaining to or of the nature of a disquisition. [L. *disquīsītiō, -ōnis*—*disquīrĕre, dis-*, inten., *quaerĕre, quaesītum*, to seek.]

disrank, *dis-rangk', v.t.* to reduce to a lower rank: to throw into confusion.

disrate, *dis-rāt', v.t.* (*naut.*) to reduce to a lower rating or rank, as a petty officer.

disregard, *dis-ri-gärd', v.t.* to pay no attention to.— *n.* want of attention: neglect: slight.—*adj.* **disregard'ful.**—*adv.* **disregard'fully.**

disrelish, *dis-rel'ish, v.t.* not to relish: to dislike the taste of: to dislike.—*n.* distaste: dislike: disgust.—*adj.* **disrel'ishing,** offensive.

disremember, *dis-ri-mem'bər, v.t.* (*vulg.*) not to remember, to forget.

disrepair, *dis-ri-pār', n.* state of being out of repair.

disrepute, *dis-ri-pūt', n.* bad repute: discredit.— Also **disreputā'tion** (*dis-rep-*).—*adj.* **disrep'utable,** in bad repute: disgraceful: not respectable: disordered and shabby.—*ns.* **disrep'utableness, disreputabil'ity** (*rare*).—*adv.* **disrep'utably.**

disrespect, *dis-ri-spekt', n.* want of respect: discourtesy: incivility.—*v.t.* (*arch.*) not to respect.— *adjs.* **disrespect'able** (*rare*), not respectable; **disrespect'ful,** showing disrespect: irreverent: uncivil.—*adv.* **disrespect'fully.**—*n.* **disrespect'fulness.**

disrobe, *dis-rōb', v.t.* and *v.i.* to undress: to uncover: to divest of robes.

disroot, *dis-rōōt', v.t.* to uproot.

disrupt, *dis-rupt', v.t.* and *v.i.* to burst asunder, to break up.—*n.* **disrup'tion,** the act of breaking asunder: the act of bursting and rending: breach: **Disruption,** in Scottish ecclesiastical history, the separation of the Free Church from the Established Church for the sake of spiritual independence (1843).—*adj.* **disrup'tive,** causing, or accompanied by, disruption. [L. *disruptus, dīruptus*—*dīrumpĕre* —*dis-*, asunder, *rumpĕre*, to break.]

diss, *dis, n.* an Algerian reedy grass (*Ampelodesma tenax*) used for cordage, etc. [Ar. *dīs.*]

dissatisfactory, *dis-sat-is-fak'tər-i, adj.* causing dissatisfaction.—*ns.* **dissatisfac'tion,** state of being dissatisfied: discontent: uneasiness: **dissatisfac'toriness.**

dissatisfy, *dis-sat'is-fī, v.t.* to fail to satisfy: to make discontented: to displease.—*adj.* **dissat'isfied,** discontented: not pleased.

disseat, *dis-sēt', v.t.* to unseat.

dissect, *di-sekt', v.t.* to cut asunder: to cut into parts for the purpose of minute examination: to divide and examine: to analyse and criticise.— *adj.* **dissect'ed,** (*bot.*) deeply cut into narrow segments: (*geol.*) cut up by valleys.—*adj.* **dissect'ible.**—*ns.* **dissect'ing; dissec'tion,** the act or the art of cutting in pieces a plant or animal in order to ascertain the structure of its parts: anatomy.—*adj.* **dissect'ive,** tending to dissect.— *n.* **dissect'or.**—**dissected map, picture,** a map or picture on a board cut up, so as to form a puzzle;

dissecting microscope, a form of microscope that allows dissection of the object under examination; **dissecting room, table,** a room in, table on, which anatomical dissection is practised. [L. *dissecāre, dissectum*—*dis-*, asunder, *secāre*, to cut.]

disseise, disseize, *dis-sēz', v.t.* to deprive of seisin or possession of an estate of freehold: to dispossess wrongfully.—*ns.* **disseis'in, disseiz'in; disseis'or, disseiz'or.**

dissemble, *di-sem'bl, v.t.* to disguise: to mask: (*obs.*) to feign.—*v.i.* to assume a false appearance: to play the hypocrite: to dissimulate.—*ns.* **dissem'blance** (*rare*), want of resemblance: the act of dissembling; **dissem'bler; dissem'bling.**— *adj.* deceiving, hypocritical.—*adv.* **dissem'blingly.** [L. *dissimulāre*—*dissimilis*, unlike—*dis-*, neg., and *similis*, like; perh. remodelled on *resemble.*]

dissembly, *dis-em'bli, n.* the breaking up of an assembly: (*Shak.*) a Dogberryism for assembly.

disseminate, *di-sem'i-nāt, v.t.* to sow or scatter abroad: to propagate: to diffuse.—*adj.* **scattered.**— *n.* **dissemina'tion.**—*adj.* **dissem'inative.**—*ns.* **dissem'inātor; dissem'inule,** any part or organ of a plant that serves for dissemination.—**disseminated sclerosis,** a chronic progressive disease in which patches of thickening appear throughout the central nervous system, resulting in various forms of paralysis. [L. *dissēminare, -ātum*—*dis-*, asunder, *sēminare*, to sow—*sēmen, sēminis*, seed.]

dissent, *di-sent', v.i.* to think differently: to disagree in opinion: to differ (with *from*).—*n.* the act of dissenting: difference of opinion: a protest by a minority: a differing or separation from an established church.—*ns.* **dissen'sion,** disagreement in opinion: discord: strife; **Dissent'er,** one (esp. a Protestant) who is separate from an established church: a nonconformist: **dissenter,** (*U.S.*) a dissentient: —*adj.* **dissent'erish.**—*n.* **dissent'erism.** —*adj.* **dissen'tient** (*-shənt*), declaring dissent: disagreeing.—*n.* one who disagrees: one who declares his dissent.—*adj.* **dissent'ing.**—*adv.* **dissent'ingly.**—*adj.* **dissen'tious** (*-shəs; Shak.*), disposed to discord, contentious. [L. *dissentīre, dissēnsum* —*dis-*, apart, *sentīre*, to think.]

dissepiment, *di-sep'i-mənt, n.* (*bot.*) a partition in an ovary: (*zool.*) a partition partly cutting off the bottom of a coral cup.—*adj.* **dissepimental** (*-ment'l*). [L. *dissaepimentum*, a partition—L. *dissaepīre*—*dis-*, apart, *saepīre*, to hedge in.]

dissertate, *dis'ər-tāt, v.i.* to discourse—(*arch.*) **dissert'.**—*n.* **dissertā'tion,** a formal discourse: a treatise.—*adjs.* **dissertā'tional, disser'tative.**— *n.* **diss'ertātor.** [L. *dissertāre*, inten. of *disserĕre*, to discuss—*dis-*, *serĕre*, to put together.]

disserve, *dis-sərv', v.t.* to do an ill turn to: to clear (a table).—*n.* **disserv'ice,** injury: mischief: an ill turn.—*adj.* **disserv'iceable.** [O.Fr. *desservir*—L. *dis-*, neg., *servīre*, to serve.]

dissever, *di-sev'ər, v.t.* to sever: to part in two: to separate: to disunite.—*ns.* **dissev'erance, disseverā'tion, dissev'erment,** a dissevering or parting.—*adj.* **dissev'ered,** disunited. [O.Fr. *dessevrer*—L. *dis-*, apart, *sēparāre*, to separate.]

dissheathe, *dis-shēdh', v.t.* to unsheathe.

disshiver, *dis-shiv'ər, v.t.* (*Spens.*) and *v.i.* to shiver in pieces.

dissident, *dis'i-dənt, adj.* dissenting.—*n.* a dissenter.—*n.* **diss'idence,** disagreement. [L. *dissidēns, -ēntis*, pr.p. of *dissidēre*—*dis-*, apart, *sedēre*, to sit.]

dissight, *di(s)-sīt', n.* an unsightly object.

dissilient, *di(s)-sil'yənt, adj.* springing asunder: (*bot.*) bursting open with force.—*n.* **dissil'ience.** [L. *dissiliēns, -entis*—*dis-*, asunder, *salīre*, to leap.]

dissimilar, *di-sim'i-lər, adj.* unlike.—*n.* **dissimilarity** (*-ar'*), unlikeness.—*adv.* **dissim'ilarly.**—*v.t.* **dissim'ilate,** to make unlike.—*n.* **dissimilā'tion,** the act of rendering dissimilar: katabolism; **dissimile** (*di-sim'i-li*), the opposite of a simile, a comparison by contrast; **dissim'ilitude.**

dissimulate, *di-sim'ū-lāt, v.t.* to pretend the contrary of: to conceal or disguise: to dissemble.— *v.i.* to practise dissimulation, play the hypocrite.— *ns.* **dissimulā'tion,** the act of dissembling: a hiding under a false appearance : false pretension : hypocrisy : **dissim'ulātor**. [L. *dissimulāre*, *-ātum*, to dissimulate—*dis*, neg., *similis*, like.]

dissipate, *dis'i-pāt*, *v.t.* to scatter : to squander : to waste : to dispel.—*v.i.* to separate and disappear : to waste away : to be dissolute in conduct : to indulge in trivial amusements.—*adj.* **diss'ipable**, that may be dissipated.—*adj.* **diss'ipated**, dissolute, esp. addicted to drinking.—*n.* **dissipā'tion**, dispersion : state of being dispersed : scattered attention : a course of frivolous amusement or of dissolute life.—*adj.* **diss'ipātive**, tending to dissipate or disperse : connected with the dissipation of energy.—**dissipation of energy**, degradation of energy, or progressive loss of availability of a portion for doing work at each transformation. [L. *dissipāre*, *-ātum*—*dis-*, asunder, and (archaic) *supāre*, to throw.]

dissociate, *di-sō'shi-āt*, *v.t.* and *v.i.* to separate from society or from association of any kind : to separate : to subject to or suffer dissociation.—*adj.* separated.—*n.* **dissōciabil'ity** (*-sh∂*).—*adjs* **dissō'ciable**, not sociable : ill associated : incongruous : capable of being dissociated ; **dissō'cial**, not social. —*v.t.* **dissō'cialise**, to make unsocial.—*ns.* **dissociality** (*-sō-shi-al'*) ; **dissociā'tion** (*-sō-shi-* or *-sō-si-*), act of dissociating : state of being dissociated : (*chem.*) separation into simpler constituents, esp. a reversible separation caused by heat, or separation into ions : (*psychology*) splitting of personality : splitting off from consciousness of certain ideas and their accompanying emotions : breaking of associations.—*adj.* **dissō'ciative** (*chem.*), tending to dissociate. [L. *dissociāre*, *-ātum*—*dis-*, asunder, *sociāre*, to associate.]

dissoluble, *dis'∂l-(y)oo-bl*, or *dis-ol'ū-bl*, *adj.* capable of being dissolved.—*ns.* **dissolubil'ity**, **dissol'ūbleness**.—*adj.* **diss'olute** (*-lōōt* or *-lūt*), loose, esp. in morals, debauched.—*n.* a dissolute person. —*adv.* **diss'olutely**.—*ns.* **diss'oluteness** ; **dissolution** (*-lōō'* or *-lū'*), the breaking up of an assembly : loosening : melting : break-up : death : (*arch.*) dissoluteness or dissolute behaviour ; **dissolu'tionism** ; **dissolu'tionist** ; **dissolvabil'ity** (*diz-*) ; **dissolv'ableness**.—*adj.* **dissolv'able**, capable of being dissolved.—*v.t.* **dissolve** (*di-zolv'*), to loose asunder : to undo : to separate or break up : to put an end to (as a parliament) : to melt in solution (formerly also in fusion) : to disperse : (*arch.*) to resolve (as doubts, riddles).—*v.i.* to go into solution : to break up : to waste away : to fade away : to melt.—*n.* **dissolv'ent**, a solvent.—*adj.* having power to melt.—*n.* and *adj.* **dissolv'ing**. [L. *dissolvĕre*, *dissolūtum*—*dis-*, asunder, *solvĕre*, *-ātum*, to loose.]

dissonant, *dis'o-n∂nt*, or *-∂-*, *adj.* not agreeing or harmonising in sound : without concord or harmony : disagreeing.—*n.* **diss'onance**, disagreement of sound : want of harmony : discord : disagreement : (*spec.*) a combination of musical sounds that calls for resolution or produces beats—also **diss'onancy**. [L. *dissonāns*, *-āntis*—*dis-*, apart, *sonāre*, to sound.]

dissuade, *di-swād'*, *v.t.* (*obs.*) to give advice against : (*obs.*) to seek to divert by advice : to divert by advice.—*ns.* **dissua'der** ; **dissua'sion** (*-zh∂n*).— *adj.* **dissua'sive** (*-siv*), tending to dissuade.—*n.* that which tends to dissuade.—*adv.* **dissua'sively**. —*n.* and *adj.* **dissua'sory** (*rare*). [L. *dis- suādēre*—*dis-*, apart, *suādēre*, *suāsum*, to advise.]

dissunder, *dis-sun'd∂r*, *v.t.* to sunder.

dissyllable, a faulty spelling of **disyllable**.

dissymmetry, *dis-sim'i-tri*, *n.* want of symmetry : enantiomorphy—the symmetry of right and left hand, object and mirror-image.—*adjs.* **dissymmetric**, **-al** (*-et'*).

distaff, *dis'tâf*, *n.* the stick that holds the bunch of flax, tow, or wool in spinning.—**distaff side**, the female part, line, side, or branch of a family or descent. [O.E. *distæf*, from the root found in L.G. *diesse*, the bunch of flax on the staff ; and *stæf*, staff ; see **dizen**.]

distain, *dis-tān'*, *v.t.* to stain : to sully. [O.Fr. *desteindre*, to take away the colour of—L. *dis-*, neg., and *tingĕre*, to colour.]

distal, *dis't∂l*, *adj.* far apart : at the outer end—opp. to *proximal*.—*adv.* **dis'tally**. [Formed from **distance** on the analogy of *central*.]

distance, *dis't∂ns*, *n.* measure of interval between : remoteness : a remote place or region : the remote part of the field of view or the part of a picture representing it : degree of remoteness : opposition : stand-offishness or aloofness of manner : in horseracing, the space measured back from the winning-post which a horse, in heat-races, must reach when the winner has covered the whole course, in order to run in the final heat.—*v.t.* to place at a distance : to leave at a distance behind.—*adj.* **dis'tanceless**, not allowing a distant view (of hazy weather) : having no indications of distance (of pictures).— *n.* **dis'tance-sig'nal**, on a railway, a signal farther from the destination than the home-signal.— **keep one at a distance**, to treat with aloofness : **keep one's distance**, to abstain from familiarity with, to keep aloof from. [See **distant**.]

distant, *dis't∂nt*, *adj.* at a certain distance : at a great distance : remote, in time, place, resemblance, or connexion : indistinct : reserved or aloof in manner.—*adv.* **dis'tantly**. [Fr.,—L. *dīstāns*, *-antis* —*dī-*, apart, *stāns*, *stantis*, pr.p. of *stāre*, to stand.]

distaste, *dis-tāst'*, *n.* disrelish : dislike : (*obs.*) unpleasant experience : (*obs.*) offence.—*v.t.* (*arch.*) to dislike : (*obs.*) to offend : (*Shak.*) to spoil the taste of.—*v.i.* (*Shak.*) to be distasteful.—*adj.* **distaste'ful**, unpleasant to the taste : unpleasant : (*Shak.*) indicating distaste : full of distaste.—*adv.* **distaste'fully**.—*n.* **distaste'fulness**.

distemper, *dis-temp'∂r*, *n.* a mode of painting in size, water-glass, or other watery vehicle giving body to the pigment : paint of this kind—for indoor walls, scenery, etc.—*v.t.* to paint in distemper.— Also **destemp'er**. [L. *dis-*, neg., *temperāre*, to regulate, mix in proportion ; cf. next word.]

distemper, *dis-temp'∂r*, *n.* a morbid or disorderly state of body or mind : disease, esp. of animals : specifically a disease of the dog and ferret families caused by a filterable virus : ill-humour.—*v.t.* to derange the temper : to disorder or disease.— *adj.* **distemp'erate**, not temperate, immoderate : diseased.—*n.* **distemp'erature** (*arch.*), want of proper temperature : intemperateness, disturbance : uneasiness of mind : indisposition.—*adj.* **distem'pered**, disordered : intemperate, ill-humoured, put out of sorts. [O.Fr. *destemprer*, to derange—L. *dis-*, apart, *temperāre*, to govern, regulate.]

distend, *dis-tend'*, *v.t.* to stretch forth or apart : to stretch in three dimensions : to swell.—*v.i.* to swell.—*n.* **distensibil'ity**, capacity for distension.—*adj.* **disten'sible**, that may be stretched ; **disten'sile** (*-sīl*), distensible : able to cause distension.—*n.* **disten'sion**, act of distending or stretching : state of being stretched : (*rare*) breadth (sometimes **disten'tion**).—*adjs.* **disten'sive**, capable of stretching or of being stretched ; **distent'** (*Spens.*), extended : distended, swollen. [L. *distendĕre*—*dis-*, asunder, *tendĕre*, *tēnsum* or *tentum*, to stretch.]

disthene, *dis'thēn*, *n.* kyanite—so called from its difference in hardness when scratched in different directions. [Gr. *di-*, twice, *sthenos*, strength.]

disthrone, *dis-thrōn'*, *v.t.* to dethrone—(*Spens.*) **disthrōn'ize**.

distich, *dis'tik*, *n.* a couple of lines or verses, making complete sense : a couplet (*pl.* **distichs**, *-tiks*).—*adj.* having two rows.—*adj.* **dis'tichous**, in or having two rows. [Gr. *distichos*—*dis*, twice, *stichos*, a line.]

distil, now rarely **distill**, *dis-til'*, *v.i.* to fall in drops : to flow gently : to use a still.—*v.t.* to let or cause to fall in drops : to convert from liquid into vapour by heat, and then to condense again : to extract by evaporation and condensation :—*pr.p.* **distill'ing** ; *pa.t.* and *pa.p.* **distilled'**.—*adj.* **distill'able**.—*ns.* **dis'tillāte**, the product of distillation ; **distillā'tion**, the act of distilling.—*adj.* **distill'atory**, of or for distilling.—*ns.* **distill'er** ; **distill'ery**, a place where distilling, esp. of alcoholic spirits, is carried on ; **distill'ing** ; **distil'ment** (*Shak.*), that which is distilled.—**destructive distillation**, the collection of volatile matters released when a substance is destroyed by heat in a close vessel (as coal in making gas); **fractional distillation**, the separation by distilling of liquids having different boiling-points, the heat being gradually increased and the receiver changed. [O.Fr. *distiller*, with substitution of prefix—L. *dēstillāre*, *-ātum—dē*, down, *stillāre*, to drop—*stilla*, a drop.]

distinct, *dis-tingkt'*, *adj.* (*Milt.*) distinguished, differentiated : separate : different : well-defined : clear : (*Spens.*, *Milt.*) marked, variegated.—*n.* **distinction** (*dis-tingk'shən*), separation or division : discrimination : a distinguishing mark or character : (*obs.*) distinctness : difference : a mark or honorific recognition of excellence : an honour : discriminating favour : noticeable eminence : outstanding merit : impressive and meritorious individuality.—*adj.* **distinct'ive**, marking or expressing difference : characteristic.—*adv.* **distinct'ively.**—*n.* **distinct'-iveness.**—*adv.* **distinct'ly.**—*ns.* **distinct'ness** ; **distinct'ure** (*-yər*), distinctness. [See **distinguish.**]

distinguish, *dis-ting'gwish*, *v.t.* to mark off, set apart (often with *from*) : to recognise by characteristic qualities : to make out : (*obs.*) to make distinctions in or concerning : to bring by drawing distinctions : to separate by a mark of honour : to make eminent or known.—*v.i.* to make or show distinctions or differences, to recognise a difference (often with *between*).—*adj.* **disting'uishable**, capable of being distinguished.—*adv.* **disting'uishably.**—*adj.* **disting'uished**, illustrious.—*n.* **disting'uisher.**—*adj.* **disting'uishing**, peculiar.—*n.* **disting'uishment** (*Shak.*), distinction. [L. *dīstinguĕre*, *distinctum—dī-*, asunder, *stinguĕre*, orig. to prick, and *-ish*, in imitation of Fr. vbs. in *-ir*.]

distort, *dis-tort'*, *v.t.* to twist aside : to put out of shape without breach of continuity : to turn aside from the true meaning : to pervert : to misrepresent.—*adj.* **distort'ed.**—*n.* **distortion** (*-tor'-shən*), a twisting awry : deformation without breaking : change of wave-form in course of transmission : crookedness : perversion.—*adj.* **distort'-ive**, causing distortion. [L. *dis-*, asunder, *torquēre*, *tortum*, to twist.]

distract, *dis-trakt'*, *v.t.* to draw aside, apart, or in different directions—esp. of the mind or attention : to confuse : to harass : to render crazy.—*adj.* (*Shak.*, *dis'*) separate : (*Milt.*, *-trakt'*) distracted.—*adj.* **distract'ed.**—*adv.* **distract'edly.**—*ns.* **distract'-edness** ; **distrac'tion**, state of being distracted : that which distracts : perplexity : agitation : madness : recreation, relaxation.—*adj.* **distract'ive**, causing perplexity. [L. *distrahĕre*, *-tractum—dis-*, apart, *trahĕre*, to draw.]

distrain, *dis-trān'*, *v.t.* to seize (esp. goods for debt, esp. for non-payment of rent or rates) : (*Spens.*) to pull apart, burst.—*v.i.* to seize the goods of a debtor.—*adj.* **distrain'able.**—*ns.* **distrain'er** ; **distrain'ment** ; **distrain'or** (*law*); **distraint'**, seizure of goods. [O.Fr. *destraindre*—L. *dī-*, asunder, *stringĕre*, to draw tight.]

distraught, *dis-trawt'*, *adj.* (*Spens.*) drawn aside : distracted : mad : perplexed. [*distract*, mod. by association with words like **caught, taught.**]

distress, *dis-tres'*, *n.* extreme pain or suffering : that which causes suffering : calamity : misfortune : acute poverty : exhaustion : peril : difficulty : (*arch.*) compulsion : act of distraining goods.—*v.t.* to afflict with pain or suffering : to harass : to grieve : to distrain.—*adj.* **distressed'.**—*adj.* **distress'ful.**—*adv.* **distress'fully.**—*n.* **distress'fulness.**—*adj.* **distress'ing.**—*adv.* **distress'ingly.** [O.Fr. *des-tresse*—L. *dīstringĕre*; see **distrain.**]

distribute, *dis-trib'ūt*, *v.t.* to divide amongst several : to deal out or allot : to classify : to disperse about a space : to spread out : (*print.*) to separate and put back in compartments : (*log.*) to use with full extension, including every individual to which the term is applicable.—*n.* **distrib'uend**, that which is to be distributed.—*adjs.* **distrib'utable**, that may be divided; **distrib'utary**, distributing.—*n.* a branch of a distributing system : an off-flow from a river that does not return to it.—*ns.* **distrib'uter**, **-or** ; **distribu'tion**, the act or process

of distributing : dispersal : division : range : allotment : classification : the application of a general term to all the objects denoted by it : (*pol. econ.*) the manner in which the products of industry are shared among the people.—*adjs.* **distribu'tional** ; **distrib'utive**, that distributes, separates, or divides : giving to each his own.—*n.* a word, like *each* or *every*, that indicates the several individuals of a number taken separately.—*adv.* **distrib'utively.**—**geographical distribution**, the department of science that treats of the range and dispersal of animals and plants about the world. [L. *distribuĕre—dis-*, asunder, *tribuĕre*, *tribūtum*, to allot.]

district, *dis'trikt*, *n.* a portion of territory defined for political, judicial, educational, or other purposes (as a registration district, a militia district, the District of Columbia) : a region : (*U.S.*) a constituency : (*India*) a subdivision of a division.—*v.t.* to divide into districts.—**district attorney** (*U.S.*) a public prosecutor for a district; **district council**, the council of an urban or rural district; **district nurse**, a nurse appointed to attend to cases in a district; **district visitor**, a church worker who visits parishioners in a district. [Fr.,—L.L. *dīstrictus*, jurisdiction—*dīstringĕre*; see **distrain.**]

distringas, *dis-tring'gas*, *n.* an old writ directing a sheriff or other officer to distrain. [Second pers. sing. pres. subj. of L. *dīstringĕre*; see **distrain.**]

distrouble, *dis-trub'l*, *v.t.* (*Spens.*) to trouble greatly, to perplex. [L. *dis-*, inten., and **trouble.**]

distrust, *dis-trust'*, *n.* want of trust : want of faith or confidence : doubt.—*v.t.* to have no trust in : to disbelieve : to doubt.—*adj.* **distrust'ful**, full of distrust : apt to distrust : suspicious : (*rare*) to be distrusted.—*adv.* **distrust'fully.**—*n.* **distrust'fulness.**—*adj.* **distrust'less.**

distune, *dis-tūn'*, *v.t.* to put out of tune.

disturb, *dis-turb'*, *v.t.* to throw into confusion : to agitate : to disquiet : to interrupt.—*n.* disturbance.—*n.* **disturb'ance**, agitation : tumult : interruption : perplexity.—*adj.* and *n.* **disturb'ant**, disturbing.—*adjs.* **disturb'ative** ; **disturbed'.**—*n.* **disturb'er**. [O.Fr. *destrouber*—L. *disturbāre*, *dis-* asunder, *turbāre*, to agitate—*turba*, a crowd.]

distyle, *dis'tīl*, *dī'stīl*, *n.* a portico with two columns. [Gr. *di-*, twice, and *stȳlos*, column.]

disulphate, *dī-sul'fāt*, *n.* a pyrosulphate : formerly, an acid sulphate.—*n.* **dīsul'phide**, a sulphide containing two atoms of sulphur to the molecule—also (*obs.*) **dīsul'phuret.**—*adj.* **disulphū'ric**, pyrosulphuric.

disunion, *dis-ūn'yən*, *n.* want of union : breaking up of union or concord : separation.—*n.* **disun'ionist**, one who favours dissolution of a union.—*v.t.* **disunite'**, to separate from union : to sever or sunder.—*v.i.* to fall asunder : to part.—*n.* **disu'nity**, state of disunion.

disuse, *dis-ūs'*, or *dis'ūs*, *n.* the state of being out of use.—*v.t.* (*dis-ūz'*) to cease to use or practise : to leave out of use.—*n.* **disusage** (*dis-ūz'ij*), gradual cessation of use or custom.

disvalue, *dis-val'ū*, *v.t.* (*Shak.*) to disparage.

disvouch, *dis-vowch'*, *v.t.* (*Shak.*) to disavow.

disworship, *dis-wur'ship*, *n.* (*Milt.*) dishonour, disgrace.

disyllable, *dis-il'ə-bl*, *n.* a word of two syllables.—*adj.* **disyllabic** (*-ab'ik*).—*n.* **disyllabificā'tion.**—*v.t.* **disyllab'ify**, to make into two syllables.—*n.* **disyll'abism**, the character of having two syllables. [Through Fr. *dissyllabe*, *dissilabe*, and L. from Gr. *di-*, twice, *syllabē*, a syllable; with *l* as in **syllable.**]

disyoke, *dis-yōk'*, *v.t.* (*Tenn.*) to free from the yoke.

dit, *ditt*, *dit*, *n.* (*arch.*) a poem : the words of a song. [Apparently formed by Spenser from **dite**, influenced by **ditty**.]

dit, *dit*, *v.t.* (now *Scot.*) to stop, block :—*pa.t.* and *pa.p.* **ditt'ed**, **ditt'it**; *pa.p.* also **dit**. [O.E. *dyttan*, to shut.]

dita, *dē'tā*, *n.* an apocynaceous tree (*Alstonia scholaris*) of India and the Philippines, with tonic bark. [Tagálog or Visayan.]

dital, *dī'təl*, *n.* a thumb key for sharpening a lute or guitar string by a semitone. [It. *dito*, finger, with *-al* after **pedal, manual**.]

ditch, *dich*, *n.* a trench dug in the ground : any long narrow depression carrying water : the border of a bowling-green : (*slang*) the sea.—*v.i.* to make, repair or clean a ditch or ditches.—*v.t.* to dig a ditch in or around : to drain by ditches : (*U.S.*) to throw into a ditch : (*slang*) to abandon, throw away : (*U.S.*) to derail : (*slang*) to bring down into the sea.—*ns.* **ditch'-dog** (*Shak.*), a dead dog rotting in a ditch; **ditch'er**, a man or machine that makes, cleans or repairs ditches; **ditch'-water**, stagnant foul water such as is found in ditches, proverbially dull. [O.E. *dic*, whence also **dike**.]

dite, *dīt*, *n.* (*obs.*) writing : a composition.—*v.t.* (*obs.*) to compose, indite : to dictate : to indict. [O.Fr. *dit*, saying, *ditier*, *diter*, to write—L. *dictum*, an utterance, *dictāre*, freq. of *dīcĕre*, to say.]

dite, *v.t.* (*Spens.*). Same as **dight.**

dithecal, *dī-thē'kl*, *adj.* having two thecae.—Also **dīthē'cous.**

ditheism, *dī'thē-izm*, *n.* the doctrine of the existence of two supreme gods.—*n.* **dī'theist.**—*adjs.* **ditheist'ic, -al.** [Gr. *di-*, twice, and *theos*, a god.]

Ditheletism, *dī-thel'et-izm*, *n.* the doctrine that Christ on earth had two wills, human and divine— opp. to **Monotheletism.**—Also **Dī'thelism, Di-, Dȳoth'elism, Dȳothel'etism, Dīthel'itism.**—*n.* **Dī'thelēte**, a believer in the doctrine.—Also **Dīo-, Dȳoth'elēte, -ite.**—*adjs.* **Dītheleŧ'ic, -al.**—Also **Dīo-, Dyotheleŧ'ic, -iŧ'ic, -al.** [Gr. *di-*, twice (or *dyo*, two), *theleŧēs*, a willer—*thelein*, to will.]

dither, *didh'ər*, *n.* (*dial.*) to tremble, shiver, quake.—*v.t.* to perturb, confuse.—*n.* a trembling condition : a quaking fit : tremulous excitement : perturbation.—Also **didd'er.** [Prob. imit.]

dithionate, *dī-thī'ən-āt*, *n.* a salt of dithionic (*-on'ik*) acid, otherwise hyposulphuric acid ($H_2S_2O_6$). [Gr. *di-*, twice, *theion*, sulphur.]

dithyramb, *dith'i-ram(b)*, *n.* an ancient Greek hymn sung in honour of Bacchus : a short poem of a like character.—*adj.* **dithyram'bic**, of, or like a dithyramb : rapturous : wild and boisterous.—*adv.* **dithyram'bically.**—*n.* **dithyram'bist.** [Gr. *dithyrambos*.]

ditokous, *dit'o-kəs*, *adj.* producing two at a birth or in a clutch. [Gr. *di-*, twice, *tokos*, birth.]

ditone, *dī'tōn*, *n.* in ancient Greek music, an interval of two major tones.

ditriglyph, *dī-trī'glif*, *n.* a space for two triglyphs in the entablature between columns.—*adj.* **ditriglyph'ic.**

ditrochee, *dī-trō'kē*, *n.* a trochaic dipody.—*adj.* **ditrochē'an.**

dittander, *di-tan'dər*, *n.* a pepperwort (*Lepidium latifolium*), a pungent cruciferous plant : dittany. [A form of **dittany.**]

dittany, *dit'ə-ni*, *n.* an aromatic rutaceous plant (*Dictamnus albus*), secreting much volatile oil. [O.Fr. *dictame*—L. *dictamnus*—Gr. *diktamnos;* prob. from Mt. *Diktē* in Crete.]

dittay, *dit'ā*, *n.* (*Scots law*) an indictment, charge. [O.Fr. *ditté*—L. *dictātum;* cf. **ditty, dictate.**]

ditto, *dit'ō*, contracted **do.**, *n.* that which has been said : the same thing.—*adv.* as before, or aforesaid : in like manner.—*v.t.* to duplicate.—*n.pl.* **ditt'os**, a suit of clothes of the same colour throughout. [It. *ditto*—L. *dictum*, said, *pa.p.* of *dīcĕre*, to say.]

dittography, *di-tog'rə-fi*, *n.* unintentional repetition of letters or words in copying a manuscript. [Gr. *dittos*, double, *graphein*, to write.]

dittology, *di-tol'ə-ji*, *n.* a double reading or interpretation. [Gr. *dittologiā*—*dittos*, double, *legein*, to speak.]

ditty, *dit'i*, *n.* a song : a little poem to be sung.— *v.t.* to set words to. [O.Fr. *ditie*—L. *dictātum*, neut. perf. part. (pass.) of *dictāre*, to dictate.]

ditty-bag, *dit i-bag*, *n.* a sailor's bag for needles, thread, etc.—Also **ditt'y-box.** [Origin unknown.]

diuretic, *dī-ū-ret'ik*, *adj.* promoting the discharge of urine.—*n.* a medicine causing this discharge.— *n.* **diurē'sis**, discharge of urine, esp. in excess. [Gr. *diourētikos*—*dia*, through, *ouron*, urine.]

diurnal, *dī-ur'nəl*, *adj.* daily : relating to or performed in or lasting a day : belonging to the daytime.—*n.* a service-book containing the day hours, except matins (a night-office) : a diary, journal.—*n.* **diur'nalist**, a journalist.—*adv.* **diur'nally.** [L. *diurnālis—diēs*, a day; see **journal.**]

diuturnal, *dī-ū-tur'nəl*, *adj.* lasting long.—*n.* **diutur'nity.** [L. *diūturnus—diū*, long.]

div, *div*, *v.t.* (*Scot.;* in *pres. indic.* only) a form of **do** (auxiliary).

div, *dēv* (Pers. *dīv*), *n.* an evil spirit of Persian mythology.

diva, *dē'vä*, *n.* a popular female singer : a prima-donna. [It.,—L. *dīva*, fem. of *dīvus*, divine.]

divagate, *dī'və-gāt*, *v.i.* to wander about : to digress. —*n.* **divagā'tion.** [L. *dīvagārī*, to wander.]

divalent, *div'əl-ənt*, or *dī-vā'lənt*, *n.* a chemical element or atom capable of uniting with two atoms of hydrogen or their equivalent.—*adj.* having two combining equivalents.—Also **bivalent.** [Gr. *di-*, twice, L. *valēre*, to be worth.]

divan, *di-van'*, *n.* a collection of poems : a council of state : a court of justice : (poetically) any council or assembly : a council-chamber with cushioned seats : an Eastern couch : a couch of similar type (without back or sides) often used as couch and bed (**divan-bed**) : a smoking-room : a dewan. [Ar. and Pers. *dīwān*, a long seat.]

divaricate, *dī-var'i-kāt*, *v.i.* to part into two branches, to fork : to diverge.—*v.t.* to divide into two branches.—*adj.* widely divergent, spreading apart.—*n.* **divaricā'tion.** [L. *dīvaricāre*, *-ātum— dis-*, asunder, *varicāre*, to spread the legs—*varus*, bent apart.]

dive, *dīv*, *v.i.* to dip or plunge into or down through water or down through the air : to go headlong into a recess, forest, etc. : to plunge or go deeply into any matter.—*v.t.* to plunge, dip.—*n.* a plunge : a swoop : a headlong descent : a refuge : (*U.S.*) a resort, generally disreputable, often underground : a subway.—*ns.* **dive'-bomber**, an aeroplane that discharges a bomb in a longitudinal direction in a steep dive; **dive'-bombing; dive-dapp'er** (*Shak.*), a didapper, dabchick; **div'er**, one who dives or can dive : one who dives for pearls : one who works from a diving-bell or in a diving-dress beneath water : a bird expert at diving, esp. the loon, loosely applied to auks, grebes, penguins, etc. : (*slang*) a pickpocket. [O.E. *dȳfan*, *dūfan;* O.N. *dȳfa*.]

divellent, *dī-vel'ənt*, *adj.* drawing asunder.—*v.t.* **divell'icate**, to pull in pieces : to pluck apart. [L. *dī-*, apart, *vellĕre*, *vellicāre*, to pluck.]

diverge, *di-* or *dī-vərj'*, *v.i.* to incline or turn apart : to tend from a common point in different directions : to vary from the standard.—*ns.* **diverge'ment; diverg'ence, diverg'ency;**—*adj.* **diverg'ent.**—*adv.* **diverg'ently.**—*adv.* **diverg'ing.**—*adv.* **diverg'ingly.** [L. *dī-*, asunder, *vergĕre*, to incline.]

divers, *dī'vərz*, *adj.* sundry : several : more than one : (*B.*) same as **diverse.**—*adv.* (*Milt.*) in different directions.—*adj.* **diverse** (*dī'vərs, div-ərs', dī-vərs'*), different : unlike : multiform : various : (*Spens.*) distracting.—*v.i.* (*Spens.*) to turn aside.— *adv.* **di'versely**, or **diverse'ly.**—*adjs.* **diversifi'-able; diver'sified.**—*n.* **diversifica'tion.**—*v.t.* **diver'sify**, to make diverse or different : to give variety to (*pr.p.* **diver'sifying;** *pa.t.* and *pa.p.* **diver'sified**).—*ns.* **diver'sion**, act of diverting or turning aside : that which diverts : amusement, recreation : something done to turn the attention of an opponent; **divers'ity**, state of being diverse : difference : unlikeness : variety.—*adv.* **dī'versly**, in divers ways.—*v.t.* **divert** (*di-vərt*, also *dī-*), to turn aside (also *arch.*, *v.i.*) : to change the direction of : to turn from business or study : to amuse.—*adj.* **divert'ible.**—*ns.* **divertibil'ity; divertimen'to** (It.; *obs.*), diversion : (*mus.*) a piece in several movements : a pot-pourri : a light piece of music : a ballet-interlude (*pl.* **divertimen'ti,** *-tē*).—*adj.* **divert'ing.**—*adv.* **divert'ingly.**—*ns.* **divertisement** (*di-vərt'iz-mənt*), diversion : a divertissement; **divertissement** (Fr.; *dē-ver-tēs'mäⁿ*), a divertimento.—*adj.* **divert'ive**, tending to divert. [Fr.—

—L. *dīvertĕre*, *dīversum*—*dī-*, aside, *vertĕre*, to turn.]

diverticulum, *dī-vər-tik'ū-ləm*, *n.* (*anat.*) a blind tubular branch.—*adjs.* **divertic'ular**, **divertic'ulate**, **-d**. [L. *dīverticulum*, a byway, retreat.]

Dives, *dī'vēz*, *n.* the rich man at whose gate Lazarus lay (Luke xvi. 19): a rich and luxurious person. [L. *dives*, rich (man), understood as a proper name.]

divest, *dī-* or *di-vest'*, *v.t.* to strip or deprive of anything.—*adj.* **divest'ible**.—*ns.* **divest'iture**, **divest'ment** (*rare*). [O.Fr. *desvestir*, with change of prefix (*dis-* for *dē-*) from L. *dēvestīre*—*dē*, away from, *vestīre*, to clothe—*vestis*, a garment.]

divide, *di-vīd'*, *v.t.* to break up, or mark off, into parts, actually or in imagination: to separate or distinguish the parts of: to classify: to share: to allot: to deal out: (*math.*) to ascertain how many times a quantity is contained in: (*mus.*) to perform with division or floridly: to be a boundary or a subject of difference between: to keep apart: to cause to vote for and against a motion: to sever.—*v.i.* to separate: to fall apart: to branch: to vote for and against a motion: to admit of or be susceptible of division.—*n.* (*coll.*) the act of dividing: (esp. in *U.S.*) a watershed.—*adjs.* **divid'able** or *div'id-*), divisible: (*Shak.*) divided; **divid'ant** (*Shak.*), distinguishable, separable.—*adv.* **divid'edly**.—*n.* **divid'er**, one who or that which divides: (*Scot.*) a soup-ladle: (*pl.*) a kind of compasses for measuring.—*adj.* **divid'ing**, separating.—*n.* separation.—*n.* **divid'ing-en'gine**, an instrument for graduating the scales of scientific apparatus.—*adjs.* **divid'ual**, divisible: (*Milt.*) separable: (*Milt.*) shared in common with others: **divid'uous**, divided, special, accidental. [L. *dīvidĕre*, *dīvīsum*—*dis-*, asunder, root *vid*, to separate.]

dividend, *div'i-dend*, *n.* that which is to be divided: the share of a sum divided that falls to each individual, by way of interest or otherwise.—*n.* **div'idend-warr'ant**, a certificate entitling to payment of dividend.—**declare a dividend**, to announce the sum per cent. a trading concern is prepared to pay its shareholders. [L. *dīvidendum*, to be divided, *dīvidĕre*.]

dividivi, *div'i-div-i*, *n.* the curved pods of *Caesalpinia coriaria*, imported for tanning and dyeing. [Carib name.]

divine, *di-vīn'*, *adj.* belonging to or proceeding from a god: holy: excellent in the highest degree: (*Milt.*) prescient, having forebodings.—*n.* one skilled in divine things: a minister of the gospel: a theologian.—*v.t.* to foresee or foretell as if divinely inspired: to guess or make out: to prognosticate: (*Spens.*) to make divine.—*v.i.* to profess or practise divination: to have forebodings.—*ns.* **divina'tion**, the act or practice of divining: seeking to know the future or hidden things by magical means: instinctive prevision: prediction: conjecture: **div'inātor**, **divin'er**, one who divines or professes divination: a conjecturer:—*fem.* **divin'eress**.—*adjs.* **divinatō'rial**, **divin'atory**, relating to divination, conjectural.—*adv.* **divine'ly**.—*ns.* **divine'ness**; **divin'ing-rod**, a rod, usually of hazel, used by those professing to discover water or metals under ground.—*v.t.* **div'inise**, **divin'ify**, to treat as divine. [O.Fr. *devin*, soothsayer, and L. *dīvīnus*—*dīvus*, *deus*, a god.]

diving, *dīv'ing*, *n.* the action of the verb to dive.—*adj.* that dives.—*ns.* **div'ing-bell**, a hollow vessel or chamber, originally bell-shaped, open at the bottom and supplied with air by a tube from above, in which one may descend into and work under water; **div'ing-board**, a board for diving from; **div'ing-dress**, the water-tight costume of a diver, with special provision for receiving air, etc. [See dive.]

divinity, *di-vin'i-ti*, *n.* godhead: the nature or essence of a god: a celestial being: a god: the science of divine things: theology.—**divinity hall** (*Scot.*), a theological college or department. [O.Fr. *devinite*—L. *dīvīnitas*, *-tātis*; see divine.]

division, *di-vizh'ən*, *n.* act of dividing: state of being divided: that which divides: a partition: a barrier: a portion or section: the taking of a vote: (*mus.*; *arch.*) a florid passage or performance in which many short notes may be regarded as taking the place of a long note: (*India*) a part of a province under a commissioner, divided into districts: an army unit (usually half an army corps) containing almost all branches of the service: separation: difference in opinion, etc.: disunion: (*math.*) the process of finding how many times one quantity is contained in another.—*n.* **divisibil'ity** (*-viz-*).—*adj.* **divis'ible**, capable of being divided or separated: capable of being divided without remainder.—*adv.* **divis'ibly**.—*adjs.* **divisional** (*-vizh'*). **divis'ionary**, pertaining to or marking a division or separation; **divisive** (*-vīz'*), forming division or separation: creating discord.—*ns.* **divis'iveness**; **divis'or** (*math.*), the number which divides the dividend.—**division of labour**, the assigning of different functions to different agents. [L. *dīvīsiō*, *-ōnis*, *dīvīsor*, *-ōris*—*dīvidĕre*, to divide.]

divorce, *di-vōrs'*, *n.* the legal dissolution of marriage.—*v.t.* to sunder: to dissolve the marriage of: to put away by divorce: to separate.—*adj.* **divorce'able**.—*ns.* **divorcee'**, a divorced person; **divorce'ment** (*B.*), divorce; **divor'cer**.—*adj.* **divor'cive**, having power to divorce. [Fr.,—L. *divortium*—*dīvortĕre*, another form of *dīvertĕre*; see divert.]

divot, *div'ət*, *n.* (*Scot.*) a thin sod, cut for roofing, &c., or accidentally by golfers.—**feal and divot** (*Scots. law*), a right of cutting sods. [Origin unknown.]

divulge, *di-* or *dī-vulj'*, *v.t.* to spread abroad among the vulgar or the people: to make public: to reveal.—*v.t.* **divul'gate** (*-gāt*), to publish.—*n.* **divulga'tion**. [L. *dīvulgāre*—*dī-*, abroad, *vulgāre*, to publish, *vulgus*, the common people.]

divulsion, *di-* or *dī-vul'shən*, *n.* act of pulling or rending asunder or away.—*adj.* **divul'sive**, tending to pull asunder. [L. *dīvulsiō*, *-ōnis*—*dī-*, *vellĕre*, *vulsum*, to pull.]

divvy, **divi**, *div'i*, *n.* (*slang*) a dividend.—*v.t.* and *v.i.* to divide: to go shares.—Also **divvy up**. [Abbrev. of **divide**, **dividend**.]

dixie, *diks'i*, *n.* a military cooking-pail or camp-kettle. [Perh. Hind. *degchi*—Pers. *degcha*, dim. of *dīg*, large metallic cooking utensil.]

dizain, *di-zān'*, *n.* a ten-line stanza or poem. [Fr. *dix*, ten—L. *decem*, ten.]

dizen, *dī'zn*, or *diz'n*, *v.t.* (*obs.*) to dress or charge (a distaff) with flax: to dress up, dress gaudily. [From root seen in distaff.]

dizzard, *diz'ərd*, *n.* a blockhead. [Perh. M.E. and O.Fr. *disour*, story-teller.]

dizzy, *diz'i*, *adj.* giddy: confused: causing giddiness.—*v.t.* to make dizzy: to confuse.—*adv.* **dizz'ily**.—*n.* **dizz'iness**, giddiness.—*adj.* **dizz'ying**, making dizzy. [O.E. *dysig*, foolish; cf. Dan. *dösig*, drowsy; also **doze**.]

djereed. See jerid.

djibbah, *jib'ä*. Same as **jubbah**.

djinn. See jinn.

do, *dōō*, *v.t.* (*obs.*) to put, place: (*obs.*) to cause: to put in some condition: to render: to confer: bestow: to perform: to accomplish: to finish: to exhaust: to work at: to perform work upon: to prepare, set in order: to cook: (*slang*) to cheat, or overreach: to treat: to make the round of, see the sights of: to spend in prison.—*v.i.* to act, be active: to behave: to fare: to thrive: to suffice: to be good enough to pass (*2nd sing.* **do'est**, **dost**, *dust*, *3rd* **does**, *duz*, also **do'eth**, **doth**, *doth*; *pa.t.* **did**; *pr.p.* **do'ing**; *pa.p.* **done**, *dun*; in *Spens. infin.* **doen**, **done**, **donne**, *3rd pl.* *pa.t.* **doen**).—*Do* serves as a substitute for a verb that has just been used. It is used as an auxiliary verb (where there is no other auxiliary) with an infinitive in negative, interrogative, emphatic, and rhetorically inverted sentences, in some dialects merely periphrastically, and in verse sometimes to gain a syllable or postpone the accent; but these uses are limited with the verbs *have* and *do*.—*n.* activity: what one has to do: (*arch.*) fuss: a feast, celebration: (*slang*) a swindle, hoax.—*adj.* **do'able** (*rare*), that can be done.—*ns.* **do'-all**, a factotum; **do'er**, one who does, or habitually does, anything: an agent.—*adj.* **do'ing**, active (as in *up and doing*).

—*n.* (*coll.*) a scolding: severe treatment: (in *pl.*) activities, behaviour, proceedings: (*U.S.* in *pl.*) fancy dishes or adjuncts: (*slang,* in *pl.*) what's-its-name.—*ns.* do′-naught, do′-nought, do-noth′ing, one who does nothing: a lazy or idle person: a fainéant (see **donnot**); **do-noth′ingism**; **do-noth′ingness.**—**be done**, to be at an end: (*Scot.*) to have done, finished; **do away with,** to abolish, destroy; **do brown,** to cook or roast to brownness: (*slang*) to make a fool of, swindle; **do down** (*obs.*), to put down, subdue: (*slang*) to cheat, to get the better of; **do for,** to suit: to provide for: to ruin: (*vulg.*) to kill; **do in,** (*coll.*) to deceive, to get the better of: to exhaust: to ruin, to murder; **do one proud** (*coll.*), to make one feel flattered: to treat lavishly; **do over,** to do again: to cover over, as with paint; **do to death,** to murder; **do up,** fasten up: put up, make tidy, arrange, tie up: dress (linen): fatigue utterly; **do well,** to be justified: to prosper; **do with,** to make use of: to meddle with: to get on with; **do without,** not to be dependent on, to dispense with; **have done,** desist: stop it: have no more dealings; **have to do with,** to have any sort of connexion with; **what's to do?** what is the matter? [O.E. *dón, dyde, gedón;* Du. *doen,* Ger. *tun;* conn. with Gr. *tithenai,* to put, place.]

do, *dō, n.* (*mus.*) a syllable representing the first note of the scale—Anglicised as **doh.** [Perh. from G.B. *Doni* (1593-1647), who is said to have substituted it for the Aretinian syllable *ut* (see **gamut**).]

doab, *dō′äb, n.* a tongue of land between two rivers (esp. the Ganges and Jumna). [Perh. *dōāb,* two waters.]

doat. Same as **dote.**

dobbin, *dob′in, n.* a workhorse. [An altered dim. of *Robert.*]

dobby, dobbie, *dob′i, n.* a dotard: a brownie: an attachment to a loom for weaving small figures. [Perh. from *Robert.*]

dobchick, *dob′chik.* Same as **dabchick.**

Doberman(n) pinscher, *dōb′ər-man pin′shər, n.* a breed of terrier—large, smooth-coated, with long forelegs. [*Dobermann,* the first breeder, and Ger. *pinscher,* terrier.]

dobhash, *dō′bash, n.* an interpreter. [Hind. *dōbāshī, dūbhāshiya*—*dō, dū,* two, *bhāshā,* language.]

docent. See **privat-dozent.**

docetism, *dō-sē′tizm, n.* a 2nd-century heresy, that Christ's body was only a semblance, or else of ethereal substance.—*ns.* do′cēte, docē′tist, a holder of this belief; *n.pl.* docē′tae (-tē).—*adjs.* **docetic** (-set′, -set′), **docetist′ic.** [Gr. *dokēsis,* phantom, semblance—*dokeein,* to seem.]

doch-an-doris, *dohh′an-dō′ris, n.* a stirrup-cup, a parting-cup.—Also **doch-an-dorach** (*-əhh*), **deuch-an-doris.** [Gael. *deoch,* drink, *an,* the, *doruis,* gen. of *dorus,* door.]

dochmius, *dok′mi-əs, n.* a foot of five syllables, typically with first and fourth short, the rest long.—*adjs.* **doch′miac, dochmī′acal.** [L.—Gr. *dochmios.*]

docile, *dō′sīl,* or *dos′il, adj.* teachable: ready to learn: easily managed.—(*obs.*) **do′cible.**—*ns.* **docibil′ity, doc′ibleness, docil′ity.** [Fr.,—L. *docilis*—*docēre,* to teach.]

docimasy, *dos′i-mə-si, n.* scrutiny: application of tests: assaying: examination of drugs.—*adj.* **docimastic** (-*mas′tik*).—*n.* **docimol′ogy,** the art of assaying. [Gr. *dokimasiā,* examination—*dokimazein,* to test—*dechesthai,* to take, approve.]

dock, *dok, n.* a polygonaceous weed (Rumex) with large leaves and a long root.—*ns.* **dock′-cress,** the nipplewort; **dock′en** (*Scot.,* perh. orig. *pl.*), a dock. [O.E. *docce.*]

dock, *dok, v.t.* to cut short: to curtail: to cut off: to clip: to deprive of pay.—*n.* the part of a tail left after clipping: (*Scot.*) the rump. [M.E. *dok,* prob.—O.N. *dokkr,* stumpy tail.]

dock, *dok, n.* an artificial basin for the reception of vessels: the waterway between two wharves or two piers: a wharf or pier: the enclosure in court for the accused: in a railway station, the place of arrival and departure of a train: in the theatre, a space for storing scenery.—*v.t.* (*Shak.*) to embed in sand or ooze: to place in a dock: to bring into dock: to equip with docks.—*v.i.* to enter a dock.—*ns.* **dock′age,** accommodation in docks for ships: dock-dues; **dock′-dues,** payments for use of a dock; **dock′er, dock′-la′bourer,** one who works in the docks; **dockīsā′tion.**—*v.t.* **dock′īse,** to convert into docks.—*ns.* **dockland,** a district about docks; **dock′-master,** the person superintending a dock; **dock′-warrant,** a warehouse receipt; **dock′yard,** a naval establishment with docks, building-slips, stores, etc. [Origin obscure; cf. Old Du. *dokke.*]

docket, *dok′it, n.* a summary of a larger writing: a bill or ticket affixed to anything indicating its contents: a label: a list or register of cases in court, or of legal judgments, or (*U.S.*) business to be transacted: an official permit to buy: a customhouse certificate of payment.—*v.t.* to make a summary of the heads of a writing: to enter in a book: to mark the contents of papers on the back (*pr.p.* **dock′eting;** *pa.t.* and *pa.p.* **dock′eted**).—Also **docq′uet** (as if French). [Perh. a dim. of **dock,** to curtail.]

doctor, *dok′tər, n.* (*arch.*) a teacher: a learned father of the church: a cleric especially skilled in theology or ecclesiastical law: one who has received from a university (or the Archbishop of Canterbury) the highest degree in any faculty (originally implying competency to teach): a physician or medical practitioner, whatever be his degree in medicine: in U.S. extended to a dentist or druggist: a mender: in some warm countries, a cool sea-breeze conducive to health: a ship's cook: a name for various contrivances for removing defects or superfluities in manufacture: material used for sophistication: brown sherry: counterfeit coin: (in *pl.*) loaded dice: a fish, the sea-surgeon: an angler's fly.—*v.t.* to treat, as a doctor does: to patch up, repair: to sophisticate, tamper with, falsify: to address as doctor: to confer a doctor's degree upon.—*v.i.* to practice medicine.—*adj.* **doc′toral.**—*n.* **doc′torand,** a candidate for the doctorate.—*v.t.* **doc′torate,** to confer the degree of doctor upon.—*n.* the degree of doctor.—*ns.* **doc′toress, doc′tress** (*facetious*), a female doctor; a doctor's wife; **doc′tor-fish,** a sea-surgeon.—*adjs.* **doctorial** (-*tō′ri-əl*); **doc′torly.**—*n.* **doc′tor-ship.**—**Doctors' Commons,** before the establishment of the Divorce Court and Probate Court in 1857, the college of the doctors of civil law in London, incorporated by royal charter in 1768; **doctor's stuff,** medicine. [L., a teacher—*docēre,* to teach.]

doctrinaire, *dok-tri-nār′, n.* an unpractical theorist, disposed to carry principles to logical but unworkable extremes: in France, in 1815-30, one of a school who desired constitutional government.—*adj.* theoretical.—*n.* and *adj.* **doctrinā′rian,** doctrinaire.—*ns.* **doctrinair′ism, doctrinā′rianism,** blind adhesion to one-sided principles. [Fr.,—L.L. *doctrīnārius.*]

doctrine, *dok′trin, n.* (*arch.*) teaching: a thing taught: a principle of belief.—*adj.* **doc′trinal** (or *-trī′nal*).—*adv.* **doc′trinally** (or *-trī′*). [L. *doctrīna, docēre,* to teach.]

document, *dok′ū-mənt, n.* (*Spens.*) instruction: (*obs.*) warning: a paper or other material thing affording information, proof, or evidence of anything.—*v.t.* (also -*ment′*), to furnish with documents: to support or prove by documents.—*adjs.* **documental** (-*ment′*), **document′ary,** relating to or found in documents: aiming at presentation of reality.—*n.* a motion-picture presenting an activity or occupation of real life without fictional colouring or professional actors.—*n.* **documentā′tion,** (*arch.*) instruction: preparation, setting forth, or use of documentary evidence and authorities: in fiction, realistic reproduction of records, real or supposed. [Fr.,—L. *documentum*—*docēre,* to teach.]

dod, *dod, v.t.* (*obs.* or *prov.*) to cut the hair of: to poll: to pollard: to clip.—*n.* (*Scot.*) a rounded hilltop, esp. a shoulder of a greater hill.—*adj.*

dodd'ed, polled : hornless : pollard.—*n.* **dodd'y** (*Scot.*), a hornless cow. [M.E. *dodden.*]

dod, *dod, n.* (*Scot.*) a slight fit of ill-humour, esp. in pl.—*adj.* **dodd'y.** [Gael. *dod,* peevishness.]

dod, *dod, n.* a minced form of **God,** in oaths.

dodder, *dod'ər, n.* a leafless, twining, pale parasitic plant (Cuscuta) of or akin to the convolvulus family. [M.E. *doder;* cf. Ger. *dotter.*]

dodder, *dod'ər, v.i.* to shake : to tremble : to totter : to potter : to ramble in talk : to be decrepit in mind or body.—*n.* **dodd'erer.**—*adj.* **dodd'ering.**—*adj.* **dodd'ery.** [Perh. conn. with **doddered.**]

doddered, doddard, *dod'ərd, adj.* orig. perh. pollard : decayed with loss of branches. [Cf. **dod** (1).]

doddypoll, dodipoll, *dod'i-pōl, n.* a blockhead.— Also **dottipoll.** [App. **dote,** and **poll.**]

dodecagon, *dō-dek'ə-gon, n.* a plane figure with twelve angles and sides. [Gr. *dōdeka,* twelve, *gōniā,* an angle.]

Dodecagynia, *dō-dek-ə-jin'i-ä, n.pl.* in some classes of the Linnaean classification an order of plants with twelve styles.—*adjs.* **dodecagyn'ian, do-decagynous** (-*aj'i-nəs*). [Gr. *dōdeka,* twelve, *gynē,* a woman, female.]

dodecahedron, *do-dek-ə-hē'dron, n.* a solid figure, having twelve faces (equal pentagons in a *regular* dedecahedron, rhombs in a *rhombic* dodecahedron). —*adj.* **dodecahē'dral.** [Gr. *dōdeka,* twelve, *hedrā,* a seat.]

Dodecandria, *dō-dek-an'dri-ä, n.pl.* a Linnaean class of plants having twelve stamens.—*adj.* **dodecan'drous.** [Gr. *dōdeka,* twelve, *anēr, andros,* a man, male.]

dodecastyle, *dō'dek-ə-stīl, adj.* (*archit.*) having twelve columns in front.—*n.* a portico so built.

dodecasyllable, *dō-dek-ə-sil'ə-bl, n.* (*pros.*) a line of twelve syllables.—*adj.* **dodecasyllabic** (-*ab'ik*).

dodge, *doj, v.i.* to start aside or shift about : to evade or use mean tricks : to shuffle or quibble.— *v.t.* to evade by a sudden shift of place : to evade : to trick.—*n.* an evasion : a trick : a quibble.—*ns.* **dodg'er,** one who dodges : a screen on a ship's bridge for shelter in rough weather : (*U.S.*) an advertising leaflet; **dodg'ery,** trickery.—*adj.* **dodg'y.** [Origin obscure.]

dodkin, *dod'kin, n.* a doit.—Also **doit'kin.** [doit.]

dodman, *dod'mən, n.* (*prov.*) a snail. [Origin unknown.]

dodo, *dō'dō, n.* a clumsy flightless bird, about the size of a turkey, a native of Mauritius, extinct about the end of the 17th century :—*pl.* **do'do(e)s.** [Port. *doudo,* silly.]

Dodonaean, *dō-dō-nē'ən, adj.* pertaining to *Dodona* in Epirus, or its oracle sacred to Zeus, situated in a grove of oaks.—Also **Dodō'nian.**

Doe, *dō.*—**John Doe** and **Richard Roe,** imaginary plaintiff and opponent in the old legal action for ejectment, proverbial as a legal fiction.

doe, *dō, n.* the female of the fallow-deer or buck : extended to the female of other deer, of antelope, rabbit, hare, and sometimes other animals.—*n.* **doe'-skin,** the skin of a doe : a smooth, close-woven, woollen cloth. [O.E. *dá;* Dan. *daa,* deer.]

doer, does. See **do.**

doff, *dof, v.t.* to take off : to put off : to remove.— *n.* **doff'er,** part of a carding machine that strips the cotton from the cylinder when carded : one who removes full bobbins from a frame machine. [**do, off.**]

dog, *dog, n.* a wild or domestic animal of the same genus (Canis) as the wolf : a male of the species : a mean scoundrel : a term of contempt : a fellow (as *a jolly dog*) : either of the two constellations, the Greater and the Lesser Dog (Canis Major and Minor) : an andiron : a hook for holding logs : a gripping appliance of various kinds : a cock, as of a gun : a dogfish : a prairie dog : (*slang*) heavy ostentation : (*coll.* in *pl.*) greyhound races.—*adj.* (and in composition) of dogs : male (opposed to *bitch*) : spurious, base, inferior.—*adv.* (esp. in composition) utterly.—*v.t.* to follow as a dog : to track and watch constantly : to hunt with dogs : to fasten with a dog : (*pr.p.* **dogg'ing;** *pa.t.* and *pa.p.* **dogged**).—*ns.* **dog'-ape,** a baboon (from the form of its head); **dog'(s)'bane,** a plant (Apocynum) said to be poisonous to dogs; **dog'-bee,** a drone;

dog'-belt, a broad belt put round the waist for hauling; **dog'berry,** the fruit of the wild cornel or dogwood : extended to many other plants and their fruits : **Dogberry,** a pompous, muddle-headed fellow (from the character in Shakespeare's *Much Ado About Nothing*); **Dog'berrydom; Dog'-berryism,** an utterance worthy of Dogberry, wordy consequential blundering and malapropism; **dog'-bis'cuit,** a biscuit for feeding dogs; **dog'bolt,** orig. a kind of arrow : (*obs.*) a contemptible fellow; **dog'cart,** a two-wheeled horse-vehicle with seats back to back, originally used for sporting dogs.—*adj.* **dog'-cheap,** extremely cheap.—*ns.* **dog'-collar,** a collar for a dog : a clerical collar fastened behind : a woman's stiff collar or neck-ornament; **dog'-crab,** a very small crab; **dog'-dai'sy,** the common daisy : the ox-eye daisy.— *n.pl.* **dog'days,** the period when the Dogstar rises and sets with the sun (generally reckoned July 3rd to August 11th)—erroneously supposed to be the time when dogs are specially liable to hydrophobia.—*n.* **dog'-ear,** a dog's-ear.—*adj.* **dog'-faced.**—*ns.* **dog'-fan'cier,** a breeder or seller of dogs; **dog'-fight,** a fight between dogs : a confused fight or mêlée; **dog'fish,** a small shark of various kinds; **dog'fox,** a male fox.—*adj.* **dog'ged,** dog-like : sullen : pertinacious.—*adv.* (*slang*) very.— *adv.* **dogg'edly.**—*ns.* **dogg'edness,** one who dogs; **dogg'ery,** doggish ways or doings : dogs collectively : rabble : (*U.S.*) a drinking resort; **dogg'ess** (*facet.*), a bitch; **dogg'iness; dogg'ing,** shooting with dogs : following like a dog.—*adj.* **dogg'ish,** doglike : characteristic of dogs : churlish : brutal.—*adv.* **dogg'ishly.**—*ns.* **dogg'ishness; dog'-grass, dog'-wheat,** couch-grass or kindred species.—*adj.* **dogg'y,** fond of dogs.—*ns.* **dog'-head,** the hammer of a gun-lock; **dog'-hip, -hep** (*dial.*), the hip or fruit of the dog-rose; **dog'hole,** a hole fit only for a dog : a wretched dwelling; **dog'-house, -kennel; dog'-Lat'in,** barbarous Latin; **dog'-leech,** one who treats diseases of dogs.—*adj.* **dog'-leg(ged),** bent like a dog's hind leg : (of stairs) having successive flights running opposite ways without a well-hole : (of a fence) made of poles laid on cross-shaped supports.—*ns.* **dog'-letter,** *r,* from its growling sound; **dog'-louse; dog'-parsley,** fool's parsley; **dog'-peri-winkle,** a species of Purpura (also **dog-whelk**); **dog'rose,** a species of wild rose, *Rosa canina;* **dog'-sal'mon,** the keta, a Pacific species of salmon : also another Pacific species, the humpback; **dog's-body** (*naut. slang*), pease-pudding : a dish of biscuit, water, and sugar : a junior naval (or other) officer; **dog'(s)'-ear,** a fold at the corner of a leaf in a book.—*v.t.* to fold at the corner.—*ns.* **dog's'-fenn'el,** may-weed; **dog'ship,** the quality or personality of a dog.—*n.pl.* **dog'shores,** pieces of timber used to shore up a vessel before launching. —*adj.* **dog-sick',** thoroughly sick, sick as a dog.— *n.* **dog'skin,** leather made of or in imitation of dog's skin.—Also *adj.*—*ns.* **dog'sleep,** a light sleep, very easily broken; **dog's'-meat,** scraps and refuse sold as food for dogs; **dog's'-mer'cury,** a euphorbiaceous plant *Mercurialis perennis;* **dog's'-nose,** gin and beer, or similar mixture; **dog's'-tail-grass',** a common British pasture grass (Cynosurus); **Dog'star,** Sirius, in the constellation of the Greater Dog, whose rising and setting with the sun gave name to the dogdays; **dog's'-tongue,** hound's-tongue; **dog's'-tooth-grass',** a seaside sand-binding grass (Cynodon); **dog'-tick.**—*adjs.* **dog'-tired, dog'-wea'ry** (*Shak.*), tired as a dog, completely worn out.—*n.* **dog'tooth,** a moulding in later Norman architecture, consisting of a series of ornamented square pyramids : a canine tooth; **dog'tooth-spar',** calcite crystals like canine teeth; **dog'tooth-vi'olet,** any plant of the liliaceous genus Erythronium; **dog'-town,** a prairie-dog community; **dog'-trick,** a low trick; **dog'trot,** a gentle trot like a dog's; a jogtrot; **dog'vane** (*naut.*), a small vane to show direction of wind; **dog'-vi'olet,** a scentless wild violet, esp. *Viola canina;* **dog'-whelk',** a gasteropod of the genus Nassa, like a small whelk : a dog-periwinkle; **dog'wood,** the wild cornel (*Cornus sanguinea*), a small tree with white flowers and purple berries, the shoots and leaves turning red in autumn : extended to many other shrubs and trees.—**dog in the manger**, one who will not let others enjoy what he has himself no use for; **dog's age** (*coll.*) a long time; **dog's chance**, a bare chance; **go to the dogs**, to be ruined; **hot dog** (*U.S.*) hot sausage sandwich; **not to lead the life of a dog**, to lead a life so wretched that even a dog would not be content with it; **throw, give**, or **send to the dogs**, to throw away or abandon. [Late O.E. *docga;* cf. Du. *dog*, a mastiff; Ger. *dogge*.]

dog, *dog, n.* (*obs.*) used in oaths for God.—*interj.* **doggone**(d) (*dog-gon*(*d*)'), **dog on it** (*U.S.*), expressing vexation.—Also *adj.*

doge, *dōj*, *n.* the chief-magistrate in republican Venice and Genoa.—*ns.* **dogaressa** (*dō-gä-res'ä*), a doge's wife; **dogate** (*dō'gāt*), **doge'ate** (*dō'jāt*), **doge'ship.** [It. (Venetian dial.) for *duce*, duke—L. *dux*, a leader.]

dogger, *dog'ər*, *n.* a two-masted Dutch fishing-vessel.—*n.* **dogg'erman.** [Du.]

dogger, *dog'ər*, *n.* a concretion, esp. of ironstone : a sandy ironstone or ferruginous sandstone : part of the Middle Jurassic. [Origin uncertain; a northern word.]

doggerel, *dog'ər-əl*, *n.* irregular measures in burlesque poetry, so named in contempt : worthless verses.—*adj.* irregular in rhythm, mean.—Also **dogg'rel.** [Origin unknown.]

doggo, *dog'ō, adj.* (*coll.*) hidden. [Poss. from **dog**.]

dogie, dogy, *dō'gi, n.* (*U.S.*) a motherless calf. [Origin obscure.]

dogma, *dog'mä, n.* a settled opinion : a principle or tenet : a doctrine laid down with authority.—*adjs.* **dogmatic** (*-mat'ik*), **-al**, pertaining to a dogma : asserting a thing as if it were a dogma : asserting positively : overbearing.—*adv.* **dogmat'ically.**—*n.* **dogmat'ics** (*theol.*), the statement of Christian doctrines, systematic theology.—*v.i.* **dog'matise** (*-mə-tīz*), to state one's opinion dogmatically or arrogantly.—*ns.* **dog'matiser; dog'matism**, dogmatic or positive assertion of opinion; **dog'matist**, one who makes positive assertions; **dogmatol'ogy**, the science of dogma.—*adj.* **dog'matory.** [Gr. *dogma, -atos*, an opinion—*dokeein*, to think, seem.]

dog-watch, *dog'-woch, n.* on shipboard, a watch 4—6 p.m. or 6—8 p.m., consisting of two hours only, instead of four.

doh. See do (2).

doilt, *doilt, adj.* (*Scot.*) crazy, foolish.—Also **doiled.** [Origin obscure.]

doily, *doi'li, n.* (*obs.*) an old kind of woollen stuff : a small ornamented napkin, often laid on or under dishes. [From *Doily* or *Doyley*, a famous haberdasher.]

doit, *doit, n.* a small Dutch coin worth about half a farthing : a thing of little or no value. [Du. *duit.*]

doited, doitit, *doit'id, -it, adj.* (*Scot.*) in dotage. [Origin obscure.]

dolabriform, *dō-lab'ri-form, adj.* like a hatchet or cleaver. [L. *dolābra*, a cleaver, *forma*, form.]

dolce, *dōl'chā, adj.* (*mus.*) sweet.—*n.* a soft-toned organ-stop.—*adv.* **dolcemen'te** (*mus.*), softly and sweetly. [It.,—L. *dulcis.*]

doldrums, *dol'drəmz, n.pl.* (*naut.*) those parts of the ocean about the equator where calms and baffling winds prevail : low spirits. [Prob. conn. with obs. *dold*, stupid, or *dol*, dull.]

dole, *dōl, n.* a share : a dealing out : something given in charity : (usu. contemptuously) state pay to unemployed : a small portion.—*v.t.* to deal out in small portions. [O.E. *dāl;* cf. **deal**.]

dole, *dōl, n.* pain : grief : (*arch.* and *poet.*) heaviness at heart.—*adj.* **dole'ful**, full of dole or grief : melancholy.—*adv.* **dole'fully.**—*n.* **dole'fulness.** —*adjs.* **do'lent** (*obs.*), **dole'some**, dismal.—*adv.* **dole'somely.** [O.Fr. *doel* (Fr. *deuil*), grief—L. *dolēre*, to feel pain.]

dole, *dōl, n.* (*obs.*) guile : (*Scots. law*) criminal intention. [L. *dolus*—Gr. *dolos*, guile.]

dolerite, *dol'ər-īt, n.* a basic igneous rock like

basalt in composition but coarser grained.—*adj.* **dolerit'ic.** [Fr. *dolérite*—Gr. *doleros*, deceptive.]

dolichocephalic, *dol-i-kō-sif-al'ik, adj.* long-headed—having a breadth of skull (from side to side) less than 75 (or 78) per cent. of the length (front to back)—opp. to *brachycephalic.*—Also **dolichocephalous** (*-sef'ə-ləs*).—*ns.* **dolichocephaly, dolichoceph'alism.** [Gr. *dolichos*, long, *kephalē*, the head.]

Dolichos, *dol'i-kos, n.* a genus of long-podded leguminous plants allied to the haricot. [Gr., long. also a plant of like nature.]

Dolichosaurus, *dol-i-kō-saw'rəs, n.* the typical genus of **Dolichosau'ria**, a group of Cretaceous fossil reptiles. [Gr. *dolichos*, long, *sauros*, lizard.]

Dolichotis, *dol-i-kō'tis, n.* a genus of long-eared S. American rodents—the mara or Patagonian hare. [Gr. *dolichos*, long, *ous, ōtos*, the ear.]

dolichurus, *dol-i-kū'rəs, n.* a dactylic hexameter with a redundant syllable at the end. [Gr. *dolichouros*, long-tailed.]

dolium, *dō'li-əm, n.* a Roman earthenware jar for wine, oil, grain, etc. :—*pl.* **dō'lia.** [L. *dōlium.*]

doll, *dol, n.* a puppet : a toy in human form : an insipid woman, esp. one who is over-dressed and silly : the smallest or pet pig in a litter.—*v.t.* and *v.i.* to dress (often with *up*).—*ns.* **doll'dom; doll'hood; doll'iness.**—*adj.* **doll'ish.**—*ns.* **doll'ishness; doll's-house; doll'y,** dim. of **doll.**—*adj.* **doll'y.** [Prob. from *Dolly*, familiar dim. of *Dorothy*.]

dollar, *dol'ər, n.* a silver coin (=100 cents) of U.S.A. and Canada, of Mexico, Hong-Kong, etc. : a thaler : (*slang*) five shillings.—*adjs.* **doll'ared; doll'arless.**—*ns.* **dollaroc'racy; doll'arship. —dollar diplomacy**, diplomacy dictated by financial interests : diplomacy that employs financial weapons to increase political power. [Ger. *t*(*h*)*aler* (L.G. *daler*), short for *Joachimsthaler*, because first coined at the silver-mines in Joachimsthal (Joachim's dale) in Bohemia.]

dollop, *dol'əp, n.* a tuft of grass or weeds : a rank patch in a field : a lump.—Also **dall'op.** [Prob. conn. with Norw. dial. *dolp*, a lump.]

dolly, *dol'i, n.* a complimentary offering of flowers, sweetmeats, etc., on a tray. [Anglo-Ind.,—Hindi *dālī.*]

dolly, *dol'i, n.* a wooden shaft attached to a disk with projecting arms, used for beating and stirring clothes in a washing-tub : somewhat similar apparatus in mining, pile-driving, etc. : a tool for holding the head of a rivet : a trolley, truck, or small platform on wheels or roller.—*v.t.* to operate upon, yield, or obtain, with a dolly : to beat with a hammer.—*adj.* **doll'ied.**—*ns.* **doll'ier; doll'y-shop,** a marine store, a low pawn-shop—often having a black doll as sign; **doll'y-tub,** a tub for washing clothes or ores with a dolly. [Prob. from *Dolly*, the familiar form of *Dorothy*.]

Dolly Varden, *dol'i var'dən, n.* a flowered muslin dress for women, with pointed bodice and tucked-up skirt : a large hat, one side bent downwards, abundantly trimmed with flowers. [Named from *Dolly Varden*, a character in Dickens's *Barnaby Rudge*.]

dolman, *dol'mən, n* a Turkish robe with slight sleeves and open in front : a hussar's jacket, worn like a cloak, with one or both sleeves hanging loose : a woman's mantle. [Turk. *dōlāmān*.]

dolmen, *dol'mən, n.* a stone table : a prehistoric sepulchral chamber of erect unhewn stones, supporting a flattish stone. [Fr. *dolmen;* usually explained as—Bret. *dol, taol*, table, *men*, stone; but *tolmên* in Cornish meant hole of stone.]

dolomite, *dol'ə-mīt, n.* a mineral, double carbonate of calcium and magnesium : a rock composed of that mineral, magnesian limestone.—*adj.* **dolomitic** (*-mit'ik*).—*n.* **dol'omitisation.**—*v.t.* **dol'omitise,** to convert into dolomite. [After the French geologist D. Guy de *Dolomieu* (1750-1801).]

dolour, *dol'ər, dōl'ər*, historically *dul'ər, n.* pain : grief : anguish.—*adjs.* **dolorif'erous, dolori'fic,** causing or conveying dolour, pain, or grief.—*adv.* **doloro'so** (*It.; mus.*), in a soft and pathetic manner.—*adj.* **dol'orous**, full of dolour, pain, or grief : doleful.—*adv.* dol′orously.—*n.* dol′orousness. [O.Fr.,—L. *dolēre*, to grieve.]

dolphin, *dol′fin, n.* an animal of the whale kind, closely resembling the porpoise, about 8 or 10 feet long : the Coryphaena, a fish about 5 feet in length, noted for the brilliancy of its colours when dying.—*ns.* dol′phinet (*Spens.*), a female dolphin; dol′phin-fly, a black aphis or plant-louse, destructive to bean-plants. [O.Fr. *daulphin*—L. *delphīnus*—Gr. *delphīs, -phinos.*]

dolt, *dōlt, n.* a dull or stupid fellow.—*adj.* dolt′ish, dull : stupid.—*adv.* dolt′ishly.—*n.* dolt′ishness. [For dulled or blunted; see dull.]

Dom, *dom, n.* the Portuguese form of *Don :* also a title given to certain Catholic dignitaries and members of some monastic orders, esp. the Benedictine. [L. *dominus,* lord.]

domain, *dō-mān′, n.* what one is master of or has dominion over : an estate : territory : ownership of land : the scope or range of any subject or sphere of knowledge.—*adjs.* domain′al, domā′nial. [Fr. *domaine*—L. *dominicum*—*dominus,* a master.]

domal, *dōm′əl, adj.* relating to a house. [L. *domus,* a house.]

domatium, *do-mā′sh(y)əm, n.* a plant structure that harbours mites or other symbiotic organisms :—*pl.* domā′tia. [Latinised form of Gr. *dōmation,* dim. of *dōma,* house.]

Domdaniel, *dom-dan′yəl, n.* (*Southey*) a hall under the sea inhabited by a sorcerer and his disciples : (*Carlyle*) an infernal cave, den of iniquity generally. [Fr.,—Gr. *dōma Daniēl,* house of Daniel; from Chavis and Cazotte's French continuation of the *Arabian Nights.*]

dome, *dōm, n.* a structure, usually hemispherical, raised above a large building : a large cupola : a cathedral : (*poet.*) a building, esp. a great or stately building : anything approaching the form of a hemispherical vault, esp. a head, the cover of a reverberatory furnace, the steam-chamber on a locomotive boiler, a clip-fastener that fits into a hold : (*cryst.*) a pair of crystal-faces parallel to a lateral axis, meeting in a rooflike edge.—*v.t.* to furnish with a dome : to form into a dome.—*v.i.* to swell or rise as a dome.—*adjs.* domed, domical (*dōm′, dom′*), having a dome; dom′y. [L. *domus,* a house; Fr. *dôme,* It. *duomo,* Ger. *dom.*]

dome (*Spens.*). Same as **doom.**—*n.* **Domesday.—**

Doomsday-book (*dōōmz′dā-book*), a book compiled by order of William the Conqueror, containing a survey of all the lands in England, their value, owners, etc.—so called from its authority in judgment (O.E. *dóm*) on the matters contained in it.

domestic, *dō-, də-mes′tik, adj.* belonging to the house : remaining much at home : private : tame : not foreign.—*n.* a servant in the house :—(in *pl.*) articles of home manufacture, esp. home-made cotton cloths.—*adj.* domes′tical (*arch.*).—*adv.* domes′tically.—*v.t.* domes′ticate, to make domestic or familiar : to tame.—*adj.* domes′ticated, adapted to or content with home life and activities : tamed.—*ns.* domesticā′tion; domes′ticātor; domesticity (*dō-, do-mis-tis′*), domestic or domesticated state : home life : (in *pl.*) home conditions and arrangements.—**domestic architecture,** the architecture of mansions, dwelling-houses, cottages, etc.; **domestic economy,** the principles of efficient ordering of a household; **domestic science,** the household arts, as catering, cookery, laundry-work, studied in the light of physiological, chemical, etc., science. [L. *domesticus*—*domus,* a house.]

domett, *dom′ət, -it, n.* a plain cloth with cotton warp and woollen weft. [Perh. a proper name.]

domicile, *dom′i-sil, -sīl, n.* a dwelling-place, abode : one's legally recognised place of residence.—*v.t.* to establish in a fixed residence.—*adjs.* dom′iciled; domiciliary (*-sil′*), pertaining to the domicile.—*v.t.* domiciliāte (*-sil′*), to establish in a permanent residence.—*n.* domiciliā′tion.— **domiciliary nurse,** a nurse visiting sick persons in their homes; **domiciliary visit,** a visit, under authority, to a private house for the purpose of searching it. [Fr.,—L. *domicilium*—*domus,* a house.]

dominant, *dom′in-ənt, adj.* prevailing : predominant : overtopping : (*Mendelism*) of an ancestral character, appearing in the first generation of cross-bred off-spring to the exclusion of the alternative character in the other parent, which may yet be transmitted to later generations.—*n.* (*mus.*) the fifth above the tonic : a dominant Mendelian character : one of the prevailing species in a plant community.—*ns.* dom′inance, dom′inancy, ascendency.—*adv.* dom′inantly. [L. *domināns, -āntis,* pr.p. of *domināri,* to be master.]

dominate, *dom′in-āt, v.t.* to be lord over : to govern : to prevail over : to tower over : to command a view of : to be the controlling position of.— Also *v.i.*—*n.* the Roman Empire in its later more avowedly absolute form.—*n.* dominā′tion, government : absolute authority : tyranny.—*adj.* dom′inative, governing : (*rare*) arbitrary.—*n.* dom′inātor (*Shak.*), a ruler or governor : a ruling influence. [L. *dominārī, -ātus,* to be master—*dominus,* master—*domāre,* to tame.]

domineer, *dom-in-ēr′, v.i.* to rule arbitrarily : to command haughtily : to be overbearing.—*adj.* domineer′ing, overbearing. [Prob. through Du. from O.Fr. *dominer*—L. *domināri.*]

dominical, *do-min′i-kl, adj.* belonging to the Lord, as the Lord's Prayer, the Lord's Day.— **dominical letter,** one of the first seven letters of the alphabet, used in calendars to mark the Sundays throughout the year. [L.L. *dominicālis*—L. *dominicus*—*dominus,* lord, master.]

Dominican, *do-min′i-kən, adj.* belonging to St. *Dominic* or to the Dominicans.—*n.* a friar or monk of the order of St. Dominic—*Fratres Predicatores,* founded in 1215, or *Black Friars,* from their black mantle.

dominie, *dom′i-ni, n.* a schoolmaster, a tutor : (*U.S.*) a clergyman. [L. *domine,* voc. of *dominus,* master.]

dominion, *dō-, də-min′yən, n.* lordship : sovereignty : a domain or territory with one ruler, owner, or government : a completely self-governing colony, not subordinate to but freely associated with the mother-country : control : (in *pl.*) a class of angelic spirits (Col. i, 16).—**Dominion Day,** a Canadian festival on the anniversary of the union of the provinces, 1st July, 1867. [L.L. *dominiō, -ōnis*—*dominus,* master.]

domino, *dom′i-nō, n.* a cape with a hood worn by a master or by a priest : a long cloak of black silk with a hood, used at masked balls, or its wearer : a mask : one of the oblong pieces with which the game of **dom′inoes** (*-nōz*) is played, usually twenty-eight in number, divided into two compartments, each of which is blank or marked with from one to six spots : a card game played in a similar way : the end. [Apparently Sp. *dominó, dómino,* in some way conn. with L. *dominus,* master.]

Don, *don, n.* a Spanish title, corresponding to English Sir, Mr., formerly applied only to noblemen, now to all classes : **don,** a Spanish nobleman, a Spaniard : a fellow of a college, a college authority : (*coll.*) a swell, adept :—*fem.* **Doña,** *dōn′yä,* Don′na (Italian form); corr. **dona(h),** *dō′nä,* a sweetheart. —*adj.* donn′ish, pertaining to a don : with the airs of a don.—*ns.* donn′ism, self-importance; don′ship, rank or dignity of a don.—**Don Juan,** a libertine of Spanish legend, subject of plays, poems, and operas in several European languages : an attractive profligate. [Sp.,—L. *dominus.*]

don, *don, v.t.* to do or put on : to assume (*pr.p.* donn′ing; *pa.t.* and *pa.p.* donned). [do on.]

dona(h). See under Don.

Donat, Donet, *dō′nət, n.* a grammar, a primer. [O.Fr. *donat,* from Aelius *Dōnātus,* author about 358 A.D. of a long famous Latin grammar.]

donation, *dō-nā′shən, n.* act of giving : that which is given, a gift of money or goods : (*law*) the act by which a person freely transfers his title to anything to another.—*ns.* dō′nary, a thing given to a sacred use; dō′natary (*Scots. law*), one to whom lands escheated to the crown are made over; dōn′atory (or *don′*), a recipient.—*v.t.* dōnāte′ (*U.S.*), a backformation from **donation**), to give.—*n.* dōn′ative (or *don′*), a gift : a gratuity : a benefice presented by the founder or patron without reference to the bishop.—*adj.* vested or vesting by donation.—*ns.* dōnā′tor, one who makes a gift, a donor; dōn′atory (or *don*′), a recipient; dōnee′, the person to whom a gift is made; dō′nor, a giver: a benefactor.—dona nobis, the last section of the mass, beginning *Dona nobis pacem,* Give us peace. [Fr.,—L. *dōnāre, -ātum—dōnum,* a gift—*dāre,* to give.]

Donatist, *dōn′, don′ə-tist, n.* a member of an African Christian sect of the 4th and 5th centuries, who protested against any diminution of the extreme reverence paid to martyrs, treated the lapsed severely, and rebaptised converts from the Catholic Church.—*n.* don′atism.—*adjs.* donatis′tic, -al. [From *Dōnātus,* one of their leaders.]

done, dun, *pa.p.* of do, often with sense of utterly exhausted: so done up, done out: (*obs.*) inf. of do.

donga, dong′gä, *n.* (*S. African*) a gully. [Zulu, bank, side of a gully.]

donjon, dun′jon, *n.* a strong central tower in ancient castles, to which the garrison retreated when hard pressed. [A doublet of dungeon.]

donkey, dong′ki, *n.* an ass: a stupid person: (*pl.* donkeys).—*ns.* don′key-en′gine, a small auxiliary engine; don′key-man, a man in charge of a donkey-engine; don′key-pump, an extra steam-pump; don′key-work, drudgery.—argue, talk, the hind-leg off a donkey, to do so with invincible pertinacity; donkey's years, a long time (a pun on *ears*). [Still regarded as slang in 1823; perh. a double dim. of *dun,* from its colour; or from *Duncan.*]

Donna. See Don.

donnered, donnerd, donnert, *don′ərd, -ərt, adj.* (*Scot.*) stupid: dull-witted.

donnot, donnat, *don′ət, n.* (*Yorkshire*) a good-for-nothing: an idler. [App. partly do-naught, partly dow-nought.]

Donnybrook, *don′i-brook, n.* a riotous assembly. [From the fair at *Donnybrook,* Dublin.]

do-nothing, do-nought. See do.

donsie, *don′si, adj.* (*Scot.*) unlucky, perverse: neat: trim: sickly. [Origin unknown.]

don't, *dōnt,* for do not.

donzel, *don′zel, n.* (*obs.*) a squire, aspirant to knighthood. [It. *donzello*—L.L. *domnicellus,* dim. of L. *dominus,* lord.]

doob, *dōōb, n.* dog's-tooth grass. [Hind. *dūb.*]

doo, *dōō, n.* Scots form of dove.—*n.* doocot, dooket (*dook′ət*), a dovecote.

doodle, *dōōd′l, v.t.* (*Scot.*) to dandle.

doodle, *dōōd′l, v.t.* (*Scot.*) to drone or play, as a bagpipe. [Ger. *dudeln.*]

doodle, *dōōd′l, v.i.* scrawl, scribble, meaninglessly.

doodlebug, *dōōd′l-bug, n.* (*U.S.*) the larva of an ant-lion or other insect (used in divination in America): any instrument, scientific or unscientific, used by prospectors to indicate pressure of minerals: (*war slang*) a flying bomb.

dook, *dōōk, n.* (*Scot.*) a plug of wood driven into a wall to hold a nail, etc.: a bung. [Origin unknown.]

dook, *dōōk, v.t.* and *v.i.* (*Scot.*) to duck: to bathe.—*n.* an act of plunging, dipping or bobbing: a bathe: an inclined mine-adit. [duck.]

dool, doole. See dole, dule.

dool, *dōōl,* dule, (*Scot.*) dül, *n.* a boundary mark: a goal.—hail the dules, to score a goal. [Cf. Du. *doel,* L. Ger. *dôle,* Fris. *dôl, dôle.*]

doolie, *dōō′li, n.* a litter or palanquin. [Hind. *dōli.*]

doom, *dōōm, n.* judgment: condemnation: destiny: ruin: final judgment: a picture of the Last Judgment.—*v.t.* to pronounce judgment on: to sentence: to condemn: to destine:—(*pr.p.* dōōm′ing; *pa.p.* dōōmed).—*adjs.* doomed, under sentence: fated; doom′ful (*Spens.*), dispensing judgment.—*adv.* dooms (*Scot.*), very, exceedingly.—*ns.* dooms′day, the day of doom, the last judgment; Dooms′day-book (see Domesday); dooms′man, one who pronounces doom or sentence, a judge; doom′ster, a judge: a dempster.—crack of doom, the last trump. [O.E. *dóm,* judgment.]

doom-palm. See doum-palm.

door, *dōr, n.* the usual entrance into a house, room, or passage: a frame for closing up the entrance: a means of approach or access.—*ns.* door′-bell; door′-case, the frame which encloses a door; door′-cheek (*Scot.*), a side-post of a door; door′-keep′er; door′knob; door′-knocker; door(s)′-man, a porter, doorkeeper; door′-mat, a mat for wiping shoes or other purpose at a door: (*coll.*) a person whom others trample upon; door′nail, a stud for a door, proverbially dead; door′-plate, a plate on or at a door with the householder's name on it; door′-post, the jamb or side-piece of a door; door′-sill, the threshold of a doorway; door′-stead, a doorway; door′-step, a step at a door: (*coll.*) a thick slice of bread; door′-stone; door′-way, an opening where there is or might be a door; door′-yard (*U.S.*) a yard about the door of a house.—next door (to), in the next house: near, bordering upon, very nearly; out of doors, in the open air; show one the door, to turn out of the house. [O.E. *duru* (fem.) and *dor* (neut.); cf. Ger. *tür, tor;* Gr. *thyrā,* L. *foris,* a door.]

doorn, *dōōrn, n.* (*S. Africa*) thorn.—*n.* doorn-boom (*dōōrn′bōōm*), a S. African acacia. [Du. *doorn,* thorn, *boom,* tree.]

dop, *dop, n.* a copper cup in which a gem is fastened for cutting or polishing: Cape brandy made from grape-skins. [Du. *dop,* shell, husk.]

dop, *dop, v.t.* and *v.i.* to dip: to dap.—*n.* (*obs.*) a curtsy: a bob.—*ns.* dopp′er, a didapper: a rod for dapping; dopp′ing, a flock of sheldrake. [O.E. *dop-* (in compounds); connected with dip.]

dope, *dōp, n.* a thick liquid, semi-liquid, or pasty material: an absorbent: lubricating grease: aeroplane varnish: a liquid added to improve the efficiency of anything: opium: a drug, esp. one administered to a racehorse or taken by an addict: drug-taking: (*U.S.*) confidential or fraudulent information in advance: information in general: a wireless news bulletin: anything supplied to dull, blind, or blunt the conscience or insight: a fool.—*v.t.* to give or apply dope to: to drug.—*v.i.* to take dope.—*ns.* dope′-fiend, a drug addict; dōp′er, one who applies, administers, deals in, or takes dope.—*adj.* dōp′y, dope′y, narcotic: stupefied. [Du. *doop,* a dipping sauce; *doopen,* to dip.]

doppel-gänger, *dop′l-geng′ər, n.* a double: a wraith.—Also doppel-gang′er. [Ger., double-goer.]

Dopper, *dop′er, n.* a Baptist or Anabaptist: a member of a rigid Calvinistic sect in S. Africa. [Du. *dooper—doopen,* to dip.]

dopplerite, *dop′lər-īt, n.* a black elastic substance (calcium salts of humus acids) found in peat beds.—Doppler's principle, the law of change of wave-length when a source of vibrations is moving towards or from the observer, explaining the fall of pitch of a railway whistle when the engine passes, and enabling astronomers to measure the radial velocity of stars by the displacement of known lines of the spectrum; Doppler effect, this observed change. [From Christian *Doppler* (1803-53) who announced the principle in 1842.]

dor, *dor, n.* (*obs.*) a scoff, mockery, as *to give* (any one) *the dor.*—*v.t.* to mock, put out of countenance. [Prob. O.N. *dár,* scoff.]

dor, dorr, *dor, n.* a kind of dung-beetle, also called dor′-beetle and dor′-fly: a cockchafer (in *U.S.* called dor′-bug): (*obs.*) a drone.—*n.* dor′-hawk, the nightjar. [O.E. *dora,* a humble-bee.]

Dora, *dō′rä, n.* (*coll.*) the Defence of the Realm Act (1914) which imposed war-time restrictions. [From the initials—Defence Of Realm Act.]

dorado, *dō-rä′dō, n.* the coryphene, so called from its beautiful colour when dying: the so-called golden salmon, a S. American river fish (*Salminus*) of the Characinidae. [Sp., from *dorar,* to gild—L. *deaurāre, -ātum;* see dory, el Dorado.]

Doras, *dō′ras, n.* a S. American genus of Siluridae, bony-plated river fish with spines, with the habit of walking overland when drought threatens.—*n.* dō′rad, any member of the genus, or of the group to which it belongs. [Gr. *dory,* spear.]

Dorcas, *dor′käs, n.* in Acts, ix, 36, the Greek translation (*Dorkas*) of *Tabitha* (Aramaic, gazelle), name of a woman famous for good works—hence **Dorcas society,** a ladies' society for making and providing clothing for the poor. [Gr. *dorkas,* gazelle.]

doree. See **dory.**

Dorian, *dō′ri-ən, adj.* belonging to *Doris* in Greece or to the Dorians : Doric.—*n.* a native of Doris : a member of one of the main divisions of the ancient Greeks who arrived about 1100 B.C. and made their home in Doris, S.E. Peloponnese, Crete, Rhodes, etc.—**Dorian mode,** a mode of ancient Greek music consisting of two tetrachords with a semitone between the two lowest notes in each, the tetrachords separated by a whole tone (as : efga; bcde—but reckoned downwards by the Greeks), traditionally of a stirring, solemn, simple and martial quality : an authentic mode of old church music, extending from d to d with d as its final. [L. *Dōrius*—Gr. *Dōrios*—*Dōris.*]

Doric, *dor′ik, adj.* belonging to *Doris* in Greece, or the Dorians, or their dialect : denoting one of the Greek orders of architecture, distinguished by its simplicity and massive strength.—*n.* a Greek dialect : any dialect imagined to resemble it, esp. Scottish.—*n.* **Doricism** (*dor′i-sizm*), a peculiarity of the Doric dialect.—*v.t.* and *v.i.* **dōr′ise,** to render or become like the Dorians, in language, manners, etc.—*n.* **Dō′rism,** Doricism : a Dorian characteristic. [L. *Dōricus*—Gr. *Dōrikos*—*Dōris.*]

Doris, *dō′ris, n.* a genus of nudibranchiate gasteropods, shell-less molluscs with a plumy tuft of gills on the back, giving name to the family **Dorid′idae.**—*n.* and *adj.* **do′ridoid.** [Gr. *Dōris,* a sea-goddess.]

Dorking, *dork′ing, n.* a square-bodied breed of poultry, variously coloured, and with five claws on each foot—so named from *Dorking* in Surrey.

dorlach, *dor′lahh, n.* a bundle, a valise. [Gael.]

dormant, *dor′mənt, adj.* sleeping : with suspended animation or development : torpid : at rest : not used, in abeyance (as a title) : (*her.*) in a sleeping posture.—*n.* a crossbeam : a joist.—*n.* **dor′mancy.** [O.Fr. *dormant,* pr.p. of *dormir*—L. *dormīre,* to sleep.]

dormer, *dor′mər, n.* (*obs.*) a dormitory or bedroom : a dormer-window.—*n.* **dor′mer-win′dow,** a small window with a gable, projecting from a sloping roof (orig. a dormitory window). [O.Fr. *dormeor*—L. *dormītōrium*—*dormīre,* to sleep.]

dormient, *dor′mi-ənt, adj.* sleeping : dormant. [L. *dormiēns, -entis,* pr.p. of *dormīre,* to sleep.]

dormition, *dor-mish′ən, n.* falling asleep : death —*n.* and *adj.* **dor′mitive,** soporific. [Fr.,—L. *dormīre,* to sleep.]

dormitory, *dor′mi-tər-i, n.* a large sleeping-room with many beds, whether in separate cubicles or not : a resting-place : (*U.S.*) a college hostel : a suburb where town workers dwell.—*n.* **dormitory-car** (*U.S.*), a railway sleeping-carriage. [L. *dormītōrium*—*dormīre,* to sleep.]

dormouse, *dor′mows, n.* any member of the Myoxidae, a family of rodents akin to mice but somewhat squirrel-like in form and habit :—*pl.* **dor′mice.** [Perh. connected with L. *dormīre,* to sleep (from their hibernation); prob. **mouse.**]

dormy, dormie, *dor′mi, adj.* in golf, as many holes up or ahead as there are yet to play. [Conjecturally connected with L. *dormīre,* to sleep; the player who is *dormy* cannot lose though he go to sleep.]

dornick, *dor′nik, n.* a kind of stout figured linen, originally made at Doornik, or Tournai, in Belgium.

dorp, *dorp, n.* a village, esp. Dutch. [Du. *dorp;* O.E. *thorp.*]

dorsal, *dor′sl, adj.* pertaining or belonging to the back.—*n.* a dorsal fin : a dorsal vertebra : a dossal.—*adv.* **dor′sally.**—*ns.* **dorse** (*obs.*), the back of a book or writing : a dossal : the back; **dor′sel,** a dossal; **dor′ser,** a dosser.—*adjs.* **dorsibranchiate** (*-brangk′*), having gills on the back; **dorsif′erous,** having sori on the back : carrying young on the back; **dor′sifixed** (*bot.*) of an anther, attached by the whole length of the back to the filament; **dor′siflex,** bent towards the back.—*n.* **dorsiflex′ion,** a bending backwards : a bending of the back, a bow.—*adjs.* **dor′sigrade,** walking

on the back of the toes; **dorsiven′tral,** possessing two sides distinguishable as upper or ventral and lower or dorsal, as a leaf.—*ns.* **dorsiventral′ity; dors′um,** back.—**dorsal suture,** the seam at the midrib of a carpel; **send to dorse,** to throw on the back. [L. *dorsum,* the back.]

dorse, *dors, n.* a small cod. [Low Ger. *dorsch.*]

dort, *dort, v.i.* (*Scot.*) to sulk.—*n.pl.* **dorts,** sulks.— *adj.* **dor′ty,** pettish : delicate. [Origin unknown.]

dorter, dortour, *dor′tər, n.* (*arch.*) a dormitory, esp. monastic. [O.Fr. *dortour*—L. *dormītōrium;* see **dormer, dormitory.**]

dory, *dō′ri, n.* a golden-yellow fish (*Zeus faber*) of the mackerel family.—Also **John Dory** and **Doree.** [Fr. *dorée,* from *dorer,* to gild—L. *deaurāre,* to gild—*dē-,* in the sense of over, *aurum,* gold.]

dory, *dō′ri, n.* (*Amer.*) a small boat, with flat bottom, sharp bow and stern, especially suited for surf riding. [Origin unknown.]

dose, *dōs,* in Scotland commonly *dōz, n.* the quantity of medicine, electric current, X-rays, etc., administered at one time : a portion, esp. a measured portion, of something given or added : anything disagreeable or medicinal that must be taken. —*v.t.* to order or give in doses : to give doses to.— *ns.* **dōs′age,** practice, act, or method of dosing : regulation of dose : addition of an ingredient : proper size of dose; **dos(i)ol′ogy,** the science of doses. [Fr.,—Gr. *dŏsis,* a giving—*didonai,* to give.]

doseh, *dō′se, n.* a religious ceremony at Cairo (abolished 1884), during the festival of the Prophet's birth, when the sheikh of the Sa′di dervishes rode on horseback over the prostrate bodies of his followers. [Ar. *dawsah,* treading.]

doss, *dos, n.* (*slang*) a bed, sleeping-place : a sleep.— *v.i.* to sleep : to go to bed.—*ns.* **doss′er,** one who lodges in a doss-house, or where he can; **doss′-house,** a very cheap lodging-house. [Perh. from *doss,* a prov. Eng. name for a hassock; or perh. **dorse** (see under **dorsal**).]

dossal, dossel, *dos′əl, n.* a cloth hanging for the back of an altar, sides of a church chancel, etc. [L.L. *dossāle, dorsāle*—L. *dorsum,* back.]

dosser, *dos′ər, n.* a rich hanging of tapestry for the walls of a hall or of a chancel : a pannier. [O.Fr. *dossier*—*dos*—L. *dorsum,* back.]

dossier, *do-syā, dos′i-ər, n.* a bundle of documents relating to a person or case : a brief. [Fr.,—*dos*— L. *dorsum,* back.]

dossil, *dos′il, n.* a plug, spigot : a cloth roll for wiping ink from an engraved plate in printing : (*surg.*) a pledget of lint for dressing a wound. [O.Fr. *dosil*—L.L. *ducillus.* a spigot.]

dost, *dust,* 2nd pers. sing. pres. indic. of **do.**

dot, *dot, n.* a very small spot : a short element in the Morse code.—*v.t.* to mark with a dot or dots : to diversify with objects : to jot.—*v.i.* to form dots : to limp : (*pr.p.* **dott′ing;** *pa.t.* and *pa.p.* **dott′ed**). —*adj.* **dott′ed,** composed of dots : marked with a dot or dots.—*adj.* **dott′y,** composed of, covered with, dots : (*coll.*) unsteady : feeble : crazed—**dot and carry,** to set down the units and carry over the tens to the next column; **dotted note,** (*mus.*) one whose length is increased by one half by a dot placed after it. [O.E. has *dott,* head of a boil; Du. *dot,* a little lump.]

dot, *dot, n.* a marriage portion.—*adj.* **dotal** (*dō′təl*), pertaining to dowry or to dower.—*n.* **dōtā′tion,** the bestowing of a dowry : an endowment. [Fr., —L. *dōs, dōtis.*]

dote, doat, *dōt, v.i.* (*arch.*) to be stupid or foolish : to be weakly affectionate : to show excessive love (with *upon, on*) : of timber, to decay.—*ns.* **dōt′age,** a doting : childishness of old age : excessive fondness; **dōt′ant** (*Shak.*), a dotard; **dōt′ard,** one who dotes : one showing the weakness of old age, or excessive fondness.—*adj.* **dōt′ed** (*Spens.*), stupid. —*n.* **dōt′er, doat′er,** one who dotes.—*adj.* and *n.* **dōt′ing, doat′ing.**—*ns.* **dōt′ing-piece, doat′ing-piece,** one who is doted on.—*adj.* **dōt′ish,** silly.— *n.* **dōtt′le** (*Scot.*), a dotard.—*adjs.* **dōtt′le, -d** (*Scot.*), in dotage; **dōt′y,** decaying (of timber). [Cf. Old Du. *doten,* to be silly; Fr. *radoter,* to rave, is from the same root.]

doth, *duth,* 3rd pers. sing. pres. indic. of **do.**

dotterel, dottrel, *dot'(ə-)rəl, n.* a kind of plover, named from its apparent stupidity in allowing itself to be approached and caught: a stupid fellow, a dupe. [dote.]

dottle, *dot'l, n.* (*Scot.*) a plug, esp. of tobacco left at the bottom of a pipe. [dot.]

douane, *dōō-än', dwän', n.* a custom-house.—*n.* **douanier** (*dwä-nyā*), a custom-house officer. [Fr.,—Ar. *diwān;* cf. **divan, diwan.**]

douar, dowar, *dōō'ār.* See **duar.**

Douay, *dōō-ā,* among Catholics often *dow'i, n.* the town of *Douai* in France (Nord), historically famous for its English and other Catholic colleges.— **Douay Bible,** an English Roman Catholic translation of the Bible, the New Testament in the Rhemish version, the Old done at Douai in 1609-10.

double, *dub'l, adj.* twofold: twice as much: of about twice the weight, size, or quality: two of a sort together: in pairs: paired: acting two parts, insincere: folded once: sounding an octave lower: having stamens in the form of petals, or having ligulate in place of tubular florets.—*adv.* to twice the extent: twice over: two together: deceitfully. —*v.t.* to multiply by two: to make twofold: to make twice as much or as many: to be the double of: to be a substitute for or counterpart of: (in bridge) to double the scoring value of: to sound in another octave: (*her.*) to line: to fold: to clench: to pass (esp. sail) round or by.—*v.i.* to increase to twice the quantity: to turn sharply back on one's course in running: to act as substitute.—*n.* a quantity twice as much: a combination of two things of the same kind (as a binary star): in tennis, a game with two players on each side: in tennis, two faults in succession: a win, or a defeat, in two events on the same programme: a combined bet on two races, stake and winnings from the first being bet on the second: a Guernsey copper coin, ⅛th of a penny: a duplicate: an actor's substitute: a quick pace (short for **double-quick**): one's wraith or apparition: an exact counterpart: a turning upon one's course: a trick: (*eccles.*) a feast on which the antiphon is said both before and after the psalms.—*adj.* **doub'le-act'ing,** applying power in two directions: producing a double result.—*n.* **doub'le-axe',** a religious symbol of Minoan Crete and the Aegean, a double-headed axe, associated with the mother-goddess and her son (Zeus).—*adjs.* **doub'le-banked',** having two men at each oar, or having two tiers of oars one above the other, as in ancient galleys.—*n.* **doub'le-bar',** a double vertical line marking the end of a movement or piece of music or one of its important divisions.—*adj.* **doub'le-barr'elled,** having two barrels: of a surname, hyphened: of a compliment, ambiguous.—*n.* **doub'le-bass',** a stringed instrument—contra-bass or *violone.*—*adjs.* **doub'le-bit'ing,** cutting on either side; **doub'le-breast'ed,** of a coat, having two breasts, one to be folded over the other.—*v.t.* **doub'le-charge',** to load with double measure.—*ns.* **doub'le-chin',** a chin with a fold of flesh; **doub'le-co'conut,** the coco-de-mer; **doub'le-cross,** a betrayal of both sides, as when one who has arranged to lose a contest sets himself to win.—*v.t.* to betray by double-cross.— *ns.* **doub'le-cross'er;** **doub'le-dagg'er,** a diesis (‡); **doub'le-deal'er,** a deceitful person; **doub'le-deal'ing,** duplicity.—*adj.* **doub'le-decked,** having two decks.—*ns.* **doub'le-deck'er,** a double-decked ship: a bus, tram-car or other structure in two stories or tiers; **doub'le-decomposi'tion,** a chemical action in which two compounds exchange some of their constituents; **doub'le-Dutch,** jargon.—*adj.* **doub'le-dyed,** twice-dyed: deeply imbued.—*n.* **doub'le-ea'gle** (*U.S.*), a gold coin worth $20: heraldic representation of an eagle with two heads, as in the old arms of Russia and Austria.—*adj.* **doub'le-edged,** having two edges: cutting or working both ways.—*ns.* **doub'le-end'er,** anything having two ends alike: a cross-cut sawing machine with two adjustable cyclical saws, for sawing both ends of timber; **doub'le-en'try** (*book-k.*), a method by which two entries

are made of each transaction.—*adjs.* **doub'le-eyed,** doubly keen of sight; **doub'le-faced,** hypocritical, false.—*ns.* **doub'le-fā'cedness;** **doub'le-first,** at Oxford, a degree with first-class honours in mathematics and classics: one who takes such a degree; **doub'le-flat',** a note already flat flattened again by a semitone: a sign indicating this.—*adjs.* **doub'le-flow'ered,** having double flowers, as a plant; **doub'le-form'd',** having, or combining, two forms; **doub'le-fount'ed,** having two sources.— *v.t.* **doub'le-gild,** to gild with double coatings of gold: to gloze over.—*n.* **doub'le-Glos'ter,** Gloucestershire cheese of extra richness.—*adjs.* **doub'le-hand'ed,** having two hands: two-handled; **doub'le-head'ed,** having two heads; **doub'le-heart'ed,** treacherous; **doub'le-hung,** (of a window) having top and bottom sashes each balanced by sash cord and weights, so as to be capable of vertical movement in its own groove; **doub'le-joint'ed,** having joints admitting some degree of movement backward; **doub'le-lived',** having two lives; **doub'le-locked',** locked with two locks or bolts: locked by two turns of the key, as in very few locks but many novels; **doub'le-manned',** furnished with twice the complement of men; **doub'le-mean'ing,** ambiguous; **doub'le-mind'ed,** undetermined, wavering.—*n.* **doub'le-mind'edness.**—*adjs.* **doub'le-mouth'd',** speaking with contradictory voices; **doub'le-nā'tured,** having a twofold nature. —*n.* **doub'leness,** the state of being double: duplicity.—*adj. and adv.* **doub'le-quick,** at a pace approaching a run.—*n.* the double-quick pace.— *n.* **doub'ler,** one who or that which doubles.—*v.t.* **doub'le-shade'** (*Milt.*), to double the darkness of. —*n.* **doub'le-sharp',** a note already sharp sharpened again by a semitone: a sign indicating this.— *adj.* **doub'le-shott'ed,** of cannon, with double charge.—*ns.* **doub'le-shuff'le,** a scraping movement made twice with each foot: a dance of such steps: a trick; **doub'le-stopp'ing,** playing on two stopped strings of an instrument at once; **doub'le-stout',** extra strong stout or porter.—*adj.* **doub'le-tongued',** having two tongues or a cleft tongue: self-contradictory: deceitful.—*ns.* **doub'le-you, -u,** the letter **w;** **doub'ling,** the act of making double: a turning back in running: a trick: (*her.*) mantling.—*adj.* shifting, manoeuvring.—*adv.* **doub'ly—double up,** to fold double: to bend over (as with laughter): to come at the double: to share with another. [O.Fr. *doble*—L. *duplus,* double—*duo* two, and the root seen in Eng. **fold,** Gr. *haploos.*]

double entendre, *dōō-blän²-tän²-dr', n.* a word or phrase with two meanings, one usually more or less indecent. [Fr. of 17th century, superseded now by (*mot*) *à double entente.*]

doublet, *dub'lit, n.* a close-fitting garment for the upper part of the body—with *hose,* the typical masculine dress in the 14th-17th c.: a thing that is repeated or duplicated: one of a pair, esp. one of two words orig. the same but varying in spelling and meaning, *e.g. balm, balsam.* [O.Fr., dim. of *double.*]

doubloon, *dub-lōōn', n.* an obsolete Spanish gold coin, orig. = 2 pistoles. [Sp. *doblón,* aug. of *doble,* double; see **double.**]

doubt, *dowt, v.i.* to be undecided in opinion: (*obs.*) to be apprehensive.—*v.t.* to hold in doubt: to hesitate or scruple: to incline to believe with fear or hesitation: to distrust: (esp. *Scot.*) to incline to think: to suspect (*arch.* also *refl.*): (*obs.*) to cause to doubt or fear.—*n.* uncertainty of opinion: suspicion: (*obs.*) fear: (*obs.*) a thing doubtful or questioned: (*Spens.*) danger.—*adj.* **doubt'able.**— *adj.* **doubt'ed** (*Spens.*), redoubted: feared: questioned.—*n.* **doubt'er.**—*adj.* **doubt'ful,** full of doubt: undetermined: subject to doubt: not clear: insecure: suspicious: not confident.—*n.* a doubtful person or thing.—*adv.* **doubt'fully.**—*n.* **doubt'fulness.**—*n. and adj.* **doubt'ing.**—*adv.* **doubt'ingly.** —*adj.* **doubt'less,** free from doubt or (*Shak.*) fear —*adv.* without doubt: certainly: no doubt (often a mere concession of possibility).—*adv.* **doubt'lessly.** [O.Fr. *douter*—L. *dubitāre,* akin to *dubius,* doubtful, moving in two (*duo*) directions.]

douc, *dook*, *n.* a variegated monkey in Cochin-China. [Fr., from Cochin name.]

douce, *dōōs*, *adj.* (*obs.*) sweet: (*Scot.*) sober, peaceable, sedate.—*adv.* douce′ly.—*ns.* douce′ness; **doucet, dowset** (*dōō′*, *dow′sit*; *obs.*), a sweet dish: (in *pl.*) a deer's testicles; **douceur** (*dōō-sər′*), sweetness of manner (*obs.*): something intended to please, a present, bribe, or tip. [Fr. *doux*, *douce*, mild—L. *dulcis*, sweet.]

douche, *dōōsh*, *n.* a jet of water directed upon the body from a pipe: an apparatus for throwing it.—*v.t.* to turn a douche upon. [Fr.,—It. *doccia*, a water-pipe—L. *dūcĕre*, to lead.]

doucine, *dōō-sēn′*, *n.* (*archit.*) a cyma recta. [Fr.]

dough, *dō*, *n.* a mass of flour or meal moistened and kneaded, but not baked: (*slang*) money.—*adj.* **dough′-baked**, half-baked, defective in intelligence.—*n.* **dough′boy** (*U.S.* and *colonial*), boiled flour dumpling: (*mil. slang*) an American infantryman.—*adj.* **dough′faced** (*U.S.*), pliable, truckling.—*n.* **dough′iness.**—*adj.* **dough′-kneaded** (*Milt.*), soft.—*n.* **dough′nut**, sweetened dough fried in fat.—*adj.* **dough′y**, like dough: soft. [O.E. *dáh*; Ger. *teig*, O.N. *deig*, dough; cf. **duff**.]

doughty, *dow′ti*, *adj.* able, strong: brave.—*adv.* **dough′tily.**—*n.* **dough′tiness.** [O.E. *dyhtig*, later *dohtig*, valiant—*dugan*, to be strong; Ger. *tüchtig*, able.]

Douglas fir, *dug′las fər*, *n.* a tall western American coniferous timber tree (*Pseudotsuga Douglasii*). [David *Douglas* (1798-1834), who introduced it to Britain.]

Doukhobor. See **Dukhobor.**

doum-palm, *dowm′*, *dōōm′-päm*, *n.* an African palm (Hyphaene), with a branched stem, and a fruit with the taste of gingerbread.—Also **doom′-, dun′-palm.** [Ar. *daum*, *dūm*.]

doup, *dowp*, *n.* (*Scot.*) the end of an egg-shell: the buttocks.—*n.* **can′dle-doup**, a candle-end. [Cf. O.N. *daup*, a hollow.]

dour, *dōōr*, *adj.* (*Scot.*) obstinate: sullen: grim.—*n.* **dour′ness.** [Apparently L. *dūrus*, hard.]

doura. See **durra.**

dourine, *dōō-rēn′*, *dōō′rēn*, *n.* a contagious disease of horses due to a trypanosome. [Fr. *dourin*.]

douroucouli, durukuli, *dōō-rōō-kōō′lē*, *n.* a night-ape, any monkey of the S. American genus *Nyctipithecus*. [S. Amer. name.]

douse, dowse, *dows*, *v.t.* to plunge into water.—*v.i.* to fall suddenly into water. [Cf. Sw. *dunsa*, fall heavily; prob. from sound; cf. *souse*.]

douse, dowse, *dows*, *v.t.* to strike: to strike or lower (a sail).—*n.* a heavy blow. [Prob. related to Old Du. *dossen*, to beat.]

douse, dowse, *dows*, *v.t.* to put out, extinguish (esp. in the *slang* **douse the glim**, put out the light).—*n.* **dous′er**, a shutter for cutting off light in a cinema projector. [Perh. connected with **dout**, or with **douse** (2).]

dout, *dowt*, *v.t.* to put out, extinguish.—*n.* **dout′er.** [do out.]

douzepers, *dōō′zə-pär*, *n.pl.* the twelve peers of Charlemagne, or similar group:—*sing.* **douzeper**, **doucepere** (*Spens.*), a champion, great knight or noble. [O.Fr. *douze pers*, twelve peers.]

dove, *duv*, *n.* a pigeon (esp. in comp., as *ring-dove*, *turtle-dove*, etc.): a word of endearment: an emblem of innocence, gentleness, also of the Holy Spirit (Matt. iii. 16).—*v.t.* to treat as a dove.—*ns.* **dove′-colour**, a greyish, bluish, pinkish colour; **dove′cot, -cote**, a small cot or box in which pigeons breed: a pigeon-house.—*adjs.* **dove′-drawn** (*Shak.*), drawn by doves; **dove′-eyed**, meek-eyed.—*ns.* **dove′-house**, a dovecot; **dove′-let**, a small dove.—*adj.* **dove′like**, like a dove: innocent.—*ns.* **dove′s-foot**, a name for some species of cranesbill (*Geranium dissectum*, *Geranium molle*, etc.); **dove′tail**, a tenon shaped like a dove's spread tail, for fastening boards: a joint of alternate tenons and mortises of that shape.—*v.t.* and *v.i.* to fit by, or as if by, dovetail.—*n.* **dove′tailing.—flutter the dove-cots**, to disturb commonplace, conventional people, as the eagle would a dovecot (see Shak., *Cor.* V,

vi, 115). [O.E. *dúfe*, found only in the compound *dúfe-doppa*, a diving bird; Ger. *taube*.]

dove, *dōv*, *v.i.* (*Scot.*) to be half asleep or stupefied.—*v.i.* to ver (*Scot.*), to snooze, doze.—*v.t.* to stun.—*n.* a snooze: a swoon: half-consciousness. [O.E. *dofian*, to be stupid.]

dove, *dōv*, *U.S. p.a.t.* of **dive**.

dovekie, *duv′ki*, *n.* the little auk or rotche: the black guillemot. [Dim. of **dove**.]

Dover's powder, *dō′vərz pow′dər*, *n.* a sudorific compounded of ipecacuanha root, opium and potassium sulphate. [First prescribed by Dr. Thomas *Dover* (1660-1742).]

dow. See **dhow.**

dow, *dow*, *v.i.* (*obs.* and *Scots*) to be good for a purpose: to avail: to be able:—3rd pers. sing. **dow, dows:** *pa.t.* **docht, dought** (*dohht*), **dowed.** [O.E. *dugan*.]

dowager, *dow′ə-jər*, *n.* a widow with a dower or jointure: a title given to a widow to distinguish her from the wife of her husband's heir: an elderly woman of imposing appearance. [O.Fr. *douagere*—L.L. *dōtārium*, dower—L. *dōtāre*, to endow.]

dowd, *dowd*, **dowdy**, *dowd′i*, *ns.* a woman who wears dull-looking clumsy ill-shaped clothes.—Also *adj.*—*adv.* **dowd′ily.**—*n.* **dowd′iness.**—*adj.* **dowd′yish.**—*n.* **dowd′yism.** [Origin unknown.]

dowel, *dow′əl*, *n.* a pin for fastening things together by fitting into a hole in each.—*v.t.* to fasten by means of dowels.—*ns.* **dow′el-joint; dow′el-pin.** [Prob. related to Ger. *döbel*, a plug.]

dower, *dow′ər*, *n.* a jointure: a dowry: an endowment.—*v.t.* to bestow a dowry upon: to endow.—*adj.* **dow′able**, that may be endowed.—*n.* **dow′erhouse**, the house set apart for the widow.—*adj.* **dow′erless.** [O.Fr. *douaire*—L.L. *dōtārium*—L. *dōtāre*, to endow.]

dowf, *dowf*, *adj.* (*Scot.*) dull, heavy, spiritless.—*n.* **dowf′ness.** [Prob. O.N. *daufr*, deaf.]

dowie, *dow′i*, *adj.* (*Scot.*) dull, low-spirited, sad: dismal. [Prob. O.E. *dol*, dull.]

dowl, dowle, *dowl*, *n.* (*Shak.*) a portion of down in a feather: a piece of fluff. [Origin obscure.]

dowlas, *dow′las*, *n.* a coarse linen cloth. [From *Daoulas* or *Doulas*, near Brest, in Brittany.]

down, *down*, *n.* soft feathers: a soft covering of fluffy hair.—*n.* **down′-bed.**—*adj.* **downed**, filled or covered with down.—*ns.* **down′iness; down′-quilt.**—*adj.* **down′y**, covered with or made of down: like down: (*slang*) knowing.—**the downy** (*old slang*), bed.—The spellings **dowlne, dowlney** (*Shak.*) show confusion with **dowl.** [O.N. *d′ūnn*; Ger. *daune*, *dune*.]

down, *down*, *n.* a bank of sand thrown up ρy the sea (same as **dune**): a treeless upland: (in *pl.*) an undulating upland tract of pasture-land, esp. in S.E. England—also the roadstead off E. Kent.—*n.* **down′land.** [O.E. *dún*, a hill—Celt. *dun*.]

down, *down*, *adv.* (passing into *adj.* in predicative use), to a lower position, level or state: away from a centre (capital, great town, university, etc.): southward: to leeward: in a low or lowered position or state: below: on or to the ground: downstairs: under the surface: from earlier to later times: to a further stage in a series: from greater to less (in size, grain, activity, intensity, etc.): to a standstill, exhaustion, or conclusion: to a final state of defeat, subjection, silence, etc.: in a fallen state: in adversity: at a disadvantage: ill: behindhand: in writing or record, in black and white: in flood: on the spot, in cash: in readiness to pounce: in a state of alert awareness and understanding: in watchful opposition or hostility (with *on*, *upon*).—Also elliptically, passing into an interjection or verb by omission of *go*, *come*, *put*, etc., often followed by *with*.—*adj.* going, reaching, or directed towards a lower position or level: depressed: low.—*prep.* in a descent along, through, or by: to or in a lower position on or in: along in the direction of the current: along.—*n.* a descent: a low place: a reverse of fortune: an act of throwing or putting down: a tendency to bear down on one.—*v.t.* to knock, throw or set down: to put down, overthrow: to dispirit.—*adj.* **down′-and-out′**, at the end of one's resources.—Also *n.*—*n.* **down′-and-**

out′er.—*adj.* down′-at-heel′, having the back of the shoe trodden down.—*ns.* down′-beat, a downward movement of the conductor's baton: an accented beat; down′bow (*mus.*), a movement of bow over strings beginning at the nut end.—*adj.* down′cast, dejected.—*n.* a current of air into a mine: a shaft carrying it (down′cast-shaft′): a downward throw: a downthrow.—*ns.* down′-come, a fall, ruin: a heavy pour of rain; down′-draught, a current of air downwards; down′-east′er, one living *down east* from the speaker, a New Englander, and esp. an inhabitant of Maine; down′fall, fall, failure, humiliation, ruin: a falling down, as of rain.—*adjs.* down′fallen, ruined; down′-going.—*ns.* down-go′ing (or *down′*); down′grade, a downward slope or course.—*adj.* and *adv.* downhill.—*adj.* down′-gyved (*Shak.*), hanging down like fetters.—*n.* down′-haul, a rope by which a jib, etc., is hauled down when set.—*adjs.* down′-heart′ed, dejected; down′hill, descending, sloping.—Also *n.*—*adv.* downhill′.—*n.* down′-line, the line of a railway leading from the capital, or other important centre, to the provinces. —*adj.* down′looked (*Dryden*), downcast, gloomy. —*n.* down′-ly′ing, time of retiring to rest: a woman's lying-in.—*adv.* and *adj.* down′most, superlative of *down*.—*n.* down′pour, a heavy fall of rain, etc.—*adj.* down′right (*obs.*), perpendicular: in plain terms: utterly.—*adj.* plain-spoken: brusque: utter, out-and-out (as in *downright madness*).—*ns.* down′rightness; down′rush, a rushing down (as of gas, hot air, etc.); down′-sett′ing, a setting down, a snub; down′-sitt′ing, sitting down, time of rest (Ps. cxxxix, 2): (*Scot.*) a sitting, session: (*Scot.*) a settlement, establishment (esp. by marriage).—*advs.* down′stage′, towards the footlights (also *adj.*); downstairs′, in, or towards, a lower story.—*adj.* down′stair(s).—*n.* a position downstairs.—*adv.* downstream′, with the current.—*adj.* down′stream, further down the stream: going with the current.—*ns.* down′stroke, a downward line made by the pen in writing; down′-throw, act of throwing down, state of being thrown down: (*geol.*) the amount of vertical displacement of the relatively lowered strata at a fault.—*v.i.* down′-tools′, to strike.—*adj.* and *adv.* down′town′, in or towards the lower part or (*U.S.*) the business and shopping centre of the town.—*n.* down′-train, a railway train proceeding from the chief terminus.—*adj.* down′-trod, -trod′den, trampled on: tyrannised over.—*advs.* down′-ward (-*wərd*), down′wards, from higher to lower: from source to outlet: from more ancient to modern: in the lower part.—*adj.* down′ward.—*adv.* down′wardly.—*n.* down′wardness, a sinking tendency: a state of being low.—**down east** (*U.S.*), in or into Maine and adjoining parts of New England; **down in the mouth**, in low spirits; **down on one's luck**, in ill-luck; **down south**, in the southern states; **down to the ground** (*coll.*), completely; **down town**, down in or towards the centre of a town; **down under**, at the antipodes; **down with**, put down: swallow; **go down with**, be acceptable to; **up and down**, often merely to and fro. [M.E. *a-down, adun*—O.E. *of dúne*, from the hill (dat. case of *dún*, hill; see foregoing and **adown**).]

Downing Street, *down′ing*, the street in London where the Prime Minister's official residence is, as well as the Foreign Office: the government.

dowry, *dow′ri*, *n.* the property which a woman brings to her husband at marriage—sometimes used for dower: sometimes a gift given to or for a wife at marriage: a natural endowment. [See dower.]

dowse, *dows*, *v.t.* and *v.i.* See **douse**.

dowse, *dowz*, *v.* . to use the divining-rod.—*n.* **dows′er**, a water-diviner. [Origin unknown.]

doxographer, *doks-og′rə-fər*, *n.* a compiler of opinions of philosophers.—*ns.* **doxog′raphy**; **doxol′ogy**, a hymn or liturgical formula ascribing glory to God. [Gr. *doxa*, opinion, reputation, glory, *graphein*, write, *legein*, speak, *logos*, discourse.]

doxy, *dok′si*, *n.* (*Shak.*) a mistress: a woman of loose character. [Origin unknown.]

doxy, *dok′si*, *n.* opinion—'Orthodoxy', said Warburton, 'is my doxy—heterodoxy is another man's doxy'. See above. [Gr. *doxa*, opinion.]

doyen, *dwä′yän⁸*, *n.* dean, senior member (of an academy, diplomatic corps, etc.). [Fr.,—L. *decānus*.]

doyley. See **doily**.

doze, *dōz*, *v.i.* to sleep lightly, or to be half-asleep: to be in a dull or stupefied state.—*v.t.* to spend in drowsiness (with *away*).—*n.* a short light sleep.—*adj.* **dōzed**, drowsy.—*v.t.* dō′zen (*Scot.*), to stupefy.—*v.i.* to become stupefied.—*ns.* dō′zer; dō′ziness; dō′zing.—*adj.* dō′zy, drowsy: beginning to decay. [Cf. O.N. *dúsa*, Dan. *döse*, to doze.]

dozen, *duz′n*, *n.* a set of twelve :—*pl.* **dozen**, when preceded by a numeral, otherwise **dozens**.—*adj.* **doz′enth**—baker's, devil's, long, dozen, thirteen. [O.Fr. *dozeine*—L. *duodecim*—*duo*, two, and *decem*, ten, and neut. pl. ending *-ēna* (as in *centēna*).]

drab, *drab*, *n.* a low, sluttish woman: a whore.—*v.i.* to associate with drabs.—*ns.* drabb′er, one who herds with drabs; drabb′iness.—*adjs.* drabb′-ish, drabb′y, sluttish. [Poss. Gael. *drabag*; Ir. *drabog*, slut; or L.G. *drabbe*, dirt.]

drab, *drab*, *n.* thick, strong, grey cloth : a grey or dull-brown colour, perh. from the muddy colour of undyed wool: uninteresting unvaried dulness.—*adj.* of the colour of drab: dull and monotonous.—*n.* drabb′et, a coarse linen fabric used for smockfrocks.—Also **drabette′**.—*adj.* drab′ly.—*n.* drab′ness. [Perh. Fr. *drap*, cloth—L.L. *drappus*, prob. Gmc.; see **drape**.]

drabble, *drab′l*, *v.t.* to besmear, bedraggle.—*n.* drabb′ling, a manner of fishing for barbels with a rod and long line passed through a piece of lead.—*n.* drabb′ler, drab′ler, an additional piece of canvas, laced to the bottom of the bonnet of a sail, to give it greater depth. [L.Ger. *drabbeln*, to wade about.]

Dracaena, *drā-sē′nä*, *n.* the dragon-tree genus. [L.L. *dracaena*, a she-dragon—Gr. *drakaina*, fem. of *drakōn*, dragon.]

drachm, *dram*, *n.* a drachma : a dram.

drachma, *drak′mä*, *n.* an ancient Greek weight, and a silver coin of different values : a modern Greek franc :—*pl.* **drach′mas**, **drach′mae** (*-mē*) **drach′mai** (*-mī*). [Gr. *drachmē*—*drassesthai*, to grasp with the hand.]

Draco, *drā′kō*, *n.* the Dragon, a northern constellation: a dragon-lizard.—*adjs.* **draconian** (*drak-, drak-ō′ni-ən*), **draconic** (*-on′ik*), of, of the nature of, a dragon.—*ns.* **draconites** (*drak-ə-nī′tēz*), a precious stone fabled to come from a dragon's brain; **dracontiasis** (*drak-ən-tī′ə-sis*), Guineaworm disease; **Dracontium** (*drə-kon′shi-əm*), a S. American araceous genus once of medical repute; **Dracunculus** (*drə-kungk′ū-ləs*), the green dragon genus of Araceae; **dracunculus**, the dragonet : the Guinea-worm. [L. *dracō*, -*ōnis*, and Gr. *drakōn*, -*ontos*, a dragon or snake, dims. L. *dracunculus*, Gr. *drakontion*, prob. from the root of Gr. *derkesthai*, to look.]

Draconian, *drə-* or *drā-kō′ni-ən*, **Dracontic** (-*kont′ik*), *adjs.* extremely severe, as the laws of *Draco* (Gr. *Drakōn*), archon at Athens 621 B.C.—*n.* **Draconism** (*drak′ən-izm*).

drad, *drad*, (*Spens.*) *pa.t.* and *pa.p.* of **dread**.—*adj.* (*Spens.*) dread.

draff, *dräf*, *n.* dregs : the refuse of malt after brewing.—*adjs.* draff′ish, draff′y, worthless. [Prob. related to Du. *draf*, Ger. *träber*.]

draft, *dräft*, *n.* anything drawn : the selecting of a smaller body (of men, animals, things) from a larger : the body so selected (esp. *mil.*): a member of it : (*U.S.*) conscription : an order for the payment of money : a demand (upon resources, credulity, patience, etc.) : a plan : a preliminary sketch : (occasional and *U.S.*) a draught (in various senses). —*v.t.* to draw an outline of : to draw up in preliminary form : to draw off : to detach.—*ns.* draft′bar, a draw-bar; draft′er, draught′er, one who drafts : a draught-horse; draft′-horse, draft′-ox,

fāte, fär, àsk ; mē, hər (her) ; *mīne ; mōte ; mūte ; mōōn ; dhen* (then)

drafts, drafts'man, drafts'manship (see **draught). [draught.]**

drag, *drag, v.t.* to draw by force: to draw slowly: to pull roughly and violently: to trail: to explore with a drag-net or hook: to apply a drag to.—*v.i.* to hang so as to trail on the ground: to be forcibly drawn along: to move slowly and heavily: to lag: to give the feeling of being unduly slow or tedious: (*pr.p.* **dragg'ing**; *pa.t., pa.p.* **dragged).**—*n.* anything dragged: an act of dragging: a dragging effect: (*aero.*) the component of the aerodynamic force on an aircraft that lies along the longitudinal axis: a net or hook for dragging along to catch things under water: a heavy harrow: a device for guiding wood to the saw: a mail-coach: a long open carriage, with transverse or side seats: a contrivance for retarding a wheel, esp. an iron shoe that drags on the ground: any obstacle to progress: a trail of scent: an artificial scent dragged on the ground for foxhounds to follow: (*billiards*) a retarded motion of the cue-ball imparted by striking somewhat under the centre.—*ns.* **drag'-bar,** a draw-bar; **drag'-chain,** a chain used as drag to a wheel: a chain for coupling railway vehicles; **drag'hound,** a foxhound trained to follow a drag; **drag'-hunt; drag'-man,** a fisherman who uses a drag-net; **drag'-net,** a net to be dragged along the bottom of water or the ground; **drag'-shot,** a shot that imparts drag to a billiard-ball; **drags'man,** the driver of a drag or coach. [Northern—O.E. *dragan* or O.N. *draga;* Ger. *tragen;* see **draw.]**

dragée, *drä-zhā, n.* a sweetmeat enclosing a drug, or a nut or fruit, etc.: a chocolate drop. [Fr.]

draggle, *drag'l, v.t.* or *v.i.* to make or become wet and dirty, as by dragging along the ground: to trail.—*n.* **dragg'le-tail,** a slut.—*adj.* **dragg'le-tailed.** [Freq. of drag, and a doublet of **drawl.]**

dragoman, *drag'ō-man, n.* an interpreter or guide in Eastern countries: (*pl.* **drag'omans).** [Fr., from Ar. *tarjumān—tarjama,* to interpret.]

dragon, *drag'ən, n.* a fabulous winged scalyarmoured fire-breathing monster, often a guardian of treasure, ravaging a country when its hoard is rifled: a fierce, intimidating, or watchful person: a paper kite: a dragon-lizard: applied to various plants, esp. Dracunculus (green dragon), and Dracontium; **Dragon,** a northern constellation (Draco).—*ns.* **drag'oness,** a she-dragon; **drag'onet,** a little dragon: a goby of the genus Callionymus; **drag'on-fish,** a dragonet: a fish of the genus Pegasus; **drag'onfly,** a predaceous long-bodied often brilliantly coloured insect of the Odonata; **drag'onhead, drag'on's-head,** a labiate garden plant (Dracocephalum)—from the shape of the corolla.—*v.t.* **drag'onise,** to turn into a dragon: to watch like a dragon.—*adjs.* **drag'onish, drag'on-like.**—*ns.* **drag'onism,** unremitting watchfulness; **drag'on-liz'ard,** a small tree-dwelling E. Indian lizard (Draco) with parachute of ribs and skin: a S. American lizard (Thorictis): a monitor, esp. a species (*Varanus komodensis*) found in Komodo (in Indonesia), reaching 10 feet in length.—*adj.* **dragonné** (*drag-o-nā´; her.*), like a dragon in the hinder part.—*ns.* **drag'on-root** (*U.S.*) an araceous plant (Arisaema) or its tuberous root, used in medicine; **drag'on's-blood,** a red resinous exudation from the dragon-tree and many other trees, used for colouring varnishes, etc.; **drag'onstand'ard,** a standard in, or bearing, the form of a dragon; **drag'on-tree',** a great tree of the Canary Islands (*Dracaena Draco*), of the Liliaceae, remarkable for its resin (a variety of dragon's blood), its growth in thickness like a dicotyledon, and the great age it attains. [Fr.,—L. *dracō, -ōnis*—Gr. *drakōn, -ontos,* perh.—root *drak,* as in *edrakon,* aorist of *derkesthai,* to see clearly.]

dragonnade, *drag-ən-ād´, n.* the persecution of French Protestants under Louis XIV by means of dragoons: any persecution by military means (usu. in *pl*). [Fr., from *dragon,* dragoon.]

dragoon, *drə-gōōn´, n.* an old fire-spitting musket: (*obs.*) a mounted infantryman armed with it: a heavy cavalryman, as opp. to hussars and lancers—surviving in the names of certain regiments.—

v.t. to harass or compel by military bullying.—*n.* **dragoon'-bird,** the umbrella-bird. [Fr. *dragon,* dragon, dragoon.]

dragsman. See **drag.**

drail, *drāl, n.* the iron bow of a plough from which the traces draw: a piece of lead round the shank of the hook in fishing.—*v.i.* to draggle. [Prob. a combination of **draggle** and **trail.]**

drain, *drān, v.t.* to draw off by degrees: to filter: to draw off water, sewage, or other liquid from: to furnish means of withdrawal of liquid from: to make dry: to drink dry: to exhaust.—*v.i.* to flow off gradually: to part with liquid by flowing, trickling or dripping: to discharge.—*n.* a watercourse: a channel for escape of liquid: a ditch: a sewer: (*slang*) a drink: exhausting expenditure.—*adj.* **drain'able.**—*ns.* **drain'age,** act, process, method, or means of draining: mode of discharge of water: the system of drains in a town; **drain'age-basin,** the area of land that drains into one river; **drain'age-tube,** a tube for discharge of pus, etc.; **drain'er,** a utensil on which articles are placed to drain; **drain'-pipe; drain'-tile; drain'-trap,** a contrivance for preventing the escape of foul air from drains, while admitting water to them. [O.E. *dréahnian.*]

drake, *drāk, n.* the male of the duck: a flat stone thrown so as to skip along the surface of water in playing *ducks and drakes* (also **drake'stone).** [Ety. obscure; cf. prov. Ger. *draak;* O.H.G. *antrahho,* Ger. *enterich,* the first element usually explained as *eend, end, anut,* duck.]

drake, *drāk, n.* a dragon: a fiery meteor: a beaked galley, or viking ship of war; an angler's name for species of Ephemera. [O.E. *draca,* dragon—L. *dracō.*]

dram, *dram, n.* a contraction of **drachm:** ⅛th of an oz. avoirdupois: formerly, with apothecaries, ⅛th of an oz.: a small drink of alcoholic liquor: a tipple.—*v.i.* to drink a dram.—*v.t.* to give a dram to.—*ns.* **dram'-drink'er; dram'-shop.** [Through Fr. and L., from Gr. *drachmē.* See **drachma.]**

drama, *dräm'ä, n.* a story of life and action for representation by actors: a composition intended to be represented on the stage: dramatic literature: theatrical entertainment: (journalistically) a series of deeply interesting events.—*adjs.* **dramat'ic** (*drə-mat'ik*), **-al,** belonging to the drama: appropriate to or in the form of drama: with the force and vividness of the drama.—*adv.* **dramat'ically.**—*n.* **dramat'icism.**—*adj.* **dramatis'able** (*dram-*).—*n.* **dramatisā'tion,** the act of dramatising: the dramatised version of a novel or story.—*v.t.* **dram'atise,** to compose in, or turn into, the form of a drama or play.—*n.* **dram'atist,** a writer of plays.—**dram'atis persō'nae** (*-ē*), the characters of a drama or play. [L.,—Gr. *drāma, drāmatos—drāein,* to do.]

dramaturgy, *dram'ə-tur-ji, n.* the principles of dramatic composition: theatrical art.—*ns.* **dram'-aturge, dram'aturgist,** a playwright.—*adj.* **dramatur'gic.** [Through Fr. from Gr. *drāmatourgiā, drāmatourgos,* playwright—*drāma,* and *ergon,* a work.]

drammock, *dram'ək, n.* meal and water mixed raw. [Cf. Gael. *dramag, dramaig,* a foul mixture.]

drank, *drangk, pa.t.* of **drink.**

drant, draunt, *dränt, drawnt, v.i.* and *v.t.* (*prov.*) to drawl, to drone.—*n.* a droning tone.

drap, *drāp, n.* and *v.* Scots form of **drop.**—*n.* **drapp'ie, drapp'y,** (*Scot.*) a little drop, esp. of spirits.

drap-de-Berry, *drä-də-ber-ē, n.* (*obs.*) a woollen cloth made in Berry, in France.—Also *adj.* [Fr., Berry cloth.]

drape, *drāp, v.t.* to cover as with cloth: to hang cloth in folds about.—*adj.* **draped.**—*n.* **drāp'er,** a dealer in cloth and cloth goods.—*adj.* **drāp'eried,** draped.—*n.* **drāp'ery,** cloth goods: hangings: the draper's business: (*art*) the representation of clothes and hanging folds of cloth: (*pl.* **draperies).**—*v.t.* to drape.—*ns.* **drapet** (*drap'it;* *Spens.*), a cloth covering; **drapier** (*drāp'i-ər; obs.*) a draper. [O.Fr. *draper,* to weave, drape, *drapier,* draper—*drap*, cloth. prob. Gmc.; see **drab**.]

drastic, *dras'tik*, *adj.* forcible, powerful in action: violent: unsparing.—*n.* a severe purgative.—*adv.* **dras'tically**. [Gr. *drastikos*—*draein*, to act, to do.]

drat, *drat*, *v.t.* a minced oath used to express vexation. [Aphetic from **God rot**.]

dratchell, *drach'l*, *n.* (*prov.*) a slut.

draught, *dräft*, *n.* drawing or pulling: a pull: attraction: the thing or quantity drawn: readiness for drawing from the cask: the act of drinking: the quantity drunk in one breath: a dose of liquor or medicine: outline of a picture: a preliminary sketch or plan (usu. **draft**): that which is taken in a net by drawing: a chosen detachment of men (usu. **draft**): a current of air: the depth to which a ship sinks in the water: (*obs.*) a move in a game: a thick disk used in the game of draughts: (in *pl.*) a game played by two persons moving draughtmen alternately on a chequered board: (*Shak.*) a cesspool or privy.—*v.t.* to sketch out, make a preliminary plan of or attempt at (also **draft**): occasionally for **draft** in sense of draw off, set apart from a larger body.—*ns.* **draught'-animal**, **-horse**, **-ox**, etc., one used for drawing heavy loads; **draught'board**, a chessboard used for playing draughts; **draught'-en'gine**, the engine over the shaft of a coal-pit.—*n.pl.* **draught'-hooks**, large iron hooks fixed on the cheeks of a cannon-carriage.—*ns.* **draught'-house** (*B.*), a sink, privy; **draught'iness**; **draught'man**, a piece used for playing draughts; **draught'-net**, a drag-net; **draught'-screen**, a screen for warding off a current of air; **draughts'man**, a piece used in playing draughts: one skilled or employed in drawing: one who draughts or draws up documents (in this sense usually **draftsman**).—*adj.* **draught'y**, full of draughts or currents of air. —**feel the draught**, to be unpleasantly conscious of difficult conditions, esp. economic. [O.E. *draht* —*dragan*, to draw; see **drag, draw**.]

drave, *dräv*, old *pa.t.* of **drive**.

Dravidian, *dra-vid'i-ən*, *adj.* belonging to a dark, long-headed, wavy-haired race of the Deccan: belonging to a group of languages in Southern India, including Tamil, Malayalam, Kanarese, Telugu, etc.—Also *n.* [Sans. *Drāvida*, an ancient province of Southern India.]

draw, *draw*, *v.t.* to pull: to drag: to pull along: to bring forcibly towards or after one: to pull into position: to pull back: to pull back the string of: to pull together or awry: to take at random from a number: to entice, attract: to coax into giving information: to stimulate to self-expression (usu. **draw out**): to inhale: to take out: to unsheathe: to withdraw: to cause to flow out: to evoke or bring out by some artifice: to extract by pulling: to extract the essence of: to eviscerate: to pull through a small hole, as in making wire: to deduce: to lengthen: to extend to the full length: to force to appear (as a badger from its hole): to receive or take from a source or store: to demand by a draft: to get by lot: to trace: to construct in linear form: to make a picture of, by lines drawn: to describe: to put into shape, frame: to write out (as a cheque): to require as depth of water for floating: to finish without winning or losing: (*cricket*) to glance.—*v.i.* to pull: to practise drawing: to move: to make one's way, betake oneself: to resort: to approach: to make a draught: to allow a free current: to act as drawer: to draw a card, a sword, lots: to infuse: to end a game without winning or losing: (*pa.t.* **drew**, *drōō*; *pa.p.* **drawn**).—*n.* the act of drawing: assignment by lot, as of prizes, opponents in a game: anything drawn: a drawn or undecided game: an attraction: (*U.S.*) a drawer (of a chest of drawers).—*adj.* **draw'able**.—*ns.* **draw'back**, a disadvantage: a receiving back some part of the duty on goods on their exportation; **draw'-bar**, a sliding bar: a bar used in coupling railway vehicles (also **drag-**, **draught-bar**); **draw'-boy**, the boy who pulls the cords of the harness in figure-weaving: a mechanical device for this purpose; **draw'bridge**, a bridge that can be drawn up or let down at pleasure: bridge played by two

persons, with two dummy hands, not exposed; **drawee'**, the person on whom a bill of exchange is drawn; **draw'er**, he or that which draws: one who draws beer or fetches liquor in a tavern: (*drawr*) a thing drawn out, as the sliding box in a **chest of drawers**: (in *pl.*) a close under-garment for the lower part of the body and the legs; **draw'-gear**, the apparatus by which railway-cars are coupled; **draw'ing**, the art of representing objects or forms by lines drawn, shading, etc.: a picture in lines: an assigning by lot: act of pulling, etc.; **draw'ing-board**, a slab on which paper can be pinned for drawing on; **draw'ing-frame**, a machine in which carded wool, cotton, or the like is drawn out fine; **draw'ing-knife**, a knife with a handle at each end, used by a cooper for shaving hoops by drawing it towards him; **draw'ing-mas'ter**; **draw'ing-paper**; **draw'ing-pen**; **draw'ing-pencil**; **draw'ing-pin**, a short broad-headed pin for fastening paper to a drawing-board; **draw'ing-room**, in engineering, a room where plans and patterns are drawn (see also separate article); **draw'ing-table**, a table which can be extended in length by drawing out sliding leaves.—*adj.* **drawn**, pulled together: closed: neither won nor lost: unsheathed: eviscerated: strained, tense: etiolated.—*ns.* **draw'-net** (same as **drag-net**); **drawn'-thread'work**, ornamental work done by pulling out some of the threads of a fabric; **draw'-plate**, a plate supporting dies for drawing wire or tubing; **draw'-sheet**, a hospital sheet that can be drawn out from under a patient; **draw'-tube**, a tube sliding within another, as in a form of telescope; **draw'-well**, a well from which water is drawn up by a bucket and apparatus.—**at daggers drawn**, openly hostile; **draw a bead on** (see **bead**); **draw a blank**, to get a lottery ticket that wins no prize: to get no result; **draw a cover** (**covert**), to send the hounds into a cover to frighten out a fox; **draw blank**, to do so, but find no fox; **draw back**, to recoil: to withdraw; **draw cuts**, to cast lots; **draw, hang, and quarter** (see **hang**); **draw in**, to reduce, contract: to become shorter; **draw it fine**, to be too precise; **draw it mild**, to refrain from exaggeration; **draw near**, to approach; **draw off**, to cause to flow from a barrel, etc.: to withdraw; **draw on**, to approach: to pull on; **draw on, upon**, to make a draught upon: to make a demand upon (one's credulity, patience, resources): to draw one's sword, pistol, against; **draw on one's imagination**, to make imaginative or lying statements; **draw on one's memory**, to try to remember: to make use of what one remembers; **draw out**, to leave the place (of an army, etc.): to lengthen: to entice into talk and self-expression; **draw rein**, to slacken speed, to stop; **draw stumps**, end a game of cricket by removing the wickets; **draw the cloth, board, table** (*arch.*), clear up after a meal; **draw the line**, to fix a limit; **draw the long-bow** (see **long**); **draw to a head**, to mature; **draw up**, to form in regular order: to compose, put into shape: to stop (as in driving a carriage); **in drawing**, correctly drawn; **out of drawing**, inaccurately drawn, or drawn in violation of the principles of drawing. [O.E. *dragan*; cf. **drag**.]

Drawcansir, *draw-kan'sər*, *n.* a blustering bully. [*Drawcansir* (parodying Dryden's *Almanzor*), who 'kills 'em all on both sides' in Buckingham's *Rehearsal* (performed 1671).]

drawing-room, *draw'ing-rōōm*, *n.* a room to which the company withdraws after dinner: a reception of company at court: (*U.S.*) a private compartment of a 'parlor-car'.—*adj.* suitable for the drawing-room. [Orig. **withdrawing-room**.]

drawl, *drawl*, *v.i.* (*obs.*) to dawdle: to speak in a slow lengthened tone.—*v.t.* to utter in a slow and sleepy manner.—*n.* a slow, lengthened utterance. —*n.* **drawl'er**.—*adv.* **drawl'ingly**.—*n.* **drawl'ingness**. [Connected with **draw**.]

drawn, *drawn*, *pa.p.* of **draw**, and *adj.*

dray, *drā*, *n.* a low strong cart for heavy goods: a timber sledge: that which is dragged or drawn.— *ns.* **dray'age**; **dray'-horse**; **dray'man**; **dray'-**

plough. [Cf. O.E. *dræge*, drag-net—*dragan*, to draw; see **drag, draw**.]

dray. Same as **drey**.

drazel, *drāz'l, n. (prov.)* a slut. [Origin unknown.]

dread, *dred, n.* great fear: awe: an object of fear or awe: (*Spens.*) fury.—*adj.* dreaded: inspiring great fear or awe.—*v.t.* to fear greatly: to reverence: (*obs.*) to cause to fear, to affright.—*n.* **dread'er.**—*adj.* **dread'ful,** (*orig.*) full of dread: producing great fear or awe: terrible.—*adv.* **dread'fully.**—*n.* **dread'fulness.**—*adj.* **dread'less,** free from dread: intrepid.—*adv.* (*Spens.*) doubtless.—*adv.* **dread'lessly.**—*n.* **dread'lessness.**—*adv.* **dread'ly.**—*n.* **dread'nought, dread'-naught,** one who dreads nothing: hence, a thick cloth or garment thereof: a powerful type of battleship or battle-cruiser (dating from 1905-6). **—penny dreadful,** a cheap sensational serial or tale. [M.E. *dreden*—O.E. *ondrǽdan,* to fear; O.N. *ondréda,* O.H.G. *intratan,* to be afraid.]

dream, *drēm, n.* (*obs.*) joy: mirth: minstrelsy: music: sound.—*n.* **dream'hole,** a hole in the wall of a steeple, tower, etc., for admitting light. [O.E. *drēam,* joy, mirth.]

dream, *drēm, n.* a train of thoughts and fancies during sleep, a vision: something only imaginary: a distant hope or ideal, probably unattainable. —*v.i.* to fancy things during sleep: to think idly (with *of*): to think (of) as possible, contemplate as imaginably possible.—*v.t.* to see or imagine in, or as in, a dream: (*pa.t.* and *pa.p.* dreamed or dreamt, *dremt*).—*ns.* **dream'er; dream'ery,** a place favourable to dreams: dreamlike fancies.—*adj.* **dream'ful** (*Tenn.*), dreamy.—*adv.* **dream'ily.**—*n.* **dream'iness.**—*n.* and *adj.* **dream'ing.**—*adv.* **dream'ingly.**—*n.* **dream'-land,** the land of dreams, reverie, or imagination.—*adj.* **dream'less.**—*adv.* **dream'lessly.** —*ns.* **dream'lessness; dream'while,** the duration of a dream; **dream'world,** a world of illusions.—*adj.* **dream'y,** full of dreams: given to dreaming: appropriate to dreams: dream-like. [M.E. *dream, drēm;* perh. the same word as the foregoing.]

dreary, *drēr'i, adj.* gloomy: cheerless.—*adj.* **drear, dreary.**—*n.* (*Spens.*) **dreare, drere)** dreariness: gloom: mishap: stroke.—*ns.* **drear'ihead, drear'iment, drear'iness, drear'ing** (all *Spens.*), **drear'ihood.**—*adv.* **drear'ily.**—*adj.* **drear'isome,** desolate, forlorn. [O.E. *drēorig,* mournful, bloody—*drēor,* gore.]

dredge, *drej, n.* a bag-net for dragging along the bottom to take oysters, biological specimens, mud, etc.: a machine for deepening a harbour, canal, river, etc., for excavating under water or on land, or for raising alluvial deposits and washing them for minerals, by means of buckets on an endless chain, pumps, grabs, or other devices.— *v.t.* to gather, explore, or deepen with a dredge.— **dredg'er,** one who dredges: a machine for dredging: a boat, ship, or raft equipped for dredging. [Conn. with **drag, draw**.]

dredge, *drej, v.t.* to sprinkle.—*ns.* **dredg'er, dredge'-box, dredg'ing-box,** a vessel with perforated lid for dredging. [O.Fr. *dragie,* sugarplum—Gr. *tragēmata,* dessert.]

dree, *drē, v.t.* (*Scot.*) to endure, bear.—**dree one's weird,** to undergo one's destiny. [O.E. *drēogan,* suffer, accomplish.]

dregs, *dregz, n.pl.* impurities in liquor that fall to the bottom, the grounds: dross: the vilest part of anything.—*n.* **dregg'iness.**—*adj.* **dregg'y,** containing dregs: muddy: foul. [O.N. *dregg.*]

dreich, *drēhh, adj.* (*Scot.*) long drawn out: tedious: dreary. [See **dree**.]

drench, *drensh, drench, v.t.* to fill with drink or liquid: to wet thoroughly: to soak: to physic by force: (*obs.*) to drown.—*v.i.* (*obs.*) to drown.—*n.* a draught: a dose of physic forced down the throat.—*n.* **drench'er.** [O.E. *drencan,* to cause to drink (*drincan,* to drink), *drenc,* drink, drowning; Ger. *tränken,* to soak. See **drink**.]

drent, *drent* (*Spens.*), obsolete *pa.p.* of **drench,** to drown.

drepanium, *dri-pā'ni-əm, n.* a cymose inflorescence in which each daughter axis is on the same side of its parent axis, and all in one plane. [Latinised from Gr. *drepanion,* dim. of *drepanon,* a reaping-hook.]

drere, dreryhead, etc. Spenserian forms of **drear,** etc.

dress, *dres, v.t.* to straighten: to flatten: to smooth: to erect: to set in order: to prepare: to finish or trim: to treat: to tend: to apply suitable materials to: to clothe: to adorn: to treat with severity: to chide: to thrash.—*v.i.* to come into line: to put on clothes: to put on finer, more elaborate, or more formal clothes: (*pa.t.* and *pa.p.* dressed, sometimes drest).—*n.* the covering or ornament of the body: a lady's gown: manner of clothing: ceremonial or formal clothing.—*adj.* pertaining to evening dress.—*ns.* **dress'-cir'cle,** part of a theatre (usually the first gallery) intended for people in evening dress; **dress'-coat,** a fine black coat with narrow or cut-away skirts, worn in full dress; **dress'er,** one who dresses: a medical student who dresses wounds: a tirewoman: a custodian of dresses in a theatre: a tool or machine for dressing: a table on which meat is dressed or prepared for use: a kitchen sideboard: (*U.S.*) a chest of drawers or dressing-table.—*n.pl.* **dress'-goods,** cloths for making women's and children's gowns, frocks, etc.—*ns.* **dress'-guard,** an arrangement of strings to protect the rider's dress from contact with a bicycle wheel; **dress'-improver,** (*obs.*) a bustle; **dress'ing,** dress or clothes: material applied to land, a wound, manufactured goods, etc.: matter used to give stiffness and gloss to cloth: sauce, stuffing, etc., used in preparing a dish for the table, etc.: an ornamental moulding: a thrashing; **dress'ing-case,** a case of toilet requisites; **dress'ing-gown,** a loose garment used in dressing, or in deshabille; **dress'ing-jack'et, dress'ing-sack,** a jacket worn by women in dressing; **dress'ing-room; dress'ing-sta'tion,** a place where wounded are collected and tended by members of a field-ambulance; **dress'ing-ta'ble; dress'-length,** enough to make a dress; **dress'maker,** a person who makes gowns or dresses for women; **dress'-reform; dress'-rehears'al,** a full rehearsal in costume, with everything as for the performance; **dress'-shield,** a device to protect the armpit of a dress against sweat; **dress'-shirt', dress'-suit', dress'-tie',** one for formal evening dress.—*adj.* **dress'y,** fond of dress: showy: indicating care in dressing.— **dress down,** to handle with severity: to reprimand: to thrash; **dressed day,** formerly, the second day of a three days' visit, between the *rest day,* and the *pressed day;* **dress up,** to dress elaborately: to dress for a part: to masquerade; **evening dress, full dress,** the costume prescribed by fashion for evening receptions, dinners, balls, etc. [O.Fr. *dresser,* to prepare—an inferred L.L. *directiāre,* to straighten; see **direct**.]

dressage, *dres-äzh, n.* training, horsemanship. [Fr.]

drest, *drest, pa.t.* and *pa.p.* of **dress**.

drevill, *drev'il, n.* (*Spens.*) a foul person. [Cf. M.Du. *drevel,* scullion.]

drew, *drōō, pa.t.* of **draw**.

drey, dray, *drā, n.* a squirrel's nest. [Ety. dub.]

drib, *drib, (obs.) v.i.* to trickle: to go little by little.—*v.t.* to let trickle: to take a little, filch: to lead gradually: to shoot (an arrow) short or wide.—*n.* a drop: a trickle: a small quantity.— *ns.* **dribb'er; drib'let, dribb'let,** a drop: a trickle: a small quantity. [Akin to **drip**.]

dribble, *drib'l, v.i.* to fall in small drops: to drop quickly: to trickle: to slaver, as a child or an idiot.—*v.t.* to let fall in drops: to give out in small portions: (*football*) to kick forward little by little: (*archery; Shak.*) to drib.—Also *n.*—*n.* **dribb'ler.** [Freq. of **drib**.]

dried, drier, dries, driest. See **dry**.

drift, *drift, n.* a driving: (*arch.*) a drove: a heap of matter driven together, as snow: floating materials driven by water: a driving shower: a streaming movement: the direction in which a thing is driven: a slow current caused by the wind: leeway: passive travel with the current: abandonment to external influences: tendency: a cattle-track, drove-road: a pin or bar driven into a hole: a drift-net: a set of nets: the object aimed at: the meaning of words used: (*geol.*) loose superficial deposits, esp. glacial or fluvio-glacial: (*mining*) a horizontal or oblique excavation or passage: (*S. Africa; Du.*) a ford.—*v.t.* to drive: to carry by drift: to cause or allow to drift: to pierce or tunnel.—*v.i.* to be floated along: to be driven into heaps: to leave things to circumstances. —*ns.* drift′age, that which is drifted: the amount of deviation from a ship's course due to leeway; drift′-anchor, an anchor for keeping the ship's head to the wind; drift′-bolt, a steel bolt used to drive out other bolts; drift′er, one who, or that which drifts: an aimless shiftless person: a fisherman or a fishing-boat that uses a drift-net; drift′-ice, floating masses of ice drifting before the wind; drift′land, an old tribute paid for the privilege of driving cattle through a manor.— *adj.* drift′less, without drift.—*ns.* drift′-mining, gold-mining by means of drifts in the gravel and detritus of old river-beds; drift′-net, a net which is allowed to drift with the tide; drift′-sail, a sail immersed in the water, used for lessening the drift of a vessel during a storm; drift′-way, a road over which cattle are driven: (*min.*) drift; drift′-weed, gulf-weed: tangle: seaweed thrown up on the beach; drift′-wood, wood drifted by water.—*adj.* drift′y, full of or forming drifts. [See **drive**.]

drill, *dril, v.t.* to bore, pierce: to make with a drill: to exercise (soldiers, pupils, etc.) by repeated practice: to sow in rows.—*n.* an instrument for boring stone, metal, teeth, or hard substances (not wood), actuated by a kind of bow, by a brace, or otherwise: a large boring instrument used in mining: training exercise: a spell of it: a drill-master: a ridge with seed or growing plants on it (turnips, potatoes, etc.): the plants in such a row: the machine for sowing the seed in drill-husbandry.—*ns.* drill′-barrow, a grain-drill driven by hand; drill′-harrow, a harrow for working between drills; drill′-husbandry, the method of sowing seed in drills or rows; drill′ing-machine′, drill′ing-lathe, drill′-press, machines for boring with a drill or drills; drill′-master, one who teaches drill, one who trains in anything, esp. in a mechanical manner; drill′-plough, a plough for sowing grain in drills; drill′-sergeant, a sergeant who drills soldiers. [Prob. borrowed from Du. *drillen,* to bore; *dril, drille,* a borer; cf. **thrill**.]

drill, *dril, n.* a W. African baboon, smaller than the mandrill. [Perh. a W. African word.]

drilling, *dril′ing, n.* a stout twilled linen or cotton cloth.—Also **drill.** [Ger. *drillich,* ticking—L. *trilix,* three-threaded; *trēs, tria,* three, *līcium,* thread.]

drily. See under **dry.**

drink, *dringk, v.t.* to swallow as a liquid: (*obs.*) to smoke (tobacco): to empty, as a glass, bowl, etc.: to absorb: to take in through the senses.— *v.i.* to swallow a liquid: to take intoxicating liquors to excess: (*pr.p.* drink′ing; *pa.t.* drank, *arch.* drunk; *pa.p.* drunk).—*n.* an act of drinking: a quantity drunk: something to be drunk: a beverage: intoxicating liquor.—*adj.* drink′able.— *ns.* drink′ableness; drink′er, one who drinks: a tippler.—*interj.* drink′-hail, an Early Middle English reply to a pledge in drinking (*waes hail,* be healthy, or lucky, was answered with *drinc hail,* drink healthy or lucky—hail being the O.N. *heill,* not O.E. *hál*).—*n.* drink′ing.—Also *adj.* fit to drink: for drinking.—*ns.* drink′ing-bout; drink′ing-foun′tain; drink′ing-horn; drink′-mon′ey, a gratuity, ostensibly given to buy liquor for drinking to the health of the giver; drink′-offering, an offering of wine, oil, blood, etc., to a god.—drink himself drunk, to drink until he is drunk; drink in, to absorb (rain, etc.), as dry land does; drink off, to quaff wholly and at a gulp; drink the others under the table, to continue drinking and remain (comparatively) sober after the others have completely collapsed;

drink to, drink to the health of, to drink wine, etc., with good wishes for one's health; drink up, to exhaust by drinking; in drink, intoxicated; strong drink, alcoholic liquor; the drink, (*slang*) the sea. [O.E. *drincan;* Ger. *trinken.*]

drip, *drip, v.i.* to fall in drops: to let fall drops.— *v.t.* to let fall in drops: (*pr.p.* dripp′ing; *pa.t.* and *pa.p.* dripped).—*n.* a falling in drops: that which falls in drops: the edge of a roof.—*ns.* dripp′ing, that which falls in drops, as fat from meat in roasting; dripp′ing-pan, a pan for receiving the dripping from roasting meat; drip′-stone, a projecting moulding over doorways, etc., serving to throw off the rain; drip′-tip (*bot.*) a prolonged leaf-tip, serving to shed rain.—dripping roast, a source of easy and continuous profit; right of drip, a right in law to let the drip from one's roof fall on another's land. [O.E. *dryppan* —*dréopan.*]

drive, *drīv, v.t.* to urge along: to hurry on: to control or guide the movements or operations of: to convey or carry in a carriage: to force in: to push briskly: to furnish motive power to: to urge, as a point of argument: to carry through, as a bargain: to impel: to compel: to send away with force, as a ball. esp. in golf, to play from the tee or with a driver, in cricket to hit strongly down the pitch, in tennis, to return forcibly underarm: to chase: to excavate: to sort out (as feathers) in a current of air.—*v.i.* to control an engine, vehicle, draught-animal, etc.: to press forward with violence: to be forced along, as a ship before the wind: to be driven: to go in a carriage: to aim or tend towards a point: to strike with a sword, the fist, etc. (with *at*):—(*pr.p.* drīv′ing; *pa.t.* drōve, *arch.* drāve, *Spens.* drive, *driv; pa.p.* driv′en). —*n.* an excursion in a carriage: a road for driving on, esp. the approach to a house within its own grounds: a driving stroke in games: impulse: impulsive force: power of getting things done: the chasing of game towards the shooters, or the sport so obtained, or the ground over which the game is driven: pushing sales by reducing prices: an organised campaign to attain any end: apparatus for driving.—*ns.* driv′er, one who or that which drives, in all senses: a club used in golf to propel the ball from the teeing-ground; drive′way, a carriage drive: a driving road; driv′ing-band, the band or strap that communicates motion from one machine, or part of a machine, to another; driv′ing-box, a box on which a driver sits; driv′ing-gear, apparatus by which power is transmitted from shaft to shaft; driv′ing-shaft, a shaft from a driving-wheel communicating motion to machinery; driv′ing-wheel, a main wheel that communicates motion to other wheels: one of the main wheels in a locomotive.—let drive, to aim a blow. [O.E. *drīfan,* to drive; Ger. *treiben,* to push.]

drivel, *driv′l, v.i.* to slaver like a child: to be foolish: to speak like an idiot:—(*pr.p.* driv′elling; *pa.t.* and *pa.p.* driv′elled).—*n.* slaver: nonsense. —*n.* driv′eller. [M.E. *drevelen, dravelen;* O.E. *dreflian.*]

drizzle, *driz′l, v.i.* to rain in small drops.—*v.t.* (*Shak.*) to shed in small drops.—*n.* a small, light rain.—*adj.* drizz′ly. [Freq. of M.E. *dresen*— O.E. *dréosan,* to fall; Goth. *driusan.*]

droger, drogher, *drō′gėr, n.* a W. Indian coasting vessel, with long masts and lateen sails. [Du. *droogen,* to dry—orig. a vessel on which fish were dried.]

drogue, *drōg, n.* the drag of boards, attached to the end of a harpoon-line, checking the progress of a running whale. [Origin obscure.]

droguet, *drō-gā′, n.* a ribbed woollen dress fabric, a variety of rep. [Fr.; cf. **drugget.**]

droich, *drōhh, n.* (*Scot.*) a dwarf.—*adj.* droich′y, dwarfish. [See **dwarf.**]

droil, *droil, v.i.* to drudge. [Perh. Du. *druilen,* to loiter.]

droit, *droit, drwä, n.* right, legal claim. [Fr.]

droll, *drōl, adj.* odd: amusing: laughable.—*n.* one who excites mirth: a jester.—*v.i.* to practise drollery: to jest.—*ns.* droll′ery, drollness: waggery : a comic show, picture, story : a jest : a puppet-show; **droll'ing.**—*adjs.* **droll'ish**, rather droll.—*adv.* **drolly** (*drōl'li*).—*n.* **droll'ness.** [Fr. *drôle*, prob. from Du. *drollig*, odd—*trold*, a hobgoblin; cf. Ger. *droll*, a short thick person.]

dromedary, *drum'i-dər-i*, *n.* a thoroughbred camel : a one-humped Arabian camel.—*Spens.*

drom'edare. [O.Fr. *dromedaire*—L.L. *dromedārius*—Gr. *dromas*, *dromados*, running—*dromos*, a course, run.]

dromond, *drom'*, *drum'ənd*, *n.* a swift mediaeval ship of war.—Also **drom'on**. [O.Fr.,—L.L. *dromō*, *-ōnis*—Byzantine Gr. *dromōn*—*dromos*, a running, *dramein* (aor.) to run.]

dromos, *drom'os*, *n.* a Greek race-course : an entrance-passage or avenue, as to a subterranean tomb, etc. :—*pl.* **drom'oi.**—*adjs.* **drom'ic**, **-al**, pertaining to a race-course : basilican. [Gr.]

drone, *drōn*, *n.* the male of the honey-bee : one who lives on the labour of others, like the dronebee : a lazy, idle fellow : a deep humming sound : a bass-pipe of a bagpipe : its note : a pedal bass : the burden of a song : a monotonous tiresome speaker.—*v.i.* to emit a monotonous humming sound.—*v.t.* to utter with such a tone.—*adj.* **dron'ish**, like a drone : lazy, idle.—*adv.* **dron'-ishly.**—*ns.* **dron'ishness; drone'-pipe**, a pipe producing a droning sound.—*adj.* **dron'y**. [O.E. *drān*, bee, but the quantity of the *a* is doubtful, and relations obscure : perh.—Old Saxon.]

drongo, *drong'gō*, *n.* any member of the family *Dicruridae*, glossy-black fork-tailed insect-catching birds of the Old World tropics.—Also **drong'o-shrike.**—*n.* **drong'o-cuck'oo**, a cuckoo that resembles a drongo. [From Malagasy.]

drool, *drōōl*, *v.i.* to slaver : to drivel.—*n.* drivel. [drivel.]

droome, *drōōm*, *n.* (*Spens.*) another form of **drum.**

droop, *drōōp*, *v.i.* to hang down : to grow weak or faint : to decline.—*v.t.* to let hang down.—*n.* a drooping position.—*adv.* **droop'ingly**. [O.N. *drúpa*, to droop; see **drop**.]

drop, *drop*, *n.* a small rounded blob of liquid that hangs or falls at one time : a very small quantity of liquid : anything hanging like a drop : a pendant : a round sweetmeat : a curtain dropped between acts (also **drop'-cur'tain**): (in *pl.*) a medicine taken in drops : a fall : a vertical descent, difference of level : an unpleasant surprise : a trap in the gallows scaffold, the fall of which allows the criminal to drop : a device for lowering goods into a ship's hold.—*v.i.* to fall in drops : to let drops fall : to fall suddenly, steeply or sheer : to let oneself fall gently : to sink : to lapse : to diminish : to subside into a condition, come gradually to be : to come casually or accidentally. —*v.t.* to let fall in drops : to let fall : to let go, relinquish, abandon : to omit : to lower : to lay : to give birth to : to spot, bespatter, sprinkle : to utter casually : to write and send (a note) in an offhand manner : to set down, part with :—(*pr.p.* **dropp'ing**; *pa.t.* and *pa.p.* **dropped**).—*ns.* **drop'-drill**, an apparatus for dropping seed and manure into the soil simultaneously; **drop'-forging**, the process of shaping metal parts by forging between two dies, one fixed to the hammer and the other to the anvil of a steam or mechanical hammer; **drop'-goal**, *n.* (*rugby*) a goal secured by a dropkick; **drop'-hamm'er, drop'-press**, a swaging, stamping, or forging machine; **drop'-kick** (*rugby football*), a kick made when the ball rebounds from the ground after dropping from the hand; **drop'let**, a little drop; **drop'-lett'er** (*U.S.*), a letter posted in any place merely for local delivery; **drop'-net**, a net suspended from a boom, to be suddenly dropped on a passing shoal of fish; **dropp'er**, one who or that which drops; a tube or contrivance for making liquid issue in drops : (*hort.*) a shoot that grows downward from a bulb and develops a new bulb : a setter or dog that drops to earth on sighting game : an artificial fly attached to the leader—a **drop'fly; dropp'ing**, that which is dropped : (in *pl.*) dung; **dropp'ing-well**, a spring where water falls in drops from

above; **dropp'le**, a trickle.—*adj.* **drop'-ripe**, so ripe as to be ready to drop from the tree.—*ns.* **drop'-scene**, a drop-curtain; **drop(ped)'-scone**, a scone made like a pancake; **drop'-stone**, a stalactitic calcite.—*adv.* **drop'wise**, by drops.— *n.* **drop'wort**, a species of spiraea (*S. Filipendula*) with bead-like root tubercles.—**a drop in the bucket**, a quantity infinitesimal in proportion; **drop a brick** (see **brick**); **drop a curtsy**, to curtsy; **drop astern** (*naut.*), to get left more and more behind; **drop away, off**, to depart, disappear; **drop down**, to sail, move, or row down a coast, or down a river to the sea; **drophead coupé**, one whose top can be opened; **drop in**, to come, fall, set, etc. in casually, unintentionally, or one by one; **drop off**, to fall asleep; **drop out**, to disappear from one's place : withdraw; **dropping fire**, unremitting irregular discharge of smallarms; **drop serene** (*Milt.*), an old medical name for amaurosis, literally translated from L. *gutta serēna*; **get the drop on one** (*U.S.*), to be ready to shoot first; hence to have at a disadvantage; (**Prince**) **Rupert's drops**, drops of glass that have fallen in a melted state into cold water, and have assumed a tadpole-like shape, the whole falling to dust with a loud report if the point of the tail be nipped off. [O.E. *dropa*, a drop, *dropian*, *droppian*, to drop; Du. *drop*, Ger. *tropfe*.]

dropsy, *drop'si*, *n.* a morbid accumulation of watery fluid in any part of the body.—*adjs.* **drop'sical**, **drop'sied** (*Shak.*), affected with dropsy. [Aphetic for **hydropsy**.]

Drosera, *dros'ə-rä*, *n.* the sundew genus of **Droserā'ceae**, a family of insectivorous plants.—*adj.* **droserā'ceous**. [Fem. of Gr. *droseros*, dewy—*drosos*, dew.]

droshky, *drosh'ki*, **drosky**, *dros'ki*, *n.* a low fourwheeled open carriage much used in Russia : a German four-wheeled cab. [Russ. *drozhki*.]

drosometer, *dros-om'i-tər*, *n.* an instrument for measuring dew. [Gr. *drosos*, dew, *metron*, measure.]

Drosophila, *dros-of'i-lä*, *n.* a genus of small yellow flies—fruit-flies—which breed in fermenting fruit juices and are utilised in experiments in heredity. [Gr. *drosos*, dew, moisture, *phileein*, to love.]

dross, *dros*, *n.* the scum of melting metals : waste matter : small or waste coal : refuse : rust : lucre.— *n.* **dross'iness.**—*adj.* **dross'y**, like dross : impure : worthless. [O.E. *drós*.]

drought, *drowt*, **drouth**, *drowth* (Scot. *drōōth*), *n.* dryness : want of rain or of water : a condition of atmosphere favourable to drying : thirst.—*ns.* **drought'iness, drouth'iness.**—*adjs.* **drought'y, drouth'y**, full of drought : very dry : wanting rain, thirsty. [O.E. *drúgath*, dryness—*drúgian*, to dry.]

drouk, drook, *drōōk*, *v.t.* (*Scot.*) to drench.—*n.* **drouk'ing, drook'ing.**—*adj.* **drouk'it, drook'it**. [Origin obscure; cf. O.N. *drukna*, to be drowned; Dan. *drukne*.]

drove, *drōv*, *pa.t.* of **drive**.—*n.* a number of cattle, or other animals, driven.—*n.* **drov'er**, one whose occupation is to drive cattle : (*Spens.*) a fishing boat, drifter; **drove'-road**, an old generally grassy track used or once used by droves of cattle. [O.E. *dráf*—*drífan*, to drive.]

drow, *drow*. See **troll**. [Possibly blended with O.N. *draugr*, dead man, ghost.]

drow, *drow*, *n.* (*Scot.*) a drizzling mist : a squall. [Origin obscure.]

drown, *drown*, *v.i.* to die of suffocation in liquid. —*v.t.* to kill by suffocation in liquid : to submerge : to flood : to extinguish : to make indistinguishable or imperceptible.—*adj.* **drownd'ed** (*Spens.*; now *illiterate*); **drowned.**—*n.* **drown'er.** —*n.* and *adj.* **drown'ing.** [M.E. *drounen*; origin obscure; the word used in O.E. was *druncnian*.]

drowse, *drowz*, *v.i.* to be heavy with sleep.—*v.t.* to make heavy with sleep : to stupefy : to pass in a half-sleeping state.—*n.* a half-sleeping state.— *ns.* **drows'ihe(a)d** (*Spens.*), drowsiness, sleepiness.—*adv.* **drows'ily.**—*n.* **drows'iness.**—*adj.* **drows'y**, sleepy : heavy : dull : inducing sleep. [Apparently O.E. *drúsian*, to be sluggish ; but not known between O.E. times and the 16th century.]

Neutral vowels in unaccented syllables : *el'ə-mənt, in'fənt, ran'dəm*

drub, *drub*, *v.t.* to beat or thrash: (*pr.p.* **drubb'ing**; *pa.t.* and *pa.p.* **drubbed**).—*n.* **drubb'ing**, a cudgelling. [Ar. *daraba*, to beat, bastinado— *darb*, a beating, has been suggested.]

drucken, *druk'ən* (*Scot.*) *adj.* drunken.—Used also as *pa.p.* of **drink**.—*n.* **druck'enness**. [O.N. *drukkinn*, pa.p. of *drekka*, to drink.]

drudge, *druj*, *v.i.* to do dull, laborious or very mean work.—*n.* one who does heavy monotonous work: a slave: a menial servant: dull task-work.— *ns.* **drudg'er**; **drudg'ery**, **drudg'ism**, the work of a drudge: uninteresting toil: hard or humble labour.—*adv.* **drudg'ingly**. [Ety. unknown; perh. from root of O.E. *dréogan*, to perform, undergo.]

drug, *drug*, *n.* any substance used in the composition of medicine: a substance used to stupefy or poison or for self-indulgence: an article that cannot be sold, generally owing to overproduction. —*v.t.* to mix or season with drugs: to administer a drug to: to dose to excess: to poison or stupefy with drugs.—*v.i.* to administer drugs or medicines: to take drugs, esp. narcotics, habitually:— (*pr.p.* **drugg'ing**; *pa.t.* and *pa.p.* **drugged**).—*ns.* **drug'-addict**, **drug'-fiend**, a habitual taker of drugs; **drugg'er** (*obs.*), a druggist: one who drugs; **drugg'ist**, one who deals in drugs; **drug'-store**, (*U.S.*) a chemist's shop (usually in America selling a variety of goods). [O.Fr. *drogue*, of uncertain origin.]

drug, *drug*, *n.* (*Shak.*) a form of **drudge**.

drugget, *drug'it*, *n.* a woven and felted coarse woollen fabric. [O.Fr. *droguet*.]

Druid, *drōō'id*, *n.* a priest among the ancient Celts of Britain, Gaul, and Germany: a member of a benefit society (founded 1781), its lodges called *groves*: an Eisteddfod official:—*fem.* **Dru'idess**. —*adjs.* **druid'ic**, **-al**.—*n.* **dru'idism**, the doctrines which the Druids taught: the ceremonies they practised.—**druidical circle**, a fanciful 18th-century name for a stone circle (not made by the Druids). [L. pl. *druidae*, from a Celtic stem *druid-*, whence O.Ir. *drai*, Ir. and Gael. *draoi*, magician.]

drum, *drum*, *n.* an instrument of percussion, a skin stretched on a frame: anything shaped like a drum: the tympanum of the ear: (*archit.*) the upright part of a cupola: a cylinder, esp. a revolving cylinder: a cylindrical barrel: (*Austr.*) a bundle: formerly, a large and tumultuous evening party (said to be so called because rival hostesses vied with each other in beating up crowds of guests): a drumfish.—*v.i.* to beat a drum: to beat rhythmically: (*U.S.*) to solicit orders.—*v.t.* to expel by beat of drum: to summon: to impress by iteration:—(*pr.p.* **drumm'ing**; *pa.t.* and *pa.p.* **drummed**).—*ns.* **drum'fish**, any fish of the *Sciaenidae;* **drum'fire**, massed artillery-fire with a rolling sound; **drum'head**, the head or skin of a drum: the top part of a capstan.—*adj.* (*mil.*) improvised in the field (see **court-martial**).— *ns.* **drum'-mā'jor**, the marching leader of a military band; **drumm'er**, one who drums: (*U.S.*) a commercial traveller: (*Austr.*) a bush tramp; **drum'stick**, the stick with which the drum is beaten: the tibia of a dressed fowl. [From a Gmc. root found in Du. *trom*, Ger. *trommel*, a drum; prob. imit.]

drum, *drum*, *n.* a ridge (in many place-names).— *n.* **drum'lin**, (*geol.*) a ridge formed under the ice-sheet of the Glacial Period (also **drum**). [Ir. and Gael. *druim*, back.]

drumble, *drum'bl*, *v.i.* (*Shak.*) to be sluggish.— *n.* **drum'bledor**, a dumbledore.

drumly, *drum'li*, *adj.* (*Scot.*) turbid, muddy: gloomy.

drummock, *drum'ək*. Same as **drammock**.

Drummond-light, *drum'ənd-līt*, *n.* the lime-light or oxy-hydrogen light invented by Captain T. Drummond (1797-1840).

drunk, *drungk*, *pa.p.* and old-fashioned *pa.t.* of **drink**.—*adj.* intoxicated: saturated.—*n.* a drunken bout: a drunk person.—*n.* **drunk'ard**, one who frequently drinks to excess: a habitual drinker.— *adj.* **drunk'en**, given to excessive drinking: worthless, besotted: resulting from intoxication:—

(sometimes) drunk.—*adv.* **drunk'enly**.—*n.* **drunk'enness**, intoxication: habitual intoxication.

drupe, *drōōp*, *n.* a fleshy fruit with a stone.—*adj.* **drupā'ceous**, producing or pertaining to drupes or stone-fruits.—*n.* **drup'el**, **drupe'let**, a little drupe, forming part of a fruit, as in the raspberry. [L. *drūpa*—Gr. *dryppā*, an olive.]

druse, *drōōz*, *n.* a rock cavity lined with crystals— by geologists usu. called a drusy cavity.—*adj.* **dru'sy**, rough with, composed of, minute crystals: miarolitic. [Ger. *druse*—Czech. *druza*, a piece of crystallised ore.]

druxy, *druk'si*, *adj.* of timber, having decayed spots concealed by healthy wood.—Also **drick'sie**. [Origin unknown.]

Druz, Druze, Druse, *drōōz*, *n.* one of a remarkable people inhabiting chiefly a mountainous district in the south of Syria, with a peculiar religion interwoven from the Bible and the Koran.—*adj.* **Drus'ian**. [Perh. from *Darazi*, an early exponent of the religion.]

dry, *drī*, *adj.* without water or liquid, contained or adhering: free from, or deficient in, moisture, sap, rain: thirsty: out of water: failing to yield water, or milk, or other liquid: of a fruit, not fleshy: not green: unbuttered: not drawing blood: of wines, etc., free from sweetness and fruity flavour: legally forbidding the liquor trade: enforcing or subjected to prohibition: uninteresting: frigid, precise, formal: of humour, quiet, restrained, and unobtrusive: of manner, distantly unsympathetic (*comp.* **drī'er**; *superl.* **drī'est**).—*v.t.* to free from or exhaust of water or moisture.—*v.i.* to become dry: to evaporate entirely: (*pr.p.* **dry'ing**; *pa.t.* and *pa.p.* **dried**; *3rd pers. sing. pr.t.* **dries**).—*n.* a prohibitionist.—*n.* **drī'er**, **dry'er**, one who or that which dries: a machine for extracting moisture from cloth, grain, etc.: a drying agent for oils, paint, etc.—*adv.* **drī'ly**, **dry'ly**, in a dry manner.—*n.* **Dry'asdust**, a character in the prefatory matter of some of Scott's novels: a dull, pedantic, learned person.—Also *adj.*—*v.t.* **dry'-beat** (*Shak.*), to drub, but without shedding blood.—*ns.* **dry'-bi'ble**, a disease of horned cattle in which the third stomach, or bible, is very dry; **dry'-bob**, at Eton a boy who plays cricket, football, etc.—opp. to the *wet-bob*, who rows.—*v.t.* **dry'-clean**, to clean without using water.—*ns.* **dry'-cell**, an electric cell in which the electrolyte is not a liquid but a paste (as a refill for an electric torch); **dry'-cupping**, application of cups without previous scarification; **dry'-dock**, a dock that can be emptied of water: a graving dock.—*v.t.* to put in dry-dock.—*n.* **dry'er**, another spelling of **drier**.—*adj.* **dry'-eyed**, tearless.—*n.* **dry'-fist**, a niggard.—*adj.* and *adv.* **dry-fist'ed**, taking payment for gains and owing for losses.—*adj.* **dry'-fly** (of fishing), without sinking the fly in the water.—*adv.* **dry'-foot** (*Shak.*), by scent of the foot alone.—*n.pl.* **dry'-goods**, drapery and the like, distinguished from groceries, hardware, etc.—*n.* and *adj.* **dry'ing**.—*adj.* **dry'ish**.—*adv.* **dry'ly**, another spelling of **drily**.—*ns.* **dry'ness**; **dry'-nurse**, a nurse who does not suckle.—Also *v.t.*—*ns.* **dry'-plate**, a sensitised photographic plate, with which a picture may be made without the preliminary use of a bath; **dry'-point**, a sharp needle by which fine lines are drawn in copper-plate engraving: a plate or impression produced with it; **dry'-rot**, a decay of timber caused by *Merulius lacrymans* and other fungi which reduce it ultimately to a dry, brittle mass: (*fig.*) a concealed decay or degeneration.—*v.t.* **dry'-salt**, to cure (meat) by salting and drying.—*ns.* **dry'-salter**, a dealer in gums, dyes, etc.: or (*obs.*) in salted or dry meats, pickles, etc.: **dry'saltery**.— *adj.* and *adv.* **dry'-shod**, without wetting the shoes or feet.—*adj.* **dry'-stone**, built of stone without mortar, as some walls.—*ns.* **dry'-stove**, a kind of hot-house with dry heat; **dry'-wall'er**, one who builds walls without mortar; **dry'-wash'**, the bed of an intermittent stream.—**cut and dried** (see **cut**); **dry farming**, a system of tillage in dry countries, surface soil being kept constantly loose, so as to retain scanty rains and reduce evaporation; **dry land**, land as opposed to sea; **dry light**, an undeceptive light : an unprejudiced view; **dry mass, service**, *Missa sicca*, a rite in which there is neither consecration nor communion; **dry measure**, a system of measure by bulk, used for grain, etc. (see **bushel, peck, pint**); **dry steam**, steam unmixed with liquid drops; **dry up**, to dry thoroughly or completely : (*slang*) to stop talking; **go dry**, to adopt liquor prohibition; **high and dry** (see **high**). [O.E. *drȳge*; cf. Du. *droog*, Ger. *trocken*.]

dryad, drī′ad, *-ad*, *n.* a wood nymph : a foresttree :—*pls.* dry′ads, **-adēs**. [Gr. *drȳas*, *-ados*, from *drȳs*, oak, tree.]

dso, dsobo, dsomo. See under **zho**.

dual, dū′al, *adj.* two-fold : consisting of two : (*gram.*) expressing or representing two things.— *n.* a grammatical form indicating duality : a word in the dual number.—*ns.* **dū′ad**, a dyad; **dū′alin**, an explosive mixture of sawdust, saltpetre, and nitroglycerine; **dū′alism** (*philos.*), that view which seeks to explain the world by the assumption of two radically independent and absolute elements— e.g. (1) the doctrine of the entire separation of spirit and matter, thus being opposed both to *idealism* and to *materialism;* (2) the doctrine of two distinct principles of good and evil, or of two distinct divine beings of these characters; **du′alist**, a believer in dualism.—*adj.* **dualis′tic**, consisting of two : relating to dualism.—*ns.* **duality** (*dū-al′i-ti*), doubleness : state of being double; **du′archy**, a faulty form for **diarchy**.—**dual control**, joint control or jurisdiction; **dual monarchy**, two (more or less) independent states with one and the same monarch : (*spec.*) Austria-Hungary (before 1918); **dual school**, one for both boys and girls. [L. *duālis—duo*, two.]

duan, dōō′an, *n.* a division of a poem, canto. [Gael.]

duar, dōō′ar, *n.* a circular Arab encampment or tent village.—Also **douar, dowar**. [Ar. *dūār*.]

dub, *dub*, *v.t.* to confer knighthood upon, from the ceremony of striking the shoulder with the flat of a sword : to confer any name or dignity upon : to smooth with an adze : to trim : to cut the comb and wattles from : to rub a softening and waterproof mixture into, as leather : to dress (a fly) for fishing :—(*pr.p.* **dubb′ing**; *pa.p.* **dubbed**). —*n.* **dubb′ing**, the accolade : (also **dubb′in**) a preparation of grease for softening leather. [O.E. *dubbian*, to dub knight.]

dub, *dub*, *n.* (*Scot.*) a pool of foul water : a puddle. [Cf. L.G. *dobbe.*]

dub, *dub*, *v.t.* to give (a film) a new sound-track, e.g. one in a different language : to add sound effects or music. [Abbrev. of **double**.]

dubious, dū′bi-əs, *adj.* doubtful : undetermined : causing doubt : of uncertain event or issue.— *n.* **dūbiety** (*-bī′i-ti*), doubt.—*adv.* **dū′biously**.— *ns.* **dūbios′ity, dū′biousness**. [L. *dubius*.]

dubitate, dū′bi-tāt, *v.i.* to doubt, hesitate.—*adj.* **dū′bitable**.—*ns.* **dū′bitancy, dūbitā′tion**.—*adj.* **dū′bitative**.—*adv.* **dū′bitatively**. [L. *dubitāre, -ātum.*]

ducal, dū′kəl, *adj.* pertaining to a duke.—*adv.* **dū′cally**. [Fr.,—L.L. *ducālis*—L. *dux*, leader.]

ducat, *duk′ət*, *n.* a gold coin formerly much used on the Continent, its commonest value being about 9s. 4d., though there were silver ducats in Italy worth 3s. 4d.—*n.* **ducatoon′**, an old silver coin in Venice and elsewhere, worth 5 to 6 shillings. [O.Fr. *ducat*—It. *ducato*—L.L. *ducātus*, a duchy.]

ducdame, *dook′da-mi, dook-dā′mi, interj.* (*Shak., As You Like It*) perh. a meaningless refrain : explained as L. *duc ad mē*, bring to me, as Welsh *dewch 'da mi*, come with me, as Romany *dukrā′mē*, I tell fortunes, etc.

duce, dōō′chā, *n.* the title assumed by the Italian dictator Mussolini. [It., leader—L. *dux*.]

duchy, *duch′i*, *n.* the territory of a duke, a dukedom.—*ns.* **duch′ess**, the consort or widow of a duke : a woman of the same rank as a duke in her own right; **duchesse** (*duch′es, dū-shes′;* Fr., duchess), a table-cover or centre-piece.—Also **duchesse cover.—duchesse lace**, Flemish pillow lace with designs in cord outline; **duchesse set**, a set of covers for a dressing table; **duch′y court**, the court of a duchy. [O.Fr. *duché*—L.L. *ducātus;* Fr. *duchesse*—L.L. *ducissa*.]

duck, *duk*, *n.* a kind of coarse cloth for small sails, sacking, etc. : (in *pl.*) garments made of duck. [Du. *doeck*, linen cloth; Ger. *tuch*.]

duck, *duk*, *v.t.* to dip for a moment in water.—*v.i.* to dip or dive : to lower the head suddenly : to cringe, yield.—*n.* a quick plunge, dip : a quick lowering of the head or body, a jerky bow.—*ns.* **duck′er**, one who ducks : a diving-bird; **duck′ing**; **duck′ing-pond** : **duck′ing-stool**, a stool or chair in which offenders were formerly tied and ducked in the water. [M.E. *douken* from an assumed O.E. *dūcan*, to duck, dive; Ger. *tauchen*, Du. *duiken*.]

duck, *duk*, *n.* any bird of the family Anatidae, the prominent marks of which are short webbed feet, with a small hind-toe not reaching the ground, the netted scales in front of the lower leg, and the long bill : the female duck as distinguished from the male **drake** : in cricket (originally **duck's egg**), the zero (O), which records in a scoring-sheet that a player made no runs : (*coll.*) a darling, sweetheart : a defaulter, bankrupt.—*ns.* **duck′-ant**, a Jamaican termite nesting in trees; **duck′bill**, an aquatic burrowing and egg-laying Australian monotreme (Ornithorhynchus), with broadly webbed feet, and duck-like bill.—*adj.* **duck′-billed**, having a bill like a duck.—*ns.* **duck′-board**, planking for swampy ground, trenches, etc.; **duck′-hawk**, the moor-buzzard or marsh-harrier : the U.S. peregrine falcon; **duck′ing**, duckhunting.—*adj.* **duck′-legged**, short-legged.—*ns.* **duck′ling**, a young duck; **duck′mole**, the duckbill; **duck′pond**; **duck′s-foot**, lady's mantle; **duck′-shot**, shot for shooting wild-duck; **duck′s meat**, duckweed; **duck′weed**, any plant of the family Lemnaceae, monocotyledons consisting of a small flat green floating plate, from which a root dangles; **duck′y**, a colloquial endearment.— Also *adj.*—**Bombay duck**, bummalo; **wild′- duck**, the mallard, esp. the hen-bird.—**break one's duck** (*cricket*), to make one's first run (see above); **lame duck**, a defaulter : bankrupt : anything disabled; **like a dying duck**, languishing; **make, play, ducks and drakes**, to make flat stones skip on the surface of water : to use recklessly : squander, waste (with *with, of*). [O.E. *dúce* (or *duce?*), a duck; cf. **duck** (2).]

duct, *dukt*, *n.* a tube conveying fluids in animal bodies or plants : a pipe for an electric cable : an air-passage.—*adj.* **duct′less.—ductless glands**, masses of glandular tissue that lack ducts and discharge their products directly into the blood. [L. *ductus—dūcěre*, to lead.]

ductile, *duk′til, -tīl, adj.* easily led : yielding : capable of being drawn out into threads.—*n.* **ductility** (*-til′*), capacity of being drawn out without breaking. [Fr.,—L. *ductilis—dūcere*, to lead.]

dud, *dud*, *n.* (*coll.*) in *pl.* poor or ragged clothes, tatters.—*n.* **dudd′ery**, a shop where old clothes are sold : rags collectively.—*adj.* **dudd′y**, ragged. [There is a M.E. *dudde*, birrus, a cloak; cf. O.N. *duthi*, swaddling-clothes.]

dud, *dud*, *n.* (*slang*) a bomb or projectile that fails to go off : a dishonoured cheque : a counterfeit : any person or thing useless or ineffective : a failure. —Also *adj.* [Origin unknown.]

dudder, *dud′ər*, *n.* (*prov.*) confusion. [Cf. **dither**.]

dude, *dūd, dōōd, n.* (*slang*, orig. *Amer.*), a fop or dandy, esp. remarkable for the exquisite make and quality of his clothes.—*adj.* **du′dish**.—*n.* **du′dism**. [Origin unknown.]

dudeen, *dōō-dēn′, -dhēn′, n.* a short clay tobaccopipe. [Ir. *dúidín*, dim. of *dúd*, pipe.]

dudgeon, *duj′ən, n.* resentment : offended indignation. [Origin unknown.]

dudgeon, *duj′ən, n.* the haft of a dagger : a small dagger. [Anglo-Fr. *digeon*, knife-handle.]

due, *dū, adj.* owed : that ought to be paid or done to another : proper : appointed, under engagement to be ready, arrive, etc.—*adv.* **exactly** :

directly.—*n.* that which is owed : what one has a right to : perquisite : fee, toll, charge, or tribute : (in *pl.*) subscription to a club or society.—*adj.* **due′ful, dewfull** (*Spens.*), proper, fit.—**due to,** caused by : (wrongly) owing to, because of ; **give the devil his due,** to give a fair hearing or fair-play to one of notorious character ; **in due course,** in the ordinary way when the time comes. [O.Fr. *deü,* pa.p. of *devoir*—L. *debēre,* to owe.]

due, *dū, v.t.* (*Shak.*) to endue.

duel, *dū′əl, n.* a combat between two persons, pre-arranged and fought under fixed conditions, generally on an affair of honour : single combat to decide a quarrel : any fight or struggle between two parties.—*v.i.* to fight in a duel :—(*pr.p.* **dū′elling** ; *pa.t.* and *pa.p.* **dū′elled**).—*ns.* **dū′eller** ; **dū′elling** ; **dū′ellist** ; **duello** (*doo-el′lō ;* It.), a duel : the laws which regulate duelling.—*adj.* **dū′elsome,** given to duelling. [It. *duello*—L. *duellum,* the original form of *bellum*—*duo,* two.]

duenna, *dū-en′ä, n.* an old lady who acts the part of governess in Spain : an old lady who watches over or chaperons a younger. [Sp. *dueña,* a form of *doña,* mistress—L. *domina,* fem. of *dominus,* lord.]

duet, duett, *dū-et′,* **duetto,** *doo-et′tō, n.* a composition in music for two performers.—*ns.* **duettino** (*-tē′nō*), a simple duet ; **duett′ist** (*dū-*). [It. *duetto,* dim. of *duo*—*due,* two—L. *duo.*]

duff, *duf, n.* dough : a stiff flour pudding boiled in a bag : decaying vegetable matter, fallen leaves : coal-dust. [A form of **dough.**]

duff, *duf, v.t.* to make to look new : to alter brands on (stolen cattle). [Perh. a back-formation from **duffer** (2).]

duff, *duf, v.t.* (*golf*) to play amiss by hitting the ground behind the ball. [Back-formation from **duffer** (1).]

duffel, *duf′l, n.* a thick, coarse woollen cloth, with a thick nap—also **duff′le:** (*U.S.*) sporting or camping kit. [Du., from *Duffel,* a town near Antwerp.]

duffer, *duf′ər, n.* an unskilful person : a fogy, useless old fellow : a counterfeit coin : an unproductive mine.—*ns.* **duff′erdom, duff′erism.** [Origin unknown.]

duffer, *duf′ər, n.* a peddler of sham jewellery, etc. : one who fakes up sham articles or duffs cattle. [Origin unknown : thieves' slang.]

dug, *dug, n.* a nipple or udder of a cow or other beast. [Cf. Sw. *dægga,* Dan. *dægge,* to suckle.]

dug, *dug, pa.t.* and *pa.p.* of **dig.**—*n.* **dug′out,** a boat made by hollowing out the trunk of a tree : a rough dwelling or shelter dug out of a slope or bank or in a trench : a superannuated person brought back to employment.

dugong, *doo′gong, n.* a herbivorous marine mammal of the order Sirenia—the supposed original of the mermaid. [Malayan *dūyong.*]

duiker, duyker, *dī′kər, n.* a small S. African antelope : (*S.Afr.*), a cormorant. [Du., diver, from plunging into the bush, or into the sea.]

duke, *dūk, n.* a sovereign prince of a small state : a nobleman of the highest order : (*B.*) a chief : (*slang*) the fist.—*v.t.* (with *it*) to play the duke.—*ns.* **duke′dom,** the title, rank, or territories of a duke ; **duke′ling,** a petty duke ; **duk′ery,** a duke's territory or ducal seat ; **duke′ship.**—**the Dukeries,** a group of ducal seats in Nottinghamshire. [O.Fr. *duc*—L. *dux, ducis,* a leader—*dūcĕre,* to lead.]

Dukhobor, Doukhobor, *doo′hhō-bor, doo′kō-bor, n.* a member of a Russian sect who trust to an inner light, reject the doctrine of the Trinity, and refuse military service, many of them settled in Canada since 1899 :—*pl.* **D(o)ukhobors, Dukhobort′sy.** [Russ. *Dukhoborets*—*dukhu,* spirit, *boroti,* to fight.]

dukkeripen, *dook-ə-rip′ən, n.* fortune-telling. [Romany *drukeriben.*]

dulcamara, *dul-kä-mä′rä, n.* the bittersweet. [L. *dulcis,* sweet, *amāra* (fem.) bitter.]

dulcet, *duls′it, adj.* sweet : melodious, harmonious.—*n.* **dulciana** (*dul-si-ä′nä*), an open diapason organ stop of pleasing tone and small scale ; **dulcifica′tion.**—*adj.* **dulcif′luous,** flowing sweet-

ly.—*v.t.* **dul′cify,** to make sweet.—*ns.* **dulcil′oquy,** a soft manner of speaking ; **dul′cite, dul′citol, dul′cose** (*-kōs*), a saccharine substance derived from various plants—in its crude form, *Madagascar manna ;* **dul′citone,** a tuning-fork piano ; **dul′-citude,** a sweetness.—**dulcified spirit,** a compound of alcohol with mineral acid. [L. *dulcis,* sweet.]

dulcimer, *dul′si-mər, n.* a musical instrument like a flat box, with sounding-board and wires stretched across bridges : a Jewish musical instrument, probably a bagpipe. [Sp. *dulcemele*—L. *dulce melos,* a sweet song—*dulcis,* sweet, Gr. *melos,* a song.]

Dulcinea, *dul-sin-ē′ä, dul-sin′i-ä, n.* sweetheart. [From *Dulcinea* del Toboso, the name given by Don Quixote to the mistress of his imagination.]

dule, *dūl, n.* (*Scot.*) woe.—*n.* **dule′-tree,** the gallows. [See **dole.**]

dulia, douleia, *d(y)oo-lī′ä, n.* (*R.C. Church*) that inferior veneration accorded to saints and angels.—*ns.* **d(o)uloc′racy,** government by slaves ; **dulō′sis,** enslavement, practised by certain ants upon other kinds.—*adjs.* **dulot′ic.** [Gr. *douleiā,* servitude, *doulōsis,* enslavement—*doulos,* a slave.]

dull, *dul, adj.* slow of learning, or of understanding: wanting in keenness of hearing or other sense : insensible : without life or spirit : uninteresting : slow of motion : drowsy : sleepy : sad : downcast : cheerless : lacking brightness or clearness : cloudy : dim, obscure : obtuse : blunt.—*v.t.* to make dull or stupid : to blunt : to damp : to cloud.—*v.i.* to become dull.—*n.* **dull′ard,** a dull and stupid person : a dunce.—*adjs.* **dull′-brained** (*Shak.*), **dull′-browed ; dull′-eyed** (*Shak.*); **dull′ish.**—*ns.* **dull′ness, dul′ness,** the state or quality of being dull.—*adjs.* **dull′-sighted ; dull′-witted ; dull′y,** somewhat dull.—*adv.* **dully** (*dul′li*). [Related to O.E. *dol,* foolish, and *dwellan,* to err ; Du. *dol,* Ger. *toll,* mad.]

dulse, *duls, n.* an edible red seaweed, esp. *Rhodymenia palmata.* [Gael. *duileasg,* poss.—*duille,* a leaf, *uisge,* water.]

duly, *dū′li, adv.* properly : fitly : at the proper time. [See **due.**]

duma, douma, *doo′mä, n.* an elected council, esp. the Russian parliament of 1906-17.—*n.* **dum′aist,** a duma member. [Russ. *duma,* of Gmc. origin ; cf. **doom.**]

dumb, *dum, adj.* without the power of speech: silent : soundless : (*U.S.* after Ger. or Du.) stupid. —*v.t.* (*Shak.*) to render dumb.—*n.* **dumb′-bell,** a double-headed weight swung in the hands to develop the muscles : any object or figure of the same shape : (*U.S.*) a stupid person.—*n.* **dumb′-cane,** a tropical American araceous plant (*Dieffenbachia Seguine*) whose acrid juice swells the tongue. —*adv.* **dumb′ly,** in silence : mutely.—*ns.* **dumb′-ness ; dumb′-pia′no,** a soundless keyboard for piano practice ; **dumb′-show,** gesture without words : pantomime ; **dumb′-wait′er,** a movable platform used for conveying food, dishes, etc., at meals : a stand with revolving top for holding dessert, etc. : (*U.S.*) a lift for food and dishes.—*vs.t.* **dum(b)found′, -er,** to strike dumb : to confuse greatly : to astonish.—*ns.* **dumm′erer** (*old slang*), a dumb person, esp. a rogue who feigns dumbness ; **dumb′iness ; dumm′y,** one who is dumb : a mere tool, man of straw : a block or lay-figure : a sham or counterfeit article taking the place of a real one : an unprinted model of a book : a rubber teat : an exposed hand of cards : a game in which a hand is exposed : the imaginary player of such a game : (*Rugby football*) a feint of passing.—**strike dumb,** to silence with astonishment. [O.E. *dumb ;* Ger. *dumm,* stupid, Du. *dom.*]

dumbledore, *dum′bl-dōr, n.* (*prov.*) the bumble-bee : the brown cockchafer.

dumdum, *dum′dum, n.* a soft-nosed expanding bullet, first made at *Dum Dum* near Calcutta.— **dumdum fever,** kala-azar.

dumka, *doom′kä, n.* (*mus.*) a lament : a slow movement or piece. [Ukrainian.]

dummy. See **dumb.**

dumose, *dū′mōs*, *adj.* bushy—also **dū′mous.**—*n.* **dumŏs′ity.** [L. *dūmus*, a thorn-bush.]

dump, *dump*, *v.t.* to set down heavily or with a thump : to unload : (*pol. econ.*) to land and sell at prices below cost of production in the exporting country—or (according to some) in the importing country.—*n.* a thud : a place for the discharge of loads, or for rubbish : a deposit : (*mil.*) store. [Cf. Dan. *dumpe*, Norw. *dumpa*, to fall plump.]

dump, *dump*, *n.* dullness or gloominess of mind, ill-humour, low spirits—now only used in the pl. : an obsolete slow dance or dance-tune in 4-4 time : (*Shak.*) a melancholy strain : any tune.— *adj.* **dump′ish**, depressed in spirits.—*adv.* **dump′-ishly.**—*n.* **dump′ishness.** [Prob. related to O.Du. *domp*, mist; or Ger. *dumpf*, gloomy.]

dump, *dump*, *n.* a deep hole in a river-bed, a pool. [Prob. Norw. *dump*, pit.]

dump, *dump*, *n.* a short thick person or thing : a marble : a counter : a small coin : (in pl.) money (*slang*). [Perh. a back-formation from **dumpy.**]

dum-palm. Same as **doum-palm.**

dumpling, *dump′ling*, *n.* a kind of thick pudding or mass of paste : a dumpling-shaped person or animal. [Origin obscure.]

dumpy, *dump′i*, *adj.* short and thick.—*n.* a dumpy person or animal, esp. one of a breed of very short-legged fowls : a short umbrella.—*n.* **dump′i-ness.**—*v.t.* **dump′le**, to make or cook, as a dumpling: to round into a dumpy shape.—*n.* **dump′y-lev′el**, a surveyor's level with rigid connexion of the telescope to the vertical spindle. [Origin unknown.]

dun, *dun*, *adj.* greyish brown : mouse-coloured : dingy : dusky.—*v.t.* (*U.S.*) to cure and brown, as cod.—*v.i.* to become dun-coloured.—*ns.* **dun′-bird**, the pochard, esp. the hen-bird; **dun′-cow**, the shagreen ray; **dun′-div′er**, the merganser; **dun′-fish**, codfish cured by dunning; **dunn′ing.** —*adj.* **dunn′ish**, somewhat dun. [O.E. *dun*, most prob. Celt.; W. *dwn*, dusky, Gael. *donn*, brown.]

dun, *dun*, *v.t.* to importune for payment :—(*pr.p.* **dunn′ing**; *pa.t.* and *pa.p.* **dunned**).—*n.* one who duns : a demand for payment. [Perh. allied to **din.**]

dun, *dun*, *n.* a hill : a fortified mound. [Celt.; in many place-names; adopted in O.E. as *dún;* see **down.**]

dunce, *duns*, *n.* one slow at learning : a stupid person.—*ns.* **dunce′dom**, the class of dunces; **dun′cery**, stupidity; **Dun′ciad**, Pope's epic of dunces. [*Duns* Scotus (died 1308), the Subtle Doctor, leader of the schoolmen, from him called *Dunses*, who opposed classical studies on the revival of learning—hence any opposer of learning, a blockhead.]

dunch, *dunsh*, *v.t.* (*Scot.*) to jog, nudge, bump : to butt.—Also *n.* [Ety. doubtful.]

dunder, *dun′dər*, *n.* lees, dregs of sugar-cane juice. [Sp. *redundar*, to overflow.]

dunderfunk, *dun′dər-fungk*, *n.* ship-biscuit, soaked in water, mixed with fat and molasses, and baked in a pan.—Also **dan′dyfunk.**

dunderhead, *dun′dər-hed*, *n.* a stupid person— also **dun′derpate.**—*adj.* **dun′derheaded.**—*n.* **dun′derheadism.** [Origin unknown.]

Dundreary, *dun-drēr′i*, *adj.* like Lord *Dundreary*, in Tom Taylor's *Our American Cousin*—in Sothern's creation of the part, a lisping and brainless dandy, wearing long side-whiskers.

dune, *dūn*, *n.* a low hill of sand esp. on the seashore. [French,—O.Du. *duna:* cf. **down.**]

dung, *dung*, *n.* excrement : manure.—*v.t.* to manure with dung.—*v.i.* to void excrement.—*ns.* **dung′-bee′tle**, the dor-beetle : a scarabaeoid beetle generally; **dung′-cart**; **dung′-fork**, a fork used for moving stable manure; **dung′-heap, dung′hill**, a heap of dung : any mean situation; **dung′-hunt′er**, a skua; **dung′mere**, a manure-pit.—*adj.* **dung′y.** [O.E. *dung;* cf. Dan. *dynge*, a heap; Ger. *dung*.]

dungaree, *dung-gə-rē′*, or *dung′*, *n.* a coarse Indian calico : (pl.) overalls made of it. [Hind. *dungrī*.]

dungeon, *dun′jən*, *n.* (*orig.*) the principal tower of a castle : a close, dark prison : a cell under ground. —*v.t.* to confine in a dungeon.—*n.* **dun′geoner, a** gaoler. [O.Fr. *donjon*—L.L. *domniō*, *-ōnis*—L. *dominus*, a lord.]

duniewassal, dunniewassal, duniwassal, *dōōn-i-wos′l*, *n.* a Highland gentleman of inferior rank. [Gael. *duine*, man, *uasal*, gentle.]

dunite, *dun′īt*, *n.* a crystalline rock composed almost entirely of olivine. [*Dun* Mountain, near Nelson, in New Zealand.]

dunk, *dungk*, *v.t.* and *v.i.* (*U.S.*) to dip cake, etc., that one is eating in one's coffee or other beverage. [Ger. *tunken*, to dip; cf. **Dunker.**]

Dunker, *dungk′ər*, *n.* a member of a sect of German-American Baptists who practise triple immersion. —Also **tunk′er.** [Ger., dipper.]

dunlin, *dun′lin*, *n.* the red-backed sandpiper. [Dim. of **dun.**]

Dunlop, *dun-lop′*, *n.* a rich cheese made of un-skimmed milk—from *Dunlop* in Ayrshire.

dunnage, *dun′ij*, *n.* loose wood of any kind laid in the bottom of the hold to keep the cargo out of the bilge-water, or wedged between parts of the cargo to keep them steady : sailor's baggage. [Ety. unknown.]

dunnock, *dun′ək*, *n.* the hedge-sparrow. [Dim. of **dun.**]

dunny, *dun′i*, *adj.* (*prov.*) deaf. [Origin obscure.]

Dunstable, *dun′stə-bl*, *n.* a kind of straw-plait, first made at *Dunstable* in Bedfordshire : a straw hat, etc. :—**Dunstable road, highway**, anything plain and direct.

dunt, *dunt*, *n.* (*Scots.*) a thump, the wound made thereby.—*v.t.* to thump, beat. [See **dint.**]

dunt, *dunt*, *n.* (*prov.*) gid or sturdy in sheep, etc. [Origin obscure.]

duo, *dōō′ō, dū′ō*, *n.* a duet. [It.—L. *duo*, two.]

duodecennial, *dū-ō-di-sen′yəl*, *adj.* occurring every twelve years. [L. *duodecim*, twelve, *annus*, year.]

duodecimal, *dū-ō-des′i-ml*, *adj.* computed by twelves: twelfth : (in *pl.*) a method of calculating the area of a rectangle when the length and breadth are stated in feet and inches.—**duo-decimal system**, a system of numbers in which each denomination is twelve times the next, in-stead of ten times, as in ordinary (decimal) arith-metic: the name given to the division of unity into twelve equal parts. [L. *duodecim*, twelve—*duo*, two, and *decem*, ten.]

duodecimo, *dū-ō-des′i-mō*, *adj.* formed of sheets folded so as to make twelve leaves.—*n.* a book of such sheets—usually written 12mo. [L. in *duodecimō*, in twelfth (abl. of *duodecimus*, twelfth) —*duo*, two, *decem*, ten.]

duodenary, *dū-ō-dē′nə-ri*, *adj.* relating to twelve, twelvefold. [L. *duodēnārius*.]

duodenum, *dū-ō-dē′nəm*, *n.* the first portion of the small intestines, so called because about twelve fingers′-breadth in length :—*pl.* **duodē′na.**—*adj.* **duodē′nal.**—*ns.* **duodēnec′tomy**, excision of the duodenum; **duodēni′tis**, inflammation of the duodenum. [Formed from L. *duodēnī*, twelve each.]

duologue, *dū′ō-log*, *n.* a piece spoken between two. [Irregularly formed from L. *duo* (or Gr. *dyo*) two, Gr. *logos*, discourse.]

duomo, *dwō′mō*, *n.* a cathedral. [It. See **dome.**]

dup, *dup*, *v.t.* (*Shak.*) to undo, open. [do up; cf. **don** and **doff.**]

dupe, *dūp*, *n.* one who is cheated.—*v.t.* to deceive : to trick.—*n.* **dūpabil′ity.**—*adj.* **dū′pable.**—*ns.* **dū′per, dū′pery**, the art of deceiving others. [Fr. *dupe;* of uncertain origin.]

duple, *dū′pl*, *adj.* double, twofold : (*mus.*) having two beats in the bar.—*n.* **dū′plet**, a like throw of two dice : a pair of electrons forming a single bond between two atoms. [L. *duplus;* cf. **double.**]

duplex, *dū′pleks*, *adj.* twofold, double : having some part doubled : communicating in both directions at the same time.—*n.* **duplicity** (*dū-plis′i-ti*), doubleness, esp. in conduct and inten-tion: insincerity : double-dealing. [L. *duplex*, *-icis*.]

duplicate, dū′pli-kit, *adj*. double : twofold : like, equivalent or alternative.—*n*. another (esp. subsidiary or spare) thing of the same kind : a copy or transcript : the condition of being in two copies.—*v.t.* (-kāt) to double : to copy : to fold.—*ns*. **dūpli-cand′** (*Scots law*), double feu-duty, due on certain occasions ; **dūplicā′tion**.—*adj*. **dū′plicative**.—*ns*. **dū′plicātor**, a copying apparatus ; **dū′plicāture**, a doubling : anything doubled : the fold of a membrane ; **dūplȳ′**, a second reply in Scots law.—*v.t.* to say in duply.—**in duplicate**, in two copies, or original accompanied by a copy ; **duplicate ratio**, ratio of the squares of the quantities ; **duplication of the cube**, the problem eagerly discussed by the early Greek geometers, of constructing a cube equal to twice a given cube, impossible by use of straight line and circle only, but soluble by means of other curves. [L. *duplicāre*, *-ātum*, *duo*, two, *plicāre*, to fold.]

duppy, dup′i, *n*. a ghost. [West Indian negro word.]

dura. See **durra.**

durable, dūr′ə-bl, *adj*. able to last or endure : hardy : permanent.—*ns*. **durabil′ity**, **dur′ableness**.—*adv*. **dur′ably.**—*ns*. **dur′ance** (*obs*.), continuance : durability : (*obs*.) a durable cloth : imprisonment ; **dur′ant**, a strong cloth in imitation of buff-leather ; **durā′tion**, continuance in time : time indefinitely : power of continuance : length of time.—**for the duration** (*coll*.), as long as the war continues. [L. *dūrāre*, to harden, endure, last.]

duraluminium, dūr-al-ūm-in′i-əm, *n*. an aluminium alloy.—Also **dural′umin.** [L. *dūrus*, hard, and **aluminium.**]

dura mater, dū′rā mā′tər, L. dōō′rā mā′ter, *n*. the exterior membrane of the brain and spinal column distinguished from the other two, the arachnoid and the pia mater. [L. *dūra māter*, hard mother, a translation of the Ar. name.]

duramen, dū-rā′mən, *n*. heartwood. [L. *dūrāmen*, hardness—*dūrus*, hard.]

durbar, dur′bär, *n*. an audience-chamber : a reception or levee : a court : the body of officials at an Indian court. [Pers. *darbār*, a prince's court, lit. a door of admittance.]

durdum. Same as **dirdum.**

dure, dūr, *v.i.* (*obs*.) to endure, last or continue.—*adj*. **dure′ful** (*Spens*.), enduring, lasting. [Fr. *durer*—L. *dūrāre*—*dūrus*, hard.]

duress, duresse, dūr′es, or dūr-es′, *n*. constraint : imprisonment : constraint illegally exercised to force a person to perform some act. [O.Fr. *duresse*—L. *dūritia*—*dūrus*, hard.]

durgan, dur′gən, *n*. a dwarf, any undersized creature.—*adj*. **dur′gy.** [Related to **dwarf.**]

Durham, dur′əm, *n*. one of a particular breed of shorthorned cattle—from the English county.

durian, dōō′ri-ən, or dū′, *n*. a lofty Indian and Malayan bombacaceous fruit-tree (*Durio Zibethinus*), with leaves like a cherry's : its large fruit, with hard rind and pulp of foul smell but fine flavour.—Also **du′rion.** [Malay *dūrī*, thorn.]

during, dū′ring, *prep*. throughout the time of : in the course of. [Orig. *pr.p.* of **dure.**]

durmast, dur′mäst, *n*. a variety of sessile-fruited oak with leaves downy below. (*Quercus lanuginosa*.) [Origin unknown : perhaps a blunder for *dun mast*.]

durn, durn, *n*. (*prov*.) a door-post.—Also **dern.** [Prob. Norse.]

duro, dōō′rō, *n*. a Spanish peso :—*pl*. **dūr′os.** [Sp. (*peso*) *duro*, hard (peso).]

duroy, dōō-roi′, *n*. an obsolete form of **corduroy.**

durra, dōō′rä, *n*. Indian millet, a grass (*Sorghum vulgare*) akin to sugar-cane, much cultivated for grain in Asia and Africa, or other species of the genus.—Also **dou′ra, dhu′rra,** and **du′ra.** [Ar. *dhurah*.]

durrie, dur′i, *n*. an Indian cotton carpet fabric with fringes, used for curtains, covers, etc. [Hind. *darī*.]

durst, durst, *pa.t.* of **dare**, to venture. [O.E. *dorste*, pa.t. of *durran*, to dare.]

dush, dush, *v.t.* (*Scot*.) to strike heavily against : to throw down.—*n*. a heavy impact.

dusk, dusk, *adj*. darkish : of a dark colour.—*n*. twilight : partial darkness : darkness of colour.—*v.t.* and *v.i.* to make or become dusky : to dim.—*v.t.* and *v.i.* **dusk′en**, to make or grow dark.—*adv*. **dusk′ily.**—*n*. **dusk′iness.**—*adj*. **dusk′ish.**—*adv*. **dusk′ishly.**—*n*. **dusk′ishness.**—*adv*. **dusk′ly.**—*n*. **dusk′ness.**—*adj*. **dusk′y**, partially dark or obscure ; dark-coloured : sad : gloomy. [Apparently connected with O.E. *dox*, dark.]

dust, dust, *n*. fine particles of solid matter : a cloud of powdery matter : powder : earth : the grave : a mean condition : gold-dust—hence money : (*slang*) turmoil : a disturbance, a brawl (also **dust′-up′**).—*v.t.* to free from dust : to sprinkle.—*ns*. **dust′-ball**, a ball of grain-dust, etc., in a horse's intestine ; **dust′-bin**, a receptacle for household rubbish ; **dust′-bowl**, a drought area subject to dust-storms, especially (**Dust Bowl**) the region of the U.S. along the western edge of the Great Plains ; **dust′-brand**, smut ; **dust′-brush**, a light brush for removing dust ; **dust′-cart**, a cart for taking away household rubbish ; **dust′-coat**, an overall : a light overcoat ; **dust′-cover**, the jacket of a book ; **dust′-devil, -storm**, a small storm in which a whirling column of dust or sand travels across a dry country ; **dust′er**, one who dusts : a cloth or brush used for removing dust : (*U.S.*) a dust-coat ; **dust′-hole**, a dust-bin : **dust′iness** ; **dust′-jack′et**, the jacket or dust-cover of a book.—*adj*. **dust′less.**—*ns*. **dust′-man**, one who removes household rubbish ; **dust′-pan**, a pan or shovel for removing dust swept from the floor ; **dust′-sheet**, a cloth for protecting furniture from dust ; **dust′-shot**, the smallest size of shot.—*adjs*. **dust′proof**, impervious or inaccessible to dust ; **dust′y**, covered or sprinkled with dust : like dust : (*slang*) contemptible, bad (in phrase *not so dusty*).—*ns*. **dust′y-foot** (see **piepowder**) ; **dust′y-mill′er**, the auricula, from the white dust upon its leaves and flowers.—**bite the dust** (see **bite**) ; **dust one's jacket**, to give him a drubbing ; **kick up (raise) a dust** (see **kick**) ; **throw dust in one's eyes**, to deceive. [O.E. *dūst* ; cf. Ger. *dunst*, vapour.]

Dutch, duch, *adj*. pertaining to Holland, its people, or language : (*obs*., except *U.S.*) German : heavy, clumsy, as in *Dutch-built*.—*n*. the language of Holland : (*obs*. and *U.S.*) German (*High and Low Dutch*, *Hoch* and *Nieder* or *Platt Deutsch*, High and Low German) : (*pl*.) the people of Holland : (*obs*. and *U.S.*) Germans.—*n*. **Dutch′man**, a native or citizen of Holland :—*pl*. **Dutch′men** ; *fem*. **Dutch′woman** ; *pl*. **Dutch′women** : a South African of Dutch origin : (*U.S.*) a German or Teuton.—**Dutch auction, courage, tiles** (see **auction, courage, tile**) ; **Dutch carpet**, a mixed material of cotton and wool for floor coverings ; **Dutch cheese**, a small round cheese made on the Continent from skim-milk ; **Dutch clinker**, a hard yellow brick for paving, etc. ; **Dutch clock**, a clock of wood and wire with brass wheels, made in the Black Forest ; **Dutch clover**, white clover ; **Dutch comfort**, 'Thank God it's no worse' ; **Dutch concert**, a concert in which singers sing their various songs simultaneously, or each one sings a verse of any song he likes between bursts of some familiar chorus ; **Dutch doll**, a wooden doll with jointed legs ; **Dutch drops**, a once popular medicine, composed of oil of turpentine, tincture of guaiacum, etc. ; **Dutch gold, leaf, metal**, a copper-zinc alloy, a substitute for gold-leaf ; **Dutch hoe**, a hoe with blade attached like a spade ; **Dutch liquid**, ethylene dichloride ($C_2H_4Cl_2$), an anaesthetic discovered by Dutch chemists ; **Dutch lunch, supper, treat**, one at which each brings or pays for his own share ; **Dutchman′s breeches**, Dicentra ; **Dutchman′s pipe**, a species of Aristolochia ; **Dutch oven**, a cooking-pot used by burying in coals : a tin for roasting before an open fire ; **Dutch pink** (see **pink**) ; **Dutch rush**, a horse-tail (*Equisetum hyemale*) with much silica in its stem, used for polishing ; **Dutch wife**, an open frame of rattan or cane used in the East Indies, to rest the limbs upon in bed; **double Dutch,** any unknown or unintelligible language; **High Dutch,** see above: also (*S. Africa*) Dutch as spoken in the Netherlands: (*obs.*) double Dutch; **Pennsylvania Dutch,** the mixed German dialect of the descendants of German settlers in Pennsylvania; **talk like a Dutch uncle,** to rebuke. [Ger. *deutsch,* (lit.) belonging to the people—O.H.G. *diutisc;* cf. O.E. *théod,* Goth. *thiuda,* nation; see Teutonic.]

dutch, *duch,* n. (*costermonger's slang*), a wife. [**duchess.**]

duty, *dū'ti,* n. that which is due: what one is bound by any (esp. moral) obligation to do: one's proper business: service: attendance: supervision of pupils out of school hours: performance of function or service: the work done by a machine under given conditions, or for a specified amount of energy supplied: respect: tax on goods, etc.—*adj.* **dū'teous,** devoted to duty: obedient.—*adv.* **dū'teously.**—*n.* **dū'teousness.**—*adjs.* **dū'tiable,** subject to custom duty; **dū'tied,** subjected to duties and customs; **dū'tiful,** attentive to duty: respectful: expressive of a sense of duty.—*adv.* **dū'tifully.**—*n.* **dū'tifulness.**—*adj.* **dū'ty-free,** free from tax or duty; **dū'ty-paid,** on which duty has been paid. [Anglo-Fr. *dueté;* see **due** (1).]

duumvir, *dū-um'vir, -vər,* n. one of two associated in the same office (*pl.* **duum'virs, duum'viri, -ī;** L. *doo-ōōm-vir-ē*).—*adj.* **duum'viral.**—*n.* **duum'virate,** an association of two men in one office: a government by duumvirs. [L. *duūmvirī,* for *duovirī—duo,* two, and *vir,* a man.]

duvet, *dü-vā',* n. a quilt stuffed with eider-down or swan's-down. [Fr.]

dux, *duks,* n. a leader: the head boy or girl in a school or class. [L., a leader.]

dvornik, *dvor'něk,* n. a Russian concierge or porter. [Russ. *dvor,* yard, court.]

dwale, *dwâl,* n. (*bot.*) deadly nightshade: a stupefying drink: (*her.*) a black colour. [O.N. *dvöl, dvali,* delay, sleep.]

dwalm, dwaum, *dwäm, dwawm,* n. (*Scot.*) a swoon, a sudden sickness.—*v.i.* to swoon: to fail in health. [O.E. *dwolma,* confusion.]

dwarf, *dwawrf,* n. a diminutive man: a small manlike mythological being, esp. a metal-worker: an animal or plant much below the ordinary height: anything very small of its kind: a small star of high density and low luminosity (**white dwarf, red dwarf,** etc. according to colour).—*adj.* dwarfed: dwarfish: very small.—*v.t.* to hinder from growing: to make to appear small.—*v.i.* to become dwarfed.—*adjs.* **dwarfed; dwarf'ish,** like a dwarf: very small: despicable.—*adv.* **dwarf'ishly.**—*n.* **dwarf'ishness.—dwarfed trees,** small trees growing in flower-pots, a characteristic ornament in Chinese and Japanese houses and gardens. [O.E. *dweorg;* Du. *dwerg,* O.N. *dvergr,* Ger. *zwerg.*]

dwell, *dwel,* v.i. to abide: to reside: to remain: to rest the attention: to continue long.—*v.t.* (*Milt.*) to inhabit: (*Milt.*) to cause to dwell:—(*pr.p.* **dwell'ing;** *pa.t.* and *pa.p.* **dwelt,** or **dwelled).**—*n.* a pause, hesitation.—*ns.* **dwell'er; dwell'ing,** the place where one dwells: a house: habitation: continuance; **dwell'ing-house,** a house used as a dwelling, in distinction from a place of business or other building; **dwell'ing-place,** a place of residence. [O.E. *dwellan,* to go astray, delay, tarry.]

dwindle, *dwin'dl,* v.i. to grow less: to waste away: to grow feeble: to become degenerate.—*v.t.* to lessen.—*n.* decline.—*n.* **dwin'dlement.** [Dim. of **dwine.**]

dwine, *dwīn,* v.i. to pine: (*Scot.*) to waste away. [O.E. *dwínan,* to fade; cf. O.N. *dvína,* Dan. *tvine,* to pine away.]

dyad, *dī'ad,* n. a pair of units treated as one: (*chem.*) a bivalent atom, radical, or element.—*adj.* **dyad'ic.** [Gr. *dyas, -ados—dyo,* two.]

dyarchy, *dī'ärk-i,* n. a common but undesirable spelling of **diarchy.**

dye, *dī,* n. (*Spens.*). Same as **die** (2).

dye, *dī, v.t.* to stain: to give a new colour to: (*pr.p.* **dye'ing;** *pa.t.* and *pa.p.* **dyed).**—*n.* colour: tinge: stain: a colouring liquid.—*adj.* **dyed.**—*ns.* **dye'-house,** a building in which dyeing is done; **dye'ing; dy'er,** one whose trade is to dye cloth, etc.; **dy'er's-green'weed,** or **dy'er's-broom,** a papilionaceous shrub (*Genista tinctoria*), a source of yellow colouring matter; **dy'er's-rock'et, -weld, -yell'owweed,** a plant (*Reseda Luteola*) akin to mignonette yielding a yellow dye; **dy'er's-weed,** a name for various plants that yield dyes—woad, weld, dyer's-greenweed, etc.; **dye-ster** (*dī'stər; Scot.*), a dyer; **dye'-stuff,** a material used in dyeing; **dye'-wood,** any wood from which material is obtained for dyeing; **dye'-work(s),** an establishment for dyeing. [O.E. *déagian,* to dye, from *déag,* or *déah,* colour.]

dying, *dī'ing, pr.p.* of **die.**—*adj.* destined for death: mortal: declining: occurring immediately before death, as dying words: pertaining to death. —*n.* death.—*adv.* **dy'ingly.**—*n.* **dy'ingness.— dying declaration** (*law*), declaration made by a dying person who does not survive the trial of the accused. [See **die** (1).]

dyke. Same as **dike.**

dynamic, -al, *din-am'ik,* or *dīn-, adj.* relating to force: relating to dynamics: relating to the effects of forces in nature: relating to activity or things in movement: relating to dynamism: causal: forceful, very energetic.—*n.* a moving force.— *adj.* **dynam'ical.**—*adv.* **dynam'ically.**—*ns.* **dynam'ics** (treated as *sing.*), the science of matter and motion, mechanics, sometimes restricted to kinetics; **dyn'amism,** a theory which explains the phenomena of the universe by some immanent energy: operation of force; **dyn'amist.**—*adj.* **dynamis'tic.** [Gr. *dynamikos—dynamis,* power —*dynasthai,* to be able.]

dynamite, *din'ə-mīt,* or *dīn', n.* a powerful explosive, consisting of absorbent matter, as porous silica, saturated with nitro-glycerine.—*v.t.* to blow up with dynamite.—*ns.* **dyn'amitard (-ärd), dyn'amiter,** a user of dynamite, esp. for political purposes. [Gr. *dynamis.*]

dynamo, *din', din'ə-mō, n.* a contraction of **dynamo-electric machine,** a machine for generating electric currents by means of the relative movement of conductors and magnets :—*pl.* **dyn'amos.** —*adjs.* **dyna'mo-elec'tric, -al.**—*ns.* **dynamo-gen'esis, dynamog'eny,** production of increased nervous activity; **dynamograph** (*-am'*), a recording dynamometer; **dynamom'eter,** an instrument for measuring force, or power.—*adjs.* **dynamo-met'ric, -al.**—*n.* **dynamom'etry.** [Gr. *dynamis,* power.]

dynast, *din'ast, -əst,* also *dīn', n.* a ruler.—*adj.* **dynas'tic,** relating to a dynasty.—*n.* **dyn'asty** (*-əs-ti*), a succession of kings of the same family. [Gr. *dynamis.*]

dyne, *dīn,* n. the C.G.S. unit of force—the force which, acting for one second on a mass of one gramme, produces a velocity of one centimetre per second. [Gr. *dynamis,* force.]

dyophysite. See **diphysite.**

dyothelete, dyotheletism, dyothelism. See **ditheletism.**

dysaesthesia, *dis-əs-thē'si-ä, -zhi-ä, -zhä,* or *-ēs-, n.* impaired sensation, partial insensibility.—*adj.* **dysaesthetic** (*-thet'ik*). [Gr. *dys-,* amiss, *aisthēsis,* sensation—*aisthanesthai,* to feel.]

dyschroa, *dis'krō-ä, n.* discoloration of the skin from disease.—Also **dyschroia** (*-kroi'*). [Gr. *dys-,* amiss, *chroä, chroiä,* complexion.]

dyscrasia, *dis-krä'si-ä, -zhi-ä, -zhä, n.* (*path.*) a disordered condition of the body attributed originally to unsuitable mixing of the body fluids. [From Gr. *dys-,* amiss, *krāsis,* a mixing.]

dyscrasite, *dis'kras-īt,* n. a mineral composed of silver and antimony. [Gr. *dys-,* ill, *krāsis,* mixture.]

dysentery, *dis'an-tər-i, -tri,* n. a term formerly applied to any condition in which inflammation of the colon was associated with the frequent passage of bloody stools: now confined to **amoebic dysentery,** the result of infection with the *Entamoeba histolytica;* and to **bacillary dysentery,** due to infection with *Bacterium dysenteriae.*—*adj.* **dysen-**

Neutral vowels in unaccented syllables: *el'ə-mənt, in'fənt, ran'dəm*

teric (*-ter'ik*). [Gr. *dysenterīa—dys-*, amiss, *enteron*, intestine.]

dysfunction, *dis-fung(k)'shən*, *n*. impairment or abnormality of the functioning of an organ. [Gr. *dys-*, ill, and **function**.]

dysgenic, *dis-jēn'ik*, *adj*. unfavourable to race-improvement. [Gr. pfx. *dys-*, ill, and the root of *gennaein*, to beget.]

dysharmonic, *dis-här-mon'ik*, *adj*. unbalanced, wanting in harmony of proportion. [Gr. *dys-*, ill, and **harmonic**.]

dyslogistic, *dis-lə-jis'tik*, *adj*. conveying censure, opprobrious.—*adv*. **dyslogis'tically**.—*n*. **dys'-logy**, dispraise. [Gr. *dys-*, ill, *logos*, discourse.]

dysmenorrhoea, *dis-men-ō-rē'ä*, *n*. difficult or painful menstruation.—*adjs*. **dysmenorrhoe'al**, **-ic**. [Gr. *dys-*, ill, *mēn*, month, *rhoiä*, flow.]

dysodyle, **-ile**, **-il**, *dis'ō-dīl*, *-dil*, *n*. a yellow or greyish laminated bituminous mineral, often found with lignite, burning vividly, with an odour of asafoetida. [Gr. *dysōdēs*, stinking—*dys-*, ill, *ozein*, to smell, *hȳlē*, matter.]

dyspathy, *dis'pə-thi*, *n*. antipathy, dislike.—*adj*. **dyspathet'ic**. [Gr. *dys-*, ill, *pathos*, feeling.]

dyspepsia, *dis-pep'si-ä*, *n*. indigestion.—Also **dys-pep'sy**.—*n*. **dyspep'tic**, a person afflicted with dyspepsia.—*adjs*. **dyspep'tic**, **-al**, afflicted with, pertaining to, or arising from indigestion.—*adv*. **dyspep'ticall ⁄**. [Gr. *dyspepsiä—dys-*, ill, *pepsis*, digestion.]

dysphagia, *dis-fā'ji-ä*, *n*. difficulty in swallowing—also **dys'phagy** (*-fə-ji*).—*adj*. **disphagic** (*-faj'ik*). [Gr. *dys-*, ill, *phagein* (aorist), to eat.]

dysphonia, *dis-fō'ni-ä*, *n*. difficulty in producing sounds. [Gr. *dys-*, ill, *phōnē*, sound.]

dysphoria, *dis-fō'ri-ä*, *n*. impatience under affliction : morbid restlessness : uneasiness : want of feeling of wellbeing. [Gr. *dysphōriä*, affliction, pain—*dys-*, ill, and the root of *pherein*, to bear.]

dyspnoea, *disp-nē'ä*, *n*. difficulty of breathing.—*adjs*. **dyspnoe'al**, **dyspnoe'ic**. [Gr. *dyspnoia—dys-*, ill, *pnoē*, breathing.]

dysprosium, *dis-prōz'i-əm*, *n*. a metal of the rare earths, the element of atomic number 66. [Gr. *dysprositos*, difficult to reach—*dys-*, ill, difficult, *pros*, to, *ienai*, to go.]

dystectic, *dis-tek'tik*, *adj*. not easily fused. [Gr. *dystēktos—dys-*, ill, *tēkein*, to melt.]

dysteleology, *dis-tel-i-ol'ə-ji*, *n*. the doctrine of purposelessness, or denial of final causes : the study of functionless rudimentary organs in animals and plants.—*adj*. **dysteleological** (*-i-ə-loj'i-kl*).—*n*. **dysteleol'ogist**. [Gr. *dys-*, ill (in a negative sense), and **teleology**.]

dysthesia, *dis-thē'si-ä*, *n*. a morbid habit of body, resulting in general discomfort and impatience.—*adj*. **dysthetic** (*-thet'ik*). [Gr. *dysthesiä—dys-*, ill, *thesis*, position.]

dystrophy, *dis'trə-fi*, *n*. (*biol*.) imperfect nutrition.—Also **distrō'phia**.—*adj*. **distrophic** (*-tro'fik*). [Gr. *dys-*, ill, *trophē*, nourishment.]

dysuria, *dis-ū'ri-ä*, *n*. a difficulty or pain in passing urine—also **dys'ūry**.—*adj*. **dysū'ric**. [Gr. *disouriä—dys-*, ill, *ouron*, urine.]

Dytiscus, *di-* or *dī-tis'kəs*, *n*. a genus of carnivorous water-beetles, including a common large British species, *D. marginalis*.—Also **Dyticus** (*dit'*)—*adj*. and *n*. **dytiscid** (*di-* or *dī-tis'id*). [Gr. *dȳtikos*, diving—*dyein*, to dive.]

dyvour, *dī'vər*, *n*. (*Scot*.) a bankrupt.—*n*. **dyv'oury**, bankruptcy. [Origin unknown.]

dzeren, *dzē'rən*, *n*. a Central Asian antelope. [Mongolian.]

dziggetai, *dzig'ə-tī*, *n*. a Central Asian wild ass (*Equus hemionus*), more horse-like than the others. [Mongolian *tchikhitei*.]

fāte, fär, ásk ; mē, hər (her) *; mīne ; mōte ; mūte ; mōōn ; dhen* (then)

E

E, e, *ē, n.* the fifth letter in our own and cognate alphabets, with various sounds (as in m*e*, g*e*t, *E*ngland, h*e*r, pr*e*y) and often mute (commonly an indication of a preceding long vowel or diphthong—cf. not, note : bit, bite) : in music the third note or sound of the natural diatonic scale, the major third above the tonic C : *e* represents the base of the natural system of logarithms, the limit, as *m* approaches infinity, of $\left(1 + \frac{1}{m}\right)^m$.

ea, *ē'ä, ē, n.* (*dial.*) a river : running water : a drainage canal in the Fens—sometimes **eau,** as if from French. [O.E. *éa;* akin to L. *aqua,* water.]

each, *ēch, adj.* and *pron.* every one separately considered.—*adv.* **each'where,** everywhere.—**each other,** a compound reciprocal pronoun, one another, by some restricted in application to two; **each way,** in betting, for a win and for a place. [O.E. *ǽlc—á,* ever, *gelíc,* alike.]

eadish, obsolete form of **eddish.**

eager, *ē'gər, adj.* excited by desire : ardent to do or obtain : (*obs.*) earnest : keen, severe : (*Shak.* aygre) sour, acid, bitter.—*adv.* **ea'gerly.**—*n.* **ea'gerness.** [O.Fr. *aigre*—L. *acer, acris,* sharp.]

eager. Same as **eagre.**

eagle, *ē'gl, n.* a name given to many large birds of prey of the family Falconidae : a military standard carrying the figure of an eagle : a lectern in the form of an eagle : the badge of certain orders, as the Prussian **black** (1701) and **red** (1705) **eagle,** the Polish, afterwards Russian, **white eagle** (1705) : a gold coin of the United States, worth ten dollars : (*U.S.*) a hole at golf played in two strokes less than par.—*adjs.* **ea'gle-eyed, ea'gle-sight'ed,** having a piercing eye : discerning; **ea'gle-flight'ed,** mounting high.—*ns.* **ea'gle-hawk,** a name applied to several eagles of comparatively small size; **ea'gle-owl,** a genus (Bubo) of large owls; **ea'gle-ray,** a large sting-ray; **ea'gle-stone,** a hard-crusted nodule of argillaceous oxide of iron; **ea'glet,** a young or small eagle.—*adj.* **ea'gle-winged,** having an eagle's wings. [O.Fr. *aigle*—L. *aquila.*]

eaglewood, *ē'gl-wood, n.* a genus (Aquilaria) of the daphne family, large spreading trees of Eastern India, whose heartwood contains a resinous substance fragrant in burning. [From the accidental resemblance of its name in some Eastern language to eagle, L. *aquila;* cf. agalloch, agila.]

eagre, *ā'gər, ē'gər, n.* a bore or sudden rise of the tide in a river. [Origin doubtful; hardly from O.E. *égor,* flood.]

ealdorman. See **alderman.**

eale, prob. *ēl, n.* (*Shak., Hamlet* I, iv, 36), generally supposed to be for **evil,** but perh. a misprint.

ean, *ēn, v.t.* and *v.i.* (*Shak.*) to bring forth.—*n.* **ean'ling,** a young lamb. [O.E. *éanian.*]

ear, *ēr, n.* a spike, as of corn.—*v.i.* to put forth ears.—*n.* **ear'-cock'le,** a disease of wheat caused by a threadworm (Tylenchus).—*adj.* **eared,** of corn, having ears. [O.E. *éar;* Ger. *ähre.*]

ear, *ēr, v.t.* (*obs.*) to plough or till.—*n.* **ear'ing** (*obs.*), ploughing. [O.E. *erian;* cf. L. *arāre,* Gr. *aroein.*]

ear, *ēr, n.* the organ of hearing, or the external part merely : the sense or power of hearing : the faculty of distinguishing sounds esp. of a different pitch : attention : anything projecting or shaped like an ear, the auricle of a leaf, lug of a vessel, a projecting part for support, attachment, etc.—*ns.* **ear'ache,** an ache or pain in the ear; **ear'bob,** an earring; **ear'-bone.**—*adj.* **ear'-bussing** (*Shak.;* another reading **ear'-kiss'ing**), whispered.—*ns.* **ear'-cap,** a covering to protect the ear from cold or injury; **ear'drop,** an ornamental pendant hanging from the ear; **ear'drum,** the drum or middle cavity of the ear, tympanum.—*adj.* **eared,** having ears, or external ears.—*ns.* **ear'-hole,** the aperture of the ear; **ear'ing** (*naut.*), one of a number of small ropes to fasten the upper corner of a sail to the yard; **ear'lap,** the tip of the ear : an ear-cap.—*adj.* **ear'less,** without ears, or external ears.—*ns.* **ear'lock,** a curl near the ear worn by Elizabethan dandies; **ear'mark,** an owner's mark on an animal's ear : a distinctive mark.—*v.t.* to put an earmark on : to set aside for a particular purpose.—*ns.* **ear'-phone,** a head-phone; **ear'-pick,** an instrument for clearing the ear.—*adj.* **ear'-pierc'ing,** shrill, screaming.—*ns.* **earring** (*ēr'ing*), an ornament hung from the ear; **ear'-shell,** any shell of the family Haliotidae; **ear'shot,** the distance at which a sound can be heard; **ear'trum'pet,** a tube to aid in hearing; **ear'wax,** a waxy substance secreted by the glands of the ear; **ear'wig** (O.E. *éarwicga, éare,* ear, *wicga,* insect, beetle), any dermapterous insect of the family Forficulidae, once supposed to creep into the ear : a flatterer.—*v.t.* to gain the ear of : to bias : to torment by private importunities.—*adj.* **ear'-wiggy.**—*n.* **ear'-witness,** a witness that can testify from his own hearing.—**about one's ears,** said of a house falling, etc.; **be all ears,** to give every attention; **give ear,** to attend; **go in at one ear and out at the other,** to make no permanent impression; **have a person's ear,** to be secure of his favourable attention; **have itching ears,** to be desirous of hearing novelties (2 Tim. iv, 3); **lend an ear,** to listen; **over head and ears,** overwhelmed : deeply engrossed or involved; **set by the ears,** to set at strife; **tickle the ear of,** to gratify, pander to the taste of, flatter; **turn a deaf ear,** to refuse to listen; **walls have ears,** there may be listeners. [O.E. *éare;* cf. Ger. *ohr,* L. *auris.*]

eard, eard-hunger. See **yird.**

earl, *ərl, n.* a British nobleman ranking between a marquis and a viscount :—*fem.* **count'ess.**—*n.* **earl'dom,** the dominion or dignity of an earl. —**Earl Marshal,** an English officer of state, president of the Heralds' College—the Scottish form **Earl Marischal.** [O.E. *eorl,* a warrior, hero; cf. O.N. *jarl.*]

early, *ər'li, adv.* near the beginning (of a time, period, series) : soon : in good time : before appointed time :—*comp.* **ear'lier;** *sup.* **earliest.**—*adj.* belonging to or happening in the first part of time, period, or series : beforehand : ready, advanced, astir, or on the spot in good time : happening in the remote past or near future.—*n.* **ear'liness.**—*adj.* **ear'ly-Victor'ian,** belonging to or characteristic of the early portion of Queen Victoria's reign (1837-1901).—**early and late,** at all times; **early bird,** the proverbial catcher of the (early) worm : an early riser; **early closing,** observance of a weekly half-holiday : closing of public houses early in the night; **early door,** an entrance to a theatre or hall open before the ordinary door at a higher price; **Early English** (*philol.* see **English**) : (*archit.*) the form of Gothic in which the pointed arch was first employed in Britain—succeeding the Norman towards the end of the 12th century, merging into the *Decorated* at the end of the 13th; **keep early hours,** to rise and go to bed betimes. [O.E. *ǽrlíce* (adv.)—*ǽr,* before.]

earn, *ərn, v.t.* to gain by labour : to acquire : to deserve : to bring to one.—*n.* **earn'er.**—*n.pl.* **earn'ings,** what one has earned : money saved. [O.E. *earnian,* to earn; cf. O.H.G. *aran,* harvest; Ger. *ernte.*]

earn, *ərn*, *v.t.* and *v.i.* (*dial.*) to curdle (of milk).— Also **yearn**. [O.E. *iernan=rinnan*, to run, and *ærnan=rennan*, to cause to run; *gerinnan*, causative *gerennan*, to curdle.]

earn, *ərn*, *v.i.* (*Spens.*, *Shak.*). See **yearn** (1).

earnest, *ər′nist*, *adj.* intent : sincere : serious.— *n.* seriousness : reality.—*adv.* **ear′nestly**.—*n.* **ear′nestness**. [O.E. *eornost*, seriousness; Ger. *ernst*.]

earnest, *er′nist*, *n.* money given in token of a bargain made (also **ear′nest-money**, **ear′nest-penny**): a pledge : first-fruits. [Ety. obscure; possibly conn. with **arles**.]

earst, obsolete form of **erst**.

earth, *ərth*, *n.* the third planet in order from the sun : the matter on the surface of the globe : soil, a mixture of disintegrated rock and organic material in which plants are rooted : dry land, as opposed to sea : the world : the inhabitants of the world : dirt : dead matter : the human body : a burrow : an electrical connexion with the earth, usually by a wire soldered to a metal plate sunk in moist earth : an old name for certain oxides of metals.— *v.t.* to hide or cause to hide in the earth : to bury : to connect to earth electrically : to clog, cover, smear, or partially cover with earth (often with *up*).—*v.t.* to burrow : to hide.—*ns.* **earth′-bag**, a sack of earth used in fortifications; **earth′-bath**, a bath of earth or mud; **earth′-board**, the board of a plough, or other implement, that turns over the earth.—*adjs.* **earth′-born**, born from or on the earth; **earth′-bound**, bound to earth; **earth′-bred**, bred from earth : mean, grovelling.—*n.* **earth′-closet**, a closet in which earth is used for the deodorisation of faecal matters.—*adjs.* **earth′-crea′ted**, made of earth; **earth′en**, made of earth or clay : earthly.—*ns.* **earth′enware**, crockery : coarse pottery; **earth′-fall**, a landslide.—*adj.* **earth′fast**, fixed in the earth; **earth′-fed**, contented with earthly things.—*ns.* **earth′flax**, asbestos; **earth′-hog**, the aardvark; **earth′-house**, an ancient underground dwelling or storehouse, also called **Picts′ house**; **earth′-hunger**, passion for acquiring land; **earth′iness**; **earth′liness**; **earth′ling**, a dweller on the earth : a worldly-minded person.—*adjs.* **earth′ly**, belonging to the earth : vile : worldly : conceivably possible on earth; **earth′ly-mind′ed**, having the mind intent on earthly things.—*ns.* **earth′ly-mind′edness**; **earth′-move′ment**, elevation, subsidence, or folding of the earth's crust; **earth′-nut**, the edible root-tuber of *Conopodium flexuosum*, a woodland umbelliferous plant : the plant itself (also *arnut*, *pig-nut*, *earth-chestnut*): the pea-nut (*Arachis*); **earth′-pea**, the peanut; **earth′-pillar**, a column of soft material protected from erosion by an overlying stone; **earth′-plate**, a buried plate of metal forming the earth-connexion of a telegraph-wire, lightning-conductor, etc.; **earth′quake**, a quaking or shaking of the earth : a heaving of the ground.—*adjs.* **earth′quaked**, shaken, destroyed or visited by an earthquake; **earth′quaking**.—*ns.* **earth′-shine**, the faint light visible on the part of the moon not illuminated by the sun; **earth′-smoke**, fumitory; **earth′-star**, a fungus (Geaster) akin to the puff balls that opens out into a starlike form; **earth′-table**, a course of stone or brick just above the ground; **earth′-tremor**, a slight earthquake.—*adv.* **earth′ward**, toward the earth.—*ns.* **earth′wax**, ozokerite; **earth′wolf**, the aardwolf; **earth′work**, a fortification of earth : an embankment : work of excavation and embanking; **earth′-worm**, the common worm : a mean person, a poor creature.—*adj.* **earth′y**, consisting of, relating to, or resembling earth : inhabiting the earth : gross : unrefined. [O.E. *eorthe*; cf. Du. *aarde*, Ger. *erde*.]

ease, *ēz*, *n.* freedom from pain or disturbance : rest from work : quiet : freedom from difficulty : naturalness : unconstrained manner.—*v.t.* to free from pain, trouble, or anxiety : to relieve : to relax : to calm : to move gently.—*adj.* **ease′ful**, ease-giving : quiet, fit for rest.—*ns.* **ease′ment**, relief : assistance : support : gratification : (*legal*) the right to use something (esp. land) not one's own

or to prevent its owner from making an inconvenient use of it.—*adv.* **eas′ily**.—*n.* **eas′iness**.— *adj.* **eas′y**, at ease : free from pain : tranquil : unconstrained : giving ease : not difficult : yielding : not straitened (in circumstances): not tight : not strict.—*interj.* a command to lower, or to go gently, to stop rowing, etc.—*n.* **eas′y-chair**, an arm-chair for ease or rest.—*adjs.* **eas′y-go′ing**, -ō′sy, indolent : placid.—**chapel of ease** (see **chapel**); **ease off**, to slacken gradually : to make or become less intense; **ease oneself**, to defecate; **easy money**, money made without much exertion or difficulty; **easy street**, (*coll.*) a situation of comfort or affluence; **honours easy**, honours evenly divided (at cards, etc.); **ill at ease**, uncomfortable; **stand at ease**, used of soldiers, when freed from attention; **stand easy**, used of a still easier position; **take it easy**, to avoid exertion : to be in no hurry; **take one's ease**, to make oneself comfortable. [O.Fr. *aise*; cog. with It. *agio*; Prov. *ais*, Port. *azo*.]

easel, *ēz′l*, *n.* the frame for supporting a picture during painting. [Du. *ezel*, or Ger. *esel*, an ass.]

easle, **aizle**, *āz′l*, *n.* (*Burns*) hot ashes. [O.E. *ysle*.]

eassel, **eassil**, *ēs′l*, *adv.* (*Scot.*) eastward : easterly. —*advs.* **eass′elgate**, **eass′elward**. [east.]

east, *ēst*, *n.* that part of the heavens where the sun rises at the equinox : one of the four cardinal points of the compass : the east part of a region : the east wind.—*adj.* toward the rising of the sun : blowing from the east.—*v.t.* and *v.i.* to move or turn east.—*ns.* **East′-end**, the eastern part of London or other town, often the habitation of the poorer classes; **east′-end′er**.—*adjs.* **east′er**, **east′ern**, toward the east : connected with the east : dwelling in the east.—*ns.* **east′erner**, a native or inhabitant of the east, esp. of the United States; **east′erling**, a native of the east : a trader from the shores of the Baltic.—*adj.* **east′erly**, situated in the east : coming from the eastward : looking toward the east.—*adv.* on the east : toward the east.—*n.* an east wind.—*adjs.* **east′ernmost**, **east′most**, situated furthest east.—Also **east′ermost** (*obs.*).—*ns.* **East′-In′diaman**, a vessel used in the East India trade; **east′ing**, the course gained to the eastward : distance eastward from a given meridian; **east′land**, the land in the East.— *adj.* **east′ling**, **-lin** (*Scot.*), easterly.—*adv.* **east′-lings**, **-lins** (*Scot.*), eastward; **east′ward**, **east′wards**, toward the east.—*adj.* **east′ward**.—**east-by-south** (**north**), 11¼ degrees south (north) from due east; **east-south** (**north**)-**east**, 22½ degrees south (north) from the east.—**about east** (*slang*), in proper manner; **the East**, the countries to the east of western Europe (*Near East*, Turkey, Balkans, etc.: *Middle East*, Turkey, Persia, India, etc.: *Far East*, China, Japan, etc.): the eastern part of the United States, used relatively and vaguely, but commonly that part between the Mississippi and the Ohio; **East Coast fever**, African coast fever : a protozoan cattle disease resembling red-water, transmitted by ticks; **Eastern Church**, the Greek Church. [O.E. *éast*; Ger. *ost*; akin to Gr. *ēōs*, the dawn.]

Easter, *ēst′ər*, *n.* a Christian festival commemorating the resurrection of Christ, held on the Sunday after Good-Friday.—*n.* **East′er-Day**, Easter Sunday.—*ns.pl.* **East′er-dues**, -**off′erings**, customary sums paid to the parson by his people at Easter.— *ns.* **East′er-egg**, a stained or artificial egg, given as a present at Easter; **East′er-tide**, **East′ertime**, either Easter week of the fifty days between Easter and Whitsuntide. [O.E. *éastre*; Ger. *ostern*. Bede derives the word from *Eostre* (*Eastre*), a goddess whose festival was held at the spring equinox.]

easy. See **ease**.

eat, *ēt*, *v.t.* to take into the body by the mouth as food : to consume : to corrode.—*v.i.* to take food : to be eatable, to taste : (*pr.p.* **eat′ing**; *pa.t.* **ate**, *et* or *āt*; *pa.p.* **eaten**, *ētn*, or, *obs.*, **eat**, *et*).—*n.* (*arch.* in *sing.*, *U.S.* *slang* in *pl.*) food.—*adj.* **eat′able**, fit to be eaten.—*n.* anything used as food (chiefly in *pl.*).—*ns.* **eat′age**, grass or fodder for horses, etc. : the right to eat; **eat'er,** one who, or that which, eats or corrodes.—*n.* and *adj.* **eat'ing.**—*n.* **eat'ing-house,** a place where provisions are sold ready dressed: a restaurant.— **eat away,** to destroy gradually: to gnaw; **eat in,** used of the action of acid; **eat its head off,** to cost as much for food as it is worth; **eat off,** to clear (a crop) by setting cattle to eat it; **eat one's hat,** an undertaking promised on conditions one thinks very improbable; **eat one's heart out,** to pine away, brooding over misfortune; **eat one's terms,** to study for the bar, with allusion to the number of times in a term that a student must dine in the hall of an Inn of Court; **eat one's words,** to retract: to recant; **eat out,** to finish eatables: to encroach upon; **eat the air** (*Shak.*), to be deluded with hopes; **eat up,** to devour entirely: to consume, absorb. [O.E. *etan;* cf. Ger. *essen,* O.N. *eta,* L. *edĕre,* Gr. *edein.*]

eatche, *ēch, n.* (*Scott*) a Scots form of adze.

eath, eathe, ethe, *ēth, eth, adj.* (*Spens.* etc.) easy. —*adv.* easily.—*adv.* **eath'ly.** [O.E. *éathe,* easy, easily.]

eau, *ō, n.* the French word for water, used in English in various combinations.—**eau des créoles** (*dā krā-ol'*), a fine Martinique liqueur, made by distilling the flowers of the mammee-apple with spirit of wine; **eau de Cologne** (see **Cologne**); **eau de vie** (*dǝ vē*), brandy.

eaves, *ēvz, n.pl.* (orig. *sing.*) the projecting edge of the roof : anything projecting.—*ns.* **eaves'drip, eaves'drop,** the water that falls from the eaves of a house : the place where the drops fall.—*v.i.* **eaves'drop,** to stand under the eaves or near the windows of a house to listen : to listen for secrets.—Also *v.t.*—*ns.* **eaves'-dropper,** one who thus listens : one who tries to overhear private conversation; **eaves'dropping.** [O.E. *efes,* the clipped edge of thatch; cf. Ice. *ups.*]

ebb, *eb, n.* the going back or retiring of the tide : a decline.—*v.i.* to flow back : to sink : to decline.— *adj.* (*obs.* or *dial.; Scott*) shallow.—*adj.* **ebb'less.** —*n.* **ebb'-tide,** the ebbing tide. [O.E. *ebba.*]

ebenezer, *eb-ǝn-ēz'ǝr, n.* a memorial stone set up by Samuel after the victory of Mizpeh (1 Sam. vii, 12): a name sometimes applied to a chapel or meeting-house. [Heb. *eben-hā-'ezer,* stone of help.]

Ebionite, *ē'bi-ǝn-īt, n.* an early Christian holding the Mosaic law binding and denying the apostolate of Paul and the miraculous birth of Jesus.—*v.t.* **e'bionise.**—*adj.* **ebionitic** (*-it'ik*).—*ns.* **e'bionitism, e'bionism.** [Heb. *ebyōn,* poor.]

Eblis, *eb'lis,* **Iblis,** *ib'lis, n.* the chief of the fallen angels in Mohammedan mythology. [Ar. *Iblīs.*]

ebon, *eb'ǝn,* **ebony,** *eb'ǝn-i, n.* a kind of wood furnished by various species of Diospyros (family **Ebenā'ceae**), almost as heavy and hard as stone, usually black, admitting of a fine polish: a tree yielding it : a negro.—*adj.* made of ebony : black as ebony.—*v.t.* and *v.i.* **eb'onise,** to make or become like ebony.—*ns.* **eb'onist,** a worker in ebony; **eb'onite,** black vulcanised rubber. [L. *(h)ebenus*—Gr. *ebenos;* cf. Heb. *hobnīm,* pl. of *hobni, obni—eben,* a stone.]

éboulement, *ā-bool'mäṅ', n.* the falling in of the wall of a fortification: a landslide or landslip. [Fr.]

ebracteate, *ē-brak'ti-āt, adj.* (*bot.*) without bracts. —*adj.* **ebract'eolate,** without bracteoles. [L. *ē-,* without, from, *bractea,* a thin plate.]

ebriate, ebriated, *ē'bri-āt, -id, adjs.* intoxicated.— *n.* **ebriety** (*ē-brī'i-ti*), drunkenness.—*adj.* **e'briōse,** drunk.—*n.* **ebrios'ity.** [L. *ēbriāre, -ātum,* to make drunk.]

ebrillade, *ā-brē-(l)yäd, n.* the sudden jerking of a horse's rein when he refuses to turn. [Fr.]

ebullient, *ǝ-bul'yǝnt, adj.* boiling up or over : agitated : enthusiastic.—*ns.* **ebull'ience, ebull'iency,** a boiling over; **ebull'ioscope,** apparatus for determining the boiling-points of liquids.— *adjs.* **ebullioscop'ic, -al.**—*ns.* **ebullios'copy;** **ebullition** (*eb-ǝ-lish'ǝn*), act of boiling : agitation : an outbreak. [L. *ēbulliēns, -entis*—*ēbullīre*—*ē,* out, and *bullīre,* to boil.]

eburnean, *eb-ur'ni-ǝn, adj.* of or like ivory—also **ebur'neous.**—*ns.* **eburna'tion** (*ēb-* or *eb-*), a morbid change of bone by which it becomes very hard and dense; **eburnifica'tion,** art of making like ivory. [L. *eburneus—ebur,* ivory.]

ecardinate, *ē-kärd'in-āt, adj.* hingeless.—*n.pl.* **Ecard'inēs,** a class of brachiopods without hinge or arm skeleton. [L. *ē-,* without, *cardō, -inis,* hinge.]

ecarté, *ā-kär'tā, n.* a game in which cards may be discarded for others. [Fr., discarded—L. *ē,* out of, from, Fr. *carte,* a card.]

ecaudate, *ē-kaw'dāt, adj.* tailless. [L. *ē-,* without, *cauda,* tail.]

ecblastesis, *ek-blas-tē'sis, n.* (*bot.*) proliferation of a floral axis. [Gr. *ekblastēsis,* budding forth— *ek,* out of, *blastos,* a sprout.]

ecbole, *ek'bo-lē, n.* (*rhet.*) a digression : (*mus.*) the raising or sharpening of a tone.—*adj.* **ecbol'ic,** promoting parturition.—*n.* a drug with this quality. [Gr. *ekbolē,* throwing out—*ek,* out of, *ballein,* to throw.]

eccaleobion, *e-kal-i-ō-bī'on, n.* a kind of incubator. [Gr. *ekkaleō bion,* I call forth life.]

eccentric, *ek-sen'trik, adj.* departing from the centre : not having the same centre as another, said of circles : out of the usual course : not conforming to common rules : odd.—*n.* a circle not having the same centre as another : (*mech.*) a contrivance for taking an alternating rectilinear motion from a revolving shaft : an eccentric fellow.—*adj.* **eccen'trical.**—*adv.* **eccen'trically.** —*n.* **eccentricity** (*-sǝn-tris'*), condition of being eccentric : in a conic section, the constant ratio of the distance of a point on the curve from the focus to its distance from the directrix (usually represented by *e*) : singularity of conduct : oddness. [Gr. *ek,* out of, *kentron,* centre.]

ecchymosis, *ek-i-mō'sis, n.* a discoloration of extravasation of blood.—*adjs.* **ecch'ymosed, ecchymot'ic.** [Gr. *ekchȳmōsis—ek,* out of, and *chȳmos,* juice.]

Eccles cake, *ek'lz kāk, n.* a cake like a Banbury cake. [*Eccles* in Lancashire.]

ecclesia, *i-klē'zi-ä, n.* a popular assembly, esp. of Athens, where the people exercised full sovereignty, and every male citizen above twenty years could vote : applied by the Septuagint commentators to the Jewish commonwealth, and from them to the Christian Church.—*adj.* **ecclē'sial.**—*ns.* **ecclē'siarch** (*-ärk*), a ruler of the church; **ecclē'siast,** the preacher—as the author of Ecclesiastes : an ecclesiastic; **Ecclesias'tes,** one of the books of the Old Testament, traditionally ascribed to Solomon; **ecclesias'tic,** one consecrated to the church, a priest, a clergyman.— *adjs.* **ecclesias'tic, -al,** relating to the church.— *adv.* **ecclesias'tically.**—*ns.* **ecclesias'ticism** (*-sizm*), attachment to ecclesiastical observances, etc. : the churchman's temper or spirit; **Ecclesias'ticus,** one of the books of the Apocrypha; **ecclesiol'atry** (Gr. *latreiā,* worship), excessive reverence for church forms and traditions.—*adj.* **ecclesiolog'ical.**—*ns.* **ecclesiol'ogist;** **ecclesiol'ogy,** the science of church forms and traditions, of building and decorating churches: the science relating to the church. [L.L.,—Gr. *ekklēsia,* an assembly called out of the world, the church—*ek,* out of, and *kaleein,* to call.]

eccoprotic, *ek-ō-prot'ik, adj.* laxative, mildly cathartic.—*n.* a laxative. [Gr. *ekkoprōtikos—ek,* out of, *kopros,* dung.]

eccrinology, *ek-ri-nol'ǝ-ji, n.* the branch of physiology that relates to the secretions. [Gr. *ek,* out of, *krinein,* to separate, secrete.]

eccrisis, *ek'ri-sis, n.* expulsion of waste or morbid matter.—*n.* **eccrit'ic,** a medicine having this property. [Gr. *ekkrisis,* secretion.]

ecdysis, *ek'di-sis, n.* the act of casting off an integument, sloughing. [Gr. *ekdysis—ek,* out of, *dyein,* to put on.]

eche, *ēch, v.t.* (*Shak.*) to eke out : to augment. [Other readings, **ech, eech, ich;** O.E. *ēcan;* akin to L. *augēre,* to increase; see **eke.**]

echelon, *esh'ə-lon*, *āsh'-lonˢ*, *n.* a stepwise arrangement of troops, ships, etc. [Fr. *échelon*, from *échelle*, a ladder or stair; see **scale**.]

Echidna, *ek-id'nä*, *n.* a genus of Australian toothless, spiny, egg-laying (burrowing) monotremes. —*n.* **echid'nine**, snake-poison. [Gr. *echidna*, a viper.]

echinus, *e-kī'nəs*, *n.* a sea-urchin: (*archit.*) the convex projecting moulding (of eccentric curve in Greek examples) supporting the abacus of the Doric capital.—*adjs.* **echinate**, **-d**, *ek'in-āt*, *-id*, prickly like a hedgehog: bristly.—*ns.* **Echi'nococ'-tus**, a large genus of ribbed, generally very spiny, cactuses; **echi'nococc'us**, the bladderworm stage (parasitic in cow, sheep, pig, man) of the dog tapeworm; **echi'noderm**, any one of the **Echinoder'ma** or **Echinoder'mata**, a phylum of radially symmetrical marine animals, having the body-wall strengthened by calcareous plates, and moving usually by tube-feet, distensible finger-like protrusions of a part of the coelom known as the watervascular system—starfishes, sea-urchins, brittle-stars, sea-cucumbers, and sea-lilies.—*adj.* **echinoder'matous**; **echi'noid**, like a sea-urchin.—*n.* a sea-urchin.—*n.pl.* **Echinoid'ea**, the sea-urchins, a class of Echinoderms. [Gr. *echīnos*, a hedgehog.]

echo, *ek'ō*, *n.* the sending back or reflection of sound or other waves: the repetition of sound by reflection: a reflected sound: a soft-toned organ forming a part of some large organs: a device in verse in which a line ends with a word which recalls the sound of the last word of the preceding line: response: repetition: imitation: an imitator: conventional play to indicate what cards one holds:—*pl.* **echoes** (*ek'ōz*).—*v.i.* to reflect sound: to be sounded back: to resound: to play a card as an echo.—*v.t.* to send back (sound or other waves): to send back the sound of: to repeat: to imitate: to flatter slavishly: (*pr.p.* **ech'öing**; *pa.t.* and *pa.p.* **ech'oed**, *-ōd*).—*n.* **ech'oer**.—*adj.* **echo'ic**, of the nature of an echo: (*philol.*) onomatopoeic.—*v.i.* **echo'ise**.—*ns.* **ech'oism**, the formation of imitative words; **ech'oist**, one who repeats like an echo; **echolalia** (*ek-ō-lā'li-ä;* Gr. *laliä*, talk), senseless repetition of words heard, occurring in disease of the brain or in insanity.—*adj.* **ech'oless**, given no echo, unresponsive.—*ns.* **echoprax'ia**, **echoprax'is** (Gr. *praxis*, doing), imitation by an insane person of postures or movements of those near him; **ech'o-sounding**, a method of measuring depth of water, locating shoals of fish, etc., by noting time for return of echo from the bottom, or bottom and shoal, etc.—**cheer to the echo**, to applaud most heartily. [L.,—Gr. *ēchō*, a sound.]

éclair, *ā-kler'*, *n.* a cake, long in shape but short in duration, with cream filling and chocolate icing. [Fr. *éclair*, lightning.]

éclaircissement, *ā-kler-sēs'mänˢ*, *n.* the act of clearing up anything: explanation.—**come to an éclaircissement**, to come to an understanding: to explain conduct that seemed equivocal. [Fr. *éclaircir*—L. *ex*, out, *clārus*, clear.]

eclampsia, *ek-lamp'si-ä*, *n.* a condition resembling epilepsy: now confined to acute toxaemia with convulsive fits about the time of childbirth.—Also **eclamp'sy**.—*adj.* **eclamp'tic**. [Gr. *ek-lampsis*—*eklampein*, to flash forth, to burst forth violently (as a fever)—*ek*, out of, *lampein*, to shine.]

éclat, *ā-klä'*, *n.* a striking effect: showy splendour: social distinction, notoriety: applause. [Fr. *éclat*, from O.Fr. *esclater*, to break, to shine.]

eclectic, *ek-lek'tik*, *adj.* selecting or borrowing: choosing the best out of everything: broad, the opposite of exclusive.—*n.* one who selects opinions from different systems, esp. in philosophy.—*adv.* **eclec'tically**.—*n.* **eclec'ticism** (*-sizm*), the practice of an eclectic: the doctrine of the **eclec'tics**, a name applied to certain Greek thinkers in the 2nd and 1st centuries B.C., later to Leibniz and Cousin. [Gr. *eklektikos*—*ek*, from, *legein*, to choose.]

eclipse, *i-klips'*, *n.* the total or partial disappearance of a heavenly body by the interposition of another between it and the spectator, or by passing into its shadow: a throwing into the shade: loss of brilliancy: darkness.—*v.t.* to hide wholly or in part: to darken: to throw into the shade, to cut out, surpass.—*n.* **eclip'tic**, the great circle in which the plane containing the centres of the earth and sun cuts the celestial sphere; hence, the apparent path of the sun's annual motion among the fixed stars: a great circle in which that plane cuts the earth's surface at any moment.—*adj.* pertaining to an eclipse or the ecliptic. [O.Fr.—L. *eclīpsis*—Gr. *ekleipsis*, failure—*ek*, out of, *leipein*, to leave.]

eclogite, **eklogite**, *ek'-lo-jīt*, *-gīt*, *n.* a crystalline rock composed of red garnet and green omphacite or smaragdite. [Gr. *eklogē*, selection (from the unusual minerals that compose it)—*ek*, out of, *legein*, to choose.]

eclogue, *ek'log*, *n.* a short pastoral poem like Virgil's *Bucolics*. [L. *ecloga*—Gr. *eklogē*, a selection, esp. of poems—*ek*, out of, *legein*, to choose.]

ecology, *ē-kol'ə-ji*, *n.* study of plants, or of animals, or of peoples and institutions, in relation to environment.—*adjs.* **ecologic** (*ē-kō-loj'ik*), **-al**.—*adv.* **ecolog'ically**.—*n.* **ecol'ogist**.—Also **oecology**, etc. [Gr. *oikos*, house, *logos*, discourse.]

economy, *i-* or *ē-kon'ə-mi*, *n.* the management of a household or of money matters: a frugal and judicious expenditure of money: thrift: saving: a system of rules or ceremonies: a dispensation, as *the Christian economy:* regular operations, as of nature.—*adjs.* **economic** (*ē-* or *ek-ən-om'ik*), **-al**, pertaining or having reference to economy or to economics: utilitarianism: conducive to thrift: frugal: careful.—*adv.* **econom'ically**.—*ns.* **econom'ics**, (*obs.*) the science of household management: pecuniary position and management: political economy; **economisa'tion**, act of economising.—*v.t.* **econ'omise**, to manage with economy: to spend money carefully: to save.—*v.t.* to use prudently: to spend with frugality.—*ns.* **economi'ser**, one who is economical: a device for saving heat, fuel, etc.; **econ'omist**, one who studies political economy: a good manager: an economiser.—[L. *oeconomia*—Gr. *oikonomiā*—*oikos*, a house, *nomos*, a law.]

écorché, *ā-kor-shā'*, *n.* a figure in which the muscles are represented stripped of the skin, for the purposes of artistic study. [Pa.p. of Fr. *écorcher*, to flay.]

écossaise, *ā-ko-sez'*, *n.* originally a dance or dance-tune of Scottish origin in 3-4 or 2-4 time: later a lively country-dance or its music in 2-4 time.—**douche écossaise**, the alternation of hot and cold douches. [Fr., fem. of *écossais*, Scottish.]

ecostate, *ē-kos'tāt*, *adj.* ribless. [L. *ē*, from, *costa*, rib.]

ecphonesis, *ek-fō-nē'sis*, *n.* (*rhet.*) exclamation: in the Greek Church, the part of the service spoken in an audible tone. [Gr. *ekphōnēsis*—*ek*, out, *phōnē*, voice.]

ecphractic, *ek-frak'tik*, *adj.* (*med.*) serving to remove obstructions.—*n.* a drug with such properties. [Gr. *ekphraktikos*—*ek*, from *phrassein*, to enclose.]

ecraseur, *ā-krä-zər*, *n.* (*surg.*) a chain or wire for removing tumours, etc. [Fr. *écraseur*, crusher.]

ecru, *ā-krōō'*, *-krü'*, *n.* unbleached linen: its colour.—*adj.* like unbleached linen. [Fr. *écru*—L. *ex* intensive, *crūdus*, raw.]

ecstasy, *ek'stə-si*, *n.* a state of temporary mental alienation and altered or diminished consciousness: excessive joy: enthusiasm, or any exalted feeling.—*v.t.* to fill with joy.—*adj.* **ec'stasied**, enraptured.—*n.* **ec'stasis**, ecstasy.—*v.t.* **ec'stasise**.—*adj.* **ecstat'ic**, causing ecstasy: amounting to ecstasy: rapturous.—*n.* one given to ecstasy: something spoken in a state of ecstasy.—*adv.* **ecstat'ically**. [Gr. *ekstasis*—*ek*, from, and root of *histanai*, to make to stand.]

ectasis, *ek'tə-sis*, *n.* the lengthening of a short syllable: dilatation. [Gr. *ektasis*, stretching.]

ecthlipsis, *ek-thlip'sis*, *n.* suppression of a sound, esp. of a syllable ending in *m* in verse before a vowel. [Gr. *ekthlīpsis*—*ek*, from, *thlībein*, to rub or squeeze.]

ecthyma, *ek-thī'mä*, *n.* a skin eruption in large pustules. [Gr. *ekthȳma*, a pustule.]

ecto-, prefix, outside, often opposed to **endo-, ento-**. [Gr. *ektos*, outside.]

ectoblast, *ek'tō-blāst*, *n.* the outer cell-layer of a gastrula, the epiblast.—*adj.* **ectoblas'tic**. [Gr. *blastos*, a shoot, bud.]

ectoderm, *ek'tō-dərm*, *n.* the external germinal layer or epiblast of the embryo, or any part of the mature animal derived from it.—*adjs.* **ectoderm'al, ectoderm'ic**. [Gr. *derma*, skin.]

ectogenesis, *ek-tō-jen'i-sis*, *n.* development outside the body: variation in response to outside conditions.—*adjs.* **ectogenetic** (*-jən-et'ik*), produced by or pertaining to ectogenesis; **ectogen'ic**, of external origin: ectogenous; **ectogenous** (*ek-toj'ə-nəs*), capable of living independently, or outside the body of the host (as some parasites).— *n.* **ectog'eny**, the effect of pollen on the tissues of a plant. [Gr. *ektos*, outside, *genesis*, generation.]

ectoparasite, *ek-tō-par'ə-sīt*, *n.* an external parasite.

ectophyte, *ek'tō-fīt*, *n.* a vegetable ectoparasite.— *adj.* **ectophytic** (*-fit'ik*). [Gr. *ektos*, outside, *phyton*, a plant.]

ectopia, *ek-tō'pi-ä*, *n.* (*path.*) morbid displacement of parts—also **ec'topy**.—*adj.* **ectop'ic**. [Gr. *ek*, from, *topos*, place.]

ectoplasm, *ek'tō-plāzm*, *n.* (*biol.*) the outer layer of cytoplasm of a cell: an emanation of bodily appearance believed by some spiritualists to come from a medium.—*adjs.* **ectoplas'mic, ectoplas'tic**. [Gr. *plasma*, mould.]

ectosarc, *ek'tō-särk*, *n.* ectoplasm. [Gr. *sarx, sarkos*, flesh.]

ectotrophic, *ek-tō-trof'ik*, *adj.* (*bot.*) of a mycorrhiza, having its hyphae mainly on the outside of the root that it feeds. [Gr. *trophē*, food.]

ectozoon, *ek-tō-zō'on*, *n.* an animal ectoparasite:— *pl.* **ectozo'a**.—*n.* and *adj.* **ectozo'an**.—*adj.* **ectozo'ic**. [Gr. *zōion*, animal.]

ectropion, -um, *ek-trōp'i-on, -əm*, *n.* eversion of the margin of the eyelid, so that the red inner surface is exposed.—*adj.* **ectrop'ic**. [Gr. *ek*, out of, *trepein*, to turn.]

ectype, *ek'tīp*, *n.* a reproduction or copy.—*adj.* **ec'typal** (*ek'ti-pəl*).—*n.* **ectypog'raphy**. [Gr. *ek*, from, and *typos*, a stamp.]

écu, *ā'kü*, or *ā-kü'*, *n.* a French silver coin, usually considered as equivalent to the English crown: also a gold coin weighing about 60 grains: a common name for the five-franc piece. [Fr.,—L. *scūtum*, a shield.]

ecumenic, oecumenic, -al, *ēk-* or *ek-ū-men'ik, -əl*, *adj.* general, universal, belonging to the entire Christian Church. [L. *oecumenicus*—Gr. *oikoumenikos*—*oikoumenē* (*gē*), inhabited (world).]

eczema, *ek'zi-mä*, *n.* a common skin disease, in which part of the skin is red, with numerous small papules, that turn into vesicles.—*adj.* **eczem'atous** (*-zem'ə-təs*). [Gr.,—*ek*, out of, *zeein*, to boil.]

edacious, *i-, ē-, e-dā'shəs*, *adj.* given to eating: gluttonous.—*adv.* **edā'ciously**.—*ns.* **edā'ciousness; edacity** (*i-das'i-ti*). [L. *edāx, edācis*—*edĕre*, to eat.]

Edam, *ē'dam*, *n.* a kind of Dutch cheese. [After *Edam* near Amsterdam.]

edaphic, *i-daf'ik*, *adj.* pertaining to the soil.—*n.* **edaphology** (*ed-əf-ol'ə-ji*). [Gr. *edaphos*, ground.]

Edda, *ed'ä*, *n.* the name of two Scandinavian books—the *Elder Edda*, a collection of ancient mythological and heroic songs (9th-11th century, or earlier); and the *Younger* or *Prose Edda*, by Snorri Sturluson (c. 1230), mythological stories, poetics, and prosody. [O.N. apparently akin to *ōdr*, mad, *ōthr*, spirit, mind, poetry; cf. **wood** (2); Ger. *wut*, fury; L. *vātēs*, poet, seer.]

eddish, *ed'ish*, *n.* pasturage, or the eatable growth of grass after mowing. [Dubiously referred to O.E. *edisc*, a park.]

eddoes, *ed'ōz*, *n.pl.* the tubers of various plants, especially of Colocasia. [Gold Coast word.]

eddy, *ed'i*, *n.* a current running back, contrary to the main stream, thus causing a circular motion:

a whirlpool: a whirlwind.—*v.i.* to move round and round:—*pr.p.* **eddy'ing**; *pa.t.* and *pa.p.* **edd'ied**. [Cf. O.N. *itha*; prob. conn. with O.E. pfx. *ed-*, back.]

edelweiss, *ā'dəl-vīs*, *n.* a small white composite (*Leontopodium alpinum*), with woolly heads, found in damp places on the Alps. [Ger. *edel*, noble, *weiss*, white.]

edema, edematose, -ous. See **oedema**.

Eden, *ē'dn*, *n.* the garden of Adam and Eve: a paradise.—*adj.* **Edenic** (*-den'*). [Heb. *ēden*, delight, pleasure.]

edentate, *ē-den'tāt*, *adj.* without teeth: wanting front teeth.—*n.* a member of the **Edentā'ta**, a not very natural order of mammals having no front teeth or no teeth at all—sloths, ant-eaters, armadillos, pangolins.—*adjs.* **eden'tal**, of the edentates; **eden'tulous**, toothless. [L. *ēdentātus*, toothless—*ē*, out of, *dēns, dentis*, a tooth.]

edge, *ej*, *n.* the border of anything: a rim: the brink: the intersection of the faces of a solid figure: a ridge or crest: the cutting edge of an instrument: something that wounds or cuts: keenness: sharpness of mind or appetite: irritability: (*slang*) advantage: (*slang*) grudge.—*v.t.* to put an edge on: to place a border on: to border: (*obs.*) to egg, urge on: to move by little and little: to thrust edgewise: to strike with the edge.—*v.i.* to move sideways: to move by little and little.— *n.* **edge'-coal**, a steeply dipping coal-seam.— *adjs.* **edged; edge'less**, without an edge: blunt. —*ns.* **edge'-rail**, a rail of such form that the carriage-wheels roll on its edges, being held there by flanges; **edge'-tool, edged tool**, a tool with a sharp edge.—*advs.* **edge'ways, edge'wise**, in the direction of the edge: sideways.—*ns.* **edg'iness**, angularity, over-sharpness of outline: state of being on edge; **edg'ing**, any border or fringe round a garment: a border of box, etc., round a flower-bed.—*adj.* **edg'y**, with edges: sharp, hard in outline: irritable, on edge.—**edge in a word**, to get a word in with difficulty; **inside, outside, edge**, a skating movement on the inner or outer edge of the skate; **on edge**, in a state of expectant irritability: all agog; **play with edge-tools**, to deal carelessly with dangerous matters; **set on edge**, to excite; **set one's teeth on edge**, to cause a strange grating feeling in the teeth: to give a feeling of abhorrent discomfort: formerly, to make eager, stimulate desire. [O.E. *ecg*; cf. Ger. *ecke*, L. *acies*.]

edge-bone. See **aitchbone**.

edh. See **eth**.

edible, *ed'i-bl*, *adj.* fit to be eaten.—*n.* something for food.—*ns.* **edibil'ity, ed'ibleness**, fitness for being eaten. [L. *edibilis*—*edĕre*, to eat.]

edict, *ē'dikt*, *n.* something proclaimed by authority: an order issued by a king or lawgiver.—*adj.* **edict'al**.—*adv.* **edict'ally**. [L. *ēdictum*—*ē*, out of, *dīcĕre, dictum*, to say.]

edify, *ed'if-ī*, *v.t.* to build: (*Spens.*) to furnish with buildings: to build up the faith of: to strengthen spiritually towards faith and holiness: to comfort: to improve the mind of: (*pr.p.* **ed'ifying**; *pa.t.* and *pa.p.* **ed'ified**).—*n.* **edifica'tion**, instruction: progress in knowledge or in goodness.—*adj.* **edif'icatory**, tending to edification.—*n.* **ed'ifice** (*-fis*), a building: a large building or house.—*adj.* **edificial** (*-fish'l*), structural.—*n.* **ed'ifier**, one who edifies.—*adj.* **ed'ifying**, instructive: improving.—*adv.* **ed'ifyingly**. [L. *aedificāre*—*aedēs*, a house, *facĕre*, to make.]

edile. See **aedile**.

edit, *ed'it*, *v.t.* to prepare for publication: to superintend the publication of: to compile, garble, or cook up into literary shape.—*ns.* **edi'tion**, (*obs.*) the publication of a book: one of the different forms in which a book is published: the form given to a text by its editor: the number of copies of a book printed at a time, or at different times without alteration; **ed'itor**, one who edits books, etc.: one who conducts a newspaper, periodical, etc., or a section of it:—*fem.* **ed'itress**.—*adj.* **edito'rial**, of or belonging to an editor.—*n.* an article in a newspaper written by an editor or leader writer.—

adv. **edito'rially.**—n. **ed'itorship.** [L. *ēděre*, *ēditum*—*ē*, from, *dāre*, to give.]

edriophthalmic, ed-ri-of-thal'mik, adj. (of crustacea) with stalkless eyes.—Also **edriophthal'-mian, edriophthal'mous.** [Gr. *hedrion*, dim. of *hedrā*, seat, *ophthalmos*, eye.]

educate, ed'ū-kāt, v.t. to bring up and instruct: to teach: to train.—adj. **ed'ucable.**—ns. **educabil'ity; educā'tion,** bringing up or training, as of a child: instruction: strengthening of the powers of body or mind: culture.—adj. **educā'tional.**— adv. **educā'tionally.**—n. **educā'tion(al)ist,** one skilled in methods of educating or teaching: one who promotes education.—adj. **ed'ucātive,** of or pertaining to education: tending to teach.—n. **ed'ucātor.** [L. *ēducāre*, -*ātum*, to rear—*ēdūcěre* —*ē*, from, *dūcěre*, to lead.]

educe, i- or ē-dūs', v.t. to draw out: to extract: to cause to appear, elicit.—n. **educe'ment.**— adj. **educ'ible.**—ns. **educt** (*ē'dukt*), what is educed; **eduction** (*ē-duk'shən*), the act of educing: exhaust of an engine; **educ'tor,** he who, or that which, educes. [L. *ēdūcěre*, *ēductum*—*ē*, from, and *dūcěre*, to lead.]

edulcorate, i-dul'kō-rāt, v.t. to sweeten: to free from soluble particles by washing.—adj. **edul'-corant.**—n. **edulcorā'tion.**—adj. **edul'corātive.** —n. **edul'corātor.** [L. *ē*-, intens., *dulcōrāre*, to sweeten—*dulcis*, sweet.]

Edwardian, ed-wawrd'i-ən, adj. belonging to or characteristic of the reign of (any) King *Edward*, esp. Edward VII.—Also n.

ee, *ē*, Scottish form of **eye**:—pl. **een.**

eel, *ēl*, n. any fish of the Anguillidae, Muraenidae, or other family of Apodes, fishes with long smooth cylindrical or ribbon-shaped bodies, scaleless or nearly, without pelvic fins: extended to various other fishes of similar form, as the **sand-eel** (launce), **electric eel** (Gymnotus): extended also to some eel-like thread-worms (also **eel'-worm**): a slippery person.—ns. **eel'-bas'ket,** a basket for catching eels; **eel'fare,** a migratory passage of young eels: a brood of young eels: a young eel; **eel'grass, eel'wrack,** grasswrack (Zostera), a grasslike flowering plant of the pondweed family, growing in sea-water; **eel'-pout** (*powt*; O.E. *ǣlepūte*), the burbot: the viviparous blenny; **eel'-set,** a net placed across a river to catch eels; **eel'-spear,** an instrument with broad prongs for catching eels; **eel'-worm,** a nematode.—**salt eel** (*obs.*), a rope's end. [O.E. *ǣl*; Ger., Du. *aal*.]

e'en, *ēn*, a contraction of **even.**

e'er, *ār*, a contraction of **ever.**

eerie, eery, *ē'ri*, adj. exciting fear: weird: affected with fear: timorous.—adv. **ee'rily.**—n. **ee'riness.** [Scot.; M.E. *arh*, *eri*—O.E. *ǣrg* (*earg*), timid.]

eeven, eevn, eev'n, **eevning,** old spellings (Milt.) of **even** (n., adj., adv.) and **evening.**

effable, ef'ə-bl, adj. capable of being expressed. [Fr.,—L. *effārī*—*ex*, out, *fārī*, to speak.]

efface, i-, e-fās', v.t. to destroy the surface of: to rub out: to obliterate, wear away.—adj. **efface'-able.**—n. **efface'ment.**—to efface oneself, to avoid notice. [Fr. *effacer*—L. *ex*, out, *faciēs*, face.]

effect, i-fekt', n. the result of an action: impression produced: reality: (in *pl.*) goods: property.— v.t. to produce: to accomplish, bring about.—n. **effec'ter.**—adjs. **effec'tible,** that may be effected; **effec'tive,** having power to effect: causing something: successful in producing a result or effect: powerful: serviceable: actual: in force.—n. a soldier, or a body of soldiers, ready for service.— adv. **effec'tively.**—n. **effec'tiveness.**—adj. **effect'less,** without effect, useless.—n. **effect'or** (*biol.*), an organ that effects a response to stimulus. —adj. **effec'tual,** successful in producing the desired effect: (*Shak.*) decisive.—n. **effectual'ity.** —adv. **effec'tually.**—v.t. **effec'tuate,** to accomplish.—n. **effectuā'tion.**—**effectual calling** (*theol.*), the invitation to come to Christ received by the elect; **for effect,** so as to make a telling impression; **general effect,** the effect produced, by a picture, etc., as a whole; **give effect to,** to carry out, perform; **in effect,** in truth, really:

substantially; **leave no effects,** to die without property to bequeath; **take effect,** to begin to operate: to come into force. [O.Fr.,—L. *effectus*— *ex*, out, *facěre*, to make.]

effeir, effere, e-fēr', n. (*Scot.*) affair: appearance, show, array. [**affair.**]

effeir, effere, e-fēr', v.i. to appertain: to suit. [O.Fr. *afferir*—L. *ad*, to, *ferīre*, to strike.]

effeminate, i-fem'in-āt, adj. womanish: unmanly: weak: soft: voluptuous: (*Shak.*) feminine.—n. an effeminate person.—v.t. to make womanish: to weaken, unman.—Also v.i.—Also **effem'inise.** —n. **effem'inacy** (*-ə-si*), womanish softness or weakness: indulgence in unmanly pleasures.— adv. **effem'inately.**—n. **effem'inateness.** [L. *effēmināre*, -*ātum*, to make womanish—*ex*, out, and *fēmina*, a woman.]

effendi, e-fen'di, n. a title for civil officials and educated persons generally (abolished in Turkey in 1934). [Turk.; from Gr. *authentēs*, an absolute master.]

efferent, ef'ə-rənt, adj. conveying outward or away. [L. *ē*, from, *ferēns*, -*entis*, pr.p. of *ferre*, to carry.]

effervesce, ef'ər-ves', v.i. to boil up: to bubble and hiss: to froth up.—ns. **effervesc'ence; effervesc'ency.**—adjs. **effervesc'ent,** boiling or bubbling from the disengagement of gas; **effervesc'-ible.** [L. *effervēscěre*—*ex*, inten., and *fervěre*, to boil.]

effete, e-fēt', adj. exhausted: spent: worn out. [L. *effētus*, weakened by having brought forth young—*ex*, out, *fētus*, a bringing forth, young.]

efficacious, ef-i-kā'shəs, adj. able to produce the result intended.—adv. **efficā'ciously.**—ns. **efficā'ciousness; efficacity** (*-kas'i-ti*), **eff'icacy** (*-kə-si*), virtue, power of producing an effect: effectiveness. [L. *efficāx*, -*ācis*—*efficěre*; see next word.]

efficient, i-fish'ənt, adj. capable of doing what may be required: effective.—n. the person or thing that effects.—ns. **effi'cience,** efficient action or power; **effi'ciency,** power to produce the result intended, adequate fitness: ratio of a machine's output of energy to input.—adv. **effi'ciently.** [Fr., L.— *efficiēns*, -*entis*, pr.p. of *efficěre*—*ex*, out, *facěre*, to make.]

effierce, e-fērs', v.t. (*Spens.*) to make fierce.

effigurate, ef-ig'ū-rāt, adj. having a definite shape. —n. **effigurā'tion,** an axial outgrowth in a flower. [L. *ef*-, *ex*-, intens., and **figurate.**]

effigy, ef'i-ji, n. a likeness or figure of a person: the head or impression on a coin—(*arch.*) **effigies** (*ef-ij'i-ēz*):—pl. **effigies** (*ef'i-jiz*; *arch. ef-ij'i-ēz*). —**burn in effigy,** to burn a figure of a person, as an expression of dislike. [L. *effigiēs*—*effingěre*— *ex*, inten., *fingěre*, to form.]

effleurage, ef-lə-räzh, n. a stroking movement in massage.—Also v.i. and v.t. [Fr., glancing, grazing.]

effloresce, ef-lo-res', v.i. to blossom forth: (*chem.*) to become covered with a powdery crust: to form such a crust.—n. **efflorescʼence,** production of flowers: the time of flowering: a redness of the skin: a powdery surface crust: the formation of such a crust.—adj. **efflorescʼent.** [L. *efflōrēscěre* —*ex*, out, *flōrēscěre*, to blossom—*flōs*, *flōris*, a flower.]

effluent, ef'loo-ənt, adj. flowing out.—n. a stream that flows out of another stream or lake.—n. **eff'luence,** a flowing out: that which flows from any body: issue: outflow of sewage at any stage of treatment. [L. *effluēns*, -*entis*, pr.p. of *effluěre* —*ex*, out, *fluěre*, to flow.]

effluvium, e-floo'vi-əm, n. minute particles that flow out from bodies: disagreeable vapours rising from decaying matter:—pl. **efflu'via.**—adj. **efflu'vial.** [L.L.,—L. *effluěre.*]

efflux, ef'luks, n. act of flowing out: that which flows out.—Also **efflux'ion** (*e-fluk'shən*). [L. *effluěre*—*ex*, out, *fluěre*, *fluxum*, to flow.]

efforce, e-fōrs', v.t. (*Spens.*) to compel: to force: to force open: to do violence to: to put forward with force. [Fr., *efforcer*—Late L. *exfortiāre*—*ex*, out, *fortis*, strong.]

effort, *ef'ərt*, *n.* a putting forth of strength: attempt: struggle: a piece of work produced by way of attempt.—*adj.* **eff'ortless**, making no effort, passive: easy, showing no sign of effort. [Fr.,—L. *ex*, out, *fortis*, strong.]

effray, **effraide**, obsolete forms of **affray, afraid.**

effrontery, *e-frunt'ər-i*, *n.* shamelessness: impudence: insolence. [Fr. *effronterie*—L. *effrōns, effrontis*—*ex*, out, without, *frōns, frontis*, forehead.]

effulge, *e-fulj'*, *v.i.* to shine forth: to beam:—*pr.p.* **efful'ging**; *pa.p.* **efful'ged'**.—*n.* **efful'gence**, great lustre or brightness: a flood of light.—*adj.* **efful'gent**, shining forth: extremely bright: splendid.—*adv.* **efful'gently**. [L. *effulgēre*, to shine out, pr.p. *effulgēns, -entis*—*ex*, out, *fulgēre*, to shine.]

effuse, *e-fūz'*, *v.t.* to pour out: to pour forth (as words): to shed (as blood): to spread : (*Thomson*) to let loose.—*v.i.* to flow out.—*n.* (*e-fūs'*; *Shak.*) effusion, shedding.—*adj.* (*e-fūs'*) poured out: loosely spreading: expanded.—*ns.* **effusiometer** (*e-fūz-i-om'i-tər*), an apparatus for comparing molecular weights of gases by observing the relative time taken to stream out through a small hole; **effusion** (*e-fū'zhən*), pouring or streaming out : emission: shedding (as of blood) : (*med.*) an abnormal outpouring of fluid into the tissues or cavities of the body: an outpouring, esp. in poetic form: effusiveness.—*adj.* **effusive** (*e-fū'ziv*), poured out abundantly: gushing: (*geol.*) poured out at the surface in a state of fusion, volcanic: expressing emotion in a copious and demonstrative manner.—*adv.* **effus'ively**.—*n.* **effus'iveness**. [L. *effundēre, effūsum*—*ex*, out, *fundēre*, to pour.]

eft, *eft*, *n.* (*obs.*) a lizard: (now) a newt. [O.E. *efeta*; see **newt**.]

eft, *eft*, *adv.* (*Spens.*) afterwards, again, forthwith, moreover.—*adv.* **eftsoons** (*eft-sōōnz'*; *obs.*), soon afterwards, forthwith. [O.E. *æft, eft*, after, again; see **aft**.]

eftest, *eft'ist*, *adj. superl.* (*Warwickshire, Worcestershire; Shak.* Much Ado, IV, ii, 38) readiest : most convenient.

egad, *i-gad'*, *interj.* a minced oath. [Perh. orig. **ah! God!**]

egal, *ē'gəl*, *adj.* (*Shak.*) equal.—*adj.* and *n.* **egalitā'rian**, equalitarian.—*ns.* **egalita'rianism**; **egality** (*-gal'*), equality.—*adv.* **e'gally**. [O.Fr. *egal*—L. *aequālis*—*aequus*, equal.]

egence, *ē'jəns*, **egency**, *-i*, *ns.* need. [L. *ēgēre*, to be in need.]

eger, *ē'gər*, *n.* Same as **eagre**.

Egeria, *ē-jē'ri-ä*, *n.* a female adviser. [L. *Ēgēria*, or *Aegēria*, the nymph who instructed Numa Pompilius.]

egest, *e-jest'*, *ē-jest'*, *v.t.* to discharge: to expel from the body in any way.—*n.pl.* **egest'a**, things thrown out: excreta: waste materials removed from the body.—*n.* **egestion** (*e-jest'yən*).—*adj.* **egest'ive**. [L. *ēgerĕre*—*ēgestum*—*ē*, out, *gerĕre*, to carry.]

egg, *eg*, *n.* an oval body laid by birds and certain other animals from which the young is hatched : an ovum or female gamete (also **egg'-cell'**): a zygote: anything shaped like a hen's egg.—*ns.* **egg'-and-anch'or, egg'-and-dart'**, ornaments on mouldings in the form of eggs alternating with anchors or darts; **egg-and-spoon'-race**, a race in which each competitor lifts and carries an egg in a spoon; **egg-apparatus** (*bot.*), the egg and the two synergidae in the embryo-sac of an angiosperm; **egg'-apple**, the egg-fruit; **egg'-binding**, inability to expel an egg; **egg'-bird**, the sooty tern.—*adj.* **egg'-bound**.—*ns.* **egg'-capsule, -case, -purse**, a protective covering in which the eggs of some animals are enclosed; **egg'-cōsy**, a cover for keeping a boiled egg hot; **egg'-cup**, a cup for holding a boiled egg at table; **egg'-dance**, a dance performed blindfold among eggs; **egg'er**, one who collects wild-fowl's eggs : any moth of the family *Lasiocampidae*, whose cocoons are egg-shaped (also **egg'ar**); **egg'ery**, a place where eggs are laid; **egg'-flip**, a drink made of ale, wine, spirits or milk, with eggs, sugar, spice, etc.; **egg'-fruit**, the fruit of the egg-plant; **egg'-glass**, a small sand-glass for regulating the boiling of eggs: **egg'ler**, a dealer in eggs; **egg'-nog**, a drink of eggs and hot beer, spirits, etc.; **egg'-plant**, the aubergine or brinjal, an East Indian annual plant (*Solanum Melongena*) with edible egg-shaped fruit; **egg'-plum**, a yellowish egg-shaped plum; **egg'-pow'der**, a powder of dried eggs, or a substitute; **egg'-shell**, the calcareous covering of a bird's egg: a very thin kind of porcelain; **egg'-slice**, a utensil for lifting fried eggs out of a pan; **egg'-spoon**, a spoon used in eating eggs from the shell; **egg'-tooth**, a point on the beak by which an unhatched bird or reptile breaks the egg-shell.—*adj.* **egg'y**, abounding in eggs : having just laid or about to lay an egg: savouring of, or marked with, eggs.—**a bad egg** (*coll.*), a worthless person; **put all one's eggs into one basket**, to risk all on one enterprise; **take eggs for money**, to be put off with mere promises of payment; **teach your grandmother to suck eggs**, spoken contemptuously to one who would teach those older and wiser than himself; **tread upon eggs**, to walk warily, to steer one's way carefully in a delicate situation. [O.N. *egg*; cf. O.E. *æg*, Ger. *ei*, perh. L. *ōvum*, Gr. *ōon*.]

egg, *eg*, *v.t.* to instigate. [O.N. *eggja*—*egg*, an edge; cog. with O.E. *ecg*; see **edge**.]

egis. See **aegis**.

eglandular, *ē-glan'dū-lər*, *adj.* having no glands.—*adj.* **eglan'dulose**.

eglantine, *eg'lən-tīn*, *n.* the sweet-brier: (*Milt.*) perhaps the honeysuckle. [Fr.,—O.Fr. *aiglent*, as if from a L. *aculentus*, prickly—*acus*, a needle, and suff. *-lentus*.]

eglatere, *eg-lə-tēr'*, *n.* (*arch.*) eglantine.

egma, *eg'mä*, *n.* Costard's attempt at **enigma** (*Shak.* Love's Lab. III, i. 73.)

ego, *ē'gō*, *n.* the 'I' or self—that which is conscious and thinks.—*adj.* **egocen'tric**, self-centred: regarding or regarded from the point of view of the ego.—*ns.* **e'gōism** (*phil.*), the doctrine that we have proof of nothing but our own existence: (*ethics*), the theory of self-interest as the principle of morality: selfishness: egotism; **e'gōist**, one who holds the doctrine of egoism: one who thinks and speaks too much of himself or 'of things as they affect himself : an egotist.—*adjs.* **egōist'ic, -al**, pertaining to or manifesting egoism.—*ns.* **egō'ity**, the essential element of the ego; **egomā'nia**, morbid egotism; **egomā'niac**; **e'gōtheism** (or *-thē'*), the deification of self : identification of oneself with God.—*v.i.* **e'gotise**, to talk much of oneself.—*ns.* **e'gotism**, a frequent use of the pronoun I : thinking or speaking too much of oneself: self-exaltation: an account of some matter concerning oneself; **e'gotist**, one full of egotism.—*adjs.* **egotist'ic, -al**, showing egotism: self-important: conceited.—*adv.* **egotist'ically**. [L. *ego, egō*, and Gr. *egō*, I.]

egregious, *i-grē'jəs*, *adj.* (*arch.*) prominent, distinguished: outrageous: notorious (in bad sense).—*adv.* **egrē'giously**.—*n.* **egrē'giousness**. [L. *ēgregius*, chosen out of the flock—*ē*, out of, *grex, gregis*, a flock.]

egress, *ē'gres*, *n.* act of going out: departure: the way out: the power or right to depart.—*n.* **egression** (*i-, ē-gresh'ən*), the act of going out. [L. *ēgredī, ēgressus*—*ē*, out of, *gradī*, to go.]

egret, *ē'gret*, *n.* a white heron of several species : an aigrette. [See **aigrette**.]

egurgitate, *ē-gur'ji-tāt*, *v.t.* to vomit: to cast forth. [L. *ēgurgitāre, -ātum*—*ē*, out of, *gurges, -itis*, a whirlpool.]

Egypt, *arch.* **Aegypt**, *ē'jipt*, *n.* a country of N.E. Africa.—*adj.* **Egyptian** (*ē-jip'shən*), belonging to Egypt: (of *type*) antique.—*n.* a native or citizen of Egypt : a gypsy.—*adj.* **Egyptolog'ical**.—*ns.* **Egyptol'ogist**; **Egyptol'ogy**, the science of Egyptian antiquities.—**Egyptian darkness**, darkness like that of Exod. x. 22.

eh, *ā*, *interj.* expressing inquiry, failure to hear, or slight surprise.—*v.i.* to say 'Eh'.

eident, *ī'dənt*, *adj.* (*Scot.*) busy, diligent. [M.E. *ithen*—O.N. *ithinn*, diligent.]

Neutral vowels in unaccented syllables : *el'ə-mənt, in'fənt, ran'dəm*

eider, ī′dər, *n.* the **ei′der-duck′**, a northern sea-duck, sought after for its fine down.—*n.* **ei′der-down′**, the soft down of the eider-duck, used for stuffing quilts. [Prob. through Sw. from O.N. *æthar*, gen. of *æthr*, an eider-duck.]

eidetic, ī-det′ik, *adj.* vividly clear: reproducing, or able to reproduce, a vividly clear visual image of what has been previously seen.—*n.* a person with this ability. [Gr. *eidētikos*, belonging to an image—*eidos*, form.]

eidograph, ī′dō-gräf, *n.* an instrument for copying drawings. [Gr. *eidos*, form, *graphein*, to write.]

eidolon, ī-dō′lon, *n.* an image: a phantom or apparition: a confusing reflection or reflected image:—*pl.* **eidō′la**. [Gr. See **idol**.]

eight, āt, *n.* the cardinal number one above seven: a symbol (8, viii, etc.) representing that number: a set of eight things or persons (syllables, leaves, oarsmen, etc.): an eight-oar boat: an eight-cylinder engine or car: a card with eight pips: a shoe or other article of a size denoted by 8: the eighth hour after midday or midnight.—*adj.* of the number eight.—*adj.* **eight′-day**, lasting or running for eight days.—*n.* **eight′foil** (*her.*), an eight-leaved flower.—*adjs.* and *advs.* **eight′fold**, in eight divisions: eight times as much; **eight′-foot**, eight feet in measure.—*adj.* (*mus.*) having the pitch of an open organ-pipe eight feet long, or having that pitch for the lowest note.—*adj.* **eighth** (*ātth*), last of eight: equal to one of eight equal parts.—*n.* an eighth part: (*mus.*) an octave. —*adv.* **eighthly** (*ātth′li*), in the eighth place.— *adjs.* **eight′-hour**, consisting of eight hours, or eight working hours; **eight′-oar**, manned by eight oarsmen.—*n.* an eight-oar boat.—*n.* **eight′-pence**, the value of eight pennies.—*adj.* **eight′-penny**, costing eightpence.—*n.* and *adj.* **eight′-score**, eight times twenty.—*ns.* **eights′man**, one of a crew or team of eight; **eight′some**, a group of eight: eight together: a lively Scottish reel for eight dancers.—Also *adj.*—*adj.* **eight′-square**, regularly octagonal.—**an eight days**, a week; **figure of eight**, a figure shaped like an 8 made in skating, etc.; **piece of eight**, an old Spanish coin worth eight reals; **the eights**, annual bumping boat-races in the summer term between the various Oxford colleges. [O.E. (Anglian) *æhta* (W.S. *eahta*); Ger. *acht*, L. *octō*, Gr. *oktō*.]

eighteen, ā-tēn′, ā′tēn, *n.* and *adj.* eight and ten.— *adj.* **eigh′teen-hole**, having eighteen golf-holes.— *adj.* and *n.* **eighteen′mo**, octodecimo.—*n.* **eigh′-teen-pence**, one shilling and sixpence.—*adj.* **eigh′teen-penn′y**.—*adj.* **eigh′teenth** (or -*tēnth′*), last of eighteen: equal to one of eighteen equal parts.—*n.* an eighteenth part.—*adv.* **eighteenth′ly**. [O.E. (Mercian) *æhtatēne* (W.S. *eahtatiene*).]

eighty, ā′ti, *n.* and *adj.* eight times ten:—*pl.* **eight′ies**, the numbers eighty to eighty-nine: the years so numbered in life or any century.— *adj.* **eigh′tieth**, last of eighty: equal to one of eighty equal parts.—*n.* an eightieth part. [O.E. *æhtatig* (W.S. *eahtatig*, or *hundeahtatig*).]

eigne, ān, *adj.* first-born. [Fr. *aîné*.]

eik, ēk, Scots form of **eke**.

eikon. Same as **icon**. **eild**. Same as **eld**.

eild, ēld, *adj.* (*Scot.*) not yielding milk. [See **yeld**.]

eilding. See **elding**.

eine, īn, ēn, *n.pl.* (*obs.*) eyes. [See **een**, under **ee**.]

eirack, ē′rək, *n.* (*Scot.*) a young hen. [Gael. *eireag*.]

eirenicon, ī-rē′ni-kon, a proposition or scheme for peace: a peace-making message: the deacon's litany at the beginning of the Greek liturgy—from its opening petitions for peace.—**eire′nic** (see **irenic**). [A partly Latinised spelling of Gr. *eirēnikon*, neut. of *eirēnikos*, peaceful, peaceable —*eirēnē*, peace.]

eisel(l), ā′səl, ī′səl, *n.* (*obs.*) vinegar. [O.Fr. *aisil*, *aissil*, from a L.L. dim. of L. *acētum*, vinegar.]

eisteddfod, ā-is-tedh′vod, *n.* a congress of Welsh bards and musicians. [W., lit. session—*eistedd*, to sit.]

either, ī′dhər, or ē′dhər, *adj.* or *pron.* the one or the other: one of two: each of two.—*conj.* correlat-ive to *or*: (*B.*) or. [O.E. *ǽgther*, contraction of *ǽghwæther*—*á*, aye, pfx. *ge-*, and *hwæther*, whether; see also **each**.]

ejaculate, i-jak′ū-lāt, *v.t.* to eject: to utter with suddenness.—*v.i.* to utter or make an ejaculation. —*n.* **ejaculā′tion**, ejection, emission: a sudden utterance in prayer or otherwise: an unpremeditated emotional prayer or remark.—*adjs.* **ejac′ulative**; **ejac′ulatory**. [L. *ē*, from, and *jaculāri*, -*ātus*—*jacĕre*, to throw.]

eject, ē-jekt′, *v.t.* to cast out: to dismiss: to turn out: to expel.—*n.* **eject** (*ē′jekt*), a mental state other than one's own, a thing thrown out of one's own consciousness, as distinguished from *object*, a thing presented in one's consciousness.—*ns.pl.* **eject′a**, **ejectament′a**, matter thrown out, esp. by volcanoes.—*n.* **ejec′tion**, discharge: expulsion: state of being ejected: vomiting: that which is ejected.—*adj.* **ejec′tive**.—*ns.* **eject′ment**, expulsion: dispossession: (*law*) an action for the recovery of the possession of land; **eject′or**, one who ejects or dispossesses another of his land: any mechanical apparatus for ejecting or discharging. [L. *ējectāre*, freq. of *ējicĕre*, *ējectum*—*ē*, from, *jacĕre*, to throw.]

eka, ā′kä, ē′kä, prefixed to the name of an element to give a provisional name for the hypothetical undiscovered element that should follow in the periodic table. [Sans. *eka*, one.]

eke (*Scot.* eik), ēk, *v.t.* to add to, increase: to lengthen: to supplement, make up to the required measure (often with *out*).—*n.* (*Scot.*) an addition, supplement. [O.E. *ēcan* (W.S. *īecan*); cf. **eche**; L. *augēre*; Gr. *auxanein*.]

eke, ēk, *adv.* in addition: likewise. [O.E. *ēac*; Ger. *auch*, perh. from root of **eke** (1).]

ekka, ek′ä, *n.* a small one-horse carriage. [Hind. —*ekka*, one—Sans. *eka*.]

el, *el*, *n.* the letter L: anything of that shape.

el, *el*, *n.* (*U.S. coll.*) an elevated railroad.

e-la, ē′lä, *n.* the highest note in old church music, E, the fourth space in the treble, sung to the syllable *la* in the highest hexachord: the highest pitch of anything.—*n.* **e-la-mi**, ē′lä′mē′, E, the third space in the bass ('in bass') or the first line in the treble ('in alt'), sung to *la* in the first and fourth hexachords respectively, and *mi* in the second and fifth.

elaborate, i-lab′ər-āt, *v.t.* to labour on: to produce with labour: to work out: to build up from raw or comparatively simple materials: to add detail to.—*v.i.* to become elaborate.—*adj.* wrought with labour: done with fullness and exactness: highly detailed: complicated.—*adv.* **elab′orately**.—*ns.* **elab′orateness**; **elaborā′tion**, act of elaborating: refinement: the process by which substances are built up in the bodies of animals or plants.—*adj.* **elab′orative**.—*ns.* **elab′orator**, one who elaborates; **elab′oratory**, a laboratory. [L. *ēlabōrāre*, -*ātum*—*ē*, from, *labōrāre*—*labor*, labour.]

Elaeagnus, el-i-ag′nəs, *n.* the oleaster genus, giving name to the fam. **Elaeagnā′ceae**. [Gr. *elaiagnos*, goat willow.]

Elaeis, el-ē′is, *n.* the oil-palm genus. [Gr. *elaion*, olive oil.]

elaeolite, el-ē′ō-līt, *n.* a greasy-looking nepheline. [Gr. *elaion*, olive oil, *lithos*, stone.]

élan, ā-län′, *n.* impetuosity, dash. [Fr.]

elance, i-läns′, *v.t.* to throw as a lance. [Fr. *élancer*.]

eland, ē′lnnd, *n.* a S. African antelope, resembling the elk in having a protuberance on the larynx. [Du.,—Ger. *elend*—Lith. *élnis*, elk.]

elanet, el′ə-net, *n.* a kite of the genus Elanus. [Gr. *elanos*, a kite.]

elaphine, el′ə-fīn, *adj.* like or belonging to a red deer. [Gr. *elaphos*, stag.]

Elaps, ē′laps, *n.* an American genus of snakes, otherwise Micrurus—coral-snake: applied by others to a South African genus, otherwise Homorelaps—garter-snake. [A form of **ellops**.]

elapse, i-laps′, *v.i.* to slip or glide away: to pass silently, as time.—*n.* passing.—*n.* **elap′sion**. [L. *ēlāpsus*, *ēlābī*—*ē*, from, *lābī*, *lāpsus*, to slide.]

elasmobranch, *i-laz'mō-brangk*, or *-las'*, *n.* any member of the **Elasmobranch'ii**, a class of fishes including sharks and skates, having a cartilaginous skeleton and plate-like gills. [Gr. *elasmos*, a beaten-metal plate, *branchia*, gills.]

elastic, *i-lăs'tik*, *adj.* having a tendency to recover the original form or size : springy : able to recover quickly a former state or condition after a shock : flexible : yielding : made of elastic.—*n.* a string or ribbon with rubber strands.—*n.* **elast'ance**, the reciprocal of the capacity of a condenser, from its electro-mechanical analogy with a spring.—*adv.* **elas'tically**.—*ns.* **elasticity** (*el-* or *ēl-əs-tis'*), power of returning to original form or size: springiness : power to recover from depression: **elas'ticness**. [Late Gr. *elastikos—elaunein*, to drive.]

elate, *i-lāt'*, *adj.* (*obs.*) lifted up : puffed up with success : exalted.—*v.t.* (*obs.*) to raise or exalt : to make exultant or proud.—*adv.* **elat'edly**.—*ns.* **elat'edness** ; **elā'tion**, pride resulting from success : exaltation, high spirits. [L. *ēlātus*, used as pa.p. of *efferre—ē*, from, *lātus*, carried.]

elater, *el'ə-tər*, *n.* an elastic filament aiding spore-dispersal in certain fungi, in liverworts and in horse-tails : a skip-jack beetle.—*ns.* **elate'rium**, a substance contained in the juice of the fruit of the squirting cucumber, yielding the purgative **elat'erin** ; **elaterite** (*i-lat'ər-īt*), elastic bitumen, a rubber-like mineral resin. [Gr. *elatēr*, driver—*elaunein*, to drive.]

elbow, *el'bō*, *n.* the joint where the arm bows or bends : any sharp turn or bend.—*v.t.* to push with the elbow : to jostle.—*ns.* **el'bow-chair**, an arm-chair ; **el'bow-grease** (humorously), vigorous rubbing : hard work ; **el'bow-room**, room to extend the elbows : space enough for moving or acting : freedom and scope.—**at one's elbow**, close at hand ; **bend, crook, or lift the elbow**, to drink too much ; **out at elbow**, with coat ragged at the elbows ; **up to the elbows**, completely engrossed. [O.E. *elnboga* ; see **ell** ; **bow**, *n.* and *v.t.*]

elchi, eltchi, elchee, *el'chē*, *chi*, an ambassador. [Turk. *ilchī*.]

eld, *eld*, *n.* age : old age, senility : former times, antiquity. [O.E. *eldo*.]

elder, *eld'ər*, *n.* a shrub or tree (Sambucus) of the Caprifoliaceae, with pinnate leaves, small flowers (the corolla wheel-shaped) and three-seeded fruits.—*ns.* **eld'er-berry**, the acidulous purple-black drupaceous fruit of the elder ; **eld'er-gun**, a popgun made of elder by extracting the pith ; **eld'er-wine**, a wine made from elder-berries.—**elder-flower water**, distilled water made from the flowers. [O.E. *ellærn*.]

elder, *eld'ər*, *adj.* older : having lived a longer time : prior in origin.—*n.* one who is older : an ancestor : one advanced to office on account of age : one of a class of office-bearers in the Presbyterian Church (*presbyter* of the New Testament).—*n.* **eld'erliness**.—*adj.* **eld'erly**, somewhat old : bordering on old age.—*n.* **eld'ership**, state of being older : the office of an elder.—*adj.* **eld'est**, oldest.—**Elder Brethren**, the governing members of Trinity House ; **elder, or eldest, hand**, the player on the dealer's left, who leads in card-playing ; **elders' hours**, respectable hours— usually not after 10 p.m. ; **Elder Statesmen**, a reactionary group of retired statesmen who exercised a power behind the throne in Japan. [O.E. *eldra* (W.S. *ieldra*, *yldra*), comp. ; *eldesta* (*ieldesta*), superl. of *ald* (*eald*), old.]

elding, *el'din(g)*, (*Scot.*) **eilding**, *ēl'din*, *n.* (Northern) fuel. [O.N.,—*eldr*, fire.]

El Dorado, *el'dō-rä'dō*, the golden land of imagination of the Spanish conquerors of America : any place where wealth is easily to be made. [Sp. *el*, the, *dorado*, pa.p. of *dorar*, to gild—the gilded man, the king of Manoa who smeared himself with gold-dust—afterwards transferred to Manoa itself.]

eldritch, *el'(d)rich*, *adj.* (*Scot.*) weird : uncanny. [Perh. connected with **elf**.]

Eleatic, *el-i-at'ik*, *adj.* belonging to *Elea*, a Greek city of Lower Italy, or to the school of philosophers connected with it, including Xenophanes, Parmenides, and Zeno.—*n.* one belonging to this school.

elecampane, *el-i-kam-pān'*, *n.* a composite plant (*Inula Helenium*) allied to Aster, formerly much cultivated for its medicinal root. [L. *enula campāna*, field, or Campanian, inula.]

elect, *i-lekt'*, *v.t.* to choose (in preference) to select for any office or purpose : to select by vote.— *adj.* chosen : taken by preference from among others : chosen for an office but not yet in it (almost always after the noun) : (*theol.*) chosen by God for salvation.—*n.* one chosen or set apart.—*n.* **elec'tion** (*-shən*), the act of electing or choosing : the public choice of a person for office, usually by the votes of a constituent body : freewill : (*theol.*) the exercise of God's sovereign will in the pre-determination of certain persons to salvation : (*B.*) the elected in this way.—*v.i.* **electioneer'**, to labour to secure the election of a candidate.— *n.* **electioneer'er**.—*n.* and *adj.* **electioneer'ing**. —*adj.* **elect'ive**, pertaining to, dependent on, or exerting the power of choice : (*U.S.*) optional.— *n.* (*U.S.*) an optional subject of study.—*adv.* **elect'ively**.—*ns.* **electiv'ity** (*ē-*, *e-*) ; **elect'or**, one who elects : one who has a vote at an election : (*U.S.*) a member of the so-called **electoral college**, which elects the President and Vice-President : the title formerly belonging to those princes and archbishops of the German Empire who had the right to elect the Emperor :—*fem.* **elect'ress**, **elect'oress**.—*adjs.* **elect'oral**, **electo'rial** (*ē-*, *e-*), pertaining to elections or to electors : consisting of electors.—*ns.* **elect'orate**, the dignity or the territory of an elector : the body of electors ; **elect'orship**.—**electoral vote**, (*U.S.*) the vote of the members of the electoral college, themselves elected by popular vote. [L. *ēligěre*, *ēlectum—ē*, from, *legěre*, to choose.]

electric, *i-lek'trik*, *adj.* pertaining to electricity : charged with or capable of being charged with electricity : producing or produced by, conveying, operated by, or making use of electricity : (*fig.*) thrilling : producing a sudden startling effect : unstable.—*n.* a non-conductor of electricity, as amber, glass, etc., capable of being electrified by friction. —*adj.* **elec'trical**.—*adv.* **elec'trically**.—*ns.* **elec'tric-eel**, Gymnotus, **electrician** (*el-ik-trish'ən*), one who studies, or is versed in, the science of electricity : one who makes, instals, or repairs electrical apparatus ; **electricity** (*el-ik-tris'i-ti*), the attractive power of amber and other substances when rubbed : an imaginary fluid supposed to explain this and related phenomena : manifestation of a form of energy attributed to the separation or movement of electrons : the branch of science that deals with this.—*adj.* **elec'trifiable**. —*n.* **electrifica'tion**.—*v.t.* **elec'trify**, to communicate electricity to : to excite suddenly : to astonish : to adapt to electricity as the motive power :—(*pr.p.* **elec'trifying** ; *pa.t.* and *pa.p.* **elec'trified**).—*n.* **electrisā'tion**.—*v.t.* **elec'trise**, to electrify.—**electric arc**, a luminous space between electrodes when a current passes across ; **electric battery**, a group of cells connected in series or in parallel for generating an electric current by chemical action ; **electric blue**, a steely blue colour ; **electric calamine**, the mineral hemimorphite, which becomes positively electrified at one end, negatively at the other, when its temperature rises, and *vice versa* as it cools ; **electric chair**, the seat on which a condemned criminal is put to death by electricity ; **electric eye**, a photo-electric cell ; **electric fire, heater, radiator**, an apparatus using an electric current, for heating a room ; **electric furnace**, an apparatus for getting very high temperatures by means of an electric current ; **electric hare**, a dummy animal electrically worked to draw on racing greyhounds ; **electric organ**, (*mus.*) an organ in which the sound is produced by electrical devices instead of wind : (*zool.*) in certain fishes, a structure that generates, stores and discharges electricity ; **electric ray**, the fish Torpedo ; **electric seal**, dyed rabbit or hare skin ; **electric**

storm, a violent disturbance in the electric condition of the atmosphere; **electric torch**, a portable electric light. [L. *electrum*—Gr. *ēlektron*, amber, in which electricity was first observed.]

electro-, *i-lek'trō-*, *el-ik-tro'-*, in composition, electric.—*ns.* **elec'tro** (*coll.*), an abbrev. of **electro-plate** and **electrotype**; **elec'troanal'ysis**, separation by electrolysis; **elec'tro-bath'**, a metallic solution used in electroplating; **elec'trobiol'ogist**; **elec'trobio'logy**, *n.* the science of the electrical phenomena in living organisms: an old name for hypnotism; **elec'trocar'diogram**, a photographic record of the electrical variations that occur during contraction of the muscle of the heart; **elec'trocar'diograph**, a galvanometer used for making such records; **elec'trocardiog'raphy**; **elec'tro-cement'**, cement made in an electric furnace, by adding lime to molten slag.—*adjs.* **elec'trochem'ic**, **-al**. — *ns.* **elec'trochem'ist**; **elec'trochem'istry**, the study of the relation between electricity and chemical change; **electrocul'ture**, cultivation of plants under stimulus of electricity.—*v.t.* **elec'trocute**, to inflict a death penalty by means of electricity: to kill by electricity.—*ns.* **electrocū'tion**; **elec'trōde** (Gr. *hodos*, way), a conductor by which a current of electricity enters or leaves an electrolytic cell, gas discharge tube, or thermionic valve; **elec'trodeposi'tion**, deposition of a layer of metal by electrolysis; **elec'trodynam'ics**, the study of electricity in motion, or of the interaction of currents and currents, or currents and magnets; **elec'tro-dynamom'eter**, an instrument for measuring currents by the attraction or repulsion between current-bearing coils; **elec'tro-engrav'ing**, an etching process in which the etched plate is placed in an electro-bath to deepen the bite; **elec'tro-extrac'tion**, **-win'ning**, recovery of a metal from its salts, by passing an electric current through a solution; **elec'tro-gild'ing**, electroplating with gold; **elec'trograph**, a recording electrometer; **elec'tro-kinet'ics**, that branch of science that treats of distribution of currents; **electrolier** (*-lēr'*), an electric-light fixture resembling a chandelier; **electrol'ogy**, the science of electricity: electrotherapy.—*v.t.* **elec'trolyse** (*-līz*), to break up by electric means: to subject to electrolysis.—**electrol'ysis** (*el-ek-trol'i-sis*; Gr. *lysis*, loosing), decomposition by electric current, with migration of ions shown by changes at the electrodes.—*n.* **elec'trolyte** (*-līt*), a substance that admits of electrolysis.—*adj.* **electrolytic** (*-lit'ik*).—*adv.* **electrolyt'ically**.—*n.* **elec'tro-mag'net**, a piece of soft iron, etc., rendered magnetic by a current of electricity passing through a coil of wire wound round it.—*adj.* **elec'tro-magnet'ic**.—*ns.* **elec'tro-mag'netism**, a branch of science which treats of the relation of electricity to magnetism.—*adj.* **electromechan'ical**, pertaining to any mechanical process or device involving the use of electricity: pertaining to electromechanics.—*ns.* **electromechan'ics**, the mechanics of the electric circuit; **elec'tromer**, a substance showing electromerism.—*adj.* **electromer'ic**.—*n.* **electrom'erism**, a form of tautomerism caused by a re-distribution of electrons among the atoms of a molecule or group.—*adj.* **electrometallur'gical**.—*ns.* **electromet'allurgist**; **electromet'allurgy**, industrial working of metals by means of electricity; **electrŏm'eter**, an instrument for measuring difference of electric potential.—*adjs.* **electromet'ric**, **-al**.—*ns.* **electrŏm'etry**, the science of electrical measurements; **electromobile** (*-bēl'*, or *-mō'*), a vehicle moved by electricity generated within itself; **electromō'tion**, motion of or produced by electricity.—*adjs.* **electromō'tive**, pertaining to the motion of electricity or the laws governing it.—*n.* **electromō'tor**, an apparatus for applying electricity as a motive power.—*adj.* **electroneg'ative**, carrying a negative charge: tending to form negative ions.—*ns.* **electrophorē'sis** (Gr. *phoreein*, to bear), migration of suspended particles, as protein macromolecules, under the influence of an electric field; **electrŏph'orus**, an instrument for obtaining statical

electricity by means of induction; **elec'trophysiol'ogy**, the study of electric phenomena of living organisms.—*v.t.* **elec'troplate**, to plate or cover, esp. with silver, by electrolysis.—*n.* electroplated ware.—*n.* **elec'troplating**.—*adjs.* **elec'tropō'lar**, having, as an electrical conductor, one end or surface positive and the other negative; **electropos'itive**, carrying a positive charge: tending to form positive ions.—*ns.* **elec'troscōpe**, an instrument for detecting the presence of electricity in a body and the nature of it.—*adjs.* **electroscŏp'ic**; **electrostat'ic**.—*ns.* **electrostat'ics**, the branch of science which treats of electricity at rest; **electrotech'nics**, electric technology; **electrotherapeu'tics**, **electrother'apy**, treatment of disease by electricity.—*adjs.* **electrotherm'al**, **electrotherm'ic**, pertaining to electricity and heat, or heat obtained electrically.—*ns.* **electrotherm'ics**; **electrotherm'y**; **elec'trotint**, a printing block produced by drawing with varnish on a metal plate, and depositing metal electrically on the parts not covered.—*adj.* **electroton'ic**.—*n.* **electrot'onus**, the state of a nerve subjected to a steady discharge of electricity; **elec'trotype**, a printing plate made by electrolytically coating a mould with copper.—*adj.* **electrotȳp'ic**.—*ns.* **elec'trotȳpist**; **elec'trotȳpy**; **elec'trovalency**, union within a chemical compound achieved by transfer of electrons, the resulting ions being held together by electrostatic attraction—cf. *covalency*.—*adj.* **elec'trovalent**.—**electromagnetic theory**, Clerk Maxwell's theory explaining light in terms of electromagnetic waves; **electromagnetic wave**, a travelling disturbance in space produced by the acceleration of an electric charge, comprising an electric field and a magnetic field at right angles to each other, both moving at the same velocity in a direction normal to the plane of the two fields; **electromotive force**, difference of potential.

electron, *i-lek'tron*, *n.* a natural alloy of gold and silver used by the ancients (also Latinised as **elec'trum**): a minute particle charged with electricity, or a unit charge having inertia, normally forming part of an atom but capable of isolation as in cathode rays.—*adj.* **electronic** (*el-ik-tron'ik*).—*ns.* **electron'ics**, the science of the behaviour of free electrons; **electron-volt**, the unit of energy associated with an electron which has freely dropped its potential by one volt.—**electron camera**, any device that converts an optical image into a corresponding electric current directly by electronic means; **electron microscope**, a microscope that makes use of a beam of electrons instead of light. [Gr. *ēlektron*, amber.]

electuary, *i-lek'tū-ar-i*, *n.* a medicine mixed with honey or the like. [L.L. *ēlectuārium*, perh.—Gr. *ekleikton*—*ekleichein*, to lick up.]

eleemosynary, *el-i-i-moz'i-nər-i*, or *-mos'*, *adj.* relating to charity or almsgiving: dependent on charity: of the nature of alms. [Gr. *eleēmosynē*, alms—*eleos*, pity. See **alms**.]

elegant, *el'i-gənt*, *adj.* pleasing to good or fastidious taste: graceful: neat: refined: foppish: pretty: (*vulg.*) excellent.—*ns.* **el'egance**, **el'egancy**, the state or quality of being elegant: the beauty of propriety: refinement: an exemplification of elegance.—*adv.* **el'egantly**. [Fr.,—L. *ēlegāns*, *-āntis*—*ē*, from, and root of *legēre*, to choose.]

elegy, *el'i-ji*, *n.* a song of mourning: a funeral-song: a poem of serious, pensive, or reflective mood: a poem written in elegiac metre.—*adj.* **elegī'ac**, belonging to elegy: mournful: used in elegies, esp. applied to classical verse in alternate hexameter and pentameter lines.—*n.* elegiac verse.—*adj.* **elegī'acal**.—*ns.* **elegiast** (*e-lē'ji-ast*; Goldsmith), **el'egist**, a writer of elegies.—*v.i.* **el'egise**, to write elegiacally.—*v.t.* to write an elegy on. [L. *elegīa*—Gr. *elegeiā*—*elegos*, a lament.]

element, *el'i-mənt*, *n.* a first principle: one of the essential parts of anything: an ingredient: the proper medium, habitat or sphere of any thing or being: any one of the four substances, fire, air, earth, and water, supposed by the ancients to be the foundation of everything: (*pl.*) the rudiments of learning : (usu. *pl.*) the bread and wine used in the Eucharist : (*chem.*) a substance that cannot be resolved by chemical means into simpler substances : a member or unit of a structure : a resistance wire in an electric heater : an electrode : a determining fact or condition in a problem : the sky : a celestial sphere : (*pl.*) the weather, the powers of nature.—*adj.* **elemental** (*-ment'l*), pertaining to the elements : belonging to or produced by or inhabiting the elements.—*n.* an elemental spirit : a nature spirit : a disembodied spirit.—*n.* **element′alism,** worship of elemental spirits : the theory which resolves the divinities of antiquity into the elemental powers.—*adv.* **element′ally.** —*adj.* **element′ary,** of a single element : primary : rudimentary : uncompounded : pertaining to the elements : treating of first principles.—**elemental spirits,** beings in mediaeval belief who presided over the four elements, living in and ruling them ; **elements of an orbit,** the data mathematically necessary to determine it. [L. *elementum,* pl. *elementa,* first principles.]

elemi, *el′im-i, n.* a fragrant resinous substance obtained from various tropical trees, esp. a species of *Canarium.*—*n.* **el′emin,** the crystallisable portion of elemi. [Perh. Ar.]

elench, *i-lengk′,* **elenchus** (*pl.* **elench′i**), *-əs, ns.* refutation : a sophism.—*adjs.* **elench′ic, -al, elenc′tic.** [L.—Gr. *elenchos—elenchein,* refute.]

elephant, *el′i-fənt, n.* a Proboscidean (*Elephas*) of several fossil and two surviving species, the largest living land mammal, having a very thick skin, a trunk, and ivory tusks : a special size of paper (writing, 23 by 28 inches ; brown, 24 by 34).—*ns.* **elephantiac** (*-fant′*), one affected with elephantiasis ; **elephanti′asis** (Gr. *elephantiāsis*), a disease chiefly of tropical climates, consisting of an overgrowth of the skin and connective tissue usually of the legs and scrotum.—*n.* **el′ephant-fo′lio,** a folio of the largest size ; *n.* **el′ephant-grass′,** a kind of reed-mace, *Typha elephantum.*—*adjs.* **elephant′ine,** pertaining to an elephant : like an elephant : very large or ungainly ; **elephant′oid,** elephant-like.—*ns.* **el′ephant-seal,** the largest of the seals, the male measuring about 20 feet in length ; **el′ephant's-ears′,** begonia ; **elephant's-foot,** Hottentot bread, a plant (*Testudinaria elephantipes*) of the yam family, whose root-stock resembles an elephant's foot, eaten by the Hottentots : a tropical composite plant, Elephantopus, from the shape of its radical leaves ; **el′ephant-shrew′,** any member of the African family Macroscelidae, long-nosed, long-legged Insectivora, agile jumpers over loose sand.—**a white elephant,** anything that gives more trouble than it is worth— a (so-called) white elephant being an honourable but onerous gift of the kings of Siam to a courtier they wished to ruin. [Remodelled after Lat. from M.E. *olifaunt*—O.Fr. *olifant,* or poss. O.E. *olfend,* camel—L. *elephantus, elephās*—Gr. *elephās, -antos.*]

Eleusinian, *el-ū-sin′i-ən, adj.* relating to *Eleusis* in Attica.—**eleusinian mysteries,** the mysteries of Demeter celebrated there.

eleutherian, *el-ū-thē′ri-ən, adj.* freedom-giving.— *n.* **eleu′therarch** (*-thər-ärk ;* Gr. *archos,* chief ; *Shelley*), chief of a feigned society of **eleu′theri.**— *adj.* **eleutherodac′tyl** (Gr. *daktylos,* toe ; of birds), having the hind-toe free. [Gr. *eleutheros,* free.]

elevate, *el′i-vāt, v.t.* to raise to a higher position : to raise in mind and feelings : to cheer : to exhilarate.—*adjs.* **el′evate, -d,** raised : lofty : exhilarated, esp. by liquor.—*ns.* **eleva′tion,** the act of elevating or raising, or the state of being raised : exaltation : an elevated place or station : a rising ground : height : (*archit.*) a representation of the flat side of a building, drawn with mathematical accuracy, but without any attention to effect : a facade : angular height above the horizon : an angle made by a line with the plane of the horizon : lifting up (of the Host) in view of the people ; **el′evātor,** a person or thing that lifts up : a lift or machine for raising grain, etc., to a higher floor : (*U.S.*) a lift : a storehouse for grain : a muscle raising a part of the body : movable control surface or surfaces at the tail of an aeroplane by which it is made to

climb or dive.—*adj.* **el′evatory,** able or tending to raise.—**elevated (railroad),** a railway borne on pillars or trestles over a roadway, as in some American towns (familiarly **el,** or **L**). [L. *ēlevāre, -ātum—ē,* from, *levāre,* to raise—*levis,* light. See **light** (2).]

eleven, *i-lev′n, n.* the cardinal number next above ten : a team of eleven (cricket, association football, etc.) : the eleventh hour after noon or midnight.— *adj.* of the number eleven.—*n.* **elev′ens, elev′-enses** (*coll.*), an eleven o'clock snack or draught : morning coffee or the like.—*adj.* **elev′enth,** next after the tenth : equal to one of eleven equal parts. —*n.* an eleventh part : (*mus.*) an octave and a fourth.—*adv.* **elev′enthly.—eleven and twenty long** (*Shak.*), exactly right (the score aimed at in the game of one-and-thirty) ; **eleventh hour,** the very last moment, referring to Matt. xx. 6, 9. [O.E. *en(d)le(o)fan ;* cf. Goth. *ainlif ;* perh. (ten and) *one left,* from the root of L. *linquĕre,* Gr. *leipein,* to leave.]

elf, *elf, n.* in European folklore, a supernatural being, generally of human form but diminutive size, sometimes more malignant than a fairy : a fairy : a dwarf : a tricky, froward, or fairy-like being, esp. a child : a wretch : (*pl.* **elves,** *elvz*).— *v.t.* (*Shak.*) of the hair, to entangle.—*ns.* **elf′-arrow, -bolt,** an elf-shot ; **elf′-child,** a changeling, or a child supposed to have been left by elves in place of one stolen by them ; **elf′hood.**—*adj.* **elf′in,** of, like, or relating to elves.—*n.* a little elf : a child.—*adjs.* **elf′ish, elv′an, elv′ish,** elf-like, mischievous : tricky : distraught : froward.—*n.* **elf′-land,** the land of the elves or fairies.—*n.pl.* **elf′-locks** (*Shak.*), locks of hair clotted together, supposedly by elves.—*v.t.* **elf′-shoot,** to shoot with an elf-arrow, bewitch.—*n.* **elf′-shot,** a prehistoric flint or stone arrow-head, supposed to be used by elves : sickness attributed to it.—*adj.* shot with an elf-arrow : bewitched. [O.E. *ælf ;* cf. O.N. *ālfr,* Sw. *elf.*]

Elian, *ē′li-ən, adj.* of, or like the work of, Charles Lamb, who wrote under the name of *Elia.*—*n.* a devotee or imitator of Lamb.

eliad. See **œiliade.**

elicit, *i-, e-lis′it, v.t.* to draw forth : to evoke.—*n.* **elicita′tion.** [L. *ēlicĕre, ēlicitum.*]

elide, *i-līd′, v.t.* to rebut : to cut off, as a syllable.— *n.* **elision** (*i-lizh′ən*), the suppression of a vowel or syllable. [L. *ēlīdĕre, ēlīsum—ē,* from *laedĕre,* to strike.]

eligible, *el′i-ji-bl, adj.* fit or worthy to be chosen : legally qualified for election or appointment : desirable.—*n.* (*coll.*) a person or thing eligible.— *n.* **eligibil′ity.**—*adv.* **el′igibly.** [Fr.,—L. *ēligĕre ;* see **elect,** *v.t.*]

eliminate, *i-, e-lim′in-āt, v.t.* to thrust out : to remove, cancel, get rid of.—*adjs.* **elim′inable ;** **elim′inant,** (*med.*) causing elimination of waste or morbid matter.—*n.* an eliminating agent.—*n.* **elimina′tion.**—*adj.* **elim′inative.**—*n.* **elim′-inator,** one who or that which eliminates ; esp. a device for substituting an electric main for a battery in a wireless receiving set.—*adj.* **elim′inatory.** [L. *ēlīmināre, -ātum—ē,* from, *līmen, -inis,* a threshold.]

elision. See **elide.**

élite, *ā-lēt, n.* a chosen or select part : the pick or flower of anything. [Fr. *élite*—L. *electa* (*pars,* part, understood) ; see **elect.**]

elixir, *i-, e-liks′ər, n.* a liquor once supposed to have the power of indefinitely prolonging life (**elixir of life**), or of transmuting metals : the quintessence of anything : a substance which invigorates : a panacea : a nostrum : a strong tincture : a compound tincture. [L.L.,—Ar. *al-iksīr,* the philosopher's stone, from *al-,* the, *iksīr,* prob. from Late Gr. *xērion,* a desiccative powder for wounds— Gr. *xēros,* dry.]

Elizabethan, *e-liz-ə-bē′thən, adj.* pertaining to a Queen *Elizabeth* or her reign, esp. to the first Queen Elizabeth (1533-1603) or her reign (1558-1603)—of dress, manners, literature, etc.—*n.* a person, esp. poet or dramatist, of that age.—*n.* **Elizabeth′anism.—Elizabethan architecture,**

the mixed style that sprang up on the decline of Gothic, marked by Tudor bow-windows and turrets decorated with classic cornices and pilasters, long galleries, enormous square windows, large apartments, plaster ceilings wrought into compartments, etc.

elk, *elk*, *n.* deer of northern Europe and Asia, identical or close akin with the moose of N. America, the largest of all living deer: (*Amer.*) the wapiti.—*ns.* **elk′horn-fern′**, a genus (Platycerium) of tropical epiphytic ferns, with large leaf like an elk's horn; **elk′-hound**, a large strong Norwegian breed of dog with thick coat and curled tail.—**Irish elk**, a giant deer now extinct, known from the remains found in the Pleistocene, esp. of Ireland. [Perh. Gmc., but apparently not O.E. *elh* (W.S. *eolh*); cf. O.H.G. *elaho*, O.N. *elgr*, Sw. *elg*, L. *alcēs*, Gr. *alkē*.]

ell, *el*, *n.* a varying measure of length originally taken from the arm: a cloth measure equal to 1¼ yd.—*n.* **ell′-wand**, a measuring rod.—**give him an inch and he′ll take an ell**, a concession will encourage the taking of liberties. [O.E. *eln*; Du. *el*, Ger. *elle*, L. *ulna*, Gr. *ōlenē*, elbow.]

ell, *el*, *n.* the letter L or anything of like shape: (*U.S.*) a wing giving a building the shape of the letter L.

ellagic, *e-laj′ik*, *adj.* pertaining to gall-nuts, applied to an acid, $C_{14}H_6O_8$. [Fr. *galle*, gall, spelt backwards.]

ellipse, *el-ips′*, *n.* (*geom.*) a figure produced by the section of one branch of a right circular cone by a plane passing obliquely and failing to meet the other branch.—*ns.* **ellip′sis** (*gram.*), a figure of syntax by which a word or words are left out and implied:—*pl.* **ellip′sēs**; **ellip′sograph**, an instrument for describing ellipses; **ellip′soid** (*math.*), a surface (or the enclosed solid) of which every plane section is an ellipse or a circle.—*adjs.* **ellipsoi′dal**; **ellip′tic**, **-al**, pertaining to an ellipse: oval: pertaining to ellipsis: having a part understood: (*bot.*) slightly acute at each end, rather narrow, and broadest in the middle.—*adv.* **ellip′tically.**—*n.* **ellipticity** (*el-ip-tis′i-ti*), deviation from the form of a circle or sphere: of the earth, the difference between the equatorial and polar diameters.—**elliptic space**, space according to Riemann's conception (see **Riemannian**). [L. *ellipsis*—Gr. *elleipsis*—*elleipein*, to fall short—*en*, in, *leipein*, to leave.]

ellops, *el′ops*, *n.* (*Milt.*) a kind of snake: a sturgeon: (*Goldsmith*) a sea-serpent. [Gr. *ellops*, also *elops*, *elaps*, perh. mute, perh. scaly, also an unknown fish, and an unknown snake; cf. **elaps**.]

elm, *elm*, *n.* a tree (Ulmus) with serrated leaves unequal at the base, and small flowers in clusters appearing before the leaves.—*adj.* of elm.—*adjs.* **elm′en**, made of elm; **elm′y**, abounding with elms. [O.E. *elm*; Ger. *ulme*, L. *ulmus*.]

elocution, *el-o-kū′shan*, *n.* the art of effective speaking, more esp. of public speaking, regarding solely the utterance or delivery: eloquence.—*adj.* **elocū′tionary.**—*n.* **elocū′tionist**, one versed in or practising elocution: a teacher of elocution: a reciter. [L. *ēlocūtiō*, *-ōnis*, *ēloquī*, *-cūtus*—*ē*, from, *loquī*, to speak.]

Elodea, *e-lō′di-ä*, *n.* an American genus of Hydrocharitaceae, to which the Canadian waterweed belongs.—Also called Helodea, Anacharis, and Phyllotria. [Gr. *helōdēs*, marshy, marsh-dwelling—*helos*, marsh, *eidos*, form.]

éloge, *ā-lōzh′*, **elogium**, *ē-lō′ji-əm*, **elogy**, *el′ə-ji*, *n.* a funeral oration: a panegyric.—*n.* **el′ogist**, one who delivers an éloge. [Fr. *éloge*, and its source L. *ēlogium*, a short statement, an inscription on a tomb, perh. confused with **eulogy**.]

Elohim, *e-lō′him*, *n.* Hebrew name for God.—*n.* **Elō′hist**, the writer or writers of the Elohistic passages of the Old Testament.—*adj.* **Elohist′ic**, relating to Elohim—said of those passages in the Old Testament in which the name Elohim is used instead of Yahweh (Jehovah). [Heb. pl. of *Eloah*—explained by Delitzsch as a plural of intensity.]

eloin, **eloign**, *e-loin′*, *v.t.* to convey to a distance, to separate and remove.—*ns.* **eloin′ment**, **eloign′-**

-ment. [O.Fr. *esloignier* (Fr. *éloigner*)—L.L. *ēlongāre*. See **elongate**.]

elongate, *ē′long-gāt*, also *-long′*, *v.t.* to make longer: to extend.—*v.i.* to grow longer.—*adjs.* **elongate**, **-d.**—*n.* **elonga′tion**, act of lengthening out: distance: the moon's or a planet's angular distance from the sun. [L.L. *ēlongāre*, *-ātum*—*ē*, from, *longus*, long.]

elope, *i-lōp′*, *v.i.* to escape privately, esp. with a lover: to run away, bolt.—*ns.* **elope′ment**; **elop′er.** [Cf. O.Du. *ontlōpen*, Ger. *entlaufen*, to run away.]

eloquent, *el′o-kwənt*, *adj.* having eloquence: persuasive: strongly expressive.—*n.* **el′oquence**, the power, art, or practice of uttering strong emotion in correct, appropriate, expressive, and fluent language: the art which produces fine speaking: persuasive speech.—*adv.* **el′oquently.** [L. *ēloquēns*, *-entis*, pr.p. of *ēloquī*.]

else, *els*, *adj.* (or *adv.*) other (in addition or instead).—*adv.* otherwise: besides: except that mentioned.—*advs.* **elsewhere′**, in or to another place; **elsewhith′er**; **else′wise**, in a different manner: otherwise. [O.E. *elles*, otherwise, orig. gen. of *el*, other; cf. O.H.G. *alles* or *elles*, L. *alius*, Gr. *allos*, other.]

elsin, *el′sin*, **elshin**, *el′shin*, *n.* (*Scot.*) an awl. [From O.Du. *elssene* (mod. *els*); cf. **awl**.]

elt, *elt*, *n.* (*prov.*) a young sow. [Cf. **yelt**, **gilt** (2).]

eltchi. Same as **elchi**.

elucidate, *e-l(y)ōō′si-dāt*, *v.t.* to make lucid or clear: to throw light upon: to illustrate.—*n.* **elucidā′tion.**—*adjs.* **elu′cidative**, **elu′cidatory**, making clear: explanatory.—*n.* **elu′cidator**. [L.L. *ēlūcidāre*, *-ātum*—*ē*-, inten., *lūcidus*, clear.]

elucubration. Same as **lucubration**. [L. *ē*-, inten.]

elude, *ē*-, *i-l(y)ōōd′*, *v.t.* to escape by stratagem: to baffle.—*adj.* **elu′dible.**—**elu′sion** (*-zhen*), act of eluding: evasion.—*adj.* **elu′sive** (*-ziv*), practising elusion: deceptive.—*adv.* **elu′sively.**—*n.* **elu′soriness.**—*adj.* **elu′sory**, tending to elude or cheat: evasive: deceitful. [L. *ēlūdĕre*, *ēlūsum*—*ē*, from, *lūdĕre*, to play.]

elul, *ē′lul*, *n.* the 12th month of the Jewish civil year, and 6th of the ecclesiastical. [Heb.,—*ālal*, to reap.]

elution, *i-l(y)ōō′shən*, *n.* (*chem.*) purification or separation by washing.—*v.t.* **elute′.**—*n.* **elu′tor**, a vessel for elution. [L. *ēlūtiō*, *-ōnis*, washing—*ēluĕre*, *ēlūtum*—*ē*, from, *luĕre*, to wash.]

elutriate, *i-l(y)ōō′tri-āt*, *v.t.* to separate by washing into coarser and finer portions.—*ns.* **elutriā′tion**, **elu′triātor**, apparatus for elutriating. [L. *ēlutriāre*, *-ātum*, to wash out, *ēluĕre*—*ē*, from, *luĕre*, to wash.]

eluvium, *ē-l(y)ōō′vi-əm*, *n.* an accumulation of rock débris formed on the spot or moved by wind only, as loess.—*adj.* **elu′vial**. [Formed on the analogy of **alluvium**, **diluvium.**—L. *ē*, from, *luĕre*, to wash.]

elvan, *elv′ən*, *n.* a granular crystalline dyke rock, composed of quartz and orthoclase.—Also **elv′anite.** [Cornish miners' name; prob. Cornish *elven*, spark.]

elvan, **elves**, **elvish.** See under **elf**.

elver, *el′vər*, *n.* a young eel. [eel-fare; see **eel**.]

Elysium, *e-liz(h)′i-əm*, *n.* (*myth.*) among the Greeks, the abode of the blessed dead: any delightful place.—*adj.* **Elys′ian.** [L.,—Gr. *ēlysion* (*pedion*), the Elysian (plain).]

elytrum, *el′it-rəm*, *n.* a beetle's fore-wing modified to form a case for the hind-wing: a dorsal plate in certain worms.—Also **el′ytron:**—*pl.* **el′ytra.**—*adjs.* **el′ytral**; **elyt′riform**; **elytrigerous** (*-trij′ər-əs*). [Latinised from Gr. *elytron*, a sheath.]

Elzevir, *el′zi-vēr*, *-vər*, *adj.* published by the *Elzevirs*, a celebrated family of printers at Amsterdam, Leyden, and other places in Holland, whose small neat editions were chiefly published between 1592 and 1681: pertaining to the type used in their 12mo and 16mo editions of the Latin classics.—*n.* a special form of printing types.

em, *em*, *n.* the name of the letter **m**: (*print.*) the unit of measurement (lower-case 'm') in estimating how much is printed in a line or page.

'em, *əm*, *pron.* them: to them. [Orig. the unstressed form of *hem*, dat. and accus. pl. of *he* (O.E. *him*, *heom*, dat. pl.); but now used coll. as if an abbreviation of **them**.]

emaciate, *i-mā′shi-āt*, *v.t.* to make meagre or lean: to deprive of flesh: to waste.—*v.i.* to become lean: to waste away.—*adjs.* **emā′ciate, -d.**—*n.* **emacia′tion**, the condition of becoming emaciated or lean: leanness. [L. *ēmaciāre*, *-ātum—ē*, inten. *maciāre*, to make lean—*maciēs*, leanness.]

emanate, *em′ə-nāt*, *v.i.* to flow out of from anything: to proceed from some source: to arise.—*adj.* **em′anant**, flowing out.—*ns.* **emana′tion**, a flowing out from a source, as the universe considered as issuing from the essence of God: the *generation* of the Son and the *procession* of the Spirit, as distinct from the origination of created beings: that which issues or proceeds from some source: a radioactive gas given off by radium, thorium and actinium—*radon*; **em′anatist.**—*adjs.* **em′anative, em′anatory, emana′tional.** [L. *ēmānāre*, *-ātum—ē*, out from, *mānāre*, to flow.]

emancipate, *i-man′si-pāt*, *v.t.* to set free from restraint or bondage or disability of any kind.—*ns.* **emancipa′tion**, the act of setting free from bondage or disability of any kind: the state of being set free: **emancipa′tionist**, an advocate of the emancipation of slaves; **eman′cipātor;** **eman′cipist**, a convict who has served his time of punishment in a penal colony. [L. *ēmancipāre*, *-ātum—ē*, away from, *mancipāre*, to transfer property—*manceps*, *-cipis*, one who gets property, from *manus*, the hand, *capēre*, to take.]

emarginate, *ē-mär′jin-āt*, *v.t.* to take away the margin of.—*adj.* (*bot.*) depressed and notched instead of pointed at the tip, as a leaf: (*min.*) having all the edges of the primitive form crossed by a face: (*zool.*) having the margin broken by a notch or segment of a circle.—*n.* **emargina′tion.** [L. *ēmargināre*, *-ātum—ē*, out, *margināre*, to provide with a margin—*margō*, a margin.]

emasculate, *i-*, *ē-mas′kū-lāt*, *v.t.* to deprive of the properties of a male: to castrate: to deprive of masculine vigour: to render effeminate.—*adj.* emasculated.—*ns.* **emascula′tion; emas′culātor.**—*adj.* **emas′culatory** (*-lə-tər-i*). [L.L. *ēmasculāre*, *-ātum—ē*, from, *masculus*, dim. of *mas*, a male.]

embace. See **embase.**

embail, *im-*, *em-bāl′*, *v.t.* to encircle: to hoop in: (*pa.p.*, Spens., **embayld′**). [Pfx. *em-* and **bail**.]

embale, *im-*, *em-bāl′*, *v.t.* to make up, as into a bale: to bind up: to enclose. [Fr. *emballer*—*em-* (L. *in*), in, *balle*, a bale.]

emball, *em-bawl′*, *v.t.* to ensphere.—*n.* **emball′ing** (*Shak.*), the receiving of the ball (of sovereignty). [**ball**.]

embalm, *im-*, *em-bäm′*, *v.t.* to preserve from decay by aromatic drugs, as a dead body: to preserve with fragrance: to preserve unchanged but lifeless: to impregnate with balm, perfume.—*ns.* **embalm′er; embalm′ing; embalm′ment.** [Fr. *embaumer*, from *em-*, in, and *baume;* see **balm**.]

embank, *im-*, *em-bangk′*, *v.t.* to enclose or defend with a bank or dike.—*ns.* **embank′er; embank′ment**, the act of embanking: a bank or mound made to keep water within certain limits: a mound constructed so as to carry a level road or railway over a low-lying place. [Pfx. *em-*, **bank**.]

embar, *im-*, *em-bär′*, *v.t.* to shut in: to hinder or stop: (*Milt.* **imbar′**) to put under embargo:— (*pr.p.* **embarr′ing;** *pa.t.* and *pa.p.* **embarred′**.)—*n.* **embarr′ing.**—Also **imbar′.**

embarcation. Same as **embarkation.**

embargo, *em-bär′gō*, *n.* a temporary order from the Admiralty to prevent the arrival or departure of ships: a stoppage of trade for a short time by authority: a prohibition, ban:—*pl.* **embar′goes.** —*v.t.* to lay an embargo on: to seize.—(*pr.p.* **embar′göing;** *pa.t.* and *pa.p.* **embar′goed,** *-gōd.*) —*n.* **embarque′ment** (*Shak.*) a placing under embargo. [Sp.,—*embargar*, to impede, to restrain —Sp. pfx. *em-*, in, L.L. (and Sp.) *barra*, a bar.]

embark, *im-bärk′*, *v.t.* to put on board ship: to engage, invest, in any affair.—*v.i.* to go on board ship: to engage in (with *on*, *in*).—*n.* **embarka′tion** (*em-*),

a putting or going on board: that which is embarked: (*obs.*) a vessel.—*adjs.* **embarked′; embark′ing.**—*n.* **embark′ment.** [Fr. *embarquer*, from *em-*, in, *barque*, bark.]

embarrass, *im-*, *em-bar′əs*, *v.t.* to encumber: to involve in difficulty, esp. in money matters: to put out of countenance, disconcert: to perplex.— *adj.* **embarr′assed**, perplexed · constrained: disconcerted.—*n.* **embarr′assment**, perplexity or confusion: difficulties in money matters. [Fr. *embarrasser*—*em-*, in, *barre*, L.L. *barra*, bar.]

embase, **imbase** (*Spens.* **embace**), *im-bās′*, *v.t.* to lower: to bring down: to degrade: to debase :— *pa.p.* and *pa.t.* **embased′;** (*Spens.*) **embaste′.**— *adj.* **embased′.**—*n.* **embase′ment.** [Pfx. *em-* and **base**, or Fr. *bas.*]

embassy, *em′bə-si*, *n.* the charge or function of an ambassador: the person or body of persons sent on an undertaking: an ambassador's residence.— *n.* **em′bassade** (*Shak.*), an embassy.—*adv.* (*Spens.* *-bas′*), on an embassy.—*ns.* **embassador** (*-bas′;* *obs.* except *U.S.*), an ambassador; **em′bassage**, embassy: the sending or business of an embassy. [See **ambassador**.]

embathe, **imbathe**, *im-bādh′*, *v.t.* to bathe: to immerse: to bedew.

embattle, *im-bat′l*, *v.t.* to furnish with battlements. —*adj.* **embatt′led**, furnished with battlements: (*her.*) having the outline like a battlement.—*n.* **embatt′lement**, battlement. [Pfx. *em-* and O.Fr. *bataillier*, to embattle; see **battlement**.]

embattle, *im-bat′l*, *v.t.* to range in order of battle: (*Spens.*) to arm.—*adj.* **embatt′led**, arranged for battle. [O.Fr. *embataillier*—pfx. *em-*, in, *bataille*, battle.]

embay, *im-bā′*, *v.t.* to enclose in a bay: to landlock.—*n.* **embay′ment**, a bay. [Pfx. *em-*, in, and **bay**.]

embay, *em-bā′*, *v.t.* (*Spens.*) to bathe, steep, imbue. [Fr. pfx. *em-*, in, and apparently *baigner;* see **bagnio**.]

embayld. See **embail.**

embed, **imbed**, *im-bed′*, to place in a mass of matter: to lay, as in a bed.—*n.* **embed′ment**, the act of embedding: state of being embedded. [Pfx. *em-* and **bed**.]

embellish, *im-bel′ish*, *v.t.* to make beautiful with ornaments: to decorate: to make graceful: to illustrate pictorially, as a book.—*n.* **embell′isher**. —*adv.* **embell′ishingly.**—*n.* **embell′ishment**, act of embellishing or adorning: decoration: ornament. [Fr. *embellir*, *embellissant*—*em-*, in, *bel* (*beau*) beautiful.]

ember, *em′bər*, *n.* a piece of live coal or wood: (chiefly in *pl.*) red-hot ashes : smouldering remains of a fire. [O.E. *æmerge;* O.N. *eimyrja*.]

Ember-days, *em′bər-dāz*, *n.pl.* the three Fast-days (Wednesday, Friday, Saturday) in each quarter, following the first Sunday in Lent, Whitsunday, Holy Cross Day (Sept. 14th), and St. Lucia's Day (Dec. 13th).—*n.* **Em′ber-week**, the week in which they occur. [O.E. *ymbryne*, a circuit—*ymb*, round (cf. Ger. *um*, L. *ambi-*), and *ryne*, a running, from *rinnan*, to run.]

ember-goose, *em′bər-gōōs*, *n.* the great northern diver. [Norw. *emmer;* Ger. *imber*.]

embezzle, *im-bez′l*, *v.t.* to appropriate fraudulently (now only what has been entrusted): (*obs.*) to impair.—*ns.* **embezz′lement**, fraudulent appropriation of property entrusted to one; **embezz′ler.** [Anglo-Fr. *enbesiler*, to make away with, perh. influenced by **imbecile**.]

embitter, **imbitter**, *im-bit′ər*, *v.t.* to make bitter or more bitter: to make more bitterly hostile.—*adj.* **embitt′ered**, soured: rendered misanthropical, cynical, or disappointed.—*n.* **embitt′erer.**—*n.* and *adj.* **embitt′ering.**—*n.* **embitt′erment.**

emblaze, *im-blāz′*, *v.t.* to light up: to set aflame. [Pfx. *em-* and **blaze** (1).]

emblaze, *im-blāz′*, *v.t.* to describe or depict heraldically: to celebrate: to adorn heraldically. [Pfx. *em-* and **blaze** (3).]

emblazon, *im-blā′zn*, *v.t.* (*her.*) to adorn with figures: to depict heraldically: to celebrate.—*ns.* **emblā′zoner; emblā′zonment**, an emblazoning;

emblā′zonry, the art of emblazoning or adorning : devices on shields. [Pfx. **em-** and **blazon**; confused with **emblaze** (1).]

emblem, em′bləm, n. a picture representing to the mind something different from itself : a symbolic device or badge : a type or symbol : (*Milton*) an inlaid ornament.—*v.t.* to symbolise.—*n.* **emblema** (em-blē′mä), an inlaid ornament :—*pl.* **emblē′-mata**.—*adjs.* **emblemat′ic, -al**, pertaining to or containing emblems : symbolical : representing.—*adv.* **emblemat′ically.**—*v.t.* **emblematise** (-blem′ə-tīz), **em′blemise**, to represent by an emblem.—*n.* **emblem′atist**, a writer or inventor of emblems. [L.—Gr. *emblēma, -atos*, a thing inserted—*en*, in, and the root of *ballein*, to throw.]

emblements, em′bli-mənts, n.pl. crops raised by the labour of the cultivator, but not tree-fruits nor grass. [O.Fr. *emblaer*, to sow with corn—L.L. *imbladāre*—*in*, in, *bladum*, wheat.]

emblic, em′blik, an East Indian tree (*Phyllanthus Emblica*) of the spurge family : its fruit, used for tanning.—Also **emblic myrobalan**. [Ar. *amlaj* —Pers. *amleh*.]

embloom, im-bloom′, v.t. to cover with bloom.

emblossom, im-blos′əm, v.t. to cover with blossom.

embody, imbody, im-bod′i, v.t. to form into a body : to make corporeal : to make tangible : to express (in words, in tangible form, etc.) : to make part of a body, to incorporate : to organise.—*v.i.* to unite in a body or mass : to become corporeal, carnal, or sensual : (*pr.p.* **embod′ying**; *pa.t.* and *pa.p.* **embod′ied**).—*adj.* **embod′ied.**—*n.* **embod′iment**, act of embodying : state of being embodied : that in which something is embodied. [*Em-*, in, and **body**.]

embog, im-bog′, v.t. to bog.

embogue, im-bōg′, v.i. to disembogue.

emboil, em-, im-boil′, v.i. (*Spens.*) to burn with anger.—*v.t.* to cause to burn with anger : irritate.

emboîtement, än²-bwät′män², n. encasement.— **emboîtement theory**, the abandoned theory of old embryologists that the egg contained the germs of all future descendants, box within box. [Fr.]

embolden, em-bōld′n, v.t. to make bold or courageous : to give the necessary courage for some action.—*n.* **embold′ener.**

embolism, em′bol-izm, -bəl-, n. an intercalation of days in the calendar to correct error : an intercalated prayer for deliverance from evil coming after the Lord's Prayer : (*med.*) the presence of obstructing clots in the blood-vessels.—*adjs.* **embolic** (-bol′), relating to an embolus or to an emboly ; **embolis′-mal, embolis′mic.**—*ns.* **em′bolus**, a clot obstructing a blood-vessel ; **em′boly**, an invagination. —**embolismic year** (see **year**). [Late Gr. *embolismos*, intercalation, Gr. *embolos*, a stopper, *embolē*, insertion, ramming—*emballein*, to throw in.]

embonpoint, än²-bon²-pwan²′, adj. stout, plump, full in figure, mostly of women : well-fed.—*n.* stoutness, plumpness, well-fed condition. [Fr.,— *en bon point*, in good form.]

emborder, em-bord′ər, v.t. (*Milt.*) to set as a border : to border.

emboscata, em-bos-kä′tä, -kä′tä, n. an erroneous form of It. *imboscata*, or Sp. *emboscada*, an ambuscade.

embosom, imbosom, im-booz′əm, v.t. to take into the bosom : to receive into the affections : to inplant in the bosom or mind : to enclose or surround.

emboss, im-bos′, v.t. to cover with bosses : to raise bosses on : to raise in relief : to ornament with raised work.—*adj.* **embossed′**, formed or covered with bosses : raised, standing out in relief : (*bot.*) having a protuberance in the centre.—*ns.* **em′-boss′er** ; **emboss′ment**, a prominence like a boss : raised work. [Pfx. *em-*, and **boss**.]

emboss, imboss, im-bos′, **imbosk**, -bosk′, v.i. to take to the depths of a wood.—*v.t.* to drive to extremity : to make to foam at the mouth : (*pa.p.* **embossed′**, *Milt.* **embost′**). [O.Fr. *embosquer*, *em-* (L. *in*, in), *bosc*, a wood ; see **ambush**.]

emboss, em-bos′, v.t. (*Spens.*) to clothe : to wrap : to enclose. [Origin obscure.]

embouchure, än²-bōō-shür′, n. the mouth of a river : the mouth-piece of a wind instrument : the disposition of the mouth in playing a wind instrument. [Fr.,—*emboucher*, to put to the mouth, to discharge—*en*, in, *bouche*, a mouth.]

embound, em-bownd′, v.t. (*Shak.*) to enclose.

embow, em-bow′, em-bō′, v.t. to bend : to arch or vault : to ensphere.—*adj.* **embowed′**, bent. [Pfx. *em-* and **bow**.]

embowel, im-bow′əl, v.t. (*obs.*) to enclose : to disembowel, to remove the entrails from : to enclose in, or (*Spens.*) thrust into, the bowels : (*pr.p.* **embow′elling**; *pa.t.* and *pa.p.* **em-bow′elled**).—*n.* **embow′elment**. [Pfx. *em-*, in, and **bowel**.]

embower, imbower, im-bow′ər, v.t. to place in a bower : to shelter, as with trees.—*v.i.* to take or give shelter.—*n.* **embow′erment.**

embox, im-boks′, v.t. to set in a box. [*Em-*, in, **box**.]

embrace, im-brās′, v.t. to take in the arms : to press to the bosom with affection : to take eagerly or willingly : to comprise : to admit, adopt, or receive.—*v.i.* to join in an embrace :—(*pr.p.* **embrac′ing**; *pa.t.* and *pa.p.* **embraced′**).—*n.* an embracing : fond pressure in the arms : (in *pl.*) sexual intercourse.—*ns.* **embrace′ment** ; **embrac′er.**—*adjs.* **embrac′ing, embrac′ive.**—*adv.* **embrac′ingly.**—*n.* **embrac′ingness.** [O.Fr. *embracer* (Fr. *embrasser*)—L. *in*, in, into, *brā(c)chium*, an arm ; see **brace**.]

embrace, em-brās′, v.t. (*Spens.*) to brace, to fasten, or bind. [Pfx. *em-*, in, and **brace**.]

embracer, embraceor, embrasor, em-brā′sər, n. (*law*) one who seeks to influence jurors by corrupt means to deliver a partial verdict.—*n.* **em-brac′ery**, the offence of an embracer. [O.Fr. *embraceor*, from *embraser*, to set on fire.]

embraid, em-brād′, v.t. (*Spens.*) to braid.

embranchment, im-brānsh′mənt, n. a branching off, as an arm of a river, a spur of a mountain, etc. [Pfx. *em-*, and **branch**.]

embrangle, imbrangle, im-brang′gl, v.t. to confuse, perplex.—*n.* **embran′glement.** [Pfx. *em-* and **brangle**.]

embrasure, em-brās′yər, n. (*Shak.*) embrace.

embrasure, im-brā′zhər, formerly em′brə-zhōōr′, n. an internally splayed recess of a door or window : the slant of such a recess : an opening in a wall for cannon.—Also **embrazure**. [Fr.,—O.Fr. *embraser*, to slope the sides of a window, *em-* (—L. *in*), *braser*, to skew.]

embrave, em-brāv′, v.t. (*Spens.*) to make brave or showy, to decorate : to inspire with bravery.

embread, em-brēd′, v.t. (*Spens.*) embraid.

embreathe, em-brēdh′, v.t. to breathe into : to breathe in. [*En-* and **breathe**.]

embrewe (*Spens.*). See **imbrue**.

embrocate, em′brō-kāt, v.t. to moisten and rub, as with a lotion.—*n.* **embrocā′tion**, act of embrocating : the lotion used. [L.L. *embrocāre, -ātum*, from Gr. *embrochē*, a lotion—*embrechein*, to soak, embrocate—*en-*, in, into, *brechein*, to wet.]

embroglio. See **imbroglio.**

embroider, im-broid′ər, v.t. to ornament with designs in needlework : to add ornament or fictitious detail to.—*ns.* **embroid′erer** ; **em-broid′ery**, the art of producing ornamental designs in needlework on textile fabrics, etc. : ornamental needlework : variegation or diversity : artificial or elaborate ornamentation : embellishment : exaggeration or invented detail. [M.E. *embrouderie*—O.Fr. *embroder* ; confused with or influenced by O.E. *bregdan*, to weave, braid.]

embroil, im-broil′, v.t. to involve in a broil, or in perplexity (with) : to entangle : to distract : to throw into confusion.—*n.* **embroil′ment**, a state of perplexity or confusion : disturbance. [Fr. *embrouiller*—pfx. *em-*, and *brouiller*, to break out.]

embrown, imbrown, im-brown′, v.t. to make brown : to darken, obscure.—*adj.* **embrown′ing.**

embrue. Same as **imbrue.**

embrute. Same as **imbrute.**

embryo, em′bri-ō, also (*archaic*) **embryon**, em′bri-on, n. a young animal or plant in its earliest stages of development: beginning of anything:—*pl.* **em′bryos, em′bryons.**—Also *adj.*—*n.* **embryogeny** (*-oj′i-ni*), the formation and development of the embryo.—*adjs.* **embryolog′ic, -al.**—*ns.* **embryol′ogist; embryol′ogy,** the science of the formation and development of the embryo.—*adjs.* **em′bryonal, em′bryonate, -d; embryon′ic, embryot′ic,** of or relating to anything in an imperfect state: rudimentary.—*ns.* **em′bryosac,** *n.* the megaspore of a flowering plant, one of the cells of the nucellus; **embryot′omy** (Gr. *tomē*, a cut), the division of a fetus to effect removal; **embryul′cia** (*-ul′shi-ä;* Gr. *holkē*, dragging), forcible extraction of a fetus. [L.L.,— Gr. *embryon—en*, in, *bryein*, to swell.]

embus, *im-bus′*, *v.t.* to put into a bus (esp. troops). —*v.i.* to mount a bus:—*pr.p.* **embuss′ing,** *pa.t.* and *pa.p.* **embussed′.**

embusy, *em-biz′i*, *v.t.* (*Spens.*) to occupy, make busy.

eme, *ēm*, *n.* (*obs.*) an uncle. [O.E. *éam;* Du. *oom*.]

emend, *ē-mend′*, *v.t.* to remove faults or blemishes from: to correct or improve.—*adj.* **emend′able,** that may be emended.—*n.pl.* **emend′als,** funds set apart for repairs in the accounts of the Inner Temple.—*v.t.* **e′mendate,** to correct errors.—*ns.* **emenda′tion,** removal of an error or fault: correction; **e′mendātor,** a corrector of errors in writings: one who corrects or improves.—*adj.* **emen′datory,** mending or contributing to correction. [L. *ēmendāre, -ātum—ē*, from, *menda*, a fault.]

emerald, *em′ər-əld*, (*Spens.* **emerande**), *n.* a very highly esteemed gem-stone, a beautiful velvety green variety of beryl.—*n.* **em′erald-copp′er,** dioptase.—**Emerald Isle,** Ireland, from its greenness; **emerald type** (*print.*), a small size of type. [O.Fr. *esmeralde*—L. *smaragdus*—Gr. *smaragdos*.]

emerge, *i-, ē-mərj′*, *v.i.* to rise out of anything: to issue or come forth: to reappear after being concealed: to come into view: to crop up.—*ns.* **emer′gence,** act of emerging: sudden appearance: (*obs.*) emergency; (*bot.*) an outgrowth of subepidermic tissue along with epidermic—an appendage more complex in structure than a hair; **emer′gency,** (*obs.*) emergence: an unexpected occurrence: pressing necessity: an emergencyman: a substitute in reserve.—Also *adj.*—*n.* **emer′gency-man,** a man called in for any special occasion.—*adj.* **emer′gent,** emerging: suddenly appearing: arising unexpectedly: urgent: coming into being in the course of evolution.— *adv.* **emer′gently.**—*adj.* **emersed** (*ē-mərst′; bot.*), rising above the surface of water (as leaves).—*n.* **emer′sion** (*-shən*), act of emerging: (*astron.*) the reappearance of a heavenly body after eclipse or occultation. [L. *ēmergēre, ēmersum—ē*, out of, *mergēre*, to plunge.]

emeritus, *i-, ē-mer′i-təs*, *adj.* honourably discharged from the performance of public duty, esp. noting a retired professor.—*n.* one who has been honourably discharged from public duties:—*pl.* **emer′itī.** [L. *ēmeritus*, having served one's time— *ēmerērī*, to earn.—*ē-*, sig. completeness, and *merērī*, to deserve.]

emerods, *em′ə-rodz*, *n.pl.* (*B.*) now **haemorrhoids.**

emery, *em′ər-i*, *n.* a very hard mineral, a variety of corundum, used as powder for polishing, etc.— *v.t.* to rub or coat with emery.—*ns.* **em′ery-bag,** a bag of emery-powder for cleaning and sharpening needles; **em′ery-cloth, -pā′per,** cloth, paper, covered with emery-powder for polishing; **em′ery-pow′der,** ground emery; **em′ery-wheel,** a wheel coated with emery for polishing. [O.Fr. *esmeril, emeril*—L.L. *smericulum*—Gr. *smēris, smȳris*.]

emetic, *i-met′ik*, *adj.* causing vomiting.—*n.* a medicine that causes vomiting.—*n.* **emesis** (*em′i-sis*), vomiting.—*adj.* **emet′ical.**—*adv.* **emet′ically.**—*n.* **em′etin, -ine,** the alkaloid forming the active principle of ipecacuanha-root, violently emetic. [Gr. *emetikos—emeein*, to vomit.]

emeu. See **emu.**

émeute, *ā-mət′*, sometimes *i-mūt′*, *n.* a popular rising or uproar. [Fr.]

emicate, *em′i-kāt*, *v.i.* to sparkle.—*adj.* **em′icant,** flashing.—*n.* **emica′tion.** [L. *ēmicāre, -ātum*.]

emiction, *i-mik′shən*, *n.* the discharging of urine.— *adj.* **emic′tory,** promoting the flow of urine. [L. *ēmingēre, ēmictum—ē*, from, *mingēre*, to urinate.]

emigrate, *em′i-grāt*, *v.i.* and *v.t.* to remove from one country (or state) to another as a place of abode.—*adj.* **em′igrant,** emigrating or having emigrated.—*n.* one who emigrates.—*n.* **emigrā′tion.**—*adj.* **emigrā′tional.**—*n.* **emigrā′tionist,** an advocate or promoter of emigration.—*adj.* **em′igratory.**—*n.* **émigré** (*ā-mē-grā′; Fr.*), a royalist who quitted France during the Revolution. [L. *ēmigrāre, ēmigrāre, -ātum—ē*, from, *migrāre*, to remove.]

eminent, *em′i-nənt*, *adj.* rising above others: conspicuous: distinguished: exalted in rank or office.—*ns.* **em′inence,** a part eminent or rising above the rest: a rising ground: a ridge or knob: height: distinction: a title given in 1631 to cardinals, till then styled Most Illustrious: (*Shak.*) advantage, upper hand; **em′inency.**—*adj.* **eminen′tial** (*-shəl*).—*adv.* **em′inently.**—**eminent domain,** the right by which the supreme authority in a state may compel a proprietor to part with what is his own for the public use. [L. *ēminēns, -entis*, pr.p. of *ēminēre—ē*, from, *minēre*, to project.]

emir, *ā-mēr′*, sometimes *ē′mər*, *n.* a title given in the East and in N. Africa to all independent chieftains, and also (perh. improperly) to all the supposed descendants of Mohammed through his daughter Fatima.—*n.* **emir′ate,** the office, jurisdiction, or state of an emir.—Also **ameer, emeer.** [Ar. *amīr*, ruler.]

emit, *i-, ē-mit′*, *v.t.* to send out: to throw or give out: to issue: to utter (a declaration):—(*pr.p.* **emit′ing;** *pa.t.* and *pa.p.* **emit′ed**).—*n.* **emissary** (*em′is-ər-i*), one sent out on a mission, esp. an underhand or secret mission: a spy: an underground outlet, esp. of a lake.—*adj.* that is sent forth: outgoing.—*adj.* **emiss′ile,** protrusible.— *n.* **emission** (*-mish′ən*), the act of emitting: that which is issued at one time:—*adj.* **emiss′ive,** emitting, sending out.—*n.* **emissiv′ity** (*ē-*), property or power of emitting or radiating.— **emission theory,** the corpuscular theory. [L. *ēmittēre, ēmissum—ē*, out of, *mittēre*, to send.]

emma, *em′ä*, *n.* a telephone operators' name for the letter *m*.

Emmanuel, Immanuel, *im-an′ū-əl*, *n.* the symbolical name of the child announced by Isaiah (Isa. vii. 14), and applied to Jesus as the Messiah in Matt. i. 23. [Heb.,—*'im*, with, *ānū*, us, *ēl*, God.]

emmarble, *e-mär′bl*, *v.t.* to turn to marble: to represent in marble: to adorn with marble. [Pfx. *em-*, and **marble.**]

emmenagogue, *em-ēn′ə-gog*, or *-en′*, *n.* medicine intended to restore, or to bring on, the menses.— *adj.* **emmenagogic** (*-goj′ik*).—*n.* **emmenol′ogy,** knowledge about menstruation. [Gr. *emmēna, menses—mēn*, a month, *agōgos*, drawing forth.]

Emmental, Emmentaler, *em′ən-täl, -ər*, *n.* and *adj.* applied to a Swiss cheese, like Gruyère, made in the Emmental or Emme valley.

emmer, *em′ər*, *n.* a species of wheat, *Triticum dicoccum.* [Ger. dial.]

emmesh. Same as **enmesh.**

emmet, *em′it*, *n.* (*arch.* and *prov.*) the ant. [O.E. *ǣmete*.]

emmetropia, *em-e-trō′pi-ä*, *n.* the normal condition of the refractive media of the eye.—*n.* **emm′etrope,** an emmetropic person.—*adj.* **emmetropic** (*-trop′ik*). [Gr. *en*, in, *metron*, measure, *ops*, the eye.]

emmew, immew, *i-mū′, em-mū′, enmew, in-mū′, v.t.* to confine, mew up.—But in *Shak.* app. for **enew.**

emmove, *e-mŏŏv′, v.t.* (*Spens.*) to move, to excite.

emollient, *i-mol′yənt*, *adj.* softening: making supple.—*n.* (*med.*) a softening application, as poultices, fomentations, etc.—*n.* **emollesc′ence,** incipient fusion.—*v.t.* **emolli′iate,** to soften: to render effeminate.—*n.* **emolli′tion,** the act of softening or relaxing. [L. *ēmollīre, ēmollītum—ē*, inten., *mollīre*, to soften—*mollis*, soft.]

emolument, *i-mol'ū-mənt*, *n.* (*obs.*) advantage : (often in *pl.*) profit arising from employment, as salary or fees.—*adjs.* **emolumen'tal, emolument'ary.** [L. *ēmolimentum*, prob. from *ēmŏlěre*, to grind out—*ē-*, and *mŏlěre* to grind, rather than from *ēmŏlīrī* to work out, *mōlīrī*, to toil.]

emong, emonges, emongest, emongst, old forms of **among, amongst.**

emotion, *i-mō'shən*, *n.* a moving of the feelings : agitation of mind : (*phil.*) one of the three groups of the phenomena of the mind—feeling, distinguished from cognition and will.—*adjs.* **emō'tionable ; emō'tional.**—*n.* **emō'tionalism,** tendency to emotional excitement, the habit of working on the emotions, the indulgence of superficial emotion.—*adv.* **emō'tionally.**—*adjs.* **emō'tionless ; emō'tive** (*-tiv*), pertaining to the emotions.—*v.t.* **emove** (*i-mōōv*), to affect 'with emotion. [L. *ēmōtiō*, *-ōnis*, *ēmovēre*, *-ōtum*, to stir up—*ē-* and *movēre*, to move.]

emp-. For words not found under this, see **imp-.**

empaestic, *em-pē'stik*, *adj.* pertaining to the art of embossing, stamped. [Gr. *empaiein*, to emboss.]

empacket, *im-pak'it*, *v.t.* (*Scott*) to pack up.

empaire, empare, empayre (*Spens.*). See **impair.**

empale, *em-pāl'*, *v.t.* to impale : (*Spens.*) to surround with a border. [**impale.**]

empanel, *im-pan'əl*, *v.t.* to enter on a panel :—*pr.p.* **empan'elling ;** *pa.t.* and *pa.p.* **empan'elled.**—*n.* **empan'elment.**—Also **impanel, impannel.**

empanoply, *im-pan'o-pli*, *v.t.* to invest in full armour.

empathy, *em'pə-thi*, *n.* power of entering into another's personality and imaginatively experiencing his experiences. [Gr. *en*, in, *pathos*, feeling.]

empatron, *em-pā'trən*, *v.t.* (*Shak.*) to patronise.

empennage, *im-pen'ij*, *än°-pen-äzh*, *n.* an aeroplane's tail as a unit, including elevator, rudder, and fin. [Fr., feathering of an arrow—L. *penna*, feather.]

empeople, *im-pē'pl*, *v.t.* (*obs.*) to fill with people : to form into a people or community.

emperish, *im-per'ish*, *v.t.* (*Spens.* etc.) to impair. [Perh. (irregularly)—Fr. *empirer* ; cf. **impair.**]

emperor, *em'pər-ər*, *n.* the head of an empire : the highest title of sovereignty : a size of paper (48 x 72 inches ; in U.S.A. 40 x 60) :—*fem.* **em'press.**—*v.i.* **em'perise,** to play the emperor. —*ns.* **em'peror-moth,** except the death's-head, the largest British moth, its expanse of wings being about three inches ; **em'peror-pen'guin,** the largest of the penguins ; **em'perorship ; em'pery,** empire, power. [O.Fr. *emperere*—L. *imperātor,* a commander (fem. *imperātrix*)—*imperāre*, to command.]

emphasis, *em'fə-sis*, *n.* (*obs.*) use of language to imply more than is said : forcible or impressive expression : insistent or vigorous way of attributing importance or thrusting upon attention : stress : accent : prominence :—*pl.* **em'phases** (*-sēz*).—*v.t.* **emphasise,** to make emphatic : to lay stress on.—*adjs.* **emphat'ic** (*im-, em-fat'ik*), **-al,** expressed or expressing with emphasis : stressed forcibly : impressive : strongly marked.—*adv.* **emphat'ically.**—*n.* **emphat'icalness.** [Gr. *emphasis,* image, outward appearance, significance, implied meaning—*en,* in, *phainein,* to show.]

emphlysis, *em'fli-sis*, *n.* a vesicular eruption. [Gr. *en,* in, *phlysis,* eruption—*phlyein,* to bubble, break out.]

emphractic, *em-frak'tik*, *adj.* stopping the pores of the skin.—*n.* a substance with this property. [Gr. *emphraktikos,* obstructive, *en,* in, *phrassein,* to stop.]

emphysema, *em-fis-ē'mä*, *n.* (*med.*) an unnatural distention of a part with air.—*adj.* **emphysē'matous.** [Gr. *emphysēma*—*emphysaein,* to inflate.]

emphyteusis, *em-fit-ū'sis*, *n.* in Roman law, a perpetual right in a piece of land, for which a yearly sum was paid to the proprietor.—*adj.* **emphyteu'tic.** [Gr.,—*emphyteuein,* to implant.]

empiecement, *em-pēs'mənt*, *n.* an insertion in a garment. [Fr. *empiècement.*]

empierce, emperce, *em-pērs', v.t.* (*Spens.*) to pierce.

empight, *em-pīt', adj.* (*Spens.*) fixed. [**pitch.**]

empire, *em'pīr*, *n.* (loosely) a widespreading dominion, or group of states, etc., under the same sovereign power—not always an emperor : supreme control or dominion : the government or office of an emperor : the time of its duration : (*hist.*) a country whose sovereign owes no allegiance to another.—**Empire day,** 24th May (Queen Victoria's birthday) ; **Empire gown,** a gown such as was worn during the first French Empire (1804-14). [Fr.,—L. *imperium.*]

empiric, *em-pir'ik,* formerly *em', adj.* empirical.— *n.* one who makes trials or experiments : one whose knowledge is got from experience only : a quack.— *adj.* **empir'ical,** resting on trial or experiment : known or knowing only by experience.—*adv.* **empir'ically.**—*ns.* **empir'icism** (*-sizm ; phil.*), the system which, rejecting all *a priori* knowledge, rests solely on experience and induction : dependence of a physician on his experience alone without a regular medical education : the practice of medicine without a regular education : quackery : **empir'icist** (*-sist*), one who practises empiricism. —*adj.* **empiricūt'ic** (*Shak.* **empirick qutique**), modelled on therapeutic), empirical.—**empirical formula** (*chem.*), a formula showing in simplest form the ratio of atoms in a molecule, not the absolute number. [Fr.,—L. *empīricus*—Gr. *empeirikos*—*en,* in, *peira,* a trial.]

emplacement, *im-plās'mənt*, *n.* the act of placing : (*mil.*) a gun-platform.—*v.t.* **emplace'** (backformation) to put in or provide with an emplacement.

emplane, *im-plān', v.t.* to put or take on an aeroplane.—*v.i.* to mount an aeroplane. [Pfx. *em-,* and **plane.**]

emplaster, *em-pläs'tər*, *n.* and *v.* same as **plaster.** —*adj.* **emplastic** (*-plas'*), glutinous : adhesive.— *n.* a medicine that stops the pores.—*ns.* **emplas'tron** (Gr.), **emplas'trum** (L.), a medicated plaster. [Gr. *emplastron.*]

emplecton, *em-plek'ton*, *n.* ashlar masonry filled up with rubble.—Also (L.) **emplec'tum.** [Gr. *emplekton*—*en,* in, *plekein,* to weave.]

emplonge (*Spens.*). See **implunge.**

employ, *im-ploy', v.t.* to occupy the time or attention of : to use as a means or agent : to give work to.—*n.* employment.—*adj.* **employ'able,** that may be employed.—*adj.* **employed',** having employment, in a job.—*ns.* **employ'ee** (or *-ē'*), a person employed ; **employ'er ; employ'ment,** act of employing : that which engages or occupies : occupation. [Fr. *employer*—L. *implicāre,* to enfold —*in,* in, and *plicāre,* to fold ; cf. **imply, implicate.**]

emplume, *im-plōōm', v.t.* to furnish with a plume.

empoison, *im-poi'zn, v.t.* to put poison in : to poison.—*adj.* **empoi'soned.**—*n.* **empoi'sonment.**

emporium, *em-pō'ri-əm*, *n.* a place to which goods are brought from various parts for sale : (*vulg.*) a big shop : a great mart :—*pl.* **empō'ria, emporiums.** [L.,—Gr. *empŏrion,* a trading station— *empŏros,* a wayfarer, trader, *en,* in, *poros,* a way.]

empoverish. See **impoverish.**

empower, *im-pow'ər, v.t.* to authorise.

empress. See **emperor.**

emprise, *em-prīz', n.* (*Spens.*) an enterprise : a hazardous undertaking. [O.Fr. *emprise*—pa.p. fem. of *emprendre*—L. *in,* in, *praehendēre,* to take.]

emption, *emp'shən, n.* act of buying, purchase.— *adj.* **emp'tional.** [L. *emptiō, -ōnis*—*emēre,* to buy.]

empty, *emp'ti, adj.* having nothing within : unoccupied : unfurnished : without effect : unsatisfactory : wanting substance : foolish.—*v.t.* to make empty : to deprive of contents : to remove from a receptacle :—*v.i.* to become empty : to discharge.— (*pr.p.* **emp'tying ;** *pa.t.* and *pa.p.* **emp'tied.**)—*n.* an empty vessel, box, sack, etc. :—*pl.* **emp'ties.**— *ns.* **emp'tier ; emp'tiness,** state of being empty : want of substance : unsatisfactoriness : inanity.— *adjs.* **emp'ty-hand'ed,** bringing nothing or no gift ; **emp'ty-head'ed,** frivolous.—*n.* **emp'tying.**

—come away empty, to come away without having received anything. [O.E. *æmetig—æmetta*, leisure, rest; the *p* is excrescent.]

emptysis, *emp'ti-sis*, *n.* spitting, esp. of blood. [Gr. *emptysis*, spitting—*en*, in, *ptyein*, to spit.]

empurple, *im-pur'pl*, *v.t.* to dye or tinge purple.

empusa, *em-pū'zä*, *n.* a goblin or spectre sent by Hecate, (also **empuse'**): **Empusa**, a genus of fungi parasitic upon houseflies and other insects. [Gr. *Empousa.*]

empyema, *em-pī-ē'mä*, or *-pi-*, *n.* a collection of pus in any cavity, esp. the pleura.—*n.* **empyesis** (*-ē'sis*), pustulous eruption. [Gr. *empyēma*, *empyēsis—en*, in, *pyon*, pus.]

empyreal, *em-pir-ē'əl*, (*Milt.*, *Pope*, *em-pir'i-əl*) *adj.* formed of pure fire or light: pertaining to the highest and purest region of heaven: sublime.— *adj.* **empyre'an**, empyreal.—*n.* the highest heaven, where the pure element of fire was supposed to subsist: the heavens. [Gr. *empyros*, fiery—*en*, in, *pȳr*, fire.]

empyreuma, *em-pir-ū'mä*, *n.* the burned smell and acrid taste that come when vegetable or animal substances are burned:—*pl.* **empyreu'mata.**— *adjs.* **empyreumat'ic, -al.**—*v.t.* **empyreu'matise.** [Gr. *empȳreuma, -atos*, embers—*en*, in, *pȳr*, fire.]

emu, emeu, *ē'mū*, *n.* an Australian running bird of the Ratitae, akin to the cassowary, largest of living birds after the ostrich.—*n.* **e'mu-wren**, a small Australian bird (Stipiturus), with tail-feathers like emu feathers in structure. [Port. *ema*, an ostrich.]

emulate, *em'ū-lāt*, *v.t.* to strive to equal or excel: to rival.—*adj.* (*Shak.*) ambitious.—*n.* **emulā'tion**, act of emulating or attempting to equal or excel: rivalry: competition: contest: (*obs.*) jealous rivalry.—*adj.* **em'ulative**, inclined to emulation, rivalry, or competition.—*n.* **em'ulātor:**—*fem.* **em'ulātress.**—*v.t.* **em'ule** (*Southey*), to emulate. —*adj.* **em'ulous**, eager to emulate: desirous of like excellence with another: engaged in competition or rivalry.—*adv.* **em'ulously.**—*n.* **em'ulousness.** [L. *aemulārī, -ātus—aemulus*, emulous.]

emulge, *i-mulj'*, *v.t.* to milk or drain out.—*n.* **emul'gence.**—*adj.* **emul'gent.** [See next.]

emulsion, *i-mul'shən*, *n.* a colloidal suspension of one liquid in another.—*ns.* **emulsifica'tion**; **emul'sifier**, apparatus for preparing emulsions.— *v.t.* **emul'sify.**—*n.* **emul'sin**, an enzyme got from bitter almonds.—*v.t.* **emul'sionise.**—*adj.* **emul'sive.**—*ns.* **emul'soid**, a colloid easily dispersed, giving a suspension readily formed again after coagulation; **emul'sor**, an emulsifying apparatus. [L. *ēmulgēre, ēmulsum*, to milk out—*ē*, from, and *mulgēre*, to milk.]

emunctory, *i-* or *ē-mungk'tər-i*, *adj.* conveying waste: pertaining to nose-blowing.—*n.* any organ or passage of the body that carries off waste: an excretory duct.—*v.t.* **emunge** (*e-munj'*), to clean. [L. *ēmunctōrium*, a pair of snuffers, a means of cleansing, *ēmungēre, ēmunctum*, to blow the nose, to cleanse.]

emure, *i-mūr'* (*Shak.*), *v.t.* a variant of **immure.**— *n.* an encircling wall.

Emys, *em'is*, *n.* a genus of freshwater and marsh tortoises:—*pl.* **em'ydēs.** [Gr. *emys, -ydos.*]

en, *en*, *n.* the name of the letter *n*: (*print.*) half of an em. See **N.**

enable, *in-ā'bl*, *v.t.* to make able: to give power, strength, or authority to: to make possible.— **enabling act, bill**, one giving or proposing to give power to act. [Pfx. *en-*, **able.**]

enact, *in-akt'*, *v.t.* to perform: to act the part of: to establish by law.—*n.* (*Shak.*) an enactment.— *adjs.* **enact'ing, enact'ive.**—*ns.* **enac'tion** (*-shən*), **enact'ment**, the passing of a bill into law: that which is enacted: a law; **enact'or**, one who practises or performs anything: one who forms decrees or establishes laws: **enact'ure** (*Shak.*), fulfilment. [Pfx. *en-*, **act.**]

enallage, *en-al'ə-jē*, *n.* (*gram.*) the exchange of one case, mood, tense, etc., for another. [Gr. *enallagē—en*, in, and *allassein*, to change.]

enamel, *in-am'əl*, *n.* a vitrified coating applied to a metal or other surface and fired: any glossy enamel-like surface or coating, esp. that of the teeth: a work of art in enamel.—*v.t.* to coat with or paint in enamel: to form a glossy surface upon, like enamel:—(*pr.p.* **enam'elling**; *pa.t.* and *pa.p.* **enam'elled.**)—*ns.* **enam'eller, enam'ellist**; **enam'elling.** [O.Fr. *enameler—en*, in, *esmail*, enamel; see **smelt, melt.**]

enamour, *in-am'ər*, *v.t.* to inflame with love: to charm.—*n.* **enamorado** (*en-äm-ō-rä'dō*; Sp.) a lover.—*adjs.* **enam'oured**; **enam'ouring.**— **enamoured of**, in love with. [O.Fr. *enamourer*— pfx. *en-*, *amour*—L. *amor, -ōris*, love.]

enantiomorph, *en-an'ti-ō-morf*, *n.* a shape or object (as a crystal, a molecule) exactly similar to another except that right and left are interchanged, each being a mirror-image of the other.—*adjs.* **enantiomorph'ic, enantiomorph'ous.** — *ns.* **enantiomorph'ism, enantiomorph'y.** [Gr. *enantios*, opposite, *morphē*, shape.]

enantiopathy, *en-an-ti-op'ə-thi*, *n.* allopathy. [Gr. *enantios*, opposite, *pathos*, suffering.]

enantiosis, *en-an-ti-ō'sis*, *n.* (*rhet.*) the expression of an idea by negation of its contrary (litotes), or by substitution of the contrary (antiphrasis, irony). [Gr. *enantiōsis*, contradiction.]

enantiostyly, *en-an-ti-ō-stī'li*, *n.* (*bot.*) a dimorphous condition in which the style projects at one side or the other in different flowers.—*adj.* **enantiostȳ'lous.** [Gr. *enantios*, opposite, *stȳlos*, a column.]

enarch. See **inarch.**

enarched, *en-ärcht'*, *adj.* (*her.*) arched, like an arch.

enarm, *en-ärm'*, *v.t.* (*obs.*) to arm: (*obs.*) to lard.— *adj.* **enarmed'**, (*her.*) having horns, hoofs, etc., of a different colour from the body.

enarration, *ē-na-rā'shən*, *n.* exposition: detailed narration.

enarthrosis, *en-är-thrō'sis*, *n.* (*anat.*) a ball-and-socket joint.—*adj.* **enarthrō'dial.** [Gr. *enarthrōsis—en*, in, *arthron*, a joint.]

enate, *ē'nāt*, *adj.* growing out.—*n.* **enā'tion**, an outgrowth. [L. *ē-*, from, *nātus*, born.]

enaunter, *en-awn'tər*, *en-än'tər*, *conj.* (*obs.*; *Spens.*) lest by chance. [Contr. from *in a(d)venture.*]

encaenia, *en-sē'ni-ä*, *n.* the annual commemoration of founders and benefactors at Oxford, held in June. [L.,—Gr. *enkainia* (pl.), a feast of dedication—*en*, in, *kainos*, new.]

encage, incage, *in-kāj'*, *v.t.* to shut up in a cage.

encalm, *in-käm'*, *v.t.* (*obs.*) to becalm.

encamp, *in-kamp'*, *v.t.* to form into a camp: to lodge in a camp.—*v.i.* to pitch tents: to make, or stay in, a camp.—*n.* **encamp'ment**, the act of encamping: the place where a camper or company is encamped: a camp.

encanthis, *en-kan'this*, *n.* a small tumour of the inner angle of the eye. [Gr. *enkanthis—en*, in, *kanthos*, a canthus.]

encarnalise, *in-kär'nəl-īz*, *v.t.* to embody: to make carnal.

encarpus, *en-kär'pəs*, *n.* a festoon of fruit ornamenting a frieze. [Gr. *enkarpa* (neut. pl.)—*en*, in, *karpos*, fruit.]

encase, incase, *in-kās'*, *v.t.* to enclose in a case: to surround, cover: to line.—*n.* **encase'ment**, the act of encasing: an enclosing substance: a covering: a lining: emboîtement.

encash, *in-kash'*, *v.t.* to convert into cash.— **encash'ment.**

encaustic, *en-kaws'tik*, *adj.* having the colours burned in.—*n.* an ancient method of painting in melted wax.—**encaustic tile**, a decorative glazed and fired tile, having patterns of different coloured clays inlaid in it and burnt with it. [Gr. *enkaustikos—enkaiein*, to burn in—*en*, in, *kaiein*, to burn.]

encave, *en-kāv'*, *v.t.* (*Shak.*) to hide. [Fr. *encaver*, to put in a cellar—*en*, in, *cave*, cellar.]

enceinte, *än²-sant'*, *n.* (*fort.*) an enclosure, generally the whole area of a fortified place. [Fr.,— *enceindre*, to surround—L. *in*, in, *cingĕre, cinctum*, to gird.]

enceinte, *än⁹-sanᵗt'*, *adj.* pregnant, with child. [Fr.,—L. *incincta*, girt about or ungirt.]

Encephalartos, *en-sef-əl-är'tos*, *n.* the Kaffir-bread genus of cycads. [Gr. *enkephalos*, within the head, palm-cabbage, *artos*, bread.]

encephalon, *en-sef'əl-on*, *n.* the brain.—*adjs.* **encephalic** (*-fal'ik*), belonging to the head or brain; **encephalit'ic**, pertaining to encephalitis.—*ns.* **encephali'tis**, inflammation of the brain; **enceph'alocele** (Gr. *kēlē*, tumour), a protrusion of portion of the brain through the skull, where the bones are incomplete in infancy; **enceph'alogram, enceph'alograph**, an X-ray photograph of the brain; **encephalog'raphy.**—*adj.* **enceph'aloid**, resembling the matter of the brain.—*n.* **encephalot'omy** (Gr. *tomē*, a cut), dissection of the brain.—*adj.* **enceph'alous**, cephalous.—**encephalitis lethar'gica**, an obscure acute disease marked by profound physical and mental lethargy —popularly but erroneously called *sleeping-sickness*, better *sleepy-sickness*. [Gr. *enkephalos—en*, in, *kephalē*, the head.]

enchafe, *en-chāf'*, *v.t.* (*obs.*) to make warm: to irritate. [Earlier *enchaufe, eschaufe*—O.Fr. *eschauffer—es*- (L. *ex*), *chauffer*; see **chafe.**]

enchain, *in-chān'*, *v.t.* to put in chains: to hold fast: to link together.—*n.* **enchain'ment**, act of enchaining: concatenation: a set of things connected in series. [Fr. *enchaîner—en*, in, *chaîne*, chain—L. *catēna.*]

enchant, *in-chänt'*, *v.t.* to act on by songs or rhymed formulas of sorcery: to cast a spell upon: to compel by enchantment: to charm: to delight in a high degree.—*adj.* **enchant'ed**, under the power of enchantment: delighted: possessed by witches or spirits.—*n.* **enchant'er**, one who enchants: a sorcerer or magician: one who charms or delights:—*fem.* **enchant'ress.**—*adj.* **enchant'ing.**—*adv.* **enchant'ingly**, with the force of enchantment: in a manner to charm or delight.— *n.* **enchant'ment**, act of enchanting: use of magic arts: enchanted state: that which enchants.— **enchanter's nightshade**, a plant (*Circaea lutetiana*) of the evening-primrose family, growing in shady places—both names transferred apparently from another plant (perhaps mandrake, or swallowwort) for no apparent reason. [Fr. *enchanter*—L. *incantāre*, to sing a magic formula over—*in*, on, *cantāre*, to sing.]

encharge, *in-chärj'*, *v.t.* to enjoin: to entrust. [O.Fr. *encharger*; see **charge.**]

encharm, *in-chärm'*, *v.t.* to cast a spell on: to charm.

enchase, *in-chās'*, *v.t.* to fix in a border or setting: to enshrine: to enclose: to enshrine in verse: to insert, let in: to set with jewels: to engrave: to adorn with raised or embossed work: (*Spens.*) prob. to fewter.—*n.* (*Spens.*) enchasing.—*adj.* **enchased'**. [Fr. *enchâsser—en*, in, *châsse*, shrine, setting—L. *capsa*, a case; see **case** (1), **chase** (3); **chase** (2) is a contraction.]

encheason, *en-chē'zn*, *n.* (*Spens.*) reason, cause, occasion. [O.Fr. *encheson—encheoir*, to fall in; influenced by L. *occāsiō, -ōnis*, occasion.]

encheer, *in-chēr'*, *v.t.* to cheer, comfort.

encheiridion, *en(g)-kī-rid'i-on*, *n.* a book to be carried in the hand for reference: a manual. [Gr. *encheiridion—en*, in, *cheir*, hand.]

enchondroma, *en-kon-drō'mä*, *n.* (*path.*) an abnormal cartilaginous growth. [Gr. *en*, in, *chondros*, cartilage.]

enchorial, *en-kō'ri-əl*, *adj.* belonging to or used in a country: used by the people, esp. (in ancient Egypt) demotic.—Also **enchoric** (*-kor'*). [Gr. *enchōrios—en*, in, and *chōrā*, a place, country.]

encincture, *in-singk'tyər*, *v.t.* to girdle.—*n.* girdling: an enclosure.

encircle, *in-sərk'l*, *v.t.* to enclose in a circle: to embrace: to pass round.—*ns.* **encirc'ling, -cir'clement.**

enclasp, *in-kläsp'*, *v.t.* to clasp.

enclave, *en'klāv*, also *en-klāv'*, or *än⁹-kläv'*, *n.* a piece of territory entirely enclosed within foreign territory: an enclosure.—*v.t.* to surround. [Fr.,— L.L. *inclāvāre*—L. *in*, and *clāvis*, a key.]

enclitic, *en-klit'ik*, *adj.* inclined: (*gram.*) without accent, as if not a separate word.—*n.* (*gram.*) a word or particle which always follows another word, so united with it as to seem a part of it.— *n.* **enclisis** (*eng'klis-is*).—*adv.* **enclit'ically**. [Gr. *enklitikos—en*, in, *klīnein*, to lean.]

encloister, *in-klois'tər*, *v.t.* to immure.

enclose, inclose, *in-klōz'*, *v.t.* to close or shut in: to confine: to surround: to put within, esp. of something sent within a letter or within its envelope: to seclude: to fence, esp. used of waste land.—*ns.* **enclos'er; enclosure** (*-klō'zhər*), the act of enclosing: state of being enclosed: that which is enclosed, esp. in a letter: a space fenced off: that which encloses; a barrier: the framing of a window. [Pfx. *en-*, in-, and **close.**]

enclothe, *in-klōdh'*, *v.t.* to clothe.

encloud, *in-klowd'*, *v.t.* to cover with clouds.

encolour, *in-kul'ər*, *v.t.* to colour, tinge.

encolpion *en-kol'pi-on*, *n.* a reliquary, cross, etc., worn on the breast.—Also (Latinised) **encol'pium**. [Gr.,—*en*, in, on, *kolpos*, bosom.]

encolure, *en(g)'kol-ūr'*, *n.* (*Browning*) a horse's mane. [Fr., horse's neck.]

encomium, *en-kō'mi-əm*, also **encō'mion** (*-on*), *n.* high commendation: a eulogy: (*pl.* **encō'miums, encō'mia.**)—*n.* **encō'miast**, one who utters or writes encomiums: a praiser.—*adjs.* **encomias'tic, -al**, bestowing praise.—*adv.* **encomias'tically**. [L.,—Gr. *enkōmion*, a song of praise—*en*, in, *kōmos*, festivity.]

encompass, *in-kum'pəs*, *v.t.* to surround or enclose: (*obs.*) to go round: to bring about.—*n.* **encom'passment.**

encore, *än⁹-*, *ong-kōr'*, *interj.* calling for repetition of a performance, or an additional item.—*n.* a call of encore: an item given in response to such a call.—*v.t.* to call encore to. [Fr., again, still.]

encounter, *in-kown'tər*, *v.t.* to meet face to face, esp. unexpectedly: to meet in contest: to oppose.— *n.* a meeting unexpectedly: an interview: a fight: (*Shak.*) manner of meeting or accosting. [O.Fr. *encontrer*—L. *in*, in, *contrā*, against.]

encourage, *en-kur'ij*, *v.t.* to put courage in: to inspire with spirit or hope: to incite: to patronise: to cherish.—*ns.* **encour'agement**, act of encouraging: that which encourages; **encour'ager.** —*n.* and *adj.* **encour'aging.**—*adv.* **encour'agingly**. [O.Fr. *encoragier* (Fr. *encourager*)—pfx. *en-, corage*, courage.]

encradle, *en-krā'dl*, *v.t.* (*Spens.*) to lay in a cradle.

encraty, *en'krə-ti*, *n.* self-control.—*ns.* **En'cratism**, the doctrine of the Encratites; **En'cratite**, one of a heretical sect in the early church who abstained from marriage, and from flesh and wine. [Gr. *enkrateia—en*, in, *kratos*, strength.]

encrease, obsolete form of **increase.**

encrimson, *en-krim'zn*, *v.t.* to tinge with a crimson colour.—*adj.* **encrim'soned.**

encrinite, *en(g)'krin-nīt*, *n.* a fossil crinoid: a crinoid.—*adjs.* **en'crinal, encrin'ic, encrini'tal, encrinitic** (*-it'ik*). [Gr. *en*, in, *krinon*, a lily.]

encroach, *in-krōch'*, *v.i.* to seize on the rights of others: to intrude beyond boundaries: to trench upon, extend into, territory, sphere, etc., of others.—*n.* **encroach'er.**—*adv.* **encroach'ingly**. —*n.* **encroach'ment**, act of encroaching: that which is taken by encroaching. [O.Fr. *encrochier*, to seize—*en-* and *croc*, a hook.]

encrust, incrust, *in-krust'*, *v.t.* to cover with a crust or hard coating: to form a crust on the surface of.—*v.i.* to form a crust.—*ns.* **encrust'ment, encrustā'tion** (*en-*; usu. **incrustā'tion, in-**), act of encrusting: a crust or layer of anything: an inlaying of marble, mosaic, etc. [L. *incrustāre, ātum—in*, on, *crusta*, crust.]

encumber, *in-kum'bər*, *v.t.* to impede the motion of: to hamper: to embarrass: to burden: to load with debts.—*ns.* **encum'berment**, the act of encumbering: the state of being encumbered; **encum'brance**, that which encumbers or hinders: a legal claim on an estate: one dependent on another, esp. a child; **encum'brancer.** [O.Fr. *encombrer*, from *en-*, and *combrer*; see **cumber.**]

encurtain, *in-kur'tin*, *v.t.* to curtain, to veil.

encyclical, *en-sīk'lik-əl,* or *-sik',* *adj.* sent round to many persons or places.—*n.* a letter addressed by the Pope to all his bishops.—Also **encyc'lic.** [Gr. *enkyklios*—*en,* in, *kyklos,* a circle.]

encyclopaedia, encyclopedia, *en-si-klō-pē'di-ä, n.* the circle of human knowledge : a work containing information on every department, or on a particular department, of knowledge, generally alphabetically arranged : esp. that by Diderot, D'Alembert, and others.—*adjs.* **encyclopae'dian,** embracing the whole circle of learning; **encyclopae'dic, -al,** pertaining to an encyclopaedia : all-comprehensive : full of information.—*ns.* **encyclopae'dism,** knowledge of everything : the rationalistic attitude of the French Encyclopaedists; **encyclopae'dist,** the compiler, or one who assists in the compilation, of an encyclopaedia : esp. (*Encyclopédiste*) a writer for the French *Encyclopédie* (1751-65). [False Gr. *enkyklopaideiā,* a wrong reading for *enkyklios paideiā,* general education (opposed to professional or special) : *enkyklios,* circular, recurring, everyday—*en,* in, *kyklos,* circle; *paideiā,* education—*pais, paidos,* boy.]

encyst, *en-sist',* *v.t.* or *v.i.* to enclose or become enclosed in a cyst or vesicle.—*ns.* **encystā'tion, encyst'ment.**—*adj.* **encyst'ed.**

end, *end, n.* the last point or portion : termination or close : death : consequence : object aimed at : a fragment, odd piece : half a unit length of cloth : a waxed thread ending in a bristle (*shoemaker's end*) : part of a game played from one end (of the bowling-green, archery-ground, etc.) : an outer district : a region (*Scot.*) a cottage room.—*v.t.* to bring to an end : to destroy.—*v.i.* to come to an end : to cease.—*n.* **end'-all,** that which ends all.—*adj.* **end'ed,** brought to an end : having ends.—*n.* **end'ing,** termination : conclusion : death : extremity : that which is at the end : (*gram.*) the terminal syllable or portion of a word.—*adj.* concluding : finishing : completing : dying.—*adj.* **end'less,** without end : returning upon itself : everlasting : incessant : objectless.—*adv.* **end'lessly.**—*n.* **end'lessness.**—*adv.* **endlong** (see separate article).—*adj.* **end'most,** farthest.—*adv.* and *adj.* **end'-on',** in the direction in which the end points.—*ns.* **end'organ,** a specialised sensory or motor structure at a nerve-end; **end'-paper,** a paper at the beginning or end of a book, pasted to the binding and leaving an additional fly-leaf; **end'-product,** the final product of a series of operations; **end'-reader,** one who peeps at the end of a novel to see if she got him; **end'ship,** (*obs.*), a village.—*adj.* **end'-stopped,** having a pause at the end of each line (of verse).—*advs.* **end'ways, end'wise,** on end : with the end forward.—**at a loose end,** with nothing to do; **at an end,** terminated : discontinued : exhausted; **at loose ends,** in disorder; **at the end of one's tether,** without further resource; **be the end of,** to cause the death of (often a coll. exaggeration); **end for end,** with the position of the ends reversed; **endless chain,** a chain whose ends are joined; **endless gearing, screw, worm,** an arrangement for producing slow motion in machinery, consisting of a screw whose thread gears into a wheel with skew teeth; **get hold of the wrong end of the stick,** to misunderstand blunderingly; **in the end,** after all : at last; **keep one's end up,** to maintain one's part : to be content to keep one's wicket standing without trying to score; **make both ends meet,** to live within one's income (both ends meaning both ends of the year); **no end** (*coll.*), very much; **on end,** erect : at a stretch. [O.E. *ende;* cf. Ger. and Dan. *ende,* Goth. *andeis;* Sans. *ánta.*]

endamage, *in-dam'ij,* *v.t.* to damage.—*n.* **endam'agement,** damage, injury, loss.

endanger, *in-dān'jər,* *v.t.* to place in danger : to expose to loss or injury.—*ns.* **endan'gerer; endan'germent,** hazard, peril.

endarch, *end'ärk,* *adj.* (*bot.*) having the protoxylem on the inner edge. [Gr. *endō,* within, *archē,* origin.]

endart, *in-därt',* *v.t.* (*Shak.*) to dart in.

endear, *in-dēr',* *v.t.* to make dear or more dear : (*Shak.*) to bind as in gratitude.—*adjs.* **endeared',** beloved; **endear'ing,** making dear : expressing love.—*adv.* **endear'ingly.**—*ns.* **endear'ingness; endear'ment,** act of endearing : state of being endeared : that which excites or increases affection : a caress or utterance of love.

endeavour, *in-dev'ər,* *v.t.* to strive or attempt.—*n.* an exertion of power towards some object : attempt or trial.—*n.* **endeav'ourment** (*Spens.*), endeavour.—**do one's endeavour,** to do one's utmost. [From such phrases as to *put oneself in devoir* (Fr. *se mettre en devoir*), to make it one's duty, do what one can :—Fr. *en,* in, *devoir,* duty.]

endecagon, a faulty form for **hendecagon.**

endeictic, *en-dīk'tik,* *adj.* showing, exhibiting, demonstrating.—*n.* **endeix'is,** an indication. [Gr. *endeiktikos.*]

endemic, *en-dem'ik,* *adj.* prevalent or regularly found in a people or a district : (*biol.*) confined to a particular area.—*n.* a disease constantly or generally present in a place.—*adjs.* **endemial** (*-dē'mi-əl*), **endem'ical.**—*adv.* **endem'ically.**—*ns.* **endemicity** (*-is'i-ti*), **en'demism,** state of being endemic; **endemiol'ogy** (*-dem-,* or *-dēm-*) knowledge of endemic diseases. [Gr. *endēmios*—*en,* in, and *dēmos,* a people, a district.]

endenizen, *en-den'i-zn,* *v.t.* to naturalise, to make a denizen.

endermic, -al, *en-dərm'ik, -əl, adj.* through or applied directly to the skin—also **endermat'ic.**—*n.* **en'deron,** the corium, derma, or true skin. [Gr. *en,* in, *derma,* and *deros,* skin.]

endew, *en-dū',* *v.t.* (*obs.*) to endue or indue : to take in (esp. into the stomach) : to digest : (*Spens.*) to endow. [**endue.**]

endiron. See **andiron.**

endite, obs. form of **indict, indite.**

endive, *en'div, -dïv, n.* a salad plant (*Cichorium Endivia*) of the chicory genus : (*U.S.*) a kind of chicory. [Fr.,—L. *intubus.*]

endlong, *end'long* (*Scot.* **endlang, -lâng**), *adv.* (*arch.*) lengthwise : continuously : straight on : on end.—*prep.* (*obs.*) along.—*adj.* set on end. [M.E. *endelong* or O.N. *endelangr* (cf. **end long**), confused with *andlang* (see **along**).]

endo-, *en'dō-, en-do'-,* *pfx.* inside, often interchanging with *ento-* and opp. to *exo-, ecto-.*—*n.* **en'doblast** (Gr. *blastos,* a shoot, bud), the inner cell-layer of a gastrula, the hypoblast.—*adjs.* **endocar'diac, endocar'dial,** within the heart.—*ns.* **endocardi'tis,** inflammation of the endocardium, esp. over the valves; **endocar'dium** (Gr. *kardiā,* heart), the lining membrane of the heart; **en'docarp** (Gr. *karpos,* fruit; *bot.*), a differentiated innermost layer of the pericarp, usu. hard, as a plum stone.—*adjs.* **endochylous** (*en-dok'i-ləs;* Gr. *chylos,* juice; *bot.*), having internal water-storing cells; **endocri'nal; en'docrine** (Gr. *krinein,* to separate; *physiol.*), secreting internally : applied esp. to certain glands that pour secretions into the blood (also *n.*); **endocrinic** (*-krin'ik*).—*n.* **endocrinol'ogy,** the science of the discharge of ductless glands.—*adj.* **endocritic** (*-krit'ik*), endocrine.—*n.* **en'doderm** (Gr. *derma,* skin), the inner layer of cells in a gastrula : the tissues derived from that layer.—*adjs.* **endoderm'al, endoderm'ic.**—*n.* **endoderm'is,** a close-set sheath, one cell thick, enclosing the central cylinder in plants.—*adjs.* **endogamic** (*-gam'ik*), **endogamous** (*-dog'ə-məs*).—*ns.* **endogamy** (*en-dog'əm-i;* Gr. *gamos,* marriage), the custom forbidding marriage outside one's own group : inbreeding : pollination between two flowers on the same plant : union of female gametes; **en'dogen** (*-jen;* Gr. *genēs,* born; *obs.*), a monocotyledon—so called because regarded as growing from within.—*adj.* **endogenous** (*en-doj'i-nəs*), monocotyledonous, increasing by internal growth : formed within.—*ns.* **endog'eny; en'dolymph,** the fluid within the membranous labyrinth of the ear; **endometri'tis,** inflammation of the endometrium; **endome'trium** (Gr. *mētra,* womb), the mucous membrane lining the cavity of the uterus; **endomix'is** (Gr. *mixis,* mingling), in Protozoa,

Neutral vowels in unaccented syllables : *el'ə-mənt, in'fənt, ran'dəm*

a nuclear reorganisation without conjugation; **en'domorph** (Gr. *morphē*, form), a mineral enclosed within another mineral, the latter being termed a perimorph.—*adj.* **endomorph'ic.**—*n.* **endopar'asite**, an internal parasite.—*adj.* **endophagous** (en-dof'*ə*-gəs).—*n.* **endoph'agy** (-*ə*-ji; Gr. *phagein*, aorist, to eat), cannibalism within the family or tribe: eating away from within.—*adj.* **endophyllous** (-fil'əs; Gr. *phyllon*, a leaf; *bot.*), being or formed within a sheathing leaf: living inside a leaf.—*n.* **endophyte** (en'dō-fīt; Gr. *phyton*, a plant), a plant living within another, whether parasitically or no.—*adj.* **endophytic** (-fit'ik).—*n.* **en'doplasm**, the inner portion of the cytoplasm of a cell.—*adjs.* **endoplas'mic, endoplast'ic.**—*ns.* **endopleura** (-plōō'rä; Gr. *pleurā*, a side; *bot.*), the inner seed coat; **endopodite** (en-dop'ə-dīt; Gr. *pous, podos*, a foot), the inner branch of a crustacean's leg.—*adj.* **endorhizal** (-rī'zəl; Gr. *rhiza*, root; *bot.*), having the radicle of the embryo enclosed within a sheath, as in monocotyledons: hence monocotyledonous. [Gr. *endon*, or *endō*, within.]

endorse, indorse, in-dors', *v.t.* to write on the back of (esp. one's signature, a note of contents, a record of an offence): to assign by writing on the back of: to give one's sanction to: to express approbation of: to lay on the back, to load.—*adj.* **endors'able.**—*ns.* **endorsee'** (en-), the person to whom a bill, etc., is assigned by endorsement; **endorse'ment**, act of endorsing: that which is written on the back: sanction; **endors'er.** [See **endosse**; changed under the influence of L.L. *indorsāre*—*in*, on, *dorsum*, the back.]

endorse, en-dors', *n.* (*her.*) a vertical band or stripe on a shield, one-fourth or one-eighth of the width of a pale.—*adj.* **endorsed'**, (of a pale) with an endorse on each side of it: (of wings) thrown back. [Origin obscure.]

endo- (continued)—*ns.* **en'dosarc** (Gr. *sarx, sarkos*, flesh), endoplasm; **en'doscope** (Gr. *skopeein*, to look), an instrument for viewing the cavities of internal organs.—*adj.* **endoscopic** (-skop'ik).—*n.* **endoscopy** (en-dos'kə-pi).—*adj.* **endoskel'etal.**—*ns.* **endoskel'eton**, the internal skeleton or framework of the body; **endosmō'sis**, osmosis inwards, i.e., towards the solution.—Also **en'dosmose** (-mōs); **endosmōm'eter**, an instrument for measuring endosmotic action.—*adjs.* **endosmomet'ric; endosmōt'ic**, pertaining to or of the nature of endosmosis.—*adv.* **endosmot'ically.**—*n.* **en'dosperm** (Gr. *sperma*, seed), in a seed, nutritive tissue formed from the embryo-sac.—*adj.* **endosper'mic.**—*n.* **en'dospore** (Gr. *sporos*, seed), the innermost layer of a spore-wall: a spore formed within a mother-cell.

endoss, en-dos', *v.t.* (*obs.*) to endorse: (*Spens.*) to inscribe. [M.E. *endosse*—O.Fr. *endosser*.]

endo- (continued)—*adj.* **endos'teal** (Gr. *osteon*, bone), within a bone.—*n.* **endos'teum** (*anat.*), the internal periosteum.—*adjs.* **endotroph'ic** (Gr. *trophē*, food), of a mycorrhiza, occurring mainly within the root of the plant it feeds; **endotherm'ic** (Gr. *thermē*, heat), accompanied by, characterised by, or formed with absorption of heat.

endow, in-dow', *v.t.* to give a dowry or marriage-portion to: to settle a permanent provision on: to provide permanent means of support for: to enrich with any gift or faculty: to present.—*ns.* **endow'er; endow'ment**, act of endowing: that which is settled on any person or institution: a quality or faculty bestowed on anyone—**endowment insurance**, a form of insurance providing for the payment of a certain sum at a certain date. [Fr. *en* (—L. *in*), *douer*, to endow—L. *dōtāre*—*dōs, dōtis*, a dowry.]

endozoon, en-dō-zō'on, *n.* an entozoon:—(*pl.* **endozo'a**).—*adj.* **endozo'ic**, entozoic: (*bot.*) having seeds dispersed by animals that swallow them. [Gr. *endon*, within, *zōion*, animal.]

endue, indue (*Spens.*, etc., **endew, indew**), in-dū', *v.t.* (*obs.*) to take into the stomach, as a hawk: to digest: (*Spens.*) to take in, digest mentally: (*Shak.*) to bring on: to put on, as clothes: to invest, clothe: to supply. [O.Fr. *enduire*—L.

indūcěre—*in*, into, *dūcěre*, to lead, with meaning influenced by *indu̅ěre*, to put on.]

endungeon, in-dun'jən, *v.t.* to shut up in a dungeon or the like.

endure, in-dūr', *v.t.* (*Spens.*) to harden: to remain firm under: to bear without sinking: to tolerate.—*v.i.* to remain firm: to last.—*adj.* **endur'able**, that can be endured or borne: lasting.—*n.* **endur'ableness.**—*adv.* **endur'ably.**—*ns.* **endur'ance**, state or power of enduring or bearing: a suffering patiently without sinking: patience: continuance: (*obs.*) duration: lasting quality: maximum performance under given conditions: (*obs.*) captivity; **endur'er.**—*adv.* **endur'ingly.** [O.Fr. *endurer*—L. *indūrāre*—*in*, in, *dūrus*, hard.]

ene. Same as **e'en** (even).

enema, en'i-mä, often e-nē'mä, *n.* a liquid medicine forced into the rectum: an instrument for doing this :—(*pl.* **en'emas, ene'mata**). [Gr. *enēma*, -*atos*—*enienai*, to send in—*en*, in, and *hienai*, to send.]

enemy, en'i-mi, *n.* one who hates or dislikes: a foe: a hostile force.—*adj.* hostile.—**how goes the enemy?** (*slang*) what o'clock is it? **the enemy, the old enemy**, the Devil; **the last enemy**, death. [O.Fr. *enemi* (Fr. *ennemi*)—L. *inimīcus*—*in*-, neg., *amīcus*, a friend.]

enemy, a prov. form of **anemone**.

energumen, en-ər-gū'mən, *n.* one possessed: a demoniac. [L.L. *energūmenus*—Gr. *energoumenos* —*energeein*—*en*, in, *ergon*, work.]

energy, en'ər-ji, *n.* power of doing work: power exerted: vigorous activity: vigour: forcefulness. —*adjs.* **energet'ic, -al**, having or showing energy: active: forcible: effective.—*adv.* **energet'ically.** —*n.pl.* **energet'ics**, the science of the general laws of energy.—*adj.* **ener'gic**, exhibiting energy. —*n.* **ener'gid**, a protoplasmic unit: a cell with or without a cell-wall.—*v.t.* **en'ergise**, to give strength or active force to: to stimulate to activity. —*v.i.* to act with force.—**conservation of energy** (see **conservation**). [Gr. *energeia*—*en*, in, *ergon*, work.]

enervate, en'ər-vāt, (still sometimes *i*-nər', *v.t.* to deprive of nerve, strength, or courage: to weaken. —*adj.* weakened: spiritless.—*adjs.* **en'ervating, ener'vative.**—*n.* **enervā'tion.**—*v.t.* **enerve'** (*obs.*) to enervate. [L. *ēnervāre*, -*ātum*—*ē*, out of, *nervus*, a nerve.]

enew, e-nū', *v.t.* in falconry, to drive or (*refl.*) plunge into water. [O.Fr. *enewer*—*en*, in, *eau*, water.]

enfeeble, in-fē'bl, *v.t.* to make feeble: to weaken. —*n.* **enfee'blement**, weakening: weakness.

enfelon, en-fel'ən, *v.t.* (*Spens.*) to make fierce.

enfeoff, in-fef', en-fēf', *v.t.* to give a fief to: to invest with a possession in fee: to surrender.—*n.* **enfeoff'ment**, act of enfeoffing: the deed which invests with the fee of an estate. [O.Fr. *enfeffer*—*en*-, and *fief*; see **fief, feoff.**]

enfested, en-fest'id, *adj.* (*Spens.*) embittered. [Perh. for **infest**, hostile, or **infestered.**]

enfestered, en-fest'ərd, *adj.* festered. [Pfx. *en*-, intens.]

enfetter, en-fet'ər, *v.t.* (*Shak.*) to bind in fetters.

enfierce, en-fērs', *v.t.* (*Spens.*) to make fierce.

enfilade, en-fi-lād', *n.* a number of things arranged as if threaded on a string: a series of rooms with the doors in line affording a continuous passage: a vista: a fire that rakes a line or position from end to end: a situation or a body open from end to end.—*v.t.* to rake, or be in position to rake, with shot through the whole length of a line.— Also *adj.*—*adj.* **enfiled** (en-fīld'; *her.*), thrust through like a sword. [Fr. *enfiler*—*en* (L. *in*), and *fil*—L. *filum*, a thread. See **file**, a line or wire.]

enfire, en-fīr', *v.t.* (*Spens.*) to set on fire, inflame.

enfix. See **infix.**

enflesh, in-flesh', *v.t.* to turn into flesh.

enflower, en-flow'ər, *v.t.* to cover with flowers.

enfold, infold, in-fōld', *v.t.* to wrap up: to encompass.—*n.* **enfold'ment**, act of enfolding: that which enfolds.

enforce, in-fōrs', *v.t.* to gain by force: to give force to: to put in force: to give effect to: to urge: **to**

impress : to drive : to compel : to apply force to : (*Spens.*) to strive.—*adj.* **enforce'able.**—*adv.* **enforc'edly,** by violence, not by choice.—*n.* **enforce'ment,** act of enforcing : compulsion : a giving effect to : that which enforces. [O.Fr. *enforcer*—en (L. *in*), and *force.*]

enforest, *in-for'əst, v.t.* to turn into forest.

enform (*Spens.*). See **inform.**

enfouldered, *en-föl'dərd, adj.* (*Spens.*) charged with or like lightning. [Pfx. *en-,* and O.Fr. *fouldre* (Fr. *foudre*)—L. *fulgur,* lightning.]

enframe, *in-frām', v.t.* to put in a frame.

enfranchise, *in-fran'chīz, -shīz, v.t.* to set free : to give a franchise or political privileges to.—*n.* **enfran'chisement** (*-chiz-, -shiz-*), act of enfranchising : liberation : admission to civil or political privileges. [O.Fr. *enfranchir*—*en,* and *franc,* free; see **franchise.**]

enfree, *en-frē', enfreedom, en-frē'dəm, vs.t.* (*Shak.*) to set free, to give freedom to.

enfreeze, *en-frēz', v.t.* to freeze : turn to ice :— *pa.p.* (*Spens.*) **enfrōs'en.**

engage, *in-gāj', v.t.* to pledge : to bind by a gage or pledge : to render liable : to secure for service : to enlist : to gain over, induce : to betroth : to bespeak, reserve : to win : to hold or occupy : to enter into contest : (*archit.*) to fasten : to interlock : to entangle.—*v.i.* to pledge one's word : to become bound : to take part : to occupy or busy oneself : to enter into conflict.—*adj.* **engaged',** pledged : promised, esp. in marriage : greatly interested : taken, booked, or bespoke : occupied : (*archit.*) partly built or sunk into, or so appearing : geared together, interlocked.—*ns.* **engage'ment,** act of engaging : state of being engaged : that which engages : betrothal : promise : appointment : employment : a fight or battle; **engage'ment-ring,** a ring given in token of betrothal, esp. by the man to the woman, worn on the third finger of the left hand; **Engag'er,** (*hist.*) an adherent of the *Engagement* of 1647, a secret treaty between Charles I and Scottish Commissioners.—*adj.* **engag'ing,** winning : attractive.—*n.* **engag'ingness.** —*adv.* **engag'ingly.**—**engage for,** to answer for. [Fr. *engager*—*en gage,* in pledge; see **gage.**]

engaol, *en-jāl', v.t.* (*Shak.*) to put in gaol.

engarland, *in-gär'lənd, v.t.* to put a garland round.

engarrison, *in-gar'i-sn, v.t.* to establish as a garrison.

engender, *in-jen'dər, v.t.* to beget : to bear : to breed : to sow the seeds of : to produce.—*v.i.* to be caused or produced.—*ns.* **engen'drure, engen'dure,** act of engendering : generation. [Fr. *engendrer*—L. *ingenerāre*—*in,* and *generāre,* to generate.]

engild, *en-gild', v.t.* (*Shak.*) to gild.

engine, *en'jin, n.* a mechanical contrivance, esp. a complex piece of machinery in which power is applied to do work : a locomotive; a military machine : (*obs.*) an instrument of torture : anything used to effect a purpose : a device, contrivance, wile : a snare : (*arch.*) a person used as a tool : (*obs.; see also* **ingine**) ability, ingenuity, genius, turn of mind.—*v.t.* to equip with an engine or engines : to contrive.—*ns.* **en'gine-driver,** a workman who controls an engine, esp. a railway locomotive; **engineer',** one who designs or makes engines or machinery : an officer who manages a ship's engines : (*obs.*) one who constructs or manages military works and engines : one who designs or constructs public works, such as roads, railways, sewers, bridges, harbours, canals, and the like : a soldier of a division of an army called *Engineers,* concerned with entrenching, road-making, and other constructive work : (esp. *U.S.*) an engine-driver.—*v.i.* to act as engineer.—*v.t.* to arrange, contrive : to manoeuvre, guide.—*ns.* **engineer'ing,** the art or profession of an engineer; **en'gine-fitter,** one who fits together the parts of an engine; **en'gine-man,** one who drives an engine; **en'giner** (*Shak.*), engineer; **en'gine-room,** the room in a vessel in which the engines are; **enginery** (en'jin-ri), the art of managing engines : engines collectively : machinery; **en'gine-turning,** a kind of ornament made by a rose-

engine, as on the backs of watches, etc. [O.Fr. *engin*—L. *ingenium,* skill; see **ingenious.**]

engird, *in-gərd', v.t.* to gird round : to encircle : *pa.p.* and *pa.t.* **engirt'.**—*v.t.* **engir'dle.**

English, *ing'glish, adj.* belonging to *England* or its inhabitants or language.—*n.* the English people (as *pl.*) : the language of the people of England, the Scottish Lowlands, etc. : 14-point type.—*v.t.* to translate into English : to make English.—*n.* **Eng'lander,** an Englishman.—*adj.* **Eng'lified,** like the English of England in speech or ways : (*Scot.*) Southroun in speech, esp. affectedly so.— *ns.* **Eng'lisher,** a translator into English : (*Scot.*) an Englishman; **Eng'lishman,** a native or naturalised inhabitant of England; **Eng'lishry,** the fact of being an Englishman : in Ireland, the population of English descent; **little Englander,** an opponent of British imperialism and empire-building; **Old English,** a kind of type—Black-letter : the English language down to about 1100 or 1150 (popularly *Anglo-Saxon*); **Middle English,** from then till about 1500; **Modern English,** from about 1500 onwards.—**Early English** often means Early Middle English; (*archit.*), see **early; presentment of Englishry,** the offering of proof that a person murdered belonged to the English race, to escape the fine levied on the hundred or township for the murder of a Norman; **Young England** (see **young**). [O.E. *Englisc*—*Engle,* Angles.]

englobe, *in-glōb', v.t.* to enclose as in a globe : to form into a globe.

engloom, *in-glōōm', v.t.* to make gloomy.

englut, *in-glut', v.t.* to glut, to fill : to swallow.

engore, *in-gōr', v.t.* (*Spens.*) to gore : to pierce : to wound : to make gory.

engorge, *in-gorj', v.t.* (*Spens.*) to devour : to glut.— *v.i.* (*Milt.*) to feed voraciously.—*adj.* **engorged',** filled to excess (with blood, etc.).—*n.* **engorge'ment,** the act of swallowing greedily : (*med.*) congestion as with blood.

engouement, engoûment, *än⁹-gōō-mäṅ⁹, n.* excessive fondness : infatuation. [Fr.]

engouled, *en-gōōld', adj.* (*her.*) of bends, crosses, etc., having ends that enter the mouths of animals. [Fr. *engoulée*—*en,* in, O.Fr. *goule* (Fr. *gueule*), a beast's mouth.]

engrace, *in-grās', v.t.* to put grace into.

engraff, obsolete form of **engraft.**

engraft, *in-gräft', v.t.* to graft : to insert : to join on (to something already existing) : to fix deeply : (*obs.*) to cuckold.—*ns.* **engrafta'tion** (en-), act of engrafting : **engraft'ment,** engrafting : the thing engrafted : a scion.—Also (*obs.*) **ingraft',** etc.

engrail, *in-grāl', v.t.* (*her.*) to border with little semicircular indents : to make rough.—*v.i.* to form an edging or border : to run in indented lines.— *n.* **engrail'ment,** the ring of dots round the edge of a medal : (*her.*) indentation in curved lines. [O.Fr. *engresler* (Fr. *engrêler*)—*gresle,* hail.]

engrain, ingrain, *in-grān', v.t.* to dye of a fast or lasting colour : to dye in the raw state : to infix deeply.—*adj.* **engrained',** more often **ingrained'** (or *in'*), dyed in grain : deeply coloured or permeated.—*n.* **engrain'er.** [Orig. to dye in grain, i.e., with grain; see **grain.**]

engram, *en'gram,* **engramma,** *en-gram'ä, ns.* a permanent impression made by a stimulus or (*psych.*) experience : a stimulus impression supposed to be inheritable : a memory trace. [Gr. *en,* in, *gramma,* that which is written.]

engrasp, *en-gräsp', v.t.* (*Spens.*) to grasp.

engrave, *in-grāv', v.t.* to cut with a graver on wood, steel, etc. : to cut into : to impress deeply : to form or represent by engraving :—(*pa.p.* **engraved', engräv'en**).—*ns.* **engräv'er; engräv'ery** (*obs.*), the art of the engraver; **engräv'ing,** act or art of cutting or incising designs on metal, wood, etc., for the purpose of printing impressions from them —in metal, the lines to be printed are sunk or incised; in wood, the lines to be printed appear in relief, the wood between them being cut away : an impression taken from an engraved plate : a print. [Pfx. *en-* and **grave,** vb.]

engrave, *in-grāv', v.t.* to deposit in the grave.

engrieve, *en-grēv', v.t.* (*Spens.*) to grieve.

Neutral vowels in unaccented syllables : *el'ə-mənt, in'fənt, ran'dəm*

engroove, ingroove, in-gr$\overline{oo}$v', v.t. to cut a groove or furrow in : to fit into a groove.

engross, in-grōs', v.t. to buy up wholesale or completely : to monopolise : to take wholly to oneself : to absorb the whole attention or powers of : to copy in a large hand or in distinct characters : to write in legal form : (obs.) to name in a list or document : (Spens.) to make thick : (Shak.) to fatten.—ns. engross'er ; engross'ing, the conduct of those who buy merchandise in large quantities to obtain command of the market ; engross'ment, act of engrossing : that which has been engrossed : a fair copy.—engrossing a deed, writing it out in full and regular form for signature. [Fr. en gros—L. in, in, grossus, large ; see gross.]

enguard, in-gärd', v.t. (Shak.) to guard or defend.

engulf, ingulf, in-gulf', v.t. to swallow up wholly, as in a gulf : to cause to be swallowed in a gulf.— Also (obs.) engulph', ingulph'.—n. engulf'ment.

engyscope, en'ji-skōp, n. (obs.) a microscope, esp. a kind of reflecting microscope.—Erroneously en'giscope. [Gr. engys, near, skopeein, to view.]

enhalo, in-hā'lō, v.t. to surround with a halo.

enhance, in-häns', v.t. to lift, raise : to heighten : to intensify : to add to, increase.—v.i. to increase : to rise in value.—n. enhance'ment.—adj. enhanc'ive. [A.Fr. enhauncer, prob. from O.Fr. enhaucer—L. in, and altus, high ; cf. hance.]

enharmonic, -al, en-här-mon'ik, -əl, adj. pertaining to music constructed on a scale containing intervals less than a semitone : pertaining to that scale of music current among the Greeks in which an interval of 2¼ tones was divided into two quarter tones and a major third : distinguishing between those tones that are identified in equal temperament.—adv. enharmon'ically.—enharmon'ic modulation, for instruments of equal temperament, change of notation without change of tone. [Gr. enarmonikos—en, in, harmoniā, harmony.]

enhearse. Same as inhearse.

enhearten, in-härt'n, v.t. to encourage : to cheer.

enhunger, en-hung'gər, v.t. to make hungry.

enhydros, en-hi'dros, n. a chalcedony nodule with water or other liquid in a cavity.—n. enhy'drite, a mineral with fluid inclusions.—adjs. enhydrit'ic, enhy'drous. [Gr. enydros, containing water—en, in, hydōr, water.]

enhypostasia, en-hī-pō-stā'zi-ä, n. substantial or personal existence : personality not existing independently but by union with another.—adj. enhypostatic (-stat'ik).—v.t. enhypostatise (-pos'ta-tīz). [Gr. en, in, and hypostasis ; see hypostasis.]

enigma, in-ig'mä, n. a statement with a hidden meaning to be guessed : anything very obscure : a riddle.—adjs. enigmat'ic, -al (en- or ēn-), relating to, containing, or resembling an enigma : obscure : puzzling.—adv. enigmat'ically.—v.t. enig'matise, to express enigmatically or symbolically.—ns. enig'matist, one who concocts or deals in riddles : one who expresses himself riddlingly ; enigmatog'raphy. [L. aenigma— Gr. ainigma—ainissesthai, to speak darkly—ainos, a fable.]

enisle, inisle, in-īl', v.t. to put on, or make into, an island : to isolate.

enjambment, enjambement, in-jam(b)'mənt, änᵍ-zhänᵍb-mänᵍ, n. in verse, the continuation of the sense without a pause beyond the end of the line. —v.t. and v.i. enjamb (in-jam'). [Fr. enjambement —enjamber, to stride, encroach—en, in, jambe, leg.]

enjoin, in-join', v.t. to lay upon, as an order : to order or direct with authority or urgency : (law and U.S.) to forbid, to prohibit by injunction.—n. enjoin'ment. [Fr. enjoindre—L. injungere—in, and jungere, to join.]

enjoy, in-joi', v.t. to joy or delight in : to feel or perceive with pleasure : to possess or use with satisfaction or delight : to have the use of : to have sexual intercourse with.—adj. enjoy'able, capable of being enjoyed : giving pleasure, delightful.—n. enjoy'ableness.—adv. enjoy'ably.—ns. enjoy'er ; enjoy'ment, state or condition of enjoying : satisfactory possession or use of anything : pleasure : happiness. [O.Fr. enjoier, to give joy

to—en (L. in), and joie, joy ; or O.Fr. enjoir, to enjoy—en, and joir—L. gaudēre, to rejoice.]

enkernel, in-kər'nəl, v.t. to enclose in a kernel.

enkindle, in-kin'dl, v.t. to kindle or set on fire : to inflame : to rouse.—adj. enkin'dled.

enlace, in-lās', v.t. to encircle : to embrace : to entwine : to entangle : to cover with a network or with lace : to lace.—n. enlace'ment.—Also inlace'.

enlard, in-lärd', v.t. (Shak.) to grease, to baste.

enlarge, in-lärj' (Spens. enlarg'en), v.t. to make wider : to increase in size or quantity : to expand : to amplify : to reproduce on a larger scale (esp. of a photograph) : to set free.—v.i. to grow large or larger : to be diffuse in speaking or writing : to expatiate.—adj. enlarged'.—adv. enlar'gedly.— ns. enlar'gedness ; enlarge'ment, act of enlarging : state of being enlarged : increase : extension : diffuseness of speech or writing : a photograph reproduced on a larger scale : a setting at large : release. [O.Fr. enlarger—en (L. in), large, large.]

enlevement, in-lēv'mənt, n. (esp. Scots law) abduction of a woman or child.—Also (as Fr.) enlèvement (änᵍ-lev'mänᵍ).

enlight, in-līt', v.t. to shed light on : to light up, kindle.—v.t. enlight'en, to lighten or shed light on : to give light to : (obs.) to make clear to the mind : to impart knowledge or information to : to elevate by knowledge or religion : to free from prejudice and superstition.—n. enlight'enment, act of enlightening : state of being enlightened : the spirit of the French philosophers of the 18th century. [O.E. inlihtan—in, in, lihtan, to light ; or independently formed later.]

enlink, in-lingk', v.t. to connect closely.

enlist, in-list', v.t. to enrol : to engage as a soldier, etc. : to employ in advancing an object.—v.i. to engage in public service, esp. as a soldier : to enter heartily into a cause.—n. enlist'ment, act of enlisting : state of being enlisted. [Pfx. en-, and list.]

enliven, in-līv'n, v.t. to put life into : to excite or make active : to make sprightly or cheerful : to animate.—ns. enliv'ener ; enliv'enment.

enlock, in-lok', v.t. to lock up, enclose.

enlumine, en-l$\overline{oo}$'min, v.t. (Spens.). See illumine.

enmesh, in-mesh', emmesh, immesh, em-(m)esh', im-(m)esh', v.t. to catch in a mesh or net, to entangle.

enmity, en'mi-ti, n. the quality of being an enemy : unfriendliness : ill-will : hostility. [O.Fr. enemistié —L. inimīcus ; see enemy.]

enmossed, in-most', adj. covered with moss.

enmove, en-m$\overline{oo}$v', v.t. (Spens.). Same as emmove.

ennea-, en'i-ä-, in composition, nine.—n. ennead (en'i-ad ; Gr. enneas, -ados), the number nine : a set of nine things.—adj. ennead'ic.—n. enn'eagon (-ə-gon ; Gr. gōniā, angle), a polygon with nine angles.—adj. enneagonal (-ag'ən-əl).— n.pl. Ennean'dria (Gr. anēr, andros, man, male), the ninth Linnaean class of plants, with nine stamens.—adjs. ennean'drian ; ennean'drous ; enn'eastyle (Gr. stŷlos, column), having nine columns. [Gr. ennea, nine.]

ennoble, i-nō'bl, v.t. to make noble : to elevate, distinguish : to raise to nobility.—n. ennō'blement, the act of making noble : that which ennobles. [Fr. ennoblir—Fr. en (L. in), and noble.]

ennui, änᵍ-nwē, on'wē, on-wē', n. a feeling of weariness or languor : boredom : the occasion of ennui.—v.t. to weary : to bore.—adj. ennuyé (-yā), bored. [Fr., distress,—O.Fr. anoi—L. in odiō, as in odiō habeō, I hold in hatred, i.e., I am tired of ; see annoy.]

enodal, ē-nō'dl, adj. without nodes.

enomoty, e-nom'o-ti, n. a band of sworn soldiers, esp. the smallest Spartan subdivision. [Gr. enōmotiā—en, in, omnynai, to swear.]

enormous, i-nor'məs, adj. (arch.) abounding, exceeding the normal, esp. in a bad sense : immense : huge : (arch.) outrageous : atrocious—(obs.) enorm'. —n. enor'mity, a great crime : great wickedness : outrage : iniquity : (obs.) abnormality : (obs.) hugeness.—*adv.* **enor'mously.**—*n.* **enor'mousness.** [L. *ēnormis*—*ē*, out of, *norma*, rule.]

enough, *i-nuf'*, *adj.* as much as need be : sufficient : giving content : satisfying want.—*adv.* sufficiently. —*n.* sufficience : as much as satisfies desire or want. [O.E. *genóh* (nom., neut. accus., and adv., for earlier *genóg*) ; Goth. *ganóhs* ; Ger. *genug* ; O.N. *gnógr*.]

enounce, *i-* or *ē-nowns'*, *v.t.* to enunciate : to proclaim : to utter or articulate. [Fr. *énoncer*— L. *ēnuntiāre*.]

enow, *i-now'*, *adj.* and *adv.* (*arch.*) enough : formerly used as plural of enough. [O.E. *genóg* (*genóh*), with *g* preserved in inflective forms ; cf. **enough.**]

enow, *ē-noo'*, *adv.* (*Scot.* and *dial.*) a moment ago, or presently. [Prob. **even now.**]

enquire (*Spens.* also **enquere**). See **inquire.**

enrace, *en-rās'*, *v.t.* (*Spens.*) to implant.

enrage, *in-rāj'*, *v.t.* to make angry.—*adj.* **enraged',** angered : furious.—*n.* **enrage'ment,** act of enraging, state of being enraged : (*Spens.*) rapture. [O.Fr. *enrager*—*en* (L. *in*), and *rage*, rage.]

enrange, *en-rānj'*, **enraunge,** *en-rawnj'*, *v.t.* (*Spens.*) to arrange : to rove over.

enranckle, *in-rang'kl*, *v.t.* (*Spens.*) to enrage.

enrank, *en-rangk*, *v.t.* (*Shak.*) to place in order.

enrapture, *in-rap'tyər*, *v.t.* to put in rapture or ecstasy : to transport with pleasure or delight.— *adjs.* **enrap'tured, enrapt',** in ecstasy.

enravish, *en-rav'ish*, *v.t.* (*Spens.*) to enrapture.

enregiment, *in-rej'(i-)mənt*, *v.t.* to form into a regiment.

enregister, *in-rej'is-tər*, *v.t.* to register : to enrol : to record : to put on record as ratified.

enrich, *in-rich'*, *v.t.* to make rich : to fertilise : to adorn : to enhance.—*n.* **enrich'ment,** act of enriching ; that which enriches : ornamentation.

enridged, *en-rij'id*, *adj.* (*Shak.*) formed into ridges.

enring, *in-ring'*, *v.t.* to encircle : to put a ring on.

enriven, *en-riv'n*, *adj.* (*Spens.*) torn.

enrobe, *in-rōb'*, *v.t.* to dress, clothe, or invest.

enrol, enroll, *in-rōl'*, *v.t.* to insert in a roll, list or register : to enter in a list as pupil, member, etc. : to enlist : to record : to put in writing : (*Spens.*) to form into a roll : (*Spens.*) to enwrap.—*v.i.* to enrol oneself—(*pr.p.* **enroll'ing** ; *pa.t.* and *pa.p.* **enrolled'.**)—*ns.* **enroll'er ; enrol'ment,** act of enrolling : that in which anything is enrolled : a register. [O.Fr. *enroller* (Fr. *enrôler*)—*en*, and *rolle*, roll.]

enroot, *in-rōōt'*, *v.t.* to fix by the root : to implant firmly : (*Shak.*) to entangle, as root by root.

enrough, *in-ruf'*, *v.t.* to make rough.

enround, *en-rownd'*, *v.t.* (*Shak.*) to surround.

ens, *enz*, *n.* an entity, as opp. to an attribute (*pl.* **entia,** *en'shi-ä*). [L.L. *ēns*, pr.p. from L. *esse*, to be.]

ensample, *en-säm'pl*, *n.* example.—*v.t.* to give an example of. [O.Fr. *essample* ; see **example.**]

ensanguine, *in-sang'gwin*, *v.t.* to stain or cover with blood.—*adj.* **ensan'guined,** bloody. [Fr. pfx. *en-*, in, L. *sanguis*, *-inis*, blood.]

ensate, *en'sāt*, *adj.* sword-shaped. [L. *ēnsis*, sword.]

enschedule, *en-shed'ūl*, *v.t.* (*Shak.*) to insert in a schedule.

ensconce, *in-skons'*, *v.t.* to cover or protect as with a sconce or earth-work : to hide safely : to settle comfortably.

enseal, *en-sēl'*, *v.t.* to put one's seal to : to seal up.

enseam, *en-sēm'*, *v.t.* to mark as with a seam.

enseam, *en-sēm'*, *v.t.* to grease : (*Shak.*) to defile : to free from superfluous fat. [Cf. **seam,** grease.]

enseam, *en-sēm'*, *v.t.* (*Spens.*) to contain : (*obs.*) to introduce to company. [Der. obscure ; cf. M.E. *in same, in seme*, O.E. *ætsomne, tosomne*, together, O.N. *semja*, to put together.]

ensear, *en-sēr'*, *v.t.* (*Shak.*) to dry up.

ensemble, *än⁹-sän⁹-bl'*, *n.* all parts of a thing taken together : (*mus.*) union of performers in a concerted number : the group of musicians so combining : the combined effect of the performance : a woman's costume consisting of different garments.—**tout**

ensemble (*tōō-tän⁹-*), general appearance or effect. [Fr. *ensemble*, together—L. *in*, in, *simul*, at the same time.]

ensepulchre, *in-sep'əl-kər*, *v.t.* to put in a sepulchre.

ensew, (*Spens.*). Same as **ensue.**

ensheathe, ensheath, insheathe, *in-shēdh'*, *v.t.* to enclose as a sheath.

enshell. Same as **inshell.**—*adj.* **enshield'** (*Shak.*), prob. **enshelled** or **inshelled.**

enshelter, *in-shel'tər*, *v.t.* (*Shak.*) to put in shelter.

enshield, *in-shēld'*, *v.t.* to shield or protect.

enshrine, *in-shrīn'*, *v.t.* to enclose in or as in a shrine.

enshroud, *en-shrowd'*, *v.t.* to cover up : to cover with a shroud.

ensiform, *en'si-form*, *adj.* sword-shaped. [L. *ēnsis*, a sword, *forma*, form.]

ensign, *en'sīn*, *n.* a badge, sign or mark : the sign or flag distinguishing a nation or a regiment (see also under **blue, red, white**) : one who carries the colours : until 1871, the officer of lowest commissioned rank in the British infantry.—*v.t.* (*-sīn'*) to mark with a badge or sign, in heraldry, with one placed above.—*ns.* **en'sign-bearer ; en'-signcy, en'signship,** the rank of commission of an ensign in the army. [O.Fr. *enseigne*—L. *insignia*, pl. of *insigne*, a distinctive mark—*in*, and *signum*, a mark.]

ensilage, *en'sil-ij*, *n.* the storing of green fodder in pits or silos.—*v.t.* **ensile** (*en-sīl'*, or *en'sīl*), to store by ensilage. [Fr.,—Sp. *en*, in, and *silo*—L. *sīrus*—Gr. *siros, sīros, seiros*, pit for corn.]

ensky, *en-skī'*, *v.t.* (*Shak.*) to place in the sky.

enslave, *in-slāv'*, *v.t.* to reduce to slavery : to subject to a dominating influence.—*adj.* **enslaved'.** —*ns.* **enslave'ment,** act of enslaving : state of being enslaved : slavery : bondage ; **enslav'er.**

ensnare, *in-snār'*, *v.t.* to catch in a snare : to entrap : to entangle.

ensnarl, *en-snärl'*, *v.t.* (*Spens.*) to entangle.

ensorcell, *in-sör'səl*, *v.t.* to bewitch. [O.Fr. *ensorceler*—*en*, and *sorcier*, a sorceror.]

ensoul, insoul, *in-sōl'*, *v.t.* to join with the soul : to animate as a soul.

ensphere, insphere, *in-sfēr'*, *v.t.* to enclose or place in a sphere : to give a spherical form to :— *pa.p.* (*Milt.*) **insphear'd.**

enstamp, *in-stamp'*, *v.t.* to mark as with a stamp.

enstatite, *en'stat-īt*, *n.* a rock-forming mineral, an orthorhombic pyroxene, magnesium silicate. [Gr. *enstatēs*, adversary, from its refractory character.]

ensteep, *en-stēp'*, *v.t.* (*Shak.*) to steep : to lay under water.

enstyle, *in-stīl'*, *v.t.* to style, call.

ensue, *in-sū'*, *v.t.* to follow, to come after : to result (with *from*).—*v.t.* (*B.*, *arch.*) to follow after :— (*pr.p.* **ensū'ing** ; *pa.t.* and *pa.p.* **ensūed'.**) [O.Fr. *ensuir* (Fr. *ensuivre*)—L. *in*, after, L.L. *sequĕre*,— L. *sequi*, to follow.]

ensure, *in-shōōr'*, *v.t.* to make sure : to make safe : (*obs.*) to betroth : (*obs.*) to insure. [See **insure.**]

enswathe, inswathe, *in-swädh'*, *v.t.* to wrap.—*n.* **enswathe'ment.**

ensweep, *in-swēp'*, *v.t.* to sweep over.

entablature, *en-tab'lat-yər*, *n.* in classic architecture that part which surmounts the columns and rests upon the capitals : an engine framework upon columns. [It. *intavolatura*—*in*, in, *tavola*—L. *tabula*, a table.]

entail, entayle, *en-tāl'*, *v.t.* and *v.i.* (*Spens.*) to carve.—*n.* cut, fashion. [O.Fr. *entailler*—L.L. *intaleāre*—*in*, into, *taleāre*, to cut.]

entail, *in-tāl'*, *v.t.* to settle on a series of heirs, so that the immediate possessor may not dispose of the estate : to bring on as an inevitable consequence. —*n.* the settlement of an entailed estate : an estate entailed : the transmission, or the rule of descent, of an estate.—*ns.* **entail'er ; entail'ment,** act of entailing : state of being entailed. [Pfx. *en-* and **tail** (2).]

entame, *en-tām'*, *v.t.* (*Shak.*) to tame.

entangle, *in-tang'gl*, *v.t.* to twist into a tangle, or so as not to be easily separated : to involve in complications or in an embarrassing or a compromising situation : to perplex : to ensnare.—*n.*

entang'lement, a confused state: perplexity: a tangled obstacle: a tangle: condition of being entangled: an entangling connexion.

entasis, *en'ta-sis, n.* (*archit.*) the swelling outline of the shaft of a column or the like. [Gr. *entásis—en*, in, *tasis*, a stretch.]

entelechy, *en-tel'ə-ki. n.* (*phil.*) actuality: distinctness of realised existence: a vital principle supposed by vitalists to direct processes in an organism towards realisation of a certain end. [Gr. *entelecheia—en*, in, *telos*, perfection, end, *echein*, to have.]

Entellus, *en-tel'əs, n.* the hanuman monkey of India. [App. from *Entellus* the old Sicilian in *Aeneid*, book V., from its old-mannish look.]

entender, intender, *in-tend'ər, v.t.* to make tender: to weaken.

entente, *ä̃n²-tän²t, n.* an understanding: a friendly agreement or relationship between states—as the **entente cordiale** (*kor-dē-äl'*) between Britain and France (1904). [Fr.]

enter, *en'tər, v.i.* to go or come in: to penetrate: to come upon the stage: to take possession: to become a member: to put down one's name (as competitor, candidate, etc.): to become a party or participator.—*v.t.* to come or go into: to penetrate: to join or engage in: to begin: to put into: to enrol or record: to admit: to inscribe or cause to be inscribed: to register (as a vessel leaving a port, a horse for a race, a pupil for a school, etc.): to insert a record of: to initiate: to become a member of: to take possession of: (*U.S.*) to obtain right of preemption to by recording one's name in a land office, etc.—*n.* (*Shak.*) ingoing.—*adj.* **en'terable.**—*n.* **en'terer.**—*n.* and *adj.* **en'tering.**—**enter a protest,** to write it in the books: thence simply, to protest; **enter into,** to become a party to: to be interested in: to participate actively or heartily: to understand sympathetically: to take up the discussion of: to be part of; **enter on,** to begin: to engage in. [Fr. *entrer—*L. *intrāre*, to go into, related to *inter*, between.]

enterchaunge, *en-tər-chawnj'*, an obs. form of interchange.

enterdeale, *en-tər-dēl', n.* (*Spens.*) interdeal.

enteron, *en'tər-on, n.* in Coelenterates the bodycavity: in higher animals the gut or alimentary canal:—(*pl.* **en'tera**).—*adjs.* **en'teral,** pertaining to, within, or by way of, the intestine; **en'terate,** having an alimentary canal.—*n.* **enterec'tomy** (Gr. *ek*, from, *tomē*, a cut), surgical removal of part of the bowel.—*adj.* **enteric** (*en-ter'ik*), pertaining to the intestines: possessing an alimentary canal.—*n.* enteric fever.—*ns.* **enteri'tis,** inflammation of the intestines, esp. the small intestine; **en'terocele** (*-sēl*; Gr. *kēlē*, tumour), a hernia containing intestine; **enterocentesis** (*-sen-tē'sis*; Gr. *kentēsis*, pricking), operative puncturing of the intestine; **en'terolith** (Gr. *lithos*, stone), a concretion of organic matter with lime, bismuth or magnesium salts formed in the intestine; **Enteromor'pha** (Gr. *morphē*, form), a genus of green seaweeds of tubular form; **en'teropneust,** any animal of the **Enteropneus'ta** (gut-breathers; Gr. *pneein*, to breathe), the Hemichordata, or a division of them including Balanaglossus; **enteros'tomy** (Gr. *stoma*, mouth), surgical formation of an opening in the intestine; **enterot'omy,** incision of the intestinal wall.—**enteric fever,** typhoid fever, an infectious disease due to a bacillus, characterised by fever, rose-red rash, enlargement of the spleen and ulceration of the intestines. [Gr. *enteron*, gut.]

enterprise, *en'tər-prīz, n.* an undertaking: a bold or dangerous undertaking: an adventure: readiness, initiative, and daring in undertaking.—*v.t.* to undertake.—*n.* **en'terpriser,** an adventurer.—*adj.* **en'terprising,** forward in undertaking: adventurous.—*adj.* **en'terprisingly.** [O.Fr. *entreprise*, pa.p. of *entreprendre—entre*, between (L. *inter*), and *prendre—*L. *praehendĕre*, to seize.]

entertain, *en-tər-tān', v.t.* (*obs.*) to maintain, keep: (*obs.*) to take on (as servant, etc.): (*obs.*) to treat: to receive: to receive and provide lodging or refreshment for: to receive and treat hospitably:

to hold the attention or thoughts of: to hold the attention of pleasurably: to amuse: to receive and take into consideration: to keep or hold in the mind: to harbour: (*Spens.*) to meet or experience.—*n.* (*Spens.; Shak.*) entertainment.—*n.* **entertain'er,** one who gives or offers entertainment in any sense: one who gives amusing performances professionally.—*adj.* **enter'taining,** affording entertainment: amusing.—Also *n.*—*adv.* **en²ertain'ingly.**—*n.* **entertain'ment,** act of entertaining: reception and provision for guests: hospitality at table: that which entertains: the provisions of the table: a banquet: amusement: a performance or show intended to give pleasure. [Fr. *entretenir—*L. *inter*, among, *tenēre*, to hold.]

entertake, *en-tər-tāk', v.t.* (*Spens.*) to receive.

entertissued. See **intertissued.**

enthrall, enthral, *in-thrawl', v.t.* to bring into thraldom or bondage: to hold in thrall: to hold spellbound:—(*pr.p.* **enthrall'ing;** *pa.t.* and *pa.p.* **enthralled').**—*ns.* **enthral'dom,** condition of being enthralled; **enthral'ment,** act of enthralling: slavery.—Also **inthrall', inthral'.**

enthrone, *in-thrōn', v.t.* to place on a throne: to exalt to the seat of royalty: to install as bishop: to exalt.—*ns.* **enthrone'ment, enthrōnisā'tion,** the act of enthroning or of being enthroned.—*v.t.* **enthrō'nise** (or *en'*), to enthrone, as a bishop: to exalt.

enthusiasm, *in-*, or *en-th(y)ōō'zi-azm, n.* (*obs.*) possession by a god, inspiration, or religious exaltation: (*obs.*) religious extravagance: intense interest: passionate zeal.—*v.t.* and *v.i.* **enthuse'** (back-formation), to make, be, become, or appear enthusiastic.—*n.* **enthu'siast,** one filled with enthusiasm.—*adjs.* **enthusias'tic, -al,** filled with enthusiasm: zealous: ardent.—*adv.* **enthusias'tically.** [Gr. *enthousiasmos*, a god-inspired zeal—*enthousiazein*, to be inspired by a god—*en*, in *theos*, a god.]

enthymeme, *en'thi-mēm, n.* (*rhet.*) an argument of probability only: (now) a syllogism in which one premise is suppressed.—*adj.* **enthymemat'ical.** [Gr. *enthȳmēma*, a consideration—*enthȳmeesthai*, to consider—*en*, in, *thȳmos*, the mind.]

entice, *in-tīs', v.t.* to induce by exciting hope or desire: to tempt: to lead astray.—*adj.* **entice'able.**—*ns.* **entice'ment,** act of enticing: that which entices or tempts: allurement; **entic'er.**—*n.* and *adj.* **entic'ing.**—*adv.* **entic'ingly.** [O.Fr. *enticier*, provoke; prob. related to L. *titiō*, a brand.]

entire, *in-tīr', adj.* whole: complete: unmingled: intact: unimpaired: (*Spens.*) untired: not castrated (esp. of a horse): (*biol.*) with untoothed and unlobed margin: (*Spens.*) inner, inward: (*arch.*) genuine.—*adv.* (*arch.*) within: (*arch.*) sincerely.—*n.* the whole: completeness: a stallion: porter or stout as delivered from the brewery.—*adv.* **entire'ly.**—*ns.* **entire'ness, entire'ty,** completeness: the whole.—**in its entirety,** in its completeness. [O.Fr. *entier—*L. *integer*, whole, from *in-*, not, and root of *tangere*, to touch; in some senses showing confusion with **interior.**]

entitle, *en-tī'tl, v.t.* to give a title to: to style: to give a right or claim to. [O.Fr. *entiteler—*L.L. *intitulāre—in*, in, *titulus*, title.]

entity, *en'ti-ti, n.* being: existence: a real substance: a thing that exists. [L.L. *entitās, -ātis—ēns;* see **ens.**]

ento-, *en'tō-, en-to'-*, **ent-,** *ent-, pfx.* inside, often interchanging with **endo-,** as *entoderm, endoderm, entophyte, endophyte,* and often opp. to **ecto-.**—*ns.* **en'toblast** (Gr. *blastos*, a shoot, bud), endoderm: a cell nucleolus; **en'toderm** endoderm. [Gr. *entos*, within.]

entoil, *in-toil', v.t.* to entangle or ensnare.—*n.* **entoil'ment.**

entomb, *in-tōōm', v.t.* to place in a tomb: to bury.—*n.* **entomb'ment,** burial. [O.Fr. *entoumber—en*, in, *tombe*, a tomb.]

entomic *en-tom'ik, adj.* pertaining to insects.—*adj.* **entomolog'ical.**—*adv.* **entomolog'ically.**—*v.t.* **entomol'ogise.**—*ns.* **entomol'ogist,** one learned in entomology.—*n.* **entomol'ogy,** the science of insects.—*adjs.* **entomoph'agous** (Gr.

phagein, to eat—aorist), insectivorous; **ento-moph'ilous** (Gr. *phileein*, to love), specially adapted for pollination by insects.—*n.* **ento-moph'ily**, pollination by insects : adaptation to pollination by insects. [Gr. *entoma*, insects—*entomos*, cut up—*en*, in, *tomē*, a cut.]

Entomostraca, *en-tō-mos'tra-kä*, *n.pl.* a general name for the lower orders of crustacea—*Phyllopods, Ostracods, Copepods,* and *Cirripedes.*—*n.* and *adj.* **entomos'tracan**.—*adj.* **entomos'tracous**. [Gr. *entomos*, cut up—*en*, in, *tomē*, a cut, *ostrakon*, a shell.]

ento- (continued)—*adj.* **entophytal** (*-fī'tl*).—*n.* **entophyte** (*-fīt;* Gr. *phyton*, plant), an endophyte.—*adjs.* **entophytic** (*-fīt'ik*), **entophytous** (*en-tof'i-təs* or *en-tō-fī'təs*); **entoplas'tral**.—*n.* **entoplas'tron**, the unpaired plate behind the epiplastra in a turtle's plastron.—*adj.* **entopt'ic** (Gr. *ōps, ōpos,* eye), within the eyeball : pertaining to the visibility to the eye of objects within itself.—*n.* **entop'tics**, the study of such appearances.—*adj.* **ento'tic** (Gr. *ous, ōtos,* ear), of the interior of the ear.

entourage, *än³-tŏŏ-räzh'*, *n.* surroundings : followers. [Fr.,—*entourer*, to surround—*en*, in, *tour*, a circuit.]

entozoon, *en-tō-zō'on*, *n.* an animal living parasitically within the body of its host :—*pl.* **entozō'a**.—*adjs.* **entozō'al** ; **entozō'ic**. [Gr. *entos*, within, *zōion*, an animal.]

entr'acte, *än³-trakt'*, *n.* the interval between acts in a play : a piece of music or other performance between acts. [Fr.,—*entre*, between, *acte*, act.]

entrail, *en-trāl'*, *v.t.* (*Spens.*) to interlace, entwine.—*n.* (*Spens.*) twisting, entanglement. [O.Fr. *entreillier*—*en*, and *treille*, trellis-work.]

entrails, *en'trālz* (*Spens.* **entralles**, *en'trawlz*), *n.pl.* the internal parts of an animal's body, the bowels : the inside of anything : (*obs.*) the seat of the emotions :—*sing.* (*rare*) **entrail** (*Spens.* **entrall**, *en-trawl'*). [O.Fr. *entraille*—L.L. *intrālia*—*inter*, within.]

entrain, *in-trān'*, *v.t.* to put into a railway train, esp. used by troops.—*v.i.* to get into a train : to take a train.—*n.* **entrain'ment**.

entrain, *in-trān'*, *v.t.* to draw after : to sweep or carry along.—*n.* **entrain'ment**. [Fr. *entrainer*.]

entrammel, *in-tram'l*, *v.t.* to trammel, fetter.

entrance, *en'trəns*, *n.* act of entering : coming upon the stage : power or right to enter : a place of entering : a door : the beginning.—*n.* **en'trant**, one who, or that which, enters. [Fr. *entrer*—L. *intrāre*, to enter.]

entrance, *in-*, *en-träns'*, *v.t.* to put into a trance : to fill with rapturous delight.—*n.* **entrance'ment**, state of trance or of excessive joy.—*adj.* **entranc'ing**, charming, transporting.

entrap, *in-trap'*, *v.t.* to catch, as in a trap : to ensnare : to entangle.—*ns.* **entrap'ment**, act of entrapping : the state of being entrapped : **entrapper**. [O.Fr. *entraper*—*en*, in, *trappe*, a trap.]

entreasure, *in-trezh'ər*, *v.t.* to lay up, as in a treasury.

entreat, *in-trēt'*, *v.t.* to ask earnestly : to beseech : to beg for : (*obs.*) to induce : (*orig.*) to treat, to deal with, to behave towards : (*Spens.*) to occupy oneself with : (*Shak.*) to pass, spend (time).—*v.i.* to sue, beseech : to ask :—*adjs.* **entreat'able** (*obs.*); **intreatful** (*Spens.*); **entreat'ing**.—*adv.* **entreat'ingly**.—*adj.* **entreat'ive**, pleading.—*ns.* **entreat'ment**, act of entreating : treatment : (*Shak.* perhaps discourse, verbal intercourse, or favours as objects of entreaty; **entreat'y**, act of entreating : earnest prayer.—Also (*Spens.*) **intreat'**, etc. [O.Fr. *entraiter*—*en*, and *traiter*, to treat, to treat.]

entrechat, *än³-tr'-shä*, *n.* a leap during which a dancer beats his heels together. [Fr.,—It. *intrecciata*, plaited, complicated (caper).]

entrée, *än³'*, *on'trä*, *n.* entry, freedom of access, admittance : a dish served at dinner between the chief courses or as a substitute : (*mus.*) an introduction or prelude : the act of entering, a formal entrance, or music for it.—*n.* **entrée-dish**, a dish, usually silver, with a cover, suitable for an entrée. [Fr.]

entremets, *än³'tra-mā*, *-me*, *n.* any dainty served at table between the chief courses—formerly **entremes, entremesse**. [O.Fr. *entremes*—*entre*, between, *mes* (Fr. *mets*), dish.]

entrench, intrench, *in-trensh'*, *-trench'*, *v.t.* to dig a trench around : to fortify with a ditch and parapet : to establish in a strong position : (*Spens.*) to cut into, wound.—*v.i.* to encroach.—*n.* **entrench'ment**, a defensive earthwork of trenches and parapets : any protection : an encroachment.

entrepas, *än³'tra-pä*, *n.* a gait between a walk and a trot, an amble. [Fr.]

entrepot, *än³'tra-pō*, *n.* a storehouse : a bonded warehouse : a seaport through which exports and imports pass. [Fr.]

entrepreneur, *än³-tra-pra-nər'*, *n.* one who undertakes an enterprise : a contractor or employer : an organiser of musical or other entertainments. [Fr.]

entresol, *en'tar-sol*, or *än³-tra-sol*, *n.* a low story between two main stories of a building, generally between the ground-floor and the first floor. [Fr.,—*entre*, between, *sol*, the ground.]

entrold, another reading **introld**, *in-trōld'*, (*Spens.*) apparently a past participle, meaning unknown—enrolled, in the sense of encircled, has been conjectured.

entropion, -um, *en-trō'pi-on*, *-əm*, *n.* inversion of the edge of the eyelid. [Gr. *en*, in, *tropē*, turning.]

entropy, *en'tra-pi*, *n.* (*phys.*) a measure of unavailable energy, energy still existing but lost for purpose of doing work : a measure of heat-content, regarded as increased in a reversible change by the ratio of heat taken in to absolute temperature. [Gr. *en*, in, *tropē*, turning, intended to represent 'transformation-content'.]

entrust, intrust, *in-trust'*, *v.t.* to give in trust : to commit as a trust : to charge trustingly.—*n.* **entrust'ment**.

entry, *en'tri*, *n.* act of entering in any sense : coming upon the stage : coming in of an instrument or performer : entrance : a narrow lane between houses : a lobby or vestibule : (*obs.*) a hostel : act of committing to writing in a record : the thing so written : a list of competitors : a young hound, or hounds collectively, old enough to begin training : (*law*) taking possession.—*n.* **en'try-money**, the money paid on entering a society, club, etc.—**card of entry** (*bridge*, etc.), a card to bring in one's hand with; **port of entry** (see **port**).

entwine, *in-twīn'*, *v.t.* to interlace : to weave.

entwist, *in-twist'*, *v.t.* to twist round.

enucleate, *in-ū'kli-āt*, *v.t.* to deprive of a kernel or nucleus : to lay bare, explain : to extract.—*adj.* without a nucleus.—*n.* **enuclea'tion**. [L. *ēnucleāre*—*ē*, from, *nucleus*, a kernel.]

enumerate, *i-nū'mər-āt*, *v.t.* to count the number of : to name over.—*n.* **enūmera'tion**, act of numbering : a detailed account : a summing-up.—*adj.* **enū'merative**.—*n.* **enū'merator**, one who enumerates. [L. *ē*, from, *numerāre*, *-ātum*, to number.]

enunciate, *i-nun's(h)i-āt*, *v.t.* to state formally : to pronounce distinctly : to utter.—*adj.* **enun'ciable** (*-shi-* or *-si-*), capable of being enunciated.—*n.* **enunciation** (*i-nun-si-ā'shən*), act of enunciating : manner of uttering or pronouncing : a distinct statement or declaration : the words in which a proposition is expressed.—*adjs.* **enun'ciative** (*-si-ā-*, *-syā-*, *-sh*(*y*)*ā-*, or *-sha-*), **enun'ciatory**, containing enunciation or utterance : declarative.—*n.* **enun'ciātor**, one who enunciates. [L. *ēnuntiāre*, *-ātum*—*ē*, from, *nuntiāre*, to tell—*nuntius*, a messenger.]

enure, *in-ūr'*, older form of **inure**.

enuresis, *en-ū-rē'sis*, *n.* incontinence of urine. [Gr. *en*, in, *ourēsis*, urination.]

envassal, *en-vas'al*, *v.t.* (*obs.*) to reduce to vassalage.

envault, *en-vawlt'*, *v.t.* (*obs.*) to enclose in a vault.

enveigle. See **inveigle**.

envelop, *in-vel'əp*, *v.t.* to cover by wrapping : to surround entirely : to hide.—*n.* **envelope** (*en'val-ōp*), that which envelops, wraps, or covers : a cover for a letter (in this sense sometimes but quite unnecessarily pronounced *on'*, *an'*, or otherwise in imitation of French) : (*bot.*) one of the coverings of a flower—calyx or corolla: the gas-bag of a balloon or airship: (*math.*) the locus of ultimate intersections of a series of curves.—*adj.*

envel'oped (*her.*), entwined, as with serpents, laurels, etc.—*n.* envel'opment, a wrapping or covering on all sides. [O.Fr. *enveloper*; origin obscure.]

envenom, *in-ven'əm, v.t.* to put venom into: to poison: to taint with bitterness or malice. [O.Fr. *envenimer*—*en,* and *venim,* venom.]

envermeil, *en-vər'mil, v.t.* (*Milt.*) to dye red, to give a red colour to. [O.Fr. *envermeiller*—*en,* in, *vermeil,* red, vermilion.]

environ, *in-vī'rən, v.t.* to surround: to encircle: to invest.—*n.* envi'ronment, a surrounding: conditions influencing development or growth.—*adj.* environment'al.—*n.pl.* environs (*in-vī'rənz,* or *en'vi-*), the places that environ: the outskirts of a city: neighbourhood. [Fr. *environner*—*environ,* around—*virer,* to turn round; cf. veer.]

envisage, *in-viz'ij, v.t.* to face: to consider: to present to view or to mental view: to visualise.—*n.* envis'agement. [Fr. *envisager*—*en,* and *visage,* the face.]

envision, *in-vizh'ən, v.t.* to see as in a vision: to visualise.

envoy, *en'voi, n.* a messenger, esp. one sent to transact business with a foreign government: a diplomatic minister of the second order.—*n.* en'voyship. [Fr. *envoyé*—pa.p. of *envoyer,* to send.]

envoy, envoi, *en'voi, n.* the concluding part of a poem or a book: the author's final words, esp. now the short stanza concluding a poem written in certain archaic metrical forms. [O.Fr. *envoye*—*envoiier,* to send—*en voie,* on the way—L. *in,* on, *via,* a way.]

envy, *en'vi, n.* (*obs.*) ill-will, hostility, odium: a feeling of mortification at another's good: a good thing contemplated with grudging or emulous feeling.—*v.t.* (formerly and dial. *in-vī'*), to feel vexation at: to feel envy towards, or on account of: to grudge: to desire with emulation or rivalry:—(*pr.p.* en'vying; *pa.t.* and *pa.p.* en'vied).—en'viable, that is to be envied.—*n.* en'viableness.—*adv.* en'viably.—*n.* en'vier, one who envies.—*adj.* en'vious, feeling envy: directed by envy: (*Spens.*) enviable.—*adv.* en'viously.—*n.* en'viousness; en'vying (*B.*), jealousy, ill-will. [Fr. *envie*—L. *invidia*—*in,* on, *vidēre,* to look.]

enwall, inwall, *in-wawl', v.t.* to enclose within a wall.

enwallow, *en-wol'ō, v.t.* (*Spens.*) to roll about wallowingly.

enwheel, *en-hwēl', v.t.* (*Shak.*) to encircle.

enwind, inwind, *in-wīnd', v.t.* to wind about, enwrap.

enwomb, *en-wōōm', v.t.* (*Spens.*) to make pregnant: (*Shak.*) to conceive or have in the womb: to contain.

enwrap, inwrap, *in-rap', v.t.* to cover by wrapping: to enfold: to perplex: to engross.—*n.* enwrap'ment.—*adj.* and *n.* enwrapp'ing.

enwreathe, inwreathe, *in-rēdh', v.t.* to wreathe: to envelop: to encircle, as with a wreath.

enzone, *in-zōn', v.t.* to engirdle: to enclose as with a zone.

enzootic, *en-zō-ot'ik, adj.* of animal diseases, prevalent in a particular district or at a particular season.—*n.* a disease of this character. [Irregularly formed from Gr. *en,* in, *zōion,* animal, in imitation of *endemic.*]

enzym, enzyme, *en'zim, -zīm, n.* any unorganised ferment: leavened bread.—*adjs.* enzymat'ic (-*zim-*, -*zīm-*), enzym'ic, enzymot'ic. [Gr. *en,* in, *zȳmē,* leaven.]

E O, *ē'-ō', n.* a mid-18th-century gambling game, depending on a ball passing an arch marked E or O.

eoan, *ē-ō'ən, adj.* of or pertaining to dawn. [L., Gr. *ēōs,* dawn.]

Eoanthropus, *ē-ō-an-thrō'pəs, n.* once supposed very early form of man represented by parts of skull found at Piltdown, Sussex (1912); in 1954 mandible was shown to be ape's. [Gr.*ēōs,*dawn,*anthrōpos,*man.]

Eocene, *ē'ō-sēn, adj.* (*geol.*) belonging to the oldest division of the Tertiary formation.—*n.* the Eocene system, period, or strata. [Gr. *ēōs,* daybreak, *kainos,* new—from the very small proportion of living species of molluscs among its fossils.]

Eohippus, *ē'ō-hip-əs, n.* the oldest known horselike animal, an Eocene fossil. [Gr. *ēōs,* dawn, *hippos,* horse.]

éolienne, *ā-ol-yen', n.* dress-material of fine silk and wool. [Fr.]

Eolian, Eolic, Eolipile, Eon. See Aeolian, Aeolic, etc.

eolith, *ē'ō-lith, n.* a very early roughly-broken stone implement, or one naturally formed but assumed to have been used by man.—*adj.* eolith'ic. [*ēōs,* dawn, *lithos,* stone.]

eosin, *ē'ō-sin, n.* a red dyestuff, $C_{20}H_8Br_4O_5$.—*adj.* eosin'ophil, readily staining with eosin. [Gr. *ēōs,* dawn.]

eothen, *ē-ō'then, adv.* from the east—the name given by Kinglake to his book of travel in the East (1844). [Gr. *ēōthen,* lit. from morn, at earliest dawn.]

Eozoon, *ē-ō-zō'on, n.* a once supposed fossil organism in the Archaean system of Canada, which would have been the oldest known living thing, or the banded arrangement of calcite and serpentine then supposed to be its remains.—*adj.* Eozō'ic. [Gr. *ēōs,* dawn, *zōion,* an animal.]

Epacris, *ep-ak'ris, ep'ə-kris, n.* a chiefly Australian genus of heath-like plants, giving name to the fam. Epacridā'ceae, close akin to the heaths.—*n.* epac'rid (or *ep'*), any member of the genus, or of the family. [Gr. *epi,* upon, *akris,* a summit.]

epact, *ē'pakt, n.* the moon's age at the beginning of the year: the excess of the calendar month or solar year over the lunar. [Fr. *épacte*—Gr. *epaktos,* brought on—*epi,* on, *agein,* to bring.]

epagoge, *ep-ə-gō'gē, -jē, n.* induction, proof by examples.—*adj.* epagōg'ic. [Gr. *epagōgē*—*epi,* on, *agōgē,* leading.]

epanadiplosis, *ep-a-nə-di-plō'sis, n.* (*rhet.*) a figure by which a sentence begins and ends with the same word, as in Phil. iv. 4. [Gr. *epanadiplōsis.*]

epanalepsis, *ep-a-nə-lep'sis, n.* (*rhet.*) repetition or resumption, as in 1 Cor. xi. 18 and 20. [Gr. *epanalēpsis.*]

epanaphora, *ep-ə-naf'o-rā, n.* beginning of several clauses or lines with the same word or phrase. [Gr. *epanaphorā;* cf. anaphora.]

epanodos, *ep-an'o-dos, n.* recapitulation of the chief points in a discourse. [Gr. *epanodos.*]

epanorthosis, *ep-an-or-thō'sis, n.* (*rhet.*) the re-tracting of a statement in order to correct or intensify it, as *For Britain's guid! for her destruction!* [Gr. *epanorthōsis.*]

eparch, *ep'ärk, n.* the governor of a modern Greek province: a metropolitan.—*ns.* ep'archate, ep'-archy, the province, territory or diocese of an eparch. [Gr. *eparchos*—*epi,* upon, *archē,* dominion.]

epaule, *e-pawl',* the shoulder of a bastion.—*n.* epaule'ment, a side-work of a battery or earth-work to protect it from a flanking fire. [Fr. *épaule,* shoulder—L. *spatula.*]

epaulet, epaulette, *ep'əl-et, n.* a shoulder-piece: a badge of a military or naval officer (now disused in the British army): an ornament on the shoulder of a lady's dress. [Fr. *épaulette*—*épaule,* the shoulder.]

epaxial, *ep-aks'i-əl, adj.* above the axis. [Gr. *epi,* on, over, and axis.]

epedaphic, *ep-e-daf'ik, adj.* pertaining to atmos-pheric conditions. [Gr. *epi,* above, *daphos,* ground.]

épée, *ā-pā', n.* a sharp-pointed, narrow-bladed sword, without a cutting edge, used for duelling, and, with a button on the point, for fencing practice. [Fr.]

Epeira, *ep-īr'ā, n.* a genus of spiders, the type of the Epeir'idae including the common garden spider.—*n.* epeir'id, a member of the family. [Perh. Gr. *epi,* on, related to, to string.]

epeirogenesis, *ep-ī-rō-jen'i-sis, n.* (*geol.*) continent-building.—Also epeirogeny (*-roj'i-ni*).—*adjs.*..

epeirogen'ic, epeirogenetic (*-jin-et'ik*). [Gr. *ēpeiros*, mainland, *genesis*, formation.]

epencephalon, *ep-en-sef'ə-lon, n.* the cerebellum.—*adj.* **epencephalic** (*-si-fal'ik*). [Gr. *epi*, on, *enkephalon*, brain.]

epenthesis, *e-pen'thə-sis, n.* the insertion of a letter or syllable within a word.—*adj.* **epenthetic** (*-thet'ik*). [Gr.]

epeolatry, *ep-i-ol'ə-tri, n.* worship of words. [Gr. *epos*, word, *latreiā*, worship.]

epergne, *i-pərn', n.* a branched ornamental centre-piece for the table. [Poss. Fr. *épargne*, saving; explanation unknown.]

epexegesis, *ep-eks-i-jē'sis, n.* the addition of words to make the sense more clear.—*adjs.* **epexeget'ic** (*-jet'ik*), **-al.**—*adv.* **epexeget'ically.** [Gr. *epexēgēsis*—*epi*, in addition, *exēgeesthai*, to explain.]

epha, ephah, *ē'fā, n.* a Hebrew measure for dry goods. [Heb.; prob. of Egyptian origin.]

ephebe, *ef-ēb'*, **ephē'bus, -os,** *n.* (*Greek antiquities*) a young citizen from 18 to 20 years of age.—*adj.* **ephēb'ic.** [L. *ephēbus*—Gr. *ephēbos*—*epi*, upon, *hēbē*, early manhood.]

Ephedra, *ef'ed-rä, ef-ēd'rä, ef-ed'rä, n.* sea-grape, a genus of jointed, all but leafless desert plants of the Gnetaceae,—*n.* **eph'edrine** (or *ef-ed'rin*), an alkaloid got from Ephedra. [Gr. *ephedrā*, horse-tail.]

Ephemera, *ef-em'ər-ä,* or *ēm', n.* a genus of insects whose adult life is very short, the may-fly: that which lasts a short time.—*adj.* **ephem'eral,** existing only for a day: daily: short-lived: fleeting.—*n.* anything very short-lived.—*ns.* **ephemeral'ity; ephem'erid,** an insect of the may-fly family, **Ephem'eridae** (*-mer'i-dē;* order Plectoptera or **Ephemerop'tera**). — *adj.* **ephemerid'ian.** — *ns.* **ephem'eris,** an account of daily transactions : a journal : an astronomical almanac :—*pl.* **ephem'erides** (*ef-e-mer'i-dēz*); **ephem'erist,** one who studies the daily motions of the planets; **ephem'-eron,** an insect that lives but by day.—*adj.* **ephem'erous.** [Gr. *ephēmeros*, living a day—*epi*, for, *hēmerā*, a day.]

Ephesian, *ef-ē'zi-ən, adj.* of or pertaining to *Ephesus.*—*n.* an inhabitant of Ephesus : (*Shak.*) a jolly companion.

ephialtes, *ef-i-al'tēz, n.* an incubus : a nightmare. [Gr. *ephialtēs.*]

ephod, *ef'od, n.* a kind of linen surplice worn by the Jewish priests : a surplice, generally. [Heb *ēphōd*—*āphad*, to put on.]

ephor, *ef'or, n.* a class of magistrates whose office apparently originated at Sparta, being peculiar to the Doric states.—*n.* **eph'oralty.** [Gr. *epi*, upon, and root of *horaein*, to see.]

epiblast, *ep'i-blāst, n.* the outer germinal layer of an embryo.—*adj.* **epiblast'ic.** [Gr. *epi*, upon, *blastos*, a germ, shoot.]

epic, *ep'ik, adj.* applied to a long narrative poem that relates heroic events in an elevated style : characteristic of an epic poem.—*n.* an epic poem : epic poetry as a genre : a story comparable to that of an epic poem : (*obs.*) an epic poet.—*adj.* **ep'ical.**—*adv.* **ep'ically.**—*ns.* **ep'icism** (*-sizm*), **ep'icist.** —**epic dialect,** Homer's Greek. [Gr. *epikos*—*epos*, a word.]

epicalyx, *ep-i-kāl'iks,* or *kal', n.* an apparent accessory calyx outside of the true calyx, composed of bracts or of fused stipules of sepals.

epicanthus, *ep-i-kan'thəs, n.* a fold of skin over the inner canthus of the eye, characteristic of the Mongolian race.—*adj.* **epican'thic.** [Gr. *epi*, on, and **canthus.**]

epicarp, *ep'i-kärp, n.* (*bot.*) the outermost layer of the pericarp or fruit. [Gr. *epi*, upon, *karpos*, fruit.]

epicede, *ep'i-sēd,* **epicedium,** *ep-i-sē'di-əm,* or *-di', n.* a funeral ode.—*adjs.* **epicē'dial, epicē'-dian,** elegiac. [L. *epicēdium*—Gr. *epikēdeion*—*epi*, upon, *kēdos,* care.]

epicene, *ep'i-sēn, adj.* common to both sexes : having characteristics of both sexes, or neither : effeminate : (*gram.*) of common gender : sometimes restricted to those words that have one grammatical gender though used for both sexes.—Also *n.* [Gr. *epi*, upon, *koinos,* common.]

epicentre, *ep'i-sen-tər, n.* that point on the earth's surface directly over the point of origin of an earthquake.—*adj.* **epicen'tral.** [Gr. *epi*, upon, over, *kentron,* a point.]

epicheirema, *ep-i-kī-rē'mä, n.* a syllogism con-firmed in its major or minor premise, or both, by an incidental proposition. [Gr. *epicheirēma,* attempt, an attempted proof short of demon-strating.—*epi*, upon, *cheir,* hand.]

epicotyl, *ep-i-kot'il, n.* the stem of an embryo plant or seedling between the cotyledons and the next leaf. [Gr. *epi*, over, and **cotyledon.**]

epicure, *ep'i-kūr, n.* (*obs.*) an Epicurean : (*obs.*) one given to sensual enjoyment : a person of refined and fastidious taste, esp. in the luxuries of the table.—*adj.* **Epicurē'an,** pertaining to Epicurus (341-270 B.C.), the Greek philosopher, who taught an atomic materialism in physics and hedonism in ethics, misrepresented by opponents as brutish sensuality : **epicurean,** given to luxury, esp. refined luxury.—*n.* **Epicurē'an,** a follower of Epicurus : (**epi-**) a hedonist : an epicure.—*n.* **Epicurē'anism,** the doctrines of Epicurus : attachment to these doctrines : epicurism.—*v.i.* **ep'icurise,** to play the epicure : to profess the philosophy of Epicurus.—*n.* **ep'icurism,** pursuit of pleasure : fastidiousness in luxury : (also *ep-i-kūr'izm*) Epicureanism. [L. *Epicūrus*—Gr. *Epikouros.*]

epicycle, *ep'i-sī-kl, n.* a circle whose centre is carried round the circumference of a greater circle.—*adj.* **epicy'clic.**—*n.* **epicy'cloid,** a curve described by a point on the circumference of a circle rolling on the outside of the circumference of another circle.—*adj.* **epicycloi'dal.** [Gr. *epi*, upon, *kyklos,* a circle.]

epideictic, -al, *ep-i-dīk'tik, -əl, adjs.* done for show or display. [Gr. *epi*, upon, *deiknynai,* to show.]

epidemic, *ep-i-dem'ik, adj.* affecting a community at a certain time : prevalent.—*n.* a disease that attacks great numbers in one place, at one time, and itself travels from place to place : a wide-spread outbreak.—*adj.* **epidem'ical**—*adv.* **epi-dem'ically.**—*n.* **epidemiol'ogy** (*-dēm-*), the science of epidemics. [Gr. *epidēmos,* general—*epi*, among, *dēmos,* the people.]

epidermis, *ep-i-dər'mis, n.* (*zool.*) scarf-skin or cuticle, forming an external covering of a pro-tective nature for the true skin or corium : (*bot.*) an outer sheath of close-set cells, usually one deep. —*adjs.* **epider'mal, epider'mic, epiderm'oid** [Gr. *epidermis*—*epi*, upon, *derma,* the skin.]

epidiascope, *ep-i-dī'ə-skōp, n.* a lantern for pro-jecting images of objects whether opaque or no. [Gr. *epi*, upon, *dia*, through, *skopeein,* to look at.]

epidiorite, *ep-i-dī'ə-rīt, n.* a dioritic or gabbroitic rock more or less metamorposed, the pyroxene being changed to amphibole. [Gr. *epi*, after, and **diorite.**]

epidote, *ep'i-dōt, n.* a greenish mineral, silicate of calcium, aluminium, and iron.—*n.* **epidosite** (*ep-id'ə-sīt*), a rock composed of epidote and quartz.—*adj.* **epidotic** (*-dot'*).—*n.* **epidotisā'tion.** —*adj.* **epid'otised,** changed into epidote. [Gr. *epidōnai,* to give in addition, superadd, from the great length of the base of the crystal.]

epifocal, *ep-i-fō-kl, adj.* above the focus (of an earthquake).

epigaeal, epigeal, *ep-i-jē'əl,* **epigaeous, epigeous, -us, epigaean, epigean,** *-ən, adjs.* growing or living close to the ground : with cotyledons above ground. [Gr. *epigaios, epigeios—epi,* on *gaia, gē,* earth.]

epigamic, *ep-i-gam'ik, adj.* attractive to the opposite sex. [Gr. *epigamos,* marriageable—*epi,* upon, *gamos,* marriage.]

epigastrium, *ep-i-gas'tri-əm, n.* the part of the abdomen extending from the sternum towards the navel—the pit of the stomach—*adj.* **epigas'tric.** [Gr. *epi*, upon, *gastēr,* the stomach.]

epigene, *ep'i-jēn, adj.* (*geol.*) acting or taking place at the earth's surface. [Gr. *epi*, upon, *gennaein*, to produce.]

epigenesis, *ep-i-jen'i-sis*, *n.* the theory, now universally accepted, that the development of an embryo consists of the gradual production and organisation of parts, as opposed to the theory of preformation, which supposed that the future animal or plant was already present complete, although in miniature, in the germ.—*ns.* **epigen'esist**, **epigenet'icist**.—*adj.* **epigenet'ic**, pertaining to epigenesis: (of minerals) formed subsequently to the enclosing rock. [Gr. *epi*, upon, after, *genesis*, formation.]

epigon, *ep'i-gon*, **epigone**, *ep'i-gōn*, *n.* one of a later generation :—*pl.* **ep'igons**, **ep'igones** (*-gōnz*), **epig'oni**, sons (esp. of the Seven against Thebes), or successors (esp. of Alexander) : undistinguished descendants of the great. [Gr. *epi*, after, *gonē*, birth.]

epiglottis, *ep-i-glot'is*, *n.* a cartilaginous flap over the glottis.—*adj.* **epiglott'ic**. [Gr. *epiglōttis*—*epi*, over, *glōttis*, glottis.]

epigram, *ep'i-gram*, *n.* any concise and pointed or sarcastic saying : a short poem expressing an ingenious thought with point, usually satirical.—*adjs.* **epigrammat'ic** (*-gram-at'ik*), **-al**, relating to or dealing in epigrams : like an epigram : concise and pointed.—*adv.* **epigrammat'ically**.—*v.t.* **epigramm'atise**, to make an epigram on.—*n.* **epigramm'atist**, one who writes epigrams. [Through Fr. and L., from Gr. *epigramma*—*epi*, upon, *gramma*, a writing—*graphein*, to write.]

epigraph, *ep'i-gráf*, *n.* an inscription, esp. on a building : a citation or motto at the beginning of a book or its part.—*v.t.* to provide with an epigraph. —*ns.* **epigrapher** (*ep-ig'ra-far*), **epig'raphist**.—*adj.* **epigraphic** (*-graf'ik*).—*n.* **epig'raphy**. [Gr. *epigraphē*—*epi*, upon, *graphein*, to write.]

epigynous, *e-pij'i-nas*, *adj.* (*bot.*) growing upon the top of the ovary : having calyx, corolla, and stamens inserted on the top of an inferior ovary.—*n.* **epig'yny**. [Gr. *epi*, upon, *gynē*, woman, female.]

epilate, *ep-i-lāt*, *v.t.* to pluck out, remove (of hair). —*n.* **epilā'tion**. [Fr. *épiler*—L. *ex*, from, *pilus*, hair.]

epilepsy, *ep'i-lep-si*, *n.* a chronic functional disease of the nervous system, manifested by recurring attacks of sudden insensibility or impairment of consciousness, commonly accompanied by peculiar convulsive seizures.—*n.* **epilep'tic**, an epileptic patient.—*adjs.* **epilep'tic**, **-al**. [Gr. *epilēpsiā*—*epi*, upon, and root of *lambanein*, to seize.]

Epilobium, *ep-i-lōb'i-am*, *n.* a willow-herb. [Gr. *epi*, upon, *lobos*, a pod, from the position of the petals.]

epilogue, *ep'i-log*, *n.* the concluding section of a book, etc. : a short poem or speech at the end of a play : the speaker thereof : the conclusion of a wireless programme.—*adjs.* **epilogic** (*-loj'ik*), **epilogistic** (*-jis'*).—*v.i.* **epilogise** (*ep-il'a-jīz*, or *ep'*), **epiloguise** (*-gīz*), to speak or write an epilogue. [Fr.,—L. *epilogus*—Gr. *epilgos*, conclusion—*epi*, upon, *legein*, to speak.]

epinasty, *ep'i-nas-ti*, *n.* (*bot.*) down-curving of an organ, caused by a more active growth on its upper side :—opposed to *hyponasty*.—*adj.* **epinas'tic**.—*adv.* **epinas'tically**. [Gr. *epi*, upon, *nastos*, pressed close.]

epinephrine, *ep-i-nef'rin*, *rēn*, *n.* adrenaline. [Gr. *epi*, upon, *nephros*, kidney.]

epinikion, *ep-i-nik'i-an*, **epinicion**, *ep-i-nis(h)'i-an*, *n.* a song of victory : an ode in honour of a victor or winner.—*adj.* **epinik'ian**, **epinic'ian**. [Gr. *epinikion*—*epi*, on, after, *nikē*, victory.]

epipetalous, *ep-i-pet'a-las*, *adj.* (*bot.*) inserted or growing on a petal or petals.

Epiphany, *e-pif'a-ni*, *n.* a church festival celebrated on Jan. 6, in commemoration of the manifestation of Christ to the wise men of the East : the manifestation of a god. [Gr. *epiphaneia*, appearance—*epi*, to, *phainein*, to show.]

epiphenomenon, *ep-i-fen-om'an-an*, *n.* an accompanying phenomenon outside the chain of causation: (*path.*) something appearing after, a

secondary symptom of a disease :—*pl.* **epiphenom'ena**.—*n.* **epiphenom'enalism**, interpretation of mind as an epiphenomenon upon the physical.—*n.* and *adj.* **epiphenom'enalist**. [Gr. *epi*, after, *phainomenon*, neut. pr.p. pass. of *phainein*, to show.]

epiphonema, *ep-i-fō-nē'mä*, *n.* (*rhet.*) an exclamation : a phrase or reflection added as a finishing touch. [Gr. *epiphōnēma*.]

epiphragm, *ep'i-fram*, *n.* the disk with which certain molluscs close the aperture of their shell. [Gr. *epiphragma*, covering—*epiphrassein*, to obstruct.]

epiphyllous, *ep-i-fil'as*, *adj.* (*bot.*) growing upon a leaf, esp. on its upper surface. [Gr. *epi*, upon, *phyllon*, a leaf.]

epiphysis, *ep-if'i-sis*, *n.* any portion of a bone having its own centre of ossification : the pineal gland (*epiphysis cerebri*) : an ossicle of Aristotle's lantern in a sea-urchin : an upgrowth around the hilum of a seed :—*pl.* **epiph'yses**. [Gr., excrescence.]

epiphyte, *ep'i-fīt*, *n.* a plant growing on another plant, without being parasitic : (*path.*) a vegetable parasite on the surface of an animal.—*adjs.* **epiphyt'al**, **epiphytic** (*-fit'ik*), **-al**.—*n.* **ep'iphytism** (or *fīt'*), the condition of being epiphytic : a similar relation among animals. [Gr. *epi*, upon, *phyton*, a plant.]

epiplastron, *ep-i-plas'tron*, *n.* the anterior lateral one of the (nine) pieces forming the plastron of a turtle :—*pl.* **epiplas'tra**.—*adj.* **epiplas'tral**.

epiploon, *e-pip'lō-on*, *n.* the great omentum.—*adj.* **epiplō'ic**. [Gr. *epiploon*—*epipleein*, to float on.]

epipolism, *e-pip'o-lizm*, *n.* fluorescence.—*adj.* **epipol'ic**. [Gr. *epipolē*, surface.]

epirrhema, *ep-i-rē'mä*, *n.* in Greek comedy the address of the Coryphaeus to the audience after the parabasis.—*adj.* **epirrhēmat'ic**. [Gr.—*epi*, on, after, *rhēma*, word.]

episcopacy, *e-pis'ka-pas-i*, *n.* church government by bishops : the office of a bishop : a bishop's period of office : the bishops, as a class.—*adj.* **epis'copal**, governed by bishops : belonging to or vested in bishops.—*adj.* **episcopā'lian**, belonging to bishops, or government by bishops, or to an episcopal church.—*n.* one who belongs to an episcopal (especially Anglican) church.—*n.* **episcopā'lianism**, episcopalian government and doctrine.—*adv.* **epis'copally**.—*ns.* **epis'copant** (*Milt.*), a holder of a bishopric ; **epis'copate**, a bishopric : the office of a bishop : a bishop's period of office : the order of bishops.—*v.i.* (*Milt.*) to act as a bishop.—*v.t.* **epis'copise**, to make a bishop of : to make episcopalian.—*v.i.* to play the bishop (also *v.t.* with *it*).—*n.* **epis'copy** (*Milt.*), survey, superintendence. [Gr. *episkopos*, an overseer.]

episcope, *ep'i-skōp*, *n.* a lantern for projecting images of opaque objects. [Gr. *epi*, on, over, *skopeein*, to look.]

episemon, *ep-i-sē'mon*, *n.* a badge or characteristic device : one of three obsolete Greek letters used as numerals—ς or ⌐, vau or digamma (6); ϙ, koppa (90); and ⅀, san, sampi (900).—*adj.* **episēmat'ic** (*zool.*) serving for recognition. [Gr. *episēmon*, a badge—*epi*, on, *sēma*, a sign.]

episepalous, *ep-i-sep'al-as*, *adj.* growing or inserted upon a sepal or sepals.

episode, *ep'i-sōd*, *n.* a story introduced into a narrative or poem to give variety : an interesting incident : (*mus.*) a passage affording relief from the principal subject.—*adjs.* **ep'isōdal**, **episō'dial**, **episodic** (*-sod'*), **episōd'ical**, pertaining to or contained in an episode : brought in as a digression : abounding in episodes.—*adv.* **episōd'ically**, by way of episode : incidentally. [Gr. *epeisodion*—*epi*, upon, *eisodos*, a coming in—*eis*, into, *hodos*, a way.]

epispastic, *ep-i-spas'tik*, *adj.* blistering.—*n.* a blistering agent. [Gr. *epispastikos*—*epi*, upon, *spaein*, to draw.]

episperm, *ep'i-sparm*, *n.* the outer seed-coat. [Gr. *epi*, upon, and *sperma*, seed.]

epispore, *ep'i-spōr*, *n.* the outermost layer of a spore-wall.

epistaxis, *ep-i-stak′sis*, *n.* bleeding from the nose. [Gr. *epistazein*, to shed in drops.]

epistemology, *ep-is-tē-mol′ə-ji*, *n.* the theory of knowledge.—*adj.* **epistemological** (*-ə-loj′*).—*n.* **epistemol′ogist**. [Gr. *epistēmē*, knowledge, *logos*, discourse.]

episternum, *ep-i-stər′nəm*, *n.* the interclavicle : the epiplastron : the presternum of mammals.—*adj.* **epister′nal**.

epistilbite, *ep-i-stil′bīt*, *n.* a zeolite close akin to stilbite. [Gr. *epi*, on, after, in addition to, and **stilbite**.]

epistle, *i-pis′l*, *n.* a writing sent to one, a letter : esp. a letter to an individual or church from an apostle, as the Epistles of Paul : the extract from one of the apostolical epistles read as part of the communion service : a verse composition in letter form.—*v.t.* (*Milt.*) to preface.—*ns.* **epistler** (*pis′* or *pist′*), **epistoler** (*i-pist′ə-lər*), a letter-writer : one who reads the liturgical epistle in the communion service ; **epistolā′rian**, a letter-writer.—*adjs.* **epistolā′rian**, **epis′tolary**, **epis′tolatory**, **epistolic** (*ep-is-tol′ik*), **-al**, pertaining to or consisting of epistles or letters : suitable to an epistle : contained in letters.—*n.* **epis′tolet**, a short letter.—*v.i.* **epis′tolise**, to write a letter.—*ns.* **epis′tolist**, a writer of letters ; **epistolog′raphy**, letter-writing.—**epistle side** of a church, the south side, opp. to *Gospel side*. [O.Fr.,—L. *epistola*—Gr. *epistolē*—*epi*, on the occasion of, *stellein*, to send.]

epistrophe, *e-pis′trə-fē*, *n.* (*rhet.*) ending of successive clauses with the same word, as in 2 Cor. xi. 22 : a refrain in music. [Gr. *epistrophē*, a return—*epi*, upon, *strephein*, to turn.]

epistyle, *ep′i-stīl*, *n.* architrave. [Gr. *epi*, upon, *stylos*, a pillar.]

epitaph, *ep′i-táf*, *n.* a tombstone inscription : a composition in the form of a tombstone inscription.—*v.t.* to compose an epitaph upon.—*ns.* **epitapher** (*ep′i-taf-ər*), **ep′itaphist**, a composer of epitaphs.—*adjs.* **epitaph′ian**, **epitaph′ic**. [Gr. *epitaphion*—*epi*, upon, *taphos*, a tomb.]

epitasis, *e-pit′ə-sis*, *n.* the main action of a Greek drama leading to the catastrophe—opp. to *Protasis*.

epithalamium, **epithalamion**, *ep-i-thə-lā′mi-əm*, *-on*, *n.* a song or poem in celebration of a marriage : *pl.* **epithalā′mia**.—*adj.* **epithalām′ic**. [L. *epithalamium*, Gr. *epithalamion*—*epi*, upon, *thalamos*, a bride-chamber.]

epithelium, *ep-i-thē′li-əm*, *n.* the cell-tissue that invests the outer surface of the body and the mucous membranes connected with it, and also the closed cavities of the body.—*adj.* **epithē′lial**.—*n.* **epithēliō′ma**, carcinoma of the skin.—*adj.* **epithēliō′matous**. [Mod.L.—Gr. *epi*, upon, *thēlē*, nipple.]

epithem, *ep′i-them*, *n.* (*med.*) a soft external application : (*bot.*) a group of cells exuding water in some leaves.—Also **epithema** (*ep-i-thē′mä*, *ep-ith′i-mä*; *pl.* **epithems**, **epithe′mata**. [Gr. *epithema*, *epithēma*, *-atos*—*epi*, on, *tithenai*, to place.]

epithesis, *ep-ith′i-sis*, *n.* paragoge. [Gr., setting on.]

epithet, *ep′i-thet*, *n.* an adjective expressing some real quality of the thing to which it is applied : a descriptive term : (*Shak.*) term, expression.—*v.t.* to term.—*adj.* **epithet′ic**, pertaining to an epithet : abounding with epithets.—*n.* **epith′eton** (*Shak.* apath′aton*), epithet. [Gr. *epitheton*, neut. of *epithetos*, added—*epi*, on, *tithenai*, to place.]

epithymetic, *ep-i-thim-et′ik*, *adj.* pertaining to desire. [Gr.,—*epi*, upon, *thýmos*, the soul.]

epitome, *i-pit′ə-mē*, *n.* an abridgment or short summary of anything, as of a book : an embodiment in little.—*adjs.* **epitomic** (*ep-i-tom′ik*), **-al**.—*v.t.* **epit′omise**, to make an epitome of : to shorten : to condense.—*ns.* **epit′omiser**, **epit′omist**, one who abridges.—**in epitome**, on a small scale. [Gr.,—*epi*, *tomē*, a cut.]

epitonic, *ep-i-ton′ik*, *adj.* overstrained. [Gr. *epi*—*tonos*—*epi*, upon, *teinein*, to stretch.]

epitrachelion, *ep-i-tra-kē′li-ən*, *n.* an Orthodox priest's or bishop's stole. [Gr.,—on the neck—*epi*, upon, *trachēlos*, neck.]

epitrite, *ep′i-trīt*, *n.* (*pros.*) a foot made up of three long syllables and one short. [Gr. *epitrītos*—*epi*, in addition to, *tritos*, third.]

epitrochoid, *ep-i-trō′koid*, *n.* a curve like an epicycloid, but generated by any point on a radius. [Gr. *epi*, on, *trochos*, wheel.]

epizeuxis, *ep-i-zūk′sis*, *n.* (*rhet.*) the immediate repetition of a word for emphasis. [Gr., joining on.]

epizoon, *ep-i-zō′on*, *n.* an animal that lives on the surface of another animal, whether parasitically or commensally : (*pl.* **epizō′a**).—*adj.* and *n.* **epizō′an**.—*adjs.* **epizō′ic**, dwelling upon an animal : having seeds dispersed by animals ; **epizootic** (*ep-i-zō-ot′ik*), pertaining to epizoa : (*geol.*, *obs.*) containing fossil remains (as subsequent to the appearance of life) : affecting animals as an epidemic does mankind.—*n.* an epizootic disease. [Gr. *epi*, upon, *zōïon*, an animal.]

epoch, *ēp′ok*, *ep′ok*, *n.* a point of time fixed or made remarkable by some great event from which dates are reckoned : (*astron.*) the particular time, used as a point of reference, at which the data had the values in question : a planet's heliocentric longitude at the epoch : a precise date : a time from which a new state of things dates : an age, geological, historical, or other.—Also (*arch.*) **ep′ocha**.—*adjs.* **epochal** (*ep′ok-l*) ; **ep′och-māking**, important enough to be considered as beginning a new age ; **ep′och-marking**. [Gr. *epochē*—*epechein*, to stop, take up a position—*epi*, upon, *echein*, to hold.]

epode, *ep′ōd*, *n.* a kind of lyric poem invented by Archilochus, in which a longer verse is followed by a shorter one : the last part of a lyric ode, sung after the strophe and antistrophe.—*adj.* **epodic** (*-od′ik*). [Gr. *epōïdos*—*epi*, on, *ōïdē*, an ode.]

eponychium, *ep-o-nik′i-əm*, *n.* a narrow band of cuticle over the base of a nail. [Gr. *epi*, on, *onyx*, *onychos*, nail.]

eponym, *ep′o-nim*, *n.* one who gives his name to something : a hero invented to account for the name of a place or people : a character who gives a play, etc., its title : a distinguishing title.—*adj.* **epon′ymous**. [Gr. *epōnymos*, eponymous—*epi*, upon, to, *onyma*, *onoma*, a name.]

epopee, *ep′o-pē*, **epopoeia**, *ep-o-pē′yä*, *n.* epic poetry : an epic poem. [Gr. *epopoiïä*—*epos*, a word, an epic poem, *poïeein*, to make.]

epopt, *ep′opt*, *n.* one initiated into the Eleusinian mysteries. [Gr. *epoptēs*—*epi*, upon, and root *op-*, to see.]

epos, *ep′os*, *n.* the elementary stage of epic poetry : an epic poem : a series of events such as are treated in epic poetry. [Gr. *epos*, a word.]

éprouvette, *ā-proo-vet′*, *n.* an apparatus for testing the strength of gunpowder. [Fr.,—*éprouver*, to try.]

epsilon, *ep-sī′lən*, *n.* fifth letter (E, ε) of the Greek alphabet, short e : as a numeral ε′ = 5, ͵ε = 5,000. [Gr. *e psīlon*, bare or mere e.]

epsomite, *ep′səm-īt*, *n.* a mineral, hydrated magnesium sulphate (MgSO₄· 7H₂O).—**ep′som-salt(s)′**, a purgative and refrigerant medicine of like composition, originally got from the springs at Epsom, in Surrey.

epulation, *ep-ū-lā′shən*, *n.* feasting. [L. *epulārī*, *-ātus*, to feast.]

epulotic, *ep-ū-lot′ik*, *adj.* cicatrising.—*n.* a cicatrising medicament. [Gr. *epoulōtikos*—*epi*, upon, *oulē*, a scar.]

epurate, *ep′ū-rāt*, *v.t.* to purify.—*n.* **epurā′tion**. [Fr. *épurer*.]

equable, *ek′wə-bl*, or *ēk′*, *adj.* even, uniform : smooth : without great variations or extremes : of even temper.—*ns.* **equabil′ity**, **e′quableness**.—*adv.* **e′quably**. [L. *aequābilis*—*aequāre*—*aequus*, equal.]

equal, *ē′kwəl*, *adj.* identical in quantity : of the same value : adequate : in just proportion : fit : equable : uniform : equitable : evenly balanced : just : (*bot.*) equally developed on each side.—*n.* one of the same age, rank, etc. : (*Spens.*) equality.—

v.t. to be, or to make, equal to: (*bot.*) to reach the same level as : (*pr.p.* e'qualling ; *pa.t.* and *pa.p.* e'qualled).—*n.* equalisa'tion, the act of making equal : state of being equalised.—*v.t.* e'qualise, to make equal or uniform : (*obs.*) to equal.—*v.i.* to become equal : (*coll.*) to make one's score equal to one's opponent's.—*n.* equali'ser, a person or thing that equalises : a score that makes both sides alike.—*adj.* equalitār'ian (*-kwol*-), of or pertaining to the equality of mankind.—*n.* one who believes in or favours political and social equality of mankind.—*ns.* equalita'rianism, equality (*ē-kwol'i-ti*), the condition of being equal : sameness : evenness :—*adv.* equally (*ē'kwa-li*).—*n.* e'qualness, equality : equability.—*v.t.* equate', to reduce to an average or to a common standard of comparison : to state as equal : to regard as equal.—*ns.* equa'tion, the act of making equal : a statement of the equality of two quantities : reduction to a common standard : correction to compensate for an error, irregularity, or discrepancy : the quantity added for this purpose : a formula expressing a chemical action and the proportions of the substances involved; equa'tor, (*geog.*), a great circle passing round the middle of the globe and equidistant from N. and S. poles : (*astron.*) the corresponding great circle of another body : the great circle in which the plane of the earth's equator intersects the celestial sphere (so called because day and night are equal when the sun reaches it) : the middle belt or line of any globular or nearly globular body that has some sort of polarity.—*adj.* equatorial (*ek-wa-tō'ri-al* or *ēk-*), of, pertaining to, of the nature of, or in the neighbourhood of an equator.—*n.* a telescope mounted on an axis, capable of moving parallel to the equator and so following a star in any part of its diurnal course.—*adv.* equatō'rially, so as to have motion or direction parallel to the equator.— **equal temperament** (see **temperament**); **equal to the occasion**, fit or able for an emergency; **equation of time**, mean solar time minus apparent solar time, or the right ascension of the true sun minus that of the mean sun; **personal equation**, a correction to be applied to the reading of an instrument on account of the observer's tendency to read too high, too low, etc.: any tendency to error or prejudice due to personal characteristics for which allowance must be made. [L. *aequālis*, equal, *aequāre*, *-ātum*, to make equal—*aequus*, equal.]

equanimity *ē-kwa-nim'i-ti*, *e-*, *n.* evenness of mind or temper.—*adj.* equanimous (*i-kwan'i-mas*).—*adv.* equan'imously. [L. *aequanimitās*—*aequus*, equal, *animus*, the mind.]

equerry, *ek'wa-ri*, *ik-wer'i*, *n.* (*obs.*) princely stables : an officer thereof : an official in attendance upon a prince or personage. [Fr. *écurie*—L.L. *scūria*, a stable.]

equestrian, *i-kwes'tri-an*, *adj.* pertaining to horsemanship, or to the Roman order of *equitēs* or knights : on horseback.—*n.* a horseman : a performer on horseback :—*fem.* (sham Fr.) equestri- enne'.—*n.* eques'trianism, horsemanship. [L. *equester*, *equestris*—*eques*, a horseman—*equus*, a horse.]

equi-, *ē'kwi*, a prefix meaning equal, from L. *aequus*.—*adj.* equian'gular, having equal angles (**equiangular spiral**), a curve whose radius vector makes a constant angle with the tangent —the *logarithmic spiral*)—*n.* equiangular'ity.— *n.* and *v.t.* equibal'ance, equipoise.—*adj.* equi- diff'erent, having equal differences.—*n.* equi- dis'tance—*adj.* equidis'tant, equally distant.— *adv.* equidis'tantly.—*adj.* equilat'eral (L. *latus*, *-eris*, side), having all sides equal.—*n.* equi- mul'tiple, a number multiplied by the same number as another.—*adjs.* equipo'tent, of equal power; equipoten'tial, of equal power, capability, potential, or potentiality.—*adj.* e'quivalve, having valves alike in size and form.

Equidae, *ek'wi-dē*, *n.pl.* a family of ungulate mammals consisting of the genus **Eq'uus** (horse, ass, zebra) and various fossil forms. [L. *equus*, horse.]

equilibrium, *ēk-*, *ek-wi-lib'ri-am*, *n.* balance : state of even balance : a state in which opposing forces or tendencies neutralise each other.—*v.t.* and *v.i.* equilibrate (*ēk-wi-lib'rāt*, or *lib'rāt*, or *-kwil'*), to balance : to counterpoise.—*ns.* equilibrā'tion ; equil'ibrator (or *-līb'*), a balancing or stability device, esp. an aeroplane fin; equil'ibrist (or *-līb'*, or *-līb'*), one who does balancing tricks; equilib'- rity. [L. *aequilībrium*—*aequus*, equal, *lībra*, balance.]

equine, *ē'kwīn*, equinal, *ē-kwīn'al*, *adj.* pertaining to, or of the nature of, a horse.—*ns.* equinia (*i-*, *ē-kwin'i-ā*), glanders; equin'ity, equine nature. [L. *equīnus*—*equus*, a horse.]

equinox, *ek'wi-noks*, *ēk'wi-noks*, *n.* the time when the sun crosses the equator, making the night equal in length to the day, about 21st March and 23rd Sept.—*adj.* equinoc'tial, pertaining to the equinoxes, the time of the equinoxes, or to the regions about the equator.—*n.* the celestial equator or *equinoctial line*—*adv.* equinoc'tially, in the direction of the equinox.—**equinoctial gales**, high gales popularly supposed to prevail about the times of the equinoxes—the belief is unsupported by observation. [L. *aequus*, equal, *nox*, *noctis*, night.]

equip, *i-kwip'*, *v.t.* to fit out : to furnish with everything needed :—(*pr.p.* equipp'ing ; *pa.t.* and *pa.p.* equipped').—*n.* equipage (*ek'wi-pāj*), that with which one is equipped : furniture required for any operation, e.g. making tea : a carriage and attendants : retinue.—*v.t.* (*obs.*) to equip.—*n.* equip'ment, the act of equipping : the state of being equipped : things used in equipping or furnishing : outfit. [Fr. *équiper*, prob. O.N. *skipa*, to set in order, *skip*, a ship; partly influenced by confusion with L. *equus*, horse.]

equipoise, *ek'wi-poiz*, *n.* a state of balance : a counterpoise.—*v.t.* to balance : to counterpoise. [L. *aequus*, equal, and **poise**.]

equipollent, *ē-kwi-pol'ant*, *adj.* having equal power or force : equivalent.—*n.* an equivalent.—*ns.* equi- poll'ence, equipoll'ency. [L. *aequus*, equal, *pollēns*, *pollentis*, pr.p. of *pollēre*, to strong, able.]

equiponderate, *ē-kwi-pon'dar-āt*, *v.i.* to be equal in weight : to balance.—*adj.* equal in weight.—*n.* equipon'derance.—*adj.* equipon'derant. [L. *aequus*, equal, *pondus*, *ponderis*, weight.]

Equisetum, *ek-wi-sē'tam*, *n.* the only surviving genus of the family **Equisetā'ceae**, constituting the **Equiseti'nae** or **Equisetā'les**, a class of pteridophytes, stiff herbaceous plants with almost leafless articulated and whorled stems and branches —also *Horse-tail*.—*adjs.* equisetā'ceous ; equi- sēt'ic ; equisēt'iform. [L.,—*equus*, a horse, *sēta*, a bristle.]

equitation, *ek-wi-tā'shan*, *n.* the art of riding on horseback.—*adjs.* eq'uitant, riding : straddling, overlapping : of leaves, folded lengthwise over succeeding leaves. [L. *equitāre*, to ride—*equus*, a horse.]

equity, *ek'wi-ti*, *n.* right as founded on the laws of nature : moral justice, of which laws are the imperfect expression : the spirit of justice which enables us to interpret laws rightly : fairness : an equitable right : (*U.S.*) the value of property in excess of any charges upon it: (in pl. **eq'uities**) ordinary shares.—*adj.* eq'uitable, possessing or showing or in accordance with equity : held or exercised in equity.—*n.* eq'uitableness.—*adv.* eq'uitably. [O.Fr. *équité*—L. *aequitās*, *-ātis*—*aequus*, equal.]

equivalent, *i-kwiv'a-lant*, *adj.* equal in value, power, meaning, etc.: interchangeable : (*chem.*) of like combining value.—*n.* a thing equivalent : (*chem.*) an equivalent weight.—*ns.* equiv'alence, equiv'al- ency.—*adv.* equiv'alently.—**equivalent weight**, (*chem.*) that weight which displaces or combines with or otherwise represents a standard unit, usu. 1 gram of hydrogen or 8 of oxygen. [Fr.,—L. *aequus*, equal, *valēns*, *valentis*, pr.p. of *valēre*, to be worth.]

equivocal, *i-kwiv'a-kl*, *adj.* capable of meaning two or more things : of doubtful meaning : capable of a double explanation : suspicious : questionable.—

adv. **equiv′ocally.**—*n.* **equiv′ocalness.**—*v.i.*
equiv′ocāte, to use equivocal or doubtful words
in order to mislead.—*ns.* **equivocā′tion; equiv′-
ocātor.**—*adj.* **equiv′ocatory,** containing or
characterised by equivocation.—*ns.* **equivoke,**
equivoque (*ek′wi-vōk*), an equivocal expression:
equivocation: a quibble. [L. *aequus*, equal, *vōx*,
vōcis, the voice, a word.]
er, *ə, interj.* expressing hesitation.
era, *ē′rä, n.* a series of years reckoned from a
particular point, or that point itself: an important
date: an age: a main division of geological time.
[L.L. *aera*, a number, orig. counters, pieces of
copper used in counting, pl. of *aes*, copper.]
eradiate, *i-, ē-rā′di-āt, v.t.* and *v.i.* to shoot out
like a ray of light.—*n.* **eradiā′tion.** [L. *ē-*, from,
radius, a ray.]
eradicate, *i-, ē-rad′i-kāt, v.t.* to pull up by the
roots: to root out: to extirpate.—*adj.* **erad′icable.**
—*adj.* **erad′icāted,** rooted up: (*her.*) of a tree, or
part of a tree, torn up by the roots.—*n.* **eradicā′-
tion,** the act of eradicating: state of being eradicated.—*adj.* **erad′icātive,** serving to eradicate or
drive thoroughly away.—*n.* **erad′icātor.** [L.
ērādicāre, -atum, to root out—*e*, from, *rādix, -īcis*,
a root.]
erase, *i-rāz′, v.t.* to rub or scrape out: to efface:
to destroy.—*adj.* **erā′sable.**—*adj.* **erased′,** rubbed
out: effaced: (*her.*) torn off, so as to leave jagged
edges.—*ns.* **erā′ser,** one who, or that which,
erases, as *ink-eraser*; **erā′sion** (*-zhər*), **erase′ment,
era′sure** (*-zhər*), the act of erasing: a rubbing
out: scraping away: the place where something
written has been rubbed out. [L. *ērādĕre—ē*,
from, *rādĕre, rāsum*, to scrape.]
Erastian, *e-rast′yən, n.* a follower of Thomas
Erastus (1524-83), a Swiss physician, who denied
the church the right to inflict excommunication
and disciplinary penalties: one who would subordinate the church jurisdiction to the state—a
position not held by Erastus at all.—*adj.* relating
to the Erastians or their doctrines.—*n.* **Erast′-
ianism,** control of church by state.
Erato, *er′ə-tō, n.* the Muse of lyric poetry. [Gr.
Eratō.]
erbium, *ər′bi-əm, n.* a rare metal (Er; at. numb. 68),
found at Ytterby, near Stockholm.
ere, *ār, adv., prep.* and *conj.* before.—*advs.* **ere-
long′, ere long,** before long: soon; **erenow′,
ere now,** before this time; **erewhile′,** formerly:
some time before. [O.E. *ǣr*; cf. Du. *eer*.]
ere. Same as **ear,** to plough.
Erebus, *er′i-bəs, n.* (*myth.*) the dark and gloomy
cavern between earth and Hades: the lower world,
hell. [L.,—Gr. *Erebos.*]
erect, *i-rekt′, adj.* upright: directed upward: right
end up, not inverted: (*bot.*) not decumbent:
(*zool.*) turgid and raised.—*v.t.* to set upright: to
set erect: to set at right angles: to raise: to build:
to exalt: to establish.—*adj.* **erect′ed.**—*ns.*
erect′er, erect′or, one who, or that which, erects
or raises: a muscle which assists in erecting a part
or an organ: an attachment to a compound microscope for making the image erect instead of
inverted.—*adj.* **erect′ile** (*-īl*), that may be erected.
—*ns.* **erectility** (*e-, ē-rek-til′i-ti*); **erec′tion,** act
of erecting: state of being erected: exaltation:
anything erected: a building of any kind.—*adj.*
erect′ive, tending to erect.—*adv.* **erect′ly.**—*n.*
erect′ness. [L. *ērigĕre, ērēctum*, to set upright—*ē*,
from, *regĕre*, to direct.]
eremacausis, *er-i-mə-kaw′sis, n.* (*chem.*) very slow
oxidation. [Gr. *ērema*, quietly, slowly, *kausis*,
burning—*kaiein*, to burn.]
eremic, *e-rē′mik, adj.* belonging to deserts. [Gr.
erēmikos—erēmiā, desert, solitude.]
eremite, *er′i-mīt, n.* a recluse who lives apart, esp.
from religious motives: a hermit.—*adjs.* **eremi′tal,**
eremitic (*-mit′ik*), **-al.**—*n.* **er′emitism.** [L.L.
*erēmīta—*Gr. *erēmītēs—erēmos*, desert.]
erepsin, *e-rep′sin, n.* an enzyme of the small
intestine, acting upon casein, gelatine, etc. [L.
ēripĕre, ēreptum—ē, from, *rapĕre*, to snatch.]
erethism, *er′e-thizm, n.* excitement or stimulation
of an organ: abnormal irritability.—*adjs.* **erethis′-**

mic, erethis′tic, erethit′ic. [Gr. *erethismos.*]
Erewhon, *er′e-hwon, n.* the imaginary country of
Samuel Butler's satirical Utopian romances
Erewhon (1872) and *Erewhon Revisited* (1901).—
n. and *adj.* **Erewhō′nian.** [Formed from *Nowhere*
spelt backwards.]
erf, erf, *n.* (*S. Afr.*) a garden plot or small piece of
ground: (*pl.* **er′ven**). [Du.; cf. O.E. *erfe,*inheritance.]
erg, *ərg, n.* the unit of work in the centimetre-
gramme-second system—that is, the quantity of
work done when the point of operation of a force
of one dyne is allowed to move one centimetre in
the direction of the force.—*ns.* **erg′-nine′, erg′ɤ
ten′,** etc., an erg multiplied by ten to the power
nine, ten, etc.; **er′gogram,** a record by ergograph;
er′gograph, an instrument for measuring and
recording muscular work; **ergonom′ics,** study
of man in relation to his working environment;
ergopho′bia, morbid dislike of work. [Gr.
ergon, work.]
ergates, *ər′ga-tēz,* **ergate,** *ər′gāt, ns.* a worker ant,
an undeveloped female.—*ns.* **ergatan′dromorph**
(Gr. *andromorphos*, of male form), an ant combining characters of males and workers; **ergatan′-
er** (Gr. *anēr*, man), a worker-like wingless male
ant; **ergatogyne** (*-jī′nē;* Gr. *gynē*, woman), a
worker-like wingless female ant.—*adj.* **er′gatoid,**
worker-like, wingless but sexually perfect.—*n.*
er′gatomorph, an ergatoid ant.—*adj.* **ergato-
morph′ic.** [Gr. *ergatēs*, workman—*ergon*, work.]
ergo, *ər′gō, adv.* (*logic*) therefore, used to introduce
the conclusion of a syllogism.—*v.i.* **er′gotise,** to
wrangle. [L. *ergō*, therefore.]
ergogram, etc. See **erg.**
ergot, *ər′got, n.* a disease of grasses (esp. rye) and
sedges due to *Claviceps purpurea:* a seed so diseased.
—*n.* **ergos′terol,** an unsaturated sterol got from
ergot.—*v.t.* **er′gotise,** to affect with ergot or with
ergotism.—*n.* **er′gotism,** poisoning caused by
eating bread made of rye diseased with ergot. [Fr.]
eric, *er′ik, n.* the blood-fine paid by a murderer to
his victim's family in old Irish law.—Also **er′iach,
er′ick.** [Ir. *eiric.*]
Erica, *e-rī′kä, n.* the heath genus.—*adjs.*
ericaceous (*e-ri-kā′shəs*), belonging to plants of
the genus Erica, or its family **Erica′ceae:** heath-
like; **er′icoid,** with heatherlike leaves. [L.,—Gr.
ereikē, heath.]
Erigeron, *e-rij′ə-ron, n.* the flea-bane genus of
composites. [Gr. *ērigĕron*, groundsel—*ēri*, early,
gerōn, old.]
eringo. Same as **eryngo.**
erinite, *er′i-nīt, n.* a basic arsenate of copper found
in Cornwall and Ireland. [*Erin*, Ireland.]
Erinys, *e-rī′nis, n.* a Fury:—*pl.* **Erinyes** (*e-rin′i-ēz*).
[Gr. *Erīnys*, pl. *Erīnyēs.*]
Eriocaulon, *er-i-ō-kaw′lon, n.* the pipewort genus,
giving name to the **Eriocaul(on)ā′ceae,** a family
of monocotyledons akin to the Bromelias. [Gr.
erion, wool, *kaulos*, stalk.]
Eriodendron, *er-i-ō-den′dron, n.* the silk-cotton
genus of trees.—*n.* **eriom′eter,** an optical instrument for measuring small diameters of fibres, etc.—
adj. **erioph′orous,** very cottony.—*n.* **Erioph′o-
rum,** the cotton-grass or cotton-sedge genus.
[Gr. *erion*, wool, *dendron*, a tree, *metron*, a measure;
phoros, carrying.]
eristic, -al, *er-is′tik, -al, adj.* of or pertaining to
controversy. [Gr. *eristikos—eris*, strife.]
erl-king, *ərl′-king, n.* for German *erl-könig*, a mis-
translation (alder-king) of the Danish *eller-konge*
(i.e. *elverkonge*, king of the elves).
ermelin, *ər′mə-lin, n.* (*arch.*) ermine (q.v.).
ermine, *ər′min, n.* the stoat: a white fur, the
stoat's winter coat in northern lands, used for the
robes of judges and magistrates with the black
tail-tip of an (imitation) attached.—*adj.* **er′mined,**
adorned with ermine. [O.Fr. *ermine* (Fr. *hermine*),
perh. from L. (*mūs*) *Armēnius*, lit. (mouse) of
Armenia, whence it was brought to Rome; but
acc. to some from O.H.G. *harmin* (Ger. *hermelin*),
ermine-fur.]
ern, an old spelling (*Milt.*) of **earn.**
erne, *ərn, n.* the eagle. [O.E. *earn;* cf. O.N. *örn,*
Du. *arend.*]

Neutral vowels in unaccented syllables: *el′ə-mənt, in′fənt, ran′dəm*

erne, *ərn* (*Spens.*). Same as **earn** (3), **yearn.**

erode, *i-,* *e-rōd',* *v.t.* to eat away, wear away: to form by wearing away.—*adjs.* **erō'ded, erose** (*-rōs'*), irregularly notched as if bitten.—*adj.* and *n.* **erō'dent,** caustic.—*n.* **erosion** (*-rō'zhən*), eating away, wearing down: (*geol.*) the denuding action of weathering, water, ice, wind, etc.—*adj.* **erosive** (*-rō'ziv*). [L. *ē,* from, *rōdĕre, rōsum,* to gnaw.]

Erodium, *e-rō'di-əm, n.* the stork's-bill genus of the geranium family. [Gr. *erōdios,* a heron.]

Eros, *er'os, -ōs, ē'ros, n.* the Greek love-god, identified by the Romans with Cupid: a minor planet discovered in 1898, notable for its near approach to the earth.—*adj.* **erotic** (*e-rot'ik*), **-al,** pertaining to sexual love; amatory: amorous.—*n.* an amatory poem or composition.—*n.pl.* **erot'ica,** a booksellers' name for erotic literature.—*ns.* **erot'icism** (*-sizm*), amorous temperament or habit: erotism; **er'otism,** sexual desire: the manifestations of sex in its widest application.—*adj.* **erotogenic** (*er-ət-ō-jen'ik*), **erotogenous** (*-oj'*), less correctly **erogen'ic, erog'enous,** productive of erotic desire or gratification.—*ns.* **erōtomā'nia,** morbid sexual passion; **erōtomā'niac.** [Gr. *Ērōs, -ōtos.*]

erostrate, *ē-ros'trāt, adj.* (*bot.*) beakless. [L. *ē,* from, *rōstrum,* a beak.]

erotema, *er-ō-tē'mä,* **eroteme,** *er'ō-tēm,* **erotesis,** *er-ō-tē'sis, ns.* a rhetorical question.—*adj.* **erotetic** (*-tet'ik*), interrogatory. [Gr. *erōtēma, erōtēsis—erōtaein,* to question.]

err, *ər, v.i.* to wander: to wander from the right way: to go astray: to miss the mark: to mistake: to sin: (*pr.p.* **erring,** *ər'ing* or *er'ing;* *pa.t.* and *pa.p.* **erred,** *ərd*).—*adjs.* **err'able** (*er'*), capable of erring; **errant** (*er'ənt*), wandering: roving: wild: (*obs.*) thorough (cf. **arrant**).—*n.* a knight-errant.—*adv.* **err'antly.**—*n.* **err'antry,** an errant or wandering state: a rambling about like a knight-errant.—*adj.* **erra'tic,** wandering: having no certain course: not stationary: irregular, capricious, irregular or unpredictable in behaviour.—*n.* a wanderer: an erratic block or boulder.—*adj.* **errat'ical.**—*adv.* **errat'ically.**—*n.* **errā'tum,** an error in writing or printing, esp. one noted in a list in a book (*pl.* **errā'ta**).—*adj.* **err'ing,** (*obs.*) wandering: straying from the truth or right conduct.—*n.* wandering: straying: making mistakes.—*adv.* **err'ingly.**—*adj.* **erroneous** (*i-rō'ni-əs*), erring: full of error: wrong: mistaken: (*obs.*) wandering, straying.—*adv.* **errō'neously.**—*ns.* **errō'neousness; error** (*er'ər*), (*arch.*) wandering, winding course: deviation from the right way: mistaken opinion: difference between a quantity obtained by observation and the true value: a blunder or mistake: wrong-doing; **err'orist—erratic block,** a mass of rock transported by ice and deposited at a distance. [L. *errāre,* to stray; cog. with Ger. *irren,* and *irre,* astray.]

errand, *er'ənd, n.* a message: a commission to say or do something: (*dial.*) marketing.—*ns.* **err'and-boy, girl.—a fool's errand, a sleeveless errand,** a futile journey; **make an errand,** to invent a reason for going; **once (yince, ance) errand** (*Scot.*), for the express purpose and nothing else; **run errands,** to be sent to convey messages or perform small pieces of business. [O.E. *ǣrende;* O.N. *eyrindi;* prob. conn. with Goth. *āirus,* O.N. *árr,* a messenger.]

errhine, *er'īn, adj.* and *n.* sternutatory. [Gr. *errīnon—en,* in, *rhīs, rhinos,* the nose.]

ers, *ərs, n.* the bitter vetch. [Fr.,—L. *ervum.*]

ersatz, *er-zäts', n.* a substitute: (*mil.*) a supplementary reserve from which waste can be made good. [Ger.]

Erse, *ers, ərs, n.* the name given by Lowland Scots to the language of the people of the West Highlands, as being of Irish origin: now sometimes used for Irish Gaelic, as opposed to Scottish Gaelic. [Variant of **Irish.**]

erst, *ərst, adv.* at first: formerly.—*adv.* **erst'while, erstwhile,** formerly.—*adj.* former. [O.E. *ǣrest,* superl. of *ǣr.* See **ere.**]

erubescent, *er-(y)oo-bes'ənt, adj.* growing red: blushing.—*ns.* **erubesc'ence, erubesc'ency; erubesc'īte,** the mineral bornite. [L. *ērubescĕre,* to grow red; see **rubescent, ruby.**]

eruciform, *e-roō'si-form, adj.* like a caterpillar. [L. *ērūca,* caterpillar, *forma,* form.]

eruct, *i-rukt',* **eructate,** *-āt, vs.t.* to belch out, as wind from the stomach.—*n.* **eructā'tion** (*ē-*). [L. *ēructāre, -ātum—ē,* from, *ructāre,* to belch forth.]

erudite, *er-(y)oo-dīt, adj.* learned.—*n.* a learned person.—*adv.* **er'uditely.**—*n.* **erudi'tion,** state of being learned: knowledge gained by study: learning, esp. in literature. [L. *ērudītus, ērudīre, ērudītum,* to free from rudeness—*ē,* from, *rudis,* rude.]

erupt, *i-rupt', v.i.* to break out or through, as a volcano.—*n.* **erup'tion,** a breaking or bursting forth: that which bursts forth: a breaking out of spots on the skin: the action of a volcano.—*adjs.* **erup'tional; erupt'ive,** breaking forth: attended by or producing eruption: produced by eruption.—*n.* **erupt'iveness.** [L. *ērumpĕre, ēruptum—ē,* from, *rumpĕre,* to break.]

eryngo, *e-ring'gō, n.* the candied root of sea-holly: the plant itself (Eryngium), a superficially thistle-like umbellifer. [Gr. *ēryngos.*]

Erysimum, *er-is'i-məm, n.* the treacle-mustard genus of Cruciferae. [Latinised from Gr. *ĕrўsimŏn,* hedge-mustard.]

erysipelas, *er-i-sip'i-las, n.* an inflammatory disease, generally in the face, marked by a bright redness of the skin.—*adj.* **erysipelatous** (*-el'ə-tas*). [Gr.; prob.—root of *erythros,* red, *pella,* skin.]

erythema, *er-i-thē'mä, n.* redness of the skin.—*adjs.* **erythemat'ic, erythem'atous.** [Gr. *erythēma—erythainein,* to redden—*erythros,* red.]

Erythrina, *er-ith-rī'nä, n.* the kaffir-boom genus of Papilionaceae, tropical and subtropical trees with brilliant red flowers. [Gr. *erythros,* red.]

erythrism, *er-ith'rizm, n.* red colouring, esp. exceptional or abnormal. [Gr. *erythros,* red.]

erythrite, *er-ith'rīt, n.* a reddish hydrous arsenate of cobalt.—*adj.* **erythrīt'ic.** [Gr. *erythros,* red.]

erythrocyte, *er-ith'rō-sīt, n.* a red blood corpuscle. [Gr. *erythros,* red, *kytos,* case.]

escalade, *es-kə-lād', n.* the scaling of the walls of a fortress by means of ladders.—Also **escalā'dō** (for Sp. *escalada*).—*v.t.* to scale: to mount and enter by means of ladders.—*n.* **es'calātor,** a moving staircase. [Fr.,—Sp. *escalada—escala,* a ladder—L. *scāla.*]

Escallonia, *es-kal-ōn'i-ä,* a South American genus of shrubs of the Saxifrage family. [*Escallon,* the discoverer.]

escallop, *is-kal'əp, n.* a variant of **scallop.**—*adj.* **escall'oped** (*her.*), covered with scallop-shells.

escape, *is-kāp', v.t.* to free oneself from: to pass out of danger from: to evade, elude.—*v.i.* to come off or come through in safety: to emerge into or gain freedom: to flee: to slip out: to issue: to leak.—*n.* act of escaping: a means of escaping: flight: flight from reality: an outlet: a leakage: an accidental or inadvertent emission: an outburst: a sally: a prank: a venial offence: a transgression: a person or thing that has escaped, esp. a garden plant maintaining itself wild.—*adj.* **escap'able.**—*ns.* **escapade** (*es-kə-pād'*), an escape: a mischievous adventure; **escapado** (*-ä'dō*), an escaped evil-doer: an escapade (Sp. *escapada*); **escapee',** one who has escaped, e.g. from prison.—*adj.* **escape'less.**—*ns.* **escape'ment,** an escape: part of a timepiece connecting the wheelwork with the pendulum or balance, and allowing a tooth to escape at each vibration; **escape'-valve,** a valve to let steam, etc., escape when wanted; **escape'-wheel,** the wheel that the pallets act upon in a clock; **escāp'ism; escāp'ist,** one who seeks escape, esp. from reality.—Also *adj.* [O.Fr. *escaper* (Fr. *échapper*)—L.L. *ex cappā,* (lit.) out of one's cape or cloak.]

escarmouche, *e-skär'moosh, n.* (*obs.*) a skirmish. [Fr.]

escarp, *is-kärp', v.t.* to make into a scarp or sudden slope.—*n.* a scarp or steep slope: (*fort.*) the side

fāte, fär, ȧsk; mē, hər (her); *mīne, mōte, mūte, mōōn; dhen* (then)

of the ditch next the rampart.—*n.* **escarp′ment,** the precipitous side of a hill or rock : escarp. [Fr. *escarper,* to cut down steep, from root of **scarp.**]

eschalot. See **shallot.**

eschar, *es′kär, n.* a slough or portion of dead or disorganised tissue, esp. an artificial slough produced by caustics.—*adj.* **escharot′ic,** tending to form an eschar : caustic.—*n.* a caustic substance. [L.,—Gr. *eschara,* a hearth, mark of a burn.]

eschatology, *es-kə-tol′ə-ji, n.* (*theol.*) the doctrine of the last or final things, as death, judgment, the state after death.—*adjs.* **eschatolog′ic, -al.**—*n.* **eschatol′ogist.** [Gr. *eschatos,* last, *logos,* a discourse.]

escheat, *is-chēt′, n.* property that falls to the feudal lord or to the state for want of an heir, or by forfeiture : plunder, gain (*Spens.* **excheat′**).—*v.t.* to confiscate.—*v.i.* to fall to the lord of the manor or the state.—*adj.* **escheat′able.**—*ns.* **escheat′age, escheat′ment ; escheat′or,** an official who watched over escheats. [O.Fr. *eschete—escheoir* (Fr. *échoir*)—L. *ex,* from, *cadēre,* to fall.]

eschew, *is-chōō′, v.t.* to shun : to flee from : to abstain from. [O.Fr. *eschever;* cog. with Ger. *scheuen,* to shun.]

Eschscholtzia, *e-sholt′si-ä, n.* a genus of Papaveraceae, including the Californian poppy, a showy garden annual. [J. F. von *Eschscholtz,* a member of the expedition that discovered the plant in 1821.]

esclandre, *es-klän₂′dr′, n.* notoriety : any unpleasantness. [Fr.,—L. *scandalum.*]

escolar, *es-kō-lär′, n.* an Atlantic and Southern fish of spectacled appearance. [Sp., scholar.]

escopette, *es-kō-pet′, n.* (*U.S.*) a carbine. [Sp. *escopeta.*]

escort, *es′kort, n.* a person or persons, ship or ships, etc., accompanying another or others for protection, guidance, or merely courtesy : an armed guard : attendance.—Also used as *adj.*—*v.t.* **escort,** to attend as escort.—*n.* **escort′age.** [Fr. *escorte*—It. *scorta—scorgere,* to guide—L. *ex,* out, *corrigère,* to set right.]

escot, *es-kot′, v.t.* (*Shak.*) to pay for, to maintain. [O.Fr. *escoter, escot,* a tax; of Gmc. origin; cf. **scot** (1), **shot** (2).]

escribe, *ē-skrīb′, v.t.* to describe so as to touch one side externally, the others (produced) internally. [L. *ē,* out of, *scribēre,* to write.]

escritoire, *es-krē-twär′, n.* a writing-desk.—*adj.* **escritō′rial.** [Fr. *escritoire*—L.L. *scriptōrium*— L. *scribēre, scriptum,* to write.]

escroll, escrol, *es-krōl′, n.* an escrow : (*her.*) a scroll.—*n.* **escrow,** *es-krō′,* a deed in the hands of a third party, to take effect when a condition is fulfilled. [A.Fr. *escroele, escroe;* see **scroll, scrow.**]

escuage, *es′kū-ij, n.* scutage. [A.Fr.; see **scutage.**]

escudo, *es-kōō′dō, n.* a coin or currency unit of various kinds, in Portugal one milreis. [Port. and Sp., shield.]

Esculapian. See **Aesculapian.**

esculent, *es′kū-lənt, adj.* eatable : fit to be used for food by man.—*n.* something that is eatable. [L. *esculentus,* eatable—*esca,* food—*edēre,* to eat.]

escutcheon, *es-kuch′ən, n.* a shield on which a coat of arms is represented : a family shield : the part of a vessel's stern bearing her name : a shield-shaped object or ornament, etc., as a shield over a keyhole.—*adj.* **escutch′eoned,** having an escutcheon.—a **blot on the escutcheon,** a stain on one's good name; **escutcheon of pretence,** an escutcheon placed with the arms of an heiress in the centre of her husband's coat. [O.Fr. *escuchon*—L. *scūtum,* a shield.]

esemplastic, *es-əm-plas′tik, adj.* unifying.—*n.* **esem′plasy** (*es-em′plə-si*), the unifying power of imagination. [Gr. *es,* into, *hen* (neut.), one, *plastikos,* moulding.]

esile. See **eisel.**

esker, *esk′ər, n.* (*geol.*) a kame, or ridge of gravel and sand laid down by a subglacial stream or one issuing from a retreating glacier. [Ir. *eiscir.*]

Eskimo, *es′ki-mō, n.* and *adj.* one of a people inhabiting arctic America with its islands, Green-

land, and the nearest Asiatic coast : their language :— *pl.* **Es′kimo, -s.**—Eskimo dog, a half-tamed variety, widely distributed in the Arctic regions, and indispensable for drawing sledges. [Said by Dr. Rink to be from an Indian word meaning eaters of raw flesh.]

esloin, esloyne, *es-loin′.* See **eloin.**

esne, *ez′ni, n.* (*hist.*) a domestic slave in O.E. times. [O.E.]

esnecy, *es′nə-si, n.* the eldest daughter's right of first choice in dividing an inheritance. [O.Fr. *aisneece* (Fr. *ainesse*).]

esophagus. See **oesophagus.**

esoteric, *es-ō-ter′ik, adj.* inner : secret : mysterious : (*phil.*) taught to a select few—opp. to *exoteric.*— *adv.* **esoter′ically.**—*ns.* **esoter′icism** (*-i-sizm*), **esoterism** (*es-ot′ər-izm*), the holding of esoteric opinions ; **es′otery,** secret doctrine.—**esoteric Buddhism** (see **theosophy**). [Gr. *esōterikos— esōterō,* comp. of *esō, eisō,* within.]

espadrille, *es-pə-dril′, n.* a rope-soled shoe. [Fr.,— Prov. *espardillo—espart,* esparto.]

espagnolette, *es-pan-yō-let′, n.* the fastening of a French window. [Fr., dim. of *espagnol,* Spanish.]

espalier, *es-pal′yər, n.* a lattice-work of wood to train trees on : a fruit-tree trained on stakes : (*obs.*) a row of trees so trained.—*v.t.* to train as an espalier. [Fr.,—It. *spalliera,* a support for the shoulders—*spalla,* a shoulder; cf. **epaulet.**]

esparto, *es-pär′tō, n.* a strong grass (*Stipa tenacissima,* and others) grown in Spain, N. Africa, etc., and used for making paper, baskets, cordage, etc. [Sp.,—L. *spartum*—Gr. *sparton,* a kind of rope.]

especial, *is-pesh′l, adj.* special : particular : principal : distinguished.—*adv.* **espec′ially.**—**in especial,** in particular. [O.Fr.,—L. *speciālis— speciēs,* species.]

esperance, *es′pər-əns, n.* (*Shak.*) hope. [Fr. *espérance*—L. *spērāre,* to hope.]

Esperanto, *es-pər-än′tō, n.* an auxiliary international language devised by Dr. Zamenhof, published 1887.—Also *adj.*—*n.* **Esperan′tist,** a speaker of Esperanto. [The inventor's pseudonym, **the** hoping one.]

espial. See **espy.**

espiègle, *es-pē-eg′l′, adj.* roguish, frolicsome : arch. —*n.* **espièg′lerie,** roguishness : frolicsomeness. [Fr.,—Ger. *Eulenspiegel;* see **owl.**]

espionage, *es-pyon-äzh′, es′pi-ə-nij, es-pī′ə-nij, n.* spying : use of spies. [Fr.,—*espionner—espion,* a spy.]

esplanade, *es-plə-nād′, n.* a level space between a citadel and the first houses of the town : any level space for walking or driving in. [Fr.,—Sp. *esplanada*—L. *explānāre—ex,* out, *plānus,* flat.]

espouse, *is-powz′, v.t.* to give or take in marriage or betrothal : to take upon oneself or embrace, as a cause.—*ns.* **espous′al,** the act of espousing or betrothing : the taking upon oneself, as a cause : (*pl.*) a contract or mutual promise of marriage : a wedding : a formal betrothal; **espous′er.** [O.Fr. *espouser* (Fr. *épouser*)—L. *spōnsāre,* to betroth— *spondēre, spōnsum,* to vow.]

esprit, *es-prē, n.* wit, liveliness.—**esprit de corps** (*es-prē də kor*), regard for the honour of the body to which one belongs : loyalty of a member to the whole; **esprit fort** (*for*), a free-thinker. [Fr. *esprit,* spirit, de, of, *corps,* body, *fort,* strong.]

espy, *es-pī′, v.t.* to watch : to see at a distance : to catch sight of : to observe : to discover unexpectedly :—*pr.p.* **espy′ing ;** *pa.t.* and *pa.p.* **espied′ ;** 3rd pers. sing. **espies′.**—*n.* **espi′al,** the act of espying : observation. [O.Fr. *espier;* see **spy.**]

Esquimau, *es′ki-mō* (*pl.* **Esquimaux,** *es′ki-mōz*), a French spelling of **Eskimo.**

esquire, *es-kwīr′,* sometimes *es′-, n.* (*orig.*) a squire or shield-bearer : an attendant on a knight : a landed proprietor : a title of dignity next below a knight : a gentleman acting as escort : a general title of respect in addressing letters. [O.Fr. *esquier* (Fr. *écuyer*)—L. *scūtārius—scūtum,* a shield.]

ess, *es, n.* the nineteenth letter of the alphabet (see **S**) : an object of the same shape.—**collar of esses,** a chain of links (also written SS) in **the**

form of the letter S, worn by various dignitaries. [O.E. *ess*, from the Latin name.]

essay, *es'ā*, *n.* an attempt; a tentative effort: a first draft: a trial: an experiment: a written composition less elaborate than a treatise.—*v.t.* **essay'**, to try: to attempt: to make experiment of:—*pr.p.* **essay'ing**; *pa.t.* and *pa.p.* **essayed'.**—*ns.* **essay'er**; **ess'ayist**, one who essays: a writer of essays; **essayette'**, **ess'aykin**, a little essay.—*adjs.* **ess'ayish**; **essayis'tic**. [O.Fr. *essai*—L. *exagium*, weighing—*exagěre*, to try, examine.]

esse, *es'i*, *n.* actual existence: essence.—**in esse**, in existence, opposed to *in posse*, in potentiality. [L. *esse*, to be.]

essence, *es'əns*, *n.* the inner distinctive nature of anything: the qualities which make any object what it is: a being: an alcoholic solution of a volatile or essential oil: a perfume of such composition: the extracted virtues of any drug: a liquid having the properties of the substance from which it is got.—*adj.* **essential** (*is-*, *es-en'shl*), relating to, constituting, or containing the essence: necessary to the existence of a thing: indispensable or important in the highest degree: highly rectified: pure.—*n.* something necessary: a leading principle.—*n.* **essentiality** (*is-en-shi-al'i-ti*), the quality of being essential: an essential quality or element.—*adv.* **essen'tially**.—*n.* **essen'tialness**. —**essential minerals**, those whose presence is considered necessary to entitle a rock to the name it bears—opp. to *accessory* minerals; **essential oils**, oils forming the odorous principles of plants, also called *ethereal oils, volatile oils;* **essential organs**, (*bot.*) stamens and carpels. [Fr.,—L. *essentia*—*essēns, -entis*, assumed p.r.p. of *esse*, to be.]

Essene, *es-ēn'*, *es'ēn*, *n.* one of a small religious fraternity among the ancient Jews leading retired ascetic lives and holding property in common.—*n.* **Ess'enism**. [Gr. *essēnos*; origin doubtful.]

essoin, essoyne, *es-oin'*, *n.* (*law*) excuse for not appearing in court. (*Spens.*) excuse.—*n.* **essoin'er**. [O.Fr. *essoine* (Fr. *exoine*), *es*—L. *ex*, out of, *soin*, care.]

essonite, *es'ən-īt*, **hessonite**, *hes'ən-īt*, *n.* cinnamon-stone. [Gr. *hēssōn*, inferior (i.e. in hardness, to hyacinth which it resembles).]

essorant, *es'ō-rənt*, *adj.* soaring. [Fr.]

establish, *is-*, *es-tab'lish*, *v.t.* to settle or fix: to set up: to place in fixed position, possession, or power: to make good: to confirm: to prove: to ordain: to found: to set up in business: to institute by law as the recognised state church, and to recognise officially.—*adj.* **estab'lished**, fixed: ratified: instituted by law and backed by the state.—*ns.* **estab'lisher**; **estab'lishment**, act of establishing: fixed state: that which is established: a permanent civil or military force: permanent staff: one's residence, household, and style of living: a business: a settlement: the church established by law.—*adj.* **establishment-ār'ian**, maintaining the principle of church establishment.—Also *n.* [O.Fr. *establir*, pr.p. *establissant*—L. *stabilīre*—*stabilis*, firm—*stāre*, to stand.]

estacade, *es-tə-kād'*, *n.* a dike of piles in a morass, river, etc., against an enemy. [Fr.,—Sp. *estacada*.]

estafette, *es-tə-fet'*, *n.* a military courier or express. [Fr.,—It. *staffetta*—*staffa*, stirrup; cf. O.H.G. *stapho*, a step.]

estaminet, *es-tam'ē-nā*, a restaurant where smoking is allowed: a small café. [Fr.]

estancia, *es-tän'syä*, *n.* a Spanish-American cattle-estate.—*n.* **estanciero** (*-syä'rō*), a farmer. [Sp., station—L. *stāre*, to stand.]

estate, *is-*, *es-tāt'*, *n.* (*arch.*) state: rank: worldly condition: total possessions: property, esp. landed: a landed property, esp. of some size: (*coll.*) a private park: an order or class of men in the body-politic: (*obs.*) a chair or canopy of state, or a dais.—*v.t.* to give an estate to: (*arch.*) to bestow upon.—*n.* **estates'man**, statesman.—**man's estate**, the state of manhood; **the estates of the realm** are three—Lords Spiritual, Lords Temporal, and Commons: often misused for the legislature—king, lords, and commons.—**The**

ancient parliament of Scotland consisted of the king and the **three estates**—viz.: (1) archbishops, bishops, abbots, and mitred priors; (2) the barons and the commissioners of shires and stewartries; (3) the commissioners from the royal burghs;—in France, the nobles, clergy, and **third estate** (*tiers état*) remained separate down to 1789; **the fourth estate** (*facet.*), the press; **real estate** (see **real**). [O.Fr. *estat* (Fr. *état*)—L. *status*, a state.]

esteem, *is-*, *es-tēm'*, *v.t.* to set a high estimate or value on: to regard with respect or friendship: to consider or think.—*n.* high estimation or value: favourable regard: estimation of worth.—*adj.* **esteemed'**, respected: in commercial correspondence, a colourless complimentary word.—*adj.* **es'timable**, that can be estimated or valued: worthy of esteem: deserving our good opinion.—*adv.* **es'timably**.—*v.t.* **es'timate**, to judge of the worth of: (*chem.*) to ascertain how much is present of: to calculate:—*n.* (*Shak.*) reputation: a valuing in the mind: judgment or opinion of the worth or size of anything: a rough calculation: a preliminary statement of the probable cost of a proposed undertaking: estimation.—*n.* **estimā'-tion**, act of estimating: a reckoning of value: esteem, honour: importance: conjecture.—*adj.* **es'timātive**.—*n.* **es'timātor**.—**hold in estimation**, to esteem highly.—**the estimates**, accounts laid before parliament, etc., showing the probable expenditure for the year. [Fr. *estimer*—L. *aestimāre*.]

ester, *es'tər*, *n.* a compound formed by the condensation of an alcohol and an acid, with elimination of water.—*n.* **esterificā'tion** (*-ter-*).—*v.t.* **ester'ify** (or *es'*). [Invented by Leopold Gmelin (1788-1853).]

esthetic. See **aesthetic.**

Est(h)onian, *es-t(h)ō'ni-ən*, *adj.* pertaining to *Est(h)onia*, a Baltic republic, till 1918 a province of Russia, admitted in 1940 as a republic of the U.S.S.R.—*n.* a native or citizen thereof: its language.—*n.* **Esth**, an Esthonian of the original Finnish stock; **Esth'lander**, an Esthonian of mixed race in which the German element preponderates.

estival, estivation. See **aestival, aestivation.**

estoc, *es-tok'*, *n.* a short sword. [Fr.]

estoile, *es-twäl'*, *n.* (*her.*) a star with wavy points. [O.Fr. *estoile* (Fr. *étoile*), a star.]

estop, *es-top'*, *v.t.* to stop or bar: (*law*) to hinder, preclude:—*pr.p.* **estopp'ing**; *pa.t.* and *pa.p.* **estopped'**.—*ns.* **estopp'age**, the state of being estopped; **estopp'el**, a conclusive admission, which cannot be denied by the party whom it affects. [O.Fr. *estoper*—*estoupe*—L. *stuppa*, tow; see **stop, stuff**.]

estover, *es-tō'vər*, *n.* a right to necessaries allowed by law, as wood to a tenant for necessary repairs, etc.—**common of estovers**, the right of taking necessary wood from another's estate for household use and the making of implements of industry. [O.Fr. *estover*, to be necessary, necessaries.]

estrade, *es-träd'*, *n.* a low platform. [Fr.,—Sp. *estrado*.]

estrange, *is-trānj'*, *v.t.* to cut off, remove: to alienate, esp. from friendship: to divert from original use or possessor.—*adj.* **estranged'**, alienated: disaffected.—*ns.* **estrang'edness**; **estrange'ment**; **estrang'er**. [O.Fr. *estranger* (Fr. *étranger*)—L. *extrāneāre*—*extrāneus*; see **strange.**]

estrang(h)elo, *es-trang'gə-lō*, *n.* a cursive form of the old Syriac alphabet.—Also *adj.* [Syr., perh.— Gr. *strongylos*, round.]

estray, *es-strā'*, *n.* a beast found within a manor or lordship, wandering from its owner.—*v.i.* to stray. [See **astray.**]

estreat, *e-strēt'*, *n.* (*law*) a true extract, copy, or note of some original writing or record, esp. of fines and amercements to be levied by bailiffs or other officers.—*v.t.* to extract from the records of a court, as a forfeited recognisance: to levy, exact. [O.Fr. *estraite*—L. *extrahěre*—*ex*, from, *trahěre*, to draw; see **extract.**]

fāte, fär, ásk; mē, hər (her)*; mīne; mōte; mūte; mōōn; dhen* (then)

estrich, *es'trich*, **estridge**, *es'trij*, *n.* (*obs.*) the ostrich.

estuary, *es'tū-ər-i*, *n.* the wide lower tidal part of a river.—*adjs.* **estūarial** (*-ā'ri-əl*), **estūā'rian**, **es'tūarine** (*-ə-rīn*). [L. *aestuārium—aestus*, burning, boiling, commotion, tide.]

esurient, *es-ū'ri-ənt*, *adj.* hungry: rapacious.—*n.* **esū'rience**, **esū'riency**, greedy hunger: needy rapacity. [L. *ēsuriēns*, *-entis*, pr.p. of *ēsurīre*, to be hungry—desiderative of *edĕre*, to eat.]

eta, *ē'tä*, *ā'tä*, *n.* the seventh letter of the Greek alphabet, long e (H, η): as a numeral η'=8. ,η=8000.—*n.* **etacism** (*ā'tä-sizm*), pronunciation of eta as close e (in this dictionary represented as ā)—opposed to *itacism*. [Gr. *ēta*.]

etaerio, *et-ē'ri-ō*, *n.* (*bot.*) an aggregated fruit, a group of achenes or drupels. [Gr. *hetaireiā*, association.]

et cetera, *et set'ər-ä* usually written etc. or &c., a Latin phrase meaning and the rest: and so on.—*n.* something in addition, which can easily be understood. [L. *et*, and, *cētera*, the rest.]

etch, *ech*, *v.t.* and *v.i.* to design on metal, glass, etc. by eating out the lines with an acid: to eat away, corrode.—*ns.* **etch'er**, one who etches; **etch'ing**, the act or art of etching or engraving: the impression from an etched plate; **etch'ing-ground**, the coating of wax or varnish on a plate prepared for etching; **etch'ing-need'le**, a fine-pointed steel instrument used in etching. [Ger. *ätzen*, to corrode by acid; from same root as Ger. *essen*. See eat.]

eten, **ettin**, *et'ən*, *n.* (*arch.*) a giant. [O.E. *eten*, *eoten*; O.N. *jötunn*.]

eternal, *i-*, *ē-tər'nl*, *adj.* without beginning or end of existence: everlasting: ceaseless: unchangeable.—(*arch.*) **eterne'**.—*v.t.* **eter'nalise**, **eter'nise** (or *ē'tər-nīz*), to make eternal: to immortalise with fame.—*n.* **eter'nalist**, one who thinks that matter has existed from eternity.—*adv.* **eter'nally**.—*n.* **eter'nity**, eternal duration: the state or time after death.—**The Eternal**, an appellation of God; the **Eternal City**, Rome; the **eternities**, the eternal reality or truth. [Fr. *eternel*—L. *aeternus—aevum*, an age.]

etesian, *e-tē'zh(y)ən*, *-zyən*, *adj.* periodical: blowing at stated seasons, as certain winds, esp. the north-west winds of summer in the Aegean. [L. *etēsius*—Gr. *etēsios*, annual—*etos*, a year.]

eth, **edh**, *edh*, *n.* a letter (Ð ð), a barred D, used in Old English without distinction from thorn for voiced or voiceless th, in Icelandic and by phoneticians set apart for the voiced sound, thorn standing for the voiceless.

ethane, *eth'ān*, *n.* a hydrocarbon (C_2H_6) of the methane series. [ether.]

ethe, *ēth.* Same as eath.

ethene. See under ethyl.

Etheostoma (*e-the-os'to-mä*), *n.* a genus of small American fresh-water fishes akin to perch.—*adj.* **etheos'tomine**. [Gr. *ētheein*, to sift, *stoma*, mouth.]

ether, *ē'thər*, *n.* the clear, upper air: a medium, not matter, that has been assumed to fill all space and transmit electro-magnetic waves—(in these senses also **aether**): a colourless transparent, volatile liquid ($C_2H_5.O.C_2H_5$) of great mobility and high refractive power, fragrant odour and a fiery, passing to a cooling, taste (specifically **ethyl ether** or **diethyl ether**): extended to the class of compounds in which two alkyl groups are united with an oxygen atom.—*adj.* **ethe'real**, **ethe'rial**, consisting of ether: heavenly: airy: spirit-like.—*n.* **ethērealisā'tion**.—*v.t.* **ethe'realise**, to convert into ether, or the fluid ether: to render spirit-like.—*n.* **ethēreal'ity**.—*adv.* **ethe'really**.—*adjs.* **ethe'reous** (*Milt.*), **etheric** (*ē-ther'ik*), **-al**, ethereal.—*n.* **etherifica'tion** (*-ther-*).—*ns.* **ethe'rion**, a very light gas once supposed to exist in air; **ethērisā'tion**.—*v.t.* **ethe'rise**, to convert into ether: to stupefy with ether.—*n.* **e'thērism**, the condition induced by using ether: addiction to the taking of ether; **e'thērist**, one who takes or who administers ether; **ethēroma'nia**, addiction to the ether habit; **etheroma'niac.**—**ethereal oils**,

essential or volatile oils. [L. *aethēr*—Gr. *aithēr*, the heavens—*aithein*, to light up.]

ethic, *eth'ik*, *adj.* (*rare*) relating to morals: treating of morality or duty.—*n.* (more commonly **eth'ics**) the science of morals, that branch of philosophy which is concerned with human character and conduct: a treatise on morals.—*adj.* **eth'ical**, relating to duties, morals, the science of ethics.—*adv.* **eth'ically**.—*v.t.* **eth'icise** (*-sīz*), to make ethical: to treat as ethical.—*n.* **eth'icism**, tendency to moralise or ethecise; *ns.* **eth'icist**, one versed in ethics: one who detaches ethics from religion.—**ethic(al) dative**, dative implying an indirect interest in the matter, used colloquially to give a livelier tone to the sentence. [Gr. *ēthikos—ēthos*, custom, character.]

ethine, *eth'īn*, *n* acetylene.

Ethiopian, *ē-thi-ō'pi-ən*, *adj.* pertaining to Ethiopia (a name given to the countries south of Egypt inhabited by negro races, and also to Abyssinia): Hamitic: Abyssinian.—*n.* a native of Ethiopia: a blackamoor: a Hamite: an Abyssinian.—(*arch.*) **E'thiop** (*-op*).—*n.* **Ethiō'pianism**, a negro nationalist movement.—*adj.* **Ethiōp'ic**, belonging to Ethiopia or to Abyssinia, or the Abyssinian church, or to a group of Semitic languages including Ge'ez, Amharic, Tigre.—*n.* the Ge'ez language.—*n.* **e'thiōps**, in old chemistry, a name given to various dull, dingy, or black compounds.—Also **Aethiopian**, etc.—**Ethiopian region**, a biological region consisting of Africa and Arabia south of the Tropic of Cancer. [Gr. *Aithiops—aithein*, to burn, *ops*, *ōps*, face.]

ethmoid, *eth'moid*, *adj.* like a sieve.—*adj.* **ethmoid'al**.—**ethmoid bone**, one of the bones forming the anterior part of the brain-case. [Gr. *ēthmos*, a sieve, and *eidos*, form.]

ethnic, **-al**, *eth'nik*, *-əl*, *adjs.* concerning nations or races: pertaining to gentiles or the heathen.—*ns.* **eth'nic**, a gentile: a heathen: a national name; **eth'narch** (*-närk*; Gr. *archos*, leader) a ruler or governor of a people; **eth'narchy**; **eth'nicism** (*-sizm*), heathenism: gentile religion; **ethnog'rapher**.—*adj.* **ethnograph'ic**.—*n.* **ethnog'raphy**, the scientific description of the races of the earth.—*adj.* **ethnolog'ical**.—*adv.* **ethnolog'ically**.—*ns.* **ethnol'ogist**; **ethnol'ogy**, the science that treats of the varieties of the human race: cultural anthropology. [Gr. *ethnos*, a nation.]

ethos, *ē'thos*, *n.* habitual character and disposition: moral significance.—*adjs.* **etholog'ic**, **-al**.—*ns.* **ethol'ogist**; **ethol'ogy**, the science of character: bionomics. [Gr. *ēthos*, custom, character.]

ethyl, *eth'il*, *n.* the base (C_2H_5) of common alcohol, ether, etc.—*ns.* **eth'ylamine** (*-ə-mēn*), a substance ($NH_2C_2H_5$) resembling ammonia with one atom of hydrogen replaced by ethyl.—*n.* **eth'ylene** (also **eth'ene**), olefiant gas, heavy carburetted hydrogen (C_2H_4).—**ethyl petrol**, petrol containing lead tetraethyl, Pb (C_2H_5)$_4$, to prevent knock. [ether, and Gr. *hŷlē*, matter.]

etiolate, *ē'ti-o-lāt*, *v.t.* (*bot.*) to cause to grow pale with long whitish internodes and small yellow leaves for want of light, to blanch: to make pale.—*v.i.* to become pale.—*ns.* **etiolā'tion**; **e'tiolin**, a yellow pigment found in etiolated plants. [Fr. *étioler*, to become pale, to grow into stubble, *éteule*, stubble—L. *stipula*, a stalk, straw.]

etiology. Same as aetiology.

etiquette, *et'i-ket*, or *-ket'*, *n.* forms of ceremony or decorum: ceremony: the conventional laws of courtesy observed between members of the same profession, players, etc. [Fr. *étiquette*; see ticket.]

etna, *et'nä*, *n.* a vessel for heating liquids in a saucer of burning alcohol.—*adjs.* **Aetnē'an**, **Etnē'an**, of, pertaining to, resembling, or characteristic of, the volcano Etna. [L. *Aetna*—Gr. *Aitnē*.]

Eton, *ē'tn*, *n.* a town opposite Windsor with an old public school: (in *pl.*) an Eton suit.—*n.* **Etonian** (*ē-tōn'i-ən*), one educated at *Eton* College.—Also *adj.*—**Eton collar**, a boy's broad starched turned-down collar: a like-shaped collar to a woman's jumper, etc.; **Eton crop**, a fashion of cutting ladies' hair short and sleeking it; **Eton jacket**, a boy's black dress-coat, untailed; **Eton suit,** an Eton jacket with waistcoat and trousers in keeping.

Etruria, *i-trōō'ri-ä, n.* an ancient state of Italy north of the Tiber: part of Hanley, Stoke-on-Trent, where Josiah Wedgwood made *Etruria ware.—n.* and *adj.* **Etru'rian.**—*adj.* **Etruscan** (*i-trus'kən*), Etrurian.—*n.* an Etruscan: the language of the Etruscans, of undetermined affinities.—*ns.* **Etruscol'ogist; Etruscol'ogy.** [L. *Etrūria, Etrūscus.*]

ettercap, *et'ər-kåp,* **ethercap,** *edh'ər-kåp, n.* Scots forms of **attercop.**

ettle, *et'l, v.t.* (*Scot.*) to purpose, intend: to aim: to aspire.—*n.* purpose, intent. [O.N. *ætla,* to think.]

étude, *ā-tüd', n.* (*mus.*) a composition intended either to train or to test the player's technical skill. [Fr., study.]

etui, etwee, *ā-twē', et-wē', n.* a small case for holding small articles. [Fr. *étui,* a case, sheath.]

etymon, *et'i-mon, n.* the true origin of a word: an original root: (*rare*) the genuine or literal sense of a word.—*adjs.* **etym'ic; etymolog'ical.**—*adv.* **etymolog'ically.**—*ns.* **etymolog'icon, -cum,** an etymological dictionary.—*v.i.* **etymol'ogise,** to inquire into or discuss etymology.—*v.t.* to trace or propound an etymology for.—*ns.* **etymol'ogist; etymol'ogy,** the science or investigation of the derivation and original signification of words: an etymon. [Neut. of Gr. *etymos,* true.]

etypic, -al, *ē-tip'ik, -əl, adj.* unconformable to type. [L. *ē,* from, Gr. *typos,* type.]

eucaine, eucain, *ū-kā'in, -kā'in, -kān, n.* a safer substitute for cocaine as a local anaesthetic. [Gr. *eu,* well, and **cocaine.**]

Eucalyptus, *ū-kə-lip'təs, n.* a large characteristically Australian genus of the myrtle family, forest trees, some gigantic, and mallee shrubs, with leathery often glaucous leaves turned edgewise to the sun and flower-buds opening lid-wise, yielding timber, oils, and gum: eucalyptus oil:—*pl.* **eucalyp'tuses, eucalyp'ti.**—*ns.* **eu'calypt,** a eucalyptus: **eucalyp'tol, eucalyp'tole,** cineol, a constituent of the various oils got from eucalyptus leaves. [Latinised from Gr. *eu,* well, *kalyptos,* covered.]

eucharist, *ū'kə-rist, n.* the sacrament of the Lord's Supper: the elements of the sacrament.—*adjs.* **eucharist'ic, -al.** [Gr. *eucharistiā,* thanksgiving— *eu,* well, and *charizesthai,* to show favour—*charis,* grace, thanks.]

euchlorine, *ū-klō'rin, n.* a very explosive green-coloured gas, a mixture of chlorine with chlorine peroxide.—*adj.* **euchlō'ric.** [Gr. *eu,* well, *chlōros,* green.]

euchologion, *ū-ko-lō'ji-on, n.* a formulary of prayers, primarily that of the Greek Church.— Also **euchology** (-*kol'ə-ji*). [Gr. *euchologion— euchē,* a prayer, *logos—legein,* to speak.]

euchre, *ū'kər, n.* an American card game for two, three, or four persons, with the 32, 28, or 24 highest cards of the pack—if a player fails to make three tricks he is *euchred,* and his adversary scores against him.—*v.t.* to score over, as above: to outwit. [Ety. unknown.]

euclase, *ū'klās, n.* a hydrated beryllium aluminium silicate occurring in pale-green transparent crystals. [Fr.,—Gr. *eu,* well, *klasis,* breaking.]

Euclidean, *ū-klid'i-ən, ū-kli-dē'ən, adj.* pertaining to Euclid, a geometrician of Alexandria *c.* 300 B.C., or to space according to his assumptions.

eucrite, *ū'krīt, n.* a gabbroitic rock composed of lime-felspar, pyroxenes, and olivine.—*adj.* **eucritic** (-*krit'ik*). [Gr. *eu,* well, *kritos,* distinguished.]

eucyclic, *ū-si'klik, adj.* (*bot.*) having the same number of floral leaves in each whorl. [Gr. *eu,* well, *kyklos,* wheel.]

eudaemonism, eudemonism, *ū-dē'mən-izm, n.* a system of ethics that makes happiness the test of rectitude—whether *egoistic,* as Hobbes's, or *altruistic,* as Mill's.—*ns.* **eudae'monist, eudē'monist.** [Gr. *eudaimoniā,* happiness—*eu,* well, *daimōn,* a spirit.]

eudialyte, *ū-dī'ə-līt, n.* a silicate of zirconium, sodium, calcium and iron, occurring in Greenland, easily dissolved by acids. [Gr. *eu,* well, *dialyein,* to dissolve.]

eudiometer, *ū-di-om'i-tər, n.* an apparatus for gas-analysis, a graduated tube holding the gas over mercury, usually with wires for sparking—early used for testing the air at different times. [Gr. *eudios,* clear, fine (as weather), *metron,* measure.]

euge, *ū'jē, interj.* well! well done! [Gr. *euge.*]

Eugenia *ū-jē'ni-ä, n.* the clove genus of the myrtle family.—**eugenol** (*ū'jin-ol*), the chief constituent of oil of cloves ($C_{10}H_{12}O_2$)—also **eugenic** (-*jen'*) acid. [Named after Prince *Eugene.*]

eugenic, *ū-jen'ik, adj.* pertaining to race improvement by judicious mating and helping the better stock to prevail.—*adv.* **eugen'ically.**—*n.* (treated as *sing.*) **eugen'ics,** the science of race improvement.—*ns.* **eu'genism** (-*jin-*), **eu'genist.** [Gr. *eugenēs,* of good stock.]

eugh, eughen, ewghen, obs. spellings (*Spens., Shak.*) of **yew, yewen.**

Eugubine, *ū'gū-bin, -bīn, adj.* pertaining to the ancient town of *Eugubium* or *Iguvium* (mod. *Gubbio*), or to its famous seven tablets of bronze, the chief monument of the ancient Umbrian tongue.

euharmonic, *ū-här-mon'ik, adj.* in just intonation. [Gr. *eu,* well, *harmoniā,* harmony.]

Euhemerism, *ū-hē'mə-rizm, n.* the system which explains mythology as growing out of real history, its deities as merely magnified men.—*v.t.* and *v.i.* **euhē'merise.**—*n.* and *adj.* **euhē'merist.**—*adj.* **euhemeris'tic.**—*adv.* **euhemeris'tically.** [From *Euhēmerus,* Gr. *Euēmeros,* a 4th-cent. (B.C.) Sicilian philosopher.]

eulachon, *ū'lə-kon, n.* the North Pacific candle-fish, so oily that it is dried for use as a candle.— Also **oolakan, oulakan, -chon, ulicon, -chon, -kon.** [Chinook jargon, *ulâkân.*]

eulogium, *ū-lō'ji-əm,* **eulogy,** *ū'lə-ji, n.* praise: a speech or writing in praise.—*v.t.* **eu'logise,** to extol.—*n.* **eu'logist,** one who extols another.— *adj.* **eulogist'ic,** full of praise.—*adv.* **eulogist'ically.** [Late L. *eulogium—*Gr. *eulogion* (classical *eulogiā*)—*eu,* well, *logos,* a speaking.]

Eumenides, *ū-men'i-dēz, n.pl.* euphemistic name for the Erinyes or Furies. [Gr. *Eumenidēs,* gracious ones—*eu,* well, *menos,* disposition.]

eumerism, *ū'mər-izm, n.* (*biol.*) aggregation of similar parts. [Gr. *eu,* well, *meros,* part.]

Eumycetes, *ū-mī-sē'tēz, n.pl.* the higher fungi, Ascomycetes and Basidiomycetes. [Gr. *eu,* well, and **mycetes.**]

eunuch, *ū'nək, n.* a castrated man, esp. one in charge of a harem, or a high-voiced singer. [Gr. *eunouchos—eunē,* bed, *echein,* to have (charge of).]

euoi. See **evoe.**

Euonymus, *ū-on'-i-məs, n.* the spindle-tree and burning bush genus of Celastraceae.—*n.* **euon'ymus,** an extract of bark of burning bush. [Gr. *euōnymos,* spindle-tree.]

eupad, *ū'pad, n.* an antiseptic powder containing hypochlorous acid. [*E*dinburgh *U*niversity *P*athological *D*epartment—where it originated.]

eupatrid, *ū-pat'rid, n.* a member of the aristocracy in ancient Greek states. [Gr. *eupatridēs—eu,* well— *patēr,* father.]

eupepsy, *ū-pep'si,* **eupepsia,** *-ä, n.* good digestion— opp. to *dyspepsia.—adj.* **eupep'tic.**—*n.* **eupepticity** (-*tis'i-ti*). [Gr. *eupepsiā,* digestibility—*eu,* well, *pepsis,* digestion—*peptein,* to digest.]

Euphausia. See **krill.**

euphemism, *ū'fim-izm, n.* a figure of rhetoric by which an unpleasant or offensive thing is designated by a milder term.—*v.t.* **eu'phemise,** to express by a euphemism.—*v.i.* to use euphemistic terms.— *adj.* **euphemist'ic.**—*adv.* **euphemist'ically.** [Gr. *euphēmismos—euphēmizein,* to speak words of good omen—*eu,* well, *phanai,* to speak.]

euphon, *ū'fə-ni, n.* an agreeable sound: a pleasing, easy pronunciation—also **euphonia** (-*fō'*).—*n.* **eu'phon,** a form of glass harmonica invented by Chladni in 1790.—*adjs.* **euphonic** (-*fon'*), **-al, eupho'nious,** agreeable in sound.—*adv.* **euphō'niously.**—*v.t.* **eu'phonise,** to make euphonious.— *n.* **euphō'nium,** the bass saxhorn: the euphon. [Gr. *euphōniā—eu,* well, *phōnē,* sound.]

fāte, fär, ásk; mē, hər (her); *mīne; mōte; mūte; mōōn; dhen* (then)

Euphorbia, *ū-for'bi-ä, n.* the spurge genus of plants, giving name to the **Euphorbiā'ceae,** an isolated family of archichlamydeous dicotyledons. —*adj.* **euphorbiā'ceous.**—*n.* **euphor'bium,** a gum resin got from some spurges. [*Euphorbos,* Greek physician to Juba, king of Mauritania.]

euphoria, *ū-fō'ri-ä,* **euphory,** *ū'fə-ri, ns.* a feeling of well-being.—*adj.* **euphoric** (*-for'*). [Gr. *euphōriā.*]

euphrasy, *ū'frə-si, -zi, n.* (*bot.*) eyebright (*Euphrasia*) once thought good for disorders of the eyes. [Gr. *euphrāsiā,* delight—*euphrainein,* to cheer—*eu,* well, *phrēn,* the mind.]

Euphrosyne, *ū-froz'i-nē,* or *-fros', n.* one of the three Charites or Graces. [Gr. *Euphrosynē*—*euphrōn,* cheerful.]

Euphuism, *ū'fū-izm, n.* the affected and bombastic literary style brought into vogue by John Lyly's romance *Euphues* (1579-80): a high-flown expression in this style.—*v.i.* **eu'phuise.**—*n.* **eu'phuist.**—*adj.* **euphuist'ic.**—*adv.* **euphuist'ically.** [Gr. *euphyēs,* graceful, goodly.]

Eurafrican, *ūr-af'ri-kən, adj.* pertaining to Europe and Africa, or Europe and North Africa, jointly: of a human race common to Europe and North Africa, the Mediterranean race: of mixed European and African parentage or descent.—*n.* a person of Eurafrican race in either sense.

Euraquilo, *ū-rak'wi-lō, n.* See **Euroclydon.**

Eurasian, *ūr-ā'zh(y)ən, -shən, adj.* of mixed European and Asiatic parentage or descent: of, or pertaining to, Europe and Asia (*Eurasia*) taken as one continent.—*n.* a Eurasian half-caste.

eureka, rarely **heureka,** (*h*)*ū-rē'kä, interj.* announcing a discovery.—*n.* a brilliant discovery. [Gr. *heurēka,* I have found, perf. tense of *heuriskein,* to find, the cry of Archimedes when he thought of a method of detecting the adulteration of the gold for Hiero's crown.]

eurhythmy, eurythmy, *ū-rith'mi,* or *ridh', n.* rhythmical movement or order: harmony of proportion.—*adj.* **eurhyth'mic.**—*n.pl.* **eurhyth'mics,** the art or system of rhythmic movement expounded by E. Jaques-Dalcroze (1865-1950). [Gr. *eurythmiā*—*eu,* well, *rhythmos,* rhythm.]

euripus, *ū-rī'pəs, n.* an arm of the sea with strong currents, spec. that between Euboea and Boeotia: a ditch round the arena in a Roman amphitheatre. [L.,—Gr. *eurīpos.*]

Euroclydon, *ū-rok'li-don, n.* the tempestuous wind by which St Paul's ship was wrecked (Acts, xxvii, 14). [Gr. *Euroklydōn,* as if—*Euros,* east wind, *klydōn,* a wave; supposed to be a wrong reading for *Eurakylōn,* L. *Euroaquilō*—*Eurus* (Gr. *Euros*) and *Aquilō,* north wind.]

European, *ū-rō-pē'ən, adj.* belonging to Europe.—*n.* a native of Europe: a member of the white race of man characteristic of Europe.—*v.t.* **europe'anise,** to assimilate to European character or ways.— **European plan** (*U.S.*) in hotels, the system of charging for lodging and service without including meals. [Gr. *Eurōpē.*]

europium, *ū-rō'pi-əm, n.* a metal of the rare earths, (Eu; at. numb. 63) discovered spectroscopically by Demarçay in 1896. [**Europe.**]

Eurus, *ū'rəs, n.* the south-east wind. [L.,—Gr. *Euros.*]

Eurypharynx, *ū-ri-far'ingks, n.* the pelican-fish. [Gr. *eurys,* wide, *pharynx, pharynx.*]

Eurypterus, *ū-rip'tər-əs, n.* a genus of Eurypterida. —*n.* **euryp'terid,** any member of the Eurypterida. —*n.pl.* **Eurypter'ida** (*-ter'i-dä*), a Palaeozoic fossil order of Arachnida, scorpion-like aquatic animals, sometimes over six feet long, with the last (sixth) pair of appendages expanded.—*adj.* **euryp'teroid,** like or of the Eurypterida.—*n.* a eurypterid. [Gr. *eurys,* broad, *pteron,* wing.]

Eusebian, *ū-sē'bi-ən, adj.* pertaining to Eusebius of Caesarea, father of ecclesiastical history (died 340), or to the Arian *Eusebius* of Nicomedia (died 342).

Euskarian, *ūs-kā'ri-ən, adj.* Basque. [Basque *Euskara,* the Basque language.]

eusol, *ū'sol, n.* an antiseptic solution got by treating eupad with water.

eusporangiate, *ū-spor-an'ji-āt, adj.* (*bot.,* of a group of ferns) having each sporangium derived from a group of cells—opp. to *leptosporangiate.* [Gr. *eu,* well, and **sporangium.**]

Eustachian, *ū-stā'ki-ən, adj.* pertaining to the Italian physician Bartolommeo *Eustachio* (died 1574).—**Eustachian tube,** the tube leading from the middle ear to the pharynx; **Eustachian valve,** the rudimentary valve at the entrance of the inferior vena cava in the heart.

eustyle, *ū'stīl, adj.* with columns spaced at about two diameters and a quarter.—*n.* a colonnade or building so proportioned. [Gr. *eustȳlos,* well intercolumniated—*eu,* well, *stȳlos,* column.]

eutaxy, *ū'tak-si, n.* good order.—*n.* **eutax'ite,** a volcanic rock with banded structure.—*adj.* **eutaxit'ic,** having such a structure. [Gr. *eu,* well, *taxis,* arrangement.]

eutectic, eutectoid. See **eutexia.**

Euterpe, *ū-tər'pē, n.* the muse of lyric poetry: a genus of palms.—*adj.* **Euter'pean,** pertaining to Euterpe, or to music. [Gr. *Euterpē*—*eu,* well, *terpein,* to delight.]

eutexia, *ū-tek'si-ä, n.* the property of being easily melted.—*n.* **eutec'tic,** a mixture in such proportions that the melting-point (or freezing-point) is a minimum, the constituents melting (or freezing) simultaneously.—*adj.* of maximum fusibility: pertaining to a eutectic.—*n.* **eutec'toid,** an alloy similar to a eutectic but involving formation of two or three constituents from another solid constituent. — Also *adj.* [Gr. *eutēktos,* easily melted—*eu,* well, *tēkein,* to melt.]

euthanasia, *ū-than-ā'zi-ä, n.* an easy mode of death: the act or practice of putting painlessly to death, esp. in cases of incurable suffering.—Also **euthanasy** (*-than'ə-si*). [Gr. *euthanasiā*—*eu,* well, *thanatos,* death.]

euthenics, *ū-then'iks, n.* (treated as *sing.*) the science concerned with the improvement of living conditions. [Gr. *euthēneein,* to flourish.]

Eutheria, *ū-thē'ri-ä, n.pl.* the placental mammals. [Gr. *eu,* well, *thēr,* a beast.]

Euthyneura, *ū-thi-nū'rä, n.pl.* a subclass of Gasteropods in which the visceral nerve-loop is not twisted. [Gr. *euthys,* straight, *neuron,* nerve.]

eutrophy, *ū'trə-fi, n.* healthy nutrition. [Gr. *eutrophiā.*]

eutropy, *ū'trə-pi, n.* regular variation of the crystal-line form of a series of compounds with the atomic number of the element.—*adjs.* **eutropic** (*-trop'ik*), according to eutropy: (*bot.*) turning sun-wise; **eu'tropous.** [Gr. *eu,* well, *tropos,* a turn.]

Eutychian, *ū-tik'i-ən, adj.* of or pertaining to the doctrine of Eutyches, a 5th-cent. archimandrite of Constantinople, who held that Christ's human nature was merged in the divine.—*n.* a follower of Eutyches.

euxenite, *ūks-ə-nīt, n.* a mineral, niobate and titanate of yttrium, erbium, cerium, and uranium. [Gr. *euxenos,* hospitable, as containing many rare elements.]

evacuate, *i-, ē-vak'ū-āt, v.t.* to throw out the contents of: to discharge: to withdraw: to remove, as from a place of danger: to clear out troops, inhabitants, etc. from: (*law*) to nullify.—*adj.* and *n.* **evac'uant,** purgative.—*n.* **evacua'tion,** act of evacuating: withdrawal: that which is discharged. —*adj.* **evac'uative.**—*ns.* **evac'uator; evac'uee,** a person removed in an evacuation. [L. *ē,* from, *vacuāre, -ātum,* to empty—*vacuus,* empty.]

evade, *i-, ē-vād', v.i.* (*rare*) to escape, slip away.— *v.t.* to escape or avoid artfully: to shirk: to baffle, elude. [L. *ēvādere*—*ē,* from, *vādere,* to go.]

evagation, *ē-,* or *e-vag-ā'shən, n.* wandering: a digression. [L. *ēvagārī*—*ē,* from, *vagārī,* wander.]

evaginate, *i-, ē-vaj'i-nāt, v.t.* to turn outside in: to evert: to remove from a sheath.—*adj.* without a sheath.—*n.* **evagina'tion.** [L. *ēvāgināre, -ātum,* to unsheathe, *ē,* from, *vāgīna,* a sheath.]

evaluate, *i-, ē-val'ū-āt, v.t.* to determine the value of.—*n.* **evalua'tion.** [Fr. *évaluer.*]

evanescent, *ev-ən-es'ənt, adj.* fleeting; vanishing.— *v.i.* **evanesce,** to fade away.—*n.* **evanesc'ence.** —*adv.* **evanesc'ently.** [L. *ēvānēscēns, -entis*—*ē, vānēscĕre,* to vanish—*vānus,* empty.]

evangel, *i-van'jəl*, *n.* (*poet.*) good news : gospel : a doctrine set up as a saving principle, esp. in morals or politics.—*ns.* **evangeliar** (*ev-ən-jel'*), **evangeliā'rion, evangeliā'rium, evangel'iary,** a book of passages from the Gospels to be used at mass or in other services.—*adjs.* **evangelic** (*ev-ən-jel'ik*), **-al,** of or pertaining to the Gospel : relating to the four Gospels : according to the doctrine of the Gospel : maintaining the teaching of the Gospel : Protestant : of the school that insists especially on the total depravity of unregenerate human nature, the justification of the sinner by faith alone, the free offer of the Gospel to all, and the plenary inspiration and exclusive authority of the Bible.—*n.* **evangel'ical,** one who belongs to the evangelical school.—*n.* **evangel'icalism.**— *adv.* **evangel'ically.**—*ns.* **evangel'icalness; evangel'icism** (*-sizm*), evangelical principles; **evangelisation** (*i-van-jəl-ī-zā'shən*), act of proclaiming the Gospel : Christianisation.—*v.t.* **evan'gelise,** to make acquainted with the Gospel : to Christianise.—*v.i.* to preach the Gospel from place to place.—*ns.* **evan'gelism,** evangelising, evangelicalism; **evan'gelist,** one who evangelises : an author of a Gospel, especially one of the canonical Gospels : an assistant of the apostles : one who is authorised to preach but who is without a fixed charge : an itinerant preacher : a lay missionary in the Catholic Apostolic Church, a minister of the third grade; **evangelis'tary,** a book of the Gospels, or of passages from them to be read at divine service : a table of such passages— also **evangelistā'rion.**—*adj.* **evangelis'tic,** tending or intended to evangelise.—*n.* **evan'gely** (*obs.*), the Gospel.—**Evangelical Union** (see **Morisonian**). [L. *evangelicus*—Gr. *euangelikos*—*eu,* well, *angellein,* to bring news.]

evanish, *i-van'ish,* *v.i.* to vanish : to die away. —*ns.* **evan'ishment, evanition** (*ev-ə-nish'ən*). [O.Fr. *evanir, evaniss-*—L. *ex,* from, *vānus,* empty; cf. **evanesce.**]

evaporate, *i-vap'ər-āt,* *v.i.* to fly off in vapour : to pass into an invisible state : to depart, vanish. —*v.t.* to convert into vapour : to dry by evaporation.—*adj.* **evap'orable,** able to be evaporated or converted into vapour.—*n.* **evaporā'tion,** act of evaporating or passing off in steam or gas : the process by which a substance changes into the state of vapour.—*adj.* **evap'orative.**—*ns.* **evap'orator; evaporim'eter,** an instrument for measuring rate of evaporation. [L. *ē,* from, *vapōrāre, -ātum—vapor,* vapour.]

evasion, *i-vā'zhən,* *n.* act of evading or eluding : an attempt to escape the force of an argument or accusation : an excuse.—*adjs.* **evasible** (*i-vā'zi-bl*), capable of being evaded; **evā'sive** (*-siv*), that evades or seeks to evade : elusive : not straightforward : shuffling.—*adv.* **evā'sively.**—*n.* **evā'siveness.**

eve. See **even** (2).

evection, *i-, ē-vek'shən,* *n.* (*astron.*) a lunar inequality, combined effect of the irregularity of the motion of the perigee and alternate increase and decrease of the eccentricity of the moon's orbit. [L. *ēvectiō, -ōnis—ē,* from, *vehĕre, vectum,* to carry.]

even, *ēv'n, ēvn, adj.* flat : level : smooth : uniform : in a straight line or plane : (*Shak.*) straightforward : balanced : equal : on an equality : exact : divisible by 2 without a remainder : denoted by such a number.—*v.t.* to make even or smooth : to put on an equality : to liken : to equal : (*Shak.*) to act up to.—*v.i.* to become even.—*adv.* exactly : nearly : indeed : so much as : still : extreme as the case may be, nevertheless.—*n.* **ev'en-Chris'tian** (*obs.*), fellow-Christian.—*adj.* **ev'en-down,** straightdown (of rain) : downright, honest.—*adv.* thoroughly.—*adj.* **ev'en-hand'ed,** with an equal, fair, or impartial hand : just.—*adv.* **ev'enly.**— *adj.* **ev'en-mind'ed,** having an even or calm mind : equable.—*n.* **ev'enness.**—**be even with,** to be revenged on : to be quits with; **even date,** the same date; **even money,** an equal sum bet on each side; **even now** (*arch.*), a very little while ago; **even on** (*Scot.*), without intermission;

even up on, to requite, come square with. [O.E. *efen;* Du. *even,* Ger. *eben.*]

even, *ēv'n, n.* (*poet.*) evening : (*obs.* or *dial.*) eve— also **e'en** (*ēn*).—*ns.* **eve** (*ēv; poet*) evening : the night, or the whole day, before a festival : the time just preceding an event; **eve'jar** (*dial.*) the nightjar; **ev'enfall,** early evening, twilight; **evening** (*ēv'ning*) the close of the daytime : the decline or end of life : an evening party, gathering or entertainment; **eve'ning-dress,** the dress conventionally appropriated to social functions in the evening; **eve'ning-prim'rose,** a N. American plant (Oenothera) with pale yellow flowers that open in the evening.—*adv.* **eve'nings** (*U.S.*), in the evening.—*ns.* **eve'ning-star',** a planet, esp. Venus, seen in the west setting soon after the sun; **ev'ensong,** evening prayer, the Anglican form appointed to be said or sung at evening : the time proper for such; **ev'en-tide,** the time of evening, evening. [O.E. *æfen, æfnung.*]

event, *i-vent', n.* that which happens : result : any incident or occurrence : contingency : an item in a programme of sports : (*obs.*) fortune or fate. —*adjs.* **event'ful,** full of events : momentous; **event'ual,** happening as a consequence : final.— *v.i.* **event'ualise,** to come to pass : to come into being.—*n.* **eventual'ity,** a contingency : (*phrenology*) propensity to take notice of events, changes, or facts.—*adv.* **event'ually,** finally : at length.— *v.i.* **event'uate,** to turn out. [L. *ēventus— ēvenīre,* to come out, happen—*ē,* from, *venīre,* to come.]

eventration, *ē-ven-trā'shən, n.* act of opening the belly : protrusion of an organ from the abdomen. [Fr. *éventration*—L. *ē,* from, *venter,* belly.]

ever, *ev'ər, adv.* always : eternally : at all times : continually : at any time : on record (as *the biggest ever,* the biggest that ever was or happened) : in any degree : at all : in the world.— As a suffix, giving complete generality to relative adverbs and pronouns.—*adj.* **ev'ergreen,** in leaf throughout the year : always fresh and green : unfading.—*n.* a tree or shrub that is green throughout the year.—*adj.* **everlast'ing,** endless : perpetual : unceasing : eternal : wearisomely long-continued.—*n.* eternity : a flower (of *Helichrysum, Antennaria,* or other genus) that may be kept for years without much change of appearance : a very durable cloth.—*adv.* **everlast'ingly.**—*n.* **everlast'ingness.**—*adj.* **ev'er-liv'ing** (*Shak.*) immortal : deathless.—*adv.* **evermore'** (or *ev'*) for all time to come (also **for evermore**) : ever : unceasingly.—**ever and anon,** from time to time; **ever so,** to any extent : to a very great extent; **for ever,** to all eternity. [O.E. *æfre.*]

everglade, *ev'ər-glād, n.* a large shallow lake or marsh : (chiefly in *pl.*) such a marsh in southern Florida, enclosing thousands of islets covered with dense thickets. [Perh. **ever,** and **glade.**]

evert, *ē-,* or *i-vərt', v.t.* to turn inside out : to turn outwards.—*n.* **ever'sion.** [L. *ēvertĕre—ē,* from, *vertĕre, versum,* to turn.]

every, *ev'ri, adj.* each of a number : all taken separately.—*prons.* **ev'erybody, ev'eryone,** every person.—*adj.* **ev'eryday,** of or belonging to every day, daily : common, usual : pertaining to weekdays, not Sunday.—*ns.* **ev'erydayness; Ev'eryman,** the hero of an old morality play, representing mankind, everybody, anybody.— *pron.* **ev'erything,** all things taken singly : all.— *advs.* **ev'eryway,** in every way or respect; **ev'erywhen, ev'erywhence, ev'erywhither** (*all rare*); **ev'erywhere,** in every place.—**every bit, whit,** the whole : quite; **every here and there,** all over dispersedly; **every man Jack, every mother's son,** every one without exception; **every now and then,** or **again,** at intervals; **every other,** every second or alternate; **every which way** (*U.S.*) every way : in disorder. [O.E. *æfre, ever,* and *ælc,* each.]

evet, *ev'it, n.* Same as **eft** (1).

evict, *i-, ē-vikt', v.t.* to dispossess by law : to expel. —*ns.* **evic'tion,** the act of evicting from house or lands : the dispossession of one person by another having a better title of property in land; **evic'tor.** [L. *ēvictus*, pa.p. of *ēvincĕre*, to overcome.]

evident, *ev'i-dənt, adj.* that can be seen: clear to the mind: obvious.—*n.* that which serves as evidence.—*n.* **ev'idence,** that which makes evident: means of proving an unknown or disputed fact: support for a belief: indication: information in a law case: testimony: a witness or witnesses collectively.—*v.t.* to render evident: to attest, prove: to indicate.—*adjs.* **evidential** (*-den'shəl*), **eviden'tiary,** furnishing evidence: tending to prove.—*advs.* **eviden'tially; ev'idently** (*N.T.*), visibly: obviously: manifestly.—**in evidence,** received by the court as competent evidence: plainly visible, conspicuous—a penny-a-liner's phrase adopted from the Fr. *en évidence;* **turn King's (Queen's) evidence,** to give evidence against an accomplice in a crime. [L. *ēvidēns, -entis—ē,* from, *vidēre,* to see.]

evil, *ē'v(i)l, adj.* wicked: bad: mischievous: disagreeable: unfortunate.—*adv.* in an evil manner: badly.—*n.* that which produces unhappiness or calamity: harm: wickedness: depravity: sin.—*ns.* **e'vil-doer,** one who does evil; **e'vil-eye,** a supposed power to cause harm by a look.—*adj.* **e'vil-fā'voured,** having a repulsive appearance: ugly.—*n.* **e'vil-fā'vouredness** (*B.*), ugliness: deformity.—*adv.* **evilly** (*ē'vil-i*) in an evil manner: not well.—*adj.* **e'vilmind'ed,** inclined to evil: malicious: wicked.—*ns.* **e'vilness,** state of being evil: wickedness; **e'vil-speak'ing,** the speaking of evil: slander.—*adj.* **e'vil-starred'** (*Tenn.*), born under the influence of an unpropitious star, unfortunate.—*n.* **e'vil-work'er,** one who works or does evil.—**the evil one,** the devil; **speak evil of,** to slander. [O.E. *yfel;* Du. *euvel;* Ger. *übel;* cf. **ill.**]

evince, *i-vins', v.t.* to prove beyond doubt: to show clearly: to make evident: to give indication of:—*n.* **evince'ment.**—*adj.* **evinc'ible.**—*adv.* **evinc'ibly.**—*adj.* **evinc'ive,** tending to evince, prove, or demonstrate. [L. *ēvincĕre,* to vanquish —*ē*-, inten., *vincĕre,* to overcome.]

evirate, *ē'-* or *e'vir-āt, v.t.* to castrate: to render weak or unmanly. [L. *ēvirāre—ē,* from, *vir,* a man.]

eviscerate, *ē-* or *i-vis'ər-āt, v.t.* to tear out the viscera or bowels of: to gut.—*n.* **eviscerā'tion.** [L. *ē,* from, *viscera,* the bowels.]

evite, *i-vīt', v.i.* to avoid.—*adj.* **evitable** (*ev'it-ə-bl*).—*v.t.* **evi'tate** (*Shak.*), to avoid.—*n.* **evitā'tion,** the act of shunning. [L. *ēvītāre, -ātum—ē,* from, *vītāre,* to shun.]

eviternal, *ēv-i-tər'nl, adj.* eternal.—*adv.* **eviter'nally.**—*n.* **eviter'nity.** [L. *aeviternus;* see **eternal.**]

evoke, *i-vōk', v.t.* to call out: to draw out or bring forth: to call up or awaken in the mind.—*v.t.* **evocate** (*ev'ō-kāt*), to evoke: to call up from the dead.—*n.* **evocā'tion.**—*adjs.* **evocative** (*i-vok'ə-tiv*), **evoc'atory.** [L. *ēvocāre—ē,* from, and *vocāre,* to call.]

evoe, evhoe, euoi, *ē-vē', ē-vō'i, ū-oi', interj.* expressing Bacchic frenzy. [L. *eu(h)oe*—Gr. *euoi, eu hoi.*]

evolution, *ēv-,* or *ev-ə-l(y)ōō'shən, n.* the act of unrolling or unfolding: gradual working out or development: a series of things unfolded: the doctrine according to which higher forms of life have gradually arisen out of lower: (*math.*) the extraction of roots: (usu. *pl.*) orderly movements as of a body of troops, flock of birds, etc.—*n.* **ev'olute** (*math.*), an original curve from which another curve (the *involute*) is described by the end of a thread gradually unwound from the former.—*adj.* rolled back.—*adjs.* **evolu'tional, evolu'tionary,** of or pertaining to evolution.—*ns.* **evolu'tionism,** the doctrine of evolution; **evolu'tionist,** one skilled in evolutions or military movements: one who believes in evolution as a principle in science.—*adj.* **ev'olutive.** [L. *ēvolūtiō, -ōnis,—ēvolvĕre;* see **evolve.**]

evolve, *i-,* or *ē-volv', v.t.* to unroll: to disclose: to develop: to unravel.—*v.i.* to disclose itself: to result.—*adj.* **evolv'able,** that can be drawn

out.—*n.* **evolve'ment.**—*adj.* **evolv'ent.** [L. *ēvolvĕre—ē*-, from, *volvĕre, volūtum,* to roll.]

evulgate, *ē-,* or *e-vul'gāt, v.t.* to divulge: to publish. [L. *ēvulgāre, -ātum—ē,* out, *vulgus,* the people.]

evulse, *i-,* or *ē-vuls', v.t.* to pluck out.—*n.* **evul'sion.** [L. *ēvellĕre, ēvulsum—ē,* from, *vellĕre, vulsum,* to pluck.]

ewe, *ū, n.* a female sheep.—*ns.* **ewe'-cheese,** cheese made from the milk of ewes; **ewe'-lamb,** a female lamb: a poor man's one possession—used in reference to 2 Sam. xii.; **ewe'-milk; ewe'-neck,** of horses, a thin hollow neck.—*adj.* **ewe'-necked.** [O.E. *ēowu;* cf. L. *ovis,* Gr. *oïs,* Sans. *avi,* a sheep.]

ewer, *ū'ər, n.* a large water jug with a wide spout. [Through Fr. from L. *aquārium—aqua,* water.]

ewest, *ū'ist, adj.* or *adv.* (*Scot.*) near. [App. from O.E. *on nēaweste,* in the neighbourhood, wrongly divided as *on ewest.*]

ewftes, *ūfts, n.pl.* (*Spens.*), efts. [See **eft** (1).]

ewghen, an old spelling of **yewen.**

ewhow, *ā'hwow', interj.* (*Scot.*) an exclamation of deploration.

ewigkeit, *ā'vihh-kīt, n.* eternity. [Ger.]

ewt. See **newt.**

ex-, *eks-, prefix,* used in words like **ex-emperor,** to signify late, but surviving.—*n.* **ex,** one who is no longer what he was (*pl.* **ex's, ex'es**).

ex, *eks, n.* the twenty-fourth letter, see **X.**

exacerbate, *eks-,* or *egz-as'ər-bāt, v.t.* to embitter: to provoke: to render more violent or severe, as a disease.—*ns.* **exacerbā'tion, exacerbesc'ence,** increase of irritation or violence, esp. the increase of a fever or disease: embitterment. [L. *exacerbāre, -ātum—ex,* and *acerbāre,* from *acerbus,* bitter.]

exact, *igz-akt', v.t.* to force out: to compel payment of: to demand and obtain: to extort: to require as indispensable.—*v.i.* to practise extortion.—*adj.* precise: rigorous: accurate: absolutely correct: finished: consummate: strict.—*adj.* **exact'ing,** compelling full payment: unreasonable in making demands: demanding much.—*ns.* **exac'tion,** act of exacting or demanding strictly: an oppressive demand: that which is exacted, as excessive work or tribute; **exact'itude,** exactness: correctness.—*adv.* **exact'ly.**—*ns.* **exact'ment; exact'ness,** quality of being exact: accuracy; **exact'or, -er,** one who exacts: an extortioner: one who claims rights, often too strictly:—*fem.* **exact'ress**—**exact sciences,** the mathematical sciences, whose results are precise or quantitative. [L. *exigĕre, exāctum,* to demand, to weigh strictly— *ex,* from, *agĕre,* to drive.]

exaggerate, *igz-aj'ər-āt, v.t.* to magnify unduly: to overstate: to represent too strongly: to intensify.—*n.* **exaggerā'tion,** extravagant representation: a statement in excess of the truth.—*adjs.* **exagg'erative, exagg'eratory,** containing exaggeration or tending to exaggerate.—*n.* **exagg'erator.** [L. *exaggerāre, -ātum—ex-, aggerāre,* to heap up—*agger,* a heap.]

exalbuminous, *eks-al-bū'min-əs, adj.* (*bot.*) without albumen.

exalt, *igz-awlt', v.t.* to set aloft: to elate or fill with the joy of success: to extol: (*old chem.*) to refine or subtilise.—*n.* **exaltā'tion** (*egz-ol-*), elevation in rank or dignity: high estate: elation: (*astrol.*) a planet's position of greatest influence: (*arch.*) a flight of larks.—*adj.* **exalt'ed,** elevated: lofty: dignified.—*n.* **exalt'edness.** [L. *exaltāre—ex-, altus,* high.]

examine, *igz-am'in, v.t.* to test: to inquire into: to question: to look closely into: to inspect.—*n.* **exā'men,** examination.—*adj.* **exam'inable.**—*ns.* **exam'inant,** an examiner: one who is being examined; **exam'inate,** one who is examined; **examinā'tion,** careful search or inquiry: close inspection: trial: a test of capacity and knowledge, familiarly contracted to **exam'; examinee',** one under examination; **exam'iner, exam'inātor,** one who examines.—*adj.* **exam'ining.** [Fr. *examiner*—L. *exāmināre—exāmen,* the tongue of a balance.]

example 370 excite

example, *igz-äm′pl*, *n.* a specimen: an illustration: a copy of a book: a person or thing to be imitated or not to be imitated: a pattern: a warning: an instance.—*v.t.* to exemplify: to instance.—*n.* **exam′plar** (*arch.*) an exemplar. [O.Fr.,—L. *exemplum—eximĕre*, to take out—*ex*, out of, *emĕre*, *emptum*, to take.]

exanimate, *egz-*, *igz-an′i-māt*, *adj.* lifeless: spiritless: depressed.—*n.* **exanimā′tion**. [L. *exanimātus—ex*, from, *anima*, breath.]

exanthem, *eks-an′thəm*, **exanthema**, *eks-an-thē′mä*. *ns.* a skin eruption, esp. accompanied by fever: a disease so characterised:—(*pl.* **exan′thems**, **exanthē′mata**).—*adjs.* **exanthēmat′ic**, **exanthēmatous**. [Gr. *exanthēma*, *-atos—ex-*, out, *antheein*, to blossom.]

exarch, *eks′ärk*, *n.* a Byzantine provincial governor, esp. of Italy: a metropolitan: (*Gr. Ch.*) a bishop of rank between a patriarch and a metropolitan: the head of the Bulgarian church: an ecclesiastical inspector: a legate.—*ns.*—*n.* **exarch′ate** (or *eks′*), the office, jurisdiction or province of an exarch; **exarch′ist** (or *eks′*), a supporter of the Bulgarian exarch. [Gr. *exarchos*, leader.]

exarch, *eks′ärk*, *n.* (*bot.*) having the protoxylem on the outer edge. [Gr. *ex-*, out, *archē*, beginning, origin.]

exasperate, *igz-äs′pər-āt*, *v.t.* to make rough, harsh: to make more grievous or painful: to make very angry: to irritate in a high degree.—*adj.* irritated: (*bot.*) rough with hard points.—*adjs.* **exas′perating**, **exas′perative**.—*ns.* **exasperā′tion**; **exas′perātor**. [L. *ex-* inten., *asperāre*, to make rough—*asper*, rough.]

Excalibur, *eks-kal′ib-ər*, *n.* the name of King Arthur's sword. [O.Fr. *Escalibor* for Caliburn; cf. *Caladbolg*, a famous sword in Irish legend.]

excambion, *eks-kam′bi-on*, *n.* (*Scots law*) exchange of lands—also **excam′bium**.—*v.t.* **excamb′**, to exchange. [L.L. *excambiāre*; cf. **cambist**, **cambium**, **exchange**.]

excavate, *eks′kə-vāt*, *v.t.* to hollow or scoop out: to dig out: to lay bare by digging.—*ns.* **excavā′tion**, act of excavating: a hollow or cavity made by excavating; **ex′cavātor**, one who excavates: a machine used for excavating. [L. *excavāre—ex-*, out, *cavus*, hollow.]

exceed, *ik-sēd′*, *v.t.* to go beyond the limit or measure of: to surpass or excel.—*v.i.* to go beyond a given or proper limit: to be intemperate.—*adj.* **exceed′ing**, surpassing: excessive: (*bot.*) projecting beyond a neighbouring member.—Also *adv.* (*arch.*) exceedingly.—*adv.* **exceed′ingly**, very much: greatly. [L. *ex-*, beyond, *cēdĕre*, *cēssum*, to go.]

excel, *ik-sel′*, *v.t.* to be superior to: to surpass: (*Milt.*) to exceed.—*v.i.* to have good qualities in a high degree: to perform very meritorious actions: to be superior:—(*pr.p.* **excell′ing**; *pa.t.* and *pa.p.* **excelled′**).—*ns.* **excellence** (*eks′ə-ləns*), **exc′ellency**, great merit: any excellent quality: worth: greatness: a title of honour given to persons high in rank or office.—*adj.* **exc′ellent**, surpassing others in some good quality: of great virtue, worth, etc.: good in a high degree.—*adv.* **exc′ellently**—*interj.* **excel′sior** (L. *comp. adj.*, taller, loftier), higher still (after Longfellow)—*n.* (*U.S.*) a trade name for wood shavings for packing. [L. *excellĕre—ex-*, out, up, *celsus*, high.]

excentric. Same as **eccentric**.

except, *ik-sept′*, *v.t.* to take out, or leave out: to exclude.—*v.i.* to object.—*prep.* leaving out: excluding: but.—*conj.* (*arch.*) unless.—*adj.* and *n.* **except′ant**.—*prep.* **except′ing**, with the exception of, except.—*n.* **excep′tion**, the act of excepting: that which is excepted: exclusion: objection: offence.—*adj.* **excep′tionable**, objectionable.—*adv.* **excep′tionably**.—*adj.* **excep′tional**, of the nature of an exception.—*adv.* **excep′tionally**.—*adjs.* **excep′tious**, disposed to take exception; **except′ive**, including, making, or being an exception; **except′less** (*Shak.*), making no exception, usual.—*n.* **except′or**.—**the exception proves the rule**, the making of an exception proves that the rule holds in cases not excepted—

thus *No smoking abaft the funnel* implies that smoking is allowed before the funnel. [L. *excipĕre*, *exceptum—ex*, from, *capĕre*, to take.]

excerpt, *ek′sərpt*, or *ek-sərpt′*, *n.* a passage selected from a book, opera, etc., an extract.—*v.t.* **excerpt′**, to select: to extract.—*ns.* **excerpt′ing**, **excerp′tion**; **excerp′tor**. [L. *excerptum*, pa.p. of *excerpĕre—ex*, from, *carpĕre*, to pick.]

excess, *ik-ses′*, *n.* a going beyond what is usual or proper: intemperance: that which exceeds: the degree or amount by which one thing exceeds another: (*Shak.*) usury.—*adj.* in excess.—*adj.* **excess′ive**, beyond what is usual or right: immoderate: extreme.—*adv.* excessively.—*adv.* **excess′ively**.—*n.* **excess′iveness**.—**carry to excess**, to do too much; **excess fare**, payment for distance travelled beyond, or in a class superior to, that allowed by the ticket; **excess luggage**, luggage above the weight allowed free. [L. *excessus—excēdĕre*, *excēssum*, to go beyond.]

exchange, *iks-chānj′*, *v.t.* to give or give up in return for something else: (*obs.*) to receive in return for something else: to give and take mutually: to barter: (*obs.*) to change.—*v.i.* to pass by exchange of office with another.—*n.* the giving and taking of one thing for another: barter: the thing exchanged: process by which accounts between distant parties are settled by bills instead of money: money-changing business: exchanging currency of one country for that of another: the difference between the value of money in different places: a stock exchange: the building where merchants, etc., meet for business: a central office where telephone lines are connected: (*U.S. slang*) a bar-room.—*n.* **exchangeabil′ity**.—*adj.* **exchange′able**, that may be exchanged.—*n.* **exchan′ger**, one who exchanges or practises exchange: (*B.*) a money-changer, a banker. [O.Fr. *eschangier* (Fr. *échanger*)—L.L. *excambiāre*—L. *ex*, from, L.L. *cambiāre*, to barter.]

excheat, *eks-chēt′*, *n.* (*Spens.*). Same as **escheat**.

exchequer, *iks-chek′ər*, *n.* a department of state having charge of revenue, so named from the chequered cloth which covered the table, and on which the accounts were reckoned: the Court of Exchequer: a national treasury: one's funds, finances, purse.—*v.t.* to proceed against in the Court of Exchequer.—**Chancellor of the Exchequer** (see **chancellor**); **Court of Exchequer**, in England originally a revenue court developed out of the judicial branch of the Exchequer, acquired a general common-law jurisdiction by a legal fiction, became a division of the High Court of Justice in 1875, and is now merged in the King's (Queen's) Bench Division: in Scotland a revenue court, abolished in 1886, its jurisdiction transferred to the Court of Session; **exchequer bill**, a bill issued at the Exchequer, as security for money advanced to the government. [See **chequer**, **check**, **chess**.]

excide, *ek-sīd′*, *v.t.* to cut off. [L. *excīdĕre—ex*, from, *caedĕre*, to cut.]

excipient, *ek-sip′i-ənt*, *n.* a substance mixed with a medicine to give it consistence, or used as a vehicle for its administration. [L. *excipiēns*, *-entis*, pr.p. of *excipĕre*, to take out, receive—*ex*, from, *capĕre*, to take.]

excise, *ek-sīz′*, *n.* a tax on certain home commodities, and on licences for certain trades: the department in the civil administration concerned with this tax.—Also *adj.*—*v.t.* to subject to excise duty.—*adj.* **excis′able**, liable to excise duty.—*n.* **excise′man**, an officer charged with collecting the excise.—**excise law**, (*U.S.*) a liquor law, licensing law. [M.Du. *excijs*—O.Fr. *acceis*, tax—L.L. *accēnsāre*, to tax—*ad*, to, *cēnsus*, tax.]

excise, *ek-sīz′*, *v.t.* to cut off or out.—*n.* **excision** (*ek-sizh′ən*), a cutting out or off of any kind: extirpation. [L. *excīdĕre*, to cut out—*ex*, from, *caedĕre*, to cut.]

excite, *ik-sīt′*, *v.t.* to call into activity: to stir up: to rouse: to energise: to produce electric or magnetic activity in: to sensitise: to stir emotionally.—*n.* **excitabil′ity**.—*adj.* **excit′able**, capable of being excited: responsive to stimulus:

easily excited.—*ns.* **excīt'ableness; excitancy** (*ek'si-tən-si*), excitant property; **excitant** (*ek'si-* or *ek-sī'*), that which excites or rouses the vital activity of the body: a stimulant: the electrolyte in an electric cell.—*adj.* exciting: stimulating.— *n.* **excitā'tion** (*ek-si-*): act of exciting: means of excitement: state of excitement.—*adjs.* **excīt'-ative, excīt'atory**, tending to excite.—*adj.* **excīt'ed**, agitated: roused emotionally: in a state of great activity.—*ns.* **excīte'ment**, agitation: that which excites; **excīt'er**, one who or that which excites: an auxiliary machine supplying current for another machine: a sparking apparatus for producing electric waves.—*adj.* **excīt'ing**, tending to excite: stirring, thrilling.—*n.* **excī'tor**, exciter: an afferent nerve stimulating a part. [Fr. *exciter*—L. *excitāre, -ātum*—*exciēre*—*ex-*, out, *ciēre*, to set in motion.]

exclaim, *iks-klām'*, *v.t.* and *v.i.* to cry out: to utter or speak vehemently.—*n.* an exclamation, outcry.— *n.* **exclamation** (*eks-klə-mā'shən*), vehement utterance: outcry: an uttered expression of surprise and the like: the mark expressing this (!): an interjection—*adjs.* **exclamative** (*eks-klam'ə-tiv*), **exclam'atory**, containing or expressing exclamation. [Fr. *exclamer*—L. *exclāmāre, -ātum*—*ex-*, out, *clāmāre*, to shout.]

exclave, *eks'klāv*, *n.* a part of a country, province, etc. disjointed from the main part—opp. to *enclave*. [See **enclave.**]

exclude, *iks-, eks-klōōd'*, *v.t.* to shut out: to thrust out: to hinder from entrance: to emit: to hinder from participation: to except: to hatch.—*adj.* **exclud'ed**, (*bot.*) exserted.—*ns.* **exclu'sion** (*-zhən*), a shutting or putting out: ejection: exception; **exclu'sionism; exclu'sionist**, one who excludes, or would exclude, another from a privilege.—*adj.* **exclu'sive** (*-siv*), able or tending to exclude: incompatible: debarring from participation: of the nature of monopoly: socially inaccessible or aloof: sole: not to be had elsewhere or from another: (*U.S.*) select, fashionable: without taking into account: not included.—*n.* one of a number who exclude others from their society: an exclusive product: a Plymouth Brother of a Darbyite section.—*adv.* **exclu'sively**.—*ns.* **exclu'siveness; exclu'sivism**.—*adj.* **exclu'sory**, exclusive.—**exclusive dealing**, the act of abstaining deliberately from any business or other transactions with persons of opposite political or other convictions to one's own—a euphemism for boycotting; **law of excluded middle**, (*log.*) that everything is either A or not-A. [L. *exclūdĕre, -clūsum*—*ex-*, out, *claudĕre*, to shut.]

excogitate, *eks-koj'i-tāt*, *v.t.* to discover by thinking: to think out earnestly or laboriously.—*n.* **excogitā'tion**, laborious thinking: invention: contrivance. [L. *excōgitāre, -ātum*—*ex-*, out, *cōgitāre*, to think.]

excommunicate, *eks-kəm-ūn'i-kāt*, *v.t.* to put out of or expel from the communion of the church: to deprive of church privileges.—*adj.* **excommun'icable**.—*ns.* **excommunicā'tion**, act of expelling from the communion of a church—(*Milt.*) **excommun'ion**.—*adj.* **excommun'icatory**, of or pertaining to excommunication. [From L.L. *excommūnicāre*—L. *ex, commūnis*, common.]

excoriate, *eks-kō'ri-āt*, *v.t.* to strip the skin from.— *n.* **excoriā'tion**, the act of excoriating: the state of being excoriated. [L. *excoriāre, -ātum*—*ex*, from, *corium*, the skin.]

excorticate, *eks-kor'ti-kāt*, *v.t.* to strip the bark off.—*n.* **excorticā'tion**. [L. *ex*, from, *cortex*, *-icis*, bark.]

excrement, *eks'kri-mənt*, *n.* dregs: useless matter discharged from the animal system: dung.—*adj.* **excremental** (*-ment'l*), **excrementitial** (*-tish'l*), **excrementi'tious**, pertaining to or containing excrement. [L. *excrēmentum*—*excernĕre*—*ex-*, out, *cernĕre*, to sift.]

excrement, *eks'kri-mənt*, *n.* (*Shak.*) an outgrowth, a moustache.—*adj.* **excremental** (*-ment'l*). [L. *excrēmentum*—*ex-*, out, *crēscĕre*, to grow.]

excrescence, *iks-kres'əns*, *n.* an outgrowth or projection, esp. abnormal, grotesque, or offensive: a wart or tumour: a superfluous part: an outbreak.—*n.* **excresc'ency**, state of being excrescent: excrescence.—*adjs.* **excresc'ent**, growing out: superfluous; **excrescential** (*eks-kri-sen'shl*). [L. *excrēscĕre*—*ex-*, out, *crēscĕre*, to grow.]

excrete, *eks-krēt'*, *v.t.* to separate and discharge: to eject.—*n.pl.* **excrē'ta**, matters discharged from the animal body.—*n.* **excrē'tion**, the excreting of matter from an organism: that which is excreted.—*adjs.* **excrē'tive**, able to excrete: concerned with excretion; **excrē'tory** (or *eks'kri-tər-i*), having the quality of excreting.—*n.* a duct that helps to receive and excrete matter. [L. *ex*, from, *cernĕre, crētum*, to separate.]

excruciate, *iks-krōō'shi-āt*, *v.t.* to torture: to rack: to pain, grieve.—*adj.* **excru'ciating**, extremely painful: racking: torturing: agonising.—*adv.* **excru'ciatingly**.—*n.* **excruciā'tion**, torture: vexation. [L. *ex-*, out, *cruciāre, -ātum*, to crucify—*crux, crucis*, a cross.]

excubant, *eks'kū-bənt*, *adj.* on guard. [L. *excubāns, -āntis*, pr.p. of *excubāre*, to sleep out, lie on guard—*ex, cubāre*, to lie.]

exculpate, *eks'kul-pāt*, also *-kul'*, *v.t.* to clear from the charge of a fault or crime: to absolve: to vindicate.—*n.* **exculpā'tion**.—*adj.* **excul'patory**, tending to free from the charge of fault or crime. [L. *ex*, from, *culpa*, a fault.]

excurrent, *eks-kur'ənt*, *adj.* having the main stem reaching to the top: having the midrib reaching beyond the lamina: flowing outwards: carrying an outgoing current. [L. *ex*, from, *currēns, -entis*, pr.p. of *currĕre*, to run.]

excursion, *iks-, eks-kur'shən*, *n.* a going forth: a raid: a sally: a deviation: an escapade: a pleasure trip: a company or collection of people on a pleasure outing: a wandering from the main subject: a digression.—Also *v.i.*—*vs.i.* **excurse'**, to digress; **excur'sionise**, to go on an excursion.—*n.* **excur'sionist**, one who goes on a pleasure-trip.—*adj.* **excur'sive**, rambling: deviating.—*adv.* **excur'sively**.—*ns.* **excur'siveness; excur'sus**, a dissertation on some particular matter appended to a book or chapter.—**excursion train**, a special train, usually with reduced fares, for persons making an excursion. [L. *ex-* out, *currĕre, cursum*, to run.]

excuse, *iks-kūz'*, *v.t.* to free from blame or guilt: to exonerate: to pass over, overlook: to pardon or condone (in small matters): to free from an obligation: to release, dispense with: to allow to absent oneself: to seek to extenuate or justify: to make an apology or ask pardon for.—*v.i.* to make excuse.—*n.* (*iks-kūs'*) a plea offered in extenuation: indulgence.—*adj.* **excūsable** (*iks-kūz'ə-bl*).—*n.* **excūs'ableness**.—*adv.* **excūs'-ably**.—*n.* **excūs'al**.—*adjs.* **excūs'atory**, making or containing excuse: apologetic; **excusive** (*eks-kūs'iv*).—**excuse me**, an expression used as an apology for any slight or apparent impropriety, or for controverting a statement that has been made. [L. *excūsāre*—*ex*, from, *causa*, a cause, accusation.]

exeat, *eks'i-at*, *n.* formal leave of absence, esp. for a student to be out of college for more than one night. [L., let him go out: 3rd pers. sing. pres. subj. of *exīre*.]

execrate, *eks'i-krāt*, *v.t.* to curse: to denounce evil against: to denounce: to detest.—*adj.* **ex'ecrable**, deserving execration: detestable: accursed.—*adv.* **ex'ecrably**.—*n.* **execrā'tion**, act of execrating: a curse pronounced: that which is execrated.—*adj.* **ex'ecrātive**, of or belonging to execration.—*adv.* **ex'ecrātively**.—*adj.* **ex'ecrātory**. [L. *exsecrārī -ātus*, to curse—*ex*, from, *sacer*, sacred.]

execute, *eks'i-kūt*, *v.t.* to perform: to give effect to: to carry into effect: to put to use, bring into action: to put to death by law.—*adj.* **execūtable** (*eg-zek'ūt-ə-bl*, or *ek-sek'*, or *eks'i-kūt-ə-bl*), that can be executed.—*ns.* **exec'ūtancy** (*eg-zek'*, or *ek-sek'*) technique in music; **exec'ūtant** (*eg-zek'* or *ek-sek'*), one who executes or performs: a technically accomplished performer of music; **execūter** (*eks'*); **execū'tion**, act of or skill in executing or performing : accomplishment : completion : carrying into effect the sentence of a court of law : the warrant for so doing : the infliction of capital punishment; **execū′tioner**, one who executes, esp. one who inflicts capital punishment.—*adj.* **executive** (*eg-zek′ū-tiv*, or *ek-sek′*) designed or fitted to execute or perform : concerned with performance, administration, or management : active : qualifying for or pertaining to the execution of the law : administrative.—*n.* the power or authority in government that carries the laws into effect : the persons who administer the government or an organisation : (*U.S.*) a person in an executive position in government or business : (*U.S.*) the head of an executive, as president, governor, mayor, etc. (also **chief executive**).—*adv.* **exec′ūtively**.—*n.* **exec′ūtor** (*eg-zek′*), one who executes or performs : a person appointed to see a will carried into effect :— *fem.* **exec′ūtress**, **exec′ūtrix** (*pl.* **execūtrī′cēs**). —*adj.* **execūtō′rial**.—*n.* **exec′ūtorship**.—*adj.* **exec′ūtory**, executing official duties : designed to be carried into effect.—*n.* **exec′ūtry**, executorship : (*Scots law*) moveable estate and effects.—**executive session**, (*U.S.*) a meeting of the Senate for executive business, usu. held in private : hence, any meeting in private. [L. *exsequī*, *exsecūtus—ex*, out, *sequī*, to follow.]

exedra, *eks′i-drä*, *eks-ed′rä*, *n.* a portico, hall, or vestibule : a seated room : a raised platform with steps, in the open air : an apse, recess, niche—also **exhedra**:—*pl.* **ex′(h)edrae**. [Gr. *exedrā—ex-*, out, *hedrā*, seat.]

exeem, **exeme**, *eks-ēm′*, *v.t.* (*obs. Scot.*) to release, exempt. [L. *eximēre—ex*, from, *emēre*, to take.]

exegesis, *eks-i-jē′sis*, *n.* interpretation, esp. Biblical. —*ns.* **ex′egēte**, **exegēt′ist**, one who interprets or expounds.—*adjs.* **exegetic** (*-jet′ik*), **-al**, pertaining to exegesis : explanatory.—*adv.* **exegēt′ically**:— *n.pl.* **exegēt′ics**, the science of exegesis. [Gr. *exēgēsis—exēgeesthai*, to explain—*ex-*, out, *hēgeesthai*, to guide.]

exemplar, *egz-em′plar*, *-plär*, *n.* a person or thing to be imitated : the ideal model of an artist : a type : an example : a copy of a book.—*adv.* **ex′emplarily** (*egz′im-plər-i-li* or *igz-em′*).—*ns.* **ex′emplariness** (or *-em′*); **exemplarity** (*-plar′*), **exemplariness** : exemplary conduct.—*adj.* **exemplary** (*egz′im-plər-i*, or *igz-em′*) worthy of imitation or notice : serving as model, specimen, illustration, or warning. [L. *exemplar—exemplum*, example.]

exemplify, *igz-em′pli-fī*, *v.t.* to illustrate by example : to make an attested copy of : to prove by an attested copy :—(*pr.p.* **exem′plifying**; *pa.t.* and *pa.p.* **exem′plified**).—*adj.* **exem′plifiable**.— *n.* **exemplificā′tion**, act of exemplifying : that which exemplifies : a copy or transcript. [L. *exemplum*, example, *facĕre*, to make.]

exempt, *igz-emt′*, *v.t.* (*Milt.*) to set apart : to free, or grant immunity (with *from*).—*adj.* taken out : not liable.—*n.* one who is exempt : an officer who commanded in absence of his superiors, exempted on this account from ordinary duties.—*n.* **exemp′tion**, act of exempting : state of being exempt : freedom from any service, duty, burden, etc. : immunity. [Fr.,—L. *eximĕre*, *exemptum—ex*, from, *emĕre*, to buy.]

exenterate, *eks-en′tər-āt*, *v.t.* to disembowel.— *adj.* (*-it*) disembowelled.—*n.* **exenterā′tion**. [L. *exenterāre*—Gr. *ex*, from, *enteron*, intestine.]

exequatur, *eks-i-kwā′tər*, *n.* an official recognition of a consul or commercial agent given by the government of the country in which he is to be. [L. *exequātur*, let him execute—the opening word.]

exequy, *eks′i-kwi*, (usu. in *pl.* **exequies**, *-kwiz*), *n.* a funeral procession : funeral rites.—*adj.* **exequial** (*eks-ē′kwi-əl*). [L. *exequiae—ex*, from, *sequī*, to follow.]

exercise, *eks-ər′sīz*, *n.* a putting in practice : exertion of the body for health or amusement or acquisition of skill : a similar exertion of the mind : a task designed or prescribed for these purposes : a written school task : a study in music : a set of problems, passages for translation, etc., in a text-

book : an academical disputation : (*Shak.*) accomplishment : (in *pl.*) military drill or manoeuvres : (*U.S.*) a ceremony or formal proceeding : an act of worship or devotion : a discourse, the discussion of a passage of Scripture, giving the coherence of text and context, etc. (the *addition* giving the doctrinal propositions, etc.) : a meeting of a presbytery for this purpose; hence formerly the presbytery itself.—*v.t.* to train by use : to improve by practice : to give exercise to : to trouble : to put in practice : to use : to wield.— *v.i.* to take exercise : to drill.—*adj.* **ex′ercisable**. —*n.* **ex′ercise-book**, a book for writing school exercises in. [O.Fr. *exercice*—L. *exercitium*—L. *exercēre*, *-citum*, pfx. *ex-*, and *arcēre*, to shut up, restrain.]

exercitation, *egz-ər-sit-ā′shən*, *n.* putting into practice : employment : exercise : a discourse. [L. *exercitātiō*, *-ōnis—exercēre*, to exercise.]

exergue, *eks′erg* or *egz-ərg′*, *n.* part on the reverse of a coin, below the main device, often filled up by the date, etc.—*adj.* **exer′gual**. [Fr.,—Gr. *ex*, out of, *ergon*, work.]

exert, *igz-ərt′*, *v.t.* (*obs.*) to put forth : to bring into active operation : (*obs.*) to do or perform.—*n.* **exer′tion**, a bringing into active operation : striving : activity.—*adj.* **exert′ive**, having the power or tendency to exert : using exertion. [L. *exserēre*, *exsertum—ex*, from, *serēre*, to put together.]

exes, *eks′əz*, *n.pl.* a slang abbreviation of **expenses**.

exeunt, *eks′i-unt*. See **exit**.

exfoliate, *eks-fō′li-āt*, *v.t.* to shed in flakes : to remove in flakes.—*v.i.* to come off in flakes : to separate into layers.—*n.* **exfoliā′tion**.—*adj.* **exfō′liative**. [L. *exfoliāre*, *-ātum*, to strip of leaves— *ex*, from, *folium*, a leaf.]

exhale, *egz-āl′*, *eks-hāl′*, *v.t.* to breathe forth : to emit or send out as vapour, smell, etc. : to cause or allow to evaporate : to emit through a membrane.—*v.i.* to breathe out : to rise or come off as a vapour, smell, emanation : to evaporate : to ooze out.—*adjs.* **exhāl′able**; **exhāl′ant**, exhaling : emitting vapour or liquid.—*n.* an organ or vessel that emits vapour or liquid.—*n.* **exhalation** (*eks-*, *egz-ə-lā′shən*, or *eks′hə-*), act or process of exhaling : evaporation : that which is exhaled, vapour, effluvium, emanation : a mist : (*arch.*) a meteoric phenomenon, a meteor. [L. *exhālāre—ex*, from, *hālāre*, *-ātum*, to breathe.]

exhale, *egz-hāl′*, *v.t.* (*Shak.*) to hale or draw out. [Pfx. *ex-*, and **hale**.]

exhaust, *igz-awst′*, *v.t.* to draw off : to draw out the whole of : to use the whole strength of : to use up : to empty : to wear or tire out : to treat of or develop completely.—*n.* an outward current, or means of producing it : the exit of used working fluid from the cylinder of an engine : the period of discharge of the fluid : the fluid so escaping (**exhaust′-gas**, **-steam**).—*adj.* **exhaust′ed**, drawn out : emptied : consumed : tired out.—*n.* **exhaust′er**, he who or that which exhausts.—*adj.* **exhaust′ible**, that may be exhausted.—*n.* **exhaustion** (*-awst′yən*), act of exhausting or consuming : state of being exhausted : extreme fatigue.—*adjs.* **exhaust′ive**, tending to exhaust : investigating all parts or possibilities : by the method of exhausting possibilities : **exhaust′less**, that cannot be exhausted.—*ns.* **exhaust′-pipe′**, **valve′**, the pipe, valve, through which exhaust gases pass out. [L. *exhaurīre*, *exhaustum—ex*, from, *haurīre*, to draw.]

exheredate, *eks-her′i-dāt*, *v.t.* (*rare*) to disinherit.— *n.* **exheredā′tion**. [L. *exhērēdāre—ex*, out, *hērēs*, *-ēdis*, heir.]

exhibit, *igz-ib′it*, *v.t.* to hold forth or present to view : to present formally or publicly : to show : (*med.*) to give as a remedy.—*n.* (*law*) a document or object produced in court to be used as evidence : something exhibited : an article at an exhibition.— *ns.* **exhib′iter** (*rare*); **exhibition** (*eks-i-bish′ən*), presentation to view : display : showing off : a public show, esp. of works of art, manufactures, etc. : that which is exhibited : a public performance at the end of a school year : a grant or gift : an allowance towards support, esp. to scholars in a university : administration of a remedy; **exhibi'-tioner,** one who enjoys an exhibition at a university; **exhibi'tionism,** morbid inclination towards display, esp. of the naked body; **exhibi'tionist.**—*adj.* **exhib'itive** (*egz-*), serving for exhibition : representative.—*n.* **exhibitor** (*egz-ib'i-tər*).—**exhib'itory,** exhibiting.—**make an exhibition of oneself,** to behave foolishly, exciting ridicule. [L. *exhibēre,* -*itum*—*ex-,* out, *habēre,* -*itum,* to have.]

exhilarate, *igz-il'ə-rāt, v.t.* to make hilarious or merry : to raise the spirits of : to enliven : to cheer.—*adj.* **exhil'arant,** exhilarating : exciting joy, mirth, or pleasure.—*n.* an exhilarating medicine.—*adj.* **exhil'arating,** cheering : gladdening.—*adv.* **exhil'aratingly.**—*n.* **exhilarā'tion,** state of being exhilarated : joyousness.—*adjs.* **exhil'arātive, ex-hil'aratory.** [L. *exhilarāre,* -*ātum*—*ex-,* inten., *hilaris,* cheerful.]

exhort, *ig-,* *eg-zort', v.t.* to urge strongly and earnestly : to counsel.—*n.* **exhortā'tion** (*eks-* or *egz-*), act of exhorting : language intended to exhort : counsel : a religious discourse.—*adjs.* **exhort'ative, exhort'atory,** tending to exhort or advise.—*n.* **exhort'er,** one who exhorts : in some churches a layman appointed to give religious exhortation. [L. *exhortārī,* -*ātus*—*ex-,* inten., *hortārī,* to urge.]

exhume, *eks-hūm', ig-zūm', v.t.* to take out of the ground or place of burial : to bring to light.—Also **exhumate** (*eks'hūm-āt*).—*ns.* **exhumā'tion** (*eks'*); **exhum'er.** [L. *ex,* out of, *humus,* the ground.]

exies, *ek'sāz, n.pl.* (*Scot.*) a fit, as of hysterics, ague. [access.]

exigent, *eks'i-jənt, adj.* pressing : urgent : exacting : demanding immediate attention or action.—*n.* extremity : strait : (*Shak.*) the last strait, the end of all : (*Browning*) a needed amount.—*adj.* **exigeant** (*eks-ē-zhän²,* Fr.), exacting (*fem.* **exigeante,** -*zhän²t*).—*ns.* **ex'igence, ex'igency** (or -*ij'*), pressing necessity : emergency : distress. [L. *exigēns,* -*entis*—pr.p. of *exigēre*—pfx. *ex-, agēre,* to drive.]

exigible, *eks'i-jib-l, adj.* capable of being exacted. [See **exact.**]

exiguous, *egz-,* *eks-ig'ū-əs, adj.* scanty : slender.—*ns.* **exigū'ity** (*eks-*); **exig'ūousness.** [L. *exiguus*—*exigēre,* to weigh strictly; see **exact.**]

exile, *eks',* or *egz'īl, n.* enforced or regretted absence from one's country or home : banishment (in these senses formerly *egz-īl'*) : one who is in exile : a banished person.—*v.t.* (formerly *egz-īl'*) to expel from one's country : to banish.—*n.* **ex'ilement,** banishment.—*adjs.* **exilic** (*egz-il'ik,* or *eks-*) pertaining to exile, esp. that of the Jews in Babylon. [O.Fr. *exil*—L. *exsilium,* banishment—*ex,* out of, and root of *salīre,* to leap; affected by L. *exsul,* an exile.]

exility, *egz-,* *eks-il'i-ti, n.* slenderness, smallness : refinement. [L. *exīlitās,* -*ātis*—*exīlis,* slender.]

eximious, *eg-zim'i-əs, adj.* excellent, distinguished. [L. *eximius*—*eximēre*—*ex,* from, *emēre,* to take.]

exine, *eks'in,* -*īn.* Same as **extine.** [L. *ex,* out of.]

exist, *igz-ist', v.i.* to have an actual being.—*n.* **exist'ence,** state of existing or being : livelihood : life : anything that exists : a being.—*adjs.* **exist'ent,** having being : at present existing; **existential** (*eks-is-ten'shəl*).—*ns.* **existen'tialism,** a term covering a number of related doctrines denying objective universal values and holding that a man must create values for himself through action and by living each moment to the full; **existen'tialist.** [L. *existēre, exsistēre,* to stand forth—*ex-,* out, *sistēre,* to stand.]

exit, *eks'it, n.* the departure of a player from the stage : any departure or passing out : a passage out : a way of departure : a quitting of the world's stage, or life : death :—(*pl.* **ex'its**).—*v.i.* to make an exit : to die :—*pa.p.* and *pa.t.* **ex'ited.** [Partly from the L. stage-direction *exit,* goes out (in pl. *exeunt,* go out)—*exīre,* to go out—*ex-,* out, and *īre, itum,* to go; partly—L. *exitus,* a way out.]

ex-libris, *eks-lī'bris, n.* a book-plate.—*ns.* **ex-li'brism; ex-li'brist,** a collector or student of book-plates. [L. *ex librīs,* from the books (of so-and-so).]

exocarp, *eks'ō-kärp, n.* the epicarp of a fruit. [Gr. *exō,* outside, *karpos,* fruit.]

exode, *ek'sōd, n.* the concluding part of a Greek drama : a farce or afterpiece. [Gr. *exōdion.*]

exodermis, *eks-ō-dər'mis, n.* the outer cortex-layer of a root. [Gr. *exō,* outside, *dermis,* skin.]

exodus, *eks'ə-dəs, n.* a going out, esp. that of the Israelites from Egypt : **Exodus,** the second book of the Old Testament.—*adj.* **exodic** (-*od'*).—*n.* **ex'odist,** one who goes out : an emigrant. [L.,—Gr. *exodos*—*ex-,* out, *hodos,* a way.]

exogamy, *eks-og'ə-mi, n.* the practice of marrying only outside of one's own group : (*biol.*) union of gametes not closely related.—*adjs.* **exogamic** (-*ō-gam'ik*), **exog'amous.** [Gr. *exō,* out, *gamos,* marriage.]

exogen, *eks'ō-jən, n.* (*obs.*) a dicotyledon—so called because its stem thickens by layers growing on the outside of the wood.—*adj.* **exogenous** (*eks-oj'i-nəs*), growing by successive additions to the outside. [Gr. *exō,* outside, and *gen-,* root of *gignesthai,* to be produced.]

exomis, *eks-ō'mis, n.* a one-sleeved or (in Rome) sleeveless garment—(*Browning*) **exo'mion.** [Gr. *exōmis*—*ex-,* out, *ōmos,* shoulder.]

exon, *eks'on, n.* un officer of the Yeomen of the Guard. [App. intended to express the pronunciation of Fr. *exempt;* see **exempt.**]

exonerate, *igz-on'ər-āt, v.t.* to free from the burden of blame or obligation : to acquit.—*n.* **exonerā'tion,** act of exonerating.—*adj.* **exon'erative,** freeing from a burden or obligation. [L. *exonerāre,* -*ātum*—*ex,* from, *onus, oneris,* burden.]

exophagy, *eks-of'ə-ji, n.* the custom among cannibals of eating only the flesh of persons not of their own kin.—*adj.* **exoph'agous** (-*gəs*). [Gr. *exō,* outside, *phagein,* to eat.]

exophthalmia, -mus, *eks-of-thal'mi-ä,* -*məs, ns.* a protrusion of the eyeballs.—*adj.* **exophthal'mic.** [Gr. *ex,* out, *ophthalmos,* eye.]

exopodite, *eks-op'o-dīt, n.* the outer branch of a crustacean limb. [Gr. *exō,* outside, *pous, podos,* foot.]

exorable, *eks'ər-ə-bl, adj.* capable of being moved by entreaty.—*n.* **exorā'tion,** entreaty. [L. *exōrāre*—pfx. *ex-* in the sense of thoroughly, *ōrāre,* to entreat.]

exorbitant, *igz-or'bi-tənt, adj.* going beyond the usual limits : excessive.—*ns.* **exor'bitance, exor'-bitancy,** great excess.—*adv.* **exor'bitantly.**—*v.i.* **exor'bitate,** to stray. [L. *exorbitāns,* -*āntis,* pr.p. of *exorbitāre*—*ex,* out of, *orbita,* a track—*orbis,* a circle.]

exorcise, *eks'or-sīz, v.t.* to adjure by some holy name : to call forth or drive away, as a spirit : to deliver from the influence of an evil spirit.—*ns.* **ex'orcism** (-*sizm*), act of exorcising or expelling evil spirits by certain ceremonies : a formula for exorcising : **ex'orcist,** one who exorcises or retends to expel evil spirits by adjuration (also **exorcīs'er**) : (*R.C. Church*) the third of the minor orders. [L.L., from Gr. *exorkizein*—*ex-,* out, *horkos,* an oath.]

exordium, *egz-or'di-əm, n.* the introductory part of a discourse or composition :—*pl.* **exor'diums, -ia.**—*adj.* **exor'dial,** pertaining to the exordium : introductory. [L.,—*exordīrī*—*ex,* out of, *ordīrī,* to begin.]

exoskeleton, *eks-sō-skel'i-tən,* a hard supporting or protective structure secreted externally by the ectoderm.—*adj.* **exoskel'etal.** [Gr. *exō,* outside, and **skeleton.**]

exosmosis, *eks-os-mō'sis, n.* osmosis outwards, i.e. away from the solution—also **ex'osmose** (-*mōs*).—*adj.* **exosmotic** (-*mot'ik*). [Gr. *ex-,* out, and **osmosis.**]

exospore, *eks'ō-spōr, n.* the outer layer of a spore wall : a spore formed by abstriction, not within a mother-cell. [Gr. *exō,* outside, *sporos,* a seed.]

Neutral vowels in unaccented syllables : *el'ə-mənt, in'fənt, ran'dəm*

13

exostosis, *eks-os-tō'sis*, *n.* (*anat.*) morbid enlargement of a bone. [Gr. *exostōsis*—*ex-*, out, *osteon*, a bone.]

exoteric, *eks-ō-ter'ik*, *adj.* external: fit to be communicated to the public or multitude—opp. to *esoteric.*—*adj.* **exoter'ical.**—*adv.* **exoter'ically.** —*n.* **exoter'icism** (*-sizm*). [Gr. *exōterikos*— *exōterō*, comp. of *exō*, outside.]

exothermic, *eks-ō-thər'mik*, *adj.* (*chem.*) involving evolution of heat. [Gr. *exō*, outside, *thermē*, heat.]

exotic, *egz-ot'ik*, *adj.* introduced from a foreign country: alien: foreign-looking: outlandish.—*n.* anything of foreign origin: something not native to a country, as a plant, a word, a custom.—*n.* **exot'icism** (*-sizm*). [Gr. *exōtikos*—*exō*, outside.]

expand, *iks-pand'*, *v.t.* to spread out: to lay open: to enlarge in bulk or surface: to develop, or bring out in fuller detail: to express at length, as in terms of a series, or without contractions.—*v.i.* to become opened: to increase in volume: to enlarge: to spread: (*fig.*) to become communicative.— *ns.* **expanse** (*-pans'*), a wide extent: a stretch: amount of spread or stretch: the firmament; **expansibil'ity.**—*adj.* **expans'ible**, capable of being expanded.—*adv.* **expans'ibly.**—*adj.* **expans'ile** (*-īl*), capable of expansion.—*n.* **expan'sion**, act of expanding: state of being expanded: enlargement: that which is expanded: amount of expanding: territorial extension: immensity: extension.—*adj.* **expan'sional.**—*ns.* **expan'sionism**, **expan'sionist**, one who favours territorial expansion.—*adj.* **expans'ive**, widely extended: diffusive.—*adv.* **expans'ively.**—*ns.* **expans'iveness**; **expansiv'ity** (*eks-*). [L. *expandĕre*—*ex-*, out, *pandĕre*, *pānsum*, to spread.]

ex-parte, *eks-pär'ti*, *adj.* on one side only: partial: prejudiced. [L. *ex*, from, *parte*, abl. of *pars*, *partis*, party, side.]

expatiate, *eks-pā'shi-āt*, *v.t.* to walk about: to range at large: to enlarge in discourse, argument, or writing.—*n.* **expatiā'tion.**—*adjs.* **expā'tiative**, **expā'tiatory**, expansive.—*n.* **expā'tiātor.** [L. *exspatiārī*, *-ātus*—*ex*, out of, *spatiārī*, to roam—*spatium*, space.]

expatriate, *eks-pā'tri-āt*, *v.t.* to send out of one's country: banish, exile.—Also *n.*—**expatriā'tion**, act of expatriating: exile, voluntary or compulsory. [L.L. *expatriāre*, *-ātum*—*ex*, out of, *patria*, fatherland.]

expect, *iks-pekt'*, *v.t.* (*obs.*) to await: to look forward to as likely to come or happen, or as due: (*coll.*) to suppose.—*v.i.* (*obs.*) to wait.—*n.* (*Shak.*) expectation.—*ns.* **expect'ance**, **expect'ancy**, act or state of expecting: that which is expected: hope.—*adj.* **expect'ant**, looking or waiting for something: in expectation: not yet but expecting to be.—*n.* one who expects: one who is looking or waiting for some benefit or office.—*adv.* **expect'antly.**—*ns.* **expecta'tion** (*eks-*), act or state of expecting: prospect of future good: that which is or may fairly be expected: degree of probability: the value of something expected: (*pl.*) prospect of fortune or profit by a will; **expecta'tion-week**, the period between Ascension Day and Whitsunday—commemorating the Apostles' expectation of the Comforter.—*adj.* **expect'ative**, giving rise to expectation: reversionary.—*n.* an expectancy: an anticipatory grant of a benefice not yet vacant.— *adj.* **expect'ed.**—*adv.* **expect'edly.**—*n.* and *adj.* **expect'ing.**—*adv.* **expect'ingly**, in a state of expectation. [L. *exspectāre*, *-ātum*—*ex*, out, *spectāre*, to look, freq. of *specĕre*, to see.]

expectorate, *eks-pek'ta-rāt*, *v.t.* to expel from the breast or lungs by coughing, etc.: (*coll.*) to spit forth.—*v.i.* to discharge or eject phlegm from the throat: (*coll.*) to spit.—*adj.* **expec'torant**, tending to promote expectoration.—*n.* a medicine that promotes expectoration.—*n.* **expectora'tion**, act of expectorating: that which is expectorated: (*coll.*) spittle.—*adj.* **expec'torative**, having the quality of promoting expectoration. [L. *expectorāre*, *-ātum*—*ex*, from, *pectus*, *pectoris*, breast.]

expedient, *iks-pē'di-ant*, *adj.* suitable: advisable: (*Shak.*) expeditious.—*n.* that which serves to promote: means suitable to an end: contrivance,

shift.—*ns.* **expē'dience** (*Shak.*), haste, despatch: (*Shak.*) enterprise: expediency; **expē'diency**, fitness: desirableness: conduciveness to the need of the moment: that which is opportune: self-interest.—*adj.* **expēdien'tial** (*-en'shl*).—*adv.* **expē'diently.** [L. *expediēns*, *-entis*, pr.p. of *expedīre*; see **expedite.**]

expeditate, *eks-ped'it-āt*, *v.t.* to deprive of three claws or of the ball of the foot, to claw.—*n.* **expeditā'tion.** [L.L. *expeditāre*, *-ātum*—*ex*, from, *pēs*, *pedis*, foot.]

expedite, *eks'pi-dīt*, *v.t.* to free from impediments: to hasten: to send forth: to despatch.—*adj.* free from impediment: unencumbered: quick: prompt. —*adv.* **ex'peditely.**—*n.* **expedition** (*-di'shən*), speed: promptness: an organised journey to attain some object, as hunting, warfare, exploration, etc.: the party undertaking such a journey.—*adjs.* **expedi'tionary**, belonging to an expedition: of the nature of an expedition; **expedi'tious**, characterised by expedition or rapidity: speedy: prompt.—*adv.* **expedi'tiously.**—*n.* **expedi'tiousness.**—*adj.* **exped'itive.** [L. *expedīre*, *ītum*—*ex*, from, *pēs*, *pedis*, a foot.]

expel, *iks-pel'*, *v.t.* to drive out: eject: to discharge: to banish: (*Shak.*) to keep off:—*pr.p.* **expell'ing**; *pa.t.* and *pa.p.* **expelled'.**—*adj.* and *n.* **expell'ant**, **-ent.** [L. *expellĕre*, *expulsum*—*ex*, *pellĕre*, to drive.]

expend, *iks-pend'*, *v.t.* to lay out: to employ or consume in any way: to spend.—*adj.* **expend'able**, that may be expended, esp. that may be sacrificed to achieve some end.—Also *n.*—*ns.* **expend'iture**, act of expending or laying out: that which is expended: the process of using up: money spent; **expense** (*-pens'*), expenditure: outlay: cost: (in *pl.*) money out of pocket, or an allowance therefor: (in *pl.*: *Scots law*) costs in a lawsuit.— *adj.* **expens'ive**, causing or requiring much expense: costly: lavish.—*adv.* **expens'ively.**—*n.* **expens'iveness**—**be at the expense of**, to pay the cost of. [L. *expendĕre*—*ex*, out, *pendĕre*, *pēnsum*, to weigh.]

experience, *iks-pē'ri-əns*, *n.* (*obs.*) test, trial, experiment: practical acquaintance with any matter gained by trial: repeated trial: long and varied observation, personal or general: wisdom derived from the changes and trials of life: the passing through of any event or course of events by which one is affected: an event so passed through: anything received by the mind, as sensation, perception, or knowledge.—*v.t.* to make trial of, or practical acquaintance with: to prove or know by use: to have experience of: to suffer, undergo.— *adj.* **expē'rienced**, taught by experience: having much experience: skilful: wise.—*adjs.* **expē'rienceless**, having little or no experience; **expērien'tial** (*-en'shl*), pertaining to or derived from experience.—*ns.* **expērien'tialism**, the doctrine that all knowledge comes from experience; **expērien'tialist.**—**experience meeting**, one for the relating of religious experiences. [Fr. *expérience* and L. *experientia*, from *experīrī*—*ex-*, inten., and old verb *perīrī*, to try.]

experiment, *iks-per'i-mənt*, *n.* (*obs.*) experience: a trial: something done to test a theory, or to discover something unknown.—*v.i.* (also *-ment'*) to make experiment or trial: to search by trial.—*v.t.* to make trial of.—*adj.* **experiment'al** (*obs.*) experienced, having experience: pertaining to experiment: based on or proceeding by experiment: tentative.—*v.i.* **experiment'alise.**—*ns.* **experiment'alism**, reliance on experiment; **experiment'alist**, **experi'menter** (or *-ment'*), **per'imentist**, one who makes experiments.—*adv.* **experiment'ally.**—*n.* **experimentā'tion.**—*adjs.* **experiment'ative**; **experiment'ed**, (*obs.*) experienced: practised. [L. *experimentum*, from *experīrī*, to try thoroughly; see **experience.**]

expert, *eks-pərt'*, *adj.* taught by practice: having a familiar knowledge: having a facility of performance: skilful, adroit.—*v.t.* (*Spens.*) to experience.— *ns.* **ex'pert**, one who is skilled in any art or science: a specialist: a scientific or professional witness; **expertise** (*-ēz'*; Fr.) expert knowledge: expertness.—*adv.* **expert'ly.**—*n.* **expert'ness.** [Fr.,—

L. *expertus—experīrī*, to try thoroughly; see **experience.**]
expiate, *eks'pi-āt, v.t.* to make complete atonement for : to make satisfaction or reparation for.—*adj.* (*Shak.*) expired, at an end.—*adj.* **ex'piable,** capable of being expiated, atoned for, or done away.—*ns.* **expia'tion,** act of expiating : the means by which atonement is made : atonement; **ex'piātor.**—*adj.* **ex'piatory** (-ə-, or -ā-tər-i). [L. *expiāre, -ātum—ex-,* inten., *piāre,* to appease, atone for.]
expire, *iks-, eks-pīr', v.t.* to breathe out : to emit : (*Spens.*) to bring to an end.—*v.i.* to breathe out : to die : to come to an end : to lapse : to become invalid by lapse of time : (*Spens.*) to fulfil a term. —*adj.* **expī'rable,** that may expire or come to an end.—*ns.* **expī'rant,** one expiring; **expirā'tion** (*eks-pi-* or -*pī-*), the act of breathing out : (*obs.*) death : end : that which is expired.—*adj.* **expī'ratory,** pertaining to expiration, or the emission of the breath.—*adjs.* **expīred',** dead : extinct : lapsed : obsolete; **expī'ring,** dying : pertaining to or uttered at the time of dying.—*n.* **expī'ry,** the end or termination, esp. by lapse of time : expiration. [Fr. *expirer* and L. *ex,* from; *spīrāre, -ātum,* to breathe.]
expiscate, *eks-pis'kāt, v.t.* to find out by skilful means or by strict examination.—*n.* **expiscā'tion.** —*adj.* **expis'cātory.** [L. *expiscārī, expiscātus—ex,* from, *piscārī,* to fish—*piscis,* a fish.]
explain, *iks-plān', v.t.* to make plain or intelligible : to unfold and illustrate the meaning of : to expound : to account for.—*v.i.* to give an explanation.—*adj.* **explain'able.**—*ns.* **explain'er;** **explana'tion** (*eks-plə-nā'shən*), act of explaining or clearing from obscurity : that which explains or clears up : the meaning or sense given to anything : a mutual clearing up of matters.—*adv.* **explan'atorily** (*iks-plan'ə-tər-i-li*).—*adj.* **explan'atory,** serving to explain or clear up : containing explanations.—**explain away,** to modify the force of by explanation, generally in a bad sense. [L. *explānāre—ex-,* out, *plānāre,* to level—*plānus,* flat, plain.]
expletive, *eks'pli-tiv, eks-plē'tiv, adj.* filling out : added merely to fill up.—*n.* a word inserted to fill up a sentence or line of verse : a meaningless word serving a grammatical purpose only : anything present merely to fill a gap : a meaningless oath.—*adj.* **ex'pletory,** serving to fill up : expletive : supplementary. [L. *explētivus—ex-,* out, *plēre,* to fill.]
explicate, *eks'pli-kāt, v.t.* to unfold, develop : to lay open or explain the meaning of.—*adj.* **ex'plicable** (by some, -*plik'*), capable of being explicated or explained.—*n.* **explica'tion,** act of explicating or explaining : explanation.—*adjs.* **ex'plicative, ex'plicatory** (also -*plik'*), serving to explicate or explain. [L. *explicāre, explicātum* or *explicitum—ex-,* out, *plicāre,* to fold.]
explicit, *eks-plis'it, adj.* not implied merely, but distinctly stated : plain in language : outspoken : clear : unreserved.—*adv.* **explic'itly.**—*n.* **explic'itness.** [See **explicate.**]
explicit, *eks'pli-sit, n.* a conclusion. [From the mediaeval custom of writing *explicit* at the end of a book or section : originally apparently for L. *explicitum est,* is completed : later taken to be 3rd sing. pres. indic., and supplied with a plural *expliciunt;* see **explicate.**]
explode, *iks-plōd', v.t.* to cry down, hoot off, as an actor : to bring into disrepute, and reject : to cause to blow up.—*v.i.* to burst with a loud report : to burst out, break forth suddenly.—*adj.* **explō'ded,** blown up : rejected, discarded.—*n.* **explō'sion** (-*zhen*), act of exploding : a sudden violent burst of feelings, etc.—*adj.* **explō'sive** (-*siv, -ziv*), liable to or causing explosion : bursting out with violence and noise.—*n.* something that will explode : a stop consonant.—*adv.* **explō'sively.**—*n.* **explō'siveness.**—**explosion shot,** a golf stroke to send a ball forcibly out of a bunker. [L. *explōdĕre, explōsum—ex,* from, *plaudĕre,* to clap the hands.]

exploit, *iks-ploit',* or *eks'ploit, n.* a deed or achievement, esp. an heroic one : a feat.—*v.t.* (*iks-ploit'*) to work, make available : to turn to use : to make gain out of or at the expense of.—*adj.* **exploit'-able.**—*ns.* **exploit'age, exploitā'tion** (*eks-*), the act of successfully applying industry to any object, as the working of mines, etc. : the act of using for selfish purposes; **exploit'er.** [O.Fr. *exploit—*L. *explicitum,* unfolded; see **explicate.**]
explore, *iks-, eks-plōr', v.t.* and *v.i.* to search or travel through for the purpose of discovery : to examine thoroughly.—*n.* **explorā'tion** (*eks-*), act of searching thoroughly : travel for the sake of discovery.—*adjs.* **explorative** (-*plor'* or -*plōr'*); **explor'atory,** serving to explore or investigate : searching out.—*n.* **explor'er.**—*adj.* **explor'ing.** [Fr.,—L. *explōrāre, -ātum,* to search out.]
explosion. See **explode.**
exponent, *eks-pō'nənt, adj.* setting forth : expounding.—*n.* an expounder : (*mus.*) an interpreter by performance : an example, illustration, type : (*math.*) a symbol showing what power a quantity is raised to, an index.—*adj.* **exponential** (*eks-pō-nen'shl*), pertaining to or involving exponents. —*n.* an exponential function.—**exponential curve,** a curve expressed by an exponential equation; **exponential equation,** one in which the variable occurs in the exponent of one or more terms; **exponential function,** a quantity with a variable exponent, esp. e^x, where *e* is the base of natural logarithms; **exponential series,** a series in which exponential quantities are developed; **exponential theorem** gives a value of any number in terms of its natural logarithm, and from it can at once be derived a series determining the logarithm. [L. *expōnēns, -entis,* setting forth—*ex-,* out, *pōnĕre,* to place.]
exponible, *eks-pō'ni-bl, adj.* able to be, or requiring to be, explained. [L. *expōnĕre;* see **exponent.**]
export, *eks-pōrt', v.t.* to carry or send out of a country, as goods in commerce.—*n.* **ex'port,** act of exporting : that which is exported : a commodity which is or may be sent from one country to another in traffic.—*adj.* **export'able.**—*ns.* **exportā'tion; export'er.—invisible exports,** such items in a national trade balance as money spent abroad by tourists, etc.; opp. to **visible exports,** goods sold abroad by traders. [L. *exportāre, -ātum—ex,* out of, *portāre,* to carry.]
expose, *iks-pōz', v.t.* to lay forth to view : to deprive of cover, protection, or shelter : to make bare : to abandon (an infant) : to submit to an influence (as of light, weather) : to put up for sale : to explain : to make liable : to disclose : to show up.—*n.* (*U.S.*) exposé.—*ns.* **expōs'al,** exposive : exposition; **exposé** (*eks-pō-zā;* Fr.), an exposing : a shameful showing up : a formal statement or exposition.—*adj.* **exposed',** unprotected; shelterless.—*ns.* **expos'edness,** the state of being exposed; **expos'er; exposure** (-*pō'zhər, -zhyər*), act of laying open or bare : subjection to an influence : (*phot.*) act of allowing access of light : duration of such access : act of showing up an evil : state of being laid bare : openness to danger : shelterless state : position with regard to the sun, influence of climate, etc. [Fr. *exposer—*L. *ex-,* out, and *pausāre,* to rest, confused with *expōnĕre,* to expose; see **exponent, exposition,** and cf. **pose, compose, repose,** etc.]
exposition, *eks-pō-zish'ən, n.* act of exposing : a setting out to public view : the abandonment of a child : a public exhibition : act of expounding : explanation : commentary : an expository discourse : enunciation of themes in a composition : that part of a sonata, fugue, etc., in which themes are presented.—*adj.* **expositive** (-*poz'*), serving to expose or explain : explanatory : exegetical.— *n.* **expos'itor,** one who, or that which, expounds : an interpreter.—*fem.* **expos'itress.**—*adj.* **expos'itory,** serving to explain : explanatory.—*n.* **exposture** (-*pos'tyər; Shak.*), exposure. [L. *expositiō, -ōnis, expositor, -ōris—expōnĕre, expositum,* to expose, set forth; see **expound.**]

expostulate, *eks-post'ū-lāt*, *v.i.* to remonstrate : (*Shak.*) to discuss : (*Milt.*) to claim.—*n.* **expostulā'tion.**—*adjs.* **expost'ūlātive** (or *-ə-tiv*), **expost'ūlatory** (*-ā-* or *-ə-tər-i*), containing expostulation.—*n.* **expost'ūlātor.** [L. *expostulāre*, *-ātum* —*ex-*, inten., *postulāre*, to demand.]

expound, *iks-pownd'*, *v.t.* to expose, or lay open the meaning of : to explain : to interpret : to explain in a certain way.—*n.* **expound'er.** [O.Fr. *espondre*—L. *expōnĕre*—*ex-*, out, *pōnĕre*, to place.]

express, *iks-pres'*, *v.t.* to press or force out : to emit : to represent or make known by a likeness, words, signs, symbols, etc. : to put into words : to symbolise : to state explicitly : to reveal : to designate : to despatch.—*adj.* clearly brought out : exactly representing : directly stated : explicit : clear : intended or sent for a particular purpose : expeditious.—*adv.* with haste : specially : by express train or messenger : by express.—*n.* a messenger or conveyance sent on a special errand : a special message : a regular and quick conveyance : a system for the speedy transmission of messages or goods : an express train : an express messenger.—*n.* **express'age**, the system of carrying by express : the charge for doing so.—*adj.* **express'ible.**—*ns.* **expression** (*-presh'ən*), act of forcing out by pressure : act, or mode, or power, of representing or giving utterance : representation or revelation by language, art, the features, etc. : the manner in which anything is expressed : a word, phrase : a symbol : intonation : due indication of feeling in performance of music.—*adj.* **express'ional**, of, or pertaining to, expression.—*ns.* **express'ionism**, in literature and painting a revolt against impressionism, turning away from the outer life to the inner ; **express'ionist.**—*adjs.* **express'ionless** ; **express'ive**, serving to express or indicate : full of expression : vividly representing : emphatic : significant.—*adv.* **express'ively.**—*n.* **express'iveness.**—*adv.* **express'ly**, explicitly : for the express purpose : definitely.—*ns.* **express'man** ; **express'ness** ; **expressure** (*eks-presh'ər*) pressing out : (*Shak.*) expression : (*Shak.*) representation.—**express agency, company,** one that undertakes speedy transmission of goods ; **express delivery,** immediate delivery by special messenger : delivery by express agency ; **express fee,** a fee for express delivery ; **expression stop,** a stop in a harmonium by which the performer can regulate the air to produce expression ; **express letter, packet, parcel,** one sent by special messenger ; **express messenger,** a special messenger ; **express rifle,** a rifle for big game at short range, with heavy charge of powder and light bullet ; **express train,** a railway-train at high speed and with few stops ; **to express oneself,** to give expression to one's thoughts. [L. *exprimĕre*, *expressum*—*ex*, from, *premĕre*, *pressum*, to press ; partly through Fr. *exprès*, etc.]

exprobrate, *eks'prō-brāt*, *v.t.* (*arch.*) to reproach with : to upbraid.—*n.* **exprobrā'tion.**—*adjs.* **expro'brative** ; **expro'bratory.** [L. *exprobrāre*, *-ātum*—pfx. *ex-*, indicating source, *probrum*, disgrace.]

expromission, *eks-pro-mish'ən*, *n.* the intervention of a new debtor, substituted for the former one, who is consequently discharged by the creditor. —*n.* **expromissor** (*-mis'ər*). [L. *exprōmittĕre*, *-missum*, to promise to pay—*ex-*, intens., *prōmittĕre*, to promise.]

expropriate, *eks-prō'pri-āt*, *v.t.* to dispossess.—*n.* **expropriā'tion.** [L. *expropriāre*, *-ātum*—*ex*, from, *proprium*, property.]

expugn, *eks-pūn'*, *v.t.* to take by storm : to storm : to overcome.—*adj.* **expugnable** (*-pug'* or *-pū'nəbl*), capable of being taken or vanquished.—*adj.* **expugnā'tion** (*-pug-*). [L. *expugnāre*.]

expulse, *eks-puls'*, *v.t.* (*obs.*) to expel forcibly, eject.—*n.* **expul'sion**, the act of expelling : banishment.—*adj.* **expul'sive**, able or serving to expel. [L. *expulsāre*, freq. of *expellĕre*. See **expel.**]

expunge, *eks-punj'*, *v.t.* to efface : to mark for deletion.—*n.* **expunc'tion** (*-pungk'shən*). [L. *expungĕre*,

-punctum, to mark for deletion by a row of dots— *ex-*, out, *pungĕre*, to prick.]

expurgate, *eks'pur-gāt*, also *-pur'*, *v.t.* to purge out or render pure : to purify from anything supposed to be offensive, noxious, or erroneous.— *ns.* **expurgā'tion**, act of expurgating or purifying : the removal of anything hurtful or evil : bowdlerising : exculpation : **expurgator** (*eks'pur-gā-tər*, or *eks-pur'gə-tər*), one who expurgates or purifies.— *adjs.* **expurgatō'rial** (*-gə-tō'ri-əl*), **expur'gatory**, pertaining to expurgation : tending to expurgate or purify.—*v.t.* **expurge** (*purj'*), to purify, expurgate. [L. *expurgāre*, *-ātum*—*ex-*, out, *purgāre*, to purge.]

exquisite, *eks'kwiz-it*, also *-kwiz'*, *adj.* (*Shak.*) far-fetched : (*obs.*) abstruse : delicious : of consummate excellence : compelling the highest admiration : of delicate perception or close discrimination : not easily satisfied : fastidious : exceeding, extreme, as pain or pleasure.—*n.* one exquisitely nice or fastidious in dress : a fop.— *adv.* **ex'quisitely.**—*n.* **ex'quisiteness.** [L. *exquīsītus*—*ex*, out, *quaerĕre*, to seek.]

exsanguinous, *eks-sang'gwin-əs*, *adj.* without blood : anaemic—also **exsang'uine, -d, exsanguin'eous.** —*n.* **exsanguin'ity.** [L. *ex-*, without, *sanguis*, *-inis*, blood.]

exscind, *ek-sind'*, *v.t.* to cut off. [L. *ex*, from, *scindĕre*, to cut.]

exsect, *ek-sekt'*, *v.t.* to cut out.—*n.* **exsec'tion.** [L. *ex*, from, *secāre*, *sectum*, to cut.]

exsert, *eks-sərt'*, *v.t.* to protrude.—*adj.* **exsert'ed**, projecting.—*adj.* **exser'tile** (*-til*, *-tīl*).—*n.* **exser'tion.** [L. *exserĕre*, *-sertum*. See **exert.**]

ex-service, *eks-sər'vis*, *adj.* formerly in one of the fighting services.—*n.* **ex-ser'viceman.**

exsiccate, *ek'si-kāt*, *v.t.* to dry up.—*adj.* **exsicc'ant.**—*n.* **exsiccā'tion.**—*adj.* **exsicc'ative** (or *-āt'*).—*n.* **ex'siccātor**, a drying agent or apparatus. [L. *exsiccāre*—*ex-*, *siccus*, dry.]

exstipulate, *ek-stip'ū-lāt*, *adj.* (*bot.*) without stipules.

exsuccous, *ek-suk'əs*, *adj.* sapless. [L. *exsuccus*— *ex-*, *succus*, juice.]

exsufflicate, *ek-suf'li-kāt*, *adj.* (*Shak.*) puffed out.—*v.t.* **exsuff'late**, to blow away : to exorcise by blowing away.—*n.* **exsufflā'tion**, expiration : forced expiration : exorcism by blowing. [L. *ex-*, out, and *sufflāre*, to blow out—*sub*, under, *flāre*, to blow.]

extant, *eks'tant*, *iks-tant'*, *adj.* standing out, or above the rest : still standing or existing. [L. *exstāns*, *-āntis*—*ex-*, out, *stāre*, to stand.]

extasy, extatic. Same as **ecstasy, ecstatic.**

extempore, *eks-tem'pə-ri*, *adv.* on the spur of the moment : without preparation : suddenly.—*adj.* sudden : rising at the moment : without help of manuscript : composed and delivered or performed impromptu.—*n.* an impromptu.—*adjs.* **extem'poral**, **extemporā'neous**—*adv.* **extemporā'neously.**—*n.* **extemporā'neousness.**—*adv.* **extem'porarily.**—*n.* **extem'porariness.**—*adj.* **extem'porary**, done on the spur of the moment : hastily prepared : speaking extempore : done without preparation : off-hand.—*n.* **extemporīsā'tion.** —*v.i.* **extem'porise**, to speak, or compose and play, extempore or without previous preparation : to discourse without notes : to speak off-hand. [L. *ex*, out of, and *tempore*, abl. of *tempus*, time.]

extend, *iks-tend'*, *v.t.* to stretch out : to prolong in any direction : to enlarge : to expand : to widen : to unfold : to straighten out : to hold out : to offer, accord : to exert to the full : (*law*; *Shak.*) to seize : to value, assess.—*v.i.* to stretch, reach : to be continued in length or breadth.— *adjs.* **extend'able** ; **extend'ant** (*her.*), displayed ; **extend'ed**, occupying space : having extension : stretched out : (*U.S.*) extensive.—*adv.* **extend'edly.**—*n.* **extend'er**, one who or that which extends : a university extension lecture : substance added to paint to give body.—*adjs.* **extend'ible** ; **extense** (*-tens'*) (*obs.*), extensive.— *n.* **extensibil'ity.**—*adjs.* **extens'ible, extensile** (*eks-ten'sīl*), that may be extended.—*n.* **extension** (*iks-*, *eks-ten'shən*), an act of extending : condition of being extended : an added piece : (*U.S.*) a wing or annex of a house : the property of occupying space : (*logic*) extent of the application of a term or the number of objects included under it—opp. *intension*: (*gram.*) word or words added to subject, predicate, or object. (**University extension, the** enlargement of the aim of a university, in providing instruction for those unable to become regular students).—*adj.* **exten′sional.**—*adv.* **exten′sionally.**—*ns.* **exten′sionist,** an advocate of extension : a university extension lecturer or student; **exten′sity,** massiveness or spatial quality in sensation from which perception of extension is derived.—*adj.* **extens′ive,** large : wide-spread : comprehensive : (*eks-*) pertaining to extension : seeking or deriving a comparatively small crop cheaply from a wide area—opp. to *intensive.*— *adv.* **extens′ively.**—*ns.* **extens′iveness; extensom′eter** (*eks-*), an instrument for measuring small strains in metal; **exten′sor,** a muscle that extends or straightens any part of the body; **extent′,** the space or degree to which a thing is extended : bulk : compass : scope : degree or amount (as *to some extent*) : a stretch or extended space : a valuation of property : (*law*) a writ directing the sheriff to seize the property of a debtor, for the recovery of debts of record due to the Crown : (*Shak.*) seizure : (*Shak.*) attack : (*Shak.*) an act of extending (justice, courtesy, etc.).—*adj.* stretched out. [L. *extendĕre, extentum,* or *extēnsum*—*ex-,* out, *tendĕre,* to stretch.]

extenuate, *eks-ten′ū-āt, v.t.* to lessen : to underrate : to weaken the force of : to palliate.—*n.* and *adj.* **exten′ūāting,** palliating.—*adv.* **exten′ūatingly.** —*n.* **extenūā′tion,** act of representing anything as less wrong or criminal than it seems : palliation : mitigation.—*adjs.* **exten′ūātive, exten′ūātory,** tending to extenuate : palliative.—*n.* **exten′ūātor.** [L. *extenuāre, -ātum*—*ex-,* inten., *tenuis,* thin.]

exterior, *eks-tē′ri-ər, adj.* outer : outward, external : on or from the outside : foreign.—*n.* the outside, outer surface : outward form or deportment : appearance : a representation of an outdoor scene : an outer part (esp. in *pl.*).—*n.* **extērior′ity** (-*or′i-ti*).—*adv.* **extē′riorly,** outwardly. [L. *exterior,* comp. of *exter, exterus,* outward—*ex,* from.]

exterminate, *eks-tər′mi-nāt, v.t.* (*obs.*) to drive out : to destroy utterly : to put an end to : to root out.—*adj.* **exter′minable,** that can be exterminated : (*Shelley*) illimitable.—*n.* **exterminā′tion,** complete destruction or extirpation.—*adjs.* **exter′minative, exter′minatory,** serving or tending to exterminate.—*n.* **exter′minātor.**—*v.t.* **exter′-mine** (*Shak.*), to exterminate. [L. *extermināre, -ātum,* to drive beyond the boundary—*ex,* out of, *terminus,* boundary.]

external, *eks-tər′nal, adj.* exterior : lying outside : outward : belonging to the world of outward things : that may be seen : not innate or intrinsic : accidental : foreign.—*n.* exterior : (in *pl.*) the outward parts : (in *pl.*) outward or non-essential forms and ceremonies.—*adj.* **extern′, externe′,** external, outward.—*n.* a non-resident, as a day-scholar, an out-patient, non-resident physician or surgeon.—*n.* **externalisā′tion.**—*v.t.* **exter′nalise,** to give form or apparent reality to.—*ns.* **exter′-nalism,** undue regard to mere externals or non-essential outward forms, esp. of religion : externality (-*nal′i-ti*), external character : superficiality : undue regard to externals.—*adv.* **exter′nally.** —*n.* **externat** (-*nä;* Fr.), a day-school.—**external student** one examined by a university in which he has not studied. [L. *externus,* outward—*exter,* outside.]

exterritorial, *eks-ter-i-tō′ri-əl.* Same as **extra-territorial.**

extinct, *iks-tingkt′, adj.* put out : extinguished : no longer existing : dead.—*adj.* **extinct′ed** (*Shak.*), extinguished.—*n.* **extinc′tion,** extinguishing, quenching or wiping out : destruction : suppression : the cutting off of polarised light at certain angles when a section of doubly refracting mineral is rotated between crossed nicols.—*adj.* **extinct′-**

ive, tending to extinguish.—*n.* **extinct′ure** (*Shak.*), extinction.

extine, *eks′tin, -tēn, -tīn, n.* (*bot.*) the outer membrane of a pollen-grain or spore.—Also **ex′ine.** [From the root of L. *exter, extimus,* outer, outmost.]

extinguish, *iks-ting′gwish, v.t.* to quench, put out : to render extinct : to put an end to : to destroy, annihilate : to obscure by superior splendour.—*v.i.* to die out.—*adj.* **exting′uishable.**—*ns.* **exting′uisher,** one who, or that which, extinguishes : a small hollow conical instrument for putting out a candle, etc. : a device for putting out fire : a conical structure resembling a candle extinguisher; **exting′uishment,** the act of extinguishing : (*law*) putting an end to a right by consolidation or union. [L. *ex*(*s*)*tinguĕre, ex*(*s*)*tinctum*—*ex-,* out, *stinguĕre,* to quench.]

extirpate, *eks′tər-pāt, v.t.* to root out : to destroy totally : to exterminate—(*Spen., Shak.,* etc.) **extirp′.**—*adj.* **extirp′able.**—*ns.* **extirpā′tion,** extermination : total destruction; **ex′tirpātor,** one who extirpates : an implement for weeding.—*adj.* **extirp′atory.** [L. *exstirpāre, -ātum*—*ex,* out, and *stirps,* a stock, root.]

extol, *iks-tol′, -tōl′, v.t.* (*Spens.*) to lift up : to praise highly :—*pr.p.* **extoll′ing;** *pa.t.* and *pa.p.* **extolled′;** *Spens.* **extold′.**—*n.* **extol′ment,** the act of extolling : the state of being extolled. [L. *extollĕre*—*ex-,* up, *tollĕre,* to lift or raise.]

extort, *iks-tort′, v.t.* to wring out : to gain or draw out by compulsion or violence.—*adj.* extorted : wrongfully obtained.—*adj.* **extors′ive,** serving or tending to extort.—*adv.* **extors′ively.**—*n.* **extor′-tion** (-*tor′shan*), illegal or oppressive exaction : that which is extorted.—*adjs.* **extor′tionary,** pertaining to or implying extortion; **extor′-tionate,** oppressive.—*n.* **extor′tioner,** one who practises extortion.—*adj.* **extort′ive.** [L. *extor-quēre, extortum*—*ex,* out, *torquēre,* to twist.]

extra, *eks-trə, adj.* beyond or more than the usual or the necessary : extraordinary : additional.— *adv.* unusually.—*n.* what is extra or additional, as an item above and beyond the ordinary school curriculum, something over and above the usual course or charge in a bill, etc. : a special edition of a newspaper containing later news : a run scored at cricket from a bye, leg-bye, wide, or no-ball (not hit).—*adj.* **ex′tra-condensed′** (*print.*), extremely narrow in proportion to the height.— *v.t.* **ex′tra-ill′ustrate** (or -*lus′*), to grangerise.— *n.* **ex′tra-illustrā′tion.**—*adj.* **ex′tra-speci′al,** much out of the way.—*n.* a special late edition of an evening newspaper called for by some news of great importance. [Prob. contracted from **extra-ordinary.**]

extra-, *eks′-trä-, -trə-.* (See **Prefixes**).—*adjs.* **ex′tra-ax′illary,** not in the axil of a leaf; **ex′tra-cellular,** outside the cell-walls; **extrado′tal,** not forming part of the dowry; **ex′traflo′ral,** not in a flower; **extraforā′neous,** outdoor; **ex′tra-galac′tic,** outside the Milky Way; **extrajudi′cial,** not made in court, beyond the usual course of legal proceeding.—*adv.* **ex′trajudi′cially.**—*adjs.* **ex′tralim′ital,** not found within a given faunal area : lying outside a prescribed area—also **extra-lim′itary;** **ex′tramet′rical,** in excess of the recognised number of syllables in the line; **ex′tra-mun′dane,** beyond the material world; **ex′tra-mū′ral,** without or beyond the walls : connected with a university but not under its direct control; **ex′trapa-rō′chial,** beyond the limits of a parish; **ex′tra-phys′ical,** not subject to physical laws; **ex′tra-profess′ional,** not belonging to a particular profession : outside the usual limits of professional duty or practice; **extr′a-provin′cial,** outside the limits of a particular province; **ex′tra-reg′ular,** unlimited by rules; **ex′tra-sō′lar,** beyond the solar system; **ex′traterritō′rial,** outside a territory or territorial jurisdiction—also **exterritōr′ial.**—*n.* **extraterritorial′ity,** the privilege of being outside the jurisdiction of the country one is in.—also **exterritorial′ity.**—*adjs.* **ex′tra-trop′ical,** outside the tropics; **ex′tra-ū′terine,** outside the uterus; **extravas′cular,**

outside of the vascular system or a vessel: not vascular. [L. *extrā*, outside.]

extract, iks-, eks-trakt'-, *v.t.* to draw out by force or otherwise: to choose out or select: to find out: to derive: to extort: (*Scots law*) to take a copy of: to copy passages from: to withdraw by chemical or physical means from containing or combined matter: to exhaust or treat by extraction.—*adj.* (*obs. except Scots law*) extracted: derived.—*n.* **extract** (*eks'*), anything drawn from a substance by heat, distillation, solvents, etc., as an essence: a passage taken from a book or writing: wool from rags from which cotton has been chemically removed.—*adjs.* **extract'able** (also **extract'ible**); —**extrac'tion**, act of extracting: derivation from a stock or family: birth: lineage: that which is extracted.—*adj.* **extract'ive**, tending or serving to extract: of the nature of an extract.—*n.* an extract.—*n.* **extract'or**, he who, or that which, extracts.—**extract the root of a quantity**, to find its root by a mathematical process; **extractive matter**, the soluble portions of any drug. [L. *extrahĕre*, *extractum*—*ex*, from, *trahĕre*, to draw.]

extradition, eks-trə-dish'ən, *n.* a delivering up of accused persons by one government to another.—*adj.* **extradi'table** (-*dīt'ə-bl*).—*v.t.* **ex'tradite**, to hand over for trial or punishment to a foreign government. [L. *ex*, from, *trāditiō*, -*ōnis*—*trā-dĕre*, *trāditum*, to deliver up.]

extrados, eks-trā'dos, *n.* the convex surface of an arch: the external curve of the voussoirs. [Fr., —L. *extrā*, outside, Fr. *dos*, back.]

extraneous, eks-trān'yəs, *adj.* external: foreign: not belonging to or dependent on a thing: not essential.—*n.* **extraneity** (-*trə-nē'i-ti*).—*adv.* **ex-trān'eously**. [L. *extrāneus*, external, *extrā*, outside.]

extraordinary, eks-trord'(i-)nər-i, or eks-trə-ord', or iks-trord', *adj.* beyond ordinary: not usual or regular: remarkable, wonderful: special or super-numerary, as 'physician extraordinary' in a royal household, and 'extraordinary professor' in a German university, both being inferior to the ordinary official.—*n.pl.* **extraord'inaries**, things that exceed the usual order, kind, or method.—*adv.* **extraord'inarily.**—*n.* **extraord'inariness.**—**extraordinary ray**, in double refraction, the ray that does not obey the ordinary law of re-fraction. [L. *extraordinārius*—*extrā*, outside, *ordō*, -*inis*, order.]

extrapolate, eks-trap'ō-lāt, -ə-lāt, eks', *v.t.* to obtain or extend by extrapolation.—*v.i.* to practise extrapolation.—*n.* **extrapolā'tion**, calculation of more or less probable values for a function outside the limits between which values are known. [L. *extrā* and **interpolate**.]

extraught, eks-trawt' (Shak.), *pa.p.* of **extract**.

extravagant, iks-trav'ə-gənt, *adj.* wandering beyond bounds: irregular: unrestrained: excessive: pro-fuse in expenses: wasteful.—*ns.* **extrav'agance**, excess: lavish expenditure: (*Milt.*) digression; **extrav'agancy** (Shak.), vagrancy: extravagance.—*adv.* **extrav'agantly.**—*v.i.* **extrav'agate**, to wander: to exceed proper bounds. [L. *extrā*, beyond, *vagāns*, -*āntis*, pr.p. of *vagārī*, to wander.]

extravaganza, eks-trav-ə-gan'zä, *n.* an extravagant or eccentric musical, dramatic, or literary pro-duction: extravagant conduct or speech. [It. (*e*)*stravaganza*.]

extravasate, eks-trav-ə-sāt, *v.t.* to let out of the proper vessels.—*adj.* let out of its proper vessel: extravasated.—*n.* **extravasā'tion**, act of extra-vasating: the escape of any of the fluids of the living body from their proper vessels. [L. *extrā*, out of, *vās*, a vessel.]

extravert, extrovert, eks-trə- or -trō-vərt', *v.t.* to turn outward or outside in: to make manifest.—*n.* (*eks'*) a person interested mainly in the world external to himself—opp. to **introvert**. —*n.* **extraver'sion, extrover'sion.** [Lat. *extrā*, outside, *vertĕre*, to turn: the *extro-* forms by analogy with **introvert**.]

extreat, eks-trēt, *n.* (Spens.) extraction. [**estreat**.]

extreme, iks-trēm' (arch. eks'), *adj.* outermost: most remote: last: highest in degree: greatest:

most violent: of opinions, etc., not moderate, going to great lengths: stringent: (*superl.*, Shak. etc., **extrēm'est**; *comp.*, rare, **extrēm'er**).—*n.* the ut-most point or verge: end: utmost of the highest limit or degree: (in *pl.*, *obs.*) great necessity.—*adv.* **extrēme'ly.**—*ns.* **extrē'mism**; **extrē'mist**, one ready to go to extremes: a holder of extreme opinions: an advocate of extreme action; **extrem-ity** (-*trem'i-ti*), the utmost limit: the highest degree: greatest necessity or distress: extreme condition: an end: hand or foot.—**extreme unction** (see **unction**); **go to extremes**, to go too far: to use extreme measures; **in the extreme**, in the last, highest degree: extremely; **the last extremity**, the utmost pitch of misfortune: death. [O.Fr. *extreme*—L. *extrēmus*, superl. of *exter*, *exterus*, on the outside.]

extricate, eks'tri-kāt, *v.t.* to free from entangle-ments or perplexities: to disentangle: to set free.—*adj.* **ex'tricable.**—*n.* **extricā'tion**, dis-entanglement: act of setting free. [L. *extrīcāre*, -*ātum*—*ex*, from, *trīcae*, hindrances.]

extrinsic, eks-trin'sik, *adj.* external: not contained in or belonging to a body: foreign: not essential: of a muscle, running from the trunk to limb or girdle—opp. to *intrinsic*.—*adj.* **extrin'sical.**—*adv.* **extrin'sically.** [Fr. *ex-trinsèque*—L. *extrīnsecus*—*exter*, outside, suff. -*in*, *secus*, beside.]

extrorse, eks-trors', *adj.* turned outward: (of an anther) opening towards the outside of the flower. [L. *extrā*, outside, *versus*, turned.]

extrovert, extroversion. Same as **extravert**, etc.

extrude, eks-trōōd', *v.t.* to force or urge out: to expel: to protrude.—*v.i.* to protrude.—*n.* **extru-sion** (-*trōō'zhən*), act of extruding, thrusting, or throwing out: expulsion.—*adjs.* **extrusive** (*trōō'-siv*), **extru'sory** (-*sər-i*). [L. *extrūdĕre*, *extrūsum* —*ex-*, out, *trūdĕre*, to thrust.]

exuberant, egz-, *igz*-(*y*)*ōō'bər-ənt*, *adj.* luxuriant: overflowing: abounding: in high spirits: lavish. —*ns.* **exu'berance, exu'berancy**, quality of being exuberant: luxuriance, an overflowing quantity: redundancy: outburst.—*adv.* **exu'ber-antly.**—*v.i.* **exu'berate**, to be exuberant. [L. *exūberāns*, -*āntis* pr.p. of *exūberāre*—*ex-*, inten., *ūber*, rich.]

exude, egz-, eks-ūd', *v.t.* to discharge by sweating: to discharge through pores or incisions.—*v.i.* to flow out of a body through the pores: to ooze out.—*ns.* **exudate** (eks'), exuded matter; **exudā'-tion** (eks-), act of exuding or discharging through pores: that which is exuded. [L. *exūdāre*—*ex*, from, *sūdāre*, to sweat.]

exul, eks'ul, *n.* (Spens.) an exile. [L. *ex*(*s*)*ul*.]

exulcerate, egz-ul'sər-āt, *v.t.* to exasperate, afflict as with an ulcer.—*n.* **exulcerā'tion**, ulceration: exasperation. [L. *exulcerāre*, -*ātum*—*ex-*, intens., *ulcerāre*, to ulcerate.]

exult, igz-ult', *v.i.* to rejoice exceedingly: to triumph.—*ns.* **exult'ance, exult'ancy**, exulta-tion: triumph.—*adj.* **exult'ant**, exulting: triumph-ant.—*n.* **exultā'tion** (egz-), triumphant delight: transport.—*adv.* **exult'ingly.** [L. *ex*(*s*)*ultāre*, -*ātum*, from *ex*(*s*)*ilīre*—*ex-*, out or up, *salīre*, to leap.]

exuviae, egz-, eks-(*y*)*ōō'vi-ē*, *n.pl.* cast-off skins, shells, or other coverings of animals: (*geol.*) fossil remains of animals.—*adj.* **exū'vial.**—*v.i.* **exū'-viate**, to shed, cast off, for a new covering or condition.—*n.* **exuviā'tion**, the act of exuviating. [L.,—*exuĕre*, to draw off.]

eyalet, ā-yä'let, *n.* a division of Turkey—a *vilayet*. [Turk.,—Ar. *iyālah*.]

eyas, i'əs, *n.* an unfledged hawk.—*adj.* (Spens.) unfledged.—*n.* **ay'as-mus'ket**, an unfledged male hawk: (Shak.) a child. [*An eyas* for *a nyas*—Fr. *niais*—L. *nidus*, nest.]

eye, ī, *n.* (obs.) a brood, esp. of pheasants. [*An eye* for *a nye*—O.Fr. *ni*—L. *nidus*, nest.]

eye, ī, *n.* the organ of sight or vision: more narrowly the globe or movable part of it: the power of seeing: sight: a tinge, suffusion: regard: aim: keenness of perception: anything resembling an eye, as an eye-spot: a central spot: the hole of a needle: the aperture for inserting the bias in a bowl: a round aperture: a mine entrance: a spring of water: a wire loop or ring for a hook: a round hole or window: the seed-bud of a potato: a spot on an egg: a spectacle lens: the central calm area of a cyclone: (*pl.*) the foremost part of a ship's bows, the hawse-holes: (*pl.* eyes; *arch.* eyne, *īn*; *Scot.* een, *ēn.*)—*v.t.* to look on: to observe narrowly.—*v.i.* (*Shak.*) to appear: (*pr.p.* ey'ing or eye'ing; *pa.t.* and *pa.p.* eyed, *īd*).—*ns.* eye'-ball, the ball or globe of the eye; eye'-bath, a cup that can be held in the orbit to bathe the eye; eye'-beam, a glance of the eye; eye'bright, a little plant of the genus Euphrasia (fam. Scrophulariaceae), formerly used as a remedy for eye diseases; eye'brow, the hairy arch above the eye.—*v.t.* to provide with artificial eyebrows.—*adj.* eye'browless, without eyebrows.—*adj.* eyed, having eyes: spotted as if with eyes.—*ns.* eye'-drop (*Shak.*), a tear; eye'-flap, a blinder on a horse's bridle; eye'ful, as much as the eye can take in: (*slang.*) something worth looking at, a fascinating sight.—*adj.* (*dial.*) sightly: (*dial.*) careful, having an eye.—*ns.* eye'-glance, a quick look; eye'glass, a glass to assist the sight, esp. such as stick on the nose by means of a spring: an eye-piece: (*Shak.*) the lens of the eye; eye'lash, the row, or one, of the hairs that edge the eyelid.—*adj.* eye'less, without eyes or sight: deprived of eyes: blind.—*ns.* eye'lid, the lid or cover of the eye: the portion of movable skin by means of which the eye is opened or closed at pleasure; eye'-opener, something that opens the eyes literally or figuratively, a startling enlightenment: a drink, esp. in the morning; eye'-piece, the lens or combination of lenses at the eye end of an optical instrument; eye'-pit, the socket of the eye; eye'-rhyme, a would-be rhyme between words that are spelt as if they rhymed but do not; eye'-salve, salve or ointment for the eyes; eye'-servant, one who does his duty only when under the eye of his master; eye'-service, service so performed: formal worship; eye'-shot, the reach or range of sight of the eye: a glance: eye'sight, power of seeing: view: observation; eye'sore, anything that is offensive to look at; eye'-splice, a kind of eye or loop formed by splicing the end of a rope into itself; eye'-spot, a spot like an eye: a rudimentary organ of vision.—*adj.* eye'-spott'ed (*Spens.*), marked with spots like eyes.—*ns.* eye'-string, the muscle that raises the eyelid; eye'-tooth, a canine tooth, esp. in the

upper jaw, below the eye; eye'-wash, a lotion for the eye: humbug: deception; eye'-water, water flowing from the eye: a lotion for the eyes; eye'-wink (*Shak.*), a rapid lowering and raising of the eyelid: a glance: the time of a wink; eye'-wit'ness, one who sees a thing done.—all my eye (*slang*), humbug; be all eyes, to give all attention; be a sheet in the wind's eye, to be intoxicated; clap, lay, set, eyes on (*coll.*), to see; cry one's eyes out, to weep copiously; cut one's eye-tooth, to cease to be a child: to be shrewd; electric eye (see electric); eye for eye, *lex talionis* (Ex. xxi. 24); eye of day, the sun; glad, green eye (see glad, green); give an eye to, to attend to; have an eye to, to contemplate: to have regard to: to incline towards; in eye, in sight; in one's mind's eye, in imagination; in the eyes of, in the estimation, opinion, of; in the wind's eye, against the wind; keep one's (or an) eye on, to observe closely: to watch; keep one's eye skinned, to be keenly watchful; make a person open his eyes, to cause him astonishment; makes eyes at, to look at in an amorous way; to ogle; mind your eye (*slang*), take care; my eye! a mild asseveration; naked eye (see naked); open a person's eyes, to make him see: to show him something of which he is ignorant; pipe, or put a finger in, the eye, to weep; put a person's eye out, blind him: supplant him in favour; see eye to eye, from Is. lii. 8, but used in the sense of to think alike; see with half an eye, to see without difficulty; throw sheep's eyes at, to ogle sheepishly; turn a blind eye on, feign not to see, wink at; under the eye of, under the observation of; up to the eyes, deeply involved. [O.E. *éage*; cf. Goth. *augo*, Ger. *auge*, Du. *oog*, O.N. *auga*.]

eyelet, *ī'lit*, *n.* a small eye or hole to receive a lace or cord, as in garments, sails, etc.: a small hole for seeing through (also eye'let-hole): a little eye.—*v.t.* to make eyelets in. [O.Fr. *oillet*—L. *oculus*, influenced by eye.]

eyeliad, eyliad, *ī'li-ad*, *n.* old variants of oeillade.

eyne, *īn*, *n.pl.* (*arch.*) eyes. [O.E. *éagan*.]

eyot, *āt*. Same as ait.

eyra, *ī'rā*, *n.* a South American wild cat. [Guaraní.]

eyre, *ār*, *n.* a journey or circuit: a court of itinerant justices. [O.Fr. *eire*, journey, from L. *iter*, a way, a journey—*ire*, *itum*, to go.]

eyry, eyrie. See aerie.

F

F, f, *ef, n.* the sixth letter in the English and Latin alphabets, derived from the Greek digamma—its sound a labio-dental fricative formed by bringing the lower lip into contact with the upper teeth: (*mus.*) the fourth note of the natural diatonic scale of C: as a mediaeval Roman numeral F=40; F=40,000: F is used as a contraction for Fahrenheit; F_1, F_2 (Mendelism) first and second filial generations: ff in mediaeval script was used instead of a capital F.—*ns.* **F'-clef,** a clef marking F, the fourth line in the bass, the bass-clef; **f'-hole,** either of a pair of holes in the belly of a violin, etc., shaped like an italic *f.*—**the three F's,** free sale, fixity of tenure, fair rent.

fa, *fä, n.* the fourth note in the sol-fa notation—also anglicised in spelling as **fah.** [See **Aretinian.**]

fa', *faw,* **fa'ard, faurd,** *färd, fawrd,* Scots for **fall, favoured.**

fabaceous, *fə-bāsh'əs, adj.* bean-like. [L. *faba,* a bean.]

Fabian, *fā'bi-ən, adj.* delaying, avoiding battle, cautious, practising the policy of delay: favouring the gradual introduction and spread of Socialism.—*n.* a member or supporter of the *Fabian Society* (founded 1884) for this purpose.—*n.* **Fā'bianism.** [From Q. *Fabius* Maximus, surnamed Cunctator (delayer), from the masterly tactics with which he wore out the strength of Hannibal, whom he dared not meet in battle.]

fable, *fā'bl, n.* a narrative in which things irrational, and sometimes inanimate, are, for the purpose of moral instruction, feigned to act and speak with human interests and passions: any tale in literary form, not necessarily probable in its incidents, intended to instruct or amuse: the plot or series of events in an epic or dramatic poem: a fiction or myth: a ridiculous story, an old wives' tale: a falsehood: subject of common talk.—*v.i.* to tell fictitious tales: (*obs.*) to tell falsehoods.—*v.t.* to feign: to invent.—*adj.* **fā'bled,** mythical: renowned in story: feigned.—*n.* and *adj.* **fā'bling.**—*n.* **fābler,** a writer or narrator of fictions.—*adj.* **fabular** (*fab'ū-lər*).—*v.i.* to write fables, or to speak in fables.—*ns.* **fab'ulist,** one who invents fables; **fabulos'ity.**—*adj.* **fab'ulous,** feigned, false: related in fable: celebrated in story: immense, amazing.—*adv.* **fab'ulously.**—*n.* **fab'ulousness.** [Fr. *fable* and L. *fābula—fāri,* to speak.]

fabliau, *fab'li-ō, n.* a metrical tale after the type of those, usually satirical in quality, produced in France in the 12th and 13th centuries:—*pl.* **fabliaux** (*fab'li-ōz*). [Fr.,—dim. of *fable.*]

fabric, *fab'rik, n.* workmanship: texture: anything framed by art and labour: a building: manufactured cloth: any system of connected parts.—*v.t.* (*Milt.*) to construct.—*n.* **fab'ricant,** a manufacturer.—*v.t.* **fab'ricate,** to put together by art and labour: to manufacture: to produce: to devise falsely.—*n.* **fabricā'tion,** construction: manufacture: that which is fabricated or invented: a story: a falsehood.—*adj.* **fab'ricātive.**—*n.* **fab'ricātor.** [L. *fābrica,* fabric—*fāber,* a worker in hard materials: partly through Fr. *fabrique.*]

faburden, *fa'bər-dən, n.* (*arch.*), harmony in thirds and sixths: an early kind of counterpoint: an undersong: a refrain. [Fr. *faux-bourdon—faux,* false, *bourdon,* bourdon.]

façade, *fā-säd', n.* the exterior front or face of a building: (*fig.*) the appearance presented to the world, esp. if showy and with little behind it. [Fr.,—*face,* after It. *facciata,* the front of a building—*faccia,* the face.]

face, *fās, n.* the front part of the head, including forehead, eyes, nose, mouth, cheeks, and chin:

the outside make or appearance: front or surface of anything: a flat surface of a solid geometrical figure, crystal, etc.: the striking surface of a golf-club, etc.: the edge of a cutting-tool, etc.: the front or upper surface, or that usually presented: the exposed surface in a cliff, mine, or quarry: a principal cleavage-plane: the dial of a watch, etc.: the printed surface of a playing card: (*print.*) a style of letter: special appearance or expression of the countenance: aspect, look, configuration: command of facial expression and bearing: boldness, effrontery: a grimace: presence: (*B.*) anger or favour.—*v.t.* to meet in the face or in front: to stand opposite to or looking towards: to confront: to stand up to: to brave: to resist: to put an additional face or surface on: to cover in front: to trim.—*v.i.* to direct or turn the face: to take or have a direction: (*obs.*) to show a face, esp. bold or false.—*ns.* **face'-ache,** neuralgia in the nerves of the face; **face'-card,** a playing-card bearing a face (king, queen, or knave); **face'-cloth,** a cloth laid over the face of a corpse or living person: a cloth used in washing the face.—*adj.* **faced,** having a face: having the outer surface dressed: with the front covered with another material.—*n.* **face'-guard,** a kind of mask to guard or protect the face.—*adj.* **face'less,** without a face.—*ns.* **face'-lifting,** an operation aiming at smoothing and firming the face; **face'-powder,** a cosmetic powder for the face; **fac'er,** one who puts on a false show: a bold-faced person: (*slang*) a severe blow on the face: an affront: anything that staggers one; **fac'ing,** a covering in front for ornament or protection.—**face down,** to abash by stern looks; **face out,** to carry off by bold looks; **face the music** (*U.S. slang*), to accept the unpleasant consequences at their worst: to brave a trying situation, hostile reception, etc.; **face to face,** opposite: in actual presence; **face value,** the value as stated on the face of a coin, etc.: nominal worth; **fly in the face of,** to set oneself directly against; **have two faces, or be two-faced,** to be disingenuous; **in the face of,** in defiance of, despite; **on the face of it,** on its own showing: palpably plain: at first glance, superficially; **pull a long face,** to look dismal; **put a good face on,** to assume a bold or contented bearing as regards; **right face! left face! right about face!** words of command, on which the soldiers turn to the side specified; **run one's face** (*U.S. slang*), to obtain things on credit by sheer impudence; **save one's face,** to avoid humiliation or appearance of climbing down; **set one's face against,** to oppose strenuously; **show (one's) face,** to appear; **to one's face,** in his presence, openly. [Fr. *face*—L. *faciēs,* form, face; perh. from *facĕre,* to make.]

facet, *fas'it, n.* a small surface, as of a crystal.—*v.t.* to cut a facet upon, or cover with facets.—*adj.* **fac'eted,** having or formed into facets. [Fr. *facette,* dim. of *face,* face.]

facetious, *fə-sē'shəs, adj.* witty, humorous, jocose: waggish: would-be funny: bawdy—(*obs.* or *arch.*) **facete** (*-sēt'*).—*n.pl.* **face'tiae** (*shi-ē*), witty or humorous sayings or writings: a bookseller's term for improper books—of all degrees of indecency.—*adv.* **facē'tiously.**—*n.* **facē'tiousness.** [L. *facētia—facētus,* merry, witty.]

facia. Same as **fascia.**

facial, *fā'shl, adj.* of or relating to the face.—*adv.* **fā'cially.—facial angle,** in craniometry, the angle formed by lines drawn from the middle of the forehead to the upper jaw above the incisor teeth and from the opening of the ear to the opening of the nose.

fāte, fär, ȧsk; mē, hər (her); mīne; mōte; mūte; mōōn; dhen (then)

facies, *fa'shi-ez*, *n.* general aspect. [L. *facies*, face.]

facile, *fas'il*, or *-il*, *adj.* (*obs.*) affable: easily persuaded: yielding: (*Scots law*) mentally weak, short of idiocy but so as to be easily persuaded to deeds to one's own prejudice: easy of accomplishment: easy: working with ease: fluent (usu. depreciatory).—*adv.* **fac'ilely.**—*n.* **fac'ileness.**—*v.t.* **facilitāte** (*fa-sil'*), to make easy or easier.—*ns.* **facilitā'tion**; **facil'ity**, ease in performance or action: fluency: easiness to be persuaded: pliancy: (*obs.*) affability: (*Scots law*) a condition of being facile: (esp. in *pl.* **facil'ities**) means or opportunities that render anything readily possible. [Fr.,—L. *facilis*, easy—*facĕre*, to do.]

facinorous, *fa-*, *fə-sin'ə-rəs*, *adj.* atrociously wicked.—Also (*Shak.*) **facinē'rious.**—*n.* **facin'orousness.** [L. *facinorōsus—facinus*, a crime—*facĕre*, to do.]

facsimile, *fak-sim'i-li*, *n.* an exact copy, as of handwriting, a coin, etc.: accurate reproduction (*pl.* **facsim'iles**).—*adj.* exactly corresponding.—*v.t.* to make a facsimile of, to reproduce.—*n.* **facsim'i-list.**—**facsimile telegraph**, the transmission of a still picture over a telegraph circuit and its reproduction. [L. *fac*, imper. of *facĕre*, to make, *simile*, neut. of *similis*, like.]

fact, *fakt*, *n.* (*arch.*) a deed, act, or anything done: anything that comes to pass: a truth: truth: reality, or a real state of things, as distinguished from a mere statement or belief: an assertion of fact: (*obs.*) a crime committed.—*adj.* **fact'ual**, pertaining to facts: actual.—*ns.* **factual'ity**; **fact'ualness**; **fact'um**, a thing done, a deed.—**as a matter of fact**, in reality; **in fact**, **in point of fact**, indeed; **the fact of the matter**, the plain truth about the subject in question. [L. *factum*, neut. pa.p. of *facĕre*, to do.]

faction, *fak'shən*, *n.* a company of persons associated or acting together, mostly used in a bad sense: a contentious party in a state or society: dissension.—*adj.* **fac'tional.**—*ns.* **fac'tionalism**; **fac'tion-ary**, a member of a faction; **fac'tionist.**—*adj.* **fac'tious**, turbulent: given to faction: proceeding from party spirit: seditious.—*adv.* **fac'tiously.**—*n.* **fac'tiousness.** [L. *factiō*, *-ōnis—facĕre*, to do.]

factitious, *fak-tish'əs*, *adj.* artificial: made: produced by artificial conditions.—*adv.* **facti'tiously.**—*n.* **facti'tiousness.**—*adjs.* **fac'titive**, causative; **fac'tive** (*obs.*), making. [L. *facticius*, *factitīvus—facĕre*, to make.]

factor, *fak'tər*, *n.* a doer or transactor of business for another: one who buys and sells goods for others, on commission: (*Scot.*) an agent managing heritable estates for another: (*math.*) one of two or more quantities, which, when multiplied together, result in the given quantity—e.g. 6 and 4 are factors of 24: an element in the composition of anything, or in bringing about a certain result: in heredity, a gene.—*ns.* **fac'torage**, the fees or commission of a factor.—*adj.* **factō'rial**, of or pertaining to a factor.—*n.* the product of all whole numbers from a given number down to one.—*v.t.* **fac'torise**, to resolve into factors: (*U.S.*), to warn not to pay or give up goods: to attach (the effects of a debtor in the hands of a third person).—*ns.* **fac'torship**; **fac'tory**, a manufactory: a trading settlement in another country.—**judicial factor**, a person appointed by the Court to manage the estate of a person under some incapacity. [L.,—*facĕre*, to do.]

factotum, *fak-tō'təm*, *n.* a person employed to do all kinds of work for another:—*pl.* **facto'tums.** [L.L.,—L. *fac*, imper. of *facĕre*, to do, *tōtum*, all.]

facture, *fak'tyər*, *n.* the act or the result of making, workmanship. [L. *factūra—facĕre*, to make.]

facula, *fak'ū-lä*, *n.* a spot brighter than the rest of the surface, sometimes seen on the sun's disk: (*pl.* **fac'ulae**, *-lē*). [L., *facula*, dim. of *fax*, torch.]

faculty, *fak'əl-ti*, *n.* facility or power to act: any particular ability or aptitude: an original power of the mind: any physical capability or function: personal quality or endowment: right, authority, or privilege to act: licence: a department of learning at a university, or the professors constituting it: the members of a profession: executive ability.—*adj.* **fac'ultātive**, optional: incidental: of or pertaining to a faculty.—**Court of Faculties**, a court established by Henry VIII., whereby authority is given to the Archbishop of Canterbury to grant dispensations and faculties. [Fr. *faculté*—L. *facultās*, *-ātis—facilis*, easy.]

facundity, *fa-kun'di-ti*, *n.* eloquence. [L. *fācunditās*, *-ātis.*]

fad, *fad*, *n.* a weak or transient hobby, crotchet, or craze: any unimportant belief or practice intemperately urged.—*n.* **fadd'iness.**—*adj.* **fadd'ish.**—*ns.* **fadd'ishness**; **fadd'ism**; **fadd'ist**, one who is a slave to some fad.—*adj.* **fadd'y.** [Ety. unknown.]

faddle, *fad'l*, *v.i.* (*prov.*) to trifle.—*n.* nonsense, trifling—usually in **fiddle-faddle.**

fade, *fād*, *v.i.* to lose strength, freshness, loudness, brightness, or colour gradually: to grow pale, dull, or faint: to die away: to disappear.—*v.t.* to cause to fade: to cause to change gradually in distinctness (as *fade out*, *fade in*).—*n.* a fading.—*adj.* (*arch.*) faded, weak: (*fād*; Fr.) insipid, dull.—*ns.* **fade'-away'**, a gradual disappearance; **fade'-out'**, a graded fading out; **fade'-in'**, in cinematography, gradual appearance and growth in distinctness.—*adv.* **fa'dedly.**—*adj.* **fade'less**, unfading: not liable to fade.—*adv.* **fade'lessly.**—*n.* and *adj.* **fād'ing.**—*adj.* **fā'dy**, wearing away. [O.Fr. *fader—fade*—L. *vapidum*, acc. to Gaston Paris.]

fadge, *faj*, *v.i.* to agree, hit it off: to succeed, turn out. [Ety. dub.; not conn. with O.E. *fēgan*, to join.]

fading, *fā'ding*, *n.* an old dance, probably Irish: (*Shak.*) the burden of a song (*with a fading*). [Origin unknown.]

faeces, *fē'sēz*, *n.pl.* sediment after infusion or distillation: dregs: excrement.—*adj.* **faecal** (*fē'kl*). [L., pl. of *faex*, *faecis*, dregs, grounds.]

faerie, **faery**, *fā'(ə-)ri*, *n.* (*arch.*) the world of fairies, fairyland: (*obs.*) a fairy. [A variant of **fairy**.]

fag, *fag*, *v.i.* to become weary or tired out: to work hard: to be a fag.—*v.t.* to weary: to use as a fag: (*pr.p.* **fagg'ing**; *pa.t.* and *pa.p.* **fagged**).—*n.* a schoolboy forced to do menial offices for another: a tiresome piece of work: drudgery: (*slang*) an inferior cigarette (for fag-end): hence, any cigarette.—*n.* **fag'-end'**, the end of a web of cloth that hangs loose: the untwisted end of a rope: the refuse or meaner part of a thing: the stump of a cigar or cigarette; **fagg'ery**, drudgery: fagging.—*n.* and *adj.* **fagg'ing.**—**to fag out**, to field, as a fag, in cricket. [Ety. dub.; perh. a corr. of **flag**, to droop, which see.]

faggot, **fagot**, *fag'ət*, *n.* a bundle of sticks for fuel, fascines, etc.: a stick: anything like a faggot: a bundle of pieces of iron or steel cut off into suitable lengths for welding: a soldier numbered on the muster-roll, but not really existing: a voter who has obtained his vote expressly for party purposes, on a spurious or sham qualification: a roll of internal organs, etc. of a pig mixed with bread and savoury herbs.—*adj.* got up for a purpose, as in *faggot vote*.—*v.t.* to tie together.—*ns.* **fagg'oting**, **fag'oting**, a kind of embroidery in which some of the cross-threads are drawn together in the middle.—**to burn one's faggot**, to recant a heresy. [Fr. *fagot*, a bundle of sticks, perh. from L. *fax*, a torch.]

fagotto, *fag-ot'ō*, *n.* a bassoon.—*n.* **fagott'ist**, one who plays on the bassoon. [It.]

Fagus, *fā'gəs*, *n.* the beech genus of trees, giving name to the fam. **Fagā'ceae.**—*adj.* **fagā'ceous.** [L. *fāgus*, beech; cf. Gr. *phēgos*, oak, O.E. *bóc*, beech.]

fah. See **fa**.

fahlband, *fäl'bänt*, *n.* in crystalline rocks, a pale band rich in metals; **fahl'erz** (*-erts*), tetrahedrite: also tennantite; **fahl'ore** (*-ōr*), tetrahedrite or tennantite. [Ger. *fahl*, dun-coloured, *band*, band, *erz*, ore, and Eng. **ore**.]

Fahrenheit, *fä'rən-hit*, or *far'ən-īt*, *adj.*, of a thermometer or thermometer scale, having the freezing-point of water marked at 32, and the boiling-point at 212 degrees (to convert F° into C°, subtract 32, and take ⅝ of remainder). [Named from the inventor, Gabriel D. *Fahrenheit* (1686-1736).]

faible, *feb'l*, *n.* a penchant, weakness, or foible (of which it is a variant): the part of a foil blade between the middle and the point—the weak part. [Fr., weak.]

faience, *fä-yän°s*, *n.* glazed coloured earthenware. [Fr.; prob. from *Faenza* in Italy.]

faik, *fāk*, *v.i.* and *v.t.* (*Scot.*) to abate: to excuse. [Fr., weak.]

fail, *fāl*, *n.* a turf, sod.—*n.* **fail'-dike** (*Scot.*), a turf-wall. [Perh. Gael. *fàl*, a sod.]

fail, *fāl*, *v.i.* to fall short or be wanting (with *in*): to fall away: to decay: to die: to prove deficient under trial, examination, pressure, etc.: to miss: to be disappointed or baffled: to become insolvent or bankrupt.—*v.t.* to be wanting to: not to be sufficient for: to leave undone, omit: to disappoint or desert: (*Spens.*) to deceive.—*n.* (*Shak.*) failure.—*adj.* **failed,** that has failed: decayed, worn out: bankrupt.—*n.* **fail'ing,** a fault, weakness: a foible: failure.—*adj.* that fails.—*prep.* in default of.—*n.* **fail'ure,** a falling short, or cessation: omission: decay: bankruptcy.—**fail of,** to come short of accomplishing any purpose; **without fail,** for certain. [O.Fr. *faillir*—L. *fallĕre*, to deceive; cf. Du. *feilen*, Ger. *fehlen*, O.N. *feila*.]

fain, *fān*, *adj.* glad or joyful: eager (with *to*): content for want of better: compelled: (*Spens.*) wont.—*v.t.* (*Spens.*) to delight in: (*Spens.*) to desire.—*adv.* gladly.—*adv.* **fain'ly,** gladly.—*n.* **fain'ness,** eagerness. [O.E. *fægen,* joyful: cf. O.N. *feginn,* glad.]

fain, faine, *fān*, *v.t.* (*Spens.*). Same as **feign.**

fainéant, *fen'ā-än°*, *adj.* and *n.* do-nothing, applied esp. to the later Merovingian kings of France, mere puppets, whose mayors of the palace governed the country.—*ns.* **fai'néance** (-*än°s*), **fai'neancy** (-*ən-si*), **fainéantise** (-*tēz'*). [Fr., as if—*faire*, to do, *néant*, nothing; really—O.Fr. *faignant*, pr.p. of *faindre*, to skulk.]

faint, *fānt*, *adj.* wanting in strength: dim: lacking distinctness: not bright or forcible: weak in spirit: lacking courage: done in a feeble way: inclined to faint: sickly-smelling, oppressive.—*v.i.* to become feeble or weak: to lose strength, colour, etc.: to swoon: to fade or decay: to vanish: to lose courage or spirit.—*v.t.* (*rare*) to render faint.—*n.* a swoon.—*adj.* **faint'ed** (*Milt.*), exhausted.—*adjs.* **faint'-heart, faint'-heart'ed,** (*obs.*) spiritless: timorous.—*adv.* **faint'-heart'edly.** —*n.* **faint'-heart'edness.**—*n.* and *adj.* **faint'ing.** —*adj.* **faint'ish,** slightly faint.—*n.* **faint'ishness.** —*adv.* **faint'ly.**—*n.* **faint'ness,** want of strength: feebleness of colour, light, etc.: dejection.—*n.pl.* **faints,** impure spirit that comes over at the beginning and end of distillation (also **feints**).—*adj.* **faint'y,** faintish. [O.Fr. *feint*, feigned—L. *fingĕre*, to feign.]

fair, *fār*, *adj.* bright: clear: clean: free from blemish: pure: pleasing to the eye: beautiful: of a light hue: free from rain, fine, dry: unobstructed: open: smoothly curving: prosperous: impartial: just: equitable: good, pleasing: plausible: specious: reasonable: likely: favourable: pretty good: passable: (*dial.*) out-and-out, veritable: also (*arch.*) a general expression of commendation or courtesy (as *fair sir*).—*n.* that which is fair; (*arch.*) a woman: (*Shak.*) beauty.—*v.t.* to make fair.—*v.i.* to clear up, as the weather from rain.—*adv.* in a fair manner (in all senses): civilly: suitably: evenly: (*dial.* and *U.S.*) full, square, directly: gently: favourably: (*dial.*) quite. —*adjs.* **fair'-and-square',** honest—also used adverbially; **fair'-bod'ing,** (*Shak.*) auspicious.—*ns.* **fair'-cop'y,** a clean copy after correction; **fair'-deal'ing.**—*adj.* **fair'-faced,** with a light complexion: beautiful: specious.—*n.* **fair'-field,** just conditions.—*adj.* **fair'-haired,** having light-coloured hair.—*n.* **fair'ing,** adjustment or testing of curves in shipbuilding: means of reducing head-resistance in an aeroplane.—*adj.* **fair'ish,** somewhat fair: pretty well: pretty drunk.—*adv.* **fair'ly,** (*arch.*) beautifully: neatly: justly: reason-

ably: plainly: (*obs.*) gently: fully, quite: tolerably. —*adj.* **fair'-mind'ed,** judging fairly.—*ns.* **fair'-ness; fair'-play,** honest dealing: justice.—*adjs.* **fair'-seem'ing,** appearing fair; **fair'-spok'en,** bland and civil in language and address.—*ns.* **fair'-trade',** euphemism for smuggling: a mild form of the protective system, in which the basis of economic policy is supposed to be reciprocity or free-trade only with such nations as grant similar privileges—also used adverbially; **fair'way,** the navigable channel or usual course of vessels in a river, etc.: (*golf*) the smooth turf between tee and putting-green, distinguished from the uncut rough and from hazards.—*adj.* **fair'-weath'er,** suitable only for fair weather or favourable circumstances.—**bid fair** (see **bid**); **fair (be)fall,** (*arch.*) good luck to; **in a fair way to,** likely to succeed in: **keep fair with,** to keep on amicable terms with; **speak fair** (see **speak**); **stand fair with,** to be in the good graces of; **the fair, the fair sex,** the female sex. [O.E. *fæger.*]

fair, *fār*, *n.* a great periodical market for one kind of merchandise, or for the general sales and purchases of a district, with or without amusements: often reduced to a collection of shows, swing-boats and similar amusements: a charity bazaar or the like.—*ns.* **fair'day**; **fair'-ground**; **fair'ing,** a present given at or from a fair: any complimentary gift.—**a day after the fair,** too late; **get one's fairing** (*Scot.*), to get one's deserts. [O.Fr. *feire*—L. *fēria,* holiday.]

fairy, *fār'i*, *n.* an imaginary being, generally of diminutive and graceful human form, capable of kindly or unkindly acts towards man: fairy-folk collectively: fairyland: an enchantress: a creature of overpowering charm.—*adj.* like a fairy, fanciful, whimsical, delicate.—*adv.* **fair'ily.**—*n.pl.* **fair'y-beads,** joints of the stems of fossil crinoids.—*ns.* **fair'y-butt'er,** a name applied in northern England to certain gelatinous fungi; **fai'ry-cy'cle,** a child's bicycle; **fair'ydom;** **fair'y-god'mother,** a benefactress such as Cinderella had; **fair'yhood;** **fair'yism;** **fair'yland,** the country of the fairies.—*adj.* and *adv.* **fair'ylike,** like fairies, or like something in fairyland: very delicate and charming. —*n.* **fair'y-mon'ey,** money given by fairies, which quickly changes into withered leaves, slate, stones, etc.: money that comes unsought.—*ns.* **fair'y-ring,** a ring of darker-coloured grass due to outward spread of a fungus (as the fairy-ring champignon, *Marasmius oreades*), attributed to the dancing of fairies; **fair'y-stone',** a fossil sea-urchin: a concretion; **fair'y-tale,** a story about fairies or other supernatural beings: a folk-tale: a romantic tale: an incredible tale: euphemistically, a lie: a marvel. [O.Fr. *faerie,* enchantment—*fae* (mod. *fée*); see **faerie, fay.**]

faith, *fāth*, *n.* trust or confidence: belief in the statement of another: belief in the truth of revealed religion: confidence and trust in God: the living reception of religious belief: that which is believed: any system of religious belief, esp. the religion one considers true: fidelity to promises: honesty: word or honour pledged: faithfulness.—*interj.* by my faith: indeed.—*v.t.* (*fādh; Shak.*) to believe.— *adj.* **faith'ful,** full of faith, believing: firm in adherence to promises, duty, friendship, love, etc.: loyal: constant: conformable to truth: worthy of belief: true: exact.—*adv.* **faith'fully,** with confidence: with fidelity: with sincerity: with scrupulous exactitude: (*coll.*) solemnly: a meaningless word used in concluding a letter.—*ns.* **faith'-fulness; faith'-heal'er; faith'-heal'ing,** or **-cure,** a system of belief based on James v. 15, that sickness may be cured without medical advice or appliances, if the prayer of Christians be accompanied in the sufferer by true faith: cure by suggestion.—*adj.* **faith'less,** without faith or belief: not believing, esp. in God or Christianity: not adhering to promises, duty, etc.: inconstant: adulterous: untrustworthy: delusive.—*adv.* **faith'-lessly.**—*ns.* **faith'lessness; faith'worthiness,** trustworthiness.—*adj.* **faith'worthy,** worthy of faith or belief.—**bad faith,** treachery; **Father of**

the **faithful,** Abraham: the caliph; **in good faith,** with sincerity; **the Faithful,** believers, esp. Mohammedans. [M.E. *feith, feyth*—O.Fr. *feid*—L. *fidēs*—*fīdĕre,* to trust.]

faitor, *fā′tər, n.* an impostor.—Often **fai′tour.** [O.Fr. *faitor*—L. *factor, -ōris,* doer.]

faix, *fāks, interj.* (*dial.*) faith. [Prob. short for *faykins*; see **fay** (2).]

fakes, faikes, *fāks, n.pl.* thin-bedded shaly or micaceous sandstone or sandy shale.

fake, *fāk, v.t.* to fold, coil.—*n.* a coil or rope, etc. [Origin obscure.]

fake, *fāk, v.t.* to rob or attack: to filch: to doctor, cook, or counterfeit.—*n.* a swindle, dodge, sham: a faked article—also **fake′ment.**—*n.* **fak′er.** [Prob. the earlier *feak, feague,* Ger. *fegen,* to furbish up.]

fakir, *fā-kēr′,* or *fā′kər, n.* a religious (esp. Mohammedan) mendicant, ascetic, or wonder-worker in India, etc.—*n.* **fakir′ism.** [Ar. *faqīr,* a poor man.]

fa-la, *fä-lä, n.* an old kind of madrigal.—**fa la (la,** etc.), syllables used as a refrain.

falange, *fä-läng′hhä, n.* a Spanish fascist group.—*ns.* **falangism** (*fə-lan′jizm*); **falan′gist.** [Sp.,—Gr. *phalanx,* phalanx.]

falbala, *fal′bə-lä, n.* a trimming or flounce: a furbelow. [Ety. dub.; cf. **furbelow.**]

falcade, *fal′kād′, n.* the motion of a horse when he throws himself on his haunches in a very quick curvet. [Fr.,—L. *falcāta* (fem.) bent.]

falcate, -d, *fal′kāt, -id, adj.* bent like a sickle.—*ns.* **falcā′tion; fal′cŭla,** a falcate claw.—*adjs.* **falciform** (*fal′si-form*), sickle-shaped; **fal′cŭlate.** [L. *falx, falcis,* a sickle.]

falchion, *fawl′(t)shən, n.* a short, broad sword, bent somewhat like a sickle. [O.Fr. *fauchon,* through L.L., from L. *falx,* a sickle.]

falcon, *faw′kən, fawl′kən, n.* a bird of prey of a kind trained to the pursuit of game: by falconers confined to the female: any of the long-winged birds of prey of the genus Falco or its kindred: a kind of cannon.—*ns.* **fal′coner,** one who sports with, or who breeds and trains, falcons or hawks for taking wild-fowl; **fal′conet,** a small field-gun in use till the 16th century.—*adj.* **fal′con-eyed,** keen-eyed.—*ns.* **fal′con-gen′til, -gen′tle,** the female of the peregrine falcon.—*adj.* **fal′conine.**—*n.* **fal′conry,** the art or practice of training, or hunting with, falcons. [O.Fr. *faucon*—L.L. *falcō, -ōnis.*]

faldage, *fawld′ij, fald′ij, n.* the right of the lord of a manor of folding his tenant's sheep in his own fields for the sake of the manure: a fee paid in commutation therefor. [Law L. *faldāgium*—O.E. *fald,* fold.]

falderal, *fal′dər-al′, n.* a meaningless refrain in songs: any kind of flimsy trifle—also **fol′derol** (*fol′dər-ol′*) and **fal de rol.**—**falderal it,** to sing unmeaning sounds.

faldetta, *fäl-det′ä, n.* a Maltese woman's combined hood and cape. [It.]

faldstool, *fawld′stōōl, n.* a folding or camp stool: a coronation stool: a bishop's armless seat: a small desk in churches in England, at which the litany is to be sung or said.—*n.* **fald′istory,** a bishop's seat within the chancel. [L.L. *faldistolium, faldistorium*—O.H.G. *faldstuol—faldan* (Ger. *falten*), to fold, *stuol* (Ger. *stuhl*), stool.]

Falernian, *fa-lər′ni-ən, adj.* pertaining to a district (*Falernus ager*) in Campania, famous of old for its wine.—*n.* **faler′no,** a modern sweet white wine, produced in Campania.

fall, *fawl, v.i.* to descend, esp. to descend freely and involuntarily by force of gravity: to drop: to drop prostrate: to throw oneself down: to be dropped in birth: to collapse: to become lower literally or figuratively (in position, degree, intensity, value, pitch, etc.): to die away: to subside: to abate: to ebb: to decline: to sink: (of the face) to relax into an expression of dismay: to flow downwards: to slope or incline down: to hang, dangle, or trail down: to be cast or shed: to drop dead or as if dead, esp. in fight: to be overthrown: to come to

ruin: to lose power, station, virtue or repute: to be degraded: to be taken or captured: to become a victim: to yield to temptation: to pass into any state or action, to become, to begin to be (as *fall asleep, fall in love, fall a-weeping*): to rush: to become involved: to betake oneself: to come to be: to befall: to come about: to come by chance or as if by chance: to come in due course: to occur: to chance, light: to issue: to come forth: to appertain: to be apportioned, assigned: to come as one's share, lot, duty, etc.: to take position or arrangement: to find place: to be disposed: to impinge: to lapse: to terminate: to revert.—*v.t.* to cause to fall: to let fall: (*obs.; Burns*) to get (as what befalls one): (*pr.p.* **fall′ing**; *pa.t.* **fell**; *pa.p.* **fallen,** *faw′ln*).—*n.* the act, manner, occasion, or time of falling or of felling: descent by gravity, a dropping down: that which falls: as much as comes down at one time: onset: overthrow: death: descent from a better to a worse position: slope or declivity: descent of water: a cascade: length of drop, amount of descent: decrease in value: a sinking of the voice: a cadence: the time when the leaves fall, autumn: a bout of wrestling: the passing of a city or stronghold into the enemy's hands: a lapse into sin, esp. that of Adam and Eve —'the Fall (of Man)': a falling-band, a hanging fringe, flap, or ornament: fortune: lot: a hoisting rope.—*n.* **fall′-cloud,** stratus.—*adj.* **fall′en,** having fallen: killed, esp. in battle: overthrown: seduced: in a degraded state, ruined.—*ns.* **fall′en-star,** a gelatinous mass of a blue-green alga (Nostoc, etc.) once popularly thought of meteoric origin; **fall′ing; fall′ing-band,** a 17th century collar turned down on the shoulders; **fall′ing-off,** decline; **fall′ing-sick′ness,** epilepsy; **fall′ing-star,** a meteor; **fall′ing-stone,** a portion of an exploded meteor; **fall′trank** (*fäl′tränk;* Ger. *fall-drink*), a medicine compounded of aromatic and astringent Swiss plants, of repute for accidents; **fall′-trap,** a trap that operates by a fall.—**fall across,** to meet by chance; **fall among,** to find oneself in the midst of; **fall away,** to decline gradually: to languish: to grow lean: to revolt or apostatise; **fall back,** to retreat, give way; **fall back, fall edge,** no matter what may happen; **fall back upon,** to have recourse to as an expedient or resource in reserve; **fall behind,** to lag: to be outstripped: to get in arrear; **fall flat,** to fail of effect; **fall for** (*U.S.*), to become enamoured of: to be taken in by; **fall foul** (see **foul**); **fall in,** (*mil.*) to (cause to) take places in ranks: to become hollowed: to revert; **fall in with,** to concur or agree with: to comply with: to meet by chance; **fall off,** to become detached and drop: to deteriorate: to die away, to perish: to revolt or apostatise: to draw back; **fall on,** to begin eagerly: to make an attack: to meet; **fall on one's feet,** to come well out of a difficulty, to gain any unexpected good fortune; **fall out,** to quarrel: to happen or befall: (*mil.*) to (cause to) quit ranks; **fall over,** (*Shak.*) to go over to the enemy: (*Scot.*) to go to sleep; **fall short,** to turn out to be short or insufficient: to become used up: to fail to attain or reach what is aimed at (with *of*); **fall through,** to fail, come to nothing; **fall to,** to begin hastily and eagerly: to apply oneself to: to begin to eat; **fall upon,** to attack: to rush against: to devolve upon: to chance upon; **try a fall,** to take a bout at wrestling. [O.E. *fallan* (W.S. *feallen*); Ger. *fallen;* prob. conn. with L. *fallĕre,* to deceive.]

fall, *fawl, n.* a trap. [O.E. *fealle—feallan,* to fall.]

fall, *fawl, n.* the cry given when a whale is sighted, or harpooned: the chase of a whale.—**loose fall,** the losing of a whale. [Perh. from the north-eastern Scottish pronunciation of **whale.**]

fallacy, *fal′ə-si, n.* something fallacious: deceptive appearance: an apparently genuine but really illogical argument: (*obs.*) deception, deceitfulness: fallaciousness: (*coll.*) a wrong but prevalent notion.—*adj.* **fallacious** (*fə-lā′shəs*), of the nature of fallacy: deceptive: misleading: not well founded: causing disappointment: delusive.—*adv.* **fallā′ciously.**—*n.* **fallā′ciousness.** [L. *fallācia—fallāx,* deceptive—*fallĕre,* to deceive.]

fallal, *fal-al'*, *n.* a streamer of ribbon : any trifling ornament.—*adj.* foppish, trifling.—*n.* **fallal'ery**.—*adv.* **fallal'ishly**.

fallible, *fal'i-bl*, *adj.* liable to error or mistake.—*n.* **fallibil'ity**, liability to err.—*adv.* **fall'ibly**. [L.L. *fallibilis,—fallĕre,* to deceive.]

Fallopian, *fə-lō'pi-ən*, *adj.* relating to the Italian anatomist Gabriele *Fallopio* (1523-62).—**Fallopian tubes**, two tubes or ducts through which the ova pass from the ovary to the uterus, perhaps discovered by him.

fallow, *fal'ō*, *adj.* left untilled or unsowed for a time.—*n.* land that has lain a year or more untilled or unsown after having been ploughed.—*v.t.* to plough without seeding.—*ns.* **fall'ow-chat**, **fall'ow-finch**, the wheatear; **fall'owness**.—**green fallow**, fallow where land is cleaned by a green crop, as turnips. [O.E. *fealgian,* to fallow; *fealh,* fallow land.]

fallow, *fal'ō*, *adj.* brownish-yellow.—*n.* **fall'ow-deer**, a yellowish-brown deer smaller than the red-deer, with broad flat antlers. [O.E. *falu* (*fealu*); cf. Ger. *fahl*, O.N. *fölr*.]

false, *fawls*, *adj.* wrong : erroneous : deceptive or deceiving : untruthful : unfaithful : untrue : not genuine or real, counterfeit : improperly so called : artificial, as opposed to natural, of teeth, etc. : incorrect, not according to rule : out of tune.—*adv.* incorrectly : untruly : dishonestly : faithlessly.—*n.* (*Spens.; Shak.*) falsehood : untruth.—*v t.* (*Spens.*) to deceive : (*Spens.*) to feign : (*Spens.*) to be false to : to falsify.—*n.* **false'-acā'cia**, Robinia.—*adj.* **false-bedd'ed**.—*n.* **false-bedd'ing**, (*geol.*) irregular lamination running obliquely to the general stratification, due to deposition in banks by varying currents.—*v.i.* **false-card'**, to play a false card.—*n.* **false'-face**, a mask.—*adjs.* **false'-faced**, (*Shak.*) hypocritical; **false'-heart'ed**, treacherous, deceitful.—*n.* **false'hood**, state or quality of being false : want of truth : want of honesty : deceitfulness : false appearance : an untrue statement : lying : a lie.—*adv.* **false'ly**.—*ns.* **false'ness**; **fals'er**, (*obs.*) a falsifier, counterfeiter : (*Spens.*) a deceiver, a liar.—*adjs.* **fals'ish**, somewhat false.—*ns.* **fals'ism**, a self-evident falsity; **fals'ity**, quality of being false : a false assertion.—**false alarm**, a warning without danger; **false bottom**, a partition cutting off a space between it and the true bottom; **false card**, the card played to deceive; **false conception**, a uterine growth consisting of some degenerate mass instead of a foetus; **false dawn**, deceptive appearance simulating dawn; **false gallop**, (*arch.*) a canter; **false imprisonment**, illegal detention by force or influence; **false leg**, a pro-leg; **false quantity**, pronunciation or use of a long vowel as short or short as long; **false relation**, (*mus.*) occurrence in different parts together or in succession of a tone and a chromatic derivative; **false rib**, one that does not reach the breastbone; **false shame**, shame for that which is not shameful; **play one false**, to act falsely or treacherously to a person; **put in a false position**, to bring any one into a position in which he must be misunderstood. [O.Fr., *fals* (mod. *faux*)—L. *falsus,* pa.p. of *fallĕre,* to deceive.]

falsetto, *fawl-set'ō*, *n.* a forced voice of a range or register above the natural, the head voice : one who uses such a voice : false or strained sentiment.—*adj.* and *adv.* in falsetto. [It. *falsetto,* dim. of *falso,* false.]

falsidical, *fawl-sid'i-kəl*, *adj.* conveying a meaning that is false. [L. *falsus,* and *dīcĕre,* to say.]

falsify, *fawls'i-fī*, *v.t.* to forge or counterfeit : to tamper with : to misrepresent : to prove or declare to be false : to be false to : to feign.—*v.i.* (*obs.*) to lie : (*pr.p.* **fals'ifying**; *pa.t.* and *pa.p.* **fals'ified**).—*adj.* **fals'ifiable**.—*ns.* **falsificā'tion**; **fals'ifier**. [Fr. *falsifier*—L.L. *falsificāre*—L. *falsus,* false, *facĕre,* to make.]

Falstaffian, *fawl-stäf'i-ən*, *adj.* like or pertaining to Shakespeare's *Falstaff*—corpulent, jovial, humorous, dissolute, and irrepressibly impudent.

falter, *fawl'tər*, *v.i.* to stumble : to go unsteadily : to hesitate in speech as if taken aback : to flinch :

to waver : to flag : to fail.—*v.t.* to utter falteringly.—*n.* unsteadiness.—*n.* and *adj.* **fal'tering**.—*adv.* **fal'teringly**. [Prob. a freq. of M.E. *falden,* to fold; conn. with *fault* (in which the *l* is late) is not possible.]

falx, *falks*, *n.* a sickle-shaped part or process, as of the dura mater : (*pl.* **falces**, *fal'sēz*). [L., a sickle.]

famble, *fam'bl*, *n.* (*slang*) the hand—also **fam**.—*v.t.* to feel or handle. [Der. obscure; perh. from the obs. verb *famble,* in its probably original sense, to grope, fumble.]

fame, *fām*, *n.* public report or rumour : renown or celebrity, chiefly in a good sense.—*v.t.* to report : to make famous.—*n.* **fā'ma** (L. *fä'mä*), report, rumour, fame.—*adjs.* **famed**, renowned; **fame'less**, without renown.—**fama clamo'sa** (*Scot.*), any notorious rumour ascribing immoral conduct to a minister or office-bearer in a church; **house of ill fame**, a brothel. [Fr.,—L. *fāma,* from *fārī,* to speak; cf. Gr. *phēmē,* from *phanai,* to say.]

familiar, *fə-mil'yər*, *adj.* well acquainted or intimate : in the manner of an intimate : free : unceremonious : having a thorough knowledge : well known or understood : private, domestic : common, plain.—*n.* one well or long acquainted : a spirit or demon supposed to attend a person at call : a member of a pope's or bishop's household : the officer of the Inquisition who arrested the suspected.—*v.t.* **famil'iarise**, to make thoroughly acquainted : to accustom : to make easy by practice or study.—*n.* **familiarity** (*-i-ar'i-ti*), intimate acquaintanceship : freedom from constraint : any unusual or unwarrantable freedom in act or speech toward another, act of licence—usu. in *pl.*—*adv.* **famil'iarly**. [O.Fr. *familier*—L. *familiāris,* from *familia,* a family.]

family, *fam'i-li*, *n.* the household, or all those who live in one house (as parents, children, servants) : parents and their children : the children alone : the descendants of one common progenitor : race : honourable or noble descent : a group of animals, plants, languages, etc. more comprehensive than a genus.—*adjs.* **famil'ial** (*fəm-*), characteristic of a family; **famil'iar** (see above).—*ns.* **familism** (*fam'*), the family feeling : the principles of the Familists; **Fam'ilist**, one of the 16th-cent. mystical sect known as the Family of Love, which based religion upon love independently of faith.—**family baker, butcher, etc.**, one who supplies families, not merely institutions; **family Bible**, a large Bible for family worship, with a page for recording family events; **family circle**, the members of the family taken collectively : one of the galleries in a theatre; **family coach**, a large carriage able to carry a whole family : a parlour game; **family man**, a man with a family : a domesticated man; **family name**, surname; **family tree**, a diagram showing the branching of a family; **in a family way**, in a familiar informal manner; **in the family way**, pregnant; **official family**, (*U.S.*) the cabinet. [L. *familia—famulus,* a servant.]

famine, *fam'in*, *n.* extreme general scarcity of food : scarcity of anything : hunger : starvation. [Fr.,—L. *famēs,* hunger.]

famish, *fam'ish*, *v.t.* to starve.—*v.i.* to die of or suffer extreme hunger or thirst.—*n.* **fam'ishment**, starvation. [Obs. *fame,* to starve—L. *famēs,* hunger.]

famous, *fā'məs*, *adj.* renowned : noted : (*slang*) excellent.—*v.t.* to make famous.—*adv.* **fā'mously**.—*n.* **fā'mousness**. [O.Fr.,—L. *fāmōsus—fāma,* fame.]

famulus, *fam'ū-ləs*, *n.* a private secretary or factotum : an attendant, esp. on a magician or scholar. [L., a servant.]

fan, *fan*, *n.* a basket for winnowing corn by throwing it in the wind : any instrument for winnowing : a broad, flat instrument esp. used by ladies to cool themselves—typically in the shape of a sector of a circle : a wing : any fan-shaped structure, as a deposit of alluvium : a small sail to keep a windmill to the wind : a whale's tail-fluke : a propeller-screw or propeller-blade : a rotating ventilating or blowing apparatus : the agitation of the air caused by a fan.—*v.t.* to winnow : to move by a fan or the like : to direct a current of air upon : to cool or to kindle with, or as with, a fan.—*v.i.* to move like a fan : to spread out like a fan : (*pr.p.* **fann'ing** ; *pa.t.* and *pa.p.* **fanned**).— *ns.* **fan'light**, a window resembling in form an open fan ; **fann'er**, a fanning apparatus for winnowing, ventilation, etc. ; **fan'-palm**, any palm with palmate leaves, esp. palmetto.—*adj.* **fan'-shaped**, forming a sector of a circle.—*ns.* **fan'tail**, a variety of domestic pigeon with tail feathers spread out like a fan ; **fan'-trāc'ery, -vault'ing**, (*archit.*) tracery rising from a capital or a corbel, and diverging like the folds of a fan over the surface of a vault ; **fan'-wheel**, a wheel with fans on its rim for producing a current of air. [O.E. *fann*, from L. *vannus*, a basket for winnowing ; cf. Fr. *van*.]

fan, *fan*, *n.* a fanatic : now (from *U.S.* use) a devotee or enthusiastic follower of some sport or hobby, or public favourite.—*n.* **fan'-mail**, letters from devotees. [From **fanatic**.]

fanal, *fā'nəl*, *n.* (*arch.*) a lighthouse, a beacon. [Fr.,—Gr. *phanos*, a lantern, *phainein*, to show.]

Fanariot. Same as **Phanariot.**

fanatic, *fə-nat'ik* (by some *fan'ə-tik*), *adj.* extravagantly or unreasonably zealous, esp. in religion : excessively enthusiastic.—*n.* a person frantically or excessively enthusiastic, esp. on religious subjects.—*adj.* **fanat'ical**, fanatic : (*Shak.*) extravagant.—*adv.* **fanat'ically.**—*v.t.* **fanat'icise** (*-i-sīz*), to make fanatical.—*v.i.* to act as a fanatic.— *n.* **fanat'icism** (*-sizm*), wild and excessive religious or other enthusiasm. [L. *fānāticus*, belonging to a temple, inspired by a god, *fānum*, a temple.]

fan-cricket. Same as **fen-cricket.**

fancy, *fan'si*, *n.* that faculty of the mind by which it recalls, represents, or makes to appear past images or impressions—imagination, esp. of a lower, passive, or more trivial kind : an image or representation thus formed in the mind : an unreasonable lightly-formed or capricious opinion : a whim : a fantasia : capricious inclination or liking : taste : (*Shak.*) love.—*adj.* pleasing to, or guided by, or originating in fancy or caprice : fantastic : capriciously departing from the ordinary, the simple, or the plain : ornate : particoloured.—*v.t.* to portray in the mind : to imagine : to be inclined to believe : to have a fancy or liking for : to be pleased with : to breed or cultivate, with a view to development of conventionally accepted points : (*pr.p.* **fan'cying** ; *pa.t.* and *pa.p.* **fan'cied**).—*adj.* **fan'cied**, formed or conceived by the fancy : imagined : favoured.—*n.* **fan'cier**, one who fancies : one who has a liking for anything and is supposed to be a judge of it : a breeder for points.—*adj.* **fan'ciful**, guided or created by fancy : imaginative : whimsical : wild : unreal.— *adv.* **fan'cifully.**—*n.* **fan'cifulness.**—*adj.* **fan'ciless**, destitute of fancy.—*ns.* **fan'cy-ball'**, a ball at which fancy-dresses in various characters are worn ; **fan'cy-bread**, bread other than plain bread ; **fan'cy-dress'**, dress arranged according to the wearer's fancy, to represent some character ; **fan'cy-fair'**, a special sale of fancy articles for some charitable purpose.—*adj.* **fan'cy-free'**, (*Shak.*) free from the power of love.—*n.pl.* **fan'cy-goods'**, fabrics of variegated rather than simple pattern, applied generally to articles of show and ornament.—*ns.* **fan'cy-man**, a prostitute's attendant or bully ; **fan'cy-monger**, (*Shak.*) one who concerns himself with love.—*adj.* **fan'cy-sick** (*Shak.*), love-sick.—*ns.* **fan'cy-stitch'**, a more intricate and decorative stitch than *plain-stitch* ; **fan'cy-wo'man**, mistress : prostitute ; **fan'cy-work**, ornamental needlework.—the **fancy**, sporting characters generally, esp. pugilists : pugilism. [Contracted from **fantasy**.]

fand, *fānd* (*Scot.*), *pa.t.* of **find.**

fand, *fand*, **fond**, *fond*, *v.i.* (*obs.*) to try, attempt : to proceed :—*pa.t.* and *pa.p* **fanded, fonded,** or (*Spens.*) **fond.** [O.E. *fandian.*]

fandango, *fan-dang'gō*, *n.* an old Spanish dance

for two or its music in $\frac{3}{4}$ time, with castanets : a gathering for dancing, a ball. [Sp.]

fane, *fān*, *n.* (*obs.*) a flag : a weathercock. [O.E. *fana*, flag ; cf. Ger. *fahne* ; cf. **vane** and L. *pannus*, a cloth.]

fane, *fān*, *n.* a temple. [L. *fānum.*]

fanfare, *fan'fār*, *fān°-fār°*, *n.* a flourish of trumpets or bugles : an elaborate style of bookbinding.— *ns.* **fanfarade** (*fan-fər-ād'*), a fanfare ; **fan'faron**, one who uses bravado : a blusterer, braggart ; **fanfarō'na** (*Scott*; Sp. *fanfarrona*, trumpery) a gold chain ; **fanfaronade'**, vain boasting : bluster : ostentation.—*v.i.* to bluster. [Fr., perh. from the sound.]

fang, *fang*, *n.* the tooth of a ravenous beast : a claw or talon : the venom-tooth of a serpent : the embedded part of a tooth, etc. : a tang : a prong : (*Shak.*) a grip, catch : (*Scot.*) grip or power of suction in a pump.—*v.t.* (*obs.*; *Shak.* **phang**) to seize upon, catch.—*adjs.* **fanged**, having fangs, clutches, or anything resembling them ; **fang'less.** [O.E. *fang*, from the same root as *fōn*, to seize.]

fangle, *fang'gl*, *n.* (*Milt.* ; *Bunyan*) fancy.—*v.t.* (*Milt.*) to fabricate, trick out.—*adj.* **fang'led**, (*Shak.*) foppish. [Mistaken back-formation from **newfangle**(d).)

fanion, *fan'yən*, *n.* a small flag, esp. for surveying. —*n.* **fan'on**, a cloth for handling holy vessels or offertory bread : a maniple : an oreale. [O.Fr. *fanion, fanon*—L.L. *fanō, -ōnis*, banner, napkin— O.H.G. *fano* ; cf. **fane, vane.**]

fank, *fangk*, *n.* a coil : a noose : a tangle.—*v.t.* **fank'le**, to entangle. [Scot. ; perh. conn. with **fang.**]

fank, *fangk*, *n.* (*Scot.*) a sheep-fold. [Gael. *fang.*]

fannel, *fannell*, *fan'əl*, *n.* a maniple. [L.L. *fanonellus, fanula*, dims. of *fanō* ; see **fanion.**]

fan-tan, *fan'-tan*, *n.* a Chinese gambling game. [Chin.]

fantasia, *fan-tä-zē'ä*, also *fan-tä'* or *-tā'zi-ä*, *n.* a musical or other composition not governed by the ordinary rules of form. [It.,—Gr. *phantasiā* ; see **fantasy.**]

fantasy, phantasy, *fan'tə-zi, -si*, *n.* fancy : imagination : mental image : love : whim, caprice : fantasia : preoccupation with thoughts associated with unobtainable desires.—*v.t.* to fancy, conceive mentally.—*adj.* **fan'tasied**, filled with fancies.— *n.* **fan'tasm** (same as **phantasm**).—*adj.* **fantasque** (*-task'*), fantastic.—*ns.* **fan'tast**, a person of fantastic ideas ; **fantas'tic**, one who is fantastical : a dandy, a fop.—*adjs.* **fantas'tic, -al**, fanciful : not real : capricious : whimsical : wild : foppish.— *adv.* **fantas'tically.**—*n.* **fantas'ticalness.**—*v.t.* and *v.i.* **fantas'ticate.**—*ns.* **fantas'ticism** (*-sizm*) ; **fantas'tico** (*Shak.* ; It.), a fantastic ; **fan'tastry.** [O.Fr. *fantasie*—through L. from Gr. *phantasiā* —*phantazein*, to make visible ; cf. **fancy, fantasia.**]

Fanti, Fantee, *fan'tē*, *n.* a Gold Coast people : their language.—**to go Fanti**, to adopt the ways of an uncivilised people.

fantoccini, *fan-to-chē'nē*, *n.pl.* marionettes : a marionette show. [It., pl. of *fantoccino*, dim. of *fantoccio*, a puppet—*fante*, a boy—L. *infāns, -āntis.*]

fantod, *fan'tod*, **fantad**, *-täd*, *n.* (*slang*), a fidgety fussy person, esp. a ship's officer : (usu. in pl.) fidgets.—*n.* **fantigue, fanteeg** (*fan-tēg'*), anxiety, unpleasant excitement.

fantom. Same as **phantom.**

fap, *fap*, *adj.* (*Shak.*) fuddled, drunk.

faquir, *fäk-ēr'*, *n.* Same as **fakir.**

far, *fär*, *adj.* remote : more distant of two (in *Shak.* as *comp.*) : advanced.—*adv.* to, at, or over a great distance or advanced stage : remotely : in a great degree : very much : long : (of an animal) off, right-hand (i.e. the side remote from one leading it).—*v.t.* (*prov.*) to remove to a distance. —*adj.* **far'-away**, distant : abstracted, absent-minded.—*adv.* by **far.**—*n.* the distant.—*adjs.* **far'-fetched** (*obs.* **far'fet**), fetched or brought from a remote place : forced, unnatural ; **far'-flung**, thrown far and wide : a fashionable word for extensive.—*advs.* **far'-forth** (*Spens.*), far ; **far'most**, most distant or remote.—*n.* **far'ness,**

the state of being far: remoteness, distance.—*adj.* and *adv.* **far′-off**, in the distance.—*adjs.* **far′-reach′ing**, having wide validity, scope, or influence; **far′-sight′ed**, seeing to a great distance: having defective eyesight for near objects: prescient; **far′-sought**, sought for at a distance; **far′-spent**, far advanced.—**by far**, in a very great degree; **far and away**, by a great deal; **far and near**, **far and wide**, everywhere, all about; **far between**, at wide intervals: rare; **far be it**, God forbid; **far cry**, a long distance; **Far East**, Eastern Asia (China, Japan, etc.); **Far North**, the Arctic regions; **Far South**, the Antarctic regions; **Far West**, the Great Plains, Rocky Mountains and Pacific side of North America; **I'll see you far (or farther) first, I** will not do it by any means; **in so far as**, to the extent that.—See also **farther**. [O.E. *feor(r)*; Du. *ver;* O.N. *fiarre.*]

farad, *far′əd*, *n.* a unit of electrical capacity—that of a conductor which when raised to a potential of one volt has a charge of one coulomb.—*n.* **far′aday**, a unit of quantity of electricity, that carried by the ions of one gramme-equivalent, or 96500 coulombs.—*adj.* **faradic** (*-ad′ik*), pertaining to Faraday, esp. in connexion with induced currents.—*n.* **faradisā′tion**.—*v.t.* **far′adise** (*med.*) to stimulate by induced currents.—*ns.* **far′adism**, treatment by induced currents; **microfar′ad**, the millionth part of a farad. [From Michael Faraday (1791-1867).]

farand, farrand, farrant, *fär′ənd, -ənt, adj.* (*Scot.*) having a certain appearance or manner, esp. in such compound forms as **auld-farand**, old-fashioned, quaint, precocious, sagacious; *fair-farand*, goodly, specious. [M.E. *farand*, comely. Origin obscure; prob. pr.p of **fare.**]

farandine, farrandine, *far′ən-dēn*, **ferrandine** *fer′, n.* (*obs.*) a cloth or a dress of silk with wool or hair. [Fr. *ferrandine.*]

farandole, *far-ən-dōl′, n.* a Provençal dance performed in a long string: music for it, in 6-8 time. [Prov. *farandoula.*]

farborough, *fär′bər-ə, n.* Goodman Dull's pronunciation of **thridborough** (*Love's Lab. Lost* I.i. 182).—Another reading, **tharborough.**

farce, *färs, v.t.* to cram: to stuff, fill with stuffing: (*Shak.*) to swell out.—*n.* stuffing, force-meat: comedy of extravagant humour, buffoonery, and improbability: ridiculous or empty show: a hollow formality.—*n.* **farceur** (*fär-sər′;* Fr.), a joker.—*adj.* **far′cical.**—*n.* **farcical′ity**, farcical quality.—*adv.* **far′cically.**—*v.t.* **far′cify**, to turn into a farce.—*n.* **farc′ing**, stuffing. [Fr. *farce*, stuffing, from L. *farcīre*, to stuff; the connecting links of meaning seem to be interpolation, theatrical gag, buffoonery; cf. **farse.**]

farcy, *fär′si, n.* chronic glanders.—(*obs.*) **far′cin.**—*adj.* **far′cied.**—*n.* **far′cy-bud**, a swollen lymphatic gland, as in farcy. [Fr. *farcin*—L.L. *farcīminum.*]

fard, *färd, n.* white paint for the face.—*v.t.* to paint with fard: to gloss over: to trick out. [Fr., of Gmc. origin.]

fardage, *fär′dij, n.* (*naut. obs.*), dunnage. [Fr.]

fardel, *fär′dl, n.* (*obs.*) a fourth part. [O.E. *féortha dǽl*, fourth deal.]

fardel, *fär′dl, n.* a pack: anything cumbersome or irksome: the manyplies or omasum.—**far′del-bag**, the omasum.—*adj.* **far′del-bound**, constipated, esp. of cattle and sheep, by the retention of food in the omasum. [O.Fr. *fardel* (Fr. *fardeau*), dim. of *farde*, a burden, possibly—Ar. *fardah*, a package.]

farden, farding, *fär′dən* (*obs.* or *dial.*). Same as **farthing.**

fare, *fār, v.i.* to travel: to get on or succeed: to happen well or ill to: to be in any particular state, to be, to go on: to be fed.—*n.* (*orig.; Spens.*) a course or passage: the price of passage: a passenger (or passengers): food or provisions for the table.—*interj.* **farewell′**, may you fare well! a parting wish for safety or success: goodbye.—*n.* well-wishing at parting: the act of departure.

—*adj.* (*fär′wel*) parting: valedictory: final. [O.E. *faran;* Ger. *fahren.*]

farina, *fə-rī′nä, fə-rē′nä, n.* ground corn: meal: starch: pollen: a mealy powder.—*adjs.* **farinaceous** (*far-i-nā′shəs*), mealy: consisting of cereals; **far′inose** (*-i-nōs*), yielding farina. [L. *farīna*—*fär*, corn.]

farl(e), farl, *färl, n.* (*Scot.*), the quarter of a round cake of flour or oatmeal: a cake. [**fardel** (1).]

farm, *färm, n.* (*obs.*) a fixed payment: (*Spens.*) a lease: a fixed payment in composition of taxes, etc.: the letting out of revenue to one who collects it in exchange for a fixed sum: a tract of land (originally one leased or rented) used for cultivation and pasturage, along with a house and other necessary buildings: a farmhouse: a farmstead: a piece of land or water used for breeding animals (as a fox-farm, oyster-farm): a place where children are handed over to be brought up.—*v.t.* to grant or receive the revenues of, for a fixed payment: to rent or lease to or from another: to cultivate: to arrange for the maintenance of at a fixed price.—*v.i.* to practise the business of a farmer.—*ns.* **farm′-bai′liff; farm′er,** one who farms or cultivates land: the tenant of a farm: one who receives taxes, etc., for a certain payment:—*fem.* **farm′eress.**—*ns.* **farm′ergen′eral,** a member of a privileged association in France, who before the Revolution, leased the public revenues; **farm′ery,** the buildings of a farm; **farm′house′,** a house attached to a farm in which the farmer lives; **farm′-hand, farm′-la′bourer,** one who works on a farm; **farm′ing,** the business of cultivating land.—*n.pl.* **farm′off′ices,** the outbuildings on a farm.—*ns.* **farm′place, farm′stead, farm′stead′ing,** a farm-house with the buildings belonging to it—*Scot.* **farm′-toun′** (*-toon*); **farm′-yard′,** the yard or enclosure surrounded by the farm buildings. [L.L. *firma*, a fixed payment—L. *firmus*, firm.]

farmost. See **far.**

faro, *fär′ō, n.* a game of chance played by betting on the order of appearance of certain cards. [Perh. from *Pharaoh;* reason unknown.]

farouche, *fä-* or *fə-rōōsh′, adj.* wild and shy or sullen. [Fr.]

farrago, *fə-rā′gō, fə-rä′gō, n.* a confused mass.—*adj.* **farraginous** (*fə-rāj′in-əs*, or *-raj′*), miscellaneous, jumbled. [L. *farrāgō, -inis*, mixed fodder—*fär*, grain.]

farrier, *far′i-ər, n.* one who shoes horses: one who cures horses' diseases: one in charge of cavalry horses.—*n.* **farr′iery**, the farrier's art: veterinary surgery. [O.Fr. *ferrier*—L. *ferrum*, iron.]

farrow, *far′ō, n.* a litter of pigs.—*v.i.* or *v.t.* to bring forth (pigs). [O.E. *fearh*, a pig; Ger. (dim.) *ferkel;* L. *porcus.*]

farrow, *far′ō, adj.* not with calf for the time being. [Ety. dub.; with *farrow cow* cf. Flem. *verwekoe, varwekoe.*]

farse, *färs, n.* an explanation of the Latin epistle in the vernacular.—*v.t.* to extend by interpolation. [**farce.**]

fart, *färt, v.i.* (*coarse*) to break wind from the anus.—Also *n.* [O.E. (assumed) *feortan;* cf. Gr. *perdesthai.*]

farthel, *fär′dhəl, n.* (*Scot.*). Same as **farl.**

farther, *far′dhər,* **far′thermore, far′thermost, farthest.** Same as **further,** etc., and sometimes preferred where the notion of distance is more prominent. [A variant (M.E. *ferther*) of **further** that came to be thought a comp. of **far.**]

farthing, *fär′dhing, n.* (*obs.*) a fourth part: the fourth of a penny: anything very small: (*B.*) the rendering of Gr. *assarion* (the L. *as*) and of *kodrantēs* (L. *quadrāns*), a fourth of an *as.*—*n.* **far′thingland,** a varying area of land.—*adj.* **far′thingless.**—*n.* **far′thingsworth,** as much as a farthing will buy. [O.E. *féorthing*, a fourth part—*féortha*, fourth, and suff. *-ing.*]

farthingale, *fär′dhing-gäl, n.* a kind of crinoline of whalebone for distending women's dress. [O.Fr. *verdugale*—Sp. *verdugado*, hooped, *verdugo*, rod.]

fasces, *fas'ēz*, *n.pl.* the bundle of rods, with or without an axe, borne before an ancient Roman magistrate of high grade. [L. *fascēs*, pl. of *fascis*, bundle.]

fascia, *fas(h)'i-ä*, *n.* (*obs.*) a band, fillet: (*archit.*) a broad flat band, as in an architrave, or over a shop-front: a board in like position, commonly bearing the shopkeeper's name: (also **fascia-board**) the instrument-board of a motor-car: (*zool.*) any bandlike structure, esp. of connective tissue ensheathing a muscle.—*adjs.* **fasc'ial**, **fasc'iated**.—*n.* **fascia'tion** (*bot.*), union of a number of parts side by side in a flat plate; **fasciola** (*fǝ-sī'ō-lä*), **fasciole** (*fas'i-ōl*), a band of colour. [L. *fascia*, band, bandage.]

fascicle, *fas'i-kl*, *n.* a bundle or bunch, esp. a bunched tuft of branches, roots, fibres, etc.: a part of a book issued in parts.—Also **fasc'icule**, **fascic'ulus**.—*adjs.* **fasc'icled**, **fascic'ular**, **fascic'ulate**, **-d**. [L. *fasciculus*, dim. of *fascis*, bundle.]

fascinate, *fas'i-nāt*, *v.t.* (*obs.*) to bewitch, enchant, cast the evil eye upon: to control by the eye like a snake: to entangle the attention of: to charm: to captivate.—*adj.* **fasc'inating**, charming, delightful: binding the attention.—*n.* **fascina'tion**, the act of charming: power to harm, control, allure, or render helpless by looks or spells: state of being fascinated; **fasc'inātor**, one who fascinates: (*arch.*) a woman's head-covering. [L. *fascināre*, *-ātum;* perh. allied to Gr. *baskainein*, to bewitch.]

fascine, *fas-ēn'*, *n.* a brushwood faggot, used to fill ditches, protect a shore, etc. [Fr.,—L. *fascīna—fascis*, a bundle.]

fascio, *fä'shō*, *n.* an organised political group or club (*pl.* **fasci** *fä'shē*)—*ns.* **Fascist**, *fas(h)'ist*, **Fascista**, *fä-shēs'tä*, a member of a political party in Italy (and elsewhere in imitation) representing a nationalist reaction against socialism and communism, that came into power by violent means in 1922 and fell in 1943 (*pl.* **Fasc'ists**, **Fascisti**, *fä-shēs'tē*)—*fascist*, when expressing attitude not official party membership—Also *adj.*—*n.* **Fasc'ism**, **Fascis'mo**, the policy or forceful methods of the Facisti. [Ital. *fascio*, bundle, group, with a hint of *fasces* (q.v.).]

fash, *fäsh*, *v.t.* (*Scot.*) to trouble, annoy.—*v.i.* to be vexed: to take trouble or pains: to annoy.—*n.* pains, trouble: annoyance.—*n.* **fash'ery**.—*adj.* **fash'ious** (*fäsh-ǝs*), troublesome, vexatious.—*n.* **fash'iousness.**—**never fash your thumb**, take no trouble in the matter. [O.Fr. *fascher* (Fr. *fâcher*)—L. *fastīdium*, disgust.]

fashion, *fash'n*, *n.* the make or cut of a thing: form or pattern: vogue: prevailing mode or shape of dress or that imposed by those whose lead is accepted: a prevailing custom: manner: genteel society: appearance.—*v.t.* to make: to mould according to a pattern: to suit or adapt.—*adj.* **fash'ionable**, according to prevailing fashion: prevailing or in use at any period: observant of the fashion in dress or living: moving in high society: patronised by people of fashion.—*n.* a person of fashion.—*adv.* **fash'ionableness.**—*adv.* **fash'ionably.**—*ns.* **fash'ioner**; **fash'ionist.**—*adjs.* **fash'ionmongering, fash'ionmonging** (*Shak.*), behaving like a fop.—*n.* **fash'ion-plate**, a pictorial representation of the latest style of dress: (*fig.*) a very smartly dressed person.—**after** or **in a fashion**, in a way: to a certain extent; **in the fashion**, in accordance with the prevailing style of dress, etc. [O.Fr. *fachon*—L. *factiō*, *-ōnis -facēre*, to make.]

fashions, *fash'ǝnz*, *n.pl.* (*Shak.*) for **farcins**, farcy.

fast, *fäst*, *adj.* firm: fixed: steadfast: fortified: (of sleep) sound: (of colours) not liable to fade or run.—*adv.* firmly, unflinchingly: soundly or sound (asleep): close: near.—*n.* **fast'-and-loose**, a cheating game practised at fairs, the dupe being invited to put a stick in the loop of a coiled belt so that it cannot be pulled away—called also *prick-the-garter.*—*adj.* **fast'-hand'ed**, close-fisted.—*adv.* **fast'ly** (*Shak.*), firmly.—*n.* **fast'ness**, fixedness: a stronghold, fortress, castle.

—**fast by**, close to, close by; **play fast and loose** (from the cheating game), to be unreliable, shifty: to behave without sense of moral obligation. [O.E. *fæst;* Ger. *fest.*]

fast, *fäst*, *adj.* quick: rapid: before time (as a clock): promoting fast play: seeking excitement: rash: dissipated.—*adv.* swiftly: in rapid succession: extravagantly.—*adj.* **fast'ish**, somewhat fast.—*n.* **fast'ness**. [A special use of fast (1), derived from the Scand. sense of urgent.]

fast, *fäst*, *v.i.* to keep from food: to go hungry: to abstain from food in whole or part, as a religious duty.—*n.* abstinence from food: special abstinence enjoined by the church: the day or time of fasting.—*ns.* **fast'-day**, a day of religious fasting: a day for humiliation and prayer, esp. before communion; **Fast'ens**, short for **Fastens-eve** (*Scot.* **Fasten-e'en** and **Fastern's-e'en**), **Fastens Tuesday**, Shrove Tuesday (O.E. *fæstenes*, gen. of *fæsten*, fast); **fast'er**, one who fasts; **fast'ing**, religious abstinence. [O.E. *fæstan*, to fast; Ger. *fasten.*]

fast, *fäst* (*Spens.*) a spelling of faced.

fasten, *fäs'n*, *v.t.* to make fast or firm: to fix securely: to attach.—*v.i.* to admit of being fastened: to remain stationary: to fix: to lay hold: to make assault.—*ns.* **fastener** (*fäsn'ǝr*), a clip, catch, or other means of fastening; **fas'tening** (*fäsn'ing*), that which fastens.—**fasten on**, to direct (one's eyes) on: to seize on, e.g. a fact: (*slang*) to fix the blame, responsibility for, on (a person). [fast (1).]

fasti, *fas'tī*, L. *fäs'tē*, *n.pl.* those days among the ancient Romans on which it was lawful to transact legal or public business—opp. to *Nefasti:* an enumeration of the days of the year, a calendar: annals. [L.]

fastidious, *fas-tid'i-ǝs*, *adj.* affecting superior taste: over-nice: difficult to please: exacting in taste: nicely critical.—*adv.* **fastid'iously.**—*n.* **fastid'iousness**. [L. *fastīdiōsus—fastīdium*, loathing.]

fastigiate, *fas-tij'i-āt*, *adj.* pointed, sloping to a point or edge: (*bot.*) with branches more or less erect and parallel: conical.—*adj.* **fastig'iated.**—*n.* **fastig'ium**, the apex of a building: gable-end: pediment. [L. *fastigium*, a gable-end, roof.]

fat, *fat*, *adj.* plump, fleshy: well-filled out: thick, full-bodied (of some kinds of printing types): corpulent: obese: having much, or of the nature of, adipose tissue or the substance it contains: oily: fruitful or profitable: rich in some important constituent: gross: fulsome: (*comp.* **fatt'er**; *superl.* **fatt'est**).—*n.* a substance found in adipose tissue: solid animal or vegetable oil: (*chem.*) any member of a group of naturally occurring substances consisting of the glycerides of higher fatty acids, *e.g.* palmitic acid, stearic acid, oleic acid: the richest part of anything: a piece of work offering more than usual profit for the trouble expended: a passage that enables an actor or musician to show what he can do: inclination to corpulency: a fat animal.—*v.t.* to make fat.—*v.i.* to grow fat: (*pr.p.* **fatt'ing**; *pa.t.* and *pa.p.* **fatt'ed**).—*adjs.* **fat'-face**, **-d**, having a fat or broad face; **fat'-brained** (*Shak.*), stupid.—*n.* **fat'-head**, a dullard.—*adj.* **fat'-head'ed.**—*ns.* **fat'-hen**, any one of various thick-leaved plants, esp. of the goosefoot family; **fat'-kidney'd** (*Shak.*); **fat'ling**, a young animal fattened for slaughter.—*adj.* small and fat.—*n.* **fat'-lute**, a mixture of pipe-clay and linseed-oil, for filling joints, etc.—*adv.* **fat'ly**, grossly: in a lumbering manner.—*n.* **fat'ness**, quality or state of being fat: fullness of flesh: richness: fertility: that which makes fertile.—*adjs.* **fat'-tailed**, having much fat in the tail, as certain Asiatic and African sheep; **fatt'ed** (fatted calf, the not always approved fare for the returned prodigal—Luke xv 23, etc.).—*v.t.* **fatt'en**, to make fat or fleshy: to make fertile.—*v.i.* to grow fat.—*ns.* **fatt'ener**; **fatt'ening**; **fatt'iness.**—*adjs.* **fatt'ish**, somewhat fat; **fatt'y**, containing fat: having qualities of fat.—*n.* a fat person (often as a nickname).—*adj.* **fat'-witt'ed**, dull, stupid.—**a fat lot** (*slang*, ironically) much; **fatty acids**, acids which with glycerine form fats; **fatty**

degeneration, morbid deposition of fat; **fatty heart,** etc., fatty degeneration of the heart, etc.; **the fat is in the fire,** a critical act has precipitated the trouble. [O.E. *fǽtt,* fatted.]

fat, *fat, n.* a vessel for holding liquids : a vat : a dry measure of nine bushels. [See **vat.**]

fata Morgana, *fä'tä mor-gä'nä,* a striking kind of mirage seen most often in the Strait of Messina. [Supposed to be caused by the fairy (It. *fata*) *Morgana* of Arthurian romance.]

fate, *fāt, n.* inevitable destiny or necessity : appointed lot : destined term of life : ill-fortune : doom : final issue : (in *pl.*) the three goddesses of fate, Clotho, Lachesis, and Atropos, who determine the birth, life, and death of men—the **fatal sisters.**—*adj.* **fāt'al,** belonging to or appointed by fate : announcing fate : causing ruin or death : mortal : calamitous.—*ns.* **fāt'alism,** the doctrine that all events are subject to fate, and happen by unavoidable necessity : acceptance of this doctrine : lack of effort in the face of threatened difficulty or disaster ; **fāt'alist,** one who believes in fatalism.—*adj.* **fātalist'ic,** belonging to or partaking of fatalism.—*n.* **fatality** (*fə-tal'i-ti*), the state of being fatal or unavoidable : the decree of fate : fixed tendency to disaster or death : mortality : a fatal occurrence.—*adv.* **fāt'ally.**— *adjs.* **fāt'ed,** doomed : destined : (*Shak.*) invested with the power of destiny : (*Dryden*) enchanted ; **fate'ful,** charged with fate.—*adv.* **fate'fully.**—*n.* **fate'fulness.** [L. *fātum,* a prediction—*fātus,* spoken—*fārī,* to speak.]

father, *fä'dhər,* a male parent : an ancestor or forefather : a fatherly protector : a contriver or originator : a title of respect applied to a venerable man, to confessors, monks, priests, etc. : a member of certain fraternities : (usu. in *pl.*) a member of a ruling body, as *conscript fathers, city fathers:* the oldest member, or member of longest standing, of a profession or body : one of a group of ecclesiastical writers of the early centuries, usually ending with Ambrose, Jerome, and Augustine : the first person of the Trinity.—*v.t.* to adopt : to ascribe to one as his offspring or production. —*ns.* **fa'therhood,** state or fact of being a father : (*arch.*) fatherly authority ; **fa'ther-in-law,** the father of one's husband or wife : (*arch.*) stepfather : (*pl.* fathers-in-law) ; **fa'therland,** native land, esp. Germany (*Vaterland*) ; **fa'ther-lash'er,** a name applied to two bull-heads found on the British coasts.—*adj.* **fa'therless,** destitute of a living father : without a known author.—*ns.* **fa'therlessness** ; **fa'therliness.**—*adj.* **fa'therly,** like a father : paternal.—*n.* **fa'thership.**—be **gathered to one's fathers** (*B.*), to die and be buried ; **Holy Father,** the Pope. [O.E. *fæder;* Ger. *vater,* L. *pater,* Gr. *patēr.*]

fathom, *fadh'əm, n.* originally, the reach of the outstretched arms : now, a nautical measure, six feet : penetration of mind : (*pl.* fathom, fathoms) —*v.t.* (*arch.*) to measure or encompass with outstretched arms : to try the depth of : to comprehend or get to the bottom of.—*adjs.* **fath'omable** ; **fath'omless.**—*n.* **fath'om-line,** sailor's line and lead for taking soundings. [O.E. *fæthm;* Du. *vadem,* Ger. *faden.*]

fatidical, *fā-, fə-tid'i-kl, adj.* having power to foretell future events : prophetical.—*adv.* **fatid'ically.** [L. *fātidicus—fātum,* fate, *dīcĕre,* to tell.]

fatigue, *fə-tēg', n.* weariness from labour of body or of mind : toil : lessened power of response to stimulus resulting from activity : failure under repeated stress : fatigue-duty (sometimes allotted as a punishment).—*v.t.* to reduce to weariness : to exhaust the strength or power of recovery of : (*pr.p.* **fatigu'ing** ; *pa.t.* and *pa.p.* **fatigued').**— *adj.* **fatig(u)able** (*fat'ig-ə-bl*), capable of being fatigued : easily fatigued.—*n.* **fat'ig(u)ableness.**— *adj.* **fatigate** (*fat'i-gāt; Shak.*), fatigued.—*v.t.* (*obs.*) to fatigue.—*ns.* **fatigue'-dress** ; **fatigue'-dū'ty,** the part of a soldier's work distinct from the use of arms ; **fatigue'-party**—*adv.* **fatigu'ingly.** [Fr. *fatigue*—L. *fatīgāre,* to weary.]

fatiscent, *fā-, fə-tis'ənt, adj.* gaping with cracks.

—*n.* **fatisc'ence.** [L. *fatīscēns, -entis,* pr.p of *fatīscĕre,* to gape.]

fattrels, *fat'rəlz, n.pl.* (*Scot.*) ends of ribbon. [O. Fr. *fatraille,* trumpery.]

fatuous, *fat'ū-əs, adj.* silly : imbecile.—*adj.* **fatū'itous.**—*ns.* **fatū'ity, fat'ūousness,** unconscious stupidity : imbecility.—**fatuous fire,** ignis fatuus, Will-o'-the-Wisp. [L. *fatuus.*]

faubourg, *fō-bōōr', n.* a suburb just beyond the walls, or a district recently included within a city. [Fr.]

fauces, *faw'sēz, n.pl.* the upper part of the throat, from the root of the tongue to the entrance of the gullet : the throat of a flower.—*adjs.* **fau'cal** (*-kl*), of, produced, in the fauces, as certain Semitic guttural sounds ; **faucial** (*faw'shl*), of the fauces. [L. *faucēs.*]

faucet, *faw'sit, n.* a pipe inserted in a barrel to draw liquid : (*U.S.*) a tap. [Fr. *fausset.*]

faugh, *fo, interj.* expressing disgust.

faulchion, faulchin, obsolete forms of **falchion.**

fault, *fawlt,* formerly *fawt, n.* a failing : error : blemish : imperfection : a slight offence : (*geol.*) a dislocation of strata or veins : (*tennis*) a stroke in which the player fails to serve the ball into the proper place : culpability for that which has happened amiss.—*v.i.* (*obs.*) to fall short : to be faulty : to commit a fault.—*v.t.* to find fault with : (*geol.*) to cause a fault in.—*ns.* **fault'-finder** ; **fault'-finding.**—*adj.* **fault'ful** (*Shak.*), full of faults or crimes.—*adv.* **fault'ily.**—*n.* **fault'iness.** —*adj.* **fault'less,** without fault or defect.—*adv.* **fault'lessly.**—*n.* **fault'lessness.**—*adj.* **fault'y,** imperfect, defective : guilty of a fault : blamable.— **at fault** (of dogs) unable to find the scent : at a loss ; **in fault,** to blame ; **find fault** (*with*), to censure for some defect. [O.Fr. *faute, falte*—L. *fallĕre,* to deceive.]

fauna, *fawn'ä, n.* the assemblage of animals of a region or period : a list or account thereof : (*pl.* **faun'as, faun'ae**).—*n.* **faun,** a Roman rural deity, protector of shepherds.—*adj.* **faun'al.**—*n.* **faun'ist,** one who studies faunas.—*adj.* **faunist'ic.** [L. *Fauna, Faunus,* tutelary deities of shepherds— *favēre, fautum,* to favour.]

fauteuil, *fō-tə'i,* also *fō'til, n.* an arm-chair, esp. a president's chair : the seat of one of the forty members of the French Academy : a theatre-stall. [Fr.]

fautor, *faw'tər, n.* a favourer : patron : abettor. L. *fautor—favēre,* to favour.]

Fauve, Fauvist, *fōv, -ist, ns.* one of a group of painters at the beginning of the 20th century, including Matisse, who viewed a painting as essentially a two-dimensional decoration in colour, not necessarily imitative of nature.—*n.* **Fauv'ism.** [Fr. *fauve,* wild beast.]

fauvette, *fō-vet', n.* a warbler. [Fr.]

fauxbourdon, *fō-bōōr-don⁹.* Same as **faburden.**

faveolate, *fəv-ē'ō-lāt, adj.* honeycombed. [L. *favus,* honeycomb.]

Favonian, *fav-ō'ni-ən, adj.* pertaining to the west wind, favourable. [L. *Favōnius,* the west wind.]

favour, or (*esp. U.S.*) **favor,** *fā'vər, n.* countenance : good-will : a kind deed : an act of grace or lenity : indulgence : partiality : advantage : a concession of amorous indulgence : a knot of ribbons worn at a wedding, election, etc. : anything worn as a token of a woman's favour : (*arch.*) appearance, face : (*commercial jargon*) a letter or written communication : (*Shak.*) an attraction or grace : (*Milt.*) an object of favour.—*v.t.* to regard with good-will : to be on the side of : to treat indulgently : to give support to ; to afford advantage to : (*coll.*) to resemble ; to choose to wear, etc.—*adj.* **fā'vourable,** friendly : propitious : conducive : advantageous : satisfactory, promising.—*n.* **fā'vourableness.**—*adv.* **fā'vourably.**—*adj.* **fā'voured,** enjoying favour or preference : wearing favours : having a certain appearance, featured—as in *ill-favoured, well-favoured.*—*ns.* **fā'vouredness** ; **fā'vourer,** *n.* **fā'vourite** (*-it*), a person or thing regarded with marked preference : one unduly loved and indulged, esp. by a king : one expected to win : a kind of curl of the hair, affected by ladies of the 18th century.—*adj.* esteemed, preferred.—*n.* fā′vouritism, inclination to partiality : preference shown to favourites.—*adj.* fā′vourless, without favour : (*Spens.*) not favouring.—**curry favour** (see **curry**) ; **favours to come**, favours still expected ; **in favour of**, for : on the side of : for the advantage of. [O.Fr.,—L. *favor—favēre*, to favour, befriend.]

favus, *fāv-ɔs*, *n.* a fungal skin disease, chiefly of the scalp, giving a honeycombed appearance.—*adjs.* **favose** (*fɔ-vōs′*, *fā′vōs*), honeycombed ; **fā′vous**, like a honeycomb : relating to favus. [L. *favus*, a honeycomb.]

faw, *faw*, *n.* a gypsy. [From the surname *Faa*.]

fawn, *fawn*, *n.* a young deer, esp. a fallow deer : its colour, light yellowish brown.—*adj.* resembling a fawn in colour.—*v.t.* and *v.i.* to bring forth (a fawn). [O.Fr. *faon*, through L.L. from L. *fētus*, offspring.]

fawn, *fawn*, *v.i.* to cringe, to flatter in a servile way (with *upon*).—*n.* (*rare*) a servile cringe or bow : mean flattery.—*n.* **fawn′er**, one who flatters to gain favour.—*n.* and *adj.* **fawn′ing**.—*adv.* **fawn′ingly**.—*n.* **fawn′ingness**. [A variant of **fain**, to rejoice—O.E. *fægen*, glad.]

fay, *fā*, *n.* a fairy. [O.Fr. *fae*—L.L. *fāta ;* see **fate**.]

fay, *fā*, *n.* (*Shak.*) faith. [O.Fr. *fei*.]

fay, same as **fey**.

fay, *fā*, *v.t.* and *v.i.* to fit, unite closely.—**fay′ing face**, prepared surface of contact. [O.E. *fēgan ;* Ger. *fügen*.]

fay, *fey*, *fā*, *v.t.* (*prov.*) to clean out, as a ditch. [O.N. *fǽgja*, to cleanse.]

fayalite, *fā′ɔ-līt*, *fā-yāl′īt*, iron-olivine, a silicate of iron found in slag and occurring naturally. [*Fayal*, in the Azores, where it was found, probably in ballast.]

fayence. See **faience**.

faze, *fāz*. See **feeze**.

feague, *fēg*, *v.t.* (*obs.*) to whip : to perplex. [Cf. Du. *vegen*, Ger. *fegen*.]

feal, *fēl*, *adj.* (*obs.*) loyal, faithful. [O.Fr. *feal*—L. *fidēlis*.]

feal, *fēl*, *v.t.* (*prov.*) to conceal. [O.N. *fela*.]

feal, *fēl*. Same as **fail** (1).

fealty, *fē′ɔl-ti*, or *fēl′ti*, *n.* the vassal's obligation of fidelity to his feudal lord : loyalty. [O.Fr. *fealte*—L. *fidēlitās*, *-tātis*,—*fidēlis*, faithful—*fidēre*, to trust.]

fear, *fēr*, *n.* a painful emotion excited by danger : apprehension of danger or pain : alarm : the object of fear : aptness to cause fear : (*B.*) deep reverence : piety towards God.—*v.t.* to regard with fear : to expect with alarm : to be regretfully inclined to think : (*obs.*) to be anxious or in fear about : (*B.*) to stand in awe of : to venerate : (*obs.*) to terrify : to make afraid.—*v.i.* to be afraid : to be in doubt.—*adjs.* **feared** (*fērd ;* arch. and *Scot.*) afraid ; **fear′ful**, timorous : exciting intense fear : terrible.—*adv.* **fear′fully**.—*n.* **fear′fulness**.—*adj.* **fear′less**, without fear : daring : brave.—*adv.* **fear′lessly**.—*ns.* **fear′lessness** ; **fear′nought**, dreadnought cloth.—*adj.* **fear′some**, causing fear, frightful.—*adv.* **fear′somely**. [O.E. *fǽr*, fear, *fǽran*, to terrify.]

fear(e). Same as **fere**.

feasible, *fē′zi-bl*, *adj.* practicable, possible : (*loosely*) probable, likely—*ns.* **feas′ibleness**, **feasibil′ity**. —*adv.* **feas′ibly**. [Fr. *faisable*, that can be done—*faire*, *faisant*—L. *facĕre*, to do.]

feast, *fēst*, *n.* a day of unusual solemnity or joy : a festival in commemoration of some event—*movable*, of varying date, as Easter ; *immovable*, at a fixed date, as Christmas : a rich and abundant repast : rich enjoyment : festivity.—*v.i.* to hold a feast : to eat sumptuously : to receive intense delight.—*v.t.* to entertain sumptuously.—*ns.* **feast′-day** ; **feast′er**.—*adj.* **feast′ful**, festive, joyful, luxurious.—*ns.* **feast′ing** ; **feast′-rite**, a rite or custom observed at feasts.—*adj.* **feast′-won** (*Shak.*), won or bribed by feasting.—**Feast of Fools**, **Feast of Asses**, mediaeval festivals held between Christmas and Epiphany, in which a mock bishop was enthroned in church, a burlesque

mass said by his orders, and an ass driven round in triumph. [O.Fr. *feste* (Fr. *fête*)—L. *fēstum*, a holiday, *fēstus*, solemn, festal.]

feat, *fēt*, *n.* (*obs.*) act, deed : a deed manifesting extraordinary strength, skill, or courage, an exploit, achievement : (*Spens.*) art, skill.—*v.t.* (*Shak.*) perh., to fashion, to make feat or neat.—*adj.* neat, deft.—*adv.* **feat′ly**, neatly : dexterously—(*Spens.*) **feat′eously**. [Fr. *fait*—L. *factum—facĕre*, to do ; cf. **fact**.]

feather, *fedh′ɔr*, *n.* one of the growths that form the covering of a bird : a feather-like appearance, ornament or flaw : the feathered end of an arrow : plumage (*birds of a feather*, birds of like plumage, or—*fig.*—persons of like character) : condition : birds collectively : anything light or trifling : a projecting longitudinal rib or strip : a wedge : a formation of hair : the act of feathering an oar : a foamy wave or wave-crest.—*v.t.* to furnish or adorn with a feather or feathers : to move edgewise (as an oar, to lessen air-resistance), or to make (a propellor-blade, etc.) rotate in such a way as to lessen resistance.—*v.i.* to take the appearance of a feather : to quiver the tail.—*ns.* **feath′er-bed**, a mattress filled with feathers ; **feath′er-board′ing** (same as **weather-boarding**) ; **feath′er-bonn′et**, a Highland soldier's feather-covered head-dress ; **feath′er-dust′er**, a brush of feathers, used for dusting.—*adj.* **feath′ered**, covered or fitted with feathers, or anything feather-like : like the flight of a feathered animal, swift : smoothed as with feathers.—*ns.* **feath′er-edge**, an edge of a board or plank thinner than the other edge ; **feath′er-grass**, a perennial grass (*Stipa*) with feathery awns ; **feath′er-head**, **feath′er-brain**, **feath′er-pate**, a frivolous person ; **feath′eriness** ; **feath′ering**, plumage : the addition of a feather or feathers : a featherlike appearance : (*archit.*) an arrangement of small arcs separated by cusps, within an arch ; **feath′er-palm′**, any palm with pinnate leaves ; **feath′er-star**, a crinoid ; **feath′er-stitch**, one of a series of stitches making a zigzag line ; **feath′erweight**, the lightest weight that may be carried by a racing-horse : a boxer (9st. or under), wrestler, etc., below a light-weight : hence anyone of small importance or ability.—*adj.* **feath′ery**, pertaining to, resembling or covered with feathers or appearance of feathers.—**a feather in one's cap**, a striking distinction ; **feather one's nest**, to accumulate wealth for oneself while serving others in a position of trust ; **in high feather**, greatly elated or in high spirits ; **make the feathers fly**, to throw into confusion by a sudden attack ; **show the white feather**, to show signs of cowardice—a white feather in a game-cock's tail being considered as a sign of degeneracy. [O.E. *fether ;* Ger. *feder ;* L. *penna*, Gr. *pteron*.]

featous, *fēt′ɔs*, **feat′eous**, *-ɔs*, **feat′uous**, *-ū-ɔs*, *adjs.* (*arch.*) shapely : well-made : handsome : dexterous : neat.—*adv.* **feat′eously** (*Spens.*) dexterously, neatly. [O.Fr. *fetis*—L. *factīcius—facĕre*, to make ; cf. **factitious**.]

feature, *fēt′yɔr*, *n.* form, appearance : (*obs.*) beauty : shape, phantom : cast of face : an element or prominent trait of anything : a characteristic : a part of the body, esp. of the face : (*pl.*) the face : a department of a newspaper : (*U.S.*) anything offered as a special attraction or distinctive characteristic.—Also *adj.*—*v.t.* (*coll.*) to have features resembling : to be a feature of : (*U.S.*) to make a feature of : to present prominently.—**feature film**, a long cinematograph film forming the basis of a programme ; **feature programme**, a wireless programme that reconstructs dramatically the life of a prominent person, or an important event, or gives a dramatic picture of an employment or activity.—*adjs.* **feat′ured**, with features well marked ; **feat′ureless**, destitute of distinct features ; **feat′urely**, handsome. [O.Fr. *faiture*—L. *factūra—facĕre*, to make.]

febrile, *fēb′*, *feb′ril*, or *-ril*, *adj.* of or like fever : feverish.—*ns.* **febril′ity** (*fi-bris′i-ti*), feverishness ; **febricula** (*fi-brik′ū-lä*), **febricule** (*feb′*), a slight short fever.—*adjs.* **febrifacient** (*fē-bri-fā′shɔnt ;* L. *faciēns*, *-entis*, making), producing fever ;

febrif'ic (*fi-*), febrifacient: feverish; **febrifugal** (*fi-brif'ū-gl, feb-ri-fū'gl; L. fugāre*, to drive off).— *ns.* **febrifuge** (*feb'* or *feb'ri-fū*), that which drives off fever; **febril'ity**. [L. *febris*, fever.]

Febronianism, *feb-rō'ni-ən-izm, n.* a system of doctrine antagonistic to the claims of the Pope and asserting the independence of national churches, propounded in 1763 by Johann Nikolaus von Hontheim under the pseudonym Justinus *Febronius*.

February, *feb'roo-ər-i, n.* the second month of the year. [L. *Februārius* (*mēnsis*), the month of expiation, *februa*, the feast of expiation.]

feces, fecal. See **faeces, faecal.**

fecht, *fehht*, **fechter,** *-ər,* Scots forms of **fight, fighter.**

fecial. See **fetial.**

feck, *fek, n.* (*obs.*) purport: substance: (*Scot.*) efficacy: quantity, number: the bulk.—*adj.* **feck'-less,** spiritless: helpless: futile.—*adv.* **feck'ly,** mostly: nearly. [Aphetic for **effect**.]

fecula, *fek'ū-lä, n.* starch got as a sediment: sediment, dregs.—*ns.* **fec'ulence, fec'ulency.**— *adj.* **fec'ulent,** containing or consisting of faeces or sediment: foul: turbid. [L. *faecula,* dim. of *faex,* dregs.]

fecund, *jek'und, fēk'und, -ənd, adj.* fruitful: fertile: prolific.—*v.t.* **fec'undāte,** to make fruitful: to impregnate.—*ns.* **fecundā'tion; fecundity** (*fi-kund'i-ti*), fruitfulness: prolificness. [L. *fēcundus,* fruitful.]

fed, *fed, pa.t.* and *pa.p.* of **feed.**

fedarie, foedarie, *fē'dər-i,* **federarie,** *fed'ər-ər-i, ns.* Shakespearian words for a confederate, accomplice. [L. *foedus, -eris,* treaty; moulded on **feudary.**]

fedelini, *fed-e-lē'nē, n.* vermicelli. [It.]

federal, *fed'ər-əl, adj.* pertaining to or consisting of a treaty or covenant: confederated, founded upon mutual agreement: of a union or government in which several states, while independent in home affairs, combine for national or general purposes, as in the United States (in the American Civil War, *Federal* was the name applied to the states of the North which defended the Union against the *Confederate* separatists of the South).— *n.* a supporter of federation: a Unionist soldier in the American Civil War.—*v.t.* **fed'eralise.**—*ns.* **fed'eralism,** the principles or cause maintained by federalists; **fed'eralist,** a supporter of a federal constitution or union; **fed'erary** (*Shak.*), a confederate.—*v.t.* and *v.i.* **fed'erate,** to join in league or federation.—*adj.* united by league: confederated.—*n.* **federā'tion,** the act of uniting in league: a federal union.—*adj.* **fed'erātive,** united in league.—**Federal Bureau of Investigation,** in the U.S., a bureau or subdivision of the Department of Justice that investigates crimes, such as smuggling and counterfeiting, that are the concern of the federal government; **federal (or covenant) theology,** that first worked out by Cocceius (1603-69), based on the idea of two covenants between God and man— of Works and of Grace (see **covenant**). [L. *foedus, foederis,* a treaty, akin to *fīdēre,* to trust.]

fedora, *fi-dō'rä, n.* (*U.S.*) a felt hat dented lengthwise, orig. with curled brim. [*Fédora,* a play by Sardou.]

fee, *fē, n.* (*obs.*) cattle, live-stock: (*obs.*) property: (*obs.*) money: price paid for services, as to a lawyer or physician: recompense, wages: the sum exacted for any special privilege: a grant of land for feudal service: feudal tenure: service: feesimple: inheritance: possession: ownership.— *v.t.* to pay a fee to: to hire (*pr.p.* **fee'ing;** *pa.t.* and *pa.p.* **feed** or **fee'd**).—*ns.* **fee'-farm** (*Shak.*) tenure by fee-simple at a fixed rent without services; **fee'-grief** (*Shak.*), a private grief; **fee'ing-mar'ket** (*Scot.*), a fair or market at which farm-servants are hired for the year or half-year following; **fee'-sim'ple,** unconditional inheritance; **fee'-tail,** an entailed estate, which on failure of heirs reverts to the donor.—**base fee,** a qualified fee, a freehold estate of inheritance to which a qualification is annexed; **conditional fee,** a fee granted on condition, or limited to particular heirs: the estate of a mortgagee of land, possession of which is conditional on payment; **great fee,** the holding of a tenant of the Crown. [Partly O.E. *feoh,* cattle, property; Ger. *vieh,* O.N. *fé;* allied to L. *pecus,* cattle, *pecūnia,* money; partly A.Fr. *fee,* probably ultimately Gmc. and of the same origin.]

feeble, *fē'bl, adj.* very weak: forceless: vacillating: faint.—*adj.* **fee'ble-mind'ed,** weak-minded to the extent of being unable to compete with others or to manage one's affairs with ordinary prudence: irresolute.—*ns.* **fee'bleness; fe'blesse** (*Spens.*)— *adv.* **fee'bly.** [O.Fr. *foible,* for *floible*—L. *flēbilis,* lamentable, from *flēre,* to weep.]

feed, *fēd, v.t.* to give, furnish, or administer food to: to nourish: to furnish with necessary material: to foster: (*U.S.*) to give as food or as material to be used progressively: to furnish (an actor) with cues or opportunities of achieving an effect.—*v.i.* to take food: to nourish oneself by eating: (*pr.p.* **feed'ing;** *pa.t.* and *pa.p.* **fed**).—*n.* an allowance of provender, esp. to cattle: fodder: feeding: pasture: a plentiful meal: material supplied progressively for any operation: the means, channel, motion or rate of such supply: rate of progress of a tool: a theatrical feeder.—*ns.* **feedback, feedback,** the interconnexion of the input and output terminals of an amplifier so that part of the output energy is returned; **feed'er,** one who feeds, in any sense: an actor who feeds another: that which supplies (water, electricity, ore, paper, etc.): a tributary: an eater: a feeding-bottle: a bib: one who fattens cattle: a shepherd: (*Shak.*) a dependant, a servant: (*obs.*) a parasite; **feed'-head,** a cistern that supplies water to a boiler; **feed'-heat'er,** an apparatus for heating water for a boiler; **feed'ing,** act of eating: that which is eaten: pasture: the placing of the sheets of paper in position for a printing or ruling machine; **feed'ing-bott'le,** a bottle for supplying liquid food to an infant; **feed'-pipe,** a pipe for supplying liquid, as water to a boiler or cistern; **feed'-pump,** a force-pump for supplying a boiler with water; **feed'-water,** water supplied to a boiler, etc.—**fed up** (*slang*), sated: jaded: nauseated; **off one's feed,** without appetite, disinclined to eat. [O.E. *fēdan,* to feed.]

feed, *fēd, pa.t.* and *pa.p.* of **fee.**

fee-faw-fum, *fē'-faw'-fum', n.* a nursery word for anything frightful. [From *Jack the Giant-killer.*]

feel, *fēl, v.t.* to perceive by the touch: to try by touch: to be conscious of: to be keenly sensible of: to have an inward persuasion of: to experience. —*v.i.* to know by the touch: to have the emotions excited: to produce a certain sensation when touched, as to feel hard or hot: (*pr.p.* **feel'ing;** *pa.t.* and *pa.p.* **felt**).—*n.* the sensation of touch.— *ns.* **feel'er,** a remark cautiously dropped, or any indirect stratagem, to sound the opinions of others: a tentacle: a jointed organ in the head of insects, etc., possessed of a delicate sense—an *antenna;* **feel'ing,** the sense of touch: perception of objects by touch: consciousness of pleasure or pain: tenderness: emotion: sensibility, susceptibility, sentimentality: opinion as resulting from emotion: (*pl.*) the affections or passions.—*adj.* expressive of great sensibility or tenderness: easily or strongly affected by emotion: sympathetic: compassionate: pitying: deeply felt.—*adj.* **feel'ingless.**—*adv.* **feel'ingly.**—**feel after** (*B.*), to search for. [O.E. *fēlan,* to feel; Ger. *fühlen;* prob. akin to L. *palpāri,* to stroke.]

feer. Same as **fere.**

feer, *fēr, v.i.* to draw the first furrow in ploughing, to mark out the rigs. [Perh. O.E. *fýrian,* to make a furrow—*furh,* furrow.]

feet, *fēt, pl.* of **foot.**—*adj.* **feet'less,** footless.

feeze, pheese, pheeze, phese, *fēz, v.t.* (*Shak.;* now *dial.*) to drive, drive off: to settle the business of: to beat: to worry, perturb, discompose.— Also (*U.S.*) **faze, phase** (*fāz*).—*n.* (*dial.*) a rush: a rub: (*U.S.*) perturbation. [O.E. *fēsian,* to drive away.]

fegary, *fi-gā'ri, n.* a variant of **vagary.**

fegs, *fegz, interj.* in faith. [See **fay, faith, faix**.]

fehmgericht. Same as **vehmgericht.**

feign (*Spens.* **fain, faine, fayne**), *fān, v.t.* to fashion: to invent: to imagine falsely: to assume fictitiously: to imagine: to make a show or pretence of, to counterfeit, simulate: (*Spens.*) to dissemble. —*adj.* **feigned,** pretended: simulating: imagined: fictitious.—*adv.* **feign′edly.**—*ns.* **feign′edness; feign′ing.** [Fr. *feindre,* pr.p. *feignant,* to feign— L. *fingĕre, fictum,* to form.]

feint, *fānt, n.* a false appearance: a pretence: a mock-assault: a deceptive movement in fencing, boxing, etc.—*v.i.* to make a feint. [Fr. *feinte,* see above.]

feint, *fānt, adj.* a printers' or stationers' spelling of **faint.**—*n.pl.* **feints** (same as **faints**).

feldgrau, *felt′grow, n.* and *adj.* field-grey, the colour of German military uniforms. [Ger. *feld,* field, *grau,* grey.]

feldspar, another form (preferred in *U.S.*) of **felspar.**

Félibre, *fā-lē′br′, n.* a member of the **Félibrige** (*-brēzh′*), a Provençal literary brotherhood, founded in 1854 by Joseph Roumanille (1818-91) and six others. [Prov., perh. doctors of the law.]

felicity, *fi-lis′i-ti, n.* happiness: delight: a blessing: a happy event: a happiness of expression.—*v.t.* **felic′itate,** to express joy or pleasure to: to congratulate.—*n.* **felicita′tion,** the act of congratulating.—*adj.* **felic′itous,** happy: prosperous: delightful: appropriate.—*adv.* **felic′itously.** [O.Fr. *felicité*—L. *felicitās, -ātis,* from *fēlix, -īcis,* happy.]

feline, *fē′lin, adj.* pertaining to the cat or the cat kind: like a cat.—*n.* any animal of the cat tribe.—*ns.* **felinity** (*fi-lin′i-ti*); **Fē′lis,** the cat genus, typical of the fam. **Fē′lidae** and sub-family **Fēli′nae.** [L. *fēlīnus—fēlēs,* a cat.]

fell, *fel, n.* a hill: an upland tract of waste, pasture, or moorland. [O.N. *fjall;* Dan. *fjeld.*]

fell, *fel, pa.t.* of **fall.**

fell, *fel, v.t.* to cause to fall: to knock down: to bring to the ground: to cut down: (*dial.*) to prostrate (as by illness): to stitch down with an overturned edge.—*n.* a quantity felled at a time: a falling of lambs: a felled hem.—*adj.* **fell′able.**—*n.* **fell′er.** [O.E. *fælla(n), fella(n)* (W.S. *fiellan*), causative of *fallan (feallan),* to fall.]

fell, *fel, n.* a skin: a membrane: covering of rough hair.—*n.* **fell′monger,** one who prepares skins for the tanner. [O.E. *fell;* cf. Ger. *fell,* L. *pellis,* Gr. *pella.*]

fell, *fel, n.* (*Spens.*) gall, bitterness. [L. *fel.*]

fell, *fel, adj.* cruel: fierce: dire: ruthless: deadly: keen: doughty: (*Scot.*) pungent: (*Scot.*) great, mighty.—*adv.* in a fell manner: (*Scot.*) very: very much.—*adj.* **fell-lurk′ing** (*Shak.*) lurking with treacherous purpose.—*n.* **fell′ness.**—*adv.* **felly** (*fel′li*). [O.Fr. *fel,* cruel—L.L. *fellō, -ōnis;* see **felon.**]

fellah, *fel′a, n.* a peasant, esp. in Egypt (*pl.* **fell′ahs, fellahin, -hēn′**). [Ar. *fellāh,* tiller.]

felloe. See **felly.**

fellow, *fel′ō, n.* an associate: a companion and equal: one of a pair, a mate: a counterpart: the like: a member of a university who enjoys a fellowship: a member of a scientific or other society: a man generally: a worthless or contemptible person.—*ns.* **fell′ow-cit′izen,** one belonging to the same city; **fell′ow-comm′oner,** at Cambridge and elsewhere, one of a privileged class of undergraduates, dining at the Fellows' table; **fell′ow-coun′tryman,** a man of the same country; **fell′ow-crea′ture,** one of the same creation, a creature like oneself; **fell′ow-feel′ing,** feeling of common interest: sympathy; **fell′ow-heir,** a joint-heir.—*adj.* **fell′owly** (*Shak.*), companionable.—*ns.* **fell′ow-man,** one who shares humanity with oneself; **fell′ow-mem′ber,** a member of the same body; **fell′ow-serv′ant,** one who has the same master; **fell′owship,** the state of being a fellow or partner: friendly intercourse: communion: an association: an endowment in a college for the support of graduates called Fellows: the position and income of a fellow: reckoning of proportional division of profit and loss among partners; **fell′ow-towns′man,** a dweller in the same town; **fell′ow-trav′eller,** one who travels in the same railway carriage, bus, etc., or along the same route: (*fig.;* used derogatorily) one who, though not a party member, takes the same political road, a sympathiser (trans. of Russ. word). —**good fellowship,** companionableness; **right hand of fellowship,** the right hand given esp. by one minister or elder to another at an ordination in some churches. [M.E. *felawe*—O.N. *félagi,* a partner in goods, from *fé* (O.E. *feoh;* Ger. *vieh*), cattle, property, and root *lag-,* a laying together, a law. Cf. **fee, law, lay.**]

felly, *fel′i,* **felloe,** *fel′i, fel′ō, n.* a curved piece in the circumference of a wheel: the circular rim of the wheel. [O.E. *felg;* Ger. *felge.*]

felon, *fel′ən, n.* one guilty of felony: a wicked person: an inflamed sore.—*adj.* wicked or cruel: fell: fierce: (*obs.*) mighty.—*adj.* **felonious** (*fi-lō′ni-əs*), wicked: depraved: done with the deliberate intention to commit crime.—*adv.* **felō′niously.**—*n.* **felō′niousness,** the quality of being felonious.—*adj.* **fel′onous** (*Spens.*), fell.—*ns.* **fel′onry,** a body of felons; **fel′ony,** (*orig.*) a crime punished by total forfeiture of lands, etc.: a grave crime, beyond a misdemeanour, as one punishable by penal servitude or death. [O.Fr.,— L.L. *fellō, -ōnis,* a traitor, prob. L. *fel,* gall.]

felsite, *fel′sīt, n.* a fine-grained intimate mixture of quartz and orthoclase: a devitrified acid igneous rock, characterised by felsitic structure.—*adj.* **felsitic** (*-sit′ik*), consisting of a fine patchy mosaic of quartz and felspar. [**felspar.**]

felspar, *fel′spär,* **feldspar,** *fel(d)′spär, n.* any member of the most important group of rock-forming minerals, anhydrous silicates of aluminium along with potassium (as *orthoclase, microcline*), sodium, calcium, or both (the *plagioclases*), or sodium and barium (*hyalophane*)—also (*obs.*) **feld′spath.**—*adj.* **feld(d)spathic** (*-spath′ik*).—*n.* **fel(d)′spathoid,** any mineral of a group chemically akin to felspar, including nepheline, leucite, sodalite, etc. [Swed. *feldtspat,* a name given in 1740 by D. Tilas—Sw. *feldt* or *fält,* field, *spat,* spar, apparently because of the abundance of felspar in tilled fields in SW. Finland; confused with Ger. *fels,* rock.]

felstone, *fel′stōn, n.* felsite—an old-fashioned name. [Ger. *felsstein,* partly anglicised.]

felt, *felt, pa.t.* and *pa.p.* of **feel.**

felt, *felt, n.* a fabric formed without weaving, using the natural tendency of the fibres of wool and certain kinds of hair to interlace and cling together.—*v.t.* to make into felt: to cover with felt.— *v.i.* to become felted.—*v.t.* **felt′er,** to mat together like felt.—*n.* **felt′ing,** the art or process of making felt or of matting fibres together: the felt itself. [O.E. *felt;* cf. Du. *vilt,* Ger. *filz.*]

felucca, *fe-luk′ä, n.* a small merchant-vessel used in the Mediterranean, with two masts, lateen sails, and often a rudder at each end. [It. *feluca; cf.* Ar. *falūkah.*]

felwort, *fel′wurt, n.* a gentian. [O.E. *feldwyrt— feld,* field, *wyrt,* wort.]

female, *fē′māl, n.* a woman or girl (now verging on the impolite): any animal or plant of the same sex as a woman.—*adj.* of the sex that produces young or eggs, fructifications or seeds: for, belonging to, characteristic of, or fancifully attributed to that sex: (*Shak.*) womanish: (*biol.*) of the sex characterised by relatively large gametes: (*mach.*) of parts of mechanism, hollow and adapted to receive a counterpart.—Also (*Milt.*) **fe′mäl.**—*ns.* **fe′māleness, femality** (*-mal′i-ti*).—**female screw,** a screw cut on the inward surface of a hole. [Fr. *femelle*—L. *femella,* a girl, dim. of *fēmina,* woman; the second syllable influenced by association with **male.**]

feme, *fem, n.* (*law*) a woman.—**feme covert** (*kuv′ərt*), a married woman; **feme sole,** a spinster, widow, or married woman legally in the position of an unmarried. [O.Fr. *feme.*]

femerell, *fem′ər-əl, n.* an outlet for smoke in a roof. [O.Fr. *fumeraille*—L. *fūmus,* smoke.]

femetary. See **fumitory.**

feminal, *fem'in-əl*, *adj.* female : feminine.—*ns.*
feminal'ity (*-al'i-ti*), **feminē'ity, feminil'ity,
fem'inineness, feminin'ity, femin'ity,** female-
ness : the quality of being female, feminine,
womanly or womanish.—*adj.* **fem'inine** (*-in*),
female : characteristic of, peculiar or appropriate
to, woman or the female sex : womanish : (*gram.*)
of that gender to which words denoting females,
and in some languages various associated classes
of words, belong.—*n.* the female sex or nature :
a word of feminine gender.—*adv.* **fem'ininely.**—
n. **fem'ininism,** an idiom or expression characteristic of woman : addiction to feminine ways.—
v.t. and *v.i.* **fem'inise,** to make or become
feminine.—*ns.* **fem'inism,** advocacy of women's
rights, of the movement for the advancement and
emancipation of women; **fem'inist,** an advocate
or favourer of feminism : a student of women.—
feminine ending, (*Fr. pros.*) ending of a line in
mute *e* (the French feminine suffix) : ending in
one unstressed syllable; **feminine caesura,** one
which does not immediately follow the ictus;
feminine rhyme, a rhyme on a feminine ending.
[L. *fēmina*, woman.]

femiter, *fem'i-tər,* **fenitar,** *fen'.* See **fumitory.**

femur, *fē'mur, n.* the thigh-bone : the third segment
of an insect's leg : (*pl.* **fē'murs, fem'ora,** *fem'ər-ä*).
—*adj.* **fem'oral,** belonging to the thigh.—
femoral artery, the main artery of the thigh.
[L. *fēmur, -ŏris,* thigh.]

fen, *fen, n.* low marshy land often, or partially,
covered with water : a morass or bog.—*ns.* **fen'-
berry,** the cranberry; **fen'-crick'et,** the mole
cricket; **fen'-fire,** the Will-o'-the-wisp; **fen'land;**
fen'man, a dweller in fen country.—*adjs.* **fenn'-
ish; fenn'y; fen'-sucked** (*Shak.*), drawn out of
bogs. [O.E. *fenn;* O.N. *fen.*]

fen, *fen, v.t.* an exclamation in boys' games, used
to bar a right or privilege. [Cf. **fend.**]

fence, *fens, n.* a barrier, esp. of wood or of wood
and wire for enclosing, bounding or protecting
land : the art of fencing : defence : (*thieves' slang*)
a receiver of stolen goods, also a receiving-house.—
v.t. to enclose with a fence : to fortify : to shield :
to keep off.—*v.i.* to guard : to practise fencing :
to conceal the truth by equivocal answers : to
answer or dispute evasively : to leap fences.—
adjs. **fenced,** enclosed with a fence; **fence'less,**
without fence or enclosure, open.—*ns.* **fence'-
liz'ard,** a small American lizard (Sceloporus);
fenc'er, one who practises fencing with a sword.—
adj. **fenc'ible,** capable of being fenced or defended.
—*n.* (*hist.*) a militiaman or volunteer enlisted at a
crisis.—*adj.* **fenc'ing,** defending or guarding.—
n. the act of erecting a fence : material for fences :
fences collectively : the leaping of fences :
(*thieves' slang*) receiving stolen goods : the act
or art of attack and defence with a sword or the
like.—*n.* **fenc'ing-master,** one who teaches
fencing.—**fence the tables,** in the ancient usage
of Scotland, to debar the unworthy from partaking
in communion; **sit on the fence,** to avoid committing oneself : to remain neutral; **sunk fence,**
a ditch or water-course. [Aphetic from **defence.**]

fend, *fend, v.t.* to ward off : to shut out : to defend.
—*v.i.* to offer resistance : to provide.—*n.* self-
support, the shift one makes for oneself.—*adj.*
fend'y, (*Scot.*) resourceful : thrifty. [Aphetic for
defend.]

fend, *fend,* (*Milt.*). Same as **fiend.**

fender, *fend'ər, n.* a guard before a hearth to
confine the ashes : a protection for a ship's side
against piers, etc., consisting of a bundle of rope,
etc. : any structure serving as a guard against
contact or impact.—*ns.* **fend'er-stool,** a long
stool placed beside a fireside fender. [**fend.**]

fenestella, *fen-is-tel'ä, n.* a small window or
window-like opening; a niche containing the
piscina : **Fenestella,** a Palaeozoic genus of lace-
like Polyzoa. [L., dim. of *fenestra,* a window.]

fenestra, *fi-nes'trä, n.* a window or other wall-
opening : a perforation : a translucent spot.—*n.*
fenes'tral, a window with some translucent
material instead of glass.—*adj.* of or like a window :
perforated : with translucent spots.—*adj.* **fenes-**

trate (*fen'is-trit, fi-nes'trit*), **-d,** having windows
or appearance of windows : pierced : perforated :
having translucent spots.— *i.* **fenestrā'tion,** the
arrangement of windows in a building : fact of
being fenestrate : perforation : the operation of
making an artificial fenestra when the fenestra
ovalis has been clogged by growth of bone.—
fenestra ovalis, rotunda, the oval and round
windows, two membrane-covered openings between the middle and the internal ear. [L.]

Fenian, *fē'nyən, n.* a member of an association of
Irishmen founded in New York in 1857 for the
overthrow of the English government in Ireland.—
adj. belonging to the legendary *fiann,* or to the
modern Fenians.—*n.* **Fē'nianism.** [Old Ir. *Féne,*
one of the names of the ancient population of
Ireland, confused in modern times with *fiann,* the
militia of Finn and other ancient Irish kings]

fenks, *fengks,* **finks,** *fingks, n.* the refuse of whale-
blubber. [Origin unknown.]

fennec, *fen'ək, n.* a little African fox with large ears.
[Ar. *fenek.*]

fennel, *fen'əl, n.* a genus (*Foeniculum*) of yellow-
flowered umbelliferous plants, allied to dill, but
distinguished by the cylindrical, strongly-ribbed
fruit.—*n.* **fenn'el-flower,** Nigella.—**giant fennel,**
an umbelliferous plant, *Ferula communis.* [O.E.
finul—L. *fēniculum, fēnuc(u)lum,* fennel—*fēnum,*
hay.]

fent, *fent, n.* a slit, crack : (*N. Engl.*) a remnant or
odd, short, or damaged piece of cloth.—*n.* **fent'-
merchant.** [O.Fr. *fente*—L. *findĕre,* to cleave.]

fenugreek, *fen'ū-grēk, n.* a plant (*Trigonella
Foenum-graecum*), allied to melilot. [L. *fēnum
graecum,* Greek hay.]

feod, feodal, feodary. Same as **feud, feudal,
feudary.**

feoff, *fef, n.* a fief.—*v.t.* to grant possession of a
fief or property in land.—*ns.* **feoffee',** the person
invested with the fief; **feoff'er, feoff'or,** he who
grants the fief; **feoff'ment,** the gift of a fief.
[O.Fr. *feoffer* or *fiefer*—O.Fr. *fief.* See **fee.**]

feracious, *fi-rā'shəs, adj.* fruitful.—*n.* **feracity**
(*fi-ras'i-ti; rare*). [L. *ferāx, -ācis—ferre,* to bear.]

feral, *fē'rəl, adj.* wild : untamed : uncultivated :
run wild : brutish.—*adjs.* **fer'alised,** run wild
from domestication; **ferine** (*-rin, -rin*), pertaining
to or like a wild beast : wild : brutish.—*n.* **ferity**
(*fer'i-ti*), wildness : uncultivated state : savagery.
[L. *fera,* a wild beast.]

feral, *fē'rəl, adj.* deadly : funereal. [L. *fērālis.*]

fer-de-lance, *fer'də-läns, n.* the lance-headed or
yellow viper of tropical America. [Fr., lance-
head (iron).]

fere, feare, feer, fiere, pheere, *fēr, n.* (*arch.*) a
companion : a mate : a spouse : an equal.—**in fere,**
or (*adv.*) **yfere',** together, in company. [O.E.
gefēra, companion, *gefēre,* company.]

fere, *fēr, adj.* (*Scot.*) able, sound. [O.E. *fēre.*]

feretory, *fer'i-tər-i, n.* a shrine for relics carried in
processions. [L. *feretrum*—Gr. *pheretron,* bier,
litter—*pherein,* to bear.]

ferial, *fē'ri-əl, adj.* pertaining to holidays : belonging
to any day of the week which is neither a fast nor
a festival. [L. *fēria,* a holiday.]

Feringhi, Feringhee, *fer-ing'gē, n.* a Hindu name
for a European.—Also **Farin'gee.** [**Frank.**]

ferly, *fər'li, adj.* fearful : sudden : singular.—*n.*
(*Scot.; fär'li*) a wonder.—*v.i.* to wonder. [O.E.
fǣrlic, sudden; cf. Ger. *gefährlich,* dangerous.]

ferm, *fərm, n.* a farm : (*Spens.*) lodging. [**farm.**]

fermata, *fer-mä'tä, n.* (*mus.*) a pause. [It.]

ferment, *fər'mənt, n.* a substance that excites
fermentation : internal motion amongst the parts
of a fluid : agitation : tumult.—*v.t.* **ferment**
(*-ment'*), to excite fermentation in : to work up,
excite.—*v.i.* to rise and swell by the action of
fermentation : to work, used of wine, etc. : to be
in excited action : to work in the mind, as emotions.
—*n.* **fermentabil'ity.**—*adj.* **ferment'able,** capable of fermentation.—*n.* **fermentā'tion,** the act
or process of fermenting : a slow decomposition
process of organic substances induced by micro-
organisms, or by complex nitrogenous organic
substances (*enzymes*) of vegetable or animal

origin, usually accompanied by evolution of heat and gas, e.g. alcoholic fermentation of sugar and starch, and lactic fermentation: restless action of the mind or feelings.—*adj.* **ferment′ative**, causing or consisting in fermentation.—*n.* **ferment′ativeness**.—*adjs.* **ferment′ed; ferment′esc′ible**, capable of being fermented; **fermentitious** (*-ish′əs*); **ferment′ive**. [Fr.,—L. *fermentum*, for *fervimentum*—*fervēre*, to boil.]

fern, *fərn*, *n.* one of the class of higher or vascular cryptogamous plants, Filices.—*ns.* **fern′-ally′** (or *-al′*), a pteridophyte other than a fern; **fern′ery**, a place for rearing ferns; **fern′-owl**, the night-jar: the short-eared owl; **fern′-seed**, the spores of ferns, once held to confer invisibility; **fern′shaw**, a thicket of ferns; **fern′tic(k)le** (*obs.* or *dial.*), also **ferni-, fairni-, ferny-, fairny-** (*Scot.*), a freckle.—*adjs.* **fern′tic(k)led; fern′y**. [O.E. *fearn;* Ger. *farn.*]

ferocious, *fə-rō′shəs*, *adj.* savage, fierce: cruel.—*adv.* **ferō′ciously**.—*ns.* **ferō′ciousness; ferocity** (*-ros′i-ti*), savage cruelty of disposition: untamed fierceness. [L. *ferōx, ferōcis*, wild—*ferus*, wild.]

ferrandine. See **farandine**.

ferrate, *fer′āt*, *n.* a salt of ferric acid.—*adjs.* **ferr′eous**, pertaining to, containing, or like iron; **ferr′ic**, of iron; (*chem.*) of trivalent iron (**ferr′ic acid**, a hypothetical acid H_2FeO_4).—*ns.* **ferricy′anide**, a salt of hydroferricyanic acid; **ferricyan′ogen**, the trivalent radical, $Fe(CN)_6$, of the ferricyanides.—*adj.* **ferrif′erous**, bearing or yielding iron.—*ns.* **ferr′ite**, a form of pure iron; **ferr′o-all′oy** (or *-oi′*), an alloy of iron and some other metal; **ferr′o-chro′mium, ferr′o-mang′-anese, ferr′o-molyb′denum, ferr′o-nick′el**, an alloy of iron with much chromium, etc. (as the case may be); **ferr′o-con′crete**, reinforced concrete; **ferrocy′anide**, a salt of hydroferrocyanic acid; **ferrocyan′ogen**, the quadrivalent radical, $Fe(CN)_6$, of the ferrocyanides.—*adjs.* **ferromagnēs′ian**, containing iron and magnesium; **ferromagnet′ic**, strongly magnetic: formerly, paramagnetic.—*ns.* **ferr′o-print**, a photograph made by means of iron salts; **ferropruss′iate**, ferrocyanide.—*adj.* **ferrosoferr′ic**, combining ferrous and ferric.—*n.* **ferr′otype**, an old form of photograph upon a film on an iron plate.—*adj.* **ferr′ous**, of bivalent iron: (*loosely*) containing iron. [L. *ferrum*, iron.]

ferret, *fer′it*, *n.* narrow silk or cotton ribbon.—Also *adj.* [It. *fioretto*, dim.—L. *flōs, flōris*, flower.]

ferret, *fer′it*, *n.* a half-tamed albino variety of the polecat, employed in unearthing rabbits.—*v.t.* to drive out of a hiding-place: to search out cunningly.—*v.t.* and *v.i.* to hunt with a ferret: (*pr.p.* **ferr′eting;** *pa.p.* **ferr′eted**).—*n.* **ferr′eter**, one who ferrets.—*adj.* **ferr′ety**, like a ferret. [O.Fr. *furet*, a ferret, dim.—L.L. *fūrō, -ōnis*, ferret, robber—L. *fūr*, a thief.]

ferro-alloy, etc. See **ferrate**.

ferruginous, *fe-, fə-rōō′jin-əs*, *adj.* of the colour of iron-rust: impregnated with iron.—Also **ferrugin′eous** (*fer-*).—*n.* **ferru′go** (*-gō*), rust disease of plants. [L. *ferrūgō, -inis*, iron-rust—*ferrum*.]

ferrule, *fer′əl*, *n.* a metal band, ring or cap on a stick, etc.—Also **ferr′el** (*Scot.* **virl**). [O.Fr. *virole*—L. *viriola*, a bracelet.]

ferry, *fer′i*, *v.t.* to carry or convey over a water, etc., in a boat, ship or aircraft.—*v.i.* to cross by ferry (*pr.p.* **ferr′ying;** *pa.t.* and *pa.p.* **ferr′ied**).—*n.* a place or route of carriage over water: the right of conveying passengers: a ferry-boat.—*ns.* **ferr′iage**, provision for ferrying: the fare paid for it; **ferr′y-boat; ferr′y-house**, a ferryman's house: a place of shelter or refreshment at a ferry; **ferr′yman**. [O.E. *ferian*, to convey, *faran*, to go; Ger. *fähre*, a ferry—*fahren*, to go, to carry.]

fertile, *fər-til*, *adj.* able to bear or produce abundantly: rich in resources: inventive: fertilising: capable of breeding, hatching, or germinating.—*adv.* **fer′tilely**.—*n.* **fertilisa′tion** (*-ti-lī-zā′shən*), the act or process of fertilising.—*v.t.* **fer′tilise**, to make fertile or fruitful: to enrich: to impregnate: to pollinate.—*ns.* **fer′tiliser**, one who, or that which, fertilises; **fertility** (*-til′i-ti*), fruitful-

ness: richness: abundance. [Fr.,—L. *fertilis—ferre*, to bear.]

ferule, *fer′(y)ōol*, *n.* a cane or rod used for punishment.—*n.* **fer′ula**, a ferule: a staff of command: **Fer′ula**, the giant fennel genus.—*adj.* **ferulā′-ceous**, like a cane, reed, or Ferula. [L. *ferula*, a giant fennel—*ferīre*, to strike.]

fervent, *fər′vənt*, *adj.* hot: ardent: zealous: warm in feeling.—*n.* **fer′vency**, heat: eagerness: emotional warmth.—*adv.* **fer′vently**.—*adjs.* **fervescent** (*-ves′ənt*), growing hot; **fer′vid**, very hot: having burning desire or emotion: glowing: zealous.—*n.* **fervid′ity**.—*adv.* **fer′vidly**.—*ns.* **fer′vidness; Fervidor′, Thermidor; fer′vour**, heat: heat of emotion: zeal.—*adj.* **fer′vorous**. [L. *fervēre*, to boil, *fervēscĕre, fervidus*.]

Fescennine, *fes′ə-nīn, -nin, adj.* scurrilous.—**Fescennine verses**, rude extempore verses, generally in Saturnian measure, in which the parties rallied and ridiculed one another. [The Etruscan town of *Fescennium*.]

fescue, *fes′kū, n.* a genus (Festuca) of grasses, very nearly allied to brome-grass, and including many valuable pasture and fodder grasses: a pointer used in teaching. [O.Fr. *festu*—L. *festūca*, a straw.]

fesse, fess, *fes, n.* (*her.*) one of the ordinaries—a horizontal band over the middle of an escutcheon, usually one-third of the whole.—*n.* **fesse′-point**, the centre of an escutcheon.—*adv.* **fess(e)′wise**. [Fr. *fasce*—L. *fascia*, a band.]

festal, *fes′tl, adj.* pertaining to a feast or holiday: joyous: gay.—*n.* a festivity.—*adv.* **fes′tally**.—*n.* **festil′ogy**, a treatise on ecclesiastical festivals. [See **feast**.]

fester, *fes′tər, v.i.* to become corrupt or malignant: to suppurate.—*v.t.* to cause to fester or rankle.—*n.* a wound discharging corrupt matter. [O.Fr. *festre*—L. *fistula*, an ulcer.]

festinate, *fes′ti-nāt, v.t.* to accelerate.—*adj.* (*Shak.*) hurried, hasty.—*adv.* **fes′tinately** (*Shak.*) hastily.—*n.* **festina′tion**. [L. *festināre, -ātum*, to hurry.]

festive, *fes′tiv, adj.* festal: mirthful.—*n.* **fes′tival**, a joyful or honorific celebration: a feast: a season of performances of music, plays, or the like.—*adv.* **fes′tively**.—*n.* **festiv′ity**, social mirth: joyfulness: gaiety.—*adj.* **fes′tivous** (or *-tī′*), festive. [L. *fēstīvus—fēstus*.]

festoon, *fes-tōōn′, n.* a garland suspended between two points: (*archit.*) an ornament like a garland.—*v.t.* to adorn, hang, or connect with festoons.—*v.i.* to hang in festoons.—*n.* **festoon′-blind**, a window-blind of cloth gathered into rows of festoons in its width. [Fr. *feston*, app. conn. with L. *fēstum*, a festival.]

festschrift, *fest′shrift, n.* a festival publication, commonly a collection of learned papers or the like, presented by their authors and published in honour of some person. [Ger., festival writing.]

fet, fett, *fet, v.t.* obsolete form of **fetch**.

fetal. See **foetus**.

fetch, *fech, v.t.* to bring: to go and get: to obtain as its price: to cause to come: to call forth: to recall from a swoon: to draw (as blood, breath): to achieve the gaining over of, to take: to derive: to strike: to perform, make, take, utter (as a leap, a sigh, a circuit): to achieve: to reach or attain.—*v.i.* to make one's way: to arrive: to be effective.—*n.* the act of bringing: space carried over: a stratagem.—*adj.* **fetch′ing**, fascinating.—**fetch a compass, circuit**, to go round in a wide curve; **fetch and carry**, to perform humble services for another; **fetch a pump**, to pour water in so as to make it draw; **fetch off**, to bring out of danger or difficulty: (*Shak.*) to make away with: (*Shak.*) to fleece; **fetch out**, to draw forth, develop; **fetch up**, to recover: to come to a stop: (*U.S.*) to bring up, rear. [O.E. *fæccan*, app. an altered form of *fetian*, to fetch; cf. Ger. *fassen*, to seize.]

fetch, *fech, n.* the apparition, double, or wraith of a living person.—*n.* **fetch′-can′dle**, a nocturnal light, supposed to portend a death. [Ety. unknown.]

fête, *fet, fāt, n.* a festival: a holiday: the festival of the saint whose name one bears.—*v.t.* to entertain at a feast: to honour with festivities. [Fr.]

fetial, *fē′shəl*, *adj.* pertaining to the Roman *fētiālēs*, a priestly college of heralds: heraldic, ambassadorial.—Also **fē′cial.**

feticide. See **foetus.**

fetid, *fē′tid*, or *fet′id*, *adj.* stinking: having a strong offensive smell.—*ns.* **fē′tidness, fē′tor.**—Less justifiable spellings are **foetid, foetor.** [L. *fētidus, fētor—fētēre*, to stink.]

fetish, fetich, fetiche, *fet′ish, fē′tish*, *n.* an object believed to procure for its owner the services of a spirit lodged within it: something regarded with irrational reverence.—*ns.* **fet′ishism, fet′ichism**, the worship of a fetish: a belief in charms; **fet′ishist, fet′ichist.**—*adjs.* **fetishist′ic, fetich-is′tic.** [Fr. *fétiche*—Port. *feitiço*, magic: a name given by the Portuguese to the gods of W. Africa—Port. *feitiço*, artificial—L. *facticius—facēre*, to make.]

fetlock, *fet′lok*, *n.* a tuft of hair that grows above a horse's hoof: the part where this hair grows.—*adj.* **fet′locked**, having a fetlock: tied by the fetlock. [History obscure; long felt as a compound of **foot** and **lock** (of hair); cf. Ger. *fiszloch.*]

fetter, *fet′ər*, *n.* a chain or shackle for the feet: anything that restrains—used chiefly in *pl.*—*v.t.* to put fetters on: to restrain.—*adj.* **fett′erless.**—*n.* **fett′erlock**, (*her.*) a shackle for a horse, as a charge. [O.E. *feter;* conn. with *fōt*, foot.]

fettle, *fet′l*, *v.t.* to make ready, set in order, arrange: (*dial.*) to tidy up: to line (a furnace).—*v.i.* to potter fussily about.—*n.* condition, trim, form: lining for a furnace.—*ns.* **fett′ler; fett′ling.** [Prob. O.E. *fetel*, a belt.]

fetus. See **foetus.**

fetwa, *fet′wä*, *n.* a Moslem legal decision. [Ar.]

feu, *fū*, *n.* (*Scot.*) a tenure where the vassal, in place of military services, makes a return in grain or in money: a right to the use of land, houses, etc., in perpetuity, for a stipulated annual payment (**feu′-dū′ty**): a piece of land held in feu.—*v.t.* to vest in one who undertakes to pay the feu-duty.—*n.* **feu′ar**, one who holds real estate in consideration of payment of feu-duty. [O.Fr. *feu;* see **fee.**]

feud, *fūd*, *n.* a war waged by private individuals, families, or clans against one another on their own account: a bloody strife: a persistent state of private enmity.—**right of feud**, the right to protect oneself and one's kinsmen, and punish injuries. [O.Fr. *faide, feide*—L.L. *faida*—O.H.G. *fēhida;* vowel change unexplained; see **foe.**]

feud, *feod*, *fūd*, *n.* a fief or land held on condition of service.—*adj.* **feud′al**, pertaining to feuds or fiefs: belonging to feudalism.—*n.* **feudalisā′tion.**—*v.t.* **feud′alise**—*ns′.* **feud′alism**, the feudal system or its principles; **feud′alist; feudal′ity**, the state of being feudal: the feudal system.—*adv.* **feud′ally.**—*adjs.* **feud′ary, feod′ary, feud′atory**, holding lands or power by a feudal tenure.—Also *ns.*—*n.* **feud′ist**, a writer on feuds: one versed in the laws of feudal tenure.—**feudal system**, the system by which vassals held lands from lords-superior on condition of military service. [L.L. *feudum;* see **fee.**]

feuilleton, *fə′i-ton⁹*, *n.* in French and other newspapers, a part ruled off the bottom of a page for a serial story, critical article, etc.: a contribution of such a kind.—*ns.* **feu′illetonism** (*-tən-izm*); **feu′illetonist.** [Fr. dim. of *feuillet*, a leaf—L. *folium.*]

feutre. Same as **fewter.**

fever, *fē′vər*, *n.* disease (esp. infectious) marked by great bodily heat and quickening of pulse: extreme excitement of the passions, agitation: a painful degree of anxiety.—*v.t.* to put into a fever.—*v.i.* to become fevered.—*adj.* **fē′vered**, affected with fever: excited.—*ns.* **fē′verfew** (O.E. *fēferfūge*), a composite perennial *Matricaria* (or *Chrysanthemum*) *Parthenium*, closely allied to camomile, so called from its supposed power as a febrifuge; **fē′ver-heat**, the heat of fever: an excessive degree of excitement.—*adj.* **fē′verish**, slightly fevered: indicating fever: restlessly excited: morbidly eager.—*adv.* **fē′verishly.**—*n.* **fē′verish-**

---

ness.—*adj.* **fē′verous**, feverish: marked by sudden changes: apt to cause fever. [O.E. *fēfor*—L. *febris.*]

few, *fū*, *adj.* small in number: not many.—*n.* **few′ness**, smallness of number: (*Shak.*) few words, brevity.—**a few**, a small number (of)—used as a noun, or virtually a compound adjective; also facetiously as an *adv.*, a little; **a good few** (*dial.*) a considerable number; **in few**, in a few words, briefly; **some few**, an inconsiderable number; **the few**, the minority. [O.E. *féa*, pl. *féawe;* cf. L. *paucus*, small.]

fewmet. Same as **fumet.**

fewter, feutre, *fū′tər*, *n.* (*obs.*) a spear-rest.—*v.t.* (*Spens.*) to set in rest. [O.Fr. *feutre*, felt, a felt-lined socket.]

fewtrils, *fū′trilz*, *n.pl.* (*prov.*) little things, trifles. [See **fattrels.**]

fey, fay, fie, *fā, fui, adj.* (*Scot.*) doomed, fated soon to die, under the shadow of a sudden or violent death—imagined to be marked by extravagantly high spirits. [M.E. *fay, fey*—O.E. *fæge*, doomed; cf. Du. *veeg*, about to die.]

fez, *fez*, *n.* a red brimless truncated conical cap of wool or felt, with black tassel, worn in Egypt, formerly in Turkey—the *tarbush* (pl. **fezz′es, fez′es**).—*adj.* **fezzed** (*fezd*). [From *Fez* in Morocco.]

fiacre, *fē-ak′r′*, *n.* a hackney-coach: a cab. [Fr., from the Hôtel de St. *Fiacre* in Paris, where first used.]

fiançailles, *fē-än⁹-sā′ē*, *n.pl.* betrothal.—*n.* **fiancé**, fem. **fiancée** (*fē-än⁹′sā*), one betrothed. [Fr.]

fianchetto, *fyäng-ket′tō*, *n.* (*chess*) the early movement of a knight's pawn to develop a bishop on a long diagonal.

Fianna Fáil, *fē′an-ä foil*, the Irish republican party. [Ir., militia of Fál (a stone monument at Tara, hence Ireland); cf. **Fenian.**]

fiars, *fē′ərz, n.pl.* (*Scot.*) the prices of grain legally **struck** or fixed for the year at the *Fiars* Court, so as to regulate the payment of stipend, rent, and prices not expressly agreed upon—usu. **fiars prices.** [O.Fr. *feor, fuer*, fixed price, standard—L. *forum*, market.]

fiasco, *fi-as′kō*, *n.* a failure in a musical performance: a complete failure of any kind. [It. *fiasco*, bottle, perh. from L. *vasculum*, a little vessel, *vas*, a vessel.]

fiat, *fī′at*, L. *fē′ät*, *n.* a formal or solemn command: a short order or warrant of a judge for making out or allowing processes, letters-patent, etc.—(*Spens.*) **fiaunt′**).—*v.t.* to sanction. [L. *fiat (fiant)*, let it (them) be done, 3rd pers. sing. (plur.) pres. subj. of *fiēri*, serving as passive of *facēre*, to do.]

fib, *fib*, *n.* something said falsely: a not very serious lie.—*v.i.* to tell a fib or lie: to speak falsely (*pr.p.* **fibb′ing;** *pa.p.* **fibbed**).—*ns.* **fibb′er**, one who fibs; **fibb′ery** (*rare*), the habit of fibbing; **fib′ster**, a fibber. [Perh. **fable.**]

fibre, *fī′bər*, *n.* any fine thread or thread-like substance: a structure or material composed of fibres: texture: stamina.—*adjs.* **fī′bred**, having fibre; **fī′breless**, without fibre, strength, or nerve.—*n.* **fī′bre-plant**, a plant yielding a commercial fibre.—*adj.* **fī′briform**, fibre-like.—*ns.* **fī′bril**, a small fibre: a root-hair: a minute thread-like structure such as the longitudinal contractile elements of a muscle-fibre; **fibrill′a**, a fibril filament (*pl.* **fibrill′ae**, -*ē*).—*adjs.* **fī′brillar, fī′brillary, fī′brillate, -d**, pertaining to, of the nature of, or having fibrils or fibrous structure.—*v.i.* **fī′brillate**, to undergo fibrillation.—**fibrillā′-tion**, formation of fibrils: a mass of fibrils: a twitching of muscle-fibres: (*med.*) uncoordinated contraction of muscle-fibres in the heart.—*adjs.* **fī′brillose**, having, or covered with small fibres or the appearance of small fibres; **fī′brillous**, pertaining to or having small fibres.—*ns.* **fī′brin**, an insoluble protein precipitated as a network of fibres when blood coagulates; **fībrin′ogen** (-*jən*), a protein that forms fibrin.—*adj.* **fī′brinous**, of or like fibrin.—*n.* **fibrocar′tilage**, cartilage with embedded fibres.—*adj.* **fī′broid**, of a fibrous character.—*n.* a fibrous tumour.—*ns.* **fibroin**

(fī'brō-in), the chief chemical constituent of silk; **fī'broline** (-lēn), a yarn of flax, hemp, and jute waste, used with linen or cotton for backs of carpets, etc.; **fī'brolite**, the mineral sillimanite, a fibrous aluminium silicate; **fibrō'ma**, a tumour composed of fibrous tissue (*pl.* **fibrō'mata**).—*v.i.* **fibrose** (*fī-brōs'*), to form fibrous tissue.—*adj.* **fibrose** (*fī'brōs*)—*ns.* **fibro'sis**, a morbid growth of fibrous tissue; **fibrosi'tis**, inflammation (*esp.* rheumatic) of fibrous tissue.—*adjs.* **fibrot'ic**, pertaining to fibrosis; **fi'brous**, composed of or like fibres; **fibrovas'cular**, composed of fibres and conducting elements. [Fr.,—L. *fibra*, thread, fibre.]

fibula, *fib'ū-lä*, *n.* a brooch; the outer of the two bones from the knee to the ankle.—*adjs.* **fib'ular**, **fib'ulate**, **fib'ulous**. [L. *fibula*, brooch.]

fichu, *fē-shū*, *n.* a three-cornered cape worn over the shoulders, the ends crossed upon the bosom: a triangular piece of muslin, etc., for the neck. [Fr.]

fickle, *fik'l*, *adj.* inconstant: changeable.—*n.* **fick'leness.** [O.E. *ficol; gefic*, fraud.]

fico, *fē'kō*, *n.* (*Shak.*) a fig, as a type of insignificance, a whit: a motion of contempt by placing the thumb between two fingers. [It., fig.]

fictile, *fik'til*, *-til*, *adj.* used or fashioned by the potter: plastic. [L. *fictilis—fingĕre*, to form or fashion.]

fiction, *fik'shən*, *n.* a feigned or false story: a falsehood: romance: the novel, story-telling as a branch of literature: a supposition of law that a thing is true, which is either certainly not true, or at least is as probably false as true.—*adj.* **fic'tional.**—*n.* **fic'tionist**, a writer of fiction.—*adj.* **fictitious** (-*tish'əs*), of the nature of fiction: imaginary: not real: feigned.—*adv.* **ficti'tiously.**—*adj.* **fic'tive**, fictitious, imaginative.—*n.* **fic'tor**, one who makes images of clay, etc. [Fr.,—L. *fictiō, -ōnis—fictus*, pa.p. of *fingĕre* to form, fashion.]

fid, *fid*, *n.* a conical pin of hard wood, used by sailors to open the strands of rope in splicing: a square bar, with a shoulder, used to support the weight of the topmast or top-gallant-mast. [Origin unknown.]

fiddious, *fid'i-əs*, *v.t.* (*Shak.*) app., to treat as Coriolanus treated *Aufidius*.

fiddle, *fid'l*, *n.* the violin: extended to other instruments of the same kind, as *bass fiddle*: a violin-player: a device to keep dishes from sliding off a table at sea.—*v.t.* and *v.i.* to play on a fiddle.—*v.i.* to be busy over trifles, to trifle.—*ns.* **fidd'le-block**, a long block having two sheaves of different diameters in the same plane; **fidd'le-bow**, a bow strung with horse-hair, with which the strings of the fiddle are set vibrating.—*interj.* **fiddle-de-dee'**, nonsense!—*v.i.* **fidd'le-fadd'le**, to trifle, to dally.—*n.* trifling talk or behaviour.—*adj.* fussy, trifling.—*interj.* nonsense!—*n.* **fidd'le-fadd'ler.**—*adj.* **fidd'le-fadd'ling.**—*ns.* **fidd'le-head**, an ornament at a ship's bow, over the cut-water, consisting of a scroll turning aft or inward; **fidd'ler**, one who fiddles: a small crab of the genus *Uca* or *Gelasimus*, also **fiddler crab** (from the attitude of its enlarged claw); **fidd'lestick**, a violin bow: derisively, a mere nothing or anything.—*interj.* **fidd'le-stick(s)**, nonsense!—*n.* **fidd'le-string**, a string for a fiddle; **fidd'le-wood**, a tropical American tree (Citharexylum; fam. Verbenaceae) yielding valuable hard wood.—*adj.* **fidd'ling**, trifling, busy about trifles.—**a face like a fiddle**, a long, or dismal face; **as fit as a fiddle**, in the best of condition; **fiddler's green**, a sailor's name for a place of frolic on shore; **fiddler's money**, small coins, as sixpences; **play first**, or **second fiddle**, to act as a first-violin or a second-violin player in an orchestra: to take a leading, or a subordinate, part in anything; **Scotch fiddle**, the itch (from the motion of the fingers against the palm). [O.E. *fithele*; Ger. *fiedel*; see **viol.**]

fiddley, *fid'li*, *n.* iron framework round a hatchway opening. [Origin obscure.]

fidelity, *fi-del'i-ti*, *n.* faithful performance of duty: faithfulness to a husband or wife: honesty: firm adherence: exactitude in reproducing. [L. *fidēlitās, -ātis—fidēlis*, faithful—*fidĕre*, to trust.]

fidget, *fij'it*, *v.i.* to be unable to rest: to move about uneasily (*pr.p.* **fidg'eting**; *pa.t.* and *pa.p.* **fidg'eted**).—*n.* one who fidgets: irregular motion: restlessness: (*pl.*) general nervous restlessness, with a desire of changing position.—*v.i.* **fidge**, to move about restlessly: to be eager.—*n.* **fidg'etiness.**—*adj.* **fidg'ety**, restless: uneasy. [Perh. related to **fike.**]

fiducial, *fi-dū'sh(y)əl*, *adj.* serving as a basis of reckoning: showing confidence or reliance: of the nature of trust.—*adv.* **fidū'cially.**—*adj.* **fidū'ciary**, of the nature of a trust: depending upon public confidence: held in trust.—*n.* one who holds anything in trust: (*theol.*) one who depends for salvation on faith without works, an Antinomian. [L. *fidūcia*, confidence—*fidĕre*, to trust.]

fie, *fī*, *interj.* denoting disapprobation or disgust real or feigned.—**fie upon**, an expression of disapprobation of the thing named. [Cf. Fr. *fi*; L. *fī*; O.N. *fy, fei*; Ger. *pfui*.]

fie. Same as **fey.**

fief, *fēf*, *n.* land held in fee or on condition of military service. [Fr.,—L.L. *feudum*; see **fee, feoff.**]

field, *fēld*, *n.* country or open country in general: a piece of ground enclosed for tillage or pasture or sport: the range of any series of actions or energies: region of space in which forces are at work: the locality of a battle: the battle itself: room for action of any kind: a wide expanse: the area visible to an observer at one time (as in a microscope, telescope): (*U.S.*) a frame in television: a region yielding a mineral: (*her.*) the surface of a shield: a ground or background: those taking part in a hunt: all the entries collectively against which a single contestant has to compete: all the parties not individually excepted (as *to bet on the field* in a horse-race): disposition of fielders.—*v.t.* at cricket and base-ball, to catch or stop and return to the fixed place.—*v.i.* to stand in position for catching or stopping the ball in cricket.—*ns.* **field'-allow'ance**, a small extra payment to officers on active service; **field'-artill'ery**, light ordnance suited for active operations in the field; **field'-batt'ery**, a battery of field-artillery; **field'-bed**, a camp or trestle bedstead: a bed in the open air; **field'-book**, a book used in surveying fields, etc.; **field'-bot'any**, **fie'ld-geol'ogy**, etc., botany, geology, etc., pursued in the open air, as opposed to laboratories, libraries, etc.; **field'-club**, a club of field-naturalists.—*n.pl.* **field'-col'ours**, small flags used for marking the position for companies and regiments, also any regimental headquarters' flags.—*ns.* **field'-cor'net** (*S. Africa*), the magistrate of a township; **field'-day**, a day when troops are drawn out for instruction in field exercises: any day of unusual bustle or activity; **field'-dew** (*Shak.*).—*adj.* **field'ed** (*Shak.*), encamped.—*ns.* **field'er**, one who fields; **field'fare** (ety. doubtful), a species of thrush, having a reddish-yellow throat and breast spotted with black; **field'-glass**, a binocular telescope for use in the field or open air; **field'-gray**, **-grey**, a grey (*feld-grau*) adopted for uniforms in the German army in the war of 1914-18: a German soldier so clad; **field'-gun**, a light cannon mounted on a carriage; **field'-hand**, an outdoor farm labourer; **field'-hos'pital**, a temporary hospital near the scene of battle; **field'-ice**, ice formed in the polar seas in large surfaces, distinguished from icebergs; **field'ing**, the acting in the field at cricket as distinguished from batting; **field'-lark**, an American bird (*Sturnella*) of the Icteridae, not a lark; **field'-mar'shal**, an army officer of highest rank; **field'-meet'ing**, a conventicle; **field'-mouse**, a name for various species of mouse and vole that live in the fields; **field'-nat'uralist**, one who studies natural history out of doors; **field'-night**, a night marked by some important gathering, discussion, etc.—*n.pl.* **field'-notes**, data noted in the field, to be worked up later.—*ns.* **field'-off'icer**, a military officer above the rank of captain, and below that of general; **field'piece**, a cannon or piece of artillery used in the field of battle; **field'-preach'er**, an open-air preacher; **field'-preach'ing**; **fields'man**, a fielder.—*n.pl.* **field'-sports**, sports of the field, as hunting, racing, etc.—*n.* **field'-train**, a department of the Royal Artillery responsible for the safety and supply of ammunition during war.—*advs.* **field'ward**, **-wards**, toward the fields; **field'-work**, farm work in fields : work (scientific surveying, etc.) in the field, opposed to laboratory, office, etc. : (often in *pl.*) a temporary fortification thrown up by troops in the field, either for protection or to cover an attack upon a stronghold.— **field of view**, **vision**, what is visible at one moment; **keep the field**, to keep the campaign open : to maintain one's ground; **take the field**, to begin warlike operations. [O.E. *feld*; cf. Du. *veld*, the open country, Ger. *feld*.]

fiend, *fēnd*, *n.* a devil : one actuated by the most intense wickedness or hate : an addict : a devotee : a person with an annoying habit or fad.—*adj.* **fiend'ish**, like a fiend : devilishly cruel.—*n.* **fiend'ishness**.—*adj.* **fiend'-like**, like a fiend : fiendish. [O.E. *féond*, enemy, orig. pr.p of *féon*, to hate; Ger. *feind*, Du. *vijand*.]

fierce, *fērs*, *adj.* savage : ferocious : violent.—*adv.* **fierce'ly**.—*n.* **fierce'ness**. [O.Fr. *fers* (Fr. *fier*) —L. *ferus*, wild, savage.]

fiery, *fīr'i*, *adj.* like or consisting of fire : ardent : impetuous : irritable : of ground in games, dry, hard, fast.—*adv.* **fier'ily**.—*ns.* **fier'iness**.—*adjs.* **fier'y-footed**, swift in motion; **fier'y-hot**, impetuous; **fier'y-new**, hot from newness; **fier'y-short**, short and passionate.—**fiery cross**, a charred cross dipped in blood, formerly carried round in the Highlands as a token calling to arms. [**fire**.]

fife, *fīf*, *n.* a smaller variety of the flute.—*v.i.* to play on the fife.—*ns.* **fife'-ma'jor** (*obs.*), the chief fifer in a regiment; **fif'er**, a fife-player; **fife'-rail**, the rail round the mainmast, where a fifer sat at heaving of the anchor. [Ger. *pfeife*, pipe, or Fr. *fifre*, fifer, both—L. *pīpāre*, to cheep.]

Fifish *fīf'ish*, *adj.* cranky : queer : like a **Fīf'er**, or inhabitant of *Fife*.

fifteen, *fif'tēn*, or *fif-tēn'*, *adj.* and *n.* five and ten : a set, group, or team of fifteen (as formerly the Court of Session).—*n.* **fifteen'er**, a verse of fifteen syllables.—*adj.* **fifteenth'** (or *fif'*), last of fifteen : equal to one of fifteen equal parts.—*n.* a fifteenth part : (*mus.*) a double octave : an organ stop sounding two octaves above the diapason.—**the Fifteen**, the Jacobite rebellion of 1715. [O.E. *fífténe*; see **five**, **ten**.]

fifth, *fifth*, *adj.* last of five : equal to one of five equal parts.—*n.* one of five equal parts : (*mus.*) an interval of four (conventionally called five) diatonic degrees : a tone at that interval from another : a combination of two tones separated by that interval.—**fifth column**, sympathisers among the enemy, awaiting their time (expression used by a Spanish insurgent general when four columns were advancing upon Madrid).—*n.* **fifth-columnist** (*kol'əm-ist*).—*adv.* **fifth'ly**, in the fifth place.—*ns.* **Fifth'-mon'archism**; **Fifth'-mon'archist**. — **Fifth-monarchy men**, an extreme sect at the time of the Puritan revolution, who looked for a new reign of Christ on earth in succession to Daniel's four great monarchies of Antichrist. [O.E. *fífta*, assimilated to other ordinals in *-th*.]

fifty, *fif'ti*, *adj.* and *n.* five tens or five times ten : *pl.* **fif'ties**, the numbers fifty to fifty-nine : the years so numbered (of a life or century).—*adj.* **fif'tieth**, last of fifty : equal to one of fifty equal parts.—*n.* a fiftieth part.—*n.* and *adj.* and *adv.* **fif'ty-fif'ty** (*U.S.*) half-and-half : fifty per cent. of each of two things : share and share alike.— *adj.* **fif'tyish**, apparently about fifty years old. [O.E. *fíftig*—*fíf*, five, and *-tig*, the suff. *-ty*.]

fig, *fig*, *n.* the fig-tree (Ficus, of the mulberry family), or its fruit, growing in warm climates : a thing of little or no consequence : (*obs.*) piles.— *v.t.* (*Shak.*) to insult by putting the thumb between

the fingers.—*ns.* **fig'-leaf**, the leaf of the fig-tree : a representation of such a leaf for veiling the private parts of a statue or picture : any scanty clothing (from Gen. iii. 7) : any prudish evasion : a makeshift; **fig'-tree**, the tree which produces figs; **fig'wort**, any species of Scrophularia (once reputed to cure piles). [Fr. *figue*—L. *fīcus*, a fig, fig-tree.]

fig, *fig*, *n.* (*coll.*) figure : dress : form.—*v.t.* to dress, get up : (*pr.p.* **figg'ing**; *pa.t.* and *pa.p.* **figged**).— *n.* **figg'ery**, dressy ornament. [Perh. **figure**.]

fight, *fīt*, *v.i.* to strive : to contend in war or in single combat.—*v.t.* to engage in conflict with : to contend against : to maintain or contend for by combat, action at law, or otherwise : to manipulate in fight : to achieve by struggle : to cause to fight : (*pr.p.* **fight'ing**; *pa.t.* and *pa.p.* **fought**, *fawt*).—*n.* a struggle : a combat : a battle or engagement : fighting spirit : inclination to fight : (*Shak.*) a screen to cover the men in a naval fight.—*n.* **fight'er**.—*adj.* **fight'ing**, engaged in or fit for war.—*n.* the act of fighting or contending. —*ns.* **fight'ing-cock**, a gamecock : a pugnacious fellow; **fight'ing-fish** (*Betta pugnax*), a small Siamese fresh-water fish, kept for its extraordinary readiness for fighting, bets being laid on the issue.—**fight it out**, to struggle on until the end; **fight shy of**, to avoid from mistrust; **live like fighting-cocks**, to get the best of meat and drink. [O.E. *fehtan* (W.S. *feohtan*); Ger. *fechten*.]

figment, *fig'mənt*, *n.* a fabrication or invention. [L. *figmentum*—*fingĕre*, to form.]

figo, *fē'gō*, *n.* (*Shak.*) a fico. [O. Sp.]

figuline, *fig'ū-lin*, *-lin*, *adj.* of earthenware : fictile. —*n.* an earthen vessel. [L. *figulīnus*—*figulus*, potter.]

figure, *fig'ər*, or (old-fashioned) *fig'ūr*, *n.* the form of anything in outline : appearance : a shape : a geometrical form : a diagram : (*Shak.*) a horoscope : a design : an illustration : bodily shape : a human form or representation of it : a personality, personage, character : an impressive, noticeable, important, ludicrous, or grotesque person : a character denoting a number : amount : value or price : (*rhet.*) a deviation from the ordinary mode of expression : (*logic*) the form of a syllogism with respect to the position of the middle term : (*mus.*) a group of notes felt as a unit : a series of steps or movements in a dance or in skating : a type or emblem.—*v.t.* to form or shape : to make an image of : to represent : to mark with figures or designs : to imagine : (*U.S.*) to reckon, to work out (often with *out*) : to symbolise : to foreshow : to note by figures.—*v.i.* to make figures : to appear as a figure, make an appearance or show.—*n.* **figurabil'ity**, the quality of being figurable.— *adjs.* **fig'urable**; **fig'ural**, represented by figure. —*n.* **fig'urant**, **figūrante** (*fig'ū-rənt*, *-rant*; It. *fig-ōō-rän'tä*) a ballet dancer, one of those who form a background for the solo dancers.—*adj.* **fig'ūrate**, of a certain determinate form : (*mus.*) florid.—*n.* **figūrā'tion**, act of giving figure or form : (*mus.*) florid treatment.—*adj.* **fig'ūrative** (*rhet.*), representing by, containing, or abounding in figures : metaphorical : flowery : typical.—*adv.* **fig'ūratively**.—*ns.* **fig'ūrativeness**; **fig'ure-cast'er**, an astrologer; **fig'ure-cast'ing**, the art of preparing casts of animal or other forms.—*adj.* **fig'ured**, having a figure : marked or adorned with figures : delineated in a figure : in the form of figures.—*ns.* **fig'ure-dance**, a dance consisting of elaborate figures; **fig'urehead**, the figure or bust under the bowsprit of a ship : a nominal head; **fig'ure-weav'ing**, the weaving of figured fancy fabrics : **fig'ūrine** (*-ēn*, *-ēn'*), a small carved or moulded figure; **fig'urist**, one who uses or interprets by figures.—**cut a figure**, to make a conspicuous appearance; **figurate numbers**, a series of numbers such that if each be subtracted from the next, and the series so formed be treated in the same way, by a continuation of the process equal differences will ultimately be obtained; **figured bass**, a bass with numerals added to indicate chords; **figure**

on, to count upon. [Fr.,—L. *figūra—fingĕre*, to form.]

fike, *fīk*, *v.i.* (*Scot.*) to fidget restlessly.—*n.* restlessness: any vexatious requirement or detail in work; a pernickety, exacting person.—*n.* fik'ery, fuss.—*adjs.* fik'ish, fik'y. [Prob. O.N. *fikja*.]

filabeg. Same as **filibeg.**

filacer, *fil'ə-sər*, *n.* formerly an officer who filed writs.—Also **fil'azer.** [O.Fr. *filacier—filace*, a file for papers—apparently L. *filum*, a thread.]

filagree. Same as **filigree.**

filament, *fil'ə-mənt*, *n.* a slender or threadlike object : a fibre : (*bot.*) the stalk of a stamen : a chain of cells : (*elec.*) a thread of high resistance in an incandescent lamp or thermionic valve.—*adjs.* **filamentary** (*-ment'ə-ri*), like a filament; **filament'ous**, threadlike. [L. *filum*, a thread.]

filander, *fil-an'dər*, threadlike intestinal worm in hawks : (in *pl.*) the disease it causes. [O.Fr. *filandre*—L. *filum*, thread.]

Filaria, *fi-lā'ri-ä*, *n.* a nematode introduced into the blood by mosquitoes.—*adj.* **filā'rial.**—*n.* **filariasis** (*-lə-rī'ə-sis*), a disease due to the presence of filaria in the blood. [L. *filum*, thread.]

filasse, *fil-äs'*, *n.* vegetable fibre ready for manufacture. [Fr.,—L. *filum*, thread.]

filature, *fil'ə-tyər*, *n.* the reeling of silk, or the place where it is done.—*n.* fil'atory, a machine for forming or spinning threads. [Fr.,—L. *filum*, a thread.]

filbert, *fil'bərt*, *n.* the nut of the cultivated hazel —(*obs.*) fil'berd. [Prob. from St. *Philibert*, whose day fell in the nutting season, Aug. 22 (O.S.).]

filch, *filch*, *v.t.* to steal: to pilfer.—*n.* filch'er, a thief.—*n.* and *adj.* filch'ing.—*adv.* filch'ingly. [Ety. unknown.]

file, *fīl*, *n.* (*obs.*) a thread : a line or wire on which papers are strung : any contrivance for keeping papers in order : a collection of papers arranged for reference : a roll or list : a line of soldiers, chessboard squares, etc., ranged one behind another : a small body of soldiers : an individual soldier.—*v.t.* to put upon a file : to arrange in an orderly way : to put on record : to bring before a court : (*U.S.*) to deposit, lodge.—*v.i.* to march in file.—*adjs.* **filaceous** (*fil-ā'shəs*), composed of threads; **filar** (*fī'lər*) having threads or wires.—*ns.* **file'-copy**, a copy filed for reference: an editor's copy of a book in which errors, possible changes, etc. are noted; **file'-lead'er.**—*adjs.* **filiform** (*fil'*), threadlike; **filipen'dulous** (*fil-*), hanging by or strung on a thread.—*ns.* **filofloss** (*fil'*), a fine soft silk thread; **fil'oplume**, a slender hairlike feather.—*adj.* **filose** (*fī'lōs*) threadlike : having a threadlike end.—**file off**, to wheel off at right angles to the first direction; **file with**, to rank with, to be equal to.—**single file**, **Indian file**, one behind another. [L. *filum*, a thread.]

file, *fīl*, *n.* an instrument with sharp-edged furrows for smoothing or rasping metals, etc. : any means adopted to polish a thing, as a literary style : a shrewd, cunning person, a deep fellow : a pickpocket.—*v.t.* to cut or smooth with, or as with, a file : to polish, improve.—*n.* file'-cutter, a maker of files.—*adj.* **filed**, polished, smooth.—*ns.* **file'-fish**, a fish of Balistes or kindred genus, the skin granulated like a file; **fil'er**, one who files; **fil'ing**, a particle rubbed off with a file. [O.E. *fíl* (W.S. *féol*): Ger. *feile*; Du. *vijl*.]

file, *fīl*, *v.t.* (*Shak.*; *Scots*) to defile, pollute. [O.E. *gefŷlan* ; cf. **foul.**]

filemot, *fil'i-mot*, *adj.* of a dead-leaf colour—*n.* the colour itself.—Also **philamot**, **philomot.** [Fr. *feuillemorte*, dead leaf.]

filial, *fil'i-əl*, *adj.* pertaining to or becoming a son or daughter : bearing the relation of a child.—*adv.* **fil'ially.** [Fr.,—L.L. *filiālis*—L. *fīlius*, a son.]

filiate, **filiation.** Same as **affiliate**, **affiliation.**

filibeg, **filabeg**, **fillibeg**, **phil(l)abeg**, **phil(l)ibeg**, *fil'i-beg*, *n.* the kilt, the dress or petticoat reaching nearly to the knees, worn by the Highlanders of Scotland. [Gael. *feileadhbeag—feileadh*, plait, fold, *beag*, little.]

filibuster, **fillibuster**, *fil'i-bus-tər*, *n.* a military or piratical adventurer : a buccaneer : one who makes unauthorised war : one who obstructs legislation by speeches, motions, etc. : obstruction in a legislative body.—*v.i.* to act as a filibuster.—*ns.* **filibus'tering**, **filibus'terism.** [Sp. *filibustero*, through Fr. *flibustier*, *fribustier*, from Du. *vrijbuiter* (cf. Eng. **freebooter**, Ger. *freibeuter*), from *vrij*, free, *buit*, booty.]

Filices, *fil'i-səz*, *n.pl.* the ferns : esp. the true (homosporous leptosporangiate) ferns.—*ns.pl.* **Filicales** (*-kā'lēz*), **Filicineae** (*-sin'i-ē*), the ferns, leptosporangiate and eusporangiate, with or without water-ferns.—*adj.* **filicin'ean.** [L. *fīlix*, *-icis*, fern.]

filigree, *fil'i-grē*, *n.* a kind of ornamental metallic lacework of gold and silver, twisted into convoluted forms, united and partly consolidated by soldering—also **fil'agree**; earlier forms, **fil'i-grain**, **fil'igrane.**—*adj.* **fil'igreed**, ornamented with filigree. [Fr. *filigrane*—It. *filigrana*—L. *fīlum*, thread, *grānum*, a grain.]

filioque, *fil-i-ō'kwi*, *n.* the clause inserted into the Nicene Creed at Toledo in 589, which asserts that the Holy Ghost proceeds from the Son, as well as from the Father—not accepted by the Eastern Church. [L., and from the son.]

Filipino, *fil-i-pē'nō*, *n.* a native of the *Philippine Islands* :—*fem.* **Filipi'na.** [Sp.]

fill, *fil*, *v.t.* to make full : to put into until all the space is occupied : to supply abundantly : to satisfy : to glut : to perform the duties of : to supply (a vacant office) : (esp. *U.S.*) to fulfil, carry out.—*v.i.* to become full : to become satiated.—*n.* as much as fills or satisfies : a full supply : the fullest extent : a single charge of anything.—*ns.* **fill'er**, he who, or that which, fills : a vessel for conveying a liquid into a bottle : a substance added to various materials to impart desired qualities; **fill'ing**, anything used to fill up, stop a hole, to complete, etc., as the woof, in weaving : supply.—**fill in**, to occupy (time) : to add what is necessary to complete, e.g. a form. [O.E. *fyllan—full*, full.]

fill, **fil**, *fil*, *n.* (*Shak.*) a thill or shaft.—*n.* **fill'-horse**, **p(h)il'-horse** (*Shak.*), a thill-horse. [See **thill.**]

fillet, *fil'ət*, *n.* a little string or band, esp. to tie round the head : meat or fish boned and rolled : a piece of meat composed of muscle, esp. the fleshy part of the thigh or the undercut of the sirloin : a thick boneless slice of fish : (*archit.*) a small space or band used along with mouldings.—*v.t.* to bind or adorn with a fillet : to make into fillets : to bone :—(*pr.p.* **fill'eting**; *pa.t.* and *pa.p.* **fill'eted**). [Fr. *filet*, dim. of *fil*, from L. *filum*, a thread.]

fillibeg. See **filibeg.**

fillip, *fil'ip*, *v.t.* to strike with the finger-nail released from the ball of the thumb with a sudden jerk : to incite, stimulate : (*pr.p.* **fill'iping** ; *pa.t.* and *pa.p.* **fill'iped**).—*n.* a jerk of the finger from the thumb : a stimulus. [A form of **flip.**]

fillister, *fil'is-tər*, *n.* a kind of rabbeting plane. [Origin unknown.]

filly, *fil'i*, *n.* a young mare : a lively, wanton girl. [Dim. of **foal** ; prob. from O.N.]

film, *film*, *n.* a thin skin or membrane : a thin layer or coating : a pellicle : a very slender thread : a mistiness : a coating of a sensitive substance for taking a photograph : a sheet or ribbon of celluloid or the like prepared with such a coating for ordinary photographs or for instantaneous photographs for projection by cinematograph : a motion-picture, or connected series of motion-pictures setting forth a story, etc. : (in *pl.*) the cinematograph.—*v.t.* to cover with a film : to make a motion-picture of : to adapt and enact for the cinematograph.—*v.i.* to become covered with a film.—*adj.* **film'able**, suitable for making a film of.—*ns.* **film'-fan**, a devotee of the cinematograph; **film'house**, a cinematograph theatre.—*adjs.* **film'ic**, pertaining to the cinematograph.—*n.* **film'iness.**—*adj.* **film'ish**, savouring of the cinematograph.—*ns.* **film'-play**, a **film'-star**, a favourite cinematograph performer.—*adj.* **film'y**, composed of or like a film : covered with a film : gauzy : clouded.—**filmy ferns**, a family of ferns with very thin leaves, the Hymenophyllaceae. [O.E. *filmen*, conn. with *fell*, skin.]

filoselle, *fil-ō-sel'*, *n.* a coarse floss silk. [It. *filosello*—L.L. *folexellus*, cocoon.—L. *folliculus*, influenced by It. *filo*, thread.]

filter, *fil'tər*, *n.* an apparatus for purifying a fluid of solid matter by pouring it through porous material : a device for wholly or partly eliminating undesirable frequencies from light or electric currents.—*v.t.* to pass through a filter : to separate by a filter (esp. with *out*).—*v.i.* to pass through a filter : to percolate : to pass gradually and dispersedly through obstacles.—*adj.* **fil'terable, fil'trable**, able to pass through a filter : capable of being filtered.—*ns.* **fil'ter-bed**, a bed of sand, gravel, clinker, etc. used for filtering water or sewage.—*ns.* **fil'ter-paper**, porous paper for use in filtering ; **fil'ter-passer**, *n.* a filterable virus, a virus that passes through any filter :—*v.t.* and *v.i.* **fil'trate**, to filter or percolate.—*n.* a liquid that has been passed through a filter.—*n.* **filtra'tion**, act or process of filtering. [O.Fr. *filtre*—L.L. *filtrum*, felt.]

filth, *filth*, *n.* foul matter : anything that defiles, physically or morally : obscenity.—*adv.* **filth'ily**.—*n.* **filth'iness**.—*adj.* **filth'y**, foul : unclean : impure. [O.E. *fylth*—*fúl*, foul.]

fimble, *fim'bl*, *n.* the male plant of hemp, weaker and shorter in fibre than *carl-hemp(q.v.)* [Du. *femel*, female.]

fimbria, *fim'bri-ā*, *n.* a fringing filament.—*adj.* **fim'briate**, fringed : (*her.*) having a narrow border.—*v.t.* **fim'briate**, to fringe : to hem.—*adj.* **fim'briated**.—*n.* **fimbria'tion**. [L. *fimbriae*, fibres, fringe.]

fimicolous, *fim-ik'ə-ləs*, *adj.* growing on dung. [L. *fimus*, dung, *colēre*, to inhabit.]

fin, *fin*, *n.* an organ by which an aquatic animal steers, balances, or swims : a fixed vertical surface on the tail of an aeroplane : a portion of a mechanism like a fish's fin in shape or purpose : a thin projecting edge or plate.—*ns.* **fin'back, finn'er, fin'-whale**, a rorqual.—*adjs.* **fin'-foot'ed**, web-footed : with fringed toes ; **fin'less**, **finned**, having fins ; **finn'y**, finned.—*n.* **fin'-ray'**, a horny rod supporting a fin.—*adj.* **fin'-toed'**, having lobate or fringed toes. [O.E. *finn* ; L. *pinna*.]

finable, *fin'ə-bl*, *adj.* liable to a fine.

final, *fi'nl*, *adj.* last: decisive, conclusive: respecting the end or motive : of a judgment ready for execution.—*n.* last of a series (as the letters of a word, games in a contest, examinations in a curriculum, etc.): in the old church modes, the key-note or tonic, the lowest note in the authentic modes, a fourth above it in the plagal.—*v.t.* **fi'nalise**, to put the finishing touches to : to put an end to completely.—*ns.* **fi'nalism**, teleology, interpretation in terms of purpose : belief that an end has been reached; **fi'nalist**, teleologist : one who reaches the final stage in a competition : one who believes that finality has been reached; **finality** (*-al'i-ti*), state of being final : completeness or conclusiveness : the principle of final cause : that which is final.—*adv.* **fi'nally.—final cause** (see cause). [Fr.,—L. *fīnālis*—*finis*, an end.]

finale, *fi-nä'lā*, *-li*, *n.* the end : the last movement in a musical composition : the concluding number of an opera or the like. [It. *finale*, final—L. *fīnālis*.]

finance, *fi-nans'* (also *fī-*), *n.* money affairs or revenue, esp. of a ruler or state: public money : the art of managing or administering the public money : (in *pl.*) money resources.—*v.t.* to manage financially : to furnish with money.—*v.i.* to engage in money business.—*adj.* **finan'cial** (*-shəl*), pertaining to finance.—*n.* **finan'cialist**, a financier.—*adv.* **finan'cially.—n.* **finan'cier** (*-si-ər*; U.S. *fin-an-sēr'*), one skilled in finance; one who administers the public revenue.—*v.i.* and *v.t.* (*-sēr'*) to finance : to swindle. [Fr.,—O.Fr. *finer*, to settle—L. *finis*, an end.]

finback. See **fin**.

finch, *fin(t)sh*, *n.* a name applied to many passerine birds, esp. to those of the genus Fringilla or family Fringillidae—bullfinch, chaffinch, goldfinch, etc.—*adjs.* **finch'-backed, finched**, striped or spotted on the back. [O.E. *finc;* Ger. *fink*.]

find, *find*, *v.t.* to come upon or meet with : to discover or arrive at : to come to perceive : to experience : to supply : to determine after judicial inquiry : to succeed in getting.—*v.i.* to come upon game : (*pr.p.* **find'ing** ; *pa.t.* and *pa.p.* **found**).—*n.* an act of finding : something found, esp. of value or interest.—*n.* **find'er**, one who finds : a small telescope attached to a larger one, or a lens attached to a camera, to facilitate the directing of it upon the object required; **find'-fault** (*Shak.*), one who finds fault with another; **find'ing**, act of one who finds : that which is found : a judicial verdict : (*pl.*) the appliances which some workmen have to supply, esp. of shoemakers—everything save leather : (*U.S.*) accessories.—**find one in**, to supply one with; **find one's account in**, to find satisfactory profit or advantage in; **find one's feet**, to become able to stand, able to cope readily with new conditions; **find oneself**, to feel, as regards health, happiness, etc.; find out, to discover, to detect. [O.E. *findan;* Ger. *finden*.]

findon-haddock. See **finnan-haddock**.

fine, *fin*, *adj.* excellent : beautiful : fair : not coarse or heavy : consisting of small particles : subtle : thin, slender : sharp : keen : exquisite : nice : delicate : sensitive : over-refined : over-elaborate : pretentious : showy : splendid : striking or remarkable : excellent (often ironically): egregious : pure : refined : containing so many parts of pure metal out of twenty-four (as 22 carats, or ounces, fine, $\frac{22}{24}$ gold or silver), or out of a thousand.—*v.t.* to make fine : to refine : to purify : to change by imperceptible degrees.—*adv.* (*Scot.* and *coll.*) well, well enough : narrowly : with little to spare. —*v.t.* **fine'-draw**, to draw or sew up so finely that no rent is seen : to draw out finely or too finely.—*adj.* **fine'-drawn**.—*adj.* **fine'ish** (also **fin'ish**), somewhat fine.—*adv.* **fine'ly**.—*ns.* **fine'ness**, state, fact, or degree of being fine : state of subdivision : of gold or silver, number of parts in a thousand; **fin'er**, refiner; **fin'ery**, spendour : showy adornments : a place where anything is fined or refined : a furnace for making iron malleable.—*adjs.* **fine'-spok'en**, using fine phrases; **fine'-spun**, finely spun out : oversubtle.—**fine and**, often almost equivalent to an adverb, enough, very; **fine arts**, as painting, sculpture, music, those chiefly concerned with the beautiful—opp. to the *useful* or *industrial arts;* **fine gentleman**, **lady**, an idle person, usu. ostentatiously fashionable, sometimes refined; **fine metal**, comparatively pure cuprous sulphide got from *coarse metal;* **fine writing**, literary matter or style pretentiously ornate. [Fr. *fin*, prob. a back-formation from L. *finītus*, finished, pa.p. of *fīnīre*, to finish—*finis*, an end.]

fine, *fin*, *n.* (*obs.* except in phrase *in fine*) end, conclusion : a final settlement : a fee paid on some particular occasion : a fictitious suit as a means of conveying property or barring an entail : a composition by money payment : a money penalty.—*v.t.* (*Shak.*) to bring to an end : to impose a fine on : to punish by fine : (*Shak.*) to pledge or pawn.—*adj.* **fine'less** (*Shak.*), endless.—**foot of fine** (see foot). [L. *finis*, end.]

fineer, *fi-nər'*, an old form of **veneer** (*n.* and *v.t.*).

fineer, *fi-nər'*, *v.i.* to get goods on credit by fraudulent artifice. [Prob. Du.; cf. **finance**.]

Fine Gael, *fē'ne gāl*, (*lit.* United Ireland) the moderate party led orig. by W. T. Cosgrave.

finesse, *fi-nes'*, *n.* subtlety of contrivance : artifice : an endeavour by a player holding a higher card to take the trick with a lower, risking loss.—*v.t.* and *v.i.* to play in finesse.—*v.i.* to use artifice.—*ns.* **finess'er**; **finess'ing**. [Fr.]

fingan, *fin-gän'*, *n.* a small coffee-cup without a handle—used with a zarf.—Also **finjan** (*-jän'*). [Egyptian *fingān*, Ar. *finjān*.]

finger, *fing'gər*, *n*. one of the five terminal parts of the hand, or of the four other than the thumb: anything shaped like a finger: part of a glove that covers a finger: a finger-breadth: touch: fingering. —*v.t.* to handle or perform with the fingers: to pilfer: to toy or meddle with: (*mus.*) to make or indicate choice of fingers in performing.—*v.t.* to use the fingers.—*ns*. **fing'er-al'phabet**, a deaf and dumb alphabet: **fing'er-and-toe'**, a disease of turnips in which the tap-root branches: another turnip disease, anbury; **fing'er-board**, the part of a violin, etc., against which the strings are stopped by the fingers; **fing'er-bowl, -glass**, a bowl for water to cleanse the fingers at table; **fing'er('s)-breadth**, the breadth of a finger, a digit, ¾ of an inch.—*adj*. **fing'ered**, having fingers, or anything like fingers, or indication of fingering.—*ns*. **fing'er('s)-end'**; **fing'er-grass**, grass of genus Digitaria, with fingerlike spikes; **fing'er-guard**, the quillons of a sword-handle; **fing'er-hole**, a hole in a wind instrument closed by the finger to modify the pitch; **fing'ering**, act or manner of touching with the fingers: the choice of fingers as in playing a musical instrument: the indication thereof.—*adj*. **fing'erless**. —*ns*. **fing'erling**, a very diminutive being: the parr; **fing'er-mark**, a mark, esp. a soil, made by the finger; **fing'er-nail**; **fing'er-plate**, a plate to protect a door from dirty fingers; **fing'er-post**, a post with a finger pointing the way; **fing'er-print**, an impression of the ridges of the finger-tip; **fing'er-stall**, a covering for protecting the finger; **fing'er-tip**.—**a finger in the pie**, a share in the doing of anything, often of vexatious meddling; **have at one's finger(s')-ends**, to be perfect master of a subject; **have one's fingers all thumbs**, to be awkward in handling. [O.E. *finger*.]

fingering, *fing'gər-ing*, *n*. a thick woollen yarn for stockings. [Perh. Fr. *fin grain*, fine grain.]

finial, *fin'i-əl*, *n*. the bunch of foliage, etc., on the top of a pinnacle, gable, spire, etc. [L. *fīnis*, end.]

finical, *fin'i-kl*, *adj*. affectedly or excessively precise in trifles: nice: foppish.—*n*. **finicality** (-*kal'i-ti*), state of being finical: something finical. —*adv*. **fin'ically**.—*ns*. **fin'icalness, fin'icking**, fussiness and fastidiousness.—*adjs*. **fin'icking**, **fin'icky, fin'ikin**, particular about trifles. [Prob. conn. with **fine**, 1.]

fining, *fīn'ing*, *n*. process of refining or purifying: a clarifying agent (often in *pl*.).—*n*. **fin'ing-pot**, a vessel used in refining. [**fine**, 1.]

finis, *fī'nis*, *n*. the end: conclusion. [L. *fīnis*.]

finish, *fin'ish*, *v.t.* to end: to complete the making of: to perfect: to give the last touches to: to complete the education of, esp. for life in society: to put an end to, to destroy.—*n*. that which finishes or completes: the end of a race, hunt, etc.: last touch, careful elaboration, polish: the last coat of plaster to a wall.—*adj*. **fin'ished**, brought to an end or to completion: complete: consummate: perfect.—*n*. **fin'isher**, one who finishes, completes, or perfects: in bookbinding, one who puts the last touches to the book in gilding and decoration.—*n*. and *adj*. **fin'ishing**. [Fr. *finir, finissant*—L. *fīnīre—fīnis*, an end.]

finite, *fī'nīt*, *adj*. having an end or limit: subject to limitations or conditions—opp. to *infinite*.— *adv*. **fī'nitely**.—*ns*. **fī'niteness, finitude** (*fin'i-tūd*). [L. *fīnītus*, pa.p of *fīnīre*, to limit.]

finjan. See **fingan**.

finks, *fingks*, same as **fenks**.

Finn, *fin*, *n*. a member of a people dwelling in Finland and adjacent regions: more generally, a member of the group of peoples to which the Finns proper belong.—*n*. **Fin'lander**, a native or citizen of Finland.—*adjs*. **Finn'ic**, pertaining to the Finns or the Finno-Ugrians; **Finn'ish**, pertaining to the Finns, or to Finland, or its language.—*n*. the Finno-Ugrian language of Finland.—*adjs*. **Finno-Ugrian, Finno-Ugric** (*fin'ō-(y)ōō'gri-ən, -grik*), belonging to the north-western group of Ural-Altaic languages and peoples— Finnish, Estonian, Lapp, Cheremiss, Mordvin,

Zyrian, Votyak, etc.—also **U'gro-Finn'ic**. [O.E. *finnas*, Finns.]

finnan, *fin'ən*, *obs*. **findram**, *fin'rəm*, *n*. a kind of smoked haddock, probably named from Findon, Kincardineshire, not from the Findhorn river.— —Also **finn'an-, fin'don-hadd'ock**.

finnesko, finnsko, finsko, *fin'(e-)skō*, *n.pl*. reindeer-skin boots with the hair on. [Norw. *finnsko—Finn*, Lapp, *sko*, shoe.]

finnock, finnack, finnac, *fin'ək*, *n*. a young sea-trout. [Gael. *fionnag—fionn*, white.]

fiord, fjord, *fyōr(d)*, *n*. a long, narrow, rock-bound inlet. [Norw. *fjord*.]

florin, *fī'ə-rin*, *n*. a variety of creeping bent-grass (*Agrostis alba*, var. *stolonifera*). [Ir. *fiorthán*.]

fioritura, *fyor-i-tōō'rä*, *n*. a florid embellishment (*pl*. **fioriture, -rä**). [It., flowering—L. *flōs, flōris*.]

fippence, *fip'əns*, a shortened form of **fivepence**.

fipple, *fip'l*, *n*. (*dial*.) the under-lip: a sharp-edged lip on which the air impinges in the recorder, etc.—*n*. **fipp'le-flute'**, a flute with a fipple, blown from the end, as the recorder, the penny-whistle. [Cf. O.N. *flipi*, a horse's lip.]

fir, *fər*, *n*. the name of several conifers, esp. of the genera Abies and Picea, resinous trees, valuable for their timber.—*n*. **fir'-cone'**.—*adj*. **firr'y**, abounding in firs: of fir.—*ns*. **fir'-tree, fir'-wood**. [O.E. *fyrh;* cf. Ger. *föhre*.]

fire, *fīr*, *n*. a once-supposed substance reckoned one of the four elements: the heat and light of burning: a mass of burning matter, as of fuel in a grate: flame or incandescence: a conflagration: firing: fuel: a heating apparatus: heat or light due to other causes than burning: (*poet.*) lightning: volcanic or plutonic heat: great heat: the heat of fever or inflammation: glowing appearance: a sparkle of light: discharge of fire-arms (also *fig.*): enthusiasm: ardour: passion: spirited vigour or animation.—*v.t.* to ignite: to cause to explode: to expose to heat: to bake: to cauterise: to fuel: to affect as if by fire: to discharge: to drive out: (*U.S.*) to dismiss (from employment, etc.): to inflame: to animate: to rouse to passion of any kind.—*v.i.* to take fire: to shoot with firearms: to become inflamed: to break out in anger.—*ns*. **fire'-alarm'**, apparatus for giving warning of fire: a warning of fire; **fire'-arm**, a weapon discharged by explosion (usu. in *pl*.); **fire'-arr'ow**, a dart or arrow carrying a combustible; **fire'-back**, a red-backed Sumatran pheasant: the back wall of a fireplace: an ornamental plate of iron so placed; **fire'-ball**, a bolide: ball-lightning: an incendiary or illuminating projectile; **fire'-balloon'**, a balloon carrying fire and raised by the heating and rarefaction of air: a balloon discharging fireworks in the air; **fire'-bar**, a bar of a fire-grate: a heating element in an electric radiator; **fire'-bas'ket**, a portable fire-grate; **fire'-bird**, the Baltimore oriole, or other bird of orange and red plumage; **fire'-blast**, a blight of hops, due to a mite, giving a scorched appearance; **fire-blight**, a bacterial disease of fruit-trees, giving a scorched appearance; **fire'-bote**, a tenant's right to cut wood for fuel; **fire'box**, a chamber for the fire in a steam-engine, etc.; **fire'brand**, a burning piece of wood: one who foments strife; **fire'brat**, a small insect found in bakehouses; **fire'brick**, a brick refractory to fire, used for furnace-linings, etc.; **fire'-brigade'**, a body of firemen; **fire'-buck'et**, a water bucket for putting out fires; **fire'bug** (*U.S.*), an incendiary; **fire'clay**, a clay poor in lime and iron, suitable for making refractory pottery and firebricks; **fire'-control'**, a system of controlling the whole gunfire of a ship from one centre; **fire'crest, or fire'-crested wren**, a bird close akin to the gold-crest, a kinglet.— *adj*. **fired**, affected, or having the appearance of having been affected, with fire: baked: ignited: kindled: discharged.—*ns*. **fire'damp**, a combustible gas given off by coal, etc., chiefly methane; **fire'dog**, an andiron; **fire'-drake**, a fire-breathing dragon: a luminous phenomenon: a kind of firework; **fire'-drill**, a primitive instrument for getting fire by twirling a stick: practice in putting

Neutral vowels in unaccented syllables : *el'ə-mənt, in'fənt, ran'dəm*

out or escaping from fire; **fire′-eat′er**, a juggler who seems to eat fire : a seeker of quarrels; **fire′-edge** (*dial.*), a cutting edge hardened by fire : crispness in a newly baked cake : first eagerness; **fire′-engine**, an engine or pump for extinguishing fires; **fire′-escape′**, a fixed or movable way of escape from a burning building; **fire′-extin-guisher**, a contrivance for ejecting chemicals to put out fires.—*adj.* **fire′-eyed** (*Shak.*) having fiery eyes.—*ns.* **fire′-fighter** (esp. *U.S.*) a fire-man; **fire′-fighting**; **fire′-flag** (*Coleridge*), **fire′-flaught** (*Swinburne*), a flash of fire, lightning, etc.; **fire′float**, a boat or raft used in harbours for extinguishing fires; **fire′fly**, an insect, generally a beetle, that emits light by night; **fire′-grate**, a grating to hold a fire; **fire′-guard**, a protective wire-frame or railing in front of a fireplace; **fire′-hook**, a hook formerly used to tear down burning buildings; **fire′-hose**, hose for extin-guishing fires; **fire′-house**, a house with a fire-place, a dwelling-house; **fire′-insu′rance**, insur-ance against loss by fire.—*n.pl.* **fire′-irons**, fireside implements—poker, tongs, shovel—not necessarily of iron.—*adj.* **fire′less**.—*ns.* **fire′-light**, the light of a domestic fire; **fire′lighter**, a readily inflammable material or other means of lighting a fire; **fire′lock**, a gun discharged by a lock with flint and steel; **fire′man**, one whose function is to assist in putting out fires and rescuing those in danger : a stoker : one who attends to conditions of safety in a mine : one who explodes charges; **fire′-mark**, a metal plate formerly placed by insurance companies to mark an insured building; **fire′-mar′shal** (*U.S.*), **fire′-mas′ter**, head of a fire-brigade.—*adj.* **fire′-new**, new from the fire : brand-new.—*ns.* **fire′-office**, a fire insurance office; **fire′-o′pal**, a flame-coloured variety of opal; **fire′pan**, a metal vessel for holding fire; **fire′place**, the place in a house appropriated to the fire : the opening of a chimney into a room : a hearth; **fire′-plug**, a hydrant for use against fires; **fire′-pol′icy**, a written instrument of insurance against fire; **fire′-pot**, an earthen pot full of combustibles, used as a missile.—*adj.* **fire′proof**, proof against fire : incombustible (see **curtain**).—*v.t.* to render fireproof.—*ns.* **fire′-proofing**; **fir′er**, one who fires, in any sense; **fire′-raiser**, an incendiary; **fire′-raising**, arson.—*adjs.* **fire′-resist′ing**, immune to effects of fire up to a required degree; **fire′-risk**; **fire′-robed** (*Shak.*) robed in fire.—*ns.* **fire′screen**, a screen for intercepting the heat of a fire; **fire′ship**, a ship carrying combustibles sent among the enemy's ships; **fire′-shovel**; **fire′side**, the side of the fireplace : the hearth : home.—*adj.* domestic : familiar.—*ns.* **fire′-step**, **fir′ing-step**, a ledge on which soldiers stand to fire over a parapet : a banquette; **fire′-stick**, a primitive implement for getting fire by friction; **fire′-stone**, a rock, esp. a sandstone, that stands much heat without injury; **fire′-tube**, a tube through which fire passes; **fire′-walk**, **-ing**, the ceremony of walking barefoot over hot stones, ashes, etc.; **fire′-walker**; **fire′-war′den** (*U.S.*), an official charged with prevention and extinction of fires; **fire′-watch′er**, one who watches against fire; **fire′-watch′ing**; **fire′-wa′ter**, ardent spirits; **fire′-weed** (*U.S.*) the rose-bay willow-herb, which springs up after forest fires; **fire′wood**, wood for fuel; **fire′-work**, (*obs.*) a combustible or explosive com-position used in warfare, or a projectile carry-ing it : a contrivance for producing sparks, jets, flares, or glowing pictorial designs in fire for amusement : (now only in *pl.*) a display of these : a florid technical display in music, talk, etc.; **fire′worm**, a glow-worm : a firefly; **fire′-wor′ship**, worship of fire : (*loosely*) homage to fire (as among Parsees) as a symbol of deity but not itself a god; **fire′-wor′shipper**; **fir′ing**, ignition : dis-charge of guns, etc. : simultaneous ringing of a peal of bells : fuelling : firewood : fuel : cautery : injury by overheating : subjection to heat; **fir′ing-line**, area or troops within range of the enemy for practical purposes; **fir′ing-par′ty**, a detach-ment told off to fire over a grave or shoot a con-

demned prisoner; **fir′ing-pin**, a pin that strikes the detonator and explodes the cartridge in a rifle; **fir′ing-point**, the temperature at which an inflammable oil takes fire spontaneously.—**catch** or **take fire**, to become ignited : to become aroused about something; **fire and brimstone**, hell—an exclamation of wrath or extreme irrita-tion; **fire and sword**, military devastation; **fire off**, to discharge : to ask, utter in rapid succession; **fire out** (*Shak.*), to expel; **fire up**, to start a fire : to fly into a passion; **on fire**, in a state of fiery combustion : St. Anthony's, St. Elmo's fire (see **Saint**) set on fire, set fire to, to ignite; **under fire**, exposed to the enemy's fire. [O.E. *fýr*; Ger. *feuer*; Gr. *pŷr*.]

firk, *fərk*, *v.t.* to drive : to rouse : (*Shak.*) to whip or beat. [O.E. *fercian*, to conduct.]

firkin, *fər′kin*, *n.* a measure equal to the fourth part of a barrel : 9 gallons : 56 lb. of butter. [With dim. suf. *-kin*, from Old Du. *vierde*, fourth.]

firlot, *fir′lət*, *n.* an old Scottish dry measure, the fourth part of a boll. [Earlier *ferthelot*; cf. O.N. *fiórthe hlotr*, fourth lot.]

firm, *fərm*, *adj.* compact : strong : not easily moved or disturbed : unshaken : resolute : decided.—*v.t.* to fix, fasten, establish, confirm.—*adj.* **firm′less**, wavering.—*adv.* **firm′ly**.—*n.* **firm′-ness**. [O.Fr. *ferme*—L. *firmus*.]

firm, *fərm*, *n.* the title under which a company transacts business : a business house or partner-ship. [It. *firma*, from L. *firmus*; see **farm**.]

firmament, *fər′mə-mənt*, *n.* the solid sphere in which the stars were thought to be fixed : the sky.—*adj.* **firmament′al** (*-ment′l*). [L. *firmā-mentum*—*firmus*, firm.]

firman, *fər′man*, or *fer-män′*, *n.* a decree. [Pers. *fermān*; Sans. *pramāna*, command.]

firn, *firn*, or *fərn*, *n.* snow on high glaciers while still granular. [Ger. *firn*, of last year; cf. obs. Eng. *fern*, former.]

firring. Same as **furring**.

first, *fərst*, *adj.* foremost : before all others : most eminent : chief : (*gram.*) referring to the speaker or writer.—*n.* one who or that which is first or of the first class : a place in the first class.—*adv.* before anything else.—*n.* **first′-aid′**, treatment of a wounded or sick person before the doctor's arrival.—*adjs.* **first′-begott′en**, begotten first : eldest; **first′-born**, born first.—*n.* the first in the order of birth : the eldest child.—*adj.* **first′-class**, of the first class, rank, or quality.—*ns.* **first′-day**, Sunday; **first′-floor′** (*adj.* **first′-floor**; see **floor**); **first′-foot′** (*Scot.*), the first person to enter a house after the beginning of the new year.—*v.t.* to visit as first-foot.—*v.i.* to go around making visits as first-foot.—*ns.* **first′-foot′er**; **first′-fruit′**, **-fruits′**, the fruits first gathered in a season : the first profits or effects of anything, a bishopric, benefice, etc. : annat.—*adj.* **first′-hand**, obtained directly, without an inter-mediary.—*adv.* **first-hand′**.—*n.* **first′ling**, the first produce or offspring, esp. of animals.—*adv.* **first′ly**, in the first place.—*ns.* **first′-night′**, the first night of a performance; **first-night′er**, one who habitually goes to the theatre on first-nights; **first′-offend′er**, one convicted for the first time.—*adj.* **first′-rate**, of the first or highest rate or excellence; pre-eminent in quality, size, or estimation.—*n.* a warship so rated.—*adv.* **first-rate′**, excellently.—**first cousin**, a full cousin, son or daughter of an uncle or aunt; **(the) first thing**, before doing anything else; **first water**, the first or highest quality, purest lustre—of diamonds and pearls. [O.E. *fyrst*, superl.; cf. *fore*, before.]

firth, *fərth*, *n.* an arm of the sea, esp. a river-mouth.—Also **frith**. [O.N. *fiörthr*; Norw. *fjord*.]

firth. See **frith** (3).

fisc, fisk, *fisk*, *n.* the state treasury : the public revenue : one's purse.—*adj.* **fisc′al**, pertaining to the public treasury or revenue.—*n.* a treasurer : a public prosecutor, chief law officer of the crown under the Holy Roman Empire : (*Scot.*) an officer who prosecutes in criminal cases in local and inferior courts—in full, *Procurator-fiscal.*—**the**

fiscal question, free trade or protection. [L. *fiscus*, a basket, a purse.]

fisgig. See **fizgig.**

fish, *fish*, *n.* a vertebrate that lives in water and breathes through gills : loosely, any exclusively aquatic animal : the flesh of fish :—*pl.* **fish**, or **fish´es.**—*v.i.* to catch or try to catch or obtain fish, or anything that may be likened to a fish (as seals, sponges, coral, compliments, information, husbands ; often with *for*) : to serve the purpose of fishing.—*v.t.* to catch and bring out of water : to bring up or out from a deep or hidden place, obscurity or the like : to elicit (with *out*) : to practise the fisher's craft in : to ransack : to hoist the flukes of.—*adj.* **fish´able.**—*ns.* **fish´-ball**, **-cake**, a ball of chopped fish and mashed potatoes, fried.—*adj.* **fish´-bell´ied**, swelled out downward like the belly of a fish.—*ns.* **fish´-bone** ; **fish´-carv´er**, **fish´-slice**, **fish´-trowel**, a large flat implement for carving fish at table ; **fish´-creel**, an angler's basket : a fishwife's basket : **fish´-day**, a day on which fish is eaten instead of meat ; **fish´er**, one who fishes for sport or gain : the pekan or wood-shock (an inappropriate name) ; **fish´erman**, a fisher ; **fish´ery**, the business of catching fish : a place for catching fish : right of fishing ; **fish´-fag**, a woman who sells fish.—*adj.* **fish´ful**, abounding in fish.—*ns.* **fish´-garth**, an enclosure on a river for the preserving or taking of fish—also **fish´-weir** ; **fish´-glue**, glue made from the sounds of fish ; **fish´-god**, a deity in form wholly or partly like a fish, like the Philistine Dagon ; **fish´-guano**, fish-manure.—*n.pl.* **fish´-guts.**—*ns.* **fish´-gutter** ; **fish´-gutting** ; **fish´-hatch´ery**, a station for artificial rearing of fish ; **fish´-hawk**, osprey ; **fish´-hook**, a barbed hook for catching fish.—*v.t.* **fish´ify** (*Shak.*), to turn to fish.—*n.* **fish´iness.**—*adj.* **fish´ing**, used in fishery.—*n.* the art or practice of catching fish.—*ns.* **fish´ing-frog**, the angler-fish ; **fish´ing-rod**, a long slender rod to which a line is fastened for angling ; **fish´ing-tack´le**, tackle—nets, lines, etc.—used in fishing ; **fish´-kett´le**, a long oval dish for boiling fish ; **fish´-ladd´er**, **fish´-way**, an arrangement of steps and shelters for enabling a fish to ascend a fall, etc. ; **fish´-louse**, a copepod or other crustacean parasitic on fishes ; **fish´-manure´**, fish used as a fertiliser ; **fish´-meal**, dried fish ground to meal : (*Shak.*) a meal of fish : abstemious diet ; **fish´-monger**, a dealer in fish ; **fish´-oil**, oil got from fishes and other marine animals ; **fish´-packing**, the process of canning fish ; **fish´-pond**, a pond in which fish are kept—formerly also **fish´-stew** ; **fish´-sales´man**, one who receives consignments of fish for sale by auction to retail dealers ; **fish´-sauce**, sauce proper to be eaten with fish ; **fish´-scrap**, fish or fish-skins from which oil or glue has been extracted ; **fish´skin**, the skin of a fish : ichthyosis ; **fish´-spear**, a spear or dart for striking fish ; **fish´-strainer**, a metal colander for taking fish from a boiler.—*adj.* **fish´-tail**, shaped like the tail of a fish.—*ns.* **fish´-torpe´do**, a self-propelling torpedo ; **fish´wife**, **fish´-woman**, a woman who carries fish about for sale.—*adj.* **fish´y**, consisting of fish : like a fish : abounding in fish : dubious, as a story : equivocal, unsafe.—**fisherman's luck**, getting wet and catching no fish ; **fisherman's ring**, a signet-ring, with the device of St. Peter fishing, used in signing papal briefs ; **fish in troubled waters**, to take advantage of disturbed times to further one's own interests ; **have other fish to fry**, to have something else to do or attend to ; **make fish of one and flesh (or fowl) of another**, to make invidious distinctions ; **neither fish nor flesh (nor good red herring), or neither fish, flesh, nor fowl**, to be neither one thing nor another ; **queer fish**, a person of odd habits, or of a nature with which one is not in sympathy. [O.E. *fisc* ; Ger. *fisch* ; O.N. *fiskr* ; L. *piscis* ; Gael. *iasg*.]

fish, *fish*, *n.* (*naut.*) a piece of wood placed alongside another to strengthen it : a counter for games.—*v.t.* to strengthen with a fish or fish-plate.—*ns.* **fish´-joint**, a joining by fish-plates ; **fish´-plate**,

an iron plate used in pairs to join railway rails. [Prob. Fr. *fiche*, peg, mark.]

fishgig. See **fizgig.**

fisk, *fisk*, *v.i.* (*obs.*) to frisk, to gad. [Prob. a freq. of O.E. *fysan*, to hurry, or of *fysian*, to feeze.]

fisnomie, *fiz´no-mi*, *n.* (*Shak.*) for **physiognomy.**

fissile, *fis´il*, *-il*, *adj.* readily split.—*adjs.* **fissicos´-tate** (L. *costa*, rib), with divided ribs ; **fissiling´ual** (L. *lingua*, tongue), with cloven tongue.—*ns.* **fissility** (*-il´*), cleavableness ; **fission** (*fish´ən*), a cleaving : reproduction by dividing : the splitting of the nucleus of an atom into two roughly equal parts.—*n.* **fiss´ionable.**—*ns.* **fissip´arism** (L. *parĕre*, to bring forth), **fissipar´ity.**—*adj.* **fissip´-arous**, reproducing by fission.—*adv.* **fissip´-arously.**—*adj.* **fiss´ipĕd**, **fiss´ipēde** (L. *pēs*, *pedis*, foot), with digits separate.—*n.* an animal with digits separate.—*adjs.* **fissiros´tral** (L. *rŏstrum*, beak), with deep-cleft or gaping beak ; **fiss´ive**, by fission.—*n.* **fissure** (*fish´ər*), a narrow opening or chasm : a cleft, slit, or furrow : any groove or sulcus, esp. one of the furrows on the surface of the brain, as the longitudinal fissure separating the hemispheres.—*adj.* **fiss´ured**, cleft, divided. [L. *findĕre*, *fissum*, to cleave.]

fissle, *fis´l*, *v.i.* (*Scot.*) to rustle. [Imitative.]

fist, *fist*, *n.* the closed or clenched hand : (*coll.*) handwriting.—*v.t.* to strike or grip with the fist.—*n.* **fistiana** (*-ā´nä*, *-ä´nä*; *facet.*) anecdotes about boxing and boxers.—*adj.* **fist´ic**, **-al** (*facet.*), puglistic.—*ns.* **fisti´cuff**, a blow with the fist ; **fist´-law**, the law of brute force.—*adj.* **fist´y.** [O.E. *fýst* ; Ger. *faust.*)

fistula, *fist´ū-lä*, *n.* a narrow passage or duct : (*med.*) an artificially-made opening : (*path.*) a long narrow pipe-like ulcer : a tube through which the wine of the eucharist was once sucked from the chalice—also *calamus.*—*adjs.* **fist´ūlar**, **fist´ūlose**, **fist´ūlous.** [L. *fistula*, a pipe.]

fit, *fit*, *adj.* suitable : in suitable condition : of suitable ability : convenient : befitting : well trained and ready : in good condition.—*n.* success in fitting : adjustment and correspondence in shape and size : a thing (esp. a garment) that fits.—*v.t.* to make suitable or able : to alter or make so as to be in adjustment : to adjust : to piece together : to be suitable or becoming for : to be of such size and shape as to adjust closely to : to be in agreement or correspondence with : to furnish, supply : (*Shak.*) to drive by fits.—*v.i.* to be suitable or becoming : to go into place with accurate adjustment to space : to be of such size and shape as to be able to do so : (*pr.p.* **fitt´ing** ; *pa.t.* and *pa.p.* **fitt´ed**).—*adv.* **fit´ly** (*comp.* **fit´lier** ; *superl.* **fit´li-est**).—*ns.* **fit´ment** (*Shak.*) due : (*Shak.*) something fitted to an end : an article of furniture or equipment : a fitting ; **fit´ness** ; **fit´-out**, outfit ; **fitt´er**, he who, or that which fits or makes fit : one who fits on clothes : one who assembles the parts of a machine, etc.—*adj.* **fitt´ing**, fit : appropriate.—*n.* anything used in fitting up, esp. in *pl.*, equipment, accessories : a fixture : the work of a fitter.—*adv.* **fitt´ingly.**—*ns.* **fitt´ing-out**, a supply of things fit and necessary ; **fitt´ing-shop**, a shop in which pieces of machinery are fitted together.—**fit on**, to try on : to try on a garment upon ; **fit out**, to furnish, equip ; **fit up**, to provide with fittings. [Origin obscure.]

fit, *fit*, *n.* (*obs.*) a crisis : (*Spens.*) the approach of death : (*Spens.*) a painful experience : an attack of illness, esp. epilepsy : a convulsion or paroxysm : an access, temporary attack, or outburst of anything, as laughter : a sudden effort or motion : a mood or passing humour.—*v.t.* (*Shak.*) to wrench, cause to start, as by a fit.—*adj.* **fit´ful**, marked by sudden impulses : capriciously intermittent : spasmodic.—*adv.* **fit´fully.**—*n.* **fit´fulness.**—**fit of the face**, a grimace ; **fits and starts**, spasmodic and irregular bursts of activity. [O.E. *fitt*, a struggle.]

fit, *fit*, *n.* a song : a division of a poem, a canto : a strain.—Also **fitt**, **fitte**, **fytte**. [O.E. *fitt*, a song.]

fitch, *fich*, *n.* vetch : in Isa. xxviii. 25, black cummin (*Nigella sativa*) : in Ezek. iv. 9, spelt. [**vetch.**]

Neutral vowels in unaccented syllables : *el´ə-mənt*, *in´fənt*, *ran´dəm*

fitch, *fich, n.* a polecat: polecat fur: a paint-brush of polecat-hair: a small hog's-hair brush.—*ns.* **fitch′et, fitchew** (*fich′ōō*), the polecat or its fur. [M.Du. *visse* and O.Fr. *fissel, fissau,* from the root of Du. *visse,* nasty.]

fitché, fitchée, *fich′ā, adj.* (*her.*) cut to a point—also **fitch′y.** [Fr. *fiché,* pa.p. of *ficher,* to fix.]

fitz, *fits, pfx.* son of: used in England, esp. of the illegitimate sons of kings and princes. as *Fitz-clarence,* etc. [A.Fr. *fiz* (Fr. *fils*)—L. *filius.*]

five, *fīv, adj.* and *n.* four and one.—*n.* a group of five: a score of five points, strokes, etc.: a card with five pips: an article of the size so numbered: the fifth hour after midnight or midday.—*n.* **five′-a-side,** a form of association football played by five men on each side, instead of eleven.—Also *adj.*—*adj.* **five′-bar,** having five bars.—*n.* **five′-finger(s),** a name for various plants (cinquefoil, oxlip, etc.): a starfish.—*adj.* **five′-finger,** for five fingers, as a piano exercise.—*adj.* and *adv.* **five′fold,** in five divisions: five times as much: folded in five thicknesses.—*adj.* **five′-parted,** in five parts: divided into five nearly to the base.—*n.* **five′pence.**—*adj.* **five′penny.**—*n.* **fiv′er** (*coll.*), a five-pound note.—*adj.* **five′-square** (*B.*), regularly pentagonal.—**bunch of fives,** the fist; **Five Articles, Five Points,** statements of the distinctive doctrines of the Arminians and Calvinists respectively—the former promulgated in 1610, the latter sustained by the Synod of Dort in 1619 (see **Calvinism**); **Five Nations,** a confederacy of five northern Iroquoian Indian tribes. [O.E. *fīf;* Ger. *fünf;* Goth. *fimf;* W. *pump;* L. *quinque;* Gr. *pente, pempe;* Sans. *pañcha.*]

fives, *fīvz, n.* (*Shak.*). Same as **vives.**

fives, *fīvz, n.pl.* a game of handball played in a roomy court against a wall, chiefly at the great public schools of England. [Origin obscure.]

fix, *fiks, v.t.* to make firm or fast: to establish: to drive in: to settle: to make or keep permanent, solid, rigid, steady, or motionless: to fasten or attach: (*U.S.*) to put to rights, mend, arrange, attend to.—*v.i.* to settle or remain permanently: to become firm, stable or permanent.—*n.* (*coll.*) a difficulty: a dilemma: the position of an aircraft as calculated from instrument readings.—*adj.* **fix′able,** capable of being fixed.—*v.t.* **fix′ate,** to fix, make stable: to direct the eyes upon: to direct (the eyes) upon an object: (*psych.*) to arrest the emotional development of.—*ns.* **fixā′tion,** act of fixing, or state of being fixed: steadiness, firmness: state in which a body does not evaporate: conversion of atmospheric nitrogen into a combined form: emotional arrest of personality, instinctive forces maintaining their earlier channels of gratification; **fix′ative,** a fixing agent; **fix′ature,** a gummy preparation for fixing the hair.—*adj.* **fixed,** settled: not apt to evaporate: steadily directed: fast, lasting, permanent: substantively for fixed stars (*Par. Lost,* III. 481).—*adv.* **fix′edly.** —*ns.* **fix′edness; fix′er; fix′ing,** act or process of making fixed: arrangement: (*U.S.* in *pl.*) adjuncts, trimmings: equipment; **fix′ity,** fixedness.— *adj.* **fix′ive.**—*ns.* **fix′ture,** fixing: a movable that has become fastened to land or to a house: a fixed article of furniture: a thing or person permanently established in a place: a fixed or appointed time or event, as a horse-race; **fix′ure** (*Shak.*), stability, position, firmness.—**fixed air,** the name given by Dr Joseph Black in 1756 to what in 1784 was named by Lavoisier carbonic acid; **fixed capital** (see **capital**); **fixed oils,** those which, on the application of heat, do not volatilise without decomposition; **fixed stars,** stars which appear always to occupy the same position in the heavens —opp. to *planets;* **fix on,** to single out, decide for; **fix up,** to arrange or make arrangements for: to settle: (*U.S.*) to put to rights, attend to. [L. *fixus, figĕre,* to fix, prob. through L.L. *fixāre.*]

fizgig, fisgig, *fiz′gig, n.* a giddy girl: a firework of damp powder: a gimcrack: a crotchet: a harpoon (also **fish′gig**). [gig.]

fizz, fiz, *fiz, v.i.* to make a hissing or sputtering sound: (*pr.p.* **fizz′ing;** *pa.t.* and *pa.p.* **fizzed**).—*n.* a sputtering sound: a frothy drink, esp. champagne.

—*n.* **fizz′er,** that which fizzes: anything excellent: a very fast ball.—*n.* and *adj.* **fizz′ing.**—*v.i.* **fizz′le,** to hiss or sputter: to go out with a sputtering sound (often with *out*): to come to nothing, be a fiasco: to fail.—*n.* a state of agitation or worry: an abortive effort.—*adj.* **fizz′y.** [Formed from the sound.]

fizzen. See **foison.**

fjord. Same as **fiord.**

flabbergast, *flab′ər-gäst, v.t.* (*coll.*) to stun, confound. [Prob. conn. with **flabby** and **gast, to** astonish.]

flabby, *flab′i, adj.* soft, yielding: hanging loose.— *n.* **flabb′iness.** [**flap.**]

flabellum, *fla-bel′əm, n.* (*eccles.*) a fan, anciently used to drive away flies from the chalice during the celebration of the eucharist: (*biol.*) a fan-like structure.—*adj.* **flabell′ate,** fan-shaped.—*n.* **flabellation** (*flab-ə-lā′shən*), the action of fanning. —*adj.* **flabell′iform.** [L., a fan.]

flaccid, *flak′sid, adj.* limp: flabby: lax: easily yielding to pressure: soft and weak: clammy.— *adv.* **flac′cidly.**—*ns.* **flac′cidness, flaccid′ity.** [L. *flaccidus*—*flaccus,* flabby.]

flacker, *flak′ər, v.i.* (*prov.*) to flap, flutter. [Cf. O.E. *flacor,* fluttering.]

flacket, *flak′it, n.* a flask, bottle. [O.Fr. *flasquet.*]

flacon, *flak-onɡ′, n.* a scent-bottle, etc. [Fr.]

flaff, *fläf, v.i.* (*Scot.*) to flap: to pant.—*n.* a flutter of the wings: a puff.—*v.i.* **flaff′er,** to flutter. [Imit.]

flag, *flag, v.i.* to droop: to flap feebly: to grow languid or spiritless: (*pr.p.* **flagg′ing;** *pa.t.* and *pa.p.* **flagged**).—*n.* **flagg′iness.**—*adj.* **flagg′y,** limp, drooping: flabby. [Perh. O.Fr. *flac*—L. *flaccus;* prob. influenced by imit. forms as **flap.**]

flag, *flag, n.* an iris: (*B.*) reed-grass.—*ns.* **flag′-bas′ket,** a reed basket for tools; **flagg′iness.**— *adj.* **flagg′y,** abounding in flags.—*n.* **flag′-worm,** a worm or grub bred among flags or reeds. [Ety. obscure; cf. Du. *flag.*]

flag, *flag, n.* a piece usually of bunting with a design, used as an emblem for military or naval purposes, signalling, decoration, display, propaganda, etc.: a conspicuous sign to mark a position, e.g. of a golf-hole, or convey information, as that a taxi is disengaged: a flag-ship: a bushy tail.—*v.t.* to decorate with flags: to inform by flag-signals.— *ns.* **flag′-cap′tain,** the captain of a flag-ship; **flag′-day,** a day on which collectors levy contributions to a fund in exchange for small flags as badges to secure immunity for the rest of the day: (*U.S.*) the 14th of June, anniversary of the adoption of the Stars and Stripes.—*adj.* **flagg′y,** like a banner: spreading.—*ns.* **flag′-lieuten′ant,** an officer in a flag-ship, corresponding to an aide-de-camp in the army; **flag′-off′icer,** a naval officer privileged to carry a flag denoting his rank—admiral, vice-admiral, rear-admiral, or commodore; **flag′-ship,** the ship in which an admiral sails, and which carries his flag; **flag′-staff,** a staff or pole for displaying a flag; **flag′-wagging,** signalling by flag: aggressive patriotism or imperialism.—**flag of distress,** a flag displayed as a signal of distress— usually upside down or at half-mast; **flag of truce,** a white flag displayed during war when some pacific communication is intended between the hostile parties; **black flag** (see **black**); **dip the flag,** to lower the flag and then hoist it—a token of respect; **red flag,** a flag used as a signal of danger, defiance, no quarter, or an auction sale: the banner of socialism or of revolution: a socialists' song; **strike, or lower, the flag,** to pull it down as a token of relinquishment of command, respect, submission, or surrender; **white flag,** an emblem of truce or of surrender; **yellow flag** (see **yellow**). [Origin unknown; cf. Dan. *flag;* Du. *vlag,* Ger. *flagge.*]

flag, *flag, n.* a stone that separates in slabs: a flat paving stone.—*v.t.* to pave with flagstones.—*ns.* **flagg′ing,** flagstones: a pavement thereof; **flag′-stone.**—*adj.* **flagg′y.** [O.N. *flaga,* a slab.]

flagellum, *fla-jel′əm, n.* a scourge: (*bot.*) a long runner: (*biol.*) a long cilium or whip-like appendage (*pl.* **flagell′a**).—*n.pl.* **Flagellata** (*flaj-ə-lā′tä*), unicellular organisms with flagella.—*v.t.* **flag′ellate,** to scourge.—*adj.* having a flagellum or flagella.—*adjs.* **flag′ellated; flag′ellant,** scourging.—*n.* one who scourges, esp. himself in religious discipline.—*ns.* **flag′ellantism; flagellā′tion, flag′ellātor.**—*adjs.* **flag′ellatory; flagellif′erous; flagell′iform.** [L. *flagellum,* dim. of *flagrum,* a whip.]

flageolet, *flaj-ō-let′, flaj′, n.* the modern form of the flûte-à-bec, or straight flute, in its simplest type a tin whistle with six holes. [Fr., dim. of O.Fr. *flageol, flajol,* a pipe; not L. *flauta,* flute.]

flageolet, *flaj-ō-let′, flā-zhō-lā, n.* a variety of kidney bean. [Corr. of Fr. *fageolet;* L. *faseolus.*]

flagitate, *flaj′i-tāt, v.t.* to entreat, importune.—*n.* **flagitā′tion.** [L. *flāgitāre, -ātum.*]

flagitious, *flə-jish′əs, adj.* grossly wicked: guilty of enormous crimes.—*adv.* **flagi′tiously.**—*n.* **flagi′tiousness.** [L. *flāgitiōsus—flāgitium,* a disgraceful act—*flagrāre,* to burn.]

flagon, *flag′ən, n.* a large, esp. wide, bottle: a liquor-jug. [Fr. *flacon—flascon*—L.L. *flascō, -ōnis;* see **flask.**]

flagrant, *flā′grənt, adj.* notorious: enormous.—*ns.* **flā′grance, flā′grancy.**—*adv.* **flā′grantly.** [L. *flagrāns, -āntis,* pr.p. of *flagrāre,* to burn.]

flail, *flāl, n.* an implement for threshing corn, consisting of a wooden bar (the *swingle*) hinged or tied to a handle: a mediaeval weapon with spiked iron swingle.—*v.t.* to strike with, or as if with, a flail. [O.E. *fligel,* influenced by O.Fr. *flaiel,* prob. from L. *flagellum,* a scourge.]

flair, *flār, n.* intuitive discernment: faculty for nosing out: (popularly and loosely) a natural aptitude. [Fr., scent.]

flak, *flak, n. (mil. slang)* anti-aircraft protection, missiles, or fragments. [Initials of Ger. *flieger*-(or *flug-)abwehrkanone,* anti-aircraft cannon.]

flake, *flāk, n.* a small flat scale or layer: a very small loose mass, as of snow: a spark or detached flame: (*Spens.*) a flash.—*v.t.* to form into flakes.—*v.i.* to come off in flakes.—*ns.* **flake′-white,** the purest white-lead for painting, made in the form of scales or plates; **flak′iness.**—*adj.* **flak′y.** [Perh. conn. with O.N. *flóke,* flock of wool; O.H.G. *floccho.*]

flake, *flāk, n.* a movable hurdle for fencing: (*naut.*) a stage hung over a ship's side for caulking, etc. [Cf. O.N. *flake;* Du. *vlaak.*]

flam, *flam, n.* a whim: an idle fancy: a falsehood.—*v.t.* to impose upon. [Perh. **flim-flam** or **flamfew.**]

flam, flamm. Same as **flawn.**

flambeau, *flam′bō, n.* a flaming torch: (*pl.* **flam′-beaux,** *-bōz*). [Fr.,—O.Fr. *flambe*—L. *flamma.*]

flamboyant, *flam-boi′ənt, adj. (archit.)* late French Gothic (15th-16th cent.) with flame-like tracery: of wavy form: gorgeously coloured: florid.—*n.* (also **flamboy′ante**) a tropical tree of the Caesal-pinia family (*Poinciana regia*) with flame-coloured flowers.—*ns.* **flamboy′ance, flamboy′ancy.**—*adv.* **flamboy′antly.**—*n.* **flamboy′ant(e)-tree.** [Fr., pr.p. of *flamboyer,* to blaze.]

flame, *flām, n.* gaseous matter undergoing com-bustion: the gleam or blaze of a fire: rage: ardour of temper: vigour of thought: warmth of affection: love or its object.—*v.i.* to burn as flame: to break out in passion.—*v.t.* to set aflame.—*adjs.* **flame′-coloured** (*Shak.*), of the colour of flame, bright reddish yellow; **flamed** (*Spens.*), inflamed.—*n.* **flame′-leaf,** Poinciana.—*adj.* **flame′less.**—*ns.* **flame′let,** a small flame; **flame′-thrower,** an apparatus for throwing jets of flame in warfare.—*adj.* **flam′ing,** brilliantly red: gaudy: violent: furious: flagrant.—*adv.* **flam′ingly.**—*adj.* **flam′y,** pertaining to, or like, flame. [O.Fr. *flambe*—L. *flamma.*]

flamen, *flā′mən, n.* in ancient Rome a priest of one particular god.—*adj.* **flamin′ical.** [L. *flāmen, -inis.*]

flamenco, *flā-meng′kō, n.* a type of gypsy song or dance from Andalusia. [Sp., Flemish, hence gypsy.]

flamfew, *flam′fū, n.* a fantastic trifle. [Fr. *fanfelue.*]

Flamingant, *flā-man²-gän²′, n.* one who favours the Flemish language or Flemish nationalism. [Fr.]

flamingo, *flə-ming′gō, n.* a tropical bird of a pink or bright-red colour, with long legs and neck (*pl.*

flaming′o(e)s). [Port. *flamengo,* Sp. *flamenco*—L. *flamma,* a flame.]

flammenwerfer, *fläm′ən-ver-fər, n.* a flame-thrower. [Ger., flame-thrower.]

flammule, *flam′ūl, n.* a little flame, as in a picture of a Japanese god.—*adj.* **flamm′ūlāted,** ruddy.—*n.* **flammūlā′tion,** flamelike marking. [L. *flammula,* dim. of *flamma,* flame.]

flan. Same as **flawn.**

flanch, *flānsh, n.* a flange: (*her.*) an ordinary formed on each side of a shield by the segment of a circle.—*adj.* **flanched,** charged with a pair of flanches. [Prob. related to **flank.**]

flanch, *flānsh, v.i.* to widen, esp. outwards or upwards: to flare. [Ety. obscure.]

flanconade, *flang-kə-nād′, n.* (*fencing*) a thrust in the flank or side. [Fr., from *flanc,* the side.]

flâneur, *flā-nər′, n.* one who saunters about, a stroller.—*n.* **flânerie** (*flän-rē*), idling. [Fr. *flâner,* to lounge.]

flange, *flanj, n.* a projecting or raised edge or flank, as of a wheel or of a rail.—*v.i.* to widen out.—*v.t.* to put a flange on.—*adj.* **flanged.** [Perh. conn. with **flank.**]

flank, *flangk, n.* the side of an animal from the ribs to the thigh: the side or wing of anything, esp. of an army or fleet: a body of soldiers on the right or left extremity.—*v.t.* to be on, pass round, attack, threaten, or protect the flank of.—*n.* **flank′er,** a fortification that commands the flank of an assailing force:—*v.t.* (*obs.*) to defend by flankers: to attack sideways. [Fr. *flanc.*]

flannel, *flan′əl, n.* a soft woollen cloth of loose texture for undergarments, etc.: the garment itself: (*pl.*) the garb of cricketers, etc.—*v.t.* to wrap in or rub with flannel.—**flannelette′,** a cotton imitation of flannel.—*adjs.* **flann′elled; flann′elly.**—*n.* **flann′en** (*obs.* or *dial.*), flannel. [Poss. O.Fr. *flaine,* blanket, or Welsh *gwlanen—gwlan,* wool.]

flap, *flap, n.* the blow or motion of a broad loose object: anything broad and flexible hanging loose, as the tail of a coat: a portion of skin or flesh detached from the underlying part for covering and growing over the end of an amputated limb.—*v.t.* to beat or move with a flap.—*v.i.* to move, as wings: to hang like a flap: (*pr.p.* **flapp′ing;** *pa.t.* and *pa.p.* **flapped**).—*ns.* **flap′doodle,** the food of fools: gross flattery, etc.; **flap′-dragon,** a play in which small edibles, as raisins, are snatched from burning brandy, and swallowed.—*adj.* **flap′-eared** (*Shak.*).—*n.* **flap′-jack** (*Shak.*) a kind of broad, flat pancake: an apple-puff: a flat face-powdering outfit.—*adj.* **flap′-mouthed.**—*n.* **flapp′er,** one who or that which flaps: a flipper: young wild duck or partridge: (*slang*) a girl nearing womanhood: a flighty young maid; **flapp′erhood.**—*adj.* **flapp′erish.** [Prob. imit.]

flare, *flār, v.i.* to spread: to wave: to widen out bell-wise: to burn with a glaring, unsteady light: to glitter, or flash: to blaze up, lit. or in anger: to display glaringly.—*n.* a widening out, as in the bell of a horn, a bowl, a skirt: an unsteady glare: an unshaded flame: a sudden blaze: a torch: a signalling light.—*n.* **flare′-up′.**—*adj.* **flar′ing.**—*adv.* **flā′ringly.**—*adj.* **flā′ry.** [Poss. conn. with Norw. *flara,* to blaze.]

flaser, *flā′zər,* an irregular streaky lenticular structure developed in metamorphic rocks. [Ger., streak.]

flash, *flash, n.* a momentary gleam of light: a sudden burst, as of merriment: a moment, an in-stant: a sudden rush of water: a board for deepen-ing or directing a stream of water: a bright garter or ribbon worn with knickerbockers or kilt, a small portion showing below the knee: a distinct-ive mark on a uniform: thieves' slang: a brief news dispatch by telegraph: in a film, a scene shown momentarily by way of explanation or comment, especially (**flash-back**) a scene of the past.—*adj.* showy: vulgar: pertaining to the criminal class and its speech: (formerly) fashionable.—*v.i.* to break forth, as a sudden light (*lit.* and *fig.*): to give forth flashes of light: to sparkle brilliantly: to blaze out: to break out into intellectual brilliancy: to burst out into violence: to move like a flash.—*v.t.* to cause to flash: to expand, as blown glass, into a disk: to send by some startling or sudden means.—*ns.* **flash'-board,** one of a set of boards set up at the sides of a water-channel to deepen it; **flash'er,** one who flashes: a device for turning off and on lights in an advertising display; **flash'-house,** a brothel.—*adv.* **flash'ily.**—*ns.* **flashi'ness; flash'ing,** the act of blazing: a sudden burst, as of water.—*adj.* emitting flashes: sparkling.—*ns.* **flash'-light,** a light that flashes periodically: a sudden light used to take photographs: an electric torch: **flash'-point,** the temperature at which a liquid gives off enough inflammable vapour to flash when a light is applied to it.—*adj.* **flash'y,** dazzling for a moment: showy but empty: (*Milt.*) vapid: gaudy: tawdry.—**flash in the pan** (see **pan**). [Prob. imit.; cf. Sw. prov. *flasa,* to blaze.]

flask, *flåsk, n.* a narrow-necked vessel for holding liquids: a bottle: a pocket-bottle: a horn or metal vessel for carrying powder.—*n.* **flask'et,** a vessel in which viands are served: (*Spens.*) a basket. [O.E. *flasce;* Ger. *flasche;* prob. from L.L. *flascō*—L. *vasculum,* a flask.]

flat, *flat, adj.* smooth: level: wanting points of prominence or interest: monotonous: uniform: vapid, insipid: no longer brisk or sparkling: failing of effect: dejected: downright, out-and-out, sheer: (of feet) having little or no arch: (*mus.*) relatively low: below the right pitch: having flats in the key-signature: (*phon.*) voiced.—*n.* a level part: a plain: a tract covered by shallow water: something broad: a story or floor of a house, esp. one, or part of one, used as a separate residence: (*naut.*) the floor of a particular compartment; a flat piece of scenery slid or lowered on to the stage: an insipid passage: a simpleton: (*mus.*) a character (♭) that lowers a note a semitone: a note so lowered: a black key on a piano.—*adv.* in or to a flat position: evenly: too low in pitch: without qualification.—*ns.* **flat'-boat,** a large flat-bottomed boat for floating goods downstream; **flat'-cap,** a low-crowned cap worn by London citizens in the 16th and 17th centuries: a London citizen or apprentice; **flat'-fish,** a marine fish that habitually lies on one side, with unsymmetrical flat body—flounder, turbot, etc.; **flat'-foot,** a condition in which the arch of the instep is flattened.—*adj.* **flat'-footed,** having flat feet: (*U.S.*) resolute.—*n.* **flat'-footedness.**—*adj.* **flat'-head,** having an artificially flattened head, as some American Indians.—Also *n.*—*n.* **flat'-iron,** an iron for smoothing cloth.—*advs.* **flat'ling, flat'lings, flat'long** (*Spens., Shak.*), with the flat side: flat side on: not edgewise: prostrate; **flat'ly.**—*ns.* **flat'ness; flat-race,** a race over open or clear ground.—*adj.* **flatt'ed,** made flat: divided into flats.—*n.* **flat'-spin',** rotation about a horizontal axis: confused excitement.—*v.t.* **flatt'en,** to make flat.—*v.i.* to become flat.—*n.* **flatt'ing,** a mode of house-painting in which the paint is left without gloss.—*adj.* **flatt'ish,** somewhat flat.—*adj.* or *adv.* **flat'ways, flat'wise,** with or on the flat side.—*n.* **flat'-worm,** a tapeworm or other member of the Platyhelminthes.—**flatten out,** to bring an aeroplane into a horizontal position; **flat rate,** a fixed or standard uniform rate; **that's flat,** I tell you plainly. [O.N. *flatr,* flat.]

flatter, *flat'ər, v.t.* to treat with insincere praise and servile attentions: to please with false hopes or undue praise: to overpraise: to represent overfavourably: to coax: to please with belief: to gratify.—*n.* **flatt'erer.**—*adj.* **flatt'ering.**—*adv.* **flatt'eringly.**—*n.* **flatt'ery,** exaggerated or insincere praise. [Conn. with O.Fr. *flater* (Fr. *flatter*); Gmc.; cf. O.N. *flathra.*]

flatus, *flā'təs, n.* a puff of wind: a blast: a breath: gas generated in the stomach or intestines.—*ns.* **flatulence** (*flat'ū-ləns*), **flat'ulency,** distension of stomach or bowels by gases formed during digestion: windiness: emptiness of utterance.—*adj.* **flat'ulent.**—*adv.* **flat'ulently.**—*adj.* **flat'uous.** [L. *flātus, -ūs,* a blowing—*flāre,* to blow.]

flaught, *flawt* (*Scot. flawhht*), *n.* a flight, a flapping.—*n.* **flaugh'ter,** a fluttering motion.—*v.i.* to flutter, flicker. [Related to **flight.**]

flaught, *flawt* (*Scot. flawhht*), *n.* a flake: a hide: a gust: a flash: a spark: a turf.—*v.t.* to pare, skin, card.—*v.i.* **flaugh'ter,** to cut turfs, etc.—*n.* a paring of turf. [Cf. **flake** (1), **flaw** (1), **flay.**]

flaunt, *flawnt, v.i.* to wave in the wind: to move ostentatiously: to carry a gaudy or saucy appearance.—*v.t.* to display ostentatiously.—*n.* (*Shak.*) anything displayed for show.—*n.* **flaunt'er.**—*adjs.* **flaunt'ing, flaunt'y.**—*adv.* **flaunt'ingly.** [Prob. Scand.]

flautist, *flawt'ist, n.* a flute player. [It. *flautista.*]

flavescent, *flə-, flā-ves'ənt, adj.* yellowish or turning yellow. [L. *flāvēscēns, -entis,* pr.p. of *flāvēscēre,* to become yellow—*flāvus,* yellow.]

Flavian, *flāv'i-ən, adj.* of or pertaining to *Flavius* Vespasian and his sons Titus and Domitian, the Flavian emperors of Rome (69–96 A.D.).

flavin, *flā'vin,* **flavine,** *flā'vēn, n.* a yellow dye made from quercitron bark. [L. *flāvus,* yellow.]

flavour, *flā'vər, n.* that quality of anything which affects the smell or taste: a smack or relish.—*v.t.* to impart flavour to.—*adj.* **flā'vorous.**—*n.* **flā'vouring,** any substance used to give a flavour.—*adjs.* **flā'vourless, flā'voursome.** [O.Fr. *flaur;* prob. influenced by **savour.**]

flaw, *flaw, n.* a gust of wind: a sudden rush: an outburst of passion: uproar. [Cf. Du. *vlaag,* Sw. *flaga.*]

flaw, *flaw, n.* (*Shak.*) a flake, fragment, splinter: a break, a crack: a defect.—*v.t.* to crack or break.—*adjs.* **flawed, flaw'less, flaw'y.** [O.N. *flaga,* a slab.]

flawn, flaune, *flawn,* **flam, flam, flan, flan,** *n.* a custard: a pancake: a flat open tart. [O.Fr. *flaon*—L.L. *fladō, -ōnis*—O.H.G. *flado.*]

flax, *flaks, n.* the fibres of the plant Linum, which are woven into linen cloth: the plant itself.—*ns.* **flax'-bush, flax-lil'y,** a New Zealand plant (Phormium) of the lily family, yielding a valuable fibre, **New Zealand flax; flax'-comb,** a toothed instrument or heckle for cleaning the fibres of flax; **flax'-dresser,** one who prepares flax for the spinner by the successive processes of rippling, retting, grassing, breaking, and scutching.—*adj.* **flax'en,** made of or resembling flax: light yellow.—*ns.* **flax'-mill,** a mill for working flax into linen; **flax'-seed,** linseed; **flax'-wench,** a female who spins flax.—*adj.* **flax'y,** like flax: of a light colour.—**purging flax,** a small wild species of flax (Linum catharticum). [O.E. *flæx* (W.S. *fleax*); Ger. *flachs.*]

flay, *flā, v.t.* to strip off the skin from: (*pr.p.* **flay'ing;** *pa.t.* and *pa.p.* **flayed**).—*ns.* **flay'er; flay'-flint,** a skinflint. [O.E. *fléan;* O.N. *flā,* to skin.]

flea, *flē, n.* a well-known wingless blood-sucking insect of great agility.—*ns.* **flea'-bane,** a name for various composite plants (Erigeron, Pulicaria, etc.), whose strong smell is said to drive away fleas; **flea'-bite,** the bite of a flea: a small mark caused by the bite: (*fig.*) a trifle.—*adjs.* **flea'-bitten,** bitten by fleas: (*fig.*) mean: having small reddish spots on a lighter ground, esp. of horses; **flea'some.**—**a flea in one's ear,** a stinging rebuff. [O.E. *fléah;* cf. Ger. *floh,* Du. *vloo.*]

fleam, *flēm, n.* an instrument for bleeding cattle. [O.Fr. *flieme* (Fr. *flamme*)—Gr. *phlebotomon,* a lancet—*phleps, phlebos,* a vein, and *tomē,* a cut.]

flèche, *flesh, n.* a spire: a slender spire rising from the intersection of the nave and transepts in some large churches: (*fort.*) a parapet with two faces forming a salient angle at the foot of a glacis: a point on a backgammon board. [Fr., arrow.]

fleck, *flek, n.* a spot or speckle: a little bit of a thing.—*vs.t.* **fleck, fleck'er,** to spot: to streak.—*adjs.* **flecked,** spotted, dappled; **fleck'less,** without spot. [O.N. *flekkr,* a spot; Ger. *fleck,* Du. *vlek.*]

flection, a bad spelling of **flexion.**

fled, *fled, pa.t.* and *pa.p.* of **flee.**

fledge, *flej, v.t.* to furnish with feathers or wings.—*v.i.* to acquire feathers for flying.—*adj.* (*Milt.*) **fledged.**—*adj.* **fledged.**—*n.* **fledg'ling** (rarely

fledge'ling, a bird just fledged.—*adj.* **fledg'y** (*Keats*), feathery. [M.E. *fligge, flegge*—an assumed O.E. (Kentish) *flecge;* cf. O.E. *unflycge*, unfledged; see **fly.**]

flee, *flē, v.i.* to run away, as from danger: to disappear.—*v.t.* to keep at a distance from: (*pr.p.* **flee'ing**; *pa.t.* and *pa.p.* **fled**).—*n.* flē'er. [O.E. *fléon;* Ger. *fliehen;* not akin to *fly*, but influenced by it, the *f* representing an earlier *th.*]

fleece, *flēs, n.* a sheep's coat of wool: the wool shorn from a sheep at one time: anything like a fleece.—*v.t.* to shear: to plunder: to cover, as with wool.—*adjs.* **fleeced**, having a fleece; **fleece'less**.—*ns.* **fleec'er**, one who strips or plunders; **fleece'-wool**, that got at clippings after the first.—*adj.* **fleec'y**, woolly: like a fleece. [O.E. *fléos;* Du. *vlies*, Ger. *fliess.*]

fleech, *flēch, v.t.* and *v.i.* (*Scot.*) to flatter, coax, beg.—*ns.* **fleech'ing, fleech'ment**. [Origin obscure.]

fleer, *flēr, v.i.* to make wry faces in contempt: to leer.—*v.t.* to mock.—*n.* mockery.—*n.* **fleer'er**.—*n.* and *adj.* **fleer'ing.**—*adv.* **fleer'ingly**. [Cf. Norw. *flira*, Sw. *flissa*, to titter.]

fleet, *flēt, n.* a number of ships (birds, aircraft, motor-cars, etc.) in company or otherwise associated: a navy: a division of a navy under an admiral. [O.E. *fléot*, a ship—*fléotan*, to float; conn. with Du. *vloot*, Ger. *flotte.*]

fleet, *flēt, adj.* swift: nimble: transient.—*adjs.* **fleet'-foot** (*Shak.*) fleet or swift of foot; **fleet'ly**. —*n.* **fleet'ness**. [Prob. O.N. *fliótr*, swift; but ult. cog. with succeeding word.]

fleet, *flēt, v.i. (obs.)* to float: (*Spens.*) to flow: to flit, pass swiftly.—*v.t.* (*Shak.*) to make to pass quickly.—*adj. (prov.)* shallow.—*adj.* **fleet'ing**, passing quickly: temporary.—*adv.* **fleet'ingly**. [O.E. *fléotan*, to float.]

fleet, *flēt, n.* a shallow creek, bay, brook or drain, as in North*fleet*, *Fleet*-ditch, etc.—**the Fleet, or Fleet Prison**, a London gaol down to 1842, near the Fleet, long a place of confinement for debtors —clandestine marriages were solemnised here down to 1754 by **Fleet parsons**, broken-down clergymen confined for debt; **Fleet Street**, journalism or its ways and traditions, from the street near the Fleet with many newspaper offices. [O.E. *fléot*, an inlet.]

fleg, *fleg, n.* (*Scot.*) a fright.—*v.t.* to frighten. [O.E. *flecgan*, to put to flight.]

fleme, *flēm, v.t.* (*Scot.*) to put to flight: (*pa.t.* and *pa.p.* **flem'it**). [O.E. *flieman*.]

Flemish, *flem'ish, adj.* of or belonging to the *Flemings* or people of Flanders, or their language. —*n.* **Flem'ing**, a native of Flanders.—**Flemish bond**, a bricklayer's bond of alternate headers and stretchers in every course; **Flemish school**, a school of painting formed by the brothers Van Eyck, reaching its height in Rubens, Vandyck, and Teniers; **Flemish stitch**, a stitch used in making certain kinds of point-lace. [Du. *Vlaamsch.*]

flench, *flensh*, **flense**, *flens*, **flinch**, *flinsh, v.t.* to cut up the blubber of, as a whale: to flay. [Dan. *flense.*]

flesh, *flesh, n.* muscular tissue: all the living substance of the body of similar composition to muscle: the soft substance that covers the bones of animals: animal food: the bodies of beasts and (sometimes) birds, not fish: the body, not the soul: animals, or animal nature: human bodily nature: mankind: kindred: bodily appetites: the soft substance of fruit, esp. the part fit to be eaten.—*v.t.* to reward with flesh: to train to an appetite for flesh, as dogs for hunting: to inure: to glut: to use upon flesh, as a sword: to use for the first time: to gratify with fleshly indulgence: to put flesh upon: to scrape flesh from.—*ns.* **flesh'-broth**, broth made by boiling flesh; **flesh'-brush**, a brush used for rubbing the skin to excite circulation; **flesh'-colour**, the natural colour of the skin of a European; **flesh'-eater**. —*adj.* **fleshed** (*flesht*), having flesh: fat.—*ns.* **flesh'er**, an instrument for scraping hides: (esp. *Scot.*) a butcher; **flesh'-fly**, a fly (esp. Sarcophaga) whose larvae feed on flesh; **flesh'-hood** (*Mrs. Browning*), the state of being in the flesh; **flesh'-hook**, a hook for drawing flesh from a pot; **flesh'iness**.—*n.pl.* **flesh'ings**, flesh-coloured tights.—*adj.* **flesh'less**, without flesh: lean.—*ns.* **flesh'liness**; **flesh'ling**, a sensualist. —*adj.* **flesh'ly**, corporeal: carnal: not spiritual. —Also *adv.*—*ns.* **flesh'-market**; **flesh'-meat**, flesh of animals used for food; **flesh'ment**, (*Shak.*) act of fleshing or initiating, excitement arising from success; **flesh'-monger**, one who deals in flesh: (*Shak.*) a whoremonger: a procurer, a pimp, a slave-dealer; **flesh'-pot**, a pot or vessel in which flesh is cooked: (*fig.*) abundance of flesh, high living; **flesh'-pottery**, sumptuous living; **flesh'-tint**, a tint or colour that represents the human body; **flesh'-worm**, a worm or maggot that feeds on flesh; **flesh'-wound**, a wound not reaching beyond the flesh.—*adj.* **flesh'y**, fat: pulpy: plump.—**an arm of flesh**, human strength or help; **flesh and blood**, human nature: one's own kindred; **in flesh**, in good condition: fat; **in the flesh**, in bodily life, alive: incarnate; **one flesh**, united in marriage. [O.E. *flǣsc;* cog. forms in all Gmc. languages; Ger. *fleisch*, etc.]

fletch, *flech, v.t.* to feather.—*n.* **fletch'er**, one who makes arrows. [Fr. *flèche*, an arrow, O.Fr. *flecher*, a fletcher.]

fleur-de-lis, -lys, *flər-də-lē', -lēs', n.* the iris: an ornament and heraldic bearing of disputed origin (an iris, three lilies, etc.), borne by the kings of France:—*pl.* **fleurs-de-lis, fleurs-de-lys,** (*flər-*). —Also **flower(-)delice, flower-de-luce, flower** (-)**deluce**.—*ns.* **fleuret** (*flōōr'et*) an ornament like a small flower: (*-et'*) a fencing foil; **fleuron** (*flə-ron²*) a flowerlike ornament, in architecture, printing, etc.—*adj.* **fleury** (*flōō'ri*), having fleurs-de-lis—also **flo'ry**. [Fr.; *lis*, being O.Fr. *liz*—L. *lilium*, lily.]

flew, *flōō, pa.t.* of **fly;** coll. used for **fled** (*pa.t.*). See also **fly.**

flew, *flōō, n.* a dog's pendulous chop (usu. in *pl.*).—*adj.* **flewed** (*Shak.*). [Ety unknown.]

flex, *fleks, v.t.* and *v.i.* to bend.—*n.* a bending: a flexible cord or line, esp. of insulated wire.—*n.* **flexibil'ity**.—*adjs.* **flexi'ble**, easily bent: pliant: docile.—*ns.* **flex'ibleness**.—*adv.* **flex'ibly**.—*adj.* **flex'ile** (*-īl*), flexible.—*ns.* **flexion** (*flek'shən*), a bend: a fold: the action of a flexor muscle: (*gram.*) inflexion; **flex'or**, a muscle that bends a joint, as opposed to *extensor*.—*adjs.* **flex'uose**, **flex'uous**, full of windings and turnings: undulating; **flexural** (*flek'shər-əl*).—*n.* **flex'ure**, a bend or turning: (*math.*) the curving of a line or surface: the bending of loaded beams: (*Shak.*) obsequious bowing. [L. *flectĕre, flexum*, to bend.]

fley, flay, *flui, flā, (Scot.) v.t.* to cause to flee: to frighten.—*v.i.* to be frightened. [M.E. *flayen*—O.E. *flégan* (as in compound *dflégan, dfliegan*, to put to flight); cf. O.N. *fleyja*, Goth. *flaugjan*.]

flibbertigibbet, *flib'ər-ti-jib'it, n.* a flighty person: an imp. [Most prob. jargon.]

flichter, *flihh'tər, n.* (*Scot.*) a flutter.—*v.t.* and *v.i.* to flutter, quiver.

flick, *flik, v.t.* to strike lightly, as with a lash or a finger-nail.—*n.* a stroke of this kind: (*slang*) a cinematograph film. [Echoic.]

flicker, *flik'ər, v.i.* to flutter and move the wings, as a bird: to burn unsteadily, as a flame.—*n.* an act of flickering, a flickering movement or light.—*adv.* **flick'eringly**. [O.E. *flicorian;* imit.]

flicker, *flik'ər, n.* an American woodpecker. [Prob. echoic.]

flier, flies. See under **fly.**

flight, *flīt, n.* a passing through the air: a soaring: distance flown: a sally: a series of steps: a flock of birds flying together: the birds produced in the same season: a volley: (*Shak.*) a long-distance arrow: the power of flying: the art or the act of flying with wings or in an aeroplane or other machine: a unit of the Air Force answering to a platoon in the army.—*n.* **flight'ed** (*Milt.*) flying.—*n.* **flight'-feather**, a quill of a bird's wing.—*adv.* **flight'ily**.—*n.* **flight'iness**.—*adj.* **flight'less**, without power of flying.—*n.* **flight'-lieuten'ant**, an Air Force officer of rank answering

14

to naval lieutenant or army captain.—*adj.* **flight'y**, (*Shak.*) swift: fanciful: changeable: giddy-minded.—**in the first, top, flight**, in the highest class. [O.E. *flyht*—*fléogan*, to fly.]

flight, *flīt*, *n.* an act of fleeing. [Assumed O.E. *flyht*; cf. *fléon*, to flee.]

flim-flam, *flim'-flam*, *n.* a trick. [Cf. **flam.**]

flimp, *flimp*, *v.t.* (*slang*) to rob while a confederate hustles. [Cf. West Flem., *flimpe*, knock, rob.]

flimsy, *flim'zi*, *adj.* thin: without solidity, strength, or reason: weak.—*n.* transfer-paper: (*slang*) a banknote: reporters' copy written on thin paper.—*adv.* **flim'sily**, in a flimsy manner.—*n.* **flim'siness**. [First in 18th century; prob. suggested by **film.**]

flinch, *flin(t)sh*, *v.i.* to shrink back: to fail.—*n.* **flinch'er.**—*n.* and *adj.* **flinch'ing.**—*adv.* **flinch'ingly.** [Prob. conn. with M.E. *fleechen*, O.Fr. *flechir*, L. *flectĕre*, to bend.]

flinch. Same as **flench.**

flinder, *flin'dər*, *n.* a splinter or small fragment—usually in pl. [Norw. *flindra*, a splinter.]

Flindersia, *flin-dər'si-ä*, *n.* an Australian genus of valuable trees of the *Rutaceae*. [From the explorer, Matthew *Flinders*, 1774–1814.]

fling, *fling*, *v.t.* to throw, cast, toss: to dart: to send forth: to send suddenly: to cause to fall.—*v.i.* to throw the body about: to kick out: to dash or rush, throw oneself impetuously: to throw missiles: (*pr.p.* **fling'ing**; *pa.t.* and *pa.p.* **flung**).—*n.* a cast or throw: a try: a passing attack: a jibe: a taunt: complete freedom, full enjoyment of pleasure: a lively Scottish country-dance.—**fling out**, break out in impetuous plain-speaking; **full fling**, at the utmost speed, recklessly. [Cf. O.N. *flengja*; Sw. *flänga*.]

flint, *flint*, *n.* a hard mineral, a variety of quartz, from which fire is readily struck with steel: a concretion of silica: a piece of flint, esp. one used for striking fire, or one manufactured into an implement before (or after) the use of metals: anything proverbially hard: (*obs. slang*) a tailor or other who refuses low wages.—*adj.* made of flint: hard.—*n.* **flint'-glass**, a very fine and pure lead glass, originally made of calcined flints.—*adjs.* **flint'-heart, -ed** (*Shak.*), having a hard heart.—*v.t.* **flint'ify**, to turn to flint.—*adv.* **flint'ily.**—*ns.* **flint'iness**; **flint'-knapp'er**, one who flakes or chips flints; **flint'-knapp'ing**; **flint'-lock**, a gun-lock or gun with a flint.—*adj.* **flint'y**, consisting or, abounding in, or like flint: hard: cruel. [O.E. *flint*; Dan. *flint*; Gr. *plinthos*, a brick.]

flip, *flip*, *v.t.* and *v.i.* to fillip: to flick: to flap.—*n.* a fillip: a flick: a hot drink of beer and spirits sweetened, or similar concoction: (*coll.*) a trip in an aeroplane: a pleasure-flight.—*n.* **flip'-dog**, an iron for heating flip.—*adv.* **flip'-flap', flip'-flop'**, with repeated flapping.—*n.* a coster's dance: a form of somersault: a cracker: the sound of regular footfall: a flighty woman: a revolving apparatus for public amusement; **flipp'er**, a limb adapted for swimming: (*slang*) hand.—*adj.* **flipp'erty-flopp'erty**, loose, dangling. [Cf. **fillip, flap.**]

flippant, *flip'ənt*, *adj.* pert and frivolous of speech: showing disrespectful levity: (*obs.*) nimble: (*obs.*) playful.—*ns.* **flipp'ancy**, **flipp'antness**, pert fluency of speech: pertness: levity.—*adv.* **flipp'antly.** [Cf. **flip**, and O.N. *fleipa*, to prattle.]

flirt, *flərt*, *v.t.* to jerk: to move about quickly like a fan, to flick, rap.—*v.i.* to trifle with love: to play at courtship: to move briskly about.—*n.* a pert, giddy girl: one who coquets for amusement, usually of a woman.—*n.* **flirta'tion**, the act of flirting.—*adj.* **flirta'tious** (*coll.*), given to flirting.—*ns.* **flirt'-gill** (*-jil; Shak.*), a pert or wanton woman; **flirt'ing.**—*adv.* **flirt'ingly.**—*adj.* **flirt'ish**, betokening a flirt. [Onomatopoeic.]

flisk, *flisk*, *v.i.* (*Scot.*) to skip or caper about: to be restive.—*n.* a whim.—*adj.* **flisk'y.** [Onomatopoeic.]

flit, *flit*, *v.i.* to move about lightly: to fly silently or quickly: to be unsteady or easily moved: (*Scot.*) to change one's abode.—*v.t.* to remove,

transfer:—*pr.p.* **flitt'ing**; *pa.t.* and *pa.p.* **flitt'ed**, *Spens.* **flitt.**—*n.* **flitt'ing.** [O.N. *flytja*; Sw. *flytta.*]

flit, flitt, *flit*, *adj.* (*Spens.*) fleet: fleeting: light. [**fleet.**]

flitch, *flich*, *n.* the side of a hog salted and cured. [O.E. *flicce*; O.N. *flikki.*]

flite. Same as **flyte.**

flitter, *flit'ər*, *v.i.* to flutter.—**flitt'er-mouse**, a bat. [**flit.**]

flittern, *flit'ərn*, *n.* (*prov.*) a young oak.

flitters, *flit'ərz*, *n.pl.* fragments, tatters.

flivver, *fliv'ər*, *n.* (*slang*), a failure: a small cheap motor-car or aeroplane: a small destroyer.

flix, *fliks*, *n.* fur, beaver-down.

flix-weed, *fliks'wēd*, *n.* a species of hedge-mustard.

float, *flōt*, *v.i.* to be supported on or suspended in a fluid: to be buoyed up: to move lightly, supported by a fluid: to seem to move in such a way: to be free from the usual attachment: to drift about aimlessly: (*Milt.*) to flow: (*Spens., Pope*) to be flooded: in weaving, to pass threads without interweaving with them: to use a float.—*v.t.* to cause to float: to cover with liquid: to convey on floats: to levitate: to separate by flotation: to smooth: to pare off (as turf): to set agoing.—*n.* state of floating: a wave: a contrivance for floating or for keeping something afloat, as a raft, the cork or quill of a fishing-line, the ball of a ball-cock, etc.: a tool for smoothing: a plasterer's trowel: a low cart for carrying cattle, etc.: a footlight or the footlights collectively.—*adj.* **float'able.**—*ns.* **float'age**, **flot'age**, buoyancy: that which floats: the part above the water-line; **floata'tion** (see **flotation**); **float'-board**, a board of an undershot water-wheel or of a paddle-wheel; **float'er.**—*adj.* **float'ing**, that floats, in any sense: not fixed: fluctuating: circulating.—*n.* action of the verb: the spreading of plaster on the surface of walls.—*adv.* **float'ingly.**—*n.* **float'stone**, a porous, sponge-like variety of silica, so light as to float for a while on water: a bricklayer's smoothing tool.—*adj.* **float'y.**—**floating battery**, a vessel or hulk heavily armed, used in the defence of harbours or in attacks on marine fortresses; **floating bridge**, a bridge supported on pontoons; **floating dock**, a floating structure that can be sunk by admitting water to its air chambers, and raised again carrying a vessel to be repaired; **floating island**, a floating aggregation of driftwood, or a mass of vegetation buoyed up from the bottom by marsh gas, or the like; **floating kidney**, an abnormally mobile kidney; **floating light**, a light-ship. [O.E. *flotian*, to float; O.N. *flota.*]

floccus, *flok'əs*, *n.* a tuft of woolly hair: a tuft, esp. at the end of a tail: the covering of unfledged birds: (*pl.* **flocci**, *flok'sī*).—*n.* **floccilla'tion** (*flok-si-*), fitful plucking at the bed-clothes by a delirious patient; **floc'cinauci'nihilipil'ifica'tion**, (*facet.*) setting little or no value (from the Latin genitives *floccī*, *naucī*, at a trifle, *nihilī*, at nothing, *pilī*, at a hair, and *facĕre*, to make.)—*adjs.* **flocc'ose** (or *-ōs'*), wooly; **flocc'ular**; **flocc'ulate.**—*v.t.* and *v.i.* **flocc'ulate**, to aggregate in tufts, flakes or cloudy masses.—*ns.* **flocccula'tion**; **flocc'ule**, a flocculus; **flocc'ulence**, flocculated condition.—*adj.* **flocc'ulent**, woolly: flaky: flocculated.—*n.* **flocc'ulus**, a small flock, tuft, or flake: a small outgrowth of the cerebellum: a cloud of calcium vapour on the sun: (*pl.* **flocculi**, *flok'ū-lī*). [L. *floccus*, a lock, a trifle; dim. *flocculus.*]

flock, *flok*, *n.* a company of animals, as sheep, birds, etc.: a company generally: a congregation.—*v.i.* to gather or go in flocks or in crowds.—*n.* **flock'-mas'ter**, an owner or overseer of a flock. [O.E. *flocc*, a flock, a company; O.N. *flokkr.*]

flock, *flok*, *n.* a lock of wool: a tuft: cloth refuse, waste wool (also in pl.): a woolly-looking precipitate (also *pl.*).—*ns.* **flock'-bed**, a bed stuffed with wool; **flock'-pa'per**, a wall-paper dusted over with flock. [O.Fr. *floc*—L. *floccus*, a lock of wool.]

floe, *flō, n.* a field of floating ice. [Prob. Norw. *flo,* layer—O.N. *fló.*]

flog, *flog, v.t.* to beat or strike: to lash: to chastise with blows: (*pr.p.* **flogg'ing;** *pa.t.* and *pa.p.* **flogged**).—*n.* **flogg'ing.** [Late; prob. an abbrev. of **flagellate**.]

flong, *flong, n.* papier-mâché for stereotyping. [Fr. *flan.*]

flood, *flud, n.* a great flow of water: an inundation: a deluge: a condition of abnormally great flow in a river: (*poet.*) a river or other water: the rise of the tide: any great inflow or outflow, as of light, tears, visitors.—*v.t.* to overflow: to inundate: to supply in excessive quantity.—*v.i.* to bleed profusely, as after parturition.—*adj.* **flood'ed.**—*ns.* **flood'gate,** a gate for allowing or stopping the flow of water, a sluice or lock-gate; **flood'ing; flood'light, -lighting,** strong illumination from many points to eliminate shadows.— *v.t.* **flood'light** (*pa.p.* **flood'lighted, flood'lit**). —*ns.* **flood'mark,** the mark or line to which the tide or a flood has risen; **flood'-tide,** the rising tide; **flood'wa'ter; flood'way,** an artificial passage for floodwater.—**the Flood,** Noah's deluge. [O.E. *flód;* Du. *vloed,* Ger. *flut;* cf. with **flow.**]

floor, *flōr, n.* the part of a room on which we stand: a platform: the rooms in a house on the same level, a story: a bottom surface: that on which anything rests or any operation is performed: a levelled area: (*S. Afr.*) the ground.—*v.t.* to furnish with a floor: to throw or place on the floor: (*coll.*) to vanquish, stump.—*n.* **floor'-cloth,** a covering for floors, esp. of linoleum or the like: a cloth for washing floors.—*adj.* **floored.** —*ns.* **floor'er,** a knock-down blow: a decisive retort, etc.: an examination question one cannot answer; **floor'head,** the upper end of a floor-timber; **floor'ing,** material for floors: a platform; **floor'-tim'ber,** a timber placed immediately across a ship's keel, on which her bottom is framed; **first'-floor',** the floor in a house above the ground-floor, the second story: (*U.S.*) usu. the ground-floor.—Also *adj.* [O.E. *flór;* Du. *vloer,* a flat surface, Ger. *flur,* flat land; W. *llawr.*]

flop, *flop, n.* a limp, heavy, flapping movement, fall, or sound: a collapse: a fiasco: a failure.— *adv.* with a flop.—*v.t.* and *v.i.* to move with a flop: to drop plump: (*U.S.*) to change over in nature or politics.—*v.i.* to collapse.—*adv.* **flopp'ily.**—*n.* **flopp'iness.**—*adj.* **flopp'y.** [A form of **flap.**]

flora, *flō'rä, n.* the assemblage of vegetable species of a region, or age: a list or descriptive enumeration of these.—*adj.* **flō'ral** (or *flor'*), pertaining to the goddess Flora, to floras, or to flowers.—*adv.* **flō'rally.**—*ns.* **Floréal** (Fr.; *flō-rā-āl'*), the 8th month of the French revolutionary calendar, about April 20—May 20; **florescence** (*flor-es'ns*), a bursting into flower: (*bot.*) time of flowering.— *adj.* **floresc'ent,** bursting into flowers.—*n.* **floret** (*flor'it*), a small flower: a single flower in a close-packed inflorescence.—*adjs.* **flō'riated, flō'reated,** decorated with floral ornament.—*adj.* **floricul'-tural** (*flōr-* or *flor-*).—*ns.* **flor'iculture,** the culture of flowers or plants; **floricul'turist.**— *adj.* **flōr'id,** abounding in flowers: flowery: bright in colour: flushed with red: characterised by flowers of rhetoric: melodic figures, or other ornament: overadorned: richly ornamental; **flōrid'ity.**—*adv.* **flōr'idly.**—*n.* **flōr'idness.**—*adjs.* **flōrif'erous,** bearing or producing flowers; **flō'riform,** flower-shaped.—*ns.* **flōrilegium** (*-lē'ji-əm; L. legère,* to gather), an anthology or collection of choice extracts (*pl.* **florilē'gia**); **flōr'ist,** a cultivator or seller of flowers: (*flō'rist*) a student of flowers or of floras.—*adj.* **flōrist'ic.**—*n.* **flōrist'ics,** the study of floras.—*adj.* **flō'ry,** fleury: (*Scott*) showy, conceited.—**floral diagram,** a figure showing the arrangement of the parts of a flower in ground-plan. [L. *Flōra,* goddess of flowers; *flōs, flóris,* a flower.]

Florentine, *flor'ən-tīn, adj.* pertaining to *Florence* in Tuscany.—*n.* a native or inhabitant thereof: a durable silk textile fabric—also **flor'ence:** a pie with no crust beneath the meat.—**Florence flask,** a long-necked round flask, for olive oil from Florence, etc. [L. *Flŏrentīnus—Flŏrentia.*]

Florideae, *flor-id'i-ē, n.pl.* (*bot.*) the Rhodophyceae or red seaweeds.—*n.* and *adj.* **florid'ean.** —*adj.* **florid'eous.** [L. *flŏridus,* florid.]

florin, *flor'in, n.* (*orig.*) a Florentine gold coin with a lily stamped on one side, first struck in the 11th century: an English silver or cupro-nickel coin worth 2s., first minted in 1849 (**double florin,** a 4s. piece, first coined, 1887): in Holland, the gulden. [Fr., from It. *fiorino—fiore,* a lily.— L. *flōs, flóris.*]

floruit, *flō'rōo-it, n.* the period during which a person flourished or guiding date when he or she was alive. [L., 3rd pers. sing. perf. indic. of *flŏrēre,* to flourish.]

floscule, *flos'kūl, n.* a floret.—*adjs.* **flos'cūlar, flos'cūlous.** [L. *flŏsculus,* dim. of *flōs,* a flower.]

floss, *flos, n.* the rough outside of the silkworm's cocoon, and other waste of silk manufacture: fine silk in spun strands not twisted together, used in embroidery and tooth-cleaning: any loose downy or silky plant substance: fluff— also **flosh.**—*n.* **floss'-silk, flox'-silk.**—*adj.* **floss'y.** [Prob. O.Fr. *flosche,* down: or from some Gmc. word cog. with **fleece;** cf. O.N. *flos,* nap.]

flota, *flō'tä, n.* a commercial fleet: formerly the fleet which annually conveyed the produce of America to Spain. [Sp.]

flote, *flōt, n.* (*Shak.*) a wave.—*n.* **flōt'age** (see **floatage**).—*adj.* **flo'tant** (*her.*), floating in air or in water.—*ns.* **flotā'tion,** the act of floating: the science of floating bodies: act of starting a business, esp. a limited liability company: a method of separating ore from gangue by forming a froth, the ore particles clinging to the bubbles; **flote'-grass,** floating meadow-grass (*Glyceria fluitans*).—**plane,** or **line, of flotation,** the plane or line in which the horizontal surface of a fluid cuts a body floating in it. [See **float.**]

flotilla, *flo-til'ä, n.* a fleet of small ships. [Sp., dim. of **flota,** a fleet.]

flotsam, *flot'sam, n.* goods lost by shipwreck and found floating on the sea (see **jetsam**). [Anglo-Fr. *floteson* (Fr. *flottaison*)—O.Fr. *floter,* to float.]

flounce, *flowns, v.i.* to move abruptly or impatiently.—*n.* an impatient fling, flop, or movement.—*adv.* with a flounce. [Prob. cog. with Norw. *flunsa,* to hurry, Sw. prov. *flunsa,* to plunge.]

flounce, *flowns, n.* a hanging strip sewed to the skirt of a dress by its upper edge.—*v.t.* to furnish with flounces.—*n.* **floun'cing,** material for flounces. [See **frounce.**]

flounder, *flown'dər, v.i.* to struggle with violent and awkward motion: to stumble helplessly in thinking or speaking.—*n.* an act of floundering. [Prob. an onomatopoeic blending of the sound and sense of earlier words like **founder, blunder.**]

flounder, *flown'dər n.* a name given to a number of species of flatfish of the family Pleuronectidae —in Europe *Platichthys flesus* in America certain species of Pseudopleuronectes, Limanda, etc. [Anglo-Fr. *floundre,* O.Fr. *flondre,* most prob. of Scand. origin; cf. O.N. *flythra;* Sw. *flundra.*]

flour, *flowr, n.* the finely-ground meal of wheat or other grain: the fine soft powder of any substance.—*v.t.* to reduce into or sprinkle with flour.—*v.i.* to break up into fine globules of mercury in the amalgamation process.—*ns.* **flour'-bolt,** a machine for bolting flour; **flour'-mill,** a mill for making flour.—*adj.* **flour'y,** covered with flour: like flour. [Same word as **flower.**]

flourish, *flur'ish, v.i.* (*obs.* and *Scot.*) to bloom: to grow luxuriantly: to thrive: to be in full vigour: to be prosperous: to use copious and flowery language: to move in fantastic figures: to display ostentatiously: (*mus.*) to play or sing ostentatious passages, or ostentatiously: to play a fanfare: to make ornamental strokes with the pen: to show off.—*v.t.* to adorn with flourishes or ornaments: (*Shak.*) to make fair: to brandish in show or triumph or exuberance of spirits.—*n.* decoration: showy splendour: a figure made by a bold stroke of the pen: the waving of a weapon or other thing: a parade of words: a showy, fantastic, or highly ornamental passage of music: (*prov.*) a mass of blossom of a fruit-tree.—*adjs.* **flour′ished**, decorated with flourishes; **flour′-ishing**, thriving: prosperous: making a show.—*adv.* **flour′ishingly.**—*adj.* **flour′ishy**, abounding in flourishes.—**flourishing thread**, thread used in fancy-work; **flourish of trumpets**, a fanfare heralding great persons; any ostentatious introduction. [O.Fr. *florir, floriss*- —L. *flōs, flōris*, flower.]

flouse, *flows*, *v.t.* and *v.i.* (*prov.*) to splash.—Also **floush** (*flowsh*). [Cf. **flush.**]

flout, *flowt*, *v.t.* to jeer at: to mock: to treat with contempt.—*v.i.* to jeer.—*n.* a jeer.—*adv.* **flout′-ingly.**—*n.* **flout′ing-stock**, (*Shak.*) an object for flouting. [Prob. a specialised use of *floute*, M.E. form of **flute**, to play on the flute; so with Du. *fluiten*.]

flow, *flō*, *v.i.* to run, as water: to move or change form like a fluid: to rise or come in, as the tide: to move in a stream: to glide smoothly: to abound, run over: to run in smooth lines: to stream or hang loose and waving: (*obs.*) to melt.—*v.t.* to cover with water: (*pa.t.* and *pa.p.* **flowed**; *pa.p.*, *Shak., Milt.*, **flown**, *flōn*).—*n.* a stream or current: movement of, or like that of, a fluid: that which flows or has flowed: mode of flowing: the setting in of the tide: copious fluency.—*n.* **flow′age**, act of flowing: state of being flooded.—*adj.* **flow′ing**, moving, as a fluid: fluent: smooth and continuous: falling in folds or in waves.—*adv.* **flow′ingly.**—*n.* **flow′ingness.** [O.E. *flōwan*.]

flow, *flō, flow, n.* a morass: (*Scot.*) a flat, moist tract of land: a quicksand: a moorland pool: a sea basin or sound. [Cf. Icel. *flói*, a marshy moor; Norw. dial. *floe*, pool in a swamp; O.N. *flóa*, to flood.]

flower, *flowr, flow′ər, n.* a growth comprising the reproductive organs of seed-plants: the blossom of a plant: the flowering state: a flowering plant, esp. one valued for its blossoms: the prime of life: the best of anything: the person or thing most distinguished: the embodiment of perfection: a figure of speech: ornament of style: (*pl.; obs.*) menstrual discharge: (*pl.*) a sublimate (as **flowers of sulphur**): (*pl.*) applied to some fungous growths, as **flowers of tan**, a slime-fungus on tan-bark.—*v.t.* to adorn with figures of flowers.—*v.i.* to blossom: to flourish.—*ns.* **flower′age**, flowers collectively: flowering state; **flower′-bed**, a garden bed for flowers; **flower′-bell**, a blossom shaped like a bell; **flower′-bud**, a bud with the unopened flower; **flower′-clock**, a collection of flowers so arranged that the time of day is indicated by their times of opening and closing; **flower-de-luce** (*-di-lōōs*), **-delice** (*-di-lēs′, -lis′, -del′is*), old names for the iris, or for the **fleur-de-lis**.—*adj.* **flowered**, decorated with figures of flowers: fleury.—*ns.* **flower′er**, a plant that flowers; **flower′et**, a little flower: a floret; **flower′-garden**; **flower′-girl**, a girl or woman who sells flowers in the street; **flower′-head**, a close inflorescence in which all the florets are sessile on the receptacle; **flower′iness.**—*n.* and *adj.* **flower′ing.**—*n.* **flower′ing-rush**, a monocotyledonous plant (Butomus), with large linear three-edged leaves and an umbel of rose-coloured flowers.—*adj.* **flower′less.**—*ns.* **flower′-pot**, a pot, usu. a truncated cone of earthenware, in which a plant is grown; **flower′-serv′ice**, a church service where offerings of flowers are made; **flower′-show**, an exhibition of flowers; **flower′-stalk**, the stem that supports the flower.—*adjs.* **flower′y**, full of, or adorned with, flowers: highly embellished, florid; **flower′y-kir′tled** (*Milt.*).—**flower of Jove**, a campion with heads of purple or scarlet flowers, and leaves silky-white with hairs; **the flowery land**, China. [O.Fr. *flour* (Fr. *fleur*)—L. *flōs, flōris*, a flower.]

flown, *flōn, pa.p.* of **fly**; old *pa.p.* of **flow.**

flox-silk. Same as **floss-silk.**

flu, flue, *flōō, n.* (*coll.*) influenza.

fluate, *flōō′āt, n.* (*obs.*) a fluoride.

fluctuate, *fluk′tū-āt, v.i.* to move like a wave: to go up and down or to and fro: to vary this way and that.—*v.t.* to throw into fluctuation.—*adjs.* **fluc′tuant; fluc′tuating.**—*n.* **fluctūā′tion**, rise and fall: motion to and fro: wavelike motion: alternate variation. [L. *fluctuāre, -ātum*—*fluctus*, a wave—*fluĕre*, to flow.]

flue, *flōō, n.* a pipe for conveying hot air, smoke, flame, etc.: a small chimney: (*mus.*) a flue-pipe: the opening by which the air escapes from the foot of a flue-pipe.—*ns.* **flue′-pipe**, a pipe, esp. in an organ, in which the sound is produced by air impinging upon an edge; **flue′-work**, in an organ, the flue-pipes collectively. [Origin doubtful.]

flue, *flōō, n.* light fluff, such as collects in unswept places: soft down or fur.—*adj.* **flu′ey.** [Origin doubtful.]

flue, *flew, flōō, adj.* (*prov.*) shallow, flat: flared: splayed. [Origin uncertain.]

fluellin, *flōō-el′in, n.* a name given to various speedwells (esp. *Veronica serpyllifolia* and *V. officinalis*) and toadflaxes (esp. *Linaria Elatine* and *L. spuria*). [W. *llysian Llewelyn*, Llewelyn's herbs.]

fluent, *flōō′ənt, adj.* ready in the use of words: voluble: marked by copiousness.—*n.* the variable quantity in fluxions.—*ns.* **flu′ence** (*Milt.*), **flu′ency, flu′entness.**—*adv.* **flu′ently.** [L. *fluēns, fluentis*, pr.p. of *fluĕre*, to flow.]

fluff, *fluf, n.* a soft down from cotton, etc.: anything downy: faulty acting: a duffed stroke at golf: (*slang*) a girl.—*v.t.* to make fluffy.—*v.t.* and *v.i.* to bungle.—*n.* **fluff′iness.**—*adj.* **fluff′y.** [Perh. conn. with **flue**, light down.]

flügel, *flü′hhəl, n.* (*Ger.*) a grand piano.—*ns.* **flügel-horn**, a hunting-horn, a kind of keyed bugle; **flugelman** (*flōō′gl-man;* see **fugleman**). [Ger., wing.]

fluid, *flōō′id, adj.* that flows: unsolidified.—*n.* a substance whose particles can move about with freedom—a liquid or gas.—*adjs.* **flu′idal; fluid′ic.**—*v.t.* **fluid′ify.**—*ns.* **fluid′ity, flu′idness.** [L. *fluidus*, fluid—*fluĕre*, to flow.]

fluke, *flōōk, n.* a flounder: a trematode worm, esp. that which causes liver-rot in sheep, so called because like a miniature flounder (also **fluke′-worm**): a variety of kidney potato. [O.E. *flóc*, a plaice; cf. O.N. *flóke*.]

fluke, *flōōk, n.* the barb of an anchor: a barb: a lobe of a whale's tail.—*adj.* **fluk′y.** [Prob. a transferred use of the foregoing.]

fluke, *flōōk, n.* an accidental success. [Origin unknown.]

flume, *flōōm, n.* an artificial channel for water to be applied to some industrial purpose: (*U.S.*) a ravine occupied by a torrent.—**be, or go, up the flume**, to come to grief, to be done for. [O.Fr. *flum*—L. *flūmen*, a river—*fluĕre*, to flow.]

flummery, *flum′ər-i, n.* an acid jelly made from the husks of oats, the Scots sowens: blancmange: anything insipid: empty compliment, humbug. [W. *llymru—llymrig*, harsh, raw—*llym*, sharp, severe.]

flummox, *flum′əks, v.t.* (*dial.*) to perplex. [Ety. unknown.]

flump, *flump, v.t.* (*coll.*) to throw down heavily.—*v.i.* to move with a flop or dump.—*n.* the dull sound so produced. [Imit.]

flung, *flung, pa.t.* and *pa.p.* of **fling.**

flunkey, *flung′ki, n.* a livery servant: a footman: a mean cringer.—*n.* **flun′keydom.**—*adj.* **flun′-keyish.**—*n.* **flun′keyism.** [Perh. orig. *flanker*, one who runs alongside.]

fluor, *flōō′ər, -or, n.* a mineral, calcium fluoride, commonly purple, also green, colourless, etc., crystallising in cubes and octahedra, found abundantly in Derbyshire—also **flu′or-spar, flu′-orite** (*flōō′ər-īt*), or Derbyshire spar.—*v.i.* **fluoresce** (*-ər-es′*).—*ns.* **fluorescein** (*-es′i-in*), a fluorescent dyestuff, $C_{20}H_{12}O_5$; **fluoresc′ence**, the property of some substances (e.g. fluor) of emitting, when exposed to radiation, rays of greater wave-length than those received.—*adjs.* **fluoresc′ent; fluoric** (*-or′ik*).—*ns.* **flu′oride**, a compound of fluorine with another element or radical; **fluorinā′tion**, introduction of fluorine; **flu′orine** (-ēn), an element (F), a pale greenish-yellow gas; **flu′orocarbon**, any of a series of compounds of fluorine and carbon (corresponding to the hydrocarbons) highly resistant to heat and chemical action; **flu′oroscope**, an instrument for X-ray examination by means of a fluorescent screen; **flu′orotype**, photography by means of fluorides.—**fluorescent lighting**, brighter lighting obtained, for the same consumption of electricity, by using fluorescent material to convert ultra-violet radiation in the electric lamp into visible light. [L. *fluor*, flow, from its use as a flux.]

flurry, flur′i, *n.* a sudden blast or gust: agitation: bustle: the death-agony of the whale: a fluttering assemblage of things, as snowflakes.—*v.t.* to agitate, to confuse: (*pr.p.* flurr′ying; *pa.t.* and *pa.p.* flurr′ied).—*v.t.* flurr, to scatter.—*v.i.* to fly up. [Prob. onomatopoeic, suggested by **flaw, hurry**, etc.]

flush, flush, *n.* a sudden flow: a flow of blood to the skin, causing redness: a suffusion of colour, esp. red: a sudden growth: a renewal of growth: a rush of feeling: a puddle: a watery place about a spring, etc.: bloom, freshness, vigour: abundance.—*v.i.* to glow: to become red in the face: to flow swiftly, suddenly, or copiously.—*v.t.* to cleanse by a copious flow of water: to clear by a blast of air: to cause to glow: to elate, excite the spirits of.—*adj.* overflowing: abounding: well supplied, as with money: (*Shak.*) in full bloom: flushed: (of weather) hot and heavy.—*n.* **flush′box**, a tank for flushing a water-closet.—*adj.* **flushed**, suffused with ruddy colour: excited.—*ns.* **flush′er**, one who flushes sewers; **flush′ing**; **flush′ness.**—*adj.* **flush′y**, reddish. [Prob. next word influenced by **flash, blush.**]

flush, flush, *v.i.* to start up like an alarmed bird.—*v.t.* to rouse and cause to start off.—*n.* the act of starting: (*Spens.*) a bird, or a flock of birds so started. [Prob. onomatopoeic; suggested by **fly, flutter, rush.**]

flush, flush, *v.t.* to make even: to fill up to the level of a surface (often with *up*).—*adj.* having the surface in one plane with the adjacent surface: of a deck, having the same level throughout the ship's length.—Also *adv.* [Prob. related to **flush**, 1.]

flush, flush, *n.* in card-playing, a hand in which all the cards or a specified number are of the same suit.—*adj.* in poker, consisting of cards all of the same suit.—**straight**, or **royal, flush**, in poker, a sequence of five cards of the same suit. [Prob. Fr. *flux*—L. *fluxus*, flow; influenced by **flush**, 1.]

fluster, flus′tər, *n.* hurrying: flurry: heat.—*v.t.* to make hot and flurried: to fuddle.—*v.i.* to bustle: to be agitated or fuddled.—*n.* **flus′terment.**—*adj.* **flus′tery**, confused.—*v.t.* **flus′trate**, to fluster.—*n.* **flustrā′tion.** [O.N. *flaustr*, hurry.]

Flustra, flus′trä, *n.* one of the commonest genera of marine Polyzoa. [Ety. unknown.]

flute, flōōt, *n.* a musical pipe with finger-holes and keys played by blowing: in organ-building, a stop with stopped wooden pipes, having a flute-like tone: a longitudinal groove, as on a pillar: a tall and narrow wine-glass: a shuttle in tapestry-weaving, etc.—*v.i.* to play the flute: to make fluty sounds.—*v.t.* to play or sing in soft flute-like tones: to form flutes or grooves in.—*ns.* **flûte-à-bec** (*flüt-ä-bek;* Fr.), a fipple flute; **flute′-bird**, a piping crow.—*adj.* **flut′ed**, ornamented with flutes, channels, or grooves.—*ns.* **flute′-mouth**, a fish (*Fistularia*) akin to the sticklebacks; **flut′er**; **flutina** (-tē′), a kind of accordion; **flut′ing**, flute-playing or similar sounds: longitudinal furrowing; **flut′ist.**—*adj.* **flut′y**, in tone like a flute. [O.Fr. *fleüte;* ety. dubious.]

flutter, flut′ər, *v.i.* to move about with bustle: to vibrate: to be in agitation or in uncertainty: (*obs.*) to be frivolous: to toss a coin.—*v.t.* to throw into disorder: to move in quick motions.—*n.* quick, irregular motion: agitation: confusion: a

hasty game at cards, etc.: a gambling transaction: a small speculation. [O.E. *flotorian*, to float about, from the root of *fléotan*, to float.]

fluvial, flōō′vi-əl, *adj.* of or belonging to rivers.—*n.* **flu′vialist**, one who calls in the agency of rivers in explanation of phenomena.—*adjs.* **fluviat′ic**, **flu′viatile** (-til, -til), belonging to or formed by rivers.—*adj.* **fluviogla′cial**, pertaining to glacial rivers. [L. *fluviālis—fluvius*, a river, *fluĕre*, to flow.]

flux, fluks, *n.* act of flowing: a flow of matter: a state of flow or continuous change: a discharge generally from a mucous membrane: matter discharged: excrement: an easily fused substance, esp. one added to another to make it more fusible.—*v.t.* to melt.—*v.i.* to flow: to fuse.—*ns.* **fluxion** (*fluk′shən*), a flowing or discharge: a difference or variation: (*math.*) the rate of change of a continuously varying quantity: (*pl.*) the name given after Newton to that branch of mathematics which with a different notation is known after Leibniz as the differential and integral calculus.—*adjs.* **flux′ional**, **flux′ionary**, variable: inconstant.—*n.* **flux′ionist**, one skilled in fluxions.—*adj.* **flux′ive**, (*Shak.*) flowing with tears. [O.Fr., —L. *fluxus—fluĕre*, to flow.]

fly, flī, *v.i.* to move through the air, esp. on wings or in aircraft: to move swiftly: to pass away: to flee: to burst quickly or suddenly: to flutter.—*v.t.* to avoid, flee from: to cause to fly, as a kite: to conduct or transport by air: to cross or pass by flying: (*pr.p.* **fly′ing**; *pa.t.* **flew**, flōō; *pa.p.* **flown**, flōn; *3rd. pers. pres. ind.* **flies**).—*n.* any insect of the *Diptera*: often so widely used, esp. in composition:—e.g. *butterfly, dragon-fly, May-fly*—as to be virtually equivalent to insect: a fish-hook dressed in imitation of a fly: (collectively) an insect pest: (*arch.*) a familiar spirit: an attendant parasite: a flight: a flap, esp. a tent-door: the free end of a flag, or the like: a fast stage-coach: a light vehicle on hire, at first drawn by a man, later by a horse: a fly-wheel: (in *pl.*) the large space above the proscenium in a theatre, from which the scenes, etc., are controlled: (*pl.* **flies**).—*adj.* (*slang*) wideawake, knowing.—*ns.* **flier**, **flyer** (flī′ər), one who flies or flees: part of a machine with rapid motion: a rectangular step in stairs; **fly′-ag′aric**, a poisonous mushroom-like fungus that has been used for killing flies.—*adjs.* **fly′-away**, streaming: flighty.—*ns.* **fly′bane**, poison for flies: a name for various plants so used; **fly′-belt**, a belt of country infested by tsetse fly.—*adj.* **fly′-bitten**, marked as by the bite of flies.—*n.* **fly′blow**, the egg of a fly.—*adj.* **fly′blown**, tainted with flies' eggs or maggots.—*ns.* **fly′boat**, a long, narrow, swift boat used on canals; **fly′book**, a case like a book for holding fishing-flies; **fly′-by-night**, one who gads about at night: an absconding debtor; **fly′catcher**, a name for various birds that catch flies on the wing, esp. of the fam. Muscicapidae; **fly′er** (see **flier**, above); **fly′-fisher**, one who uses artificial flies as bait; **fly′-fishing**; **fly′-flap**, a device for driving away flies; **fly′-flapp′er**; **fly′ing**; **fly′ing-boat**, a seaplane with boat body; **fly′ing-bomb**, a bomb in the form of a jet-propelled aeroplane; **fly′ing-bridge**, a ferry-boat moving under the combined forces of the stream and the resistance of a long cable: a pontoon: the highest bridge of a ship; **fly′ing-butt′ress**, an arch-formed prop; **fly′ing-camp**, -col′umn a body of troops for rapid motion from one place to another.—*n.pl.* **fly′ing-col′ours**, flags unfurled: triumphant success.—*ns.* **Fly′ing-Corps**, the precursor (1912-18) of the Royal Air Force; **Fly′ing-Dutch′man**, a black spectral Dutch ship, or its captain, condemned to sweep the seas around the Cape of Storms for ever; **fly′ing-fish**, a fish that can leap from the water and sustain itself in the air for a short time by its long pectoral fins, as if flying; **fly′ing-fox**, a large frugivorous bat; **fly′ing-lē′mur**, an animal (*Cynocephalus* or *Galeopithecus*) of the Eastern Archipelago, whose fore and hind limbs are connected by a fold of skin—included in the Insectivora or made a separate order Dermoptera; **fly′ing-liz′ard**, a dragon-lizard: **fly′ing-machine**, a dirigible contrivance to convey human beings into and through the air: an aircraft (esp. one heavier than air); **fly′ing-off′icer**, an officer in the Air Force of rank answering to sub-lieutenant in the navy and lieutenant in the army (formerly called **observer**); **fly′ing-par′ty**, a small body of soldiers, equipped for rapid movements, used to harass an enemy; **fly′ing-phalan′ger**, a general name for animals akin to the phalangers with a parachute of skin between fore and hind legs; **fly′ing-shore**, a horizontal baulk or shore; **fly′ing-shot**, a shot at something in motion; **fly′ing-squad**, a rapidly moving body of police, ticket-examiners, or the like; **fly′ing-squid**, a squid with broad lateral fins by which it can spring high out of the water; **fly′ing-squirr′el**, a name for several kinds of squirrels with a parachute of skin between the fore and hind legs: also applied to a flying-phalanger; **fly′ing-start**, in a race, a start given after the competitors are in motion; **fly′ing-wing**, an arrow-head-shaped aircraft designed to minimise drag at very high speeds; **fly′leaf**, a blank leaf at the beginning or end of a book; **fly′-line**, a line for angling with an artificial fly; **fly-maker**, one who ties artificial flies for angling; **fly′man**, one who works the ropes in theatre flies: one who drives a fly; **fly′-or′chis**, an orchid (*Ophrys muscifera* or *insectifera*) with a flylike flower; **fly′-paper**, a sticky or poisonous paper for destroying flies; **fly′-past**, a ceremonial flight analogous to a march past; **fly′-powder**, a powder used for killing flies; **fly′-rail**, a flap that turns out to support the leaf of a table; **fly′-rod**, a light flexible rod used in fly-fishing, usually in three pieces—butt, second-joint, and tip.—*adj.* **fly′-slow** (*Shak.*; doubtful reading and sense), slow-flying.—*ns.* **fly′-trap**, a trap to catch flies : (*bot.*) a plant that traps flies, esp. the American dog-bane, and Venus's fly-trap; **fly′-weight**, a boxer of eight stone or less; **fly′wheel**, a large wheel with a heavy rim applied to machinery to equalise the effect of the driving effort.—**a fly in the ointment**, some slight flaw which corrupts a thing of value (Eccles. x.i.); **fly a kite**, to send up and control a kite: to obtain money as by accommodation bills esp. when the endorser himself has no money: to put out a feeler to try how people will take anything; **fly at, upon**, to attack suddenly; **fly in the face of**, to insult: to oppose, defy; **fly open**, to open suddenly or violently; **fly out**, to break out in a rage; **let fly**, to attack: to throw or send off; **make the feathers fly** (see **feathers**); **no flies on**, no want of alertness in: no flaw in. [O.E. *fléogan*, to fly, p.a.t. *fléah*; *fléoge*, fly, insect; Ger. *fliegen, fliege*.]

flype, *flīp*, *v.t.* to strip back: to turn partly outside in. [Prob. Scand.; *cf.* Dan. *flip*, a flap.]

Flysch, *flish*, *n.* a great Alpine mass of Cretaceous and Lower Tertiary sandstone with shales. [Swiss Ger.]

flyte, flite, *flīt*, *v.i.* (*Scot.*) to scold, to brawl.—*ns.* **flyte, flyt′ing**, a scolding-match, esp. as a poetical exhibition. [O.E. *flītan*, to strive; Ger. *befleissen.*]

foal, *fōl*, *n.* the young of the horse family.—*v.i.* and *v.t.* to bring forth (a foal).—*ns.* **foal′foot**, coltsfoot. [O.E. *fola*; Ger. *fohlen*, Gr. *pōlos*; L. *pullus*.]

foam, *fōm*, *n.* froth: bubbles on the surface of liquor: a suspension of gas in a liquid.—*v.i.* to gather or produce foam: to come in foam.—*v.t.* to pour out in foam: to fill or cover with foam. —*n.* and *adj.* **foam′ing**.—*adv.* **foam′ingly**.—*adjs.* **foam′less; foam′y**, frothy. [O.E. *fám*; Ger. *feim*, prob. akin to L. *spūma*.]

fob, *fob*, *v.t.* a trick.—*v.t.* to cheat, to put off (with *with*): to foist, palm. [Cf. Ger. *foppen*, to jeer.]

fob, *fob*, *n.* a small watch pocket in the waistband of trousers: a chain with seals, etc., hanging from the fob.—*v.t.* to pocket. [Perh. conn. with L. Ger. *fobke*, little pocket, H.Ger. dial. *fuppe*, pocket.]

fo′c′sle, *fōk′sl*, contr. form of **forecastle**.

focus, *fō′kəs*, *n.* (*geom.*) a fixed point such that the distances of a point on a conic section from it and from the directrix have a constant ratio : (*opt.*) a point in which rays converge after reflection or refraction, or from which (*virtual focus*) they seem to diverge: any central point: the point or region of greatest activity: the point of origin (as of an earthquake): the position, or condition, of sharp definition of an image: (pl. **foci**, *fō′sī*, **fo′cuses**).—*v.t.* to bring to a focus: to adjust to focus: to adjust so as to get a sharp image of: to concentrate (*pr.p.* **fo′cusing**; *pa.t.* and *pa.p.* **fo′cused**; some double the *s*).—*adj.* **fō′cal**, of or belonging to a focus.—*v.t.* **fō′calise**, to focus.—*n.* **focimeter** (*fō-sim′i-tər*), apparatus to help in focusing.—**conjugate foci**, two points such that each is focus for rays proceeding from the other; **focusing cloth**, a cloth thrown over a photographic camera and the operator's head and shoulders to exclude extraneous light in focusing; **in focus**, placed or adjusted so as to secure distinct vision, or a sharp, definite image; **principal focus**, the focus for rays parallel to the axis. [L. *fŏcus*, a hearth.]

fodder, *fod′ər*, *n.* food supplied to cattle.—*v.t.* to supply with fodder.—*ns.* **fodd′erer; fodd′ering**. [O.E. *fōdor*; Ger. *futter*; cf. **food, feed**.]

foe, *fō*, *n.* an enemy: (*pl.* **foes**; *Spens.* **fone, foen**, *fōn*).—*n.* **foe′man**, an enemy in war (*pl.* **foe′men**). [M.E. *foo*—O.E. *fáh, fá* (adj.) and *gefá* (noun).]

foedarie. See **fedarie.**

foetid, foetor. See **fetid, fetor.**

foetus, the usual but etymologically unsatisfactory form of **fetus**, *fē′təs*, *n.* the young animal in the egg or in the womb, after its parts are distinctly formed.—*adj.* **foe′tal**, **fē′tal**.—*n.* **foe′ticide, fē′ticide**, destruction of a foetus.—*adj.* **foetici′dal, fē′-**. [L. *fētus*, offspring.]

fog, *fog*, *n.* a thick mist: watery vapour condensed about dust particles in drops: cloudy obscurity. —*v.t.* to shroud in fog: to obscure.—*v.i.* to become coated, clouded.—*ns.* **fog′-bank**, a dense mass of fog like a bank of land; **fog′-bell**, a bell rung by waves or wind to warn sailors in fog.— *adj.* **fog′-bound**, impeded by fog.—*ns.* **fog′-bow**, a whitish arch like a rainbow, seen in fogs; **fog′-dog**, a whitish spot seen near the horizon in fog. —*adj.* **fogged** (*fogd*) clouded, obscured.—*ns.* **fogg′er, fog′man**, one who sets fog-signals on a railway.—*adv.* **fogg′ily**.—*n.* **fogg′iness**.— *adj.* **fogg′y**, misty: damp: fogged: clouded in mind: stupid.—*n.* **fog′-horn**, a horn used as a warning signal by or to ships in foggy weather: a siren: a big bellowing voice.—*adj.* **fog′less**, without fog, clear.—*ns.* **fog′-signal**, a detonating cap or other audible warning used in fog; **fog′-smoke, fog**. [The origin of the word is hopelessly misty; perh. conn. with next word; perh. with Dan. *fog*, as in *snee-fog*, thick falling snow.]

fog, *fog*, **foggage**, *fog′ij*, *n.* grass that grows after the hay is cut: (*Scot.*) moss.—*v.i.* to become covered with fog.—*adj.* **fogg′y**. [Origin unknown; W. *ffwg*, dry grass, is borrowed from English.]

fogash, *fog′osh*, the pike-perch. [Hung. *fogas*.]

fogy, fogey, *fō′gi*, *n.* a dull old fellow: one with antiquated notions.—*adj.* **fō′gram**, antiquated. —*n.* a fogy.—*ns.* **fō′gramite; fogram′ity; fō′gydom.**—*adj.* **fō′gyish**.—*n.* **fō′gyism**. [Prob. from **foggy**, moss-grown.]

foh, *fo*, *interj.* expressing disgust or contempt.

föhn, foehn, *fən*, *n.* a hot dry wind blowing down a mountain valley. [Ger.,—Rumansch *favugn*— Lat. *Favōnius*, the west wind.]

foible, *foi′bl*, *n.* a weakness: a penchant: a failing: a faible. [O.Fr. *foible*, weak; cf. **faible, feeble**.]

foil, *foil*, *v.t.* to defeat: to baffle: to frustrate: to beat down or trample with the feet.—*n.* a check, repulse, frustration: an incomplete fall in wrestling: a blunt fencing sword with a button on the point.—**put on the foil**, to overcome, bring to naught. [O.Fr. *fuler*, to stamp or crush—L. *fullō*, a fuller of cloth.]

foil, *foil*, *n.* a leaf or thin plate of metal, as tinfoil: a mercury coating on a mirror: metal-coated paper: a thin leaf of metal put under a precious stone to show it to advantage: anything that serves to set off something else: a small arc in tracery.—*adj.* **foiled.**—*n.* **foil′ing.** [O.Fr. *foil* (Fr. *feuille*)—L. *folium*, a leaf.]

foin, *foin, v.i.* to thrust with a sword or spear.— *n.* a thrust with a sword or spear.—*adv.* **foin′-ingly.** [O.Fr. *foine*—L. *fuscina*, a trident.]

foison, *foi′zn, n.* plenty: plentiful yield: strength, vitality, essential virtue (esp. *Scot.* **fushion,** *fəzh′ən, fizh′ən,* **fizz′en**).—*adj.* **foi′sonless,** weak, feeble—(*Scot.* **fush′ionless, fizz′enless**). [O.Fr. —L. *fŭsiŏ, -ŏnis*—*fundĕre, fūsum*, to pour forth.]

foist, *foist, v.t.* to bring in by stealth: to insert wrongfully: to pass off (*in* or *into* the thing affected, *upon* the person).—*n.* **foist′er.** [Prob. Du. prov. *vuisten*, to take in hand; *vuist,* fist.]

fold, *fōld, n.* a doubling of anything upon itself: a crease: the concavity of anything folded: a part laid over on another.—*v.t.* to lay in folds, double over: to enclose in a fold or folds, to wrap up: to embrace.—*v.i.* to become folded: to be capable of folding: (*obs.*) to yield.—*suff.* **-fold** (with numerals), times, as in **ten′-fold.**—*n.* **fold′er,** the person or thing that folds: a flat knife-like instrument used in folding paper: a folding case for loose papers: a folded circular.— *adj.* **fold′ing,** that folds, or that can be folded.— *ns.* **fold′ing,** a fold or plait: (*geol.*) the bending of strata, usu. as the result of compression; **fold′ing-door,** a door consisting of two parts hung on opposite jambs; **fold′ing-machine,** a mechanism that automatically folds printed sheets.—**folded mountains,** mountains produced by folding processes. [O.E. *faldan* (W.S. *fealdan*), to fold; Ger. *falten.*]

fold, *fōld, n.* an enclosure for protecting domestic animals, esp. sheep; a flock of sheep: (*fig.*) a church: the Christian Church.—*v.t.* to confine in a fold.—*n.* **fold′ing.** [O.E. *falod, fald,* a fold, stall.]

folderol, *fol′də-rol.* See **falderal.**

folic acid. See **folium.**

folio, *fō′li-ō, n.* a leaf (two pages) of a book: a sheet of paper once folded: a book of such sheets: the size of such a book: one of several sizes of paper adapted for folding once into well-proportioned leaves: (*book-k.*) a page in an account-book, or two opposite pages numbered as one: (*law*) a certain number of words taken as a basis for computing the length of a document: (*print.*) page number in a book: a wrapper for loose papers.—*adj.* consisting of paper only once folded: of the size of a folio.—*v.t.* to number the leaves or the pages of: to mark off the end of every folio of, in law copying.—**in folio,** in sheets folded but once: in the form of a folio. [L. *in foliō,* on leaf (so-and-so), used in references; L. *folium,* a leaf, a sheet of paper.]

folium, *fō′li-əm, n.* a leaf, lamina, or lamella (*pl.* **fō′lia**).—*adj.* **fōliāceous** (-*ā′shəs*), leaflike: like a foliage leaf: leaf-bearing: laminated.—*n.* **fō′liage,** leaves collectively: a mass of leaves: plant forms in art.—*adjs.* **fō′liaged,** having foliage: worked like foliage; **fō′liar,** pertaining to leaves: resembling leaves.—*v.t.* **fō′liate,** (*orig.*) to beat into a leaf: to cover with leaf-metal: to number the leaves (not pages) of.—*adj.* **fō′liated,** beaten into a thin leaf: decorated with leaf ornaments or foils: consisting of layers or laminae.— *ns.* **fō′liātion,** the leafing, esp. of plants: the act of beating a metal into a thin plate, or of spreading foil over a piece of glass to form a mirror: the numbering of leaves in a book: (*geol.*) the alternation of more or less parallel layers or folia of different mineralogical nature, of which the crystalline schists are composed: (*archit.*) decoration with cusps, lobes, or foliated tracery; **fō′liature,** foliation; **fō′liole** (*bot.*) a leaflet of a compound leaf: a small leaflike structure. —*adjs.* **fō′liolate, fō′liolose,** composed of or pertaining to leaflets; **fō′liose,** leafy: leaflike.— **foliage leaf,** an ordinary leaf, not a petal, bract, etc.; **foliage plant,** one grown for the beauty of its foliage; **fo′lic acid,** an acid in the Vitamin

B_2 complex, found in leaves, liver, etc., or a similar acid which cures some of the symptoms of pernicious anaemia (see article **pterin**). [L. *folium,* a leaf; cf. **blade**; Gr. *phyllon.*]

folk, *fōk, n.* people, collectively or distributively: a nation or people: (*arch.*) the people, commons: (often in *pl.*) those of one's own family, relations (*coll.*):—generally used as a pl., **folk** or **folks** (*fōks*).—*ns.* **folk′-dance,** a dance handed down by tradition of the people; **Folketing** (Dan. *fōl′ke-ting*), the lower house of the Danish parliament or Rigsdag; **folk′-etymol′ogy,** popular unscientific attempts at etymology.—*adj.* **folk′-free,** having the rights of a freeman.—*ns.* **folk′land** (O.E. *folcland*), in old English times, probably land held by folk-right, opposed to *bócland* (bookland); **folk′lore,** the study of ancient observances and customs, the notions, beliefs, traditions, superstitions, and prejudices of the common people—the science of the survival of archaic belief and custom in modern ages (a name suggested by W. J. Thoms in 1846); **folk′lörist,** one who studies folklore; **folk′moot,** an assembly of the people among the Old English; **folk′-right,** the common law or right of the people; **folk′-song,** any song or ballad originating among the people and traditionally handed down by them; **folk′-speech,** the dialect of the common people of a country, in which ancient idioms are embedded; **folk′-tale,** a popular story handed down by oral tradition from a more or less remote antiquity; **folk′-tune,** a tune handed down by tradition among the people. [O.E. *folc;* O.N. *folk;* Ger. *volk.*]

follicle, *fol′i-kl, n.* (*bot.*) a fruit formed from a single carpel containing several seeds, splitting along the ventral suture only: (*zool.*) any small saclike structure, as the pit surrounding a hair-root.—*adjs.* **follic′ulated, follic′ular, follic′ū-lose, follic′ūlous.** [L. *folliculus,* dim. of *follis,* a wind-bag.]

follow, *fol′ō, v.t.* to go after or behind: to keep along the line of: to come after, succeed: to pursue: to attend: to imitate: to obey: to adopt, as an opinion: to keep the eye or mind fixed on: to grasp or understand the whole course or sequence of: to result from, as an effect from a cause: (*B.*) to strive to obtain.—*v.i.* to come after: to result: to be the logical conclusion.—*n.* (*billiards;* commonly **follow-through′**) a stroke that causes the ball to follow the one it has struck: a second helping.—*ns.* **foll′ow-board,** in moulding, the board on which the pattern is laid; **foll′ower,** one who comes after, esp. in pursuit: a copier: a disciple: a servant-girl's sweetheart: a part of a machine driven by another part: (*Dickens;* also **foll′erer**) a bailiff; **foll′owing,** the whole body of supporters.—*adj.* coming next after: to be next mentioned.—*ns.* **follow-my-lead′er,** a game in which all have to mimic whatever the leader does; **follow-on′, -through′,** an act of following on or through.—**follow home,** follow out, to follow to the end; **follow on,** (*B.*) to continue endeavours: (*cricket*) to take a second innings immediately after one's first, as compulsory result of being short in number of runs; **follow suit,** in card-playing, to play a card of the same suit as the one which was led: to do what another has done; **follow through,** to complete the swing of a stroke after hitting the ball; **follow up,** to pursue an advantage closely: to pursue a question that has been started. [O.E. *folgian, fylgan;* Ger. *folgen.*]

folly, *fol′i, n.* silliness or weakness of mind: a foolish thing: (*obs.*) sin: a monument of folly, as a great useless structure, or one left unfinished, having been begun without a reckoning of the cost.—*v.i.* to act with folly. [O.Fr. *folie—fol,* foolish.]

Fomalhaut, *fō′mal-howt, -hawt, n.* a first-magnitude star in the constellation of the Southern Fish. [Ar. *fam-al-hût,* the whale's mouth.]

foment, *fō-ment′, v.t.* to apply a warm lotion to: to cherish with heat: to foster (usu. evil).—*ns.* **fomentā′tion,** a bathing or lotion with warm water (extended sometimes to a dry or cold application): instigation; **foment'er**. [L. *fōmentum* for *fovimentum*—*fovēre*, to warm.]

fomes, *fō'mēz*, *n.* a substance capable of carrying infection (*pl.* **fomites**, *fō'mi-tēz*). [L. *fōmes*, -*ĭtis*, touchwood.]

fon, *fon*, *n.* (*Spens.*) a fool.—*v.i.* (*obs.*) to be foolish, play the fool.—*v.t.* (*obs.*) to befool: to toy with. —*adv.* **fon'ly**, foolishly. [See **fond.**]

fond, *fond*, *adj.* foolishly tender and loving: weakly indulgent: prizing highly (with *of*): very affectionate: kindly disposed: foolish.—*v.i.* to dote.—*v.t.* **fond'le**, to handle with fondness: to caress.—*ns.* **fond'ler**; **fond'ling**, a pet: (*obs.*) a fool.—*adv.* **fond'ly**, in a fond manner, foolishly: credulously: in vain.—*n.* **fond'ness**. [Pa.p. of **fon**—M.E. *fonnen*, to act foolishly, *fon*, a fool.]

fond (*Spens.*) *pa.t.* of **fand** (2) and *pa.t.* and *pa.p.* of **find**.

fondant, *fon'dant*, *n.* a soft sweetmeat that melts in the mouth. [Fr.,—*fondre*, to melt—L. *fundēre*.]

fone, *fōn*, *n.* (*Spens.*) *pl.* of **foe**.

font, *font*, *n.* a vessel for baptismal water: (*poet.*) a fount, fountain.—*adj.* **font'al**, pertaining to a font or origin.—*ns.* **font'let**, a little font; **font'-stone**, a baptismal font of stone. [O.E. *font*—L. *fōns*, *fontis*, a fountain.]

font, *font*. See **fount** (1).

fontanelle, **fontanel**, *fon-tə-nel'*, *n.* a gap between the bones of the skull of a young animal: an opening for discharge. [Fr. dim.,—L. *fōns*, *fontis*, fountain.]

fontange, *fonᵍ-tänᵍzh'*, *n.* a tall head-dress worn in the 17th and 18th centuries. [Fr., from *Fontanges*, the territorial title of one of Louis XIV's drabs.]

Fontarabian, *fon-tə-rā'bi-ən*, *adj.* pertaining to *Fontarabia* or *Fuenterrabia* at the west end of the Pyrenees (confused by Milton with *Roncesvalles*.)

fonticulus, *fon-tik'ū-ləs*, *n.* the depression just over the top of the breast-bone. [L. *fonticulus* dim. of *fōns*, fountain.]

Fontinalis, *fon-tin-ā'lis*, *n.* a genus of aquatic mosses allied to *Hypnum*. [L. *fontinālis*, of a spring—*fōns*.]

food, *fōōd*, *n.* what one feeds on: that which, being digested, nourishes the body: whatever sustains or promotes growth: (*bot.*) substances elaborated by the plant from raw materials taken in.—*ns.* **food'-card**, a card entitling its holder to obtain his quota of rationed food-stuffs; **food'-controll'er**, an official who controls the storing, sale, and distribution of food in time of emergency. —*adjs.* **food'ful**, able to supply food abundantly; **food'less**, without food.—*n.* **food'-stuff**, a substance used as food.—**food values**, the relative nourishing power of foods. [O.E. *fóda*; Goth. *deins*, Sw. *föda*.]

food, *fōōd*, *n.* (*Spens.*). Same as **feud** (1).

fool, *fōōl*, *n.* one wanting in wisdom: a person of weak mind: a jester: a tool or victim, as of untoward circumstances: a vague term of endearment: nothing in comparison.—*v.t.* to deceive: to treat as a fool: to make to appear foolish: to squander: to get by fooling.—*v.i.* to play the fool: to trifle.—*adj.* (*Scot.* and *U.S.*) foolish.—*adjs.* **fool'-begged** (*Shak.*), perh., foolish enough to be begged for a fool (in allusion to the custom of seeking the administration of a lunatic's estate for one's own advantage); **fool'-born** (*Shak.*), born of a fool or of folly.—*n.* **fool'ery**, an act of folly: habitual folly: fooling.—*adj.* **fool'-happ'y**, happy or lucky without contrivance or judgment. —*ns.* **fool'hard'iness**, **fool'hardise**, -**ize** (-*īz'*, or -*härd'*; *Spens.*).—*adj.* **foolhard'y**, foolishly bold: rash or incautious.—*n.* **fool'ing**, playing the fool: acting the jester: vein of jesting: trifling. —*adj.* **fool'ish**, weak in intellect: wanting discretion: unwise: ridiculous: marked with folly: paltry.—*adv.* **fool'ishly**.—*ns.* **fool'ishness**. —*adjs.* **fool'ish-witt'y** (*Shak.*), wise in folly and foolish in wisdom; **fool'proof**, not liable to sustain or inflict injury by wrong usage: infallible.—*ns.* **fool's'-err'and**, a silly or fruitless enterprise: search for what cannot be found;

fool's'-gold', iron pyrites; **fool's'-pars'ley**, a poisonous umbelliferous plant (*Aethusa Cynapium*) that a great enough fool might take for parsley. —**All Fools' Day** (see **all**); **fool away**, to squander to no purpose or profit; **fool's cap**, a jester's head-dress, usu. having a cockscomb hood with bells; **fool's mate** (*chess*), the simplest of the mates (in four moves); **fool's paradise**, a state of happiness based on fictitious hopes or expectations; **fool with**, to meddle with officiously; **make a fool of**, to bring a person into ridicule: to disappoint; **play the fool**, to behave as a fool: to sport. [O.Fr. *fol* (Fr. *fou*)—L. *follis*, a windbag.]

fool, *fōōl*, *n.* crushed fruit or the like scalded or stewed, mixed with cream and sugar, as *gooseberry fool*. [Prob. a use of preceding suggested by *trifle*.]

foolscap, *fōōlz'kap*, *n.* a long folio writing or printing paper, generally 17 × 13½ in., originally bearing the water-mark of a *fool's cap* and bells.

foot, *foot*, *n.* the part of its body on which an animal stands or walks: a muscular development of the ventral surface in molluscs: (*bot.*) the absorbent and attaching organ of a young sporophyte: the part on which a thing stands: the base: the lower or less dignified end: a measure = 12 in., (*orig.*) the length of a man's foot: the corresponding square or cubic unit (sq. ft. 144 sq. inches; cu. ft. 1728 cu. inches): foot-soldiers: a division of a line of poetry: (*pl.* **feet**; also, as a measure, **foot**; in some compounds and in sense of dregs, or footlights, **foots**).—*v.t.* and *v.i.* to dance: to walk: to sum up.—*v.t.* to kick: to pay: to add a foot to: to grasp with the foot (*pr.p.* **foot'ing**; *pa.t.* and *pa.p.* **foot'ed**).—*ns.* **foot'age**, measurement or payment by the foot: length of organ pipe giving the lowest note; **foot'ball**, a large ball for kicking about in sport: a game played with this ball; **foot'baller**, **foot'-ballist**, a football player; **foot'-bar**, the bar controlled by the pilot's feet, for operating the rudder in air-craft; **foot'-bath**, act of bathing the feet: a vessel for this purpose; **foot'board**, a support for the foot in a carriage or elsewhere: the foot-plate of a locomotive engine; **foot'boy**, an attendant in livery; **foot'breadth**, the breadth of a foot; **foot'bridge**, a bridge for foot-passengers; **foot'cloth**, a sumpter-cloth reaching to the feet of the horse.—*adj.* **foot'ed**, provided with a foot or feet: (*Shak.*) having gained a foothold.—*ns.* **foot'er** (*slang*), football; **foot'fall**, the sound of setting the foot down; **foot'fault** (*lawn-tennis*), an overstepping of the line in serving.—Also *v.t.* and *v.i.*—*n.* **foot'gear**, shoes and stockings. —*n.pl.* **foot'guards**, guards that serve on foot; **foot'hill**, a minor elevation below a higher mountain or range (usually in *pl.*); **foot'hold**, a place to fix the foot in: a grip, establishment, often insecure; **foot'ing**, place for the foot to rest on: standing: terms: installation: an installation fee or treat: foundation: lower part: position: settlement: track: tread: dance: plain cotton lace; **foot'-jaw**, a maxilliped; **foot'-land-raker** (*Shak.*) a footpad.—*adj.* **foot'less**, having no feet or no footing: (*U.S.*) futile.—*ns.* **foot'-licker**, a fawning, slavish flatterer; **foot'light**, one of a row of lights along the front of the stage.—*adj.* **foot'-loose**, free, unhampered.—*ns.* **foot'man**, one who goes on foot: a servant or attendant in livery: a foot soldier: a servant running before a coach or rider (*pl.* **foot'men**); **foot'mark**, **foot'print**, the mark or print of a foot: a track; **foot'-muff**, a muff for keeping the feet warm; **foot'note**, a note of reference at the foot of a page; **foot'pace**, a walking pace: a dais; **foot'pad**, a highwayman on foot; **foot'page**, a boy attendant; **foot'-pass'enger**, one who goes on foot; **foot'path**, a way for foot-passengers only: a side pavement; **foot'plate**, the platform on which the driver and stoker of a locomotive engine stand; **foot'-post**, a post or messenger that travels on foot; **foot'-pound**, the energy needed to raise a mass of one pound through the height of one foot; **foot'-pump**, a pump held or operated by the foot; **foot'-race**, a race on foot; **foot'-racing**; **foot'rest**, a support for the foot; **foot'-rope**, a rope stretching along under a ship's yard for the men to stand on when furling the sails : the rope to which the lower edge of a sail is attached; **foot'rot**, ulceration of the coronary band, or other affection of the feet in sheep; **foot'rule**, a rule or measure a foot in length or measured off in feet.—*v.i.* **foot'-slog**, to march, tramp.—*ns.* **foot'slogger**; **foot'-slogging**; **foot'-soldier**, a soldier serving on foot.—*adj.* **foot'sore**, having sore or tender feet, as by much walking.—*ns.* **foot'stalk** (*bot.*), the stalk or petiole of a leaf; **foot'-stall**, a side-saddle stirrup; **foot'step**, a tread : a footfall : a footprint : a raised step for ascending or descending : (in *pl.*, *fig.*) course, example.—*n.* **foot'stool**, a stool for placing one's feet on when sitting.—*adj.* **foot'-stooled.**—*ns.* **foot'-warm'er**, a contrivance for keeping the feet warm; **foot'way**, a path for passengers on foot; a mine shaft with ladders; **foot'wear**, a shopkeeper's word for boots and shoes; **foot'-work**, use or management of the feet, as in games.—*adj.* **foot'worn**, worn by many feet : footsore.—**at the feet of**, in submission. homage, supplication, or devotion to; **cover the feet** (*B.*), to defecate; **foot-and-mouth disease**, murrain; **foot it**, to walk : to dance; **foot of fine**, the bottom part (preserved in the records) of a tripartite indenture in case of a fine of land; **foot the bill**, to pay up; **have one foot in the grave**, to be not far from death; **on foot**, walking or running : in activity or being; **put one's best foot foremost**, to make one's best effort; **put one's foot in it**, to spoil anything by some indiscretion; **set on foot**, to originate; **the ball is at his feet**, he has nothing to do but seize his opportunity. [O.E. *fót*, pl. *fét*; Ger. *fuss*, L. *pēs, pedis*, Gr. *pous, podos*, Sans. *pād.*]

footle, *foot'l*, *v.i* to trifle, to show foolish incompetence, to bungle.—*n.* silly nonsense.—*n.* and *adj.* **foot'ling**. [Origin obscure.]

footy, *foot'i*, *adj.* (*prov.*) mean. [Origin obscure.]

foozle, *fōōz'l*, *n.* (*coll.*) a tedious fellow : a bungled stroke at golf, etc.—*v.i.* to fool away one's time : —*v.i.* and *v.t.* to bungle.—*n.* **fooz'ler.**—*n.* and *adj.* **fooz'ling.** [Cf. Ger. prov. *fuseln*, to work badly, to potter.]

fop, *fop*, *n.* an affected dandy.—*ns.* **fop'ling**, a vain affected person; **fopp'ery**, vanity in dress or manners : affectation : folly.—*adj.* **fopp'ish**, vain and showy in dress : affectedly refined in manners.—*adv.* **fopp'ishly.**—*n.* **fopp'ishness.** [Cf. Ger. *foppen*, to hoax.]

for, *for*, *for*, *prep.* in the place of : in favour of : on account of : in the direction of : with respect to : in respect of : by reason of : appropriate or adapted to, or in reference to : beneficial to : in quest of : notwithstanding, in spite of : in recompense of : during : in the character of : to the extent of :—*conj.* because.—**as for**, as far as concerns; **for all** (that), notwithstanding; **for that** (*obs.*) because; **for to** (now *vulg.*) in order to : to; **for why** (*obs.*) why : because; **nothing for it but**, nothing else to be done in the case; **to be** (in) **for it**, to have something unpleasant impending; **what is he for a man?** (*obs.*), what kind of man is he? [O.E. *for.*]

for-. See Prefixes.

forage, *for'ij*, *n.* fodder, or food for horses and cattle : provisions : the act of foraging.—*v.i.* to go about and forcibly carry off food for horses and cattle : to rummage about for what one wants.—*v.t.* to plunder.—*ns.* **for'age-cap**, the undress cap worn by infantry soldiers; **for'ager**. [Fr. *fourrage*, O.Fr. *feurre*, fodder, of Gmc. origin; cf. **fodder**.]

foramen, *fō-rā'men*, *n.* a small opening (*pl.* **foramina**, *-ram'i-nä*).—*adjs.* **foram'inated**, **foram'inous**, pierced with small holes : porous.—*n.* **foraminifer** (*for-ə-min'i-fər*; L. *ferre*, to bear), any member of the **Foraminif'era** (*-am-*, or *-ām-*), an order of Rhizopods with a shell usu. perforated by pores (*foramina*).—*adjs.* **foraminif'eral**, **foraminif'erous.**—**foramen mag-**

num, the great hole in the occipital bone through which the spinal column joins the medulla oblongata. [L. *forāmen—forāre*, to pierce.]

forane, *for-ān'*, *adj.* a form of **foreign**, outlying, rural, as in **vicar forane** (q.v.).

forasmuch, *for-*, *fər-əz-much'*, *conj.* because, since (with *as*).

foray, *for'ā*, *n.* a raid.—*v.t.* and *v.i.* to raid : to forage.—*n.* **for'ayer**. [Ety. obscure, but ult. identical with **forage** (q.v.).]

forbad(e). See **forbid**.

forbear, *for-*, *fər-bār'*, *v.i.* to keep oneself in check : to abstain.—*v.t.* to abstain from : to avoid voluntarily : to spare, to withhold : (*Spens.*) to give up (*pa.t.* **forbore'**; *pa.p.* **forborne'**).—*n.* **forbear'ance**, exercise of patience : command of temper : clemency.—*adjs.* **forbear'ant**, **forbear'-ing**, long-suffering : patient.—*adv.* **forbear'ingly.** [O.E. *forberan*, pa.t. *forbær*, pa.p. *forboren;* see pfx. *for-* and **bear**.]

forbear, *fōr'bār*. Same as **forebear**.

forbid, *far-*, *for-bid'*, *v.t.* to prohibit : to command not to : (*pa.t.* **forbade**, *-bad'*, by some *-bād'*, or **forbad'** ; *pa.p.* **forbidd'en**).—*ns.* **forbidd'al**, **forbidd'ance**, prohibition : command or edict against a thing.—*adj.* **forbidd'en**, prohibited : unlawful. —*adv.* **forbidd'enly**, (*Shak.*) in a forbidden or unlawful manner.—*n.* **forbidd'ing.**—*adj.* uninviting : sinister : unprepossessing : threatening or formidable in look.—*adv.* **forbidd'ingly.**—*n.* **forbidd'ingness.**—**forbidden degrees** (see **degree**); **forbidden fruit**, that forbidden to Adam (Gen. ii. 17): anything tempting and prohibited : (or *Adam's apple*) a name fancifully given to the fruit of various species of Citrus, esp. to one having tooth-marks on its rind.—*n.* **forbode** (*for-bōd'; arch.*) prohibition.—**over God's forbode**, God forbid. [O.E. *forbēodan*, pa.t. *forbéad*, pa.p. *forboden;* see pfx. *for-* and **bid**; cf. Ger. *verbieten.*]

forby, *fər-bī'*, *adv.* and *prep.* (*Spens.*) near : past : by : (*Scot.*) besides. [**fore-, by.**]

forçat, *for'sä*, *n.* in France, a convict condemned to hard labour. [Fr.]

force, *fōrs*, *n.* strength, power, energy : efficacy : validity : influence : vehemence : violence : coercion or compulsion : group of men assembled for collective action (as *Air Force, police force*): an armament : any cause which changes the direction or speed of the motion of a portion of matter. — *v.t.* to draw or push by main strength : to thrust : to compel : to constrain : to overcome the resistance of by force : to do violence to : to achieve or bring about by force : to ravish : to take by violence : to strain : (*hort.*) to cause to grow or ripen rapidly : to work up to a high pitch : (*cards*) to induce to play in a particular way : to cause the playing of : (*Shak.*) to strengthen : (*obs.*) to attribute importance to.—*v.i.* (*Spens.*) to strive : to make way by force : (*obs.*) to care.—*adj.* **forced**, accomplished by great effort, as a forced march : strained, excessive, unnatural : artificially produced.—*adv.* **forc'edly.**—*n.* **forc'edness**, the state of being forced : constraint : unnatural or undue distortion.—*adj.* **force'ful**, full of force or might : energetic : driven or acting with power.—*adv.* **force'fully.**—*adj.* **force'less**, weak.—*ns.* **force'-pump**, **forc'ing-pump**, a pump that delivers liquid under pressure greater than its suction pressure : a pump for cleaning out pipes by blowing air through; **forc'er**, the person or thing that forces, esp. the piston of a force-pump.—*adj.* **forc'ible**, having force : done by force.—*n.* **forc'ibleness.**—*adv.* **forc'ibly.**—*ns.* **forc'ing**; **forc'ing-house**, a hothouse for forcing plants; **forc'ing-pit**, a frame sunk in the ground over a hotbed for forcing plants.—**force and fear** (*Scot.*), that amount of constraint or compulsion which is enough to annul an engagement or obligation entered into under its influence; **force the pace**, to bring and keep the speed up to a high pitch by emulation; **forcible detainer**, detaining property or forcing an entry into it by violence or intimidation; **forcible Feeble**, a weak man with show of valour (in allusion to Francis Feeble in II. Hen. IV., III. ii. 180). [Fr.,—L.L. *fortia*—L. *fortis*, strong.]

force, *fōrs*, **foss**, *fos*, *n*. a waterfall. [O.N. *fors*.]

force, *fōrs*, *v.t.* (*cook*.) to stuff, as a fowl.—*n*. **force′meat**, meat chopped fine and highly seasoned, used as a stuffing or alone. [For farce.]

forceps, *for′seps*, *n*. a pincer-like instrument or organ for holding, lifting, or removing (*pl.* **for′ceps**, also **for′cepses**, **for′cipēs**, *-si-pēz*).—*adj*. **for′cipated**, formed and opening like a forceps. —*n*. **forcipā′tion**, torture by pinching with forceps. [L.,—*formus*, hot, *capĕre*, to hold.]

ford, *fōrd*, *n*. a place where water may be crossed by wading.—*v.t.* to wade across.—*adj*. **ford′able**. [O.E. *ford-faran*, to go; cf. Ger. *furt-fahren*, Gr. *poros*, L. *portus*, and **fare**, **ferry**, **far**.]

fordo, *for-*, *far-dōō′*, *v.t.* (*arch*.) to destroy: to ruin: to overcome: to exhaust: (*pr.p.* **fordo′ing**; *pa.t.* **fordid′**; *pa.p.* **fordone**, *-dun′*).—*adj*. **fordone′**, exhausted.—from **fordonne** (*Spens*.), from being **fordone**. [O.E. *fordón*; Ger. *vertun*, to consume.]

fore, *fōr*, *adj*. in front: (*obs*.) former, previous.— *adv*. at or towards the front: previously.—*n*. the front: the foremast.—*interj*. (*golf*) a warning cry to anybody in the way of the ball.—*adj*. and *adv*. **fore′-and-aft′**, lengthwise of a ship: without square sails.—*ns*. **fore-and-aft′er**, a vessel of fore-and-aft rig: a hat peaked before and behind; **fore′bitt**, one of the bitts at the foremast; **fore′bitter**, a ballad sung at the forebitts. —**at the fore**, displayed on the foremast (of a flag); **to the fore**, at hand: (*Scot*.) in being, alive: (loosely) prominent. [O.E. *fore*, radically the same as **for**, *prep*.]

fore-, *fōr-*, *pfx*. before: beforehand: in front.— *vs.t.* **fore-admon′ish**, to admonish beforehand; **fore-advise′**, to advise beforehand.—*n*. **fore′arm**, the part of the arm between the elbow and the wrist.—*v.t.* **forearm′**, to arm or prepare beforehand.—*n*. **forebear**, **forbear** (*fōr′bār*), (*Scot*.) an ancestor (from **be** and suff. **-er**).—*v.t.* **forebode′**, to prognosticate: to have a premonition of (esp. of evil).—*ns*. **forebode′ment**, feeling of coming evil; **forebod′er**; **forebod′ing**, a boding or perception beforehand; apprehension of coming evil.—*adv*. **forebod′ingly**.—*ns*. **fore′-body**, the part in front of the mainmast; **fore′-brace**, a rope attached to the fore yard-arm, for changing the position of the foresail; **fore′brain**, the front part of the brain.—*prep*. **foreby′**, (*Spens*) same as **forby**).—*ns*. **fore′cabin**, a cabin in a ship's forepart; **fore′-caddy**, a caddy posted where he may see where the balls go; **fore′car**, a small car carrying a passenger in front of a motor-cycle; **fore′carriage**, the front part of a carriage, with arrangement for independent movement of the fore-wheels.—*v.t.* **forecast′**, to contrive or reckon beforehand: to foresee: to predict.—*v.i.* to form schemes beforehand:—*pa.t.* and *pa.p.* **forecast′**, sometimes **forecast′ed**.— *ns*. **fore′cast**, a previous contrivance: foresight: a prediction; **forecast′er**; **forecastle**, **fo′c′sle** (*fōk′sl*, sometimes *fōr′kās-l*), a short raised deck at the fore-end of a vessel: the forepart of the ship under the maindeck, the quarters of the crew.—*adjs*. **forechos′en**, chosen beforehand; **fore-ci′ted**, quoted before or above.

foreclose, *fōr-klōz′*, *v.t.* to preclude: to prevent: to stop: to bar the right of redeeming.—*n*. **fore′closure** (*-klō′zhər*), a foreclosing: (*law*) the process by which a mortgagor, failing to repay the money lent on the security of an estate, is compelled to forfeit his right to redeem the estate. [O.Fr. *forclos*, pa.p. of *forclore*, to exclude —L. *foris*, outside, and *claudĕre*, *clausum*, to shut.]

fore-, continued.—*ns*. **fore′course**, a foresail; **fore′court**, a court in front of a building: an outer court.

fore-damned, *for-dam′ned*, *adj*. (*Spens*.) utterly damned (or poss. damned beforehand). [Pfx. **for-** (or poss. **fore-**).]

fore-, continued.—*v.t.* **foredate′**, to date before the true time.—*ns*. **fore′day**, (*Scot*.) forenoon;

fore′deck, the forepart of a deck or ship.—*v.t.* **foredoom′**, to doom beforehand.—*ns*. **fore′edge**, the outer edge of a book, furthest from the back—placed outward in a mediaeval library; **fore′-end**, the early or fore part of anything; **fore′father**, an ancestor.—*v.t.* **forefeel′**, to feel beforehand.—*adv*. **forefeel′ingly**.—*adj*. **forefelt′**. —*ns*. **fore′finger**, the finger next the thumb; **fore′foot**, one of the anterior feet of a quadruped: (*naut*.) the foremost end of the keel, whereon rests the stem: (*pl.* **forefeet**); **fore′front**, the front or foremost part; **fore′gleam**, a glimpse into the future.—*v.t.* and *v.i.* **forego′**, to go before, precede: chiefly in its *pr.p.* **foregō′ing** (or *fōr′*) and *pa.p.* **foregone′** (or *fōr′*); **forewent′** (*rare*) serves as *pa.t.*, formerly also as *pa.p.*—*ns*. **foregō′er** (or *fōr′*); **foregoing**.—*adj*. **foregone** (**foregone conclusion**, a conclusion come to before examination of the evidence: an obvious or inevitable conclusion or result).—*n*. **fore′gone′ness**.

forego, better **forgo**.

fore-, continued.—*ns*. **fore′ground**, the part of a picture or field of view nearest the observer's eye, as opp. to the *background* or *distance*; **fore′hammer**, a sledge-hammer; **fore′hand**, the front position or its occupant: the upper hand, advantage, preference: the part of a horse that is in front of its rider: (*tennis*) the part of the court to the right of a right-handed player, or to the left of a left-handed player: a stroke played forehand.—*adj*. done beforehand (*Shak*.) anticipating, of anticipation: with the palm in front— opp. to *backhand*: (of an arrow; *Shak*.) for shooting point-blank.—*adv*. with hand in forehand position. —*adj*. **fore′handed**, forehand, as of payment for goods before delivery, or for services before rendered: seasonable: (*U.S.*) well off: shapely in the foreparts.—*ns*. **forehead** (*for′id*, *-ed*), the forepart of the head above the eyes, the brow: confidence, audacity; **fore′-horse**, the foremost horse of a team.

foreign, *for′in*, *adj*. belonging to another country: from abroad: alien: extraneous: not belonging: unconnected: not appropriate.—*adj*. **for′eign-built**, built in a foreign country.—*ns*. **for′eigner**, a native of another country; **for′eigness**, the quality of being foreign: want of relation to something: remoteness. [O.Fr. *forain*—L.L. *forāneus*—L. *forās*, out of doors.]

fore-, continued.—*v.t.* **forejudge′**, to judge before hearing the facts and proof.—*ns*. **forejudg′ment**; **fore′king**, (*Tenn*.) a preceding king.—*v.t.* **foreknow′** (*fōr-nō′*) to know beforehand: to foresee. —*adj*. **foreknow′ing**.—*adv*. **foreknow′ingly**.— *n*. **foreknowl′edge** (*-nol′ij*).—*adj*. **foreknown′**.

forel, *for′əl*, *n*. a kind of parchment for covering books. [O.Fr. *forrel*, dim. of *forre*, *fuerre*, sheath.]

fore-, continued.—*n*. **fore′land**, a point of land running forward into the sea, a headland: a front region.—*vs.t.* **forelay′**, to contrive antecedently: to lay wait for in ambush: to hinder; **forelay′**, *pa.t.* of **forelie**.—*n*. **fore′leg**, a front leg.—*vs.t.* **forelend′**, to grant or resign beforehand (*pa.p.*, *Spens*., **forelent′**); **forelie′**, to lie before (*pa.t.*, *Spens*., **forelay′**); **forelift′** (*Spens*.), to raise in front.—*ns*. **fore′lock**, the lock of hair on the forehead (**take time by the forelock**, to seize an opportunity betimes); **fore′man**, the first or chief man, one appointed to preside over, or act as spokesman for, others : an overseer :— *pl.* **fore′men**; **fore′mast**, the mast that is forward, or next the bow of a ship; **fore′mastman**, any sailor below the rank of petty officer.—*v.t.* **foremean′**, to intend beforehand.—*adjs*. **fore′men′tioned**, mentioned before in a writing or discourse; **foremost** (*fōr′mōst*, *-məst*; double superl.—O.E. *forma*, first, superl. of *fore*, and superl. suffix *-st*), first in place: most advanced: first in rank or dignity.—*n*. **fore′name**, the first or Christian name.—*adj*. **fore′-named**, mentioned before.—*ns*. **fore′night**, (*Scot*.) the early part of the night before bedtime, the evening; **forenoon** (*fōr-nōōn′*, *fōr′nōōn*; chiefly *Scot*. and *Ir*.), the part of the day before midday, distinguished from morning.—*adj.* (*for'*) pertaining to this time.—*n.* fore'no'tice, notice of anything in advance of the time.

forensic, *fə-ren'sik, adj.* belonging to courts of law, held by the Romans in the forum: used in law pleading: appropriate to, or adapted to, argument.—**forensic medicine**, medical jurisprudence, the application of medical knowledge to the elucidation of doubtful questions in a court of justice. [L. *forēnsis—forum*, marketplace, forum.]

fore-, continued.—*v.t.* fore'-ordain', to arrange beforehand: to predestinate.—*ns.* fore'-ordinā'tion; fore'part, the front: the early part.—*adj.* fore'past, bygone.—*ns.* fore'pay'ment, payment beforehand.; fore'peak, the contracted part of a ship's hold, close to the bow.—*vs.t.* foreplan', to plan beforehand; forepoint', to foreshadow. —*adj.* fore-quo'ted, quoted or cited before.— *v.t.* foreran', *pa.t.* of forerun.—*n.* fore'-rank, the front rank.—*v.i.* forereach', (*naut.*) to glide ahead, esp. when going in stays (with *on*).—*v.t.* to sail beyond.—*v.t.* foreread', to foretell:— *pa.t.* foreread (-*red'*).—*n.* fore'-reading.—*adj.* fore-reci'ted, (*Shak.*) recited or named before. —*v.t.* forerun', to run or come before: to precede.—*n.* fore'runner, a runner or messenger sent before: a precursor: a prognostic.—*adj.* fore'said, already mentioned (see also foresay). —*n.* foresail (*for'sl, -sāl*) the chief and lowest square sail on the foremast: a triangular sail on the forestay.—*v.t.* fore-say', to predict or foretell: (*Shak.*) to ordain (see also forsay).—*v.t.* and *v.i.* foresee', to see or know beforehand:— *pa.t.* foresaw'; *pa.p.* foreseen'.—*adj.* foresee'-ing.—*adv.* foresee'ingly.—*v.t.* foreshad'ow, to shadow or typify beforehand: to give, or have, some indication of in advance.—*ns.* foreshad'ow-ing; fore'ship, the forepart of a ship; fore'shore, the space between high and low water marks.—*v.t.* foreshort'en, to draw or cause to appear as if shortened, by perspective.—*n.* fore-short'ening.—*v.t.* foreshow, foreshew (*for-shō'*), to show or represent beforehand: to predict (*pa.t.* foreshowed, foreshewed, -*shōd'*; *pa.p.* foreshown, foreshewn, -*shōn'*, also *Spens.* fore-shewed').—*ns.* fore'side, the front side: (*Spens.*) outward appearance; fore'sight, act or power of foreseeing: wise forethought, prudence: the sight on the muzzle of a gun: a forward reading of a levelling staff.—*adjs.* fore'sighted; fore'sightful; fore'sightless.—*v.t.* foresig'nify, to betoken beforehand: to foreshow: to typify.—*ns.* fore'skin, the skin that covers the glans penis, the prepuce; fore'skirt, (*Shak.*) the loose part of a coat before.—*vs.t.* forespeak', to predict: (*Scot.*) to engage beforehand (see also forspeak); fore-spend', to spend beforehand (*pa.p.* forespent'; see also forspend).—*n.* forespurr'er, (*Shak.*) one who rides before.

forest, *for'ist, n.* a large uncultivated tract of land covered with trees and underwood: woody ground and rude pasture: a preserve for big game: a royal preserve for hunting, governed by a special code called the **forest law**.—*adj.* pertaining to a forest: silvan: rustic.—*v.t.* to cover with trees.—*n.* for'estage, an ancient service paid by foresters to the king: the right of foresters.—*adj.* for'estal.—*n.* foresta'tion, afforestation.—*adjs.* for'est-born (*Shak.*) born in a wild; for'est-bred; for'ested.—*ns.* for'ester, one who has charge of a forest: one who has care of growing trees: a member of the Ancient Order of Foresters or similar friendly society: an inhabitant of a forest; for'est-fly, a dipterous insect (*Hippobosca equina*) that annoys horses.— *adj.* for'estine.—*ns.* For'est-Mar'ble, a Middle Jurassic fissile limestone of which typical beds are found in Wychwood Forest, Oxfordshire; for'est-oak, Australian beefwood (*Casuarina*); for'estry, the art of planting, tending, and managing forests: forest country: an extent of trees; for'est-tree, a tree, esp. a timber-tree, that grows in forests. [O.Fr. *forest* (Fr. *forêt*)— L.L. *forestis* (*silva*), the outside wood, as opposed

to the *parcus* (park) or walled-in wood—L. *forīs*, out of doors.]

fore-, continued.—*n.* fore'stair (*Scot.*) an outside stair in front of a house.—*v.t.* forestall (*fōr-stawl'*; O.E. *foresteall*, ambush, lit. a place taken beforehand—*steall*, stand, station), to buy up before reaching the market, so as to sell again at higher prices: to anticipate: to hinder by anticipating: to bar.—*ns.* forestall'er; forestall'ing; forestal'ment; fore'stay, a rope reaching from the foremast-head to the bowsprit end to support the mast.—*v.t.* foretaste', to taste before possession: to anticipate: to taste before another.—*n.* fore'taste, a taste beforehand: anticipation— *vs.t.* foreteach', to teach beforehand: (*pa.t.* and *pa.p.* foretaught'); foretell', to tell before: to prophesy.—*v.i.* to utter prophecy: (*pa.t.* and *pa.p.* foretold').—*n.* foretell'er.—*v.t.* forethink', to anticipate in the mind: to have prescience of: (*pa.t.* and *pa.p.* forethought').—*ns.* forethinker; fore'thought, thought or care for the future: anticipation: thinking beforehand.—*adj.* fore-thought'ful.—*n.* fore'token, a token or sign beforehand.—*v.t.* foretō'ken, to signify before-hand.—*n.* and *adj.* foretō'kening.—*ns.* fore'-tooth, *n.* a tooth in the forepart of the mouth (*pl.* fore'teeth); fore'top, (*naut.*) the platform at the head of the foremast: (*obs.*) the forepart of the crown of the head: a lock (usu. upright) over the forehead: (*obs.*) an appendage to a shoe.— *n.* foretop'mast, the mast erected at the head of the foremast, at the top of which is the **fore'top-gall'ant-mast.**

forever, *fər-ev'ər, adv.* for ever, for all time to come: eternally: everlastingly.—*adv.* forev'er-more', for ever hereafter.

fore-, continued.—*adj.* forevouched', (*Shak.*) affirmed or told before.—*n.* fore'ward, advance-guard: (*Shak.*) the front.—*v.t.* forewarn', to warn beforehand: to give previous notice (see also forwarn).—*n.* forewarn'ing.—*vs.t.* fore-weigh', to estimate beforehand; forewent', used as *pa.t.* (*Spens. pa.p.*) of forego (see also forgo).— *ns.* fore'wind, a favourable wind; fore'woman, a woman overseer, a headwoman: (*pl.* fore'-women); fore'word, a preface.

forfair, *for-fār', v.i.* (*obs.*) to perish, decay.—*adj.* (*Scot.*) forfairn', worn out: exhausted. [O.E. *forfaran*.]

forfeit, *for'fit, n.* that to which a right is lost: a penalty for a crime, or breach of some condition: a fine: something deposited and redeemable by a sportive fine or penalty, esp. in *pl.*, a game of this kind.—*adj.* forfeited.—*v.t.* to lose the right to by some fault or crime: (*arch.*) to confiscate: to penalise by forfeiture: (*loosely*) to give up voluntarily.—*adj.* for'feitable.—*ns.* for'feiter (*Shak.*), one who incurs punishment by forfeiting his bond; forfeiture, act of forfeiting: state of being forfeited: the thing forfeited.—Also (*obs.*) for-fault, etc., by association with fault. [O.Fr. *forfait*—L.L. *forisfactum*—L. *forīs*, outside, *facĕre*, to make.]

forfend, *fər-fend', v.t.* (*arch.*) to ward off, avert. [Pfx. *for-*, denoting prohibition, and fend.]

forfex, *for'feks, n.* a pair of scissors, or pincers: the pincers of an earwig, etc.—*n.* Forfic'ula, the common genus of earwigs.—*adj.* forfic'ulate, like scissors. [L. *forfex, -icis*, shears, pincers.]

forfoughten, *fər'faw'tən*, (*Scot.* forfoughen, *fər-fohh'ən*, forfeuchen, *-fyoohh'*), *adj.* exhausted, as by struggling.

forgat, *fər-gat'*, old *pa.t.* of forget.

forgather, *fər-gadh'ər, v.i.* (*Scot.*) to meet.

forgave, *fər-gāv', pa.t.* of forgive.

forge, *forj, n.* the workshop of a workman in iron, etc.: a furnace, esp. one in which iron is heated: a smithy: a place where anything is shaped or made.—*v.t.* to form by heating and hammering: to form: to make falsely: to fabricate: to counterfeit or imitate for purposes of fraud.—*v.i.* to commit forgery.—*ns.* forge'man; forg'er, one who forges or makes: one guilty of forgery; forg'ery, fraudulently making or altering anything, esp. a writing: that which is forged or counterfeited:

(obs.) deceit.—*adj.* forg'etive (*Shak.*), creative.—*n.* forg'ing, a piece of metal shaped by hammering : act of one who forges. [O.Fr. *forge*—L. *fabrica*—*faber*, a workman.]

forge, *forj, v.t.* to move steadily on (usu. with *ahead*). [Origin obscure.]

forge, *forj, v.i.* in a horse, to click the hind shoe against the fore. [Origin obscure.]

forget, *for-get', v.t.* to lose or put away from the memory : to fail to remember or think of : (*pr.p.* forgett'ing ; *pa.t.* forgot' ; *arch.* forgat' ; *pa.p.* forgott'en ; *arch.* forgot').—*adj.* forget'ful, apt to forget : inattentive.—*adv.* forget'fully.—*ns.* forget'fulness : forget'-me-not, any plant of the genus Myosotis, regarded as an emblem of loving remembrance.—*adj.* forgett'able.—*n.* forgett'er.—*n.* and *adj.* forgett'ing.—*adv.* forgett'ingly.—*adj.* forgott'en.—*n.* forgott'enness—forget oneself to lose one's self-control or dignity, to descend to words and deeds unworthy of oneself. [O.E. *forgetan* (*forgietan*)—pfx. *for-*, away, *getan* (*gietan*), to get.]

forgive, *for-giv', v.t.* to pardon : to overlook : (*Spens.*) to give up.—*v.i.* to be merciful or forgiving : (*pa.t.* forgave', *pa.p.* forgiv'en).—*adj.* forgiv'able, capable of being forgiven.—*n.* forgive'ness, pardon : remission : disposition to pardon.—*adj.* forgiv'ing, ready to pardon : merciful : compassionate. [O.E. *forgiefan*—pfx. *for-*, away, *giefan*, to give ; cf. Ger. *vergeben*.]

forgo, forego, *for-, for-gō', v.t.* to leave : to give up : to relinquish : to do without : to forbear the use or advantage of : (*arch.*) to forfeit.—*v.i.* to forbear : (*pr.p.* for(e)go'ing ; *pa.p.* for(e)gone' ; for(e)went. serves as *pa.t.*). See also forego. [O.E. *forgán*, to pass by, abstain from—pfx. *for-*, *gán*, to go.]

forgot, forgotten. See forget.

forhaile, *for-hāl', v.t.* (*Spens.*) to distract. [Pfx. *for-*, hale.]

forhent, *for-hent', v.t.* to overtake (*pa.p., Spens.*, forhent').

forhow, *for-how', v.t.* (*obs.*) to despise : (*Scot.; for-hōō'*), to desert or abandon. [O.E. *forhogian*, pfx. *for-*, away, *hogian*, to care.]

forinsec, *for-in'sek, adj.* (of feudal service) due to the lord's superior.—*adj.* forin'secal, foreign : alien : extrinsic. [L. *forīnsecus*, from without—*forīs*, out of doors, *secus*, following.]

forisfamiliate, *for-, fōr-is-fə-mil'i-āt, v.t.* to emancipate from paternal authority : to put in possession of land which is accepted as the whole portion of the father's property, said of a father.—*v.i.* to renounce one's title to a further share, said of a son.—*n.* forisfamiliā'tion. [L.L. *forisfamiliāre, -ātum*—L. *forīs*, out of doors, *familia*, a family.]

forjeskit, *for-jes'kit*, forjaskit, *-jás', adj.* (*Scot.*) tired out. [Pfx. *for-*; cf. disjaskit.]

fork, *fork, n.* a pronged instrument : anything that divides into prongs or branches : a branch or prong : the space or angle between branches, esp. on a tree or between the legs : a confluent, tributary, or branch of a river : one of the branches into which a road divides : a bifurcation : a place of bifurcation : a barbed arrowhead : part of a bicycle to which a wheel is attached : the appearance of a flash of lightning : the bottom of a sump in a mine.—*v.i.* to branch : to follow a branch road.—*v.t.* to form as a fork : to move with a fork : to stab with a fork : (*chess*) to menace simultaneously : to pump dry.—*n.* fork'chuck, a forked lathe-centre used in wood-turning.—*adj.* forked, shaped like a fork.—*adv.* fork'edly.—*ns.* fork'edness ; fork'er ; fork'head, (*Spens.*) an arrowhead : the forked end of a rod ; fork'iness ; fork'it-tail, fork'y-tail (*dial.*), an earwig ; fork'-tail, a name for various fishes and birds, as the kite.—*adj.* fork'y.—fork out, over (*slang*), to hand or pay over. [O.E. *forca*—L. *furca*.]

forlana, *for-lä'nä*, furlana, *fōōr-, n.* a Venetian dance in 6-8 time. [It. *Furlana*, Friulian.]

forlend, *for-lend', v.t.* to give up entirely (*pa.t.*, Spens. forlent').

forlorn, *for-lorn', adj.* quite lost : forsaken : neglected : wretched.—*n.* (*Shak.*) a forsaken person : a forlorn hope—orig. *pa.p.* of the *obs.* forlese (*for-lēz'), v.t.* to lose : to forsake (*pa.t.* and *pa.p.*, Spens. forlore, *-lōr').—adv.* forlorn'ly.—*n.* forlorn'ness. [O.E. *forloren*, pa.p. of *forléosan*, to lose—pfx. *for-*, away, and *léosan*, to lose ; Ger. *verloren*, pa.p. of *verlieren*, to lose.]

forlorn-hope, *for-lorn'-hōp', n.* a body of soldiers selected for some service of uncommon danger : a desperate enterprise of last resort : a vain or faint hope (from association with hope=expectation). [Du. *verloren hoop*, lost troop.]

form, *form, n.* shape : a mould : species : pattern : mode of being : mode of arrangement : order : regularity : system, as of government : (*obs.*) beauty : style and arrangement : structural unity in music, literature, etc. : a prescribed set of words or course of action : ceremony : behaviour : condition of fitness or efficiency : a schedule to be filled in with details : a specimen document for imitation : (*phil.*) the inherent nature of an object : that which the mind itself contributes as the condition of knowing : that in which the essence of a thing consists : (*crystal.*) a complete set of crystal faces similar with respect to the symmetry of the crystal : (*print.*) the type from which an impression is to be taken arranged and secured in a chase—often forme : a long seat, a bench : a class : the bed of a hare, shaped by the animal's body.—*v.t.* to give form or shape to : to bring into being : to make : to contrive : to conceive in the mind : to go to make up : to constitute : to establish.—*v.i.* to assume a form.—*adj.* form'al, according to form or established mode : relating to form : ceremonious, punctilious, methodical : having the form only : (*Shak.*) sane : having the power of making a thing what it is : essential : proper.—*v.t.* and *v.i.* form'alise.—*ns.* form'alism, excessive observance of form or conventional usage, esp. in religion : stiffness of manner ; form'alist, one having exaggerated regard to rules or established usages ; formal'ity, the precise observance of forms or ceremonies : a matter of form : a ceremonious observance : established order : sacrifice of substance to form.—*adv.* form'ally.—*n.* formā'tion, a making or producing : structure : (*geol.*) a stratigraphical group of strata : (*bot.*) a plant community.—*adj.* form'ative, giving form, determining, moulding : capable of development : growing : (*gram.*) serving to form, not radical.—*n.* a derivative.—*adj.* formed.—*n.* form'er.—*adj.* form'less.—*adv.* form'lessly.—*n.* form'lessness.—formal logic (see logic) ; good, or bad, form, according to good or recognised social usage, or the opposite. [L. *fōrma*, shape.]

formaldehyde, formalin. See under formic.

format, *for'mä, -mät, n.* of books, etc., the size, form, shape in which they are issued. [Fr.]

former, *form'ər, adj.* (*comp.* of fore) before in time : past : first mentioned (of two) : (*Spens.*) beforehand, first (of two).—*adv.* form'erly, in former times : heretofore. [Formed late on analogy of M.E. *formest*, foremost, by adding comp. suff. *-er* to base of O.E. *forma*, first, itself superlative.]

formic, *for'mik, adj.* pertaining to ants.—*ns.* formal'dehyde, a formic aldehyde, formalin ; for'malin, a formic aldehyde used as an antiseptic, germicide, or preservative ; for'mate, a salt of formic acid.—Also for'miate.—*adj.* for'micant, crawling like an ant : very small and unequal, of a pulse.—*ns.* formicā'rium, for'micary, an ant-hill, ants' nest, or colony.—*adj.* for'micate, resembling an ant.—*n.* formicā'tion, a sensation like that of ants creeping on the skin.—formic acid, a fatty acid H.CO.OH, found in ants and nettles. [L. *formīca*, an ant.]

formidable, *for'mid-ə-bl*, by some *-mid', adj.* causing fear : adapted to excite fear : redoubtable.—*ns.* formidabil'ity ; for'midableness.—*adv.* for'midably. [Fr.,—L. *formīdābilis*—*formīdō*, fear.]

formula, *form'ū-lä, n.* a prescribed form : a formal statement of doctrines : (*math.*) a general expression for solving problems : (*chem.*) a set of symbols expressing the composition of a body : a list of ingredients of a patent medicine :(*pl.* **formulae,** *form'ū-lē,* **form'ūlas**).—*adjs.* **form'ūlar, formū-laris'tic.**—*ns.* **formūlarisā'tion, formūlā'tion** ; **form'ūlary,** a formula : a book of formulae or precedents.—*adj.* prescribed : ritual.—*vs.t.* **form'ū-late, form'ūlise,** to reduce to or express in a formula : to state or express in a clear or definite form. [L. *förmula* dim. of *förma.*]

fornent, *för-nent'*, *adv.* and *prep.* (*Scot.*) right opposite to.—Also **foreanent', fornenst'.**

fornicate, *for'ni-kāt*, *adj.* arched : (*bot.*) arching over.—*n.* **fornicā'tion.** [L. *fornicātus—fornix,* a vault, arch.]

fornicate, *for'ni-kāt*, *v.i.* to commit fornication.— *ns.* **fornicā'tion,** voluntary sexual intercourse of the unmarried : sometimes extended to cases where one is unmarried : (*B.*) adultery, or (*fig.*) idolatry ; **for'nicātor ; for'nicātress.** [L. *forni-cārī, -ātus—fornix,* a vault, brothel.]

fornix, *for'niks, n.* something resembling an arch : an arched formation of the brain. [L.]

forpine, *for-pīn', v.i.* (*Spens.*) to waste away.

forpit, forpet, *for'pit, n.* (*Scot.*) a fourth part (now of a peck). **[fourth part.]**

forrad, *for'əd,* **forrit** (*Scot.*), *for'it, adv.* forms of **forward.**—*comp.* **forr'ader.**

forray, *for-ā', n.* Spenser's form of **foray.**

forren (*Milt.*). Same as **foreign.**

forsake, *fər-sāk', v.t.* to desert : to abandon: (*pr.p.* **forsak'ing ;** *pa.t.* **forsook' ;** *pa.p.* **forsāk'en**).— *adj.* **forsāk'en.**—*adv.* **forsāk'enly.**—*ns.* **for-sāk'enness ; forsāk'ing,** abandonment. [O.E. *forsacan—for-,* away, *sacan,* to strive.]

forsay, foresay, *fər-sā', v.t.* to forbid : (*Spens.*) to renounce : (*Spens.*) to banish. [O.E. *forsecgan— for-,* against, *secgan,* to say.]

forset-seller. See **fossit-seller.**

forslack, *for-slak', v.t.* (*Spens.*) to injure by slackness.

forslow, forsloe, foreslow, *for-slō', v.t.* (*Spens.*) to delay.—*v.i.* (*Shak.*) to delay.

forsooth, *fər-sōōth', adv.* in truth : certainly (now only ironically). **[for sooth.]**

forspeak, forespeak, *fər-spēk', v.t.* (*Shak.*) to forbid : (*Shak.*) to speak against : (now *Scot.*) to bewitch.

forspend, *fər-spend', v.t.* to wear out (*pa.t.* and *pa.p.* **forspent'**).—Also **forespend.**

forswatt, *fər-swat', adj.* (*Spens.*) covered with sweat. [Pfx. *for-,* inten., and *swat,* old pa.p. of **sweat.**]

forswear, *fər-swār', v.t.* to deny or renounce upon oath.—*v.i.* to swear falsely: (*pa.t.* **forswore' ;** *pa.p.* **forswōrn'**).—*adj.* **forsworn',** perjured, having forsworn oneself.—*n.* **forsworn'ness.**— **forswear oneself,** to swear falsely.

forswink, *fər-swingk', v.t.* to exhaust by labour.— *adi.* **forswunk'** (*Spens.* **forswonck'**), over-worked.

Forsythia, *for-sī'thi-ä, n.* a genus of oleaceous shrubs with flowers like jasmine. [After William Forsyth (1737-1804), botanist.]

fort, *fört, n.* a small fortress : an outlying trading-station.—*v.t.* to fortify. [Fr.,—L. *fortis,* strong]

fortalice, *fort'ə-lis, n.* a fortress : a small outwork of a fortification. [L.L. *fortalitia*—L. *fortis.*]

forte, fort, n. that in which one excels : the upper half of a sword or foil blade—the strong part. [Fr. *fort,* strong.]

forte, *for'te, adj.* and *adv.* (*mus.*) loud (*superl.* **fortis'simo,** *double superl.* **fortissis'simo,** as loud as possible).—*n.* a loud passage in music.—*n.* **fortepia'no,** an old name for the pianoforte.— *adj.* and *adv.* loud with immediate relapse into softness. [It.]

forth, *förth, adv.* forward : onward : out : into the open : progressively, in continuation : abroad.— *prep.* (*Shak.*) out of, forth from.—*v.i.* **forthcome',** to come forth.—*adj.* **forthcom'ing,** just coming forth : about to appear : approaching : at hand, ready to be produced.—*ns.* **forth'going,** a going forth ; **forth'-putting,** action of putting forth : (*U.S.*) undue forwardness.—*adj.* forward.—*adv.*

forth'right (or *-rīt'*), straightforward : straight-way.—*n.* (*Shak.*) a straight path.—*adj.* straight-forward : downright.—*adv.* **forthwith** (*-with', -widh',* or *förth'*), immediately.—**and so forth,** and so on. [O.E. *forth—fore,* before ; Du. *voort,* Ger. *fort.*]

forthink, *fər-thingk', v.t.* (*Spens.*) to be sorry for : to change one's mind about.

forthy, for-dhi', adv. (*Spens.*) therefore : for that. [O.E. *forthȳ—for,* and *thȳ,* instrumental case of *thæt,* that.]

forties, fortieth. See **forty,** and under **roar.**

fortify, *for'ti-fī, v.t.* to strengthen with forts, etc., against attack : to invigorate : to confirm : to strengthen (esp. certain wines) by adding alcohol : to enrich (a food) by adding e.g. vitamins : (*pr.p.* **for'tifying ;** *pa.t.* and *pa.p.* **for'tified**).—*adj.* **for'tifiable.**—*ns.* **fortificā'tion,** the art of strengthening a military position by means of defensive works : the work so constructed : that which fortifies ; **for'tifier.** [Fr. *fortifier*—L.L. *fortificāre*—*fortis,* strong, *facĕre,* to make.]

fortilage, *för'ti-lāj, n.* (*Spens.*) a variant of **fortalice.**

fortissimo. See **forte.**

fortitude, *for'ti-tūd, n.* courage in endurance : (*obs.*) strength.—*adj.* **fortitū'dinous.** [L. *forti-tūdō, -inis—fortis,* strong.]

fortlet, *fört'let, n.* a little fort.

fortnight, *fort'nīt, n.* two weeks or fourteen days.— *adj.* and *adv.* **for'nightly,** once a fortnight. [O.E. *féowertȳne niht,* fourteen nights.]

fortress, *for'tris, n.* a fortified place : a defence.— *v.t.* (*Shak.*) to guard. [O.Fr. *forteresse,* another form of *fortelesce* (see **fortalice**).]

fortuitous, *for-tū'i-təs, adj.* happening by chance.— *ns.* **fortū'itism,** belief in evolution by fortuitous variation ; **fortū'itist.**—*adv.* **fortū'itously.**—*ns.* **fortū'itousness, fortū'ity.** [L. *fortuītus.*]

fortune, *for'tūn, n.* whatever comes by lot or chance : luck : the arbitrary ordering of events : the lot that falls to one in life : success : a great accumulation of wealth : (*obs.*) an heiress.—*v.i.* to befall.—*v.t.* to determine the fortune of.—*adj.* **for'tunate,** happening by good fortune : lucky : auspicious : felicitous.—*adv.* **for'tunately.**—*ns.* **for'tunateness ; for'tūne-book,** a book for use in fortune-telling.—*adj.* **for'tuned,** supplied by fortune.—*n.* **for'tune-hunter,** one who hunts for a wealthy marriage.—*adj.* **for'tuneless,** without a fortune: luckless.—*v.i.* **for'tune-tell** (back-forma-tion).—*ns.* **for'tune-teller,** one who professes to foretell one's fortune ; **for'tune-telling.**—*v.t.* **for'tunize** (*Spens.*), to make fortunate or happy. [Fr.,—L. *fortūna.*]

forty, *for'ti, adj.* and *n.* four times ten :—*pl.* **for'ties,** esp. the fortieth to forty-ninth years (of life, a century)—see also **roaring forties.**—*adj.* **for'tieth,** the last of forty : equal to one of forty equal parts.—*n.* one of forty equal parts.—*adj.* **for'tyish,** apparently about forty years old.—*n.* **forty-nin'er,** a gold-seeker in the 1849 rush in California.—**forty winks,** a short nap, esp. after dinner ; **the Forty,** the French Academy ; **the Forty-five,** the Jacobite rebellion of 1745. [O.E. *féowertig—féower,* four, *-tig,* ten (as suffix).]

forum, *fō'rəm, n.* a market-place, esp. that in Rome where public business was transacted and justice dispensed : the courts of law as opposed to Parliament. [L. *fŏrum,* akin to *forās,* out of doors.]

forwander, *fər-won'dər, v.i.* (*Spens.*) to wander till wearied : to stray far.—*adj.* **forwan'dered,** strayed.

forward, *for'wərd, adj.* near or at the forepart : in advance : well advanced : ready : too ready : presumptuous : officious : earnest : early ripe.— *v.t.* to help on : to send on.—*advs.* **for'ward, for'wards,** towards what is in front : onward : progressively.—*ns.* **for'ward,** in football, etc., a player in the front line ; **for'warder ; for'warding,** the act of sending forward merchandise, etc.— *adv.* **for'wardly.**—*n.* **for'wardness.** [O.E. *fore-ward* (W.S. *foreweard*)—*fore-,* and *-ward* (*-weard*) sig. direction ; the *s* of *forwards* is a gen. ending (cf. Ger. *vorwärts*).]

forwarn, forewarn, *fɔr-, for-wawrn′, v.t.* to forbid. —See also **forewarn.** [Pfx. *for-,* against, and *warn.*]

forwaste, *for-wāst′, v.t.* (*Spens.*) to waste utterly.

forweary, *fɔr-, for-wē′ri, v.t.* (*Spens.*) to weary out.

forwent, *fɔr-, for-went′.* See **forgo.**

forwhy, *fɔr-hwī′, conj.* (*arch.*) because.

forworn, *fɔr-wōrn′, adj.* (*Spens.*) much worn.

forzando, *for-tsän′dō,* **forzato,** *-tsä′tō, adjs.* and *advs.* sforzando. [It., forcing, forced.]

foss, fosse, *fos, n.* a ditch, moat, trench, or canal.— *adj.* **fossed.**—*ns.* **fossette′,** a small fossa; **Foss(e)′- way,** a Roman road, esp. that from Lincoln to Exeter, with a ditch on each side. [Fr. *fosse*—L. *fossa*—*fodĕre, fossum,* to dig.]

fossa, *fos′ä, n.* (*anat.*) a pit or depression.—*ns.* **foss′ula,** a small depression or groove.—*adj.* **foss′ulate.** [L., a ditch.]

fossa, *fos′ä,* **foussa,** *fōōs′ä, n.* a Madagascan animal more or less akin to the civets. [Malagasy.]

fosset-seller, *fos′it-sel′ər, n.* (*Shak.*) apparently one who sells faucets.—Another reading for **set′-seller.** [*Fosset, forset,* obs. forms of **faucet.**]

fossick, *fos′ik, v.i.* to be troublesome: to undermine another's diggings, or work over waste-heaps for gold: to search about for any kind of profit: to prospect.—*v.t.* to dig out.—*ns.* **foss′icker** a mining gleaner who works over old diggings, and scratches about in the beds of creeks; **foss′icking.** [Australian; ety. dub.]

fossil, *fos′l,* or *-il, n.* (*obs.*) a rock or mineral dug from the earth: (*geol.*) a relic or trace of a former living thing preserved in the rocks: an antiquated, out-of-date, or unchanging person or thing.— *adj.* dug out of the earth: in the condition of a fossil: antiquated.—*adj.* **fossilif′erous,** bearing or containing fossils.—*n.* **fossilisā′tion.**—*v.t.* **foss′ilise,** to convert into a fossil.—*v.i.* to become fossil. [Fr. *fossile*—L. *fossilis*—*fodĕre,* to dig.]

fossor, *fos′or, n.* a grave-digger.—*adj.* **fossorial** (*-ō′ri-al*), adapted for digging. [L. *fossor*—*fodĕre,* to dig.]

foster, *fos′tər, v.t.* to bring up or nurse: to encourage: to promote: to cherish.—*ns.* **fos′terage,** the act or custom of fostering or nursing: the condition or relation of foster-child: **fos′terbrother,** a male child of different parents brought up along with one; **fos′ter-child,** a child nursed or brought up by one who is not its parent; **fos′ter-daughter; fos′terer; fos′ter-father,** one who brings up a child in place of its father; **fos′terling,** a foster-child; **fos′ter-mother,** one who brings up a child not her own: an apparatus for rearing chickens; **fos′ter-nurse; fos′terparent; fos′ter-sister; fos′ter-son; fos′tress.** [O.E. *fóstrian,* to nourish, *fóstor,* food.]

foster, *fos′tər, n.* (*Spens.*) a forester.

fother, *fodh′ər, v.t.* to cover (a sail, etc.) with yarn and oakum, as stopping for a leak. [Perh. Du. *voederen* (mod. *voeren*), or L.G. *fodern,* to line.]

fother, *fodh′ər, n.* a load, quantity: a cart-load: a definite weight—of lead, 19½ cwt. [O.E. *fóther;* Ger. *fuder.*]

fou, *fōō, adj.* (*Scot.*) full: drunk.

fou, *fōō, n.* (*Scot.*) a bushel. [Perh. **full.**]

fouat, fouet, *fōō′ət, n.* (*Scot.*) the house-leek.

foud, *fowd, n.* a bailiff or magistrate in Orkney and Shetland.—*n.* **foud′rie,** his jurisdiction. [O.N. *fógeti;* Ger. *vogt;* from L. *vocātus—vocāre,* to call.]

foudroyant, *fōō-droi′ənt, -drwä′yän′, adj.* thundering: sudden and overwhelming. [Fr., pr.p. of *foudroyer—foudre,* lightning.]

fougade, *fōō-gäd′,* **fougasse,** *fōō-gäs′, ns.* (*mil.*) a small mine loaded with stones. [Fr.]

fought, *fawt, pa.t.* and *pa.p.,* **foughten,** *fawt′n,* old *pa.p.,* of **fight.**

foughty, *fow′ti, fōō′ti, adj.* (*dial.*) musty. [O.E. *fúht,* moist.]

foul, *fowl, adj.* filthy: dirty: disfigured: untidy: loathsome: obscene: impure: shameful: gross: in bad condition: stormy: unfavourable: unfair: little worth: choked up: entangled: (*Shak.*) ugly.— *v.t.* to make foul: to soil: to collide with, come in accidental contact with.—*v.i.* to collide.—*n.* act of fouling: any breach of the rules in games or contests.—*adv.* in a foul manner: unfairly.—*n.* **foul′-brood,** a bacterial disease of bee larvae.— *adj.* **foul′-faced** (*Shak.*), ugly-faced.—*n.* **foul′- fish,** fish during the spawning season.—*adv.* **foul′ly.**—*n.* **foul′mart** (see **foumart**).—*adjs.* **foul′-mouthed, foul′-spok′en,** addicted to the use of foul or profane language.—*ns.* **foul′mouth′edness; foul′ness; foul′-play′,** unfair action in any game or contest: dishonest dealing generally: violence or murder.—**claim a foul,** to assert that a rule has been broken, and claim the penalty; **fall foul of,** to come against: to clash with: to assail; **foul (be)fall,** bad luck to; **make foul water,** to come into such shallow water that the keel raises the mud. [O.E. *fúl;* Ger. *faul,* Goth. *fúls.*]

foulard, *fōō-lär′, -lärd′, n.* a soft untwilled silk fabric: a silk handkerchief. [Fr.]

foulder, *fowl′dər, v.i.* (*Spens.*) to thunder. [O.Fr. *fouldre*—L. *fulgur,* lightning.]

foumart, *fōō′märt, -mart, n.* a polecat. [M.E. *fulmard*—O.E. *fúl,* foul, *mærth,* bad luck to; *marten.*]

found, *pa.t.* and *pa.p.* of **find.**—*n.* **found′ling,** a little child found deserted.

found, *fownd, v.t.* to lay the bottom or foundation of: to establish on a basis: to originate: to endow. —*v.i.* to rely.—*ns.* **foundā′tion,** the act of founding: the base of a building: the groundwork or basis: a permanent fund for a benevolent purpose or for some special object; **foundā′tioner,** one supported from the funds or foundation of an institution; **foundā′tion-mus′lin, -net,** gummed fabrics used for stiffening dresses and bonnets; **foundā′tion-stone,** one of the stones forming the foundation of a building, esp. a stone laid with public ceremony; **foundā′tion-stop,** any organ stop whose sounds are those belonging to the keys, or differing by whole octaves only: a fundamental flue stop; **found′er,** one who founds, establishes, or originates: an endower (*fem.* **found′ress**). [Fr. *fonder*—L. *fundāre, -ātum,* to found—*fundus,* the bottom.]

found, *fownd, v.t.* to melt: to make by melting: to cast.—*ns.* **found′er; found′ing; found′ry,** the art of founding or casting: a place where founding is carried on. [Fr. *fondre*—L. *fundĕre, fūsum,* to pour.]

founder, *fownd′ər, v.i.* to subside: to collapse: to go to the bottom: to fill with water and sink: to stumble: to go lame: to stick in mud.—*v.t.* to cause to founder.—*n.* a collapse: laminitis.—*adj.* **found′erous,** causing to founder. [O.Fr. *fondrer,* to fall in, *fond,* bottom—L. *fundus,* bottom.]

fount, *fownt, n.* a complete assortment of types of one sort, with all that is necessary for printing in that kind of letter.—Also (esp. in U.S.) **font.** [Fr. *fonte—fondre*—L. *fundĕre,* to cast.]

fount, *fownt, n.* a spring of water: a source.—*adj.* **fount′ful,** full of springs. [L. *fōns, fontis.*]

fountain, *fownt′in, n.* a spring of water, a jet: a structure for supplying drinking water or other liquid: an ornamental structure with jets, spouts, and basins of water: a reservoir from which oil, ink, etc., flows, as in a lamp, a pen: the source; **fount′ain-head,** the head or source: the beginning.—*adj.* **fount′ainless.**—*n.* **fount′ain-pen′,** a pen with a reservoir for ink. [Fr. *fontaine*— L.L. *fontāna*—L. *fōns, fontis,* a spring.]

four, *fōr, n.* the cardinal number next above three: a symbol representing that number: a set of four things or persons (leaves, oarsmen, etc.): a four-oar boat: a four-cylinder engine or car: a shoe or other article of a size denoted by 4: a card with four pips: a score of four points, tricks, strokes, etc.: the fourth hour after midday or midnight: (in *pl.*) a snack taken at 4 o'clock (also **fours′es**): (in *pl.*) the four extremities (in the phrase *on all fours*).—*adj.* of the number four.—*n.* **four′-ale′,** ale sold at fourpence a quart.—*adj.* **four′-ball** (*golf*), played two against two with four balls, best ball counting.—*n. sing.* **four′-eyes,** the fish *Anableps.*—*adj.* **four′-figure,** running into four figures: to four places of decimals.—*n.* **four′-flush′** (*poker*), a hand with four cards of the same suit.—*v.i.* to bluff with a four-flush: to bluff.—*adj.* bluffing: not genuine.—*adj.* and *adv.* **four'-fold**, in four divisions: folded in four thicknesses: four times as much.—*n.* **four'foldness.**—*adjs.* **four'-foot**, measuring four feet (**four-foot way** in railways, a space of 4 ft. 8½ in. between the rails): having the pitch of an open organ pipe four feet long, or having that pitch for its lowest note; **four'-foot'ed**, having four feet; **four'-hand'ed**, having four hands: (*cards*) played by four players; **four'-horse**, drawn by four horses.—*n.* **four'-hours** (Scot. *fowr-ōōrz*), a refreshment about four o'clock.—*adj.* **four'-inched** (*Shak.*) four inches wide.—*n.* **four'-in-hand**, a coach drawn by four horses, two by two, driven by one person: the team drawing it: a necktie tied with a flat slip-knot, with dangling ends.—Also *adj.* and *adv.*—*adjs.* **four'-leaved**, with four leaves or leaflets; **four'-legged'.**—*ns.* **four'-oar**, a boat rowed with four oars; **four'-o'clock**, marvel of Peru: the friar-bird.—*adjs.* **four'-part, four-part'ed**, in four parts: divided into four nearly to the base.—*n.* **four'-pence**, the value of four pennies; **four'penny**, an old silver coin worth fourpence.—*adj.* sold or offered for fourpence.—*n.* **four'-post'er**, large bed with four curtain posts; **four'-pound'er**, a gun that throws a four-pound shot: a four-pound loaf.—*adj.* **four'score**, eighty; **four'-scorth** (*Addison*), eightieth.—*ns.* **four'-seat'er**, a vehicle seated for four; **four'-some**, a group of four: anything in which four act together, esp. a game of golf (two against two, partners playing the same ball) or a reel—also *adj.*—*adjs.* **four'square**, square: presenting a firm bold front to all; **four'-wheeled**.—*n.* **four'-wheel'er**, a cab or other vehicle with four wheels. —**four-stroke cycle**, in an internal-combustion engine, a recurring series of four strokes of the piston—an out-stroke drawing the mixed gases into the cylinder, an in-stroke compressing them, an out-stroke impelled by their explosion and working the engine, and an in-stroke driving out the burnt gas; **on all fours**, on four feet or hands and feet, hands and knees: analogous, strictly comparable; **the four seas** (see **sea**). [O.E. *féower;* Ger. *vier.*]

fourchette, *fŏŏr-shet'*, *n.* anything forked: a forked piece between glove fingers, uniting the front and back parts: a combination of the card next above and that next below the one just played: part of the external female genitals. [Fr., dim. of *fourche*—L. *furca*, fork.]

Fourcroya, *fŏŏr-kroi'ä.* Same as **Furcraea.**

fourgon, *fŏŏr-gon²'*, *n.* a baggage-wagon. [Fr.]

Fourierism, *fŏŏ'ri-ər-izm*, *n.* the socialistic system of F. M. Charles *Fourier* (1772-1837), based on the harmony educed by the free play of his twelve radical passions.

fourteen, *fŏr-tēn'*, or *fŏr'tēn*, *n.* and *adj.* four and ten.—*n.* **fourteen'er**, a verse line of fourteen syllables.—*adj.* **four'teenth** (or *-tēnth'*), last of fourteen: equal to one of fourteen equal parts.—*n.* a fourteenth part.—*adv.* **fourteenth'ly.** [O.E. *féowerténe (-tiene);* see **four** and **ten**.]

fourth, *fōrth*, *adj.* last of four: equal to one of four equal parts.—*n.* one of four equal parts: an interval of three (conventionally called four) diatonic degrees: a tone at that interval from another: a combination of two tones separated by that interval.—*adv.* **fourth'ly.**—*adj.* **fourth'-rate**. [O.E. *féowertha, féortha.*]

fouter, fou'tre, *fŏŏ'tər,* (*Shak.*) foot'ra, -trä, *n.* a fig (as a type of worthlessness). [O.E. *foutre*—L. *futuĕre*, to copulate with.]

fouth, fowth, *footh, n.* (*Scot.*) abundance. [**full**, suff. *-th*.]

fovea, *fō'vi-ä*, *n.* (*anat.*) a depression or pit (*pl.* **foveae,** *-ē*).—*adjs.* **fo'veal**; **fo'veate**, pitted.—*n.* **fovē'ola**, a small depression—also **fo'veole.** [L. *fŏvea.*]

fowl, *fowl*, *n.* a bird: a bird of the barn-door or poultry kind, a cock or hen: the flesh of fowl (*pl.* **fowls, fowl**).—*v.i.* to kill or try to kill wildfowl.—*ns.* **fowl'er**, one who takes wildfowl; **fowl'ing;** **fowl'ing-net**, a net for catching birds; **fowl'ing-**

piece, a light gun for small-shot, used in fowling. [O.E. *fugol;* Ger. *vogel.*]

fox, *foks*, *n.* a cunning animal akin to the dog (*fem.* **vix'en**): any one notorious for cunning: extended to other animals, as black-fox (pekan), flying-fox: (*obs.*) a kind of sword.—*v.t.* (*slang*) to baffle, deceive, cheat.—*v.i.* (*coll.*) to act cunningly, to cheat.—*ns.* **fox'-bat**, a flying-fox, a fruit-bat; **fox'berry**, the bearberry: the cowberry; **fox'-brush**, the tail of a fox; **fox'-earth**, a fox's burrow.—*adj.* **foxed**, (of books) discoloured, spotted: drunk.—*ns.* **fox'-ē'vil**, alopecia; **fox'-glove**, a plant (Digitalis) with flowers like glove-fingers; **fox'-grape**, an American grape (*Vitis Labrusca;* also *V. rotundifolia*); **fox'hound**, a hound used for chasing foxes; **fox'-hunt; fox'-hunt'er; fox'-hunting; fox'iness**, craftiness: decay: a harsh, sour taste: spotted state as in books; **fox'ing**, act of one who foxes; **fox'-shark**, a large long-tailed shark, the thresher; **fox'ship** (*Shak.*), the character of a fox, craftiness; **fox'-tail**, a fox's brush: a genus (Alopecurus) of grasses, with head like a fox's tail; **fox'-terr'ier**, a kind of terrier trained to unearth foxes; **fox'-trap; fox'-trot**, a horse's pace with short steps, as in changing from trotting to walking: an American shuffling dance to syncopated music.—*adj.* **fox'y**, of foxes: fox-like: cunning: reddish brown.—**fox and geese**, a game played with pieces on a board, where the object is for certain pieces called the geese to surround or corner one called the fox or prevent him from passing. [O.E. *fox;* Ger. *fuchs.*]

foy, *foi*, *n.* (*Spens.*) allegiance. [Fr. *foi*, faith.]

foy, *foi*, *n.* (*prov.*) a parting entertainment or gift. [Du. *fooi.*]

foyer, *fwä-yä, n.* in theatres, a public room opening on the lobby. [Fr.,—L. *focus*, hearth.]

foyle, foyne, Spenserian spellings of **foil, foin.**

fozy, *fō'zi, adj.* (*Scot.*) spongy: wanting in freshness: fat: dull-witted.—*n.* **foz'iness**, softness, want of spirit. [Cf. Du. *voos.* spongy.]

frab, *frab, v.t.* (*dial.*) to worry.—*adj.* **frabb'it**, peevish.

frabjous, *frab'jəs, adj.* perh. joyous: surpassing. [Invented by Lewis Carroll.]

fracas, *frak'ä, frä-kä', n.* uproar: a noisy quarrel (*pl.* **fracas,** *-käz*). [Fr.,—It. *fracasso—fracassare*, to make an uproar.]

frack, *fräk, adj.* (*Scot.*) prompt: eager: lusty. [O.E. *fræc, frec.*]

fract, *frakt, v.t.* (*Shak.*) to break, to violate.—*adj.* **fract'ed**, broken: violated: (*her.*) having a part displaced, as if broken.—*n.* **frac'tion** (*-shən*), a fragment or small piece: (*arith.*) any part of a unit (see **decimal** and **vulgar, proper** and **improper**): (*Shak.*) a breach of amity: a portion separaſed by fractionation: the breaking of the bread in the Eucharist.—*adjs.* **frac'tional**, belonging to a fraction or fractions: of the nature of a fraction: **frac'tionary**, fractional: fragmentary.—*v.t.* **frac'tionate**, to separate the components of by distillation or otherwise.—*n.* **fractiona'tion.**—*v.t.* **frac'tionise**, to break up into fractions.—*n.* **frac'tionlet**, a small fraction.—*adj.* **frac'tious**, ready to quarrel: cross.—*adv.* **frac'-tiously.**—*ns.* **frac'tiousness; frac'ture** (*-tyər*), breaking: the breach or part broken: the surface of breaking, other than cleavage: the breaking of a bone.—*v.t.* and *v.i* to break through: to crack.—**fractional distillation,** a distillation process for the separation of the various constituents of liquid mixtures by means of their different boiling points; **simple fracture,** a fracture of bone without wound in the skin. [L. *frangĕre, frāctum,* to break (partly through Fr.).]

frae. See **fro.**

fraenum. Same as **frenum.**

Fragaria, *frə-gā'ri-ä, n.* the strawberry genus. [L. *frāgum,* the strawberry.]

fragile, *fraj'il,* also *-īl, adj.* easily broken: frail: delicate.—*n.* **fragility** (*frə-jil'*), the state of being fragile. [Fr.,—L. *fragilis—frangĕre, frāctum.*]

fragment, *frag'mənt, n.* a piece broken off: an unfinished portion.—*adj.* **fragmental** (*-ment'*;

also *frag'mən-təl*), composed of fragments of older rocks: in fragments.—*adv.* frag'mentarily.—*n.* frag'mentariness.—*adjs.* frag'mentary, frag'ment'ed, consisting of fragments or pieces: broken.—*n.* fragmentā'tion, division into fragments: (*biol.*) cell division without mitosis. [L. *fragmentum—frangĕre, frāctum*, to break.]

fragor, *frā'gor, n.* a crash. [L. *frăgor*.]

fragrant, *frā'grənt, adj.* sweet-scented.—*ns.* fra'grance, fra'grancy, pleasantness of smell: sweet or grateful influence.—*adv.* fra'grantly.—*n.* fra'grantness. [L. *frăgrāns, -āntis*, pr.p. of *frăgrāre*, to smell.]

frail, *frāl, adj.* very easily shattered: (*esp. Scot.*) feeble and infirm: decrepit: morally weak: (euphemistically) unchaste: (*Spens.*) tender.—*n.* (*slang*) a woman.—*adj.* frail'ish, somewhat frail.—*adv.* frail'ly.—*ns.* frail'ness, frail'ty (*Spens.* fra'iltee), weakness: infirmity. [O.Fr. *fraile*—L. *fragilis*, fragile.]

frail, *frāl, n.* a rush: a rush-basket. [O.Fr. *frayel*.]

fraim. See frem.

fraise, *frāz, n.* (*fort.*) a horizontal or nearly horizontal palisade: a tool for enlarging a drillhole: a 16th-cent. ruff.—*v.t.* to fence with a fraise. [Fr.]

fraise, *frāz, n.* (*prov.*) commotion.

fraise, *frāz.* See froise.

fraktur, *fräk-tŏŏr', n.* German type. [Ger.—L. *frāctūra*, breaking.]

framboesia, *fram-bē'zi-ä, n.* yaws. [Fr. *framboise*, raspberry.]

frame, *frām, v.t.* to form: to shape: to put together: to plan, adjust, or adapt: to contrive or devise: to concoct: to bring about: to articulate: to direct (one's steps): to set about: to enclose in a frame or border: to make victim of a frame-up.—*v.i.* to make one's way: to resort: (*dial.*) to pretend: to make a move: to give promise of progress or success: (*B.*) to contrive.—*n.* the body: a putting together of parts: structure: a case made to enclose, border or support anything: the skeleton of anything: the rigid part of a bicycle: a structure on which embroidery is worked: a stocking-making machine: (*obs.*) a loom: a structure on which bees build a honeycomb: in gardening, a structure used for the cultivation or the sheltering of plants: state (of mind), humour, mood: (*Shak.*) the act of devising: a unit picture in a cinematograph film: in television, one of the interlaced sets of scanning lines (*U.S. field*): (snooker, etc.) the triangular support in which the balls are grouped for the break: the balls so grouped: a game of snooker, etc.—*ns.* frame'-breaker, one who broke stocking-frames on their introduction; frame'-bridge, a bridge constructed of pieces of timber framed together; frame'-house, a house consisting of a skeleton of timber, with boards or shingles laid on; frame'-maker, a maker of picture-frames; fram'er, one who forms or constructs: one who makes frames for pictures, etc.; frame'-saw, a thin saw stretched in a frame; frame'-up (*U.S.*) a trumped-up affair: a staged or preconcerted event; frame'-work, the work that forms the frame: the skeleton or outline of anything; fram'ing, the act of constructing: a frame or setting. [O.E. *framian*, to be helpful, *fram*, forward.]

frampold, *fram'pōld, -pəld, adj.* (*Shak.*) peevish, cross-grained: fiery.—Also fram'pal.—*n.* fram'pler (*Scott*), a brawler. [Ety. obscure.]

franc, *frangk, n.* a coin (100 centimes), forming since 1795 the unit of the French monetary system, and used also in Belgium, Switzerland, etc., long worth about 9½d. [O.Fr. *franc*, from the legend *Francorum rex* on the first coins.]

franchise, *fran'(t)shīz, n.* liberty: a privilege or exemption by prescription or grant: the right of voting, esp. for an M.P.: a voting qualification: (*U.S.*) a commercial concession.—*v.t.* (*obs.*) to enfranchise.—*ns.* fran'chisement (*-shiz-, -chiz-*; *Spens.*), liberation; fran'chiser, a voter. [O.Fr.,—*franc*, free.]

Franciscan, *fran-sis'kən, adj.* belonging to the order of mendicant friars in the R.C. Church,

founded by St. *Francis* of Assisi (1182-1226).—*n.* a monk of this order. [L. *Franciscus*, Francis.]

francium, *fran'si-əm, n.* the chemical element of atomic number 87, discovered by a Frenchwoman, Mlle. Perey. [France.]

Franco-, *frangk'ō-*, in composition, French: French and, as Franco-German, Franco-Russian, etc.—Francomania, -phil(e), -phobe, see Gallomania, etc.

francolin, *frang'kō-lin, n.* a genus (*Francolinus*) of partridges. [Fr.]

frangible, *fran'ji-bl, adj.* easily broken.—*n.* frangibil'ity. [L. *frangĕre*, to break; see fraction.]

frangipani, *fran-ji-pä'nē, n.* the red jasmine or other species of Plumieria, tropical American apocynaceous shrubs with scented flowers: a perfume from or in imitation of red jasmine: (also frangipane, *fran'ji-pān*), a pastry-cake filled with cream, almonds, and sugar. [From the name *Frangipani*.]

franion, *fran'yən, n.* a paramour: a boon-companion: (*Spens.*) a loose woman. [Origin obscure.]

frank, *frangk, adj.* free, open: (*obs.*) liberal: open or candid in expression: (*Spens.*) unrestrained: (*med.*) unmistakable, true (as *frank pus, asthma*).—*v.t.* to sign so as to ensure free carriage: to send free of expense, as a letter.—*n.* the signature of a person who had the right to frank a letter: a franked cover.—*n.* frank'-fee, tenure in fee-simple.—*adv.* frank'ly.—*ns.* frank'ness; frank'-pledge, a mutual suretyship by which the members of a tithing were made responsible for one another; frank'ten'ement, freehold. [O.Fr. *franc*—L.L. *francus*; O.H.G. *Franko*, Frank, hence a free man.]

Frank, *frangk, n.* a German of a confederation in Franconia of which a branch conquered Gaul in the 5th century, and founded France: in the East, a Western European.—*adj.* Frank'ish. [See foregoing.]

frank, *frangk, n.* (*Shak.*) a pig-sty.—*v.t.* (*Shak.*) to shut up in a sty: to cram, to fatten. [O.Fr. *franc*.]

frankalmoign, *frangk'al-moin, n.* (*Eng. law*) a form of land-tenure in which no obligations were enforced except religious ones, as praying, etc. [O.Fr. *franc*, free, *almoigne*, alms.]

Frankenia, *frang-kē'ni-ä, n.* the sea-heath genus, constituting a family Frankeniā'ceae, akin to the tamarisk family. [Named after John *Frankenius* (1590-1661), Swedish physician and botanist.]

Frankenstein, *frangk'ən-stīn, n.* the hero of Mrs. Shelley's romance so named, who by his skill forms an animate creature like a man, only to his own torment: hence, by confusion, any creation that brings disaster to its author.

frankincense, *frangk'in-sens, n.* olibanum, a sweet-smelling resin from Arabia, used as incense: spruce resin.—herb frankincense, laser. [O.Fr. *franc encens*, pure incense.]

franklin, *frangk'lin, n.* (*hist.*) an English freeholder, free from feudal servitude to a subject-superior. [L.L. *francus*; see frank.]

franklinite, *frangk'lin-īt, n.* a zinc-manganese spinel, mined at *Franklin Forge*, New Jersey.]

frantic, *fran'tik, adj.* mad, furious: wild.—*advs.* fran'tically, fran'ticly (*Shak.*)—*adj.* fran'ticmad, raving mad.—*n.* fran'ticness, the state of being frantic. [O.Fr. *frenetique*—L. *phrenēticus*—Gr. *phrenētikos*, mad—*phrēn*, the mind; see phrenetic, frenzy.]

franzy, *fran'zi, adj.* (*prov.*) cross: peevish. [frenzy.]

frap, *frap, v.t.* (now *dial.*) to strike: (*naut.*) to secure by many turns of a lashing. [Fr. *frapper*, to strike.]

frass, *fras, n.* excrement or other refuse of boring larvae. [Ger.,—*fressen*, to eat; cf. fret.]

fratch, *frach, n.* (*prov.*) a quarrel or brawl.—*adjs.* fratch'ety, fratch'y; fratch'ing. [Perh. imit.]

frater, *frā'tər, n.* a refectory: sometimes applied in error to a monastic common-room or to a chapter-house (by confusion with next word).—Also frā'ter-house, frā'try. [O.Fr. *fraitur* for *refreitor*—L.L. *refectōrium*.]

frater, *frā'tər, n.* a friar : a comrade.—*n.* **Fratercula** (*fra-tər'kū-lä*), the puffin genus.—*adj.* **frater'nal** (*fra-tər'nl*), belonging to a brother or brethren : brotherly.—*adv.* **frater'nally.**—*n.* **fraternisā'tion** (*frat-*), the associating as brethren.—*v.i.* **frat'ernise,** to associate as brothers : to seek brotherly fellowship : to come into friendly association.—*ns.* **frat'erniser ; frater'nity,** the state of being brethren : a brotherhood : a society formed on a principle of brotherhood : an American college **association** : any set of people with something in common ; **fratry** (*frāt'ri*), **frāt'ery** : a fraternity : a convent of friars (see also foregoing article). [L. *frāter,* a brother ; cf. **brother,** Gr. *phrātēr,* a clansman, Sans. *bhrāta.*]

fratricide, *frat'ri-sīd,* or *frāt', n.* one who kills his brother : the murder of a brother.—*adj.* **fratrici'dal.** [Fr.,—L. *frāter, frātris, caedĕre,* to kill.]

frau, Frau, *frow, n.* a woman : a wife : Mrs.—*n.* **fräulein, Fräulein** (*froi'līn*), an unmarried woman : often applied to a German governess : Miss. [Ger.]

fraud, *frawd, n.* deceit : imposture : (*Milt.*) a snare : a deceptive trick : (*coll.*) a cheat, swindler : a fraudulent production.—*adj.* **fraud'ful,** deceptive. —*adv.* **fraud'fully.**—*ns.* **fraud'ulence, fraud'ulency.**—*adj.* **fraud'ulent,** using fraud : dishonest. —*adv.* **fraud'ulently.**—**fraudulent bankruptcy,** a bankruptcy in which the insolvent is accessory, by concealment or otherwise, to the diminution of the funds divisible among his creditors. [O.Fr. *fraude*—L. *fraus, fraudis,* fraud.]

fraught, *frawt, n.* a load, cargo : the freight of a ship.—*v.t.* to fill, store.—*v.i.* (*Shak.*) to form the freight of a vessel.—*adj.* **freighted,** laden : filled.— *n.* **fraught'age** (*Shak.*), loading cargo. [Prob. Old Du. *vracht.* Cf. **freight.**]

Fraxinus, *frak'si-nəs, n.* the ash genus.—**Fraxinell'a,** dittany (from its ashlike leaves). [L., an ash-tree.]

fray, *frā, n.* an affray : a brawl.—*v.t.* to frighten. [Aphetic from **affray.**]

fray, *frā, v.t.* to wear off by rubbing : to ravel out the end or edge of.—*v.i.* to become frayed : to rub off the velvet from the new antlers.—*n.* **fray'ing,** the action of the verb : frayed off material. [Fr. *frayer*—L. *fricāre,* to rub.]

frazil, *frāz'il, frā'zil, n.* ground-ice : ice in small spikes and plates in rapid streams. [Canadian Fr. *frasil* ; prob. Fr. *fraisil,* cinders.]

frazzle, *fraz'l, v.t.* (*U.S.*) to fray, wear out.—*n.* state of being worn out. [Origin unknown.]

freak, *frēk, n.* caprice : sport : an abnormal production of nature, a monstrosity.—*ns.* **freak'iness, freak'ishness.**—*adjs.* **freak'ish, freak'ful, freak'y,** apt to change the mind suddenly : capricious.—*adv.* **freak'ishly.** [A late word ; cf. O.E. *frícian,* to dance.]

freak, *frēk, v.t.* (*Milt.*) to spot or streak : to variegate.—*n.* a streak of colour. [Perh. the same as the foregoing.]

freckle, *frek'l, v.t.* to spot : to colour with spots.— *n.* a yellowish or brownish-yellow spot on the skin, esp. of fair-haired persons : any small spot.— *n.* **freck'ling,** a little spot.—*adjs.* **freck'ly, freck'led,** full of freckles. [O.N. *freknur* (pl.), Dan. *fregne.*]

free, *frē, adj.* not bound : at liberty : not under arbitrary government : not strict, or bound by rules : not literal : unimpeded : unconstrained : readily cut, separated or wrought : ready (esp. in phrase *free to confess*) : guiltless : frank : lavish : uncombined : unattached : exempt (with *from*) : having a franchise (with *of*) : without payment : bold : indecent : (*compar.* **freer,** *frē'ər* ; *superl.* **freest,** *frē'ist*).—*adv.* freely : without payment : without obstruction.—*v.t.* to set at liberty : to deliver from what confines : to rid (with *from, of*) : (*pr.p.* **free'ing** ; *pa.t.* and *pa.p.* **freed**).—*ns.* **free'agency,** state or power of acting freely, or without necessity or constraint upon the will ; **free'agent ; free'-and-eas'y,** a public-house club where good fellows gather to smoke and sing.— *adj.* informal in manners, without ceremonious restraint.—*adj.* **free'-arm,** with unsupported arm.

—*ns.* **free'-bench,** a widow's right to dower out of her husband's lands ; **free'-board,** the distance between waterline and deck : a strip of land outside a fence, or a right thereto ; **free'booter** (Du. *vrijbuiter*), one who roves about freely in search of booty ; **free'bootery.**—*adj., n.* **free'-booting.**— *n.* **free'booty.**—*adj.* **free'born,** born free.—*ns.* **free'-cit'y,** a city constituting a state in itself ; **free'-cost,** freedom from charges ; **freed'man,** a man who has been a slave and has been freed (*pl.* **freed'men** ; *fem.* **freed'woman** ; *pl.* **freed'women**) ; **free'dom,** liberty : frankness : outspokenness : unhampered boldness : separation : privileges connected with a city (often granted as an honour merely) : improper familiarity : licence ; **free'-fish'er,** one who has a right to take fish in certain waters ; **free'-food'er,** an opponent of taxes on food.—*adj.* **free-foot'ed** (*Shak.*), not restrained in movement.—*n.* **free'-for-all'** (*U.S.*) a contest open to anybody : a free fight.—*adjs.* **free'-hand,** executed by the unguided hand ; **free'-hand'ed,** open-handed : liberal ; **free'-heart'ed,** open-hearted : liberal.—*ns.* **free'-heart'edness ; free'hold,** a property held free of duty except to the king ; **free'holder,** one who possesses a freehold ; **free'-lā'bour,** voluntary, not slave, labour ; **free'-lance,** one of the mercenary knights and men-at-arms who after the Crusades wandered about Europe : an unattached journalist, politician, etc. : anyone who works for himself, without an employer ; **free'-liv'er,** one who freely indulges his appetite for eating and drinking : a glutton ; **free'-love,** the claim to freedom in sexual relations, unshackled by marriage or obligation to aliment.—*adv.* **free'ly.**—*ns.* **free'man,** a man who is free or enjoys liberty : one who holds a particular franchise or privilege : (*pl.* **free'men** ; *fem.* **free'-woman** ; *pl.* **free'women**) ; **free'mā'son,** in the Middle Ages, a stone-mason of a superior grade : a member of a secret fraternity, united in lodges for social enjoyment and mutual assistance.—*adj.* **freemason'ic.**—*n.* **freemā'sonry,** the institutions, practices, etc. of Freemasons.—*adj.* **free'-mind'ed,** with a mind free or unperplexed : without a load of care.—*ns.* **free'ness ; free'-port,** a port where no duties are levied on articles of commerce ; **freer** (*frē'ər*), liberator.—*adj.* **free'-reed** (*mus.*) having a reed that does not touch the side of the aperture.—*ns.* **free'-school,** a school where no tuition fees are exacted.—*v.i.* **free'-select',** (*Austr.*) to take up crown-land under the Land Laws.—*ns.* **free'-selec'tion,** the process of doing so : the land so taken ; **free'-selec'tor** (also **selec'tion, selec'tor**) ; **free'-shot** (Ger. *Freischütz*), a legendary hunter and marksman who gets a number of bullets (*Freikugeln*) from the devil, six of which always hit the mark, while the seventh remains at the devil's disposal.—*adj.* **free'-soil,** in favour of free territory, opposed to slavery.—*n.* **free-soil'er.**—*adj.* **free'-spök'en,** accustomed to speak without reserve.—*ns.* **free'-spök'enness ; free'stone,** any easily wrought building stone without tendency to split in layers.— *adj.* having a stone from which the pulp easily separates, as a peach—opp. to **clingstone.**—*adjs.* **free'-swimm'ing,** swimming about, not attached. —*ns.* **free'thinker,** one who rejects authority in religion : a rationalist ; **free'thinking ; free'-thought.**—*adj.* **free'-tongued,** free-spoken.—*ns.* **free'-trade,** free or unrestricted trade : free interchange of commodities without protective duties ; **free'-trad'er,** one who practises or advocates this : a smuggler : a smuggling vessel ; **free'-vers'er,** a writer of free verse, a verslibrist ; **free'-wheel',** the mechanism of a bicycle by which the hind-wheel may be temporarily disconnected and set free from the driving-gear.— *v.i.* to cycle with wheel so disconnected.—*n.* **free'-will',** freedom of the will from restraint : liberty of choice : power of self-determination.— *adj.* **free'-will,** spontaneous.—**free atom, radical,** short-lived atom, radical, assumed to exist during certain chemical reactions ; **Free Church,** that branch of the Presbyterians in Scotland which left the Established Church in the Disruption of

1843: the small minority thereof who refused to combine with the United Presbyterians in the **United Free Church** (see under **presbyter**): in England, a Nonconformist church generally; **free companion**, a member of a **free company**, or mediaeval band of mercenaries ready for any service; **free fight**, a confused or promiscuous fight; **free hand**, complete freedom of action; **free kick**, a kick allowed without interference; **free list**, the list of persons admitted without payment to a theatre, etc., or of those to whom a book, etc., is sent; **free on board (f.o.b.)**, delivered on a vessel or other conveyance without charge; Free States, in America, before the Civil War of 1861-65, those of the United States in which slavery did not exist, as opposed to *Slave States;* **free verse**, verse defying usual metrical laws in length of lines, etc.: rhythmic prose arranged as irregular verses; **make free with**, to be familiar with, to take liberties with. [O.E. *fréo;* Ger. *frei;* O.N. *fri.*]

freemartin, *frē'mär-tin, n.* a calf (twin with a bull) with internal male organs and external and rudimentary internal female: a similar animal of another species. [Ety. unknown; perh. conn. with Ir. *mart,* a heifer.]

Freesia, *frē'zi-ä,* a South African genus of the iris family, scented greenhouse plants. [E. M. *Fries* (1794-1878), Swedish botanist.]

freeze, *frēz, v.i.* to become ice: to become solid by fall of temperature: to be at a temperature at which water would freeze: to be very cold: to become motionless, stiff, fixed, attached, or stopped by, or as if by, cold.—*v.t.* to cause to freeze: to fix: to stabilise: to prevent the use of or dealings in: (*pr.p.* **freez'ing;** *pa.t.* **frōze,** (*Milt.*) **freez'd;** *pa.p.* **frōz'en;** *obs.* **frōze, frōre, frōrn**).—*n.* a frost: a stoppage.—*adj.* **freez'able.**—*ns.* **freeze'-dry'ing,** freezing by rapid evaporation at low pressure, and subsequent drying by evaporation of moisture from the ice; **freez'er,** a freezing apparatus: anything that freezes; **freez'-ing-mixture,** a mixture, as of pounded ice and salt, producing cold enough to freeze a liquid by the rapid absorption of heat; **freez'ing-point,** the temperature at which a liquid solidifies—that of water being 32° Fahrenheit, 0° centigrade. [O.E. *frēosan,* pa.p. *froren;* Du. *vreizen,* Ger. *frieren.*]

freight, *frāt, n.* the lading or cargo, esp. of a ship: the charge for transporting goods by water or land. —*v.t.* to load (esp. a ship): to hire, let out.—*adj.* (*obs.*) freighted: fraught.—*ns.* **freight'age,** money paid for freight; **freight'-car,** (*U.S.*) a luggage-van: a goods van or wagon; **freight'er,** one who freights a vessel: a cargo-boat, etc.: (*U.S.*) a transporting agent: (*U.S.*) a goods wagon; **freight'-shed,** a goods shed or warehouse. [Prob. Old Du. *vrecht,* a form of *vracht.*]

freischütz. See free-shot.

freit, freet, *frēt, n.* (*Scot.*) an omen.—*adj.* **freit'y, freet'y,** superstitious. [O.N. *frétt,* news.]

frem, fremd, *frem(d), frām(d),* **fremit,** *frem'it, frām'it,* **fraim,** *frām, adj.* (*Scot.*) foreign: strange: not akin: estranged, cold, unfriendly.—*n.* a stranger: strange folk, other than kindred.—*Spens.* **frenne** (*fren*). [O.E. *fremde;* cf. Ger. *fremd.*]

fremescent, *frəm-es'ənt, adj.* growling, muttering. —*n.* **fremesc'ence.** [L. *fremĕre,* to growl.]

fremitus, *frem'i-təs, n.* a palpable vibration, as of the walls of the chest. [L., a murmur.]

French, *fren(t)sh, adj.* belonging to *France* or its people: originating in France (in names of commodities now sometimes spelt without *cap.*).—*n.* the people or language of France.—*ns.* **French'-bean,** the common kidney-bean (*Phaseolus vulgaris*) eaten, pods and all, as a table vegetable; **French'-berr'y,** the berry of species of buckthorn, used in dyeing yellow; **French'-chalk',** soapstone; **French'ery,** French fashions collectively; **French'-horn',** the orchestral horn; **Frenchifica'tion.**—*v.t.* **French'ify,** to make French or Frenchlike: to infect with the manner of the French.—*ns.* **French'iness; French'man,** a native or citizen of France (*pl.* **French'men;** *fem.* **French'woman;** *pl.* **French'women**);

French'-pol'ish, a varnish for furniture, consisting chiefly of shellac dissolved in spirit.—*v.t.* to treat with French-polish.—*ns.* **French'-pol'isher; French'-pol'ishing.**—*adj.* **French'y,** with an exaggerated French manner.—*n.* a contemptuous name for a Frenchman.—**French pitch** (*mus.*), a standard pitch established by the French government in 1859, and later widely adopted—435 cycles per second at 15°C for A (see **international concert pitch**); **French plum,** a prune, a dried plum; **French pox** (*obs.*), syphilis; **French roof,** a modified mansard-roof—really American; **French sash, window,** a door-like window; **take French leave,** to depart without notice or permission, to disappear suspiciously. [O.E. *Frencisc*—L. *Francus*—O.H.G. *Franko.*]

frenetic. See phrenetic.

frenne, *fren, n.* (*Spens.*) a stranger. [See **frem.**]

frenum, fraenum, *frē'nəm, n.* a ligament restraining the motion of a part. [L. *frēnum,* a bridle.]

frenzy, *fren'zi, n.* a violent excitement: a paroxysm of madness.—*v.t.* to drive to frenzy.—*adjs.* **fren'zical, fren'zied.** [O.Fr. *frenesie*—L. and late Gr. *phrenēsis*—Gr. *phrenītis;* see **phrenetic.**]

frequent, *frē'kwənt, adj.* coming or occurring often: crowded: (*Shak.*) addicted.—*v.t.* (*fri-kwent'*), to visit often: to associate with: to resort to: to crowd.—*ns.* **frē'quence** (*Milt.*), a crowd, an assembly: frequency; **frē'quency** (*obs.*) resort: commonness of recurrence: number of vibrations, cycles, or other recurrences in unit time; **frē-quenta'tion,** the act of visiting often.—*adj.* **frequentative** (*fri-kwent'ə-tiv; gram.*), denoting the frequent repetition of an action.—*n.* (*gram.*) a verb expressing this repetition.—*n.* **frequent'er.**—*adv.* **frē'quently.**—*n.* **frē'quentness.** [L. *frequēns, frequentis;* conn. with *farcīre,* to stuff.]

frescade, *fres-kād', n.* a cool walk. [Fr.,—It. *frescata.*]

fresco, *fres'kō, n.* a mode of painting upon walls covered with damp freshly-laid plaster (*true fresco*), or partly dried plaster (*dry fresco*): a picture so painted: (*pl.* **fres'coes,fres'cos**).—*v.t.* to paint in fresco.—*adj.* **fres'coed** (-*kōd*).—*ns.* **frescoer** (*fres'kō-ər*); **fres'coing; fres'coist.** [It. *fresco,* fresh.]

fresh, *fresh, adj.* in a state of activity and health: in new condition, not stale, faded or soiled: new, recently added: raw, inexperienced: in youthful bloom: cool, invigorating: brisk: (*slang*) tipsy: without salt: of food, not treated as by pickling, drying, addition of preservatives, etc.: (*Scot.*) not frosty: (*U.S.*) cheeky, pert.—*adv.* freshly: afresh: newly.—*n.* time of freshness: (*Shak.*) a small stream of fresh water: (*Scot.*) a thaw, open weather.—*v.t.* to freshen.—*adj.* **fresh'-blown,** newly blown, as a flower.—*v.t.* **fresh'en,** to make fresh: to take the saltness from.—*v.i.* to grow fresh.—*ns.* **fresh'ener; fresh'er,** a student in his or her first year, a freshman; **fresh'erdom; fresh'et,** a stream of fresh water: a flood.—*adj.* **fresh'ish.**—*adv.* **fresh'ly,** with freshness: newly: anew.—*ns.* **fresh'man,** a newcomer: a student in his first year; **fresh'manship; fresh'ness.**—*adjs.* **fresh'-new** (*Shak.*), quite new; **fresh'-run,** newly come up from the sea, as a salmon; **fresh'-water,** of or pertaining to water not salt: accustomed to sail only on fresh water—hence unskilled, raw.—**freshwater college** (*U.S.*) a small college. [O.E. *fersc;* cf. Ger. *frisch.*]

fret, *fret, v.t.* to eat into: to eat out: to corrode: to wear away by rubbing: to rub, chafe: to ripple, disturb: to vex, to irritate.—*v.i.* to wear away: to vex oneself: to worry: to chafe: to work, ferment: (*pr.p.* **fret'ing;** *pa.t.* and *pa.p.* **fret'ed**).—*n.* agitation of the surface of a liquid: irritation: worry: a worn or eroded spot.—*adj.* **fret'ful,** peevish.—*adv.* **fret'fully.**—*n.* **fret'fulness.**—*adj.* **fretting,** vexing.—*n.* peevishness. [O.E. *fretan,* to gnaw—pfx. *for-,* inten., and *etan,* to eat; Ger. *fressen.*]

fret, *fret, v.t.* to ornament with interlaced work: to variegate: (*pr.p.* **fret'ting;** *pa.t.* and *pa.p.* **fret'ed**).—*n.* ornamental net-work: (*archit.*) an ornament consisting of small fillets meeting usually at right angles—a key pattern : (*her.*) bendlets, dexter and sinister, interlaced with a mascle.—*ns.* fret′-saw, a saw with a narrow blade and fine teeth, used for fret-work, scroll-work, etc.; **frette**, a strengthening hoop shrunk on a cannon breech.—*adjs.* frett′ed, frett′y, ornamented with frets.—*n.* fret′-work, ornamental work consisting of a combination of frets : perforated wood-work. [O.Fr. *freter*, to adorn with interlaced work, *frete*, trellis-work; prob. influenced by or confused with O.E. *frætwa*, ornament.]

fret, *fret, n.* a ridge on the finger-board of a guitar or other instrument.—*v.t.* to furnish with frets. [Prob. same as the above.]

Freudian, *froid′i-ən, adj.* pertaining to Sigmund *Freud* (1856-1939), his theory of the libido, or his method of psychoanalysis—*n.* a follower of Freud.

friable, *frī′ə-bl, adj.* apt to crumble : easily reduced to powder.—*ns.* fri′ableness, friabil′ity. [Fr.,—L. *friābilis*—*friāre, friātum*, to crumble.]

friar, *frī′ər, n.* a member of one of the mendicant monastic orders in the R.C. Church—the Franciscans (*Friars Minor* or *Grey Friars*), Dominicans (*Friars Preachers*, or *Black Friars*), Carmelites (*White Friars*), Augustinians (*Austin Friars*), and others : a pale patch on a printed page.—*n.* fri′ar-bird, an Australian honey-eater with featherless head.—*adj.* fri′arly, like a friar.—*n.* fri′ary, a convent of friars.—friar′s balsam, a tincture of benzoin, storax, tolu and aloes; friar′s cap, wolf's-bane; friar′s cowl, wake-robin; friar′s lantern, the Will-o'-the-wisp. [O.Fr. *frere*—L. *frāter*, a brother.]

fribble, *frib′l, v.i.* to trifle.—*n.* a trifler.—*ns.* fribb′ledom; fribb′leism; fribb′ler.—*adj.* fribb′lish, trifling. [Onomatopoeic; prob. influenced by frivol.]

fricandeau, *frik-ən-dō′,* or *frik′, n.* a thick slice of veal, etc., larded (*pl.* fricandeaux, *-dōz*).

fricassee, *frik-ə-sē′, n.* a dish of fowl, rabbit, etc. cut into pieces and cooked in sauce.—*v.t.* to dress as a fricassee (*pr.p.* fricassee′ing; *pa.t.* and *pa.p.* fricasseed′). [Fr. *fricassée*; origin unknown.]

friction, *frik′shən, n.* rubbing : (*statics*) a force acting in the tangent plane of two bodies, when one slides or rolls upon another, in direction opposite to that of the movement : disagreement, antagonism, jarring.—*adj.* fric′ative, produced by friction.—*n.* a consonant produced by the breath being forced through a narrow opening.—*adjs.* fric′tional; friction′less. [L. *fricāre, frictum*, to rub.]

Friday, *frī′dā, n.* the sixth day of the week.—**Black Friday,** Good Friday, from the black vestments of the clergy and altar in the Western Church : any Friday marked by a great calamity; **Good Friday,** the Friday before Easter, kept in commemoration of the Crucifixion; **Holy Friday,** Friday in an ember-week—also **Golden Friday,** sometimes put for Good Friday itself. [O.E. *Frīgedæg*, day of (the goddess) Frig.]

fridge, *frij, v.t.* (*Sterne*) to rub or fray.

fried. See fry.

friend, *frend, n.* one loving or attached to another : an intimate acquaintance : a favourer, well-wisher : one of a society so named; (*Scot.*) a relative.—*v.t.* (*obs.*) to befriend.—*adj.* friend′ed, supplied with friends.—*n.* friend′ing (*Shak.*), friendliness.—*adj.* friend′less, without friends : destitute.—*n.* friend′lessness.—*adv.* friend′lily.—*n.* friend′liness.—*adj.* friend′ly, like a friend : having the disposition of a friend : favourable : amicable : for amusement only, not money : pertaining to the Friends or Quakers.—*n.* friend′ship, attachment from mutual esteem : friendly assistance.—**friendly lead,** an entertainment for the benefit of one in need; **friendly society,** benefit society, an association for relief in sickness, old age, widowhood, by provident insurance; **be friends with,** to be on good terms with, well disposed towards; **have a friend at court,** to have a friend in a position where his influence is likely to prove useful; **Society of Friends,** the designation proper of a sect of Christians better known as

Quakers. [O.E. *fréond* (orig. a pr.p.; cf. *fréon*, to love); Ger. *freund*.]

frier, *frī′ər, n.* (*Milt.*) a friar.

frier, fries. See fry.

Friesian. See Frisian.

frieze, *frēz, n.* a rough, heavy woollen cloth.—*adj.* friezed, napped. [Fr. *frise*.]

frieze, *frēz, n.* (*archit.*) the part of the entablature between the architrave and cornice, often ornamented with figures : a decorated band along the top of a room wall.—*v.t.* to put a frieze on. [O.Fr. *frise*; It. *fregio*; perh. L. *Phrygium* (*opus*), Phrygian (work).]

frig, *frij, n.* (*coll.*) short for **refrigerator.**

frigate, *frig′it, n.* formerly a vessel in the class next to ships of the line: now denoting an escort vessel.—*ns.* frig′ate-bird, a large tropical sea-bird (*Fregata*) with very long wings; friga-toon′, a small Venetian vessel with square stern and two masts. [O.Fr. *fregate*—It. *fregata*; ety. dub.]

fright, *frīt, n.* sudden fear : terror : (*coll.*) a figure of grotesque or ridiculous appearance.—*vs.t.* fright (now *rare*, except as Scot. **fricht,** *frihht*) fright′en, to make afraid : to alarm : to drive by fear.—*adjs.* fright′ened; fright′ening.—*adv.* fright′eningly.—*adj.* fright′ful, terrible : horrible.—*adv.* fright′fully.—*n.* fright′fulness, the quality of being frightful : terrorism.—*adj.* fright′some, frightful : feeling fright. [O.E. *fyrhto*; cf. Ger. *furcht*, fear.]

frigid, *frij′id, adj.* frozen or stiffened with cold : cold : chillingly stiff : without spirit or feeling : unanimated : leaving the imagination untouched.—*n.* frigid′ity, coldness : coldness of affection : want of animation : sexual irresponsiveness.—*adv.* frig′idly.—*n.* frig′idness.—frigid zones, the parts of the earth's surface within the polar circles. [L. *frīgidus*—*frīgēre*, to be cold—*frīgus*, cold.]

frigorific, *frig-ər-if′ik, adj.* causing cold : freezing.—*n.* frigorif′ico (*Sp.*) a slaughtering and meat-freezing establishment. [L. *frīgus, -oris*, cold, *facĕre*, to make.]

frigot, *frig′ət, n.* (*Spens.*). Same as **frigate.**

frijol, frijole, *frē′hhōl, n.* the kidney-bean, or any species of Phaseolus : *pl.* **frijoles** (*-les*). [Sp. *frijol, fréjol.*]

frill, *fril, v.i.* to ruffle, as a hawk its feathers, when shivering.—*v.t.* to furnish with a frill.—*n.* a ruffle : a ruffled or crimped edging : superfluous ornament.—*ns.* frilled′-liz′ard, a large Australian lizard (Chlamydosaurus) with an erectile frill about its neck; frill′ing.—*adj.* frill′y. [Origin unknown.]

Frimaire, *frē-mār′, n.* the third month of the French revolutionary calendar, about Nov. 21-Dec. 20. [Fr. *frimas*, hoar-frost.]

fringe, *frinj, n.* a border of loose threads : hair falling over the brow : a border, margin.—*v.t.* to adorn with fringe : to border.—*adjs.* fringed; fringe′less.—*n.* fringe′-tree, a large American shrub (*Chionanthus virginica*) of the olive family, whose very numerous snow-white flowers have long narrow corolla-segments.—*adj.* fring′y, ornamented with fringes. [O.Fr. *frenge*—L. *fimbria*, threads, fibres, akin to *fibra*, a fibre.]

fringillaceous, *frin-ji-lā′shəs, adj.* pertaining to the finches or Fringill′idae.—*adjs.* fringill′iform, fringill′ine. [L. *fringilla*, a finch.]

frippery, *frip′ər-i, n.* (*obs.*) cast-off clothes : (*obs.*) an old-clothes shop, or the old-clothes trade : tawdry finery : foppish triviality : useless trifles.—*adj.* useless : trifling.—*n.* fripp′er, fripp′erer, an old-clothes dealer. [O.Fr. *freperie*—*frepe*, a rag.]

fris, *frish,* **friska,** *frish′kaw, ns.* the quick movement of a csárdás. [Hung.]

Frisian, *friz′i-ən, n.* a native of *Friesland* : the Low German language of Friesland.—*adj.* of Friesland, its people, or their language.—*adj.* **Friesian** (*freez′*), Frisian, esp. of a heavy breed of dairy-cattle.—*n.* a Frisian : a Friesian bull or cow.—*adjs.* Friesic, Fries′ish.

frisk, *frisk, v.i.* to gambol : to leap playfully.—*v.t.* (*slang*) to search (a person or pockets).—*n.* a frolicsome movement.—*n.* frisk′er.—*adj.* frisk′-ful, brisk, lively.—*adv.* frisk′ily.—*n.* frisk′iness.

—*n.* and *adj.* **frisk'ing.**—*adv.* **frisk'ingly.**—*adj.* **frisk'y,** lively: jumping with gaiety: frolicsome. [O.Fr. *frisque.*]

frisket, *frisk'it, n.* (*print.*) the light frame between the tympan and the form, to hold in place the sheet to be printed. [Fr. *frisquette.*]

frist, *frist, n.* (*obs.*) delay, respite.—*v.t.* (*Scott*) to postpone: to grant time, as for payment. [O.E. *first,* time, respite.]

frit, *frit, n.* the mixed materials for making glass, pottery glazes, etc.—*v.t.* to fuse partially: (*pr.p.* **fritt'ing;** *pa.t.* and *pa.p.* **fritt'ed**).—*n.* **fritt'ing-furnace.**—**frit porcelain,** an artificial soft-paste English porcelain (from its vitreous nature). [Fr. *fritte*—It. *fritta*—L. *frīgĕre, frīctum,* to roast.]

frit, *frit, n.* a small fly destructive to wheat. [Ety. unknown.]

frith, *frith.* Same as **firth** (1).

frith, *frith, n.* (*obs.* or *hist.*) peace: sanctuary.—*ns.* **frith'borh** (*-borhh*), a surety for keeping the peace, frankpledge; **frith'gild,** a union of neighbours pledged to one another for the preservation of peace; **frith'soken** (O.E. *frith-sócn*) sanctuary, asylum; **frith'stool** (O.E. *frithstól*) a chair of sanctuary, placed near the altar in a church—as at Hexham and Beverley. [O.E. *frith,* peace; Ger. *friede.*]

frith, *frith, n.* wooded country: brushwood: underwood. [O.E. (*ge*)*fyrhthe.*]

fritillary, *frit'il-ər-i,* or *-il',* *n.* a genus (Fritillaria) of the lily family, the best-known species with chequered purple flowers: a name for several butterflies of similar pattern. [L. *fritillus,* a dice-box.]

fritter, *frit'ər, n.* a piece of fruit, etc., fried in batter. [O.Fr. *friture*—L. *frīgĕre, frīctum,* to fry.]

fritter, *frit'ər, n.* a fragment.—*v.t.* to break into fragments: to squander piecemeal.—*n.* **fritt'erer,** one who wastes time. [Perh. O.Fr. *freture*—L. *frāctūra*—*frangĕre, frāctum,* to break.]

frivolous, *friv'ə-ləs, adj.* trifling: silly.—*v.t.* and *v.i.* **friv'ol** (back-formation), to trifle.—*n.* **frivolity** (*-ol'*), trifling habit or nature: levity.—*adv.* **friv'olously.**—*n.* **friv'olousness.** [L. *frīvolus.*]

frize, *frīz* (*Spens.*). See **freeze, frieze.**

frizz, friz, *friz, v.t.* to curl: to render rough and tangled.—*n.* a curl: a wig.—*adjs.* **frizzed,** having the hair crisped into frizzes; **frizz'y.** [O.Fr. *friser,* to curl; perh. conn. with **frieze,** cloth.]

frizzle, *friz'l, v.t.* to form in small short curls.—*v.i.* to go into curls.—*n.* a curl.—*adj.* **frizz'ly.** [Related to **frizz** and **frieze.**]

frizzle, *friz'l, v.t.* and *v.i.* to fry: to scorch. [Perhaps onomatopoeic adaptation of **fry,** from sputtering noise.]

fro, *frō, prep.* (*obs.* except in Scots form **frae,** *frā*) from.—*adv.* away: back or backward. [O.N. *frá.*]

frock, *frok, n.* a monk's wide-sleeved garment: a long coat: a smock-frock: a sailor's jersey: a woman's or child's gown: an undress regimental coat: a wearer of a frock.—*v.t.* to furnish with a frock: to invest with priestly office.—*n.* **frock'-coat,** a double-breasted full-skirted coat for men.—*adj.* **frocked,** clothed in a frock.—*n.* **frock'ing,** cloth suitable for frocks, coarse jean.—*adj.* **frock'less,** wanting a frock. [O.Fr. *froc,* a monk's frock—L.L. *frocus*—L. *floccus,* a flock of wool; or from L.L. *hrocus*—O.H.G. *hroch* (Ger. *rock*), a coat.]

frog, *frog, n.* a tailless web-footed amphibian, esp. one of the genus Rana, more agile than a toad: a swelling in the throat.—*ns.* **frog'-bit,** a small aquatic plant (*Hydrocharis Morsus-ranae*), allied to the water-soldier, but with floating leaves; **frog'-eater,** one who eats frogs, a Frenchman; **frog'-fish,** a name for various fishes, esp. the angler; **frogg'ery,** frogs collectively: a place where frogs abound or are kept; **frogg'y,** a frog: a contemptuous name for a Frenchman.—*adj.* **froggy,** froglike: having or abounding in frogs.—*ns.* **frog'-hopper,** a froth-fly; **frog'ling,** a little frog; **frog'-man,** a diver with swimming appendages on his feet; **frog(s)'-march,** a method of carrying a refractory or drunken prisoner face downwards between four men, each holding a limb.—*v.t.* to

carry in such a way.—*n.* **frog'mouth,** any bird of the mopoke family or subfamily (Australian and S. Asian) akin to or included in the goatsuckers; **frog'-spit,** cuckoo-spit. [O.E. *frogga;* also *frox;* cog. with O.N. *froskr;* Ger. *frosch.*]

frog, *frog, n.* a V-shaped band of horn on the underside of a horse's hoof. [Perh. the same word as the preceding.]

frog, *frog, n.* on a railway or tramway, a structure in the rails allowing passage across or to another track. [Possibly the same as **frog** (1).]

frog, *frog, n.* an ornamental fastening or tasselled or braided button: an attachment to a belt for carrying a weapon.—*adj.* **frogged,** having ornamental stripes or workings of braid or lace, mostly on the breast of a coat. [Perhaps Port. *froco*—L. *floccus,* a flock, lock.]

froise, *froiz,* **fraise,** *frāz, n.* a thick pancake, often with slices of bacon. [Origin unknown.]

frolic, *frol'ik, adj.* merry: pranky.—*n.* gaiety: a prank: a gambol: a merry-making.—*v.i.* to play wild pranks or merry tricks: to gambol: (*pr.p.* **frol'icking;** *pa.t.* and *pa.p.* **frol'icked**).—*adj.* **frol'icsome,** gay: sportive.—*adv.* **frol'icsomely.** —*n.* **frol'icsomeness.** [Du. *vrolijk,* merry; cf. Ger. *fröhlich,* joyful, gay.]

from, *from, frəm, prep.* forth of: out of: away, to or at a greater distance relatively to: springing out of: beginning at: apart relatively to: by reason of. [O.E. *fram, from;* akin to Goth. *fram,* O.N. *frá.*]

frond, *frond, n.* a leaf, esp. of a palm or fern: a leaflike thallus, or a leaflike organ of obscure morphological nature.—*n.* **frond'age,** fronds collectively.—*adjs.* **frond'ed,** having fronds; **frond'ent,** leafy.—*n.* **frondesc'ence,** development of leaves.—*adjs.* **frondesc'ent,** leaflike: leafy: springing into leaf; **frondif'erous,** bearing or producing fronds; **frond'ose,** leaflike: leafy. [L. *frōns, frondis,* a leaf.]

Fronde, *frōnᵈ, n.* the opposition to Mazarin and the court in France during Louis XIV's minority. —*n.* **frondeur** (*fronᵍ-dər'*), a member of the Fronde: an irreconcilable. [Fr., sling—L. *funda,* sling.]

front, *frunt, n.* the forehead: the face: the forepart of anything: the side presented to view: the face of a building, esp. the principal face: the part facing the sea or other water: a seaside promenade or pleasure ground: the foremost line: the scene of hostilities: a combined face presented against opponents: a wig for the forehead: an attachment or addition to the front of anything: the middle part of the tongue: boldness: impudence.—*adj.* of, relating to, in, the front: articulated with the front of the tongue.—*v.t.* to stand in front of or opposite: to face towards: to meet, or to oppose, face to face: to add a front to: to serve as a front to: to change into or towards a front sound.—*v.i.* (*Shak.*) to be foremost: to face.—*n.* **front'age,** the front part of a building: extent of front: ground in front.—*adj.* **front'al** (*frunt'l,* also *front'l*), of or belonging to the front, or the forehead.—*n.* a front-piece: something worn on the forehead or face: (*archit.*) a pediment over a door or window: a hanging of silk, satin, etc., embroidered for an altar—now usually covering only the top, the *superfrontal*—formerly covering the whole of the front, corresponding to the *antependium.*—*adj.* **front'-bench,** sitting on a front bench, as a minister, or an opposition member of like standing.—*ns.* **front'-bench'er;** **front'-door'.**—*adjs.* **front'ed,** formed with a front: changed into or towards a front sound; **front'less,** void of shame or modesty.—*adv.* **front'lessly.**—*ns.* **front'let,** a band worn on the forehead; **front'-page',** the outside page of a newspaper.—*adj.* suitable for a front-page, important.—*adj.* **front'-rank.**—*n.* **front-rank'er.**—*advs.* **front'ward, -s,** towards the front; **front'ways, -wise,** with face or front forward.—**come to the front,** to become noticeable: to attain an important position; **in front (of),** before. [L. *frōns, frontis,* the forehead.]

frontier, *frunt'* or *front'ēr, -yər,* or *-ēr', n.* the border of a country: the border of settled country:

(*Shak.*) an outwork.—*adj.* belonging to a frontier: bordering.—*v.t.* (*Spens.*) to border.—*n.* front'iersman (or *-tērz'*), a dweller on a frontier. [O.Fr. *frontier*—L. *frōns, frontis.*]

frontispiece, *frunt'is-pēs* (or *front'*), *n.* (*archit.*) the principal face of a building: a figure or engraving at the front of a book.—*v.t.* to put as a frontispiece: to furnish with one. [Fr. *frontispice*—L.L. *frontispicium*—*frōns, frontis*, forehead, *specĕre, spicĕre*, to see; not conn. with piece.]

fronton, *frun'tɔn, n.* (*archit.*) a pediment.—Also frontoon (*-tōōn'*). [Fr.,—It. *frontone.*]

frore, *frōr*, froren, frorne, frorn, *frōr'ɔn*, frorn, *adj.* frozen, frosty.—*adj.* frō'ry (*Spens.*), frozen. [O.E. *froren*, pa.p. of *frēosan*, to freeze.]

frost, *frost*, *n.* a state of freezing: temperature at or below the freezing-point of water: frozen dew, or hoar-frost: (*slang*) a disappointment, a cheat.—*v.t.* to affect with frost: to cover with hoar-frost: to make like hoar-frost: to sharpen (the points of a horse's shoe) that it may not slip on ice.—*v.i.* to assume a frostlike appearance.—*n.* frost'-bite, injury, sometimes ending in mortification, in a part of the body by exposure to cold.—*v.t.* to affect with frost.—*adjs.* frost'-bitten, bitten or affected by frost; frost'-bound, bound or confined by frost; frost'ed, covered by frost: having a frost-like appearance (as a cake or Christmas card by sprinkling, glass by roughening): injured by frost.—*adv.* frost'ily.—*ns.* frost'iness; frost'ing, coating with hoar-frost: material or treatment to give appearance of hoar-frost.—*adj.* frost'less, free from frost.—*n.* frost'-nail, a projecting nail in a horse-shoe serving as an ice-calk.—*v.t.* to furnish with frost-nails.—*ns.* frost'-smoke, vapour frozen in the atmosphere, and having a smoke-like appearance; frost'-work, tracery wrought by frost, as on windows: work resembling frost tracery, etc.—*adj.* frost'y, producing, attended with, covered with, frost: chill: frost-like. [O.E. *frost, forst*—*frēosan*; cf. Ger. *frost.*]

froth, *froth*, *n.* foam: (*fig.*) chatter.—*v.t.* to cause froth on.—*v.i.* to throw up froth.—*ns.* froth'-blower, a beer-drinker; froth'ery, mere froth; froth'-fly, froth'-hopper, a frog-hopper, any insect of the family Cercopidae, whose larvae live surrounded by froth (cuckoo-spit) on plants.—*adj.* froth-fō'my (*Spens.*), foaming.—*adv.* froth'ily.—*n.* froth'iness.—*adjs.* froth'less; froth'y, full of or like froth or foam: empty: unsubstantial. [O.N. *frotha;* Dan. *fraade.*]

froughy. Same as frowy.

frounce, *frowns, v.t.* to plait: to curl: to wrinkle up.—*v.i.* to wrinkle: (*obs.*) to frown.—*n.* (*obs.*) a wrinkle, a plait or curl: affected ornament. [O.Fr. *froncier;* see flounce (2).]

frounce, *frowns, n.* a disease of the mouth in hawks. [Origin unknown.]

frow, *frow, n.* a Dutchwoman. [Du. *vrouw.*]

froward, *frō'ərd, adj.* (*Spens.*) turned away: self-willed: perverse: unreasonable—opp. to *toward.* —*adv.* in an averse direction.—*prep.* (also *fro'-wards*) in a direction away from.—*adv.* fro'wardly.—*n.* fro'wardness. [fro, and suffix. *-ward.*]

frown, *frown, v.i.* to wrinkle the brow as in anger: to look angry, gloomy, threatening: to show disapprobation.—*v.t.* to express, send, or force by a frown.—*n.* a wrinkling or contraction of the brow in displeasure, etc.: a stern look.—*adj.* frown'ing, gloomy: disapproving: threatening.—*adv.* frown'ingly. [From O.Fr. *froignier* (Fr. *refrogner*), to knit the brow; origin unknown.]

frowst, *frowst, v.i.* to luxuriate in hot stuffiness and stupefaction.—*n.* hot stuffy fustiness: a spell of frowsting.—*ns.* frowst'er; frowst'iness.—*adj.* frowst'y, fusty: close-smelling: ill-smelling. [Origin unknown.]

frowy, froughy, (*Spens.* frowie), *frō'i, frow'i, adj.* (*Spens.*) musty, rancid: of timber, soft and brittle. [Prob. O.E. *thróh*, rancidity.]

frowzy, frowsy, *frow'zi, adj.* fusty: stuffy, offensive. [Origin unknown.]

frozen, *frōz'n*, pa.p. of freeze.

Fructidor, *frük-tē-dor', n.* the twelfth month in the French revolutionary calendar, about Aug. 18-

Sept. 16. [Fr.,—L. *frūctus*, fruit; Gr. *dōron*, a gift.]

fructed, *fruk'tid, adj.* (*her.*) bearing fruit.—*adj.* fructif'erous, bearing fruit.—*n.* fructificā'tion, fruit-production: (*bot.*) a structure that contains spores or seeds.—*v.t.* fruc'tify, to make fruitful: to fertilise.—*v.i.* to bear fruit.—*adj.* fructiv'orous (L. *vorāre*, to devour), frugivorous.—*ns.* fruc'tose, fruit sugar or laevulose; fruc'tūary, one enjoying the fruits of anything.—*v.i.* fruc'tūate, to come to fruit: to fructify.—*n.* fructūā'tion, coming to fruit, bearing fruit.—*adj.* fruc'tūous, fruitful. [L. *frūctus*, fruit.]

frugal, *frōō'gl, adj.* economical in the use of means: sparing: spare: thrifty.—*ns.* fru'galist, one who is frugal; frugality (*-gal'*), economy: thrift.—*adv.* fru'gally. [L. *frūgālis—frūx, frūgis*, fruit.]

frugiferous, *frōō-jif'ə-rəs, adj.* (L. *ferre*, to bear) fruit-bearing.—*adj.* frugiv'orous (L. *vorāre*, to eat), feeding on fruits or seeds. [L. *frūx, frūgis*, fruit.]

fruit (*obs.* fruict), *frōōt, n.* the produce of the earth, which supplies the wants of men and animals: an edible part of a plant, generally sweet, acid, and juicy, *esp.* a part that contains the seed, but sometimes extended to include other parts (e.g. the leaf-stalk in rhubarb): (*bot.*) a fructification, esp. the structure that develops from the ovary and its contents after fertilisation, sometimes including also structures formed from other parts of the flower or axis: the offspring of animals: product, effect, advantage.—*v.i.* to produce fruit.—*ns.* fruit'age, fruit collectively: fruits; fruitā'rian, one who lives on fruit.—Also *adj.;* fruit'-bat, any bat of the suborder Megacheiroptera, large fruit-eating bats of the Old World; fruit'-bud, a bud that produces fruit; fruit'-cake, a cake containing raisins, etc.; fruit'erer, one who deals in fruit—also (now *dial.*) fruit'er; (*fem.* fruit'eress); fruit'ery, a place for storing fruit: fruitage; fruit'-fly, an insect of genus Drosophila.—*adj.* fruit'ful, productive.—*adv.* fruit'fully.—*ns.* fruit'fulness; fruit'ing, process of bearing fruit; fruit'-knife, a knife with a blade of silver, etc., for cutting fruit.—*adj.* fruit'less, barren: without profit: useless: in vain.—*adv.* fruit'lessly.—*ns.* fruit'lessness; fruit'-sal'ad, a mixture of pieces of fruit, fresh or preserved; fruit'-tree, a tree of a kind yielding edible fruit.—*adj.* fruit'y, like, or tasting like, fruit: rich.—bush fruits, small fruits growing on woody bushes; first-fruits (see first, annat); small fruits, strawberries, currants, etc. [O.Fr. *fruit, fruict*—L. *frūctus—frui, frūctus*, to enjoy.]

fruition, *frōō-ish'ən, n.* enjoyment: use or possession, esp. accompanied with pleasure: often wrongly used for fruiting, bearing of, coming into, fruit.—*adj.* fru'itive. [O.Fr. *fruition*—L. *frui*, to enjoy.]

frumentation, *frōō-mən-tā'shən, n.* a largess of grain bestowed on the starving or turbulent people in ancient Rome.—*adjs.* frumentā'ceous, made of or resembling wheat or other grain; frumentā'rious, pertaining to corn. [L. *frūmentātiō, -ōnis—frūmentārī*, to provide with corn—*frūmentum*, corn.]

frumenty, *frōō'mən-ti, n.* hulled wheat boiled in milk.—Also fur'menty, fur'mety, fur'mity (*fur'*). [O.Fr. *frumentee—frument*—L. *frūmentum.*]

frump, *frump, n.* a dowdy and cross-grained woman: (*obs.*) a flout or snub.—*v.t.* (*obs.*) to snub. —*adjs.* frump'ish, frump'y, sour-tempered: ill-dressed.

frumple, *frum'pl, v.t.* (*prov.*) to wrinkle.

frush, *frush, v.t.* (*Shak.*) to break or bruise.—*adj.* brittle.—*n.* a crash: splinters. [O.Fr. *froissier*, to bruise—L. *frustum*, fragment.]

frush, *frush, n.* (*prov.*) the frog of a horse's foot: a disease in that part of a horse's foot. [Cf. O.E. *forsc*, frog (animal); Gr. *batrachos* means frog in both senses.]

frust, *frust, n.* (*Sterne*) a fragment.—*ns.* frust'ule, the siliceous two-valved shell of a diatom, with its contents; frust'um, a slice of a solid body: the part of a cone or pyramid between the base and a

Neutral vowels in unaccented syllables: *el'ə-mənt, in'fənt, ran'dəm*

parallel plane, or between two planes : (*pl.* **frust′a**). [L. *frustum*, a bit.]

frustrate, *frus′trāt*, *-trāt′*, *v.t.* to make vain of or no effect : to bring to naught : to balk : to thwart.—*adj.* (*frus*′) vain, ineffectual : balked.—*n.* **frustrā′-tion**. [L. *frustrārī*, *frustrātus—frustrā*, in vain.]

frutex, *froo′teks*, *n.* a shrub (*pl.* **fru′tices**, *-ti-sēz*).—*adj.* **fru′ticose**, shrubby. [L. *frutex*, *-icis*, a shrub.]

frutify, *froo′ti-fī*, *v.t.* (*Shak.*) Launcelot Gobbo's blunder for **notify** or **specify**.

fry, *frī*, *v.t.* to cook in oil or fat in a pan : to burn or scorch : to torture with heat or passion.—*v.i.* to undergo frying : (*Spens.*) to foam : (*pr.p.* **fry′ing**; *pa.t.* and *pa.p.* **fried** ; *3rd pers. pres. indic.* **fries**).—*n.* a dish of anything fried.—*ns.* **fried′cake**, (*U.S.*) a cake fried in deep fat : a doughnut ; **fri′er** (**fry′er**), one who fries (esp. fish) : a vessel for frying : a fish suitable for frying.—*n.* and *adj.* **fry′ing**.—*n.* **fry′ing-pan**, a flat pan for frying with.—**out of the frying-pan into the fire**, out of one evil into a greater. [Fr. *frire*—L. *frīgĕre* ; cf. Gr. *phrȳgein*.]

fry, *frī*, *n.* young, collectively : a swarm of young, esp. of fishes just spawned : a number of small things.—**small fry**, small things collectively, persons or things of little importance. [O.N. *frió*, seed ; Dan. and Sw. *fro*.]

fub, *fub*, *v.t.* (*Shak.*) to put off : to fob.—*n.* **fubb′ery** (*obs.*), a deception.—**fub off**, to put off or evade by a trick or a lie. [See **fob**.]

fubby, *fub′i*, **fubsy**, *fub′zi*, *adj.* chubby. [Ety. dub.]

fuchsia, *fū′shi-ä*, *-shä*, *n.* any plant of a S. American genus (Fuchsia) of the evening primrose family, with long pendulous flowers.—*n.* **fuchsine** (*fooks′-ēn*), the dye-stuff magenta, a green solid, purplish red in solution (from its colour). [Named after Leonard *Fuchs*, a German botanist, 1501-66.]

fuchsite, *fooks′īt*, *n.* a brilliant green chromium mica. [J. N. von *Fuchs* (1774-1856), German mineralogist.]

fucus, *fū′kos*, *n.* (*obs.*) paint for the face, cosmetic (*pl.* **fūci**, *-sī*, **fūcuses**): Fucus, the bladder-wrack genus of seaweeds.—*adj.* **fū′coid**, like, pertaining to, or containing bladder-wrack, or seaweed, or seaweed-like markings.—*n.* a marking like a fossil seaweed.—*adjs.* **fūcoid′al** ; **fū′cused**, painted. [L. *fūcus*, orchil, rouge; Gr. *phȳkos*.]

fud, *fud*, *n.* (*Scot.*) a rabbit's or hare's tail : the buttocks.

fuddle, *fud′l*, *v.t.* to stupefy, as with drink.—*v.i.* to drink to excess or habitually : (*pr.p.* **fudd′ling**; *pa.t.* and *pa.p.* **fudd′led**).—*n.* intoxicating drink.—*ns.* **fudd′le-cap**, a hard drinker; **fudd′ler**, a drunkard.—*n.* and *adj.* **fudd′ling**, tippling. [Origin obscure.]

fudge, *fuj*, *n.* stuff: nonsense: humbug: an in-serted patch in a newspaper, or space reserved for it : a soft sweetmeat.—*inter.* bosh.—*v.t.* to patch up, fake : to botch : to foist.—*v.i.* to fadge.—*adj.* **fudg′y**, irritable : awkward.

fuel, *fū′əl*, *n.* material for a fire.—*v.t.* to furnish with fuel.—*v.i.* to take or get fuel : (*pr.p.* **fu′elling**; *pa.t.* and *pa.p.* **fū′elled**).—*n.* **fū′eller**. [O.Fr. *fowaille*—L.L. *focāle*—L. *focus*, a fireplace.]

fuero, *fwā′rō*, *n.* a code or body of law or privileges, esp. in the Basque provinces, a constitution. [Sp.,—L. *forum*.]

fuff, *fuf*, *n.* (*Scot.*) a puff: the spitting of a cat : a burst of anger.—*v.t.* and *v.i.* to puff: to spit as a cat.—*adj.* **fuff′y**, light and soft. [Imit.]

fug, *fug*, *n.* a very hot close state of atmosphere: sitting in such an atmosphere: one who fugs : dusty fluff.—*v.i.* to sit or revel in a fug.—*adj.* **fugg′y**. [Origin unknown.]

fugacious, *fū′gā-shəs* *adj.* apt to flee away : fleeting : readily shed.—*ns.* **fugā′ciousness**, **fugacity** (*-gas′*). [L. *fugāx*, *-ācis*, from *fugĕre*, to flee.]

fugitive, *fū′ji-tiv*, *adj.* apt to flee away : fleeing : fleeting : evanescent : occasional, written for some passing occasion.—*n.* one who flees or has fled : one hard to be caught : an exile.—*ns.* **fū′gie** (*Scot.*) a cock that will not fight : a runaway; **fū′gie-warr′ant**, a warrant to apprehend a debtor supposed to be about to abscond, prob. from the phrase *in meditatione fugae;* **fūgitā′tion** (Scots

law), absconding from justice: sentence of out-lawry.—*adv.* **fū′gitively.**—*n.* **fū′gitiveness.** [L. *fugitivus—fugĕre*, to flee.]

fugleman, *fū′gl-mən*, *n.* a soldier who stands before a company at drill as an example : a ringleader, mouthpiece of others.—*v.i.* **fū′gle** (Carlyle), to act like a fugleman. [Ger. *flügelmann*, the leader of a file—*flügel*, a wing, *mann*, man.]

fugue, *fūg*, *n.* (*mus.*) a form of composition in which the subject is given out by one part and im-mediately taken up by a second (in *answer*), during which the first part supplies an accompaniment or counter-subject, and so on : wandering with loss of memory.—*adj.* **fū′gal.**—*adv.* **fū′gally.**—*adj.* and *adv.* **fugato** (*foo-gä′tō*; It.) in the manner of a fugue without being strictly a fugue.—Also *n.*—*n.* **fughetta** (*foo-get′tä*), a short fugue.—*n.* **fuguist** (*fūg′ist*), one who writes or plays fugues. [Fr.,—It. *fuga*—L. *fuga*, flight.]

Führer, *fü′rər*, *n.* the title taken by Hitler as dictator of Nazi Germany. [Ger., leader, guide.]

fulcrum, *ful′krəm*, *n.* (*mech.*) the prop or fixed point on which a lever moves : a support (*pl.* **ful′crums**, **ful′cra**).—*adj.* **ful′crate**, supported with fulcrums. [L. *fulcrum*, a prop—*fulcīre*, to prop.]

fulfil, *fool-fil′*, *v.t.* (arch.) to fill full : to complete : to accomplish : to carry into effect : to bring to consummation : (*pr.p.* **fulfill′ing**; *pa.t.* and *pa.p.* **fulfilled′**).—*ns.* **fulfill′er** ; **fulfill′ing**, **fulfil′ment**, full performance : completion : accomplishment. [O.E. *fullfyllan—full*, full, *fyllan*, to fill.]

fulgent, *ful′jənt*, *adj.* shining : bright.—*n.* **ful′gency.**—*adv.* **ful′gently.**—*adj.* **ful′gid**, flashing.—*ns.* **ful′gor**, **ful′gour** (*-gor*, *-gər*), splendour.—*adj.* **ful′gorous**, flashing. [L. *fulgēns*, *-ĕntis*, pr.p. of *fulgēre*, to shine, *fulgidus*, shining, *fulgor*, bright-ness.]

fulgurate, *ful′gū-rāt*, *v.i.* to flash as lightning.—*adjs.* **ful′gūral**, pertaining to lightning; **ful′gūrant**, flashing like lightning.—*ns.* **fulgūrā′tion**, flashing : in assaying, the sudden and final brightening of the fused globule; **ful′gūrite**, a tube of vitrified sand formed by lightning.—*adj.* **ful′gūrous**, resembling lightning. [L. *fulgur*, lightning.]

fulham, *fool′əm*, *n.* a die loaded at the corner.—Also **full′am**, **full′an**. [Prob. the place-name *Fulham*.]

fuliginous, *fū-lij′i-nəs*, *adj.* sooty: dusky.—*n.* **fūliginos′ity.**—*adv.* **fūlig′inously.** [L., *fūlīgō*, *-inis*, soot.]

full, *fool*, *adj.* holding all that can be contained : having no empty space : replete : abundantly supplied or furnished : abounding : copious : filling : containing the whole matter : complete : perfect : strong : clear : intense : swelled or rounded : protuberant : having excess of material : at the height of development or end of course : having thoughts completely engrossed : (*coll.*) drunk : (*compar.* **full′er** ; *superl.* **full′est**).—*n.* completest extent, as of the moon : highest degree : the whole : time of full-moon.—*v.t.* to make with gathers or puckers.—*v.i.* to become full.—*adv.* quite : thoroughly, veritably : directly.—*adjs.* **full′-a′corned** (Shak.), full-fed with acorns ; **full′-aged**, having reached majority.—*ns.* **full′-back** (see **back**) ; **full′-blast**, full operation (*adv.* with maxi-mum energy and fluency); **full′-blood**, an indivi-dual of pure blood.—*adjs.* **full′-blood′ed**, having a full supply of blood : vigorous : thoroughbred, of unmixed descent : related through both parents; **full′-blown**, fully expanded, as a flower : beyond the first freshness of youth : fully qualified or admitted : puffed out to fullness; **full′-bod′ied**, with much body or substance.—*n.* **full′-bottom**, a full-bottomed wig.—*adjs.* **full′-bott′omed**, having a full or large bottom, as a wig; **full′-bound**, with the boards covered as well as the back; **full′-charged**, fully loaded (*lit.* and *fig.*).—*adv.* **full′-cir′cle**, round in a complete revolution.—*n.* **full′-cock′**, the posi-tion of a gun cock drawn fully back, or of a tap fully open.—*adv.* in that position.—*adjs.* **full′-cocked** ; **full′-dress**, in the dress worn on occasions of state or ceremony (**full-dress debate**, a set debate of some importance in which the leaders take part).—*adjs.* **full'-eyed**, with large prominent eyes; **full'-face**, **full'-faced**, having a full or broad face: (of type) bold-faced: showing the face in direct front view; **full'-fash'ioned**, or **fully fashioned**, of garments, esp. stockings, conforming to the body contour; **full'-fed**, fed to plumpness or satiety; **full'-fledged'**, completely fledged: having attained full membership; **full'-fraught** (*Shak.*), fully charged, equipped, endowed, all-round; **full'-grown**, grown to full size.—*ns.* **full'-hand'**, **full'-house'**, at poker, three cards of a kind and a pair.—*adjs.* **full'-hand'ed**, bearing something valuable, as a gift; **full'-heart'ed**, full of heart or courage: fraught with emotion; **full'-hot** (*Shak.*), heated to the utmost; **full'ish**, inclining to fullness; **full'-length'**, extending the whole length.—*n.* a portrait showing the whole length.—*adv.* stretched out to the full extent; **full'-manned** (*Shak.*), having a full crew.—*ns.* **full'-moon**, the moon with its whole disk illuminated, when opposite the sun: the time when the moon is full; **full'-mouthed**, having a full set of teeth: having food in plenty: loud: sonorous; **full'ness**, **ful'ness**, the state of being full: moment of fulfilment: (*Shak.*) plenty, wealth.—*adjs.* **full'-orbed**, having the orb or disk fully illuminated, as the full-moon: round; **full'-page**, occupying a whole page.—*advs.* **full'-pelt**, **full'-speed**, **full'-split**, **full'-tilt'**, with highest speed and impetus.—*adv.* **full'-sail'**.—*adj.* **full'-sailed**, having all sails set: having sails filled with wind: advancing with speed and momentum.—*n.* **full'-stop'**, a point marking the end of a sentence.—*adjs.* **full'-summed**, complete in all its parts; **full'-throat'ed**, **full'-voiced**, singing with the whole power of the voice; **full'-time**, occupied during or extending over the whole working day.—*n.* **full'-tim'er.**—*adj.* **full'-winged** (*Shak.*), having perfect or strong wings.—*adv.* **full'y**, completely: entirely: quite.—**at the full**, at the height, as of one's good fortune, etc.; **full and by**, closehauled to the wind; **full brother**, **sister**, **son**, daughter, of the same parents; **full cousin**, son or daughter of an uncle or aunt, first cousin; **full of years**, at a good old age; **full organ**, the organ, or great organ, with all or most of the stops in use; **full pitch** (*cricket*), a ball which does not or would not pitch before passing or hitting the batsman's wicket—also **full toss**; **full score**, a complete musical score with a staff for every part; **full up**, full to the limit; (*slang*) sated, wearied; **in full**, without reduction; **in full cry**, in chase together, giving tongue; **in full rig**, with maximum number of masts and sails; **in full swing**, at the height of activity; **in the fullness of time**, at the due or destined time; **to the full**, in full measure, completely. [O.E. *full*; Goth. *fulls*, O.N. *fullr*, Ger. *voll*.]

full, *fool*, *v.t.* to scour and beat, as a means of finishing or cleansing woollens: to scour and thicken in a mill.—*ns.* **full'age**, the charge for fulling cloth; **full'er**, one who fulls cloth; **fuller's-earth**, an earthy hydrous aluminium silicate, capable of absorbing grease: a division of the English Jurassic; **fuller's-herb**, soapwort; **full'-ing-mill**, a mill in which woollen cloth is fulled. [O.Fr. *fuler* (see **foil**, 1) and O.E. *fullere*, fuller, both—L. *fullō*, a cloth-fuller.]

fulmar, *fool'mär*, *-mər*, *n.* a gull-like bird of the petrel family. [Perh. O.N. *fúll*, foul, *már*, gull.]

fulminate, *ful'min-āt*, *v.i.* to thunder or make a loud noise: to detonate: to issue decrees with violence, or threats: to inveigh: to flash.—*v.t.* to cause to explode: to send forth, as a denunciation: to denounce.—*n.* a salt of fulminic acid (often dangerously detonating).—*adj.* **ful'minant**, fulminating: (*path.*) developing suddenly.—*n.* a thunderbolt: an explosive.—*adj.* **ful'minating**, detonating.—*n.* **fulminā'tion**, act of thundering, denouncing, or detonating: a denunciation.—*adj.* **ful'minatory.**—*v.t.* and *v.i.* **fulmine** (*ful'min*), to fulminate (*Spens.*, *Milt.*).—*adjs.* **fulmin'eous**, **ful'minous**, pertaining to thunder and lightning.— **fulminating gold**, a green powder made from

auric oxide and ammonium hydroxide; **fulminating mercury**, mercuric fulminate; **fulminating silver**, a black solid made from silver oxide and ammonium hydroxide; **fulmin'ic acid**, an acid isomeric with cyanic acid. [L. *fulmināre*, *-ātum—fulmen*, *-inis*, lightning—*fulgēre*, to shine.]

fulsome, *fool'səm*, also *ful'*, *adj.* cloying or causing surfeit: nauseous: offensive: gross: rank: disgustingly fawning.—*adv.* **ful'somely.**—*n.* **ful'someness.** [**full** and affix *-some.*]

fulvous, *ful'vəs*, *adj.* dull yellow: tawny.—*adj.* **ful'vid.** [L. *fulvus*, tawny.]

fum. See **fung.**

fumado, *fū-mä'dō*, *n.* a smoked fish, esp. a pilchard. [Sp., smoked—L. *fūmāre*, to smoke.]

Fumaria, *fū-mā'ri-ä*, the fumitory genus, giving name to the **Fumaria'ceae**, a family akin to the poppies.—**fumaric** (*fū-mar'ik*) **acid**, an acid isomeric with maleic acid, found in Fumaria and other plants. [L. *fūmus*; see **fumitory**.]

fumarole, *fūm'ə-rōl*, *n.* a hole emitting gases in a volcano or volcanic region. [Fr. *fumerolle* or It. *fumaruola*—L. *fūmus*, smoke.]

fumble, *fum'bl*, *v.i.* to grope about awkwardly: to make bungling or unsuccessful attempts: to mumble.—*v.t.* to handle, manage, or effect awkwardly or bunglingly: to huddle: to mumble.— *n.* **fum'bler.**—*adv.* **fum'blingly.** [Cf. Du. *fommelen*, to fumble; Dan. *famle*; O.N. *fálma*, to grope about.]

fume, *fūm*, *n.* smoke or vapour: any volatile matter: heat of mind, rage, fretful excitement: a passionate person: anything unsubstantial, vain conceit.—*v.i.* to smoke: to throw off vapour: to come off or pass in fumes: to be in a rage.—*v.t.* to treat with fumes: to give off: to offer incense to.—*n.* **fūm'age**, hearth-money; **fūm'atory**, a place for smoking or fumigation; **fume'-cham'ber**, **-cup'board**, a case for laboratory operations that give off fumes; **fūmos'ity**, a fuming condition: an exhalation: breath stinking of food or drink.— *adjs.* **fūm'ous**, **fūm'y**.—**fumed oak**, oak darkened by ammonia fumes. [L. *fūmus*, smoke.]

fumet, **fewmet**, *fū'mit*, *n.* (*arch.*, usu. in *pl.*) the dung of deer, hares, etc. [Appar. Anglo-Fr.—L. *fimāre*, to dung.]

fumet, **fumette**, *fū-met'*, *n.* the scent of game when high. [Fr. *fumet.*]

fumigate, *fūm'i-gāt*, *v.t.* to expose to fumes, esp. for purposes of disinfecting, or destroying pests: to perfume.—*ns.* **fūm'igant**, a source of fumes, esp. a substance used for fumigation; **fūmigā'tion**, **fūm'igātor**, a fumigating apparatus.—*adj.* **fum'i-gatory.** [L. *fūmigāre*, *-ātum.*]

fumitory, *fūm'i-tər-i*, *n.* a plant of the genus Fumaria.—Also (*Shak.*) **fem'iter** or **fen'itar**, **fem'etary.** [O.Fr. *fume-terre*, lit. earth-smoke— L. *fūmus*, smoke, *terra*, earth; reason for name not obvious.]

fun, *fun*, *n.* (*obs.*) a hoax, trick: merriment: sport: a source of merriment or amusement.—*v.t.* (*obs.*) to trick.—*v.i.* to make sport: (*pr.p.* **fun'ing**).— **be great fun**, to be very amusing; **in fun**, in joke, not seriously; **like fun** (*coll.*), in a rapid manner; **make fun-of**, poke fun at, to ridicule. [Prob. a form of obs. *fon*, to befool.]

funambulist, *fū-nam'bū-list*, *n.* a rope-walker or rope-dancer.—*v.i.* **fūnam'būlate.**—*ns.* **fūnambū-lā'tion**; **fūnam'būlātor.**—*adj.* **fūnam'būlatory.** [L. *fūnambulus*, a rope walker—*fūnis*, rope, *ambulāre*, to walk.]

function, *fung(k)'shən*, *n.* the doing of a thing: performance: activity: duty peculiar to any office: faculty, exercise of faculty: the peculiar office of anything: (*obs.*) a profession: a solemn service: a ceremony: a social gathering: (*math.*) a quantity so connected with another that any change in the one produces a corresponding change in the other: the technical term in physiology for the vital activity of organ, tissue, or cell.—*v.i.* to perform a function: act: operate: work.—*adj.* **func'tional**, pertaining to or performed by functions: of disease, characterised by impairment of function, not of organs: designed with special regard to purpose: serving a function.—*adv.* **func'tionally.**

—*n.* **func'tionary,** one who discharges any duty : one who holds an office.—*v.i.* **func'tionate,** to perform a function.—*adj.* **func'tionless,** having no function. [O.Fr.,—L. *functiō, -ōnis—fungī, functus,* to perform.]

fund, *fund, n.* a sum of money on which some enterprise is founded or expense supported : a supply or source of money : a store laid up : supply : (*pl.*) permanent debts due by a government and paying interest.—*v.t.* to form into a stock charged with interest : to place in a fund.—*adj.* **fund'able,** capable of being converted into a fund or into bonds.—*adj.* **fund'ed,** invested in public funds : existing in the form of bonds.—*n.* **fund'-holder,** one who has money in the public funds.—*adj.* **fund'less,** destitute of supplies or money. [L. *fundus,* the bottom.]

fundamental, *fun-də-ment'əl, adj.* basal : serving as foundation : essential : primary : important.—*n.* that which serves as a groundwork : an essential : (*mus.*) the root of a chord or of a system of harmonics.—*ns.* **fund'ament** (-*mənt*), the lower part or seat of the body; **fundament'alism,** belief in the literal truth of the Bible, against evolution, etc.; **fundament'alist,** one who professes this belief; **fundamental'ity.**—*adv.* **fundament'ally.** [L. *fundāmentum,* foundation, *fundāre,* to found.]

fundus, *fun'dəs, n.* the bottom of anything : (*anat.*) the rounded bottom of a hollow organ. [L.]

funeral, *fū'nər-l, n.* disposal of the dead, with any ceremonies or observances connected therewith : a procession to the place of burial or cremation, etc. : (*Spens., Shak.*) death : (*Spens.*) tomb.—*adj.* pertaining to the disposal of the dead.—*adjs.* **fūne'bral, fūne'brial,** funereal; **fū'nerary,** pertaining to or suiting a funeral; **fūne'real,** pertaining to a funeral : dismal : mournful.—**your, my** (etc.) **funeral,** your, my (etc.) affair, or lookout. [L.L. *fūnerālis* and L. *fūnerārius, fūnebris, fūnēreus—*L. *fūnus, fūnĕris,* a funeral procession.]

funest, *fū-nest', adj.* deadly : lamentable. [Fr.,—L. *fūnestus,* destructive.]

fung, *fung,* **fum,** *fum, n.* a fabulous Chinese bird, sometimes called phoenix. [Chin. *fung, fêng.*]

fungibles, *fun'ji-blz, n.pl.* (*law*) movable effects which perish by being used, and which are estimated by weight, number, and measure. [L.L. *fungibilis*—L. *fungī,* to perform; see **function.**]

fungus, *fung'gəs, n.* a plant of one of the lowest groups, thallophytes without chlorophyll, including mushrooms, toadstools, mould, etc. : proud-flesh formed on wounds : (*pl.* **fungi,** *fun'jī,* or **funguses**).—*adj.* **fung'al,** pertaining to fungus.—*n.* **fungicide** (*fun'ji-sīd*), a means of killing fungi.—*adjs.* **fungiform** (*fun'ji-form*), mushroom-shaped; **fung'oid** (-*goid*), **-al,** fungus-like : of the nature of a fungus.—*n.* **fungos'ity,** quality of being fungous.—*adj.* **fung'ous,** of or like fungus : soft : spongy : growing suddenly : ephemeral. [L. *fungus,* a mushroom; cf. Gr. *sphongos, spongos,* a sponge.]

funicle, *fū'ni-kl, n.* a small cord or ligature : a fibre : (*bot.*) the stalk of an ovule.—*adjs.* **fūnic'ū-lar; fūni'cūlate.**—*n.* **fūnic'ūlus,** the umbilical cord : a funicle.—**funicular railway,** a cable-railway. [L. *fūniculus,* dim. of *fūnis,* a rope.]

funk, *fungk, n.* (*coll.*) a state of fear : panic : shrinking or shirking from loss of courage : one who funks.—*v.i.* to flinch : to draw back or hold back in fear.—*v.t.* to balk at or shirk from fear.—*ns.* **funk'hole** (*mil. slang*), a place of refuge, dug-out, retreat; **funk'iness.**—*adj.* **funk'y.** [Poss. Flem. *fonck.*]

funk, *fungk, n.* touchwood : a spark. [Cf. Du. *vonk.*]

funk, *fungk, v.t.* to stifle with smoke. [Ety. dub.]

Funkia, *fungk'i-ä, n.* an E. Asiatic genus allied to the day lilies. [From the German botanist, H. C. *Funck,* 1771–1839.]

funnel, *fun'l, n.* a vessel, usually a cone ending in a tube, for pouring fluids into bottles, etc. : a passage for the escape of smoke, etc.—*adj.* **funn'elled,** with a funnel : funnel-shaped.—*n.* **funn'el-net,** a net shaped like a funnel. [Prob. through Fr. or Port. from L. *infundibulum—fundĕre,* to pour.]

funnel, *fun'l, n.* (*prov.*) the offspring of a stallion and a she-ass. [Origin unknown.]

funny, *fun'i, adj.* full of fun : droll : mirth-provoking : (*coll.*) queer, odd.—*n.pl.* **funn'ies,** (*U.S.*) the comic section of a newspaper.—*adv.* **funn'ily.** —*n.* **funn'iness.—funny bone** (a punning translation of L. *humerus*), the bone at the elbow with the comparatively unprotected ulnar nerve which, when struck, shoots a tingling sensation down the forearm to the fingers.

funny, *fun'i, n.* a light clinker-built pleasure-boat, with a pair of sculls. [Perh. from the foregoing.]

Funtumia, *fun-tū'mi-ä, n.* an African genus of apocynaceous trees, yielding Lagos rubber. [From a Gold Coast name.]

fur, *fur, n.* the thick, soft fine hair of certain animals : the skin with this hair attached : a garment of fur : furred animals (opposed to *feather*) : (*her.*) a patched or tufted tincture : a coating on the tongue : a crust in boilers, etc. : a strengthening piece nailed to a rafter.—*v.t.* to clothe, cover, coat, trim or line with fur : to coat.—*v.i.* to become coated : (*pr.p.* **furr'ing**; *pa.t.* and *pa.p.* **furred**).—*adj.* **furred.**—*ns.* **furr'ier,** a dealer or worker in furs; **furr'iery,** furs in general : trade in furs; **furr'ing,** fur trimmings : a coating on the tongue : (also **firr'ing**) strips of wood fastened to joists, etc. : a lining to a wall to carry lath, provide an air-space, etc.; **fur'-seal,** a sea-bear, an eared seal with close fur under its long hairs.—*adj.* **furr'y,** consisting of, like, covered with, or dressed in fur. [O.Fr. *forrer* (Fr. *fourrer*), to line, encase—*forre, fuerre,* sheath.]

fur, furr, *fur, n.* (*Scot.*) a form of **furrow.**

furacious, *fū-rā'shəs, adj.* thievish.—*ns.* **fūrā'-ciousness, fūrac'ity** (-*ras'i-ti*). [L. *fūrāx, -ācis—fūr,* thief.]

furbelow, *fur'bi-lō, n.* a plaited border or flounce : a superfluous ornament.—*v.t.* to flounce. [Fr., It., and Sp. *falbala;* of unknown origin.]

furbish, *fur'bish, v.t.* to purify or polish : to rub up until bright : to renovate.—*n.* **fur'bisher.** [O.Fr. *fourbir, fourbiss-,* from O.H.G. *furban,* to purify.]

furcate, furcated, *fur'kāt, -id, adj.* forked.—*adj.* **fur'cal.—*n.* **furca'tion.—*adj.* **furcif'erous** (-*sif'*), bearing a forked appendage : rascally (in allusion to the *furca* or yoke of criminals).—*n.* **fur'cūla,** the united clavicles of a bird—the merry-thought.—*adj.* **fur'cūlar,** furcate : shaped like a fork. [L. *furca,* fork.]

Furcraea, *fur-krē'ä,* **Fourcroya,** *fōōr-kroi'ä, n.* a tropical American genus of plants akin to **Agave,** yielding Mauritius hemp. [After A. F. de *Fourcroy* (1755-1809), French chemist.]

furder, *fur'dər,* an obs. form (*Milt.*) of **further.**

furfur, *fur'fur, -fər* (*Browning,* **furfair**), *n.* dandruff, scurf.—*adj.* **furfuraceous** (*fur-fū-rā'shəs*), branny : scaly : scurfy.—*ns.* **furfural** (*fur'fū-ral, -fə-ral*), in full **furfural'dehyde;** also called **fur'al, fur'furol(e), fūr'ol(e),** a liquid (C₄H₃O·CHO) got by heating bran with dilute sulphuric acid; **fur'furan** (also called **fūr'an**), a colourless liquid (C₄H₄O) got from wood-tar.—*adj.* **fur'furous** (*fur'fū-rəs, -fə-rəs*), furfuraceous. [L. *furfur,* bran.]

furibund, *fū'ri-bund, adj.* raging. [L. *furibundus—furia,* rage.]

furious, *fū'ri-əs, adj.* full of fury : violent.—*n.* **fūrios'ity,** madness.—*adv.* **fū'riously.**—*n.* **fū'riousness.** [O.Fr. *furieus*—L. *furiōsus—furia,* rage.]

furioso, *fōō-ri-ō'sō, n.* a furious person, madman.—*adj.* and *adv.* (*mus.*) with fury. [It.; cf. **furious.**]

furl, *furl, v.t.* to roll up. [Perh. **fardel.**]

furlana, *fōōr-lä'nä.* Same as **forlana.**

furlong, *fur'long, n.* 40 poles, one-eighth of a mile. [O.E. *furlang—furh,* furrow, *lang,* long.]

furlough, *fur'lō, n.* leave of absence.—*v.t.* to grant furlough to. [Du. *verlof;* cf. Ger. *verlaub.*]

furmenty, furmety, furmity. See **frumenty.**

furnace, *fur'nis, n.* an enclosed structure in which great heat is produced : a time or place of grievous affliction or torment.—*v.t.* to exhale like a furnace : to subject to the heat of a furnace. [O.Fr. *fornais*—L. *fornāx, -ācis—fornus,* an oven.]

furniment, *fur'ni-ment, n.* (*Spens.*) furnishing.

furnish, *fur′nish, v.t.* to fit up or supply completely, or with what is necessary: to supply, provide: to equip.—*adj.* **fur′nished,** equipped: stocked with furniture.—*n.* **fur′nisher.**—*n.pl.* **fur′nishings,** fittings of any kind, esp. articles of furniture, etc., within a house: (*Shak.*) any incidental part.—*n.* **fur′nishment.** [O.Fr. *furnir, furniss-*; of Gmc. origin; cf. O.H.G. *frummen,* to further.]

furniture, *fur′ni-tyər, n.* movables, either for use or ornament, with which a house is equipped: (*Shak.*) equipment: the trappings of a horse: (*Shak.*) decorations: the necessary appliances in some arts: accessories: metal fittings for doors and windows: (*print.*) the pieces of wood or metal put round pages of type to make margins and fill the spaces between the pages and the chase. [Fr. *fourniture.*]

furor, *fū′ror, n.* fury: excitement, enthusiasm. [L.]

furore, *foo-ror′ā, n.* a craze: wild enthusiasm. [It.]

furrow, *fur′ō, n.* the trench made by a plough: a groove: a wrinkle.—*v.t.* to form furrows in: to groove: to wrinkle.—*n.* **furr′ow-weed** (*Shak.*), a weed of ploughed land.—*adj.* **furr′owy.** [O.E. *furh;* cf. Ger. *furche,* L. *porca,* ridge.]

furth, *furth, adv.* (*Scot.*) forth: outside of.—**furth of,** outside: beyond the bounds of. [Variant of **forth.**]

further, *fur′dhər, adv.* at or to a greater distance or degree: in addition.—*adj.* more distant: additional.—*adv.* **fur′thermore,** in addition to what has been said, moreover, besides.—*adj.* **fur′thermost,** most remote.—*adv.* **fur′thest,** at or to the greatest distance.—*adj.* most distant.—**see one further,** see one hanged, or the like. [O.E. *furthor* (adv.), *furthra* (adj.)—*fore* or *forth* with comp. suffix *-ther.*]

further, *fur′dhər, v.t.* to help forward, promote.—*ns.* **fur′therance,** a helping forward; **fur′therer,** a promoter, advancer.—*adj.* **fur′thersome,** helpful: advantageous: rash. [O.E. *fyrthran.*]

furtive, *fur′tiv, adj.* stealthy: secret.—*adv.* **fur′-tively.** [L. *furtivus—fūr,* a thief.]

furuncle, *fū′rung-kl, n.* a boil.—*adjs.* **furun′cular, furun′culous.** [L. *furunculus,* lit. a little thief.]

fury, *fū′ri, n.* rage: violent passion: madness: (**Fury,** *myth.*) one of the three goddesses of vengeance, the Erinyes, or euphemistically Eumenides—Tisiphone, Alecto, and Megaera (in *Milt.* a Fate): hence a passionate, violent woman. [Fr. *furie*—L. *furia—furĕre,* to be angry.]

furze, *furz, n.* whin or gorse.—*adj.* **furz′y,** overgrown with furze. [O.E. *fyrs.*]

fusain, *fū-zān′, n.* an important constituent of coal, resembling charcoal and consisting of plant remains from which the volatiles have been eliminated (also *fū′zān*): artists′ fine charcoal. [Fr., the spindle-tree, or charcoal made from it.]

fusarole, fusarol, *fū′sə-rōl,* or *-zə-, n.* (*archit.*) an astragal moulding. [Fr. *fusarolle*—It. *fusaruolo,* spindle-whorl—L. *fūsus,* spindle.]

fuscous, *fus′kəs, adj.* brown: dingy.—Also (*Lamb*) **fusc.** [L. *fuscus.*]

fuse, *fūz, v.t.* to melt: to liquefy by heat: to join by, or as if by, melting together.—*v.i.* to be melted: to be reduced to a liquid: to melt together: to blend or unite: of an electric light, to go out by melting of a fuse.—*n.* a bit of fusible metal, with its mounting, inserted as a safeguard in an electric circuit.—*n.* **fūsibil′ity,** the degree of ease with which a substance can be fused.—*adjs.* **fū′sible,** able to be fused or easily fused; **fū′sil** (*fū′zil; Milt.*), cast: fusible: molten.—Also **fūsile** (*fū′zil, -sil, -zil*).—*ns.* **fūsing-point,** melting point; **fū′sion** (*-zhən*), melting: the state of fluidity from heat: a close union of things, as if melted together: (*U.S.*) coalition; **fū′sionism,** a policy that favours union or coalition; **fū′sionist.—fusible metal,** an alloy of bismuth, lead, and tin (sometimes with mercury or cadmium) that melts at temperatures of 60° to 180° C. [L. *fundĕre, fūsum,* to melt.]

fuse, *fūz, n.* a tube filled with combustible matter for firing mines, discharging shells, etc.—Also **fuze.** [It. *fuso*—L. *fūsus,* a spindle.]

fusee, fuzee, *fū-zē′, n.* the spindle in a watch or clock on which the chain is wound: a match with

long, oval head for outdoor use: a fuse for firing explosives. [O.Fr. *fusée,* a spindleful—L. *fūsus,* a spindle.]

fusee. Same as **fusil** (2).

fuselage, *fū′zil-ij,* or *fū-zə-läzh′, n.* the body of an aeroplane. [Fr. *fuseler,* to shape like a spindle —L. *fūsus,* spindle.]

fusel-oil, *fū′zl-oil, n.* a nauseous oil in spirits distilled from potatoes, grain, etc. [Ger. *fusel,* bad spirits.]

fushion, fusion. See foison.

fusiform, *fū′zi-form, adj.* spindle-shaped. [L. *fūsus,* spindle, *forma,* shape.]

fusil, *fū′zil, n.* (*her.*) an elongated rhomboidal figure. [O.Fr. *fusel*—L. *fūsus,* a spindle.]

fusil, *fū′zil, n.* a flint-lock musket.—*ns.* **fusilier′, fusileer′,** formerly a soldier armed with fusil, now simply a historical title borne by a few regiments; **fusillade** (*-ād′*), simultaneous or continuous discharge of firearms.—*n.* **fusillā′tion,** death by shooting. [O.Fr. *fuisil,* a flint-musket, same as It. *focile*—L.L. *focile,* steel (to strike fire with), dim. of L. *focus,* a fireplace.]

fusil, fusile, fusion. See under **fuse** (1).

fuss, *fus, n.* a bustle: flurry: commotion, esp. over trifles: petty ostentatious activity or attentions.—*v.i.* to be in a fuss, agitate about trifles.—*v.t.* to agitate, flurry.—*n.* **fuss′er.**—*adv.* **fuss′ily.**—*ns.* **fuss′iness;** **fuss′-pot,** one who fusses.—*adj.* **fuss′y.** [Origin obscure.]

fust, *fust, n.* a mouldy or musty smell: the shaft of a column.—*v.i.* to mould: to smell mouldy: to taste of the cask.—*ns.* **fustilā′rian, fustil(l)ir′ian,** (*Shak.*) a term of abuse; **fust′ilugs,** a gross overgrown person, esp. a woman; **fust′iness.**—*adj.* **fust′y,** smelling of the cask: musty: stale: stuffy: wanting in freshness. [O.Fr. *fust* (Fr. *fût*), cask— L. *fūstis,* cudgel.]

fustanella, *fus-tə-nel′ä, n.* a white kilt worn by Greek men. [Mod. Gr. *phoustanella,* dim. of *phoustani,* Albanian *fustan*—It. *fustagno,* fustian.]

fustet, *fus′tat, n.* Venetian sumach (*Rhus Cotinus*), or its wood, source of the dye called young fustic. [Fr.,—Prov. *fustet*—Ar. *fustuq;* see fustic.]

fustian, *fust′yən, n.* a kind of coarse, twilled cotton fabric, including moleskin, velveteen, corduroy, etc.: a pompous and unnatural style of writing or speaking: bombast: a liquor made of white wine with yolk of eggs, lemon, spices, etc.—*adj.* made of fustian: bombastic.—*v.i.* **fust′ianise** (*Holmes*), to write bombastically.—*n.* **fust′ianist,** one who writes bombast. [O.Fr. *fustaigne* (Fr. *futaine*)— It. *fustagno*—L.L. *fustāneum,* prob. from *El-Fustāt* (Old Cairo) where it may have been made.]

fustic, *fus′tik, n.* formerly, fustet (now called **young fustic**): now, the wood of a tropical American tree (*Chlorophora tinctoria*), yielding a yellow dye.—Also **fus′toc.** [Fr. *fustoc*—Sp. *fustoc* —Ar. *fustuq*—Gr. *pistakē,* pistachio.]

fustigate, *fus′ti-gāt, v.t.* to cudgel.—*n.* **fustigā′tion.** [L. *fūstigāre, -ātum—fūstis,* a stick.]

Fusus, *fū′səs, n.* a genus of gasteropods, allied to whelks—the spindle-shells. [L. *fūsus,* spindle.]

futchel, *fuch′əl, n.* a piece of timber lengthwise of a carriage, supporting the splinter-bar and the pole.

futhork, futhorc, futhark, *foo′thork, -thärk, n.* the Runic alphabet. [From the first six letters, *f, u, þ (th), o* or *a, r, k.*]

futile, *fū′til, adj.* ineffectual: trifling: (*obs.*) tattling. —*adv.* **fu′tilely.**—*ns.* **futilitā′rian,** one who gives himself to profitless pursuits: one who believes all to be futile; **futil′ity,** uselessness. [L. *fūtilis,* leaky, futile—*fundĕre,* to pour.]

futtock, *fut′ək, n.* one of the crooked timbers of a wooden ship.—*n.* **futt′ock-plate,** an iron plate with dead-eyes, for the topmast or topgallant rigging.—*n.pl.* **futt′ock-shrouds,** short pieces of rope or chain securing the futtock-plates to a band round a lower mast. [Perh. for **foot-hook.**]

future, *fū′tyər, adj.* about to be: that is to come: (*gram.*) expressive of time to come.—*n.* time to come: life, fate, or condition in time to come: (*gram.*) the future tense: (in *pl.*) goods bought and sold to be delivered at a future time.—*adjs.* **fut′ureless**, without prospects; **fut′ure-per′fect** (*gram.*), expressive of action viewed as past in reference to an assumed future time.—*n.* the future-perfect tense: a verb in that tense.—*ns.* **fut′urism** (*art*), a movement claiming to anticipate or point the way for the future, esp. a 20th-century revolt against tradition; **fut′urist**, one whose chief interests are in what is to come: a believer in futurism.—*adj.* **futurist′ic**; **futurition** (*-ish′ən*), future existence: accomplishment: futurity; **futurity** (*fū-tū′ri-ti*), time to come: an event, or state of being, yet to come. [Fr. *futur* —L. *futūrus*, used as fut.p. of *esse*, to be.]

fuze. See fuse (2).

fuzz, *fuz, n.* fine light particles or fibres, as dust,

down, etc.: fluff: blurr.—*v.i.* to disintegrate in fuzz.—*n.* **fuzz′-ball**, **fuss′-ball**, a puff-ball.—*adv.* **fuzz′ily.**—*n.* **fuzz′iness.**—*adj.* **fuzz′y**, covered with fuzz: fluffy: blurred. [Origin doubtful.]

fuzzle, *fuz′l, v.t.* (*prov.*) to fuddle.

fy, *fī, interj.* Same as fie.

fyke. Same as fike.

fyke, *fīk, n.* (*U.S.*) a bag-net. [Du. *fuik*.]

fyle (*Spens.*). See file.

fylfot, filfot, *fil′fot, n.* a swastika, esp. one turned counter-clockwise. [Prob. from misunderstanding of a manuscript, *fylfot*=fill-foot, really meaning a device for filling the foot of a painted window.]

fyrd, fard, fürd, *n.* the militia of Old English times. [O.E. *fyrd*, army.]

fytte. See fit (3).

G

G, g, *jē, n.* the seventh letter of our alphabet, and of the Roman ; originally a form of C, inserted in the place of the disused Z, its ordinary sound (as in Latin) a voiced guttural stop, but in some words in English the same as J : (*mus.*) the fifth note of the diatonic scale of C major—also *sol* : the scale or key having that note for its tonic : a symbol (*g*) for acceleration due to gravity, which is about 32 feet per second per second : as a mediaeval Roman numeral G=400, Ḡ=400,000.—*ns.* **G′-clef,** a clef on the second line of the treble stave, marking G, the treble clef ; **G′-man,** (*U.S.*) an agent of the Federal Bureau of Investigation (for Government-man).

gab, *gab, v.i.* (*coll.*) to chatter, prate.—*n.* idle or fluent talk, prattle.—*n.* **gabb′er,** a chatterer.—*adj.* **gabb′y,** garrulous.—**gift of the gab,** a talent (or propensity) for talking. [Origin doubtful.]

gab, *gab, n.* (*obs.*) mockery : a jest : a vaunt.—*v.i.* to brag. [O.Fr. *gabber,* to mock.]

gab, *gab, n.* a Scots form of **gob.**

gabbart, *gab′art, n.* a barge.—Also **gabb′ard.** [Fr. *gabare*—Prov. and It. *gabarra.*]

gabble, *gab′l, v.i.* to talk inarticulately : to chatter : to cackle like geese.—*ns.* **gabb′le,** gabbling ; **gabb′ler** ; **gabb′ling, gabb′lement.** [Perh. freq. of **gab** (1).]

gabbro, *gab′rō, n.* a coarsely crystalline igneous rock composed of labradorite or similar plagioclase and pyroxene, often with olivine and magnetite.—*adj.* **gabbroitic** (*-it′ik*). [It.]

gabelle, *gäb-el′, n.* a tax, esp. formerly in France, on salt.—*n.* **gabell′er,** a collector of gabelle. [Fr. *gabelle*—L.L. *gabella, gablum* ; of Gmc. origin.]

gaberdine, gabardine, *gab′ər-dēn, n.* a loose cloak, esp. a Jew's : a closely woven twill fabric, esp. of cotton and wool. [O.Fr. *gauvardine* ; perh. M.H.G. *wallevart,* pilgrimage, whence also Sp. *gabardina,* &c.]

gaberlunzie, *gab′ər-lün′i, -lun′zi, -yi, n.* (*Scot.*) a beggar's pouch : a strolling beggar.

gabion, *gä′bi-ən, n.* (*fort.*) a bottomless basket of earth, used in fortification and engineering : (*Scott*) a small curiosity.—*ns.* **gä′bionade,** a work formed of gabions ; **gä′bionage,** gabions collectively.—*adj.* **gä′bioned,** furnished with gabions. [Fr.,—It. *gabbione,* a large cage—*gabbia*—L. *cavea,* cage.]

gable, *gä′bl, n.* (*archit.*) the triangular part of an exterior wall of a building between the top of the side-walls and the slopes on the roof—(*Scot.*) **gä′vel.**—*adj.* **gä′bled.**—*ns.* **gä′ble-end,** the end-wall of a building on the side where there is a gable ; **gä′blet,** (*dim.*) a small gable over a niche, buttress, tabernacle, &c. ; **gä′ble-win′dow,** a window in a gable-end : a window with its upper part shaped like a gable. [The northern form *gavel* is prob. O.N. *gafl* ; Sw. *gafvel,* Dan. *gavl* ; the southern form *gable* is prob. through O.Fr. *gable,* from O.N. *gafl.*]

gabnash, *gab′nash, n.* (*Scot.*) prattle : chatter : a pert prattler. [Cf. *nashgab.*]

gaby, *gä′bi, n.* a simpleton. [Origin unknown.]

gad, *gad, n.* a metal spike or pointed bar : a miner's wedge or chisel : (*obs.* ; also **gade, gaid,** *gäd*) a spear : (*Shak.*) a graver : a rod or stick : a goad : the bar across a Scottish condemned cell, on which the iron ring ran which fastened the shackles. —*n.* **gad′ling,** one of the spikes on the knuckles of a gauntlet.—**upon the gad,** (*Shak.*) upon the spur of the moment. [O.N. *gaddr,* a spike ; confused with O.E. *gád* ; see **goad.**]

gad, *gad, interj.* a minced form of **God.**—*interj.* **gad-zooks′,** an obs. minced oath (app. for *God's hooks*).

gad, *gad, v.i.* to rush here and there in a wayward uncontrolled manner : to straggle : (*pr.p.* **gadd′-ing ;** *pa.t.* and *pa.p.* **gadd′ed**).—*n.* the move, gadding about.—*ns.* **gad′about, gadd′er,** one who rushes from place to place. [Prob. back-formation from **gadling ;** or from **gadfly.**]

gadfly, *gad′flī, n.* a blood-sucking fly (Tabanus) that distresses cattle : sometimes applied to a bot-fly : a mischievous gadabout. [**gad** (1) or O.E. *gád* (see **goad**) and **fly.**]

gadge, *gaj, n.* an instrument of torture (*Browning*).

gadget, *gaj′it, n.* any small ingenious device : a what-d'ye-call-it.

Gadhel, *gad′el, n.* a Gael, a Celt of the branch to which the Irish, the Scottish Highlanders, and the Manx belong.—*adj.* **Gadhelic** (*-el′ik, -ēl′ik,* or *gad′*). [Ir. *Gaedheal* (pl. *Gaedhil*).]

gadi, *gäd′ē, gud′ē, n.* an Indian throne. [Marathi *gādī,* Bengali *gadī.*]

gadling, *gad′ling, n.* (*obs.*) a vagabond. [O.E. *gædeling,* orig. companion.]

gadling. See **gad** (1).

gadoid. See under **Gadus.**

gadolinite, *gad′ə-lin-īt, n.* a silicate of yttrium, beryllium, and iron.—*n.* **gadolin′ium,** a metal of the rare earths (Gd ; at. numb. 64). [From the Finnish chemist *Gadolin* (1760-1852).]

gadroon, *gə-drōōn′, n.* a boss-like ornament, used in series in plate, &c.—*adj.* **gadrooned′.**—*n.* **gad-roon′ing.** [Fr. *godron.*]

gadsman, *gadz′mən, n.* (*Scot.*) one who drives horses at the plough. [**gad** (1), or O.E. *gád* (see **goad**), and **man.**]

gadso, *gad′sō, interj.* expressing surprise. [Origin obscene,—It. *cazzo,* assimilated to **gad** (2).]

Gadus, *gä′dəs, n.* the cod genus, typical of the family Gadidae (*gad′i-dē*).—*ns.* **gäde, gäd′oid,** a fish of the family.—*adj.* **gad′oid,** codlike. [Latinised from Gr. *gados,* the hake or similar fish.]

gadwall, *gad′wawl, n.* a northern freshwater duck.

gae, *gā,* a Scots form of **go** :—*pr.p.* **gaun ;** *pa.t.* **gaed ;** *pa.p.* **gane.**

Gaekwar, *gik′wär, n.* the prince of Baroda in India. —Also **Gaikwar, Guicowar.** [Marathi *gāekwār,* cowherd.]

Gael, *gāl, n.* one whose language is Gadhelic, esp. a Scottish Highlander.—*adj.* **Gaelic** (*gāl′ik,* also *gäl′ik*), pertaining to the Gaels. — *n.* Gadhelic, the Scottish Highland language.—*v.t.* **gael′icise** (*-sīz*).—*n.* **gael′icism** (*-sizm*). [Gael. *Gaidheal.*]

gaff, *gaf, n.* a hook used esp. for landing large fish : (*naut.*) the spar to which the head of a fore-and-aft sail is bent.—*v.t.* to hook or bind by means of a gaff.—*n.* **gaff′-top-sail,** a small sail, the head of which is extended on a small gaff which hoists on the top-mast, and the foot on the lower gaff. [Fr. *gaffe.*]

gaff, *gaf, n.* (*slang*) a low theatre : a fair.

gaff, gaffe, *gaf, n.* a blunder. [Fr. *gaffe.*]

gaff, *gaf, v.i.* (*slang*) to gamble.—*ns.* **gaff′er ; gaff′ing.**

gaff, *gaf, n.* (*slang*) humbug, nonsense.—**to blow the gaff,** to disclose a secret, to blab. [Prob. connected with **gab** (2) or **gaff** (3) ; cf. O.E. *gegaf-spræc,* scurrility.]

gaffer, *gaf′ər, n.* originally a word of respect applied to an old man, now familiar (*fem.* **gam-mer**) : the foreman of a squad of workmen. [grandfather, or godfather.]

gag, *gag, v.t.* to stop the mouth of forcibly : to silence : to choke up : to introduce gag into.—*v.i.* to interpolate gag : to choke : to retch : (*pr.p.* **gagg′ing ;** *pa.t.* and *pa.p.* **gagged**).—*n.* something thrust into the mouth or put over it to enforce silence, or to distend the jaws during an operation :

Neutral vowels in unaccented syllables : *el′ə-mənt, in′fənt, ran′dəm*

the closure applied in a debate : (*Lamb*) a nauseous mouthful, boiled fat beef : (*slang*) an actor's interpolation : a joke or hoax.—*n.* **gagg'er**, one who gags. [Prob. imitative of sound made in choking.]

gag, *gag*, *v.t.* (*slang*) to deceive.—*v.i.* to practise imposture.—*n.* a made-up story, lie : (*U.S.*) a laughing-stock.

gaga, *gä'gä*, *adj.* (*slang*) fatuous : in senile dotage. [Fr.]

gage, *gäj*, *n.* a pledge : something thrown down as a challenge, as a glove.—*v.t.* to bind by pledge or security : offer as a guarantee : to stake, wager. [O.Fr. *guage*; Gmc.; see **wage, wed.**]

gage. See **gauge.**

gage, *gäj.* See **greengage.**

gaggle, *gag'l*, *n.* a flock of geese, or of women.— *v.i.* to cackle. — *n.* **gagg'ling**, cackling. — *adj.* garrulous. [Prob. imit.]

gag-tooth, *gag'-tōōth*, *n.* a projecting tooth.—*adj.* **gag'-toothed.**

gahnite, *gän'it*, *n.* a zinc spinel. [J. G. *Gahn* (1745-1818), Swedish chemist.]

gaiety, gaily. See **gay.**

Gaikwar. See **Gaekwar.**

gain, *gān*, *v.t.* to obtain to one's advantage : to earn : to win : to be successful in : to draw to one's own party : to reach.—*v.i.* to profit : to become or appear better : to progress.—*n.* that which is gained : profit : an instance of gaining, a win.—*adj.* **gain'able.**—*n.* **gain'er.**—*adj.* **gain'ful**, lucrative : profitable : engaged in for pay, paid.—*adv.* **gain'fully.**—*n.* **gain'fulness.**—*n.pl.* **gain'ings.**—*adj.* **gain'less.**—*n.* **gain'lessness.**— **gain ground** (see **ground**); **gain on, upon,** to overtake by degrees : to increase one's advantage against : to encroach on. [O.Fr. *gain*, *gaain*, *gaigner*, *gaaignier*, from Gmc., as in O.H.G. *weidenen*, to graze, to seek forage, *weida*, pasture.]

gain, *gān*, *adj.* (*prov.*) near, straight : (*obs.*) convenient. [O.N. *gegn.*]

gaingiving, *gän'giv-ing*, *n.* (*Shak.*) misgiving.

gainly, *gān'li*, *adj.* shapely : comely : graceful. [**gain** (2).]

gainsay, *gān-sā'*, *gān'sā*, *v.t.* to contradict : to deny : to dispute : (*pr.p.* **gainsay'ing**, or *gān'*; *pa.t.* and *pa.p.* **gainsaid**, *gān-sād'*, *-sed'*; *3rd pers. sing. pres. indic.* **gainsays**, *-sāz*).—*n.* **gain'say** (or *-sā'*), denial.—*ns.* **gainsay'er**, (*B.*) an opposer; **gainsay'ing.** [O.E. *gegn*, against, and **say.**]

gainst, 'gainst, *genst*, a poetic abbreviation of **against.**

gainstrive, *gān-strīv'*, *v.t.* (*obs.*) to strive against.— *v.i.* to resist.

gair, *gār*, *n.* (*Scot.*) gore (of cloth or land). [See **gore.**]

gairfowl. See **garefowl.**

gait, *gāt*, *n.* way or manner of walking : a horse's pace.—*adj.* **gait'ed**, having a particular gait. [**gate** (2).]

gait, *gāt*, *n.* (*prov.*) a sheaf of corn set on end.

gaiter, *gāt'ər*, *n.* a covering for the ankle, fitting down upon the shoe. [Fr. *guêtre.*]

gal, *gal*, *n.* (*prov.*) for **girl.**

gala, *gä'lä*, *gā'lä*, *n.* festivity.—*n.* **ga'la-dress**, gay costume for a gala-day. [Fr. *gala*, show—It. *gala*, finery.]

galactic, *gə-lak'tik*, *adj.* pertaining to or obtained from milk : (*astron.*) pertaining to the Milky Way. —*ns.* **galac'tagogue** (*-tə-gog*; Gr. *agōgos*, bringing), a medicine that promotes secretion of milk; **galactom'eter** (Gr. *metron*, measure), an instrument for finding the specific gravity of milk.—*adjs.* **galactoph'orous** (Gr. *phoros*, bringing), milk-carrying; **galactopoiet'ic** (Gr. *poiētikos*, productive), milk-producing. — *ns.* **galactorrhoea** (*-rē'ä*; Gr. *rhoiā*, a flow), a too abundant flow of milk; **galac'tose**, a sugar, ($C_6H_{12}O_6$), got by hydrolysis from lactose. [Gr. *gala*, *galaktos*, milk.]

galage, *gäl-äj'*, an obs. form of **galosh.**

Galago, *gä-lā'gō*, *n.* a genus of large-eared, long-tailed nocturnal African lemurs.

Galam butter, *gä'läm*, shea butter. [*Galam*, a district on the Senegal.]

galangal. See **galingale.**

galantine, *gal'ən-tēn*, *-tin*, *n.* a dish of poultry, veal, &c., served cold in jelly. [Fr.; see **gelatine.**]

galanty show, *gäl-an'ti shō*, a shadow pantomime. [Perh. It. *galanti*, pl. of *galante*; see **gallant.**]

Galaxy, *gal'ək-si*, *n.* the Milky Way, the luminous band of stars stretching across the heavens : any similar system or 'universe' : a splendid assemblage. [Through Fr. and L., from Gr. *galaxias*— *gala*, *-aktos*, milk.]

galbanum, *gal'bə-nəm*, *n.* a gum-resin got from Eastern species of Ferula. [L.,—Gr. *chalbanē*, prob. an Eastern word.]

galdragon, *gal'drə-gən*, *n.* (*Scott*) an obs. Shetland word for a sorceress, witch. [O.N. *galdra-kona* —*galdr*, crowing, incantation, witchcraft, *kuna*, woman.]

gale, *gāl*, *n.* a strong wind between a stiff breeze and a hurricane : in old poetic diction, a gentle wind : a wafted smell : (*U.S.*) a state of excitement. [Origin obscure.]

gale, *gāl*, *n.* (usu. **sweet'-gale**) bog-myrtle. [Prob. O.E. *gagel*; cf. Ger. *gagel.*]

gale, *gāl*, *n.* a periodic payment of rent : a mining licence. [Perh. **gavel.**]

galea, *gal'i-ä*, *gāl'i-ä*, *n.* (*biol.*) a helmet-shaped structure.—*adjs.* **gal'eate, -d.** [L. *galea*, a skin helmet.]

galena, *gə-lē'nä*, *n.* lead-glance, native sulphide of lead.—Also **gale'nite.**—*adj.* **gale'noid.** [L. *galēna*, lead-ore.]

Galenic, *gə-len'ik*, *adj.* pertaining to *Galen* (*Galēnos*), the 2nd-cent. Greek physician, or to his methods and theories.—*adj.* **Galen'ical.**—*n.* a remedy such as Galen prescribed, a vegetable simple.—*ns.* **Galenism** (*gā'lən-izm*); **Ga'lenist.**

Galeopithecus, *gā-li-ō-pi-thē'kəs*, *n.* the so-called flying-lemur.—*adjs.* **galeopithē'cine** (*-sīn*), **galeopithē'coid.** [Gr. *galeē*, weasel, marten, *pithēkos*, ape.]

Galilean, *gal-i-lē'ən*, *adj.* of or pertaining to *Galileo*, the great Italian mathematician (1564-1642).

Galilean, *gal-i-lē'ən*, *adj.* of or pertaining to *Galilee* (L. *Galilaea*, Gr. *Galilaiā*), one of the Roman divisions of Palestine.—*n.* a native of Galilee : a Christian.

galilee, *gal'i-lē*, *n.* (*archit.*) a porch or chapel at the west end of some churches, in which penitents were placed, and where ecclesiastics met women who had business with them.—**galilee porch**, a galilee in direct communication with the exterior. [Perh. suggested by Mark, xvi. 7, or Matt. iv. 15.]

galimatias, *gal-i-mat'i-äs*, *-mä'shi-əs*, *n.* nonsense : any confused mixture of unlike things. [Fr.]

galingale, *gal'ing-gāl*, *n.* the aromatic rootstock of certain E. Indian plants of the ginger family (Alpinia and Kaempferia), formerly much used like ginger : the rootstock of a sedge (*Cyperus longus*), of ancient medicinal repute : also the whole plant.—Also **gal'angal**, **gal'engale**, **galang'a.** [O.Fr. *galingal*—Ar. *khalanjān*—Chin. *ko-liang-kiang*—*Ko*, a district near Canton, *liang*, mild, and *kiang*, ginger.]

galiongee, *gal-yən-jē'*, *n.* a Turkish sailor. [Turk. *qālyūnjī*, deriv. of *qālyūn*—It. *galeone*, galleon.]

galipot, *gal'i-pot*, *n.* the turpentine that exudes from the cluster-pine. [Fr.]

gall, *gawl*, *n.* bile, the greenish-yellow fluid secreted from the liver : bitterness : malignity : (*U.S.*) assurance, presumption.—*ns.* **gall'-bladder**, a reservoir for the bile; **gall'-duct**, a tube for conveying bile or gall.—*adj.* **gall'-less**, without gall : mild : free from rancour.—*n.* **gall'-stone**, a concretion in the gall-bladder or biliary ducts. [O.E. *galla*, *gealla*, gall; cf. Ger. *galle*, Gr. *cholē*, L. *fel*.]

gall, *gawl*, *n.* an abnormal growth on a plant owing to attack by a parasite (fungus, insect, &c.).—*ns.* **gallate** (*gal'āt*), a salt of gallic acid; **gall-fly** (*gawl'-*), **gall'-wasp**, an insect of the hymenopterous family Cynipidae that causes galls by depositing its eggs in plants; **gall'-midge**, a Cecidomyia or kindred gall-making midge; **gall'-nut**, a nutlike gall produced on an oak by a gall-wasp, used for making ink.—**gallic** (*gal'ik*) **acid**, a crystalline substance obtained from gall-nuts, and used in making ink. [Fr. *galle*—L. *galla*, oak-apple.]

gall, *gawl*, *n.* a painful swelling, esp. in a horse: a sore due to chafing: a state or cause of irritation: a chafed place: a bare place: a flaw: (*mining*) a fault or a dyke.—*v.t.* to fret or hurt by rubbing: to irritate.—*v.i.* to become chafed: (*Shak.*) to scoff.—*adj.* **gall'ing**, irritating.—*adv.* **gall'ingly**. [O.E. *galla*, *gealla*, a sore place.]

gallant, *gal'ənt*, *adj.* brave: noble: (*rare*) gay, splendid, magnificent: attentive (esp. formally or obsequiously) to ladies: amorous, erotic (sometimes *gə-lant'* in these two senses).—*n.* a gay, dashing person: a man of fashion: suitor: seducer (also *gə-lant'* in this sense).—*adv.* **gall'antly**.—*ns.* **gall'antness**; **gall'antry**, bravery: intrepidity: attention or devotion to ladies, often in a bad sense, amorous intrigue: (*Shak.*) gallants collectively.— **the honourable and gallant member**, a mode of referring in parliament to a member who is an officer in the fighting services. [Fr. *galant*—O.Fr. *gale*, a merrymaking; prob. Gmc.; cf. **gala**.]

galleass, *gal'i-as*, *n.* (*Shak.*) a vessel of the same construction as a galley, but larger and heavier.— —Also **gall'iass**. [O.Fr. *galeace*—It. *galeazza*, augmentative from *galea*, galley.]

galleon, *gal'i-ən*, *n.* a large vessel with lofty stem and stern, mostly used formerly by Spaniards for carrying treasure. [Sp. *galeón*; cf. **galley**.]

gallery, *gal'ə-ri*, *n.* a covered walk: a long balcony: a long passage: an upper floor of seats, esp. in a theatre, the highest: the occupants of the gallery: a room for the exhibition of works of art: an underground passage, drift, or level.—*v.t.* to tunnel.—*adj.* **gall'eried**, furnished with, or arranged like, a gallery.—**play to the gallery**, to play for the applause of the least cultured. [O.Fr. *galerie* (It. *galleria*).]

galley, *gal'i*, *n.* a long, low-built ship with one deck, propelled by oars and sails: a Greek or Roman warship: a large open rowing-boat: the cooking place on board ship: (*print.*) a flat oblong tray for type that has been set up: a galley-proof.—*ns.* **gall'ey-foist**, (*obs.*) a state barge; **gall'ey-proof**, an impression taken from type on a galley, a slip-proof; **gall'ey-slave**, one condemned to work as a slave at the oar of a galley; **gall'ey-worm**, a myriapod. [O.Fr. *galie*, *galee*—L.L. *galea*.]

galley-west, *gal-i-west'*, *adv.* (*U.S. slang*) into confusion.

galliambic, *gal-i-am'bik*, *adj.* in or of a metre (◡◡—◡—◡— |◡◡—◡◡◡—) said to have been used by the Phrygian priests of Cybele, best known from the *Attis* of Catullus.—*n.pl.* **galliam'bics**, galliambic verses. [Gr. *galliambikos*—*Gallos*, a priest of Cybele, *iambos*, an iamb.]

galliard, *gal'yərd*, *adj.* (*arch.*) brisk, lively.—*n.* a spirited dance for two, in triple time, common in the 16th and 17th centuries: a gay fellow.—*n.* **gall'iardise** (*-ēz*, *-īz*), gaiety: a merry trick. [O.Fr. *gaillard*.]

gallic. See **gall** (2).

Gallic, *gal'ik*, *adj.* and *n.* Gaulish.—*adj.* **Gall'ican**, of or pertaining to France: esp. pertaining to the Roman Catholic Church in France, regarded as national and more or less independent.—*n.* one holding Gallican doctrines.—*n.* **Gall'icanism**, the spirit of nationalism within the French Church— as opposed to *Ultramontanism*, or the absolute subjection of everything to the personal authority of the pope.—*adv.* **Gallice** (*gal'i-sē*; L. *gäl'i-kā*), in French.—*v.t.* and *v.i.* **Gall'icise**, to assimilate or conform to French habits, &c.—*ns.* **Gall'icism**, the use in another language of an expression or idiom peculiar to French; **Gallomā'nia**, a mania for French ways; **Gall'ophil(e)**, one who is friendly to France; **Gall'ophobe**, one who dislikes or fears France or what is French; **Gallopho'bia**. [L. *Gallus*, a Gaul; *Gallicus*, Gaulish.]

galligaskins, *gal-i-gas'kinz*, *n.pl.* wide hose or breeches: leggings. [O.Fr. *garguesque*—It. *grechesco*, Greekish—L. *graecus*, Greek.]

gallimaufry, *gal-i-maw'fri*, *n.* (*Shak.*) any inconsistent or absurd medley: a miscellaneous gathering. [Fr. *galimafrée*, a ragout, hash.]

gallinaceous, *gal-in-ā'shəs*, *adj.* akin to the domestic fowl. [L. *gallīna*, a hen—*gallus*, a cock.]

gallinazo, *gal-i-nä'zō*, *n.* a turkey-buzzard or other vulture. [Sp.,—*gallina*—L. *gallīna*, hen.]

gallinule, *gal'i-nūl*, *n.* a water-hen. [L. *gallīnula*, a chicken—*gallīna*, a hen.]

Gallio, *gal'i-ō*, *n.* one who keeps himself free from trouble and responsibility. [From *Gallio*, Acts xviii. 12-17.]

galliot, **galiot**, *gal'i-ət*, *n.* a small galley: an old Dutch cargo-boat. [Fr. *galiote*—L.L. *galea*, galley.]

gallipot, *gal'i-pot*, *n.* a small glazed pot, esp. for medicine. [Prob. a pot brought in galleys.]

gallise, *gal'īz*, *v.t.* in wine-making, to bring to standard proportions by adding water and sugar to inferior must.—Also **gall'isise**. [Ger. *gallisieren*, from the name of the inventor, Dr L. *Gall*.]

gallium, *gal'i-əm*, *n.* a rare metallic element (atomic number 31). [L. *gallus*, a cock, from the discoverer's name, *Lecoq* de Boisbaudran, or *Gallia*, Gaul, France, his country.]

gallivant, *gal-i-vant'*, *v.i.* to spend time frivolously, esp. in flirting: to gad about. [Perh. **gallant**.]

gallivat, *gal'i-vat*, *n.* a large two-masted Malay boat. [Port. *galeota*; see **galliot**.]

galliwasp, *gal'i-wosp*, *n.* a W. Indian lizard.

galloglass, **gallowglass**, *gal'ō-glas*, *n.* a soldier or armed retainer of a chief in ancient Ireland and other Celtic countries. [Ir. *gallóglách*—Ir. *gall*, foreign, *óglách*, youth.]

gallon, *gal'ən*, *n.* the standard measure of capacity =4 quarts. [O.N.Fr. *galun*, *galon* (O.Fr. *jalon*).]

galloon, *gə-lōōn'*, *n.* a kind of lace: a narrow tapelike trimming or binding material, sometimes made with gold or silver thread.—*adj.* **gallooned'**, adorned with galloon. [Fr. *galon*, *galonner*; prob. cog. with **gallant**.]

galloon, *gə-lōōn'*, *n.* a variant of **galleon**.

gallop, *gal'əp*, *v.i.* to go at a gallop: to ride a galloping animal: to move very fast.—*v.t.* to cause to gallop.—*n.* the pace at which an animal runs when the forefeet are lifted together and the hind-feet together: a ride at a gallop: a track for galloping.—*n.* **gall'oper**, one who, or that which, gallops.—*adj.* **gall'oping**, proceeding at a gallop: (*fig.*) advancing rapidly, as *galloping consumption*.— **Canterbury gallop**, a moderate gallop of a horse (see **canter**). [O.Fr. *galoper*, *galop*; prob. Gmc.; cf. **wallop**.]

gallopade, *gal-əp-ād'*, *n.* a quick kind of dance: the music appropriate to it: a sidewise gallop.— *v.i.* to move briskly: to perform a gallopade. [Fr.]

Gallovidian, *gal-ō-vid'i-ən*, *adj.* belonging to Galloway.—*n.* a native thereof. [*Gallovidia*, Latinised from Welsh *Gallwyddel*.]

gallow, *ga'lō*, *v.t.* (*Shak.*) to frighten. [O.E. *ā-gælwan*, to frighten, to astonish.]

Galloway, *gal'ō-wā*, *n.* a small strong horse, 13-15 hands high: a breed of large black hornless cattle, orig. from *Galloway* in Scotland.

gallows, *gal'ōz*, or (old-fashioned) *gal'əs*, *n.* orig. *pl.*, treated as *sing.* a wooden frame for hanging criminals: (*Shak.*) one who deserves the gallows: (*Shak.*) the look of one destined to hang: any contrivance with posts and cross-beam for suspending things: a frame for the tympan of a hand printing-press: the main frame of a beam-engine: (also **gallus**, **gallace**, *dial.*) one of a pair of braces (*double pl.*, Shak. gal(l)'owses; used also, *Scot.* and *dial.*, in sense of braces).—*adj.* deserving the gallows: villainous: mischievous: in *dial.* a mere intensive.—*adv.* (*dial.*) damnably, confoundedly.— *ns.* **gall'ows-bird**, one who deserves hanging or has been hanged; **gall'ows-foot**.—*adj.* **gall'ows-free**, free from the danger of hanging.—*ns.* **gall'ows-lee**, the place of hanging; **gall'ows-maker**; **gall'owsness**, (*slang*) recklessness.— *adj.* **gall'ows-ripe**, ready for the gallows.—*n.* **gall'ows-tree'**, a gallows.—**cheat the gallows**, to deserve but escape hanging. [M.E. *galwes* (pl.) —O.E. *galga*; Ger. *galgen*.]

gally, *gal'i*, *v.t.* (*prov.*) to scare, daze.—*ns.* **gall'y-bagg'er**, **-begg'ar**, **-crow** (also galli-), a scarecrow. [See **gallow**.]

galoot, gə-lōōt', *n.* (*slang*) a soldier: a marine: a clumsy fellow.

galop, gə-lop', gal'əp, *n.* a lively dance or dance-tune in duple time.—*v.i.* to dance a galop. [Fr.; cf. **gallop**.]

galopin, gal'ə-pin, *n.* (*Scott*) an errand boy: a kitchen boy. [Fr.]

galore, gə-lōr', *adv.* in abundance. [Ir. *go*, an adverbialising participle, *leór*, sufficient.]

galosh, golosh, galoche, gə-losh', *n.* (*obs.*) a rustic shoe, sandal, or clog: a piece running round a shoe or boot above the sole: an overshoe.—*v.t.* to furnish with a galosh. [Fr. *galoche*—Gr. *kalopodion*, dim. of *kalopous*, a shoemaker's last—*kalon*, wood, *pous*, foot.]

galravage. See **gilravage**.

galumph, gə-lumf', *v.i.* to march along boundingly and exultingly. [A coinage of Lewis Carroll.]

galvanism, gal'vən-izm, *n.* current electricity: medical treatment by electric currents.—*adj.* **galvanic** (-van'), of, producing, produced by, galvanism: also *fig.*—*n.* **galvanisā'tion.**—*v.t.* **gal'vanise**, to subject to the action of an electric current: to stimulate to spasmodic action by, or as if by, an electric shock: to confer a false vitality upon: to coat with metal by an electric current: to coat with zinc without using a current.—*ns.* **gal'vaniser, gal'vanist; galvanom'eter**, an instrument for measuring electric currents; **galvanom'etry.**—*adj.* **galvanoplas'tic.**—*ns.* **galvanoplas'ty**, electrodeposition; **galvan'oscope**, an instrument for detecting electric currents.—**galvanic battery, cell**, an electric battery, cell; **galvanic belt**, a belt supposed to benefit the wearer by producing an electric current; **galvanised iron**, iron coated with zinc. [From Luigi *Galvani*, of Bologna, the discoverer (1737-98).]

Galwegian, gal-wē'ji-ən, *adj.* belonging to Galloway.—*n.* a native thereof.—Also **Gallowe'gian**. [On the analogy of *Norwegian*.]

gam, gam, *n.* a school of whales: social intercourse or visit at sea.—*v.i.* to associate in a gam.—*v.t.* to call on, exchange courtesies with. [Ety. dub.]

gam, gâm, *n.* (*Scot.*) a tooth or tusk: the mouth.

gama-grass, gä'mä-gräs, *n.* a tall N. American forage grass (*Tripsacum dactyloides*). [Perh. Sp. *grama*.]

gamash, gəm-ash', *n.* a kind of legging.—Also **gramash, gramosh**. [Fr. (now *dial.*) *gamache*, Prov. *garamacha*, apparently from *Ghadames*, famous for leather.]

gamb, gamb, *n.* (*her.*) a beast's whole foreleg.—*n.* **gam**, (*slang*) a leg. [L.L. *gamba*, a leg.]

gamba, gam'bä, *n.* short for *viola da gamba*: an organ-stop of string-like quality.—*n.* **gam'bist**, a gamba-player.

gambado, gam-bā'dō, *n.* a leather covering or boot attached to a saddle. [It. *gamba*, leg.]

gambado, gam-bā'dō, *n.* a bound or spring of a horse: a fantastic movement, a caper. [Sp. *gambada*; cf. **gambol**.]

gambeson, gam'bi-sən, *n.* an ancient leather or quilted cloth coat worn under the habergeon. [O.Fr.,—O.H.G. *wamba*, belly.]

gambet, gam'bit, *n.* the redshank: (*U.S.*) any sandpiper. [It. *gambetta*, ruffe, *gambetta fosca*, spotted redshank.]

gambir, gambier, gam'bēr, *n.* an astringent substance prepared from the leaves of *Uncaria Gambir*, a rubiaceous climbing shrub of the East Indies, used in tanning and dyeing. [Malay.]

gambit, gam'bit, *n.* (*chess*) the offer of a sacrifice for the sake of an advantage in timing or position in the opening stages of a game: (*fig.*) an initial move in anything, esp. one with an element of trickery.—*ns.* **gam'bit-pawn', -piece'**, one so offered. [Sp. *gambito*—It. *gambetto*, a tripping up—*gamba*, leg.]

gamble, gam'bl, *v.i.* to play for money, esp. for high stakes: to engage in wild financial speculations: to take great risks for the sake of possible advantage.—*v.t.* to squander or lose by staking.—*n.* a transaction depending on chance.—*ns.* **gam'bler**, one who gambles, esp. one who makes it his business; **gam'bling-house, -hell**, a house kept for the accommodation of people who play at games of hazard for money. [Freq. of **game**.]

gamboge, gam-bōōzh', -bōj', -bōōj', *n.* a yellow gumresin, chiefly got from *Garcinia Morella*, used as a pigment and in medicine.—*adjs.* **gambogian** (-bōj', -bōōj'), **gambogic** (-bōj'). [From *Cambodia*, whence it was brought about 1600.]

gambol, gam'bl, *v.i.* to leap: to frisk in sport: (*pr.p.* **gam'bolling**; *pa.t.* and *pa.p.* **gam'bolled**).—*n.* a frisk: a frolic. [Formerly *gambold*—O.Fr. *gambade*—It. *gambata*, a kick—L.L. *gamba*, leg.]

gambrel, gam'brəl, *n.* the hock of a horse: a crooked stick for hanging a carcass, &c.—**gambrel roof**, a mansard roof. [O.Fr. *gamberel*; cf. Fr. *gambier*, a hooked stick; connexion with *cambrel* obscure.]

gambroon, gam-brōōn', *n.* a twilled cloth of worsted and cotton, or linen. [Prob. *Gambrun*, in Persia.]

game, gām, *n.* sport of any kind: (in *pl.*) athletic sports: a contest for recreation: a competitive amusement according to a system of rules: the stake in a game: manner of playing a game: form in playing: the requisite number of points to be gained to win a game: jest, sport, trick: any object of pursuit: scheme or method of seeking an end, or the policy that would be most likely to attain it: fighting spirit: (*Shak.*) gallantry: (*slang*) prostitution: (*slang*) thieving: the spoil of the chase: wild animals hunted by sportsmen: the flesh of such animals: a flock of swans (formerly of other animals) kept for pleasure.—*adj.* of or belonging to animals hunted as game: (*slang*) having the spirit of a fighting cock: plucky, courageous: having the necessary spirit and willingness for some act.—*v.i.* to gamble.—*ns.* **game'-bag**, a bag for holding a sportsman's game; **game'-chick'en, game'cock**, a cock of a breed trained to fight; **game'-dealer; game'-fish**, a fish that affords sport to anglers—opp. to *coarse fish*; **game'keeper**, one who has the care of game.—*n.pl.* **game'-laws**, laws relating to the protection of game.—*n.* **game'-li'cence**, a licence to kill, or to sell, game.—*adv.* **game'ly.**—*ns.* **game'ness; game'-preserve'**, a tract of land stocked with game preserved for sport; **game'preserv'er**, one who preserves game on his land.—*adj.* **game'some**, playful.—*ns.* **game'someness; game'ster**, a gambler: (*Shak.*) a lewd person: (*Shak.*) a maker of sport; **game'tenant**, one who rents the privilege of shooting or fishing over a particular area; **gam'ing, gambling; gam'ing-house**, a gambling-house, a hell; **gam'ing-tā'ble**, a table used for gambling.—*adj.* **gam'y**, having the flavour of game, esp. that kept till tainted: (*coll.*) spirited, plucky.—**big game**, the larger animals hunted; **die game**, to keep up courage to the last; **make game of**, to make sport of, to ridicule; **play a waiting game** (see **wait**); **play the game**, to act in a fair, sportsmanlike, straightforward manner; **red game**, grouse; **round game**, a game, as at cards, in which the number of players is not fixed; **the game is not worth the candle** (see **candle**); **the game is up**, the game is started: the scheme has failed. [O.E. *gamen*, play; O.N. *gaman*, Dan. *gammen*.]

game, gām, *adj.* lame. [Origin obscure.]

gamete, gam'ēt, gam-ēt', *n.* a sexual reproductive cell—an egg-cell or sperm-cell.—*adjs.* **gam'etal** (or -ēt'), **gametic** (-et' or -ēt').—*ns.* **gametangium** (*gam-it-an'ji-əm*), a cell or organ in which gametes are formed (*pl.* **gametan'gia**); **gametogen'esis**, the formation of gametes; **game'tophyte** (or *gam'*; Gr. *phyton*, plant), a plant of the sexual generation, producing gametes. [Gr. *gametēs*, husband, *gametē*, wife—*gameein*, to marry.]

gamic, gam'ik, *adj.* sexual: sexually produced. [Gr. *gamikos*—*gamos*, marriage.]

gamin, gä-man^g, gam'in, *n.* a street Arab, a precocious and mischievous imp of the pavement (*fem.* **gamine**, -mēn). [Fr.]

gamma, gam'ä, *n.* the third letter of the Greek alphabet (Γ, γ=G, g): as a numeral γ'=3, ,γ=3000.—*ns.* **gammād'ion, gammā'tion** (-ti-on),

a figure composed of capital gammas, esp. a swastika.
—**gamma rays**, a penetrating radiation given off by radium and other radio-active substances. [Gr.]

gammer, *gam'ər, n.* an old woman (*masc.* **gaffer**). [grandmother, or godmother.]

gammerstang, *gam'ər-stang, n.* (*prov.*) a tall, awkward person, esp. a woman: a wanton girl. [Perh. **gammer** and **stang**.]

gammexane, *gam-eks'ān, n.* a powerful insecticide. [γ-hexachlorocyclohexane.]

gammock, *gam'ək, n.* (*prov.*) a frolic, fun.—*v.i.* to frolic, to lark.

gammon, *gam'ən, n.* (*rare*) backgammon: a double game at backgammon, won by bearing all one's men before one's opponent bears any: (*slang*) patter, chatter, esp. that of a thief's confederate to divert attention: (mostly *coll.*) a hoax: nonsense, humbug.—*v.t.* to defeat by a gammon at backgammon: to hoax, impose upon.—*v.i.* to talk gammon: to feign.—*ns.* **gamm'oner; gamm'oning.** [Prob. O.E. *gamen*, a game.]

gammon, *gam'ən, n.* the ham of a hog, esp. when cured, now usually with the adjacent parts of the side. [O.N.Fr. *gambon, gambe,* leg.]

gammon, *gam'ən, n.* (*naut.*) the lashing of the bowsprit.—*v.t.* to lash (the bowsprit).

gamo-, *gam'ō-, gam-o'-,* in composition, united, uniting.—*n.* **gamogen'esis,** sexual reproduction. —*adjs.* **gamopet'alous,** with petals united: **gamophyll'ous,** with perianth leaves united: **gamosep'alous,** with sepals united: **gamotrop'ic.**— *n.* **gamot'ropism** (Gr. *tropos*, a turning), tendency of gametes to attract each other. [Gr. *gamos,* marriage.]

gamp, *gamp, n.* (*slang*) a large, clumsy, or untidily tied up umbrella: an umbrella.—*adj.* **gamp'ish,** bulging. [From Mrs Sarah *Gamp,* in Dickens's *Martin Chuzzlewit.*]

gamut, *gam'ət, n.* (*hist. mus.*) the note G on the first line of the bass stave: Guido of Arezzo's scale of six overlapping hexachords, reaching from that note up to E in the fourth space of the treble: any recognised scale or range of notes: the whole compass of a voice or instrument: the full extent of anything. [From *gamma,* the Greek letter G, adopted when it was required to name a note added below the A with which the old scale began, and *ut,* the Aretinian (q.v.) syllable.]

gan, *gan, pa.t.* of **gin.**

ganch, gaunch, *gān(t)sh, gawn(t)sh, v.t.* to impale: to lacerate.—*n.* impaling apparatus: a wound from a boar's tusk. [O.Fr. *gancher*—It. *gancio,* a hook.]

gander, *gan'dər, n.* the male of the goose: a simpleton: (*U.S.*) a man living apart from his wife.—*ns.* **gan'derism; gan'der-moon, -month,** the month of a wife's lying-in; **gan'der-mooner,** a husband during his gander-moon: **gan'der-par'ty,** a social gathering of men only. [O.E. *ganra, gandra;* Du. and L.G. *gander.*]

gane, *gān, pa.p.* of **gae.**

Ganesa, *gun-ā'shä, n.* the elephant-headed Hindu god of foresight.

gang, *gang, n.* a band of roughs or criminals: a number of persons or animals (esp. elk) associating together, often in a bad sense: a number of labourers working together: (*U.S.*) a set of boys who habitually play together: the range of pasture allowed to cattle: a set of tools, &c., used together. —*v.t. and v.i.* to associate in a gang or gangs.— *v.t.* to adjust in coordination.—*ns.* **ganger** (*gang'ər*), **gangs'man,** the foreman of a gang; **gang'ing; gang'-mill,** a sawmill with gang-saws; **gang'-saw,** a saw fitted in a frame with others; **gang'ster,** a member of a gang of roughs or criminals; **gang'sterism.** [O.E. *gang* (Dan. *gang,* Ger. *gang*) —*gangan,* to go.]

gang, *gang, v.i.* and *v.t.* (*Scot.*) to go:—*pr.p.* **gang'-ing** (*rare*); *pa.p.* and *pa.t.* not in use.—*ns.* **gang'-board,** (*naut.*) a gangway, plank, or platform for walking on; **gang'-bye,** (*Scot.*) the go-by.—*n.pl.* **Gang'-days,** (*obs.*) Rogation Days.—*n.* **gang'er,** a walker: a fast horse.—*n.* and *adj.* **gang'rel,** (*Scot.*) vagrant: (a child) beginning to walk.—*adj.* **gang'-there-out,** (*Scot.*) vagrant.—*n.* **gang'way**

(O.E. *gangweg*), a passage into, out of, or through any place, esp. a ship: a way between rows of seats, esp. the cross-passage about halfway down the House of Commons (ministers and ex-ministers with their immediate followers sitting *above the gangway*).—*interj.* make way: make room to pass. [O.E. *gangan,* to go.]

ganglion, *gang'gli-ən, n.* a tumour in a tendon sheath: a nerve-centre: (*pl.* **gang'lia, gang'-lions**).—*adjs.* **gang'liar, ganglionic** (*-on'ik*), pertaining to a ganglion; **gang'liate, -d,** provided with ganglion or ganglia; **gang'liform.** [Gr.]

gangrel. See **gang** (2).

gangrene, *gang'grēn, n.* death of part of the body: the first stage in mortification.—*v.t.* to mortify: to cause gangrene in.—*v.i.* to become gangrenous. —*adj.* **gangrenous** (*gang'-grin-əs*), mortified. [Gr. *gangraina,* gangrene.]

gangue, gang, *gang, n.* rock in which ores are embedded. [Fr.,—Ger. *gang,* a vein.]

gangway. See under **gang** (2).

ganister, gannister, *gan'is-tər, n.* a hard, closegrained siliceous stone, found in the Lower Coal Measures of N. England. [Origin unknown.]

ganja, *gän'jä, n.* an intoxicating preparation, the female flowering tops of Indian hemp. [Hind. *gānjhā.*]

gannet, *gan'ət, n.* the solan goose or other bird of the family Sulidae. [O.E. *ganot,* a sea-fowl; Du. *gent.*]

ganoid, *gan'oid, adj.* (of fish scales) having a glistening outer layer over bone: (of fishes) belonging to an order **Ganoid'ei** (*-i-ī*) in some classifications, variously defined, having commonly such scales, including many fossil forms.—*n.* a ganoid fish.— *n.* **ganoin** (*gan'ō-in*), a calcareous substance, forming an enamel-like layer on ganoid scales. [Gr. *ganos,* brightness, *eidos,* appearance.]

gant, gaunt, *gänt, gawnt, v.i.* (*Scot.*) to yawn.—*n.* a yawn. [Prob. freq. of O.E. *gánian,* to yawn.]

gantlet. Same as **gauntlet** (1 and 2).

gantlope, *gant'lōp.* Same as **gauntlet** (2).

gantry, *gan'tri, n.* a stand for barrels: a platform or bridge for a travelling-crane, railway signals, &c.— Also (in first sense) **gauntry** (*gawn'tri*), **gaun'tree.** [Perh. O.Fr. *gantier*—L. *cantērius,* a trellis—Gr. *kanthēlios,* a pack-ass.]

Ganymede, *gan'i-mēd, n.* a cup-bearer, pot-boy, from *Ganymēdēs,* the beautiful youth who succeeded Hebe as cup-bearer to Zeus: a catamite.

gaol, gaoler. Same as **jail, jailer.**

gap, *gap, n.* an opening or breach: a cleft: a passage: a notch or pass in a mountain-ridge: a breach of continuity.—*v.t.* to notch: to make a gap in.— *adjs.* **gapp'y,** full of gaps; **gap'-toothed,** with teeth set wide apart. [O.N. *gap.*]

gape, *gāp, v.i.* to open the mouth wide: to yawn: to stare with open mouth: to be wide open: (*obs.*; *prob. Shak.*) to bawl.—*n.* act of gaping: the extent to which the mouth can be opened: the angle of the mouth: a wide opening, parting, fissure, chasm, or failure to meet: (**the gapes,** a yawning fit: a disease of poultry of which gaping is a symptom, caused by a threadworm, Syngamus, or **gape'worm,** in the windpipe and bronchial tubes). —*ns.* **gāp'er,** one who gapes: a mollusc (Mya) with shell gaping at each end: a sea-perch (Serranus): (*cricket*) an easy catch; **gape'-seed,** an imaginary commodity that the gaping starer is supposed to be looking for or sowing: hence, the act of staring open-mouthed, or the object stared at.—*n.* and *adj.* **gāp'ing.**—*adv.* **gāp'ingly.** [O.N. *gapa,* to open the mouth; Ger. *gaffen,* to stare.]

gapó, *gä-pō', n.* riverside forest periodically flooded. [Port. (*i*)*gapó*—Tupí *igapó, ygapó.*]

gar, shortened from **garfish.**

gar, *gär, v.t.* (chiefly *Scot.*) to cause, to compel:— *pa.t.* and *pa.p.* **garred,** (*Scot.*) **gart.**—Also (*Spens.*) **garre.** [Norse *ger*(*v*)*a,* to make; cf. **yare.**]

garage, *gar'ij, gar'äzh, gä-räzh', n.* a building where motor-vehicles are housed or tended.—*v.t.* to put into or keep in a garage. [Fr.,—*garer,* to secure; cf. **wary.**]

Garamond, *gar'ə-mənd, n.* a form of type-face like that designed by Claude *Garamond* (d. 1561).

Neutral vowels in unaccented syllables: *el'ə-mənt, in'fənt, ran'dəm*

garb, *gärb*, *n.* (*obs.*) external appearance : fashion of dress : dress.—*v.t.* to clothe, array. [It. *garbo*, grace ; of Gmc. origin ; cf. **gear**.]

garb, garbe, *gärb*, *n.* (*her.*) a sheaf. [O.Fr. *garbe* ; of Gmc. origin.]

garbage, *gär'bij*, *n.* refuse, as animal offal : any worthless matter : (*U.S.*) household food and other refuse.—*n.* **gar'bage-man**, (*U.S.*) a dustman. [Of doubtful origin.]

garble, *gär'bl*, *v.t.* (*obs.*) to cleanse, sift : to select what may serve one's own purpose from, esp. in a bad sense : to misrepresent or falsify by suppression and selection.—*ns.* **gar'bler ; gar'blership ; gar'bling**. [It. *garbellare*—Ar. *ghirbāl*, a sieve, perh.—L.L. *crībellum*, dim. of *crībrum*, a sieve.]

garboard, *gär'bōrd*, *n.* the first range of planks or plates laid on a ship's bottom next the keel.—Also **gar'board-strake'**. [Du. *gaarboord*.]

garboil, *gär'boil*, *n.* (*Shak.*) disorder, uproar. [O.Fr. *garbouil*—It. *garbuglio*, conn. with L. *bullīre*, to boil.]

Garcinia, *gär-sin'i-ä*, *n.* a tropical genus of Guttiferae, trees yielding gamboge, kokum butter, and mangosteen. [After the French botanist Laurent *Garcin*.]

gardant (*her.*). Same as **guardant**. See **guard**.

garden, *gär'dn*, *n.* a piece of ground on which flowers, &c., are cultivated : a pleasant spot : a fertile region : (in *pl.*) used in street-names.—*adj.* of, used in, grown in, a garden or gardens.—*v.i.* to cultivate or work in a garden.—*ns.* **gar'dencit'y, -sub'urb, -vill'age**, a model town, suburb, village, laid out with broad roads, trees, and much garden ground between the houses ; **gar'dener**, one who gardens, or is skilled in gardening : one employed to tend a garden ; **gar'den-glass**, a bell-glass for covering plants ; **gar'den-house**, (*Shak.*) a summer-house : a house in a garden : (*obs.*) a house kept for sensual indulgence ; **gar'dening**, the laying out and cultivation of gardens ; **gar'den-par'ty**, a social gathering held in the garden of a house ; **gar'den-patch' ; gar'denpath' ; gar'den-stuff'**, garden produce for the table.—**gardener's garters**, variegated garden ribbon-grass ; **hanging garden**, a garden formed in terraces rising one above another ; **lead one up the garden (path)**, to draw one on insensibly, to mislead one ; **market garden**, a garden in which vegetables, fruits, &c., are raised for sale ; **market gardener ; philosophers of the garden**, followers of Epicurus, who taught in a garden. [O.Fr. *gardin* (Fr. *jardin*) ; from Gmc. ; cf. **yard**, **garth**.]

Gardenia, *gär-dē'ni-ä*, *n.* a genus of the madder family, Old World tropical and sub-tropical trees and shrubs, with beautiful and fragrant flowers. [Named from the American botanist Dr Alex. *Garden* (*c.* 1730-91).]

garderobe, *gärd'rōb*, *n.* (*archit.*) a wardrobe : an armoury : a private room : a privy. [Fr. ; cf. **wardrobe**.]

gardyloo, *gär'di-loo*, *interj.* the old warning cry in Edinburgh before throwing slops out of the window into the street. — *n.* the slops so thrown, or the act of throwing. [Recorded in this form by Smollett ; supposed to be would-be Fr. *gare de l'eau* for *gare l'eau*, beware of the water ; Sterne has *garde d'eau* (*Sent. Journey*), for Paris.]

gare, *gār*, *adj.* (*Scot.*) greedy, miserly. [O.N. *gerr* ; cf. **yare**.]

garefowl, *gār'fowl*, *n.* the great auk. [O.N. *geirfugl*.]

garfish, *gär'fish*, *n.* a pike-like fish (Belone) with long slender beaked head : the bony pike, an American ganoid river-fish (Lepidosteus) : an Australian half-beak.—Also **gar, gar'-pike**. [O.E. *gár*, spear.]

garganey, *gär'gə-ni*, *n.* a bird akin to the teal, the summer teal. [It. *garganello*.]

Gargantuan, *gär-gan'tū-ən*, *adj.* like or worthy of Rabelais's hero *Gargantua*, a giant of vast appetite : enormous : prodigious.—*ns.* **Gargan'tuism ; Gargan'tuist**.

gargarism, *gär'gə-rizm*, *n.* a gargle.—*v.t.* and *v.i.* **gar'garise**.

garget, *gär'git*, *n.* inflammation of the throat or udder in cows, swine, &c. : (*U.S.*) pokeweed.

gargle, *gär'gl*, *v.t.* and *v.i.* to wash (the throat) preventing the liquid from going down by expelling air against it.—*n.* a liquid for washing the throat. [O.Fr. *gargouiller*—*gargouille*, the throat.]

gargoyle, *gär'goil*, *n.* a projecting spout, usually grotesquely carved, from a roof-gutter.—Also **gur'goil**. [O.Fr. *gargouille*—L.L. *gurguliō*, throat.]

garial. See **gavial**.

garibaldi, *gar-i-bawl'di*, *-bal'di*, *n.* a woman's loose blouse, an imitation of the red shirts worn by followers of the Italian patriot *Garibaldi* (1807-1882).

garish, *gār'ish*, *adj.* showy : gaudy : glaring.—*adv.* **gar'ishly**. — *n.* **gar'ishness**. [Formerly also *gaurish, gawrish*, perh.—obs. *gaure*, to stare, perh. a freq. of obs. *gaw*, to stare ; cf. O.N. *gá*, to heed.]

garish. See **guarish**.

garjan. Same as **gurjun**.

garland, *gär'land*, *n.* (*obs.*) a crown : a wreath of flowers or leaves : a book of selections in prose or poetry : (*Spens.* ; *Shak.*) ornament, glory.—*v.t.* to deck with a garland.—*n.* **gar'landage**, (*Tenn.*) a decoration of garlands.—*adj.* **gar'landless**.—*n.* **gar'landry**, garlands collectively. [O.Fr. *garlande*.]

garlic, *gär'lik*, *n.* a bulbous liliaceous plant (*Allium sativum*) having a pungent taste and very strong smell : extended to others of the genus, as **wild garlic** (ramsons).—*n.* **gar'lic-mustard**, a tall cruciferous hedge plant (*Sisymbrium Alliaria*) with garlicky smell.—*adj.* **gar'licky**, like garlic. [O.E. *gárléac—gár*, a spear, *léac*, a leek.]

garment, *gär'mənt*, *n.* any article of clothing.—*v.t.* to clothe as with a garment.—*adjs.* **gar'mented ; gar'mentless**.—*n.* **gar'menture**, clothing. [O.Fr. *garniment—garnir*, to furnish.]

garner, *gär'nər*, *n.* a granary : a store of anything. —*v.t.* to store.—*v.i.* (*Tenn.*) to accumulate. [O.Fr. *gernier* (Fr. *grenier*)—L. *grānārium* (usu. in *pl.*), a granary.]

garnet, *gär'nit*, *n.* a mineral, in some varieties a precious stone, generally red, crystallising in dodecahedra and icositetrahedra, an orthosilicate of a bivalent and a tervalent metal.—*adj.* **garnetif'erous**.—*n.* **gar'net-rock**, a rock composed of garnet with hornblende and magnetite. [O.Fr. *grenat*—L.L. *grānātum*, pomegranate ; or L.L. *grānum*, grain, cochineal, red dye.]

garnet, *gär'nit*, *n.* a hoisting tackle. [Origin obscure.]

garnet, *gär'nit*, *n.* a T-shaped hinge. [Possibly O.Fr. *carne*—L. *cardō*, *-inis*, hinge.]

garnierite, *gär'ni-ər-īt*, *n.* a green hydrated nickel magnesium silicate. [Jules *Garnier*, who discovered it in New Caledonia.]

garnish, *gär'nish*, *v.t.* to adorn : to furnish : to surround with ornaments, as a dish.—*n.* entrancemoney : a gift of money, esp. that formerly paid to fellow-prisoners on entering : something placed round a principal dish at table, whether for embellishment or relish.—*n.* **gar'nishee**, a person warned not to pay money owed to another, because the latter is indebted to the garnisher who gives the warning.—*v.t.* to attach in this way.—*ns.* **garnishee'ment ; gar'nisher**, one who garnishes ; **gar'nishing, gar'nishment, gar'niture**, that which garnishes or embellishes : ornament : apparel : trimming ; **gar'nishry**, adornment. [O. Fr. *garniss-*, stem of *garnir*, to furnish (old form *warnir*), from a Gmc. root seen in O.E. *warnian*, Ger. *warnen* ; cf. **warn**.]

garotte. See **garrotte**.

gar-pike. See **garfish**.

garret, *gar'it*, *n.* a turret or watch-tower : a room just under the roof of a house.—*adj.* **garr'eted**, provided with garrets : lodged in a garret.—*ns.* **garreteer'**, one who lives in a garret : a poor author ; **garr'et-master**, a cabinet-maker, locksmith, &c., working on his own account for the dealers. [O.Fr. *garite*, a place of safety, *guarir, warir*, to preserve (Fr. *guérir*), from the Gmc. root seen in **ware**.]

garrison, *gar'i-sn*, *n.* a supply of soldiers for guarding a fortress : a fortified place.—*v.t.* to furnish with troops : to defend by fortresses manned with troops.—**garrison town**, a town in which a garrison is stationed. [O.Fr. *garison—garir, guerir,* to furnish ; Gmc. ; see foregoing.]

garron, garran, *gar'ən, n.* a small horse. [Ir. *gearran.*]

garrot, *gar'ət, n.* a name for various ducks. [Fr.]

garrot, *gar'ət, n.* (*surg.*) a tourniquet. [Fr.]

garrotte, garotte, *gä-rot', gə-rot', n.* a Spanish mode of putting criminals to death : apparatus for the purpose—originally a string round the throat tightened by twisting a stick, later a brass collar tightened by a screw, whose point enters the spinal marrow.—*v.t.* to execute by the garrotte : suddenly to render insensible by semi-strangulation in order to rob :—*pr.p.* **garrott'ing, garott'ing** ; *pa.t.* and *pa.p.* **garrott'ed, garott'ed.**—*ns.* **gar(r)ott'er** ; **gar(r)ott'ing.** [Sp. *garrote* ; cf. Fr. *garrot,* a stick.]

garrulous, *gar'(y)oo-ləs, adj.* talkative : loquacious. —*n.* **garrulity** (*-ōō'li-ti,* or *-ū'*), loquacity.—*adv.* **garr'ulously.**—*n.* **garr'ulousness.** [L. *garrulus— garrīre,* to chatter.]

garter, *gär'tər, n.* a band used to support a stocking : the badge of the highest order of knighthood in Great Britain.—*v.t.* to put a garter on : to support, bind, decorate, or surround with a garter.—*ns.* **gar'ter-snake,** in N. America, any snake of the genus Eutaenia, non-venomous, longitudinally striped : in S. Africa applied to two venomous snakes, with black and red rings (see Elaps) : **gar'ter-stitch,** a plain stitch in knitting : ribbed knitting made by using plain stitches only.— **Garter King-of-Arms,** the chief herald of the Order of the Garter. [O.Fr. *gartier* (Fr. *jarretière*) —O.Fr. *garet* (Fr. *jarret*), ham of the leg, prob. Celt. as Bret. *gar,* shank of the leg.]

garth, *gärth, n.* an enclosure or yard : a garden : a weir in a river for catching fish. [O.N. *garthr,* a court ; cf. **yard, garden.**]

garuda, *gur ōō-dä, n.* a Hindu demigod, part man, part bird. [Sans.]

garvie, *gär'vi, n.* (*Scot.*) a sprat.—Also **gar'vock.** [Gael. *garbhag* is perh. from Scots.]

gas, *gas, n.* a substance in a condition in which it has no definite boundaries or fixed volume, but will fill any space : often restricted to such a substance above its critical temperature : a substance or mixture which is in this state in ordinary terrestrial conditions : esp. coal-gas, or other gas for lighting or heating, or **one** used for attack in warfare : gas-light : laughing gas (see **laughing**) : (*coll.*) empty, boastful, frothy, garrulous, or pert talk : (*U.S.*) short for gasoline (petrol) : (*pl.* **gas'es**).—*v.t.* to supply, attack, poison, light, inflate, or treat with gas : (*U.S.*) to impose on by talking gas.—*v.i.* to emit gas : to talk gas :—*pr.p.* **gass'ing** ; *pa.t.* and *pa.p.* **gassed.**—*ns.* **gasalier', gaselier',** a hanging frame with branches for gas-jets (formed on false analogy after *chandelier*) ; **gas'-bag,** a bag for holding gas, esp. in a balloon or airship : a talkative person ; **gas'-bott'le,** a steel cylinder for holding compressed gas ; **gas'-bracket,** a gas-pipe projecting from the wall of a room for lighting purposes ; **gas'-buoy,** a floating buoy carrying a supply of gas to light a lamp fixed on it ; **gas'-burn'er,** the perforated part of a gas-fitting where the gas issues and is burned ; **gas'-car'bon,** a hard dense carbon deposited in coal-gas retorts ; **gas'-coal,** any coal suitable for making gas : cannel coal ; **gas'-coke',** coke made in gas retorts ; **gas'-condens'er,** an apparatus for freeing coal-gas from tar ; **gas'-cook'er,** a gas cooking - stove ; **gasē'ity** ; **gas' - en'gine,** an engine worked by the explosion of gas.—*adj.* **gaseous** (*gāz', gās', gas', gaz'i-əs*), in a state of gas : of gas.—*ns.* **gas'eousness** ; **gas'-escape',** a leakage of gas ; **gas'-field,** a region in which natural gas occurs.—*adj.* **gas'-filled,** filled with gas.—*n.* **gas'-fire,** a heating-stove in which gas is burned.—*adj.* **gas'-fired,** fuelled or heated by gases.—*n.* **gas'-fitter,** one who fits up the pipes and brackets for gas-lighting.—*n.pl.* **gas'-fittings,** gas pipes and brackets for lighting a building.— *ns.* **gas'-fur'nace,** a furnace of which the fuel is

gas ; **gas'-globe,** a glass used to enclose and shade a gas-light ; **gas'-heat'er,** any heating apparatus in which gas is used ; **gas'-hel'met,** a gas-mask in the form of a helmet completely covering the head ; **gas'holder,** a large vessel for storing gas : a gasometer ; **gasificā'tion,** conversion into gas. —*v.t.* **gas'ify,** to convert into gas.—*ns.* **gas'-jar,** a jar for collecting and holding a gas in chemical experiments ; **gas'-jet,** a jet of gas : a gas-flame : a burner ; **gas'-lamp,** a lamp that burns gas ; **gas'-light,** light produced by combustion of gas : a gas jet, burner, or lamp.—*adj.* of, concerned with, for use by, gaslight.—*ns.* **gas'-lime,** lime that has been used in purifying gas ; **gas'-liquor,** a solution of ammonia and ammonium salts got in gas-making.—*adj.* **gas'-lit,** lighted by gas.—*ns.* **gas'-main,** a principal gas-pipe from the gas-works ; **gas'-man,** a man employed in gas-making or in the reading of meters ; **gas'-man'tle,** a gauze covering, chemically prepared, enclosing a gas-jet, and becoming incandescent when heated ; **gas'-mask,** a respiratory device (covering nose, mouth, and eyes) as a protection against poisonous gases ; **gas'-mē'ter,** an instrument for measuring gas consumed ; **gas'-mo'tor,** a gas-engine ; **gas'-ogene** (see **gazogene**) ; **gas'olene, -oline** (*-ə-lēn*), a low-boiling petroleum distillate : (*U.S.*) the ordinary name for petrol ; **gasom'eter,** a storage tank for gas.—*adjs.* **gasomet'ric, -al,** pertaining to the measurement of gas.—*ns.* **gasom'etry ; gas'-pipe,** a pipe for conveying gas ; **gas'-plant,** dittany (see **burning-bush**) ; **gas'-po'ker,** a gas-jet that can be inserted among fuel to kindle a fire ; **gas'-retort,** a closed heated chamber in which gas is made ; **gas'-ring,** a hollow ring with perforations serving as gas-jets ; **gas'-shell',** a shell that gives off a poisonous gas or vapour on bursting ; **gass'-ing,** poisoning by gas : idle talking ; **gas'-stove,** an apparatus in which coal-gas is used for heating or cooking.—*adj.* **gass'y,** full of gas : abounding in or emitting gas : gaseous : (*slang*) given to vain and boastful talk.—*ns.* **gas'-tank,** a reservoir for coal-gas ; **gas'-tap ; gas'-tar,** coal-tar.—*adj.* **gas'-tight,** impervious to gas.—*ns.* **gas'-trap,** a trap in a drain to prevent escape of foul gas ; **gas'-turbine,** a machine consisting of a combustion chamber, to which air is supplied by a compressor and heated at constant pressure by oil fuel, and a turbine in which the hot gases expand and do work ; **gas'-water,** water through which coal-gas has been passed in scrubbing : gas-, or ammoniacal, liquor ; **gas'-well,** a boring from which natural gas issues ; **gas'-works,** a factory where gas is made.—**gas-discharge tube,** any tube in which an electric discharge takes place through a gas ; **natural gas,** a mixture of gases, chiefly hydrocarbons, occurring naturally in rocks ; **step on the gas** (i.e. gasoline), to press the accelerator pedal of a motor-car : to speed up. [A word invented by J. B. van Helmont (1577–1644) ; suggested by Gr. *chaos.*]

Gascon, *gas'kən, n.* a native of Gascony : a boaster. —*adj.* of Gascony.—*n.* **Gasconade',** boasting talk.—*v.i.* to boast extravagantly.—*ns.* **Gascon-ād'er ; Gas'conism,** boastfulness. [Fr.]

gash, *gash, v.t.* to cut deeply into.—*n.* a deep, open cut. [Formerly *garse*—O.Fr. *garser,* to scarify— L.L. *garsa,* scarification, possibly—Gr. *charassein,* to scratch.]

gash, *gash, adj.* (*Scot.*) talkative.—*v.i.* to talk.

gash, *gash, adj.* (chiefly *Scot.*) ghastly, hideous.— Also **gash'ful, gash'ly.**—*n.* **gash'liness.**—*adv.* **gash'ly.** [Perh. ghastful, ghastly.]

gasket, *gas'kit, n.* (*naut.*) a canvas band used to bind the sails to the yards when furled : a strip of tow, &c., for packing a piston, &c.—Also **gas'kin.** [Cf. Fr. *garcette,* It. *gaschetta* ; ety. dub.]

gaskins, *gas'kinz, n.* (*Shak.*). See **galligaskins.**

gasolene, gasoline. See under **gas.**

gasp, *gäsp, v.i.* to gape for breath : to catch the breath : to desire eagerly.—*v.t.* to breathe : to utter with gasps.—*n.* the act of gasping.—*ns.* **gasp'er,** one who gasps : (*slang*) a cheap cigarette ; **gasp'iness.**—*n.* and *adj.* **gasp'ing.**—*adv.* **gasp'-ingly.**—*adj.* **gasp'y.—the last gasp,** the point of death. [O.N. *geispa,* to yawn ; cf. *geip,* idle talk.]

gaspereau, *gas'pə-rō̄, n. (Canada)* the alewife (fish). [Fr. *gasparot*, a kind of herring.]

gast, *gäst, v.t. (Shak.)* to make aghast, to frighten or terrify.—*adj.* **gastfull** (*Spens.*; see **ghastful**).— *n.* **gast'ness(e)**, (*obs.*; *Shak.*) dread. [O.E. *gǽstan*; cf. **aghast.**]

gastero-, gastro-, gastr-, in composition, belly.— *n.pl.* **Gasteromycetes** (*gas'tər-ō-mī-sē'tēz*; Gr. *mykētes,* pl. of *mykēs,* mushroom), an order of fungi—Basidiomycetes with fructification closed till the spores ripen—puff-balls, stink-horns, &c.— *n.* **gas'teropod, gas'tropod** (Gr. *pous, podos,* foot), any member of the **Gast(e)rop'oda,** a class of asymmetrical molluscs in which the foot is broad and flat, the mantle undivided, the shell in one piece, usually conical—limpets, whelks, snails, slugs, &c. —*adj.* **gast(e)rop'odous.**—*ns.* **gæstraea** (*gas-trē'ä*), Haeckel's hypothetical ancestor of the Metazoa, like a gastrula; **gastraeum** (*gas-trē'əm*), the under surface of the body, esp. in birds; **gastralgia** (*gas-tral'ji-ä*; Gr. *algos,* pain), pain in the stomach. —*adj.* **gastral'gic.**—*n.* **gastrectomy** (*gas-trek'-tə-mi*; Gr. *ek,* out, *tomē,* cutting), surgical removal of the stomach, or part of it.—*adj.* **gas'tric,** belonging to the stomach.—*ns.* **gastri'tis,** inflammation of the stomach; **gastrocnemius** (*gas-trok-nē'mi-əs*; Gr. *knēmē,* leg), the muscle that bulges the calf of the leg (*pl.* -mii); **gastrol'-oger.** — *adj.* **gastrolog'ical.** — *ns.* **gastrol'ogy,** cookery, good eating; **gastromancy** (*gas'trō-man-si*; Gr. *manteiā,* soothsaying), divination by ventriloquism: divination by large-bellied glasses; **gastronome** (*gas'trə-nōm*; Gr. *nomos,* law), **gastronomer** (-*tron'ə-mər*), an epicure.—*adjs.* **gastronomic** (-*nom'ik*), **-al.**—*ns.* **gastron'omist; gastron'omy,** the art or science of good eating; **gas'trosoph** (Gr. *sophos,* wise), one skilled in matters of eating; **gastros'opher; gastros'ophy; gastros'tomy** (Gr. *stoma,* mouth), the making of an opening to introduce food into the stomach; **gastrot'omy** (Gr. *tomē,* a cut), the operation of cutting open the stomach or abdomen; **gastrula** (*gas'troo-lä*), an embryo at the stage in which it forms a two-layered cup by the invagination of its wall; **gastrula'tion,** formation of a gastrula.— **gastric fever,** typhoid; **gastric juice,** the acid liquid secreted by the stomach for digestion. [Gr. *gastēr,* belly.]

gat, *gat, (B.) p.a.t.* of **get.**

gat, *gat, n.* an opening between sandbanks: a strait. [Perh. O.N.]

gate, *gāt, n.* a passage into a city, enclosure, or any large building: a narrow opening or defile: a frame for closing an entrance: an entrance, passage, or channel: the people who pay to see a game: the total amount of money paid for entrance— (also **gate'-money**).—*v.t.* to supply with a gate: at Oxford and Cambridge, to punish by requiring the offender to be within the college gates by a certain hour.—*v.i.* **gate'-crash,** to enter without paying or invitation: also *fig.*—*n.* **gate'-crasher.** —*adj.* **gāt'ed,** having a gate or gates (often in composition, as **hun'dred-gated**): punished by gating.—*ns.* **gate'-fine,** the fine imposed upon the gated for disobedience; **gate'-house,** (*archit.*) a building over or at a gate; **gate'-keeper, gate'-man,** one who watches over the opening and shutting of a gate.—*adjs.* **gate'-legged,** of a table, having a hinged and framed leg that can swing in to let down a leaf; **gate'less.**—*ns.* **gate'-post,** a post from which a gate is hung or against which it shuts; **gate'-tower,** a tower beside or over a gate; **gate'-vein,** the great abdominal vein; **gate'way,** the way through a gate: a structure at a gate: any entrance; **gāt'ing.**—**break gates,** at Oxford and Cambridge, to enter college after the prescribed hour; **gate of justice,** a gate as of a city, temple, &c., where a sovereign or judge sat to dispense justice; **ivory gate, gate of horn** (or in *Spenser* silver), in Greek legend and poetical imagery, the gates through which false and true dreams respectively come; **stand in the gate,** (*B.*) to occupy a position of defence. [O.E. *geat,* a way; Du. *gat,* O.N. *gat.*]

gate, *gāt, n.* (chiefly *Scot.*) a way, path, street (often in street-names, as *Cowgate, Kirkgate*): manner of doing. See also **gait.** [O.N. *gata*; Dan. *gade,* Ger. *gasse.*]

gate, *gāt, n. (Spens.)* a Northern form of **goat.** ̄ᵃteau, *gät-ō̄, n.* a cake.—**veal gâteau,** minced veal made up like a pudding, and boiled in a shape or mould. [Fr.]

gather, *gadh'ər, v.t.* to collect: to assemble: to amass: to cull: to pick up: to draw together: in sewing, to draw into puckers by passing a thread through: to learn by inference.—*v.i.* to assemble or muster: to increase: to suppurate: to make way.—*n.* a plait or fold in cloth, made by drawing the thread through (*pl.* that part of the dress which is gathered or drawn in).—*ns.* **gath'erer,** one who collects, amasses, assembles, or culls: a workman who collects molten glass on the end of a rod preparatory to blowing; **gathering,** the action of one who gathers: a crowd or assembly: a narrowing: a number of leaves of paper folded one within another: the assembling of the sheets of a book: a suppurating swelling; **gath'ering-coal, -peat,** a coal, peat, put into a fire, to keep it alive till morning; **gath'ering-cry,** a summons to assemble for war; **gath'ering-ground,** catchment area.—**gather breath,** to recover wind; **gather ground,** to gain ground; **gather oneself together,** to collect all one's powers, like one about to leap; **gather to a head,** to ripen: to come into a state of preparation for action or effect; **gather way,** to get headway by sail or steam so as to answer the helm. [O.E. *gaderian, gæderian*; (*tō*)*gædere,* together; *geador,* together, *gæd,* fellowship.]

gatling-gun, *gat'ling-gun, n.* a machine-gun invented by R. J. *Gatling* about 1861.

gau, *gow, n.* a district.—*n.* **gauleiter** (*gow'lī-tər*), head of a district organisation of the German Nazi Party. [Ger.]

gauche, *gōsh, adj.* clumsy: tactless.—*n.* **gaucherie** (*gōsh'ə-rē, -rē'*), clumsiness: social awkwardness. [Fr., left.]

gaucho, *gow'chō̄, n.* a cowboy of the pampas. [Sp.]

gaucie, gaucy, gawcy, gawsy, *gaw'si, adj. (Scot.)* portly, jolly. [Origin unknown.]

gaud, *gawd, n. (obs.)* a large ornamental bead on a rosary: (*obs.*) a prank: an ornament: a piece of finery: showy ceremony: festivity.—*v.i. (Shak.)* make merry.—*v.t. (Shak.)* to adorn with gauds: to paint, as the cheeks.—*ns.* **gaudea'mus** (in Scotland *gow-di-ä'moos*; L., let us be glad: opening word of a students' song), a rejoicing, students' merrymaking, **gaud'ery,** finery.—*adv.* **gaud'ily.** —*ns.* **gaud'iness**; **gaud'y,** an English college or other festival.—*adj.* showy: gay: vulgarly bright.—*ns* **gaud'y-day, gaud'y-night.** [In part app.—O.Fr. *gaudir*—L. *gaudēre,* to be glad, *gaudium,* joy; in part directly from L.]

gaudy-green, *gaw'di-grēn, n.* and *adj. (obs.)* yellowish green. [O.Fr. *gaude,* weld.]

gauge (also **gage**), *gāj, n.* a measuring apparatus: a standard of measure: a means of limitation or adjustment to a standard: a measurement, as the diameter of a wire, calibre of a tube, width of a row of slates: distance between a pair of wheels or rails: a means of estimate: relative position of a ship (in this sense usu. **gage**; see **lee, weather**).—*v.t.* to measure: to estimate: to adjust to a standard.—*v.i.* to measure the contents of casks.—*adj.* **gauge'able,** capable of being gauged.—*ns.* **gauge'-glass,** a tube to show height of water; **gaug'er,** one who gauges: an excise man; **gaug'ing,** the measuring of casks holding excisable liquors; **gaug'ing-rod,** an instrument for measuring the contents of casks.—*adjs.* **broad'-, narr'ow-gauge,** in railroad construction greater or less than standard gauge, 56½ inches. [O.Fr. *gauge* (Fr. *jauge*).]

Gaul, *gawl, n.* a name of ancient France: an inhabitant of Gaul.—*adj.* **Gaul'ish.**—*n.* the Celtic (Brythonic) language of the Gauls. [Fr. *Gaule*— L. *Gallia, Gallus*; perh. conn. with O.E. *wealh,* foreign.]

Gault, *gawlt, n.* a series of beds of clay and marl between the Upper and the Lower Greensand:

gault, brick earth : a brick of gault clay.—*n.* **gault'er**, one who digs gault. [Origin obscure.]

Gaultheria, *gawl-thē'ri-ä, n.* a genus of evergreen aromatic plants of the heath family, including the American wintergreen and salal. [From the Swedish-Canadian botanist Hugues *Gaulthier.*]

gaum, *gawm, v.t.* to smear : to daub : to clog : (*obs.*) to handle clumsily.—*n.* a smear : a daub : a shiny lustre as on new varnish : stickiness : a sticky mass. —*adj.* **gaum'y**, dauby.

gaun, *gawn*, Scots for **going** and **go**.

gaunt. See **gant**.

gaunt, *gawnt, adj.* thin : of a pinched appearance : grim.—*adv.* **gaunt'ly.**—*n.* **gaunt'ness**. [Origin obscure.]

gauntlet, *gawnt'lit, n.* the iron glove of armour, formerly thrown down in challenge and taken up in acceptance : a long glove covering the wrist : an extension of a glove covering the wrist.— *adj.* **gaunt'leted**, wearing a gauntlet or gauntlets.— *n.* **gaunt'let-guard**, a guard of a sword or dagger, protecting the hand very thoroughly.—**throw down, take up, the gauntlet**, to give, to accept a challenge. [Fr. *gantelet*, dim. of *gant*, glove, of Gmc. origin ; cf. Sw. *vante*, a mitten, glove, O.N. *vöttr*, a glove, Dan. *vante*.]

gauntlet, *gawnt'lit*, **gantlope**, *gant'lōp, n.* the military punishment of having to run through a lane of soldiers who strike as one passes.—**run the gauntlet**, to undergo the punishment of the gauntlet : to be exposed to unpleasant remarks or treatment. [Sw. *gatlopp—gata*, lane (cf. **gate**, 2), *lopp*, course (cf. **leap**) ; confused with **gauntlet** (1).]

gauntry. See **gantry**.

gaup, gawp, *gawp, v.i.* (*prov.*) to gape in astonishment.—*ns.* **gaup'us, gawp'us**, a silly person. [From obs. *galp* ; cog. with **yelp**.]

gaur, *gowr, n.* a species of ox inhabiting some of the mountain jungles of India. [Hindustani.]

gauss, *gows, n.* the unit intensity of magnetic field, one maxwell per square centimetre.—*adj.* **Gauss'ian**, pertaining to or due to Karl Friedrich *Gauss* (1777-1855), German mathematician and physicist.

gauze, *gawz, n.* a thin, transparent fabric : material slight and open like gauze.—*n.* **gauze'-tree**, the lace-bark.—*adj.* **gauze'-winged**, having gauzy wings.—*n.* **gauz'iness**.—*adj.* **gauz'y**. [Fr. *gaze*, dubiously referred to *Gaza* in Palestine.]

gavage, *gä-väzh', n.* feeding by stomach-tube : cramming of poultry. [Fr. *gaver—gave*, bird's crop.]

gave, *gāv, pa.t.* of **give**.

gavel, *gā'vl*, a prov. form of **gable**.

gavel, *gav'l, n.* (*hist.*) tribute or rent.—*ns.* **gav'el-kind**, a tenure long prevailing in Kent by which lands descended from the father to all sons (or, failing sons, to all daughters) in equal portions, and not by primogeniture ; **gav'elman**, a tenant holding land in gavelkind. [O.E. *gafol*, tribute ; conn. with *giefan*, to give.]

gavel, *gav'l, n.* a mallet : a chairman's hammer.

gavelock, *gav'ə-lək, n.* a javelin : a crow-bar. [O.E. *gafeluc*.]

gavial, *gā'vi-əl*, **garial**, *gur'i-əl, n.* an Indian crocodile (*Gavialis*) with very long slender muzzle. [Hindustani *ghariyāl*, crocodile.]

gavotte, *gä-vot', n.* a dance, somewhat like a country-dance, originally a dance of the Gavots, people of the French Upper Alps : the music for such a dance in common time, often occurring in suites.

gawd, *gawd, n.* (*Shak.*). Same as **gaud**.

gawk, *gawk, n.* an awkward or ungainly person, esp. from tallness, shyness, or simplicity : one who stares and gapes.—*v.i.* to stare and gape.—*ns.* **gawk'ihood** ; **gawk'iness**.—*adj.* **gawk'y**, awkward : ungainly.—*n.* a tall awkward person : a gawk. [Ety. obscure : perh. of various origin : most prob. not related to Fr. *gauche*, left.]

gawsy. Same as **gaucie**.

gay, *gā, adj.* lively : bright : sportive, merry : dissipated : of loose life : showy : (*prov.*) spotted : (*Scot.* ; usu. **gey, gui**) considerable : often by hendiadys instead of an adv., as *gey and easy*, easy enough : (*U.S.*) unduly familiar : (*compar.* **gay'er** ;

superl. **gay'est**).—*adv.* (*Scot.* ; **gey**) rather, fairly, considerably.—*n.* **gai'ety**.—*adv.* **gai'ly.**—*n.* **gay'ness.**—*adj.* **gay'some**, gladsome.—**gay science**, a rendering of *gai saber*, the Provençal name for the art of poetry. [O.Fr. *gai*—perh. O.H.G. *wâhi*, pretty.]

gayal, gyal, *gī'al, n.* an Indian domesticated ox, akin to the gaur, with curved horns. [Hindi *gayāl*.]

gay-you, *gī'ū, gā'ū, n.* a narrow flat-bottomed Anamese boat with outrigger and masts. [Anamese *ghe hâu*.]

gaze, *gāz, v.i.* to look fixedly.—*n.* a fixed look : the object gazed at—(*Spens.*) **gaze'ment**.—*adj.* **gaze'-ful**, (*Spens.*) looking intently.—*ns.* **gaze'-hound**, a hound that pursues by sight ; **gaz'er** ; **gaz'ing-stock**, one exposed to public view, generally unpleasantly.—*adj.* **gaz'y**, affording a wide prospect : given to gazing.—**at gaze**, in the attitude of gazing. [Prob. cog. with obs. *gaw*, to stare ; cf. O.N. *gá*, to heed ; Sw. dial. *gasa*, to stare.]

gazebo, *gə-zē'bō, n.* a belvedere. [Ety. dub.]

gazelle, gazel, *gə-zel', n.* a small antelope (*Gazella Dorcas*) of N. Africa and S.W. Asia, with large eyes, or kindred species. [Fr.,—Ar. *ghazāl*, a wild-goat.]

gazette, *gə-zet', n.* a newspaper : **Gazette**, an official newspaper containing lists of government appointments, legal notices, despatches, &c.—*v.t.* to publish or mention in a gazette :—*pr.p.* **gazett'-ing** ; *pa.t.* and *pa.p.* **gazett'ed**.—*n.* **gazetteer'** (*gaz-*), a geographical dictionary : (*orig.*) a writer for a gazette, official journalist.—*v.t.* to describe in gazetteers.—*adj.* **gazetteer'ish**—**appear, have one's name in the Gazette**, to be mentioned in one of the official newspapers, esp. of bankrupts. [Fr.,—It. *gazzetta*, a small coin ; or from It. *gazzetta*, dim. of *gazza*, magpie.]

gazogene, *gaz'ə-jēn*, **gasogene**, *gas', n.* an apparatus for making aerated waters. [Fr. *gazogène—gaz*, gas, Gr. suff. *-genēs*—root of *gennaein*, to generate.]

gazon, *gazoon*, *gə-zōōn', n.* a sod in fortification : used erroneously by Hogg for a compact body of men. [Fr., turf.]

geal, *jēl, v.t.* and *v.i.* to congeal. [Fr. *geler*.]

gealous, gealousy, Spenser's spellings of **jealous, jealousy**.

gean, *gēn, n.* the European wild cherry. [O.Fr. *guigne.*]

geanticline, *jē-an'ti-klīn, n.* an anticline on a great scale.—*adj.* **geanticli'nal**. [Gr. *gē*, earth, and **anticline**.]

gear, *gēr, n.* equipment : accoutrements : tackle : clothes : armour : harness : apparatus : a set of tools or a mechanism for some particular purpose : household stuff : possessions : stuff : matter : affair, business, doings (often contemptuous) : any moving part or system of parts for transmitting motion : connexion by means of such parts : working connexion : working order : the diameter in inches of a wheel whose circumference equals the distance a bicycle would go for one turn of the pedals.—*v.t.* to harness : to put in gear, as machinery : to connect in gear : (*fig.* ; with *to*) to make to work in accordance with requirements of (a project or a larger organisation).—*v.i.* to be in gear.—*ns.* **gear'-box**, the box containing the apparatus for changing gear ; **gear'-case**, a protective case for the gearing of a bicycle, &c.—*adj.* **geared**.—*n.* **gear'-ing**, harness : working implements : means of transmission of motion, esp. a train of toothed wheels and pinions.—*adj.* **gear'less**.—*n.* **gear'-wheel**, a wheel with teeth or cogs which impart or transmit motion by acting on a similar wheel or a chain. —*adjs.* **high'-gear, low'-gear**, geared to give a high or a low number of revolutions of the driven part relatively to the driving part.—**gear down, up**, to make the speed of the driven part lower, higher, than that of the driving part ; **multiplying gearing**, a combination of cog-wheels for imparting motion from wheels of larger to wheels of smaller diameter, by which the rate of revolution is increased ; **straight gearing**, the name given when the planes of motion are parallel—opposed to

bevelled gearing (see **bevel**); **three-speed gear, two-speed gear, variable gear,** a contrivance for changing gear at will. See also **synchromesh.** [M.E. *gere*, prob. O.N. *gervi*; cf. O.E. *gearwe*, O.H.G. *garawi*; **yare, gar** (vb.).]

geare, (*Spens.*) for **gear, jeer.**

geasou, *ge̅'zn, adj.* (*Spens.*) rare: out of the way: wonderful. [O.E. *gǣsne, gésne,* wanting, barren.]

geat, *je̅t, n.* the hole in a mould through which the metal is poured in casting. [**jet.**]

gebur, *gə-bo̅o̅r', yə-bo̅o̅r', n.* (*hist.*) a tenant-farmer. [O.E. *gebúr.*]

geck, *gek, n.* a dupe: object of scorn: a derisive gesture: scorn.—*v.t.* to mock.—*v.i.* to scoff: to toss the head: to show disdain. [Prob. L.G. *geck*; Du. *gek,* Ger. *geck.*]

gecko, *gek'o̅, n.* any lizard of the genus Gecko or the subclass **Gecko'nes,** mostly thick-bodied, dull-coloured animals with adhesive toes and vertebrae concave at both ends. [Malay *ge̅koq*; imit.]

ged, *ged, n.* (*prov.*) the pike or luce. [O.N. *gedda.*]

gee, *ie̅, n.* the seventh letter of the alphabet. See G.

gee, *ge̅, n.* (*prov.*) a fit of perversity.

gee, *je̅, v.i.* of horses, to move to the right or to move on: to go, to suit, get on well.—*n.* **gee'-gee,** a child's word for a horse.—*v.i.* **gee up, gee-hup',** to proceed faster.

gee, *je̅, n.* an air-navigation radar system in which three ground stations A (master), B and C (slave), give for AB and AC two sets of intersecting hyperbolae which, charted, give an equipped aircraft its geographical position over a few hundred miles' range from A.

gee, *je̅, interj.* (*U.S.*) expressing strong emotion. [Perh. **Jesus.**]

geebung, *je̅'bung, n.* an Australian proteaceous tree (Persoonia) or its fruit. [Native name.]

geese, *pl.* of **goose.**

gee-string, *je̅'string, n.* a string or strip worn round the waist and between the legs by American Indians. —Also **G-string.** [Origin obscure.]

Geëz, *ge̅-ez', ge̅'ez,* **Giz,** *ge̅z, n.* the ancient language of Ethiopia, a Semitic tongue closely related to Arabic.

geezer, *ge̅z'ər, n.* (*slang*) a queer elderly person. [**guiser.**]

gegenschein, *ga̅'gən-shi̅n, n.* a glow of zodiacal light seen opposite the sun. [Ger.]

Gehenna, *gi-hen'ä, n.* the valley of Hinnom, near Jerusalem, in which the Israelites sacrificed their children to Moloch, and to which, at a later time, the refuse of the city was conveyed to be slowly burned: hence (*N.T.*) hell: a place of torment. [Heb. *Ge-hinnom,* village of Hinnom.]

Geiger-Müller counter, *gi̅'gər mül'ər kown'tər,* an instrument for detecting radio-activity by means of the ionising effect of the charged particles and counting the particles mechanically. [*Geiger* and *Müller,* German physicists.]

geisha, *ga̅'shä, n.* a Japanese dancing-girl. [Jap.]

geist, *gi̅st, n.* spirit, any inspiring or dominating principle. [Ger.]

geitonogamy, *gi̅-tən-og'ə-mi, n.* pollination from another flower on the same plant.—*adj.* **geitonog'-amous.** [Gr. *geito̅n,* neighbour, *gamos,* marriage.]

gel, *jel, n.* a jelly-like apparently solid colloidal solution.—*v.i.* to form a gel:—*pr.p.* **gell'ing,** *pa.t.* and *pa.p.* **gelled.**—*n.* **gela'tion** (see separate article). [**gelatine.**]

gelastic, *jel-as'tik, adj.* pertaining to or provoking laughter. [Gr. *gelastikos*—*gelaein,* to laugh.]

gelatine, gelatin, *jel'ə-tin, -te̅n, n.* colourless, odourless, and tasteless glue, prepared from albuminous substances, e.g. bones and hides, used for food-stuffs, photographic films, glues, &c.—*vs.t.* **gelatinate** (*ji-lat'i-na̅t*), **gelat'inise,** to make into gelatine or jelly.—*v.i.* to be converted into gelatine or jelly.—*ns.* **gelatina'tion, gelatinisa'tion.**— *adj.* **gelat'inous,** resembling or formed into jelly. —**blasting gelatine,** a violently explosive rubbery substance composed of nitroglycerine and nitrocotton. [Fr.,—It. *gelatina, gelata,* jelly—L. *gela̅re,* to freeze.]

gelation, *jel-a̅'shən, n.* solidification by cooling:

formation of a gel from a sol. [Partly L. *gela̅tio̅, -o̅nis*—*gela̅re,* to freeze; partly **gel.**]

geld, geld, *n.* (*hist.*) a tax.—*v.t.* to tax. [O.E. *geld, gyld,* payment; O.N. *giald,* money; cf. **yield.**]

geld, geld, *v.t.* to emasculate, castrate: to spay: to deprive of anything essential, to enfeeble, to deprive: to expurgate:—*pa.t.* and *pa.p.* **gelt, geld'ed.**—*ns.* **geld'er; geld'ing,** act of castrating: a castrated animal, esp. a horse. [O.N. *gelda*; Dan. *gilde.*]

gelder(s)-rose. See **guelder-rose.**

gelid, *jel'id, adj.* icy cold: cold.—*adv.* **gel'idly.**— *ns.* **gel'idness, gelid'ity.** [L. *gelidus*—*gelu̅,* frost.]

gelignite, *jel'ig-ni̅t, n.* a powerful explosive used in mining, made from nitroglycerine, nitrocotton, potassium nitrate, and wood-pulp. [**gelatine** and L. *ignis,* fire.]

gelliflowre (*Spens.*). Same as **gillyflower.**

gelly, *jel'i, adj.* (*Spens.*) jellied.

gelosy (*Spens.*). Same as **jealousy.**

Gelsemium, *jel-se̅'mi-əm, n.* the so-called yellow or Carolina jasmine, an American climbing-plant of the Loganiaceae.—*ns.* **gel'semine** (-*səm-e̅n*) and **gelseminine** (-*sem'*), two alkaloids yielded by its rhizome and rootlets. [It. *gelsomino,* jasmine.]

gelt, *galt, pa.t.* and *pa.p.* of **geld.**

gelt, *gelt, n.* (*Spens.*) a madman. [Ir. *geilt.*]

gelt, *gelt, n.* (*obs.*) money: pay: profit. [Ger. and Du. *geld.*]

gelt, *gelt,* an obsolete erroneous form of **geld** (1): (*Spens.*) apparently for **gilt.**

gem, *jem, n.* any precious stone, esp. when cut: anything extremely admirable or flawless: a size of type smaller than diamond: (*obs.*) a bud.—*v.t.* (*obs.*) to bud: to adorn with gems: to bespangle:— *pr.p.* **gemm'ing;** *pa.t.* and *pa.p.* **gemmed.**—*ns.* **gem'-cutting,** the art of cutting and polishing precious stones; **gem'-engraving,** the art of engraving figures on gems.—*adj.* **gemm'eous** (-*i-əs*), pertaining to gems: like a gem.—*ns.* **gemm'ery,** gems generally; **gemmol'ogy,** the science of gems.—*adj.* **gemm'y,** full of gems: brilliant.—*n.* **gem'stone.** [O.E. *gim*; O.H.G. *gimma*—L. *gemma,* a bud; later remodelled on L. or reintroduced.]

Gemara, *gə-mä'rä, n.* the second part of the Talmud, consisting of commentary and complement to the first part, the Mishna. [Aramaic, completion.]

gematria, *gə-mä'tri-ä, n.* a cabbalistic method of interpreting the Hebrew Scriptures by interchanging words whose letters have the same numerical value when added. [Rabbinical Heb. *ge̅matriya̅*— Gr. *geo̅metria̅,* geometry.]

gemel, *jem'əl, n.* (*obs.*) a twin: a gimmal: a gimbal: a hinge.—*n.* **gem'el-ring** (see **gimmal**). [O.Fr. *gemel* (Fr. *jumeau*)—L. *gemellus,* dim. of *geminus,* twin.]

geminate, *jem'in-a̅t, v.t.* to double.—*adj.* (*bot.*) in pairs.—*n.* **gemina'tion,** a doubling.—*n.pl.* **Gemini** (*jem'i-ni̅*), the twins, a constellation containing the two bright stars Castor and Pollux: the third sign of the zodiac.—*adj.* **gem'inous,** (*bot.*) double, in pairs.—*n.* **gem'iny,** (*Shak.*) a pair, esp. of eyes. —*interj.* expressing surprise—spelt also **gemini,** **jiminy, jiminy.** [L. *geminus,* twin.]

gemma, *jem'ä, n.* (*rare*) a plant bud, esp. a leaf-bud: (*bot.*) a small multicellular body produced vegetatively, capable of separating and becoming a new individual: (*zool.*) a bud or protuberance from the body that becomes a new individual:— *pl.* **gemm'ae** (-*e̅*).—*adj.* **gemma'ceous,** bud-like: relating to gemmae.—*n.* **gemm'a-cup,** a liverwort cupule.—*adj.* **gemm'ate,** having or reproducing by buds or gemmae.—*v.t.* to deck with gems.—*v.i.* to reproduce by gemmae.—*n.* **gemma'tion,** budding or gemma-formation.—*adjs.* **gemm'-ative,** pertaining to gemmation; **gemmif'erous,** bearing gemmae; **gemmip'arous,** reproducing by gemmae.—*ns.* **gemmula'tion,** formation of gemmules; **gemm'ule,** Darwin's hypothetical particle produced by each part of the body, as a vehicle of heredity: (*obs.*) a plumule: an internal bud in sponges. [L. *gemma,* a bud.]

gemman, *jem'ən, n.* (*vulg.*) a gentleman:—*pl.* **gemmen** (*jem'ən*). [**gentleman.**]

fa̅te, fär, àsk; me̅, hər (her); *mi̅ne; mo̅te; mu̅te; mo̅o̅n; dhen* (then)

gemot, gə-mōt', yə-mot', n. a meeting or assembly. [O.E. gemót; cf. **moot.**]

gemsbok, gemz'bok, n. (Oryx gazella) a S. African antelope, about the size of a stag, with long straight horns. [Du., male chamois—Ger. gemsbock—gemse, chamois, bock, buck.]

gen, jen, n. (slang) general information: the low-down or inside information.

gena, jē'nä, n. the cheek or side of the head.—adj. **gē'nal**. [L. gĕna.]

genappe, jə-nap', n. a smooth worsted yarn used with silk in fringes, braid, &c. [Genappe in Belgium.]

gendarme, zhän°'-, zhən°'-därm', n. originally man-at-arms, horseman in full armour: since the French Revolution one of a corps of French military police: a similar policeman elsewhere: a rock-pillar on a mountain:—pl. **gen'darmes'**, **gens'darmes'.**—n. **gendarm'erie** (-ə-rē), an armed police force. [Fr. gendarme, sing. from pl. gens d'armes, men-at-arms —gens, people, de, of, armes, arms.]

gender, jen'dər, n. (obs.) kind: (gram.) a distinction of words roughly answering to sex: (loosely or jocularly) sex. [Fr. genre—L. genus, generis, a kind, kin.]

gender, jen'dər, v.t. to beget: to generate.—v.i. to copulate. [Fr. gendrer—L. generāre.]

gene, jēn, n. a material unit whose transmission determines (along with other conditions) the in-heritance of a given unit character.—n. **genotype** (jen'ō-tip), the actual constitution of a zygote in genes (opp. to phaenotype): a type or group having the same gene-constitution.— adj. **genotypic** (-tip'ik). [Gr. genos, a race.]

genealogy, jē-mi-al'ə-ji, or jen'i-, n. history of the descent of families: the pedigree of a particular person or family.—adj. **genealogical** (-ə-loj'i-kl).—adv. **genealog'ically.**—v.i. **geneal'ogise**, to investigate or treat of genealogy.—n. **geneal'ogist**, one who studies or traces genealogies or descents. —**genealogical tree**, a table of descent in the form of a tree with branches. [Gr. geneālogiā—geneā, race, logos, discourse.]

genera, pl. of **genus**.

general, jen'ə-rəl, adj. relating to a genus or whole class: including various species: not special: not restricted or specialised: relating to the whole or to all or most: universal: nearly universal: common: prevalent: widespread: public: vague: (after an official title, &c.) chief, of highest rank, at the head of a department (as director-general, post-master-general): (obs.) socially accessible and familiar with all.—adv. (Shak.) generally.—n. a class embracing many species: an officer who is head over a whole department: a general officer: the chief commander of an army in service: one skilled in leadership, tactics, management: (R.C. Church) the head of a religious order, responsible only to the Pope: the head of the Salvation Army: a general servant: (Shak.) the public, the vulgar.—v.t. to act as general of.—n. **generāl'e** (L. gen-er-ā'lä), general principles, esp. in pl. **generāl'ia.**—adj. **gen'eralisable.**—n. **generalīsā'tion.**—v.t. **gen'eralise**, to make general: to include under a general term: to reduce to a general form: to comprehend as a particular case within a wider concept, proposition, definition, &c.: to represent or endow with the common characters of a group without the special characters of any one member: to bring to general use or knowledge: to infer inductively.—v.i. to make general statements: to form general concepts: to depict general character: to reason inductively.—ns. **generaliss'imo** (It. superl.), supreme commander of a great or combined force; **general'ity.**—adv. **gen'erally**, in a general or collective manner or sense: in most cases: upon the whole.—n. **gen'eralship**, the position of a military commander: the art of manipulating armies: tactical management and leadership.— **General Assembly** (see **assembly**); **general election**, an election of all the members of a body at once; **general epistle** (see **catholic**): **general line**, the party line: **general officer**, an officer above rank of colonel: **general post**, formerly, dispatch of mail to all parts, opp. to local twopenny

or penny post: the first morning delivery of letters: a general change of positions, &c. (from a parlour game); **general post-office**, formerly, an office receiving letters for the general post: the head post-office of a town or district; **general prac-titioner**, a physician who devotes himself to general practice rather than to special diseases; **general principle**, a principle to which there are no excep-tions within its range of application; **general servant**, a servant whose duties are not special, but embrace domestic work of every kind; **in general**, as a generalisation: mostly, as a general rule. [O.Fr.,—L. generālis—genus.]

generate, jen'ər-āt, v.t. to produce: to bring into life or being: to evolve: to originate: (geom.) to trace out.—adj. **gen'erable**, that may be generated or produced.—ns. **gen'erant**, a begetter, producer, parent: (geom.) a line, point, or figure that traces out another figure by its motion; **generā'tion**, production or originating: a single stage in natural descent: the people of the same age or period: descendants removed by the same number of steps from a common ancestor: the ordinary time interval between the births of successive generations—usu. reckoned at 30 or 33 years: offspring, progeny, race: (B. in pl.) genealogy, history; **generā'tion-ism**, traducianism.—adj. **gen'erative**, having the power of, or concerned with, generating or pro-ducing.—n. **gen'erātor**, begetter or producer: apparatus for producing gases, &c.: apparatus for turning mechanical into electrical energy: (mus.) a fundamental tone:—fem. **gen'erātrix**, a mother: a generator: a generant.—**alternation of generations** (see **alternation**); **motion gen-erative**, (Shak.) a male puppet: or perh. one who is a mere puppet so far as engendering is con-cerned; **spontaneous generation**, the origina-tion of living from non-living matter. [L. generāre, -ātum—genus, a kind.]

generic, **-al**, **generically**. See **genus**.

generous, jen'ə-rəs, adj. of a noble nature: courage-ous: liberal: bountiful: invigorating in its nature, as wine: (obs.) nobly born.—adv. **gen'er-ously.**—ns. **gen'erousness**, **generos'ity**, noble-ness or liberality of nature: (arch.) nobility of birth. [L. generōsus, of noble birth—genus, birth.]

genesis, jen'i-sis, n. generation, creation, or pro-duction: **Genesis**, the first book of the Bible:— pl. (L.) **gen'esēs.**—adjs. **Genesiac** (ji-nē'si-ək), **-al**, **Genesit'ic**, pertaining to Genesis. [Gr.]

genet, **gennet**. Same as **jennet**.

genet, **genette**, jen'it, ji-net', n. a carnivorous animal (Genetta) allied to the civet: its fur, or an imitation. [Fr. genette—Sp. gineta—Ar. jarnait.]

genethliac, ji-neth'li-ək, adj. relating to a birthday or to the casting of nativities.—n. a caster of nativities: a genethliacon.—adj. **genethliacal** (jen-ith-li'ə-kl).—adv. **genethli'acally.**—n. **gen-ethli'acon**, a birthday ode.—adjs. **genethlialog'ic**, **-al.**—n. **genethlial'ogy** (Gr. genethliālogiā), the art of casting nativities. [Gr. genethlē, birth.]

genetic, **-al**, ji-net'ik, əl, adjs. pertaining to origin. —adv. **genet'ically.**—ns. **genet'icist** (-i-sist), a student of genetics; **genetics** (treated as sing.), the branch of biology that deals with descent, variation, and heredity.—**genetic spiral**, a line through the insertions of successive leaves on a stem. [Im-properly formed from **genesis**.]

genetrix. See **genitor**.

geneva, ji-nē'vä, n. a spirit distilled from grain and flavoured with juniper-berries, also called Hollands. —n. **genevrette** (jen-əv-ret'), a wine made from wild fruits flavoured with juniper-berries. [Du. genever, jenever, O.Fr. genevre (Fr. genièvre)—L. jūniperus, juniper: confused with the town of Geneva; see **gin**.]

Genevan, ji-nē'vən, adj. pertaining to Geneva.—n. an inhabitant of Geneva: an adherent of Genevan or Calvinistic theology.—adj. and n. **Genevese** (jen'i-vēz).— n. **Genē'vanism**, Calvinism.— **Geneva Bible**, a version of the Bible with racy notes produced by English exiles at Geneva in 1560; **Geneva Convention**, an international agreement of 1865 providing for the neutrality of hospitals, and the security of sanitary officers, naval and military chaplains ; **Geneva cross,** a red cross on a white ground displayed for protection in war of persons serving in hospitals, &c. ; **Geneva gown,** the dark, long preaching gown of the early Geneva reformers, and still the common form of pulpit-gown among Presbyterians ; **Genevan theology,** so called from Calvin's residence in Geneva and the establishment of his doctrines there.

genial, jē'ni-əl, *adj.* pertaining to marriage and generation : favouring growth : cheering : kindly : sympathetic : healthful.—*v.t.* **gē'nialise,** to impart geniality to.—*ns.* **gēniality** (-*al'i-ti*), **gē'nialness.**—*adv.* **gē'nially.** [L. *geniālis—genius,* the tutelary spirit.]

genial, ji-nī'əl, *adj.* of or pertaining to the chin. [Gr. *geneion,* chin—*genys,* under jaw.]

geniculate, -d, je-nik'ū-lāt, -*id, adjs.* bent like a knee : jointed : knotted.—*v.t.* **genic'ulate,** to form joints in.—*n.* **geniculā'tion.** [L. *geniculātus—geniculum,* a little knee—*genū,* the knee.]

genie, jē'ni, *n.* a jinnee. [Fr. *génie*—L. *genius,* adopted because of its similarity to the Arabic word.]

genipap, jen'i-pap, *n.* a large West Indian tree (*Genipa americana*; Rubiaceae): its excellent fruit. [From Tupi.]

Genista, je-nis'tä, *n.* a genus of shrubby, papilionaceous plants, with simple leaves and yellow flowers—green-weed and petty whin. [L. *genista,* broom.]

genital, jen'i-təl, *adj.* belonging to generation or the act of producing.—*n.pl.* **gen'itals** (also **genitä'lia),** the organs of generation, esp. external.—*adj.* **genito-ūr'inary,** pertaining to genital and urinary organs or functions. [L. *genitālis—gignĕre, genitum,* to beget.]

genitive, jen'i-tiv, *adj.* (*obs.*) pertaining to generation : (*gram.*) of or belonging to case expressing origin, possession, or similar relation.—*n.* the genitive case : a word in the genitive case.—*adj.* **geniti'val.**—*advs.* **geniti'vally, gen'itively.** [L. *genitīvus* (—*gignĕre, genitum,* to beget) for ˈGr. *genikē* (*ptōsis*), properly, generic (case)—*genos,* a class.]

genitor, jen'i-tər, *n.* a father : a parent : a progenitor :—*fem.* **gen'etrix, gen'itrix.**—*n* **gen'-iture,** engendering : birth. [L.]

genius, jēn'yəs, or jē'ni-əs, *n.* the special inborn faculty of any individual : special taste or natural disposition : consummate intellectual, creative, or other power, more exalted than talent : one so endowed : a good or evil spirit, supposed to preside over every person, place, and thing, and esp. to preside over a man's destiny from his birth : prevailing spirit or tendency : type or generic exemplification :—*pl.* **ge'niuses** ; in sense of spirit, **genii** (jē'ni-ī). [L. *genius—gignĕre, genitum,* to beget.]

gennet. Same as **jennet.**

genocide, jen'ō-sīd, *n.* deliberate extermination of a race or people. [Gr. *genos,* race, and L. *caedĕre,* to kill.]

Genoese, jen'ō-ēz, or -ēz', **Genovese,** -vēz', *adjs.* relating to Genoa.—*ns.* an inhabitant, citizen, or native of Genoa :—*pl.* **Genoese, Genovese.** [L. *Genua,* It. *Genova,* Genoa.]

genotype. See gene.

genouillère, zhə-noo-yer, *n.* the knee-piece in armour. [Fr.]

genre, zhän⁰r', *n.* kind : a literary species : a style of painting scenes from familiar or rustic life. —Also *adj.* [Fr.,—L. *genus.*]

Genro, gen-rō', *n.* the Japanese Elder Statemen. [Jap.]

gens, jenz (L. *gāns*), *n.* in ancient Rome, a clan including several families descended from a common ancestor : a tribe :—*pl.*gen'tēs.—*adj.* gen'tile (q.v.). [L. *gēns, gentis.*]

gent, jent, *adj.* (*Spens.*) noble : gentle. [O.Fr.,— L. *genitus,* born.]

gent, jent, *n.* vulg. abbrev. of **gentleman** : one who apes the manners of a gentleman :—*pl.* **gents.**

genteel, jən-tēl', *adj.* well-bred : graceful in manners or in form : fashionable. (Now used mainly with

mocking reference to a standard of obsolete snobbery or false refinement.)—*adj.* **genteel'ish.**—*n.* **genteel'ism,** a would-be refined substitute for the right word or phrase.—*adv.* **genteel'ly.**—*n.* **genteel'ness.** [Fr. *gentil*—L. *gentīlis* ; see gentle.]

gentian, jen'shən, any plant of the genus Gentiana, herbs, usually blue-flowered, abounding chiefly in alpine regions, typical of the family **Gentianä'ceae** (sympetalous dicotyledons with corolla twisted in bud and unilocular ovary) : the root and rhizome of the yellow gentian used as a tonic and stomachic. —*n.* **gentianell'a,** a name for several species of gentian, esp. *Gentiana acaulis,* with deep-blue flowers.—**gentian violet,** a mixture of three dyes, methyl rosaniline, methyl violet, and crystal violet, which is antiseptic and bactericidal. [L. *gentiāna,* acc. to Pliny from *Gentius,* king of Illyria, who introduced it in medicine (2nd cent. B.C.).]

Gentile, gentile, jen'til, *n.* (*B.*) anyone not a Jew, or (now *rare*) not a Christian, or (*U.S.*) not a Mormon. —*adjs.* **gentile,** of or belonging to a *gens* or clan : belonging to the Gentiles : (*gram.*) denoting a race or country ; **gentilic** (-*til'ik*), tribal ; **gen'tilish,** heathenish.—*n.* **gen'tilism** (-*til-,* or -*til-*), paganism.—*adjs.* **gentilitial** (jen-ti-lish'l), **gentili'tian, gentili'tious,** pertaining to a gens. [L. *gentīlis*— —*gēns,* a nation, clan.]

gentle, jen'tl, *adj.* (*arch.*) well-born : mild and refined in manners : mild in disposition or action : amiable : soothing : moderate : gradual.—*v.t.* (*Shak.*) to make gentle.—*n.* (*arch.*) a person of good family : a trained falcon : hence a peregrine falcon (*masc.* **ter'cel-gen'tle**) ; *fem.* **fal'con-gen'tle**) : a soft maggot, used as a bait in angling.—*n.* **gentilesse** (-*til-es'*), the quality of being gentle, courtesy.— *v.t.* **gen'tilise,** to raise to the class of gentleman.—*n.* **gentil'ity,** good birth or extraction : good breeding : politeness of manners : genteel people : marks of gentility.—*n.pl.* **gen'tlefolk,** people of good family.—*adj.* **gen'tle-heart'ed,** having a gentle or kind disposition.—*n.* **gen'tlehood,** position or character attaching to gentle birth ; **gen'tleman,** a man of good birth : one who without a title bears a coat of arms : more generally every man above the rank of yeoman, including the nobility : one above the trading classes : a man of refined manners : a well-to-do man of no occupation : a man of good feeling and instincts, courteous and honourable : a polite term used for man in general : (*Shak.*) a body-servant :—*pl.* **gen'tlemen**—also a word of address :—*fem.* **gen'tle-woman** (usu. lady) :—*pl.* **gen'tlewomen.**—*ns.* **Gen'tleman-at-arms,** a member of the royal bodyguard, instituted in 1509, and now composed of military officers of service and distinction only ; **gen'tleman-cadet',** a student in a military college ; **gen'tleman-comm'oner,** a member of the higher class of commoners at Oxford University ; **gen'tle-manhood, gen'tlemanship,** the condition or character of a gentleman.—*adjs.* **gen'tlemanlike,** like or characteristic of a gentleman ; **gen'tlemanly,** befitting a gentleman : well-bred, refined, generous.—*ns.* **gen'tlemanliness** ; **gen'tleness** ; **gent'-lesse,** (*obs.*) same as **gentilesse.**—*adj.* **gen'tle-womanly,** like a refined and well-bred woman.— *n.* **gen'tlewomanliness.** — **gentle craft,** shoemaking : angling ; **gentleman farmer,** a landowner who resides on his estate and superintends the cultivation of his own soil : a farmer who owns his farm : a farmer who deputes the harder work of his farm to others ; **Gentleman of the Chapel-royal,** a lay-singer who assists the priests in the choral service of the royal chapel ; **gentleman's (-men's) agreement,** an agreement resting on honour, not on formal contract ; **gentleman's gentleman,** a valet ; **gentleman usher** (*pl.* **gentlemen ushers),** a gentleman who serves as an usher at court, or as an attendant on a person of rank ; **gentle reader,** courteous reader, an old-fashioned phrase common in the prefaces of books. [O.Fr. (Fr.) *gentil*—L. *gentīlis,* belonging to the same *gens* or clan, later, well-bred ; see genteel.]

Gentoo, jen-too', *n.* a Telugu-speaker : a pagan of India : a Hindu : **gentoo,** a Falkland Island penguin.—Also *adj.* [Port. *gentio,* a Gentile.]

gentry, *jen'tri*, *n.* the class of people next below the rank of nobility: (*coll.*) people of a particular, esp. an inferior, stamp: rank by birth: the rank of gentleman: (*Shak.*) good manners and courtesy.—*n.* **gen'trice** (*-tris*), gentle birth: good breeding. [O.Fr. *genterise, gentelise*, formed from adj. *gentil*, gentle.]

genty, *jen'ti*, *adj.* (*Scot.*) neat, dainty: graceful.

genuflect, *jen'ū-flekt*, *v.i.* to bend the knee in worship or respect.—*n.* **genūflex'ion** (also **genū-flec'tion**). [L. *genū*, the knee, *flectĕre, flexum*, to bend.]

genuine, *jen'ū-in*, *adj.* natural: native: not spurious: real: pure: sincere.—*adv.* **gen'uinely**. —*n.* **gen'uineness**. [L. *genuīnus—gignĕre*, to beget.]

genus, *jē'nəs*, *n.* (*biol.*) a taxonomic group of lower rank than a family, consisting of closely related species, in extreme cases of one species only: (*log.*) a class of objects comprehending several subordinate species: — *pl.* **genera** (*jen'ə-rä*). — *adjs.* **generic, -al** (*ji-ner'ik, -əl*).—*adv.* **gener'ically**.— **generic name**, (*biol.*) the name of the genus, placed first in naming the species, thus *Equus caballus* (horse), *Equus asinus* (ass), *Equus zebra*, &c., are species of the genus Equus, and Equus is the generic name. [L. *gĕnus, generis*, birth; cog. with Gr. *genos*.]

geo, gio, *gyō*, *n.* (*Orkney, Shetland*) a gully, creek. [O.N. *gjá*.]

geocarpy, *jē-ō-kär'pi*, *n.* production, or ripening, of fruit underground.—*adj.* **geocarp'ous**. [Gr. *gē*, earth, *karpos*, fruit.]

geocentric, *jē-ō-sen'trik*, *adj.* having the earth for centre: (*astron.*) as viewed or reckoned from the centre of the earth.—Also **geocen'trical**.—*adv.* **geocen'trically**.— *n.* **geocen'tricism** (*-sizm*), belief that the earth is the centre of the universe. [Gr. *gē*, the earth, *kentron*, point, centre.]

geode, *jē'ōd*, *n.* (*geol.*) a rock cavity lined with crystals that have grown inwards: (*mining*) a rounded hollow nodule of ironstone.—*adj.* **geōd'ic**. [Fr. *géode*—Gr. *geōdēs*, earthy—*gē*, earth, *eidos*, form.]

geodesy, *jē-od'i-si*, *n.* earth measurement on a large scale: surveying with allowance for the earth's curvature.—*adjs.* **geodesic** (*jē-ō-des'ik, -dēs'ik*), **-al**, **geodet'ic, -al**, pertaining to or determined by geodesy.—*n.* **geod'esist**, one skilled in geodesy.— **geodesic** or **geodetic (line)**, the shortest line on a surface between two points on it. [Gr. *geōdaisiā* —*gē*, the earth, *daisis*, division.]

geognosy, *jē-og'nə-si*, *n.* knowledge of the general structure, condition, and materials of the earth.— Also (*rare*) **geognosis** (*jē-əg-nō'sis*).—*n.* **gē'ognost**. —*adjs.* **gēognostic** (*-nos'tik*), **-al**.—*adv.* **gēognost'ically**. [Fr. *géognosie*—Gr. *gē* the earth, *gnōsis*, knowledge.]

geogony, *jē-og'ə-ni*, *n.* the science or theory of the formation of the earth.—Also **geogeny** (*-oj'*).— *adj.* **geogonic** (*jē-ō-gon'ik*). [Gr. *gē*, the earth, *gonē*, generation.]

geography, *jē-og'rə-fi*, *n.* the science of the surface of the earth and its inhabitants: a book containing a description of the earth.—*n.* **geog'rapher**.—*adjs.* **geographic** (*jē-ō-graf'ik*), **-al**.—*adv.* **geograph'ically**.—**geographical distribution** (see distribution); **geographical mile** (see mile); **physical, political geography** (see physical, political). [Gr. *geōgraphiā*—*gē*, earth, *graphein*, to write.]

geoid, *jē'oid*, *n.* the figure of the earth's mean sea-level surface assumed to be continued across the land, approximately an oblate ellipsoid of revolution.—*adj.* **geoid'al**. [Gr. *geōdēs, geoeidēs*, earth-like—*gē*, earth, *eidos*, form.]

geolatry, *jē-ol'ə-tri*, *n.* earth-worship. [Gr. *gē*, earth, *latreiā*, worship.]

geology, *jē-ol'ə-ji*, *n.* the science relating to the history and development of the earth's crust, with its successive floras and faunas.—*ns.* **geologian** (*jē-ə-lō'ji-ən*), **geol'ogist**.—*adjs.* **geologic** (*-loj'ik*), **-al**.—*adv.* **geolog'ically**.—*v.i.* **geol'ogise**, to work at geology in the field.—*v.t.* to investigate the geology of.—**dynamical geology**, the study of the work of natural agents in shaping the earth's crust

—**wind, frost, rivers, volcanic action, &c.**; **structural geology**, the study of the arrangement and structure of rock masses. [Fr. *géologie*—Gr. *gē*, earth, *logos*, a discourse.]

geomancy, *jē'ō-man-si*, *n.* divination by figures of or on earth.—*n.* **gē'omancer**.—*adj.* **gēoman'tic**. [Gr. *gē*, earth, *manteiā*, divination.]

geometry, *jē-om'i-tri*, *n.* that branch of mathematics which treats of spatial magnitudes: a textbook of geometry.—*ns.* **geom'eter**, a geometrician: a geometrid; **geometrician** (*-me-trish'ən*), one skilled in geometry.—*adjs.* **geometric** (*-met'*), **-al**, relating to or according to geometry: consisting of or using simple figures such as geometry deals with.—*adv.* **geomet'rically**.—*n.* **geom'etrid**, any moth of the family or superfamily **Geomet'ridae**, whose caterpillars are loopers.—*v.t.* and *v.i.* **geom'etrise**, to work geometrically.—*n.* **geom'etrist**.—**geometrical progression**, a series of quantities each of which has the same ratio to its predecessor. [Gr. *geōmetriā—gē, metron*, a measure.]

Geomys, *jē'ō-mis*, *n.* the typical genus of **Geomyidae** (*-mī'i-dē*), the pouched rats.—*adj.* **Geomy'oid**. [Gr. *gē*, earth, *mys*, mouse.]

geomorphology, *jē-ō-mor-fol'ə-ji*, *n.* morphology of the earth's surface. [Gr. *gē*, earth, **morphology**.]

geophagy, *jē-of'ə-ji*, *n.* earth-eating.—Also **geoph'agism.** — *n.* **geoph'agist**. — *adj.* **geoph'agous** (*-gəs*). [Gr. *gē*, earth, *phagein*, to eat.]

geophilous, *gē-of'il-əs*, *adj.* living in or on the ground: geocarpic: having a short stem with leaves at ground-level. — *adj.* **geophil'ic**. [Gr. *gē*, earth, *phileein*, to love.]

geophysics, *gē-ō-fiz'iks*, *n.* the physics of the earth. —*adj.* **geophys'ical**.—*n.* **geophys'icist** (*-i-sist*). [Gr. *gē*, earth, and **physics**.]

geophyte, *jē'ō-fīt*, *n.* a plant that survives the winter by subterranean buds.—*adj.* **geophytic** (*-fit'ik*). [Gr. *gē*, earth, *phyton*, plant.]

geoponic, -al, *jē-ō-pon'ik, -əl*, *adjs.* agricultural.— *n.* **geopon'ics** (treated as *sing.*), the science of agriculture. [Gr. *geōponikos—gē*, earth, *ponos*, labour.]

geordie, *jor'di*, *n.* a guinea, from the figure of St *George*: a safety-lamp for miners invented by *George* Stephenson: a coal-pitman: a collier-boat: a native of Tyneside.

George, *jorj*, *n.* a jewelled figure of St *George* slaying the dragon, worn by Knights of the Garter: the automatic pilot of an aircraft.—**George Cross**, an award for outstanding courage or heroism given in cases where a purely military honour is not applicable—instituted during the Second World War; **George Medal**, an award for gallantry given to civilians and members of the armed forces; **St George's cross**, the Greek cross of England, red on a white ground.

georgette, *jor-jet'*, *n.* a thin silk stuff. [Named after a milliner.]

Georgian, *jorj'i-ən*, *adj.* relating to or contemporary with any of the various *Georges*, kings of Great Britain: relating to or following Henry *George*, Lloyd *George*, or other of the name: belonging to *Georgia* (*Gurjestan, Gruzia*) in the Caucasus, its people, language, &c.: of or pertaining to the American State of *Georgia*.—Also *n.*—**Georgian planet**, Uranus, named after George III. by its discoverer, Sir William Herschel.

georgic, *jorj'ik*, *adj.* relating to agriculture or rustic affairs.—*n.* a poem on husbandry. [L. *geōrgicus*—Gr. *geōrgikos—geōrgiā*, agriculture—*gē*, earth, *ergon*, work.]

geosphere, *jē'ō-sfēr*, *n.* the solid part of the earth, distinguished from *atmosphere* and *hydrosphere*. [Gr. *gē*, earth, *sphaira*, sphere.]

geostatic, *jē-ō-stat'ik*, *adj.* capable of sustaining the pressure of earth from all sides.—*n.* **geostat'ics** (treated as *sing.*), the statics of rigid bodies. [Gr. *gē*, the earth, *statikos*, causing to stand.]

geosyncline, *jē-ō-sin'klīn*, *n.* a syncline on a great scale.—*adj.* **geosyncli'nal**. [Gr. *gē*, earth, and **syncline**.]

geotaxis, *jē-ō-taks'is*, *n.* response of an organism to the stimulus of gravity.—*adjs.* **geotact'ic, -al**. [Gr. *gē*, earth, *taxis*, arrangement.]

Neutral vowels in unaccented syllables : *el'ə-mənt, in'fənt, ran'dəm*

geotectonic, *jē-ō-tek-ton'ik*, *adj.* relating to the structure of rock masses.—*n.* **geotecton'ics** (treated as *sing.*), structural geology. [Gr. *gē*, earth, *tektōn*, a builder.]

geothermic, *jē-ō-thər'mik*, **geothermal**, *-əl*, *adjs.* pertaining to the internal heat of the earth.—*n.* **geothermom'eter**, an instrument for measuring subterranean temperatures. [Gr. *gē*, earth, *thermē*, heat.]

geotropism, *jē-ot'rop-izm*, *n.* (*bot.*) geotaxis (positive downwards, negative upwards).—*adj.* **geotrop'ic**. [Gr. *gē*, earth, *tropos*, a turning.]

gerah, *gē'rä*, *n.* (*B.*) the smallest Hebrew weight and coin, $\frac{1}{20}$ of a shekel, worth about $1\frac{1}{4}$d. [Heb. *gērāh*.]

geranium, *ji-rān'yəm*, *n.* a plant of a genus (Geranium) with seed-vessels like a crane's bill, typical of the family **Geraniaceae** (*-i-ā'si-ē*): (loosely) a pelargonium. [L.,— Gr. *geranion* — *geranos*, a crane.]

gerbe, *jərb*, *n.* (*her.*) a wheat-sheaf : a fountain or firework resembling a wheat-sheaf. [Fr. *gerbe* ; cf. **garb** (2).]

gere (*Spens.*). Same as **gear**.

gerent, *jē'rənt*, *n.* controller, ruler. [L. *gerēns*, *-entis*, pr.p. of *gerĕre*, to manage.]

gerfalcon, gyrfalcon, jerfalcon, *jər'faw(l)-kn*, *n.* a large northern falcon. [O.Fr. *gerfaucon*—L.L. *gyrofalcō*, most prob. O.H.G. *gīr*, a vulture (Ger. *geier*) ; see **falcon**.]

geriatrics, *jer-i-at'riks*, *n.* medical care of the old. —*adj.* **geriat'ric**.—*ns.* **geriatrician** (*-ə-trish'ən*) **geriatry** (*jer-i'ətri*), care of the old, old people's welfare. [Gr. *gēras*, old age, *iātros*, physician.]

gerle (*Spens.*). Same as **girl**.

germ, *jərm*, *n.* a rudimentary form of a living thing, whether plant or animal : (*obs.*) a plant ovary : a shoot : that from which anything springs, the origin or beginning : a first principle : that from which a disease springs : a micro-organism, esp. a malign one.—*v.i.* to put forth buds, sprout.— *ns.* **germ'-cell**, a sperm or ovum, a gamete, or cell from which it springs ; **ger'men, ger'min** (*Shak.* **ger'main, ger'maine**), a rudiment : a shoot : (*obs.*) the ovary in a flower ; **germ'icide**, that which kills germs.—*adjs.* **germ'inal**, pertaining to a germ or rudiment : in the germ ; **germ'inant**, sprouting : budding : capable of developing.—*v.i.* **germ'inate**, to begin to grow (esp. of a seed or spore).—*v.t.* to cause to sprout.— *n.* **germinā'tion**.—*adj.* **germ'inative**.—*ns.* **germ'-lay'er**, a primary layer in an embryo—ectoderm, mesoderm, or endoderm ; **germ'-plasm**, that part of the nuclear protoplasmic material which, according to Weismann, is the vehicle of heredity, and maintains its continuity from generation to generation. [Partly through Fr. *germe*, from L. *germen*, *-inis*, a sprout, bud, germ, *germināre*, *-ātum*, to sprout.]

german, *jər'mən*, *adj.* of the first degree: full (see **brother, cousin**): closely allied.—*n.* a full brother or sister : a near relative.—*adj.* **germane** (*-mān'*), nearly related : relevant, appropriate. [O.Fr. *germain*—L. *germānus*.]

German, *jər'mən*, *n.* a native or citizen of *Germany*, or one of the same linguistic or ethnological stock (*pl.* **Ger'mans**) : the German language, esp. High German.—*adj.* of or from Germany, or the Germans: German-speaking.—*n.* **Ger'man-band'**, street-musicians, orig. from Germany.—*adjs.* **Germanesque'**, marked by German characteristics ; **Germanic** (*-man'ik*), of Germany : of the linguistic family to which German, English, Norwegian, &c., belong—Teutonic.—*n.* an extinct Indo-Germanic tongue which differentiated into **East Germanic** (Gothic and other extinct languages), **North Germanic** or Scandinavian (Norwegian, Danish, Swedish, Icelandic), and **West Germanic** (English, Frisian, Dutch, Low German, High German).— *adv.* **German'ically**.—*v.t.* **Ger'manīse**, to make German.—*v.i.* to become German : to adopt German ways.—*n.* **Germanisā'tion**.—*adj.* **Ger'-manish**, somewhat German.—*ns.* **Ger'manism**, a German idiom : German ideas and ways ; **Ger'-manist**, one learned in German philology or other matters relating to Germany.—*adj.* **Ger-manis'tic**, pertaining to the study of German.— *ns.* **German'ophil**, a lover of the Germans and things German ; **German'ophobe**, one who fears or hates the Germans and things German.— **German flute**, the ordinary modern flute ; **German measles**, rubella ; **German silver**, an alloy of copper, nickel, and zinc, white like silver, and first made in Germany ; **German sixth**, a chord with major third, perfect fifth, and augmented sixth ; **High German**, the speech, originally of High or Southern Germany, the literary language throughout Germany ; **Low German**, **Platt-Deutsch**, the language of Low or Northern Germany : formerly applied to all the West Germanic dialects except High German. [L. *Germānus*, German.]

germander, *jər-man'dər*, *n.* a labiate herb (Teucrium) with aromatic, bitter, and stomachic properties.—**germander speedwell**, a bright blue-flowered veronica (*V. Chamaedrys*). [L.L. *germandra*—Late Gr. *chamandrya*—Gr. *chamaidrys*—*chamai*, on the ground, *drȳs*, oak.]

germanium, *jər-mā'ni-əm*, *n.* a metallic element (atomic number 32) discovered in 1885 by Clemens Winkler (1838–1904), a German.

Germinal, *zher-mē-nal'*, *n.* the seventh month of the French revolutionary calendar, about March 21-April 19. [See **germ**.]

germinate. See **germ**.

gerne, *gərn*, *v.i.* (*Spens.*) to grin or gape. [**grin**.]

gerontocracy, *ger-* or *jer-on-tok'rə-si*, *n.* government by old men.—*ns.* **gerontol'ogy**, scientific study of the processes of growing old ; **gerontotherapeut'ics**, the science of medical treatment of the diseases of old age. [Gr. *gerōn*, *-ontos*, an old man, *kratos*, power.]

geropiga, *jer-ō-pē'gä*, *n.* a mixture of grape-juice, brandy, &c., used to sophisticate port-wine. [Port.]

gerrymander, *ger'i-man-dər*, also *jer'*, *v.t.* (*U.S.*) to rearrange (voting districts) in the interests of a particular party or candidate : to manipulate (facts, arguments, &c.) so as to reach undue conclusions. —*n.* an arrangement of the above nature. [Formed from the name of Governor Elbridge *Gerry* (1744–1814) and sala*mander*, from the likeness to that animal of the gerrymandered map of Massachusetts in 1811.]

gerund, *jer'ənd*, *n.* a part of the Latin or other verb with the value of a verbal noun, as *amandum*, loving.—*n.* **ger'und-grind'er**, a pedantic teacher. —*adjs.* **gerundial** (*ji-rund'i-əl*), **gerundival** (*jer-ən-dī'vl*), **gerundive** (*ji-rund'iv*).—*n.* **gerund'ive**, a Latin verbal adjective, as *amandus*, *-a*, *-um*, deserving or requiring to be loved. [L. *gerundium*—*gerĕre*, to bear.]

Gesneria, *jes-nē'ri-ä*, *n.* a tropical American genus typical of the **Gesneriā'ceae**, a family close akin to the Scrophulariaceae. [Named after Konrad von *Gesner* (1516-65), Swiss botanist and scholar.]

gessamine (*Milt.*). Same as **jasmine**.

gesse (*Spens.*). Same as **guess**.

gesso, *jes'ō*, *n.* plaster of Paris : a plaster surface, prepared as a ground for painting. [It.,—L. *gypsum* ; see **gypsum**.]

gest, jest, *n.* (*Shak.*) time fixed for a stay in a place. [O.Fr. *giste*, a stopping-place.]

gest, geste, *jest*, *n.* an exploit : a tale of adventure, a romance. [O.Fr. *geste*—L. *gesta*, things done—*gerĕre*, *gestum*, to bear, behave ; cf. **jest**.]

gest, geste, *jest*, *n.* bearing : gesture.—*adj.* **gest'ic**. [Fr. *geste*—L. *gestus*—*gerĕre*, *gestum*, to bear, behave.]

gestalt, *gə-shtält'*, *n.* form : structure : organised whole. — **gestalt psychology**, a revolt from the atomistic outlook of the orthodox school, starts with the organised whole as something not a mere sum of the parts into which it can be logically analysed. [German.]

gestapo, *gə-stä'pō*, *n.* the Nazi secret police in Germany. [From Ger. *geheime staats polizei*, secret state police.]

gestation, *jes-tā'shən*, *n.* (*arch.*) being carried in a vehicle, a boat, &c. : the act of carrying the young in the womb.—*adjs.* ges'tant, laden ; gestato'rial, ges'tatory, pertaining to carriage. [L. *gestāre*, *-ātum*, to carry—*gerĕre*, to bear.]

gesticulate, *jes-tik'ū-lāt, v.i.* to make vigorous gestures.—*ns.* gesticulā'tion ; gestic'ulātor.— *adj.* gestic'ulatory. [L. *gesticulāri, -ātus—gesticulus,* dim. of *gestus,* gesture—*gerĕre,* to carry, behave.]

gesture, *jes'tyər, n.* (*obs.*) a posture, or movement of the body : an action expressive of sentiment or passion or intended to show inclination or disposition : the use of such movements : an action dictated by courtesy or diplomacy, or by a desire to impress : (*Shak.*) behaviour.—*adj.* ges'tural. [L.L. *gestūra*—L. *gestus,* from L. *gerĕre,* to carry, behave.]

get, *get, v.t.* to obtain : to acquire : to procure : to receive : to attain : to come to have : to catch : to grasp or take the meaning of : to learn : to commit to memory : to hit : to descry : to make out : to succeed in coming into touch or communication with (e.g. a wireless station) : to worst, have the better of, gain a decisive advantage over : to baffle : to irritate : to grip emotionally, take, captivate, hit the taste of exactly : to induce : to cause to be, go, or become : to betake : to beget.— *v.i.* to arrive, to bring or put oneself (in any place, position, or state) : to become : to grow richer : (*U.S.*) to clear out : (*pr.p.* get'ing ; *pa.t.* got, *obs.* gat ; *pa.p.* got, *arch., Scot.,* and *U.S.* got'en). —*n.* (*obs.*) that which is got : output : offspring : (*Scot.* contemptuously) a child, brat : begetting.— *adj.* get-at'-able, easily accessible.—*ns.* get'away, an escape : a start : breaking cover ; gett'er ; gett'ing, a gaining : anything gained : procreation ; get'-up', equipment : general appearance. —get ahead, along, to make progress, advance ; get at, to reach, attain : (*slang*) to poke fun at ; get away with it, pull it off : carry a thing through successfully or with impunity ; get off, to escape ; get on, to proceed, advance : to prosper : to agree, consort harmoniously ; get out, to produce : to extricate oneself : to take oneself off ; get over, to surmount : to recover from ; get round, to circumvent : to persuade, talk over ; get there, (*slang*) to achieve one's object, succeed ; get through, to finish : to be put in telephonic communication ; get up, to arise : to ascend : to arrange : to prepare : to learn up for an occasion : to commit to memory ; to have got, (*coll.*) to have ; to have got to, to be obliged to. [O.N. *geta* ; cog. with O.E. *-gietan* (in compounds).]

Geum, *jē'əm, n.* the avens genus of the rose family. [L. *gĕum.*]

gewgaw, *gū'gaw, n.* a toy : a bauble.—*adj.* showy without value. [Origin unknown.]

gey (*Scot.*). See gay.—*adv.* geyan (*gui'ən*), for gey and.

geyser, *gā'* or *gī'zər,* or *-sər, gē'zər, n.* a spring that spouts hot water into the air : a heater for bathwater.—*n.* gey'serite, sinter. [*Geysir,* a geyser in Iceland—Ice. *geysa,* O.N. *göysa,* to gush.]

gharri, gharry, *ga'ri, n.* in India, a wheeled vehicle, generally for hire. [Hind. *gārī,* a cart.]

ghast, *gāst, v.t.* (*Shak.*) to strike aghast : to affright. —*adj.* ghast'ful (*Spens.* gastfull), dreary, dismal. —*adv.* ghast'fully, frightfully.—*n.* ghast'liness. —*adj.* ghast'ly, death-like : hideous : (*coll.*) deplorable.—Also *adv.*—*n.* ghastness (see gastness). [O.E. *gǣstan* ; cf. gast.]

ghat, ghaut, *gawt, n.* in India, a mountain-pass : a landing-stair : a place of cremation (*burning ghat*). [Hind. *ghāt,* descent.]

ghazal, *gaz'al, n.* a Persian and Arabic verse-form, of not more than 18 couplets, the first two lines and the even-numbered lines thereafter rhyming together, mainly amatory and bacchanalian.—Also gazal, ghazel. [Ar. *ghazal.*]

ghazi, *gā'zē, n.* a veteran Mohammedan warrior : a slayer of infidels : a high Turkish title. [Ar. *ghāzi,* fighting.]

gheber, ghebre. Same as guebre.

ghee, ghi, *gē, g'hē, n.* clarified buffalo butter. [Hind. *ghi.*]

gherkin, *gər'kin, n.* a small cucumber used for pickling. [From an earlier form of Du. *a(u)gurkje,* a gherkin ; app. from Slavonic ; cf. Byzantine Gr. *angourion,* a water-melon.]

ghesse (*Spens.*). Same as guess : (*pa.t.* and *pa.p.* ghest, ghessed).

ghetto, *get'ō, n.* the Jews' quarter in an Italian or other city, where they used to be strictly confined. [It.]

Ghibeline, *gib'ə-lēn, -lin, -lin, n.* one of a party in Italy in the Middle Ages, originally supporters of the Hohenstaufen emperors against the Guelfs and the pope. [It. *Ghibellino,* apparently—*Waiblingen* in Württemberg, a Hohenstaufen possession.]

ghost, *gōst, n.* a spirit : the soul of a man : a spirit appearing after death : (*Shak.*) a dead body : (*slang*) one who does another's work for him, as writing speeches or the like : a faint or false appearance : a semblance.—*v.t.* to haunt as a ghost. —*v.i.* (*slang*) to play the ghost for another.—*adj.* ghost'-like. — *n.* ghost'liness. — *adj.* ghost'ly, spiritual : religious : pertaining to apparitions : ghost-like : faint. —*ns.* ghost'-moth, a moth (*Hepialus humuli*), the male of ghostly white appearance, the caterpillar destructive to hop-gardens ; ghost'-story, a story in which ghosts figure ; ghost'-word, a word that has originated in the blunder of a scribe or printer—common in dictionaries.—*adj.* ghost'y.—give up the ghost, (*B.*) to die ; Holy Ghost, the Holy Spirit, the third person in the Christian Trinity. [O.E. *gāst* ; Ger. *geist* ; the *h* from Caxton's Flemish habit.]

ghoul, *gōōl,* now often gowl, *n.* an Eastern demon that preys on the dead : a gruesome fiend : a person of gruesome or revolting habits or tastes.— *adj.* ghoul'ish. [Ar. *ghūl.*]

ghyll, *gil,* an unnecessary variant of gill, a ravine.

giambeux, (*Spens.*) for jambeaux.

giant, *gī'ənt, n.* a huge mythical being of more or less human form : a person of abnormally great stature : anything much above the usual size of its kind : a person of much greater powers than his fellows.—*adj.* gigantic.—*ns.* gi'antess ; gi'anthood, gi'antism, the quality or character of a giant : the occurrence of giants : gigantism. —*adj.* gi'antly, giantlike.—*n.* gi'ant-pow'der, a kind of dynamite.—*adj.* gi'ant-rude, (*Shak.*) enormously rude or uncivil.—*ns.* gi'antry, giants collectively : giant stories or mythology ; gi'antship ; giant's-kett'le, a great pot-hole believed to have been formed by subglacial water ; giant('s)-stride, a gymnastic apparatus enabling one to take great strides around a pole. [O.Fr. *geant* (Fr. *géant*)—L. *gigās*—Gr. *gigās, gigantos.*]

giaour, *jowr, n.* infidel, a term applied by the Turks to all who are not of their own religion. [Through Turk.—Pers. *gaur* ; see guebre.]

gib, *jib, gib, n.* wedge-shaped piece of metal holding another in place, &c.—*v.t.* to fasten with a gib. [Origin obscure.]

gib, *gib, n.* a tom-cat, esp. one castrated : a term of reproach.—Also gib'-cat (*Shak.*). [From the name *Gilbert.*]

gibber, *jib'ər, v.i.* to utter senseless or inarticulate sounds. [Imit.]

gibberish, *gib'ər-ish, n.* rapid, gabbling talk : unmeaning words.—*adj.* unmeaning. [Imit.]

gibbet, *jib'it, n.* a gallows, esp. one on which criminals were suspended after execution : the projecting beam of a crane.—*v.t.* to expose on, or as on, a gibbet. [O.Fr. *gibet,* a stick ; origin unknown.]

gibble-gabble, *gib'l-gab'l, n.* senseless chatter. [gabble.]

gibbon, *gib'ən, n.* an E. Indian anthropoid ape (of several species) with very long arms. [Origin unknown.]

gibbous, *gib'əs, adj.* hump-backed : humped : unequally convex on two sides, as the moon between half and full.—Also gibb'ose.—*ns.* gibbos'ity, gibb'ousness.—*adv.* gibb'ously. [L. *gibbōsus—gibbus,* a hump.]

gibe, jibe, *jīb, v.i.* to scoff : to flout.—*v.t.* to scoff at : to taunt.—*n.* a flout : a sneer.—*n.* gib'er.— *adv.* gib'ingly. [Origin obscure.]

gibel, *gib'əl, n.* the Prussian carp, without barbules.

Gibeonite, gib′i-ən-īt, n. a slave's slave—from Josh. ix.

giblets, jib′lits, n.pl. the internal eatable parts of a fowl, &c.: entrails.—adj. gib′let, made of giblets. [O.Fr. gibelet; origin unknown; not a dim. of gibier, game.]

gibus, jī′bəs, n. a crush-hat, opera-hat. [Fr.]

gid, gid, n. sturdy in sheep. [giddy.]

giddy, gid′i, adj. unsteady, dizzy: causing giddiness: whirling: light-headed: flighty. — adv. **gidd′ily.**—n. **gidd′iness.**—adjs. **giddy-head′ed,** thoughtless, wanting reflection; **giddy-paced,** (Shak.) moving irregularly. [O.E. gidig, gydig, insane, possessed by a god.]

gie, gē, vb. a Scots form of give:—pa.t. gied, gēd, gae, gā; pa.p. gien, gēn.

gier-eagle, jēr′-ē′gl, n. (B.) a vulture. [Du. gier.]

gif, gif, conj. an obsolete form (except in Scots) of if.

giff-gaff, gif′-gâf′, n. (Scot.) give and take. [give.]

gift, gift, n. a thing given: a bribe: a quality bestowed by nature: the act of giving.—v.t. to endow, esp. with any power or faculty: to present. —n. **gift′-book,** a book suitable or intended for presentation.—adj. **gift′ed,** highly endowed by nature.—ns. **gift′-horse,** a horse given as a present; **gift′ling,** a little gift.—**look a gift-horse in the mouth,** to criticise a gift. [See give.]

gig, gig, n. a whip-top: a flighty girl: a light, two-wheeled carriage: a long, light boat: a machine for raising the nap on cloth (in full, **gig′-mill**): (dial.) sport, fun.—v.t. and v.i. **gigg′it,** (U.S.) to convey or move rapidly.—n.pl. **gig′-lamps,** (slang) spectacles.—n. **gig′man,** one who drives or keeps a gig: (Carlyle) a narrow middle-class philistine—whence ns. **gig′maness,** **gigman′ity,** **gig′mānia.** [M.E. gigge, a whirling thing (cf. **whirligig**); origin obscure.]

giggle, gig′l, v.i. to laugh with short catches of the breath, or in a silly manner.—n. a laugh of this kind—ns. **gigg′ler;** **gigg′ling.**—adjs. **gigg′le-some,** **gigg′ly.** [Echoic.]

giglet, giglot, gig′lit, -lət, n. a giddy girl: a wanton. —adj. (Shak.) inconstant. [Perh. conn. with **gig;** later associated with **giggle.**]

gigolo, jig′ō-lō, n. a professional male dancing partner. [Fr.]

gigot, jig′ət, n. a leg of mutton, &c.: a leg-of-mutton sleeve. [Fr.]

gigue, zhēg, n. (mus.) a lively dance-form in triple time, common in old suites.—Also (It.) **giga** (jē′gä). [Fr.: cf. jig.]

gila, hhē′lä (in full **gila monster),** n. either of the two Heloderma species, the only venomous lizards known. [Gila River, Arizona.]

Gilbertian, gil-bərt′i-ən, adj. whimsically or para-doxically humorous. [Sir W. S. Gilbert (1836-1911), librettist, playwright, poet, &c.]

Gilbertine, gil′bərt-īn, -in, n. a member of the order of canons and nuns founded (c. 1148) by St Gilbert of Sempringham.—Also adj.

gilcup. Same as **giltcup.**

gild, gild, v.t. to cover or overlay with gold or with any gold-like substance: (obs.) to smear with blood: (obs.) to flush: to furnish with gold: to gloss over, give a specious appearance to: to adorn with lustre:—pr.p. **gild′ing;** pa.t. and pa.p. **gild′ed** or **gilt.**—ns. **gild′er,** one who coats articles with gold; **gild′ing,** act or trade of a gilder: gold or imitation thereof laid on a surface.—**Gilded Chamber,** the House of Lords; **gilded spurs,** an emblem of knighthood; **gilded youth,** rich young people of fashion; **guild the pill,** to make a disagreeable thing seem less so. [O.E. gyldan—gold; see gold.]

gild. See **guild.**

gilden, gylden, gil′dən, orig. adj. golden, adopted later (as Spens.) as a pa.p. of **gild.** [O.E. gylden.]

gill, gil, n. an organ for breathing in water: the flesh under the jaw: the wattle below the bill of a fowl: one of the radiating plates under a mush-room or toadstool cap: a projecting rib of a heating surface.—n. **gill′-cover,** a fold of skin, usu. with bony plates, protecting the gills. [Cf. Dan. giælle; Sw. gäl.]

gill, jil, n. a measure, now=¼ pint.—n. **gill′-house,** a dram-shop. [O.Fr. gelle.]

gill, jil, n. a girl (also jill): a female ferret (jill): ground-ivy: beer with an infusion of ground-ivy (in full **gill′-ale, gill′-beer).**—ns. **gill′et, gill′ot,** a skittish, flighty, or loose young woman; **gill′-flirt,** a wanton girl. [Gillian or Juliana (from Julius), a woman's name.]

gill, ghyll, gil, n. a small ravine, a wooded glen: a brook. [O.N. gil.]

gillaroo, gil-ə-roo′, n. an Irish trout with thickened muscular stomach. [Ir. giolla ruadh, red lad.]

gillie, gil′i, n. an attendant, esp. on a sportsman.—v.i. to act as gillie.—ns. **gillie-wet′-foot, -white′-foot,** a barefoot Highland lad, esp. a messenger or chief's attendant. [Gael. gille, a lad, Ir. giolla.]

gillyflower, jil′i-flowr (Shak. **gillyvor,** -vər), n. a flower that smells like cloves, esp. **clove-gilly-flower, stock-gillyflower** (see clove, stock, 1). [O.Fr. girofle—Gr. karyophyllon, the clove-tree—karyon, a nut, phyllon, a leaf.]

gilpy, gilpey, gil′pi, n. (Scot.) a boisterous girl or (formerly) boy.

gilravage, gillravage, galravage, -itch, gəl-räv′ij, -ich, or räv′, n. (Scot.) a noisy frolic: riotous merrymaking.—v.i. to behave riotously.—n. **gil-rav′ager.**

gilt, gilt, pa.t. and pa.p. of **gild.**—adj. gilded: gold-coloured.—n. gilding: (Shak.) money.—adj. **gilt′-edged,** having the edges gilt: of the highest quality (**gilt-edged securities,** those stocks whose interest is considered perfectly safe).—ns. **gilt′cup,** **gil′cup,** a buttercup; **gilt′-head,** a name for several fishes, esp. a sparoid fish with a half-moon-shaped gold spot between the eyes; **gilt′-tail,** a yellow-tipped worm (Dendrobaena subrubicunda) of old dunghills.

gilt, gilt, n. (prov.) a young sow (in various con-ditions locally). [O.N. gyltr; cf. O.E. gilte.]

gimbal, jim′bl, n. (obs.) a gimmal: (in pl.) a con-trivance for keeping a hanging object level (sing. in composition, as **gim′bal-ring′).** [See gemel.]

gimblet. Same as **gimlet.**

gimcrack, jimcrack, jim′krak, n. a trumpery knick-knack: a paltry, ill-made frail article: a trivial mechanism. — adj. trumpery. — n. **gim-crack′ery.** [Origin obscure.]

gimlet, gim′lit, n. a small tool for boring holes by turning it with the hand.—v.t. to pierce as with a gimlet: to turn like a gimlet.—adj. **gim′let-eyed′,** very sharp-sighted. [O.Fr. gumbelet, from Gmc.; cf. **wimble.**]

gimmal, jim′l, n. a gimbal: a ring (also **gimm′al-ring′)** that can be divided into two (or three) rings: a joint or part in a piece of mechanism (also **gimm′er;** Shak. **gimm′or).**—adj. **gimm′alled** (Shak. **jymold),** jointed, hinged. [See gemel.]

gimmer, gim′ər, n. a young ewe: (contemptuously) a woman. [O.N. gymbr; cf. Sw. gimmer, Dan. gimmer.]

gimp, gimp, n. a yarn with a hard core: a trimming thereof: a fishing-line bound with wire: a coarse thread in lace-making.—v.t. to make or furnish with gimp.—Also **guimp, gymp.** [Fr. guimpe, app. from O.H.G. wimpal, a light robe; cf. **wimple;** perhaps confused with Fr. guipure; see **guipure.**]

gimp, jimp, v.t. to scallop, notch: to corrugate.

gin, jin, n. Same as **geneva.**—ns. **gin′-fizz,** a drink of gin, lemon-juice, effervescing water, &c.; **gin′-palace, gin′-shop,** a shop where gin is sold; **gin′-sling,** a cold gin and water, sweetened and flavoured. [Contr. from **geneva.**]

gin, jin, n. (Spens.) a scheme, artifice, contrivance: a snare or trap: a machine, esp. one for hoisting:

a cotton-gin : (*Spens.*) an instrument of torture.—
v.t. to trap or snare : to clear of seeds by a cotton-
gin :—*pr.p.* **ginn'ing** ; *pa.t.* and *pa.p.* **ginned.**—
ns. **gin'-horse**, a mill-horse ; **gin'-house**, **ginn'-
ery**, a place where cotton is ginned ; **ginn'er**, one
who gins cotton. [**engine.**]

gin, *jin, n.* an Australian black woman. [Native
word.]

gin, *jin, n.* a type of rummy in which a player whose
unmatched cards count ten or less may stop the
game.—Also **gin rummy**. [Origin uncertain.]

gin, *gin, v.t.* and *v.i.* to begin :—*pa.t.* **gan**, used
poetically in the sense of *did*. [Aphetic from O.E.
beginnan or *onginnan*, to begin.]

gin, *gin, prep.* (*Scot.*) by (the time of). [M.E. *gain*,
app.—O.N. *gegn*, against.]

gin, *gin, conj.* (*Scot.*) if. [Perh. pa.p. of give as a
substitute for *gif* ; perh. from **gin**, prep.]

ging, *ging, n.* a gang or company. See **gang**.

gingal, **gingall**. Same as **jingal**.

gingelly. Same as **gingili**.

ginger, *jin'jər, n.* the root-stock of *Zingiber officinale*,
or other species of the genus (family Zingiberaceae)
with a hot taste, used as a condiment or stomachic :
ginger-beer : stimulation : mettle.—*adj.* (*coll.*)
sandy, reddish.—*v.t.* to put ginger into : to make
spirited.—*ns.* **gingerāde'**, **ginger-ale'**, an aerated
drink flavoured with ginger ; **ginger-beer'**, an
effervescent drink made with fermenting ginger ;
gin'ger-cor'dial, a cordial made of ginger, lemon-
peel, raisins, water, and sometimes spirits ; **gin'ger-
nut'**, a small thick ginger-snap.—*adj.* **gin'gerous**,
like ginger.—*ns.* **gin'ger-pop'**, (*coll.*) weak ginger-
beer ; **gin'ger-snap'**, a gingerbread biscuit ;
gin'ger-wine', liquor made by the fermentation
of sugar and water, and flavoured with various
spices, chiefly ginger.—**ginger-beer plant**, a
symbiotic association of a yeast and a bacterium,
by which ginger-beer can be prepared (also called
Californian bees). [M.E. *gingivere*—O.Fr. *gen-
gibre*—L.L. *gingiber*—L. *zingiber*—Gr. *zingiberis*,
perh. Sans. *çriṅga*, horn, *vera*, shape—Malay *inchi-
ver*.]

gingerbread, *jin'jər-bred, n.* a cake flavoured with
treacle and usually ginger.—**gingerbread ware**,
or **work**, cheap and tawdry ornamental work ;
take the gilt off the gingerbread, to destroy the
glamour. [O.Fr. *gingimbrat*—L.L. *gingiber* ; see
ginger ; confused with **bread**.]

gingerly, *jin'jər-li, adv.* with soft steps : with
extreme wariness and delicate gentleness.—Also
adj. [Possibly O.Fr. *gensor*, compar. of gent ; see
gent (1).]

gingham, *ging'əm, n.* a kind of cotton cloth, woven
from coloured yarns into stripes or checks : (*coll.*)
an umbrella. [Fr. *guingan*, orig. from Malay
ginggang, striped.]

gingili, **gingelly**, **jinjili**, *jin'ji-li, n.* a species of
sesamum : an oil got from its seeds. [Hind.
jinjalī, prob.—Ar. *juljulān*.]

gingival, *jin-jī'vəl, adj.* pertaining to the gums.—
n. **gingivitis** (*jin-ji-vī'tis*), inflammation of the
gums. [L. *gingīva*, gum.]

gingle. Same as **jingle**.

ginglymus, *jing'gli-məs* (or *ging'-*), *n.* a joint that
permits movement in one plane only :—*pl.* **ging'-
lymī**.—*adj.* **ging'limoid**. [Latinised from Gr.
ginglymos.]

ginkgo, *gingk'gō, n.* the maidenhair tree, holy in
Japan, perhaps still wild in China, with leaves
like maidenhair fern, forming by itself an order
(**Ginkgoā'les**) of Gymnosperms.—Also **ging'ko**.
[Jap. *gingko*—Chin. *yin*, silver, *hing*, apricot.]

ginseng, *jin'seng, n.* a species of *Panax* or *Aralia* :
its root, a Chinese panacea. [Chin. *jên-shên*, perh.
image of man.]

gip, *jip, n.* Same as **gyp**.

gipsen, *jip'sən, n.* (*Spens.*) an obs. form of gypsy.

gipsy. See **gypsy**.

giraffe, *ji-räf', n.* the camelopard, an African
ruminant with remarkably long neck and fore-legs.
—*adj.* **giraff'ine**, [Ar. *zarāfah*.]

girandole, *jir'ən-dōl, n.* a branched chandelier or
similar structure : a pendant, &c., with small
jewels attached around it : a rotating firework.

[Fr.,—It. *girandola*—*girare*—L. *gȳrāre*, to turn
round—*gȳrus*—Gr. *gȳros*, a circle.]

girasol, **girasole**, *jir'ə-sol, -sōl, n.* a fire-opal or
other stone that seems to send a fire-like glow
from within in certain lights : the plant heliotrope :
the sunflower. [It.,—*girare* (see foregoing), and
sole—L. *sōl*, the sun.]

gird, *gərd, v.i.* to gibe, jeer (with *at*).—*v.t.* to taunt.
—*n.* a taunt, dig, gibe. [Origin obscure ; not from
O.E. *gyrd*, *gierd*, rod.]

gird, *gird, n.* (*Scot.*) a hoop.—Also **girr** (*gir*). [A
form of **girth**.]

gird, *gərd, v.t.* to bind round : to make fast by a
belt or girdle : to encompass : to surround : to
clothe, furnish :—*pa.t.* and *pa.p.* **gird'ed** and **girt**.
—*ns.* **gird'er**, a great beam, simple or built up, of
wood, iron, or steel, to take a lateral stress, e.g. to
support a floor, wall, roadway of a bridge : (*bot.*)
a strip of strengthening tissue ; **gird'ing**, that
which girds.—**girder bridge**, a bridge whose
load is sustained by girders resting on supports ;
gird oneself, to tuck up loose garments under the
girdle : to brace the mind for any trial or effort.
[O.E. *gyrdan* ; cf. Ger. *gürten*.]

girdle, *gərd'l, n.* a waist-belt : a cord worn about
the waist by a monk, &c. : anything that encloses
like a belt : a bony arch to which a limb is attached :
a worm's clitellum : a ring-shaped cut around a
tree : the rim of a brilliant-cut gem.—*v.t.* to bind,
as with a girdle : to enclose : to cut a ring round.
—*n.* **gird'le-belt**, a belt for girding the waist.—
adj. **gird'led**.—*ns.* **gird'ler**, one who girdles : a
maker of girdles ; **gird'lestead**, the waist. [O.E.
gyrdel—*gyrdan*, to gird.]

girdle, *gird'l, n.* a Scottish form of **griddle**.

girkin, *gər'kin, n.* Same as **gherkin**.

girl, *gərl, n.* a female child : a young unmarried
woman : a woman irrespective of age : (*coll.*) a
sweetheart : (*U.S.*) a coloured woman : a maid-
servant.—*n.* **girl'hood**, the state or time of being
a girl.—*adj.* **girl'ish**, of or like a girl.—*adv.* **girl-
ishly**.—*n.* **girl'ishness**.—**Girl Guide**, a member
of an organisation for girls, analogous to the Boy
Scouts' Association ; **Girl Scout**, a member of a
similar American organisation ; **old girl**, a female
former pupil : a kindly disrespectful mode of
address or reference to a female of any age or
species. [Origin obscure.]

girlond, obsolete form of **garland**.—In Spens.
Faerie Queene, IV. x. 51, 9, *girlonds* may be a
misprint for *guardians* (or *guerdons*).

girn, *girn, v.i.* (*Scot.*) to grin, snarl, whimper.—
n. an act or manner of girning. [**grin**.]

girnel, *gir'nl, n.* (*Scot.*) a granary, meal-chest.
[Variant of **garner**.]

Girondist, *ji-rond'ist, n.* a member of the moderate
republican party during the French Revolution,
so called because its earliest leaders, Vergniaud,
Guadet, &c., were sent up to the Legislative
Assembly (Oct. 1791) by the *Gironde* department.
—Also **Giron'din**.

girr. See **gird** (2).

girt, *gərt, pa.p.* of **gird** in all senses : of a ship,
moored so taut by her cables to two oppositely
placed anchors as to be prevented from swinging
to the wind or tide.—*v.t.* to gird : to girth.—*v.i.* to
girth.

girth. See **grith**.

girth, *gərth, n.* belly-band of a saddle : circumferential measure of thickness.—*v.t.* to put a girth
on : to measure the girth of.—*v.i.* to measure in
girth.—Also **girt**. [O.N. *gjǫrth*.]

gist, *jist, n.* the main point or pith of a matter.
[O.Fr. *gist* (Fr. *gît*)—O.Fr. *gesir* (Fr. *gésir*), to
lie—L. *jacēre*.]

gite, *zhēt, n.* a resting-place. [Fr. *gîte*—O.Fr. *giste* ;
see gest (1).]

gittern, *git'ərn, n.* a kind of guitar, a cithern.—
v.i. to play on the gittern. [O.Fr. *guiterne*, conn.
Gr. *kitharā* ; see **cithern, guitar, zither**.]

giust, *just, n.* and *v.i.* (*Spens., Scott*). Same as
joust.

giusto, *joos'tō, adj.* (*mus.*) suitable : regular : strict.
[It.,—L. *jūstus*, just.]

give, *giv, v.t.* to bestow : to impart : to yield : to

grant : to permit : to afford : to furnish : to pay or render, as thanks : to pronounce, as a decision : to show, as a result : to apply, as oneself : to allow or admit.—*v.i.* to yield to pressure: to begin to melt: to grow soft: to open, or give an opening or view, to lead (with *upon, on, into,* a gallicism): (*pr.p.* giv′ing; *pa.t.* gāve; *pa.p.* given, giv′n).—*n.* yielding: elasticity.—*adj.* giv′en, bestowed: specified: addicted, disposed: granted: admitted.—*ns.* giv′enness; giv′er, one who or that which gives or bestows; giv′ing, the act of bestowing: the thing given.—*adj.* that gives.—give and take, reciprocity in concession: mutually compensatory variations: fair exchange of repartee; give away, to give for nothing: to betray: to bestow ceremonially (as a bride); give birth to, to bring forth: to originate; give chase, to pursue; give ear, to listen; give forth, to emit: to publish; give ground, place, to give way, to yield; give in to (*obs.* give into), to yield to; give it to one, (*coll.*) to scold or beat anybody severely; give line, head, rein, &c., to give more liberty or scope—the metaphors from angling and driving; given name, the name bestowed upon the individual, not that of the family—the first or Christian name, distinguished from the *surname* ; give oneself away, to betray one's secret unawares; give out, to report: to emit: to run short: (*Shak.*) to relinquish; give over, to cease ; give the lie to, to charge openly with falsehood; give tongue, to bark; give up, to abandon; give way, to fall back, to yield, to withdraw : to break, snap, collapse, under strain : to begin rowing—usually as a command to a crew. [O.E. *gefan* (W.S. *giefan*), the back *g* prob. owing to Scand. influence : O.N. *gefa,* Sw. *gifva,* Dan. *give,* Goth. *giban,* Ger. *geben.*]

gives. Same as gyves.

gizz, jiz, *jiz, n.* (*Scot.*) a wig. [Origin unknown.]

gizzard, *giz′ərd, n.* a muscular stomach, esp. the second stomach of a bird.—to stick in one's gizzard, to be more than one can accept or tolerate. [M.E. *giser*—O.Fr. *guiser,* supposed to be—L. *gigeria* (pl.), cooked entrails of poultry.]

gizzen, *giz′n, v.i.* (*Scot.*) to shrink from dryness so as to leak: to wither.—*adj.* leaky. [O.N. *gisna.*]

glabella, *glə-bel′ä, n.* part of the forehead between the eyebrows and just above their level.—*adj.* glabell′ar. [L. *glaber* bald, smooth.]

glabrous, *glā′brəs, adj.* hairless. [L. *glāber.*]

glacé, *glä′sä, adj.* iced with sugar : glossy, lustrous, esp. of a thin silk material or kid leather. [Fr.]

glacial, *glā′shi-əl, -si-əl, -shəl, adj.* icy : frozen : readily or ordinarily solidified (as glacial acetic acid, practically pure acetic acid): pertaining to ice or its action.—*ns.* glā′cialist, glaciol′ogist, one who studies the geological action of ice.—*v.t.* glaciate (*glāsh′, glās′, glas′*), to polish by ice-action : to subject to the action of land-ice.—*ns.* glacia′tion ; glaciol′ogy.—Glacial Period, the Ice Age, or any ice age. [L. *glaciālis,* icy, *glaciāre, -ātum,* to freeze —*glaciēs,* ice.]

glacier, *glas′i-ər, -yər* (also *glāsh′*), *n.* a mass of ice, fed by snow on a mountain, slowly creeping downhill to where it melts or breaks up into icebergs. [Fr.,—*glace,* ice—L. *glaciēs,* ice.]

glacis, *gläs-ē, glas′is, glās′is, n.* a gentle slope, esp. in fortification :—*pl.* glacis (*gläs-ē, glas′iz, glās′iz*), glacises. [Fr., orig. a slippery place—L. *glaciēs,* ice.]

glad, *glad, adj.* pleased : cheerful : bright : giving pleasure.—*v.t.* to make glad :—*pr.p.* gladd′ing ; *pa.t.* and *pa.p.* gladd′ed.—*v.t.* gladd′en, to make glad : to cheer : to animate.—*adj.* glad′ful (*Spens.*). — *n.* glad′fulness. — *adv.* glad′ly. — *n.* glad′ness.—*adj.* ᵷlad′some, glad : joyous : gay. —*adv.* glad′somely.—*n.* glad′someness—glad eye, (*slang*) an ogle; glad neck, a neck exposed in front : a low neck; glad of, glad to have : glad because of ; glad rags, (*coll.*) best clothes, dress clothes. [O.E. *glæd* ; Ger. *glatt,* smooth, O.N. *glathr,* bright, Dan. *glad.*]

gladdon, *glad′ən, n.* an iris. [Origin obscure.]

glade, *glād, n.* an open space in a wood.—*adj.*

glā′dy, having glades. [Origin obscure ; poss. conn. with glad.]

gladius, *glad′i-əs, glād′, n.* (*rare*) a sword : a cuttlefish pen. — *adj.* gladiate (*glad′, glād′*) swordshaped. — *n.* gladiator (*glad′i-ā-tər*), in ancient Rome, a professional combatant with men or beasts in the arena.—*adjs.* gladiatorial (*-ə-tō′ri-əl*), gladiato′rian, glad′iatory.—*ns.* glad′iatorship; glad′iole, gladiolus (*glad′yō-ləs, glə-dī′o-ləs,* very commonly *glad-i-ō′ləs*), any plant of a genus (Gladiolus) of the Iris family, with sword-shaped leaves : the middle part of the sternum : (*pl.* gladiolī, gladioluses). [L. *glădius,* sword, dim. *glădīolus ; glădiātor,* a gladiator.]

Gladstone-bag, *glad′stən-bag′, n.* a travelling bag or small portmanteau, opening out flat, named in honour of the statesman W. E. *Gladstone* (1809-98). —*adj.* Gladstonian (*-stō′ni-ən*), pertaining to Gladstone.—*n.* a follower of Gladstone, esp. after the split in the Liberal party in 1886.

gladwellise, *glad′wəl-īz, v.t.* to treat with tar, &c., to prevent formation of dust. [*Gladwell,* the inventor (1908).]

Glagolitic, *glag-ō-lit′ik, adj.* of or pertaining to Glagol, an ancient Slavonic alphabet, apparently derived from the cursive Greek of the 9th century. [Old Slav. *glagolu,* a word.]

glaik, *glāk, n.* (*Scot.*) a flash : (*usu.* in *pl.*) dazzling : illusion : mocking deception : jilting : scoffs : pranks : tricks : a puzzle-game.—*adj.* glaik′it, giddy : foolish.—*n.* glaik′itness, levity.—fling the glaiks in folk's een, (*Scot.*) to throw dust in people's eyes, dazzle. [Origin obscure.]

glair, *glār, n.* the clear part of an egg used as varnish : any viscous, transparent substance : mud. —*v.t.* to varnish with white of eggs.—*adjs.* glair′y, glair′eous, glār′eous.—*n.* glair′in, organic matter in mineral waters. [Fr. *glaire,* perh.—L.L. *clāra* (*ōvī*), white (of egg)—L. *clārus,* clear.]

glaive, *glāv, n.* (*arch.*) a sword : a spear : a longshafted weapon like a halberd, its edge on the outer curve. [O.Fr. *glaive.*]

glamour, *glam′ər, n.* the supposed influence of a charm on the eyes, making them see things as fairer than they are : fascination : enchantment : witchery : groomed beauty and studied charm.— *v.t.* to enchant, bewitch, cast a spell over.—*adjs.* glam′orous, bewitching : deceptively alluring ; glam′oury, glamorous.—*n.* glamour. [gramary.]

glance, *gläns, v.i.* to fly off obliquely on striking : to make a passing allusion, esp. unfavourable (with *at*) : to dart a reflected ray : to flash : to snatch a momentary view.—*v.t.* to cause to glance : to direct glancingly : to deflect : to glance at.—*n.* an oblique impact or movement : (*cricket*) a stroke by which the ball is allowed to glance off an upright bat to fine leg : a passing allusion, esp. satirical : a sudden shoot of reflected light : a darting of the eye : a momentary look. — *n.* and *adj.* glanc′ing.—*adv.* glanc′ingly. [Origin obscure.]

glance, *gläns, n.* a black or grey mineral with metallic lustre, usually a sulphide, selenide, or telluride, e.g. redruthite or copper-glance, galena or lead-glance, argentite or silver-glance.— *n.* glance′-coal, anthracite. [Ger. *glanz,* glance, lustre.]

gland, *gland, n.* a secreting structure in plant or animal.—*adjs.* glandif′erous, bearing acorns or nuts ; gland′iform, resembling a gland : acornshaped ; gland′ular, gland′ulous, containing, consisting of, or pertaining to glands.—*n.* gland′ūle, a small gland.—*adj.* glandūlif′erous.—*n.* glans (*glanz*), an acorn or similar fruit : a glandular structure. [L. *glāns, glandis,* an acorn.]

glanders, *gland′ərz, n.* a malignant, contagious, and fatal disease of the horse and ass (and man), showing itself esp. on the mucous membrane of the nose, upon the lungs, and on the lymphatic system.—*adj.* gland′ered, affected with glanders. [O.Fr. *glandre,* a gland.]

glare, *glār, n.* an oppressive or unrelieved dazzling light : overpowering lustre : a glassy or icy surface : a fierce stare.—*adj.* (*U.S.*) glassy.—*v.i.* to emit a hard, fierce, dazzling light : to be obtrusively

noticeable, to shine dazzlingly : to stare fiercely.
—*v.t.* to send forth or express with a glare.—*adj.*
glar′ing, bright and dazzling : flagrant.—*adv.*
glar′ingly.—*n.* **glar′ingness.** [M.E. *glären,* to
shine ; cf. **glass,** O.E. *glær,* amber, L.Ger.
glaren, to glow.]
glareous, *glā′ri-əs, adj.* gravelly : growing on
gravel.—*adj.* **glā′real,** growing on dry exposed
ground. See also **glair.** [L. *glārea,* gravel.]
glass, *glås, n.* a hard, amorphous, brittle substance,
a bad conductor of electricity, usually transparent,
made by fusing together one or more of the oxides
of silicon, boron, or phosphorus with certain basic
oxides (e.g. sodium, magnesium, calcium, potassium), and cooling the product rapidly to prevent
crystallisation : an article made of or with glass,
esp. a drinking-vessel, a mirror, a lens, the cover
of a watch-face, a weather-glass, a telescope, &c. :
the quantity of liquid a glass holds : any fused
substance like glass, with a vitreous fracture : a
rock, or portion of rock, without crystalline
structure : (*pl.*) spectacles.—*adj.* made of glass.—
v.t. to glaze : to polish highly : to put in, under,
or behind glass : to furnish with glass : to reflect
in glass.—*ns.* **glass′-blower ; glass′-blowing,** the
process of making glassware by inflating a viscid
mass ; **glass′-cloth,** a cloth for drying glasses :
a material woven from glass threads : a polishing
cloth covered with powdered glass ; **glass′-
coach,** (*obs.*) a coach (esp. one for hire) having
glazed windows ; **glass′-crab,** the transparent
larva of the spiny lobster ; **glass′-cutter,** a tool
for cutting sheets of glass : one who does cut-glass
work ; **glass′-cutting,** the act or process of cutting,
shaping, and ornamenting the surface of glass.—*adj.*
glass′en, (*arch.*) of or like glass.—*n.* **glass′-eye,**
an artificial eye made of glass : (*obs.* ; *pl.*) spectacles :
a form of blindness in horses.—*adj.* **glass′-faced,**
(*Shak.*) reflecting the sentiments of another, as
in a mirror.—*ns.* **glass′ful,** as much as a glass will
hold (*pl.* **glass′fuls**) ; **glass′-gall,** a scum formed
on fused glass.—*adj.* **glass′-gaz′ing,** (*Shak.*)
addicted to looking in a mirror.—*ns.* **glass′-
grinding,** the ornamenting of glass by rubbing
with sand, emery, &c. ; **glass′-house,** a glass
factory : a house made of glass or largely of glass,
esp. a greenhouse : (*slang*) military detention
barracks (from one with a glass roof at Aldershot).
—*adv.* **glass′ily.**—*ns.* **glassine** (*-en′*), a transparent paper ; **glass′iness.**—*adj.* **glass′-like.**—
ns. **glass′-man,** a maker or seller of glass : (*arch.*)
a beggar hawking glass as a pretext ; **glass′-
painting,** the art of producing pictures on glass
by means of staining it chemically ; **glass′-paper,**
paper coated with finely pounded glass, used
like sand-paper ; **glass′-rope,** a silicious sponge
(Hyalonema) with a long anchoring tuft ; **glass′-
snake,** a legless lizard (Ophisaurus) with brittle
tail ; **glass′-soap,** manganese dioxide or other
substance used by glass-makers to remove colouring
from glass ; **glass′ware,** articles made of glass ;
glass′-wool, glass spun into woolly fibres ; **glass′-
work,** a glass factory : furnishings or articles
made of glass ; **glass′wort,** a name for plants
of the genera Salicornia and Salsola yielding soda,
once used in making glass.—*adjs.* **glass′y,** like
glass : of the nature of glass : (*Shak.*) frail ; **glass′y-
headed,** (*Tenn.*) shiny-pated.—**live in a glass
house,** to be open to attack or retort ; **musical
glasses** (see **harmonica**) ; **water, or soluble,
glass,** sodium or potassium silicate. [O.E. *glæs.*]
Glassite, *glås′īt, n.* a Sandemanian, or follower of
John *Glas* (1695-1773), deposed in 1730 from the
ministry of the Church of Scotland for maintaining
that a congregation with its eldership is, in its
discipline, subject to no jurisdiction but that of
Jesus Christ.
Glaswegian, *glås-wēj′(y)ən, n.* a native or citizen of
Glasgow.—Also *adj.* [Modelled on Norwegian.]
glauberite, *glaw′bər-īt, n.* a greyish-white mineral,
sodium calcium sulphate found chiefly in rock-
salt, named after the German chemist Johann
Rudolf *Glauber* (1604-68).—**Glauber('s) salt**
(*glow′bər, glaw′bər*), hydrated sodium sulphate,
discovered by him.

glaucoma, *glaw-kō′mä, n.* an insidious disease of
the eye, marked by increased tension within the
eyeball and growing dimness of vision.—*adj.*
glaucomatous (*-kōm′ə-təs, -kom′*). [Gr. *glaukōma,*
cataract ; see **glaucous.**]
glauconite, *glawk′ə-nīt, n.* a mineral now forming
in the sea, a hydrated potassium iron and aluminium silicate, which gives a green colour to
some of the beds of the Greensand.—*adj.* **glauco-
nitic** (*-nit′ik*).—*n.* **glauconītīsā′tion,** conversion
into glauconite. [Gr. *glaukos,* bluish-green.]
glaucous, *glaw′kəs, adj.* sea-green : greyish-blue :
(*bot.*) covered with a fine greenish or bluish bloom.
—*n.* **glaucescence** (*-ses′əns*).—*adj.* **glaucesc′ent,**
somewhat glaucous. [L. *glaucus*—Gr. *glaukos,*
bluish green or grey (orig. gleaming).]
Glaucus, *glaw′kəs, n.* a genus of translucent blue
nudibranch gasteropods of warm seas. [Gr.
glaukos, bluish-green.]
glaum, *glawm, v.i.* (*Scot.*) to clutch (with *at*).
glaur, *glawr, n.* (*Scot.*) mire.—*adj.* **glaur′y.** [Origin
unknown.]
Glaux, *glawks, n.* the generic name of sea milkwort
or black saltwort, a fleshy seaside plant of the
primrose family, with pink sepals and no petals,
once used in soda-making. [Gr. *glaux,* wart-
cress.]
glaze, *glāz, v.t.* to furnish or set with glass : to
cover with a thin surface of glass or something
glassy : to give a glassy surface to.—*n.* the glassy
coating put upon pottery : a thin coat of transparent colour : any shining exterior.—*v.i.* to
become glassy.—*adj.* **glāz′en,** glassy : glazed.—
ns. **glāz′er,** a workman who glazes pottery, paper,
&c. ; **glā′zier** (*-zyər*), one who sets glass in
window-frames, &c. ; **glāz′ing,** the act or art of
setting glass : the art of covering with a vitreous
substance : (*paint.*) semi-transparent colours put
thinly over others to modify the effect. [M.E.
glasen—*glas,* glass ; see **glass.**]
gleam, *glēm, v.i.* to glow or shine, usu. not very
brightly.—*v.t.* to flash.—*n.* a faint or moderate
glow ; a small stream of light : a beam : brightness. — *n.* **gleam′ing.** —*adj.* **gleam′y,** casting
gleams or rays of light. [O.E. *glæm,* gleam, brightness ; see **glimmer.**]
glean, *glēn, v.t.* to gather in handfuls after the
reapers : to collect (what is thinly scattered,
neglected, or overlooked).—*v.i.* to gather the corn
left by a reaper or anything that has been left by
others.—*n.* that which is gleaned : the act of
gleaning. — *ns.* **glean′er ; glean′ing.** [O.Fr.
glener (Fr. *glaner*), through L.L. *glenāre, glena* ;
origin unknown.]
glebe, *glēb, n.* (*arch.*) the soil : a clod : a field : the
land attached to a parish church.—*n.* **glebe′-house,**
a manse.—*adjs.* **gleb′ous, gleb′y,** cloddy, turfy.
[L. *glēba,* a clod.]
glede, *glēd, gled, gled, n.* (*B.*) the common kite.
[O.E. *glida,* from *glīdan,* to glide.]
gledge, *glej,* (*Scot.*) *v.i.* to squint : to cast an eye
around : to look cunningly.—*n.* a knowing look :
a side-glance : a glimpse. [Cf. **gley.**]
glee, *glē, n.* joy : mirth and gaiety : impish enjoyment : (*mus.*) a song or catch in parts, strictly,
one without an accompaniment : (proverbially
coupled with *gold* ; *Spens.*) app. glitter.—*adj.*
glee′ful, merry.—*ns.* **glee′-maiden,** a female
minstrel ; **glee′man,** a minstrel.—*adj.* **glee′some,**
merry. [O.E. *gléo, glīw,* mirth ; O.N. *glý.*]
glee. Same as **gley.**
gleed, *glēd, n.* a hot coal or burning ember. [O.E.
gléd ; cf. Du. *gloed,* Ger. *glut,* Sw. *glöd.*]
gleek, *glēk, n.* (*Shak.*) a jest or scoff, a trick.—*v.i.*
(*Shak.*) to gibe : to jest.—*v.t.* to play a trick upon.
[Cf. **glaik.**]
gleek, *glēk, n.* an old game at cards for three, each
having twelve, and eight being left for the stock.
[O.Fr. *glic, ghelicque,* possibly—M.Du. *ghelic,*
alike.]
Gleep, *n.* the first British atomic pile. [**G**raphite
Low **E**nergy **E**xperimental **P**ile.]
gleet, *glēt, n.* a glairy discharge from a mucous
surface.—*v.i.* to discharge gleet.—*adj.* **gleet′y.**
[O.Fr. *glette, glecte,* a flux.]

Neutral vowels in unaccented syllables : *el′ə-mənt, in′fənt, ran′dəm*

gleg, *gleg*, *adj*. (*Scot.*) clever : apt : alert : keen. [O.N. *gleggr*, clever ; cf. O.E. *gléav*, wise, Ger. *glau*, clear.]

glen, *glen*, *n*. a narrow valley with a stream, often with trees : a depression, usu. of some extent, between hills. [Gael. *gleann* ; cf. W. *glyn*.]

glendoveer, *glen-dō-vēr'*, *n*. (*Southey*) a heavenly spirit. [Fr. *grandouver*, app.—Sans. *gandharva*.]

glengarry, *glen-gar'i*, *n*. a Highlander's cap of thick-milled woollen, generally rising to a point in front, with ribbons hanging down behind. [*Glengarry* in Inverness-shire.]

Glenlivet, *glen-lēv'it*, *-liv'it*, *n*. a noted whisky. [*Glenlivet*, a valley in Banffshire.]

glenoid, **-al**, *glē'-noid*, *-əl*, *adjs*. socket-shaped : slightly cupped.—Also *n*. [Gr. *glēnoeidēs*—*glēnē*, a socket.]

glent, *glent*, *v.t.*, *v.i.*, and *n*. an earlier form of **glint**.

gley, *glī*, *glē*, *v.i*. to squint.—*adj*. **gleyed**, (*Scot.*) squint-eyed.—Also **glee**, **gleed**. [Origin obscure ; cf. **gledge**.]

gliadin, *glī'ə-din*, *n*. glutin, a protein in gluten. [Fr. *gliadine*—Gr. *glia*, glue.]

glib, *glib*, *adj*. smooth : slippery : easy : facile : fluent and plausible.—*adv*. **glibly**.—*v.t*. to make **glib**.—*adj*. **glibb'ery**, (*obs.*) slippery.—*adv*. **glib'ly**.—*n*. **glib'ness**. [Cf. Du. *glibberig*, slippery.]

glib, *glib*, *n*. (*Spens.*) a bush of hair over the eyes. [Ir.]

glib, *glib*, *v.t*. (*Shak.*) to castrate. [Cf. **lib**.]

glidder, *glid'ər*, *adj*. slippery.—Also **glid** (*Scot.*), **glidd'ery** (*prov.*). [O.E. *glidder*.]

glide, *glīd*, *v.i*. to slide smoothly and easily : to flow gently : to pass smoothly or stealthily : to travel through the air without expenditure of power : to travel by glider : to play a glide stroke. —*n*. act of gliding : (*phon.*) a transitional sound produced in passing from one position to another : (*cricket*) a glance stroke : a smooth and sliding dance-step : an inclined plane or slide : a gliding stream or part of a stream.—*ns*. **glid'er**, one who, or that which, glides : an aircraft like an aeroplane without engine : a hydroplane ; **glid'ing**, the action of the verb in any sense : the sport of flying in a glider.—*adv*. **glid'ingly**. [O.E. *glīdan*, to slip ; Ger. *gleiten*.]

gliff, *glif*, *n*. (*Scot.*) a fright, a scare : (*Scot.*) a glimpse or other transient experience, a moment.— Also **gliff**.—*n*. **gliff'ing**, a moment. [Ety. dub.]

glike, *glīk*, *n*. (*Shak.*). Same as **gleek**.

glim, *glim*, *n*. a glimpse : (*slang*) a light : (*slang*) an eye. [Cf. **gleam**, **glimmer**, and Ger. *glimm*, a spark.]

glimmer, *glim'ər*, *v.i*. to burn or appear faintly.— *n*. a faint light : feeble rays of light.—*ns*. **glimm'er-gowk**, (*Tenn.*) an owl ; **glimm'ering**, a glimmer : an inkling.—*adv*. **glimm'eringly**.—*adj*. **glimm'ery**. [M.E. *glemern*, freq. from root of **gleam**.]

glimmer, *glim'ər*, *n*. mica. [Ger.]

glimpse, *glimps*, *n*. a short gleam : a passing appearance : a momentary view.—*v.i*. to glimmer : to appear by glimpses.—*v.t*. to get a glimpse of. [M.E. *glymsen*, to glimpse.]

glint, *glint*, *v.i*. to flash a glittering light.—*v.t*. to reflect.—*n*. a gleam. [Earlier *glent* ; prob. Scand.]

glisk, *glisk*, *n*. (*Scot.*) a glimpse. [Perh. from the same root as O.E. *glisian*, to shine.]

glissade, *glēs-äd'*, *v.i*. to slide or glide down.— *n*. act of sliding down a slope : a gliding movement in dancing.

glissando, *glēs-än'dō*, *n*. (*mus.*) a passage played by sliding the finger along the keyboard, string, or strings.—Also *adj*. and *adv*. [It., sliding.]

glisten, *glis'n*, *v.i*. to shine, esp. somewhat dully or subduedly.—*n*. gleam. [M.E. *glistnen*—O.E. *glisnian*, to shine ; cf. Du. *glinsteren*.]

glister, *glis'tər*, *v.i*. to sparkle, glitter.—*adj*. **glis'tering**. [M.E. *glistren* ; cf. **glisten**, and Du. *glisteren*.]

glit, *glit*, *n*. shiny, sticky, or slippery material : gleet. [A Scots form of **gleet**.]

glitter, *glit'ər*, *v.i*. to sparkle with light : to be splendid : to be showy.—*n*. sparkle : showiness.— *adj*. **glitt'erand**, (*Spens.*) glittering.—*n*. and *adj*. **glitt'ering**.—*adv*. **glitt'eringly**. [M.E. *gliteren* ; cf. O.N. *glitra*, Ger. *glitzern*.]

gloaming, *glōm'ing*, *n*. twilight, dusk. [Apparently from a short-vowelled derivative of O.E. *glōmung*— *glōm*, twilight.]

gloat, *glōt*, *v.i*. to gaze exultingly, esp. with a wicked or malicious joy.—*n*. an act of gloating. [Perh. O.N. *glotta*, to grin.]

globe, *glōb*, *n*. a ball : a round body, a sphere : the earth : a sphere representing the earth (terrestrial globe), or one representing the heavens (celestial globe) : an orb, emblem of sovereignty : a lamp glass : a nearly spherical glass vessel : (*obs.*) a group.—*v.t*. and *v.i*. to form into a globe.—*adjs*. **glob'al**, spherical : world-wide : affecting, or taking into consideration, the whole world or all peoples ; **glob'ate**, **-d**, globe-shaped ; **globed**, globe-shaped : having a globe.—*ns*. **globe'-fish**, any fish of the families Diodontidae and Tetrodontidae, capable of blowing itself up into a globe ; **globe'-flower**, a ranunculaceous plant (Trollius) with a globe of large showy sepals enclosing the small inconspicuous petals ; **globe'-trotter**, one who goes sight-seeing about the world ; **globe'-trotting**.—*adjs*. **glob'oid**, **globose** (or *glob'* ; *Milt*. also as *n*., globosity).—*n*. **globos'ity**.—*adjs*. **glob'ous** ; **globular** (*glob'ū-lər*), spherical.—*n*. **globularity** (*glob-ū-lar'i-ti*).—*adv*. **glob'ūlarly**.— *ns*. **glob'ūle**, a little globe or round particle : a drop : a small pill ; **glob'ūlet** ; **glob'ūlin**, any one of a class of proteins soluble in dilute salt solutions but not in pure water ; **glob'ūlite**, a minute spheroidal crystallite occurring esp. in glassy rocks.—*adjs*. **globūlous** ; **glob'y**, (*Milt.*) round. [L. *globus*.]

Globigerina, *glob-i-jə-rī'nä*, *n*. a genus of foraminifers with calcareous shell of globose chambers in a spiral.—**globigerina ooze**, a deep-sea deposit of globigerina shells. [L. *globus*, globe, *gerĕre*, to carry.]

glockenspiel, *glok'ən-shpēl*, *n*. an orchestral instrument consisting of a set of bells or bars, struck by hammers with or without a keyboard. [Ger. *glocke*, bell, *spiel*, play.]

glode, *glōd*, (*Spens.*) *pa.t.* of **glide**.

glomerate, *glom'ər-āt*, *v.t*. to gather into a ball. —*adj*. balled : clustered in heads.—*n*. **glomerā'tion**.—*adj*. **glomerular** (*glom-er'ū-lər*).—*n*. **glomerule** (*glom'ər-ool*), a little ball of spores : a cluster of short-stalked flowers. [L. *glomerāre*, *-ātum* —*glomus*, *glomeris*, a clew of yarn.]

gloom, *glōōm*, *n*. partial darkness : cloudiness : a dark place : heaviness of mind : hopelessness : sullenness : (*Scot.*) a scowl, sullen look.—*v.i*. to be or look sullen or dejected : to be or become cloudy, dark, or obscure : to scowl : to dusk.—*v.t*. to fill with gloom.—*adj*. **gloom'ful**.—*adv*. **gloom'ily**.— *n*. **gloom'iness**.—*adj*. **gloom'ing**, (*Spens.*) shining obscurely.—*n*. twilight : gloaming : scowling.— *adj*. **gloom'y**, dim or obscure : dimly lighted : depressed in spirits : dismal. [Perh. partly—O.E. *glōm*, twilight, partly from root of **glum**.]

glorify, *glō'ri-fī*, *v.t*. to make glorious : to cast glory upon : to honour : to exalt to glory or happiness : to ascribe honour to : to worship :—*pr.p*. **glō'rifying** ; *pa.t*. and *pa.p*. **glō'rified**.—*n*. **glōrificā'tion**, an act of glorifying : a doxology : (*coll.*) riotous festivity. [L. *glōria*, glory, *facĕre*, to make.]

glory, *glō'ri*, *n*. renown : exalted or triumphant honour : the occasion of praise : an object of supreme pride : splendour : resplendent brightness : summit of attainment, prosperity or gratification : in religious symbolism, a combination of the nimbus and the aureola, but often erroneously used for the nimbus : a burst of sunlight : a ring or glow of light about the moon, the Brocken spectre, or other object or phenomenon : (*obs.*) boastful or self-gratulatory spirit : (*B.*) the presence of God : the manifestation of God to the blessed in heaven : a representation of the heavens opened : heaven.—*v.i*. to boast : to exult proudly.—*v.t*. (*obs.*) to glorify :—*pr.p*. **glō'rying** ; *pa.t*. and *pa.p*. **glō'ried**.—*ns*. **glō'riole**, a halo or glory ; **Glōriō'sa**, a tropical genus of leaf-climbers of the lily family.—*adj*. **glō'rious**, noble : splendid : conferring renown : (*coll.*) elated, tipsy : (*obs.*) boastful.—*adv*. **glō'riously**.—*ns*. **glō'riousness** ;

glō'ry-pea', the papilionaceous genus Clianthus, consisting of Sturt's desert-pea (in Australia) and the parrot-bill (in New Zealand).—**glory be**, a devout ascription of Glory to God: hence, an ejaculation of exultation; **glory of the snow**, the plant Chionodoxa; **Old Glory**, the Stars and Stripes. [O.Fr. *glorie* and L. *glōria*.]

glory-hole, *glō'ri-hōl*, *n.* a glass-maker's supplementary furnace: a hole for viewing the inside of a furnace: a nook or receptacle for miscellaneous odds and ends: a steward's room on a ship: a hiding-place: an excavation. [Perh. M.E. *glory*, to defile, or **glaury**, or **glory**, and **hole**.]

gloss, *glos*, *n.* brightness or lustre, as from a polished surface: external show.—*v.t.* to give a superficial lustre to: to render plausible: to palliate.—*adv.* **gloss'ily.**—*n.* **gloss'iness.**—*adj.* **gloss'y,** smooth and shining: highly polished. [Cf. O.N. *glossi*, blaze, *glóa*, to glow; see **glass**.]

gloss, *glos*, *n.* a marginal or interlinear explanation of a hard word: an explanation: a sophistical explanation: a collection of explanations of words. —*v.t.* to give a gloss on: to explain away.—*v.i.* to comment or make explanatory remarks.—*adj.* **glossa'rial,** relating to a glossary: containing explanation.—*ns.* **gloss'arist** (*-ə-rist*), a writer of a gloss or of a glossary; **gloss'ary,** a collection of glosses: a partial dictionary for a special purpose; **glossa'tor, gloss'er,** a writer of glosses or comments, a commentator; **Gloss'ic,** a phonetic alphabet devised by A. J. Ellis (1814-90); **Gloss'i'na,** the tsetse fly genus; **glossi'tis,** inflammation of the tongue; **glosso'grapher.**—*adj.* **glosso-graph'ical.**—*ns.* **glossog'raphy,** the writing of glosses or comments; **glossolā'lia** (Gr. *laleein*, to talk), the 'gift of tongues,' abnormal utterance under religious emotion.—*adj.* **glossolog'ical.**—*ns.* **glossol'ogist; glossol'ogy,** (*obs.*) comparative philology (also **glottol'ogy**): terminology. [Gr. *glōssa, glōtta,* tongue, a word requiring explanation.]

glottis, *glot'is*, *n.* the opening of the larynx or entrance to the windpipe.—*adj.* **glott'al,** of the glottis; **glott'ic,** pertaining to the glottis or to the tongue: linguistic.—**glottal stop,** a consonant sound produced by opening or shutting the glottis, recognised in Hebrew and Arabic, and often substituted for *t* by careless speakers in Scotland and England. [Gr. *glōttis—glōtta*, the tongue.]

glottology. See **glossology.**

glout, *glowt*, *v.i.* to be sulky.—*n.* a sulky look, the sulks. [Perh. a variant of **gloat**.]

glove, *gluv*, *n.* a covering for the hand, with a sheath for each finger: a boxing-glove.—*v.t.* to cover with, or as with, a glove.—*adj.* **gloved.**—*ns.* **glove'-fight,** a boxing-match in which the hands are gloved; **glove'-money,** a gratuity given to servants, officers of a court, &c.; **glov'er,** one who makes or sells gloves; **glove'-shield,** a shield worn by a knight on the left-hand gauntlet to parry blows; **glove'-stretcher,** a scissors-shaped instrument for stretching the fingers of gloves. [O.E. *glóf,* perh. conn. with **loof**.]

glow, *glō*, *v.i.* to shine with an intense heat: to burn without flame: to emit a steady light: to flush: to tingle with bodily warmth or with emotion: to be ardent.—*n.* a shining with heat: a luminous appearance: a feeling of warmth: brightness of colour: warmth of feeling.—*adj.* **glow'ing.**—*adv.* **glow'ingly.**—*ns.* **glow'-lamp,** an incandescent lamp, usually electric; **glow'-worm,** a beetle, esp. *Lampyris noctiluca*, whose larvae and wingless females are luminous. [O.E. *glówan,* to glow; Ger. *glühen,* O.N. *glóa*, to glow.]

glower, *glow'ər, glowr, v.i.* to stare frowningly: to scowl.—*n.* a fierce or threatening stare. [Origin obscure.]

Gloxinia, *glok-sin'i-ä, n.* a tropical American genus of Gesneraceae, with bright bell-shaped flowers: generally applied to the allied Sinningia. [*Gloxin*, a German botanist.]

gloze, *glōz, v.i.* to flatter: to comment.—*v.t.* (*arch.*) to make glosses on, explain: to palliate by specious explanation: to flatter: to deceive with smooth words.—*n.* (*arch.*) an explanation: a false show.—

n. glō'zing, flattery, deceit. [O.Fr. *glose*—L. *glossa*—Gr. *glōssa*; see **gloss** (2).]

glucinum, *gloo-si'nəm,* also **glucinium,** *gloo-sin'i-əm, ns.* beryllium.—*n.* **gluci'na,** beryllia. [Gr. *glykys*, sweet, from the taste of its salts.]

glucose, *gloo'kōs, n.* grape-sugar or dextrose.— *ns.* **glu'coside,** a vegetable product which, on treatment with acids or alkalies, yields glucose or kindred substance; **glucosū'ria,** glycosuria. [Gr. *glykys*, sweet.]

glue, *gloo, n.* an impure gelatine got by boiling animal refuse, used as an adhesive substance.— *v.t.* to join with glue or other adhesive:—*pr.p.* **glu'ing;** *pa.t.* and *pa.p.* **glued.**—*ns.* **glue'-pot,** a vessel for melting or holding glue: a sticky place; **glu'er,** one who cements with glue.—*adj.* **glu'ey,** containing glue: sticky: viscous.—*n.* **glu'ey-ness.**—*adj.* **glu'ish,** (*obs.*) having the nature of glue.—**marine glue,** not a glue, but a composition of rubber, shellac, and oil, that resists sea-water. [Fr. *glu*—L.L. *glūs, glūtis*.]

glum, *glum, adj.* sullen: gloomy.—*adv.* **glum'ly.**— *n.* **glum'ness.** — *adj.* **glump'ish,** glum. — *n.pl.* **glumps,** the sulks.—*adj.* **glump'y,** sulky. [M.E. *glombe, glome,* to frown.]

glume, *gloom, n.* an outer sterile bract which, alone or with others, encloses the spikelet in grasses and sedges.—*adj.* **glumā'ceous,** like a glume, thin, brownish and papery.—*n.* **glumell'a,** a palea. —*adj.* **glumif'erous,** having glumes.—*n.pl.* **Glumi-flō'rae,** an order of monocotyledons consisting of grasses and sedges. [L. *glūma,* husk—*glūbĕre,* to peel.]

glut, *glut, v.t.* to swallow greedily: to feed to satiety: to saturate: (*pr.p.* **glutt'ing;** *pa.t.* and *pa.p.* **glutt'ed**).—*n.* a giutting: a surfeit: an over-supply. [L. *gluttire,* to swallow.]

glutaeus, gluteus, *gloo-tē'əs, n.* one of the natal or buttock muscles. — *adj.* **glutae'al, glutē'al.** [Gr. *gloutos,* the rump.]

gluten, *gloo'tən, n.* the nitrogenous part of the flour of wheat and other grains, insoluble in water.—*adj.* **glu'tinous,** gluey: tenacious: sticky.—*adv.* **glu'-tinously.**—**glutam'ic acid,** an important amino-acid, $HOOC \cdot CH_2 \cdot CH_2 \cdot CH(NH_2) \cdot COOH$. [L. *glūten, -īnis,* glue; cf. **glue**.]

glutton, *glut'n, n.* one who eats to excess: a northern carnivore (Gulo) of the weasel family, reputed a great eater: (*fig.*) a devourer, e.g. of books.—*v.i.* to eat to excess.—*adjs.* **glutt'onous, glutt'onish,** given to, or consisting in, gluttony.— *adv.* **glutt'onously.**—*n.* **glutt'ony,** excess in eating. [Fr. *glouton*—L. *glūtō, -ōnis—glūtīre, gluttire,* to devour.]

glycerine, glycerin, *glis'ə-rēn, -in,* **glycerol,** *-ol, ns.* a trihydric alcohol, a colourless, viscid, neutral inodorous fluid, of a sweet taste, soluble in water and alcohol.—*ns.* **glyc'eride,** an ester of glycerol; **gly'ceryl,** a radical of which glycerine is the hydroxide. [Gr. *glykeros,* sweet—*glykys*.]

glycin, glycine, *glis'in, glī'sin, -sēn, -sēn', n.* amino-acetic acid or glycocoll, $CH_2(NH_2) \cdot COOH$, a sweetish colourless crystalline solid first prepared from glue. [Gr. *glykys,* sweet.]

glycocoll, *glik'ō-kol,* or *glīk', n.* glycin. [Gr. *glykys,* sweet, *kolla,* glue.]

glycogen, *glik'ō-jən,* or *glīk', n.* animal starch, a starch found in the liver, yielding glucose on hydrolysis. [Gr. *glykys,* sweet, and the root of *gennaein,* to produce.]

glycol, *glik'ol, glīk'ol, n.* the type of a class of compounds forming a link between alcohol and glycerine. [From *glycerine* and *alcohol.*]

glyconic, *glī-kon'ik, adj.* (*Greek pros.*) consisting of four feet—one a dactyl, the others trochees. —*n.* a glyconic verse. [The poet *Glycon* (Gr. *Glykōn*).]

glycose, *glī'kōs, n.* glucose.—*n.* **glycosū'ria** (*ouron,* urine), the presence of sugar in the urine. [Gr. *glykys,* sweet.]

glyph, *glif, n.* (*archit.*) an ornamental channel or fluting, usually vertical: a sculptured mark.— *adjs.* **glyph'ic,** carved; **glyphograph'ic.**—*n.* **glyphog'raphy,** a process of taking a raised copy of an engraved plate by electrotype; **glyph'ograph,**

a plate formed by this process. [Gr. *glyphē*—*glyphein*, to carve.]

glyptal resins, *glip'təl rez'inz*, almost colourless, tacky, adhesive resins made by heating glycerol or other polyhydric alcohol with a polybasic acid, used as bonding materials for mica, and (modified) in the paint and varnish trades.

glyptic, *glip'tik*, *adj.* pertaining to carving, esp. gem-carving.—*n.* **glyp'tics** (treated as *sing.*), the art of gem-engraving.—*adj.* **glyptograph'ic.**—*ns.* **glyp-tog'raphy**, the art of engraving on precious stones ; **glyptothē'ca** (Gr. *thēkē*, receptacle), a place for keeping sculpture. [Gr. *glyptos*, carved.]·

Glyptodon, *glip'tō-don*, *n.* a gigantic Post-Tertiary fossil edentate of S. America with fluted teeth. [Gr. *glyptos*, carved, *odous*, *odontos*, tooth.]

gmelinite, *(g)mel'in-īt*, *n.* (*min.*) a sodium aluminium zeolite. [After C. G. *Gmelin* (1792–1860), German chemist.]

Gnaphalium, *na-fā'li-əm*, *n.* the cudweed genus of composites. [Latinised from Gr. *gnaphallion*, cottonweed.]

gnar, *när*, *v.i.* to snarl or growl.—Also **gnarr**, **knar**, **gnarl**. [Onomatopoeic ; cf. O.E. *gnyrran*, to grind the teeth, creak, Ger. *knurren*, Dan. *knurre*, to growl.]

gnarl, **knarl**, *närl*, *n.* a lump or knot in a tree.—*adjs.* **gnarled**, **gnarl'y**, knotty : contorted. [After Shakespeare's *gnarled* for **knurled**.]

gnash, *nash*, *v.t.* and *v.i.* to strike (the teeth) together in rage or pain : to bite with a snap or clash of the teeth.—*n.* a snap of the teeth.—*adv.* **gnash'-ingly**. [M.E. *gnasten* ; prob. from O.N., ultimately onomatopoeic.]

gnat, *nat*, *n.* any small fly of the family Culicidae, of which the females are commonly blood-suckers—a mosquito : extended to other small insects.—*n.* **gnat'ling**, a little gnat : an insignificant person. [O.E. *gnæt*.]

gnathic, *nath'ik*, *adj.* of the jaws.—*n.* **gnath'ite**, in arthropods, an appendage used as a jaw.—*n.pl.* **Gnathobdell'ida** (Gr. *bdella*, leech), an order of leeches with (usu.) jaws but no proboscis. [Gr. *gnathos*, jaw.]

gnathonic, -al, *na-thon'ik*, *-əl*, *adjs.* flattering. [From *Gnathō*, a character in Terence's *Eunuchus*—Gr. *gnathos*, jaw.]

gnaw, *nav*, *v.t.* and *v.i.* to bite with a scraping or mumbling movement: to wear away: to bite in agony or rage : (*fig.*) to distress persistently :—*pa.t.* **gnawed** ; *pa.p.* **gnawed**, **gnawn**. — *n.* **gnaw'er**, one who gnaws: a rodent. [O.E. *gnagan* ; cf. **nag** (2) ; Du. *knagen*, Mod. Ice. *naga*.]

gneiss, *nīs*, *n.* coarse-grained foliated metamorphic rock, usually composed of quartz, felspar, and mica.—*adjs.* **gneiss'ic**, **gneissit'ic**, of the nature of gneiss ; **gneiss'oid**, like gneiss ; **gneiss'ose**, having the structure of gneiss. [Ger. *gneis*.]

Gnetum, *nē'təm*, *n.* a tropical genus of trees and shrubs constituting with Ephedra and Welwitschia the family **Gnetā'ceae** and order **Gnetā'lēs**, gymnosperms differing from conifers in having a perianth, vessels in secondary wood, and no resin canals. [Said to be from *gnemon*, a name used in Ternate.]

gnocchi, *nyok'kē*, *n.* a dish of semolina or other cereal with cheese, &c. [It., pl. of *gnocco*.]

gnome, *nōm*, *(g)nō'mē*, *n.* a pithy and sententious saying, generally in verse, embodying some moral sentiment or precept.—*adj.* **gnōm'ic**—**gnomic aorist**, a past tense of the Greek verb, used in proverbs, &c., for what once happened and is generally true. [Gr. *gnōmē*, an opinion, maxim.]

gnome, *nōm*, *n.* a sprite guarding the inner parts of the earth and its treasures : a dwarf or goblin.—*adj.* **gnōm'ish**. [Paracelsus's Latin *gnomus*.]

gnomon, *nō'mon*, *n.* the pin of a dial, whose shadow points to the hour : an upright rod for taking the sun's altitude by its shadow : an index or indicator : (jocularly) the nose : (*geom.*) that which remains of a parallelogram when a similar parallelogram within one of its angles is taken away : a geometrical figure which, added to or subtracted from another, gives a figure similar to the original one.—*adjs.* **gnomonic, -al** (*-mon'*), pertaining to

a gnomon or to the art of dialling.—*adv.* **gnomon'-ically.**—*ns.* **gnomon'ics** (treated as *sing.*), the art of dialling ; **gnomonol'ogy**, a treatise on dialling. [Gr. *gnōmōn*, a gnomon, a carpenter's square—*gnōnai* (aorist), to know.]

Gnostic, *nos'tik*, *n.* (*theol.*) an adherent of Gnosticism.—*adj.* having knowledge : knowing, cunning : pertaining to the Gnostics.—*ns.* **gnō'sis**, knowledge : mystical knowledge ; **Gnos'ticism**, the eclectic doctrines of the Gnostics, a syncretistic religious philosophy, esp. in early Christian times, that taught the redemption of the spirit from matter by knowledge, and a process of emanation from the original essence. [Gr. *gnōstikos*, good at knowing—*gignōskein*, to know.]

gnu, *noo*, *nū*, *n.* a large African antelope (Connochaetes or Catoblepas), superficially like a horse or buffalo. [From Hottentot.]

go, *gō*, *v.i.* to pass from one place to another : to be in motion: to proceed : to run (in words or notes) : (*obs.*) to walk : to depart : to work, to be in operation: to sound (as a bell, gun): to take a direction : to extend : to tend : to be about (usu. in participle): to be current : to be valid : to be reckoned : to be known : to be on the whole or ordinarily : to be pregnant : to become, or become as if : to happen in a particular way : to turn out : to fare : to contribute towards a whole or a result : to be contained : to be able to pass : to give way.——*v.t.* to go through or over : to stake, bet : to call, bid, declare : (*pr.p.* **gō'ing**; *pa.t.* **went** (supplied from **wend**) ; *pa.p.* **gone**, *gon*).—*n.* a going: affair, matter (as in *a pretty go*): fashion (as in *all the go*): avail (as in *no go*): energy, activity: a spell, turn, bout : a portion supplied at one time: an attempt : failure to play in cribbage : a score for an opponent's failure to play.—*adj.* **go'-ahead**, dashing, energetic : enterprisingly progressive.—*ns.* **go'-between**, an intermediary ; **go'-by'**, escape by artifice : evasion : any intentional disregard : in coursing, the act of passing by or ahead in motion ; **go'er** ; **go-gett'er**, (*U.S. slang*) a forceful enterprising person who knows how to get what he wants.—For **going** and **gone**, see these articles.—**go about**, (*B.*) to set oneself about : to seek : to endeavour ; **go about one's business**, to attend to one's own affairs : to be off ; **go abroad**, to go to a foreign country or out-of-doors : to circulate ; **go against**, to turn out unfavourably for : to be repugnant to ; **go along with you**, (*coll.*) none of that ; **go aside**, to err : to withdraw, retire ; **go at**, to attack ; **go back on**, to betray : to draw back from ; **go bail**, to give security for ; **go black, brown, native**, to adopt the ways of life of, assimilate oneself to, the blacks, Polynesians, natives ; **go down**, to sink, decline : to be swallowed, believed, or accepted : (*bridge*) to fail to fulfil one's contract ; **go far**, to last long : to go a long way (*lit.* and *fig.*): to come to importance ; **go for**, to assail : to set out to secure, to go to get or fetch ; **go for nothing**, to have no value ; **go halves**, to share equally ; **go hard with**, to turn out ill for ; **go in**, to assemble : to admit the audience or congregation ; **go in and out**, to come and go freely ; **go in for**, to make a practice of : devote oneself to ; **go in unto**, (*B.*) to have sexual intercourse with ; **go it**, to act in a striking or dashing manner—often in *imper.* by way of encouragement ; **go off**, to leave : to die : to explode : to fade, deteriorate ; **go on**, to proceed (often *coll.* in derisive irony) ; **go one better**, to take a bet and add another more to it : to excel : to cap a performance ; **go one's way**, to depart ; **go out**, to be extinguished ; **go over**, to pass in review : to recall : to revise ; **go slow policy**, deliberately restricting output or effort so as to force the hands of opponents ; **go the whole hog**, to go to the fullest extent ; **go through**, to perform to the end, often perfunctorily : to examine in order : to undergo ; **go through fire and water**, to undertake any trouble or risks (from the usage in ancient ordeals) ; **go to**, come now (a kind of interjection, like the L. *agedum*, the Gr. *age nyn*) ; **go to pieces**, to break up entirely (*lit.* and *fig.*) : to lose completely ability to cope with the situation; **go to the wall**, to be pushed aside, passed by; **go under**, to be called by some title or character: to be submerged, overwhelmed, or ruined: to die; **go with**, to accompany: to agree with: accord with: to court; **go without**, suffer the want of; **go without saying**, to be plainly self-evident (a Gallicism; Fr. *cela va sans dire*); **great go**, a degree examination, compared with **little go**, a preliminary examination in Cambridge University; **let go**, to release, to quit hold of; **no go**, not possible: futile: in vain. [O.E. *gán*, to go; cf. Ger. *gehen*, Du. *gaan*.]

Goa, gō'ä, *n.* a Portuguese possession in India.— **Goa bean**, a papilionaceous plant (Psophocarpus) of tropical Asia and Africa, grown for its beans and root: its bean; **Goa butter**, kokum butter; **Goa powder**, araroba.

goad, gōd, *n.* a sharp-pointed stick, often shod with iron, for driving oxen: a stimulus.—*v.t.* to drive with a goad: to urge forward.—*ns.* **goads'man**, **goad'ster**, one who uses a goad. [O.E. *gǣd*.]

goaf, gōf, *n.* (*prov.*) a rick in a barn. [O.N. *gólf*, floor.]

goaf, gōf, *n.* (*mining*) the space left by the extraction of a coal-seam, into which waste is packed.

goal (*Milt.* **gole**), gōl, *n.* a mark set up to bound a race: the turning-point: the winning-post: also the starting-post: the end aimed at: the structure or station into which the ball is driven in some games: the sending of the ball between the goal-posts or over the cross-bar: a score for doing so: an end or aim.—*ns.* **goal'-keeper**, a player charged with defence of the goal (*coll.* **goal'ie**); **goal'-post**, one of the upright posts at the goal. [Origin obscure.]

goanna, gō-an'ä, *n.* (*Austr.*) any large lizard. [iguana.]

goary, Milton's spelling of **gory**.

goat, gōt, *n.* a ruminant (Capra) allied to the sheep: the sign or the constellation Capricorn.—*ns.* **goat'-ant'elope**, a goatlike antelope, or animal inter-mediate between goat and antelope, as the chamois, the goral; **goatee'**, a tuft on the chin; **goat'-fig**, the wild fig; **goat'-fish**, red mullet; **goat'-herd**, one who tends goats.—*adj.* **goat'ish**, re-sembling a goat, esp. in smell: lustful: wanton.— *ns.* **goat'ishness**; **goat'-moth**, a large moth whose larva, feeding on willow-wood, &c., gives forth a goatlike smell; **goat'-sall'ow**, **-will'ow**, the great sallow (*Salix caprea*); **goat's'-beard**, the com-posite plant Tragopogon, or John-go-to-bed-at-noon; **goat's'-hair**, cirrus clouds; **goat's'-rue**, a papilionaceous border and fodder plant, *Galega officinalis*; **goat'-skin**, the skin of the goat: leather, or a wine-skin, made from it; **goat'sucker**, the nightjar, a bird akin to the swift falsely thought to suck goats; **goat's'-thorn**, an Astragalus shrub; **goat'weed**, goutweed.—**get one's goat**, enrage. [O.E. *gát*; Ger. *geiss*, Du. *geit*.]

gob, gob, *n.* the mouth: a mouthful, lump: a space left in a mine by extraction of coal: waste packed into it. [O.Fr. *gobe*, mouthful, lump; cf. Gael. *gob*, mouth; perh. partly from **goaf**.]

go-bang, gō-bang', *n.* a game played on a board of 256 squares, with fifty counters, the object being to get five in a row. [Jap. *goban*.]

gobbelines, gob'ə-lēnz, *n.pl.* Same as **goblins**.

gobbet, gob'it, *n.* a mouthful: a lump to be swal-lowed: a clot: a lump, esp. of flesh hacked or vomited: an extract, esp. for translation or com-ment. [O.Fr. *gobet*, dim. of *gobe*; see **gob**.]

gobble, gob'l, *v.t.* to swallow in lumps: to swallow hastily: (*golf*) to play with a gobble.—*v.i.* to make a noise in the throat, as a turkey.—*n.* (*golf*) a rapid straight putt so strongly played that if the ball had not gone into the hole, it would have gone a good way past.—*n.* **gobb'ler**, a turkey-cock. [O.Fr. *gober*, to devour.]

Gobelins, gob'ə-linz, *-lanz*, *n.* a rich French tapestry. —*adj.* **Gob'elin**. [From the *Gobelins*, a famous family of French dyers settled in Paris as early as the 15th century.]

goblet, gob'lit, *n.* a large drinking-cup, properly one without a handle: (*Scot.*) a kind of saucepan. [O.Fr. *gobelet*, dim. of *gobel*, of doubtful origin.]

goblin, gob'lin, *n.* a frightful sprite: a bogy or bogle. [O.Fr. *gobelin*—L.L. *gobelinus*, perh.— *cobălus*—Gr. *kobălos*, a mischievous spirit.]

gobony, gob-ō'ni. Same as **compony**.

goburra, gō-bur'ä. Same as **kookaburra**.

goby, gō'bi, *n.* any fish of the genus Gobius or the family Gobī'idae, small fishes with ventral fins forming a sucker. [L. *gōbius*—Gr. *kōbios*, a fish of the gudgeon kind.]

go-cart, gō'-kärt, *n.* a wheeled apparatus for teach-ing children to walk: a form of child's carriage.

god, god, *n.* a superhuman being, an object of wor-ship: (as a proper name, God) the Supreme Being of monotheist religions, the Creator: an idol: an object of excessive devotion or reverence: (usu. in *pl.*) an occupant of the gallery of a theatre: (*fem.* **godd'ess**).—*v.t.* (*Spens. Shak.*) to deify:—*pa.t.* **godd'ed**.—*interj.* **God'-a-mer'cy**, (*Shak.*) prob-ably for *God have mercy*.—*ns.* **god'child**, a person to whom one is godfather or godmother; **god'-daughter**; **godd'ess-ship**, state or quality of a goddess; **god'father**, one who, at baptism, guarantees a child's religious education: (*slang*) one who pays the reckoning.—*adj.* **God'-fearing**, reverencing God; **God'-forgotten**, **God'-for-saken**, remote, miserable, behind the times, as if forgotten or forsaken by God; **God'-gift'ed**; **God'-given**.—*n.* **god'head**, state of being a god: deity: divine nature—also rarely **god'hood**.— *adj.* **god'less**, without a god: living without God. —*adv.* **god'lessly**.—*n.* **god'lessness**.—*adj.* **god'-like**, like a god: divine.—*ns.* **god'liness**; **god'-ling**, (*Dryden*) a little god.—*adj.* **god'ly**, like God in character: pious: according to God's laws.— *advs.* **god'ly**, **god'lily**.—*ns.* **god'mother**; **god'-send**, a very welcome piece of good fortune; **god'-ship**, the rank or character of a god: a divinity; **god'-smith**, (*Dryden*) a maker of idols.—*interj.* **god'so** (see **gadso**).—*ns.* **god'son**, a male godchild; **god'speed**, an expressed wish that God may speed one.—*advs.* **god'ward**, **-s**, toward God: in relation to God.—**God's acre**, a burial-ground (imitated from Ger. *Gottesacker*); **God's truth**, an absolute truth—an emphatic asseveration; **household gods**, among the Romans, the special gods presiding over the family: anything bound up with home interests. [O.E. *god*; Ger. *gott*, Goth. *guth*, Du. *god*; all from a Gmc. root *guth-*, God, and quite distinct from *good*.]

god day, (*Spens.*) for **good-day**.

god-den, god-en', a variant of **good even**.

godet, gō-dā', *-det'*, *n.* a triangular piece inserted in a skirt, &c., to make a flare. [Fr.]

Godetia, go-dē'sh(y)ä, *n.* an American genus close akin to the evening primrose. [C. H. *Godet*, Swiss botanist.]

godown, gō-down', *n.* a warehouse in the East. [Malay *godong*.]

go-down, gō'down, *n.* a cutting in the bank of a stream allowing animals to get to the water. [go, down.]

godroon, go-drōōn', *n.* (*archit.*) an inverted fluting or beading. [Fr. *godron*, a plait.]

godwit, god'wit, *n.* a bird (Limosa) of the plover family, with long slightly up-curved bill ar 1 long slender legs, with a great part of the ti' ᴧ bare. [Origin obscure.]

goe, go (*Spens.*). Same as **go**, **gone**.

goel, gō'äl, *n.* the avenger of blood among the Hebrews, the nearest relative whose duty it was to hunt down the murderer. [Heb.]

goety, gō'ə-ti, *n.* black magic.—*adj.* g.etic (*-et'*). [Gr. *goēteiä*, witchcraft.]

gofer, **gopher**, **gaufer**, **gaufre**, gō' or gaw'fər, *n.* a wafer with pattern in crossed lines. [Fr. *gaufre*, honeycomb.]

goff, a variant of **golf**.

goffer, gof'ər, *v.t.* to plait or crimp.—*n.* **goff'ering**, plaits or ruffles, or the process of making them: indented tooling on the edge of a book. [O.Fr. *gauffrer*—*goffre*, a wafer.]

gog, gog, *n.* (*obs.*, in oaths) for **God**.

go-getter. See **go**.

goggle, gog'l, *v.i.* to strain or roll the eyes.—*v.t.* to turn about (the eyes).—*adj.* rolling: staring:

prominent.—*n.* a stare or affected rolling of the eye: (*pl.*) spectacles with projecting eye-tubes: protective spectacles: conspicuous spectacles.—*adj.* **gogg′le-eyed**, having prominent, distorted, or rolling eyes.—*n.* **gogg′ler**, (*slang*) an eye. [Possibly related to Ir. and Gael, *gog*, to nod.]

goglet, *gog′lit, n.* a water-cooler. [Port. *gorgoleta.*]

Goidel, *goi′dəl, n.* a Gael in the general sense.—*adj.* **Goidelic** (*-del′*), Gadhelic. [O.Ir. *Góidel.*]

going, *gō′ing, n.* the act of moving: departure: (*B.*) course of life: conditions of travel: progress: gait.—*adj.* (for earlier **a-go′ing**) in motion or activity: about, to be had: in existence.—**going forth**, (*B.*) an outlet: **goings on**, behaviour, esp. reprehensible behaviour; **goings out**, (*arch.*) expenditure. [**go**.]

going, *gō′ing, pr.p.* of **go**, in any sense: about: approaching (the age of).—**going concern**, a business in actual activity; **going strong**, in full activity, flourishing.

goitre, *goi′tər, n.* morbid enlargement of the thyroid gland: a swelling in front of the throat.—*adjs.* **goi′tred**; **goi′trous**. [Fr. *goître*—L. *guttur*, the throat.]

Golconda, *gol-kon′dä, n.* a rich source of wealth. [Ruined city near Haidarabad (Hyderabad) once famous for diamond-cutting.]

gold, *gōld, n.* a heavy yellow element (Au; atomic number 79), one of the precious metals, used for coin, &c.: articles made of it: money: riches: anything very precious: yellow, gold colour.—*adj.* made of or like gold.—*ns.* **gold′-beater**, one whose trade is to beat gold into gold-leaf; **gold′-beaters′-skin**, the outer coat of the caecum of the ox; **gold′-beating**· **gold′-brick′**, a block of gold or (*U.S.*) of pretended gold, hence a sham; **gold′-bug**, (*U.S.*) a beetle of the family Chrysomelidae or of the Cassididae: a plutocrat: one who favours a gold standard; **gold′-cloth**, cloth of gold; **gold′crest**, a golden-crested bird of the genus Regulus—also **golden-crested wren**; **gold′-digger**, one who digs for gold, esp. a placer-miner: a woman who treats a man as a source of money for nothing; **gold′-digging**; **gold′-dust′**, gold in fine particles, as found in some rivers.—*adj.* **gold′en**, of gold: of the colour of gold: bright: most valuable: happy: most favourable.—*v.t.* to gild.—*v.i.* to become golden.—*n.* **gold′enberry**, the Cape gooseberry.—*adj.* **gold′en-crest′ed**.—*n.pl.* **gold′-ends′**, (*arch.*) broken remnants of gold.—*ns.* **gold-end′-man**, a dealer in these; **gold′en-eye**, a northern sea duck (Clangula): the lace-wing fly.—*adv.* **gold′enly**.—*ns.* **gold′en-seal**, a N. American ranunculaceous plant, *Hydrastis canadensis*: its yellow rhizome, used in medicine; **gold′enrod**, any plant of the composite genus Solidago, with rodlike stems and yellow heads crowded along the branches; **gold′eye**, a N. American freshwater fish (Hyodon); **gold′-fe′ver**, a mania for seeking gold; **gold′field**, a region in which gold is got; **gold′finch**, a beautiful finch, black, red, yellow and white, an eater of thistle seeds; **gold′finny**, same as **gold′sinny**; **gold′-fish**, a Chinese and Japanese freshwater fish near allied to the carp, golden or (*silverfish*) pale in its domesticated state, brownish when wild; **gold′-foil**, gold beaten into thin sheets, but not so thin as gold-leaf; **gold′ilocks**, a golden-haired person: a species of buttercup, *Ranunculus auricomus*.—*adj.* **gold′ish**, somewhat golden.—*n.* **gold′-lace**, lace made with gold-thread.—*adj.* **gold′-laced**.—*n.* **gold′-leaf**, gold beaten extremely thin.—*adj.* **gold′less**.—*ns.* **gold′-mine**, a mine for gold: a source of great profit; **gold′-miner**; **gold′-of-pleas′ure**, a cruciferous plant of the genus Camelina; **gold′-plate**, vessels and utensils of gold collectively; **gold′-rush**, a rush to a new goldfield; **gold′sinny**, a kind of wrasse, the cork-wing; **gold′-size**, an adhesive, of various kinds, used to attach gold-leaf to a surface; **gold′smith**, a worker in gold and silver; **gold′smithry, -ery**; **gold′spink** (*Scot.*, also **gowd′spink**), the gold-finch; **gold′stick**, a colonel of Life Guards who carries a gilded wand before the sovereign; **gold′-thread**, gold-wire used in weaving: silk wound with gilded wire: a European ranunculaceous plant (Coptis) with yellow roots; **gold′-washer**, one who gets gold by washing from sand and gravel: a cradle or other implement for washing gold; **gold-wasp**, any wasp of a family (Chrysididae) with brilliant metallic colouring and telescopic abdomens, whose larvae feed on those of wasps and bees—cuckoo-flies or ruby-tails, ruby-wasps; **gold′-wire′**, wire made of or covered with gold.—*adj.* **gold′y**, somewhat gold-like.—**golden age**, an imaginary past time of innocence and happiness: any time of highest achievement; **golden bough**, the bough plucked by Aeneas before visiting the underworld; **golden bull** (L. *bulla aurea*), an edict issued by the Emperor Charles IV. in 1356, mainly for the purpose of settling the law of imperial elections; **golden calf** (see **calf**); **golden eagle**, the common eagle, from a slight golden gleam about the head and neck; **golden fleece**, in Greek mythology, the fleece of the ram Chrysomallus, the recovery of which was the object of the famous expedition of the Argonauts—it gave its name to a celebrated order of knighthood in Austria and Spain, founded in 1429; **golden goose**, the fabled layer of golden eggs, slain by its over-greedy owner; **golden horde**, the Kipchaks, a Turkic people, whose empire was founded in central and southern Russia by Batu in the 13th century; **Golden Legend** (L. *Legenda Aurea*), a celebrated mediaeval collection of saints' lives, by Jacobus de Voragine (1230-98); **golden mean**, the middle way between extremes: moderation; **golden mole**, a bronzy S. African insectivore (Chrysochloris) superficially like a mole; **golden number**, a number marking the position of a year in the Metonic Cycle of nineteen years; **golden pheasant**, a golden-crested Chinese pheasant; **golden plover**, a plover with feathers speckled with yellow; **golden rose**, a rose of wrought gold, blessed by the Pope on the 4th Sunday in Lent; **golden rule**, to do as one would be done by; **golden salmon**, the S. American dorado; **golden saxifrage**, a greenish-yellow plant (Chrysosplenium) of the saxifrage family; **golden section**, division of a line so that one segment is to the other as that to the whole; **golden wedding** (see **wedding**); **gold ink**, a writing fluid in which gold or an imitation is in suspension; **gold paint**, bronze powders mixed with transparent varnish or amyl acetate; **gold standard**, a standard consisting of gold or of a weight in gold in relation to which money values are assessed; **on, off, the gold standard**, using, or not using, gold as standard. [O.E. *gold*, O.N. *gull*, Ger. *gold*, Goth. *gulth*.]

gold, *gōld, n.* the marigold: the corn-marigold.—Also (*Scot.*) **gool, gule** (*gōōl*), (*Spens.*) **goold** (*gōōld*). [O.E. *golde*, apparently related to **gold** (1), **gollan, gowan**; cf. **marigold**.]

golf, *golf* (*Scot. gowf*; by some Englishmen *gof*), *n.* a game played with a club or set of clubs over a prepared stretch of land, the aim being to propel a small ball into a series of holes.—*v.i.* to play golf.—*ns.* **golf′-bag**, a bag for carrying golf-clubs; **golf′-ball**, a small ball used in golf; **golf′-club**, a club used in golf; a golfing society; **golf′-course**, **golf′-links**, the ground on which golf is played; **golf′er, golf′ing**. [Origin obscure; Du. *kolf*, a club has been suggested.]

Golgi (*gol′jē*) **bodies**, easily stained bodies around the centrosome in animal cells, studied by Camillo *Golgi* (1884-1926).

Golgotha, *gol′go-thä, n.* a burial-ground: a charnel-house: a place littered with bones. [See under **Calvary**.]

goliard, *gō′li-ärd*, or *-lyərd, n.* a disreputable vagrant mediaeval cleric given to revelry, buffoonery, and satirical Latin versifying, follower of an imaginary Bishop Golias.—*adj.* **goliardic** (*-ärd′ik*). — *ns.* **go′liardy, goliard′ery**. — *v.i.* **go′lias**, (*Tenn.*) to play Golias. [O.Fr., glutton—L. *gūla*, gluttony.]

Goliath, *gō-lī′ath, n.* a giant.—*n.* **goli′ath-bee′tle**, a tropical beetle (Goliathus) reaching four inches in length.—*v.i.* **goli′athise**, to play Goliath, exaggerate extravagantly. [From *Goliath*, the Philistine giant in 1 Sam. xvii.]

gollan, golland, *gol'ən(d),* **gowland,** *gow'lənd, n.* a northern name for various yellow flowers (marigold, corn-marigold, globeflower, &c.). [Perh. conn. with **gold** (2) ; see **gowan**.]

gollar, *gol'ər, n.* (*Scot.*) a loud inarticulate gurgling sound : a thick or guttural bawl.—Also *v.i.* [Imitative.]

gollop, *gol'əp, v.t.* and *v.i.* to gulp greedily or hastily. [Perh. **gulp**.]

golly, *gol'i, interj.* expressing surprise. [Negro modification of **God**.]

gollywog, *gol'i-wog, n.* a fantastical doll with black face, staring eyes, and bristling hair.

goloe-shoes. See **galosh**.

golomynka, *go-lo-ming'kä, n.* a very oily fish found in Lake Baikal, resembling the gobies. [Russ.]

golosh. Same as **galosh**.

goluptious, *gol-up'shəs, adj.* (*jocular*) delicious : voluptuous.

gombeen, *gom-bēn', n.* (*Ir.*) usury.—*n.* **gombeen'-man,** a grasping usurer. [Ir. *gaimbín.*]

gombo, gombro. Same as **gumbo**.

gomeril, gomeral, *gom'ər-l, n.* (*Scot.*) a simpleton : a dunderhead. [Origin obscure.]

gomphosis, *gom-fō'sis, n.* an immovable articulation, as of the teeth in the jaw. [Gr. *gomphōsis— gomphos,* a bolt.]

gomuti, *gō-mōō'ti, n.* a palm, *Arenga saccharifera :* the black fibre it yields.—Also **gomu'to.** [Malay *gumuti.*]

gonad, *gon'ad, n.* (*biol.*) an organ that produces sex-cells.—*adjs.* **gonadial** (*-ād'i-əl*), **gonadic** (*-ad'*). [Gr. *gonē,* generation.]

gondola, *gon'də-lä, n.* a long, narrow boat used chiefly on the canals of Venice : (*U.S.*) a lighter : (*U.S.*) a flat railway wagon : the car of an airship. —(*Spens.*) **gon'delay.**—*n.* **gondolier** (*-lēr'*), one who rows a gondola. [It. ; origin obscure.]

Gondwanaland, *gond-wä'nä-land, n.* an ancient continent held to have connected India with S. Africa, S. America, Antarctica and Australia from Carboniferous times to Jurassic. [*Gondwana* district in India, i.e. forest of the Gonds.]

gone, *gon, pa.p.* of **go,** in an advanced stage : lost, passed beyond help : departed : dead : weak, faint, feeling a sinking sensation : wide of the mark, of an arrow : (*slang*) enamoured of (with *on*).— *ns.* **gone'ness,** a sinking sensation ; **gon'er,** (*slang*) one dead or ruined beyond recovery : a thing beyond hope of recovery.—**gone under,** ruined beyond recovery.

gonfalon, *gon'fə-lon, n.* an ensign or standard with streamers.—*ns.* **gonfalonier** (*-ēr'*), one who bears a gonfalon : the chief magistrate in some Italian republics ; **gon'fanon,** a gonfalon : a pennon. [It. *gonfalone* and O.Fr. *gonfanon*—O.H.G. *gund-fano—gund,* battle, *fano* (Ger. *fahne*), a flag ; cf. O.E. *gúthfana.*]

gong, *gong, n.* a metal disk, usu. rimmed, that sounds when struck or rubbed with a drumstick : an instrument of call, esp. to meals : a steel spiral for striking in a clock : a bell sounded by a hammer : (*slang*) a medal.—*v.t.* to call upon to stop by sounding a gong.—*ns.* **gong'ster,** one who gongs, esp. an American motoring policeman ; **gong'-stick.** [Malay.]

Gongorism, *gong'gor-izm, n.* a florid, inverted, and pedantic style of writing, introduced by the Spanish poet Luis de Góngora y Argote (1561-1627), some of whose distinctive features reappeared in Euphuism.

goniatite, *gō'ni-ə-tīt, n.* a fossil cephalopod of a group with comparatively simple angular septa.— *n.* and *adj.* **goniati'toid.** [Gr. *gōniā,* an angle.]

gonidium, *gon-id'i-əm, n.* an algal cell in a lichen :— *pl.* **gonid'ia.**—*adj.* **gonid'ial.** [Gr. *gonē,* generation, seed.]

gonimoblast, *gon'i-mō-bläst, n.* in the red seaweeds, a spore-bearing filament that springs from the fertilised carpogonium. [Gr. *gonimos,* productive, *blastos,* a shoot.]

goniometer, *gōn-, gon-i-om'i-tər, n.* an instrument for measuring angles, esp. between crystal-faces :

a direction-finding apparatus.—*adjs.* **goniometric** (*-ə-met'rik*), **-al.**—*n.* **goniom'etry.** [Gr. *gōniā,* an angle, *metron,* measure.]

gonococcus, *gon-ō-kok'əs, n.* the bacterium that causes gonorrhoea.—*adj.* **gonococc'al.** [Gr. *kokkos,* a berry.]

gonophore, *gon'ə-fōr, n.* (*bot.*) a prolongation of the axis bearing stamens or carpels : (*zool.*) a reproductive zooid of a hydrozoan, answering to a medusa but remaining fixed. [Gr. *gonos,* seed, *phoreein,* to bear.]

gonorrhoea, *gon-ō-rē'ä, n.* a contagious infection of the mucous membrane of the genital tract.— *adj.* **gonorrhoe'al.** [Gr. *gonorroiā—gonos,* seed, *rheein,* to flow, from a mistaken notion of its nature.]

goo, *gōō, n.* (*U.S. slang*) a sticky substance : sentimentality.—*adj.* **goo'ey.** [Origin unknown.]

good, *good, adj.* having suitable or desirable qualities : promoting health, welfare, or happiness : virtuous : pious : kind : benevolent : well-behaved : not troublesome : of repute : doughty : worthy : commendable : suitable : adequate : thorough : competent : sufficient : valid : sound : serviceable : beneficial : genuine : pleasing : favourable : ample, moderately estimated : considerable, as in *a good deal, a good mind :* to be counted on : (*comp.* **bett'er** ; *superl.* **best**).—*n.* the end of ethics : that which is good : prosperity : welfare : advantage, temporal or spiritual : benefit : avail : virtue : (*arch.*) possessions : (in *pl.*) movable property, chattels, merchandise, freight.—*interj.* well : right : be it so.—*adv.* well.—*ns.* **good'-breed'ing,** polite manners formed by a good bringing-up ; **good-broth'er, -fath'er, -moth'er, -sis'ter, -son',** (*Scot.* ; also **gude-**) a brother-in-law, father-in-law, &c.—*n.* or *interj.* **good-bye',** for *God be with you :* farewell, a form of address at parting.—*adjs.* **good'-cheap,** (*arch.*) cheap (lit. good-bargain) ; **good'-condi'tioned,** in a good state.—*n.* **good-dame'** (**gude-dame'**, **güd-, gid-** ; *obs. Scot.*), a grandmother.—*ns.* or *interjs.* **good-day',** a common salutation at meeting or parting ; **good-den'** (from *good-e'en*), **good-e'en', good-ev'en, good-eve'ning,** a salutation on meeting or parting in the evening.—*adj.* **good'-faced,** (*Shak.*) having a handsome face.—*ns.* **good'-fell'ow,** a jolly or boon companion : a reveller ; **good-fell'owship,** merry or pleasant company : conviviality.—*adj.* **good'-for-nothing,** worthless, useless.—*n.* an idle person.—*ns.* **Good-Fri'day,** the Friday of Passion-week ; **good-hū'mour,** a cheerful, tolerant mood.—*adj.* **good-hū'moured.**—*adv.* **good-hū'mouredly.**— *n.* **good'iness,** weak, priggish, or canting goodness. —*adj.* **good'ish,** pretty good, of fair quality or quantity.—*n.* **good'-King-Hen'ry,** a goosefoot formerly grown as a pot-herb.—*interj.* **good-lack',** an expression of surprise or pity (prob. a variation of *good Lord,* under the influence of **alack**).—*n.* **good'liness.**—*adj.* **good'-look'ing,** handsome.— *adv.* **good'ly,** (*Spens.*) graciously : excellently, kindly.—*adj.* comely: good-looking: fine: excellent: ample.—*comp.* **good'lier** ; *superl.* **good'liest.**— *ns.* **good'lyhead, good'lihead,** (*Spens.*) goodness ; **good'man,** (*arch.*) a yeoman : formerly prefixed to name of a man of yeoman's rank : (*good-man',* chiefly *Scot.* ; also **gude-**) a householder or husband (*fem.* **good'wife'**) or euphemistically the devil.—*ns.* and *interjs.* **good-morn'ing** or (*arch.*) **good-morr'ow,** a salutation at meeting or parting early in the day.—*n.* **good-na'ture,** natural goodness and mildness of disposition.—*adj.* **good'-na'tured.**—*adv.* **good'-na'turedly.**—*n.* **good'-ness,** virtue : excellence : benevolence : substituted for God in certain expressions and as *interj.*—*n.* and *interj.* **good-night',** a common salutation on parting at night or well on in the day. —*interj.* **good'-now,** an exclamation of wonder, surprise, or entreaty.—*ns.* **goods'-en'gine,** an engine used for drawing goods-trains ; **good'-sense',** sound judgment ; **goodsire'** (**gudesire'**, **güd-, gid-** ; **gutcher,** *gut'shər ; obs. Scot.*), a grandfather.—*n.* and *interj.* **good'-speed',** a contraction of *I wish you good speed* (i.e. success).—*n.* **goods'-**

Neutral vowels in unaccented syllables : *el'ə-mənt, in'fənt, ran'dəm*

train, a train of goods wagons.—*adj.* **good'-tem'pered**, possessing a good temper.—*ns.* **good-wife'** (or *good'*), the *fem.* of goodman: **good'will'**, benevolence: well-wishing: the established custom or popularity of any business or trade—often appearing as one of its assets, with a marketable money value.—*adjs.* **good'-will**; (*Scot.*) **good-will'y**, well-wishing: expressive of good-will.—*n.* **good'y**, good-wife: good-woman (probably formed from *good-wife*): a sweetmeat. — *adj.* **good'y**, **good'y-good'y**, mawkishly good: weakly benevolent or pious.—**as good as**, the same as, no less than: virtually; **be as good as one's word**, to fulfil one's promise; **for good (and all)**, permanently: irrevocably; **good for anything**, ready for any kind of work; **goodman's croft**, a patch once left untilled in Scotland to avert the malice of the devil from the crop; **good offices**, mediation; **good people, good folk**, the fairies (euphemistically); **good sailor**, a person not liable to seasickness; **Good Templar**, a member of a temperance society, modelled on the Freemasons; **make good**, to fulfil, perform: to compensate: to come to success, esp. unexpectedly: to do well, redeeming a false start: to justify; **no good**, useless: unavailing: worthless; **stand good**, to be lastingly good: to remain; **the goods**, (*slang*) the real thing; **think good**, to be disposed, to be willing. [O.E. *gód*; Du. *goed*, Ger. *gut*, O.N. *góthr*, Goth. *gōths.*]

goodyear, -s, *good'yēr*(*z*), *n.* (*Shak.*) the devil, the plague, or the like—a meaningless imprecation. [Of obscure origin. Perh. orig. as I hope for a *good year*.]

goof, *goof*, *n.* a stupid or awkward person.—*adj.* **goof'y**. [Perh. Fr. *goffe.*]

googly, *goog'li*, *n.* (*cricket*) an off-breaking ball with an apparent leg-break action on the part of the bowler, or conversely.—Also *adj.*—*v.i.* **goog'le**, to behave or bowl in such a manner. [Ety. dub.]

gool, goold. See **gold** (2).

goon, *goon*, *n.* (*U.S. slang*) hired thug: stupid person.

goop, *goop*, *n.* a fool: a fatuous person.—*adj.* **goop'y**. [Cf. **goof**.]

Goorkha, gooroo. See **Gurkha, guru**.

goosander, *goos-an'dər*, *n.* a large duck of the merganser genus. [Perh. **goose**, and O.N. *önd*, pl. *ander*, duck.]

goose, *goos*, *n.* any one of a group of birds of the duck family, intermediate between ducks and swans: a domesticated member of the group, descended mainly from the grey-lag: the female of such a bird (*masc.* **gander**): a tailor's smoothing-iron, from the likeness of the handle to the neck of a goose: a stupid, silly person: a game of chance once common in England, in which the players moved counters on a board, with right to a double move on reaching a picture of a goose: (*pl.* **geese**, *gēs*, or, of tailor's goose, **goos'es**).—*v.t.* (*slang*) to hiss off the stage.—*ns.* **goose'-cap**, a silly person; **goose'-club**, a combination for saving to buy geese for Christmas, or to raffle for a goose; **goose'-egg**, the egg of a goose: (*U.S.*) a zero score; **goose'-fish**, (*U.S.*) the angler-fish; **goose'-flesh**, a puckered condition of the skin, like that of a plucked goose: the bristling feeling in the skin due to erection of hairs through cold, horror, &c.; **goose'-flower**, the pelican-flower, a gigantic Aristolochia; **goose'foot**, any plant of a genus (Chenopodium) of the beet family, from the shape of the leaf (*pl.* **goose'foots**); **goose'-girl**, a girl who herds geese; **goose'herd**, one who herds geese; **goose'-grass**, cleavers: silverweed; **goose'-neck**, a hook, bracket, pipe, &c., bent like a goose's neck; **goose'-quill**, one of the quills or large wing-feathers of a goose, esp. one used as a pen; **goos'ery**, a place for keeping geese: stupidity; **goose'-skin**, goose-flesh, horripilation; **goose'-step**, (*mil.*) a method of marching (resembling a goose's walk) with knees stiff and soles brought flat on the ground; **goose'-wing**, one of the clews or lower corners of a ship's mainsail or foresail when the middle part is furled or tied up to the yard.—*adj.* **goose'-winged**, having only one clew set: in fore-and-aft rigged vessels,

having the mainsail on one side and the foresail on the other, so as to sail wing-and-wing.—*n.* **goos'ey**, a goose: a blockhead. [O.E. *gós* (pl. *gés*); O.N. *gás*, Ger. *gans*, L. *anser* (for *hanser*), Gr. *chēn*.]

gooseberry, *gooz'bə-ri*, *n.* the fruit of the **goose'-berry-bush** (*Ribes Grossularia*), a prickly shrub of the saxifrage family: a fermented effervescing drink (also **goose'berry-wine**) made from gooseberries: an imitation champagne: an unwanted third person.—*ns.* **goose'berry-cat'erpillar**, a creamy looper with orange spots and black dots, feeding on gooseberry leaves, the larva of the **goose'berry-moth'** or magpie moth (*Abraxas grossulariata*), a yellow-bodied moth with black-spotted white wings; **goose'berry-fool'** (see **fool** (2)); **goose'berry-stone'**, grossular; **goose'-gog**, (*coll.* and *dial.*) a gooseberry.—**Cape gooseberry**, or **gooseberry tomato** (see **cape**); **Coromandel gooseberry** (see **carambola**). [Perh. **goose** and **berry**; or *goose* may be from M.H.G. *krus* (Gr. *kraus*, crisp, curled); cf. O.Fr. *groisele*, *grosele*, gooseberry, Scot. *grossart*.]

gopher, *gō'fər*, *n.* a name in America applied to various burrowing animals—the pouched rat, the ground squirrel, the land tortoise of the Southern States, and a burrowing snake.—*v.i.* to burrow: to mine in a small way. [Perh. Fr. *gaufre*, honey-comb.]

gopher, *gō'fər*, *n.* (*B.*) a kind of wood, generally supposed to be cypress: (*U.S.*) yellow-wood (Cladastris). [Heb.]

gopura, *gō'poō-rä*, *n.* in Southern India, a pyramidal tower over the gateway of a temple. [Sans. *gōpura.*]

goral, *gō'rəl*, *n.* a Himalayan goat-antelope.

goramy, gourami, gurami, *gō'*, *goo'ra-mi*, or *-rä'mi*, *n.* a large freshwater food-fish (*Osphromenus olfax*) of the Eastern Archipelago. [Malay *gurāmī.*]

gor-belly, *gor'-bel-i*, *n.* a big belly: a big-bellied person.—*adj.* (*Shak.*) **gor'-bellied**. [Perh. O.E. *gor*, filth, and belly.]

gorblimy, *gaw-blī'mi*, *interj.* (*Cockney*) for *God blind me.*

gorcock, *gor'kok*, *n.* the red grouse cock. [Origin obscure.]

gorcrow, *gor'krō*, *n.* the carrion-crow. [O.E. *gor*, filth, and **crow**.]

Gordian, *gord'yən*, *adj.* pertaining to *Gordium* the capital, or *Gordius* the king, of ancient Phrygia, or to the intricate knot he tied: intricate: difficult.—*v.t.* (*Keats*) to tie up, knot.—*n.* **Gordius**, a genus of hairworms.—**cut the Gordian knot**, to overcome a difficulty by violent measures as Alexander with his sword.

gore, *gōr*, *n.* (*obs.*) filth: clotted blood: blood.—*n.* **gore'-blood** (*Spens.*).—*adv.* **gor'ily**.—*adj.* **gor'y**, like gore: covered with gore: bloody.—**gory dew**, a dark-red slimy film sometimes seen on damp walls, &c., a simple form of vegetable life, *Porphyridium cruentum*. [O.E. *gor*, filth, dung; O.N. *gor*, cud, slime.]

gore, *gōr*, *n.* a triangular piece of land: a triangular piece let into a garment to widen it: (*obs.*) a skirt: a sector of a curved surface.—*v.t.* to shape like or furnish with gores: to pierce with anything pointed, as a spear or horns.—*n.* **gor'ing**, an angular, tapering, or obliquely-cut piece.—*adj.* forming a gore. [O.E. *gára*, a pointed triangular piece of land, and *gár*, a spear.]

gorge, *gorj*, *n.* the throat: a ravine: (*fort.*) the entrance to an outwork: a hawk's crop: the maw: the contents of the stomach: a gluttonous feed: a fish-catching device, to be swallowed by the fish.—*v.t.* to swallow greedily: to glut.—*v.i.* to feed gluttonously.—*adj.* **gorged**, having a gorge or throat: glutted: (*her.*) having a crown or coronet about the neck.—*n.* **gor'get**, a piece of armour for the throat: a metal badge formerly worn on the breast by army officers: a wimple: a neck ornament.—**have one's gorge rise**, to be filled with loathing; **heave the gorge**, to retch. [O.Fr.]

gorgeous, *gor'jəs*, *adj.* showy: splendid: magnificent. — *adv.* **gor'geously**. — *n.* **gor'geousness**. [O.Fr. *gorgias*, gaudy.]

fāte, fär, ásk; mē, hər (her); *mīne; mōte; mūte; mōōn; dhen* (then)

Gorgio, *gor'ji-ō*, *n.* one who is not a gypsy. [Romany *gacho*, *gatscho*.]

Gorgon, *gor'gon*, *n.* one of three fabled female monsters (Stheno, Euryale, and Medusa), of horrible and petrifying aspect, winged, with hissing serpents for hair : anybody, esp. a woman, very ugly or formidable.—*adjs.* **gor'gon, gor-gō'nian**.—*n.* **gorgoneion** (*-ī'on*), a mask of the gorgon.—*v.t.* **gor'gonise**, to turn to stone. [Gr. *Gorgō*, pl. *-ŏnĕs—gorgos*, grim.]

Gorgonia, *gor-gō'ni-ä*, *n.* a genus of sea-fans or horny corals.—*adj.* **gorgo'nian**.—*n.* a horny coral. [L. *gorgōnia*, coral—*Gorgō*, Gorgon (from hardening in the air).]

Gorgonzola, *gor-gon-zō'lä*, *n.* a highly esteemed cheese. [From *Gorgonzola*, a small Italian town near Milan.]

gorilla, *gor-il'ä*, *n.* a great African ape, the largest anthropoid.—*adj.* **gorill'ine**. [Gr. *Gorillai* (pl.), reported by Hanno the Carthaginian as a tribe of hairy women; supposed to be an African word.]

gorm, a variant of **gaum**.

gormand, *gor'mand*, *n.* older form of **gourmand**.— *v.i.* **gor'mandise**, to eat hastily or voraciously.— *n.* gourmandise : gluttony : gormandising.—*ns.* **gor'mandīser ; gor'mandīsing ; gor'mandism**, gluttony. [See **gourmand**.]

gorse, *gors*, *n.* furze or whin, a prickly papilionaceous shrub (Ulex).—Also **gosse** (*Shak.*).—*adj.* **gors'y**. [O.E. *gorst*.]

gorsedd, *gor'sedh*, *n.* a meeting of bards and druids. [W.]

gosh, *gosh*, *interj.* (*vulg.*) for **God**.

goshawk, *gos'hawk*, *n.* a short-winged hawk, once used for hunting wild-geese and other fowl, not having a toothed bill like the falcons proper. [O.E. *gōshafoc—gós*, goose, *hafoc*, hawk.]

Goshen, *gō'shɔn*, *n.* a happy place of light and plenty. [From the abode of the Israelites during the plague of darkness in Egypt, Exod. x. 23.]

goslarite, *gos'lɔr-īt*, *n.* a mineral, hydrated zinc sulphate, found at *Goslar*.

gosling, *goz'ling*, *n.* a young goose.—*n.* **gos'let**, an Eastern dwarf goose (Nettapus). [O.E. *gós*, goose, double dim. *-l-ing*.]

gospel, *gos'pɔl*, *n.* the teaching of Christ : a narrative of the life of Christ, esp. one of those included in the New Testament, Matthew, Mark, Luke, and John : the principles set forth therein : the stated portion of these read at service : any strongly advocated principle or system : (*coll.*) absolute truth.—*v.t.* (*Shak.*) to instruct in the gospel.—*v.t.* **gos'pel(l)ise**, to evangelise : to square with the gospel.—*n.* **gos'peller**, a preacher : an evangelist : a Wycliffite, Protestant, or Puritan (often in derision) : one who reads the gospel in church.— **gospel side**, the north side or gospeller's side of the altar. [O.E. *godspel(l)*, a translation of L. *evangelium—gōd*, good (with shortened vowel being understood as *God*, God) and *spel(l)*, story.]

gospodar. Same as **hospodar**.

gossamer, *gos'ɔ-mɔr*, *n.* very fine spider-threads that float in the air or form webs on bushes in fine weather : any very thin material.—*adj.* **light, flimsy**.—*adj.* **goss'amery**, like gossamer : flimsy. [M.E. *gossomer* ; perh. goose-summer, a St Martin's summer, when geese are in season and gossamer abounds ; cf. Ger. *sommerfäden*, summer-threads, also *mädchensommer*, maiden-summer.]

gossan, gozzan, *gos'*, *goz'ɔn*, *n.* decomposed rock, largely quartz impregnated with iron compounds, at the outcrop of a vein esp. of metallic sulphides. [Cornish miner's term ; origin unknown.]

gosse, *gos*, *n.* (*Shak.*) a form of **gorse**.

gossip, *gos'ip*, *n.* (*arch.*) a sponsor at baptism (in relation to child, parent, or other sponsor) : a woman friend who comes at a birth : a familiar friend (*Spens.*). **goss'ib**) : one who goes about telling and hearing news, or idle, malicious, and scandalous tales: idle talk: tittle-tattle: scandalous rumours : easy familiar writing.—*v.i.* to run about telling idle or malicious tales : to talk much : to chat.—*v.t.* (*Shak.*) to stand godfather to.—*n.* and *adj.* **goss'iping**. — *n.* **goss'ipry**. — *adj.* **goss'ipy**.

[O.E. *godsibb*, godfather, one who is sib in God spiritually related.]

gossoon, gorsoon, *go-*, *gor-sōōn'*, *n.* a boy or boy-servant. [Anglo-Ir.,—Fr. *garçon*, boy.]

Gossypium, *go-sip'i-ɔm*, *n.* a tropical genus of the mallow family, yielding cotton.—*adj.* **goss'ypine**, cottony.—*n.* **goss'ypol**, a poisonous principle in cotton-seed. [L. *gossypion*.]

got, gotten. See under **get**.

Goth, *goth*, *n.* one of an ancient Germanic nation, originally settled on the southern coasts of the Baltic, migrating to Dacia in the 3rd century, and later founding kingdoms in Italy, southern France, and Spain : a rude or uncivilised person, a barbarian.—*adj.* **Goth'ic**, belonging to the Goths or their language : barbarous : romantic : denoting a style of architecture with high-pointed arches, clustered columns, &c. (applied in reproach at the time of the Renaissance) : (*print.*) black-letter.— *n.* the language of the Goths, an East Germanic tongue : Gothic architecture. — *v.t.* **goth'icise** (*-sīz*), to make Gothic.—*n.* **Goth'icism** (*-sizm*), a Gothic idiom or style of building : rudeness of manners. [The native names *Gutans* (sing. *Guta*) and *Gutôs* (sing. *Guts*), and *Gutthiuda*, people of the Goths ; Latinised as *Gothī, Gotthī* ; Gr. *Gothoi, Gotthoi* ; O.E. *Gotan* (sing. *Gota*).]

Gothamite, *got'ɔm-īt*, **Gothamist**, *-ist*, *ns.* a simpleton : a wiseacre : (*U.S.* ; *goth', gōth'*) a New Yorker. [From *Gotham*, a village in Nottinghamshire, with which name are connected many of the simpleton stories of immemorial antiquity.]

göthite, *got'īt*, *n.* a mineral, hydrated ferric oxide. [Named in honour of the poet *Goethe*.]

gouache, *gwäsh*, *goo-äsh*, *n.* a method of watercolour painting with opaque colours, mixed with water, honey, and gum, presenting a matt surface : work painted according to this method. [Fr.]

Gouda, *gow'dä*, *n.* a kind of cheese from *Gouda*.

gouge, *gowj*, also *gōōj*, *n.* a chisel with a hollow blade for cutting grooves or holes.—*v.t.* to scoop out, as with a gouge : to force out, as the eye with the thumb. [O.Fr.,—L.L. *gubia*, a kind of chisel.]

gouge, *gōōj*, *n.* (*Scott*) a wench. [O.Fr.]

goujeers, an editor's would-be improvement upon **goodyear** (q.v.), from a spurious Fr. *goujère*, the French disease.

goulash, *gōō'läsh*, *n.* a stew of beef, vegetables, and paprika : (*bridge*) a re-deal of cards that have been arranged in suits and order of value. [Hung. *gulyás* (*hús*), herdsman (meat).]

Goura, *gow'rä*, *n.* a New Guinea genus of beautifully crested, ground-loving pigeons. [From a native name.]

gourami. See **goramy**.

gourd, *gōrd*, or *gōōrd*, *n.* a large hard-rinded fleshy fruit characteristic of the cucumber family : rind of one used as a bottle, cup, &c. : a gourd-bearing plant.—*n.* **gourd'-worm**, a fluke-worm resembling a gourd-seed, esp. the liver-fluke. [O.Fr. *gourde*, contr. from *cougourde*—L. *cucurbita*, a gourd.]

gourds, *gōrdz, gōōrdz, n.pl.* a kind of false dice. [Cf. O.Fr. *gourd*, swindle.]

gourdy, *gōrd'i, gōōrd'i, adj.* swollen in the legs (of a horse).—*n.* **gourd'iness**. [O.Fr. *gourdi*, swollen.]

gourmand, *gōōr'mand*, *-mänᵈ', n.* one who eats greedily : a glutton : a lover of good fare.—*adj.* voracious : gluttonous.—*n.* **gourmandise** (*gōōr'-mɔn-dīz, gōōr-mänᵈ-dēz*), skill or indulgence in good eating : (*Spens.*) voracious greed. [Fr. ; cf. **gormand**.]

gourmet, *gōōr-mā', -me, n.* an epicure, originally one with a delicate taste in wines. [Fr., a wine-merchant's assistant.]

goustrous, *gows'trɔs, adj.* (*Scot.*) boisterous, rude.

gousty, *gows'ti, adj.* (*Scot.*) dreary : desolate : empty.

gout, *gowt*, *n.* (*arch.*) a drop, spot : a disease in which excess of uric acid in the blood is deposited as sodium biurate in the joints, &c., with swelling esp. of the great toe : a kindred disease of poultry : a swelling of the stalk in wheat and other grasses.— *n.* **gout'fly**, a fly (Chlorops) whose larvae cause gout by boring in wheat, &c.—*ns.* **gout'iness ; gout'weed, -wort**, bishopweed or goatweed (*Aegopodium Podagraria*), an umbelliferous weed,

Neutral vowels in unaccented syllables : *el'ɔ-mɔnt, in'fɔnt, ran'dɔm*

long supposed to be good for gout.—*adj.* **gout'y**, relating to gout : diseased with or subject to gout. [O.Fr. *goutte*—L. *gutta*, a drop, the disease supposed to be caused by a defluxion of humours.]

gout, *gōō, n.* taste : relish. [Fr.,—L. *gustus*, taste.]

gouvernante, *gōō-ver-näns t, n.* (*obs.*) a female ruler : a house-keeper : a duenna : a governess. [Fr.]

govern, *guv'ərn, v.t.* to direct : to control : to rule with authority : to determine : (*gram.*) to determine the case of : to require as the case of a noun or pronoun.—*v.i.* to exercise authority : to administer the laws. — *adj.* **gov'ernable.** — *ns.* **gov'ernall,** (*Spens.*) government ; **gov'ernance,** (*arch.*) government : control : direction : behaviour ; **gov'ernante,** (*obs.*) a gouvernante ; **gov'erness,** a female governor : a lady who has charge of the instruction of the young at home or in school : a tutoress (**nur'sery-gov'erness,** one having charge of young children only, tending as well as teaching them).—*v.i.* to act as governess.— *v.t.* to be governess to.—*ns.* **gov'erness-car, -cart,** a light low two-wheeled vehicle with face-to-face seats at the sides.—*adj.* **gov'erning,** having control. — *n.* **government** (*guv'ər(n)-mənt*), a ruling or managing : control : system of governing : the body of persons authorised to administer the laws, or to govern a state : tenure of office of one who governs : an administrative division : territory : (*gram.*) the power of one word in determining the case of another : (*Shak.*) conduct.—*adj.* of or pursued by government.—*adj.* **governmental**(-*ment'l*), pertaining to government.—*ns.* **gov'ernor,** a real or titular ruler, esp. of a state, province, colony : the head of an institution or a member of its ruling body : the commander of a fortress : a tutor : (*slang,* usu. *guv'nər*) a father, chief, or master, applied more generally in kindly, usually ironically respectful, address : (*mach.*) a regulator, or contrivance for maintaining uniform velocity with a varying resistance : (*B.*) a pilot ; **gov'ernor-gen'eral,** the supreme governor in a country : a viceroy : (*pl.* **gov'ernors-gen'eral**) ; **gov'ernor-gen'eralship** ; **gov'ernorship.** [O.Fr. *governer* —L. *gubernāre*—Gr. *kybernaein,* to steer.]

gowan, *gow'ən, n.* (*Scot.*) the wild daisy : the ox-eye daisy (also **horse'-gow'an**).—*adj.* **gow'any.**—*n.* **luck'en-gow'an,** the globe-flower. [Apparently a form of **gollan**(d).]

gowd. Scots form of **gold.**

gowf, *gowf, v.t.* (*Scot.*) to strike, cuff.—*v.i.* to golf.— *n.* golf.—*ns.* **gowf'-ba'**, golf-ball ; **gowf'er,** golfer. [See **golf.**]

gowk, gouk, gowk, *n.* (*Scots.*) a cuckoo : a fool : an April fool. [O.N. *gaukr* ; O.E. *géac.*]

gowl, *gowl, v.i.* (*Scot.*) to cry or howl. [O.N. *gaula.*]

gown, *gown, n.* a loose flowing outer garment : a woman's dress : an academic, clerical, or official robe.—*v.t.* and *v.i.* to dress in a gown.—*v.t.* to invest or furnish with a gown.—*n.* **gown'boy,** a school foundationer, wearing a gown.—*adj.* **gowned.**—*ns.* **gown'man, gowns'man,** one who wears a gown, as a divine or lawyer, and esp. a member of an English university : a civilian. [O.Fr. *goune*—L.L. *gunna* ; origin unknown.]

gowpen, *gowp'ən, n.* (*Scot.*) the hollow of the two hands held together : a double handful.—*n.* **gow'-penful.** [O.N. *gaupn.*]

goy, *goi, n.* a non-Jew, Gentile. [Heb., nation.]

Graafian, *grä'fi-ən, adj.* pertaining to the Dutch anatomist Regnier de *Graaf* (1641-73) who discovered the **Graafian follicles,** in which the ova are contained in the ovary of higher vertebrates.

graal. Same as **grail** (dish).

grab, *grab, n.* an Eastern coasting vessel. [Ar. *ghurāb.*]

grab, *grab, v.t.* (*coll.*) to seize or grasp suddenly : to lay hands on.—*v.i.* to clutch : (*pr.p.* **grabb'ing** ; *pa.t.* and *pa.p.* **grabbed**).—*n.* a sudden grasp or clutch : unscrupulous seizure : a double scoop hinged like a pair of jaws : a simple card-game depending upon prompt claiming.—*ns.* **grab'-bag,** (*U.S.*) a lucky-bag ; **grabb'er,** one who grabs : an avaricious person. [Cf. Sw. *grabba,* to grasp.]

grabble, *grab'l, v.i.* to grope. [Freq. of **grab.**]

grace, *grās, n.* easy elegance in form or manner : what adorns and commends to favour : embellishment : favour : kindness : pardon : the undeserved mercy of God : divine influence : eternal life or salvation : a short prayer at meat : an act or decree of the governing body of an English university : a ceremonious title in addressing a duke, an archbishop, or formerly a king : (*pl.*) favour, friendship (with *good*) : **Graces,** (*myth.*) the three sister goddesses in whom beauty was deified (the Greek Charites), Euphrosyne, Aglaia, Thalia. —*v.t.* to mark with favour : to adorn.—*n.* **grace'-cup,** a cup or health drunk at the end of the feast. —*adjs.* **graced,** (*Shak.*) favoured, endowed with grace or graces, virtuous, chaste ; **grace'ful,** elegant and easy : marked by propriety or fitness, becoming : having or conferring grace, in any sense. — *adv.* **grace'fully.** — *n.* **grace'fulness.** — *adj.* **grace'less,** wanting grace or excellence : without mercy or favour : depraved : wicked : indecorous. — *adv.* **grace'lessly.** — *n.* **grace'lessness.** — *ns.* **grace'-note,** (*mus.*) a note introduced as an embellishment, not being essential to the harmony or melody ; **grace'-stroke,** a finishing stroke, *coup de grâce* ; **graciosity** (*grā-shi-os'i-ti*), graciousness, esp. with duplicity ; **gracioso** (*grä-shi-ō'sō* ; Sp. *grä-thyō'sō*), a favourite : a clown in Spanish comedy.—*adj.* **gracious** (*grā'shəs*), abounding in grace or kindness : proceeding from divine favour : acceptable : affable : becoming in demeanour : favourable.—*n.* used as substitute for God.—*adv.* **grā'ciously.**—*n.* **grā'ciousness.—days of grace,** (three) days allowed for the payment of a note or bill of exchange after it falls due ; **fall from grace,** to backslide, to lapse from the state of grace and salvation or from favour ; **good gracious, an** exclamation of surprise ; **saving grace,** (*Christian theology*) divine grace so bestowed as to lead to salvation : a compensating virtue or quality ; **take heart of grace,** to take courage from favour shown ; **with good** (**bad**) **grace,** in amiable (ungracious) fashion ; **year of grace,** year of Christian era, A.D. [Fr. *grâce*—L. *grātia,* favour —*grātus,* agreeable.]

gracile, *gras'il, adj.* slender : gracefully slight in form.—*n.* **gracil'ity.** [L. *gracilis,* slender.]

grackle, grakle, *grak'l, n.* a myna (hill myna) or kindred bird : an American 'blackbird' of the family Icteridæ. [L. *grāculus,* jackdaw.]

graddan, *grad'ən, n.* parched grain.—*v.t.* to parch in the husk. [Gael. *gradan.*]

grade, *grād, n.* a degree or step in quality, rank, or dignity : a stage of advancement : rank : (*U.S.*) a yearly stage in education : (*U.S.*) a pupil's mark of proficiency : (*U.S.,* in *pl., the grades*) the elementary school : position in a scale : a class, or position in a class, according to value : (*philol.*) position in an ablaut series : (*math.*) one-hundredth part of a right angle : gradient or slope : (*U.S.*) an inclined stretch of road or railway : a class of animals produced by crossing a breed with one purer.—*v.t.* to arrange acc. to grade : to assign a grade to : to adjust the gradients of.—*v.i.* to shade off.—*adj.* cross-bred.—*v.t.* and *v.i.* **gradate** (*gra-dāt'*), to shade off imperceptibly. — *adv.* **grädā'tim** (L. *grä-dä'tim*), step by step.—*n.* **grädā'tion,** a degree or step : a rising step by step : progress from one degree or state to another : position attained : state of being arranged in ranks : (*mus.*) a diatonic succession of chords : insensible shading off : (*philol.*) ablaut.—*adjs.* **grädā'tional** ; **grädā'tioned,** formed by gradations or stages ; **gradatory** (*grad'ət-ə-ri*), proceeding step by step : adapted for walking ; **gradient** (*grā'di-ənt, -dyənt*), walking.—*n.* the degree of slope as compared with the horizontal : rate of change in any quantity with distance (e.g. in barometer readings) : an incline.—*ns.* **grad'ienter,** a surveyor's instrument for determining grades ; **gradin, gradine** (*grā'din, grə-dēn'*), a rising tier of seats, as in an amphitheatre : a raised step or ledge behind an altar ; **gradino** (*grä-dē'nō* ; It.), a decoration for an altar gradin.—*adj.* **gradual** (*grad'ū-əl*), advancing by grades or degrees : gentle and slow.—*n.* in the R.C. Church, the portion of the mass between the epistle and the gospel, formerly always sung from the steps of the altar: the book containing such anthems—also **grail.**— *ns.* **grad´ūalism,** the principle or policy of proceeding by degrees; **gradūal´ity.**—*adv.* **grad´ūally.**—*n.* **grad´ūand,** one about to receive a university degree.—*v.t.* **grad´ūate,** to divide into regular intervals: to mark with degrees: to proportion: (*arch.* and *U.S.*) to admit to a university degree.—*v.i.* to pass by grades: to receive a university degree.—*n.* one admitted to a degree in a university: (*U.S.*) one who has completed a course in any educational institution.—*adj.* **grad´ūated,** marked with degrees, as a thermometer. —*ns.* **grad´ūate-ship; gradūā´tion; grad´ūātor,** an instrument for dividing lines at regular intervals; **grā´dus,** a dictionary of Greek or Latin prosody— for *Gradus ad Parnassum.* — **grade crossing,** (*U.S.*) a level crossing; **make the grade** (*U.S.*), to succeed in climbing a steep hill: to overcome obstacles: to stand a test: to be up to standard. [L. *gradus,* a step—*gradī,* to step.]

gradely, *grād´li, adj.* (*prov.*) decent: proper: fit: fine. — *adv.* properly: readily: very. — Also **graith´ly.** [See **graith.**]

Gradgrind, *grad´grind, n.* one who regulates all human things by rule and compass and the mechanical application of statistics, allowing nothing for sentiment, emotion, and individuality. [From Thomas *Gradgrind* in Dickens's *Hard Times.*]

Graecise, *grē´sīz, v.t.* to make Greek: to hellenise. —*v.i.* to become Greek: to conform to Greek ways or idioms: to use the Greek language.—*n.* **Grae´cism,** a Greek idiom: the Greek spirit: a following of the Greeks.—*adj.* **Graeco-Ro´man** (*grē´kō-*), of or pertaining to both Greece and Rome, esp. the art of Greece under Roman domination: applied to a mode of wrestling imagined to be that of the Greeks and Romans.—Also **Grecise,** &c. [L. *Graecus*—Gr. *Graikos,* Greek; *graikizein,* to speak Greek.]

graf, *gräf, n.* a count, earl:—*fem.* **gräfin** (*gref´in*). [Ger.]

graff, *gräf, n.* (*Scot.*) a variant of **grave.**

graff, *gräf, n.* and *vb.* an older form of **graft.**

graffito, *gräf-fē´tō, n.* (*ant.*) a mural scribbling or drawing, as by schoolboys and idlers at Pompeii, Rome, and other ancient cities: sgraffito:—*pl.* **graffiti** (*-fē´tē*). [It.,—Gr. *graphein,* to write.]

graft, *gräft, n.* a small piece of a plant or animal inserted in another individual or another part so as to come into organic union: the act of inserting a part in this way: the place of junction of stock and scion: the double plant composed of stock and scion: a sucker: a branch: a plant.—*v.t.* to insert a graft in: to insert as a graft: (*fig., arch.*) to cuckoldise.—*v.i.* to insert grafts.—*ns.* **graft´er; graft´-hy´brid,** a hybrid form produced, as some have bel:´ved, by grafting: a patchwork compound of two species propagated from the junction of tissues in a graft, each part retaining the specific character proper to the cells from which it arose; **graft´ing.** [From older **graff**—O.Fr. **graffe** (Fr. **greffe**)—L. *graphium*—Gr. *graphion, grapheion,* a style, pencil—*graphein,* to write.]

graft, *gräft, n.* (*dial.*) a ditch, excavation: a spade's depth: a ditching spade: (*slang*) hard work: a craft: a criminal's special branch of practice: (*U.S.*) illicit profit by corrupt means, esp. in public life: corruption in official life: thieving.—*v.i.* (*dial.*) to dig: (*slang*) to work hard: (*U.S.*) to engage in graft or corrupt practices.—*n.* **grafter.** [Cf. O.N. *gröftr,* digging: perh. the Amer. use may belong to **graft** (1).]

grail, *grāl, n.* gravel.—Also (*Spens.*) **graile, grayle.** [Perh. **gravel**; or O.Fr. *graile* (Fr. *grêle*), hail— L. *gracilis,* slender.]

grail. See **gradual.**

grail, *grāl, n.* in mediaeval legend, the platter used by Christ at the Last Supper, in which Joseph of Arimathaea caught his blood. — Also **graal, grayle.** [O.Fr. *graal* or *grael,* a flat dish—L.L. *gradāle,* a flat dish, ultimately from Gr. *krātēr,* a bowl.]

grain, *grān, n.* a single small hard seed: corn, in general: a hard particle: a very small quantity: the smallest British weight (the average weight of a seed of corn) $= \frac{1}{7000}$ of a pound avoirdupois: (in *pl.*) refuse malt after brewing or distilling: the arrangement and size of the particles, fibres, or plates of anything, as stone or wood: texture: a granular surface: dried bodies of kermes or of cochineal insects, once thought to be seeds: the red dye made from these: any fast dye—to *dye in grain* is to dye deeply, also to dye in the wool: dye in general: innate quality or character.—*v.t.* to form into grains, cause to granulate: to paint in imitation of grain: to dye in grain: in tanning, to take the hair off.—*n.* **grain´age,** duties on grain. —*adj.* **grained,** granulated: subjected to graining: having a grain: rough: furrowed.—*ns.* **grain´er,** one who grains: a paint-brush for graining; **grain´ing,** specif., painting to imitate the grain of wood: a process in tanning in which the grain of the leather is raised.—*adj.* **grain´y,** having grains or kernels.—**against the grain,** against the fibre of the wood—hence against the natural temper or inclination; **grains of Paradise,** the aromatic and pungent seeds of an African Amomum; **in grain,** in substance, in essence; **with a grain of salt,** with reservation, as of a story that cannot be admitted (L. *cum grānō salis*). [Fr. *grain,* collective *graine*—L. *grānum,* seed and *grāna,* orig. pl.; akin to **corn.**]

grain, *grān,* a branch: a prong: a fork: (in *pl.,* used as *sing.*) a kind of harpoon. [O.N. *grein.*]

graine, *grān, n.* silkworm eggs. [Fr.]

graining, *grān´ing, n.* dace (in Lancashire)—once thought a different species. [Origin unknown.]

graip, *grāp, n.* (*Scot.*) a three- or four-pronged fork used for lifting dung or digging potatoes. [A form of **grope**; cf. Sw. *grep,* Dan. *greb.*]

graith, *grāth, n.* apparatus: equipment.—*v.t.* (*Scot.*) to make ready, to dress. [O.N. *greithr,* ready; cf. O.E. *geréde,* ready.]

grakle. See **grackle.**

Grallae, *gral´ē,* **Grallatores,** *gral-ə-tō´rēz, ns.pl.* in old classifications, an order of wading birds.—*adj.* **grallato´rial.** [L. *grallātor,* a stilt-walker—*grallae,* stilts—*gradus,* a step.]

gralloch, *gral´əhh, n.* a deer's entrails.—*v.t.* to disembowel (deer). [Gael. *grealach.*]

gram, *gram, n.* (*obs.*) anger: (*arch.*) grief, trouble. [O.E. *grama,* anger.]

gram, *gram, n.* chick-pea: pulse generally. [Port. *grão* (*gram*)—L. *grānum,* a grain.]

gram, gramme, *gram, n.* the unit of mass in the metric system—formerly that of a cubic centimetre of water at 4° C., now a thousandth part of the International Prototype Kilogram (see **kilogram**). — *ns.* **gram´-at´om, gram´-mol´ecule,** the quantity of an element, a compound, whose mass in grams is equal to its atomic weight, molecular weight. [Fr. *gramme*—L. *gramma*—Gr. *gramma,* a letter, a small weight.]

grama, *grä´mä, n.* an American pasture grass (Bouteloua) with one-sided spikes. [Sp.,—L. *grāmen,* grass.]

gramary, gramarye, *gram´ə-ri, n.* magic: enchantment. [M.E. *gramery,* skill in grammar, hence magic; see **grammar, glamour.**]

gramercy, *grə-mər´si, interj.* (*arch.*) great thanks. —*n.* thanks. [O.Fr. *grammerci, grantmerci,* great thanks.]

gramicidin, *grə-mis´i-dēn, gram-i-sī´dēn, n.* an antibiotic obtained from certain bacteria, used against Gram-positive bacteria. — *adjs.* **Gramneg´ative** (*gram´-*), losing a stain of methyl violet and iodine on treatment with alcohol; **Grampos´itive,** retaining the stain. [H. J. C. *Gram,* deviser of the method, L. *caedēre,* to kill.]

Gramineae, *grə-, gra-, grā-min´i-ē, n.pl.* the grass family.—*adjs.* **graminā´ceous** (*gra-*), **gramin´eous; graminiv´orous,** grass-eating. [L. *grāmen, grāminis,* grass.]

grammalogue, *gram´ə-log, n.* a word represented by a single sign: a sign for a word in shorthand. [Gr. *gramma,* a letter, *logos,* a word.]

grammar, *gram´ər, n.* the science of language, from

the points of view of pronunciation, inflexion, syntax, and historic development : the art of the right use of language : a book that teaches these subjects : any elementary work.—*ns.* **gramma′-rian**, one versed in grammar, a teacher of or writer on grammar ; **gramm′ar-school**, a school in which grammar, *esp.* Latin grammar, is taught : a higher school, in which Latin and Greek are taught.—*adjs.* **grammat′ic, -al**, belonging to, or according to the rules of, grammar.—*adv.* **gram-mat′ically.**—*n.* **grammat′icaster**, a piddling grammarian.—*v.t.* **grammat′icise** (*-sīz*), to make grammatical.—*v.i.* to act the grammarian.—*ns.* **grammat′icism**, a point of grammar ; **gramm′-atist**, a grammarian. [Gr. *gramma, -atos,* a letter ; partly through O.Fr. *gramaire.*]

gramme. See **gram.**

gramoche, *gra-mosh′, n.* (*Scott*) a legging. [See **gamash.**]

gramophone, *gram′ə-fōn, n.* an instrument for recording and reproducing sounds by means of a disk—invented by E. Berliner.—*adj.* **gramo-phonic** (*-fon′ik*).—*adv.* **gramophon′ically.**—*ns.* **gramophonist** (*gram-of′ə-nist, gram′ə-fōn-ist*) ; **gramoph′ony.** [Ill formed from Gr. *gramma,* letter, record, *phōnē,* sound.]

grampus, *gram′pəs, n.* a popular name for many whales, *esp.* the killer : technically, Risso's dolphin (*Grampus griseus*) : one who puffs. [16th century *graundepose,* earlier *grapays*—O.Fr. *graspeis*—L. *crassus,* fat, *piscis,* fish, confused with Fr. *grand,* big.]

granadilla, *gran-ə-dil′ä,* **grenadilla,** *gren′, n.* an edible passion-flower fruit.—**granadilla tree,** the cocus-wood tree. [Sp.]

granary, *gran′ə-ri, n.* a storehouse for grain or threshed corn : (*fig.*) a rich grain-growing region. [L. *grānārium—grānum.*]

grand, *grand, adj.* pre-eminent : supreme : chief : main : exalted : magnificent : dignified : sublime : imposing : would-be imposing : on a great scale : in complete form : in full proportions : (in com-position) of the second degree of parentage or descent, as **grand′father,** a father's or mother's father (*adj.* **grand′fatherly**), **grand′child,** a son's or daughter's child ; so **grand′mother, grand′son, grand′daughter,** &c.—*n.* a grand piano : (*U.S. slang*) a thousand dollars.—*ns.* **grand-(d)ad,** an old man : a grandfather ; **gran′dam, grann′am,** an old dame or woman : a grand-mother ; **grand′-aunt,** a grandparent's sister, a great-aunt. — *adj.* **grand′-du′cal.** — *ns.* **grand′-duke′,** a title of sovereignty over a **grand′-duch′y,** first created by the Pope in 1569 for the rulers of Florence and Tuscany, assumed by certain German and Russian imperial princes (*fem.* **grand′-duch′ess**) ; **grandee′,** from the 13th century a noble of the most highly privileged class in the kingdom of Castile, the members of the royal family being included : a man of high rank or station ; **grandee′ship** ; **grandeur** (*grand′yər*), vastness : splendour of appearance : loftiness of thought or deportment ; **grand′father('s)-clock′,** an old-fashioned clock with a long case standing on the ground—larger than a **grand′mother-clock′** ; **grandil′oquence.**—*adj.* **grandil′oquent** (L. *loquēns, -entis,* speaking), speaking, expressed, grandly or bombastically—(*rare*) **grandil′oquous.** —*adv.* **grandil′oquently.**—*adj.* **gran′diose,** grand or imposing : bombastic.—*adv.* **gran′diosely.**— *ns.* **grandios′ity** ; **grand′-ju′ror,** member of a **grand′-ju′ry,** a special jury which (till 1933) decided whether there was sufficient evidence to put an accused person on trial.—*adv.* **grand′ly.** —*ns.* **grand′mamma, grand′ma,** a grandmother ; **Grand′-Mas′ter,** the head of a religious order of knighthood (Hospitallers, Templars, and Teutonic Knights), or of the Freemasons, &c.—*adj.* **grand′-motherly,** like a grandmother, over-anxious to direct the whole life of another.—*ns.* **grand′-neph′ew,** a great-nephew, the grandson of a brother or sister ; **grand′ness** ; **grand′-niece,** a great-niece, the granddaughter of a brother or sister ; **grand′papa, grand′pa,** a grandfather ; **grand′parent,** a grandfather or grandmother ;

grand′-pia′no, a large harp-shaped piano, with horizontal strings ; **grand′sire,** a grandfather : any ancestor ; **grand′-slam′,** the winning of every trick at bridge ; **grand′stand,** an elevated erection on a racecourse, &c., affording a good view ; **grand′-un′cle,** the brother of a grandfather or grandmother—also **great′-un′cle.—grand con-cert,** one that need not be taken too seriously ; **grand opera,** one without spoken dialogue ; **grand style,** a style adapted to lofty or sublime subjects ; **grand total,** the sum of all subordinate sums. [Fr. *grand*—L. *grandis,* great.]

Grandisonian, *gran-di-sō′ni-ən, adj.* like the novelist Richardson's hero, Sir Charles *Grandison,* benefi-cent, polite, and chivalrous.

granfer, *gran′fər, n.* (*prov.*) a contracted form of grandfather.

grange, *grānj, n.* (*Milt.*) a granary : a farm-house with its stables and other buildings : a country house : (*Spens.*) an abiding place : (*U.S.*) a lodge of the order of Patrons of Husbandry.—*n.* **gran′ger,** the keeper of a grange : a member of a grange. [O.Fr. *grange,* barn—L.L. *grānea*—L. *grānum,* grain.]

Grangerism, *grān′jər-izm, n.* the practice of cutting plates and title-pages out of many books to illus-trate one book.—*v.t.* **gran′gerise,** to practise Grangerism on. [From James *Granger* (1716-76), whose *Biographical History of England* (1769) gave an impetus to this.]

granite, *gran′it, n.* a coarse-grained igneous crystal-line rock, composed of quartz, felspar, and mica. —*adj.* of granite : hard like granite.—*adj.* **granit′ic,** pertaining to, consisting of, or like granite.—*n.* **granitifica′tion.**—*adj.* **granit′iform.**—*n.* **gran′-itite,** muscovite granite.—*adj.* **gran′itoid,** of the form of or resembling granite.—*n.* **granodi′-orite,** a rock resembling diorite but containing quartz.—*adj.* **granolith′ic** (Gr. *lithos,* stone), com-posed of cement and granite chips.—Also *n.*—*n.* **gran′ophyre** (*-fīr* ; with *-phyre* after *porphyry*), a quartz-porphyry with graphic intergrowth of quartz and orthoclase for groundmass.—*adj.* **granophyric** (*-fir′ik, -fīr′ik*). [It. *granito,* granite, lit. grained— L. *grānum,* grain.]

granivorous, *gran-iv′ər-əs, adj.* grain-eating : feed-ing on seeds. [L. *grānum,* grain, *vorāre,* to devour.]

grannam, *gran′əm, n.* (*arch.*) a grandmother.—*n.* **grann′y, grann′ie,** a grandmother : an old woman : an old-womanish person : a revolving cap on a chimney-pot.—*n.* **grann′y-knot,** a knot like a reef-knot, but unsymmetrical, apt to slip or jam. [grandam.]

grant, *grânt, v.t.* to bestow : to admit as true : to concede.—*v.i.* (*Shak.*) to consent.—*n.* a bestowing : something bestowed, an allowance : a gift : (*Eng. law*) conveyance of property by deed.—*adj.* **grant′-able.**—*ns.* **grantee′,** (*law*) the person to whom a grant, gift, or conveyance is made ; **grant′er, grant′or** (*law*), the person by whom ⌐ grant or conveyance is made.—**take for granted,** to pre-suppose, assume, esp. tacitly or unconsciously. [O.Fr. *graanter, craanter, creanter,* to promise— L. *crēdĕre,* to believe.]

Granth, *grunt, n.* the holy book of the Sikhs. [Hind.]

granule, *gran′ūl, n.* a little grain : a fine particle.— *adjs.* **gran′ular, gran′ulary, gran′ulose, gran′-ulous,** consisting of or like grains or granules.— *adv.* **gran′ularly.**—*v.t.* **gran′ulate,** to form or break into grains or small masses : to make rough on the surface.—*v.i.* to be formed into grains.— *adj.* **gran′ular :** having the surface covered with small elevations.—*n.* **granūlā′tion,** act of forming into grains, esp. of metals by pouring them through a sieve into water while hot : (*pl.*) the materials of new texture as first formed in a wound or on an ulcerated surface.—*adjs.* **granūlif′erous ; gran′-ūliform.**—*n.* **gran′ūlite,** a schistose but sometimes massive aggregate of quartz and felspar with garnets : a granular-textured metamorphic rock.— *adj.* **granūlit′ic,** of the texture of granulite.—*n.* **granūlitisā′tion,** reduction of the components of a rock to crystalline grains by regional meta-morphism. [L. *grānulum,* dim. of *grānum,* grain.]

grape, *grāp, v.i.* a Scottish form of **grope.**

grape, *grāp, n.* the fruit of the grape-vine : a mangy tumour on the legs of horses : grapeshot.—*ns.* **grape'-fruit,** a fine variety of the shaddock, the pompelmoose, with sometimes a slightly grapelike taste ; **grape'-hy'acinth,** (Muscari) a near ally to the hyacinth, with clusters of small grapelike flowers.—*adj.* **grape'less,** without the flavour of the grape, said of wine.—*ns.* **grape'-louse** (see **phylloxera**) ; **grap'ery,** a place where grapes are grown ; **grape'seed,** the seed of the vine ; **grape'seed-oil,** an oil expressed from it ; **grape'-shot,** shot that scatters ; **grape'-stone,** the pip of the grape ; **grape'-su'gar,** glucose or dextrose ; **grape'tree,** a tropical American tree (*Coccoloba uvifera*) of the dock family, or its edible fruit ; **grape'-vine,** *Vitis vinifera* or other species of *Vitis.*—*adj.* **grap'y,** made of or like grapes.—**sour grapes,** things decried because they cannot be attained (from Aesop's fable of the fox and the grapes).—See also **Ephedra.** [O.Fr. *grape, grappe,* a cluster of grapes—*grape,* a hook ; orig. Gmc.]

graph, *grāf, n.* a symbolic diagram : a curve representing the variation of a quantity : -**graph,** is used as a terminal in many Greek compounds to denote an agent that writes, records, &c., as *telegraph, seismograph,* or the thing written, as in *autograph,* &c.—*adjs.* **graphic** (*graf'ik*), **-al,** pertaining to writing, describing, delineating, or diagrammatic representation : picturesquely described or describing : vivid.—*adv.* **graph'ically.** —*ns.* **graph'icness** ; **graph'ics,** the art or science of mathematical drawing, and of calculating stresses, &c., by geometrical methods ; **Graph'is,** a genus of lichens, with fructifications like writing ; **graph'ite,** a mineral, commonly called blacklead or plumbago, though composed of carbon.—*adjs.* **graphit'ic, graph'itoid.**—*v.t.* **graph'itise,** to convert wholly or partly into graphite.—*ns.* **graph'ium,** a stylus ; **graphol'ogy,** the art of estimating character, &c., from handwriting.—**graphic arts,** painting, drawing, engraving, as opposed to music, sculpture, &c. ; **graphic formula,** a chemical formula in which the symbols for single atoms are joined by lines representing valency bonds ; **graphic granite,** a granite with markings like Hebrew characters, owing to intergrowth of quartz and felspar. [Gr. *graphē,* a writing—*graphein,* to write.]

grapnel, *grap'nǝl, n.* a small anchor with several claws or arms : a grappling-iron : a hooking or grasping instrument. [Dim. of O.Fr. *grapin*—*grape,* a hook ; of Gmc. origin.]

grapple, *grap'l, n.* an instrument for hooking or holding : a grasp, grip, hold, or clutch : a state of being held or clutched.—*v.t.* to seize : to lay fast hold of.—*v.i.* to contend in close fight.—Also (*Spens.*) **graple.**—*ns.* **graplement,** (*Spens.*) a grappling, close fight ; **grapp'le-plant',** a S. African plant (*Harpagophytum procumbens*) of the sesame family, with strongly hooked fruits ; **grapp'ling-i'ron,** an instrument for grappling : a large grapnel for seizing hostile ships in naval engagements. [Cf. O.Fr. *grappil*—*grape,* a hook.]

graptolite, *grap'tǝ-līt, n.* one of a group of fossil Hydrozoa with one or two rows of hydrothecae on a simple or branched polypary—characteristic Silurian fossils like writing upon shales.—*adj.* **graptolit'ic.** [Gr. *graptos,* written, *graphein,* to write, *lithos,* a stone.]

grasp, *grāsp, v.t.* to seize and hold : to comprehend.—*v.i.* to endeavour to seize : to catch (with *at, after*).—*n.* grip : power of seizing : mental power of apprehension.—*adj.* **grasp'able.**—*n.* **grasp'er.** — *adj.* **grasp'ing,** seizing : avaricious. — *adv.* **grasp'ingly.** — *n.* **grasp'ingness.** — *adj.* **grasp'less,** feeble, relaxed. [M.E. *graspen, grapsen,* from the root of *grápian,* to grope.]

grass, *grās, n.* common herbage : any plant of the monocotyledonous family Gramineae, the most important to man in the vegetable kingdom, with long, narrow leaves and tubular stems, including wheat and other cereals, reeds (but not sedges), bamboo, sugar-cane : pasture grasses : pasturage : time of grass, spring or summer : the surface of a mine.—*v.t.* to cover with grass : to feed with grass : to bring to the grass or ground.—*ns.* **grass'-cloth,** a name for various coarse cloths rarely made of grass, esp. ramie ; **grass'-cloth-plant',** ramie ; **grass'-cutter,** a mowing machine : in India, one who provides provender for baggage-cattle (perh. really Hindustani *ghāskatā*) ; **grass'er,** an extra or temporary worker in a printing-office.—*adjs.* **grass'-green,** green with grass : green as grass ; **grass'-grown,** grown over with grass.—*ns.* **grass'hopper,** a name for various saltatorial, orthopterous insects akin to locusts and crickets, that lurk among grass and chirp by rubbing their wing-covers ; **grass'iness ; grass'ing,** bleaching by exposure on grass ; **grass'land,** permanent pasture ; **grass'-moth,** a small light-coloured moth that frequents grass, a veneer-moth ; **grass'-of-Parnass'us** (see **Parnassus**) ; **grass'-oil,** a name for several volatile oils derived from widely different plants, some of them grasses ; **grass'-plot,** a plot of grassy ground ; **grass'-snake,** the harmless common ringed snake ; **grass'-tree,** an Australian plant (Xanthorrhoea) of the lily family, with shrubby stems, tufts of long wiry foliage at the summit, and a tall flower-stalk, with a dense cylindrical spike of small flowers ; **grass'-wid'ow,** a wife temporarily separated from or deserted by her husband ; **grass'-wrack,** eel-grass. — *adj.* **grass'y,** covered with or resembling grass, green.— **go to grass,** to be turned out to pasture, esp. of a horse too old to work : to go into retirement, to rusticate : to fall violently (of a pugilist) ; **let the grass grow under one's feet,** to loiter, linger. [O.E. *gærs, græs* ; O.N., Ger., Du., and Goth. *gras* ; prob. allied to **green** and **grow**.]

grass, *grās, n.* for **sparr'ow-grass,** a corruption of **asparagus.**

grassum, *gräs'ǝm, n.* (*Scots law*) a lump sum paid by persons who take a lease of landed property— in England, 'premium' and 'fine.' [O.E. *gærsum,* treasure, rich gift, &c.]

graste, *grāst,* (*Spens.*) pa.p. of **grace.**

grate, *grāt, n.* a framework of bars with interstices, esp. one for holding a fire or for looking through a door, &c. : a cage : a grid.—*adj.* **grāt'ed,** having a grating.—*ns.* **graticulā'tion** (*gra- or grǝ-tik-ū-lā'shǝn*), the division of a design into squares for convenience in making an enlarged or diminished copy ; **graticule** (*grat'i-kūl*), a ruled grating for identification of points in a map, the field of a telescope, &c. ; **grāt'ing,** the bars of a grate : a perforated cover for a drain or the like : a partition or frame of bars : a surface ruled closely with fine lines to give a diffraction spectrum. [L.L. *grāta,* a grate— L. *crātis,* a hurdle ; see **crate**.]

grate, *grāt, v.t.* to rub hard or wear away with anything rough : to irritate or jar on : to fret into anger or sorrow : to grind jarringly : to emit or utter jarringly.—*v.i.* to make a harsh sound : to jar : to be jarred : to fret.—*n.* **grat'er,** an instrument with a rough surface for pulverising.—*adj.* **grāt'ing,** rubbing hard on the feelings : harsh : irritating. — *adv.* **grāt'ingly.** [O.Fr. *grater,* through L.L., from O.H.G. *chrazzōn* (Ger. *kratzen*), to scratch, akin to Sw. *kratta.*]

grateful, *grāt'fǝl, adj.* causing pleasure : acceptable : delightful : thankful : having a due sense of benefits.—*adv.* **grate'fully.**—*ns.* **grate'fulness ; gratificā'tion** (*grat-*), a pleasing or indulging : that which gratifies : delight, feeling of satisfaction : a recompense, tip, or bribe ; **grat'ifier.**—*v.t.* **grat'ify,** to do what is agreeable to : to please : to soothe : to indulge :—*pr.p.* **grat'ifying ;** *pa.t.* and *pa.p.* **grat'ified.** — *adj.* **grat'ifying.** — *adv.* **grat'ifyingly.** [O.Fr. *grat*—L. *grātus,* pleasing, thankful.]

graticule. See **grate** (1).

gratility, *grǝ-til'i-ti, n.* (*Shak.*) a small gratuity.

gratis, *grā'tis, adv.* for nothing : without payment or recompense. [L. *grātīs,* contr. of *grātiīs,* abl. pl. of *grātia,* favour—*grātus.*]

gratitude, *grat'i-tūd, n.* warm and friendly feeling towards a benefactor : thankfulness. [Fr.,—L.L. *grātitūdō*—L. *grātus.*]

grattoir, *grät-wär, n.* (*archaeol.*) a scraper. [Fr.]

gratuity, *grǝ-tū'i-ti, n.* a present : an acknowledg-

ment of service, usu. pecuniary : a tip : a bounty : a payment to a soldier on discharge, &c.— *adj.* **gratū′itous,** done or given for nothing : voluntary : (*law*) benefiting one party only : without reason, ground, or proof : uncalled for.—*adv.* **gratū′-itously.** [Fr. *gratuité*—L.L. *grātuitās, -ātis*—L. *grātus.*]
gratulatory, *grat′ū-lə-tər-i,* or *-lā-,* adj. congratulatory. — *adj.* **grat′ūlant,** congratulatory. — *v.t.* **grat′ūlate,** to congratulate : to welcome : to express joy at.—*adj.* (*Shak.*) gratifying.—*n.* **gratūlā′tion,** congratulation.
gravamen, *grəv-ā′men, n.* grievance : the substantial or chief ground of complaint or accusation : a statement of abuses grievances, &c., sent by the Lower to the Upper House of Convocation : —*pl.* **gravā′mina.** [L. *gravāmen*—*gravis,* heavy.]
grave, *grāv, v.t.* (*obs.*) to dig : to carve or cut on a hard substance : to engrave : (*obs.*) to bury.—*v.i.* to engrave : (*pa.p.* **graved** or **grav′en**).—*n.* a pit graved or dug out, esp. one to bury the dead in : any place of burial : (*B.*) the abode of the dead : (*fig.*) death, destruction : a deadly place.—*n.pl.* **grave′-clothes,** the clothes in which the dead are buried. — *n.* **grave′-digger.** — *adj.* **grave′less** (*Shak.*).—*ns.* **grave′-maker,** (*Shak.*) a grave-digger ; **grav′er,** an engraver : a burin ; **grave′-stone,** a stone placed as a memorial at a grave ; **grave′yard,** a burial-ground ; **grav′ing.—with one foot in the grave,** on the brink of death. [O.E. *grafan,* to dig, *græf,* a cave, grave, trench ; Du. *graven,* Ger. *graben.*]
grave, *grāv, v.t.* to clean (by burning, &c.) and pay with tar (a wooden ship's bottom).—*n.* **grav′ing-dock,** a dry-dock for cleaning and repair of ships. [Perh. Fr. *grave, grève,* beach.]
grave, *grāv, adj.* of importance : serious : not gay or showy : sedate : sober : solemn : weighty : calling for anxiety : low in pitch.—*n.* grave accent.—*adv.* **grave′ly.** — *n.* **grave′ness.** — **grave accent,** a mark (‵), originally indicating a pitch falling somewhat, or failing to rise, now used for various purposes. [Fr.,—L. *gravis.*]
grave, *grāv, n.* a count, prefect, a person holding office (now only in compounds, as *landgrave, margrave, burgrave*). [Du. *graaf,* Ger. *graf.*]
gravel, *grav′l, n.* an assemblage of small rounded stones : small collections of gravelly matter in the kidneys or bladder.—*v.t.* to cover with gravel : to run aground on gravel : to impede with gravel : to puzzle, perplex :—*pr.p.* **grav′elling** ; *pa.t.* and *pa.p.* **grav′elled.**—*adjs.* **grav′el-blind** or **high′-gravel-blind′,** after Shakespeare, punningly, between sand-blind and stone-blind ; **grav′elly.**—*ns.* **grav′el-pit,** a pit from which gravel is dug ; **grav′el-walk′,** a footpath covered with gravel. [O.Fr. *gravele* (Fr. *gravier*) ; prob. Celt., as in Bret. *grouan,* sand, W. *gro,* pebbles.]
graven, *grāv′n, pa.p.* of **grave,** to carve, engrave.
graveolent, *grəv-ē′ō-lənt,* or *grav′i-,* rank-smelling. [L. *graveolēns, -ēntis*—*gravis,* heavy, *olēns,* pr.p. of *olēre,* to smell.]
graves. Same as **greaves.**
gravid, *grav′id, adj.* pregnant.—*n.* **gravid′ity.** [L. *gravidus*—*gravis,* heavy.]
gravimeter, *grə-vim′i-tər, n.* a kind of hydrometer. —*adjs.* **gravimetric** (*grav-i-met′rik*), **-al,** pertaining to measurement by weight.—*n.* **gravim′etry.** [L. *gravis,* heavy, Gr. *metron,* measure.]
gravity, *grav′i-ti, n.* weightiness : gravitational attraction or acceleration : graveness : lowness of pitch.—*v.i.* **grav′itāte,** to be acted on by gravity : to tend towards the earth or other body : to be attracted, or move, by force of gravitation : to sink or settle down : to be strongly attracted towards anything.—*n.* **gravitā′tion,** act of gravitating : the force of attraction between bodies, the acceleration being directly proportional to the product of the masses and inversely to the square of the distances.—*adjs.* **gravitā′tional** ; **grav′itā-tive.** — **specific gravity** (see **specific**). [L. *gravitās, -ātis*—*gravis,* heavy.]
gravy, *grāv′i, n.* the juices from meat while cooking. —*ns.* **grav′y-boat,** a vessel for gravy ; **grav′y-soup,** soup like gravy, made from fresh meat.

[Perh. *gravé,* a copyist's mistake for O.F. *grané*—*grain,* a cookery ingredient.]
gray. Same as **grey.**—*ns.* **gray′fly,** (*Milt.*) an unknown insect ; **gray′ling,** a silvery-grey fish (Thymallus) of the salmon family, with a smaller mouth and teeth, and larger scales : a grey butterfly of the Satyridae.
grayle. See **grail** (1) and (3).
graywacke. Same as **greywacke.**
graze, *grāz, v.t.* to eat or feed on (growing grass or pasture) : to feed or supply with grass.—*v.i.* to eat grass : to supply grass.—*ns.* **graz′er,** an animal that grazes ; **gra′zier,** one who pastures cattle and rears them for the market ; **graz′ing,** the act of feeding on grass : the feeding or raising of cattle. [O.E. *grasian*—*græs,* grass.]
graze, *grāz, v.t.* to pass lightly along the surface of.—*n.* a passing touch or scratch. [Ety. dub. ; perhaps only a special use of **graze** above ; perh. from *rase* (Fr. *raser*), the *g* due to the analogy of *grate.*]
grease, *grēs, n.* soft thick animal fat : oily matter of any kind : condition of fatness : an inflammation in the heels of a horse, marked by swelling, &c.—*v.t.* (sometimes pron. *grēz*) to smear with grease : to lubricate.—*ns.* **grease′-gun,** a lubricating pump ; **grease′-heels,** grease in horses ; **grease′-paint,** a tallowy composition used by actors in making up.—*adj.* **grease′-proof,** resistant or impermeable to grease.—*ns.* **greaser** (*grēs′ər,* or *grēz′ər*), one who greases : (*U.S. slang*) a Mexican or a Spanish American ; **grease′wood,** a name for various oily American shrubs of the goosefoot family.—*adv.* **greas′ily.**—*n.* **greas′iness.**—*adj.* **greas′y** (sometimes *grēz′i*), of or like grease or oil : smeared with grease : having a slippery coating : fatty : oily : obscene.—**grease one's palm,** to bribe ; **hart of grease,** a fat hart. [O.Fr. *gresse,* fatness, *gras,* fat—L. *crassus.*]
great, *grāt, adj.* big : large : of a high degree of magnitude of any kind : capital (of letters) : elevated in power, rank, station, &c. : pre-eminent in genius : highly gifted : chief : sublime : weighty : outstanding : pregnant, teeming : swelling with emotion : much addicted or given to, or excelling in the thing in question : favourite : habitual : in high favour or intimacy : in a high degree : on a large scale : (*slang*) excellent : in composition indicating one degree more remote in the direct line of descent (as **great′-grand′father, great′-grand′son,** and similarly **great′-great′-grand-father,** and so indefinitely).—*n.* bulk, mass : whole : wholesale.—*n.* **great′-aunt,** a grand-parent's sister. —*adjs.* **great′-bellied,** (*Shak.*) pregnant ; **great′-circle,** of or along a great circle of the earth (see **circle**).—*n.* **great′coat,** an overcoat.—*v.t.* **great′en,** to make great or greater.—*v.i.* to become great.—*adj.* **great′er,** comp. of **great** : (with geographical names) in an extended sense (as *Greater Britain,* Britain and the dominions ; *Greater London*).—*ns.* **great′-grand′child,** the child of a grandchild ; **great′-grand′mother,** the mother of a grandparent.—*adj.* **great′-hearted,** having a great or noble heart : high-spirited : magnanimous.—*adv.* **great′ly.**—*ns.* **great′-nephew, -niece,** a brother's or sister's grandson, granddaughter ; **great′ness ;** **great′-prim′er** (see **primer**).—*n.pl.* **Greats,** the final honour School of Literae Humaniores (*Classical Greats*) or of Modern Philosophy (*Modern Greats*) at Oxford.—*n.* **great′-uncle,** a grand-parent's brother.—**Great Dane,** a large close-haired dog ; **great schism,** the division between the Latin and Greek Churches, culminating in 1054 ; **Great Sea,** the Mediterranean ; **great unwashed,** a contemptuous term for the populace. [O.E. *gréat ;* Du. *groot,* Ger. *gross.*]
greave, *grēv, n.* (*Spens.*) a thicket. [O.E. *græfa, græfe ;* cf. **grove.**]
greave. See **grieve.**
greave, *grēv, n.* armour for the leg below the knee. [O.Fr. *greve,* shin, greave.]
greaves, *grēvz,* **graves,** *grāvz, n.pl.* dregs of melted tallow. [L.G. *greven ;* cf. Ger. *griebe,* greaves ; O.E. *gréofa,* pot.]
grebe, *grēb, n.* a short-winged almost tailless freshwater diving bird (Podiceps). [Fr. *grèbe.*]

grece. See gree (2).

Grecian, *grēsh'(y)ən, adj.* Greek.—*n.* a Greek: one well versed in the Greek language and literature: (*B.*) a hellenising Jew: a senior boy of Christ's Hospital: (*slang*) an Irish labourer newly over.—**Grecian bend,** a foolish mode of walking with a slight bend forward, at one time affected by a few women who fondly thought to imitate the pose of a figure like the Venus of Milo. [L. *Graecia,* Greece —Gr. *Graikos,* Greek.]

grecise, grecism, greco-roman. See graecise, &c.

grecque, *grek, n.* a Greek fret. [Fr. (*fem.*), Greek.]

gree, *grē, n.* (*Spens.*) good-will, favour.—*v.i.* (*Shak., Scot.*) to agree. [O.Fr. *gré*—L. *grātus,* pleasing; the vb. may be from O.Fr. *gréer* or aphetic from agree.]

gree, *grē, n.* degree, rank: a step: superiority: victory: prize.—*n.* grece (*grēs, obs.* or *dial.*; from the Fr. plur.), a flight of steps: a step: a degree— also spelt **grees, grese, greece, greese, grice, griece, grise, grize** (grees'ing, grees'ing, and even **grē'cian,** are obs. forms).—*adj.* **grieced,** having steps. [O.Fr. *gré*—L. *gradus*; see grade.]

greedy, *grēd'i, adj.* having a voracious appetite: inordinately desirous of increasing one's own share: covetous: eagerly desirous.—*n.* **greed,** an eager desire or longing: covetousness.—*adv.* **greed'ily.** —*n.* **greed'iness.** [O.E. *grǣdig*; Du. *gretig.*]

Greek, *grēk, adj.* of Greece, its people, or its language.—*n.* a native or citizen of Greece, of a Greek state, or of a colony elsewhere of a Greek state: the language of Greece: a member of the Greek Church: (*B.*) a hellenising Jew: a cunning rogue, a merry fellow: (*slang*) an Irishman: any language of which one is ignorant, jargon, anything unintelligible.—*n.* **Greek'dom,** the Greek world: a Greek community.—*adjs.* **Greek'ish; Greek'- less,** without knowledge of Greek.—*n.* **Greek'ling,** a contemptible Greek.—**the Greek calends,** never, the Greeks having no calends; **Greek architecture,** that developed in ancient Greece (Corinthian, Doric, Ionic); **Greek Church,** the church that follows the ancient rite of the East and accepts the first seven councils, rejecting papal supremacy—(*Greek*) *Orthodox* or *Eastern* Church; **Greek cross,** an upright cross with arms of equal length; **Greek fire,** a composition that took fire when wetted, used in war, long a secret of the Byzantine Greeks; **Greek gift,** a treacherous gift (from Virgil's *Aeneid,* ii. 49); **Greek nose,** a straight nose. [O.E. *Grécas, Crécas,* Greeks, or L. *Graecus*—Gr. *Graikos,* Greek.]

green, *grēn, adj.* of the colour usual in leaves, be-tween blue and yellow in the spectrum: growing: vigorous: hale: new: young: unripe: fresh: undried: raw: incompletely prepared: immature: unseasoned: inexperienced: easily imposed on.— *n.* the colour of green things: a grassy plat, esp. that common to a village or town or for bowling, bleaching, drying of clothes: a golf-course: the prepared ground (*putting-green*) round a golf-hole: a green pigment: (*pl., U.S.*) fresh leaves: green vegetables for food, esp. of the cabbage kind: (**Greens**) a political party at Constantinople, under Justinian, opposed to the Blues.—*v.t.* and *v.i.* to make or become green.—*ns.* **green'back,** an American note (often printed in green on the back), first issued in 1862; **green'-bag,** a lawyer's bag: (*old slang*) a lawyer; **green'-bone,** a gar-fish: a viviparous blenny; **green'-bottle,** a metallic green fly (Lucilia); **green'-cloth,** a gaming-table: a department of the royal household chiefly concerned with the commissariat—from the green cloth on the table round which its officials sat; **green'-crop,** a crop of green vegetables, as grasses, turnips, &c.; **green'-drag'on,** a European aroid (Dracunculus): (*U.S.*) dragon-root; **green'- drake,** a mayfly; **green'-earth,** glauconite or similar green earthy mineral, used as a pigment; **green'ery,** green plants or boughs: verdure.—*adjs.* **green'ery-yall'ery,** in or favouring greens and yellows, hence decadently aesthetic; **green'-eyed,** having green eyes: (*fig.*) jealous (**green-eyed monster,** jealousy).—*ns.* **green'finch, green**

linnet, a finch of a green colour, with some grey and brown; **green'-fly,** a plant-louse or aphis; **green'-goose,** a young goose: a simpleton; **green'grocer,** a dealer in fresh vegetables; **green'-hand,** an inferior sailor; **green'-heart,** bebeeru (*Nectandra Rodiei*), a S. American tree of the laurel family with very hard wood; **green'- horn,** a raw, inexperienced youth; **green'house,** a glass-house for plants, esp. one with little or no artificial heating; **green'ing, a** becoming or making green: a kind of apple green when ripe.— *adj.* **green'ish.**—*ns.* **green'ishness; green'- keeper,** one who has the care of a golf-course or bowling-green: **green'let,** any bird of the American family Vireonidae.—*adv.* **green'ly,** immaturely, unskilfully.—*ns.* **green'ness; green'room,** the retiring-room of actors in a theatre, which origin-ally had the walls coloured green; **green'sand,** a sandstone containing much glauconite: **Green-sand,** two divisions (Lower and Upper) of the Cretaceous system, separated by the Gault; **green'shank,** a large sandpiper with long, some-what greenish legs; **green'-sickness,** chlorosis; **green'-snake,** a harmless colubrine snake com-mon in the southern United States; **green'stone,** nephrite: a vague name for any compost basic or intermediate igneous rock; **green'-stuff,** green vegetables, esp. of the cabbage kind; **green'sward,** sward or turf green with grass; **green'-tea** (see tea); **greenth,** greenness, verdure; **green'- tur'tle** (see turtle); **green'-vit'riol,** ferrous sulphate; **green'-weed,** a name given to certain half-shrubby species of Genista; **green'wood,** a leafy wood or forest: wood newly cut.—Also *adj.* —*adj.* **green'y.**—**green algae** or **seaweeds,** the Chlorophyceae; **green in my eye,** mark of credulity; **Green,** or **Emerald, Isle,** Ireland; **green flash** or **ray,** a flash of green light sometimes seen at the moment of sunrise or sunset; **green fingers** (or **thumb**), a knack of making plants grow well; **green gown,** a roll on the grass (sometimes but not always understood to imply loss of virginity); **green-stick fracture,** a fracture where the bone is partly broken, partly bent, occurring in limbs of children. [O.E. *gréne*; Ger. *grün,* Du. *groen,* green; O.N. *grœnn.*]

green, grein, *grēn, v.i.* (*Scot.*) to long, yearn. [Cf. O.N. *girna.*]

greengage, *grēn'gāj', n.* a green and very sweet variety of plum. [Said to be named from Sir W. *Gage* of Hengrave Hall, near Bury, before 1725.]

greenockite, *grēn'ak-īt, n.* a rare mineral, cadmium sulphide, discovered by Lord *Greenock* (1783–1859), Earl Cathcart.

greese, greesing. See gree (2).

greet, *grēt, v.t.* to accost with salutation or kind wishes: to send kind wishes to: to congratulate: (*Spens.*) to offer congratulations on: to meet, become evident to.—*v.i.* to meet and salute:— *pr.p.* **greet'ing;** *pa.p.* **greet'ed.**—*n.* **greet'ing,** expression of kindness or joy: salutation. [O.E. *grétan,* to greet, to meet; Du. *groeten,* Ger. *grüssen,* to salute.]

greet, *grēt, v.i.* (*Scot.; Spens.* **greete**) to weep (*pa.t., Scot.,* **grat;** *pa.p., Scot.,* **grutt'en**).—*n.* weeping: a spell of weeping.—**greeting meeting** the last meeting of a town-council before an election. [O.E. (Anglian) *grétan*; Goth. *grétan.*]

greffier, *gref'yā, n.* a registrar: a notary. [Fr.]

gregale, *grā-gä'lā, n.* a north-east wind in the Mediterranean. [It.,—L. *graecus,* Greek.]

gregarious, *gri-gā'ri-əs, adj.* associating in flocks and herds: (*bot.*) growing together but not matted. —*adj.* **gregā'rian,** of the common rank.—*ns.* **gregā'rianism,** gregariousness; **Gregarina** (*greg-ə-rī'nä*), a genus of Protozoa, typical of the **Grega-rinida** (*-rin'*), a group of parasites; **greg'arine** (*-rīn, -rin*), a member of the Gregarinida.—*adv.* **gregā'riously.**—*n.* **gregā'riousness.** [L. *gregā-rius*—*grex,* gregis, a flock.]

grego, *grā'gō, grē'gō, n.* a Levantine hooded jacket or cloak: an overcoat. [Port. *grego* or other deriv. of L. *graecus,* Greek.]

Gregorian, *gri-gō'ri-ən, adj.* belonging to or estab-lished by *Gregory*—as the Gregorian chant or tones, introduced by Pope Gregory I. (6th cent.), the calendar, reformed by Gregory XIII. (1582), the reflecting telescope of James Gregory (1638-75), a wig attributed to a barber Gregory.—*n.* a follower of any Gregory: a member of an 18th-century English brotherhood.—*n.* **gregory** (*greg'ər-i* ; *coll.*), **Gregory's mixture or powder,** rhubarb, magnesia and ginger, compounded by Dr. James *Gregory* (1753-1821), great-grandson of the first James.

greisen, *grī'zən, n.* a rock composed of quartz and mica, often with topaz, formed from granite by fluorine exhalations.—*v.t.* **greisenīsā'tion. — *v.t.* greis'enise.** [Ger.]

greisly (*Spens., Milt.*). Same as **grisly.**

gremial, *grē'mi-əl, adj.* pertaining to the lap or bosom: intimate: resident: in full membership. —*n.* a full or resident member: a cloth laid on a bishop's knees to keep his vestments clean from oil at ordinations. [L. *gremium,* the lap.]

gremlin, *grem'lin, n.* a goblin accused of vexing airmen.

gren, *gren, v.i.* (*Spens.*). Same as **grin.**

grenade, *gri-nād', n.* a small bomb thrown by the hand or shot from a rifle: a glass projectile containing chemicals for putting out fires, testing drains, &c.—*ns.* **grenadier** (*gren-ə-dēr'*), orig. a soldier who threw grenades: then, a member of the first company of every battalion of foot: now used as the title of the first regiment of foot-guards (Grenadier Guards); **grenadine** (*-dēn'*), a pomegranate (or other) syrup. [Fr., — Sp. *granada,* pomegranate—L. *grānātus,* full of seeds (*grāna*).]

grenadilla, *gren-ə-dil'ä.* Same as **granadilla.**

grenadine. See under **grenade.**

grenadine, *gren'ə-dēn, n.* a thin silk or mixed fabric. [Fr., perh. *Granada.*]

gressorial, *gres-ō'ri-əl, adj.* adapted for walking. [L. *gressus,* pa.p. of *gradī,* to walk.]

greve, a variant of **greave.**

grew, *grōō, pa.t.* of **grow.**

grew. See **gruesome.**

grew, *grōō,* **grewhound,** *grōō'hownd, ns.* a greyhound. [By confusion with obs. *Grew,* Greek.]

grey, gray, *grā, adj.* of a mixture of black and white with little or no hue: dull: grey-haired, old, mature.—*n.* a grey colour: a grey or greyish animal, esp. a horse: (*obs.*) a badger.—*v.t.* to make grey or dull.—*v.i.* to become grey or dull.—*ns.* **grey'beard,** one whose beard is grey: an old man: a stoneware jar for liquor, a bellarmine; **grey'coat,** one who wears a grey coat, esp. a pupil in certain schools: a Confederate soldier.—Also *adj.* —*adjs.* **grey'-coat'ed; grey'-eyed.**—*ns.* **grey'fish,** a dogfish: a young coalfish; **Grey'-Fri'ar,** a Franciscan; **grey'-goose, grey'lag,** the common wild goose (perh. from its lateness in migrating).— *adjs.* **grey'-haired, grey'-headed.**—*n.* **grey'hen,** the female of the blackcock.—*adj.* **grey'ish,** somewhat grey.—*adv.* **grey'ly.**—*ns.* **grey'ness; grey'weth'er,** a block of sandstone or quartzite, a relic of denudation, like a grazing sheep at a distance.— **grey-goose quill, shaft, wing,** an arrow; **grey mare** (see **mare**); **grey matter,** the ashen grey active part of the brain and spinal cord; **grey owl,** the tawny owl; **grey parrot,** a red-tailed grey African parrot; **grey squirrel,** a N. American squirrel naturalised in Britain; **grey wolf,** the N. American timber wolf; **the Greys,** the Scots Greys (see **Scot**). [O.E. *græg;* cf. Ger. *grau.*]

greyhound, *grā'hownd, n.* a tall and slender dog with great speed and keen sight. [O.E. *grīghund* (cf. O.N. *greyhundr*—grey, bitch), *hund,* dog.]

greywacke, *grā-wak'i, n.* an indurated sedimentary rock composed of grains (round or angular) and splinters of quartz, felspar, slate, &c., in a hard matrix.—*n.* **greywack'e-slate',** a fine-grained fissile greywacke. [Ger. *grauwacke,* partly translated, partly adopted.]

grice, *grīs, n.* a little pig:—*pl.* **grices, grice.** [O.N. *gríss.*]

grice. See **gree** (2).

grid. See **gridiron.**

griddle, *grid'l, n.* a flat iron plate for baking cakes. —Also (*Scot.*) **gird'le.** [Anglo-Fr. *gridil,* from a dim. of L. *crātis,* a hurdle.]

gride, *grīd, v.t.* and *v.i.* to pierce: to cut, esp. with a grating sound: to graze: to grate.—*n.* a harsh grating sound. [**gird.**]

gridelin, *grid'ə-lin, n.* and *adj.* violet-grey. [Fr. *gris de lin,* grey of flax.]

gridiron, *grid'ī-ərn, n.* a frame of iron bars for broiling over a fire: a frame to support a ship during repairs: a network: (*U.S.*) a football field.—*v.t.* to cover with parallel bars or lines.—*n.* **grid** (back formation), a grating: a gridiron: a framework: a network: a network of power-transmission lines: a perforated screen or spiral of wire between the filament and the plate of a thermionic valve: a grated luggage-carrier on a motor-car: a network of lines for finding places on a map, or for other purpose. [M.E. *gredire,* a griddle; from the same source as **griddle,** but the term. *-ire* became confused with M.E. *ire,* iron.]

griece. See **gree** (2).

grief, *grēf, n.* sorrow: distress: great mourning: affliction: (*Shak.*) bodily pain: cause of sorrow.— *adjs.* **grief'ful,** full of grief; **grief'less; grief'-shot,** (*Shak.*) pierced with grief.—**come to grief,** meet with reverse, disaster, mishap. [O.Fr.,—L. *gravis,* heavy.]

griesie, griesy, griesly, Spenserian forms of **grisy** (see under **gris, grise**), **grisly.**

grieve, *grēv, v.t.* to cause grief or pain of mind to: to make sorrowful: to vex: (*obs.*) to inflict bodily pain on: (*poet.*) to show grief for.—*v.i.* to feel grief: to mourn.—*ns.* **griev'ance,** cause or source of grief: ground of complaint: condition felt to be oppressive or wrongful: distress: burden: hardship: injury: grief; **griev'er.**—*adv.* **griev'ingly.** —*adj.* **griev'ous,** causing grief: burdensome: painful: severe: hurtful. — *adv.* **griev'ously.** — *n.* **griev'ousness.** [O.Fr. *grever* — L. *gravāre* — *gravis,* heavy.]

grieve, *grēv, n.* (*Scot.*) a farm overseer: (*hist.*) a governor or sheriff. [O.Northumbrian *græfa* (W.S. *geréfa*) ; cf. **reeve.**]

griff, griffe, *grif, n.* a claw: a clawlike architectural ornament. [Fr. *griffe.*]

griffin, griffon, gryphon, *grif'in, -ən, n.* an imaginary animal with lion's body and eagle's beak and wings: a newcomer in the East, a novice: a pony never before entered for a race: a watchful guardian, esp. over a young woman: a duenna.— *adj.* **griff'inish.**—*n.* **griff'inism.**—**griffon vulture,** a European vulture, *Gyps fulvus.* [Fr. *griffon*— L. *grȳphus*—Gr. *gryps,* a bird, probably the *lämmergeier,* a griffin—*grȳpos,* hook-nosed.]

griffon, *grif'ən, n.* a French dog like a coarse-haired terrier.—**Brussels griffon,** a toy dog with a stub nose. [Prob. from **griffin.**]

grig, *grig, n.* a cricket: a grasshopper: a small lively eel, the sand-eel. [Origin obscure.]

grill, *gril, v.t.* to broil on a gridiron or scallop-shell: to torment: (*U.S.*) to cross-examine harassingly. —*v.i.* to undergo grilling.—*n.* a grating: a gridiron: a grill-room: a grilled dish: an act of grilling.—*ns.* **grillade',** anything grilled; **grill'age,** a foundation of cross-beams on marshy grounds.— *adj.* **grilled,** embossed with small rectangular indentations.—*n.* **grill'-room,** part of a restaurant where beefsteaks, &c., are served grilled to order. [Fr. *griller*—*gril,* a gridiron, from a dim. of L. *crātis,* a grate.]

grille, *gril, n.* a lattice, or grating, or screen, or openwork of metal, generally used to enclose or protect a window, shrine, &c.: a grating in a convent or jail door, &c. [Fr. ; see **grill.**]

grilse, *grils, n.* a young salmon on its first return from salt water. [Origin unknown.]

grim, *grim, adj.* of forbidding aspect: ferocious: ghastly: sullen: stern: unyielding.—*adj.* **grim'-looked,** (*Shak.*) having a grim or dismal aspect.— *adv.* **grim'ly.**—*n.* **grim'ness.** [O.E. *grim(m)* ; Ger. *grimmig*—*grimm,* fury, Du. *grimmig,* O.N. *grimmr.*]

grimace, *gri-mās', n.* a distortion of the face, in jest, &c.: a smirk.—*v.i.* to make grimaces. [Fr.]

grimalkin, *gri-mal'kin, -mawl'kin, n.* an old cat: a cat generally. [**grey** and **Malkin,** a dim. of *Maud.*]

grime, *grīm, n.* sooty or coaly dirt: ingrained dirt

—*v.t.* to soil deeply.—*adv.* **grim'ily.**—*n.* **grim'-iness.**—*adj.* **grim'y.** [Cf. Flem. *grijm.*]
Grimm's law. See **law.**

grin, *grin, v.i.* to set the teeth together and withdraw the lips : to smile with some accompanying distortion of the features, expressive of pain, derision, clownish admiration, glee, &c.—*v.t.* to set in a grin : to express by grinning : (*pr.p.* **grinn'ing** ; *pa.t.* and *pa.p.* **grinned**).—*n.* act of grinning : a grinning smile : a forced or sardonic smile. [O.E. *grennian* ; O.N. *grenja,* Ger. *greinen,* Du. *grijnen,* to grumble, Scot. **girn** ; allied to **groan.**]

grin, *grin, n.* a snare or trap. [O.E. *grín.*]

grind, *grind* (*Spens.*). Same as **grinned.**

grind, *grīnd, v.t.* to reduce to powder by friction or crushing : to wear down, sharpen, smooth or roughen by friction : to rub together : to oppress or harass : to work by a crank.—*v.i.* to be moved or rubbed together : to jar or grate : to drudge at any tedious task : to read hard : (*pr.p.* **grind'ing** ; *pa.t.* and *pa.p.* **ground,** *grownd*).—*n.* the act, sound, or jar of grinding : drudgery : laborious study for a special examination, &c. : (*U.S.*) a student who gives all his time to study.—*ns.* **grind'er,** one who, or that which, grinds : a tooth that grinds food : a coach or crammer of students for examination : a hard student ; **grind'ery,** a place where knives, &c., are ground : shoemakers' materials ; **grind'-ing,** act or process of reducing to powder.—*adj.* harassing.—*n.* **grind'stone,** a circular revolving stone for grinding or sharpening tools.—*adj.* (*arch.*) **ground'en,** sharpened. — **ground glass,** glass obscured by grinding, sandblast, or etching ; **keep one's nose to the grindstone,** to subject one to severe *continuous* toil or punishment ; **take a grinder,** (*Dickens*) to put the left thumb to the nose, and to work a visionary coffee-mill round it with the right hand—a gesture of derision. [O.E. *grindan.*]

gringo, *gring'gō, n.* in Spanish-speaking America, one whose language is not Spanish. [Sp., gibberish, prob.—*Griego,* Greek.]

grip, *grip, n.* a small ditch, gutter, or trench, a drain.—*v.t.* to trench.—Also **gripe** (*grip*). [O.E. *grype,* cf. L.G. *gruppe, grüppe.*]

grip, *grip, n.* a grasp or firm hold with the hand or mind : strength of grasp : the handle or part by which anything is grasped : a mode of grasping : a particular mode of grasping hands for mutual recognition : (*U.S.*) a gripsack, travelling bag : a holding or clutching device : power : pinch of distress : mastery : power of holding the mind or commanding the emotions : gripe : grippe.—*v.t.* to take or maintain fast hold of : to hold fast the attention or interest of : to command the emotions of.—Also *v.i.*—*pr.p.* **gripp'ing** ; *pa.t.* and *pa.p.* **gripped** (*gript*).—*n.* **gripp'er,** one who, that which, grips : a clutch : a claw.—*adj.* **gripp'le** (*Spens.*) **grip'le**), griping, grasping : greedy.—*n.* a gripe.—*adj.* **gripp'y,** (*Scot.*) inclining to avarice : having grip.—*n.* **grip'sack,** (*U.S.*) a bag for travel. [O.E. *gripe,* grasp, *gripa,* handful.]

gripe, *grīp, v.t.* to grasp : to seize and hold fast : to squeeze : to afflict : to oppress : to give pain to the bowels of.—*v.i.* to clutch.—*n.* fast hold : grasp : forcible retention : (*slang*) a usurer : lashing for a boat on deck : pain : (esp. in *pl.*) severe spasmodic pain in the intestines.—*n.* **grip'er.**—*adj.* **grip'ing,** avaricious : of pain, seizing acutely.—*adv.* **grip'ingly.** [O.E. *grípan* (*gráp, gripen*) ; O.N. *grípa,* Ger. *greifen,* Du. *grijpen.*]

gripe, *grīp, n.* a griffin : vulture.—**gripe's egg,** a cup like a large egg. [Gr. *gryps.*]

grippe, *grēp, n.* influenza. [Fr.,—*gripper,* to seize.]

Griqua, *grēk'wä, n.* one of a mixed Hottentot and European race (Hottentot prevailing).

gris, grise, *grīs, adj.* (*obs.*) grey.—*n.* (*arch.*) a grey fur.—*adjs.* **griseous** (*griz', gris'i-as*), grey : blue-grey or pearl-grey ; **grisly** (*Spens.* **griesie, gryesy** ; all *griz'zi*), grey.

grisaille, *grē-zäl', -zä'ē, n.* a style of decorative painting in greyish tints in imitation of bas-reliefs : a work in this style.—Also *adj.* [Fr.,—*gris,* grey.]
gris-amber, *gris'-am'bər, n.* ambergris.—*adj.* **gris-amb'er-steam'd'** (*Milt.*).

grise, *grīz, v.t.* (*obs.*) to shudder at : to affright.—*v.i.* to shudder.—*adj.* **gri'sy** (*Spens.* **griesy grysie** ; *Shak.* **grizy),** grim : horrible : grisly. [From the verb of which O.E. *á-grísan* is a compound ; cf. **agrise.**]

grise, grice, gris. See **gree** (2).

Griselda, *griz-el'dä, n.* a woman of excessive meekness and patience, from the heroine of a tale retold by Boccaccio, Petrarch, and Chaucer.

grisette, *gri-zet', n.* a gay young working-class Frenchwoman. [Fr. *grisette,* a grey gown, which used to be worn by that class—*gris,* grey.]

griskin, *gris'kin, n.* (*prov.*) lean from the spine of a hog. [**grice.**]

grisled, *griz'ld.* Same as **grizzled.**

grisly, *griz'li, adj.* frightful : hideous (*Spens., Milt.* **greisly** ; *Spens.* **griesly, grisely, gryesly).** —Also *adv.* (*rare*).—*n.* **gris'liness.** [O.E. *grislic* ; cf. **grise.**]

grison, *griz'ən, grīz'ən, -on, n.* a large grey S. American weasel : a grey S. American monkey. [Fr.,—*gris,* grey.]

grist, *grist, n.* corn for grinding, or ground, at one time : malt for one brewing : (*U.S.*) supply, portion, quantity : (*fig.*) profit.—*n.* **grist'-mill,** a mill for grinding grain.—**bring grist to the mill,** to be a source of profit. [O.E. *grist* ; cf. **grind.**]

gristle, *gris'l, n.* cartilage.—*n.* **grist'liness.**—*adj.* **grist'ly.** [O.E. *gristle.*]

grisy. See **grise.**

grit, *grit, n.* (*obs.*) gravel : hard particles : small woody bodies in a pear : a coarse sandstone, often with angular grains : firmness of character, spirit. —*ns.* **grit'stone** ; **gritt'iness.**—*adj.* **gritt'y,** having or containing hard particles : sandy : of the nature of grit : scratchy : grating : determined, plucky. —*v.t.* and *v.i.* to grind : to grate. [O.E. *gréot* ; Ger. *griess,* gravel.]

grit, *grit,* a Scottish form of **great.**

grith, *grith, girth, girth, n.* (*hist.*) sanctuary, asylum. — *n.* **grith'-stool,** a seat in which a fugitive was in sanctuary. [O.E. *grith.*]

grits, *grits, n.pl.* coarsely ground grain, esp. oats. [O.E. *grytta* ; cf. **groats.**]

grivet, *griv'it, n.* a north-east African guenon monkey. [Fr. ; origin unknown.]

grize. See **gree** (2).

grizzle, *griz'l, n.* a grey colour.—*adjs.* **grizz'led,** grey, or mixed with grey ; **grizz'ly,** of a grey colour.—*n.* the grizzly bear (*Ursus horribilis*) of the Rocky Mountains. [M.E. *grisel*—Fr. *gris,* grey.]

grizzle, *griz'l, v.i.* to grumble : to whimper : to fret.—*n.* a bout of grizzling.—*n.* **grizz'ler.** [Origin unknown.]

groan, *grōn, v.i.* to utter a deep rumbling or voiced sound as in distress or disapprobation : (*fig.*) to be afflicted.—*n.* a deep moan : a grinding rumble. —*adj.* **groan'ful** (*Spens.* **grone'full).**—*n.* and *adj.* **groan'ing.—groaning board,** a table laid with very generous supplies of food. [O.E. *gránian.*]

groat, *grōt* (formerly *gravt*), *n.* an English silver coin, worth fourpence—after 1662 coined only as Maundy money—the silver fourpenny-piece, coined 1836-56, was not officially called a groat : a very small sum, proverbially.—*n.* **groats'worth.** [O.L.G. *grote,* or Du. *groot,* lit, great, i.e. thick.]

groats, *grōts, n.pl.* the grain of oats deprived of the husks. [O.E. *grotan* (pl.).]

Grobian, *grō'bi-ən, n.* a boorish rude sloven.—*n.* **Gro'bianism.** [Ger. *Grobianus,* a character in German satire of the 15th and 16th centuries—*grob,* coarse.]

grocer, *grōs'ər, n.* a dealer in tea, sugar, &c.—*ns.* **groc'ery** (generally used in *pl.*), articles sold by grocers : (*U.S.*) a grocer's shop or liquor shop : **grocete'ria,** a self-service grocery store. [Earlier **grosser,** a wholesale dealer ; O.Fr. *grossier*—L.L. *grossárius—grossus* ; cf. **gross.**]

grog, *grog, n.* a mixture of spirits and cold water, without sugar.—*ns.* **grog'-bloss'om,** a redness of the nose due to drinking ; **grogg'ery,** (*U.S.*) a low public-house ; **grogg'iness,** state of being groggy ; **grogg'ing,** extracting the spirit from the wood of empty spirit-casks with water.—*adj.* **grogg'y,** affected by grog, partially intoxicated : (*boxing*)

Neutral vowels in unaccented syllables : *el'ə-mənt, in'fənt, ran'dəm*

weak and staggering from blows : applied to a horse that bears wholly on his heels in trotting.—*n.*

grog'-shop, a dram-shop. [From Old *Grog*, the nickname (apparently from his *grogram* cloak) of Admiral Vernon, who in 1740 ordered that sailors' rum should be mixed with water.]

grogram, *grog'rəm, n.* a kind of coarse cloth of silk and mohair. [O.Fr. *gros grain*, coarse grain.]

groin, *groin, n.* the fold between the belly and the thigh : (*archit.*) the line of intersection of two vaults : a rib along the intersection.—*v.t.* to form into groins, to build in groins.—*n.* **groin'-cen'tring**, the centring of timber during construction.—*adj.* **groined.** — *n.* **groin'ing.** [Early forms *grind*, *grine*, perh.—O.E. *grynde*, abyss.]

groin, *groin, v.i.* (*obs.*) to grunt, to growl. [O.Fr. *grogner*—L. *grunnīre*, to grunt.]

Grolier, *grō'lyā, n.* a book or a binding from the library of the French bibliophile Jean *Grolier* (1479-1565).—*adj.* **Grolieresque** (*grō-lyər-esk'*), after the style of Grolier's bindings, with geometrical or arabesque figures and leaf-sprays in gold lines.]

gromet, grommet. Same as **grummet** (1).

gromwell, *grom'wəl, n.* any plant of the genus Lithospermum : the oyster-plant (Mertensia)—both of the borage family. [O.Fr. *gromil.*]

grone, obs. form of **groan.**

groof. See under **grovelling.**

groom, *groom, n.* (*obs.*) a boy, young man, esp. a servant : one who has the charge of horses : a title of several household officers (groom of the stole, grooms-in-waiting) : a bridegroom.—*v.t.* to tend, esp. a horse : to smarten.—*n.* **grooms'man**, the attendant on a bridegroom. [Origin obscure ; cf. Du. *grom*, fry, offspring, O.Fr. *gromet*, boy (see **gourmet, grummet,** 2) ; encroaching on O.E. *guma* (as in bride*groom*), a man.]

groove, *groov, n.* a furrow, or long hollow, such as is cut with a tool.—*v.t.* to grave or cut a groove or furrow in. [Prob. Du. *groef, groeve*, a furrow ; cog. with Ger. *grube*, a pit, O.N. *gróf*, Eng. **grave.**]

grope, *grōp, v.i.* to search, feel about, as if blind or in the dark.—*v.t.* to search by feeling.—*adv.* **grop'ingly.** [O.E. *grápian* ; allied to **grab, gripe.**]

groper. Same as **grouper.**

grosbeak, *grōs'bēk, n.* the hawfinch, or other finch of the same subfamily, with thick, heavy, seed-crushing bill : extended to various more or less related birds, as the cardinal and the rose-breasted grosbeak. [Fr. *grosbec—gros*, thick, *bec*, beak.]

groschen, *grō'shən, n.* a small silver coin till 1873-76 current in the north of Germany, in value ³⁄₁₀th of a thaler : a ten-pfennig piece. [Ger.]

groser, *grō'zər*, **grosert, grossart, -zərt, groset, -zit, n.** (*Scot.*) a gooseberry. [Fr. *groseille.*]

gross, *grōs, adj.* coarse : rough : dense : palpable : flagrant, glaring : shameful : whole : coarse in mind : stupid : sensual : obscene : total, including everything.—*n.* the main bulk : the whole taken together : twelve dozen : — *pl.* **gross.** — *adv.* **gross'ly.**—*n.* **gross'ness.**—**great gross**, a dozen gross ; **in gross**, in bulk, wholesale. [Fr. *gros*—L. *grossus*, thick.]

grossular, *gros'ū-lər*, **grossularite, -īt, ns.** gooseberry-stone, a lime alumina garnet, often green. [Fr. *groseille*, gooseberry, Latinised as *grossulāria.*]

grot, *grot, n.* a grotto.

grotesque, *grō-tesk', adj.* extravagantly formed : fantastic.—*n.* (*art*) extravagant ornament, containing animals, plants, &c., not really existing : a bizarre figure or object.—*adv.* **grotesque'ly.**—*ns.* **grotesque'ness** ; **grotesqu'ery.** [Fr. *grotesque*—It. *grottesca—grotta*, a grotto.]

Grotian, *grō'shi-ən, adj.* of or pertaining to Hugo *Grotius*, or Huig van *Groot* (1583-1645), founder of the science of international law.—**Grotian theory**, the theory that man is essentially a social being, and that the principles of justice are of perpetual obligation and in harmony with his nature ; **Grotian, or governmental, theory of the Atonement**, a divine acquittal for Christ's sake, rather than a real satisfaction on the part of Christ.

grotto, *grot'ō, n.* a cave : an imitation cave, usu. fantastic :—*pl.* **grott'oes, grott'os.**—*n.* **grott'o-work.** [It. *grotta* (Fr. *grotte*)—L. *crypta*—Gr. *kryptē*, a crypt, vault.]

grouch, *growch, v.i.* (*U.S.*) to grumble.—*n.* a grumbling : sulks : a grumbler.—*adv.* **grouch'ily.** —*n.* **grouch'iness.**—*adj.* **grouch'y.** [See **grutch, grudge.**]

ground, grounden. See **grind.**

ground, *grownd, n.* (*arch.*) bottom, esp. sea-bottom : the solid surface of the earth : a portion of the earth's surface : land : soil : the floor, &c. : (*elect.*) earth : position : field or place of action : (*lit.* or *fig.*) that on which something is raised : foundation : sufficient reason : (*art*) the surface on which the figures are represented : a first coat of paint : (*mining*) surrounding rock : (*cricket*) the space behind the popping-crease with which the batsman must be in touch by bat or person if he is not to be stumped or run out : in *pl.*—an ornamental enclosure attached to a building : dregs or sediment : basis of justification.—*v.t.* to fix on a foundation or principle : to put or rest on the ground : to cause to run aground : to instruct in first principles : to cover with a layer of plaster, &c., as a basis for painting : to coat with a composition, as a surface to be etched : (*elect.*) to put to earth : to keep on the ground, prevent from flying : to attach to the ground-staff.—*v.i.* to come to the ground : to strike the bottom and remain fixed.—*ns.* **ground'age**, a charge on a ship in port ; **ground'-ang'ling**, fishing without a float, with a weight placed a few inches from the hook—bottom-fishing ; **ground'-ann'ual**, (*Scots law*) an annual payment forming a burden on land ; **ground'-ash**, a sapling of ash ; **ground'-bait**, bait dropped to the bottom to bring fish to the neighbourhood ; **ground'-bass**, a bass constantly repeated with varying melody and harmony ; **ground'-beetle**, any beetle of the Carabidae, a family akin to the tiger-beetles ; **ground'-cherry**, Cape gooseberry ; **ground'-cuckoo**, a name for several ground-running birds akin to the cuckoo as the chaparral cock, the coucal ; **ground'-dove, -pigeon**, various small American pigeons of terrestrial habits.—*adj.* **ground'ed.**—*adv.* **ground'edly**, on good grounds.—*ns.* **ground'er**, a ball that keeps low ; **ground'-feed'er**, a fish that feeds at the bottom ; **ground'-floor, -story**, the floor on or near a level with the ground ; **ground'-game**, hares, rabbits, as distinguished from winged game ; **ground'-hog**, the woodchuck : the aardvark ; **ground'-hold**, (*Spens.*) ground-tackle ; **ground'-ice**, the ice formed at the bottom ; **ground'ing**, foundation : sound general knowledge of a subject : the background of embroidery, &c. : act or process of preparing or laying a ground : act of laying or of running aground ; **ground'-i'vy**, a British labiate creeping-plant (Nepeta) whose leaves when the edges curl become ivy-like.—*adj.* **ground'less**, without ground, foundation, or reason. — *adv.* **ground'lessly.** — *ns.* **ground'lessness** ; **ground'ling**, a fish that keeps near the bottom of the water, esp. the spinous loach : a spectator in the pit of a theatre—hence one of the common herd.—*adj.* (*Lamb*) base.—*ns.* **gr(o)und'-mail**, (*Scot.*) payment for right of burial ; **ground'mass**, the fine-grained part of an igneous rock, glassy or minutely crystalline, in which the larger crystals are embedded ; **ground'-moraine'**, a mass of mud, sand, and stones dragged along under a glacier or ice-sheet ; **ground'-nut**, the peanut or monkey-nut (Arachis) : the earth-nut ; **ground'-oak**, a sapling of oak ; **ground'-off'icer**, one who has the charge of the grounds of an estate ; **ground'-plan**, plan of the horizontal section of the lowest or ground story of a building ; **ground'-plot**, the plot of ground on which a building stands ; **ground'-rent**, rent paid to a landlord for the use of the ground for a specified term, usually in England ninety-nine years ; **ground'-robin**, the chewink ; **ground'sel, ground'sell, ground'sill**, the lowest timber of a structure ; **ground'sheet**, a waterproof sheet spread on the ground by campers, &c. ; **ground'-**

sloth, a heavy extinct ground-going sloth; **grounds′man, ground′man,** a man charged with the care of a cricket-ground or a sports-field: an aerodrome mechanic; **ground′-squirr′el,** the chipmunk or hackee; **ground′-staff,** aircraft mechanics, &c., whose work is on the ground: (*cricket*) paid staff of players; **ground′-swell,** a broad, deep undulation of the ocean; **ground′-tack′le,** tackle for securing a vessel at anchor; **ground′-work,** that which forms the ground or foundation of anything: the basis: the essential part: the first principle.—**break ground,** to take the first step in any project; **fall to the ground,** to come to nothing; **gain ground,** to advance, to obtain an advantage; **give ground, lose ground,** fall back, to lose advantage; **hold, or stand, one′s ground,** to stand firm; **let in on the ground-floor,** admit on the same terms as the original promoters. [O.E. *grund*; cog. with Ger. *grund*, O.N. *grunnr*.]

groundsel, *grown(d)′sl, n.* a very common yellow-flowered composite weed of waste ground (*Senecio vulgaris*). [O.E. *gundeswilge*, appar.—*gund*, pus, *zwelgan*, to swallow, from its use in poultices, influenced by *grund*, ground.]

group, *grōōp, n.* a number of persons or things together: a number of individual things related in some definite way differentiating them from others: a clique, school, section of a party: (*art*) a combination of figures forming a harmonious whole.—*v.t.* to form into a group or groups.—*v.i.* to fall into harmonious combination. — *ns.* **group′-captain,** an air-force officer answering to a colonel or naval captain; **group′ing,** (*art*) the act of disposing and arranging figures or objects in a group; **group′ist,** an adherent of a group; **group′-marriage,** a hypothetical primitive relation by which every man of a group is husband to every woman of a group. [Fr. *groupe*—It. *groppo,* a bunch, knot—Gmc.; cf. Ger. *kropf,* protuberance.]

grouper, *grōōp′ər* (*Amer.*), **groper,** *grōp′ər* (*Austr.*), *ns.* names given to many fishes, esp. various kinds resembling bass. [Port. *garoupa.*]

grouse, *grows, n.* the heathcock or moorfowl (*Lagopus scoticus*), a plump bird with a short curved bill, short legs, and feathered feet, which frequents Scottish moors and hills, close akin to the ptarmigan: extended to other birds of the sub-family Tetraoninae, esp. the *black grouse* or black-cock and the *willow-grouse:—pl.* **grouse.**—*n.* **grouse′-disease′,** a nematode infection of grouse. [Origin unknown.]

grouse, *grows, v.i.* to grumble.—*n.* a grumble.—*n.* **grous′er.** [Cf. **grutch.**]

grout, *growt, n.* coarse meal: the sediment of liquor: lees: a thin coarse mortar: a fine plaster for finishing ceilings.—*v.t.* to fill and finish with grout.—*n.* **grout′ing,** filling up or finishing with grout: the material so used.—*adj.* **grout′y,** thick, muddy: sulky. [O.E. *grūt,* coarse meal; or perh. in part Fr. *grouter,* to grout.]

grout, *growt, v.i.* to root or grub with the snout. [Perh. conn. with O.E. *grēot,* grit.]

grove, *grōv, n.* a wood of small size, generally of a pleasant or ornamental character: an avenue of trees: often used (quite fancifully) in street-names: (*B.*) an erroneous translation of *Asherah,* the wooden image of the goddess Ashtoreth; also of Heb. *eshel,* tamarisk, in Gen. xxi. 33: a lodge of a benefit society called Druids. [O.E. *gráf,* possibly tamarisk.]

grovelling, *gruv′, grov′(ə)-ling, adv.* and *adj.* prone: face-down: later felt to be the pr.p. or verbal noun of the new *v.i.* **grov′el,** to crawl on the earth, esp. in abject fear, &c.: to be base or abject:—*pa.t.* and *pa.p.* **grov′elled.**—*n.* **grov′eller.**—*n.* **groof, grouf** (*groof; Scot.*), the front of the body. [M.E. *groveling, grofling,* prone—O.N. *grúfa,* and suff. *-ling.*]

grow, *grō, v.i.* to have life: to have a habitat: to become enlarged by a natural process: to advance towards maturity: to increase in size: to develop: to become greater in any way: to extend: to pass from one state to another: to become.—*v.t.* to cause or allow to grow: to produce: to cultivate:

(in *pass.*) to cover with growth:—*pa.t.* **grew,** *grōō*; *pa.p.* **grown,** *grōn.*—*n.* **grow′er.**—*n.* and *adj.* **grow′ing.** — *n.pl.* **grow′ing-pains′,** neuralgic pains in young persons (also *fig.*).—*ns.* **grow′ing-point,** (*bot.*) the meristem at the apex of an axis, where active cell-division occurs and differentiation of tissues begins; **grown′-up,** an adult.—Also *adj.*—*n.* **growth,** a growing: gradual increase: progress: development: that which has grown: a morbid formation: product.—**grow on, upon,** to gain a greater hold on: to gain in the estimation of; **grow out of,** to issue from, result from: to pass beyond in development: to become too big for; **grow to,** to advance to, come to: of milk, to stick to the pan and develop a bad taste in heating (so prob. Shak. *Merch. of Ven.*, II. ii.); **grow together,** to become united by growth; **grow up,** to advance in growth, become full-grown, mature, or adult: to spring up. [O.E. *grówan*; O.N. *gróa.*]

growl, *growl, v.i.* to utter a deep rough murmuring sound like a dog: to grumble surlily.—*v.t.* to utter or express by growling.—*n.* a murmuring, snarling sound, as of an angry dog: a surly grumble.—*ns.* **growl′er,** one who growls: a N. American river fish, the large-mouthed black-bass, so named from the sound it emits: a small iceberg: (*slang*) a four-wheeled cab: (*Amer.*) a jug or pitcher used for carrying beer; **growl′ery,** a retreat for times of ill-humour; **growl′ing.**—*adv.* **growl′ingly.**—*adj.* **growl′y.** [Cf. Du. *grollen,* to grumble: allied to Gr. *gryllizein,* to grunt.]

groyne, *groin, n.* a breakwater, usu. wooden, to check erosion and sand-drifting. [Prob. O.Fr. *groign,* snout—L. *grumīre,* to grunt.]

grub, *grub, v.i.* to dig in the dirt: to be occupied meanly: (*slang*) to eat.—*v.t.* to dig or root out of the ground (generally followed by *up* or *out*): (*slang*) to supply with victuals: (*pr.p.* **grubb′ing;** *pa.t.* and *pa.p.* **grubbed**).—*n.* an insect larva, esp. one thick and soft: (*slang*) food.—*n.* **grubb′er,** he who, or that which, grubs: an implement for grubbing or stirring the soil.—*adj.* **grubb′y,** dirty: infested with grubs.—*n.* **grub′-stake,** (*Amer.*) outfit, provisions, &c., given to a prospector for a share in any finds.—*v.t.* to provide thus.—**Grub Street,** a former name of Milton Street, Moor-fields, London, once inhabited by booksellers' hacks and shabby writers generally: applied adjectivally to any mean literary production. [M.E. *grobe*; origin uncertain.]

grubble, *grub′l, v.t.* and *v.i.* to grope. [Variant of **grabble.**]

grudge, *gruj, v.t.* to murmur at: to look upon with envy: to give or allow unwillingly: to be loth: (*Shak.*) to thank with ill-will.—*v.i.* to murmur, to show discontent.—*n.* secret enmity or envy: an old cause of quarrel.—*adj.* **grudge′ful** (*Spens*).—*n.* and *adj.* **grudg′ing.**—*adv.* **grudg′ingly.** [**grutch.**]

gruel, *grōō′əl, n.* a thin food made by boiling oat-meal in water: (*coll.*) punishment, severe treatment.—*v.t.* to subject to severe or exhausting experience.—*n.* and *adj.* **gru′elling.** [O.Fr. *gruel* (Fr. *gruau*), groats—L.L. *grūtellum,* dim. of *grūtum,* meal, of Gmc. origin; cf. O.E. *grūt.*]

gruesome, *grōō′səm, adj.* horrible: grisly: macabre. —*n.* **grue, grew** (*Scot.*), a creeping of the flesh: a shiver: a shudder: a pellicle of ice.—*v.i.* **grue, grew,** to shudder: to feel the flesh creep: to creep (as the flesh): to curdle (as the blood).—*n.* **grue′someness.** [Cf. Du. *gruwzaam,* Ger. *grausam.*]

gruff, *gruf, adj.* rough, or abrupt in manner or sound.—*adj.* **gruff′ish.**—*adv.* **gruff′ly.**—*n.* **gruff′ness.** [Du. *grof*; cog. with Sw. *grof,* Ger. *grob,* coarse.]

gru-gru, **groo-groo,** *grōō′grōō, n.* a name for several tropical American palms akin to the coconut palm, yielding oil-nuts: an edible weevil grub (also **gru-gruworm**) found in their pith.

grum, *grum, adj.* morose: surly: deep in the throat, as a sound.—*adv.* **grum′ly.**—*n.* **grum′ness.** [Cf. Dan. *grum.*]

grumble, *grum′bl, v.i.* to murmur with discontent: to express discontent: to mutter, mumble, murmur: to growl: to rumble.—*n.* the act of grumbling.— *ns.* **grum′bler; Grumbletō′nian,** one of the country party as opposed to the court party, after 1689.—*n.* and *adj.* **grum'bling.**—*adv.* **grum'-blingly.**—*adj.* **grum'bly,** inclined to grumble. [Cf. Du. *grommelen,* freq. of *grommen,* to mutter ; Ger. *grummeln.*]

grume, *grōōm, n.* a thick fluid : a clot.—*adjs.* **grum'ous, grum'ose,** composed of grains. [O.Fr. *grume,* a bunch—L. *grūmus,* a little heap.]

grummet, grommet, gromet, *grum'it, n.* a ring of rope : a hole edged with rope : a washer of hemp and red-lead putty : a metal ring lining an eyelet : an eyelet.—*n.* **grumm'et-hole.** [Perh. 15th-cent. Fr. *gromette,* curb of a bridle.]

grummet, *grum'it, n.* a cabin-boy. [O.Fr. *gromet ;* see **gourmet.**]

grumph, *grumf, n.* (*Scot.*) a grunt.—*v.i.* to grunt. —*n.* **grumph'ie,** a swine.

grumpy, *grum'pi, adj.* surly.—*adv.* **grum'pily.**—*n.* **grump'iness.** [Obs. *grump,* snub, sulkiness.]

Grundyism, *grun'di-izm, n.* conventional prudery, from the question ' But what will Mrs *Grundy* say? ' in Thomas Morton's play, *Speed the Plough* (1798).

grunt, *grunt, v.i.* to make a sound like a pig.—*n.* a sound made by a pig : a fish (Haemulon, &c.) of a family akin to the snappers, that grunts when taken from the sea.—*n.* **grunt'er,** one who grunts : a pig : a grunting fish of various kinds.—*n.* and *adj.* **grunt'ing.**—*adv.* **grunt'ingly.**—*v.i.* **grunt'le,** to grunt, keep grunting.—*n.* a grunt : a snout. [O.E. *grunnettan,* freq. of *grunian.*]

grutch, *gruch, v.t.* or *v.i.* (*Spens.*) to grudge.—*n.* a grudge. [O.Fr. *groucher, grocher, gruchier,* to grumble.]

Gruyère, *grü' or groo'yer, or -yer', n.* a famous whole-milk cheese, made at *Gruyère* (Switzerland) and elsewhere.

gryde ; gryfon, gryphon ; grype ; grysely ; grysie. See **gride, griffin, gripe, grisly, grisy.**

grypt, *gript, (Spens.)* prob. for **griped** or **gripped,** in the sense of bitten, pierced.

grysbok, *grīs'bok, n.* a small S. African antelope, ruddy chestnut with white hairs. [Du., *grey-buck*—*grys,* grey, *bok,* buck.]

guacharo, *gwä'chä-rō, n.* the oil-bird, a S. American nocturnal frugivorous oily bird (Steatornis) allied to the goatsuckers. [Sp. *guacharo.*]

guaco, *gwä'kō, n.* a tropical American name for plants reputed antidotes against snakebite, esp. species of Mikania (climbing composites), and of Aristolochia : the medicinal substance got from them. [Amer. Sp.]

Guaiacum, *gwī'ə-kəm, n.* a tropical American genus of trees of the bean-caper family, yielding lignum-vitae : their greenish resin, used in medicine. [Sp. *guayaco,* from a Haitian word.]

guan, *gwän, n.* a large noisy American arboreal game-bird.

guana, *gwä'nä, n.* any large lizard. [For **iguana.**]

guanaco, *gwä-nä'kō, n.* a wild llama. — Also **huana'co** (*wä-*). [Quichua *huanaco.*]

guano, *gwä'nō, n.* the long-accumulated dung of sea-fowl, much used for manure.—*adj.* **guanif'-erous.**—*n.* **gua'nin(e),** a yellowish-white, amorphous substance, a constituent of guano, also of the liver and pancreas of mammals. [Sp. *guano,* or *huano,* from Peruv. *huanu,* dung.]

guaraná, *gwä-rä-nä', n.* a Brazilian liana (*Paullinia Cupana ;* Sapindaceae) : a paste of its seeds (**guaraná bread**) : a drink or drug made therefrom. [Tupí.]

Guaraní, *gwä-rä-nē', n.* an Indian of a group of tribes of southern Brazil and Paraguay (*pl.* **Guaraní**) : their language, derived from Tupí : **guarani** (*pl.* **guaranies**), the monetary unit of Paraguay.—Also *adj.*

guarantee, *gar-ən-tē', n.* a person who makes a contract to see performed what another has undertaken : such a contract : surety or warrant : one responsible for the performance of some action, the truth of some statement, &c.—*v.t.* to undertake as surety for another : to secure : to engage, undertake :— *pr.p.* **guarantee'ing ;** *pa.t.* and *pa.p.* **guaranteed'.** —*ns.* **guar'antor** (or *-tor'*), one who makes a guaranty ; **guar'anty,** a securing, guarantee-

ing : a written undertaking to be responsible : a person who guarantees : a security.—*v.t.* to guarantee.—**guarantee association, company, society,** a joint-stock company on the insurance principle, which becomes security for the integrity of cashiers, &c. [Anglo-Fr. *garantie—garant,* warrant and prob. Sp. *garante ;* see **warrant.**]

guard, *gärd, v.t.* to ward, watch, or take care of : to protect from danger or attack : to escort : to protect the edge of, as by an ornamental border : to furnish with guards : to trim : to stripe.—*v.i.* to watch : to be wary.—*n.* ward, keeping : protection : watch : that which guards from danger : a man or body of men stationed to watch, protect, or keep in custody : one who has charge of a coach or railway train : state of caution : posture of defence : (*cricket*) the position in which a batsman grounds his bat in facing the bowling : a trimming : a stripe : part of the hilt of a sword : a watch-chain : a cricketer's pad : in a book, a strip for attachment of a plate, map, or additional leaf : (*pl.*) household troops (Foot, Horse, and Life Guards).—*adj.***guard'able.**—*n.* **guard'age,** (*Shak.*) wardship.—*adj.* **guard'ant, gardant,** (*her.*) having the face turned towards the beholder.—*n.* (*Shak.*) protector.—*ns.* **guard'-book,** a blank book with guards ; **guard'-cell,** (*bot.*) one of the lips of a stoma.—*adj.* **guard'ed,** wary : cautious : uttered with caution : trimmed : striped.—*adv.* **guard'-edly.**—*ns.* **guard'edness ; guard'-house, guard'-room,** a house or room for the accommodation of a guard of soldiers, where defaulters are confined ; **guard'ian,** one who guards or takes care : (*law*) one who has the care of a person, property, and rights of another, as a minor, a lunatic : a member of a board (in England till 1930) administering the poor laws.—*adj.* protecting.—*n.* **guard'ianship.**— *adj.* **guard'less,** without a guard : defenceless.— *ns.* **guard'-ring,** a keeper, or finger-ring that serves to keep another from slipping off ; **guard'-ship,** a ship of war that superintends marine affairs in a harbour and protects it : (*Swift*) guardianship ; **guards'man,** a soldier of the guards. —**guardian angel,** an angel supposed to watch over a particular person : a person specially devoted to the interests of another ; **mount guard,** to go on guard ; **on,** or **off, one's guard,** on the watch, or the opposite ; **run the guard,** to get past a guard or sentinel without detection. [O.Fr. *garder*—O.H.G. *warten ;* O.E. *weardian,* mod. Eng. **ward.**]

guarish, garish, *gär'ish, v.t.* (*Spens.*) to heal. [O.Fr. *guarir* (Fr. *guérir*), to heal.]

guava, *gwä'vä, n.* a small tropical American myrtaceous tree (Psidium) : its yellow, pear-shaped fruit, often made into jelly. [Sp. *guayaba,* guava fruit ; of S. Amer. origin.]

guayule, *gwä-ū'lā, n.* a Mexican composite plant (*Parthenium argentatum*) : the rubber yielded by it. [Sp. ; of Nahuatl origin.]

gubernator, *gū'bər-nā-tər, n.* a governor.—*n.* **gubernā'tion,** control, rule.—*adj.* **gubernatorial** (*-nə-tō'ri-əl*). [L. *gubernātor,* a steersman.]

guddle, *gud'l, v.t.* and *v.i.* (*Scot.*) to fish with the hands by groping under the stones or banks of a stream.

gude, guid, güd, gid, Scottish form of **good.**— **gudesire** (see under **good**).

gudgeon, *guj'ən, n.* an easily caught small carp-like freshwater fish (Gobio) : a person easily cheated.—*adj.* foolish.—*v.t.* to impose on, cheat. [O.Fr. *goujon*—L. *gōbiō, -ōnis,* a kind of fish—Gr. *kōbios ;* see **goby.**]

gudgeon, *guj'ən, n.* the bearing of a shaft, esp. when made of a separate piece : a metallic journal-piece let into the end of a wooden shaft : a pin. [O.Fr. *goujon,* the pin of a pulley.]

gue, gu, gju, *gōō, gū, n.* a rude kind of violin used in Shetland. [O.N. *gigja.*]

Guebre, Gueber, *gā'bər, gē'bər, n.* a Zoroastrian. [Fr. *guèbre*—Pers. *gaur ;* see **giaour.**]

guelder-rose, *gel'dər-rōz, n.* the snowball-tree, Viburnum with large white balls of flowers. [From *Geldern* or from *Gelderland.*]

Guelf, Guelph, *gwelf, n.* one of a papal and popular

party in mediaeval Italy, opposed to the Ghibellines and the emperors.—*adj.* **Guelf'ic,** pertaining to the Guelf family or party. [*Guelfo,* Italian form of the German family name *Welf,* said to have been the war-cry of Henry the Lion at the battle of Weinsberg (1140) against the Emperor Conrad III.]

guenon, *gə-non²,* gen'*on, n.* any species of the genus Cercopithecus, long-tailed African monkeys. [Fr.]

guerdon, *gər'dən, n.* a reward or recompense.—*v.t.* to reward. [O.Fr. *guerdon, gueredon* (It. *guidardone*)—L.L. *widerdonum* — O.H.G. *widarlôn* (O.E. *witherléan*)—*widar,* against, and *lôn,* reward; or more probably the latter part of the word is from L. *dōnum,* a gift.]

guereza, *ger'ə-zä, n.* a large, long-haired, black-and-white African monkey, with a bushy tail: any species of the same genus (Colobus). [App. of Somali origin.]

guernsey, *gərn'zi, n.* a close-fitting knitted upper garment, worn by sailors: **Guernsey,** one of a breed of dairy cattle from *Guernsey,* in the Channel Islands.

guerrilla, guerilla, *gər-il'ä, n.* harassing an army by small bands: petty warfare: (loosely) one who takes part in such warfare (properly **guerrillero,** -*yā'ro).*—Also *adj.* [Sp. *guerrilla,* dim. of *guerra,* war—O.H.G. *werra;* cf. **war;** Fr. *guerre.*]

guess, *ges, v.t.* (*arch.* and *U.S.*) to think, believe, suppose: to judge upon inadequate knowledge or none at all: to conjecture: to hit on or solve by conjecture.—*v.i.* to make a conjecture or conjectures.—*n.* judgment or opinion without sufficient evidence or grounds: a random surmise: (*Scot.*) a riddle, conundrum.—*adj.* **guess'able.**—*n.* **guess'er.**—*n.* and *adj.* **guess'ing.**—*adv.* **guess'ingly.**—*n.* **guess'work,** process or result of guessing. [M.E. *gessen;* cog. with Du. *gissen;* Dan. *gisse,* mod. Ice. *giska, gizka,* for *gitska*—*geta,* to get, think; see **get, forget.**]

guess. See **othergates.**

guest, *gest, n.* a visitor received and entertained gratuitously or for payment: an animal inhabiting or breeding in another's nest.—*ns.* **guest'-chamber** (*B.*), **guest'-room,** a room for the accommodation of a guest.—*v.i.* **guest'en,** (*Scott*) to stay as a guest.—*ns.* **guest'-house,** a hospice: a boarding-house; **guest'night,** a night when non-members of a society are entertained.—*adv.* **guest'wise,** in the manner or capacity of a guest. [O.E. (Anglian) *gest* (W.S. *giest*), perh. influenced by O.N.; allied to Du. and Ger. *gast,* L. *hostis,* stranger, enemy.]

Gueux, *gə, n.pl.* the name assumed by the confederation (1565) of nobles and others to resist the introduction of the Inquisition into the Low Countries by Philip II. of Spain. [Fr., beggars.]

guffaw, *guf-aw', v.i.* to laugh loudly.—*n.* a loud laugh. [From the sound.]

guggle, *gug'l, v.i.* to gurgle.—*n.* a gurgle. [Cf. **gurgle.**]

guichet, *gē'shā, n.* a small opening, door, grating, or window—esp. at a booking-office. [Fr.; cf. **wicket.**]

Guicowar. See **Gaekwar.**

guide, *gīd, v.t.* to lead, conduct, or direct: to regulate: to influence.—*n.* he who, or that which, guides: one who conducts travellers, tourists, mountaineers, &c.: one who directs another in his course of life: a soldier or other employed to obtain information for an army: a Girl Guide (see **girl**): a guide-book: anything serving to direct, show the way, determine direction of motion or course of conduct.—*adj.* **guid'able.**—*ns.* **guid'age,** guidance; **guid'ance,** direction: leadership; **guide'-book,** a book of information for tourists.—*adj.* **guide'less.**—*ns.* **guide'-post,** a post to guide the traveller; **guid'er,** one who guides: a device for guiding: a captain or lieutenant in the Girl Guides; **guide'-rail,** an additional rail to keep rolling-stock on the rails at a bend; **guide'-rope,** a rope for guiding the movement of a thing hoisted or hauled; **guide'ship.**—*n.* and *adj.* **guid'ing.**—*n.* **guid'on,** a pennant carried by a cavalry company or mounted battery: the officer bearing it.—**guided missile,** one that can be guided in flight by remote control, as by radio or radar. [O.Fr.

guider; prob. from a Gmc. root, as in O.E. *witan,* to know, *wis,* wise, Ger. *weisen,* to show, conn. with **wit, wise.**]

guild, gild, *gild, n.* an association for mutual aid: a corporation: (*hist.*) a mediaeval association providing for masses for the dead, maintenance of common interests, mutual support and protection: (*obs.;* *Spens.* **gyeld**) meeting-place of a guild; —*ns.* **guild'brother,** a fellow-member of a guild: **guild'hall,** the hall of a guild: a town-hall; **guild'ry,** (*Scot.*) the corporation of a royal burgh: membership thereof.—**Guild Socialism,** a form of socialism that would make trade unions or guilds the authority for industrial matters. [O.E. *gield,* influenced by O.N. *gildi.*]

guilder, gilder, *gild'ər, n.* an old Dutch and German gold coin: a modern Dutch gulden: (*Shak.*) a coin vaguely. [Du. *gulden.*]

guile, *gīl, n.* wile, jugglery: cunning: deceit.—*v.t.* (*Spens.*) to beguile. — *adjs.* **guiled,** armed with deceit: treacherous; **guile'ful,** crafty: deceitful.—*adv.* **guile'fully.**—*n.* **guile'fulness.**—*adj.* **guile'less,** without deceit: artless.—*adv.* **guile'lessly.** — *ns.* **guile'lessness;** **guil'er, guyler** (*Spens.*), a deceiver. [O.Fr. *guile,* deceit, perh. Gmc.; cf. **wile.**]

guillemot, *gil'i-mot, n.* a diving bird (Uria) of the auk family. [Fr., dim. of *Guillaume,* William, perh. suggested by Bret. *gwelan,* gull.]

guilloche, *gi-lōsh', n.* an ornament formed of interlacing curved bands enclosing circles.—*v.t.* to decorate with intersecting curved lines. [Fr., a guilloching tool; said to be named from one *Guillot.*]

guillotine, *gil'ə-tēn, -tēn', n.* an instrument for beheading by descent of a heavy oblique blade—adopted during the French Revolution, and named after Joseph Ignace *Guillotin* (1738-1814), a physician, who first proposed its adoption: a machine for cutting paper, straw, &c.: a surgical instrument for cutting the tonsils: a specially drastic rule or closure for shortening discussion.—*v.t.* to behead, crop, or cut short by guillotine.

guilt, *gilt, n.* the state of having done wrong: sin, sinfulness: the state of having broken a law: liability to a penalty.—*adv.* **guilt'ily.**—*n.* **guilt'iness.**—*adj.* **guilt'less,** free from crime: innocent. — *adv.* **guilt'lessly.** — *n.* **guilt'lessness.** — *adj.* **guilt'y,** justly chargeable: wicked: involving, indicating, burdened with, or pertaining to guilt.— *adv.* **guilt'y-like,** (*Shak.*) guiltily.—**guilty of,** (sometimes in *B.*) deserving. [Orig. a payment or fine for an offence; O.E. *gylt.*]

guilt (*Spens.*). Same as **gilt** (gilded).

guimp. Same as **gimp.**

guinea, *gin'i, n.* an obsolete English gold coin first made of gold brought from *Guinea,* in Africa: its value, finally 21s.—*adj.* priced at a guinea.— *ns.* **guin'ea-corn,** durra (*Sorghum vulgare*): pearl millet (*Pennisetum typhoideum*), a cereal; **guin'ea-fowl,** an African bird (Numida) of the pheasant family, dark-grey with white spots; **guin'ea-grass,** a tall African grass of the millet genus (Panicum); **guin'ea-hen,** a guinea-fowl: formerly, a turkey: (*Shak.*) a courtesan; **guin'ea-pig,** a small S. American rodent, the cavy: (*slang*) a fainéant company director: a person used as the subject of an experiment—as the cavy commonly is in the laboratory; **guin'ea-worm,** a very slender threadlike parasitic nematode worm (Filaria) common in tropical Africa.

guipure, *gē-pōōr', n.* a kind of lace having no ground or mesh, the pattern fixed by interlacing threads: a species of gimp. [Fr. *guipure*—O.Fr. *guiper,* prob. Gmc.; cf. Goth. *weipan,* to weave.]

guise, *gīz, n.* manner, behaviour: custom: external appearance: dress.—*v.t.* (*arch.*) to dress.—*v.i.* to act as a guiser.—*ns.* **guis'er** (*Scot.*), **guis'ard,** a person in disguise: a Christmas (or other) mummer. [O.Fr. *guise;* cf. O.H.G. *wisa* (Ger. *weise*), a way, guise, O.E. *wise,* way, *wis,* wise.]

guitar, *gi-tär', n.* a fretted musical instrument, now six-stringed—like the lute, but flat-backed.—*n.* **guitar'ist.** [Fr. *guitare*—L. *cithara*—Gr. *kithará;* see **cithern.**]

gula, *gū′lä*, *n.* the upper part of the throat: in some insects a plate on the under side of the head.—*adj.* **gū′lar**. [L. *gŭla*, throat.]

gulch, *gulch*, *gulsh*, *n.* (*U.S.*) a ravine or narrow rocky valley, a gully.—*v.t.* (*prov.*) to swallow greedily. [Origin doubtful.]

gulden, *gōōl′dan*, *n.* a gold or silver coin in Germany in the Middle Ages: the old unit of account in Austria, worth about 2s.: a florin: a Dutch coin, the guilder or florin. [Ger., lit. golden.]

gule (*Scot.*). See gold (2).

gules, *gūlz*, *n.* (*her.*) a red colour, marked in engraved figures by perpendicular lines.—*adj.* **gū′ly**. [O.Fr. *gueules*, perh.—L. *gŭla*, the throat.]

gulf (*arch.* **gulph**), *gulf*, *n.* an indentation in the coast: a deep place: an abyss: anything insatiable: in Oxford and Cambridge examinations, the place of those candidates for honours who are allowed a pass without honours.—*v.t.* to engulf.—*v.i.* to flow like a gulf.—*n.* **gulf′-weed**, a large olive-brown seaweed (Sargassum) that floats unattached in great 'meadows' at the branching of the Gulf Stream and elsewhere in tropical oceans.—*adj.* **gulf′y**, full of gulfs or whirlpools. [O.Fr. *golfe*—Late Gr. *kolphos*—Gr. *kolpos*, the bosom.]

gull, *gul*, *n.* a sea-mew, a sea-bird of the family Laridae, esp. of the genus Larus. [Prob. W. *gwylan*.]

gull, *gul*, *n.* (*Shak.*) an unfledged bird. [Perh. O.N. *gulr*, yellow.]

gull, *gul*, *n.* a dupe: an easily duped person: a hoax.—*v.t.* to beguile, hoax.—*ns.* **gull′-catcher**, (*Shak.*) a cheat; **gull′er**; **gull′ery**, deception; **gullibil′ity**.—*adjs.* **gull′ible** (also **gull′able**); **gull′ish**. [Perh. from gull (1 or 2).]

gullet, *gul′it*, *n.* the passage in the neck by which food is taken into the stomach: the throat: a narrow trench, passage, water-channel, or ravine. [O.Fr. *goulet*, dim. of *goule* (Fr. *gueule*)—L. *gŭla*, the throat.]

gully, **gulley**, *gul′i*, *n.* (*Scot.*) a big knife.

gully, **gulley**, *gul′i*, *n.* a channel worn by running water, as on a mountain-side: a ravine: a ditch: a groove: a grooved rail, as for a tramway: (*cricket*) the position between point and slips: (*pl.* **gull′ies**, **gull′eys**).—*v.t.* to wear a gully or channel in.—*adj.* **gull′ied**.—*ns.* **gull′y-hole**, a passage by which a gutter discharges into a drain; **gull′y-hunt′er**, one who picks up things from gutters. [Prob. gullet.]

gulosity, *gū-los′i-ti*, *n.* gluttony. [L. *gŭlōsus*, gluttonous—*gŭlō*, glutton—*gŭla*, throat.]

gulp, *gulp*, *v.t.* to swallow spasmodically or in large draughts.—*v.i.* to make a swallowing movement.—*n.* a spasmodic or copious swallow: a movement as if of swallowing: a quantity swallowed at once: capacity for gulping. [Cf. Du. *gulpen*, *gulp*.]

gum, *gum*, *n.* the firm fleshy tissue that surrounds the bases of the teeth: (*slang*) insolence.—*n.* **gum′boil**, a small abscess on the gum. [O.E. *gōma*, palate; O.N. *gōmr*, Ger. *gaumen*, palate.]

gum, *gum*, *n.* a substance that collects in or exudes from certain plants, and hardens on the surface, dissolves or swells in water, but does not dissolve in alcohol or ether: a plant gum or similar substance used as an adhesive, a stiffener, or for other purpose: any gum-like or sticky substance: chewing-gum: a hard gelatinous kind of sweet: a gum-tree: gummosis: (*U.S.*) a rubber overshoe: (*U.S.*) a bee-hive, orig. one made from a hollow gum-tree: (*U.S.*) a humbug.—*v.t.* to smear, coat, treat, or unite with gum: (*U.S.*) to humbug.—*v.i.* to become gummy: to exude gum:—*pr.p.* **gumm′ing**; *pa.t.* and *pa.p.* **gummed**.—*ns.* **gum′-ammō′niac**, -**ammonī′acum**, a gum-resin, inspissated juice of a Persian umbelliferous plant (Dorema), used in medicine and manufactures: that of an African species of Ferula; **gum′-ar′abic**, a gum obtained from various acacias; **gum′-boot′**, a rubber boot; **gum′-drag′on**, -**trag′acanth**, tragacanth; **gum′-elas′tic**, -ubber; **gum′-ju′niper**, sandarac; **gumm′a**, a gummy tumour (*pl.* **gumm′ata**).—*adjs.* **gumm′-atous**; **gummif′erous**, producing gum.—*ns.*

gumm′iness; **gumm′ing**, act of fastening with gum: application of gum-water to a lithographic stone: gummosis: becoming gummy; **gummo′sis**, pathological conversion of cell-walls into gum; **gummos′ity**, gumminess.—*adjs.* **gumm′ous**; **gumm′y**, consisting of or resembling gum: producing or covered with gum.—*ns.* **gum′-res′in**, a resin mixed with gum; **gum′-shoe**; **gum′-tree**, a tree that exudes gum, or gum-resin, kino, &c., esp. a Eucalyptus tree, or an American tree of the cornel family (Nyssa).—**up a gum-tree**, in straits (from the opossum's refuge). [O.Fr. *gomme*—L. *gummi*—Gr. *kommi*; prob.—Egyptian *kemai*.]

gum, *gum*, *n.* material that gathers in the corner of the eye.—*n.* **gum′-rash**, red-gum. [Perh. O.E. *gund*, matter, pus.]

gum, *gum*, *n.* used in oaths for God.

gumbo, *gum′bō*, *n.* the okra or its mucilaginous pods: a soup of which okra is an ingredient: a dish of okra pods seasoned: a negro patois in Louisiana, &c. [Angolan negro (*ki*)*ngombo*.]

gump, *gump*, *v.t.* and *v.i.* (*Scot.*) to guddle.

gumphion, *gum′fi-ən*, *n.* a funeral banner. [gonfanon.]

gumple-foisted, *gum′pl-foist′id*, *adj.* (*Scott*) sulky.

gumption, *gum(p)′shən*, *n.* sense: shrewdness: common-sense: art of preparing colours.—*adj.* **gump′tious**. [Poss. conn. with O.N. *gaumr*, heed.]

gun, *gun*, *n.* a tubular weapon from which projectiles are discharged, usually by explosion: a cannon, rifle, or, (*U.S.*) revolver: a device for spraying, squirting, or otherwise propelling material: a signal by gun: one who carries a gun, a member of a shooting-party.—*v.t.* to shoot: to shoot at: to provide with guns.—*v.i.* to shoot: to go shooting.—*ns.* **gun′-barrel**, the tube of a gun; **gun′-boat**, a small vessel of light draught, fitted to carry one or more guns; **gun′-carriage**, a carriage on which a cannon is mounted; **gun′cotton**, an explosive prepared by saturating cotton with nitric and sulphuric acids; **gun′-deck**, a deck carrying guns below the main deck (formerly below the spar-deck); **gun′-dog**, a dog trained to follow guns; **gun′fire**, the firing of guns: the hour at which the morning or evening gun is fired: an early cup of tea; **gun′-flint**, a piece of flint fitted to the hammer of a flint-lock musket; **gun′-layer**, one who lays a gun; **gun′-maker**; **gun′man**, a man who carries a gun, esp. a ruffian with a revolver; **gun′metal**, an alloy of copper and tin in the proportion of about 9 to 1, once used in making cannon: an imitation thereof: the colour of the alloy; **gunn′age**, the number of guns carried by a ship of war; **gunn′er**, one who works a gun: a private in the Artillery: (*naut.*) a warrant officer in charge of naval ordnance; **gunn′ery**, the art of managing guns, or the science of artillery; **gunn′ing**; **gun′-port**, a port-hole for a gun; **gun′powder**, an explosive mixture of saltpetre, sulphur, and charcoal; **gun′-room**, the apartment on board ship occupied by the gunner, or by the lieutenants as a mess-room; **gun′-runner**; **gun′-running**, smuggling guns into a country; **gun′shot**, the distance to which shot can be thrown from a gun.—*adj.* caused by the shot of a gun.—*adj.* **gun′-shy**, frightened by guns.—*ns.* **gun′smith**, a smith or workman who makes or repairs guns or small-arms; **gun′stick**, a ramrod; **gun′stock**, the piece on which the barrel of a gun is fixed; **gun′stone**, (*Shak.*) a stone shot.—**as sure as a gun**, quite sure, certainly; **blow great guns**, to blow tempestuously—of wind; **great gun**, (*obs.*) a cannon: (*coll.*) a person of great importance; **gunning for**, out to compass the downfall of; **kiss the gunner's daughter**, to be tied to a gun for a flogging; **son of a gun**, a soldier's bastard: a rogue, rascal; **stand, stick, to one's guns**, maintain one's position staunchly. [M.E. *gonne*, poss. from the woman's name *Gunhild*.]

gunnel, *gun′l*, *n.* Same as gunwale.

gunnel, *gun′l*, the butter-fish (Centronotus), a small long coast fish of the blenny family. [Origin unknown.]

Gunnera, *gun′ər-ä*, *n.* a gigantic-leaved herb of the

mare's-tail family. [After J. E. *Gunner* (1718-73), Norwegian botanist.]

gunny, *gun'i*, *n.* a strong coarse jute fabric. [Hind. *gōn*, *gōnī*, sacking—Sans. *gōnī*, a sack.]

gunter, *gun'tər*, *n.* a Gunter's scale: a rig with topmast sliding on rings (from its resemblance to a sliding variety of Gunter's scale).—**Gunter's chain**, a surveyor's chain of 100 links, 66 feet long (10 chains = 1 furlong; 10 sq. chains = 1 acre); **Gunter's scale**, a scale graduated in several lines for numbers, logarithmic sines, &c., so arranged that trigonometrical problems can be roughly solved by use of a pair of compasses, or in another form by sliding. [From the inventor, Edmund *Gunter* (1581-1626), astronomer.]

gunwale, **gunnel**, *gun'l*, *n.* the *wale* or upper edge of a ship's side next to the bulwarks, so called because the upper *guns* were pointed from it.

Günz, *günts*, *n.* the first (Pliocene) stage of glaciation in the Alps.—*adjs.* **Günz**, **Günz'ian.** [From a Bavarian tributary of the Danube.]

gup, *gup*, *interj.* (*obs.*) expressing remonstrance or derision. [Prob. **go up.**]

gup, *gup*, *n.* gossip : prattle. [Urdu *gap*.]

guppy, *gup'i*, *n.* a small West Indian fish (Lebistes), called also millions. [From R. J. L. *Guppy*, who sent it to the British Museum.]

gurge, *gurj*, *n.* (*Milt.*) a whirlpool. [L. *gurges*.]

gurgitation, *gur-ji-tā'shən*, *n.* surging. [L. *gurges -itis*, whirlpool.]

gurgle, *gur'gl*, *v.i.* to flow in an irregular noisy current : to make a bubbling sound.—*n.* the sound of gurgling. [Cf. It. *gorgogliare*.]

gurgoyle. See **gargoyle**.

gurjun, *gur'jun*, *n.* an East Indian dipterocarp yielding timber and a balsamic liquid used against leprosy. [Hind. *garjan*.]

Gurkha, **Goorkha**, *gōōr'kä*, *n.* one of the dominant people of Nepal, a broad-chested fighting race claiming Hindu origin, but Mongolised.

gurl, *gurl*, *n.* (*Scot.*) a growl.—*v.i.* to growl.—*adj.* **gur'ly**, grim : lowering : rough : surly. [Cf. **growl.**]

gurnard, *gur'nərd*, **gurnet**, *-nit*, *n.* a fish (Trigla ; of many species) with large angular head and three finger-like walking rays in front of the pectoral fin. [O.Fr. *gornard*, related to Fr. *grogner*, to grunt—L. *grunnīre*, to grunt ; from the sound they emit when taken.]

gurrah, *gur'ä*, *n.* a coarse Indian muslin. [Hind. *gārhā*, thick.]

gurry, *gur'i*, *n.* whale-offal : fish-offal.

guru, **gooroo**, *gōō'rōō*, *n.* a spiritual teacher : a venerable person. [Hind. *gurū*—Sans. *guru*, venerable.]

gush, *gush*, *v.i.* to flow out with violence or copiously : to be effusive, or highly sentimental.—*n.* that which flows out : a violent issue of a fluid.—*n.* **gush'er**, one who gushes : an oil-well not needing to be pumped.—*adj.* **gush'ing.**—*adv.* **gush'ingly.**—*adj.* **gush'y**, effusively sentimental. [M.E. *gosshe*, *gusche* ; the connexion, if any, with O.N. *gusa*, *gjósa*, Du. *gudsen*, is not clear.]

gusla, *gōōs'lä*, **gusle**, *-le*, **gusli**, *-lē*, *n.* a one-stringed Balkan musical instrument : a Russian instrument with several strings.—*n.* **guslar'**, a performer on it. [Bulg. *gusla*, Serb. *gusle*, Russ. *gusli*.]

gusset, *gus'it*, *n.* the piece of chainmail covering a joint in armour, as at the armpit : an angular piece inserted in a garment to strengthen or enlarge some part of it or to give freedom of movement.—*v.t.* to make with a gusset : to insert a gusset into. [O.Fr. *gousset—gousse*, a pod, husk.]

gust, *gust*, *n.* a sudden blast of wind : a violent burst of passion.—*adjs.* **gust'ful**, **gust'y**, stormy : irritable.—*n.* **gust'iness.** [O.N. *gustr*, blast.]

gust, *gust*, *n.* sense of pleasure of tasting : relish : gratification : (*obs.*) taste, experience : (*arch.*) flavour.—*adj.* and *n.* **gust'able.**—*n.* **gustā'tion**, the act of tasting : the sense of taste.—*adjs.* **gust'ative**, **gust'atory**, of or pertaining to the sense of taste ; **gust'ful**, savoury : enjoyable.— *n.* **gust'o** (It.), taste : zest.—*adj.* **gust'y**, savoury : appetisingly flavoured. [L. *gustus*, taste ; cf. Gr. *geuein*, to make to taste.]

gut, *gut*, *n.* the alimentary canal : sheep's or other intestines or silkworm's glands prepared for violin-strings, &c. : a narrow passage : a strait : a channel : a lane : (in *pl.*) the viscera : the inner or essential parts : (*coll.*) stamina, toughness of character, tenacity, staying power, endurance, forcefulness.—*v.t.* to take out the guts of : to remove the contents of : to reduce to a shell (by burning, dismantling, plundering, &c.) : to extract what is essential from :—*pr.p.* **gutt'ing** ; *pa.t.* and *pa.p.* **gutt'ed.** — *ns.* **gut'-scrap'er**, a fiddler ; **guts'iness** (*Scot.*).—*adj.* **guts'y** (*Scot.*), gluttonous. —*n.* **gutt'er.**—*v.t.* and *v.i.* **gutt'le**, to eat greedily. [O.E. *guttas* (pl.) ; cf. *geotan*, to pour ; prov. Eng. *gut*, Ger. *gosse*, a drain.]

gutta, *gut'ä*, *n.* a drop : a small drop-like ornament on the under side of a mutule or a regula of the Doric entablature : a small vacuole: (*zool.*) a small round colour-spot :—*pl.* **gutt'ae** (*-ē*).— *adjs.* **gutt'ate**, **-d**, containing drops : spotted.— *n.pl.* **Guttif'erae**, a family of archichlamydeous dicotyledons with abundant oil-glands and passages, and entire exstipulate opposite leaves, including mangosteen, mammee-apple, and according to some St John's wort.—*adj.* **guttif'erous**, exuding drops : of the Guttiferae.—**gutta serena**, amaurosis. [L. *gutta*, drop.]

gutta, *gut'ä*, *n.* the coagulated latex of sapotaceous and other trees, esp. gutta-percha : a hydrocarbon (empirically $C_{10}H_{16}$) found in gutta-percha : a solid gutta-percha golf-ball, used in the 19th century—(*coll.*)**gutt'y.**—*n.* **gutta-percha**-(*-per'chä*), a substance like rubber, but harder and not extensible, got chiefly from the latex of Malaysian trees of the Sapotaceae (Palaquium, Payena, &c.). —Also *adj.* [Malay *getah*, gum, *percha*, a tree producing it.]

gutter, *gut'ər*, *n.* a channel for conveying away water, esp. at the roadside or at the eaves of a roof : a furrow, groove : (*print.*) a grooved piece, used to separate pages of type in a form : (*fig.*) slum-life, social degradation : (*pl.* ; *Scot.*) mud, dirt.— *v.t.* to cut or form into small hollows.—*v.i.* to become hollowed : to trickle : to run down in drops, as a candle.—*ns.* **gutt'er-blood**, a low-born person : an indigenous town-dweller ; **gutt'er-man**, **-mer'chant**, a pavement-side vendor ; **gutt'er-snipe**, a neglected child, a street Arab. — *adj.* [O.Fr. *goutiere—goute*—L. *gutta*, a drop.]

guttiferous, **Guttiferae**. See under **gutta** (1).

guttural, *gut'ər-əl*, *adj.* pertaining to the throat : formed in the throat : throaty in sound.—*n.* (*phon.*) a sound pronounced in the throat or (loosely) by the back part of the tongue : a letter representing such a sound.—*v.t.* **gutt'uralise**, to sound gutturally : to make guttural.—*adv.* **gutt'urally.** [L. *guttur*, the throat.]

guy, *gī*, *n.* (*naut.*) a rope, rod, &c., used to steady anything, or hold it in position.—*v.t.* to keep in position by a guy.—*n.* **guy'-rope.** [O.Fr. *guis*, *guie* ; Sp. *guia*, a guide.]

guy, *gī*, *n.* an effigy of *Guy* Fawkes, dressed up grotesquely on the anniversary of the Gunpowder Plot (5th Nov.): an odd figure : (*U.S.*) a fellow : (*slang*) a joke, lark : (*slang*) flight, decamping.— *v.t.* to turn to ridicule.—*v.i.* to decamp.

guyle, **guyse**, (*Spens.*) forms of **guile**, **guise**.

guzzle, *guz'l*, *v.t.* and *v.i.* to swallow (esp. liquor, in Scotland food) greedily.—*n.* a bout of guzzling.— *n.* **guzz'ler.** [Perh. conn. with Fr. *gosier*, throat.]

gwyniad, **gwiniad**, *gwin'i-ad*, *n.* a whitefish (*Coregonus pennanti*), found in Bala Lake. [W. *gwyniad—gwyn*, white.]

gybe, *jīb*, *v.i.* (of a sail) to swing over from one side to the other : to alter course in this way.— *v.t.* to cause to gybe.—*n.* a gybing. [Origin obscure ; see **jib.**]

gyeld, a Spenserian form of **guild** (-hall).

gylden. See **gilden**.

gym, *jim*, *n.* and *adj.* a familiar abbreviation of **gymnasium**, **gymnastic**, **gymnastics**.

gymkhana, *jim-kä'nä*, *n.* a place of public resort for athletic games, &c. : a meeting for such sports. [Hind. *gend-khāna* (ball-house), racket-court, remodelled on *gym*nastics.]

gymmal. Same as **gimmal**.

gymnasium, *jim-nā'zi-əm*, *n.* a place, hall, building, or school for gymnastics : (*orig.*) a public place or building where the Greek youths exercised themselves, with running and wrestling grounds, baths, and halls for conversation : (usu. *gim-nā'zi-oom*) a (German) secondary school :—*pl.* **gymna'siums, -ia**, for continental schools **gymnasien** (*gim-nä-zi-ən.*—*adj.* **gymnā'sial.**—*ns.* **gymnas'iarch** (*-ärk* ; Gr. *archos*, chief), head of a gymnasium ; **gymnās'iast**, a pupil in a gymnasium : a gymnast. —*adj.* **gymnā'sic.**—*ns.* **gym'nast** (*-nast*), one skilled in gymnastics ; **gymnas'tic**, a system of training by exercise : (usu. **gymnas'tics**, used as *sing.*) exercises devised to strengthen the body : feats or tricks of agility.—*adjs.* **gymnas'tic, -al**, pertaining to athletic exercises : athletic, vigorous. —*adv.* **gymnas'tically.** [Latinised from Gr. *gymnasion—gymnos*, naked.]

gymnic, *jim'nik*, *adj.* (*Milt.*) gymnastic. [Gr. *gymnikos—gymnos*, naked.]

gymnorhinal, *gim-*, *jim-nō-rī'nl*, *adj.* with un-feathered nostrils. [Gr. *gymnos*, naked, *rhis*, *rhinos*, nose.]

gymnosoph, *gim'*, *jim'nō-sof*, **gymnosophist**, *-nos'ə-fist*, *ns.* an ancient Hindu philosopher who wore little or no clothing, and lived solitarily in mystical contemplation.—*n.* **gymnos'ophy.** [Gr. *gymnos*, naked, *sophos*, wise.]

gymnosperm, *gim'*, *jim'nō-spərm*, *n.* any of the lower or primitive group of seed-plants whose seeds are not enclosed in an ovary.—*adj.* **gymnosper'mous.** [Gr. *gymnos*, naked, *sperma*, seed.]

gymp. See gimp.

gynaeceum, *gīn-*, *jīn-*, *jin-ē-sē'əm*, *n.* women's quarters in a house : (*bot.*) the female organs of a flower. [Gr. *gynaikeion*, women's quarters.]

gynaeco-, *gīn-*, *jīn-*, *jin-ē'kō-*, or *-i-ko'-*, **gyno-**, *gīn'-*, *jīn'-*, or *jin'ō-*, or *-o'-*, in composition, woman, female.—*n.* **gyn(aec)oc'racy** (Gr. *kratos*, power), government by women or a woman. — *adjs.* **gyn(aec)ocrat'ic** ; **gynaecolog'ical.**—*ns.* **gyn-aecol'ogist** ; **gynaecol'ogy**, that branch of medicine which treats of the diseases of women ; **gynand'rism** (Gr. *anēr*, *andros*, man, male), hermaphroditism.—*adj.* **gynan'drous**, with stamen concrescent with the carpels, as in orchids.—*n.* **gynan'dromorph** (Gr. *morphē*, form), an animal combining male and female secondary characters. —*adjs.* **gynandromorph'ic, gynandromorph'-ous.** — *ns.* **gynandromorph'ism, gynan'dro-morphy.**—*adj.* **gynodioe'cious** (see dioecious), having hermaphrodite and female flowers on different plants. — *ns.* **gynodioe'cism** ; **gynoe-cium** (*jin-*, *jin-ē'si-əm* ; *bot.*), a wrong spelling of gynaeceum. — *adj.* **gynomonoe'cious**, having hermaphrodite and female flowers on the same plant.—*ns.* **gynomonoe'cism** ; **gyn'ophore** (Gr. *phoros*, carrying), an elongation of the receptacle of a flower carrying carpels only ; **gynostē'mium** (Gr. *stēma*, stamen), a united gynaeceum and androecium, as the column of an orchid. [Gr. *gynē*, *-aikos*, woman.]

gynn(e)y, Shakespearian spellings of guinea **(-hen).**

gyp, *jip*, *n.* a college servant at Cambridge and Durham. [Perh. **gypsy** ; **or** perh. obs. *gippo*, a short jacket, a varlet—obs. Fr. *jupeau*.]

gyp, *jip*, *n.* (*slang* ; *U.S.*) a swindle : a cheat.—*v.t.* to swindle :—*pr.p.* **gypp'ing** ; *pa.t.* and *pa.p.* **gypped.**

gyp, *jip*, *n.* (*slang*) pain, torture. [gee up.]

Gypsophila, *jip-sof'i-lä*, *n.* a hardy perennial akin to the pinks, but of more chickweed-like aspect. [Gr. *gypsos*, chalk, *phileein*, to love.]

gypsum, *jip'səm*, *gip'səm*, *n.* a soft mineral, hydrated calcium sulphate, source of plaster of Paris.—*adjs.* **gyp'seous** ; **gypsif'erous**, producing or con-taining gypsum. [L.,—Gr. *gypsos*, chalk.]

gypsy, **gipsy**, *jip'si*, *n.* a Romany, a member of a wandering people of Indian origin : a cunning rogue : a dark-skinned person.—*adj.* of the Gypsies : out-of-door : unconventional.—*v.i.* to live like a gypsy, camp out, or picnic.—*ns.* **gyp'sydom, gyp'syism** ; **gyp'sy-moth**, a kind of tussock-moth ; **gyp'sywort**, a labiate plant (Lycopus) with which gypsies were reputed to stain their skin. [Egyptian, because once thought to have come from Egypt.]

gyre, *jīr*, *n.* a ring, circle : a circular or spiral turn or movement.—*v.t.* and *v.i.* (in Lewis Carroll pronounced *gīr*) to spin round, gyrate.—*adjs.* **gyr'al, gyr'ant.**—*adv.* **gyr'ally.**—*v.i.* **gyr'ate** (or *-āt'*), to revolve, spin, whirl.—*adj.* **gyr'ate**, curved round in a coil.—*n.* **gyrā'tion**, a whirling motion : a whirl : a whorl.—*adjs.* **gyra'tional** ; **gyr'ātory**, revolving : spinning round : of traffic, revolving in one-way lines.—*ns.* **gyr'ō-car**, a monorail car balanced by a gyroscope ; **gyr'ō-com'pass**, a compass which indicates direction by the freely moving axis of a rapidly spinning wheel—owing to the earth's rotation, the axis assuming and main-taining a north and south direction.—*adj.* **gyroid'al**, spiral : rotatory.—*ns.* **gyr'omancy** (Gr. *manteiā*, divination), divination by walking in a circle and falling from giddiness ; **gyr'oplane, gyrop'ter**, a rotaplane ; **gyr'oscope, gyr'ostat**, an apparatus in which a heavy fly-wheel or top rotates at high speed, the turning movement resisting change of direction of axis, used as a toy, an educational device, a compass, a stabiliser of ships, &c.—*adjs.* **gyroscop'ic, gyrostat'ic** ; **gyr'ose**, having a folded surface : marked with wavy lines or ridges ; **gyr'ous.**—*n.* **gyr'us**, a convoluted ridge between two grooves : a convolution of the brain. [L. *gyrus*—Gr. *gyros*, a circle, ring.]

gyre-carlin, *gīr-kär'lin*, *n.* (*Scot.*) a witch. [O.N. *gýgr*, a witch, ogress, and **carline.**]

gyrfalcon. See gerfalcon.

gyron, giron, *ji'ron*, *n.* (*her.*) two lines drawn from the edge of the escutcheon and meeting at right angles in the fesse-point.—*adj.* **gyronn'y.** [Fr. *giron*, older *geron* ; O.H.G. *gēro* ; cf. **gore.**]

gyte, *gīt*, *adj.* (*Scot.*) crazy, mad.

gyte, *git*, *n.* (*Scot.*) a child : a first year's boy at Edinburgh High School or Academy. [Perh. **get**, offspring.]

gytrash, *gi'trash*, *n.* (*prov.*) a ghost.

gyve, *jīv*, earlier *gīv*, *v.t.* to fetter.—*n.* a shackle : a fetter. [M.E. *gives*, *gyves*.]

H

H, h, *āch*, sometimes spelt out **aitch**, *n.* the eighth letter in our alphabet, representing in Old English a guttural sound, gradually softened down to a spirant, and now often silent: (*mus.*) in German notation=B natural: in mediaeval Roman notation=200, H̄=200,000.

ha, *hä, interj.* denoting surprise, joy, or grief, and, when repeated, laughter: often an involuntary expression of hesitation. [Spontaneous utterance.]

ha', *hä, hǝ,* a shortened form of **have**.

ha', *haw, n.* Scots form of **hall**.

haaf, *häf, n.* (*Orkney* and *Shetland*) a deep-sea fishing-ground.—*n.* **haaf'-fish'ing**. [O.N. *haf*, sea.]

haanepoot, *hä'nǝ-pōt.* See **honeypot**.

haar, *här, n.* (*East Coast*) a raw sea-mist. [O.N. *härr*, hoary; cf. **hoar**.]

habanera, *(h)ä-bä-nā'rä, n.* a Cuban negro dance or dance-tune in 2-4 time. [*Habana* or Havana, in Cuba.]

habeas-corpus, *hä'bi-as-kor'pǝs, n.* a writ to a jailer to produce a prisoner in person, and to state the reasons of detention. [L., lit. have the body (*ad subjiciendum*, to be brought up).]

haberdasher, *hab'ǝr-dash-ǝr, n.* a seller of small-wares, as ribbons, tape, &c.: (*U.S.*) a men's outfitter.—*n.* **hab'erdashery**, a haberdasher's goods, business, or shop. [O.Fr. *hapertas*; origin unknown.]

haberdine, *hab'ǝr-dēn, -dīn, -din, n.* dried salt cod. [Old Du. *abberdaen*, also *labberdaen*; prob. from Le *Labourd*, or *Lapurdum*, Bayonne.]

habergeon, *hab'ǝr-jǝn (Milt. hab-ǝr'ji-on), n.* a sleeveless mail-coat, orig. lighter than a hauberk. [O.Fr. *haubergeon*, dim. of *hauberc*.]

habiliment, *hǝ-bil'i-mǝnt, n.* attire (esp. in *pl.*).—*adjs.* **hab'ilable**, (*Carlyle*) capable of being clothed; **habil'atory**, of clothes or dressing. [Fr. *habiller*, to dress—L. *habilis*, fit, ready—*habēre*.]

habilitate, *hǝ-bil'i-tāt, v.t.* to qualify: to equip or finance (as a mine, *U.S.*): to attire.—*v.i.* to qualify, esp. as a German university lecturer (Ger. *habilitieren*).—*ns.* **habilitā'tion**; **habil'itātor**. [L.L. *habilitāre*, to enable—L. *habilis*, able.]

habit, *hab'it, n.* ordinary course of behaviour: tendency to perform certain actions: custom: accustomedness: familiarity: bodily constitution: characteristic mode of development: outward appearance: dress, esp. official or customary: a garment, esp. a riding-habit.—*v.t.* to dress: (*arch.*) to inhabit.—*adj.* **hab'itable**, that may be dwelt in.—*ns.* **habitabil'ity**, **hab'itableness.**—*adv.* **hab'itably.**—*ns.* **hab'itant**, an inhabitant: (*āb-ē-tän᷉*; Fr.) a native of Canada or Louisiana of French descent (*pl.* in this sense sometimes **habitans**); **habitā'tion**, act of inhabiting: a dwelling or residence: a lodge of a society; **hab'itaunce**, (*Spens.*) dwelling-place; **hab'it-cloth**, a light broadcloth; **hab'it-mak'er**, a maker of riding-habits.—*adj.* **hab'itual**, customary: usual: confirmed by habit.—*n.* one who has a habit: a habitual drunkard, drug-taker, frequenter, &c.—*adv.* **habit'ually.**—*v.t.* **habit'uāte**, to accustom.—*ns.* **habituā'tion**; **hab'itūde**, constitution: characteristic condition: habit: (*obs.*) relation: (*obs.*) familiar acquaintance; **habitué** (*hab-it'ū-ā, ä-bē-tü-ā*), a habitual frequenter.—**habit and repute**, (*Scots law*) notoriety that affords strong and generally conclusive evidence of fact. [L. *habitus*, state, dress—*habitāre*, to dwell.]

habitat, *hab'i-tat, n.* (*biol.*) the normal abode or locality of an animal or plant. [L., (it) dwells.]

hable, *hā'bl, adj.* (*Spens.*). Same as **able**.

haboob, *hä-boob', n.* a sand-storm. [Ar. *habūb*.]

hachis, *(h)ä-shē, n.* hash. [Fr.]

hachure, *hash'ūr, ä-shür, n.* a hill-shading line on a map. [Fr.]

hacienda, *as-i-en'dä, n.* (*Sp. Amer.*) an estate or ranch: establishment: factory. [Sp.,—L. *facienda*, things to be done.]

hack, *hak, v.t.* to cut with rough blows: to chop or mangle: to notch: to roughen with a hammer: to kick the shins of.—*v.i.* to slash, chop.—*n.* an act of hacking: a gash: a notch: a chap in the skin: a kick on the shin.—*n.* **hack'ing.**—*adj.* short and interrupted, as a broken, troublesome cough.—*ns.* **hack'-log**, a chopping-block; **hack'-saw**, a saw for metals. [Assumed O.E. *haccian*, found in composition *tó-haccian*; cf. Du. *hakken*, Ger. *hacken*.]

hack, *hak, n.* a horse (or formerly, still in *U.S.*, a vehicle) kept for hire, esp. a poor one: an ordinary riding-horse: any person overworked on hire: a literary drudge: (*obs.*) anything hackneyed.—*adj.* hired: mercenary: hackneyed.—*v.t.* to make a hack of: to use as a hack: to hackney.—*n.* **hack'work**, literary drudgery for publishers. [**hackney**.]

hack, *hak, n.* a grating or rack, as for feeding cattle: a bank for drying bricks. [O.E. *hæcc, hæc,* grating, hatch; cf. **hatch** (1) and **heck.**]

hack, *hak, v.i.* (Shak., *M.W. of W.*) meaning unknown—poss. to take to the highway (or the street), or to have spurs hacked off.

hackberry, *hak'ber-i, n.* the hagberry: an American tree (Celtis) allied to the elm. [See also **hagberry.**]

hackbolt, *hak'bōlt, n.* the greater shearwater.—Also **hag'bolt**, **hag'den**, **hag'don**, **hag'down.** [Origin obscure.]

hackbut, *hak'but,* **hagbut**, *hag', n.* an arquebus.—*n.* **hackbuteer'.** [O.Fr. *haquebute*, from O.Du. *hakebus*; see **arquebus.**]

hackee, *hak'ē, n.* the chipmunk. [Imit.]

hackery, *hak'ǝr-i, n.* an Indian bullock-cart. [Perh. Hind. *chhakrā*, a cart.]

hackle, *hak'l, n.* a comb for flax or hemp: a cock's neck feather: the hair of a dog's neck: hair, whiskers: an angler's fly made of a cock's hackle, or its frayed-out part.—*v.t.* to dress with a hackle.—*n.* **hack'ler.**—*adj.* **hack'ly**, rough and broken, as if hacked or chopped: (*min.*) jagged and rough. [Cf. **hatchel**, **heckle**; Du. *hekel*; Ger. *hechel*; perh. partly from O.E. *hacele, hæcele*, cloak, vestment.]

hacklet, *hak'lit,* **haglet**, *hag', n.* prob. the shearwater: the kittiwake. [Origin unknown.]

hackmatack, *hak'mǝ-tak, n.* an American larch. [Indian word.]

hackney, *hak'ni, n.* a horse for general use, esp. for hire: ('s.) a person hired for drudgery.—*v.t.* to carry in a hackney-coach: to use overmuch: to make commonplace.—*adjs.* **hack'ney**, let out for hire; **hack'neyed**, devoted to common use: trite: dulled by overmuch use.—*ns.* **hack'ney-carr'iage**, **-coach**, a vehicle let out for hire; **hack'ney-coach'man**; **hack'neyman**, one who keeps hackney horses. [O.Fr. *haquenée*, an ambling nag: further history unknown.]

hacqueton. Same as **acton.**

had, *had, pa.t.* and *pa.p.* of **have**.

had, *häd, hawd, hud,* a Scots form of **hold**:—*pa.p.* **hadden** (*häd'n, hud'n*).

haddock, *had'ǝk, n.* a sea-fish of the cod family—(*Scot.*) **hadd'ie**. [M.E. *haddok*; ety. unknown.]

hade, *hād, n.* (*min.*) the angle between the plane of a fault, &c., and a vertical plane.—*v.i.* to incline from the vertical. [Origin obscure.]

Hades, *hā'dēz, n.* the underworld: the abode of the dead: hell. [Gr. *Aïdēs, Haïdēs,* the god of the underworld: the abode of the dead.]

hadith, *had'ith, hä-dēth', n.* the body of traditions

about Mohammed, supplementary to the Koran. [Ar. *hadīth*.]

had-I-wist, *had-ī-wist'*, *n.* (*obs.*) vain regret : remorse. [had I wist.]

hadj, hajj, *häj*, *n.* a Mohammedan pilgrimage to Mecca.—*n.* hadj′i, hajj′i (-*ē*, -*i*), one who has performed a hadj : a Christian who has visited Jerusalem. [Ar. *hajj*, pilgrimage.]

hadrome, *had′rōm*, *n.* (*bot.*) xylem. [Gr. *hadros*, thick.]

Hadrosaurus, *had-rō-saw′rəs*, *n.* a great Cretaceous dinosaur. [Gr. *hadros*, thick, *sauros*, a lizard.]

hae, *hā*, a form of **have**, esp. Scots.

haecceity, *hek-sē′i-ti*, *hēk-*, *n.* Duns Scotus's word for that element of existence on which individuality depends, hereness-and-nowness. [Lit. thisness, L. *haec*.]

haem-, *hēm-*, **hem-**, **haemat-**, **haemo-**, in composition, blood.—*n.* **haem** (also **hem, heme**), the pigment combined with the protein (globin) in haemoglobin.—*adj.* **haemal, hemal** (*hē′məl*), of the blood or blood-vessels : ventral — opp. to *neural.*—*ns.* **Haeman′thus** (Gr. *anthos*, flower), blood-flower, a S. African amaryllid ; **haematem′esis** (Gr. *emesis*, vomiting), vomiting of blood from the stomach.—*adj.* **haemat′ic**, pertaining to blood.—*ns.* **hae′matin**, a brown substance containing ferric iron obtainable from oxyhaemoglobin or from dried blood ; **hae′matite**, a valuable iron ore, Fe₂O₃, often blood-red, with red streak—also **hem′atite** ; **hae′matoblast** (Gr. *blastos*, a germ), a blood platelet.—*adj.* **hae′matoid**, bloodlike.—*ns.* **hae′matocele**, or **hem-** (Gr. *kēlē*, a tumour), a cavity containing blood ; **haematogen′esis**, blood formation ; **haematol′ogy**, the study of blood ; **haematol′ysis, haemol′ysis** (Gr. *lysis*, dissolution), breaking up of red bloodcorpuscles ; **haemato′sis**, the formation of blood : conversion of venous into arterial blood ; **Haematox′ylon** (Gr. *xylon*, wood), the logwood genus ; **haematox′ylin**, a dye got from logwood ; **haematū′ria** (Gr. *ouron*, urine), presence of blood in the urine ; **hae′min**, the chloride of haematin ; **haemoco′nia** (Gr. *kōniā*, dust), blood-dust, small colourless granules in the blood ; **haemoglo′bin**, or **hem-** (L. *globus*, a ball), the red oxygencarrying pigment in the red blood-corpuscles ; **hae′mony** (prob. Gr. *haimōnios*, blood-red), a plant with sovereign properties against magic, &c., in Milton's *Comus* ; **haemophil′ia** (Gr. *phileein*, to like), a constitutional tendency to excessive bleeding when any blood-vessel is even slightly injured ; **haemophil′iac**, a bleeder ; **haemop′tysis** (Gr. *ptysis*, a spitting), spitting of blood from the lungs ; **haemorrhage, hem-** (*hem′ər-ij* ; Gr. *haimorragiā*—*rhēgnynai*, to burst), a discharge of blood from the blood-vessels.—*adj.* **haemorrhagic** (-*raj′*).—*n.* **haemorrhoid**, or **hem-** (*hem′ər-oid*; Gr. *haimorrois*, -*idos*—*rheein*, to flow), dilatation of a vein about the anus—usu. in *pl.* piles.—*adj.* **haemorrhoid′al.**—*n.* **hae′mostat**, an instrument for stopping bleeding.—*n.* and *adj.* **haemostat′ic** (Gr. *statikos*, causing to stand), styptic. [Gr. *haima*, -*atos*, blood.]

haet, **ha′it**, *hāt*, *n.* (*Scot.*) a whit. [From the phrase *deil ha′ it*, devil have it.]

haffet, *hâf′it*, *n.* (*Scot.*) the side of the head : the temple : locks of hair on the temple. [**half-head** ; cf. O.E. *healf-hēafod*, the sinciput.]

hafflin, *hâf′lin* (*Scot.*). See **halfling**.

hafnium, *haf′ni-əm*, *n.* an element (Hf ; at. numb. 72) discovered in 1922 by Profs. Coster and Hevesy of Copenhagen. [L. *Hafnia*, Copenhagen.]

haft, *hâft*, *n.* a handle : a winged leaf-stalk.—*v.t.* to set in a haft : to establish firmly. [O.E. *hæft* ; Ger. *heft*.]

hag, *hag*, *n.* an ugly old woman, originally a witch : one of the round-mouths, allied to the lamprey (also hag′fish).—*adjs.* **hagg′ed**, haglike : haggard ; **hagg′ish.**—*adv.* **hagg′ishly.**—*adj.* **hag′-ridd′en**, ridden by witches, as a horse : troubled by nightmare.—*v.t.* **hag′-ride.**—*ns.* **hag′-seed**, a witch's offspring ; **hag′-ta′per**, the great mullein ; **hag′-weed**, the common broom-plant—a broomstick being a witch's usual aircraft. [Perh. O.E. *hægtesse*, a witch ; cf. Ger. *hexe*.]

hag, *hag*, *v.t.* and *v.i.* (*Scot.*) to hack, hew. [O.N. *höggva*.]

hag, hagg, *hag*, *n.* (*Scot.*) any broken ground in a moss or bog : a place from which peat has been dug : a pool or hole in a bog : a relatively high and firm place in a bog : the rough overhanging edge of a peat-hole or stream-bank : brushwood to be cut down. [O.N. *högg*, a gash, ravine, a cutting of trees.]

hagberry, *hag′ber-i*, **hackberry**, *hak′*, *n.* the birdcherry : the American hackberry. [Cf. O.N. *heggr*.]

hagbolt, hagden, hagdon, hagdown, *hag′dən*. See **hackbolt**.

hagbut. See **hackbut**.

Haggada, *hä-gä′dä*, *n.* a free Rabbinical homiletical commentary on the whole Old Testament, forming, with the Halacha, the Midrash : the Passover ritual.—Also **Hagga′dah, Aga′dah.**—*adjs.* **Haggad′ic, Haggadist′ic.**—*n.* **Hagga′dist.** [Heb.]

haggard, *hag′ərd*, *n.* an untamed hawk, or one caught when adult, esp. a female.—*adj.* untamed : intractable : lean : hollow-eyed.—*adv.* **hagg′ardly.** [O.Fr. *hagard*.]

haggis, *hag′is*, *n.* a Scottish dish made of the heart, lungs, and liver of a sheep, calf, &c., chopped up with suet, onions, oatmeal, &c., seasoned and boiled in a sheep's stomach-bag. [Ety. unknown.]

haggle, *hag′l*, *v.t.* to cut unskilfully : to mangle.—*v.i.* to bargain contentiously or wranglingly : to stick at trifles : to cavil.—*n.* **hagg′ler.** [Freq. of **hag**, at least in part.]

hagi-, *hag′i-* (sometimes *haj′i-*), in composition, holy : saint.—*ns.* **hag′iarchy**, rule or order of saints or holy persons ; **hagioc′racy** (Gr. *kratos*, power), government by holy ones.—*n.pl.* **Hagiog′rapha**, those books which with the Law and the Prophets make up the Old Testament.—*ns.* **hagiog′rapher**, a writer of the Hagiographa : a sacred writer : a writer of saints' lives.—*adjs.* **hagiograph′ic, -al.**—*ns.* **hagiog′raphist** ; **hagiog′raphy** ; **hagiol′ater**, a worshipper of saints ; **hagiol′atry** (Gr. *latreiā*, worship).—*adjs.* **hagiol′ogic, -al.**—*ns.* **hagiol′ogist**, a writer of, or one versed in, saints' legends ; **hagiol′ogy** ; **hag′ioscope**, a squint in a church, giving a view of the high altar.—*adj.* **hagioscop′ic.** [Gr. *hagios*, holy.]

haglet. Same as **hacklet**.

hah, *hä*, *interj.* Same as **ha**.

ha-ha, *hä-hä*, *interj.* in representation of a laugh.—*n.* the sound of laughter.—*v.i.* to laugh. [Imit.]

ha-ha, *hä′hä*, **hawhaw**, *haw′haw*, *n.* a sunk fence. [Fr. *haha*.]

haiduk, heyduck, *hī′dook*, *n.* a brigand : a guerrilla warrior : a liveried servant. [Hung. *hajduk*, pl. of *hajdú*.]

haik, haick, haique, hyke, *hīk*, *n.* an oblong cloth worn by Arabs on head and body. [Ar. *hayk*.]

Haikh, *hīhh*, *n.* and *adj.* Armenian. [Armenian.]

hail, *hāl*, *n.* (*obs.*) health : a call from a distance : a greeting : earshot.—*adj.* (*obs.*) sound, hale.—*v.t.* to greet : to address, accost : to call to from a distance : to summon to stop or come.—*interj.* of greeting or salutation.—*adj.* **hail′-fellow** (**-well-met′**), readily friendly and familiar.—Also *n.* and *adv.*—**hail from**, to come from. [O.N. *heill*, health, sound ; cf. **hale, heal.**]

hail, *hāl*, *n.* frozen rain or grains of ice falling from the clouds : a shower of hail or the like.—*v.i.* and *v.t.* to shower hail : to shower vigorously or abundantly.—*ns.* **hail′shot**, small shot that scatters like hail ; **hail′stone**, a ball of hail ; **hail′-storm.**—*adj.* **hail′y.** [O.E. *hægl* (*hagol*) ; Ger. *hagel*.]

hail, *hāl*, *n.* (*Scot.*) in ball-games, a goal : a score.—*v.t.* to score (a goal) : to put into the goal. [App. from **hail** (1), from the shout with which the player claimed a goal.]

hain, *hān*, *v.t.* (*Scot.*) to save, preserve : to spare.—*adj.* **hained.**—*n.* **hain′ing**, an enclosure. [O.N. *hegna*, to enclose, protect ; cf. Sw. *hägna* ; Dan. *hegne*.]

hainch, *hänsh*, Scots form of **haunch**.

hair, *hār*, *n.* a filament growing from the skin of an animal : an outgrowth of the epidermis of a plant : a fibre : a mass or aggregate of hairs, esp. that covering the human head: anything very small and fine : a hair's-breadth : type or character : a locking spring or other safety contrivance in a firearm.—*v.t.* to free from hair : to furnish with hair.—*ns.* **hair'-ball**, a concretion of hair in the stomach ; **hair'bell** (see **harebell**) ; **hair('s)'-breadth**, the breadth of a hair : a minute distance. —*adj.* extremely close or narrow.—*ns.* **hair'-brush**, a brush for the hair ; **hair'cloth**, cloth made wholly or partly of hair ; **hair'-cut**, a cutting of the hair ; **hair'-do**, (*coll.*) act or style of hairdressing ; **hair'dresser**, one whose occupation is the cutting and dressing of hair : a barber ; **hair'-dressing**, a dressing of the hair ; **hair'-eel**, a hairworm ; **hair'-grass**, a genus (Aira) of coarse grasses (perh. only a modification of the generic name) ; **hair'iness**.—*adj.* **hair'less**.—*ns.* **hair'line**, a line made of hair : a very fine line in writing, type, &c. : a finely striped cloth ; **hair'-net**, a net for confining a woman's hair ; **hair'-oil**, a scented oil for dressing the hair ; **hair'-pen'cil**, a fine paint-brush ; **hair'pin**, a bent wire or the like used for fastening up the hair.—*adj.* narrowly U-shaped, as a bend on a road.—*ns.* **hair'-powd'er**, powdered starch formerly dusted on the hair or wig ; **hair'-rais'er**, a tale of terror.—*adj.* **hair'-rais'ing**.—*ns.* **hair-restor'er**, a preparation claiming to make hair grow on bald places ; **hair'-seal**, a sea-lion, or eared seal with coarse hair only ; **hair'-shirt**, a penitent's garment of haircloth ; (*fig.*) an intimate or secret affliction ; **hair'-space**, the thinnest metal space used by compositors ; **hair'splitt'er**, a maker of over-fine distinctions ; **hair'splitt'ing** ; **hair'spring**, a slender spring regulating a watch balance ; **hair'streak**, a butterfly (Thecla, &c.) with fine white band under the wing ; **hair'stroke**, a hairline in penmanship ; **hair'-tail**, a fish of the family Trichiuridae, with whiplike tail ; **hair'-trigg'er**, a trigger that releases the hair of a gun ; **hair'-work**, work done or something made with hair, esp. human ; **hair'-worm**, a worm, like a horse-hair, which when young lives in the bodies of insects.—*adj.* **hair'y**, or of or like hair : covered with hair.—*against the hair*, against the grain : contrary to inclination ; *a hair of the dog that bit him*, a smaller dose of that which caused the trouble : a morning glass after a night's debauch—a homoeopathic dose ; *keep one's hair on*, (*slang*) to keep cool ; *lose one's hair*, to grow angry ; *make one's hair stand on end*, to give the greatest astonishment or fright to another ; *not to turn a hair*, to show no sweat : not to be ruffled or disturbed ; *put up the hair*, to dress the hair up on the head instead of wearing it hanging— once the mark of passage from girlhood to womanhood ; *split hairs*, to make superfine distinctions ; *to a hair, to the turn of a hair*, exactly, with perfect nicety. [O.E. *hǽr*, Ger., Du., and Dan. *haar*, &c. ; vowel perh. influenced by Fr. *haire*, a hair-shirt.]

hairst, *hārst*, a Scottish form of **harvest**.—*n.* **hairst-rig'**, a harvest-field, or a section of it, formerly cut in competition.

haith, *hāth*, *interj.* (*Scot.*) by my faith. [**faith.**]

hajj, hajji. See **hadj, hadji**.

hake, *hāk*, *n.* a gadoid fish resembling the cod. [Prob. Scand. ; cf. Norw. *hake-fisk*, lit. hook-fish.]

hakenkreuz, *hä'kən-kroits*, *n.* the swastika. [Ger., hook-cross.]

hakim, *hä-kēm'*, *n.* a physician. [Ar. *hakīm*.]

hakim, *hä'kim*, *n.* a judge, governor, or official in Pakistan. [Ar. *hakim*.]

Halachah, Halakah, Halacha, *hä-lä'hhä, -kä, n.* the legal element in the Midrash.—*adj.* **Halach'ic**. [Heb.,—*hālak*, to walk.]

halal, *hāl-äl'*, *v.t.* to slaughter according to Mohammedan law.—*n.* an animal that may lawfully be eaten as so slaughtered. [Ar. *halāl*, lawful.]

halation, *hə-, ha-lā'shən, n.* blurring in a photograph by reflection and dispersion of light. [**halo.**]

halberd, *hal'bərd, n.* an axe-like weapon with a hook or pick on its back, and a long shaft, used in the 15th and 16th centuries, in the 18th century denoting the rank of sergeant.—Also **hal'bert**.—*n.* **halberdier** (*-dēr'*), one armed with a halberd. [O.Fr. *halebard*—M.H.G. *helmbarde* (Ger. *hellebarde*)—*halm*, handle, or *helm*, helmet ; O.H.G. *barta* (Ger. *barte*), axe.]

halcyon, *hal'si-ən, n.* the kingfisher, once believed to make a floating nest on the sea, which remained calm during hatching.—*adj.* calm : peaceful: happy.—**halcyon days**, a time of peace and happiness. [L. *halcyōn*—Gr. *alkyōn*, fancifully changed to *halkyōn* as if from *hals*, sea, *kyōn*, conceiving.]

hale, *hāl*, *adj.* healthy : robust : sound of body : (*Scot.*) whole.—*n.* (*Spens.*) welfare.—*n.* **hale'ness**. [Northern from O.E. *hāl* ; see **whole** ; cf. **hail** (1), **heal**.]

hale, *hāl*, *v.t.* to drag. [O.Fr. *haler* ; Germanic in origin.]

half, *häf*, *n.* one of two equal parts : a half-year, term : a half-back : a halved hole in golf : (*pl.* **halves**, *hävz*).—*adj.* having or consisting of one of two equal parts : being in part : incomplete, as measures.—*adv.* to the extent of one-half: in part : imperfectly.—*n.* **half'-and-half**, a mixture of two things in equal proportions, esp. beer or porter and ale.—*adj.* and *adv.* in the proportion of one to one, or approximately : in part one thing, in part another.—*ns.* **half'-ape**, a lemur ; **half'-back**, in football, a player or position directly behind the forwards—in Rugby (*scrum half* and *stand-off* half), a link between forwards and three-quarters.—*adj.* **half'-baked**, underdone : incomplete : crude : immature : half-witted.—*v.t.* **half'-baptise'**, to baptise privately and hastily.—*ns.* **half'-beak**, a fish (Hyporhynchus, &c.) with spear-like under jaw ; **half'-bind'ing**, a bookbinding with only backs and corners of leather or the like ; **half'-blood**, relation between those who have only one parent in common : a half-breed.—*adj.* **half'-blood'ed**.—*ns.* **half'-blue'**, at Oxford and Cambridge, a substitute for a full blue, or the colours awarded him ; **half'-board**, (*naut.*) a manoeuvre by which a sailing-ship gains distance to windward by luffing up into the wind ; **half'-boot**, a boot reaching half-way to the knee.—*adjs.* **half'-bound**, bound in half-binding ; **half'-bred**, poorly bred or trained : mongrel. — *ns.* **half'-breed**, one of mixed breed (esp. a mixture of white and coloured races) ; **half'-brother, half'-sister**, a brother or sister by one parent only ; **half'-cap**, (*Shak.*) a cap only partly taken off : a slight salute ; **half'-caste**, a half-breed, esp. a Eurasian.—*adj.* **half'-checked**, (*Shak.*) with reins attached half-way up the side-piece of the bit, giving little leverage.—*ns.* **half'-cheek**, (*Shak.*) a face in profile ; **half'-close**, (*mus.*) an imperfect cadence ; **half'-cock'**, the position of the cock of a gun drawn back half-way and retained by the first notch : (*cricket*) a stroke made by playing neither forward nor back.—*adv.* in that position.—*adj.* **half'-cocked'**.—*ns.* **half'-crown'**, a coin worth **half'-a-crown'**, or two shillings and sixpence ; **half'-doll'ar**, an American coin worth 50 cents.—Also *adjs.*—*adj.* **half'-done**, partly done : partly cooked. —*n.* **half'-door**, the lower part of a divided door.— *n.* and *adj.* **half'-doz'en**, six.—*adjs.* **halfe'-hors'y**, (*Spens.*) of the Centaurs, partly of the nature of horses ; **half'en**, (*Spens.*) half.—*adv.* **half'endeale**, (*Spens.*) half.—*n.* **half'-face**, profile.—*adjs.* **half'-faced**, (*Shak.*) showing only part of the face: wretched-looking ; **half'-hard'y**, able to grow in the open air except in winter ; **half'-heart'ed**, lacking in zeal.—*adv.* **half'-heart'edly**.—*ns.* **half'-heart'edness** ; **half'-hitch**, a simple knot tied around an object ; **half'-hol'iday**, half of a working day for recreation ; **half'-kir'tle**, a kind of jacket worn by women in the 16th and 17th centuries ; **half'-length**, a portrait showing the upper part of the body.—*adj.* of half the whole or ordinary length.—*ns.* **half'-life**, the period of time in which the activity of a radioactive substance falls to half its original value ; **half'ling, half'lin**, (*Scot.*) a half-grown person, between boy and man : half a silver penny.—*adj.* half-grown.—*adv.* **half'-lin(g)s**, half : partially.—*adj.* half-grown.—*ns.*

half'-loaf', a loaf of half the standard weight; **half'-mast'**, the position of a flag partly lowered, in respect for the dead or in signal of distress.— Also *adv.* and *v.t.*—*ns.* **half'-meas'ure**, any means inadequate for the end proposed; **half'-moon**, the moon at the quarters when half the disk is illuminated: anything semicircular; **half'-mourn'ing**, mourning attire less than deep or full mourning: (*slang*) the condition of having one black eye; **half'-nel'son**, a hold in wrestling, one arm under arm, hand on back of the neck: (*fig.*) a disabling restraint; **half'-note**, (*mus.*) a minim; **half'-one'**, (*golf*) a handicap of one stroke every second hole; **half'-pay'**, reduced pay, as of an officer not on active service.—*adj.* **half'-pay**, on half-pay.—*n.* **halfpenny** (*hāp'ni*), a coin worth half a penny: its value : (*Shak.*) anything very small: (*pl.* **halfpence**, *hā'pəns*, also **halfpennies**, *hāp'niz*).—*adj.* valued at a halfpenny.— *ns.* **halfpennyworth** (*hāp'ni-wərth*—also **hap'orth**, *hāp'ərth*), as much as is sold for a halfpenny or is worth a halfpenny; **half'-pike**, a short-shafted pike: a spontoon; **half'-plate** (see **plate**); **half'-pound**, half a pound.—*adj.* weighing half a pound. —*ns.* **half-pound'er**, a fish or other thing weighing half a pound: a gun that throws a half-pound shot; **half'-price**, a charge reduced to half.—*adj.* and *adv.* at half the usual price.—*n.* **half-round'**, a semicircle.—*adj.* (*Milt.*) semicircular.—*n.* **half'-roy'al**, a kind of millboard.—*adj.* and *adv.* **half'-seas-o'ver**, halfway across the sea: half-drunk.— *ns.* **half'-shell**, one shell or valve of a bivalve; **half'-shift'**, a position of the hand in violin-playing giving notes a semitone above the open-string position; **half'-sove'reign**, a gold coin worth half'-a-sove'reign, or ten shillings.—*adj.* **half'-starved**, very inadequately fed.—*n.* **half'-sword**, fighting within half a sword's length: close fight. —*adj.* **half'-term**, about the middle of a term.— *ns.* **half'-text**, handwriting half the size of text (also *adj.*); **half'-tide**, the stage midway between flood and ebb.—*adj.* uncovered at half-tide.—*adj.* **half'-tim'bered**, built of a timber frame, with spaces filled in.—*n.* **half'-time'**, half of full or whole time: the middle of the whole time.—*adj.* **half'-time**, at or for half-time.—*ns.* **half'-tim'er**, one who works half the full time, esp. a school pupil; **half'-tint**, an intermediate tint; **half'-ti'tle**, a short title preceding the title-page or before a section of a book.—*adj.* **half'-tone**, representing light and shade photographically by dots of different sizes.—*n.* (*mus.*) a semitone.—*ns.* **half'-truth**, a belief containing an element of truth : a statement conveying only part of the truth; **half'-voll'ey** (see **volley**).—*adv.* **halfway'** (sometimes *häf'wā*), midway: at half the distance: imperfectly.—*adj.* **half'way**, equidistant from two points.—*n.* **half'-wit**, a would-be wit: an idiot. —*adj.* **half'-witt'ed**, mentally defective.—*n.* **half'-year**, half of a year, six months.—*adj.* **half'-year'ly**, occurring or appearing every half-year.— *adv.* twice a year.—*n.* a half-yearly publication.— **cry halves**, to claim half; **go halves**, to share equally; **not half**, (*slang*) not moderately: not even half: not at all: very much, exceedingly. [O.E. (Anglian) *half* (W.S. *healf*), side, half; cf. Ger. *halb* ; Dan. *halv*.]

halfa, alfa, (*h*)*al'fä*, *n.* N. African esparto-grass. [Ar. *halfä*.]

halfpace, *häf'pās*, *n.* a landing or broad step: a raised part of a floor. [O.Fr. *halt* (Fr. *haut*), high, *pas*, step.]

halibut, *hal'i-bət*, *n.* a large flatfish, more elongated than flounder or turbot.—Also **hol'ibut**. [App. **holy butt**, as much eaten on holy days; see **holy**, **butt** (5) ; cf. Du. *heilbot*, Ger. *heilbutt*.]

Halicore, *hal-ik'o-rē*, *n.* the dugong. [Gr. *hals*, sea, *korē*, girl.]

halide, *hal'īd*, *n.* a compound of a halogen with a metal or radical—a chloride, bromide, iodide, or fluoride. [Gr. *hals*, salt.]

haliidom, *hal'i-dəm*, *n.* (*arch.*) holiness : a holy place or thing—esp. in an oath. [O.E. *hāligdóm*— *hālig*, holy.]

halieutic, *hal-i-ū'tik*, *adj.* pertaining to fishing.

—*n.* **halieu'tics**, the art of fishing: a treatise thereon. [Gr. *halieutikos*—*halieus*, fisher—*hals*, sea.]

halimot(e), *häl'i-mōt*, *n.* an erroneous form of **hall-moot** (as if a holy or church court).

Haliotis, *hal-i-ō'tis*, *n.* earshell or ormer, a genus of gasteropods with ear-shaped shell with perforations, belonging to the family **Haliōt'idae**. [Gr. *hals*, sea, *ous*, *ōtos*, ear.]

halite, *hal'īt*, *n.* rock-salt. [Gr. *hals*, salt.]

halitus, *hal'i-təs*, *n.* a vapour.—*n.* **halitō'sis**, foul breath.—*adj.* **hal'itous**, vaporous. [L.]

hall, *hawl*, *n.* the main room in a great house : a building containing such a room : a manor-house : the main building of a college : in some cases the college itself : an unendowed college : a licensed residence for students : a college dining-room : hence, the dinner itself : a place for special professional education, or the conferring of diplomas, licences, &c.: the headquarters of a guild, society, &c. : a servants' dining-room and sitting-room (*servants' hall*) : a building or large chamber for meetings, concerts, exhibitions, &c.: a large room entered immediately by the front door of a house : a passage or lobby at the entrance of a house : (*arch.*) a clear space.—*ns.* **hall'-bed'room**, (*U.S.*) a bedroom over an entrance-hall; **hall'-door**, front-door; **hall'-mark**, the authorised stamp impressed on gold or silver articles at Goldsmiths' Hall or other place of assaying, indicating date, maker, fineness of metal, &c. : any mark of authenticity or good quality.—*v.t.* to stamp with such a mark.—*ns.* **hall'-moot**, the court of the lord of a manor : the court of a guild; **hall'way**, (*U.S.*) an entrance hall.—**a hall, a hall**, (*arch.*) a cry at a masque for room for the dance, &c.; **bachelor's hall**, a place free from the restraining presence of a wife; **Liberty Hall**, a place where everyone may do as he pleases. [O.E. *hall* (*heall*) ; Du. *hal*, O.N. *höll*, &c.]

hallal. Same as **halal**.

hallali, *hal'ə-lē*, *n.* a bugle-call.

hallaloo, *hal-ə-lōō'*, *n.* (*Fielding*) halloo.

hallan, *häl'ən*, *n.* (*Scot.*) a partition or screen between the door and fireplace in a cottage.—*n.* **hallan-shāk'er** (or -*shäk'ēr*), a sturdy beggar. [Perh. **hall**.]

hälleflinta, *hel'ə-flin-tä*, *n.* a very compact rock composed of minute particles of quartz and felspar. [Sw., hornstone.]

hallelujah, halleluiah, *hal-ə-lōō'yə*, *n.* and *interj.* the exclamation 'Praise Jehovah': a song of praise to God : a musical composition based on the word.—Also **alleluia**. [Heb. *hallelū*, praise ye, and *Jāh*, Jehovah.]

halliard. See **halyard**.

halling, *hal'ing, hawl'ing*, *n.* a Norwegian country dance in 2-4 time, or its tune. [Perh. *Hallingdal*, N.W. of Oslo.]

hallion, hallian, hallyon, *häl'yən*, *n.* a lout: a lazy rascal. [Origin unknown.]

hallo, halloa, *hə-lō', hu-lō', interj.* expressing surprise, discovery, becoming aware: used also in greeting, accosting, calling attention.—*n.* a call of hallo.—*v.i.* to call hallo.—Also **hullo** and other forms. [Imit.]

halloo, *hə-lōō'*, *n.* a cry to urge on a chase or to call attention.—*v.i.* to cry dogs on: to raise an outcry.—*v.t.* to encourage with halloos: to hunt with halloos.—**don't halloo till you 're out of the wood**, keep quiet till you are sure you are safe. [Imit.]

hallow, *hal'ō*, *v.t.* to make holy: to consecrate: to reverence.—*n.* (*obs.*) a saint.—*ns.* **Hallowe'en'**, (esp. *Scot.*) the eve of, or the evening before, All Hallows; **Hall'owmas**, the feast of All Hallows or All Saints, 1st November. [O.E. *hālgian*, to hallow, *hālga*, a saint—*hālig*, holy.]

halloysite, *hal-oiz'īt*, *n.* a clayey mineral, a hydrated aluminium silicate. [Omalius d'*Halloy* (1783-1875), Belgian geologist.]

Hallstatt, *häl'shtät*, *adj.* of the transition from the Bronze to the Iron Age. [From finds at *Hallstatt* in Upper Austria.]

hallucinate, *hal-(y)ōō'sin-āt*, *v.t.* to affect with

fāte, fär, ȧsk ; mē, hȧr (her) ; *mīne ; mōte ; mūte ; mōōn ; dhen* (then)

hallucination.—*v.i.* to experience hallucination.— *n.* **hallucinā'tion,** a perception without objective reality : (loosely) delusion.—*adjs.* **hallu'cinative, hallu'cinatory.** [L. *hallūcinārī* (better *ālūcinārī*), *-ātus,* to wander in the mind.]

hallux, *hal'uks, n.* the innermost digit of the hind-limb : the great toe : a bird's hind-toe :—*pl.* **halluces** (*hal-ū'sēz*). [Wrong form of L. (*h*)*allex, -icis.*]

halm, *häm.* Same as **haulm.**

halma, *hal'mä, n.* in the Greek pentathlon, a long jump with weights in the hands : a game played on a board of 256 squares, in which the men move by jumps. [Gr., a jump.]

halo, *hā'lō, n.* a ring of light or colour, esp. one round the sun or moon caused by refraction by ice-crystals, or one round the head of a holy person : an ideal or sentimental glory or glamour attaching to anything : (*pl.* **hā'lo(e)s,** rarely **hālō'nēs**).—*v.t.* to surround with a halo :—*pa.p.* **ha'loed, ha'lo'd.** [Gr. *halōs,* a threshing-floor, disk, halo.]

haloid, *hal'oid, n.* a halide.—*adj.* having the composition of a halide.—*n.* **halogen** (*hal'ə-jən*), any member of a group of elements (chlorine, bromine, iodine, fluorine) that form with metals compounds like common salt.—*v.t.* **halogenate** (*-oj'*), to combine with a halogen.—*adjs.* **halog'enous; hal'ophile** (*-fil, -fīl ;* Gr. *phileein,* to like), **haloph'-ilous,** tolerant of salt : capable of living in salt water.—*ns.* **haloph'ily,** adaptation to life in the presence of much salt ; **halophyte** (*hal'ō-fīt ;* Gr. *phyton,* a plant), a plant adapted to life in soil or water containing much salt.—*adj.* **halophytic** (*-fit'*). [Gr. *hals,* salt.]

Haloragis, *hal-ō-rā'jis, n.* sea-berry, an Australasian genus of plants giving name to the family **Halo-ragidā'ceae,** a reduced offshoot of the evening primrose family, including mare's-tail and water milfoil. [Gr. *hals,* sea, *rhäx, rhāgos,* a berry.]

halse, *hawls, Scot.* and *Northern* **hause, hawse,** *haws, n.* (*obs.* or *dial.*) the neck : the throat : a pass, defile, or connecting ridge.—*v.t.* (*obs.* or *arch.*) to embrace :—*pa.t.* **halsed,** (*Spens.*) **haulst.**—*ns.* **hause'-bane,** (*Scot.*) collar-bone ; **hause'-lock,** the wool of a sheep's neck. [O.E. *hals* (*heals*), neck ; Ger. *hals.*]

halse, *häls, haws, v.t.* (*obs.*) to salute, greet. [O.E. *halsian.*]

halser, *hawz'ər, n.* See **hawser.**

halt, *hawlt, v.i.* to come to a standstill : to make a temporary stop.—*v.t.* to cause to stop.—*n.* a standstill : a stopping-place : a railway station not fully equipped. [Ger. *halt,* stoppage.]

halt, *hawlt, v.i.* to be lame, to limp : to walk un-steadily : to vacillate : to proceed lamely or im-perfectly, to be at fault, as in logic, rhythm, &c.— *adj.* lame, crippled, limping.—*n.* a limp : foot-rot : (*Scot.*) an impediment in speech.—*n.* and *adj.* **halt'ing.**—*adv.* **halt'ingly.** [O.E. *halt* (*healt*) ; Dan. *halt.*]

halter, *hawlt'ər, n.* a rope for holding and leading an animal, or for hanging criminals.—*v.t.* to put a halter on. [O.E. *hælftre ;* Ger. *halfter.*]

halteres, *hal-tēr'ēz, n.pl.* the rudimentary hind-wings of flies. [Gr. *haltēres,* dumb-bells held by jumpers—*hallesthai,* to jump.]

halve, *häv, v.t.* to divide in half : in golf, to draw : in carpentry, to join by cutting away half the thickness of each.—*n.* **halv'er,** one who halves : a half-share.—*interj.* **halv'ers,** used in claiming half of a find. [half.]

halyard, halliard, *hal'yərd, n.* a rope or purchase for hoisting or lowering a sail, yard, or flag. [For *halier*—**hale,** by association with **yard.**]

ham, *ham, n.* the back of the thigh or hough : the thigh of an animal, esp. of a hog salted and dried.— *adj.* **hamm'y.** [O.E. *hamm ;* cf. dial. Ger. *hamme.*]

ham, *ham, n.* (*slang*) an actor who rants and over-acts : overacting : a part that lends itself to over-acting : an inexpert boxer : an amateur.—Also *adj.* [Prob. **hamfatter.**]

hamadryad, *ham-ə-drī'ad, n.* a wood-nymph who died with the tree in which she dwelt : a large poisonous Indian snake, *Naja hamadryas* : a large baboon of Abyssinia :—*pl.* **hamadry'ads, hama-dry'ades** (*-ēz*). [Gr. *hamadryas*—*hama,* together, *drÿs,* (oak) tree.]

Hamamelis, *ham-ə-mē'lis, n.* the American witch-hazel genus, giving name to a family, **Hamamel-idā'ceae,** akin to the planes. [Gr. *hamamēlis,* medlar—*hama,* together with, *mēlon,* an apple.]

hamarthritis, *ham-är-thrī'tis, n.* gout in all the joints. [Gr. *hama,* together, *arthrītis,* gout.]

hamartiology, *ham-är-ti-ol'ə-ji, n.* that section of theology which treats of sin. [Gr. *hamartiā,* sin, *logos* discourse.]

hamate, *hā'māt, adj.* hooked. [L. *hāmātus—hāmus,* hook.]

hamble, *ham'bl, v.t.* to mutilate, make useless for hunting (by cutting the balls of a dog's feet). [O.E. *hamelian.*]

Hamburg, Hamburgh, *ham'bərg, -bə-rə, n.* a black variety of grape (often *black Hamburg*) : a small blue-legged domestic fowl. — *n.* **ham'-burg(h)er,** Hamburg steak, finely chopped meat : a large sausage. [*Hamburg* in Germany, actual or imagined place of origin.]

hame, *hām, n.* one of the two curved bars of a draught-horse's collar. [Cf. Du. *haam,* L.G. *ham.*]

hame, *hām, Scots* form of **home.**—*adv.* **hame'-with,** homewards.

hamesucken, *hām'suk-n, n.* (*Scots law*) the assault-ing of a man in his own house. [O.E. *hām-sōcn—hām,* home, *sōcn,* seeking, attack ; cf. Ger. *heim-suchung.*]

hamfatter, *ham'fat-ər, n.* a third-rate minstrel, variety artist, actor.—*v.t.* and *v.i.* to act badly or ineffectively. [Perh. from an old negro minstrel song, *The Hamfat Man.*]

Hamiltonian, *ham-il-tō'ni-ən, adj.* pertaining to James *Hamilton* (1769-1831), or his method of teaching languages without grammar, to the philosopher Sir William *Hamilton* (1788-1856), to Sir William Rowan *Hamilton* (1805-65), Irish mathematician, or other of the name.

Hamite, *ham'īt, n.* a descendant or supposed de-scendant of *Ham,* son of Noah : a member of a dark-brown long-headed race of N.E. Africa (Galla, Hadendoa, &c.), sometimes understood more widely to cover much of N. Africa : a speaker of any language of a N. African family distantly related to Semitic (ancient Egyptian, Berber, &c.). —*adj.* **Hamitic** (*-it'ik*).

hamlet, *ham'lit, n.* a cluster of houses in the country : a small village. [O.Fr. *hamelet,* dim. of *hamel* (Fr. *hameau*), from Gmc. ; cf. **home.**]

hammal, hamal, *hum-äl', n.* an Eastern porter. [Ar. *hammāl.*]

hammam, *hum-äm', hum'um, ham'am, n.* an Ori-ental bathing establishment, a Turkish bath.— Also **humm'aum, humm'um.** [Ar. *hammām.*]

hammer, *ham'ər, n.* a tool for beating metal, breaking rock, driving nails, or the like : a striking-piece in the mechanism of a clock, piano, &c. : the apparatus that causes explosion of the charge in a firearm : the mallet with which an auctioneer announces that an article is sold : a small bone of the ear, the malleus.—*v.t.* to beat, drive, shape, or fashion with or as with a hammer : to contrive by intellectual labour, to excogitate (with *out*) : to trounce or criticise severely : to declare a defaulter on the Stock Exchange : to beat down the price of (a stock), to depress (a market).—*v.i.* to use a hammer : to make a noise as of a hammer : to persevere pertinaciously. — *adv.* **hamm'er-and-tongs',** with great noise and violence. — *ns.* **hamm'er-beam,** a horizontal piece of timber in place of a tie-beam at or near the feet of a pair of rafters ; **hamm'er-brace,** a curved brace sup-porting a hammer-beam ; **hamm'erhead,** a shark with hammer-shaped head (also **hamm'er-fish, hamm'er-head'ed shark**) : the umbrette (also **hamm'erkop,** Du.). — *adj.* **hamm'er-head'ed,** with a head shaped like a hammer : dull in intellect, stupid.—*n.* and *adj.* **hamm'ering.** —*adj.* **hamm'erless.**—*ns.* **hamm'erman,** one who wields a hammer, as a blacksmith, goldsmith, &c. ; **hamm'er-toe,** a condition in which a toe is permanently bent upwards at the base and

---

Neutral vowels in unaccented syllables : *el'ə-mənt, in'fənt, ran'dəm*

doubled down upon itself.—**bring to the hammer**, to sell, or cause to sell, by auction. [O.E. *hamor* ; Ger. *hammer*, O.N. *hamarr*.]

hammercloth, *ham'ər-kloth*, *n.* a cloth covering a coach-box. [Origin unknown.]

hammock, *ham'ok*, *n.* a cloth or netting hung by the ends, for use as a bed or couch. [Sp. *hamaca*, from Carib.]

hamose, *hā'mōs*, *adj.* hooked—also **hā'mous.**—*adjs.* **hamular** (*ham'ū-lər*), like a small hook ; **hăm'ūlate**, tipped with a small hook.—*n.* **hăm'ūlus**, a small hook or hook-like process. [L. *hāmus*, hook.]

hamper, *ham'pər*, *v.t.* to impede : to derange.—*n.* (*obs.*) a shackle : that which impedes. [First, about 1350, in Northern writers ; cf. O.N. and Mod. Ice. *hemja*, to restrain, Ger. *hemmen*.]

hamper, *ham'pər*, *n.* a large basket.—*v.t.* to give a hamper to, to bribe.—*ns.* **han'ap**, a large drinking-cup ; **han'aper**, (*obs.*) a case for a hanap : a receptacle for treasure, paper, &c.: a former department of Chancery. [O.Fr. *hanapier—hanap*, drinking-cup ; cf. O.H.G. *hnapf* ; O.E. *hnæpp*, a bowl.]

hamshackie, *ham'shak-l*, *v.t.* to shackle by tying head to fore-leg : to fetter, restrain. [**shackle** ; otherwise obscure.]

hamster, *ham'stər*, *n.* a rodent (Cricetus) with cheek-pouches reaching almost to the shoulders. [Ger.]

hamstring, *ham'string*, *n.* the great tendon at the back of the knee or hock of the hind-leg.—*v.t.* to lame by cutting the hamstring :—*pa.t.* and *pa.p.* **ham'stringed, ham'strung** (*Milt.*). [**ham, string.**]

han, *han*, an old *pl.* (*Spens.*) of **have.**

hanap, hanaper. See **hamper** (2).

hance, *hăns*, *n.* (*naut.*) a curved rise from a lower to a higher part : (*archit.*) the arc of smaller radius at the springing of an elliptical or many-centred arch —also **haunch.** [O.Fr. *hauce, haulce*, rise ; cf. **enhance.**]

hanch, *hănsh*, *v.i.* and *v.t.* to snap (at) with the jaws. [Older Fr. *hancher*.]

hand, *hand*, *n.* the extremity of the arm below the wrist : the forefoot : the extremity of the hind-limb when it is prehensile : a pointer or index : a measure of four inches ; a division of a bunch of bananas : side, direction, quarter : a worker, esp. in a factory or a ship : a performer : a doer, author, or producer : instrumentality : influence : share in performance : power or manner of performing : style : skill : handiwork : touch : stroke : control : keeping, custody : possession : style of handwriting : sign-manual : pledge or trothplight : consent to or promise of marriage, or fulfilment of such promise : the set of cards held by a player at one deal : the play of a single deal of cards : (loosely) a game of cards : a turn, round, or innings in a game : a round of applause.—*v.t.* to lay hands on, set hand to, manipulate, handle : to join hands with : to pass with the hand : to lead, escort, or help, esp. in entering a carriage : to transfer or deliver (often with *over*).—**hand-**, in composition, by hand, or direct bodily operation (as **hand'-knitt'ed, hand'-made, hand'paint'ed, hand'-set, hand'-sewn, hand'-weed'ed**) : operated by hand (as **hand'-or'gan**) : held in the hand (as **hand'-bask'et**).—*ns.* **hand'bag,** a bag for small articles, carried in the hand by ladies : a light travelling-bag ; **hand'-ball,** the sport of throwing and catching a ball ; **hand'-bar'row,** a wheelless barrow, carried by handles ; **hand'bell,** a small bell with a handle, rung by hand ; **hand'bill,** a light pruning-hook : a bill or loose sheet bearing an announcement ; **hand'-book,** a manual : (*U.S.*) a bookmaker's book of bets ; **hand(s)'breadth,** the breadth of a hand ; **hand'car,** (*U.S.*) a workman's vehicle driven by hand on a railway ; **hand'-cart,** a light cart drawn by hand ; **hand'craft,** handicraft ; **hand'cuff,** (esp. in *pl.*) a shackle locked upon the wrist.—*v.t.* to put handcuffs on. —*adj.* **hand'ed,** having hands : (*Milt.*) with hands joined.—*ns.* **hand'er,** one who hands : a blow on the hand ; **hand'fast,** a firm grip : custody : (*prov.*) a handle : a contract, esp. a betrothal.—*adj.*

bound : espoused : tight-gripping.—*v.t.* to betroth : to join by handfasting.—*ns.* **hand'fasting,** betrothal : probationary marriage : private marriage ; **hand'feeding,** feeding of animals or machinery by hand ; **hand'ful,** enough to fill the hand : a small number or quantity : a charge that taxes one's powers : (*pl.* **hand'fuls**) ; **hand'gall'op,** an easy gallop, restrained by the bridle-hand ; **hand'-glass,** a glass or glazed frame to protect plants : a mirror or a lens with a handle ; **hand'-grenade',** a grenade to be thrown by hand ; **hand'grip,** a grasp with the hand : something for the hand to grasp : (in *pl.*) close struggle ; **hand'-hold,** a hold by the hand : a place or part that can be held by the hand.—*n.pl.* **hand'icuffs,** fisticuffs. —*adv.* **hand'-in-hand',** with hands mutually clasped : in close association : conjointly.—Also *adj.*—*adj.* **hand'less,** without hands : awkward.— *ns.* **hand'-line,** a fishing-line without a rod ; **hand'list,** a list without detail, for handy reference ; **hand'loom,** a hand-worked weaving loom.—*adj.* **hand'made.**—*ns.* **hand'maid, hand'maiden,** a female servant.—*adj.* **hand'-me-down',** ready-made : second-hand.—*n.* a ready-made or second-hand garment.—*ns.* **hand'mill,** a quern : a coffee-mill, pepper-mill, &c., worked by hand ; **hand'-off,** act or manner of pushing off an opponent in Rugby football.—*v.t.* and *v.i.* **hand-off'.**—*ns.* **hand'-out,** (*U.S.*) a portion handed out, esp. to a beggar : an issue : a prepared statement issued to the press ; **hand'-pa'per,** paper with a hand for watermark.—*v.t.* **hand'-pick,** to pick by hand : to select one by one, e.g. a packed jury.—*ns.* **hand'play,** dealing of blows ; **hand'-post,** a finger-post ; **hand'-press,** a printing or other press worked by hand ; **hand'-prom'ise,** a solemn form of betrothal among the Irish peasantry ; **hand'rail,** a rail to hold by, as on stairs.—*adv.* **hand'-runn'ing,** (*dial.*) consecutively.—*ns.* **hand'saw,** a saw worked by hand : a small saw : (*Shak.*) perh. for **heronshaw** ; **hand'-screen,** a screen against fire or sun, held in the hand ; **hand'-screw,** a clamp : a jack for raising weights ; **hand'shake, hand'shaking,** a shaking of hands ; **hand'spike,** a bar used as a lever ; **hand'spring,** a cartwheel or somersault with hands on the ground ; **hand'-staff,** a staff-like handle, as of a flail : a staff as a weapon : a javelin : (*pl.* **hand'staves, hand'-staffs**) ; **hands'turn,** a single or least act of work. —*adjs.* and *advs.* **hand'-to-hand',** at close quarters ; **hand'-to-mouth',** with provision for immediate needs only.—*n.* **hand'work,** work done by hand. —*adjs.* **hand'worked, hand'wrought,** done by hand.—*n.* **hand'writing,** writing, script : style of writing.—**at any hand, in any hand,** (*Shak.*) at any rate, in any case ; **at first hand,** directly from the source ; **at hand,** conveniently near : within easy reach : near in time : (*Shak.*) at the beginning ; **at the hand of,** by the act of ; **bear a hand,** to take part, lend aid ; **bloody, or red hand,** the arms of Ulster, a sinister hand erect couped at the wrist gules, borne by baronets in a canton or inescutcheon ; **by hand,** by use of the hands, or tools worked by the hand, not by machinery or other indirect means ; **by the strong hand,** by force ; **change hands,** to pass to other ownership or keeping ; **come to hand,** to arrive : to be received ; **come to one's hand,** to be found easy : to come to close quarters ; **for one's own hand,** on one's own account ; **get one's hand in,** to get control of the play so as to turn one's cards to good use : to get into the way or knack ; **good hands,** a trustworthy source : good keeping : care of those who may be trusted to treat one well ; **hand and foot,** with respect to hands and feet : with assiduous attention ; **hand and (or in) glove,** on very intimate terms : in close co-operation ; **hand down,** or **on,** transmit in succession or by tradition ; **hand it to one,** (*slang*) admit his superiority, esp. as shown by his success in a difficult matter ; **hand of God,** unforeseen and unavoidable accident, as lightning, tempest ; **hand over hand,** by passing the hands alternately one before or above another, as in climbing a rope or swimming with a certain stroke : progressively :

with steady and rapid gain (also **hand over fist**); **hand over head**, headlong; **hands down**, with utter ease (as in winning a race); **hands off**, keep off: do not touch or strike; **hands up**, hold the hands above the head in surrender; **handwriting on the wall**, a foreshadowing of disaster (from Dan. v. 5); **in hand**, as present payment: in preparation: under control: (*billiards*) of a ball that has to be played from balk; **lay hands on**, to seize: to obtain or find: to subject physically to rough treatment: to bless or to ordain by touching with the hand(s)—also to **lay on hands**; **laying on of hands**, the touch of a bishop or presbyters in ordination; **lend a hand**, to give assistance; **off one's hands**, no longer under one's responsible charge; **old hand**, one experienced, as opposed to **young hand**; **on all hands**, on all sides, by everybody; **on hand**, ready, available: in one's possession; **on one's hands**, under one's care or responsibility: remaining as a burden or encumbrance; **out of hand**, at once, immediately, without premeditation: out of control; **poor hand**, an unskilful one; **set one's hand to**, to engage in, undertake: to sign; **show of hands**, a vote by holding up hands; **show one's hand**, to expose one's purpose; **stand one's hand**, (*slang*) to pay for a drink to another; **strike hands**, to make a contract; **take in hand**, to undertake; **take off one's hands**, to relieve one of; **to one's hand**, in readiness; **under one's hand**, with one's proper signature attached; **upper hand**, mastery; **wash one's hands (of)**, to disclaim responsibility (Matt. xxvii. 24). [O.E. *hand*; in all Gmc. tongues, perh. rel. to Goth. *hinthan*, to seize.]

handicap, *hand'i-kap*, *v.t.* to impose special disadvantages or impediments upon, in order to offset advantages and make a better contest: (*fig.*) to place at a disadvantage.—*n.* any contest so adjusted, or the condition imposed: (*golf*) amount added to or subtracted from one's score in stroke competitions: (*fig.*) a disadvantage.—*n.* hand'icapper, one who handicaps. [App. *hand i' cap*, from the drawing from a cap in an old lottery game.]

handicraft, *hand'i-krȧft*, *n.* a manual craft or trade. —*n.* **hand'icraftsman**, a man skilled in a manual art:—*fem.* **hand'icraftswoman.** [O.E. *handcræft*—*hand* and *cræft*, craft, assimilated to **handiwork.**]

handiwork, handywork, *hand'i-wərk*, *n.* work done by the hands, performance generally: work of skill or wisdom: creation: doing. [O.E. *handgewerc*—*hand* and *gewerc* (*geweorc*), work.]

handjar, hanjar, *han'jär*, *n.* a Persian dagger. [Pers. and Ar. *khanjar*.]

handkerchief, *hang'kər-chif*, *-chēf*, *n.* a cloth or paper for wiping the nose, &c.: a neckerchief.— Also (*Shak.*, &c.; now *vulg.*) **handk'ercher.**— **throw the handkerchief**, to summon to pursuit, call upon to take one's turn—as in children's games and royal harems. [hand, kerchief.]

handle, *hand'l*, *v.t.* to hold, move about, feel freely, with the hand: to make familiar by frequent touching: to manage: to discuss: to deal with, treat: to cope with: pass through one's hands: to trade or do business in.—*ns.* **hand'ler; hand'ling.** [O.E. *handlian*—*hand*, a hand.]

handle, *hand'l*, *n.* a part by which a thing is held: anything affording an advantage or pretext to an opponent.—*n.* **hand'le-bar**, the steering-bar of a cycle, or one half of it.—*adj.* **hand'led**, having a handle.—**a handle to one's name**, a title. [O.E. *handle*—*hand*.]

hand of glory, *hand əv glō'ri*, *n.* a charm made originally of mandrake root, afterwards of a murderer's hand from the gallows. [A translation of Fr. *main de gloire*—O.Fr. *mandegloire*, mandrake —*mandragore*.]

handsel, hansel, *han(d)'səl*, *n.* an inaugural gift, e.g. a present on Handsel Monday, a coin put in the pocket of a new coat, or the like: an inauguration or beginning, as the first money taken, earnest-money, a first instalment, the first use of anything: (*Spens.*) app. payment, penalty.—*v.t.* to give a handsel to: to inaugurate: to make a beginning

on: (*Chatterton*, from a blundering reading of a dictionary explanation, to cut off a first slice) to cut off, kill:—*pr.p.* **han(d)'selling**; *pa.p.* and *pa.t.* **han(d)'selled.—Handsel Monday**, the first Monday after New Year's Day, when handsels are given. [O.E. *handselen*, hand-gift, giving; or O.N. *handsal*.]

handsome, *han'səm*, *adj.* (*obs.*) convenient, handy: (*arch.*) suitable, becoming, gracious: good-looking: well-proportioned: dignified: liberal or noble: generous: ample.—*adv.* **hand'somely.—*n.* hand'someness.** [hand and suff. *-some*; cf. Du. *handzaam*.]

handy, *han'di*, *adj.* dexterous: ready to the hand: convenient: near.—*adv.* **hand'ily.—*ns.* hand'iness; hand'y-man**, a man for odd jobs: a bluejacket. [hand.]

handy-dandy, *hand'i-dand'i*, *n.* a children's game of guessing which hand a thing is in.—*interj.* (*Shak.*) the formula used in the game. [hand.]

hang, *hang*, *v.t.* to support from above against gravity: to suspend: to decorate with pictures, tapestry, &c., as a wall: to put to death by suspending by the neck: (in the *imper.*) a euphemism for damn.—*v.i.* to be suspended, so as to allow of free lateral motion: to drag: to hover: to impend: to be in suspense: to linger: to hold back: to depend: to have things hanging: to remain in close attention:—*pa.t.* and *pa.p.* **hanged** (by the neck), or **hung** (in all senses).—*n.* hang, action or mode of hanging: principle of connexion, plan: knack of using: a declivity: a slackening of motion: a hanging mass: (euphemistically) a damn.—*n.* hangabil'ity.—*adj.* hang'able, liable to be hanged: punishable by hanging.—*ns.* hang'-bird, a Baltimore oriole (from its pensile nest); hang'-dog, a low fellow.—*adj.* with a sneaking look.—*ns.* hang'er, one who hangs: that on which anything is hung: a wood on a hillside: a short sword; hang'er-on', one who hangs on or sticks to a person or place: an importunate acquaintance: a dependent; hang'fire, delay in explosion.—*adj.* hang'ing, suspending: suspended: drooping: downcast: deserving or involving death by hanging.—*n.* death by the halter: (esp. in *pl.*) that which is hung, as drapery.—*n.* hang'man, a public executioner.—*adj.* rascally.—*ns.* hang'-nest, a hangbird; hang'-over, a survival: after-effects of drinking.—**hang about**, to loiter; **hang back**, to show reluctance; **hang by a thread**, to depend upon very precarious conditions (from the sword of Damocles); **hang, draw, and quarter, to** hang, cut down while still alive, disembowel and cut in pieces for exposure at different places; **draw, hang, and quarter**, to drag on a hurdle or otherwise to the place of execution, then hang and quarter; **hang fire**, to be long in exploding or discharging: to be slow in taking effect: to hesitate; **hanging buttress**, a buttress supported by a corbel or the like; **hang in the balance**, to be in doubt or suspense; **hang off**, to let go: to hold off; **hang on**, to cling: to persist: to linger, wait about: to give close admiring attention to (esp. *to hang on one's lips*): to depend upon: to weigh down or oppress; **hang one's head**, to look ashamed or sheepish; **hang out**, to display, as a sign: (*slang*) to lodge or reside; **hang over**, to project over or lean out from; **hang together**, to keep united: to be consistent: to connect; **hang up**, to suspend: to delay: to replace a telephone receiver, break off communication; **hang up one's hat**, to take up one's abode. [O.E. *hangian*, pa.t. *hangode*, pa.p. *hangod* (intrans.) and *hón*, pa.t. *heng*, pa.p. *hangen* (trans.), and O.N. *hanga* and *hengja*; cf. Du. and Ger. *hangen*.]

hangar, *hang'ar, hang'gär*, *n.* a shed for carriages, aircraft, &c. [Fr.]

hang-nail, *hang'nāl.* See **agnail.**

hank, *hangk*, *n.* a coil or skein (840 yds. of cotton, 560 of worsted): a loop: a restraining hold.— *v.t.* to catch, as on a loop.—*v.i.* to catch, be entangled. [O.N. *hanki*, a hasp.]

hanker, *hangk'ər*, *v.i.* to linger about: to yearn (with *after, for*).—*n.* a yearning.—*n.* hank'ering. [Perh. conn. with hang; cf. Du. *hunkeren*.]

hankie, **hanky**, *hangk'i*, *n.* a coll. dim. of **handkerchief**.

hanky-panky, *hangk'i-pangk'i*, *n.* jugglery, underhand trickery. [Arbitrary.]

Hanoverian, *han-ə-vē'ri-ən*, *adj.* pertaining to *Hanover* (Ger. *Hannover*): of the dynasty that came thence to the British throne in 1714.—*n.* a native of Hanover: a supporter of the house of Hanover, opp. to a Jacobite.

Hansard, *han'särd*, *n.* the printed reports of debates in parliament, from Luke *Hansard* (1752-1828), whose descendants continued to print them down to 1889.—*v.t.* han'sardise, to confront with one's former recorded opinions.

Hanse, *hans*, *n.* a league, esp. one of German commercial cities.—*adjs.* **Hanse**, **Hanseatic** (*han-si-at'ik*). [O.H.G. *hansa*, a band of men (Ger. *hanse*).]

hansel. See **handsel**.

hansom, *han'səm*, *n.* a light two-wheeled cab with driver's seat raised behind.—Also **han'som-cab**. [From the inventor, Joseph A. *Hansom* (1803-82).]

ha'n't, *hänt*, a coll. contr. for **have not** or **has not**.

hantle, *hän'tl*, *n.* (*Scot.*) a good many : a good deal. [Poss. **hand** and **tale**, number.]

hanuman, *han-ōō-män'*, *n.* a long-tailed sacred monkey of the East Indies—the entellus monkey. [*Hanumān*, Hindu monkey god.]

hap, *hap*, *n.* chance : fortune : accident.—*v.i.* to chance, happen :—*pr.p.* **happ'ing** ; *pa.t.* and *pa.p.* **happed**.—*n.* and *adj.* **hap'haz'ard**, random : chance.—*adv.* at random.—*n.* **haphaz'ardness**.—*adj.* **hap'less**, unlucky : unhappy.—*adv.* **hap'lessly**.—*n.* **hap'lessness**.—*adv.* **hap'ly**, by hap, chance, or accident : perhaps : it may be. [O.N. *happ*, good luck.]

hap, *hap*, *v.t.* (*Scot.* and *E. Angl.*) to wrap up from the cold or rain.—*n.* a cloak or other covering. [Origin unknown.]

haplo–, in composition, single.—*ns.* **haplography** (*hap-log'rə-fi*), the inadvertent writing once of what should have been written twice ; **haplol'ogy**, omission in utterance of a sound resembling a neighbouring sound (as *idolatry* for *idololatry*).—*adj.* **hap'loid**, (*biol.*) having the reduced number of chromosomes characteristic of the species, as in germ-cells (opp. to *diploid*).—*n.* **haploid'y**.—*adj.* **haplostē'monous** (Gr. *stēmōn*, thread ; *bot.*), with one whorl of stamens. [Gr. *haploos*, single, simple.]

hap'orth, *hā'pərth*, for **halfpennyworth**.

happen, *hap'ən*, *v.i.* to fall out : to come to pass : to take place : to chance.—*adv.* (*N. Engl.*) perhaps.—*n.* **happ'ening**, event.—**if anything should happen**, in case of death. [hap.]

happy, *hap'i*, *adj.* lucky : fortunate : expressing, or characterised by, content, wellbeing, pleasure, or good : apt : felicitous.—*v.t.* (*Shak.*) to make happy.—*adv.* **happ'ily**, in a happy manner : in happiness : by chance : perhaps.—*n.* **happ'iness**.—*adj.* **happ'y-go-luck'y**, easy-going : taking things as they come.—*adv.* in any way one pleases.—**happy dispatch**, a euphemism for hara-kiri. [hap.]

hapteron, *hap'tər-on*, *n.* a holdfast or attachment organ of a plant thallus.—*adj.* **haptotrop'ic**, curving in response to touch, as a tendril.—*n.* **haptot'ropism**. [Gr. *haptein*, to fasten, *tropos*, turning.]

haqueton, *hak'tən*. Same as **acton**.

hara-kiri, *hä'rä-kē'rē*, *n.* ceremonious Japanese suicide by ripping the belly. [Japanese *hara*, belly, *kiri*, cut.]

harangue, *hə-rang'*, *n.* a loud speech addressed to a multitude : a pompous or wordy address.—*v.i.* to deliver a harangue.—*v.t.* to address by a harangue :—*pr.p.* **haranguing** (*-rang'ing*) ; *pa.t.* and *pa.p.* **harangued** (*-rangd'*).—*n.* **harangu'er**. [O.Fr. *arenge*, *harangue*—O.H.G. *hring* (Ger. *ring*), ring (of auditors).]

harass, *har'əs*, *v.t.* to distress, wear out : to annoy, pester.—*adj.* **har'assed**.—*adv.* **har'assedly**.—*n.* **har'asser**.—*n.* and *adj.* **har'assing**.—*adv.* **har'assingly**.—*n.* **har'assment**. [O.Fr. *harasser*; prob. from *harer*, to incite a dog.]

harbinger, *här'bin-jər*, *n.* (*obs.*) a host : (*obs.*) one sent before to provide lodging : a forerunner, pioneer.—*v.t.* to precede as harbinger. [M.E. *herbergeour* ; see **harbour**.]

harbour, *här'bər*, *n.* a refuge or shelter : a shelter, natural or artificial, for ships : a haven.—*v.t.* to lodge, shelter, entertain, or give asylum to : to trace to its lair.—*v.i.* to take shelter.—*ns.* **har'bourage**, place of shelter : entertainment ; **har'bour-bar'**, a sandbank at a harbour's mouth.—*n.pl.* **har'bour-dues**, charges for the use of a harbour.—*n.* **har'bourer**.—*adj.* **har'bourless**.—*ns.* **har'bour-light'**, a guiding light into a harbour ; **har'bour-master**, an officer who has charge of a harbour.—**harbour of refuge**, a harbour constructed to give shelter to ships : protection in distress. [M.E. *herberwe*—O.E. *hereboorg*—*here*, army, *beorg*, protection ; cf. Ger. *herberge*, O.N. *herbergi*.]

hard, *härd*, *adj.* not easily penetrated or broken : unyielding to pressure : firm, solid : (*min.*) difficult to scratch : difficult : strenuous : laborious : vigorous : fit, in good bodily condition : coarse and scanty : stingy, niggardly : difficult to bear : difficult to please : unfeeling : insensitive : severe : rigorous : stiff : constrained : intractable : obdurate : (of water) difficult to lather owing to calcium or magnesium salt in solution : harsh : brilliant and glaring : over-sharply defined : lacking in finer shades : (*U.S.*) spirituous : (of silk) retaining the natural gum : (of news) definite, substantiated : (of letters) representing a guttural, not a sibilant, sound : (*obs. phon.*) voiceless : (of radiation) penetrating.—*n.* hardship : hard state : hard ground : a firm beach or foreshore : hard labour.—*adv.* with urgency, vigour, &c. : earnestly, forcibly : uneasily : in excess : severely : to the full extent (as **hard aport**) : with difficulty : harshly : close, near, as in **hard by**.—*adv.* **hard'-a-lee'**, close to the lee-side, &c.—*adj.* **hard'-and-fast**, rigidly laid down and adhered to.—*ns.* **hard-and-fast'ness** ; **hard'-bake**, almond toffee ; **hard'beam**, the hornbeam.—*adjs.* **hard'-billed**, having a hard bill or beak ; **hard'-bitt'en**, given to hard biting, tough in fight ; **hard'-boiled**, boiled until solid : callously or cynically immovable : practical ; **hard'-cured**, thoroughly cured, as fish, by drying in the sun ; **hard'-drawn**, of wire, &c., drawn when cold to give the required thickness ; **hard'-earned**, earned with toil or difficulty.—*v.t.* **hard'en**, to make hard or harder or hardy : to make firm : to strengthen : to confirm in wickedness : to make insensitive.—*v.i.* to become hard or harder, *lit.* or *fig.*—*adj.* **hard'ened**, made hard : unfeeling : obdurate.—*ns.* **hard'ener** ; **hard'face**, a soullessly relentless person.—*adjs.* **hard'-fav'oured**, **hard'-feat'ured**, of hard, coarse, or forbidding features.—*ns.* **hard'-fav'ouredness** ; **hard'-feat'uredness** ; **hard'-fern**, the northern fern (Lomaria or Blechnum).—*adjs.* **hard'-fist'ed**, having hard or strong fists or hands : close-fisted : niggardly ; **hard'-fought**, sorely contested ; **hard'-got**, **hard'-gotten**, obtained with difficulty ; **hard'-grained**, having a close firm grain : forbidding.—*ns.* **hard'-grass**, cock's-foot or other coarse grass ; **hard'-hack**, an American Spiraea.—*adj.* **hard'-hand'ed**, having hard hands : rough : severe.—*n.* **hard'head**, knapweed : a fish of various kinds (gurnard, menhaden, fatherlasher).—*adjs.* **hard'-head'ed**, shrewd ; **hard'-heart'ed**, unfeeling : cruel.—*adv.* **hard'-heart'edly**.—*n.* **hard'-heart'edness**.—*adjs.* **hard'-hit**, seriously hurt, as by a loss of money : deeply smitten with love ; **hard'ish**, somewhat hard.—*adv.* **hard'ly**, with difficulty : scarcely, not quite : severely, harshly.—*adj.* **hard'-mouthed**, with mouth insensible to the bit : not easily managed.—*ns.* **hard'ness**, quality of being hard : (*min.*) power of, and resistance to, scratching ; **hard'-pan**, a hard layer often underlying the superficial soil : the lowest level.—*adjs.* **hard'-paste**, (of porcelain) made of china-clay and altered granite ; **hard'-pressed**, **hard'-pushed**, in difficulties ; **hard'-rid'ing**, strenuously riding ; **hard'-ruled**, (*Shak.*) ruled with difficulty ; **hard'-run**, greatly pressed ; **hard'-set**, beset by difficulty : rigid ; **hard'shell**, having a hard shell : rigidly orthodox : uncompromising.—*ns.* **hard'ship**, a thing, or conditions, hard to bear : privation : (*obs.*) an instance of hard treatment ; **hard'tack**, ship-biscuit.—*adjs.* **hard'-up'**, short of money, or of anything else ; **hard'-vis'aged**, of a hard, coarse, or forbidding visage. —*ns.* **hard'ware**, goods made of the baser metals, such as iron or copper ; **hard'wareman.**—*adj.* **hard'-won**, won with toil and difficulty.—*n.* **hard'wood**, timber of deciduous trees, whose comparatively slow growth produces compact hard wood.—*adj.* **hard'work'ing.**—**die hard**, to die only after a desperate struggle for life : to survive obstinately : (*obs.*) to die impenitent ; **go hard but**, will not easily fail that ; **go hard with**, turn out ill for ; **hard case**, a person difficult to deal with or reform ; **hard cash**, specie : ready money ; **hard currency**, metallic money : a term without precise meaning applied to the currency of any country with which one has an adverse balance of payments ; **hard drinker**, one who drinks persistently and excessively ; **hard facts**, undeniable, stubborn facts ; **hard lines**, a hard lot ; **hard money**, (*U.S.*) coin ; **hard of hearing**, pretty deaf ; **hard pad** (**disease**), a neurotropic virus disease of young dogs, sometimes characterised by hardening of the pads of the feet ; **hard put to it**, in great straits or difficulty ; **hard swearing**, persistent and reckless swearing (by a witness) : (often) perjury ; **hard words**, words that give difficulty to a half-educated reader : harsh words : angry words ; **hold hard**, stop ; **Mohs's scale of hardness**, a series of minerals each of which will scratch the one before it : (1) talc, (2) gypsum, (3) calcite, (4) fluorite, (5) apatite, (6) orthoclase, (7) quartz, (8) topaz, (9) corundum, (10) diamond. [O.E. *hard* (*heard*) ; Du. *hard*, Ger. *hart*, Goth. *hardus* ; allied to Gr. *kratys*, strong.]

hard, *härd*, (*Spens.* and *Scot.*) for **heard**.

hardoke, *här'dok*, *n.* (Shak., *King Lear*, folio) perhaps burdock.—The quartos have **hor'dock**. [Prob. O.E. *hár*, hoary, and **dock**.]

hards, *härdz*, **hurds**, *hərdz*, *n.pl.* coarse or refuse flax or hemp : (*Scott*) tarred rags used as torches. —*n.* **hard'en**, **herd'en**, **hurd'en**, a coarse fabric made from hards. [O.E. *heordan*.]

hardy, *härd'i*, *adj.* daring, brave, resolute : confident : impudent : able to bear cold, exposure, or fatigue.—*ns.* **hard'ihead** (*arch.*), **hard'ihood**, boldness : audacity : (*rare*) robustness.—*adv.* **hard'ily.**—*ns.* **hard'iment**, (*arch.*) hardihood : a deed of hardihood ; **hard'iness**. [O.Fr. *hardi*—O.H.G. *hartjan*, to make hard.]

hare, *här*, *n.* a common very timid and very swift rodent.—*v.i.* (*slang*) to run like a hare, hasten.—*ns.* **hare'-and-hounds'**, a paper-chase ; **hare'-bell**, the Scottish bluebell (*Campanula rotundifolia*). —*adjs.* **hare'-brained**, giddy : heedless : headlong ; **hare'-foot**, swift of foot ; **har'ish**, somewhat like a hare.—*n.* **hare'-lip**, a fissured upper lip like that of a hare.—*adj.* **hare'-lipped.**—*ns.* **hare's'-ear**, an umbelliferous plant (Bupleurum, various species) with yellow flowers ; **hare's'-foot** (**tre'foil**), a clover with long soft fluffy heads.—**first catch your hare**, make sure you have a thing first before you think what to do with it—from a direction in Mrs Glasse's cookery-book, where catch was a misprint for case, skin ; **hold** (**run**) **with the hare and run** (**hunt**) **with the hounds**, to play a double game, to be with both sides at once. [O.E. *hara* ; Du. *haas*, Dan. *hare*, Ger. *hase*.]

hareld, *har'ld*, *n.* a long-tailed northern sea-duck. [Mod. Ice. *havella*—*hav*, sea.]

harem, *hā'rem*, *hä-rēm'*, *n.* women's quarters in a Mohammedan house : a set of wives and concubines.—Also **haram'**, **harim** (*-ēm'*).—**harem skirt**, an early 20th-century divided skirt in imitation of Turkish trousers. [Ar. *harīm*, *haram*, anything forbidden—*harama*, to forbid.]

haricot, *har'i-kō*, *-kot*, *n.* a kind of ragout or stew of mutton and beans or other vegetables : the kidney-bean or French bean (plant or seed). [Fr. *haricot*.]

harigal(d)s, *har'i-glz*, *n.pl.* (*Scot.*) viscera.

hari-kari, *här'ē-kär'ē*, an incorrect form of **hara-kiri**.

hariolate, *har'i-ō-lāt*, *v.i.* to divine.—*n.* **hariolā'-tion**. [L. *hariolārī*, *-ātus*.]

hark, *härk*, *v.i.* to listen : to enquire : to go in quest.—*v.t.* to listen to.—*n.* a whisper.—*n.* **hark'-back**, a backward move.—**hark away, back, forward**, cries to urge hounds and hunters ; **hark back**, to revert. [See **hearken**.]

harken, *här'kən*, *v.i.* Same as **hearken**.

harl, *härl*, *n.* the fibre of flax, feathers, &c. [L.G.] **harl**, *härl*, *v.t.* (*Scot.*) to drag along the ground : to roughcast.—*v.i.* to drag oneself : to troll for fish.—*n.* act of dragging : a small quantity, a scraping of anything : a haul : roughcast.

Harleian, *här-lē'ən*, *här'li-ən*, *adj.* pertaining to Robert *Harley*, Earl of Oxford (1661-1724), and his son Edward, or the library collected by them. —**Harley Street**, in London, a favourite abode of physicians and surgeons, hence symbolically.

harlequin, *här'lə-kwin*, *n.* a pantomime character, in tight spangled dress, with visor and magic wand : a buffoon : a breed of small spotted dogs. —*v.i.* to play the harlequin.—*n.* **harlequināde'**, part of a pantomime in which the harlequin plays a chief part.—**harlequin duck**, a variegated northern sea-duck. [Fr. *harlequin*, *arlequin* (It. *arlecchino*), prob. the same as O.Fr. *Hellequin*, a devil in mediaeval legend, perh. of Gmc. origin.]

harlot, *här'lət*, *n.* (*obs.*) a general term of opprobrium applied to man or woman : a whore : a prostitute.—*adj.* lewd : base—*n.* **har'lotry**, prostitution : unchastity : meretriciousness : (*obs.*) a harlot.—*adj.* base, foul. [O.Fr. *herlot*, *arlot*, a base fellow ; origin unknown.]

harm, *härm*, *n.* injury : moral wrong.—*v.t.* to injure.—*n.* **harm-do'ing** (*Shak.*).—*adj.* **harm'ful**, hurtful.—*adv.* **harm'fully.**—*n.* **harm'fulness.**—*adj.* **harm'less**, not injurious, innocent : unharmed.—*adv.* **harm'lessly.**—*n.* **harm'lessness**. [O.E. *herm* (*hearm*) ; Ger. *harm*.]

harmala, *här'mä-lä*, *n.* the so-called African or Syrian rue (*Peganum Harmala*) of the bean-caper family.—Also **har'mel.**—*ns.* **har'malin(e)**, **har'min(e)**, alkaloids derived from its seeds. [Gr., from Semitic ; cf. Ar. *harmil*.]

harman, *här'mən*, *n.* (*old thieves' slang*) a constable : (in *pl.*) the stocks.—*n.* **har'man-beck**, a constable. [Origin obscure ; see **beak**.]

harmattan, *här-mä-tan'*, *här-mat'ən*, *n.* a dry dusty N.E. wind from the desert in W. Africa. [Fanti *haramata*.]

harmonic, *här-mon'ik*, *adj.* in harmony : in harmonious proportion : pertaining to harmony : musical : concordant : (*math.*) in accordance with the physical relations of sounds in harmony or bodies emitting such sounds.—*n.* a component whose frequency is an integral multiple of the fundamental frequency : an overtone : a flutelike sound produced on a violin, &c., by lightly touching a string at a node and bowing : one of the components of what the ear hears as a single sound : (in *pl.* form treated as *sing.*) musical acoustics.—*n.* **harmon'ica**, the musical glasses, Benjamin Franklin's instrument, revolving bell-glasses touched on the rim by a wet finger : an instrument composed of a sound-box and hanging strips of glass or metal, struck by a hammer : a mouthorgan.—*adj.* **harmon'ical.**—*adv.* **harmon'ically.** —*ns.* **harmon'ichord**, a keyboard instrument of violin tone, in which the strings are rubbed by rosined wheels ; **harmon'icon**, a harmonica : an orchestrion : a pyrophone (*chemical harmonicon*).— *adj.* **harmonious** (*-mō'ni-əs*), in, having, or producing harmony : in agreement : justly proportioned : concordant : congruous.—*adv.* **harmon'iously.**—*ns.* **harmon'iousness** ; **harmoniphon(e)** (*-mon'i-fon*, *-fōn*), a keyboard wind instrument with reeds ; **harmonisation** (*här-mən-ī-zā'shən*, or *-i-*).— *v.i.* **har'monise**, to be in harmony : to agree : to be compatible.—*v.t.* to bring into harmony : to reconcile : (*mus.*) to provide parts to.—*ns.* **harmonīs'er** ; **har'monist**, one skilled in harmony (in theory or composition) : a reconciler : one who seeks to reconcile apparent inconsistencies : **Harmonist**, member of a Second Adventist celibate sect (also **Har'monite**) founded by George Rapp (*d.* 1847), from its settlement at *Harmony*, Pennsylvania; **harmōn′ium**, a reed-organ, esp. one in which the air is forced (not drawn) through the reeds; **harmōn′iumist**; **harmonogram** (-*mon′*), a curve drawn by a harmonograph; **harmon′-ograph**, an instrument for tracing curves representing vibrations; **harmonom′eter**, an instrument for measuring the harmonic relations of sounds; **harmony** (*härʹmən-i*), a fitting together of parts so as to form a connected whole: agreement in relation: in art, a normal and satisfying state of completeness and order in the relations of things to each other: (*mus.*) a simultaneous and successive combination of accordant sounds: the whole chordal structure of a piece, as distinguished from its melody or its rhythm: concord: music in general: a collation of parallel passages with a view to demonstrate agreement—as of the Gospels. —**harmonic mean**, the middle term of three in harmonic progression; **harmonic minor**, a minor scale with minor sixth and major seventh, ascending and descending; **harmonic motion**, the motion along a diameter of a circle of the foot of a perpendicular from a point moving uniformly round the circumference; **harmonic pencil**, (*math.*) a pencil of four rays that divides a transversal harmonically; **harmonic progression**, a series of numbers whose reciprocals are in arithmetic progression, such numbers being proportional to the lengths of strings that sound harmonics; **harmonic proportion**, the relation of successive numbers in harmonic progression; **harmonic range**, a set of four points in a straight line such that two of them divide the line between the other two internally and externally in the same ratio; **harmonic receiver**, a receiver for electric waves, in harmony with the impulses producing them; **harmonic triad**, (*mus.*) the common chord; **harmony of the spheres** (see **sphere**); **pre-established harmony**, the divinely established relation, according to Leibniz, between body and mind—the movements of monads and the succession of ideas being in constant agreement like two clocks. [Gr. *harmoniā*—*harmos*, a joint, fitting.]

harmost, *härʹmost*, *n.* a Spartan governor of a subject city or province.—*n.* **harʹmosty**, the office of harmost. [Gr. *harmostēs*.]

harmotome, *härʹmo-tōm*, *n.* a zeolite, hydrated silicate of aluminium and barium. [Gr. *harmos*, joint, *tomē*, a cut.]

harn, *härn*, *n.* a coarse linen fabric. [See **harden**, under **hards**.]

harness, *härʹnis*, *n.* tackle: gear: equipment, esp. now of a draught animal: (*arch.*) armour for man or horse: equipment for any task.—*v.t.* to equip with armour: to put harness on: to attach by harness.—*ns.* **harʹness-cask**, (*naut.*) a cask for salt meat for daily use; **harʹness-makʹer**; **harʹness-room.**—**harnessed antelope**, any antelope of the striped genus Tragelaphus; **in harness**, occupied in the routine of one's daily work, not on holiday or retired. [O.Fr. *harneis*, armour.]

harns, *härnz*, *n.pl.* (*Scot.*) brains.—*n.* **harnʹ-pan**, brain-pan. [O.E. *hærn*, prob.—O.N. *hjarne*; cf. Ger. *hirn*; Gr. *krānion*.]

haro. See **harrow** (2).

harp, *härp*, *n.* a musical instrument played by plucking strings stretched from a curved neck to an inclined sound-board.—*v.i.* to play on the harp: to dwell tediously.—*v.t.* to render on or to the harp: to lead, call, or bring by playing the harp: to give voice to, esp. by surmise.—*ns.* **harpʹer**, **harpʹist**, a player on the harp.—*n.pl.* **harpʹings**, (*naut.*) the foreparts of the wales at the bow.—*ns.* **harpʹ-seal**, the Greenland seal, a grey animal with dark bands curved like an old harp; **harpʹ-shell**, a genus (Harpa) of gasteropods with ribs suggesting harp-strings.—**harp on one string**, to dwell constantly on one topic. [O.E. *hearpe*; Ger. *harfe*.]

harpoon, *här-pōōnʹ*, *n.* a barbed dart, esp. for killing whales.—*v.t.* to strike with a harpoon.—*ns.* **harpoonʹer**, **harpooneerʹ**; **harpoon-gunʹ**. [Fr. *harpon*, a clamp—L. *harpa*—Gr. *harpē*, sickle.]

harpsichord, *härpʹsi-kord*, *n.* a keyboard instru-

ment in which the strings are twitched by quills or leather points. [O.Fr. *harpechorde*; see **harp,** **chord.**]

harpy, *härʹpi*, *n.* (*myth.*) a rapacious and filthy monster, part woman, part bird: a large South American eagle (also **harʹpy-eaʹgle**): a rapacious person. [Gr. *harpyia*, lit. snatcher, in Homer a personification of the storm-wind—*harpazein*, to seize.]

harquebus, **harquebuse**, **harquebuss**, *härʹkwibus*, *n.* Same as **arquebus**.

harridan, *harʹi-dən*, *n.* a vixenish old woman. [Prob. O.Fr. *haridelle*, a lean horse, a jade.]

harrier, *harʹi-ər*, *n.* a small keen-scented dog for hunting hares: a cross-country runner. [**hare**, or **harry.**]

harrier. See **harry.**

Harrovian, *har-ōʹvi-ən*, *adj.* pertaining to *Harrow*. —*n.* one educated at Harrow school.

harrow, *harʹō*, *n.* a spiked frame or other contrivance for smoothing and pulverising land and covering seeds.—*v.t.* to draw a harrow over: to tear or harass.—*adj.* **harrʹowing**, acutely distressing.—*adv.* **harrʹowingly.** [M.E. *harwe.*]

harrow, **haro**, *harʹō*, *har-ōʹ*, *interj.* (*arch.*) alas: out upon it: in the Channel Islands a cry announcing a claim to legal redress. [O.Fr. *haro, harou*; not an appeal to *Rou* or Rollo.]

harry, *harʹi*, *v.t.* to plunder: to ravage: to destroy: to harass:—*pr.p.* **harrʹying**; *pa.t.* and *pa.p.* **harrʹied.**—*n.* **harrʹier**, one who, or that which, harries: a kind of hawk (Circus) that harries small animals.—**harrying**, or **harrowing, of hell**, Christ's delivery of the souls of patriarchs and prophets. [O.E. *hergian—here*, army; Ger. *heer.*]

harsh, *härsh*, *adj.* rough: jarring on the senses or feelings: rigorous.—*v.t.* **harshʹen.**—*adv.* **harshʹly.** —*n.* **harshʹness.** [M.E. *harsk*, a Northern word; cf. Sw. *härsk* and Dan. *harsk*, rancid, Ger. *harsch*, hard.]

harslet. See **haslet.**

hart, *härt*, *n.* a male deer (esp. red deer) from the age of six years, when the crown or sur-royal antler begins to appear:—*fem.* **hind.**—*ns.* **hartsʹhorn**, the antler of the red deer: a solution of ammonia in water, orig. a decoction of the shavings of a hart's horn (*spirit of hartshorn*); **hartʹs-tongue**, a fern (*Scolopendrium vulgare*) with strap-shaped leaves. [O.E. *heort.*]

hart, **hartely**, **harten**, **hartlesse**, (*Spens.*) for **heart**, **heartly**, **hearten**, **heartless**.

hartal, *härʹtal*, *hurʹtäl*, *n.* (*India*) a stoppage of work in protest or boycott. [Hind. *hartāl*, for *hattāl*.]

hartebeest, *härʹtə-bēst*, *n.* a large South African antelope. — **bastard hartebeest**, the sassaby [S.Afr.Du., hart-beast.]

harum-scarum, *häʹrəm-skāʹrəm*, *adj.* flighty: rash. —*n.* a giddy, rash person. [Prob. from obs. **hare**, to harass, and **scare**.]

haruspex, *ha-rusʹpeks*, *n.* one (among the Etruscans) who foretold events from inspection of entrails of animals:—*pl.* **harusʹpices** (*-pi-sēz*).—*ns.* **haruspication** (*-kāʹshən*), **harusʹpicy** (*-si*). [L., perh. from an Etruscan word and L. *specēre*, to view.]

harvest, *härʹvist*, *n.* (*obs.* and *dial.*) autumn: the time of gathering in crops: crops gathered in: fruits: product of any labour or act.—*v.t.* to reap and gather in.—*v.i.* to gather a crop.—*ns.* **harʹvest-bug**, **-louse**, **-mite**, **-tick**, a minute larval form of a mite (Trombidium) abundant in late summer, a very troublesome biter; **harʹvester**, a reaper: a reaping-machine: any member of the Opiliones, a class of Arachnida with very long legs (also **harʹvestman**, **harʹvest-spiʹder**); **harʹvest-feast**; **harʹvest-field**; **harʹvest-fly**, in U.S. a cicada of various kinds; **harʹvest-goose**, a goose eaten at a harvest-home feast; **harʹvest-home**, a celebration of the bringing home of the harvest; **harʹvest-laʹdy**, **harʹvest-lord**, the head-reapers at the harvest; **harʹvestman**, a harvester; **harʹvest-moon**, the full moon nearest the autumnal equinox, rising nearly at the same hour for several days; **harʹvest-mouse**, a very small mouse that nests in the stalks of corn; **harʹvest-queen**, the

fāte, fär, ȧsk; mē, hər (her); *mīne; mōte, mūte, mōōn; dhen* (then)

corn-maiden : the harvest-lady. [O.E. *hærfest* ; Ger. *herbst*, Du. *herfst*.]

has, *haz*. See **have**.—*n.* **has'-been**, a person or thing whose day is over :—*pl.* **has'-beens**.

hash, *hash*, *v.t.* to hack : to mince : to chop small. —*n.* that which is hashed : a mixed dish of meat and vegetables in small pieces : a mixture and preparation of old matter : a mess : (*Scot.*) a stupid fellow.—*adj.* **hash'y**.—**settle one's hash**, (*slang*) to silence or make an end of him. [Fr. *hacher*—*hache*, hatchet.]

hashish, hasheesh, *hash'ish, -ēsh*, *n.* leaves, shoots, or resin of hemp, smoked, or swallowed as an intoxicant. [Ar. *hashīsh*.]

hask, *hask*, *n.* (*Spens.*) a fish-basket. [Cf. **hassock**.]

haslet, *hāz'lit*, also **hās', hās', harslet, hārs'**, *n.* edible entrails, esp. of a hog. [O.Fr. *hastelet*, roast meat—*haste*, spit—L. *hasta*, a spear.]

hasp, *hāsp*, *n.* a clasp : a slotted part that receives a staple, as for a padlock : a spindle : a skein of yarn.—*v.t.* to fasten with a hasp. [O.E. *hæpse* ; Dan. and Ger. *haspe*.]

hassar, *has'ər*, *n.* a South American nest-building land-walking cat-fish (in the American sense). [Amer. Indian origin.]

hassock, *has'ək*, *n.* a tuft or tussock of grass, rushes, &c. : a stuffed stool : in Kent a soft calcareous sandstone.—*adj.* **hass'ocky**. [O.E. *hassuc*.]

hast, *hast*. See **have**.

hastate, -d, *hast'āt, -id*, *adjs.* spear-shaped : (*bot.*) with basal lobes turned outward. [L. *hastātus*—*hasta*, spear.]

haste, *hāst*, *n.* urgency calling for speed : hurry : inconsiderate speed.—*vs.t.* **haste, hasten** (*hās'n*), to put to speed : to hurry on : to drive forward.— *vs.i.* to move with speed : to hurry.—*n.* **hastener** (*hās'n-ər*).—*adv.* **hastily** (*hāst'i-li*).—*n.* **hast'iness**, hurry : rashness : irritability.—*adj.* **hast'y**, speedy : quick : rash : eager : passionate.—*n.* **hast'y-pudd'ing**, flour, milk, or oatmeal and water porridge. — *adj.* **hast'y-witt'ed**, rash. — **make haste**, to hasten. [O.Fr. *haste* (Fr. *hâte*), from Gmc. ; cf. O.E. *hæst*, Du. *haast*, Ger. *hast*.]

hat, *hat*, *n.* a covering for the head, generally with crown and brim : the dignity of cardinal, from the red hat : (*Scot.* or *obs.*) a salutation by lifting the hat.—*v.t.* to provide with or cover with a hat : to lift one's hat to.—*v.i.* (*Austr.*) to work alone :— *pa.t.* and *pa.p.* **hatt'ed.**—*ns.* **hat'band**, a ribbon round a hat ; **hat'box** ; **hat'brush** ; **hat'ful**, as much as will fill a hat (*pl.* **hatfuls**) ; **hat'-guard**, a string for keeping a hat from being blown away. —*adj.* **hat'less**.—*ns.* **hat'lessness** ; **hat'-peg**, a peg for hanging a hat on ; **hat'pin**, a long pin for fastening a hat to the hair ; **hat'-plant**, the sola plant, used for making topees ; **hat'rack**, a set of hat-pegs ; **hat'stand**, a piece of furniture with hat-pegs.—*adj.* **hatt'ed**, provided or covered with a hat.—*ns.* **hatt'er**, a maker or seller of hats : (*Austr.*) a miner or other who works by himself, one whose ' hat covers his family ' ; **hatt'ing** ; **hatt'ock**, (*Scot.*) a little hat ; **hat'-trick**, a con-jurer's trick with a hat : the taking of three wickets by consecutive balls (deserving a new hat) in cricket, or corresponding feat (as three goals) in other games.—**a bad hat**, (*slang*) a rascal ; **hang up one's hat** (see **hang**) ; **hats off to**, all honour to ; **horse and hattock** (*arch.*), to horse : boot and saddle ; **mad as a hatter**, quite mad ; **my hat**, an exclamation of surprise ; **pass, send, round the hat**, to take up a collection, solicit contributions ; **talk through one's hat**, to talk wildly or at random ; **under one's hat**, in con-fidence. [O.E. *hæt* ; Dan. *hat*.]

hatch, *hach*, *n.* a half-door : a wicket : the covering of a hatchway : a hatchway.—*v.t.* to close as with a hatch.—*ns.* **hatch'-boat**, a kind of half-decked fishing-boat ; **hatch'way**, an opening in a deck, floor, or roof.—**under hatches**, below deck : off duty : under arrest : in confinement. [O.E. *hæcc, hæc*, grating, half-gate, hatch ; cf. **hack** (3), **heck** ; Du. *hek*, gate.]

hatch, *hach*, *v.t.* to bring out from the egg : to breed : to originate, develop or concoct.—*v.i.* to bring young from the egg : to come from the egg :

to develop into young.—*n.* act of hatching : brood hatched.—*ns.* **hatch'er** ; **hatch'ery**, a place for artificial hatching, esp. of fish eggs.—**count one's chickens before they are hatched**, to depend too securely on some uncertain future event. [Early M.E. *hacchen*, from an assumed O.E. *hæccean*.]

hatch, *hach*, *v.t.* to mark with fine lines, incisions, or inlaid or applied strips.—*n.* **hatch'ing**, shading in fine lines. [O.Fr. *hacher*, to chop.]

hatchel, *hach'əl*, *n.* and *vb.* Same as **hackle**.

hatchet, *hach'it*, *n.* a small axe for one hand.—*adjs.* **hatch'et-faced**, having a narrow face with profile like a hatchet ; **hatch'ety**, like a hatchet.—**bury the hatchet**, to end war, from a habit of North American Indians. [Fr. *hachette*—*hacher*, to chop.]

hatchettite, *hach'it-īt*, *n.* mountain tallow, a natural waxy hydrocarbon. [After Charles *Hatchett* (d. 1847), English chemist.]

hatchment, *hach'mənt*, *n.* the arms of a deceased person within a black lozenge-shaped frame, formerly placed on the front of his house. [achievement.]

hate, *hāt*, *v.t.* to dislike intensely.—*n.* extreme dislike : hatred.—*adjs.* **hat'able, hate'able**, de-serving to be hated ; **hate'ful**, exciting hate : odious : detestable : feeling or manifesting hate.— *adv.* **hate'fully**.—*n.* **hate'fulness**.—*adj.* **hate'-less**.—*ns.* **hate'lessness** ; **hāt'er** ; **hate'rent**, (*Scot.*) hatred.—*adj.* **hate'worthy**.—*n.* **hāt'red**, extreme dislike : enmity : malignity. [O.E. *hete*, hate, *hatian*, to hate ; Ger. *hasz*.]

hate. Same as **haet**.

hath, *hath*, (*arch.*). See **have**.

hatter. See **hat**.

hatter, *hat'ər*, *v.t.* to trouble, annoy : to batter.

Hatteria, *hat-ē'ri-ä*, *n.* the sphenodon or tuatara. [Origin unknown.]

hatti-sherif, *hā'ti-she-rēf'*, *n.* (*hist.*) a decree signed by the Sultan of Turkey. [Pers. *khatt-i-sharif*, noble writing, from Ar.]

hattock. See under **hat**.

hauberk, *haw'bərk*, *n.* a long coat of chain-mail sometimes ending in short trousers, originally armour for the neck. [O.Fr. *hauberc*—O.H.G. *halsberg*—*hals*, neck, *bergan*, to protect.]

haud, *hawd*, *n.* and *vb.* a Scottish form of **hold** :— *pa.p.* **hudd'en**.

haugh, *hawhh*, *n.* (*Scot.*) a riverside meadow or flat. [O.E. *halh* (W.S. *healh*), corner.]

haughty, *haw'ti*, *adj.* proud : arrogant : con-temptuous : (*arch.*) bold : (*Spens.*) high.—*adj.* **haught, hault, haut** (*hawt* ; *Shak., Spens., Milt.*), haughty : exalted.—*adv.* **haught'ily**.—*n.* **haught'-iness**. [O.Fr. *halt, haut*, high—L. *altus*, high.]

haul, *hawl*, *v.t.* to drag : to pull with violence or effort : (*U.S.*) to transport.—*v.i.* to tug, to try to draw something : to alter a ship's course : to sail generally.—*n.* a pulling : a draught, as of a net : the contents of a hauled-in net : a catch, take, or gain : a hauled load.—*ns.* **haul'age**, act of hauling : transport, esp. heavy road transport : charge for hauling ; **haul'er, haulier** (*hawl'yər*), this form is used esp. for a man who conveys coal from the workings to the foot of the shaft, or for one who engages in road haulage business).— **haul over the coals** (see **coal**) ; **haul round** or **off**, to turn a ship's course away from an object ; **haul up**, to come or bring to rest after hauling : to call to account. [A variant of **hale**.]

hauld, *hawld*, *n.* a Scottish form of **hold**, as in the prov. phrase *out of house and hauld*, homeless.

haulm, halm, *hawm, hām*, *n.* straw, esp. of gathered plants : a strawy stem : a culm : straw or stems of plants collectively. [O.E. *halm* (*healm*).]

haulst, *hawlst*, (*Spens.*) for **halsed**.

hault, *hawt*, *adj.* (*Spens.*). See **haughty**.

haunch, *hawnsh*, also (old-fashioned) **hanch, hänsh**, *n.* the expansion of the body and near the pelvis : the hip with buttock : the leg and loin of venison, &c. : the side or flank of an arch between the crown and the springing : (*Shak.*) the rear : a jerked underhand throw.—*v.t.* to throw with an under-hand movement.—*n.* **haunch'-bone**, the innominate bone. [O.Fr. *hanche*, prob. of Gmc. origin; cf. O.H.G. *anchâ*, leg.]

haunt, *hawnt*, *v.t.* to frequent : to associate with : to follow importunately : to intrude upon continually : to inhabit or visit (as a ghost) : to cling, or keep recurring, to the memory of.—*v.i.* to be much about : to appear or visit frequently.—*n.* a place much resorted to : (*Shak.*) resort, habit of frequenting : (*U.S.*) a ghost.—*adj.* **haunt'ed,** frequented, infested, esp. by ghosts or apparitions. —*n.* **haunt'er.**—*n.* and *adj.* **haunt'ing.**—*adv.* **haunt'ingly.** [O.Fr. *hanter.*]

haurient, hauriant, *haw'ri-ənt, adj.* (*her.*) rising as if to breathe. [L. *hauriēns, -entis,* pr.p. of *haurīre,* to draw up, drink.]

hause. See **halse.**

haussmannise, *hows'mən-īz, v.t.* to open out, generally rebuild as Baron *Haussmann* did Paris as prefect of the Seine (1853-70).—*n.* **haussmannīsā′- tion.**

haustellum, *haws-tel'əm, n.* a sucking proboscis or its sucking end, as in flies :—*pl.* **haustell'a.**—*adj.* **haus'tellate,** having a haustellum.—*n.* **haustō′- rium,** the part by which a parasitic plant fixes itself and derives nourishment from its host:—*pl.* **haustō′ria.** [L. *haurīre, haustum,* draw up, drink.]

haut. See **haughty.**

hautboy, *(h)ō′boi, n.* same as **oboe:** a large kind of strawberry. [Fr. *hautbois—haut,* high, *bois,* wood.]

haute école, *ōt-ā-kol, n.* horsemanship of the most difficult kind. [Fr., high school.]

hauteur, *ō-tər′, n.* haughtiness : arrogance. [Fr.]

haüyne, *haw'in, hā′win, n.* a blue mineral, in composition like nosean, with calcium. [After the French mineralogist René J. Haüy (1743-1822).]

Havana, *hə-van′ä, n.* a fine quality of cigar, fondly supposed to be made at *Havana* (Habana).—Also **Havann′a(h).**

have, *hav, v.t.* to hold : to keep : to possess : to own : to hold in control : to bear : to be in a special relation to (analogous to, if short of, ownership) : to be characterised by : to be in enjoyment of : to experience : to know : to entertain in the mind : to grasp the meaning or point of : to have received as information : to put, assert, or express : to suffer, endure, tolerate : to hold or esteem : to cause or allow to be : to convey, take, cause to go : to accept, take : to get : to obtain : to give birth to : to be obliged : to get the better of, hold at a disadvantage or in one's power in a dilemma : to take in, deceive : as an auxiliary verb, used with the *pa.p.* in forming the perfect tenses : (*2nd pers.* *sing.* **hast ;** *3rd* **has,** *arch.* **hath ;** *pl.* **have ;** *pres. subj.* **have ;** *pa.t.* and *pa.p.* **had,** *2nd pers. pa.t.* **hadst ;** *pa.subj.* **had ;** *pr.p.* **hav′ing**).—*n.* one who has possessions (*pl.* **haves**).—*ns.* **have-at′- him,** (*Shak.*) a thrust ; **have′-not,** one who lacks possessions (*pl.* **have′-nots**) ; **have-on′,** a deception, a hoax : a piece of humbug or chaff ; **hav′er,** one who has or possesses, a holder : (*Scots law*) the person in whose custody a document is ; **hav′ing,** act of possessing : possession, estate : behaviour : (*Scot.* esp. in *pl. hāv′ingz*) good manners.—*adj.* greedy.—**had as good,** might as well ; **had as lief,** would as willingly ; **had better, best,** would do best to ; **had like to** (see **like**) ; **have at,** (let me) attack : here goes ; **had rather,** would prefer ; **have done, have to do with** (see **do**) ; **have it,** to prevail : to exceed in any way : to get punishment, unpleasant consequences ; **have it out,** to discuss or express explicitly and exhaustively ; **have on,** to wear : to take in, hoax, chaff ; **have up,** to call to account before a court of justice, &c. ; **have with you,** (*arch.*) I am ready to go with you ; **he's had it,** (*slang*) there is nothing for him : it's all up with him : he's been killed. [O.E. *habban,* pa.t. *hæfde,* pa.p. *gehæfd* ; Ger. *haben,* Dan. *have.*]

havelock, *hav′lək, n.* a white cover for a military cap, with a flap over the neck. [From Gen. Henry *Havelock,* 1795-1857.]

haven, *hā′vn, n.* an inlet affording shelter to ships : a harbour : any place of retreat or asylum.—*v.t.* to shelter.—*adj.* **hā′vened.** [O.E. *hæfen* ; Du. *haven,* Ger. *hafen.*]

haver, *hāv′ər, v.i.* (*Scot.*) to talk nonsense, or foolishly.—*n.* (usu. in *pl.*) foolish talk : nonsense. —*n.* **hav′erel,** a foolish person.

haver, *hav′ər, n.* (*Northern*) oats : the wild oat (grass).—*n.* **hav′ersack,** a bag for carrying food (orig. horse's oats) on a journey. [O.N. (pl.) *hafrar* ; cf. Ger. *hafer, haber,* oats, Fr. *havresac*—Ger. *habersack.*]

havildar, *hav′il-där, n.* an Indian sergeant. [Pers. *hawāl-dār.*]

haviour, haveour, *hāv′yər, n.* (*obs.*) possession : (*Spens.*) behaviour. [Partly O.Fr. *aveir,* possession, partly **behaviour.**]

havoc, *hav′ək, n.* general destruction : devastation. —*v.t.* to lay waste (*pr.p.* **hav′ocking** ; *pa.t.* and *pa.p.* **hav′ocked**). — *interj.* an ancient warcry, signal for plunder. [A.Fr. *havok*—O.Fr. *havot,* plunder ; prob. Gmc.]

haw, *haw, n.* a hedge : an enclosure : a messuage : the fruit of the hawthorn.—*ns.* **haw′buck,** a clown ; **haw′finch,** the common grosbeak ; **haw′- thorn,** a small tree of the rose family, much used for hedges. [O.E. *haga,* a yard or enclosure, a haw ; Du. *haag,* a hedge, Ger. *hag,* a hedge, O.N. *hagi,* a field.]

haw, *haw, v.i.* to speak with hesitation or drawl, natural or affected.—*adj.* **haw′-haw′,** pompously superior in enunciation.—*n.* a hesitation or affectation of superiority in speech : loud vulgar laughter. —*v.i.* to guffaw, to laugh boisterously. [Imit.]

haw, *haw, n.* the nictitating membrane : a disease of the nictitating membrane. [Origin unknown.]

hawhaw. See **ha-ha, haw.**

hawk, *hawk, n.* any bird of the falcon family other than the eagles, esp. of the sparrow-hawk (Accipiter) or the goshawk genus (Astur) : a predatory or a keen-sighted person : a hawk-moth.—*v.t.* and *v.i.* to hunt with trained hawks : to hunt on the wing. —*adj.* **hawk′-beaked, -billed,** with a beak, or nose, like a hawk's bill.—*ns.* **hawk′-bell,** a small bell attached to a hawk's leg ; **hawk′bit,** a plant (Leontodon) close akin to the dandelion ; **hawk′er.** —*adj.* **hawk′-eyed.**—*n.* **hawk′ing,** falconry.— *adj.* practising falconry : (*Shak.*) hawklike, keen. —*adj.* **hawk′ish.**—*n.* **hawk′-moth,** any member of the Sphinx family, heavy moths with hovering flight. —*adj.* **hawk′-nosed,** hook-beaked. — *ns.* **hawks′beard,** a plant (Crepis) very like hawkweed ; **hawks′bill,** a hawk-beaked turtle ; **hawk′- weed,** a genus (Hieracium) of yellow-headed ligulate-flowered composites.—**know a hawk from a hand-saw** (prob. for *hernshaw*), to be able to judge between things pretty well. [O.E. *hafoc* ; Du. *havik,* Ger. *habicht,* O.N. *haukr.*]

hawk, *hawk, v.t.* to force up from the throat.—*v.i.* to clear the throat noisily.—*n.* the act of doing so. [Prob. imit.]

hawk, *hawk, n.* a plasterer's slab with handle below. [Origin unknown.]

hawked, *hawkt,* (*Scot.*) **hawk′it,** *adj.* streaked : white-faced.—*ns.* **hawk′ey, hawk′ie,** a cow with white-striped face.

hawker, *hawk′ər, n.* one who goes about offering goods for sale : now confined to one who uses a beast of burden or vehicle (distinguished from a pedlar, who carries his wares bodily).—*v.t.* **hawk,** to convey about for sale : to cry for sale. [Cf. L.G. and Ger. *höker,* Du. *heuker.*]

hawm, *hawm, v.i.* (*prov.*) to lounge about. [Origin unknown.]

hawse, *hawz, n.* part of a vessel's bow in which the hawse-holes are cut.—*n.* **hawse′-hole,** a hole for a ship's cable. [O.N. *hāls,* neck.]

hawse. See **halse.**

hawser, *haw′zər, n.* a small cable, a large rope used in warping : a hawser-laid rope.—*adj.* **haw′ser- laid,** composed of strands with a left-handed twist twisted together to the right hand. [O.Fr. *haucier, haulser,* to raise.—L.L. *altiāre*—L. *altus,* high.]

hawthorn. See **haw.**

hay, *hā, n.* grass, &c., cut down and dried for fodder or destined for that purpose.—*ns.* **hay′-band,** a rope of twisted hay ; **hay′box,** an air-tight box of hay used to continue the cooking of dishes already begun ; **hay′cock,** a conical pile of hay in the field ; **hay'-fe'ver,** irritation by pollen of the nose, throat, &c., with sneezing and headache — also **hay'-asth'ma ; hay'-field,** a field where hay is made ; **hay'-fork,** a long-handled fork used in turning and lifting hay ; **hay'ing,** the making or harvesting of hay ; **hay'-knife,** a broad knife, with a handle set crosswise at one end, used for cutting hay from a stack ; **hay'-loft,** a loft in which hay is kept ; **hay'-maker,** one who makes hay : (*slang*) a wild swinging blow : (in *pl.*) a kind of country-dance ; **hay'-making ; hay'-mow,** a rick of hay : a mass of hay stored in a barn ; **hay'-rick,** a haystack ; **hay'seed,** grass seed dropped from hay : (*U.S.*) a rustic ; **hay'sel** (O.E. *sǽl,* season ; *prov.*), the hay season ; **hay'stack ; hay'-wire,** wire for binding hay.—*adj.* (*U.S. slang*) tangled : crazy : all amiss.—Also *adv.*—**hit the hay,** (*slang*) go to bed ; **make hay,** to toss and turn cut grass : to throw things into confusion ; **make hay while the sun shines,** to seize an opportunity while it lasts. [O.E. *hieg, hig, hég* ; Ger. *heu,* Du. *hooi* ; O.N. *hey.*]

hay, *hā, n.* a hedge, fence.—*ns.* **hay'-bote,** hedgebote ; **hay'-ward,** one who had charge of fences and enclosures and prevented cattle from breaking through : one who herded the common cattle of a town. [O.E. *hege—haga,* a hedge.]

hay, *hā, interj.* used on hitting in fencing.—*n.* (*Shak.*) a hit or home-thrust. [It. *hai,* thou hast (it)—*avere*—L. *habēre,* to have.]

hay. See hey.

hayle (*Spens.*). See hale.

hazard, *haz'ərd, n.* an old dicing game : chance : accident : risk : the thing risked : (*billiards*) the pocketing of the object ball (*winning* hazard), of the player's own ball after contact (*losing* hazard) : (*tennis*) the side of the court into which the ball is served : (*golf*) any difficulty on golf-links— bunker, long grass, road, water, whins, &c.—*v.t.* to expose to chance : to risk : to venture : to venture to say or utter.—*adj.* **haz'ardable.**—*n.* **haz'ardize,** (*Spens.*) hazard.—*adj.* **haz'ardous,** dangerous : perilous : uncertain.—*adv.* **haz'ardously.**—*ns.* **haz'ardousness ; haz'ardry,** (*Spens.*) playing at games of hazard or chance : rashness. [O.Fr. *hasard* ; prob. through the Sp. from Arab. *al zār,* the die ; according to William of Tyre from *Hasart,* a castle in Syria, where the game was invented during the Crusades.]

haze, *hāz, n.* vapour or mist, often shining and obscuring vision : mistiness : lack of definition or precision.—*v.t.* to make hazy.—*v.i.* to form a haze.—*adv.* **haz'ily.**—*n.* **haz'iness.**—*adj.* **haz'y,** thick with haze : ill-defined : not clear : confused (of the mind). [App. not O.E. *hasu, haswe,* grey.]

haze, *hāz, v.t.* to vex with needless or excessive tasks, rough treatment, practical jokes : to rag : to bully.—*ns.* **haz'er ; haz'ing.** [O.Fr. *haser,* to annoy.]

hazel, *hā'zl, n.* a tree (Corylus) of the birch family. —*adj.* of hazel : light-brown, like a hazel-nut.— *adj.* **hā'zelly.**—*ns.* **hā'zel-grouse, -hen,** the ruffed grouse ; **hā'zel-nut,** the edible nut of the hazel-tree. [O.E. *hæsel* ; Ger. *hasel,* O.N. *hasl,* L. *corulus, corylus.*]

he, *hē* (or when unemphatic *hi, ē, i*), *nom.* (irregularly or ungrammatically *accus.* or *dat.*) *masc. pron. of 3rd pers.* the male (or thing spoken of as if male) named before, indicated, or understood (*pl.* **they**).—*n.* a male (*pl.* **hes, he's**).—*adj.* male (esp. in composition).—*n.* **he'-man,** a man of exaggerated or extreme virility, or what some women take to be virility. [O.E. *hé, he.*]

head, *hed, n.* the uppermost or foremost part of an animal's body : the brain : the understanding : self-possession : a chief or leader : a headmaster, principal : the place of honour or command : the front or top of anything : a rounded or enlarged end or top : a capitulum : a mass of leaves, flowers, hair, &c. : a head-dress or dressing for the head : the peg-box and scroll of a violin, &c. : the membrane of a drum : the essential part of an apparatus : in a bicycle, the tube in which the front-fork is socketed : an individual animal or person : a title, heading : that which is or may be treated under a

heading : a topic or chief point of a discourse : source : energy of a fluid owing to height, velocity, and pressure : strength : insurrectionary force : highest point of anything : culmination : a cape : a froth on liquor poured out : point of suppuration : headway : a head's length or height : a mine tunnel : (in *pl.*) the obverse of a coin.—*v.t.* to remove the head or top from : (*obs.*) to behead : to supply with a head, top, or heading : to be the head, or at the head, of : to get ahead of and turn : to go round the head of : to face : to meet in the face : to cause to face or front : to strike with the head.—*v.i.* to form a head : to face, front : to shape one's course, make (for).—*n.* **head'ache,** a pain in the head.—*adj.* **head'achy.**—*ns.* **head'-band,** a band or fillet for the head : a band round the head of anything, even breeches : the band at each end of a book : a thin slip of iron on the tympan of a printing-press ; **head'-boom,** a jibboom or a flying jib-boom ; **head'borough** (see **borrow**), the head of a frank-pledge, tithing, or decennary : a petty constable ; **head'-boy,** the senior boy in a school ; **head'-chair,** a highbacked chair with head-rest ; **head'-cheese,** (*U.S.*) brawn ; **head'-cloth,** a kerchief worn instead of a hat ; **head'-dress,** a covering for the head : a mode of dressing the hair.—*adj.* **head'ed,** having a head : (*Shak.*) come to a head.—*ns.* **head'er,** one who heads : a dive head foremost : a brick or stone at right angles to the wall surface : a headed ball : a blow on the head ; **head'-fast,** a mooring rope at the bows ; **head'-frame,** the structure over a mine-shaft supporting the winding machinery ; **head'gear,** gear, covering, or ornament of the head : apparatus at the head of a mineshaft ; **head'-hunter ; head'-hunt'ing,** the practice of collecting human heads.—*adv.* **head'ily.**— *ns.* **head'iness ; head'ing,** the action of the verb head in any sense : a part forming a head : a small passage to be enlarged into a tunnel : words placed at the head of a chapter, paragraph, &c. ; **head'-land,** a point of land running out into the sea : a cape : the border of a field where the plough turns, ploughed separately afterwards.—*adj.* **head'-less.**—*ns.* **head'light,** a light carried in front ; **head'line,** line at the top of a page containing title, folio, &c. : title in a newspaper, caption : (in *pl.*) the sails and ropes next the yards ; **head'-lin'er,** one whose name is made most prominent in a bill or programme.—*adv.* **head'long,** with the head foremost or first : without thought, rashly : precipitately.—*adj.* rash : precipitate : precipitous.—*adj.* **head'-lugged,** (*Shak.*) dragged by the head.—*ns.* **head'man,** a chief, a leader ; **head'-mark,** a peculiar characteristic ; **headmas'ter,** the principal master of a school ; **headmis'tress ; head'-money,** a poll tax : prize-money by head of prisoners : a reward for a proscribed outlaw's head.—*adj.* **head'most,** most advanced, or forward.—*ns.* **head'-note,** a note placed at the head of a chapter or page, esp. a condensed statement of points of law involved introductory to the report of a legal decision : a tone produced in the head register.—*adj.* and *adv.* **head'-on',** head to head : with head pointing directly forward.—*ns.* **head'phone,** (usu. in *pl.*) a telephone receiver worn in pairs on a head-band, esp. for wireless listening : a hairdressing of similar form ; **head'piece,** a helmet : a hat : a head : a skull (*Spens.* **head'-peace**) : a brain : a man of intelligence : a top part : (*print.*) a decorative engraving at the beginning of a book, chapter, &c.—*n.pl.* **headquar'ters,** the quarters or residence of a commander-in-chief or general : a central or chief office, &c.—*ns.* **head'-race,** the race leading to a water-wheel ; **head'rail,** one of the rails at a ship's head ; **head'-reach,** the distance made to windward in tacking.—*v.i.* to shoot ahead, in tacking.—*ns.* **head'-rest,** a support for the head ; **head'-rhyme,** alliteration ; **head'-rig,** (*Scot.*) a headland in a ploughed field ; **head'-ring,** a palm-leaf ornament worn by Kaffir men in their hair after marriage ; **head'room,** uninterrupted space below a ceiling, bridge, &c. : space overhead ; **head'-rope,** a rope for tying or leading an animal ; **head'-sea,** a sea running directly against a ship's course ; head'-shake, a significant shake of the head ; head'ship, the position or office of head or chief ; heads'man, an executioner who cuts off heads ; head'-square, a square cloth worn as a covering for the head ; head'stall, the part of a bridle round the head : head-harness without a bit : a choir-stall with back to screen ; head'-sta'tion, the dwelling-house, &c., on an Australian sheep or cattle station ; head'-stick, (print.) a straight piece of furniture placed at the head of a form, between the chase and the type ; head'stock, (mach.) a device for supporting the end or head of a member or part ; head'stone, the principal stone of a building : corner-stone : gravestone ; head'-stream, a head-water : a high tributary : the stream forming the highest or remotest source.—adj. head'strong, obstinately self-willed.—ns. head'-tire, a head-dress ; head'-voice, the highest register : falsetto ; head'-wait'er, a person placed over the waiters of a restaurant or hotel ; head'-wat'er, the highest part of a stream, before receiving affluents ; head'-way, motion ahead, esp. of a ship : progress ; head'-wind, a directly opposing wind ; head'-work, mental work ; head'-work'er. — adj. head'y, affecting the brain : intoxicating : inflamed : rash : violent.—come to a head, to reach a climax ; eat one's head off (see eat) ; give a horse his head, to let him go as he chooses ; go by the head, to sink head foremost ; go to one's head, to disturb one's sobriety or good sense ; have a head on one's shoulders, to have ability and balance ; head and shoulders, very much, as if taller by a head and shoulders : violently ; head first, foremost, with the head first ; head off, to get ahead of so as to turn back : to deflect from path or intention ; heads or tails, an invitation to guess how a coin will fall ; head over heels, in a somersault ; keep, lose, one's head, to keep, lose, one's self-possession ; lay heads together, to confer and co-operate ; off one's head, crazy ; out of one's own head, spontaneously : of one's own invention ; over head and ears, deeply submerged or engrossed ; show one's head, to allow oneself to be seen ; take it into one's head, to conceive the notion ; turn one's head (see turn). [O.E. héafod ; cf. Du. hoofd, Ger. haupt.]

heal, hēl, v.t. to make whole and healthy : to cure : to restore to soundness : to remedy, amend.—v.i. to grow sound.—n. (arch. and Scot.) health : soundness : welfare.—adj. heal'able.—n. heal'er. —n. and adj. heal'ing.—adv. heal'ingly.—adj. heal'some, (Scot.) wholesome. [O.E. hǽlan (vb.), hǽlu (n.).—hál, whole ; cf. Ger. heil, Du. heel ; O.N. heill ; hail, hale, whole.]

heal. Same as hele.

heald, hēld, n. the same as heddle.—Also an old form of heel (2).

health, helth, n. sound bodily condition : soundness : condition of wholesomeness : wellbeing : state with respect to soundness : a toast.—adj. health'ful, enjoying, indicating, or conducing to health.—adv. health'fully.—n. health'fulness.—adv. health'ily.—n. health'iness.—adj. health'less.—ns. health'lessness ; health'-resort'.—adjs. health'some, (Shak.) healthy, wholesome ; health'y, in good health : conducive to or indicative of good health. [O.E. hǽlth—hál, whole.]

heame, hēm, adv. (Spens.) for home.

heap, hēp, n. a mass of things resting one above another : a mound : (Shak.) a company : a great number, a great deal (often in pl.), a collection : (B.) a ruin.—v.t. to throw in a heap : to amass : to load with a heap or heaps : to pile high, or above the rim or brim.—n. heap'stead, the buildings and works around a mine-shaft.—adj. heap'y, full of heaps.—knock all of a heap, to confound utterly. [O.E. héap ; cf. O.N. hópr, Ger. haufe, Du. hoop.]

hear, hēr, v.t. to perceive by the ear : to accede to : to listen to : to listen to in trial of ability to repeat : to try judicially : to be informed : to be called.— (Milt., a Latinism) to be called.—v.i. to have or exercise the sense of hearing : to listen : to have

news : (Spens., a Graecism) to be spoken of :—pa.t. and pa.p. heard (hǝrd).—adj. heard (hǝrd).—ns. hear'er ; hear'ing, power or act of perceiving sound : opportunity to be heard : audience : audition : judicial investigation and listening to evidence and arguments, esp. without a jury : earshot : news : (coll.) a scolding ; hear'say, common talk : report.—adj. of the nature of, or based on, report given by others.—hear, hear ! an exclamation of approval from the hearers of a speech ; hear tell of, to hear some one speak of. [O.E. (Anglian) héran (W.S. hieran, hýran) ; Du. hooren, O.N. heyra, Ger. hören, Goth. hausjan.]

heard, heare, hēr, hearie, (Spens.) forms of herd, hair, hairy.

hearken, härk'n, v.i. to hear attentively : to listen. —v.t. to listen to : (obs.) to seek by enquiry.—n. heark'ener. [O.E. hercnian (heorcnian) ; cf. hark, hear ; Ger. horchen.]

hearse, (Spens.) herse, hǝrs, n. (orig.) a framework for candles, esp. at a funeral service : (Spens.) a funeral service : (obs.) a bier : a car for carrying the dead.—v.t. to put on or in a hearse.—n. hearse'-cloth, a pall.—adj. hearse'-like, hears'y. [O.Fr. herse (It. erpice)—L. hirpex, -icis, a harrow.]

heart, härt, n. the organ that circulates the blood : (obs.) the stomach : the innermost part : the core : the chief or vital part : the (imagined) seat of the affections : courage : inmost feelings : vigour, spirit : cordiality : a term of endearment or encouragement : a heart-shaped figure or object : a playing-card with heart-shaped pips : a diseased state of the heart.—v.t. to hearten.—v.i. to form a compact head or inner mass, as a lettuce.—ns. heart'ache, sorrow : anguish ; heart'-beat, a pulsation of the heart : a throb ; heart'-block, a condition in which the ventricle does not keep time with the auricle ; heart'(s)'-blood, blood of the heart : life, essence ; heart'-bond, in masonry, a bond in which two headers meet in the middle of a wall and one header overlaps them ; heart'-break, a crushing sorrow or grief.—v.t. (Burns) to break the heart of.—n. heart'-brea'ker, a flirt : a curl, love-lock.—adjs. heart'-brea'king ; heart'-broken.—ns. heart'burn, a burning, acrid feeling in throat or breast ; heart'burning, discontent : secret grudging ; heart'-cam, a heart-shaped cam in a stop-watch, &c.; heart'-cockle, heart'-shell, a mollusc (Isocardia) or its shell, like a cockle coiled at the bosses.—adj. heart'-dear, (Shak.) dear to the heart, sincerely beloved.—n. heart'-disease', any morbid condition of the heart.—adjs. heart'-eas'ing, giving peace to the mind ; heart'ed, having a heart, esp. of a specified kind (hard-hearted, &c.) : seated or fixed in the heart, laid up in the heart.—v.t. heart'en, to encourage, stimulate : to add strength to.—v.i. to take courage. —adjs. heart'-felt, felt deeply : sincere ; heart'-free, having the affections disengaged.—ns. heart'-grief, deep-seated affliction ; heart'-heav'iness, depression of spirits ; heart'ikin, a little heart (in a minced oath).—adv. heart'ily.—n. heart'iness. —adj. heart'less, without heart, courage, or feeling : callous.—adv. heart'lessly.—ns. heart'-lessness ; heart'let, a little heart ; heart'ling, (Shak.) little heart, used in a minced oath (ods heartlings, God's heart).—adv. heart'ly (Spens. heart'ly), heartily.—n. heart'-quake, trembling, fear. — adj. heart'-rend'ing, agonising. — ns. heart'-rot, decay in the hearts of trees, caused by various fungi ; heart'-search'ing, examination of one's feelings ; heart's'-ease, the pansy ; heart'-seed, or heart'-pea, balloon-vine, from the heart-shaped scar left by the seed ; heart'-ser'vice, sincere devotion, as opp. to eye-service.—adjs. heart'-shaped, shaped like the conventional representation of the human heart ; heart'-sick, despondent.—n. heart'-sick'ness.—adjs. heart'-some, exhilarating : merry ; heart'-sore, sore at heart : (Shak.) caused by soreness of heart.—n. grief : (Spens.) cause of grief.—n. heart'-spoon, the depression in the breastbone : the breastbone. — adj. heart'-stirr'ing, rousing : exhilarating.— v.t. heart'-strike, to strike to the heart : to dismay :

to drive into the heart:—*pa.p.* **heart'-stricken**, **heart'-struck** (*obs.* **-strook**).—*n.* **heart'-string**, a nerve or tendon imagined to brace and sustain the heart: (*pl.*) affections.—*adj.* **heart'-to-heart'**, candid, intimate, and unreserved.—*n.* **heart'-ur'chin**, a sea-urchin of the Spatangoidea, typically heart-shaped.—*adj.* **heart'-whole**, whole at heart: sincere: with affections disengaged: undismayed: out-and-out.—*n.* **heart'-wood**, the duramen or hard inner wood of a tree.—*adj.* **heart'y**, full of heart: heart-felt: sincere: cordial: robust: lusty: in, or indicating, good spirits, appetite, or condition: sound: in good heart.—*n.* a hearty fellow, esp. a sailor: a student who goes in for sports, distinguished from an *aesthete*. — *adj.* **hart'ie-hale**, (*Spens.*) good for the heart.—**after one's own heart**, exactly to one's own liking; **at heart**, in real character: substantially; **break one's heart**, to die of, or be broken down by, grief or disappointment: to cause deep grief to anyone; **by heart**, by rote: in the memory; **eat one's heart** (see **eat**); **find in one's heart**, to be able to bring oneself; **from the bottom of one's heart**, most sincerely; **have at heart**, to cherish as a matter of deep interest; **have one's heart in one's boots**, to feel a sinking of the heart; **have one's heart in one's mouth**, to be in trepidation; **heart and hand, heart and soul**, with complete heartiness, with complete devotion to a cause; **heart of heart(s)**, the inmost feelings or convictions: deepest affections; **heart of oak**, heart-wood of the oak-tree: a brave, resolute heart; **in good heart**, in sound or fertile condition: in good spirits or courage; **lay, take, to heart**, to store up in the mind for future guidance: to be deeply moved by something; **set the heart at rest**, to render easy in mind; **set the heart upon**, to come to desire earnestly; **speak to the heart**, (*B.*) to comfort, encourage; **take heart**, to be encouraged; **take heart of grace** (see **grace**); **take to heart**, to come to feel in earnest; **wear one's heart on one's sleeve**, to show the feelings openly; **with all one's heart**, most willingly. [O.E. *heorte*; cf. Du. *hart*, Ger. *herz*; L. *cor*, *cordis*; Gr. *kardiā*.]

hearth, *härth*, *n.* the part of the floor on which the fire is made: the fireside: the house itself: the home circle: the lowest part of a blast-furnace: a brazier, chafing-dish, or fire-box.—*ns.* **hearth'-brush**, a brush for sweeping the hearth; **hearth'-mon'ey, -penn'y, -tax**, a tax on hearths; **hearth'-rug**, a rug laid over the hearth-stone; **hearth'-stone**, a stone forming a hearth: a soft stone used for whitening hearths, doorsteps, &c. [O.E. *heorth*; Du. *haard*, Ger. *herd*.]

heast, heaste, *hēst*, *n.* (*Spens.*). Same as **hest**.

heat, *hēt*, *n.* that which excites the sensation of warmth: sensation of warmth, esp. in a high degree: a heating: exposure to intense heat: a high temperature: the hottest time: redness of the skin: vehemence, passion: sexual excitement, or its period, esp. in the female, corresponding to *rut* in the male: a single course in a race: animation. —*v.t.* to make hot: to agitate: (*Shak.*) perh., to run over, as if in a race.—*v.i.* to become hot.—*n.* **heat'-ap'oplexy**, sunstroke.—*adj.* **heat'ed**.—*ns.* **heat'-en'gine**, an engine that transforms heat into mechanical work; **heat'er**, one who, or that which, heats: apparatus for heating a room or building: means of heating a flat-iron, &c.; **heat'er-shield**, a triangular shield, like the heater of a flat-iron.—*n. and adj.* **heat'ing**.—*ns.* **heat'-pump**, a device (on the refrigerator principle) for drawing heat from water, air, or the earth, and giving it out to warm e.g. a room; **heat'-spot**, an area of skin with nerve-ends sensitive to heat: a spot or blotch on the skin caused by heat: a freckle; **heat'-stroke**, exhaustion, illness, or prostration due to exposure to heat: sunstroke; **heat'-ū'nit**, amount of heat required to raise a pound of water one degree Fahrenheit in temperature (*British thermal unit*), or one gramme one degree Centigrade (*calorie*) or a kilogram (*large calorie*); **heat'-wave**, a heated state of the atmosphere passing from one locality to another: a hot spell.—**latent heat**, the heat required to change solid to liquid, or liquid to gas, without change of temperature; **mechanical equivalent of heat**, the energy required to produce one heat-unit; **specific heat**, the number of heat-units necessary to raise the unit of mass of a given substance one degree in temperature; **turn on the heat**, (*slang*) to use brutal treatment, mental or physical, esp. in order to coerce. [O.E. *hǣto*, heat; *hát*, hot; Ger. *hitze*.]

heath, *hēth*, *n.* barren open country, esp. covered with ericaceous and other low shrubs: any shrub of genus Erica, sometimes extended to Calluna (heather) and others of the family Ericaceae: a butterfly of the Satyridae.—*ns.* **heath'-bell**, heather bell: harebell; **heath'-bird, heath'-fowl**, the black grouse; **heath'cock**, the male black grouse; **heath'-hen**, the grey-hen or female black grouse: an extinct American bird akin to the prairie-chicken; **heath'-poult**, the black grouse, esp. the female or young.—*adj.* **heath'y**, abounding with heath. [O.E. *hǣth*; Ger. *heide*, Goth. *haithi*, a waste.]

heathen, *hē'dhn*, *n.* one who belongs to a people of some lower form of religion, esp. polytheistic, or of no religion: a pagan: (*coll.*) one who is ignorant or unmindful of religion: (*coll.*) an uncivilised person: (*pl.* **heath'en** (collectively), **heath'ens** (individually)). — *adj.* pagan: irreligious. — *ns.* **hea'thendom, heath'enesse** (suff. *-ness*), heathenism: the condition of a heathen: those regions of the world where heathenism prevails.—*v.t.* **hea'thenise**, to make heathen or heathenish.—*adj.* **hea'thenish**, relating to the heathen: rude: uncivilised: cruel. — *adv.* **hea'thenishly**. — *ns.* **hea'thenishness; hea'thenism**, the religious system of the heathens: paganism: barbarism; **hea'thenry**, heathenism: heathendom. [O.E. *hǣthen*; Du. *heiden*.]

heather, *hedh'∂r*, *n.* ling, a common low shrub (*Calluna vulgaris*) of the heath family: sometimes extended to the heaths (Erica): an assemblage of heather plants.—*adj.* of the colour of (red) heather: composed of or from heather.—*ns.* **heath'er-ale**, a famous liquor traditionally brewed in Scotland from the bells of heather—a lost art; **heath'er-bell**, the flower of the cross-leaved heath (*Erica tetralix*) or of the common heath (*Erica cinerea*); **heath'er-mix'ture**, a woollen fabric speckled in colours like heather.—*adj.* **heath'ery**.—**set the heather on fire**, to create a disturbance or a sensation; **take to the heather**, to become an outlaw. [Older Scots *hadder*; origin unknown; prob. influenced by **heath**.]

heather-bleat, heather-bleater, *hedh'∂r-blēt'*, *-∂r*, *ns.* (*Scot.*) a snipe.—Also **heather-bluiter**, **-blutter** (*-blüt'*, *-blut'*). [O.E. *hǣfer-blǣte*—*hǣfer*, goat, *blǣtan*, to bleat, from its cry; influenced by **heather**; cf. also Scots *bluiter*, bittern.]

heaume, *hōm*, *n.* (*arch.*) a massive helmet. [Fr.]

heave, *hēv*, *v.t.* to lift up, esp. with great effort: to throw: to haul: to swell or puff out: to force from the breast (as a sigh): (*mining*) to displace (as a vein).—*v.i.* to be raised: to rise like waves: to retch: to strive or strain to lift or move something: (*pa.t.* and *pa.p.* **heaved**, (*naut.*) **hōve**: *pa.p.* in sense of swollen, **hōv'en**).—*n.* an effort upward: a throw: a swelling: an effort to vomit: (*Shak.*) a sigh: (*mining*) horizontal displacement: (in *pl.*) broken wind in horses.—*ns.* **heave'-off'er-ing**, **heave'-shoul'der**, (*B.*) an offering, an animal's shoulder, elevated in sacrifice; **heav'er**; **heav'ing**.—**heave ho!** an exclamation used by sailors in putting forth exertion, as in heaving the anchor; **heave in sight**, to come into view; **heave the log**, to cast the log into the water in order to ascertain the ship's speed; **heave to**, to bring a vessel to a standstill, to make her lie to. [O.E. *hebban*, pa.t. *hóf*, pa.p. *hafen*; Ger. *heben*.]

heaven, *hev'n*, *hevn*, *n.* the vault of sky overhanging the earth (commonly in *pl.*): the upper regions of the air: a very great and indefinite height: any one of the concentric revolving spheres imagined by the old astronomers: the dwelling-place of God or the gods, and the blessed: the Deity as inhabiting heaven: supreme happiness. — *adjs.* **heav'en-born,** descended from heaven; **heav'en-bred,** (*Shak.*) bred or produced in heaven; **heav'en-direct'ed,** pointing to the sky: divinely guided; **heaven-fallen** (*hevn-fawln'*; *Milt.*), fallen from heaven; **heaven-gift'ed,** bestowed by heaven; **heav'en-kiss'ing,** (*Shak.*) as it were, touching the sky.—*n.* **heavenliness** (*hevn'*).—*adj.* **heavenly** (*hevn'*), of or inhabiting heaven: celestial: pure: supremely blessed: very excellent.—*adv.* in a manner like that of heaven: by the influence of heaven.—*adj.* **heaven'ly-mind'ed,** with mind set upon heavenly things: pure.—*n.* **heaven'ly-mind'edness.** — *adjs.* **heaven'-sent,** sent by heaven; **heaven'ward,** **heaven'ward.**—*advs.* **heaven'-ward,** **heaven'wards.**—**heavenly bodies,** the sun, moon, planets, comets, stars, &c.; **heavenly host,** a multitude of angels; **heaven of heavens,** (*B.*) the highest of the heavens, the abode of God; **in the seventh heaven,** in a state of the most exalted happiness—from the Cabbalists, who divided the heavens into seven in an ascending scale of happiness up to the abode of God; **tree of heaven,** ailanto. [O.E. *heofon*.]

Heaviside layer. See **Kennelly-Heaviside layer.**

heavy, *hev'i,* *adj.* weighty: ponderous: laden: abounding: of high specific gravity: not easy to bear: grievous: oppressive: grave: dull, lacking brightness and interest: wanting in sprightliness: pedantic: pompous: laborious: sad: in low spirits: drowsy: with great momentum: deep-toned: massive: thick: not easily digested: doughy: impeding the feet in walking: heavy-armed: strong, as liquor: dark with clouds: gloomy: (*theat.*) pertaining to grave or serious rôles : (*compar.* **heav'ier ;** *superl.* **heav'iest**).—*adv.* heavily.—*adj.* **heav'ier-than-air',** of aircraft, not sustained by a gas-bag.—*adv.* **heav'ily.** —*n.* **heav'iness.**—*adjs.* **heav'y-armed,** bearing heavy armour or arms; **heav'y-hand'ed,** clumsy, awkward: oppressive; **heav'y-head'ed,** having a heavy or large head: dull: stupid: drowsy; **heav'y-heart'ed,** weighed down with grief; **heav'y-lâd'en,** with a heavy burden.—*ns.* **heav'y-spar,** barytes; **heav'y-weight,** a person or thing well above the average weight: in sporting language one placed in the highest class in ascending weight (*boxing*; **light heavy-weight,** 12 st. 7 lb., or under; **heavy-weight,** any weight above this).—**heavy chemicals,** those produced on a large scale for use in industry (e.g. sulphuric acid and sodium carbonate); **heavy hydrogen,** deuterium: also tritium; **heavy marching order,** the condition of troops fully equipped for field service; **heavy metal,** a metal of high specific gravity, usu. above 5: guns or shot of large size: great influence or power: a person to be reckoned with; **heavy water,** water in which deuterium takes the place of ordinary hydrogen; **heavy wet,** a drink of strong ale or ale and porter mixed; **the heavies,** (*mil.*) the heavy cavalry: those who play heavy parts. [O.E. *hefig—hebban,* to heave; O.H.G. *hebig.*]

hebdomad, *heb'dō-mad, n.* a set of seven: a week: in some Gnostic systems, a group of superhuman beings. — *adj.* **hebdomadal** (*-dom'a-dl*), weekly. —*adv.* **hebdom'adally.** — *adj.* **hebdom'adary,** weekly.—*n.* a member of a chapter or convent taking weekly turn to officiate.—**hebdomadal council,** an administrative board of Oxford university, meeting weekly. [Gr. *hebdomas,-ados,* a set of seven, a week—*hepta,* seven.]

Hebe, *hē'bē, n.* a daughter of Zeus and Hera, cup-bearer of Olympus, a personification of youth.—*n.* **hebephrenia** (*hē-bi-frē'ni-ä*), a form of insanity beginning in late childhood, arresting intellectual development, and ending in complete dementia. —*adjs.* and *ns.* **hebephrē'niac, hebephrenic** (*-fren'ik*). [Gr. *hēbē,* youth, puberty (*Hēbē,* the goddess), *phrēn,* mind.]

heben, *heb'n, n.* and *adj.* (*Spens.*). See **ebony.**

hebenon, *heb'a-non,* **hebona,** *-nä, n.* (*Shak.*) something with a poisonous juice. [Perh. **ebony** or **henbane,** or Ger. *eibenbaum,* yew-tree.]

hebetate, *heb'i-tāt, v.t.* to dull or blunt.—*v.i.* to

become dull.—*adj.* dull: blunt: soft-pointed.— *adj.* **heb'etant,** making dull. —*ns.* **hebetā'tion,** **heb'etude;** **hebetūdinos'ity.** — *adj.* **hebetū'-dinous.** [L. *hebetāre, -ātum—hebes, -etis,* blunt.]

Hebrew, *hē'brōō, n.* a Jew (*fem.* **Hē'brewess,** *B.*): the Semitic language of the Hebrews: (*coll.*) unintelligible speech.—*adj.* of the Hebrews or their language.—*adjs.* **Hebraic** (*hē-brā'ik*), **-al,** relating to the Hebrews or to their language.—*adv.* **Hebrā'ically,** after the manner of the Hebrew language: from right to left.—*n.* **Hebrā'icism.**— *v.t.* **Hē'brāise,** to make Hebrew.—*v.i.* to use a Hebrew idiom: to conform or incline to Hebrew ways or ideals.—*ns.* **Hē'braiser;** **Hē'brāism,** a Hebrew idiom; **Hē'brāist,** one skilled in Hebrew. —*adjs.* **Hebrāist'ic, -al,** of or like Hebrew.—*adv.* **Hebrāist'ically.**—*n.* **Hē'brewism.** [O.Fr. *Ebreu* and L. *Hebraeus*— Gr. *Hēbraios*— Aram. *'ebrai* (Heb. *'ibri*), lit. one from the other side (of the Euphrates).]

Hebridean, *heb-ri-dē'an,* **Hebridian,** *-rid'i-an, adj.* of the Hebrides (*heb'ri-dēz*).—*n.* a native of the Hebrides.—*adj.* **Heb'rid.** [Due to a misprint of L. *Hebūdēs*—Gr. *Heboudai.*]

Hecate, *hek'a-tē, Shak.* **Hecat(e),** *hek'at, n.* a mysterious goddess, in Hesiod having power over earth, heaven, and sea—afterwards identified with Artemis, Persephone, and other goddesses: in Shakespeare, &c., the chief or goddess of witches. [Gr. *Hekatē.*]

hecatomb, *hek'a-tom, -tōm* (sometimes *-tōōm*), *n.* a great public sacrifice: any large number of victims. [Gr. *hekatombē—hekaton,* a hundred, *bous,* an ox.]

hech, *hehh, interj.* (*Scot.*) an exclamation of surprise or weariness.

hecht, *hehht,* Scottish form of the verb **hight.**

heck, *hek, n.* (*Scot.*) a rack : a grating.—**heck and manger,** rack and manger. [O.E. *hec* (*hæc*), grating, hatch; cf. **hack** (3), **hatch** (1); Du. *hek,* gate.]

heck, *hek, n.* and *interj.* euphemistic for **hell.**

heckle, *hek'l, v.i.* to comb: to ply with embarrassing questions (as at an election).—*n.* a hackle.—*n.* **heck'ler.** [Cf. **hackle, hatchel.**]

hectare. See under **hecto-.**

hectic, *hek'tik, adj.* pertaining to the constitution or habit of body: affected with hectic fever: (*coll.*) feverish: (*Shelley*) flushed.—*n.* a hectic fever: a consumptive: a flush.—*adj.* **hec'tical.** —**hectic fever,** fever occurring in connexion with certain wasting diseases of long duration. [Gr. *hektikos,* habitual—*hexis,* habit.]

hecto-, *hek'tō-,* **hect-,** in composition (esp. in the metric system) 100 times.—*ns.* **hectare** (*hek'tär*), 100 ares or 10,000 sq. metres (about 2·471 acres); **hec'togram(me),** 100 grammes (*c.* 3·527 oz.); **hec'tograph,** a gelatine pad for printing copies.— *v.t.* to reproduce in this way.—*adj.* **hectograph'ic.** —*ns.* **hec'tolitre,** 100 litres (*c.* 22·01 imperial gallons); **hec'tometre,** 100 metres (*c.* ·0621 mile); **hec'tostere,** 100 cubic metres or steres (*c.* 3531·56 cu. ft.). [Fr. contraction of Gr. *hekaton,* a hundred.]

hector, *hek'tar, n.* a bully, a blusterer.—*v.t.* to treat insolently: to annoy.—*v.i.* to play the bully: to bluster.—*ns.* **hec'torer;** **hec'torism.**—*adv.* **hec'torly.**—*n.* **hec'torship.** [Gr. *Hektōr,* the Trojan hero.]

heddle, *hed'l, n.* a series of vertical cords or wires, each having in the middle a loop (**hedd'le-eye**) to receive a warp-thread, and passing round and between parallel bars.—*v.t.* to draw through heddle-eyes. [An assumed O.E. *hefedl,* earlier form of *hefeld* ; cf. **heald.**]

Hedera, *hed'ar-ä, n.* the ivy genus of the Aralia family. — *adjs.* **hed'eral; hed'erated,** ivy-crowned. [L.]

hedge, *hej, n.* a close row of bushes or small trees serving as a fence : (*fig.*) a barrier : an act of hedging.—*v.t.* to enclose with a hedge : to obstruct : to surround : to guard : to protect oneself from loss on, by compensatory transactions, e.g. bets on the other side.—*v.i.* to make hedges : to shuffle, as in argument : to be shifty.—*adj.* living in or frequenting hedges : wayside : used by, or only fit for, vagrants: low: debased.—*ns.* **hedge'-accen'tor,** the hedge-sparrow; **hedge'bill, hedg'-ing-bill,** a bill for dressing hedges.—*adj.* **hedge'-born,** born under a hedge, low-born.—*ns.* **hedge'-bote,** a tenant's right to cut wood for repairing hedges or fences; **hedge'-creep'er,** a sneaking rogue; **hedge'hog,** a small prickly-backed insectivorous animal that lives in hedges and bushes, and has a snout like a hog: a prickly fruit, or prickly-fruited plant: one whose manners keep others at a distance: an offensive person: a small, strongly fortified, defensive position.—*v.i.* **hedge'-hop,** (*aeronauts' slang*) to fly low as if hopping over hedges.—*ns.* **hedge'-hyss'op,** a plant (Gratiola) of the figwort family; **hedge'-mar'riage,** a clandestine marriage; **hedge'-mus'tard,** a tall stiff cruciferous roadside weed (*Sisymbrium officinale*) with small yellow flowers, or kindred species; **hedge'-pars'ley,** an umbelliferous roadside weed (Torilis or Caucalis) with leaves somewhat like parsley; **hedge'-par'son, hedge'-priest,** a disreputable, vagrant, or illiterate parson or priest; **hedge'pig,** a hedge-hog; **hedg'er,** one who hedges or dresses hedges; **hedge'row,** a line of hedge, often with trees; **hedge'-school,** an open-air school: a mean school; **hedge'-spar'row, hedge'-war'bler,** a warbler, superficially like a sparrow, that frequents hedges; **hedge'-wri'ter,** a Grub Street author; **hedg'ing,** the work of a hedger.—*adj.* **hedg'y.** [O.E. *hecg*; Du. *hegge*, Ger. *hecke*.]

hedonism, *hē'dən-izm, n.* in ethics, the doctrine that pleasure is the highest good.—*ns.* **hedonic** (-*don'*), **hedonist'ic.**—*n.* (treated as *sing.*) **hedon'-ics,** that part of ethics or of psychology that treats of pleasure.—*n.* **hē'donist.** [Gr. *hēdonē*, pleasure.]

hedyphane, *hed'i-fān, n.* a white variety of green lead ore, arsenate, phosphate, and chloride of lead and calcium with barium. [Gr. *hēdys*, sweet, pleasant, and the root of *phainein*, to show.]

heed, *hēd, v.t.* to observe: to look after: to attend to.—*v.i.* to mind, care.—*n.* notice: caution: attention.—*adj.* **heed'ful,** attentive: cautious.—*adv.* **heed'fully.**—*ns.* **heed'fulness; heed'iness.** —*adj.* **heed'less.**—*adv.* **heed'lessly.**—*n.* **heed'-lessness.**—*adj.* **heed'y,** (*Spens.*) heedful, careful. [O.E. *hēdan*; Du. *hoeden*, Ger. *hüten*.]

heehaw, *hē'haw, v.i.* to bray.—*n.* a bray. [Imit.]

heel, *hēl, n.* the part of the foot projecting behind: the whole foot (esp. of beasts): the covering or support of the heel: a spur: the hinder part of anything, as a violin bow: a heel-like bend, as on a golf-club: a knob: the top, bottom, or end of a loaf or a cheese.—*v.t.* to execute or perform with the heel: to strike with the heel: to furnish with a heel: to arm with a spur, as a fighting cock: to seize by the heels: to follow at the heels of: (*U.S.*) to supply with a weapon, money, &c.—*v.i.* to follow well (of a dog).—*n.* **heel'-ball,** a black, waxy composition for blacking the edges of heels and soles of shoes and boots, and for taking rubbings. —*adj.* **heeled,** provided with a heel, shod: (*U.S.*) comfortably supplied with money, &c.—*ns.* **heel'er,** one who heels, in any sense: one who follows at heel, as (*U.S.*) an unscrupulously faithful follower of a party boss; **heel'ing.** (*Spens.*) a heelpiece: the act of making or attaching a heel; **heel'piece,** a piece or cover for the heel; **heel'-tap,** a layer of material in a shoe-heel: a small quantity of liquor left in the glass after drinking.—**at, on, upon, a person's heels,** close behind; **come to heel,** come in behind: to obey or follow like a dog; **cool or kick one's heels,** to be kept waiting for some time; **down at heel,** having the heels of one's shoes trodden down: slovenly: in poor circumstances; **heel and toe,** with strict walking pace, as opposed to running; **heel of Achilles** (see under Achillean); **heels o'er gowdy** (*Scot.*), **heels over head,** upside down; **kick up one's heels,** to frisk; **lay, set, clap, by the heels,** to fetter: to put in confinement; **out at heel,** having one's heels showing through holes in the socks or stockings; **show a clean pair of heels,** to run off; **take to one's heels,** to flee; **tread on one's heels,** to come crowding behind; **trip up one's**

heels, to trip up or overthrow; **turn on (upon) one's heel,** to turn sharply round, to turn back or away; **two for his heels,** in cribbage, a score for turning up the knave; **under the heel,** crushed, tyrannised over. [O.E. *héla*; Du. *hiel*.]

heel, *hēl, v.i.* to incline: to lean on one side, as a ship.—*v.t.* to tilt. [Earlier *heeld, hield*; O.E. *hieldan*, to slope; cf. Du. *hellen*.]

heel. Same as **hele.**

heeze, *hēz, v.t.* (*Scot.*) a form of **hoise.**—*n.* a lift: a heave upward.—*n.* **heez'ie,** a lift.

heft, *heft, n.* heaving: (*Shak.*) retching: (*U.S.*) weight: the greater part.—*v.t.* to lift: to try the weight of.—*adj.* **heft'y,** rather heavy: muscular: vigorous: violent.—*adv.* very. [heave.]

heft, hefte (*Spens.*), obsolete forms of **heaved.**

heft, *heft, v.t.* to accustom: (*Scot.*) to attach: to restrain: to hold back. [Cf. O.N. *hefta*, to bind, and **haft.**]

heft, *heft, n.* a number of sheets fastened together: an instalment of a serial publication. [Ger.]

Hegelian, *hā-gēl'i-ən, adj.* of or pertaining to Wilhelm Friedrich *Hegel* (1770-1831) or his philosophy.—*n.* a follower of Hegel.—*n.* **Hegel'ian-ism.**

hegemony, *hi-gem'ən-i,* or *-jem', n.* leadership: preponderant influence, esp. of one state over others.—*adjs.* **hegemonic** (*hē-gi-mon'*, or *-ji-*), **-al.** [Gr. *hēgemoniā*—*hēgemōn,* leader—*hēgeesthai,* to lead.]

hegira, hejira, hejra, hijra, *hej', hij'(i-)rä, n.* the flight of Mohammed from Mecca, 622 A.D., from which is dated the Mohammedan era: any flight. [Ar. *hijrah,* flight, *hajara,* to leave.]

he-he, *hē-hē, interj.* representing a high-pitched or gleeful laugh.—*n.* such a laugh.—*v.i.* to laugh so. [Imit.]

heifer, *hef'ər, n.* a young cow. [O.E. *héahfore, héahfru, -fre*: lit. prob. high-goer—*faran,* to go.]

heigh, *hā* (or *hī*), *interj.* a cry of enquiry, encouragement, or exultation—also **hey, ha.**—*interj.* **heigh'-ho,** an exclamation expressive of weariness.—*n.* (*Scot.* also **heich-how,** *hēhh'-how'*) routine: familiar jog-trot. [Imit.]

height, *hīt, n.* the condition of being high: degree of highness: distance upwards: angle of elevation: that which is elevated: a hill: a high place: elevation in rank or excellence: utmost degree.—*v.t.* and *v.i.* **height'en,** to make or become higher: to advance or improve: to make or become brighter or more conspicuous: (*obs.*) to elate.—**height of land,** a watershed, esp. if not a range of hills; **height to paper,** the standard length (11/12 inch) of type, from foot to face. [From **highth**—O.E. *híehtho, héahthu*—*héah,* high.]

heinous, *hā'nəs, adj.* wicked in a high degree, enormous, odious, atrocious.—*adv.* **hei'nously.**—*n.* **hei'nousness.** [O.Fr. *haïnos* (Fr. *haineux*)—*haïr,* to hate.]

heir, *ār, n.* (*law*) one who actually succeeds to property, title, &c., on the death of its previous holder: (popularly) one entitled to succeed when the present possessor dies: a successor: a child, esp. a first-born son.—*v.t.* to inherit.—*ns.* **heir'-appä'rent,** the one by law acknowledged to be heir, no matter who may subsequently be born; **heir'-at-law,** an heir by legal right; **heir'dom, heir'ship; heir'ess,** a female heir: a woman who has succeeded or is likely to succeed to a considerable fortune.—*adj.* **heir'less,** without an heir. —*ns.* **heir'loom,** any piece of furniture or personal property which descends to the heir-at-law by special custom; **heir'-por'tioner,** (*Scots law*) a joint-heiress or her representative; **heir'-pre-sump'tive,** one who will be heir if no nearer relative should be born.—**heir by custom,** one whose right as heir is determined by customary modes of descent, as gavelkind, &c. [O.Fr. *heir*—L. *hērēs* (vulgar accus. *hērem*), an heir.]

hejira, hejra. See **hegira.**

Hel, *hel, n.* in Northern mythology, the goddess of the dead, sister of the wolf Fenrir, and daughter of Loki.

helcoid, *hel'koid, adj.* ulcerous. [Gr. *helkos,* an ulcer.]

held, *pa.t.* and *pa.p.* of hold.

hele, **heel**, **heal**, *hēl*, *v.t.* (*Spens.*; now *dial.*) to hide, conceal: to cover.—**hele in**, to cover the roots of temporarily with earth. [O.E. *helian* from *hellan* (weak vb.) blended with *helan* (strong), to hide; Ger. *hehlen*; L. *celāre*; Gr. *kalyptein*.]

heliac, *hē'li-ak*, **heliacal**, *hē-lī'ak-əl*, *adjs.* solar: coincident with that of the sun, or as nearly as could be observed (**heliacal rising**, the emergence of a star from the light of the sun; **heliacal setting**, its disappearance in it).—*adv.* **heli'acally**. [Gr. *hēliakos*—*hēlios*, the sun.]

Helianthemum, *hē-li-anth'ə-məm*, *n.* the rock-rose genus. [Gr. *hēlios*, sun, *anthemon*, flower.]

Helianthus, *hē-li-an'thəs*, *n.* the sunflower genus. [Gr. *hēlios*, sun, *anthos*, flower.]

helical, &c. See **helix**.

Heliconian, *hel-i-kō'ni-ən*, *adj.* pertaining to Helicon (Gr. *Helikōn*), a mountain-range in Boeotia, favourite seat of the Muses, by some modern poets made a fountain.

helicopter, *hel-i-kop'tər*, or *hel'*, *n.* a flying-machine sustained by a power-driven screw or screws revolving on a vertical axis. [Gr. *helix*, screw, *pteron*, wing.]

helio-, *hē'li-ō-*, *hē-li-o'-*, in composition, sun.—*adj.* **heliocen'tric** (*-sen'trik*; Gr. *kentron*, centre; *astron.*), referred to the sun as centre.—*adv.* **heliocen'trically**.—*n.* **he'liochrome** (*-krōm*; Gr. *chrōma*, colour), a photograph in natural colours. — *adj.* **heliochrō'mic**. — *ns.* **he'liochrŏmy**; **he'liograph** (Gr. *graphē*, a drawing), an apparatus for signalling by flashing the sun's rays: an engraving obtained photographically: an apparatus for photographing the sun: an instrument for measuring intensity of sunlight.—*v.t.* and *v.i.* to communicate by heliograph.—*n.* **heliog'rapher**.—*adjs.* **heliograph'ic**, **-al**.—*adv.* **heliograph'ically**. —*ns.* **heliog'raphy**; **heliogravure** (*-grəv-ūr'*, *-grăv'yər*; Fr. *héliogravure*), photo-engraving; **heliol'ater**, a sun-worshipper.—*adj.* **heliol'atrous**. —*ns.* **heliol'atry** (Gr. *latreiā*, worship), sun-worship; **heliol'ogy**, the science of the sun; **heliom'eter**, an instrument for measuring angular distances, as the sun's diameter.—*adjs.* **heliomet'ric**, **-al**; **helioph'ilous** (Gr. *phileein*, to love), fond of the sun; **heliopho'bic** (Gr. *phobos*, fear), fearing or shunning sunlight.—*ns.* **he'liophyte** (Gr. *phyton*, a plant), a plant that can live in full exposure to sunlight; **heliosciophyte** (*hē-li-ō-sī'ō-fīt*; Gr. *skiā*, shadow), a plant that can live in shade but does better in the sun; **he'lioscope** (*-skōp*; Gr. *skopeein*, to look at), an apparatus for observing the sun without injury to the eye. —*adj.* **helioscopic** (*-skop'ik*).—*ns.* **heliō'sis** (Gr. *hēliōsis*), exposure to the sun: spotting of leaves by raindrops or greenhouse glass flaws, &c., acting as burning-glasses; **he'liostat** (Gr. *statos*, fixed), an instrument on the principle of the coelostat by means of which a beam of sunlight is reflected in an invariable direction, for study of the sun or for signalling; **heliotax'is** (Gr. *taxis*, arrangement), response of an organism to the stimulus of the sun's rays; **heliother'apy** (Gr. *therapeiā*, healing), medical treatment by exposure to the sun's rays; **heliotrope** (*hē'li-ō-trōp*, *hel'i-ō-trōp*; Gr. *hēliotropion*), any plant of the genus Heliotropium of the borage family, many species with fragrant flowers, esp. the *Peruvian heliotrope*, with small fragrant lilac-blue flowers: the colour of its flowers: a kind of perfume imitating that of the flower: (*min.*) a bloodstone: a surveyor's heliograph.—*adjs.* **heliotropic** (*-trop'ik*), **-al**.—*adv.* **heliotrop'ically**.—*ns.* **heliotropism** (*-ot'rə-pizm*), **heliŏt'ropy**, the tendency of stem and leaves to bend towards (*positive heliotropism*), and roots from (*negative heliotropism*), the light; **he'liotype** (Gr. *typos*, impression), a photograph by heliotypy.—*adj.* **heliotypic** (*-tip'ik*).—*n.* **he'liotypy** (*-ti-pi*), a photo-mechanical process in which the gelatine relief is itself used to print from. —*n.pl.* **Heliozo'a** (Gr. *zōion*, an animal), sun-animalcules, an order of Protozoa, spherical with radiating processes of living matter.—*adj.* and *n.* **heliozō'an**.—*adj.* **heliozō'ic**. [Gr. *hēlios*, the sun.]

helium, *hē'li-əm*, *n.* an element (He; at. numb. 2), a very light inert gas, discovered (1868) by Lockyer in the sun's atmosphere, isolated (1895) by Ramsay from cleveite, and found in certain natural gases. [Gr. *hēlios*, sun.]

helix, *hē'liks*, *n.* a screw-shaped coil: (*math.*) a curve on a developable surface (esp. a right circular cylinder) which becomes a straight line when the surface is unrolled into a plane—distinguished from a *spiral*, which is a plane curve: (*anat.*) the rim of the ear: (*archit.*) a small volute or twist in the capital of a Corinthian column: a screw-propeller: **Helix**, (*zool.*) a genus of molluscs including the best-known land-snails:—*pl.* **hē'lixes** or **helices** (*hel'i-sēz*).—*adj.* **helical** (*hel'ik-əl*). —*adv.* **hel'ically**.—*n.pl.* **Helicidae** (*-is'i-dē*), a large family of terrestrial, air-breathing gasteropods, including the common snails.—*n.* **hel'icograph**, a drawing instrument for describing spirals on a plane.—*adjs.* **hel'icoid**, **-al**, like a helix, screw-shaped; **helispher'ic**, **-al**, loxodromic.—**helicoid cyme**, a bostryx. [Gr. *hĕlix*, a spiral—*helissein*, to turn round.]

Hell, *hel*, *n.* the place of the dead in general: the place or state of punishment of the wicked after death: the abode of evil spirits: the powers of Hell: **hell**, any place of vice or misery: a gambling-house: a space under a tailor's board, or other receptacle for waste: the den in certain games.—*adj.* and *adv.* **hell'-bent**, (*U.S.*) with reckless determination.—*adjs.* **hell'-black**, (*Shak.*) black as hell; **hell'-born**, born in hell: of hellish origin; **hell'-bred**.—*ns.* **hell'-box**, a receptacle for broken type; **hell'-broth**, (*Shak.*) a composition boiled up for malignant purposes; **hell'-cat**, a malignant hag; **hell'-fire**, the fire of hell: punishment in hell; **hell'-gate**, the entrance into hell.—*adj.* **hell'-hat'ed**, (*Shak.*) hated or abhorred as hell.—*ns.* **hell'-hole**, the pit of hell; **hell'hound**, a hound of hell: an agent of hell.—*adj.* **hell'ish**, pertaining to or like hell: very wicked.—*adv.* **hell'ish(ly)**.—*ns.* **hell'ishness**; **hell'-kite**, (*Shak.*) a kite of infernal breed.—*adj.* and *adv.* **hell'ward**, towards hell.—*adv.* **hell'wards**.—**hell for leather**, at a furious pace. [O.E. *hel*, *hell*; O.N. *hel*, Ger. *hölle*; cf. **Hel**.]

hell, *hel*, *v.t.* (*obs.*) same as **hele**.—*n.* **hell'ier**, a slater: a tiler: a thatcher. [See **hele**.]

he'll, *hēl*, contraction for **he will**.

Helladic, *hel-ad'ik*, *adj.* Greek: of the Greek mainland Bronze Age, answering roughly to Minoan. [Gr. *Helladikos*, Greek—*Hellas*, Greece.]

hellbender, *hel'bend-ər*, *n.* a large American salamander. [**Hell**, and **bender**.]

hellebore, *hel'i-bōr*, *n.* any plant of the genus Helleborus, of the buttercup family (as *black hellebore* or Christmas rose, *stinking hellebore*, *green hellebore*): any plant of the genus Veratrum of the lily family (*American*, *false*, or *white hellebore*, known also as Indian poke or itch weed): the winter aconite (*winter hellebore*): the rhizome and roots of these prepared as a drug.—*n.* **hell'eborine** (*-īn*, *-in*), an orchid of the genus Epipactis. [Gr. *helleboros*.]

Hellene, *hel'ēn*, *n.* a Greek.—*adj.* **Hellēn'ic** (or *-en'*), Greek.—*v.i.* **hell'enise** (*-in-īz*), to conform, or tend to conform, to Greek usages.—*v.t.* to make Greek.—*ns.* **Hell'enism**, a Greek idiom: the Greek spirit: Greek nationality: conformity to Greek ways, esp. in language; **Hell'enist**, one skilled in the Greek language: one who adopted Greek ways and language, esp. a Jew.—*adjs.* **Hellenist'ic**, **-al**, pertaining to the Hellenists: pertaining to the Greeks, the Greek language and Greek culture, affected by foreign influences after the time of Alexander.—*adv.* **Hellenist'ically**. [Gr. *Hellēn*, a Greek: also the son of Deucalion.]

heller, *hel'ər*, *n.* a small coin probably first made at Hall in Swabia, in Austria and Czechoslovakia once worth a hundredth part of a crown.

hellgrammite, **hellgramite**, *hel'grə-mīt*, *n.* a large American neuropterous larva, used as bait by bass-fishers.

hellicat, *hel'i-kat*, *adj.* giddy-headed: flighty.—*n.* a wicked creature. [Scot.; origin obscure.]

hellier. See **hell** (2).

hello. Same as **hallo.**

helm, *helm, n.* steering apparatus.—*v.t.* to direct, steer.—*adj.* **helm'less.**—*n.* **helms'man,** a steersman. [O.E. *helma*; O.N. *hjálm,* a rudder, Ger. *helm,* a handle.]

helm, *helm,* **helmet,** *hel'mit, ns.* a covering of armour for the head: anything resembling a helmet, as a cloud on a mountain top, the top of a guinea-fowl's head, the hooded upper lip of certain flowers.—*adjs.* **helmed,** **hel'meted.**—*n.* **hel'met-shell,** a gasteropod of the genus Cassis, having a thick heavy shell with bold ridges. [O.E. *helm*; Ger. *helm*; cf. **hele.**]

helminth, *hel'minth, n.* a worm.—*n.* **helminthi'asis,** infestation with worms.—*adjs.* **helmin'thic; helmin'thoid,** worm-shaped; **helmintholog'ic, -al.**—*ns.* **helminthol'ogist; helminthol'ogy,** the study of worms, esp. parasitic.—*adj.* **helminth'ous,** infested with worms. [Gr. *helmins, -inthos,* a worm.]

helot, *hel'ət, n.* one of a class of serfs among the ancient Spartans, deliberately humiliated and liable to massacre: a serf: a plant or animal living symbiotically with another in a subject relationship.—*ns.* **hel'otage,** the state of a helot; **hel'otism; helotry,** the whole body of the helots: any class of slaves. [Gr. *Heilōtēs,* also *Heilōs, -ōtos.*]

help, *help, v.t.* to contribute towards the success of, aid, or assist: to give means for doing anything: to relieve the wants of: to provide or supply with a portion: to deal out: to remedy: to mitigate: to prevent, to keep from.—*v.i.* to give assistance: to contribute: (with an adv. or prep. phrase) to contribute towards bringing into the condition in question: (*pa.t.* **helped,** *arch.* **hōlp**; *pa.p.* **helped,** *arch.* **hōlp'en**).—*n.* means or strength given to another for a purpose: assistance: relief: one who assists: (*Amer.*) a hired servant, esp. domestic. —*n.* **help'er,** one who helps: an assistant: (*old-fashioned*) an assistant minister.—*adj.* **help'ful,** giving help: useful.—*n.* **help'fulness.**—*n.* **help'-ing,** a portion served at a meal.—*adj.* **help'less,** without ability to do things for oneself: wanting assistance: giving no help: (*Spens.*) that cannot be helped.—*adv.* **help'lessly.**—*ns.* **help'lessness; help'mate,** a modification of **help'meet,** itself formed from the phrase in Gen. ii. 18, ' an help meet for him,' *specif.* a wife.—**help off with,** to aid in taking off, disposing or getting rid of; **help on with,** to help to put on; **help oneself (to),** to take for oneself without waiting for offer or authority; **help out,** to eke out: to supplement; **more than one can help,** (illogically but idiomatically) more than is necessary; **so help me God,** a form of solemn oath. [O.E. *helpan,* pa.t. *healp* (pl. *hulpon*), pa.p. *holpen*; O.N. *hjálpa,* Ger. *helfen.*]

helter-skelter, *hel'tər-skel'tər, adv.* in a confused hurry: tumultuously.—*n.* a confused medley: disorderly motion: a fair-ground spiral slide.— *adj.* confused.—*n.* **hel'ter-skel'teriness.** [Imit.]

helve, *helv, n.* the handle of an axe or similar tool.— *v.t.* to furnish with a helve.—*n.* **helve'-ham'mer,** a trip-hammer. [O.E. *helfe* (*hielfe*), a handle.]

Helvetic, *hel-vet'ik,* **Helvetian,** *hel-vē'shən, adjs.* Swiss.—*n.* **helvē'tium,** a superseded name for astatine.—**Helvetic Confessions,** two confessions of faith drawn up by the Swiss theologians in 1536 and 1566. [L. *Helvētia,* Switzerland.]

hem, *hem, n.* an edge or border: a border doubled down and sewed.—*v.t.* to form a hem on: to edge: —*pr.p.* **hemm'ing**; *pa.t.* and *pa.p.* **hemmed.**— *n.* **hem'-stitch,** the ornamental finishing of the inner side of a hem, made by pulling out several threads adjoining it and drawing together in groups the cross-threads by successive stitches.— *v.t.* to embroider with such stitches.—**hem in,** to surround. [O.E. *hemm,* a border.]

hem, *hem, hm, n.* and *interj.* a sort of half-cough to draw attention.—*v.i.* to utter the sound *hem* :—*pr.p.* **hemm'ing**; *pa.t.* and *pa.p.* **hemmed.** [Sound of clearing the throat.]

hem, (*h)əm,* (*obs.*) them: to them. See **'em.**

he-man. See **he.**

hematite, &c. See **haematite,** &c.

heme, *hēm, adv.* (*Spens.*). Same as **home.**

hemeralopia, *hem-ər-ə-lō'pi-ä, n.* day-blindness : vision requiring dim light : sometimes misapplied to night-blindness. [Gr. *hēmerā,* day, *alaos,* blind, *ōps,* eye.]

Hemerobaptist, *hem-ər-ō-bap'tist, n.* a member of an ancient Jewish sect that practised daily baptism : also a Mandaean. [Gr. *hēmerā,* day, *baptistēs,* a baptiser.]

Hemerocallis, *hem-ər-ō-kal'is, n.* a day-lily. [Gr. *hēmerā,* day, *kallos,* beauty.]

hemi-, *hem'i-,* in composition, half.—*n.* **hemianops'ia** (Gr. *an-,* priv., *opsis,* sight), blindness in half of the field of vision.—Also **hemianōp'ia, hemiō'pia, hemiop'sia.**—*adjs.* **hemianop'tic, hemiop'ic.**—*ns.pl.* **Hemichordata** (-*kor-dā'tä*), **hemichorda** (-*kor'dä*), a group of worm-like marine animals with rudimentary notochord, including Balanoglossus, believed by many to represent the ancestors of the vertebrates.—*n.* **hemicrania** (-*krā'ni-ä*; Gr. *hēmikrāniā—krānion,* skull, head), headache confined to one side.—*adj.* **hemicrys'talline,** (*petrol.*) consisting of crystals in a glassy or partly glassy groundmass.—*n.* **hem'icycle** (Gr. *kyklos,* wheel), a semicircle : a semicircular structure.—*adj.* **hemicyc'lic,** (*bot.*) having some parts in whorls, some in spirals.—*ns.* **hemihē'drism, hemihē'dry** (-*dri* ; Gr. *hedrā,* a seat), a property of crystals of being **hemihē'dral,** or having half the number of symmetrically arranged planes occurring on a holohedron.—*n.* **hemihē'dron.**—*adj.* **hemimorph'ic** (Gr. *morphē,* form), having a polar axis, dissimilar at the two ends.—*ns.* **hemimorph'ism ; hemimorph'ite,** the mineral electric calamine, hydrous zinc silicate, which forms crystals whose ends are different in form and pyroelectric property; **hemiō'lia** (Gr. *hēmiōlios,* half as much again—*holos,* whole), in mediaeval music, a perfect fifth : also, a triplet. —*adj.* **hemiolic** (-*ol'*), in or based on the ratio of 3 to 2, as the paeonic foot.—*ns.* **hemionus** (*hi-mī'-on-əs*), **hemione** (*hem'i-ōn* ; Gr. *hēmionos,* mule— *onos,* as ass), an Asiatic wild ass, the kiang or the dziggetai ; **hemipar'asite,** an organism that is partly parasitic, partly independent : a saprophyte capable of living parasitically.—*adj.* **hemiparasit'ic.**—*adv.* **hemiparasit'ically.**—*n.* **hemiplegia** (-*plē'ji-ä,* or -*gi-ä* ; Gr. *plēgē,* a blow), paralysis of one side only.—*adj.* **hemiplegic** (-*plej'* or -*plēj'*).— *n.pl.* **Hemip'tera** (Gr. *pteron,* a wing), an order of insects, variously defined, with wings (when present) often half leathery, half membranous— the bugs, cicadas, greenfly, cochineal insect, &c.— *adjs.* **hemip'teral, hemip'teran, hemip'terous.** —*n.* **hem'isphere** (Gr. *hēmisphairion—sphaira,* a sphere), a half-sphere divided by a plane through the centre : half of the globe or a map of it : one of the two divisions of the cerebrum—**Eastern** and **Western hem'ispheres,** the eastern and western halves of the terrestrial globe, the former including Europe, Asia, and Africa ; the latter, the Americas. — *adjs.* **hemispher'ic, -al.** — *n.* **hemisphē'roid,** the half of a spheroid.—*adj.* **hemisphēroi'dal.**—*n.* **hemistich** (*hem'i-stik* ; Gr. *hēmistichion—stichos,* a line), one of the two divisions of a line of verse : half a line, an incomplete or unfinished line : an epodic line or refrain. —*adj.* **hem'istichal** (or -*is'*).—*n.* **hem'itrope** (Gr. *tropos,* a turn), a form of twin crystal in which one twin is as if rotated through two right angles from the position of the other.—*adjs.* **hem'itrope, hemitropal** (*hem-it'rə-pl*), **hemitropic** (-*trop'*), **hemit'ropous.** [Gr. *hēmi-,* half.]

hemlock, *hem'lok, n.* a poisonous spotted umbelliferous plant (*Conium maculatum*): the poison got from it : extended to other umbelliferous plants, e.g. water-hemlock (Cicuta): a N. American tree (hemlock spruce, Tsuga) whose branches are fancied to resemble hemlock leaves. [O.E. *hymlíce* (Kentish *hemlíc*).]

hemo-. See **haemo-.**

hemp, *hemp, n.* a plant (*Cannabis sativa*) of the mulberry family, yielding a coarse fibre, a narcotic drug, and an oil : the fibre itself : the drug : a similar fibre got from various other plants (e.g. *Manila*, sisal, *sunn hemp*).—*ns.* hemp'-ag'rimony, a composite plant (*Eupatorium cannabinum*) with hemp-like leaves; hemp'bush, an Australian fibre-plant (*Plagianthus*) of the mallow family.— *adj.* hemp'en, made of hemp.—*ns.* hemp'nett'le, a coarse bristly labiate weed (*Galeopsis*); hemp'-palm, a palmetto (yielding fibre); hemp'seed, the oil-yielding seed of hemp, a bird's food: (*Shak.*) gallows-bird.—*adj.* hemp'y, like hemp: roguish: romping.—*n.* (*Scot.*) a rogue: a romp: a tomboy.—hempen widow, the widow of a man who has been hanged. [O.E. *henep*, *hænep*; cf. Gr. *kannabis*.]

hen, hen, *n.* a female bird: a female domestic fowl: applied loosely to any domestic fowl: the female of certain fishes and crustaceans: (facetiously, disrespectfully, or endearingly) a woman or girl: a faint-hearted person.—*v.i.* (*Scot.*) to lose courage or resolution: to balk.—*v.t.* (*Scot.*) to challenge to an act of daring.—*adj.* female: composed of females.—*ns.* hen-and-chick'ens, a name for various plants, esp. a garden daisy with small heads surrounding the main head; hen'bane, a poisonous plant (*Hyoscyamus niger*) of the nightshade family; hen'-bit, the ivy-leaved speedwell: a species of dead-nettle; hen'-coop, a coop for a hen; hen'-court, an enclosure for fowls; hen'driv'er, a hen-harrier; hen'flesh, gooseflesh; hen'-harr'ier, the common harrier.—*adj.* hen'-heart'ed, faint-hearted: timid.—*ns.* hen'-house, a house for fowls; hen'-huss'y, a man who meddles with women's affairs; henn'er, (*Scot.*) a challenge to an act of daring; henn'ery, a place where fowls are kept; henn'y, a hen-like cock.— *adj.* hen-like. — *ns.* hen'-pad(d)'le, -paid'le (see paddle (2)); hen'-par'ty, a gathering of women only.—*v.t.* hen'peck, to domineer over (said of a wife).—*ns.* hen'peck, henpeck'ery; hen'-pen', (*Scot.*) fowl-house manure; hen'-roost, a roosting-place for fowls; hen'-run, an enclosure for fowls. —*adj.* hen'-toed, with toes turned in.—*n.* hen'-wife, a woman with charge of poultry. [O.E. *henn*, fem. of *hana*, a cock; Ger. *henne* (*hahn*, cock).]

hence, hens, *adv.* from this place: from this time onward: in the future: from this cause or reason: from this origin.—*interj.* away! begone!—*advs.* hence'forth, hencefor'ward, from this time forth or forward. [M.E. *hennes*, formed with genitive ending from *henne*—O.E. *heonan*, from the base of he; Ger. *hinnen*, *hin*, hence: so L. *hinc*, hence—*hic*, this.]

henchman, hen(t)sh'mən, *n.* a servant: a page: a right-hand man: (*U.S.*) an active political partisan, esp. from self-interest: a thick-and-thin supporter:—*pl.* hench'men. [O.E. *hengest*, a horse (Ger. *hengst*), and *man*; not connected with haunch.]

hend, hend, *adj.* (*obs.*) convenient: skilful: gracious: courteous. [App. O.E. *gehende*, handy—*hand*.]

hend, hend, *v.t.* (*Spens.*) to seize, to grasp. [O.E. *gehendan* or O.N. *henda*; cf. hand.]

hendecagon, hen-dek'ə-gon, *n.* a plane figure of eleven angles and eleven sides.—*adj.* hendecagonal (-*ag'ən-l*). [Gr. *hendeka*, eleven, *gōniā*, an angle.]

hendecasyllable, hen'dek-ə-sil'ə-bl, *n.* a metrical line of eleven syllables.—*adj.* hendecasyllabic (-*ab'ik*). [Gr. *hendeka*, eleven, *syllabē*, a syllable.]

hendiadys, hen-dī'ə-dis, *n.* a rhetorical figure in which one and the same notion is presented in two expressions, as with *might and main*. [Gr. *hen dia dyoin*, lit. one by two.]

henequen, hen'ə-kən, *n.* a Mexican Agave: its leaf-fibre, sisal-hemp used for cordage.—Also hen'equin, hen'iquin. [Sp. *henequén, jeniquén*.]

henge, *henj*, *n.* (*Spens.*) axis. [hinge.]

henna, hen'ä, *n.* a small Oriental shrub (*Lawsonia*) of the loosestrife family, with fragrant white flowers: a pigment made from its leaves for dyeing the nails and hair.—*adj.* hennaed (hen'äd), dyed with henna. [Ar. *hinnā'*.]

henotheism, hen'ō-thē-izm, *n.* belief in one god, supreme or specially venerated but not the only

god — a stage between polytheism and monotheism. — *n.* henothe'ist. — *adj.* henotheist'ic. [Gr. *heis, henos*, one, *theos*, god.]

henotic, hen-ot'ik, *adj.* tending to unify or reconcile. [Gr. *henōtikos*—*heis, henos*, one.]

henry, hen'ri, *n.* (*elect.*) the practical unit of inductance, 10^9 electromagnetic units. [Named in honour of Joseph *Henry*, American physicist (1797-1878).]

hent, hent, *v.t.* (*arch.*) to grasp: to take: to snatch away, carry off: (*Shak.*) to reach: (*pa.t.* and *pa.p.* hent).—*n.* a grasp: (*Shak.*) perh. a conception, intention, perh. an opportunity. [O.E. *hentan*, to seize.]

heortology, hĕ-ort-ol'ə-ji, *n.* the study of religious feasts.—*adj.* heortological (-ə-*loj'i-kl*).—*n.* heortol'ogist. [Gr. *heortē*, a feast, *logos*, discourse.]

hep, hep, *n.* See hip (the fruit of the dog-rose).

hepar, hē'pär, *n.* the name given by the older chemists to various compounds of sulphur, from their brown, liver-like colour—*n.* heparin (*hep'ə-rin*), any of certain substances formed in the tissues of liver, lung, kidney, muscle, &c., that prevent the clotting of blood.—*adj.* hepatic (*hi-pat'ik*), pertaining to, or like, liver, or a hepar, or the liverworts: liver-coloured.—*n.* a liverwort: a medicine that acts on the liver.—*n.* hepat'ica, an anemone with liver-like leaves: the common liverwort *Marchantia polymorpha*: in *pl.* Hepat'-icae (-*sē*), liverworts.—*adjs.* hepat'ical; hepati-colog'ical. — *ns.* hepaticol'ogist, a student of liverworts; hepaticol'ogy; hepatisation (*hep-ət-ī-zā'shən*), a liver-like solidification of tissue as of the lungs in pneumonia.—*v.t.* hep'atise, to convert into a substance resembling liver: (*obs.*) to impregnate with sulphuretted hydrogen.—*ns.* hep'atite, a variety of barytes with a sulphureous stink; hepati'tis, inflammation of the liver; hepatol'ogist, a specialist in liver diseases; hepatol'ogy; hepatos'copy, divination by inspection of the livers of animals. [Gr. *hēpar, hēpatos*, liver.]

hephthemimer, hef-thi-mim'ər, *n.* (*Gr.* and *Lat.* pros.) seven half-feet.—*adj.* hephthemim'eral, of a caesura, occurring in the middle of the fourth foot. [Gr. *hepta*, seven, *hēmi-*, half, *meros*, part.]

Hepplewhite, hep'l-hwīt, *adj.* belonging to a light and graceful school of furniture design that began with George Hepplewhite (d. c. 1786).

hept, hept, (*Spens.*) for heaped.

hepta-, hep'tə-, hep-ta'-, in composition, seven.— *ns.* hep'tachord (Gr. *chordē*, string), in Greek music, a diatonic series of seven tones, containing five whole steps and one half-step: an instrument with seven strings: an interval of a seventh; hep'tad (Gr. *heptas, heptados*), a group of seven: (*chem.*) an atom, radical, or element having a combining power of seven.—*adj.* hep'tagiot (Gr. *heptaglōttos*—*glōtta*, tongue), in seven languages.— *n.* a book in seven languages.—*n.* hep'tagon (Gr. *heptagōnos*—*gōniā*, an angle), a plane figure with seven angles and seven sides.—*adj.* heptag'onal. —*n.pl.* Heptagynia (-*jin'i-ä*; Gr. *gynē*, woman, female), in Linnaean classification an order of plants (in various classes) having seven styles. — *adj.* heptag'ynous. — *n.* Heptam'eron (Gr. *hēmerā*, a day), a book containing the transactions of seven days, esp. the collection of stories told in seven days bearing the name of Queen Margaret of Navarre (1492-1549).—*adj.* heptam'erous (Gr. *meros*, part), having parts in sevens.—*n.* hepta'-meter (Gr. *metron*, measure), a verse of seven measures or feet.—*n.pl.* Heptan'dria (Gr. *anēr, andros*, a man, male), a Linnaean class of plants having seven stamens.—*adj.* heptan'drous, with seven stamens.—*n.* hep'tane, a hydrocarbon (C_7H_{16}), seventh of the methane series.—*adj.* heptapod'ic.—*ns.* heptap'ody (Gr. *pous, podos*, foot), a verse of seven feet; hep'tarch, hep'-tarchist, ruler in a heptarchy.—*adj.* heptar'chic. —*n.* heptarchy (hep'tär-ki; Gr. *archē*, sovereignty), a government by seven persons: a country governed by seven: a misleading term for a once supposed system of seven English kingdoms —Wessex, Sussex, Kent, Essex, East Anglia,

Mercia, and Northumbria.—*adj.* heptasyllab′ic, seven-syllabled. — *n.* Hep′tateuch (-*tūk*; Gr. *teuchos*, instrument, volume), the first seven books of the Old Testament. [Gr. *hepta*, seven.]

her, *hər*, *pron.*, *gen.* (or *poss. adj.*), *dat.*, and *acc.* of the *pron.* she: (*refl.*, *poetic* only) herself: (*coll. nom.*) she. [O.E. *hire*, gen. and dat. sing. of *héo*, she.]

her, *hər*, *pron.* or *poss. adj.* (*obs.*; *Spens.*) their. [O.E. *hiera*, *hira*, *heora*, gen. pl. of **he**.]

her, *ər*, *pron.* See a (3).

Heraclean, Heracleian, *her-ə-klē′ən*, *adj.* pertaining to *Heracles* (Gr. *Hēraklēs*).—*adj.* Heracli′dan, Heraclei′dan, pertaining to the Heracleidae or descendants of Heracles (Hercules), the aristocracy of Sparta.—*n.* Her′aclid, one claiming such descent.

herald, *her′əld*, *n.* in ancient times, an officer who made public proclamations and arranged ceremonies : in mediaeval times, an officer who had charge of all the etiquette of chivalry, keeping a register of the genealogies and armorial bearings of the nobles : an officer whose duty is to read proclamations, to blazon the arms of the nobility, &c. : a proclaimer : a forerunner : a name given to many newspapers : the red-breasted merganser, usually her′ald-duck.—*v.t.* to usher in : to proclaim.—*adj.* heraldic (*her-*, *hər-al′dik*), of or relating to heralds or heraldry.—*adv.* heral′dically. —*ns.* her′aldry, the art or office of a herald : the science of recording genealogies and blazoning coats of arms ; her′aldship. [O.Fr. *herault*; of Gmc. origin.]

herb, *hərb* (old-fashioned *ərb*), *n.* a plant with no woody stem above ground, distinguished from a tree or shrub : a plant used in medicine : an aromatic plant used in cookery.—*adj.* herbā′ceous, pertaining to, composed of, containing, or of the nature of, herbs : like ordinary foliage leaves : (*hort.*) usu. understood as of tall herbs that die down in winter and survive in underground parts.— *n.* herb′age, herbs collectively : herbaceous vegetation covering the ground : right of pasture.— *adjs.* herb′aged, covered with grass ; herb′al, composed of or relating to herbs.—*n.* a book containing descriptions of plants with medicinal properties, orig. of all plants.—*ns.* herb′alist, one who studies, collects, sells, or administers herbs or plants : an early botanist ; herb′ar (*Spens.*; see arbour); herbā′rian, a herbalist ; herbā′rium, a classified collection of preserved plants (*pl.* herbā′riums, herbā′ria); herb′ary, a garden of herbs ; herb′-beer, a substitute for beer made from herbs ; herb′-benn′et (L. *herba benedicta*, blessed herb), avens ; herb′-Chris′topher, baneberry ; herb′ist, a herbalist.—*n.pl.* herbiv′ora (*-ə-rä*), grass-eating animals, esp. ungulates.— *n.sing.* herb′ivore (*-vōr*).—*adjs.* herbiv′orous, eating or living on grass or herbage ; herb′less. —*ns.* herb′let, herb′elet (*Shak.*), a small herb ; herb′-(of-)grace′, or of-repent′ance, the common rue ; herborisā′tion.—*v.i.* herb′orise, to botanise.—*n.* herb′orist, a herbalist.—*adjs.* herb′ous, herb′ose, abounding with herbs.—*ns.* herb′-Par′is, a tetramerous plant (*Paris quadrifolia*) of the lily family; herb′-Pē′ter, cowslip ; herb′-Rob′ert, stinking crane′s-bill (*Geranium Robertianum*), a plant with small reddish-purple flowers ; herb′-tea′, a drink made from aromatic herbs ; herb′-trin′ity, the pansy.—*adj.* herb′y, of or pertaining to herbs.—herbaceous border, a bed of usually tall stiff herbaceous plants. [Fr. *herbe*—L. *herba*.]

Herbartian, *hər-bärt′i-ən*, *adj.* of Johann Friedrich *Herbart* (1776-1841), German philosopher and paedagogic psychologist.

hercogamy, herkogamy, *hər-kog′ə-mi*, *n.* (*bot.*) an arrangement of the flower preventing self-pollination.—*adj.* hercog′amous. [Gr. *herkos*, fence, *gamos*, marriage.]

Herculean, *hər-kū′li-ən*, also *-lē′ən*, *adj.* of or pertaining to *Hercules* (the Greek *Hēraklēs*): extremely difficult or dangerous, as the twelve labours of Hercules : of extraordinary strength and size.—Hercules beetle, a gigantic S. American lamellicorn beetle, 6 inches long, with a long horn on the thorax of the male and a smaller one on the head ; Hercules' choice, toil and duty chosen in preference to ease and pleasure—from a famous story in Xenophon's *Memorabilia*; Hercules' club, a stick of great size and weight : a West Indian tree (*Xanthoxylum*): a kind of gourd : a species of Aralia ; Pillars of Hercules, two rocks flanking the entrance to the Mediterranean at the Strait of Gibraltar.

Hercynian, *hər-sin′i-ən*, *adj.* of or pertaining to the forest-covered mountain region between the Rhine and the Carpathians or the mountain chains running NW. and SE. between Westphalia and Moravia, of Upper Carboniferous to Cretaceous date.—*n.* her′cynite, black spinel, aluminate of iron. [L. *Hercynia* (*silva*), the Hercynian (forest).]

herd, *hərd*, *n.* a company of animals, esp. large animals, that habitually keep together : a group of domestic animals, esp. cows or swine, with or without a guardian : a stock of cattle : the people regarded as a mass, as acting from contagious impulse, or merely in contempt : the rabble.—*v.i.* to associate as in herds : to live like a beast in a herd.—*v.t.* to put in a herd : to drive together.— *ns.* herd′-book, a pedigree book of cattle or pigs ; herd′-in′stinct, the instinct that urges men or animals to act upon contagious impulses or follow the herd ; herds′man, keeper of a herd. [O.E. *heord* ; Ger. *herde* ; cf. herd (2).]

herd, *hərd*, *n.* a herdsman : keeper of a herd or flock. —*v.t.* to tend : to harbour.—*v.i.* to act as herd.— *ns.* herd′boy, a boy who acts as shepherd, cowherd, &c. : a cowboy ; herd′ess (*rare*) ; herd′-groom, (*arch.*) a herdsman : a shepherd boy ; herd′-man, (*obs.*) a herdsman. [O.E. *hirde*, *hierde* ; Ger. *hirte* ; cf. herd (1).]

herden, *hərd′ən*. See under hards.

herd grass, herd's grass, *hərd(z)* *gräs*, (*U.S.*) timothy : redtop. [From John *Herd*, who observed timothy in New Hampshire, 1700.]

herdic, *hər′dik*, *n.* a low-hung two- or four-wheeled carriage with back entrance and side seats. [From the inventor, Peter *Herdic* (1824-88) of Pennsylvania.]

here, *hēr*, *adv.* in this place : hither : in the present life or state.—*advs.* here′about, -s, about this place ; hereaf′ter, after this, in some future time, life, or state.—*n.* a future state.—*advs.* hereat′, at or by reason of this ; here′away, (*coll.*) hereabout ; hereby′, not far off : by this ; herefrom′, from this : from this place ; herein′, in this ; hereinaf′ter, afterward in this (document, &c.)—opp. to hereinbefore′.—*n.* here′ness, fact of being here.—*advs.* hereof′, of this ; hereon′, on or upon this ; hereto′, to this : (*Shak.*) till this time : for this object ; here′tofore′, before this time : formerly ; hereund′er, under this ; here′unto (also -*un*′), to this point or time ; here′upon′, on this : immediately after this ; herewith′, with this.—here and there, in this place, and then in that : thinly : irregularly ; here goes! an exclamation indicating that the speaker is about to do something ; here′s to, I drink the health of ; here you are, (*coll.*) this is what you want : this is something for you : this way ; neither here nor there, of no special importance. [O.E. *hér*, from base of *hé*, he ; Du. and Ger. *hier*, Sw. *här*.]

heredity, *hi-red′i-ti*, *n.* transmission of characters to descendants : heritability.—*n.* hereditabil′ity. —*adj.* hered′itable, that may be inherited.—*n.* heredit′ament (*her-id-*), any property that may pass to an heir.—*adv.* hered′itarily.—*n.* hered′itariness, the quality of being hereditary.—*adj.* hered′itary, descending or coming by inheritance : transmitted to offspring : succeeding by inheritance : according to inheritance. [L. *hērēditās*, -*ātis*—*hērēs*, -*ēdis*, an heir.]

Hereford, *her′i-fərd*, *adj.* of a breed of white-faced red cattle, originating in *Herefordshire*.

heresy, *her′i-si*, *n.* belief contrary to the authorised teaching of one's natural religious community : an opinion opposed to the usual or conventional belief : heterodoxy.—*ns.* heresiarch (*he-rē′zi-ərk*), a leader in heresy ; heresiog′rapher, one who writes about heresies ; heresiog′raphy ; heresiol′ogist, a student of, or writer on, heresies ;

heresiol′ogy; **her′esy-hunt**, vexatious pursuit of a supposed heretic; **her′esy-hunt′er**; **heretic** (*her′ə-tik*), the upholder of a heresy.—*adj.* **heretical** (*hi-ret′i-kl*). — *adv.* heret′ically. — *v.t.* heret′icate, to denounce as heretical. [O.Fr. *heresie*—L. *haeresis*—Gr. *hairesis*, a taking, choice, set of principles, school of thought—*haireein*, to take.]

heriot, *her′i-ət*, *n.* a fine due to the lord of a manor on the death of a tenant—originally his best beast or chattel.—*adj.* **her′iotable**. [O.E. *heregeatu*, a military preparation—*here*, an army, *geatwe*, equipment.]

herisson, *her′i-sən*, *n.* a spiked beam turning on a pivot, for defence: (*her.*) a hedgehog.—*adj.* **hérissé** (*her′is-ā*, *ā′-rē-sā*; *her.*), bristled. [Fr.; see **urchin**.]

heritable, *her′it-ə-bl*, *adj.* that may be inherited.— *n.* heritabil′ity.—*adv.* her′itably.—*n.* her′itor, one who inherits: in Scotland, a landholder in a parish, liable to public burdens:—*fem.* her′itress, her′itrix (*pl.* her′itrixes, heritri′cēs).—**heritable property**, (*Scots law*) real property, as opposed to movable property or chattels; **heritable security**, same as English mortgage. [Fr. *héritable*, *heredit-able*—L.L. *hērēditābilis*—*hērēs*, heir.]

heritage, *her′it-ij*, *n.* that which is inherited: inherited lot, condition of one's birth: anything transmitted from ancestors or past ages: (*B.*) the children (of God). [O.Fr. *heritage*, *heriter*—L.L. *hērēditāre*, to inherit.]

herkogamy. See **hercogamy**.

herling, **hirling**, *hər′ling*, *n.* (*dial.*) a young sea-trout, a finnock.

herm, **herma**, *hərm*, *-ā*, *n.* a head or bust (originally of *Hermes*) on a square base, often double-faced:—*pl.* herms, hermae (*-ē*).

hermandad, *ər-män-dād′*, *n.* a confederation of the entire burgher class of Spain for police and judicial purposes, formed in 1282, and formally legalised in 1485. [Sp., brotherhood—*hermano*, brother— L. *germānus*.]

hermaphrodite, *hər-maf′rod-īt*, *n.* an animal or plant with the organs of both sexes, whether normally or abnormally: a compound of opposite qualities.—*adj.* uniting the characters of both sexes: combining opposite qualities.—*n.* **hermaph′roditism**, the union of the two sexes in one body.— *adjs.* hermaphrodit′ic, -al.—hermaphrodite brig, a brig square-rigged forward and schooner-rigged aft. [Gr. *Hermaphrodītos*, the son of *Hermēs* and *Aphroditē*, who grew together with the nymph Salmacis into one person.]

hermeneutic, -al, *hər-mə-nū′tik*, *-əl*, *adjs.* interpreting: concerned with interpretation.—*adv.* hermeneu′tically.—*ns.* hermeneu′tics, the science of interpretation (treated as *sing.*); hermeneu′tist. [Gr. *hermēneutikos*—*hermēneus*, an interpreter, from *Hermēs*.]

Hermes, *hər′mēz*, *n.* the herald of the Greek gods, patron of herdsmen, arts, eloquence, and thieves: the Egyptian Thoth, identified with the Greek Hermes: a herm. [Gr. *Hermēs*, identified by the Romans with Mercury.]

hermetic, -al, *hər-met′ik*, *-əl*, *adjs.* belonging in any way to the beliefs current in the Middle Ages under the name of *Hermes*, the Thrice Great: belonging to magic or alchemy, magical: perfectly close.—*adv.* hermet′ically.—*n.* (treated as *sing.*) hermet′ics, the philosophy wrapped up in the hermetic books, esoteric science: alchemy.— **hermetically sealed**, closed completely: made air-tight by melting the glass. [From *Hermēs Trismegistos*, Hermes the thrice-greatest, the Greek name for the Egyptian Thoth, god of science, esp. alchemy.]

hermit, *hər′mit*, *n.* a solitary religious ascetic: one who lives a solitary life: a beadsman: a kind of humming-bird: a hermit-crab.—*ns.* **her′mitage**, a hermit's cell: a retired abode: a wine produced near Valence (Drôme) in France, where there was a supposed hermit's cell; **her′mit-crab**, a soft-bodied crustacean that inhabits a mollusc shell; **her′mitess**, a female hermit.—*adj.* **hermit′ical**. [M.E. *eremite*, through Fr. and L. from Gr. *erēmitēs*—*erēmos*, solitary.]

hern, *hern*. Same as **heron**.

hern, *ərn*, a provincial form for **hers**. [App. from **her**, on the analogy of **mine**, **thine**.]

hernia, *hər′ni-ä*, *n.* a protrusion through a weak place of part of the viscera, rupture.—*adjs.* **her′nial**; **her′niäted**.—*n.* **herniot′omy** (Gr. *tomē*, a cut), cutting for hernia. [L.]

hernshaw, *hərn′shaw*, *n.* See **heronshaw**.

hero, *hē′rō*, *n.* a man of distinguished bravery: any illustrious person: a person reverenced and idealised: the principal male figure, or the one whose career is the thread of the story, in a history or work of fiction: (*orig.*) a man of superhuman powers, a demigod: —*pl.* hē′roes (formerly, as *Spens.*, who never uses the singular, hērō′ēs, from which a singular form, hērō′ē, was formed): *fem.* **heroine** (*her′ō-in*).—*adj.* **heroic** (*hi-rō′ik*), befitting a hero: of or pertaining to heroes: epic: supremely courageous.—*n.* a heroic verse: (*pl.*) extravagant phrases, bombast.—*adj.* **herō′ical**.—*adv.* herō′ically (*Milt.* herō′icly). — *ns.* herō′icalness, herō′icness.—*adjs.* herō′i-com′ic, -al, consisting of a mixture of heroic and comic: high burlesque.—*ns.* **heroism** (*her′ō-izm*), the qualities of a hero: courage: boldness; **hērō′on**, a temple dedicated to a hero: a temple-shaped tomb or monument; **hē′roship**, the state of being a hero; **hē′ro-worship**, the worship of heroes: excessive admiration of great men, or of anybody.—**heroic age**, any semi-mythical period when heroes or demigods were represented as living among men; **heroic couplet**, a pair of rhyming lines of heroic verse; **heroic poem**, an epic: a compromise between epic and romance which flourished in the 16th and 17th centuries; **heroic remedy**, one that may kill or cure; **heroic size**, in sculpture, larger than life, but less than colossal; **heroic verse**, the form of verse in which the exploits of heroes are celebrated (in classical poetry, the hexameter; in English, the iambic pentameter, esp. in couplets; in French, the alexandrine). [Through O.Fr. and L. from Gr. *hērōs*; akin to L. *vir*, O.E. *wer*, a man, Sans. *vīra*, a hero.]

heroin, *her′ō-in*, hi-rō′in, *n.* a derivative of morphine used by drug-addicts. [Said to be from Gr. *hērōs*, a hero, from its effect.]

heron, *her′ən*, *hərn*, *hern*, *n.* a large screaming wading-bird (Ardea or kindred genus).—*n.* **her′onry**, a place where herons breed. [O.Fr. *hairon*— O.H.G. *heigir*.]

heronshaw, **heronsew**, **hernshaw**, *her′ən-* or *hern′-*, *hərn′-shaw*, *-shōō*, *n.* a young heron: a heron. [O.Fr. *herounçel*, confounded with shaw (wood).]

herpes, *hər′pēz*, *n.* a skin disease of various kinds, with spreading clusters of vesicles on an inflamed base—esp. *herpes zoster* or shingles.—*adj.* **herpetic** (*-pet′ik*), relating to or resembling herpes: creeping. [Gr. *herpēs*—*herpein*, to creep.]

Herpestes, *hər-pes′tēz*, *n.* the ichneumon or mongoose genus. [Gr. *herpēstēs*—*herpein*, to creep.]

herpetology, *hər-pi-tol′ə-ji*, *n.* the study of reptiles. —*adjs.* **her′petoid**, reptile-like; **herpetolog′ic**, -al.—*adv.* herpetolog′ically.—*n.* herpetol′ogist, [Gr. *herpeton*, a reptile—*herpein*, to creep.]

herr, *her*, *n.* lord, master, the German term of address equivalent to sir, or (prefixed) Mr :—*pl.* **herr′en**. [Ger.]

herring, *her′ing*, *n.* a common small sea-fish (*Clupea harengus*) of great commercial value, found moving in great shoals or multitudes.—*adj.* **herr′ing-bone**, like the spine of a herring, applied to a kind of masonry in which the stones slope in different directions in alternate rows, to a zigzag stitch crossed at the corners, to a crossed strutting, &c. —*v.t.* to make in herring-bone work, or mark with herring-bone pattern.—*ns.* **herr′ing-buss** (*hist.*; see **buss**, 2); **herr′inger** (*-ing-ər*), a man or boat employed in herring fishing; **herr′ing-fish′ery**; **herr′ing-gull**, a large white gull with black-tipped wings; **herr′ing-pond**, (*facet.*) the ocean, esp. the Atlantic.—**dead as a herring**, quite certainly dead—a herring out of water soon dies; **neither fish nor flesh nor good red herring** (see **fish**); **packed like herring** (in a barrel), very closely packed ; **red herring** (see red). [O.E. *hǣring*, *héring* ; cf. Ger. *häring*, *heer*.]

Herrnhuter, *hern'hōōt-ər*, *n.* one of the Moravians or United Brethren, so called from their settlement in 1722 at *Herrnhut* in Saxony.

herry. See **hery.**

herry, *her'i*, *v.t.* (*Scot.*) to harry.—*n.* **herr'iment**, **herr'yment**, spoliation : plunder. [harry.]

hers, *hərz*, *pron.* possessive of **she** (used without a noun).

hersall, *hər'səl*, *n.* (*Spens.*) rehearsal.

herse, *hərs*, *n.* (*obs.*) a harrow : a spiked portcullis : a form of battle-array : a hearse in various senses.— *adj.* **hersed**, arranged in harrow form. [**hearse.**]

herself, *hər-self'*, *pron.* an emphatic form for **she** or **her** : in her real character : reflexive for **her** : predicatively (or *n.*) one having the command of her faculties, sane, in good form or (*Scot.*) alone, by herself. [See **her, self.**]

hership, *hər'ship*, *n.* (*Scot.*) plundering : plunder. [O.E. *here*, army, or *hergan*, to harry ; cf. O.N. *herskapr*, warfare.]

Hertzian, *hert'si-ən*, *hərt'*, *adj.* connected with Heinrich *Hertz* (1857–94), German physicist.— **Hertzian waves**, electric waves, used in wireless communication.

hery, herye, herry, *her'i*, *v.t.* (*Spens.*) to praise, to regard as holy. [O.E. *herian*, to praise.]

Heshvan. See **Hesvan.**

hesitate, *hez'i-tāt*, *v.i.* to stop in making a decision : to be in doubt : to stammer.—*v.t.* (*rare*) to express or utter with hesitation.—*ns.* **hes'itancy, hesitā'-tion**, wavering : doubt : stammering : a faltering motion in dancing : a kind of waltz (**hesitation waltz**) with such motion.—*adj.* **hes'itant**, hesitating.—*adv.* **hes'itatingly.**—*adj.* **hes'itative**, showing hesitation.—*n.* **hes'itātor.**—*adj.* **hes'itātory**, hesitating. [L. *haesitāre*, *-ātum*, freq. of *haerēre*, *haesum*, to stick.]

hesp, *hesp*, a Scots form of **hasp.**

Hesper, *hes'pər*, **Hesperus**, *-əs*, *ns.* Venus as the evening-star.—*adj.* **Hesperian** (*-pē'ri-ən*), western : Italian (from the Greek point of view) : Spanish (from the Roman) : of the Hesperides : of the skipper butterflies.—*n.* a westerner : a skipper butterfly.—*ns.* **hes'perid** (*-pər-id*), one of the Hesperides : a skipper butterfly :—*pl.* **Hesperides** (*-per'i-dēz*), the sisters who guarded in their delightful gardens in the west the golden apples which Hera, on her marriage with Zeus, had received from Gaea ; **Hesperid'ium**, (*bot.*) a fruit of the orange type.—*n.pl.* **Hesperiidae** (*-i'i-dē*), a family of moth-like butterflies, the skippers.—*n.* **Hes'peris**, the dame's violet genus of Cruciferae, generally fragrant in the evening. [Gr. *hesperos*, evening, western.]

Hessian, *hes'i-ən*, sometimes *hesh'(i-)ən*, *adj.* of or pertaining to Hesse : (*U.S.*) mercenary (from the use of Hessian mercenaries by the British against the Revolutionaries).—*n.* a native or citizen of Hesse : a cloth made of jute : short for **Hessian boot**, a kind of long boot first worn by Hessian troops.—**Hessian fly**, a midge whose larva attacks wheat stems in America, once believed to have been introduced in straw for the Hessian troops. [*Hesse*, Ger. *Hessen*, in Germany.]

hessonite, an amended form of **essonite.**

hest, *hest*, *n.* (*arch.*) behest, command : vow.— Also (*Spens.*) **heast** (*hēst*). [O.E. *hǣs*, a command —*hátan*, to command.]

hesternal, *hes-tər'nəl*, *adj.* of yesterday. [L. *hesternus*.]

Hesvan, *hes'vän*, **Heshvan**, *hesh'*, *n.* the second month of the Jewish civil year. [Heb.]

Hesychast, *hes'i-kast*, *n.* one of a 14th-century quietist sect of the Greek Church.—*n.* **Hes'ychasm**, their doctrines and practice. [Gr. *hēsychastēs*— *hēsychos*, quiet.]

het, *het*, a Scots form of **hot.** [O.E. *hát*.]

het, *het*, *pa.p.* (*U.S.* and *prov.*) for **heated.**—**het up**, agitated.

hetaira, *he-tī'rä*, *n.* in Greece, a woman employed in public or private entertainment, as flute-playing, dancing, &c. : a paramour : a concubine : a

courtesan, esp. of a superior class :—*pl.* **hetai'rai** (*-rī*).—*ns.* **hetai'ria**, a club or society ; **hetai'rism**, concubinage : the system of society that admitted hetairai : a supposed primitive communal marriage ; **hetai'rist.**—Also (Latinised) **hetaera** (*-tē'* ; L. *-tī'*), Gr. *hetairā*, fem. of *hetairos*, companion ; *hetair(e)iā*, a club.]

heter-, hetero-, *het'ər-*, *-ō-*, or *-o'-*, in composition, other, different : one or other (often opposed to *homo-*, *auto-*).—*n.* **heterauxē'sis** (Gr. *auxēsis*, growth ; *bot.*), unsymmetrical growth. — *adj.* **heteroblast'ic** (Gr. *blastos*, bud, germ), derived from different kinds of cells : showing indirect development. — *n.* **het'eroblasty**, heteroblastic condition. — *adj.* **heterocarp'ous** (Gr. *karpos*, fruit), bearing fruit of more than one kind.—*n.pl.* **Heterocera** (*-os'ər-ä* ; Gr. *keras*, horn), a loose term for moths, distinguished from *Rhopalocera* (butterflies). — *adj.* **heterocercal** (*-sər'kəl* ; Gr. *kerkos*, tail), having the vertebral column passing into the upper lobe of the tail, which is usually larger than the lower, as in sharks.—*n.* **het'erocercy** (*-sər-si*).—*adjs.* **heterochlamydeous** (*-klə-mid'i-əs* ; Gr. *chlamys*, *-ydos*, mantle), having calyx and corolla distinctly different ; **heterochromous** (*-krō'məs* ; Gr. *chrōma*, colour), having different or varying colours ; **heterochron'ic.**—*n.* **heteroch'ronism.**—*adjs.* **heterochronist'ic** ; **heteroch'ronous.**—*n.* **heterochrony** (*-ok'rə-ni* ; Gr. *chronos*, time ; *biol.*), divergence from the normal time-sequence in development.—*adj.* **het'eroclite** (*-klīt* ; Gr. *heteroklitos*—*klitos*, inflected—*klinein*, to inflect ; *gram.*), irregularly inflected : irregular : having forms belonging to different declensions.— *n.* a word irregularly inflected : anything irregular. —*adjs.* **heteroclit'ic, heteroc'litous ; hetero-cyclic** (*-sī'klik* ; Gr. *kyklos*, wheel ; *chem.*), having a closed chain in which the atoms are not all alike : (*bot.*) having different numbers of parts in different whorls.—*n.* **heterodactyl** (*-dak'til* ; Gr. *daktylos*, toe), a heterodactylous bird.—*adj.* **heterodactylous.** —*adjs.* **heterodac'tylous**, having the first and second toes turned backwards (as trogons—not the first and fourth as parrots) ; **het'erodont** (Gr. *odous*, *odontos*, a tooth), having different kinds of teeth ; **het'erodox** (Gr. *heterodoxos*—*doxa*, opinion —*dokeein*, to think), holding an opinion other than or different from the one generally received, esp. in theology : heretical.—*n.* **het'erodoxy**, heresy.— *adjs.* **het'erodyne** (*-ō-dīn* ; Gr. *dynamis*, strength), in wireless communication applied to a method of imposing on a continuous wave another of slightly different length to produce beats ; **heteroecious** (*-ē'shəs*).—*n.* **heteroecism** (*-ē'sizm* ; Gr. *oikos*, a house), parasitism upon different hosts at different stages of the life-cycle.—*adj.* **heterog'amous.**— *ns.* **heterog'amy** (Gr. *gamos*, marriage), alternation of generations : reproduction by unlike gametes : presence of different kinds of flower (male, female, hermaphrodite, neuter, in any combination) in the same inflorescence : indirect pollination ; **hetero-genē'ity.**—*adj.* **heterogeneous** (*-jē'ni-əs* ; Gr. *heterogenēs*—*genos*, a kind), different in kind : composed of parts of different kinds—opp. to *homogeneous.*—*adv.* **heteroge'neously.** — *ns.* **hetero-ge'neousness ; heterogenesis** (*-jen'i-sis* ; Gr. *genesis*, generation ; *biol.*), spontaneous generation : alternate generation.—*adj.* **heterogenetic** (*-ji-net'ik*).—*n.* **heterogeny** (*-oj'ən-i*), a heterogeneous assemblage : heterogenesis.—*adj.* **heterogonous** (*-og'ə-nəs* ; Gr. *gonos*, offspring, begetting), having flowers differing in length of stamens : having alternation of generations. — *ns.* **heterog'ony ; het'erokont, het'erocont** (Gr. *kontos*, a punting pole), any member of the **Heterocont'ae** or yellow-green algae (e.g. the common Conferva), a class usually characterised by the pair of unequal cilia on the motile cells.—*adjs.* **heterokont'an ; het-erom'erous** (Gr. *meros*, part ; *bot.*), having different numbers of parts in different whorls : (of lichens) having the algal cells in a layer : (*zool.*) having unlike segments ; **heteromor'phic** (Gr. *morphē*, form), deviating in form from a given type : of different forms—also **heteromor'phous.** —*ns.* **heteromor'phism, het'eromorphy.**—*adj.*

Neutral vowels in unaccented syllables : *el'ə-mənt*, *in'fənt*, *ran'dəm*

heteron'omous (Gr. *nomos*, law), subject to different laws: subject to outside rule or law—opp. to *autonomous*.—*n.* heteron'omy.—*adj.* hetero-ousian (*het-ər-ō-ōō'si-ən*, or -*ow'*; Gr. *ousiā*, being), **heterousian** (-*ōō'*, -*ow'*, or -*ō-ōō'*), of unlike essence: believing the Father and Son to be of different substance.—*n.* a holder of such belief.—*adj.* **heterophyllous** (-*fil'əs*; Gr. *phyllon*, a leaf), having different kinds of foliage leaf.—*ns.* **het'erophylly**; **heteroplasia** (-*plā'z*(*h*)*i-ä*, -*si-ä*; Gr. *plasis*, a forming), development of abnormal tissue or tissue in an abnormal place.—*adj.* **heteroplastic** (-*plas'tik*). — *ns.* **het'eroplasty**, heteroplasia: grafting of tissue from another person; **het'eropod**. — *ns.pl.* Heterop'oda (Gr. *pous*, *podos*, a foot), pelagic gasteropods in which the foot has become a swimming organ; **Heterop'tera** (Gr. *pteron*, a wing), a suborder of insects, the bugs, Hemiptera with fore and hind wings (when present) markedly different. — *n.* **heterop'terous**. — *n.* **heteroscian** (*het-ər-osh'i-ən*; Gr. *skiā*, a shadow), a dweller in a temperate zone, whose noon-shadow is always thrown one way, either north or south.—*adj.* **heterosex'ual**, normally sexual.—*ns.* **heterosexual'ity**; **heterō'sis**, cross-fertilisation.—*n.pl.* **Heterosō'mata** (Gr. *sōma*, pl. *sōmata*, a body), the flat-fishes.—*adjs.* **heterosō'matous**; **heterosporous** (-*os'por-əs*, or -*pōr'*), having different kinds of asexually produced spores.—*n.* **heteros'pory**.—*adj.* **heterostroph'ic** (Gr. *strophē*, a turning), consisting of unequal strophes: coiled contrary to the usual direction.—*n.* **heteros'trophy**.—*adjs.*het'erostyled, heterosty'lous, having styles of different length in different flowers.—*ns.* **heterostyl'ism**; **het'erostyly**.—*adj.* **heterotact'ic**.—*ns.* **heterotax'is**, het'erotaxy (Gr. *taxis*, arrangement), anomalous arrangement. — *adj.* **heterothall'ic** (Gr. *thallos*, a shoot; *bot.*), having (as certain fungi) two physiologically different types of mycelium, called plus and minus, comparable to male and female.—*ns.* **heterothall'ism**, het'erothally.—*adj.* **heterother'mal** (Gr. *thermos*, heat), taking the temperature of the surroundings.—*n.* **het'erotroph**, a heterotrophic organism.—*adj.* **heterotroph'ic**.—*n.* **heterot'rophy** (Gr. *trophē*, livelihood; *bot.*), dependence (immediate or ultimate) upon green plants for carbon (as in parasites and saprophytes).—*adj.* **heterousian**, same as heteroousian.—*n.* **heterozygote** (-*zī'gōt*; Gr. *zygōtos*, yoked—*zygon*, yoke), a zygote or individual formed from gametes differing with respect to some pair of alternative characters (one dominant and one recessive).—*adj.* **heterozy'gous**. [Gr. *heteros*, other, one or other.]

hether, hetherward (*Spens.*). Same as hither, hitherward.

hetman, *het'man*, *n.* (*hist.*) a Polish officer: the head or general of the Cossacks:—*pl.* **het'mans**. —*ns.* **het'manate**, **het'manship**. [Pol.,—Ger. *hauptmann*, captain.]

heugh, heuch, *hühh*, *n.* (*Scot.*) a crag: a ravine or steep-sided valley: a quarry-face: an excavation, esp. for coal. [O.E. *hōh*, heel; cf. hoe (2).]

heulandite, *hū'lan-dīt*, *n.* a zeolite like stilbite. [After H. *Heuland*, an English mineralogist.]

heuristic, *hū-ris'tik*, *adj.* serving or leading to find out.—*n.* the art of discovery in logic: the method in education by which the pupil is set to find out things for himself.—*ns.* **heuret'ic**, (*logic*) heuristic; **heur'ism**, the heuristic method or principle in education. [Irreg. formed from Gr. *heuriskein*, to find; cf. eureka.]

hew, *hū*, *v.t.* to cut with blows: to shape, fell or sever with blows of a cutting instrument.—*v.i.* to deal blows with a cutting instrument: (*pa.t.* hewed; *pa.p.* hewed, or hewn).—*n.* (*Spens.*) hacking.—*n.* hew'er, one who hews.—*n.* and *adj.* hew'ing.—*adj.* hewn. [O.E. *hēawan*; Ger. *hauen*.]

hew (*Spens.*). Same as hue.

hewgh, *hū*, *interj.* (*Shak.*) imitating the whistling of an arrow.

hex-, hexa-, *heks-, heks'ə-, heks-a'-*, in composition, six.—*n.* hex'achord (-*kord*), a diatonic series of six notes having a semitone between the third and fourth.—*adj.* hex'act (-*akt*; Gr. *aktīs*, -*īnos*,

ray), six-rayed.—*n.* a six-rayed sponge spicule.—*adj.* **hexactī'nal** (or -*akt'i-nl*), six-rayed.—*n.* and *adj.* **hexactinell'id**.—*n.pl.* Hexactinell'ida, a class of sponges whose spicules have three axes and therefore (unless some are suppressed) six rays.—*n.* **hexad** (*heks'ad*; Gr. *hexas*, -*ados*), a series of six numbers: a set of six things: (*chem.*) an atom, element, or radical with a combining power of six units. — *adjs.* **hexad'ic**; **hexadactyl'ic**, **hexadact'ylous** (Gr. *daktylos*, finger, toe), six-fingered: six-toed.—*n.* **hexaëmeron** (*heks-ə-ē'mer-on*; Gr. *hēmerā*, day), a period of six days, esp. that of the creation, according to Genesis : a history of the six days of creation.—*adj.* hex'aglot (Gr. *glōtta*, tongue), in six languages.—*n.* hex'agon (Gr. *hexagōnon—gōniā*, an angle), a figure with six sides and six angles.—*adj.* **hexagonal** (-*ag'ən-əl*), of the form of a hexagon : (*cryst.*) of the hexagonal system, a crystal system with three axes at 60° to each other and a fourth perpendicular to their plane.—*adv.* **hexag'onally**.—*n.* **hex'agram** (Gr. *gramma*, figure), a figure of six lines, esp. a stellate hexagon.—*n.pl.* Hexagynia (-*jin'i-ä*; Gr. *gynē*, woman), a Linnaean order of plants (in various classes) having six styles.—*adjs.* **hexagyn'ian, hexagynous** (-*aj'i-nəs*); **hexahē'dral**.—*n.* **hexahē'dron** (Gr. *hēdrā*, a base), a solid with six sides or faces, esp. a cube.—*adj.* **hexam'erous** (Gr. *meros*, part), having six parts, or parts in sixes. —*n.* **hexam'eter** (Gr. *metron*, measure), a verse of six measures or feet : in Greek and Latin verse such a line where the fifth is almost always a dactyl and the sixth a spondee or trochee, the others dactyls or spondees.—*adj.* having six metrical feet. — *adjs.* **hexamet'ric, -al.** — *v.i.* **hexam'etrise**, to write hexameters.—*n.* **hexam'etrist**, a writer of hexameters.—*n.pl.* Hexan'dria (Gr. *anēr, andros*, a man, male), a Linnaean class of plants having six stamens.—*adjs.* hexan'drian; hexan'drous, having six stamens.—*ns.* **hexane** (*heks'ān*), a hydrocarbon (C_6H_{14}), sixth member of the methane series; **hex'apla** (Gr. *hexaplā*, contracted pl. neut. of *hexaploos*, sixfold), an edition (esp. of the Bible) in six versions.—*adjs.* **hex'aplar, hexaplār'ian, hexaplär'ic**; **hex'aploid**, of, or having, six times the ordinary number of chromosomes.—*n.* a hexaploid cell, individual, species, &c.—*n.* hex'apod (Gr. *pous, podos*, a foot), an animal with six feet.—*n.pl.* Hexap'oda, insects.—*n.* **hexap'ody**, a line or verse of six feet.—*adj.* **hexarch** (*heks'ärk*; Gr. *archē*, beginning; *bot.*), having six vascular strands.—*n.* **hexastich** (*heks'ə-stik*; Gr. *hexastichos*, adj.—*stichos*, a line), a poem or stanza of six lines.—*adjs.* **hexastichal** (-*as'tik-l*), having six lines or rows; **hexastyle** (*heks'ə-stīl*; Gr. *hexastylos—stylos*, a pillar), having six columns.—*n.* a building or portico having six columns in front.—*n.* **Hexateuch** (*heks'ə-tūk*; Gr. *teuchos*, tool, afterwards book), the first six books of the Old Testament.—*adj.* **hexateuch'al**.—*n.* **hexylene** (*heks'i-lēn*; Gr. *hylē*, matter), hex'ene, an unsaturated hydrocarbon (C_6H_{12}) of the ethylene series. [Gr. *hex*, six; cf. L. *sex*, and six.]

hey, *hā*, *interj.* expressive of joy or interrogation, or calling attention.—*interjs.* hey'day, expressive of frolic, exultation, or wonder; hey'-go-mad, expressing a high degree of excitement.—Also *n.*, as like hey-go-mad, helter-skelter.—*interjs.* and *ns.* (hey'-pass, hey'-pres'to, a conjuror's command in passing objects.—hey for, now for: off we go for. [Imit.]

hey, hay, *hā*, *n.* a winding country-dance.—*v.i.* to dance the hay.—*n.* hey'- or hay-de-guy (-*gī*), -guise, -guyes, a hay popular in the 16th and 17th centuries. [Obs. Fr. *haye*.]

heyday, *hā'dā*, *n.* exaltation of spirits: culmination or climax of vigour, prosperity, gaiety, &c.: flush or full bloom. [Origin obscure.]

heyduck. See haiduk.

hi ! *hī*, *interj.* calling attention: hey. [Cf. hey (1).]

hiant, *hī'ənt*, *adj.* gaping. [L. *hiāns*, -*āntis*, pr.p. of *hiāre*, to gape.]

hiatus, *hi-ā'təs*, *n.* a gap: an opening: a chasm: a break in continuity, a defect: (*gram.*) a concurrence of vowel sounds in two successive syllables :—*pl.* **hīā′tuses.** [L. *hĭātus, -ūs—hĭāre, hĭātum,* to gape.]

hibernate, *hī′bər-nāt, v.i.* to winter : to pass the winter in a resting state.—*ns.* **hī′bernacle,** winter quarters : a hibernaculum ; **hībernac′ūlum,** a winter retreat : (*zool.*) a bud in Polyzoa that regenerates the colony after winter : (*bot.*) a winter-bud, bulb, &c., by which a plant survives the winter :—*pl.* **hībernac′ūla.**—*adj.* **hīber′nal,** belonging to winter : wintry.—*n.* **hībernā′tion.** [L. *hibernāre, -ātum — hibernus,* wintry — *hiems,* winter.]

Hibernian, *hī-bər′ni-ən, adj.* relating to Hibernia or Ireland : Irish : characteristic of Ireland.—*n.* an Irishman.—*ns.* **Hiber′nianism, Hiber′nicism** (*-sizm*), an Irish idiom or peculiarity : a bull in speech.—*adv.* **Hiber′nically.**—*v.t.* **hiber′nicise** (*-sīz*), to render Irish.—*n.* **hibernisā′tion,** a making Irish.—*v.t.* **hi′bernise,** to hibernicise. [L. *Hibernia,* Ireland.]

Hibiscus, *hib-is′kəs, n.* a genus of malvaceous plants, mostly tropical. [L.,—Gr. *ibiskos,* marshmallow.]

hic, *hik, interj.* representing a drunken hiccup.

hiccatee, hicatee, *hik-ə-tē′, n.* a West Indian freshwater tortoise. [From a native name.]

hiccup, *hik′əp, n.* the involuntary contraction of the diaphragm while the glottis is spasmodically closed : the sound caused by this.—*v.i.* to make a hiccup.—*v.t.* to say with a hiccup :—*pr.p.* **hicc′-uping ;** *pa.t.* and *pa.p.* **hicc′uped.**—*adj.* **hicc′upy,** marked by hiccups. [Imit. ; an early form was *hicket* ; cf. Du. *hik,* Dan. *hik,* Bret. *hik.* The spelling *hiccough* is due to a confusion with *cough.*]

hick, *hik, n.* a lout : a booby. [A familiar form of *Richard.*]

hickery-pickery (*hik′ər-i-pik′ər-i*)=**hiera-picra.**

hickory, *hik′ər-i, n.* a North American genus (Carya) of the walnut family, yielding edible nuts and heavy strong tenacious wood. [Earlier *po-hickery* ; of Indian origin.]

hickwall, *hik′wawl, n.* the green woodpecker. [Origin obscure.]

hid, hidden. See hide (1).

hidage. See hide (3).

hidalgo, *hi-dal′gō, n.* a Spanish nobleman of the lowest class : a gentleman :—*pl.* **hidal′gōs ;** *fem.* **hidal′ga,** *pl.* **hidal′gas.**—*adj.* **hidal′gōish.**—*n.* **hidal′gōism.** [Sp. *hijo de algo,* son of something.]

hiddenite, *hid′ən-īt, n.* a green spodumene, discovered by W. E. *Hidden* (1853-1918).

hidder, *hid′ər, n.* (*Spens.*) a young male sheep :— *fem.* **shidder.** [Perh. **he,** and **deer** in the sense of animal.]

hide, *hīd, v.t.* to conceal : to keep in concealment : to keep secret or out of sight.—*v.i.* to go into, or to stay in, concealment : (*pa.t.* **hid,** *hid* ; *pa.p.* **hidden,** *hid′n,* **hid**).—*n.* a hiding-place : a hidden store.—*adj.* **hidd′en,** concealed : unknown.—*adv.* **hidd′enly,** in a hidden or secret manner : privily. —*adj.* **hidd′enmost,** most hidden.—*ns.* **hidd′enness ; hide′-and-seek′,** a game in which one seeks the others, who have hidden themselves ; **hide′-away,** a fugitive : concealment.—*adj.* that hides away.—*ns.* **hide′out,** a retreat ; **hid′ing,** concealment : a place of concealment ; **hid′ing-place ;** **hid′y-hole,** (*Scot.* and *U.S.*) a hiding-place. [O.E. *hȳdan* ; cf. M.L.G. *hûden,* and (doubtfully) Gr. *keuthein.*]

hide, *hīd, n.* the skin of an animal, esp. the larger animals, sometimes used derogatorily for human skin.—*v.t.* to flog or whip : to skin.—*adj.* **hide′-bound,** having the hide closely bound to the body, as in animals : in trees, having the bark so close that it impedes the growth : stubborn, bigoted, obstinate.—*n.* **hīd′ing,** a thrashing. [O.E. *hȳd* ; Ger. *haut,* L. *cutis.*]

hide, *hīd, n.* in old English law, a variable unit of area of land, enough for a household.—*n.* **hid′age,** a tax once assessed on every hide of land. [O.E. *hīd,* contracted from *higid* ; cf. *hīwan, hīgan,* household.]

hideous, *hid′i-əs, adj.* frightful : horrible : ghastly : extremely ugly : (*obs.*) huge.—*ns.* **hideos′ity, hid′eousness.**—*adv.* **hid′eously.** [O.Fr. *hideus,*

hisdos—hide, hisde, dread, poss.—L. *hispidus,* rough, rude.]

hidrosis, *hid-rō′sis, n.* sweating, esp. in excess.—*n.* and *adj.* **hidrotic** (*-rot′ik*), sudorific. [Gr. *hidrōs, -ōtos,* sweat.]

hie, *hī, v.i.* to hasten.—*v.t.* to urge on : pass quickly over (one's way) : (*pr.p.* **hie′ing ;** *pa.t.* and *pa.p.* **hied**).—*n.* (*obs.*) haste. [O.E. *higian.*]

hie, high, *hī, n.* and *interj.* the call to a horse to turn to the left—opp. to *hup.*—*v.t.* and *v.i.* to turn to the left (of or to a horse or plough-ox).

hielaman, *hē′la-man, n.* the native Australian narrow shield of bark or wood. [Native word *hīlaman.*]

Hieland, *hēl′ən(d), -ənt, adj.* a Scots form of **High-land.**—no sae **Hielant,** not altogether absurd : not so bad as might be.

hiems, *hī′emz, n.* (*Shak.*) winter.—*adj.* **hī′emal.** [L. *hiems.*]

Hieracium, *hī-ər-ā′shi-əm, n.* the hawkweed genus of Compositae. [Latinised from Gr. *hierākion,* hawkweed—*hierāx,* hawk.]

hiera-picra, *hī′ər-ə-pik′rä, n.* a purgative drug from aloes and canella bark.—Also **hick′ery-pick′ery, hig′ry-pig′ry.** [Gr. *hierā* (fem.), sacred, *pikrā* (fem.), bitter.]

hierarch, *hī′ər-ärk, n.* a ruler in holy things : a chief priest : a prelate : (*Milt.*) an archangel.—*adjs.* **hī′erarchal, -arch′ic, -al.**—*adv.* **hierarch′ically.** —*ns.* **hī′erarchism ;** **hī′erarchy,** the collective body of angels, grouped in three divisions and nine orders of different power and glory : (1) seraphim, cherubim, thrones ; (2) dominations or dominions, virtues, powers ; (3) principalities, archangels, angels : each of the three main classes of angels : classification in graded subdivisions : a body classified in successively subordinate grades : priestly government. [Gr. *hierarchēs — hieros,* sacred, *archein,* to rule.]

hieratic, *hī-ər-at′ik, adj.* priestly : applying to a certain kind of ancient Egyptian writing which consisted of abridged forms of hieroglyphics ; also to certain styles in art bound by religious convention.—*n.* **hierat′ica,** the finest papyrus. [L. *hierāticus*—Gr. *hierātikos—hieros,* sacred.]

hierocracy, *hī-ər-ok′rə-si, n.* priestly government. —*n.* **hī′erocrat.**—*adj.* **hierocrat′ic.** [Gr. *hieros,* sacred, *krateein,* to rule.]

hierodule, *hī′ər-ō-dūl, n.* a temple slave. [Gr. *hieros,* sacred, *doulos,* a slave.]

hieroglyph, *hī′ər-ō-glif, n.* a sacred character used in ancient Egyptian picture-writing or in picture-writing in general.—*v.t.* to represent by hieroglyphs. —*adjs.* **hieroglyph′ic, -al.**—*n.* **hieroglyph′ic,** a hieroglyph : any written character difficult to read. — *adv.* **hieroglyph′ically.** — *n.* **hieroglyphist** (*-og′*), one skilled in hieroglyphics. [Gr. *hiero-glyphikon—hieros,* sacred, *glyphein,* to carve.]

hierogram, *hī′ər-ō-gram, n.* a sacred or hiero-glyphic symbol.—*n.* **hierogramm′at(e),** a writer of sacred records.—*adjs.* **hierogrammat′ic, -al.**— *ns.* **hierogramm′atist ; hī′erograph,** a sacred symbol ; **hierog′rapher,** a sacred scribe.—*adjs.* **hierograph′ic, -al,** pertaining to sacred writing. —*n.* **hierog′raphy,** a description of sacred things. [Gr. *hieros,* sacred, *gramma,* a character, *graphein,* to write.]

hierolatry, *hī-ər-ol′ə-tri, n.* the worship of saints or sacred things. [Gr. *hieros,* sacred, *latreiā,* worship.]

hierology, *hī-ər-ol′ə-ji, n.* the science of sacred matters, esp. ancient writing and Egyptian in-scriptions.—*adj.* **hierologic** (*-ō-loj′ik*).—*n.* **hierol′ogist.** [Gr. *hieros,* sacred, *logos,* discourse.]

hieromancy, *hī-ər-ō-man′si, n.* divination by ob-serving the objects offered in sacrifice. [Gr. *hieros,* sacred, *manteiā,* divination.]

Hieronymic, *hī-ər-on-im′ik, adj.* of or pertaining to St Jerome.—Also **Hieronym′ian.**—*n.* **Hieron′-ymite,** a member of any of a number of hermit orders established in the 13th and 14th centuries. [L. *Hierōnymus,* Gr. *Hierōnymos,* Jerome.]

hierophant, *hī′ər-ō-fant, n.* one who shows or re-veals sacred things : a priest : an expounder.—*adj.* **hierophant′ic.** [Gr. *hierophantēs—hieros,* sacred, *phainein,* to show.]

hieroscopy, *hī-ar-os'ka-pi*, *n*. hieromancy. [Gr. *hieros*, sacred, *skopeein*, to look at.]

Hierosolymitan, *hī-a-rō-sol'i-mī-tan*, *adj*. of or pertaining to Jerusalem. [L. and Gr. *Hierosolyma*, Jerusalem.]

hierurgy, *hī'ar-ar-ji*, *n*. a sacred performance.—*adj*. hierur'gical. [Gr. *hierourgiā—hieros*, sacred, *ergon*, work.]

higgle, *hig'l*, *v.i*. to make difficulty in bargaining: to chaffer.—Also higg'le-hagg'le (reduplicated variant).—*n*. higg'ler.—*n*. and *adj*. higg'ling. [Prob. a form of haggle.]

higgledy-piggledy, *hig'l-di-pig'l-di*, *adv*. and *adj*. haphazard: in confusion. [Origin obscure.]

high, *hī*, *adj*. elevated: lofty: tall: far up from a base, as the ground, sea-level, low-tide, the mouth of a river, the zero of a scale, &c.: advanced in a scale, esp. the scale of nature: reaching far up: expressible by a large number: of a height specified or to be specified: of advanced degree of intensity: advanced or full (in time, as *high summer*): of grave importance: advanced: exalted: excellent: eminent: dignified: chief: noble: haughty: arrogant: extreme in opinion: powerful: angry: loud: violent: tempestuous: acute in pitch: luxurious: elated: drunk: standing out: difficult: dear: for heavy stakes: remote in time: (of game, &c.) slightly tainted: (*phon*.) pronounced with some part of the tongue much raised in the mouth: (of latitude) far from the equator: (of an angle) approaching a right angle.—*adv*. aloft: shrilly: arrogantly: eminently: powerfully: luxuriously: dear: for heavy stakes.—*n*. that which is high: the highest card: (*U.S.*) the maximum, high level.—*ns*. high'-ad'miral, a high or chief admiral of a fleet; high'-al'tar, the principal altar in a church.—*adj*. high'-and-dry', high-dried.—*ns*. high'-bail'iff, an officer who serves writs, &c., in certain franchises, exempt from the ordinary supervision of the sheriff; high'ball, (*U.S.*) whisky and soda or the like with ice in a tall glass.—*adj*. high'-batt'led (hye-battel'd; *Shak*.), app. in command of proud battalions.—*n*. high'-bind'er, (*U.S.*) a member of a Chinese criminal secret society: a conspirator: a rowdy, ruffian, blackmailer.—*adjs*. high-blest', (*Milt*.) supremely blest or happy; high'-blood'ed, of noble lineage; high'-blown, swelled with wind: (*Shak*.) inflated, as with pride; high'-born, of high or noble birth; high'-bred, of high or noble breed, ‖training, or family.—*n*. high'brow, (*slang*) an intellectually exalted person: a lofty intellectual.—Also *adj.*-*n*. high'browism.—*adj*. high'-church, of a party within the Church of England that exalts the authority of the episcopate and the priesthood, the saving grace of sacraments, &c.: of similar views in other churches.—*ns*. high'-church'ism; high'-church'man.—*adjs*. high'-class, superior; high'-col'oured, having a strong or glaring colour: ruddy: over-vivid.—*ns*. high'-court, a supreme court; high'-cross, a town or village cross; high'-day, a holiday or festival: (*-dā'*) broad daylight: (*hī'*) heyday (erroneously).—*adj*. befitting a festival.—*adjs*. high'-dried, brought to an advanced stage of dryness: of fixed and extreme opinions; high'er, *comp*. of high.—*v.t*. to raise higher: to lift.—*v.i*. to ascend. —*adjs*. high'ermost (*rare*), high'est, *superl*. of high.—*ns*. high'-explos'ive, a detonating (disruptive) explosive (e.g. dynamite, T.N.T.) of great power and exceedingly rapid action—also *adj*.; high-falutin(g) (*-lōōt'*), bombastic discourse.—*adj*. bombastic: pompous.—*adj*. high'-fed, fed highly or luxuriously: pampered.—*ns*. high'-feed'ing; high'-fli'er, a bird that flies high: one who runs into extravagance of opinion or action: High'-fli'er (*hist*.), a High-churchman, or, in Scotland, an Evangelical.—*adjs*. high'-flown, extravagant: elevated: turgid; high'-fly'ing, extravagant in conduct or opinion; high'-fre'quency, of many oscillations a second; high'-geared (see gear); high'-grade, superior: rich in metal.—*v.t*. to steal rich ore from.—*adjs*. high'-grown, (*Shak*.) covered with a high growth; high'-hand'ed, overbearing: violent: arbitrary. — *ns*. high'-

hand'edness; high'-hat', a wearer of a top-hat: a snob or aristocrat: one who puts on airs.—*adj*. affectedly superior.—*v.i*. to put on airs.—*v.t*. to adopt a superior attitude towards or to ignore socially.—*adjs*. high'-heart'ed, full of courage; high'-heeled, having or wearing high heels; high'ish, somewhat high.—*ns*. high'jacker (see hijacker); high'-jinks, boisterous play or jollity: an old Scottish tavern game in which persons played various parts under penalty of a forfeit.— *adj*. high'-kilt'ed, having the skirt much kilted up: indecorous.—*n*. high'land, a mountainous district, esp. (in *pl*. Highlands) the north-west of Scotland, bordered geologically by the great fault running from Dumbarton to Stonehaven, ethnologically the considerably narrower area in which Gaelic is or was recently spoken.—*adj*. belonging to or characteristic of a highland, esp. the Highlands of Scotland.—*ns*. High'lander, High'landman, an inhabitant or native of a mountainous region, esp. the Highlands of Scotland: a cow or bull of Highland breed; High'land-fling', a lively dance of the Scottish Highlands, danced by one person; high'-light, outstanding feature. — *v.t*. to throw into relief by strong light: also *fig*.— *n.pl*. high'-lights, the most brightly lighted spots. —*adv*. high'-lone, (*Shak*.) quite alone.—*n*. high'-low, a high shoe fastened in front.—*adv*. high'ly, in a high degree: in a high position.—*n*. high'man, a loaded die: — *pl*. high'men. — *adjs*. high'-mett'led, high-spirited, fiery; high'-mind'ed, having a high, proud, or arrogant mind: having honourable pride: lofty: magnanimous. — *n*. high'-mind'edness.—*adjs*. high'most, highest; high'-necked, of a dress, cut so as to cover the shoulders and neck.—*n*. high'ness, the state of being high: dignity of rank: a title of honour given to princes.—*adj*. high'-pitched, acute in sound, tending towards treble: steep (as a roof): lofty-toned.—*n*. high'-place, (*B*.) an eminence on which idolatrous rites were performed by the Jews —hence the idols, &c., themselves.—*adjs*. high'-placed, having a high place: placed high; high'-press'ure, making or allowing use of steam or other gas at a pressure much above that of the atmosphere: involving intense activity; high'-priced, costly.— *ns*. high'-priest (see priest); high'-priest'ess; high-priest'hood.—*adjs*. high-priest'ly; high'-prin'cipled, of high, noble, or strict principle; high'-proof, proved to contain much alcohol: highly rectified; high'-raised, -reared, raised aloft: elevated; high'-reach'ing, reaching upwards: ambitious.—*ns*. high'-road, one of the public or chief roads: a road for general traffic; high'-roll'er, a plunging spendthrift; high'-roll'ing.—*adjs*. high'-sea'soned, made rich or piquant with spices or other seasoning; high'-set, placed or pitched high; high'-sight'ed, (*Shak*.) looking upwards, supercilious; high'-souled, having a high or lofty soul or spirit; high'-sound'ing, pompous: imposing; high'-speed, working, or suitable for working, at a great speed; high'-spir'ited, having a high spirit or natural fire: bold: daring: irascible.—*n*. high'-stepp'er, a horse that lifts its feet high from the ground: a person of imposing bearing or fashionable pretensions.—*adjs*. high'-stepp'ing; high'-stom'-ached, (*Shak*.) proud-spirited, lofty, obstinate; high'-strung, nervously sensitive.—*ns*. hight (*hīt*), highth (*hīth*), obsolete forms of height; high'-ta'per (see hag-taper).—*adj*. high'-tast'ed, having a strong, piquant taste or relish.—*ns*. high'-tide; high-water: a tide higher than usual: (*hī'tīd; rare*) a great festival; high-to'by, (*thieves' slang*) highway robbery on horseback.—*adj*. high'-toned, high in pitch: morally elevated: (*U.S.*) superior, fashionable.—*ns*. high'-top, (*Shak*.) a mast-head; high'-trea'son, treason against the sovereign or state.—*adjs*. high-veloc'ity, (of shells) propelled at a high velocity with a low trajectory; high'-viced, (*Shak*.) enormously wicked.—*ns*. high'-wa'ter, the time at which the tide or other water is highest: the greatest elevation of the tide; high'-wa'ter-mark, the highest line so reached: a tide-mark; high'way, a public road on which all have right to go: the main or usual way or course; **high′wayman**, a robber who attacks people on the public way.—*adj.* **high′wrought**, wrought with exquisite skill: highly finished: elaborate: worked up, agitated.—**high and dry**, up out of the water, stranded; **high and low**, rich and poor: up and down: everywhere; **high and mighty** (*ironically*), exalted: arrogant; **High Dutch**, High German: pure Dutch of Holland (as opp. to *Cape Dutch*); **high feather**, high spirits: happy trim; **High German**, of upper or southern Germany: that form of Germanic language affected by the second consonant shift, including the literary language of Germany; **high hand**, arbitrary arrogance; **Highland cattle**, a shaggy breed with very long horns; **Highland costume**, kilt, plaid, and sporran; **high life**, the life of fashionable society: the people of this society; **high life below stairs**, servants' imitation of the life of their employers; **high living**, luxurious feeding; **high mass**, a mass celebrated with music, ceremonies, and incense; **high relief**, bold relief, standing out well from the surface; **high school**, a secondary school; **high seas**, the open ocean; **high shoe**, (*arch.*) a boot not reaching far above the ankle; **high-speed steel**, an alloy that remains hard when red-hot, suitable for metal-cutting tools; **high spot**, an outstanding feature; **High Street**, a common name for the main, or former main, street of a town; **high table**, the dons' table in a college dining-hall; **high tea**, a tea with meat, &c., as opposed to a plain tea; **high (old) time**, (*coll.*) a time of special jollity or enthusiasm; **high time**, quite time (that something were done); **high words**, angry altercation; **hit the high spots**, to go to excess: to reach a high level; **on high**, aloft: in heaven; **on one's high horse**, in an attitude of fancied superiority: very much on one's dignity; **on the high ropes**, (*coll.*) in an elated or highly excited mood; **how's that for high?** (*U.S.*) beat that if you can (from a card game). [O.E. *héah*; Goth. *hauhs*, O.N. *hár*, Ger. *hoch*.]

hight, *hīt*, *Scot.* **hecht**, *hehht*, *obs.* **hete**, *hēt*, *v.t.* (*obs.*) to command: to promise, assure, vow: (*arch.*) to call, name: (*Spens.*) to mention: (*Spens.*) to commit: (*Spens.*) to direct, determine, intend. —*v.i.* (*orig. passive*) to be called or named, to have as a name—*pa.t.* (*arch.*) **hight**, (*Scot.*) **hecht**, (*Spens.*) **hote**; *pa.p.* **hight**, (*Scot.*) **hecht**, (*obs.*) **ho′ten.** [O.E. *hēht* (*hét*), redup. pa.t. of *hátan* (pa.p. *háten*), substituted for the present and for the last surviving trace of the inflected passive in English, *hátte*, is or was called; cf. Ger. *ich heisse*, I am named, from *heissen*, to call.]

highty-tighty, *hī′ti-tī′ti.* Same as **hoity-toity.**

higry-pigry, *hig′ri-pig′ri.* Same as **hiera-picra.**

hijacker, highjacker, *hī′jak-ər*, *n.* a highwayman: a robber or blackmailer of rum-runners and boot-leggers.—*v.t.* and *v.i.* **hi′jack, high′jack.** [Origin obscure.]

hijra, hijrah. Same as **hegira.**

hike, *hik*, *v.t.* (*coll.*) to hoist, shoulder.—*v.i.* to hitch: to tramp: to go walking and camping with equipment on back.—*ns.* **hike**, a walking tour or outing, esp. of the self-conscious kind; **hi′ker.** [Perh. **hitch.**]

hiiar. See **hilum.**

hilarious, *hi-lā′ri-əs*, *adj.* gay: extravagantly merry. —*adv.* **hilā′riously.**—*n.* **hilarity** (*hi-lar′*), gaiety: pleasurable excitement. [L. *hilaris*—Gr. *hilaros*, cheerful.]

Hilary, *hil′ər-i*, *adj.* a term or session of the High Court of Justice in England: also one of the university terms at Oxford and Dublin—from St *Hilary* of Poitiers (d. c. 367; festival, Jan. 13).

hilch, *hilsh*, *v.t.* (*Scot.*) to hobble.—*n.* a limp.

hild, *hild* (*Shak.*, *Spens.*). Same as **held.**

Hildebrandism, *hil′də-brand-izm*, *n.* the spirit and policy of *Hildebrand* (Pope Gregory VII., 1073-85), unbending assertion of the power of the Church, &c.—*adj.* **Hildebrand′ic.**

hilding, *hild′ing*, *n.* (*arch.*) a mean, cowardly person, a dastard: a worthless beast.—*adj.* cowardly, spiritless. [Prob. conn. with **heel** (2).]

hill, *hil*, *n.* a high mass of land, less than a mountain: a mound: an incline on a road.—*v.t.* to form into a hill: to bank up (sometimes for **hele**).—*ns.* **hill′-billy**, (*U.S.*) a rustic of the hill country; **hill′-digg′er**, a rifler of sepulchral barrows, &c.—*adj.* **hilled**, having hills.—*ns.pl.* **hill′-folk, hill′men**, people living or hiding among the hills: the Scottish sect of Cameronians: the Covenanters generally.—*ns.* **hill′-fort**, a fort on a hill: a pre-historic stronghold on a hill; **hill′iness**; **hill′ock**, a small hill.—*adj.* **hill′ocky.**—*ns.* **hill′-pasture**; **hill′side**, the slope of a hill; **hill′top**, the summit of a hill.—*adj.* **hill′y**, full of hills.—**up hill and down dale**, vigorously and persistently. [O.E. *hyll*; cf. L. *collis*, a hill, *celsus*, high.]

hillo. Same as **hallo.**

hilt, *hilt*, *n.* the handle, esp. of a sword or dagger (sometimes in *pl.*).—*v.t.* to furnish with a hilt.—**up to the hilt**, completely, thoroughly, to the full. [O.E. *hilt*; M.Du. *hilte*; O.H.G. *helza*; not conn. with **hold.**]

hilum, *hī′ləm*, *n.* the scar on a seed where it joined its stalk: (*anat.*) the depression where ducts, vessels, &c., enter an organ.—*adj.* **hī′lar.** [L. *hílum*, a trifle, ' that which adheres to a bean.']

him, *him*, *pron.* the dative and accusative (objective) case of **he**: the proper character of a person. [O.E. *him*, dat. sing. of *hé*, *he*, he, *hit*, it.]

himation, *hi-mat′i-on*, *n.* the ancient Greek outer garment, oblong, thrown over the left shoulder, and fastened either over or under the right. [Gr.]

himself, *him-self′*, *pron.* the emphatic form of **he**, **him**: in his real character: having command of his faculties: sane: in normal condition: in good form: (*Scot.*) alone, by himself: the reflexive form of **him** (*dat.* and *accus.*). [See **him, self.**]

Himyarite, *him′yär-īt*, *n.* a member of an ancient South Arabian people.—*n.* and *adj.* **Himyaritic** (*-it′ik*). [*Himyar*, a traditional king of Yemen.]

hin, *hin*, *n.* a Hebrew liquid measure containing about four or six English quarts. [Heb. *hin*.]

hind, *hīnd*, *n.* the female of the stag or red-deer.— *n.* **hind′berry**, the raspberry. [O.E. *hind*; Du. and Ger. *hinde*.]

hind, *hīnd*, *n.* a farm-servant, esp. one having charge of a pair of horses, with cottage on the farm, formerly bound to supply a female field-worker (*bondager*): a rustic. [O.E. *hina*, *hiwna*, gen. pl. of *hiwan*, members of a household.]

hind, *hīnd*, *adj.* placed in the rear: pertaining to the part behind: backward—opp. to *fore*.—*n.* **hind′-brain**, the cerebellum and medulla oblong-ata.—*adj.* **hinder** (*hīn′dər*; *Scot.* *hin′ər*), hind: (*Scot.*) last (as *this hinder night*, last night).—*n.* **hin′der-end′** (*Scot.* *hin′ər-en′*, *-end′*), the latter end: buttocks.—*n.pl.* **hind′erlin(g)s**, less correctly **hinderlan(d)s** (*hin′ər-lanz*; *Scot.*), the buttocks.—*adjs.* **hind′ermost, hind′most**, superlative of **hind**, farthest behind.—*n.* **hind′-foot.**— *adv.* **hindfore′most**, (*U.S.*) with the back part in the front place.—*ns.* **hind′-gut**, the posterior part of the alimentary canal; **hind′head**, the back of the head, the occiput; **hind′-leg**.—*n.pl.* **hind′-quar′ters**, the rear parts of an animal.—*n.* **hind′-sight**, (*facet.*) wisdom after the event.—*adj.* and *adv.* **hind′ward**.—*ns.* **hind′-wheel**; **hind′-wing**. [O.E. *hinder*, backwards; Goth. *hindar*, Ger. *hinter*, behind: cf. O.E. *hindan* (adv.), back; **behind**.]

hinder, *hin′dər*, *v.t.* to keep back: to stop, or prevent, progress of.—*v.i.* to be an obstacle.—*ns.* **hin′derer**; **hin′drance**, act of hindering: that which hinders: prevention: obstacle.—Also **hin′-derance.** [O.E. *hindrian*; Ger. *hindern*.]

hinderland, *hin′dər-land*, an Anglicised form of **hinterland.** See also under **hind-**.

Hindi, *hin′dē*, *n.* an Indo-Germanic language of Northern India.—Also *adj.* [Urdu *Hindī*—*Hind*, India.]

Hindu, Hindoo, *hin-dōō′*, or *hin′*, *n.* (*arch.*) a member of any of the races of Hindustan or India: a believer in a form of Brahminism.—*v.t.* and *v.i.* **Hin′duise.**—*n.* **Hindu′ism** (or *hin′*), the religion and customs of the Hindus. [Pers. *Hindu*—*Hind*, India.]

Hindustani, Hindoostanee, *hin-dōō-stä′nē, n.* Urdu, an impure form of Hindi, chief official and commercial language of India.—Also *adj.*

hinge, *hinj, n.* the hook or joint on which a door or lid turns: a joint as of a bivalve shell: (*Milt.*) the earth's axis: a cardinal point: a principle or fact on which anything depends or turns.—*v.t.* to furnish with hinges: to bend.—*v.i.* to hang or turn as on a hinge: to depend:—*pr.p.* **hinging** (*hinj′ing*); *pa.t.* and *pa.p.* **hinged** (*hinjd*).—*adj.* **hinge′-bound,** unable to move easily on a hinge.—*n.* **hinge′-joint,** (*anat.*) a joint that allows movement in one plane only.—**off the hinges,** disorganised: out of gear. [Related to **hang.**]

hinny, *hin′i, n.* the offspring of a stallion and she-ass. [L. *hinnus*—Gr. *ginnos*, later *hinnos*, a mule.]

hinny, *hin′i, n.* a Scottish variant of **honey.**

hinny, *hin′i, v.i.* to neigh, whinny. [Fr. *hennir*—L. *hinnīre.*]

hint, *hint, n.* (*obs.*) moment, opportunity: a distant or indirect indication or allusion: slight mention: insinuation: a helpful suggestion, tip.—*v.t.* to intimate or indicate indirectly.—*v.i.* to give hints.—*adv.* **hint′ingly.**—**hint at,** to give a hint, suggestion, or indication of. [O.E. *hentan*, to seize.]

hinterland, *hint′ər-land, -länt, n.* a region lying inland from a port or centre of influence. [Ger.]

hip, *hip, n.* the haunch or fleshy part of the thigh: the hip-joint: (*archit.*) the external angle formed by the sides of a roof when the end slopes backwards instead of terminating in a gable.—*v.t.* to sprain or hurt the hip of: to throw over the hip: (*U.S.*) to carry on the hip: to construct with a hip:—*pr.p.* **hipp′ing**; *pa.t.* and *pa.p.* **hipped, hipt.**—*adv.* **hip′-and-thigh′,** unsparingly.—*ns.* **hip′-bath,** a bath to sit in; **hip′-belt,** the 14th-century sword-belt, passing diagonally from waist to hip; **hip′-bone,** the innominate bone; **hip′-flask,** a flask carried in a hip-pocket; **hip′-gir′dle,** the pelvic girdle: a hip-belt; **hip′-gout,** sciatica; **hip′-joint,** the articulation of the head of the thigh-bone with the ilium; **hip′-knob,** an ornament placed on the apex of the hip of a roof or of a gable; **hip′-lock,** a trick in wrestling by which one throws a leg and hip before the other to throw him.—*adj.* **hipped,** having a hip or hips: of a roof, sloping at the end as well as at the sides.—*ns.* **hipp′ing,** (*Scot.*) a napkin wrapped about an infant's hips; **hip′-pock′et,** a trouser pocket behind the hip; **hip′-roof′,** a hipped roof.—*adj.* **hip′-shot,** having the hip out of joint.—**have, catch, on the hip,** to get an advantage over someone (from wrestling); **hip-joint disease,** a disease of the hip-joint with inflammation, fungous growth, caries, and dislocation. [O.E. *hype*; Goth. *hups*, Ger. *hüfte.*]

hip, *hip, hep, hep, n.* the fruit of the dog-rose or other rose. [O.E. *héope.*]

hip, *hyp, hip, n.* hypochondria.—*v.t.* to render melancholy.—*adjs.* **hipped,** melancholy; **hipp′ish,** somewhat hypochondriac. [**hypochondria.**]

hip, *hip, interj.* an exclamation to invoke a united cheer—**hip′-hip′-hurrah′.**

Hipparion, *hi-pā′ri-on, n.* a fossil genus of Equidae. [Gr. *hipparion*, dim. of *hippos*, a horse.]

hippety-hoppety, *hip′ə-ti-hop′ə-ti, adv.* hopping and skipping.—*n.* and *adv.* **hipp′ety-hop′.**

hippiatric, *hip-i-at′rik, adj.* relating to the treatment of the diseases of horses.—*n.pl.* **hippiat′rics.**—*ns.* **hippiatrist** (*-i′ət-rist*); **hippiatry** (*-i′ət-ri*). [Gr. *hippiātrikos*—*hippos*, horse, *iātros*, a physician.]

hippic, *hip′ik, adj.* relating to horses. [Gr. *hippikos*—*hippos*, horse.]

hippo, *hip′ō, n.* a shortened form of **hippopotamus.**

hippocampus, *hip-ō-kam′pəs, n.* (*myth.*) a fish-tailed horse-like sea-monster: a genus of small fishes (family Syngnathidae) with horse-like head and neck, the sea-horse: (*anat.*) a raised curved trace on the floor of the lateral ventricle of the brain:—*pl.* **hippocamp′i.** [Gr. *hippokampos*—*hippos*, a horse, *kampos*, a sea-monster.]

Hippocastanaceae, *hip-ō-kast-ə-nā′si-ē, n.pl.* the horse-chestnut family. [Gr. *hippos*, horse, *kastanon*, chestnut tree.]

hippocentaur, *hip-ō-sent′awr, n.* Same as **centaur.** [Gr. *hippokentauros*—*hippos*, a horse, and *kentauros.*]

hippocras, *hip′ō-kras, n.* spiced wine, formerly much used as a cordial.—*adj.* **Hippocrat′ic,** pertaining to the Greek physician *Hippocrates* (*Hippokratēs*; born about 460 B.C.).—*v.i.* **Hippocratise** (*-ok′rə-tīz*), to imitate, follow, Hippocrates.—*n.* **Hippoc′ratism.**—**Hippocratic oath,** an oath taken by a doctor binding him to observe the code of medical ethics contained in it—first drawn up (perhaps by Hippocrates) in the 4th or 5th century B.C.

Hippocrene, *hip-ō-krē′nē, hip′ō-krēn, n.* a fountain on the northern slopes of Mount Helicon, sacred to the Muses and Apollo, attributed to a kick of Pegasus. [Gr. *hippokrēnē*—*hippos*, a horse, *krēnē*, a fountain.]

hippocrepian, *hip-ō-krē′pi-ən, adj.* horse-shoe shaped. [Gr. *hippos*, a horse, *krēpis*, a shoe.]

hippodame, *hip′ō-dām, n.* (*Spens.*, wrongly) the sea-horse. — *n.* **hippodamist** (*hip-od′ə-mist*), a horse-tamer.—*adj.* **hippod′amous,** horse-taming. [Gr. *hippos*, horse, *damaein*, to tame.]

hippodrome, *hip′ə-drōm, n.* (*ant.*) a racecourse for horses and chariots: a circus.—*adj.* **hippodromic** (*-drom′*). [Gr. *hippodromos*—*hippos*, a horse, *dromos*, a course.]

hippogriff, hippogryph, *hip′ō-grif, n.* a fabulous mediaeval animal, a griffin-headed winged horse. [Fr. *hippogriffe*—Gr. *hippos*, a horse, *gryps*, a griffin.]

hippomanes, *hip-om′ən-ēz, n.* an ancient philtre obtained from a mare or foal. [Gr. *hippos*, a horse, *maniā*, madness.]

hippophagy, *hip-of′ə-ji, -gi, n.* feeding on horse-flesh.—*n.* **hippoph′agist,** an eater of horse-flesh.—*adj.* **hippoph′agous** (*-gəs*), horse-eating. [Gr. *hippos*, a horse, *phagein* (aor.), to eat.]

hippopotamus, *hip-ō-pot′ə-məs, n.* a large African artiodactyl ungulate of aquatic habits, with very thick skin, short legs, and a large head and muzzle:—*pl.* **-muses** or **-mi.**—*adjs.* **hippopotamian** (*-tām′*), **hippopotamic** (*-tam′*, also *-pot′*), like a hippopotamus, clumsy. [L.,—Gr. *hippopotamos*—*hippos*, a horse, *potamos*, a river.]

hippuric, *hip-ū′rik, adj.* denoting an acid first obtained from the urine of horses. [Gr. *hippos*, a horse, *ouron*, urine.]

Hippuris, *hip-ū′ris, n.* the mare's-tail genus of Haloragidaceae.—*n.* **hipp′ūrite,** a Cretaceous fossil lamellibranch (*Hippuri′tes*) with a conical valve and a flat one.—*adj.* **hippurit′ic.** [Gr. *hippos*, a horse, *ourā*, a tail.]

hippus, *hip′əs, n.* clonic spasm of the iris. [Gr. *hippos.*]

hircine, *hər′sīn, adj.* goat-like: having a strong goatish smell.—*ns.* **hircocervus** (*hər-kō-sər′vəs*), a fabulous creature, half goat, half stag; **hircosity** (*-kos′*), goatishness. [L. *hīrcus*, a he-goat.]

hirdy-girdy, *hər′di-gər′di, adv.* (*Scot.*) in confusion or tumult.

hire, *hīr, n.* wages for service: the price paid for the use of anything: an arrangement by which use or service is granted for payment.—*v.t.* to procure the use or service of, at a price: to engage for wages: to bribe: to grant temporary use of for compensation. — *adjs.* **hir′able, hire′able, hired.**—*ns.* **hire′ling,** a hired servant: a mercenary: a prostitute—also *adj.*; **hir′er,** one who obtains use or service for payment: (now *Scot.* or *obs.*) one who lets out on hire; **hire′-pur′chase,** a system by which a hired article becomes the hirer's property after a stipulated number of payments—also *adj.*; **hir′ing,** the act of contract by which an article or service is hired: a fair or market where servants are engaged—also *adj.*—**on hire,** for hiring: for hire. [O.E. *hýr*, wages, *hýrian*, to hire.]

hirple, *hir′pl, v.i.* (*Scot.*) to walk or run as if lame.—*n.* a limping gait.

hirrient, *hir′i-ənt, adj.* roughly trilled.—*n.* a trilled sound. [L. *hirriēns, -entis,* pr.p. of *hirrīre,* to snarl.]

hirsel, *hir′sl, n.* a stock of sheep: a multitude: the ground occupied by a hirsel of sheep.—*v.t.* to put in different groups. [O.N. *hirzla*, safe-keeping—*hirtha*, to herd.]

hirsle, *hir'sl, v.i.* (*Scot.*) to slide, wriggle, or hitch on the hams : to move forward with a rustling sound. [Cf. O.N. *hrista*, to shake.]

hirsute, *hər'sūt,* or -*sūt', adj.* hairy : rough : shaggy : (*bot.*) having long, stiffish hairs. [L. *hirsūtus—hirsus, hirtus,* shaggy.]

Hirudinea, *hir-ood-in'i-ä, n.pl.* a class of worms, the leeches. [L. *hirūdō, -inis,* a leech.]

hirundine, *hi-run'dīn, -din, adj.* of or pertaining to the swallow. [L. *hirundō, -inis,* a swallow.]

his, *hiz, pron. gen.* (possessive) form of **he,** or (*B., Shak.,* &c.) **it.—hisn, his'n,** dialectal forms on the analogy of **mine, thine.** [O.E. *his,* gen. of *hé, he,* he, and of *hit,* it.]

hish, *hish,* a by-form of hiss.

Hispanic, *his-pan'ik, adj.* Spanish.—*adv.* **Hispan'-ically.—***vs.t.* **hispan'icise** (*-i-sīz*), **hispan'iolise,** to render Spanish.—*n.* **hispan'icism,** a Spanish phrase. [L. *Hispānia,* Spain.]

Hispano-, *his-pā'nō-,* in composition, Spanish, as *Hispano-American,* Spanish-American. [L. *Hispānus.*]

hispid, *his'pid, adj.* (*bot.*) rough with, or having, strong hairs or bristles.—*n.* **hispid'ity.** [L. *hispidus.*]

hiss, *his, v.i.* to make a sibilant sound like that represented by the letter *s,* as a goose, snake, gas escaping from a narrow hole, a disapproving audience, &c.—*v.t.* to condemn by hissing : to drive by hissing.—*n.* a sibilant.—*n., adj.,* and *adv.* **hiss'ing.** [Imit.]

hist, *hist, st, interj.* demanding silence and attention : hush : silence.—*v.t.* (*hist*) to urge or summon, as by making the sound.—*v.i.* to be silent. [Imit.]

hist-, histio-, histo-, *hist'-, -(i-)ō-, -o'-,* in composition, tissue : sail.—*ns.* **hist'amine** (*-ə-mēn*), a base used in medicine obtained from ergot, from histidine, &c. ; present also in all tissues of the body, being liberated into the blood, e.g. when the skin is cut or burnt; **hist'idine** (*-i-dēn*), an amino-acid derived from proteins.—*adjs.* **hist'ioid, hist'oid,** like ordinary tissue.—*ns.* **histiol'ogy** (same as **histology**) ; **Histioph'orus, Istioph'orus** (Gr. *phoros,* bearer), a genus of swordfishes with sail-like dorsal fin.—*adj.* **histioph'-oroid.**—*n.* **histogenesis** (*-jen'i-sis*), (*biol.*) the formation or differentiation of tissues.—*adj.* **histogenetic** (*-ji-net'ik*).—*adv.* **histogenet'ically.**—*ns.* **histogeny** (*his-toj'i-ni*), histogenesis ; **hist'ogram,** a statistical graph in which frequency distribution is shown by means of rectangles.—*adjs.* **histolog'ic, -al.**—*ns.* **histologist** (*-tol'*) ; **histol'ogy,** the study of the minute structure of the tissues of organisms ; **histol'ysis** (Gr. *lysis,* loosing), the breakdown of organic tissues.—*adj.* **histolytic** (*-ō-lit'ik*). [Gr. *histos* and *histion,* a web.]

histie, *his'ti, adj.* (*obs. Scot.*) dry : barren.

history, *hist'ər-i, n.* an account of an event : a systematic account of the origin and progress of the world, a nation, an institution, a science, &c. : the knowledge of past events : a course of events : a life-story : an eventful life, a past of more than common interest : a drama representing historical events.—*v.t.* (*Shak.*) to record.—*n.* **historian** (*his-tō'ri-ən*), a writer of history.—*adjs.* **histō'riāted,** adorned with figures ; **historic** (*-tor'ik*), **-al,** pertaining to history : containing history : derived from history : famous in history : associated with history : according to history : authentic.—*adv.* **histor'ically.**—*v.t.* **histor'icise** (*-sīz*), to make, or represent as, historic.—*ns.* **historicity** (*hist-ər-is'i-ti*), historical truth or actuality ; **histor-iette',** a short history or story.—*v.t.* **histor'ify,** to record in history.—*n.* **histōriog'rapher,** a writer of history : a professed or official historian.—*adjs.* **historiograph'ic, -al,** pertaining to the writing of history.—*adv.* **historiograph'ically.**—*ns.* **historiŏg'raphy,** the art or employment of writing history ; **historiol'ogy,** the knowledge or study of history.—**historical method,** the study of a subject in its historical development ; **historical painting,** the painting of historic scenes, or scenes in which

historic figures are introduced ; **historical present,** the present tense used for the past, to add life and reality to the narrative ; **make history,** to do that which will mould the future or have to be recognised by future historians. [L. *historia—* Gr. *historiā—historō,* knowing.]

histrionic, -al, *his-tri-on'ik, -əl, adjs.* relating to the stage or stage-players : stagy, theatrical : feigned.—*ns.* **his'triŏ** (L.), **his'triŏn** (Fr.), a stage-player.—*adv.* **histrion'ically.**—*ns.* **histrion'icism, his'trionism,** acting : theatricality.—*n.pl.* **histrion'ics,** play-acting : stagy action or speech. [L. *histriōnicus—histriō,* an actor.]

hit, *hit, v.t.* to strike : to reach with a blow or missile : to light upon : to chance to attain : to succeed in reaching or attaining straightway or to a nicety : to suit : fit : conform to : to hurt, affect painfully.—*v.i.* to strike : to make a movement of striking : to come in contact : to alight : to chance luckily : to succeed : (*pr.p.* **hitt'ing** ; *pa.t.* and *pa.p.* **hit**).—*n.* an act or occasion of striking : a successful stroke or shot : a lucky chance, a surprising success : a happy turn of thought or expression : something that takes the public or an audience : at backgammon, a move that throws one of the opponent's men back to the entering point, or a game won after one or two men are removed from the board.—*adjs.* **hit'-and-miss',** hitting or missing, doing one thing or another, according to circumstances ; **hit'-and-run',** lasting only a very short time (e.g. of an air-raid) ; **hit'-or-miss',** random.—*n.* **hitt'er.**—*adj.* **hitt'y-miss'y,** random, haphazard.—**a hit or a miss,** a case in which either success or complete failure is possible ; **hard hit,** gravely affected by some trouble, or by love ; **hit a blot,** to capture an exposed man in backgammon : to find a weak place ; **hit at,** to aim a blow, sarcasm, jibe, &c., at ; **hit below the belt,** to deal a blow disallowable in the rules of the ring : to do an injury to another unfairly ; **hit it (off),** to agree ; **hit off,** to imitate or describe felicitously ; **hit out,** to strike out, esp. with the fist ; **hit the nail on the head** (see nail) ; **hit upon,** to come upon, discover, devise ; **hit wicket,** (*cricket*) i.e. of a batsman, with bat or person in playing a ball, thus being out. [O.E. *hyttan,* app. O.N. *hitta,* to light on, to find ; Sw. *hitta,* to find, Dan. *hitte,* to hit upon.]

hitch, *hich, v.i.* to move jerkily : to catch on an obstacle : (*orig. U.S.*) to connect with a moving vehicle so as to be towed : to travel by getting lifts : to hike.—*v.t.* to jerk : to hook : to catch : to fasten : to tether : to harness to a vehicle : to make fast : to throw into place : to bring in (to verse, a story, &c.), esp. with some violence.—*n.* a jerk : a catch or anything that holds : a stoppage owing to a small or passing difficulty : (*naut.*) a species of knot by which one rope is connected with another, or to some object : a means of connecting a thing to be dragged : (*U.S.*) a mode or act of harnessing a horse or horses, a team, or a vehicle with horses : a lift in a vehicle.—*n.* **hitch'er.**—*v.i.* **hitch'-hike,** to hike with the help of lifts in vehicles.—*ns.* **hitch'-hike** ; **hitch'-hi'ker.**—*adv.* **hitch'ily.**—*adj.* **hitch'y.**—**hitch up,** to harness a horse to a vehicle : to jerk up : (*slang*) to marry. [Ety. obscure.]

hithe, *hīdh, n.* a small haven. [O.E. *hȳth.*]

hither, *hidh'ər, adv.* to this place.—*adj.* toward the speaker : nearer.—*v.i.* to come—chiefly in phrase *to hither and thither,* i.e. to go to and fro.—*adj.* **hith'ermost,** nearest on this side.—*n.* **hith'er-side,** the nearer side.—*advs.* **hith'erto,** up to this time : (*arch.*) to this point or place ; **hith'er-ward(s),** towards this place.—**hither and thither,** to and fro : this way and that. [O.E. *hider* ; Goth. *hidrē,* O.N. *hethra.*]

Hitlerism, *hit'lər-izm, n.* the principles, policy, and methods of Adolf *Hitler* (1889–1945), German Nazi dictator, militant anti-Semitic nationalism, subordinating everything to the state.—*ns.* and *adj.* **Hit'lerist, Hit'lerite.**

Hitopadesa, *hē-tō-pä-dä'shä, n.* a collection of fables and stories in Sanskrit literature, a popular summary of the *Panchatantra.* [Sans. *Hitopadeśa.*]

Hittite, *hit'īt*, *n*. one of the Khatti or Heth, an ancient and powerful people of Syria and Asia Minor: their language, of obscure affinities.— Also *adj*. [Heb. *Hitti*; Gr. *Chettaios*.]

hive, *hīv*, *n*. a box or basket in which bees live and store up honey: a scene of great industry: a teeming multitude or breeding-place: a hat like an old beehive.—*v.t.* to collect into a hive: to lay up in store.—*v.i.* to take shelter together: to reside in a body.—*ns*. **hive'-bee**, the common honey-producing bee, *Apis mellifica*; **hive'-hon'ey**; **hive'-nest**, a large nest built and occupied by several pairs of birds in common; **hīv'er**, one who hives.—*adj*. and *adv*. **hive'ward.**—*adv*. **hive'-wards.** [O.E. *hyf*.]

hives, *hīvz*, *n*. a popular term for nettle-rash and similar diseases: laryngitis. [Origin unknown.]

hizz, *hiz*, *v.i.* (*Shak*.) to hiss. [Echoic.]

ho, hoa, *hō*, *interj*. a call to excite attention, to announce destination or direction, to express exultation, surprise, or (repeated) derision: hullo: hold: stop.—*n*. cessation: moderation.—*v.i.* (*obs*.) to stop. [Cf. O.N. *hó*, Fr. *ho*.]

hoar, *hōr*, *adj*. white or greyish-white, esp. with age or frost: (*obs*.) mouldy.—*n*. hoariness: age.—*v.i.* (*Shak*.) to become mouldy.—*v.t.* (*Shak*.) to make hoary.—*ns*. **hoar'-frost**, rime or white frost, the white particles formed by the freezing of the dew; **hoar'head**, a hoary-headed old man.—*adj*. **hoar'-head'ed.**— *adv*. **hoar'ily.**— *ns*. **hoar'iness**; **hoar-stone** (*Scot*. **hare'stane**), an old hoary stone: a standing-stone or ancient boundary stone.—*adj*. **hoar'y**, white or grey with age: ancient: (*bot*.) covered with short, dense, whitish hairs. [O.E. *hár*, hoary, grey; O.N. *hárr*.]

hoard, *hōrd*, *n*. a store: a hidden stock: a treasure: (*obs*.) a place for hiding anything.—*v.t.* to store, esp. in excess: to treasure up: to amass and deposit in secret.—*v.i.* to store up: to collect and form a hoard.—*n*. **hoard'er**. [O.E. *hord*; O.N. *hodd*, Ger. *hort*.]

hoard, *hōrd*, **hoarding**, *hōrd'ing*, *ns*. a screen of boards, esp. for enclosing a place where builders are at work, or for display of bills. [O.Fr. *hurdis* —*hurt, hourt, hourd*, a palisade.]

hoarhound. Same as **horehound**.

hoarse, *hōrs*, *adj*. rough and husky: having a rough husky voice, as from a cold: harsh: discordant.— *adv*. **hoarse'ly.** — *v.t.* and *v.i.* **hoars'en.** — *n*. **hoarse'ness**. [M.E. *hors, hoors*—O.E. *hás*, inferred *hárs*.]

hoast, *hōst*, *n*. (*prov*.) a cough.—*v.i.* to cough. [O.N. *hóste*; cf. O.E. *hwósta*; Du. *hoest*.]

hoastman, *hōst'man*, *n*. a member of an old merchant guild in Newcastle, with charge of coal-shipping, &c. [O.Fr. *hoste*—L. *hospes*, stranger, guest.]

hoatzin, *hō-at'sin*, **hoactzin**, *-akt'*, *n*. the stink-bird (Opisthocomus), a S. American bird forming an order by itself, with occipital crest, great crop, peculiar sternum, and, in the tree-climbing and swimming young, clawed wings. [Nahuatl *uatsin*.]

hoax, *hōks*, *n*. a deceptive trick played as a practical joke.—*v.t.* to trick, by a practical joke or fabricated tale, for sport, or without malice.—*n*. **hoax'er**. [App. **hocus**.]

hob, *hob* *n*. a hub: a surface beside a fireplace, on which anything may be laid to keep hot: a game in which stones are thrown at coins on the end of a short stick—also the stick used: a gear-cutting tool.—*n*. **hob'nail**, a nail with a thick strong head, used in horse-shoes, &c.: a clownish fellow.— *v.t.* to furnish with hobnails: to trample upon with hobnailed shoes.—*adj*. **hob'nailed**. [Cf. **hub**.]

hob, *hob*, *n*. a clownish fellow: a rustic: a fairy or brownie (as Robin Goodfellow): a male ferret.— *n*. **Hobb'inoll**, a rustic (from Spenser's *Shepheards Calender*).—*adj*. **hobb'ish**, clownish.—*ns*. **hob'-goblin**, a mischievous fairy: a frightful apparition; **hobgob'linism, hobgob'linry—play hob**, to make confusion. [For *Robert*.]

hob-a-nob, hob-and-nob. Same as **hobnob**.

Hobbesian, *hobz'i-ən*, **Hobbian**, *hob'i-ən*, *adjs*. relating to Thomas *Hobbes* (1588-1679) or his political philosophy.—*ns*. a follower of *Hobbes*.— *ns*. **Hobbes'ianism, Hobb'ianism, Hobb'ism**; **Hobb'ist**, a Hobbian.—*adjs*. **Hobb'ist, Hobbist'-ical**.

hobble, *hob'l*, *v.i.* to walk with short unsteady steps: to walk awkwardly: to move irregularly.—*v.t.* to fasten the legs of loosely together: to hamper: to perplex.—*n*. an awkward hobbling gait: a difficulty, a scrape: anything used to hamper the feet of an animal, a clog or fetter.—*ns*. **hobb'ler**, one who hobbles: an unlicensed pilot, a casual labourer in docks, &c.: a man who tows a canal-boat with a rope; **hobb'ling.**—*adv*. **hobb'lingly.—hobble skirt**, a narrow skirt that hampers the legs. [Cf. Du. *hobbelen, hobben*, to toss; and **hopple**.]

hobbledehoy, *hob'l-di-hoi'*, *n*. an awkward youth, a stripling, neither man nor boy.—*ns*. **hobbledehoy'-dom, hobbledehoy'hood, hobbledehoy'ism.**— *adj*. **hobbledehoy'ish**. [Origin obscure.]

hobbler, *hob'lər*, *n*. one bound to keep a hobby (horse) for military service: a horseman employed for light work, as reconnoitring, &c.: a horse. [O.Fr. *hobeler—hobin*, a small horse.]

hobby, *hob'i*, *n*. a small or smallish strong, active horse: a pacing horse: a subject on which one is constantly setting off, as in *to ride* or *to mount a hobby*: a favourite pursuit followed as an amusement: a hobby-horse: an early form of bicycle.—*n*. **hobb'y-horse**, a stick or figure of a horse bestridden by children: one of the chief parts played in the ancient morris-dance: the wooden horse of a merry-go-round: a rocking-horse: a dandy-horse: (*Shak*.) a loose and frivolous person, male or female: a hobby.—*adj*. **hobby-hors'ical**, whimsically given to a hobby.—*ns*. **hobb'yism**; **hobb'yist**, one who rides a hobby.—*adj*. **hobb'y-less**. [M.E. *hobyn, hoby*, prob. *Hob*, a by-form of *Rob*. O.Fr. *hobin, hobi* (Fr. *aubin*), is from the English.]

hobby, *hob'i*, *n*. a small species of falcon. [O.Fr. *hobé*; *hobet*—L.L. *hobētus*; prob. O.Fr. *hober*, to move.]

hobgoblin. See **hob** (2).

hobjob, *hob'job*, *n*. (*prov*.) an odd job.—*v.i.* to do odd jobs.—*ns*. **hob'jobber; hob'jobbing**.

hobnail. See **hob** (1).

hobnob, *hob'nob*, *adv*. at a venture: hit-or-miss: with alternate or mutual drinking of healths.—*v.i.* to associate or drink together familiarly: (*pr.p.* **hob'nobbing**).—*n*. (*obs*.) a sentiment in drinking: mutual health-drinking: a familiar private talk.— *adj*. **hob'nobby**. [Prob. *hab nab*, have or have not (ne-have); cf. *Twelfth Night*, III. iv. 'Hob, nob, is his word; give 't or take 't.']

hobo, *hō'bō*, *n*. (*U.S.*) a vagrant workman: a tramp, esp. of the arrogant type: (*pl*. **ho'boes**).—*v.t.* to wend as a hobo.—*ns*. **ho'bodom, ho'boism**. [Origin unknown.]

Hobson-Jobson, *hob'sən-job'sən*, *n*. festal excitement, esp. at the Moharram ceremonies: the modification of names and words introduced from foreign languages, which the popular ear assimilates to already familiar sounds, as in the case of the word Hobson-Jobson itself. [Ar. *Yā Hasan! Yā Hosain!* a typical phrase of Anglo-Indian argot, adopted as a concise alternative title for Yule and Burnell's *Glossary of Anglo-Indian Colloquial Words and Phrases* (1886).]

hock, *hok*, *n*. and *vb*. See **hough**.

hock, *hok*, *n*. properly, the wine made at *Hochheim*, on the Main, in Germany: now applied to all white Rhine wines. [Obs. *Hockamore*—Ger. *Hochheimer*.]

hock, *hok*, *v.t.* to subject to Hock-tide customs.— *v.i.* to observe Hock-tide.—*ns*. **Hock'-day (Hock Tuesday)**, an old English festival held on the second Tuesday after Easter Sunday, one of the chief customs being the seizing and binding of men by women until they gave money for their liberty: (in *pl*.) Hock Tuesday and the preceding day **(Hock Monday)** on which the men seized the women in like manner; **Hock'-tide**, the two Hock-days. [Origin unknown.]

hockey, *hok'i*, *n*. a ball game played with a club or stick curved at one end, a development of shinty:

(U.S.) a hockey stick: ice-hockey.—Also **hook'ey**. [Prob. O.Fr. *hoquet*, a crook.]

hockey, *hok'i*, *n.* (*prov.*) harvest-home, the harvest-supper.—Also **hawk'ey, hork'ey**.—*n.* **hock'-cart**, the cart that brings home the last load of the harvest. [Origin unknown.]

hocus-pocus, *hō'kəs-pō'kəs*, *n.* (*obs.*) a juggler: a juggler's trick or formula: jugglery: deception: mumbo-jumbo.—*v.t.* **hō'cus**, to cheat: to stupefy with drink: to drug:—*pr.p.* **hō'cusing**; *pa.t.* and *pa.p.* **hō'cused**. [Sham Latin.]

hod, *hod*, *n.* a V-shaped stemmed trough for carrying bricks or mortar on the shoulder: a coal-scuttle: a pewterer's blowpipe.—*n.* **hod'man**, a man who carries a hod: a mason's labourer. [Cf. prov. *hot, hott*, Ger. *hotte*, obs. Du. *hodde*, Fr. *hotte*, a basket.]

hod, *hod*, *v.i.* (*Scot.*) to bob: to jog.—*v.i.* **hodd'le**, (*Scot.*) to waddle.

hodden, *hod'n*, *n.* coarse, undyed homespun woollen cloth.—*adj.* of or clad in hodden: rustic.—*n.* **hodd'en-grey**, hodden made of mixed black and white wool.—Also *adj.* [Origin unknown.]

Hodge, *hoj*, *n.* a countryman, rustic. [For *Roger*.]

hodgepodge, *hoj'poj*, *n.* (see **hotchpotch**).—*n.* **hodge'-pudd'ing**, (*Shak.*) a pudding made of a mass of ingredients mixed together.

hodiernal, *hō-di-ərn'əl*, *adj.* of or pertaining to the present day. [L. *hodiernus*—*hodiē*, to-day=*hōc diē*, on this day.]

hodmandod, *hod'mən-dod*, *n.* a snail.—*n.* **hodd'y-dodd'y**, a dumpy person: a duped husband: a noodle. [Cf. **dodman**.]

hodograph, *hod'ə-gräf*, *n.* a curve whose radius vector represents the velocity of a moving point. [Gr. *hodos*, a way, *graphein*, to write.]

hodometer, *hod-om'i-tər*, *n.* an instrument attached to a wheel for measuring distance travelled. [Gr. *hodos*, a way, *metron*, a measure.]

hoe, *hō*, *n.* an instrument for scraping or digging up weeds and loosening the earth.—*v.t.* to scrape, remove, or clean with a hoe: to weed.—*v.i.* to use a hoe:—*pr.p.* **hoe'ing**; *pa.t.* and *pa.p.* **hoed**.—*ns.* **hoe'-cake**, (*U.S.*) a thin cake of Indian meal (originally baked on a hoe-blade): **hō'er**. [O.Fr. *houe*—O.H.G. *houwâ* (Ger. *haue*), a hoe.]

hoe, *hō*, *n.* a promontory or projecting ridge. [O.E. *hóh*, heel; cf. **heugh**.]

hog, *hog*, *n.* a general name for swine: a castrated boar: a pig: a yearling sheep not yet shorn (also **hogg**): a yearling of other species: formerly slang for a shilling: a low filthy fellow: a greedy person: an inconsiderate boor: a person of coarse manners. —*v.t.* and *v.i.* to eat or seize hoggishly: to arch or hump like a hog's back.—*v.t.* to cut like a hog's mane: to behave like a hog or a road-hog towards: —*pr.p.* **hogg'ing**; *pa.t.* and *pa.p.* **hogged**.—*ns.* **hog'back**, a hill-ridge, an ancient monument, or other object, shaped like a hog's back, i.e. curving down towards the ends; **hog'-chol'era**, swine-fever; **hog'-deer**, a small Indian deer; **hog'-frame**, a frame built to resist vertical flexure.—*adj.* **hogged** (*hogd*).—*ns.* **hogg'erel**, a yearling sheep; **hogg'ery**, hogs collectively: hoggishness of character: coarseness; **hogg'et**, a yearling sheep or colt.—*adj.* **hogg'ish**, resembling a hog: brutish: filthy: selfish.—*adv.* **hogg'ishly**.—*ns.* **hogg'ishness**; **hogg'hood**, the nature of a hog; **hog'-mane**, a mane clipped short or naturally short and upright.—*adj.* **hog'-maned**.—*ns.* **hog'-nose**, an American snake (Heterodon: various species); **hog'-pen**, a pig-sty; **hog'-plum**, a West Indian tree (Spondias) of the cashew family, the fruit relished by hogs; **hog'-rat**, the hutia, a West Indian rodent (Capromys); **hog'-reeve**, **-con'stable**, an officer charged with the care of stray swine; **hog'-ring'er**, one who puts rings into the snouts of hogs.—*v.t.* **hog'-shouther** (*shoo'dhər*; *Scot.*), to jostle with the shoulder.—*ns.* **hog'-skin**, leather made of the skin of swine; **hog'-wash**, the refuse of a kitchen, brewery, &c., given to pigs: thin worthless stuff; **hog'weed**, the cow-parsnip: applied also to many other coarse plants. —**bring one's hogs to a fine market**, to make a complete mess of something; **go the whole hog**,

to do a thing thoroughly or completely: to commit oneself to anything unreservedly. [O.E. *hogg*.]

hog, *hog*, *n.* in curling, a stone that does not pass the hog-score.—*v.t.* to play a hog.—*n.* **hog'-score**, a line drawn across the rink short of which no stone counts. [Perh. **hog** (1).]

hogen-mogen, *hō'gən-mō'gən*, *n.* (*obs.*) high-mightiness: (usu. *pl.*) the Dutch States General. —*adj.* high and mighty: Dutch: (of liquor) strong.—*n.* **hō'gan, ho'gen**, strong liquor. [Du. *hoog en mogend*, high and mighty.]

hogg, hoggerel, hogget. See under **hog**.

hogger, *hog'ər*, *n.* (*Scot.*) a footless stocking worn as a gaiter: a short connecting-pipe. [Origin obscure.]

hoggin, hogging, *hog'in*, *n.* sifted gravel: a mixture containing gravel. [Origin uncertain.]

hogh, a Spenserian spelling of **hoe** (2).

Hogmanay, *hog-mə-nā'*, *n.* (*Scot.*) the last day of the year: a refection or gift begged or bestowed then. [Origin unknown.]

hogshead, *hogz'hed*, *n.* (*Shak.*) a large cask: a measure of capacity=52½ imperial gallons, or 63 old wine gallons; *of beer*=54 gallons; *of claret*=46 gallons; *of tobacco* (*U.S.*), 750 to 1200 lb. [App. **hog's**, and **head**; reason unknown.]

hoick, hoik, *hoik*, *n.* a jerk.—*v.t.* and *v.i.* (esp. of aeroplanes) to jerk upwards. [Cf. **hike**.]

hoicks, hoiks, *hoiks*, *interj.* a cry to urge hounds.—*v.t.* to urge on with cries.—*v.i.* to shout hoicks: to hark back.

hoiden. See **hoyden**.

hoise, *hoiz*, (*arch.*) *v.t.* to hoist:—*pa.t.* and *pa.p.* **hoised, hoist**.—**hoist with his own petar(d)**, (*Shak.*) beaten with his own weapons, caught in his own trap. [Perh. Old Du. *hijssen*, Du. *hijschen*, to hoist.]

hoist, *hoist*, *v.t.* to lift: to heave upwards: to raise or move with tackle.—*n.* act of lifting: the height of a sail: that part of a flag next to the mast: a lift for heavy goods.—*ns.* **hoist'man**, one who works a hoist; **hoist'way**, a hoist shaft. [**hoise**.]

hoisting, *hōst'ing* (*Scott*). Same as **hosting**.

hoity-toity, *hoi'ti-toi'ti*, *interj.* an exclamation of surprise or disapprobation.—*adj.* giddy, noisy: huffy: superciliously haughty.

hokum, *ho'kəm*, *n.* (*U.S. slang*) something done for the sake of applause: claptrap. [App. **hocus-pocus** combined with **bunkum**.]

hoky-poky, hokey-pokey, *hō'ki-pō'ki*, *n.* hocus-pocus: a kind of ice-cream sold on the streets.

Holarctic, *hol-ärk'tik*, *adj.* of the north temperate and Arctic biological region, including Palaearctic and Nearctic. [Gr. *holos*, whole, *arktikos*, northern —*arktos*, a bear, the Great Bear constellation.]

hold, *hōld*, *v.t.* to keep: to have: to grasp: to have in one's possession, keeping, or power: to sustain: to defend successfully: to maintain: to assert authoritatively: to occupy: to derive title to: to bind: to confine: to restrain: to detain: to retain: to keep the attention of: to catch: to stop: to continue: to persist in: to contain: to celebrate: to conduct: to carry on: to convoke and carry on: to esteem: to endure: (*arch.*) to bet.—*v.i.* to grasp: to remain fixed: to be true or unfailing: to continue unbroken or unsubdued: to adhere: to derive right: (*pr.p.* **hōld'ing**; *pa.t.* **held**; *pa.p.* **held**, obs. **hōld'en**).—*n.* act or manner of holding: grip: power of gripping: tenacity: a thing held: a place of confinement: custody: stronghold: (*mus.*; *obs.*) a pause.—*ns.* **hold'-all**, an accommodating receptacle for clothes, &c., esp. a canvas wrapper; **hold'-back**, a check: a strap joining the breeching to the shaft of a vehicle; **hold'er**; **hold'-fast**, that which holds fast: a long nail: a catch: a plant's fixing organ other than a root; **hold'ing**, anything held: a farm held of a superior: hold: influence: (*Scots law*) tenure: (*Shak.*) the burden of a song; **hold'-up**, an attack with a view to robbery: a highwayman: an act or state of holding up: a stoppage.— **hold forth**, to put forward: to show: to speak in public, to declaim; **hold hard!** stop; **hold in**, to restrain, check: to restrain oneself; **hold of**,

hold

(*Pr.Bk.*) to regard; **hold off**, to keep at a distance; **hold on**, to persist in something: to continue: to cling: (*imper.*) stop: wait a bit; **hold one in hand**, to amuse in order to gain some advantage; **hold one's own**, to maintain one's position; **hold one's peace, tongue**, to keep silence; **hold out**, to endure, last: to continue resistance: to offer; **hold over**, to postpone, to keep possession of land or a house beyond the term of agreement; **hold together**, to remain united: to cohere; **hold up**, to raise: to keep back: to endure: to bring to, or keep at, a standstill: to stop and rob: to rob by threatening assault; **hold up one's head**, to face the world with self-respect; **hold water** (see **water**); **hold with**, to take sides with: to approve of. [O.E. *haldan* (W.S. *healdan*); O.H.G. *haltan*, Goth. *haldan*.]

hold, *hōld*, *n.* the interior cavity of a ship used for the cargo. [**hole**, with excrescent *d*.]

hole, *hōl*, *n.* a hollow place: a cavity: an aperture: a gap: a breach: a pit: a subterfuge: a means of escape: a difficult situation: a scrape: a place of hiding, a mean lodging, a secret room for some disreputable business: an animal's excavation or place of refuge: a miserable or contemptible place: a cavity 4¼ inches in diameter, into which golf-balls are played: the distance, or the part of the game, between tee and hole: the score for playing a hole in fewest strokes.—*v.t.* to form holes in: to put, send, play into a hole.—*v.i.* to go, play, into a hole.—*adjs.* **hole'-and-cor'ner**, secret: underhand: in obscure places; **holey** (*hōl'i*), full of holes.—*n.* and *adj.* **hol'ing**.—*ns.* **hōl'ing-axe**, a narrow axe for cutting holes in posts; **hol'ing-pick**, a pick used in under-cutting coal.—**a hole in one's coat**, a stain on a person's reputation; **in holes**, full of holes; **toad in the hole**, meat baked in batter, &c.; **to hole out**, (*golf*) to play the ball into the hole. [O.E. *hol*, a hole, cavern; Du. *hol*, Dan. *hul*, Ger. *hohl*, hollow; conn. with Gr. *koilos*, hollow.]

hole, an earlier (and etymological) spelling (*Spens.*) of **whole**.—*adj.* **hole'som(e)**, wholesome.

holibut. See **halibut**.

holiday, *hol'i-dā*, *n.* (*orig.*) a religious festival: a day or season of idleness and recreation.—*adj.* befitting a holiday: cheerful. [**holy, day**.]

holism, *hol'izm*, *hōl'izm*, *n.* the theory that the fundamental principle of the universe is the creation of wholes, i.e. complete and self-contained systems from the atom and the cell by evolution to the most complex forms of life and mind.—*n.* **hol'ist**.—*adj.* **holist'ic**. [Gr. *holos*, whole; coined by General Smuts.]

holla, *hol'ä*, *interj.* ho, there! attend! (*naut.*) the usual response to *ahoy!*—*n.* a loud shout.—*interj.* **holl'a-ho(a)!** [Fr. *holà*—*ho* and *là*—L. *illāc*, there.]

holland, *hol'ənd*, *n.* a coarse linen fabric, unbleached or dyed brown, which is used for covering furniture, &c.: (*orig.*) a fine kind of linen first made in *Holland*.—*n.* **Holl'ander**, a native or citizen of *Holland*: a Dutch ship.—*adj.* **Holl'andish**.—*n.* **holl'ands**, gin made in Holland.

holler, *hol'ər*, *n.* and *vb.* (*U.S.* and *dial.*) for **hollo**.

hollo, *hol'ō*, *n.* and *interj.* a shout of encouragement or to call attention: a loud shout.—*v.t.* and *v.i.* to shout. [Cf. **holla, hallo**.]

holloa, *hol-ō'*. Same as **hallo**.

hollow, *hol'ō*, *n.* a hole: a cavity: a depression: a vacuity: a groove: a channel.—*adj.* having an empty space within or below: concave: sunken: unsound, unreal, fleeting, deceptive: insincere: muffled, as if coming from a hollow.—*v.t.* to make a hole in: to make hollow: to excavate.—*adv.* completely: clean.—*adjs.* **holl'ow-eyed**, having sunken eyes; **holl'ow-ground**, ground concave on both sides; **holl'ow-heart'ed**, having a hollow or untrue heart: faithless: treacherous.—*adv.* **holl'owly**, (*Shak.*) in a hollow or insincere manner.—*ns.* **holl'owness**, the state of being hollow: cavity: insincerity: treachery; **holl'owware**, trade name for hollow articles of iron, as pots and kettles. [O.E. *holh*, a hollow place—*hol*; see **hole**.]

holly, *hol'i*, *n.* an evergreen shrub (*Ilex Aquifolium*; family Aquifoliaceae) having leathery, shining, and spinous leaves and scarlet or yellow berries, much used for Christmas decorations.—*ns.* **holl'y-fern**, a spiny-leaved fern; **holl'y-oak**, the holm-oak. [O.E. *holegn*; cf. W. *celyn*, Ir. *cuileann*.]

hollyhock, *hol'i-hok*, *n.* a plant (Althaea) of the mallow family brought into Europe from the Holy Land. [M.E. *holihoc*—*holi*, holy, and O.E. *hoc*, mallow.]

holm, *hōm*, *n.* an islet, esp. in a river: rich flat land beside a river. [O.E. *holm*; Ger. *holm*, &c.]

holm, *hōm*, *n.* (*Spens.*) holly: the holm-oak.—*n.* **holm'-oak**, the evergreen oak (*Quercus Ilex*), not unlike holly. [M.E. *holin*; see **holly**.]

holmium, *hōl'mi-əm*, *n.* a metallic element (Ho; at. numb. 67).—*n.* **hol'mia**, its oxide. [Mod. L. *Holmia*, Stockholm.]

holo-, *hol'ō*, **hol-**, *hol-*, in composition, whole: wholly.—*adj.* **holoblast'ic** (Gr. *blastos*, a shoot, bud), segmenting throughout the mass.—*n.* **hol'ocaust** (*-kawst*; Gr. *holokauston*—*kaustos*, burnt), a sacrifice, in which the whole of the victim was burnt: a huge slaughter or destruction of life.—*adj.* **holocrys'talline**, wholly crystalline in structure—without glass.—*n.* **hol'ograph** (*-gräf*), a document wholly written by the person from whom it proceeds.—Also *adj.*—*adj.* **holographic** (*-graf'ik*).—*adj.* **holohē'dral** (Gr. *hedrā*, base).—*ns.* **holohēd'rism**, (*math.*) the property of having the full number of symmetrically arranged planes crystallographically possible; **holohē'dron**, a form possessing this property.—*adj.* **holometabol'ic**.—*n.* **holometab'olism**, complete metamorphosis.—*adj.* **holophōt'al** (Gr. *phōs, phōtos*, light).—*n.* **hol'ophote**, an apparatus by which all the light from a lighthouse is thrown in the required direction.—*adj.* **holophytic** (*-fit'ik*; Gr. *phyton*, a plant), obtaining nutriment wholly in the manner of a green plant.—*n.* **holophytism** (*-fit'izm*).—*adj.* **holop'tic**, having the eyes meeting in front.—*n.pl.* **Holostei** (*hol-os'ti-ī*; Gr. *osteon*, bone), an order of fishes including Lepidosteus.—*adjs.* **holosteric** (*-ster'ik*; Gr. *stereos*, solid), wholly solid: having no liquids (as an aneroid barometer); **holozoic** (*-zō'ik*; Gr. *zōion*, an animal), obtaining nutrition wholly in the manner of an animal, i.e. from other organisms live or dead. [Gr. *holos*, whole.]

holothurian, *hol-ō-th(y)ōō'ri-ən*, *n.* any member of the **Holothuroid'ea**, a class of wormlike unarmoured echinoderms—the sea-cucumbers.—Also *adj.* [Gr. *holothourion*, a kind of sea animal.]

holp, *hōlp*, **holpen**, *-ən*, old *pa.t.* and *pa.p.* of **help**.

holster, *hōl'stər*, *n.* a pistol-case, on saddle or belt.—*adj.* **hol'stered**. [Perh. Du. *holster*, pistol-case; cf. O.E. *heolster*, hiding-place.]

holt, *hōlt*, *n.* a wood or woody hill: an orchard. [O.E. *holt*, a wood; O.N. *holt*, a copse, Ger. *holz*.]

holt, *hōlt*, *n.* (*U.S.* and *dial.*) a hold: a refuge: an otter's den. [**hold** (1).]

holus-bolus, *hōl'əs-bōl'əs*, *adv.* all at a gulp: altogether. [Sham L.; perh.—Eng. *whole bolus* or Gr. *holos* and *bōlos*, lump, bolus.]

holy, *hō'li*, *adj.* perfect in a moral sense: pure in heart: religious: set apart to a sacred use: regarded with awe (often ironically): saintly: sanctimonious.—*n.* a holy object, place, or person.—*adv.* **ho'lily**.—*ns.* **ho'liness**, sanctity: a title of the pope; **ho'ly-ale**, (conjectured in Shak., *Pericles*, Prol., 9, for rhyme's sake) a church festival.—*adj.* **ho'ly-cru'el**, (*Shak.*) cruel through holiness.—*ns.* **holyday(e)**, **hollidam**, (*Shak.*) for **halidom**; **ho'ly-day**, a religious festival (see also **holiday**); **ho'ly-rood** (as a place-name, *hol'*), Christ's cross: a cross, esp. in R.C. churches over the entrance to the chancel (for **Holy-rood Day**, see **rood**); **ho'lystone**, a sandstone used by seamen for cleansing the decks, said to be named from cleaning the decks for Sunday, or from kneeling in using it.—*v.t.* to scrub with a holystone.—**Holy Alliance**, a league formed after the fall of Napoleon (1815) by the sovereigns of Austria, Russia, and Prussia, professedly to regulate all national and international relations in accordance with the principles of Christian charity; **holy city**, Jeru salem: Rome: Mecca: Benares: Allahabad, &c.; **holy coat**, the seamless coat of Jesus, claimed to be kept at Trier; **Holy Family**, the infant Christ with Joseph, Mary, &c.; **Holy Ghost, Spirit**, the third person of the Christian Trinity; **holy grail** (see **grail**, 3); **holy grass**, a sweet-smelling grass sometimes strewed on church floors on festival days; **Holy Land**, Palestine; **Holy Office**, the Inquisition; **holy of holies**, the inner chamber of the Jewish tabernacle; **Holy One**, God: Christ: the one who is holy, by way of emphasis: one separated to the service of God; **holy orders** (see **order**); **Holy Roman Empire**, the official denomination of the German Empire from 962 to 1806; **Holy Thursday**, Maundy Thursday: Ascension Day; **holy war**, a war for the extirpation of heresy or a rival religion: a Crusade; **holy water**, water blessed for religious uses; **Holy Week**, the week before Easter; **holy writ**, the holy writings: the Scriptures. [O.E. *hálig*, lit. whole, perfect, healthy—*hál*, sound, whole; conn. with **hail, heal, whole**.]

homage, *hom'ij*, *n.* a vassal's acknowledgment that he is the man of his feudal superior: anything done or rendered as such an acknowledgment: reverence, esp. shown by outward action: a body of vassals or tenants.—*v.t.* to do homage to.—*n.* **hom'ager**, one who does homage. [O.Fr. *homage*—L.L. *homināticum*—L. *homō*, a man.]

homaloid, *hom'al-oid*, *n.* Euclidean space, analogous to a plane.—*adj.* **homaloid'al**, flat: of the nature of a plane. [Gr. *homalos*, even, *eidos*, form.]

Homburg-hat, *hom'bərg-hat'*, *n.* a man's hat, of felt, with narrow brim and crown, dinted in at the top: a deer-stalker hat. [First worn at *Homburg*.]

home, *hōm*, *n.* habitual abode, or the place felt to be such: residence of one's family: the scene of domestic life, with its emotional associations: (*U.S.*) a separate building occupied by a family: one's own country: the mother-country: seat: habitat: natural or usual place of anything: the den or base in a game: the goal: the inner table in backgammon: the plate in baseball: an institution affording refuge, asylum, or residence for strangers, the afflicted, poor, &c.: a private hospital: a place where cats, dogs, &c., are received and boarded.—*adj.* pertaining or belonging to or being in one's own dwelling, country, or playing-ground: domestic: near the dwelling or headquarters: coming or reaching home: effective, searching.—*adv.* to home: to the innermost or final position: effectively.—*v.i.* to go home: to find the way home: to dwell.—*v.t.* to send home: to set up in a home.—*adjs.* **home'-and-home'**, played alternately on different home grounds; **home'-born**, originating at home or in the home: native, not foreign; **home'-bound**, homeward bound: fixed to the home; **home'-bred**, bred at home: native: domestic: plain: unpolished; **home'-brewed**, brewed at home or for home use.—*ns.* **home'-com'er**; **home'-com'ing**, arrival at home: return home (also *adj.*); **home'craft**, household arts: arts practised at home or concerned with home-life; **home'-croft**, a cottage with a small piece of land for an industrial worker to grow his own food; **home'-croft'er**; **home'-croft'ing**; **home'-defence'**, defence of a country by a force of its own people within it; **home'-farm**, the farm attached to and near a great house.—*adj.* **home'felt**, felt in one's own breast: inward: private.—*n.* **home'-fire**, the domestic hearth, with its activities and connexions.—*adj.* **home'-grown**, produced in one's own country.—*n.* **home'-guard'**, a member of a volunteer force for home-defence: a force of the kind (first in war of 1939-45, **Home Guard**).—*adj.* **home'-keeping**, staying at home.—*n.* **home'land**, native land, fatherland: mother-country.—*adj.* **home'less**, without a home.—*ns.* **home'lessness**; **home'-life**, domestic life.—*adj.* **home'like**, like a home: familiar: easy: comfortable.—*adv.* **home'lily** (-*li-li*).—*n.* **home'liness**.—*adjs.* **home'ly**, pertaining to home: familiar: plain: unpretentious: (*U.S.*) ugly; **home'-made**, made at home: made in one's own country: plain.—*n.* **hom'er**, a pigeon of a breed

that can readily be trained to find its way home from a distance: any person or animal so skilled: a stroke in itself enabling a baseball-player to make a complete circuit.—*n.* **home'-rul'er**, an advocate of Home Rule.—*adj.* **home'sick**, pining for home. — *n.* **home'sickness**. — *adj.* **home'spun**, spun or wrought at home: not made in foreign countries: plain: inelegant.—*n.* cloth made at home: (*Shak.*) an unpolished person.—*ns.* **home'-stall**, (*obs.*) a homestead: a farmyard; **home'-stead**, a dwelling-house with outhouses and enclosures immediately connected with it: (*U.S.*) a piece of public land allotted under special laws to a settler; **home'steader**; **home'stretch'**, the last stretch of a racecourse; **home'-town**, the town where one's home is or was; **home'-truth**, a pointed, effective, and usually unanswerable statement that strikes home.—*advs.* **home'ward**, **home'wards**.—*adj.* **home'ward**, in the direction of home.—*adj.* **home'ward-bound**, bound homeward or to one's native land.—*n.* **home'work**, work to be done at⸗home, esp. for school.—*n.* and *adj.* **hom'ing**.—*adj.* **hom'y**, home-like.—**at home**, in one's own house: at ease: familiar: ready to receive a visitor; **at-home'**, a reception (**not at home**, out of one's house or not receiving a visitor); **bring home to**, to prove to, in such a way that there is no way of escaping the conclusion: to impress upon; **eat out of house and home**, to live at the expense of another so as to ruin him; **home circuit**, the south-eastern circuit of Assize, with boundaries changed at various times; **home counties**, the counties over and into which London has extended—Middlesex, Essex, Kent, Surrey (Herts, Sussex); **Home Department**, that part of government which is concerned with the maintenance of the internal peace of England—its headquarters the **Home Office**, its official head the **Home Secretary**; **home market**, the market for goods in the country that produces them; **Home Rule**, self-government such as was claimed by Irish Nationalists, including a separate parliament to manage internal affairs; **home thrust**, a pointed remark that goes home; **long home**, the grave; **make one's self at home**, to be as free and unrestrained as in one's own house; **pay home**, to strike to the quick: to retaliate. [O.E. *hám*; Du. and Ger. *heim*, Goth. *haims*.]

homelyn, *hom'əl-in*, *hōm'iin*, *n.* the spotted ray. [Origin unknown.]

homeopathy, &c. Same as **homoeopathy**, &c.

homer, *hō'mər*, *n.* a Hebrew measure of capacity, roughly 11 bushels. [Heb. *khōmer*, a heap—*khāmar*, to swell up.]

Homeric, *hō-mer'ik*, *adj.* pertaining to *Homer*, the great poet of Greece (*c.* 850 B.C.): attributed to Homer: resembling Homer or his poetry: worthy of Homer: in the heroic or epic manner.—*n.* **Homerid** (*hō'mər-id*), one of the **Homer'idae** (*-i-dē*), Chian reciters of the Homeric poems, claiming descent from him.—**Homeric laughter**, loud inextinguishable laughter; **Homeric question**, the question of Homer's authorship of the *Iliad* and the *Odyssey*, disputed by Wolf (1795). [Gr. *hōmērikos*—*Hōmēros*, Homer.]

homicide, *hom'i-sīd*, *n.* manslaughter: one who kills another.—*adj.* **homici'dal**, pertaining to homicide: murderous: bloody. [L. *homicīdium*, manslaughter, and *homicida*, a man-slayer—*homō*, a man, *caedĕre*, to kill.]

homily, *hom'i-li*, *n.* a plain expository sermon, practical rather than doctrinal: a hortatory discourse.—*adjs.* **homilet'ic, -al**.—*n.* **homilet'ics**, the art of preaching.—*n.* **hom'ilist**. [Gr. *homīliā*, an assembly, a lecture or sermon — *homos*, the same, *īlē*, a company.]

hominid, *hom'in-id*, *n.* (*zool.*) an animal of the human family (Homin'idae).—*n.* and *adj.* **hom'inoid**. [L. *homō*, -*inis*, man.]

hominy, *hom'i-ni*, *n.* maize hulled, or hulled and crushed, boiled with water—a kind of Indian-corn porridge. [Amer. Ind. origin.]

hommock. See **hummock**.

homo, *hō'mō*, *n.* man generically: (*zool.*) Homo, the human genus.—**Ho'mo sa'piens**, the one existing species of man. [L. *hŏmō*, *-inis*, man, human being.]

homo-, *hom'ō-*, *hom-ō'-*, in composition, same.—**homoeo-**, **homeo-**, **homoio-**, *hom'i-ō-*, *-oi'ō-*, or *-o'-*, like, similar.—*n.* and *adj.* **homo** (*hō'mō*, *slang*), abbreviation of *homo*sexual.—*adj.* **homoblast'ic** (Gr. *blastos*, a germ), derived from similar cells : showing direct development.—*n.* **hom'oblasty.**—*adjs.* **homocentric** (*-sen'trik* ; Gr. *homokentros—kentron*, centre, point), concentric : proceeding from the same point ; **homocercal** (*-sər'kəl* ; Gr. *kerkos*, tail), having the upper and lower lobes of the tail alike ; **homochlamydeous** (*-klə-mid'i-əs* ; Gr. *chlamys*, *-ydos*, cloak), with calyx and corolla similar ; **homochromous** (*-krō'məs* ; Gr. *chrōma*, colour), alike in colour.—*n.* **homochromy** (*-ok'*, or *-krōm'*), protective coloration.—*adjs.* **homocyclic** (*-sīk'lik* ; Gr. *kyklos*, a ring ; *chem.*), having a closed chain of like atoms ; **homodont** (*hom'ə-dont* ; Gr. *odous*, *odontos*, tooth), having teeth all alike ; **homodyne** (*hom'ə-dīn* ; Gr. *dynamis*, power ; *wireless telephony*), applied to the reception of waves strengthened by he imposition of a locally generated wave of the same length ; **homoeom'erous**, **homoiom'erous** (Gr. *meros*, part), composed of similar parts : of lichens, having the algal cells distributed throughout the thallus—also **homoeomeric** (*-mer'ik*).—*ns.* **homoeom'ery** ; **hom'oeomorph** (Gr. *morphē*, form), a thing similar in form to another but essentially different, esp. a different chemical substance with similar crystalline form.— *adj.* **homoeomorph'ic.** — *adj.* **homoeomorph'ism.**— *adj.* **homoeomorph'ous.**—*ns.* **homoeomorph'y** ; **homoeopath** (*hom'* or *hōm'i-ə-päth* ; Gr. *pathos*, feeling), **homoeopathist** (*-op'ə-thist*), one who believes in or practises homoeopathy.—*adj.* **homoeopathic** (*-path'*).—*adv.* **homoeopath'ically.**—*ns.* **homoeopathy** (*-op'ə-thi*), the system of treating diseases by small quantities of drugs that excite symptoms similar to those of the disease ; **homoeosis** (*hom-i-ō'sis* ; Gr. *homoiōsis*, a becoming like ; *biol.*), assumption of the character of a corresponding member of another whorl or somite ; **homoeoteleuton** (*hom-i-ō-tel-ū'ton* ; Gr. *homoioteleuton—teleutē*, ending), the use, or occurrence, of similar endings.—*adjs.* **homoeotherm'al**, **-ic**, **-ous**, homothermous.—Also **homoi'other'-mal**, &c. ; **homogamic** (*-gam'ik*), **homogamous** (*hom-og'ə-məs*).—*ns.* **homogamy** (*hom-og'ə-mi* ; Gr. *gamos*, marriage), breeding of like with like : in-breeding : (*bot.*) the condition of having all the flowers of an inflorescence sexually alike : simultaneous ripening of stamens and stigmas ; **homogeneity** (*hom-ō-ji-nē'i-ti*), the state or fact of being homogeneous.—*adj.* **homogeneous** (*hom-ō-jēn'i-əs*, also *hōm-*, *-jen'* ; Gr. *homogenēs—genos*, kind), of the same kind or nature : having the constituent elements similar throughout : (*math.*) of the same degree or dimensions in every term.—*n.* **homogē'neousness.**—*adj.* **homogenous** (*hom-oj'ən-əs*), similar owing to common descent.—*n.* **homogenesis** (*-jen'i-sis* ; Gr. *genesis*, birth ; *biol.*), a mode of reproduction in which the offspring is like the parent, and passes through the same cycle of existence.—*adjs.* **homogenet'ic**, **-al**, homogenous.—*v.t.* **homog'enise** (or *hom-ō-jən-īz*), to make homogeneous : to make (milk) more digestible by breaking up fat globules, &c. : to produce (milk) synthetically by mixing its constituents.—*ns.* **homogenisation** ; **homogeniser** ; **homog'eny**, similarity owing to common descent ; **homograph** (*hom'ō-gräf* ; Gr. *graphein*, to write), a word of the same spelling as another, but of different meaning and origin.—*adj.* **homoiousian** (*hom-oi-ōō'si-ən*, or *-otv'* ; Gr. *ousiā*, being), of similar (as distinguished from identical) essence : believing the Father and Son to be of similar essence.—*n.* a holder of such belief, a semi-Arian.—*v.t.* **homol'ogate** (L.L. *homologāre*, *-dātum*—Gr. *homologeein*, to agree—*logos*, speech), to confirm : to approve : to consent to : to ratify.—*v.i.* to agree.—*n.* **homologā'tion**, (*Scots. law*) confirming and ratifying by subsequent act.—*adj.* **homological** (*-loj'*).—*v.t.* and *v.i.* **homol'ogise** (*-jīz*).—*adj.* **hom-**

ologous (*hom-ol'ə-gəs*), agreeing : corresponding in relative position, general structure, and descent.—*n.* **hom'ologue** (*-ə-log*), that which is homologous to something else, as a man's arm, a whale's flipper, a bird's wing.—*n.pl.* **homolog(o)umena** (*hom-ol-o-gōō'mi-nä* ; Gr. *homologoumena*, things granted, neut. pl. of pr.p. pass. (contracted) of *homologeein*), the books of the New Testament whose authenticity was universally acknowledged in the early Church—opp. of *antilegomena*.—*ns.* **homol'ogy** (*-ə-ji* ; Gr. *homologos*), the quality of being homologous : affinity of structure and origin, apart from form or use ; **hom'omorph** (Gr. *morphē*, form), a thing having the same form as another.—*adjs.* **homomorph'ic**, **homomorph'-ous**, alike in form, esp. if essentially different : uniform.—*ns.* **homomorph'ism** ; **homomorphō'-sis**, regeneration of a lost part in the original form ; **hom'onym** (Gr. *homōnymos — onyma*, *onoma*, name), a word having the same sound as another, but a different meaning and origin : (*biol.*) a name rejected as preoccupied by another genus or species : a namesake.—*adjs.* **homonym'ic**, pertaining to homonyms ; **homon'ymous**, having the same name : having different significations and origins but the same sound : ambiguous : equivocal.—*adv.* **homon'ymously.**—*n.* **homon'ymy.**—*adj.* **homoousian**, **homousian** (*hom-(ō-)ōō'si-ən*, or *-otv'* ; Gr. *ousiā*, being), of the same essence : believing the Son to be of the same essence as the Father.—*n.* a holder of such belief (according to the Nicene Creed).—*n.* **homophone** (*hom'ə-fōn* ; Gr. *phōnē*, sound), a character representing the same sound as another : a word pronounced alike with another but different in meaning.—*adjs.* **homophonic** (*-fon'*), sounding alike in unison : in the monodic style of music ; **homophonous** (*-of'*).—*n.* **homoph'ony.**—*adj.* **homoplastic** (Gr. *plastikos*, plastic, *plasma*, a mould ; *biol.*), similar in structure and development owing to parallel or convergent evolution (*ns.* **hom'oplasmy**, *-plaz-mi*, **homop'lasy**).—*n.pl.* **Homoptera** (*-op'* ; Gr. *pteron*, a wing), an order of insects (or suborder of Hemiptera) having the wings alike—cicadas, frog-hoppers, green-fly, scale-insects, &c.—*adjs.* **homop'terous** ; **homosex'ūal**, having, or pertaining to, sexual propensity to one's own sex.—Also *n.*—*ns.* **homosex'ualist** ; **homosexual'ity.**—*adjs.* **homosporous** (*-os'por-əs*, or *-ō-spō'rəs* ; Gr. *sporos*, seed), having spores all of one kind ; **homotax'ial**, **homotax'ic.**—*n.* **homotax'is** (Gr. *taxis*, arrangement ; *geol.*), coincidence in order of organic succession but not necessarily in time.—*adj.* **homothall'ic**, having only one type of mycelium (opp. to *heterothallic*).—*ns.* **homothall'ism**, **hom'othally.**—*adjs.* **homotherm'ic**, **homotherm'ous** (Gr. *thermē*, heat), keeping the same temperature, warm-blooded ; **homotonic** (*-ton'*), **homot'onous** (Gr. *tonos*, tone), of the same tenor or tone.—*n.* **homot'ony.**—*adjs.* **homotypal** (*-tīp'*), **homotypic** (*-tip'ik*), conforming to normal type.—*ns.* **hom'otype** (Gr. *typos*, type), that which has the same fundamental structure with something else ; **homotypy** (*hom'ō-tī-pi*, *hom-ot'i-pi*) ; **homozy'gote**, a zygote formed from gametes that are alike with respect to some pair of alternative characters (both dominant or both recessive), therefore breeding true.—*adj.* **homozy'gous.** [Gr. *homos*, same, *homoios*, like, similar.]

homunculus, *hŏ-mung'kū-ləs*, *n.* a tiny man capable of being produced artificially, according to Paracelsus, endowed with magical insight and power : a dwarf, manikin : a minute human form believed by the spermatist school of preformationists to be contained in the spermatozoon.—Also **homunc'-ūle**, **homunc'le**.—*adj.* **homunc'ūlar.** [L., dim. of *homō*.]

hond, *hond*, an obs. form of **hand.**

hone, *hōn*, *n.* a smooth stone used for sharpening instruments.—*v.t.* to sharpen as on a hone.—*n.* **hone'-stone**, a hone : any hard fine-grained stone suitable for honing, esp. novaculite. [O.E. *hān* ; O.N. *hein* ; allied to Gr. *kōnos*, a cone.]

hone, *hōn*, *v.i.* to pine, moan, grieve. [Perh. Fr. *hogner*, to grumble.]

honest, on'ist, *adj.* full of honour: just: fair-dealing: upright: the opposite of thievish: free from fraud: candid: truthful: ingenuous: seemly: (now only patronisingly) respectable: (*arch.*) chaste: honourable.—*adv.* hon'estly, in an honest way: in truth.—*n.* hon'esty, the state of being honest: integrity: candour: a cruciferous garden-plant (*Lunaria biennis*) with shining silvery or satiny white dissepiments: (*obs.*) decorum: (*Shak.*) chastity.—honest Injun (Indian), upon my honour; make an honest woman of, to marry, where the woman has been dishonoured first. [O.Fr. honeste—L. honestus—honor.]

honey, hun'i, *n.* a sweet, thick fluid elaborated by bees from the nectar of flowers: nectar of flowers: anything sweet like honey: a term of endearment.—*v.t.* to sweeten: to make agreeable.—*v.i.* (*Shak.*) to talk endearingly: (*pr.p.* hon'eying; *pa.t.* and *pa.p.* hon'eyed, -id).—*adj.* (*Shak.*) sweet.—*ns.* hon'ey-badg'er, the ratel; hon'ey-bag, an enlargement of the alimentary canal of the bee in which it carries its load of honey; hon'ey-bear, the kinkajou, which robs the nests of wild bees: the sloth-bear: the Malayan bear; hon'ey-bee, the hive-bee; hon'ey-bird, a honey-guide: a honey-sucker; hon'ey-buzz'ard, a buzzard or falcon (*Pernis apivora*) that feeds on bees, wasps, &c.; hon'eycomb (-kōm), a comb or mass of waxy cells formed by bees, in which they store their honey: anything like a honeycomb.—*v.t.* to make like a honeycomb.—*adj.* hon'eycombed (-kōmd).—*ns.* hon'eycomb-moth', a bee-moth; hon'ey-crock, a crock or pot of honey; hon'ey-dew, a sugary secretion from aphides or plants: ambrosia: a fine sort of tobacco moistened with molasses; hon'ey-eat'er, a honey-sucker.—*adj.* hon'eyed, hon'ied, covered with honey: sweet: seductive: flattering.—*n.* hon'ey-guide, a bird of a mainly African family (Indicatoridae) supposed to guide men to honey by hopping from tree to tree with a peculiar cry: a marking on a flower showing the way to the nectaries.—*adj.* hon'eyless.—*ns.* hon'ey-lō'cust, an ornamental N. American tree (Gleditsia); hon'eymoon (*obs.* hon'eymonth), the first weeks after marriage, commonly spent on holiday, before settling down to the business of life.—Also *v.i.*—*ns.* hon'eymooner; hon'ey-mouse, a long-snouted Australian marsupial (Tarsipes) that feeds on honey and insects.—*adj.* hon'ey-mouthed, having a honeyed mouth or speech: soft or smooth in speech.—*ns.* hon'ey-stalk, (*Shak.*) prob. the stalk or flower of the clover; hon'ey-stone, mellite, a very soft yellow mineral found with lignite; hon'ey-suck'er, any bird of a large Australian family, Meliphagidae; hon'eysuckle, a climbing shrub (Lonicera) with beautiful cream-coloured flowers, so named because honey is readily sucked from the flower (by long-tongued insects only): applied also to clover and many other plants.—*adj.* hon'(e)y-suckle, and *adj.* and *n.* hon'(e)y-seed, (*Shak.*) the Hostess's blunders for homicidal, homicide.—*adjs.* hon'ey-sweet, sweet as honey; hon'ey-tongued, soft, pleasing, persuasive, or seductive in speech: eloquent.—virgin honey, honey that flows of itself from the comb; wild honey, honey made by wild bees. [O.E. hunig; Ger. honig; O.N. hunang.]

honey-pot, hun'i-pot, *n.* (*S.Afr.*) a kind of grape. [Du. haane-poot—haan, cock, poot, foot.]

hong, hong, *n.* a Chinese warehouse: a foreign mercantile establishment in China. [Chin. hang, row, range.]

hong, hong, obs. form of hang, hung.

honied. See honeyed.

Honiton, usu. hon'i-tən, locally hun', *adj.* applied to a kind of pillow lace with sprigs, made at *Honiton* in Devon.

honk, hongk, *n.* the cry of the wild goose: the noise of a motor horn.—Also *v.i.* [Imit.]

honorarium, hon-ə-rā'ri-əm, *n.* a voluntary fee paid, esp. to a professional man for his services.—*adj.* honorary (on'(ə-)rə-ri), conferring honour: holding a title or office without performing services or without reward.—*n.* a fee. [L. honōrārius,

honōrārium (dōnum), honorary (gift)—*honor*, -ōris, honour.]

honorific, (h)on-ə-rif'ik, *adj.* attributing or doing honour.—*n.* an honorific form of address or mention. — *adj.* honorif'ical. — *adv.* honorif'ically. [L. honōrificus—honor, -ōris, honour, and facĕre, to do, make.]

honorificabilitudinity, hon-or-if-ik-ab-il-i-tū-din'-i-ti, *n.* honourableness. [L.L. honōrificābilitū-dinitās, preserved in the abl. pl. honōrificābilitū-dinitātibus as a superlatively long word, in Love's Labour's Lost, V. i. 44 and elsewhere; the gen. sing. is used by Albertino Mussato (early 14th cent.).]

honour, in U.S. honor, on'ər, *n.* the esteem due or paid to worth: respect: high estimation: veneration: that which rightfully attracts esteem: that which confers distinction or does credit: self-respecting integrity: a fine and scrupulous sense of what is due: chastity: virginity: distinction: exalted rank: any mark of esteem: a title or decoration: a title of respect in addressing or referring to judges, &c. (in Ireland quite generally): a prize or distinction: (*pl.*) privileges of rank or birth: (*poet.*) an ornament or decoration: (*pl.*) civilities paid: (*pl.*) in universities, &c., a higher grade of distinction for meritorious, advanced, or specialised work: (*golf*) the right to play first from the tee: any one of four (in whist) or five (in bridge) best trumps, or an ace in a no-trump hand: (*pl.*) a score for holding these: a group of manors held by one lord.—*v.t.* to hold in high esteem: to respect: to adorn: to exalt: to do honour to: to confer honour upon: to grace: to accept and pay when due.—*adj.* hon'ourable, worthy of honour: illustrious: actuated by principles of honour: conferring honour: becoming men of exalted station: Honourable (written Hon.), prefixed to names of various persons as a title of distinction.—*n.* hon'ourableness, eminence: conformity to the principles of honour: fairness.—*adv.* hon'ourably.—*adjs.* hon'oured; hon'ourless.—*ns.* hon'ourer; hon'our-point, (her.) the point just above the fesse-point; hon'ours-man, one who has taken a university degree with honours. —affair of honour, a duel; birthday honours, honours granted to mark the monarch's birthday; Companions of Honour, an order instituted in 1917 for those who have rendered conspicuous service of national importance; Court of Honour, a court regulating affairs of honour; debt of honour (see debt); do the honours, to render civilities, esp. as host; honour bright, a kind of interjectional minor oath or appeal to honour; honours easy (see ease); honours of war, the privileges granted to a capitulating force of marching out with their arms, flags, &c.; last honours, funeral rites; laws of honour, the conventional rules of honourable conduct, esp. in the conduct of duels; maid of honour, a lady in the service of a queen or princess: a kind of cheese-cake: (U.S.) a bridesmaid; person of honour, (obs.) a titled person; point of honour, any scruple caused by a sense of duty: the obligation to demand and to receive satisfaction for an insult, esp. in the duel; upon my honour, an appeal to one's honour in support of a statement; word of honour, a promise which cannot be broken without disgrace. [A.Fr. (h)onour—L. honor, honōs, -ōris.]

hoo, hōō, *interj.* (*Shak.*) expressing boisterous emotion.—Also hoo-oo' (*Shak.*).

hooch, hōōhh, *interj.* a Highland dancer's shout.

hooch, hōōch. See hootch.

hood, hood, *n.* a flexible covering for the head and back of the neck: a covering for a hawk's head: a distinctive ornamental fold worn on the back over an academic gown: a folding roof for a carriage, &c.: a chimney-cowl: an overhanging or protective cover: the expansion of a cobra's neck: a hood-moulding: (U.S.) a motor-car bonnet.—*v.t.* to cover with a hood: to blind.—*adj.* hood'ed.—*n.* hood'ie-crow, the hooded crow (*Corvus cornix*).—*adj.* hood'less, having no hood.—*ns.* hood'man, the person blind-folded in blindman's buff; hood'man-blind, (*Shak.*) blindman's buff; hood'-mould, hood'-mould'ing, an uppermost projecting moulding over a door, window, or arch. [O.E. *hód*; Du. *hoed*, Ger. *hut*.]

hood, *hood*, *n.* (*Spens.*) condition. [O.E. *hád*; see *Suffixes*.]

hoodlum, *hood'ləm*, *n.* (*U.S.*) a rowdy, street bully.

hoodoo, *hōō'dōō*, *n.* (*U.S.*) voodoo: a bringer of bad luck: foreboding of bad luck: bad luck: a rock-pinnacle.—*v.t.* to bewitch: to bring bad luck to. [App. **voodoo**.]

hoodwink, *hood'wingk*, *v.t.* to blindfold: (*Shak.*) to cover: to deceive, impose on. [**hood, wink**.]

hoof, *hōōf*, *n.* the horny part of the feet of certain animals, as horses, &c.: a hoofed animal: (*coll.*) a foot: (*pl.* **hoofs, hooves**).—*v.t.* to strike with the hoof: to kick: to expel.—*v.i* to walk: (*slang*) to dance.—*adjs.* **hoof'-bound**, having a contraction of the hoof causing lameness; **hoofed**; **hoof'less**. —*ns.* **hoof'-mark**, **hoof print**, the mark of a hoof on the ground, &c.; **hoof'rot**, foot-rot.—**on the hoof**, alive (of cattle). [O.E. *hóf*; Ger. *huf*; O.N. *hófr*.]

hook, *hook*, *n.* an object of bent form, such as would catch or hold anything: a sharply bent line: a snare: an advantageous hold: a curved instrument for cutting grain, branches, &c.: a spit of land with hooked end: a boxer's blow with bent elbow: an act of hooking.—*v.t.* to catch, fasten, or hold with or as with a hook: to form into or with a hook: to ensnare: (*golf and cricket*) to pull abruptly: (*Rugby*) to obtain possession of (the ball) in the scrum.—*v.i.* to bend: to be curved: to pull abruptly: (*Rugby*) to act as hooker.—*n.* **hook'-climber**, a climbing-plant that clings to its support by means of hooks. —*adj.* **hooked** (*hookt*).—*n.* **hook'edness**; **hook'er**, one who hooks: (*Rugby*) one whose part it is to hook the ball.—*adj.* **hook'-nosed**.—*ns.* **hook'-pin**, an iron pin with hooked head used for pinning the frame of a floor or roof together; **hook'-up**, a connexion; **hook'-worm**, a parasitic nematode with hooks in the mouth: the disease it causes, ankylostomiasis or miner's anaemia.— *adj.* **hook'y**, full of, or pertaining to, hooks.—**by hook or by crook**, one way if not another; **hook and eye**, a contrivance for fastening dresses by means of a hook that catches in a loop or eye; **hook it**, (*slang*) to decamp, make off; **off the hooks**, out of gear: superseded: dead; **on one's own hook**, on one's own responsibility, initiative, or account. [O.E. *hóc*; Du. *hoek*.]

hookah, hooka, *hook'ä*, *n.* the water tobacco-pipe of Arabs, Turks, &c. [Ar. *huqqah*, bowl, casket.]

hooker, *hook'ər*, *n.* a two-masted Dutch vessel, a small fishing-smack. [Du. *hoeker*.]

hookey, hooky, *hook'i*, *n.* (*U.S.*) truant (in the phrase *play hookey*).—**blind hookey**, a gambling card-game; **hookey walker** (see under **walk**).

hooligan, *hōōl'i-gən*, *n.* a street rough.—*n.* **hool'-iganism**. [Said to be the name of a leader of a gang.]

hoolock, *hōō'lək*, *n.* a small Assamese gibbon. [Said to be native name, *hulluk*.]

hooly, *hūl'i*, *həl'i*, *adv.* (*Scot.*) softly, carefully.— Also *adj.*—**hooly and fairly**, fair and soft. [Perh. O.N. *hófliga*, fitly, or *hógliga*, gently.]

hoop, *hōōp*, *n.* a ring or band for holding together the staves of casks, &c: a large ring for a child to trundle, for carrying pails, for leaping through, for expanding a skirt, or other purpose: a ring: a croquet arch.—*v.t.* to bind with hoops: to encircle.—*ns.* **hoop'-ash**, a kind of ash used for making hoops: the nettle-tree (Celtis); **hooped'-pot**, a drinking-pot with hoops to mark the amount each man should drink; **hoop'er**, one who hoops casks: a cooper. [O.E. *hóp*; Du. *hoep*.]

hoop, hooper, hooping-cough. See under **whoop**.

hoopoe, *hōōp'ōō*, *n.* a crested bird (*Upupa epops*), an occasional visitor in Britain. [Earlier *hoop*—O.Fr. *huppe*, partly remodelled on L. *upupa*; cf. Gr. *epops*.]

hoord, an obs. form of **hoard**.

hoosh, *hōōsh*, *interj.* used in driving away animals. —*v.t.* to drive or shoo away animals. [Imit.]

hoosh, *hōōsh*, *n.* a thick soup.

hoot, *hōōt*, *v.i.* to shout in derision: to cry like

an owl: to sound a motor-horn, siren, or the like. —*v.t.* to greet or drive with such sounds.—*n.* the sound of hooting: the note of an owl, motor-horn, &c.: a whit (often *two hoots*).—*interj.* (*Scot.*) tut.—*n.* **hoot'er**, one who hoots: a factory or mine siren or steam whistle.—*interj.* **hoots**, (*Scot.*) tut.—Also **hoot'-toot', hoots'-toots'**. [Imit., prob. immediately Scand.; cf. Sw. *hut*, begone.]

hootch, hooch, *hōōch*, *n.* a drink made by the Indians of N.W. America from fermented dough and sugar: whisky: illicitly got liquor. [Said to be from *Hootchino*, an Alaskan tribe.]

hoove, *hōōv*, *n.* a disease of cattle and sheep, marked by distention of the abdomen by gas—also *wind-dropsy*, *drum-belly*.—*adjs.* **hoov'en**, **hō'ven**. [Cf. **heave**.]

hoove. See **hove** (2).

hooves. See **hoof**.

hop, *hop*, *v.i.* to leap on one leg: to move in jumps like a bird: to walk lame: to limp: to fly (in aircraft).—*v.t.* to cause to hop: to jump or fly over: to jump from: to board when in motion: (*pr.p.* **hopp'ing**; *pa.t.* and *pa.p.* **hopped**).—*n.* a leap on one leg: a jump: a spring: a dance, dancing-party: a stage in a flying journey.—*ns.* **hop-off**, the start of a flight; **hop'-o'-my-thumb** (i.e. on my thumb), a pygmy; **hopp'er**, one who hops: a hopping or leaping animal, esp. (*U.S.*) a grasshopper: a jack or sticker of a piano: a shaking or conveying receiver, funnel, or trough (originally a shaking one) in which something is placed to be passed or fed, as to a mill: a barge with an opening in its bottom for discharging refuse: a vessel in which seed-corn is carried for sowing; **hopp'ing**; **hop'-scotch**, a game in which children hop over lines scotched or traced on the ground.—**hop it**, to take oneself off; **hop, skip, and jump**, a leap on one leg, a skip, and a jump with both legs; **hop the twig**, (*slang*) to escape one's creditors: to die; **on the hop**, in the act: unawares: at the very moment. [O.E. *hoppian*, to dance; Ger. *hopfen*, *hüpfen*.]

hop, *hop*, *n.* a plant (*Humulus Lupulus*) of the mulberry family with a long twining stalk: (in *pl.*) its bitter catkin-like fruit-clusters used for flavouring beer and in medicine.—*v.t.* to mix or flavour with hops.—*v.i.* to gather hops:—*pr.p.* **hopp'ing**; *pa.t.* and *pa.p.* **hopped**.—*ns.* **hop'bind, hop'bine**, the stalk of the hop; **hop'-bitt'ers**, a drink like ginger-beer, flavoured with hops; **hop'dog**, the tussock-moth caterpillar: a tool for pulling out hop-poles; **hop'-flea**, a small beetle injurious to hops; **hop'-fly**, a greenfly injurious to hops; **hop'-garden**, a field of hops; **hop'-oast**, a kiln for drying hops.—*adj.* **hopped**, impregnated with hops.—*ns.* **hop'per, hop'-pick'er**, one who picks hops: a mechanical contrivance for stripping hops from the bines; **hopp'ing**, the act of gathering hops: the time of the hop harvest; **hop'-pock'et**, a coarse sack for hops—as a measure, about 1½ cwt. of hops; **hop'-pole**, a slender pole supporting a hop-bine.—*adj.* **hopp'y**, tasting of hops.—*ns.* **hop'-tree**, an American rutaceous shrub (*Ptelea trifoliata*) with bitter fruit, a poor substitute for hops; **hop'-tre'foil**, a clover with hop-like heads; **hop'-vine**, the hop-plant: its stock or stem; **hop'-yard**, a field where hops are grown. [Du. *hop*; Ger. *hopfen*.]

hope, *hōp*, *v.i.* to cherish a desire of good with some expectation of fulfilment: to have confidence: to be hopeful.—*v.t.* to desire with some expectation or with belief in the prospect of fulfilment: (*obs.*) to expect, fear.—*n.* a desire of some good, with some expectation of obtaining it: confidence: anticipation: that on which hopes are grounded: an embodiment of hope: that which is hoped for.— *n.* **hope'-chest**, (*U.S.*) a repository of things stored by a woman against marriage—a bottom drawer.—*adj.* **hope'ful**, full of hope: having qualities which excite hope: promising good or success.—*n.* a promising young person.—*adv.* **hope'fully**.—*n.* **hope'fulness**.—*adj.* **hope'less**, without hope: giving no ground to expect good or success: incurable: (*Spens.*) unhoped-for. —*adv.* **hope'lessly**.—*n.* **hope'lessness.**—*adv.*

hōp′ingly.—hope against hope, to continue to hope when all ground is gone. [O.E. *hopian—hopa*, hope; Du. *hopen*, Ger. *hoffen*.]

hope, *hōp, n.* an enclosure: the upper end of a narrow mountain-valley: a combe—common in Border place-names (usu. pron. *-əp*): an inlet. [O.E. *-hop* (in compounds), or O.N. *hóp*.]

hope. See **forlorn hope.**

hoplite, *hop′līt, n.* a heavy-armed Greek foot soldier. [Gr. *hoplītēs*.]

hoplology, *hop-lol′ə-ji, n.* the study of weapons.— *n.* **hoplol′ogist.** [Gr. *hoplon*, tool, weapon.]

hopple, *hop′l, v.t.* to restrain by tying the feet together.—*n.* (chiefly in *pl.*) a fetter for horses, &c., when left to graze. [Cf. obs. Flem. *hoppelen*; also **hop, hobble.**]

horal, *hō′rəl, adj.* relating to hours.—*adj.* **ho′rary,** pertaining to an hour: noting the hours: hourly: continuing an hour. [L. *hōra*, an hour.]

Horatian, *hor-ā′shən, adj.* pertaining to *Horace*, the Latin poet (65-8 B.C.), or to his manner or verse.

horde, *hōrd, n.* a migratory or wandering tribe or clan: a multitude.—*v.i.* to live together as a horde. **—Golden Horde** (see **golden**). [Fr.,—Turk. *ordū*, camp.]

Hordeum, *hor′di-əm, n.* the barley genus.—*ns.* **hordein** (*hor′di-in*), a protein found in barley grains; **hordeolum** (*-dē′*), a sty on the eyelid. [L., barley.]

hore (*Spens.*). Same as **hoar.**

horehound, hoarhound, *hōr′hownd, n.* a hoary labiate plant (*Marrubium vulgare*) once popular as a remedy for coughs.—Also called **white horehound.** — **black horehound, stinking horehound,** a darker-coloured kindred weed (*Ballota nigra*); **water horehound,** gypsywort. [O.E. *hār*, hoar, *hūne*, horehound.]

horizon, *hor-ī′zən, n.* the circle in which earth and sky seem to meet (*sensible, apparent,* or *visible horizon*): a plane through the earth's centre parallel to the sensible horizon (*rational horizon*), or the great circle in which it meets the heavens: a horizontal reflecting surface, as of mercury, used as a substitute for the horizon in taking an observation (*artificial horizon*): (*geol.*) a stratigraphical level, characterised generally by some particular fossil or fossils: (*anat.*) a level line or surface: the limit of one's experience or apprehension.— *adj.* **horizontal** (*hor-i-zont′l*), pertaining to the horizon: parallel to the horizon: level: near the horizon: measured in the plane of the horizon.—*n.* a horizontal line, position, or object.—*n.* **horizontal′ity.**—*adv.* **horizon′tally.** [Fr.,—L.,—Gr. *horizōn* (*kyklos*), bounding (circle), *horizōn, -ōntos,* pr.p. of *horizein*, to bound—*horos*, a limit.]

hormone, *hor′mōn, n.* an internal secretion which on reaching some part of a plant or animal body exercises a specific physiological action. [Gr. *hormōn*, contracted pr.p. of *hormaein*, to stir up.]

horn, *horn, n.* a hard outgrowth on the head of an animal, sometimes confined to the hollow structure on an ox, sheep, goat, &c., sometimes extended to a deer's antler, the growth on a giraffe's head, on a rhinoceros's snout, &c.: a beetle's antenna: a snail's tentacle: any projection resembling a horn: a cusp: a crescent tip: an outgrowth visible only to the eye of faith on a cuckold's forehead: the material of which horns are composed, keratin: an object made of or like a horn, as a drinking vessel: a funnel-shaped mouthpiece: a wind instrument orig. made from a horn, now of brass, &c.: a sounding apparatus on motor vehicles: a Jewish symbol of strength.—*adj.* made of horn.— *v.t.* to furnish with horns, real or visionary: to dishorn: to outlaw: to gore: to butt or push.— *v.i.* to play or blow the horn: to butt.—*ns.* **horn′-beak,** the garfish; **horn′beam,** a tree (Carpinus) resembling a beech, with hard tough wood; **horn′-bill,** a bird (of family Bucerotidae) with a horny excrescence on its bill; **horn′book,** a first book for children, which consisted of a single leaf set in a frame, with a thin plate of transparent horn in front to preserve it; **horn′bug,** (*U.S.*) a stag-beetle.—*adj.* **horned,** having a horn or horns: curved like a horn.—*ns.* **horned′-horse,** the gnu;

horned′-owl, horn′owl, an owl with hornlike tufts of feathers on its head; **horned′-popp′y,** a poppy (Glaucium) with horned seed-vessel; **horned′-toad,** a spiny American lizard (Phrynosoma): a S. American toad (Ceratophrys) with a bony shield on the back; **horn′er,** one who works or deals in horns: a horn-player: a cuckold-maker; **horn′fels** (*-fels*; Ger. *fels*, rock), a compact rock composed of lime silicates produced by contact metamorphism.—*adj.* **horn′-foot′ed,** hoofed.—*ns.* **horn′ful;** **horn′-gate,** gate of horn (see **gate**); **horn′geld** (*hist.*), cornage; **Horn′ie,** (*Scot.*) the devil, usu. represented with horns; **horn′i-ness;** **horn′ing,** appearance of the moon when in its crescent form: (*U.S.*) a mock serenade with tin horns and any discordant instruments: (*Scots law*) putting to the horn: (*obs.*) cuckold-making.— *adj.* **horn′ish,** like horn: hard.—*n.* **horn′ist,** a horn-player.—*adj.* **horn′less,** without horns.—*n.* **horn′let,** a little horn.—*adj.* **horn′-mad,** mad to the point of goring anybody: enraged like a cuckold.—*ns.* **horn-mad′ness** (*Browning*); **horn′-mak′er,** (*Shak.*) a cuckold-maker; **horn′-mer′-cury,** native mercurous chloride or calomel; **horn′-nut,** water-chestnut.—*adj.* **horn′-rimmed,** having rims of horn.—*ns.* **horn′-sil′ver,** cerargyrite; **horn′-spoon,** a spoon made of a sheep's horn; **horn′stone,** a flinty chalcedony; **horn′tail,** a hymenopterous insect, often with a stout ovipositor; **horn′work,** (*fort.*) an outwork having angular points or horns, and composed of two demi-bastions joined by a curtain: work in horn: cuckoldry; **horn′worm,** a hawkmoth caterpillar; **horn′wort,** a rootless water-plant (Ceratophyllum) with much-divided submerged leaves that turn translucent and horny; **horn′wrack,** the sea-mat. —*adjs.* **horn′y,** like horn: of horn: hard: callous: **horn′y-hand′ed,** with hands hardened by toil.—*n.* **horn′y-head,** an American cyprinoid fish with hornlike processes on its head.—**horn in,** (*U.S.*) interpose, butt in; **horn of plenty** (see **cornucopia**); **horns of a dilemma** (see **dilemma**); **horns of the altar,** the projections at the four corners of the Hebrew altar; **letters of horning,** (*Scots law*) letters running in the sovereign's name, and passing the signet, instructing messengers-at-arms to charge the debtor to pay, on his failure a caption or warrant for his apprehension being granted; **make a spoon or spoil a horn,** to attempt something at the risk of failure; **pull,** or **draw, in one's horns,** to abate one's ardour or pretensions; **put to the horn,** (old *Scots law*) to outlaw by three blasts of the horn at the Cross of Edinburgh. [O.E. *horn*; Scand. and Ger. *horn*, Gael. and W. *corn*, L. *cornū*, Gr. *keras*.]

hornblende, *horn′blend, n.* a rock-forming mineral, one of the amphiboles, essentially silicate of calcium, magnesium and iron, generally green to black, with cleavage angle about 56°. [Ger.; cf. **horn, blende.**]

hornet, *horn′it, n.* a large kind of wasp. [O.E. *hyrnet*, app.—*horn*.]

hornito, *hor-nē′tō, n.* a low oven-shaped fumarole. [Sp., dim. of *horno*—L. *furnus*, an oven.]

hornpipe, *horn′pip, n.* an old Welsh musical instrument like a clarinet, prob. sometimes with a horn mouthpiece or bell: a lively English dance, usually by one person, popular amongst sailors: a tune for the dance. [horn, pipe.]

horography, *hor-og′rə-fi, n.* the art of constructing sundials, clocks, &c.—*n.* **horog′rapher.** [Gr. *hōrā*, an hour, *graphein*, to describe.]

horologe, *hor′ə-loj, n.* any instrument for telling the hours.—*ns.* **horologer** (*-ol′ə-jər*), **horol′ogist,** a maker of clocks, &c.—*adjs.* **horolog′ic, -al.**— *n.* **horol′ogy,** the science of time-measurement: the art of clock-making: the office-book of the Greek Church for the canonical hours. [L. *hōrologium*—Gr. *hōrologion*—*hōrā*, an hour, *legein*, to tell.]

horometry, *hor-om′it-ri, n.* time-measurement.— *adj.* **horometrical** (*-met′*). [Gr. *hōrā*, an hour, *metron*, a measure.]

horoscope, *hor′ə-skōp, n.* an observation of the heavens at the hour of a person's birth, by which the astrologer predicted the events of his life: a representation of the heavens for this purpose.—*adj.* **horoscopic** (-*skop'*).—*ns.* **horoscopist** (-*os'kə-pist*), an astrologer; **horos'copy**, the art of predicting the events of a person's life from his horoscope: aspect of the stars at the time of birth. [Gr. *hōroskopos*—*hōrā*, an hour, *skopeein*, to observe.]

horrent, *hor'ənt, adj.* bristling. [L. *horrēns, -ēntis,* pr.p. of *horrēre,* to bristle.]

horrible, *hor'i-bl, adj.* exciting horror: dreadful: (*coll.*) detestable.—*n.* **horr'ibleness.**—*adv.* **horr'-ibly.** [L. *horribilis*—*horrēre,* to shudder.]

horrid, *hor'id, adj.* (*arch.* or *poet.*) shaggy, bristling, rough: (*arch.*) horrible: (*coll.*) repellent, detestable.— *adv.* **horr'idly.**—*n.* **horr'idness.** [L. *horridus*—*horrēre,* to bristle.]

horrify, *hor'i-fī, v.t.* to strike with horror:—*pr.p.* **horr'ifying;** *pa.t.* and *pa.p.* **horr'ified.**—*adj.* **horrif'ic,** exciting horror: frightful. [L. *horrificus* —root of *horrēre, facĕre,* to make.]

horripilation, *hor-i-pi-lā'shən, n.* a contraction of the cutaneous muscles causing erection of the hairs and goose-flesh.—*adj.* **horrip'ilant.**—*v.t.* and *v.i.* **horrip'ilate.** [L. *horripilātiō, -ōnis*—root of *horrēre,* to bristle, *pilus,* a hair.]

horrisonant, *hor-is'ən-ənt, adj.* sounding dreadfully.—Also **horris'onous.** [From root of L. *horrēre,* to bristle, *sonāns, -āntis,* sounding.]

horror, *hor'ər, n.* (*obs.*) shagginess, raggedness: a shuddering: excessive repugnance and loathing: the power of exciting such feeling: a source of such feeling: (*coll.*) anything mildly objectionable, ridiculous, grotesque, or distasteful.—*adjs.* **horr'or-stricken, -struck.—the horrors,** extreme depression: delirium tremens. [L. *horror,* a shudder, bristling, &c.]

hors-d'oeuvre, *or'dəvr', n.* a whet (olives, sardines, or the like) before a meal or after soup. [Fr.]

horse, *hors, n.* a solid-hoofed ungulate (*Equus caballus*) with flowing tail and mane: any member of the genus Equus (horse, ass, zebra, &c.) or the family Equidae: a male adult of the species: (*collec.*) cavalry: a wooden frame on which soldiers used to be mounted as a punishment—also *timber-mare*: a gymnastic apparatus for vaulting, &c.: a horselike apparatus or support of various kinds (as *saw-horse, clothes-horse*): a crib or translation: a mass of barren country interrupting a lode: (*pl.* **horses,** sometimes **horse**).—*v.t.* to mount or set as on a horse: to provide with a horse: to sit astride: to carry on the back: (of a stallion) to cover: to urge at work tyrannically: to construe by means of a crib.—*v.i.* to get on horseback: to travel on horseback: to hasten (also *v.t.* with *it*): to charge for work before it is done.—*ns.* **horse'-artill'ery,** field artillery with comparatively light guns and the gunners mounted; **horse'back,** the back of a horse; **horse'-bean,** a large bean given to horses; **horse'-block,** a block or stage for mounting and dismounting by; **horse'-boat,** a boat for carrying horses, or towed by a horse; **horse'-bot,** a botfly; **horse'-box,** a railway car for horses: a stall on shipboard: a high-sided church pew; **horse'-boy,** a stable-boy; **horse'-bread,** a coarse bread for feeding horses; **horse'-break'er, -tam'er,** one who breaks or tames horses, or teaches them to draw or carry: a court-esan who appears on horseback; **horse'-car,** a car drawn by horses; **horse-chest'nut,** a smooth, brown, bitter seed or nut, perh. so called from its coarseness contrasted with the edible chestnut: the tree that produces it (*Aesculus Hippocastanum*); **horse'-cloth,** a cloth for covering a horse; **horse'-collar,** a stuffed collar for a draught-horse, carrying the hames, used also for grinning through in rustic sports; **horse'-co'per** or (*Scot.*) **horse'-couper** (*kow', kōō'*), **horse'-deal'er,** one who deals in horses; **horse'-doc'tor,** a veterinary surgeon; **horse'-drench,** a dose of physic for a horse.—*adj.* **horse'-faced,** having a long horselike face.—*ns.* **horse'-fair,** a fair or market for sale of horses; **horse'flesh,** the flesh of a horse: horses collectively. — *adj.* of reddish-bronze colour. — *ns.* **horse'flesh-ore,** bornite or erubescite, from its

colour; **horse'-fly,** the forest-fly or other large fly that stings horses; **horse'-foot,** coltsfoot: a kingcrab; **horse'-god'mother,** a fat clumsy woman; **horse'-gow'an,** (*Scot.*) the ox-eye daisy.—*n.pl.* **horse'-guards,** horse-soldiers employed as guards: the cavalry brigade of the British household troops, esp. the *Royal Horse Guards,* or *Blues,* a regiment raised in 1661: their headquarters in Whitehall, London, once seat of the departments of the army commander-in-chief: the military authorities.—*n.* **horse'-hair,** a hair from a horse's mane or tail: a mass of such hairs: a fabric woven from horse-hairs.—*adj.* made of or stuffed with horse-hair. — *ns.* **horse'-hide;** **horse'-hoe,** a hoe drawn by horses; **horse'-knack'er,** one who buys and slaughters worn-out horses; **horse'-lat'itudes,** two zones of the Atlantic Ocean (about 30° N. and 30° S., esp. the former) noted for long calms; **horse'-laugh,** a harsh, boisterous laugh; **horse'-leech,** (*obs.*) a horse-doctor: a large species of leech, so named from its fastening on horses: a bloodsucker (Prov. xxx. 15).—*adj.* **horse'less,** without a horse: mechanically driven.—*ns.* **horse'-litt'er,** a litter or bed borne between two horses: bedding for horses; **horse'-mack'erel,** the scad or allied fish: the tunny: applied to various other fishes; **horse'man,** a rider: one skilled in managing a horse: a mounted soldier: one who has charge of horses: a kind of carrier pigeon: a kind of land-crab; **horse'manship,** the art of riding and of training and managing horses; **horse'-marine',** a person quite out of his element: a member of an imaginary corps; **horse'-meat,** food for horses; **horse'-mill,** a mill turned by horses; **horse'-mill'iner,** one who provides the trappings for horses; **horse'-mint,** any wild mint: the American *Monarda punctata*: (sweet horse-mint, the common dittany); **horse'-mush'room,** a large coarse mushroom; **horse'-muss'el,** a mollusc (Modiolus) akin to the common mussel but much bigger; **horse'-nail,** a nail for fastening a horse-shoe to the hoof; **horse'-pis'tol,** a large pistol carried in a holster; **horse'-play,** rough, boisterous play; **horse'-pond,** a pond for watering horses at; **horse'-power,** the power a horse can exert, or its conventional equivalent=that required to raise 33,000 lb. avoirdupois one foot in one minute—a standard for estimating the power of engines; **horse'-race,** a race by horses; **horse'-rac'ing,** the practice of racing or running horses in matches; **horse'-rad'ish,** a kind of scurvy-grass with a pungent root, used as a condiment: (**horse'-radish tree,** a tree, *Moringa pterygosperma,* cultivated in tropical countries for its edible capsules and its seeds, ben-nuts, which yield oil of ben—the roots tasting like horse-radish: an Australian tree, *Codonocarpus cotinifolius,* with leaves of horse-radish flavour); **horse'-rake,** a rake drawn by horses; **horse'-rid'ing; horse'-sense,** plain robust sense; **horse'-shoe,** a shoe for horses, consisting of a curved piece of iron: anything of like shape.—*adj.* shaped like a horse-shoe.—*ns.* **horse'-shoer** (-*shōō'ər*), one who makes or affixes horse-shoes; **horse'-shoe'ing; horse'-sick'ness,** an African disease of horses, due to a filterable virus; **horse'-sol'dier,** a cavalry soldier; **horse'-tail,** a horse's tail: a Turkish standard, marking rank by number: any plant of the genus Equisetum (scouring-rush) with hollow rush-like stems, constituting with kindred fossils a class of fern-allies, Equisetinae; **horse'-thief; horse'-train'er,** one who trains horses for racing, &c.; **horse'-way,** a road by which a horse may pass; **horse'-whip,** a whip for driving horses.—*v.t.* to thrash with a horse-whip: to lash.—*ns.* **horse'-wom'an,** a woman who rides on horseback, or who rides well; **hors'iness; hors'ing,** birching a schoolboy mounted on another's back. — *adj.* **hors'y,** of or pertaining to horses: horselike: devoted to horses, horse-racing, or breeding.— **a dark horse** (see **dark**); **flog a dead horse,** to try to work up excitement about a threadbare subject; **gift horse** (see **gift**); **high horse** (see **high**); **horse and hattock** (see **hattock**):

horseless carriage, an old name for a motor-car; **put the cart before the horse** (see **cart**); **take horse,** to mount on horseback; **white horse** (see **white**). [O.E. *hors*; O.N. *hross*; O.H.G. *hros* (Ger. *ross*).]

horson (*Shak.*). Same as **whoreson**.

horst, *horst, n.* (*geol.*) a block of the earth's crust that has remained in position while the ground around it has either subsided or been folded into mountains by pressure against its solid sides. [Ger.]

hortative, *hort'ə-tiv, adj.* inciting: encouraging: giving advice.—Also **hort'atory.**—*n.* **hortā'tion.** [L. *hortārī, -ātus,* to incite.]

horticulture, *hor'ti-kult-yər, n.* the art of gardening. —*adj.* **horticul'tural.**—*n.* **horticul'turist,** one versed in the art of cultivating gardens. [L. *hortus,* a garden, *cultūra—colēre,* to cultivate.]

hosanna, *hō-zan'ä, n.* an exclamation of praise to God, or a prayer for blessings. [Gr. *hōsanna*—Heb. *hōshi'āh nnā, hōshiā',* save, *nā,* I pray.]

hose, *hōz, n.* a covering for the legs or feet: stockings: socks (*half-hose*): close-fitting breeches or drawers: a flexible pipe for conveying water, so called from its shape: a socket for a shaft: (*pl.* hose; (*arch.*) **hos'en;** in sense of pipe, *pl.* **hos'es**).—*v.t.* to provide with hose: to play a hose on.—*adj.* **hosed.**—*ns.* **hose'man,** a fireman who directs the stream of water; **hose'-net,** a stocking-shaped net; **hose'pipe;** **hose'-reel,** a large revolving drum for carrying hose; **hosier** (*hōzh'(y)ər, hōz'yər*), a dealer in or a maker of hosiery; **hō'siery,** hose collectively: knitted goods. [O.E. *hosa,* pl. *hosan,* Du. *hoos,* Ger. *hose.*]

hospice, *hos'pis, n.* a house of entertainment for strangers, esp. one kept by monks: a hostel: a home of refuge. [Fr.,—L. *hospitium—hospes, -itis,* a stranger, guest.]

hospitable, *hos'pit-ə-bl, adj.* kind to strangers: welcoming and generous towards guests.—*n.* **hos'-pitableness.** — *adv.* **hos'pitably.** — *n.* **hospitage** (*hos'pit-āj; Spens.*), that which is due from a guest. [L.L. *hospitāgium*—L. *hospes, -itis,* stranger, guest.]

hospital, *hos'pit-l, n.* a building for the reception and treatment of the old, the sick, and hurt, &c., or for the support and education of the young.— *ns.* **hos'pitale** (*-āl; Spens.*), lodging; **hospital-ity** (*-al'i-ti*), the practice of one who is hospitable: friendly welcome and entertainment of guests; **hos'pitaller,** one of a charitable brotherhood for the care of the sick in hospitals: one of the Knights of St John (otherwise called Knights of Rhodes, and afterwards of Malta), an order which built a hospital for pilgrims at Jerusalem; **hos'pital-ship',** a ship fitted out exclusively for the treatment and transport of the sick and wounded. [O.Fr. *hospital* —L.L. *hospitāle—hospes, -itis,* a guest.]

hospitium, *hos-pish'i-əm, n.* a hospice:—*pl.* **hos-pit'ia.** [L.; cf. **hospice.**]

hospodar, *hos'po-där, n.* (*hist.*) a prince or governor, esp. of Moldavia or Wallachia.—Also **gos'podar.** [Rum. *hospodār,* of Slav. origin.]

hoss, *hos, n.* (*U.S.* and *vulg.*) for **horse.**

host, *hōst, n.* one who entertains a stranger or guest at his house without (or with) reward: an innkeeper: an organism on which another lives as a parasite.—*v.t.* (*Spens.*) to receive and entertain as one's guest.—*v.i.* (*Spens., Shak.*) to lodge, to be a guest.—*ns.* **hōst'ess,** *fem.* of **host;** **air'-hostess,** one appointed to look after the comfort, and keep up the morale, of aircraft passengers; **hōst'ess-ship,** (*Shak.*) the character or office of a hostess.— *adj.* **hōst'lesse,** (*Spens.*) inhospitable.—*n.* **hōst'ry,** (*Spens.*) lodging.—**lie at host,** (*Shak.*) to be lodged; **reckon,** or **count, without one's host,** to count up one's bill without reference to the landlord: fail to take account of some important possibility, as the action of another. [O.Fr. *hoste*—L. *hospes, hospitis.*]

host, *hōst, n.* an army: a great multitude.—*n.* **hōst'ing,** (*Milt.*) a battle: (*Spens.*) a muster, a military expedition.—**a host in himself,** one of great strength, skill, or resources, within himself; **heavenly host,** the angels and archangels; **Lord**

of hosts, a favourite Hebrew term for Jehovah, considered as head of the hosts of angels, the hosts of stars, &c. [O.Fr. *host*—L. *hostis,* an enemy.]

host, *hōst, n.* (*obs.*) a sacrificial victim: in the R.C. Church, the consecrated wafer of the eucharist. [L. *hostia,* a victim.]

hostage, *hos'tij, n.* one kept in the hands of an enemy as a pledge.—**hostages to fortune,** wife, children, &c. [O.Fr. *hostage* (Fr. *ôtage*)—L. *obses, obsidis,* a hostage.]

hostel, *hos'tal, n.* an inn: in some universities an extra-collegiate hall for students: a residence for students or for some class or society of persons, esp. one not run commercially: a lodging for (esp.) young persons on tour (as **youth hostel**).—*ns.* **hos'teler, hos'teller,** hospitaller: keeper of a hostel: one who lives in, or uses, a hostel; **hos'telling,** making sojourns in hostels; **hos'telry,** an inn. [O.Fr. *hostel, hostellerie*—L. *hospitāle;* cf. **hospital.**]

hostile, *hos'tīl, -til, adj.* belonging to an enemy: showing enmity: adverse: engaged in hostilities: pertaining to hostilities.—*adv.* **hos'tilely.**—*n.* **hostility** (*-til'*), enmity:—*pl.* **hostil'ities,** acts of warfare. [L. *hostīlis—hostis.*]

hostler. Same as **ostler.**

hot, *hot, adj.* having a high temperature: very warm: fiery: pungent: giving a feeling suggestive of heat: animated: ardent: vehement: violent: passionate: sexually excited: lustful: dangerously charged with electricity: dangerous: near the object sought: played with interpolations suggestive of excitement: good enough to excite: recently obtained dishonestly.—*adv.* **hotly.** —*v.t.* (*coll.*) to heat. — *adjs.* **hot'-air,** making use of heated air: boastful, idly-talking; **hot'-and-hot',** cooked and served up at once in hot dishes. — Also *n.*—*ns.* **hot'bed,** a glass-covered bed heated by a layer of fermenting manure for bringing forward plants rapidly: (*fig.*) a place favourable to rapid growth or development; **hot'blast,** a blast of heated air. — *adj.* **hot'-blood'ed,** having hot blood: homothermous: passionate: ardent: high-spirited: irritable. — *n.* **hot'-brain,** a hothead. — *adj.* **hot'-brained.** — *ns.* **hot'-cock'les,** an old game in which one with eyes covered guesses who strikes him; **hot'-dog',** (*U.S.*) a hot sausage sandwich; **hot'-flue,** a drying-room.—*adv.* **hot'foot,** in hot haste.—*ns.* **hot'-gos'peller,** a revivalist preacher; **hot'head,** an impetuous headstrong person.—*adj.* **hot'-head'ed.**—*n.* **hot'house,** a house kept hot for the rearing of tropical or tender plants: any heated chamber or drying-room, esp. that where pottery is placed before going into the kiln: (*arch.*) a hot-bathing establishment: (*Shak.*) a brothel.—*adj.* **hot'-liv'ered,** (*Milt.*) hot-tempered.—*adv.* **hot'ly.** —*adj.* **hot'-mouthed,** restive, as when the bit hurts.—*ns.* **hot'ness;** **hot'-plate,** the flat top surface of a stove for cooking: a similar plate, independently heated, for keeping things hot; **hot'pot,** a dish of chopped mutton seasoned and stewed in a pot, with sliced potatoes, or similar mixture.—*v.t.* **hot'press,** to press between hot plates to produce a glossy surface.—*adjs.* **hot'-short,** brittle when heated; **hot'-spir'ited,** having a fiery spirit.—*n.* **Hot'spur,** a violent, rash man like Henry Percy (1364-1403), so nicknamed.— *adjs.* **hot'-tem'pered,** having a quick temper; **hott'ish.**—*ns.* **hot'-trod,** the hot pursuit in old Border forays; **hot'-wall,** a wall enclosing passages for hot air, affording warmth to fruit-trees; **hot'-well,** a spring of hot water: in a condensing engine, a reservoir for the warm water drawn off from the condenser.—**go (sell) like hot cakes,** to sell off or disappear promptly; **hot air,** empty talk; **hot coppers** (see **copper**); **hot cross-bun** (see **cross**); **hot stuff,** any person, thing, or performance that is outstandingly remarkable, excellent, vigorous, or reprehensible; **hot water,** a state of trouble; **make a place too hot for one,** to make it impossible for him to stay there. [O.E. *hát;* Ger. *heiss,* Sw. *het.*]

hot, hote, or **hote,** *hōt,* (*Spens.*) named: was called. [Pa.t. act. and pass. of **hight.**]

hotch, *hoch*, *v.t.* and *v.i.* (*Scot.*) to hitch. [Cf. Du. *hotsen*, Fr. *hocher*.]

hotchpotch, *hoch'poch*, **hotchpot**, *hoch'pot*, **hodgepodge**, *hoj'poj*, *n.* a confused mass of ingredients shaken or mixed together in the same pot : a kind of mutton-broth with vegetables of many kinds : a jumble.—*n.* **hotchpot**, a commixture of property in order to secure an equable division amongst children. [Fr. *hochepot*—*hocher*, to shake, and *pot*, a pot ; cf. Du. *hutspot*.]

hotel, *hō-tel'* (old-fashioned *ō-tel'*), *n.* a superior house for the accommodation of strangers : an inn : in France, also a public office, a private town-house, a palace.—*ns.* **hotel'-keeper, hôtelier** (Fr. *hôtelier* ; *ōt'ə-lyā*). [Fr. *hôtel*—L. *hospitālia*, guest-chambers—*hospes*.]

Hottentot, *hot'n-tot*, *n.* one of a dwindling, nomad, pastoral, pale-brown race in S.-W. Africa (orig. a Bushman-Bantu cross), calling themselves *khoikhoin* (men of men) : their language : a barbarian. — Also *adj.* — **Hottentot fig**, the edible fruit of a Mesembrianthemum ; **Hottentot's bread**, elephant-foot. [Du. imit.—from their staccato gibberish.]

hotter, *hot'er*, *v.i.* (*Scot.*) to vibrate : to tremble : to clatter : to totter : to jolt : to swarm.—*n.* vibration : commotion : swarming. [Cf. Flem. *hotteren*.]

houdah. See **howdah**.

houdan, *hōō'dan*, *n.* a black and white five-toed domestic fowl of a breed orig. from *Houdan* in Seine-et-Oise.

hough, *hok* (*Scot.* *hohh*), *n.* the joint on the hindleg of a quadruped, between the knee and fetlock, corresponding to the ankle-joint in man : a piece of meat extending from the hough-joint upward : in man, the back part of the knee-joint : the ham.—*v.t.* to hamstring :—*pr.p.* **hough'ing** ; *pa.t.* and *pa.p.* **houghed** (*hokt*).—Also **hock**.—*n.* **hough'er**. [O.E. *hóh*, the heel.]

hound, *hovnd*, *n.* (*arch.*) a dog : a dog of a kind used in hunting : a pursuer in a paper-chase : a contemptible scoundrel : a hunter, tracker, or assiduous seeker of anything.—*v.t.* to set on in chase : to drive by harassing.—*ns.* **hound'-fish**, a dog-fish ; **hounds'-berry**, dogwood ; **hounds'-foot** (Ger. *hundsfott*, -*futt*, vulva canina), a scoundrel. —*adj.* (*Scott*) scoundrelly.—*n.* **hound's'-tongue**, a plant (*Cynoglossum*) of the borage family (from its leaf).—**Gabriel('s) hounds**, (*coll.*) the yelping noise made by flights of wild-geese, ascribed to damned souls whipped on by the angel Gabriel ; **master of hounds**, the master of a pack of hounds. [O.E. *hund* ; Gr. *kyōn, kynos*, L. *canis*, Sans. *çvan.*]

hour, *owr*, *n.* 60 minutes, or the 24th part of a day : the time as indicated by a clock, &c. : an hour's journey, or three miles : a time or occasion : an angular unit (15°) of right ascension : (in *pl.*, *myth.*) the goddesses of the seasons and the hours : set times of prayer, the *canonical hours*, the offices or services prescribed for these, or a book containing them.—*ns.* **hour-ang'le**, (*astron.*) the angle (usu. measured as time) between the declination circle of a body observed and the observer's meridian ; **hour'-cir'cle**, a great circle passing through the celestial poles : the circle of an equatorial which shows the right ascension ; **hour'-glass**, an instrument for measuring the hours by the running of sand through a narrow neck.—*adj.* having the form of an hour-glass : constricted.—*n.* **hour'-hand**, the hand which shows the hour on a clock, &c.—*adj.* **hour'ly**, happening or done every hour : frequent.—*adv.* every hour : frequently.—*n.* **hour'plate**, a timepiece dial.—**at the eleventh hour**, at the last moment (Matt. xx. 6, 9) ; **in a good, or evil, hour**, under a fortunate, or an unfortunate, impulse—from the old belief in astrological influences ; **keep good hours**, to go to bed and to rise early : to lead a quiet and regular life ; **the small hours**, the hours from 1 to 3 or 4 a.m. [O.Fr. *hore* (Fr. *heure*)—L. *hōra*—Gr. *hōrā*.]

houri, *hōō'ri, hov'ri, n.* a nymph of the Mohammedan paradise : a voluptuously alluring woman. [Pers. *hūrī*—Ar. *hūriya*, a black-eyed girl.]

house, *hows, n.* a building for dwelling in : a building in general : a dwelling-place : an inn : a public-house : a household : a family in line of descent : kindred : a trading establishment : one of the twelve divisions of the heavens in astrology : a legislative or deliberative body or its meeting-place : a convent : a school boarding-house : the pupils of such a boarding-house collectively : a section of a school where no such boarding-house exists : an audience, auditorium, or performance : (*coll.*) the workhouse : (**the House**) at Oxford, Christ Church (*Aedes Christi*) : in London, the Stock Exchange : (*pl.* **houses**, *howz'iz*).—*adj.* domestic.—*v.t.* **house** (*howz*), to protect by covering : to shelter : to store : to provide houses for.—*v.i.* to take shelter : to reside. —*ns.* **house-a'gent** (*hows'*), one who arranges the buying, selling, and letting of houses ; **house'-boat**, a barge with a deck-cabin that may serve as a dwelling-place ; **house'-bote**, a tenant's right to wood to repair his house ; **house'-break'er**, one who breaks open and enters a house for the purpose of stealing, esp. by day : one who demolishes old houses ; **house'-break'ing** ; **house'-carl**, a member of a king's or a noble's bodyguard ; **house'-coat**, a woman's long dress, formed like a coat, worn at home ; **house'craft**, skill in domestic activities ; **house'-dog**, a dog kept in a house : a watch-dog ; **house'-du'ty, -tax**, a tax laid on inhabited houses ; **house'-fac'tor**, (*Scot.*) a house-agent ; **house'-fa'ther**, the male head of a household or community ; **house'-flag**, the distinguishing flag of a shipowner or shipping company ; **house'-fly**, the common fly universally distributed ; **house'ful** (*pl.* **house'fuls**) ; **house'hold**, those who are held together in the same house, and compose a family.—*adj.* pertaining to the house and family.—*ns.* **house'holder**, the holder or tenant of a house ; **house'keeper**, a person employed to keep house : one who has the chief care of a house : one who stays much at home : (*obs.*) a dispenser of hospitality : (*obs.*) a watch-dog ; **house'keeping**, the keeping or management of a house or of domestic affairs : (*obs.*) hospitality.—*adj.* domestic.—*n.* **house'-leek**, a plant (*Sempervivum tectorum*) of the stonecrop family with succulent leaves, often growing on roofs.—*adj.* **house'less**, without a house or home : having no shelter.—*ns.* **house'-line**, (*naut.*) a small line of three strands, for seizings, &c. ; **house'maid**, a maid employed to keep a house clean, &c. ; **house'-mas'ter**, the head of a boarding-house in connexion with a public school ; **house'-mate**, one sharing a house with another ; **house'-moth'er**, the mother of a family, the female head of a family ; **house'-par'ty**, a company of guests spending some days in a country-house.— *adj.* **house'-proud**, taking a pride in the condition of one's house.—*ns.* **house'-room**, room or place in a house ; **house'-stew'ard**, a steward who manages the household affairs of a great family ; **house'-sur'geon**, a resident surgeon in a hospital — so also **house'-physi'cian**.— *adj.* **house'-to-house**, performed or conducted by calling at house after house.—*n.* **house'top**, the top or roof of a house.—*adj.* **house'-trained**, (of animals) taught to be cleanly indoors.—*ns.* **house'-warm'ing**, an entertainment given after moving into a new house ; **housewife** (*hows'wif*, or *huz'if*), the mistress of a house : a female domestic manager : (*huz'if*) a pocket sewing-outfit.—*adj.* **house'wifely**.—*ns.* **house'wifery** (*huz'if-ri, hows'wif-ri, -wif-ri*)—(*Scot.*) **house'-wifeskep** ; **house'work**, domestic work, such as cooking, dusting, scrubbing, washing-up ; **housing** (*howz'ing*), houses, accommodation, or shelter, or the provision thereof : a cavity into which a timber fits.—Also *adj.*—**bring down the house**, to evoke very loud applause in a place of entertainment ; **household gods**, one's favourite domestic things—a playful use of the Roman *penates* ; **household suffrage**, or **franchise**, the right of householders to vote for members of parliament ; **household troops**, Guards regiments whose peculiar duty is to attend the sovereign and defend the metropolis ; **household word**, a familiar saying or name ; **housemaid's knee**, an inflammation of the sac between the knee-pan and the skin, to which housemaids are specially liable through kneeling on damp floors ; **house of call**, a house where the journeymen of a particular trade call when out of work : a house that one often visits ; **house of correction**, a jail ; **house of God, prayer, or worship**, a place of worship ; **house of ill-fame**, a brothel ; **House of Lords, Peers, Representatives** (see **lord**, **peer**, **represent**); **House of the People**, the lower house of the Indian parliament ; **housing scheme**, a plan for the designing, building, and provision of houses, esp. by a local authority: sometimes applied to an area coming under such a plan ; **Inner House**, the higher branch of the Court of Session, its jurisdiction chiefly appellate ; **Outer House**, the lower branch of the Court of Session ; **keep a good house**, to keep up a plentifully supplied table ; **keep house**, to maintain or manage an establishment ; **keep open house**, to give entertainment to all comers ; **keep the house**, to remain indoors : to take charge of the house or be on watch for the time being : to be confined to the house ; **like a house afire**, with astonishing rapidity ; **the Household**, the royal domestic establishment. [O.E. *hús* ; Goth, *hūs*, Ger. *haus*.]

housel, *howz'əl, n.* the eucharist : the act of taking or administering it.—*v.t.* to administer the eucharist to :—*pa.p.* **houselled**.—*n.* **hous'elling**.—*adj.* (*Spens.*) **hous'ling**, sacramental. [O.E. *hūsel*, sacrifice.]

housing, *howz'ing, n.* an ornamental covering for a horse : a saddle-cloth : (*pl.*) the trappings of a horse. [O.Fr. *houce*, a mantle, of Gmc. origin.]

hout, hout-tout, houts-touts. Same as **hoot**, &c.

Houyhnhnm, *hwin'əm, n.* one of the noble rational horse race in *Gulliver's Travels*. [Perh. **whinny**.]

Hova, *huv'ä, hōv'ä, n.* one of the dominant race in Madagascar, esp. of the middle class :—*pl.* **Hova, Hovas.**

hove, *hōv, hōōv*, Scot. *hüv, v.t.* to swell.—*v.i.* to swell : (*Spens.*) to rise. [Perh. a form of **heave**.]

hove, hoove, *hōōv, v.i.* (*Spens.*) to hover : to loiter, linger. [Origin unknown.]

hove, *pa.t.* and *pa.p.* of **heave**.

hovel, *hov'əl, huv'əl, n.* a small or wretched dwelling : a shed: (*dial.*) a framework for a corn-stack.—*v.t.* to put in a hovel : to shelter : to build like a hovel or shed, as a chimney with side opening.—*n.* **hov'el-post**, a post for supporting a corn-stack. [Origin doubtful.]

hoveller, *hov', huv'(ə-)lər, n.* a boatman acting as an uncertificated pilot or doing any kind of occasional work on the coast : a small coasting-vessel. [Origin doubtful.]

hoven, *hō'vən.* See **hoove**.

hover, *huv'ər, hov'ər, v.i.* to remain aloft flapping the wings : to remain suspended : to linger : to move about near.—*v.t.* to brood over.—*n.* act or state of hovering : (*U.S.*) a helicopter : an apparatus for keeping chicks warm.—*n.* **hov'er-fly**, a syrphid or other wasp-like fly that hovers and darts.—*adv.* **hov'eringly.** [Perh.—**hove** (2).]

how, *how, adv.* and *conj.* in what manner : to what extent : by what means : in what condition : how comes it that : to what an extent, in what a degree : that.—**and how** (*U.S. slang*), yes, certainly : very much indeed : I should think so indeed ; **how now**, what is this : why is this so ; **how's that** (*howzat'* ; *cricket*), the appeal of the fielding side to the umpire to give the batsman out ; **the how and the why**, the manner and the cause. [O.E. *hú*, prob. an adverbial form from *hwá*, who.]

how, howe, *how, n.* (*Scot.*) a hollow. [**hole.**]

how, *how, n.* (*prov.*) a low hill. [O.N. *haugr* ; cf. O.E. *héah*, high.]

howbeit, *how-bē'it, conj.* be it how it may : notwithstanding: yet: however—(*Spens.*) **howbe'**, [**how, be, it.**]

howdah, houdah, *hov'dä, n.* a pavilion or seat fixed on an elephant's back. [Ar. *haudaj*.]

howdie, howdy. *how'di, n.* (*Scot.*) a midwife. [Poss. O.E. *hold*, gracious.]

howdy, *how'di, interj.* a colloquial form of the common greeting, *How do you do?*—*n.* **how'-d' ye-do', how'dy-do'**, a troublesome state of matters.

however, *how-ev'ər, adv.* and *conj.* in whatever manner or degree: nevertheless: at all events. [**how, ever.**]

howff, houff, *howf, n.* (*Scot.*) a haunt, resort.—*v.i.* to resort to a place. [Poss. O.E. *hof*, a house.]

howitzer, *how'its-ər, n.* a short, squat gun, used for shelling at a steep angle, esp. in siege and trench warfare. [Ger. *haubitze*—Czech *houfnice*, a sling.]

howk, *howk, v.t.* and *v.i.* (*Scot.*) to dig, burrow. [Earlier *holk* ; cf. L.G. *holken.*]

howker, *how'kər, n.* Same as **hooker.**

howl, *howl, v.i.* to yell or cry, as a wolf or dog : to utter a long, loud, whining sound : to wail : to roar.—*v.t.* to utter with outcry : (*pr.p.* **howl'ing** ; *pa.t.* and *pa.p.* **howled**).—*n.* a loud, prolonged cry of distress : a mournful cry : a loud sound like a yell, made by the wind, a wireless receiver, &c.—*n.* **howl'er**, one who howls : a S. American monkey, with prodigious power of voice : (*slang*) a glaring and amusing blunder.—*adj.* **howl'ing**, filled with howlings, as of the wind, or of wild beasts : (*slang*) tremendous.—*n.* a howl. [O.Fr. *huller*—L. *ululāre*, to shriek or howl—*ulula*, an owl ; cf. Ger. *heulen*, Eng. **owl.**]

howlet, *how'lit, n.* an owlet : (*Scot. hool'it*) an owl. [**owlet.**]

howre, an obs. form of **hour.**

howso, *how'sō, adv.* (*obs.*) howsoever.

howsoever, *how-sō-ev'ər, adv.* in what way soever : although : however.—Provincial forms are **howsomev'er** and **howsomdev'er**. [**how, so, ever** ; and M.E. *sum*, as.]

hox, *hoks, v.t.* (*Shak.*) to hough or hamstring. [O.E. *hóhsinu*, hough-sinew.]

hoy, *hoi, n.* a large one-decked boat, commonly rigged as a sloop. [M.Du. *hoei* ; Du. *heu*, Flem. *hui.*]

hoy, *hoi, interj.* ho! stop!—*v.t.* to incite, drive on.

hoyden, hoiden, *hoi'dən, n.* a tomboy, a romp : formerly also *masc.*—*ns.* **hoy'denhood, hoy'denism.**—*adj.* **hoy'denish.** [Perh. Du. *heiden*, a heathen, a gypsy, *heide*, heath.]

huanaco. Same as **guanaco.**

hub, *hub, n.* the nave of a wheel : a mark at which quoits, &c., are cast.—*n.* **hub'-brake**, a brake acting on the hub of a wheel.—**hub of the universe**, Boston, U.S.A. [Prob. a form of **hob** (1) ; origin unknown.]

hubble-bubble, *hub'l-bub'l, n.* a bubbling sound : tattle : confusion : a crude kind of hookah. [Reduplic. from **bubble.**]

hubbub, *Shak.* **whoobub**, *hub'ub, n.* a confused sound of many voices : riot : uproar.—Also **hubb'uboo**. [App. of Irish origin.]

hubby, *hub'i, n.* (*vulg.*) a diminutive of **husband.**

hubris, *hū'bris, n.* (*academic slang*) insolence : arrogance, such as invites disaster : overweening.—*adj.* **hubris'tic.**—*adv.* **hubris'tically.** [Gr. *hybris.*]

huckaback, *huk'ə-bak, n.* a coarse linen or cotton with raised surface, used for towels, &c. [Origin unknown.]

huckle, *huk'l, n.* a hunch : the hip.—Also **huck.**—*adjs.* **huck'le-backed, -shoul'dered**, having the back or shoulders round.—*n.* **huckle'-bone**, the hip-bone : the astragalus. [Poss. conn. with **hook.**]

huckleberry, *huk'l-bər-i, -ber-i, n.* a N. American shrub (Gaylussacia) akin to whortleberry : its fruit: extended to species of whortleberry.—*n.* **huck'leberrying**. [App. for **hurtleberry.**]

huckster, *huk'stər, n.* a retailer of smallwares, a hawker or pedlar : a mean, haggling fellow.—*v.i.* to deal in small articles : to higgle meanly.—*ns.* **huck'sterage** ; **huck'steress, huck'stress** ; **huck'stery.** [Origin obscure.]

huddle, *hud'l, v.t.* (*obs.*) to hustle out of sight, hush up : to jumble : to hustle, bundle : to drive, draw, throw or crowd together in disorder : to put hastily : to perform perfunctorily and hastily.—*v.i.* to crowd in confusion.—*n.* a confused mass : a jumble : confusion : perfunctory haste.—*adj.* **hudd'led**, jumbled : crowded : in a heap : crouching. [Poss. conn. with **hide.**]

Neutral vowels in unaccented syllables : *el'ə-mənt, in'fənt, ran'dəm*

huddup, *hud-up′*, *interj*. (*U.S.*) get up (to a horse).
Hudibrastic, *hū-di-bras′tik*, *adj*. similar in style to *Hudibras*, a metrical burlesque on the Puritans by Samuel Butler (1612-80).—*n.pl*. **Hudibras′tics**, verses of the form used in *Hudibras*, a burlesque cacophonous octosyllabic couplet with extravagant rhymes.]

hue (*Spens*. hew), *hū*, *n*. appearance: colour: tint: dye.—*adjs*. **hued**, having a hue; **hue′less**. [O.E. *hīow*, *hēow* (W.S. *hīw*, *hīew*); Sw. *hy*, complexion.]

hue, *hū*, *n*. a shouting, clamour.—*n*. **hu′er**, a pilchard fishermen's look-out man.—**hue and cry**, an outcry calling upon all to pursue one who is to be made prisoner: a proclamation or publication to the same effect: the pursuit itself: a loud clamour about something. [Imit.; perh. Fr. *huer*.]

huff, *huf*, *n*. (*obs*.) a puff of wind: (*obs*.) bluster: (*obs*.) a blusterer: a fit of anger, sulks, or offended dignity: an act of huffing in draughts.—*v.t*. (*obs*.) to puff up: to hector: to give offence: (in draughts) to remove from the board for omitting capture.—*v.i*. (*obs*.) to blow, puff, swell: to take offence: to bluster.—*adj*. **huff′-cap**, (*obs*.) of liquor, heady: blustering.—*n*. (*obs*.) a bully, blusterer.—*adjs*. **huff′ish**, **huff′y**, given to huff: touchy: ready to take offence.—*advs*. **huff′ishly**, **huff′ily**.—*ns*. **huff′ishness**, **huff′iness**. [Imit.]

hug, *hug* *v.t*. to clasp close with the arms: to cherish: to keep close to, skirt: (*pr.p*. **hug′ging**; *pa.t*. and *pa.p*. **hugged**).—*n*. a close embrace: a particular grip in wrestling.—*n*. **hug′-me-tight**, a close-fitting knitted garment.—**hug oneself**, to congratulate oneself. [Ety. obscure.]

huge, *hūj*, *adj*. vast: enormous.—*adv*. **huge′ly**.—*n*. **huge′ness**.—*adj*. **huge′ous**, (*arch*.) huge.—*adv*. **huge′ously**. — *n*. **huge′ousness**. — *adj*. **hug′y** (*arch*.). [O.Fr. *ahuge*.]

hugger-mugger, *hug′ər-mug′ər*, *n*. secrecy: confusion.—*adj*. secret: disorderly. [Origin obscure.]

Huguenot, *hū′gə-not*, or *-nō*, *n*. (*hist*.) a French Protestant.—Also *adj*. [Fr.,—earlier *eiguenot*— Ger. *eidgenoss*, confederate, assimilated to the name *Hugues*, Hugh.]

huia, *hōō′yä*, *n*. a New Zealand bird akin to the crows and starlings. [Maori; imit.]

huitain, *wē-tān′*, *n*. a group of eight lines of verse. [Fr.,—*huit*, eight.]

hula-hula, *hōō′lä-hōō′lä*, *n*. a Hawaiian women's dance.—Also **hu′la**. [Hawaiian.]

hule. Same as **ule**.

hulk, *hulk*, *n*. an unwieldy ship: a dismantled ship: a big lubberly fellow: anything unwieldy: often by confusion, a hull.—*pl*. **the hulks**, old ships formerly used as prisons.—*adjs*. **hulk′ing**, **hulk′y**, clumsy. [O.E. *hulc*, perh. Gr. *holkas*, a towed ship—*helkein*, to draw.]

hull, *hul*, *n*. a husk or outer covering.—*v.t*. to separate from the hull: to husk.—*adj*. **hull′y**, having husks or pods. [O.E. *hulu*, a husk, as of corn—*helan*, to cover; Ger. *hülle*, a covering, *hehlen*, to cover.]

hull, *hul*, *n*. the frame or body of a ship: part of a flying-boat in contact with the water.—*v.t*. to pierce the hull of.—*v.i*. (*Shak*.) to float or drift, as a mere hull, to float about.—*adv*. **hull′-down′**, so far away that the hull is below the horizon. [Perh. same word as above, modified in meaning by confusion with Du. *hol*, a ship's hold, or with **hulk**.]

hullabaloo, *hul-ə-bə-lōō′*, *n*. an uproar. [Perh. **halloo**.]

hullo, *hu-lō′*, *vb*., *n*., and *interj*. Same as **hallo**.

Hulsean, *hul′si-ən*, *adj*. of or pertaining to John Hulse (1708-89), founder of the Hulsean divinity lectures at Cambridge.

hum, *hum*, *v.i*. to make a sound like bees or that represented by *m*: to sing with closed lips without words or articulation: to pause in speaking and utter an inarticulate sound: to stammer through embarrassment: to be audibly astir.—*v.i*. to be busily active.—*v.t*. to render by humming: (*obs*.) to applaud: (*pr.p*. **humm′ing**; *pa.t*. and *pa.p*. **hummed**).—*n*. the noise of bees: a murmurous sound: an inarticulate murmur: the sound of humming.—*n*. **humm′er**, a person or thing that hums, as a bee, a humming-bird, a top: one who

makes things hum.—*n*. and *adj*. **humm′ing**.—*ns*. **humm′ing-bird**, any member of the tropical family Trochilidae, very small birds of brilliant plumage and rapid flight (from the humming sound of the wings); **humm′ing-top**, a top that gives a humming sound as it spins.—**hum and haw** (or ha), to make inarticulate sounds when at a loss: to shilly-shally; **humming ale**, ale that froths up well, or that makes the head hum; **make things hum**, to set things agoing briskly. [Imit.; cf. Ger. *hummen*, *humsen*.]

hum, *hum*, *v.t*. to impose on.—*n*. an imposition. [Contr. of **humbug**.]

hum, *hum*, *interj*. expressing doubt or reluctance to agree.

huma, *hōō′mä*, *n*. a fabulous restless bird. [Pers. *humā*, phoenix.]

human, *hū′man*, *adj*. belonging or pertaining to or of the nature of man or mankind: having the qualities of a man or the limitations of man: humane: not invidiously superior: genial.—*n*. (*coll*.) a human being.—*n*. **hū′mankind**, the human species.—*adj*. **hū′manlike**.—*adv*. **hū′manly**, in a human manner: by human agency: having regard to human limitations: humanely.—*ns*. **hū′manness**; **hū′manoid**, one of the immediate kindred of man (closer than *anthropoid*). [Fr. *humain*—L. *hūmānus*—*homō*, a human being.]

humane, *hū-mān′*, *adj*. having the feelings proper to man: kind: tender: merciful, humanising, as *humane letters*, i.e. classical, elegant, polite.—*adv*. **humane′ly**.—*n*. **humane′ness**, kindness: tenderness.

humanise, *hū′mən-īz*, *v.t*. to render human or humane: to soften: to impart human qualities to, make like that which is human or of mankind.— *v.i*. to become humane or civilised.—*n*. **human′isā′tion**.

humanist, *hū′mən-ist*, *n*. a student of polite literature: at the Renaissance, a student of Greek and Roman literature: a student of human nature: a pragmatist.—Also *adj*.—*n*. **hū′manism**, literary culture: any system which puts human interests paramount: (*phil*.) pragmatism: a critical application of the logical method of pragmatism to all the sciences.—*adj*. **humanist′ic**.

humanitarian, *hū-man′i-tā′ri-ən*, *n*. one who denies Christ's divinity, and holds him to be a mere man: a philanthropist.—*adj*. of or belonging to humanity, benevolent.—*n* **humanitā′rianism**.

humanity, *hū-man′it-i*, *n*. the nature peculiar to a human being: humanness: humaneness: the kind feelings of man: mankind collectively:—*pl*. **human′ities**, in Scotland, grammar, rhetoric, Latin, Greek, and poetry, so called from their humanising effects.—**professor of humanity**, in Scottish universities, the professor of Latin. [Fr. *humanité*—L. *hūmānitās*—*hūmānus*—*homō*, a man.]

humble, *hum′bl* (old-fashioned *um′bl*), *adj*. low: lowly: modest: unpretentious: having a low opinion of oneself or of one's claims: abased.— *v.t*. to bring down to the ground: to lower: to abase: to mortify: to degrade.—*adj*. **hum′ble-mouthed**, humble in speech.—*ns*. **hum′bleness**; **hum′blesse** (*Spens*.)—*adj*. and *n*. **hum′bling**.—*advs*. **hum′blingly**, **hum′bly**.—**your humble servant**, old formula used in subscribing a letter. [Fr.,—L. *humilis*, low—*humus*, the ground.]

humble, *hum′bl*. Same as **hummel**.

humble-bee, *hum′bl-bē*, *n*. the bumble-bee (Bombus), a large noisy wild bee. [Perh. from *humble*, freq. of **hum**; cf. Ger. *hummel*.]

humbles, see **umbles**.—*n*. **hum′ble-pie′**, a pie made from the umbles of a deer.—**eat humble-pie**, punningly, to humiliate oneself, eat one's own words.

humbug, *hum′bug*, *n*. an imposition under fair pretences: hollowness, pretence: one who so imposes: a lump of toffee, peppermint drop, or the like.—*v.t*. to deceive: to hoax: to cajole.— *v.i*. to potter about:—*pr.p*. **hum′bugging**; *pa.t*. and *pa.p*. **hum′bugged**.—*adj*. **humbug′able**.— *ns*. **hum′bugger**; **hum′buggery**. [Appears about 1750; origin unknown.]

humbuzz, *hum'buz*, *n*. (*local*) a cockchafer : a bull-roarer. [hum, buzz.]

humdrum, *hum'drum'*, *adj*. dull : droning : monotonous : commonplace.—*n*. a stupid fellow : monotony : tedious talk. [hum, and perh. drum.]

humdudgeon, *hum-duj'ən*, *n*. (*Scot*.) an unnecessary outcry.

Humean, Humian, *hū'mi-ən*, *adj*. pertaining to David *Hume*, or his philosophy.—*n*. a follower of Hume.—*ns*. **Hūm'ism, Hūm'ist**.

humect, *hū-mekt'*, *v.t.* and *v.i.* to make or become moist.—Also **humect'ate**.—*adjs*. and *ns*. **humect'-ant, humect'ive**. — *n*. **humectā'tion**. [L. (*h*)*ūmectāre—ūmēre*, to be moist.]

humerus, *hū'mər-əs*, *n*. the bone of the upper arm : —*pl*. **hū'meri**.—*adj*. **hū'meral**, belonging to the shoulder or the humerus.—*n*. an oblong vestment worn on the shoulders. [L. (*h*)*umerus*, shoulder.]

humgruffin, *hum-gruf'in*, **humgruffian**, (*-i-ən*), *n*. a terrible person. [App. hum and griffin.]

humhum, *hum'hum*, *n*. a kind of plain, coarse cotton cloth used in the East Indies.

humic. See under humus.

humid, *hū'mid*, *adj*. moist : damp : rather wet. —*v.t.* **humid'ify**, to moisten. — *n*. **humid'ity**, moisture : a moderate degree of wetness.—*adv*. **hu'-midly**.—*ns*. **hu'midness ; hum'idor**, a chamber, &c., for keeping anything moist, as cigars : a contrivance for keeping the air moist. [L. (*h*)*ūmidus*—(*h*)*ūmēre*, to be moist.]

humify, *hū'mi-fī*, *v.i.* to moisten.—Also (*obs*.) **hu'mefy**.—*n*. **humificā'tion**. [L. (*h*)*ūmificāre*.]

humify, *hū'mi-fī*, *v.t.* and *v.i.* to make or turn into humus.—*n*. **humificā'tion**. [humus.]

humiliate, *hū-mil'i-āt*, *v.t.* to humble. — *adjs*. **humil'iant**, humiliating ; **humil'iāting ; humil'-iative ; humil'iatory** (*-ə-tər-i*).—*ns*. **humiliā'-tion ; humil'iātor**. [L. *humiliāre, -ātum*.]

humility, *hū-mil'i-ti*, *n*. the state or quality of being humble : lowliness of mind : modesty. [O.Fr. *humilite*—L. *humilitās, -ātis—humilis*, low.]

hummel, *hum'l*, **humble**, *hum'(b)l*, *adj*. hornless : awnless.—*n*. a hornless stag.—*v.t.* to make hummel. —*ns*. **hum'lie**, a polled or hornless cow, ox, &c.: **humm'eller**, a machine for removing barley awns.—**hummel** (usu. **humble**) **bonnet**, a type of Scotch cap worn by Highland regiments before the introduction (1851) of the glengarry. [Cf. L.G. *hummel, hommel*.]

hummer, humming. See under hum.

hummock, *hum'ək*, *n*. a hillock : a pile or ridge of ice.—*adjs*. **humm'ocked, humm'ocky**. [Origin unknown : at first nautical.]

hummum. Same as hammam.

humogen, *hū'mō-jən*, *n*. a fertiliser composed of peat treated with a culture of nitrogen-fixing bacteria. [L. *humus*, soil, Gr. *gennaein*, to produce.]

humour, *ū'mər*, by some *hū'mər*, *n*. moisture : a fluid : a fluid of the animal body, esp. any one of the four that in old physiology were supposed to determine temperament : temperament or disposition of mind : state of mind (*good* or *ill humour*) : disposition : caprice : (*Shak*.) in Corporal Nym's vocabulary (also as *adj*. and *v.t.*, and *adj*. **humoured**) a word of any meaning, down to no meaning at all : a mental quality which apprehends and delights in the ludicrous and mirthful : playful fancy.—*v.t.* to go in with the humour of : to gratify by compliance.—*adj*. **hū'moral**, pertaining to or proceeding from the humours.—*ns*. **hū'moral-ism**, the state of being humoral : the doctrine that diseases have their seat in the humours ; **hū'mor-alist**, one who favours the doctrine of humoralism ; **hūmoresk'**, **hūmoresque'**, a musical caprice ; **hū'morist**, one whose conduct and conversation are regulated by humour or caprice : one who studies or portrays the humours of people : one possessed of humour : a writer of comic stories. —*adjs*. **hūmoris'tic**, humorous ; **hū'morous**, governed by humour : capricious : irregular : full of humour : exciting laughter.—*adv*.**hū'morously**.—*n*. **hū'morousness**.—*adjs*. **hū'mourless** ; **hū'mour-some**, capricious, petulant.—*n*. **hū'moursome-ness**.—**comedy of humours**, the comedy of Ben Jonson and his school in which the characters

instead of being conceived in the round are little more than personifications of single qualities ; **out of humour**, out of temper, displeased. [O.Fr. *humor* (Fr. *humeur*)—L. (*h*)*ūmor*—(*h*)*ūmēre*, to be moist.]

humous. See under humus.

hump, *hump*, *n*. a hunch on the back : a protuberance : (*Austr*.) a walk with swag on back : (*slang*) despondency : sulks.—*v.t.* to bend in a hump : (*U.S. slang*) to prepare for a great exertion : (*slang*) to vex or annoy : (*Austr*.) to shoulder, to carry on the back.—*v.i.* to put forth effort.—*n*. **hump'back**, a back with a hump or hunch : a person with a humpback : a Pacific species of salmon : a whale with a humplike dorsal fin.—*adjs*. **hump'back, hump'-backed**, having a humpback ; **humped**, having a hump ; **hump'y**, full of humps or protuberances. [Origin obscure.]

humph, *hmh*, *interj*. expressive of reserved doubt or dissatisfaction.

Humphrey, to dine with Duke. See dine.

Humpty-dumpty, *hum'ti-dum'ti*, *n*. a short, squat, egg-like being of nursery folklore : a gypsy drink, ale boiled with brandy.—*adj*. short and broad.

humpy, *hum'pi*, *n*. (*Austr*.) a hut. [Native *oompi*.]

humstrum, *hum'strum*, *n*. a hurdy-gurdy or other musical instrument. [hum, strum, with imit. effect.]

humus, *hūm'əs*, *n*. decomposed organic matter in the soil.—*adjs*. **hū'mic, hū'mous**. [L. *humus* ; cf. Gr. *chamai*, on the ground.]

Hun, *hun*, *n*. one of a powerful, squat, swarthy, and savage nomad race of Asia who moved westwards, and under Attila (433-453) overran Europe : a Hungarian : a barbarian (*war slang* of 1914) a German.—*adjs*. **Hunn'ic, Hunn'ish**. [O.E. (*pl*.) *Hūne, Hūnas* ; L. *Hunnī* ; Gr. *Ounnoi, Chounnoi*.]

hunch, *hunsh*, *n*. a hump : a lump : (*U.S.*) a premonition : a hint.—*v.t.* to hump, bend.—*n*. **hunch'back**, one with a hunch or lump on his back.—*adj*. **hunch'backed**. [Origin obscure.]

hundred, *hun'drəd*, *n*. the number of ten times ten : applied also to various other numbers used in telling : a set of a hundred things : a hundred pounds, dollars, &c.: a division of a county in England orig. supposed to contain a hundred families : (*pl*. **hundreds**, or, preceded by a numeral, **hundred**).—*adj*. to the number of a hundred : (*obs*. or *dial*.) hundredth.—*n*. **hun'-dreder, -or**, (*hist*.) the bailiff, or an inhabitant, of a hundred.—*adj., adv.,* and *n*. **hun'dredfold**, folded a hundred times : in a hundred divisions : a hundred times as much.—*adj*. **hun'dred-per-cent'**, out-and-out : thorough-going.—*n*. **hun'-dred-per-cent'er**, (*U.S.*) an uncompromising patriot.—*n.pl*. **hun'dreds-and-thou'sands**, little sweets used as an ornamental dressing.—*adj*. **hun'dredth**, last of a hundred : equal to one of a hundred equal parts.—*n*. one of a hundred equal parts.—*n*. **hun'dredweight**, the twentieth part of a ton, or 112 lb. avoirdupois : orig. a hundred lb., abbreviated *cwt*. (*c* standing for L. *centum, wt*. for weight).—**Chiltern Hundreds**, a district of Bucks, whose stewardship is a nominal office under the Crown, the temporary acceptance of which by a member of parliament enables him to vacate his seat ; **great, or long, hundred**, usually six score : sometimes some other number greater than ten tens (as of herrings, 132 or 126) ; **Hundred Days**, the time between Napoleon's return from Elba and his final downfall after Waterloo (the reign lasted exactly 95 days, March 20-June 22, 1815) ; **Hundred Years' War**, the struggle between England and France, from 1337 down to 1453 ; **not a hundred miles from**, at ; **Old Hundred** (see old). [O.E. *hundred*—old form *hund*, a hundred, with the suffix *-red*, a reckoning.]

hung, *pa.t.* and *pa.p.* of **hang**.—*n*. **hung'-beef**, beef cured and dried.

Hungarian, *hung-gā'ri-ən*, *adj*. pertaining to Hungary or its inhabitants.—*n*. a person of Hungarian birth, descent, or citizenship : the Magyar or Hungarian language.—**Hungary** (*hung'gə-ri*) **water**, oil of rosemary distilled with alcohol (said to have been used by a queen of Hungary). [Cf. Ugrian.]

hunger, *hung'gər*, *n*. craving for food : need or

lack of food : strong desire for anything.—*v.i.* to crave food : to long.—*adjs.* **hung′er-bitten**, bitten, pained, or weakened by hunger ; **hung′erful**, hungry ; **hung′erly**, (*Shak.*) hungry.—*adv.* (*Shak.*) hungrily.—*ns.* **hung′er-march**, a procession of unemployed or others in need, as a demonstration ; **hunger′-march′er** ; **hung′er-strike**, prolonged refusal of all food by a prisoner as a form of protest, or a means to ensure release.—Also *v.i.*—*n.* **hung′er-strik′er.**—*adv.* **hung′rily.**—*adj.* **hung′ry**, having eager desire for food (or anything else): greedy: lean: poor. [O.E. *hungor* (n.), *hyngran* (vb.) ; cf. Ger. *hunger*, Du. *honger*, &c.]

hunk, *hungk*, *n.* a lump. [Same as **hunch.**]

hunk, *hungk*, *n.* (*U.S.*) goal or base in boys' games.—*n.* **hunk′er**, a conservative.—*adj.* **hunk′y**, in good position or condition. [Du. *honk.*]

hunker, *hungk′ər*, *v.i.* (*Scot.*) to squat down.—*n.pl.* **hunk′ers**, the hams. [Origin obscure ; perh. conn. with O.N. *húka*, to squat.]

hunks, *hungks*, *n.sing.* a miserly curmudgeon. [Origin unknown.]

hunt, *hunt*, *v.t.* to chase or go in quest of for prey or sport: to seek or pursue game over: to ransack: to use in the hunt: to search for: to pursue: to hound, drive.—*v.i.* to go out in pursuit of game: to search: (*mech.*) to oscillate or vary in speed.—*n.* a chase of wild animals: search: a pack of hunting hounds: an association of huntsmen: the district hunted by a pack: (*Shak.*) game killed in a hunt: (*obs.*) a huntsman.—*ns.* **hunt′-count′er**, (*Shak.*) perh. one who hunts counter ; **hunt′er**, one who hunts (*fem.* **hunt′ress**): a horse used in the chase: a watch whose face is protected with a metal case (**a half′-hunt′er**, if that case has a small circle of glass let in) ; **hun′ter's-moon**, full moon following harvest-moon ; **hunt′ing**, the pursuit of wild game, the chase.—Also *adj.*—*ns.* **hunt′ing-box, -lodge, -seat**, a temporary abode for hunting ; **hunt′ing-cap**, a form of cap much worn in the hunting-field ; **hunt′ing-cog**, an extra cog in one of two geared wheels, by means of which the order of contact of cogs is changed at every revolution ; **hunt′ing-crop, -whip**, a short whip with a crooked handle and a loop of leather at the end, used in the hunting-field ; **hunt′ing-field**, the scene or sphere of hunting, esp. fox-hunting: the assemblage of huntsmen ; **hunt′ing-ground**, a place or region for hunting ; **hunt′ing-horn**, a horn used in hunting, a bugle ; **hunt′ing-knife, -sword**, a knife or short sword used to despatch the game when caught, or to skin and cut it up ; **hunt′ing-song**, a song about hunting ; **hunt′ing-tide**, the season of hunting ; **hunts′man**, one who hunts: a servant who manages the hounds during the chase ; **hunts′manship**, the qualifications of a huntsman ; **hunt′s′-up**, (*Shak.*) a tune or song intended to arouse huntsmen in the morning—hence, anything calculated to arouse ; **hunt′-the-gowk**, the making of an April fool: a fool's errand, a deception, or a hoax, appropriate to the First of April.—Also *adj.*—*v.t.* to make an April fool of. — *n.* **hunt-the-slipp′er**, a game in which one in the middle of a ring tries to catch a shoe passed around by the others.—**happy hunting-grounds**, the paradise of the Red Indian ; **hunt after**, to seek for ; **hunt counter**, to follow the scent backwards ; **hunt down**, to pursue to extremities: to persecute out of existence ; **hunting mass**, a hasty and abridged mass said for impatient hunters ; **hunt the letter**, to affect alliteration ; **hunt up**, to seek out. [O.E. *huntian* ; prob. conn. with *hentan*, to seize.]

Hunterian, *hun-tē′ri-ən*, *adj.* of or pertaining to the surgeon John *Hunter* (1728-93), to his anatomical collection, nucleus of the Hunterian Museum in London, or to the annual Hunterian Oration at the Royal College of Surgeons: of or pertaining to his elder brother, William *Hunter* (1718-83), or his museum in Glasgow.

Huntingdonian, *hun-ting-dō′ni-ən*, *n.* a member of the Countess of Huntingdon's Connexion, a denomination of Calvinistic Methodists founded by Whitefield with Selina, Countess of *Huntingdon* (1707-91).—Also *adj.*

Huon-pine, *hū′ən-pīn′*, *n.* a Tasmanian conifer (*Dacrydium Franklinii*), found first on the *Huon* river.

hup, *hup*, *v.i.* to shout hup: of a horse, to go on: (*Scot.*) to turn to the right.—*v.t.* to turn (a horse or plough ox) to the right.—*n.* and *interj.* a cry of 'hup'—opp. to *hie* or *wind.*—**neither hup nor wind**, (*Scott*) neither do one thing nor another.

hupaithric, *hū-pāth′rik*, *adj.* hypaethral (q.v.).

hurcheon, *hur′chən*, Scots form of **urchin.**

hurdies, *hur′diz*, *n.pl.* (*Scot.*) the buttocks. [Origin unknown.]

hurdle, *hur′dl*, *n.* a frame of twigs or sticks interlaced: (*agri.*) a movable frame of timber or iron for gates, &c.: a rude sledge on which criminals were drawn to the gallows: (in *pl.*) a hurdle-race.—*v.t.* to enclose with hurdles.—*v.i.* to jump as over a hurdle: to run a hurdle-race.—*ns.* **hurd′ler**, a maker of hurdles: a hurdle-racer ; **hur′dle-race**, a race in which hurdles have to be cleared ; **hur′dle-rac′er** ; **hur′dle-rac′ing** ; **hur′dling.** [O.E. *hyrdel* ; Ger. *hürde.*]

hurds, hurden. Same as **hards, harden** (see **hards**).

hurdy-gurdy, *hur′di-gur′di*, *n.* a musical stringed instrument, like a rude violin, whose strings are sounded by the turning of a wheel: a hand-organ: a water-wheel driven by impact. [Imit.]

hurl, *hurl*, *v.t.* to fling with violence: (*Scot.*) to wheel: (*Scot.*) to convey in a wheeled vehicle.—*v.i.* to dash: (*Scot.*) to travel in a wheeled vehicle: to play hurley.—*n.* act of hurling: (*Scot.*) a trip or journey in a wheeled vehicle.—*ns.* **hurl′-barrow**, (*Scot.*) a wheelbarrow ; **hurl′er** ; **hurl′ey**, in Ireland, hockey, or a hockey-stick ; **hurl′ing**, in Ireland, hockey ; **hur′ley-house**, (*Scott*) a house in a state of disrepair ; **hurl′y**, (*Scot.*) a large two-wheeled barrow ; **hurl′y-hack′et**, (*Scot.*) a carriage, gig: an improvised sledge: sledging. [Cf. L.G. *hurreln*, to hurl, precipitate ; influenced by **hurtle** and **whirl.**]

hurly, *hur′li*, *n.* commotion: tumult.—*n.* **hurly-burly** (*hur′li-bur′li*), tumult: confusion.—Also *adj.* and *adv.* [Perh. from **hurl.**]

Huronian, *hū-rō′ni-an*, *n.* and *adj.* (*geol.*) upper Pre-Cambrian of Canada, well exemplified north of lake *Huron.*

hurrah, hurra, *hur-ä′, hoor-ä′*, **hurray, -ä′**, *interj.* an exclamation of approbation or joy.—Also *n.* and *v.i.* [Cf. Norw., Sw., Dan. *hurra*, Ger. *hurrah*, Du. *hoera.*]

hurricane, *hur′i-kin, -kān*, *n.* a West Indian cyclonic storm of great violence: a wind of extreme violence (over 75 miles an hour): (*fig.*) anything tempestuous: (*obs.*) a social party, a rout: a type of fighting aeroplane.—*ns.* **hurr′icane-deck**, a light partial deck over the saloon of some steamers ; **hurr′icane-lamp**, a lamp designed to defy strong wind ; **hurrica′no**, (*obs.*) a hurricane: (*Shak.*) a waterspout. [Sp. *huracán*, from Carib.]

hurry, *hur′i*, *v.t.* to urge forward: to hasten.—*v.i.* to move or act with haste, esp. perturbed or impatient haste: (*pr.p.* **hurr′ying** ; *pa.t.* and *pa.p.* **hurr′ied**).—*n.* a driving forward: haste: flurried haste: flurry: commotion: a rush: need for haste: (*mus.*) a tremolo passage for strings, or drum roll, in connexion with an exciting situation. — *adj.* **hurr′ied.** — *adv.* **hurr′iedly.** — *n.* **hurr′iedness.** — *n.* and *adj.* **hurr′ying.** — *adv.* **hurr′yingly.**—*n.* **hurr′y-skurr′y, -scurr′y**, confusion and bustle.—*adv.* confusedly.—**hurry up**, make haste. [Prob. imit. ; cf. Old Sw. *hurra*, to whirl round.]

hurst, *hurst*, *n.* a wood, a grove. [O.E. *hyrst.*]

hurt, *hurt*, *v.t.* to cause pain to: to damage: to injure: to wound, as the feelings.—*v.i.* to give pain: to be the seat of pain: to be injured: (*pa.t.* and *pa.p.* **hurt**).—*n.* a wound: injury.—*adj.* injured: pained in body or mind.—*n.* **hurt′er**, that which hurts: a beam, block, &c., to protect a wall from wheels: the shoulder of an axle against which the hub strikes.—*adj.* **hurt′ful**, causing hurt or loss: mischievous.—*adv.* **hurt′fully.**—*n.* **hurt′fulness.**—*adj.* **hurt′less**, without hurt or injury, harmless.—*adv.* **hurt′lessly.**—*n.*

hurt′lessness. [O.Fr. *hurter* (Fr. *heurter*), to knock, to run against.]

hurtle, *hurt′l*, *v.t.* to dash: to hurl: (*Spens.*) to brandish.—*v.i.* to clash: to rattle: to move rapidly with a clattering sound. [Freq. of *hurt* in its original sense.]

hurtleberry, a form of **whortleberry.**

husband, *huz′bond*, *n.* a man to whom a woman is married: (*obs.*) a husbandman: a manager: a thrifty manager.—*v.t.* to supply with a husband: to become, be, or act as, a husband to: to manage with economy: to economise: to cultivate.—*ns.* **hus′bandage,** allowance or commission of a ship's husband; **hus′bandland,** (*hist.*) a manorial tenant's holding: two oxgangs.—*adjs.* **hus′bandless; hus′bandlike; hus′bandly,** frugal, thrifty, pertaining to or befitting a husband.—*ns.* **hus′bandman,** a working farmer: one who labours in tillage; **hus′bandry,** the business of a farmer: tillage: economical management: thrift.—**ship′s husband,** an owner's agent who manages the affairs of a ship in port. [O.E. *húsbonda*, O.N. *húsbóndi*—*hús*, a house, *búandi*, inhabiting, pr.p. of O.N. *búa*, to dwell; cf. **boor, bower,** and Ger. *bauen*, to till.]

hush, *hush*, *interj.* or *imper.* silence: be still.—*n.* a silence, esp. after noise: a rush of water or its sound: (*min.*) the washing away of surface soil to lay bare bedrock.—*adj.* silent: quiet.—*v.i.* to become silent or quiet.—*v.t.* to make quiet: to calm: to procure silence or secrecy about: to pour in a stream: (*min.*) to wash away or to pour in order to expose bedrock.—*n.* **hush′aby** (*-ə-bī*), a lullaby used to soothe babies to sleep.—Also *v.t.* and *interj.*—*n.* **hush′-boat,** (*coll.*) a mystery-ship.—*adj.* **hushed,** silent, still.—*adj.* **hush′-hush,** (*coll.*) secret, esp. of an armament designed to take an enemy by surprise.—*n.* **hush′-mon′ey,** a bribe for silence.—**hush up,** to stifle, suppress: to be silent. [Imit.; cf. **hist** and **whist.**]

husher, *hush′ər*. See **usher.**

husk, *husk*, *n.* the dry, thin covering of certain fruits and seeds: a case, shell, or covering, esp. one that is worthless or coarse: (*pl.*) refuse, waste: **huskiness:** bronchitis in cattle caused by parasitic nematodes.—*v.t.* to remove the husk or outer integument from.—*adj.* **husked,** covered with a husk: stripped of husks.—*n.* **husk′er,** one who husks Indian corn, esp. at a husking-bee: apparatus (as a glove) for the same purpose.—*adv.* **husk′ily.**—*ns.* **husk′iness; husk′ing,** the stripping of husks: a festive gathering to assist in husking Indian corn (maize)—also **husk′ing-bee.**—*adj.* **husk′y,** full of husks: of the nature of husks: like a husk: dry: (*U.S.*) sturdy like a corn-husk: with a dry, almost whispering voice, as if there were husks in the throat.—*n.* (*U.S.*) a sturdy fellow. [Perh. conn. with **house.**]

husky, *hus′ki*. See **husk.**

husky, *hus′ki*, *n.* a Canadian sledge-dog: an Eskimo: the Eskimo language. [App.—*Eskimo.*]

huso, *hū′so*, *n.* the great sturgeon. [O.H.G. *húso.*]

hussar, *hoo-zär′*, *n.* a light-armed cavalry soldier: (*orig.*) a soldier of the national cavalry of Hungary. [Hung. *huszar*, through Old Serb.—It. *corsaro*, a freebooter.]

hussif. See **housewife.**

Hussite, *hus′īt*, *hoos′īt*, *n.* a follower of the Bohemian reformer John *Hus*, martyred in 1415.

hussy, *hus′i*, *huz′i*, *n.* a pert girl: a worthless wench: (*obs.*) a housewife: (*obs.*) a hussif. [**housewife.**]

hustings, *hus′tingz*, *n.sing.* the principal court of the city of London: formerly the booths where the votes were taken at an election of an M.P., or the platform from which the candidates gave their addresses. [O.E. *hústing*, a council (used in speaking of the Danes)—O.N. *hústhing*—*hús*, a house, *thing*, an assembly.]

hustle, *hus′l*, *v.t.* to shake or push together: to crowd with violence: to jostle: to thrust hastily: to hasten roughly.—*v.i.* to act strenuously.—*n.* frenzied activity.—*n.* **hus′tler,** an energetic fellow. [Du. *hutselen*, to shake to and fro; cf. **hotchpotch.**]

huswife. See **housewife.**

hut, *hut*, *n.* a small or mean house: a small tempor-

ary dwelling or similar structure.—*v.t.* to quarter in or furnish with a hut or huts.—*v.i.* to dwell in a hut or huts:—*pr.p.* **hutt′ing;** *pa.t.* and *pa.p.* **hutt′ed.**—*ns.* **hut′-cir′cle,** (*ant.*) the remains of a prehistoric circular hut, a pit lined with stones, &c.; **hut′ment,** an encampment of huts: lodging in huts. [Fr. *hutte*—O.H.G. *hutta* (Ger. *hütte*); cf. **hide.**]

hutch, *huch*, *n.* a box, a chest: a coop for rabbits: a baker's kneading-trough: a trough used with some ore-dressing machines: a low wagon in which coal is drawn up out of the pit.—*v.t.* (*Milt.*) to hoard up. [Fr. *huche*, a chest—L.L. *hūtica*, a box; prob. Gmc.]

Hutchinsonian, *huch-in-sōn′i-ən*, *n.* a follower of John *Hutchinson* (1674-1737), who held that the Hebrew Scriptures contain typically the elements of all rational philosophy, natural history, and true religion.

hutia, *hōō-tē′ä*, *n.* the hog-rat. [Sp. *hutia*, from Taino.]

Huttonian, *hut-ō′ni-ən*, *adj.* relating to the teaching of James *Hutton* (1720-97), esp. expounding the importance of geological agencies still at work, and the igneous origin of granite and basalt.—*n.* a follower of Hutton.

huzoor, *huz-ōōr′*, *n.* a respectful title used by Indians to a person of rank or a European. [Ar. *hudūr*, the presence.]

huzza, *hooz-ä′*, *huz-ä′*, *interj.* and *n.* hurrah: a shout of joy or approbation.—*v.t.* to attend with shouts of joy.—*v.i.* to utter shouts of joy or acclamation:—*pr.p.* **huzza′ing;** *pa.t.* and *pa.p.* **huzzaed, huzza′d** (*-zäd′*). [Perh. Ger. *hussa*; cf. **hurrah.**]

hyacine, *hī′ə-sīn*, *n.* (*Spens.*) for **hyacinth** (the purple stone).

hyacinth, *hī′ə-sinth*, *n.* (*myth.*) a flower that sprang from the blood of Hyacinthus, a youth accidentally killed by Apollo: a bulbous genus (Hyacinthus) of the lily family, much cultivated: extended to others of the family, as **wild hyacinth** (the English bluebell), **grape hyacinth** (Muscari): a blue stone of the ancients (perh. aquamarine): a red, brown, or yellow zircon—jacinth: cinnamon-stone: a purple colour, of various hues.—*adj.* **hyacin′thine,** consisting of or resembling hyacinth: very beautiful, like Hyacinthus: of a colour variously understood as golden, purple-black, or a blue or purple of some kind. [Gr. *hyakinthos*, a species of Scilla, blue larkspur, a blue stone; cf. **jacinth.**]

Hyades, *hī′ə-dēz*, **Hyads,** *hī′adz*, *n.pl.* a cluster of five stars in the constellation of the Bull, supposed by the ancients to bring rain when they rose with the sun. [Gr. *Hyădēs*, *Hyădĕs*, explained by the ancients as from *hyein*, to rain; more prob. little pigs, *hўs*, a pig.]

hyaena, hyena, *hī-ē′nä*, *n.* a carrion-feeding carnivore (genus **Hyae′na,** constituting a family **Hyae′nidae**) with long thick neck, coarse mane, sloping body, and hysterical-sounding laugh, of three existing species, *striped* (Africa and Asia), *spotted*, and *brown* or *woolly* (Africa).—*n.* **hyae′na-dog,** an African wild dog, blotched like a hyaena. [L. *hyaena*—Gr. *hyaina*—*hўs*, a pig.]

hyaline, *hī′ə-lin*, *-līn*, *adj.* glassy: of or like glass: clear: transparent: free from granules.—*n.* (*Milt.*) a glassy transparent surface.—*adj.* **hy′alite,** transparent colourless opal.—*adj.* **hy′aloid,** hyaline, transparent.—*ns.* **hyalom′elan(e)** (*-ăn, -an*; Gr. *melas, -anos,* black), tachylite; **hyalonē′ma** (Gr. *nēma,* thread), the glass-rope sponge; **hy′alophane** (root of Gr. *phainesthai,* to seem), a felspar containing barium; **hy′aloplasm,** the clear fluid part of protoplasm. [Gr. *hyalos,* glass.]

hybernate, &c. See **hibernate, &c.**

Hyblaean, *hī-blē′ən*, *adj.* pertaining to ancient *Hybla* in Sicily, noted for its honey.

hybrid, *hī′brid*, *n.* the offspring of parents of two different species: a mongrel: a mule: a word formed of elements from different languages.—*adjs.* **hy′brid, hyb′ridous,** produced from different species: mongrel.—*adj.* **hybridīs′able.**—*n.* **hybridīsā′tion.**—*v.t.* **hy′bridise,** to cause to interbreed.—*v.i.* to interbreed.—*ns.* **hybridīs′er;**

hy'bridism, hybrid'ity, state of being hybrid. [L. *hibrida*, offspring of a tame sow and wild boar; with associations of Gr. *hybris*, insolence, overweening.]

hydathode, *hī'də th-ōd, n.* (*bot.*) an epidermal water-excreting organ. [Gr. *hydōr, hydatos,* water, *hodos,* way.]

hydatid, *hī'də-tid, n.* a water cyst or vesicle in an animal body, esp. one containing a tapeworm larva: the larva itself. [Gr. *hydatis, -idos,* a watery vesicle—*hydōr, hydatos,* water.]

hydatoid, *hī'də-toid, adj.* watery. [Gr. *hydōr, -atos,* water, *eidos,* form.]

Hydnocarpus, *hid-nō-kär'pəs, n.* a genus of trees akin to the chaulmoogra, yielding an oil containing chaulmoogric acid. [Gr. *hydnon,* a truffle, *karpos,* a fruit.]

hydr-. See **hydro-**.

Hydra, *hī'drä, n.* (*myth.*) a water-monster with many heads, which when cut off were succeeded by others: any manifold evil: a freshwater hydrozoon remarkable for power of multiplication on being cut or divided.—*adj.* **hy'dra-head'ed,** difficult to root out, springing up vigorously again and again. [Gr. *hydrā—hydōr,* water, akin to Sans. *udras,* an otter.]

hydraemia, hydragogue, Hydrangea, &c. See **hydro-**.

hydro-, *hī'drō-, -dro'-,* **hydr-,** in composition, water.—*n.* **hydraemia** (*hī-drē'mi-ä;* Gr. *haima,* blood), wateriness of the blood.—*adj.* **hydragogue** (*hī'dro-gog, -gōg;* Gr. *agōgos,* bringing; *med.*), removing water or serum.—*n.* a drug with that effect.—*ns.* **Hydrangea** (*hī-drän'jä, -jyä;* Gr. *angeion,* vessel), a genus of shrubby plants of or akin to the saxifrage family with large globular clusters of showy flowers, natives of China and Japan; **hydrant** (*hī'drənt*), a connexion for attaching a hose to a water-main, a fire-plug; **hydranth** (*hī'dranth;* Gr. *anthos,* flower), a nutritive polyp in a hydroid colony; **hydrargyrism** (*hī-drär'jir-izm;* Gr. *hydrargyros,* mercury—*argyros,* silver), mercurial poisoning; **hydrar'gyrum** (mod. L. on analogy of *argentum,* &c.; L. *hydrargyrus*), mercury.—*adj.* **hydrar'gyral.**—*n.* **hy'drate,** a compound containing water chemically combined yet somehow retaining its identity: an old word for a hydroxide.—*v.t.* to combine with water.—*n.* **hydra'tion.**—*adj.* **hydraulic** (*hī-drawl'ik;* Gr. *aulos,* a pipe), relating to hydraulics: conveying water: worked by water or other liquid in pipes: setting in water: (**hydraulic belt,** an endless belt of absorbent material for raising water; **hydraulic jack,** a lifting apparatus in which oil, &c., is pumped against a piston; **hydraulic mining, hydraulicking; hydraulic press,** a press operated by forcing water into a cylinder in which a ram or plunger works; **hydraulic ram,** a device whereby the pressure head produced when a moving column of water is brought to rest is caused to deliver some of the water under pressure).—*v.t.* (*min.*) to excavate and wash out by powerful jets of water:—*pr.p.* **hydraul'icking;** *pa.t.* and *pa.p.* **hydraul'icked.**—*adv.* **hydraul'ically.**—*n.pl.* **hydraul'ics,** used as *sing.,* the science of hydrodynamics in general, or its practical application to water-pipes, &c.—*n.* **hydria** (*hī'dri-ä, hid'ri-ä;* Gr. *hydriä*), a large Greek water-vase.—*adj.* **hy'dric,** of or containing hydrogen.—*n.* **hy'dride,** a compound of hydrogen with an element or radical.—*adj.* **hydriodic** (*hī-dri-od'ik*), applied to an acid composed of hydrogen and iodine, hydrogen iodide.—*ns.* **hy'drō,** an abbreviation of **hydropathic** (establishment), or (*U.S.*) **hydro-airplane** (*hī-drō-lē);* **hydro-a'eroplane,** or (*U.S.*) **hydro-air'plane,** a seaplane.—*adj.* **hydrobrō'mic,** applied to an acid composed of hydrogen and bromine, hydrogen bromide.—*ns.* **hydrocar'bon,** a compound of hydrogen and carbon with nothing else; **hy'drocele** (*-sēl;* Gr. *kēlē,* a swelling; *med.*), a swelling containing serous fluid, esp. in the scrotum; **hydrocephalus** (*-sef'ə-ləs;* Gr. *kephalē,* head), an accumulation of serous fluid within the cranial cavity, either in the sub-dural space or the ventricles: water in the head: dropsy of the brain;

Hydrocharis (*hī-drok'ə-ris;* Gr. *charis, -itos,* grace), the frogbit genus, giving name to the **Hydrocharitā'ceae,** a family of water-plants akin to the pondweeds.—*adj.* **hydrochloric** (*-klor'ik, -klōr'*), applied to an acid composed of hydrogen and chlorine, hydrogen chloride, still sometimes called muriatic acid.—*n.* **hy'drochore** (*-kōr;* Gr. *chōreein,* to make room, spread about), a plant disseminated by water.—*adj.* **hydrochoric** (*-kor'ik*).—*n.pl.* **Hydrocoralli'nae,** an order of Hydrozoa, massive reef-builders, the millepores, &c.—*n.* and *adj.* **hydrocor'alline.**—*adjs.* **hydrocyanic** (*-sī-an'ik*), denoting an acid (*prussic acid*) composed of hydrogen and cyanogen; **hydrodynamic** (*-dinam'ik;* Gr. *dynamis,* power), **-al.**—*n.* (treated as *sing.*) **hydrodynam'ics,** the science of the motions and equilibrium of a material system partly or wholly fluid (called *hydrostatics* when the system is in equilibrium, *hydrokinetics* when it is not).—*adj.* **hydroelec'tric.**—*ns.* **hydroelectric'ity,** electricity produced by means of water, esp. by water-power; **hydro-extract'or,** a drying-machine that works centrifugally.—*adjs.* **hydroferricyanic** (*-fer-i-sī-an'ik*), **hydroferrōcyan'ic,** applied to two acids composed of hydrogen, iron, and cyanogen, hydroferricyanic acid, $H_5Fe(CN)_6$, having an atom of hydrogen less than hydroferrocyanic, $H_4Fe(CN)_6$; **hydrofluor'ic,** applied to an acid composed of fluorine and hydrogen, hydrogen fluoride.—*n.* **hydrogen** (*hī'drō-jən;* a word coined by Cavendish (1766) from Gr. *hydōr,* water, and *gennaein,* to produce), a gas which in combination with oxygen produces water, an elementary gaseous substance, the lightest of all known substances, and very inflammable (**heavy hydrogen,** see **heavy**; **hydrogen bomb,** or H-bomb, a bomb in which an enormous release of energy would be achieved by converting hydrogen nuclei into helium nuclei, and in which an atomic bomb would probably be used to provide the necessary great heat; **hydrogen-ion concentration,** the concentration of hydrogen ions in a solution, in gram-atoms per litre, a measure of acidity or alkalinity, expressed by pH=minus the logarithm of the concentration).—*v.t.* **hydrogenate** (*hī'drō-jən-āt,* or *hī-droj'ən-āt*), to cause to combine with hydrogen, as in the hardening of oils by converting an olein into a stearin by addition of hydrogen in the presence of a catalyst such as nickel or palladium.—*n.* **hydrogenā'tion.**—*adj.* **hydrog'enous.**—*n.* **hydrog'rapher** (Gr. *graphein,* to write).—*adjs.* **hydrographic** (*-graf'ik*), **-al.**—*adv.* **hydrograph'ically.**—*n.* **hydrog'raphy,** the investigation of seas and other bodies of water, including charting, sounding, study of tides, currents, &c.—*adj.* **hy'droid,** like a Hydra: polypoid.—*n.* a hydrozoan: a hydrozoan in its asexual generation.—*n.* (treated as *sing.*) **hydrokinet'ics,** a branch of *hydrodynamics* (q.v.).—*adjs.* **hydrolog'ic, -al.**—*ns.* **hydrol'ogist; hydrol'ogy,** the science of water, esp. underground waters, or of medical treatment by baths.—*v.t.* **hydrolyse** (*hī'drō-līz*), to subject to hydrolysis.—*ns.* **hydrolysis** (*hī-drol'i-sis;* Gr. *lysis,* loosing), chemical decomposition or ionic dissociation caused by water; **hy'drolyte** (*-līt*), a body subjected to hydrolysis.—*adj.* **hydrolytic** (*-lit'ik*).—*n.* **hy'dromancy** (Gr. *manteiä,* divination), divination by water.—*adj.* **hydromant'ic.**—*n.* (treated as *sing.*) **hydromechan'ics,** hydrodynamics. — *n.* **hydromedū'sa,** a hydrozoan in its sexual generation:—*pl.* **Hydromedū'sae,** the class Hydrozoa.—*adjs.* **hydromedū'san, hydromedū'soid** (also *ns.*).—*ns.* **hy'dromel** (Gr. *hydromeli—meli,* honey), a beverage made of honey and water; **hydromē'teor** (Gr. *meteōron,* a meteor), any weather phenomenon depending on the moisture-content of the atmosphere; **hydrometeorol'ogy; hydrom'eter** (Gr. *metron,* a measure), a float for measuring specific gravity.—*adjs.* **hydrometric** (*-met'*), **-al.** —*ns.* **hydrom'etry; Hydromys** (*hī'drō-mis;* Gr. *mȳs,* mouse), an Australasian genus of aquatic rodents; **hydrop'athy,** the treatment of disease by water.—*adj.* **hydropathic** (*hī-drō-path'ik;* Gr, *pathos,* suffering), of, for, relating to, practising.

hydropathy.—*n.* (in full **hydropathic establishment**; *coll.* **hy'dro**), a hotel (with special baths, &c.) where the guests can have hydropathic treatment if desired, virtually a hotel with social life.— *adj.* **hydropath'ical**.—*adv.* **hydropath'ically**.— *ns.* **hydrop'athist**, one who practises hydropathy; **hydrophane** (*hī'drō-fān*; Gr. *phānos*, bright), a translucent opal transparent in water. — *adj.* **hydrophanous** (*-drof'an-as*), transparent on immersion.—*n.pl.* **Hydrophidae** (*hī-drof'i-dē*; Gr. *ophis*, snake), a family of venomous sea-snakes.— *n.* **hydroph'ilite**, native calcium chloride (a very hygroscopic substance). — *adj.* **hydroph'ilous**, water-loving : (*bot.*) pollinated by agency of water. —*ns.* **hydroph'ily** (Gr. *phileein*, to love), water-pollination; **hydrophō'bia** (Gr. *phobos*, fear), horror of water : inability to swallow water owing to a contraction in the throat, a symptom of rabies : rabies itself.—*adjs.* **hydrophobic** (*-fob'ik*), **hydrophobous** (*-drof'a-bas*).—*ns.* **hy'drophone** (*-fōn*; Gr. *phōnē*, voice), an apparatus for listening to sounds conveyed by water; **hy'drophyte** (*-fīt*; Gr. *phyton*, plant), a water-plant.—*adj.* **hydrophytic** (*-fit'ik*).—*n.* **hydrophyton** (*hī-drof'i-ton*),the coenosarc of a hydroid colony.—*adj.* **hydroph'ytous**.—*ns.* **hy'droplane**, a light, flat-bottomed motor-boat which, at high speed, skims along the surface of the water : (erroneously) a *hydroaeroplane* or seaplane; **hydropol'yp**, a hydrozoan polyp.—*n.* (treated as *sing.*) **hydroponics** (*hī-drō-pon'iks*; Gr. *ponos*, toil), the art or practice of growing plants in a chemical solution without soil.— *adj.* **hydrop'ic** (erroneously **hydrop'tic**) dropsical : thirsty : charged or swollen with water.—*n.* **hy'dropsy** (Gr. *hydrōps*, dropsy), dropsy.—*n.pl.* **Hydropterid'eae** (*-i-ē*; Gr. *pteris*, *-idos*, male-fern), the water-ferns or heterosporous ferns.—*ns.* **hy'dropult** (modelled on catapult), a hand force-pump; **hydroquinone** (*-kwin-ōn'*, or *-kwin'*, or *-kwīn'*), quinol; **hy'droscope** (Gr. *skopeein*, to view), a kind of water-clock, a graduated tube, from which the water escaped : an instrument for viewing the sea-bottom; **hydrosō'ma**, **hy'drosome** (*-sōm*; Gr. *sōma*, body), a hydroid colony :— *pl.* **hydrosō'mata**, **hy'drosomes**.—*adjs.* **hydrosō'mal**, **hydrosō'matous**.—*ns.* **hydrosphere** (*hī'-drō-sfēr*; Gr. *sphaira*, sphere), the water-envelope of the earth—the seas and oceans; **hy'drostat** (Gr. *statos*, standing), a contrivance for indicating or regulating height of water.—*adjs.* **hydrostat'ic** **(hydrostatic balance**, a balance for weighing bodies in water to determine their specific gravity; **hydrostatic paradox**, the principle that—disregarding molecular forces—any quantity of fluid, however small, may balance any weight, however great; **hydrostatic press**, the hydraulic press); **hydrostat'ical**. — *adv.* **hydrostat'ically**. — *n.* (treated as *sing.*) **hydrostat'ics**, a branch of hydrodynamics (q.v.).—*ns.* **hydrosul'phide**, a compound formed by action of hydrogen sulphide on a hydroxide; **hydrosul'phite**, a hyposulphite (esp. sodium hyposulphite). — *adjs.* **hydrosul-phū'ric**, formed by a combination of hydrogen and sulphur; **hydrotac'tic**.—*ns.* **hydrotax'is** (Gr. *taxis*, arrangement), response of an organism to the stimulus of water; **hydrothē'ca** (Gr. *thēkē*, case), the horny cup of a hydranth; **hydrother'apy**, **hydro-therapeu'tics**, treatment of disease by water. — *adjs.* **hydrotherapeu'tic**; **hydrother'mal**, pertaining to, or produced by, action of heated or super-heated water, esp. in dissolving, transporting, and redepositing mineral matter.—*n.* **hydrothō'rax** (Gr. *thōrax*, chest), dropsy in the chest.—*adj.* **hydrotrop'ic**.—*n.* **hydrot'ropism** (Gr. *tropos*, a turn), the turning of an organ towards (*positive hydrotropism*) or away from (*negative*) moisture.—*adj.* **hydrous** (*hī'dras*; *chem.*, *min.*), containing water.—*ns.* **hydrox'ide**, a chemical compound which contains one or more hydroxyl groups; **hydrox'yl** (Gr. *hȳlē*, matter), a compound radical consisting of one atom of oxygen and one of hydrogen : sometimes loosely applied to hydrogen peroxide; **hydroxyl'amine**, a basic substance composed of a hydroxyl group and an amino group (NH_2OH); **hydrozincite** (*-zingk'īt*), basic zinc carbonate.—*n.pl.* **Hydrozō'a**; Gr. *zōion*, an animal), a class of Coelenterata, chiefly marine organisms in which alternation of generations typically occurs, the hydroid phase colonial, giving rise to the medusoid phase by budding—the zoophytes, millepores, &c. : sometimes extended to include the true jellyfishes.—*sing.* **hydrozō'on**. —*n.* and *adj.* **hydrozō'an**. [Gr. *hydōr*, water.]

hye (*Spens.*) for **hie**, **high**.

hyena, *hī-ē'nä*, **hyen** (*Shak.*), *hī'en*, *n.* a hyaena.

hyetal, *hī'i-tl*, *adj.* rainy : pertaining to rain.—*n.* **hy'etograph**, a rain-chart : a self-registering rain-gauge.—*adjs.* **hyetograph'ic**, **-al**.—*ns.* **hyetog'raphy**; **hyetol'ogy**; **hyetom'eter**; **hye-tomet'rograph**. [Gr. *hȳetos*, rain.]

Hygeian, *hī-jē'an*, *adj.* relating to Hygeia or to health and its preservation. [Gr. *Hygieia*, later *Hygeia*, goddess of health, daughter of Asklēpios (Aesculapius).]

hygiene, *hī'ji-ēn*, also *-jēn*, *n.* the science or art of preserving health: sanitary principles.—*adj.* **hygienic** (*hī-ji-en'ik*, also *-jēn'*).—*adv.* **hygien'-ically**.—*n.* (treated as *sing.*) **hygien'ics**, principles of hygiene.—*n.* **hygienist** (*hī'ji-an-ist*), one skilled in hygiene. [Fr. *hygiène*—Gr. *hygieinē* (*technē*), hygienic (art)—*hygieia*, health, *hygiēs*, healthy.]

hygro-, *hī'grō-*, *-gro'*, in composition, wet, moist.— *ns.* **hygrochasy** (*hī-grok'a-si*; Gr. *chasis*, a gape), dehiscence on moistening; **hy'grodeik** (*-dīk*; Gr. *deiknynai*, to show), a psychrometer with an index and scale; **hygrom'eter**, an instrument for measuring the relative humidity of the atmosphere or of other gases.—*adjs.* **hygrometric** (*-met'rik*), **-al**, belonging to hygrometry : hygroscopic.—*n.* **hygrom'etry**.—*adjs.* **hy'grophil**, **hy-grophilous** (*-grof'*; Gr. *phileein*, to love), moisture-loving : living where there is much moisture; **hy'grophobe** (Gr. *phobeein*, to fear), growing best where moisture is scanty.—*n.* **hy'grophyte** (*-fīt*; Gr. *phyton*, plant), a plant adapted to plentiful water-supply. — *adj.* **hygrophytic** (*-fit'ik*). — *n.* **hy'groscope**, an instrument that shows. without measuring, changes in the humidity of the atmosphere.—*adjs.* **hygroscopic** (*-skop'ik*), **-al**, relating to the hygroscope: readily absorbing moisture from the atmosphere : indicating or caused by absorption or loss of moisture, as some movements of plants : (**hygroscopic salt**, any salt, esp. chloride of calcium, used to withdraw moisture from other substances). — *n.* **hygroscopicity** (*-skop-is'i-ti*). [Gr. *hygros*, wet.]

hyke, *hīk*, *n.* Same as **haik**.

Hyksos, *hik'sōs*, *n.* a foreign line of kings (the xv. and xvi. dynasties, called the shepherd kings) who ruled Egypt for centuries. [Gr. *Hyksōs*—Egypt. *Hiku-khasut*, princes of the desert, app. misunderstood as shepherd princes.]

hylding (*Spens.*). Same as **hilding**.

hyle, *hī'lē*, *n.* wood, matter.—*adj.* **hy'lic**, material : corporeal.—*ns.* **hy'licism**, **hy'lism**, materialism; **hy'licist**, **hy'list** (wrongly **hy'loist**); **hy'lobate**, a gibbon (genus Hylob'atēs) : from the root of Gr. *bainein*, to go); **hylogen'esis**, the origin of matter; **hylop'athism** (Gr. *pathos*, feeling), the doctrine that matter is sentient; **hylop'athist**.— *adj.* **hyloph'agous** (Gr. *phagein*, to eat), wood-eating.—*ns.* **hy'lophyte** (Gr. *phyton*, plant), a woodland plant; **hy'lotheism** (Gr. *theos*, god), the doctrine that there is no God but matter and the universe; **hy'lotheist**.—*adjs.* **hylot'omous** (Gr. *tomē*, a cut), wood-cutting; **hylozō'ical**, **hylo-zois'tic**.—*ns.* **hylozō'ism** (Gr. *zōē*, life), the doctrine that all matter is endowed with life; **hylozō'ist**. [Gr. *hȳlē*, wood, matter.]

hyleg, *hī'leg*, *n.* the ruling planet at the hour of birth. [Origin obscure; cf. Pers. *hailāj*, nativity.]

Hymen, *hī'men*, *n.* (*myth.*) the god of marriage: marriage.—*adjs.* **hymenē'al**, **hymenē'an**.—*n.pl.* **hymenē'als**, nuptials. [Gr. *Hymēn*, *Hȳmēn*, a wedding-cry, perh. also a god.]

hymen, *hī'men*, *n.* a membrane : a thin membrane partially closing the virginal vagina.—*adjs.* **hy'-menal**, pertaining to the hymen; **hymē'nial**, pertaining to the hymenium.—*n.* **hymē'nium**, the spore-bearing surface in fungi.—*ns.pl.* **Hymeno-**

mycetes (hī-mən-ō-mī-sē´tēz), an order of fungi with exposed hymenium from an early stage—toadstools, &c. ; **Hymenophyllā´ceae**, the filmy ferns. — adj. **hymenophyllā´ceous**. — n.pl. **Hymenop´tera**, an order of insects with four transparent wings—ants, bees, wasps, &c.—adj. **hymenop´terous**. [Gr. hȳmēn, membrane.]

hymn, him, n. a song of praise.—v.t. to celebrate in song: to worship by hymns.—v.i. to sing in adoration :—pr.p. **hymning** (him´ing, him´ning); pa.t. and pa.p. **hymned** (himd, him´nid).—ns. **hym´nal**, **hym´nary**, a hymn-book.—adj. **hym´nic**.—ns. **hym´nody**, hymns collectively : hymnsinging : hymnology ; **hymnog´rapher** ; **hymnog´raphy**, the art of writing hymns : the study of hymns ; **hymnol´ogist** ; **hymnol´ogy**, the study or composition of hymns. [Gr. hymnos.]

hynde, a Spenserian spelling of **hind** (2).

hyoid, hī´oid, adj. having the form of the Greek letter upsilon (υ), applied to a bone at the base of the tongue. [Gr. hyoeidēs—hȳ, the letter upsilon, and eidos, form.]

hyoplastron, hī-ō-plas´tron, n. in a turtle's plastron a plate between the hypoplastron and the entoplastron :—pl. **hyoplas´tra**.—adj. **hyoplas´tral**. [Gr. hȳ, the letter upsilon.]

Hyoscyamus, hī-ō-sī´ə-məs, n. the henbane genus.—ns. **hy´oscine**, **hyoscy´amine**, poisonous alkaloids similar to atropine, got from henbane. [Gr. hyoskyamos.]

hyp. See **hip** (3).

hypabyssal, hip-ə-bis´l, adj. (petr.) moderately deep-seated, not quite abyssal, intermediate between plutonic and eruptive. [Gr. hypo, beneath.]

hypaethral, hip-ē´thrəl, or hīp-, adj. roofless, open to the sky.—n. **hypae´thron**, an open court. [Gr. hypo, beneath, aithēr, upper air, sky.]

hypalgesia, hip-al-jē´si-a, -zi-ä, or hīp´, n. diminished susceptibility to pain.—Also **hypal´gia**.—adj. **hypalgē´sic**. [Gr. hypo, under, algēsis, algos, pain.]

hypallage, hip-, hīp-al´ə-jē, n. (rhet.) a figure in which the relations of words in a sentence are mutually interchanged.—adj. **hypallact´ic**. [Gr. hypo, under, allassein, to exchange.]

hypanthium, hip-, hīp-an´thi-əm, n. the flat or concave receptacle of a perigynous flower. [Gr. hypo, under, anthos, flower.]

hypate, hip´a-tē, n. (Gr. mus.) the lowest string of the lyre or its tone. [Gr. hypatē, highest (fem.), prob. as having the longest string.]

hyper-, hī´pər-, in composition, over: excessive: more than normal.—ns. **hyperacid´ity**, excessive acidity, esp. in the stomach; **hyperacusis** (-ə-kū´sis ; Gr. akousis, hearing), abnormally increased power of hearing.—adj. **hyperacute´**.—ns. **hyperacute´ness**; **hyperadre´nalism**, excessive activity of the adrenal gland; **hyperaemia** (-ē´mi-ä; Gr. haima, blood), congestion or excess of blood in any part.—adj. **hyperae´mic**.—n. **hyperaesthesia** (-ēs- or -es-thē´si-ä, -zi-ä; aisthēsis, perception), excessive sensitivity to stimuli: an abnormal extension of the bodily senses assumed to explain telepathy and clairvoyance: exaggerated aestheticism.—adjs. **hyperaesthe´sic**, **hyperaesthetic** (-thet´ik), overaesthetic: abnormally or morbidly sensitive.—n. **hyperalgesia** (-al-jē´si-ä, -zi-ä; Gr. algēsis, pain), heightened sensitivity to pain.—adj. **hyperalgē´sic**.—adj. **hyperbat´ic**.—adv. **hyperbat´ically**.—ns. **hyper´baton** (Gr.,—root of bainein, to go ; rhet.), a figure by which words are transposed from their natural order ; **hyper´bola** (Gr. hyperbolē, overshooting — hyperballein — ballein, to throw ; geom.), one of the conic sections, the intersection of a plane with a cone when the plane cuts both branches of the cone ; **hyperbole** (hī-pər´bo-lē), a rhetorical figure which produces a vivid impression by extravagant and obvious exaggeration.—adjs. **hyperbol´ic**, **-al**, of a hyperbola or hyperbole: (**hyperbolic functions**, a set of six functions (sinh, cosh, tanh, &c.) analogous to the trigonometrical functions ; **hyperbolic logarithms**, natural logarithms ; **hyperbolic spiral**, a spiral whose polar equation is $\rho\theta = k^2$).—adv. **hyperbol´-**

ically.—v.t. **hyper´bolise**, to represent hyperbolically.—v.i. to speak hyperbolically or with exaggeration.—ns. **hyper´bolism** ; **hyper´boloid**, a solid figure certain of whose plane sections are hyperbolas.—adj. **hyperbō´rean** (Gr. Hyperboreoi, a people supposed to live in sunshine beyond the north wind—Boreas, the north wind), belonging to the extreme north.—n. an inhabitant of the extreme north.—adj. **hypercatalect´ic**, (pros.) having an additional syllable or half-foot after the last complete dipody. — ns. **hypercatalex´is**; **hypercrit´ic**, one who is over-critical : a carper.—adjs. **hypercrit´ic**, **-al**.—adv. **hypercrit´ically**.—v.t. **hypercrit´icise** (-sīz).—n. **hypercrit´icism**.—adj. **hyperdac´tyl** (Gr. daktylos, finger, toe).—n. **hyperdac´tyly**, possession of more than five fingers or toes.—adj. **hyperdō´rian** (Gr. hyperdōrios ; mus.), above the Dorian mode : applied in ancient Greek music to a mode having as its lower tetrachord the upper tetrachord of the Dorian (as : b c d e ; e f g a ; b).—ns. **hyperdulia** (-dōō-lī´ä ; Gr. douleiā, service), the special kind of worship paid by Roman Catholics to the Virgin Mary, being higher than that paid to other saints (dulia), and distinct from that paid to God alone (latria) ; **hyperem´esis** (Gr. emesis, vomiting), excessive vomiting.—adj. **hyperemet´ic**.—ns. **hyperē´mia** (same as **hyperaemia**) ; **hypergamy** (hī-pər´gə-mi ; Gr. gamos, marriage), a custom that allows a man but forbids a woman to marry a person of lower social standing. [Gr. hyper, over.]

Hypericum, hī-per´i-kəm, n. the St John's wort genus of plants, giving name to a family **Hypericā´ceae**. [Gr. hyperīkon or hypereikos—hypo, under, ereikē, heath.]

hyperinosis, hī-pər-i-nō´sis, n. excess of fibrin in the blood.—adj. **hyperinot´ic**. [Gr. īs, īnos, strength, fibre.]

Hyperion, hī-pēr´i-on, n. a Titan, son of Uranus and Ge, and father of Helios, Selene, and Eos : Helios himself, the incarnation of light and beauty. [Gr. Hypēriōn.]

hyper- (continued).—adjs. **hyperlydian** (-lid´i-ən ; Gr. hyperlȳdios), above the Lydian mode : applied in ancient Greek music to a mode having as its lower tetrachord the upper tetrachord of the Lydian (as : g a b c ; c d e f ; g) ; **hypermet´rical**, beyond or exceeding the ordinary metre of a line : having or being an additional syllable.—n. **hypermetrō´pia** (Gr. metron, measure, ōps, eye), longsightedness. — Also **hyperō´pia**. — adjs. **hypermetrōp´ic**; **hyperphrygian** (-frij´i-ən, -frij´ən ; Gr. hyperphrȳgios), above the Phrygian : applied to a mode of ancient Greek music having as its lower tetrachord the upper tetrachord of the Phrygian (as : a b c d ; d e f g ; a) ; **hyperphys´ical**, beyond physical laws: supernatural.—n. **hyperplasia** (-plā´zi-ä, -zhä ; Gr. plasis, a forming ; path.), overgrowth of a part due to excessive multiplication of its cells.—adjs. **hyperplastic** (-plaz´), **hyperplastic** (-plas´) ; **hyperpyretic** (-pir-et´ik ; Gr. pyretikos, feverish).—ns. **hyperpyrex´ia**, abnormally high body temperature ; **hypersarcō´ma**, **hypersarcō´sis** (Gr. hypersarkōma, hypersarkōsis—sarx, flesh ; path.), proud or fungous flesh.—v.t. **hypersens´itise**, to increase the sensitivity of.—adj. **hypersens´itive**, excessively sensitive.—ns. **hypersens´itiveness** ; **hypersensitiv´ity**.—adjs. **hypersen´sual**, beyond the scope of the senses : **hyperson´ic** (L. sonus, sound), supersonic : ultrasonic.—ns. **hyperson´ics** ; **hypersthene** (hī´pər-sthēn ; Gr. sthenos, strength, because harder than hornblende), a rock-forming orthorhombic pyroxene, an anhydrous silicate of magnesium and iron, generally dark green, brown, or raven-black with metallic lustre ; **hypersthe´nia**, (path.) a morbid condition marked by excessive excitement of all the vital phenomena.—adj. **hypersthenic** (-sthen´ik), of hypersthene or of hypersthenia.—ns. **hypersthē´nite**, a rock consisti.g almost entirely of hypersthene : (obs.) an aggregate of labradorite and hypersthene ; **hyperten´sion**, blood-pressure higher than normal ; **hyperthyroidism** (-thī´roid-izm), over-activity of the thyroid gland, and the resulting condition.—adjs. **hypertroph´ic**, **-al**,

hyper'trophied, hyper'trophous (Gr. *trophē,* nourishment).—*ns.* **hyper'trophy,** overnourishment: abnormal enlargement; **hypervitaminos'is,** the condition resulting from too much of any vitamin. [Gr. *hyper,* over.]

hypha, *hī'fä, n.* a thread of fungus mycelium :— *pl.* **hy'phae** (*-fē*).—*adj.* **hy'phal.** [Gr. *hyphē,* web.]

hyphen, *hī'fən, n.* a short stroke (-) joining two syllables or words.—*v.t.* to join by a hyphen.— *v.t.* **hy'phenate,** to hyphen.—*adj.* hyphened : hyphenated.—*n.* a hyphenated American.—*adj.* **hy'phenated,** hyphened : of nationality expressed by a hyphened word, as Irish-American : of divided, or alien, national sympathies.—*n.* a hyphenated American.—*n.* **hyphena'tion.**—*adj.* **hyphenic** (*-fen'ik*).—*v.t.* **hy'phenise.**—*ns.* **hyphenīsā'tion,** hyphening ; **hy'phenism,** state of being a hyphenate. [Gr. *hŷphĕn*—*hypo,* under, *hen,* one.]

hypinosis, *hip-i-nō'sis, n.* defect of fibrin in the blood. [Gr. *hypo,* under, *īs, īnos,* fibre.]

Hypnos, *hip'nos, n.* the Greek god of sleep.—*adjs.* **hypnagogic** (*-goj'ik, -gog'ik* ; Gr. *agōgos,* bringing), sleep-bringing : ushering in sleep ; **hyp'nic,** pertaining to or inducing sleep.—*n.* a soporific.— *ns.* **hyp'no-anal'ysis,** analysis of a patient's psychological troubles by obtaining information from him while he is in a state of hypnosis ; **hypnogen'esis, hypnogeny** (*-noj'i-ni*), production of the hypnotic state.—*adjs.* **hypnogenet'ic, hypnog'enous, hypnogen'ic,** inducing the hypnotic state, or sleep ; **hyp'noid, -al,** like sleep : like hypnosis : esp. of a state between hypnosis and waking.—*v.t.* **hyp'noidise,** to put in the hypnoidal state.—*ns.* **hypnol'ogy,** the scientific study of sleep ; **hyp'none,** an aromatic ketone used in medicine as a hypnotic.—*adj.* **hypnopomp'ic** (Gr. *pompē,* a sending), dispelling sleep.—*n.* **hypnō'sis,** a sleeplike state in which the mind responds to external suggestion and can recover forgotten memories.—*adj.* **hypnŏt'ic,** of or relating to hypnosis : soporific.—*n.* a soporific : a person subject to hypnotism or in a state of hypnosis.—*adv.* **hypnot'ically.**—*adj.* **hypnotīs'able.**—*ns.* **hypnotīsabil'ity ; hypnotīsā'tion.**—*v.t.* **hyp'notise,** to put in a state of hypnosis : (*fig.*) to fascinate, dazzle, overpower the mind of.—*ns.* **hypnotīs'er ; hyp'notism,** the science of hypnosis : the art or practice of inducing hypnosis : hypnosis ; **hyp'notist,** one who hypnotises.—*adjs.* **hypnotist'ic ; hyp'notoid,** like hypnosis. [Gr. *hypnos,* sleep.]

Hypnum, *hip'nəm, n.* a large genus (often divided) of mosses, with capsules on special lateral branches. [Latinised from Gr. *hypnon,* a kind of lichen.]

hypo-, *hī'pō-, hip'ō-,* or *-o'-,* in composition, under : defective : inadequate.—*n.* **hy'po,** (*phot.*) an abbreviation of *hypo*sulphite, in the sense of sodium thiosulphate.—*adj.* **hypoaeolian** (*hī-pō-ē-ō'li-ən*), below the Aeolian mode : applied in old church music to a plagal mode extending from *e* to *e,* with *a* for its final.—*n.* **hypoblast** (*hip', hip'ō-blast* ; Gr. *blastos,* bud), the inner germ-layer of a gastrula.— *adj.* **hypoblast'ic.**—*ns.* **hypobole** (*hip-ob'o-lē* ; Gr. *hypobolē,* throwing under, suggestion—*ballein,* to throw ; *rhet.*), anticipation of objections ; **hypocaust** (*hip', hip'ō-kawst* ; Gr. *hypokauston*—*hypo,* under, *kaiein,* to burn), a space under a floor for heating by hot air or furnace gases ; **hypochlorite** (*hī-pō-klō'rīt*), a salt of **hypochlō'rous acid,** an acid (HClO) with less oxygen than chlorous acid ; **hypochondria** (*hip-, hip-ō-kon'dri-ä*), originally the *pl.* of *hypochondrium* (see below) : a nervous malady, often arising from indigestion, and tormenting the patient with imaginary fears (once supposed to have its seat in the abdomen) : morbid anxiety about health : imaginary illness.—*adj.* **hypochon'driac,** relating to or affected with hypochondria : melancholy.—*n.* a sufferer from hypochondria. — *adj.* **hypochondrī'acal.** — *ns.* **hypochondrī'asis, hypochondrī'acism, hypochon'driasm,** hypochondria ; **hypochon'driast,** one suffering from hypochondria ; **hypochon'drium** (Gr. *hypochondrion*—*chondros,* cartilage ;

---

anat.), the region of the abdomen on either side, under the costal cartilages and short ribs ; **hypocist** (*hī'pō-sist* ; Gr. *hypokistis*—*kistos,* cistus), an inspissated juice from the fruit of *Cytinus hypocistis* (Rafflesiaceae), a plant parasitic on cistus roots ; **hypocorism** (*hip-, hip-ok'ər-izm*), **hypocorisma** (*-iz'mä* ; Gr. *hypokorisma*—*hypokorizesthai,* to use child-talk—*koros,* boy, *korē,* girl), a pet-name : a diminutive or abbreviated name.— *adjs.* **hypocorist'ic, -al.**—*adv.* **hypocorist'ically.** —*n.* **hypocotyl** (*hip-, hip-ō-kot'il*), that part of the axis of a plant which is between the cotyledons and the primary root.—*adj.* **hypocotylē'donary.**— *ns.* **hypocrisy** (*hi-pok'ri-si* ; Gr. *hypokrisiä,* acting, playing a part), a feigning to be better than one is, or to be what one is not : concealment of true character or belief (not necessarily conscious) ; **hypocrite** (*hip'ə-krit* ; Gr. *hypokritēs,* actor), one who practises hypocrisy.—*adj.* **hypocrit'ical** (also **hypocrit'ic**), practising hypocrisy : of the nature of hypocrisy.—*adv.* **hypocrit'ically.**—*n.* **hypocycloid** (*hī-pō-sī'kloid*), a curve generated by a point on the circumference of a circle which rolls on the inside of another circle.—*adj.* **hypocycloid'al.**—*ns.* **hypoderm** (*hip'* or *hip'ō-dərm*), **hypoder'ma, hypoder'mis** (Gr. *derma,* skin ; *bot.*), the tissue next under the epidermis.—*adjs.* **hypoderm'al, hypoderm'ic,** pertaining to the hypodermis : under the epidermis : under the skin, subcutaneous, esp. of a method of injecting a drug in solution under the skin by means of a fine hollow needle to which a small syringe is attached. —*n.* **hypoder'mic,** a hypodermic injection : a drug so injected : a syringe for the purpose.—*adv.* **hypoder'mically.** — *adjs.* **hypodorian** (*hī-pō-dō'ri-ən* ; Gr. *hypodōrios*), below the Dorian : applied in ancient Greek music to a mode whose upper tetrachord is the lower tetrachord of the Dorian (as. *a; b c d e; e f g a*): in old church music to a plagal mode extending from *a* to *a,* with *d* as its final ; **hypogastric** (*hip-* or *hip-ō-gas'trik* ; Gr. *gastēr,* belly), belonging to the lower median part of the abdomen.—*n.* **hypogas'trium,** the lower gastric region.—*adjs.* **hypogeal, -gaeal** (*-jē'əl*), **-ge'an, -gae'an, -ge'ous, -gae'ous** (Gr. *hypogeios, -gaios—gē* or *gaia,* the ground), underground : germinating with cotyledons underground ; **hypogene** *hip'* or *hip'ō-jēn* ; Gr. *gennaein,* to engender ; *geol.*), of or pertaining to rocks formed, or agencies at work, under the earth's surface, plutonic—opp. to *epigene*).—*n.* **hypogeum, hypogaeum** (*hip-, hip-ō-jē'əm*), an underground chamber :—*l.* **hypoge'a, -gae'a.**—*adj.* **hypoglossal** (*hīp-* or *hip-ō-glos'əl* · Gr. *glōssa,* the tongue), under the tongue.— *n.* **hypog'nathism.**—*adjs.* **hypognathous** (*hip-* or *hip-og'na-thəs*), having the lower jaw or mandible protruding ; **hypogynous** (*hī-poj'i-nəs* ; Gr. *gynē* a woman, female ; *bot.*), growing from beneath the ovary : having the other floral parts below the ovary.—*n.* **hypog'yny.**—*adjs.* **hypolydian** (*hī-pō-lid'i-ən*), below the Lydian mode : applied in ancient Greek music to a mode having as its upper tetrachord the lower tetrachord of the Lydian (as . *f ; g a b c ; c d e f*): in old church music to a plagal mode extending from *c* to *c* with *f* as its final , **hypomixolydian** (*hī-pō-mik-sō-lid'i-ən*), applied in old church music to a mode extending from *d* to *d* with *g* as its final.—*ns.* **hyponasty** (*hīp'* or *hip'ō-nas-ti* ; Gr. *nastos,* pressed close ; *bot.*), increased growth on the lower side causing an upward bend—opp. to *epinasty* ; **hypophosphite** (*hī-pō-fos'fīt*), a salt of **hypophos'phorous acid,** an acid (H₃PO₂) with less oxygen than phosphorous acid.—*adj.* **hypophrygian** (*-frij'i-ən*), below the Phrygian mode : applied in ancient Greek music to a mode having its upper tetrachord the lower tetrachord of the Phrygian (as, *g ; a b c d ; d e f g*): in old church music to a plagal mode extending from *b* to *b,* with *e* for its final.—*ns.* **hypophysis** (*hīp-, hip-of'i-sis* ; Gr. *hypophysis,* an attachment underneath—*phyein,* to grow), a down-growth : the pituitary body of the brain : (*bot.*) an inflated part of the pedicel under the capsule, in mosses : in flowering plants, a cell at the end of the suspensor ; **hypoplastron** (*hīp-, hip-ō-plas'tron*), the

plate behind the hyoplastron in a turtle's plastron ;
hypostasis (*hip-*, *hip-os′ta-sis*; Gr. *hypostasis*—
stasis, setting), a substance : the essence or real
personal subsistence or substance of each of the
three divisions of the Trinity: sediment, deposit:
passive hyperaemia in a dependent part owing
to sluggishness of circulation.—*adjs.* **hypostatic**
(*-stat′ik*), **-al.**—*adv.* **hypostat′ically.**—*v.t.* **hypos′-**
tatise, to treat as hypostasis : to personify.—*n.*
hypostrophe (*hip-*, *hip-os′tro-fi*; Gr. *hypostrophē*,
turning back ; *med.*), relapse : (*rhet.*) reversion
after a parenthesis.—*adj.* **hypostyle** (*hip′*, *hip′ō-*
stīl ; Gr. *stylos,* a pillar ; *archit.*), having the roof
supported by pillars.—Also *n.*—*ns.* **hyposul′phate,**
a dithionate ; **hyposul′phite,** an old name for a
thiosulphate : a salt of **hyposul′phurous acid**
($H_2S_2O_4$).—*adjs.* **hyposulphūr′ic,** dithionic; **hypo-**
tac′tic.—*ns.* **hypotaxis** (*hip-*, *hip-ō-tak′sis* ; Gr.
taxis, arrangement ; *gram.*), dependent construction—opp to *parataxis* ; **hypotenuse** (*hip-*, *hip-*
ot′on-ūs, or *-ūz*), **hypothenuse** (*-oth′* ; Fr. *hypo-*
ténuse—L. *hypotēnūsa*—Gr. *hypoteinousa,* fem. part.,
subtending or stretching under—*teinein,* to stretch),
the side of a right-angled triangle opposite to the
right angle ; **hypoten′sion,** low blood-pressure ;
hypothec (*hip-oth′ik,* *hip-oth′ik* ; Gr. *hypothēkē,*
a pledge), in Scots law, a lien or security over
goods in respect of a debt due by the owner
of the goods—**the whole** (*Scot.* hale) **hypothec,**
the whole affair, collection, concern.—*adj.* **hy-**
poth′ecary, pertaining to hypothecation or mortgage.—*v.t.* **hypoth′ecate,** to place or assign as
security under an arrangement : to mortgage.—
ns. **hypothecā′tion ; hypoth′ecātor ; hypothe-**
sis (*hī-poth′i-sis* ; Gr. *hypothesis*—*thesis,* placing),
a supposition : a proposition assumed for the sake
of argument : a theory to be proved or disproved
by reference to facts : a provisional explanation of
anything :—*pl.* **hypoth′esēs.**—*vs.t.* and *vs.i.* **hy-**
poth′esise, hypoth′etise.—*adjs.* **hypothet′ic, -al.**
—*adv.* **hypothet′ically.**—*ns.* **hypotrochoid** (*hip-,*
hip-ō-trō′koid ; Gr. *trochos,* wheel, *eidos,* form), the
curve traced by a point on the radius, or radius
produced, of a circle rolling within another circle ;
hypotyposis (*hip-*, *hip-ō-tip-ō′sis* ; *rhet.*), vivid
description of a scene. [Gr. *hypo,* under.]
hypsometry, *hip-som′o-tri, n.* the art of measuring
the heights of places on the earth's surface.—*n.*
hypsom′eter, an instrument for doing this by
taking the boiling-point of water.—*adj.* **hyp-**
somet′ric. [Gr. *hypsos,* height, *metron,* a measure.]
hypsophyll, *hips′ō-fil, n.* (*bot.*) a bract.—*adj.*

hypsophyll′ary. [Gr. *hypsos,* height, *phyllon,* leaf.]
hypural, *hī-pū′rol, adj.* situated beneath the tail.
[Gr. *hypo,* under, *ourā,* tail.]
Hyrax, *hī′raks, n.* a genus (also called Procavia) of
mammals superficially like marmots but really
closer akin to the ungulates, living among rocks
in Africa and Syria—the daman, the dassie or
rock-rabbit, the cony of the Bible—constituting
the order **Hyracoid′ea.** [Gr. *hyrax,* a shrew.]
hyson, *hī′son, n.* a very fine sort of green tea.—*n.*
hy′son-skin, the refuse of hyson tea. [From
Chin.]
hyssop, *his′op, n.* an aromatic labiate (*Hyssopus*
officinalis) : (*B.*) an unknown wall-plant used as a
ceremonial sprinkler: a sprinkler. [L. *hyssōpus,*
-um—Gr. *hyssōpos, -on* ; cf. Heb. *′ēzōb.*]
hysteranthous, *his-tor-an′thos, adj.* having the
leaves appearing after the flowers. [Gr. *hysteros,*
later, *anthos,* flower.]
hysteresis, *his-to-rē′sis, n.* a lag in variation behind
the variation of the cause.—*adjs.* **hysterē′sial,**
hysterĕt′ic. [Gr. *hysterēsis,* a deficiency, coming
late—*hysteros,* later.]
hysteria, *his-tē′ri-ä, n.* a psychoneurosis in which
repressed complexes become split off or dissociated
from the personality, forming independent units,
partially or completely unrecognised by consciousness, giving rise to hypnoidal states (amnesia,
somnambulisms), and manifested by various
physical symptoms, such as tics, paralysis, blindness, deafness, &c., general features being an
extreme degree of emotional instability and an
intense craving for affection : an outbreak of wild
emotionalism.—*adjs.* **hysteric** (*his-ter′ik*), **-al,** pertaining to, of the nature of, or affected with,
hysterics or hysteria : like hysterics : fitfully and
violently emotional. — *adv.* **hyster′ically.**— *adj.*
hyster′icky (*coll.*).—*n.pl.* **hyster′ics,** hysteric fits :
popularly, alternate paroxysms of laughing and
crying, often with a choking sensation in the
throat.—*n.* **hysteri′tis,** inflammation of the uterus.
—*adjs.* **hys′teroid, -al,** like hysteria.—*ns.* **hys-**
teromān′ia, hysterical mania, often marked by
erotic delusions and an excessive desire to attract
attention ; **hysterot′omy** (Gr. *tomē,* a cut),
surgical incision of the uterus. [Gr. *hysterā,* the
womb, with which hysteria was formerly thought
to be connected.]
hysteron-proteron, *his′tor-on-prot′or-on, n.* a figure
of speech in which what would ordinarily follow
comes first : an inversion. [Gr., lit. latter-former.]
hythe. Same as **hithe.**

fāte, fär, ȧsk ; mē, hȯr (her) *; mīne ; mōte ; mūte ; mōōn ; dhen* (then)

I

I, i, ī, *n.* the ninth letter of our alphabet, answering to Greek ῐŏta, has in most European languages the sound of the Latin long *i*, as in our *machine, marine.* This sound in Old English has changed to a diphthong in modern English. The normal sound in English is that in *bit, dip,* the Latin short *i.* In Roman numerals I represents one; in chemistry, iodine; in mathematics *i* represents the imaginary square root of −1.

I, ī, *pron.* the nominative singular of the first personal pronoun: the word used in mentioning oneself.—*n.* the object of self-consciousness, the ego. [M.E. *ich*—O.E. *ic*; Ger. *ich*, O.N. *ek*, L. *ego*, Gr. *egō.*]

I, i, *adv.* same as **ay.**

i', i, *prep.* a form of **in.**

iambus, ī-am'bos, *n.* a foot of two syllables, a short followed by a long, or an unstressed by a stressed: (*pl.* **iam'buses, iam'bī**). — Also **i'amb.** — *adj.* **iam'bic,** consisting of iambuses: of the nature of an iambus: using iambic verse: satirical in verse.—*n.* an iambus: (in *pl.*) iambic verse, esp. satirical.—*adv.* **iam'bically,** in the manner of an iambic.—*ns.* **iam'bist, iambog'rapher,** a writer of iambics. [L. *iambus*—Gr. *iambos*—*iaptein,* to assail, this metre being first used by satirists.]

ianthine, ī-an'thīn, *adj.* violet-coloured. [Gr. *ianthinos*—*ion,* violet, *anthos,* flower.]

Iastic, ī-ast'ik, *adj.* (*mus.*) Ionian.—**Iastic mode,** the Ionian, Hypophrygian, or Hyperdorian mode of ancient Greek music. [Gr. *Iastikos,* Ionian.]

iatric, -al, ī-at'rik, -əl, *adj.* relating to medicine or physicians. — *adj.* **iatrochem'ical.** — *ns.* **iatrochem'ist, iatrochem'istry,** an application of chemistry to medical theory introduced by Franciscus Sylvius (1614-72) of Leyden. [Gr. *iātros,* a physician.]

Iberian, ī-bē'ri-ən, *adj.* of Spain and Portugal: of Iberia (now Georgia) in the Caucasus: of the ancient inhabitants of either of these, or their later representatives: of a Mediterranean people of Neolithic culture in Britain, &c.—*n.* a member of any of these peoples. [L. *Ibēria*—Gr. *Ibēria.*]

Iberis, ī-bē'ris, *n.* the candytuft genus of Cruciferae. [Gr. *ibēris,* pepperwort.]

ibex, ī'beks, *n.* a large-horned mountain wild-goat: —*pl.* **i'bexes,** also **ibices (ī'bi-sēz).** [L. *ibex, -icis.*]

ibis, ī'bis, *n.* a wading bird with curved bill, akin to the spoonbills, one species worshipped by the ancient Egyptians. [L. and Gr. *ibis,* prob. Egyptian.]

Iblis. See **Eblis.**

Icarian, ī-kā'ri-ən, *adj.* of or like *Icarus* (Gr. *Ikäros*), who fell into the sea as he flew from Crete.

ice, īs, *n.* frozen water: concreted sugar on a cake, &c.: a frozen confection of sweetened cream, fruit-juice, &c.—*adj.* of ice.—*v.t.* to cover with ice: to freeze: to cool with ice: to cover with concreted sugar :—*pr.p.* **ic'ing;** *pa.t.* and *pa.p.* **iced.**
—*ns.* **ice'-action,** the work of land-ice in grinding the earth's surface; **ice'-age,** (*geol.*) any time when a great part of the earth's surface has been covered with ice, esp. that in Pleistocene times; **ice'-anchor,** a one-armed anchor for mooring to an ice-floe; **ice'-a'pron,** a structure on the up-stream side of a bridge pier to break or ward off floating ice; **ice'-axe,** an axe used by mountain-climbers to cut steps in ice; **ice'-bird,** the little auk or sea-dove; **ice'blink,** a gleam reflected from distant masses of ice; **ice'boat,** a boat for forcing a way through or sailing or being dragged over ice.—*adj.* **ice'-bound,** bound, surrounded, or fixed in with ice.—*ns.* **ice'-box,** (*U.S.*) kind of refrigerator; **ice'-breaker,** ship for breaking channel through ice: anything for breaking ice; **ice'-cap,** a covering of ice over a convexity, as a mountain top, the polar regions of a planet.—*adj.* **ice'-cold,** cold as, or like, ice.—*ns.* **ice'craft,** skill in travelling over or through ice; **ice'-cream',** cream, or a substitute, sweetened or flavoured, and frozen (**ice'-cream soda,** soda-water with ice-cream added).—*adj.* **iced (īst),** covered or cooled with ice: encrusted with sugar.—*ns.* **ice'-fall,** a fall of ice: a steep broken place in a glacier; **ice'-fern,** a fern-like encrustation on a window in frost; **ice'-field,** a large area covered with ice, esp. floating ice; **ice'-floe,** a large sheet of floating ice; **ice'-foot,** a belt of ice forming round the shores in Arctic regions—also **ice'-belt, ice'-ledge.**—*adj.* **ice'-free,** without ice.—*ns.* **ice'-front,** the front face of a glacier; **ice'-hill,** a slope of ice for tobogganing; **ice'-hill'ing; ice'-hock'ey,** a form of hockey played on ice by skaters with a puck; **ice'-house,** a house for keeping ice in; **ice'man,** a man skilled in travelling upon ice: a dealer in ice: a man in attendance on skaters, &c.; **ice'pack,** drifting ice packed together: a pack prepared with ice; **ice'-pail,** a pail with ice for cooling wine; **ice'-pan,** a slab of floating ice; **ice'-plant,** a plant (Mesembrianthemum) whose leaves glisten like ice in the sun; **i'cer,** one who makes icing; **ice'-rink,** a skating rink of ice; **ice'-run,** a tobogganing slide; **ice'-sheet,** land-ice covering a whole region; **ice'-spar,** a clear glassy orthoclase; **ice'-stone,** cryolite; **ice'-water,** water from melted ice: iced water; **ice'-worm,** a species of oligochaete stated by some to be found on glaciers in Alaska, &c.; **ice'-yacht,** a ship on runners and with sails for sailing over smooth ice; **ice'-yacht'ing.**—*adv.* **ic'ily.**—*ns.* **ic'iness; ic'ing,** covering with or of ice or concreted sugar.—*adjs.* **ic'y,** composed of, abounding in, or like ice: frosty: cold: chilling: without warmth of affection; **ic'y-pearl'ed,** (*Milt.*) studded with pearls or spangles of ice.—**break the ice** (see **break**); **cut no ice,** to count for nothing; **dry ice,** solid carbon dioxide. [O.E. *is*; O.N. *iss*; Ger. *eis,* Dan. *is.*]

iceberg, īs'bərg, *n.* a huge mass of floating ice. [From Scand. or Du.; see **ice, berg.**]

Iceland, īs'lənd, *adj.* belonging to, originating in, *Iceland.*—*ns.* **Ice'land-dog',** a shaggy white dog, sharp-eared, imported from Iceland; **Ice'lander,** a native or citizen of Iceland: an Iceland-falcon; **Ice'land-fal'con,** a white gerfalcon of Iceland.—*adj.* **Icelandic (īs-land'ik),** of Iceland.—*n.* the modern language of the Icelanders: Old Norse.—*ns.* **Ice'land-moss',** a lichen of northern regions, used as a medicine and for food; **Ice'land-popp'y,** a dwarf poppy (*Papaver nudicaule*) with grey-green pinnate leaves and flowers varying from white to orange-scarlet; **Ice'land-spar',** a transparent calcite with strong double refraction.

ich, ich, *v.t.* (*Shak.*). Same as **eke.**

ichabod, ik'ə-bod, *interj.* the glory is departed. [From Heb.; see 1 Sam. iv. 21.]

ichneumon, ik-nū'mon, *n.* any animal of the mongoose genus (Herpestes) of the civet family, esp. the Egyptian species that destroys crocodiles' eggs: (in full **ichneu'mon-fly**) any insect of a large family of Hymenoptera whose larvae are parasitic in or on other insects. [Gr. *ichneumōn,* lit. tracker, *ichneuein,* to hunt after—*ichnos,* a track.]

ichnography, ik-nog'rəf-i, *n.* a ground-plan: the art of drawing ground-plans.—*adjs.* **ichnographic (-nō-graf'ik), -al.**—*adv.* **ichnograph'ically.**—*n.* **ichnol'ogy,** footprint lore: the science of fossil footprints. [Gr. *ichnos,* a track, footprint.]

ichor, ī'kor, *n.* (*myth.*) the ethereal juice in the veins of the gods: a watery humour: colourless matter from an ulcer.—*adj.* **i'chorous.** [Gr. *ichōr.*]

Neutral vowels in unaccented syllables : **el'ə-mənt, in'fənt, ran'dəm**

ichthy-, *ik'thi-*, in composition, fish.—*adj.* **ich'thic.** —*ns.* **ichthyocoll'a** (Gr. *kolla*, glue), fish-glue: isinglass; **ichthyodor'ulite, ichthyodor'ylite** (*-i-līt*; Gr. *dory*, a spear, *lithos*, a stone), a fossil fish-spine; **ichthyog'raphy,** a description of fishes.—*adjs.* **ich'thyoid, -al,** fishlike.—*n.* **ichthyol'atry** (Gr. *latreiā*, worship), fish-worship.—*adj.* **ichthyol'atrous.**—*n.* **ich'thyolite** (Gr. *lithos*, a stone), a fossil fish or fish-fossil.—*adjs.* **ichthyolitic** (*-lit'ik*); **ichthyolog'ical.**—*ns.* **ichthol'ogist;** **ichthyol'ogy,** the branch of natural history that treats of fishes; **ichthyophagist** (*-of'ə-jist*; Gr. *phagein*, to eat), a fish-eater.—*adj.* **ichthyoph'agous** (*-ə-gəs*).—*ns.* **ichthyophagy** (*-of'ə-ji*), the practice of eating fish; **ichthyop'sid, -an** (Gr. *opsis*, appearance).—*n.pl.* **Ichthyop'sida,** a group of vertebrates in Huxley's classification comprising amphibians, fishes, and fishlike vertebrates; **Ichthyopterygia** (*-op-tər-ij'i-ā*; Gr. *pterygion*, a fin, dim. of *pteryx*, wing), the Ichthyosauria.—*ns.* **Ichthyor'nis** (Gr. *ornis*, a bird), a Cretaceous fossil bird with vertebræ like those of fishes, and with teeth set in sockets; **ichthyosaur** (*ik'thi-ō-sawr*; Gr. *sauros*, lizard), any member of the genus **Ichthyosaur'us** or of the order **Ichthyosaur'ia,** gigantic Mesozoic fossil fishlike marine reptiles.—*adj.* **ichthyosaur'ian.**—*n.* **ichthyō'sis,** a disease in which the skin becomes hardened, thickened, and rough.—*adj.* **ichthyŏt'ic.**—*n.* **ich'thys,** an emblem or motto (IXΘΥΣ), supposed to have a mystical connexion with Jesus Christ, being the first letters of the Greek words meaning 'Jesus Christ, Son of God, Saviour.' [Gr. *ichthys*, fish.]

icicle, *īs'i-kl*, *n.* a hanging, tapering piece of ice formed by the freezing of dropping water. [O.E. *īsesgicel—īses*, gen. of *īs*, ice, *gicel*, icicle.]

icker, *ik'ər*, *n.* (*Scot.*) an ear of corn. [O.E. (Northumbrian) *eher, æhher*; cf. **ear.**]

icon, *ī'kon*, *n.* a figure: image: a portrait, carved, painted, &c.: in the Greek Church a figure representing Christ, or a saint, in painting, mosaic, &c. (not sculpture).—*adj.* **icon'ic,** of images or icons: conventional in type.—*ns.* **iconog'raphy** (Gr. *graphiā*, a writing), the art of illustration: the study, description, cataloguing, or collective representation of portraits; **iconol'ater,** an image-worshipper; **iconol'atry** (Gr. *latreiā*, worship), image-worship; **iconol'ogist;** **iconol'ogy,** the study of icons: symbolism; **iconomachist** (*-om'ə-kist*), one who contends against the use of icons in worship; **iconom'achy** (Gr. *machē*, fight), opposition to image-worship.—*adj.* **iconomat'ic,** using pictures of objects to represent not the things themselves but the sounds of their names, as in a transition stage between picture-writing and a phonetic system.—*ns.* **iconomat'icism** (*-i-sizm*); **iconom'eter,** an instrument for inferring distance from size or size from distance of an object, by measuring its image: a direct photographic view-finder; **iconom'etry; iconoph'ilism,** a taste for pictures, &c.; **iconoph'ilist,** a connoisseur of pictures, &c.; **icon'oscope,** a form of photographic view-finder: **Icon'oscope,** a form of electron camera; **iconos'tasis** (Gr. *eikonostasis — stasis*, placing), in Eastern churches, a screen shutting off the sanctuary, on which the icons are placed. [L. *īcōn*—Gr. *eikōn*, an image.]

iconoclasm, *ī-kon'ō-klazm*, *n.* act of breaking images: opposition to image-worship.—*n.* **icon'oclast,** a breaker of images: one opposed to image-worship, esp. those in the Eastern Church, from the 8th century: one who assails old cherished errors and superstitions.—*adj.* **iconoclast'ic.** [Gr. *eikōn*, an image, *klaein*, to break.]

icosahedron, *ī-kos-a-hē'drən*, *n.* (*geom.*) a solid with twenty plane faces: — *pl.* **icosahē'dra.**—*adj.* **icosahē'dral.**—*n.* **icositetrahē'dron,** a solid figure with twenty-four plane faces. [Gr. *eikosi*, twenty, *hedrā*, a seat.]

Icosandria, *ī-kos-an'dri-ā*, *n.pl.* a Linnæan class of plants with twenty or more free stamens.—*adjs.* **icosan'drian, icosan'drous.** [Gr. *eikosi*, twenty, *anēr, andros*, a man (male).]

icterus, *ik'tər-əs*, *n.* jaundice: **Icterus,** a genus of birds with much yellow in their plumage, including the Baltimore oriole, giving name to the American family **Icteridae** (*-ter'i-dē*; hang-nests, bobolinks, troupials, grakles).—*adjs.* **icteric** (*-ter'ik*), **-al,** relating to or affected with jaundice.—*ns.* a medicine for jaundice.—*adjs.* **ic'terine** (*-tər-īn, -in*), of or like the family Icteridae: yellowish or marked with yellow; **icteritious** (*ik-tər-ish'əs*), jaundiced: yellow. [Gr. *ikteros*, jaundice, also a yellowish bird (acc. Pliny the golden oriole) the sight of which cured jaundice.]

ictus, *ik'tos*, *n.* a stroke: rhythmical or metrical stress: a pulsation:—*pl.* **ic'tuses** (or L. **ic'tūs**).—*adj.* **ic'tic.** [L., a blow.]

I'd, *īd*, contracted from *I would*, or *I had*: also used for *I should*.

id, *id*, **ide,** *īd*, *n.* a fish of the same family as the carp, inhabiting the fresh waters of Northern Europe. [Sw. *id*.]

id, *id*, *n.* (*biol.*) in Weismann's theory, an element in a chromosome carrying all the hereditary characters.—*n.* **idant** (*ī'dənt*), an aggregation of ids: a chromosome. [Gr. *idios*, own, private; appar. suggested by **idioplasm.**]

id, *id*, *n.* (*psych.*) the sum total of the primitive instinctive forces in an individual subserving the pleasure-pain principle. [L. *id*, it.]

Idaean, *ī-dē'ən*, *adj.* of Mount Ida in Crete, or that near Troy.—**Idaean vine,** the cowberry (*Vaccinium Vitis-Idaea*). [Gr. *Idaios—Idē*.]

Idalian, *ī-dā'li-ən*, *adj.* pertaining to *Idalium* (Gr. *Idālion*), in Cyprus, or to Aphrodite, to whom it was sacred.

idea, *ī-dē'ä*, *n.* an image of an external object formed by the mind: a notion, thought, any product of intellectual action, of memory and imagination: an archetype of the manifold varieties of existence in the universe, belonging to the supersensible world, where reality is found and where God is (*Platonic*): one of the three products of the reason (the Soul, the Universe, and God) transcending the conceptions of the understanding—*transcendental ideas*, in the functions of mind concerned with unification of existence (*Kantian*): the ideal realised, the absolute truth of which everything that exists is the expression (*Hegelian*).—*adjs.* **idē'aed, idē'a'd,** provided with an idea or ideas; **idē'al,** existing in idea: mental: existing in imagination only: highest and best conceivable: perfect, as opposed to the real, the imperfect: theoretical, conforming absolutely to theory.—*n.* the highest conception of anything, or its embodiment: a standard of perfection.—*adj.* **idē'aless,** devoid of ideas.—*n.* **idēalisā'tion.**—*v.t.* **idē'alise,** to regard or represent as ideal.—*v.i.* to form ideals: to think or work idealistically.—*ns.* **idē'aliser;** **idē'alism,** the doctrine that in external perceptions the objects immediately known are ideas, that all reality is in its nature psychical: any system that considers thought or the idea as the ground either of knowledge or existence: tendency towards the highest conceivable perfection, love for or search after the best and highest: the imaginative treatment of subjects; **idē'alist,** one who holds the doctrine of idealism: one who strives after the ideal: an unpractical person.—*adj.* **idēalist'ic,** pertaining to idealists or to idealism.—*adv.* **idēalist'ically.**—*n.* **idēality** (*-al'i-ti*), ideal state: ability and disposition to form ideals of beauty and perfection.—*adj.* **idē'alless,** having no ideals.—*adv.* **idē'ally,** in an ideal manner: mentally.—*n.* **idē'alogue** (a misspelling of **ideologue**).—*v.t.* **idē'ate,** to form or have an idea of: to imagine: to preconceive.—*v.i.* to form ideas.—*adj.* produced by an idea.—*n.* the correlative or object of an idea. —*n.* **idēā'tion,** the power of the mind for forming ideas: the exercise of such power.—*adjs.* **idēā'tional, idē'ative.**—*adv.* **idēā'tionally.** [L. *idea* —Gr. *idēā*; cf. *idein* (aor.), to see.]

identify, *ī-den'ti-fī*, *v.t.* to make, reckon, ascertain or prove to be the same: to ascertain the identity of: to assign to a species: to bind up or associate closely.—*v.i.* to become the same:—*pr.p.* **iden'tifying;** *pa.p.* **iden'tified.**—*adj.* **iden'tifīable.**—*n.* **identificā'tion.** [L.L. *identificāre — idem*, the same, *facěre*, to make.]

identity, *ī-den′ti-ti, n.* state of being the same: sameness: sameness of a thing with itself: individuality: personality: who or what a person or thing is: (*math.*) an equation true for all values of the symbols involved.—*adj.* **iden′tical,** the very same: not different: expressing or resulting in identity.—Also **iden′tic.**—*adv.* **iden′tically.**—*n.* **iden′ticalness.**—**identical twins,** twins developing from₁one zygote; **identity card, disk, a** card, disk, &c., bearing the owner's or wearer's name, &c., used to establish his identity. [L.L. *identitās, -ātis*—L. *idem,* the same.]

ideogram, *id′i-ō-gram,* or *id′,* **ideograph,** *-gråf, ns.* a written character or symbol that stands not for a word or sound but for the thing itself directly. —*adjs.* **ideographic** (*-graf′ik*), **-al.**—*adv.* **ideograph′ically.**—*n.* **ideography** (*-og′rə-fi*). [Gr. *idĕā,* idea, *gramma,* a drawing, *graphein,* to write.]

ideology, *id-,* *id-i-ol′ə-ji, n.* the science of ideas, metaphysics: abstract speculation: visionary speculation: body of ideas: way of thinking.— *adjs.* **ideologic** (*-loj′*), **-al,** of or pertaining to an ideology: arising from, concerned with, rival ideologies.—*n.* **ideol′ogist,** one occupied with ideas or an idea: a mere theorist or visionary.— Also **ideologue** (*ī-dē′ō-log*). [Gr. *idĕā,₁*idea, *logos,* discourse.]

ideopraxist, *id-,* *id-i-ō-prak′sist, n.* one who is impelled to carry out an idea. [Gr. *idĕā,* idea, *prāxis,* doing.]

Ides, *īdz, n.pl.* in ancient Rome, the 15th day of March, May, July, October, and the 13th of the other months. [Fr. *ides*—L. *īdūs* (pl.).]

idiocy. See **idiot.**

idiograph, *id′i-ō-gråf, n.* a private mark: trademark.—*adj.* **idiographic** (*-graf′ik*). [Gr. *idios,* own, private, *graphein,* to write.]

idiom, *id′i-əm, n.* a mode of expression peculiar to a language: an expression characteristic of a particular language not logically or grammatically explicable: a form or variety of language: a dialect: a characteristic mode of expression.— *adjs.* **idiomat′ic, -al.**—*adv.* **idiomat′ically.**—*ns.* **idioticon** (*-ot′i-kon*), a vocabulary of a particular dialect or district; **id′iotism** (*-ə-tizm*), an idiom: an idiomatic expression: idiomatic character: (see also under **idiot**). [Gr. *idiōma, idiōtikon*—*idios,* own.]

idiomorphic, *id-i-ō-mor′fik, adj.* having the faces belonging to its crystalline form, as a mineral that has had free room to crystallise out. [Gr. *idios,* own, *morphē,* form.]

idiopathy, *id-i-op′ə-thi, n.* a state or experience peculiar to the individual: (*med.*) a primary disease, one not occasioned by another.—*adj.* **idiopathic** (*-path′ik*).—*adv.* **idiopath′ically.** [Gr. *idios,* own, *pathos,* suffering.]

idioplasm, *id′i-ō-plazm, n.* that part of the protoplasm that determines hereditary character. [Gr. *idios,* own, private, *plasma,* mould.]

idior(r)hythmic, *id-i-ō-ridh′mik,* or *rith′, adj.* self-regulating: allowing each member to regulate his own life. [Gr. *idios,* own, *rhythmos,* order.]

idiosyncrasy, *id-i-ō-sing′krə-si, n.* peculiarity of temperament or mental constitution: any characteristic of a person.—*adjs.* **idiosyncratic** (*-krat′ik*), **-al.** [Gr. *idios,* own, *synkrāsis,* a mixing together—*syn,* together, *krāsis,* a mixing.]

idiot, *id′i-ət, id′yət, n.* a person so defective in mind from birth as to be unable to protect himself against ordinary physical dangers: one afflicted with the severest grade of feeble-mindedness: a flighty fool: a blockhead: a foolish or unwise person.— *adj.* afflicted with idiocy: idiotic.—*ns.* **id′iocy** (*-ə-si*), **id′iotcy** (*rare*), state of being an idiot: imbecility: folly.—*adjs.* **idiotic** (*-ot′ik*), **-al,** pertaining to or like an idiot: foolish.—*adv.* **idiot′ically.**—*n.* **idiot′icon** (see under **idiom**).—*adj.* **id′iotish,** idiotic.—*n.* **id′iotism,** the state of being an idiot: (see also under **idiom**). [Fr.,—L. *idiōta*—Gr. *idiōtēs,* a private person, ordinary person, one who holds no public office or has no professional knowledge—*idios,* own, private.]

idiothermous, *id-i-ō-thər′məs, adj.* warm-blooded, i.e. having a temperature of one's own, independent of surroundings. [Gr. *idios,* own, *thermē* heat.]

idle, *ī′dl, adj.* vain: baseless: trifling: unemployed: averse to labour: not occupied: useless: unimportant: unedifying.—*v.t.* to spend in idleness: to cause to be idle.—*v.i.* to be idle or unoccupied: of machinery, to run without doing work. —*adj.* **i′dle-head′ed,** foolish.—*ns.* **i′dlehood, i′dleness; i′dler; id′lesse,** idleness; **i′dle-wheel,** a wheel placed between two others for transferring the motion from one to the other without changing the direction.—*n.pl.* **i′dle-worms,** worms once jocularly supposed to be bred in the fingers of lazy maid-servants.—*adv.* **i′dly.** [O.E. *idel*; Du. *ijdel,* Ger. *eitel.*]

Ido, *ē′dō, n.* an auxiliary international language developed (since 1907) from Esperanto.—*ns.* **Id′ist, I′doist.** [Ido, offspring.]

idocrase, *īd′, id′ō-krās, -krāz, n.* the mineral vesuvianite. [Gr. *eidos,* form, *krāsis,* mixture.]

idol, *ī′dl, n.* a figure: an image: a phantom: (*Spens.*) a counterfeit: an image of a god: an object of worship: an object of love, admiration, or honour in an extreme degree: (also **Idō′lon, Idō′lum**; *pl.* **Idō′la**) a false notion or erroneous way of looking at things to which the mind is prone, classified by Bacon (*Novum Organum,* i. § 39) as *Idols of the tribe* (due to the nature of man's understanding); *Idols of the den* or *cave* (due to personal causes); *Idols of the forum* (due to the influence of words or phrases); *Idols of the theatre* (due to misconceptions of philosophic system or demonstration).—*v.t.* **i′dolise,** to make an idol of.—*ns.* **idolīs′er; i′dolism,** idol-worship: idolising: (*Milt.*) a false notion; **i′dolist** (*Milt.*) an idolater; **idoloclast** (*-dol′*), a breaker of images. [L. *idōlum* —Gr.*eidōlon—eidos,* form—*idein* (aor.), to see.]

idolater, *ī-dol′ə-tər, n.* a worshipper of idols: a great admirer:—*fem.* **idol′atress.**—*v.t.* and *v.i.* **idol′atrise,** to worship as an idol: to adore.— *adj.* **idol′atrous.**—*adv.* **idol′atrously.**—*n.* **idol′atry,** the worship of an image held to be the abode of a superhuman personality: excessive love. [Fr. *idolâtre*—Gr. *eidōlolatrēs—eidōlon,* idol, *latreuein,* to worship.]

idyll, *id′il, ī′dil, -əl, n.* a short pictorial poem, chiefly on pastoral subjects: a story of happy innocence or rusticity: a work of art of like character in any medium.—Also **idyl.**—*adjs.* **idyll′ian, idyll′ic.**—*n.* **i′dyllist.** [L. *īdyllium*—Gr. *eidyllion,* dim. of *eidos,* image.]

if, *if, conj.* on condition that: provided that: in case that: supposing that: whether.—*n.* a condition: a supposition.—**as if,** as it would be if. [O.E. *gif*; cf. Du. *of,* O.N. *ef.*]

igad, *i-gad′.* Same as **egad.**

igapó, Same as **gapó.**

igarapé, *i-gä-rä-pā′, n.* a canoe waterway in Brazil. [Tupí.]

igloo, *ig′loo, n.* a snow-hut. [Eskimo.]

ignaro, *ig-nä′rō, ēn-yä′rō, n.* an ignorant person. [Prob. from Spenser's character (*Faerie Queene,* I. viii.) whose only answer is 'He could not tell'— It. *ignaro*—L. *ignārus,* ignorant.]

Ignatian, *ig-nā′shən, adj.* of or pertaining to St *Ignatius,* first-century bishop of Antioch (applied to the Epistles attributed to him): or *Ignatius* Loyola. —*n.* a Jesuit.—**Ignatius's bean** (see under **Saint**).

igneous, *ig′ni-əs, adj.* of or like fire: (*geol.*) produced by solidification of the earth's internal molten magma.—*adj.* **ignip′otent,** (*Pope*) presiding over fire. [L. *ignis,* fire.]

ignis-fatuus, *ig′nis-fat′ū-əs,* L. *fät′oo-oos, n.* Will-o'-the-wisp: the light of combustion of marsh-gas, apt to lead travellers into danger: any delusive ideal that leads one astray:—*pl.* **ignes-fatui** (*ig′nēz-fat′ū-ī*; L. *ig′nās-fät′oo-ē*). [L. *ignis,* fire, *fatuus,* foolish.]

ignite, *ig-nīt′, v.t.* to set on fire: to heat to the point at which combustion occurs.—*v.i.* to take fire.—*adj.* **ignīt′able** (also **ignīt′ible**).—*ns.* **ignīt-abil′ity** (**ignītibil′ity**); **ignīt′er,** one who ignites: apparatus for firing an explosive or explosive mixture; **ignition** (*-nish′ən*), act of igniting: means of igniting: state of being ignited: the firing system of an internal-combustion engine. [L. *ignīre, ignītum*, to set on fire, to make red-hot—*ignis*, fire.]

ignoble, *ig-nō'bl, adj.* of low birth : mean or worthless : unworthy : base : dishonourable.—*v.t.* to degrade.—*ns.* **ignōbil'ity**, **ignō'bleness**.—*adv.* **ignō'bly**. [Fr.,—L. *ignōbilis—in-*, not, *(g)nōbilis*, noble.]

ignominy, *ig'nō-min-i*, or *-nƏ-*, *n.* loss of good name : public disgrace : infamy—formerly also (as *Shak.*) **ig'nomy**.—*adj.* **ignomin'ious**, deserving or marked with ignominy.—*adv.* **ignomin'iously**. [L. *ignōminia, in-*, not, *(g)nōmen, -inis*, name.]

ignoramus, *ig-nō-rā'mƏs, n.* the word formerly written by a grand-jury on the back of a rejected indictment : an ignorant person, esp. one pretending to knowledge :—*pl.* **ignorā'muses**. [L. *ignōrāmus*, we are ignorant, in legal use, we ignore, take no notice, 1st per. pl. pres. indic. of *ignōrāre*.]

ignorant, *ig'nƏr-Ənt, adj.* without knowledge, in general or particular : uninstructed : uninformed : unaware : showing, arising from, want f knowledge : (*Shak.*) keeping back knowledge : (*obs.*) unknown. —*n.* an ignorant person.—*n.* **ig'norance**, want of knowledge—in R.C. theol. *vincible* or *wilful* ignorance is such as one may be fairly expected to overcome ; *invincible* ignorance is that which one cannot help or abate : the time of ignorance, i.e. before Mahommed : an instance of ignorance : an act committed in ignorance.—*adv.* **ig'norantly**. [Fr.,—L. *ignōrāns, -āntis*, pr.p. of *ignōrāre* ; see **ignore**.]

Ignorantine, *ig-nō-ran'tīn, -tin, n.* (*R.C.*) a member of a religious congregation of men devoted to the instruction of the poor—inaccurately applied to *Brethren of the Christian Schools.*

ignore, *ig-nōr', v.t.* wilfully to disregard : to set aside.—*adj.* **ignor'able**.—*ns.* **ignorā'tion**, ignoring ; **ignor'er**. [L. *ignōrāre*, not to know—*in-*, not, and the root of *(g)nōscĕre*, to know.]

Iguana, *i-gwä'nä, n.* a genus of large thick-tongued arboreal lizards in tropical America : loosely extended to others of the same family (**Iguan'idae**) : **iguana**, in South Africa a monitor lizard. [Sp., from Carib.]

Iguanodon, *i-gwä'nƏ-don, n.* a large Jurassic and Cretaceous herbivorous dinosaur, with teeth like those of the iguana. [**iguana**, and Gr. *odous, odontos*, tooth.]

Iguvine, *ig'ū-vīn, adj.* Eugubine.

ihram, *ē-räm', ēhh'räm, n.* the scanty garb worn by Mahommedan pilgrims on drawing near Mecca : the holy state it betokens. [Ar. *ihrām.*]

ikon. Same as icon.

ilang-ilang. Same as ylang-ylang.

ileac. See ileum, ileus.

ileum, *il', il'i-Əm, n.* the posterior part of the small intestine.—*adj.* **il'eac, il'iac**. [L.L. *īleum*, L. *īlia* (pl.), the groin, flank, intestines.]

ileus, *il', il'i-Əs, n.* obstruction of the intestine with severe pain, vomiting, &c.—Also **ileac** or **iliac passion**.—*adj.* **il'eac, il'iac**. [L. *īleos*—Gr. *īleos* or *eileos*, colic.]

ilex, *i'leks, n.* the holm-oak (*Quercus Ilex*) : **Ilex**, the holly genus :—*pl.* **i'lexes, ilices** (*i'li-sēz*). [L. *īlex*, holm-oak.]

Iliac, iliac. See ileum, ileus, Ilium, ilium.

Iliad, *il'i-ad, -Əd, n.* a Greek epic ascribed to Homer, on the siege of Troy : a long story or series of woes. [Gr. *Ilias, -ados—Ilios* or *Ilion*, Ilium, Troy.]

ilium, *il', il'i-Əm, n.* the bone that unites with the ischium and pubis to form the innominate bone :—*pl.* **il'ia**, the flanks.—*adj.* **il'iac**. [L. *ilium* (in classical L. only in pl. *īlia*) ; see **ileum**.]

Ilium, *il'i-Əm, n.* Troy.—*adjs.* **Il'iac, Il'ian**. [L. *Ilium*—Gr. *Ilion*, Troy.]

ilk, *ilk, adj.* same.—**of that ilk**, of that same, that is, of the estate of the same name as the family—often used ignorantly for ' of that kind.' [O.E. *ilca*, same.]

ilk, *ilk, adj.* (*Scot.*) each : usu. compounded with the article as **ilk'a** (*-Ə, -ā*).—*n., adj., adv.* **ilk'aday**, every day, every day but Sunday. [O.E. *ǽlc*, each.]

ill, *il, adj.* (*comp.* **worse** ; *superl.* **worst**) evil, bad : wicked : producing evil : hurtful : unfortunate : unfavourable : difficult : reprehensible : sick : diseased : incorrect : cross, as temper : (*Scot.*) grieved, distressed : (*Scot.*) severe.—*adv.* (*comp.* **worse** ; *superl.* **worst**) badly : not well : not rightly : wrongfully : unfavourably : amiss : with hardship : with difficulty.—*n.* evil : wickedness : misfortune : harm : ailment.—*adjs.* **ill'-advised'**, imprudent : ill-judged ; **ill'-affect'ed**, not well disposed ; **ill'-beseem'ing**, (*Shak.*) unbecoming. —*ns.* **ill'-blood'**, **ill'-feel'ing**, resentment, enmity. — *adjs.* **ill'-bod'ing**, inauspicious ; **ill'-bred'**, badly bred or educated : uncivil.—*n.* **ill'-breed'ing**.—*adjs.* **ill'-condit'ioned**, in bad condition : churlish ; **ill'-deed'y**, (*Scot.*) mischievous ; **ill'-disposed'**, unfriendly : inclined to evil ; **ill'-faced** (*Spens.*) **ill-faste**), ugly-faced.—*n.* **ill'-fame'**, disrepute (see **house**).—*adjs.* **ill'-fat'ed**, unlucky ; **ill'-faurd'** (*Scot.*), **ill'-fā'voured**, ill-looking : deformed : ugly.—*adv.* **ill'-fā'vouredly**. —*n.* **ill'-fā'vouredness**.—*adjs.* **ill'-got'**, **-gott'en**, procured by bad means ; **ill'-haired'**, (*Scot.*), cross-grained ; **ill'-head'ed** (*Spens.* -hedd'ed), not clear in the head ; **ill'-hu'moured**, bad-tempered ; **ill'-judged'**, not well judged ; **ill'-look'ing**, having a bad look ; **ill'-manned'**, insufficiently provided with men ; **ill'-mann'ered**, rude : ill-bred ; **ill'-nā'tured**, of a bad temper : cross : peevish.—*adv.* **ill'-nā'turedly**.—*ns.* **ill'-nā'turedness** ; **ill'ness**, sickness : disease.—*adjs.* **ill'-off**, in bad circumstances ; **ill'-ō'mened**, having bad omens : unfortunate ; **ill'-spent**, spent amiss ; **ill'-starred'**, born under the influence of an unlucky star : unlucky ; **ill'-tem'pered**, having a bad temper : morose : (*Shak.*) badly tempered, ill-mixed, distempered.—*n.* **illth**, (*Ruskin*, &c.) the contrary of wealth or well-being.—*adj.* **ill'-timed**, said or done at an unsuitable time.—*v.t.* **ill-treat'**, to treat ill : to abuse.—*ns.* **ill-treat'ment** ; **ill'-turn'**, an act of unkindness or enmity ; **ill-us'age**. —*v.t.* **ill-use'**, to ill-treat.—*adj.* **ill-used'**, badly used or treated.—*ns.* **ill'-will'**, unkind feeling : enmity ; **ill'-wisher**, one who wishes harm to another.—*adj.* **ill'-wrest'ing**, misinterpreting to disadvantage.—*adv.* **illy** (*il'li* ; *rare*), ill.—**go ill with**, to result in danger or misfortune ; **take it ill**, to be offended. [O.N. *illr* ; not connected with O.E. *yfel*, evil, but formerly confused with **it**, so that **ill** is to be read where *evil* is written.]

illapse, *il-aps', n.* a sliding in.—*v.i.* to glide in. [L. *illābī, illāpsus—il-* (*in-*), in, *lābī*, to slip, to slide.]

illaqueate, *i-lak'wi-āt, v.t.* to ensnare.—*adj.* **illaq'ueable**.—*n.* **illaquea'tion**. [L. *illaqueāre*, *-ātum—il-* (*in-*), into, *laqueus*, a noose.]

illation, *il-ā'shƏn, n.* act of inferring from premises : inference : conclusion.—*adj.* **illative** (*il'Ə-tiv*, also *il-ā'tiv*), pertaining 'to, of the nature of, expressing, or introducing an inference.—*adv.* **illa'tively**. [L. *illātiō, -ōnis—illātus*, used as pa.p. of *inferre*, to infer—*il-* (*in-*), in, *lātus*, carried.]

illaudable, *il-aw'dƏ-bl, adj.* not praiseworthy.—*adv.* **illau'dably**. [L. *il-* (*in-*), not.]

Illecebrum, *il-es'i-brƏm, n.* a genus of plants of one species found in Devon and Cornwall, giving name in some classifications to a family **Illecebrā'ceae**, corresponding more or less to the Paronychiaceae or Corregiolaceae of others, by others again placed in Caryophyllaceae. [Said to be from L. *illecebra*, allurement, ' as enticing the simpler into bogs and marshes.']

illegal, *il-ē'gl, adj.* contrary to law.—*v.t.* **illē'galise**, to render unlawful.—*n.* **illegality** (*-gal'i-ti*), the quality or condition of being illegal.—*adv.* **illē'gally**.

illegible, *il-ej'i-bl, adj.* that cannot be read : indistinct.—*ns.* **illeg'ibleness**, **illegibil'ity**.—*adv.* **illeg'ibly**.

illegitimate, *il-i-jit'i-mit, adj.* not according to law : not in the legal position of those born in wedlock : not properly inferred or reasoned : not genuine : not recognised by authority or good usage : (of racing) other than flat-racing.—*n.* a bastard.—*v.t.* (*-māt*) to pronounce or render illegitimate.—*n.* **illegit'imacy** (*-mƏ-si*).—*adv.* **illegit'im-**

ately.—*n.* **illegitima′tion,** the act of pronouncing or rendering, or state of being, illegitimate.— **illegitimate pollination,** in dimorphic flowers, pollination of long style from short stamen, or short from long.

illiad, a Shakespearian form of oeillade.

illiberal, *il-ib′ər-əl, adj.* niggardly : mean, narrow in opinion or culture.—*v.t.* **illib′eralise.**—*n.* **illiberality** (-*al′i-ti*).—*adv.* **illib′erally.**

illicit, *il-is′it, adj.* not allowable : unlawful : unlicensed.—*adv.* **illic′itly.**—*n.* **illic′itness.**—**illicit process of the major, or minor,** (*log.*) the fallacy of distributing the major or minor term in the conclusion when it is not distributed in the premise. [L. *illicitus—il-* (*in-*), not, *licitus,* pa.p. of *licēre,* to be allowed.]

illimitable, *il-im′it-ə-bl, adj.* that cannot be bounded: infinite.—*n.* **illim′itableness.**—*adv.* **illim′itably.** —*n.* **illimitā′tion.**—*adj.* **illim′ited.**

illinium, *il-in′i-əm, n.* a name proposed for element No. 61.—See **prometheum.** [*Illinois* University, where its discovery was claimed.]

illipe, *il′i-pi,* **illupi,** *il′oo-pi, n.* the mahwa tree (Sapotaceae) yielding **illipe nuts** and **oil.** [Tamil *illuppai.*]

illiquation, *il-i-kwā′shən, n.* the melting of one thing into another. [L. *in,* into, *liquāre, -ātum,* to melt.]

illision, *il-izh′ən, n.* the act of striking against something. [L. *illīsiō, -ōnis—illidēre—in,* into, *laedēre,* to strike.]

illiterate, *il-it′ər-it, adj.* unacquainted with literature : without book-learning : uneducated : ignorant : unable to read : of or characteristic of those who are without literary education.—*n.* an illiterate person : one who cannot read.—*adv.* **illit′erately.** —*ns.* **illit′erateness, illit′eracy** (-*ə-si*).

illogical, *il-oj′i-kəl, adj.* contrary to the rules of logic : regardless or incapable of logic.—*adv.* **illog′ically.**—*n.* **illog′icalness.**

illude, *il-(y)ōōd′, v.t.* to trick. [L. *illūdēre—in,* on, *lūdēre, lūsum,* to play.]

illume, *il-(y)ōōm′, v.t.* a shortened poetic form of **illumine.**—*v.t.* **illum′inate** (-*in-āt*), to light up : to enlighten : to illustrate : to adorn with coloured lettering or illustrations : to confer power of vision upon.—*adj.* (-*āt,* -*it*) enlightened : pretending to enlightenment : admitted to a mystery. —*n.* an initiate.—*adj.* **illu′minable,** that may be illuminated.—*adj.* **illu′minant,** enlightening.—*n.* a means of lighting.—*n.pl.* **Illuminā′ti** (L. *il-lōō-mi-nā′tē*), the enlightened, a name given to various sects, and especially to a society of German Freethinkers at the end of the 18th century.—*n.* **illuminā′tion,** lighting up : enlightenment : intensity of lighting up : splendour : brightness : a decorative display of lights : adorning of books with coloured lettering or illustrations : inspiration.— *adj.* **illu′minative** (-*ə-tiv,* -*ā-tiv*), tending to give light : illustrative or explanatory.—*n.* **illu′minātor.**—*v.t.* **illu′mine,** to make luminous or bright : to enlighten : to adorn.—*ns.* **illu′miner,** an illuminator ; **illu′minism,** the principles of the Illuminati : belief in or claim to an inward spiritual light. [L. *illūmināre, -ātum, in,* in, upon, *lūmināre,* to cast light.]

illupi. Same as **illipe.**

illusion, *il-(y)ōō′zhən, n.* (*obs.*) a mocking : deceptive appearance : an apparition : false conception : delusion : (*psych.*) a false sense-impression of something actually present.—*ns.* **illu′sionism,** the doctrine that the external world is illusory : the production of illusion ; **illu′sionist,** a believer in or practitioner of illusionism : one who produces illusions, a conjurer or prestidigitator.—*adjs.* **illu′sive** (-*siv*), **illu′sory** (-*sər-i*), deceiving by false appearances : false.—*adv.* **illu′sively.**—*n.* **illu′siveness.** [See illude.]

illustrate, *il′əs-trāt* (old-fashioned *il-us′trāt*), *v.t.* (*obs.*) to make bright, adorn : to show in a favourable light : to give distinction or honour to : to make clear to the mind : to exemplify : to explain and adorn by pictures : to execute pictures for.— *adj.* (-*lus′* ; *Shak.*) illustrious : renowned.—*n.* **illustrā′tion,** act of making lustrous or clear : (*obs.*) lighting up : act of explaining : that which

illustrates : exemplification, example : a picture or diagram elucidating, or at least accompanying, letterpress.—*adj.* **ill′ustrated** (or -*us′*), having pictorial illustrations.—*n.* an illustrated periodical. —*adjs.* **illustrā′tional, illustrative** (*il′əs-trā-tiv* or -*trə-,* or *il-us′trə-tiv*), **illus′tratory,** having the quality of making clear or explaining.—*adv.* **ill′ustratively** (or *il-us′*).—*n.* **ill′ustrātor.**—*adj.* **illus′trious,** (*obs.*) luminous : highly distinguished : noble : conspicuous. — *adv.* **illus′triously.** — *n.* **illus′triousness.** [L. *illūstris* ; *illūstrāre, -ātum, lūstrāre,* to light up, prob.—*lūx,* light.]

illustrous, *il-us′tri-əs, adj.* (*Shak.*) dull. [L. *il-* (*in-*), not.]

ilmenite, *il′mən-īt, n.* a black mineral composed or iron, titanium, and oxygen. [From the *Ilmen* Mountains in the Urals.]

I'm, *īm,* a contraction of **I am.**

image, *im′ij, n.* likeness : a statue : an idol : a representation in the mind, an idea : a picture or representation (not necessarily visual) in the imagination or memory : an appearance : that which very closely resembles anything : a type : (*geom.*) a figure got from another figure by joining every point in it with a fixed point, or dropping a perpendicular from it to a fixed straight line or plane, and producing to the same distance : (*opt.*) the figure of any object formed by rays of light reflected or refracted (*real* if the rays converge upon it, *virtual* if they appear to diverge from it) : an analogous figure formed by other rays : (*rhet.*) a metaphor or simile.—*v.t.* to form an image of : to form a likeness of in the mind : to mirror : to imagine : to portray : to typify.—*adj.* **im′ageable.** —*n.* **im′age-breaker,** an iconoclast.—*adj.* **im′ageless,** having no image.—*ns.* **imagery** (*im′ij-ri,* -*ə-ri*), the work of the imagination : mental pictures : figures of speech : images in general or collectively ; **im′age-wor′ship** ; **im′agism** ; **im′agist,** one of a twentieth-century school of poetry aiming at concentration, the exact word, and hard clearness.— Also *adj.* [O.Fr.,—L. *imāgō,* image ; cf. *imitārī,* to imitate.]

imagine, *im-aj′in, v.t.* to form an image of in the mind : to conceive : to think : to think vainly or falsely : to conjecture : to contrive or devise. —*v.i.* to form mental images : to exercise imagination.—*adj.* **imag′inable.**—*n.* **imag′inableness.**— *adv.* **imag′inably.**—*adj.* **imag′inary,** existing only in the imagination : not real : non-existent.—*n.* **imaginā′tion,** act of imagining : the faculty of forming images in the mind : the artist′s creative power : that which is imagined : contrivance.— *adj.* **imag′inative** (-*ə-tiv,* or -*ā-tiv*), full of imagination : suffused with imagination.—*ns.* **imag′inativeness ; imag′iner ; imag′ining,** that which is imagined ; **imag′inist,** (*Jane Austen*) a person of active imagination and speculative temper.— **imaginary point, line,** &c., a non-existent point, &c., whose co-ordinates are **imaginary quantities,** non-existent quantities involving the square roots of negative quantities. [O.Fr. *imaginer* — L. *imāginārī—imāgō,* an image.]

imago, *i-mā′gō, n.* the last or perfect state of insect life : an image or optical counterpart of a thing : (*psych.*) an elaborated type, founded on a parent or other, persisting in the unconscious as an influence :—*pl.* **imagines** (*i-mā′jin-ēz*), **imā′gos.**— *adj.* **imaginal** (*i-maj′*). [L. *imāgō, -inis,* image.]

imâm, *i-mäm′,* **imaum,** *i-mawm′, n.* the officer who leads the devotions in a mosque : **Imâm,** a title for various Mohammedan potentates, founders, and leaders.—*n.* **imam′ate.** [Ar. *imām,* chief.]

imb-, for many words see **emb-.**

imbalance, *im-bal′əns, n.* (*med.*) a lack of balance, as between the ocular muscles, or between the activities of the endocrines, or between the parts of the involuntary nervous system, or between the elements of a diet : temporary lack of balance in a self-adjusting system.

imbark, *im-bärk′, v.t.* to enclose in bark.

imbecile, *im′bi-sil,* -*sēl,* formerly *im-bi-sēl′,* *im-bes′il, adj.* feeble (now generally in mind) : fatuous. —*n.* one who is imbecile : one whose defective mental state (from birth or an early age) does not

Neutral vowels in unaccented syllables : *el′ə-mənt, in′fənt, ran′dəm*

amount to idiocy, but who is incapable of managing his own affairs.—*n.* **imbecil'ity.** [Fr. *imbécille* (now *imbécile*)—L. *imbēcillus*; origin unknown.]

imbibe, *im-bīb'*, *v.t.* to drink in: to absorb: to receive into the mind.—*v.i.* to drink, absorb.—*ns.* **imbīb'er**; **imbibition** (*im-bib-ish'ən*). [L. *im-bibĕre*—*in*, in, into, *bibĕre*, to drink.]

imbrast, (*Spens.*) for **embraced.**

imbricate, *im'bri-kāt*, *v.t.* to lay one over another, as tiles in a roof.—*v.i.* to be so placed.—*adj.* overlapping like roof-tiles.—*n.* **imbrica'tion.** [L. *imbricāre*, *-ātum*, to tile—*imbrex*, a tile—*imber*, a shower.]

imbroccata,*im-bro-kä'tä,n.* in fencing,a thrust. [It.]

imbroglio, *im-brōl'yō*, *n.* a confused mass: a tangle: an embroilment: (*mus.*) an ordered confusion. [It., confusion—*imbrogliare*, to confuse, embroil.]

imbrue, *im-brōō'*, *v.t.* to wet or moisten: to soak: to drench: to stain or dye.—Also **embrue'.**—*n.* **imbrue'ment.** [O.Fr. *embreuver*—*bevre* (Fr. *boire*)—L. *bibĕre*, to drink.]

imbrute, *im-brōōt'*, *v.t.* or *v.i.* to reduce, or sink, to the state of a brute.—Also **embrute.**

imbue, *im-bū'*, *v.t.* to moisten: to tinge deeply: to cause to imbibe, as the mind. [O.Fr. *imbuer*—L. *imbuĕre*—*in*, and root of *bibĕre*, to drink.]

imburse, *im-burs'*, *v.t.* to put in a purse or in one's purse: to pay: to repay.

imitate, *im'i-tāt*, *v.t.* to strive to be like or produce something like: to copy, not necessarily exactly: to mimic.—*n.* **imitability** (*-ə-bil'i-ti*).—*adj.* **im'itable,** that may be imitated or copied: (*obs.*) inviting or worthy of imitation.—*ns.* **im'itancy,** the tendency to imitate; **im'itant,** a counterfeit; **imitā'tion,** act of imitating: that which is produced as a copy, or counterfeit: a performance in mimicry: (*mus.*) the repeating of the same passage, or the following of a passage with a similar one in one or more of the other parts or voices.—*adj.* sham, counterfeit: machine-made (as lace).—*adj.* **im'itātive,** inclined to imitate: formed after a model: mimicking.—*adv.* **im'itātively.**—*ns.* **im'itātiveness;** **im'itātor.** [L. *imitārī*, *-ātus.*]

immaculate, *im-ak'ū-lit*, *adj.* spotless: unstained: pure.—*n.* **immac'ulacy,** state of being immaculate.—*adv.* **immac'ulately.**—*n.* **immac'ulateness.**—**Immaculate Conception,** the R.C. dogma that the Virgin Mary was conceived without original sin—first proclaimed as an article of faith in 1854—not the same as the Virgin Birth. [L. *immaculātus*—*in*-, not, *maculāre*, to spot.]

immanacle, *im-(m)an'ə-kl*, *v.t.* (*Milt.*) to put in manacles, to fetter or confine.

immanation, *im-ə-nā'shən*, *n.* inflow. [L. *in*, in, *mānāre*, *-ātum*, to flow.]

immane, *im-ān'*, *adj.* huge: cruel, savage.—*adv.* **immane'ly.**—*n.* **immanity** (*im-an'i-ti*), cruelty. [L. *immānis*, huge, savage.]

immanent, *im'ə-nənt*, *adj.* indwelling: pervading: inherent.—*ns.* **imm'anence,** **imm'anency,** the pervasion of the universe by the intelligent and creative principle—a fundamental conception of Pantheism. — *adj.* **immanental** (*-ent'l*). — *ns.* **imm'anentism,** belief in an immanent God; **imm'anentist.** [L. *in*, in, *manēre*, to remain.]

immantle, *im-(m)an'tl*, *v.t.* to envelop in a mantle.

Immanuel, Emmanuel, *i-man'ū-el*, *n.* a name given to Jesus (Matt. i. 23) in allusion to Is. vii. 14. [Gr. *Emmanouēl*—Heb. *'Immānūēl*, God-with-us.]

immarcescible, *im-är-ses'i-bl*, *adj.* never-fading: imperishable.—Less correctly **immarcess'ible.** [L. *in*-, not, *marcēscĕre*, to languish.]

immarginate, *im-är'jin-āt*, *-it*, *adj.* without distinct margin.

immask, *im-mäsk'*, *v.t.* (*Shak.*) to mask, disguise.

immaterial, *im-ə-tē'ri-əl*, *adj.* not consisting of matter: incorporeal: unimportant. — *v.t.* **immatē'rialise,** to separate from matter.—*ns.* **immatē'rialism,** the doctrine that there is no material substance; **immatē'rialist;** **immatēriality** (*-al'*), the quality of being immaterial or of not consisting of matter.—*adv.* **immatē'rially.**

immature, *im-ə-tūr'*, **immatured,** *-tūrd'*, *adjs.* not ripe: not perfect: come before the natural time.

—*adv.* **immature'ly.**—*ns.* **immature'ness, immatur'ity.**

immeasurable, *im-ezh'ər-ə-bl*, *adj.* that cannot be measured: very great.—*n.* **immeas'urableness.** — *adv.* **immeas'urably.** — *adj.* **immeas'ured,** (*Spens.*) beyond the common measure, immeasurable.

immediate, *im-ē'di-āt*, *-dyət*, *-dyit*, *adj.* with nothing between: not acting by second causes: direct: present: without delay.—*n.* **imme'diacy.** —*adv.* **imme'diately.** — *ns.* **imme'diateness;** **imme'diatism,** immediateness: the policy of action at once, esp. (*U.S. hist.*) in abolition of slavery.

immedicable, *im-(m)ed'i-kə-bl*, *adj.* incurable.

immemorial, *im-i-mōr'i-əl*, *adj.* ancient beyond the reach of memory.—*adv.* **immemō'rially.**

immense, *i-mens'*, *adj.* that cannot be measured: vast in extent: very large: (*slang*) vastly amusing. —*adv.* **immense'ly.**—*ns.* **immense'ness;** **immens'ity,** an extent not to be measured: infinity: greatness. [Fr.,—L. *immēnsus*—*in*-, not, *mēnsus*, pa.p. of *metīrī*, to measure.]

immensurable, *im-(m)ens'ūr-ə-bl*, *adj.* that cannot be measured.—*n.* **immensurabil'ity.**

immerge, *im-(m)ərj'*, *v.t.* and *v.i.* to plunge in. [L. *in*, into, *mergĕre*, *mersum*, to plunge.]

immeritous, *im-mer'it-əs*, *adj.* (*Milt.*) undeserving. [L. *immeritus*—*in*-, not, *meritus*, deserving.]

immerse, *im-(m)ərs'*, *v.t.* to dip under the surface of a liquid: to baptise by dipping the whole body: to engage or involve deeply.—*adj.* **immersed'**, (*bot.*) embedded in the tissues.—*ns.* **immer'sion,** act of immersing: state of being immersed: deep absorption or involvement: baptism by immersing: (*astron.*) entry into a position of invisibility as in eclipse or occultation: application of liquid to a microscope object-glass; **immer'sionism**; **immer'sionist,** one who favours or practises baptism by immersion.—**immersion heater,** an electrical apparatus for heating water by direct immersion in it; **immersion lens,** a microscope object-glass that works with a drop of oil or water between it and the cover-glass. [See **immerge.**]

immesh. See **enmesh.**

immethodical, *im-(m)i-thod'ik-əl*, *adj.* without method or order: irregular.—*adv.* **immethod'ically.**

immew. See **emmew.**

immigrate, *im'i-grāt*, *v.i.* to migrate or remove into a country with intention of settling in it.— *ns.* **imm'igrant,** one who immigrates; **immigrā'tion.** [L. *immigrāre*—*in*, into, *migrāre*, *-ātum*, to remove.]

imminent, *im'i-nənt*, *adj.* overhanging: intent: threatening: impending.—*ns.* **imm'inence,** fact or state of being imminent: (*Shak.*) impending evil; **imm'inency.**—*adv.* **imm'inently.** [L. *imminēns*, *-ēntis*—*in*, upon, *minēre*, to project, jut.]

immingle, *im-(m)ing'gl*, *v.t.* and *v.i.* to mingle together, to mix. [L. *in*, into.]

immiscible, *im-(m)is'i-bl*, *adj.* not capable of being mixed.—*n.* **immiscibil'ity.** [L. *in*-, not.]

immit, *im-(m)it'*, *v.t.* to insert: to introduce: to inject:—*pr.p.* **immitt'ing;** *pa.t.* and *pa.p.* **immitt'ed.**—*n.* **immission** (*-ish'ən*). [L. *immittĕre*—*in*, into, *mittĕre*, *missum*, to send.]

immitigable, *im-it'i-gə-bl*, *adj.* incapable of being mitigated.—*adv.* **immit'igably.**

immix, *im-(m)iks'*, *v.t.* (*Milt.*) to mix in: to mix in mixture. [L. *in*, into.]

immobile, *im-(m)ō'bil*, *-bil*, *-bēl*, *adj.* immovable: not readily moved: motionless: stationary.—*n.* **immobilisā'tion.**—*v.t.* **immob'ilise,** to render immobile: to put or keep out of action or circulation.—*n.* **immobil'ity.**

immoderate, *im-od'ər-it*, *adj.* exceeding due bounds: extravagant: unrestrained.—*ns.* **immod'eracy, immod'erateness.**—*adv.* **immod'erately.**—*n.* **immoderā'tion,** want of moderation: excess.

immodest, *im-od'ist*, *adj.* wanting restraint: exceeding in self-assertion: impudent: wanting shame or delicacy: indecent.—*adv.* **immod'estly.** —*n.* **immod'esty.**

immolate, *im'ō-lāt, im'əl-āt, v.t.* to offer in sacrifice : (*obs.*) to dedicate to the church or church uses.—*ns.* **immolā'tion, imm'olātor.** [L. *immolāre, -ātum,* to sprinkle meal (on a victim), hence to sacrifice—*in,* upon, *mola,* meal.]

immoment, *im-mō'mənt, adj.* (*Shak.*) of no value.

immoral, *im-(m)or'əl, adj.* inconsistent with or disregardful of morality : sometimes esp. of sexual morality : wicked : licentious.—*ns.* **immor'alism,** denial or rejection of morality ; **immor'alist ; immorality** (*im-or-, im-ər-al'i-ti*), quality of being immoral : an immoral act or practice.—*adv.* **immor'ally.**

immortal, *im-or'tl, adj.* exempt from death : imperishable : never to be forgotten (as a name, poem, &c.).—*n.* one who will never cease to exist : one whose works will always retain their supremacy : one of the forty members of the French Academy.—*n.* **immortalisā'tion.**—*v.t.* **immor'talise,** to make immortal.—*n.* **immortality** (*im-or-, im-ər-tal'i-ti*).—*adv.* **immor'tally.**

immortelle, *im-or-tel', n.* an everlasting flower. [Fr. (*fleur*) *immortelle,* immortal (flower).]

immovable, *im-ōōv'ə-bl, adj.* impossible to move : steadfast : unyielding : impassive : motionless : unalterable : (*law* ; commonly **immove'able**) not liable to be removed : real, not personal.—*n.* (*law* ; usu. in *pl.* **immove'ables**) immoveable property.—*ns.* **immov'ableness, immovabil'ity.**—*adv.* **immov'ably.**

immune, *im-ūn', adj.* free from obligation : exempt : not liable to danger, esp. infection.—*n.* one who is immune.—*n.* **immunisā'tion.**—*v.t.* **imm'unise,** to render immune, esp. to make immune from a disease by injecting disease germs, or their poisons (either active or rendered harmless).—*ns.* **immun'ity ; immunol'ogist ; immunol'ogy,** the scientific study of immunity. [L. *immūnis—in-,* not, *mūnis,* serving.]

immure, *im-ūr', v.t.* to wall in : to shut up : to imprison.—*n.* (*Shak.* **emure'**) an enclosing wall.—*n.* **immure'ment,** imprisonment : walling up. [L. *in,* in, *mūrus,* a wall.]

immutable, *im-ūt'ə-bl, adj.* unchangeable.—*ns.* **immūtabil'ity, immūt'ableness.**—*adv.* **immūt'ably.**

imp, *imp, n.* (*obs.*) a shoot, scion, graft : a scion of a family : (*obs.*) a young man : a child : a teasing or taunting mischievous child : a little devil or wicked spirit.—*v.t.* to graft, engraft : (*falconry*) to engraft feathers in (to mend a wing).—*adj.* **imp'ish,** like or characteristic of an imp, teasingly mischievous. [O.E. *impa*—L.L. *impotus,* a graft—Gr. *emphytos,* engrafted.]

imp-, for words beginning thus see also **emp-.**

impacable, *im'pak-ə-bl, adj.* (*Spens.*) not to be quieted or appeased. [L. *in-,* not, *pācāre,* to quiet.]

impact, *im-pakt', v.t.* to press firmly together : to drive close : to strike or collide.—*ns.* **im'pact,** the blow of a body in motion impinging on another body : the impulse resulting from collision ; **impac'tion.**—**impacted fracture,** (*surg.*) one where part of the bone is forcibly driven into the other part ; **impacted tooth,** one wedged between the jawbone and another tooth, and thus unable to come through the gum. [L. *impactus,* pa.p. of *impingĕre* ; see **impinge.**]

impaint, *im-pānt', v.t.* (*Shak.*) to paint.

impair, *im-pār'* (*Spens.* **empaire'**)*, v.t.* to diminish in quantity, value, or strength : to injure : to weaken.—*v.i.* to become worse : to decay.—*n.* impairing.—*n.* **impair'ment.** [O.Fr. *empeirer* (Fr. *empirer*), from L. *im-* (*in-*), intensive, *pējōrāre,* to make worse—*pējor,* worse.]

impair, *im-pār', adj.* (*Shak.*) perhaps, unsuitable. [Fr.,—L. *impār—in-,* not, *pār,* equal.]

impala, *im-pā'lä, n.* a large African antelope (*Aepyceros melampus*). [Zulu *i-mpǎlaj.*]

impale, *im-pāl', v.t.* to fence in with stakes : to shut in : to surround with a border : to put to death by spitting on a stake : to transfix : (*her.*) to combine palewise.—Also **empale'.**—*n.* **impale'ment,** an enclosed space : the act or punishment of impaling : (*her.*) the marshalling side by side of two escutcheons combined in one. [Fr. *empaler*—L. *in,* in, *pālus,* a stake.]

impalpable, *im-pal'pə-bl, adj.* not perceivable by touch : extremely fine-grained : eluding apprehension.—*n.* **impalpabil'ity.**—*adv.* **impal'pably.**

impanation, *im-pə-nā'shən,* or *-pā-, n.* local union of the body of Christ with the consecrated bread in the Eucharist : later specially used of Luther's consubstantiation. — *adj.* **impanate** (*im-pān'āt, im'pən-āt*), embodied in bread. [From L.L. *im-pānāre, -ātum—in,* in, *pānis,* bread.]

impanel, impannel. See **empanel.**

imparadise, *im-par'ə-dīs, v.t.* (*Milt.*) to put in a paradise or state of extreme felicity : to make a paradise of.—Also **empar'adise.**

imparity, *im-par'i-ti, n.* inequality : (*arith., obs.*) oddness.—*adjs.* **imparipin'nate,** pinnate with a terminal leaflet ; **imparisyllab'ic,** having a syllable more in the other cases than in the nominative. [L. *impār—in-,* not, *pār,* equal.]

impark, *im-pärk', v.t.* to enclose in, or as, a park.—*n.* **imparkā'tion.**

imparl, *im-pärl', v.i.* to hold a consultation.—*v.t.* to talk over.—*n.* **imparl'ance** (*Spens.* **emparlaunce**), parleying, conference : delay in pleading, ostensibly for amicable adjustment. [Obs. Fr. *emparler—em-* (L. *in-*), *parler,* to talk.]

impart, *im-pärt'* (*Spens.* **empart'**)*, v.t.* to bestow a part of : to give : to communicate : to make known.—*v.i.* to give a part.—*ns.* **impartā'tion ; impart'er ; impart'ment** (*Shak.*). [O.Fr. *empartir*—L. *impartīre—in,* on, *pars, partis,* a part.]

impartial, *im-pär'shl, adj.* not favouring one more than another : just : (*Shak.*) partial.—*ns.* **impartiality** (*-shi-al'i-ti*), **impar'tialness.**—*adv.* **impar'tially.**

impartible, *im-pärt'i-bl, adj.* capable of being imparted.—*n.* **impartibil'ity.** [**impart.**]

impartible, *im-pärt'i-bl, adj.* not partible : indivisible.—*n.* **impartibil'ity.** [L. *im-* (*in-*), not.]

impassable, *im-päs'ə-bl, adj.* not capable of being passed.—*ns.* **impassabil'ity, impass'ableness.**—*adv.* **impass'ably.**—*n.* **impasse** (*an^'pās^'* ; Fr.), a place from which there is no outlet : a deadlock.

impassible, *im-pas'i-bl, adj.* incapable of suffering, injury, or emotion.—*ns.* **impassibil'ity, impass'ibleness.** [Church L. *impassibilis—in-,* not, *patī, passus,* to suffer.]

impassion, *im-pash'ən, v.t.* to move with passion : to make passionate.—*adjs.* **impass'ionate, impass'ioned** (*Spens.* **empass'ionate, empass'ioned**), moved by strong passion : animated : informed with passion. [It. *impassionare*—L. *in,* in, *passiō, -ōnis,* passion.]

impassive, *im-pas'iv, adj.* not susceptible of feeling : not showing feeling : imperturbable.—*adv.* **impass'ively.**—*ns.* **impass'iveness, impassiv'ity.** [L. *im-* (*in-*), not.]

impaste, *im-pāst', v.t.* (*Shak.*) to knead into a paste : to lay on thick.—*ns.* **impastation** (*im-pas-tā'shən*), **impasto** (*im-päs'tō* ; It.), in painting and pottery, 'the thick laying on of pigments.—*adj.* **impast'oed, impast'o'd.** [L.L. *impastāre—in,* into, *pasta,* paste.]

impatient, *im-pā'shənt, adj.* not able to endure or to wait : fretful : restless.—*n.* **impā'tience.**—*adv.* **impā'tiently.** [L. *im-* (*in-*), not.]

impave, *im-pāv', v.t.* (*Wordsworth*) to depict in pavement. [L. *in,* in.]

impavid, *im-pav'id, adj.* fearless.—*adv.* **impav'idly.** [L. *impavidus—im-* (*in-*), not, *pavidus,* fearing.]

impawn, *im-pawn', v.t.* to put in pawn : to pledge : to risk. [L. *in,* in.]

impeach, *im-pēch'* (*Spens.* **empeach**)*, v.t.* (*obs.*) to hinder, impede : (*obs.*) to beset : to impair : to disparage : to find fault with : to call in question : to arraign (esp. when a lower legislative house charges a high officer with grave offences before the upper house as judges) : to turn king's evidence against, peach upon.—*n.* (*Spens.*) hindrance : (*Spens.*) damage, injury, impairment, detriment : (*Shak.*) calling in question.—*adj.* **impeach'able.**—*ns.* **impeach'er ; impeach'ment.** [O.Fr. *empech(i)er,* to hinder (Fr. *empêcher*)—L. *impedicāre,* to fetter—*in,* in, *pēdīca,* fetter—*pēs, pĕdis,* foot ;

influenced by O.Fr. *empachier*, to hinder, accuse, from the root of L. *pangĕre*, to fasten, and by L. *impetĕre*, to accuse.]

impearl, *im-pərl'*, *v.t.* to adorn with or as with pearls: to make like pearls.

impeccable, *im-pek'ə-bl*, *adj.* not liable to sin: faultless.—*n.* one who is impeccable.—*ns.* **impeccabil'ity**, **impecc'ancy**.—*adj.* **impecc'ant**, without sin. [L. *in-*, not, *peccāre*, to sin.]

impecunious, *im-pi-kū'ni-əs*, *-nyəs*, *adj.* without money: short of money.—*n.* **impecunios'ity**. [L. *in-*, not, *pecūnia*, money.]

impede, *im-pēd'*, *v.t.* to hinder or obstruct.—*n.* **impē'dance**, hindrance: (*elect.*) an apparent increase of resistance to an alternating current owing to induction in a circuit.—*n.* **impediment** (*-pĕd'*), obstacle: a defect preventing fluent speech.—*n.pl.* **impediment'a** (L. *impedīmenta*), military baggage: baggage generally.—*adjs.* **impedimen'tal**, **imped'itive**, hindering. [L. *impedīre—in*, in, *pēs*, *pedis*, a foot.]

impel, *im-pel'*, *v.t.* to urge forward: to excite to action: to instigate :—*pr.p.* **impell'ing**; *pa.t.* and *pa.p.* **impelled**.—*adj.* **impell'ent**, impelling or driving on.—*n.* an impelling agent or power.—*n.* **impell'er**. [L. *impellĕre*, *impulsum—in*, on, *pellĕre*, to drive.]

impend, *im-pend'*, *v.i.* to overhang: to threaten: to be about to happen.—*ns.* **impend'ence**, **impend'ency**.—*adj.* **impend'ent**. [L. *impendēre—in*, on, *pendēre*, to hang.]

impenetrable, *im-pen'i-trə-bl*, *adj.* not to be penetrated: occupying space exclusively: impervious: inscrutable. — *n.* **impenetrabil'ity**. — *adv.* **impen'etrably**. [L. *in-*, not.]

impenetrate, *im-pen'i-trāt*, *v.t.* to permeate: penetrate thoroughly.—*n.* **impenetrā'tion**. [L. *in*, in, into.]

impenitent, *im-pen'i-tənt*, *adj.* not repenting.—*n.* one who does not repent: a hardened sinner.—*ns.* **impen'itence**; **impen'itency**.—*adv.* **impen'itently**. [L. *in-*, not.]

imperative, *im-per'ə-tiv*, *adj.* expressive of command, advice, or request: authoritative: peremptory: obligatory: urgently necessary: calling out for action.—*n.* that which is imperative: the imperative mood: a verb in the imperative mood. —*adv.* **imper'atively**.—**imperative mood**, the form of a verb expressing command, advice, or request; **categorical imperative** (see under **category**). [L. *imperātīvus—imperāre*, to command—*in*, in, *parāre*, to prepare.]

imperator, *im-pər-ä'tər* ; L. *im-per-ä'tor*, *n.* a commander: a ruler: an emperor. — *adj.* **imperatorial** (*im-per-ə-tō'ri-əl*). [L. *imperātor*, a general, later an emperor—*imperāre*, to command.]

imperceable, *im'pərs-ə-bl*, *adj.* (*Spens.*) unpierceable.

imperceptible, *im-pər-sep'ti-bl*, *adj.* not discernible. —*n.* an imperceptible thing.—*ns.* **impercep'tibleness**, **imperceptibil'ity**.—*adv.* **impercep'tibly**. —*adjs.* **impercep'tive**, **impercip'ient**, not perceiving: having no power to perceive. [L. *in-*, not.]

imperfect, *im-pər'fikt*, *adj.* incomplete: defective: falling short of perfection: wanting any normal part, or the full normal number of parts : (*gram.*) expressing continued or habitual action in past time : (*mus.*) diminished, less by a semitone: (*old mus.*) duple.—*n.* the imperfect tense: a verb in the imperfect tense.—*n.* **imperfection** (*-fek'shən*), the state of being imperfect : a defect : that which is wanting : that which is got to make good a deficiency.—*adv.* **imper'fectly**.—*n.* **imper'fectness**.—**imperfect cadence**, any cadence other than a perfect cadence, esp. one passing from tonic to dominant chord.

imperforate, *im-pər'fə-rit*, **-d**, *-rā-tid*, *adjs.* not pierced through or perforated: having no opening: abnormally closed : without perforations for tearing apart, as a sheet of postage stamps.—*adj.* **imper'forable**.—*n.* **imperforā'tion**.

imperial, *im-pē'ri-əl*, *adj.* pertaining to, or of the nature of, an empire or emperor: sovereign, supreme: commanding, august.—*n.* (*obs.*) an emperor or empress : a supporter of an emperor : a tuft of hair on the lower lip (earlier than the reign of Napoleon III.) : a pointed dome of ogee section : the top of a diligence : a size of paper, 22×30 in. (*U.S.* 23×31) : a size of slates, 33×24 in. : an obsolete Russian gold coin.—*v.t.* **impē'rialise**, to make imperial.—*ns.* **impē'rialism**, the power or authority of an emperor : the spirit of empire ; **impē'rialist**, a soldier or partisan of an emperor : a believer in the policy of developing and utilising the spirit of empire.—*adj.* **impērialist'ic**.—*n.* **impēriality** (*-al'i-ti*), imperial power, right, or privilege.—*adv.* **impē'rially**.—*adj.* **impē'rious**, assuming command : haughty : tyrannical : domineering: peremptory: authoritative : (*obs.*) imperial.—*adv.* **impē'riously**.—*ns.* **impē'riousness**; **impē'rium** (L. *impĕrium*), a military chief command: empire.—**imperial cap**, a size of brown paper, 22×29 in.; **imperial city**, Rome : in the older German Empire one of those cities that owed allegiance only to the emperor, exercised suzerainty within their own bounds, and had the right of voting in the imperial diet ; **Imperial Conference**, a periodical conference (orig. *Colonial Conference*) of the prime ministers and other representatives of the United Kingdom and the self-governing Dominions ; **imperial federation**, a scheme to federate or bind the self-governing parts of the British Empire ; **imperial measure**, **weight**, the standard of measure, weight, fixed by parliament for the United Kingdom ; **imperial octavo**, a book size, 8¼×11 in. ; **Imperial Parliament**, the parliament of the United Kingdom ; **imperial preference**, the favouring of trade within the empire by discriminating tariffs. [L. *imperium*, sovereignty.]

imperil, *im-per'il*, *v.* . to endanger :—*pa.p.* **imper'illed**.—*n.* **imper'ilment**.

imperishable, *im-per'ish-ə-bl*, *adj.* indestructible : everlasting.—*ns.* **imper'ishableness**, **imperishabil'ity**.—*adv.* **imper'ishably**.

impermanence, *im-pər'man-əns*, *n.* want of permanence. — *n.* **imper'manency**. — *adj.* **imper'manent**.

impermeable, *im-per'mi-ə-bl*, *adj.* not permitting passage, esp. of fluids : impervious.—*ns.* **impermeabil'ity**, **imper'meableness**.—*adv.* **imper'meably**.

imperseverant, *im-pər-sev'ər-ənt*, *adj.* (*Shak.*) perh. unseeing, wanting in power to perceive what is before one, or perh. stubborn. [Pfx. *im-* (*in-*), not, and **perceive**, or *im-* (*in-*), intens., and **persevere**, with suff. *-ent*.]

impersistent, *im-pər-sist'ənt*, *adj.* not persistent : not enduring.

impersonal, *im-pər'sən-əl*, *adj.* not having personality: used only in the third person singular (in English usu. with *it* as subject) : without reference to any particular person: objective, uncoloured by personal feeling.—*n.* **impersonality** (*-al'i-ti*).—*adv.* **imper'sonally**. [L. *im-* (*in-*), not.]

impersonate, *im-pər'sən-āt*, *v.t.* to invest with personality or the bodily substance of a person : to ascribe the qualities of a person to : to personify : to assume the person or character of, esp. on the stage.—*adj.* (*-it*, *-āt*) personified.—*ns.* **impersonā'tion** ; **imper'sonātor**. [L. *in*, in, *persōna*, person ; see **personate**.]

impertinent, *im-pər'ti-nənt*, *adj.* not pertaining to the matter in hand : trifling: intrusive : saucy: impudent.—*n.* an impertinent person : one whose presence is not to the purpose.—*ns.* **imper'tinence**, **imper'tinency**, that which is impertinent : intrusion: impudence, overforwardness : (*law*) matter introduced into an affidavit, &c., not pertinent to the matter.—*adv.* **imper'tinently**.

imperturbable, *im-pər-tur'bə-bl*, *adj.* that cannot be disturbed or agitated : permanently quiet.— —*n.* **imperturbabil'ity**.—*adv.* **impertur'bably**.— *n.* **imperturbā'tion**. [L. *imperturbābilis—in-*, not, *perturbāre*, to disturb ; see **perturb**.]

imperviable, *im-pər vi-ə-bl*, **impervious**, *im-pər'vi-əs*, *adjs.* not to be penetrated.—*ns.* **imper'viableness**, **imperviabil'ity**, **imper'viousness**. —*adv.* **imper'viously**.

impeticos, *im-pet'i-kos*, *v.t.* (*Shak.*) a word coined by the fool in *Twelfth Night* (II. iii.) perh. meaning **impocket**, or perh. bestow on (the wearer of) a petticoat.

impetigo, *im-pi-ti'gō*, *n.* a skin disease characterised by thickly-set clusters of pustules :—*pl.* **impetigines** (*-tij'i-nēz*).—*adj.* **impetiginous** (*-tij'*). [L. *impetīgō—impetēre*, to rush upon, attack.]

impetrate, *im'pi-trāt*, *v.t.* to obtain by entreaty *ɪ* petition.—*n.* **impetrā'tion.**—*adjs.* **im'petrātive**, **im'petrātory**. [L. *impetrāre, -ātum—in*, on, *patrāre*, to bring about.]

impetus, *im'pi-təs*, *n.* momentum : impulse : incentive :—*pl.* **im'petuses.**—*adj.* **impetuous** (*impet'ū-əs*), rushing on with impetus or violence : vehement : acting with headlong energy.—*n.* **impetuosity** (*-os'i-ti*).—*adv.* **impet'uously.**—*n.* **impet'uousness**. [L. *impetus* (pl. *impetūs*)—*in*, into, on, *petēre*, seek.]

impi, *im'pi*, *n.* a body of Kaffir warriors. [Zulu.]

impictured, *im-pik'tyərd*, *adj.* (*Spens.*) painted.

impierceable, *im-pērs'ə-bl* (*Spens.* **imperceable**, *im'pərs-ə-bl*), *adj.* incapable of being pierced.

impiety, *im-pī'ə-ti*, *n.* want of piety or veneration. [L. *impietās, -ātis—in-*, not ; cf. **piety**.]

impignorate, *im-pig'nər-āt*, *v.t.* to pledge or pawn. —*n.* **impignorā'tion**. [L. *in*, in, into, *pignus, -ōris, -ĕris*, pledge.]

impinge, *im-pinj'*, *v.i.* (with *on, upon, against*) to strike : to encroach.—*v.t.* to drive, strike :—*pr.p.* **imping'ing.**—*n.* **impinge'ment.**—*adj.* **imping'ent**. [L. *impingĕre—in*, against, *pangĕre*, to fix, drive in.]

impious, *im'pi-əs*, *adj.* irreverent : wanting in veneration, as for gods, parents, &c. [L. *impius—im-* (*in-*), not, *pius* ; cf. **pious**.]

implacable, *im-plak'ə-bl*, *-plāk'* (*Spens. im*), *adj.* not to be appeased : inexorable : irreconcilable. — *ns.* **implac'ableness, implacabil'ity**. — *adv.* **implac'ably.**

implacental, *im-plə-sen'tl*, *adj.* having no placenta.

implant, *im-plānt'*, *v.t.* to engraft : to plant firmly : to fix in : to insert : to instil or inculcate : to plant (*with* anything).—*n.* **implantā'tion.**

implate, *im-plāt'*, *v.t.* to put a plate or covering upon : to sheathe.

implausible, *im-plawz'i-bl*, *adj.* not plausible.—*n.* **implausibil'ity.**

impleach, *im-plēch'*, *v.t.* (*Shak.*) to intertwine.

implead, *im-plēd'*, *v.t.* to plead : to sue.—*n.* **implead'er.**

impledge, *im-plej'*, *v.t.* to pledge.

implement, *im'pli-mənt*, *n.* (*obs.*) a piece of equipment, a requisite : a tool or instrument of labour : (*Scots law*) fulfilment.—*v.t.* (often *-ment'*) to give effect to : to fulfil or perform.—*adj.* **implemen'tal**, instrumental : effective.—*n.* **implementā'tion**. [L.L. *implēmentum—*L. *in*, in, *plēre*, to fill.]

implete, *im-plēt'*, *v.t.* to fill.—*adj.* replete.—*n.* **impletion** (*-plē'shən*), filling : fulness : fulfilment. [L. *implēre, -ētum—in*, in, *plēre*, to fill.]

implex, *im'pleks*, *adj.* not simple : complicated.— *n.* in Arthropoda, an in-turning of the integument for attachment of muscles.—*n.* **implexion** (*im-plek'shən*).—*adj.* **implex'uous**. [L. *implexus—in*, into, *plectĕre*, to twine.]

implicate, *im'pli-kāt*, *v.t.* to entwine together : to enfold : to involve : to entangle : to imply.—*n.* a thing implied. (*-kit*) intertwined.—*n.* **implicā'tion**, the act of implicating or implying : entanglement : that which is implied.—*adj.* **im'plicātive** (or *im-plik'ə-tiv*), tending to implicate. —*adv.* **im'plicātively.**—*adj.* **implicit** (*im-plis'it*), implied : relying entirely, unquestioning : (*rare*) entangled, involved.—*adv.* **implic'itly.**—*n.* **implic'itness**. [L. *implicāre, -ātum*, also *-ĭtum—in*, in, *plicāre, -ātum* or *-ĭtum*, to fold.]

implode, *im-plōd'*, *v.t.* and *v.i.* to burst inwards : to sound by implosion.—*ns.* **implōd'ent**, an implosive sound ; **implosion** (*-plō'zhən*), bursting inward : (*phon.*) simultaneous stopping by the mouth parts and the glottis : stopping without an off-glide.—*adj.* **implosive** (*-plōs'iv*, or *-plōz'*). [L. *in*, in, *plōdĕre* (*plaudĕre*), to clap.]

implore, *im-plōr'*, *v.t.* to ask earnestly : to entreat.—

Also *v.i.*—*n.* (*Spens.*) entreaty.—*ns.* **implorā'tion** ; **implor'ator**, (*Shak.*) one who implores or entreats. —*adj.* **imploratory** (*-plor'ə-tə-ri*).—*n.* **implōr'er**. —*adv.* **implōr'ingly**, in an imploring manner. [L. *implōrāre*, to invoke with tears—*in*, in, *plōrāre*, to weep.]

implunge, *im-plunj'*, *v.t.* to plunge, submerge.— Also (*Spens.*) **emplonge.**

impluvium, *im-plōō'vi-əm*, *n.* in ancient Roman houses, the square basin in the atrium that received the rain-water :—*pl.* **implu'via**. [L. *impluvium— in*, in, into, *pluĕre*, to rain.]

imply, *im-plī'*, *v.t.* (*Spens.*) to enfold : to involve the truth or reality of : to express indirectly : to insinuate : to mean : to signify :—*pr.p.* **imply'ing** ; *pa.t.* and *pa.p.* **implied'.**—*adv.* **impli'edly**. [O.Fr. *emplier*—L. *implicāre*.]

impocket, *im-pok'it*, *v.t.* to put in the pocket.

impolder, *im-pōl'dər*, *v.t.* to make a polder of. [Du. *impolderen* ; see **polder**.]

impolite, *im-pə-līt'*, *adj.* of unpolished manners : uncivil.—*adv.* **impolite'ly.**—*n.* **impolite'ness.**

impolitic, *im-pol'i-tik*, *adj.* not politic : inexpedient.—Also (*obs.*) **impolit'ical.**—*n.* **impol'icy**. —*advs.* **impolit'ically** (*rare*) ; **impol'iticly.**

imponderable, *im-pon'dər-ə-bl*, *adj.* not able to be weighed or estimated : without weight, immaterial : without sensible weight.—Also *n.*—*ns.* **impon'derableness, imponderabil'ity.**—*n.pl.* **impon'derables**, once-supposed fluids without sensible weight, as heat, light, electricity, and magnetism, considered as material—still used of ether.—Also (L.) **imponderabil'ia.**—*adj.* **impon'derous**, weightless : very light.

impone, *im-pōn'*, *v.t.* and *v.i.* to impose : to lay on : (*Shak.*—perh. an error for *impawn*) to stake, as a wager.—*adj.* **impōn'ent**, competent to impose an obligation.—*n.* one who imposes. [L. *impōnĕre —in*, on, *pōnĕre*, to place.]

import, *im-pōrt'*, *v.t.* to bring in : to bring from abroad : to convey, as a word : to signify : to betoken : to portend : to be of consequence to : to interest : to behove.—*v.i.* to be important.— *n.* **im'port** (formerly *-pōrt'*), that which is brought from abroad : meaning : importance : tendency.— *adj.* **import'able**, that may be imported or brought into a country.—*ns.* **import'ance**, the fact of being important : extent to which anything is important : weight, consequence : appearance of dignity : (*Shak.*) import, significance ; **import'ancy** (*Shak.*). —*adj.* **import'ant**, of great import or consequence : momentous : pompous : (*Shak.*) urgent, importunate.—*adv.* **import'antly.**—*ns.* **importā'tion**, the act of importing : a commodity imported ; **import'er.**—*adj.* **import'less**, (*Shak.*) without consequence.—**invisible imports**, such items in a national trade balance as money spent by tourists from abroad, &c. ; opp. to **visible imports**, goods bought from foreign countries by traders. [L. *importāre, -ātum—in*, in, *portāre*, to carry.]

importable, *im-pōrt'ə-bl* (*Spens. im'*), *adj.* (*obs.*) unbearable : irresistible. [L. *importābilis—im-* (*in-*), not, *portāre*, to bear.]

importune, *im-por-tūn'*, *-por'*, *adj.* (*obs.*) inopportune, untimely : (*obs.*) burdensome : importunate : (*Spens.*) urgent, passing into resistless.—*v.t.* (*obs.*) to be troublesome to : to urge or crave with troublesome application : (*Spens.* ; wrongly) to import, signify.—*v.i.* to be important.—*ns.* **importunacy** (*Shak.* *-tūn'*), **import'unateness.**— *adj.* **impor'tunate** (*-it, -āt*), (*obs.*) inopportune : (*obs.*) burdensome : troublesomely urgent : pressing : pertinacious.—*v.i.* to solicit pertinaciously.— *advs.* **impor'tunately** ; **importune'ly** (or *-por'*).— *ns.* **importun'er** ; **importun'ing** ; **importun'ity**. [L. *importūnus*, inconvenient—*im-* (*in-*), not, *portus*, a harbour ; cf. **opportune**.]

impose, *im-pōz'*, *v.t.* to place upon something : to lay on : to enjoin : to set as a burden or task : to set up in or by authority : to pass off unfairly : (*print.*) to arrange or place in a chase, as pages of type.—*v.i.* (with *upon*) to mislead or deceive : to lay a burden, as by encroaching, taking undue advantage of one's good nature : act with constraining effect.—*n.* (*Shak.*) command, injunction.

—*adj.* **impos'able,** capable of being imposed or laid on.—*n.* **impos'er.**—*adj.* **impos'ing,** commanding : adapted to impress forcibly : specious : deceptive.—*adv.* **impos'ingly.**—*n.* **impos'ingness.** [Fr. *imposer* ; see **compose.**]

imposition, *im-pəz-ish'ən, n.* a laying on : laying on of hands in ordination : a tax, a burden : a deception : a punishment task : (*print.*) assembling of pages and locking them into a chase. [L. *impositiō, -ōnis—in,* on, *pōnĕre, pŏsitum,* to place.]

impossible, *im-pos'i-bl, adj.* that cannot be : that cannot be done or dealt with : that cannot be true : out of the question : hopelessly unsuitable : beyond doing anything with.—*n.* a person or thing that is impossible.—*ns.* **imposs'ibilism,** belief in or advocacy of an impracticable policy ; **imposs'ibilist ; impossibil'ity.**

impost, *im'pōst, n.* a tax, esp. on imports. [O.Fr. *impost* (Fr. *impôt*)—L. *impōnĕre, impŏsitum,* to lay on.]

impost, *im'pōst, n.* (*archit.*) the upper part of a pillar in vaults and arches, on which the weight of the building is laid : a horizontal block resting on uprights. [Fr. *imposte*—It. *imposta*—L. *impōnĕre, impŏsitum.*]

impostor, *im-post'ər, n.* one who assumes a false character or personates another.—Also **impost'er.** —*n.* **impost'ure** (*-yər,*) an imposition, fraud. [L.L., —L. *impōnĕre, impŏsitum,* to impose.]

imposthume, imposthume, *im-pos'tūm, n.* (*arch.*) an abscess.—*v.t.* and *v.i.* **impos't(h)ūmate.**— *n.* **impost(h)ūmā'tion.** — *adj.* **impos't(h)ūmed.** [O.Fr. *empostume* from *aposteme*—Gr. *apostēma,* abscess—*apo,* from, and the root of *histanai,* to set ; the form due to confusion with *posthumous,* which itself is due to confusion.]

impot, *im'pot, n.* (*school slang*) an imposition.

impotent, *im'pə-tənt, adj.* powerless : helpless : without sexual power : (*obs.*) without self-control : (*Spens.*) ungovernable.—*ns.* **im'potence, im'-potency.**—*adv.* **im'potently.**

impound, *im-pownd', v.t.* to confine, as in a pound : to restrain within limits : to hold up in a reservoir : to take legal possession of.—*adj.* **impound'able.**— *ns.* **impound'age ; impound'er ; impound'ment.** [Pfx. *im-* (*in-*), in, and **pound** (2).]

impoverish, *im-pov'ər-ish, v.t.* to make poor.—*n.* **impov'erishment.** [From O.Fr. *empovrir, -iss-* —L. *in,* in, *pauper,* poor.]

impracticable, *im-prak'tik-ə-bl, adj.* not able to be done : not able to be used or traversed : unmanageable.—*ns.* **impracticabil'ity, imprac'ticableness.**—*adv.* **imprac'ticably.**

impractical, *im-prak'ti-kl, adj.* (*U.S.*) unpractical. —*ns.* **impracticality** (*-kal'i-ti*) ; **imprac'ticalness.**

imprecate, *im'pri-kāt, v.t.* to call down by prayer (esp. something evil) : to pray for or to : to invoke evil upon, to curse.—*v.i.* to curse.—*n.* **impreca'tion.**—*adj.* **im'precatory** (*-kə-tə-ri,* or *-kā-tə-ri* or *-kā'*). [L. *imprecāri—in,* upon, *precāri, -ātus,* to pray.]

impregn, *im-prēn', v.t.* (*Milt.*) to impregnate.—*adj.* **impregnant** (*-preg'nant*), impregnating : (*obs.*) impregnated.—*v.t.* **impreg'nate,** to make pregnant : to fecundate : to fill or imbue (with the particles or qualities of another thing) : to saturate. —*n.* **impregna'tion.** [L.L. *impraegnāre, -ātum—in,* in, *praegnāns,* pregnant.]

impregnable, *im-preg'na-bl, adj.* that cannot be taken : proof against attack.—*n.* **impregnabil'ity.** —*adv.* **impreg'nably.** [Fr. *imprenable*—L. *in-,* not, *prendĕre, prehendĕre,* to take ; *g,* a freak of spelling, has come to be pronounced.]

impresa, *in-prā'zä, n.* (*obs.*) an emblematic device, often with a motto : a motto.—Also **imprese** (*im'prēz,* or as *Milt. -prēz'*). [It.]

impresario, *im-pre-sä'ri-ō,* or *-zä', n.* the manager of an opera company, &c. :—*pl.* **impresa'rios, impresa'ri** (*-rē*). [It.,—*impresa,* enterprise.]

imprescriptible, *im-pri-skrip'ti-bl, adj.* not liable to be lost by prescription, or lapse of time : inalienable.—*n.* **imprescriptibil'ity.**

impress, *im-pres', v.t.* to press : to apply with pressure, esp. so as to leave a mark : to mark by

pressure : to produce by pressure : to stamp or print : to fix deeply in the mind : to affect the mind : to produce a profound effect upon, or upon the mind of.—*ns.* **im'press,** that which is made by pressure : stamp : distinctive mark ; **impressibil'-ity.**—*adj.* **impress'ible,** susceptible.—*ns.* **impression** (*im-presh'ən*), the act or result of impressing : pressure : a difference produced in a thing by action upon it : a single printing of a book : the effect of anything on the mind : a profound effect on the emotions : a vague uncertain memory or inclination to believe : belief, generally ill-founded ; **impressionabil'ity.**—*adj.* **impress'ion-able,** able to receive an impression : very susceptible to impressions.—*n.* **Impress'ionism,** a nineteenth-century movement in painting, originating in France, aiming at the realistic representation of the play of light in nature, purporting to render faithfully what the artist actually saw, dispensing with the academic rules of composition and colouring : any similar tendency in other arts.—*n.* and *adj.* **impress'ionist.**—*adj.* **impressionis'tic.**—*adv.* **impressionist'ically.**—*adj.* **impressive** (*-pres'*), exerting or tending to exert pressure : capable of making a deep impression on the mind : solemn. — *adv.* **impress'ively.** — *ns.* **impress'iveness ; impressure** (*im-presh'ər*), (*Shak.*) impression. [L. *imprimĕre, -pressum — in, premĕre* ; see **press** (1).]

impress, *im-pres', v.t.* to force into service, esp. the public service.—*ns.* **im'press** (*Shak. im-pres'*) ; **impress'ment,** the act of impressing or seizing for service, esp. in the navy. [Pfx. *im-* (*in-*), in, and **prest** ; cf. **press** (2).]

impress, impresse, *im'pres, n.* (*Shak.*) an impresa.

impress, a variant of **imprest.**

imprest, *im'prest, n.* earnest-money : money advanced.—*v.t.* **imprest',** to advance on loan. [Pfx. *im-* (*in-*), in, and **prest.**]

imprimatur, *im-pri-mā'tər, n.* a licence or permission to print a book, &c. [L. *imprimātur,* let it be printed, subj. pass. of *imprimĕre—in,* on, *premĕre,* to press.]

imprimis, *im-pri'mis, adv.* in the first place. [L. *imprīmīs—in prīmīs* (abl. pl.), *in,* in, *primus,* first.]

imprint, *im-print', v.t.* to print : to stamp : to impress : to fix in the mind.—*n.* **im'print,** that which is imprinted : the name of the publisher, time and place of publication of a book, &c., pr.nted usu. on the title-page : the printer's name on the back of the title-page or at the end of the book.

imprison, *im-priz'n, v.t.* to put in prison : to shut up : to confine or restrain.—*n.* **impris'onment.**

improbable, *im-prob'ə-bl, adj.* unlikely.—*n.* **improb-abil'ity.**—*adv.* **improb'ably.**

improbation, *im-prō-bā'shən, n.* in Scots law, an action for the purpose of declaring some instrument false or forged.—*adj.* **improbative** (*-prob'ə-tiv*), disapproving—also **improb'atory.**

improbity, *im-prōb'i-ti, -prob', n.* want of probity.

impromptu, *im-promp'tū, adj.* improvised : off-hand.—*adv.* without preparation : on the spur of the moment.—*n.* an extempore witticism or speech : an improvised composition : a musical composition with the character of an extemporisation. [L. *impromptū* for *in promptū* (abl.), *in,* in, *promptus,* readiness.]

improper, *im-prop'ər, adj.* not strictly belonging : not properly so called : not suitable : unfit : unbecoming : unseemly : indecent : (**improper fraction,** a fraction not less than unity).—*adv.* **improp'erly.**—*n.* **impropri'ety.** [L. *im-* (*in-*), not, *proprius,* own.]

impropriate, *im-prō'pri-āt, v.t.* to appropriate to private use : to place (ecclesiastical property) in the hands of a layman.—*adj.* (*-it*) devolved into the hands of a layman.—*ns.* **impropriā'tion ; im-prō'priator,** a layman who is in possession of a benefice or its revenues. [L.L. *impropriātus*—L. *in,* in, *proprius,* one's own.]

improve, *im-prōōv', v.t.* (*rare*) to turn to good use : (*U.S.*) to make use of, occupy : (*obs.*) to increase (whether good or ill) : to raise in value (esp. by cultivating or building) : to raise in price :

to make better.—*v.i.* (*obs.*) to increase : to grow in price or value : to grow better : to make progress : to make improvements : to follow up with something better (with *on*).—*ns.* **improvabil′ity**, **improv′ableness**. — *adj.* **improv′able**. — *adv.* **improv′ably**.—*ns.* **improve′ment**, the act of improving : a change for the better : a thing changed, or introduced in changing, for the better : a better thing substituted for or following one not so good (often with *on*) ; **improv′er**, one who improves : a worker who is in part a learner : one who sets himself to the improvement of land : a pad or bustle.—*pr.p.* and *adj.* **improv′ing**, tending to cause improvement : instructive : edifying : uplifting.—*adv.* **improv′ingly**.—**improve the occasion**, to seize an opportunity for edification or other purpose : to draw a moral from what has happened. [A.Fr. *emprower*—O.Fr. *en prou*, *preu*, into profit.]

improvident, *im-prov′i-dənt*, *adj.* not provident or prudent : wanting foresight : thoughtless.—*ns.* **improvidence** (*im-prə-vī′did*), unprovided : (*Spens.*) unforeseen.—*n.* **improv′idence**.—*adv.* **improv′idently**.

improvise, *im-prō-*, *-prə-vīz′*, or *im′*, **improvisate**, *im-prov′i-zāt*,*vs.t.* to compose and recite, or perform, without preparation : to bring about on a sudden : to make or contrive offhand or in emergency.—*v.i.* to perform extempore : to do anything offhand. (The spelling with *z* is wrong.)—*ns.* **improvisā′tion** (or *-prov′iz-*), act of improvising : that which is improvised ; **improvisator** (*im-prov′iz-ā-tər*, or *im′prov-īz-* ; It. **improvvisatore**, *im-prov-vē-sä-tō′rä*) ; sometimes *fem.* **improv′isātrix** (It. **improvvisatrice**, *-trē′chä*), one who improvises : one who composes and performs or speaks without preparation.—*adjs.* **improvisatō′rial** (*-iz-ə-*), **improvisatory** (*-iz′* or *-īz′*).—*n.* **improvīs′er**. [Fr. *improviser*—L. *in-*, not, *prōvīsus*, foreseen ; see **provide**.]

imprudent, *im-prōō′dənt*, *adj.* wanting foresight or discretion : incautious : inconsiderate.—*n.* **impru′dence**.—*adv.* **impru′dently**.

impudent, *im′pū-dənt*, *adj.* wanting shame or modesty : brazen-faced : shamelessly bold : pert : insolent.—*n.* **im′pudence**.—*adv.* **im′pudently**.—*n.* **impudicity** (*-dis′i-ti*). [L. *im-* (*in-*), not, *pudēns*, *-ēntis*, pr.p. of *pudēre*, to be ashamed ; and *pudīcus*, modest.]

impugn, *im-pūn′*, *v.t.* to oppose : to attack by words or arguments : to call in question.—*adj.* **impugn′able** (*-pūn′* ; distinguished from obs. or rare **impug′nable**, unassailable, from L. *in-*, not).—*ns.* **impugn′er** ; **impugn′ment**. [L. *impugnāre*—*in*, against, *pugnāre*, to fight.]

impuissant, *im-pwis′ənt*, also *-pū′is-*, *-pū-is′*, *adj.* (*arch.*) powerless.—*n.* **impuiss′ance** (or *-pū′*). [Pfx. *im-* (*in-*), not, and **puissant**.]

impulse, *im′puls*, *n.* the act of impelling : effect of an impelling force : force suddenly and momentarily communicated : a beat : a single blow, thrust, or wave : a disturbance travelling along a nerve (**nervous impulse**) or a muscle : an outside influence on the mind : a sudden inclination to act.—*n.* **impul′sion** (*-shən*), impelling force : instigation.—*adj.* **impuls′ive**, having the power of impelling : acting or actuated by impulse : not continuous : given to acting upon impulse.—*adv.* **impuls′ively**.—*ns.* **impuls′iveness** ; **impulsiv′ity**.—*adj.* **impuls′ory**. [L. *impulsus*, pressure—*impellĕre* ; see **impel**.]

impunity, *im-pūn′i-ti*, *n.* freedom or safety from punishment or ill consequences. [L. *impūnitās*, *-ātis*—*in-*, not, *poena*, punishment.]

impure, *im-pūr′*, *adj.* mixed with something else : defiled : unholy : unchaste : unclean materially, morally, or ceremonially.—*adv.* **impure′ly**.—*ns.* **impure′ness**, **impur′ity**.

impurple, *im-pur′pl*. Same as **empurple**.

impute, *im-pūt′*, *v.t.* to ascribe (usu. of evil) : to charge (*theol.*) to attribute vicariously : (*obs.*) to reckon : (*obs.*) to impart.—*adj.* **imput′able**, capable of being imputed or charged : open to accusation : attributable.—*ns.* **imput′ableness**, **imputabil′ity**.—*adv.* **imput′ably**.—*n.* **imputā′tion**, act of imputing or charging : censure : re-

proach : the reckoning as belonging.—*adjs.* **imput′ative**, imputed ; **imput′atively**. — *n.* **imput′er**. [Fr. *imputer*—L. *imputāre*, *-ātum*—*in*, in′ *putāre*, to reckon.]

in, *in*, *prep.* expressing the relation of a thing to that which surrounds, encloses, includes, or conditions it, with respect to place, time, or circumstances, or to that which is assumed, held, maintained, or the relation of a right or possession to the person who holds or enjoys it : at : among : into : within : during : consisting of : by way of : because of : by or through : by the medium or method of : (*obs.*) with : among the characteristics or possibilities of.—*adv.* within : not out : at home : on the spot : in or to a position within or inward : in or into office, parliament, &c. : in favour : in mutual favour : in intimacy : in fashion : in the market : in season : at the bat : as an addition : alight : in pocket.—*n.* a member of the party in office or the side that is having its innings : a re-entrant or inward turn.—*adj.* inward : proceeding inwards.—*v.t.* to take in : to enclose : to gather in harvest.—*adj.* and *adv.* **in′-and-in**, from parents that are near akin : with constant and close interaction.—*n.* a game with four dice.—*n.* **in′-off**, (*billiards*) a losing hazard.—**in as far as, in so far as, insofar as**, to the extent that ; **in as much as, inasmuch as**, considering that ; **in for**, doomed to receive (esp. unpleasant consequences) : involved to the extent of : entered for : (see also **go**) ; **in it**, in enjoyment of success : in the running ; **nothing in it**, no truth, no importance, no difficulty in the matter : no important difference—six of one and half a dozen of the other ; **in itself**, intrinsically, apart from relations ; **in on**, (*slang*) participating in ; **ins and outs** (or **outs and ins**), turnings this way and that : nooks and corners : the whole details of any matter : those who repeatedly enter and leave (esp. the workhouse) ; **in that**, for the reason that. [O.E. *in* ; Du., Ger. *in*, O.N. *í* ; W. *yn*, L. *in*, Gr. *en*. O.E. also had *innan*, within ; cf. O.H.G. *innana*, Sw. *innan*.]

in, *in*, *n.* (*Spens.*). See **inn**.

inability, *in′ə-bil′i-ti*, *n.* want of sufficient power : incapacity.

inabstinence, *in-ab′sti-nəns*, *n.* want of abstinence.

inaccessible, *in-ak-ses′i-bl*, or *-ək-*, *adj.* not to be reached, obtained, or approached.—*ns.* **inaccessibil′ity**, **inaccess′ibleness**.—*adv.* **inaccess′ibly**.

inaccurate, *in-ak′ūr-it*, *adj.* not accurate : incorrect : erroneous.—*n.* **inacc′uracy** (*-ə-si*), want of exactness : mistake.—*adv.* **inacc′urately**.

inactive, *in-akt′iv*, *adj.* not active : inert : having no power to move : sluggish : idle : lazy : having no effect : (*chem.*) not showing any action : not rotating the plane of polarised light.—*n.* **inac′tion**, absence of action : idleness : rest.—*v.t.* **inact′ivate**, to render inactive.—*n.* **inactivā′tion**.—*adv.* **inact′ively**.—*n.* **inactiv′ity**, inaction : inertness : idleness.

inadaptable, *in-ə-dap′tə-bl*, *adj.* that cannot be adapted.—*n.* **inadaptā′tion** (*-ad-*).—*adj.* **inadap′tive**.

inadequate, *in-ad′i-kwit*, *adj.* insufficient : short of what is required : incompetent.—*ns.* **inad′equacy** (*-kwə-si*), **inad′equateness**, insufficiency.—*adv.* **inad′equately**.

inadmissible, *in-əd-mis′i-bl*, *adj.* not allowable.—*n.* **inadmissibil′ity**.—*adv.* **inadmiss′ibly**.

inadvertent, *in-əd-vərt′ənt*, *adj.* inattentive : unintentional.—*ns.* **inadvert′ence**, **inadvert′ency**, negligence : oversight.—*adv.* **inadvert′ently**.

inadvisable, *-ability*, &c. See **unadvisable**, &c.

inaidable, *in-ād′ə-bl*, *adj.* (*Shak.*) that cannot be aided.

inalienable, *in-āl′yən-ə-bl*, *-i-ən-ə-bl*, *adj.* not capable of being transferred or removed.—*n.* **inalienabil′ity**.—*adv.* **inal′ienably**.

inalterable, *-ability*. Same as **unalterable**, &c.

inamorata, *in-am-o-rä′tä*, *n.fem.* a woman in love or beloved :—*masc.* **inamora′to**. [It. *innamorata*, *-to*—L.L. *inamorāre*, to cause to love—L. *in*, in, *amor*, love.]

inane, *in-ān′*, *adj.* empty, void : vacuous : senseless : characterless.—*n.* the void of space.—*ns.*

inanition (*in-ə-nish'ən*), exhaustion from want of food; **inanity** (*in-an'i-ti*), senselessness : mental vacuity : emptiness : an insipid empty-headed utterance. [L. *inānis*.]

inanimate, *in-an'i-mit,* **-d,** **-māt-id,** *adjs.* without animation : without life : dead : spiritless : dull. —*ns.* **inan'imateness, inanimā'tion.**

inappeasable, *in-ə-pēz'ə-bl, adj.* that cannot be appeased.

inapplicable, *in-ap'lik-ə-bl, adj.* not applicable.—*n.* **inapplicabil'ity.**

inapposite, *in-ap'ə-zit, adj.* not apposite, suitable, or pertinent.—*adv.* **inapp'ositely.**—*n.* **inapp'-ositeness.**

inappreciable, *in-ə-prē'sh(y)ə-bl, adj.* not appreciable or able to be valued.—*n.* **inappreciation** (*-shi-ā'shən*).—*adj.* **inappre'ciative** (*-shi-ə-tiv,* or *-shi-ā-tiv*), not valuing justly or at all.

inapprehensible, *in-ap-ri-hen'si-bl, adj.* not apprehensible or intelligible.—*n.* **inapprehen'sion.**—*adj.* **inapprehen'sive.**

inapproachable, *in-ə-prōch'ə-bl, adj.* unapproachable : inaccessible.—*adv* **inapproach'ably.**

inappropriate, *in-ə-prō'pri-it, adj.* not suitable.—*adv.* **inappro'priately.**—*n.* **inappro'priateness.**

inapt, *in-apt', adj.* not apt : unfit, or unqualified.—*ns.* **inapt'itude, inapt'ness,** unfitness, awkwardness.—*adv.* **inapt'ly.**

inarable, *in-ar'ə-bl, adj.* not arable.

inarch, *in-ärch', v.t.* to graft by uniting without separating from the original stem.—Also **enarch'.**

inarm, *in-ärm', v.t.* to embrace. [Pfx. *in-,* **arm.**]

inarticulate, *in-ər-tik'ū-lit, adj.* not jointed or hinged : not uttered with the distinct sounds of spoken language : indistinctly uttered or uttering : incapable of clear and fluent expression.—*n.* **inartic'ulacy.**—*adv.* **inartic'ulately.**—*ns* **inartic'ulateness, inarticulā'tion,** indistinctness of sounds in speaking.

inartificial, *in-ärt-i-fish'əl, adj.* not done by art : simple.—*adv.* **inartific'ially.**

inartistic, -al, *in-är-tis'tik, -əl, adjs.* not artistic : deficient in appreciation of art.—*adv.* **inartis'tically.**

inasmuch, *in-az-much'.* See **in.**

inattentive, *in-ə-ten'tiv, adj.* careless : not fixing the mind to attention : neglectful.—*ns.* **inatten'tion, inatten'tiveness.**—*adv.* **inatten'tively.**

inaudible, *in-awd'i-bl, adj.* not able to be heard.—*ns.* **inaudibil'ity, inaud'ibleness.**—*adv.* **inaud'ibly.**

inaugurate, *in-aw'gūr-āt, v.t.* to induct formally into an office : to cause to begin : to make a public exhibition of for the first time.—*adj.* **inau'gural,** pertaining to, or done at, an inauguration.—*n.* (*U.S.*) an inaugural address, esp. the President's.—*ns.* **inaugurā'tion ; inau'gurator**—*adj.* **inau'guratory** (*-ə-tər-i*). [L. *inaugurāre, -ātum,* to inaugurate with taking of the auspices ; see **augur.**]

inaurate, *in-aw'rāt, adj.* gilded : having a golden lustre. [L. *inaurāre, -ātum,* to gild—*in,* in, on, *aurum,* gold.]

inauspicious, *in-aw-spish'əs, adj.* not auspicious : ill-omened : unlucky.—*adv.* **inauspic'iously.**—*n.* **inauspic'iousness.**

inbeing, *in'bē-ing, n.* inherent existence : inherence : inner nature.

inbent, *in'bent, adj.* bent inwards.

in-between, *in-bi-twēn', adj.* intervening : intermediate.—*n.* an interval : an intermediary : any thing or person that is intermediate.

inboard, *in'bōrd, adv.* and *adj.* within the hull or interior of a ship : toward or nearer to the centre.

inborn, *in'bawrn, adj.* born in or with one : innate : implanted by nature.

inbreak, *in'brāk, n.* a violent rush in : irruption.

inbreathe, *in-brēdh', in'brēdh, v.t.* to breath in.

inbreed, *in'brēd, in-brēd', v.t.* to breed or generate within : to breed in-and-in.—*pa.p.* and *adj.* **in'bred,** innate : bred in-and-in.—*n.* **in'breeding.**

inbring, *in-bring', v.t.* to bring in : to bring into court.—*pa.p.* and *adj.* **inbrought'.**—*n.* **in'bringing.**

inburning, *in-burn'ing, adj.* (*Spens.*) burning within.

inburst, *in'burst, n.* an irruption.

inby, inbye, *in-bī', adv.* (*Scot.*) toward the interior : near : near the house.—Also *adj.* [**in, by.**]

Inca, *ing'kä, n.* an Indian of Peru : a member of the old royal family of Peru : a Peruvian king or emperor.—Also *adj.* [Quichua, prince.]

incage, *in-kāj'.* Same as **encage.**

incalculable, *in-kal'kū-lə-bl, adj.* not calculable or able to be reckoned : too great to calculate : unpredictable.—*ns.* **incalculabil'ity, incal'culableness.**—*adv.* **incal'culably.**

incalescent, *in-ka-les'ənt,* or *-kə-, adj.* growing warm.—*n.* **incalesc'ence.** [L. *incalēscēns, -entis,* pr.p. of *incalēscēre*—*in,* in, *calēscēre,* inceptive of *calēre,* to be warm.]

in-calf, *in-käf', adj.* pregnant (with calf). [**in, calf.**]

incandesce, *in-kan-des', v.i.* to be luminous by heat.—*n.* **incandesc'ence,** a white heat.—*adj.* **incandesc'ent,** white-hot.—*n.* an **incandescent lamp,** one whose light is produced by heating something to white heat, as a filament resisting an electric current in a glow-lamp, or a mantle heated by a flame. [L. *in,* in, *candēscēre*—*candēre,* to glow.]

incantation, *in-kan-tā'shən, n.* a formula of words said or sung for purposes of enchantment : the use of spells.—*n.* **in'cantător.**—*adj.* **incan'tatory** (*-tə-tə-ri*). [L. *incantāre,* to sing a magical formula over.]

incapable, *in-kāp'ə-bl, adj.* not capable : (*obs.*) unable to receive or take in : unable (with *of*) : incompetent : helplessly drunk : disqualified.—*n.* an incompetent person : one who is helplessly drunk.—*n.* **incapabil'ity.**—*adv.* **incap'ably.**

incapacious, *in-kə-pā'shəs, adj.* not large, narrow : of small capacity.—*n.* **incapā'ciousness.**—*v.t.* **incapacitate** (*-pas'*), to deprive of capacity : to make incapable : to disqualify.—*ns.* **incapacitā'-tion,** a disqualifying ; **incapac'ity,** want of capacity : inability : disability : legal disqualification. [L. *incapāx, -ācis.*]

incapsulate, *in-kap'sūl-āt, v.t.* to enclose as in a capsule : to enclose (a modifying element) between other elements of a word.

incarcerate, *in-kär'sər-āt, v.t.* to imprison : to confine.—*n.* **incarcerā'tion,** imprisonment : (*surg.*) obstinate constriction or strangulation. [L. *in,* in, *carcer,* a prison.]

incardinate, *in-kär'di-nāt, v.t.* to attach as a cardinal part, as a priest to his church.—*adj.* Sir Andrew Aguecheek's blunder for *incarnate* (*Twelfth Night,* V. i.). [L. *in,* in, into, *cardō, -inis,* a hinge.]

incarnadine, *in-kär'nə-dīn, -din, v.t.* to dye red.—*adj.* carnation-coloured : flesh-colour, blood-red. [Fr. *incarnadin*—It. *incarnadino,* carnation, flesh-colour.]

incarnate, *in-kär'nāt,* or *in', v.t.* to embody in flesh.—*v.i.* to form flesh, heal.—*adj.* (*-kär'nit, -nāt*) invested with flesh.—*n.* **incarnā'tion,** act of embodying in flesh, esp. of Christ : an incarnate form : manifestation, visible embodiment : (*surg.*) the process of healing, or forming new flesh. [L.L. *incarnāre, -ātum*—L. *in,* in, *carō, carnis,* flesh.]

incase, incasement. See **encase, encasement.**

incatenation, *in-kat-i-nā'shən, n.* harnessing : chaining together : linking. [L. *in, catēna,* chain.]

incautious, *in-kaw'shəs, adj.* not cautious or careful.—*ns.* **incau'tion, incau'tiousness.**—*adv.* **incau'tiously.**

incavo, *in-kä'vō, n.* the incised part in an intaglio. [It.,—L. *in,* in, *cavus,* hollow.]

incede, *in-sēd', v.i.* to advance majestically.—*adv.* **inced'ingly.** [L. *incēdĕre ;* see Virg. *Aen.* I. 46.]

incendiary, *in-sen'di-ər-i, n.* one who maliciously sets fire to property : one who enflames passions or promotes strife : an incendiary bomb.—*adj.* relating to incendiarism : adapted or used for setting buildings, &c., on fire : tending to excite strife.—*n.* **incen'diarism.** [L. *incendiārius*—*incendium*—*incendĕre,* to kindle.]

incendivity, *in-sen-div'i-ti, n.* power of causing ignition. [L. *incendĕre,* to set on fire.]

incense, *in-sens', v.t.* (*obs.*) to kindle : to inflame with anger : to incite, urge.—*ns.* **incense'ment,** (*Shak.*) anger ; **incens'or,** instigator : inciter. [O.Fr. *incenser*—L. *incendĕre, incēnsum,* to kindle.]

incense, *in'sэns, n.* material burned or volatilised to give fragrant fumes, esp. in religious rites—usu. a mixture of resins and gums, &c. (olibanum, benzoin, styrax, cascarilla bark): the fumes so obtained: any pleasant smell: (*fig.*) homage, adulation.—*v.t.* (*in'sэns, in-sens'*) to perfume or fumigate with incense: to offer incense to.—*n.* **in'cense-boat,** a boat-shaped vessel for feeding a censer with incense.—*adj.* **in'cense-breathing,** exhaling fragrance. — *ns.* **in'cense-burner,** a stationary vessel for burning incense; **in'censer, in'sensor** (or *-sens'*), a burner or offerer of incense: a flatterer; **in'sensory** (or *-sens'*), a censer or thurible. [O.Fr. *encens*—L. *incēnsum—incendēre*, to set on fire.]

incentive, *in-sent'iv, adj.* inciting, encouraging: (*Milt.*) igniting.—*n.* that which incites to action. [L. *incen:ivus*, striking up a tune—*incinēre—in*, in, *canēre*, to sing.]

incentre, *in'sen-tэr, n.* the centre of the inscribed circle or sphere.

incept, *in-sept', v.t.* (*obs.*) to begin: to take into the body.—*v.i.* (*Cambridge*) to complete the taking of a master's or doctor's degree.—*n.* **incep'tion,** beginning.—*adj.* **incep'tive,** beginning or marking the beginning: (*gram.*) inchoative.—*n.* an inchoative verb.—*n.* **incep'tor.** [L. *incipēre, inceptum*, to begin—*in*, in, on, *capēre*, to take.]

incertain, *in-sэr'tэn, adj.* (*Shak.*) uncertain.—*ns.* **incer'tainty** (*Shak.*), **incer'titude.**

incessant, *in-ses'эnt, adj.* uninterrupted: continual. —*adv.* **incess'antly,** unceasingly: (*obs.*) immediately. [L. *incessāns, -āntis—in-*, not, *cessāre*, to cease.]

incest, *in'sest, n.* sexual intercourse within the prohibited degrees of kindred.—*adj.* **incest'uous.**—*adv.* **incest'uously.**—*n.* **incest'uousness.** [L. *incestum—in-*, not, *castus*, chaste.]

inch, *in(t)sh, n.* the twelfth part of a foot: proverbially, a small distance or degree: (in *pl.*) stature.—*v.t.* and *v.i.* to move by slow degrees.— *adj.* **inched,** containing inches: marked with inches.—*adv.* **inch'meal,** inch by inch.—*n.* **inch'-worm,** a looper caterpillar.—**at an inch,** (*Shak.*) ready at hand; **by inches, inch by inch,** by small degrees; **every inch,** entirely, thoroughly. [O.E. *ynce*, an inch—L. *uncia*, a twelfth part; cf. **ounce.**]

inch, *insh, n.* an island. [Gael. *innis*, island.]

incharitable, *in-char'it-э-bl, adj.* (*Shak.*) uncharitable.

inchase, *in-chās'.* See **enchase.**

inchoate, *in-kō'āt, in'kō-āt, adj.* only begun: unfinished, rudimentary: not established.—*v.t.* (*in'*) to begin.—*adv.* **inchoately** (*-kō'*, or *in'*).—*n.* **inchoa'tion,** beginning: rudimentary state.—*adj.* **inchoative** (*in-kō'э-tiv* or *in-kō-ā'tiv*), incipient: (*gram.*) denoting the beginning of an action, inceptive.—*n.* an inchoative verb. [L. *inchoāre* (for *incohāre*), *-ātum*, to begin.]

inchpin, *in(t)sh'pin, n.* (*obs.*) a deer's sweetbread. [Perh. **inch, pin.**]

incident, *in'si-dэnt, adj.* falling upon something: liable to occur: naturally belonging, or consequent. —*n.* that which happens: an event: a subordinate action: an episode.—*n.* **in'cidence,** the fact or manner of falling: bearing or onus, as of a tax: the falling of a ray on a surface: (*geom.*) the falling of a point on a line, or a line on a plane.—*adj.* **incidental** (*-dent'l*), incident: striking or impinging: liable to occur: naturally attached: accompanying: concomitant: occasional, casual.— *n.* anything that occurs incidentally.—*adv.* **incident'ally,** in an incidental way: (loosely) by the way, parenthetically, as a digression.—*n.* **incident'alness.—angle of incidence,** the angle between an incident ray and the normal to the surface it falls on; **incidental music,** music accompanying the action of a play. [L. *incidēns, -entis—in*, on, *cadēre*, to fall.]

incinerate, *in-sin'эr-āt, v.t.* to reduce to ashes.—*ns.* **incinera'tion; incin'erātor,** a furnace for consuming anything. [L. *incinerāre, -ātum—in*, in, *cinis, cineris*, ashes.]

incipient, *in-sip'i-эnt, adj.* beginning: nascent.—

ns. **incip'ience, incip'iency.**—*adv.* **incip'iently.** [L. *incipiēns, -entis*, pr.p. of *incipēre*, to begin.]

incise, *in-sīz', v.t.* to cut into: to cut or gash: to engrave.—*adjs.* **incised',** (*bot.*) cut to about the middle; **incīs'iform,** shaped like an incisortooth.—*n.* **incision** (*in-sizh'эn*), the act of cutting in: a cut: a gash.—*adj.* **incisive** (*-sīs'*), having the quality of cutting in: trenchant: acute: sarcastic.—*adv.* **inci'sively.**—*ns.* **inci'siveness; incisor** (*-sīz'эr*), a cutting or fore tooth.—*adjs.* **incisorial** (*-sis-ō'ri-эl, -sīz-*), **incisory** (*-sīs', -sīz'эr-i*).—*n.* **incisure** (*-sizh'эr*), a cut, incision. [Fr. *inciser*—L. *incīdēre, incīsum—in*, into, *caedēre*, to cut.]

incite, *in-sīt', v.t.* to move to action: to instigate.— *ns.* **incitant** (*in'sit-эnt, in-sīt'эnt*), that which incites: a stimulant; **incitā'tion** (*-sit-, -sīt-*), the act of inciting or rousing: an incentive.—*adj.* and *n.* **incitative** (*-sīt'э-tiv*).—*ns.* **incite'ment; incit'er.**—*adv.* **incit'ingly.** [Fr.,—L. *incitāre—in*, in, *citāre*, to rouse—*ciēre*, to put in motion.]

incivil, *in-siv'il, adj.* (*Shak.*) uncivil.—*n.* **incivil'ity,** want of civility or courtesy: impoliteness: an act of discourtesy (in this sense *pl.* **incivil'ities**).

incivism, *in'siv-izm, n.* neglect of duty as a citizen, conduct unbecoming a good citizen. [Fr. *incivisme.*]

inclasp, *in-klâsp'.* Same as **enclasp.**

inclement, *in-klem'эnt, adj.* severe: stormy: harsh. —*n.* **inclem'ency.**—*adv.* **inclem'ently.**

incline, *in-klīn', v.i.* to lean forward or downward: to bow or bend: to deviate or slant: to slope: to tend: to be disposed: to have some slight desire. —*v.t.* to cause to bend downwards: to turn: to cause to deviate: to slope: to tilt: to direct: to dispose.—*n.* (*in'klīn, in-klīn'*) a slope: (*min.*) a sloping tunnel or shaft.—*adj.* **inclīn'able,** leaning, capable of being tilted or sloped: tending: somewhat disposed.—*ns.* **inclīn'ableness; inclīnā'tion** (*-klin-*), a bend or bow: a slope or tilt: a deviation: angle with the horizon or with any plane or line: tendency: disposition of mind: natural aptness: favourable disposition, preference, affection.—*adj.* **inclīnā'tional.**—*n.* **inclīnatō'rium,** the dipping-needle.—*adjs.* **inclīn'atory; inclīned',** bent: sloping: oblique: having a tendency: disposed.—*n.* **inclīn'ing,** inclination: (*Shak.*) side, party.—*n.* **inclinom'eter** (*-klin-*), an instrument for measuring slopes (clinometer), the magnetic dip (dipping-needle), or the inclination of the axis of an aeroplane.—**inclined plane,** one of the mechanical powers, a slope or plane up which one can raise a weight one could not lift. [L. *inclīnāre*, to bend towards—*in*, into, *clīnāre*, to lean.]

inclip, *in-klip', v.t.* (*Shak.*) to embrace, enfold. [in. clip.]

inclose, inclosure. See **enclose.**

include, *in-klōōd', v.t.* to enclose: to comprise as a part: to classify, or reckon as part: to take in: (*Shak.*) to conclude.—*adj.* **includ'ed,** (*bot.*) not protruding.—*prep.* (or *pr.p.* merging in *prep.*) with the inclusion of.—*adj.* **includ'ible.**—*n.* **inclusion** (*-klōō'zhэn*), act of including: that which is included: a foreign body enclosed in a crystal, or the like.—*adj.* **inclusive** (*-klōō'siv*), shutting in: enclosing: comprehensive: including everything: (with *of*) comprehending the stated limit or extremes, including: (*obs.* or *loose*) included.—*adv.* **inclu'sively.** [L. *inclūdēre, inclūsum—in*, in, *claudēre*, to shut.]

incoagulable, *in-kō-ag'ū-lэ-bl, adj.* incapable of coagulation.

incoercible, *in-kō-эrs'i-bl, adj.* that cannot be coerced: that cannot be liquefied by pressure.

incog, *in-kog', adv.* an abbreviation for **incognito.**

incogitable, *in-koj'i-tэ-bl, adj.* unthinkable.—*ns.* **incogitabil'ity, incog'itancy.**—*adjs.* **incog'itant,** unthinking: without power of thought; **incog'itative.** [L. *in-*, not, *cōgitāre*, to think.]

incognisable, incognizable, *in-kog'niz-э-bl,* or *in-kon'iz-э-bl, adj.* that cannot be known or distinguished.—*adj.* **incog'nisant, incog'nizant,** not cognisant.—*ns.* **incog'nisance, incog'nizance,** failure to recognise; **incognoscibil'ity** (*-kog-*

nos-i-).—adj. **incognosc'ible.** [See **cognition, cognosce, recognise.**]

incognito, *in-kog'ni-tō, adj.* unknown : disguised : under an assumed title.—*adv.* under an assumed name : with concealment, or feigned concealment, of identity.—*n.* a man unknown (*fem.* **incog'nita**) : concealment, real or feigned. [It.,—L. *incognitus* —*in-,* not, *cognitus,* known—*cognōscĕre,* to recognise, come to know.]

incoherent, *in-kō-hēr'ɘnt, adj.* not coherent: loose : rambling.—*ns.* **incohēr'ence, -ency.**— *adv.* **incohēr'ently.**—*n.* **incohē'sion.**—*adj.* **incohē'sive** (*-siv*).

incombustible, *in-kɘm-bust'i-bl, adj.* incapable of combustion.—*ns.* **incombustibil'ity, incombust'- ibleness.**—*adv.* **incombust'ibly.**

income, *in'kɘm, ing'kɘm, in'kum, n.* (*Shak.*) coming in, advent : that which comes in : profit, or interest from anything : revenue : (*Scot.*) a disease coming without known cause.—*n.* **incomer** (*in'kum-ɘr*), one who comes in : one who takes possession of a farm, house, &c., or who comes to live in a place, not having been born there; **in'come-tax,** a tax directly levied on income or on income over a certain amount. — *adj.* **in'coming,** coming in : accruing : (*Scot.*) ensuing, next to follow.—*n.* the act of coming in : revenue. [**in, come.**]

incommensurable, *in-kɘm-en'sū-rɘ-bl, adj.* having no common measure : incommensurate.—*n.* a quantity that has no common measure with another, esp. with rational numbers.—*ns.* **incommensurabil'ity, incommen'surableness.**—*adv.* **incommen'surably.** — *adj.* **incommen'surate,** disproportionate : not adequate : incommensurable. — *adv.* **incommen'surately.** — *n.* **incommen'surateness.**

incommiscible, *in-kɘm-is'i-bl,* that cannot be mixed together. [L. *in-,* not, *commiscĕre,* to mix.]

incommode, *in-kɘm-ōd', v.t.* to cause trouble or inconvenience to.—*adj.* **incommō'dious,** inconvenient : troublesome : unsuitable. — *adv.* **incommō'diously.**—*ns.* **incommō'diousness ; incommodity** (*-od'*), inconvenience : anything that causes inconvenience. [Fr. *incommoder*—L. *incommodāre*—*in-,* not, *commodus,* commodious.]

incommunicable, *in-kɘm-ūn'i-kɘ-bl, adj.* that cannot be communicated or imparted to others.—*ns.* **incommunicabil'ity, incommun'icableness.**— *adv.* **incommun'icably.**—*adj.* **incommun'icative,** uncommunicative.—*adv.* **incommun'icatively.**—*n.* **incommun'icativeness.**

incommutable, *in-kɘm-ūt'ɘ-bl, adj.* that cannot be commuted or exchanged.—*ns.* **incommutabil'ity, incommut'ableness.**—*adv.* **incommut'ably.**

incomparable, *in-kom'pɘr-ɘ-bl, adj.* not admitting comparison : matchless.—*ns.* **incomparabil'ity, incom'parableness.**—*adv.* **incom'parably.**—*adj.* **incompared** (*in-kom-pār'ed ; Spens.*), peerless.

incompatible, *in-kɘm-pat'i-bl, adj.* not consistent : contradictory : incapable of existing together in harmony or at all : incapable of combination, co-operation, functioning together : mutually intolerant or exclusive : irreconcilable.—*n.* a thing incompatible with another : (in *pl.*) things which cannot coexist.—*ns.* **incompatibil'ity, incompat'- ibleness.**—*adv.* **incompat'ibly.**

incompetent, *in-kom'pi-tɘnt, adj.* wanting adequate powers : unable to function : wanting the proper legal qualifications : grossly deficient in ability for one's work.—*n.* an incompetent person.—*ns.* **incom'petence, incom'petency.**—*adv.* **incom'- petently.**

incomplete, *in-kɘm-plēt', adj.* imperfect: unfinished : wanting calyx, corolla, or both.—*n.pl.* **Incomplē'- tae** (*-tē*), an artificial group of dicotyledons with perianth absent or incomplete, the Monochlamydeae.—*adv.* **incomplete'ly.**—*ns.* **incomplete'- ness, incomplē'tion.**

incompliance, *in-kɘm-plī'ɘns, n.* refusal to comply : an unaccommodating disposition.—*adj.* **incompli'- ant.**

incomposed, *in-kɘm-pōzd', adj.* (*Milt.*) discomposed.

incomposite, *in-kom'pɘz-it, adj.* simple : ill-constructed.—**incomposite numbers,** prime numbers.

incompossible, *in-kɘm-pos'i-bl, adj.* incapable of coexisting.—*n.* **incompossibil'ity.**

incomprehensible, *in-kom-pri-hens'i-bl, adj.* not capable of being understood : not to be contained within limits.—*ns.* **incomprehensibil'ity, incomprehens'ibleness.**—*adv.* **incomprehens'ibly.**— *n.* **incomprehen'sion,** lack of comprehension.— *adj.* **incomprehens'ive,** not comprehensive.— *n.* **incomprehens'iveness.**

incompressible, *in-kɘm-pres'i-bl, adj.* not to be compressed into smaller bulk.—*ns.* **incompressibil'ity, incompress'ibleness.**

incomputable, *in-kɘm-pūt'ɘ-bl,* or *in-kom', adj.* that cannot be computed or reckoned.

inconceivable, *in-kɘn-sēv'ɘ-bl, adj.* that cannot be conceived by the mind : incomprehensible : involving a contradiction in terms : physically impossible : (*coll.*) taxing belief or imagination.—*n.* an inconceivable thing.—*ns.* **inconceivabil'ity, inconceiv'ableness.**—*adv.* **inconceiv'ably.**

inconcinnity, *in-kɘn-sin'i-ti, n.* want of congruousness or proportion.—*adj.* **inconcinn'ous.**

inconclusive, *in-kɘn-klōōs'iv, adj.* not settling a point in debate, indeterminate, indecisive.—*n.* **inconclusion** (*-klōō'zhɘn*).—*adv.* **inconclus'ively.** —*n.* **inconclus'iveness.**

incondensable, *in-kɘn-dens'ɘ-bl, adj.* not condensable.

incondite, *in-kon'dīt, -dit, adj.* not well put together, irregular, unfinished. [L. *inconditus*—*in-,* not, *condĕre, conditum,* to build.]

incongruous, *in-kong'grōo-ɘs, adj.* inconsistent : not fitting well together, disjointed : unsuitable.— Also **incong'ruent.**—*ns.* **incongruity** (*-kong-* or *-kɘn-grōō'*), **incong'ruousness.**—*adv.* **incong'ruously.**

inconscient, *in-kon'sh*(*y*)*ɘnt, adj.* unconscious.—*adv.* **incon'sciently.**—*adj.* **incon'scious,** unconscious.

inconscionable, *in-kon'shɘn-ɘ-bl, adj.* unconscionable.

inconsecutive, *in-kɘn-sek'ū-tiv, adj.* not succeeding or proceeding in regular order.—*n.* **inconsec'- utiveness.**

inconsequent, *in-kon'si-kwɘnt, adj.* not following from the premises : illogical : irrelevant : disconnected : unrelated : unimportant.—*n.* **incon'- sequence.**—*adj.* **inconsequential** (*-kwen'shl*), not following from the premises : of no consequence or value.—*advs.* **inconsequen'tially, incon'sequently.**

inconsiderable, *in-kɘn-sid'ɘr-ɘ-bl, adj.* not worthy of notice : unimportant : of no great size.—*n.* **inconsid'erableness.**—*adv.* **inconsid'erably.**

inconsiderate, *in-kɘn-sid'er-it, adj.* not considerate : thoughtless : inattentive.—*adv.* **inconsid'erately.** —*ns.* **inconsid'erateness, inconsidera'tion.**

inconsistent, *in-kɘn-sist'ɘnt, adj.* not consistent : not suitable or agreeing : intrinsically incompatible : self-contradictory : changeable, fickle.—*ns.* **inconsist'ence, inconsist'ency.**—*adv.* **inconsist'ently.**

inconsolable, *in-kɘn-sōl'ɘ-bl, adj.* not to be comforted.—*n.* **inconsol'ableness.**—*adv.* **inconsol'ably.**

inconsonant, *in-kon'sɘn-ɘnt, adj.* not consonant.— *n.* **incon'sonance.**—*adv.* **incon'sonantly.**

inconspicuous, *in-kɘn-spik'ū-ɘs, adj.* not conspicuous. — *adv.* **inconspic'uously.** — *n.* **inconspic'uousness.**

inconstant, *in-kon'stɘnt, adj.* subject to change : fickle.—*n.* **incon'stancy.**—*adv.* **incon'stantly.**

inconsumable, *in-kɘn-sūm'ɘ-bl, adj.* that cannot be consumed or wasted.—*adv.* **inconsum'ably.**

incontestable, *in-kɘn-test'ɘ-bl, adj.* too clear to be called in question : undeniable.—*n.* **incontestabil'- ity.**—*adv.* **incontest'ably.**

incontiguous, *in-kɘn-tig'ū-ɘs, adj.* not adjoining or touching.—*adv.* **incontig'uously.**—*n.* **incontig'- uousness.**

incontinent, *in-kon'ti-nɘnt, adj.* not restraining the passions or appetites : unchaste : (*med.*) unable to restrain natural discharges or evacuations.—*ns.* **incon'tinence, incon'tinency.** — *adv.* **incon'- tinently.** [L. *incontinēns, -entis*—*in-,* not, *continēns ;* see **continent.**]

incontinent, *in-kon'ti-nənt, adv. (arch.)* straightway.—Also **incon'tinently.** [Fr.,—L.L. *in continēnti (tempore),* in unbroken (time).]

incontrollable, *in-kən-trōl'ə-bl, adj.* uncontrollable.—*adv.* **incontroll'ably.**

incontrovertible, *in-kon-trə-vərt'i-bl, adj.* too clear to be called in question.—*n.* **incontrovertibil'ity.** —*adv.* **incontrovert'ibly.**

inconvenient, *in-kən-vēn'yənt, adj.* unsuitable: causing trouble or uneasiness: increasing difficulty: incommodious.—*v.t.* **inconvēn'ience,** to trouble or incommode.—*ns.* **inconvēn'ience, inconvēn'iency.**—*adv.* **inconvēn'iently.**

inconversable, *in-kən-vərs'ə-bl, adj.* indisposed to conversation, unsocial.

inconversant, *in-kon'vər-sənt, adj.* not versed (with *with* or *in*).

inconvertible, *in-kən-vərt'i-bl, adj.* that cannot be changed or exchanged.—*n.* **inconvertibil'ity.**— *adv.* **inconvert'ibly.**

inconvincible, *in-kən-vin'si-bl, adj.* not capable of being convinced.

incony, inconie, *in-kun'i, adj. (Shak.)* fine, delicate, pretty. [Origin unknown.]

incoordinate, *in-kō-ord'(i-)nit, adj.* not coordinate. —*n.* **incoordination** (-*i-nā'shən*), want or failure of coordination.

incoronate, *in-kor'ə-nāt, -nit, -d, -nāt-id, adjs.* crowned.—*n.* **incorona'tion.** [L. *in,* in, *corōna,* crown.]

incorporate, *in-kor'pər-āt, v.t.* to form into a body: to combine into one mass, or embody: to take or put into the body: to merge: to absorb: to form into a corporation: to admit to a corporation: to incarnate.—*v.i.* to unite into one mass: to become part of another body.—*adj.* (*-it*) united in one body: constituted as an incorporation.— *adj.* **incor'porāting,** (*philol.*) combining the parts of a sentence in one word.—*n.* **incorpora'tion,** act of incorporating: state of being incorporated: formation of a legal or political body: an association: an incorporated society: an embodiment. —*adj.* **incor'porative** (-*ə-tiv, -ā-tiv*).—*n.* **incor'porātor,** one who incorporates : (*U.S.*) a member, or original member, of an incorporated company : a member of a university admitted to membership of another. [L. *incorporāre, -ātum—in,* in, into, *corpus, -oris,* body.]

incorporate, *in-kor'pər-āt, -it, adj.* without a body: unembodied.—*adjs.* **incor'poral(1)** (*Shak.*), **incorporeal** (-*pō'ri-əl*), not having a body: spiritual: intangible.—*ns.* **incorpō'realism, incorporē'ity, incorporeality** (-*kor-por-i-al'i-ti*).—*adv.* **incorpō'really.** [L. *incorporātus, incorporālis,* bodiless— *in-,* not, *corpus, -oris,* body.]

incorpse, *in-korps', v.t.* (*Shak.*) to incorporate.

incorrect, *in-kər-əkt', adj.* containing faults : not accurate : not correct in manner or character : (*Shak.*) not regulated.—*adv.* **incorrect'ly.**—*n.* **incorrect'ness.**

incorrigible, *in-kor'i-ji-bl, adj.* beyond correction or reform.—Also *n.*—*ns.* **incorr'igibleness, incorrigibil'ity.**—*adv.* **incorr'igibly.**

incorrosible, *in-kə-rō'si-bl,* **incorrodible,** *in-kə-rō'di-bl, adjs.* incapable of being corroded : not readily corroded.

incorrupt, *in-kər-upt', adj.* sound : pure : not depraved : not to be influenced by bribes.—*adj.* **incorrupt'ible,** not capable of decay : that cannot be bribed : inflexibly just.—*ns.* **incorrupt'ibleness, incorruptibil'ity.**—*adv.* **incorrupt'ibly.**—*ns.* **incorrup'tion, incorrupt'ness.**—*adj.* **incorrupt'ive.** —*adv.* **incorrupt'ly.**

incrassate, *in-kras'āt, v.t.* and *v.i.* to thicken.— *adjs.* **incrass'ate, -d,** thickened.—*n.* **incrassā'tion.** —*adj.* **incrass'ative** (-*ə-tiv*). [L.L. *incrassāre, -ātum*—L. *in,* in, *crassus,* thick.]

increase, *in-krēs', v.i.* to grow in size, number, or (*arch.*) wealth : (*L. gram.*) to have a syllable more in the genitive than in the nominative.—*v.t.* to make greater in size, number, or (*arch.*) wealth.— *n.* **in'crease,** growth : addition to the original stock : profit : produce : progeny.—*adjs.* **increas'able ; increase'ful,** (*Shak.*) abundant of produce.—*n.* **increas'er.**—*n.* and *adj.* **increas'-**

ing.—*adv.* **increas'ingly.** [M.E. *encressen*—A.Fr. *encresser*—L. *incrēscĕre—in,* in, *crēscĕre,* to grow.]

increate, *in-krē-āt', adj.* (*arch.*) uncreated.

incredible, *in-kred'i-bl, adj.* surpassing belief.— *ns.* **incredibil'ity ; incred'ibleness.**—*adv.* **incred'ibly.**

incredulous, *in-kred'ū-ləs, adj.* hard of belief : not believing : (*Shak.*) incredible.—*ns.* **incredū'lity** (-*krid-*), **incred'ulousness.**—*adv.* **incred'ulously.**

incremate, *in'kri-māt,* to burn : to cremate.—*n.* **incremā'tion.** [L. *in-,* inten., *cremāre, -ātum,* to burn.]

increment, *ing'* or *in'kri-mənt, n.* increase : amount of increase : an amount or thing added : (*math.*) the finite increase of a variable quantity : (*rhet.*) an adding of particulars towards a climax : (*gram.*) a syllable in excess of the number of the nominative singular or the second pers. sing. present indicative. —*adj.* **incremental** (-*ment'l*).—**unearned increment,** any exceptional increase in the value of land, houses, &c., not due to the owner's labour or outlay. [L. *incrēmentum—incrēscĕre,* to increase.]

increscent, *in-kres'ənt, adj.* (*her.*) waxing (of the moon).

incriminate, *in-krim'in-āt, v.t.* to charge with a crime or fault, to criminate : to involve in a charge. —*adj.* **incrim'inatory.**

incrust, incrustation. See **encrust, encrustation.**

incubate, *in'* or *ing'kū-bāt, v.i.* to sit on eggs : to hatch : to undergo incubation : (*fig.*) to brood, meditate.—*v.t.* to hatch : to foster the development of (as bacteria) : (*fig.*) to brood or ponder over.—*n.* **incuba'tion,** the act of sitting on eggs to hatch them : hatching (natural or artificial) : fostering (as of bacteria) : sleeping in a holy place to obtain dreams from the gods : (*fig.*) meditation on schemes : (*med.*) the period between infection and appearance of symptoms.—*adjs.* **in'cubātive, in'cubatory.**—*n.* **in'cubātor, a** brooding hen : an apparatus for hatching eggs by artificial heat, for rearing prematurely born children, or for developing bacteria.—*adj.* **in'cubous,** (*bot.*) having the upper leaf-margin overlapping the leaf above. [L. *incubāre, -ātum* (usu. *-itum*)—*in,* on, *cubāre,* to lie, recline.]

incubus, *in'* or *ing'kū-bəs, n.* the nightmare : a devil supposed to assume a male body and consort with women in their sleep : any oppressive influence :— *pl.* **in'cubuses, in'cubi** (-*bī*). [L. *incūbus,* nightmare—*in,* on, *cubāre,* to lie.]

inculcate, *in'kul-kāt* or *-kul', v.t.* to enforce by frequent admonitions or repetitions.—*n.* **inculcā'tion.**—*adj.* **inculc'ative** (-*ə-tiv*).—*n.* **in'culcātor.** —*adj.* **inculc'atory.** [L. *inculcāre, -ātum—in,* into, *calcāre,* to tread—*calx,* heel.]

inculpable, *in-kul'pə-bl, adj.* blameless.—*adv.* **incul'pably.** [L. *inculpābilis—in-,* not, *culpābilis,* see **culpable.**]

inculpate, *in'kul-pāt,* or *-kul', v.t.* to involve in a charge or blame : to charge.—*n.* **inculpā'tion.**— *adj.* **incul'patory** (-*pə-tə-ri*). [L.L. *inculpāre, -ātum*—L. *in,* in, *culpa,* a fault.]

incult, *in-kult', adj.* (*rare*) uncultivated.

incumbent, *in-kum'bənt, adj.* lying or resting : weighing on something : overlying : leaning over : overhanging : imposed or resting as a duty : lying along a surface, as a moth's wings at rest : (*bot.*) of a radicle, lying along the back of one cotyledon.— *n.* one who holds an ecclesiastical benefice.—*n.* **incum'bency,** a lying or resting on something : the state or fact of being incumbent or an incumbent : a duty or obligation : the holding of an office : an ecclesiastical benefice.—*adv.* **incum'bently.** [L. *incumbēns, -entis,* pr.p. of *incumbĕre,* to lie down.]

incunabula, *in-kū-nab'ū-la, n.pl.* books printed in the early period of the art, before the year 1500 : the cradle, birthplace, origin of a thing :—*sing.* **incūnab'ūlum,** also **incūnab'ūlum,** also **incūn'able.**—*adj.* **incūnab'ular.**—*n.* **incūnab'ūlist,** a student or collector of incunabula. [L. *incūnābŭla,* swaddling-clothes, infancy, earliest stage—*in,* in, *cūnābŭla,* dim. of *cūnae,* a cradle.]

incur, *in-kur', v.t.* to become liable to : to bring

upon oneself : to suffer :—*pr.p.* **incurr'ing** ; *pa.t.* and *pa.p.* **incurred'.**—*adj.* **incurr'able.** [L. *incurrĕre, incursum—in*, into, *currĕre*, to run.]

incurable, *in-kū'rə-bl, adj.* not admitting of cure or correction.—*n.* one beyond cure.—*ns.* **incur'ableness, incurabil'ity.**—*adv.* **incur'ably.**

incurious, *in-kū'ri-əs, adj.* not curious or inquisitive : inattentive : free of care : without curiousness : not exquisite : deficient in interest.—*adv.* **incū'riously.**—*ns.* **incū'riousness, incūrios'ity.**

incurrent, *in-kur'ənt, adj.* running in : carrying an inflowing current. [L. *in*, into, *currens, -entis,* pr.p. of *currĕre*, to run.]

incursion, *in-kur'shən, n.* a hostile inroad.—*adj.* **incur'sive,** making inroads. [L. *incursiō, -ōnis—incurrĕre.*]

incurve, *in-kurv', v.t.* and *v.i.* to curve : to curve inward.—*n.* **in'curve,** a curve inwards : (*baseball*) a ball that curves in, or towards the batsman.—*v.t.* and *v.i.* **incur'vate** (or *in'*), to bend, esp. inwards.—*adj.* curved, esp. inward—also **incur'vated.**—*ns.* **incurva'tion,** bending : bowing, kneeling, &c. : an inward bend or growth ; **incur'vature,** curve or curvature, esp. inward.—*adj.* **incurved'** (or *in'*), curved : curved inward.—*n.* **incur'vity.** [L. *incurvāre,* to bend in, *incurvus,* bent.]

incus, *ing'kəs, n.* one of the bones in the middle ear, so called from its fancied resemblance to an anvil :—*pl.* **incudes** (*ing-kū'dēz,* or *ing'*). [L. *incūs, incūdis,* an anvil.]

incuse, *in-kūz', v.t.* to impress by stamping, as a coin.—*adj.* hammered.—*n.* an impression, a stamp. [L. *incūsus,* pa.p. of *incūdĕre—in,* on, *cūdĕre,* to strike.]

incut, *in'kut, adj.* set in by, or as if by, cutting, esp. in printing, inserted in spaces left in the text.

Ind, *ind, īnd, n.* (*poet.*) India.

indaba, *in-dä'bä, n.* an important native council meeting. [Kaffir, news.]

indagate, *in'də-gāt, v.t.* to search out.—*n.* **indagā'tion.**—*adj.* in **dagātive.**—*n.* **in'dagātor.**—*adj.* **in'dagātory.** [L. *indāgāre, -ātum,* to trace.]

indart. Same as **endart.**

indebted, *in-det'id, adj.* being in debt : obliged by something received.—*ns.* **indebt'edness, indebt'ment.**

indecent, *in-dē'sənt, adj.* offensive to common modesty : unbecoming : gross, obscene.—*n.* **indē'cency,** quality of being indecent : anything violating modesty or seemliness.—*adv.* **indē'cently.**

indeciduous, *in-di-sid'ū-əs, adj.* not deciduous.—*adj.* **indecid'uate,** not deciduate.

indecipherable, *in-di-sī'fər-ə-bl, adj.* incapable of being deciphered.

indecision, *in-di-sizh'ən, n.* want of decision or resolution : hesitation.—*adj.* **indecisive** (*-sī'siv*), unsettled : inconclusive.—*adv.* **indeci'sively.**—*n.* **indeci'siveness.**

indeclinable, *in-di-klīn'ə-bl, adj.* (*gram.*) not varied by inflection.—*adv.* **indeclin'ably.**

indecomposable, *in-dē-kəm-pōz'ə-bl, adj.* that cannot be decomposed.

indecorous, *in-di-kō'rəs,* sometimes *in-dek'ə-rəs, adj.* unseemly : violating good manners.—*adv.* **indecō'rously.**—*ns.* **indecō'rousness, indecō'rum,** want of propriety of conduct : a breach of decorum. [L. *indĕcōrus.*]

indeed, *in-dēd', adv.* in fact : in truth : in reality. It emphasises an affirmation, marks a qualifying word, or clause, a concession or admission, or, used as an interj., it expresses surprise or interrogation, disbelief, or mere acknowledgment. [in, deed.]

indefatigable, *in-di-fat'i-gə-bl, adj.* not to be wearied out : unremitting in effort.—*n.* **indefat'igableness.**—*adv.* **indefat'igably.** [Fr. (obs.),—L. *indēfatigābilis—in-,* not, *dē,* from, *fatīgāre,* to tire.]

indefeasible, *in-di-fēz'i-bl, adj.* not to be made void.—*n.* **indefeasibil'ity.**—*adv.* **indefeas'ibly.**

indefectible, *in-di-fekt'i-bl, adj.* incapable of defect : unfailing.

indefensible, *in-di-fens'i-bl, adj.* untenable, that cannot be maintained or justified.—*n.* **indefensibil'ity.**—*adv.* **indefens'ibly.**

indefinable, *in-di-fīn'ə-bl, adj.* that cannot be defined.—*adv.* **indefin'ably.**

indefinite, *in-def'i-nit, adj.* without clearly marked outlines or limits : of a character not clearly distinguished : not precise : undetermined : (*gram.*) not referring to a particular person or thing (see also **article**) : not distinguishing between complete and incomplete active (as the Greek aorist) : (*bot.*) not fixed in number : not terminating in a flower : racemose or centripetal.—*adv.* **indef'initely.**—*n.* **indef'initeness.**

indehiscent, *in-di-his'ənt, adj.* not dehiscent.—*n.* **indehisc'ence.**

indelible, *in-del'i-bl, adj.* that cannot be blotted out or effaced.—*ns.* **indelibil'ity, indel'ibleness.**—*adv.* **indel'ibly.** [L. *indēlēbilis—in-,* not, *dēlēre,* to destroy : influenced by words ending in *-ible.*]

indelicate, *in-del'i-kit, adj.* immodest or verging on the immodest : wanting in fineness of feeling or tact : coarse.—*n.* **indel'icacy.**—*adv.* **indel'icately.**

indemnify, *in-dem'ni-fī, v.t.* to secure (with *against*) : to compensate :—*pr.p.* **indem'nifying ;** *pa.t.* and *pa.p.* **indem'nified.**—*n.* **indemnification** (*-fi-kā'shən*). [L. *indemnis,* unhurt (—*in-,* not, *damnum,* loss), and *facĕre,* to make.]

indemnity, *in-dem'ni-ti, n.* security from damage, loss, or punishment : compensation for loss or injury.—**Act of Indemnity,** an act or decree for the protection of public officers from any technical or legal penalties or liabilities they may have been compelled to incur. [Fr. *indemnité*—L. *indemnis,* unharmed—*damnum,* loss.]

indemonstrable, *in-dem'ən-strə-bl,* or *in-di-mon', adj.* that cannot be demonstrated or proved.—*n.* **indemonstrabil'ity.**

indene, *in'dēn, n.* a hydrocarbon (H₉C₈) got from coal-tar. [indigo.]

indent, *in-dent', v.t.* to cut into zigzags : to divide along a zigzag line : to notch : to indenture, apprentice : to make out a written order with counterfoil for : to order (esp. from abroad) : to requisition : to begin farther in from the margin than the rest of a paragraph : to impress : to dent or dint.—*v.i.* (*Shak.*) to move in a zigzag course : to bargain : to make a compact.—*n.* (*in'dent,* also *in-dent'*) a cut or notch : a recess like a notch : an indenture : an order for goods (from abroad) : (*orig.* Indian) an official requisition for goods : a dint.—*n.* **indenta'tion,** a hollow or depression : act of indenting or notching : notch : recess.—*adj.* **indent'ed,** having indentations : serrated : zigzag.—*ns.* **indent'er,** a person or thing that indents ; **inden'tion,** indentation : blank space at the beginning of a line ; **indent'ure,** the act of indenting, indentation : (*law*) a deed under seal, with mutual covenants, where the edge is indented for future identification : a written agreement between two or more parties : a contract.—*v.t.* to bind by indentures : to indent. [Two different words fused together : (1)—L.L. *indentāre*—L. *in,* in, *dens, dentis,* a tooth ; (2)—English **in** and **dint, dent.**]

independent, *in-di-pend'ənt, adj.* (with *of*) not dependent or relying on others : not subordinate : completely self-governing : thinking or acting for oneself : too self-respecting to accept help : not subject to bias : having or affording a comfortable livelihood without necessity of working or help from others : (*math.*) not depending on another for its value, said of a quantity or function : **Independent,** belonging to the Independents.—*n.* one who in ecclesiastical affairs holds that every congregation should be independent of every other and subject to no superior authority—a Congregationalist : a politician or other who commits himself to no party.—*ns.* **independ'ence,** the state of being independent : a competency ; **independ'ency,** independence : a sovereign state : an independent income : **Independency,** Congregationalism.—*adv.* **independ'ently.**—**Declaration of Independence,** the document (1776) proclaiming with reasons the secession of the thirteen colonies of America from the United Kingdom, reported to the Continental Congress, July 4, 1776—observed in the U.S. as a national holiday, **Independence Day**; **Independent Labour Party**, a Socialist party founded by Keir Hardie in 1893.

indescribable, *in-di-skrīb'ə-bl*, *adj.* that cannot be described.—*n.* (*old slang*, in *pl.*) trousers.—*adv.* **indescrib'ably**.

indesignate, *in-dez'ig-nāt*, *adj.* (*log.*) without any indication of quantification.

indestructible, *in-di-struk'ti-bl*, *adj.* that cannot be destroyed. — *ns.* **indestructibil'ity**, **indestruc'- tibleness.**—*adv.* **indestruc'tibly.**

indetectable, *in-di-tekt'ə-bl*, *adj.* not to be detected. —Also **indetect'ible.**

indeterminable, *in-di-tər'min-ə-bl*, *adj.* not to be ascertained or fixed.—*n.* **indeter'minableness.** —*adv.* **indeter'minably.**—*n.* **indeter'minacy.**— *adj.* **indeter'minate**, not determinate or fixed: uncertain: having no defined or fixed value.— *adv.* **indeter'minately.** — *ns.* **indeter'minate- ness, indetermina'tion**, want of determination: want of fixed direction.—*adj.* **indeter'mined**, not determined: unsettled.—*ns.* **indeter'minism**, the theory that denies determinism; **indeter'minist.**

indew, a Spenserian form of **endue**.

index, *in'deks*, *n.* the forefinger (also **in'dex-fing'er**), or the digit corresponding: a pointer or hand on a dial or scale, &c.: a moving arm, as on a surveying instrument: the gnomon of a sun-dial: the finger of a finger-post: (*print.*) a figure of a pointing hand, used to draw attention: (*slang*) the nose: anything that gives an indication: (*obs.*) a table of contents or other preliminary matter in a book: hence (*Shak.*; *fig.*) a preface, prologue, introduc- tion: an alphabetical register of subjects dealt with, usu. at the end of a book, with page or folio references: a similar list of other things: a list of prohibited books: (*mus., obs.*) a direct, or indi- cation of the first notes of next page or line: (*math.*) a symbol denoting a power: a number, commonly a ratio, expressing some relation (as *refractive index*, ratio of sines of angles of incidence and refraction; *cranial index*, breadth of skull as percentage of length): (*crystal.*) reciprocal of in- tercept with parameter as unit: (*pl.*, of a book usu. **in'dexes**; other senses **indices**, *in'di-sēz*).—*v.t.* to provide with or place in an index.—*n.* **in'dexer.** —*adj.* **index'ical.**—*n.* **in'dex-learn'ing**, super- ficial knowledge got together from the indexes of books.—*adj.* **in'dexless.**—**index number**, a num- ber indicating the general cost of living, taking the prices of various commodities into account. [L. *index, indicis*—*indicāre*, to show.]

indexterity, *in-deks-ter'i-ti*, *n.* want of dexterity.

Indian, *in'di-ən*, *adj.* belonging to India (with various boundaries), or to the birds, East or West, or to the aborigines of America.—*n.* a member of one of the races of India: (formerly) a European long resident in India: an aboriginal of America.—*n.* **In'diaman**, a large ship employed in trade with India.—*v.t.* **In'dianise**, to make Indian: to assimilate to what is Indian.—*v.i.* to become Indian or like an Indian.—*ns.* **In'dianist**, one who has a scholarly knowledge of Indian languages, history, &c.; **in'dia-rubb'er**, an elastic gummy substance, the inspissated juice of various tropical plants: a piece of this material, esp. one used for rubbing out pencil-marks.—*adj.* **In'dic**, originating or existing in India: of the Indian branch of the Indo-Germanic languages.—**East India Company**, a great chartered company formed for trading with India and the East Indies, more especially applied to the English Company, incorporated in 1600 and abolished in 1858; **East Indian**, an inhabitant or a native of the East Indies, usually applied to a Eurasian; **Indian berry**, the fruit of *Anamirta Cocculus* (see **cocculus indicus**); **Indian bread**, a Virginian fungus said to have been eaten by the Indians: maize bread; **Indian club**, a bottle- shaped block of wood, swung in various motions by the arms to develop the muscles; **Indian corn**, maize, so called because brought from the West Indies; **Indian cress**, a garden plant (*Tropaeolum majus*), popularly nasturtium) from Peru, with orange flowers; **Indian fig**, the banyan-tree: the prickly pear; **Indian file** (see **file**); **Indian fire**,

a firework used as a signal-light, consisting of sulphur, realgar, and nitre; **Indian gift**, a gift that is asked back or for which a return gift is expected; **Indian hemp**, a kind of hemp which is used in medicine, and from which hashish (used for smok- ing and chewing) is got: (*U.S.*) a species of Apocynum; **Indian ink** (see **ink**); **Indian liquorice**, the jequirity or crab's-eye plant; **Indian meal**, ground maize; **Indian-millet**, durra; **Indian pink**, Spigelia; **Indian pipe**, an American Monotropa with a solitary drooping flower, not unlike a tobacco-pipe; **Indian poke**, an American liliaceous plant, white hellebore; **Indian red**, red ochre, or native ferric oxide, formerly imported from the East as a red pigment, also made artificially; **Indian rice** (see **Zizania**); **Indian shot**, a cosmopolitan tropical plant of the genus Canna, much cultivated for its flowers; **Indian summer**, (originally in America) a period of warm, dry, calm weather in late autumn, with hazy atmosphere; **Indian tobacco**, an American lobelia; **Indian turnip**, an American araceous plant with a starchy tuber; **India Office**, a govern- ment office in London where till 1947 were managed the affairs of the Indian government; **India paper**, a thin soft absorbent paper, of Chinese or Japanese origin, used in taking the finest proofs (**India proofs**) from engraved plates: a thin tough opaque paper used for printing Bibles; **India shawl**, a Cashmere shawl; **Red Indian**, one of the aborigines of America (from the coppery- brown colour of some tribes); **West Indian**, a native or an inhabitant of the West Indies. [L. *India*— *Indus* (Gr. *Indos*), the Indus (Pers. *Hind*, Sans. *sindhu*, a river).]

indican. See under **indigo.**

indicate, *in'di-kāt*, *v.t.* to point out: to show: to give some notion of: to be a mark or token of: to give ground for inferring: (*med.*) to suggest or point to as suitable treatment.—*adj.* **in'dicant**, indicating.—*n.* that which indicates.—*n.* **indi- cā'tion**, act of indicating: mark: token: sug- gestion of treatment: symptom.—*adj.* **indicative** (*in-dik'ə-tiv*), pointing out: giving intimation: (*gram.*) applied to the mood of the verb that expresses matter of fact.—*n.* the indicative mood: a verb in the indicative mood.—*adv.* **indic'- atively.**—*ns.* **in'dicator**, one who or that which indicates: a pointer: a diagram showing names and directions of visible objects, as on a mountain top: a substance showing chemical condition by change of colour: a measuring contrivance with a pointer or the like: any device for exhibiting condition for the time being: **Indicator**, a genus of birds, the honey-guides; **in'dicator-dia'gram**, a graphical representation of the pressure and volume changes undergone by a fluid in performing a work-cycle in the cylinder of an engine on com- pression, the area representing, to scale, the work done during the cycle.—*adj.*(**in'dicatory** (or *dik'*).— **indicated horse-power**, of a reciprocating engine, the horse-power developed by the pressure-volume changes of the working agent within the cylinder, exceeding the useful or brake horse-power at the crankshaft by the power lost in friction and pump- ing. [L. *indicāre, -ātum—in*, in, *dicāre*, to proclaim.]

indict, *in-dīt'*, *v.t.* to charge with a crime formally or in writing.—*adj.* **indict'able.**—*n.* **indictee'**, one who is indicted; **indict'ment**, formal accusa- tion: the written accusation against one who is to be tried by jury: (*Scots law*) the form under which one is put to trial at the instance of the Lord Advocate.—**find an indictment**, of a grand-jury, to be satisfied that there is a *prima facie* case, and endorse the bill *a true bill*. [With Latinised spell- ing (but not pronunciation) from A.Fr. *enditer*—L. *in*, in, *dictāre*, to declare.]

indiction, *in-dik'shən*, *n.* a proclamation: (*Rom. hist.*) a decree of the emperor, fixing land-tax valuation: the tax itself: a cycle of fifteen years, instituted by Constantine the Great for fiscal purposes, and adopted by the popes as part of their chronological system: a year bearing a number showing its place in a fifteen years' cycle, reckoning

Neutral vowels in unaccented syllables : *el'ə-mənt, in'fənt, ran'dəm*

from 24th September (or other day), A.D. 312. [L. *indictiō*, *-ōnis*—*indīcĕre*, to appoint.]

indifferent, *in-dif'ər-ənt, adj.* without importance : uninteresting : of a middle quality : not very good, inferior : (*dial.*) in poor health : neutral : unconcerned.—*n.* one who is indifferent or apathetic : that which is indifferent. — *ns.* **indiff'erence**, **indiff'erency**; **indiff'erentism**, indifference : (*theol.*) the doctrine that religious differences are of no moment : (*metaph.*) the doctrine of absolute identity—i.e. that to be in thought and to exist are one and the same thing ; **indiff'erentist**.—*adv.* **indiff'erently**, in an indifferent manner : tolerably : passably : without distinction, impartially.

indigenous, *in-dij'in-əs, adj.* native born : originating or produced naturally in a country—opp. to *exotic.*—*adj.* and *n.* **in'digene** (*-jēn*), native, aboriginal.—*adv.* **indig'enously**. [L. *indigena*, a native—*indu-*, in, and *gen-*, root of *gignĕre*, to produce.]

indigent, *in'di-jənt, adj.* in need, esp. of means of subsistence.—*ns.* **in'digence**, **in'digency**.— *adv.* **in'digently**. [Fr.,—L. *indigēns*, *-ēntis*, pr.p. *indigēre*—*indu*- (see *Prefixes*), in, *egēre*, to need.]

indigest, *in-di-jest', adj.* not digested, shapeless.— *n.* a crude mass, disordered state of affairs.—*adj.* **indigest'ed**, not digested : unarranged : not methodised.—*ns.* **indigestibil'ity**; **indigestion** (*in-di-jest'yən*), want of digestion : painful digestion. —*adj.* **indigest'ible**, not digestible : not easily digested : not to be received or patiently endured. —*adv.* **indigest'ibly**.—*adj.* **indigest'ive**, dyspeptic. [L. *indigestus*, unarranged—*in-*, not, *dīgĕrĕre*, to arrange, digest.]

indign, *in-dīn', adj.* (*arch.*) unworthy : disgraceful. [L. *in-*, not, *dignus*, worthy.]

indignant, *in-dig'nənt, adj.* affected with anger and disdain.—*n.* **indig'nance**, (*arch.*) indignation : contemptuous impatience.—*adv.* **indig'nantly**.— *n.* **indigna'tion**, the feeling caused by what is unworthy or base : anger mixed with contempt : effect of indignant feeling.—*v.t.* **indig'nify**, (*Spens.*) to treat insultingly : to disgrace (with inadequate praise).—*n.* **indig'nity**, (*obs.*) unworthiness : disgrace : dishonour : unmerited contemptuous treatment : incivility with contempt or insult : (*Spens.*) indignation. [L. *indignus*, unworthy—*in-*, not, *dignus*, worthy.]

indigo, *in'di-gō, n.* a violet-blue dye obtained from the leaves of the indigo-plant, from woad, or synthetically : indigotin : the indigo-plant, any of various species of **Indigof'era**, a tropical genus of Papilionaceae.—*adj.* deep blue.—*ns.* **in'dican**, a glucoside found in indigo leaves ; **in'digotin** (or *in-dig'*), **indigo blue**, the blue colouring matter of indigo got from indican by hydrolysis ; **indirubin** (*in-di-rōō'bin*), **indigo red**, an isomer of indigotin, got from natural indigo.—**indigo bird**, an American finch, of which the male is blue. [Sp. *índico*, *índigo*—L. *indicum*—Gr. *Indikon*, Indian (neut. adj.).]

indirect, *in-di-rekt', adj.* not direct or straight : not lineal or in direct succession : not related in the natural way, oblique : not straightforward or honest. — *adv.* **indirect'ly**. — *ns.* **indirect'ness**; **indirec'tion**, (*Shak.*) indirect course or means, dishonest practice.—**indirect evidence**, or **testimony**, circumstantial or inferential evidence ; **indirect object**, (*gram.*) a substantive word dependent on a verb less immediately than an accusative governed by it ; **indirect speech** (L. *ōrātiō oblīqua*), speech reported with adjustment of the speaker's words to change of persons and time.

indiscernible, *in-di-sərn'i-bl*, or *-zərn', adj.* not discernible.—*adv.* **indiscern'ibly**.

indiscerptible, *in-di-sərp'ti-bl, adj.* not discerptible. —*n.* **indiscerptibil'ity**.

indiscipline, *in-dis'i-plin, n.* want of discipline.— *adj.* **indisc'iplinable**.

indiscoverable, *in-dis-kuv'ər-ə-bl, adj.* not discoverable.

indiscreet, *in-dis-krēt', adj.* not discreet : imprudent : injudicious.—*adv.* **indiscreet'ly**.—*ns.* **discreet'ness**; **indiscretion** (*-kresh'ən*), want of discretion : rashness : an indiscreet act.

indiscrete, *in-dis-krēt'*, or *-dis', adj.* not separated or distinguishable in parts : homogeneous.—*adv.* **indiscrete'ly**.—*n.* **indiscrete'ness**.

indiscriminate, *in-dis-krim'i-nit, adj.* not distinguishing : promiscuous.—*adv.* **indiscrim'inately**. —*adjs.* **indiscrim'inating**, undiscriminating ; **indiscrim'inative** (*-ə-tiv*), not discriminative.—*n.* **indiscriminā'tion**.

indispensable, *in-dis-pens'ə-bl, adj.* that cannot be dispensed with : absolutely necessary.—*ns.* **indispensabil'ity**, **indispens'ableness**.—*adv.* **indispens'ably**.

indispose, *in-dis-pōz', v.t.* to render indisposed, averse, or unfit.—*pa.p.* and *adj.* **indisposed'**, averse : slightly disordered in health.—*ns.* **indispos'edness**; **indisposition** (*-pə-zish'ən*), state of being indisposed : disinclination : slight illness.

indisputable, *in-dis'pū-tə-bl*, also *-pū', adj.* beyond dispute.—*n.* **indis'putableness**.—*adv.* **indis'putably**.

indissociable, *in-dis-ō'sh(y)ə-bl, adj.* incapable of being separated.

indissoluble, *in-dis'ol-(y)ōō-bl*, or *-əl-*, or *-ol', adj.* that cannot be broken or violated : inseparable : binding for ever.—*ns.* **indiss'olubleness**, **indissolubility** (*-ol-ū-bil'*).—*adv.* **indiss'olubly**.

indissolvable, *in-di-zol'və-bl, adj.* that cannot be dissolved.

indissuadable, *in-dis-wād'ə-bl, adj.* not to be dissuaded.—*adv.* **indissuad'ably**.

indistinct, *in-dis-tingkt', adj.* not plainly marked : confused : not clear to the mind : dim.—*adj.* **indistinct'ive**, not constituting a distinction.— *adv.* **indistinct'ively**, indiscriminately. — *n.* **indistinct'iveness**.—*adv.* **indistinct'ly**.—*ns.* **indistinct'ness**; **indistinc'tion**, confusion : absence of distinction, sameness.

indistinguishable, *in-dis-ting'gwish-ə-bl, adj.* that cannot be distinguished.—*n.* **indistin'guishableness**.—*adv.* **indistin'guishably**.

indistributable, *in-dis-trib'ū-tə-bl, adj.* not distributable.

indite, *in-dīt', v.t.* to compose or write : (*Shak.*) to invite.—*v.i.* to compose.—*ns.* **indite'ment**; **indit'er**. [O.Fr. *enditer* ; see **indict**.]

indium, *in'di-əm, n.* a soft malleable silver-white metallic element (In ; at. numb. 49). [From two *indigo*-coloured lines in the spectrum.]

indivertible, *in-di-vərt'i-bl, adj.* not capable of being turned aside out of a course.

individable, *in-di-vīd'ə-bl, adj.* (*Shak.*) that cannot be divided.

individual, *in-di-vid'ū-əl, adj.* not divisible without loss of identity : subsisting as one : pertaining to one only or to each one separately of a group : single, separate : (*Milt.*) inseparable.—*n.* a single person, animal, plant, or thing considered as a separate member of its species or as having an independent existence : (*vulg.*) a person.—*n.* **individualisā'tion**.—*v.t.* **individ'ualise**, to stamp with individual character : to particularise.—*ns.* **individ'ualism**, individual character : independent action as opposed to co-operation : that theory which opposes interference of the state in the affairs of individuals, opp. to *socialism* or *collectivism* : the theory that looks to the rights of individuals not the advantage of an abstraction such as the state : the doctrine that individual things alone are real : the doctrine that nothing exists but the individual self ; **individ'ualist**.—*adj.* **individualist'ic**.—*n.* **individuality** (*-al'i-ti*), separate and distinct existence : oneness : distinctive character.—*adv.* **individ'ually**.—*v.t.* **individ'uate**, to individualise : to give individuality to.—*adj.* **undivided** : inseparable : individuated.—*n.* **individuā'tion**, the act or process of individuating or individualising : individual existence : essence : continued identity : the sum of the processes of individual life : synthesis into an organic unity.—*n.* **individ'uum**, an indivisible entity : an individual person or thing : a member of a species. [L. *individuus*—*in-*, not, *dīviduus*, divisible—*dīvidĕre*, to divide.]

indivisible, *in-di-viz'i-bl, adj.* not divisible.—*n.* (*math.*) an indefinitely small quantity.—*ns.* **indivisibil'ity**, **indivis'ibleness**.—*adv.* **indivis'ibly**.

Indo-Chinese, *in'dō-chī-nēz'*, *adj.* of or pertaining to Indo-China, the south-eastern peninsula of Asia.

indocile, *in-dō'sīl*, or *in-dos'il*, *adj.* not docile: not disposed to be instructed.—Also **indō'cible**.—*n.* **indocil'ity**.

indoctrinate, *in-dok'trin-āt*, *v.t.* to instruct in any doctrine: to imbue with any opinion.—*ns.* **indoctrinā'tion; indoc'trinātor.**

Indo-European, *in'dō-ū-rō-pē'ən*, *adj.* (*philol.*) Indo-Germanic.

Indo-Germanic, *in-dō-jər-man'ik*, *adj.* (*philol.*) of the family of languages, also called Indo-European and sometimes Aryan, whose great branches are Aryan proper or Indian, Iranian, Armenian, Greek or Hellenic, Italic, Celtic, Tocharian, Balto-Slavonic, Albanian, and Germanic.

indole, *in'dōl*, *n.* a substance (C_8H_7N) related to indigo.—Also **indol**. [**indigo** and L. *oleum*, oil.]

indolent, *in'dəl-ənt*, *adj.* indisposed to activity: (*med.*) not painful.—*ns.* **in'dolence, in'dolency.**—*adv.* **in'dolently.** [L. *in-*, not, *dolēns, -ēntis*, pr.p. of *dolēre*, to suffer pain.]

indomitable, *in-dom'it-ə-bl*, *adj.* not to be overcome.—*adv.* **indom'itably.**

Indonesian, *in-do-nē'zi-ən, -zh(y)ən, -sh(y)ən*, *adj.* of the East Indian or Malay Archipelago: of a short, mesocephalic, black-haired, light-brown race distinguishable in the population of the East Indian Islands: of a branch of the Austronesian family of languages chiefly found in the Malay Archipelago and Islands (Malay, &c.).—*n.* a member of the race or speaker of one of the languages. [Gr. *Indos*, Indian, *nēsos*, island.]

indoor, *in'dōr*, *adj.* practised, used, or being within a building.—*adv.* **indoors'**, within doors.—**indoor relief**, support given to paupers in public buildings, as opposed to *outdoor relief*, or help given them at their own homes.

indorse. See **endorse.**

Indra, *in'drä*, *n.* the Hindu god of the firmament and of rain. [Sans.]

indraught, indraft, *in'dräft*, *n.* a drawing in: an inward flow of current. [**in, draught.**]

indrawn, *in'drawn, in-drawn'*, *adj.* drawn in.

indrench, *in-dren(t)sh'*, *v.t.* (*Shak.*) to submerge in water.

indubious, *in-dū'bi-əs*, *adj.* not dubious: certain.

indubitable, *in-dū'bit-ə-bl*, *adj.* that cannot be doubted: certain.—*n.* **indū'bitableness.**—*adv.* **indū'bitably.**

induce, *in-dūs'*, *v.t.* to bring in: to draw on: to prevail on: to bring into being: (*phys.*) to cause, as an electric state, by mere proximity: to infer inductively.—*v.i.* to reason or draw inferences inductively.—*ns.* **induce'ment**, that which induces: (*Shak., Milt.*) persuasion: incentive, motive: (*law*) a statement of facts introducing other important facts; **induc'er**.—*adj.* **indu'cible**.—**induced current** (*elect.*) a current set in action by the influence of the surrounding magnetic field, or by the variation of an adjacent current. [L. *indūcĕre, inductum—in*, into, *dūcĕre*, to lead.]

induct, *in-dukt'*, *v.t.* to introduce: to put in possession, as of a benefice, to install.—*ns.* **induct'ance**, the property of inducing an electromotive force by variation of current in a circuit: self-induction: coefficient of self-induction.—*n.* **induc'tion**, bringing or drawing in: installation in office, benefice, &c.: a prelude, introductory section or scene: the act of inducing: magnetising by proximity without contact: the production by one body of an opposite electric state in another by proximity: production of an electric current by magnetic changes in the neighbourhood: (*log.*) reasoning from particular cases to general conclusions. — *adj.* **induc'tional.** — *ns.* **induc'tion-coil'**, an electrical machine consisting of two coils of wire, in which every variation of the current in one induces a current in the other; **induc'tion-pipe', -valve'**, a pipe, valve, by which steam, or an explosive mixture, is admitted to the cylinder of an engine.—*adj.* **induct'ive**.—*adv.* **induct'ively.**—*n.* **induct'or.**—**induction by simple enumer-**

ation, logical induction by enumeration of all the cases singly. [See **induce.**]

inductile, *in-duk'til*, *adj.* not ductile.—*n.* **inductility** (*-til'i-ti*). [L. *in-*, not, *ductilis*, ductile.]

indue. See **endue.**

indulge, *in-dulj'*, *v.t.* to yield to the wishes of: to favour or gratify: to treat with favour or undue favour: not to restrain: to grant an indulgence to or on: (*hist.*) to grant some measure of religious liberty.—*v.i.* (with *in*) to gratify one's appetites freely.— *n.* **indulg'ence**, gratification: excessive gratification: favourable or unduly favourable treatment: a grant of religious liberty: forbearance of present payment: in the R.C. Church, a remission, to a repentant sinner, of the temporal punishment which remains due after the sin and its eternal punishment have been remitted (*plenary* indulgences, such as remit all; *partial*, a portion of the temporal punishment due to sin; *temporal*, those granted only for a time; *perpetual* or *indefinite*, those which last till revoked; *personal*, those granted to a particular person or confraternity; *local*, those gained only in a particular place): exemption of an individual from an ecclesiastical law.—Also **indulg'ency**.—*adj.* **indulg'ent**, ready to gratify the wishes of others: compliant: not severe.—*adv.* **indulg'ently**.—*ns.* **indulg'er: indult'**, a licence granted by the Pope, authorising something to be done which the common law of the Church does not sanction.—**Declaration of Indulgence**, a name given to proclamations of Charles II. and (esp.) James II. declaring laws restraining religious liberty suspended by the king's will. [L. *indulgēre*, to be kind to, indulge—*in*, in, and prob. *dulcis*, sweet.]

induline, *in'dū-lin, -lēn, -līn*, *n.* any one of a class of coal-tar dye-stuffs, giving blues, &c. [**indigo.**]

indumentum, *in-dū-men'tam*, *n.* a general covering of hair, feathers, &c.: woolly pubescence. [L. *indūmentum*, garment—*induĕre*, to put on.]

induna, *in-dōō'nä*, *n.* a native councillor in South Africa. [Zulu, person of rank.]

induplicate, *in-dū'pli-kāt*, *adj.* (*bot.*) folded inwards.—*n.* **induplicā'tion.** [L. *in*, in, *dūplicāre, -ātum*, to double.]

indurate, *in'dū-rāt*, *v.t.* and *v.i.* to harden.—*n.* **indurā'tion**.—*adj.* **in'durative.** [L. *indūrāre, -ātum—in*, in, *dūrāre*, to harden.]

indusium, *in-dū'zi-əm*, *n.* a protective membrane or scale, esp. that covering a fern sorus: an insect larva-case:—*pl.* **indu'sia**.—*adjs.* **indu'sial**, containing fossil insect indusia; **indu'siate**, having indusia. [L. *indūsium*, an under-garment—*induĕre*, to put on.]

industry, *in'dəs-tri*, *n.* quality of being diligent: assiduity: steady application: habitual diligence: systematic economic activity, or any branch thereof: a trade or manufacture.—*adj.* **industrial** (*-dus'*), relating to or consisting in industry.—*n.* **industrialisā'tion**.—*v.t.* **indus'trialise**, to give an industrial character, or character of industrialism to.—*ns.* **indus'trialism**, devotion to labour or industrial pursuits: that system or condition of society in which industrial labour is the chief and most characteristic feature; **indus'trialist**, a manufacturer: an industrial worker.—*adv.* **indus'trially**.—*adj.* **indus'trious**, diligent or active in one's labour: laborious: diligent in a particular pursuit.—*adv.* **indus'triously**.—**industrial council** (see **Whitley Council**); **industrial revolution**, the economic and social changes arising out of the change from industries carried on in the home with simple machines to industries in factories with power-driven machinery—esp. such changes (from about 1760) in Britain, the first country to be industrialised; **industrial school**, a school in which some industrial art is taught: a school where neglected or delinquent children are taught mechanical arts. [L. *industria*, perh. from the old word *indu*, in, within, and *struĕre*, to build up.]

induviae, *in-dū'vi-ē*, *n.pl.* (*bot.*) withered leaves persistent on the stems of some plants.—*adjs.* **indū'vial; indū'viate**. [L. *induviae*, clothes.]

indwell, *in-dwel'*, *v.i.* to dwell or abide in:—*pr.p.*

indwell'ing; *pa.t.* and *pa.p.* **indwelt'**.—*n.* **in'-dweller**, an inhabitant.—*adj.* **in'dwelling**, dwelling within, abiding permanently in the mind or soul.—*n.* residence within, or in the heart or soul. [**in, dwell**.]

inearth, *in-arth'*, *v.t.* to inter.

inebriate, *in-ē'bri-āt*, *v.t.* to make drunk, to intoxicate : to exhilarate greatly.—*adj.* (*-it, -at*) drunk : intoxicated.—*n.* a drunk person : a drunkard.—*adj.* **inē'briant**, intoxicating.— Also *n.* — *ns.* **inēbriā'tion, inebriety** (*in-ē-brī'i-ti*, or *in-i-*), drunkenness : intoxication. — *adj.* **inē'brious**, drunk : (*obs.*) causing intoxication. [L. *inēbriāre*, *-ātum*—*in-*, inten., *ēbriāre*, to make drunk—*ēbrius*, drunk.]

inedible, *in-ed'i-bl*, *adj.* unfit to be eaten.—*n.* **inedibil'ity**.

inedited, *in-ed'it-id*, *adj.* not edited : unpublished.

ineducable, *in-ed'ū-ka-bl*, *adj.* incapable of education.—*n.* **ineducabil'ity**.

ineffable, *in-ef'a-bl*, *adj.* that cannot be described, inexpressible.—*n.* **ineff'ableness**.—*adv.* **ineff'ably**. [L. *ineffābilis*—*in-*, not, *effābilis*, effable.]

ineffaceable, *in-i-fās'a-bl*, *adj.* that cannot be rubbed out.—*adv.* **ineffac'ably**.

ineffective, *in-i-fek'tiv*, *adj.* not effective : useless.—*adv.* **ineffec'tively**.—*adj.* **ineffec'tual**, fruitless.—*ns.* **ineffectual'ity, ineffec'tualness**.—*adv.* **ineffect'ually**. — *adj.* **inefficacious** (*in-ef-i-kā'shas*), not having power to produce an effect.—*adv.* **inefficā'ciously**.—*n.* **ineff'icacy** (*-ef'i-ka-si*), want of efficacy.—*n.* **inefficiency** (*in-i-fish'an-si*).—*adj.* **ineffic'ient**, not efficient.—*adv.* **ineffic'iently**.

inelaborate, *in-il-ab'ar-āt*, *-it*, *adj.* unlaboured : simple.—*adv.* **inelab'orately**.

inelastic, *in-i-las'tik*, *adj.* not elastic : incompressible.—*n.* **inelasticity** (*in-el-as-tis'i-ti*).

inelegance, *in-el'i-gans*, *n.* want of gracefulness or refinement.—Also **inel'egancy**.—*adj.* **inel'egant**.—*adv.* **inel'egantly**.

ineligible, *in-el'i-ji-bl*, *adj.* not qualified for election : not suitable for choice : not rich enough to be chosen as a husband : unsuitable.—Also *n.*—*n.* **ineligibil'ity**.—*adv.* **inel'igibly**.

ineloquent, *in-el'a-kwant*, *adj.* not eloquent.—*n.* **inel'oquence**.

ineluctable, *in-i-luk'ta-bl*, *adj.* not to be escaped from. [L. *inēluctābilis*—*in-*, not, *ē*, from, *luctārī*, to struggle.]

inenarrable, *in-en'ar-a-bl*, *in-ē-nar'a-bl*, *adj.* incapable of being narrated or told. [L. *inēnarrābilis*—*in-*, not, *ē-*, out, *narrāre*, to tell.]

inept, *in-ept'*, *adj.* unfit : irrelevant and futile : fatuous : (*law*) void.—*ns.* **inept'itude, inept'ness**.—*adv.* **inept'ly**. [L. *ineptus*—*in-*, not, *aptus*, apt.]

inequable, *in-ek'wa-bl*, *-ēk'*, *adj.* not equable, changeable.

inequality, *in-ē-kwol'i-ti*, or *in-i-*, *n.* want of equality : difference : inadequacy : incompetency : unevenness : dissimilarity : an uneven place.

inequitable, *in-ek'wi-ta-bl*, *adj.* unfair, unjust.—*adv.* **ineq'uitably**.—*n.* **ineq'uity**, lack of equity : an unjust action.

ineradicable, *in-i-rad'i-ka-bl*, *adj.* not able to be eradicated or rooted out.—*adv.* **inerad'icably**.

inerasable, *in-i-rāz'a-bl*, *adj.* impossible to erase.—Also **ineras'ible**.—*adv.* **ineras'ably, -ibly**.

inerm, *in-arm'*, *adj.* unarmed : without thorns. [L. *inermis*—*in-*, not, *arma* (pl.), arms.]

inerrable, *in-er'a-bl*, or *-ar'*, *adj.* incapable of erring.—*adv.* **inerr'ably**.—*n.* **inerr'ancy**, freedom from error.—*adj.* **inerr'ant**, unerring.

inert, *in-art'*, *adj.* without inherent power of moving, or of active resistance to motion : passive : chemically inactive : sluggish : disinclined to move or act.—*n.* **inertia** (*in-ar'shi-ä, -shyä, -shä*), inertness : the inherent property of matter by which it continues, unless constrained, in its state of rest or uniform motion in a straight line.—*adv.* **inert'ly**.—*n.* **inert'ness**. [L. *iners, inertis*, unskilled, idle—*in-*, not, *ars, artis*, art.]

inerudite, *in-er'ū-dīt*, or *-oo-*, *adj.* not erudite : unlearned.

inescapable, *in-is-kā'pa-bl*, *adj.* unescapable : inevitable.

inesculent, *in-es'kū-lant*, inedible.

inescutcheon, *in-is-kuch'an*, *n.* (*her.*) a single shield borne as a charge.

inessential, *in-is-en'shl*, *adj.* not essential : not necessary : immaterial.

inestimable, *in-es'tim-a-bl*, *adj.* not able to be estimated or valued : priceless.—*adv.* **ines'timably**.

inevitable, *in-ev'it-a-bl*, *adj.* not to be evaded or avoided : certain to happen : consummate, giving the feeling that the thing could not have been other than it is.—*ns.* **inevitabil'ity ; inev'itableness**.—*adv.* **inev'itably**. [L. *inēvītābilis*—*in-*, not, *ē*, from, *vītāre*, to avoid.]

inexact, *in-igz-akt'*, *adj.* not precisely correct or true : lax.—*ns.* **inexact'itude, inexact'ness**.—*adv.* **inexact'ly**.

inexcitable, *in-ek-sīt'a-bl*, *adj.* not excitable : (*obs.*) from which one cannot be roused.

inexcusable, *in-iks-kūz'a-bl*, *adj.* not justifiable : unpardonable. — *ns.* **inexcusabil'ity, inexcus'ableness**.—*adv.* **inexcus'ably**.

inexecrable, *in-eks'i-kra-bl*, *adj.* in Shak., *Merchant of Venice*, IV. i. 128, perh. a misprint for *inexorable*, perh. an intensive form of *execrable*.

inexecutable, *in-igz-ek'ūt-a-bl*, or *in-eks-ek'*, or *in-eks-i-kūt'a-bl*, *adj.* incapable of being executed.—*n.* **inexecū'tion**, fact or state of not being executed.

inexhausted, *in-igs-aws'tid*, *adj.* unexhausted, not used up or spent.—*n.* **inexhaustibil'ity**.—*adj.* **inexhaust'ible**, not able to be exhausted or spent : unfailing. — *adj.* **inexhaust'ibly**. — *adj.* **inexhaust'ive**, unfailing : not exhaustive.

inexistence, *in-ig-zist'ans*, *n.* non-existence.—*adj.* **inexist'ent**. [L. *in-*, not.]

inexistence, *in-ig-zist'ans*, *n.* inherence.—*adj.* **inexist'ent**, indwelling. [L. *in*, in.]

inexorable, *in-eks'ar-a-bl*, *adj.* not to be moved by entreaty : unrelenting : unyielding.—*ns.* **inex'orableness, inexorabil'ity**.—*adv.* **inex'orably**. [L.L. *inexōrābilis*—*in-*, not,—*exōrāre*—*ex*, out of, *ōrāre*, to entreat.]

inexpansible, *in-iks-pan'si-bl*, *adj.* incapable of being expanded.

inexpectant, *in-iks-pek'tant*, *adj.* not expecting.—*n.* **inexpec'tancy**.

inexpedient, *in-iks-pē'di-ant*, *adj.* contrary to expediency : impolitic.—*n.* **inexpe'dience**, **inexpe'diency**.—*adv.* **inexpe'diently**.

inexpensive, *in-iks-pens'iv*, *adj.* not costly : not inclined to spend much.—*adv.* **inexpens'ively**.—*n.* **inexpens'iveness**.

inexperience, *in-iks-pē'ri-ans*, *n.* want of experience.—*adj.* **inexpe'rienced**, not having experience : unskilled or unpractised.

inexpert, *in-iks-part'*, *adj.* unskilled.—*n.* **inexpert'-ness**.

inexpiable, *in-eks'pi-a-bl*, *adj.* not able to be expiated or atoned for : not to be appeased.—*n.* **inex'piableness**.—*adv.* **inex'piably**.

inexplicable, *in-eks'pli-ka-bl*, *adj.* (*obs.*) that cannot be disentangled : incapable of being explained or accounted for.—*ns.* **inexplicabil'ity, inex'plicableness**.—*adv.* **inex'plicably**.

inexplicit, *in-iks-plis'it*, *adj.* not explicit : not clear.

inexpressible, *in-iks-pres'i-bl*, *adj.* that cannot be expressed : unutterable : indescribable : (in *pl.* ; *arch.* *would-be humorous*) trousers.—*adv.* **inexpress'ibly**.—*adj.* **inexpress'ive**, inexpressible : unexpressive.—*n.* **inexpress'iveness**.

inexpugnable, *in-iks-pug'na-bl*, *adj.* not to be taken by assault : unassailable.—*adv.* **inexpug'nably**.

inextended, *in-iks-tend'id*, *adj.* not extended : without extension.—*n.* **inextensibil'ity**.—*adj.* **inexten'sible**.—*n.* **inexten'sion**.

inextinguishable, *in-iks-ting'gwish-a-bl*, *adj.* that cannot be extinguished, quenched, or destroyed.—*adv.* **inextin'guishably**.

inextricable, *in-eks'tri-ka-bl*, *adj.* not able to be extricated or disentangled.—*adv.* **inex'tricably**.

infall, *in'fawl*, *n.* an inroad : falling in : confluence, inlet, or junction. [**in, fall**.]

infallible, *in-fal'i-bl*, *adj.* incapable of error : certain to succeed : inevitable.—*ns.* **infall′ibilism**, the doctrine of the Pope's infallibility ; **infall′ibilist** : **infallibil′ity**.—*adv.* **infall′ibly**.—**the doctrine of infallibility** in the R.C. Church, since 1870, is that the Pope, when speaking *ex cathedra*, is kept from error in all that regards faith and morals.

infame, in-fām′, *v.t.* to defame.—*adj.* **infamous** (in′fa-mas, formerly in-fā′mas), having a reputation of the worst kind : publicly branded with guilt : notoriously vile : disgraceful.—*vs.t.* **infamise** (in′fa-mīz), **infamonise** (in-fam′on-īz ; *Shak.*), to defame, to brand with infamy.—*adv.* **in′famously**. —*n.* **in′famy**, ill fame or repute : public disgrace : extreme vileness : (*law*) a stigma attaching to the character of a person so as to disqualify him from being a witness. [L. *infāmāre*—*in-*, not, *fāma*, fame.]

infangthief, in′fang-thēf, *n.* in old English law, the right of taking and fining a thief within the boundary of one's own jurisdiction. [O.E. *infangenetheóf*—*in*, in, the root of *fón*, to seize, *théof*, thief.]

infant, in′fant, *n.* a babe : (*Eng. law*) a person under twenty-one years of age : (*Spens.*) a noble youth : an infante or infanta.—*adj.* of or belonging to infants : of or in infancy.—*v.t.* (*obs.*) to give birth to.—*n.* **in′fancy**, the state or time of being an infant : childhood : the beginning of anything : (*Milt.*) want of distinct utterance.—*adj.* **infantile** (in′fant-īl, also -*fant′*), pertaining to infancy or to an infant : having characteristics of infancy : no better than that of an infant : undeveloped.— *n.* **infant′ilism**, persistence of infantile characters : an utterance or trait worthy of an infant :—*adj.* **in′fantine** (-*īn*), of infancy or an infant : infantlike.—**infantile paralysis**, poliomyelitis ; **infant school**, a school for children up to about the age of seven. [L. *infāns*, *infāntis*—*in-*, not, *fāns*, pr.p. of *fāri*, to speak ; cf. Gr. *phanai*.]

infante, in-fan′tā, *n.* (*hist.*) a prince of the blood royal of Spain or Portugal, esp. a son of the king other than the heir-apparent :—*fem.* **infant′a**, a princess likewise defined : the wife of an infante. [Sp. and Port. from the root of **infant**.]

infanticide, in-fant′i-sīd, *n.* the killing of new-born children as a social institution in some states of society : the murder of a new-born child by, or with consent of, a parent : the murderer of an infant.—*adj.* **infantici′dal** (or -*fant′*). [L. *infanticīdium*, child-killing, *infanticīda*, child-killer— *infāns*, an infant, *caedĕre*, to kill.]

infantry, in′fant-ri, *n.* foot-soldiers : infants or children collectively.—Also *adj.*—*n.* **in′fantryman**. [Fr. *infanterie*— It. *infanteria*—*infante*, youth, servant, foot-soldier—L. *infāns*, -*āntis*.]

infare, in′fār, *n.* (*obs.*) entrance : ingoing : (*Scot.* and *U.S.*) a house-warming after a wedding. [O.E. *innfær* ; cf. **in**, **fare**.]

infatuate, in-fat′-ū-āt, *v.t.* to turn to folly : to deprive of judgment : to inspire with foolish passion.—*adj.* **infatuated**.—*n.* **infatuā′tion**. [L. *infatuāre*, -*ātum*—*in*, in, *fatuus*, foolish.]

infaust, in-fawst′, *adj.* unlucky : ill-omened. [L. *infaustus*—*in-*, not, *faustus*, propitious.]

infeasible, in-fēz′i-bl, *adj.* not feasible.—*n.* **infeasibil′ity**.

infect, in-fekt′, *v.t.* to impart some quality to : to taint, especially with disease : to introduce pathogenic micro-organisms into : to corrupt : to spread to : to affect successively.—*adj.* (*Shak.*) tainted.—*n.* **infec′tion** (-*shan*), act of infecting : that which infects or taints : an infectious disease. —*adjs.* **infec′tious** (-*shas*), **infec′tive** (-*tiv*), having the quality of infecting : corrupting : apt to spread. — *adv.* **infec′tiously**. — *ns.* **infec′tiousness** ; **infect′iveness** ; **infect′or**. [L. *inficĕre*, *infectum*—*in*, into, *facĕre*, to make.]

infecundity, in-fi-kun′di-ti, *n.* want of fecundity or fertility : unfruitfulness.—*adj.* **infecund** (-*fek′*).

infeft, in-feft′, *v.t.* (*Scots law*) to invest with heritable property :—*pa.p.* **infeft′**, rarely **infeft′ed**.—*n.* **infeft′ment**, (*Scots law*) the symbolical giving possession of land in completion of the title. [enfeoff.]

infelicitous, in-fi-lis′i-tas, *adj.* not felicitous or happy : inappropriate, inapt.—*n.* **infelic′ity**.

infelt, in′felt, *adj.* felt deeply, heart-felt.

infer, in-far′, *v.t.* (*Spens.*, *Shak.*) to bring on : (*Milt.*) to render : to derive as a consequence : to arrive at as a logical conclusion : to conclude : to entail or involve as a consequence : to imply :— *pr.p.* **inferr′ing** ; *pa.t.* and *pa.p.* **inferred′**.—*adj.* **in′ferable** (or -*far′* ; also **inferr′able**, **-ible**), that may be inferred or deduced.—*n.* **in′ference**, that which is inferred or deduced : the act of drawing a conclusion from premises : consequence : conclusion.—*adj.* **inferential** (-*en′shl*), relating to inference : deducible or deduced by inference.— *adv.* **inferen′tially**. [L. *inferre*—*in*, into, *ferre*, to bring.]

infere, in-fēr′, *adv.* (*obs.*) for **in fere**, together. [See **fere** (1).]

inferior, in-fē′ri-ar, *adj.* lower in any respect : subordinate : poor or poorer in quality : (*print.*) somewhat below the line : (*bot.*) of an ovary, having the other parts above it : of the other parts, below the ovary : of a planet, revolving within the earth's orbit.—*n.* one lower in rank or station.—*n.* **inferiority** (-*or′*).—*adv.* **infe′riorly**, in an inferior manner.—**inferior conjunction**, conjunction when the planet is between the sun and the earth ; **inferiority complex**, (*psych.*) a complex involving a suppressed sense of personal inferiority : popularly, a feeling of inferiority. [L. *inferior*, comp. of *inferus*, low.]

infernal, in-far′nal, *adj.* belonging to the lower regions : resembling or suitable to hell, devilish : outrageous.—*n.* **infernality** (-*nal′*).—*adv.* **infer′nally**.—*n.* **Infer′no**, (*It.*) hell : the title and the subject of one of the divisions of Dante's great poem, *La Divina Commedia*.—**infernal machine**, a contrivance made to resemble some ordinary harmless object, but charged with a dangerous explosive. [L. *infernus*—*inferus*.]

infertile, in-far′til, *adj.* not productive : barren.— *n.* **infertility** (-*til′*).

infest, in-fest′, *v.t.* to disturb : to harass : to molest : to haunt, beset, or swarm about, in a troublesome or injurious way.—*adj.* (*Spens.*) hostile : troublesome. — *n.* **infestā′tion**, (*Milt.*) molestation : attack, or condition of being attacked, esp. by parasites. [L. *infestāre*, from *infestus*, hostile.]

infeudation, in-fū-dā′shan, *n.* the putting of an estate in fee : the granting of tithes to laymen. [L. *in*, in ; see **feud** (2).]

infibulate, in-fib′ū-lāt, *v.t.* to fasten with a clasp.— *n.* **infibulā′tion**, act of confining, esp. the sexual organs. [L. *in*, in, *fibula*, a clasp.]

inficete, in-fi-sēt′, *adj.* not facetious : rudely jesting. [L. *inficētus*—*in-*, not, *facētus*, courteous, witty.]

infidel, in′fi-dl, *adj.* unbelieving : sceptical : disbelieving Christianity or whatever be the religion of the user of the word.—*n.* one who rejects Christianity, &c.—*n.* **infidel′ity**, want of faith or belief : disbelief in Christianity, &c. : unfaithfulness, esp. to the marriage contract : treachery. [O.Fr. *infidèle*—L. *infidēlis*—*in-*, not, *fidēlis*, faithful—*fidēs*, faith.]

infield, in′fēld, *n.* in baseball, the space enclosed within the base-lines : (*Scot.*) formerly, land near the farm-house, kept constantly manured and under tillage (also *adj.*)—opp. to **outfield**.—*n.* **in′fielder**, a player on the infield. [**in**, **field**.]

infighting, in′fīt-ing, *n.* boxing at close quarters when blows from the shoulder cannot be given.

infilling, in′fil-ing, *n.* filling up or in : material used to fill up or level. [**in**, **fill**.]

infiltrate, in-fil′trāt, *v.t.* to cause to percolate : to cause to percolate into : to sift into : to permeate.— *v.i.* to permeate by degrees : to sift or filter in.—*v.t.* **infil′ter**, to filter or sift in.—*n.* **infiltrā′tion**, the process of infiltrating : gradual permeation or interpenetration : gradual accession or introduction of a new element, as of population or troops : a deposit or substance infiltrated.

infinite, in′fin-it, in church singing also in′fi-nīt, *adj.* without end or limit : (*math.*) greater than any quantity that can be assigned : extending to infinity : vast : in vast numbers : inexhaustible : (*log.*) infinitated.—*n.* that which is not only without determinate bounds, but which cannot possibly admit of bound or limit : the Absolute, the Infinite Being or God.—*adjs.* **infin'itant**, denoting merely negative attribution ; **infin'itary**, pertaining to infinity.—*v.t.* **infin'itate**, to make infinite : (*log.*) to turn into a negative term.—*adv.* **in'finitely.**— *n.* **in'finiteness.**—*adj.* (orig. ordinal numeral) **infinitesimal** (-*es*'), infinitely small: (loosely) extremely small.—*n.* an infinitely small quantity.— *adv.* **infinites'imally.**—*ns.* **infin'itude, infin'ity,** boundlessness : an infinite quantity : an infinite distance : vastness, immensity : countless or indefinite number.—**infinite canon,** (*mus.*) a canon that can be repeated indefinitely.

infinitive, *in-fin'it-iv, adj.* (*gram.*) expressing, in the mood that expresses, the idea without person or number.—*n.* the infinitive mood : a verb in the infinitive mood.—*adj.* **infiniti'val.**—*adv.* **infin'itively.** [L. *infinitivus* — *in-,* not, *finire,* to limit.]

infirm, *in-ferm', adj.* feeble : sickly : weak : frail : unstable.—*ns.* **infirmā'rian,** an officer in a monastery having charge of the quarters for the sick ; **infirmary** (*in-ferm'er-i*), a hospital or place for the treatment of the sick ; **infirm'ity.**—*adv.* **infirm'ly.**—*n.* **infirm'ness.** [L. *infirmus* — *in-,* not, *firmus,* strong.]

infix, *in-fiks', v.t.* to fix in : to drive or fasten in : to set in by piercing.—Also **enfix** (*Shak.*).—*n.* **in'fix,** (*philol.*) an element inserted within a root, as *m* in the Gr. *lambanō,* from the root *lab.* [L. *infixus*—*in,* in, *figere, fixum,* to fix.]

inflame, *in-flām', v.t.* to cause to flame : to cause to burn : to make hot : to make red : to cause inflammation in : to arouse passions in : to excite : to exacerbate.—*v.i.* to burst into flame : to become hot, painful, red or excited : to undergo inflammation.—*adjs.* **inflām'able,** (*obs.*) inflammable ; **inflamed'.**—*n.* **inflām'er.** [O.Fr. *enflammer*—L. *inflammāre* ; see next.]

inflammable, *in-flam'ə-bl, adj.* that may be set on fire : easily kindled or excited.—*ns.* **inflammabil'ity ; inflamm'ableness.**—*adv.* **inflamm'ably.**—*n.* **inflammation** (-*fla-mā'shən*), state of being in flame : heat of a part of the body, with pain, redness, and swelling : kindling of the passions.—*adj.* **inflamm'atory,** tending to inflame : inflaming : exciting. [L. *inflammāre*—*in,* into, *flamma,* a flame.]

inflate, *in-flāt', v.t.* to swell with air or gas : to puff up : to elate : to expand unduly.—*adjs.* **inflat'able ; inflat'ed,** swollen or blown out : turgid. — *adv.* **inflat'ingly.** — *n.* **inflation** (*in-flā'shən*), the act of inflating : the condition of being inflated : (*rare*) afflatus, inspiration : turgidity of style : undue increase in quantity of money in proportion to buying power, as on an excessive issue of fiduciary money.—*adj.* **infla'tionary.**— *ns.* **infla'tionism,** the policy of inflating currency ; **infla'tionist.**—*adj.* **inflat'ive,** causing inflation : tending to inflate.—*ns.* **inflat'or,** one who inflates : a cycle-pump ; **inflat'us** (L.), inspiration. [L. *inflāre, -ātum*—*in,* into, *flāre,* to blow.]

inflect, *in-flekt', v.t.* to bend in : to turn from a direct line or course : to modulate, as the voice: (*gram.*) to vary in the terminations.—*n.* (**inflec'tion), inflex'ion,** a bending or deviation : modulation of the voice : (*gram.*) the varying in termination to express the relations of case, number, gender, person, tense, &c.—*adjs.* **(inflec'tional), inflex'ional ; (inflec'tionless), inflex'ionless ; in-flect'ive,** subject to inflection ; **inflexed',** bent inward : bent : turned.—*n.* **inflexure** (*in-flek'shər*), an inward bend or fold. [L. *inflectĕre*—*in,* in, *flectĕre, flexum,* to bend, *flexiō, -ōnis,* a bend.]

inflexible, *in-flek'si-bl, adj.* that cannot be bent : unyielding : rigid : unbending.—*ns.* **inflexibil'ity, inflex'ibleness.**—*adv.* **inflex'ibly.** [L. *in-,* not.]

inflict, *in-flikt', v.t.* to lay on : to impose (as punishment, pain).—*n.* **inflic'tion,** act of inflicting or imposing : that which is inflicted.—*adj.* **in-flict'ive,** tending or able to inflict. [L. *infligĕre, inflictum*—*in,* against, *fligĕre,* to strike.]

inflorescence, *in-flor-es'əns, n.* mode of branching of a flower-bearing axis : aggregate of flowers on an axis. [L. *inflōrēscĕre,* to begin to blossom.]

inflow, *in'flō, n.* the act of flowing in, influx : that which flows in.—*adj.* **in'flowing,** flowing in.

influence, *in'floo-əns, n.* (*obs.*) inflow : (*astrol.*) the power or virtue supposed to flow from planets upon men and things : a spiritual influx : power of producing an effect, esp. unobstrusively : effect of power exerted : that which has such power : a person exercising such power : ascendency, often of a secret or undue kind : exertions of friends at court, wire-pulling, and the like.—*v.t.* to have or exert influence upon : to affect.—*adjs.* **in'fluent,** inflowing: exerting influence ; **influential** (-*en'shl*), of the nature of influence : having much influence : effectively active.—*adv.* **influentially.** [O.Fr.,— L.L. *influentia*—L. *in,* into, *fluĕre,* to flow.]

influenza, *in-floo-en'zä, n.* an epidemic virus disease attacking esp. the upper respiratory tract. —*adj.* **influen'zal.** [It., influence, influenza (as a supposed astral visitation) ; see **influence.**]

influx, *in'fluks, n.* a flowing in : accession : that which flows in.—*n.* **influxion** (*in-fluk'shən*). [L. *influxus*—*influĕre.*]

in-foal, *in-fōl', adj.* pregnant (with foal). [**in, foal.**]

infold. See **enfold.**

infold, *in'fold', n.* fold inwards.

inform, *in-form', v.t.* to give form to : to animate or give life to : to impart a quality to : to impart knowledge to : to tell : (*Milt.*) to direct.—*v.i.* (*Shak.*) to take shape or form : to give information, make an accusation (with *against* or *on*).—*ns.* **inform'ant,** one who informs or gives intelligence ; **information** (*in-fər-mā'shən*), intelligence given : knowledge : an accusation given to a magistrate or court.—*adjs.* **inform'ative,** having power to form : instructive ; **inform'atory,** instructive : giving information.—*n.* **inform'er,** one who gives information : one who informs against another : an animator. [O.Fr. *enformer*—L. *infōrmāre*—*in,* into, *fōrmāre,* to form, *fōrma,* form.]

inform, *in-form', adj.* without form : unformed : ill-formed.—*adj.* **inform'al,** not in proper form : irregular : unceremonious. — *n.* **informal'ity.**— *adv.* **inform'ally.**—*adj.* **informed',** (*Spens.*) unformed : (*astron.*) of stars not included within the figures of any of the ancient constellations. [L. *in-,* not, *fōrma,* form ; *infōrmis,* formless, misshapen.]

informidable, *in-for'mi-də-bl, adj.* (*Milt.*) not formidable.

infortune, *in-for'tūn, n.* misfortune. [L. *in-,* not.]

infracostal, *in-fra-kos'tl, adj.* beneath the ribs. [L. *infrā,* below, *costa,* a rib.]

infraction, *in-frak'shən, n.* violation, esp. of law : breach.—*v.t.* **infract',** to infringe.—*adjs.* **infract'** (*obs.*), **infract'ed,** broken : interrupted : bent in.— *n.* **infrac'tor,** one who infracts. [L. *infringĕre, infrāctum*—*in,* in, *frangĕre, frāctum,* to break.]

infragrant, *in-frā'grənt, adj.* not fragrant.

infrahuman, *in-frə-hū'mən, adj.* lower than human.

Infralapsarian, *in-frə-lap-sā'ri-ən, n.* a believer in Infralapsarianism. — Also *adj.*—*n.* **Infralapsā'-rianism,** the common Augustinian and Calvinist doctrine, that God for his own glory determined to create the world, to permit the fall of man, to elect some and leave the rest to punishment— distinct both from *Supralapsarianism* and *Sublapsarianism* : also used as equivalent to Sublapsarianism. [L. *infrā,* below, after, *lāpsus,* a fall.]

inframaxillary, *in-frə-mak'si-lə-ri, adj.* situated under the jaw : belonging to the lower jaw. [L. *infrā,* below, *maxilla,* jaw.]

infrangible, *in-fran'ji-bl, adj.* that cannot be broken : not to be violated.—*ns.* **infrangibil'ity, infran'-gibleness.** [L. *in-,* not, *frangĕre,* to break.]

infraorbital, *in-frə-or'bi-tal, adj.* situated below the orbit of the eye.

infra-red, *in'frə-red', adj.* beyond the red end of the visible spectrum. [L. *infrā,* below, and **red.**]

infrequent, *in-frē'kwənt, adj.* seldom occurring : rare : uncommon.—*ns.* **infrē'quence, infrē'-quency.**—*adv.* **infrē'quently.**

infringe, *in-frinj', v.t.* to violate, esp. law : to neglect to obey.—*n.* **infringe'ment.** [L. *infringĕre*—*in,* in, *frangĕre,* to break.]

infructuous, *in-fruk'tū-əs, adj.* not fruitful.—*adv.*

infruc'tuously. [L. *infrŭctuōsus—in-*, not, *frŭctūosus*, fruitful.]

infula, *in'fū-lä, n.* a white-and-red fillet or band of woollen stuff, worn by the ancient Romans upon the forehead in religious rites : a lappet in a mitre : —*pl.* **in'fulae** (*-ē*). [L. *infula.*]

infundibular, *in-fun-dib'ū-lər, adj.* funnel-shaped.— Also **infundib'ulate, infundib'uliform.** [L. *infundibulum,* a funnel—*in,* in, *fundĕre,* to pour.]

infuriate, *in-fū'ri-āt, v.t.* to enrage : to madden.— *adj.* (*-āt, -it*) enraged : mad. [L. *in,* in, *furiāre, -ātum,* to madden—*furĕre,* to rave.]

infuscate, *in-fus'kāt, -kit, adj.* clouded with brown. [L. *in,* in, *fuscus,* brown.]

infuse, *in-fūz', v.t.* to pour in : to instil : to steep in liquor without boiling : (*Shak.*) to shed, to pour : to imbue.—*v.i.* to undergo infusion.—*n.* (*Spens.*) infusion. — *adj.* **infus'ible.** — *n.* **infusion** (*in-fū'zhən*), pouring in : something poured in or introduced : the pouring of water over any substance in order to extract its active qualities : a solution in water of an organic, esp. a vegetable, substance : the liquor so obtained : inspiration : instilling.—*adj.* **infusive** (*-fū'siv*), having the power of infusion, or of being infused. [L. *infundĕre, infūsum—in,* into, *fundĕre, fūsum,* to pour.]

infusible, *in-fūz'i-bl, adj.* that cannot be fused.

infusoria, *in-fū-zō'ri-ä, -sō'ri-ä, n.pl.* (originally) minute organisms found in stagnant infusions of animal or vegetable material : **Infusoria,** the Ciliophora, a class of Protozoa with cilia throughout life (Ciliata) or in early life (Suctoria).—*adjs.* **infūsō'rial, infū'sory,** composed of or containing infusoria.—*n.* and *adj.* **infūsō'rian—infusorial earth,** diatomite. [Neut. pl. of modern L. *infūsōrius* ; see **infuse.**]

ingan, *ing'ən, n.* a Scots and dialectal form of **onion.**

ingate, *in'gāt, n.* an inlet for molten metal in founding. [**in, gate** (1).]

ingate, *in'gāt, n.* (*Spens.*) a way in : entrance : ingress. [**in, gate** (2).]

ingathering, *in'gadh-ər-ing, n.* collection : securing of the fruits of the earth : harvest.—**Feast of Ingathering** (see **Tabernacles, Feast of**).

ingeminate, *in-jem'in-āt, v.t.* to reiterate : to double.—*n.* **ingeminā'tion.** [L. *ingemināre, -ātum —in,* in, *geminus,* twin.]

ingener, *in'jən-ər, n.* (*Shak.*). Same as **engineer.**

ingenerate, *in-jen'ər-āt, v.t.* to generate or produce within.—*adj.* (*-it*) inborn : innate. [Pfx. *in-,* in.]

ingenerate, *in-jen'ər-āt, -it, adj.* not generated, self-existent. [L. pfx. *in-,* not.]

ingenious, *in-jē'nyəs, -ni-əs, adj.* (*obs.*) of good natural abilities : skilful in invention or contriving : skilfully contrived.—*adv.* **ingē'niously.**—*ns.* **ingē'niousness,** power of ready invention : facility in combining ideas : curiousness in design ; **ingē'nium,** bent of mind. [L. *ingenium,* mother-wit.]

ingenuity, *in-ji-nū'i-ti, n.* (*orig.*) ingenuousness (by confusion with foregoing) ingeniousness. [L. *ingenuĭtas, -ātis* ; see next word.]

ingenuous, *in-jen'ū-əs, adj.* (*obs.*) free-born : frank : honourable : free from deception.—*adv.* **ingen'uously.**—*ns.* **ingen'uousness** ; **ingenu'ity** (see previous word). [L. *ingenuus,* free-born, ingenuous.]

ingest, *in-jest', v.t.* take into the body.—*n.pl.* **ingest'a,** materials taken into the body.—*n.* **ingestion** (*in-jest'yən*). [L. *ingerĕre, ingestum,* to carry in—*in,* in, *gerĕre,* to carry.]

ingine, *in-jin', n.* (*obs.*) ability : genius. [L. *ingenium.*]

ingle, *ing'gl, n.* (Scot. *ing'l*) a fire : fireplace.— *ns.* **ing'le-cheek,** the jamb of a fireplace ; **ing'le-nook,** a chimney-corner ; **ing'le-side,** a fireside. [Possibly Gael. *aingeal* ; or L. *igniculus,* dim. of *ignis,* fire.]

ingle, *ing'gl, n.* a catamite : (wrongly) a friend. [Origin obscure.]

inglobe, *in-glōb', v.t.* (*Milt.*) to englobe, form into a sphere.

inglorious, *in-glō'ri-əs, adj.* not glorious : unhonoured : shameful. — *adv.* **inglō'riously.** — *n.* **inglō'riousness.**

ingluvies, *in-gloō'vi-ēz, n.* the crop or craw of birds.—*adj.* **inglu'vial.** [L. *inglŭviēs.*]

ingoing, *in'gō-ing, n.* a going in : entrance : (*Scot.*) a reveal.—*adj.* going in : entering as an occupant : thorough, penetrating. [**in, go.**]

ingot, *ing'gət, -got, n.* a mass of unwrought metal, esp. gold or silver, cast in a mould.—Also (*Spens., pl.*) **ingowes, ingoes.** [Perh. O.E. *in,* in, and the root *got,* as in *goten,* pa.p. of *géotan,* to pour ; Ger. *giessen,* Goth. *giutan.*]

ingraft. See **engraft.**

ingrain, *in-grān', v.t.* the same as **engrain.**—*adj.* (pron. *in'grān* when attributive) dyed in the yarn or thread before manufacture : deeply fixed : through and through.—*adj.* **ingrained'** (attrib. *in'grānd*).

ingram, ingrum, *ing'rəm, adj.* (*obs.*) ignorant. [**ignorant.**]

ingrate, *in-grāt', in'grāt, adj.* (*obs.*) unpleasing : (*arch.*) ungrateful.—*n.* one who is ungrateful.—*adj.* **ingrate'ful,** unthankful. [L. *ingrātus—in-,* not, *grātus,* pleasing, grateful.]

ingratiate, *in-grā'shi-āt, v.t.* to commend to grace or favour (used reflexively, and followed by *with*).—*adj.* **ingra'tiating.** [L. *in,* into, *grātia,* favour.]

ingratitude, *in-grat'i-tūd, n.* unthankfulness. [L.L. *ingrātitūdō*—L. *ingrātus,* unthankful.]

ingredient, *in-grē'di-ənt, n.* that which enters into a compound : a component. [L. *ingrediēns, -entis,* pr.p. of *ingredī—in,* into, *gradī,* to walk.]

ingress, *in'gres, n.* entrance : power, right, or means of entrance.—*n.* **ingression** (*in-gresh'ən*). [L. *ingressus—ingredī* ; see preceding.]

ingroove. See **engroove.**

ingross, *in-grōs', v.t.* (*Shak*). Same as **engross.**

ingrowing, *in'grō-ing, adj.* growing inward : growing into the flesh : growing within.—*adj.* **in'grown.**—*n.* **in'growth,** growth within or inward : a structure so formed.

inguinal, *ing'gwin-əl, adj.* relating to the groin. [L. *inguinālis—inguen, inguinis,* the groin.]

ingulf, ingulph. See **engulf.**

ingurgitate, *in-gur'ji-tāt, v.t.* to swallow up greedily, as in a gulf.—*n.* **ingurgitā'tion.** [L. *ingurgitāre, -ātum—in,* into, *gurges, -itis,* a whirlpool.]

inhabit, *in-hab'it, v.t.* to dwell in : to occupy.—*v.i.* (*arch.*) to dwell.—*adj.* **inhab'itable,** that may be inhabited (see also next word).—*ns.* **inhab'itance, inhab'itancy,** the act of inhabiting : abode ; **inhab'itant,** one who inhabits : a residence.—*adj.* resident.—*ns.* **inhabitā'tion,** the act of inhabiting : dwelling-place : (*Milt.*) population, or perh. the inhabited world ; **inhab'itor,** (B.) an inhabitant : (*obs.*) a colonist, settler ; **inhab'itiveness,** (*phrenol.*) love of locality and home ; **inhab'itress,** a female inhabitant. [L. *inhabitāre—in,* in, *habitāre,* to dwell.]

inhabitable, *in-hab'it-ə-bl, adj.* not habitable, uninhabitable. See also under **inhabit.** [L. *inhabitābilis—in-,* not, *habitābilis.*]

inhale, *in-hāl', v.t.* and *v.i.* to breathe in : to draw in.—*adj.* **inha'lant,** inhaling : drawing in.—*ns.* **inha'lant,** an inhaling organ, structure, or apparatus : a medicinal preparation to be inhaled ; **inhalation** (*in-hə-lā'shən*), the act of drawing into the lungs : something to be inhaled ; **inhalator** (*in'hə-lā-tər,* or *-lā'*), apparatus for enabling one to inhale a gas, &c. ; **inhalatorium** (*in-hāl-ə-tō'ri-əm*), an institution or department for administering inhalations ; **inhā'ler,** one who inhales : one who habitually inhales tobacco smoke : an inhalator : a respirator or gas-mask. [L. *in,* upon, *hālāre,* to breathe [L. *inhālāre* means to breathe upon].]

inharmonious, *in-här-mō'ni-əs, adj.* discordant, unmusical : disagreeing.—*adjs.* **inharmonic** (*in-här-mon'ik*), **-al,** wanting harmony : inharmonious.—*adv.* **inharmō'niously.**—*ns.* **inharmō'niousness ; inharmony** (*in-här'mən-i*).

inhaust, *in'hawst, v.t.* (*humorous*) to drink in. [L. *in,* in, *haurīre, haustum,* to draw.]

inhearse, inherce, *in-hərs', v.t.* (*Shak.*) to enclose as in a hearse : to bury.—Also **enhearse.**

inhere, *in-hēr', v.i.* to stick, remain firm in something : to be inherent.—*ns.* **inhēr'ence, inhēr'ency,** a sticking fast : existence in something else : a fixed state of being in another body or substance.

—*adj.* **inhēr′ent**, sticking fast : existing in and inseparable from something else : innate : natural.—*adv.* **inhēr′ently.** [L. *inhaerēre, inhaesum—in,* in, *haerēre,* to stick.]

inherit, *in-her′it, v.t.* (*Shak.*) to make heir : (*arch.*) to be the heir of, succeed as heir : to get as heir : to possess by transmission from past generations : to have by natural transmission from ancestors.— *v.i.* to succeed.—*adj.* **inher′itable,** same as **heritable.**—*ns.* **inher′itance,** that which is or may be inherited : hereditary descent ; **inher′itor,** one who inherits or may inherit : an heir :—*fem.* **inher′itress, inher′itrix.** [O.Fr. *enheriter,* to put in possession as heir—L.L. *inhērēditāre,* to inherit—L. *in,* in, *hērēs, hērēdis,* an heir.]

inhesion, *in-hē′zhən.* Same as **inherence.**

inhibit, *in-hib′it, v.t.* to hold in or back : to keep back : to check.—*ns.* **inhibi′tion,** the act of inhibiting or restraining : the state of being inhibited : prohibition : a writ from a higher court to an inferior judge to stay proceedings : a restraining action of the unconscious will : the blocking of a mental or psychophysical process by another set up at the same time by the same stimulus ; **inhib′itor.**—*adj.* **inhib′itory,** prohibitory. [L. *inhibēre, -hibitum—in,* in, *habēre,* to have.]

inholder, *in-hōld′ər, n.* (*Spens.*) an inhabitant.

inhoop, *in-hōōp′, v.t.* (*Shak.*) to confine, as in a hoop or enclosure.

inhospitable, *in-hos′pit-ə-bl, adj.* affording no kindness to strangers.—*ns.* **inhos′pitableness, inhospital′ity,** want of hospitality or courtesy to strangers.—*adv.* **inhos′pitably.**

inhuman, *in-hū′mən, adj.* barbarous : cruel : unfeeling.—*n.* **inhumanity** (*in-hū-man′i-ti*), the state of being inhuman : barbarity : cruelty.—*adv.* **inhū′manly.**

inhume, *in-hūm′, v.t.* to bury in the earth.—Also **inhumate** (*in′,* or *-hūm′*).—*n.* **inhumā′tion,** the act of depositing in the ground : burial. [L. *inhumāre—in,* in, *humus,* the ground.]

inimical, *in-im′i-kl, adj.* unfriendly : hostile : unfavourable : opposed.—*adv.* **inim′ically.**—*adj.* **inimicitious** (*-sish′əs, Sterne*), unfriendly. [L. *inimīcālis — inimīcus,* enemy — *in-,* not, *amīcus,* friend.]

inimitable, *in-im′it-ə-bl, adj.* that cannot be imitated : surpassingly excellent.—*ns.* **inimitabil′ity, inim′itableness.**—*adv.* **inim′itably.**

inion, *in′i-ən, n.* the external occipital protuberance :—*pl.* **in′ia.** [Gr. *īnion,* the occiput.]

iniquity, *in-ik′wi-ti, n.* want of equity or fairness : injustice : wickedness : a crime : **Iniquity,** one of the names of the Vice, the established buffoon of the old Moralities.—*adj.* **iniq′uitous,** unjust : scandalously unreasonable : wicked.—*adv.* **iniq′uitously.** [Fr. *iniquité—L. iniquitās, -ātis— inīquus,* unequal—*in-,* not, *aequus,* equal.]

inisle. Same as **enisle.**

initial, *in-ish′l, adj.* beginning : of, at, or serving as, the beginning : original.—*n.* the letter beginning a word, esp. a name.—*v.t.* to put the initials of one's name to :—*pr.p.* **init′ialling ;** *pa.t.* and *pa.p.* **init′ialled.**—*vs.t.* **init′ialise,** to designate by initial letters ; **initiate** (*-ish′i-āt*), to begin, start : to introduce (e.g. to knowledge) : to admit esp. with rites (as to a secret society, a mystery).—*v.i.* to perform the first act or rite.—*n.* (*-it*) one who is initiated.—*adj.* **begun :** initiated : belonging to one newly initiated.—*n.* **initiā′tion,** act or process of initiating : act of admitting to a society or the like.— *adj.* **init′iative** (*-i-ə-tiv*), serving to initiate : introductory.—*n.* the lead, first step, considered as determining the conditions for others : the right or power of beginning : energy and resourcefulness enabling one to act without prompting from others : the right of the sovereign people to originate legislation, or a constitutional method of doing so. — *adj.* **init′iatory** (*-i-ə-tə-ri*), tending to initiate : introductory.—*n.* introductory rite.—**initial cell,** (*bot.*) a cell that remains meristematic and gives rise to many daughter-cells from which permanent tissues are formed ; **initiation fee,** (*U.S.*) entrance fee of a society. [L. *initiālis—*

initium, a beginning, *inīre, initum—in,* into, *īre, itum,* to go.]

inject, *in-jekt′, v.t.* (*obs.*) to throw in or on : to force in : to inspire or instil : to fill by injection.—*ns.* **injec′tion** (*-shən*), act of injecting or forcing in, esp. a liquid : a liquid injected into the body : a magma injected into a rock ; **injec′tor,** one who injects : something used for injecting, especially an apparatus for forcing water into a boiler. [L. *injicĕre, injectum—in,* into, *jacĕre,* to throw.]

injelly, *in-jel′i, v.t.* (*Tenn.*) to place as if in jelly.

injoint, *in-joint′, v.t.* (*Shak.*) to join.

injudicious, *in-joo-dish′əs, adj.* not judicious : ill-judged.—*adj.* **injudic′ial,** not according to law-forms.—*advs.* **injudic′ially, injudic′iously.**—*n.* **injudic′iousness.**

Injun, *in′jən, n.* (*coll. U.S.*) an (American) **Indian.**— Also *adj.*

injunction, *in-jungk′shən, n.* act of enjoining or commanding : an order : a precept : exhortation : an inhibitory writ by which a superior court stops or prevents some inequitable or illegal act being done—called in Scotland an **interdict :** (*Milt.*) conjunction. [L.L. *injunctiō, -ōnis—in,* in, *jungĕre, junctum,* to join.]

injure, *in′jər, v.t.* to wrong : to harm : to damage : to hurt.—*n.* **in′jurer.**—*adj.* **injurious** (*in-joō′ri-əs*), tending to injure : unjust : wrongful : hurtful : damaging to reputation.—*adv.* **inju′riously.**—*ns.* **inju′riousness ; injury** (*in′jər-i*), that which injures : wrong : damage : hurt : impairment : annoyance : (*obs.*) insult, offence. [L. *injūria,* injury—*in-,* not, *jūs, jūris,* law.]

injustice, *in-jus′tis, n.* violation or withholding of another's rights or dues : wrong : iniquity.

ink, *ingk, n.* a black or coloured liquid used in writing, printing, &c. : a dark liquid ejected by cuttle-fishes, &c.—*v.t.* to daub, cover, blacken, or colour with ink.—*ns.* **ink′-bag, -sac,** a sac in some cuttle-fishes, containing a black viscid fluid ; **ink′-bottle,** a bottle for holding ink ; **ink′er,** one who inks : a pad or cushion for inking type, &c. ; **ink′-erā′ser,** india-rubber treated with fine sand, used for rubbing out ink-marks ; **ink′-feed,** the passage by which the nib of a fountain-pen is fed with ink ; **ink′holder,** a container for ink : the reservoir of a fountain-pen ; **ink′horn,** (*obs.*) an ink-holder, formerly of horn : a portable case for ink, &c.— *adj.* pedantic, bookish.—*n.* **ink′horn-mate,** (*Shak.*) a bookish man ; **ink′iness.**—*ns.* **ink′ing-ta′ble,** a table or flat surface used for supplying the inking-roller with ink during the process of printing ; **ink′ing-roll′er,** a roller covered with a composition for inking printing type ; **ink′pencil,** a copying-pencil, a pencil made from a composition whose marks when moistened look like ink and can be copied by a printing-press ; **ink′-pot,** an ink-bottle, or pot for dipping a pen in ; **ink′-slinger,** a professional author : a scribbler : a controversialist ; **ink′-stand,** a stand or tray for ink-bottles and (usually) pens ; **ink′-stone,** a kind of stone containing sulphate of iron, used in making ink ; **ink′-well,** a reservoir for ink let into a desk.— *adj.* **ink′y,** consisting of or resembling ink : very black : blackened with ink.—**China ink, Indian ink** (sometimes without capital letters), a mixture of lampblack and size or glue, kept in solid form and rubbed down in water for use ; **invisible** or **sympathetic ink,** a kind of ink that remains invisible on the paper until it is heated ; **marking ink** (see **mark**) ; **printing ink** (see **print**) ; **sling ink** (*slang*), to write : to earn one's bread by writing : to engage in controversy. [O.Fr. *enque* (Fr. *encre*)—L.L. *encaustum,* the purple-red ink used by the later Roman emperors—Gr. *enkauston—enkaiein,* to burn in. See **encaustic.**]

inkle, *ingk′l, n.* (*Shak.*) a kind of broad linen tape. [Poss. Du. *enkel,* single.]

inkling, *ingk′ling, n.* a hint or whisper : intimation : a dim notion or suspicion.—*v.i.* **ink′le,** to have or give a hint of. [M.E. *inclen,* to hint at ; origin unknown.]

in-kneed, *in′-nēd′, adj.* bent inward at the knees : knock-kneed.

inlace. Same as **enlace.**

Inlaid. See **inlay.**

Inland, *in'land, in'lənd, n.* the interior part of a country: (*arch.*) the peopled part, or part near the capital.—*adj.* remote from the sea: carried on, or produced, within a country: confined to a country: (*Shak.*) refined, polished.—*adv.* (also *in-land'*) landward: away from the sea: in an inland place.—*n.* in'lander, one who lives inland.—**inland navigation,** passage of boats or vessels on rivers, lakes, or canals within a country; **inland revenue,** internal revenue, derived from excise, stamps, income-tax, &c. [O.E. *inland,* a domain—*in* and *land.*]

in-law, *in-law', n.* (*coll.*) a relative by marriage, e.g. mother-in-law, brother-in-law:—*pl.* **in-laws'.**

inlay, *in-lā', in'lā', v.t.* to insert, embed: to insert for preservation in a larger leaf, serving as margin: to ornament by laying in or inserting pieces of metal, ivory, &c:—*pr.p.* **in'lay'ing**; *pa.t.* and *pa.p.* **in'laid'.**—*n.* in'lay (or *in'lā'*), inlaying: inlaid work: material inlaid.—*adj.* **in'laid'** (or *in'lād,* or *in-lād'*), inserted by inlaying: decorated with inlay: consisting of inlay: having a pattern penetrating the thickness.—*ns.* **inlayer** (*in'lā-ər, in-lā'ər*); **inlay'ing.**

inlet, *in'let, n.* entrance: a passage by which anything is let in: place of ingress: a small bay or opening in the land: a piece let in. [**in, let.**]

inlier, *in'lī-ər, n.* (*geol.*) an outcrop of older rock surrounded by younger. [**in, lie.**]

inlock, *in-lok', v.t.* Same as **enlock.**

inly, *in'li, adj.* inward: secret.—*adv.* inwardly: in the heart: thoroughly, entirely.

inmate, *in'māt, n.* (now rare) one who lodges in the same house with another: one of those who live in a house, esp. an institution.—*adj.* (*obs.*) dwelling in the same place. [**in** or **inn, mate.**]

inmost. See **innermost.**

inn, *in, n.* (*obs.*) abode (formerly often in *pl.*): a house open to the public for lodging and entertainment of travellers: a hostel: a hotel: (loosely) a public-house.—*v.t.* and *v.i.* to lodge, put up.—*ns.* inn'-hold'er (*Bacon; U.S.*), inn'keeper, one who keeps an inn; inn'-yard, the courtyard round which an old-fashioned inn was built.—**Inns of Court,** the buildings of four voluntary societies that have the exclusive right of calling to the English bar (Inner Temple, Middle Temple, Lincoln's Inn and Gray's Inn): hence the societies themselves; the **Inns of Chancery** were the buildings of minor societies, residences of junior students of law. [O.E. *inn,* an inn, house—*in, inn,* within (adv.), from the prep. *in,* in.]

innate, *in'āt, in-nāt', adj.* inborn: natural to the mind: inherent: (*bot.*) of an anther, attached by the base to the tip of the filament.—*adv.* inn'ately (or *-nāt'*).—*n.* inn'ateness (or *-nāt'*).—*adj.* innā'tive, native. [L. *innātus—in-,* in, *nāscī, nātus,* to be born.]

innavigable, *in-nav'i-gə-bl, adj.* unnavigable.—*adv.* innav'igably.

inner, *in'ər, adj.* (comp. of **in**) farther in: interior.—*n.* (a hit on) that part of a target next the bull's eye.—*adjs.* inn'ermost, in'most (superl. of **in**), farthest in: most remote from the outside.—**inner part, voice,** a voice part intermediate between the highest and the lowest. [O.E. *in,* comp. *innera,* superl. *innemest=inne-m-est*—thus a double superlative.]

innervate, *in'ər-vāt, in-ər'vāt, v.t.* to supply with nerves or nervous stimulus.—Also **innerve'.**—*n.* innervā'tion.

inning, *in'ing, n.* ingathering, esp. of crops: (in *pl.*; in *U.S.,* in *sing.*) a team's turn of batting in cricket, &c.: hence, the time during which a person or a party is in possession of anything, a spell or turn: (in *pl.*) lands recovered from the sea. [**in** or **inn.**]

innocent, *in'ə-sənt, adj.* not hurtful: inoffensive: blameless: harmless: guileless: simple: ignorant of evil: imbecile: not guilty: (*med.*) not malignant or cancerous.—*n.* one free from fault: one with no knowledge of evil: a child: a simpleton: an idiot.—*ns.* inn'ocence, harmlessness: blamelessness: guilelessness: simplicity: imbecility:

freedom from legal guilt; inn'ocency, the quality of being innocent.—*adv.* inn'ocently.—**Innocents' Day** (see **Childermas**). [O.Fr.,—L. *innocēns, -entis—in-,* not, *nocēre,* to hurt.]

innocuous, *in-ok'ū-əs, adj.* harmless.—*adv.* innoc'uously.—*ns.* innoc'uousness, innocu'ity. [L. *innocuus—in-,* not, *nocuus,* hurtful—*nocēre,* to hurt.]

innominate, *i-nom'i-nāt, -nit, adj.* having no name.—*adj.* innom'inable, unnamable.—*n.* (in *pl.; obs. facetious*) trousers.—**innominate artery,** the first large branch given off from the arch of the aorta; **innominate bone** (*os innōminātum*), the haunch-bone, hip-bone, formed by fusion in the adult of the ilium, ischium, and pubis. [L. *in-,* not, *nōmināre, -ātum,* to name.]

innovate, *in'o-vāt, in'ə-vāt, v.t.* (*rare*) to renew, alter: to introduce as something new.—*v.i.* to introduce novelties: to make changes.—*ns.* innovā'tion, the act of innovating: a thing introduced as a novelty: (*Shak.*) revolution: (*Scots law*) substitution of one obligation for another: (*bot.*) a season's new growth; innovā'tionist; inn'ovātor. [L. *innovāre, -ātum—in,* in, *novus,* new.]

innoxious, *in-ok'shəs, adj.* not noxious.—*adv.* innox'iously.—*n.* innox'iousness.

innuendo, *in-ū-en'dō, n.* insinuation: an indirect reference or intimation: a part of a pleading in cases of libel and slander, pointing out what and who was meant: (*pl.* innuen'do(e)s.—*v.t.* to insinuate by innuendo: to interpret as insinuation.—*v.i.* to make insinuations. [L. *innuendō,* by nodding at (i.e. indicating, to wit—used in old legal documents to introduce a parenthetic indication), ablative gerund of *innuĕre,* to nod to, indicate—*in,* to, *nuĕre,* to nod.]

innumerable, *in-(n)ū'mər-ə-bl, adj.* that cannot be numbered: countless.—*ns.* innūmerabil'ity; innū'merableness.—*adv.* innū'merably.—*adj.* innū'merous (*Milt.*), without number: innumerable.

innutrition, *in-(n)ū-trish'ən, n.* want of nutrition: failure of nourishment.—*adjs.* innū'trient, not nutrient; innūtritious (*-trish'əs*), not nutritious.

inobedient, *in-ō-bē'dyənt, adj.* disobedient.—*n.* inobe'dience.—*adv.* inobe'diently.

inobservant, *in-əb-zər'vənt, adj.* unobservant: heedless.—*adj.* inobser'vable, incapable of being observed.—*n.* inobser'vance, lack of observance; inobservā'tion (*-ob-*).

inobtrusive, *in-əb-trōō'siv, adj.* unobtrusive.—*adv.* inobtru'sively.—*n.* inobtru'siveness.

inoccupation, *in-ok-ū-pā'shən, n.* lack of occupation.

inoculate, *in-ok'ū-lāt, v.t.* to insert as a bud or graft: to graft: to imbue: to introduce (e.g. a disease, a virus, germs) into the body: to make an inoculation upon, esp. for the purpose of safeguarding against subsequent infection.—*v.i.* to practise inoculation.—*n.* inoculabil'ity.—*adj.* inoc'ulable.—*n.* inoculā'tion, act or practice of inoculating: insertion of the buds of one plant into another: the communication of disease by the introduction of a germ or virus, esp. that of a mild form of the disease to produce immunity: the analogous introduction of anything else, e.g. nitrogen-fixing bacteria into soil, a crystal into a supersaturated solution to start crystallisation.—*adjs.* inoc'ulative (*-ə-tiv,* or *-ā-tiv*); inoc'ula-tory (*-ə-tər-i*).—*ns.* inoc'ulātor; inoc'ulum, material used for inoculating. [L. *inoculāre, -ātum—in,* into, *oculus,* an eye, a bud.]

inodorous, *in-ō'dər-əs, adj.* without smell.—*adv.* ino'dorously.—*n.* ino'dorousness.

inoffensive, *in-ə-fen'siv, adj.* giving no offence: harmless.—*adv.* inoffen'sively.—*n.* inoffen'siveness.

inofficious, *in-ə-fish'əs, adj.* (*obs.*) disobliging: regardless of duty: inoperative.

inoperable, *in-op'ər-ə-bl, adj.* not to be operated on.—*adj.* inop'erative, not in action: producing no effect.

inoperculate, *in-o-pər'kū-lāt, adj.* without an operculum or lid.

inopinate, *in-op'in-āt, adj.* unexpected. [L. *in-opinatus.*]

inopportune, *in-op'ǝr-tūn, -tūn', adj.* unseasonable in time.—*adv.* **inopp'ortūnely** (or *-tūn').*—*ns.* **inopp'ortūnist** (or *-tūn'),* one who thinks a policy inopportune; **inopportūn'ity.**

inorb, *in-orb', v.t.* to set in an orb.

inordinate, *in-ord'(i-)nit, adj.* unrestrained: excessive: immoderate.—*ns.* **inor'dinacy, inor'-dinateness.**—*adj.* **inor'dinately.**—*n.* **inordinā'-tion,** deviation from rule: irregularity. [L. *inordinātus—in-,* not, *ordināre, -ātum,* to arrange, regulate.]

inorganic, *in-or-gan'ik, adj.* not organic: not organised: not belonging to an organism: of accidental origin, not normally developed.—*adv.* **inorgan'ically.**—*n.* **inorganisā'tion,** want of organisation.—*adj.* **inor'ganised,** unorganised.— **inorganic chemistry,** the chemistry of all substances but carbon compounds, generally admitting a few of these also (as oxides of carbon, carbonates).

inornate, *in-or-nāt',* or *-or'nit, adj.* not ornate: simple.

inosculate, *in-os'kū-lāt, v.t.* and *v.i.* to unite by mouths or ducts, as two vessels in an animal body: to anastomose.—*n.* **inosculā'tion.** [L. *in,* in, and *osculārī, -ātus,* to kiss.]

inositol, *in-os'i-tol, n.* a member of the vitamin B_2 complex, occurring in practically all plant and animal tissues. [Gr. *īs, ínos,* a sinew, muscle, and suffixes *-ite* and *-ol.*]

in-patient, *in'pā-shǝnt, n.* a patient lodged and fed as well as treated in a hospital—opp. to *out-patient.*

inphase, *in-fāz', adj.* in the same phase. [in, phase.]

inpouring, *in'pōr-ing, n.* a pouring in: addition.

input, *in'poot, n.* (*Scot.*) contribution: amount, material, or energy, that is put in.

inquere, enquere, *in-kwēr', v.i.* and *v.t.* (*Spens.*) to inquire.

inquest, *in'kwest,* formerly *in-kwest', n.* act of inquiring: search: judicial inquiry before a jury into any matter, esp. any case of violent or sudden death. [O.Fr. *enqueste*—L.L. *inquesta*—L. *inquisīta* (*rēs*)—*inquīrĕre,* to inquire.]

inquietude, *in-kwī'i-tūd, n.* disturbance: uneasiness.—*adj.* **inqui'et,** unquiet.—*v.t.* to disturb.

inquiline, *in'kwi-līn, adj.* living in the abode of another.—*n.* an animal so living.—*adj.* **inquili'-nous.** [L. *inquilīnus,* tenant, lodger—*incola,* inhabitant—*in,* in, *colĕre,* to inhabit.]

inquinate, *in'kwin-āt, v.t.* to defile.—*n.* **inquinā'-tion.** [L. *inquināre, -ātum.*]

inquire, enquire, *in-kwīr', v.i.* to ask a question: to make an investigation.—*v.t.* to ask: to seek: (*obs.*) to make an examination regarding: (*Spens.*) to call.—*n.* (*Shak.*) inquiry.—*ns.* **inquirā'tion** (*Dickens*), **enquirā'tion,** inquiry; **inquiren'do,** (*law*) an authority to inquire; **inquir'er,** en-**quir'er.**—*adj.* **inquir'ing,** given to inquiry: eager o acquire information.—*adv.* **inquir'ingly.**—*n.* **inquir'y, enquir'y,** act of inquiring: search for knowledge: investigation: a question.—**writ of inquiry,** a writ appointing an inquest. [O.Fr. *enquerre* (Fr. *enquérir*)—L. *inquīrĕre—in,* in, *quaerĕre, quaesītum,* to seek.]

inquisition, *in-kwi-zish'ǝn, n.* searching examination: investigation: judicial inquiry: **Inquisition,** a tribunal in the R.C. Church, called also 'the Holy Office,' for the discovery, repression, and punishment of heresy, unbelief, and other offences against religion.—*v.t.* (*Milt.*) to subject to inquisition.— *adjs.* **inquisit'ional,** searching or vexatious in making inquiry: relating to inquisition or the Inquisition; **inquisitive** (*-kwiz'i-tiv*), eager to know: apt to ask questions, esp. about other people's affairs: curious.—*adv.* **inquis'itively.**— *ns.* **inquis'itiveness; inquis'itor,** one who inquires, esp. with undue pertinacity or searchingness: an official inquirer: a member of the Court of Inquisition. — *adj.* **inquisitō'rial.** — *adv.* **inquisitō'rially.**—*n.* **inquis'itress,** an inquisitorial woman.—*adj.* **inquisit'rient,** (*Milt.*) eager to act as inquisitor.—**Grand Inquisitor,** the chief

in a Court of Inquisition. [L. *inquīsītiō, -ōnis.* See **inquire.**]

inro, *in'rō, n.* a small Japanese medicine-chest. [Jap., seal-box.]

inroad, *in'rōd, n.* an incursion into an enemy's country: a raid: encroachment. [in, and **road,** in sense of riding; cf. **raid.**]

inrush, *in'rush, n.* an inward rush.

insalivate, *in-sal'i-vāt, v.t.* to mix with saliva.—*n.* **insalivā'tion.**

insalubrious, *in-sa-l(y)ōō'bri-ǝs, adj.* unhealthy.— *n.* **insalu'brity.**

insalutary, *in-sal'ū-tǝr-i, adj.* unwholesome.

insane, *in-sān', adj.* not sane or of sound mind: crazy: mad: utterly unwise: senseless: causing insanity (*Shak.* **insane root,** prob. a root mentioned by Plutarch, *Life of Antony,* perh. hemlock, henbane, or belladonna).—*adv.* **insane'ly.**—*ns.* **insane'ness,** insanity: madness; **insa'nie** (*Shak.*; an emendation of the reading *infamie*), insanity; **insanity** (*in-san'i-ti*), want of sanity: mental disorder causing one to act against the social or legal demands of society: madness. [L. *insānus.*]

insanitary, *in-san'i-tǝr-i, adj.* not sanitary.

insatiable, *in-sā'sh(y)ǝ-bl, adj.* that cannot be satiated or satisfied.—*ns.* **insā'tiableness, in-sātiabil'ity.**—*adv.* **insā'tiably.**—*adj.* **insā'tiate,** not sated: insatiable.—*n.* **insatiety** (*in-sǝ-tī'i-ti*), unsated or insatiable state.

inscient, *in'sh(y)ǝnt, -shi-ǝnt, adj.* ignorant.—*n.* **in'science.** [L. *insciēns, -entis—in-,* not, *scīre,* to know.]

inscient, *in'sh(y)ǝnt, adj.* having insight or inward knowledge. [L. *in,* in, *sciēns, -entis,* pr.p. of *scīre,* to know.]

inscribe, *in-skrīb', v.t.* to engrave or otherwise mark: to engrave or mark on: to enter in a book or roll: to dedicate: (*geom.*) to describe within another figure so as either to touch all sides or faces of the bounding figure or to have all angular points on it.—*adj.* **inscrīb'able.**—*ns.* **inscrīb'er; inscription** (*in-skrip'shǝn*), the act of inscribing: that which is inscribed: dedication: a record inscribed on stone, metal, clay, &c.—*adjs.* **inscrip'-tional, inscrip'tive.** [L. *inscrībĕre, inscriptum—in,* upon, *scrībĕre,* to write.]

inscroll, *in-skrōl', v.t.* (*Shak.*) to write on a scroll.

inscrutable, *in-skrōōt'ǝ-bl, adj.* that cannot be scrutinised or searched into and understood: inexplicable.—*ns.* **inscrutabil'ity, inscrut'able-ness.**—*adv.* **inscrut'ably.** [L. *inscrūtābilis—in-,* not, *scrūtārī,* to search into.]

insculp, *in-skulp', v.t.* (*Shak.*) to engrave, to cut or carve upon something: to carve: to form by carving.—*adj.* **insculpt',** (*Shak.*) engraved: (*bot.*) having depressions in the surface.—*n.* **insculp'-ture,** (*Shak.*) anything engraved: inscription.— *v.t.* to carve on something. [L. *insculpĕre—in,* in, *sculpĕre,* to carve.]

inseam. Same as **enseam** (3).

insect, *in'sekt, n.* a word loosely used for a small invertebrate creature, esp. one with a body as if cut into, or divided into sections: (*zool.*) an arthropod sharply divided into head, thorax, and abdomen, with three pairs of legs attached to the thorax, usually winged in adult life, breathing air by means of tracheae, and commonly having a metamorphosis in the life-history.—*adj.* of insects: like an insect: small: mean.—*ns.* **insectār'ium,** a vivarium for insects; **insec'ticide** (*-i-sīd*), killing of insects: an insect-killing substance: an insect-killer.—*adjs.* **insec'tiform; insec'tile,** having the nature of an insect.—*n.* **insec'tifuge,** a substance that drives away insects.—*n.pl.* **Insectiv'ora,** an order of mammals, mostly terrestrial, insect-eating, nocturnal in habit, and small in size— shrews, moles, hedgehogs, &c.—*n.* **insect'ivore,** a member of the Insectivora.—*adj.* **insectiv'orous,** living on insects.—*ns.* **insection** (*in-sek'shǝn*), an incision: notch: division into segments; **in'sect-net,** a light hand-net for catching insects; **in'sect-pow'der,** powder for stupefying and killing insects: an insecticide or insectifuge.—*adj.* **in'-secty,** abounding in insects. [L. *insectum,* pa.p. of *insecāre—in,* into, *secāre,* to cut.]

Insecure, *in-si-kūr'*, *adj.* apprehensive of danger or loss : exposed to danger or loss : unsafe : uncertain : not fixed or firm.—*adv.* **insecure'ly.**—*n.* **insecur'ity.**

inseem (*Shak.*). See **enseam** (2).

inseminate, *in-sem'in-āt*, *v.t.* to sow : to implant : to introduce : to impregnate, esp. artificially.—*n.* **insemina'tion.** [L. *insēmināre—in*, in, *sēmen*, *-inis*, seed.]

insensate, *in-sen'sāt*, *adj.* wanting power of sensation, good sense, or sensibility.—*n.* **insen'sateness.** [L. *insēnsātus—in-*, not, *sēnsātus*, intelligent—*sēnsus*, feeling.]

insensible, *in-sen'si-bl*, *adj.* not having feeling : not susceptible of emotion : callous : dull : unconscious : imperceptible by the senses.—*ns.* **insensibil'ity**, **insen'sibleness.** — *adv.* **insen'-sibly.**

insensitive, *in-sen'si-tiv*, *adj.* not sensitive.

insensuous, *in-sen'sū-əs*, *adj.* not sensuous.

insentient, *in-sen'sh(y)ənt*, *adj.* not having perception.

inseparable, *in-sep'ər-ə-bl*, *adj.* that cannot be separated.—*n.* an inseparable companion (usu. in *pl.*). — *ns.* **insep'arableness, inseparabil'ity.**—*adv.* **insep'arably.**—*adj.* **insep'arate**, (*Shak.*) not separate or separable.

insert, *in-sərt'*, *v.t.* to put in.—*n.* **in'sert**, something additional inserted into a proof, &c. : a paper placed within the folds of a periodical or leaves of a book.—*adj.* **insert'ed**, (*bot.*) attached to or growing out of some part.—*n.* **insertion** (*in-sər'shən*), act of inserting : mode or condition of being inserted : point of place of attachment : that which is inserted : lace or the like suitable for letting into another material. [L. *inserĕre*, *insertum—in*, in, *serĕre*, to join.]

Insessores, *in-ses-ō'rēz*, *n.pl.* perching birds, in old classifications an order answering roughly to Passeriformes.—*adj.* **insessō'rial**, of the Insessores : adapted for perching. [L. *insessor*, pl. *-ōrēs*, besetter (of the roads), highwayman, adopted with the meaning percher—*insidēre—in*, on, *sedēre*, to sit.]

inset, *in'set*, *n.* something set in, an insertion or insert, a leaf or leaves inserted between the folds of other leaves : a small map or figure inserted in a spare corner of another : a piece let in : the setting in of a current.—*v.t.* **inset'**, to set in, to infix or implant.

inseverable, *in-sev'ər-ə-bl*, *adj.* that cannot be severed or separated.

inshallah, *in-shä'lä*, *interj.* (among Mohammedans) if God will. [Ar. *in shā 'llāh*.]

inshell, *in-shel'*, *v.t.* (*Shak.*) to draw in or withdraw, as into a shell.

inshelter, *in-shel'tər*, *v.t.* to place in shelter.

inship, *in-ship'*, *v.t.* (*Shak.*) to ship, to embark.

inshore, *in'shōr'*, *adv.* near or toward the shore. —*adj.* (*in'shōr*) situated near the shore, as fishings.

inshrine, *in-shrīn'*. Same as **enshrine.**

inside, *in'sīd'*, *in'sīd*, *in-sīd'*, *n.* the side, space, or part within : the entrails : inner nature : that which is not visible at first sight : a passenger in the interior part of a vehicle : (in *pl.*) the inner quires of a ream of paper.—*adj.* being within : interior : indoor : working indoors : from within : from a secret or confidential source.—*adv.* in or to the interior : on the inner side.—*prep.* within : on the inner side of.—*ns.* **in'side-car**, an Irish jaunting-car in which the passengers face one another ; **insi'der**, one who is inside : an inside passenger : one within a certain organisation, &c. : one possessing some particular advantage.—**inside edge** (see **edge**) ; **inside left, right**, in some games a forward between the centre and outside ; **inside of**, (esp. *U.S.*) in less than ; **inside out**, with the inner side turned outwards ; **inside track**, the inner side in a race-course : the advantage in position.

insidious, *in-sid'i-əs*, *adj.* watching an opportunity to ensnare : intended to entrap : deceptive : advancing imperceptibly : treacherous.—*adv.* **insid'iously.**—*n.* **insid'iousness.** [L. *insidiōsus—insidiae*, an ambush—*insidēre—in*, in, *sedēre*, to sit.]

insight, *in'sīt*, *n.* power of seeing into and under-

standing things : imaginative penetration : practical knowledge : enlightenment : a view into anything.

insight, *in'sīt*, *in'sihht*, *n.* (*Scot.*) household goods, furniture.—Also *adj.* [Origin unknown.]

insignia, *in-sig'ni-ä*, *n.pl.* signs or badges of office, honour, membership, occupation, &c. : marks by which anything is known. [L., neut. pl. of *insignis —in*, in, *signum*, a mark.]

insignificant, *in-sig-nif'i-kənt*, *adj.* destitute of meaning : without effect : unimportant : petty.—*ns.* **insignif'icance, insignif'icancy.**—*adv.* **insignif'icantly.**—*adj.* **insignif'icative**, not significative or expressing by external signs.

insincere, *in-sin-sēr'*, *adj.* not sincere.—*adv.* **insincere'ly.**—*n.* **insincerity** (*-ser'i-ti*).

insinew, *in-sin'ū*, *v.t.* (*Shak.*) to impart vigour to.

insinuate, *in-sin'ū-āt*, *v.t.* to introduce gently or artfully : to hint, esp. a fault : to work into favour. —*v.i.* to creep or flow in : to enter gently : to obtain access by flattery or stealth.—*adj.* **insin'uating.**—*adv.* **insin'uatingly.**—*n.* **insinuā'tion.** —*adj.* **insin'uative**, insinuating or stealing on the confidence : using insinuation.—*n.* **insin'uator.**—*adj.* **insin'uatory** (*-ə-tər-i*). [L. *insinuāre*, *-ātum —in*, in, *sinus*, a curve.]

insipid, *in-sip'id*, *adj.* tasteless : without satisfying definite flavour : wanting spirit or interest : dull.—*adv.* **insip'idly.**—*ns.* **insip'idness, insipid'ity.** [L.L. *insipidus—L. in-*, not, *sapidus*, well-tasted—*sapĕre*, to taste.]

insipience, *in-sip'i-əns*, *n.* lack of wisdom.—*adj.* **insip'ient.** [L. *insipientia—in-*, not, *sapiēns*, wise.]

insist, *in-sist'*, *v.i.* to dwell emphatically in discourse : to persist in pressing : (*Milt.*) to persevere.—*v.t.* to maintain persistently.—*n.* **insist'ence.**—*adj.* **insist'ent**, urgent : prominent : (of bird's hindtoe) touching the ground with the tip only.—*adv.* **insist'ently.**—*n.* **insist'ure**, persistence : (*Shak.*) prob., uniformity of motion. [L. *insistĕre*, *in*, upon, *sistĕre*, to stand.]

insnare. See **ensnare.**

insobriety, *in-sō-brī'ə-ti*, *n.* want of sobriety.

insociable, *in-sō'shə-bl*, *adj.* unsociable : (*obs.*) incompatible.—*n.* **insociabil'ity.**

insolate, *in'sō-lāt*, *in-sō'lāt*, *v.t.* to expose to the sun's rays.—*n.* **insolā'tion**, exposure to the sun's rays : radiation received from the sun : injury caused by the sun. [L. *insolāre*, *-ātum—in*, in, *sōl*, the sun.]

insole, *in'sōl*, *n.* the inner sole of a boot or shoe—opp. to *outsole* : a sole of some material placed inside a shoe for warmth or dryness.

insolent, *in'səl-ənt*, *adj.* overbearing : insulting : rude.—*n.* **in'solence.**—*adv.* **in'solently.** [L. *insolēns*, *-ēntis—in-*, not, *solēns*, pa.p. of *solēre*, to be wont.]

insolidity, *in-so-lid'i-ti*, *n.* want of solidity.

insoluble, *in-sol'ū-bl*, *adj.* not capable of being dissolved : not to be solved or explained.—*v.t.* **insol'ubilise**, to render insoluble (*-ser'i-ti*).—*ns.* **insolubil'ity**, **insol'ubleness.**

insolvable, *in-solv'ə-bl*, *adj.* not solvable.

insolvent, *in-solv'ənt*, *adj.* not able to pay one's debts : bankrupt : pertaining to insolvent persons. —*n.* one unable to pay his debts.—*n.* **insolv'ency**, bankruptcy.

insomnia, *in-som'ni-ä*, *n.* sleeplessness : prolonged inability to sleep.—*adj.* **insom'nious.**—*n.* **insom'-nolence.** [L. *insomnis*, sleepless.]

insomuch, *in-sō-much'*, *adv.* to such a degree : inasmuch : so.

insooth, *in-sōōth'*, *adv.* (*arch.*) in sooth, indeed.

insouciant, *in-sōō'si-ənt*, *an*-*sōō-sē-än²*, *adj.* indifferent : unconcerned.—*n.* **insouciance** (*an²-sōō-sē-än²s*, *in-sōō'si-əns*). [Fr.,—*in-*, not, *souciant*, pr.p. of *soucier—L. sollicitāre*, to disturb.]

inspan, *in-span'*, *in'span*, *v.t.* to yoke to a vehicle. —*v.i.* to prepare to depart :—*pr.p.* **inspan'ing** ; *pa.t.* and *pa.p.* **inspanned'.** [Du. *inspannen*, to yoke—*in*, in, *spannen*, to tie.]

inspect, *in-spekt'*, *v.t.* to look into : to examine : to look at narrowly, officially, or ceremonially.—*n.* **in'spect**, (*obs.*) inspection.—*adv.* **inspect'ingly.** —*n.* **inspec'tion**, the act of inspecting or looking into: careful or official examination.—*adjs.* **inspec′tional**; **inspec′tive**.—*ns.* **inspec′tor**, one who inspects: an examining officer: a police officer ranking below a superintendent; **inspec′torate**, a district under charge of an inspector: the office of inspector: a body of inspectors.—*adj.* **inspecto′rial**.—*ns.* **inspec′torship**, the office of inspector; **inspec′tress**, a female inspector. [L. *inspectāre*, freq. of *inspicĕre*, *inspectum*—*in*, into, *specĕre*, to look.]

insphere, inspheare. See **ensphere.**

inspire, *in-spīr′*, *v.t.* to breathe or blow into: to breathe or blow in: to draw or inhale into the lungs: to infuse as if by breathing: to infuse into the mind: to instruct by divine influence: to instruct or affect with a superior influence.—*v.i.* to draw in the breath: (*obs.*; *Spens.* **inspyre**) to blow.—*adj.* **inspir′able**, able to be inhaled.—*n.* **inspirā′tion** (*in-spər-*, *-spīr-*, *-spīr-*), the act of inspiring or breathing in: a breath: instruction, dictation, or stimulation of a divinity, genius, an idea or passion: unacknowledged prompting by authorities: an inspired condition: an inspired thought.—*adjs.* **inspirā′tional**; **inspirative** (*in-spīr′ə-tiv*, *in′spīr-ā-tiv*), tending to inspire.—*n.* **inspirator** (*in′spir-ā-tər*), apparatus for injecting or drawing in vapour, liquid, &c.—*adj.* **inspiratory** (*in-spīr′ə-tar-i*, or *in-spīr′*, or *in′spīr-*), belonging to or aiding inspiration or inhalation.—*n.* **inspirā′tionist**, one who maintains the direct inspiration of the Scriptures.—*adj.* **inspired′**, actuated or directed by divine influence: influenced by elevated feeling: prompted by superior, but not openly declared, knowledge or authority: actually authoritative.—*n.* **inspir′er.**—*adv.* **inspir′ingly.** [L. *inspīrāre*—*in*, into, *spīrāre*, to breathe.]

inspirit, *in-spir′it*, *v.t.* to infuse spirit into.

inspissate, *in-spis′āt*, *v.t.* to thicken, condense.—*n.* **inspissā′tion.** [L. *in*, in, *spissāre*—*spissus*, thick.]

instability, *in-stə-bil′i-ti*, *n.* want of steadiness.—*adj.* **instā′ble**, unstable.

install (also **instal**), *in-stawl′*, *v.t.* to place in a stall or official seat: to place in an office or order: to invest with any charge or office with the customary ceremonies: to set up and put in use:—*pr.p.* **install′ing**; *pa.t.* and *pa.p.* **installed′.**—*ns.* **installā′tion**, the act of installing or placing in an office with ceremonies: a placing in position for use: the complete apparatus for electric lighting, or the like; **instal′ment** (sometimes **install′ment**), (*Shak.*) a knight's stall: (*arch.*) installation: one of a series of partial payments: a portion supplied or completed at one time, as of a serial story. [L.L. *installāre*—*in*, in, *stallum*, a stall—O.H.G. *stal* (Ger. *stall*, Eng. **stall**).]

instance, *in′stəns*, *n.* quality of being urgent: solicitation: occurrence: occasion: example: (*Shak.*) evidence, proof: (*law*) process, suit.—*v.t.* to mention as an example.—*n.* **in′stancy**, insistency: urgency: imminence.—*adj.* **in′stant**, pressing, urgent: immediate: without delay: present, current, as the passing month.—*n.* the present moment of time: any moment or point of time.—*n.* **instantaneity** (*in-stant-ə-nē′i-ti*).—*adj.* **instantaneous** (*in-stənt-ā′ni-əs*), done in an instant: momentary: occurring or acting at once or very quickly: for the instant.—*adv.* **instantān′eously.**—*n.* **instantān′eousness.**—*adv.* **instanter** (*in-stan′ter*; L.), immediately.—*adj.* **instantial** (*in-stan′shl*; *rare*).—*adv.* **in′stantly**, on the instant or moment: immediately: (*Shak.*) at the same time: (*B.*) importunately, zealously.—**at the instance of,** at the motion or sollicitation of; **for instance,** as an example. [L. *instāns*, *instantis*, pr.p. of *instāre*, to be near, press upon, urge—*in*, upon, *stāre*, to stand.]

instar, *in-stär′*, *v.t.* to adorn with stars: to set as a star.

instar, *in′stär*, *n.* the form of an insect between moult and moult. [L. *instar*, image.]

instate, *in-stāt′*, *v.t.* to put in possession: to install. [Pfx. *in-* and state.]

instauration, *in-stawr-ā′shən*, *n.* restoration: renewal. [L. *instaurātiō*, *-ōnis*.]

instead, *in-sted′*, *adv.* in the stead, place, or room

(of): as an alternative or substitute. [in and stead.]

instep, *in′step*, *n.* the prominent upper part of the human foot near its junction with the leg: the corresponding part of a shoe, stocking, &c.: in horses, the hind-leg from the ham to the pastern joint.—*n.* **in′step-rais′er**, an arched device to support the instep and counteract a tendency to flat feet. [Origin obscure.]

instigate, *in′sti-gāt*, *v.t.* to urge on: to set on: to foment.—*ns.* **instigā′tion**, the act of inciting: impulse, esp. to evil; **in′stigātor**, an inciter, generally in a bad sense. [L. *instīgāre*, *-ātum*.]

instil, *in-stil′*, *v.t.* to drop in: to infuse slowly into the mind:—*pr.p.* **instil′ling**; *pa.p.* **instilled′.**—Also **instill.**—*ns.* **instillā′tion**, **instil′ment**, the act of instilling or pouring in by drops: the act of infusing slowly into the mind: that which is instilled or infused. [L. *instillāre*—*in*, in, *stillāre*, to drop.]

instinct, *in′stingkt*, formerly *in-stingkt′*, *n.* impulse: an involuntary prompting to action: intuition: the mental aspect of those actions which take rank between unconscious reflex activities and intelligent conduct: the natural impulse by which animals are guided apparently independently of reason or experience.—*adj.* (*in-stingkt′*) instigated or incited: moved: animated: charged: imbued.—*adj.* **instinct′ive**, prompted by instinct: involuntary: acting according to or determined by natural impulse.—*adv.* **instinc′tively.**—*n.* **instinctiv′ity** (*rare*). — *adj.* **instinctual**, pertaining to instincts. [L. *instinctus*—*instinguĕre*, instigate.]

institorial, *in-sti-tō′ri-əl*, *adj.* (*law*) pertaining to an agent or factor. [L. *institōrius*—*institor*, an agent, broker.]

institute, *in′sti-tūt*, *v.t.* to set up: to set on foot: (*obs.*) to order: to establish: to appoint: to educate.—*n.* anything instituted or formally established: (*obs.*) the act of instituting: established law: precept or principle: an institution: a literary and philosophical society or organisation for education, research, &c.: the building in which such an organisation is housed: (*U.S.*) a temporary school, esp. for teachers: (*Scots law*) the person first nominated as heir (distinguished from the *substitutes* who follow, failing the institute): (*pl.*) a book of precepts, principles, or rules.—*n.* **institution** (*-tū′shən*), the act of instituting or establishing: that which is instituted or established: foundation: established order: enactment: a society or organisation established for some object, esp. cultural, charitable, or beneficent, or the building housing it: a custom or usage, esp. one familiar or characteristic: that which institutes or instructs: a system of principles or rules: the appointment of an heir: the act by which a bishop commits a cure of souls to a priest.—*adj.* **institū′tional**, pertaining to institution, institutions, or institutes: of the nature of an institution: depending on or originating in institution: characterised by the possession of institutions.—*v.t.* **institū′tionalise**, to make an institution of.—*ns.* **institū′tionalism**, the system or characteristics of institutions or institution life: belief in the nature of institutions; **institū′tionalist**, a writer on institutes: one who sets a high value on institutionalism. — *adj.* **institū′tionary**, institutional: (*obs.*) educational.—*n.* **in′stitūtist**, a writer of institutes or elementary rules.—*adj.* **in′stitutive**, able or tending to establish: depending on an institution.—*n.* **in′stitūtor**, one who institutes: an instructor.—**institutional church,** one that is active through social organisations. [L. *instituĕre*, *-ūtum*—*in*, in, *statuĕre*, to cause to stand—*stāre*, to stand.]

instreaming, *in′strēm-ing*, *n.* an influx.—Also *adj.*

instruct, *in-strukt′*, *v.t.* (*obs.*) to prepare: to inform: to teach: to direct: to order or command.—*adj.* (*Milt.*) instructed.—*adj.* **instruct′ible**, able to be instructed.—*n.* **instruc′tion**, the art of instructing or teaching: information: direction: command: (*pl.*) special directions, commands.—*adjs.* **instruc′tional**, relating to instruction: educational; **instruc′tive**, affording instruction: conveying

knowledge.—*adv.* **instruc′tively.**—*ns.* **instruc′-tiveness**; **instruc′tor,** a teacher, esp. (*U.S.*) a college lecturer:—*fem.* **instruc′tress.** [L. *īn-struĕre, īnstructum—in,* in, *struĕre,* to pile up.]
instrument, *in′stroo-mənt, n.* a tool or utensil: a contrivance for producing musical sounds: a writing containing a contract: a formal record: one who, or that which, is made a means.—*v.t.* (*-ment′*) to score for instruments.—*adj.* **instrumental** (*-ment′l*), acting as an instrument or means: serving to promote an object: helpful: of, for, belonging to, or produced by musical instruments: (*gram.*) serving to indicate the instrument or means.—*n.* the instrumental case.—*ns.* **instrument′alism,** a form of pragmatism associated with John Dewey; **instrument′alist,** one who plays on a musical instrument; **instrumentality** (*-ment-al′i-ti*), agency.—*adv.* **instrument′-ally.**—*n.* **instrumenta′tion,** (*mus.*) the arrangement of a composition for performance by different instruments. [L. *īnstrūmentum — īnstruĕre,* to instruct.]
insubjection, *in-səb-jek′shən, n.* want of subjection.
insubordinate, *in-səb-ord′(i-)nit, adj.* not subordinate or submissive.—*n.* **insubordina′tion.**
insubstantial, *in-səb-stan′shəl, adj.* (*Shak.*) not substantial: not real. — *n.* **insubstantiality** (*-shi-al′i-ti*).
insucken, *in′suk-n, adj.* in Scots law, pertaining to a district astricted to a certain mill. [in, sucken.]
insufferable, *in-suf′ər-ə-bl, adj.* that cannot be endured: detestable.—*adv.* **insuff′erably.**
insufficient, *in-səf-ish′ənt, adj.* inadequate: (*obs.*) lacking.—*ns.* **insuffic′ience** (*rare*), **insuffic′iency.** —*adv.* **insuffic′iently.**
insufflate, *in′suf-lāt* (or *-suf′*), *v.t.* to blow in: to breathe on.—*ns.* **insufflā′tion,** the act of breathing on anything, esp. in baptism or exorcism: the act of blowing air, powder, &c., into a cavity or on a surface; **in′sufflātor,** an instrument for insufflation. [L. *īnsufflāre—in,* in, on, *sufflāre,* to blow upon.]
insula, *in′sū-lä* (L. *ēn′soo-lä*), *n.* (*Rom. ant.*) a block of buildings: an apartment house: (*anat.*) Reil's island, a small lobe of the cerebrum hidden in the fissure of Sylvius.—*ns.* **in′sūlance,** resistance between electric conductors separated by insulating material; **in′sūlant,** insulating material. —*adj.* **in′sūlar,** belonging to an island: surrounded by water: standing or situated alone: narrow, prejudiced.—*ns.* **in′sūlarism,** **insularity** (*-lar′i-ti*), the state of being insular.—*adv.* **in′sūlarly.**—*v.t.* **in′sūlate,** to place in a detached situation: to cut off from connexion or communication: (*elect.*) to separate, esp. from the earth, by a non-conductor.—*ns.* **insūlā′tion;** **insūlā′tor,** one who, or that which, insulates: a non-conductor of electricity: a contrivance for insulating a conductor: a stand for a piano leg; **in′sūlin,** an extract got from the islands or islets of Langerhans in the pancreas of animals, used for treating diabetes and also mental diseases. [L. *īnsula,* island.]
insulse, *in-suls′, adj.* insipid: stupid.—*n.* **insul′-sity,** (*Milt.*) stupidity. [L. *īnsulsus—in-,* not, *salĕre,* to salt.]
insult, *in-sult′, v.t.* (*obs.*) to assail: to triumph insolently or exultantly over: to treat with indignity or contempt: to affront.—*v.i.* (*obs.*) to make an attack: to behave with boastful insolence.—*n.* **in′sult,** abuse: affront: contumely.—*adjs.* **insult′able,** capable of being insulted; **insult′ant,** (*rare*) insulting.—*n.* **insult′er.**—*adj.* **insult′ing.**—*adv.* **insult′ingly.**—*n.* **insult′ment,** (*Shak.*) insult. [L. *īnsultāre—īnsilīre,* to spring at—*in,* upon, *salīre,* to leap.]
insuperable, *in-s(y)ōō′pər-ə-bl, adj.* that cannot be overcome or surmounted.—*n.* **insuperabil′ity.**— *adv.* **insu′perably.** [L. *īnsuperābilis—in-,* not, *superāre,* to pass over—*super,* above.]
insupportable, *in-səp-ōrt′ə-bl, adj.* unbearable: insufferable (*Spens.*; *-sup′*) irresistible.—*n.* **in′support′ableness.**—*adv.* **insupport′ably.**
insuppressible, *in-sə-pres′i-bl, adj.* not to be suppressed or concealed.—*adj.* **insuppress′ive,** (*Shak.*) insuppressible.

insure, *in-shōōr′, v.t.* to make sure or secure: to guarantee: to make an arrangement for the payment of a sum of money in the event of loss or injury to: to make such an arrangement for the payment of.—*v.i.* to effect or undertake insurance. —*adj.* **insur′able,** that may be insured.—*ns.* **insur′ance,** the act or system of insuring: a contract of insurance, a policy: the premium paid for insuring: the sum to be received; **insur′-ancer** (*obs.*); **insur′er,** either party to a contract of insurance. [O.Fr. *enseurer—en,* and *seur,* sure; see ensure, sure.]
insurgent, *in-sur′jənt, adj.* rising: rising in revolt. —*n.* one who rises in opposition to established authority: a rebel.—*ns.* **insur′gence, insur′-gency,** a rising up or against: rebellion: insurrection. [L. *īnsurgēns, -entis—in,* upon, *surgĕre,* to rise.]
insurmountable, *in-sər-mownt′ə-bl, adj.* not surmountable: that cannot be overcome.—*n.* **insurmountabil′ity.**—*adv.* **insurmount′ably.**
insurrection, *in-sər-ek′shən, n.* a rising or revolt.— *adjs.* **insurrec′tional, insurrec′tionary.**—*ns.* **insurrec′tionary, insurrec′tionist.** [L. *īnsurrēctiō, -ōnis—īnsurgĕre;* see insurgent.]
insusceptible, *in-səs-ep′ti-bl, adj.* not susceptible.— Also **insuscep′tive.**—*n.* **insusceptibil′ity.**
inswathe. Same as enswathe.
inswing, *in′swing, n.* an inward swing or swerve.— *n.* **inswinger** (*in′swing-ər* ; *cricket*), a ball bowled so as to swerve to leg.
intact, *in-takt′, adj.* untouched: unimpaired: whole: undiminished.—*n.* **intact′ness.** [L. *in-tactus—in-,* not, *tangĕre, tactum,* to touch.]
intaglio, *in-tāl′yō, n.* a figure cut into any substance: a stone or gem in which the design is hollowed out —opp. to cameo.—Also *v.t.*—*adj.* **intagl′iated,** incised, engraved. (See cavo-rilievo.) [It.,—*in,* into, *tagliare,* to cut—L. *tālea,* a cutting, layer.]
intake, *in′tāk, n.* that which is taken in: a tract of land enclosed: an airway in a mine: a place where water is taken in: a narrowing in a pipe: decrease in width as in a stocking-leg by knitting two stitches together: the place where contraction occurs: the setting back of a wall-face: (*prov.*) a cheat or cheater. [in, take.]
intangible, *in-tan′ji-bl, adj.* not tangible or perceptible to touch: insubstantial: eluding the grasp of the mind.—*ns.* **intan′gibleness, intangibil′ity.**—*adv.* **intan′gibly.** [See intact.]
intarsia, *in-tär′si-ä, intarsio, -ō, n.* and *adj.* tarsia. [It. *intarsio.*]
integer, *in′ti-jər, n.* a whole: (*arith.*) a whole number, as opposed to a fraction.—*adjs.* **in′-tegrable** (*-grə-bl*), capable of being integrated; **in′tegral** (*-grəl*), entire or whole: not fractional: not involving fractions: relating to integrals: unimpaired: intrinsic, belonging as a part to the whole.—*n.* a whole: the value of a function of a variable whose differential coefficient is known.—*adv.* **in′tegrally.**—*n.* **in′tegrand,** an expression to be integrated.—*adj.* **in′tegrant,** making part of a whole: necessary to form an integer or an entire thing.—*v.t.* **in′tegrate,** to make up as a whole: to make entire: to find the integral of: to find the total value of.—*v.i.* to become integral: to perform integration.—*adj.* made up of parts: complete: whole.—*n.* **integrā′tion,** the act of integrating: tending to integrate.—*ns.* **in′-tegrātor,** one who integrates: an instrument for finding the results of integrations; **integrity** (*in-teg′ri-ti*), entireness, wholeness: the unimpaired state of anything: uprightness: honesty: purity.—**integral calculus** (see calculus); **integral function,** (*alg.*) a function which does not include the operation of division in any of its terms. [L. *integer—in-,* not, root of *tangĕre,* to touch.]
integument, *in-teg′ū-mənt, n.* an external covering: (*bot.*) either of the two coats of an ovule.—*adj.* **integumentary** (*-ment′ər-i*). [L. *integumentum— in,* upon, *tegĕre,* to cover.]
intellect, *in′ti-lekt, n.* the mind, in reference to its rational powers: the thinking principle: (*Shak.*) meaning: (in *pl.*; *arch.*) mental powers.—*adj.* **in′-**

tellected, (*Cowper*) endowed with intellect.—*n.* intellec′tion, the act of understanding: (*phil.*) apprehension or perception.—*adjs.* intellec′tive, able to understand: produced or perceived by the understanding; intellectual (-*lek′tū-əl*), of or relating to the intellect: perceived or performed by the intellect: having the power of understanding: well endowed with intellect.—*n.* a person of superior intellect or enlightenment (often used to suggest doubt as to practical sagacity): (*obs.*) intellect: (in *pl.*; *arch.*) mental powers: (in *pl.*; *obs.*) things of the intellect.—*v.t.* intellect′ualise, to reason intellectually: to endow with intellect: to give an intellectual character to.—*ns.* intellect′ualism, the doctrine that derives all knowledge from pure reason: the culture (esp. exclusive or unbalanced) of the intellect; intellect′ualist; intellectuality (-*al′i-ti*), intellectual power.—*adv.* intellect′ually. [L. *intellēctus*, -*ūs*—*intelligěre*, *intellēctum*, to understand—*inter*, between, *legěre*, to choose.]

intelligent, *in-tel′i-jənt*, *adj.* having intellect: endowed with the faculty of reason: alert, bright, quick of mind: well-informed: cognisant: bringing intelligence: (*Shak.*) communicative.—*ns.* intell′igence, intellectual skill or knowledge: mental brightness: information communicated: news: a footing or mutual understanding: a spiritual being; intell′igencer, a spy: a newsmonger: an avenue of intelligence: a newspaper.—*adj.* intelligential (-*jen′shl*), pertaining to the intelligence: consisting of spiritual being.—*adv.* intell′igently.—*adj.* intell′igible, that may be understood: clear: (*phil.*) capable of being apprehended by the understanding only.—*ns.* intell′igibleness, intelligibil′ity.—*adv.* intell′igibly.—intelligence (department), a department of state or armed service for securing information; intelligence quotient, the ratio, commonly expressed as a percentage, of a person's mental age to his actual age, the mental age being the age for which he scores, on the average, 100% when tested in a specified manner; intelligence test, a test by questions and tasks to determine a person's mental capacity, or the age at which his capacity would be normal. [L. *intelligēns*, -*entis*, pr.p. of *intelligěre*.]

intelligentsia, intelligentzia, *in-tel-i-gent′si-ä*, or -*jent′*, *n.* the intellectual or cultured classes, originally esp. in Russia. [Russ.,—L. *intelligentia*.]

intemperance, *in-tem′pər-əns*, *n.* want of due restraint: excess of any kind: habitual over-indulgence in intoxicating liquor.—*n.* intem′perant, one who is intemperate.—*adj.* intem′perate, indulging to excess any appetite or passion: given to an immoderate use of intoxicating liquor: passionate: exceeding the usual degree: immoderate.—*adv.* intem′perately.—*n.* intem′perateness.

intempestive, *in-tem-pest′iv*, *adj.* unseasonable: untimely.—*n.* intempestiv′ity. [L. *intempestivus* —*in-*, not, *tempestas*, season—*tempus*, time.]

intenable, *in-ten′ə-bl*, *adj.* untenable.

intend, *in-tend′*, *v.t.* (*Spens.*) to stretch forth: (*Milt.*) to expand: (*obs.*) to strain: (*obs.*) to intensify: (*Shak.*) to direct, turn: to fix the mind upon: to design: to purpose: to mean: (*Spens.*) to designate: to superintend.—*v.i.* (*Shak.*) to direct one's course: to purpose a journey: (*obs.*) to be in attendance: (*obs.*) to attend, listen.— *ns.* intend′ancy, the office, term of office, or sphere of an intendant: a body of intendants; intend′ant, an officer who superintends some public business, a title of many public officers in France and other countries. — *adj.* intend′ed, purposed: (*obs.*) stretched. — *n.* (*coll.*) betrothed.—*adv.* intend′edly, with intention or design.—*ns.* intend′iment, (*Spens.*) attentive consideration, understanding, meaning; intend′ment (*Shak.*), intention, design: meaning. [O.Fr. *entendre*—L. *intenděre*, *intentum* and *intēnsum*—*in*, towards, *tenděre*, to stretch.]

intenerate, *in-ten′ər-āt*, *v.t.* to make tender: to soften.—*n.* intenerā′tion. [L. *in*, in, to, *tener*, tender.]

intenible, *in-ten′i-bl*, *adj.* (*Shak.*) irretentive. [L. *in-*, not, *tenēre*, to hold.]

intense, *in-tens′*, *adj.* strained: concentrated: dense: extreme in degree: earnestly or deeply emotional, or affecting such a manner.—*v.t.* intens′ate, (*Carlyle*) to intensify.—*adv.* intense′ly. —*ns.* and *adjs.* intens′ative, intens′itive, intensive. —*ns.* intense′ness, intens′ity; intensificā′tion, the act of intensifying; intens′ifier.—*v.t.* intens′ify, to make more intense.—*v.i.* to become intense:—*pr.p.* intens′ifying; *pa.t.* and *pa.p.* intens′ified.—*n.* intension (-*ten′shən*), straining: intentness: intensity: intensification: (*logic*) the sum of the qualities implied by a general name.— *adj.* intens′ive, concentrated, intense: strained: unremitting: relating to intensity or to intension: intensifying: intensified: (*gram.*) giving force or emphasis.—*n.* an intensive word.—*adv.* intens′-ively.—*n.* intens′iveness.—intensive culture, getting the very most out of the soil of a limited area. [See intend.]

intent, *in-tent′*, *adj.* having the mind bent: fixed with close attention: diligently applied.—*n.* the thing aimed at or intended: purpose, intention, design: (*obs.*) intentness: (*obs.*) meaning.—*n.* intention (*in-ten′shən*), (*obs.*) application or direction of the mind: design: purpose: application of thought to an object: a concept: (*med.*) a plan of treatment: (in *pl.*; *coll.*) purpose with respect to marriage.—*adj.* inten′tional, with intention: intended: designed.—*adv.* inten′tionally, with intention: on purpose.—*adjs.* inten′tioned, having such and such intention; intent′ive, (*Bacon*) attentive.—*adv.* intent′ly, earnestly: diligently.—*n.* intent′ness.—healing by first intention, healing of a wound by immediate union, without granulation; by second intention, with granulation; to all intents and purposes, in every important respect: virtually; well- (or ill-) intentioned, having good (or ill) designs: meaning well (or ill). [See intend.]

inter, *in-ter′*, *v.t.* to bury:—*pr.p.* interr′ing; *pa.t.* and *pa.p.* interred′.—*n.* inter′ment. [Fr. *enterrer* —L.L. *interrāre*—L. *in*, into, *terra*, the earth.]

interact, *in′tər-akt*, *n.* an interlude: an entr′acte: the interval between acts.—*v.i.* interact′, to act on one another.—*ns.* interaction (-*ak′shən*), mutual action; interac′tionism, the theory that mind and body act on each other (distinguished from *psychophysical parallelism* and *epiphenomenalism*); interac′tionist.—*adj.* interac′tive. [L. *inter*, between, act.]

interallied, *in-tər-al′īd*, or -*īd′*, *adj.* between or among allies.

interambulacrum, *in-tər-am-bū-lā′krəm*, *n.* in sea-urchins, a radial band between two ambulacra:— *pl.* interambulā′cra.—*adj.* interambulā′cral.

inter-arts, *in′tər-ärts′*, *adj.* belonging to the examination between matriculation and B.A. of London University. [For intermediate arts.]

interbedded, *in-tər-bed′id*, *adj.* interstratified.—*n.* interbedd′ing.

interbreed, *in-tər-brēd′*, *v.t.* and *v.i.* to breed together, esp. of different races:—*pa.t.* and *pa.p.* interbred′.—*n.* interbreed′ing.

intercalate, *in-tər′ka-lāt*, *v.t.* to insert between others, as a day in a calendar: to interpolate.— *adjs.* inter′calar (-*lər*; *obs.*), inter′calary, inserted between others.—*n.* intercalā′tion.—*adj.* inter′calative (-*lā-tiv*, -*lə-tiv*). [L. *intercalāre*, -*ātum*—*inter*, between, *calāre*, to proclaim; see calends.]

intercede, *in-tər-sēd′*, *v.i.* to act as peacemaker between two: to plead for one.—*adj.* intercēd′ent. —*n.* intercēd′er. [L. *intercēděre*, -*cessum*—*inter*, between, *cēděre*, to go.]

intercellular, *in-tər-sel′ū-lər*, *adj.* placed among cells.

intercensal, *in-tər-sen′səl*, *adj.* between censuses. [Irreg., formed from L. *inter* and census.]

intercept, *in-tər-sept′*, *v.t.* to stop and seize in passage: to cut off: (*math.*) to take or comprehend between.—*ns.* in′tercept, (*math.*) that part of a line that is intercepted; intercep′ter, intercep′tor; intercep′tion.—*adj.* intercep′tive. [L. *intercipěre*, -*ceptum*—*inter*, between, *capěre*, to seize.]

Intercession, *in-tər-sesh'ən, n.* act of interceding or pleading for another.—*adj.* **intercess'ional.**—*n.* **intercessor** (*-ses'ər*), one who intercedes : a bishop who acts during a vacancy in a see.—*adjs.* **intercesso'rial, intercess'ory,** interceding. — **intercession of saints,** prayer offered in behalf of Christians on earth by saints. [See **intercede.**]

interchain, *in-tər-chān', v.t.* to chain together.

interchange, *in-tər-chānj', v.t.* to give and take mutually : to exchange.—*v.i.* to succeed alternately. —*n.* **in'terchange,** mutual exchange: alternate succession.—*adj.* **interchange'able,** that may be interchanged : (*obs.*) following each other in alternate succession.—*ns.* **interchange'ableness, interchangeabil'ity.**—*adv.* **interchange'ably.**—*ns.* **interchange'ment,** (*Shak.*) exchange, mutual transfer ; **interchang'er.**

interchapter, *in'tər-chap-tər, n.* an intercalary chapter in a book, not numbered in the general sequence.

intercipient, *in-tər-sip'i-ənt, adj.* intercepting.—*n.* the person or thing that intercepts. [L. *intercipiēns, -entis,* pr.p. of *intercipĕre* ; see **intercept.**]

intercity, *in-tər-sit'i, adj.* between cities.

interclavicular, *in-tər-klə-vik'ū-lər, adj.* situated between clavicles.

interclude, *in-tər-klōōd', v.t.* to block : to enclose : to cut off.—*n.* **interclusion** (*-klōō'zhən*). [L. *interclūdĕre*—*inter,* between, *claudĕre,* to shut.]

intercollegiate, *in-tər-kə-lē'ji-āt, -ət, adj.* between colleges.

intercolline, *in-tər-kol'īn, adj.* lying between hills.

intercolonial, *in-tər-kə-lō'ni-əl, adj.* between colonies.—*adv.* **intercolo'nially.**

intercolumniation, *in-tər-kə-lum-ni-ā'shən, n.* (*archit.*) spacing of, or distance between, columns, in terms of the lower diameter.—*adj.* **inter-colum'nar,** placed between columns.

intercom, *in-tər-kom', n.* a telephone system within an aeroplane, tank, &c. [*Internal communication.*]

intercommune, *in-tər-kə-mūn', v.i.* to commune mutually or together : to hold intercourse, have dealings.—*adj.* **intercommun'icable.**—*v.t.* and *v.i.* **intercommun'icate,** to communicate mutually or together : to have free passage from one to another.—*ns.* **intercommunica'tion** ; **intercommun'ion,** mutual communion or relation, esp. between churches ; **intercommun'ity,** state of being or having in common.—**letters of intercommuning,** an ancient writ issued by the Scottish Privy Council warning persons not to harbour or have any dealings with those named, on pain of being held accessory.

interconnect, *in-tər-kə-nekt', v.t.* to connect mutually and intimately, or by a multitude of ways.—*n.* **interconnex'ion, interconnec'tion.**

intercontinental, *in-tər-kon-ti-nen'təl, adj.* between or connecting different continents.

interconvertible, *in-tər-kən-vərt'i-bl, adj.* mutually convertible : interchangeable : exactly equivalent.

intercostal, *in-tər-kost'əl, adj.* between the ribs or the leaf-veins. [L. *inter,* between, *costa,* a rib.]

intercourse, *in'tər-kōrs, n.* connexion by dealings : communication : commerce : communion : coition. [O.Fr. *entrecours*—L. *intercursus,* a running between —*inter,* between, *currĕre, cursum,* to run.]

intercrop, *in-tər-krop', v.t.* and *v.i.* to grow or cultivate in alternate rows :—*pr.p.* **intercropp'ing** ; *pa.t.* and *pa.p.* **intercropped.**—*n.* **in'tercrop.**

intercross, *in-tər-kros', v.t.* and *v.i.* to cross and recross : to cross mutually : to place or lie crosswise : to interbreed.—*n.* **in'tercross,** a crossing of breeds.

intercurrent, *in-tər-kur'ənt, adj.* running between, intervening : supervening.—*n.* **intercurr'ence.** [L. *inter,* between, *currĕre,* to run.]

interdash, *in'tər-dash', v.t.* to intersperse with dashes.

interdeal, *in'tər-dēl, n.* (*arch.*) mutual dealings : intercourse : negotiations.—Also (*Spens.*) **enterdeale.**—*v.i.* **interdeal',** (*arch.*) to have mutual dealings.—*n.* **interdeal'er.**

interdenominational, *in-tər-di-nom-i-nāsh'(ə-)nl, adj.* common to, with participation of, various religious denominations : independent of denomination.

interdental, *in-tər-dent'əl, adj.* between the teeth : pronounced with the tip of the tongue between upper and lower teeth.—*adv.* **interdent'ally.**

interdepartmental, *in-tər-dē-pärt-ment'l, adj.* between departments.—*adv.* **interdepartment'ally.**

interdependence, *in-tər-di-pend'əns, n.* mutual dependence : dependence of parts one on another. —*adj.* **interdepend'ent.**

interdict, *in-tər-dikt', v.t.* to prohibit : to forbid : to forbid communion.—*n.* **in'terdict,** prohibition : a prohibitory decree : a prohibition of the pope restraining the clergy from performing divine service.—*n.* **interdic'tion** (*-shən*).—*adjs.* **interdic'-tive, interdic'tory,** containing interdiction : prohibitory. [L. *interdīcĕre, -dictum*—*inter,* between, *dīcĕre,* to say.]

interdigital, *in-tər-dij'i-tl, adj.* between digits.—*v.i.* **interdig'itate,** to interlock by finger-like processes.—*n.* **interdigitā'tion.**

interess, *in'tər-es,* or *-es', n.* (*obs.*) interest.—*v.t.* to interest :—*pa.p.* (*Shak.*) **interest'.** [A.Fr. *interesse*—L.L. *interesse,* compensation, interest—L. *interesse* (inf.), to concern.]

interest, *int'(ə-)rest, -rist, n.* advantage : premium paid for the use of money : any increase : concern : personal influence : a right to some advantage : claim to participate or be concerned in some way : stake : share : behalf : partisanship or side : the body of persons whose advantage is bound up in anything : regard to advantage : a state of engaged attention and curiosity : disposition towards such a state : power of arousing it : that in which one has interest or is interested.—*v.t.* to concern deeply : to cause to have an interest : to engage the attention of : to awaken concern in : to excite (in behalf of another).—*adj.* **in'terested,** having an interest or concern : affected or biased by personal considerations, self-interest, &c.—*adv.* **in'terestedly.** — *n.* **in'terestedness.** — *adj.* **in'teresting** (old-fashioned *-est'*), engaging or apt to engage the attention or regard : exciting emotion or passion.—*adv.* **in'terestingly.**—*n.* **in'teresting-ness.**—**compound interest,** interest added to the principal at the end of each period (usually a year) to form a new principal for next period ; **in an interesting condition,** a vulgar euphemism for pregnant ; **make interest for,** secure favour for. [From **interess,** influenced by O.Fr. *interest,* L. *interest,* it concerns, 3rd pers. sing. pres. ind. of *interesse*—*inter,* between, among, *esse,* to be.]

interface, *in'tər-fās, n.* a surface forming a common boundary : (*chem.*) the surface of separation between phases.—*adj.* **interfacial** (*-fā'shl*), between plane faces : of an interface.

interfascicular, *in-tər-fə-sik'ū-lər, adj.* between vascular bundles.

interfemoral, *in-tər-fem'ər-əl, adj.* situated between the thighs, connecting the hind limbs.

interfenestration, *in-tər-fen-is-trā'shən, n.* spacing of windows. [L. *inter,* between, *fenestra,* a window.]

interfere, *in-tər-fēr', v.i.* to strike the foot against the opposite leg when walking : to intervene : to come in the way : to interpose : to intermeddle : to act reciprocally—said of waves, rays of light, &c.—*n.* **interfēr'ence,** the act of interfering : the effect of combining similar rays of light, &c. : the spoiling of a wireless signal by others or by natural disturbances.—*adj.* **interferential** (*-fər-en'shl*).—*n.* **interfēr'er.**—*adv.* **interfēr'ingly.**—*ns.* **interfērom'eter,** an instrument for measuring wavelengths by observing interference fringes ; **interfērom'etry.**—**interference figure,** a figure observed when a crystal section is viewed between crossed nicols ; **interference fringes,** alternate light and dark bands seen when similar beams of light interfere. [O.Fr. *entreferir*—L. *inter,* between, *ferīre,* to strike.]

interflow, *in'tər-flō, n.* intermingling.—*v.i.* **inter-flow',** to flow into one another or between.

interfluent, *in-tər'floo-ənt, adj.* flowing between or together.—Also **inter'fluous.**—*n.* **inter'fluence.** [L. *interfluēns, -entis*—*inter,* between, *fluĕre,* to flow.]

Neutral vowels in unaccented syllables : *el'ə-mənt, in'fənt, ran'dəm*

interfold, *in-tər-fōld′*, *v.t.* to fold one into the other.

interfoliate, *in-tər-fō′li-āt*, *v.t.* to interleave. [L. *inter*, between, *folium*, a leaf.]

interfretted, *in-tər-fret′id*, *adj.* interlaced.

interfrontal, *in-tər-frun′tl*, *-fron′tl*, *adj.* between the frontal bones.

interfuse, *in-tər-fūz′*, *v.t.* to pour between or through: to permeate: to fuse together: to associate.—*n.* **interfusion** (*-fū′zhən*).

intergatory, *in-tər′gə-tə-ri*, *n.* (*arch.*; usu. in *pl.*) a shortened form of **interrogatory.**

interglacial, *in-tər-glā′sh(y)əl*, *adj.* (*geol.*) occurring between two periods of glacial action.

Interglossa, *in′tər-glos′ä*, *n.* an international language largely based on well-known Greek roots, devised by Lancelot Hogben (1943). [L. *inter*, between, Gr. *glōssa*, tongue.]

intergrade, *in-tər-grād′*, *v.i.* to merge in or shade off into something else through a series of intermediate forms.—*n.* **in′tergrade,** an intermediate grade.—*n.* **intergradation** (*-grə-dā′shən*).

intergrow, *in-tər-grō′*, *v.i.* to grow into or among each other.—*adj.* **intergrown′.**—*n.* **in′tergrowth.**

interim, *in′tər-im*, *n.* the time between or intervening: the meantime: in the history of the Reformation, the name given to certain edicts of the German emperor for the regulation of religious and ecclesiastical matters, till they could be decided by a general council—as the Augsburg Interim (1548), &c.—*adj.* temporary.—*adv.* (*rare*) meanwhile. [L.]

interior, *in-tē′ri-ər*, *adj.* inner: remote from the frontier or coast: inland: situated within or further in (sometimes with *to*).—*n.* the inside of anything: the inland part of a country: a picture of a scene within a house: home affairs of a country.—*n.* **interiority** (*-or′i-ti*).—*adv.* **inter′iorly.**—**interior grate,** an open grate with built-in boiler. [L., comp. of assumed *interus*, inward.]

interjacent, *in-tər-jā′sənt*, *adj.* lying between: intervening.—*n.* **interjā′cency.** [L. *interjacēns*, *-entis*, pr.p. of *interjacēre*—*inter*, between, *jacēre*, to lie.]

interjaculate, *in-tər-jak′ū-lāt*, *v.t.* to ejaculate in interruption.—*adj.* **interjac′ulatory** (*-ū-lə-tə-ri*). [L. *inter*, between, *jaculārī*, to throw.]

interject, *in-tər-jekt′*, *v.t.* to throw between: to interpose: to exclaim in interruption or parenthesis: to insert.—*v.i.* to throw oneself between.—*n.* **interjec′tion** (*-shən*), a throwing between: (*gram.*) a word thrown in to express emotion.—*adjs.* **interjec′tional, interjec′tionary, interjec′tural.**—*adv.* **interjec′tionally.** [L. *inter-(j)icĕre, interjectum—inter*, between, *jacĕre*, to throw.]

interjoin, *in-tər-join′*, *v.t.* (*Shak.*) to join together.

interknit, *in-tər-nit′*, *v.t.* to knit into each other.

interlace, *in-tər-lās′*, *v.t.* to lace, weave, or entangle together.—*v.i.* to intermix.—*n.* **interlace′ment.**—**interlaced scanning,** in television, the alternate scanning of an image in two sets of alternate lines.

interlard, *in-tər-lärd′*, *v.t.* to mix in, as fat with lean: to diversify by mixture.

interleave, *in-tər-lēv′*, *v.t.* to put a leaf between: to insert blank leaves in.—*n.* **in′terleaf,** a leaf so inserted :—*pl.* **in′terleaves.**

interline, *in-tər-līn′*, *v.t.* to write in alternate lines: to insert between lines: to write between the lines of.—*adj.* **interlinear** (*-lin′i-ər*), written between lines.—*ns.* **interlineation** (*-lin-i-ā′shən*), **inter-lin′ing.**

interlink, *in-tər-lingk′*, *v.t.* and *v.i.* to link together.

interlobular, *in-tər-lob′ū-lər*, *adj.* between lobes.

interlocation, *in-tər-lo-kā′shən*, *n.* a placing between.

interlock, *in-tər-lok′*, *v.t.* to lock or clasp together: to connect so as to work together.—*v.i.* to be locked together.—*n.* **in′terlock,** an interlocked condition: synchronising mechanism.

interlocution, *in-tər-lo-kū′shən*, *n.* conference: an intermediate decree before final decision.—*n.* **interlocutor** (*-lok′ū-tər*), one who speaks in dialogue: (*Scots law*) an intermediate decree before final decision.—*adj.* **interloc′utory.**—*ns.* **interloc′utress, interloc′utrice, interloc′utrix,** a female interlocutor. [L. *interlocūtiō*, *-ōnis—inter*, between, *loquī, locūtus*, to speak.]

interloper, *in′tər-lō-pər*, *n.* one who trades without licence: an intruder.—*v.i.* and *v.t.* **interlope′,** to intrude into any matter in which one has no fair concern. [Prob. L. *inter*, between, and *lope.*]

interlude, *in′tər-l(y)ōōd*, *n.* a short piece introduced between the acts of the mysteries and moralities, or between meals or courses: an early form of modern drama: a short piece of music played between the parts of a drama, opera, hymn, &c.: an interval.—*v.t.* and *v.i.* to interrupt, as an interlude.—*adj.* **interlu′dial.** [L. *inter*, between, *lūdus*, play.]

interlunar, *in-tər-l(y)ōō′nər*, *adj.* belonging to the moon's monthly time of invisibility.—Also **interlu′nary.**—*n.* **interlunā′tion** (*-lōō-*), the dark time between old moon and new. [L. *inter*, between, *lūna*, the moon.]

intermarry, *in-tər-mar′i*, *v.i.* to marry, esp. of different races or groups, or of near kin: to mingle by repeated marriages.—*n.* **intermarr′iage.**

intermaxilla, *in-tər-maks-il′ä*, *n.* the premaxilla.—*adj.* **intermax′illary** (or *-il′*), of the intermaxilla: between the maxillaries.—*n.* the intermaxilla. [L. *inter*, between, *maxilla*, a jawbone.]

intermeddle, *in-tər-med′l*, *v.i.* to meddle: to interfere improperly.—*n.* **intermedd′ler.**

intermediate, *in-tər-mē′dyit*, *-di-it*, *adj.* placed, occurring, or classified between others, extremes, limits, or stages: of igneous rocks, between acid and basic in composition: intervening.—*n.* that which is intermediate: (*chem.*) any compound manufactured from a primary that serves as a starting material for the synthesis of some other product.—*v.i.* (*-di-āt*) to interpose: to act between others.—*n.* **intermē′diacy** (*-ə-si*), state of being intermediate.—*adjs.* **intermē′dial** (*rare*), intermediate: intermediary; **intermē′diary,** acting between others: intermediate.—*n.* an intermediate agent.—*adv.* **intermē′diately.**—*ns.* **intermēdiā′tion,** act of intermediating; **intermē′diator.**—*adj.* **intermē′diatory** (*-ə-tə-ri*).—*n.* **intermē′dium,** an intervening agent or instrument.

interment, *in-tər′mənt*, *n.* burial. [**inter.**]

intermezzo, *in-tər-med′zō* (or *-met′sō*), *n.* a short dramatic or musical entertainment as entr'acte: (*mus.*) a short intermediate movement or the like :—*pl.* **intermez′zi** (*-zē*), or **-os.** [It.,—L. *intermedius.*]

intermigration, *in-tər-mī-grā′shən*, *n.* reciprocal migration.

interminable, *in-tər′min-ə-bl*, **interminate,** *in-tər′min-āt*, *-it*, *adjs.* without termination or limit: boundless: endless.—*n.* **inter′minableness.**—*adv.* **inter′minably.**—**interminate decimal,** a decimal fraction that runs to an infinity of places.

intermingle, *in-tər-ming′gl*, *v.t.* and *v.i.* to mingle or mix together.

intermit, *in-tər-mit′*, *v.t.* and *v.i.* to stop for a time.—*v.t.* (*obs.*) to interpose.—*n.* **intermission** (*-mish′en*), act of intermitting: interval: pause: respite: (*Shak.*) perh., occupation, recreation interposed, something to do.—*adj.* **intermissive** (*-mis′iv*), coming and going: intermittent.—*ns.* **intermitt′ence, intermitt′ency.**—*adj.* **intermitt′ent,** intermitting or ceasing at intervals.—*adv.* **intermitt′ingly.** [L. *intermittĕre*, *-missum—inter*, between, *mittĕre*, to cause to go.]

intermix, *in-tər-miks′*, *v.t.* and *v.i.* to mix together.—*n.* **intermix′ture,** a mass formed by mixture: something added and intermixed. [L. *inter-miscēre*, *-mixtum—inter*, among, *miscēre*, to mix.]

intermolecular, *in-tər-mol-ek′ū-lər*, *adj.* between molecules.

intermundane, *in-tər-mun′dān*, *adj.* between worlds.

intermure, *in-tər-mūr′*, *v.t.* (*obs.*) to wall in. [L. *inter*, within, *mūrus*, a wall.]

intern, interne, *in-tərn′*, *adj.* internal.—*n.* an inmate, as of a boarding-school: a resident assistant surgeon or physician in a hospital.—*v.t.* to send into the interior of a country: to confine within fixed bounds without permission to leave the district, camp, port, or like limits.—*ns.* **in-**

ternee', one so restricted; **intern'ment**, confinement of this kind. [Fr. *interne*—L. *internus*, inward.]

internal, *in-tər'nəl*, *adj.* in the interior : domestic as opposed to foreign : intrinsic : pertaining to the inner nature or feelings :—opp. to *external.*—*n.* (in *pl.*) inner parts.—*n.* **internality** (*-nal'i-ti*).—*adv.* **inter'nally.**—**internal-combustion engine**, an engine in which the fuel is burned within the working cylinder ; **internal evidence**, evidence afforded by the thing itself ; **internal student**, one who has studied at the university that examines him. [L. *internus*—*inter*, within.]

international, *in-tər-nash'ən-əl*, *adj.* between nations or their representatives : transcending national limits : extending to several nations : pertaining to the relations between nations.—*n.* **International**, a short-lived association formed in London in 1864 to unite the working classes of all countries in efforts for their economic emancipation : a second organisation of socialists of all countries formed in 1889 as a successor to the first International— also (Fr.) **Internationale** : a rival organisation (third International) operating from Moscow from 1919 to 1943 : (*coll.*) a game or contest between players chosen to represent different nations : a player who takes (or has taken) part in an international match.—*n.* **Internationale** (*an'-tər-nä-syō-näl'*), an international communist song, composed in France in 1871.—*v.t.* **interna'tionalise**, to make international : to put under international control.—*ns.* **interna'tionalism ; interna'tionalist**, one who favours the common interests, or action, of all nations : one who favours the principles of the International.—*adv.* **interna'tionally.** — **international concert pitch**, since 1939, 440 cycles per second at 20° C. for A in the treble clef ; **international law**, the law regulating the relations of states (**public international law**), or that determining what nation's law shall in any case govern the relations of private persons (**private international law**).

internecine, *in-tər-nē'sīn*, *adj.* deadly : murderous : (loosely) mutually destructive, intestine. — Also **interne'cive**. [L. *internecīnus*, *-īvus*—*internecāre* —*inter*, between (used intensively), *necāre*, to kill —*nex*, *necis*, murder.]

interneural, *in-tər-nū'rəl*, *adj.* (*anat.*) situated between the neural spines or spinous processes of successive vertebrae.

internode, *in'tər-nōd*, *n.* the space between two nodes. — *adjs.* **interno'dal**, **interno'dial**. [L. *internōdium*—*inter*, between, *nōdus*, a knot.]

internuncio, *in-tər-nun'shi-ō*, *n.* a messenger between two parties : the Pope's representative at minor courts.—*adj.* **internun'cial**. [It. *internunzio*, Sp. *internuncio*, L. *internuntius* — *inter*, between, *nuntius*, a messenger.]

interoceanic, *in-tər-ō-shi-an'ik*, *adj.* between oceans.

interocular, *in-tər-ok'ū-lər*, *adj.* between the eyes.

interorbital, *in-tər-or'bit-əl*, *adj.* between the orbits.

interosculation, *in-tər-os-kū-lā'shən*, *n.* interconnexion by, or as if by, osculation : possession of characters common to different groups : dovetailing into one another.—*adj.* **interos'culant.**— *v.t.* **interos'culate.**

interosseous, *in-tər-os'i-əs*, *adj.* situated between bones.—Also **inteross'eal**.

interpage, *in-tər-pāj'*, *v.t.* to insert on intermediate pages.

interparietal, *in-tər-pə-rī'ə-təl*, *adj.* situated between the right and left parietal bones of the skull.

interpellation, *in-tər-pel-ā'shən*, *n.* a question raised during the course of a debate : interruption : intercession : a summons : an earnest address.— *v.t.* **inter'pellate** (or *-pel'*), to question. [Fr.,— L. *interpellāre*, *-ātum*, to disturb by speaking— *inter*, between, *pellĕre*, to drive.]

interpenetrate, *in-tər-pen'i-trāt*, *v.t.* to penetrate thoroughly.—*v.t.* and *v.i.* to penetrate mutually.— *n.* **interpenetrā'tion.**—*adj.* **interpen'etrātive.**

interpetiolar, *in-tər-pet'i-ō-lər*, *adj.* (*bot.*) between the petioles.

interphase, *in'tər-fāz*, *n.* (*chem.*) an interface : (*biol.*) an interval between stages of mitosis.

interphone, *in'tər-fōn*, *n.* intercom. [Gr. *phonē*, voice.]

interpilaster, *in-tər-pil-as'tər*, *n.* (*archit.*) space between two pilasters.

interplanetary, *in-tər-plan'it-ə-ri*, *adj.* between planets.

interplant, *in-tər-plânt'*, *v.t.* to plant among another crop.

interplay, *in'tər-plā*, *n.* mutual action : interchange of action and reaction.

interplead, *in-tər-plēd'*, *v.i.* (*law*) to discuss adverse claims to property by bill of interpleader.—*n.* **interplead'er**, one who interpleads : a form of process in the English courts, by a bill in equity, intended to protect a defendant who claims no interest in the subject-matter of a suit, while at the same time he has reason to know that the plaintiff's title is disputed by some other claimant.

interpleural, *in-tər-plōō'rəl*, *adj.* situated between the right and left pleural cavities.

interpolar, *in-tər-pō'lər*, *adj.* between or connecting the poles.

interpolate, *in-tər'pō-lāt*, *-pə-lāt*, *v.t.* to insert unfairly, as a spurious word or passage in a book or manuscript, to foist in : to corrupt by spurious insertions : to insert, intercalate : (*math.*) to fill in as an intermediate term of a series : to interject. — *adj.* **inter'polable.**—*n.* **interpolā'tion.** — *adj.* **inter'polātive.** — *n.* **inter'polātor**. [L. *interpolāre*, *-ātum*—*inter*, between, *polīre*, to polish.]

interpone, *in-tər-pōn'*, *v.t.* (*Scots law*) to interpose. [L. *interpōnĕre*.]

interpose, *in-tər-pōz'*, *v.t.* to place between : to thrust in : to offer, as aid or services : to put in by way of interruption.—*v.i.* to come between : to mediate : to interfere.—*ns.* **interpos'al**; **interpos'er**; **interposition** (*in-tər-poz-ish'ən*), act of interposing : intervention : anything interposed. [Fr. *interposer*—L. *inter*, between, Fr. *poser*, to place ; see **pose**.]

interpret, *in-tər'prit*, *v.t.* to explain the meaning of, to elucidate, unfold, show the purport of : to translate into intelligible or familiar terms.—*v.i.* to practise interpretation.—*adj.* **inter'pretable**, capable of being explained.—*n.* **interpretā'tion**, act of interpreting : the sense given by an interpreter : (*obs.*) the power of explaining : the representation of a dramatic part, performance of a piece of music, or the like, according to one's conception of it.—*adj.* **inter'pretative** (*-āt-iv*, *-ət-iv*), inferred by or containing interpretation.— *adv.* **inter'pretatively.**—*ns.* **inter'preter**, one who translates between two parties : an expounder : a translator ; **inter'pretership ; inter'pretress**, a female interpreter (sometimes **inter'pretess**). [L. *interpretārī*, *-ātus*—*interpres*, *-etis*.]

interprovincial, *in-tər-prə-vin'shl*, *adj.* between provinces.

interpunction, *in-tər-pungk'shən*, *n.* the insertion of points in writing.—Also **interpunctuā'tion.**— *v.t.* **interpunc'tuate.**

interracial, *in-tər-rā'sh(y)əl*, *-shi-əl*, *adj.* between races.

interradial, *in-tər-rā'di-əl*, *adj.* between radii or rays : pertaining to an interradius.—*adv.* **interrā'dially.**—*n.* **interrā'dius**, an interradial part : a radius midway between primary radii or perradii.

interramal, *in-tər-rā'məl*, *adj.* situated between the rami or branches, esp. of the lower jaw.—*n.* **interramificā'tion** (*-ram-*), interweaving of branches. [L. *rāmus*, a branch.]

interregal, *in-tər-rē'gəl*, *adj.* between kings.

interregnum, *in-tər-reg'nəm*, *n.* the time between two reigns : the time between the cessation of one and the establishment of another government : any breach of continuity in order, &c. :—*pl.* **interreg'na**, **interreg'nums.**—*n.* **in'terreign** (Bacon). [L. *inter*, between, *regnum*, rule.]

interrelation, *in-tər-ri-lā'shən*, *n.* reciprocal relation.—*n.* **interrelā'tionship.**

interrex, *in'tər-reks*, *n.* one who rules during an interregnum : a regent :—*pl.* **interreges** (*-rē'jēz*). [L. *inter*, between, *rēx*, a king.]

interrogate, *in-tər'ō-gāt*, *v.t.* to question : to examine by asking questions : of a radar set, &c.,

Neutral vowels in unaccented syllables : *el'ə-mənt*, *in'fənt*, *ran'dəm*

to send out signals to (a radio-beacon) in order to ascertain position.—*v.i.* to ask questions : to inquire.—*adj.* **interr'ogable.**—*ns.* **interr'ogant**, a questioner ; **interroga'tion**, act of interrogating : a question put : the mark placed after a question (*?*). —*adj.* **interrogative** (*in-tər-og'ə-tiv*), denoting a question : expressed as a question.—*n.* a word used in asking a question.—*adv.* **interrog'atively.** —*ns.* **interr'ogator ; interrog'atory**, a question or inquiry.—*adj.* expressing a question. [L. *interrogāre, -ātum—inter*, between, *rogāre*, to ask.]

interrupt, *in-tər-upt'*, *v.t.* to break in between : to stop or hinder by breaking in upon : to divide : to break continuity in.—*v.i.* to make an interruption.—*adj.* (*obs.*) interrupted : (*Milt.*) gaping apart. —*adj.* **interrupt'ed**, broken in continuity : (*biol.*) irregular in spacing or size of parts.—*adv.* **interrupt'edly**, with interruptions : irregularly.— *ns.* **interrup'ter** (also **interrup'tor**), one who interrupts : apparatus for interrupting, e.g. for breaking an electric circuit, for preventing the firing of a gun from an aircraft when the screw is in line of fire ; **interrup'tion**, act of interrupting : hindrance : cessation.—*adj.* **interrup'tive**, tending to interrupt.—*adv.* **interrup'tively.** [L. *interrumpĕre, -ruptum—inter*, between, *rumpĕre*, to break.]

interscapular, *in-tər-ska'pū-lər*, *adj.* (*anat.*) between the shoulder-blades.

interscholastic, *in-tər-skə-las'tik*, *adj.* between schools.

inter-science, *in-tər-sī'əns*, *adj.* belonging to the examination between matriculation and B.Sc. of London University.

interscribe, *in-tər-skrīb*, *v.t.* to write between. [L. *interscrībĕre—inter*, between, *scrībĕre*, to write.]

intersect, *in-tər-sekt'*, *v.t.* to cut across : to cut or cross mutually : to divide into parts.—*v.i.* to cross each other.—*ns.* **in'tersect**, point of intersection ; **intersec'tion**, intersecting : (*geom.*) the point or line in which lines or surfaces cut each other.—*adj.* **intersec'tional.** [L. *inter*, between, *secāre, sectum*, to cut.]

interseptal, *in-tər-sep'tl*, *adj.* between septa.

intersert, *in-tər-sərt'*, *v.t.* (*obs.*) to insert between other things, interpolate.—*adj.* **intersert'al**, (*petr.*) having interstitial crystalline or glassy matter between felspar laths. [L. *interserĕre, -sertum*, to interpose—*inter*, between, *serĕre*, to plant.]

intersex, *in'tər-seks*, *n.* (*biol.*) an animal that develops some of the characters of the other sex.— *adj.* **intersex'ual**, between the sexes : intermediate between the sexes.—*n.* **intersexual'ity.**

intersidereal, *in-tər-sī-dē'ri-əl*, *adj.* between or among the stars.

interspace, *in'tər-spās*, *n.* an interval.—*v.t.* (*-spās'*) to put intervals between. — *adj.* **interspatial** (*-spā'shl*).—*adv.* **interspa'tially.**

interspecific, *in-tər-spis-if'ik*, *adj.* between species.

intersperse, *in-tər-spərs'*, *v.t.* to scatter or set here and there : to diversify.—*ns.* **interspers'al** (*rare*) ; **interspersion** (*-spər'shən*). [L. *interspergĕre, -spersum—inter*, among, *spargĕre*, to scatter.]

interspinal, *in-tər-spī'nəl*, *adj.* between spines of the vertebrae.—Also **interspi'nous.**

interstate, *in'tər-stāt*, or *-stāt'*, *adj.* between states.

interstellar, *in-tər-stel'ər*, *adj.* beyond the solar system or among the stars : in the intervals between the stars.—Also **interstell'ary.** [L. *inter*, between, *stella*, a star.]

interstice, *in-tər'stis*, *n.* a small space between things closely set, or between the parts which compose a body : (*R.C.*) the time interval required by canon law before receiving higher orders.—*adj.* **interstitial** (*-stish'l*), occurring in interstices. [L. *interstitium—inter*, between, *sistĕre, stătum*, to stand, set.]

interstratification, *in-tər-strat-i-fi-kā'shən*, *n.* the state of lying between, or alternating with, other strata.—*adj.* **interstrat'ified.**

intertangle, *in-tər-tang'gl*, *v.t.* and *v.i.* to tangle together.—*n.* **intertang'lement.**

intertarsal, *in-tər-tär'sl*, *adj.* between tarsal bones.

intertentacular, *in-tər-ten-tak'ū-lər*, *adj.* between tentacles.

interterritorial, *in-tər-ter-i-tō'ri-əl*, *adj.* between territories.

intertexture, *in-tər-teks'tyər*, *n.* interwoven state.

intertidal, *in-tər-tī'dl*, *adj.* between low-water and high-water mark.

intertie, *in'tər-tī*, *n.* in roofing, &c., a short timber binding together upright posts. [Origin obscure.]

intertissued, *in-tər-tish'(y)ōōd*, *adj.* interwoven.— Also (*Shak.*) **entertiss'ued.**

intertraffic, *in-tər-traf'ik*, *n.* traffic between two or more persons or places.

intertribal, *in-tər-trī'bl*, *adj.* between tribes.

intertrigo, *in-tər-trī'gō*, *n.* an inflammation of the skin from chafing or rubbing. [L. *intertrīgō—inter*, between, *terĕre, trītum*, to rub.]

intertropical, *in-tər-trop'i-kl*, *adj.* between the tropics.

intertwine, *in-tər-twīn'*, *v.t.* and *v.i.* to twine or twist together.—*ns.* **in'tertwine**, intertwining ; **intertwine'ment**.—*n.* and *adj.* **intertwin'ing.**— *adv.* **intertwin'ingly.**

intertwist, *in-tər-twist'*, *v.t.* to twist together.—*adv.* **intertwist'ingly.**

interunion, *in-tər-ūn'yən*, a blending together.

interurban, *in-tər-ur'bən*, *adj.* between cities. [L. *inter*, between, *urbs, urbis*, a city.]

interval, *in'tər-vəl*, *n.* time or space between : any dividing tract in space or time : a break, or free spell between lessons : (*mus.*) the difference of pitch between any two musical tones.—*n.* **in'tervale** (*U.S.*; influenced by **vale**), a level tract along a river.—*adj.* **intervallic** (*-val'ik*).—*n.* **intervall'um**, an interval. [L. *intervallum—inter*, between, *vallum*, a rampart.]

intervein, *in-tər-vān'*, *v.t.* to intersect, as with veins.

intervene, *in-tər-vēn'*, *v.i.* to come or be between : to occur between points of time : to happen so as to interrupt : to interpose : (*law*) to interpose in an action to which one was not at first a party. —*v.t.* (*rare*) to separate.—*n.* **interven'er**, one who intervenes.—Also (*law*) **interven'or**.—*adj.* **intervenient** (*-vēn'yənt*), being or passing between : intervening.—*ns.* **intervention** (*-ven'shən*), intervening : interference : mediation : interposition ; **interven'tionism ; interven'tionist**, one who advocates interference ; **interven'tor**, a mediator in ecclesiastical controversies. [L. *inter*, between, *venīre*, to come.]

interview, *in'tər-vū*, *n.* a mutual view or sight : a formal meeting : a conference, now esp. with a view to ascertaining suitability before entering on an engagement : a conference with a notable or notorious person with a view to publishing a report of his conversation : a report supposed to be founded on such a conference.—*v.t.* to confer with for this purpose.—*n.* **in'terviewer**, a journalist or other who interviews. [O.Fr. *entrevue—entre*, between, *voir*, to see.]

intervital, *in-tər-vī'tl*, *adj.* between lives, between death and resurrection. [L. *inter*, between, *vīta*, life.]

intervocalic, *in-tər-vō-kal'ik*, *adj.* between vowels.

intervolve, *in-tər-volv'*, *v.t.* and *v.i.* to entwine or roll up one with or within another. [L. *inter*, within, *volvĕre*, to roll.]

interweave, *in-tər-wēv'*, *v.t.* and *v.i.* to weave together : to intermingle.

interwind, *in-tər-wīnd'*, *v.t.* and *v.i.* to wind together or around and among one another :—*pa.t.* and *pa.p.* **interwound** (*-wownd'*).

interwork, *in-tər-wurk'*, *v.t.* and *v.i.* to work together : to work into another or one another.— *adj.* **interwrought** (*-rawt'*).

interwreathe, *in-tər-rēdh'*, *v.t.* to wreathe together or into one another.

intestate, *in-tes'tāt*, *-tit*, *adj.* dying without having made a valid will : not disposed of by will.—*n.* a person who dies without making a valid will.— *n.* **intes'tacy** (*-tə-si*), the state of one dying without having made a valid will. [L. *intestātus—in-*, not, *testāri, -ātus*, to make a will.]

intestine, *in-tes'tin*, *adj.* internal : contained in the animal body : domestic : not foreign.—*n.* (commonly in *pl.*) a part of the digestive system, divided into the smaller intestine (comprising duodenum, jejunum, and ileum) and the greater intestine.— *adj.* **intes'tinal** (also -*tīn'*), pertaining to the intestines of an animal body. [L. *intestīnus—intus,* within.]

inthral, inthrall, obsolete forms of **enthrall.**

intil, *in-til',* prep. (*Scot.*) into, in, or unto. [in, till.]

intimate, *in'ti-mit, -māt, adj.* innermost : internal : close : deep-seated : private : personal : closely acquainted : familiar : in illicit sexual connexion. —*n.* a familiar friend : an associate.—*v.t.* (-*māt*) to hint : to announce.—*n.* **in'timacy** (-*mə-si*), state of being intimate : close familiarity : illicit sexual intercourse.—*adv.* **in'timately.**—*n.* **intimā'tion,** indication : hint : announcement. [L. *intimāre,* -*ātum—intimus,* innermost—*intus,* within.]

intimidate, *in-tim'i-dāt, v.t.* to strike fear into : to influence by threats or violence.—*n.* **intimidā'-tion,** act of intimidating : use of violence or threats to influence the conduct or compel the consent of another : state of being intimidated.— *adj.* **intim'idatory.** [L. *in,* into, *timidus,* fearful.]

intinction, *in-tingk'shən, n.* an Eastern mode of administering communion by dipping the bread into the wine. [L.L. *intinctiō, -ōnis—*L. *intingĕre, intinctum,* to dip in.]

intine, *in'tin, -tēn, -tīn, n.* the inner membrane of a pollen grain or spore. [L. *intus,* within.]

intire, an obsolete form of **entire.**

intitule, *in-tit'ūl.* Same as **entitle.**

into, *in'too, prep.* to a position within : to a state of : multiplied by : (*obs.*) unto. [in, to.]

intoed, in-toed, *in'tōd', adj.* having the toes more or less turned inwards.

intolerable, *in-tol'ər-ə-bl, adj.* not to be endured. —*ns.* **intolerabil'ity, intol'erableness.**—*adv.* **intol'erably.**—*ns.* **intol'erance, intolera'tion,** state of being intolerant.—*adj.* **intol'erant,** not able or willing to endure : not enduring difference of opinion : persecuting.—*n.* one opposed to tolera-tion.—*adv.* **intol'erantly.**

intomb, *in-tōōm',* obsolete form of **entomb.**

intonate, *in'tōn-āt, v.t.* and *v.i.* to thunder. [L. *intonāre, -ātum,* to thunder ; cf. next word.]

intonate, *in'tōn-āt, v.t.* and *v.i.* to intone.—*ns.* **intona'tion,** the opening phrase of any plain-song melody, sung usually either by the officiating priest alone, or by one or more selected choristers : pitching of musical notes : modulation or rise and fall in pitch of the voice : intoning ; **in'tonātor,** a monochord.—*v.t.* **intone** (*in-tōn'*) to chant, read, or utter in musical tones, singsong, or monotone : to begin by singing the opening phrase : to utter with a particular intonation.—*n.* **intōn'er.**—*n.* and *adj.* **intōn'ing.**—*adv.* **intōn'ingly.** [L.L. *intonāre, -ātum—*L. *in,* in, *tonus,* tone.]

intorsion, intortion, *in-tor'shən, n.* a twist : a twine. —*adj.* **intort'ed,** twisted inwards : involved. [Fr. *intorsion,* L. *intortiō, -ōnis—in,* in, *torquēre, tortum,* to twist.]

intown, *in'tōōn, adj.* (*Scot.*) infield, near the farm-house.—**intown multure,** payment to the miller by those who are thirled to the mill.

intoxicate, *in-toks'i-kāt, v.t.* (*obs.*) to poison : to make drunk : to excite to enthusiasm or madness.— *n.* **intox'icant,** an intoxicating agent.—*adj.* **in-tox'icating.**—*n.* **intoxica'tion,** (*med.*) poisoning : state of being drunk : high excitement or elation. [L.L. *intoxicāre, -ātum—toxicum—*Gr. *toxikon,* arrow-poison—*toxon,* a bow.]

intra-, *in'trā-, -trə-, pfx.* within, as in **intra-abdom'inal,** situated within the cavity of the abdomen ; **intra-arte'rial,** within an artery ; **intra-cap'sular,** lying within a capsule ; **intra-car'diac,** within the heart ; **intracell'ular,** inside a cell ; **intramercū'rial,** within Mercury's orbit ; **intramolec'ular,** within the limits of the mole-cule ; **intramun'dane,** within this world ; **intra-mū'ral,** within walls : included within the college ; **intraparī'etal,** within walls, private : situated in the parietal lobe of the brain ; **intrapet'iolar,** between petiole and stem ; **intraterritō'rial,** within a territory ; **intratropi'cal,** within the tropics ; **intra-ur'ban,** within a city ; **intra-ū'terine,** within the uterus ; **intravē'nous,** within,

or introduced into, a vein or veins. [L. *intrā,* within.]

intractable, *in-trakt'ə-bl, adj.* unmanageable : ob-stinate.—*ns.* **intractabil'ity, intract'ableness.**— *adv.* **intract'ably.** [L. pfx. *in-,* not.]

intrados, *in-trā'dos, n.* (*archit.*) the soffit or under surface of an arch. [Fr.,—L. *intrā,* within, *dorsum,* the back.]

intransigent, *in-trān'si-jənt,* or -*zi-, adj.* refusing to come to any understanding, irreconcilable.— *ns.* **intran'sigence** ; **intran'sigency** ; **intran'-sigentism** ; **intran'sigentist,** one who practises such a method of opposition. [Fr. *intransigeant—* Sp. *intransigente—*L. *in-,* not, *transigēns, -entis,* pr.p. of *transigēre,* to transact ; see **transact.**]

intransitive, *in-trān'si-tiv,* or -*zi-, adj.* not passing over or indicating passing over : (*gram.*) repre-senting action confined to the agent, i.e. having no object.—*adv.* **intran'sitively.**

intransmissible, *in-trāns-mis'i-bl, -trānz-, adj.* that cannot be transmitted.

intransmutable, *in-trāns-mūt'ə-bl, -trānz-, adj.* that cannot be changed into another substance.— *n.* **intransmutabil'ity.**

intrant, *in'trənt, adj.* entering : penetrating.—*n.* one who enters, esp. on membership, office, or possession. [L. *intrāns, -āntis—intrāre,* to enter.]

intreat, *in-trēt', v.t.* (*Spens.*) same as **entreat.**—*adj.* **intreat'full,** (*Spens.*) full of entreaty.

intrench, intrenchment. See **entrench.**

intrenchant, *in-trensh'ənt, adj.* (*Shak.*) not to be cut or wounded, indivisible.

intrepid, *in-trep'id, adj.* without trepidation or fear : undaunted : brave.—*n.* **intrepid'ity,** firm, un-shaken courage.—*adv.* **intrep'idly.** [L. *intrepidus* —*in-,* not, *trepidus,* alarmed.]

intricate, *in'tri-kit, -kāt* (also -*trik'it*), *adj.* involved : entangled.—*ns.* **in'tricacy** (-*kə-si* ; also -*trik'*), **in'tricateness.**—*adv.* **in'tricately.** [L. *intrīcātus —in,* in, *trīcāre,* to make difficulties—*trīcae,* hindrances.]

intrigue, *in-trēg', n.* indirect or underhand scheming or plot : a private or party scheme : the plot of a play or romance : a secret illicit love affair.— *v.i.* to engage in intrigue.—*v.t.* to puzzle, to fas-cinate (a Gallicism).—*n.* **intrigu'er.**—*ns.* and *adjs.* **intrig(u)ant** (*in'tri-gant, anº-trē-gänº*), (*fem.*) **intrig(u)ante** (*in-tri-gant', anº-trē-gänºt*).—*adj.* **in-trigu'ing.**—*adv.* **intrigu'ingly.** [Fr. ; see **intri-cate.**]

intrince, *in-trins', adj.* (*Shak.*) intricate. [See **intrinsicate.**]

intrinsic, -al, *in-trin'sik, -əl, adjs.* inward : genuine : inherent : essential, belonging to the point at issue : (of muscles) entirely contained within the limb and girdle.—*n.* **intrinsicality** (-*al'i-ti*).—*adv.* **in-trin'sically.**—*n.* **intrin'sicalness.** [Fr. *intrin-sèque—*L. *intrīnsecus—intrā,* within, suff. -*in, secus,* following.]

intrinsicate, *in-trins'i-kāt, adj.* (*Shak.*) intricate. [App. It. *intrinsecato,* familiar, confused with **intricate.**]

introduce, *in-trə-dūs', v.t.* to lead or bring in : to conduct into a place : formally to make known or acquainted : to bring into notice or practice : to preface.—*n.* **introduc'er.**—*adj.* **introduc'ible.**— *n.* **introduction** (-*duk'shən*), act of introducing : preliminary matter to a book : (*mus.*) preliminary passage or section leading up to a movement : a treatise introductory to a science or course of study. —*adj.* **introductive** (-*duk'tiv*), promoting intro-duction.—*adv.* **introduc'torily.**—*adj.* **introduc'-tory,** serving to introduce : preliminary : introduc-tory. [L. *intrōdūcĕre, -ductum—intrō,* inward, *dūcĕre,* to lead.]

introit, *in-trō'it,* or *in', n.* (R.C.) an anthem sung at the beginning of the Mass, immediately after the *Confiteor,* and when the priest has ascended to the altar : (in other churches) an introductory hymn, psalm, or anthem.—*n.* **intrō'itus,** an entrance to a cavity, esp. the vagina : an introit. [L. *intrŏitus—intrŏīre—intrō,* inwards, *īre, ĭtum,* to go.]

introld. See **entrold.**

intromit, *in-trō-mit',* or -*trə-, v.t.* to send within :

to admit : to permit to enter : to insert.—*v.i.*
(*Scots law*) to have dealings : (esp. *Scots law*) to
interfere, esp. with the effects of another :—*pr.p.*
intromitt'ing ; *pa.t.* and *pa.p.* **intromitt'ed.**—*ns.*
intromission (*-mish'ən*), sending within : insertion : (*Scots law*) the assumption of authority to
deal with another's property (*legal*, where the party
is expressly or impliedly authorised to interfere,
vicious, where an heir or next of kin, without any
authority, interferes with a deceased person's
estate) : proceeds of such interference.—*adjs.*
intromiss'ive, pertaining to intromission : intromitting ; **intromitt'ent**, intromitting : adapted
for insertion, esp. (*zool.*) in copulation.—*n.* **intromitt'er.** [L. *intrō*, inward, *mittĕre*, *missum*, to
send.]
introrse, *in-trors'*, *adj.* turned or facing inward : (of
an anther) opening towards the centre of the flower.
—*adv.* **introrse'ly.** [L. *introrsus*, toward the
middle.]
introspect, *in-trō-spekt'*, or *-trə-*, *v.t.* to look into
(esp. the mind).—*v.i.* to practise introspection.—*ns.*
introspection (*-spek'shən*), a viewing of the inside
or interior : the act of directly observing the
processes of one's own mind ; **introspec'tionist.**
—*adj.* **introspec'tive.** [L. *intrō*, within, *specĕre*,
to look at.]
introsusception, *in-trō-sə-sep'shən*, *n.* intussusception. [L. *intrō*, inwards.]
introvert, *in-trō-vərt'*, or *-trə-*, *v.t.* to turn inwards :
to turn in upon itself : to turn inside out : to
withdraw part within the rest of.—*n.* **in'trovert**,
anything introverted : (*psych.*) a person interested
mainly in his own inner states and processes—
opp. to *extravert*, *extrovert*.—*adj.* **introvers'ible.**
—*n.* **introver'sion** (*-shən*).—*adjs.* **introver'sive** ;
introver'tive. [L. *intrō*, inwards, *vertĕre*, *versus*,
to turn.]
intrude, *in-trōōd'*, *v.i.* to thrust oneself in : to
enter uninvited or unwelcome.—*v.t.* to force in.—
ns. **intrud'er** ; **intrusion** (*-trōō'zhən*), act of
intruding : encroachment : an injection of rock
in a molten state among and through existing
rocks : a mass so injected ; **intru'sionist**, one who
intrudes, esp. of those who, before the Scottish
Disruption of 1843, refused a parish the right of
objecting to the settlement of an obnoxious minister
by a patron—opp. to *non-intrusionist.*—*adj.* **intru'-
sive** (*-siv*), tending or apt to intrude : intruded :
inserted without etymological justification : entering without welcome or right.—*n.* an intrusive
rock.—*adv.* **intru'sively.**—*n.* **intru'siveness.** [L.
in, in, *trūdere*, *trūsum*, to thrust.]
intrust. A variant of **entrust.**
intubate, *in'tū-bāt*, *v.t.* to insert a tube in : to treat
by intubation.—*n.* **intubā'tion**, insertion of a tube.
[L. *in*, in, *tubus*, a tube.]
intuition, *in-tū-ish'ən*, *n.* the power of the mind by
which it immediately perceives the truth of things
without reasoning or analysis : a truth so perceived, immediate knowledge in contrast with
mediate.—*v.t.* and *v.i.* **intuit** (*in'tū-it*), to know
intuitively. — *adj.* **intu'ited.** — *adj.* **intuitional**
(*-ish'ən-əl*).—*ns.* **intuit'ionalism**, the doctrine that
the perception of truth is by intuition ; **intuit'ionalist.**—*adj.* **intu'itive**, perceived or perceiving by
intuition : received or known by simple inspection.
—*adv.* **intu'itively.**—*n.* **intu'itivism.** [L. *in*,
into or upon, *tuērī*, *tuitus*, to look.]
intumesce, *in-tū-mes'*, *v.i.* to swell up.—*n.* **intumesc'ence**.—*adj.* **intumesc'ent.** [L. *in*, in,
tumēscĕre, to swell.]
inturbidate, *in-tur'bi-dāt*, *v.t.* to render turbid.
[L. *in*, in, *turbidāre*, *-ātum*, to trouble.]
intuse, *in'tūs*, *n.* (*Spens.*) a bruise. [L. *in*, in,
tundĕre, *tūsum*, to thump.]
intussusception, *in-təs-sə-sep'shən*, *n.* the passing of
part of a tube (esp. the intestine) within the adjacent part : growth by intercalation of particles.—
v.t. **intussuscept'**, to receive or take in thus.—
adjs. **intussuscept'ed**, **intussuscep'tive.** [L.
intus, within, *susceptiō*, *-ōnis*—*suscipĕre*, to take up.]
intwine, **intwist.** Same as **entwine**, **entwist.**
Inula, *in'ū-lä*, *n.* the elecampane genus of Compositae.—*ns.* **in'ulase** (*-lās*), an enzyme that forms

fructose from inulin ; **in'ulin**, a carbohydrate got
from elecampane roots. [L. *inula*, prob.—Gr.
helenion, elecampane.]
inumbrate, *in-um'brāt*, *v.t.* to cast a shadow upon :
to shade. [L. *inumbrāre*, *-ātum*—*in*, on, *umbrāre*,
to shade—*umbra*, a shadow.]
inunction, *in-ungk'shən*, *n.* anointing : smearing
or rubbing with an ointment or liniment. [L.
inunctiō, *-ōnis*—*in*, in, on, *ung(u)ĕre*, to smear.]
inundate, *in'un-dāt*, formerly *in-un'dāt*, *v.t.* to flow
upon or over in waves (said of water) : to flood :
(*fig.*) to overwhelm : to fill with an overflowing
abundance. — *adj.* **inun'dant**, overflowing. — *n.*
inundā'tion. [L. *inundāre*, *-ātum*—*in*, in, *undāre*,
to rise in waves—*unda*, a wave.]
inurbane, *in-ur-bān'*, *adj.* not urbane.—*adv.* **inurbane'ly.**—*n.* **inurbanity** (*-ban'i-ti*).
inure, *in-ūr'*, *v.t.* to use or practise habitually : to
accustom : to habituate : to harden : (*Spens.*,
Milt. in the form **enure'**) to put into operation :
to commit.—*v.i.* (*law*) to come into use or effect :
to serve to one's use or benefit.—Also **enure'.**—
n. **inure'ment**, act of inuring : state of being
inured : habituation. [Pfx. *in-*, *en-*, in, and **ure.**]
inure, *in-ūr'*, *v.t.* (*obs.*) to burn in. [L. *inūrĕre*—
in, in, *ūrĕre*, to burn.]
inurn, *in-urn'*, *v.t.* to place in an urn : to entomb.
inusitation, *in-ū-zi-tā'shən*, *n.* (*obs.*) disuse.—*adj.*
inu'sitate, unwonted.
inust, *in-ust'*, *adj.* (*obs.*) burned in.—*n.* **inustion**
(*in-ust'yən*), burning in : cauterisation. [L. *inūrĕre*,
inūstum ; see **inure** (2).]
inutility, *in-ū-til'i-ti*, *n.* want of utility : uselessness : unprofitableness : something useless.
inutterable, *in-ut'ər-ə-bl*, *adj.* unutterable.
invade, *in-vād'*, *v.t.* to enter as an enemy : to
attack : to encroach upon : to violate : to seize
or fall upon : to enter : to penetrate : to come
upon : to rush into.—*ns.* **invad'er** ; **invasion**
(*-vā'zhən*), the act of invading : an attack : an
incursion : an attack on the rights of another : an
encroachment : a violation.—*adj.* **invasive** (*vā'siv*),
making invasion : aggressive : encroaching : in-
fringing another's rights. [L. *invādĕre*, *invāsum*—
in, in, *vādĕre*, to go.]
invaginate, *in-vaj'in-āt*, *v.t.* to ensheath : to draw
inwards, push or withdraw within, introvert.—*v.i.*
to be introverted : to form a hollow ingrowth.—
n. **invaginā'tion.** [L. *in*, in, *vagīna*, a sheath.]
invalid, *in-val'id*, *adj.* without validity, efficacy,
weight, or cogency : having no effect : void : null.
—*adj.* **invalid** (*in'və-lēd*, *-lid*), deficient in health,
sick, weak : disabled : suitable for invalids.—*n.*
in'valid (*-ēd*, *-id*, *-ēd'*), one who is weak : a sickly
person : one disabled for active service, esp. a
soldier or sailor.—*v.t.* **in'valid** (*-ēd*, *-id*, *-ēd'*), to
make invalid or affect with disease : to enrol or
discharge as an invalid.—*v.i.* to become an invalid :
to be discharged as an invalid.—*v.t.* **invalidate**
(*-val'*), to render invalid : to make of no effect.—
ns. **invalidā'tion** ; **invalidhood** (*in'və-lid-hŏŏd*, or
-lēd-, or *-lēd'*) ; **in'validing**, the sending or return
home, or to a more healthy climate, of those
rendered incapable of active duty by wounds,
sickness, &c.—*adj.* **in'validish** (*-id-*, *-ēd-*, or *-ēd'*).
—*ns.* **in'validism** (*-id-*, *-ēd-*, or *-ēd'*) ; **invalid'ity**,
inval'idness, want of cogency or force.—*adv.*
inval'idly.
invaluable, *in-val'ū-ə-bl*, *adj.* that cannot have a
value set upon it : priceless : (*obs.*) valueless.—*adv.*
inval'uably.
invar, *in'vär*, *in-vär'*, *n.* an alloy of iron and nickel
very slightly expanded by heat, much used in the
making of scientific instruments. [Trade-mark,
from **invariable.**]
invariable, *in-vā'ri-ə-bl*, *adj.* not variable : without
alteration or change : unalterable : constantly in
the same state.—*ns.* **invā'riableness**, **invāriabil'-
ity.**—*adv.* **invā'riably.**
invasion, **invasive.** See **invade.**
invecked, *in-vekt'*, *adj.* invected.
invected, *in-vek'tid*, *adj.* (*her.*) having or consisting
of a border-line of small convex curves—opp. to
engrailed. [L. *invehĕre*, *invectum*, to enter.]
invective, *in-vek'tiv*, *n.* a severe or reproachful

accusation brought against anyone : an attack with
words : a violent utterance of censure : sarcasm
or satire.—*adj.* railing : abusive : satirical.—*adv.*
invec′tively (*Shak.*). [See **inveigh.**]

inveigh, *in-vā′,* *v.i.* to make an attack with words :
to rail : to revile. [L. *invehĕre, invectum—in,* in,
vehĕre, to carry.]

inveigle, *in-vē′gl, in-vā′gl, v.t.* to entice : to ensnare
by cajolery : to wheedle—older forms **invea′gle,
envei′gle.** — *ns.* **invei′glement ; invei′gler.**
[Prob. altered from A.Fr. *enveogler* (Fr. *aveugler*),
to blind—L. *ab,* from, *oculus,* the eye.]

invendible, *in-ven′di-bl, adj.* unsaleable.—*n.* in-
vendibil′ity.

invent, *in-vent′, v.t.* (*Spens.*) to find : to devise or
contrive : to design for the first time, originate : to
frame by imagination : to fabricate (something
false). — *adj.* **inven′tible.** — *n.* **inven′tion,** that
which is invented : contrivance : a deceit : faculty
or power of inventing : ability displayed by any
invention or effort of the imagination : (*mus.*) a
short piece working out a single idea.—*adj.* **inven′-
tive,** able to invent : ready in contrivance.—*adv.*
inven′tively.—*ns.* **inven′tiveness ; inven′tor :**—
fem. **inven′tress.—Invention of the Cross,** a
festival observed on May 3, in commemoration of
the alleged discovery of the true cross at Jerusalem
in 326 by Helena, mother of Constantine the Great.
[L. *invenīre, inventum—in,* upon, *venīre,* to come.]

inventory, *in′vən-tər-i, n.* a list or schedule of
articles comprised in an estate, &c. : a catalogue :
stock, equipment : (*U.S.*) stock of a commodity :
(*U.S.*) stocktaking.—*v.t.* to make an inventory of :
to amount to.—*v.i.* to sum up.—*adj.* **inventō′rial.**
—*adv.* **inventō′rially.** [L.L. *inventōrium* for L.
inventārium, a list of things found—*invenīre,* to
find.]

Inverness, *in-vər-nes′, in′vər-nes, adj.* of or named
after the town of *Inverness,* as a cloak or overcoat
with cape or tippet.

inverse, *in′vərs, in-vərs′, adj.* inverted : upside
down : in the reverse or contrary order : opposite
—opp. to *direct* : (*math.*) opposite in effect, as
subtraction to addition, &c. : related by inversion.
—*n.* an inverted state : the result of inversion : a
direct opposite : (*log.*) a proposition formed by
immediate inference from another, its subject being
the negative of the original subject : (*geom.*) a
point so related to another point that the rectangle
contained by their distances from a fixed point
collinear with them is constant, or related in some
analogous manner.—*v.t.* **inverse′,** to invert.—*adv.*
inverse′ly.—*n.* **inver′sion** (*-shən*), the act of inverting : the state of being inverted : a change of
order or position : that which is got by inverting.
—*adj.* **inver′sive.—inverse ratio,** the ratio of
reciprocals. [L. *inversus,* pa.p. of *invertĕre* ; see
invert.]

invert, *in-vərt′, v.t.* to turn in or about : to turn
upside down : to reverse : to change the customary order or position of : to form the inverse of :
(*mus.*) to change by placing the lowest note an
octave higher : to modify by reversing the direction of motion : (*chem.*) to break up (cane-sugar)
into dextrose and laevulose, thereby (the laevulose
prevailing) reversing the direction of rotation of
polarised light.—*n.* **in′vert,** an inverted arch :
inverted sugar : a homosexual.—*n.* **in′vertase** (or
-vər′), an enzyme that inverts cane-sugar.—*adj.* **in-
ver′ted,** turned inwards : upside down : reversed :
pronounced with tip of tongue turned up and back
(as *r* in S.W. England).—*adv.* **inver′tedly.—*n.*
inver′ter, inver′tor.—inverted arch, an arch
with its curve turned downwards ; **inverted
commas** (see **comma**) ; **invert sugar,** the
mixture got by hydrolysis of cane-sugar. [L.
invertĕre, inversum—in, in, *vertĕre,* to turn.]

invertebrate, *in-vərt′i-brit, -brāt, adj.* without a
vertebral column or backbone : weak, irresolute :
characterless : formless.—*n.* a member of the
Invertebrata.—*n.pl.* **Invertebrā′ta,** a collective
name for all animals other than vertebrates.

invest, *in-vest′, v.t.* to clothe : to envelop : (*Spens.*)
to put on : to clothe with insignia of office : to
settle or secure : to place in office or authority

(with *with* or *in*) : to adorn : to surround : to
block up : to lay siege to : to lay out for profit,
as by buying property, shares, &c.—*v.i.* (*coll.*) to
lay out money, make a purchase (with *in*).—*adj.*
inves′titive.—*ns.* **inves′titure,** investing : ceremony of investing : in feudal and ecclesiastical
history, the act of giving corporal possession of a
manor, office, or benefice, accompanied by a
certain ceremonial, such as the delivery of a branch,
a banner, &c., to signify the authority which it is
supposed to convey ; **invest′ment,** the act of
investing : putting on : clothes : covering : investiture : a blockade : the act of surrounding or
besieging : any placing of money to secure income
or profit : that in which money is invested ;
inves′tor, one who invests, esp. money. [L.
investīre, -ītum—in, on, *vestīre,* to clothe.]

investigate, *in-vest′i-gāt, v.t.* to search or inquire
into with care and accuracy.—*v.i.* to make investigation.—*adj.* **invest′igable,** able to be investigated.
—*n.* **investigā′tion,** act of examining : research.
—*adjs.* **invest′igative, invest′igatory.**—*n.* **in-
vest′igator.** [L. *investigāre,-ātum—in,* in,*vestīgāre,*
to track.]

inveterate, *in-vet′ər-it, adj.* firmly established by
long continuance : deep-rooted, confirmed in any
habit : rootedly hostile.—*adv.* **invet′erately.—
ns. **invet′erateness, invet′eracy** (*-ə-si*), firmness
produced by long use or continuance. [L. *in-
veterātus,* stored up, long continued—*in,* in, *vetus,
veteris,* old.]

invexed, *in-vekst′, adj.* (*her.*) arched : concave. [L.
in, in, and the root of *vehēre,* to carry.]

inviable, *in-vī′ə-bl, adj.* not viable : unable to
survive.—*n.* **inviabil′ity.**

invidious, *in-vid′i-əs, adj.* likely to incur or provoke
ill-will : likely to excite envy, enviable : offensively
discriminating. — *adv.* **invid′iously.**—*n.* **invid′-
iousness.** [L. *invidiōsus—invidia,* envy.]

invigilate, *in-vij′i-lāt, v.t.* and *v.i.* to supervise (at
examinations).—*ns.* **invigilā′tion ; invig′ilātor.**
[L. *in,* on, *vigilāre, -ātum,* to watch.]

invigorate, *in-vig′ər-āt, v.t.* to give vigour to : to
strengthen : to animate.—*ns.* **invig′orant,** an
invigorating agent ; **invigorā′tion ; invig′orātor.**

invincible, *in-vin′si-bl, adj.* that cannot be overcome : insuperable.—*ns.* **invin′cibleness, in-
vincibil′ity.** — *adv.* **invin′cibly.** — **invincible
ignorance** (see **ignorance**) ; **the Invincible
Doctor,** William of Occam (*d. c.* 1349).

inviolable, *in-vī′ə-la-bl, adj.* that must not be pro-
faned : that cannot be injured.—*ns.* **inviolabil′ity,
invī′olableness,** the quality of being inviolable.—
adv. **invī′olably.—*adjs.* **invī′olate** (*-lit, -lāt*), **-d**
(*-lāt-id*), not violated : unprofaned : uninjured.—
adv. **invī′olately.—*n.* **invī′olateness.**

invious, *in-vi′əs, adj.* (*rare*) impassable : trackless.
[L. *invius—in,* not, *via,* a way.]

invis′d, *in′vizd, adj.* (*Shak.*) prob., unseen or inscrutable. [L. *invīsus,* unseen.]

invisible, *in-viz′i-bl, adj.* incapable of being seen :
unseen : (*finance*) not shown in regular statements,
as *invisible* assets (see **export, import**).—*ns.* **in-
visibil′ity, invis′ibleness.** — *adv.* **invis′ibly.** —
Invisible Church (see **visible**) ; **invisible green,**
green that is almost black ; **invisible ink** (see **ink**).

invite, *in-vīt′, v.t.* to ask hospitably or graciously to
come : to express gracious willingness to receive
or to have done : to be of such a kind as to encourage or tend to bring on : to offer inducement :
to attract.—*n.* (*coll.* or *vulg.*) an invitation.—*n.*
invitation (*in-vi-tā′shən*), the act of inviting : an
asking or solicitation : the written or verbal form
with which a person is invited : the brief exhortation introducing the confession in the Anglican
communion office.—*adj.* **invitatory** (*in-vīt′ə-tə-ri*),
using or containing invitation.—*n.* a form of
invitation to worship, esp. the antiphon to the
Venite or 95th Psalm.—*ns.* **invite′ment,** (*Lamb*)
allurement, temptation ; **invīt′er.**—*adj.* **invīt′ing,**
alluring : attractive.—*n.* (*Shak.*) invitation.—*adv.*
invīt′ingly.—*n.* **invīt′ingness,** attractiveness. [L.
invītāre, -ātum.]

invocate, *in′vō-kāt, v.t.* to invoke.—*n.* **invocā′tion,**
the act or the form of invoking or addressing in

prayer or supplication: an appellation under which one is invoked: any formal invoking of the blessing or help of a god, a saint, &c.: an opening prayer in a public religious service or in the Litany: a call for inspiration from a Muse or other deity as at the beginning of a poem: an incantation or calling up of a spirit: (*law*) a call or summons, esp. for evidence from another case.—*adj.* **invoca-tory** (*in-vok'ə-tə-ri*), making invocation. [See **invoke.**]

invoice, *in'vois*, *n.* a letter of advice of the despatch of goods, with particulars of their price and quantity.—*v.t.* to make an invoice of. [Prob. pl. of Fr. *envoi*.]

invoke, *in-vōk'*, *v.t.* to call upon earnestly or solemnly: to implore assistance of: to address in prayer: to conjure up: to call to help, resort to. [Fr. *invoquer*—L. *invocāre*, *-ātum*—*in*, on, *vocāre*, to call.]

involucre, *in'və-l(y)ōō-kər*, *n.* (*anat.*) an envelope: (*bot.*) a ring or crowd of bracts around a capitulum, umbel, &c.—Also **involū'crum.**—*n.* **involucel** (*in-vol'ū-sel*), the group of bracts below a partial umbel.—*adjs.* **involūcell'ate**, having an involucel; **involu'cral**, of the nature of, pertaining to, an involucre; **involu'crate**, having an involucre. [L. *involūcrum*—*involvĕre*, to involve.]

involuntary, *in-vol'ən-tər-i*, *adj.* not voluntary: not having the power of will or choice: not under control of the will: not done voluntarily.—*adv.* **invol'untarily.**—*n.* **invol'untariness.**

involute, *in'vol-(y)ōōt*, *adj.* involved: (*bot.*) rolled inward at the margins: turned inward: closely rolled.—*n.* that which is involved or rolled inward: a curve traced by the end of a string unwinding itself from another curve (the *evolute*).—*v.t.* and *v.i.* to make or become involute.—*adj.* **in'voluted.** —*n.* **involu'tion**, the action of involving: state of being involved or entangled: complicated gram-matical construction: (*math.*) raising to a power: (*geom.*) the condition satisfied by a system of pairs of points in a straight line such that the rectangle contained by their distances from a fixed point in that line (the *centre of involution*) is constant. [See **involve.**]

involve, *in-volv'*, *v.t.* to coil: to wrap up: to envelop: to entangle: to complicate: to im-plicate: to comprehend: to entail or imply, bring as a consequence: to be bound up with: to con-cern: (*math.*) to raise to a power.—*n.* **involve'-ment.** [L. *involvĕre*—*in*, in, *volvĕre*, *volūtum*, to roll.]

invulnerable, *in-vul'nər-ə-bl*, *adj.* that cannot be wounded: not vulnerable (as in bridge).—*ns.* **invulnerabil'ity**, **invul'nerableness.**—*adv.* **in-vul'nerably.**

invultuation, *in-vul-tū-ā'shən*, *n.* the making or use of an image of a person for purpose of witchcraft. [L.L. *involtuātiō, -ōnis*.—L. *in*, in, *vultus*, the face.]

inwall. See **enwall.**

inward, *in'ward*, *adj.* placed or being within: internal: seated in the mind or soul, not per-ceptible to the senses: uttered as if within, or with closed mouth: (*arch.*) confidential: secret, private.—*n.* (*Shak.*) inside: interior: (*Shak.*) an intimate friend: (in *pl.*) entrails.—*adv.* toward the interior: into the mind or thoughts.—*adv.* **in'-wardly**, within: in the heart: privately: toward the centre. — *n.* **in'wardness**, internal state: inner meaning or significance: (*Shak.*) intimacy, familiarity.—*adv.* **in'wards**, same as **inward.** [O.E. *inneweard* (adv.).]

inweave, *in-wēv'*, *v.t.* to weave in: to complicate: —*pa.t.* **inwove'**; *pa.p.* **inwo'ven** (*Milt.*, &c., **inwove'**).

inwick, *in'wik*, *n.* in curling, a stroke in which the stone glances off the edge of another stone, and then slides close to the tee.—*v.i.* **inwick'**, to make an inwick. [**in**, **wick** (4).]

inwit, *in'wit*, (*obs.*) inward knowledge: conscience. [**in**, **wit**.]

inwith, *in'with*, *in-widh'*, *prep.* and *adv.* (*Scot.*) within. [**in**, **with**.]

inwork, *in-wurk'*, *v.t.* and *v.i.* to work in.—*adj.* **in'-working**, energy exerted inwardly.—*adj.* **in'-**

wrought (as *pa.p. in-rawt'*), wrought in or among other things: adorned with figures.

inworn, *in'wōrn*, *in-wōrn'*, *adj.* worn or worked in, inwrought.

inwrap. Same as **enwrap.**

inwreathe. Same as **enwreathe.**

inyala, *in-yä'lä*, *n.* a S. African antelope. [Bantu.]

io, *ī'ō*, *interj.* of invocation, or expressing joy or triumph or grief.—*n.* a cry of 'Io':—*pl.* **i'os.** [Gr. *iō*.]

iodine, *ī'ə-dēn*, or *ī'ō-dēn*, also *-dīn*, *-din*, *n.* a halogen element (I; atomic number 53) giving a violet-coloured vapour.—*n.* **i'odate**, a salt of iodic acid.—*adj.* **iodic** (*ī-od'ik*), pertaining to or caused by iodine: applied to an acid (HIO₃) and its anhydride (I₂O₅).—*n.* **i'odide**, a salt of hydriodic acid.—*v.t.* **i'odise**, to treat with iodine.—*ns.* **i'odism**, a morbid condition due to iodine; **iodo-form** (*ī-od', -ōd'ə-form*), a lemon-yellow crystalline compound of iodine (CHI₃) with a saffron-like odour, used as an antiseptic.—*adjs.* **iodomet'ric**, (*chem.*) measured by iodine; **iod'ophile** (*-fil*, *-fīl*), staining intensely with iodine.—*n.* **iod'ūret**, (*obs.*) an iodide. [Gr. *īoeidēs*, violet-coloured—*ion*, a violet, *eidos*, form.]

iodyrite, *ī-od'ir-īt*, *n.* a mineral, silver iodide. [**iodine**, **argyrite**.]

iolite, *ī'ō-līt*, *n.* cordierite or dichroite, a strongly dichroic transparent gem, a silicate of aluminium, magnesium, and iron, violet-blue, grey, or yellow according to direction of view by transmitted light. [Gr. *ion*, violet, *lithos*, stone.]

ion, *ī'ən*, *ī'on*, *n.* an electrically charged particle formed by the loss or gain of electrons, effecting by its migration the transport of electricity.—*adj.* **ionic** (*ī-on'ik*).—*v.t.* **ionise** (*ī'ən-īz*), to produce ions in: to turn into ions.—*ns.* **ionisa'tion**; **ion'osphere**, the region of the upper atmosphere that includes the highly ionised Appleton and Kennelly-Heaviside layers. [Gr. *ĭōn*, neut. pr.p. of *ienai*, to go.]

Ionic, *ī-on'ik*, *adj.* relating to the Ionians, one of the main divisions of the ancient Greeks, to their dialect, to Ionia, the coastal district of Asia Minor settled by them, to a foot of two long and two short syllables (*Ionic a majore*) or two short and two long (*Ionic a minore*), to verse characterised by the use of that foot, to a style of Greek architecture character-ised by the volute of its capital, to a mode of ancient Greek music (the same as the Iastic, Hypophrygian, or Hyperlydian), or to an old ecclesiastical mode extending from C to C with C for its final.—*n.* the Ionic dialect: an Ionic foot or verse: an Ionic philosopher.—*adj.* and *n.* **Ionian** (*ī-ō'ni-ən*), Ionic: an Ionic Greek.—*vs.t.* and *vs.i.* **Ionicise** (*ī-on'i-sīz*), **Ionise** (*ī'ən-īz*), to make or become Ionian: to use the Ionic dialect.—*ns.* **I'onism**; **I'onist.**— **Ionic dialect**, the most important of the three main branches of the ancient Greek language (Ionic, Doric, Aeolic), the language of Homer and Herodotus, of which Attic is a development; **Ionic school**, the representative philosophers of the Ionian Greeks, such as Thales, Anaximander, Heraclitus, Anaxagoras, who debated the question what was the primordial constitutive principle of the cosmical universe. [Gr. *Iōnikos*, *Iōnios*.]

ionium, *ī-ōn'i-əm*, *n.* a radioactive isotope of thorium. [**ion**.]

ionosphere. See **ion.**

iota, *ī-ō'tä*, *n.* the Greek letter I, ι, answering to I: as a numeral ι' = 10, ͺι = 10,000: a jot.—*n.* **iot'acism**, excessive use of the Greek letter iota or i or of its sound: the conversion of other vowel sounds into that (Eng. *ē*) of iota, as in modern Gr. of η, υ, ει, η, οι, υι. [Gr. *iōta*, the smallest letter in the alphabet, I, ι; Heb. *yōd*.]

I O U, *ī-ō-ū'*, *n.* a memorandum of debt given by a borrower, requiring no stamp, but holograph, and usually dated, and addressed to the lender.

ipecacuanha, *ip-i-kak-ū-an'ä*, *n.* a valuable medicine or the Brazilian plant (*Cephaelis* or *Uragoga*; fam. *Rubiaceae*) whose root produces it—used as an emetic: applied to other roots used as substitutes. — Familiarly abbrev. **ipecac'**. [Port. from Tupí.]

fāte, fär, ȧsk; mē, hər (her); *mīne; mōte; mūte; mōōn; dhen* (then)

Ipomoea, ip-ō-mē´ä, *n.* the jalap and morning-glory genus of the Convolvulus family. [Gr. *ĭps, ĭpos,* a worm, *homoios,* like.]

iracund, ī´ra-kund, *adj.* inclined to anger.—*n.* **iracund´ity.** — *adj.* **iracund´ulous,** somewhat iracund. [L. *īrācundus—īra,* anger.]

irade, i-rä´de, *n.* a written decree of the Sultan of Turkey. [Turk.,—Ar. *irādah,* will.]

Iranian, ī-rān´i-ən, or *-rän´, adj.* and *n.* Persian : (of) a branch of the Indo-Germanic tongues including Persian and Ossetic.—Also **Iranic** (ī-ran´ik). [Pers. *Īrān,* Persia.]

irascible, ir-as´i-bl, or *īr-, adj.* susceptible of ire or anger : irritable. — *n.* **irascibil´ity.** — *adv.* **irasc´ibly.** [Fr.,—L. *īrāscibilis—īrāscī,* to be angry—*īra,* anger.]

ire, īr, *n.* anger : rage : keen resentment.—*adjs.* **irate** (ī-rāt´ or īr´āt), enraged, angry : **ire´ful,** full of ire or wrath : resentful.—*adv.* **ire´fully.**—*n.* **ire´fulness.** [L. *īra,* anger.]

irenic, ī-rēn´ik, *adj.* tending to create peace : pacific. —Also **irēn´ical.**—*ns.*|**irēn´icon** (see **eirenicon**); **irēn´ics,** (treated as *sing.*) irenical theology—opp. to *polemics.* [Gr. *eirēnē,* peace.]

Iricism. See **Irish. iridium,** etc. See **iris.**

Iris, ī´ris, *n.* the Greek rainbow goddess, messenger of the gods : **iris,** the rainbow : an appearance resembling the rainbow : the contractile curtain perforated by the pupil, and forming the coloured part of the eye : the fleur-de-lis, or flagflower (Iris) : an iris diaphragm : (*pl.* **i´rides, i´rises**).— *v.t.* to make iridescent : to form into a rainbow : to work an iris diaphragm.—*n.* **i´rid,** the iris of the eye : any plant of the iris family.—*n.pl.* **Iridā´ceae** (´-si-ē), the iris family, distinguished from lilies by their inferior ovary and single whorl of stamens. — Also **Irid´eae.** — *adjs.* **iridaceous** (-ā´shəs), **irid´eal,** belonging to the Iridaceae ; **i´ridal, irid´ial,** **irid´ian,** pertaining to the rainbow or the iris of the eye : rainbow-like.—*n.* **iridescence** (ir-i-des´əns), play of rainbow colours, caused by interference, as on bubbles, mother-of-pearl, some feathers.—*adjs.* **iridesc´ent, i´risated,** coloured like the rainbow : glittering with changing colours. —*n.* **iridisation** (ī-rid-īz-ā´shən, or ir-id-, or *-iz-*), iridescence.—*v.t.* **iridise** (ir´ or ir´).—*ns.* **irid´ium** (īr- or ir-), a very heavy steel-grey metallic element (**Ir** ; atomic number 77), with very high melting-point ; **iridosmine** (ir-id-oz´min, or *īr-,* or *-os´,* a native alloy of iridium and osmium used for pen-points, also called *osmiridium.—v.t.* **i´risate,** to make iridescent.—*n.* **irisation** (ī-ri-sā´shən).— *adjs.* **irised** (ī´rist), showing colours like the rainbow ; **īrit´ic,** having iritis : affecting the iris.— *n.* **irit´is,** inflammation of the iris of the eye.—**iris diaphragm,** an adjustable stop for a lens, giving a continuously variable hole. [Gr. *Iris, -idos.*]

iriscope, ī´ri-skōp, *n.* an instrument for exhibiting the prismatic colours. [Gr. *iris,* and *skopeein,* to see.]

Irish, ī´rish, *adj.* relating to, or produced in, or derived from Ireland : (*obs.*) Highland Scottish : characteristic of Ireland, esp. blundering, self-contradictory, bull-making.—*n.* the Celtic language of Ireland or (*obs.*) of the Scottish Highlands (Gaelic) : an Irish commodity, esp. linen or whisky : (*coll.*) temper, passion : (*pl.*) the natives or people of Ireland.—*ns.* **I´risher,** (*Scot.,* often slightly contemptuous) an Irishman ; **I´rishism** (also **I´ricism,** *-sizm,* a faulty form), a Hibernicism, an Irish phrase, idiom, or characteristic, esp. a bull ; **I´rishman ; I´rishry,** the people of Ireland collectively ; **I´rishwoman.—Irish car,** a jaunting car ; **Irish Guards,** a regiment formed in 1900 to represent Ireland in the Foot Guards ; **Irish moss,** carrageen ; **Irish stew,** mutton, onions, and potatoes stewed with flour ; **Irish terrier,** a breed of dog with rough, wiry, reddish-brown coat.

irk, ərk, *v.t.* to weary : to trouble : to distress (now used only impersonally).—*adj.* **irk´some,** causing uneasiness : tedious : burdensome.—*adv.* **irk´-somely.**—*n.* **irk´someness.** [M.E. *irken.*]

iron, ī´ərn, *n.* the most widely used of all the metals, the element (Fe) of atomic number 26 : a weapon, instrument, or utensil made of iron, as a

hand-harpoon, flat-iron, branding instrument, &c. : a golf-club with an iron head (formerly limited to certain types) : strength : a medicinal preparation of iron : (in *pl.*) fetters : chains.—*adj.* formed of iron : resembling iron : rude : stern : fast-binding : not to be broken : robust : dull of understanding.—*v.t.* to smooth with a flat-iron : to arm with iron : to fetter.—*n.* **i´ronbark,** eucalyptus of various species.—*adjs.* **i´ron-bound,** bound with iron : rugged, as a coast ; **i´ron-cased ; i´ronclad,** clad in iron : covered or protected with iron.—*n.* a ship defended with iron plates.—*ns.* **i´ron-clay,** clay-ironstone ; **i´roner,** one who irons ; **i´ron-founder,** one who founds or makes castings in iron ; **i´ron-foundry ; i´ron-glance,** specular iron.—*adj.* **i´ron-gray´, -grey´,** of a grey colour like that of iron freshly cut or broken.— *n.* this colour.—*adjs.* **i´ron-hand´ed,** rigorous ; **i´ron-heart´ed,** having a heart as hard as iron : unfeeling.—*ns.* **i´roning,** the act or process of smoothing with hot irons ; **i´roning-board,** a smooth board covered with cloth, on which clothes are ironed ; **i´ron-liq´uor,** iron acetate, a dyers' mordant ; **i´ronmaster,** a proprietor of iron-works ; **i´ron-mine ; i´ron-miner ; i´ron-mining ; i´ronmonger,** a dealer in articles made of iron ; **i´ronmongery,** articles made of iron : hardware ; **i´ron-mould** (earlier **-mole,** *Scot.* **-mail** ; O.E. *māl,* mole, spot), a spot left on wet cloth after touching iron ; **i´ron-ore ; i´ron-pan´,** a hard layer in sand or gravel, due to percolation of water precipitating iron salts ; **i´ron-sand,** sand containing particles of iron-ore : steel filings used in fireworks.—*adj.* **i´ron-sick,** (*naut.*) having the iron bolts and spikes much corroded.—*n.* **I´ronside,** (as King Edmund, Oliver Cromwell) : (in *pl.*) a name given to Cromwell's irresistible cavalry : (in *sing.*) a Puritan cavalryman : a Puritan.—*adj.* **i´ron-sid´ed,** having a side of, or as hard as, iron : rough : hardy.—*ns.* **i´ronsmith,** a worker in iron, blacksmith ; **i´ronstone,** any iron-ore, esp. carbonate ; **i´ronware,** wares or goods of iron.—*adj.* **i´ron-witt´ed,** (*Shak.*) unfeeling, insensible.—*n.* **i´ronwood,** timber of great hardness, and many kinds of trees producing it.—*adj.* **i´ron-word´ed,** (*Tenn.*) in words as strong as iron.—*n.* **i´ronwork,** the parts of a building, &c., made of iron : anything of iron, esp. artistic work : (often in *pl.*) an establishment where iron is smelted or made into heavy goods.—*adj.* **i´rony,** made, consisting of, rich in, iron : like iron : hard. — **Iron Age,** (*myth.*) the age in which the ancient Greeks and Romans themselves lived, regarded by them as a third step in degeneracy from the Golden Age : (*archaeol.*) the stage of culture of a people using iron as the material for their tools and weapons ; **Iron Cross,** a Prussian war-medal, instituted in 1813 and revived in 1870 ; **Iron Crown,** the crown of Lombardy, so named from a thin band of iron said to be made from one of the nails of the Cross ; **iron horse,** a worn-out circumlocution for a railway engine ; **iron lung,** an apparatus consisting of a chamber that encloses a patient's chest, the air pressure within the chamber being varied rhythmically so that air is forced into and out of the lungs ; **iron pyrites,** common pyrites, sulphide of iron ; **iron ration,** a ration of concentrated food, esp. for an extreme emergency ; **rule with a rod of iron,** to rule with stern severity ; **too many irons in the fire,** too many things on hand at once. [O.E. *īren* (*isern, īsen*) ; Ger. *eisen.*]

irony, ī´rən-i, *n.* the Socratic method of discussion by professing ignorance : conveyance of meaning (generally satirical) by words whose literal meaning is the opposite : a situation or utterance (as in a tragedy) that has a significance unperceived at the time, or by the person involved : a condition in which one seems to be mocked by fate or the facts.—*adjs.* **ironic** (ī-ron´ik), **iron´ical.**— *adv.* **iron´ically.** [L. *—īrōnia*—Gr. *eirōneiā,* dissimulation—*eirōn,* a dissembler, perh.—*eirein,* to talk.]

irradiate, i-rā´di-āt, *v.t.* to shed light or other rays upon or into : to treat by exposure to rays : to light up : to brighten : to radiate.—*v.i.* to radiate : to shine.—*adj.* adorned with rays of light or with lustre.—*ns.* **irra′diance, irra′diancy.**—*adj.* **irra′- diant.**—*n.* **irradiā′tion,** act of irradiating : exposure to rays : that which is irradiated : brightness : apparent enlargement of a bright object by spreading of the excitation of the retina, or in a photograph by reflections within the emulsion : intellectual light.—*adj.* **irra′diative.**

irradicate, *i-rad′i-kāt, v.t.* to fix firmly.

irrational, *ir-ash′ən-əl, adj.* not rational : not commensurable with natural numbers : (*pros.*) long treated as short, or having such a syllable (indicated >).—*n.* an irrational being or number.—*ns.* **irra′- tionalism,** an irrational system : irrationality ; **irra′tionalist.** — *adj.* **irrationalist′ic.** — *n.* **irrational′ity.**—*adv.* **irra′tionally.**

irrealisable, *ir-ē-ə-līz′ə-bl, adj.* not realisable.—*n.* **irreality** (-*al′i-ti*), unreality.

irrebuttable, *ir-i-but′ə-bl, adj.* not to be rebutted.

irreceptive, *ir-i-sep′tiv, adj.* not receptive.

irreciprocal, *ir-i-sip′rə-kəl, adj.* not reciprocal.— **irreciprocity** (*ir-es-i-pros′i-ti*).

irreclaimable, *ir-i-klām′ə-bl, adj.* that cannot be claimed back, brought into cultivation, or reformed : incorrigible.—*n.* **irreclaim′ableness.**—*adv.* **irreclaim′ably.**

irrecognisable, *ir-ək-əg-nīz′ə-bl,* or *ir-ek′, adj.* unrecognisable.—*n.* **irrecognition** (-*nish′ən*), lack of recognition.

irreconcilable, *ir-ek-ən-sīl′ə-bl,* or *ir-ek′, adj.* incapable of being brought back to a state of friendship or agreement : inconsistent.—*n.* an irreconcilable opponent : an intransigent.—*ns.* **irreconcil′ableness, irreconcilabil′ity.**—*adv.* **irreconcil′ably.**—*adj.* **irrec′onciled,** not reconciled, esp. (*Shak.*) with God : not brought into harmony.— *n.* **irreconcile′ment.**

irrecoverable, *ir-i-kuv′ər-ə-bl, adj.* irretrievable : not reclaimable : beyond recovery.—*n.* **irrecov′erableness.**—*adv.* **irrecov′erably.**

irredeemable, *ir-i-dēm′ə-bl, adj.* not redeemable : not subject to be paid at the nominal value.—*ns.* **irredeem′ableness, irredeemabil′ity.** — *adv.* **irredeem′ably.**

Irredentist, *ir-e-dent′ist, n.* one of an Italian party formed in 1878, its aims to gain or regain for Italy various regions claimed on language and other grounds : one who makes similar claims for any nation.—Also *adj.*—*n.* **Irredent′ism,** the programme of the Irredentist party : the doctrine of ' redeeming ' territory from foreign rule. [It. (*Italia*) *irredenta,* unredeemed (Italy)—L. *in-,* not, *redemptus,* pa.p. of *redimĕre,* to redeem.]

irreducible, *ir-i-dūs′i-bl, adj.* that cannot be reduced or brought from one degree, form, or state to another : not to be lessened : not to be overcome : not to be reduced by manipulation, as a hernia, &c.—*n.* **irreduc′ibleness.**—*adv.* **irreduc′ibly.**— *ns.* **irreducibil′ity, irreductibility** (-*duk-ti-bil′i-ti*) ; **irreduction** (-*duk′shən*).

irreflective, *ir-i-flek′tiv, adj.* not reflective.—*n.* **irreflec′tion, irreflex′ion.**

irreformable, *ir-i-form′ə-bl, adj.* not subject to revision or improvement.

irrefragable, *ir-ef′rə-gə-bl, adj.* that cannot be refuted : unanswerable. — *ns.* **irrefragabil′ity, irref′ragableness.** — *adv.* **irref′ragably.** — the **Irrefragable Doctor,** Alexander Hales (died 1245). [L. *irrefrāgābilis—in-,* not, *re-,* backwards, *frangĕre,* to break.]

irrefrangible, *ir-i-fran′ji-bl, adj.* incapable of refraction.

irrefutable, *ir-ef′ūt-ə-bl,* also -*ūt′, adj.* that cannot be refuted.—*adv.* **irref′utably** (also -*ūt′*).

irregular, *ir-eg′ū-lər, adj.* not regular : not conforming to rule or to the ordinary rules : disorderly : uneven : unsymmetrical : variable : (of troops) not trained under authority of a government : (of a marriage) not celebrated by a minister after proclamation of banns or of intention to marry.—*n.* an irregular soldier.—*n.* **irregularity** (-*lar′i-ti*).— *adv.* **irreg′ularly.** — *adj.* **irreg′ulous,** (*Shak.*) lawless.

irrelative, *ir-el′ə-tiv, adj.* not relative : irrelevant.

—*adj.* **irrelated** (*ir-i-lā′tid*).— *n.* **irrelā′tion.**— *adv.* **irrel′atively.**

irrelevant, *ir-el′ə-vənt, adj.* not relevant.—*ns.* **irrel′evance, irrel′evancy.**—*adv.* **irrel′evantly.**

irreligious, *ir-i-lij′əs, adj.* destitute of religion : regardless of religion : opposed to religion : (*Shak.*) false in religion : ungodly.—*adv.* **irrelig′iously.**— *ns.* **irrelig′iousness, irrelig′ion,** want of religion : hostility to or disregard of religion.

irremeable, *ir-em′i-ə-bl,* or -*ēm′, adj.* not admitting of return. [L. *irremeābilis in-,* not, *re-,* back, *meāre,* to go, come.]

irremediable, *ir-i-mē′di-ə-bl, adj.* beyond remedy or redress.—*n.* **irremē′diableness.**—*adv.* **irremē′diably.**

irremissible, *ir-i-mis′i-bl, adj.* not to be remitted or forgiven.—*ns.* **irremiss′ibleness, irremission** (-*mish′ən*).—*adj.* **irremiss′ive,** unremitting.

irremovable, *ir-i-mōōv′ə-bl, adj.* not removable : not liable to be displaced.—*ns.* **irremovabil′ity, irremov′ableness.**—*adv.* **irremov′ably.**

irrenowned, *ir-i-nown′id, adj.* (*Spens.*) inglorious.

irreparable, *ir-ep′ər-ə-bl, adj.* that cannot be made good or rectified : beyond repairing.—*ns.* **irreparabil′ity, irrep′arableness.** — *adv.* **irrep′arably.**

irrepealable, *ir-i-pēl′ə-bl, adj.* that cannot be repealed or annulled.—*adv.* **irrepeal′ably.**

irreplaceable, *ir-i-plās′ə-bl, adj.* whose loss cannot be made good : without possible substitute.

irreprehensible, *ir-ep-ri-hens′i-bl, adj.* beyond blame. — *n.* **irreprehens′ibleness.**—*adv.* **irreprehens′ibly.**

irrepressible, *ir-i-pres′i-bl, adj.* not to be put down or kept under.—*adv.* **irrepress′ibly.**

irreproachable, *ir-i-prōch′ə-bl, adj.* free from blame : faultless.—*n.* **irreproach′ableness.**—*adv.* **irreproach′ably.**

irreproducible, *ir-ē-pro-dūs′i-bl, adj.* that cannot be reproduced.

irreprovable, *ir-i-prōōv′ə-bl, adj.* blameless.—*n.* **irreprov′ableness.**—*adv.* **irreprov′ably.**

irresistance, *ir-i-zist′əns, n.* want of resistance : passive submission.—*adj.* **irresist′ible,** not to be opposed with success : resistless : overpowering : overmastering.—*ns.* **irresist′ibleness, irresistibil′- ity.**—*adv.* **irresist′ibly.**

irresoluble, *ir-ez′əl-(y)ōō-bl, adj.* that cannot be resolved into parts : that cannot be solved : that cannot be loosed or got rid of.

irresolute, *ir-ez′əl-(y)ōōt, adj.* not firm in purpose. —*adv.* **irres′olutely.**—*ns.* **irres′oluteness, irresolution** (-*ōō′shən,* -*ū′shən*), want of resolution.

irresolvable, *ir-i-zolv′ə-bl, adj.* that cannot be resolved.—*ns.* **irresolvabil′ity, irresolv′ableness.**

irrespective, *ir-i-spek′tiv, adj.* not having regard (with *of*).—Also *adv.*—*adv.* **irrespec′tively.**

irrespirable, *ir-es′pir-ə-bl,* or -*pīr′, adj.* unfit for respiration.

irresponsible, *ir-i-spons′i-bl, adj.* not responsible : without sense of responsibility : free from feeling of responsibility, light-hearted, carefree : done without feeling of responsibility.—*n.* **irresponsibil′ity.**—*adv.* **irrespons′ibly.**—*adj.* **irrespons′ive,** not responding : not readily responding.—*n.* **irrespons′iveness.**

irrestrainable, *ir-i-strān′ə-bl, adj.* not restrainable.

irresuscitable, *ir-i-sus′i-tə-bl, adj.* incapable of being resuscitated or revived.—*adv.* **irresusc′itably.**

irretention, *ir-i-ten′shən, n.* absence of retention or power to retain.—*adj.* **irreten′tive.**

irretrievable, *ir-i-trēv′ə-bl, adj.* not to be recovered : irreparable.—*n.* **irretriev′ableness.**—*adv.* **irretriev′ably.**

irreverent, *ir-ev′ər-ənt, adj.* not reverent : proceeding from irreverence.—*n.* **irrev′erence,** want of reverence or veneration, esp. for God.—*adj.* **irreverential** (-*en′shəl*).—*adv.* **irrev′erently.**

irreversible, *ir-i-vərs′i-bl, adj.* not reversible : that cannot proceed in the opposite direction or in both directions : incapable of changing back : not alike both ways : that cannot be recalled or annulled. —*ns.* **irreversibil′ity, irrevers′ibleness.**—*adv.* **irrevers′ibly.**

fāte, fär, ȧsk ; mē, hėr (her) *; mīne ; mōte ; mūte ; mōōn ; ᵭhen* (then)

irrevocable, *ir-ev′ǎk-ǎ-bl*, *adj.* that cannot be recalled or revoked.—*n.* **irrev′ocableness.**—*adv.* **irrev′ocably.**

irrigate, *ir′i-gāt*, *v.t.* to wet or moisten : to water by means of canals or watercourses : to cause a stream of liquid to flow upon.—*v.i.* (*slang*) to drink. —*adj.* **irr′igable.**—*ns.* **irrigā′tion**; **irr′igātor**, one who, or that which, irrigates : an appliance for washing a wound, &c.—*adj.* **irrig′ūous**, watered : wet : irrigating. [L. *irrigāre, -ātum*, to water, and *irriguus*, watering, watered—*in*, upon, *rigāre*, to wet.]

irrision, *ir-izh′ǎn*, *n.* act of laughing at another.— *adj.* **irrisory** (*ir-ī′sǎr-i*), mocking, derisive. [L. *irrīsĭō, -ōnis—in*, on, at, *rīdēre, rīsum*, to laugh.]

irritate, *ir′i-tāt*, *v.t.* to excite or stimulate : to rouse : to make angry or fretful : to excite a painful, uncomfortable, or unhealthy condition (as heat and redness) in.—*n.* **irritabil′ity**, the quality of being easily irritated : the peculiar susceptibility to stimuli possessed by living matter.—*adj.* **irr′itable**, that may be irritated : easily annoyed : susceptible of excitement or irritation.—*n.* **irr′itableness.**—*adv.* **irr′itably.**—*n.* **irr′itancy.**—*adj.* **irr′itant**, irritating.—*n.* that which causes irritation.—*n.* **irritā′tion**, act of irritating or exciting : excitement : (*med.*) the term applied to any morbid excitement of the vital actions not amounting to inflammation, often, but not always, leading to that condition.—*adj.* **irr′itātive**, tending to irritate or excite : accompanied with or caused by irritation. [L. *irrītāre, -ātum.*]

irritate, *ir-i-tāt*, *v.t.* (*Scots law*) to make void.— *n.* **irr′itancy.**—*adj.* **irr′itant**, rendering void. [L. *irrītāre—in*, not, *ratus*, valid.]

irrupt, *ir-upt′*, *v.i.* to break in : to make irruption. —*n.* **irruption** (*ir-up′shǒn*), a breaking or bursting in : a sudden invasion or incursion.—*adj.* **irrup′tive**, rushing suddenly in.—*adv.* **irrup′tively.** [L. *irrumpĕre, irruptum—in*, in, *rumpĕre*, to break.]

Irvingite, *ǎr′ving-īt*, *n.* a popular name for a member of the Catholic Apostolic Church.—Also *adj.*—*n.* **Ir′vingism**, the doctrine and practice of the Irvingites. [From Edward *Irving* (1792-1834).]

is, *iz*, used as third pers. sing. pres. indic. of **be.** [O.E. *is*; Ger. *ist*, L. *est*, Gr. *esti*, Sans. *asti.*]

isabel, *iz′ǎ-bel*, *n.* and *adj.* dingy yellowish-grey or drab. — Also **isabell′a**, **isabell′ine** (*-in*, *-īn*). [Origin unknown : too early in use to be from *Isabella*, daughter of Philip II., who did not change her linen for three years until Ostend was taken.]

isagogic, *ī-sa-goj′ik*, *-gog′ik*, *adj.* introductory.—*n.* (treated as *sing.*) **isagog′ics**, that part of theological study introductory to exegesis. [Gr. *eisagōgē*, an introduction—*eis*, into, *agein*, to lead.]

isapostolic, *ī-sap-ǎs-tol′ik*, *adj.* equal to the apostles, as bishops of apostolic creation, the first preachers of Christ in a country, &c. [Gr. *isos*, equal, *apostolikos*, apostolic.]

Isatis, *ī′sa-tis*, *n.* the woad genus of Cruciferae.—*n.* **i′satin**, a substance (C₈H₅O₂N) got by oxidising indigo. [Gr. *isatis*, woad.]

ischium, *is′ki-ǎm*, *n.* a posterior bone of the pelvic girdle. — *adjs.* **ischiad′ic**, **is′chial**, **ischiat′ic.** [Latinised from Gr. *ischion*, the hip-joint.]

ischuria, *is-kū′ri-ä*, *n.* a stoppage of urine.—*adj.* and *n.* **ischuretic** (*is-kū-ret′ik*). [Gr. *ischein*, to hold, *ouron*, urine.]

isenergic, *īs-en-ǎr′jik*, *adj.* in physics, denoting equal energy. [Gr. *isos*, equal, *energeia*, energy.]

Isengrim, *ī′zǎn-grim*, **Isegrim**, *ī′zǎ-grim*, *n.* the wolf in the beast-epic of *Reynard the Fox.*

isentropic, *ī-sen-trop′ik*, *adj.* (*phys.*) of equal entropy. [Gr. *isos*, equal, *entropē*, a turning about—*en*, in, *trepein*, to turn.]

ish, *ish*, *n.* (*Scots law*) issue, liberty of going out : expiry. [O.Fr. *issir*, to go out—L. *exīre—ex*, out of, *īre*, to go.]

Ishmael, *ish′mā′ǎl*, *n.* one like Ishmael (Gen. xvi. 12), at war with society.—*n.* **Ish′maelīte**, a descendant of Ishmael : a Bedawi Arab : an Ishmael. —*adj.* **Ishmaelīt′ish.**

Isiac, *ī-si-ak*, *adj.* relating to Isis.

Isidorian, *is-i-dō′ri-ǎn*, or *iz-*, *adj.* of or pertaining to St *Isidore* of Seville (*c.* 560-636), or the collection

of canons and decretals adopted by him ; but esp. applying to the forged *Pseudo-Isidorian* or *False Decretals*, published (*c.* 845) by *Isidore* Mercator, and fathered upon St Isidore.

isinglass, *ī′zing-glâs*, *n.* a material, mainly gelatine, got from sturgeons' air-bladders and other sources. [App. from obs. Du. *huizenblas—huizen*, a kind of sturgeon, *blas*, a bladder ; Ger. *hausenblase*; cf. **huso.**]

Isis, *ī′sis*, *n.* an Egyptian goddess, wife and sister of Osiris.—*adjs.* **I′siac**; **Isī′acal.** [Gr. *Isis.*]

Islam, *iz′lâm*, or *is′*, or *-lām′*, **Is′lamism**, *n.* the Mohammedan religion : the whole Mohammedan world.—*adjs.* **Islamic** (*-lam′ik*), **Islamitic** (*-lǎ-mit′ik*).—*n.* **Is′lamite.**—*v.t.* and *v.i.* **Islamīse′**, to convert or conform to Mohammedanism. [Ar. *islām*, surrender (to God).]

island, *ī′land*, *n.* a mass of land (not a continent) surrounded with water : anything isolated, detached, or surrounded by something of a different nature, e.g. a wood among prairies, a hill in a marsh or plain, a show-case, a building or building-site with a clear space around it : a small raised area for pedestrians crossing streets or awaiting trams : tissue or cells detached and differing from their surroundings.—*adj.* of an island : forming an island.—*v.t.* to cause to appear like an island : to isolate : to dot as with islands.—*n.* **islander** (*ī′land-ǎr*), an inhabitant of an island.—**island universe**, a spiral nebula regarded as forming a separate stellar system ; Reil's island (see **insula**). [M.E. *iland*—O.E. *īegland, igland, égland—īeg, ig, ég*, island (from a root which appears in Angles-*ea*, Alder-*ey*, &c., O.E. *éa*, L. *aqua*, water) and *land.* The *s* is due to confusion with *isle.*]

isle, *īl*, *n.* an island.—*v.t.* to make an isle of : to set in an isle.—*v.i.* to dwell in an isle.—*ns.* **isles′-man**, an islander, esp. an inhabitant of the Hebrides —also **isle′man**; **islet** (*ī′lit*), a little isle.—**Isle of Wight disease**, a disease of bees caused by a mite in the spiracles, that appeared in the Isle of Wight in 1906, and spread to other regions ; **islets of Langerhans** (*läng′ǎr-häns*), groups of epithelial cells discovered by Paul *Langerhans*, a German anatomist (1849-88), in the pancreas, producing a secretion whose want causes diabetes. [M.E. *ile, yle*—O.Fr. *isle* (Fr. *île*)—L. *insula.*]

ism, *izm*, *n.* any distinctive doctrine, theory, or practice—usually in disparagement.—*adjs.* **ismat′ic**, **-al**, **ism′y**, addicted to isms or faddish theories.— *n.* **ismat′icalness.** [From the suffix *-ism.*]

Ismaili, *is-mā-ē′lē*, or *is-mā′i-li*, *n.* one of a sect of Shiite Mohammedans who claim that *Ismail* (*c.* 770) was the seventh and last of the Imâms.— Also *adj.*—*n.* and *adj.* **Ismailian** (*is-mā-il′i-ǎn*).— *n.* **Is′mailism.**—*adj.* **Ismailit′ic.**

iso-, *ī′sō-*, in composition, equal : (*chem.*) denoting an isomeric substance—e.g. **iso-oc′tane**, one of the isomers of normal octane. [Gr. *isos*, equal.]

isobar, *ī′sō-bär*, *n.* a curve running through places of equal pressure : esp. (*meteor.*) one connecting places, or their representations on a map, of equal barometric pressure.—*adjs.* **isobaric** (*-bar′ik*), **isobaromet′ric.** [Gr. *baros*, weight.]

isobare, *ī′sō-bär*, *n.* either of two atoms of different chemical elements but of identical atomic mass (e.g. an isotope of titanium and an isotope of chromium both of atomic mass 50).—Also **i′sobar.** [Same as **isobar** above.]

isobase, *ī′sō-bās*, *n.* (*geol.*) a contour line of equal upheaval of the land. [Gr. *basis*, step.]

isobath, *ī′sō-bath*, *n.* a contour line of equal depth. —*adj.* **isobath′ic.** [Gr. *bathos*, depth.]

isobilateral, *ī-sō-bī-lat′ǎr-ǎl*, *adj.* (*bot.*) bilaterally symmetrical with upper and under surfaces alike : symmetrical about two planes : having the flanks of the organ flattened surfaces. [Gr. *isos*, equal, **bilateral.**]

isobront, *ī′sō-bront*, *n.* a contour line marking simultaneous development of a thunderstorm. [Gr. *brontē*, thunder.]

isochasm, *ī′sō-kazm*, *n.* a contour line of equal frequency of auroral displays.—*adj.* **isochasm′ic.** [Gr. *chasma*, a gap, expanse.]

isocheim, *ī′sō-kīm*, *n.* a contour line of mean winter temperature.—*adjs.* and *ns.* **isocheim'al, isocheim'enal.**—*adj.* **isocheim'ic.** [Gr. *cheima,* winter weather, *cheimainein,* to be stormy.]

isochor, isochore, *ī'sō-kōr, n.* a curve representing variation of some quantity under conditions of constant volume.—*adj.* **isochoric (-kor'ik).** [Gr. *chōrā,* space.]

isochromatic, *ī-sō-krō-mat'ik, adj. (optics)* having the same colour: (*phot.*) orthochromatic. [Gr. *chrōma, -atos,* colour.]

isochronal, *ī-sok'rən-əl,* **isoch'ronous, -əs,** *adjs.* of equal time: performed in equal times: in regular periodicity.—*advs.* **isoch'ronally, isoch'ronously.** —*n.* **isoch'ronism.** [Gr. *chronos,* time.]

isoclinal, *ī-sō-klī'nəl, adj. (geol.)* folded with nearly the same dip in each limb: (in terrestrialmagnetism) having the same magnetic dip.—*n.* an isoclinal line, or contour line of magnetic dip.—*adj.* and *n.* **isoclinic (-klin'ik),** isoclinal. [Gr. *klīnein,* to bend.]

isocryme, *ī'sō-krīm, n.* a contour line of equal temperature during the coldest time.—*adj.* and *n.* **isocrym'al.** [Gr. *krȳmos,* cold.]

isocyclic, *ī'sō-sī-klik, adj.* homocyclic. [**iso-, cyclic.**]

Isodia, *ī-sō'di-ə, n.pl.* the feast of the presentation of the Virgin in the temple at the age of three. [Gr., neut. pl. of adj. *eisodios—eisodos,* entrance.]

isodiametric, -al, *ī-sō-dī-ə-met'rik, -əl, adjs.* of equal diameters: about as broad as long.

isodicon, *ī-sod'i-kon, n. (Gr. Ch.)* a troparion or short anthem sung while the Gospel is being carried through the church. [Dim. of Gr.*eisodos,* entrance.]

isodimorphism, *ī-sō-dī-morf'izm, n. (crystal.)* isomorphism between each of the two forms of a dimorphous substance and the corresponding forms of another dimorphous substance.—*adjs.* **isodimorph'ic, isodimorph'ous.**

isodomon, *ī-sod'o-mon, n.* masonry of uniform blocks, the vertical joints placed over the middle of the blocks below.—Also (Latinised) **isod'omum:** —*pl.* **isod'oma.**—*adj.* **isod'omous.** [Gr., neut. of *isodomos,* equal-coursed—*isos,* equal, *domos,* a course—*demein,* to build.]

isodynamic, *ī-sō-din-am'ik,* or *-dīn-, adj.* of equal strength, esp. of magnetic intensity.—*n.* an isodynamic line on the earth or the map, a contour line of magnetic intensity. [Gr. *dynamis,* strength.]

isoelectric, *ī-sō-i-lek'trik, adj.* having the same potential.—**isoelectric point,** the *p*H-value at which the ionisation of an ampholyte is at a minimum. [**iso-, electric.**]

Isoetes, *ī-sō'e-tēz, n.* the quillwort genus constituting a family (**Isoetā'ceae**) of pteridophytes, with short stem, a bunch of quill-shaped leaves in which the sporangia are sunk, and branching roots. [Gr. *isoetes,* houseleek (an evergreen)—*isos,* equal, *etos,* a year.]

isogamy, *ī-sog'ə-mi, n. (bot.)* the conjugation of two gametes not clearly differentiated into male and female.—*n.* **isogamete** (*ī-sō-gam'ēt,* or *-ēt').*—*adjs.* **isogam'ic, isog'amous.** [Gr. *gamos,* marriage.]

isogeny, *ī-soj'ə-ni, n.* likeness of origin.—*adjs.* **isogenetic** (*ī-sō-ji-net'ik*), **isog'enous.** [Gr. *genos,* kind.]

isogeotherm, *ī-sō-jē'ō-thərm, n.* a subterranean contour of equal temperature. — *adj.* **isogeotherm'al.**—*n.* an isogeotherm. [Gr. *gē,* the earth, *thermē,* heat—*thermos,* hot.]

isogonic, *ī-sō-gon'ik, adj.* of equal angles, esp. of magnetic declination.—*n.* an isogonic line or contour line of magnetic declination. [Gr. *gōniā,* an angle.]

isohel, *ī'sō-hel, n.* a contour line of equal amounts of sunshine. [Gr. *hēlios,* sun.]

isohyet, *ī-sō-hī'ət, n.* a contour line of equal rainfall.—*adj.* **isohy'etal.**—*n.* an isohyet. [Gr. *hyetos,* rain—*hyein,* to rain.]

Isokontae, *ī-sō-kont'ē, n.pl.* the green algae, whose zoospores have usually equal cilia.—*n.* **i'sokont.**—*adj.* **isokont'an.** [Gr. *kontos,* a (punting) pole.]

isolate, *ī'sō-lāt, v.t.* to place in a detached situation, like an island : to detach : to insulate : to separate (esp. from those who might be infected): to seclude: to segregate: to obtain in an uncompounded state.—*adj.* **is'olable.**—*ns.* **isolā'tion;**

isolā'tionism, the policy of avoiding political entanglements with other counⱭries ; **isolā'tionist.** —*adj.* **i'solātive,** tending towards isolation : occurring without influence from outside.—*n.* **i'solātor.** —**isolating languages,** those in which each word is a bare root, not inflected or compounded. [It. *isolare—isola—*L. *īnsula,* an island.]

isomer, *ī'sō-mər, n. (chem.)* a substance isomeric with another.—*n.* **i'somēre,** (*zool.*) an organ or segment corresponding to or homologous with another.—*adj.* **isomeric (-*mer'ik ; chem.*),** identical in percentage composition and molecular weight but different in constitution or the mode in which the atoms are arranged.—*v.t.* and *v.i.* **isomerise** (*ī-som'ər-īz*), to change into an isomer.—*ns.* **isomerisā'tion ; isom'erism,** the property of being isomeric : the existence of isomers.—*adj.* **isom'erous,** having the same number of parts (esp. in floral whorls). [Gr. *meros,* part.]

isometric, -al, *ī-sō-met'rik, -əl, adjs.* having equality of measure : having the plane of projection equally inclined to three perpendicular axes : (*crystal.*) of the cubic system, or referable to three equal axes at right angles to one another.—*adv.* **isomet'rically.** [Gr. *metron,* measure.]

isomorph, *ī'sō-morf, n.* that which shows isomorphism.—*adj.* **isomorph'ic,** showing isomorphism.— *n.* **isomorph'ism,** (*biol.*) similarity in unrelated forms : (*crystal.*) close similarity in crystalline form combined with similar chemical constitution.—*adj.* **isomorph'ous.—isomorphous mixture,** a mixed crystal or solid solution in which isomorphous substances are crystallised together by vicarious substitution. [Gr. *morphē,* form.]

isonomy, *ī-son'ə-mi, n.* equal law, rights, or privileges. [Gr. *isonomiā—isos,* equal, *nomos,* law.]

isoperimeter, *ī-sō-pər-im'i-tər, n.* a figure with perimeter equal to another.—*adj.* **isoperimetrical** (*ī-sō-per-i-met'ri-kəl*). — *n.* **isoperim'etry.** [Gr. *perimetron,* circumference.]

isopod, *ī'sō-pod, n.* a member of the Isopoda.—*n.pl.* **Isopoda** (*ī-sop'ə-dä*), an order of Crustacea with no carapace, depressed body, sessile eyes, seven pairs of nearly equal thoracic legs, and usually lamellar uropods—woodlice, fishlice, &c.—*adj.* **isop'odous.** [Gr. *pous, podos,* a foot.]

isopolity, *ī-sō-pol'i-ti, n.* reciprocity of rights of citizenship in different communities. [Gr. *politeiā,* citizenship.]

isoprene, *ī'sō-prēn, n.* a hydrocarbon of the terpene group, which may be polymerised into synthetic rubber. [Etymology obscure.]

Isoptera, *ī-sop'tər-ä, n.pl.* an order of insects having the two pairs of wings (when present) closely alike— the termites.—*adj.* **isop'terous.** [Gr. *pteron,* a wing.]

isorrhythmic, *ī-sō-ridh'mik, -rith'mik, adj.* in ancient prosody, equal in the number of time-units for thesis and arsis, as dactyl, spondee, anapaest. [Gr. *rhythmos,* rhythm.]

isosceles, *ī-sos'i-lēs, adj. (geom.)* having two equal sides, as a triangle. [Gr. *isoskelēs—skelos,* a leg.]

isoseismal, *ī-sō-sīs'məl, n.* a curve or line connecting points at which an earthquake shock is felt with equal intensity.—*adjs.* **isoseis'mal, isoseis'mic.** [Gr. *seismos,* a shaking.]

isosporous, *ī-sos'pər-əs,* or *ī-sō-spō'rəs, adj.* having spores of one kind only—opp. to *heterosporous.*— *n.* **isos'pory.** [Gr. *sporos,* seed.]

isostasy, *ī-sos'tə-si, n. (geol.)* a condition of equilibrium held to exist in the earth's crust, equal masses of matter underlying equal areas, whether of sea or land.—*adj.* **isostatic** (*ī-sō-stat'ik*), in hydrostatic equilibrium from equality of pressure : in a state of isostasy : pertaining to isostasy.—*adv.* **isostat'ically.** [Gr. *stasis,* setting, weighing ; *statikos,* pertaining to weighing.]

isostemonous, *ī-sō-stēm'ən-əs, adj.* having as many stamens as petals. [Gr. *stēmōn,* a thread.]

isothere, *ī'sō-thēr, n.* a contour line of equal mean summer temperature.—*adj.* **isotheral** (*ī-soth'ər-əl, ī-sō-thēr'əl*).—*n.* an isothere. [Gr. *theros,* summer —*therein,* to make warm.]

isotherm, *ī'sō-thərm, n.* a contour line of equal temperature.—*adj.* **isotherm'al,** at constant temperature: pertaining to isotherms.—*n.* an isothermal line, isotherm. [Gr. *thermē,* heat—*thermos,* hot.]

isotonic, *ī-sō-ton'ik, adj.* having the same tone, tension, or osmotic pressure. [Gr. *tonos,* tone.]

isotope, *ī'sō-tōp, n.* an atom of an element having a different nuclear mass, and hence atomic weight, from other atoms of the same element: a form of an element distinguished by the nuclear mass of its atoms though chemically identical with other forms.—*adj.* isotopic (*-top'ik*).—*n.* isotopy (*ī-sot'-ə-pi*), fact or condition of being isotopic. [Gr. *topos,* place (*scil.* in the periodic table).]

isotropic, *ī-sō-trop'ik, adj.* having the same properties irrespective of direction: (*biol.*) without predetermined axes.—Also **isotropous** (*ī-sot'rə-pəs*).—*ns.* **isot'ropism, isot'ropy.** [Gr. *tropos,* turn, direction.]

I-spy, *ī'-spī', n.* a children's game of hide-and-seek, so called from the cry when one is spied. [I, spy.]

Israeli, *iz-rā'lē, n.* a citizen of the modern state of Israel.—Also *adj.* [See **Israelite.**]

Israelite, *iz'ri-əl-īt, n.* a descendant of Israel or Jacob: a Jew: (*fig.*) one of the elect: a member of a Christian sect that observes the Jewish law.—*adjs.* **Israelit'ic, Israelit'ish.** [Gr. *Isrāēlitēs—Isrāēl,* Heb. *Yisrāēl,* perh. contender with God—*sara,* to fight, *El,* God.]

issue, *ish'(y)ōō, is'ū, n.* a going or flowing out: an outlet: act of sending out: that which flows or passes out: fruit of the body, children: produce, profits: (*obs.*) a fine: a putting into circulation, as of banknotes: publication, as of a book: a giving out for use: a set of things put forth at one time: (chiefly *mil.*) a single thing given out or supplied: ultimate result, outcome: upshot: critical determination: (*Shak.*) luck or success in conclusion: (*Shak.*) an act, deed: point in dispute: a point on which a question depends: a question awaiting decision or ripe for decision: (*med.*) a discharge or flux: an ulcer produced artificially—*v.i.* (in *Spens.* usu. **issue'**) to go, flow, or come out: to proceed, as from a source: to spring: to be produced: (*law*) to come to a point in fact or law: to turn out, result, terminate.—*v.t.* to send out: to put forth: to put into circulation: to publish: to give out for use: (*mil. jargon*) to supply.—*adj.* **iss'uable,** capable of issuing, admitting of an issue.—*n.* **iss'uance,** act of giving out, promulgation.—*adjs.* **iss'uant,** (*her.*) issuing or coming up from another, as a charge or bearing; **iss'ueless,** without issue: childless.—*n.* **iss'uer,** one who issues or emits.—**at issue,** in quarrel or controversy: in dispute; **feigned issue,** (*law*) an issue made up for trial by agreement of the parties or by an order of court, instead of by the ordinary legal procedure; **general issue,** a simple denial of the whole charge, as 'Not guilty,' instead of a **special issue,** an issue taken by denying a particular part of the allegations; **immaterial issue,** an issue which is not decisive of any part of the litigation, as opp. to a **material issue,** one which necessarily involves some part of the rights in controversy; **join,** or **take, issue,** to take an opposite position, or opposite positions, in dispute: to enter into dispute: to take up a point as basis of dispute; **side issue,** a subordinate issue arising from the main business. [O.Fr. *issue—issir,* to go or flow out—L. *exīre—ex,* out, *īre,* to go.]

isthmus, *is(th)'məs, n.* a narrow neck of land connecting two larger portions: a constriction.—*adj.* **isth'mian,** pertaining to an isthmus, esp. the Isthmus of Corinth.—The **Isthmian Games** were on that isthmus, near the Saronic Gulf shore. [L., —Gr. *isthmos,* from root of *ienai,* to go.]

istle, *ist'li,* **ixtle,** *ikst'li, n.* a valuable fibre obtained from Agave, Bromelia, and other plants. [Mexican Sp. *ixtle*—Nahuatl *ichtli.*]

it, *it, pron.* the neut. of **he, him** (and formerly **his**), applied to a thing without life, a lower animal, a young child, rarely (except as an antecedent or in contempt) to a man or woman: used as an impersonal, indefinite, or anticipatory or provisional subject or object, as the object of a transitive verb

that is normally an intransitive, or a noun: (*obs.* and *dial.*) as gen., its: in children's games, the player chosen to oppose all others: (*coll.*) the *ne plus ultra,* that which answers exactly to what one is looking for: an indefinable crowning quality by which one carries it off—personal magnetism:—*gen.* its (*obs.* his, it); *pl.* they, them. [O.E. *hit,* neut. (nom. and acc.) of *he;* Du. *het,* Goth. *hita,* this; akin to Goth. *ita,* Ger. *es,* L. *id,* Sans. *i,* pronominal root=here. The *t* is an old neuter suffix, as in *that, what,* and cognate with *d* in L. *illud, istud, quod.*]

ita, *ē'tä, it'ä, n.* the miriti palm. [Arawak *ité.*]

itacism, *ē'tə-sizm, n.* the pronunciation of Greek *ēta* as in Modern Greek, like English long *e* (opp. to *etacism*): iotacism in pronunciation of various vowels and diphthongs. [Gr. *ēta,* eta, η.]

itacolumite, *it-ə-kol'ūm-īt, n.* a schistose quartzite containing scales of mica, talc, and chlorite, often having a certain flexibility. [*Itacolumi* mountain, Brazil.]

Italian, *i-tal'yən, adj.* of or relating to Italy or its people or language.—*n.* a native or citizen of Italy, or person of the same race: the language of Italy.—*adj.* **Ital'ianate,** Italianised. — *v.s.t.* **Ital'ianate, Ital'ianise,** to make Italian: to give an Italian character to.—*v.s.i.* to become Italian: to play the Italian: to speak Italian: to use Italian idioms: to adopt Italian ways.—*ns.* **Ital'ianism, Ital'icism** (*-sizm*), an Italian idiom or habit: Italian sympathies; **Ital'ianist,** one who has a scholarly knowledge of Italian: a person of Italian sympathies.—*adj.* **Ital'ic,** pertaining to Italy, esp. ancient Italy: (without capital) of a sloping type introduced by the Italian printer Aldo Manuzio in 1501, used esp. for emphasis or other distinctive purpose, indicated in MS. by single underlining.—*n.* (usu. in *pl.*) an italic letter.—*n.* **italicisā'tion.**—*v.t.* **ital'icise,** to put in italics: to mark for italics.—*n.* **Ital'iot, Ital'iote,** a Greek of ancient Italy.—Also *adj.*—**Italian architecture,** the style practised by Italian architects of the 15th-17th centuries, which originated in a revival of the ancient architecture of Rome; **Italianate Englishman,** an Englishman of the Renaissance, full of Italian learning and vices, proverbially equivalent to a devil incarnate; **Italian garden,** a formal garden with statues; **Italian iron,** a smoothing iron for fluting; **Italian sixth,** a chord of a note with its major third and augmented sixth; **Italian warehouseman,** a dealer in such groceries as macaroni, olive oil, dried fruits, &c.; **Italic dialects,** languages of ancient Italy akin to Latin; **Italic version,** or **It'ala,** a translation of the Bible into Latin, based on the 'Old Latin' version, and made probably in the time of Augustine. [L. *Italiānus* and Gr. *Italikos*—L. *Italia,* Gr. *Italiā,* Italy.]

itch, *ich, n.* an uneasy, irritating sensation in the skin: an eruptive disease in the skin, caused by a parasitic mite: a constant teasing desire.—*v.i.* to have an uneasy, irritating sensation in the skin: to have a constant, teasing desire.—*ns.* **itch'iness;** **itch'-mite,** a mite that burrows in the skin, causing itch or scabies; **itch'weed,** Indian poke.—*adj.* **itch'y,** pertaining to or affected with itch or itching. —**itching palm,** a greed for gain. [O.E. *giccan,* to itch; Scot. *youk, yuck,* Ger. *jucken,* to itch.]

item, *ī'təm, adv.* likewise: also.—*n.* a separate article or particular in an enumeration: a piece of news or other matter in a newspaper.—*v.t.* to set down in enumeration: to make a note of.—*v.t.* **i'temise,** to give by items. [L. *item,* likewise.]

iterate, *it'ər-āt, v.t.* to do again: to say again, repeat. —*ns.* **it'erance, iterā'tion,** repetition. — *adjs.* **it'erant, it'erative** (*-ə-tiv* or *-ā-tiv*), repeating. [L. *iterāre, -ātum—iterum,* again.]

ithyphallus, *ith-i-fal'əs, n.* an erect phallus: **Ithyphallus,** the stinkhorn genus of fungi.—*adj.* **ithyphall'ic,** of or with an ithyphallus: pertaining to the processions in honour of Dionysos in which an ithyphallus was carried, or to the hymns sung or the metres used: shameless. [Gr. *ithyphallos—ithys,* straight, *phallos,* a phallus.]

itinerant, *i-tin'ər-ənt,* also *ī-., adj.* making journeys from place to place: travelling.—*n.* one who travels from place to place, esp. a judge, a Methodist preacher, a strolling musician, or a peddler: a wanderer.—*ns.* itin'eracy (*-ə-si*), itin'erancy.—*adv.* itin'erantly.—*adj.* itin'erary, travelling: relating to roads or journeys.—*n.* a plan or record of a journey: a road-book: a route: an itinerant. —*v.i.* itin'erate, to travel from place to place, esp. for the purpose of judging, preaching, or lecturing. [L. *iter*, *itiner*s, a journey.]

its, *its*, possessive or genitive of it. [The old form was *his*, *its* not being older than the end of the 16th century. *Its* does not occur in the English Bible of 1611, or in Spenser, rarely in Shakespeare, and is not common until the time of Dryden.]

itself, *it-self'*, *pron.* the emphatic and reflexive form of it.—by itself, alone, apart; in itself, by its own nature.

ivory, *i'və-ri*, *n.* dentine, esp. the hard white substance composing the tusks of the elephant, walrus, hippopotamus, and narwhal: an object of that material, as a billiard-ball, a piano-key: (*slang*) a tooth or the teeth.—*adj.* made of, or resembling, ivory.—*adj.* i'voried, made like ivory: furnished with teeth.—*ns.* i'vorist, a worker in ivory; i'vory-black, a black powder, originally made from burnt ivory, but now from bone; i'vory-gate' (*myth.*; see gate); i'vory-nut,

the nut of Phytelephas or other palm, yielding vegetable ivory, a substance like ivory; i'vory-palm; i'vory-por'celain, a fine ware with an ivory-white glaze; i'vory-tower, (*fig.*) a place of retreat from the world and one's fellows; i'vory-tree, the palay.—show one's ivories, to show the teeth. [O.Fr. *ivurie* (Fr. *ivoire*)—L. *ebur*, *eboris*, ivory; Coptic *ebu*; Sans. *ibhas*, an elephant.]

ivy, *i'vi*, *n.* an araliaceous evergreen plant (*Hedera Helix*) that climbs by roots on trees and walls.—*adjs.* i'vied (also i'vy'd), i'vy-man'tled, overgrown or mantled with ivy.—*n.* i'vy-bush, a bush or branch of ivy, esp. formerly one hung at a tavern-door, the ivy being sacred to Bacchus.—*adj.* i'vy-leaved, having five-lobed leaves like ivy (as the *ivy-leaved* toadflax).—*n.* i'vy-tod', a bush of ivy. — ground - ivy, poison - ivy (see ground, poison). [O.E. *īfig*, O.H.G. *ebah*.]

iwis, ywis, *i-wis'*, *adv.* certainly—sometimes ignorantly written *I wis*, as if 'I know.' [M.E. *ywis*, *iwis*—O.E. *gewis*, certain; Ger. *gewiss* (adv.).]

ixtle. See istle.

iynx. Same as jynx.

Iyyar, *ē'yär*, *n.* the eighth month of the Jewish year (second of the ecclesiastical year). [Heb.]

izard, *iz'ərd*, the Pyrenean ibex. [Fr. *isard*.]

izzard, *iz'ərd*, izzet, *iz'it*, *n.* (*arch.* or *dial.*) the letter Z.

fāte, fär, âsk; mē, hər (her); mīne; mōte; mūte; mōōn; dhen (then)

J

J, j, *jā, n.* the tenth letter in our alphabet, developed from I, specialised to denote a consonantal sound (*dzh* in English, *y* in German and other languages, *zh* in French, an open guttural in Spanish), I being retained for the vowel-sound—a differentiation not general in English books till about 1630: as a numeral, used in old MSS. and in medical prescriptions instead of i when final, as *vj*, six : **J** represents the mechanical equivalent of heat—from Joule.—*n.* **J′-pen,** a pen with a short broad point.

jab, *jab, v.t.* and *v.i.* to poke, stab.—*n.* a sudden thrust or stab. [Cf. **job** (1).]

jabber, *jab′ər, v.i.* to gabble or talk rapidly.—*v.t.* to utter indistinctly.—*n.* rapid indistinct speaking.—*n.* **jabb′erer.**—*n.* and *adj.* **jabb′ering.**—*adv.* **jabb′-eringly.** [Imit.]

jabble, *jab′l, n.* (*Scot.*) an agitation in liquid : a rippling : a quantity of liquid enough to dash about or jumble.—*v.t.* and *v.i.* to splash : to ripple : to dash : to jumble. [Imit.]

jabers, *jā′bərz, n.* in the Irish oath *be jabers*, prob. for **Jesus.**

jabiru, *jab′i-rōō, -rōō′, n.* a large Brazilian stork : extended to other kinds. [Tupi *jabirú.*]

jaborandi, *jab-ō-ran′di, n.* a Brazilian drug with sialogogue and diaphoretic properties, got from the leaflets of rutaceous shrubs (Pilocarpus) and other sources. [Tupi.]

jabot, *zhā′bō, n.* a frill of lace, &c., worn in front of a woman's dress or (formerly) on a man's shirt-front. [Fr.]

jacamar, *jak′ə-mär, n.* any one of a South American family (Galbulidae) of long-billed insect-catching birds with metallic plumage and reversible fourth toe. [Fr.,—Tupi *jacamá-ciri.*]

jaçana, *zhä-sä-nä′,* **jacana,** *jak′ə-nä, n.* a South American long-toed swamp bird. [Port., from Tupi.]

jacaranda, *jak-ə-ran′dä, n.* a South American tree of the Bignoniaceae, with hard, heavy, brown wood. [Port. and Tupi *jacarandá.*]

jacchus, *jak′əs, n.* a South American marmoset (Callithrix). [L. *Iacchus*—Gr. *Iakchos,* Bacchus.]

jacent, *jā′sənt, adj.* lying at length : sluggish. [L. *jacēns, -ēntis,* pr.p. of *jacēre,* to lie.]

jacinth, *jas′inth, jās′, n.* originally, a blue gem-stone, perhaps sapphire : (*min.*) an orange or a red variety of zircon, a hyacinth : (*jewellery*) a variety of garnet, topaz, quartz, or other stone : a reddish-orange colour : a slaty-blue fancy pigeon. [hyacinth.]

Jack, *jak, n.* used as a familiar name or diminutive of John : (*obs.*) contemptuously, a fellow, a knave : a saucy or paltry fellow : a sailor : an attendant : **jack,** any instrument serving to supply the place of a boy or helper, as a boot-jack for taking off boots, a contrivance for turning a spit (smoke-jack, roasting-jack), an apparatus for raising heavy weights : a winch : a figure that strikes the bell in clocks : the male of some animals : a jackass : a jack-rabbit : a jackdaw : a young pike : in keyboard instruments, part of the action that moves the hammer or carries the quill or tangent : (*Shak.*) the key itself : a contrivance for guiding threads in a loom : a saw-horse : a flag displayed from the bowsprit of a ship : a leather pitcher or bottle : a knave in cards : the small white ball aimed at in bowls.—*v.t.* to raise with a jack (with *up*) : to act upon with a jack : (*slang*) to throw up or abandon promptly (with *up*).—*v.i.* to give in (with *up*).—*ns.* **Jack′-a-dan′dy,** a dandy or fop, esp. if diminutive ; **Jack′-a-lan′tern, Jack′-o′-lan′tern,** Will-o′-the-wisp ; **Jack′-a-Lent′,** (*Shak.*) a boy (for Jack of Lent, a kind of puppet formerly thrown at in sport at Lent) ; **jack′-block,** a block of pulleys used for raising and lowering topgallant-masts ;

jack′boot, a large boot reaching above the knee, to protect the leg, formerly worn by cavalry and covered with plates of iron : (*fig.*) military rule, esp. when brutal ; **Jack′-by-the-hedge′,** garlick-mustard ; **jack′-cross′tree,** the crosstree at the head of a topgallant-mast ; **jack′-flag,** a flag which is hoisted at the spritsail topmast-head ; **Jack′-fool′,** a fool ; **Jack′-go-to-bed-at-noon′,** the plant goat's-beard.—*adj.* and *adv.* **jack′-high,** (in bowls) as far as the jack.—*ns.* **Jack′-in-off′ice,** a vexatiously self-important petty official ; **Jack′-in-the-box′,** a figure that springs up from a box when the lid is released ; **Jack′-in-the-green′,** a May-Day dancer enclosed in a green shrubby frame-work ; **Jack′-in-the-pul′pit,** an American plant (*Arisaema triphyllum*) like cuckoo-pint ; **jack′-knife,** a large clasp-knife ; **jack′-has′ty,** a sneak : a sloven ; **Jack′-of-all′-trades,** one who can turn his hand to anything ; **jack′-pine,** a name for several North American species of pine ; **jack′-plane,** a large strong plane used by joiners ; **jack′pot,** (*poker*) a game played for the pot or pool, consisting of equal stakes from all the players, which must be opened by a hand holding two jacks or better : (*Amer. slang*) a mess or tangle ; **Jack′-priest′,** (in contempt) a parson ; **Jack′-pudd′ing,** a merry-andrew, buffoon ; **jack′-rabb′it,** a long-eared American hare ; **jack′-raft′er,** a rafter shorter than the rest, as in hip-roofs ; **Jack′-sauce′,** (*Shak.*) a saucy fellow ; **Jack′-slave,** (*Shak.*) a low servant, a vulgar fellow ; **jack′smith,** a maker of jacks for the kitchen ; **jack′-snipe,** a small species of snipe ; **jack′-staff,** the staff on which the jack is hoisted.—*n.pl.* **jack′-stays,** ropes or strips of wood or iron stretched along the yards of a ship to bind the sails to.—*ns.* **Jack′-straw′, jack′straw,** a straw effigy : a man of straw, of no real significance : a straw or slip used in the game of **jack′-straws′,** or spillikins ; **jack′-tar′,** a sailor ; **jack′-tow′el,** a long endless towel passing over a roller.—**cheap Jack** (see **cheap**) ; **every man Jack,** one and all ; **Jack Frost,** frost personified ; **Jack Ketch,** a public hangman—from one so named under James II. ; **Jack Sprat,** a diminutive fellow ; **poor Jack,** poor-John ; **steeple-jack** (see **steeple**) ; **Union Jack** (not properly a jack : see **union**) ; **yellow Jack,** (*slang*) yellow fever. [App. Fr. *Jacques,* the most common name in France, hence used as a substitute for *John,* the most common name in England ; really=*James* or *Jacob*—L. *Jacōbus* ; but possibly partly from *Jackin, Jankin,* dim. of *John.*]

jack, *jak, n.* a mediaeval defensive coat, esp. of leather.—*n.* **jack′man,** a soldier clad in a jack : a retainer. [Fr. *jaque,* perh. from *Jacques,* James.]

jack, *jak, jāk, n.* a tree of the East Indies of the bread-fruit genus (Artocarpus).—*ns.* **jack′-fruit ; jack′-tree.** [Port. *jaca*—Malayalam *chakka.*]

jackal, *jak′awl, n.* a wild, gregarious animal closely allied to the dog—erroneously supposed to act as a lion's provider or hunting scout : hence, one who does another's dirty work : a drudge : one who would share the spoil without sharing the danger.—*v.i.* to play the jackal :—*pa.p.* **jack′alled.** [Pers. *shaghāl.*]

jackanapes, *jak′ə-nāps, n.* an ape or monkey : an impudent fellow : a coxcomb : a forward child. [Origin uncertain.]

jackaroo, *jak-ə-rōō′, n.* (*Austr.*) a newcomer from England, or other person, gaining experience on a sheep-station.—*v.i.* to be a jackaroo. [App. an imitation of **kangaroo** with **Jack.**]

jackass, *jak′ās, n.* a he-ass : a blockhead.—**laughing jackass,** an Australian kingfisher that laughs, the kookaburra. [Jack, ass.]

Neutral vowels in unaccented syllables : *el′ə-mənt, in′fənt. ran′dəm*

jackdaw, *jak'daw*, *n.* a daw, a small species of crow with greyish neck. [Jack, daw.]

jacket, *jak'it*, *n.* a short coat: an animal's coat: skin (of potatoes): a loose paper cover: outer casing of a boiler, pipe, &c., as a steam-jacket, water-jacket.—*v.t.* to furnish or cover with a jacket: (*slang*) to beat.—*adj.* **jack'eted**, wearing a jacket.—dust one's jacket, to beat him. [O.Fr. *jaquet*, dim. of *jaque*; see jack (2).]

Jacobean, *jak-o-bē'ən*, *adj.* of or characteristic of the period of James I. of England (1603-25). [L. *Jacōbus*, James.]

Jacobin, *jak'o-bin*, *n.* a French Dominican monk, so named from their original establishment being that of St *Jacques*, Paris: one of a society of revolutionists in France, so called from their meeting in the hall of the Jacobin convent: a demagogue: a hooded pigeon.—*adjs.* **Jacobin'ic**, **-al.**—*v.t.* **Jac'obinise.**—*n.* **Jac'obinism**, the principles of the Jacobins or French revolutionists. [Fr.,—L. *Jacōbus*, James.]

Jacobite, *jak'o-bīt*, *n.* an adherent of James II. and his descendants: in Church history, a Syrian monophysite, named after the 6th-century monk *Jacobus* Baradaeus.—*adjs.* **Jac'obite**, **Jacobit'ic**, **-al.**—*n.* **Jac'obitism.** [L. *Jacōbus*, James.]

Jacob's-ladder, *jā'kəbz-lad'ər*, *n.* (*naut.*) a ladder of ropes with wooden steps for climbing the rigging: a wild or garden plant (Polemonium) with ladder-like leaves: an endless chain of buckets used as an elevator. [From the *ladder* seen by *Jacob* in his dream, Gen. xxviii. 12.]

Jacob's-staff, *jā'kəbz-stäf*, *n.* a pilgrim's staff: a staff with a cross-head used in surveying: a sword-cane. [Prob. from the pilgrimage to St James (L. *Jacōbus*) of Compostela.]

jacobus, *jə-kō'bəs*, *n.* a gold coin of James I. worth 20s. to 25s. [L. *Jacōbus*, James—Gr. *Iakōbos*—Heb. *Ya'aqōb*.]

jaconet, *jak'ə-net*, *n.* a cotton fabric, rather stouter than muslin—different from that originally made at *Jagannāthī* in India: a thin material of rubber and linen used for medical dressings.

Jacquard, *jak'ärd, jak-ärd'*, *n.* an apparatus with perforated cards for controlling the movement of the warp threads in weaving a pattern: a fabric so woven.—*n.* **Jacq'uard-loom**, a loom with Jacquard. [Joseph Marie *Jacquard* (1752-1824), the inventor.]

Jacqueminot, *jak'mi-nō*, *n.* a deep-red hybrid perpetual rose.—Also **Jacque** and **Jack**. [From General *Jacqueminot* of Paris.]

Jacquerie, *zhäk'rē*, *n.* the revolt of the French peasants in 1358. [From *Jacques* Bonhomme, Goodman Jack, a name applied in derision to the peasants.]

jactation, *jak-tā'shən*, *n.* act of throwing: extreme restlessness in disease: bodily agitation: boasting. [L. *jactātiō*, *-ōnis*, tossing, boasting—*jactāre*, to throw.]

jactitation, *jak-ti-tā'shən*, *n.* restless tossing in illness: twitching or convulsion: tossing or bandying about: bragging: public assertion, esp. ostentatious and false.—**jactitation of marriage**, pretence of being married to another. [L.L. *jactitātiō*, *-ōnis*—L. *jactitāre*, *-ātum*, to toss about, put about, make a display of, freq. of *jactāre*, to throw.]

jaculation, *jak-ū-lā'shən*, *n.* the act of throwing or hurling, as a dart.—*v.t.* **jac'ulate**, to dart, throw. —*n.* **jac'ulator**, a dart-thrower: an archer-fish.— *adj.* **jac'ulatory** (*-ət-ər-i*), darting or throwing out suddenly: ejaculatory. [L. *jaculārī*, *-ātus*, to throw as a dart—*jaculum*, a dart—*jacēre*, to throw.]

jade, *jād*, *n.* a sorry horse: a worthless nag: a woman, esp. perverse, ill-natured, or not to be trusted, often in irony.—*v.t.* to make a jade of: to weary, dull, cause to flag: to play the jade with. —*adv.* **jad'edly.**—*n.* **jad'ery**, the tricks of a jade. —*adj.* **jad'ish.** [Origin unknown; cf. O.N. *jalda*, a mare; Scot. *yaud*.]

jade, *jād*, *n.* a hard dark-green ornamental stone— esp. *nephrite* (silicate of calcium and magnesium) and **jade'ite** (silicate of aluminium and sodium)— once held to cure side pains.—*adj.* **jade**, of jade, of the colour of jade. [Fr.,—Sp. *ijada*, the flank— L. *ilia*.]

Jaffa, *jaf'ä*, *n.* an orange from *Jaffa* in Palestine (Jaffa orange).

jag, *jag*, *n.* a notch, slash, or dag in a garment, &c.: a ragged protrusion: (*bot.*) a cleft or division: (*Scot.*) a prick.—*v.t.* to cut into notches: to prick or pierce:—*pr.p.* **jagg'ing**; *pa.p.* **jagged** (*jagd*).— *adj.* **jagg'ed**, notched, rough-edged, uneven.— *adv.* **jagg'edly.**—*ns.* **jagg'edness**; **jagg'er**, a brass wheel with a notched edge for cutting cakes, &c., into ornamental forms—also **jagg'ing-i'ron.**— *adj.* **jagg'y**, notched: slashed: (*Scot.*) prickly. [Origin unknown.]

jag, *jag*, *n.* a load: a saddle-bag or other bag: a quantity: (*U.S.*) one's fill of liquor.—*v.t.* to cart: to transport by pack-horse.—*adj.* **jagged** (*jagd*; *U.S.*), drunk.—*n.* **jagg'er**, a carter: a pack-horse-man: a pedlar.

Jagannath, *jug-un-ät'*, *n.* a corrected form of Juggernaut.

jäger, jaeger, *yā'gər*, *n.* a (German) huntsman: a German rifleman or sharpshooter: a skua that chases and robs other gulls. [Ger., hunter— *jagen*, to hunt.]

jaggery, *jag'ə-ri*, *n.* a coarse, dark sugar made from palm-sap or otherwise. [Hind. *shakkar*, Sans. *çarkarā*; cf. **sugar, saccharum.**]

jaghir, jaghire, jagir, *jä-gēr'*, *n.* the government revenues of a tract of land assigned with power to administer.—*n.* **jaghir'dar**, the holder of a jaghir. [Hind. and Pers. *jāgīr.*]

jaguar, *jag'wär*, or *jag'ū-är*, *n.* a powerful beast of prey, allied to the leopard, found in South America. [Tupí *jaguára.*]

Jah, *jä*, *n.* Jehovah.—*n.* **Jah'veh** (same as **Yahwe**). [Heb. *Yah.*]

jail, gaol, *jāl*, *n.* a prison.—*ns.* **jail'-bird, gaol'-bird**, a humorous name for one who is, has been, or should be much in jail; **jail'-deliv'ery, gaol'-deliv'ery**, clearing of a jail by sending all prisoners to trial: delivery from jail; **jail'er, gaol'er**, one who has charge of a jail or of prisoners: a turnkey:—*fem.* **jail'eress**, &c.; **jail'-fē'ver, gaol'-fē'ver**, typhus fever, once common in jails.— **break jail**, to force one's way out of prison; **Commission of Jail Delivery**, one of the commissions issued to judges of assize and judges of the Central Criminal Court in England. [O.Fr. *gaole* (Fr. *geôle*)—L.L. *gabiola*, a cage—L. *cavea*, a cage— *cavus*, hollow.]

Jain, *jīn, jān*, **Jaina**, *jī'nä*, *n.* an adherent of an Indian religion allied to Brahmanism and Buddhism. —Also *adjs.*—*n.* **Jain'ism.** [Hind. *jina*, a deified saint.]

jak, jak, *n.* Same as jack (3).

jake, *jāk*, *n.* (*U.S.*) a country lout: a yokel. [Perh. from the name *Jacob.*]

jakes, *jāks*, *n.* (*Shak.*) a privy. [Origin unknown.]

jalap, *jal'əp*, *n.* the purgative root of an Ipomoea or Exogonium, first brought from *Jalapa* or Xalapa, in Mexico.—*adj.* **jalap'ic.**—*n.* **jal'apin**, a glucoside resin, one of the purgative principles of jalap.— **false jalap**, marvel of Peru, formerly used as a substitute.

jalop(p)y, *jə-lop'i*, *n.* an old motor-car.

jalouse, *jə-looz'*, *v.t.* (*Scot.*) to suspect. [See jealous.]

jalousie, *zhal-oo-zē'*, or *zhal'*, *n.* an outside shutter with slats.—*adj.* **jal'ousied.** [Fr., —*jalousie*, jealousy.]

jam, *jam*, *n.* a conserve of fruit boiled with sugar.— *v.t.* to spread with jam: to make into jam.—*adj.* **jamm'y**, smeared or sticky with jam: like jam.— *n.* **jam'-pot**, a jar for keeping jam in: a high collar, esp. a clergyman's. [Perh. from next.]

jam, *jam*, *v.t.* to press or squeeze tight: to crowd full: to block by crowding: to bring to a standstill by crowding or interlocking: (*wireless*) to interfere with by emitting signals of similar wavelength: (*pr.p.* **jamm'ing**; *pa.t.* and *pa.p.* **jammed**). —*n.* a crush, squeeze: a block or stoppage due to crowding or squeezing together: a jammed mass (as of logs in a river): a jamming of wireless messages. [Cf. **champ.**]

jamadar, *jum'ä-där.* Same as **jemadar.**

Jamaica, *jə-mā'kä*, **Jamaican**, *-kən*, *adjs.* of the island of Jamaica.—*n.* **Jamai′can,** a native or inhabitant of Jamaica.—**Jamaica bark,** Caribbee bark; **Jamaica cedar,** bastard Barbados cedar; **Jamaica ebony,** cocus-wood; **Jamaica pepper,** allspice; **Jamaica plum,** hog-plum.

jamb, *jam, n.* the sidepiece or post of a door, fireplace, &c.: leg-armour (in this sense also **jambe,** *jam*).—*ns.* **jambeau** (*jam′bō; obs.*), leg-armour: legging:—*pl.* **jambeaux, jambeux** (*Spens.* giambeux); **jam′ber, jam′bier,** (*obs.*) leg-armour. [Fr. *jambe,* leg; cf. **gamb.**]

jambee, *jam-bē′, n.* an 18th-century light cane. [*Jambi* in Sumatra.]

jambok. See **sjambok.**

jambolana. See **jambu.**

jambone, *jam′bōn, n.* a lone hand in euchre, played only by agreement, in which the player lays his cards on the table and must lead one chosen by his opponent, scoring 8 points if he takes all the tricks. [Origin unknown.]

jamboree, *jam-bō-rē′, n.* in euchre, a lone hand of the 5 highest cards, by agreement scoring 16 points for the holder: (*slang*) a boisterous frolic, a spree: a great boy scout rally. [Origin unknown.]

jambu, *jum′, jam′bōō, n.* the rose-apple tree or other Eugenia. — Also **jambul, jambool** (*jum-bōōl′*), **jam′bolan, jambolana** (*-bō-lä′nä*). [Sans. *jambu, jambula.*]

jamdani, *jäm-dä′nē, n.* a variety of Dacca muslin woven in design of flowers. [Pers. *jämdänī.*]

Jamesian, *jāmz′i-ən, adj.* relating to William *James* (1842–1910), American psychologist, or other of the name of James.

Jamesonite, *jim′i-sən-īt,* or *jām′sən-īt, n.* a mineral compound of lead, antimony, and sulphur. [Robert *Jameson* (1772–1854), Scottish mineralogist.]

Jamestown-weed. See **Jimson-weed.**

jampan, *jam′pan, n.* an Indian sedan-chair.—*n.* **jampanee, jampani** (*-ē′*), its bearer. [Beng. *jhāmpān.*]

jane, *jān, n.* (*Spens.*) a small silver Genoese coin: jean (cloth). [L.L. *Janua,* L. *Genua,* Genoa.]

Janeite, *jān′īt, n.* an ardent admirer of *Jane* Austen.

jangle, *jang′gl, v.t.* and *v.i.* to sound with unpleasant tone, as bells.—*v.i.* to wrangle or quarrel.—*n.* dissonant clanging: contention.—*ns.* **jang′ler; jang′-ling.**—*adj.* **jang′ly.** [O.Fr. *jangler.*]

janitor, *jan′i-tər, n.* a doorkeeper: an attendant or caretaker:—*fem.* **jan′itrix, jan′itress.**—*adj.* **jani-tō′rial.**—*n.* **jan′itorship.** [L. *jānitor—jānua,* a door.]

janizary, *jan′i-zər-i, n.* a soldier of the old Turkish foot-guards (*c.* 1330–1826), formed originally of renegade prisoners and of a tribute of children taken from Christian subjects.—Also **jan′issary** (*-zər-i*), **jan′izar.**—*adj.* **janizā′rian.**—**janizary music,** military music with much percussion. [Fr. *Janissaire,* supposed to be—Turk. *yeni,* new, *tsheri,* soldiery.]

janker, *jang′kər, n.* (*Scot.*) a long pole on wheels for transporting logs. [Origin unknown.]

jann, *jän, n.pl.* the least powerful order of jinn: (*sing.*) a jinni. [Ar. *jānn.*]

jannock, *jan′ək, adj.* (*prov.*) straightforward. [Origin obscure.]

jannock, *jan′ək, n.* (*N.* of England) oaten bread: a cake thereof. [Origin obscure.]

Jansenism, *jan′sən-izm, n.* a system of evangelical doctrine deduced from Augustine by Cornelius *Jansen* (1585–1638), Roman Catholic Bishop of Ypres, essentially a reaction against the ordinary Catholic dogma of the freedom of the will and that of merely sufficient grace, maintaining that interior grace is irresistible, and that Christ died for all.—*n.* **Jan′senist,** a believer in Jansenism.

jantee, janty. See **jaunty.**

January, *jan′ū-ər-i, n.* now the first month of the year, dedicated by the Romans to Janus. [L. *Jānuārius.*]

Janus, *jā′nəs, n.* the ancient Italian two-faced god of doors, whose temple in Rome was closed in time of peace.—*adjs.* **Jān′iform** (wrongly **Jān′uform**), two-faced; **Jān′ian, Jān′us-faced,** two-faced. [L. *Jānus.*]

Jap, *jap, n.* and *adj.* (*coll.*) for *Japanese.*—*n.* **Jap′-silk,** a thin kind of silk.

jap. Same as **jaup.**

japan, *jə-pan′, adj.* of Japan: japanned.—*n.* Japanese ware or work: varnish or lacquer for japanning: japanned work.—*v.t.* to varnish after the manner or in imitation of the Japanese: to make black and glossy: (*old slang*) to ordain:—*pr.p.* **japann′ing;** *pa.t.* and *pa.p.* **japanned′.**—*n.* **japan′-earth,** or *terra japonica,* gambier.—*adj.* **Japanese** (*jap-ə-nēz′,* or *jap′*), of Japan, of its people, or of its language.—*n.* a native or citizen of Japan: the language of Japan:—*pl.* **Japanese** (formerly **Japaneses**).—*ns.* **Japanes′ery,** Japanese decoration: a Japanese ornament: Japanese bric-à-brac; **Japanesque** (*-esk′*), a design in Japanese style.—*adj.* **Japanesque′, Japanes′y,** savouring of the Japanese.—*n.* **japann′er.**—**Japanese cedar,** a very tall Japanese conifer (*Cryptomeria japonica*), often dwarfed by Japanese gardeners; **Japanese medlar,** the loquat; **Japanese paper,** a fine soft paper made from paper-mulberry bark; **Japan lacquer, Japan varnish,** a varnish got from a species of sumach (*Rhus vernicifera*): extended to various other similar varnishes; **Japan laurel,** a shrub (*Aucuba japonica*) of the dogwood family, with spotted yellow leaves; **japanned leather,** patent leather (see **patent**); **Japan wax,** a fat got from the berries of species of sumach.

jape, *jāp, v.i.* to jest, joke.—*v.t.* to mock: (*obs.*) to seduce.—*n.* a jest, joke, trick. [O.Fr. *japer,* to yelp.]

Japhetic, *jə-fet′ik, adj.* (*obs.*) of European race: Indo-European in language. [From supposed descent from *Japhet.*]

Japonic, *jə-pon′ik, adj.* Japanese.—*n.* **japon′ica,** the Japanese quince (*Pyrus,* or *Cydonia, japonica*) or other Japanese plant.

jar, *jär, v.i.* to make a harsh discordant sound or unpleasant vibration: to give an unpleasant shock: to grate: to be discordant or distasteful: (*Shak.*) to tick: to clash: to quarrel: to be inconsistent.—*v.t.* to shake, as by a blow: to cause to vibrate unpleasantly: to grate on: to make dissonant: (*pr.p.* **jarr′ing;** *pa.t.* and *pa.p.* **jarred**).—*n.* a harsh sudden vibration: a dissonance: a grating sound or feeling: (*Shak.*) a tick of a clock: clash of interests or opinions: dispeace, conflict.—*n.* and *adj.* **jarr′ing.**—*adv.* **jarr′ingly.** [Imit.]

jar, *jär, n.* a wide-mouthed wide vessel: as much as a jar will hold: a Leyden jar (q.v.).—*v.t.* to put in jars.—*n.* **jar′ful:**—*pl.* **jar′fuls.** [O.Fr. *jarre* or Sp. *jarra*—Ar. *jarrah.*]

jar, *jär, n.* a turn, used only in the phrase *on the jar, ajar.* [Earlier *char*—O.E. *cerr;* cf. **char** (3), **ajar.**]

jardinière, *zhär-dē-nyer′, n.* a vessel for the display of flowers, growing or cut: a dish including a mixture of vegetables: a lappet forming part of an old head-dress. [Fr., gardener (fem.)—*jardin,* garden.]

jargon, *jär′gən, n.* chatter, twittering: confused talk: slang: artificial or barbarous language.—*v.i.* to twitter, chatter: to speak jargon.—*ns.* **jargoneer′, jar′gonist,** one who uses jargon. [Fr. *jargon.*]

jargoon, *jär-gōōn′,* **jargon,** *jär′-gən, n.* a brilliant colourless or pale zircon.—*n.* **jargonelle′,** an early pear (orig. a gritty kind). [See **zircon.**]

jark, *järk, n.* (*cant*) a seal: a pass, safe-conduct.—*n.* **jark′man,** a swindling beggar, a begging-letter writer.

jarl, *yärl, n.* a noble, chief, earl. [O.N.; cf. **earl.**]

jarrah, *jär′ä, n.* a Western Australian timber tree, *Eucalyptus marginata.* [From a native name.]

jarta, yarta, *yär′tä, n.* (*Shetland*) lit. heart, used as an endearment.—Also *adj.*—Also (*Scott*) **yar′to.** [O.N. *hjarta,* heart.]

jarul, jarool, *jə-rōōl′, n.* the Indian bloodwood (*Lagerstroemia*), a taller-grown tree. [Beng. *jārūl.*]

jarvey, *jär′vi, n.* (*slang*) a hackney-coach driver: a jaunting-car driver. [Earlier *Jarvis,* poss. from St *Gervase,* whose emblem is a whip.]

jasey, jasy, jazy, *jā′zi, n.* a wig, orig. of worsted. [jersey.]

Jasher, Jashar, *jäsh′ər, n.* one of the lost books of

the ancient Hebrews, quoted twice (Josh. x. 13; 2 Sam. i. 18), most probably a collection of heroic ballads.

jasmine, *jas′min*, **jessamine**, *jes′ə-min*, *ns.* a genus (Jasminum) of oleaceous shrubs, many with very fragrant flowers.—**red jasmine**, a tropical American shrub akin to periwinkle—frangipani (Plumieria). [Fr. *jasmin, jasemin*—Ar. *yāsmīn, yāsamīn*—Pers. *yāsmīn.*]

jasp, *jasp* (*Spens.*), **jasper**, *jas′pər*, *ns.* a precious stone: an opaque quartz containing clay or iron compounds: a fine hard porcelain (also **jas′perware**).—*adj.* of jasper.—*adj.* **jaspe, jaspé** (*jasp, -ā*), mottled, variegated, or veined.—*v.t.* **jasp′erise**, to turn into jasper.—*adjs.* **jasp′erous, jasp′ery.** —*n.* jas′pis, jasper.—*adjs.* **jaspid′ean, jaspid′eous.** [O.Fr. *jaspe, jaspre*—L. *iaspis, -idis*; and directly from Gr. *iaspis, -idos*, of Eastern origin.]

jataka, *jä′tə-kə*, *n.* a nativity, the birth-story of Buddha. [Sans. *jātaka—jāta*, born.]

jaunce, jaunse, *jawns, jäns, v.i.* (*Shak.*) to prance: to cause a horse to prance.—*n.* (*Shak.; prob.*) prancing: a wearisome journey. [Perh. from a doubtful O.Fr. *jancer*, to cause to prance.]

jaundice, *jawn′dis* (also *jän′dis*), *n.* a disease, characterised by a yellowing of the eyes, skin, &c., by bile pigment, the patient in rare cases seeing objects as yellow: extended to other diseases with discolorations: a disposition to take an unfavourable view: prejudice: jealousy.—*v.t.* to affect with jaundice, in any sense.—*adj.* **jaun′diced**, affected with jaundice: prejudiced: jealous. [Fr. *jaunisse —jaune*, yellow—L. *galbīnus*, yellowish, *galbus*, yellow.]

jaunt, *jawnt* (also *jänt*), *v.i.* to go from place to place, formerly with fatigue, now chiefly for pleasure: to make an excursion.—*n.* an excursion: a ramble.—*adj.* **jaunt′ing**, strolling: making an excursion.—*n.* **jaunt′ing-car**, a low-set, two-wheeled, open vehicle used in Ireland, with side-seats usu. back to back. [Origin obscure; cf. **jaunce.**]

jaunty, janty, *jawn′ti* (also *jän′ti*), *adj.* (*obs.*) gentlemanly (formerly **jantee, jauntee**): having an airy or sprightly manner approaching swagger.—*adv.* **jaunt′ily.**—*n.* **jaunt′iness.** [Fr. *gentil.*]

jaunty. See **jonty.**

jaup, *jawp*, or *jäp*, **jap**, *jäp, v.t.* and *v.i.* (*Scot.*) to spatter: to splash.—*n.* a splash: a spattering. [Origin unknown.]

Java, *jä′vä*, *adj.* of the island of Java.—*adjs.* and *ns.* **Ja′van, Javanese′.**—**Java plum**, the jambolana (*Eugenia jambolana*); **Java sparrow**, a kind of weaver-bird.

javel, *jav′əl*, *n.* (*Spens.*) a worthless fellow. [Origin unknown.]

javelin, *jav′(ə-)lin*, *n.* a throwing-spear.—*n.* **jav′elinman**, an armed member of a sheriff's retinue or a judge's escort at assizes: a soldier armed with a javelin. [Fr. *javeline*; prob. Celt.]

jaw, *jaw*, *n.* a mouth-structure for biting or chewing: the bone of a jaw: one of a pair of parts for gripping, crushing, cutting, grinding, &c.: (*pl.*) a narrow entrance: (*slang*) talkativeness, scolding.— *v.t.* (*slang*) to scold.—*v.i.* to talk, esp. in excess.— *ns.* jaw′bone, the bone of the jaw; jaw′-break′er, (*slang*) a word hard to pronounce.—*adj.* jawed, having jaws.—*n.* jaw′fall, a falling of the jaw: (*fig.*) depression of spirits.—*adj.* jaw′-fallen, depressed in spirits: dejected.—*ns.* jaw′-foot, a foot-jaw, maxilliped; jaw′ing, (*slang*) talk, esp. unrestrained, abusive, or reproving; jaw′-lē′ver, an instrument for opening the mouth of a horse or cow to admit medicine; jaw′-tooth, a molar.— hold one's jaw, to cease from talking or scolding. [Perh. chaw, modified by Fr. *joue*, cheek.]

jaw, *jaw*, *n.* (*Scot.*) a dash or surge of liquid: a portion of liquid so dashed.—*v.t.* and *v.i.* to pour suddenly in a body.—*ns.* jaw′box, a sink; jaw′-hole, a cesspool: an entrance to a sewer. [Origin unknown.]

jawbation, *jaw-bā′shən, n.* for jobation. [Influenced by jaw; see Job.]

jay, *jā*, *n.* a bird of the crow family with gay plumage: a wanton woman: an indifferent actor: a

stupid or awkward fellow.—*adj.* (*U.S.*) stupid: inferior.—*v.i.* jay′walk.—*ns.* jay′walker, a careless pedestrian whom motorists are expected to avoid running down; jay′walking. [O.Fr. *jay.*]

jay, *jā*, *n.* the tenth letter of the alphabet (J, j): an object or mark of that shape. [Named on the analogy of *kay* (K).]

jazerant, *jaz′ə-rənt.* See **jesserant.**

jazy. Same as **jasey.**

jazz, *jaz*, *n.* obstreperous rag-time dancing or music: garish colouring: a quality, impulse, or manner analogous to jazz music.—*adj.* of or characterised by jazz.—*v.t.* to impart a jazz character to.—*adv.* **jazz′ily.**—*n.* jazz′iness.—*adj.* jazz′y. [Perh. negro jargon.]

jealous, *jel′əs*, *adj.* suspicious of or incensed at rivalry: envious: solicitous: anxiously heedful: mistrustfully vigilant: brooking no unfaithfulness.—*v.t.* jealouse (*jə-lōōz′*; *obs.* except *Scot.*; see jalouse).—*adv.* jeal′ously.—*ns.* jeal′ousy, jeal′oushood (*Shak.*), jeal′ousness. [O.Fr. *jalous* —L. *zēlus*—Gr. *zēlos*, emulation.]

Jeames, *jēmz*, *n.* a flunkey. [From Thackeray's *Jeames* (James) de la Pluche.]

jean, *jān* (*U.S. jēn*), *n.* a twilled-cotton cloth: (*pl.*) a suit or garment of jean.—*n.* jeanette (*jā-net′*), a light or coarse jean.—**satin jean**, a smooth, glossy fustian. [O.Fr. *Janne*—L. *Genua*, Genoa.]

jeat, *jet* (*Milt.*). Same as **jet.**

Jebusite, *jeb′ū-zīt*, *n.* one of a Canaanitish people, predecessors of the Israelites at Jerusalem: an old nickname for a Roman Catholic.—*adj.* **Jebusitic** (*-zit′ik*).

Jeddart, *jed′ərt*, **Jethart**, *jedh′ərt*, *n.* Jedburgh.— **Jethart justice**, hanging first and trying afterwards; **Jethart staff**, a sort of battle-axe with a long head. [O.E. *Gedwearde.*]

jee. See **gee** (1 and 3).

jee, *jē, v.i.* (*Scot.*) to stir: to budge.—*v.t.* to disturb: to set on one side or ajar.—*n.* a displacement to the side: a condition of being ajar.—**jee one's ginger**, to show perturbation.

jeel, *jēl*, **jeely**, -*i, ns.* and *vs.i.* (*Scot.*) jelly: to jelly.

jeep, *jēp*, *n.* a light military vehicle with great freedom of movement. [From G.P., for general purpose; perh. with reminiscence of a comic-strip animal character.]

jeer, *jēr, v.t.* to make sport of: to treat with derision. —*v.i.* to scoff: to deride: to make a mock.— *n.* a railing remark: biting jest: mockery.—*n.* jeer′er.—*n.* and *adj.* jeer′ing.—*adv.* jeer′ingly. [Origin unknown.]

jeff, *jef, v.i.* to gamble with printers' quadrats thrown like dice.

jeff, *jef*, *n.* a rope, in circus slang.

Jeffersonian, *jef-ər-sōn′i-ən*, *adj.* pertaining to Thomas *Jefferson* (1743–1826), U.S. President 1801–09: of the American Democratic party.—*n.* a Democrat.

jehad. Same as **jihad.**

Jehovah, *ji-hō′vä*, *n.* Yahweh, the Hebrew God, a name used by Christians.—*n.* **Jeho′vist**, one who holds that the vowel-points annexed to the word *Jehovah* in the Hebrew are the proper vowels of the word: a writer of passages in the Pentateuch in which the name applied to God is Yahweh, a Yahwist.—*adj.* **Jehovist′ic.—Jehovah's Witnesses**, the International Bible Students' Association, followers of Pastor Russell. [Heb.; for *Yĕhōwāh*, i.e. *Yahweh* with the vowels of *Ădōnāi.*]

Jehu, *jē′hū*, *n.* (*coll.*) a driver, esp. a furious whip. [A reference to 2 Kings ix. 20.]

jeistiecor, *jēs′ti-kōr*, *n.* (*obs. Scot.*) a close-fitting garment. [Fr. *juste au corps*, close-fitting to the body.]

jejune, *ji-jōōn′*, *adj.* empty: void of interest: barren: spiritless, meagre, arid.—*adv.* **jejune′ly.** —*ns.* **jejune′ness**; **jeju′num**, the part of the small intestine between the duodenum and the ileum. [L. *jējūnus*, hungry.]

jelly, *jel′i*, *n.* anything gelatinous: the juice of fruit boiled with sugar: a gelatinous preparation for the table: a glass for jelly: a jellyfish.—*v.i.* to set as a jelly: to congeal.—*v.t.* to make into a jelly.— *v.i.* jell, to jelly.—*adjs.* jell′ied, in a state of jelly:

enclosed in jelly; **jell'iform.**—*v.t.* **jell'ify,** to make into a jelly.—*v.i.* to become gelatinous.—*ns.* **jell'y-bag,** a bag through which fruit juice is strained for jelly; **jell'yfish,** a marine coelenterate with jelly-like body; **jell'ygraph,** a copying appliance that uses a plate of jelly.—*v.t.* to copy by this means. [Fr. *gelée*, from *geler*—L. *gelāre*, to freeze; cf. **gel.**]

jelutong, *jel'oo-tong, n.* pontianac, a substitute for gutta-percha: the Bornean apocynaceous tree (*Dyera costulata*) yielding it. [Malay.]

jemadar, *jem'ə-där, n.* an Indian army officer below a subahdar: an officer of police, customs, &c.— Also **jamadar** (*jum'*), **jem'idar.** [Urdu *jama'där.*]

jemima, *ji-mī'mä, n.* an elastic-sided boot. [An appropriate woman's name.]

jemmy, *jem'i, n.* a burglar's short crowbar: (*slang*) a baked sheep's head: a greatcoat. [A form of the name *James*.]

jemmy, *jem'i, adj.* neat, smart, handy.—Also **gemm'y.**—*n.* **jemm'iness,** neatness. [Cf. **jimp.**]

Jenkins, *jengk'inz, n.* (*coll.*) a society reporter: a toady.

jennet, *jen'it, n.* a small Spanish horse.—Also **genn'et, gen'et.** [O.Fr. *genet*—Sp. *jinete,* a light horseman, perh. of Arab origin.]

jenneting, *jen'it-ing, n.* a kind of early apple. [Prob. St John's apple—Fr. *Jeannet,* dim. of *Jean,* John; not from *June-eating*.]

Jenny, *jen'i, n.* a country lass: a womanish man: a wren or owl regarded as female: a she-ass: a travelling crane: a spinning-jenny: a portable electric generator: (*billiards*) an in-off into a middle pocket from near the cushion.—*ns.* **Jenny-long'-legs** (*Scot.*), **Jenn'y-spinner** (*dial.*), a crane-fly; **Jenny-wren',** a wren. [From the name *Jenny*.]

jeofail, *jef'āl, n.* an error in pleadings, or the acknowledgment of a mistake. [A.Fr. *jeo fail,* I mistake.]

jeopardy, *jep'ər-di, n.* hazard, danger.—*vs.t.* **jeop'ard** (*rare* and *U.S.*), **jeop'ardise, jeop'ardy** (*rare*), to put in jeopardy.—*n.* **jeop'arder.**—*adj.* **jeop'ardous,** (*obs.*) dangerous: (*obs.*) venturesome.— *adv.* **jeop'ardously.** [Fr. *jeu parti,* a divided or even game—L.L. *jocus partitus*—L. *jocus,* a game, *partitus,* divided—*partīri,* to divide.]

jequirity, *jə-kwir'i-ti, n.* Indian liquorice: its seed, otherwise jequirity bean, crab's-eye, prayer-bead. [Origin obscure.]

jerboa, *jər-bō'ä, n.* a desert rodent (family Dipodidae) that jumps like a kangaroo. [Ar. *yarbū'*.]

jeremiad, *jer-i-mī'ad, n.* a lamentation: a tale of grief: a doleful story. [From *Jeremiah,* reputed author of the *Book of Lamentations*.]

jerfalcon. Same as **gerfalcon.**

Jericho, *jer'i-kō, n.* a remote place, to which one is humorously consigned. [Supposed to refer to 2 Sam. x. 4, 5.]

jerid, jereed, *jər-ēd', n.* a blunt Oriental javelin: a tournament in which it is used. [Ar. *jarīd.*]

jerk, *jərk, n.* (*obs.*) a stroke: a short movement begun and ended suddenly: a twitch: an involuntary spasmodic contraction of a muscle: a movement in physical exercises: a short burst of bird-song: (*slang*) vigour, haste.—*v.t.* (*obs.*) to thrash: to throw or move with a jerk.—*v.i.* to move with a jerk: to utter a jerk.—*ns.* **jerk'er,** one who jerks: a horny-head (fish); **jerk'iness;** **jerk'in-head,** (*archit.*) the combination of a truncated gable with a hipped roof.—*adj.* **jerk'y,** moving or coming by jerks or starts, spasmodic: capricious, impatient. [An imit. word, akin to **yerk.**]

jerk, jerker. See **jerque, jerquer.**

jerk, *jərk, v.t.* to make into charqui.—*n.* charqui.— Also **jerk'ed-meat, jerk'y.** [**charqui.**]

jerkin, *jər'kin, n.* a young salmon.

jerkin, *ər'kin, n.* a jacket, a short coat or close waistcoat.—*n.* **jirkinet',** (*obs. Scot.*) a woman's bodice. [Origin unknown.]

jeroboam, *jer-ō-bō'əm, n.* a very large bowl or bottle. [Allusion to 1 Kings xi. 28.]

jerque, jerk, *jərk, v.t.* to search (as a vessel) for concealed or smuggled goods: to examine (as a

ship's papers).—*ns.* **jerqu'er, jerk'er; jerqu'ing, jerk'ing.** [Origin obscure; poss. It. *cercare,* to search.]

Jerry, *jer'i, n.* (*war-slang*) a German.

jerry, *jer'i, n.* a jerry-builder.—*adj.* hastily made of bad materials.—*n.* **jerr'y-builder,** one who builds flimsy houses cheaply and hastily: a speculative builder.—*n.* **jerr'y-building.**—*adj.* **jerr'y-built.** —*ns.* **jerr'y-come-tum'ble,** a tumbler, circus performer; **jerr'y-shop,** a low dram-shop. [Prob. the personal name.]

jerrymander, a mistaken form of **gerrymander.**

jersey, *jər'zi, n.* the finest part of wool: combed wool: a close-fitting woollen upper garment: a cow of Jersey breed. [From the island of *Jersey.*]

Jerusalem artichoke, *jər-ōōs'ə-ləm.* See **artichoke.**—**Jerusalem cross,** a cross potent: **Jerusalem letters,** tattooed letters on one who has made a pilgrimage to Jerusalem; **Jerusalem pony,** an ass.

jess, *jes, n.* a short strap round the leg of a hawk.— *adj.* **jessed,** having jesses on. [O.Fr. *ges*—L. *jactus,* a cast—*jacēre,* to throw.]

jessamine. See **jasmine.**

jessamy, *jes'ə-mi, n.* (*obs.*) jasmine: a dandy.

jessant, *jes'ənt, adj.* (*her.*) overlying: also app. for **issuant.** [App. O.Fr. *gesant,* pr.p. of *gesir*—L. *jacēre,* to lie.]

Jesse, *jes'i, n.* a genealogical tree of Christ's descent from *Jesse*: a large branched church candlestick. —**Jesse window,** one showing Christ's genealogy in stained glass or carved on the mullions.

jesserant, *jes'ə-rənt,* **jazerant,** *jaz',* n. splint armour. [O.Fr. *jaseran*(t), *jazeran*—Sp. *jacerina.*]

jest, *jest, n.* something ludicrous: object of laughter: joke: fun: something uttered in sport.—*v.i.* to make a jest: to joust.—*ns.* **jest'-book,** a collection of funny stories; **jestee'** (*Sterne*), the object of a jest; **jest'er,** one who jests: (*obs.*) a reciter of romances: a buffoon: a court-fool.—*adj.* **jest'ful,** given to jesting.—*n.* and *adj.* **jest'ing.**—*adv.* **jest'ingly.**—*n.* **jest'ing-stock,** a butt for jests. [Orig. a deed, a story, M.E. *geste*—O.Fr. *geste*—L. *gesta,* things done, doings—*gerĕre,* to do.]

Jesuit, *jez'ū-it, n.* a member of the famous religious order, the Society of *Jesus,* founded in 1534 by Ignatius Loyola: (opprobriously) a crafty person, an intriguer, a prevaricator.—*adjs.* **Jesuit'ic, -al.** —*adv.* **Jesuit'ically.**—*ns.* **Jes'uitism, Jes'uitry,** the principles and practices of or ascribed to the Jesuits.—**Jesuits' bark,** cinchona (brought to Rome by Jesuit missionaries); **Jesuits' drops,** friar's balsam.

Jesus, *jē'zəs, n.* the founder of Christianity—also (in hymns, &c., esp. in the vocative) **Jesu** (*jē'zū*). [Gr. *Iēsous* (voc. and oblique cases *Iēsou*)—Heb. *Yēshūa',* contr. of *Yehōshūa',* Joshua.]

jésus, *zhā'zü, n.* a size of paper in France, approximately super-royal.—**grand jésus,** imperial size.

jet, *jet, n.* a rich black variety of lignite, very hard and compact, taking a high polish, used for ornaments: jet-black.—*adj.* of jet: jet-black.—*adj.* **jet'-black',** black as jet.—Also *n.*—*n.* **jett'iness.**— *adj.* **jett'y,** of the nature of jet, or black as jet. [O.Fr. *jaiet*—L. and Gr. *gagātēs*—*Gagas* or *Gangai,* a town and river in Lycia, where it was obtained.]

jet, *jet, n.* a narrow spouting stream: a spout, nozzle, or pipe emitting a stream or spray of fluid: a strutting movement: a jet-plane.—*v.t.* and *v.i.* to spout.—*v.i.* (*obs.*) to jut: (*Shak.*) to encroach: to strut.—*n.* **jet'-drive.**—*adj.* **jet'-driven,** driven by the backward emission of a jet of gas, &c. —*n.* **jet'(-)plane,** a jet-driven aeroplane.—*adj.* **jet'-propelled.**—*ns.* **jet'-propulsion; jet'(-)stream,** very high winds more than 20,000 feet above the earth. [O.Fr. *jetter*—L. *jactāre,* to fling.]

jetsam, *jet'səm, n.* (*obs.*) jettison: the goods so thrown away and washed up on shore: according to some, goods from a wreck that remain under water (see **flotsam**).—Also **jet'som, jet'son.**— *n.* **jett'ison,** the act of throwing goods overboard. —*v.t.* to throw overboard, as goods in time of danger: (*fig.*) to abandon, reject.—**flotsam and jetsam,** often, unclaimed odds and ends. [A.Fr. *jetteson*—L. *jactātiō, -ōnis,* a casting—*jactāre,* to cast.]

Neutral vowels in unaccented syllables: *el'ə-mənt, in'fənt, ran'dəm*

jettatura, *jet-ə-tōō'rä*, *n.* the spell of the evil eye. [It. *iettatura*, a Neapolitan word—L. *ĕjectāre*—*jactāre*, freq. of *jacĕre*, to throw.]

jettison. See **jetsam**.

jetton, jeton, *jet'ən*, *n.* a piece of stamped metal used as a counter in card-playing, casting accounts, &c. [Fr. *jeton—jeter*, to throw—L. *jactāre*, freq. of *jacĕre*, to throw.]

jetty, *jet'i*, *n.* a projection: a pier. [O.Fr. *jettee*, thrown out; see **jet** (2).]

Jew, *jōō*, *n.* a person of Hebrew descent or religion: an Israelite: opprobriously used for a usurer, miser, &c.: (*fem.* **Jew'ess**).—*v.t.* (*coll.*) to overreach: to cheat.—*ns.* **Jew'-bait'ing**, the persecuting of Jews; **jew'fish**, a name for several very large American and Australian fishes. — *adj.* **Jew'ish**, of the Jews or their religion.—*adv.* **Jew'ishly**.—*ns.* **Jew'ishness**; **Jew's'-ear**, an ear-like fungus (*Auricularia*) parasitic on elder and other trees; **Jew's'-frank'incense**, benzoin; **Jew's'-harp, Jews'-harp', -trump'**, a small lyreshaped instrument played against the teeth by twitching a metal tongue with the finger; **Jew's'-mall'ow**, a kind of jute cultivated as a pot-herb in Syria; **Jew's'-myr'tle**, butcher's broom; **Jew's'-pitch**, asphaltum; **Jew's'-stone**, a large fossil sea-urchin spine.—**Jew's eye**, proverbially, something of very high value—from the custom of torturing Jews for money; **Jews' houses, leavings**, in Cornwall, remains of prehistoric miners' dwellings, mine refuse, and tin furnaces; **Jews' thorn**, Christ's thorn; **wandering Jew** (see **wander**). [O.Fr. *Jueu*—L. *Jūdaeus*—Gr. *Ioudaios* —Heb. *Yehūdāh*, Judah.]

jewel, *jōō'əl*, *n.* a precious stone: a personal ornament of precious stones, gold, &c.: a hard stone (ruby, &c.) used for pivot bearings in a watch: an imitation of a gem-stone: a glass boss: anything or anyone highly valued.—*v.t.* to adorn with jewels: to fit with a jewel:—*pr.p.* **jew'elling**; *pa.t.* and *pa.p.* **jew'elled**.—*ns.* **jew'el-case**, a casket for holding jewels; **jewel'-house**, a room in the Tower of London where the crown-jewels are kept; **jew'eller**, one who makes or deals in jewels; **jewellery** (*jōō'əl-ri*), **jew'elry**, jewels in general. [O.Fr. *jouel* (Fr. *joyau*); either a dim. of Fr. *joie*, joy, from L. *gaudium*, joy—*gaudēre*, to rejoice—or derived through L.L. *jocāle*, from L. *jocāri*, to jest.]

Jewry, *jōō'ri*, *n.* Judaea: a district inhabited by *Jews*: the Jewish world, community, or religion.

jezail, *jez-īl', -āl'*, *n.* a heavy Afghan gun. [Pers. *jazā'il*.]

Jezebel, *jez'ə-bəl*, *n.* a shameless painted woman. [From Ahab's wife.]

jib, *jib*, *n.* a triangular sail borne in front of the foremast in a ship: the boom of a crane or derrick: (*dial.*) the under-lip: the face: a jibbing horse: an act of jibbing: a standstill.—*v.t.* to cause to gybe.—*v.i.* to gybe: (of a horse) to balk or shy: (*fig.*) to refuse, show objection, boggle:—*pr.p.* **jibb'ing**; *pa.t.* and *pa.p.* **jibbed**.—*ns.* **jibb'er**, a jibbing horse; **jib'-boom'**, a boom or extension of the bowsprit, on which the jib is spread; **jib'-crane'**, a crane with an inclined arm fixed to the foot of a rotating vertical post, the upper ends connected. —**the cut of one's jib**, appearance. [Origin obscure; perh. several different words; cf. **gibbet, gybe**; the j sound stands in the way of connecting with Dan. *gibbe*, Du. *gijpen*.]

jib, *jib*, *v.t.* (*Scot.*) to milk closely, strip: to fleece.—*n.pl.* **jibb'ings**, the last milk drawn from a cow.

jibbah, *jib'ä*. See **jubbah**.

jibber. See **gibber**.

jib-door, *jib'-dōr*, *n.* a disguised door, flush with the wall. [Origin unknown.]

jibe. Same as **gibe**.

jiffy, *jif'i*, *n.* (*coll.*) an instant.—Also **jiff**. [Origin unknown.]

jig, *jig*, *n.* a jerky movement: a lively dance usu. in 6-8 time: a dance-tune of like kind—a giga or gigue: (*obs.*) a mocking ballad: (*obs.*) a jingle or piece of doggerel: (*obs.*) a farcical afterpiece or interlude sung and danced to popular tunes: (*obs.*) a jest: a contrivance of various kinds, esp. one for

catching fish by jerking hooks into its body, an appliance for guiding a tool, a miner's jigger.—*v.t.* and *v.i.* to jerk: to perform as a jig.—*v.t.* to work upon with a jig :—*pr.p.* **jigg'ing**; *pa.t.* and *pa.p.* **jigged**.—*ns.* **jigamaree'**, a what's-its-name': a gadget; **jigg'er**, one who jigs in any sense: anything that jigs: one of many kinds of subsidiary appliances, esp. with reciprocating motion, as an oscillation transformer, an apparatus for separating ores by jolting in sieves in water, a simple potter's wheel or a template or profile used with it, a warehouse crane, the bridge or rest for the cue in billiards: a small sail at the stern: a form of ironheaded golf-club: an old-fashioned sloop-rigged boat: an odd person: an odd or despised contrivance: (*slang*) a drink.—*v.t.* to jerk or shake: to form with a jigger.—*v.i.* to tug or move with jerks.—*ns.* **jigg'er-mast**, a four-masted ship's aftermost mast: a small mast astern; **jigg'ing**.—*adj.* **jigg'ish**.—*v.t.* and *v.i.* **jigg'le**, to move with vibratory jerks.—*n.* a jiggling movement.—*ns.* **jigg'umbob**, a jigamaree; **jig'saw**, a narrow reciprocating saw: a jigsaw puzzle.—*v.t.* and *v.i.* to cut with a jigsaw.—**jiggered up**, (*slang*) exhausted; **jigsaw puzzle**, a picture cut up into pieces, as by a jigsaw, to be fitted together. [Origin obscure.]

jigger, *jig'ər*, *n.* a form of **chigoe**.

jiggered, *jig'ərd*, *adj.* (*coll.*) confounded. [Origin doubtful.]

jiggery-pokery, *jig'ə-ri-pō'kə-ri*, *n.* trickery: deception. [Cf. **joukery-pawkery**.]

jigjog, *jig'jog'*, *adv.* with a jolting, jogging motion.— *n.* a jolting motion: a jog.—Also **jick'ajog', jig'jig', jick'ajig', jig'ajog', jigg'ety-jog'.** [jig, jog.]

jigot. Same as **gigot**.

jihad, jehad, *jē-häd', n.* a holy war (for the Mohammedan faith): a stunt campaign. [Ar. *jihād*, struggle.]

jill, jillet, &c. Same as **gill** (a woman, a female ferret), **gillet**, &c.

jilt, *jilt*, *n.* one, esp. a woman, who encourages and then rejects a lover.—*v.t.* to discard (a lover) after encouragement. [Possibly **jillet** or **gillet**.]

jimcrack. See **gimcrack**.

Jim Crow, *jim krō, n.* a generic name for the negro.— *n.* **jim'-crow**, a tool for bending or straightening iron rails or bars: a plane or other tool that works in both directions.—**Jim Crow car, school**, &c., one for negroes only. [From a negro minstrel song with the refrain 'Wheel about and turn about and jump *Jim Crow*.']

jiminy, jim'in-i. See **gemini**.

jimjam, *jim'jam*, *n.* a gimcrack: a gadget: an oddity: (in *pl.*) delirium tremens: (in *pl.*) the fidgets. [Origin unknown.]

jimmy, *jim'i, n.* (*U.S.*) a burglar's jemmy. [**James**.]

jimp, *jimp, adj.* (*Scot.*) slender: elegant: scant.— *advs.* **jimp, jimp'ly**, neatly: hardly: scant.—*n.* **jimp'ness**.—*adj.* **jimp'y**, neat. [Origin unknown.]

Jimson-weed, Jimpson-weed, Jamestown-weed, *jim'sən-wēd, n.* thorn-apple. [*Jamestown*, Virginia, where it established itself.]

jingal, gingall, gingal, *jin(g)'gawl, -gawl', n.* a large Chinese or Indian swivel-musket. [Hind. *janjāl*.]

jingbang, *jing-bang', n.* (*slang*) company: collection: lot. [Origin unknown.]

jingle, *jing'gl*, *n.* a succession of clinking sounds: that which makes a tinkling sound, esp. a metal disk on a tambourine: a thin or paltry correspondence of sounds in verse: a verse or set of verses of such a kind: a covered two-wheeled vehicle.— *v.t.* and *v.i.* to sound with a jingle.—*ns.* **jing'lejang'le**, a dissonant continued jingling: a jingling trinket; **jing'ler**; **jing'let**, a ball serving as the clapper of a sleigh-bell; **jing'ling**, a game in which blindfolded players within a ring try to catch a player with a bell tied to him.—*adj.* **jing'ly**. [Imit.]

Jingo, *jing'gō*, *n.* a name used in the mild oaths 'By Jingo!', 'By the living Jingo!' (*Scot.* 'By Jing!', 'By Jings!'): from its occurrence in a music-hall song of 1878 that conveyed a threat against Russia, a (British) Chauvinist.—*adjs.* **Jing'o, Jing'oish,**

Chauvinist.—*n.* **Jing'oism.** [Appears first as a conjurer's summoning call; possible from Basque *Jinkoa, Jainko,* God.]

jingo-ring, *jing'gō-ring, n.* a children's game in which the players dance round one of their number singing 'Here we go round the jingo-ring.' [Conn. with **jink.**]

jink, *jingk, v.i.* (*Scot.*) to dodge nimbly.—*v.t.* to elude: to cheat.—*n.* a quick, illusory turn.—**high jinks** (see **high**). [Perh. a natural expression of the movement.]

jinn, *jin, n.pl.* (*sing.* **jinnee, jinni, djinni, genie** (*jin-ē', jēn'i*)) a class of spirits in Mohammedan mythology, formed of fire, living chiefly on the mountains of Káf which encircle the world, assuming various shapes, sometimes as men of enormous size and portentous hideousness.—Also **djinn, ginn.** The *jinn* are often called *genii* by a confusion. A plural **jinns** is sometimes erroneously used. [Ar. *jinn,* sing. *jinnī.*]

jinricksha, *jin-rik'shä, -shaw, n.* a small, two-wheeled, hooded carriage drawn by a man or men. —Also **jinrick'shaw, jinrik'isha, rick'shaw, rick'sha.** [Jap. *jin,* man, *riki,* power, *sha,* carriage.]

jinx, *jingks, n.* (*U.S. slang*) a bringer of bad luck.

jirble, *jir bl, v.t.* and *v.i.* (*Scot.*) to pour splashingly or unsteadily.

jirkinet. See **jerkin.**

jitney, *jit'ni, n.* (*U.S.*) a five-cent piece: a bus, &c., with low fares: anything cheap or paltry.—*adj.* cheap: paltry. [Perh. Fr. *jeton,* counter.]

jitter, *jit'ər, v.i.* (*U.S. slang*) to behave in a flustered way.—*n.* **jitt'erbug,** (*U.S.*) a violent spasmodic type of dancing to jazz music: one who dances so: (in Britain, by misunderstanding or extension) a scaremonger, alarmist.—*v.i.* to dance wildly and grotesquely.—*n.pl.* **jitt'ers,** a flustered state.—*adj.* **jitt'ery.**

jiu-jitsu. Same as **ju-jitsu.**

jive, *jīv, n.* (*slang*) a style of jazz music: dancing thereto.—*v.i.* to play or dance jive.

jo, *jō, n.* (*Scot.*) a beloved one. [An old form of **joy.**]

job, *job, n.* a sudden thrust with anything pointed, as a beak.—*v.t.* to prod or peck suddenly :—*pr.p.* **jobb'ing;** *pa.t.* and *pa.p.* **jobbed.** [App. imit.; cf. **jab.**]

job, *job, n.* any definite piece of work, esp. of a trifling or temporary nature: any undertaking or employment with a view to profit: an appointment or situation: (*coll.*) a troublesome affair: a transaction in which private gain is sought under pretence of public service: the accomplishment of an end by intrigue or wire-pulling: a criminal enterprise: a hired horse or carriage: a job-lot.—*adj.* employed, hired, or used by the job or for jobs: bought or sold lumped together.—*v.i.* to work at jobs: to buy and sell, as a broker: to practise jobbery.—*v.t.* to perform as a job: to put or carry through by jobbery: to deal in, as a broker: to hire or let out, esp. horses.—*ns.* **jobb'er,** one who jobs: one who buys and sells, as a broker: one who turns official actions to private advantage: one who engages in a mean lucrative affair; **jobb'ery,** jobbing: unfair means employed to secure some private end. —*adj.* **jobb'ing,** working by the job.—*n.* the doing of jobs: miscellaneous printing-work: buying and selling as a broker: stock-jobbing: jobbery.—*ns.* **job'-lot,** a collection of odds and ends, esp. for sale as one lot: any collection of inferior quality; **job'-mas'ter,** a livery-stable keeper who jobs out horses and carriages.—**a bad, good, job,** a piece of work ill, or well, done: an unlucky, or lucky, fact; **job of work,** a task, bit of work; **odd jobs,** occasional pieces of work; **on the job,** at work, in activity. [Origin unknown.]

Job, *jōb, n.* a person of great patience—from *Job* in the *Book of Job.*—*n.* **jobā'tion** (also **jawbā'tion**), a tedious scolding.—*v.t.* **jobe** (*jōb*), to reprimand tediously.—**Job's comforter,** one who aggravates the distress of the unfortunate man he has come to comfort; **Job's news,** bad news; **Job's post,** the bearer of bad news; **Job's tears,** the stony involucres of an Indian grass, *Coix Lachryma,* used as beads: round grains of chrysolite.

jobernowl, *job'ər-nōl, n.* a dull head: a blockhead. [App. Fr. *jobard,* a noodle, and **nowl, noll.**]

Jock, *jok, n.* (*Scot.*) Jack: (*Scot.*) a jack or knave in cards: a country fellow: (*slang*) a Scottish soldier. [Jack.]

jockey, *jok'i, n.* a man (orig. a boy) who rides in a horse-race: a horse-dealer: one who takes undue advantage in business.—*v.t.* to jostle by riding against: to trick by manoeuvring.—*ns.* **jock'ey-ism, jock'eyship,** the art or practice of a jockey.—**Jockey Club,** an association for the promotion and ordering of horse-racing: a perfume composed of rose, orris, cassia, tuberose, bergamot, &c. [Dim. of **Jock.**]

jocko, *jok'ō, n.* a chimpanzee. [Fr., from a W. African word *ncheko.*]

Jock Scott, *jok skot, n.* a kind of artificial fly.

jockteleg, *jok'tə-leg, n.* (*Scot.*) a large clasp-knife. [The suggested *Jacques de Liége* lacks confirmation.]

joco, *jō-kō', adj.* (*Scot.*) cheerfully complacent. [jocose.]

jocose, *jō-kōs', adj.* full of jokes: facetious: merry. — *adv.* **jocose'ly.** — *ns.* **jocose'ness, jocosity** (*-kos'i-ti*), the quality of being jocose.—*adj.* **jocosē'-rious,** half in jest, half in earnest. [L. *jocōsus*—*jocus,* a joke.]

jocular, *jok ū-lər, adj.* given to jokes: inclined to joke: of the nature of, intended as, a joke.—*n.* **jocularity** (*-lar'i-ti*).—*adv.* **joc'ularly.**—*n.* **joc'-ulātor,** a professional jester or minstrel. [L. *joculāris*—*jocus.*]

jocund, *jok'und, jōk'und, -ənd, adj.* mirthful: merry: cheerful: pleasant.—*ns.* **jocundity** (*-kund'i-ti*), **joc'undness.**—*adv.* **joc'undly.** [O.Fr.,—L.L. *jocundus* for L. *jūcundus,* pleasant, modified by association with *jocus.*]

jodel, *yō'dl.* Same as **yodel.**

jodhpurs, *jod'purz, n.pl.* riding-breeches with a tight extension to the ankle. [*Jodhpur* in India.]

joe, *jō, joey, jō'i, n.* (*slang*) a fourpenny-bit—from *Joseph* Hume, M.P., their author, 1836.—**Joe Miller,** an old or stale jest, a jest-book; **Joe Millerism,** the habit of retailing stale jests—from *Joe Miller* (1684-1738), a comedian but a notoriously dull fellow, on whom a jest-book was fathered; **not for Joe** (see **Joseph**).

joe. Same as **jo.**

joey, *jō i, n.* (*Austr.*) a young animal, esp. kangaroo. [Australian *joè.*]

jog, *jog, v.t.* to shake: to push with the elbow or hand: to stimulate, stir up, as the memory.—*v.i.* to move by jogs: to trudge:—*pr.p.* **jogg'ing;** *pa.t.* and *pa.p.* **jogged.**—*n.* a slight shake: a push or nudge.—*ns.* **jogg'er,** (*Dryden*) one who moves slowly and heavily; **jog'-trot',** a slow jogging trot: humdrum routine.—**be jogging,** to move on: to depart. [Perh. akin to **shog.**]

joggle, *jog'l, n.* a tooth, notch, or pin to prevent sliding of surfaces in contact: a joint so made.—*v.t.* to join with a joggle. [Perh. conn. with **jag,** a projection.]

joggle, *jog'l, v.t.* to jog or shake slightly: to jostle.—*v.i.* to shake:—*pr.p.* **jogg'ling;** *pa.t.* and *pa.p.* **jogg'led.** [App. dim. or freq. of **jog.**]

johannes, *jō-(h)an'ēz, n.* a gold coin of *John* V. of Portugal.—Also **joann'es.**—*adjs.* **Johann'ean, Johann'ine,** of or pertaining to John, esp. the Apostle. [L. *Jōhannēs* from *Jōannēs*—Gr. *Iōannēs*—Heb. *Yōchānān,* John.]

Johannisberger, *jō-han'is-bərg-ər, n.* a white Rhenish wine grown at *Johannisberg* (' St John's Mountain '), near Wiesbaden.

John, *jon, n.* a proper name, one of whose diminutives, **Johnn'y, Johnn'ie,** is sometimes used in slang for a simpleton, an empty-headed man about town, or a fellow generally.—*ns.* **John'-a-dreams',** (*Shak.*) a dreamy fellow; **John'-apple,** a kind of apple, otherwise apple-john; **John'-go-to-bed-at-noon',** the goat's-beard (from its early closing); **Johnian** (*jōn'i-ən*), a member of St *John's* College, Cambridge; **Johnn'y-cake,** a cake of Indian meal toasted; **Johnn'y-raw,** a beginner: a greenhorn. —**John a-Nokes, John a-Stiles, -Styles,** fictitious persons in English law-suits, or generally; **John Barleycorn,** malt liquor personified; **John**

Bull, a generic name for an Englishman, from Arbuthnot(t)'s *History of John Bull,* 1712; **John Bullism,** the typical English character, or any act or word expressive of it; **John Chinaman,** a Chinaman: the Chinese generically; **John Company,** the East India Company; **John Doe** (see doe); **John Dory** (see **dory**). [L. *Jōhannĕs*; see preceding word.]

Johnsonian, *jon-sō′ni-ən, adj.* of, in the manner of, Dr Samuel *Johnson,* the lexicographer (1709-84).— *ns.* **Johnsō′nianism, John′sonism** (*-sən-izm*); **John′sonese,** Johnsonian style, idiom, diction, or an imitation of it—ponderous English, full of antitheses, balanced triads, and words of classical origin.—*n.pl.* **Johnsōniana** (*-ā′nä, -ā′nä*), matters, miscellaneous items, connected with Johnson.

join, *join, v.t.* to connect: to unite: to associate: to add or annex: to become a member of: to come into association with or the company of: to go to and remain with, in, or on: (*geom.*) to draw a straight line between.—*v.i.* to be connected: to combine, unite: to run into one: to grow together: to be in, or come into, close contact. —*n.* a joining: a place where things have been joined: a mode of joining.—*ns.* **joind′er,** joining; **join′er,** one who joins or unites: a worker in wood, esp. one who makes smaller structures than a carpenter: (*U.S.*) one who joins many societies; **join′ery,** the art of the joiner: joiner's work; **join′-hand,** running hand; **join′ing,** the act of joining: a seam: a joint; **joint,** a joining: the place where, or mode in which, two or more things join: a place where two things (esp. bones) meet with power of movement as of a hinge: a node, or place where a stem bears leaves, esp. if swollen: a segment: a piece of an animal's body as cut up for the table: the flexible hinge of cloth or leather connecting the back of a book with its sides: (*geol.*) a crack intersecting a mass of rock: the place where adjacent surfaces meet: condition of adjustment at a joint (in the phrase *out of joint,* dislocated): a place of resort for tramps: (*U.S.*) a low resort.— *adj.* joined, united, or combined: shared among more than one: sharing with another or others.— *v.t.* to unite by joints: to fit closely: to provide with joints or an appearance of joints: to fill the joints of: to divide into joints.—*v.i.* to fit like or by joints.—*adj.* **joint′ed,** having joints: composed of segments: constricted at intervals.—*ns.* **joint′er,** the largest kind of plane used by a joiner: a bricklayer's tool for putting mortar in joints; **joint′-fir,** any plant of the family Gnetaceae; **joint′-heir,** one who inherits jointly with another or others; **joint′ing-rule,** a long straight-edged rule used by bricklayers for keeping their work even.—*adj.* **joint′less.**—*adv.* **joint′ly,** in a joint manner: unitedly or in combination: together.—*ns.* **joint′-ness; joint′-oil,** synovia; **joint′-stock,** stock held jointly or in company; **joint′-stool,** (*Shak.*) a stool made of parts inserted in each other; **joint′-ten′ancy; joint′-ten′ant,** one who is owner of land or goods along with others; **joint′ure,** property settled on a woman at marriage to be enjoyed after her husband's death.—*v.t.* to settle a jointure upon.—*ns.* **joint′uress, joint′ress,** a woman on whom a jointure is settled; **joint′-worm,** (*U.S.*) a hymenopterous larva that attacks grain-stalks near the first joint.—**join battle,** to begin a fight or contest; **join issue,** to begin to dispute: to take up the contrary view or side; **join up,** to enlist, esp. in participation in a general movement; **out of joint,** dislocated: (*fig.*) disordered; **put one's nose out of joint,** to supplant in another's love or confidence: to disconcert: to rebuff; **second joint,** the middle piece of a fly fishing-rod: the thigh of a fowl—opp. to the leg or drumstick, the first joint; **universal joint,** a contrivance by which one part is able to move freely in all directions, as in the ball-and-socket joint. [O.Fr. *joindre*—L. *jungĕre, junctum,* to join.]

joist, *joist, n.* a beam supporting the boards of a floor or the laths of a ceiling.—*v.t.* to fit with joists. [O.Fr. *giste—gesir*—L. *jacēre,* to lie.]

joke, *jōk, n.* a jest: a witticism: anything said or done to excite a laugh: anything provocative of

laughter: an absurdity.—*v.t.* to cast jokes at: to banter: to make merry with.—*v.i.* to jest: to be merry: to make sport.—*ns.* **jok′er,** one who jokes or jests: a fifty-third card in the pack, used at euchre, poker, &c.: (*U.S.*) an innocent-looking clause insidiously introduced to cripple the effect of a bill or document: (*slang*) a fellow; **joke′-smith,** a maker of jokes.—*adj.* **joke′some.**—*adv.* **jok′ingly,** in a joking manner.—**no joke,** a serious or difficult matter. [L. *jocus.*]

jokol, *yō′kawl, adv.* (*Shetland*; *obs.*) yes (lit. yes carl). —Also **yo′kul.** [Shetland Norn *jo,* yes, and (inferred) *koll*—O.N. *karl,* carl.]

jole, joll, other forms of **jowl** (1 and 2).

jolly, *jol′i, adj.* merry: expressing or exciting mirth, jovial: comely, robust: (*coll.*) used as an indefinite expression of approbation.—*v.t.* to make fun of: to keep in good humour, to beguile.—*adv.* (*coll.*) uncommonly.—*n.* (*slang*) a marine: a jollification. —*n.* **jollifica′tion,** a making jolly: noisy festivity and merriment.—*adv.* **joll′ily.**—*ns.* **joll′iment,** (*Spens.*) merriment; **joll′iness, joll′ity, joll′yhead** (*Spens.*).—**Jolly Roger,** the pirates' black flag with white skull and cross-bones. [O.Fr. *jolif, joli,* very doubtfully referred to O.N. *jól,* Yule.]

jollyboat, *jol′i-bōt, n.* a ship's boat. [Origin obscure.]

jolt, *jōlt, v.i.* to shake or proceed with sudden jerks. —*v.t.* to shake with a sudden shock.—*n.* a sudden jerk: a shock: a stimulating shock.—*n.* **jolt′er.**— *adv.* **jolt′ingly,** in a jolting manner. [Ety. obscure.]

jolterhead, *jolt′ər-hed,* **jolthead,** *jōlt′hed, ns.* a large clumsy head: a blockhead. [Ety. obscure.]

jomo, or **dsomo.** See **zho.**

Jonah, *jō′nä, n.* a bringer of ill-luck on shipboard or elsewhere. [From the prophet *Jonah.*]

Jonathan, *jon′ə-thən, n.* the people of the United States, collectively, or a typical specimen (**Brother Jonathan**): an American variety of apple. [Perh. from the sagacious Governor *Jonathan* Trumbull, 1710-85.]

jongleur, *zhon͡g′-glər′, n.* a wandering minstrel: a mountebank. [Fr.,—O.Fr. *jogleor*—L. *joculător*; cf. **juggler.**]

jonquil, *jong′kwil,* formerly *jung-kwil′, n.* a name given to certain species of narcissus with rush-like leaves. [Fr. *jonquille*—L. *juncus,* a rush.]

jonty, *jon′ti,* **jaunty, jauntie, janty,** *jawn′ti, jän′ti, n.* (*slang*) a naval master-at-arms.

Jordan, *jor′dn, n.* the great river of Palestine: (*fig.*) death (as a passage into the Promised Land, Numb. xxxiii. 51): (*Shak.*) a chamber-pot (according to some, from *Jordan*-bottle, a pilgrim's bottle containing *Jordan* water).

jordeloo, *jor-di-lōō′.* See **gardiloo.**

jorum, joram, *jōr′əm, n.* a large drinking-bowl: a great drink. [Ety. unknown; poss. from *Joram* in 2 Sam. viii. 10.]

Joseph, *jō′zif, n.* one whose chastity is above temptation—from the story of *Joseph* and Potiphar's wife in Gen. xxxix.: a caped overcoat worn by women in the 18th century for riding—possibly in allusion to *Joseph's* coat, Gen. xxxvii.—**not for Joseph,** not on any account (the particular Joseph, if any, is unknown).

josh, *josh, v.t.* (*U.S.*) to ridicule.—*n.* a hoax: a derisive jest.—*n.* **josh′er.**

joskin, *jos′kin, n.* a clown, yokel. [Thieves' cant.]

joss, *jos, n.* a Chinese idol: luck: fate.—*ns.* **joss′er,** (*Austr.*) a clergyman: (*slang*) a fellow: a blunderer; **joss′-house,** a temple; **joss′-stick,** a stick of gum burned by the Chinese as incense to their gods. [Port. *deos,* god—L. *deus.*]

joss-block, *jos′-blok, n.* (*prov.*) a horse-block.

jostle, *jos′l,* **justle,** *jus′l, v.i.* (*obs.*) to tilt, joust.— *v.t.* and *v.i.* to shake or jar by collision: to hustle: to elbow.—*n.* an act of jostling.—*ns.* **jos′tlement, jos′tling.** [Freq. of **joust, just.**]

jot, *jot, n.* an iota, a whit, a tittle.—*v.t.* to set down briefly: to make a memorandum of:—*pr.p.* **jott′-ing;** *pa.t.* and *pa.p.* **jott′ed.**—*ns.* **jott′er,** one who jots: a book or pad for rough notes; **jott′ing,** a memorandum: a rough note. [L. *iōta* (read as *jōta*)—Gr. *iōta,* the smallest letter in the alphabet, equivalent to i; Heb. *yōd.*]

jota, hō'tä, n. a Spanish dance in triple time. [Sp.]

jotun, yō'tən, **jötunn**, yə'tən, n. a giant. [O.N. jötunn.]

jougs, joogz, jugz, n.pl. an iron neck-ring—the old Scottish pillory. [Prob. O.Fr. joug, a yoke—L. jugum.]

jouisance, jouysaunce, jōō'is-əns, n. (Spens.) joyousness. [Fr. jouissance—jouir, to enjoy—L. gaudēre, to rejoice.]

jouk, jook, jōōk, v.i. (Scot.) to duck: to dodge: to bow.—n. an elusive duck or dodging movement: a bow.—ns. **jouk'ery, jook'ery, jouk'ery-pawk'ery**, trickery, roguery. [Ety. obscure.]

joule, jōōl, jowl, n. the practical unit of electrical energy—the work done in one second by one ampere flowing through one ohm; roughly= 10 million ergs: now also used as the unit of heat. [After the physicist J. P. Joule (said to be pronounced jowl; 1818-89).]

jounce, jowns, v.t. and v.i. to jolt, shake. [Origin unknown.]

journal, jər'nəl, n. a daily register or diary: a book containing a record of each day's transactions: a newspaper published daily (or otherwise): a magazine: the transactions of any society.—adj. (Shak.) diurnal.—n. **journalese'**, the jargon of bad journalism.—v.i. **jour'nalise**, to write for or in a journal.—v.t. to enter in a journal.—ns. **journ'alism**, the profession of conducting or writing for public journals: writing of fleeting interest or hasty character; **jour'nalist**, one who writes for or conducts a newspaper or magazine: one who keeps a journal.—adj. **journalist'ic**. [Fr., —L. diurnālis; see diurnal.]

journal, jər'nəl, n. (mech.) that part of a shaft or axle which rests in the bearings.—v.t. to provide with or fix as a journal.—n. **jour'nal-box**, a box or bearing for a journal. [Origin unexplained.]

journey, jər'ni, n. (obs.) a day's work or travel: (obs.) a campaign: any travel: tour: excursion: movement from end to end of a fixed course: the weight of finished coins delivered at one time to the Master of the Mint—also **jour'ney-weight**: a train of colliery trucks:—pl. **jour'neys**.—v.i. **jour'ney**, to travel:—pr.p. **jour'neying**; pa.t. and pa.p. **jour'-neyed** (-nid).—adj. **jour'ney-bat'ed**, (Shak.) wayworn.—ns. **jour'neyer**; **jour'neyman**, one who works by the day: any hired workman: one whose apprenticeship is completed: an electrically controlled clock or dial; **jour'ney-work**, work done by a journeyman or for hire. [Fr. journée—jour, a day—L. diurnus.]

joust, just, just (jōōst and jowst are recent pronunciations due to the spelling), n. the encounter of two knights on horseback at a tournament.—v.i. to tilt. [O.Fr. juste, jouste, joste—L. juxtā, nigh to.]

jovial, jō'vi-əl, adj. joyous: full of jollity and geniality: **Jovial**, of Jupiter: influenced by Jupiter.—ns. **joviality** (-al'i-ti), **jo'vialness**.—adv. **jo'vially**. [L. joviālis—Jovis (in the nom. usu. Juppiter, Jupiter), the god Jove or Jupiter, or the planet Jupiter, an auspicious star.]

jovysaunce, a misreading of **jouysaunce**. See **jouisance**.

jow, jow, v.t. and v.i. (Scot.) to ring, toll: to rock.— n. a stroke of a bell.—n. and adj. **jow'ing-in'**, ringing in. [jowl (2).]

jowar, jow-är', **jowari, jawari**, -ē, n. durra. [Hind. jawär, javärī.]

jowl, jōl, jowl, n. the jaw: the cheek: a pendulous double chin: a dewlap: a head: the head and shoulders of a salmon, sturgeon, or ling.—n. **jowl'er**, a heavy-jawed hound. [Prob. several different words. The development and relations of M.E. chaul, O.E. ceafl, jaw, M.E. chol, O.E. ceolu, ceolur, &c., and the modern forms with j are difficult to make out. Fr. joue, cheek, or some other word may have added to the confusion.]

jowl, joll, jole, joule, jōl, v.t. and v.i. to bump: to beat: to toll.—n. a stroke: a knock. [Ety. obscure.]

joy, joi, n. intense gladness: rapture: mirth: a cause of joy: a beloved one.—v.i. to rejoice: to be glad: to exult.—v.t. to give joy to: (Milt.) to enjoy:—pr.p. **joy'ing**; pa.t. and pa.p. **joyed**.—n. **joy'ance**, (Spens.) gaiety, festivity.—adj. **joy'ful**, full of joy: feeling, expressing, or giving joy.— adv. **joy'fully**.—n. **joy'fulness**.—adj. **joy'less**, without joy: not giving joy.—adv. **joy'lessly**.—n. **joy'lessness**.—adj. **joy'ous**, joyful.—adv. **joy'-ously**.—ns. **joy'ousness**; **joy'-ride**, (slang) a pleasure-drive, esp. reckless or surreptitious, often in a stolen car; **joy'-riding**; **joy'-stick**, (slang) the control-lever of an aeroplane; **joy'-wheel**, a great wheel that carries passengers high in the air in pleasure-grounds. [Fr. joie (cf. It. gioja)—L. gaudium.]

juba, jōō'bä, n. a negro breakdown or rustic dance, in which the spectators clap hands, slap their thighs, and sing verses with juba as a refrain.

jubate, jōō'bät, adj. maned. [L. jubātus—juba, mane.]

jubbah, joob'ä, jub'ä, n. a long loose outer garment worn by Mohammedans.—Also **jibbah, djibbah**. [Ar. jubbah.]

jube, jōō bē, n. a rood-loft. [L., imper. of jubēre, to command.]

jubilant, jōō'bi-lənt, adj. shouting for joy: uttering songs of triumph: rejoicing.—n. **ju'bilance**, exultation.—adv. **ju'bilantly**.—v.i. **ju'bilate**, to exult, rejoice.—ns. **jubilate** (yōō-bi-lä'tä, jōō-bi-lä'tē), the third Sunday after Easter, so called because the church service began on that day with the 66th Psalm, 'Jubilate Deo,' &c.: also the 100th Psalm, which in the English Prayer Book is a canticle used as an alternative for the Benedictus; **jubilä'tion**, a shouting for joy: the declaration of triumph. [L. jūbilāre, to shout for joy. Not conn. with jubilee.]

jubilee, jōō'bi-lē, n. among the Jews, every fiftieth year, a year of release of slaves, cancelling of debts, return of property to its former owners, proclaimed by the sound of a trumpet: the celebration of a fiftieth anniversary—e.g. of a king's accession, a bishop's consecration, &c.: in the R.C. Church, a year (every twenty-fifth—ordinary jubilee) of indulgence for pilgrims and others, an extraordinary jubilee being specially appointed by the Pope: any season or condition of great joy and festivity: joyful shouting: exultant joy.—**diamond jubilee**, a sixtieth anniversary. [Fr. jubilé—L. jūbilaeus—Heb. yōbēl, a ram, ram's horn.]

jud, jud, n. a mass of coal holed or undercut so as to be thrown down by wedges. [Origin unknown.]

Judaean, Judean, jōō-dē'ən, adj. belonging to Judaea or the Jews.—n. a native of Judaea: a Jew. [L. Judaea.]

Judaic, -al, jōō-dā'ik, -əl, adjs. pertaining to the Jews.—adv. **Judä'ically**.—n. **Judäisä'tion**.—v.t. **Ju'daïse**, to conform to, adopt, or practise Jewish customs or Judaism.—ns. **Judäï'ser**; **Ju'daïsm**, the doctrines and rites of the Jews: conformity to the Jewish rites; **Ju'daïst**, one who holds the doctrines of Judaism.—adj. **Judäist'ic**.—adv. **judaist'-ically**. [L. Jūdaicus—Jūda, Judah, a son of Israel.]

Judas, jōō'dəs, n. a traitor: a spy-hole in a door.— adj. **Ju'das-coloured**, red, of hair (Judas traditionally being red-haired).—ns. **Ju'das-hole**, a spy-hole; **Ju'das-kiss**, any act of treachery under the guise of kindness (Matt. xxvi. 48, 49); **Ju'das-tree**, a tree (Cercis) of the Caesalpinia family, with rose-coloured flowers that appear before the leaves (Judas having traditionally hanged himself on one): also the elder (for the same reason). [Judas Iscariot.]

judge, juj, v.i. to exercise the office of judge: to point out or declare what is just or law: to try and decide questions of law or guiltiness, &c.: to pass sentence: to compare facts to determine the truth: to form or pass an opinion: to distinguish. —v.t. to hear and determine authoritatively: to sit in judgment on: to pronounce on the guilt or innocence of: to sentence: to decide the merits of: to be censorious towards: (B.) to condemn: to decide: to award: to estimate: to form an opinion on: to conclude.—n. one who judges: one appointed to hear and settle causes, and to try accused persons: one chosen to award prizes, to decide doubtful or disputed points in a competition, &c.: an arbitrator: one who can decide upon the merit of anything: in Jewish history, a supreme magistrate having civil and military powers: one capable of discriminating well: **Judges** (*pl.*), title of 7th book of the O.T.—*n.* **judge'-ad'vocate**, the crown-prosecutor at a court-martial.—*adj.* **judge'-made'**, based on decisions of judges (as law).—*ns.* **judge ship**, the office of a judge; **judg'ment** (also **judge'ment**), act of judging: the comparing of ideas to elicit truth: faculty by which this is done, the reason: opinion formed: discrimination: good taste: sentence: condemnation: doom: a misfortune regarded as sent by Providence in punishment; **judg'ment-day**, a day of final judgment on mankind; **judg'ment-debt**, a debt evidenced by legal record; **judg'ment-hall**, a hall where a court of justice meets; **judg'ment-seat**, seat or bench in a court from which judgment is pronounced.—**judgment reserved**, decision delayed after the close of a trial (in Scotland, ' avizandum made '); **judgment respited**, execution of sentence delayed. [A.Fr. *juger*—L. *jūdicāre*—*jūs*, law, *dīcĕre*, to declare.]

Judica, *jŏŏ'di-kä*, *n.* Passion Sunday—from the opening words of the introit, ' *Judica* me, Deus ' (43rd Psalm).

judicature, *jŏŏ'di-kət-yər*, *n.* power of dispensing justice by legal trial: jurisdiction: the office of judge: the body of judges: a court: a system of courts.—*adj.* **ju'dicable**, that may be judged or tried.—*n.* **judica'tion**, judgment.—*adj.* **ju'dicative**, having power to judge.—*ns.* **ju'dicator**, one who judges; **ju'dicatory** (*-kə-tər-i*), judicature: a court.—*adj.* pertaining to a judge: distributing justice. [L. *jūdicāre, -ātum*, to judge.]

judicial, *jŏŏ-dish'əl*, *adj.* pertaining to a judge or court of justice: established by statute: of the nature of judgment: critical.—*adv.* **judic'ially**.—**judicial astrology**, the would-be science of the influence of the planets on human affairs; **judicial combat**, trial by battle; **Judicial Committee**, an offshoot of the Privy Council, forming a court of appeal; **judicial separation**, the separation of two married persons by order of the Divorce Court; **judicial trustee** (or **factor**, in Scotland), an administrator appointed by the courts to manage the estate of someone under some imperfection. [L. *jūdiciālis*—*jūdicium*.]

judiciary, *jŏŏ-dish-*(y)*ər-i*, *adj.* pertaining to judgment, judges, or courts of law.—*n.* a body of judges: a system of courts. [L. *jūdiciārius*.]

judicious, *jŏŏ-dish'əs*, *adj.* according to sound judgment: possessing sound judgment: discreet.—*adv.* **judic'iously.** — *n.* **judic'iousness.** [Fr. *judicieux*—L. *jūdicium*.]

judo, *jŏŏ'dō*, *n.* a variety of ju-jitsu. [Jap.]

Judy, *jŏŏ'di*, *n.* Punch's wife in the puppet-show: a frump, an odd-looking woman. [From the name *Judith*.]

jug, *jug*, *n.* a vessel with a handle and a spout or lip for pouring liquids: a jugful.—*v.t.* to boil or stew as in a closed jar :—*pr.p.* **jugg'ing**; *pa.t.* and *pa.p.* **jugged**.—*n.* **jug'ful**, as much as a jug will hold :—*pl.* **jug'fuls**.—**jugged hare**, hare cut in pieces and stewed with wine and other seasoning. [Origin unknown.]

jug, *jug*, *n.* (*slang*) prison. [Cf. **jougs**.]

jug, *jug*, *n.* a note of the nightingale.—*v.i.* to utter the sound.—Also **jug'-jug'**. [Imit.]

jugal, *jŏŏ'gəl*, *adj.* relating to a yoke, esp. that of marriage: malar.—*n.* the malar bone. [L. *jugālis*—*jugum*, a yoke.]

jugate, *jŏŏ'gāt*, *adj.* (*bot.*) paired: having the leaflets in pairs: joined side by side or overlapping, as heads shown on a coin, &c. [L. *jugāre, -ātum*, to join—*jugum*, a yoke.]

Juggernaut, *jug'ər-nawt*, **Jagannath**, *jug'ə-nät*, *n.* an incarnation of Vishnu, beneath whose car devotees were supposed by Europeans to immolate themselves; hence the ' car of Juggernaut ' stands metaphorically for any relentless destroying force or object of devotion and sacrifice. [Sans. *Jagannātha*, lord of the world.]

juggins, *jug'inz*, *n.* (*slang*) a simpleton. [Origin unknown.]

juggle, *jug'l*, *v.i.* (*obs.*) to perform as an entertainer:

to amuse by sleight-of-hand: to conjure: to practise artifice or imposture: to tamper or manipulate.—*v.t.* to transform, render, put by jugglery.—*n.* a trick by sleight-of-hand: an imposture.—*ns.* **jugg'ler**, one who performs tricks by sleight-of-hand: a trickish fellow; **jugg'lery** (*-lə-ri*), art or tricks of a juggler: legerdemain: trickery.—*n.* and *adj.* **jugg'ling**.—*adv.* **jugg'lingly**, in a deceptive manner, a jest.] [O.Fr. *jogler*—L. *joculāri*, to jest—*jocus*, a jest.]

Juglans, *jŏŏ'glanz*, *n.* the walnut genus. [L. *jūglāns*—*Jovis glāns*, Jove's acorn.]

Jugoslav. Same as **Yugoslav.**

jugular, *jug'*, *jŏŏg'ū-lər*, *adj.* pertaining to the neck.—*n.* one of the large veins on each side of the neck.—*v.t.* **jug'ŭlate**, to cut the throat of: to strangle. [L. *jugulum*, the collar-bone—*jungĕre*, to join.]

juice, *jŏŏs*, *n.* the sap of vegetables: the fluid part of animal bodies: interesting quality: piquancy: (*slang*) electric current, petrol vapour, or other source of power.—*adj.* **juice'less.**—*n.* **juic'iness.**—*adj.* **juic'y.**—**step on the juice**, to accelerate a motor-car. [Fr. *jus*—L. *jūs*, broth, lit. mixture.]

ju-jitsu, jiu-jitsu, *jŏŏ-jit'soo*, *n.* a system of wrestling and athletic exercises in vogue in Japan. [Jap. *jū-jutsu.*]

ju-ju, *jŏŏ'jŏŏ*, *n.* an object of superstitious worship in West Africa: a fetish or charm. [App. Fr. *joujou*, a toy.]

jujube, *jŏŏ'jŏŏb*, *n.* a spiny shrub or small tree (Zizyphus) of the buckthorn family: its fruit, which is dried as a sweetmeat: a lozenge made of sugar and gum in imitation of the fruit. [Fr. *jujube* or L.L. *jujuba*—Gr. *zizyphon.*]

juke, *jŏŏk*, *v.i.* (*U.S. slang*) to dance.—*ns.* **juke'-box**, a slot machine that plays gramophone records; **juke'-joint**, a resort for dancing and drinking.

julep, *jŏŏ lep*, *n.* a sweet drink, often medicated: an American drink of spirits, sugar, ice, and mint. [Fr.,—Sp. *julepe*—Ar. *julāb*—Pers. *gulāb*—*gul*, rose, *āb*, water.]

Julian, *jŏŏl'yən*, *adj.* pertaining to *Julius* Caesar (B.C. 100-44).—**Julian year** (see **year**).

julienne, *jŏŏ-li-en'*, *zhü-lyen*, *n.* a clear soup, with shredded herbs. [Fr. name.]

July, *jŏŏ-lī'*, formerly and still by some *jŏŏ'li*, *n.* the seventh month of the year. [L. *Jūlius*, from Gaius Julius Caesar, who was born in it.]

July-flower, a mistaken form of **gillyflower.**

jumart, *jŏŏ'märt, -mərt*, *n.* the fabled offspring of a bull and a mare, or horse and cow. [Fr.]

jumbal, jumble, *jum'bl*, *n.* a thin, crisp, sweet cake, formerly made in the shape of a ring. [Perh. **gimmel, gimbal.**]

jumble, *jum bl*, *v.t.* to mix confusedly: to throw together without order: to shake up, jolt.—*v.i.* to be mixed together confusedly: to be agitated: to flounder.—*n.* a confused mixture: confusion: jolting.—*n.* **jum'ble-sale**, a sale of miscellaneous articles, rubbish, &c., often for charity.—*adv.* **jum blingly**, in a confused or jumbled manner.—*adj.* **jum'bly**. [Origin obscure.]

jumbo, *jum bō*, *n.* an elephant: anything very big of its kind.—*adj.* huge: colossal. [Name of a huge elephant.]

jumby, jumbie, *jum'bi*, *n.* a West Indian negro's word for a ghost or evil spirit. [Congolese *zumbi*.]

jumelle, *jŏŏ-mel'*, *zhü-mel*, *n.* a paired or twinned article, esp. opera-glasses. [Fr., twin; cf. **gemel**, **gimmal**.]

jump, *jump*, *v.i.* to spring or bound: to move suddenly: to bounce: to rise suddenly: to pass discontinuously: to throb: to agree, coincide (*with*).—*v.t.* to cause or help to leap: to toss: to leap over, from, or on to: to skip over: to spring or start, as game : (*Shak.*) to risk: to appropriate, as when the owner has failed to satisfy conditions or has abandoned his claim: (*obs.*) to make up hastily, patch up: (*pr.p.* **jump'ing**; *pa.t.* and *pa.p.* **jumped**).—*n.* act of jumping: a bound: a sudden rise: a sudden movement: a start: (in *pl.*) convulsive movements, chorea, delirium tremens, or the like: a bounce: a discontinuity: (*Shak.*) a venture, a hazard.—*adv.* (*Shak.*) exactly.—*ns.* **jump'er**, one who jumps: a long iron drill used in quarries,

&c.: one of certain Welsh Methodists (*c.* 1760), who jumped about in worship; **jump′iness.**—*adj.* **jump′y,** nervy, inclined to start.—*ns.* **jump′ingbean,** the seed of a Mexican euphorbiaceous plant (Sebastiania), which an enclosed larva causes to move or jump; **jump′ing-deer′,** the blacktailed American deer; **jump′ing-hare′,** a South African rodent akin to the jerboa; **jump′ing-jack,** a toy figure whose limbs can be moved by pulling a string; **jump′ing-mouse′,** a genus (Zapus) of jumping rodents, American and Chinese; **jumping-off′-place,** the terminus of a route: the point where one sets forth into the wilds, the unknown, &c.; **jump′-off,** (*U.S.*) the start: starting-place; **jump′-seat,** a movable carriage-seat: a carriage with a movable seat.—**jump at,** to accept with eagerness; **jump down one′s throat,** to assail with violent rating; **jump on,** to jump so as to come down heavily upon: to censure promptly and vigorously; **jump one′s bail,** to abscond, forfeiting one's bail; **jump to conclusions,** to form inferences prematurely. [Prob. onomatopoeic.]

jump, *jump, n.* a short coat: (in *pl.*) stays: clothes.—*n.* **jump′er,** an overall, slipped over the head: a woman's knitted garment like a blouse, originally one loose at the waist. [Perh. from Fr. *juppe,* now *jupe,* a petticoat.]

juncate, (*Spens.*) a form of **junket.**

junco, *jung′kō, n.* (*obs.*) the reed-bunting: a North American snow-bird. [Sp. *junco*—L. *juncus,* rush.]

junction, *jung(k)′shən, n.* a joining, a union or combination: place or point of union, esp. of railway lines. [L. *junctiō,* -*ōnis*; see **join.**]

juncture, *jungk′tyər, n.* a joining, a union: a critical or important point of time. [L. *junctūra*; see **join.**]

Juncus, *jungk′əs, n.* the typical genus of rushes, giving name to the **Junca′ceae,** the rush family.—*adj.* **junca′ceous.** [L. *juncus,* a rush.]

June, *jōōn, n.* the sixth month.—*n.* **June′berry,** the fruit of the shad-bush. [L. *Jūnius.*]

juneating, *jōōn′ēt-ing,* an erroneous form of **jenneting.**

Jungermanniales, *yoong-ər-man-i-ā′lēs, n.pl.* one of the main divisions of the Hepaticae, with thallus or leafy stem, and usually capsule opening by four valves. [Ludwig *Jungermann* (1572-1653), German botanist.]

jungle, *jung′gl, n.* originally waste ground: a dense tropical growth of thickets, brushwood, &c.: dense tropical forest.—*ns.* **jung′le-fever,** a severe malarial fever; **jung′le-fowl,** the wild parent of the barndoor fowl.—*adj.* **jungli** (*jung′gli*), inhabiting a jungle: wild and boorish.—*n.* an inhabitant of a jungle: an uneducated peasant.—*adj.* **jung′ly.** [Sans. *jaṅgala,* desert.]

junior, *jōōn′yər, adj.* younger: less advanced: of lower standing.—*n.* one younger, less advanced, or of lower standing: a latecomer: a young person: a bridge-player on the declarer's right: an American student in his third year (of four).—*n.* **juniority** (*-i-or′i-ti*).—**junior optime** (see **optime**); **junior service,** the Army; **junior soph,** an undergraduate of the second year at Cambridge. [L. *jūnior,* compar. of *jŭvenis,* young.]

juniper, *jōō′ni-pər, n.* an evergreen coniferous shrub (**Juniperus**), whose berries are used in making gin. [L. *jūniperus.*]

junk, *jungk, n.* a Chinese vessel, with high forecastle and poop, sometimes large and three-masted. [Port. *junco,* app.—Javanese *djong.*]

junk, *jungk, n.* pieces of old cordage: rubbish generally: a thick piece, chunk: salt meat, perh. because it becomes as hard as old rope.—*ns.* **junk′-bottle,** (*U.S.*) a thick strong bottle of green or black glass; **junk′-dealer, junk′man,** a dealer in junk; **junk′-ring,** a metal ring confining the packing of a piston; **junk′-shop,** a place where junk is sold. [Origin doubtful.]

junker, *yŏŏngk′ər, n.* a young German noble or squire: an overbearing, narrow-minded, reactionary aristocrat.—*ns.* **junk′erdom; junk′erism.** [Ger.,—*jung,* young, *herr,* lord.]

junket, *junk′it, n.* (*dial.*) a rush-basket: a cream-

cheese: any sweetmeat or delicacy: curds mixed with cream, sweetened and flavoured: a feast or merrymaking, a picnic, an outing, a spree.—*v.i.* to feast, banquet, take part in a convivial entertainment or spree.—*v.t.* to feast, regale, entertain:—*pr.p.* **junk′eting**; *pa.p.* **junk′eted.**—*n.* **junk′eting,** a merry feast or entertainment, picnicking. [A.Fr. *jonquette,* rush-basket—L. *juncus,* a rush.]

Juno, *jōō′nō, n.* in Roman mythology, the wife of Jupiter, identified with the Greek Hera, special protectress of marriage and guardian of woman from birth to death: a queenly woman.—*adj.* **Junō′nian.** [L. *Jŭnō,* -*ōnis.*]

junta, *jun′tä, n.* a meeting, council: a Spanish grand council of state. [Sp.,—L. *jungĕre, junctum,* to join.]

junto, *jun′tō, n.* a body of men joined or united for some secret intrigue: a confederacy: a cabal or faction:—*pl.* **jun′tos.** [Sp. *junta.*]

jupati, *jōō′pa-tē* or -*tē′, n.* a species of raphia palm. [Tupí.]

Jupiter, *jōō′pi-tər, n.* the chief god among the Romans, the parallel of the Greek Zeus—also **Jove**: the largest and, next to Venus, the brightest of the planets.—**Jupiter's beard,** the house-leek: a kidney-vetch: a fungus (Hydnum Barba-Jovis). [L. *Jŭpiter, Juppiter,* Father (*pater*) Jove.]

jupon, *jōō′pon, n.* a sleeveless jacket or close-fitting coat, extending down over the hips: a petticoat. [Fr.]

jural, *jōō′rəl, adj.* pertaining to natural or positive right.—*adv.* **ju′rally.** [L. *jūs, jūris,* law.]

jurant, *jōō′rənt, adj.* taking an oath.—*n.* one who takes an oath.—*adj.* **ju′ratory,** pertaining to an oath. [L. *jūrāre,* -*ātum,* to swear.]

Jurassic, *jōō-ras′ik, adj.* (*geol.*) of the middle division of the Mesozoic rocks, well-developed in the *Jura* Mountains.—*n.* the Jurassic period or system.—Also **Ju′ra.**

jurat, *jōō′rat, n.* the official memorandum at the end of an affidavit, showing the time when and the person before whom it was sworn. [L. *jūrātum,* sworn—*jūrāre,* to swear.]

jurat, *jōō′rat, n.* a sworn officer, as a magistrate. [Fr.,—L. *jūrāre,* -*ātum,* to swear.]

juridical, *jōō-rid′ik-əl, adj.* relating to the distribution of justice: pertaining to a judge: used in courts of law.—*adv.* **jurid′ically.** [L. *jūridicus*—*jūs, jūris,* law, *dicĕre,* to declare.]

jurisconsult, *jōō′ris-kon-sult′, n.* one who is consulted on the law: a lawyer who gives opinions on cases put to him: one learned in law. [L. *jūris cōnsultus*—*jūs, jūris,* law, *cōnsulĕre, cōnsultus,* to consult.]

jurisdiction, *jōō-ris-dik′shən, n.* the distribution of justice: legal authority: extent of power: district over which any authority extends.—*adjs.* **jurisdic′tional, jurisdic′tive.** [L. *jūrisdictiō,* -*ōnis.*]

jurisprudence, *jōō-ris-prōō′dəns, n.* the science or knowledge of law.—*adj.* **jurispru′dent,** learned in law.—*n.* one who is learned in law.—*adj.* **jurisprudential** (*-den′shl*).—**medical jurisprudence,** forensic medicine (see **forensic**). [L. *jūrisprūdentia*—*jūs, jūris,* law, *prūdentia,* knowledge.]

jurist, *jōō′rist, n.* one who is versed in the science of law, esp. Roman or civil law: a student of law: a graduate in law: (*U.S.*) a lawyer.—*adjs.* **jurist′ic, -al.**—*adv.* **jurist′ically.** [Fr. *juriste.*]

jury, *jōō′ri, n.* a body of persons sworn to declare the truth on evidence before them: a committee of adjudicators or examiners.—*ns.* **ju′ror,** one who serves on a jury—also **ju′ryman, ju′rywoman** (*pl.* **ju′rymen, ju′rywomen**); **ju′ry-box,** the place in which the jury sit during a trial; **ju′ry-pro′cess,** a writ summoning a jury—**jury of matrons,** a jury of women impanelled to try a question of pregnancy. [A.Fr. *juree*—*jurer*—L. *jūrāre,* to swear.]

jurymast, *jōō′ri-mäst, -məst, n.* a temporary mast raised instead of one lost.—*adj.* **ju′ry-rigged,** rigged in a temporary way.—*n.* **ju′ry-rudd′er,** temporary rudder for one lost. [Not *injury-mast,* but perh. O.Fr. *ajurie,* aid—L. *adjūtāre,* to aid.]

Neutral vowels in unaccented syllables: *el′ə-mənt, in′fənt, ran′dəm*

jussive, *jus'iv, adj.* expressing command.—*n.* a grammatical form or construction expressing command. [L. *jubēre, jussum,* to command.]

just, *just.* Same as **joust.**

just, *just, adj.* righteous: upright: fair: impartial: according to justice: due: in accordance with facts: well-grounded: accurately true: exact: (*obs.*) normal: (*obs.*) close-fitting.—*adv.* precisely: exactly: so much and no more: barely: only: merely: (*coll.*) quite.—*adv.* **just'ly,** in a just manner: equitably: uprightly: accurately: by right.—*n.* **just'ness,** equity: fittingness: exactness.—**just intonation,** observance of the true mathematical theoretical pitch, without compromise or temperament; **just now,** precisely at this moment: hence, a little while ago, or very soon. [Fr. *juste,* or L. *jūstus—jūs,* law.]

justice, *jus'tis, n.* quality of being just: integrity: impartiality: rightness: the awarding of what is due: a judge: a magistrate.—*ns.* **jus'ticer,** a vindicator or administrator of justice; **jus'ticeship,** the office or dignity of a justice or judge.—*adj.* **justiciable** (*jus-tish'i-ə-bl*), liable to trial.—*ns.* **justiciar** (*-tish'i-ər; hist.*), an administrator of justice: a chief-justice; **justiciary** (*-tish'i-ə-ri*), a judge: a chief-justice: jurisdiction of a justiciar or justiciary.—*adj.* pertaining to the administration of justice.—**High Court of Justice,** a section of the English Supreme Court, comprising Chancery and King's (Queen's) Bench Divisions; **High Court of Justiciary,** the supreme criminal court in Scotland; **Justice of the Peace (J.P.),** a local minor magistrate commissioned to keep the peace; **justices' justice,** the kind of justice sometimes administered by the unpaid and amateur magistracy of England; **Lord Chief-justice,** the chief judge of the King's (or Queen's) Bench Division of the High Court of Justice; **Lord Justice-clerk,** the Scottish judge ranking next to the Lord Justice-general, presiding over the Second Division of the Inner House of the Court of Session, vice-president of the High Court of Justiciary; **Lord Justice-general,** the highest judge in Scotland, called also the Lord President of the Court of Session. [Fr.,—L. *jūstitia.*]

justify, *jus'ti-fī, v.t.* to make just: to prove or show to be just or right: to vindicate: to absolve: (*obs.*) to punish, esp. to hang: (*print.*) to adjust by spacing:—*pr.p.* **jus'tifying;** *pa.t.* and *pa.p.* **jus'tified.**—*adj.* **jus'tifiable** (or *-fī'*), that may be justified or defended.—*n.* **jus'tifiableness** (or *-fī'*).

—*adv.* **jus'tifiably** (or *-fī'*). — *n.* **justification** (*jus-ti-fi-kā'shən*), act of justifying: that which justifies: vindication: absolution: a plea of sufficient reason.—*adjs.* **jus'tificātive, justificatory** (*jus-tif'i-ka-tə-ri* or *jus'ti-fi-kā-tə-ri,* or *-kā'*), having power to justify.—*ns.* **jus'tificātor, jus'tifier,** one who defends or vindicates: he who pardons and absolves from guilt and punishment. —**justifiable homicide,** the killing of a person in self-defence, or to prevent an atrocious crime; **justification by faith,** the doctrine that men are justified by faith in Christ. [Fr. *justifier* and L. *jūstificāre—jūstus,* just, *facĕre,* to make.]

justle. Same as **jostle.**

jut, *jut, n.* a projection: a jetting movement.—*v.i.* to project:—*pr.p.* **jutt'ing;** *pa.t.* and *pa.p.* **jutt'ed.** —*adj.* **jutt'ing.**—*adv.* **jutt'ingly.**—*n.* **jut'-win'dow,** a bay window. [A form of **jet** (2).]

jute, *jōōt, n.* the fibre of *Corchorus capsularis* and *C. olitorius,* Indian plants of the lime family, used for making coarse bags, mats, &c.: the plant itself. —Also *adj.*—**China jute,** a species of Abutilon: its fibre. [Bengali *jhuto*—Sans. *jūta,* matted hair.]

jutty, *jut'i, n.* a projecting part of a building: a pier, a jetty.—*v.t.* (*Shak.*) to project beyond.—*v.i.* to jut. [Cf. **jetty.**]

juvenal, *jōō'vən-əl, n.* (*Shak.*) a youth. [L. *juvenālis,* belonging to youth—*juvenis,* young.]

Juvenalian, *jōōv-i-nā'li-ən, adj.* of the Roman satirist *Juvenal* (Decimus Junius Juvenalis, 1st-2nd cent. A.D.): lurid and denunciatory rather than humorous.

juvenescent, *jōō-vən-es'ənt, adj.* becoming youthful. —*n.* **juvenesc'ence.** [L. *juvenēscĕre,* to grow young.]

juvenile, *jōō'və-nīl, adj.* young: pertaining or suited to youth or young people: having or retaining characteristics of youth.—*n.* a young person: a book written for the young: an actor who plays youthful parts.—*n.* **ju'venileness.**—*n.pl.* **juvenilia** (*-il'yā*), writings or works of one's childhood or youth.—*n.* **juvenility** (*-il'i-ti*), juvenile character. [L. *juvenīlis—juvenis,* young.]

juxtaposition, *juks-tə-pə-zish'ən, n.* a placing or being placed close together.—*v.t.* **jux'tapose** (or *-pōz'*), to place side by side.—**juxtaposition twin,** crystals twinned as if set together face to face without interpenetration. [L. *juxtā,* near, and **position, pose.**]

jymold. See **gimmal.**

Jynx, *jingks, n.* the wryneck genus: a wryneck. [L. *iynx*—Gr. *iynx* or *īynx.*]

fāte, fär, ȧsk; mē, hȯr (her); *mīne; mōte; mūte; mōōn; dhen* (then)

K

K, k, *kā, n.* the eleventh letter in our alphabet, derived from Greek kappa, representing a back voiceless stop, formed by raising the back of the tongue to the soft palate : as a mediaeval numeral, K=250 : in mathematics *k* often stands for a constant quantity : in thermometry K stands for the Kelvin scale.

ka, *kā, n.* in ancient Egyptian religion, the double or genius, or individuality. [Egypt.]

ka, kae, *kā, v.t. (obs.)* serve (in the phrase *ka me, ka thee,* one good turn deserves another). [Origin unknown.]

Kaaba, *kä'bä, n.* the holy building at Mecca into which the Black Stone is built. [Ar. *ka'bah—ka'b,* cube.]

kaama, *kä'mä, n.* the hartebeest. [Of Hottentot or Bantu origin.]

kabala. Same as **cabbala.**

kabaya, *kä-bä'yä, n.* a loose tunic. [Malay, from Pers. or Ar.]

kabeljauw, *käb'əl-yow, n.* a codfish, esp. partly dried : (*S.Afr.*) the maigre. [Du., cod.]

kabob. Same as **cabob.**

Kabyle, *ka-bīl', n.* one of a branch of the great Berber people of North Africa : a dialect of Berber. [Fr.,—Ar. *qabā'il,* pl. of *qabīlah,* a tribe.]

kachahri, kacheri, *kuch'ə-ri, kuch-er'i, n.* an Indian magistrate's office or courthouse.—Also **cutcherry.** [Hind. *kachahri, kachērī.*]

Kaddish, *kad'ish, n.* a Jewish form of thanksgiving and prayer, used at funerals, &c. [Aramaic *qaddīsh.*]

kade. See **ked.**

kadi, *kä'di, n.* Same as **cadi.**

kae, *kā, n.* (*Scot.*) a jackdaw.—Also **ka.** [Cf. Du. *ka,* Dan. *kaa.*]

Kaffir, *kaf'ər, n.* a S. African Bantu (including Zulus) : their language: (*pl.*) S. African mining and other stocks.—Also **Kaf'ir, Caff're.**—Also *adj.*—*ns.* **kaff'ir-boom** (Du. *boom,* tree), the coral-tree (*Erythrina caffra*; Papilionaceae) : a boom in kaffirs (South African stocks) ; **kaffir bread,** the pith of S. African cycads (*Encephalartos*) ; **kaffir corn,** sorghum. [Kafir.]

kaffiyeh, *käf-ē'ye, n.* a Bedouin shawl for the head. [Ar. *kaffīyah.*]

kafila, *käf'i-lä, n.* a camel train, caravan. [Ar. *qāfilah.*]

Kafir, *käf'ər, n.* a native of Kafiristan : a Kaffir. [Ar. *kāfir,* unbeliever.]

kaftan. Same as **caftan.**

kago, *käg'ō, n.* a Japanese basket-work palanquin. [Jap. *kango.*]

kai, *kä'ē, kī, n.* (*N. Zealand,* &c.) food.—*n.* **kai'kai,** food : feast.—*v.t.* to eat. [Maori.]

kaiak. Same as **kayak.**

kaid, *kä-ēd', käd, n.* a North African chief. [Ar. *qā'id ;* cf. **alcaid.**]

kaie, *kā,* an obsolete form of **key.**

kaif, *kīf, n.* an undisturbed quiescence. [Ar.]

kail, *kāl, n.* a ninepin.—*n.* **kails,** the game of nine-pins : skittles. [Cf. Du. and Ger. *kegel.*]

kail, kaim. See **kale, kame.**

kaimakam, *kī-mä-käm', n.* a Turkish lieutenant-colonel or lieutenant-governor. [Turk. *qāimaqām.*]

kain. Same as **cain** (2).

kainite, *kī'nīt, kä'nīt, kä'in-īt, n.* hydrous magnesium sulphate with potassium chloride, found in salt deposits, used as a fertiliser. [Ger. *kainit—* Gr. *kainos,* new, recent.]

Kainozoic. Same as **Cainozoic.**

kaisar-i-Hind, *kī'sär-i-hind', n.* title from 1876 to 1947 of the British monarch as emperor of India. [Pers. *qaysari-Hind—*L. *Caesar.*]

kaiser, *kī'zər, n.* an emperor, esp. a German

Emperor.—Also (as *Spens.*) **kesar, keasar** (*kē'zər*). —*ns.* **kai'serdom; kai'serism; kai'sership.** [Ger.,—L. *Caesar.*]

kajawah, *kä-jä'wä, n.* a camel litter or pannier. [Pers.]

kaka, *kä'kä, n.* a New Zealand parrot (*Nestor meridionalis*).—*ns.* **ka'ka-beak, -bill,** the New Zealand glory-pea (Clianthus) ; **ka'kapo,** the New Zealand owl-parrot, large-winged but almost flight-less. [Maori *kaka,* parrot, *po,* night.]

kakemono, *kak-i-mō'nō, n.* a Japanese wall-picture with roller. [Jap. *kake,* to hang, *mono,* thing.]

kaki, *kä'kē, n.* the Japanese persimmon, or Chinese date-plum. [Jap.]

kakistocracy, *kak-is-tok'rə-si, n.* government by the worst. [Gr. *kakistos,* superl. of *kakos,* bad, *kratos,* power.]

kakodyl. See **cacodyl.**

kala-azar, *kä'lä-ä-zär', n.* a tropical fever, charac-terised by bloodlessness, and ascribed to a protozoan parasite. [Assamese *kālā,* black, *āzār,* disease.]

kalamdan, *kal'am-dan, n.* a Persian writing-case. [Pers. *qalamdan—qalam,* a pen, *dān,* holding.]

kalamkari, *kal-am-kä'rē, n.* a method of colouring and decorating by several dyeings or printings : a chintz so treated. [Pers. *qalamkārī,* writing, painting, &c.—*qalam,* pen.]

kale, kail, *kāl, n.* a cabbage with open curled leaves : cabbage generally : broth of which kale is a chief ingredient : hence (*Scot.*) dinner.—*ns.* **kail'-pot** (*Scot.* -pat') ; **kail'-runt',** a cabbage stem ; **kail'-yard, -yaird',** a cabbage-patch. — **kailyard school,** a set of Scottish sentimental story-writers (from the allusion of Ian Maclaren's *Beside the Bonnie Brier Bush,* 1894, to the Jacobite song). [Northern form of **cole.**]

kaleidophone, *kə-lī'də-fōn, n.* an instrument for exhibiting sonorous vibrations by lines of light on a screen. [Gr. *kalos,* beautiful, *eidos,* form, *phōnē,* voice.]

kaleidoscope, *kə-lī'də-skōp, n.* an optical toy in which one sees an ever-changing variety of beautiful colours and forms.—*adj.* **kaleidoscopic** (-*skop'ik*). [Gr. *kalos,* beautiful, *eidos,* form, *skopeein,* to look.]

kalendar, kalends=calendar, calends.

Kalevala, *kä'le-vä-lä, n.* the great Finnish epic, in eight-syllabled trochaic verse (from which Long-fellow's *Hiawatha* is imitated) pieced together from oral tradition by Dr Elias Lönnrot in 1835-49. [Finnish *kaleva,* a hero, -*la,* denoting place.]

kali, *kal'i,* or *kā'lī, n.* the prickly saltwort or glass-wort (*Salsola Kali*): (*obs.*) its ash : (*obs.*) alkali, esp. potash.—*ns.* **kalinite** (*kal'in-īt*), native potash alum ; **kā'lium,** potassium. [See **alkali.**]

kali, *kä'lē, n.* a carpet with long nap : the large carpet covering the centre of a Persian room. [Pers. *kālī.*]

Kali, *kä'lē, n.* a Hindu goddess, Durga, wife of Siva, as goddess of destruction. [Sans. *kālī,* black.]

kalian, *käl-yän', n.* a Persian hookah. [Pers.]

kalif. See **caliph.**

Kaliyuga, *käl-i-yōō'gä, n.* in Hindu mythology, the present (fourth) age of the world, of universal degeneracy. [Sans.]

Kallima, *kal'i-mä, n.* an Oriental genus of butter-flies, mimicking dead leaves. [Gr. *kallimos,* beautiful.]

kallitype, *kal'i-tīp, n.* a photographic process in which ferric are reduced to ferrous salts. [Gr. *kallos,* beauty, *typos,* type.]

Kalmia, *kal'mi-ä, n.* a genus of North American evergreen shrubs of the heath family, including the mountain laurel or calico-bush. [From Peter *Kalm,* pupil of Linnaeus.]

Neutral vowels in unaccented syllables : *el'ə-mənt, in'fənt, ran'dəm*

Kalmuck, *kal'muk, n.* a member of a Mongolian race in China and Russia : their language.—Also *adj.* [Turki and Russ.]

kalong, *kä'long, n.* a large fruit-bat. [Malay *kälong.*]

kalotype. Same as **calotype.**

kalpa, *kal'pə, n.* a day of Brahma, a period of 4320 million years.—Also **cal'pa.** [Sans., formation.]

kalpak, *kăl'păk,* or *-păk', n.* a triangular Turkish or Tatar felt cap.—Also **calpac, calpack.** [Turk. *qălpâq.*]

kalpis, *kal'pis, n.* a water-vase. [Gr.]

kalsomine, a wrong form of **calcimine.** See **calcium.**

kalumpit, *kă-loom-pēt', n.* a Philippine tree of the myrobalan genus : its edible fruit. [Tagálog.]

kalyptra, *ka-lip'trä, n.* a veil worn by Greek women. [Gr. ; see also **calyptra.**]

kam, kamme, cam, *kam, adj.* and *adv.* (*Shak.*) awry. [Cf. W., Gael., Ir. *cam.*]

Kama, *kä'mä, n.* the god of love in the Purânas : impure desire.—Also **Cama, Ka'madeva** (*-dä-vä*). [Sans. *Kāma.*]

kamala, *kä'mä-lä, n.* an orange dye-stuff got from the fruit-hairs of an East Indian tree of the spurge family (*Mallotus philippinensis*) : the tree itself.—Also **kamela, kamila** (*kä-mä'lä, -mē'lä*). [Sans. *kamala*; Hind. *kamēlā, kamīlā.*]

kame, kaim, *kām, n.* (*Scot.*) a comb : a low irregular ridge like a cock's comb : (*geol.*) an eskar, a bank or ridge of gravel, sand, &c., associated with the glacial deposits of Scotland : (*Scott*) a fortified site. [Northern form of **comb.**]

kame, came, *kām, n.* a lead rod for framing a pane in a lattice or stained-glass window.

kamerad, *kam-ər-äd', interj.* comrade (said to have been a German form of surrender or appeal for quarter).—*v.i.* to surrender. [Ger.,—Fr. *camarade,* comrade.]

kami, *kä'mi, n.* a Japanese lord, national god, demigod, or deified hero, or any of their supposed descendants, as the mikados and the imperial family. [Jap., superior.]

kamichi, *kä'mē-shē, n.* the horned screamer. [Fr. from Carib.]

kamila, kamela. See **kamala.**

kamis, kamees, *ka-mēs'.* Same as **camise.**

kampong, *kam'pong, kam-pong', n.* an enclosed space : a village. [Malay.]

kamsin. See **khamsin.**

kana, *kä'nä, n.* Japanese syllabic writing, as distinguished from Japanese written in Chinese characters. [Jap.]

kanaka, *kan'ə-kä,* in Australia *kən-ak'ä, n.* a South Sea Islander, esp. an indentured or forced labourer. [Hawaiian, a man.]

Kanarese, Canarese, *kan-ər-ēz', adj.* of Kanara in western India.—*n.* one of the people thereof : their Dravidian language, akin to Telugu.

kandy, *kan'di, n.* Same as **candy** (2).

kaneh, caneh, *kä'ne, n.* a Hebrew measure of 6 cubits' length. [Heb. *qāneh,* reed, cane.]

kang, *kang, n.* a large Chinese water-jar : a platform (e.g. of brick) for sleeping on that can be warmed by a fire underneath. [Chin.]

kangaroo, *kang-gə-rōō', n.* a large marsupial of Australia, with very long hind-legs and great power of leaping : (in *pl.*) Australian mining shares.—*ns.* **kangaroo'-app'le,** the edible fruit of a species of Solanum : the plant that yields it ; **kangaroo'-grass,** a valuable Australian fodder grass (Anthistiria or Themeda) ; **kangaroo'-rat',** the potoroo or rat-kangaroo, a marsupial of various species about the size of a rabbit, akin to the kangaroo : a North American rodent (Dipodomys) akin to the jerboa ; **kangaroo'-thorn',** a prickly Australian acacia (*Acacia armata*).—**kangaroo closure,** the method of allowing the chairman to decide which clauses shall be discussed and which passed or leaped over. [Supposed to be a native name.]

kans, *käns, n.* an Indian grass allied to sugar-cane.

kant. Same as **cant** (2).

kantar, cantar, *kăn-tär', n.* a varying weight in Turkey, Egypt, &c., approximately a hundred-weight. [Ar. *qintār*; see **quintal.**]

kanten, *kăn'ten, n.* agar-agar jelly. [Jap.]

Kantian, *kant'i-ən, adj.* pertaining to the great German philosopher Immanuel Kant (1724-1804) or his philosophy.—*ns.* **Kan'tianism, Kant'ism,** the doctrines or philosophy of Kant ; **Kant'ist,** a disciple or follower of Kant.

kantikoy, canticoy, *kan'ti-koi, cantico, -kō, n.* an American Indian religious dance : a dancing-match.—*v.i.* to dance as an act of worship. [From Algonquian.]

Kanuck. Same as **Canuck.**

kaoliang, *kä-ō-li-ang', n.* sorghum grain of various varieties : a spirituous liquor made from it. [Chin., tall grain.]

kaolin, *kā'ō-lin, n.* Chinese clay, esp. that composed of kaolinite.—*v.t.* and *v.i.* **ka'olinise,** to turn into kaolin.—*n.* **ka'olinite,** a hydrated aluminium silicate occurring in minute monoclinic flakes, a decomposition product of felspar, &c. [From the mountain *Kao-ling* (high ridge) in China.]

kapellmeister, *kə-pel'mīs-tər, n.* the director of an orchestra or choir, esp. formerly of the band of a ruling prince in Germany. [Ger. *kapelle,* chapel, orchestra, *meister,* master.]

kapok, *kăp'ok, n.* a very light, waterproof, oily fibre covering the seeds of a species of silk-cotton tree, used for stuffing pillows, life-belts, &c. [Malay *kăpoq.*]

kappa, *kap'ä, n.* the tenth (earlier eleventh) letter of the Greek alphabet (K, κ) : as a numeral κ' = 20, ͵κ = 20,000.

karait, *kăr-īt'.* Same as **krait.**

Karaite, *kā'rä-īt, n.* one of a stricter sect of Jews who cling to the literal interpretation of Scripture as against oral tradition. [Heb. *qārā,* to read.]

karakul, caracul, *kăr'ə-kool, -kool', n.* an Asiatic breed of sheep : a fur prepared from the skin of very young lambs of the Karakul or Bukhara breed, or of kids : a cloth imitating it. [Russ. *kara'kul,* from *Karakul,* near Bukhara.]

karite, *kar'i-ti, n.* the shea-tree. [Native African name.]

Karling, *kär'ling, n.* and *adj.* Carlovingian. [Ger. *Karl.* Charles, and patronymic suffix *-ing.*]

karma, *kär'mä, n.* the conception (Buddhist, etc.) of the quality of actions, including both merit and demerit, determining the future condition of all sentient beings : the theory of inevitable consequence generally : the result of the actions of a life. —*adj.* **kar'mic.** [Sans. *karma,* act.]

Karmathian, *kär-mä'thi-ən, n.* a member of a pantheistic socialistic Mohammedan sect which arose in Turkey about the close of the 9th century. [*Karmat,* its founder.]

Karoo, Karroo, *kä-rōō', n.* (*S.Afr.*) a high inland pastoral tableland : (*geol.*) a series of strata in South Africa of Permian and Trias age. [Believed to be of Hottentot origin.]

kaross, *kä-ros', n.* a S. African skin blanket. [Perh. a Hottentot modification of Du. *kuras,* cuirass.]

karri, *kar'ē, n.* a Western Australian gum-tree (*Eucalyptus diversicolor*) : its red timber. [Native name.]

karst, *kärst, n.* rough limestone country with underground drainage. [From the *Karst* district, east of the Adriatic.]

kartell, *kär-tel', n.* a German form of **cartel.**

karyokinesis, *ka-ri-ō-kin-ē'sis, n.* (*biol.*) mitosis—a complicated process of division of the cell-nucleus, involving the arrangement of protoplasmic fibres in definite figures. [Gr. *karyon,* kernel, and *kinēsis,* movement.]

karyoplasm, *ka'ri-ō-plazm, n.* the protoplasm of a cell-nucleus. [Gr. *karyon,* kernel, and *plasma,* that which is formed.]

Kashmir. Same as **Cashmere.**

kat, *kăt, n.* a shrub (*Catha edulis*) of the spindle-tree family, used like tea by the Arabs. [Ar. *qat.*]

kat, *kăt, n.* the chief ancient Egyptian unit of weight, $\frac{1}{10}$ lb. avoirdupois.

katabasis, *kat-ab'ə-sis, n.* a going down.—*adj.* **katabatic** (*-ə-bat'ik*). [Gr.]

katabolism, catabolism, *kat-ab'ə-lizm, n.* (*biol.*) the disruptive processes of chemical change in organisms—destructive metabolism, opposed to

fāte, fär, àsk; mē, hər (her); *mīne; mōte; mūte; mōōn; dhen* (then)

anabolism.—adj. **katabolic** (*kat-ə-bol'ik*). [Gr. *katabolē—kataballein*, to throw down—*kata*, down, *ballein*, to throw.]

katabothron, katavothron, *kat-ə-both'ron, kat-av'oth-ron, n.* an underground water-channel. [Mod. Gr. *katabothron*—Gr. *kata*, down, *bothros*, hole.]

katadromous. Same as **catadromous.**

katakana, *kat-ä-kä'nä, n.* a Japanese syllabary. [Jap.]

katharsis, kathode, kation. Same as **catharsis, cathode, cation.**

katydid, *kā'ti-did, n.* an American insect akin to the grasshopper. [Imit. of its note.]

kaugh. See **kiaugh.**

kauri, *kow'ri,* or **kauri-pine,** *n.* a splendid coniferous forest-tree (*Agathis australis*), source of the well-known kau'ri-gum, a resin used in making varnish. [Maori.]

kava, *kä'vä, n.* a species of pepper (*Piper methysticum*): a narcotic drink prepared from its root and stem.—Also **a'va.** [Polynesian.]

kavass, *kä-väs', n.* an armed attendant in Turkey. [Ar. *qawwās*.]

kayak, *ki'ak, n.* an Eskimo seal-skin canoe. [Eskimo.]

kayle. Same as **kail** (1).

kazoo, *kä-zoo', n.* a would-be musical instrument, a tube with a strip of catgut that resonates to the voice. [Prob. imit.]

kea, *kā'ä, kē'ä, n.* a New Zealand parrot that sometimes kills sheep. [Maori.]

keasar, *kēz'ər.* See **kaiser.**

keb, *keb, v.i.* (*Scot.*) to cast a lamb prematurely.—*n.* a ewe that has cast its lamb. [Cf. Ger. *kibbe, kippe,* ewe.]

kebbie, *keb'i, n.* (*Scot.*) a shepherd's crook: a crook-handled walking-stick.

kebbock, kebbuck, *keb'ək, n.* (*Scot.*) a cheese. [Origin unknown; Gael. *cabag*, a cheese, may be derived from this word.]

keblah. See **kiblah.**

keck, *kek, v.i.* to retch, feel loathing.—*n.* a retching. [Imit.]

keck, kecksy. See **kex.**

keckle, *kek'l, v.t.* to protect by binding with rope or chains.—*n.* **keck'ling,** rope, chains, &c., used to keckle cables or hawsers. [Origin unknown.]

keckle, *kek l, v.i.* (chiefly *Scot.*) a form of **cackle.** [Origin unknown.]

ked, *ked,* **kade,** *kād, n.* a sheep-tick. [Origin unknown.]

keddah. Same as **kheda.**

kedge, *kej, n.* a small anchor for keeping a ship steady, and for warping the ship.—*v.t.* to move by means of a kedge, to warp.—*n.* **kedg'er,** a kedge. [Origin doubtful.]

kedge, *kej, adj.* (*prov.*) brisk, lively: pot-bellied.— Also **kedg'y, kidge.** [Cf. **cadgy.**]

kedgeree, *kej'ə-rē, n.* an Indian mess of rice, cooked with butter and dal, flavoured with spice, shred onion, &c.: a similar European dish made with fish. [Hind. *khichrī.*]

keech, *kēch, n.* (*Shak.*) a lump of fat. [Perh. conn. with **cake.**]

keek, *kēk, v.i.* (*Scot.*) to peep.—*n.* a peep.—*ns.* **keek'er,** one who peeps or spies: an inspector of coal: an eye: a black eye; **keek'ing-glass,** a mirror. [M.E. *kyke*; cf. Du. *kijken*, Ger. *kucken.*]

keel, *kēl, n.* the part of a ship extending along the bottom from stem to stern, and supporting the whole frame: a longitudinal member running along the under side of an airship's hull or gasbag: (*bot.*) the two lowest petals of a papilionaceous flower, arranged like a ship's keel: any narrow prominent ridge.—*v.t.* or *v.i.* to plough with a keel, to navigate: to turn keel upwards. — *n.* **keel'age,** dues for a keel or ship in port.—*adj.* **keeled,** (*bot.*) keel-shaped: having a ridge on the back.—*v.t.* **keel'haul,** to punish by hauling under the keel of a ship by ropes from the one side to the other: to treat in a galling manner.— *n.* **keel'hauling.**—*adj.* **keel'less.** [O.N. *kjölr.*]

keel, *kēl, n.* a low flat-bottomed boat: a coal-lighter: a ship.—*ns.* **keel'er, keel'man,** one who works on a barge. [Du. *kiel*, ship, prob.—O.E. *cēol*, ship.]

keel, *kēl, v.t.* (*Shak.*) to cool. [O.E. *cēlan*, to chill.]

keel, *kēl, n.* (*Scot.*) red ochre, ruddle.—*v.t.* to mark with ruddle. [Origin obscure: Gael. *cil*, ruddle, may be from this word.]

keelie, *kē'li, n.* (*Scot.*) the kestrel or other hawk: a town rough: a boorish vulgarian. [Perh. imit.; some connect with **gillie.**]

keeling, *kē'ling, n.* (*Scot.*) a codfish. [Origin unknown.]

keelivine, keelyvine, *kē'li-vīn, n.* (*Scot.*) a lead pencil. [**keel** (4); ety. otherwise unknown.]

keelson, kelson, *kel'sən, n.* a ship's inner keel, which binds the floor-timbers to the outer keel. [**keel** (1); the forms in kindred languages suggest that the second syllable is equivalent either to **sill,** or to **swine,** animal names being sometimes used in similar ways.]

keen, *kēn, adj.* eager: sharp, having a fine edge: piercing: acute of mind: penetrating: intense. —*adv.* **keen'ly.**—*n.* **keen'ness.**—**keen on,** (*coll.*) devoted to: fond of: much interested in: very desirous of; **keen prices,** very low prices. [O.E. *cēne,* bold, fierce, keen; Ger. *kühn,* bold; O.N. *kœnn,* expert.]

keen, *kēn, n.* a lamentation over the dead.—*v.i.* to wail over the dead.—*n.* **keen'er,** a professional mourner. [Ir. *caoine.*]

keep, *kēp, v.t.* (*obs.*) to reck of, care for: to tend: to have the care of: to guard: to maintain: to manage, conduct, run: to attend to the making of records in: to retain: to retain as one's own: to have in one's custody: to have habitually in stock for sale: to support, supply with necessaries: to have in one's service: to remain in or on: to adhere to: to continue to follow or hold to: to continue to make: to maintain hold upon: to restrain from departure, to hold back: to prevent: to reserve: to preserve in a certain state: to observe: to celebrate: to conform to the requirements of: to fulfil. —*v.i.* (*obs.*) to care, reck: to remain: to continue to be or go: to remain fresh or good: to last or endure: to continue: (*obs.*) to lodge: to refrain: to have rooms at college (Cambridge): to refrain: to confine or restrict oneself: to keep wicket: (*pr.p.* **keep'ing;** *pa.t.* and *pa.p.* **kept,** *kept*).—*n.* (*arch.*) care: a charge: condition: that which keeps or protects: subsistence: food: the innermost and strongest part of a castle, the donjon: a stronghold.—*ns.* **keep'er,** one who or that which keeps, in any sense: an attendant, esp. upon the insane, or upon animals in captivity: a custodian: a gamekeeper: the title of certain officials as *Lord Keeper* (*of the Great Seal*), whose office since 1757 has been merged in that of Lord Chancellor: (*obs.*) one who keeps a mistress: a wicket-keeper: the socket that receives the bolt of a lock: the armature of a magnet: a guard-ring; **keep'ership,** office of a keeper; **keep'ing,** care: preservation: reservation: retention: observance: custody: charge: (*Shak.*) maintenance, support: (*obs.*) maintenance of, or as, a mistress: just proportion: harmonious consistency; **keep'ing-room,** a sitting-room, parlour; **keep'sake,** something given to be kept for the sake of the giver: an annual gift-book (such as *The Keepsake* itself, 1827-56).—*adj.* (also **keep'-saky**) sumptuously inane.—**for keeps,** as a permanent possession: for good, permanently: (*Austr.*) on the defensive (in cricket); **keep an act,** to hold an academical disputation; **keep an eye on, keep chapel, company, counsel, distance, hours, house, the peace, a term,** &c. (see the nouns); **keep at it,** to persist in anything; **keep back,** to withhold: keep down, to repress; **keep body and soul together,** to maintain life; **keep down,** to restrain: to repress: to remain low: to set in lower-case type, avoiding capitals; **keep from,** to abstain from: to remain away from; **keep going in** (a thing), to keep one supplied with it; **keep in,** to prevent from escaping: to confine in school after school hours: to conceal: to restrain; **keep in with,** to maintain the confidence or friendship of someone, often with the suggestion of unworthy means; **keep off,** to hinder from approaching or making an attack; **keep one's breath to cool one's porridge**, to hold one's peace when further talk is clearly in vain; **keep one's countenance**, to avoid showing one's emotions; **keep one's hand in**, to retain one's skill by practice; **keep one's powder dry**, to keep one's energies ready for action: to observe all practical precautions; **keep tab(s) on**, to keep a check on, to keep account of; **keep time**, to observe rhythm accurately, or along with others: to go accurately (as a clock); **keep to**, to stick closely to: to confine oneself to; **keep under**, to hold down in restraint; **keep up**, to retain one's strength or spirit: to support, prevent from falling: to continue, to prevent from ceasing: to maintain in good condition: to continue to be in touch: to keep pace, keep abreast: (*obs.*) to stop; **keep wicket**, to act as wicket-keeper. [O.E. *cépan*.]

keeshond, *kās'hond*, *n.* a dog like a Pomeranian, common on Dutch barges. [Du.,—*kees*, terrier, *hond*, dog.]

keeve, *kēv*, *n.* a large tub. [O.E. *cyf*, vat.]

keffel, *kef'l*, *n.* (Scott) a horse, nag. [W. *ceffyl*; cf. **caple**.]

keg, *keg*, *n.* a small cask. [Earlier *cag*—O.N. *kaggi*.]

keight, *kit*, *v.t.* (*Spens.*) for **caught** (*pa.t.* of **catch**).

keir. See **kier**.

keitloa, *kāt'lō-ä*, *n.* a two-horned rhinoceros. [Bechuana *kgetlwa*.]

kell, *kel*, *n.* (Northern) a woman's head-dress or hair-net: a film, network: a caul. [caul.]

kellaut. See **killut**.

kelp, *kelp*, *n.* any large brown seaweed, wrack: the calcined ashes of seaweed, a source of soda, iodine, &c.—Also **kilp**. [M.E. *culp*; origin unknown.]

kelpie, **kelpy**, *kel'pi*, *n.* (Scot.) a malignant water-sprite haunting fords in the form of a horse. [Origin uncertain.]

kelson. Same as **keelson**.

kelt, *kelt*, *n.* a salmon, &c., that has just spawned. [Origin unknown.]

kelt, *kelt*, *n.* (Scot.) coarse cloth usu. made of black and white wool mixed and not dyed.—*n.* and *adj.* **kelt'er**. [Origin obscure.]

Kelt, Keltic. Same as **Celt, Celtic**.

kelter, *kelt'ər*, **kilter**, *kilt'ər*, *n.* (mainly *prov.* and *U.S.*) good condition. [Origin unknown.]

keltie, **kelty**, *kel'ti*, *n.* (Scot.) a bumper, esp. one imposed as a penalty on one who does not drink fair.

Kelvin, *kel'vin*, *adj.* applied to a thermometer scale with absolute zero for zero and centigrade degrees. [Sir William Thomson, Lord *Kelvin* (1824-1907), Irish physicist.]

kemb, *kem*, *v.t.* (obs. and dial.) to comb.—*adj.* **kempt** (*kemt, kempt*), combed. [O.E. *cemban*, to comb.]

kemp, *kemp*, *n.* the coarse, rough hairs of wool: (*pl.*) knotty hair that will not felt. [O.N. *kampr*, beard.]

kemp, *kemp*, *n.* (arch.) a champion: (*Scot.*) a contest in reaping or other work.—*v.i.* to strive for mastery.—*ns.* **kem'per**, **kem'pery-man**, a champion, a knight-errant; **kemp'ing**. [O.E. *cempa*, a warrior; cf. **champion**.]

kemple, *kem'pl*, *n.* (Scot.) forty bottles of hay or straw. [Origin obscure.]

ken, *ken*, *v.t.* (obs.) to cause to know, direct: (arch.) to see and recognise at a distance: (mainly *Scot.*) to know: (*pa.t.* and *pa.p.* **kenned, kent**).—*n.* range of sight or knowledge.—*ns.* **kenn'er**; **kenn'ing**, range of vision: (Scot.) a small portion, a little bit: a periphrastic formula in Old Norse or other old Germanic poetry; **kenno** (*ken'ə*; Scot., know not), a cheese prepared in ostensible secrecy for the gossips at a birth.—*adj.* **kent**, known. [O.E. *cennan*, causative of *cunnan*, and O.N. *kenna*; cf. **can, con**.]

ken, *ken*, *n.* (slang) a house, esp. disreputable. [Perh. Pers. *khān*, a caravansarai; or **kennel**; or conn. with preceding word.]

Kendal-green, *ken'dl-grēn*, *n.* green cloth for foresters made at *Kendal* in Westmorland.

kennel, *ken'l*, *n.* a house for dogs: a pack of hounds: the hole of a fox, &c.: a haunt.—*v.t.* to keep in a kennel.—*v.i.* to live in a kennel:—*pr.p.* **kenn'elling**; *pa.t.* and *pa.p.* **kenn'elled**.—*ns.* **kenn'el-maid, kenn'el-man**, an attendant upon dogs. [From an O.N.Fr. form answering to Fr. *chenil*—L. *canīle*—*canis*, a dog.]

kennel, *ken'l*, *n.* a street gutter. [M.E. *canel*—O.N.Fr. *canel*—L. *canālis*; see **canal**.]

kennel-coal. Same as **cannel-coal**.

Kennelly-Heaviside layer or **region**, *ken'ə-li-hev'i-sīd*, a strongly ionised region of the upper atmosphere about 60 miles up, in which wireless waves are deflected.—Also **Heaviside layer**. [From A. E. *Kennelly* and O. *Heaviside*, who inferred its existence.]

kennet, *ken it*, *n.* (obs.) a small hunting dog. [O.N.Fr. *kennet*, dim.—L. *canis*, dog.]

Kennick, *ken'ik*, *n.* the jargon of tramping tinkers.

kenning, **kenno**. See **ken** (1).

kenosis, *ken-ō'sis*, *n.* the self-limitation of the Logos in incarnation.—*adj.* **kenotic** (*-ot'ik*).—*n.* **kenot'icist** (*-i-sist*), a believer in kenosis. [Gr. *kenōsis*, emptying, from Phil. ii. 7.]

kenspeckle, *ken'spek-l*, *adj.* easily recognised: conspicuous.—Also (*N. of England*) **ken'speck**. [Appar. O.N. *kennispeki*, power of recognition.]

kent, *kent*, *n.* (Scot.) a leaping or punting pole.—*v.t.* and *v.i.* to punt or pole. [Cf. **quant**.]

kent. See **ken** (1).

kent-bugle, *kent'-bū'gl*, *n.* an obsolete key-bugle. [Supposed to be named after a Duke of Kent.]

Kentish, *kent'ish*, *adj.* of *Kent*.—*n.* the dialect of Kent, Essex, &c.—*ns.* **Kent'ish-fire'**, synchronised volleys of applause—probably from anti-Catholic demonstrations in Kent, 1828-29; **Kent'ish-man**, a native of W. Kent (one born east of the Medway being a *Man of Kent*); **Kent'ish-rag'**, a rough limestone in the Lower Greensand of Kent.

kentledge, *kent'lij*, *n.* pig-iron laid in a ship's hold for ballast.—Also **kint'ledge**. [Origin unknown.]

kep, *kep*, *v.t.* (Scot.) to catch (an approaching object): (*pa.t.* and *pa.p.* **kepp'it**).—*n.* a catch: act or opportunity of catching. [keep.]

kephalic, *ki-fal'ik*. Same as **cephalic**.

kepi, *kāp'ē*, *n.* a flat-topped forage-cap with a straight peak. [Fr. *képi*.]

Keplerian, *kep-lē'ri-ən*, *adj.* pertaining to the German astronomer Johann *Kepler*. See **law**.

kept, *pa.t.* and *pa.p.* of **keep**.

keramic, *ki-ram'ik*. Same as **ceramic**.

keratin, *ker'ə-tin*, *n.* a nitrogenous compound, the essential ingredient of horny tissue, as of horns, nails, &c.—*v.t.* and *v.i.* **ker'atinise**, to make or become horny.—*n.* **keratinisā'tion**, formation of keratin: becoming horny.—*adj.* **keratinous** (*kə-rat'i-nəs*), horny.—*n.* **kerati'tis**, inflammation of the cornea.—*adj.* **keratogenous** (*-oj'i-nəs*), producing horn or keratin.—*n.* **ker'atŏplasty**, grafting of part of a healthy cornea to replace a piece made opaque by disease, &c. [Gr. *keras, -atos*, a horn.]

keratophyre, *ker'ət-ō-fīr*, *n.* a fine-grained soda trachyte. [Gr. *keras, -atos*, horn, and *-phyre* from **porphyry**.]

kerb, *kərb*, *n.* the edging of a pavement: a domestic fender.—*ns.* **kerb'-mer'chant, -tra'der, -ven'dor**, one who sells by the side of the pavement; **kerb'-side** (also *adj.*); **kerb'stone**.—**kerbstone broker, -market**, one outside the stock exchange. [**curb**.]

kerchief, *kər'chif*, *n.* a square piece of cloth worn to cover the head, neck, &c.: a handkerchief.—*v.t.* to cover with a kerchief.—*adj.* **ker'chiefed**. [O.Fr. *cuevrechief* (Fr. *couvrechef*)—*covrir*, to cover, *chef*, the head.]

kerf, *kərf*, *n.* a cut: a notch: the groove made by a saw: a cut place, face of a cut: the place where a cut is made: a quantity cut at once, as of wool, &c.: a single layer of hay, turf, &c., cut. [O.E. *cyrf*, a cut.]

kermes, *kər'mēz*, *n.* the female bodies of a coccus insect (*Kermes*, or *Coccus, ilicis*), used as a red dye-stuff: the oak (**kermes oak**; *Quercus coccifera*) on which they breed: a cherry-red mineral, antimony oxysulphide (also **kermes mineral**, *ker'mesite*). [Pers. and Ar. *qirmiz*.]

kermis, *ker'mis*, *n.* a fair in the Low Countries: in

America an indoor fair.—Also **ker′mess, kir′mess.** [Du. *kermis*—*kerk*, church, *mis*, mass.]

kern. See **quern**, and **kirn.**

kern, kerne, *kərn, n.* an Irish foot-soldier : a boor. —*adj.* **ker′nish.** [Ir. *ceithern* ; see **cateran.**]

kern, *kərn, v.i.* to granulate. [Cf. **corn.**]

kern, *kərn, n.* (*print.*) part of a type that projects beyond the body and rests on an adjoining letter. [Fr. *carne*, a projecting angle—L. *cardō*, *-inis*.]

kernel, *kər′nl, n.* a seed within a hard shell : the edible part of a nut : (*rare*) a gland : a nucleus : the important part of anything.—*adj.* **ker′nelly,** full of, or resembling, kernels. [O.E. *cyrnel*—*corn*, grain, and dim. suffix *-el* ; Ger. *kern*, a grain.]

kernite, *kərn′īt, n.* hydrated oxide of sodium and boron. [*Kern* Co., California, where much is mined.]

kerogen, *ker′ō-jen, n.* the organic matter in oil-shale that gives oil on distillation. [Gr. *kēros*, wax, and root of *gennaein*, to generate.]

kerosene, *ker′o-sēn, n.* paraffin-oil obtained from shale or by distillation of petroleum. [Gr. *kēros*, wax.]

kersantite, *kər′sən-tīt, n.* a dyke-rock of black mica and plagioclase. [*Kersanton*, a locality in Brittany.]

kersey, *kər′zi, n.* a coarse woollen cloth. [Perh. from *Kersey* in Suffolk.]

kerseymere, *kər′zi-mēr*, or *-mēr′, n.* twilled cloth of the finest wools. [For **cassimere, cashmere.**]

kerve, *kərv′, v.t.* (*Spens.*) a form of **carve.**

kesar, *kē′zər, n.* See **kaiser.**

kest, *kest,* an obs. form of **cast.**

kestrel, *kes′trəl, n.* a small species of falcon. [O.Fr. *quercerelle.*]

ket, *ket, n.* (*Scot.*) carrion. [O.N. *kjöt.*]

ket, *ket, n.* (*Scot.*) matted wool. [A.Fr. *cot.*]

keta, *kē′tä, n.* a Pacific salmon, the dog-salmon. [Russ. *keta.*]

ketch, *kech, n.* a small two-masted vessel. [Earlier *catch*, perh. from the vb. **catch.**]

ketch, *kech,* an obs. form of **catch.**

ketchup, *kech′əp, n.* a sauce made from mushrooms, &c.—Also **catch′up, cat′sup.** [Malay *kēchap*, perh. from Chinese.]

ketone, *kē′tōn, n.* an organic compound consisting of a carbonyl group united to two like or unlike alkyl radicals. [Modified from **acetone.**]

kettle, *ket′l, n.* a vessel for heating or boiling liquids, esp. one with a spout and a lid for domestic use : a cauldron : a cavity like a kettle in rock (see **giant's kettle**) : (*Shak.*) a kettledrum. — *ns.* **kett′ledrum,** a musical instrument, consisting of a hollow metal hemisphere with a parchment head, tuned by screws : a tea-party ; **kett′ledrumm′er** (*coll.*) **kett′leful ; kett′le-holder,** a little cloth, &c., for lifting a hot kettle.—**a kettle of fish** (cf. **kiddle**), a riverside picnic at which new-caught salmon are cooked on the spot : (ironically—often **a pretty kettle of fish**) an awkward mess. [O.E. *cetel* ; Ger. *kessel*, Goth. *katils* ; all perh. from L. *catillus*, dim. of *catīnus*, a deep cooking-vessel.]

kettle-pins. Same as **kittle-pins.**

Keuper, *koi′pər, n.* (*geol.*) the uppermost division of the Trias.—Also *adj.* [Ger. miners' term.]

kevel, *kev′l.* Same as **cavel.**

kex, *keks, n.* a dry, often hollow, herbaceous (usu. umbelliferous) stalk : any tall umbelliferous plant. —Also **kecks,** and (false singulars) **keck, kecks′y, keks′ye.** [Origin unknown.]

key, *kē,* formerly *kā, n.* an instrument for locking or unlocking, winding up, turning, tuning, tightening or loosening : a wedge : a piece inserted to prevent relative motion : a tapered piece of metal for fixing the boss of a wheel, &c., to a shaft : a spanner : the middle stone of an arch : a piece of wood let into another piece crosswise to prevent warping : in musical instruments, a lever or piston-end pressed to produce the sound required : a similar part in other instruments for other purposes, as in a typewriter or linotype : a lever for closing or breaking an electrical circuit : a dry winged fruit, as of ash or maple, often hanging in bunches like door-keys : a fret pattern : preparation of a surface to take plaster, glue, or the like :

(*obs.*) a keynote : a system of tones definitely related to one another in a scale : that which gives command of anything or upon which success turns : a scheme or diagram of explanation or identification : a set of answers to problems : a crib translation : that which leads to the solution of a problem : a leading principle : general tone of voice, emotion, morals, &c.—*v.t.* to lock or fasten with a key : to furnish with a key : to give (a particular advertisement) a keyword or other distinctive feature that will enable replies to it to be identified : to tune : to stimulate, raise, increase (also **key up**).—*ns.* **keyboard,** a range of keys or levers in a musical or other instrument ; **key′-bugle,** a bugle with keys, giving a chromatic scale of two octaves.—*adjs.* **key′-cold,** (*Shak.*) cold as a key, lifeless ; **keyed,** furnished with a key or keys : set to a particular key : in a state of tension or readiness.—*ns.* **key′-fruit,** a winged fruit ; **key′hole,** the hole in which a key of a lock is inserted ; **key′hole-lim′pet,** a mollusc (*Fissurella*) with perforated conical shell ; **key′-in′dustry,** an industry indispensable to others and essential to national economic welfare and independence.—*adj.* **key′less,** without a key : not requiring a key.—*ns.* **key′-man,** an indispensable worker, essential to the continued conduct of a business, &c. : (*U.S.*) a telegraphist ; **key′-money,** a premium, fine, or sum additional to rent, demanded for the grant, renewal, or continuance of a tenancy ; **key′-note,** the fundamental note or tonic : any central principle or controlling thought ; **key′-pin,** the pivot on which a pipe-key turns : a pin serving as fulcrum for a key of an organ, &c. ; **key′-plate,** a keyhole escutcheon ; **key′-ring,** a ring for holding a bunch of keys ; **key′-seat,** a groove for receiving a key, to prevent one piece of machinery from turning on another ; **key′-sig′nature,** the indication of key by marking sharps, flats or naturals where the key changes or at the beginning of a line ; **key′stone,** the stone at the apex of an arch : the chief element or consummation : that on which all else depends ; **key′-way,** a groove cut in a shaft or boss to accommodate a key.—**have the key of the street,** (*coll.*) to be locked out : to be homeless ; **keyed to,** made to harmonise, or fit exactly, with ; **keyed up,** raised in pitch or standard : stimulated : in a state of nervous tension and excitement ; **power of the keys,** the power to loose and bind, conferred by Christ on Peter (Matt. xvi. 19), and claimed by the popes. [O.E. *cǣg.*]

key, an old spelling of **quay.**

key, *kē, n.* a low island or reef.—Also **cay.** [Sp. *cayo.*]

Keys, *kēz, n.pl.* in full **House of Keys,** the lower house of the Manx Court of Tynwald. [App. **key** (1), not Manx *kiare-as-feed*, four-and-twenty.]

khaki, *kä′ki, adj.* dust-coloured, dull brownish or greenish yellow : militaristically imperialist.—*adv.* with war-spirit.—*n.* a light drab cloth used for military uniforms. [Urdu and Pers. *khākī*, dusty.]

khalif. See **caliph.**—*ns.* **khalifa, khalifah, *kä*-*lē′fä*,** a caliph : a Senusi leader : the Mahdi's successor ; **khalifat, khalifate, *kāl′i-fat, -fāt*,** the caliphate : the headship of Islam. [Ar. *khalīfah.*]

khamsin, *kam′sin, -sēn′, n.* a hot S. or S.E. wind in Egypt, blowing for about fifty days from mid-March. [Ar. *khamsīn*—*khamsūn*, fifty.]

khan, *kän, n.* an Eastern inn, a caravansarai. [Ar. *khān.*]

khan, *kän, n.* in N. Asia, a prince or chief : in Persia, a governor.—*ns.* **khan′ate,** a khan's dominion or jurisdiction ; **khan′um** (*-oom*), lady : Mrs. [Turki (and thence Pers.) *khān*, lord or prince.]

khat. Same as **kat** (1).

Khaya, *kä′yä, n.* a genus of African trees akin to mahogany. [Wolof *khaye.*]

kheda, keddah, *ked′ä, n.* an enclosure for catching wild elephants : the operation of catching wild elephants. [Hind. *khedā.*]

khedive, *ke-dēv′, n.* the title (1867–1914) of the viceroy of Egypt.—*ns.* **khedi′va,** his wife ; **khedi′-v(i)ate,** the khedive's office or territory.—*adjs.*

Neutral vowels in unaccented syllables : *el′ə-mənt, in′fənt, ran′dəm*

khedi′v(i)al. [Fr. *khédive*—Turk. *khidīv, hudív*—Pers. *khidīw*, prince.]

khidmutgar, *kid′mut-gär*, **khitmutgar,** *kit′*, *n.* a table-servant. [Hind.,—Pers. *khidmat*, service, and agent suffix -*gär*.]

khilafat, *kil′ä-fat, kil-ä′fat*, *n.* caliphate, spiritual leadership of Islam.—*adj.* of an anti-British agitation in India in the 20th century. [Ar. *khilāfat*; cf. **caliph.**]

khoja, khodja, *kō′jä*, also **hodja,** *hō′*, *n.* an Eastern title of respect: a professor or teacher. [Turk. and Pers. *khōjah, khwājah.*]

khor, *kōr*, *n.* a dry watercourse: a ravine. [Ar. *khurr, khorr*.]

khud, *kud*, *n.* a pit, hollow: a ravine. [Hind. *khad*.]

khuskhus. Same as **cuscus** (3).

khutbah, *koot′bä*, *n.* a Mohammedan prayer and sermon delivered in the mosques on Fridays.—Also **khot′bah, khot′beh.** [Ar.]

kiang, kyang, *kyang, ki-ang′*, *n.* a Tibetan wild ass. [Tibetan *rkyang*.]

kia-ora, *kē′ä-ō′rä*, *interj.* (*N.Zealand*) good health. [Maori.]

kiaugh, *kyawhh, kyähh*, *n.* (*Scot.*) care, trouble.—Also **kaugh** (*kawhh, kähh*).

kibble, *kib′l*, *n.* the bucket of a draw-well.—*n.* **kibb′le-chain,** the chain for drawing up a bucket. [Cf. Ger. *kübel*.]

kibe, *kīb*, *n.* chilblain, esp. on heel. [Cf. W. *cibwst*.]

kibitka, *ki-bit′kä*, *n.* a Russian covered wagon or sledge: a Central Asian felt tent. [Russ.]

kibitzer, *kib′it-sər*, *n.* onlooker (at cards, etc.) who gives unwanted advice. [Yiddish.]

kiblah, *kib′lä*, *n.* the point toward which Mohammedans turn in prayer.—Also **keb′lah.** [Ar. *qiblah*.]

kibosh, *kī′bosh, ki-bosh′*, *n.* (*coll.*) nonsense, rot.—*v.t.* to dispose of finally.—**put the kibosh on,** to kibosh. [Ety. obscure.]

kick, *kik*, *v.t.* to hit with the foot: to put or drive by blows with the foot: to start or work by foot on a pedal: to achieve by a kick or kicking.—*v.i.* to thrust out the foot with violence: to show opposition or resistance: to recoil violently: to jerk violently: to move as if kicked: to be exposed to kicking.—*n.* a blow or fling with the foot: the recoil of a gun: a jerk: kicking power: resistance: resilience: (*slang*) fashion: (*slang*) the depression in the bottom of a bottle: (*slang*) stimulus, pungency: (*slang*) dismissal.—*adj.* **kick′able.**—*ns.* **kick′er,** one who kicks, esp. a horse; **kick′ing-strap′,** a strap behind a draught-horse's hindquarters to prevent kicking; **kick′-off′,** the first kick in a game of football; **kick′-start′,** the starting of an engine by a treadle; **kick′-up′,** a disturbance: a dance: a depression in the bottom of a bottle.—**kick over the traces,** to throw off control; **kick, or strike, the beam,** to rise, as the lighter scale of a balance, so as to strike against the beam—hence to be of little weight or importance; **kick the bucket** (see **bucket**); **kick up a dust or row,** to create a disturbance. [M.E. *kiken*: origin unknown: W. *cicio*, to kick, comes from Eng.]

kickie-wickie, *kik′i-wik′i*, *n.* (*Shak.*) a wife. [Altered by editors to **kicksy-wicksy**; perh. conn. with **kickshaws.**]

kickshaws, *kik′shawz*, **kickshaw,** -*shaw*, *n.* something fantastical: (*cook.*) a fantastical dish. [Fr. *quelque chose*, something.]

kid, *kid*, *n.* a young goat: extended to young antelope, &c.: (*slang*) a child or young person: leather of kidskin, or a substitute: a glove, shoe, or boot of kid.—*adj.* made of kid leather or imitation kid leather.—*v.t.* and *v.i.* to bring forth (of a goat):—*pr.p.* **kidd′ing;** *pa.t.* and *pa.p.* **kidd′ed.** —*ns.* **kidd′y,** dim. of *kid*: a flashy thief:—*pl.* **kiddi′es; kid′-fox,** (*Shak.*) a young fox; **kid′-glove′,** a glove of kid.—*adj.* as if done by one wearing kid-gloves: overnice, delicate.—*ns.* **kid′ling,** a young kid; **kid′skin.** [O.N. *kith*; cf. Dan. *kid*; Ger. *kitze*, a young goat.]

kid, *kid*, *n.* a small tub. [Perh. a variant of **kit.**]

kid, *kid*, *n.* a faggot. [Origin unknown: W. *cedys*, faggots, is prob. from Eng.]

kid, *kid*, *v.t.* and *v.i.* (*slang*) to hoax: to pretend,

esp. banteringly (also **kidd′y**).—*n.* a deception.—*n.* **kidd′er.** [Perh. conn. with **kid**, a child.]

kidder, *kid′ər*, **kiddier,** -*i-ər*, *ns.* a forestaller: a huckster. [Origin obscure.]

Kidderminster, *kid′ər-min-stər*, *n.* a two-ply or ingrain carpet formerly made at *Kidderminster.*

kiddle, *kid′l*, *n.* a stake-fence set in a stream for catching fish.—Also **kid′el, kett′le.** [O.Fr. *quidel*; cf. Bret. *kidel*.]

kidnap, *kid′nap*, also -*nap′*, *v.t.* to steal, as a human being:—*pr.p.* **kidnapping;** *pa.t.* and *pa.p.* **kidnapped.**—*n.* **kidnapper.** [**kid**, a child, **nap** (4).]

kidney, *kid′ni*, *n.* one of two flattened glands that secrete urine: temperament, humour, disposition —hence, sort or kind.—*ns.* **kid′ney-bean′,** the French-bean; **kid′ney-ore′,** haematite in kidney-shaped masses; **kid′ney-potā′to,** a kidney-shaped variety of potato; **kid′ney-stone′,** nephrite: a septarian nodule: a hard deposit in the kidney; **kid′ney-vetch′,** any plant of the papilionaceous genus Anthyllis, including lady's fingers. [M.E. *kidenei* (pl. *kideneiren*), perh. a comp. of *ei* (pl. *eiren*), egg, confused sometimes with *nere*, kidney.]

kie-kie, *kē′ä-kē-ä, kē′kē*, *n.* a New Zealand high-climbing shrub (*Freycinetia Banksii*) of the screw-pine family. [Maori.]

kier, keir, *kēr, n.* a bleaching vat. [Cf. O.N. *ker*, tub.]

kieselguhr, *kē′zl-gōōr*, *n.* diatomite. [Ger.,—*kiesel*, flint, *guhr*, fermentation.]

kieserite, *kēz′ər-īt*, *n.* a mineral, hydrated magnesium sulphate (MgSO₄·H₂O), a source of Epsom salts. [After Professor Dietrich Georg *Kieser* (1779–1862) of Jena.]

kight (*Spens.*). Same as **kite.**

kikumon, *kik′oo-mon*, *n.* the chrysanthemum badge of the Japanese imperial family. [Jap. *kiku*, chrysanthemum, *mon*, badge.]

kikuyu, *kē-kōō′ū*, *n.* an African grass (*Pennisetum clandestinum*) grown in Australia and S. America.

kild, kild, a Spenserian form of **killed.**

kilderkin, *kil′dər-kin*, *n.* a small barrel: a liquid measure of 18 gallons. [Old Du. *kindeken, kinneken* (Scot. *kinken*), dim. of *kintal*—L.L. *quintāle*, quintal, associated with Du. *kind*, child.]

kilerg, *kil′org*, *n.* a thousand ergs. [Gr. *chilioi*, thousand, **erg.**]

kiley. Same as **kylie.**

kilfud-yoking, *kil-fud′-yōk′ing*, *n.* (*Scot.*) a fireside disputation. [Scot. *kilfuddie*, the aperture for feeding a kiln, and **yoking.**]

kill, *kil*, *v.t.* to put to death, to slay: to deprive of life: to destroy: to nullify or neutralise, to render inactive, to weaken or dilute: to reject, discard: to fascinate, overcome: (*Ir.*) to injure seriously.—*n.* the act of killing: prey or game killed: (*lawn tennis*) a ball impossible to return. —*ns.* **kill′-court′esy,** (*Shak.*) a discourteous person; **kill′cow,** a butcher: a bully; **kill′er,** one who kills: one who murders readily or habitually: a slaughterer or butcher: an instrument for killing: a neutralising agent: the grampus, or other ferocious delphinid (also **killer whale**).—*adj.* **kill′ing,** depriving of life: destructive: deadly, irresistible: completely fascinating: irresistibly funny.—*n.* slaughter: a severe handling.—*n.* **kill′joy,** a mar-sport.—*adj.* austere.—**kill by inches,** by gradual means, as by torture; **kill off,** to exterminate; **kill time,** to consume spare time, as with amusements, &c.; **kill two birds with one stone,** to effect one thing by the way, or by the same means with which another thing is done; **kill up,** (*Shak.*) to exterminate; **killing time,** the days of the persecution of the Covenanters; **to kill,** in an irresistible manner. [M.E. *killen* or *cullen.*]

killadar, *kil′ə-där*, *n.* the commandant of a fort or garrison. [Hind. (Pers.) *qil′adär*.]

killas, *kil′əs*, *n.* clay slate. [Cornish miners' term.]

killcrop, *kil′krop*, *n.* an insatiate child: a changeling. [L.G. *kilkrop*; cf. Ger. *kielkropf*.]

killdee, *kil′dē*, *n.* the largest North American ring-plover.—Also **kill′deer.** [Imit.]

killick, killock, *kil′ik*, -*ək*, *n.* a small anchor: its fluke.

killogie, ki-lō′gi, n. (Scot.) the space before the fireplace of a kiln. [kiln, logie.]

killut, kil′ut, n. in India, a robe of honour or other ceremonial present.—Also kell′aut, khil′at. [Hind. and Pers. khil′at.]

Kilmarnock, kil-mär′nək, n. a kind of closely woven broad blue cap, originally made at Kilmarnock.—Kilmarnock cowl, a kind of nightcap.

kiln, kil, kiln, n. a large oven for drying, baking, or calcining corn, hops, bricks, pottery, limestone, &c.: bricks placed for burning.—v.t. kiln′-dry, to dry in a kiln:—pa.p. and adj. kiln′-dried.—n. kiln′-hole, the mouth of a kiln. [O.E. cyln, cylen—L. culīna, a kitchen.]

kilo, kil′ō, n. a shortened form of kilogram(me), kilometre, or other word with the prefix kilo-, used in the metric system to indicate multiplication by a thousand.—ns. kil′ocycle, a frequency of 1000 cycles or vibrations a second; kil′odyne, 1000 dynes; kil′ogram(me), the mass of a platinum-iridium cylinder kept at the International Bureau of Weights and Measures near Paris—roughly 2¼ lb.; kil′olitre, 1000 litres; kil′ometre, 1000 metres, or nearly ⅝ of a mile (square kilometre, a million square metres, over ⅓ of a square mile); kil′ovolt, 1000 volts; kil′owatt, 1000 watts, about 1⅓ horse-power; kil′owatt-hour, the commercial (Board of Trade) unit of electrical energy =1000 watts an hour. [Gr. chilioi, a thousand.]

kilp, kilp, n. Same as kelp.

kilt, kilt, n. a man's short petticoat or plaited skirt, part of the Highlandman's dress.—v.t. to truss up: to pleat vertically.—v.i. to go lightly, trip.—adj. kilt′ed, dressed in a kilt: tucked up: vertically pleated.—n. kilt′y, kilt′ie, a wearer of a kilt. [Scand.; cf. Dan. kilte, to tuck up; O.N. kilting, a skirt.]

kilt, kilt, (Spens. and Ir., esp. hyperbolically) pa.p. of kill.

kilter, kil′tər. Same as kelter.

kimberlite, kim′bər-līt, n. a mica-peridotite, an eruptive rock, the matrix of the diamonds found at Kimberley and elsewhere in South Africa.

kimbo, kim′bō, n. Same as akimbo.

Kimeridgian, kim-ə-rij′i-ən, adj. (geol.) of the lowest division of the Upper Jurassic, named from a clay well developed at Kimeridge in Dorset.—Also n.

kimmer. See cummer.

kimono, ki-mō′nō, n. a loose robe, fastening with a sash, the principal outer garment in Japan: a dressing-gown of similar form. [Jap.]

kin, kin, n. persons of the same family: relatives: relationship: affinity.—adj. related.—adj. kin′less, without relations.—next of kin, the relatives (lineal or collateral) of a deceased person, among whom his personal property is distributed if he dies intestate; of kin, of the same kin. [O.E. cynn; O.N. kyn, Goth. kuni, family, race; cog. with L. genus, Gr. genos.]

kin, kin, n. a Japanese and Chinese weight, the catty. [Jap. kin, Chin. chin.]

kina, kinakina. See quina.

kinaesthesis, kin-ēs-thē′sis, n. sense of movement or of muscular effort.—Also kinaesthē′sia (si-ä).—adj.—kinaesthetic (-thet′ik), pertaining to kinaesthesis. [Gr. kinein, to move, aisthēsis, sensation.]

kinchin, kin′chin, n. a child in thieves' slang.—ns. kin′chin-cove, a boy; kin′chin-lay, the robbing of children; kin′chin-mort, a girl. [Appar. Ger. kindchen, little child.]

kincob, king′kob, n. a rich silk-stuff embroidered with gold or silver thread, made in India. [Hind. and Pers. kimkhāb.]

kind, kīnd, n. those of kin, a race: sort or species, a particular variety: nature: character: (obs.) sex: produce, as distinguished from money: a eucharistic element.—adj. having or springing from the feelings natural for those of the same family: disposed to do good to others: benevolent.—adj. kind′-heart′ed.—n. kind′-heart′edness.—adj. kind′less, (Shak.) unnatural, destitute of kindness.—adv. kind′ly, in a kind manner: often no more than a substitute for please (for the adj.,

see sep. art.).—n. kind′ness, the quality or fact of being kind: a kind act.—adj. kind′-spok′en, spoken kindly: given to speaking kindly.—after kind, according to nature; do one's kind, (Shak.) to act according to one's nature; in a kind, in a way, to some extent; in kind, in goods instead of money: tit for tat; kind of, (coll.) of a kind, somewhat, to some extent, as it were—used adjectively and adverbially; take it kind, feel it as a kindness. [O.E. (ge)cynde—cynn, kin.]

kind, kīnd, v.t. to beget: (Spens., pa.p. kynd′ed).

kindergarten, kin′dər-gär-tn, n. an infant school on Froebel's principle (1826), in which object-lessons and games figure largely.—n. kindergart′ener, a teacher in a kindergarten.—Also kindergärtner (-gert′nər). [Ger., kinder, children, garten, garden.]

kinderspiel, kin′dər-spēl, n. a children's cantata or play. [Ger., children's sport, child's play—kinder, children, spiel, game, play.]

kindle, kin′dl, v.t. to set fire to: to light: to inflame, as the passions: to provoke: to incite.—v.i. to take fire: to begin to be excited: to be roused.—ns. kin′dler; kin′dling, the act of causing to burn: materials for starting a fire. [Cf. O.N. kyndill, a torch—L. candēla, candle.]

kindle, kin′dl, v.t. (Shak.) and v.i. to bring forth.—n. (obs.) brood, litter.—in kindle, with young. [M.E. kindlen; cf. kind.]

kindly, kīnd′li, adj. natural: (orig.) belonging to the kind or race: native: native-born: inclined to kindness: benign: genial: comfortable.—adv. in a kind or kindly manner (see also under kind).—adv. kind′lily (rare).—n. kind′liness.—adj. kind′ly-nä′tured.—kindly tenant, (Scot.) a tenant of the same stock as his landlord, or one whose family has held lands in succession, from father to son, for several generations. [O.E. gecyndelic; cf. kind.]

kindred, kin′drid (Spens. kin′red), n. relationship by blood, less properly, by marriage: relatives: a group of relatives, family, clan.—adj. akin: cognate: congenial.—ns. kin′dredness; kin′dredship. [M.E. kinrede—O.E. cynn, kin, and the suffix -ræden, expressing mode or state.]

kine, kīn, n.pl. (B.) cows. [M.E. kyen, a doubled plural of O.E. cū, a cow, the plural of which is cȳ; cf. Scots kye.]

kinema, kinematograph. See cinematograph.

kinematics, kin-i-mat′iks, or kīn-, n. the science of motion without reference to force.—adjs. kinemat′ic, -al. [Gr. kīnēma, motion—kīneein, to move.]

kinesipathy, kin-ē-sip′ə-thi, n. a mode of treating disease by muscular movements, movement-cure—also kinesither′apy.—adjs. kinesiat′ric, kinesipath′ic.—ns. kine′sipath, kinesip′athist. [Gr. kīnēsis, movement.]

kinetics, kī-net′iks or kī-, n. the science of the action of force in producing or changing motion.—adjs. kinet′ic, -al, pertaining to motion or to kinetics: due to motion.—ns. kinet′ograph, a camera for taking motion-pictures; kinet′oscope, an early form of cinematograph: an instrument for the production of curves by combination of circular movements.—kinetic energy, energy possessed by a body in virtue of its motion. [Gr. kīnētikos—kīneein, to move.]

king, king, n. a hereditary chief ruler or titular head of a nation: a monarch: (obs.) a queen bee: a playing-card having the picture of a king: the most important piece in chess: a crowned man in draughts: one who is pre-eminent among his fellows: Kings, the title of two historical books of the Old Testament:—fem. queen.—king, in composition, most important.—v.t. to make king: to furnish with a king: to play king (with object it).—ns. king′-app′le, a large red variety of apple; king′-archon, the second of the nine archons in Athens, successor to the abolished kings in religious functions; king′-bird, an American tyrant fly-catcher; king′-bolt, -rod, a metal rod in a roof connecting the tie-beam and the ridge; king′-co′bra, a large Asiatic species of cobra; king′-crab (Limulus), a curious large marine arachnoid, with convex horseshoe-shaped buckler, the last of its race (Xiphosura); **king'-craft**, the art of governing, mostly in a bad sense; **king'-crow**, a kind of drongo; **king'cup**, the buttercup: the marsh-marigold; **king'dom**, the state or attributes of a king: a monarchical state: a region that was once a monarchical state: one of the three grand divisions of natural history (animal, vegetable, mineral).—*adj.* **king'domed**, (*Shak.*) constituted like a kingdom.—*ns.* **king'fish**, the opah; **king'fisher**, a fish-eating bird with very brilliant plumage, the halcyon; **king'hood**, kingship: kingliness.—*adj.* **king'less**.—*ns.* **king'let**, a little or petty king: the golden-crested wren; **king'lihood**.—*adj.* **king'-like**.—*ns.* **king'liness**; **king'ling**, a petty king.—*adj.* **king'ly**, belonging or suitable to a king: royal: king-like.—Also *adv.* —*ns.* **king'-maker**, one who has the creating of kings in his power; **king'-of-arms'** (sometimes **-at-arms'**), a principal herald (those of England having the designations Garter, Clarencieux, Norroy, and Bath, of Scotland, Lyon, of Ireland, Ulster); **king'-peng'uin**, a large penguin, smaller than the emperor; **king'-pin**, a tall pin, or one prominently placed: a pin on which swivels an axle of the type of that of an automobile front-wheel: the most important person of a group engaged in an undertaking; **king'post**, a perpendicular beam in the frame of a roof rising from the tie-beam to the ridge; **king'-sal'mon**, the largest Pacific salmon, the quinnat; **king's-chair**, **-cush'ion**, a seat formed by two persons clasping wrists; **king's-e'vil**, a scrofulous disease formerly supposed to be healed by the touch of the king; **king'ship**, the state, office, or dignity of a king; **king's'-hood**, the second stomach of a ruminant, sometimes humorously for the human stomach; **king's'-man**, a royalist: a custom-house officer; **king's'-spear**, an asphodel; **king's'-yell'ow**, orpiment as a pigment; **king'-vul'ture**, a large brilliantly-coloured tropical American vulture; **king'wood**, a beautiful Brazilian wood—also *violet-wood*: the papilionaceous tree yielding it, a species of Dalbergia.—**King Charles's head**, a matter that persists in obtruding itself, as did King Charles's head in the thoughts of Mr Dick in *David Copperfield*; **King Charles spaniel** (see **spaniel**); **kingdom come**, (*slang*) the state after death; **King Log**, a do-nothing king, as opp. to **King Stork**, one who devours his frog-subjects —from Aesop's fable; **king mob**, the vulgar multitude; **king of beasts**, the lion; **king of birds**, the eagle; **king of metals**, gold; **king of terrors**, death; **king of the forest**, the oak; **king of the herrings**, the shad: the oarfish: applied also to various other fishes, as the opah, the rabbit-fish or chimaera; **King's Bench** (**Queen's Bench** in a queen's reign), formerly a court in which the king sat: now a division of the High Court of Justice; **king's counsel** (or **queen's counsel**), an honorary rank of barristers and advocates; **king's English**, correct standard speech; **king's peace**, orig. the peace secured by the king for certain persons (as those employed on his business): the peace of the kingdom generally; **king's speech**, the sovereign's address to parliament at its opening and closing; **three kings of Cologne**, the three Wise Men of the East, Gaspar, Melchior, and Balthazar; **turn king's (queen's) evidence**, to become a witness against an accomplice, on the understanding that one will be pardoned. [O.E. *cyning—cynn*, a tribe, with suffix *-ing*; cog. with **kin**.]

kingle, *king'l*, *n.* (*Scot.*) very hard rock, esp. sandstone.

kink, *kingk*, *n.* a twisted loop in a string, rope, &c.: a mental twist.—*v.i.* to form a kink.—*v.t.* to cause a kink in.—*n.* **kink'le**, a slight kink.—*adj.* **kink'y**, twisted: curly. [Prob. Du. *kink*; but cf. Ger., Sw., and Norw. *kink*.]

kink, *kingk*, *v.i.* (*Scot.*) to cough loudly: to gasp for breath.—*n.* a convulsive cough or gasp.—*ns.* **kink'-cough**, **kink'-ho(a)st**, whooping-cough, chin-cough. [Northern form of **chink** (3).]

kinkajou, *king'ka-jōō*, *n.* a South American animal allied to the raccoon. [Appar. from a North American Indian word misapplied.]

kinnikinick, *kin-i-kin-ik'*, *n.* a mixture used by American Indians as a substitute for tobacco: a species of cornel or other plant entering into it. [From Algonquin, mixture.]

kino, *kē'nō*, *n.* an astringent exudation from various tropical trees. [Appar. of W. African origin.]

kinsfolk, *kinz'fōk*, *n.* folk or people kindred or related to one another.—Also **kins'folks**.—*ns.* **kin'ship**, relationship; **kins'man**, a man of the same kin or race with another:—*fem.* **kins'-woman**.

kintledge. See **kentledge**.

kiosk, *ki-osk'*, *n.* an Eastern garden pavilion: a small out-of-doors roofed stall for sale of papers, sweets, &c.: a bandstand: a public telephone box. [Turk. *kiōshk*, *keushk*—Pers. *kūshk*.]

kip, *kip*, *v.i.* (*Scot.*) to play truant.—Also *n.* in the phrase *to play the kip*, to play truant.

kip, *kip*, *n.* the skin of a young animal.—*n.* **kip'skin**, leather made from the skin of young cattle, intermediate between calf-skin and cow-hide.

kip, *kip*, *n.* a level or slight incline at the end of an underground way, on which the tubs of coal stand till hoisted up the shaft.

kip, *kip*, *n.* (*slang*) a house of ill-fame: a lodging-house: a bed.—*v.i.* to go to bed: to lie.—*n.* **kip'-shop**, a brothel: a tramps' lodging-house. [Cf. Dan. *kippe*, a low alehouse.]

kip, **kipp**, *kip*, *n.* (*Scot.*) anything beaked: a pointed hill. [Cf. Ger. (Low Ger.) *kippe*, point, tip.]

kip, *kip*, *n.* (*Austr.*) a short flat stick used to throw up pennies in the game of two-up.

kipe, *kip*, *n.* (*prov.*) an osier basket for catching pike. [O.E. *cȳpe*.]

kipp, *kip*, *n.* a form of generator for hydrogen sulphide or other gas.—Also **Kipp's apparatus**. [P. J. *Kipp* (19th cent.), Dutch founder of a firm of manufacturers of scientific apparatus.]

kippage, *kip'ij*, *n.* (*Scot.*) a state of displeasure or anger. [Fr. *équipage*; see **equipage**.]

kipper, *kip'ər*, *n.* a male salmon after the spawning season: a salmon or (esp.) herring split open, seasoned, and dried: (*slang*) a person (often *giddy kipper*).—*v.t.* to cure or preserve, as a salmon or herring.—*n.* **kipp'erer**. [Perh. O.E. *cypera*, a spawning salmon; or perh. from **kip** (5), from the beaked lower jaw of the male salmon after spawning.]

kirbeh, *kir'be*, *n.* a skin for holding water. [Ar. *qirba*.]

kiri, *kir'i*, *n.* (*S.Afr.*) a stick. [Prob. Hottentot.]

kirimon, *kē'ri-mon*, *n.* one of the two imperial crests of Japan, bearing three leaves and three flowers of paulownia. [Jap.]

kirk, *kirk*, *kərk*, *n.* (*Scot.*) church, in any sense: by English Episcopalians sometimes specially applied to the Church of Scotland.—*v.t.* to church. —*ns.* **kirk'ing**, **kirk'in'**, the first attendance of a pair after marriage, or of a magistrate after election; **kirk'-sess'ion**, the lowest court in Presbyterian churches, ministers and elders as the governing body of a particular congregation; **kirk'ton**, **-town**, (*Scot.*) the village in which the parish church stands.—*adj.* and *adv.* **kirk'ward**.—*n.* **kirkyard**, **-yaird** (-*yārd'*: or *kirk'*), a churchyard. —**Auld Kirk**, in Scotland the Established Church: (*coll.*) by association of ideas the whisky bottle, whisky; **make a kirk or a mill of it**, do what you please or can with it. [A Northern Eng. form of **church**.]

kirn, *kirn*, *kern*, *kern*, *kərn*, *n.* (*Scot.*) the cutting of the last sheaf or handful of the harvest: a harvest-home.—*ns.* **kirn'-ba'by**, **corn'-ba'by**, **kirn'-doll'ie**, **corn'-maid'en**, a dressed-up figure made of the last handful of corn cut. [Origin unknown.]

kirn, *kirn*, *n.* a Northern form of **churn**.—*n.* **kirn'-milk'**, buttermilk.

kirschwasser, *kērsh'väs-ər*, *n.* a liqueur made from the wild cherry.—Also **kirsch**. [Ger., cherry water.]

kirtle, *kər'tl*, *n.* a sort of gown or outer petticoat: a mantle.—*adj.* **kir'tled**. [O.E. *cyrtel*; Dan. *kjortel*; O.N. *kyrtill*; appar.—L. *curtus*, short.]

fāte, fär, ȧsk; mē, hȧr (her); *mīne; mōte; mūte; mōōn; dhen* (then)

Kisleu, *kis'li-ōō,* **Kislev,** *kis'lef, n.* the third (ecclesiastically ninth) Jewish month, parts of November and December. [Heb.]

kismet, *kiz'met,* or *kis', n.* fate, destiny. [Turk. *qismet*—Ar. *qisma.*]

kiss, *kis, v.t.* to caress or salute with the lips: to touch gently.—*v.i.* to salute with the lips: to collide.—*n.* a caress or salute with the lips: a drop of sealing-wax.—*ns.* **kiss'-curl,** a small curl at the side of the forehead; **kiss'er,** one who kisses: (*pugilistic slang*) the mouth; **kiss'ing-com'fit,** a perfumed comfit for sweetening the breath; **kiss'ing-crust,** that part of the upper crust of the loaf which overhangs and touches another.—*n.pl.* **kiss'ing-strings,** cap or bonnet strings tied under the chin.—*ns.* **kiss'-in-the-ring,** an old game in which one kisses another after a chase round a ring of players; **kiss'-me,** the wild pansy or other plant: a short veil: a small bonnet—also **kiss'-me-quick.**—**kiss hands,** to kiss the sovereign's hands on acceptance of office; **kiss of peace,** a kiss of greeting between the members of the early Church; **kiss the book,** to kiss a Bible or New Testament, in England, after taking a legal oath; **kiss the gunner's daughter,** to get a flogging, tied to the breech of a cannon; **kiss the rod,** to submit to punishment. [O.E. *cyssan,* to kiss—*coss,* a kiss; Ger. *küssen,* Dan. *kys*; allied to **choose** and **gust** (2).]

kist, *kist, n.* (*Scot.*) a chest.—*v.t.* to coffin.—**kist o' whistles,** an organ. [O.E. *cist,* chest, or O.N. *kista.*]

kistvaen, *kist'vīn, n.* a chest-shaped burial-chamber made of flat stones. [W. *cist,* chest, *maen,* stone.]

kit, *kit, n.* a small wooden tub: an outfit: (*coll.* or *slang*) a set of persons.—*n.* **kit'-bag,** a strong bag for holding one's kit or outfit. [Prob. Middle Du. *kitte,* a hooped beer-can.]

kit, *kit, n.* a small pocket violin. [Origin obscure; cf. O.E. *cytere,* Gr. *kithara.*]

kit, *kit, n.* a contraction of **kitten.**—*n.* **kit'-cat,** the game of tip-cat (see also below).

Kitcat, *kit'kat, n.* the name of a London Whig literary club, which existed from about 1688 or 1703 to about 1720, meeting for some time at the pie-shop of Christopher (*Kit*) Cat (or Catling): a portrait 36 by 28 inches in size, like those of the Kitcat Club painted by Kneller to fit their later low-ceiled clubroom.

kitchen, *kich'ən, n.* a place where food is cooked: cooking department or equipment: (*obs. Scot.*) a tea-urn: (chiefly *Scot.*) anything eaten as a relish with other food.—*v.t.* (*Shak.*) to regale in the cook-room: to serve as relish to: to make palatable: to use sparingly, make to last.—*ns.* **kitch'endom,** the domain of the kitchen; **kitch'ener,** a person employed in the kitchen: a cooking-stove; **kitchenette',** a tiny kitchen: a compact combined kitchen and pantry; **kitch'en-fee,** the fat that falls from meat in roasting—the cook's perquisite; **kitch'en-fur'niture,** the furniture of a kitchen: the percussion instruments of an orchestra; **kitch'en-gar'den,** a garden where vegetables are cultivated for the kitchen; **kitch'enknave,** a scullion; **kitch'en-maid,** a maid or servant whose work is in the kitchen; **kitch'enmidd'en** (Dan. *kjökkenmödding*), a prehistoric rubbish-heap; **kitch'en-range,** a kitchen grate with oven, boiler, &c., attached, for cooking; **kitch'en-stuff,** material used in kitchens: kitchen refuse, esp. fat from pots, &c.; **kitch'en-wench,** a kitchen-maid.—**kitchen Dutch, kitchen Kaffir,** (*S.Afr.*) a mixture of Dutch or Kaffir with English, used in speaking to native servants; **kitchen physic,** substantial fare (*Milt.*). [O.E. *cycene*—L. *coquina*—*coquĕre,* to cook.]

kite, *kīt, n.* a rapacious bird of the hawk kind: a rapacious person: a light frame covered with paper or cloth for flying in the air: a more complicated structure built up of boxes (*box-kite*) for carrying recording instruments or a man in the air: a light and lofty sail: a rumour or suggestion given out to see how the wind blows, test public opinion, or the like: an accommodation bill, esp. a mere paper credit.—*ns.* **kite'-balloon',** an observation-balloon designed on the principle of the kite to prevent revolving, &c.; **kite'-flying,** the dealing in fictitious accommodation paper to raise money: testing public opinion. [O.E. *cyta*; cf. W. *cud,* Bret. *kidel,* a hawk.]

kite, kyte, *kīt, n.* (*Scot.*) a paunch, belly. [Ety. obscure.]

kith, *kith, n.* knowledge: native land: acquaintance—obsolete except in **kith and kin,** friends (originally home-country) and relatives. [O.E. *cȳth*—*cunnan,* to know.]

kithara, *kith'ə-rä.* Same as **cithara.** [Gr.]

kithe. Same as **kythe.**

kitten, *kit'n, n.* a young cat: sometimes the young of another animal.—*v.t.* and *v.i.* (of a cat) to bring forth. — *adj.* **kitt'enish,** frolicsome: skittish: affectedly playful.—*ns.* **kitt'en-moth,** any of the smaller kindred of the puss-moth; **kitt'ling,** (*Scot.*) a kitten.—*v.t.* and *v.i.* **kitt'le,** (*Scot.*) to kitten: to come into being. [M.E. *kitoun,* dim. of **cat.**]

kittiwake, *kit'i-wāk, n.* a species of gull with long wings and rudimentary hind-toe. [Imit.]

kittle, *kit'l, adj.* (*Scot.*) ticklish, intractable.—*v.t.* (*Scot.*) to tickle: to puzzle.—*adj.* **kitt'ly,** easily tickled, sensitive.—*n.* **kitt'ly-bend'ers,** (*Amer.*) running on thin bending ice. [Ety. obscure.]

kittle-pins, *kit'l-pinz, n.pl.* skittles.—Also **kett'le-pins.** [Origin obscure.]

kittul, *kit-ōōl', n.* the jaggery palm (*Caryota urens*): its fibre. [Sinhalese *kitūl.*]

kitty, *kit'i, n.* (*Northern* and *slang*) a jail: a pool or fund.

kiwi, *kē'wi, n.* the Apteryx: (*mil. slang*) a New Zealander. [Maori, from its cry.]

klang, *klang, n.* (*mus.*) a complex tone, composed of fundamental and harmonics: timbre.—Also **clang.** —*n.* **klang'farbe** (*-fär-bə*), tone-colour, timbre. [Ger.]

klaxon, *klaks'ən, n.* orig. mechanical horn with rasping sound: electric horn. [Registered trade-name.]

klepht, *kleft, n.* a Greek or Albanian brigand.—*adj.* **klepht'ic.**—*n.* **klepht'ism.** [Mod. Gr. *klephtēs* —anc. Gr. *kleptēs,* thief—*kleptein,* to steal.]

kleptomania, *klep-tō-mā'ni-ä, n.* a mania for stealing: a morbid impulse to secrete things.—*n.* **kleptomā'niac.** [Gr. *kleptein,* to steal, *maniā,* madness.]

Klieg light, *klēg līt,* a type of incandescent floodlighting lamp for film studio use.—**klieg eyes,** the effect of strain on the eyes caused by the brilliance of floodlights in film production. [From *Kliegl* brothers, the inventors.]

klinker, *klingk'ər, n.* a very hard paving-brick. [Du.]

klinostat, *klī'nō-stat, n.* a revolving stand for experimenting with growing plants. [Gr. *klīnein,* to incline, *statos,* standing.]

klipdas, *klip'das, n.* the Cape hyrax. [Du., lit. rock-badger.]

klipspringer, *klip'spring-ər, n.* a small South African antelope. [Du. *klip,* rock, *springer,* jumper.]

Klondike, Klondyke, *klon'dīk, n.* a very rich source of wealth: a card game, a form of patience. —*v.t.* and *v.i.* to export (fresh herring) direct from Scotland to the Continent. [From the gold-rush to *Klondike* in the Yukon, in 1896, &c.]

kloof, *klōōf, n.* a mountain ravine. [Du., cleft.]

knack, *nak, n.* a petty contrivance: a toy: a nice trick: dexterity, adroitness.—*n.* **knack'iness.**— *adjs.* **knack'ish, knack'y,** cunning, crafty. [Orig. imit.; cf. Du. *knak,* a crack, Ger. *knacken,* to crack.]

knacker, *nak'ər, n.* anything that makes a snapping or cracking sound: (*pl.*) castanets or clappers, bones. [Imit.]

knacker, *nak'ər, n.* a horse-slaughterer: one who buys and breaks up old houses, ships, &c.: a wornout horse.—*n.* **knack'ery,** a knacker's yard. [Origin obscure.]

knag, *nag, n.* a knot in wood: a peg.—*n.* **knagg'iness.**—*adj.* **knagg'y,** knotty: rugged. [Cf. Dan. *knag,* Ger. *knagge.*]

knap, *nap, v.t.* to snap or break with a snapping noise: to break in pieces with blows, as stones: to pronounce or utter with a snapping effect: to rap: bite off, nibble:—*pr.p.* **knapp'ing**; *pa.t.* and *pa.p.* **knapped.**—*ns.* knap'bottle, the bladder-campion; **knapp'er**, one who breaks stones, esp. one who breaks up flint-flakes for gun-flints; **knapp'ing-hammer**, (*Scot.*) a hammer for breaking stones.—*v.i.* **knapp'le**, to nibble. [Du. *knappen*, to crack or crush.]

knap, *nap*, *n.* (*Bacon*) a protuberance: a hillock: a hill-crest. [O.E. *cnæpp*.]

knapsack, *nap'sak*, *n.* a case for necessaries borne on the back: a rucksack. [Du. *knappen*, to crack, eat.]

knapskull, **knapscull**, **knapscal**, *nap'skəl*, *n.* (*Scot. obs.*) a kind of helmet. [Origin unknown.]

knapweed, *nap'wēd*, *n.* a composite plant of the genus Centaurea, like a spineless thistle. [Earlier *knopweed*; see **knop**.]

knar, **gnar**, *när*, *n.* a knot on a tree.—*adj.* **knarred**, **gnarred**, gnarled, knotty. [Cf. L.G. *knarre*, Du. *knar*; also **knur**.]

knar, *när*, **knarl.** See **gnar, gnarl.**

knave, *nāv*, *n.* (orig., as in *Shak.*) a boy: a serving-boy: a false, deceitful fellow: a playing-card bearing the picture of a servant or soldier.—*ns.* **knave'-bairn**, (*Scot.*) a male child; **knav'ery**, dishonesty; **knave'ship**, (*Scot.*) a certain quantity of grain, the due of the miller's servant.—*adj.* **knav'ish**, fraudulent: rascally.—*adv.* **knav'ishly.** —*n.* **knav'ishness.** [O.E. *cnafa, cnapa,* a boy, a youth; Ger. *knabe, knappe.*]

knawel, *naw'əl*, *n.* a cornfield weed (Scleranthus) of the chickweed family. [Ger. *knauel* or *knäuel*.]

knead, *nēd*, *v.t.* to work and press together into a mass, as flour into dough: to operate upon in massage.—*ns.* **knead'er**; **knead'ing-trough**, a trough for kneading. [O.E. *cnedan*; O.N. *knotha,* Ger. *kneten,* to knead.]

knee, *nē*, *n.* the joint between the thigh and shin bones: in a horse's fore-leg, the joint answering to the wrist: in a bird the joint answering to the ankle: part of a garment covering the knee: a root upgrowth by which swamp-growing trees breathe: a piece of timber or metal like a bent knee: (*Shak.*) a genuflection.—*v.t.* (*Shak.*) to kneel to: (*Shak.*) to achieve by kneeling, or pass over on the knees: to furnish with a knee: to press with the knee: to make baggy at the knee.—*v.i.* to kneel.—*n.pl.* **knee'-breech'es**, breeches extending to just below the knee, as in court-dress. —*n.* **knee'-cap**, the knee-pan: a cap or strong covering for the knees, used chiefly for horses, to save their knees in case of a fall.—*n.pl.* **knee'-cords**, knee-breeches of corduroy.—*adjs.* **knee'-crooking**, obsequious: fawning; **kneed, knee'd**, having knees or angular joints: baggy at the knees, as trousers; **knee'-deep**, rising to the knees: sunk to the knees.—*n.* **knee'-drill**, directed devotional exercises.—*adj.* **knee'-high**, rising or reaching to the knees.—*ns.* **knee'-holl'y**, butcher's broom; **knee'-jerk**, a reflex throwing forward of the leg when tapped below the knee-cap; **knee'-joint**, the joint of the knee: a joint with two pieces at an angle, so as to be very tight when pressed into a straight line; **knee'-pan**, the patella, a flat, round bone on the front of the knee-joint; **knee'-stop, -swell**, a lever worked by the performer's knee, for regulating the wind-supply of a reed-organ, &c.; **knee'-tim'ber**, timber bent into a shape suitable for a knee in shipbuilding, &c.; **knee'-trib'ute**, (*Milt.*) the homage of kneeling. —**give, or offer, a knee**, to act as second or bottle-holder in a fight, the principal resting on the second's knee during the pauses between the rounds; **on the knees of the gods**, awaiting the decision of fate (after Homer). [O.E. *cnéow, cnéo;* Ger. *knie,* L. *genu,* Gr. *gony.*]

kneel, *nēl*, *v.i.* to rest or fall on the bended knee:— *pa.t.* and *pa.p.* **kneeled, knelt** (*nelt*).—*n.* **kneel'er.** [O.E. *cnéowlian.*]

knell, *nel*, *n.* the stroke of a bell: the sound of a bell at a death or funeral.—*v.i.* to sound as a bell: toll.—*v.t.* to summon as by a tolling bell. [O.E. *cnyllan,* to beat noisily; Du. and Ger. *knallen.*]

knelt, *nelt*, *pa.t.* and *pa.p.* of **kneel.**

knevell, a form of **nevel.**

knew, *nū*, *pa.t.* of **know.**

knicker. Same as **nicker** (3).

knickerbockers, *nik'ər-bok-ərz*, *n.pl.* loose breeches gathered in at the knee.—Also *n.pl.* **knick'ers**, knickerbockers: a woman's garment of similar form.—*adj.* **knick'ered**, clad in knickers. [From the wide-breeched Dutchmen in Knickerbocker's (Washington Irving's) humorous *History of New York*, whence *Knickerbocker* has come to mean the descendant of one of the original Dutch settlers of New York.]

knick-knack, *nik'-nak*, *n.* a small, trifling ornamental or would-be ornamental article—dim. knick-knack'et.—*ns.* knick-knack'atory, a collection of knick-knacks; knick-knack'ery, knick-knacks collectively.—*adj.* **knick'-knacky.**—Also **nick'-nack, &c.** [A doubling of **knack.**]

knife, *nīf*, *n.* an instrument for cutting: (*pl.* **knives**, *nīvz*).—*v.t.* to cut: to convey, or apply with a knife: to stab: (*U.S.*) to try to defeat by treachery within the party.—*n.* **knife'-and-fork'**, a trencher-man.—*adj.* involving or relating to the use of knife and fork.—*ns.* **knife'-board**, a board on which knives are cleaned: (*coll.*) a seat running along the top of an old form of bus; **knife'-box**, a box for keeping table cutlery in; **knife'-boy**, a boy employed in cleaning knives; **knife'-edge**, a sharp-edged ridge: (*mech.*) a sharp piece of steel like a knife's edge serving as the axis of a balance, &c.; **knife'-grinder**, one who grinds or sharpens knives.—*adj.* **knife'less**, without a knife: without use of the knife.—*ns.* **knife'-money**, a knife-shaped bronze currency formerly used in China; **knife'-rest**, a rest for a carving knife or fork.— **have one's knife in**, to be persistently hostile or vindictive towards; **under the knife**, undergoing a surgical operation; **war to the knife**, unrelenting conflict. [O.E. *cnīf;* Ger. *kneif,* knife, *kneifen,* to nip.]

knight, *nīt*, *n.* (orig.) a lad, servant: one of gentle birth and bred to arms, admitted in feudal times to a certain honourable military rank: one of the rank, with the title 'Sir,' next below baronets: a member of the equestrian order in ancient Rome: one devoted to the service of a lady, her 'servant' or champion: a chess-man, usually with a horse's head, that moves one square laterally and one diagonally at each move.—*v.t.* to create a knight.— *ns.* **knight'age**, the collective body of knights; **knight'-bach'elor**, a knight not a member of any order; **knight'-bann'eret**, a knight who carried a banner, and who was superior in rank to the knight-bachelor; **knight'-err'ant**, a knight who travelled in search of adventures:—*pl.* **knights-errant; knight'-err'antry; knight'hood**, the rank, title, or status of knight: the order or fraternity of knights; **knight'hood-err'ant**, (*Tenn.*) the body of knights-errant.—*adj.* **knight'less**, (*Spens.*) unbecoming a knight.—*n.* **knight'liness.** —*adj.* **knight'ly**, like a knight: befitting a knight: chivalrous: of a knight or knights.—Also *adv.*—*ns.* **knight'-mar'shal**, formerly an officer who had cognisance of offences within twelve miles of the king's abode; **knight'-service**, tenure by a knight on condition of military service.—**knight of industry**, a footpad, thief, or sharper; **knight of St Crispin**, a shoemaker; **knight of the pestle**, an apothecary; **knight of the post** (i.e. possibly the whipping-post), a professional false witness and offerer of bail; **knight of the rainbow**, a flunkey (from his livery); **knight of the road**, a highwayman: a commercial traveller: a tramp; **knight of the shears**, a tailor; **knight of the shire**, a member of parliament for a county; **knight of the spigot**, a tapster, a publican; **knight of the stick**, a compositor; **knight of the whip**, a coachman; **knight's fee**, a holding of land for which knight-service was required; **Knights of Labour**, in the United States, a national labour organisation; **Knights of Malta** (see **Hospitaller**); **knight's progress**, a series of moves in which a knight may visit every square on the chess-board; **Knights Templars** (see **Templar**). [O.E. *cniht,* youth, servant, warrior; Ger. and Du. *knecht,* servant.]

Kniphofia, *nip-hŏf'i-ä*, *n.* an African genus of the lily family, otherwise called Tritoma, the red-hot poker or torch-lily. [Named after J. H. *Kniphof* (1704-65), German botanist.]

knit, *nit*, *v.t.* (*arch.*) to form into a knot : (*arch.*) to tie together : to intertwine : to unite into network by needles or machinery : to make by means of knitting-needles or knitting-machine : to unite closely, to draw together : to contract.—*v.i.* to interweave with needles : to grow together : (*pr.p.* **knit'ting**; *pa.t.* and *pa.p.* **knit'ted** or **knit**).—*n.* (*Shak.*) a style of knitting.—*ns.* **knitt'er ; knitt'ing**, the work of a knitter : union, junction : the network formed by knitting.—Also *adj.*—*ns.* **knitt'ing-machine'**, a machine for knitting ; **knitt'ing-needle**, a long needle or wire used for knitting ; **knit'wear**, knitted clothing. [O.E. *cnyttan*— *cnotta*, a knot.]

knitch, *nich*, *n.* (*prov.*) a faggot. [O.E. *gecnycc*, bond.]

knittle, *nit'l*, *n.* (*naut.*) a small line made of two or three yarns twisted with the fingers : (*pl.*) the halves of two yarns in a rope, twisted for joining. [O.E. *cnyttels*, sinew, string.]

knive, *niv*, *v.t.* to knife.—**knives**, *pl.* of knife.

knob, *nob*, *n.* a hard protuberance : a hard swelling : a round ornament or handle.—*adj.* **knobbed**, containing or set with knobs.—*ns.* **knobb'er**, a stag in its second year ; **knobb'iness**.—*adj.* **knobb'y**, full of knobs : knotty.—*n.* **knob'stick**, a stick with knobbed head : (*slang*) a blackleg or scab. [Cf. Low Ger. *knobbe* ; **knop**.]

knobkerrie, *nob'ker-i*, *n.* a round-headed stick used as a club and a missile by Kaffirs.—Also **knob'kiri**. [**knob** and **kiri**, on the model of Cape Du. *knopkierie*.]

knock, *nok*, *v.i.* to strike with something hard or heavy : to drive or be driven against something : to strike for admittance : to rap : to make a noise by, or as if by, striking : (of machinery) to rattle : (of internal-combustion engine) to give noise of detonation.—*v.t.* to strike : to drive against : to render, put, make, or achieve by blows : (*slang*) to impress strongly, stun, daze, confound : (*U.S.*) to find fault with : (*U.S.*) to surpass.—*n.* a sudden stroke : a rap : the noise of detonation in an internal-combustion engine : (*Scot.*) a clock.— *n.* **knock'-about**, a boisterous performance with horse-play : a performer of such turns : (*Austr.*) a doer of odd jobs : (*U.S.*) a small yacht without bowsprit : a small motor-car suitable for going here and there.—*adj.* of the nature of knockabout : suitable for rough use.—*adj.* **knock'-down**, such as to overthrow : adapted for being taken to pieces.—*ns.* **knock'er**, one who knocks : a hammer suspended to a door for making a knock : a goblin inhabiting a mine who points out the presence of ore by knocks : (*U.S.*) a carper ; **knock er-up**, a person employed to rouse workers in the morning ; **knock'ing**, a beating on a door : a rap : a noise as if of something that knocks : knock in an internal-combustion engine : a piece knocked off ; **knock'-knee**, the condition of being knock-kneed.—*adj.* **knock'-kneed**, having knees that knock or touch in walking.—*n.* **knock'-out'**, the act of knocking out : a blow that knocks out : a combination among dealers at an auction : any person or thing that surpasses.—*adj.* (of a competition) eliminating losers at each round.—*ns.* **knock'-rating**, the measurement of freedom from detonation of a fuel in an internal-combustion engine in terms of the percentage of octane in an octane-heptane mixture of equivalent knock-proneness ; **knock'-up'**, (*lawn tennis*) practice immediately before a match.—**knock about**, (*slang*) to saunter, loaf about : to travel about, roughing it and having varied experiences ; **knock down**, to fell with a blow : assign to a bidder with a tap of the auctioneer's hammer : (*U.S.*) to embezzle (passengers' fares) ; **knock into a cocked hat** (see **cock**) ; **knock off**, to leave off (work) : to accomplish hastily : to strike off : to deduct : (*slang*) to steal ; **knock on**, (*Rugby football*) to knock forward with the hand (an infringement of the rules ; *n.* **knock'-on'**) ; **knock on the head**, to

suppress, put an end to ; **knock out**, to dislodge by a blow : to strike insensible or incapable of recovering in time, in boxing : to overcome : to lose the scent ; **knock-out auction**, an auction where the bidders are largely swindling confederates ; **knock-out drops**, (*U.S.*) a drug put in liquor by robbers ; **knock together**, to get together or construct hastily ; **knock the bottom out of**, to make, or show to be, invalid : to make ineffectual, bring to naught ; **knock under**, to give in, yield ; **knock up**, to rouse by knocking : to weary out : to be worn out : to construct or arrange hastily : (*cricket*) to score (so many runs) : (*U.S.*) to get with child ; **up to the knocker**, (*slang*) up to the required standard of excellence or fashion. [O.E. *cnocian* ; perh. imit.]

knoll, *nōl* (*Scot.* **knowe**, *now*), *n.* a round hillock : (*prov.*) the top of a hill. [O.E. *cnol* ; Ger. *knollen*, a knob, lump.]

knoll, *nōl.* Same as **knell**.

knop, *nop*, *n.* a knob : a bud : a loop : a tuft. [Cf. O.N. *knappr* ; Du. *knop*, Ger. *knopf*.]

knosp, *nosp*, *n.* the unopened bud of a flower : an architectural ornament resembling that. [Ger. *knospe*.]

knot, *not*, *n.* a snipe-like shore bird of the sandpiper family. [Origin unknown : the connexion with King Cnut is a fancy of Camden's.]

knot, *not*, *n.* an interlacement of parts of a cord or cords, &c., by twisting the ends about each other, and then drawing tight the loops thus formed : a piece of ribbon, lace, &c., folded or tied upon itself in some particular form, as *shoulder-knot*, *breast-knot*, &c. : anything like a knot in form : a bond of union : an elaborately designed flower-bed : a tangle : a difficulty : the main point or central part of a tangle, intricacy, problem, or difficulty : a complex of lines, mountains, &c. : the base of a branch buried in a later growth of wood : a node or joint in a stem, esp. of a grass : a lump : a concretion : a swelling : a knob : a boss : a bud : a hill : a clump or cluster : a division of the knot-marked log-line : a nautical mile per hour : (loosely) a nautical mile.—*v.t.* to tie in a knot : to unite closely : to make knotty : to make by knotting : to remove knots from : to cover knots in (before painting wood).—*v.i.* to form a knot or knots : to knit knots for a fringe :—*pr.p.* **knott'-ing**; *pa.t.* and *pa.p.* **knott'ed**.—*ns.* **knot'fulness**, (*geom.*) the number of simpler knots of which a complex knot is made up ; **knot'-grass**, a much-jointed species of Polygonum, a common weed: applied also to various grasses ; **knot'-herbs** (*Shak.* **not herbs**), flower-garden herbs ; **knot'-hole**, a hole in wood where a knot has fallen out.— *adjs.* **knot'less**, without knots ; **knott'ed**, full of, or having, knots : having intersecting lines or figures.—*ns.* **knott'er**, a person or contrivance that makes or removes knots ; **knott'iness**, the quality of being knotty : (*geom.*) the minimum number of intersections in the projection of a knot on a plane ; **knott'ing**, formation or removal of knots : covering of knots before painting : material for the purpose : fancy-work done by knitting threads into knots.—*adj.* **knott'y**, containing knots : hard, rugged : difficult : intricate.—*n.* **knot'work**, ornamental work made with knots : carving or decoration in interlaced forms.—**bowline knot** (see **bow**) ; **granny knot** (see **granny**) ; **porters' knot**, a shoulder-pad with loop for the forehead. [O.E. *cnotta* ; Ger. *knoten*, Dan. *knude*, L. *nōdus*.]

knotenschiefer, *knō'tan-shē-fər*, *n.* spotted slate, spotted schist, slightly altered argillaceous rock spotted with little concretions. [Ger., knot slate or schist.]

knout, *knoōt*, also *nowt*, *n.* a whip formerly used as an instrument of punishment in Russia : punishment inflicted by the knout.—*v.t.* to flog. [French spelling of Russ. *knut.*]

know, *nō*, *v.t.* to be informed of : to be assured of : to be acquainted with : to recognise : (*B.*) to approve : to have sexual commerce with.—*v.i.* to possess knowledge : (*pr.p.* **know'ing**; *pa.t.* **knew**, *nū* ; *pa.p.* **known**, *nōn*).—*n.* (*Shak.*) knowledge : possession of the relevant facts.—

adj. **know'able,** capable of being known, discovered, or understood.—*ns.* **know'ableness;** **know'-all,** one who thinks he knows everything; **know'er.**—*adj.* **know'ing,** intelligent: skilful: cunning.—*adv.* **know'ingly,** in a knowing manner: consciously: intentionally.—*ns.* **know'ingness,** the quality of being knowing or intelligent: shrewdness; **know'-noth'ing,** one who is quite ignorant: a member of the native American party (1854-56), originally secret.—*adj.* completely ignorant.—*n.* **know-noth'ingism.—in the know,** in possession of private information: initiated; **know better,** to be too wise, well-instructed (to do this or that); **knowing to** (*obs.* and *U.S.*), aware, informed, of; **known as,** going by name of; **know the ropes,** to understand the detail or procedure, as a sailor does his rigging; **know what's o'clock, know what's what,** to be wide awake; **know which side one's bread is buttered on,** to be fully alive to one's own interest. [O.E. *cnáwan;* O.N. *kná,* L. (*g*)*nōscere,* Gr. gignōskein.]

knowledge, *nol'ij, n.* assured belief: that which is known: information, instruction: enlightenment, learning: practical skill: acquaintance: (*law*) cognisance: (*arch.*) sexual intimacy.—*v.t.* (*obs.*) to acknowledge.—*adj.* **knowl'edgeable,** (*coll.*) possessing knowledge: intelligent. — *n.* **knowl'edge-box,** (*slang*) the head.—**to one's knowledge,** so far as one knows. [M.E. *knowleche,* where -*leche* is unexplained; see **know.**]

knub, nub, *nub, n.* a knob: a small lump: the waste or refuse of silk-cocoons.—*n.* **knubb'le,** **nubb'le,** a small lump.—*adjs.* **knubb'ly, nubb'ly, knubb'y, nubby.** [Cf. Low Ger. *knubbe.*]

knubble, nubble, *nub'l,* **knobble,** *nob'l, v.t.* to beat with the fists: to knock. [**knob.**]

knuckle, *nuk'l, n.* projecting joint of a finger: (*cook.*) the knee-joint of a calf or pig.—*v.i.* (in marbles) to touch the ground with the knuckles (usu. with *down*): to touch the forehead as a mark of respect: to yield (usu. with *down* or *under*): to bend the knuckles or knee.—*v.t.* to touch with the knuckle: to shoot from the thumb knuckle.—*ns.* **knuck'le-bone,** any bone with a rounded end: (in *pl.*) the game of dibs; **knuck'le-bow,** the curved part of a sword-guard that covers the fingers; **knuck'le-duster,** a metal covering for the knuckles, like a cestus, for attack or defence; **knuck'le-joint,** a joint where the forked end of a connecting-rod is joined by a bolt to another piece of the machinery. [M.E. *knokel,* not recorded in O.E.; cf. Du. *knokkel* (dim. of *knok*), Ger. *knöchel,* ankle-bone, knuckle (dim. of *knochen,* bone).]

knur, knurr, nur, nurr, *nur, n.* an excrescence on a tree: a hard ball or knot of wood.—**knur and spell,** a game played with a knur, trap (*spell*), and stick, in vogue chiefly in the North of England. [M.E. *knurre;* cf. Du. *knor,* Ger. *knorre, knorren.*]

knurl, nurl, *nurl, n.* a small excrescence or protuberance: a ridge or bead, esp. in series, as in the milling of a screw-head: a kink: (*Burns*) a dwarfish person.—*v.t.* to make knurls on, to mill.—*n.* **knurling,** mouldings or other woodwork elaborated into a series of knobs. [Prob. a dim. of **knur,** or perh. conn. with **gnarl, knarl.**]

knut, *knut, nut* (*slang*). See **nut.**

koa, *kō'ä, n.* a Hawaiian acacia. [Hawaiian.]

koala, *kō-ä'lä, kōō'lä, n.* an Australian marsupial, like a small bear, and therefore called also native bear. [Australian *kūlā.*]

kob, *kob, n.* an African water-antelope. [Wolof.]

koban, *kō'ban,* **kobang,** *kō'bang, n.* an obsolete Japanese oblong gold coin, rounded at the corners. [Jap. *ko-ban.*]

kobold, *kō'bold, n.* in German folklore, a spirit of the mines: a domestic brownie. [Ger.]

Kodak, *kō'dak, n.* a small portable photographic camera with a continuous roll of sensitised film.—*v.t.* and *v.i.* to photograph with a Kodak. [The trade-mark name of the Eastman *Kodak* Company.]

koff, *kof, n.* a small Dutch sailing-vessel. [Du. *kof.*]

koftgar, *koft'gär, n.* one who inlays steel with gold. —*n.* **koftgari** (*koft-gur-ē'*), such work—sometimes **koft'work.** [Hind. from Pers. *koftgar.*]

kohl, *kōl, n.* a fine powder of antimony used in the East for staining the eyelids. [Ar. *koh'l.*]

kohlrabi, *kōl'rä'bi, n.* a cabbage with a turnip-shaped stem. [Ger.,—It. *cavolo rapa,* cole-turnip.]

Koine, *koi'nē, n.* a Greek dialect developed from Attic, in use in the Eastern Mediterranean in Hellenistic and Byzantine times. [Gr. *koinē* (*dialektos*), common (dialect).]

kokra, *kok'rä, n.* the wood of an Indian tree (*Aporosa*) of the spurge family, used for making flutes, clarinets, &c.

kokum, *kō'kam, n.* an East Indian tree (*Garcinia indica*).—**kokum butter,** an edible fat got from its nuts. [Marathi *kokamb,* mangosteen.]

kola, *kō'lä, n.* an African tree (*Cola acuminata;* family Sterculiaceae) whose seeds (**ko'la-nuts**) have stimulant properties: an aerated non-alcoholic beverage. [West African name.]

Kolarian, *kō-lä'ri-ən, n.* and *adj.* Munda (language).

kolinsky, *ko-lin'ski, n.* the fur of the polecat or mink. [Russ. *kolinski,* of the Kola Peninsula.]

kolkhoz, *kol-hhoz', n.* a collective or co-operative farm. [Russ.]

kolo, *kō'lō, n.* a Serbian dance or dance-tune. [Serb., wheel.]

Komintern, Comintern, *kom-in-tern', n.* the Communist *International.*—*n.* **Kominform, Cominform, -form'**, the Central *Inform*ation Bureau of European *Com*munist parties. [From the Russian form of these words.]

komissar. See **commissar.**

komitaji, *kō-mē-tä'jē, n.* orig. a member of the Bulgarian Revolutionary Committee in Macedonia: any Balkan guerrillero. [Turk. *qomitaji,* committee-man, bandit—*qomite*—Fr. *comité,* committee.]

kommers, *kom-ers', n.* a German students' gathering.—*n.* **kommers'buch** (*-bōōhh*), a songbook for such occasions. [Ger.,—L. *commercium,* commerce.]

Komsomol, *kom-som-ol', n.* the Communist Youth Organisation. [Russ.]

kon, (*Spens.*) form of **con** (know):—*p.a.t.* **kond.**

konfijt, *kon-fät', n.* a preserve of fruit, in syrup or candied. [Du.]

konimeter, *kon-im'i-tər, n.* an instrument for measuring dust in air.—*n.* **kon'iscope,** an instrument for estimating the dustiness of air. [Gr. *konis,* dust, *metron,* measure, *skopeein,* to look at.]

konk. Same as **conk.**

koodoo, kudu, *kōō'dōō, n.* an African antelope with long spiral horns. [From Hottentot.]

kookaburra, *kōōk'ə-bur'ä, n.* the laughing jackass. [Native Australian name.]

koolah, *kōō'lä.* See **koala.**

kop, *kop, n.* (*S.Afr.*) a hill, generally round-topped. [Du.; lit. head.]

kopeck, copeck, *kō-pek', kō'pek, n.* a Russian coin, the hundredth part of a ruble. [Russ. *kopeika.*]

kopje, *kop'i, n.* a low hill. [Cape Du.,—*kop,* head.]

koppa, *kop'ä, n.* a Greek letter (Ϙ) between Pi and Rho in the alphabet, answering to Q, dropped by most dialects but retained as a numeral Ϙ'=90, ͵Ϙ=90,000. [Gr.; cf. Hebr. *qōph.*]

kora, *kō'rä, n.* the water-cock (Gallicrex).

Koran, *kō-rän',* sometimes *kō'rən, n.* the Mohammedan Scriptures. — *adj.* **Koranic** (*kō-rän'ik*). [Ar. *qurän,* reading.]

korkir. Same as **corkir.**

kos, koss. Same as **coss.**

kosher, *kō'shər, adj.* pure, clean, according to the Jewish ordinances—as of meat killed and prepared by Jews. [Heb. *kāshēr,* right.]

kosmos. Same as **cosmos.**

koto, *kō'tō, n.* a Japanese musical instrument consisting of a long box with thirteen silk strings. [Jap.]

kotow, *kō-tow', n.* the Chinese ceremony of prostration.—*v.i.* to perform that ceremony, to abase oneself.—Usually **kowtow'.** [Chin. *k'o,* knock, *t'ou,* head.]

kottabos, *kot'ə-bos.* Same as **cottabus.**

Kotytto, *kot-it'ō,* or **Kotys,** *kot'is, ns.* a Thracian goddess worshipped with wild orgies. [Gr. *Kotyttō, Kotys.*]

---

fāte, fär, ăsk; mē, hər (her); *mīne; mōte; mūte; mōōn; dhen* (then)

koulan, koumiss, kourbash, kouskous. See **kulan, kumiss, kurbash, couscous.**

kowhai, *kō'hī, -hwī, n.* a papilionaceous shrub (*Sophora tetraptera*) of New Zealand, &c.: the New Zealand glory-pea (Clianthus). [Maori.]

kowtow, *kow-tow', n.* the more usual form of kotow.

kraal, *krāl, n.* a S. African native village: a corral. —*v.t.* to pen. [Du. *kraal*—Port. *curral*—L. *currēre*, to run.]

krait, *krīt, n.* a deadly Indian rock snake (*Bungarus caeruleus*). [Hind. *karait*.]

kraken, *krä'kən, n.* a fabled sea-monster. [Norw.; the -*n* is the def. art.]

Krameria, *krä-mē'ri-ä, n.* the rhatany genus of Caesalpiniaceae, or according to some, constituting a family **Krameriā'ceae.** [J. G. H. and W. H. *Kramer*, 18th-century German botanists.]

krang, *krang.* Same as **kreng.**

krantz, *kränts, n.* (*S.Afr.*) a crown of rock on a mountain-top: a precipice.—Also **krans, kranz.** [Du. *krans*, a wreath.]

kreasote, kreatine. Same as **creosote, creatine.**

kreese. Same as **kris.**

kremlin, *krem'lin, n.* a citadel, specially that of Moscow: the Russian government. [Russ. *kreml*.]

kreng, *kreng, n.* the carcass of a whale after the blubber has been removed.—Also **krang.** [Du.]

kreosote. Same as **creosote.**

kreutzer, *kroit'sər, n.* an obs. copper coin of Austria, South Germany, &c., 100 to the florin or gulden. [Ger. *kreuzer*—*kreuz*, cross, because at one time stamped with a cross.]

k'ri, *krē, n.* a marginal reading in the Hebrew Bible. [Heb. *qerē*, read (imper.).]

kriegspiel, kriegsspiel, *krēg'spēl, n.* a war-game played on a map to train officers. [Ger. *kriegsspiel* —*krieg*, war, *spiel*, game.]

krilium, *kril'i-əm, n.* improver of soil structure, consisting of synthetic polymers. [Trade name.]

krill, *kril, n.* whaler's name for species of Euphausia (fam. Euphausiaceae), phosphorescent shrimps.

kris, *krēs, n.* a Malay dagger with wavy blade: (*pl.* **kris'es**).—*v.t.* to stab with a kris.—Also **crease, creese, kreese.** [Malay.]

Krishna, *krish'nä, n.* a deity in later Hinduism, a form of Vishnu.

kromesky, *krō'mis-ki, n.* a croquette fried in bacon or calf's udder. [Russ. *kromochka*.]

krone, *krō'ne, n.* (*pl.* **kro'ner**) in Denmark and Norway, and **krona** (*pl.* **krō'nä**) (*pl.* **kro'nor**) in Sweden, a silver coin and monetary unit equal to 100 öre.—*n.* **krone** (*krō'nə; pl.* **kro'nen**), a former silver coin of Austria, equal to 100 heller: in Germany a former gold coin of 10 marks. [Cf. **crown.**]

Kronos, *kron'os, n.* supreme god of the Greeks, son of Ouranos and Gaia, dethroned by his son Zeus.

Kru, Kroo, *krōō, n.* a West African of a people of the coast of Liberia, noted as seamen.—Also *adj.* —*ns.* **Kru'-** or **Kroo'-boy, -man.**

krummhorn, *krōōm'horn, n.* an old clarinet-like instrument: an organ reed-stop. [Ger., curved horn.]

kryometer, &c. Same as **cryometer,** &c.

krypsis, *krips'is, n.* the 17th cent. doctrine that Christ secretly exercised divine powers. [Gr., concealment.]

krypton, crypton, *krip'ton, n.* a curious gas discovered in the air by Sir W. Ramsay in 1898 (Kr; atomic number 36). [Gr. *kryptein*, to hide.]

ksar, *ksär, n.* a Miltonic form of tsar.

Kshatriya, *kshät'ri-yä, n.* a member of the second or military caste among the Brahmanic Hindus. [Sans.]

k'thibh, *kthēv, n.* a textual reading in the Hebrew Scriptures: originally a marginal note calling attention to the textual form. [Heb. *kethībh*, written.]

kudos, *kū'dos, Gr. kū'dos, n.* credit, fame, renown, prestige. [Gr. *kȳdos*, glory.]

kudu. Same as **koodoo.**

Kufic, Cufic, *kū'fik, adj.* of Al *Kūfa*, south of Babylon: esp. of the lettering of its coins, inscriptions, and MSS., mainly early copies of the Koran.

kuh-horn, *kōō'horn, n.* an alpenhorn. [Ger.]

Ku-Klux Klan, Ku-Klux Klan, or **Ku-Klux,** *n.* (*U.S.*) a secret organisation in several Southern states after the Civil War of 1861-65, to oppose Northern influence, and prevent negroes from enjoying their rights as freemen—revived in 1916 to deal drastically with Jews, Catholics, negroes, &c. [Gr. *kyklos*, a circle, and **clan.**]

kukri, *kook'rē, n.* a sharp, curved Gurkha knife or short sword. [Hind. *kukrī*.]

kulak, *kōō-lak', n.* a rich peasant: an exploiter. [Russ., fist.]

kulan, koulan, *kōō'län, n.* the onager, or a nearly related wild ass of the Kirghiz Steppe. [Kirghiz.]

kultur, *kool-toor', n.* culture: civilisation: a type of civilisation: sometimes used ironically.—*ns.* **kultur'geschichte** (-*gə-shehh'tə*), history of civilisation; **kultur'kreis** (-*krīs*), an area regarded as a centre of diffusion of culture elements. [Ger.]

kumiss, koumiss, *kōō'mis, n.* fermented mares' milk. [Russ. *kumis*—Tatar, *kumiz*.]

kümmel, *küm'l, kim'l, kooml, n.* a liqueur flavoured with cumin and caraway seeds. [Ger.,—L. *cumīnum*—Gr. *kymīnon*, cumin.]

kumquat, *kum'kwot, n.* a small kind of orange. [Cantonese, gold orange.]

Kuomintang, *kwō'min-tang, n.* the Chinese nationalist people's party. [Chin.]

kupferschiefer, *koop'fər-shē-fər, n.* a shale rich in copper in the Permian of Germany. [Ger., copper shale.]

kurbash, kourbash, *kōōr'bash, n.* a hide whip used in the East.—*v.t.* to whip with a kurbash. [Ar. *qurbāsh*.]

Kurd, *koord, kurd, n.* one of the people of Kurdistan, Iranian in speech, often blond, Xenophon's *Kardouchoi*.—*adj.* and *n.* **Kurd'ish.**

kurgan, *koor-gän', n.* a sepulchral barrow. [Russ. from Tatar.]

kurrajong, *kur'ə-jong, n.* an Australian name for various trees with fibrous bark. [Native name.]

kurre (*Spens.*). Same as **cur.**

kursaal, *koor'zäl, n.* the reception-room of a spa. [Ger., lit. cure-saloon.]

kurvey, *kur-vä', v.i.* (*S.Afr.*) to transport goods. —*n.* **kurvey'or,** transport rider. [Du. *karwei*, work—Fr. *corvée*; cf. **corvée.**]

kutch. Same as **cutch** (2).

kutcha. Same as **cutcha.**

kvass, kväs, *n.* rye-beer. [Russ. *kvas*.]

kyang. See **kiang.**

kyanise, *kī'ə-nīz, v.t.* to preserve from dry-rot by injecting corrosive sublimate (into the pores of wood). [From John H. *Kyan* (1774-1830).]

kyanite, *kī'ə-nīt, n.* a mineral, an aluminium silicate, generally sky-blue.—Also **cyanite** (*sī'*). [Gr. *kyanos*, blue.]

kye, ky, *kī, n.pl.* (*Scot.*) cows. [See **kine.**]

kyle, *kil, n.* a narrow strait. [Gael. *caol*.]

kylie, kiley, kyley, *kī'li, n.* a boomerang. [Western Australian word.]

kylix, *kil'* or *kil'iks.* Same as **cylix.**

kyllosis, *ki-lō'sis, n.* club-foot. [Gr.]

kyloe, *kī'lō, n.* one of the cattle of the Hebrides. [Origin unknown.]

kymograph, *kī'mō-gräf, n.* an instrument for recording the pressure of fluids, esp. of blood in a blood-vessel.—*adj.* **kymographic** (-*graf'ik*). [Gr. *kȳma*, a wave, *graphein*, to write.]

kynd, kynde, *kīnd, n., adj.,* and *v.t.* (*Spens.*). Same as **kind.**

kyne (*Spens.*). Same as **kine.**

kyphosis, *kī-fō'sis, n.* a hunchbacked condition.— *adj.* **kyphotic** (-*fot'ik*). [Gr. *kȳphōsis*—*kȳphos,* a hump.]

Kyrie eleison, *kēr'i-e el-ā'i-son, kir', kēr', kīr'i-e el-e-ē'son, el-e-ā'son,* &c., abbrev. **Kyrie,** *n.* a form of prayer in all the ancient Greek liturgies, retained in the R.C. mass, following immediately after the introit (including both words and music): one of the responses to the commandments in the Anglican ante-communion service. [Gr. *Kȳrie, eleēson,* Lord, have pity.]

kyrielle, *kēr-i-el', n.* a string of short lines in

stanzas all ending with the same word. [Fr., litany, rigmarole, kyrielle—Gr. *Kÿrie eleëson*; see preceding.]

kyte, *kīt*, *n*. (*Scot.*) a paunch, belly. [Origin obscure.]

kythe, kithe, *kīdh*, *v.t.* (*Scot.*) to make known:— 2nd pers. sing. **kydst**, in Spenser blunderingly used in the sense of knowest.—*v.i.* to show oneself, to appear. [O.E. *cȳthan*, to make known. See uncouth.]

fāte, fär, ȧsk; mē, hȯr (her); *mīn : mōte; mūte; mōōn; dhen* (then)

L

L, l, *el, n.* the eleventh letter in the Roman, the twelfth in our alphabet, representing a lateral liquid sound, the breath passing the side or sides of the tongue: anything shaped like the letter: used as a sign for pound (L. *libra*): as a Roman numeral L=50, L̄=50,000: (*U.S.*) an elevated railway, or train.

la, *lä, interj.* lo! see! behold! ah! indeed! [Cf. **lo, law** (5).]

la, *lä, n.* the sixth note of the scale in sol-fa notation —also spelt **lah.** [See Aretinian.]

laager, lager, *lä′gər, n.* in South Africa, a defensive ring of ox-wagons: any extemporised fortification: an encampment.—*v.t.* and *v.i.* to arrange or camp in a laager. [Cape Du. *lager*—Ger. *lager,* a camp; Du. *leger*; cf. **lair, layer, leaguer.**]

lab, *lab, n.* a familiar contraction of **laboratory.**

labarum, *lab′ə-rəm, n.* a Roman military standard, the imperial standard after Constantine's conversion—with a monogram of the Greek letters XP (ChR)—for Christ: a similar ecclesiastical banner borne in processions: any moral standard or guide. [L.,—Late Gr. *labaron,* origin unknown.]

labda, labdacism, labdanum. See **lambda, lambdacism, ladanum.**

labefactation, *lab-i-fak-tā′shən,* **labefaction,** *-fak′-shən, ns.* a weakening decay: overthrow. [L. *labefactātiō, -ōnis*—*labāre,* to totter, *facĕre,* to make.]

label, *lā′bl, n.* (*arch.*) an attached band or strip: a small slip placed on or near anything to denote its nature, contents, ownership, destination, &c.: (*law*) a paper annexed to a will, as a codicil: (*her.*) a fillet with pendants (an eldest son's cadency mark): (*archit.*) a dripstone: (*fig.*) a characterising or classificatory designation.—*v.t.* to affix a label to: to describe by or on a label:—*pr.p.* **lā′belling;** *pa.t.* and *pa.p.* **lā′belled.** [O.Fr. *label,* perh.—O.H.G. *lappa* (Ger. *lappen*), flap.]

labellum, *lə-bel′əm, n.* the lower petal, morphologically the upper, of an orchid: applied also to other lip-like structures in flowers:—*pl.* **labell′a.**—*adj.* **labell′oid.** [L., dim. of *labrum,* a iip.]

labial, *lā′bi-al, adj.* of or formed by the lips: (*mus.*) sounded by impact of air on a lip-like projection, as an organ flue-pipe.—*n.* a sound formed by the lips. —*v.t.* **lā′bialise,** to make labial: to pronounce with lip action.—*n.* **lā′bialism,** a tendency to labialise.—*adv.* **lā′bially.**—*n.pl.* **Lābiatae** (*-ā′tē*), a family of sympetalous dicotyledons with lipped flowers, four-cornered stems, and opposite branches —the dead-nettles, mints, &c.— *adj.* **lā′biate,** lipped: having a lipped corolla: belonging to the Labiatae.—*n.* any plant of the Labiatae.—*adj.* and *n.* **lā′biodent′al,** (a sound) pronounced both by the lips and teeth.—*n.* **lā′bium,** a lip or lip-like part: in insects the underlip, formed by the partial fusion of the second maxillae:—*pl.* **lā′bia.** [L. *labium,* a lip.]

labile, *lā′bil, adj.* unstable: apt to slip or change. [L. *lābilis*—*lābī,* to slip.]

labis, *lā′bis, n.* the cochlear or eucharistic spoon. [Gr. *labis,* handle—root of *lambanein,* to take.]

lablab, *lab′lab, n.* a tropical bean (*Dolichos Lablab*) with edible pods. [Ar. *lablāb.*]

laboratory, *lab′ə-rə-tə-ri,* also *lə-bor′, n.* a chemist's workroom: a place for experimental work or research. [L. *labōrāre*—*labor,* work.]

labour, *lā′bər, n.* toil: work: bodily work: pains: duties: a task requiring hard work: effort toward the satisfaction of needs: workers collectively: supply or services of workers, esp. bodily workers: the Labour Party or its cause, principles, or interest: (*arch.*) the outcome of toil: distressing difficulty: trouble taken: exertion of influence: the pangs and efforts of childbirth: heavy pitching or rolling of a ship.—*adj.* of labour or the Labour Party.—*v.i.* to undergo labour: to work: to take pains: to be oppressed: to move slowly: to be in travail: (*naut.*) to pitch and roll heavily.—*v.t.* to spend labour on: to cultivate: to operate, work: to elaborate, work out in detail: to strain, over-elaborate.—*adj.* **laborious** (*lə-bō′-ri-əs*), involving or devoted to labour: strenuous: arduous: —*adv.* **labō′riously.**—*n.* **labō′riousness.**—*adj.* **lā′boured,** cultivated: worked: bearing marks of effort in execution: strained: over-elaborated.— *ns.* **lā′bourer,** one who labours: one who does work requiring little skill; **lā′bourism**; **lā′bourist,** one who contends for the rights of workers.— *adjs.* **lā′bour-sav′ing,** intended to supersede or lessen labour; **lā′boursome,** (*Shak.*) laborious.— **hard labour,** compulsory work imposed in addition to imprisonment; **Labour Day,** in many countries the 1st of May, a day of labour demonstrations; **labour of love,** work undertaken without hope of emolument; **Labour Party,** a party aiming at securing for workers by hand or brain the fruits of their industry and equitable distribution thereof: its representatives in parliament: a local organisation of the party; **labour with,** to take pains to convince. [O.Fr. *labour, labeur*—L. *labor.*]

Labrador, *lab′rə-dör,* or *-dör′, n.* a mainland region of Newfoundland and Quebec.—Also *adj.*—*n.* **lab′radorite** (or *-dör′*), a plagioclase felspar with fine play of colours found on the Labrador coast.— **Labrador** (**dog, retriever**), a sporting dog about twenty-two inches in height, either black or (**yellow, or golden, Labrador**) from red to fawn in colour; **Labrador tea,** a shrub of the heather family (Ledum) used in Labrador as a substitute for tea.

labrum, *lā′brəm, n.* a lip: a lip-like part:—*pl.* **lā′bra.**—*n.* **lā′bret,** a lip ornament.—*adj.* **lā′brose,** thick-lipped. [L. *lābrum,* a lip.]

Labrus, *lā′brəs, n.* the wrasse genus of fishes, of the family **La′bridae.**—*adj.* **la′broid.** [L. *lābrus, lābros,* a kind of fish.]

labrys, *lab′ris, lāb′ris, n.* the double-headed axe, a religious symbol of ancient Crete, &c. [Gr., from Lydian; perh. conn. with **labyrinth.**]

laburnum, *lə-bur′nəm, n.* a small poisonous papilionaceous tree of the Alps. [L.]

labyrinth, *lab′i-rinth, n.* (*orig.*) a building with intricate passages: an arrangement of tortuous paths or alleys (usually between hedges) in which it is difficult to find the way out: a maze: a tangle of intricate ways and connexions: a perplexity: (*anat.*) the cavities of the internal ear.—*adjs.* **labyrinth′al, labyrinth′ian, labyrinth′ic, -al, labyrinth′ine** (*-in, -īn*).—*n.* **labyrinth′odont,** an extinct stegocephalian amphibian of Carboniferous, Permian, and esp. Triassic times, so called from the mazy pattern of a section of the teeth (Gr. *odous, odontos,* tooth) in some. [Gr. *labyrinthos,* perh. conn. with *labrys,* the double axe; see **labrys.**]

lac. Same as **lakh.**

lac, *lak, n.* a dark-red transparent resin produced on the twigs of trees in the East by coccid insects.— *ns.* **lac′-dye, lac′-lake,** scarlet colouring matters obtained from it. [Hind. *lākh*—Sans. *laksha,* 100,000, hence the (teeming) lac insect.]

laccolite, *lak′ō-līt, n.* a mass of igneous rock that has risen in a molten condition and bulged up the overlying strata to form a dome.—Also **lacc′olith** (*-lith*).—*adjs.* **laccolitic** (*-lit′ik*), **laccolith′ic.** [Gr. *lakkos,* a reservoir, *lithos,* a stone.]

lace, *lās, n.* a string for passing through holes: an ornamental fabric made by looping, knotting,

plaiting, or twisting threads into definite patterns.
—*v.t.* to fasten with a lace: to compress or pinch
by lacing: to adorn with lace: to streak: to mark
with the lash: to intermix, as coffee with brandy,
&c.: to intertwine.—*v.i.* to have lacing as mode of
fastening: to practise tight-lacing.—*ns.* **lace′bark**,
a lofty West Indian tree of the Daphne family,
the inner bark like coarse lace; **lace′-boot**, a boot
fastened by a lace.—*adj.* **laced**.—*ns.* **lace′-frame**,
a machine used in lace-making; **lace′-leaf** (see
lattice-leaf); **lace′-man**, a dealer in lace;
lace′-paper, paper stamped or cut like lace;
lace′-pill′ow, a cushion held on the knees by
lace-makers; **lacet** (*lās-et′*), a kind of braidwork;
lace′-wing, the golden-eye, a neuropterous insect
with gauzy wings and brilliant golden eyes.—*n.*
and *adj.* **lac′ing**.—*adj.* **lac′y**, like lace.—**laced**
mutton, (*Shak.*) a prostitute. [O.Fr. *las*, a noose
—L. *laqueus*.]
lacerate, *las′ə-rāt*, *v.t.* to tear: to rend: to wound:
to afflict.—*adjs.* **lac′erable**; **lac′erant**, harrowing;
lac′erate, **-d**, rent, torn: (*bot.*) with edges cut
into irregular segments.—*n.* **lacerā′tion**.—*adj.*
lac′erative, tearing: having power to tear. [L.
lacerāre, *-ātum*, to tear—*lacer*, torn.]
Lacerta, *lə-sər′tä*, *n.* a genus of lizards, including
the common lizard.—*adj.* **lacertian** (*-sər′shyən*),
of lizards: lizard-like.—*n.pl.* **Lacertil′ia**, the
lizard order or suborder of reptiles. — *adjs.*
lacertil′ian; **lacer′tine**. [L.]
laches, *lach′iz*, *n.* (*law*) negligence or undue delay,
esp. such as to disentitle to remedy. [A.Fr.
lachesse.]
Lachesis, *lak′i-sis*, *n.* that one of the three Fates
who assigned to each mortal his destiny—she
spun the thread of life from the distaff held by
Clotho: a genus of snakes including the bushmaster. [Gr.]
lachrymal, *lak′ri-məl*, *adj.* of or for tears.—*n.* a
tear-bottle: a bone near the tear-gland: (in *pl.*)
lachrymal organs: (in *pl.*) weeping fits.—*adjs.*
lach′rymary, **lach′rymatory**, lachrymal: causing tears to flow.—*ns.* a tear-bottle.—*n.* **lach′ry-**
mātor, a substance that causes tears to flow, as
tear-gas: a contrivance for letting it loose.—*adj.*
lach′rymose, shedding tears: given to weeping:
lugubrious.—*adv.* **lach′rymosely**.—Also **lacry-**
mal, **lacrimal**, &c.—**lachryma Christi** (*lak′ri-mä*
kris′tē; L., Christ's tear), a sweet but piquant wine
from grapes grown on Vesuvius; **lachrymal**
duct, a duct that conveys tear-water from the inner
corner of the eye to the nose; **lachrymal gland**,
a gland at the outer angle of the eye that secretes
tears. [From *lachryma*, a mediaeval spelling of
L. *lacrima*, tear; cf. Gr. *dakry*: Eng. **tear**; Gr.
dakrȳma may have influenced the spelling.]
lacinia, *la-sin′i-ä*, *n.* a long narrow lobe in a leaf,
&c.: (*entom.*) the inner lobe of the maxilla:—*pl.*
lacin′iae (*-ē*).—*adjs.* **lacin′iate**, **-d**, cut into narrow
lobes, slashed.—*n.* **laciniā′tion**. [L., a lappet, tag.]
lack, *lak*, *n.* want, deficiency: a thing wanting.—
v.t. to be in want of: to miss: to need.—*v.i.* to
be wanting: to be in want.—*ns.* **lack′-all**, one
who is destitute; **lack′-beard**; **lack′-brain**,
(*Shak.*) a fool.—*adj.* **lack′ing**.—*ns.* **lack′land**;
lack′-Latin (*obs.*; often *Sir John Lack-Latin*), an
ignorant priest.—*adj.* **lack′-linen**, (*Shak.*) wanting
linen.—*n.* **lack′-love**, one who is deficient in love.
—*adj.* **lack′-lus′tre**, dull. [Cf. M.L.G. and Du.
lak, blemish.]
lack, *lak*, *n.* See **good-lack** under **good**.
lackadaisical, *lak-ə-dā′zi-kl*, *adj.* affectedly pensive: sentimental: listless: languishing.—*interjs.*
lack′adai′sy, **lack′aday**. [See **alack-a-day**.]
lacker. See **lacquer**.
lackey, **lacquey**, *lak′i*, *n.* a footman or valet: a
servile follower:—*pl.* **lack′eys**, **lacq′ueys**.—*v.t.*
and *v.i.* to serve or attend as or like a footman.—
lackey moth, a moth (*Malacosoma neustria*) of the
egger group with gaudily striped caterpillar, like a
footman in livery. [O.Fr. *laquay* (Fr. *laquais*)—
Sp. *lacayo*, a lackey; perh. Ar. *luka′*, servile.]
lacmus, *lak′məs*, *n.* the same as **litmus** (q.v.).
Laconian, *lə-kō′ni-ən*, **Laconic**, *lə-kon′ik*, *adjs.* of
Laconia or Lacedaemonia, Spartan.—*adjs.* **laconic**,

-al, expressing or expressed in few words after
the manner of the Laconians: sententiously brief.
—*adv.* **lacon′ically**.—*ns.* **laconism** (*lak′*), **lacon′-**
icism, a concise style: a short, pithy phrase. [Gr.
lakōnikos.]
lacquer, **lacker**, *lak′ər*, *n.* a solution of film-
forming substances in a volatile solvent, esp. a
varnish of lac and alcohol: the juice of the lacquer-
tree (*Japan lacquer*) or similar product: a covering
of one of these: an article, or ware, so coated.—
v.t. to cover with lacquer: to varnish.—*ns.*
lacq′uerer; **lacq′uering**, varnishing with lacquer:
a coat of lacquer varnish.—*n.* **lacq′uer-tree′**, a
tree of the genus Rhus. [Fr. *lacre*—Port. *lacre*,
laca; see **lac** (2).]
lacrimal, &c. See **lachrymal**, &c.
lacrosse, *lä-kros′*, *n.* a Canadian game played by
two sets of twelve, the ball being driven through the
opponents' goal by means of a crosse. [Fr.]
lacteal, *lak′ti-əl*, *adj.* of milk: conveying chyle.—
n. a lymphatic conveying chyle from the intestines
to the thoracic ducts.—*ns.* **lactase** (*lak′tās*), an
enzyme that acts on lactose; **lac′tate**, a salt of
lactic acid; **lactā′tion**, secretion or yielding of
milk: the period of suckling.—*adj.* **lac′teous**,
milky. — *n.* **lactesc′ence**. — *adjs.* **lactesc′ent**,
turning to milk: producing milky juice; **lac′tic**,
pertaining to milk; **lactif′erous**, conveying or
producing milk or milky juice; **lactif′ic**, producing milk or milky juice; **lactif′luous**, flowing
with milk.—*n.* **lac′tose**, milk-sugar ($C_{12}H_{22}O_{11}$),
obtained by evaporating whey.—**lactic acid**, an
acid obtained from milk, $CH_3CH(OH)CO_2H$. [L.
lac, lactis, milk; Gr. *gala, galaktos*, milk.]
Lactuca, *lak-tū′kä*, *n.* the lettuce genus of composite plants, with milky juice. [L. *lactūca*—*lac*,
lactis, milk.]
lacuna, *la-*, *lə-kū′nä*, *n.* a gap or hiatus: (*biol.*) an
intercellular space: a cavity: a depression in a
pitted surface:—*pl.* **lacū′nae** (*-nē*).—*n.* **lacū′nar**,
a sunken panel or coffer in a ceiling or a soffit:
a ceiling containing these:—*pl.* **lacū′nars**, **la-**
cunaria (*lak-ū-nā′ri-ä*).—*adjs.* **lacū′nar**, **lacū′-**
nose, having lacunae: pitted. [L. *lacūna*, hollow,
gap, and *lacūnar*, *-āris*, a fretted ceiling.]
lacustrine, *lə-kus′trīn*, *adj.* pertaining to lakes:
dwelling in or on lakes: formed in lakes. [L.
lacus, a lake.]
lad, *lad*, *n.* a boy: a youth: a stable-man: (*Scot.*)
a lover.—*n.* **ladd′ie**, a little lad: a boy.—**lad's**
love, (*prov.*) southernwood. [M.E. *ladde*, youth,
servant; origin obscure.]
lad, obs. form of **led**.
ladanum, *lad′ə-nəm*, *n.* a resin exuded from Cistus
leaves in Mediterranean countries.—Also **lab′-**
danum. [L. *lādanum*, *lēdanum*—Gr. *lādanon*,
lēdanon—*lēdon*, the Cistus plant, prob.—Pers.
lādan.]
ladder, *lad′ər*, *n.* a contrivance, generally portable,
with rungs between two supports, for going up
and down: anything of similar form, as a run
in a knitted fabric where the breaking of a thread
gives an appearance of rungs: a contrivance for
enabling fish to ascend a waterfall (*fish-ladder*,
salmon-ladder).—*v.t.* to furnish with a ladder: to
scale with a ladder.—*v.i.* to develop a ladder.—
adjs. **ladd′ered**, **ladd′ery**. [O.E. *hlæder*; Ger.
leiter.]
lade, *lād*, *v.t.* to load: to burden: to put on
board: to ladle or scoop: to empty, drain, as
with a ladle.—*v.i.* to take cargo aboard:—*pa.t.*
lād′ed; *pa.p.* **lād′en**, **lād′ed**.—*adj.* **lād′en**,
loaded: burdened.—*n.* **lād′ing**, the act of loading:
that which is loaded: cargo: freight. [O.E. *hladan*,
pa.t. *hlód*; *pa.p.* *hlæden*, *hladen*, to load, to draw
out water.]
lade, **laid**, *lād* (*Scot.*). See **load**.
lade, *lād*, *n.* (*Scot.*) a mill-stream. [Perh. O.E.
lád, way, course; cf. **lode**, **lead** (1).]
Ladin, *lä-dēn′*, *n.* a Romance tongue spoken in the
upper Inn valley: a general name for the Rhaeto-
Romanic languages or dialects.—Also **Ladi′no**.—
n. **Ladinity** (*-din′i-ti*). [L. *Latīnus*, Latin.]
Ladino, *lä-dē′nō*, *n.* the old Castilian tongue: the
Spanish jargon of Macedonian Jews: a Spanish-

American of mixed white and Indian blood. [Sp.,—L. Latīnus, Latin.]

ladle, *lād′l*, *n.* a large spoon for lifting liquid: the float-board of a mill-wheel: (*Scot.*) a church collection-box on a long handle.—*v.t.* to transfer or distribute with a ladle.—*n.* **lad′leful**, as much as a ladle will hold :—*pl.* **lad′lefuls**. [O.E. *hlædel* —*hladan*, to lade.]

ladrone, *la-drōn′*, *n.* a robber. [Sp. *ladrón*—L. *latrō, -ōnis.*]

lady (Lady when prefixed), *lā′di*, *n.* the mistress of a house: used as the feminine of **lord** and of **gentleman**, and ordinarily as a less formal substitute for **dame**: any woman of refinement of manners and instincts, or more generally: (*arch.*) a consort, a term formerly preferred to wife by some who liked to stand upon their dignity: a lady-love or object of chivalric devotion: a size of slates, 16×8 inches: used also as a feminine prefix :—*pl.* **ladies** (*lā′diz*); old genitive **la′dy.**— *ns.* **la′dybird**, any member of the family Coccinellidae, little round beetles, often brightly spotted, preying on green-fly, &c.—also **la′dybug, la′dycow, la′dy-fly**; **La′dy-chap′el**, a chapel dedicated to the Virgin Mary, usually behind the high altar, at the end of the apse; **la′dy-fern**, a pretty British fern (*Athyrium Filix-foemina*), with long bipinnate fronds (imagined by the old herbalists to be the female of the male-fern).—*adj.* **la′dified, la′dified**, inclined to affect the lady.—*v.t.* **la′dyfy, la′dify**, to make a lady of : to call My Lady or Your Ladyship.—*ns.* **la′dy-help**, one paid to assist in house-work, but treated more or less as one of the family; **la′dyhood**, condition, character, of a lady.—*adj.* **la′dyish**, having the airs of a fine lady. —*ns.* **la′dyism**, affectation of the airs of a fine lady; **la′dy-killer**, a man who fancies himself irresistible to women : a general lover; **la′dykin**, an endearing term. of **lady**.—*adj.* **la′dylike**, like a lady in manners : refined : soft, delicate : often implying want of touch with reality and sincerity —genteel.—*ns.* **la′dy-love**, a lady or woman loved : a sweetheart; (**our**) **la′dy′s-bed′straw** (see **bedstraw**); **la′dy′s-cu′shion**, the mossy saxifrage; **la′dy′s-fing′er, -fing′ers**, a name for many plants, esp. the kidney-vetch : a finger-shaped cake; **la′dyship**, the title of a lady; **la′dy′s-maid**, a female attendant on a lady, esp. for the toilet; **la′dy′s-mantle**, a ger us (Alchemilla) of rosaceous plants with small, yellowish-green flowers and leaves like folded drapery; **la′dy′s-slipp′er**, a genus (Cypripedium) of orchids with large slipper-like lip; **la′dy′s-smock, la′dy-smock**, the cuckoo-flower (*Cardamine pratensis*), a cruciferous meadow-plant, with whitish, blush-coloured flowers; **la′dy′s-thist′le**, the milk thistle; **la′dy-trifles**, (*Shak.*) trifles befitting a lady.—**ladies′ companion**, a small bag used for carrying women's work; **ladies′ gallery**, a gallery in the House of Commons, once screened off by a grille; **ladies′ man**, one fond of women's society; **Lady Day**, 25th March, the day of the Annunciation of the Virgin.—**her, your ladyship, my lady**, forms of expression used in speaking of, or to, one who has the title of Lady; **our Lady**, the Virgin Mary. [O.E. *hlǣfdige*, lit. app. the bread-kneader—*hlāf*, loaf, and a lost word for the root of **dough**.]

laeotropic, *lē-ō-trop′ik*, *adj.* turning to the left. [Gr. *laios*, left, *tropos*, a turn.]

laesie, (*Spens.*) for **lazy.**

laetare, *lē-tā′ri*, *n.* the fourth Sunday in Lent. [*Laetāre* (first word of the introit), imper. sing. of L. *laetārī*, to rejoice—*laetus*, joyful.]

laevigate, a faulty spelling of **levigate.**

laevorotatory, *lē-vō-rō′tə-tə-ri*, *adj.* rotating the plane of polarisation of light to the left.—*n.* **laevorotā′tion**. [L. *laevus*, left, *rotāre*, to rotate.]

laevulose, *lēv′ū-lōs*, or *lev′*, *n.* fructose, a laevorotatory sugar (C₆H₁₂O₆).—Also **levulose.** [L. *laevus*, left.]

lag, *lag*, *adj.* hindmost : behindhand : late : tardy. —*n.* he who, or that which, comes behind : the fag-end: (esp. in *pl.*) dregs : a retardation or falling behind : the amount by which one pheno-menon is delayed behind another : delay.—*v.i.* to move or walk slowly : to loiter : to fall behind : —*pr.p.* **lagg′ing**; *pa.t.* and *pa.p.* **lagged**.—*n.* **lag′-end**, (*Shak.*) the last or long-delayed end.—*adj.* **lagg′ard**, lagging.—*ns.* **lagg′ard, lagg′er**, one who lags behind.—*n.* and *adj.* **lagg′ing**.—*adv.* **lagg′ingly.—lag of the tides**, the progressive lengthening of the interval between tides as neap-tide is approached — opp. to **priming.** [Origin unknown.]

lag, *lag*, *n.* a stave : a lath : boarding : a wooden lining : a non-conducting covering : a perforated wooden strip used instead of a card in weaving. —*v.t.* to furnish with a lag.—*n.* **lagg′ing**, boarding, as across the framework of a centre for an arch, or in a mine to prevent ore falling into a passage. [Prob. O.N. *lögg*, barrel-rim; cf. Sw. *lagg*, stave.]

lag, *lag*, *v.t.* (*slang*) to steal : to carry off : to arrest : to transport or send to penal servitude.— *n.* a convict : an old convict : a term of penal servitude or transportation. [Origin unknown.]

lagan, *lag′ən*, *n.* wreckage or goods at the bottom of the sea : later taken to mean such goods attached to a buoy with a view to recovery.—Also **ligan** (*lī′gən*). [O.Fr. *lagan*, perh. Scand. from the root of **lay, lie**; falsely associated with L. *ligāmen*, a tying.]

lagena, *lə-jē′nä*, *n.* (*ant.*) a narrow-necked bottle. —*adj.* **lageniform**, flask-shaped. [L. *lagēna*— Gr. *lagȳna*.]

lager, *lä′gər*, *n.* See **laager.**

lager, *lä′gər*, *n.* (in full **lager beer**) a light beer very much used in Germany. [Ger. *lager-bier*— *lager*, a store-house.]

laggen, laggin, *läg′ən*, *n.* (*Burns*) the angle between the side and bottom of a wooden dish.—*n.* **lagg′en-gird**, a hoop at the bottom of a wooden vessel. [Cf. **lag** (2), **leglin**.]

lagoon, *lə-gōōn′*, *n.* a shallow lake, esp. one communicating with the sea or a river, or just cut off from it.—Also (old-fashioned) **lagune**. [It. *laguna*—L. *lacūna*.]

lagrimoso, *läg-ri-mō′sō*, *adj.* and *adv.* (*mus.*) plaintive(ly). [It.,—L. *lacrimōsus*, tearful—*lacrima*, a tear.]

Lagthing, Lagting, *läg′ting*, *n.* (*obs.*) the upper house of the Norwegian parliament. [Norw. *lag*, law, *ting* (*thing*), court, parliament.]

lah. Same as **la** (2).

laic, laical, laicise. See **lay**, *adj.*

laid, *lād*, *pa.t.* and *pa.p.* of **lay.**—*adj.* put down, prostrate : pressed down.—**laid paper**, such as shows the marks of the close parallel wires on which the pulp was laid—opp. to *wove*; **laid work**, in embroidery, couching of the simplest kind.

laidly, *lād′li*, *adj.* Northern (*Scot.*) form of **loathly.**

laigh, *lāhh*, *adj.* and *adv.* a Scots form of **low** : low-lying : sunken.—*n.* a tract of low-lying land.

laik. Same as **lake** (4).

lain, *pa.p.* of **lie**, to rest.

lair, *lār*, *n.* a lying-place, esp. the den or retreat of a wild beast : an enclosure for beasts : (*Scot.*) the ground for one grave in a burying-place.—*v.t.* to put in a lair.—*v.i.* to lie : to go to a lair.—*n.* **lair′age**, a place where cattle are housed or laired, esp. at markets and docks. [O.E. *leger*, a couch—*licgan*, to lie down; Du. *leger*, Ger. *lager*.]

lair, *lār*, *v.t.* and *v.i.* (*Scot.*) to mire.—*n.* mire.— *adj.* **lair′y.** [O.N. *leir*, mud.]

lair, *lār*, *n.* Scots form of **lore.**

laird, *lārd*, *n.* (*Scot.*) a landed proprietor.—*n.* **laird′ship.** [Northern form of **lord.**]

laisse, *les*, *n.* a tirade or string of verses on one rhyme. [Fr.]

laissez-aller, *les′ä-al′ā*, *n.* unconstraint. — Also **laiss′er-all′er.** [Fr., let go.]

laissez-faire, *les′ä-fer′*, *n.* a general principle of non-interference.—Also **laiss′er-faire′.** [Fr., let do.]

laith, *lāth*, a Scots form of **loth.**—*adj.* **laithfu′** (*lāth′fə*), bashful.

laity. See **lay**, *adj.*

lake, *lāk*, *n.* a reddish pigment originally got from lac : a coloured substance got by combination of a dye with a metallic hydroxide : its colour :

carmine.—*v.t.* and *v.i.* to make or become lake-coloured.—*adj.* lak′y. [lac (2).]

lake, *lāk, n.* a large or considerable body of water within land.—*ns.* lake′-basin, a hollow now or once containing a lake: the area drained by a lake; lake′-dweller; lake′-dwelling, a settlement, esp. prehistoric, built on piles in a lake; lake′-law′yer, (*U.S.*) the bowfin: the burbot; lake′let, a little lake; lāk′er, a fish found in lakes: a boat for lakes: one who sails on lakes: a Lake poet: a visitor to the Lake District.—*adjs.* lāk′ish, savouring of the Lake school; lāk′y.—Lake District, a picturesque mountainous region in Cumberland, Westmorland, and Lancashire, with many lakes; Lake poets, Lake school, Wordsworth, Coleridge, and Southey, dwellers in the Lake District. [M.E. *lac*, either—O.E. *lacu*, stream (see next word), confused in sense with L. *lacus*, lake, or from *lacus* itself, directly or through Fr. *lac.*]

lake, *lāk, n.* (*obs.*) a small stream or water-channel. [O.E. *lacu.*]

lake, laik, *lāk, v.i.* (*N. England*) to sport, play. [O.E. *lācan.*]

lakh, lac, *lak, n.* the number 100,000: 100,000 rupees. [Hind. *lākh*—Sans. *laksha*, a mark, 100,000.]

lakin, *lā′kin, n.* (*Shak.*) a shortened form of ladykin, dim. of lady.

Lakshmi, *luksh′mē, n.* in Hindu mythology, Vishnu's consort. [Sans. *Lakshmī.*]

lalang, *lä′läng, n.* a coarse grass, *Imperata arundinacea*, of the Malay archipelago. [Malay.]

lallan, *lāl′ən, adj.* and *n.* a form of lawland, lowland.—*n.* Lall′ans, Broad Scots: a form of Scots developed by modern Scottish writers.

lallation, *lal-ā′shən, n.* childish speech: pronouncing of *r* like *l*.—*n.* lall′ing, babbling. [L. *lallāre*, to sing lullaby.]

lam, *lam, v.t.* to beat. [Cf. O.E. *lemian*, to subdue, lame, O.N. *lemja*, to beat, lit. lame.]

lama, *lä′mä, n.* a Buddhist priest in Tibet.—*ns.* Lamaism (*lä′mä-izm*), the religion prevailing in Tibet and Mongolia, being Buddhism corrupted by Sivaism, and by Shamanism or spirit-worship; La′maist; la′masery (or *lä-mä′sə-ri*), lamaserai (*-ri*), a Tibetan monastery. [Tibetan, *blama*, the *b* silent.]

lamantin, *lä-man′tin, n.* the manatee. [Fr.]

Lamarckism, *lä-märk′izm, n.* the theory of the French naturalist J. B. P. A. de Monet de *Lamarck* (1744-1829) that species have developed by the efforts of organisms to adapt themselves to new conditions—also Lamarck′ianism.—*adj.* and *n.* Lamarck′ian.

lamb, *lam, n.* the young of a sheep: its flesh as a food: lambskin: one simple, innocent or gentle as a lamb.—*v.t.* and *v.i.* to bring forth as sheep: to tend at lambing.—*ns.* lamb′-ale, a feast at lamb-shearing; lamb′kin, lamb′ling, lamb′ie (*Scot.*), a little lamb.—*adj.* lamb′-like, like a lamb: gentle.—*ns.* lamb′skin, the skin of a lamb dressed with the wool on: the skin of a lamb dressed as leather: a woollen cloth resembling this: a cotton cloth with raised surface and deep nap; lamb′s′-lett′uce, corn-salad; lamb′s-wool, fine wool: a wholesome old English beverage composed of ale and the pulp of roasted apples, with sugar and spices.—the Lamb, Lamb of God, applied to Christ, in allusion to the paschal lamb and John i. 29. [O.E. *lamb*; Ger. *lamm*, Du. *lam.*]

lambast, *lam-bast′, v.t.* to thrash.—Also lambaste (*lam-bāst′*). [Perh. lam and baste.]

lambda, *lam′dä*, also (more correctly) labda, *lab′dä, n.* the Greek letter (Λ, λ) corresponding to Roman *l*: as a numeral, λ′ = 30, ͵λ = 30,000: used as a symbol for wave-length: the meeting of the sagittal and lambdoid sutures of the skull.—*n.* lamb′dacism, lab′dacism, a too frequent use of words containing *l*-sounds: faulty pronunciation of the sound of *l*: a defective pronunciation of *r*, making it like *l*.—*adjs.* lamb′doid, -al, shaped like the Greek capital Λ—applied in anatomy to the suture between the occipital and the two parietal bones of the skull. [Gr. *lambda*, properly *labda*—Heb. *lāmedh.*]

lambent, *lam′bənt, adj.* licking: moving about as if touching lightly: gliding over: flickering.—*n.* lam′bency, the quality of being lambent: a flicker.—*adj.* lam′bitive, (*obs.*) taken by licking.—*n.* a medicine so taken. [L. *lambēre*, to lick.]

lambert, *lam′bərt, n.* a unit of brightness, one lumen per square centimetre. [After J. H. Lambert (1728-77), German physicist, &c.]

lamboys, *lam′boiz, n.pl.* (*ant.*) kilted flexible steel-plates worn skirt-like from the waist. [Perh. Fr. *lambeaux*, flaps; or a blunder for *jambeaux*.]

lambrequin, *lam′bər-kin*, or *-bri-kin, n.* a veil over a helmet: mantling: a strip of drapery over a window, doorway, from a mantelpiece, &c. [Fr.]

lame, *lām, adj.* disabled, esp. in the use of a leg: hobbling: unsatisfactory: imperfect.—*v.t.* to make lame: to cripple: to render imperfect.—*adv.* lame′ly.—*n.* lame′ness.—*adj.* lam′ish, a little lame: hobbling. — lame duck (see duck, 3). [O.E. *lama*, lame; Du. *lam*, Ger. *lahm.*]

lame, *lām, n.* a thin plate, esp. of metal, as in armour.—*n.* lamé, *lä′mā*, a fabric in which metal threads are interwoven. [Fr.,—L. *lāmina*, a thin plate.]

lamella, *lə-mel′ä, n.* a thin plate or layer:—*pl.* lamell′ae (*-ē*).—*adjs.* lamell′ar (or *lam′i-lər*), lam′ellate (or *-el′*), -d, lamell′iform, lamell′oid, lamell′ose.—*n.* lamell′ibranch (*-brangk*; L. *branchiae*, gills), any member of the Lamellibranch′ia, Pelecypoda, or bivalve molluscs, from their plate-like (nutritive) gills.—*adj.* lamellibranch′iate.—*n.* lamell′icorn (L. *cornū*, horn), a member of the Lamellicor′nes, a very numerous group of beetles—the cockchafer, &c., with the ends of the antennae expanded in flattened plates.—*adj.* lamellliros′tral (L. *rōstrum*, beak), having transverse lamellae within the edge of the bill. [L. *lāmella*, dim. of *lāmina.*]

lament, *lə-ment′, v.i.* to utter grief in outcries: to wail: to mourn.—*v.t.* to mourn for: to deplore.—*n.* sorrow expressed in cries: an elegy or dirge: a musical composition of like character.—*adj.* lamentable (*lam′ənt-ə-bl*), deserving or expressing sorrow: sad: pitiful.—*adv.* lam′entably.—*n.* lamentā′tion, act of lamenting: audible expression of grief: wailing: Lamentations, a book of the Old Testament traditionally attributed to Jeremiah.—*adj.* lament′ed.—*n.* and *adj.* lament′ing.—*adv.* lament′ingly. [L. *lāmentārī.*]

lameter, lamiter, *lām′i-tər, n.* (*Scot.*) a cripple. [Obscurely derived from lame.]

lamia, *lā′mi-ä, n.* in Greek and Roman mythology, a blood-sucking serpent-witch. [Gr. and L. *lāmiā.*]

lamiger, lammiger, *lam′i-jer, n.* (*prov.*) a cripple. [Cf. lameter.]

lamina, *lam′i-nä, n.* a thin plate or layer: a leaf-blade: a thin plate of bone: a plate of sensitive tissue within a hoof:—*pl.* laminae (*-nē*).—*adjs.* lam′inar, lam′inary.—*n.* Laminā′ria, the tangle genus of brown seaweeds, with large expanded leathery fronds.—*adjs.* laminār′ian; lam′inate, -d, in laminae or thin plates: consisting of scales or layers, over one another.—*n.* laminā′tion, arrangement in thin layers: a thin layer.—laminar flow, viscous flow. [L. *lāmina*, a thin plate.]

Lammas, *lam′əs, n.* the feast of first-fruits on 1st August.—*n.* Lamm′as-tide, season of Lammas. [O.E. *hláf-mæsse*, *hlámmæsse*—*hláf*, loaf, *mæsse*, feast.]

lammer, *lăm′ər, n.* (*Scot.*) amber. [Fr. *l'ambre*, the amber.]

lammergeier, lammergeyer, *lam′ər-gī-ər, n.* the great bearded vulture of southern Europe, &c. [Ger. *lämmergeier*—*lämmer*, lambs, *geier*, vulture.]

lammy, lammie, *lam′i, n.* a thick quilted jumper worn in cold weather by sailors. [Perh. lamb.]

lamp, *lamp, n.* a vessel for burning oil with a wick, and so giving a light: any structure containing a source of artificial light: any source of light: (*arch.* and *slang*) an eye.—*v.i.* (*Spens.*) to shine.—*v.t.* to illumine: to supply with lamps.—*ns.* lamp′ad, a lamp, candlestick, or torch; lamp′-adary, in the Greek Church, one who looks after the lamps and carries a lighted taper before the patriarch: a candelabrum; lampaded′romy,

lampadephor'ia (Gr. *lampadēdromiā*, *lampadē-phoriā*), an ancient Greek torch-race; **lamp'adist**, a runner in a torch-race; **lamp'adomancy** (Gr. *manteiā*, divination) divination by flame; **lamp'-black**, soot from a lamp, or from the burning of bodies rich in carbon (mineral oil, turpentine, tar, &c.) in a limited supply of air: a pigment made from it.—*v.t.* to blacken with lampblack.—*ns.* **lamp'-burner**, that part of a lamp from which the flame proceeds; **lamp'-chimney**, **lamp'-glass**, a glass funnel placed round the flame of a lamp; **lamp'-fly**, (*Browning*) perh. a glow-worm, or a firefly; **lamp'holder**, a socket for an electric bulb; **lamp'hole**, a shaft for lowering a lamp into a sewer; **lamp'-hour**, the energy required to maintain a lamp for an hour.—*adj.* **lamp'ing**, shining.—*ns.* **lamp'ion**, a coloured glass pot for illuminations; **lamp'light**, the light shed by a lamp or lamps; **lamp'lighter**, a person employed to light street-lamps: (*U.S.*) a spill or other means of lighting a lamp; **lamp'-post**, the pillar supporting a street-lamp; **lamp'-shade**, a structure for moderating or directing the light of a lamp; **lamp'-shell**, a brachiopod, esp. Terebratula or kindred genus, from its shell like an antique lamp.—**smell of the lamp**, to show signs of great elaboration or study. [Fr. *lampe*, and Gr. *lampas*, *-ados*—*lampein*, to shine.]

lamp, *lamp*, *v.i.* (*Scot.*) to run wild, to scamper: to go jauntily, stride along.

lampas, *lam'pas*, *n.* a material of silk and wool used in upholstery. [Fr.]

lampas, **lampasse**, *lam'pas*, *n.* (*Shak.*) a swelling of the roof of the mouth in horses. [Fr. *lampas*.]

lampern, *lam'pərn*, *n.* a river lamprey. [O.Fr. *lamprion*.]

lampoon, *lam-pōōn'*, *n.* a personal satire.—*v.t.* to assail with personal satire.—*ns.* **lampoon'er**; **lampoon'ery**. [O.Fr. *lampon*, perh. from a drinking-song with the refrain *lampons*, let us drink.]

lamprey, *lam'pri*, *n.* a genus (Petromyzon) of Cyclostomes that fix themselves to stones by their mouths :—*pl.* **lam'preys**. [O.Fr. *lamproie*—L.L. *lamprēda*, *lampetra*—explained as from L. *lambēre*, to lick, *petra*, rock, but found also as *naupreda*, *nauprida*.]

lamprophyre, *lam'prō-fīr*, *n.* a compact intrusive rock with phenocrysts of black mica, hornblende, &c., but not of felspar. — *adj.* **lamprophyric** (*-fir'ik*). [Gr. *lampros*, bright, and *-phyre* from *porphyry*.]

lana, *lä'nä*, *n.* genipap wood. [S. American word.]

lanate, *lā'nāt*, *adj.* woolly. [L. *lānātus*—*lāna*, wool.]

Lancasterian, *lang-kəs-tē'ri-ən*, *adj.* pertaining to Joseph *Lancaster* (1778–1838), or his method of teaching by means of monitors.

Lancastrian, *lang-kas'tri-ən*, *adj.* pertaining to *Lancaster*, or Lancashire, or the dukes or house of Lancaster.—*n.* a native of Lancaster or Lancashire: an adherent of the house of Lancaster.

lance, *läns*, *n.* a cavalry weapon with a long shaft, a spearhead, and a small flag: a similar weapon for other purposes: a surgeon's lancet: a blade in a cutting tool to sever the grain in advance of the main blade: the bearer of a lance.—*v.t.* (*obs.*) to shoot out, fling: to pierce, as with a lance: to open with a lancet.—*v.i.* (*obs.*) to rush, dart, fling oneself. — Also **launce**. — *ns.* **lance'-corporal** (formed on **lance prisado**, an acting corporal (*army slang*, **lance'-jack**); **lance'let**, the amphioxus ; lanc'er, a light cavalry soldier armed with a lance, or of a regiment formerly so armed: (*pl.*) a popular set of quadrilles, first in England about 1820, or its music ; **lance'-wood**, a wood of various kinds, strong and elastic, brought from Jamaica, Guiana, &c. [Fr.,—L. *lancea*; Gr. *lonchē*, a lance; cf. **launch**.]

lance. See **launce** (3).

lancegay, *läns'gā*, *n.* (*obs.*) a kind of spear. [O.Fr., —*lance*, a lance, *zagaye*, a pike; see **assagai**.]

lance-knight, **-knecht**, erroneous forms of **lands-knecht**.

lanceolate, **-d**, *län'si-ə-lāt*, *-id*, *adjs.* shaped like a

lance-head : lancet-shaped : (*bot.*) tapering toward both ends and two or three times as long as broad. —*adv.* **lan'ceolately**. [L. *lanceolātus*—*lanceola*, dim. of *lancea*.]

lance prisado, *läns pri-zä'dō*, **prisade**, *pri-zäd'*, **pesade**, *pi-zäd'*, **speisade**, *spē-zäd'*, *n.* (*obs.*) a lance-corporal. [It. *lancia spezzata*, broken lance, as if meaning an experienced soldier.]

lancet, *län'sit*, *n.* a surgical instrument used for opening veins, abscesses, &c.: a lancet window: a lancet arch.—**lancet arch**, high and narrow pointed arch ; **lancet window**, a tall, narrow, acutely arched window. [O.Fr. *lancette*, dim. of **lance** ; see **lance**.]

lancinate, *län'sin-āt*, *v.t.* to lacerate : to pierce.— *adj.* **lan'cinating**, (of pain) shooting, darting.—*n.* **lancina'tion**, sharp, shooting pain. [L. *lan-cināre*, *-ātum*, to tear.]

land, *land*, *n.* the solid portion of the surface of the globe : a country : a district : a nation or people : a constituent part of an empire or federation : real estate : ground : soil : (*Scot.*) a group of dwellings or tenements under one roof and having a common entry.—*v.t.* to set on land or on shore : to set down : to deposit, drop, or plant : to cause to arrive : to bring ashore : to capture : to secure : to attach to one's interest : to earth (*up*) : to silt, to block with earth.—*v.i.* to come on land or on shore : to alight : to arrive, find oneself, end by being.—*adj.* of or on the land : land-dwelling : terrestrial.—*ns.* **land'-agent**, a person employed to let farms, collect rents, &c.: (esp. *U.S.*) an agent or broker for buying and selling of land ; **land'-army**, a body of women organised for farm-work in wartime ; **land'-breeze**, a breeze setting from the land towards the sea ; **land'-bridge**, (*geol.*) a connexion by land allowing terrestrial plants and animals to pass from one region to another ; **land'-crab**, any crab that lives much or chiefly on land.—*adj.* **land'ed**, possessing land or estates : consisting in or derived from land or real estate.—*ns.* **land'er**, one who lands : (*coll.*) a heavy blow ; **land'fall**, an approach to land after a journey by sea or air : the land so approached ; **land'-fish**, (*Shak.*) a fish on land, one who is more fish than man ; **land'-flood**, an overflowing of land by water : inundation ; **land'-force**, a military force serving on land ; **land'-girl**, a girl who does farm-work ; **land'-grabber**, one who acquires land by harsh and grasping means : one who is eager to occupy land from which others have been evicted ; **land'-grabbing** ; **land'-herd**, a herd of land animals ; **land'-holder**, a tenant or proprietor of land.—*adj.* **land'-holding**.—*ns.* **land'-hunger**, desire to possess land ; **land'ing**, disembarkation : a coming to ground : alighting : putting ashore : setting down : a place for getting on shore or upon the ground : the level part of a staircase between flights of steps or at the top.— *adj.* relating to the unloading of a vessel's cargo, or to disembarking, or to alighting from the air. —*ns.* **land'ing-carriage**, the wheeled structure on which an aeroplane runs when starting or landing ; **land'ing-craft**, a small, low, open vessel, or vessels, for landing troops and equipment on beaches ; **land'ing-field**, a field that allows aircraft to land and take-off safely ; **land'ing-gear**, wheels, floats, &c., of an aircraft used in alighting ; **land'ing-ground**, a piece of ground prepared for landing aircraft as required ; **land'ing-net**, a kind of scoop-net for landing a fish that has been hooked ; **land'ing-place**, a place for landing ; **land'ing-ship**, a ship whose forward part can be let down in order to put vehicles ashore ; **land'ing-stage**, a platform, fixed or floating, for landing passengers or goods ; **land'ing-strip**, a narrow hard-surfaced runway ; **land'-jobber**, a speculator in land ; **land'-jobbing** ; **land'lady**, a woman who has tenants or lodgers : the mistress of an inn : (*obs.*) a hostess ; **land'-law**, (usu. *pl.*) a law concerning property in land.—*adjs.* **land'less** ; **land'-locked**, almost or quite shut in by land : cut off from the sea.—*ns.* **land'lord**, a man who has tenants or lodgers : the master of an inn ; **land'lordism**, the authority, policy, behaviour, or united action of the land-owning class: the system of land-ownership; **land'-lubber,** (*naut.*; in contempt) a landsman. —*adj.* **land'lubberly.**—*ns.* **land'man,** a country-man: a landsman; **land'mark,** anything serving to mark the boundaries of land: any object on land that serves as a guide to seamen or others: any distinguishing characteristic; **land'-measure** a system of square measure used in the measure-ment of land; **land'-measuring,** determination of superficial extent of land; **land'-mine,** a mine laid on or near the surface of the ground, to explode when an enemy is over it: a large bomb dropped by parachute; **land'-owner,** one who owns land; **land'-ownership.**—*adj.* **land'-owning.**—*ns.* **land'-pilot,** (*Milt.*) one skilled in finding his way by land; **land'-pirate,** a highway robber: one who swindles sailors in port: (*obs.*) a piratical publisher; **land'-plane,** an aeroplane that rises from and alights on land; **land'rail,** the corn-crake; **land'-rat,** a rat properly so called, not a water-rat: a thief by land, distinguished from a pirate; **land'-reeve,** a land-steward's assistant; **land'-roll,** a clod-crusher; **land'-scrip,** (*U.S.*) negotiable government certificate entitling to acquisition of public land; **land'-shark,** a land-grabber: one who plunders sailors on shore: (*U.S.*) a lean breed of hog; **land'-ship,** a land vehicle having certain properties of a ship—e.g. a tank; **land'skip** (same as **landscape**); **land'-slide,** (esp. *U.S.*) a landslip: a great transference of votes; **land'slip,** a fall of land or rock from a hillside or cliff: a portion so fallen; **lands'man,** one who lives or serves on land: one inexperienced in seafaring; **land'-spring,** a shallow intermittent spring; **land'-steward,** a person who manages a landed estate; **land'-survey'ing,** measurement and mapping of land; **land'-survey'or; land'-tax,** a tax upon land; **land'-val'ue,** (usu. in *pl.*) the economic value of land, a basis of taxation; **land'-waiter,** a custom-house officer who attends on the landing of goods from ships.—*advs.* **land'ward, -s,** towards the land: (*Scot.*) in the country. —*adj.* **land'ward,** lying toward the land: inland: (*Scot.*) rural.—*n.* **land'wind,** a wind blowing off the land.—**Land League,** an association founded in Ireland by Michael Davitt in 1879, and organised by C. S. Parnell, to procure reduction of rents and to promote peasant-proprietorship—condemned as an illegal conspiracy in 1881; **landed interest,** the combined interest of the land-owning class in a community. [O.E. *land*; Du., Ger. *land*.]

land, *land, n.* (*obs.*) Same as **laund.**

land, *land, n.* and *interj.* an American euphemism for **lord.**

landamman(n), *land'am-an* (Ger. *länt'äm-än*), *n.* the chief magistrate in some Swiss cantons. [Ger. *landammann*—*land,* land, and *amtmann,* bailiff—*amt,* office, and *mann,* man.]

landau, *land'daw, n.* a carriage with folding top. —*n.* **landaulet'**, **-ette'**, a motor-car whose en-closed part can be uncovered: a small landau. [*Landau* in Germany, where it is said to have been first made.]

landdamne, *land-dam', v.t.* (*Shak.*) said to mean to abuse with violence (perh. a misprint for *lam-damn* or *lame-damn*).

landdrost, *land'drōst, n.* (*S.Afr.*) a district magis-trate or sheriff. [Du.—*land,* land, *drost,* a bailiff.]

lande, *län'd, n.* a heathy plain or sandy tract (now forested) along the coast in S.W. France. [Fr.]

landgrave, *land'grāv, n.* a German count with jurisdiction over a territory: later a mere title:— *fem.* **landgravine** (*land'grə-vēn*).—*n.* **landgrā'-viate,** the territory of a landgrave. [Ger. *land-graf*—*land,* land, *graf,* count.]

ländler, *lent'lər, n.* a South German dance, or its tune, like a slow waltz. [Ger.,—'*s Landl,* a nick-name for Upper Austria.]

land-louper, *land'lowp-ər,* **land-loper,** *-lōp-ər, n.* a vagabond or vagrant. [Du. *landlooper*—*land,* land, *loopen,* to ramble; cf. Ger. *landläufer.*]

landscape, *land'skāp, n.* the appearance of that portion of land which the eye can view at once: the aspect of a country, or a picture representing

it: the painting of such pictures.—*ns.* **land'scape-gar'dening,** the art of laying out grounds so as to produce the effect of a picturesque landscape; **land'scape-mar'ble,** a limestone with dendritic markings; **land'scape-paint'er, land'scapist,** a painter of landscapes; **land'scape-paint'ing.** [Du. *landschap,* from *land* and *-schap,* suffix= *-ship.*]

landsknecht, *länts'knehht, n.* a mercenary foot-soldier of the 17th or 18th century. [Ger.,—*lands,* gen. of *land,* country, *knecht,* servant, soldier.]

Landsmaal, -mål, *läns'mawl, n.* a literary language based on Norwegian dialects by Ivar Aasen (1850), now called Nynorsk, new Norse. [Norw.,—*land,* land, *maal,* speech.]

Landsting, Landsthing, *läns'ting, n.* the upper house of the Danish Rigsdag or parliament: a Swedish provincial council. [Dan. and Sw.— *land,* land, *t(h)ing,* parliament.]

Landsturm, *länt'shtöörm, n.* a general levy in time of national emergency: the force so called out. [Ger.,—*land,* land, *sturm,* alarm.]

Landtag, *länt'tähh, n.* the legislative assembly of a German state or land: the Diet of the Holy Roman Empire, or of the German Federation: formerly the provincial assembly of Bohemia or Moravia. [Ger.,—*land,* country, *tag,* diet, day.]

Landwehr, *länt'vär, n.* an army reserve. [Ger.,— *land,* land, *wehr,* defence.]

lane, *län, n.* a narrow passage or road: a narrow street: a passage through a crowd or among obstructions: a channel: (*Scot.*) a sluggish stream: a prescribed course.—**Red Lane,** the throat, gullet. [O.E. *lane, lone.*]

lane, *län,* a Scottish form of **lone.**—**my lane, his lane,** &c., alone.

lang, a Scottish form of **long.**—*adv.* **lang'syne', lang syne,** long ago.—*n.* time long past.

langaha, *läng-gä'hä, n.* a Madagascan wood-snake, with a long flexible snout. [Perh. Malagasy.]

Langobard, *lang'gō-bärd.* See **Lombard.**

langouste, *län°-gōost', n.* the spiny lobster. [Fr.]

langrage, langridge, *lang'grij, n.* shot consisting of a canister containing irregular pieces of iron, formerly used to damage sails and rigging.—Also (*obs.*) **langrel** (*lang'grəl*). [Origin unknown.]

Langshan, *lang'shan, n.* a small black Chinese hen. [From a place near Shanghai.]

langspel, langspiel, *läng'späl, -spēl, n.* an old Shetland cithern. [Norw. *langspill*—*lang,* long, *spill,* play, instrument.]

language, *lang'gwij, n.* human speech: a variety of speech or body of words and idioms, esp. that of a nation: mode of expression: diction: any manner of expressing thought: a national branch of the Hospitallers.—*v.t.* to express in language.— *adjs.* **lang'uaged,** skilled or rich in, endowed with, having, language; **lang'uageless,** (*Shak.*) speech-less, silent. — **dead language,** one no longer spoken, as opp. to **living language.** [Fr. *langage* —*langue*—L. *lingua,* the tongue.]

langued, *langd, adj.* (*her.*) having a tongue (of this or that tincture). [Fr. *langue*—L. *lingua,* tongue.]

Langue d'oc, *län°g-dok, n.* collective name for the Romance dialects of southern France—the tongue of the troubadours, often used as synonymous with Provençal, one of its chief branches. The name itself survived in the province *Languedoc,* giving name to a class of wines.—*adj.* **Langue-docian** (*lang-gə-dō'shi-ən*). — *n.* **Langue d'oil** (*län°g-do-ēl, -doil*), also **Langue d'oui** (*-dwē*), the Romance dialect of northern France, the language of the trouvères, the main element in modern French. [O.Fr. *langue*—L. *lingua,* tongue; *de,* of; Prov. *oc,* yes—L. *hōc,* this; O.Fr. *oil, oui,* yes—L. *hōc illud,* this (is) that, yes.]

languet, languette, *lang'gwet, -get, -get', n.* a tongue-like object or part. [Fr. *languette,* dim. of *langue,* tongue.]

languid, *lang'gwid, adj.* slack: flagging: inert: listless: faint: relaxed: spiritless.—*adj.* **lan-guescent** (*-gwes'ənt*), growing languid. — *adv.* **lang'uidly.**—*n.* **lang'uidness.** [L. *languidus*— *languēre,* to be weak.]

languish, *lang'gwish, v.i.* to become or be languid,

inert, depressed: to lose strength and animation: to pine: to flag, droop: to look languishingly.—*n.* (*Shak.*) languishing: languishment.—*adj.* **lang′-uished,** sunken in languor.—*ns.* **lang′uisher; lang′uishing.**—*adj.* expressive of languor, or merely sentimental emotion: lingering.—*adv.* **lang′uishingly.**—*n.* **lang′uishment,** the act or state of languishing: tenderness of look. [Fr. *languiss-* (serving as part. stem of *languir*)—L. *languēscĕre*—*languēre,* to be faint.]

languor, *lang′g(w)ər, n.* (*obs.*) affliction: pining: languidness: listlessness: lassitude: dreamy inertia: tender softness.—*adj.* **lang′uorous,** full of or expressing languor: languishing. [L. *languor, -ōris.*]

langur, *lung-gōōr′, n.* the entellus monkey or other of its genus. [Hind. *langūr.*]

laniary, *lā′ni-ər-i, adj.* fitted for tearing. [L. *laniārius,* of a butcher—*lanius,* a butcher.]

laniferous, *lan-if′ər-əs, adj.* wool-bearing.—Also **lanigerous** (*-ij′*). [L. *lānifer, lāniger—lāna,* wool, *ferre, gerĕre,* to bear.]

lank, *langk, adj.* flabby: drooping: flaccid: limp: thin: (of hair) straight and flat.—*v.t.* and *v.i.* (*Shak.*) to make or become lank.—*n.* **lank′iness.**—*adv.* **lank′ly.**—*n.* **lank′ness.**—*adj.* **lank′y,** lean, tall, and ungainly: long and limp. [O.E. *hlanc.*]

lanner, *lan′ər, n.* a kind of falcon, esp. the female.—*n.* **lann′aret,** the male lanner. [Fr. *lanier,* possibly—L. *laniārius,* tearing, or from *lānārius,* a weaver (a mediaeval term of reproach).]

lanolin(e), *lan′ō-lēn, -lin, n.* fat from wool, a mixture of palmitate, oleate, and stearate of cholesterol. [L. *lāna,* wool, *oleum,* oil.]

lansquenet, *läns′kə-net, n.* a landsknecht: a card game. [Fr.,—Ger. *landsknecht.*]

lant, *lant, n.* stale urine, used in wool-scouring. [O.E. and O.N. *hland.*]

lant, *lant.* Same as **launce** (3).

Lantana, *lan-tā′nä,* or *-tä′, n.* a showy-flowered genus of shrubs of the vervain family.

lanterloo, *lant′ər-lōō, n.* a card game, ancestral form of loo. [Fr. *lanturlu* (a meaningless refrain).]

lantern, *lant′ərn, n.* a case for holding or carrying a light: the light-chamber of a lighthouse: a magic lantern: an open structure like a lantern, esp. one surmounting a building, giving light and air.—*v.t.* to furnish with a lantern.—*ns.* **lant′ern-fly,** any insect of the homopterous family Fulgoridae, with a lantern-like proboscis, formerly thought to give out light; **lant′ernist,** one who works a magic lantern.—*adj.* **lan′tern-jawed,** hollow-faced.—*n.pl.* **lant′ern-jaws,** thin long jaws.—*n.* **lant′ern-slide,** a transparent slip with a picture to be projected by a magic lantern.—**lantern of the dead,** a lighted tower, once common in French cemeteries. [Fr. *lanterne*—L. *lanterna*—Gr. *lamptēr—lampein,* to give light.]

lanthanum, *lan′thə-nəm, n.* the metallic element of atomic number 57 (La). [Gr. *lanthanein,* to escape notice, because it lay hid in rare minerals till 1839.]

lanthorn, an obs. spelling of **lantern,** based on folk-etymology, from the use of horn for the sides of lanterns.

lantskip, *lant′skip, n.* (*Milt.*). Same as **landscape.**

lanugo, *lan-ū′gō, n.* down: an embryonic woolly coat of hair.—*adjs.* **lanū′ginose** (*-jin-*), **lanū′-ginous,** downy: covered with fine soft hair. [L. *lānūgō, -inis,* down—*lāna,* wool.]

lanx, *langks, n.* (*ant.*) a platter—*pl.* **lances** (*lan′sēz*). [L.]

lanyard, laniard, *lan′yərd, n.* (*naut.*) a short rope used as a fastening or handle: a cord for hanging a knife, whistle, or the like about the neck. [Fr. *lanière,* origin doubtful; confused with **yard.**]

lanzknecht, an erroneous form of **landsknecht** (as if from Ger. *lanze,* lance).

Laodicean, *lā-od-i-sē′ən, adj.* lukewarm in religion, like the Christians of *Laodicea* (Rev. iii. 14-16).—*n.* **Laodicē′anism.** [Gr. *Lāodikeia,* Laodicea.]

lap, *lap, v.t.* to scoop up with the tongue: (*fig.*) to take in greedily or readily: to wash or flow against.—*v.i.* to drink by licking up: to make a sound or movement as of lapping: (*pr.p.* **lapp′ing;** *pa.t.* and *pa.p.* **lapped**).—*n.* a motion or sound of lapping: that which may be lapped: thin liquor.—*n.* and *adj.* **lapp′ing.** [O.E. *lapian;* L.G. *lappen;* L. *lambĕre,* to lick; Gr. *laptein.*]

lap, *lap, n.* a flap: a lobe: a fold: part of a garment disposed to hold or catch: the fold of the clothes and body of a person sitting: a round, as of a racecourse, or of anything coiled: an overlap: amount of overlap (in slating, over the next but one): in a steam-engine, the distance the valve has to move from mid position to open the steam or exhaust port: in euchre, &c., points carried over to another game: a polishing disk, cylinder, or the like.—*v.t.* to wrap, enfold, surround: to lay overlappingly: to polish with a lap: to unite accurately: to be a lap ahead of: to traverse as a lap or in laps: to hold in the lap.—*v.i.* to lie with an overlap: to overlap: to extend beyond some limit.—*ns.* **lap′-board,** a flat wide board resting on the lap, used by tailors and seamstresses; **lap′-dog,** a small dog fondled in the lap: a pet dog; **lap′ful.**—*adj.* **lap′-joint′ed,** having joints formed by overlapping edges.—*ns.* **lapp′er,** one who wraps or folds: a machine that compacts scutched cotton into a fleece upon a roller called a **lap-roller.**—*n.* and *adj.* **lapp′ing.**—*ns.* **lap′-stone,** a stone held in the lap to hammer leather on; **lap′-streak,** a clinker-built boat.—Also *adj.*—*n.* **lap′-work,** work containing lap-joints. [O.E. *læppa,* a loosely hanging part; Ger. *lappen,* a rag.]

lap, *lap,* Scots *pa.t.* of **leap.**

laparotomy, *lap-ə-rot′ə-mi, n.* surgical cutting of the abdominal wall. [Gr. *laparā,* flank, *tomē,* cutting.]

lapel (*obs.* **lappel**), *la-, lə-pel′, n.* part of a coat folded back continuing the collar.—*adj.* **lapelled′.** [Dim. of **lap.**]

lapis, *lap′is, n.* a stone (the Latin word, used in certain phrases only, as *lapis philosophicus,* the philosophers' stone, *lapis ollaris,* potstone).—*adj.* **lapidār′ian,** pertaining to stones: inscribed on stones: learned in stones.—*ns.* **lap′idarist** (*-ə-rist*), a gem-cutter; **lap′idary** (*-ə-ri*), a cutter of stones, esp. gem-stones: (*obs.*) a treatise on gems: an expert in gems.—*adj.* pertaining to stones: dwelling in stone-heaps (as a kind of bee): inscribed on stone: suitable for inscription.—*v.t.* **lap′idate,** (*rare*) to pelt with stones.—*n.* **lapidā′tion,** stoning.—*adj.* **lapid′eous,** stony.—*n.* **lapidesc′ence.**—*adj.* **lapidesc′ent,** becoming stone: petrifying.—*adjs.* **lapidic′olous** (L. *colĕre,* to inhabit), living under or among stones; **lapidif′ic.**—*n.* **lapidificā′-tion.**—*v.t.* and *v.i.* **lapid′ify,** to turn into stone:—*pr.p.* **lapid′ifying;** *pa.t.* and *pa.p.* **lapid′ified.**—*n.pl.* **lapilli** (*lä-pil′lē*), small fragments (in size from a pea to a walnut) of lava ejected from a volcano (*pl.* of It. *lapil′lo;* also of L. *lapill′us*).—*adj.* **lapill′iform.**—*n.* **lap′is-laz′ūlī,** a beautiful stone consisting of calcite and other minerals coloured ultramarine by lazurite, hauyne, and sodalite, commonly spangled with iron pyrites (see **azure, lazulite, lazurite**).—**lapis-lazuli blue,** a deep blue, sometimes veined with gold, used in decoration and in porcelain; **lapis-lazuli ware,** a pebble ware veined with gold upon blue. [L. *lapis, -idis,* a stone.]

lapje, *lap′i, n.* (*S.Afr.*) a rag or clout. [Du. *lap,* rag, patch.]

Lapp, *lap,* **Lap′lander,** *-ləndər, ns.* a native or inhabitant of Lapland: one of the race or people inhabiting Lapland.—*adjs.* **Lapp, Lap′landish; Lapp′ish.**—*n.* the language of the Lapps.

lapper, a Scots form of **lopper.**

lappet, *lap′it, n.* a little lap or flap.—*adj.* **lapp′eted.**—*ns.* **lapp′et-head,** a head-dress with lappets; **lapp′et-moth,** a moth of the Lasiocampidae whose caterpillar has lappets on its sides. [Dim. of **lap.**]

lapse, *laps, v.i.* to slip or glide: to pass by degrees: to fall away by cessation or relaxation of effort or cause: to fall from the faith: to fail in virtue or duty: to pass into disuse: to pass or fail owing to some omission or non-fulfilment: to become void.—*v.t.* (*Shak.*) to catch in a lapse (perh. with associations of *lap* or *latch*).—*n.* a slip: a gliding: passage (of time): a falling away: a failure (in virtue, attention, memory, &c.): a vertical gradient as of atmospheric temperature.—*adjs.* **laps′able,** liable to lapse; **lapsed,** having slipped or passed or been let slip: fallen away (esp. in the early Christian Church, from the faith). [L. *lāpsāre,* to slip, *lāpsus,* a slip—*lābī, lāpsus,* to slip.]

Laputa, *lā-pū′tä, n.* a flying island in Swift's *Gulliver's Travels* inhabited by ridiculous projectors.—*ns.* **Lapu′tan, Lapu′tian** (-*shən*), an inhabitant of Laputa.—*adjs.* absurd: chimerical.

lapwing, *lap′wing, n.* a bird of the plover family, the peewit. [M.E. *lappewinke*—O.E. *læpewince, hléapewince, hléapewince*; modified by folketymology.]

lar, *lär, n.* the god of a house (orig. prob. a field god):—*pl.* **lares** (*lā′rēz*; L. *lä′rās*). [L. *lar.*]

larboard, *lär′bōrd, lä′bərd, n.* and *adj.* (*obs.*) port or left. [M.E. *laddeborde,* influenced by **star-board**; origin unknown.]

larceny, *lär′sə-ni, n.* the legal term in England and Ireland for stealing: theft.—*ns.* **lar′cener, lar′-cenist,** a thief.—*adj.* **lar′cenous.**—*adv.* **lar′-cenously.**—**grand larceny,** in England, larceny of property of the value of one shilling or more; **petty larceny,** larceny of property less in value than one shilling; **simple larceny,** as opposed to **compound larceny,** is larceny uncombined with aggravating circumstances. [O.Fr. *larrecin* (Fr. *larcin*)—L. *latrōcinium*—*latrō,* a robber.]

larch, *lärch, n.* any tree of the coniferous genus Larix, distinguished from cedar by the deciduous leaves.—*adj.* (*rare*) **larch′en.** [Ger. *lärche*—L. *larix, -īcis.*]

lard, *lärd, n.* the rendered fat of the hog.—*v.t.* to smear or enrich with lard: to stuff with bacon or pork: to fatten: to mix with anything: to stuff or load: to interlard, interpenetrate: to garnish, strew.—*v.i.* (*Shak.*) to be intimately mixed.—*adj.* **lardā′ceous.** — *n.* **lar′don, lardoon′,** a strip of bacon used for larding.—*adj.* **lar′dy.** [O.Fr.,—L. *lāridum, lārdum;* cf. Gr. *lārīnos,* fat, *lāros,* pleasant to taste.]

lardalite. See **laurdalite.**

larder, *lärd′ər, n.* a place where food is kept: stock of provisions.—*n.* **lard′erer,** one in charge of a larder. [O.Fr. *lardier,* bacon-tub; see **lard.**]

lare, *lär,* a Northern form of **lore**; also a Spenserian form of **lair** (pasture).

large, *lärj, adj.* great in size: extensive: bulky: broad: copious: abundant: generous: magnanimous: loftily affected or pretentious: in a great way: (*obs.*) diffuse: (*Shak.,* of language) free, licentious: (*naut.,* of the wind) having a favouring component.—*adv.* (*naut.*) before the wind: ostentatiously.—*n.* (*mus.*) an obsolete note, equal to two (or in 'perfect' time three) longs.—*adjs.* **large′-hand′ed,** having large hands: (*Shak.*) grasping: profuse: **large′-heart′ed,** having a large heart: of liberal disposition or comprehensive sympathies: generous.—*adv.* **large′ly,** in a large manner: in great measure.—*adj.* **large′-mind′ed,** magnanimous: characterised by breadth of view.—*n.* **large′ness.**—*adj.* **larg′ish,** fairly large, rather big.—**at large,** at liberty: at random: in general: in full: (*U.S.*) representing the whole area, not a division; **large paper edition,** a special edition with wider margins. [Fr.,—L. *largus,* abounding.]

largess, largesse, *lärj′es, n.* a bestowal or distribution of gifts.—*n.* **largition** (*lär-jish′ən*), giving of largess. [Fr. *largesse* and L. *largītiō, -ōnis*—*largus.*]

largo, *lär′gō, adj.* (*mus.*) broad and slow.—Also *adv.*—*n.* a movement to be so performed.—*adj.* **larghet′to,** somewhat slow: not so slow as largo.—*n.* a somewhat slow movement. [It.,—L. *largus.*]

lariat, *lar′i-ət, n.* a picketing rope, a lasso. [Sp. *la,* the, *reata,* picketing rope.]

lark, *lärk, n.* a well-known bird (Alauda) that flies high as it sings: extended to various similar birds.—*v.i.* to catch larks.—*adj.* **lark′-heeled,** having a long hind-claw.—*ns.* **lark′ing-glass,** an instrument with mirrors used by bird-catchers to dazzle larks; **lark's′-heel,** the Indian cress: the larkspur; **lark′spur,** any plant of the genus Delphinium,

from the spurred flowers. [M.E. *laverock*—O.E. *lǽwerce, lǽwerce*; Ger. *lerche.*]

lark, *lärk, n.* a frolic.—*v.i.* to frolic.—*ns.* **lark′er; lark′iness.**—*adjs.* **lark′ish; lar′ky** (*coll.*). [Perh. from the preceding (cf. **skylarking**); some connect it with **lake** (4).]

larmier, *lär′mi-ər, n.* (*archit.*) a corona or other course serving as a dripstone: (*zool.*) a tear-pit. [Fr.,—*larme*—L. *lacrima,* a tear.]

larrikin, *lar′i-kin, n.* (*Austr.*) a rough or hooligan.—Also *adj.*—*n.* **larr′ikinism.** [Origin doubtful.]

larrup, *lar′əp, v.t.* (*coll.*) to flog, thrash. [Cf. Du. *larpen,* thresh with flails.]

larum, *lar′əm, n.* alarm: a noise giving notice of danger.—*n.* **lar′um-bell.** [alarm.]

Larus, *lā′rəs, lär′əs, n.* the principal genus of the gull family (Laridae, *lar′i-dē*). — *adj.* **lar′oid.** [L.,—Gr. *lāros,* a bird, prob. a gull.]

larva, *lär′vä, n.* a spectre or ghost: an animal in an immature but active state markedly different from the adult, e.g. a caterpillar:—*pl.* **larvae** (*lär′vē*; L. *-vī*).—*adjs.* **lar′val; lar′vate, -d,** clothed as with a mask; **larvici′dal,** destroying larvae.—*n.* **lar′vicide.**—*adjs.* **lar′viform;** **larvip′-arous,** giving birth to larvae. [L. *lārva, lārua,* a spectre, a mask.]

larvikite. See **laurvikite.**

larynx, *lar′ingks, n.* the upper part of the windpipe:—*pl.* **larynges** (*lar′in-jēs,* or *lar-in′jēs*) or **lar′ynxes.** — *adjs.* **laryngal** (*lar-ing′gl*), **lar-yngeal** (*lar-in′ji-əl*).—*n.* **laryngismus** (*-jiz′məs*), spasm of the larynx.—*adj.* **laryngitic** (*-jit′ik*).—*n.* **laryngitis** (*-jī′tis*), inflammation of the larynx. —*adj.* **laryngological** (*-ing-gə-loj′*).—*ns.* **laryn-gol′ogist; laryngology** (*-gol′ə-ji*), the science of the larynx; **laryngophony** (*-gof′*), the sound of the voice as heard through the stethoscope applied over the larynx; **laryng′oscope,** a mirror for examining the larynx and trachea.—*adj.* **laryngo-scop′ic.** —*ns.* **laryngos′copist; laryngos′copy; laryngot′omy,** the operation of cutting into the larynx. [Gr. *larynx, -yngos.*]

lascar, *las′kər, -kär,* or *las-kär′, n.* an Oriental (originally Indian) sailor or camp-follower. [Hind. and Pers. *lashkar,* army, or *lashkarī,* a soldier.]

lascivious, *la-siv′i-əs, adj.* wanton: inclining or tending to libidinousness.—*adv.* **lasciv′iously.**—*n.* **lasciv′iousness.** [L.L. *lascīviōsus*—L. *lascivus,* playful.]

laser, *lā′sər, n.* (*hist.*) silphium: (now) the juice of laserwort.—*ns.* **Laserpicium** (*las-ər-pish′i-əm*), a genus of umbelliferous perennial herbs of Europe, Asia, and North Africa; **laserwort** (*lās′ər-wurt*), any plant of the genus, esp. herb frankincense (L. *latifolium*): also applied to species of Ferula and Thapsia. [L. *lāser,* the juice of *lāserpīcium,* the silphium plant.]

lash, *lash, n.* the flexible part of a whip, or its terminal piece of whipcord: a scourge: an eyelash: a stroke with a whip or anything pliant: a sweep or flick: a stroke of satire.—*v.t.* to strike with, or as if with, a lash: to dash against: drive, urge, or work by blows of anything flexible, or figuratively: to whisk or flick with a sweeping movement: to secure with a rope or cord: to scourge with sarcasm or satire: (*obs.*) to lavish, squander.—*v.i.* to dash: to make a rapid sweeping movement or onset: to use the whip.—*ns.* **lash′er,** one who lashes or whips: a rope for binding one thing to another; **lash′ing,** act of whipping: a rope for making things fast: (Anglo-Irish, esp. in *pl.*) a great plenty of anything.—**lash out,** to kick out, fling out, hit out without restraint. [Perh. several different words, with possible connexions with **latch** and **lace.**]

lash, *lash, adj.* (*obs.*) slow, slack: soft: insipid.—*n.* **lash′er,** a weir: a waterfall from a weir: a pool below a weir. [M.E. *lasche,* slack—O.Fr. *lasche* (Fr. *lâche,* cowardly)—L. *laxus,* lax.]

lashkar, *lash′kär, n.* (*obs.*) a camp of Indian soldiers: a body of armed Indian tribesmen, a force. [Hind., army, camp; cf. **lascar.**]

Lasiocampidae, *laz-i-ō-kamp′i-dē,* or *lā-si-, n.pl.* a family of moths including eggers and lackeymoths. [Gr. *lasios,* woolly, *kampē,* a caterpillar.]

fāte, fär, ȧsk; *mē, hər* (her); *mīne; mōte; mūte; mōōn; dhen* (then)

lasket, *las'kit, n.* a loop at the foot of a sail, to fasten an extra sail. [Perh. **latchet.**]

lass, *lâs, n.* a girl: a sweetheart: (*Scot.*) a maid-servant.—*ns.* (dims.) **lassie** (*las'i*), the ordinary Scots word for a girl; **lass'ock.**—*adj.* **lass'lorn,** (*Shak.*) forsaken by one's mistress. [Origin obscure; the association with **lad** may be accidental.]

lassitude, *las'i-tūd, n.* faintness: weakness: weariness: languor. [L. *lassitūdo—lassus,* faint.]

lasso, *las'ō,* also *lă-sōō', n.* a long rope with a running noose for catching wild horses, &c.:—*pl.* **lass'o(e)s.**—*v.t.* to catch with the lasso:—*pr.p.* **lass'ōing** (or *-ōō'*); *pa.p.* **lassoed** (*las'od,* or *-ōōd'*). [S. Amer. pron. of Sp. *lazo*—L. *laqueus,* a noose.]

lassu, *losh'oo, n.* the slow movement of a csárdás. [Hung.]

last, *lâst, n.* a shoemaker's model of the foot on which boots and shoes are made or repaired.—*v.t.* to fit with a last.—*n.* **last'er,** one who fits the parts of shoes to lasts: a tool for doing so. [O.E. *lǽste,* last, *lást,* footprint.]

last, *lâst, v.i.* to continue, endure: to escape failure: remain fresh, unimpaired: to hold out: to survive.—*n.* lasting power or quality.—*n.* **last'er,** one who has staying power: a thing that keeps well.—*adj.* **last'ing,** enduring: durable.—*n.* **endurance.**—*adv.* **last'ingly.**—*n.* **last'ingness.**—**last out,** to last as long as or longer than: to last to the end or as long as is required. [O.E. *lǽstan,* to follow a track, keep on, suffice, last; see foregoing word.]

last, *lâst, n.* a load, cargo: a varying weight, generally about 4000 lb.—*n.* **last'age,** the lading of a ship: room for stowing goods in a ship: a duty formerly paid for the right of carrying goods, &c. [O.E. *hlǽst—hladan,* to lade; Ger. *last,* O.N. *hlass.*]

last, *lâst, adj.* latest: coming or remaining after all the others: final: immediately before the present: utmost: ending a series: most unlikely, least to be preferred.—Also *adv.*—*adv.* **last'ly,** in the last place, finally.—**at last,** in the end: after long delay; **breathe one's last,** to die; **die in the last ditch,** to fight to the bitter end; **first and last,** altogether; **last heir,** the person to whom lands escheat for want of other heirs; **last post** (*mil.*), second of two bugle-calls denoting the hour of retiring for the night: farewell bugle-call at military funerals; **last straw** (that breaks the camel's back), that beyond which there can be no possible endurance; **on one's last legs,** on the verge of utter failure or exhaustion; **put the last hand to,** to finish, put the finishing touch to; **the Last Day,** the Day of Judgment; to the **last,** to the end: till death. [O.E. *latost,* superl. of *lǽt,* slow, late.]

lat, *lât, n.* in India an isolated pillar. [Hind. *lāt.*]

Latakia, *lat-ä-kē'ä, n.* a Syrian tobacco from Latakia. [L. *Lāodicēa ad Mare,* Gr. *Lāodikeia,* named after Lāodikē, mother of Seleucus Nicator.]

latch, *lach, v.t.* (*Shak.*) probably to moisten, but possibly to fasten (next word).—*n.* (*Scot.*) a mire: a boggy water-channel. [**leach.**]

latch, *lach, n.* a door catch lifted from without by a lever or string: a light door-lock, opened from without by a key.—*v.t.* (*obs.*) to seize, take, receive.—*v.t.* and *v.i.* to fasten with a latch.—*ns.* **latch'key, latch'string,** a key, string, for opening a latched door.—**on the latch,** not locked, but to be opened by a latch. [O.E. *lǽccan,* to catch.]

latchet, *lach'it, n.* (*obs.*) a loop: a thong or lace. [O.Fr. *lachet,* a form of *lacet,* dim. of *laz*; see **lace.**]

late, *lāt, adj.* (*comp.* **lāt'er**; *superl.* **lāt'est**) slow, tardy: behindhand: coming, remaining, flowering, ripening, producing, &c., after the due, expected, or usual time: long delayed: far advanced towards the close: last in any place or character: deceased: departed: out of office: not long past.—Also *adv.*—*adj.* **lāt'ed,** (*Shak.*) belated.—*adv.* **late'ly,** recently.—*v.t.* and *v.i.* **lāt'en,** to make or grow late.—*n.* **late'ness.**—*adj.* and *adv.* **lāt'ish.**—**of late,** recently. [O.E. *lǽt,* slow; Du. *laat,* O.N. *latr,* Ger. *lass,* weary; L. *lassus,* tired.]

lateen, *lȧ-tēn', adj.* applied to a triangular sail, common in the Mediterranean, the Lake of Geneva, &c. [Fr. (*voile*) *latine*—L. *Latīnus,* Latin.]

La Tène, *lä ten, adj.* of a division of the Iron Age exemplified at *La Tène* near Neuchâtel, later than Hallstatt.

latent, *lā'tȧnt, adj.* hid: concealed: not visible or apparent: dormant: undeveloped, but capable of development.—*ns.* **lā'tence, lā'tency.**—*adv.* **lā'tently.**—*n.* **lātesc'ence.**—*adj.* **lātesc'ent,** becoming latent.—**latent heat** (see **heat**); **latent period,** the time between stimulus and reaction: that between contracting a disease and appearance of symptoms. [L. *latēns, -ēntis,* pr.p. of *latēre,* to lie hid; Gr. *lanthanein,* to be hidden.]

lateral, *lat'ȧ-rȧl, adj.* belonging to the side.—*n.* **laterality** (*-ral'i-ti*).—*adv.* **lat'erally.** — **lateral line,** in fishes, a line along the side of the body, marking the position of a sensory organ. [L. *laterālis—latus, latĕris,* a side.]

Lateran, *lat'ȧ-rȧn, adj.* pertaining to the Church of St John Lateran at Rome, the Pope's cathedral church, on the site of the splendid palace or basilica of Plautius Lateranus (executed A.D. 66). —**Lateran Councils,** five general councils of the Western Church, held in the Lateran basilica (1123, 1139, 1179, 1215, and 1512-17), regarded by Roman Catholics as oecumenical; **Lateran Treaty,** restored the papal state (1929). [L. *Laterānus.*]

laterigrade, *lat'ȧ-ri-grād, adj.* running sideways, like a crab. [L. *latus, -eris,* side, *gradus,* step.]

laterite, *lat'ȧ-rīt, n.* a clay formed by weathering of rocks in a tropical climate, composed chiefly of iron and aluminium hydroxides.—*n.* **laterīsā'tion,** conversion into laterite. [L. *later, latĕris,* a brick.]

lateritious, *lat-ȧ-rish'ȧs, adj.* brick-red. [L. *laterīcius—later, latĕris,* a brick.]

latewake, *lāt'wāk, n.* a mistaken form of **lykewake.**

latex, *lā'teks, n.* (*bot.*) the milky juice of plants.—*adj.* **laticiferous** (*lat-i-sif'ȧ-rȧs*), containing or conveying latex. [L. *lātex, lāticis.*]

lath, *lȧth, n.* a thin slip of wood: a substitute for such a slip, used in slating, plastering, &c.: anything long and thin: (*pl.* **laths,** *lȧdhz,* **laths**).—*v.t.* to cover with laths.—*adj.* **lathen** (*lȧth'ȧn*).—*ns.* **lath'ing,** the act or process of covering with laths: a covering of laths; **lath'-splitter,** one who splits wood into laths.—*adj.* **lath'y,** like a lath.—**dagger of lath,** the Vice's weapon in the old morality plays. [O.E. *lætt.*]

lathe, *lādh, n.* a machine for turning and shaping articles of wood, metal, &c.: the swing-frame of a loom carrying the reed for separating the warp threads and beating up the weft. [Origin doubtful.]

lathe, *lādh, n.* a division of Kent. [O.E. *lǽth,* a district; O.N. *lāth,* landed property.]

lather, *lȧdh'ȧr, n.* a foam made with water and soap: froth from sweat.—*v.t.* to spread over with lather.—*v.i.* to form a lather.—*adj.* **lath'ery.** [O.E. *lēathor*; O.N. *lauthr.*]

lathi, lathee, *lȧ-tē', n.* a heavy stick. [Hind. *lāthī.*]

Lathyrus, *lath'i-rȧs, n.* the sweet-pea genus of Papilionaceae.—*n.* **lath'yrism,** a disease with stiffness and paralysis of the legs among eaters of chickling, but apparently due to admixture of seeds of cultivated vetch. [L.,—Gr. *lathyros,* the chickling vetch.]

laticlave, *lat'i-klāv, n.* a broad stripe on a Roman senator's tunic. [L. *lātus,* broad, *clāvus,* a stripe.]

latifundia, *lat-i-fun'di-ä, n.pl.* great landed estates.—Also in *sing.* **latifun'dium,** and as It. *pl.* **latifondi** (*lȧ-tē-fon'dē*). [Pl. of L. *lātifundium—lātus,* wide, *fundus,* an estate.]

Latin, *lat'in, adj.* pertaining to ancient Latium (esp. Rome) or its inhabitants, or its language, or to those languages that are descended from Latin, or to the peoples speaking them: written or spoken in Latin: Roman Catholic.—*n.* an inhabitant of ancient Latium: the language of ancient Latium, and esp. of Rome: a speaker of a language derived from ancient Latin: a Roman Catholic.—*adj.* **Latian** (*lā'shyȧn, -shȧn*), of Latium. —*n.* **Lat'iner,** one who knows Latin: (*obs.*) an interpreter.—*v.t.* **Lat′inise,** to turn into or make Latin or like to Latin.—*v.i.* to use Latin idioms or derivatives.—*ns.* **Lat′inism,** a Latin idiom: use or inclination towards use of Latin idioms, words, or ways; **Lat′inist,** one skilled in Latin; **Latin′ity,** the quality of one's Latin.—**classical Latin,** the Latin of the writers who flourished from about 75 B.C. to about A.D. 200; **dog Latin,** barbarous Latin; **Late Latin,** the Latin written by authors between A.D. 200 and (*circ.*) 600; **Latin America,** those parts of America where Spanish, Portuguese, and French are spoken; **Latin Church,** the Church that uses Latin and recognises the primacy of Rome—the Roman Catholic Church; **Latin cross,** an upright cross with the lowest limb longest; **Latin Empire,** that portion of the Byzantine Empire seized in 1204 by the Crusaders (French and Venetian), and overthrown by the Greeks in 1261; **Latin kingdom,** the Christian kingdom of Jerusalem ruled by French or Latin kings, and lasting from 1099 to 1187; **Latin Quarter,** the educational and students' quarter of Paris around the Sorbonne (where Latin was spoken in the Middle Ages; Fr. *quartier latin*), famous for its unconventional way of life; **Latin Union,** a monetary union (1865-1926) of France, Belgium, Italy, and Switzerland, with Greece from 1868; **Low Latin,** Mediaeval, or Late and Mediaeval Latin; **Middle or Mediaeval Latin,** the Latin of the middle age between A.D. 600 and 1500; **New, Modern, Latin,** Latin as written between 1500 and the present time, mostly used as a scientific medium; **thieves' Latin,** thieves' cant. [L. *Latīnus,* belonging to *Latium,* the district round Rome.]

latirostral, *lat-i-ros′trəl, adj.* broad-billed.—Also **latiros′trate.** [L. *lātus,* broad, *rōstrum,* beak.]

latiseptate, *lat-i-sep′tāt, adj.* having a broad partition. [L. *lātus,* broad, *saeptum,* a fence (used in pl.).]

latitant, *lat′i-tənt, adj.* lurking: lying in wait: hibernating: dormant.—*n.* **lat′itancy.**—*ns.* **lat′itat,** a writ based on the supposition that the person summoned is in hiding; **latitā′tion.** [L. *latitāre, -ātum* (3rd pers. sing. *latitat*), freq. of *latēre,* to be in hiding.]

latitude, *lat′i-tūd, n.* (now chiefly playful) width: a wide extent: range: scope: allowance: breadth in interpretation: extent of signification: freedom from restraint: laxity: (*geog.*) angular distance from the equator: a place of specified angular distance from the equator: (*astron.*) angular distance from the ecliptic (*celestial latitude*).—*adjs.* **latitūd′inal,** pertaining to latitude: in the direction of latitude; **latitūdinā′rian,** broad or liberal, esp. in religious belief: lax.—*n.* a member of a school of liberal and philosophical theologians within the English Church in the later half of the 17th century: one who regards specific creeds, methods of church government, &c., with indifference.—*n.* **latitūdinā′rianism.**—*adj.* **latitūd′inous,** broad, wide, esp. in interpretation. [L. *lātitūdō, -inis—lātus,* broad.]

latration, *lə-trā′shən, n.* barking.—*adj.* **latrant** (*lā′trənt*). [L. *latrāre, -ātum,* to bark.]

la trenise. See **trenise.**

latria, *lā-trī′ä, n.* the kind of supreme worship due to God alone—distinguished from *dulia* and *hyperdulia.* [Gr. *latreiā—latreuein,* to serve.]

latrine, *lə-trēn′, n.* a privy, esp. in barracks, factories, hospitals, &c. [L. *lātrīna—lavātrīna—lavāre,* to wash.]

latrocinium, *lat-rō-sin′i-əm, n.* highway-robbery: Pope Leo I.'s name for the 'Robber-Council' at Ephesus in 449, which upheld Eutychianism. [L. *latrōcinium,* robbery.]

latron, *lā′tron, n.* a robber. [L. *latrō, -ōnis.*]

latten, *lat′ən, n.* brass or similar alloy in former use: tin-plate: metal in thin plates. [O.Fr. *laton* (Fr. *laiton*); of Gmc. origin; cf. **lath.**]

latter, *lat′ər, adj.* later: coming or existing after: second-mentioned of two: modern: recent: (*Shak.*) last.—*adjs.* **latt′er-born,** (*Shak.*) younger; **latt′er-day,** modern: recent.—*adv.* **latt′erly,** towards the latter end: of late.—*ns.* **latt′ermath,**

aftermath; **latt′er-mint,** (*Keats*) apparently a late kind of mint.—*adj.* **latt′ermost,** last (O.E. *lætemest*).—*n.* **latt′er-wit,** (*U.S.*) a witty thought after the occasion has passed.—**Latter-day Saint,** a Mormon; **latter end,** the final part: the end of life. [O.E. *lætra,* compar. of *læt,* slow, late.]

lattice, *lat′is, n.* a network of crossed laths or bars, called also **latt′ice-work:** anything of like pattern: a window with lozenge-shaped panes set in lead: a space-lattice.—*v.t.* to form into open work: to furnish with a lattice.—*ns.* **latt′ice-bridge,** a bridge of lattice-girders; **latt′ice-gird′er,** a girder composed of upper and lower members joined by a web of crossing diagonal bars; **latt′ice-leaf,** the lace-leaf or ouvirandra (*Aponogeton fenestrale*), a water-plant of Madagascar with leaves like open lattice-work.—**red lattice,** (*Shak.*) the sign of an ale-house. [Fr. *lattis—latte,* a lath.]

latus rectum, *lā′təs rek′təm* (L. *lā′toos rek′toom*), *n.* a focal chord parallel to the directrix of a conic. [L. *lātus rectum,* right or perpendicular side.]

Latvian, *lat′vi-ən, adj.* Lettish.—*n.* a native or citizen of Latvia or Lettland. [Lettish *Latvija,* Latvia, Lettland.]

lauch, *lawhh,* a Scots form of **law** (*Scott*) and of **laugh,** *n.* and *vb.* :—*pa.t.* **leuch,** **leugh** (*lūhh, lŏhh*); *pa.p.* **leuch′en, leugh′en.**

laud, *lawd, v.t.* to praise: to celebrate.—*n.* praise: (in *pl.*) in the R.C. Church, the prayers immediately following matins.—*adj.* **laud′able,** praiseworthy. —*n.* **laud′ableness.**—*adv.* **laud′ably.**—*n.* **laudā′tion,** praise: honour paid.—*adjs.* **laud′ative, laud′atory,** containing praise: expressing praise. —*ns.* eulogy.—*n.* **laud′er.** [L. *laudāre—laus, laudis,* praise.]

laudanum, *lawd′(ə-)nəm, n.* tincture of opium. [Coined by Paracelsus; perh. **ladanum,** transferred to a different drug.]

laugh, *läf, v.i.* to emit explosive inarticulate sounds of the voice, generally, with a smile, heaving of the sides, and other bodily movements, under the influence of amusement, joy, scorn, or other emotion, or of bodily stimulus as tickling: make merry (with *at*): to flout: (*fig.*) to have a cheerful appearance.—*v.t.* to render, put, or drive with laughter: to express by laughter: (*Spens.*) to laugh at, deride.—*n.* an act or sound of laughing. —*adj.* **laugh′able,** ludicrous.—*n.* **laugh′ableness.** —*adv.* **laugh′ably.**—*n.* **laugh′er,** one who laughs: a breed of pigeon with laughing note.—*adj.* **laugh′ful,** mirthful.—*n., adj.* **laugh′ing.**—*ns.* **laugh′ing-gas,** nitrous oxide, which may excite laughter when breathed, used as an anaesthetic, esp. in dentistry; **laugh′ing-jack′ass,** the great kingfisher of Australia.—*adv.* **laugh′ingly.**—*n.* **laugh′ing-stock,** an object of ridicule.—*adj.* **laugh′some,** inclined to laugh: provocative of laughter.—*n.* **laugh′ter,** the act or sound of laughing.—*adjs.* **laugh′worthy,** deserving to be laughed at; **laugh′y,** inclined to laugh.—**laugh and lie (or lay) down,** an old card-game in which a player lays down his hand on attaining his object; **laugh in one's sleeve,** to laugh inwardly; **laugh on the wrong side of the mouth,** to be made feel disappointment or sorrow, esp. after boasting, &c.; **laugh to scorn,** to deride or jeer at. [O.E. (Anglian) *hlæhhan* (W.S. *hliehhan*); Ger. *lachen,* Goth. *hlahjan.*]

launce, *lawns, läns* (*Spens.*). Same as **lance.**

launce, *lawns, läns, n.* (*Spens.*) a balance. [L. *lanx, lancis,* a plate, a scale of a balance.]

launce, lance, *lawns, läns, n.* a sand-eel (*Ammodytes*), an eel-like fish that buries itself in wet sand at ebb-tide.—Also **lant.** [Perh. conn. with **lance** (1).]

launcegaye, *lawns′gā, läns′gā.* Same as **lancegay.**

launch, lanch, *lawn(t)sh, län(t)sh, v.t.* to throw or hurl: to dart: to send forth: to set going: to initiate: to cause or allow to slide into water or to take off from land: (*Spens.*) to pierce: (*obs.*) to lance.—*v.i.* to rush, dart, plunge, fling oneself: to be launched: to take off: to throw oneself freely or venturesomely into some activity.—*n.* the act or occasion of launching: (*Spens.*) a lancing.— *n.pl.* **launch′ing-ways,** the timbers on which a

fāte, fär, ȧsk; mē, hėr (her); *mīne; mōte; mūte; mōŏn; dhen* (then) ship is launched. [O.Fr. *lanchier, lancier* (Fr. *lancer*); see **lance**.]

launch, *lawn*(*t*)*sh*, *län*(*t*)*sh*, *n.* the largest boat carried by a man-of-war: a large power-driven boat for pleasure or short runs. [Sp. *lancha*, perh. from Malay *lanchār*, swift.]

laund, *lawnd*, *n.* (*Shak.*) a glade: a grassy place. [O.Fr. *launde, lande*; prob. Celt.; see **lawn**.]

launder, *lawn'dər*, *län'*, *n.* (*obs.*) a washerwoman or washerman: a trough for conveying water.—*v.t.* and *v.i.* to wash and iron, as clothes.—*v.i.* to admit of laundering.—*ns.* **laund'erer**; **laun'dress**, a woman who washes and irons clothes; **laun'dry**, a place where clothes are washed and dressed: clothes for or from the laundry, a wash; **laund'ry-maid**; **laun'dry-man**, a male worker in a laundry: one who runs a laundry. [M.E. *lavander*—O.Fr. *lavandier*—L. *lavandārius*, from the ger. of *lavāre*, to wash.]

laura, *law'rä*, **lavra**, *läv'rä*, *n.* a group of recluses' cells. [Gr. *laurā* (mod. *labra*, with *b* as v), alley, lane, monastery.]

laurdalite, lardalite, *lawr'*, *lär'dəl-īt*, *n.* a coarse nepheline syenite. [*Laurdal* or *Lardal* in Norway.]

laureate, *law'ri-it*, *adj.* crowned with laurel.—*n.* one crowned with laurel: a poet-laureate.—*v.t.* (*-āt*) to crown with laurel, in token of literary merit: to confer a degree upon.—*ns.* **lau'reate-ship**; **laurea'tion**, crowning with laurel: graduation.—**Poet Laureate**, formerly one who received a degree in grammar (i.e. poetry and rhetoric) at the English universities: a poet bearing that title in the royal household or in a society. [L. *laureātus*, laurelled—*laurus*, laurel.]

laurel, *lor'əl*, *lawr'əl*, *n.* sweet bay tree (*Laurus nobilis*), used by the ancients for making honorary wreaths: another species of Laurus found in Madeira and the Canaries: the cherry-laurel: in America any species of Rhododendron or of Kalmia: extended to various trees and shrubs of similar appearance: a crown of laurel: honours gained (often in *pl.*).—*adjs.* **lau'rel**; **lau'relled**, crowned, adorned or covered with laurel.—*n.* **lau'rel-wa'ter**, a sedative and narcotic water distilled from cherry-laurel leaves.—**cherry-laurel**, **Japan laurel**, **spurge-laurel** (see under **cherry, Japan, spurge**). [Fr. *laurier*—L. *laurus*.]

Laurentian, *law-ren'sh(y)ən*, *adj.* pertaining to *Lorenzo* or *Laurentius* de' Medici, or to the library founded by him at Florence: of or pertaining to the river St *Lawrence*: applied to a series of Pre-Cambrian rocks covering a large area in the region of the Upper Lakes of North America.

Laurus, *law'rəs*, *n.* the laurel genus, giving name to the family **Laurā'ceae**, leathery-leaved archichlamydeous dicotyledons.—*adj.* **laurā'ceous**. [L.]

laurustine, laurustinus, *law'rəs-tīn*, *-tī'nəs*, *ns.* a winter-flowering shrub (*Viburnum Tinus*). [L. *laurus*, laurel, *tinus*, laurustine.]

laurvikite, larvikite, *lawr'*, *lär'vik-īt*, *n.* a soda syenite composed mainly of felspar with schiller structure. [*Laurvik* or *Larvik* in Norway.]

lauwine, *law'win*, *n.* (*Byron*) an avalanche. [Ger. *la*(*u*)*wine*, perh.—*lau*, tepid.]

lava, *lä'vä*, *n.* matter discharged in a molten stream from a volcano or fissure, whether still molten or subsequently solidified:—*pl.* **la'vas**.—*adj.* **la'va-form**, in the form of lava. [It.,—L. *lavāre*, to wash.]

lave, *läv*, *v.t.* and *v.i.* to wash: to bathe.—*ns.* **lavabo** (*lav-ā'bō*), in the mass the ritual act of washing the celebrant's fingers while he says *Lavabo inter innocentes*: a monastic lavatory: a fixed basin or washstand; **lavage** (*lav'ij*, *läv-äzh'*; *med.*), irrigation or washing out; **lavation** (*lav-ā'shən*), washing; **lav'atory**, a place, room, fixture, or vessel for washing: a laundry: (euphemistically) a privy: a ritual washing: (*obs.*) a lotion; **lavement** (*läv'mənt*), a washing: a lavage; **läv'er**, a large vessel for washing, esp. ritual washing: (*Spens.*) the basin of a fountain: (*Milt.*) an ablution. [L. *lavāre, -ātum*; Gr. *louein*, to wash.]

lave, *läv*, *n.* (*Scot.*) remainder. [O.E. *láf*; O.N. *leif*; see **leave**.]

lave, *läv*, *v.t.* to pour out: to bale. [O.E. *lafian*, to pour; fused with L. *lavāre*, to wash.]

laveer, *lä-vēr'*, *v.i.* (*arch.*) to beat to windward. [Du. *laveeren*; cf. **luff**.]

lavender, *lav'ən-dər*, *n.* a labiate plant (*Lavandula vera*) with fragrant pale-lilac flowers, yielding a volatile oil: sprigs of it used for perfuming and preserving linen, &c.: the colour of its blossoms.—*adj.* of the colour of lavender flowers.—*v.t.* to sprinkle with lavender.—*ns.* **lav'ender-cott'on**, a species of Santolina; **lav'ender-wa'ter**, a perfume composed of spirits of wine, essential oil of lavender, and ambergris.—**lay in lavender**, to lay by carefully, with sprigs of lavender; **oil of lavender**, an aromatic oil distilled from lavender flowers and stems, used as a stimulant and tonic. [A.Fr. *lavendre* (Fr. *lavande*)—L.L. *lavendula*, earlier *livendula*, perh. conn. with *līvidus*, livid.]

laver. See **lave** (1).

laver, *läv'ər*, *n.* edible seaweed of various kinds, esp. Porphyra (*purple laver*) and Ulva (*green laver*). [L. *laver*, a kind of water-plant.]

laverock, *lav'ə-rək*, Scot. *läv'(ə-)rək*, an archaic and dialectal form of **lark**.

lavish, *lav'ish*, *n.* (*obs.*) profusion: over-abundance: extravagant outpouring.—*v.t.* to expend or bestow profusely: to waste.—*adj.* bestowing profusely: prodigal: extravagant: unrestrained.—*adv.* **lav'ishly**.—*ns.* **lav'ishment**; **lav'ishness**. [O.Fr. *lavasse, lavache*, deluge of rain—*laver*—L. *lavāre*, to wash.]

lavolt, *lä-volt'*, **lavolta**, *-ä*, *n.* (*Shak.*) an old dance in which there were much turning and high leaping.—*v.i.* to dance the lavolta. [It. *la volta*, the turn.]

lavra. See **laura**.

law, *law*, *n.* a rule of action established by authority: statute: the rules of a community or state: jurisprudence: established usage: that which is lawful: the whole body of persons connected professionally with the law: litigation: a rule or code in any department of action, as morality, art, honour, arms (including heraldry), a game: a theoretical principle educed from practice or observation: a statement or formula expressing the constant order of certain phenomena: (*theol.*) the Mosaic code or the books containing it: (*sport*) a start: indulgence.—*v.t.* to go to law with: (*Burns*) to determine: to expediate.—*v.i.* (*obs.*) to go to law.—*adj.* **law'-abiding**, obedient to the law.—*ns.* **law'-agent**, (*Scots law*) a solicitor; **law'-book**, a book treating of law or law cases; **law'-breaker**, one who violates a law; **law'-burrows**, (*Scots law*) a writ requiring a person to give security against doing violence to another; **law'-calf**, a book-binding in smooth, pale-brown calf; **law'-day**, a day of open court.—*adj.* **law'ful**, allowed by law: rightful: legitimate.—*adv.* **law'fully**.—*ns.* **law'fulness**; **law'-giver**, one who enacts or imposes laws.—*adj.* **law'giving**.—*n.* **law'ing**, going to law: litigation: (*obs.*) expeditation.—*adj.* **law'less**, not subject to or controlled by law: unruly: unbridled.—*adv.* **law'lessly**.—*ns.* **law'lessness**; **law'-list**, an annual book of information about lawyers, courts, &c.; **law'-lord**, a peer in parliament who holds or has held high legal office: in Scotland, a judge of the Court of Session; **law'-maker**, a legislator; **law'-man**, one of a select body with magisterial powers in some of the Danish towns of early England; **law'-mer'chant**, the customs that have grown up among merchants in reference to mercantile documents and business; **law'-monger**, a low pettifogging lawyer; **law'-officer**, a legal functionary and adviser of the government, esp. Attorney-General, Solicitor-General, or Lord Advocate; **law'-sta'tioner**, one who sells parchment and other articles needed by lawyers; **law'suit**, a suit or process in law; **law'-writer**, a writer on law: a copier or engrosser of legal papers; **law'yer**, a practitioner in the law, esp. a solicitor: one learned or skilled in law: (*N.T.*) an interpreter of the Mosaic law: a brier, bramble, or other tenacious trailing or climbing plant (see also **Penang-lawyer**).—*adj.* **law'yerly**.—**Boyle's**, or **Mariotte's, law**, the law that, for a gas at a given temperature, pressure varies inversely as volume—announced by Robert *Boyle* in

1662, and confirmed by Mariotte; **go to law with**, resort to litigation against; **Gresham's law**, the law that of two forms of currency the inferior or more depreciated tends to drive the other from circulation, owing to the hoarding and exportation of the better form; **Grimm's law**, the law formulating certain changes undergone by Indo-Germanic stopped consonants in Germanic, stated by Jacob *Grimm* (1785-1863); **have the law of**, (*coll.*) to enforce the law against; **Kepler's laws**, three laws of planetary motion discovered by Johann *Kepler* (1571-1630)—(1) the orbits of the planets are ellipses with the sun at one focus; (2) the areas described by their *radii vectores* in equal times are equal; (3) the squares of their periodic times vary as the cubes of their mean distances from the sun; **lawful day**, one on which business may be legally done—not a Sunday or a public holiday; **law Latin**, Latin as used in law and legal documents, being a mixture of Latin with Old French and Latinised English words; **law of nations**, now international law, originally applied to those ethical principles regarded as obligatory on all communities; **law of nature**, the invariable order of nature: natural law; **law of the land**, the established law of a country; **laws of motion** (see **motion**); **lay down the law**, to state authoritatively or dictatorially; **Verner's law**, a law stated by Karl *Verner* in 1875, showing the effect of accent in the shifting of Indo-Germanic stopped consonants and *s* in Germanic, and explaining the most important anomalies in the application of Grimm's law. [M.E. *lawe*—late O.E. *lagu*, of O.N. origin, from the same root as **lie, lay**.]

law, *law*, *n.* (*obs.*) score, share of expense.—*n.* **law'ing**, (*Scot.*) a tavern reckoning. [O.N. *lag*, market-price.]

law, *law*, *n.* (*Scot.*) a hill, esp. rounded or conical. [Northern form of **low** (3), O.E. *hlāw*.]

law, *law*, *adj.* (*Scot.*) low.—*n.* and *adj.* **law'land**, lowland. [Northern form of **low** (2).]

law, *law*, *interj.* (*obs.*) expressing asseveration: (now *vulg.*) expressing surprise. [Partly for **la** or **lo**, partly **lord**.]

lawk, *lawk*, **lawks**, *lawks*, *interj.* (*vulg.*) implying surprise. [**lord** or **lack**.]

lawn, *lawn*, *n.* a sort of fine linen or cambric: extended to some cottons.—*adj.* made of lawn.—*adj.* **lawn'y.**—**lawn sleeves**, wide sleeves of lawn worn by Anglican bishops. [Prob. from *Laon*, near Rheims.]

lawn, *lawn*, *n.* an open space between woods: a smooth space of ground covered with grass, generally beside a house.—*ns.* **lawn'-mower**, a machine for cutting grass on a lawn; **lawn'-par'ty**, (*U.S.*) a garden-party; **lawn'-sprink'ler**, a machine for watering a lawn by sprinkling; **lawn-tenn'is**, a game derived from tennis, played by one or two a side on an unwalled court (hard or of turf), the aim being to hit the ball over the net and within the court, if possible so as to prevent like return.—*adj.* **lawn'y.** [**laund.**]

lax, *laks*, *adj.* slack: loose: soft, flabby: not strict in discipline or morals: loose in the bowels. —*adj.* **lax'ative**, having the power of loosening the bowels: (*arch.*) giving freedom: (*obs.*) speaking, expressing itself, freely.—*n.* a purgative or aperient medicine.—*ns.* **lax'ativeness**; **laxā'tor**, a muscle that relaxes an organ or part; **lax'ism**, the view that in morals an opinion only slightly probable may be safely followed; **lax'ist**, one holding loose notions of moral laws, or of their application; **lax'ity**, **lax'ness.**—*adv.* **lax'ly.** [L. *laxus*, loose.]

lay, *lā*, *n.* a form of **lea** (1, 2, 3).

lay, *lā*, *pa.t.* of **lie** (2).

lay, *lā*, *v.t.* to cause to lie: to place or set down: to beat down: (*obs.*) to deliver of a child: to spread on a surface: to spread something on: to cover: to apply: to cause to subside: to exorcise: to put below the horizon by sailing away: to deposit: to set on the table: to wager: to put forward: to cause to be: to set: to produce and deposit: to station: to locate: to set in position: to waylay:

(*Shak.*) to beset: to impose: to attribute, impose as a charge: to set material in position for making: to form by setting in position and twisting (as a rope): to design, plan: (*hort.*) to layer.—*v.i.* to produce eggs: to wager, bet: to deal blows: (*arch.*, *naut.*, and *illit.*) to lie: (*pr.p.* **lay'ing**; *pa.t.* and *pa.p.* **laid**).—*n.* situation: a lying-place: an oyster-bed: mode of lying: disposition, arrangement or plan: a layer: mode of twisting: laying activity: (*Shak.*) a bet: a share of profit, esp. in whaling: (*slang*) a field or method of operation, esp. in thieving.—*n.* **lay'er**, one who or that which lays—e.g. a hen, a bricklayer: a course, bed, or stratum: a distinctively coloured space between contour-lines on a map: a shoot bent down to earth in order to take root.—*v.t.* and *v.i.* to propagate by layers.—*v.t.* to put in layers.—*v.i.* to be laid flat, lodge.—*n.* **lay'er-cake**, a cake built up in layers.—*adj.* **lay'ered**, in or with layers. —*ns.* **lay'ering**; **lay'ing**, the first coat of plaster: the act or time of laying eggs: the eggs laid; **lay'-off**, (*U.S.*) an act or time of discontinuing work; **lay-out**, that which is laid out: a display: an outfit: disposition, arrangement, plan, esp. of buildings or ground: the general appearance of a printed page: (*U.S.*) a set, unit, organisation; **lay'-stall**, a place for depositing dung, rubbish, &c.; **lay'-up**, time or condition of being laid up.—**lay aboard**, to run alongside, esp. in order to board; **lay about one**, to deal blows vigorously or on all sides; **lay a course**, to succeed in sailing to the place required without tacking; **lay aside, away**, to discard: to put apart for future use; **lay at**, to endeavour to strike; **lay away**, (*Scot.*, &c.) to lay eggs in out-of-the-way places; **lay bare**, to make bare, disclose; **lay before**, to submit to, as of plans; **lay by**, to keep for future use: to dismiss: to put off; **lay by the heels** (see **heel**); **lay down**, to give up: to deposit, as a pledge: to apply, as embroidery: to delineate, describe: to affirm, assert: to store: to plant (with grass, &c.); **lay hands on** (see **hand**); **lay heads together**, to confer together; **lay hold of**, or **on**, to seize; **lay in**, to get in a supply of; **lay into**, to beat thoroughly; **lay it on**, to charge exorbitantly: to do anything, as to exaggerate, or to flatter, with profuseness; **lay off**, to mark off: to doff: to harangue, discourse or set forth volubly: (*U.S.*) to discontinue work or activity: (*U.S.*) to dismiss temporarily; **lay on**, to install a supply of: to deal blows with vigour; **lay on hands** (see **hand**); **lay oneself out to**, to make it one's professed object or practice, take great pains, to; **lay on load**, (*Spens.*) to belabour; **lay on the table** (see **table**); **lay open**, to make bare, to show, expose: to cut open; **lay out**, to display: to expend: to plan: to dispose according to a plan: to prepare for burial: to fell: to take measures, seek; **lay siege to**, to besiege: to importune; **lay to**, to apply with vigour: to bring a ship to rest; **lay to heart** (see **heart**); **lay under**, to subject to; **lay up**, to store up, preserve: (*usu.* in *pass.*) to confine to bed or one's room: to put in dock after dismantling; **lay upon**, to wager upon; **lay wait**, to lie in wait, or in ambush; **lay waste**, to devastate; **on a lay**, on shares instead of wages. [O.E. *lecgan*, to lay, causative of *licgan*, to lie; cf. O.N. *leggja*, Ger. *legen*.]

lay, *lā*, *n.* a short narrative poem: a lyric: a song. [O.Fr. *lai*; origin obscure.]

lay, *lā*, *n.* (*arch.*) law: religious faith. [O.Fr. *lei* (Fr. *loi*)—L. *lēx*, *lēgis*, law.]

lay, *lā*, *adj.* pertaining to the people: not clerical: unprofessional: (*cards*) not trumps.—*n.* the laity: (*obs.*) a layman.—*adj.* **laic** (*lā'ik*), **lay.**—*n.* a layman.—*adj.* **lā'ical.**—*v.t.* **laicise** (*lā'i-sīz*), to make laical: to open to the laity.—*ns.* **lā'ity**, the people as distinguished from some particular profession, usu. the clerical; **lay'-bap'tism**, baptism administered by a layman; **lay'-brother, -sister**, one under vows of celibacy and obedience, who serves a religious house, but is exempt from the studies and choir duties of monks or nuns; **lay'-commu'nion**, the state of being in the communion of the church as a layman; **lay'-impro'-**

priator, an impropriator who is a layman ; **lay'-man,** one of the laity : a non-professional man : one not an expert ; **lay'-read'er,** in the Anglican Church, a layman authorised to read part of the service ; **lay'-vic'ar,** a layman who is vicar-choral in an Anglican cathedral. [O.Fr. *lai*—L. *lāicus*—Gr. *lāikos*—*lāos*, the people.]

lay-day, *lā'dā, n.* one of a number of days allowed for loading and unloading. [Perh. **delay,** and **day.**]

layer. See **lay.**

layette, *lā-yet', n.* a baby's complete outfit. [Fr.]

lay-figure, *lā'-fig'ər, n.* a jointed model used by painters : a living person or a fictitious character wanting in individuality.—Also (earlier) **lay'-man.** [Du. *leeman*—*led* (now *lid*), joint, *man*, man.]

laylock, *lā'lək, n.* an obsolete form of lilac.

lazar, *laz'ər, n.* one afflicted with a loathsome and pestilential disease like *Lazarus*, the beggar.—*ns.* **la'zar-house,** a lazaretto ; **Laz'arist,** a member of the Roman Catholic Congregation of the Priests of the Mission, founded by St Vincent de Paul in 1624.—*adj.* or *adv.* **la'zar-like.**

lazaretto, *laz-ə-ret'ō, n.* a hospital for infectious diseases, esp. leprosy : a prison hospital : a place of quarantine : a place for keeping stores on a ship.—Also **laz'aret.** [It. *lazzeretto.*]

lazuli, *laz'ū-lī.* See **lapis-lazuli.**

lazulite, *laz'ū-līt, n.* a blue mineral, hydrated phosphate of aluminium, magnesium, and iron. [L.L. *lazulum*—Pers. *lājward* ; cf. **azure, lapis-lazuli, lazurite.**]

lazurite, *laz'ū-rīt, n.* a blue cubic mineral, sodium aluminium silicate with some sulphur, a constituent of lapis-lazuli. [L.L. *lazur*—Pers. *lājward* ; cf. **azure, lapis-lazuli, lazulite.**]

lazy, *lā'zi, adj.* disinclined to exertion : averse to labour : sluggish : tedious.—*v.i.* **laze,** to be idle (back-formation).—*adv.* **la'zily.**—*ns.* **la'ziness ;** **la'zy-bed,** a bed for growing potatoes, the seed being laid on the surface and covered with earth dug out of trenches along both sides ; **la'zy-bones,** (*coll.*) a lazy person, an idler ; **la'zy-jack,** a jack constructed of compound levers pivoted together.—*n.pl.* **la'zy-tongs,** a series of diagonal levers pivoted together at the middle and ends, capable of being extended by a movement of the scissors-like handles so as to pick up objects at a distance.—*adj.* constructed on the model of lazy-tongs. [Origin unknown.]

lazzarone, *lād-zä-rō'nā,* or *laz-ə-rō'ni, n.* a Nea-politan beggar :—*pl.* **lazzaro'ni (-nē).** [It.]

lea, *lē, n.* open country—meadow, pasture, or arable.—Also **lay, lee, ley** (*lā, lē*). [O.E. *léah* ; prov. Ger. *lohe, loh* ; perh. Flem. *-loo* in place-names, as Water*loo* ; confused with **lease** (4).]

lea, *lē, adj.* and *n.* fallow : arable land under grass or pasture.—Also **lay** (*lā*), **ley** (*lē, lā*).—*ns.* **lea'-rig,** an unploughed rig or grass field ; **ley'-farm'ing,** pasturing and cropping in alternating periods. [O.E. *lǣge,* found in *lǣghrycg,* lea-rig.]

lea, *lē,* **lay, ley,** *lā, n.* a measure of yarn—80 yards of worsted, 120 of cotton, 300 of linen. [Perh. conn. with Fr. *lier*—L. *ligāre,* to bind.]

leach, *lēch, v.t.* to allow liquid to percolate through : to drain away by percolation.—Also **letch.**—*ns.* **leach'-trough, -tub,** a trough or tub in which ashes are leached.—*adj.* **leach'y,** liable to be leached. [O.E. *leccan,* to water, irrigate, moisten.]

leach, leachour, (*Spens.*) for **leech, lecher.**

lead, *lēd, v.t.* to show the way by going first : to precede : to guide by the hand : to direct : to guide : to conduct ; to convey : (*dial.*) to cart : to induce : to live : to cause to live or experience : (*Scots law*) to adduce : to have a principal or guiding part or place in : (*cards*) to play as the first card of a round.—*v.i.* to be first or among the first : to be guide or chief : to act first : to cart crops to the farmyard (often with *in*) : to afford a passage (to), or (*fig.*) tend towards : (*pa.t.* and *pa.p.* led).—*n.* first place : precedence : amount by which one is ahead : direction : guidance : indication : precedent or example : chief rôle : the player of a chief rôle : leadership : initiative : the act or right of playing first, or the play of him who plays first : (*curling,* &c.) the first

player of a side : a leash : a watercourse leading to a mill : a channel among ice : the course of a running rope from end to end : a main conductor in electrical distribution.—*ns.* **lead'er,** one who leads or goes first : a chief : the principal first violin : the head of a party, expedition, &c. : the leading editorial article in a newspaper (also **leading article**) : the principal upward-growing shoot of a tree : a horse in a front place in a team : a tendon : (*U.S.*) a translucent connexion between a fishing-line and bait : (*print.*) a line of dots to guide the eye : principal wheel in any machinery ; **lead'er-ca'ble,** a cable on the sea-bottom by which ships with induction-receiving apparatus can find their way into port ; **leaderette',** a brief newspaper leader ; **lead'ership,** office of leader or conductor : ability to lead ; **lead'ing,** guidance : spiritual guidance : leadership : carting (crops, &c.).—*adj.* acting as leader : directing, controlling : principal : preceding.—*n.pl.* **lead'ing-strings,** strings used to lead children beginning to walk : vexatious care or custody.—**lead apes in hell** (see **ape**) ; **lead astray,** to draw into a wrong course, to seduce from right conduct ; **lead by the nose,** to make one follow submissively ; **lead in,** (*Scot.*) to house the harvest ; **lead in prayer,** to offer up prayer in an assembly, uniting the prayers of others ; **leading business,** the acting of the principal parts or rôles in plays (by the **leading lady** and the **leading man**) ; **leading counsel,** counsel who takes precedence of another in conducting a case ; **leading edge,** the edge first met : the foremost edge of an aerofoil or propeller blade ; **leading light,** a very influential member ; **leading note,** the seventh tone of a major or minor scale, which leads the hearer to expect the tonic to follow ; **leading question,** a question so put as to suggest the desired answer ; **lead off,** to begin or take the start in anything ; **lead on,** to persuade to go on, to draw on ; **lead one a dance** (see **dance**) ; **lead out,** to conduct to execution or a dance : (*cards*) to proceed to play out ; **lead the way,** to go first and guide others ; **lead up to,** to bring about by degrees, to prepare for by steps or stages : (*cards*) to play in challenge to, or with a view to weakness in. [O.E. *lǣdan,* to lead, *lād,* a way ; Ger. *leiten,* to lead.]

lead, *led, n.* a well-known soft bluish-grey metal (Pb ; at. numb. 82) : a plummet for sounding : a thin plate of lead separating lines of type : a pan or cauldron of lead, or of a kind once made of lead : a leaden frame for a window-pane : extended loosely to blacklead : a stick of blacklead for a pencil : (*pl.*) sheets of lead for covering roofs, a flat roof so covered.—*adj.* made of lead.—*v.t.* to cover, weight, or fit with lead : (*print.*) to separate the lines of with leads.—*n.* **lead'-arm'ing,** tallow, &c., placed in the hollow of a sounding-lead, to ascertain the nature of the bottom.—*adjs.* **lead'ed,** fitted or weighted with or set in lead : (*print.*) separated by leads ; **lead'en,** made of lead : lead-coloured : inert : depressing : heavy : dull.—*v.t.* and *v.i.* to make or become leaden.—*adv.* **lead'enly.**—*n.* **lead'enness.**—*adj.* **lead'en-stepping',** (*Milt.*) moving slowly.—*n.* **lead'-glance',** galena.—*adj.* **lead'less.**—*ns.* **lead'-line,** a sounding-line ; **lead'-paint',** paint with white lead as base ; **lead'-pencil,** a blacklead pencil for writing or drawing ; **lead'-poi'soning,** plumbism, poisoning by the absorption of lead into the system, its commonest form **lead colic,** or painter's colic ; **leads'man,** a seaman who heaves the lead.—*adj.* **lead'y,** like lead.—**red lead, white lead** (see **red, white**) ; **swing the lead,** (*slang*) to malinger ; **tree of lead** (see **Saturn**). [O.E. *léad* ; Ger. *lot.*]

leaf, *lēf, n.* one of the lateral organs developed from the stem or axis of the plant below its growing-point, esp. one of those flat green structures that perform the work of transpiration and carbon-assimilation, but also more generally any homologous structure, as a scale, a petal : condition of having leaves : leaves collectively : anything beaten thin like a leaf : two pages of a book on opposite sides of the same paper : a broad thin

Neutral vowels in unaccented syllables : *el'ə-mənt, in'fənt, ran'dəm*

part or structure, hinged, sliding, or inserted at will, as of folding doors, window-shutters, table-tops, drawbridges, &c.: (*pl.* **leaves**, *lēvz*).—*v.i.* (also **leave**) to produce leaves: (*pr.p.* **leaf'ing**; *pa.p.* **leafed**).—*adj.* in the form of leaves.—*ns.* **leaf'age**, foliage; **leaf'-base**, the base of a leaf-stalk, where it joins the stem; **leaf'-bridge**, a drawbridge with rising leaf or leaves swinging on hinges; **leaf'-bud**, a bud producing a shoot with foliage leaves only (not flowers); **leaf'-climb'er**, a plant that climbs by means of its leaves (petioles or tendrils); **leaf'-curl**, a plant disease of various kinds characterised by curling of the leaves; **leaf'-cushion**, a swollen leaf-base: a pulvinus that serves as a hinge for leaf movements: a raised scar marking the position of a leaf; **leaf'-cutter**, an insect (ant or bee) that cuts pieces out of leaves; **leaf'-cutt'ing**, a leaf used as a cutting for propagation.—*adj.* **leafed** (*lēft*), having leaves (also **leaved**, *lēvd*).—*ns.* **leaf'-fall**, the shedding of leaves: the time of the shedding of leaves, usu. autumn: premature fall of leaves; **leaf'-green**, chlorophyll; **leaf'-hopper**, a name for various hopping orthopterous insects that suck plant juices; **leaf'iness**; **leaf'-in'sect**, an orthopterous insect of family Phasmidae with wing-covers like leaves.—*adj.* **leaf'less**, destitute of leaves.—*n.* **leaf'let**, a little leaf: a division of a compound leaf: a single unstitched leaf of printed matter: a tract.—*adj.* **leaf'like**.—*ns.* **leaf'-met'al**, metal, especially alloys imitating gold and silver, in very thin leaves, for decoration; **leaf'-mosa'ic**, the arrangement of leaves so as to avoid shading one another: a name for various virus diseases of potato, tobacco, &c., in which the leaf is mottled; **leaf'-mould**, earth formed from decayed leaves, used as a soil for plants.—*adj.* **leaf'-nosed**, having a leaflike structure on the nose, as certain bats.—*ns.* **leaf'-scar**, the scar left by the fall of a leaf; **leaf'-sheath**, a leaf-base more or less completely enveloping the stem; **leaf'-stalk**, the petiole of a leaf; **leaf'-trace'**, a branch from the vascular system of the stem destined to enter a leaf.—*adj.* **leaf'y**, **leav'y**, covered with or abounding in leaves: leaflike.—**take a leaf out of one's book** (see **book**); **turn over a new leaf**, to begin a new and better course of conduct. [O.E. *léaf*; Ger. *laub*, Du. *loof*, a leaf.]

league, *lēg*, *n.* a nautical measure, $\frac{1}{20}$th of a degree, 3 geographical miles, 3·456 statute miles: an old measure of length, varying from the Roman league, 1·376 mod. Eng. miles, to the French, 2·764 miles, and the Spanish, 4·214 miles. [L.L. *leuga*, *leuca*, a Gallic mile of 1500 Roman paces; said to be Gaulish.]

league, *lēg*, *n.* a bond or alliance: union for mutual advantage: an association or confederacy: an association of clubs for games.—*v.t.* and *v.i.* to join in league.—*n.* **lea'guer**, a member of a league, esp. (**Leaguer**) that against the Huguenots in the time of Henry III. of France, the Anti-Corn-Law League, or the Irish Land League.—**league match**, a match between two clubs in the same league; **League of Nations**, an international body, under a covenant drawn up in 1919, to secure peace, justice, scrupulous observance of treaties, and international co-operation generally—superseded in 1945 by the United Nations. [Fr. *ligue*—L.L. *liga*—L. *ligāre*, to bind.]

leaguer, *lēg'ər*, *n.* a camp, esp. of a besieging army: siege: (by confusion with **ledger**) an ambassador.—*v.t.* to beleaguer.—*ns.* **lea'guer-la'dy**, **lea'guer-lass'**, a female camp-follower. [Du. *leger*, a lair.]

leaguer, *lēg'ər*, *n.* an old Dutch liquid measure: a large cask. [Du. *ligger*, a tun.]

leak, *lēk*, *n.* a crack or hole in a vessel ┼through which liquid may pass: passage through such an opening: a place or means of unintended or undesirable admission or escape of anything: (*elect.*) a high resistance, esp. serving as a dis-charging path for a condenser.—*adj.* (*obs.*) leaky.—*v.i.* to have a leak: to pass through a leak.—*v.t.* to cause to leak: (*rare*) to let out or in by, or as if by, a leak.—*ns.* **leak'age**, a leaking: that

which enters or escapes by leaking: an allowance for leaking: unauthorised divulgation; **leak'iness**.—*adj.* **leak'y**.—**leak out**, to find vent, to get to the public ears; **spring a leak**, to become leaky. [O.E. *hlec*, leaky; or perh. reintroduced from Du. or L.G. *lek*, leak; or O.N. *leka*, to leak.]

leal, *lēl*, *adj.* true-hearted, faithful.—*n.* **lealty** (*lē'əl-ti*).—**Land o' the Leal**, the home of the blessed after death—heaven, not Scotland. [O.F. *leel*, *leiel*; doublet of **loyal**.]

leam, **leme**, *lēm*, *n.* (*arch.*) a gleam of light, a glow.—*v.i.* to shine. [O.E. *léoma*.]

leam, *lēm*. Same as **lyam**.

lean, *lēn*, *v.i.* to incline: to be or become inclined to the vertical: to rest sideways against some-thing: to bend over: to swerve: to abut: to have an inclination: to rely.—*v.t* to cause to lean: (*pa.t.* and *pa.p.* **leaned**, *lēnd*, or **leant**, *lent*).—*n.* an act or condition of leaning: slope: (*arch.*) a thing to lean on.—*n.* and *adj.* **lean'ing**.—*n.* **lean'-to**, a shed or penthouse propped against another building or wall. [O.E. *hleonian*, *hlinian*, and causative *hlǽnan*; Du. *leunen*.]

lean, *lēn*, *adj.* thin, wanting flesh: not fat: with-out fat: unproductive: unprofitable, taking extra time—a printer's word.—*n.* flesh without fat.— *adj.* **lean'-faced**, having a thin face: (*print.*) slender and narrow, as letters.—*adv.* **lean'ly**.—*n.* **lean'ness**.—*adjs.* **lean'-witt'ed**, of little sense; **lean'y**, (*Spens.*) lean. [O.E. *hlǽne*; L.G. *leen*.]

leap, *lēp*, *v.i.* to move with bounds: to spring upward or forward: to jump: to rush with vehemence: to pass abruptly or over a wide interval.—*v.t.* to bound over: to cause to take a leap: to cover (of male animals)]: (*pr.p.* **leap'ing**; *pa.t.* and *pa.p.* **leaped**, *lēpt*, or **leapt**, *lept*).— *n.* act of leaping: bound: space passed by leaping: a place of leaping: an abrupt transition: a wide gap or interval.—*ns.* **leap'-day**, an intercalary day in the calendar (29th February); **leap'-frog**, a sport in which one places his hands on the back of another stooping in front of him, and vaults over him.—*v.t.* to advance by passing each other alternately.—*ns.* **leap'ing-house**, (*Shak.*) a brothel; **leap'ing-time**, (*Shak.*) active youth; **leap'-year**, a year with an intercalary day (perh. because any anniversary after February misses or leaps over a day of the week).—**leap in the dark**, an act of which we cannot foresee the consequences. [O.E. *hléapan*; cf. *lope*, *loup*, Ger. *laufen*, to run.]

leap, *lēp*, *n.* a basket: a wicker net. [O.E. *léap*.]

leaprous, **leaperous**, **leaporous**, old spellings of **leprous**.

lear, **leare**, **lere**, **leir**, *lēr*, *v.t.* (*arch.* and *Scot.*) to teach: (*Spens.*) to learn.—*n.* that which is learned, a lesson: lore: (*Scot.*) learning. [O.E. *lǽran*, to teach.]

lear, **leer**, **lehr**, *lēr*, a *n.* glass-annealing oven. [Origin unknown.]

learn, *lərn*, *v.t.* to be informed: to get to know: to gain knowledge, skill, or ability in: (now *vulg.*) to teach.—*v.i.* to gain knowledge or skill:—*pa.t.* and *pa.p.* **learned** (*lərnd*) or **learnt** (*lərnt*).—*adjs.* **learn'able**, that may be learned; **learned** (*lərn'id*), having learning: versed in literature, &c.: skilful.—*adv.* **learn'edly**.—*ns.* **learn'edness**; **learn'er**, one who learns: one who is yet in the rudiments; **learn'ing**, what is learned: knowledge: scholar-ship: skill in languages or science.—**New Learn-ing**, the awakening to classical learning in the 16th century, led (in England) by Colet, Erasmus, Warham, More, &c. [O.E. *leornian*; Ger. *lernen*; cf. O.E. *lǽran* (Ger. *lehren*), to teach.]

lease, *lēs*, *n.* a contract letting a house, farm, &c., for a term: tenure or rights under such a contract: duration of such tenure: a hold upon, or prospect of continuance of, life, enjoyment, health, &c.— *v.t.* to grant or take under lease.—*adj.* **leas'able**. —*ns.* **leas'er**, a lessee; **lease'hold**, a tenure by lease: land, &c., so held.—*adj.* held by lease.— *n.* **lease'holder**.—*n.* and *adj.* **lease'-lend'** (see **lend-lease**). [Fr. *laisser*, to leave—L. *laxāre*, to loose, *laxus*, loose.]

lease, *lēz*, *v.i.* (*prov.*) to glean.—*n.* **leas'ing**, glean-ing. [O.E. *lesan*, to gather.]

lease, *lēs, n.* place or mode of separating warp threads at the ends.—*ns.* **lease'-band, lease'-rod,** a band, rod, above and below which the warp threads are placed. [Perh. conn. with **leash.**]

lease, leaze, *lēz, v.* pasture. [See **leasow.**]

leash, *lēsh, n.* a line for holding a hawk or hound: control by a leash, or as if by a leash: a set of three, especially animals.—*v.t.* to hold by a leash: to bind. [O.Fr. *lesse* (Fr. *laisse*), a thong to hold a dog by—L. *laxus*, loose.]

leasing, *lēz'ing, n.* falsehood, lies: lying.—*ns.* **leas'ing-mak'er,** a speaker of seditious words; **leas'ing-mak'ing.** [O.E. *léasung*—*léasian*, to lie—*léas*, false, loose; Goth. *laus*, O.H.G. *los*.]

leasow, leasowe, *lē'sō, -zō, n.* pasture.—*v.t.* and *v.i.* to pasture. [Same word as **lease** (4)—O.E. *lǽs*, a meadow, in oblique cases *lǽswe*; cf. **mead, meadow.**]

least, *lēst, adj.* (serving as superl. of **little**) little beyond all others: smallest.—*adv.* in the smallest or lowest degree.—*n.* the smallest amount: the lowest degree.—*advs.* **least'ways** (*dial.*), **-wise** (*rare*), at least: however—used to tone down a preceding statement.—**at least,** or **at the least,** at the lowest estimate: at any rate. [O.E. *lǽst* (adj. and adv.); compar. *lǽssa* (adj.), *lǽs* (adv.); no positive.]

least, *lēst, conj.* (*Spens.*) Same as **lest.**

leasure, (*Spens.*) an obsolete spelling of **leisure.**

leat, leet, *lēt, n.* (*prov.*) a trench for bringing water to a mill-wheel, &c. [O.E. *gelǽt*.]

leather, *ledh'ər, n.* a tanned, tawed, or otherwise dressed skin: a strap or other piece of leather.—*adj.* of leather.—*v.t.* to apply leather to: to thrash.—*ns.* **leath'er-back,** a large variety of sea-turtle; **leath'er-cloth,** a fabric coated on one face so as to resemble leather—called also *American cloth*; **leath'er-coat,** (*Shak.*) an apple with a rough coat, the golden russet; **leatherette',** cloth or paper made to look like leather; **leath'er-head,** a blockhead: an Australian friar-bird with a bare head; **leath'ering,** a thrashing; **leath'er-jacket,** one of various fishes: a grub of the crane-fly; **leath'er-knife,** a curved knife for cutting leather.—*adjs.* **leath'ern,** of or like leather; **leath'er-lunged,** strong lunged, able to shout vigorously; **leath'er-mouthed** (*-mowdhd*), of certain fish, having a mouth like leather, smooth, and toothless.—*n.* **leath'er-neck,** sailor's name for a soldier or marine (from the leather stock he once wore).—*adjs.* **leath'er-winged,** (*Spens.*) having wings like leather; **leath'ery,** resembling leather: tough.—**fair leather,** leather not artificially coloured; **morocco leather** (see **morocco**); **patent leather**—also japanned or lacquered leather (see **patent**); **Russia leather** (see **Russia**); **split leather,** leather split by a machine, for trunk-covers, &c.; **white leather,** tawed leather, having its natural colour. [O.E. *lether*, leather; Du. and Ger. *leder*.]

leave, *lēv, n.* permission: liberty granted: formal parting: farewell: permission to depart or be absent: permitted absence from duty: time of such absence: holidays.—**French leave** (see **French**); **take leave,** to assume permission: to part, say farewell. [O.E. *léaf*, permission, cog. with *léof*, dear; see **lief.**]

leave, *lēv, v.t.* to allow to remain: to abandon, resign: to quit or depart from: to have remaining at death: to bequeath: to refer for decision.—*v.i.* to desist: to cease: to depart:—*pr.p.* **leav'ing;** *pa.t.* and *pa.p.* **left.**—*n.pl.* **leav'ings,** things left: relics: refuse.—*n.* **leav'ing-shop,** an unlicensed pawnshop.—**leave alone,** to let remain undisturbed; **leave off,** to desist, to terminate: to give up using; **leave out,** to omit. [O.E. *lǽfan.*]

leave, *lēv, v.t.* (*Spens.*) to levy, to raise. [Fr. *lever.*]

leave, leaved, leaves, leavy. See **leaf.**

leaven, *lev'n, n.* the ferment that makes dough rise: anything that makes a general change.—*v.t.* to raise with leaven: to permeate with an influence.—*n.* **leav'ening.**—*adj.* **leav'enous,** containing leaven. [Fr. *levain*—L. *levāmen*—*levāre*, to raise—*levis*, light.]

leaze. Same as **lease** (4).

lebbek, *leb'ek, n.* an Old World tropical mimosaceous timber tree (*Albizzia Lebbek*). [Origin unknown.]

Lecanora, *lek-ə-nō'rä, n.* a genus of lichens, including the edible manna lichen of the steppes and deserts of Asia and Africa. [Gr. *lekanē*, a dish.]

lecher, *lech'ər, n.* a man addicted to lewdness.—*v.i.* to practise lewdness.—*adj.* **lech'erous,** lustful: provoking lust.—*adv.* **lech'erously.**—*ns.* **lech'erousness, lech'ery.** [O.Fr. *lecheor*—*lechier,* to lick; O.H.G. *leccón,* Ger. *lecken,* Eng. **lick.**]

lecithin, *les'i-thin, n.* a very complex substance containing phosphorus, found in yolk of egg, brain, blood, &c. [Gr. *lekithos,* egg-yolk.]

lectern, *lek'tərn, n.* a church reading-desk from which the lessons are read.—Also (*obs.*) **lec'turn, lett'ern.** [L.L. *lectrīnum*—*lectrum,* a pulpit—Gr. *lektron,* a couch.]

lection, *lek'shən, n.* a reading: a lesson read in church.—*n.* **lec'tionary,** a book of church lessons for each day. [L. *lectiō, -ōnis*—*legĕre, lectum,* to read.]

lectisternium, *lek-ti-stər'ni-əm, n.* an ancient Roman religious observance at which images of gods were placed on couches as at a feast. [L.,—*lectus,* a couch, *sternĕre,* to spread.]

lector, *lek'tor, -tər, n.* a reader, esp. in a college: an ecclesiastic in one of the minor orders, lowest in the Orthodox, next above doorkeeper in the Roman Catholic.—*ns.* **lec'torate, lec'torship; lec'tress,** a female reader. [L. *lector, -ōris*—*legĕre, lectum,* to read.]

lecture, *lek'tyər, n.* (*arch.*) reading: a lesson or period of instruction: a discourse on any subject, esp. a professorial or tutorial discourse: an expository and discursive religious discourse: an endowed lectureship, as the Bampton, Hulsean, &c.: a formal reproof.—*v.t.* to instruct by discourses: to instruct authoritatively: to reprove.—*v.i.* to give a lecture or lectures.—*ns.* **lec'turer,** one who lectures: a college or university instructor of lower rank than a professor: one of a class of preachers in the Church of England, supported by voluntary contributions; **lec'tureship,** the office of a lecturer: the foundation of a course of lectures. [L. *lectūra*—*legĕre, lectum,* to read.]

lecythus, *les'i-thəs, n.* the Latinised form of **lekythos.**—*n.* **Lec'ythis,** the monkey-pot genus of **Lecythidā'ceae,** a family of tropical trees, including Brazil-nut, cannon-ball tree, and anchovy pear. [See **lekythos.**]

led, *led, pa.t.* and *pa.p.* of **lead,** to show the way.—*adj.* under leading or control, esp. of a farm or place held along with another by a non-resident.—**led captain,** an obsequious attendant, a henchman; **led horse,** a spare horse led by a servant, a sumpter-horse or pack-horse.

ledden, *led'n, n.* (*Spens.*) language, dialect, speech. [O.E. *léden, léoden,* language—*léode,* people, confused with *lǽden,* Latin—L. *Latīnum,* Latin.]

ledge, *lej, n.* an attached strip: (*obs.*) a raised edge: a shelf-like projection: a ridge or shelf of rocks: a lode.—*adj.* **ledg'y,** abounding in ledges. [M.E. *legge,* prob. from the root of **lay** (3).]

ledger, *lej'ər,* formerly also **lidger,** *lij'ər, n.* (*obs.*) a book that lies permanently in one place: (*U.S.*) a register: the principal book of accounts among merchants, in which the entries in all the other books are entered: a horizontal timber in scaffolding: a flat grave-slab: (*obs.*; also **lieger, leiger**) a resident, esp. an ambassador.—*adj.* resident, stationary.—*v.i.* to fish with a ledger-line.—*n.* **ledger-line,** (*angling*) a line fixed in one place: (*mus.*) a short line added above or below the stave where required (often **leger-line**). [App. from O.E. *licgan,* to lie, *lecgan,* to lay.]

Ledum, *lē'dəm, n.* the Labrador tea genus of ericaceous plants. [Latinised from Gr. *lēdon,* ladanum.]

lee, *lē, n.* shelter: the sheltered side: the quarter toward which the wind blows: (*obs.*) tranquillity.—*adj.* (opp. to *windward* or *weather*) sheltered: on or towards the sheltered side.—*ns.* **lee'-board,**

Neutral vowels in unaccented syllables : *el'ə-mənt, in'fənt, ran'dəm*

a board lowered on the lee-side of a vessel, to lessen drift to leeward; **lee′-gage**, position to leeward—opp. to *weather-gage*; **lee′-shore**, a shore on a ship's lee-side; **lee′-side**, the sheltered side; **lee′-tide**, a tide in the same direction as the wind.—*adj.* **lee′ward** (*naut. lū′ərd, lōō′ərd*; cf. **lew**), pertaining to, or in, the direction toward which the wind blows.—*adv.* toward the lee.—*n.* **lee′way**, leeward drift.—**lee licht of the mune**, (in Scottish ballads) perh. the pleasant moonlight; **make up leeway**, to make up for lost time, ground, &c. [O.E. *hléo(w)*, gen. *hléowes*, shelter; O.N. *hlé*, L.G. *lee*; see also **lew**.]

lee, *lē, n.* (*Spens.*) a river. [Poss. from the River *Lee.*]

lee. See **lea, lees, lie** (1).—*n.* **leear**, *lē′ər*, Scots form of **liar.**

leech, *lēch, n.* the side edge of a sail. [Cf. O.N. *lik*; Dan. *lig*; Sw. *lik*, a bolt-rope.]

leech, *lēch, n.* a blood-sucking worm: a physician.—*v.t.* to apply leeches to.—*ns.* **leech′craft**, (*arch.*) the art of medicine; **leech′dom**, (*arch.*) a remedy or prescription. [O.E. *lǽce*, perh. orig. two different words.]

leechee. Same as **litchi.**

leek, *lēk, n.* a well-known vegetable (*Allium Porrum*) of the onion genus—national emblem of Wales. —**eat the leek**, to be compelled to take back one's words or put up with insulting treatment— *Henry V.*, V. i. [O.E. *léac*, leek, plant; cf. **charlock, garlic, hemlock.**]

lee-lane, *lē′-lān′, n.* (*Scot.*) used only in phrases (by) my, his, &c., **lee-lane**, quite alone.—Also **lee′some-lane.** [**lee** of obscure origin; see **lone.**]

leer, *lēr, n.* a sly, sidelong, or lecherous look: (*Shak.*) complexion, colour.—*v.i.* to look askance: to look archly or obliquely.—*n.* and *adj.* **leer′ing.**—*adv.* **leer′ingly.** [O.E. *hléor*, face, cheek.]

leer. Same as **lear** (2).

Leerie, *lē′ri, n.* (*Scot.*) a nickname for a lamplighter—in full **Lee′rie-licht′-the-lamp.**

lees, *lēz, n.pl.* sediment or dregs of liquor.—*sing.* (*rare*) **lee.** [Fr. *lie*—L.L. *lia.*]

leese, *lēz, v.t.* (*Spens., Shak.*) to lose:—*pa.t.* **lore** (*lōr*); *pa.p.* **lore, lorn** (in *Spens.* in the sense of left). [O.E. *léosan* (in compounds), to lose.]

leet, *lēt, n.* (*Scot.*) a selected list of candidates for an office.—**short leet**, a select list for the final choice. [Perh. **élite**; but cf. O.E. *hlét*, lot.]

leet, *lēt, n.* a court-leet: its jurisdiction or district: the right to hold it. [A.Fr. *lete* or Anglo-Latin *leta*, possibly—O.E. *láeth*, lathe (of a county).]

leetle, *lē′tl*, an old-fashioned affectation for **little.**

leeze. See under **lief.**

left, *left, pa.t.* and *pa.p.* of **leave.**—*adjs.* **left′-off**, laid aside, discarded; **left′-o′ver**, remaining over from a previous occasion.—*n.* a thing left over: a survival.

left, *left, adj.* on, for, or belonging to that side which in man has normally the weaker and less skilful hand (opposed to *right*): on that side from the point of view of a person looking downstream, a soldier looking at the enemy, a president looking at an assembly, an actor looking at the audience: relatively liberal, democratic, progressive, innovating in politics.—*n.* the left side: the region to the left side: the left hand: a blow with the left hand: a shot on the left side or a bird so killed: a glove, shoe, &c., for the left hand or foot, &c.: the more progressive or actively innovating party or wing (from its sitting in some legislatures to the president's left).—*adv.* on or towards the left.—*adjs.* **left′-bank**; **left′-hand**, on the left side: performed with the left hand; **left′-hand′ed**, having the left hand stronger and readier than the right: for the left hand: counterclockwise: forming a mirror-image of the normal or right-handed form: awkward: unlucky: dubious (as a *left-hand compliment*): morganatic. —*adv.* **left′-hand′edly.**—*ns.* **left′-hand′edness**; **left′-hand′er**, a blow with the left hand: a lefthanded person; **left′-hand′iness**, awkwardness; **left′ism**, the principles of the political left; **left′ist.**—*adj.* and *adv.* **left′ward**, towards the

left: on the left side.—*advs.* **left′wardly, left′-wards.**—*adj.* **left′-wing**, playing on the left wing: belonging to the more leftwardly inclined section.—**over the left (shoulder)**, (*obs. slang*) contrariwise. [M.E. *lift, left*—O.E. (Kentish) *left*, weak, worthless; cf. O.E. *lyftádl*, paralysis.]

lefte, *left, pa.t.* (*Spens.*) lifted.

leg, *leg, n.* a walking limb: the human hind-limb, or sometimes the part between knee and ankle: a long, slender support of anything, as of a table: in cricket, that part of the field, or that fielder, on or behind a line straight out from the batsman on the on side (also *adj.*): a branch or limb of anything forked or jointed, as a pair of compasses: part of a garment that covers the leg: (*arch.*) a backward movement of the leg in bowing: a blackguard (for *blackleg*): a distinct part or stage of any course, e.g. of a flight: (*sports*) one event or part won in a contest consisting of two or more parts or events.—*v.t.* (with *it*; also *v.i.*) to walk vigorously: to propel through a canal tunnel by pushing with the feet on wall or roof.— *ns.* **leg′-bail** (see **bail** (1)); **leg′-break**, a ball that breaks inwards from the leg side; **leg′-bus′iness**, ballet-dancing; **leg′-bye**, in cricket, a run made when the ball touches any part of the batsman's person except his hand.—*adj.* **legged**, having legs.—*ns.* **legg′er**, a bargeman who legs: a worker or machine that makes stocking-legs; **legg′iness**, **legg′ing**, an outer and extra gaiterlike covering for the lower leg; **legg′ism**, character of a blackleg; **leg′-guard**, a cricketer's pad. —*adj.* **legg′y**, having noticeably long and lank legs.—*n.* **leg′-iron**, a fetter for the leg.—*adj.* **leg′less.** — *ns.* **leg′lessness**; **leg′let**, a leg ornament.—*adj.* **leg-of-mutt′on**, shaped like a leg of mutton, as a triangular sail, a sleeve tight at the wrist and full above.—*ns.* **leg′-pull**, a bantering attempt to impose on one's credulity; **leg′-puller**; **leg′-pulling**; **leg′rest**, a support for the legs.—**a leg up**, a help or hoist in mounting, climbing, or generally; **change the leg** (of a horse), to change the gait; **feel one's legs**, to begin to support oneself on the legs; **find one's legs**, to become habituated, to attain ease; **fine, long, short, square leg**, (*cricket*) fielding positions respectively fine from, far from, near to, square to, the batsman on the leg side; **in high leg**, in great excitement; **leg before (wicket)**, in cricket, a way of being given out as penalty for stopping with the leg a straight or off-break ball that would have hit the wicket (**l.b.w.**); **leg side (or the leg;** *cricket*), that half of the field nearest the batsman's legs (opp. to *off side*); **leg theory**, (*cricket*) the policy of bowling on the striker's legs with a trap of leg-side fielders: body-line; **not a leg to stand on**, no case at all; **on one's last legs** (see **last**); **on one's legs**, standing, esp. to speak; **pull one's leg**, to make a playful attempt to impose upon one's credulity; **show a leg**, make an appearance: get up; **upon one's legs**, in an independent position. [O.N. *leggr*, a leg; Dan. *læg*, Sw. *lägg*.]

legacy, *leg′ə-si, n.* that which is left to one by will: a bequest of personal property.—*ns.* **leg′acy-hunt′er**, one who courts those likely to leave legacies; **leg′atary**, a legatee; **legatee**, one to whom a legacy is left; **legator** (*li-gā′tər*), a testator. —**cumulative legacy**, an additional legacy to the same person; **demonstrative legacy**, a general legacy with a particular fund named from which it is to be satisfied; **general legacy**, a sum of money payable out of the assets generally; **legacy duty**, a duty levied on legacies, varying according to degree of relationship; **residuary legatee**, the person to whom the remainder of the property is left after all claims are discharged; **specific legacy**, a legacy of a definite thing, as jewels, pictures, a sum of stock in the funds, &c.; **substitutional legacy**, a second legacy to the same person instead of the first. [L. *lēgāre, -ātum*, to leave by will.]

legal, *lē′gl, adj.* pertaining to, or according to, law: lawful: created by law: (*theol.*) according to the Mosaic law or dispensation.—*n.* **lēgalisā′tion.**—

v.t. lē'galise, to make lawful.—*ns.* lē'galism, strict adherence to law: (*theol.*) the doctrine that salvation depends on strict adherence to the law, as distinguished from the doctrine of salvation by grace: the tendency to observe letter or form rather than spirit, or to regard things from the point of view of law; lē'galist, one inclined to legalism: one versed in law; lēgality (-gal'i-ti). —*adv.* lē'gally.—*legal tender*, that which a creditor cannot refuse in payment of a debt. [L. *lēgālis—lēx, lēgis,* law.]

legate, *leg'it, n.* an ambassador, esp. from the Pope: a delegate, deputy, esp. a Roman general's lieutenant: the governor of a Papal province.— *n.* leg'ateship.—*adj.* leg'atine (-*ə-tīn*), of or relating to a legate.—*n.* legation (*li-gā'shən*), a diplomatic mission, body of delegates, or its official abode: the office or status of legate: a Papal province. [L. *lēgātus—lēgāre,* to send with a commission.]

legatee. See legacy.

legato, *le-gä'tō, adj.* and *adv.* (*mus.*) smooth, smoothly, the notes running into each other without a break (*superl.* legatis'simo).—*n.* a legato passage or manner. [It., bound, tied—L. *ligāre, -ātum,* to tie.]

legend, *lej'ənd,* sometimes *lēj', n.* a story of a saint's life: a traditional story: a body of tradition: a myth: an untrue, unhistorical, or marvellous tale: a tale: a writing: a motto: an inscription: words accompanying an illustration or picture: (*obs.*) a book of readings from the Bible and saints' lives.—*adj.* leg'endary, a book or writer of legends.—*adj.* pertaining to, consisting of, or of the nature of legend: romantic: fabulous. —*ns.* leg'endist, a writer of legends; leg'endry. —Golden Legend (see golden). [Fr. *légende*— L.L. *legenda,* to be read, a book of chronicles of the saints read at matins—*legēre,* to read.]

legend, *lej'ənd, n.* (*Shak.*) for legion.

leger, *lej'ər, n.* (*obs. cant*) one who sells short weight in charcoal: one who swindles by scamping work, using bad materials, or the like.—*n.* leg'ering. [Poss. Fr. *léger,* light.]

legerdemain, *lej-ər-də-mān', n.* sleight-of-hand: jugglery.—*adj.* juggling: tricky. [Lit. light of hand—Fr. *léger,* light, de, of, *main,* hand.]

legerity, *li-jer'i-ti, n.* lightness: nimbleness. [Fr. *légèreté*—*léger,* light—assumed L.L. *leviārius*—L. *levis,* light.]

leger-line—better ledger-line. See ledger.

legge, *leg, n.* (*Shak.*) dregs of the people. [lag (1).]

leghorn, *leg'horn, n.* fine straw plait made in Tuscany: a hat made of it: (also *-orn'*) a small breed of domestic fowl. [*Leghorn* (It. *Legorno,* now *Livorno,* L. *Liburnus*) in Italy.]

legible, *lej'i-bl, adj.* clear enough to be deciphered: easy to read: (*rare*) readable.—*ns.* leg'ibleness, legibil'ity.—*adv.* leg'ibly. [L. *legibilis—legēre,* to read.]

legion, *lē'jən, n.* in ancient Rome, a body of three to six thousand soldiers: a military force: applied esp. to several in French history: a great number: a national association of those who have served in war.—*adj.* (*rare*) multitudinous.—*adj.* le'gionary, of, relating to, or consisting of, a legion or legions: containing a great number.—*n.* a member of a legion.—*adj.* le'gioned, arrayed in legions.— Foreign Legion, a body of foreigners, esp. that in the French army organised in 1831: Legion of Honour, an order instituted in 1802 by Napoleon I.: their name is Legion, they are beyond numbering (from Mark v. 9); Thundering Legion, in Christian tradition a body of soldiers under Marcus Aurelius, whose prayers brought down a thunderstorm and destroyed the enemy. [L. *legiō, -ōnis— legēre,* to levy.]

legislate, *lej'is-lāt, v.i.* to make laws.—*n.* legisla'tion. — *adj.* leg'islative, law-making: having power to make laws: pertaining to legislation.— *n.* law-making power: the law-making body.— *adv.* leg'islatively.—*n.* leg'islator, a lawgiver: a member of a legislative body:—*fem.* (*rare*) leg'islatress.—*adj.* legislatorial (-*lə-tō'ri-əl*), of or pertaining to, or of the nature of, a legislator, legis-

lature, or legislation.—*ns.* leg'islatorship; leg'islature, a law-making body. [L. *lēx, lēgis,* law, *latum,* serving as supine to *ferre,* to bear.]

legist, *lē'jist, n.* one skilled in the laws. [Fr. *légiste.*]

legitim, *lej'i-tim, n.* (*Scots law*) that which children are entitled to out of a deceased father's moveable estate—also *bairn's-part.* [L. *legitima (pars),* lawful (part)—*lēx,* law.]

legitimate, *li-jit'i-mit, -māt, adj.* lawful: lawfully begotten, born in wedlock, or having the legal status of those born in wedlock: related, derived, or transmitted by birth in wedlock or subsequently legitimated: as used by believers in the theory of divine right, according to strict rule of heredity and primogeniture: logically inferred: following by natural sequence: genuine: conforming to an accepted standard.—*v.t.* (-*māt*) to make lawful: to give the rights of a legitimate child to.—*n.* legit'imacy (-*mə-si*), fact or state of being legitimate.—*adv.* legit'imately.—*ns.* legit'imateness; legitima'tion, act of rendering legitimate, esp. of conferring the privileges of lawful birth.—*v.t.* legit'imise, to legitimate.—*n.* legit'imist, one who believes in the right of royal succession according to the principle of heredity and primogeniture.—legitimate drama, drama of permanent value: drama of typical form, normal comedy and tragedy, distinguished from opera, melodrama, farce, &c.; legitimate pollination, in heterostyled plants, pollination of long styles from long stamens, short from short. [L.L. *lēgitimāre, -ātum*—L. *lēgitimus,* lawful—*lēx,* law.]

leglin, leglan, leglen, *leg'lən, n.* (*Scot.*) a milking-pail.—to cast a leglin girth, to have an illegitimate child. [Cf. laggen.]

legume, *leg'ūm, li-gūm', n.* a pod (as in pea, bean, &c.) of one carpel: a vegetable used as food.—*n.* legū'min, a globulin got in peas, beans, &c.—*n.pl.* Legūminō'sae (-*sē*), an order of angiosperms characterised by the legume, including Papilionaceae, Mimosaceae, and Caesalpiniaceae.—*adj.* legū'minous, pertaining to pulse: of or pertaining to the Leguminosae: bearing legumes. [L. *legūmen,* pulse, prob.—*legēre,* to gather.]

lehr. Same as lear (2). lei, *pl.* of leu.

lei, *lā'ē, n.* a garland, wreath. [Hawaiian.]

Leibni(t)zian, *lib-nit'si-ən, adj.* pertaining to the great German philosopher and mathematician Gottfried Wilhelm *Leibniz* (1646-1716).—*n.* Leibni(t)z'ianism, the philosophy of Leibniz—the doctrine of primordial monads, pre-established harmony, fundamental optimism on the principle of sufficient reason.

Leicester, *les'tər, adj.* of a long-woolled breed of sheep that originated in *Leicestershire.*—*n.* a sheep of that breed.

leidger, leiger, *lej'ər, n.* (*Shak.*) a resident ambassador: a resident. [See ledger.]

leiotrichous, *li-ot'ri-kəs, adj.* straight-haired.—*n.* leiot'richy (-*ki*), straight-hairedness. [Gr. *leios,* smooth, *thrix,* hair.]

Leipoa, *li-pō'ä, n.* a genus of Australian mound-birds. [Gr. *leipein,* to leave, forsake, *ōon,* egg.]

leir. See lear (1).

Leishmania, *lēsh-mān'i-ä, -man'i-ä, n.* a genus of Protozoa. — *ns.* leishmaniasis (*lēsh-mən-ī'ə-sis*), leishmaniō'sis, kala-azar, due to infection with Leishmania. [Named after Sir William *Leishman* (1865-1926), who discovered the cause of the disease.]

leister, *lēs'tər, n.* (*Scot.*) a salmon-spear.—*v.t.* to spear with a leister. [O.N. *ljóstr;* Dan. *lyster.*]

leisure, *lezh'ər,* or (old-fashioned) *lēzh'ər, -ūr, n.* time free from employment: freedom from occupation: convenient opportunity.—*adj.* free from necessary business.—*v.i.* to have leisure.— *v.t.* to make leisurely.—*adj.* leis'urable, leisured: leisurely.—*adv.* leis'urably.—*adj.* leis'ured, having much leisure.—*adj.* and *adv.* leis'urely, not hasty or hastily.—at (one's) leisure, free from occupation: at one's ease or convenience. [O.Fr. *leisir*—L. *licēre,* to be permitted.]

leitmotiv, *līt'mō-tēf', n.* (*mus.*) a theme associated with a person or a thought, recurring when the person appears on the stage or the thought becomes prominent in the action.—Also **leitmotif.** [Ger., —*leiten*, to lead, and *motiv*, a motif.]

leke (*Spens.*). Same as **leak** (*adj.*).

lekythos, *lē'ki-thos, n.* (*ant.*) a narrow-necked Greek flask. [Gr. *lēkythos.*]

leman, *lem'ən,* or *lēm', n.* (*arch.*) a lover: a sweetheart: a paramour: now chiefly *fem.* and in a bad sense:—*pl.* **lem'ans.** [O.E. *léof,* lief, *mann,* man.]

lemma, *lem'ä, n.* (*math.*) a preliminary proposition: a premise taken for granted: a theme, argument, heading, or head-word :—*pl.* **lemm'as, lemm'ata.** [Gr. *lĕmma, -atos,* from the root of *lambanein,* to take.]

lemming, *lem'ing, n.* a northern rodent (*Lemmus* and other genera) near allied to voles. [Norw. *lemming.*]

Lemna, *lem'nä, n.* the duckweed genus, giving name to the family **Lemnā'ceae,** free-floating spathifloral monocotyledons. [Gr. *lemna,* water starwort.]

Lemnian, *lem'ni-ən, adj.* pertaining to *Lemnos* in the Aegean Sea.—**Lemnian earth,** a bole from Lemnos; **Lemnian ruddle,** a red ochre found in Lemnos.

lemniscate, *lem-nis'kāt, n.* the locus of the foot of the perpendicular from the centre of a conic upon the tangent. [L. *lĕmniscātus,* ribboned— Gr. *lĕmniskos,* a ribbon, bandage.]

lemon, *lem'ən, n.* an oval citrus fruit like the orange, with acid pulp: the tree that bears it: a pale yellow.—*adj.* pale yellow.—*v.t.* to flavour with lemon.—*ns.* **lemonade',** a drink (still or aerated) made with lemon juice or more or less flavoured with lemon; **lem'on-cheese', -curd',** a soft paste of lemons, eggs, and butter.—*adj.* **lem'on-coloured.**—*ns.* **lem'on-grass,** a fragrant perennial grass (*Cymbopogon* or *Andropogon*) of India, &c., smelling like lemon and yielding an essential oil; **lem'on-peel',** the skin of lemons, candied or not; **lem'on-squash',** a lemon drink, often effervescent; **lem'on-squeezer,** a small hand-press for extracting the juice of lemons; **lem'on-weed,** sea-mat.—*adj.* **lem'ony.**—*n.* and *adj.* **lem'on-yell'ow.** [Fr. *limon* (now the lime); cf. Pers. *līmūn*; cf. **lime** (2).]

lemon, *lem'ən, n.* a species of sole differing in its markings from the common sole (**lem'on-sole,** or **sand sole**): a kind of dab resembling a sole (**lem'on-dab', lem'on-sole',** also called smear-dab or smooth dab). [Fr. *limande.*]

lemur, *lē'mər, n.* any member of the **Lemuroidea** (*lem-ū-roid'i-ä*) or Prosimiae, a group of mammals akin to the monkeys, forest dwellers, mainly nocturnal in habits, common in Madagascar: an ancient Roman ghost of the dead :—*pl.* **lē'murs** (animals), **lemures** (*lem'ū-rēz*; spectres).—*n.* **Lemuria** (*li-mū'ri-ä*; *pl.*), an ancient Roman festival (9th, 11th, and 13th of May) when ghosts were exorcised : (*sing.*) a hypothetical vanished continent where the Indian Ocean now is, posited to explain the distribution of lemurs.—*ns.* and *adjs.* **lemurian** (*li-mū'ri-ən*), **lemurine** (*lem'ū-rīn*), **lem'ūroid.** [L. *lĕmūrēs,* ghosts.]

lend, *lend, v.t.* to give the use of for a time: to afford, grant, or furnish, in general: to let for hire.—*v.i.* to make a loan: (*pr.p.* **lend'ing;** *pa.t.* and *pa.p.* **lent**).—*n.* (*Scot.*) a loan (often **len'**).—*ns.* **lend'er;** **lend'ing,** the act of giving in loan: (*Shak.*) that which is lent or supplied; **lend'-lease,** an arrangement authorised by Congress in 1941 by which the President could supply war materials to other countries whose defence he deemed vital to the United States.—Also *adj.* [O E. *lǣnan—lǣn, lǎn,* a loan.]

leng, *leng, v.i.* (*obs.*) to lengthen: (*obs.*) to tarry: (*Spens.*) to long. [O.E. *lengan.*]

lenger, *leng'gər, adj.* and *adv.* (*Spens.*) longer.—*adj.* and *adv.* **leng'est,** (*obs.*) longest. [O.E. *lengra,* compar. of *lang* (adj.), *lengest,* superl. of *lang* and of *lange* (adv.).]

length, *length, n.* quality of being long: extent from end to end: the longest measure of anything: long continuance: prolixity: time occu-

pied in uttering a vowel or syllable: the quantity of a vowel: any definite portion of a known extent: a stretch or extent: (chiefly *Scot.*) distance: a suitable distance for pitching a cricket ball.—*v.t.* and *v.i.* **length'en,** to increase in length.—*adj.* (*obs.*) **length'ful.**—*adv.* **length'ily.**—*n.* **length'-iness.**—*advs.* **lengthways', length'wise,** in the direction of the length.—*adj.* **length'y,** of great or tedious length: rather long.—**at length,** in full: fully extended: at last; **go great lengths, go to all lengths,** to go to extremities; **length of days,** prolonged life. [O.E. *lengthu—lang,* long.]

lenient, *lē'ni-ənt, -nyənt, adj.* softening: soothing: mild: merciful.—*n.* (*med.*) that which softens: an emollient.—*ns.* **lē'nience, lē'niency.**—*adv.* **lē'niently.**—*v.t.* **lenify** (*len', lēn'*), to mitigate: to assuage.—*adj.* **lenitive** (*len'*), mitigating: laxative.—*n.* any palliative: (*med.*) an application for easing pain: a mild purgative.—*n.* **lenity** (*len'*), mildness: clemency. [L. *lĕniēns, -entis,* pr.p. of *lēnīre,* to soften—*lēnis,* soft.]

leno, *lē'nō, n.* a thin muslin-like fabric. [Perh. Fr. *linon.*]

lenocinium, *lē-nō-sin'i-əm, n.* (*Scots law*) connivance at one's wife's adultery. [L. *lēnōcinium,* enticement—*lēnō,* a pander.]

lens, *lenz, n.* (*opt.*) a piece of transparent matter causing regular convergence or divergence of rays passing through it: the refracting structure (*crystalline lens*) between the crystalline and vitreous humours of the eye: **Lens,** the lentil genus :—*pl.* **lens'es.**—*adjs.* **lent'iform, lent'old.** —**electron lens,** any arrangement of electrodes designed to influence the direction of cathode rays. [L. *lēns, lentis,* lentil.]

Lent, *lent, n.* (*obs.*) spring: the time from Ash-Wednesday to Easter observed as a time of fasting in commemoration of Christ's fast in the wilderness (Matt. iv. 2).—*adj.* **Lent'en,** of Lent: sparing: fleshless. — *n.* **lent'-lil'y,** the daffodil. [O.E. *lencten,* the spring; Du. *lente,* Ger. *lenz.*]

lent, *pa.t.* and *pa.p.* of **lend.**

Lentibulariaceae, *len-tib-ū-lā-ri-ā'si-ē, n.pl.* the bladderwort and butterwort family of tubifloral dicotyledons. [Origin obscure.]

lenticel, *lent'i-sel, n.* a breathing pore in bark.—*adj.* **lenticell'ate.**—*n.* **lent'icle,** (*geol.*) a lenticular mass.—*adj.* **lentic'ular,** shaped like a lens or lentil seed: double-convex.—*adv.* **lentic'ularly.** [L. *lēns, lentis,* a lentil.]

lentigo, *len-tī'gō, n.* a freckle: (usu.) freckles :—*pl.* **lentigines** (*len-tij'i-nēz*).—*adjs.* **lentig'inose, lentig'inous,** (*bot.*) minutely dotted. [L. *lentīgō, -inis,* a freckle—*lēns,* a lentil.]

lentil, *len'til, n.* an annual papilionaceous plant (*Lens esculenta,* or *Ervum Lens*) common near the Mediterranean: its seed used for food. [O.Fr. *lentille*— L. *lēns, lentis,* the lentil.]

lentisk, *len'tisk, n.* the mastic tree. [L. *lentiscus.*]

lento, *len'tō, adj.* (*mus.*) slow.—*adv.* slowly.—*n.* a slow passage or movement.—*adv.* **lentamen'te** (*-tā*).—*adj.* and *adv.* **lentan'do,** slowing. [It.,— L. *lentus,* slow.]

lentor, *len'tor, n.* sluggishness: viscidity.—*adj.* **len'tous.** [L. *lentus,* slow.]

lenvoy, *len-voi'.* See **envoy** (2). [Fr. *l'* for *le,* the.]

Leo, *lē'ō, n.* the Lion, a constellation between Cancer and Virgo: the 5th sign of the zodiac, in which it used to be (the constellation is now in the sign Virgo).—*n.* **Lē'onid** (*-ə-nid*), a meteor of a swarm whose radiant is in the constellation Leo. —*adj.* **lē'onine,** lionlike: **Leonine,** pertaining to any of the Popes named Leo: of a kind of Latin verse, generally alternate hexameter and pentameter, rhyming at the middle and end (prob. from some unknown poet named Leo, Leoninus, or Leonius). [L. *leō, -ōnis,* lion.]

leontiasis, *lē-ont-ī'ə-sis, n.* a form of leprosy giving a lionlike appearance. [Gr. *leontiāsis—leōn, -ontos,* lion.]

leopard, *lep'ərd, n.* a large spotted animal of the cat kind found in Africa and Asia: in America, the jaguar: (*her.*) a lion passant gardant: (*fem.* or *rare*) **leop'ardess.**—*ns.* **leop'ard-cat,** a spotted wild cat of India; **leop′ard's-bane**, a composite plant, *Doronicum*; **leop′ard-wood**, letter-wood. —hunting leopard, the cheetah; **snow leopard**, the ounce. [O.Fr.,—L. *leopardus*—Gr. *leopardos* (for *leontopardos*)—*leōn*, lion, *pardos*, pard.]

lep, *lep*, *v.i.* (*dial.*, esp. *Ir.*) for **leap**: also *dial.* for the *pa.t.*—*pa.t.* (*Spens.*) **lepp′ed.**

leper, *lep′ər*, *n.* (*obs.*) leprosy: one affected with leprosy: (*fig.*) a tainted person: an outcast.—*n.* **lep′ra**, leprosy: (*bot.*) a scurfy, mealy substance on some plants.—*adj.* **lep′rose** (*-rōs*), scaly: scurfy.—*ns.* **leprosity** (*-ros′i-ti*), scaliness; **lep′rosy** (*-rə-si*), a name formerly widely applied to chronic skin diseases: now to one caused by a bacillus and occurring in two forms, tubercular, beginning with spots and thickenings of the skin, and anaesthetic, attacking the nerves, with loss of sensation in areas of skin: (*fig.*) corruption.—*adj.* **lep′rous**, or affected with leprosy: scaly: scurfy. [O.Fr. *lepre* and Gr. *leprā*—*lepros*, scaly—*lepos*, or *lepis*, a scale, *lepein*, to peel.]

lepid, *lep′id*, *adj.* pleasant, jocose. [L. *lepidus*.]

lepid-, lepido-, *lep′id-*, *-ō-*, *-o′-*, in composition, scale.—*n.* **Lepidoden′dron** (Gr. *dendron*, tree), a genus of fossil trees, mainly Carboniferous of the **Lepidodendrā′ceae**, akin to Lycopodiaceae, the stem covered with ovate leaf-scars arranged spirally. —*adj.* and *n.* **lepidoden′droid**.—*ns.* **lepid′olite** (Gr. *lithos*, stone), a lithia mica, usu. pink; **lepid-omelane′** (Gr. *melas*, *-anos*, black), a black mica rich in iron, occurring in scales.—*n.pl.* **Lepidop′tera** (Gr. *pteron*, wing), an order of insects, with four wings covered with fine scales—butterflies and mot'hs.—*n.* **lepidop′terist**, a student of butterflies and moths. —*adj.* **lepidop′terous**. — *ns.* **Lepidosi′ren** (Gr. *Seirēn*, a Siren), an Amazon mudfish; **Lepidos′teus** (Gr. *osteon*, a bone), a genus of fishes with rhomboid scales hard like bone, the bony pike; **Lepidos′trobus** (Gr. *strobos*, twist), the fossil fructification of Lepidodendron.—*adj.* **lep′idote** (Gr. *lepidōtos*), scaly: scurfy. [Gr. *lepis*, *-idos*, a scale.]

leporine, *lep′ə-rīn*, *adj.* pertaining to or resembling the hare. [L. *leporīnus*—*lepus*, *lepŏris*, the hare.]

lepped. See **lep.**

leprechaun, leprechawn, *lep-re-hhawn′*, *n.* a little brownie who helps Irish housewives, mends shoes, grinds meal, &c. [Prob. Old Ir. *luchorpán*, *lu*, small, *corpan*, *corp*, a body.]

leprosy. See **leper.**

lepton, *lep′ton*, *n.* the smallest ancient Greek coin, translated mite in the N.T.: a modern Greek coin, ₁₀₀th of a 'drachma':—*pl.* **lep′ta.**—*adj.* **leptocephal′ic** (Gr. *kephalē*, head), narrow-skulled.—*n.* **leptoceph′alus**, the larva of an eel.— *adj.* **leptocerc′al** (Gr. *kerkos*, tail), slender-tailed. —*n.* **leptodac′tyl** (Gr. *daktylos*, finger, toe).— *adj.* **leptodac′tylous**, slender-toed.—*n.* **lep′tome**, phloem or bast.—*adjs.* **lep′torrhine** (Gr. *rhis*, *rhīnos*, nose), narrow-nosed; **lep′tosome** (Gr. *sōma*, body), slender-bodied: asthenic; **leptosporan′giate**, having each sporangium derived from a single cell (opposed to *eusporangiate*). [Gr. *leptos*, neut. *lepton*, slender.]

lere. Same as **lear.**

Lesbian, *lez′bi-ən*, *adj.* of the island of *Lesbos*, Mitylene, or Mytilene, home of Alcaeus and Sappho: amatory, erotic: (of women) homosexual. — *n.* **Les′bianism.** — **Lesbian rule,** an adaptable standard, from the pliable leaden rule of Lesbian masons.

lese-majestie, leze-majesty, *lēz′-maj′is-ti*, *n.* an offence against the sovereign power, treason. [Fr. *lèse majesté*, transl. of L. *laesa mājestās*, injured majesty—*laedĕre*, to hurt.]

lesion, *lē′zhən*, *n.* a hurt: (*med.*) an injury or wound. [Fr. *lésion*—L. *laesiō*, *-ōnis*—*laedĕre*, *laesum*, to hurt.]

less, *les*, *adj.* (used as *comp.* of *little*) smaller (not now used of material things): in smaller quantity: minor: (*arch.* and *coll.*) fewer: inferior, lower in estimation: younger: (*Shak.*, with an expressed or implied negative) more.—*adv.* not so much: in a lower degree.—*n.* a smaller portion or quantity.— *conj.* (*Milt.*) unless (often written **'less**).—*prep.* without: with diminution of, minus.—**much less,**

often used by confusion for much more **nothing less than,** (formerly) anything rather than: (now) quite as much as. [O.E. *lǣssa*, less, *lǣs* (adv.); apparently not conn. with **little.**]

lessee, *les-ē′*, *les′ē*, *n.* one to whom a lease is granted. [**lease.**]

lessen, *les′n*, *v.t.* to make less, in any sense: to lower in estimation: to disparage: to belittle.— *v.i.* to become less, shrink. [**less.**]

lesser, *les′ər*, *adj.* less: smaller: inferior: minor. —*adv.* (*Shak.*) less. [Double comp. from **less.**]

lesson, *les′n*, *n.* a portion of Scripture read in divine service: a spell, instalment, or prescribed portion of instruction: an exercise: (*obs.*) a piece or performance of music: an instructive or warning experience or example: a severe reproof.—*v.t.* to instruct: to train: to rebuke.—*n.* **less′oning.** [Fr. *leçon*—L. *lectiō*, *-ōnis*—*legĕre*, to read.]

lessor, *les′or*, *n.* one who grants a lease. [**lease.**]

lest, *lest*, *conj.* that not: for fear that. [M.E. *les te*—O.E. *thȳ lǣs the*, the less that—*thȳ* instrum. case; see **the** (2).]

lest, *lest*, *v.i.* (*Spens.*) for **list**, to listen.

let, *let*, *v.t.* (*Shak.*) to leave: (*Shak.*) to omit: (*arch.*) to allow to escape: to allow to go or come: to give leave or power to, to allow, permit, suffer (usu. with infin. without *to*): to grant to a tenant or hirer: in the imper. with accus. and infin. without *to*, often used virtually as an auxiliary with imperative or optative effect: (*obs.*; also *v.i.*) to behave so as to give an impression, make it appear: (*pr.p.* **lett′ing**; *pa.t.* and *pa.p.* **let**).—*n.* a letting for hire.—*n.* **let′-alone,** (*Shak.*) absence of restraint, freedom.—*adj.* refraining from interference: leaving things to themselves.—*ns.* **let′-down,** an act or occasion of letting down: a disappointment; **let′-off,** a festivity: an outlet: (in games) a failure to take advantage of an opportunity; **let′er,** one who lets, esp. on hire; **lett′er-gae′,** (*Scot.*) one who lets go, a precentor; **lett′ing.** —**let alone,** not to mention: to refrain from interference with: (*imper.*) trust; **let be** (*dial.* **let-a-be**), to leave undisturbed: (*Scot.*) not to mention, to say nothing of; **let blood,** to bleed; **let down,** to allow to fall: to lower: to leave in the lurch, fail to back up at need; **let drive,** to aim a blow: to discharge a missile; **let fall,** to drop; **let fly,** to fling, discharge, shoot: **let go,** to cease holding: (*naut.*) to slacken; **let in,** to allow to enter: to take in or swindle: to betray into or involve in (*for*) anything vexatious: to insert: to leak inwards; **let into,** to admit to the knowledge of: to throw into one with; **let off,** to allow to go free or without exacting all: to fire off, discharge; **let on,** (*dial.*) to allow to be believed, to pretend: to betray awareness: to reveal, divulge; **let one know,** to inform him; **let oneself loose,** to let go restraint, to indulge in extravagant talk or conduct; **let out,** to allow to get free, or to become known: to strike out or kick out: to widen, slacken, enlarge: to put out to hire: to leak outwards; **let well alone,** to let things remain as they are from fear of making them worse. [O.E. (Anglian) *lētan* (W.S. *lǣtan*), to permit, pa.t. *lēt*; pa.p. *lǣten*; Ger. *lassen*.]

let, *let*, *v.t.* (*arch.*) to hinder: to prevent:—*pa.t.* and *pa.p.* **lett′ed** or **let.**—*adj.* **let,** obstructed.— *n.* (*arch.*) hindrance, obstruction: delay: (*lawn-tennis*, &c.) obstruction by the net, or other ground for cancelling a service: a service so affected.—*n.* **lett′er.** [O.E. *lettan*, to hinder—*lǣt*, slow.]

letch, lech. See **latch** (1), **leach** (1).

letch. See **latch** (1), **leach** (1).

lethal, *lē′thal*, *adj.* death-dealing: deadly: mortal. —*n.* **le′thee,** (*Shak.*) app. life-blood, or death; prob. with some reminiscence of Lethe (see below). —*adj.* **lethif′erous,** carrying death. [L. *lēt(h)ālis* —*lēt(h)um*, death.]

lethargy, *leth′ər-ji*, *n.* heavy unnatural slumber: torpor.—*adjs.* **lethargic** (*-är′*), **-al,** pertaining to lethargy: unnaturally sleepy: torpid. — *adv.* **lethar′gically.** — *adj.* **leth′argied.** — *v.t.* **leth′-argise.** [Gr. *lēthargiā*, drowsy forgetfulness— *lēthē*, forgetfulness, *ārgos*, idle.]

Lethe, *lē'thē, n.* a river of the underworld causing forgetfulness of the past to all who drank of it: oblivion.—*adjs.* **lethē'an; leth'ied** (*Shak.*). [Gr. *lēthē,* forgetfulness (*lēthēs hydōr,* the water or river of forgetfulness)—*lēthein,* a collateral form of *lanthanein,* to be hidden.]

Lett, *let, n.* a member of a people inhabiting **Lett'-land** or Latvia: a native or citizen of Latvia.—*adjs.* **Lett'ic,** of the group (also called *Baltic*) of languages to which Lettish belongs, including Lithuanian and Old Prussian; **Lett'ish.**—*n.* the language of the Letts. [Ger. *Lette*—Lettish *Latvi.*]

letter, *let'ər, n.* a conventional mark primarily used to express a sound of speech: often loosely applied to the sound itself: a written or printed message: literal meaning: printing-type: (in *pl.*) learning, literary culture.—*v.t.* to stamp letters upon: to mark with a letter or letters.—*ns.* **lett'er-board,** a board on which matter in type is placed for keeping or convenience in handling; **lett'er-book,** a book in which letters or copies of letters are kept; **lett'er-box,** a box for receiving letters for or from the post; **lett'er-card,** a card folded and gummed like a letter, with perforated margin for opening; **lett'er-carrier,** a postman; **lett'er-clip,** an appliance for gripping letters or papers to keep them together.—*adj.* **lett'ered,** marked with letters: educated: versed in literature: literary.—*ns.* **lett'erer; lett'er-file,** an arrangement for holding letters for reference; **lett'er-founder,** one who casts type; **lett'ering,** the act of impressing or marking with letters: the letters impressed: their style or mode of formation.—*adjs.* **lett'erless,** without letters: illiterate; **lett'er-perfect,** (of an actor, &c.) having the words of the part committed accurately to memory.—*n.* **lett'erpress,** printed reading matter: a copying-press.—*n.pl.* **lett'ers-pat'ent,** a writing conferring a patent or privilege, so called because written on open sheets of parchment.—*ns.* **lett'er-stamp,** an instrument for cancelling postage-stamps: a stamp for imprinting dates, &c.; **lett'er-weight,** a paper-weight; **lett'er-wood,** leopard-wood, a South American tree of the bread-nut genus, with dark brown mottled heart-wood; **lett'er-writer,** one who writes letters, esp. for hire: a book of forms for imitation in writing letters.—**letter of credit,** a letter authorising credit or cash to a certain sum to be given to the bearer; **letter of indication,** a banker's letter requesting foreign bankers to accept the bearer's circular notes; **letters requisitory,** or **rogatory,** an instrument by which a court of one country asks that of another to take certain evidence on its behalf. [Fr. *lettre*—L. *littera, litera.*]

lettern, *let'ərn.* Same as **lectern.**

lettuce, *let'is, n.* a composite plant (*Lactuca sativa*) with milky juice: its leaves used as a salad: extended to other (inedible) plants of the genus.—**frog's lettuce,** a kind of pondweed; **lamb's lettuce,** corn-salad. [Appar. from some form (perh. the pl.) of A.Fr. *letue* (Fr. *laitue*)—L. *lactūca*—*lac,* milk.]

leu, *le'ōō, n.* the monetary unit or franc of Rumania. —Also **ley** (*lā*):—*pl.* **lei** (*lā*). [Rum., lion.]

leuc-, leuco-, leuk-, *l(y)ōōk-, l(y)ōōs-, l(y)ōō'kō-, -ko'-,* in composition, white.—*ns.* **leu'co-base, leu'co-compound,** a colourless reduction product of a dye that can be converted back to the dye by oxidation. [Gr. *leukos,* white.]

leucaemia, *l(y)ōō-sē'mi-ä, n.* leucocythaemia.—Also **leukaemia,** or (more strictly formed) **leuchaemia** (*-kē'*). [Gr. *haima,* blood.]

leuch. See **lauch.**

leucin(e), *l(y)ōō'sin, -sēn, n.* a decomposition product of proteins. [Gr. *leukos,* white.]

Leuciscus, *l(y)ōō-sis'kos, n.* a genus of freshwater cyprinoid fishes, including the roach, dace, chub, minnow, &c. [Gr. *leukiskos,* white mullet.]

leucite, *l(y)ōō'sīt, n.* a whitish mineral (silicate of aluminium and potassium).—*adj.* **leucitic** (*-sit'ik*). —*n.* **leucitohē'dron,** the cubic icositetrahedron, simulated by typical leucite crystals. [Gr. *leukos,* white.]

leucocyte, *l(y)ōō'kō-sīt, n.* a white corpuscle of the

blood or lymph.—*adj.* **leucocytic** (*-sit'ik*).—*ns.* **leucocythaemia** (*-sī-thē'mi-ä;* Gr. *haima,* blood), a disease in which there is a great excess of white corpuscles in the blood, associated with changes in the lymphatic system and enlargement of the spleen; **leucocytol'ysis** (Gr. *lysis,* dissolution), breaking down of the leucocytes; **leucocytopē'nia** (Gr. *peniā,* poverty), poverty in leucocytes; **leucocytō'sis,** the presence of an excessive number of white corpuscles in the blood. [Gr. *kytos,* container, used as if cell.]

Leucojum, *l(y)ōō-kō'jəm, n.* the snowflake genus of amaryllids. [Gr. *leukoïon,* snowdrop, &c.—*leukos,* white, *ion,* violet.]

leucoma, *(l)ōō-kō'mä, n.* a white opacity of the cornea. [Gr. *leukōma*—*leukos.*]

leucoplast, *l(y)ōō'kō-plast, n.* (*bot.*) a starch-forming body in protoplasm. [Gr. *plastos,* formed—*plassein,* to form.]

leucorrhoea, *l(y)ōō-kō-rē'ä, n.* an abnormal mucous or muco-purulent discharge from the vagina, the whites. [Gr. *rhoiā*—*rheein,* to flow.]

leucotomy, *l(y)ōō-kot'ə-mi, n.* surgical scission of the white association fibres between the frontal lobes of the brain and the thalamus to relieve cases of severe schizophrenia and manic-depression.—*n.* **leu'cotome** (*-kō-tōm*), a needle used for the purpose. [Gr. *leukos,* white, *tomē,* a cutting.]

leukaemia. Same as **leucaemia.**

lev, lew, *lef, n.* the monetary unit or franc of Bulgaria:—*pl.* **leva** (*lev'ä*). [Bulg., lion.]

Levant, *li-vant', n.* (*obs.*) the East: the eastern Mediterranean and its shores: **levant,** the levanter wind: a kind of morocco leather.—*adj.* **levant** (*lev'ənt*), eastern.—*n.* **Levant'er,** an inhabitant of the Levant: **levanter,** a boisterous easterly wind in the Levant.—*adj.* **Levant'ine** (or *lev'ən-tīn*), of the Levant. [Fr. *levant* or It. *levante,* east, lit. rising—L. *levāre,* to raise.]

levant, *li-vant', v.i.* to decamp.—*n.* **levant'er,** one who absconds, esp. with bets unpaid. [Sp. *levantar,* to move.—L. *levāre,* to raise.]

levator, *le-vā'tor, n.* a muscle that raises—opp. to *depressor.* [L. *levātor,* a lifter—*levāre.*]

levee, *lev'i,* also *li-vē', n.* getting out of bed: a morning (or comparatively early) reception of visitors, esp. by a personage.—*v.t.* to attend the levee of. [Fr. *levée, lever*—L. *levāre,* to raise.]

levee, *lev'i, li-vē', n.* a natural or artificial riverside embankment, esp. on the Lower Mississippi: a quay. [Fr. *levée,* raised; see the foregoing.]

level, *lev'l, n.* an instrument for testing horizontality: a horizontal position: a condition of horizontality: a horizontal plane or line: a nearly horizontal surface or region with no considerable inequalities: the horizontal plane, literal or figurative, that anything occupies or reaches up to: height: a horizontal mine-gallery: (*Shak.*) the act of aiming: (*Spens.*) the thing aimed at: an ascertainment of relative elevation: a levelling survey: natural or appropriate position or rank: a condition of equality.—*adj.* horizontal: even, smooth: even with anything else: uniform: well-balanced, sound of judgment: in the same line or plane: filled to a level with the brim: equal in position or dignity.—*adv.* in a level manner: point-blank.—*v.t.* to make horizontal: to make flat or smooth: to lay low: to raze: to aim: to make equal: to direct: survey by taking levels.—*v.i.* to make things level: to aim: to guess, estimate:—*pr.p.* **lev'elling;** *pa.t.* and *pa.p.* **lev'elled.**—*n.* **lev'el-cross'ing,** a place at which a road crosses a railway at the same level.—*adj.* **lev'el-head'ed,** having sound common sense.—*ns.* **lev'eller,** one who levels in any sense: one who would remove all social or political inequalities, esp. **(Leveller)** one of an ultra-republican party in the parliamentary army, crushed by Cromwell in 1649; **lev'elling; lev'elling-rod, -staff,** a graduated rod used in levelling.—*adv.* **lev'elly,** (*rare*) evenly.—*n.* **lev'elness.**—**level best,** (*coll.*) one's utmost; **level down** or **up,** to lower or raise to the same level or status; **find one's level,** come to equilibrium in one's natural position or rank; **on the level,** fair: (*U.S.*) honestly speaking..

[O.Fr. *livel*, *liveau* (Fr. *niveau*)—L. *lībella*, a plummet, dim. of *lībra*, a balance.]

level-coil, *lev'l-koil*, *n.* (*arch.*) an old Christmas game in which the players changed seats : a hubbub. [Fr. *lever le cul*, to lift the buttocks.]

lever, *lē'vǝr*, *n.* a bar turning on a support or fulcrum for imparting pressure or motion from a source of power to a resistance.—*v.t.* to move with a lever. —*ns.* **le'verage**, the mechanical power gained by the use of the lever : advantage gained for any purpose ; **le'ver-watch**, a watch having a vibrating lever in the mechanism of the escapement. [O.Fr. *leveor*—*lever*—L. *levāre*, to raise.]

leveret, *lev'ǝ-rit*, *n.* a hare in its first year. [O.Fr. *levrette* (Fr. *lièvre*)—L. *lepus*, *lepǒris*, a hare.]

leviable, *lev'i-ǝ-bl*, *adj.* able to be levied or assessed.

leviathan, *le-vī'ǝ-thǝn*, *n.* (*B.*) a water animal, in Job xli., apparently a crocodile : a huge sea-monster : anything of huge size, esp. a ship or a man : (after Hobbes's book, 1651) the state : (*obs.*) Satan.—*adj.* gigantic. [Heb. *livyāthān*.]

levigate, *lev'i-gāt*, *v.t.* to smooth : to grind to fine powder, esp. with a liquid.—*adj.* smooth.—*adj.* **lev'igable**—*n.* **leviga'tion**. [L. *lēvigāre*, *-ātum*—*lēvis*, smooth ; Gr. *leios* ; akin to **level**.]

levigate, *lev'i-gāt*, *v.t.* to lighten. [L. *lēvigāre*, *-ātum*—*lēvis*, light.]

levin, *lev'in*, *n.* (*arch.*) lightning. [Origin obscure.]

levirate, *lēv'* or *lev'i-rāt*, *n.* the (ancient Hebrew and other) custom of compulsory marriage with a childless brother's widow. — *adjs.* **lev'irate**, **leviratical** (*-rat'i-kl*).—*n.* **levirā'tion**. [L. *lēvir*, a brother-in-law.]

levitation, *lev-i-tā'shǝn*, *n.* the act of rising by virtue of lightness : act of rendering light : the floating of heavy bodies in the air, according to spiritualists.—*v.t.* **lev'itate**, to cause to float. [On the model of *gravitate*—L. *levis*, light.]

Levite, *lē'vīt*, *n.* a descendant of *Levi* : an inferior priest of the ancient Jewish Church : (*slang*) a clergyman.—*adjs.* **levitic** (*li-vit'ik*), **-al.**—*adv.* **levit'ically.**—*n.* **Levit'icus**, the third book of the Old Testament.—**Levitical degrees**, the degrees of kindred within which marriage was forbidden in Lev. xviii. 6-18.

levity, *lev'it-i*, *n.* lightness of weight : lightness of temper or conduct : thoughtlessness : disposition to trifle : vanity. [L. *levitās*, *-ātis*—*levis*, light.]

levulose. Same as **laevulose**.

levy, *lev'i*, *v.t.* to raise, collect; as an army or tax : to call for : to impose : to begin to wage : (*pr.p.* **lev'ying**; *pa.t.* and *pa.p.* **lev'ied**).—*n.* the act of levying : a contribution called for from members of an association : a tax : the amount collected : troops levied.—**to levy war**, to make war ; **levy in mass** (Fr. *levée en masse*), a levy of all able-bodied men for military service. [Fr. *levée*—*lever*—L. *levāre*, to raise.]

lew, *l(y)ōō*, *adj.* tepid, lukewarm. [O.E. *hléow.*]

lewd, *l(y)ōōd*, *adj.* (*obs.*) ignorant : (*B.*) bare : (*obs.*) bad : lustful : unchaste. — *adv.* **lewd'ly.** — *ns.* **lewd'ness**; **lewds'by**, **lewd'ster**, one addicted to lewdness. [O.E. *lǽwede*, ignorant.]

lewis, *lōō'is*, *n.* a dovetail iron tenon for lifting blocks of stone (also **lew'isson**): a freemason's son. [Ety. dub.]

Lewis gun, *lōō'is gun*, a light machine-gun invented by Col. Isaac Newton *Lewis*.

Lewisian, *lōō-iz'i-ǝn*, or *-is'*, *adj.* of *Lewis* in the Outer Hebrides : (*geol.*) Pre-Cambrian.

lewisite, *lōō'is-īt*, *n.* a yellow cubic mineral, calcium titanium antimonate. [Named after W. J. *Lewis* (1847-1926), English mineralogist.]

lewisite, *lōō'is-īt*, *n.* a vesicant liquid, an arsine derivative, used in chemical warfare. [Named after W. L. *Lewis*, American chemist.]

lexicon, *leks'i-kǝn*, *n.* a word-book or dictionary.— *adj.* **lex'ical**, belonging to a lexicon.—*adv.* **lexi'cally.** — *n.* **lexicographer** (*-kog'rǝ-fǝr*). — *adjs.* **lexicographic** (*-kǝ-graf'ik*), **-al.**—*ns.* **lexicog'raphist**; **lexicog'raphy**, dictionary-making : **lexicol'ogist**; **lexicol'ogy**, the study of the history and meaning of words. [Gr. *lexikon*, a dictionary —*lexis*, a word, *legein*, to speak.]

lexigraphy, *leks-ig'rǝ-fi*, *n.* a system of writing in which each sign represents a word.—*adj.* **lexigraphic** (*-graf'ik*), **-al.** [Gr. *lexis*, word, *graphein*, to write.]

ley. Same as **lea** (1, 2, 3).—*n.* **ley-farming** (see **lea** (2)).

Leyden jar, *lā'dǝn jär*, a condenser for electricity, a glass jar coated inside and outside with tinfoil or other conducting material. [*Leyden* in Holland, where it was invented.]

leze-majesty. See **lese-majesty.**

lherzolite, *lǝr'zǝ-līt*, *n.* peridotite, consisting essentially of olivine with monoclinic and orthorhombic pyroxenes. [From Lake *Lherz* in the Pyrenees (Ariège).]

liable, *lī'ǝ-bl*, *adj.* subject to an obligation : exposed to a possibility or risk : (*Shak.*) subject : responsible : tending : apt : (*Shak.*) fitting, suitable : (*U.S.*) likely.—*n.* **liabil'ity**, state of being liable : that for which one is liable, a debt, &c.—**employers' liability**, responsibility of employers to their servants for the negligence of those to whom they have delegated their authority ; **limited liability**, a principle of modern statute law which limits the responsibilities of shareholders in a partnership, joint-stock company, &c., by the extent of their personal interest therein. [App.— Fr. *lier*—L. *ligāre*, to bind.]

liaison, *lē-ā'zn*, *-zon⁰*, *lyez-on⁰*, *n.* union, or bond of union : connexion : illicit union between the sexes : in French, the linking in pronunciation of a final (and otherwise silent) consonant to a vowel beginning the next word : (*mil.*) effective conjunction with another unit or force.—**liaison officer**, an officer forming a link with another unit or force. [Fr.,—L. *ligātiō*, *-ōnis*—*ligāre*, to bind.]

liana, *lē-ä'nä*, **liane**, *lē-ân'*, *n.* any climbing plant, especially any contorted woody kind festooning tropical forests. [Fr. *liane*, Latinised or Hispanicised as *liana*, app.—*lier*—L. *ligāre*, to bind.]

liang, *lyang*, *n.* a Chinese ounce or tael. [Chinese.]

liar, *lī'ǝr*, *n.* one who tells lies, esp. habitually. [**lie** (1).]

liard, *lī'ǝrd*, *adj.* grey : dapple-grey (*Scot.* **li'art**, **ly'art**).—*n.* (*lyär*) an old French coin of little worth. [O.Fr. *liard*, *liart*.]

Lias, *lī'ǝs*, *n.* and *adj.* (*geol.*) Lower Jurassic.—*adj.* **Liassic** (*lī-as'ik*). [A Somerset quarryman's word, app.—O.Fr. *liois* (Fr. *liais*), a kind of limestone.]

lib, *lib*, *v.t.* (now *dial.*) to geld. [Cf. Du. *lubben.*]

libation, *lī-bā'shǝn*, *n.* the pouring forth of wine or other liquid in honour of a god, or (facetiously) for other purpose : the liquid poured.—*adj.* **li'bant**, sipping : lightly touching.—*v.t.* **li'bate** (*rare*) to make a libation to.—*adj.* **li'batory.** [L. *libāre*, *-ātum*, to pour, sip, touch; Gr. *leibein*, to pour.]

libbard, *lib'ǝrd*, *n.* (*arch.*). Same as **leopard.**

libeccio, *li-bet'chō*, *n.* the south-west wind.—Also (*Milt.*) **libecchio**. [It.,—L. *Libs* ; Gr. *Lips*, *Libos*.]

libel, *lī'bl*, *n.* a written accusation : any malicious defamatory publication or statement : (*English law*) written defamation (distinguished from *slander* or spoken defamation ; in Scots law both are slander): the statement of a plaintiff's grounds of complaint.—*v.t.* to defame by libel : to satirise unfairly : (*law*) to proceed against by producing a written complaint :—*pr.p.* **li'belling**; *pa.t.* and *pa.p.* **li'belled.**—*ns.* **li'bellant**, one who brings a libel ; **li'beller**, a defamer ; **li'belling.**—*adj.* **li'bellous**, containing a libel : defamatory.—*adv.* **li'bellously.** [L. *libellus*, dim. of *liber*, a book.]

liber, *lī'bǝr*, *n.* bast. [L. *liber*, bast, book.]

liberal, *lib'ǝ-rl*, *adj.* befitting a freeman or a gentleman : directed towards the cultivation of the mind for its own sake, disinterested (opposed to *technical* and *professional*): generous : noble-minded : broad-minded : not bound by authority or traditional orthodoxy : looking to the general or broad sense rather than the literal : candid : free : free from restraint : (*obs.*) licentious in speech or action : ample : of the Liberal Party (see below).—*n.* one who advocates greater freedom in political institutions : one whose views in theology are liberal.—*n.*

Neutral vowels in unaccented syllables : *el'ǝ-mǝnt*, *in'fǝnt*, *ran'dǝm*

liberalisā′tion.—*v.t.* and *v.i.* **lib′eralise,** to make or become liberal, or enlightened.—*ns.* **lib′eralism,** the principles of a Liberal in politics or religion; **lib′eralist.**—*adj.* **liberalist′ic.**—*n.* **liberality** (*-al′i-ti*), the quality of being liberal: generosity: largeness or nobleness of mind: candour: freedom from prejudice.—*adv.* **lib′erally.**—**liberal arts,** the studies that make up a liberal education: in the Middle Ages, the *trivium* and *quadrivium*; **Liberal Party,** successors of the Whigs, including the Radicals, advocates of democratic reform and liberty; **Liberal Unionists,** a section of the Liberal Party that opposed Gladstone's Home Rule policy (1886) and joined the Conservatives. [L. *liberālis,* befitting a freeman—*liber,* free.]

liberate, *lib′ə-rāt, v.t.* to set free: to release from restraint, confinement, or bondage: to give off.—*ns.* **liberā′tion;** **liberā′tionism;** **liberā′tionist,** one who is in favour of church disestablishment; **lib′erātor.**—*adj.* **lib′eratory** (*-ə-tə-ri*), tending to liberate. [L. *liberāre, -ātum—liber,* free.]

liberty, *lib′ər-ti, n.* freedom from constraint, captivity, slavery, or tyranny: freedom to do as one pleases: the unrestrained enjoyment of natural rights: power of free choice: privilege: permission: free range: leisure: disposal: the bounds within which certain privileges are enjoyed: (often in *pl.*) a limited area outside a prison in which prisoners were allowed to live: presumptuous or undue freedom: speech or action violating ordinary civility.—*ns.* **libertā′rian,** a believer in free-will; **libertā′rianism;** **liber′ticide,** a destroyer of liberty: destruction of liberty; **lib′ertinage** (also *-ərt′*), debauchery; **lib′ertine** (*-tīn, -tin, -tēn*), originally, a freedman: formerly one who professed free opinions, esp. in religion: one who leads a licentious life, a rake or debauchee.—*adj.* belonging to a freedman: unrestrained: licentious.—*ns.* **lib′ertinism;** **lib′erty-boat,** a boat for liberty-men; **liberty-man,** a sailor with permission to go ashore.—**at liberty,** free: unoccupied: available; **liberty cap** (see **cap**); **Liberty Hall,** a place where one may do as one likes; **liberty of indifference,** freedom of the will; **liberty of the press,** freedom to print and publish without government permission; **take the liberty,** venture, presume; **take liberties with,** to treat with undue freedom or familiarity, or indecently: to falsify. [Fr. *liberté*—L. *libertās, -ātis,* liberty: L. *libertīnus,* a freedman—*liber,* free.]

libido, *li-bē′dō, li-bī′dō, n.* (*psych.*) vital urge, either in general or as of sexual origin: sexual impulse.—*adjs.* **libidinal** (*-bid′*), pertaining to the libido; **libid′inous,** lustful, lascivious, lewd.—*ns.* **libid′inist,** a lewd person; **libidinos′ity, libid′inousness.**—*adv.* **libid′inously.** [L. *libīdō, -inis,* desire —*libet, lubet,* it pleases.]

libken, *lib′ken, n.* (*old slang*) a place of abode. [Old slang *lib,* to sleep, **ken** (2).]

libra, *lī′brä,* L. *lē′, n.* (*ant.*) a Roman pound (used in contraction lb. for the British pound, and £ for a pound in money): **Libra,** the Balance, a constellation between the Virgin and the Scorpion: the seventh sign of the zodiac in which it used to be (it is now in Scorpio). [L. *lībra.*]

library, *lī′brə-ri, n.* a collection of books: a building or room containing it: a publisher's series.—*ns.* **librā′rian,** the keeper of a library; **librā′rianship.** [L. *lībrārium,* a bookcase—*liber,* a book.]

librate, *lī′brāt, v.t.* to poise: to balance.—*v.i.* to oscillate: to be poised.—*n.* **librā′tion,** balancing: a state of equipoise: a slight swinging motion.—*adj.* **lī′bratory.**—**libration of the moon,** a slight turning of the moon to each side alternately so that more than half of its surface is visible one time or other. [L. *lībrāre, -ātum—lībra,* balance.]

libretto, *li-bret′ō, n.* the text or book of words of an opera or oratorio, &c.:—*pl.* **librett′i** (*-ē*), **librett′os.**—*n.* **librett′ist,** a writer of libretti. [It., dim. of *libro*—L. *liber,* a book.]

Libyan, *lib′i-ən, adj.* of Libya in North Africa.—*n.* a native thereof. [Gr. *Libyē,* Libya.]

lice, *līs,* plural of **louse.**

licence, *lī′səns, n.* a being allowed: leave: grant

of permission, as for manufacturing a patented article or for the sale of intoxicants: the document by which authority is conferred: excess or abuse of freedom: licentiousness, libertinage, debauchery: a departure for effect from a rule or standard in art or literature: tolerated freedom. —Also (esp. *U.S.*) **license.**—*v.t.* **li′cense,** to grant licence to: to permit to depart, dismiss: to authorise or permit.—Also **licence.**—*adjs.* **li′censable; li′censed,** holding a licence: permitted, tolerated.—*ns.* **licensee′,** one to whom a licence is granted; **li′censer,** one who grants licence or permission: one authorised to license; **li′censure,** act of licensing; **licentiate** (*lī-sen′shi-āt*), among Presbyterians, a person authorised by a Presbytery to preach: a holder of an academic diploma of various kinds: in some European universities a graduate ranking between bachelor and doctor.—*adj.* **licentious** (*-sen′shəs*), indulging in excessive freedom: given to the indulgence of the animal passions: dissolute.—*adv.* **licen′tiously.** —*n.* **licen′tiousness.** — **licensed victualler,** a victualler who holds a licence to sell intoxicating liquors; **special licence,** licence given by the Archbishop of Canterbury permitting the marriage of two specified persons without banns, and at a place and time other than those prescribed by law—loosely applied in Scotland to marriage by consent registered by warrant of the sheriff. [Fr. *licence*—L. *licentia—licēre,* to be allowed.]

lich, *lich, adj.* (*Spens.*) a Southern form of **like.**

lich, *lich, n.* (*obs.*) a body, living or dead.—*ns.* **lich′gate,** a roofed churchyard gate to rest the bier under; **lich′-owl,** a screech-owl, deemed a death-portent; **lich′wake,** (see **lykewake**); **lich′way,** a path by which the dead are carried to burial. [M.E. *lich* (Southern), *like* (Northern)—O.E. *līc;* Ger. *leiche,* corpse.]

lichanos, *lich′a-nos, n.* (*anc. Gr. mus.*) the string or the note struck by the forefinger. [Gr. *lichanos,* forefinger, lichanos—*leichein,* to lick.]

lichen, *lī′ken,* rarely *lich′ən, n.* a compound plant consisting of a fungus and an alga living symbiotically, forming crusts and tufts on stones, trees, and soil: an eruption on the skin.—*adj.* **li′chened,** covered with lichens.—*ns.* **li′chenin,** a starch got from Iceland moss; **li′chenism,** the consorting of fungus and alga as a lichen; **li′chenist, lichenol′ogist,** one versed in lichenol′ogy, the study of lichens.—*adj.* **li′chenous,** abounding in, or pertaining to, of the nature of, lichens, or lichen. [L. *līchēn*—Gr. *leichēn, -ēnos.*]

lichgate, &c. See **lich.**

licht, *liħt,* the Scots form of **light** (1, 2, 3).

licit, *lis′it, adj.* lawful, allowable.—*adv.* **lic′itly.** [L. *licitus.*]

lick, *lik, v.t.* to pass the tongue over: to take in by the tongue: to lap: to put or render by passing the tongue over: to pass over or play upon in the manner of a tongue: to smear: (*slang*) to beat.— *v.i.* (*slang*) to go at full speed.—*n.* an act of licking: a quantity licked up, or such as might be imagined to be licked up: a slight smearing or wash: a place where animals lick salt: a blow, flick (esp. *Scot.* in *pl.,* a thrashing): (*coll.*) vigorous speed: (*Scot.*) a wag.—*ns.* **lick′er; lick′er-in,** a toothed cylinder that takes in material to a carding engine; **lick′ing,** a thrashing; **lick′penny,** that which licks up, or is a drain upon, one's money; **lick′-platter, lick′-trencher,** a parasite; **lick′spittle,** a toady.—**a lick and a promise,** a perfunctory wash; **lick into shape,** to mould into due form, from the notion that the she-bear gives form to her shapeless young by licking them; **lick one's boots,** to toady; **lick the dust,** to be slain: to be abjectly servile. [O.E. *liccian;* Ger. *lecken,* L. *lingĕre,* Gr. *leichein.*]

lickerish, liquorish, *lik′ər-ish, adj.* dainty: tempting: eager to taste or enjoy: lecherous.—*adv.* **lick′erishly.**—*n.* **lick′erishness.** [Variant of **lecherous.**]

licorice. Same as **liquorice.**

lictor, *lik′tor, -tər, n.* an officer who attended a Roman magistrate, bearing the fasces. [L. *lictor.*]

lid, *lid, n.* a cover, hinged or separate, for the

opening of a receptacle : the movable cover of the eye : (*fig.*) an effective restraint : (*slang*) a hat.—*adjs.* **lidd'ed**, having a lid or lids ; **lid'less.**—**put the lid on it**, to end the matter : to be a culminating injustice, misfortune, &c. [O.E. *hlid* (Du. *lid*)—*hlidan*, to cover.]

lidger. See **ledger.**

lido, *lē'dō*, *n.* a bathing beach. [From the *Lido* at Venice—L. *lītus*, shore.]

lie, *lī*, *n.* a false statement made with the intention of deceiving : anything misleading or of the nature of imposture : (with *the*) an accusation of lying.—*v.i.* to utter falsehood with an intention to deceive : to give a false impression :—*pr.p.* **ly'ing** ; *pa.t.* and *pa.p.* **lied.**—(*Scot.*) **lee** (*lē*), *n.* and *v.i.* often of an unintentional false statement.—(*dial.*) **lig.**—**give one the lie (in one's throat)**, to charge one to one's face of lying ; **give the lie to**, to charge with lying : to prove false ; **lie in one's throat**, to lie shamelessly ; **white lie**, a conventional phrase not strictly true : a well-meant falsehood. [O.E. *lyge* (noun), *lēogan* (strong vb.) ; Du. *liegen*, Goth. *liugan*, Ger. *lügen*, to lie.]

lie, *lī*, *v.i.* to be in a horizontal or nearly horizontal posture : to assume such a posture : to lean : to press : to be situated : to have a position or extent : to remain : to be or remain passively : to abide : to be still : to be incumbent : to depend : to consist : (*law*) to be sustainable : (*Shak.*) to be imprisoned : to lodge, pass the night : (*pr.p.* **ly'ing** ; *pa.t.* **lay** ; *pa.p.* **lain**, (*B.*) **li'en**—erroneously **laid**, by confusion with **lay**).—*n.* mode or direction of lying : slope and disposition : relative position : general situation : a spell of lying : an animal's lurking-place or favourite station : position from which a golfball is to be played : a layer : a railway siding.—*ns.* **lī'er** ; **lie'-abed'**, one who lies late—also *adj.*—**lie along**, to be extended at full length ; **lie at one's door**, to be directly imputable to one ; **lie at one's heart**, to be an object of interest or affection to one ; **lie by**, to be inactive : to keep out of the way : (*naut.*) to lie to ; **lie by the heels**, to be in prison ; **lie hard** or **heavy on, upon, to**, to oppress, burden ; **lie in**, to be in childbed ; **lie in one**, to be in one's power ; **lie in the way**, to be ready, at hand : to be an obstacle ; **lie in wait**, to lie in ambush ; **lie low**, to keep quiet or hidden : to conceal one's actions or intentions ; **lie on, upon**, to be incumbent on ; **lie on one's hands**, to remain unwanted, unclaimed, or unused ; **lie on the oars** (see **oars**) ; **lie out of**, to remain without the good of, without payment of ; **lie over**, to be deferred to a future occasion ; **lie to**, to be or become nearly stationary with head to wind ; **lie under**, to be subject to or oppressed by ; **lie up**, to abstain from work : to take to or remain in bed : to go into or be in dock ; **lie with**, to lodge or sleep with : to have carnal knowledge of ; **lying-in hospital**, a maternity hospital ; **take it lying down**, to endure tamely. [O.E. *licgan* ; Ger. *liegen* ; Goth. *ligan.*]

Liebig, *lē'big*, *n.* a beef extract first prepared by the great German chemist J. von *Liebig* (1803-73).

lied, *lēt*, *n.* a German lyric or song, esp. an art-song : —*pl.* **lieder** (*lē'dər*). [Ger. ; cf. O.E. *lēoth*, a song.]

lief, *lēf*, *adj.* and *n.* (*arch.*) beloved, dear.—*adv.* willingly.—Also *adj.* and *adv.* **lieve, leve** (*lēv*) :—*compar.* **liefer, liev'er** (*Scot.* **loor**) ; *superl.* **lief'est, liev'est.**—**had as lief**, should like as well to ; **had liefer, liever**, had rather ; **leeze me**, (*Scot.*) for **lief is me**, an expression of affection (usu. with *on*). [O.E. *lēof* ; Ger. *lieb.*]

liege, *lēj*, *adj.* free, except as within the relations of vassal and feudal lord : under a feudal tenure.—*n.* one under a feudal tenure : a vassal : a loyal vassal, subject : a lord or superior (also in this sense, **liege'-lord**).—*n.* **liege'dom**, allegiance.—*adj.* **liege'less**, not subject to a superior.—*n.* **liege'man**, a vassal : a subject. [O.Fr. *lige*, prob. from O.H.G. *ledic*, free, *līdan*, to depart.]

lien, *lē'ən*, *lēn*, *n.* (*law*) a right to retain possession of another's property until the owner pays a debt. [Fr.,—L. *ligāmen*, tie, band.]

lien, *lī'ən*, (*B.*) *pa.p.* of **lie** (2).

lien, *lī'ən*, *n.* the spleen.—*adj.* **li'enal.** [L. *liēn.*]

lientery, *lī'ən-tə-ri*, *n.* a form of diarrhoea with liquid evacuations of undigested food.—*adj.* **lienteric** (*-ter'ik*). [Gr. *leios*, smooth, *enteron*, an intestine.]

lierne, *li-ərn'*, *n.* a cross-rib or branch-rib in vaulting.

lieu, *l(y)ōō*, *n.* place, stead, chiefly in the phrase ' in lieu of.' [Fr.,—L. *locus*, place.]

lieutenant, *lef-*, *lif-*, *ləf-ten'ənt*, in the navy *lə'*, in U.S. *l(y)ōō-*, *n.* one representing or performing the work of another : an officer holding the place of another in his absence : a commissioned officer in the army next below a captain, or in the navy next below a lieutenant-commander and ranking with captain in the army : one holding a place next in rank to a superior, as in the compounds **lieuten'ant-col'onel, lieuten'ant-comman'der, lieuten'ant-gen'eral.** — *ns.* **lieuten'ancy, lieuten'antship**, office or commission of a lieutenant : the body of lieutenants ; **lieuten'ant-col'onelcy ; lieuten'ant - command'ership ; lieuten'ant - gen'eralship ; lieuten'ant-gov'ernor**, a State governor's deputy (*U.S.*, *Australia*) : a governor subordinate to a governor-general : a governor (Isle of Man, Jersey, Guernsey) ; **lieuten'ant-gov'ernorship**, **lieuten'antry**, (*Shak.*) lieutenancy.—**Lord Lieutenant**, the title of the viceroy of Ireland (till 1922) : a permanent governor of a county, head of the magistracy and the chief executive authority :—*pl.* **lords lieutenant, lord lieutenants, lords lieutenants.** [Fr. ; see **lieu** and **tenant.**]

life, *līf*, *n.* state of being alive : conscious existence : animate or vegetative existence : the sum of the activities of plants and animals : continuation or possession of such a state : continued existence, activity, or validity of anything : vitality : union of soul and body : the period between birth and death : a continued opportunity of remaining in the game : career : present state of existence : manner of living : moral conduct : animation : liveliness : appearance of being alive : a living being : living things : social state : human affairs : narrative of a life : eternal happiness : a quickening principle : that on which continued existence depends : one who imparts animation : the living form and expression, living semblance : an insured person : (*pl.* **lives**, *līvz*).—*interj.* used as an oath, abbreviated from *God's life.*—*adj.* (and in composition) for the duration of life : of life.—*adj.* **life'-and-death'**, critical : determining between life and death.—*ns.* **life'-annū'ity**, a sum paid to a person yearly during life ; **life'-assur'ance**, **life'-insur'ance**, insurance based on a person's life ; **life'-belt**, a buoyant belt for sustaining a person in the water ; **life'-blood**, the blood necessary to life : that which gives strength or life : a twitching, as of the eyelid ; **life'boat**, a boat for saving shipwrecked persons ; **life'-buoy**, a buoy for supporting a person in the water till he can be rescued ; **life'-cycle**, (*biol.*) the round of changes in the life and generations of an organism, from zygote to zygote ; **life'-estate'**, an estate held during the life of the possessor ; **life'-force'**, a directing principle supposed to be immanent in living things, turning their activities to nature's own purposes. — *adjs.* **life'ful** (*Spens.*) **lyfull, lifull**), full of vital energy ; **life'-giving**, imparting life : invigorating.—*ns.* **life'-guard**, a body-guard : (*U.S.*) one employed to rescue bathers in difficulties ; **life'-his'tory**, the history of a life : the succession of changes from zygote to maturity and death : the life-cycle.—*adj.* **life'hold**, held for life.—*ns.* **life'-in'terest**, an interest lasting during a life ; **life'-jack'et**, a buoyant jacket, a life-belt.—*adj.* **life'less**, dead : insensible : without vigour : insipid : sluggish.—*adv.* **life'lessly.**—*n.* **life'lessness.**—*adj.* **life'like**, like a living person or the original.—*n.* **life'-line**, a rope for saving or safeguarding life.—*adj.* **life'long**, lasting throughout life.—*ns.* **life'-mor'tar**, a mortar for throwing a line to a ship in distress ; **life'-peer**, a peer whose title is not hereditary ; **life'-peer'age** ; **life'-preserv'er**, an apparatus for saving from drowning : a loaded cane ; **lif'er**, a person sentenced for life : a life sentence.—*adj.* **life'-ren'dering**, (*Shak.*)

yielding up life.—*ns.* life′rent, (*Scots law*) a right to use for life ; life′renter, one who enjoys a liferent :—*fem.* life′rentrix ; life′-rock′et, a rocket for carrying a line to a ship in distress ; life′-sav′ing.—*adj.* designed to save life, esp. from drowning.—*n.* life′-school, a school where artists work from living models.—*adjs.* life′-size(d), of the size of the object represented ; life′some, full of life : gay, lively.—*ns.* life′-table, a table of statistics of probability of life ; life′-tenant, the holder of a life-estate ; life′time, time during which one is alive.—*adj.* life′-wea′ry, (*Shak.*) weary of life : wretched.—*n.* life′-work, the work to which one's life is or is to be devoted.—bring to life, to confer life upon : to reanimate ; come to life, to become alive : to be reanimated ; for life, for the whole period of one's existence : (as if) to save one's life : for the life of him, though it were to save his life : do what he might ; high life, fashionable society or its manner of living ; Life Guards, two horse regiments formed in 1660 ; line of life, a crease in the palm in which palmists see a promise of longevity ; see life, to see how other people live, esp. the disreputable ; take one's life, to kill him ; to the life, very closely like the original : exactly drawn. [O.E. *líf* ; O.N. *líf*, Sw. *lif*, Du. *lijf*, body, life ; Ger. *leib*, body, *leben*, to live, life.]

lift, *lift*, *n.* (*Scot.*) the air, heavens, sky. [O.E. *lyft* ; Ger. *luft*, O.N. *lopt*, Goth. *luftus*, the air.]

lift, *lift*, *v.t.* to bring to a higher position : to elevate : to take up : (*Scot.*) to take up for burial : (*U.S.*) to increase : to elate : to take and carry away : to hold up, support : (*slang*) to arrest : to steal.—*v.i.* to rise.—*n.* act of lifting : lifting power : vertical distance of lifting : the component of the aerodynamic force on an aircraft acting upwards at right angles to the drag : that which is to be raised : that which assists to lift : an enclosed platform moving in a well to carry persons or goods up and down : the well in which it works : a contrivance for raising or lowering a vessel to another level of a canal : a step in advancement : help on one's way by taking upon a vehicle.—*adj.* lift′able.—*ns.* lift′er, one who, or that which, lifts : (*Shak.*) a thief ; lift′ing-bridge, a bridge whose roadway can be raised bodily ; lift′-pump, any pump that is not a force-pump.—lift one's hand, to raise it in hostility ; lift the face, perform an operation for smoothing and firming it. [O.N. *lypta*—*lopt*, the air.]

lig, ligge, *lig*, *v.i.* (*Spens.* and *Northern dialect*) a form of lie (2).—*infin.* and *pl.* (*Spens.*) also ligg′en. Lig is also a dialect form of lie (1).

ligament, *lig′ə-mənt*, *n.* anything that binds : (*anat.*) the bundle of fibrous tissue joining bones or cartilages : a bond of union.—*adjs.* ligamental (-ment′l), ligament′ary, ligament′ous.—*v.t.* ligate (*lī′gāt*), to tie up.—*ns.* liga′tion, act of binding : state of being bound ; ligature (*lig′ə-tyər*), anything that binds : a bandage : (*mus.*) a tie or slur : (*print.*) a type of two or more letters (e.g. ff, ffi) : (*med.*) a cord for tying the blood-vessels, &c. : impotence produced by magic.—*v.t.* to bind with a ligature. [L. *ligāre*, to bind.]

ligan. See lagan.

ligger, *lig′ər*, *n.* the horizontal timber of a scaffolding : a nether millstone : a plank bridge : a coverlet for a bed : a kelt or spent salmon : a night-line with float and bait for pike-fishing. [lig, Northern form of lie (2).]

light, *līt*, *n.* the agency by which objects are rendered visible : electromagnetic radiation capable of producing visual sensation : that from which it proceeds, as the sun, a lamp : a high degree of illumination : day : a gleam or shining from a bright source : a gleam or glow in the eye or on the face : the power of vision : (*arch.*) an eye : the brighter part of a picture : means of igniting or illuminating : a lighthouse : (*fig.*) mental or spiritual illumination : enlightenment : a hint, clue, keyword, help towards understanding : knowledge : open view : aspect : a conspicuous person : an aperture for admitting light : a vertical division of a window.—*adj.* not dark : bright :

whitish : well lighted.—*v.t.* to give light to : to set fire to : to attend with a light.—*v.i.* to become light or bright :—*pr.p.* light′ing ; *pa.t.* and *pa.p.* light′ed or lit.—*n.* light′-ball, a combustible ball used to give light in warfare.—*n.pl.* light′-dues, tolls from ships, for maintenance of lighthouses.—*n.* light′er, one who sets alight : a spill, mechanical device, or other means of igniting.—*adj.* light′ful, full of light.—*ns.* light′house, a building with a light to guide or warn ships or aircraft ; light′houseman, light(house)keep′er, the keeper of a lighthouse ; light′ing, illumination : ignition, kindling : disposal or quality of lights. — Also *adj.* — *n.* and *adj.* light′ing-up (lighting-up time, the time from which vehicles must show lights).—*adjs.* light′ish ; light′less.—*ns.* light′-mill, a radiometer ; light′ness ; light′-or′gan, a keyboard instrument that gives a play of light as an organ gives sound.—*adj.* light′proof, light-tight.—*n.* light′ship, a ship carrying a light and serving the purpose of a lighthouse.—*adjs.* light′some, full of light ; light′-tight, impervious to light.—*ns.* light′-tower ; light′-year, the distance light travels in a year. —according to one's lights, as far as one's knowledge, spiritual illumination, &c., enable one to judge ; between the lights, in the twilight ; between two lights, under cover of darkness ; bring to light, to reveal : come to light, to be revealed ; fixed light, in lighthouses, an unchanging light ; floating light, a light at the masthead of a lightship ; inner light, spiritual illumination, light divinely imparted ; in one's (the) light, between one and the source of illumination or chance of success, &c. ; light of nature, intellectual perception or intuition : (*theol.*) man's capacity of discovering truth unaided by revelation ; lights out, (*mil.*) a bugle-call for extinction of lights ; light up, to light one's lamp, pipe, &c. : to turn on the illumination : to make or become light or bright ; northern (southern) lights, aurora borealis (australis) ; see the light, to come into view or being : (*U.S.*) to be converted ; stand in one's own light, to hinder one's own advantage. [M.E. *liht*—O.E. (Anglian) *leht*, *léht* (W.S. *léoht*) ; Ger. *licht*.]

light, *līt*, *adj.* not heavy : of short weight : easily suffered or performed : easily digested : well risen, as bread : containing little alcohol : not heavily armed : active : not heavily burdened : unimportant : not dense or copious or intense : slight : scanty : gentle : delicate : nimble : facile : frivolous : unheeding : gay, lively : amusing : unchaste : loose, sandy : giddy, delirious : idle : worthless : (in *compar.* ; *obs.*) delivered of a child.—*adv.* lightly.—*v.t.* (*obs.*) to lighten (see also next article).—*adj.* light′-armed, armed in a manner suitable for activity.—*v.t.* light′en, to make lighter.—*v.i.* to become lighter.—*ns.* light′er, a large open boat used in unloading and loading ships ; light′erage, unloading by lighters : the payment for such unloading ; light′erman.—*adjs.* light′er-than-air, (of aircraft) sustained by a gas-bag ; light′-faced, of type, having thin lines ; light′-fing′ered, light or active with one's fingers : thievish ; light′-foot, -ed, nimble, active ; light′-hand′ed, with light, delicate, or dexterous touch : having little in the hand : empty-handed : insufficiently manned ; light′-head′ed, giddy in the head : delirious : thoughtless : unsteady.—*n.* light′-head′edness.—*adj.* light′-heart′ed, unburdened or merry of heart : free from anxiety : cheerful : inconsiderate.—*adv.* light′-heart′edly. — *n.* light′-heart′edness. — *adj.* light′-heeled, swift of foot : (*obs.*) loose, unchaste.—*ns.* light′horse, light-armed cavalry ; light′-horse′man ; light′-in′fantry, light-armed infantry. — *adjs.* light′ish ; light′-legged, swift of foot.—*adv.* light′ly, in a light manner : slightly : (*Shak.*) easily, readily, unthinkingly : (*arch.*) not improbably : promptly.—*v.t.* (esp. in Scots form lichtly, *liht′li*) to slight.—*adj.* light′-mind′ed, frivolous or unstable : inconsiderate.—*ns.* light′-mind′edness ; light′ness ; light′-o′-love, a fickle or wanton woman : in *Shak.* the name of an old dance tune.—*n.pl.* **lights**, the lungs of an animal (as lighter than adjoining parts).—*adj.* **light′some**, light, gay, lively, cheering.—*n.* **light′-someness.**—*adj.* **light′-spir′ited**, having a cheerful spirit.—*n.* **light′-weight**, a man or animal intermediate between the middle-weight and the feather-weight, as a boxer weighing 9 st. 9 lb. and under : a person of little importance or influence : a light article of any kind, esp. a motor-cycle.— *adj.* light in weight.—*adj.* **light′-winged**, having light wings : volatile.—**light literature, music,** &c., such as calls for little mental effort ; **light out,** (*U.S. slang*) to make off ; **light railway,** a railway of light construction ; **make light of,** to treat as of little consequence. [O.E. (Anglian) *líht* (W.S. *lioht*, *leóht*) ; Ger. *leicht*, O.N. *léttr* ; L. *lĕvis*.]

light, *lit*, *v.i.* dismount : to come down as from a horse or vehicle or from fall or flight : to alight : to settle : to rest : to come by chance :—*pr.p.* **light′ing;** *pa.t.* and *pa.p.* **light′ed** or **lit.**—Also (*Pr.Bk.*) **light′en.** [O.E. *líhtan*, to dismount, lit. make light ; see preceding.]

lighten. See **light** (2 and 3).

lightsome. See **light** (1 and 2).

lignage, *lin′ij* (*Spens.*). Same as **lineage.**

lign-aloes, lignaloes, *lin-al′ōz*, *lig-nal′ōz*, *n.* (*B.*) aloes-wood. [L. *lignum*, wood, and *aloēs*, gen. of L. and Gr. *aloē*, aloe.]

lignum, *lig′nəm*, *n.* wood.—*adj.* **lig′neous**, woody : wooden.—*n.* **significa′tion.**—*v.t.* and *v.i.* **lig′nify**, to turn into wood or woody :—*pr.p.* **lig′nifying;** *pa.t.* and *pa.p.* **lig′nified.**—*n.* **lig′nin**, a complicated mixture of substances deposited in thickened cell-walls of plants.—*adj.* **ligniper′dous** (L. *perdĕre*, to destroy), destructive of wood.—*n.* **lig′nite** (-*nīt*), brown coal, a stage in the conversion of vegetable matter into coal.—*adjs.* **lignitic** (-*nit′ik*) ; **ligniv′orous** (L. *vorāre*, to devour), feeding on wood.—*n.* **lig′num-vitae** (*vī′tē* ; L. pron. *lig′-noom vē′tī* ; wood of life), the wood of Guaiacum. [L. *lignum*, wood.]

lignum, *lig′nəm*, *n.* (*Austr.*) a wiry shrub (*Muehlenbeckia Cunninghamii*) or other shrub of the Polygonum family, forming dense masses in swamps and plains in Australia.—*ns.* **lig′num-scrub′, lig′num-swamp′.** [For **Polygonum.**]

ligroin, *lig′rō-in*, *n.* a petroleum fraction boiling between 80° and 120° C. [Origin unknown.]

ligule, *lig′ūl*, *n.* (*bot.*) a scale at the top of the leaf-sheath in grasses : a similar scale on a petal : a strap-shaped corolla in composite plants.—*n.* **lig′ula**, a tongue-like part or organ : the anterior part of an insect's labium or lower lip.—*adjs.* **lig′ular ; lig′ulate,** (*bot.*) like a strap : having ligules.—*n.pl.* **Liguliflo′rae**, a division of the Compositae having all flowers ligulate.—*adj.* **liguliflo′ral.** [L. *ligula*, dim. of *lingua*, a tongue.]

Liguorian, *li-gwō′ri-ən*, *n.* and *adj.* Redemptorist.

ligure, *lig′ūr*, -*yər*, *n.* (*B.*) an unknown precious stone—jacinth or amber according to R.V. [Gr. *ligýrion*.]

like, *lik*, *adj.* identical, equal, or nearly equal in any respect : similar : suiting, befitting, according, such as characterises : (*coll.*) inclined, likely, probable.—*n.* one of the same kind : the same thing : (*golf*) a stroke bringing the total to the same as the other side's : an exact resemblance. —*adv.* (tending to become a *prep.* by usual omission of *to*) in the same manner : alike : probably : (*vulg.*) as it were : (now *vulg.*) as if about.—*conj.* (*Shak.* ; another reading *as* ; now *vulg.*) as : as if.

—*v.t.* (*Shak.*) to compare, liken.—*v.i.* to be or seem likely, to come near.—*ns.* **like′lihood**, similitude : semblance : resemblance : probability : promise of success or of future excellence ; **like′liness**, likelihood : (*Spens.*) likeness.—*adj.* **like′ly**, (*Spens.*) similar : like the thing required : promising : probable : credible : pleasing : comely.— *adv.* probably.—*adj.* **like′-mind′ed**, having a similar disposition or purpose.—*v.t.* **lik′en**, to represent as like or similar : to compare.[— *n.* **like′ness**, resemblance : semblance : guise : one who or that which has a resemblance : a portrait.— *adv.* **like′wise**, in like wise or manner : also : moreover : too.—**feel like,** to be disposed or inclined towards ; **had like,** was likely, came near : was in danger ; **look like,** to show a likelihood of : to appear similar to ; **something like a,** a fine specimen, a model of what the thing should be ; **such like,** of that kind. [O.E. *líc*, seen in *gelíc* ; O.N. *líkr*, Du. *gelijk*, Ger. *gleich* (=*geleich*).]

like, *lik*, *v.t.* (*obs.*) to please : to be pleased with : to approve : to enjoy.—*n.* a liking, chiefly in phrase ' likes and dislikes.'—*adj.* **lik(e)′able**, lovable : amiable.—*ns.* **lik′er**, one who likes ; **lik′ing**, affection, taste, inclination : satisfaction : (*Milt.*) beloved : (*obs.*) condition, plight.—*adj.* pleasing : in good condition (also **good′-liking, well′-liking**).—**on liking**, on approval. [Orig. impersonal—O.E. *lícian*, to please, to be suitable— *líc*, like, suitable, likely.]

like, *lik*, *n.* (*Scot.*) a corpse : a lykewake.—*n.* **like′wake, -walk** (see **lykewake**). [Northern form of **lich.**]

likin, *lē-kēn′*, *n.* a Chinese transit duty. [Chin.]

lilac, *lī′lək*, *n.* a European tree (*Syringa vulgaris*) of the olive family, with light-purple or white flowers, or other species of the genus : a light-purple colour.—*adj.* of that colour. [Fr. (*obs.*) and Sp.,— Ar. *lilāk*, *lilāk*—Pers. *lilak*, *nīlak*, bluish.]

lill, *lil*, *v.t.* (*Spens.*) to loll (the tongue). [Cf. **loll.**]

lill, *lil*, *n.* (*Scot.*) a finger-hole of a wind instrument. [Cf. Du. *lul.*]

Lillibullero, *lil-i-boo-lē′rō*, *n.* the famous ballad in mockery of the Irish Catholics, which ' sung James II. out of three kingdoms.'—Also **Lilliburlē′ro.** [From the meaningless refrain.]

Lilliputian, *lil-i-pū′sh(y)ən*, *n.* an inhabitant of **Lill′iput** (-*put*), an imaginary country described by Swift in his *Gulliver's Travels*, inhabited by pygmies : a midget, pygmy.—*adj.* diminutive.

lilt, *lilt*, *v.i.* to do anything briskly or adroitly, as to hop about : to sing or play, esp. merrily, or vaguely and absent-mindedly, giving the swing or cadence rather than the structure of the melody : to hum.—*v.t.* to sing or play in such a manner.— *n.* a cheerful song or air : cadence, movement of a tune or the like : a lill. [M.E. *lulte* ; origin unknown.]

lily, *lil′i*, *n.* any plant or flower of the genus **Lil′ium,** typical genus of **Liliā′ceae,** a family of monocotyledons differing from rushes chiefly in the large conspicuous flowers : extended to others, of the same family, of the kindred Amaryllidaceae, or unrelated : the fleur-de-lis : a person or thing of great purity or whiteness.—*adj.* white : pale :— *adjs.* **liliā′ceous ; lil′ied**, adorned with lilies : resembling lilies ; **lil′y-liv′ered**, white-livered : cowardly ; **lil′y-white.**—**lily of the Nile,** Richardia or Zantedeschia ; **lily of the valley,** Convallaria. [O.E. *lilie*—L. *lilium*—Gr. *leirion*, lily.]

Lima, *lē′mä*, *n.* (in full **Li′ma-bean′**) a bean (*Phaseolus lunatus*) akin to the French bean.—*n.* **li′ma-wood,** a kind of Brazil-wood. [*Lima* in Peru.]

limation, *lī-mā′shən*, *n.* filing. [L. *līma*, a file.]

Limax, *lī′maks*, *n.* the common genus of slugs, giving name to the slug family **Limā′ceae** :—*pl.* **limaces** (*lī-mā′sēz*).—*adj.* **limaceous** (*lī-mā′shos*). —*n.* **limacel** (*lim-ə-sel′*), a slug's reduced, usually embedded, shell.—*adj.* **limaciform** (*lim-as′*, or *lī-mās′*), slug-like.—*n.* **limaçon** (*lim′ə-son* ; Fr. *lē-mä-son°*), a curve whose polar equation is $r = a \cos \theta + b$. [L. *līmāx*, a slug.]

limb, *lim*, *n.* a member or organ of the body, now only an arm, leg, or wing : (esp. *U.S.*) a prudish euphemism for leg: a projecting part: a main branch of a tree or of anything else: a member of a body of people, as 'a limb of the law': an imp, scapegrace, as 'a limb of Satan.'—*v.t.* (*Milt.*) to supply with limbs: to dismember.—*adj.* **limbed**, furnished with limbs.—*n.* **limb'-girdle**, a bony arch with which a limb articulates.—*adj.* **limb'less**.—*adv.* **limb'meal**, (*Shak.*) limb by limb. [O.E. *lim*: O.N. *limr*, Sw. *lem*.]

limb, *lim*, *n.* an edge or border, as of the sun, &c.: the edge of a sextant, &c.: (*bot.*) the free or expanded part of a floral or other leaf.—*adjs.* **lim'bate**, bordered; **lim'bous**, overlapping. [L. *limbus*, a border.]

limbeck, limbec, *lim'bek*, *n.* (*Spens., Shak.*) aphetic for alembic.

limber, *lim'bər*, *n.* (*prov.*) the shaft of a vehicle: (*mil.*) the detachable fore-part of a gun-carriage. —*v.t.* to attach to the limber. [Poss. Fr. *limonière*, of doubtful origin.]

limber, *lim'bər*, *adj.* pliant, flexible.—*v.t.* to make limber.—*ns.* **lim'ber-neck**, botulism in birds; **lim'berness**. [Origin obscure.]

Limbo, limbo, *lim'bō*, *n.* the borderland of Hell, assigned to the unbaptised (*Limbus patrum* for the righteous who died before Christ, *Limbus infantum* for children): any unsatisfactory place of consignment or oblivion: prison.—Also **Lim'-bus** (-*bəs*). [From the Latin phrase *in limbo, in*, in, and abl. of *limbus*, border.]

limburgite, *lim'bər-gīt*, *n.* a volcanic rock composed of olivine and augite, &c., in a fine-grained or glassy groundmass. [*Limburg* in Baden, a typical locality.]

lime, *lim*, *n.* any slimy or gluey material: bird-lime: the white caustic earth (calcium oxide, quicklime, caustic lime) got by calcining calcium carbonate (as limestone): calcium hydroxide (slaked lime) got by adding water to quicklime: (loosely) limestone or calcium carbonate.—*adj.* of lime.—*v.t.* to cover with lime: to cement: to treat with lime: to manure with lime: to ensnare. —*v.i.* (*Shak.*) to adulterate wine with lime.—*ns.* **lime'-burner**, one who calcines limestone, &c., to form lime; **lime'kiln**, a kiln or furnace in which calcium carbonate is calcined to lime; **lime'light**, Drummond light, light produced by a blowpipe-flame directed against a block of quick-lime: the glare of publicity; **lime'stone**, a sedimentary rock of calcium carbonate, sometimes (*magnesian* limestone) with much dolomite; **lime'-twig**, a twig smeared with bird-lime: a snare; **lime'-wash**, a milky mixture of slaked lime and water, used for coating walls, &c.; **lime'-wat'er**, a suspension of calcium hydroxide in water; **lim'iness**; **lim'ing**, the soaking of skins in lime-water to remove hair: application of lime.—*adjs.* **lim'ous**, muddy: slimy; **lim'y**, glutinous: sticky: smeared with, containing, like, of the nature of lime. [O.E. *lim*; Ger. *leim*, glue, L. *limus*, slime.]

lime, *lim*, *n.* a kind of lemon tree: its small nearly globular fruit.—*n.* **lime'-juice**, the acid juice of the lime, or often in use that of the lemon, used at sea as a specific against scurvy. [Fr.,—Sp. *lima*; cf. **lemon**.]

lime, *lim*, *n.* the linden tree (*Tilia europaea*), or other of the genus.—*ns.* **lime'-tree**; **lime'-wood**. [**lind**.]

lime. Same as **lyam**.

limen, *lī'men*, *n.* (*psych.*) the threshold of consciousness: the limit below which a stimulus is not perceived.—*adj.* **liminal** (*lim'*, *lim'in-əl*). [L. *limen, -inis*, threshold.]

limerick, *lim'ə-rik*, *n.* nonsense verse in a five-line stanza. [Said to be from a refrain formerly used, referring to *Limerick* in Ireland.]

limes, *lī-mēz*, L. *lē-mes*, *n.* a boundary or boundary work, esp. of the Roman Empire:—*pl.* **limites** (*li'mit-ēz*, L. *lē'mi-tās*). [L. *limes, -itis*.]

limicolous, *lī-mik'ə-ləs*, *adj.* living in mud. [L. *līmus*, mud, *colēre*, to dwell.]

limit, *lim'it*, *n.* boundary: that which may not be passed: restriction: (*math.*) a value, position, or figure, that can be approached indefinitely: (*Shak.*) a prescribed time: that which is bounded,

a region or division: (*coll.*) the unspeakable extreme of endurability.—*v.t.* (*Shak.*) to appoint, specify: to confine within bounds: to restrict: to bound: to fix within limits.—*adj.* **lim'itable**. —*n.* **limitā'rian**, one who limits salvation to part of mankind.—*adj.* **lim'itary** (-*ə-ri*), of a boundary: placed at the boundary: confined within limits: licensed as a limiter.—*n.* **limitā'tion**.—*adjs.* **lim'-itātive**, tending to limit; **lim'ited**, within limits: narrow: restricted.—*n.* a limited company. —*adv.* **lim'itedly**.—*ns.* **lim'itedness**; **lim'iter**, the person or thing that limits or confines: a friar who had a licence to beg within certain bounds.—*n.* and *adj.* **lim'iting**.—*adj.* **lim'itless**, having no limits: boundless: immense: infinite.— *adv.* **lim'itlessly**.—*n.* **lim'itlessness**.—**limited company, liability** (see **liability**); **limited express**, (*U.S.*) a railway train carrying a limited number of passengers; **limited monarchy**, one in which the monarch shares the supreme power with others. [L. *limes, -itis*, boundary.]

limitrophe, *lim'i-trōf*, *adj.* near the frontier: border. [L. *limitrophus*—*limes, -itis*, border, Gr. *trophos*, feeder.]

limma, *lim'ä*, *n.* (*pros.*) a pause of one mora: in Pythagorean music, the difference between two whole tones and a perfect fourth: applied also to other minute intervals. [Gr. *leimma*, a remnant.]

limmer, *lim'ər*, *n.* (*obs.*) a rogue or thief: (esp. *Scot.*) a hussy, a jade. [Origin obscure.]

limn, *lim*, *v.t.* and *v.i.* to draw or paint, esp. in water-colours: (*orig.*) to illuminate with ornamental letters, &c.:—*pr.p.* **limning** (*lim'ing, lim'-ning*).—*n.* **limner** (*lim'nər*), a painter on paper or parchment: a portrait-painter. [O.Fr. *luminer* or *enluminer*—L. *lūmināre* or *illūmināre*.]

Limnaea, *lim-nē'ä*, *n.* a genus of pond-snails.— *n.* **limnae'id**, any member of the family **Limnae'idae**, to which it belongs.—*adj.* **limnetic** (-*net'ik*), living in fresh water.—*n.* **limnol'ogy**, the scientific study of lakes.—*adj.* **limnoph'ilous**, living in ponds or marshes. [Gr. *limnē*, a pool or marsh.]

limonite, *lī'mən-īt*, *n.* brown iron ore, hydrated ferric oxide, a deposit in bogs and lakes (*bog-iron*), or a decomposition product in rocks.—*adj.* **limonitic** (-*it'ik*). [Gr. *leimōn*, a meadow.]

limosis, *lī-mō'sis*, *n.* a morbidly ravenous appetite. [Gr. *limos*, hunger.]

limousine, *lim-oo-zēn'*, *n.* a closed motor-car, somewhat resembling a landaulet, but not opening at the top. [*Limousin*, a district in France.]

limp, *limp*, *adj.* wanting stiffness: flaccid: drooping. [Origin obscure.]

limp, *limp*, *v.i.* to halt: to drag a leg.—*n.* a limping gait: a halt.—*n.* and *adj.* **limp'ing**.—*adv.* **limp'ingly**. [There is an O.E. adj. *lemp-healt*, halting.]

limpet, *lim'pit*, *n.* a gasteropod (Patella, &c.) with conical shell, that clings to rocks: one not easily ousted. [O.E. *lempedu*, lamprey.]

limpid, *lim'pid*, *adj.* clear: transparent.—*n.* **limpid'ity**.—*adv.* **lim'pidly**. [L. *limpidus*.]

Limulus, *lim'ū-ləs*, *n.* the king-crab genus. [L. *limulus*, dim. of *limus*, looking sideways.]

lin, *lin*, *v.i.* (*Spens.*) to cease, to give over.—*v.t.* to cease from. [O.E. *linnan*, to cease.]

linage. See **lineage** under **line** (2).

linch, *linsh*, *n.* a boundary ridge or unploughed strip: a terrace or ledge.—Also **linch'et, lynch'et**. [O.E. *hlinc*, ridge; cf. **link** (3).]

linchpin, *lin(t)sh'pin*, *n.* a pin used to keep a wheel on its axle. [O.E. *lynis*, axle, and **pin**.]

Lincoln-green, *lingk'ən-grēn*, *n.* a bright green cloth once made at *Lincoln*: its colour.

linctus, *lingk'təs*, *n.* a medicine to be licked up:— *pl.* **linc'tuses**.—*n.* **linc'ture**. [L. *linctus, -ūs*, a licking.]

lind, *lind*, **linden**, *lin'dən*, *ns.* the lime-tree (Tilia— not the lime-fruit tree). [O.E. *lind*; cf. O.N. *lind*, Ger. *linde*.]

lindworm, *lind'wurm*, *n.* a wingless dragon. [Adapted from Sw. and Dan. *lindorm*.]

line, *lin*, *n.* (*obs.*) flax, its fibre, or its seed: heckled flax: yarn spun from good flax: (*obs.*) linen thread or cloth.—*v.t.* to cover on the inside, occasionally on the outside: to pad, stuff, or face: to reinforce, strengthen: to be placed along the side of.—*adj.* **lined,** having a lining.—*n.* **lin′ing,** the action of one who lines: material applied to a surface, esp. material on the inner surface of a garment, &c.: contents: (in *pl.*, *obs.* or *dial.*) underclothing, esp. drawers. [O.E. *lín*, flax, cognate with or derived from L. *līnum*; cf. next word.]

line, *līn*, *n.* a thread, string, cord, rope, esp. one for fishing, sounding, hanging clothes, or guidance: (*math.*) that which has length without breadth or thickness: a long narrow mark: a streak, stroke, or narrow stripe: draughtsmanship: a row: a row of printed or written characters, ships, soldiers, &c.: a verse, such as is usually written in one line: a series or succession, as of progeny: a service of ships, buses, &c., or a company running them: a course, route, system: a railway or tramway track or route: a stretch or route of telegraph, telephone, or power wires or cables: an order given to an agent for goods: such goods received: trade in, or the stock on hand of, any particular goods: a lineament: a rank: a short letter or note: a wrinkle: a trench: limit: method: a rule or canon: the equator: lineage: direction: occupation: course: province or ordinary sphere of life, interest, or taste: regular army: line of battle (see below): the twelfth part of an inch:—in *pl.* a marriage certicate: a certificate of church membership: lot in life: outlines: military field-works: rows of huts: a school imposition: (*Shak.*) fits of bad temper.—*v.t.* to mark out with lines: to cover with lines: to put in line: to form a line along: to give out for public singing, as a hymn, line by line: (*rare*) to delineate, paint: to measure.—*v.i.* to take a place in a line.—*ns.* **linage, lineage** (*līn′ij*), aligning: measurement or payment by the line; **lineage** (*lin′i-ij*), earlier **linage, lignage, lynage** (*līn′ij*), ancestry.— *adj.* **lineal** (*lin′i-əl*), of or belonging to a line or lines or one dimension: composed of lines: in the direction of a line: in, of, or transmitted by direct line of descent, or legitimate descent.—*n.* **lineality** (*-al′i-ti*).—*adv.* **lin′eally.**—*n.* **lineament** (*lin′i-ə-mənt*), feature: distinguishing mark in the form, esp. of the face.— *adj.* **linear** (*lin′i-ər*), of or belonging to a line: of one dimension: consisting of, or having the form of, lines: long and very narrow, with parallel sides.—*n.* **linearity** (*lin-i-ar′i-ti*).—*adv.* **lin′early.** —*adjs.* **lin′eate, -d,** marked with lines.—*n.* **linea′tion,** marking with lines: arrangement of or in lines.—*adi.* **lined** (*līnd*), marked with lines: having a line — *ns.* **line′-engrav′er; line′-engrav′ing,** the process of engraving in lines, steel or copperplate engraving: an engraving so done; **line′-fence,** (*U.S.*) a farm-boundary fence; **line′-fish,** one taken with the line; **line′-fish′er, -fish′erman; line′-fish′ing; line′man,** one who attends to lines of railway, telegraph, telephor.e, or electric-light wires, &c.; **line′-of-batt′le-ship,** a ship fit for the line of battle, a battleship.—*adj.* **lineolate** (*lin′i-ə-lāt*), marked with fine lines.— *ns.* **line′-out,** a formation of Rugby football players when the ball is thrown from touch; **lin′er,** one who makes, marks, draws, paints, or writes lines: a paint-brush for making lines: a line-fisher: a line-fishing boat: a vessel or aircraft of a line; **linesman** (*līnz′*), a soldier in a regiment of the line: in Association football, one who marks the spot at which the ball goes into touch: in lawn-tennis, one who decides on which side of a line the ball falls; **line′-squall,** one of a chain of squalls occurring along a travelling line, with rise and sudden change of wind, rise of pressure and fall of temperature; **line′-storm,** (*U.S.*) an equinoctial storm; **line′-up′,** an arrangement in line: putting or coming into line: a queue; **lin′ing,** alignment: the making of a line: use of a line: marking with lines.—**a line on,** (*U.S.*) some idea or knowledge of; **draw the line** (see **draw**); **Fraunhofer's lines,** dark lines crossing the spectrum—from the Bavarian optician Joseph von *Fraunhofer* (1787-1826); **give line,** (from

angling) to allow apparent freedom in order to secure at last; **hard lines,** hard luck; **in line,** in a straight line: in agreement or harmony: (*U.S.*) in the running; **linear accelerator,** an apparatus in which electrons are accelerated while travelling down (a) metal tube(s), e.g. by means of electromagnetic waves; **linear perspective,** that part of perspective which regards only the positions, magnitudes, and forms of the objects delineated; **line of battle,** arrangement in line to meet the enemy; **line of beauty (Hogarth's),** a curve like a drawn-out S; **on the line,** (*paint.*) hanging on the level of the eyes; **read between the lines,** infer what is not explicitly stated. [Partly from O.E. *líne,* cord (from or cognate with L. *línum,* flax), partly through Fr. *ligne,* and partly directly from L. *línea*; cf. preceding word.]

line, *līn,* *v.t.* (esp. of a dog or wolf) to copulate with. [Fr. *ligner.*]

line, *lin, n.* a form of **lind** (linden, lime-tree).—*n.* (*Shak.*) **line-grove.**

lined. See **line** (1 and 2).

linen, *lin′ən,* *n.* cloth made of lint or flax: underclothing, esp. of linen: articles of linen, or of linen and cotton—table-linen, bed-linen, body-linen.—*adj.* of or like linen.—*ns.* **lin′en-draper,** a dealer in linens; **lin′en-fold, lin′en-scroll′,** a decoration in mouldings like parallel folds of linen.—**wash one's dirty linen at home, in public,** to keep secret, to expose, sordid family affairs. [O.E. *línen* (adj.)—*lín,* flax; see **line** (1).]

ling, *ling, n.* a fish (Molva) of the cod family. [Prob. conn. with **long.**]

ling, *ling, n.* heather.—*adj.* **ling′y.** [O.N. *lyng.*]

ling, *ling, n.* Scots form of **line** (2).—**sting and ling,** (see **sting,** 2).

lingam, *ling′gam, n.* the Hindu phallus, a symbol of Siva.—Also **ling′a.** [Sans.]

lingel, lingle, *ling′gl* (now chiefly *Scot.,* *ling′l*), *n.* a shoemaker's waxed thread. [O.Fr. *lignoel*—a dim. from L. *línea.*]

linger, *ling′gər,* *v.i.* to remain long: to delay in reluctance: to tarry: to loiter: to be protracted. —*v.t.* (*Shak.*) to prolong, protract: to pass in tedium or dawdling.—*n.* **ling′erer.**—*n.* and *adj.* **ling′ering.**—*adv.* **ling′eringly.** [Freq. from O.E. *lengan,* to protract—*lang,* long.]

lingerie, *lan″zh-rē, lan″zh-rē′,* *n.* linen goods: women's underclothing. [Fr., —*linge,* flax — L. *línum.*]

lingo, *ling′gō, n.* language, esp. one despised or not understood. [Prov. *lengo, lingo,* or some other form of L. *lingua,* language.]

lingoa geral, *ling′gwä zher-äl′,* a trade jargon used in Brazil based on Tupí-Guaraní. [Port., general language.]

lingot, *ling′gət, n.* an ingot. [Fr. *lingot*—Eng. **ingot,** with the def. art. *l′.*]

lingua, *ling′gwä, n.* the tongue: a tongue-like structure. — *adj.* **ling′ual.** — *adv.* **ling′ually.** — *adj.* **ling′uiform,** tongue-shaped.—*ns.* **ling′uist,** one who has a good knowledge of languages; **ling′uister,** (*U.S.*) an interpreter.—Also **link′ster,** **ling′ster.**—*adjs.* **linguist′ic, -al,** pertaining to languages or knowledge or study of languages. — *adv.* **linguist′ically.** — *n.* (treated as *sing.*) **linguist′ics,** the study of language in its widest sense, in every aspect and in all its varieties.—*ns.* **ling′uistry; lingula** (*ling′gū-lä*), a little tongue-like part: **Lingula,** a narrow-shelled genus of brachiopods: extended loosely to kindred genera, as **Linguiell′a,** the characteristic fossil of the Upper Cambrian *Lingula Flags.*—*adjs.* **ling′ular,** pertaining to a lingula; **ling′ulate,** tongue-shaped. —**lingua franca** (*ling′gwä frangk′ä*; It., Frankish language), a mixed Italian trade jargon used in the Levant: any international jargon. [L. *lingua* (for *dingua*), the tongue.]

linhay, linny, *lin′i, n.* a shed, open in front. [Origin obscure.]

liniment, *lin′i-mənt, n.* a thin ointment: an embrocation. [L. *linīmentum—linīre, linĕre,* to smear.]

linin, *lī′nin, n.* a substance which forms the network of a cell-nucleus. [L. *línum,* thread, net.]

lining. See **line** (1 and 2).

link, *lingk*, *n.* a ring of a chain or of chain-mail, or the like: anything connecting: the ₁₀₀th part of the surveyor's chain, 7·92 inches: a segment or unit in a connected series: (*Scot.*) a winding of a river.—*v.t.* to connect.—*v.i.* to be or become connected: to go arm-in-arm.—*ns.* **link'age**, an act or mode of linking: the fact of being linked: a system of links: a chemical bond: (*elect.*) product of magnetic flux by number of coils: (*math.*) a system of lines pivoted together, describing definite curves: (*biol.*) a tendency of certain characters to be inherited together: **link'-mo'tion**, reversing gear of a steam-engine: a system of pieces moving as a linkage; **link'work**.—**missing link**, any point or fact needed to complete a series or a chain of argument: an intermediate form in the evolution of man from simian ancestors. [Prob. from an O.N. form cogn. with O.E. *hlencan* (pl.), armour; Ice. *hlekkr*, Ger. *gelenk*, a joint.]

link, *lingk*, *n.* a torch of pitch and tow: (*Shak.*) burnt links used as blacking.—*ns.* **link'boy**, **link'man**, an attendant carrying a link in dark streets. [Origin doubtful.]

link, *lingk*, *n.* (*obs.*) a bank: (in *pl.* often treated as *sing.*) a stretch of flat or gently undulating ground along a sea-shore, hence a golf-course. [O.E. *hlinc*, a ridge of land, a bank; cf. **linch**.]

link, *lingk*, *v.i.* (*Scot.*) to move nimbly: to trip along briskly. [Cf. Norw. *linke*, to hobble, limp.]

linn, **lin**, *lin*, *n.* a waterfall: a cascade pool: a deep ravine. [O.E. *hlynn*, a torrent, combined with Gael. *linne*, Ir. *linn*, W. *llyn*, pool.]

Linnaean, **Linnean**, *lin-ē'an*, *adj.* pertaining to Linnaeus or Linné, the Swedish botanist (1707–1778), or to his artificial system of classification.

linnet, *lin'it*, *n. Linota cannabina*, a common finch, feeding on flax-seed.—**green linnet**, the greenfinch. [O.Fr. *linette*, *linot*—*lin*, flax—L. *linum*; cf. O.E. *linece* or *linete*, and **lintie**.]

linoleic, *lin-ō-lē'ik*, **linolenic**, *lin-ō-lēn'ik* (or *-len'*), **acid**, *ns.* highly unsaturated fatty acids obtained from the glycerides of certain fats and oils, as linseed oil, and constituting Vitamin F.

linoleum, *lin-ō'li-əm*, *n.* a floor-covering made by impregnating a fabric with a cement of oxidised linseed-oil, resins, and fillers (esp. cork).—Also *adj.*—Also (*coll.*) **lino** (*lī'nō*).—**linocut** (*lī'nō-kut*), a design cut in relief in linoleum: a print from such a block. [L. *linum*, flax, *oleum*, oil.]

Linotype, *lin'ō-tīp*, *n.* a machine for producing stereotyped lines: a slug or line of printing-type cast in one piece. [**line o' type** (trade mark).]

linsang, *lin'sang*, *n.* a civet-like animal of Borneo and Java: applied also to kindred animals of the Himalaya, Burma, and West Africa. [Javanese *linsan*.]

linseed, *lin'sēd*, *n.* lint or flax seed—also **lint'seed**.—*ns.* **lin'seed-cake**, the cake remaining when the oil is pressed out of lint or flax seed, used as a food for sheep and cattle; **lin'seed-meal**, the meal of linseed, used for poultices and as a cattlefood; **lint'seed-oil**, oil from flax seed. [O.E. *lin*, flax, *sēd*, seed.]

linsey, *lin'zi*, *n.* cloth made of linen and wool.—Also *adj.*—*n.* **lin'sey-woolsey** (*-wool'zi*), a thin coarse stuff of linen and wool mixed, or inferior wool with cotton: (*Shak.*) gibberish.—*adj.* of linen and wool: neither one thing nor another. [Perh. **line** (1), wool, and possibly **say** (3).]

linstock, *lin'stok*, *n.* a staff to hold a lighted match for firing cannon.—Also **lint'stock**. [Du. *lontstok*—*lont*, a match (cf. **lunt**), *stok*, a stick.]

lint, *lint*, *n.* (now *Scot.*) flax: scraped linen or a cotton substitute for dressing wounds: cotton fibre: raw cotton.—*ns.* **lint'er**, (*U.S.*) a machine for stripping off short cotton fibre from the ginned seeds: (in *pl.*) the fibre so removed; **lint'seed**, (*Scot.*) flax seed for sowing.—*adj.* **lint'white**, flaxen. [M.E. *lynt*, *lynet*, perh.—L. *linteus*, of linen—*linum*, flax.]

lintel, *lint'l*, *n.* a timber or stone over a doorway or window. — *adj.* **lint'elled**. [O.Fr. *lintel* (Fr. *linteau*)—a dim. of L. *limes*, *-itis*, border.]

lintie, *lin'ti*, **lintwhite**, *lint'hwīt*, *ns.* a linnet. [O.E. *linetwige*, lit. perh. flax-twitcher.]

lion, *lī'ən*, *n.* a large, fierce, tawny, loud-roaring animal of the cat family, the male with shaggy mane: (*fig.*) a man of unusual courage: (*astron.*) the constellation or the sign Leo: any object of interest, esp. a famous or conspicuous person much sought after (from the lions once kept in the Tower, one of the sights of London): an old Scots coin, with a lion on the obverse, worth 74 shillings Scots (James VI.):—*fem.* **li'oness**.—*ns.* **li'oncel**, **li'oncelle**, **li'onel**, (*her.*) a small lion used as a bearing; **li'onet**, a young lion; **li'on-heart**, one with great courage. — *adj.* **li'on-heart'ed**.—*n.* **li'on-hunter**, a hunter of lions: one who runs after celebrities.—*v.t.* **li'onise**, to treat as a lion or object of interest: to go around the sights of: to show the sights to.—*n.* **li'onism**, lionising: lion-like appearance in leprosy.—*adjs.* **li'on-like**, **li'only**.—**lion's provider**, the jackal, supposed to attend upon the lion, really his hanger-on; **lion's share**, the whole or greater part; **twist the lion's tail**, to harass Great Britain. [A.Fr. *liun*—L. *leō*, *-ōnis*—Gr. *leōn*, *-ontos*.]

lip, *lip*, *n.* either of the muscular flaps in front of the teeth: any similar structure, as each of the two divisions of a labiate corolla: the edge or rim of an orifice, cavity, or vessel: part of such a rim bent outwards like a spout: (*slang*) impudent talk, insolence.—*v.t.* to touch with the lips: to kiss: to wash, overflow, or overrun the edge of: to lap or lave: to form a lip on: to edge: (*Scot.*) to turn or notch the edge of: to utter with the lips.—*v.i.* to manage the lips in playing a wind-instrument: to lap at the brim: to have water lapping over: (*pr.p.* **lipp'ing**; *pa.t.* and *pa.p.* **lipped**).—*adj.* of the lip: formed or sounded by the lips: (in composition) from the lips only, not sincere.—*adjs.* **lip'-deep**, insincere: immersed to the lips; **lip'less**; **lipped** (*lipt*), having a lip or lips: labiate; **lipp'y**, with hanging lip: (*slang*) saucy.—*v.i.* **lip'-read**.—*ns.* **lip'-reader**; **lip'-read'ing**, gathering what a person says by watching the movement of the lips; **lip'-rounding**, rounding of the lips, as in pronouncing *o*; **lip'salve**, ointment for the lips: blandishment; **lip'-service**, insincere professions or worship; **lip'-stick**, red paint for the lips in the form of a stick.—*v.t.* and *v.i.* to paint with lipstick.—**in Lipsburie pinfold**, (*Shak.*) perh. between the teeth; **keep a stiff upper lip**, to show a face of resolution; **make a lip**, (*Shak.*) to pout in sullenness or derision. [O.E. *lippa*; Du. *lip*, Ger. *lippe*, L. *labium*.]

liparite, *lip'ə-rīt*, *n.* rhyolite. [From the *Lipari* Islands, where it occurs.]

lipase, *lip'ās*, *līp'ās*, *-āz*, *n.* an enzyme that breaks up fats.—*adj.* **lipoid** (*lip'* or *līp'*), fat-like.—*n.* one of a class of substances resembling fat. [Gr. *lipos*, fat.]

lipochrome, *lip'ō-krōm*, or *līp'*, *n.* a pigment of butter fat, &c. [Gr. *lipos*, fat, *chrōma*, colour.]

lipogram, *lip'ō-gram*, or *līp'*, *n.* a writing, esp. in verse, from which all words are omitted which contain a particular letter.—*adj.* **lipogrammat'ic**. — *ns.* **lipogramm'atism**; **lipogramm'atist**; **lipog'raphy**, accidental omission of a letter or letters in writing. [Gr. *leipein*, to leave, *gramma*, a letter, *graphein*, to write.]

lipoma, *lip-ō'mā*, *n.* a fatty tumour:—*pl.* **lipo'mata**.—*n.* **lipomatō'sis**, the excessive growth of fat.—*adj.* **lipo'matous**. [Gr. *lipos*, fat.]

lippen, *lip'n*, *v.i.* (*Scot.*) to trust, rely, depend (with *to*, *on*).—*v.t.* to expect.—*adj.* **lipp'ening**, (*Scott*) unguarded. [Origin obscure.]

lippitude, *lip'i-tūd*, *n.* soreness of the eyes. [L. *lippitūdō*—*lippus*, blear-eyed.]

lippy, **lippie**, *lip'i*, *n.* an old Scottish dry measure, the fourth part of a peck. [Dim. from O.E. *léap*, a basket; cf. **leap** (2).]

liquate, *līk'wāt*, *v.t.* to melt: to subject to liquation.—*adj.* **liq'uable**.—*n.* **liqua'tion**, melting: separation of metals with different melting-points. [L. *liquāre*, *-ātum*, to liquefy.]

liquefy, *lik'wi-fī*, *v.t.* to make liquid.—*v.i.* to become liquid: (*facet.*) to drink:—*pr.p.* **liq'uefying**; *pa.t.* and *pa.p.* **liq'uefied**.—*n.* and *adj.* **liquefacient**

(-fə'shənt). — *n.* **liquefaction** (-fak'shən). — *adj.* **liq'uefiable.**—*n.* **liq'uefier.** [L. *liquefacēre*—*liquēre*, to be liquid, *facĕre*, to make.]

liquesce, *lik-wes'*, *v.i.* to become liquid : to merge. —*ns.* **liquesc'ence, liquesc'ency.**—*adj.* **liquesc'-ent.** [L. *liquēscĕre*—*liquēre*, to be liquid.]

liqueur, *lik-ūr'*, or *lē-kər'*, *n.* an alcoholic preparation flavoured or perfumed and sweetened—as chartreuse, cherry brandy, curaçao, benedictine, kümmel, maraschino.—*v.t.* to flavour with a liqueur.—*v.i.* to drink liqueur.—*adj.* (of brandy or whisky) that may be drunk as a liqueur. — *n.* **liqueur'-glass,** a very small drinking-glass. [Fr., —L. *liquor*; see **liquor.**]

liquid, *lik'wid*, *adj.* flowing : fluid : watery : (*phys.*) in a state between solid and gas, in which the molecules move freely about one another but do not fly apart : clear : indisputable : unfixed : readily converted into cash.—*n.* a liquid substance : a flowing consonant sound, as *l, r.*—*v.t.* **liq'uidate,** to clear up or off : to arrange or wind up : to dispose of : (*slang*) to wipe out, do away with : to kill off.—*v.i.* to go into liquidation.—*ns.* **liquidā'-tion**; **liq'uidator.**—*v.t.* **liq'uidise,** to render liquid.—*n.* **liquid'ity.**—*adv.* **liq'uidly.**—*n.* **liq'uid-ness.** [L. *liquidus*, liquid, clear—*liquēre*, to be clear.]

Liquidambar, *lik-wid-am'bər*, *n.* a genus of balsam-iferous trees of the family Hamamelidaceae, found in North America and Asia. [L. *liquidus*, liquid, L.L. *ambar*, amber.]

liquor, *lik'ər*, *n.* anything liquid, esp. the product of cooking or other operation : a liquid secretion : a beverage, esp. alcoholic : strong drink : a strong solution : any prepared solution.—*v.t.* to apply liquor or a solution to : (*Shak.*) to rub with oil or grease.—*v.i.* (*slang*) to drink (esp. with *up*).—*n.* **liquor,** drunk; **liquor laws,** laws controlling the sale of intoxicating drinks. [O.Fr. *licur, licour* (Fr. *liqueur*)—L. *liquor, -ōris*.]

liquorice, licorice, *lik'ə-ris*, *n.* a papilionaceous plant (*Glycyrrhiza glabra*, or other species) of Europe and Asia : its long sweet root used in medicine : an extract from the root : confectionery made from it.—**Indian liquorice,** Abrus (also *liquorice-vine*); **wild liquorice,** a kind of milk-vetch (*Astragalus glycyphyllus* — also *liquorice-vetch*): rest-harrow. [A.Fr. *lycorys*—L.L. *liquīrītia*, a corr. of Gr. *glykyrrīza*—*glykys*, sweet, *rhīza*, root.] **liquorish,** another spelling of **lickerish**: also used to mean inclined towards liquor.

lira, *lē'rä*, *n.* an Italian coin and monetary unit worth 100 centesimi :—*pl.* **lire** (*lē'rä*), **lir'as.** [It.,—L. *libra*, a pound.]

Liriodendron, *lir-i-ō-den'dron*, *n.* the tulip-tree genus. [Gr. *leirion*, a lily, *dendron*, a tree.]

liripoop, *lir'i-ρoop*, *n.* (*obs.*) the long tail of a graduate's hood : a part or lesson committed to memory : a silly person.—Also **lir'ipipe** (*-pīp*). [L.L. *liripipium*; origin unknown.]

lirk, *lirk*, *n.* (*Scot.*) a fold : a wrinkle.—*v.i.* to wrinkle. [Origin unknown.]

lis, *lēs*, *n.* (*her.*) a fleur-de-lis (q.v.) :—*pl.* **lis, lisses** (*lēs'iz*).

Lisbon, *liz'bən*, *n.* a light-coloured wine from Estremadura in Portugal, shipped from *Lisbon*.

lisle, *līl*, *n.* a long-stapled, hard-twisted cotton yarn.—Also *adj.* [Old spelling of *Lille*, France.]

lisp, *lisp*, *v.i.* to speak with the tongue against the upper teeth or gums, as in pronouncing *th* for *s* or *z*: to articulate as a child : to utter imperfectly.—*v.t.* to utter with a lisp.—*n.* the act or habit of lisping : a defect of speech by which one lisps.—*n.* **lisp'er.**—*adj.* and *n.* **lisp'ing.** —*adv.* **lisp'ingly.** [O.E. *wlisp* (adj.), stammering ; Du. *lispen*, Ger. *lispeln.*]

lispound, lispund, *lis'pownd, ləs'pŏnd*, *n.* (*Orkney* and *Shetland*) a varying weight, 12 to 34 pounds. [L.G. or Du. *lispund*, for *livschpund*, Livonian pound.]

lissencephalous, *lis-ən-sef'ə-ləs*, *adj.* with smooth cerebral hemispheres. [Gr. *lissos*, smooth, *en-kephalon*, brain.]

lissome, lissom, *lis'əm*, *adj.* lithesome, nimble, flexible.—*n.* **liss'om(e)ness.** [lithesome.]

lissotrichous, *lis-ot'ri-kəs*, *adj.* smooth-haired. [Gr. *lissos*, smooth, *thrix, trichos*, hair.]

list, *list*, *n.* the selvage on woven textile fabrics : a border : a stripe : a strip : (*U.S.*) a ridge or furrow made with a lister : a strip cut from an edge : material composed of cut-off selvages : a boundary : (*Shak.*) a destination : (in *pl.*) the boundary of a tilting-ground or the like, hence the ground itself, combat.—*adj.* made of strips of woollen selvage.—*v.t.* to border : to put list on : to remove the edge from : (*U.S.*) to plough with a lister.—*adj.* **list'ed,** enclosed for tilting or the like : fought in lists.—*n.* **list'er,** (*U.S.*) a double-mould-board plough.—**enter the lists,** to come forward for contest. [O.E. *līste*; Ger. *leiste*; affected in some senses by O.Fr. *lisse* (Fr. *lice*, It. *lizza*)—L.L. *liciae*, barrier.]

list, *list*, *n.* a catalogue, roll, or enumeration.—*v.t.* to place in a list or catalogue : to enrol (as soldiers). —*v.i.* to enlist (also *'list*, as if for **enlist**).—**active list,** the roll of those liable for active service. [O.Fr. *liste*, of Gmc. origin, ultimately same word as above, from the sense of a strip of paper.]

list, *list*, *n.* (*archit.*) a fillet : a division of parted hair.—*n.* **list'el,** a small fillet. [It. *lista, listello*; ult. the same as **list** (1 and 2).]

list, *list*, *v.t.* (*impers., arch.*) to please : (*pers.*) to have pleasure in : to desire : to like or please : to choose : (*naut.*) to cause to heel over.—*v.i.* to heel over : (*pa.t.* **list'ed,** list ; *pa.p.* **list'ed**; 3*rd pers. sing. pr.t.* **list, lists, listeth**).—*n.* (*obs.*) joy : desire : inclination : choice : heeling over.—*adj.* **list'less,** having no desire or wish : uninterested : languid.—*adv.* **list'lessly.**—*n.* **list'lessness.** [O.E. *lystan*, impers., to please—*lust*, pleasure.]

list, *list*, *v.i.* (*arch.* or *poet.*) to listen.—*v.t.* to listen to.—*adj.* **list'ful,** attentive. [O.E. *hlystan.*]

listen, *lis'n*, *v.i.* to give ear or hearken : to follow advice.—*n.* act of listening.—*ns.* **listener** (*lis'nər*), one who listens or hearkens; **list'ener-in** (*pl.* **list'eners-in**); **list'ening-in; list'ening-post,** a post where men are stationed to hear what the enemy is doing.—**listen in,** to listen to a wireless broadcast : to overhear intentionally a message intended for another. [O.E. *hlysnan*, recorded in the Northumbrian form *lysna.*]

Listerism, *lis'tər-izm*, *n.* an antiseptic method of operating introduced by the English surgeon Lord *Lister* (1827-1912).—*adj.* **Listerian** (*-tē'ri-ən*), pertaining to Lister or his system.—*v.t.* **Lis'terise,** to treat by Listerism.

lit, *pa.t.* and *pa.p.* of **light** (1 and 3).

litany, *lit'ə-ni*, *n.* a prayer of supplication, esp. in processions : an appointed form of responsive prayer in public worship in which the same thing is repeated several times.—*ns.* **lit'any-desk, -stool,** in the English Church, a movable desk at which a minister kneels, facing the altar, while he recites the litany.—**lesser litany,** the common formula, 'Kyrie eleison, Christe eleison, Kyrie eleison.' [L.L. *litania*—Gr. *litaneiā*—*litesthai*, to pray.]

litchi, leechee, *lē'chē'*, *n.* a Chinese fruit, a nut or berry with a fleshy aril : the tree (*Litchi chinensis*; fam. Sapindaceae) that bears it. [Chin. *li-chi.*]

lite, lyte, *līt*, *n., adj., adv.* (*dial.*, also **leet,** otherwise *obs.*) little. [O.E. *lyt.*]

lite (*Spens.*). Same as **light** (3) : also as **light** (2) in phrase *lungs and lites.*

liter, American spelling of **litre.**

literal, *lit'ə-rəl*, *adj.* pertaining to letters of the alphabet : of the nature of a letter : according to the letter : not figurative or metaphorical : following word for word : inclined to use or understand words in a matter-of-fact sense.—*n.* a wrong letter in printed or typed matter : a misprint of a letter.—*v.t.* **lit'eralise.**—*ns.* **lit'eraliser; lit'eralism,** strict adherence to the letter : interpretation that is merely verbal : (*art*) exact and unimaginative rendering ; **li'teralist; literality** (*-al'i-ti*).—*adv.* **lit'erally** (often used by no means literally). —*n.* **lit'eralness.** [L. *litterālis*—*littera* (*litera*), a letter.]

literary, *lit'ər-ər-i*, *adj.* (*obs.*) pertaining to letters of the alphabet : (*obs.*) epistolary : pertaining to, of the nature of, versed in, or practising literature

---

Neutral vowels in unaccented syllables : *el'ə-mənt, in'fənt, ran'dəm*

or the writing of books: bookish.—*adv.* **lit′er-
arily**.—*ns.* **lit′erariness**; **lit′eraryism**, a bookish
expression. [L. *literārius*—*litera* (*littera*), a letter.]
literate, *lit′ər-it*, *-āt*, *adj.* learned: able to read and
write.—*n.* one who is literate: an educated person
without a university degree, esp. a candidate for
orders, or formerly a lady holding a certificate from
St Andrews University (*L.L.A.*, *Lady Literate in
Arts*).—*n.* **lit′eracy**, condition of being literate.—
n.pl. **literā′tī** (L., *obs.* It., *-ā′tē*), men of letters, the
learned:—*sing.* **literā′tus** (L.), **literato** (*-ä′tō*; It.).
—*adv.* **literā′tim** (L. *-ā′*), letter for letter: without
the change of a letter.—*n.* **lit′erātor**, a dabbler in
learning: a man of letters, a literary man.—*adj.*
lit′erose, affectedly or spuriously literary.—*n.*
literos′ity. [L. *litera*, *līterātus*, *līterātim*, *līterōsus*
—*lītera* (*littera*), letter.]
literature, *lit′(ə-)rə-tyər*, *n.* the art of composition
in prose and verse: the whole body of literary
compositions universally, or in any language, or
on a given subject, &c.: literary matter: printed
matter: humane learning: literary culture or
knowledge.—*adj.* **lit′eratured**, (*Shak.*) learned,
having literary knowledge. [L. *literātūra*—*litera*
(*littera*), a letter.]
lith, *lith*, *n.* (*arch.* and *Scot.*) a joint or segment.
[O.E. *lith*, a member; Ger. *glied*.]
lith-, **litho-**, *lith-*, *-lith-*, *-ō-*, *-ə-*, *-o′-*, in composition, stone:
calculus: lithium.—*ns.* **lith′ate**, (*obs.*) a urate;
lith′ia, oxide of lithium (from its mineral origin,
unlike soda and potash).—Also *adj.*—*n.* **lithi′asis**
(Gr. *lithiāsis*), formation of calculi in the body.—
adj. **lith′ic**, pertaining to or got from stone,
calculi, or lithium.—*ns.* **lithist′id**, any of the
Lithist′ida, hard stony sponges; **lith′ite**, a calcareous body secreted in an animal cell, esp. with
a sensory function; **lith′ium**, the lightest metallic
element (Li; at. numb. 3).—*adj.* **lithochromatic**
(*-ə-krō-mat′ik*, or *-krə-*).—*n.* (treated as *sing.*)
lithochromat′ics.—*ns.* **lith′ochromy** (*-krō-mi*;
Gr. *chrōma*, *-atos*, colour), painting on stone:
chromolithography: **lith′oclast** (Gr. *klaein*, to
crush), an instrument for crushing bladder-
stones; **lith′ocyst** (*-ō-sist*; Gr. *kystis*, a bladder),
a sac containing a lithite.—*adj.* **lithodomous**
(*-od′ə-məs*; Gr. *lithodomos*, a mason—*domos*, a
dwelling), living in burrows in rocks.—*n.* **Lithod′-
omus**, the date-shell genus.—*adj.* **lithogenous**
(*-oj′i-nəs*), rock-building.—*ns.* **lith′oglyph** (*-ə-glif*;
Gr. *glyphein*, to carve), an engraving on stone, esp.
a precious stone; **lith′ograph** (*-gräf*; Gr. *graphein*,
to write), a print from stone (**lithographic stone**
or **slate**, a fine-grained slaty limestone), or a
substitute (as zinc or aluminium), with greasy ink.
—*v.t.* and *v.i.* to print so.—*n.* **lithographer**
(*-og′rə-fər*).—*adjs.* **lithographic** (*-ə-graf′ik*), **-al**.—
adv. **lithograph′ically**.—*n.* **lithog′raphy**.—*adjs.*
lith′oid, **lithoid′al**, like stone.—*n.* **lith′olapaxy**
(Gr. *lapaxis*, evacuation), the operation of crushing
stone in the bladder and working it out.—*adj.*
lithol′atrous.—*n.* **litholatry** (*-ol′ə-tri*; Gr. *latreiā*,
worship), stone-worship.—*adjs.* **litholog′ic**, **-al**.—
ns. **lithol′ogist**; **lithol′ogy**, the science of rocks
as mineral masses: the department of medicine
concerned with calculi; **lith′omancy** (*-man-si*;
Gr. *manteiā*, divination), divination by stones;
lith′omarge (*-ō-märj*; L. *marga*, marl), a compact china-clay.—*adj.* **lithophagous** (*-of′ə-gəs*;
Gr. *phagein*, to eat), stone-swallowing: rock-
boring.—*n.* **lith′ophane** (*-ō-fān*; Gr. *phainesthai*,
to appear), porcelain with pictures showing through
transparency.—*adj.* **lithophilous** (*-of′i-ləs*; Gr.
philos, friend), growing, living, or sheltering
among stones.—*ns.* **lithophysa** (*-ō-fī′sä*; Gr.
physa, bubble), a bladder-like spherulite (also
lith′ophyse): — *pl.* **lithophy′sae** (*-sē*); **lith′-
ophyte** (*-fīt*; Gr. *phyton*, plant), a plant that
grows on rocks or stones: a stony organism, as
coral.—*adj.* **lithophytic** (*-fit′ik*).—*ns.* **lith′opone**
(*-ō-pōn*; perh. L. *pōnere*, to set, apply), a white
pigment of barium sulphate and zinc sulphide;
lith′osphere (*-ō-sfēr*; Gr. *sphaira*, sphere), the
rocky crust of the earth; **lith′otome** (*-ō-tōm*; Gr.
tomos, cutting), an instrument for lithotomy.—
adjs. **lithotomic** (*-tom′*), **-al**.—*n.* **lithotomist**

(*-ot′əm-ist*), one who cuts for stone in the bladder.
—*adj.* **lithot′omous**, boring in rocks, as some
molluscs.—*n.* **lithot′omy**, cutting for stone in the
bladder. [Gr. *lithos*, stone.]
litharge, *lith′ärj*, *n.* lead monoxide, such as is got
in refining silver. [Fr.,—Gr. *lithargyros*—*lithos*,
a stone, *argyros*, silver.]
lithe, *līdh*, *adj.* supple, limber.—*adv.* **lithe′ly**.—*n.*
lithe′ness. — *adj.* **lithe′some**. — *n.* **lithe′some-
ness**. [O.E. *līthe*, soft, mild; Ger. *lind* and
gelinde.]
lithe, *līdh*, *v.i.* (*obs.*) to listen. [O.N. *hlýtha*, to
listen.]
lither, *līdh′ər*, *adj.* (*obs.*) bad: lazy: (*Shak.*) soft,
yielding.—*adj.* **lith′erly**, mischievous.—*adv.* idly.
[O.E. *lýthre*, bad; influenced by **lithe**.]
lithotrity, *lith-ot′ri-ti*, **lithotripsy**, *lith′ō-trip-si*, *ns.*
the operation of crushing a stone in the bladder, so
that its fragments may be removed through the
urethra.—*ns.* **lith′otrite**, **lithotrī′tor**, **lithotrip′tor**,
lithontrip′tor, an instrument of the purpose.—
adjs. **lithotritic** (*-trit′ik*), **lithotrip′tic**, **lithontrip′-
tic**, **lithonthryp′tic**.—*ns.* a medicine producing the
like result.—*v.t.* **lithot′ritise**.—*ns.* **lithot′ritist**,
lithotrip′tist, **lithontrip′tist**, one who performs
the operation. [Gr. *lithōn* (gen. pl.) *thryptika*,
breakers of stones; reconstructed as from Gr.
tripsis, rubbing, or L. *trītus*, rubbing.]
litigate, *lit′i-gāt*, *v.t.* and *v.i.* to dispute, esp. by a
lawsuit.—*adjs.* **lit′igable**; **lit′igant**, contending
at law: engaged in a lawsuit.—*n.* a person engaged
in a lawsuit.—*n.* **litigā′tion**.—*adj.* **litigious** (*-ij′əs*),
pretaining to litigation: inclined to engage in
lawsuits: disputable: open to contention: (*Shak.*)
perh. depending on results of negotiation.—*adv.*
litig′iously. — *n.* **litig′iousness**. [L. *lītigāre*,
-ātum—*līs*, *lītis*, strife, *agĕre*, to do.]
litmus, *lit′məs*, *n.* a substance obtained from certain
lichens, turned red by acids, blue by alkalies.—
litmus paper, a test-paper dipped in litmus
solution. [M.Du. *leecmos* (Du. *lakmoes*: lak, lac,
moes, pulp); or O.N. *litr*, colour, *mos*, moss.]
litotes, *lī′* or *lit′ō-tēz*, *n.* (*rhet.*) meiosis or understatement: esp. affirmation by negation of the
contrary. [Gr. *lītotēs*, simplicity—*litos*, plain.]
litre, *lē′tər*, *n.* the metric unit of capacity, orig.
1000 cubic centimetres, now the volume of a kilogram of water at 4° C., or about ·220 British
imperial gallon—4½ litres being roughly equal to
a gallon. [Fr.,—L.L. *lītra*—Gr. *lītrā*, a pound.]
litter, *lit′ər*, *n.* a heap of straw, bracken, &c., esp.
for animals to lie upon: materials for a bed: any
scattered or confused collection of objects, esp.
of little value: a state of confusion and untidiness
with things strewn about: a couch carried by
men or beasts: a stretcher: a brood of animals:
an occasion of birth of animals.—*v.t.* to cover or
supply with litter: to scatter carelessly about: to
give birth to (said of animals).—*v.i.* to produce a
litter or brood.—*adj.* **litt′ered**.—*adj.* **litt′ery**,
in condition of litter: addicted to litter. [O.Fr.
litiere—L.L. *lectāria*—L. *lectus*, a bed.]
littérateur, *lē-tā-rä-tər′*, *n.* a literary man. [Fr.]
little, *lit′l*, *adj.* small in size, extent, quantity, or
significance: petty: small-minded.—*n.* (or *adj.*
with a noun understood) that which is small in
quantity or extent: a small quantity: a small
thing.—*adv.* in a small quantity or degree: not
much.—**less**, **least**, serve as comp. and superl. to
the adv. and to some extent, along with **lesser**,
to the adj.—*ns.* **litt′le-ease**, a narrow prison: the
pillory: the stocks: **Litt′le-end′ian**, one of the
Lilliputian party who opposed the *Big-endians*,
maintaining that boiled eggs should be cracked at
the little end; **litt′le-go** (see go); **litt′leness**.—
adj. **litt′leworth**, worthless.—*n.* **litt′ling** (*Scot.*
litt′lin, **litt′leane**; O.E. *lýtling*), a child.—**by
little and little**, **little by little**, by degrees; **in
little**, on a small scale; **little Englander**, an
opponent of British imperialism and empire-
building; **little Mary**, (*J. M. Barrie*) the stomach;
little office, a short service of psalms, hymns,
collects, &c.; **little people**, the fairies, or a traditional race of pygmies. [O.E. *lýtel*.]
littoral, *lit′ər-əl*, *adj.* belonging to the sea-shore, to

lands near the coast, the beach, the space between high and low tidemarks, or water a little below low-water mark.—*n.* the strip of land along it. [L. *littorālis* for *lītorālis*—*lītus, lītoris*, shore.]

liturgy, *lit´ər-ji, n.* the form of service or regular ritual of a church—strictly, that used in the celebration of the eucharist: in ancient Greece, personal service to the state.— *adjs.* **liturgic** (*-urj´ik*), **-al.**—*adv.* **litur´gically.**—*ns.* **litur´gics,** the doctrine of liturgies; **liturgiol´ogist**; **liturgiol´ogy,** the study of liturgical forms; **lit´urgist,** a leader in public worship: one who adheres to, or who studies, liturgies. [Gr. *leitourgiā.*]

lituus, *lit´ū-əs, n.* an augur's curved staff: a J-shaped Roman trumpet: a curve of similar form with the polar equation $r^2\theta = a$. [L. *lituus.*]

live, *liv, v.i.* to have, or continue in, life, temporal, spiritual, or figurative: to last: to enjoy life: to direct one's course of life: to be supported, subsist, get a living: to escape destruction or oblivion: to dwell.—*v.t.* to spend or pass: to act in conformity to: to express by one's life, make one's life the same thing as:—*pr.p.* **liv´ing**; *pa.t.* and *pa.p.* **lived** (*livd*).—*adjs.* **liv´able, live´able,** worth living, capable of being lived: habitable; **liv´able-with,** such as one could endure to live with.—*n.* **liv´er.**—**live and let live,** give and expect toleration or forbearance; **live down,** live so as to allow to be forgotten; **live in, out,** dwell in, away from, one's place of employment; **live on,** live by feeding upon, or with expenditure limited to; **live out,** to survive: (*U.S.*) to be in domestic service; **live to,** live long enough to, come at last to; **live under,** to be tenant to; **live up to,** to rule one's life in a manner worthy of: to spend up to the scale of. [O.E. *lifian* (W.S. *libban*).]

live, *liv, adj.* having life: alive, not dead: active: stirring: unquarried or unwrought: charged with energy (as by electricity, explosives or other chemicals, &c.) and still capable of discharge: burning: vivid.—**lived** (*livd*; sometimes *līvd*) in composition, having life (as *long-lived*).—*ns.* **live´-ax´le,** driving-axle; **live´-bait,** a living animal as bait; **live´-birth´,** birth in a living condition (opposed to *still-birth*).—*adj.* **live´-born.** —*ns.* **live´-box,** a glass box for examining living objects under the microscope: a box for live fish; **live´-car´tridge,** one containing a bullet, opposed to a *blank* or a *spent* cartridge; **live´-cir´cuit,** a circuit through which an electric current is flowing. —*n.pl.* **live´-feath´ers,** those plucked from the living fowl.—*v.t.* **liv´en,** to enliven.—*v.i.* to become lively.—*ns.* **live´-oak,** an American evergreen oak, with durable wood; **live´-rail, live´-wire,** one carrying electric current; **live´-wire,** (*fig.*) a man of intense energy; **live´-shell,** a shell still capable of exploding; **live´-stock,** domestic animals, esp. horses, cattle, sheep, and pigs; **live´-weight,** weight of living animals; **live´-well,** the well in a fishing-boat where fish are kept alive. [**alive.**]

livelihood, *liv´li-hood, n.* means of living: support.—Also (*Spens.*) **live´lod, live´lood.** [O.E. *líflád—líf,* life, *lád,* course.]

livelong, *liv´long,* also *līv´long, adj.* very long: protracted: enduring. [**lief,** used intensively, **long.**]

livelong, *liv´long, n.* the orpine, a plant difficult to kill. [**live** (vb.), **long.**]

lively, *līv´li, adj.* (*obs.*) vital: lifelike: (*obs.*) oral: brisk: active: sprightly: spirited: vivid.— *adv.* vivaciously: vigorously.—*n.* **live´lihead,** liveliness: life: living form: livelihood.—*adv.* **live´lily.** —*n.* **live´liness.** [O.E. *líflíc—líf,* life.]

liver, *liv´ər, n.* a large gland that secretes bile, formerly regarded as seat of courage, love, &c.: its substance as food : (*coll.*) a disordered state of the liver : in old chemistry a sulphide or other liver-coloured substance (*liver of sulphur*, mixture got by heating potassium carbonate with sulphur).—*adj.* **liver-colour.**—*n.* and *adj.* **liv´er-col´our,** dark reddish brown.—*adjs.* **liv´er-coloured**; **liv´ered,** having a liver, as *white-livered, lily-livered=* cowardly.—*n.* **liv´er-fluke,** a trematode worm that infects the bile-ducts of sheep and other animals.

—*adjs.* **liv´er-grown,** having a swelled liver; **liv´erish, liv´ery,** suffering from disordered liver: irritable.—*ns.* **liv´er-rot,** a disease caused by liver-flukes; **liv´er-wing,** a fowl's right wing, which is cooked with the liver; **liv´erwort** (*-wurt*), any plant of the Hepaticae, forming with the mosses the Bryophyta, some kinds having once been used medicinally in diseases of the liver. [O.E. *lifer*; Ger. *leber,* O.N. *lifr.*]

liver, *li´vər, n.* a fanciful bird on the arms of the city of Liverpool. [Formed from *Liverpool.*]

livery, *liv´ər-i, n.* (*obs.*) a delivery or handing over : (*hist.*) a dispensing or allowance of food or clothes to servants and retainers : the feeding, care, and stabling of a horse at a certain rate : (*hist.*) the distinctive dress or badge of a great man's household : the distinctive garb of a person's servants, esp. men-servants, or of a body, e.g. a trade-guild : any characteristic garb : a body of liverymen or of livery-servants : (*arch.*) a livery-servant. — *adj.* **liv´eried,** clothed in livery.—*ns.* **liv´ery-com´-pany,** a guild of the city of London ; **liv´eryman,** a man who wears a livery : a freeman of the city of London entitled to wear the livery and enjoy other privileges of his company : one who keeps or works at a livery-stable; **liv´ery-servant,** a servant who wears a livery; **liv´ery-stable,** a stable where horses are kept at livery and for hire. —**sue one's livery,** (*Shak.*) to ask for the writ delivering a freehold into the possession of its heir. [A.Fr. *liveré,* lit. handed over—*livrer—* L. *līberāre,* to free.]

lives, *līvz, n.* plural of **life.**

livid, *liv´id, adj.* black and blue : of a lead colour : discoloured. — *ns.* **livid´ity, liv´idness, livor** (*lī´vor*). [L. *lividus—līvēre,* to be of a lead colour.]

living, *liv´ing, adj.* live : alive : having vitality : lively : in present life, existence, activity, or use.— *n.* means of subsistence: manner of life: a property : a benefice.—*n.* **liv´ing-room,** a sitting-room for all-round use.—**living memory,** the memory of anybody or somebody still alive ; **living rock,** rock still in its natural position ; **living wage,** a wage on which it is possible for a workman and his family to live fairly.

livraison, *lē-vrez-on⁰, n.* a number of a book published in parts. [Fr.,—L. *līberātiō, -ōnis,* delivery.]

livre, *lē´vr´, n.* an old French coin, superseded by the franc in 1795: an old French weight about 1 lb. avoirdupois. [Fr.,—L. *lībra,* a pound.]

lixiviation, *liks-iv-i-ā´shən, n.* leaching. — *adjs.* **lixiv´ial, lixiv´ious.**—*v.t.* **lixiv´iate.**—*n.* **lixiv´ium,** lye. [L. *lixivium,* lye.]

lizard, *liz´ərd, n.* any member of the Lacertilia, an order of scaly reptiles, usually differing from snakes in having four legs, movable eyelids, and non-expansible mouths. [O.Fr. *lesard* (Fr. *lézard*) —L. *lacerta.*]

llama, *lä´mä, n.* a S. American transport animal of the camel family, a domesticated guanaco : its wool : cloth made thereof. [Sp., from Quechua.]

llano, *lyä´nō,* or *lä´nō, n.* one of the vast steppes or plains in the northern part of South America :— *pl.* **lla´nos.**—*n.* **llanero** (*lyä-nā´rō*), an inhabitant of the llanos. [Sp.,—L. *plānus,* plain.]

lo, *lō, interj.* look : behold. [O.E. *lá.*]

loach, *lōch, n.* a small river-fish of a family (Cobitidae) akin to the carps. [Fr. *loche.*]

load, *lōd, n.* that which is carried : that which may or can be carried at one time or journey : a burden : a charge : a freight or cargo : a definite quantity, varying according to the goods : weight carried : power output of an engine, &c. : work imposed or expected : power carried by an electric circuit : a large quantity borne : a burden sustained with difficulty : that which burdens or grieves : a weight or encumbrance : (*Spens.*) weight of blows : (*coll.,* esp. in *pl.*) abundance.—*v.t.* to lade or burden : to charge : to put a load on or in : to put on or in anything as a load : to put on overmuch : to weigh down : to overburden : to supply, present, or assail overwhelmingly or lavishly : to weight : to give weight or body to, by adding something : to mix with white : (*painting*) to lay on in masses : (*insurance*) to add charges to : (of wine) to doctor,

Neutral vowels in unaccented syllables : *el´ə-mənt, in´fənt, ran´dəm*

drug, adulterate, or fortify.—*v.i.* to put or take on a load : to charge a gun : to become loaded or burdened :—*pa.t.* load'ed ; *pa.p.* load'ed or (*arch.*) load'en.—*v.t.* load'en, (*obs.* or *dial.*) to load.—*ns.* load'er ; load'ing, the act of lading : that with which anything is loaded ; load'-line, a line on a ship's side to mark the depth to which her cargo may be allowed to sink her ; load'-shedding, (*elect.*) discarding part of the load. — load dice, to make one side heavier than the other so as to influence their fall for purposes of cheating ; loading coil, a coil inserted in an electric circuit to increase inductance ; loading gauge, a suspended bar that marks how high a railway truck may be loaded. [O.E. *lád*, course, journey, conveyance ; meaning affected by the unrelated lade ; cf. lode, lead.]

loadstar, loadstone. Same as lodestar, lodestone.

loaf, *lōf*, *n.* (formerly, still *Scot.*) bread : a portion of bread baked in one mass, esp. of standard weight : a conical mass of sugar : any lump : a cabbagehead :—*pl.* loaves (*lōvz*).—*v.i.* loaf, loave (*lōv*), to form a head, as a cabbage.—*ns.* loaf'-bread, (*Scot.*) ordinary plain bread ; loaf'-cake, (*U.S.*) a plain cake like a loaf in form ; loaf'-sug'ar, refined sugar moulded in the form of a great cigar. —half loaf, a loaf of half the standard weight ; loaves and fishes, temporal benefits, the main chance (John vi. 26). [O.E. *hláf*, bread.]

loaf, *lōf*, *v.i.* to loiter or stand idly about, pass time idly.—*n.* loaf'er.—*adj.* loaf'erish.—*n.* and *adj.* loaf'ing. [Origin obscure.]

loam, *lōm*, *n.* a muddy soil, of clay, sand, and animal and vegetable matter.—*v.t.* to cover with loam.—*adj.* loam'y. [O.E. *lám* ; Ger. *lehm* ; cf. lime.]

loan, *lōn*, *n.* a lane : an open space for passage left between fields of corn : a place for milking cows. —Also loan'ing. [O.E. *lone, lane* ; see lane.]

loan, *lōn*, *n.* anything lent, esp. money at interest : the act of lending : the condition of being lent : an arrangement for lending : permission to use.— *v.t.* to lend.—*adj.* loan'able.—*ns.* loan'-office, a public office at which loans are negotiated, received, or recorded : a pawnshop ; loan'-shark, a usurer ; loan'-society, a society organised to subscribe money to be lent ; loan'-word, one borrowed from another language. [O.N. *lán* ; cf. lend, O.E. *lǽnan* ; Dan. *laan.*]

loast, *lōst*, (*Spens.*) *pa.p.* of loose.

loath. Same as loth.

loathe, *lōdh*, *v.t.* to dislike intensely : to feel disgust at. — *adj.* loathed. — *ns.* loath'edness ; loath'er.—*adj.* loath'ful, exciting loathing or disgust : (*Spens.*) lothefull, lothfull) loathsome : reluctant.—*ns.* loath'fulness ; loath'ing, extreme hate or disgust : abhorrence.—*adj.* hating.—*adv.* loath'ingly. — *n.* loath'liness.—*adjs.* loath'ly, (*arch.*) hideous ; loathsome ; loathsome (*lōth', lōdh'sam*), exciting loathing or abhorrence : detestable.—*adv.* loath'somely.—*n.* loath'someness. —*adj.* loathy (*lōdh'i*). [O.E. *láthian* ; cf. loth.]

loave, loaves. See loaf (1).

lob, *lob*, *n.* a lump : a clumsy person : a lout : something thick and heavy : a pollack : a lobworm : in cricket, a slow, high underhand ball : in lawn-tennis, a ball high overhead, dropping near the back of the court.—*v.t.* (*Shak.*) to droop : to bowl or strike as a lob :—*pa.p.* lobbed.—*n.* Lob'-lie'-by-the-fire, a brownie who works by night for his bowl of cream : a Puck. — Lob's pound, prison : difficulty. [Cf. Fris. and Du. *lob.*]

lobby, *lob'i*, *n.* a small hall or waiting-room : a passage serving as a common entrance to several apartments : the ante-chamber of a legislative hall : a corridor into which members pass as they vote.—*v.t.* to seek to influence in the lobby.— *v.i.* to frequent the lobby in order to influence members or to collect political intelligence.—*ns.* lobb'ying ; lobb'yist, lobb'y-mem'ber, (*U.S.*) a journalist, &c., who frequents a lobby in the interest of some cause or of a newspaper. [L.L. *lobia*—M.H.G. *loube* (Ger. *laube*), a portico, arbour—*laub*, a leaf ; cf. lodge.]

lobe, *lōb*, *n.* a broad, esp. rounded, segmental division, branch, or projection : the soft lower part of the ear : a division of the lungs, brain, &c. : a division of a leaf.—*adjs.* lōb'ar, lōb'ate, lōbed, lōb'ose.—*ns.* lōbā'tion, lobing ; lōbe'-foot, a phalarope.—*adjs.* lōbe'-foot'ed, lō'biped, having lobate feet, i.e. with lobes along the sides of the toes, as a coot.—*ns.* lōbe'let, lobule (*lob'ūl*), small lobe ; lōb'ing, division into lobes : formation of, possession of, or provision with, lobes ; lobot'omy, leucotomy. — *adjs.* lōb'ular, -ulate(d).— *ns.* lōbulā'tion ; lōb'ulus, a small lobe or lobelike structure : — *pl.* lōb'uli (-*ī*) ; lō'bus, a lobe : —*pl.* lō'bī.— lobar pneumonia, inflammation of a whole lobe of the lungs, as distinguished from lobular pneumonia, which attacks the lungs in patches. [Gr. *lobos*, lobe.]

Lobelia, *lō-bē'lyä*, *n.* a genus of plants giving name to a family, Lobeliā'ceae, differing from Campanulaceae in having two carpels and zygomorphic flowers, twisted upside-down, including favourite blue-flowered garden plants : a drug got from an American species (*L. inflata*). [Named after the botanist Matthias de Lobel (1538-1616).]

loblolly, *lob'lol-i*, *n.* thick gruel : ship's medicine : a lout : (*U.S.*) a puddle : a name for various American pines (also loblolly pine).—*ns.* lob'-lolly-bay, an American tree of the tea family (*Gordonia Lasianthus*), its bark used in tanning ; lob'lolly-boy, a ship-surgeon's attendant ; lob'lolly-tree, a name for several American leathery-leaved trees. [Perh. lob and lolly.]

lobscouse, *lob'skows*, *n.* a stew or hash with vegetables or biscuit, a sea dish.—Also lob's course. [Origin obscure ; cf. lob, loblolly.]

lobster, *lob'stər*, *n.* a large strong-clawed edible crustacean (Homarus), red when boiled : extended to kindred kinds, as the Norway lobster (Nephrops), spiny or rock lobster (Palinurus) : (*obs. slang*) a British soldier.—*n.* lob'ster-pot, a basket for trapping lobsters. [O.E. *loppestre*—L. *locusta*, a lobster ; cf. locust.]

lobworm, *lob'wurm*, *n.* a lugworm : sometimes an earthworm. [lob, worm.]

local, *lō'kl*, *adj.* pertaining to position in space : of or belonging to a place : confined to a place or places.—*n.* someone or something local, as an inhabitant, a public-house, an examination, an item of news, a railway train, in U.S. a trade union branch : a place : (*lō-käl'*) erroneously locale, for Fr. *local*) the scene of some event.—*n.* localīsā'tion. —*v.t.* lo'calise, to assign, limit, refer to a place. —*ns.* lo'calism, the state of being local : affection for a place : provincialism ; locality (*lō-kal'i-ti*), place : position : district.—*adv.* lo'cally.—*v.t.* locate', to place : to set in a particular position : to designate or find the place of.—*v.i.* (*U.S.*) to settle, take up one's abode.—*n.* locā'tion, act of locating : a farm : a claim or place marked off (for native occupation, &c.) : position : (*U.S.*) site : (*U.S.*) taking up residence : (*law*) a leasing on rent. —*adj.* locative (*lok'ə-tiv*), pertaining to location : (*gram.*) denoting place where.—*n.* the locative case : a word in the locative case.—local authorities, elected bodies for local government, e.g. town councils, county councils ; local colour, colour of individual items as apart from general colour-scheme in a picture : faithful, characteristic details of particular scenery, manners, &c., giving verisimilitude in works of art and fiction ; local examinations, examinations of school pupils held in various local centres by universities ; local government, self-administration (in local affairs) by towns, counties, and the like, as opp. to national or central government ; local option, the right of a town or district to decide whether liquor licences shall be granted within its bounds, or to decide whether or not to enforce (locally) permissive laws and regulations ; local preacher, a Methodist layman authorised to preach in his district ; local time, the time of a place as shown by the sun ; local veto, the power of a district to prohibit the sale of liquors in its own area ; on location, (*cinematography*) anywhere outside the film-studio. [L. *locális*—*locus*, a place.]

locellate, *lō-sel′āt*, *adj.* divided into small compartments. [L. *locellus*, dim. of *locus*, a place.]

loch, *lohh*, *n.* a lake : an arm of the sea.—*n.* **loch′an** (*Gael.*), a lakelet. [Gael. *loch*; O.E. (Northumbrian) *luh*.]

Lochaber-axe, *lohh-ä′bər-aks*, *n.* a long-handled Highland variety of halbert. [*Lochaber* district in Inverness-shire.]

lochia, *lok′i-ä*, or *lōk′*, *n.pl.* a discharge after childbirth.—*adj.* **lō′chial**. [Gr. *lochia* (pl.).]

lock, *lok*, *n.* a fastening device, esp. one in which a bolt is moved by mechanism, with or without a key : an enclosure for raising or lowering boats : the part of a firearm by which it is discharged : a grapple in wrestling : a state of being jammed, or immovable : an assemblage of things mutually engaged : a lockful : a lock-keeper : any narrow, confined place : a lock-hospital : locking up.— *v.t.* to fasten with a lock : to fasten so as to impede motion : to engage : to jam : to shut up : to close fast : to embrace closely : to furnish with locks.— *v.i.* to become fast : to unite closely : to become locked.—*ns.* **lock′age**, the locks of a canal : the difference in the levels of locks : materials used for locks : water lost by the use of a lock : tolls paid for passing through locks ; **lock′-chain**, a chain for fastening the wheels of a vehicle by tying the rims to some part which does not rotate ; **lock′er**, a box or receptacle, properly one that may be locked ; **locket** (*lok′it*), a little ornamental case usually containing a miniature or memento, and hung from the neck.—*adj.* **lock′fast**, firmly fastened by locks. —*ns.* **lock′ful**, enough to fill a lock ; **lock′-gate**, a gate for opening or closing a lock in a canal, river, or dock-entrance ; **lock′-hos′pital**, a hospital for venereal diseases (from one in Southwark, originally a lazar-house, probably as specially isolated) ; **lock′house**, a lock-keeper's house ; **lock′-jaw**, tetanus : loosely, trismus ; **lock′-keeper**, the attendant at a lock ; **lock′man**, a lock-keeper : (*Scot.*, *obs.*) a hangman : (*Isle of Man*) an undersheriff, or a coroner's summoner ; **lock′out′**, the act of locking out, esp. used of the locking out of a teacher by the pupils, pupils by teacher, or employees by employer ; **locks′man**, a turnkey : a lock-keeper ; **lock′smith**, one who makes and mends locks ; **lock′stitch**, a stitch formed by the locking of two threads together ; **lock′-up**, a place for locking up prisoners, motor-cars, &c. : a locking up.—*adj.* capable of being locked up.— **a shot in the locker** (see **shot**) ; **lock in, out,** to confine, keep out, by locking doors ; **lock, stock, and barrel,** the whole : altogether ; **lock up,** to confine : to lock securely : to lock whatever is to be locked. [O.E. *loc*.]

lock, *lok*, *n.* a tuft or ringlet of hair, wool, &c. : a small quantity, as of hay : (*Scots law*) a quantity of meal, the perquisite of a mill-servant : (*Shak.*) a love-lock. [O.E.*locc* ; O.N.*lokkr*, Ger. *locke*, a lock.]

Lockian, *lok′i-ən*, *adj.* pertaining to the philosophy of John Locke (1632-1704). — *ns.* **Lock′ian**, **Lock′ist**.

lockram, *lok′rəm*, *n.* a coarse linen said to have been made at Locronan (Ronan's cell) in Brittany.

loco, *lō′kō*, *adj.* (*U.S.*) mad.—*n.* (also **lo′co-plant**, -**weed**) Astragalus or other leguminous plant.— *adj.* **locoed** (*lō′kōd*), poisoned by loco : mad. [Sp. *loco*, mad.]

locofoco, *lō-kō-fō′kō*, *n.* (*U.S.*) a friction match : one of the extreme section of the Democratic party of 1835, known as the Equal Rights Party. [Origin unknown.]

locomotive, *lō-kə-mō′tiv*, *adj.* moving from place to place : capable of, or assisting in, locomotion. —*n.* a locomotive machine : a railway engine.— *adj.* **locomo′bile** (-*bil*), having power of changing place : self-propelling.—*n.* a locomobile vehicle.— *v.i.* **lo′comote**, to move from place to place (back formation).—*ns.* **locomotion** (-*mō′shən*) ; **locomotiv′ity** ; **locomo′tor**. — *adjs.* **locomo′tor**, **locomo′tory.**—**locomotor ataxy,** tabes dorsalis, a chronic degenerative disease of the nervous system of which want of power to co-ordinate the muscles is a characteristic symptom. [L. *lŏcus*, a place, *movēre*, *mōtum*, to move.]

locorestive, *lō-kō-res′tiv*, *adj.* (*Lamb*) staying in one place. [Humorously modelled on preceding— L. *restāre*, to stay still.]

Locrian, *lō′kri-ən*, *adj.* of Locris in Greece, or its people, the Locri.—*n.* one of the Locri.—**Locrian mode,** in ancient Greek music, the same as the Hypodorian. [Gr. *Lokros*, Locrian.]

loculus, *lok′ū-ləs*, *n.* (*bot.*, *anat.*, *zool.*) a small compartment : in ancient catacombs, a small recess for holding an urn :—*pl.* **loc′uli** (-*lī*).—*n.* **loc′ulament**, (*bot.*) loculus.—*adjs.* **loc′ular**, **loc′ulate**, having loculi ; **loculicidal** (*lok-ū-li-sī′dl*), dehiscing along the back of the carpel (L. *caedĕre*, to cut). [L. *loculus*, dim. of *locus*, a place.]

locum-tenens, *lō′kəm-tēn′enz*, *n.* a deputy or substitute (*coll.* **lo′cum**).—*n.* **lō′cum-tēn′ency**, the holding by a temporary substitute of a post. [L. *lŏcum*, accus. of *lŏcus*, a place, *tĕnēns*, pr.p. of *tenēre*, to hold.]

locuplete, *lok′ū-plēt*, *adj.* well-stored. [L. *locuplēs*, -*ētis*.]

locus, *lō′kəs*, L. *lok′oos*, *n.* a place, locality, location : a passage in a writing : the position of a gene in a chromosome : (*math.*) the line or surface constituted by all positions of a point or line satisfying a given condition :—*pl.* **loci** (*lō′sī* ; L. *lok′ē*). [L. *lŏcus*, place.]

locust, *lō′kəst*, *n.* a name for several kinds of migratory winged insects of the family Acridiidae, akin to grasshoppers, highly destructive to vegetation : extended to various similar insects : (*fig.*) a devourer or devastator : a locust-bean : a locust-tree.—*v.i.* (*rare*) to lay waste like locusts. —*ns.* **locust′a**, a grass spikelet : **Locusta**, a genus of grasshoppers of the family **Locust′idae** (not usually reckoned locusts) :—*pl.* **locust′ae** (-*ē*) ; **lo′cust-bean**, the carob-bean ; **lo′cust-tree′**, the carob : the false acacia (*Robinia Pseudo-acacia*) : a large West Indian tree (*Hymenaea Courbaril*) of the Caesalpinia family, with buttress roots, valuable wood, bark exuding anime. [L. *locusta*, lobster, locust ; cf. **lobster**.]

locution, *lok-ū′shən*, *n.* act or mode of speaking : expression, word, or phrase.—*n.* **loc′utory**, a room for conversation, esp. in a monastery. [L. *loqui*, *locūtus*, to speak.]

lode, *lōd*, *n.* a vein containing metallic ore : a reach of water : an open ditch.—*ns.* **lodes′man**, a pilot ; **lode′star**, **load′star**, the star that guides, the Pole Star—often used figuratively ; **lode′-stone**, **load′stone**, magnetic iron ore, esp. in the state in which it shows polar magnetism : a magnet —often figuratively. [O.E. *ldd*, a course ; cf. **load**.]

lodge, *loj*, *n.* an abode, esp. if secluded, humble, small, or temporary : a house in the wilds for sportsmen : a gate-keeper's cottage : a college head's residence : a porter's room : the meeting-place of a branch of some societies, as freemasons : the branch itself : an American Indian's abode : the dwelling-place of a beaver, otter, &c. : a retreat : often, a villa (as part of its name) : an accumulation : a loggia : a box in a theatre.—*v.t.* to furnish with a temporary dwelling : to place : to deposit : to infix : to vest : to settle : to drive to covert : to lay flat, as grain.—*v.i.* to dwell, esp. for a time, or as a lodger : to pass the night : to take covert : to come to rest in a fixed position : to lie flat, as grain.—*ns.* **lodge′-gate′**, a gate with a lodge ; **lodge′-keeper** ; **lodge′pole**, a pole used in making an Indian lodge ; **lodg′er**, one who lodges : one who lives in a hired room or rooms ; **lodg′ing**, temporary habitation : a room or rooms hired in the house of another (often in *pl.*) : harbour ; **lodg′ing-house**, a house where lodgings are let : a house other than a hotel where travellers lodge : a house where vagrants may lodge ; **lodg′-ment** (sometimes **lodge′ment**), act of lodging, or state of being lodged : accumulation of something that remains at rest : (*mil.*) the occupation of a position by a besieging party, and the works thrown up to maintain it. [O.Fr. *loge*—O.H.G. *lauba*, shelter ; cf. **lobby, loggia.**]

lodicule, *lod′i-kūl*, *n.* a small scale in a grass flower. —Also **lodic′ula** ; *pl.* **lodic′ulae** (-*ē*). [L. *lōdicula*, dim. of *lōdix*, -*īcis*, coverlet.]

Neutral vowels in unaccented syllables : *el′ə-mənt, in′fənt, ran′dəm*

lo'e, *lōō,* Scots form of love (verb).

loess, löss, *ləs,* or *lō'es, n.* a loamy deposit of Aeolian origin. [Ger. *löss.*]

loft, *loft, n. (Spens.)* upper region, sky, height : a room or space immediately under a roof : a gallery in a hall or church : an upper room : (*U.S.*) an upper floor : (*Spens.*) a floor or ceiling : a room for pigeons (*Milt.*) a layer : a stroke that causes a golf-ball to rise : a backward slope on a golf-club head for the purpose of lofting : a lifting action.—*v.t.* to furnish with a loft : to put or keep in a loft : (*golf*) to strike up : to toss.—*n.* **loft'er,** a golf iron for lofting.—*adv.* **loft'ily.**—*n.* **loft'iness.** —*adj.* **loft'y,** very high in position, character, sentiment, manner, or diction : stately : haughty : of wool, bulky, springy, supple, and soft.—**cock of the loft,** the head or chief of a set ; **lofted house,** (*Scot.*) a house of more than one story. [Late O.E. *loft*—O.N. *loft,* sky, an upper room ; O.E. *lyft,* Ger. *luft,* the air.]

log, *log, n.* abbreviation for **logarithm.**

log, *lōg, log, n.* a Hebrew liquid measure, believed to be very nearly an English pint. [Heb. *lōg.*]

log, *log, n.* a bulky piece of wood : a clog or impediment : (*fig.*) an inert or insensitive person : an apparatus (originally a block of wood) for ascertaining a ship's speed : a record of a ship's, or other, performance and experiences, a log-book. —*adj.* consisting of logs.—*v.t.* to cut or haul in the form of logs : to enter in a log-book : to cover a distance of, according to the log : to record the name and punishment of : to punish.— *ns.* **log'board,** a hinged board for noting particulars for the log-book ; **log'-book,** a book containing an official record of a ship's progress and proceedings on board : a headmaster's record of attendances and other details connected with a school, or similar matter ; **log'-cab'in,** a hut built of hewn or unhewn logs ; **log'-canoe',** a boat made by hollowing out the trunk of a tree ; **log'-chip,** the quadrant-shaped board attached to a logline ; **logg'at,** a small log or piece of wood : a stake : (in *pl.*) old game of throwing loggats at a stake.—*adj.* **logged** (*logd*), reduced to the inactivity or helplessness of a log : waterlogged : cleared of logs.—*ns.* **logg'er,** a lumberman ; **logg'erhead,** a blockhead : a dunce : (*naut.*) a round piece of timber in a whale-boat, over which the line is passed : a large sea-turtle : a round mass of iron with a long handle, heated for various purposes. —*adj.* **logg'erheaded.**—*ns.* **log'-glass,** a 14- or 28-second sand-glass, used with the logline to ascertain the speed of a ship ; **logg'ing ; log'-head,** a blockhead ; **log'-house, log'-cabin :** (*U.S.*) a prison ; **log'-hut' ; log'-juice,** (*slang*) bad port wine, as if coloured with logwood ; **log'line,** the line fastened to the log, and marked for finding the speed of a vessel ; **log'-man,** (*Shak.*) a man who carries logs : (*U.S.*) one who cuts and removes logs ; **log'-reel,** a reel on which the logline is wound.—*v.t.* and *v.i.* **log'-roll.**— *ns.* **log'-roller ; log'-rolling,** a combination for facilitating the collection of logs after the clearing of a piece of land, or for rolling logs into a stream : mutual aid among politicians or reviewers ; **log'-slate,** a double slate used as a logboard ; **log'wood,** a tropical American tree (*Haematoxylon campechianum*) of the Caesalpinia family, exported in logs : its dark-red heartwood : an extract from it used in dyeing.—**at loggerheads,** at issue, quarrelling. [Origin obscure.]

logan, *log'ən, n.* a rocking-stone.—Also **log'an-stone, logg'an-stone, logg'ing-stone.** [Dialect word *log,* to rock ; poss. conn. with Dan. *logre,* to wag the tail.]

loganberry, *lō'gən-ber-i, n.* a supposed hybrid between raspberry and a Pacific coast blackberry, obtained by Judge J. H. Logan.

Logania, *lō-gā'ni-ä, n.* a genus of Australian plants giving name to the **Loganiā'ceae,** akin to the gentians. [Named after James Logan (1674-1751), American botanist, scholar, and statesman.]

logaoedic, *log-ə-ē'dik, adj.* (*ancient prosody*) combining dactyls with trochees. [Gr. *logos,* prose, *aoidē,* song.]

logarithm, *log'-ə-rithm, -ridhm, n.* the power of a fixed number (called the base of the system, usu. 10 or *e*) that equals the number in question.—*adjs.* **logarith'mic, -al.** — *adv.* **logarith'mically.**— **logarithmic sine, cosine,** &c., the logarithm of the sine, cosine, &c., increased by 10 ; **logarithmic spiral,** the path of a point travelling along a radius vector with a velocity increasing as its distance, from the pole, its polar equation being $r = a^\theta,$ or $\theta = k \log r$. [Gr. *logos,* ratio, reckoning, *arithmos,* number.]

loggat, logger, &c. See **log** (2).

loggia (*loj'(y)ä, n.* a covered open arcade :—*pl.* **loggie** (*loj'ä*), **loggias.** [It. ; cf. **lodge.**]

logia (*log'i-ä, n.pl.* sayings, esp. early collections of those attributed to Jesus :—*sing.* **log'ion.** [Gr.]

logic, *loj'ik, n.* the science and art of reasoning correctly : the science of the necessary laws of thought.—*adj.* **log'ical,** of or according to logic : rightly reasoning.—*ns.* **logical'ity, log'icalness.** —*adv.* **log'ically.**—*n.* **logician** (*loj-ish'ən*), one skilled in logic.—*v.i.* **log'icise** (*-sīz*), to argue.— **chop logic** (see **chop**). [Gr. *logikē* (*technē*), logical (art)—*logos,* speech, reason.]

logie, *lō'gi, n.* (*Scot.*) the space before a kiln fire. [Origin unknown ; cf. **killogie.**]

logistic, -al, *loj-is'tik, -əl, adjs.* pertaining to reasoning, to calculation, or to logistic : proportional.— *n.* **logis'tic,** the art of calculation : sexagesimal arithmetic : (*pl.*) art of movement and supply of troops. [Gr. *logistikos—logixesthai,* to compute ; influenced by Fr. *loger,* to lodge.]

loglog, *log'log, n.* the logarithm of a *log*arithm.— Also **lō'log.**

logodaedalus, *log-ō-dē'də-ləs, n.* an artificer in words.—*n.* **logodae'daly,** verbal legerdemain. [Latinised from Gr. *logodaidalos—logos,* word, *Daidalos,* Daedalus ; see **Daedal.**]

logogram, *log'ō-gram, n.* a single sign for a word : a logogriph. [Gr. *logos,* word, *gramma,* letter.]

logographer, *log-og'rə-fər, n.* in Greek literature, one of the earliest annalists, esp. those before Herodotus : a professional speech-writer.—*adjs.* **logographic** (*-graf'ik*), **-al.**—*adv.* **logograph'ically.**—*n.* **logog'raphy,** a method of printing with whole words cast in a single type. [Gr. *logos,* word, *graphein,* to write.]

logogriph, *log'ō-grif, n.* a riddle in which a word is to be found from other words made up of its letters, or from synonyms of these. [Gr. *logos,* word, *grīphos,* a net, riddle.]

logomachy, *log-om'ə-ki, n.* contention about words or in words merely.—*n.* **logom'achist.** [Gr. *logomachiā—logos,* word, *machē,* fight.]

logorrhoea, *log-ō-rē'ä, n.* excessive flow of words. [Gr. *rhoiā,* flow.]

Logos, *log'os, n.* in the Stoic philosophy, the active principle living in and determining the world : (*Christian theol.*) the Word of God incarnate. [Gr. *logos,* word.]

logothete, *log'ō-thēt, n.* a chancellor, esp. in the Byzantine Empire and in Norman Sicily. [Gr. *logothetēs,* an auditor.]

logotype, *log'ō-tīp, n.* a type of a word or several letters cast in one piece. [Gr. *logos,* word, *typos,* an impression.]

loin, *loin, n.* the back of a beast cut for food : (usually in *pl.*) the reins, or the lower part of the back : (in *pl.*) generating source.—*n.* **loin'-cloth,** a piece of cloth for wearing round the loins. —**gird up the loins,** to prepare for energetic action, as if by tucking up one's clothes. [O.Fr. *loigne*—L. *lumbus,* loin.]

loiter, *loi'tər, v.i.* to proceed lingeringly : to dawdle : to linger.—*n.* **loi'terer.**—*n.* and *adj.* **loi'tering.**—*adv.* **loi'teringly.** [Du. *leuteren,* to dawdle ; Ger. prov. *lottern,* to waver.]

Loki, *lō'ki, n.* an evil god in Norse mythology.

Loligo, *lō-lī'gō, n.* the typical genus of Loliginidae (*lol-i-jin'i-dē*) including the common squid. [L. *lōlīgō, -inis.*]

Lolium, *lō'li-əm, n.* a genus of grasses including darnel and rye-grass. [L. *lōlium,* darnel, ' tares.']

loll, *lol, v.i.* to lie lazily about, to lounge, sprawl : to dangle, hang (now mainly of the tongue).—

v.t. to let hang out.—*n.* **loll´er**.—*adv.* **loll´ingly**.—*v.i.* **loll´op**, to lounge, idle: to bound floppily along. [Perh. imit.; cf. Du. *lollen*, to sit over the fire.]

Lollard, *lol´ərd*, *n.* a follower of Wycliffe: an idler.—*ns.* **Loll´ardy**, **Loll´ardry**, **Loll´ardism**. [M.Du. *lollaerd*, mutterer, droner—*lollen*, to mew, bawl, mutter; combined with *loller* (see **loll**).]

lollipop, *lol´i-pop*, *n.* a sweetmeat made with sugar and treacle: a large sweetmeat impaled on a stick: (usu. in *pl.*) a sweetmeat in general.—Also (*Australia*) **loll´y**. [Perh. Northern dial. *lolly*, tongue.]

loll-shraub, **loll-shrob**, *lol´-shrawb´, -shrob´*, *n.* (*India*) claret. [Hind. *lāl sharāb*—Pers. *lāl*, red, Ar. *sharāb*, wine.]

loma, *lō´mä*, *n.* (*zool.*) a membranous fringe or flap. [Gr. *lōma, -atos*.]

Lombard, *lom´bərd, lum´bərd*, *n.* an inhabitant of *Lombardy* in Italy: one of the Langobardi, a Germanic tribe, which founded a kingdom in Lombardy (568), overthrown by Charlemagne (774): (*obs.*) a banker or money-lender, so called from the number of Lombard bankers in London.—*adjs.* **Lom´bard**, **Lombardic** (*-bärd´ik*).—**Lombard architecture**, the Romanesque style of Northern Italy, superseded by the Pointed in the 13th century; **Lombardic script**, a mediaeval Italian style of handwriting; **Lombard Street**, the chief centre of the banking interest in London; **Lombardy poplar**, a variety of black poplar with erect branches. [O.Fr.,—L. *Langobardus*.]

lome, (*Spens.*) for **loam**.

lomentum, *lō-ment´əm*, *n.* a pod that breaks in pieces at constrictions between the seeds:—*pl.* **loment´a**. — Also **lo´ment** (*-mənt*). [L. *lōmentum*, bean-meal (used as a cosmetic)—*lavāre*, *lōtum*, to wash.]

lompish, (*Spens.*) for **lumpish**.

Londoner, *lun´dən-ər*, *n.* a native or citizen of *London*.—*adjs.* **Londonese´**, **Londonian** (*-dō´ni-ən*), **Lon´donish**, **Lon´dony**.—*n.* **Londonese´**, cockney speech.—*v.t.* and *v.i.* **Lon´donise**.—*n.* **Lon´donism**, a mode of speech, &c., peculiar to London.—**London Clay**, a Lower Eocene formation in south-eastern England; **London ivy**, smoke; **London pride**, a hardy perennial saxifrage (*Saxifraga umbrosa*)—also *none-so-pretty* and *St Patrick's cabbage*: formerly applied to other plants.

lone, *lōn*, *adj.* alone: solitary: retired: standing by itself: uncomfortably conscious of being alone.—*ns.* **lone´liness**, **lone´ness**.—*adj.* **lone´some**, solitary: feeling lonely.—*adv.* **lone´somely**.—*n.* **lone´someness**. [alone.]

long, *long*, *adj.* and *adv.* (*Shak.* and *prov.*) on account. [**along** (2).]

long, *long*, *v.i.* (*arch.*) to belong, pertain, be fitting. [Not found as a vb. in O.E.: perh.—*gelang*, along, beside (as if to go along with).]

long, *long*, *adj.* not short: of a specified (or to be specified) length: extended in space in the direction of greatest extension: far-extending: extended in time: of extended continuance: distant in time: of distant date: requiring much time in utterance or performance: (loosely) accented: (loosely) in a long syllable: numerically extensive: of more than average number (as a suit of cards): exceeding the standard value (see **dozen, hundred**): tedious: (*comp.* **longer**, *long´gər*, *obs.* **leng´er**; *superl.* **longest**, *long´gist*, *obs.* **leng´est**).—*n.* a long time: (*pros.*) a long syllable: (*coll.*) the long summer university vacation: (*mus.*) a long note equal to two (in ' perfect ' time three) breves: (in *pl.*) long trousers.—*adv.* for, during, or by a great extent of time: throughout the whole time: (*rare*) far in space: (*comp.* and *superl.* as for *adj.*).—*v.i.* to yearn.—*n.* **long´a** (*mus.*), a long.—*adj.* **long´-ago´**, of the far past.—*n.* the far past.—*ns.* **long´boat**, the largest and strongest boat of a ship; **long´-bow**, a bow drawn by hand—opp. to *cross-bow.*—*adj.* **long´-breathed** (*bretht´*), able to continue violent exercise of the lungs for a long time.—*n.* **long´-cloth**, a cotton made in long pieces.—*ns.pl.* **long´-clothes**, **long´-coats**, a baby's first dress.—*adjs.*

long´-descend´ed, of ancient lineage; **long´-dist´ance**, going or extending to or over a long distance.—*n.* **long´-divi´sion**, (*arith.*) division in which the working is shown in full.—*adjs.* **long´-drawn** (*-out´*), prolonged: unduly protracted; **long´-eared**, with long ears or earlike feathertufts; **long´-field**, (*cricket*) a fielder or station near the boundary on the bowler's side; **long´-firm**, a company of swindlers who obtain goods on pretence of being established in business, and then decamp without payment; **long´hand**, ordinary writing—opp. to *shorthand*; **long´-head**, a dolichocephal.—*adj.* **long´-head´ed**, dolichocephalous: having good intellectual powers: sagacious.—*ns.* **long´-head´edness**; **long´horn**, an animal with long horns or antennae, as a longicorn beetle (**house longhorn beetle**, a beetle whose larvae are very destructive to house timbers): a long-eared owl; **long´-house**, a long communal house, esp. of American Indians; **long´ing**, an eager desire, craving, esp. of the whimsical desires sometimes felt in pregnancy.—*adj.* yearning.—*adv.* **long´ingly**.—*adj.* **longish** (*long´ish, -gish*).—*n.* **long´-leg**, (*cricket*) a fieldsman, or his station, far out behind the batsman and a little to his left.—*adj.* **long´-legged**, having long legs.—*n.* **long´-legs**, a crane-fly.—*adj.* **long´-lived** (*-livd´*; also *-livd´*), having a long life.—*adv.* **long´ly**, (*Shak.*) long.—*ns.* **long´-meas´ure**, lineal measure: quatrains of eight-syllable lines; **long´ness** (*rare*); **long´-nine**, (*U.S.*) a cheap cigar; **long´-off**, **long´-on**, (*cricket*) the fielders in the long-field to the off and on of the batsman respectively: their position; **long´-pig**, human flesh as food; **long´-prim´er**, a size of type intermediate between small pica and bourgeois; **long´-pur´ples**, the early purple orchis: purple loosestrife.—*adj.* **long´-range**, long in range.—*n.pl.* **longs´-and-shorts´**, Greek or Latin verses: masonry of alternate vertical and horizontal blocks, as in quoins and jambs.—*n.* **long´ship**, (*hist.*) a long vessel of the old Norsemen.—*adj.* **long´-sight´ed**, able to see far but not close at hand: hypermetropic: presbyopic: having foresight: sagacious. — *n.* **long´-sight´edness**.—*n.pl.* **long´-six´es**, candles weighing six to a pound.—*n.* **long´-slip**, (*cricket*) a fielder some distance behind the batsman on the off side.—*adjs.* **long´some**, long and tedious; **long´-spun**, long-drawn, tedious; **long´-stand´ing**, of long standing or continuance; **long´-sta´ple**, having a long fibre.—*n.* **long´-stop**, (*cricket*) one who stands behind the wicket-keeper to stop balls missed by him.—*v.i.* to field as long-stop.—*adj.* **long´-suff´ering**, enduring long and patiently.—*n.* long endurance or patience.—*n.* **long´-tail**, an animal, esp. a dog, with uncut tail: a greyhound.—Also *adj.*—*adjs.* **long´-tongued**, having a long tongue: talkative, babbling; **long´-vis´aged**, longfaced: of rueful countenance; **long´-waist´ed**, having a long waist: long from the armpits to the hips.—*n.* **long´wall**, a long working face in a coalmine.—*advs.* **long´ways**, **-wise**, lengthwise.—*adj.* **long´-wind´ed**, long-breathed: tediously wordy and lengthy.—*n.* **long´-wind´edness**.—**a long figure**, (*slang*) a high price or rate; **a long purse**, abundance of money; **before long, ere long**, soon; **draw the long bow**, to exaggerate extravagantly; **in the long run** (see **run**); **long home**, the grave; **long hop**, (*cricket*) a short-pitched, and so long-bounding, ball, easy to hit; **long moss**, a tropical American rootless epiphyte (*Tillandsia usneoides*) of the pineapple family, resembling bunches of hair; **long robe**, **ten, Tom, ton, whist**, &c. (see **robe**, &c.); **long sheep**, long-woolled sheep; **make a long arm**, (*prov.*) to help oneself freely at table; **make a long nose**, to cock a snook or put a thumb to the nose; **no longer**, not now as formerly; **not long for this world**, near death; **so long as**, provided only that; **the long and the short (of it)**, or (*Shak.*) **the short and the long (of it)**, the sum of the matter in a few words. [O.E. *lang*, *long* (adj.), *lange*, *longe* (adv.); Ger. *lang*, O.N. *langr*; L. *longus*.]

longa, *long´gä*, *n.* See **long** (3).

longan, *long'gan, n.* a tree (*Nephelium Longana*) akin to the litchi : its fruit. [Chin. *lung-yen*, dragon's eye.]

longanimity, *long-gə-nim'i-ti, n.* forbearance.—*adj.* **longanimous** (-*gan'*). [L. *longanimitās, -ātis*—*longus,* long, *animus,* spirit.]

longe. Same as **lunge** (2).

longeron, *lon'(d)zhə-ron, lonᵍ-zhə-ronᵍ, n.* a longitudinal member of an aeroplane. [Fr.]

longevity, *lon-jev'i-ti, n.* great length of life.—*adjs.* **longaeval** -**eval,** **longaevous,** -**evous** (-*jēv'*). [L. *longaevitās, -ātis*—*longus,* long, *aevum,* age.]

longicorn, *lon'ji-korn, n.* any beetle of the family Cerambycidae, with very long antennae (the larvae feed on wood).—Also *adj.* [L. *longus, cornū,* horn.]

longinquity, *lon-jingk'wi-ti, n.* remoteness. [L. *longinquitās, -ātis*—*longus,* long.]

longitude, *lon'ji-tūd, n.* length : arc of the equator between the meridian of a place and a standard meridian (usually that of Greenwich) expressed in degrees E. or W. : (*astron.*) the arc of the ecliptic between a star's circle of latitude and the first point of Aries or vernal equinox, measured eastwards.—*adj.* **longitūd'inal,** of or in length or longitude : lengthwise.—*adv.* **longitūd'inally.** [L. *longitūdō, -inis,* length—*longus,* long.]

longshore, *long'shōr, adj.* existing or employed along the shore.—*n.* **long'shoreman,** a stevedore : one who makes a living along the shore. [alongshore.]

loo, *lōō, n.* a card game.—*v.t.* to subject to a forfeit at loo :—*pr.p.* **lōō'ing ;** *pa.t.* and *pa.p.* **lōōed.**—*n.* **loo'-table,** a form of round table, orig. one for playing loo. [See **lanterloo.**]

looby, *lōōb'i, n.* a clumsy, clownish fellow.—*adv.* **loob'ily.** [Cf. **lob.**]

loof, *lōōf.* Same as **luff.**

loof, *lōōf, Scot. ləf, n.* the palm of the hand :—*pl.* **loofs, looves.**—*n.* **loof'ful** (Scot. *ləf'fə*), an open handful. [O.N. *lófi.*]

loofa, loofah. See **luffa.**

look, *look, v.i.* to direct the sight with attention : to give attention : to face : to seem : to seem to be : to have an appearance : to tend.—*v.t.* to make sure : to see to it : to ascertain by a look : to look at : to expect : to seem likely : to render by a look : to express by a look : to refer to, turn up (with *up*) : give (a look, as cognate object).—*n.* the act of looking : view : air : appearance : (in *pl.*) beauty, comeliness (also *good looks*).—*imper.* or *interj.* see : behold.—*ns.* **look'er,** one who looks : an observer : one who has good looks ; **look'er-on',** an on-looker : a mere spectator (*pl.* **look'ers-on'**) ; **look'-in',** a chance of doing anything effectively or of sharing : a short casual call ; **look'ing.**—*adj.* (in composition) having the appearance of.—*ns.* **look'ing-for,** (*B.*) expectation ; **look'ing-glass,** a mirror ; **lookout',** a careful watch : a place to observe from : one set to watch : prospect : concern ; **look'-see,** (*slang*) a look around.—**look after,** to attend to or take care of : to seek : (*B.*) to expect ; **look alive,** (*coll.*) to bestir oneself ; **look down on,** to despise ; **look for,** to search for : to expect ; **look here !** I say ! attend to this ! ; **look in,** make a short call ; **look into,** to inspect closely : to investigate ; **look on,** to regard, view, think : to be a spectator ; **look out,** to be watchful : to be on one's guard : to look for and select : (*Shak.*) to show, appear ; **look over,** to examine cursorily : to overlook or pass over ; **look sharp,** (*coll.*) be quick about it ; **look to,** to take care of : to depend on, expect ; **look up,** to search for, refer to : to take courage : to improve, to have taken a turn for the better : (*coll.*) to seek out and call upon, visit ; **look up to,** feel respect or veneration for ; **look you,** (*arch.* and *Welsh*) observe, take notice of this. [O.E. *lōcian,* to look.]

loom, *lōōm, n.* (*obs.*) a tool, implement : (*Scot.*) a receptacle : a machine for weaving : the shaft of an oar. [O.E. *gelōma,* a tool.]

loom, *lōōm, v.i.* to appear indistinctly or as in a mirage.—*n.* an indistinct or mirage-like appearance. [Origin obscure.]

loon, *lōōn,* also **lown(e)** (*Shak.*), *n.* a low-born fellow : a rascal : a harlot : the ordinary word

for boy in the N.E. of Scotland (also **loon'ie**). [Origin unknown.]

loon, *lōōn, loun, lōōm, n.* the diver (bird).—*n.* **loon'ing,** the cry of a loon. [O.N. *lómr.*]

loony, *lōōn'i, n.* and *adj.* for **lunatic.**—*n.* **loon'y-bin,** a lunatic asylum.

loop, *lōōp, n.* a doubling of a cord, chain, &c., leaving a space : an ornamental doubling in fringes : anything of like form, as an element in finger-prints : a branch of anything that returns to the main part.—*v.t.* to fasten in or with a loop : to ornament with loops : to make a loop of.—*v.i.* to travel in loops.—*adj.* **looped.**—*n.* **loop'er,** a geometrid caterpillar, from its mode of walking by forming the body in a loop and planting its hinder legs close behind the six 'true' legs : one who loops the loop in an aeroplane.—*n.* and *adj.* **loop'ing.**—*n.* **loop'-line,** a branch railway that returns to the main line.—*adj.* **loop'y,** having loops : (*Scot.*) crafty : (*slang*) slightly crazed.—**loop the loop,** to move in a complete vertical loop or circle, head downwards at the top of the curve. [Origin doubtful.]

loop, *lōōp,* **loophole,** *lōōp'hōl, n.* a slit in a wall : a means of escape or evasion.—*adjs.* **looped,** (*Shak.*) full of small openings.—*v.t.* **loop'hole,** to make loopholes in.—*n.* **loop'-light,** a small narrow window. [Perh. M.Du. *lûpen,* to peer.]

loord, *lōōrd, n.* (*Spens.*) a lout. [Fr. *lourd,* heavy.]

loos (*Spens.*). See **los.**

loose, *lōōs, adj.* slack : free : unbound : not confined : not compact : unattached : untied : not close-fitting : not tight : relaxed : inexact : indefinite : vague : not strict : unrestrained : lax : licentious : inattentive : dispersedly or openly disposed : not serried.—*adv.* **loosely.**—*n.* an act or mode of loosing, esp. an arrow : the loose state : unrestraint : freedom : abandonment : an outbreak of self-indulgence : (*obs.*) a course or rush : (*Shak.*) event, upshot, end (as in *at the very loose*).—*v.t.* to make loose : to set free : to unfasten : to untie : to disconnect : to relax : to slacken : to discharge : (*Spens.*) to solve.—*v.i.* to shoot : (*arch.*) to weigh anchor.—*adj.* **loose'-bod'ied,** flowing, loose-fitting : loose in behaviour.—*ns.* **loose'-box,** a part of a stable where horses are kept untied ; **loose'-cover,** a detachable cover, as for a chair.—*adj.* **loose'-leaf,** having a cover such that leaves may be inserted or removed.—*adv.* **loose'ly.**—*v.t.* **loos'en,** to make loose : to relax : to make less dense : to open, as the bowels.—*v.i.* to become loose : to become less tight.—*ns.* **loos'ener,** a laxative ; **loose'ness,** the state of being loose : diarrhoea.—**at a loose end,** without anything to do for the moment ; **break loose,** to escape from confinement ; **give a loose to,** to give rein or free vent to ; **let loose,** to set at liberty ; **on the loose,** indulging in a bout of unrestraint. [O.N. *lauss ;* O.E. *léas ;* see **less.**]

loosestrife, *lōōs'strīf, n.* a plant (*Lysimachia vulgaris*) of the primrose family, or other member of the genus (as yellow pimpernel, creeping Jenny) : a tall waterside plant (*Lythrum Salicaria,* purple loosestrife). [Intended as a translation of Gr. *lȳsimacheion,* common loosestrife (as if from *lyein,* to loose, *machē,* strife), which may be from the personal name *Lȳsimachos.*]

loot, *lōōt, n.* plunder.—*v.t.* or *v.i.* to plunder. [Hindi *lūt.*]

loot, *lüt, loot, Scots pa.t.* of **let :**—*pa.p.* **loot'en, litt'en, lutt'en.**

lop, *lop, v.i.* to hang down loosely.—*adj.* **lop'-eared,** having drooping ears.—*n.* **lop'grass** (or **lob**), soft brome-grass.—*adj.* **lop'-sid'ed,** ill-balanced : heavier, bigger, on one side than the other. [Perh. conn. with **lob.**]

lop, *lop, v.t.* to cut off the top or ends of, esp. of a tree : to cut away, as superfluous parts : (*pr.p.* **lopp'ing ;** *pa.t.* and *pa.p.* **lopped**).—*n.* twigs of trees cut off : an act of lopping.—*ns.* **lopp'ing,** a cutting off ; **lopp'ing,** a cutting off : that which is cut off. [O.E. *loppian.*]

lope, *lōp, v.i.* to leap : to run with a long stride. [O.N. *hlaupa ;* cf. **leap, loup.**]

lope, *lōp,* (*Spens.*) *pa.t.* of **leap.**

lophobranch, *lŏf'* or *lof'ō-brangk, n.* any fish of the seahorse and pipefish group, characterised by tufted gills.—Also *adj.—adjs.* **lophobranch'iate;** **loph'odont,** having transversely ridged molar teeth. [Gr. *lophos,* a crest, *branchia,* gills, *odous, odontos,* a tooth.]

lopper, *lop'ər (Scot.* **lapper,** *lăp'ər), v.i.* to curdle. —*v.t.* to curdle: to clot.—*n.* a clot: slush.—*n. (Scot.)* **lapp'er(ed)-milk'.** [O.N. *hlöypa,* to curdle.]

loquacious, *lō-kwā'shəs, adj.* talkative.—*adv.* **loquā'-ciously.**—*ns.* **loquā'ciousness, loquacity** (*-kwas').* [L. *loquāx, -ācis—loquī,* to speak.]

loquat, *lō'kwat, n.* a Chinese and Japanese tree (*Eriobotrya japonica*) of the rose family: its fruit. [Chinese *luh kwat.*]

loran, *lō'răn, n.* a long-range radar navigation system. [*Long-range Aid to Navigation.*]

lorcha, *lor'chä, n.* a light vessel of European build, but rigged like a Chinese junk. [Port.]

lord (**Lord,** when prefixed), *lawrd, n.* a master: a feudal superior (also **lord'-supe'rior**): a ruler: the proprietor of a manor: an owner: a dominant person: a husband: a titled nobleman—duke (not prefixed), marquess, earl, viscount or (esp.) baron: a peer: by courtesy the son of a duke or marquis, or the eldest son of an earl: a bishop, **esp.** if a member of the House of Lords: a judge of the Court of Session: used as part of various official titles: God: Christ.—*v.t.* to make a lord: to address as lord: (with *it*) to play the lord, tyrannise.—*interj.* expressing surprise (*vulg.* **lor'**, **law**).—*n.* **lord'ing,** (*arch.*) sir (usu. in pl., gentlemen): a petty or contemptible lord.—*adj.* **lord'-less.**—*ns.* **lord'liness; lord'ling,** a little lord: a would-be lord—also **lord'kin.**—*adj.* **lord'ly,** like, becoming, or pertaining to a lord: magnificent: lavish: lofty: haughty: tyrannical.— Also *adv.*—*ns.* **lordol'atry,** (*jocular*) worship of nobility; **lords'-and-la'dies,** the common arum or cuckoo-pint; **Lord's'-day,** Sunday; **lord'-ship,** state or condition of being a lord: the territory belonging to a lord: dominion: authority: used (with *possessive pronoun*) in referring to or addressing a lord (or jocularly another); **Lord's'-supp'er,** the sacrament of communion. —**drunk as a lord,** very drunk; **House of Lords,** the upper house of the British parliament; **Lord knows** (who, what, &c.), I don't know, and I question if anybody does; **Lord Lieutenant, Lord Mayor, Lord of Misrule, Lord Provost** (see **lieutenant, mayor, misrule, provost**); **Lord of Session,** a judge of the Court of Session; **Lords Ordinary,** the judges forming the Outer House of the Court of Session; **lords spiritual,** the archbishops and bishops (and formerly mitred abbots) in the House of Lords; **lords temporal,** the lay peers; **My Lord** (*mi-lawrd', mi-lud'*), used in addressing a judge or other lord: formerly also prefixed. [M.E. *loverd, laverd*—O.E. *hláford*—*hláf,* bread, *ward* (W.S. *weard*), keeper, guardian.]

lordosis, *lor-dō'sis, n.* abnormal curvature of the spinal column, the convexity towards the front. [Gr. *lordōsis*—*lordos,* bent back.]

lore, *lōr, n.* that which is learned: teaching: doctrine: learning: now esp. learning of a special, traditional, or out-of-the-way miscellaneous kind.— *n.* **lor'ing,** (*Spens.*) teaching. [O.E. *lár.*]

lore, *lōr, n.* (*obs.*) a thong: (*ornith.*) the side of the head between eye and bill.—*adjs.* **lor'al; lor'ate,** strap-like. [L. *lōrum,* thong.]

lore. See **leese.**

lorel, *lor'əl.* See **losel.**

lorette, *lor-et', n.* a showy strumpet. [Fr., from the church of their district in Paris, Notre Dame de Lorette.]

lorgnette, *lorn-yet', n.* eye-glasses with a handle: an opera-glass.—*n.* **lorgnon** (*lorn'yonᵍ'*), an eye-glass: eye-glasses. [Fr. *lorgner,* to squint.]

lorica, *lō-rī'kä, n.* a leather corslet: the case of a protozoan, rotifer, &c:—*pl.* **lori'cae** (*-sē*).—Also **loric** (*lō'rik*).—*v.t.* **loricate** (*lor'i-kāt*), to coat or armour protectively.—*adj.* armoured with plates or scales.—*n.* **lorica'tion.** [L. *lōrīca,* a leather corslet—*lōrum,* a thong.]

lorikeet, *lor-i-kēt', n.* a small lory. [From **lory,** on analogy of para*keet.*]

lorimer, *lor'i-mər,* **loriner, -nər,** *n.* a maker of the metal parts of horse-harness. [O.Fr. *loremier,* *lorenier*—L. *lōrum,* a thong.]

loriot, *lō'ri-ət, n.* the golden oriole. [Fr. *loriot—l',* the, O.Fr. *oriol*—L. *aureolus,* dim. of *aureus,* golden —*aurum,* gold.]

loris, *lō'ris, n.* the slender lemur of Ceylon: an East Indian lemur (*Nycticebus* or *Bradycebus tardigradus,* the slow *loris*). [Fr. *loris*; said to be from Du.]

lorn, *lorn, adj.* (*arch.*) lost: forsaken: (*Spens.*) left. [O.E. *loren,* pa.p. of *léosan* (found in compounds), to lose; see **leese.**]

lorrell. See **losel.**

lorry, *lor'i, n.* a four-wheeled wagon without sides. —*v.i.* (or *v.t.* with *it*) **lorr'y-hop,** to proceed by help of lifts on lorries.—*n.* **lorr'y-hopping.** [Origin obscure.]

lory, *lō'ri, n.* any parrot of a family with brushlike tongues, natives of New Guinea, Australia, &c.: in South Africa a turaco. [Malay *lūrī.*]

los, loos, *lōs, n.* (*arch.*) praise, reputation. [O.Fr., —L. *laudēs,* pl. of *laus,* praise.]

lose, *lōōz, v.t.* to fail to keep or get possession of: to be deprived of: to cease to have: to mislay: to waste, as time: to miss: to be defeated in: to cause the loss of: to cause to perish: to ruin. —*v.i.* to fail, to be unsuccessful: to suffer waste or loss:—*pr.p.* **los'ing;** *pa.t.* and *pa.p.* **lost** (*lost*). —*adj.* **los'able.**—*n.* **los'er.**—*n.* and *adj.* **los'ing.** —*adv.* **los'ingly.**—*adj.* **lost** (*lost*), parted with: no longer possessed: missing: thrown away: squandered: ruined.—**lose oneself,** to lose one's way: to become bewildered or rapt; **losing game,** a game that is going against one: a game played with reversal of the usual aim; **lost to,** insensible to; **lost tribes,** the tribes of Israel that never returned after deportation by Sargon of Assyria in 721 B.C. [O.E. *losian,* to be a loss: apparently influenced in sense by **leese** and in pronunciation by **loose.**]

losel, *lō'zl, lōō'zl,* **lorel,** *lō'rəl (Spens.* **lozell,** **lorrell**), *n.* a sorry, worthless fellow: a scamp. —*adj.* good-for-nothing. [Apparently from the past participle *losen, loren,* of **leese.**]

losh, losh, *interj.* (*Scot.*) for **lord.**

loss, *los, n.* losing: diminution: (*Shak.*) default: bereavement: destruction: defeat: deprivation: detriment: that which is lost.—**at a loss,** off the scent: at fault: nonplussed: perplexed. [O.E. *los,* influenced by **lost.**]

löss. See **loess.**

los'te, *lōst,* a Spenserian *pa.p.* of **loose.**

lot, *lot, n.* an object, as a slip of wood, a straw, drawn or thrown out from among a number in order to reach a decision by chance: decision by this method: sortilege: a prize so to be won: destiny: that which falls to any one as his fortune: a separate portion: a parcel of ground: a set: a set of things offered together for sale: the whole: (*U.S.*) a plot of ground allotted or assigned to any person or purpose, esp. for building: (*obs.*) a turn: a tax or due (see **scot**): a large quantity or number.—*v.t.* to allot: to separate into lots: to cast lots for: to catalogue:—*pr.p.* **lott'ing;** *pa.t.* and *pa.p.* **lott'ed.**—**across lots,** (*U.S.*) by short cuts; **bad lot,** a person of bad moral character; **cast, or throw, in one's lot with,** share the fortunes of; **cast, or draw, lots,** to draw from a set alike in appearance in order to reach a decision; **lots to blanks,** (*Shak.*) any odds. [O.E. *hlot, lot—hléotan,* to cast lots.]

lota, lotah, *lō'tä, n.* (in India) a small brass or copper pot. [Hind. *lota.*]

lote. See **lotus.**

loth, loath, *lōth, n.* (*obs.*) hateful, repulsive, ugly: reluctant, unwilling.—**nothing loth,** not at all unwilling. [O.E. *láth,* hateful; cf. **loathe.**]

Lothario, *lō-thā'ri-ō, -thä', n.* a gay seducer. [From *Lothario,* in Rowe's play, *The Fair Penitent.*]

lotion, *lō'shən, n.* (*obs.*) a washing: a wash, medicinal or cosmetic. [L. *lōtiō, -ōnis*, a washing—*lavāre, lōtum*, to wash.]

lottery, *lot'ər-i*, *n.* an arrangement for distribution of prizes by lot : a matter of chance : a card game of chance.—*n.* **lott'o**, *lō'to*, a game played by covering on a card each number drawn till a line of numbers is completed. [It. *lotteria, lotto*, of Gmc. origin ; cf. lot.]

lotus, *lō'təs*, *n.* an Egyptian or Indian water-lily of various species of Nymphaea and Nelumbium : a tree (possibly the jujube) in North Africa, whose fruit made strangers forget their home : an architectural ornament like a water-lily : Lotus, the bird's-foot trefoil genus.—Also **lote** (*lōt*), **lō'tos** (Gr.).—*ns.pl.* **Lotophagi** (*lō-tof'ə-jī* ; Gr. *phagein*, to eat), **Lo'tus-eat'ers**, a people who ate the fruit of the lotus, among whom Ulysses lived for a time.—*ns.* **lo'tus-eat'er**, an eater of the lotus : one given up to indolence ; **Lo'tus-land**, the country of the Lotus-eaters. [Latinised Gr. *lōtos*.]

loud, *lowd*, *adj.* making a great sound : noisy : obtrusive : vulgarly showy.—*advs.* **loud**, **loud'ly**.—*v.t.* and *v.i.* **loud'en**, to make or grow louder.—*adjs.* **loud'ish** ; **loud'-lunged** ; **loud'-mouthed**.—*ns.* **loud'ness** ; **loud'-speak'er**, an instrument for making wireless messages or other sounds audible to many at once.—*adj.* **loud'-voiced**. [O.E. *hlúd* ; Ger. *laut* ; L. *inclytus, inclutus*, Gr. *klytos*, renowned.]

lough, *lohh*, *n.* the Irish form of loch.

louis, *lōō'i*, *n.* a French gold coin superseded in 1795 by the 20-franc piece :—*pl.* **lou'is** (*-iz*).—*n.* **lou'is-d'or'**, a louis : a 20-franc piece :—*pl.* **louis-d'or** (*lōō-i-dor'*).—*adjs.* **Louis-Quatorze** (*-kä-torz*), characteristic of the reign (1643-1715) of Louis XIV., as in architecture and decoration ; **Lou'is-Quinze** (*-kaṇ²z*), of that of Louis XV. (1715-74) ; **Lou'is-Seize** (*-sez*), of that of Louis XVI. (1774-92) ; **Lou'is-Treize** (*-trez*), of that of Louis XIII. (1610-43).

loun, lound. See lown.

lounder, *lōōn'dər, lown'dər*, *v.t.* (*Scot.*) to beat, to bethump.—*n.* a heavy blow.—*n.* **loun'dering**, a beating.

lounge, *lownj*, *v.i.* to loll : to idle.—*v.t.* to idle (away).—*n.* an act, spell, or state of lounging : an idle stroll : a resort of loungers : a public room for lounging : a kind of sofa, esp. with back and one raised end : an easy chair suitable for lolling in.—*ns.* **lounge'-liz'ard**, one who loafs with women in hotel lounges, &c. ; **loung'er** ; **lounge'-suit'**, one for ordinary use, with coat cut short.—*n.* and *adj.* **loung'ing**.—*adv.* **loung'ingly**. [Origin doubtful.]

loup, *lowp, n.* (*Scot.*) a leap.—*v.i.* to leap : to dance : to flee : to burst :—*pa.t.* **loup'it** ; *pa.p.* **loup'en**, **loup'it**—for *pa.t.* **lap** and *pa.p.* **lapp'en** see leap.—*ns.* **loup'ing-ill**, a disease causing sheep to spring up in walking, due to a filterable virus transmitted by ticks ; **loup'ing-on'-stane'**, a stone to mount a horse from ; **loup'-the-dyke**, runaway : flighty : wayward. [O.N. *hlaup* ; cf. **lope, leap**.]

loup, a variant (*Scott*) of **loop** (1), and (*Spens.*) of **loop** (2).

lour, lower, *lowr, low'ər, v.i.* to look sullen or threatening : to scowl.—*n.* a scowl, glare : a gloomy threatening appearance.—*n.* and *adj.* **lour'ing, lower'ing**.—*adv.* **lour'ingly, lower'ingly**.—*adj.* **lour'y, lower'y**. [M.E. *louren* ; cf. Du. *loeren*.]

loure, *lōōr, n.* an old slow dance, or its tune, usu. in 6-4 time, sometimes included in suites. [Fr., bagpipe.]

louse, *lows, n.* a wingless parasitic insect (Pediculus), with a flat body, and short legs : extended to similar animals related and unrelated (see bird-louse, fish-louse,&c.) : (*pl.* **lice, līs**).—*v.t.* (*lowz*) to remove lice from.—*n.* **louse'wort**, any plant of the genus Pedicularis, marsh-growing scrophulariaceous herbs popularly supposed to cause grazing animals to become lousy.—*adv.* **lou'sily** (*-zi-*).—*n.* **lous'iness**.—*adj.* **lousy** (*low'zi*), infested with lice (*slang*) swarming or full (with *with*) : (*slang*) inferior, bad, unsatisfactory. [O.E. *lús*, pl. *lýs* ; Ger. *laus.*]

lout (*obs.* **lowt**), *lowt, n.* a bumpkin : an awkward boor.—*v.t.* (*Shak.*) to treat with contempt, **to** flout.—*v.i.* to play the lout.—*adj.* **lout'ish**, clownish : awkward and boorish.—*adv.* **lout'ishly**.—*n.* **lout'ishness**. [Perh. conn. with next word.]

lout (*obs.* **lowt**), *lowt, v.i.* to bow : to stoop.—*n.* a bow. [O.E. *lútan*, to stoop.]

louver, louvre, *lōō'vər, n.* a turret-like structure on a roof for escape of smoke or for ventilation : (*obs.*) a dovecote : an opening or shutter with louver-boards : a louver-board.—*ns.* **lou'ver-board, lou'vre-board**, a sloping slat placed across an opening ; **lou'ver-win'dow, lou'vre-win'dow**, an open window crossed by a series of sloping boards. [O.Fr. *lover, lovier* ; origin obscure.]

lovage, *luv'ij, n.* an umbelliferous salad plant (*Levisticum officinale*) of Southern Europe akin to Angelica : a liquor made from its roots and seeds : any plant of the kindred genus Ligusticum, including *Scottish* lovage. [O.Fr. *luvesche*—L.L. *levisticum*, L. *ligusticum*, lit. Ligurian.]

love, *luv, n.* fondness : an affection of the mind caused by that which delights : strong liking : devoted attachment to one of the opposite sex : sexual attachment : a love-affair : the object of affection : the god of love, Cupid, Eros : (*Shak.*) a kindness, a favour done : the mere pleasure of playing without stakes : hence, in some games, no score.—*v.t.* to be fond of : to regard with affection : to delight in with exclusive affection : to regard with benevolence.—*v.i.* to have the feeling of love.—*adj.* **lov'able**, worthy of love : amiable.—*ns.* **love'-affair'**, an amour, honourable or dishonourable ; **love'-apple**, the tomato ; **love'-arrow**, a hair-like crystal of rutile enclosed in quartz : a calcareous dart protruded by a snail, supposed to have a sexual function ; **love'bird**, a small African parrot (Agapornis), strongly attached to its mate : extended to other kinds ; **love'-bro'ker**, (*Shak.*) a go-between in love-affairs ; **love'-charm**, a philtre ; **love'-child**, a bastard ; **love'-day**, (*Shak.*) a day for settling disputes ; **love'-favour**, something given to be worn in token of love ; **love'-feast**, the Agape of the early Christians, or a religious feast held periodically in imitation of it ; **love'-feat**, an act of courtship ; **love'-game**, (*lawn-tennis*) a game in which the loser has not scored ; **love'-in-a-mist'**, a fennel-flower (*Nigella damascena*) a West Indian passion-flower ; **love'-in-i'dleness**, the heart's-ease ; **love'-juice**, a concoction dropped in the eye to excite love ; **love'-knot**, an intricate knot, used as a token or emblem of love.—*adj.* **love'less**.—*ns.* **love'-letter**, a letter of courtship ; **love'-lies-bleed'ing**, a kind of amaranth with drooping red spike ; **love'light**, a lustre in the eye expressive of love ; **love'lihead**, loveliness.—*adv.* **love'lily**.—*ns.* **love'liness** ; **love'lock**, a long or prominent lock of hair, esp. one hanging at the ear, worn by men of fashion in the reigns of Elizabeth and James I.—*adj.* **love'lorn**, forsaken by one's love : pining for love.—*n.* **love'lornness**.—*adj.* **love'ly**, (*Shak.*) loving, amorous : exciting love or admiration : amiable : pleasing : delightful : extremely beautiful : (*coll.*) delightful.—*adv.* (*Spens.*) lovingly : beautifully : delightfully.—*ns.* **love'-maker** ; **love-making**, amorous courtship ; **love'-match**, a marriage for love, not money ; **love'-monger**, one who deals in affairs of love ; **love'-potion**, a philtre ; **lov'er**, one who loves, esp. one in love with a person of the opposite sex (in the singular usually of the man) : a paramour : one who is fond of anything : (*Shak.*) a friend.—*adjs.* **lov'ered**, (*Shak.*) having a lover ; **lov'erless** ; **lov'erly**, like a lover.—*ns.* **love'-seat**, an armchair for two ; **love'-shaft**, a dart of love from Cupid's bow.—*adjs.* **love'sick**, languishing with amorous desire ; **love'some**, lovely : loving.—*ns.* **love'-song**, a song expressive of or relating to love ; **love'-story**, a story whose subject-matter is love ; **love'-suit**, (*Shak.*) courtship ; **love'-token**, a gift in evidence of love.—*adj.* **love'worthy**, worthy of being loved.—*n.* and *adj.* **lov'ing**.—*n.* **lov'ing-cup**, a cup passed round at the end of a feast for all to drink from ; **lov'ing-kind'ness**, kindness

full of love : tender regard : mercy : favour.—
adv. **lov'ingly.**—*n.* **lov'ingness.**—**for love or
money,** in any way whatever ; **in love,** enamoured ; **make love to,** to try to gain the
affections of ; **of all loves,** (*Shak.*) for any sake,
by all means ; **play for love,** to play without
stakes ; **there's no love lost between them,**
they have no liking for each other. [O.E. *lufu,*
love ; Ger. *liebe* ; cf. L. *libet, lubet,* it pleases.]
Lovelace, *luv'lās, n.* a well-mannered libertine.
[From *Lovelace,* in Richardson's *Clarissa.*]
lover, an obsolete form of **louver.**
low, *lō, v.i.* to make the noise of oxen.—*n.* sound
made by oxen.—*n.* **low'ing.** [O.E. *hlōwan* ; Du.
loeien.]
low, *lō, adj.* occupying a position far downward or
not much elevated : of no great upward extension :
not reaching a high level : depressed : not tall :
(of type or blocks) below the level of the forme
surface : reaching far down : (of clothes) cut so
as to expose the neck : quiet, soft, not loud : grave
in pitch, as so ds produced by slow vibrations :
(*phon.*) produced with part of the tongue low in the
mouth : in shallow relief : expressed in measurement by a small number : (of numbers) small : of
small value, intensity, quantity, or rank : weak in
vitality or nutrition : scanty, deficient : attributing
lowness : for stakes of no great value : dejected :
debased : base : mean : vulgar : humble : socially depressed : little advanced in organisation
or culture : (of latitude) near the equator : (of
dates) comparatively recent : attaching little value
to priesthood, sacraments, &c. : (*comp.* **lower,** *lō'ər;*
superl. **lowest,** *lō'ist,* **low'ermost**).—*n.* that which
is low or lowest : an area of low barometrical
pressure : (*U.S.*) a low or minimum level.—*adv.*
in or to a low position, state, or manner : humbly :
with a low voice or sound : at low pitch : at a low
price : late.—*adj.* **low'-born,** of humble birth.—
n. **low'boy,** (*obs.*) a low-churchman : (*U.S.*) a
short-legged dressing-table with drawers.—*adj.*
low'-bred, ill-bred : unmannerly.—*n.* **low'-
brow,** one who is not intellectual or makes no
pretensions to intellect.—Also *adj.*—*adj.* **Low'-
Church,** of a party within the Church of England
setting little value on sacerdotal claims, ecclesiastical constitutions, ordinances, and forms, holding
evangelical views of theology—opp. to *High-Church.*
—*ns.* **low'-church'ism** ; **low'-church'man.**—
adjs. **low'-country,** lowland (**the Low Countries,**
Holland and Belgium) ; **low'-down,** (*coll.*) mean :
base : dishonourable.—*n.* (*U.S. slang*) information,
esp. of a confidential or damaging nature : base
behaviour.—*n.* **low-down'er,** (*U.S.*) a poor white.—
v.t. **low'er,** to make lower : to let down : to lessen :
(*obs.*) to dilute.—*v.i.* to become lower or less.—
adjs. **low'er-case,** (*print.*) lit. kept in a lower case,
small as distinguished from capital ; **low'er-class,**
pertaining to persons of the humbler ranks.—*n.*
low'er-deck, deck immediately above the hold :
ship's crew (as opposed to officers).—Also *adj.*—
ns. **low'-gear** (see **gear**) ; **low'ering,** the act of
bringing low or reducing.—*adj.* letting down :
sinking : degrading.—*adj.* **low'ermost, lowest.**—
ns. **low'land,** land low with respect to higher
land (also *adj.*) ; **low'lander, Low'lander,** a
native of lowlands, esp. the Lowlands of Scotland ;
low'-life, humble life, especially sordid life ;
low'lihead, humility.—*adv.* **low'lily** (-*li-li*).—*n.*
low'liness. — *adjs.* **low'-lived** (-*līvd*), vulgar :
shabby ; **low'ly,** humble : modest : low in stature
or in organisation ; **low'-mind'ed,** moved by
base or gross motives : vulgar ; **low'-necked,**
cut low in the neck and away from the shoulders,
décolleté.—*n.* **low'ness.**—*adjs.* **low'-pitched,** of
sound, low in pitch : of a roof, gentle in slope :
having a low ceiling ; **low'-press'ure,** employing
or exerting a low degree of pressure (viz. less than
50 lb. to the sq. inch), said of steam and steamengines : having low barometric pressure ; **low'-
spir'ited,** having the spirits low or cast down :
not lively : sad.—*n.* **low'-spir'itedness.**—*adj.*
low'-thought'ed, having the thoughts directed to
low pursuits.—*ns.* **low'-tide, -wa'ter,** the lowest
point of the tide at ebb.—**in low water,** short

of money ; **lay low,** to overthrow, fell, kill ; **lie
low** (see **lie,** 2) ; **low comedy,** comedy of farcical situation, slapstick, low life ; **Low Dutch,** (*obs.*)
Low German, including Dutch ; **Low German,
Low Latin** (see **German, Latin**) ; **low life,**
sordid social circumstances : persons of low
social class ; **low mass,** mass without music
and incense ; **low side window,** a narrow window
(or lower part of a window) near the ground,
sometimes found in old churches, esp. in the
chancel ; **Low Sunday,** the first Sunday after
Easter, so called in contrast to the great festival
whose octave it ends ; **low wines,** the weak spirit
produced from the first distillation of substances
containing alcohol. [O.N. *lágr,* Du. *laag,* low ;
allied to O.E. *licgan,* to lie.]
low, *lō, n.* (*arch.* except in place-names) a hill : a
tumulus. [O.E. *hlāw* ; cf. **law** (3).]
low, lowe, *low, n.* (*Scot.*) a flame.—*v.i.* to blaze.—
n. **low-bell** (*low', lō', lōō'bel* ; *dial.*), a small bell :
a bell used by night along with a light, to frighten
birds into a net. [O.N. *logi* ; cf. Ger. *lohe.*]
lower, *lowr.* See **lour.** **lower,** *lō'ər.* See **low** (2).
lown, lowne, *lown, n.* variants of **loon** (1).
lown, lownd, loun, lound, *lown(d), adj.* (*Scot.*)
sheltered : calm : quiet.—*adv.* quietly.—*n.* calm :
quiet : shelter.—*v.i.* to calm. [O.N. *logn* (noun).]
Lowrie, *low'ri, n.* (*Scot.*) a nickname for the fox.—
Also **Low'rie-tod, Tod-low'rie.** [Laurence.]
lowse, *lows, adj.* (*Scot.*) loose.—*v.t.* (*lows,* or *lowz*)
to loose : to unyoke : to redeem.—*v.i.* to unyoke
the horses : to knock off work :—*pa.t.* and *pa.p.*
lows'it. [See **loose.**]
loxodrome, *loks'ə-drōm, n.* a line on the surface of
a sphere which makes equal oblique angles with all
meridians, a rhumb-line—also **loxodromic curve,
line,** or **spiral.**—*adjs.* **loxodromic** (-*drom'ik*), **-al.**
—*n.* **loxodrom'ics,** the art of sailing on rhumblines. [Gr. *loxos,* oblique, *dromos,* a course.]
loyal, *loi'əl, adj.* faithful : true as a lover : firm in
allegiance : personally devoted to a sovereign or
would-be sovereign : (*Shak.*) legitimate : manifesting loyalty.—*n.* **loy'alist,** a loyal adherent,
esp. of a king or of an established government :
in English history, a partisan of the Stuarts : in
the American war, one that sided with the British.
—*adv.* **loy'ally.**—*n.* **loy'alty.** [Fr.,—L. *lēgālis—
lēx, lēgis,* law.]
lozenge, *loz'inj, n.* a diamond-shaped parallelogram
or rhombus : a small sweetmeat, medicated or
not, originally diamond-shaped : (*her.*) a diamondshaped shield for the arms of a widow, spinster,
or deceased person.—*n.* **loz'en,** (*Scot.*) a windowpane.—*adjs.* **loz'enged,** divided into lozenges ;
loz'enge-shaped ; **loz'engy,** (*her.*) divided into
lozenge-shaped compartments. [Fr. *losange* (of
unknown origin).]
lubber, *lub'ər,* **lubbard,** *lub'ərd, n.* an awkward,
clumsy fellow : a lazy, sturdy fellow.—*adj.* **lubberly.**
—*adj.* and *adv.* **lubb'erly.**—**lubber fiend,** a
beneficent goblin or drudging brownie, Lob-lieby-the-fire ; **lubber's hole,** (*naut.*) a hole between
the head of the lower mast and the edge of the top
through which lubbers may climb, instead of going
round the futtock shroud. [Origin doubtful.]
lubfish, *lub'fish, n.* a kind of stockfish. [**lob.**]
lubra, *lōō'brä, n.* (*Austr.*) a black woman. [Tasmanian.]
lubricate, *l(y)ōō'bri-kāt, v.t.* to make smooth or
slippery : to supply with oil or other matter to
overcome friction.—*adjs.* **lu'bric, -al, lubricious**
(-*brish'əs*), **lu'bricous** (-*kəs*), slippery : lewd.—
adj. **lu'bricant,** lubricating.—*n.* a substance used
to reduce friction.—*n.* **lubrica'tion.**—*adj.* **lu'brica-
tive.**—*ns.* **lu'bricātor** ; **lubricity** (-*bris'*), slipperiness : smoothness : instability : lewdness. [L.
lūbricus, slippery.]
lucarne, *l(y)ōō-kärn', n.* a dormer-window, esp. in a
church spire. [Fr. (of unknown origin).]
luce, *l(y)ōōs, n.* a freshwater fish, the pike. [O.Fr.
lus—L.L. *lūcius.*]
lucent, *l(y)ōō'sənt, adj.* shining : bright.—*n.* **lu'-
cency.** [L. *lūcēns, -ēntis,* pr.p. of *lūcēre,* to shine—
lūx, lūcis, light.]
lucerne, *l(y)ōō-sərn', n.* purple medick (in *U.S.*

Neutral vowels in unaccented syllables : *el'ə-mənt, in'fənt, ran'dəm*

called alfalfa), a valuable forage-plant. — Also **lucern'** (*Browning* lu'zern); formerly often la **lucerne**. [Fr. *luzerne*.]

lucid, *l(y)ōō'sid*, *adj.* shining: transparent: easily understood: intellectually bright: not darkened with madness.—*ns.* lucid'ity, lu'cidness.—*adv.* **lu'cidly**.—lucid intervals, times of sanity in madness, of quietness in fever, turmoil, &c. [L. *lūcidus*—*lūx*, *lūcis*, light.]

Lucifer, *l(y)ōō'si-far*, *n.* the planet Venus as morning-star: Satan: lucifer, a match of wood tipped with a combustible substance to be ignited by friction—also lu'cifer-match'.—*adj.* Lucife'rian, pertaining to Lucifer.—*ns* lucif'erase, an oxidising enzyme in the luminous organs of certain animals that acts on luciferin to produce luminosity; lucif'erin, a protein-like substance in the luminous organs of certain animals.—*adj.* lucif'erous, light-bringing: light-giving. [L. *lūcifer*, light-bringer—*lūx*, *lūcis*, light, *ferre*, to bring.]

lucifugous, *l(y)ōō-sif'ū-gas*, *adj.* shunning light. [L. *lūx*, *lūcis*, light, *fugĕre*, to flee.]

lucigen, *l(y)ōō'si-jen*, *n.* a lamp burning oil mixed with air in a spray. [L. *lūx*, *lūcis*, light, and root of L. *gignĕre*, *genitum*, to beget.]

Lucina, *l(y)ōō-sī'nä*, *n.* the Roman goddess of childbirth, Juno: also Diana: hence, the moon. [L. *Lūcīna*, thought by the Romans to be from *lūx*, light, as if the bringer to light.]

luck, *luk*, *n.* fortune: good fortune: an object with which a family's fortune is supposed to be bound up.—*adv.* luck'ily.—*n.* luck'iness.—*adj.* luck'less, without good luck: unhappy.—*adv.* luck'lessly.—*ns.* luck'lessness; luck'-penny, a trifle returned for luck by a seller: a coin carried for luck.—*adj.* luck'y, having, attended by, portending, or bringing good luck.—*n.* luck'y-bag, a bag sold without disclosing its contents: a bag in which one may dip and draw a prize: a receptacle for lost property on board a man-of-war.—down on one's luck, unfortunate; worse luck, more's the pity. [Prob. L.G. or Du. *luk*; cf. Ger. *glück*, prosperity.]

lucken, *luk'an*, *adj.* (*Scot.*) closed.—*n.* luck'en-gow'an, the globe-flower. [O.E. *locen*, pa.p. of *lúcan*, to lock.]

lucky, **luckie** (prefixed or vocative, **Lucky**), *luk'i*, *n.* (*Scot.*) an elderly woman: an ale-wife.—*n.* luck'ie-dad, a grandfather. [Perh. from adj. lucky.]

lucky, *luk'i*, *n.* (*slang*) departure.—cut, or make, one's lucky, to bolt.

lucre, *l(y)ōō'kar*, *n.* sordid gain: riches.—*adj.* lu'-crative (*-kra-tiv*), profitable.—*adv.* lu'cratively. [L. *lucrum*, gain.]

luctation, *luk-tā'shan*, *n.* struggle. [L. *luctātiō*, *-ōnis*.]

lucubrate, *l(y)ōō'kū-brāt*, *v.i.* to study by lamplight: to discourse learnedly or pedantically.—*ns.* lucū-brā'tion, study or composition protracted late into the night: a product of such study: a composition that smells of the lamp; lu'cūbrātor. [L. *lūcu-brāre*, *-ātum*—*lūx*, light.]

luculent, *lōō'kū-lant*, or *lū'*, *adj.* bright: clear: transparent: evident.—*adv.* lu'culently. [L. *lūculentis*—*lūx*.]

Lucuma, *lōō'kū-mä*, *n.* a genus, mostly South American, of sapotaceous trees with edible fruit. [Quechua.]

lucumo, *l(y)ōō'kū-mō*, *n.* an Etruscan prince and priest. [L. *lúcúmo*, from Etruscan.]

lud, *lud*, *n.* a minced form of lord (trivial and forensic).—*n.* lud'ship.

Luddite, *lud'it*, *n.* a member of a band of destroyers of machinery in northern England about 1812-18. —Also *adj.*—*n.* Ludd'ism. [Said to be from Ned *Lud* who had smashed stocking-frames about 1779.]

ludicrous, *l(y)ōō'di-kras*, *adj.* (*obs.*) sportive: (*obs.*) humorous: adapted to excite laughter: laughable. —*adv.* lu'dicrously.—*n.* lu'dicrousness. [L. *lūdicrus*—*lūdĕre*, to play.]

ludo, *l(y)ōō'dō*, *n.* a game in which counters are moved on a board according to the fall of dice. [L. *lūdō*, I play.]

lues, *l(y)ōō'ēz*, *n.* a pestilence: now confined to syphilis.—*adj.* luetic (*-et'ik*; a bad formation). [L. *lūēs*.]

luff, *luf*, *n.* the windward side of a ship: the act of sailing a ship close to the wind: the loof, or the after-part of a ship's bow where the planks begin to curve in towards the cut-water.—*v.i.* to turn a ship towards the wind.—*v.t.* to turn nearer to the wind. [Origin obscure.]

luffa, **loofah**, **loofa**, *luf'ä*, *lōōf'ä*, *n.* a tropical genus (Luffa) of the gourd family: the fibrous network of its fruit, used as a flesh-brush. [Ar. *lúfan*.]

luffer-board, *luf'ar-bōrd*. Same as **louver-board**.

lug, *lug*, *v.t.* to pull: to drag heavily.—*v.i.* to pull. —*pr.p.* lugg'ing; *pa.t.* and *pa.p.* lugged.—*ns.* lugg'age, the trunks and other baggage of a traveller; lugg'age-carrier, a structure fixed to a bicycle, motor-car, &c., for carrying luggage; lugg'age-van, a railway wagon for luggage.—lug in, to introduce without any apparent connexion. [Cf. Sw. *lugga*, to pull by the hair—*lugg*, the forelock; per. conn. with **lug** (4).]

lug, *lug*, **lugsail**, *lug'säl*, *lug'sl*, *ns.* a square sail bent upon a yard that hangs obliquely to the mast. —*n.* lugg'er, a small vessel with lugsails.

lug, *lug*, *n.* a pole or stick: (*Spens.*) a perch or rod of land. [Origin obscure.]

lug, *lug*, *n.* the flap or lappet of a cap: (chiefly *Scot.*) the ear: an earlike projection or appendage: a handle: a loop: (*Scot.*) a chimney corner.—*n.* lug'-chair, an easy-chair with side head-rests.— *adj.* lugged (*lugd*), having lugs or a lug.—*n.* lugg'ie, (*Scot.*) a hooped dish with one long stave. [Perh. conn. with **lug** (1).]

lug, *lug*, **lugworm**, *lug'warm*, *ns.* a sluggish worm found in the sand on the seashore, much used for bait. [Origin doubtful.]

luge, *lōōzh*, *lüzh*, *n.* a light hand-sledge for one.— *v.i.* to glide on such a sledge.—*pa.p.* and *n.* lug'ing, luge'ing. [Swiss Fr.]

lugubrious, *lōō-gū'bri-as*, *adj.* mournful: dismal. —*adv.* lugū'briously. [L. *lūgubris*—*lūgēre*, to mourn.]

luit, *lüt*, *lit*, luit'en, *Scots* *pa.t.* and *pa.p.* of let (1).

luke, *lōōk*, *adj.* moderately warm: tepid.—*adjs.* luke'warm, luke: half-hearted; luke'warmish.— *adv.* luke'warmly.—*ns.* luke'warmness, luke'-warmth. [M.E. *luek*, *luke*; doubtful whether related to lew, or to Du. *leuk*.]

lull, *lul*, *v.t.* to soothe: to compose: to quiet.—*v.i.* to become calm: to subside.—*n.* an interval of calm: a calming influence.—*n.* lull'aby (*-a-bī*), a song to lull children to sleep, a cradle-song.— *v.t.* to lull to sleep. [Cf. Sw. *lulla*.]

lum, *lum*, *n.* (*Scot.*) a chimney: a chimney-pot hat (also lum'-hat).—*n.* lum'head', the top of a chimney. [Origin obscure: O.Fr. *lum*, light, and W. *llumon*, chimney, have been suggested.]

lumbago, *lum-bā'gō*, *n.* a rheumatic affection of the muscles or fibrous tissues in the lumbar region.— *adjs.* lumbaginous (*-baj'i-nas*); lumbar (*lum'bar*), of, or near, the loins. [L. *lumbāgō*, lumbago, *lumbus*, loin.]

lumbang, *loom-bäng'*, *n.* the candle-nut tree or other species of Aleurites, whose nuts yield lum-bang'-oil'. [Tagálog.]

lumber, *lum'bar*, *n.* furniture stored away out of use: anything cumbersome or useless: (*U.S.* and *Canada*) timber, esp. sawed or split for use.—*v.t.* to fill with lumber: to heap together in confusion: to cumber: to cut the timber from.—*v.i.* to work as a lumberman.—*ns.* lum'ber-camp, a lumberman's camp; lum'berer, lum'ber-jack, lum'-berman, one employed in lumbering; lum'bering, felling, sawing, and removal of timber; lum'ber-mill, a sawmill; lum'ber-room, a room for storing things not in use; lum'ber-yard, a timber-yard. [Perhaps from lumber (2), or from lumber (3) influenced by lumber (2).]

lumber, *lum'bar*, *n.* pawn: a pawnshop: (*slang*) prison.—*v.t.* to pawn: (*slang*) to imprison.—*ns.* lum'berer, (now *slang*) a pawnbroker; lum'ber-pie', a pie of meat or fish, with eggs. [See Lombard.]

lumber, *lum'bar*, *v.i.* to move heavily and clumsily:

to rumble. — *n.* **lum'berer.** — *adjs.* **lum'berly, lum'bersome.**—*n.* **lum'bersomeness.** [M.E. *lomeren*, perh. a freq. formed from *lome*, a variant of *lame* ; but cf. prov. Sw. *lomra*, to resound.]

Lumbricus, *lum-bri'cas, n.* a very common genus of earthworms, giving name to the family **Lumbricidae** (-*bris'i-dē*) to which all British earthworms belong.—*adj.* **lum'brical** (or -*brī'*), wormlike.—*n.* (for **lumbrical muscle**) one of certain muscles of the hand and foot used in flexing the digits.—*adjs.* **lumbriciform** (-*bris'*), **lum'bricoid** (or -*brī'*), worm-like. [L. *lumbricus*.]

lumen, *lōō'men* (or *lū'*), *n.* a unit of light-flux—the light emitted in one second in a solid angle of one steradian from a point-source of intensity of one international candle : the cavity of a tube : (*bot.*) the space within the cell-wall :—*pl.* **lu'mina, lu'mens.**—*adj.* **lu'minal,** of a lumen.—*n.* **lu'minance,** luminousness.—*adj.* **lu'minant,** giving light. —*n.* an illuminant.—*ns.* **lu'minarism ; lu'minarist,** one who paints luminously, or with skill in lights: an impressionist or plein-airist; **lu'minary,** a source of light, esp. one of the heavenly bodies: one who illustrates any subject or instructs mankind ; **luminā'tion,** a lighting up.—*v.t.* **lumine** (-*in*), to illumine.—*n.* **luminescence** (-*es'∂ns*), emission of light otherwise than by incandescence. —*adj.* **luminesc'ent.**—*adj.* **luminif'erous,** giving, yielding, being the medium of, light.—*ns.* **lu'minist,** a luminarist ; **luminosity** (-*os'i-ti*), luminousness: quantity of light emitted.—*adj.* **lu'minous,** giving light: shining: lighted: clear: lucid.— *adv.* **lu'minously.**—*n.* **lu'minousness.**—**luminous paint,** a varnish or other medium containing a sulphide of calcium, barium, or strontium. [L. *lūmen*, -*inis*, light—*lūcēre*, to shine.]

lumme, lummy, *lum'i, interj.* (*Cockney*) for (Lord) *love me.*

lummy, *lum'i, adj.* (*slang*) excellent.

lump, *lump, n.* a shapeless mass : a protuberance : a swelling : a feeling as if of a swelling in the throat : a considerable quantity : the whole together : the gross : an inert, dull, good-natured, or fair-sized person : a lumpfish.—*v.t.* to throw into a confused mass : to take in the gross : to include under one head : to endure willy-nilly : to put up with : to be lumpish about : to dislike.— *v.i.* to be lumpish : to gather in a lump : to stump along.—*ns.* **lump'er,** a labourer employed in the lading or unlading of ships : (*prov.*) a militiaman : one inclined to lumping in classification—opp. to *hair-splitter* ; **lump'fish, lump'sucker,** a clumsy sea-fish (Cyclopterus) with pectoral fins transformed into a sucker.—*adv.* **lump'ily.**—*n.* **lump'iness.**— *adjs.* **lump'ing,** in a lump : heavy : bulky ; **lump'-ish,** like a lump : heavy : gross : dull : sullen.— *adv.* **lump'ishly.**—*ns.* **lump'ishness ; lump'kin,** a lout ; **lump'-su'gar,** loaf-sugar broken in small pieces or cut in cubes.—*adj.* **lump'y,** full of lumps : like a lump.—*n.* **lump'y-jaw',** actinomycosis affecting the jaw in cattle.—**if you don't like it you may lump it,** take it as you like, but there is no remedy ; **in the lump,** in gross ; **lump sum,** a single sum of money in lieu of several. [Origin doubtful ; found in various Gmc. languages.]

lunar, lunate, lunatic, &c. See **lune.**

lunch, *lun*(*t*)*sh, n.* (*dial.*) a thick slice, a lump : a slight repast between breakfast and dinner : a restaurateur's name for an ordinary man's dinner : (*U.S.*) a snack.—*v.i.* to take lunch.—*n.* **lunch'eon,** lunch.—*v.i.* to lunch.—*ns.* **lunch'eon-bar,** a counter where luncheons are served ; **lunch'eonbasket,** basket for carrying lunch, with or without cutlery, &c. ; **lunch'er ; lunch'-hour, lunch'-time,** the time of, or time set apart for, lunch : an interval allowed for lunch. [Perh. altered from **lump** ; or from Sp. *lonja*, a slice of ham, &c.]

lune, *l*(*y*)*ōōn, n.* anything in the shape of a half-moon : a lunule : (*Shak.*) a fit of lunacy.—*n.* **lunacy** (usu. *lōō'n∂-si*), a form of insanity once believed to come with changes of the moon : insanity generally : extreme folly.—*adj.* **lunar** (usu. *lōō'n∂r*), belonging to the moon : measured by the moon's revolutions : caused by the moon : like the moon : (*old chem.*) of silver.—*n.* a lunar

distance.—*ns.* **lunā'rian,** an inhabitant of the moon : a student of the moon ; **lu'narist,** one who thinks the moon affects the weather ; **lu'nary,** the moonwort fern : the plant honesty.—*adj.* lunar.— *adjs.* **lu'nate, -d,** crescent-shaped ; **lunatic** (*lōō'n∂-tik*), affected with lunacy.—*n.* a person so affected : a madman.—*ns.* **luna'tion,** a synodic month ; **lunette',** a crescent-shaped ornament : a semi-circular or crescent-shaped space where a vault intersects a wall or another vault, often occupied by a window or by decoration : an arched opening in a vault : (*fort.*) a detached bastion : a small horseshoe : a watch-glass flattened more than usual in the centre : in the R.C. Church, a moon-shaped case for the consecrated host.—*adj.* **luniso'-lar,** pertaining to the moon and sun jointly.—*n.* **lu'nūla,** a lunule : a crescent-like appearance, esp. the whitish area at the base of a nail.—*adjs.* **lu'nūlar ; lu'nūlate, -d,** (*bot.*) shaped like a small crescent.— *n.* **lu'nūle,** anything in form like a small crescent : a geometrical figure bounded by two circular arcs. —**lunar caustic,** fused crystals of silver nitrate, applied to ulcers, &c. ; **lunar cycle** (see **metonic cycle**) ; **lunar distances,** a method of finding the longitude by comparison of the observed angular distance of the moon from a star at a known local time, with the tabulated angular distance at a certain Greenwich time ; **lunar month** (see **month**) ; **lunar theory,** the *a priori* deduction of the moon's motions from the principles of gravitation ; **lunar year** (see **year**). [L. *lūna*, the moon—*lūcēre*, to shine.]

lung, *lung, n.* a respiratory organ in animals that breathe atmospheric air : (*fig.*) an open space in a town.—*n.* **lung'-book,** a breathing organ in spiders and scorpions, constructed like the leaves of a book.—*adj.* **lunged.**—*n.* **lung'-fish,** one of the Dipnoi, having lungs as well as gills.—*adj.* **lung'-grown,** having an adhesion of the lung to the pleura.—*n.* **lung'wort** (a genus (Pulmonaria) of the borage family, once thought good for lung diseases because of its spotted leaves : a lichen (*Lobaria pulmonaria*) on tree-trunks, used as a domestic remedy for lung diseases. [O.E. *lungen*.]

lunge, *lunj, n.* a sudden thrust as in fencing : a forward plunge.—*v.i.* to make a lunge : to plunge forward.—*v.t.* to thrust with a lunge :—*pr.p.* **lunge'ing, lung'ing.** [Fr. *allonger*, to lengthen— L. *ad*, to, *longus*, long.]

lunge, longe, *lunj, n.* a long rope used in horse-training : training with a lunge : a training-ground for horses.—*v.t.* to train or cause to go with a lunge. [Fr. *longe*—L. *longus*, long.]

lungi, *lōōn'gē, n.* a long cloth used as loincloth, sash, turban, &c. [Hind. and Pers. *lungī*.]

lungie, *lung'i, n.* (*Scot.*) the guillemot. [Norw. dial. *longivie*.]

lungie, lunyie, *lung'i, lun'yi, n.* Scottish forms of loin.

lunisolar, lunulate, lunule, &c. See **lune.**

lunt, *lunt, n.* (*Scot.*) a slow-match or means of setting on fire : a sudden flame, blaze : smoke.— *v.t.* to kindle : to smoke.—*v.i.* to blaze up : to emit smoke : to smoke tobacco. [Du. *lont*, a match ; cf. Ger. *lunte*.]

Lupercal, *lōō'par-kal, -kl,* or *lū', n.* the grotto, or the festival (Feb. 15), of *Lūpercus*, Roman god of fertility and flocks.—Also (*pl.*) **Luperca'lia.** [Perh. *lupus,* wolf, *arcēre*, to ward off.]

lupin, lupine, *lōō'pin* (or *lū'*), *n.* a genus (Lupinus) of Papilionaceae, with flowers on long spikes : its seed. [L. *lupīnus*.]

lupine, *lōō'pin* (or *lū'*), *adj.* of a wolf : like a wolf : wolfish. [L. *lupīnus—lupus,* a wolf.]

luppen, *lup'n,* Scots *pa.p.* of **leap.**

lupulin, *lōō'pū-lin, n.* a yellow powder composed of glands from hop flowers and bracts.—*adjs.* **lu'-puline, lupulinic** (-*lin'ik*). [L. *lupus,* the hop-plant.]

lupus, *lōō'pas,* or *lū', n.* a chronic tuberculosis of the skin, often affecting the nose. [L. *lupus,* a wolf.]

lurch, *lurch, n.* an old game, probably like back-gammon : in various games, a situation in which one side fails to score at all, or is left far behind : discomfiture.—*v.t.* to defeat by a lurch : (*Shak.*)

to outdo so as to deprive of all chance : to leave in the lurch.—**leave in the lurch**, to leave in a difficult situation without help. [O.Fr. *lourche*.]

lurch, *lurch*, *n.* wait, ambush.—*v.i.* to lurk, prowl about.—*v.t.* (*arch.*) to get the start of, forestall : to defraud : to overreach : (*arch.*) to filch.—*n.* **lurch'er**, one who lurches : (*obs.*) a glutton : a dog with a distinct cross of greyhound, esp. a cross of greyhound and collie. [Connexion with **lurk** difficult ; influenced apparently by foregoing.]

lurch, *lurch*, *v.i.* to roll or pitch suddenly forward or to one side.—*n.* a sudden roll or pitch. [Origin obscure.]

lurdan, **lurdane**, **lurden**, *lur'dən*, *n.* a dull, heavy, stupid or sluggish person.—Also *adj.* [O.Fr. *lourdin*, dull—*lourd*, heavy.]

lure, *l(y)ōōr*, *n.* any enticement : bait : decoy : a bunch of feathers used to recall a hawk.—*v.t.* to entice : decoy. [O.Fr. *loerre* (Fr. *leurre*)—M.H.G. *luoder* (Ger. *luder*), bait.]

lure, **lur**, *lōōr*, *n.* a long curved Bronze Age trumpet still used in Scandinavian countries for calling cattle, &c. [O.N. *lúthr* ; Dan. and Norw. *lur*.]

lurid, *l(y)ōō'rid*, *adj.* glaringly, wanly, or dingily reddish-yellow or yellowish-brown : (*bot.*) dingy brown or yellow : gloomily threatening : ghastly pale, wan : ghastly : melodramatically sensational : brimstony.—*adv.* **lu'ridly.**—*n.* **lu'ridness.** [L. *lūridus*.]

lurk, *lurk*, *v.i.* to lie in wait : to be concealed : to skulk : to go or loaf about furtively.—*n.* a prowl : a lurking-place : a swindling dodge.—*n.* **lurk'er.** — *n.* and *adj.* **lurk'ing.** — *n.* **lurk'ing-place.** [Perh. freq. from **lour.**]

lurry, *lur'i*, *n.* (*Milt.*) gabbled formula : confusion. [liripoop.]

luscious, *lush'əs*, *adj.* sweet in a great degree : delightful : fulsome : voluptuous.—*adv.* **lusc'iously.** —*n.* **lusc'iousness.** [Origin unknown; **delicious**, influenced by **lush**, has been suggested.]

lush, *lush*, *adj.* rich and juicy : luxuriant.—*adv.* **lush'ly.**—*n.* **lush'ness.** [Perh. a form of **lash** (2).]

lush, *lush*, *n.* liquor : a drink : a drinking bout : a drinker or drunkard.—*v.t.* to ply with liquor.— *v.t.* and *v.i.* to drink.—*n.* **lush'er.**—*adj.* **lush'y**, tipsy. [Perh. from foregoing.]

Lusiad, *l(y)ōō'si-ad*, *n.*, and **Lusiads** (-*adz*), *n.pl.*, a Portuguese epic by Camoens, celebrating Vasco da Gama's voyage to India by the Cape.—*n.* and *adj.* **Lusita'nian**, Portuguese. [Port. *Os Lusiadas*, the Lusitanians ; L. *Lūsitānia*, approximately, Portugal.]

lusk, *lusk*, *n.* (*obs.*) a lazy fellow.—*adj.* (*obs.*) lazy.— *v.i.* (*obs.*) to skulk : to lie about lazily.—*adj.* **lusk'ish** (*obs.*).—*n.* **lusk'ishness.** [Origin obscure.]

lust, *lust*, *n.* (*Spens.*, *Shak.*) pleasure : appetite : relish : longing : eagerness to possess : sensual desire : sexual desire, now always of a degraded kind.—*v.i.* to desire eagerly (with *after*, *for*) : to have carnal desire : to have depraved desires.— *adjs.* **lust-breathed** (-*brēdh'id* ; *Shak.*), animated by lust ; **lust-di'eted**, (*Shak.*) pampered by lust.— *n.* **lust'er.**—*adj.* **lust'ful**, having lust : inciting to lust : sensual.—*adv.* **lust'fully.**—*n.* **lust'fulness.** — *adj.* **lust'ick**, **lust'ique**, (*Shak.* 'as the Dutchman says ' ; for Du. *lustig*) lusty, healthy, vigorous.—*ns.* **lust'ihead**, **lust'ihood**, **lust'iness.** —*adv.* **lust'ily.**—*adjs.* **lust'less**, (*Spens.*) listless, feeble ; **lust'y**, vigorous : healthful : stout : bulky : (*Milt.*) lustful : (*obs.*) pleasing, pleasant. [O.E. *lust*, pleasure.]

lustre, *lus'tər*, *n.* characteristic surface appearance in reflected light : sheen : gloss : brightness : splendour : (*fig.*) renown : a candlestick, vase, &c., ornamented with pendants of cut-glass : a dress material with cotton warp and woollen weft, and highly finished surface : a glaze applied to porcelain.—*v.t.* to impart a lustre to.—*v.i.* to become lustrous. — *adj.* **lus'treless.** — *n.* **lus'tring.** — *adj.* **lus'trous**, bright : shining : luminous. — *adv.* **lus'trously.** [Fr.,—L. *lūstrāre*, to shine on.]

lustre, *lus'tər*, **lustrum**, *lus'trəm* *n.* a purification of the Roman people made every five years, after the taking of the census : a period of five years :— *pl.* **lus'tres**, **lus'tra**, **lus'trums.**—*adj.* **lus'tral.**—

v.t. **lus'trate**, to purify by sacrifice : to perambulate. —*n.* **lustra'tion**, a purification by sacrifice : act of purifying. [L. *lūstrum*, prob.—*luĕre*, to wash, to purify.]

lustring, *lus'tring*, *n.* a glossy silk cloth.—Also **lus'trine**, **lutestring** (*loot'*, *lūt'string*). [Fr. *lustrine* —It. *lustrino*.]

lusty. See **lust.**

lute, *lōōt*, or *lūt*, *n.* an old stringed instrument shaped like half a pear.—*v.i.* to play on the lute.— *v.t.* and *v.i.* to sound as if on a lute.—*ns.* **lut'anist**, **lut'enist**, **lut'er**, **lut'ist**, a player on the lute ; **lute'-string**, the string of a lute (but see also **lustring**). [O.Fr. *lut* (Fr. *luth*) ; like Ger. *laute*, from Ar. *al*, the, *'ūd*, wood, the lute.]

lute, *lōōt*, *lūt*, *n.* clay, cement or other material used as a protective covering, an airtight stopping, or the like . a rubber packing-ring for a jar.—*v.t.* to close or coat with lute.—*n.* **lut'ing.** [L. *lutum*, mud—*luĕre*, to wash.]

lute, *lōōt*, *lūt*, *n.* a straight-edge for scraping off excess of clay in a brick mould. [Du. *loet*.]

lutecium. Same as **lutetium.**

lutein, *l(y)ōō'tē-in*, *n.* a yellow colouring-matter in yolk of egg.—*n.* **lutē'olin**, the yellow colouring-matter of weld or dyer's weed.—*adjs.* **lutē'olous**, yellowish ; **lu'teous** (-*i-əs*), golden-yellow ; **lutescent** (-*es'ənt*), yellowish. [L. *lūteus*, yellow, *lūteum*, egg-yolk, *lūtum*, weld.]

lutestring. See **lustrine**, **lute.**

Lutetian, *lū-tē'shən*, *adj.* Parisian. [L. *Lutetia Parīsiōrum*, the mud town of the Parisii, Paris— *lutum*, mud.]

lutetium, *l(y)ōō-tē'shi-əm*, *n.* a metallic element (Lu ; at. numb. 71) first separated from ytterbium by Georges Urbain, a Parisian. [L. *Lutetia*, Paris.]

Lutheran, *lōō'thər-ən*, *adj.* pertaining to Martin Luther, the great German Protestant reformer (1483-1546), or to his doctrines.—*n. a.* follower of Luther.—*ns.* **Lu'ther(an)ism;** **Lu'therist.**

lux, *luks*, *n.* a unit of illumination, that of a surface one metre distant from a point of unit intensity. [L. *lūx*, light.]

luxate, *luks'āt*, *v.t.* to put out of joint : to displace. —*n.* **luxa'tion**, a dislocation. [L. *luxāre*, -*ātum*— *luxus*—Gr. *loxos*, slanting.]

luxulyanite, **luxul(l)ianite**, *luks-ūl'yən-īt*, *n.* a tourmaline granite found at *Luxulyan*, Cornwall.

luxury, *luk'shə-ri*, also *lug'zhə-ri*, *n.* abundant provision of means of ease and pleasure : free indulgence in costly pleasures : anything delightful, but not necessary : a dainty : (*Shak.*) wantonness.— *ns.* **luxuriance** (*lug-zhōō'ri-əns*, -*ziū'*, -*zhū'*, or *luk-*, &c.), **luxu'riancy**, growth in rich abundance or excess : exuberance : overgrowth : rankness.— *adj.* **luxu'riant**, exuberant in growth : overabundant : profuse : erroneously, for luxurious.—*adv.* **luxu'riantly.**—*v.i.* **luxu'riate**, (*obs.*) to be luxuriant : to live luxuriously : to enjoy luxury : to enjoy free indulgence.—*n.* **luxuria'tion.**—*adj.* **luxu'rious**, of luxury : given to luxury : ministering to luxury : furnished with luxuries : softening by pleasure : (*Milt.*) luxuriant : (*Shak.*) lustful.— *adv.* **luxu'riously.**—*ns.* **luxu'riousness ; luxurist** (*luk'shə-rist*, -*sū-*), one given to luxury. [O.Fr. *luxurie*—L. *luxuria*, luxury—*luxus*, excess.]

luz, *luz*, *n.* a bone supposed by Rabbinical writers to be indestructible, probably the sacrum.

Luzula, *l(y)ōō'zū-lä*, *n.* the woodrush genus, with flat generally hairy leaves. [Old It. *luzziola* (mod. *lucciola*), firefly, glow-worm, from its shining capsules.]

lyam, *li'əm*, **lime**, **lyme**, *līm*, *n.* a leash : a lyam-hound.—*n.* **ly'am-hound**, **lime'-hound**, **lyme'-hound**, a bloodhound. [O.Fr. *liem* (Fr. *lien*)—L. *ligāmen*—*ligāre*, to tie.]

lyart. See **liard.**

Lycaena, *li-sē'nä*, *n.* a genus of butterflies giving name to the family **Lycae'nidae**, usu. small and blue or coppery. [Gr. *lykaina*, she-wolf.]

lycanthropy, *li-kan'thrə-pi*, *n.* power of changing oneself into a wolf : a kind of madness, in which the patient fancies himself to be a wolf.—*ns.* **lycanthrope** (*li'kan-thrōp*, or *-kan'*), **lycan'-thropist**, a wolf-man or were-wolf : one affected with lycanthropy. — *adj.* **lycanthropic** (-*throp'*). [Gr. *lykos*, a wolf, *anthrōpos*, a man.]

lycée, *lē-sā, n.* a state secondary school in France. [Fr., lyceum.]

Lyceum, *lī-sē'əm, n.* a gymnasium and grove beside the temple of Apollo at Athens, in whose walks Aristotle taught : **lyceum,** a college : a place or building devoted to literary studies and lectures : (*U.S.*) an organisation for instruction by lectures : a lycée :—*pl.* **lyce'ums.** [L. *Lycēum* —Gr. *Lykeion*—*Lykeios,* an epithet of Apollo (perh. wolf-slayer, perhaps the Lycian).]

lychee. Same as **litchi.**

lychgate. Same as **lichgate.**

Lychnic, *lik'nik, n.* the first part of the vespers of the Greek Church.—*ns.* **Lychnap'sia** (Gr. *haptein,* to touch, light), a series of seven prayers in the vespers of the Greek Church ; **lych'noscope,** a low side window (named on the theory that it was intended to let lepers see the altar lights). [Gr. *lychnos,* a lamp.]

Lychnis, *lik'nis, n.* the campion genus of the pink family. [Gr. *lychnis,* rose-campion.]

lycopod, *lī'kə-pod, n.* a clubmoss, any plant of the genus Lycopodium or of the Lycopodiales.—*ns.pl.* **Lycopōdiā'ceae,** a homosporous family of Lycopodiales ; **Lycopōdiā'les, Lycopodi'nae,** Lycopodī'nae, Lyco- **podin'eae,** one of the main branches of the Pteridophytes, usually with dichotomously branched stems and axillary sporangia, commonly in cones.—*n.* **Lycopō'dium,** the typical genus of Lycopodiaceae, clubmoss, or stag's horn : **lycopodium,** a powder consisting of the spores of Lycopodium. [Gr. *lykos,* a wolf, *pous, podos,* a foot.]

Lycosa, *lī-kō'sä, n.* a genus of hunting spiders, including the true tarantula, typical of the family **Lycosidae** (-*kos'i-dē*) or wolf-spiders. [L. *lykos,* a wolf, also a kind of spider.]

lyddite, *lid'īt, n.* a powerful explosive made in Kent from picrate of potash. [Tested at *Lydd.*]

Lydford law, *lid'ford,* the same as Jeddart justice. [*Lydford* in Devon.]

Lydian, *lid'i-ən, adj.* pertaining to *Lydia* in Asia Minor : (of music) soft and slow, luxurious and effeminate.—*n.* native of Lydia : the language of ancient Lydia, apparently akin to Hittite.—**Lydian mode,** in ancient Greek music, a mode of two tetrachords with a semitone between the two highest notes in each and a whole tone between the tetrachords (as : *c d e f* ; *g a b c*) ; but reckoned downwards by the Greeks) : in old church music, an authentic mode, extending from *f* to *f,* with *f* for its final ; **Lydian stone,** touchstone. [Gr. *Lȳdiā,* Lydia.]

lye, *lī, n.* a short side-branch of railway. [**lie** (2).]

lye, *lī, n.* a strong alkaline solution : a liquid used for washing : a solution got by leaching. [O.E. *léah, léag* ; Ger. *lauge* ; allied to L. *lavāre,* to wash.]

lying, *lī'ing, adj.* addicted to telling lies.—*n.* the habit of telling lies.—*adv.* **ly'ingly.** [**lie** (1).]

lying, *lī'ing, adj.* being in a horizontal position.—*n.* **ly'ing-in',** confinement during child-bearing.— Also *adj.*—**take it lying down,** to make no resistance or protest. [**lie** (2).]

lyke-wake, *līk'-wāk, n.* (*arch.*) a watch over the dead, often with merrymaking. [Northern form of **lich,** and **wake.**]

lym, *lim, n.* a conjectural Shakespearian form of **lyme,** a lyme-hound. See **lyam.**

Lymantriidae, *lī-man-trī'i-dē, n.pl.* the tussock-moths, a family akin to the eggers. [Gr. *lȳmantēr,* destroyer.]

lyme-grass, *līm'-gräs, n.* a coarse sand-binding grass, *Elymus arenarius* or other of the genus. [Origin unknown.]

lymiter (*Spens.*). Same as **limiter.**

Lymnaea. See **Limnaea.**

lymph, *limf, n.* pure water : a colourless or faintly-yellowish fluid in animal bodies, of a rather saltish taste, and with an alkaline reaction : a vaccine.—

n. **lymphangitis** (-*an-jī'tis*), inflammation of a lymphatic vessel.—*adj.* **lymphat'ic,** (*obs.*) mad : pertaining to lymph : of a temperament or bodily habit once supposed to result from excess of lymph. —*n.* a vessel that conveys lymph.—*n.* **lymphocyte** (-*ō-sīt*), a kind of leucocyte formed in the lymph-glands and spleen. [L. *lympha,* water ; *lymphāticus,* mad.]

lymphad, *lim'fad, n.* a Highland galley. [Gael. *longfhada.*]

lynage (*Spens.*). Same as **lineage.**

lynch, *lin(t)sh, v.t.* to judge and put to death without the usual forms of law.—*n.* **lynch'-law.** [Captain William *Lynch* of Virginia.]

lynchet. See **linch.**

lyne (*Spens.*). Same as **line** (linen).

lynx, *lingks, n.* an animal (genus Lynx) of the cat family, high at the haunches, with short tail and tufted ears :—*pl.* **lynx'es.**—*adjs.* **lyncean** (*lin-sē'ən*), lynx-like : sharp-sighted ; **lynx'-eyed.** [L., —Gr. *lynx, lynkos.*]

lyomerous, *lī-om'ə-rəs, adj.* relating to the **Lyom'- erī,** or loose-jointed fishes. [Gr. *lȳein,* to loosen, *meros,* part.]

Lyon, *lī'ən, n.* the chief herald of Scotland.—Also **Lord Lyon, Lyon King-of-arms** (or **-at-arms**). —**Lyon Court,** the court over which he presides, having jurisdiction in questions of coat-armour and precedency. [From the heraldic *lion* of Scotland.]

lyophil, lyophile, *lī'ō-fil,* **liophilic,** -*fil'ik, adjs.* of a colloid, readily dispersed in a suitable medium.— *adjs.* **ly'ophobe** (-*fōb*), **lyophobic** (-*fob'*), of a colloid, not readily dispersed. [Gr. *lȳē,* separation, *phileein,* to love, *phobeein,* to fear.]

lyre, *līr, n.* a musical instrument like the harp, anciently used as an accompaniment to poetry— a convex sound-chest with a pair of curved arms connected by a cross-bar, from which the strings were stretched over a bridge to a tailpiece.—*n.* **Ly'ra,** one of the northern constellations.—*adjs.* **ly'rate, -d,** lyre-shaped : (*bot.*) having the terminal lobe much larger than the lateral ones.—*n.* **ly'ra-vi'ol,** an obsolete instrument like a viola da gamba adapted for playing from lute tablature.—*advs.* **ly'ra-way, ly'ra-wise,** according to lute tablature. —*n.* **lyre'-bird,** an Australian passerine bird about the size of a pheasant, having the 16 tail-feathers of the male arranged in the form of a lyre.—*adjs.* **lyric** (*lir'*), **-al,** pertaining to the lyre : fitted to be sung to the lyre : of poetry, expressing individual emotions : songlike : that composes lyrics.—*ns.* **lyric** (*lir'ik*), a lyric poem : a song : (*obs.*) a composer of lyric poetry ; **lyricism** (*lir'i-sizm*), a lyrical expression : lyrical quality ; **lyr'ism** (*lir', lir'*), lyricism : singing ; **lyrist** (*līr'* or *lir'*), a player on the lyre or harp : (*lir'*) a lyric poet. [L. *lyra*— Gr. *lyrā.*]

lysis, *lī'sis, n.* the gradual abatement of a disease, as distinguished from *crisis* : (*biol.*) breaking down, as of a cell : the action of a lysin.—*v.t.* **lyse** (*līz*), to cause to undergo lysis.—*adjs.* **lysigenic** (*lī-* or *lī-si-jen'ik*), **lysigenet'ic, lysigenous** (-*sij'i-nəs*), caused by breaking down of cells.—*ns.* **lysim'eter,** an instrument for measuring percolation of water through the soil ; **lysin** (*lī'sin*), a substance that causes breakdown of cells ; **ly'sine** (-*sin,* -*sēn*), an amino-acid, a decomposition product of proteins ; **ly'sol,** a solution of cresol in soap, a poisonous disinfectant (a trade-mark in some countries). [Gr. *lysis,* dissolution—*lyein,* to loose.]

lyte, lythe (*Spens.*). See **light** (3), **lithe.**

lythe, *lidh, n.* (*Scot.*) the pollack.

Lythrum, *lith'rəm, n.* the purple loosestrife genus, giving name to a family of archichlamydeous dicotyledons, **Lythrā'ceae,** commonly hexamerous, heterostyled, with epicalyx. [Latinised from Gr. *lythron,* gore, from the colour of its flowers.]

lytta, *lit'ä, n.* a cartilaginous or fibrous band on the under surface of the tongue in carnivores—the worm of a dog's tongue. [Gr.]

M

M, m, *em, n.* the twelfth letter of the Roman, the thirteenth of our alphabet, representing a labial nasal consonant: an object or figure shaped like the letter: as a Roman numeral M = 1000; M = 1,000,000; in chem. *m* = *meta-.*—*n.* **M'-roof,** a roof formed by the junction of two common roofs, so that its section is like the letter M. See also **em.**

ma, *mä, n.* a childish or vulgar contraction for **mamma.**

ma'am, *mam, məm, n.* a colloquial contraction of **madam**—vulgarly **marm** (*mäm*), **mum.**

Mab, *mab, n.* the name of a female fairy, bringer of dreams: the queen of the fairies.

Mabinogion, *mab-i-nō'gi-on, n.* a title applied to four tales in the *Red Book of Hergest,* a Welsh MS. of the 14th century: extended to the whole collection in Lady Charlotte Guest's edition and translation in 1838. [W., juvenilities.]

Mac, *mak, mək,* a Gaelic prefix in names, meaning *son* (of). [Gael. and Ir. *mac,* son; W. *mab,* O.W. *map.*]

macabre, *ma-, mə-kä'br', -bər, adj.* gruesome: like the Dance of Death. — *adj.* **macaberesque** (*-bər-esk'*). [Fr. *macabre,* formerly also *macabré*—app.—Heb. *meqabēr,* grave-digger.]

macadamise, *mək-ad'əm-īz, v.t.* to cover with small broken stones, so as to form a smooth, hard surface.—*ns.* **macad'am,** macadamised road surface: material for macadamising; **macadamīsā'tion.** [From John Loudon *Macadam* (1756-1836).]

macaque, *mə-käk', n.* a monkey of genus Macacus, to which belong the rhesus and the Barbary ape. [Fr.,—Port. *macaco,* a monkey.]

macarise, *mak'ə-rīz, v.t.* to pronounce happy.—*n.* **mac'arism,** a beatitude. [Gr. *makar,* happy.]

macaroni, *mak-ə-rō'ni, n.* a paste of hard wheat flour pressed through perforations into long tubes, and dried: a medley: something fanciful and extravagant: in the 18th century, a dandy: a rockhopper or crested penguin:—*pl.* **macarō'ni(e)s.**—*adj.* **macaronic** (*-ron'ik*), in a kind of burlesque verse, intermixing modern words Latinised, or Latin words modernised, with genuine Latin—loosely, verse in mingled tongues.—*n.* (often in *pl.*) macaronic verse.—**macaroni cheese,** macaroni cooked with cheese. [It. *maccaroni* (now *maccheroni*), pl. of *maccarone,* prob.—*maccare,* to crush.]

macaroon, *mak-ə-rōōn', n.* a sweet biscuit made of almonds. [Fr. *macaron*—It. *maccarone* (see above).]

macassar-oil, *mə-kas'ər-oil, n.* an oil once used for the hair, got from the seeds of a sapindaceous tree *Schleichera trijuga,* or from ylang-ylang flowers, or other Eastern source. [*Macassar* or Mangkasara in Celebes.]

macaw, *mə-kaw', n.* any of the large, long-tailed, showy tropical American parrots of the genus Ara. [Port. *macao.*]

macaw-tree, -palm, *mə-kaw'trē, -päm, ns.* a South American palm (Acrocomia) whose nuts yield a violet-scented oil.—Also **maco'ya, macahuba** (*mä-kä-ōō'bä*). [Sp. *macoya,* from Arawak; Port. *macauba,* from Tupí.]

Maccabaean, Maccabean, *mak-ə-bē'ən, adj.* pertaining to Judas *Maccabaeus,* or to his family the Hasmonaeans or *Macc'abees,* who freed the Jewish nation from the persecutions of Antiochus Epiphanes, king of Syria, about 166 B.C.—as related in two *Books of Maccabees* of the Apocrypha.

macchie, *mäk'kyā, n.pl.* Italian form of **maquis.**

mace, *mās, n.* a metal or metal-headed war-club, often spiked: a somewhat similar staff used as a mark of authority: a mace-bearer: a light, flat-headed stick formerly used in billiards: a mallet used by a currier in dressing leather.—*ns.* **mace'-bearer,** one who carries the mace in a procession,

or before men in authority; **mac'er, a** mace-bearer: in Scotland, an usher in a law-court. [O.Fr. *mace* (Fr. *masse*)—hypothetical L. *matea,* whence L. dim. *mateola,* a kind of tool.]

mace, *mās, n.* the aril or inner coat of the nutmeg.—*n.* **mace'-ale,** ale flavoured with mace. [Fr. *macis,* possibly—L. *maccis, -idis,* a word supposed to have been invented by Plautus for an imaginary spice.]

macédoine, *mä-sā-dwän', n.* a mixture, esp. of vegetables or fruit embedded in jelly: a medley. [Fr., lit. Macedonia.]

maceranduba. Same as **massaranduba.**

macerate, *mas'ər-āt, v.t.* to steep: to soften, or remove the soft parts of, by steeping: to wear down, esp. by fasting: to mortify.—*v.i.* to undergo maceration: to waste away.—*ns.* **macerā'tion; mac'erātor,** one who macerates: a paper-pulping apparatus. [L. *mācerāre, -ātum,* to steep.]

machair, *mä'hhər, n.* low-lying sandy beach or boggy links affording some pasturage. [Gael.]

Machairodus, *ma-kī'rə-dəs,* **Machaerodus,** *-kē', n.* the sabre-toothed tiger of prehistoric times.—*n.* and *adj.* **machair'odont.** [Gr. *machaira,* a sword, *odous, odontos,* a tooth.]

machan, *mu-chän', n.* a shooting-platform up a tree. [Hind. *machān.*]

machete, *mä-chā'tä, n.* a heavy knife or cutlass used by the Cubans, &c. [Sp.]

Machiavellian, *mak-i-ə-vel'yən, adj.* destitute of political morality, following expediency rather than right: cunning, crafty, perfidious.—*n.* one who imitates Niccolo *Machiavelli,* statesmen and writer, of Florence (1469-1527): any cunning and unprincipled statesman.—*ns.* **Machiavell'ianism, Machiavell'ism,** the principles taught by Machiavelli, or conduct regulated by them: cunning statesmanship.

machicolation, *ma-chik-ō-lā'shən, n.* (*archit.*) a space between the corbels supporting a parapet, or an opening in the floor of a projecting gallery, for dropping solids or liquids on an attacking enemy: a structure with such openings: the provision of such openings or structures.—*v.t.* **machic'olate,** to provide or build with machicolations.—*adj.* **machic'olated.** [Fr. *mâchicoulis.*]

machinate, *mak'i-nāt, v.i.* to form a plot or scheme esp. for doing harm.—*ns.* **machinā'tion,** act of machinating: an intrigue or plot; **mach'inātor,** one who machinates. [L. *māchinārī, -ātus*—*māchina*—Gr. *mēchanē,* contrivance.]

machine, *mə-shēn', n.* any artificial means or contrivance: any instrument for the conversion of motion: an engine: (*obs.* or *Scot.*) a vehicle: one who can do only what he is told: a contrivance by which a god might descend upon the stage: a supernatural agent employed in carrying on the action of a poem: an organised system: (*U.S.*) a political party organisation.—*v.t.* to use machinery for: to print, sew, or make by machinery.—*n.* **machine'-gun,** an automatic quick-firing gun on a stable but portable mounting.—*v.t.* to shoot at with a machine-gun.—*n.* **machine'-gunner.**—*adj.* **machine'-made,** made by machinery.—*ns.* **machine'man,** a man who manages the working of a machine; **machine'-rul'er,** an instrument for ruling lines on paper; **machin'ery,** machines in general: the working parts of a machine: combined means for keeping anything in action, or for producing a desired result: supernatural agents in a poem; **machine'-shop,** a workshop where machines are made; **machine'-tool,** an adjustable machine for doing work with cutting-tools, or one utilising minor tools, as a planing-, drilling-machine, &c.; **machine'-work,** work done by a

fāte, fär, ȧsk; mē, hər (her); mīne; mōte; mūte; mōōn, dhen (then)

machine; **machin′ist**, a constructor of machines: one well versed in machinery: one who works a machine. [Fr.,—L. *māchina*—Gr. *mēchanē*, akin to *mēchos*, contrivance.]
Mach number, *mähh num′bər*, the ratio of the air speed (i.e. speed in relation to the air) of an aircraft to the velocity of sound under the given conditions. [Named after Ernst *Mach*, Austrian physicist and philosopher (1838-1916).]
mackerel, *mak′ər-əl*, *n.* a food fish (Scomber), bluish green, with wavy cross-streaks above, and silvery below: (*obs.*) a bawd.—*ns.* **mack′erel-breeze′**, a breeze that ruffles the surface of the sea and so favours mackerel fishing; **mack′erel-guide′**, the common garfish, which visits the coasts just before the mackerel; **mack′erel-midge′**, a small rockling; **mack′erel-shark′**, the porbeagle; **mack′erel-sky′**, a sky with clouds broken into long, thin, white, parallel masses. [O.Fr. *makerel* (Fr. *maquereau*).]
mackinaw, *mak′in-aw*, *n.* an American Indian's blanket: a short heavy woollen coat: a flat-bottomed lake-boat. [*Mackinaw*, an island between Lakes Huron and Michigan.]
mac(k)intosh, *mak′in-tosh*, *n.* waterproof cloth: a waterproof overcoat:—*contr.* **mack.** [From Charles *Macintosh* (1766-1843), the patentee.]
mackle, *mak′l*, *n.* a spot or blemish in printing, by a double impression, wrinkling, &c.—*v.t.* to spot, blur. [See next.]
macle, *mak′l*, *n.* a dark spot in a crystal: chiastolite: a twin crystal.—*adj.* **macled** (*mak′ld*), spotted. [Fr. *macle*—L. *macula*, spot.]
Macmillanite, *mək-mil′ən-īt*, *n.* a Cameronian or Reformed Presbyterian. [From John *Macmillan* (1670-1753), the first ordained minister who associated himself with the ′suffering remnant.′]
maconochie, *mə-kon′ə-hhi*, *n.* (*mil.*) tinned meat and vegetable stew: tinned food. [Packer's name.]
macramé, macrami, *mə-krä′mi*, *n.* a fringe or trimming of knotted thread: knotted threadwork. [App. Turk. *maqrama*, towel.]
macro-, *mak′rō-*, *-rο′*, in composition, long, great, sometimes interchanging with *mega-*.—*n.* **macro-axis** (*mak′rō-aks′is*; *crystal.*), the longer lateral axis. —*adj.* **macro′bian** (Gr. *bios*, life), long-lived.—*n.* **macrobiote** (*-bī′ōt*), a long liver.—*adj.* **macro-biotic** (*-bī-ot′ik*) prolonging life: relating to longevity.—*n.* (*pl.* in form) **macrobiot′ics**, the art or science of prolonging life.—*adjs.* **macrocephalic** (*-si-fal′ik*), **macrocephalous** (*-sef′ə-ləs*). — *ns.* **macrocephaly** (*-sef′ə-li*; Gr. *kephalē*, head) largeness, or abnormal largeness, of head; **mac′-rocosm** (*-kɔzm*; Gr. *kosmos*, world), the great world: the whole universe—opp. to *microcosm*.— *adj.* **macrocos′mic**.—*n.* **mac′rocyte** (*-sīt*; Gr. *kytos*, a vessel), a large uninuclear leucocyte with great powers of mobility and phagocytosis.—*adjs.* **macrodactyl** (*-dak′til*), **macrodactylic** (*-til′ik*), **macrodactylous** (*-dak′til-əs*; Gr. *daktylos*, finger, toe), long-fingered, long-toed.—*ns.* **macrodac′tyly**, condition of being macrodactylous; **macro-diag′onal**, (*crystal.*) the longer lateral axis; **mac′rodome**, **macropin′akoid**, **mac′roprism**, a dome, pinakoid, prism, parallel to the macro-diagonal; **macrogamete′** (or *-gam′ēt*), a female gamete; **macrol′ogy**, much talk with little to say; **macromol′ecule**, a large molecule, esp. one formed from a number of simpler molecules; **mac′ron** (Gr., neut. of *makros*), a straight line placed over a vowel to show it is long (as in *ē*)— opp. to *breve*, the mark of a short vowel (*ĕ*).—*adjs.* **macrop′terous** (Gr. *pteron*, a wing), long-winged: long-finned; **macroscop′ic**, visible to the naked eye — opp. to *microscopic.*—*adv.* **macroscop′-ically.**—*ns.* **macrosporan′gium**, **mac′rospore** (see **megasporangium, megaspore**).—*n.pl.* **Macrura** (*mak-rōō′rä*; Gr. *ourā*, tail), a group of decapod crustaceans including lobsters, shrimps, prawns, &c.—*adjs.* **macru′ral, macru′rous**, long-tailed. [Gr. *makros*, long, also great.]
mactation, *mak-tā′shən*, *n.* slaying, esp. of a sacrificial victim. [L. *mactātiō, -ōnis*.]
macula, *mak′ū-lä*, *n.* a spot, as on the skin, the sun, a mineral, &c.:—*pl.* **maculae** (*-lē*).—*v.t.* **mac′-**

ulate, to spot, to defile.—*adj.* spotted: soiled.— *ns.* **macula′tion**, act of spotting, a spot; **mac′-ulāture**, an impression taken from an engraved plate to remove the ink before inking afresh; **mac′ule**, a macula: a mackle.—*adj.* **mac′ulose**, spotted. [L. *macula*, a spot.]
mad, *mad*, *adj.* (*comp.* **madd′er**; *superl.* **madd′est**) disordered in intellect: insane: proceeding from madness: extremely and recklessly foolish: infatuated: frantic with pain, violent passion, or appetite: (*coll.*, esp. *U.S.*) furious with anger: extravagantly playful or exuberant: rabid.—*v.t.* (*Shak.*) to drive mad.—*v.i.* to be mad: to act madly.—*adjs.* **mad′brain**, **mad′brained**, (*Shak.*) disordered in brain or mind: rash: hot-headed; **mad′-bred**, (*Shak.*) bred in madness or heat of passion.—*n.* **mad′cap**, a person who acts madly: a wild, rash, hot-headed person: an exuberantly frolicsome person.—*adj.* fond of wild and reckless or extravagantly merry action.—*v.t.* **madd′en**, to make mad: to enrage.—*v.i.* to become mad: to act as one mad.—*adj.* **madd′ing**, distracted, acting madly.—*advs.* **madd′ingly**, **mad′ly**.—*ns.* **mad′-doc′tor**, a doctor who studies and treats the diseases of mad people; **mad′house**, a house for mad persons: a lunatic asylum; **mad′ling**, a mad person; **mad′man**, a man who is mad: a maniac; **mad′ness**; **mad′wort**, a plant believed to cure canine madness—Alyssum, Asperugo, &c.—**go mad**, to become demented: like mad, madly, furiously. [O.E. *gemǣd(e)d*; O.Sax. *gimēd*, foolish.]
madam, *mad′əm*, *n.* a courteous form of address to a lady, esp. an elderly or a married one: a woman who might be addressed as madam: a woman of rank, station, pretension, or affectation: (*arch.* and *U.S.*) the mistress of a household: a formidable woman: a general term of opprobrium for a woman: (*obs.*) a concubine: (*arch.*) prefixed to a name instead of Mrs or Miss (in *U.S.* to distinguish mother-in-law from daughter-in-law): (*pl.* **mad′ams**).—*v.t.* to address as madam.—*n.* **Madame** (*mä-däm′*, *mad′əm*) prefixed instead of Mrs to a French or other foreign woman's name: used also of palmists, milliners, and musicians:—*pl.* **mesdames** (*mā-däm′*). [Fr. *ma*, my, *dame*, lady —L. *mea domina*.]
mad-apple, *mad′-ap-l*, *n.* the fruit of the egg-plant: the Dead Sea apple: a gall produced by a gall-wasp (*Cynips insana*) on an oak in the East. [From some form of mod. L. *melongēna*, It. *melanzana* (ultimately from Sans. *vātingāna*); *mālum insānum*, transl. as mad apple.]
madarosis, *mad-ə-rō′sis*, *n.* loss of hair, esp. of the eyebrows or eyelashes. [Gr. *madarōsis*—*madaros*, bald, *madaein*, to fall off.]
madder, *mad′ər*, *n.* a plant (*Rubia tinctorum*) whose root affords a red dye, or other species of Rubia. —*n.* **madd′er-lake**, a colour mixed either with oil or water, made from madder.—**field madder**, a minute lilac-flowered plant (*Sherardia arvensis*) of the same family. [O.E. *mæddre, mædere*; O.N. *mathra*, Du. *mede*, later *meed, mee.*]
made, *mād*, *pa.t.* and *pa.p.* of **make**, and *adj.*— **made dish**, a dish of various ingredients, often recooked; **made ground**, ground formed by artificial filling in; **made man**, one whose prosperity is assured; **made road**, one with deliberately made surface, not merely formed by traffic; **made up**, put together, finished: parcelled up: dressed for a part, disguised: painted and powdered: meretricious: artificial, invented: consummate.
madefy, *mad′i-fī*, *v.t.* to moisten.—*n.* **madefac′-tion**. [L. *madefacĕre*, *-factum*—*madēre*, to be wet, *facĕre*, to make.]
Madeira, *mə-dē′rä*, *mä-dā′rä*, *n.* a rich wine of the sherry class produced in *Madeira*.—*n.* **Madei′ra-cake**, a variety of sponge-cake.
Madelenian. Same as **Magdalenian.**
mademoiselle, *mad-mwə-zel′*, *n.* a form of address to an unmarried French or other foreign woman: (with capital) prefixed to a name, Miss (*pl.* **Mesdemoiselles**, *mād-*): a French governess. [Fr. *ma*, my, and *demoiselle*; see **damsel.**]
madge, *maj*, *n.* a leaden hammer.

madge, *maj*, *n*. the barn owl: the magpie. [App. from the woman's name.]

madid, *mad'id*, *adj*. wet, dank. [L. *madidus*—*madēre*, to be wet; akin to Gr. *madaein*.]

Madonna, *mə-don'ä*, *n*. (*Shak*.) my lady: the Virgin Mary, esp. as seen in works of art.—*adj*. **madonn'-aish.**—*n*. Madonn'a-lil'y, the white lily.—*adv*. **madonn'awise**, after the fashion of the Madonna, esp. in the arrangement of a woman's hair. [It., lit. my lady—L. *mea domina*.]

madoqua, *mad'ō-kwä*, *n*. a very small Abyssinian antelope. [Amharic *midaqua*.]

madras, *mə-dräs'*, *n*. a large handkerchief, usually in bright colours, worn on the head by West Indian negroes, formerly exported from *Madras*.

madrasa, madrasah, madrassah, medresseh, *mä-dras'ä, mə-dres'ə*, *n*. a Mohammedan college: a mosque school. [Ar. *madrasah*.]

madrepore, *mad'ri-pōr*, *n*. a coral of the common reef-building type.—*adj*. **madreporic** (*-por'ik*).—*n*. **mad'reporite**, or **madreporic plate**, in Echinoderms, a perforated plate serving as opening to the stone canal. [It. *madrepora*—*madre*, mother—L. *māter*, and Gr. *pōros*, a soft stone, stalactite, &c., or L. *porus*, a pore.]

madrigal, *mad'ri-gəl*, *n*. (*mus*.) an unaccompanied song in several parts in counterpoint: a lyrical poem suitable for such treatment.—*adj*. **madrigā'lian.**—*n*. **mad'rigalist.** [It. *madrigale*, perh. from *mandr(i)a*, a cattle-shed—Gr. *mandrā*.]

madroño, *mä-drō'nyō*, *n*. a handsome evergreen Arbutus tree of North California.—Also **madrō'ña**. [Sp. *madroño*.]

Maecenas, *mē-sē'nas*, *n*. a Roman knight who befriended Virgil and Horace: any rich patron of art or literature. [L. *Maecēnās*, *-ātis*.]

Maelstrom, maelstrom, *mäl'strom*, *n*. a fabled whirlpool off the coast of Norway: any resistless overpowering influence for destruction. [Du. (now *maalstroom*), a whirlpool.]

maenad, *mē'nad*, *n*. a female follower of Bacchus: a woman beside herself with frenzy.—*adj*. **maenad'ic**, bacchanalian: furious. [Gr. *mainas*, *-ados*, raving—*mainesthai*, to be mad.]

Maeonian, *mē-ō'ni-ən*, *adj*. and *n*. Lydian.—*n*. **Maeonides** (*mē-on'i-dēz*), Homer, as a supposed native of Lydia. [Gr. *Maiōnia*, an old name for Lydia.]

maestoso, *mä-es-tō'sō*, *adj*. and *adv*. (*mus*.) with dignity or majesty. [It.]

maestro, *mä-es'trō*, *n*. a master, esp. an eminent musical composer or conductor. [It.]

maffick, *maf'ik*, *v.i.* to rejoice with hysterical boisterousness. — *ns*. **maff'icker, maff'icking**. [By back-formation from *Mafeking*, treated jocularly as a gerund or participle, from the scenes in the streets of London on the news of the relief of the town (1900).]

maffled, *maf'ld*, *adj*. (*prov*.) confused in the intellect. —*n*. **maff'lin(g)**, a simpleton.

mafia, maffia, *mä'fē-ä*, *n*. an unorganised opposition to law in Sicily: a preference for private and unofficial rather than legal justice. [Sicilian Italian *mafia*.]

mag, *mag*, *n*. (*slang*) a halfpenny.—Also **maik**, **make** (*māk*).

mag, *mag*, *v.i.* (*prov*.) to chatter.—*v.t.* to tease: (*Scott* **magg**) to steal.—*n*. chatter: the magpie: the long-tailed titmouse.—*n*. **mags'man**, a street swindler. [From the name *Margaret*.]

magazine, *mag-ə zēn'*, also *mag'*, *n*. a storehouse: a place for military stores: a ship's powder-room: a compartment in a rifle for holding extra cartridges: a periodical publication containing articles, stories, &c., by various writers.—*ns*. **magazine'-gun, -rifle**, one from which a succession of shots can be fired without reloading. [Fr. *magasin*—It. *magazzino*—Ar. *makhāzin*, pl. of *makhzan*, a storehouse.]

Magdalen, Magdalene, *mag'də-lən*, *-lēn* in the names of Oxford and Cambridge colleges, *mawd'lin*), *n*. (**magdalen, -e**) a repentant prostitute: an institution for receiving such persons (*Magdalene hospital, asylum*). [From Mary Magdalene, i.e. (Gr.) *Magdalēnē*, of Magdala (Luke viii. 2), on

the assumption that she was the woman of Luke vii. 37-50.]

Magdalenian, Madelenian, *ma(g)d-ə-lē'ni-ən*, *adj*. belonging to an upper Palaeolithic culture that succeeded the Solutrean and preceded the Azilian. [La *Madeleine*, a cave on the Vézère.]

Magdeburg hemispheres, *mag'de-bōōrg hem'i-sfērz*, two hemispherical cups held together by atmospheric pressure when the air is pumped out from between them. [Invented at *Magdeburg* in Germany.]

mage, *māj*. See **Magus**.

magenta, *mə-jen'tä*, *n*. the dye-stuff fuchsin: its colour, a reddish purple.—*adj*. reddish purple. [From its discovery about the time of the battle of *Magenta* in North Italy, 1859.]

maggot, *mag'ət*, *n*. a legless grub, esp. of a fly: a fad or crotchet: (*obs*.) a whimsical tune or impromptu. — *adj*. **magg'oty**, full of maggots: crotchety. [Poss. a modification of M.E. *maddok*, *mathek*, dim., sees **mawk**.]

Magi, Magian. See **Magus**.

magic, *maj'ik*, *n*. the pretended art of producing marvellous results by compelling the aid of spirits, or by using the secret forces of nature, such as the power supposed to reside in certain objects as 'givers of life': enchantment: sorcery: a secret or mysterious power over the imagination or will.—*adjs*. **mag'ic, -al**, pertaining to, used in, or done by magic: causing wonderful or startling results.—*adv*. **mag'ically.**—*n*. **magician** (*mə-jish'ən*), one skilled in magic: a wizard: an enchanter: a wonder-worker.—**black magic**, the black art, magic by means of evil spirits; **magic lantern**, an apparatus for projecting pictures on slides upon a screen; **magic square**, a square filled with rows of figures so arranged that the sums of all the rows will be the same, perpendicularly or horizontally—as 2, 7, 6; 9, 5, 1; 4, 3, 8; **magic circles, cubes, cylinders, spheres** are similarly arranged; **natural magic**, the art of working wonders by a superior knowledge of the powers of nature: power of investing a work of art with an atmosphere of imagination: legerdemain; **sympathetic magic**, magic aiming at the production of effects by mimicry, as bringing rain by libations, injuring a person by melting his image or sticking pins in it; **white magic**, magic without the aid of the devil. [Gr. *magikē* (*technē*), magic (art). See **Magus**.]

magilp, megilp, *mə-gilp'*, *n*. a vehicle used by oil-painters, consisting of linseed-oil and mastic varnish. [Origin unknown.]

magister, *mə-jis'tər*, *n*. a master of a university (originally one licensed to teach).—*adj*. **magisterial** (*maj-is-tē'ri-əl*), pertaining or suitable to, or in the manner of, a teacher, master artist, or magistrate: of the rank of a magistrate: authoritative: dictatorial: of a magistery.—*adv*. **magis-tē'rially.**—*ns*. **magistē'rialness ; magistē'rium**, the philosopher's stone: teaching authority or function ; **magistery** (*maj'is-tə-ri*), in alchemy, a transmuting agent, as the philosopher's stone: a product of transmutation: a precipitate: any sovereign remedy: magisterium ; **mag'istracy** (*-trə-si*), the office or dignity of a magistrate: a body of magistrates.—*adj*. **magistral** (*mə-jis'trəl*, or *maj'is-*), of or pertaining to a master: masterly: authoritative: specially prescribed for a particular case as a medicine: effectual: (*fort*.) guiding or determining the chief points.—Also *n*.—*ns*. **magistrand'** (or *maj'*), an arts student ready to proceed to graduation, esp. now at Aberdeen ; **mag'istrate**, one who has power of putting the law in force, esp. a justice of the peace, a provost, or a bailie, or one who sits in a police court.—*adjs*. **magistratic** (*-trat'ik*), **-al.**—*n*. **mag'istrature.** [L. *magister*, master.]

Maglemosian, *mag-li-mō'zi-ən*, *adj*. (*archaeol*.) of a culture represented by finds at *Maglemose* in Denmark, transitional between Palaeolithic and Neolithic.

magma, *mag'mä*, *n*. a pasty or doughy mass: molten or pasty rock material: a glassy base of a rock:—*pl*. **mag'mata** (*-mə-tä*), **mag'mas.**—

adj. **magmatic** (-mat'ik). [Gr. magma, -atos, a thick unguent.]

Magna Carta (**Charta**), mag'nä kär'tä, the Great Charter obtained from King John, 1215. [L.]

magnanimity, mag-nə-nim'i-ti, n. greatness of soul: that quality of mind which raises a person above all that is mean or unjust: generosity.—adj. **magnanimous** (-nan').—adv. **magnan'imously**. [L. magnanimitās—magnus, great, animus, the mind.]

magnate, mag'nāt, n. a noble: a man of rank or wealth, or of power. [L. magnās, -ātis—magnus, great.]

magnes, mag'nēz, n. (arch.) lodestone.—n. **mag'nesstone** (Spens.). [L. and Gr. magnēs.]

magnesium, mag-nē'z(h)i-əm, -z(h)yəm, -shi-əm, -shyəm, n. (obs.) manganese: a metallic element (Mg; at. numb. 12) of a bright, silver-white colour, burning with a dazzling white light.—n. **magnē'sia**, (obs.) an imagined substance sought by the alchemists: (obs.) manganese: a light white powder, oxide of magnesium: basic magnesium carbonate, used as a medicine.—adj. **magnē'sian**, belonging to, containing, or resembling magnesia.—n. **magnesite** (mag'nəs-īt), native magnesium carbonate.— **Magnesian Limestone**, dolomite rock: a division of the Permian of England. [See **magnet**.]

magnet, mag'nit, n. the lodestone· a bar or piece of steel, &c., to which the properties of the lodestone have been imparted. — adjs. **magnetic** (-net'ik), -al, pertaining to the magnet: having, or capable of acquiring, the properties of the magnet: attractive: strongly affecting others by personality: hypnotic.—adv. **magnet'ically.**—n. **magnetician** (-ish'ən), one versed in magnetism.—n.pl. (or sing.) **magnet'ics**, the science of magnetism.— adj. **magnetīs'able.**—n. **magnetīsā'tion.**—v.t. **mag'netise**, to render magnetic: to attract as if by a magnet: to hypnotise.—ns. **mag'netīser**; **mag'netism**, the cause of the attractive power of the magnet: the phenomena connected with magnets: the science which treats of the properties of the magnet: attraction: influence of personality (**animal magnetism**, Mesmer's name for hypnotism; **terrestrial magnetism**, the magnetic properties possessed by the earth as a whole); **mag'netist**, one skilled in magnetism; **mag'netite**, magnetic iron ore (Fe_2O_4), called lodestone when polar; **magneto** (mag-nē'tō), a small generator with permanent magnet, used for ignition in an internal-combustion engine, &c. — adjs. **magnē'to-elec'tric**, -al, pertaining to magnetoelectricity.—ns. **magnē'to-electric'ity**, electricity produced by the action of magnets: the science thereof; **magnē'tograph**, an instrument for recording the variations of the magnetic elements; **magnetometer** (mag-ni-tom'i-tər), an instrument for measuring the strength of a magnetic field, esp. the earth's.—adj. **magnētomō'tive**, producing a magnetic flux.—ns. **magnē'ton** (or mag'ni-ton), a natural unit of magnetic moment; **magnētoop'tics**, study of the influence of magnetism on light; **magnēto-stric'tion** (or -net-), the change in dimensions produced in a magnetic material, esp. nickel, when it is magnetised; **mag'netron**, a vacuum tube combined with a magnetic field to deflect electrons.—**artificial magnet**, a magnet made by rubbing with other magnets; **bar magnet**, a magnet in the form of a bar; **horse-shoe magnet**, a magnet bent like a horseshoe; **magnetic battery**, several magnets placed with their like poles together, so as to act with great force; **magnetic curves**, the curves formed by iron-filings around the poles of a magnet; **magnetic equator**, the line round the earth where the magnetic needle remains horizontal; **magnetic field**, the space over which magnetic force is felt; **magnetic fluid**, a hypothetical fluid formerly assumed to explain the phenomena of magnetism; **magnetic meridian**, the vertical plane through the magnetic needle; **magnetic mine**, a mine sunk to the sea-bottom, detonated by a pivoted magnetic needle when a ship approaches; **magnetic needle**, the light bar in the mariner's compass which, because it is magnetised, points always

to the north; **magnetic north**, the direction indicated by the magnetic needle; **magnetic poles**, two nearly opposite points on the earth's surface, where the dip of the needle is 90°; **magnetic storm**, a disturbance in the magnetism of the earth; **permanent magnet**, a magnet that keeps its magnetism after the force which magnetised it has been removed; **personal magnetism**, power of a personality to make itself felt and to exercise influence. [Through O.Fr. or L., from Gr. magnētis (lithos), Magnesian (stone), from Magnēsiā, in Lydia or Thessaly.]

magnific, mag-nif'ik, **magnifical**, -əl, adjs. magnificent: exalted: pompous.—adv. **magnif'ically.**—n. **magnif'ico**, (It.; Shak.) a Venetian noble: a grandee. [L. magnificus; cf. **magnify.**]

Magnificat, mag-nif'i-kat, n. the song of the Virgin Mary, Luke i. 46-55, beginning in the Vulgate with this word. [L., '(my soul) doth magnify,' 3rd pers. sing. pres. ind. of magnificāre.]

magnificence, mag-nif'i-səns, n. (arch.) well-judged liberality: the quality of being magnificent.—adj. **magnif'icent**, great in deeds or in show: grand: noble: pompous: displaying greatness of size or extent.—adv. **magnif'icently**. [L. magnificēns, -entis, lit. doing great things.]

magnify, mag'ni-fī, v.t. to make great or greater: to enlarge: to cause to appear greater: to exaggerate: to praise highly.—v.i. (old slang) to signify:— pr.p. **mag'nifying**; pa.t. and pa p. **mag'nified**. —adj. **mag'nifiable**, that may be magnified.— ns. **magnification** (-fi-kā'shən), act or power of magnifying: state of being magnified: enlarged appearance or state or copy: extolling; **mag'nifier** (-fī-ər), one who, or that which, magnifies or enlarges, esp. a pocket-lens: one who extols. [L. magnificāre—magnus, great, facĕre, to make.]

magniloquent, mag-nil'ə-kwənt, adj. speaking in a grand or pompous style: bombastic.—n. **magnil'oquence**.—adv. **magnil'oquently**. [L. magnus, great, loquēns, -entis, pr.p. of loquī, to speak.]

magnitude, mag'ni-tūd, n. greatness: size: extent: importance: (astron.) brightness, according to a scale in which the brightest stars are of the first magnitude.—**absolute magnitude** (see **absolute**). [L. magnitūdō—magnus.]

Magnolia, mag-nōl'i-ä, or -yä, n. an American and Asiatic genus of trees with beautiful foliage, and large solitary flowers, giving name to the family **Magnoliā'ceae**, with petaloid perianth and spirally arranged stamens and carpels.—adj. **magnoliā'ceous**. [From Pierre Magnol (1638-1715), a Montpellier botanist.]

magnum, mag'nəm, n. a two-quart bottle or vessel: two quarts of liquor:—pl. **mag'nums**.—n. **mag'num bōn'um**, a large good variety, esp. of plums or potatoes:—pl. **mag'num bōn'ums**. [L. magnum (neut.), big, bŏnum (neut.), good.]

magot, mag'ət, mä-gō', n. the Barbary ape, a macaque, the only European monkey: a small grotesque figure, in Chinese or Japanese workmanship. [Fr.]

magpie, mag'pī, n. the pie (Pica rustica), a blackand-white chattering bird allied to the crow: extended to other black-and-white or pied birds (in Australia a piping crow): a chattering person: (obs.) an Anglican bishop: (a hit on) the target space between an outer and an inner: (slang) a halfpenny—(Shak.) **mag'ot-pie**, **magg'ot-pie.**— magpie moth, the moth of the gooseberry caterpillar. [Mag, Magot, for Margaret, and **pie** (1).]

maguey, mag'wä, mä-gā'i, n. agave. [Sp.]

Magus, mā'gəs, n. an ancient Persian priest or member of a priestly class: an Eastern magician: (magus) a magician: a Wise Man of the East:—pl. **Ma'gi** (-jī).—ns. **mage** (māj), a magus or sorcerer; **mage'ship**.—adj. **Ma'gian**, pertaining to the Magi or to a sorcerer.—n. a magus: a sorcerer.— ns. **Ma'gianism**, **Ma'gism**, the philosophy or teaching of the Magi. [L.,—Gr. magos—O.Pers. magus.]

Magyar, moj'or or mag'yär, n. one of the prevailing people of Hungary: the Finno-Ugric speech of Hungary.—adj. (**magyar**) of a garment, cut with the sleeves in a piece with the rest.—v.t. and v.i.

Mag′yarise, to make or become Magyar.—*n.*
Mag′yarism, Hungarian national spirit. [Magyar.]
Mahabharata, *mu-hä-bä′ru-tu, n.* one of the great epics of ancient India. [Sans. *Mahābhārata.*]
Mahadeva, *mu-hä-dä′vu, n.* Siva. [Sans. *mahā*, great, *deva*, god.]
maharaja, maharajah, *mä-hä-rä′jä, mu-hä-rä′ju, n.* a great Indian prince :—*fem.* maharani, maharanee (-*rä′nē*). [Hind., from Sans. *mahā-*, great, *rājan*, king, *rājnī*, queen.]
mahatma, *mə-hat′mä, n.* one skilled in mysteries or religious secrets : an adept : a wise and holy leader. [Sans. *mahātman*, high-souled.]
Mahdi, *mä′dē, n.* the great leader of the faithful Mohammedans, who is to appear in the last days : a title of various insurrectionary leaders, esp. one who overthrew the Egyptian power in the Sudan in 1884-85.—*ns.* Mah′diism, Mah′dism ; Mah′-diist, Mah′dist. [Ar. *mahdīy.*]
mah-jongg, *mä-jong′, n.* an old Chinese table game for four, played with small painted bricks or ' tiles.' [Chin.]
mahlstick. See maulstick.
mahmal, *mä′mäl, n.* the empty litter sent to Mecca in the hadj.
mahogany, *mə-hog′ə-ni, n.* a tropical American tree (*Swietenia Mahogoni*) of the Meliaceae : its timber, valued for furniture-making : the colour of the timber, a dark reddish brown : (*coll.*) a dining-table : (*slang*) gin and treacle : brandy and water.—Also *adj.* [Origin unknown.]
Mahommedan, Mahometan. See Moham-medan.
Mahonia, *mə-hō′ni-ä, n.* a pinnate-leaved genus (or section of Berberis) of the barberry family. [Named after Bernard *McMahon*, Irish-American gardener and botanist (*d.* 1816).]
Mahoun, Mahound, *mə-hown(d)′, -hōōn(d)′,* or *mä′, n.* (*arch.*) Mohammed, imagined in the Middle Ages to be a pagan god : (*Scot. mə-hōōn′*) the devil.
mahout, *mä-howt′, n.* the keeper and driver of an elephant. [Hind. *mahāut, mahāwat.*]
Mahratta. See Maratha.
mahseer, mahsir, *mä′sēr, n.* a large fish found in the rivers of Northern India. [Hind. *mahāsir.*]
mahwa, mahua, *mä′(h)wä, n.* a kind of butter-tree (*Bassia*, or *Illipe, latifolia*) with edible flowers.—mahwa butter, a fat got from its seeds.—Also mowa, mowra. [Hind. *mahwā.*]
maid, *mäd, n.* an unmarried woman, esp. one young : a virgin : a female servant : a young skate.—*v.i.* to work as a maid-servant.—*ns.* maid′-child, (*B.*, *Shak.*) a female child ; maid′hood.—*adjs.* maid′ish ; maid′less, without a maid ; maid′-pale, (*Shak.*) pale, like a sick girl.—*n.* maid′-servant, a female servant.—maid of all work, a maid who does general housework ; maid of honour (see honour) ; old maid, a woman left unmarried : a card game. [Shortened from maiden.]
maidan, *mī-dän″, n.* an open plain : an open space, an esplanade or parade-ground near a town, in Persia and India. [Pers. *maidān.*]
maiden, *mäd′n, n.* a maid : (*Scot.*) a corn-maiden : (*N. England*) a washing dolly : (*hist.*) a Scottish beheading machine.—*adj.* unmarried : virgin : female : pertaining to a virgin or young woman : consisting of maidens : (*fig.*) unpolluted : fresh : new : unused : in the original or initial state : grown from a seed : that has never been captured, climbed, trodden, penetrated, pruned, &c. : that has never won a race (of a horse) : first.—*ns.* maid′enhair, a fern (Adiantum), with fine foot-stalks : extended to species of spleenwort (maid′en-hair-spleenwort) ; maid′enhair-tree, the ginkgo ; maid′enhead, virginity : the first assay, experience, or use of anything ; maid′enhood, the state or time of being a maiden : maidenhead.—*adjs.* maid′enish (depreciatorily), like a maiden ; maid′enlike.—Also *adv.*—*n.* maid′enliness.—*adj.* maid′enly, maidenlike : becoming a maiden : gentle : modest.—Also *adv.*—*adjs.* maid′en-meek, meek as a maiden ; maid′en-tongued, gentle in voice like a girl.—*n.* maid′enweed, mayweed.—*adj.* maid′en-wid′owed, widowed while still a virgin.

—maiden assize, an assize at which there are no criminal cases ; maiden battle, a first contest ; maiden castle, a common name for a prehistoric earthwork (probably originally of some other meaning) : a castle never taken ; maiden fortress, a fortress that has never been captured ; maiden name, the family name of a married woman before her marriage ; maiden over, in cricket, an over in which no runs are made ; maiden pink, a wild species of pink, *Dianthus deltoides* ; maiden speech, one's first speech, esp. in Parliament ; maiden stakes, in horse-racing, the prize in a race between horses that have not won before the date of entry · maiden voyage, a first voyage. [O.E. *mægden.*]
maidism, *mä′id-izm, n.* pellagra (attributed to a maize diet). [maize.]
maieutic, *mī-* or *mä-ūt′ik, adj.* helping birth, esp. of thoughts.—*n.* (treated as *sing.*) maieut′ics, the Socratic art. [Gr. *maieutikos—maia*, good woman, a midwife ; Socrates, son of a midwife, called himself a midwife to men's thoughts.]
maigre, *mä′gər, meg′r′, adj.* made without flesh : belonging to a fast-day or to a fast.—*adv.* (*obs.*) without using flesh.—*n.* (also meagre, *mē′gər*) a large Mediterranean fish (*Sciaena aquila*) noted for the sounds it emits. [Fr. *maigre*, lean—L. *macer.*]
maik, *mäk, n.* Same as mag (1), or make (3).
mail, *mäl, n.* defensive armour for the body formed of steel rings or network : armour generally : protective covering of an animal.—*v.t.* to clothe in mail.—*adjs.* mail′-clad, clad with a coat of mail ; mailed, protected by mail.—mailed fist, physical force. [Fr. *maille*—L. *macula*, a spot or a mesh.]
mail, *mäl, n.* (*obs.*) a travelling bag : a bag for the conveyance of letters, &c. : the contents of such a bag : post (esp. for long distances ; *U.S.* generally) : correspondence : a batch of letters, &c. : the person or the carriage by which the mail is conveyed.—*v.t.* (esp. *U.S.*) to post : to send by post.—*adj.* mail′able, (*U.S.*) capable of being sent by mail.—*ns.* mail′-bag, a bag in which letters are carried ; mail′-boat, a boat that carries the public mails ; mail′-box, (*U.S.*) a letter-box ; mail′-cart, a cart in which mails are carried : a small hand-cart, with long handles, for the conveyance of children ; mail′-catcher, an apparatus for catching up mail-bags by a train in motion ; mail′-coach, -car, -carriage, -drag, -gig, -van, a conveyance that carries the public mails ; mail′-guard, an officer who guards the public mails ; mail′ing-card, (*U.S.*) a postcard ; mail′ing-table, a table used in a post-office in sorting letters ; mail′man, a postman ; mail′-plane, mail′-train, one that carries the public mails.—mail order, an order for goods sent by post. [O.Fr. *male*, a trunk, a mail—O.H.G. *malha, malaha*, a sack.]
mail, *mäl, n.* (*Scot.*) payment : rent.—*ns.* mail′er, one who pays rent : a cottager ; mail′ing, a rented farm : rent. [Late O.E. *māl*—O.N. *māl*, speech, agreement ; cf. O.E. *mǽl.*]
mail, maile, *mäl, n.* (*obs.*) a halfpenny. [A.Fr. *mayle*—assumed L.L. *metallea* ; see medal.]
mail, *mäl, n.* (*Scot.*) a spot, esp. one caused by ironing cloth.—*v.t.* to spot. [O.E. *māl* ; see mole (1).]
mail, *mäl, v.t.* (*Shak.*) to wrap up (a hawking word).
maim, *mäm, n.* a serious bodily injury : a lameness : the loss of any essential part.—*v.t.* to disable : to mutilate : to lame or cripple : to render defective.—*adj.* maimed.—*adj.* maimed.—*ns.* maimed-ness (*mämd′* or *mäm′id-nis*) ; maim′ing. [O.Fr. *mahaing.*]
main, *mān, n.* might : strength : the principal part : the mainland : the high sea : (*Shak., Milt.*) a great expanse : a principal pipe or conductor in a branching system : that which is essential : the most part : (*obs.*) purpose.—*adj.* (*Milt.*) strong : sheer (as in *main force*) : great : extensive : important : chief, principal : first in importance or extent : leading : general.—*adv.* (*dial.*) exceedingly.—*ns.* main′boom, the spar that extends the foot of a fore-and-aft mainsail ; main′brace, the

brace attached to the mainyard (see **splice**); **main'-course**, mainsail; **main'-deck**, the principal deck of a ship; **main'door**, a door giving independent access to a house, distinguished from one opening upon a common passage: (*Scot.*) a ground-floor house in a tenement building or villa-block, entered from the front by a door of its own; **main'land** (*-land, -land*), the principal or larger land, as opposed to neighbouring islands; **main'-lander.**—*adv.* **main'ly**, chiefly, principally: (*obs.* or *dial.*) much.—*ns.* **main'mast** (*-məst, -mâst*), the principal mast, usually second from the prow; **main'sail** (*-sl, -sāl*), the principal sail, generally attached to the mainmast; **main'-sheet**, the sheet or rope attached to the lower corner of the mainsail; **main'spring**, the spring that gives motion to any piece of machinery, esp. that of a watch or a clock: (*fig.*) principal motive; **main'stay**, a rope stretching forward and down from the top of the mainmast: chief support; **main'top**, a platform on the top of the lower mainmast; **maintop-gall'ant-mast**, the mast above the maintopmast; **maintop'mast**, the mast next above the lower mainmast; **main-top'sail**, the sail above the mainsail, in square-rigged vessels; **main'yard**, the lower yard on the mainmast.—**in the main**, for the most part: on the whole; **main chance** (see **chance**); **might and main**, utmost strength; **Spanish Main** (see **Spanish**). [Partly O.E. *mægen*, strength, partly O.N. *megin*, strong; influence of O.Fr. *maine*, *magne* (—L. *magnus*), great, is questioned.]

main, *mān*, *n.* a banker's shovel. [O.Fr. *main*—L. *manus*, hand.]

main, *mān*, *n.* in hazard, a number (5 to 9) called before throwing the dice: a game of hazard: a cockfighting match: a set of cocks engaged in a match: a match in some other sports. [Perh. same as preceding.]

main, *mān*, *v.t.* (*dial.*; *Shak.*) to lame, maim.

mainor, mainour, manner, *mān'ər, man'ər, n.* act or fact, esp. of theft: that which is stolen.—**in, with, the manner**, in the act: in possession of the thing stolen. [A.Fr. *meinoure, mainoure, mainoevere*; see **manoeuvre**.]

mainprise, *mān'prīz, n.* (*law*) suretyship, esp. for the appearance of a prisoner.—*n.* **mainpernor** (*-pər'nər*), one who gives mainprise. [A.Fr. *mainprise, mainpernour—main*, hand, *prendre*, to take.]

mains, *mānz, n.pl.* (*Scot.*) a home farm. [**demesne, domain.**]

maintain, *men-tān', mən-, mān-, v.t.* to observe or practise: to keep in existence or in any state: to preserve from capture, loss, or deterioration: to uphold: to carry on: to keep up: to support: to make good: to support by argument: to affirm: to defend: (*law*) to support in an action in which one is not oneself concerned.—*adj.* **maintain'able.**—*ns.* **maintain'er**; **maintenance** (*mān'tən-əns*), the act of maintaining, supporting, or defending: continuance: the means of support: defence, protection: (*law*) an interference in a lawsuit, &c., in favour of one of the parties, by one who has no right or interest.—*v.t.* to keep in working order, as a machine or piece of apparatus.—**cap of maintenance**, a cap of dignity borne by or before a noble or other person of rank. [Fr. *maintenir*—L. *manū* (abl.) *tenēre*, to hold in the hand.]

maisonnette, maisonette, *mez-on-et', n.* a small house or flat. [Fr. *maisonnette.*]

maister, *mās'tər* (*obs.* and *Scot.*). Same as **master.**—*ns.* **mais'terdome**; **mais'tring** (both *Spens.*).

maize, *māz, n.* a staple cereal (*Zea Mays*) in America, &c., with large ears (corn-cobs)—called also *Indian corn*, or *mealies*: the yellow colour of maize.—Also *adj.*—**water maize**, *Victoria regia.* [Sp. *maiz*—from Haitian.]

maize, *māz.* Same as **mease** (of herrings).

majesty, *maj'is-ti, n.* greatness and glory of God: grandeur: dignity: elevation of manner or style: royal state: a title of monarchs (*His, Her, Your, Majesty, Their, Your, Majesties*): a representation of God (sometimes Christ) enthroned: the canopy of a hearse.—*adjs.* **majestic** (*mə-jes'tik*), **-al**, having

or exhibiting majesty: stately: sublime.—*adv.* **majes'tically**, in a majestic manner.—*ns.* **majes'-ticalness, majes'ticness**, (*obs.*) majesty. [Fr. *majesté*—L. *mājestās, -ātis—mājor, mājus*, comp. of *magnus*, great.]

Majlis, *māj-lis', n.* the Persian parliament: an assembly.—Also **Mejlis'.** [Pers. *majlis.*]

majolica, *mə-jol'i-kā*, or *-yol'*, *n.* glazed or enamelled earthenware. [Perh. from *Majorca.*]

major, *mā'jər, adj.* greater in number, quantity, size, value, importance, dignity: in boys' schools, senior: (*mus.*) greater (than minor) by a semitone: involving a major third (see below).—*n.* a person of full age (21 years): an officer in rank between a captain and lieutenant-colonel: by courtesy, a sergeant-major: anything that is major opposed to minor: (*U.S.*) a student's special subject: (*obs.*) a kind of wig.—*v.i.* to play the major, strut: (*U.S.*) to specialise at college.—*ns.* **majorat** (*mā-zhō-rä'*; Fr.), primogeniture; **mā'jor-dōmō** (Sp. *mayordomo*, L. *mājor domūs*), an official who has the general management in a large household: a general steward; **mā'jor-gen'eral**, an officer in the army next in rank below a lieutenant-general; **mā'jor-gen'eralcy, mājor-gen'eralship; majoritaire** (*mā-zhor-ē-ter'*; Fr.), a member of a majority section of a party, esp. of socialists; **majority** (*mə-jor'i-ti*), pre-eminence: the greater number: the difference between the greater and the less number: full age (at 21): the office or rank of major.—Also *adj.*—*n.* **mā'jorship.—go over to,** or **join, the majority,** to die; **major axis,** in conic sections, that passing through the foci; **major key, mode, scale,** one with its third a major third above the tonic; **major premise,** (*log.*) that in which the major term occurs; **major suit,** (*bridge*) spades or hearts; **major term,** the term which is the predicate of the conclusion; **major third,** an interval of four semitones; **major tone,** an interval of vibration ratio 8:9. [L. *mājor*, comp. of *magnus.*]

majuscule, *mə-jus'kūl*, or *maj'əs-kūl, n.* (*palaeog.*) a large letter whether capital or uncial.—Also *adj.* —*adj.* **majus'cular.** [L. (*littera*) *mājuscula*, somewhat larger (letter).]

mak, māk, Scots form of **make.**—*n.* **makar** (see **maker**).

make, māk, v.t. to fashion, frame, construct, compose, or form: to create: to bring into being: to produce: to conclude, contract: to bring about: to perform: to force: to cause: to result in: to cause to be: to convert or turn: to appoint: to render: to represent as doing or being: to reckon: to get as result or solution: to occasion: to bring into any state or condition: to establish: (in the navy) to promote: to prepare: (*Shak.*) to shut (as a door): (*cards*) to shuffle: to declare as trumps: to obtain, gain, earn: to score: to constitute: to amount to: to count for: to turn out: to be capable of turning or developing into or serving as: to arrive in sight of: to reach, succeed in reaching: to accomplish, achieve: to attempt, offer, or start: to be occupied with: to do.—*v.i.* behave, esp. deceptively: to proceed: to tend: to contribute: to flow: (*arch.*) to versify: to be in condition for making: (*Scot.*) to matter (as *it maksna*, it does not matter): (*pr.p.* **māk'ing**; *pa.t.* and *pa.p.* **māde**).—*n.* form or shape: structure, texture: build: formation: manufacture: brand: type: making: quantity made: establishment of an electric circuit or contact: trump declaration.—*adj.* **make'-and-break'**, making and breaking a circuit.—*n.* **make'bate**, a mischiefmaker.—*v.i.* **make'-believe**, to pretend, feign: to play at believing.—*n.* feigning.—*adj.* feigned.—*adj.* **make'-do**, makeshift.—*n.* **make'-peace**, (*Shak.*) a peace-maker; **māk'er**, one who makes: the Creator: (*arch.*) esp. in Scots form, **makar**, *māk'ər*) a poet: (*bridge*) the declarer: (*obs.*) a knave in cards: a calker's tool; **make'shift**, a temporary expedient or substitute.—*adj.* of the nature of or characterised by temporary expedient.—*ns.* **make'-up,** the way anything is arranged, composed, or constituted, or the ingredients in *its* constitution: one's character, temperament, mental qualities:

Neutral vowels in unaccented syllables: *el'ə-mənt, in'fənt, ran'dəm*

an actor's or woman's materials for personating a part or being in the fashion : the effect produced thereby : (*print*.) the arrangement of composed types into columns or pages, as in imposition ; **make'-weight,** that which is thrown into a scale to make up the weight : something of little value added to supply a deficiency ; **māk'ing,** the act of forming : structure : form : (in *pl*.) gains : (in *pl*.) that from which something can be made.— **make account of** (see **account**) ; **make a figure,** to be conspicuous ; **make after,** to follow or pursue ; **make a fool of** (see **fool**) ; **make against,** to militate, tell, against ; **make a (good) meal, dinner,** &c., to dine, &c. (plentifully or heartily) ; **make amends,** to render compensation or satisfaction ; **make an ass of oneself,** to behave like a fool ; **make a night of it,** to keep it up (esp. pleasure) for the night ; **make as if,** or **though,** to act as if, to pretend that ; **make at,** to make a hostile movement against ; **make away (with),** to put out of the way, get rid of, destroy, kill ; **make believe** (see **make-believe** above) ; **make bold** (see **bold**) ; **make down,** to re-fashion so as to fit a smaller person : (*Scot*.) to turn down the sheets and blankets of ; **make eyes at** (see **eye**) ; **make for,** to set out for, seek to reach : to favour ; **make free with** (see **free**) ; **make friends,** to become friendly : to acquire friends ; **make good, make head, make light of, make little of, make love to, make merry** (see **good, head,** &c.) ; **make head or tail of,** to find any sense in ; **make much of,** to treat with fondness, to cherish, to foster : to turn to great account : to find much sense in, succeed in understanding ; **make no doubt,** to have no doubt, to be confident ; **make nothing of,** to think it no great matter, have no hesitation or difficulty : to be totally unable to understand ; **make of,** to construct from (as material) : to understand by : (*obs.* and *Scot*.) to make much of, to pet : (*obs*.) to esteem ; **make off with,** to run away with ; **make on,** (*Shak.*) to make much of ; **make one's way,** to proceed : to succeed ; **make or meddle with,** to have to do with, interfere with ; **make out,** to descry : to discern : to decipher : to prove : to seek to make it appear : to draw up : (*obs*.) to achieve : to fill up : to make shift, get along somehow : to succeed ; **make over,** to remake, reconstruct : to transfer ; **make sail,** to increase the quantity of sail : to set sail ; **make sure (of),** to ascertain : to put beyond doubt or risk : to secure : to feel certain : (*obs*.) to betroth ; **make the best of,** to turn to the best advantage : take in the best spirit ; **make the most of,** to use to the best advantage ; **make up,** to fabricate : to feign : to collect : to put together : to parcel : to put into shape : to arrange : to compose (quarrels) : to constitute : to repair : to complete, supplement : to adjust one's appearance (as an actor for a part) : to paint and powder the face : to put type, &c., into columns and pages : to make good : to compensate : (*Shak*.) to decide ; **make up one's mind,** to come to a decision ; **make up to,** to make friendly, adulatory, or amorous approaches to : to compensate ; **make way** (see **way**) ; **on the make,** (*coll*.) bent on self-advancement or promotion. [O.E. *macian* ; Ger. *machen*.]

make, *māk*, *n.* Same as **mag** (1).

make, *māk*, *n.* (*arch*.) a mate, consort, equal.—*adj.* **make'less,** (*Shak*.) without a make or mate. [O.E. (*ge*)*mæcca* ; see **match.**]

makimono, *māk-i-mō'nō*, *n.* a roll, as of silk, esp. a long picture or writing rolled up and not hung. [Jap.]

Malabar-rat, *mal-ə-bär'rat'*, *n.* the bandicoot rat. [*Malabar* in India.]

Malacca-cane, *māl-ak'ə-kān*, *n.* a brown walking-cane made from a rattan. [*Malacca*, a centre of the trade.]

malachite, *mal'ə-kīt*, *n.* a green mineral, basic copper carbonate. [Gr. *malachē*, mallow, as of the colour of a mallow leaf.]

malacia, *mal-ā'shi-ä*, *n.* pathological softening : perverted appetite. [Gr. *malakiā*, softness.]

malacology, *mal-ə-kol'ə-ji*, *n.* the study of mol-

luscs.—*adj.* **malacological** (-*kə-loj'*).—*n.* **malacol'ogist.** [Gr. *malakos*, soft, *logos*, discourse.]

malacophilous, *mal-ə-kof'i-ləs*, *adj.* (*bot*.) pollinated by snails. [Gr. *malakos*, soft, *phileein*, to love.]

Malacopterygii, *mal-ə-kop-tər-ij'i-ī*, *n.pl.* a soft-finned suborder of bony fishes—herrings, salmon, &c.—*adj.* and *n.* **malacopteryg'ian.** [Gr. *malakos*, soft, *pteryx, pterygos*, a wing, fin.]

Malacostraca, *mal-ə-kos'trə-kä*, *n.pl.* the best-known class of crustaceans — crabs, lobsters, shrimps, prawns, &c.—*adj.* and *n.* **malacos'tracan.**—*adj.* **malacos'tracous.** [Gr. *malakos*, soft, *ostrakon*, a shell.]

maladaptation, *mal-ad-ap-tā'shən*, *n.* faulty adaptation. [Fr. *mal*, ill, and **adaptation.**]

maladdress, *mal-ə-dres'*, *n.* awkwardness : clumsiness. [Fr. *maladresse.*]

maladjustment, *mal-ə-just'mənt*, *n.* wrong adjustment. [Fr. *mal*, ill, and **adjustment.**]

maladministration, *mal-əd-min-is-trā'shən*, *n.* bad management, esp. of public affairs.

maladroit, *mal'ə-droit* (or -*droit'*), *adj.* not dexterous : unskilful : clumsy.—*adv.* **maladroit'ly.**—*n.* **maladroit'ness.** [Fr.]

malady, *mal'ə-di*, *n.* illness : disease, either of the body or of the mind : a faulty condition. [Fr. *maladie—malade*, sick—L. *male habitus*, in ill condition—*male*, badly, *habitus*, pa.p. of *habēre*, to have, hold.]

Malaga, *mal'ə-gä*, *n.* a white wine imported from *Málaga.*

Malagasy, *mal-ə-gas'i*, *adj.* of or pertaining to Madagascar or its inhabitants.—*n.* a native of Madagascar : the language of Madagascar.—Also **Malagash'** (or *mal'*).

malaguetta, *mal-ə-get'ä*, *n.* grains of paradise (also **malaguetta pepper**). [Origin obscure.]

malaise, *mal'āz'*, *n.* uneasiness : a feeling of discomfort or of sickness. [Fr. *malaise.*]

malander, mallender, *mal'ən-dər*, *n.* an eruption of the skin behind a horse's knee—often *pl.* [Fr. *malandre*—L. *malandria* (sing. or pl.).]

malapert, *mal'ə-pərt*, *adj.* bold : forward : saucy : impudent. — *adv.* **mal'apertly.** — *n.* **mal'apert'ness.** [O.Fr. *mal* (L. *malus*), bad, *appert* for *espert* (L. *expertus*), but understood in English as if—Fr. *apert*, open, outspoken—L. *apertus*, open.]

malappropriate, *mal-ə-prō'pri-āt*, *v.t.* to misuse.—*n.* **malappropria'tion.** [Fr. *mal*, ill, and **appropriate.**]

malapropism, *mal'ə-prop-izm*, *n.* misapplication of words without mispronunciation, from Mrs *Malaprop* in Sheridan's play, *The Rivals,* who uses words *malapropos.*

malapropos, *mäl-ä-prō-pō'*, *adj.* out of place : unsuitable : inapt.—*adv.* not, or ill, apropos : not suited to the purpose : unseasonably. [Fr. *mal*, ill, and **apropos.**]

malar, *mā'lər, adj.* pertaining to the cheek.—*n.* the cheek-bone. [L. *māla*, the cheek—*mandēre*, to chew.]

malaria, *mə-lā'ri-ä*, *n.* poisonous air arising from marshes, once believed to produce fever : miasma : the fever once attributed thereto, actually due to a protozoan parasite transmitted by mosquitoes.—*adjs.* **malā'rial, malā'rian, malā'rious.** [It. *mal' aria*—L. *malus*, bad, *āēr, āēris*, air.]

malassimilation, *mal-ə-sim-i-lā'shən*, *n.* imperfect assimilation or nutrition. [Fr. *mal*, ill, and **assimilation.**]

malate. See **malic.**

Malay, -an, *mə-lā', -ən, ns.* a member of a race inhabiting Malacca and the Malay Archipelago : the language of the Malays.—*adjs.* of the Malays, their language, or of their countries.—*adj.* **Malay'sian** (-*si-ən, -shən, -zhən*), relating to the Malay Archipelago. [Malay *malāyu.*]

Malayalam, *mä-lä-yä'läm*, *n.* the Dravidian language of Malabar.—Also *adj.*

malconformation, *mal-kon-for-mā'shən*, *n.* bad conformation or form. [Fr. *mal*, ill, and **conformation.**]

malcontent, *mal'kən-tent*, *adj.* discontented, dissatisfied, esp. in political matters.—*n.* one discontented. — *adj.* **malcontent'ed.** — *adv.* **malcontent'edly.**—*n.* **malcontent'edness.** [O.Fr. *malcontent.*]

male, *māl*, *n.* (*Spens.*) for mail (armour).

male, *māl*, *adj.* masculine: of or pertaining to the sex that begets (not bears) young, or produces relatively small gametes: (*bot.*) staminate: (*mach.*) adapted to fit into a corresponding hollow part.— *n.* one of the male sex: (*Shak.*) apparently, a father.—*n.* **male'-fern**, an elegant woodland fern once fancied to be the male of the lady-fern.— **male orchis**, the early purple orchis (cf. **Orchis**); **male order**, in architecture, the Doric order: **male rhymes**, those in which only the final syllables correspond. [O.Fr. *male*—L. *masculus*, *male*—*mās*, a male.]

Malebolge, *mä-lä-bol'jä*, *n.* the eighth circle of Dante's Hell. [It., bad holes or pits, lit. pockets.]

malediction, *mal-i-dik'shən*, *n.* evil-speaking: a calling down of evil.—*adjs.* **maledicent** (*-dī'sənt*), cursing· **mal'edict** (*-dikt*), accursed.—*v.t.* and *v.i.* to curse.—*adj.* **maledic'tory**. [L. *maledīcĕre*, *-dictum*—*male*, ill, *dīcĕre*, to speak.]

malefactor, *mal'i-fak-tər*, *n.* an evil-doer: a criminal.—*n.* **malefac'tion**, (*Shak.*) a crime, an offence.—*adj.* **malefac'tory**, **malefic** (*mal-ef'ik*), doing mischief: producing evil.—*adv.* **malef'ically.**—*ns.* **mal'efice** (*-i-fis*; *arch.*), an evil deed: enchantment: **maleficence** (*-ef'i-səns*). — *adjs.* **malef'icent**, **maleficial** (*mal-i-fish'l*; *rare*), hurtful: wrong-doing. [L. *male*, ill, *facĕre*, to do.]

maleic. See under **malic.**

malemute, *mäl'ə-mūt*, *n.* an Eskimo dog.—Also **mal'amute.** [From a tribe on the Alaskan coast.]

malengine, *mal-en'jin*, *n.* (*Spens.*) evil device: deceit. [O.Fr. *malengin*—L. *malus*, bad, *ingenium*, ingenuity.]

malevolent, *mal-ev'ə-lənt*, *adj.* wishing evil: ill-disposed towards others: rejoicing in another's misfortune. — *n.* **malev'olence.** — *adv.* **malev'olently.** [L. *male*, ill, *volēns*, *-entis*, pr.p. of *velle*, to wish.]

malfeasance, *mal-fē'zəns*, *n.* evil-doing: the doing of what one ought not to do: an illegal deed, esp. of an official.—*adj.* **malfea'sant.** [Fr. *malfaisance* —L. *male*, ill, *facĕre*, to do.]

malformation, *mal-for-mā'shən*, *n.* faulty structure: deformity.—*adj.* **malformed'.** [Fr. *mal*, ill, and **formation.**]

malgrado, *mal-grä'dō*, *prep.* (*obs.*) in spite of. [It.]

malgre. Same as **maugre.**

malic, *mā'lik*, *mal'ik*, *adj.* obtained from apple juice—applied to an acid ($H_6C_4O_5$) found in unripe fruits.—*n.* **ma'late**, a salt of malic acid.— *adj.* **maleic** (*mə-lē'ik*).—**maleic acid**, an acid, isomeric with fumaric acid, got from malic acid. [L. *mālum*, an apple; Gr. *mēlon*.]

malice, *mal'is*, *n.* ill-will: spite: disposition or intention to harm another or others: a playfully mischievous attitude of mind.—*v.t.* to have ill-will against: to wish to injure (*pa.p.* in *Spens.*) **mal'ist**).—*adj.* **malicious** (*mə-lish'us*), bearing ill-will or spite: moved by hatred or ill-will: mischievous.—*adv.* **malic'iously.**—*n.* **malic'iousness.** [Fr.,—L. *malitia*—*malus*, bad.]

malicho, *mal'i-chō*, *n.* (*Shak.*) mischief. [Conjectured to be for Sp. *malhecho*, mischief.]

malign, *mə-lin'*, *adj.* baleful: injurious: malignant.—*v.t.* to speak evil of, especially falsely and rancorously, to defame: (*obs.*) to regard with malice, envy, or hatred: to grudge.—*ns.* **malign'er**; **malignity** (*mə-lig'ni-ti*), state or quality of being malign: great hatred, virulence: deadly quality.—*adv.* **malign'ly.**—*n.* **malign'ment.** [Fr. *malin*, fem. *maligne*—L. *malignus* for *maligenus*, of evil disposition—*malus*, bad, and *gen-*, root of *genus.*]

malignant, *mə-lig'nənt*, *adj.* disposed to do harm or cause suffering: actuated by great hatred: (*hist.*) Royalist or Cavalier: (*med.*) tending to cause death, or to go from bad to worse: esp. cancerous.—*n.* a Royalist or Cavalier.—*ns.* **malig'nance**, **malig'nancy.**—*adv.* **malig'nantly.** [L. *malignāns*, *-āntis*, pr.p. of *malignāre*, to act maliciously.]

malinger, *mə-ling'gər*, *v.i.* to feign sickness in order to avoid duty.—*ns.* **maling'erer**; **maling'ery,** feigned sickness. [Fr. *malingre*, sickly.]

malison, *mal'i-zn*, *-sn*, *n.* a curse—opp. to **benison.** [O.Fr. *maleison*; a doublet of **malediction.**]

malkin, *maw'kin*, *n.* (*Shak.*) a dirty or lewd woman: a mop: a scarecrow: (*Scot.*) a hare.—Also **maw'kin.** [Dim. of *Matilda*, *Maud.*]

mall, *mawl*, or *mal*, *n.* a maul, large wooden beetle or hammer: a mallet for the old game of pall-mall: the game itself: a pall-mall alley: (from a former alley of the kind in London) a level shaded walk: a public walk.—*v.t.* to maul or beat. [See **maul** and **pall-mall.**]

mallard, *mal'ərd*, *n.* the male of the common wild duck. [O.Fr. *mallart*, *malart*; origin obscure.]

malleate, *mal'i-āt*, *v.t.* to hammer: to beat thin.— *adj.* **mall'eable**, capable of being beaten, rolled, &c., into a new shape.—*ns.* **mall'eableness,** **malleabil'ity**; **mallea'tion,** hammering: a hammer-mark.—*adj.* **malleiform** (*mal'ē-i-form*), hammer-shaped.—*n.* **malleus** (*mal'i-əs*), one of the small bones of the middle ear in mammals. [L. *malleus*, a hammer.]

malicho, an editorial emendation of **malicho** (*Shak.*).

mallee, *mal'ē*, *n.* dwarf Eucalyptus, esp. *E. dumosa.* —*ns.* **mall'ee-bird, -fowl, -hen**, an Australian mound-bird; **mall'ee-scrub'**, a thicket formation of mallee. [Australian word.]

mallemaroking, *mal'i-mə-rō'king*, *n.* the visiting and carousing of seamen in Greenland ships. [Du. *mallemerok*, a romping woman—*mal*, foolish, *marok*—Fr. *marotte*, a favoured object.]

mallemuck, *mal'i-muk*, *n.* the fulmar or similar bird. [Du. *mallemok*—*mal*, foolish, *mok*, gull; Ger. *mallemuck.*]

malleolus, *mə-lē'ə-ləs*, *n.* a bony protuberance on either side of the ankle.—*adj.* **mallē'olar** (or *mal'i-*). [L. *malleolus*, dim. of *malleus*, hammer.]

mallet, *mal'it*, *n.* a small wooden hammer: a long-handled hammer for playing croquet or polo. [Fr. *maillet*, dim. of *mail*, a mall.]

Mallophaga, *mal-of'gä*, *n.pl.* an order of wingless parasitic insects, bird-lice or biting-lice.—*adj.* **malloph'agous.** [Gr. *mallos*, a flock of wool, *phagein*, to eat.]

mallow, *mal'ō*, *n.* any plant of the genus *Malva*, from its emollient properties or its soft downy leaves: extended to other genera of Malvaceae. [O.E. *m(e)alwe*—L. *malva*; Gr. *malachē*—*malassein*, to soften.]

malm, *mäm*, *n.* calcareous loam, earth specially good for brick: an artificial mixture of clay and chalk. [O.E. *m(e)alm* (*-stán*), a soft (stone).]

malmag, *mal'mag*, *n.* the tarsier. [Philippine word.]

malmsey, *mäm'zi*, *n.* a sort of grape: a strong and sweet wine, first made in Greece and exported from *Monembasia.*—Also **malvasia** (*mäl-vä-sē'ä*), **malvesie**, **malvoisie** (*mäl'və-zi, -voi-zi*). [L.L. *malmasia*; cf. O.Fr. *malvesie*, Fr. *malvoisie*, It. *malvasia*, Sp. *malvasía.*]

malnutrition, *mal-nū-trish'ən*, *n.* imperfect or faulty nutrition. [Fr. *mal*, ill, and **nutrition.**]

malodour, *mal-ō'dər*, *n.* an ill smell.—*adj.* **malo'dorous.**—*n.* **malo'dorousness.** [Fr. *mal*, ill, and **odour.**]

Malpighia, *mal-pig'i-ä*, *n.* the Barbados cherry genus of tropical American trees, shrubs, and lianes, giving name to the family **Malpighiā'ceae**, of the geranium cohort.—*adj.* **Malpigh'ian**, applied to several structures, esp. in the kidney, investigated by Marcello *Malpighi* (1628-94).

malposition, *mal-po-zish'ən*, *n.* a wrong position, misplacement.

malpractice, *mal-prak'tis*, *n.* evil practice or conduct: professional misconduct: treatment falling short of reasonable skill or care: illegal attempt of a person in trust to benefit himself at others' cost.—*n.* **malpractitioner** (*-tish'ən-ər*).

malpresentation, *mal-prez-ən-tā'shən*, *n.* abnormal presentation in childbirth.

malstick. See **maul-stick.**

malt, *mawlt*, *n.* barley or other grain steeped in water, allowed to sprout, and dried in a kiln, used in brewing ale, &c.: malt liquor.—*v.t.* to make into malt: to treat or combine with malt.—*v.i.* to become malt: (*facet.*) to drink malt liquor.—*adj.* containing or made with malt.—*ns.* **malt′ase,** an enzyme that produces grape-sugar from maltose; **malt′-dust,** grain-sprouts produced and 'screened off' in malt-making; **malt′-ex′tract,** a fluid medicinal food made from malt; **malt′-floor,** a perforated floor in the chamber of a malt-kiln, through which heat rises; **malt′-horse,** a heavy horse, such as used by brewers—hence (*Shak.*) a dull, stupid person; **malt′-house, malt′-ing,** a building where malt is made; **malt′-kiln**; **malt′-mill,** a mill for grinding malt; **malt′ose,** a hard, white crystalline sugar, formed by the action of malt or diastase on starch; **malt′-ster, malt′man,** one whose occupation it is to make malt; **malt′worm,** (*Shak.*) a lover of malted liquors, a tippler.—*adj.* **malt′y.**—**malt liquor,** a liquor, as ale or porter, formed from malt; **malt tea,** the liquid infusion of the mash in brewing. [O.E. *m(e)alt*; cf. Ger. *malz*.]

Malta, *mawl′tä,* adj. of the island of Malta.—*adj.* **Maltese** (*-tez′,* or *mawl′*), of Malta, its people, or language.—*n.* one of the people of Malta (*pl.* **Maltese**): the language of Malta—Arabic with a strong Italian infusion.—**Malta fever,** undulant fever, once common in Malta; **Maltese cross,** the badge of the Knights of Malta, a cross with two-pointed expanding limbs; **Maltese dog,** a very small spaniel with long silky hair. [L. *Melita,* Gr. *Melitē.*]

maltalent, *mal′tal-ənt, n.* (*Spens.*) ill-will. [Fr. *mal,* ill, *talent,* disposition; see **talent.**]

maltha, *mal′thä, n.* a thick mineral pitch: an ancient cement. [Gr.]

Malthusian, *mal-thūz′i-ən, adj.* relating to Thomas Robert *Malthus* (1766-1834), or to his teaching concerning the increase of population outstripping that of the means of living.—*n.* a disciple of Malthus.—*n.* **Malthus′ianism.**

maltreat, *mal-trēt′, v.t.* to use roughly or unkindly. —*n.* **maltreat′ment.** [Fr. *maltraiter*—L. *male,* ill, *tractāre,* to treat.]

Malva, *mal′vä, n.* the mallow genus, giving name to the family **Malvā′ceae,** including hollyhock, cotton, &c., akin to the lime family.—*adj.* **malvā′-ceous.** [L.; cf. **mallow.**]

malversation, *mal-vər-sā′shən, n.* evil conduct: misbehaviour in office: corrupt administration (of funds): corruption: extortion. [Fr.,—L. *male,* badly, *versāri, -ātus,* to occupy oneself.]

malvoisie. Same as **malmsey.**

mamba, *mäm′bä, n.* (*S.Afr.*) a large, deadly African snake (Dendraspis), black or green. [Kaffir *im mamba,* large snake.]

mamelon, *mam′ə-lən, n.* a rounded hill or pro-tuberance. [Fr., nipple.]

mameluco, *mam-e-lōō′kō, n.* in Brazil the offspring of white and Indian. [Port.; cf. **Mameluke.**]

Mameluke, *mam′e-lōōk, n.* one of a military force originally of Circassian slaves—afterwards the ruling class and sultans of Egypt: a slave, esp. white. [Ar. *mamlûk,* a purchased slave—*malaka,* to possess.]

mamilla, *mam-il′ä, n.* the nipple of the mammary gland: a nipple-shaped protuberance:—*pl.* **mam-ill′ae** (*-ē*).—*adjs.* **mam′illar, mam′illary,** per-taining to the breast: nipple-shaped: studded with rounded projections; **mam′illate, mam′il-lated,** having mamillae: nipple-shaped.—*n.* **mam-illā′tion.**—*adj.* **mamill′iform.** — Also **mam-mill′a,** &c. [L. *mam(m)illa,* dim. of *mamma.*]

mamma, mama, *mä-mä′* (*U.S.* *mä′mä*), *n.* mother —once considered genteel, now used chiefly by young children.—*n.* **mammy** (*mam′i*), a child's word for mother: (*U.S.*) a black nurse. [Repeti-tion of *ma,* a child's natural utterance.]

mamma, *mam′ä, n.* the milk gland: the breast:— *pl.* **mammae** (*-ē*).—*adjs.* **mamm′ary,** of the nature of, relating to, the mammae or breasts; **mamm′ate,** having breasts.—*n.* **mamm′ifer,** a mammal.—*adjs.* **mammif′erous,** having mammae; **mamm′iform,** having the form of a breast.—*n.* **mammill′a** (see **mamilla**). [L. *mamma.*]

mammal, *mam′əl, n.* a member of the **Mammalia** (*ma-mā′li-ä*), the class of animals that suckle their young.—*adjs.* **mammā′lian**; **mammalif′erous,** (*geol.*) bearing remains of mammals; **mammalog′-ical.** — *ns.* **mammalogist** (*-al′ə-jist*); **mam-mal′ogy,** the scientific knowledge of mammals. [L. *mammālis,* of the breast—*mamma,* the breast.]

mammee, *mam-ē′, n.* a highly esteemed fruit (also **mammee apple**) of the West Indies, &c., having a sweet taste and aromatic odour: the tree producing it (*Mammea americana*; family Guttiferae).—*n.* **mammee′-sapo′ta,** the marmalade tree or its fruit. [Sp. *mamey,* from Haitian.]

mammer, *mam′ər, v.i.* (*Shak.*) to hesitate, to stand muttering and in doubt. [Prob. imit.]

mammet, *mam′it,* **maumet, mawmet,** *mawm′it,* **mommet,** *mom′it,* n. an idol: (*Shak.*) a puppet, a figure dressed up.—*n.* **mamm′etry, maum′-etry, maw′metry,** idolatry: idols collectively: Mohammedanism. [**Mohammed**; cf. **Mahound.**]

mammilla, &c. See **mamilla.**

mammock, *mam′ək, n.* a shapeless piece, shred.— *v.t.* (*Shak.*) to tear to pieces, to mangle. [Origin obscure.]

mammon, *mam′ən, n.* riches: (**Mammon**) the god of riches.—*adj.* **mamm′onish,** devoted to money-getting.—*ns.* **mamm′onism,** devotion to gain; **mamm′onist, mamm′onite,** a person devoted to riches: a worldling.—*adj.* **mammon-ist′ic.** [L.L. *mam(m)ōna* — Gr. *mam(m)ōnās* — Aramaic *māmōn,* riches.]

mammoth, *mam′əth, n.* an extinct species of elephant. — *adj.* resembling the mammoth in size: gigantic.—*n.* **mamm′oth-tree′,** a Sequoia. [Former Russ. *mammot* (now *mamont*).]

man, *man, n.* a human being: mankind: a grown-up human male: a male attendant or servant: a workman employed by a master: a vassal: a common soldier: one possessing a distinctively manly character: a husband: a piece used in playing chess or draughts or similar game: a cairn or rock pillar: a hill with such a man: a ship, as in **man-of-war:** a word of familiar address: formerly in the Highlands, a layman of peculiar holiness and austerity: (*pl.* **men**).—*adj.,* also in composition (as **man′-cook′**), male. — *v.t.* to furnish with a man or men: to strengthen or put manhood into:—*pr.p.* **mann′ing;** *pa.t.* and *pa.p.* **manned** (*mand*).—*ns.* **man′-at-arms′,** a soldier, esp. mounted and heavy-armed; **man′-body,** (*Scot.*) a male man; **man′-child,** a male child: a boy:—*pl.* **men′-children; man′dom,** (*rare*) humanity, men collectively; **man′-eater,** a canni-bal: a tiger or other beast that has acquired the habit of eating men.—*adjs.* **man′-en′tered,** (*Shak.*) entered upon manhood; **man′ful,** having the good qualities of a man: full of manliness: bold: courageous: vigorous: stout: noble-minded.— *adv.* **man′fully,** in a manful manner: stoutly.— *n.* **man′fulness.**—*v.t.* **man′handle,** to move by man-power: (*slang*) to handle roughly, knock about.—*ns.* **man′hole,** a hole large enough to admit a man, esp. to a sewer, cable-duct, or the like; **man′hood,** state of being a man: manly quality: human nature; **man′-hour,** an hour's work of one man; **man′-jack,** **man jack′,** in-dividual man (as *every man-jack*); **man′kind′,** the human race: the mass of human beings: (*man′-kind*) human males collectively.—*adj.* (*Shak.*) man-like, viragoish. — *adj.* **man′-like,** having the appearance or qualities of a human being or of an adult human male.—*adv.* in the manner of a man: as might be expected of a male man: manfully. —*n.* **man′liness.**—*adj.* **man′ly,** becoming a man: brave: dignified: noble: pertaining to manhood: not childish or womanish; **man′-made,** made by man, humanly made or originated.—*n.* **man′-mill′iner,** a man engaged in millinery—often in contempt.—*adjs.* **man′-mind′ed,** having the mind or qualities of a man; **manned** (*mand*); **mann′-ish,** like or savouring of a male or grown-up man (usu. depreciatory): masculine.—*ns.* **mann′ish-ness; man′-of-war′,** a warship: (*arch.* or *facet.*) a soldier: (in full **man-of-war bird**) the frigate-bird: (Portuguese **man-of-war,** see **Physalia**);

man'-of-war's'-man, a man who serves on board a war-ship; **man'-or'chis,** an orchid (*Aceras anthropophora*) whose flowers are like little men; **man'-power,** the agency or energy of man in doing work: the rate at which a man can work: available resources in population or in able-bodied men; **man'-queller,** (*Shak.*) a man-killer, a murderer; **man'-servant,** a male servant:—*pl.* **men'-servants; man'slaughter,** the slaying of a man: (*law*) criminal or culpable homicide— without malice aforethought; **man'-slayer,** one who kills a man; **man'stealer,** one who steals human beings, especially to make slaves of them; **man'trap,** a trap for catching trespassers: any insidious danger to passengers; **men'folk(s),** male people.—**man about town,** a fashionable idler, dangling about clubs, theatres, &c.; **man alive!** an exclamation of surprise; **Man Friday,** a factotum or servile attendant—from Robinson Crusoe's man; **manhood suffrage,** right to vote accorded to male citizens in general; **man in the moon,** a fancied semblance of a man seen in the moon; **man in the street,** the ordinary, every-day man—Tom, Dick, or Harry; **man of business,** an agent or a lawyer; **man of God,** a holy man: a clergyman; **man of his hands,** a man of prowess; **man of law,** a lawyer; **man of letters,** a scholar: a writer; **man of sin,** the devil: Antichrist: **man of straw,** a person of no substance (esp. financially): one nominally, but not really, responsible; **man of the world,** one accustomed to the ways and dealings of men; **man to man,** one man to another as individuals in fight or talk: frank and confidential; **to a man,** without exception. [O.E. *mann*; Ger. *mann*, Du. *man*.]

mana, *mä'nä, n.* (*anthrop.*) a mysterious power associated with persons and things. [Maori.]

manacle, *man'ə-kl, n.* a handcuff.—*v.t.* to handcuff: to shackle. [O.Fr. *manicle*—L. *manicula,* dim. of *manica,* sleeve, glove, handcuff—*manus,* hand.]

manage, *man'ij, n.* manège.—*v.t.* to train by exercise, as a horse: to handle: to wield: to conduct: to control: to administer, be at the head of: to deal tactfully with: (*obs.*) to husband, use sparingly: to contrive successfully: to be able to cope with: to manipulate: to contrive.—*v.i.* to conduct affairs: to get on, contrive to succeed.—*n.* **manageabil'ity,** the quality of being manageable.—*adj.* **man'ageable,** that can be managed: governable.—*n.* **man'ageableness.**—*adv.* **man'ageably.**—*ns.* **man'agement,** art or act of managing: manner of directing or of using anything: administration: skilful treatment: a body of managers; **man'ager,** one who manages: a person who controls a business or other concern: one who organises other people's doings: a domestic contriver: (*U.S.*) a party leader:—*fem.* **man'ageress; man'agership.** — *adjs.* **manage'rial,** of or pertaining to a manager, or to management; **man'aging.**—Also *n.* [It. *maneggio*—L. *manus,* the hand.]

manakin, *man'ə-kin, n.* a small tropical American bird of various species of or akin to the Cotinga family: a manikin. [See **manikin.**]

manatee, manati, *man-ə-tē', n.* a sirenian (Manatus or Trichechus) of the warm parts of the Atlantic and the rivers of Brazil. [Sp. *manati*—Carib *manatoui*; not connected with L. *manus,* hand.]

mancando, *mangk-an'dō, adj.* and *adv.* (*mus.*) fading away. [It., lacking.]

manche, *mänsh, n.* (*her.*) a sleeve. [Fr.]

Manchester, *man'chis-tər, adj.* belonging to or made in *Manchester,* or similar to goods made in Manchester, applied esp. to cotton cloths.—**Manchester school,** the followers of Bright and Cobden, advocates of free-trade and of individual freedom of action.

manchet, *man'chit, n.* (*arch.*) the finest bread of wheat: a loaf of manchet. [Origin obscure.]

manchineel, *manch-i-nēl', n.* a tropical American tree (Hippomane) of the spurge family, with poisonous latex. [Sp. *manzanilla,* dim. of *manzana,* apple.]

Manchu, Manchoo, *man-chōō', or man', n.* one of the race from which Manchuria took its name, and which governed China from the 17th to the 20th century: their language.—*adj.* of or pertaining to Manchuria or to its inhabitants.—*n.* **Manchu'ria** (Jap. **Manchukuo,** *-kwō').—adj.* **Manchur'ian.** [Manchu, pure.]

mancipation, *man-si-pā'shən, n.* (*Rom. hist.*) a legal transfer by actual or symbolic sale.—*v.t.* **man'cipate.**—*adj.* **man'cipatory** (*-pə-tə-ri*). [L. *mancipātiō, -ōnis*—*manus,* hand, *capēre,* to take.]

manciple, *man'si-pl, n.* a steward: a purveyor, particularly of a college or an inn of court. [O.Fr., —L. *manceps, -cipis,* a purchaser; see foregoing.]

Mancunian, *man(g)-kūn'i-ən, adj.* belonging to Manchester.—*n.* a Manchester man. [Doubtful L. *Mancunium,* a Roman station in Manchester. *Mamucium* is probably right.]

mancus, *mang'kus, n.* (*hist.*) an old English coin or its value, thirty pence:—*pl.* **manc'uses.** [O.E. *mancus.*]

mand, (*Spens.*) for **manned.** See **man.**

Mandaean, *man-dē'ən, n.* and *adj.* one of an ancient and surviving sect in southern Babylonia, their religion a corrupt Gnosticism, with many Jewish and Parsee elements.—Also *Mendaites, Nasoraeans, Sabians,* or (misleadingly) *Christians of St John*: the Aramaic dialect of their sacred books.—Also *adj.* [Mandaean *mandayyā,* knowledge, gnosis.]

mandamus, *man-dā'məs, n.* a writ or command issued by a higher court to a lower:—*pl.* **manda'-muses.** [L. *mandāmus,* we command.]

mandarin, *man'da-rin, -rēn, n.* a European name for a Chinese official, civil or military: the official form of the Chinese language: a man in office, person of importance, big-wig: a small kind of orange, thought to be of Chinese origin: the colour thereof: a liqueur.—Also **man'darine** (*-ēn*).—*n.* **man'darinate**—**mandarin duck,** a crested Asiatic duck (*Aix galericulata*). [Port. *mandarim*—Malay (from Hind.) *mantrī,* counsellor —Sans. *mantra,* counsel.]

mandate, *man'dāt, n.* a charge: a command from a superior official or judge to an inferior, ordering him how to act, esp. from the Pope to a legate, &c.: a right given to a person to act in name of another: a rescript of the Pope: the sanction held to be given by the electors to members of parliament to deal with a question that was before the country at the election: power conferred upon a state by the League of Nations to govern a region elsewhere.—*v.t.* to assign by mandate.—*ns.* **man'datary, man'datory** (*-də-tə-ri*), the holder of a mandate: a mandate; **mandā'tor,** the giver of a mandate.—*adj.* **man'datory,** containing a mandate or command: of the nature of a mandate: bestowed by mandate: (*U.S.*) compulsory: preceptive: directory. [L. *mandātum*—*mandāre*—*manus,* hand, *dāre,* give.]

mandible, *man'di-bl, n.* a jaw or jaw-bone, esp. the lower: either part of a bird's bill: an organ performing the functions of a jaw in the lower animals, as one of the first pair of mouth appendages in insects or crustaceans.—*adjs.* **mandib'ular,** relating to the jaw; **mandib'ulate, -d.** [L. *mandibula*—*mandēre,* to chew.]

mandioc, mandioca, mandiocca. Same as **manioc.**

mandoline, mandolin, *man'də-lin, -lēn, n.* a round-backed instrument like a guitar.—*ns.* **mandō'la, mandō'ra,** a large mandoline. [It. *mandola, mandora,* dim. *mandolino.*]

mandorla, *män'dor-lä, n.* an oval panel, or a work of art filling one: the *vesica piscis.* [It., almond.]

mandrake, *man'drāk, n.* a poisonous plant (Mandragora) of the potato family, subject of many strange fancies: extended to various other plants, as white bryony.—(*Shak.*) **mandragora** (*-drag'ə-rä*). [L. *mandragora*—Gr. *mandragorās.*]

mandrel, mandril, *man'drəl, n.* a bar of iron fitted to a turning-lathe on which articles to be turned are fixed: the axle of a circular saw. [Fr. *mandrin.*]

mandrill, *man'dril, n.* a large West African baboon. [Prob. **man,** and **drill** (baboon).]

manducate, *man'dū-kāt, v.t.* to chew or eat.—*adj.*

man'ducable.—*n.* **manduca'tion.**—*adj.* **man'-ducatory** (-kə-tə-ri). [L. *mandūcāre*—*mandĕre*, to chew.]

mane, măn, *n.* long hair on the back of the neck and neighbouring parts, as in the horse and the lion: a long bushy head of hair.—*adjs.* **maned; mane'less.**—*n.* **mane'-sheet,** a covering for the upper part of a horse's head. [O.E. *manu*; O.N. *mön*; Ger. *mähne.*]

manège, *man-ezh'*, *n.* the managing of horses: the art of horsemanship or of training horses: a horse's actions and paces as taught him: a riding-school.—*v.t.* to train, as a horse. [Fr.; cf. **manage.**]

maneh. See **mina.**

manes, *mā'nēz, n.pl.* (*Roman myth.*) the spirits of the dead. [L. *mānēs.*]

maneuver. See **manoeuvre.**

mangabeira, *mang-gä-bā'rä,* *n.* a Brazilian apocynaceous rubber tree (*Hancornia speciosa*). [Port., —Tupi *mangaba.*]

mangabey, *mang'gə-bā,* *n.* the white-eyelid monkey, any species of the mainly West African genus *Cercocebus,* esp. the sooty mangabey. [From a district in Madagascar, where they are not found.]

mangal, *mang-gäl',* *n.* a brazier. [Turk.]

manganese, *mang'gə-nēz,* or *nēz',* *n.* a hard brittle greyish-white metallic element (Mn; at. numb. 25): (originally and commercially) its dioxide (*black manganese*) or other ore.—*n.* **mang'anate,** a salt of manganic acid.—*adjs.* **manganic** (-*gan'ik*), of manganese of higher valency; **manganif'erous,** containing manganese.—*ns.* **mang'anin,** an alloy of copper with manganese and some nickel; **mang'anite,** (*chem.*) a salt of manganous acid: (*min.*) a grey ore, hydrated oxide of manganese.—*adj.* **mang'anous,** of manganese of lower valency. —**manganese bronze,** a bronze or brass with a little manganese; **manganese spar,** rhodochrosite. [Fr. *manganèse* — It. *manganese* — L. *magnēsia.*]

mange. See **mangy.**

mangel - wurzel, mangold - wurzel, *mang'gl-wur'zl,* *n.* a variety of beet cultivated as cattle food.—Also **mang'el, mang'old.** [Ger. *mangold,* beet, *wurzel,* root.]

manger, *mānj'ər,* *n.* a trough in which food is laid for horses and cattle.—**dog in the manger,** one who will neither enjoy something himself nor let others do so—also adjectively. [O.Fr. *mangeoire* —L. *mandūcāre,* to chew, eat.]

mangle, *mang'gl,* *v.t.* to hack to raggedness: to tear in cutting: to mutilate: to bungle grossly.— *n.* **mang'ler.** [A.Fr. *mangler, mahangler,* prob. a freq. of O.Fr. *mahaigner,* to maim—*mahaing,* a hurt.]

mangle, *mang'gl,* *n.* a rolling-press for smoothing linen.—*v.t.* to smooth with a mangle: to calender. —*n.* **mang'ler.** [Du. *mangel*—Gr. *manganon*; cf. **mangonel.**]

mango, *mang'gō,* *n.* an East Indian tree (*Mangifera indica*) of the cashew-nut family: its fleshy fruit, smacking of turpentine: a green musk-melon pickled:—*pl.* **mang'oes.**—**wild mango,** Irvingia (Simarubaceae). [Port. *manga*—Malay *manggā*— Tamil *mān-kāy,* mango-fruit.]

mangold, mangold-wurzel. See **mangel-wurzel.**

mangonel, *mang'gə-nel,* *n.* a mediaeval engine for throwing stones, &c. [O.Fr.,—L.L. *mangonum*— Gr. *manganon.*]

mangosteen, *mang'gə-stēn,* *n.* a tree (*Garcinia Mangostana*) of the Malay Peninsula and Archipelago: its dark brown, orange-shaped fruit, with thick rind and delicious rose-coloured pulp. —Also **mang'ostan.** [Malay *mangustan.*]

mangrove, (*mang'grōv,* *n.* a tree, esp. species of Rhizophora, that grows in muddy swamps covered at high tide or on tropical coasts and estuary shores. [Origin obscure.]

mangy, *mānj'i,* *adj.* scabby: affected with mange. —*ns.* **mange** (*mānj*; a back-formation), inflammation of the skin of animals caused by mites; **mang'iness.** [Fr. *mangé,* eaten, pa.p. of *manger*— L. *mandūcāre,* to chew.]

Manhattan, *man-hat'ən,* *n.* an American cocktail containing vermouth, whisky, bitters, &c. [*Manhattan,* New York.]

mania, *mā'ni-ä,* *n.* violent madness: insanity: excessive or unreasonable desire: a craze.—*n.* **mā'niac,** a person affected with mania: a madman.—*adj.* raving mad.—*adj.* **maniacal** (*mə-nī'ə-kl*).—*adv.* **mani'acally.**—*adj.* **manic** (*man'ik*), of or affected by mania.—**manic-depressive insanity,** a form in which there are phases of depression and elation, either alone or alternately, with lucid intervals. [L.,—Gr. *maniā.*]

Manichaean, Manichean, *man-i-kē'ən, adj.* pertaining to the *Manichees* or followers of *Mani,* a native of Ecbatana (*c.* 216-*c.* 276 A.D.), who taught that everything sprang from two chief principles, light and darkness, or good and evil.—*n.* a believer in Manichaeanism—also **Man'ichee.**—*ns.* **Manichae'anism, Man'ichaeism, Maniche'anism, Man'icheism.**

manicure, *man'i-kūr,* *n.* the care of hands and nails: one who practises this.—*v.t.* to apply manicure to.—*n.* **man'icurist.** [L. *manus,* hand, *cūra,* care.]

manifest, *man'i-fest, adj.* that may be easily seen by the eye or perceived by the mind: clear: apparent: evident.—*v.t.* to make clear or easily seen: to show plainly: to put beyond doubt: to reveal or declare.—*n.* an open or public statement: a list or invoice of a ship's cargo to be exhibited at the custom-house.—*adj.* **manifest'-able, manifest'ible,** that can be manifested or clearly shown.—*n.* **manifesta'tion,** act of disclosing what is dark or secret: that by which something is manifested: display: revelation: mass-meeting, procession, demonstration.—*adj.* **manifest'ative.**—*adv.* **man'ifestly.**—*n.* **man'-ifestness,** state of being manifest. [L. *manifestus,* prob. *manus,* the hand, *festus,* pa.p. of obs. *fendĕre,* to dash against (as in *offendĕre*).]

manifesto, *man-i-fest'ō,* *n.* a public written declaration of the intentions, opinions, or motives of a sovereign or of a leader, party, or body (*pl.* -o(e)s). —*v.i.* (*rare*) to issue a manifesto. [It.; see **manifest.**]

manifold, *man'i-fōld, adj.* various in kind or quality: many in number: multiplied.—*n.* a pipe with several lateral outlets to others: (*math.*) aggregate: a carbon-copy: (*dial.*; also in *pl.*) manyplies.—*v.t.* to multiply: to make simultaneous copies of.—*n.* **man'ifolder.**—*adv.* **man'ifoldly.**— *ns.* **man'ifoldness; man'ifold-pa'per,** thin paper for making copies; **man'ifold-writ'er,** a copying apparatus. [many, and suff. **-fold.**]

maniform, *man'i-form, adj.* having the form of a hand. [L. *manus,* the hand, *forma,* a shape.]

Manihot, *man'i-hot,* *n.* a tropical American genus of the spurge family, including manioc. [manioc.]

manikin, mannikin, *man'i-kin,* *n.* a dwarf: an anatomical model: a mannequin: a manakin. [Du. *manneken,* a double dim. of *man*; Eng. **man.**]

manila, manilla, *mə-nil'ä,* *n.* a cheroot made in *Manila*: abaca. — **Manil(l)a hemp,** abaca; **Manil(l)a rope,** rope of Manila hemp.

manilla, *mə-nil'ä,* *n.* a West African bracelet, serving as money. [Sp.,—L.L. *manilia,* a bracelet —L. *manus,* the hand, or L. *monīlia* (pl. of *monīle*), necklace, influenced by *manus.*]

manille, *mə-nil',* *n.* in ombre and quadrille, the highest card but one. [Sp. *malilla.*]

manioc, *man'i-ok,* *n.* manihot or cassava: meal therefrom.—Also **man'dioc, mandio'c(c)a, man'-ihoc.** [Tupi *mandioca.*]

maniple, *man'i-pl,* *n.* a company of foot-soldiers in the Roman army: in the Western Church, a eucharistic vestment, a narrow strip worn on the left arm.—*adj.* and *n.* **manipular** (*mə-nip'ū-lər*). [L. *manipulus*—*manus,* the hand, *plēre,* to fill.]

maniplies. Same as **manyplies.**

manipulate, *mə-nip'ū-lāt, v.t.* to work with the hands: to handle or manage: to give a false appearance to: to turn to one's own purpose or advantage.—*v.i.* to use the hands, esp. in scientific experiments.—*n.* **manipulā'tion.**—*adjs.* **manip'-ular, manip'ulative, manip'ulatory.**—*n.* **manip'-ulātor.** [L.L. *manipulāre, -ātum*; see **maniple.**]

Manis, *mā′nis, n.* the pangolin or scaly ant-eater. [App. intended as sing. of **manes.**]

manito, *man′i-tō, n.* a spirit or object of reverence among American Indians.—Also **manitou** (*-tōō*). [Algonkin.]

manjack, *man′jak, n.* a West Indian boraginaceous tree (*Cordia macrophylla*) : its fruit.

mankind, manly. See **man.**

manna, *man′ä, n.* the food of the Israelites in the wilderness : delicious food for body or mind : a sugary exudation from the **mann′a-ash** (*Fraxinus Ornus*), -larch (Briançon **manna**), and other trees, from a species of tamarisk, from Alhagi, &c. : edible fragments of the **mann′a-li′chen** (Lecanora) : flote-grass seeds : honey-dew.—*adj.* **mannif′-erous.**—*ns.* **mann′a-croup** (*krōōp′* ; Russ. *krupa*), -groats, grains of manna-grass ; **mann′a-dew,** manna imagined to be solidified dew ; **mann′a-grass′,** an aquatic grass (Glyceria) with edible seeds, flote-grass ; **mann′ite, mann′itol,** a sweet alcohol, $C_6H_8(OH)_6$, got from manna, from seaweeds of the genus Laminaria, &c. ; **mann′ose,** a sugar ($C_6H_{12}O_6$) got by oxidising mannitol. [Heb. *mān hū,* what is it? or from *man,* a gift.]

mannequin, *man′i-kin, n.* a person, usu. a woman, employed to wear and display clothes. [Fr.,—Du ; see **manikin.**]

manner, *man′ər, n.* the way in which anything is done : method : fashion : personal style of acting or bearing : habit : custom : style of writing or of thought : sort (formerly often with omission of following *of*) : style : (*pl.*) morals : good behaviour : character : courteous deportment.—*adj.* **mann′ered,** having manners (esp. in compounds, as *well-* or *ill-mannered*) : affected with mannerism : artificial : stilted.—*ns.* **mann′erism,** a constant sameness of manner : a marked peculiarity or trick of style or manner, esp. in literary composition : manner or style becoming wearisome by its sameness ; **mann′erist,** one addicted to mannerism.—*adj.* **manneris′tic.**—*adv.* **manneris′tically.**—*n.* **mann′erliness.**—*adj.* **mann′erly,** showing good manners : well-behaved : complaisant : not rude.—*adv.* with good manners : civilly : respectfully : without rudeness.—**by no manner of means,** under no circumstances whatever ; **in a manner,** in a sense ; **make one's manners,** to salute a person on meeting by a bow, curtsy, &c. ; **shark's manners,** rapacity ; **to the manner born,** accustomed from birth. [Fr. *manière*—*main*—L. *manus,* the hand.]

manner, *man′ər, n.* Same as **mainor (in or with the manner).**

manning. See **man.**

mannitol. See **manna.**

manoeuvre, (*U.S.*) **maneuver,** *mä-nōō′vər,* or *-nū′, n.* a piece of dexterous management : a stratagem : a skilful and clever movement in military or naval tactics.—*v.i.* and *v.t.* to perform a manoeuvre : to manage with art : to change the position of troops or of ships : to effect or to gain by manoeuvres.—*n.* **manoeu′vrer.** [Fr. *manœuvre*—L.L. *manuopera*—L. *manū* (abl.), by hand, *opera,* work ; cf. **manure.**]

manometer, *man-om′i-tər, n.* an instrument for measuring the pressure of gases.—*adjs.* **manometric** (*man-ō-met′rik*), **-al.** [Gr. *manos,* rare, thin, *metron,* measure.]

manor, *man′ər, n.* the land belonging to a nobleman, or so much as he formerly kept for his own use : the district over which the court of the lord of the manor had authority : a tract of land in America for which a fee-farm rent was paid.—*ns.* **man′or-house,** -seat, the house or seat belonging to a manor.—*adj.* **manorial** (*ma-nō′-ri-əl*), pertaining to a manor. [O.Fr. *manoir*—L. *manēre, mānsum,* to stay.]

manred, *man′red, n.* (*obs.*) homage : a body of vassals.—(*Scot.*) **man′rent.** [O.E. *mannrǽden ;* see **man** and suff. **-red.**]

mansard, *man′särd, n.* a roof having the lower part steeper than the upper.—Usually **man′sard-roof′.** [Employed by François *Mansard* or *Mansart* (1598-1666).]

manse, *mans, n.* an ecclesiastical residence, esp. that of a parish minister of the Church of Scotland.—**son of the manse,** a minister's son. [L.L.

mansus, mansa, a dwelling—*manēre, mānsum,* to remain.]

mansion, *man′shən, n.* abode, stay : a resting-place : a dwelling-place : an apartment : a house, esp. a large one : a manor-house : the dwelling of a nobleman or a landholder : (*astrol.*) a house : (in *pl.*) a large building let in flats.—*ns.* **man′sion-house,** a mansion (Mansion House, the official residence of the Lord Mayor of London) ; **man′-sionry** (*Shak.* **man′sonry**), residence : construction. [O.Fr.,—L. *mānsiō, -ōnis*—*manēre, mānsum,* to remain.]

mansuete, *man′swēt, adj.* gentle : mild : tame.—*n.* **man′suetude** (*-swi-tūd*). [L. *mānsuētus*—*manus,* hand, *suēscěre,* to accustom.]

mansworn, *man′swōrn, adj.* (*arch.*) perjured. [O.E. *mānswerian*—*mān,* evil, *swerian,* to swear.]

manta, *man′tä, n.* a blanket : a cloak : a horse-cloth : **Manta,** a genus of gigantic rays or sea-vampires. [Sp.]

manteau, *manto, man′tō, n.* (17th-18th cent.) a woman's loose gown. [Fr. *manteau*—L. *mantellum.*]

manteel, *man-tēl′, n.* (*obs.*) a soldier's cloak : a lady's cape. [Fr. *mantile*—Sp. *mantilla.*]

mantel, *man′tl, n.* a mantletree : a mantelpiece : a mantelshelf.—*ns.* **man′telet,** a mantlet ; **man′tel-piece,** the ornamental structure over and in front of a fireplace : a mantelshelf ; **man′telshelf,** the ornamental shelf over a fireplace ; **man′teltree,** the lintel or arch of a fireplace. [**mantle.**]

mantic, *man′tik, adj.* relating to divination : prophetic. [Gr. *mantikos*—*mantis,* a prophet.]

manticore, *man′ti-kōr,* **manticora,** *-kō′rä, n.* a fabulous compound of lion and scorpion with a human head. [L. *manticora*—Gr. *mantichōrās,* a wrong reading for *martichōrās,* from an Old Persian word for man-eater.]

mantilla, *man-til′ä, n.* a small mantle : a kind of veil covering the head and falling down upon the shoulders. [Sp. ; dim. of *manta.*]

Mantis, *man′tis, n.* a genus of orthopterous insects carrying their large spinous forelegs in the attitude of prayer.—*n.* **man′tid,** any member of the genus.—**mantis shrimp,** a stomatopod crustacean with claws like the mantis. [Gr. *mantis, -eōs.*]

mantissa, *man-tis′ä, n.* the fractional part of a logarithm. [L., make-weight.]

mantle, *man′tl, n.* a cloak or loose outer garment : a covering : spirit (in allusion to Elijah) : a fold of the integument of a mollusc or a brachiopod secreting the shell : the back and folded wings of a bird : a scum on a liquid : a hood or network of refractory material that becomes incandescent when exposed to a flame.—*v.t.* to cover : to obscure : to form a scum upon : to suffuse : to disguise.—*v.i.* to spread like a mantle : to develop a scum : to froth : to be suffused : to stretch the wings over the legs, as a hawk.—*ns.* **man′tlet,** **man′telet,** a small cloak for women : (*fort.*) a movable shield or screen ; **man′tling,** cloth suitable for mantles : (*her.*) the drapery of a coat-of-arms. [Partly through O.E. *mentel,* partly through O.Fr. *mantel* (Fr. *manteau*),—L. *mantellum.*]

manto. See **manteau.**

mantra, *man′trä, n.* a Vedic hymn : a sacred text used as an incantation. [Sans., instrument of thought.]

mantua, *man′tū-ä, n.* (17th-18th cent.) a woman's loose outer gown—(*Scot.*) **mant′y.**—*n.* **man′tua-mak′er,** a dressmaker. [*manteau,* confused with *Mantua,* in Italy.]

Mantuan, *man′tū-ən, adj.* of Mantua in Italy.—*n.* a native or inhabitant of Mantua, esp. Virgil.—Also the name of the Latin pastoral poet Baptista *Mantuanus* (1448-1516).

manual, *man′ū-əl, adj.* of the hand : done, worked, or used by the hand : working with the hands.—*n.* drill in the use of weapons, &c. : a handbook or handy compendium of a large subject or treatise : an old office-book like the modern R.C. *Rituale* : a key or keyboard played by hand : a primary feather.—*adv.* **man′ually.**—**manual alphabet,** the signs for letters made by the deaf and dumb ;

manual exercise, drill in handling arms. [L. *manuālis—manus*, the hand.]

manubrium, *mā-nū'bri-əm*, *n.* any handle-like structure: the presternum or anterior part of the breast-bone in mammals :—*pl.* **manū'bria.**—*adj.* **manū'brial.** [L. *manūbrium*, a handle.]

manufacture, *man-ū-fakt'yər*, *v.t.* to make, originally by hand, now usu. by machinery and on a large scale: to fabricate, concoct: to produce unintelligently in quantity.—*v.i.* to be occupied in manufactures.—*n.* the practice, act, or process of manufacturing: anything manufactured.—*n.* **manufact'ory**, a factory or place where goods are manufactured.—*adj.* **manufact'ural.**—*n.* **manufact'urer**, one who manufactures.—*adj.* **manufact'uring**, pertaining to manufactures. [Fr.,—L. *manū* (abl.), by hand, *factūra*, a making, from *facĕre*, *factum*, to make.]

manuka, *mä'noo-kä*, *n.* an Australian and New Zealand tree (Leptospermum) of the myrtle family, with hard wood, its leaves a substitute for tea. [Maori.]

manul, *mä'nool*, *n.* a Central Asian wild cat. [Mongolian.]

manumit, *man-ū-mit'*, *v.t.* to release from slavery: to set free :—*pr.p.* **manumitt'ing**; *pa.t.* and *pa.p.* **manumitt'ed.**—*n.* **manumission** (*-mish'ən*). [L. *mānūmittere* or *manū mittĕre* or *ēmittĕre*, to send from one's hand or control—*manus*, the hand, *mittĕre*, *missum*, to send.]

manure, *män-ūr'*, formerly *man'ūr*, *v.t.* (*obs.*) to hold, occupy: (*obs.*) to manage : (*obs.*) to cultivate : to enrich with any fertilising substance.—*n.* any substance applied to land to make it more fruitful. —*ns.* **manur'ance**, (*arch.*) cultivation; **manur'er.** — *adj.* **manur'ial.** — *n.* **manur'ing.** [A.Fr. *maynoverer* (Fr. *manœuvrer*); see **manoeuvre**.]

manus, *mä'nəs*, L. *mä'noos*, *n.* the hand or corresponding part of an animal. [L. *mănus*, pl. *-ūs*.]

manuscript, *man'ū-skript*, *adj.* written by hand.— *n.* a book or document written by hand : copy for a printer, in handwriting or typed : handwritten form. [L. *manū* (abl.), by hand, *scrībĕre*, *scrīptum*, to write.]

Manx, *mangks*, *n.* the language of the Isle of *Man*, belonging to the Gadhelic branch of Celtic.—*adj.* pertaining to the Isle of Man or to its inhabitants. —*n.* **Manx'man** :—*fem.* **Manx'woman.—Manx cat**, a breed of cat with only a rudimentary tail.

many, *men'i*, *adj.* (*comp.* **more**, *mōr*; *superl.* **most**, *mōst*) consisting of a great number : numerous.—*n.* many persons : a great number (usu. with omission of *of*): (*Spens.*) company, retinue (perh. for **meinie**).—*adjs.* **man'y-coloured**, **man'y-eyed'**, having many colours, eyes; **man'y-fold'ed**, (*Spens.*) having many layers : having many folds; **man'y-head'ed**, having many heads : consisting of many.—*n.* **man'y-root**, Ruellia.—*adj.* **man'y-sid'ed**, having many qualities or aspects : having wide interests or varied abilities.—*n.* **man'y-sid'edness.**—*adj.* **man'y-tongued'.—many a**, many (with singular noun and verb); **many-headed beast**, the people (after Horace); **the many**, the crowd. [O.E. *manig*.]

manyplies, *men'i-plīz*, *n.sing.* and *pl.* the third stomach of a ruminant—the *omasum* or *psalterium*. —Also **man'iplies** and (*dial.*) **moniplies**, **monyplies** (*mon'*, *mun'*). [many, **ply**.]

manzanilla, *man-zə-nil'ä*, *n.* a very dry, light sherry. [Sp. *manzanilla*, camomile; cf. **manchineel**.]

manzanita, *man-zə-nē'tä*, *n.* bearberry of Californian species. [Sp., dim. of *manzana*, apple.]

Maori, *mow'ri*, *mä'ō-ri*, *n.* a member of the brown race of New Zealand : the language of this race :— *pl.* **Mao'ris.**—Also *adj.*—**Maori hen**, the weka. [Maori.]

maormor, *mär'mōr*, a wrong form of **mormaor**.

map, *map*, *n.* a representation in outline of the surface features of the earth, the moon, &c., or of part of it, usu. on a plane surface : a similar plan of the stars in the sky : a representation, scheme, or epitome of the disposition or state of anything.—*v.t.* to make a map of :—*pr.p.* **mapp'ing**; *pa.t.* and *pa.p.* **mapped.**—*ns.* **map'-**

measurer, an instrument for measuring distances on a map; **map'-mounter**, one who mounts maps, or backs them with cloth and fixes them on rollers, &c.; **mappemonde** (*map'ə-mônd*, *map-mônd'*; L.L. *mappa mundī*; *hist.*), a map of the world: (*obs.*) the world itself; **mapp'er**; **map'pery**, (*Shak.*) perhaps working with, or making, maps, or planning out; **mapp'ist**; **map'-reading**, the interpretation of what one sees in a map.—*adv.* **map'wise**, in the manner of a map.—**map out, to** plan, divide up, and apportion; **off the map**, out of existence : negligible; **on the map**, to be taken into account. [L. *mappa*, a napkin, a painted cloth, orig. Punic.]

maple, *mä'pl*, *n.* any tree of the genus Acer, some species of which yield sugar and syrup from their sap : its timber.—*adj.* of maple.—*n.* **ma'ple-su'gar.—maple leaf**, the emblem of Canada. [O.E. *mapul*, maple.]

mappemond. See **map**.

mapstick. See **mopstick**.

maqui, *mä'kē*, *n.* a Chilean evergreen shrub (*Aristotelia Maqui*; Elaeocarpaceae) whose berry yields a medicinal wine. [Araucan.]

maquis, *mä'kē'*, *n.sing.* and *pl.* (*bot.*) a thicket formation of shrubs, as in Corsica : French guerrilla bands (1940-45). [Fr.,—It. *macchia*—L. *macula*, mesh.]

mar, *mär*, *v.t.* (*obs.*) to interfere with : to spoil : to impair : to injure : to damage : to disfigure :— *pr.p.* **marr'ing**; *pa.t.* and *pa.p.* **marred** (*Spens.* *mard*).—*ns.* **mar'plot**, one who defeats or mars a plot by unwarranted interference; **mar'-sport**, a spoil-sport; **mar'-text**, an ignorant preacher. [O.E. *merran*.]

mara, *mä'rä*, *n.* the so-called Patagonian hare or Dolichotis.

marabou(t), *mar'ə-bōō(t)*, *n.* an adjutant bird, esp. an African species : its feathers : a plume or trimming of its feathers : a feather necklet : a very white raw silk. [See next word.]

marabout, *mar'ə-bōōt*, *n.* a Mohammedan hermit, esp. in N. Africa : a Moslem shrine. [Fr.,—Ar. *murābit*, hermit.]

marah, *mä'rä*, *n.* bitterness : something bitter. [Heb.]

maranatha, *mar-ə-nä'thä*. See **anathema**.

Maranta, *mä-ran'tä*, *n.* the arrowroot genus of monocotyledons giving name to the family **Marantā'ceae**, akin to the banana and ginger families. [After Bartolommeo *Maranta*, 16th-cent. Italian herbalist.]

maraschino, *mar-ə-skē'nō*, *n.* a liqueur distilled from a cherry grown in Dalmatia. [It.,—*marasca*, *amarasca*, a sour cherry—L. *amārus*, bitter.]

marasmus, *mə-raz'məs*, *n.* a wasting away of the body.—*adj.* **maras'mic.**—*n.* **Maras'mius**, a common genus of toadstools, including the fairy-ring champignon, drying up in sunshine but recovering in damp. [Latinised—Gr. *marasmos—marainein*, to decay.],

Maratha, Mahratta, *mä-rät'ä*, *n.* a member of a once dominant people of S.W. India. — *n.* **Marathi** (*mä-rät'ē*), their Sanskritic language. [Sans. *Mahārāshtra*, great kingdom.]

Marathon, *mar'ə-thon*, *-thən*, *n.* scene of the Greek victory over the Persians, 490 B.C., 22 miles from Athens : a Marathon race : a test of endurance.— *adj.* and *n.* **Marathōn'ian**—**Marathon race**, a long-distance foot-race (about 26 miles), commemorating the tradition that a Greek ran to Athens with the news. [Gr. *Marathōn*.]

Marattia, *ma-rat'i-ä*, *n.* a genus of ferns giving name to the **Marattiā'ceae**, a tropical family of very large primitive eusporangiate ferns. [Named after G. F. *Maratti* (d. 1777), Italian botanist.]

maraud, *mə-rawd'*, *v.i.* to rove in quest of plunder. —*v.t.* to harry.—*n.* raiding : plundering.—*n.* **maraud'er.** [Fr. *maraud*, rogue; origin obscure.]

maravedi, *mar-ə-vä'di*, *n.* an obsolete Spanish copper coin of little value. [Sp. *maravedí*—Ar. *Murābitīn*, the dynasty of the Almoravides (11th and 12th cent.).]

marble, *mär'bl*, *n.* a granular crystalline limestone : loosely, any rock of similar appearance taking a high polish : a slab, work of art, tombstone, tomb, or other object made of marble : a little hard ball (originally of marble) used by boys in play : marbling : (*fig.*) anything hard, cold, polished, white, or otherwise like marble : (in *pl.*) a game played with little balls.—*adj.* composed of marble : shining : unyielding : hard : insensible : marbled.—*v.t.* to stain or vein like marble.—*adjs.* mar′ble-breast′ed, hard-hearted, cruel ; mar′ble-con′stant, constant or firm as marble, immovable.—*n.* mar′ble-cutter, one who hews marble : a machine for cutting marble.—*adj.* mar′bled, irregularly mottled and streaked like some kinds of marble : wrought in marble : furnished with marble.—*n.* mar′bled-white′, a butterfly of the Satyridae.—*adjs.* mar′ble-edged, having the edges marbled, as a book ; mar′ble-heart′ed, hard-hearted, insensible.—*ns.* mar′ble-paper, paper coloured in imitation of variegated marble ; mar′bler ; mar′bling, a marbled appearance or colouring : the act of veining or painting in imitation of marble.—*adv.* mar′bly, like marble. —Elgin marbles, a collection of marbles obtained chiefly from the Parthenon by Lord *Elgin* in 1811, now in the British Museum. [O.Fr. *marbre*—L. *marmor* ; cf. Gr. *marmaros*—*marmairein*, to sparkle.]

marc, *märk, n.* fruit-refuse in wine- or oil-making.—marc brandy, brandy made from marc. [Fr.]

marcantant, *mär′kɒn-tant, n.* (*Shak.*) a merchant. [It. *mercatante.*]

marcasite, *mär′ka-sīt, n.* sulphide of iron in orthorhombic crystals. [L.L. *marcasīta* ; origin unknown.]

marcato, *mär-kä′tō, adj.* marked : emphatic : strongly accented :—*superl.* marcatis′simo.—Also *adv.* [It.,—*marcare*, to mark.]

Marcel, marcel, *mär-sel′, n.* (in full Marcel wave), an artificial wave imparted to hair by a hot iron, a comb, and manipulation.—*v.t.* to wave with a marcel.—*adj.* marcelled′. [*Marcel*, a French hairdresser, the inventor (1872).]

marcescent, *mär-ses′ɒnt, adj.* withering without falling off.—*adj.* marcesc′ible. [L. *marcēscēns, -entis*, pr.p. of *marcēscĕre*—*marcēre*, to fade.]

Marcgravia, *märk-grä′vi-ä, n.* a tropical American genus of climbing epiphytic shrubs, with pitcher-like bracts developed as nectaries, visited by hummingbirds, giving name to the family Marc-graviä′ceae, akin to the tea family. [After Georg *Markgraf* (1610–44), German traveller, naturalist, and astronomer.]

March, *märch, n.* (now) the third month of the year. —March beer, strong beer brewed in March ; March hare, a hare gambolling in the breeding season, proverbially mad. [L. *Martius* (*mēnsis*), (the month) of Mars.]

march, *märch, n.* a boundary : border : a border district—used chiefly in *pl.* march′es.—*v.i.* to have a common boundary.—*ns.* march′-dyke, -dike, a boundary wall, usu. of turf ; march′-man, a borderer ; march′-stone, a boundary stone ; march′-trea′son, an offence against the laws of the marches, e.g. raiding the neighbouring country in time of peace.—riding the marches, a ceremony of riding round the bounds of a municipality. [Fr. *marche* ; of Gmc. origin ; cf. mark, O.E. *mearc.*]

march, *märch, v.i.* to walk in a markedly rhythmical military manner, or in a grave, stately, or resolute manner : to advance steadily or irresistibly. —*v.t.* to cause to march : to force to go.—*n.* a marching movement : an act of marching : distance traversed at a stretch by marching : regular advance : a piece of music fitted for marching to, or similar in character and rhythm, usu. with a trio.—forced march, a march vigorously pressed forward for combative or strategic purposes ; marching orders, orders to march ; marching regiment, one without permanent quarters ; march past, the march of a body in front of one who reviews it ; on the march, afoot and journeying ; rogue's march, music played in derision of a person expelled. [Fr. *marcher*, to walk, prob.—L. *marcus*, a hammer.]

Marchantia, *mär-kan′shi-ä, -ti-ä, n.* a well-known

genus of liverworts with flat, lobed and branched thallus, growing in damp places, giving name to the family Marchantiä′ceae. [Named after Nicolas *Marchant* (*d.* 1678), French botanist.]

märchen, *mer′hhyɒn, n.sing.* and *pl.* a story or fable, a folk-tale. [Ger.]

marchioness, *mär′shɒn-es, -is, n.* fem. of marquis, marquess.—*n.* marchesa (*mär-kä′za*), It. fem. of marchese (*mär-kā′ze*), a marquis. [L.L. *marchiōnissa*, fem. of *marchiō, -ōnis*, a lord of the marches.]

marchpane, *märch′pān, n.* (*Shak.*) a sweet almond paste. [It. *marzapane* ; cf. marzipan.]

Marcionite, *mär′shɒn-īt, n.* a follower of *Marcion* of Sinope (*d.* A.D. 165), who, partly under Gnostic influences, constructed an ethico-dualistic philosophy of religion.—Also *adj.*—*ns.* Mar′cionist ; Mar′cionītism.

Marcobrunner, *mär′kō-brōōn-ɒr, n.* a remarkably fine white wine, produced in Erbach, near Wiesbaden. [From the *Markbrunnen* fountain hard by.]

Marconi, *mär-kō′ni, adj.* connected with Guglielmo *Marconi* (1874–1937), or his system of wireless telegraphy.—*v.t.* and *v.i.* (marconi) to communicate by wireless telegraphy.—*n.* marco′nigram, a message so transmitted.—*v.t.* and *v.i.* marco′nigraph.

mard, a Spenserian spelling of marred.

mare, *mär, n.* the female of the horse.—*ns.* mare's′-nest, a supposed discovery that turns out to be a fiasco ; mare′s′-tail, a tall, erect marsh plant of the genus *Hippuris* : also applied to the horsetail : (in *pl.*) long straight fibres of grey cirrus cloud.—the grey mare is the better horse, the wife rules her husband, or is the abler. [O.E. *mere*, fem. of *mearh*, a horse ; cog. with Ger. *mähre*, O.N. *merr*, W. *march*, a horse.]

mare, *mär, n.* (*Shak.*) the nightmare (q.v.).

maremma, *mär-em′ä, n.* seaside marshland. [It.,—L. *maritima*, seaside.]

mareschal, *mär′shl.* Same as marshal.

margarin, *mär′gɒr-in, n.* a mixture of palmitin and stearin once thought a compound : a glyceryl ester of margaric acid.—*ns.* margarine (*mär′gɒr-ēn* ; popularly pron. *mär′jɒr-ēn*, and contracted marge, *märj.*), oleo-margarine : any imitation butter ; mar′garite, a pearly-lustred mineral sometimes reckoned a lime-alumina mica.—*adjs.* margaric (-*gar′*) ; margarit′ic ; margaritif′erous, pearl-bearing.—margaritic acid, an acid intermediate between palmitic and stearic. [Gr. *margaritēs*, a pearl.]

margay, *mär′gä, n.* a spotted S. American tiger-cat. [Fr. (or Sp.),—Tupí *mbaracaïa.*]

marge, *märj, n.* margin, brink. [Fr.,—L. *margō, -inis.*]

margin, *mär′jin, poet.* margent, *mär′jɒnt, n.* an edge, border : the blank edge on the page of a book : something allowed more than is needed : a deposit to protect a broker against loss.—*v.t.* to furnish with margins : to enter on the margin.—*adj.* mar′ginal, pertaining to a margin : in or on the margin.—*n.* marginä′lia, notes written on the margin.—*v.t.* mar′ginalise, to furnish with notes. —*adv.* mar′ginally.—*adjs.* mar′ginate, -d, having a well-marked border ; mar′gined.—marginal land, less fertile land which will be brought under cultivation only if economic conditions justify it. [L. *margō, marginis* ; cf. mark, march (2).]

margosa, *mär-gō′sä, n.* the tree that yields nim oil. [Port. *amargosa* (fem.), bitter.]

margrave, *mär′grāv, n.* a German nobleman of rank equivalent to an English marquis :—*fem.* margravine (*mär′grɒ-vēn*).—*ns.* mar′gravate, margrä′viate, the jurisdiction or dignity of a margrave. [M.Du. *markgrave* (Du. *markgraaf*, Ger. *markgraf*)—*mark*, a border, *grave* (mod. *graaf*), a count ; cf. Ger. *graf*, O.E. *geréfa*, Eng. reeve, sheriff.]

marguerite, *mär-gɒ-rēt′, n.* the ox-eye daisy or other single chrysanthemum. [Fr., daisy—Gr. *margaritēs*, pearl.]

marialite, *mā′ri-ɒ-līt, n.* a variety of scapolite rich in sodium, chlorine, and silica, poor in calcium. [*Maria* Rose vom Rath, a mineralogist's wife.]

Marian, mā′ri-ən, adj. relating to the Virgin Mary or to Queen Mary (Tudor or Stewart).—n. a devotee, follower, or defender of Mary: an English Roman Catholic of Mary Tudor's time. [L. Maria.]

Marian, mar′i-ən, mā′ri-ən, adj. relating to the great Roman general Gaius Marius (d. 86 B.C.).

marid, mar′id, mä-rēd′, n. a jinni of the most powerful class. [Ar. mārid, marīd.]

marigold, mar′i-gōld, n. a yellow-flowered composite (Calendula) or its flower: extended to other yellow flowers (see corn, marsh).—African, French marigold, Mexican composites (Tagetes). [From the Virgin Mary and gold (flower).]

marigraph, mar′i-gräf, n. a recording tide-gauge.— n. mar′igram, a record given by one. [L. mare, sea, Gr. graphein, to write.]

marihuana, marijuana, mä-ri-(hh)wä′nä, n. hemp: its dried flowers smoked as an intoxicant. [Amer. Sp.]

marimba, mə-rim′bä, n. an African xylophone, adopted by Central Americans and jazz-bandsmen. [Of African origin.]

marine, mə-rēn′, adj. of, in, near, concerned with, or belonging to the sea: done or used at sea: inhabiting, found in or got from the sea.—n. a soldier serving on shipboard: shipping, naval or mercantile, fleet: nautical service: naval affairs: a sea-piece in painting.—ns. **marinade** (mar-i-nād′), a liquor or pickle in which fish or meat is steeped before cooking, to improve the flavour.—v.t. mar′inate, to salt or pickle.—n. **mar′iner,** a sailor.—**marine acid,** hydrochloric acid; **marine boiler,** a steamship boiler; **marine engine,** a ship's engine; **marine glue** (see glue); **marine insurance,** insurance of ships or cargoes; **marine soap,** a coconut-oil soap, for washing with sea-water; **marine store,** a place where old ships' materials are dealt in; **marine stores,** old ships' materials: supplies for ships; **marine trumpet,** the tromba marina; **tell that to the marines,** a phrase expressive of disbelief and ridicule, from the sailor's contempt for the marine's ignorance of seamanship. [Fr.,—L. marīnus—mare, sea.]

Marinist, mə-rē′nist, n. a follower or imitator of the Italian poet Giambattista Marini (1569-1625). —n. Marin′ism, his manner, full of strained conceits.

Mariolatry, mā-ri-ol′ə-tri, n. undue worship of the Virgin Mary—the veneration paid to her being strictly hyperdulia.—n. Mariol′ater, one who practises Mariolatry.—adj. Mariol′atrous. [Gr. Maria, Mary, latreiā, worship.]

marionette, mar-i-ə-net′, n. a puppet moved by strings. [Fr., dim. of the name Marion.]

Mariotte's law. See law.

marischal, a Scots spelling of marshal.

marish, mar′ish, n. and adj. Same as marsh.

Marist, mar′ist, n. a member of a modern R.C. congregation for teaching, preaching, and foreign missions.—adj. devoted to the service of the Virgin. [Fr. Mariste.]

maritage, mar′it-ij, n. (hist.) the feudal superior's right to dispose of a vassal's heiress (or heir) in marriage, or exact a fine. [L.L. marītāgium.]

marital, mar′i-tal, mə-rī′tal, adj. pertaining to a husband: of the nature of a marriage.—adv. mar′itally (or mə-rī′). [L. marītālis—marītus, a husband.]

maritime, mar′i-tīm, adj. pertaining to the sea: relating to sea-going or sea-trade: having a sea-coast: situated near the sea: living on the shore, littoral: having a navy and sea-trade. [L. maritimus—mare, sea.]

Marivaudage, mā-rē-vō-däzh, n. preciosity in writing. [Fr., from Pierre de Marivaux (1688-1763), French author.]

marjoram, mär′jə-ram, n. an aromatic labiate plant (Origanum) used as a seasoning. [O.Fr. majorane; origin doubtful.]

mark, märk, n. a boundary: a limit: a standard: a territory, esp. a border territory: (hist.) a tract of common land belonging to a village community: a boundary stone, post, or the like: an object indicating position or serving as a guide: an object

to be aimed at, striven for, or attained, as a butt, a goal, the jack at bowls, the pit of the stomach in boxing: (obs.) a hawk's quarry: (slang) a suitable victim: (slang) that which exactly suits one: a visible indication or sign: a symbol: a distinctive device: a brand: a set, group, or class, marked with the same brand: a stamp: a token: a substitute for a signature: a distinguishing characteristic: an impression or trace: a discoloured spot, streak, smear, or other local modification of appearance: note: distinction: noteworthiness: a point awarded for merit: a footprint: the impression of a Rugby football player's heel on the ground on making a fair catch: the starting-line in a race: a groove indicative of youth in a horse's incisor (as in mark of mouth): a tag on a lead-line indicating so many fathoms, feet, &c.—v.t. to make a mark on: to indicate: to record: to make emphatic, distinct, or prominent: to impress with a sign: to note: to regard.—v.i. to take particular notice.—adj. **marked,** having marks: indicated: noticeable: prominent: emphatic: watched and suspected: doomed.—adv. mark′-edly, noticeably.—ns. mark′er, a person or tool that marks: one who marks the score at games, as at billiards: a counter or other device for scoring: a bookmark: a recorder of attendances: a kind of school monitor: (U.S.) a memorial tablet: the soldier who forms the pivot round which a body of soldiers wheels; mark′ing, act of making a mark: (esp. in pl.) disposition of marks.—Also adj.—ns. mark′ing-ink, indelible ink, used for marking clothes; mark′ing-nut, the fruit of an East Indian tree (Semecarpus) of the cashew family, yielding a black juice used in marking clothes; mark′man, one of the community owning a mark: a marksman; marks′man, marks′-woman, one good at hitting a mark: one who shoots well; mark′-white, (Spens.) the centre of a target.—beside the mark, not properly referring to the matter in hand; (God) bless, or save, the mark, a phrase expressing ironical astonishment or scorn, from the usage of archery; make one's mark, to make a notable impression: to gain great influence; mark down, set down in writing: to label at a lower price: lower the price of: to note the position of: to destine for one's own; mark off, to lay down the lines of: to graduate: to mark as attended to, disposed of; mark of the Beast, a stamp on the forehead or right hand of a worshipper of the Beast of the Book of Revelation, chap. xiii.: hence a mark of whatever was considered to be of Antichrist; a mark on, (slang) one who has a great liking for; mark out, to lay out the plan or outlines of: to destine; mark time, to move the feet alternately in the same manner as in marching, but without changing ground: to keep things going without progressing; mark up, to raise the price of; off the mark, well away from the start in a race; pass the mark, pass on the badge of demerit to the next offender (as formerly in some schools); soft mark, an easy dupe: one easy to cope with; up to the mark, satisfactory, up to standard: fit and well. [O.E. (Mercian) merc (W.S. mearc), a boundary; Ger. mark, Goth. marka.]

mark, märk, n. (obs.) a weight of 8 ounces (for gold and silver): (obs.) its value in money at 20 pennies to an ounce=13s. 4d.: a coin of Germany (at par=11¾d.; superseded in 1924 by the reichsmark; in 1948 the Deutsche mark), of Finland (the markka, originally equivalent to a franc), and formerly of various countries. [O.E. marc, of doubtful origin.]

market, mär′kit, n. a periodic concourse of people for the purposes of buying and selling: a building, square, or other public place used for such meetings: (U.S.) a shop: a region in which there is a demand for goods: buying and selling: opportunity for buying and selling: demand: state of being on sale: bargain: sale: rate of sale: value.—v.i. to deal at a market: to buy and sell.—v.t. to put on the market:—pr.p. mar′keting; pa.t. and pa.p. mar′keted.—ns. marketabil′ity, mar′ketableness.—adj. mar′ketable, fit for the market : saleable.—*ns.* **mar´ket-bell**, (*Shak.*) a bell to give notice of the time of market ; **mar´ket-cross´**, a cross or similar structure anciently set up where a market was held ; **mar´ket-day**, the fixed day on which a market is held ; **mar´keter**, one who goes to market, buys or sells at a market ; **mar´ket-gar´den**, a garden in which fruit and vegetables are grown for market ; **mar´ket-gar´dener** ; **mar´ket-gar´dening** ; **mar´ket-hall**, **mar´ket-house**, a building in which a market is held ; **mar´keting**, the act or practice of buying and selling in market ; **mar´ket-man**, one who sells, buys, or works in a market ; **mar´ket-place**, **mar´ket-square**, the open space in a town where markets are held ; **mar´ket-price**, **mar´ket-val´ue**, the current price ; **mar´ket-town**, a town having the privilege of holding a public market ; **mar´ket-woman**.—**on the market**, available for buying : on sale. [Late O.E. *market*—O.N.Fr. *market* (Fr. *marché*, It. *mercato*), from L. *mercātus*, trade, a market—*merx*, merchandise.]

markhor, *mär´kor*, *n.* a wild goat of the mountains of Asia. [Pers. *märkhōr*.]

marl, *märl*, *n.* a limy clay often used as manure : (*poet.*) the ground.—*v.t.* to cover with marl.—*ns.* **marl´-pit**, a pit where marl is dug ; **marl´stone**, a Middle Lias series of argillaceous limestones with ironstones, &c.—*adj.* **marl´y**, like marl : abounding in marl. [O.Fr. *marle* (Fr. *marne*)—L.L. *margila*, a dim. of L. *marga*, marl.]

marl, *märl*, *v.t.* to bind with marline. [Du. *marlen*, app. a freq. of *marren*, to bind.]

marl, **marle**, *märl*, an obs. form of **marvel**.

marl, *märl*, a dial. form of **marble**.—*adj.* mottled. — *adj.* **marled**, marbled. — *n.* **marl´ing**. — *adj.* **marl´y**, **mirl´y**, marbled.

marline, *mär´lin*, *n.* a small rope for winding round a larger one to keep it from wearing.—*n.* **mar´line-spike**, a spike for separating the strands of a rope in splicing. [Du. *marling*, vbl. n. from *marlen* (see **marl** (2)), or *marlijn*—*marren*, and *lijn*, rope (cf. **moor**, **line**).]

marm. See **ma´am**.

marmalade, *mär´mə-lād*, *n.* a jam or preserve generally made of the pulp (and rind) of oranges, originally of quinces.—**marmalade tree**, a tropical American sapotaceous tree (*Vitellaria*, or *Lucuma*, *mammosa*) cultivated for its fruit, the marmalade plum. [Fr. *marmelade*—Port. *marmelada*—*marmelo*, a quince—L. *melimēlum*—Gr. *melimēlon*, a sweet apple—*meli*, honey, *mēlon*, an apple.]

marmarosis, *mär-mə-rō´sis*, *n.* conversion of limestone into marble.—*v.t.* **mar´marise**. [Gr. *marmaros*, crystalline rock—*marmairein*, to sparkle.]

marmoreal, *mär-mōr´i-əl*, *adj.* of, or like, marble. [L. *marmor*, marble ; Gr. *marmaros* ; see preceding.]

marmose, *mar´mōs*, *n.* a small South American opossum. [Fr., app. from *marmouset* ; see next.]

marmoset, *mär´mə-zet*, *n.* a very small American monkey. [Fr. *marmouset*, grotesque figure.]

marmot, *mär´mət*, *n.* a stout burrowing rodent (*Marmota* or *Arctomys*) in America called wood-chuck. [It. *marmotto*—Romansch *murmont*—L. *mūs*, *mūris*, mouse, *mōns montis*, mountain.]

marocain, *mar´ə-kān*, *n.* a dress material finished with a grain surface like morocco-leather. [Fr. *maroquin*, morocco-leather ; cf. **maroquin**.]

Maronian, *ma-rō´ni-ən*, *adj.* Virgilian. [Publius Vergilius *Marō* (*-ōnis*.)]

Maronite, *mar´ə-nīt*, *n.* one of a former Monothelite sect, now Uniats, living around Lebanon. [St *Marōn*, about A.D. 400, or John *Marōn*, a patriarch of the sect in the 7th century.]

maroon, *mə-rōōn´*, *n.* a brownish crimson : a detonating firework.—*adj.* of the colour maroon. [Fr. *marron*, a chestnut—It. *marrone*, a chestnut.]

maroon, *mə-rōōn´*, *n.* a fugitive slave : a marooned person.—*v.t.* to put and leave ashore on a desolate island : to isolate uncomfortably.—*ns.* **maroon´er** ; **maroon´ing**. [Fr. *marron*—Sp. *cimarrón*, wild.]

maroquin, *mar-ə-kēn´*, *mar´ə-k(w)in*, *n.* goat-leather : morocco-leather. [Fr. ; cf. **marocain**.]

marplot. See **mar**.

marque, *märk*, *n.* (obs.) reprisals : a privateer.—

letter(s)-of-marque, a privateer's licence **to** commit acts of hostility. [Fr.]

marquee, *mär-kē´*, *n.* a large tent. [From **mar´quise**, as if pl.]

marquetry, **marqueterie**, *märk´i-tri*, *n.* **work** inlaid with pieces of various-coloured wood. [Fr. *marqueterie*—*marqueter*, to inlay—*marque*, a mark.]

marquis, **marquess**, *mär´kwis*, *n.* a title of nobility next below that of a duke :—*fem.* **marchioness** (*mär´shən-es*, *-is*).—*ns.* **mar´quisate**, **-quessate**, the lordship of a marquis ; **marquise** (*mär-kēz´*), in France, a marchioness : a style of parasol about 1850 : an entrance canopy : a marquee. [O.Fr. *marchis*, assimilated later to Fr. *marquis*—L.L. *marchēnsis*, a prefect of the marches.]

marram, **marrum**, *mar´əm*, *n.* a seaside grass (*Ammophila*, or *Psamma*, *arenaria*), a binder **of** sand-dunes. [O.N. *marr*, sea, *halmr*, haulm.]

marriage, *mar´ij*, *n.* the ceremony, act, or contract by which a man and woman become husband and wife : the union of a man and woman as husband and wife : a declaration of king and queen in bezique, &c.—*adj.* **marr´iageable**, suitable, or at a proper age, for marriage. — *ns.* **marr´iageableness** ; **marr´iage-bed**, the bed of a married couple **:** marital intercourse : the rights and obligations of marriage ; **marr´iage-bone**, a merry-thought **;** **marr´iage-con´tract**, an agreement to be married : an agreement respecting property by persons about to marry.—*ns.* **marr´iage-fa´vour**, a knot or decoration worn at a marriage ; **marr´iage-li´cence**, a licence to marry without proclamation of banns in a church.—*n.pl.* **marr´iage-lines**, a certificate of marriage.—*ns.* **marr´iage-por´tion**, a dowry ; **marr´iage-ring**, a wedding ring **;** **marr´iage-sett´lement**, an arrangement of property, &c., before marriage, by which something is secured to the wife or her children if the husband dies. [O.Fr. *mariage*; see **marry**.]

marrow, *mar´ō*, *n.* the soft tissue in the hollow parts of the bones : (*obs.*) pith or pulp of plants : a vegetable marrow (see under **vegetable**) : the essence or best part of anything : the inner meaning or purpose.—*ns.* **marr´ow-bone**, a bone containing marrow : (*pl.*) the knees or the **bones** of the knees ; **marr´owfat**, a rich kind of pea, called also Dutch admiral pea.—*adjs.* **marr´owish**, of the nature of, or resembling, marrow ; **marr´owless**, having no marrow.—*n.pl.* **marr´ow-men**, those who in the Church of Scotland supported the teaching of *The Marrow of Modern Divinity* (1645) after its republication in 1718.—*n.* **marr´ow-squash**, (*U.S.*) vegetable marrow.—*adj.* **marr´owy**, full of marrow : strong : forcible : pithy.—**spinal marrow**, the spinal cord. [O.E. (Anglian) *merg*, *mærh* (W.S. *mearg*) ; Ger. *mark*.]

marrow, *mar´ō*, *n.* (*arch.*) a mate : a companion : **a** match, equal, like : one of a pair.—*v.i.* to be **a** marrow.—*v.t.* to be a marrow to : to couple.—*adj.* **marr´owless**. [Origin unknown.]

marrowsky, *mar-ow´ski*, *n.* a spoonerism.—*v.i.* tu utter a spoonerism. [Said to be from the name of **a** Polish count.]

marry, *mar´i*, *v.t.* to take for husband or wife : to give in marriage : to unite in matrimony.—*v.i.* to enter into the married state : to take a husband or a wife :—*pr.p.* **marr´ying** ; *pa.t.* and *pa.p.* **marr´ied**.—*adj.* **marr´ied**.—*n.* **marr´ier**, one who marries in any sense : the sort of person likely to marry.—*n.* and *adj.* **marr´ying**. [Fr. *marier*—L. *marītāre*, to marry, *marītus*, a husband—*mās*, *maris*, a male.]

marry, *mar´i*, *interj.* (*arch.*) indeed ! forsooth !—**marry come up**, an exclamation of defiant protest. [By *Mary*.]

Mars, *märz*, *n.* the Roman god of war : the planet next after the earth in the order of distance from the sun : (*old chem.*) iron. [L. *Mārs*, *Mārtis*.]

Marsala, *mär-sä´lä*, *n.* a light wine resembling sherry, from *Marsala* in Sicily.

Marseillaise, *mär-sə-lāz´*, *n.* the French revolutionary hymn composed by Rouget de Lisle in 1792, sung by the volunteers of *Marseilles* as they entered Paris, 30th July, and when they marched to the storming of the Tuileries.

Neutral vowels in unaccented syllables : *el´ə-mənt*, *in´fənt*, *ran´dəm*

marsh, *märsh, n.* a tract of wet land : a morass, swamp, or fen.—*adj.* inhabiting or found in marshes.—*ns.* **marsh'-fe'ver,** malaria ; **marsh'-gas,** methane ; **marsh'-harr'ier,** a harrier frequenting marshes ; **marsh'iness ; marsh'land,** marshy country ; **marsh'lander ; marsh'locks,** a marsh-growing species of cinquefoil (Potentilla or Comarum)—also **marsh'-cinq'uefoil ; marsh'-mall'ow,** a maritime marsh-growing plant (*Althaea officinalis*) close akin to hollyhock : a gelatinous sweetmeat, originally made from its root ; **marsh'-man,** a marsh-dweller ; **marsh'-mar'igold,** the king-cup (*Caltha palustris*), a marsh-plant of the buttercup family with flowers like big buttercups ; **marsh'-sam'phire,** Salicornia ; **marsh'wort,** a small umbelliferous marsh-plant akin to celery.—*adj.* **marsh'y,** of the nature of marsh : abounding in marshes. [O.E. *mersc, merisc,* orig. adj. ; see **mere** (1).]

marshal, *mär'shl, n.* (*obs.*) a farrier : an officer in a royal household, originally the king's farrier, later having care of military arrangements, the regulation of ceremonies, preservation of order, points of etiquette, &c. : any official with like functions : a law-court officer with charge of prisoners : a prison-keeper : (Oxford) a proctor's attendant or bulldog : the chief officer who regulated combats in the lists : in France, &c., an officer of the highest military rank : (*U.S.*) a civil officer appointed to execute the process of the courts : (*U.S.*) a police or fire-brigade head.—*v.t.* to arrange in order : to usher : to combine in one coat of arms, or with a coat.—*v.i.* to come together in order :—*pr.p.* **mar'shalling ;** *pa.t.* and *pa.p.* **mar'shalled.**—*ns.* **mar'shalcy,** the rank, office, or department of a marshal : esp. (in the form **Mar'shalsea**) till 1842 a prison in Southwark, under the marshal of the royal household ; **mar'shaller ; mar'shalling ; mar'shalship. — air-marshal,** &c. (see **air**) ; **field-marshal** (see **field**) ; **marshalling yard,** a place where railway wagons are sorted out and made up into trains ; **marshal of the Royal Air Force,** an officer of supreme rank in the Royal Air Force, ranking with an admiral of the fleet or a field-marshal. [O.Fr. *mareschal* (Fr. *maréchal*) ; from O.H.G. *marah,* a horse, *schalh* (Ger. *schalk*), a servant.]

Marsilea, *mär-sil'i-ä, n.* a genus of aquatic leptosporangiate ferns, with four-lobed leaves and bean-like stalked sporocarps, giving name to a family **Marsileä'ceae.**—Also **Marsilia.** [Named after L. F. *Marsigli* (1658-1730), Italian naturalist, &c.]

Marsipobranchii, *mär'sip-ō-brangk'i-ī, n.pl.* the Cyclostomata.—*n.* **mar'sipobranch.**—*adj.* **marsipobranch'iate.** [Gr. *marsipos,* pouch, *branchia,* gills.]

marsupium, *mär-sū'pi-əm, n.* (*zool.*) a pouch.—*adj.* **marsū'pial,** pertaining to a pouch or to the Marsupialia : of the nature of a pouch : of the Marsupialia.—*n.* a member of the Marsupialia.—*n.pl.* **Marsupiä'lia,** an order of mammals co-extensive with the subclass Metatheria, animals whose young are born in a very imperfect state and are usually carried in a pouch by the female. [L. *marsūpium*—Gr. *marsip(p)ion, marsyp(p)ion,* a pouch.]

mart, *märt, n.* a place of trade.—*v.i.* (Shak.) to traffic.—*v.t.* (Shak.) to vend. [Du. *markt,* mart ; cf. **market.**]

mart, *märt, n.* (*Scot.*) a cow or ox fattened, killed (usu. about Martinmas), and salted for winter use. [Gael. *mart,* cow, ox.]

martagon, *mär'tə-gən, n.* the Turk's-cap lily. [Turk. *martagān,* a kind of turban.]

martel, *mär'təl, n.* a war-hammer.—*v.i.* (Spens.) to hammer :—*pa.t.* **mar'telled.** [O.Fr. *martel.*]

martellato, *mär-tel-lä'tō, adj.* played with a hammering touch, or with short quick detached strokes of the bow.—Also *adv.* [It., hammered.]

martello, *mär-tel'ō, n.* (in full **martello tower**) a circular fort for coast defence. [From *Mortella* Point in Corsica, where one withstood a British cannonade in 1794.]

marten, *mär'tən, n.* an animal (pine-marten) closely akin to the weasels, or other species of Mustela. [Fr. *martre,* from the Gmc. root seen in Ger. *marder,* and O.E. *mearth,* marten.]

martial, *mär'shl, adj.* belonging to Mars, the god of war, or to the planet Mars : of or belonging to war, or to the army and navy : warlike.—*ns.* **mar'tialism ; mar'tialist,** a soldier.—*adv.* **mar'tially.—martial law,** exercise of arbitrary power by the supreme authority in time of emergency (war, riot, &c.), ordinary administration ceasing to be operative. [Fr. *martial*—L. *mārtiālis*—*Mārs.*]

Martian, *mär-shən, adj.* of Mars (god or planet) : of battle.—*n.* an imagined inhabitant of Mars. [L. *Mārtius*—*Mārs.*]

martin, *mär'tin, n.* a bird of the swallow kind.—Also **mar'tinet.** [The name *Martin* ; cf. **robin,** &c.]

martinet, *mär-ti-net', or mär', n.* (*obs.*) a system of drill drawn up by *Martinet,* an officer of Louis XIV. : a strict disciplinarian.—*n.* **martinet'ism.**

martingale, *mär'tin-gāl, n.* a strap passing between a horse's forelegs, fastened to the girth and to the bit, noseband, or reins, to keep his head down : a short spar under the bowsprit : in gambling, the policy of doubling the stake on losing. [Fr., perh. from a kind of breeches worn at *Martigues* in Provence.]

Martini, *mär-tē'nē, n.* a cocktail of vermouth, gin, bitters, and other ingredients.

Martini-Henry, *mär-tē'nē-hen'ri, n.* a rifle with the action of that designed by Frederic *Martini* (1832-1897) and the barrel by *Henry* (d. 1894).

Martinmas, *mär'tin-məs, n.* the mass or feast of St *Martin,* 11th Nov., a term-day in Scotland.—Also (*obs.*) **Mar'tlemas.**

martlet, *märt'lit, n.* the martin : (her.) a martin or swallow without feet, used as a bearing, a crest, or a mark of cadency for a fourth son. [From Fr. *martinet,* dim. of *martin,* martin.]

martyr, *mär'tər, n.* one who by his death bears witness to his belief : one who suffers for his belief : one who suffers greatly from any cause, a victim.—*v.t.* to put to death for one's belief : to torture.—*n.* **mar'tyrdom,** state of being a martyr : the sufferings or death of a martyr : torment generally.—*v.t.* **mar'tyrise,** to offer as a sacrifice : to cause to suffer martyrdom : to make a martyr of : to torture.—*adj.* **martyrolog'ical.**—*ns.* **martyrol'ogist ; martyrol'ogy,** a history of martyrs : a discourse on martyrdom. [O.E.,—L.,—Gr., a witness.]

marvel, *mär'vl, n.* a wonder : anything astonishing or wonderful : (*arch.*) astonishment. — *v.i.* to wonder : to feel astonishment.—*v.t.* to wonder at (the fact) :—*pr.p.* **mar'velling ;** *pa.t.* and *pa.p.* **mar'velled.** — *adj.* **mar'vellous,** astonishing : almost or altogether beyond belief : improbable.—*adv.* **mar'vellously.**—*n.* **mar'vellousness.—marvel of Peru** (*pə-rōō'*), a showy garden flower (*Mirabilis Jalapa* ; family Nyctaginaceae) from Mexico, open and scented in the evening. [Fr. *merveille*—L. *mīrābilis,* wonderful—*mīrārī,* to wonder.]

Marxian, *märks'i-ən, adj.* pertaining to Karl *Marx* (1818-83) or his socialism, esp. as interpreted in Russia.—*n.* a follower of Marx.—*ns.* **Marx'ianism, Marx'ism.**—*n.* and *adj.* **Marx'ist.**

marybud, *mā'ri-bud, n.* a marigold bud.

marzipan, *mär-zi-pan', n.* marchpane. [Ger. form of the word.]

mascara, mascaron. See **mask.**

mascle, *mas'kl, n.* (her.) a bearing, lozenge-shaped and perforated : a lozenge-shaped plate for scale-armour.—*adj.* **mas'cled,** mas'cūly. [App. O.Fr. *mascle*—L.L. *mascula*—L. *macula,* mesh, influenced by O.H.G. *masca,* mesh.]

mascot, *mas'kət, n.* a talisman : a supposed bringer of good luck. [Fr. *mascotte.*]

masculine, *mas'kū-lin, adj.* (rare) male : characteristic of, peculiar to, or appropriate to, a man or the male sex : mannish : (*gram.*) of that gender to which belong words denoting males and, in some languages, various associated classes of words.—*n.* the male sex or nature : a male : a word of masculine gender. — *adv.* **mas′culinely.** — *n.* **mas′culineness.**—*v.t.* **mas′culinise,** to cause to develop masculine characters.—*v.i.* to develop such characters.—*n.* **masculin′ity.**—**masculine rhyme,** a rhyme on a final stressed syllable : in French one without a final mute e. [Fr.,—L. *masculīnus*—*masculus,* male—*mās,* a male.]

mash, *mash, n.* in brewing, a mixture of crushed malt and hot water : a mixture, as of bran with meal or turnips, beaten and stirred as a food for animals : any material beaten or crushed into a soft or pulpy state : crushed condition : a muddle, hash, or bungle.—*v.t.* to make into a mash : to pound down or crush : (*prov.*) to infuse.—*ns.* **mash′er; mash′ing; mash′-tub, -tun, -vat, mash′ing-tub,** a vessel in which the mash in breweries is mixed. — *adj.* **mash′y,** produced by mashing : of the nature of a mash. [O.E. *masc(-wyrt),* mash(-wort).]

mash, *mash, v.t.* (*obsolescent slang*) to seek to fascinate (one of the other sex) : to treat as a sweetheart.—*v.i.* to flirt.—*n.* one who mashes or is mashed : a masher : mashing.—*n.* **mash′er,** a fellow who dresses showily to attract the attention of silly young women : a dandy.—**mashed on,** enamoured of.

mashallah, *mä-shä′lä, interj.* (among Mohammedans) what God will. [Ar. *mä shä′llāh.*]

mashie, mashy, *mash′i, n.* an iron golf-club for lofting.—*n.* **mash′ie-nib′lick,** a club intermediate between mashie and niblick. [Perh. Fr. *massue,* club.]

mashlam, mashlin, &c. See **maslin.**

masjid, *mus′jid, n.* a mosque. [Ar.]

mask, *mäsk, n.* a covering for the face, or the upper part of it, for concealment, disguise, or protection : a false-face : a grotesque representation of a face worn in the ancient drama, or used as an architectural ornament, &c. : a fox's (or other beast's) face or head : a mould of a face : a masque : (*fig.*) a disguise, pretence, or concealment : any means of screening or disguising : (*phot.*) a screen to cover part of a sensitive surface.—*v.t.* to cover the face of with a mask : to hide, cloak, screen, or disguise.—*v.i.* to masquerade : to be disguised in any way.—*ns.* **mascara** (-kä′rä ; Sp. *máscara*), colouring for the eyelashes ; **mas′caron,** (*archit.*) a grotesque face on a keystone, door-knocker, &c. —*adj.* **mask′ed,** wearing a mask : concealed : (*bot.*) personate.—*ns.* **masked′-ball,** a ball in which the dancers wear masks ; **mask′er,** one who wears a mask : a masquerader. [Fr. *masque*—Sp. *máscara* or It. *maschera,* of doubtful origin, app. conn. in some way with L.L. *mascus, masca,* a ghost, and with Ar. *maskharah,* a jester, man in masquerade.]

mask, *mäsk, v.t.* (*Scot.*) to steep, infuse.—*v.i.* to be infusing. [See **mash.**]

maslin, *mas′lin, n.* a mixed grain, esp. rye and wheat. — Also (*Scot.*) **mash′lam, mash′lim, mash′lin, mash′loch** (-*lohh*), **mash′lum.** [O.Fr. *mesteillon*—L.L. *mistiliō, -ōnis*—L. *mistus,* mixed —*miscēre,* to mix.]

masochism, *maz′ə-kizm, n.* a sexual perversion with pleasure in being dominated or treated cruelly by the other sex : (loosely) morbid gratification in suffering pain, physical or mental.—*n.* **mas′ochist.** —*adj.* **masochist′ic.** [From the novelist Sacher-*Masoch,* who described it.]

mason, *mā′sn, n.* one who cuts, prepares, and lays stones : a builder in stone : a member of the society of freemasons. — *v.t.* to build. — *adjs.* **masonic** (*mə-son′ik*), relating to freemasonry ; **mä′sonried,** constructed of masonry.—*n.* **mä′sonry,** the art, skill, or practice of a mason : the work of a mason : building-work in stone : freemasonry. — *adj.* consisting of mason-work. — *n.* **mas′ter-mä′son** (see under **master**).—**mason′s mark,** a device carved on stones by a mason to identify his share in the work. [O.Fr. *masson* (Fr. *maçon*)—L.L. *maciō, -ōnis,* prob. Gmc. ; cf. M.H.G. *mezzo,* a mason, whence *steinmetz,* a stone-mason ; O.H.G. *meizan,* to hew, whence Ger. *meissel,* a chisel.]

masoolah, massoola, masula, *mä-soo′lä, n.* a high many-oared Indian surf-boat. [Origin obscure.]

Masora, Masorah, *mä-sō′rä, n.* a collection of critical notes on the text of the Old Testament.— Also **Massora(h), Maso′reth.**—*n.* **Mas(s)′orete** (-*rēt*), a compiler of the Masora.—*adj.* **Mas(s)o-retic** (-*ret′ik*). [Heb. *māsoreth,* mod. *māsōrāh.*]

masque, *mäsk, n.* a masked person : a company of maskers : a masquerade or masked ball : a form of courtly spectacle in vogue in the 16th and 17th centuries, in which masked performers danced and acted, developing into a form of drama with scenery and music : a literary composition for the purpose : (*obs.*) a mask.—*n.* **masqu′er,** a masker. [See **mask.**]

masquerade, *mäsk-ər-ād′, n.* an assembly of persons wearing masks, generally at a ball : disguise.— *v.i.* to wear a mask : to join in a masquerade : to go in disguise.—*n.* **masquerad′er.** [Fr. *mascarade* ; see **mask.**]

mass, *mäs, n.* a lump of matter : (*obs.*) matter, material : a quantity : a collected or coherent body : an unbroken expanse : the aggregate : the main body : the greater part : the principal part : quantity of matter in any body, measured by its resistance to change of motion : (in *pl.*) the lower classes of the people.—*v.t.* to form into mass : to bring together in masses.—*v.i.* to assemble in masses.—*adj.* **massive** (*mas′iv*), bulky : weighty : giving an impression of weight : not separated into parts or elements : without crystalline form.—*adv.* **mass′ively.** — *ns.* **mass′iveness, mass′iness; mass′-meet′ing,** a large meeting for a public protest or assertion ; **mass′-produc′tion,** production on a huge scale by a standardised process. —*adj.* **mass′y,** massive, made up of masses.— **mass number,** the atomic weight of an isotope ; **mass spectrograph,** an instrument by means of which a positive ray spectrum can be obtained, the images due to particles of different masses being spaced according to the masses, so that the atomic weights of the particles can be deduced ; **in mass,** as a body : all together ; **in the mass,** in the aggregate : as a whole : indiscriminately ; **law of mass action,** (*chem.*) rate of chemical change is proportional to the product of the concentrations of the reacting substances. [Fr. *masse*—L. *massa,* a lump, prob.—Gr. *mäza,* a barley cake—*massein,* to knead.]

mass (often **Mass**), *mäs, n.* the celebration of the Lord's Supper or Eucharist in R.C. churches : the office for it : a musical setting of certain parts of the R.C. liturgy : a church festival or feast-day, as in *Candlemas, Christmas, Martinmas,* &c. —*ns.* **mass′-bell,** a sacring bell ; **mass′-book,** the R.C. missal or service-book ; **mass′-priest,** formerly a R.C. secular priest, as distinct from one living under a rule—later, a priest retained in chantries, &c., to say masses for the dead : a R.C. priest generally. [O.E. *mæsse*—L.L. *missa* —L. *mittère,* to send away, perh. from the phrase at the close of service, *ite, missa est (ecclesia),* go, (the congregation) is dismissed.]

Mass, Mas, *mäs,* **Mess, Mes,** *mes, n.* (*obs.*) shortened forms of **Master.**—**Mas(s)-John, Mes(s)-John,** (*obs.*) a contemptuous name for a Scottish parish minister.

massa, *mas′ə, n.* a negro corruption of **master.**

massacre, *mas′ə-kər* (*Spens.* sometimes *-ak′*), *n.* indiscriminate slaughter, esp. with cruelty : carnage.—*v.t.* to kill with violence and cruelty : to slaughter. [Fr. ; origin doubtful.]

massage, *mä-säzh′, n.* a system of treatment by stroking, pressing, tapping, kneading, friction, &c.—*v.t.* to subject to massage.—*ns.* **massa′gist,** **masseur** (-*ər′*) :—*fem.* **masseuse** (-*əz′*). [Fr., from Gr. *massein,* to knead.]

massaranduba, *mas-ä-ran-dōō′bä, n.* the Brazilian milk-tree (*Mimusops elata*). — Also **masseran-duba, macaranduba.** [Port. *maçaranduba,* from Tupí name.]

massé, *mas′ā, n.* in billiards, a sharp stroke made with the cue vertical or nearly so. [Fr.]

masseter, *mas-ē′tər, n.* a muscle that raises the under jaw. [Gr. *masētēr* (not *massētēr*), chewer— *masaesthai,* to chew.]

massicot, *mas′i-kot, n.* yellow lead monoxide. [Fr.]

massif, *mä-sēf'*, *mas'if*, *n.* a central mountain-mass: an orographic fault-block. [Fr.]

Massora(h). See Masora.

massymore, *mas-i-mōr'*, *n.* (Scott) a subterranean prison. [Perh. Sp. *mazmorra*.]

mast, *mäst*, *n.* a long upright pole, esp. one for carrying the sails of a ship.—*v.t.* to supply with a mast or masts.—*adj.* **mast'ed.**—*n.* **mast'-head,** the top of a mast.—*v.t.* to raise to the mast-head: to punish by sending to the mast-head.—*n.* **mast'-house,** the place where masts are made or stored. —*adj.* **mast'less.**—before the mast, as a common sailor (whose quarters are in the forecastle). [O.E. *mæst*; Ger. *mast*.]

mast, *mäst*, *n.* the fruit of the oak, beech, chestnut, and other forest trees, on which swine feed: nuts, acorns.—*adjs.* **mast'-fed; mast'ful; mast'less; mast'y,** of the nature of mast: as if well fed on mast. [O.E. *mæst*; Ger. *mast*, whence *mästen*, to feed.]

mastaba, *mas'tə-bä*, *n.* an ancient Egyptian tomb in which offerings were made in an outer chamber communicating with an inner one where was the figure of the dead man, with a shaft descending to the actual grave. [Ar. *mastabah*, a bench.]

master, *mäs'tər*, *n.* one who commands or controls: a lord or owner: a leader or ruler: a teacher: an employer: the commander of a merchant-ship: formerly the navigator or sailing-master of a ship-of-war: one eminently skilled in any-thing, esp. art: one who has complete knowledge: a workman who has set up on his own account, or is qualified to do so: formerly prefixed to a name or designation as Mr is now: now only of a boy in this use: a title of dignity or office— a degree conferred by universities, as *Master of Arts*, &c., the title of the heir apparent of a Scottish viscount or baron, the head of some corporations, as Balliol College, &c., of a lodge of freemasons, &c.: *(dial.)* a husband.—*adj.* chief: principal: controlling: predominant: of a master: of the rank of a master.—*v.t.* to become master of: to overcome: to gain control over: to acquire a thorough knowledge of: to become skilful in: to rule as master: to furnish with a master or masters: to temper: to season: to treat with lye.—*v.i.* (also *v.t.* with *it*) to act the master or be a schoolmaster.—*ns.* **mas'ter-at-arms',** a ship's chief police officer: **mas'terate; mas'ter-build'er,** a chief builder: one who directs or employs others; **mas'ter-card,** the card that commands a suit; **mas'ter-clock,** one that regu-lates other clocks electrically; **mas'terdom,** power of control: masterfulness.—*adj.* **mas'terful,** exer-cising the authority or power of a master: im-perious: *(rare)* masterly.—*adv.* **mas'terfully.** —*ns.* **mas'terfulness; mas'ter-hand,** the hand of a master: a person highly skilled; **mas'ter-hood;** **mas'tering,** action of verb master: lye.— *ns.* **mas'ter-joint,** a joint of the most marked system of those by which a rock is intersected; **mas'ter-key,** a key that opens many locks: a clue fitted to guide one out of many difficulties.— *adj.* **mas'terless,** without a master or owner: ungoverned: unsubdued: beyond control.—*n.* **mas'terliness.**—*adj.* **mas'terly,** like a master: with the skill of a master: *(obs.)* overbearing.— *adv.* with the skill of a master.—*ns.* **mas'ter-mar'iner,** the captain of a merchant-vessel or fishing-vessel; **mas'ter-ma'son,** a freemason who has attained the third degree; **mas'ter-mind; mas'ter-pass'ion; mas'terpiece,** a piece of work worthy of a master: one's greatest achievement; **mas'tership,** the condition, authority, status, office, or term of office of master: rule or dominion: superiority; **mas'terstroke,** a stroke or perform-ance worthy of a master: superior performance; **mas'ter-wheel,** the wheel in a machine which imparts motion to other parts; **mas'ter-work,** work worthy of a master: masterpiece; **mas'ter-wort,** a plant (*Peucedanum,* or *Imperatoria, Ostru-thium*) akin to parsnip, once used as a pot-herb and in medicine: applied also to Astrantia and other plants; **mas'tery,** the power or authority of a master: upper hand: control: masterly skill or

knowledge.—**master of ceremonies, of the rolls,** &c. (see **ceremonies, rolls,** &c.); **master of the horse,** the Roman *Magister Equitum*, an official appointed by the dictator to act next under him-self: an equerry, esp. a high official of the British court; **Master of the Temple,** the preacher of the Temple Church in London; **masters of the schools,** at Oxford, the conductors of the first examination (*Responsions*) for the degree of B.A.; **masterly inactivity,** the position or part of a neutral or a Fabian combatant, carried out with diplomatic skill, so as to preserve a predominant influence without risking anything; **passed master,** one who has passed as a master: a thorough proficient (see **pastmaster**); **little masters,** a 16th-17th cent. group of followers of Dürer, notable for fine work on wood and copper; **old masters,** a term applied collectively to the great painters about the time of the Renaissance, esp. the Italians. [Partly O.E. *mægester*, partly O.Fr. *maistre* (Fr. *maître*), both from L. *magister*, from root of *magnus*, great.]

mastic, mastich, *mas'tik, n.* a pale yellow gum-resin from the lentisk and other trees, used for varnish, cement, liquor: a tree exuding mastic, esp. the lentisk (*Pistachia Lentiscus*; cashew-nut family): a bituminous or oily cement of various kinds. [Fr. *mastic*—L.L. *mastichum*—Gr. *mas-tichē*.]

masticate, *mas'ti-kāt, v.t.* to chew: to knead mechanically, as in rubber manufacture.—*adj.* **mas'ticable,** that may be chewed.—*ns.* **mas-tica'tion; mas'ticator,** one who masticates: *(facet.)* a tooth or jaw: a machine for cutting up meat for people unable to chew: a machine for kneading india-rubber.—*adj.* **mas'ticatory** (*-kə-tə-ri*), chewing: adapted for chewing.—*n.* a substance chewed to increase the saliva. [L. *masticāre, -ātum*; cf. Gr. *mastax*, jaw, *mastichaein*, to grind the teeth.]

masticot. Same as **massicot.**

mastiff, *mäs'tif, n.* a thick-set and powerful variety of dog much used as a watch-dog. [O.Fr. *mastin*, app.—L. *mansuētus*, tame; perh. confused with O.Fr. *mestif*, mongrel.]

Mastigophora, *mas-ti-gof'ə-rä, n.pl.* (*zool.*) the flagellates, in a wide sense.—*adjs.* **mastigophoric** (*-gof'ik*); **mastigophorous** (*-gof'ə-rəs*), of the Mastigophora: whip-carrying. [Gr. *mastix, -īgos,* whip, *phoreein,* to carry.]

mastitis, *mas-tī'tis, n.* inflammation of the mammary gland.—*adj.* **mas'toid,** like a nipple or teat.—*n.* a process of the temporal bone behind the ear (also **mastoid bone, process**): *(coll.)* mastoiditis.— *adj.* **mastoid'al.**—*n.* **mastoidi'tis,** inflammation of the air cells of the mastoid process. [Gr. *mastos,* a nipple.]

Mastodon, *mas'tə-don, n.* a genus of extinct ele-phants, so named from the teat-like prominences on the molar teeth of some species. [Gr. *mastos,* breast, *odous, odontos,* a tooth.]

masturbation, *mas-tər-bä'shən, n.* self-defilement, onanism. —*v.i.* **mas'turbate,** to commit self-abuse.—*n.* **mas'turbator.** [L. *masturbāri*.]

masu, *mä'soo, n.* a Japanese salmon (*Oncorhynchus masou*). [Jap.]

masula. See **masoolah.**

masurium, *mə-s(y)ōō'ri-əm, n.* a name proposed for element No. 43 when its discovery was prematurely claimed—see **technetium.** [*Masurenland,* in East Prussia.]

mat, *mat, n.* a piece of fabric of sedge, rushes, straw, coarse fibre, &c., or of rubber, wire, or other material, for cleaning shoes, for covering a floor, hearth, threshold, for protection, packing, for standing, sleeping, &c., on, or for other purpose: a rug: a small piece of strawplait, cloth, slab of cork or wood, &c., for placing under a vase, dish, or other object: a sack of matting used to cover a chest of tea, coffee, &c.: a certain weight held by such a sack: a closely interwoven or tangled mass, as of hair, of vegetation, or brushwood protecting a river-bank: a web of rope-yarn.— *v.t.* to cover with mats: to interweave: to tangle closely.—*v.i.* to become tangled in a mass:—*pr.p.*

matt'ing; *p.a.t.* and *p.a.p.* **matt'ed.**—*ns.* **mat'-grass, mat'weed,** a small, tufted, rushlike moorland grass (*Nardus stricta*): marram-grass; **matt'-ing,** mat-making: becoming matted: covering with mats: material used as mats. [O.E. *matt(e),* *meatte*—L. *matta,* a mat; perh. of Punic origin.]

mat, *mat, adj.* dull or lustreless.—Also **matt, matte.**—*n.* **mat,** a dull uniform finish or surface: a border of dull gold or of white or colour round a picture: a punch for roughening a surface: a stereotype matrix.—*v.t.* to produce a dull surface on: to frost (glass). [Fr. *mat;* Ger. *matt,* dull; cf. **checkmate; amate** (2), **mate** (2).]

matachin, *mat-ə-chēn', -shēn', n.* (*arch.*) a masked sword-dancer or sword-dance. [Fr. (obs.) *matachin* and Sp. *matachín,* perh.—Ar. *mutawajjihīn,* masked.]

matador, matadore, *mat'ə-dor, n.* the man who kills the bull in bull-fights: one of the three chief cards at ombre and quadrille: a form of dominoes. [Sp. *matador*—*matar,* to kill—L. *mactāre,* to kill, to honour by sacrifice—*mactus,* honoured.]

matamata, *mä-tä-mä'tä, n.* a South American river-turtle. [Port., from Tupí *matamatá.*]

match, *mach, n.* a piece of inflammable material which easily takes or carries fire: a prepared cord for firing a gun, an explosive, &c.: a short stick of wood or other material tipped with an easily ignited material.—*ns.* **match'-box,** a box for holding matches; **match'lock,** the lock of a musket containing a match for firing it: a musket so fired; **match'-maker; match'wood,** touch-wood: wood suitable for matches: splinters. [O.Fr. *mesche* (Fr. *mèche*): origin obscure.]

match, *mach, n.* that which tallies or exactly agrees with another thing: an equal: one able to cope with another: a condition of exact agreement or close resemblance, esp. in colours: equality in contest: (*obs.*) a compact: a formal contest or game: a pairing: a marriage: one to be gained in marriage.—*v.i.* to be exactly or nearly alike: to correspond: to form a union: to compete or encounter (esp. on equal terms).—*v.t.* to be equal to: to be a counterpart to: to be exactly like in colour, &c.: to be able to compete with: to find an equal or counterpart to: to pit or set against another in contest or as equal: to treat as equal: to fit in with: to suit: to join in marriage. —*adj.* **match'able.**—*ns.* **match'board,** a board with a tongue cut along one edge and a groove in the opposite edge; **matchboard'ing; match'-er; match'-joint,** the junction of matchboards.— *adj.* **match'less,** having no match or equal: superior to all: peerless: (*Spens.*) not matching. — *adv.* **match'lessly.** — *ns.* **match'lessness; match'maker,** one who plans to bring about marriages; **match'making; match'-point,** the stage at which another point wins the match: the point that wins the match.—**to match,** in accordance, as in colour. [O.E. *gemæcca;* cf. **make** (3).]

mate, *māt, n.* a companion: an equal: a fellow-workman: a friendly form of address among workmen: a husband or wife: an animal with which another is paired: a ship's officer under the captain or master: in the navy, formerly a rank to which a warrant-officer might be promoted— now sub-lieutenant: an assistant, deputy (as *surgeon's mate*).—*v.t.* to be equal to: to rival: to cope with: to marry: to pair: to couple: to fit. —*v.i.* to claim equality: to marry: to pair: to consort.—*adjs.* **mate'less,** without a mate or companion; **mat(e)'y,** (*coll.*) friendly and familiar, esp. in a studied or overdone manner. [Prob. M.L.G. *mate* or earlier Du. *maet* (now *maat*); cf. O.E. *gemetta,* a messmate, and **meat.**]

mate, *māt, adj.* (*arch.*) checkmated: confounded: baffled: exhausted: daunted.—*v.t.* to check-mate: to subdue: to baffle: to confound.—*n.* and *interj.* checkmate. [O.Fr. *mat,* checkmated; see **checkmate, mat** (2).]

mate, *māt, n.* a South American species of holly (*Ilex paraguayensis*): an infusion of its leaves and green shoots (Paraguay tea). [Sp. *mate*—Quechua *mati,* a gourd (in which it is made).]

matelassé, *mȧt-lä-sā, adj.* and *n.* having a raised pattern as if quilted, of silks. [Fr.,—*matelas,* a mattress.]

matelot. See **matlo.**

matelote, *mat'ə-lōt, n.* fish stewed with wine-sauce, onions, &c.: a sort of hornpipe. [Fr.,—*matelot,* a sailor.]

mater, *mā'tər,* L. *mä'ter, n.* (*slang*) a mother: either of the two membranes of the brain, outer and inner, separated by the arachnoid—the *dura mater,* or *dura,* and *pia mater,* or *pia.* [L. *māter;* cf. Gr. *mētēr;* **mother.**]

material, *mə-tē'ri-əl, adj.* relating to matter: consisting of matter: (*Shak.*) being the substance of the thing: (*Shak.*) matterful: corporeal, not spiritual: bodily: physical: gross, lacking spirituality: relating to subject-matter: relevant: of serious importance, esp. of legal importance: (*phil.*) pertaining to matter as opposed to form.— *n.* that out of which anything is or may be made: that which may be made use of for any purpose: a fabric, esp. woollen.—*n.* **materialisā'tion.**— *v.t.* **mate'rialise,** to render material: to cause to assume bodily form: to reduce to or regard as matter: to render materialistic.—*v.i.* to take bodily form: (*coll.*) to become actual.—*ns.* **mate'rialism,** the doctrine that denies the independent existence of spirit, and maintains that there is but one substance—matter: the explanation of history as the working out of economic conditions: blindness to the spiritual: exclusive or excessive devotion to bodily or physical wants; **mate'rialist.**—Also *adj.*—*adjs.* **materialist'ic, -al.**—*advs.* **materialist'ically; mate'rially,** in a material manner: in respect of matter or material conditions, or material cause: in a considerable or important degree. — *ns.* **mate'rialness, materiality** *(-al'i-ti).* — **dialectical materialism,** Karl Marx's view of history as a conflict between opposites, present conditions being due to a class struggle between the capitalists, whose aim is private profit, and the workers, who resist exploitation; **material distinction,** the distinction between individuals of the same species; **material evidence,** evidence tending to prove or to disprove the matter under judgment; **material fallacy,** a fallacy in the matter or thought, rather than in the logical form. [L. *māteriālis*—*māteria,* matter.]

materia medica, *mə-tē'ri-ä med'i-kä,* substances used in medicine: the science of their properties and use. [L.L., medical material.]

matériel, *mȧ-tā-ri-el', -ryel', n.* material: equipment: esp. the baggage and munitions of an army. [Fr.]

maternal, *mə-tər'nəl, adj.* of a mother: motherly: on the mother's side: of the nature, or in the person, of a mother.— *adv.* **mater'nally.**—*n.* **mater'nity,** the fact of being in the relation of mother: motherhood: maternal nature: a maternity hospital.—*adj.* of or for women at or near the time of childbirth. [Fr. *maternel* (It. *maternale*) and *maternité*—L. *māternus*—*māter,* mother.]

matfelon, *mat'fel-ən, n.* the greater knapweed. [O.Fr. *matefelon;* cf. **mate** (2) and **felon.**]

math, *math, n.* a mowing. [O.E. *mæth.*]

mathematic, -al, *math-i-mat'ik, -al, adjs.* pertaining to, or done by, mathematics: very accurate.—*adv.* **mathemat'ically.** — *ns.* **mathematician** *(-ma-tish'ən),* one versed in mathematics; **mathemat'ics** (treated as *sing.:* *coll.* maths), the science of magnitude and number, and of all their relations. [Gr. *mathēmatikē* (*epistēmē,* skill, knowledge) relating to learning—*mathēma*—root of *manthanein,* to learn.]

mathesis, *mä-thē'sis* (*obs.* *math'i-sis*), *n.* mental discipline, esp mathematical. [Gr. *mathēsis.*]

Mathurin, Mathurine, *math'ū-rin, -rēn, n.* a Trinitarian canon. [Perh. from their house near St *Mathurin's* chapel in Paris.]

matico, *mä-tē'kō, n.* a Peruvian pepper shrub, used as a styptic. [Sp. dim. of *Mateo,* Matthew.]

matin, *mat'in, n.* (*Shak.*) morning: (*Milt.*) a morning song: (in *pl.:* often **Matins**) one of the seven canonical hours of the R.C. Church, usually sung between midnight and daybreak, or now by anticipation the afternoon or evening before : (in *pl.*) the daily morning service of the Church of England.—*adj.* of the morning : of matins.—*adj.* **mat′inal.**—*n.* matinée (*mat′i-nā* ; Fr.), a public entertainment or reception held in the day-time, usually in the afternoon : a woman's dress for morning wear. [Fr. *matines* (fem. pl.)—L. *mātūtīnus*, belonging to the morning—*Mātūta*, goddess of morning, prob. akin to *mātūrus*, early.]

matlo, matlow, *mat′lō, n.* (*slang*) a bluejacket.— Also **matelot** (*mat′lō*). [Fr. *matelot*.]

matrass, *mat′ras, n.* a long-necked chemical flask : a hard-glass tube closed at one end. [Fr. *matras*.]

matriarchy, *mā′tri-är-ki, n.* government by a mother or by mothers : an order of society in which descent is reckoned in the female line.—*n.* **ma′triarch,** a woman in whom matriarchy rests : a patriarch's wife : a woman of like status to a patriarch.—*adj.* **matriar′chal.**—*ns.* **matriar′chalism,** a condition of society with matriarchal customs : the theory of such a society ; **matriar′chate,** the position of a matriarch : a matriarchal condition or community. [Formed on the analogy of **patriarchy**—L. *māter* (or Doric Gr. *mātēr*), mother.]

matrice, *mā′tris, mat′ris, n.* Same as **matrix.**

matricide, *mat′* or *mat′ri-sīd, n.* a murderer of his (or her) own mother : the murder of one's own mother.—*adj.* **matrici′dal.** [L. *mātrīcīda, mātrīcīdium*—*māter*, mother, *caedere*, to kill.]

matricula, *mǝ-trik′ū-lä, n.* a register of members, students, &c.—*adj.* **matric′ular,** pertaining to a register : contributed to the federal fund (as formerly by German states).—*v.t.* **matric′ulate,** to admit to membership by entering one's name in a register, esp. in a college.—*v.i.* to become a member of a college, university, &c., by being enrolled.—*n.* one admitted to membership in a society.—*n.* **matriculā′tion,** act of matriculating : state of being matriculated : an entrance examination (familiarly **matric′**). [L.L. *mātrīcula*, a register, dim. of L. *mātrīx*.]

matrilineal, *mat-ri-lin′i-ǝl,* **matrilinear,** *-ǝr, adjs.* reckoned through the mother or through females alone.—*adv.* **matrilin′eally.**—*n.* **mat′riliny** (or *-lī′ni*). [L. *māter*, a mother, *līnea*, a line.]

matrilocal, *mat-ri-lō′kl, adj.* (of a form of marriage) in which the husband goes to live with the wife's group. [L. *māter*, mother, *locālis*—*locus* place.]

matrimony, *mat′ri-man-i, n.* wedlock : a card game of chance in which one of the winning combinations is that of king and queen : the combination of king and queen in that and in various other games.—*adj.* **matrimonial** (*-mō′ni-ǝl*).—*adv.* **matrimo′nially.** [L. *mātrimōnium*—*māter, mātris,* mother.]

matrix, *mā′triks,* or *mat′riks, n.* (*anat.*) the womb : the cavity in which anything is formed : that in which anything is embedded, as ground-mass, gangue, intercellular substance, cementing material : the bed on which a thing rests, as the cutis under a nail, the hollow in a slab to receive a monumental brass : a mould : (*math.*) a rectangular array of quantities or symbols :—*pl.* **ma′trices** (*-tris-ēz,* or *-iz* : by strict adherence to L. quantities it would be *mā-trī′sēz*), or **ma′trixes.** [L. *mātrīx, -īcis,* a breeding animal, later, the womb—*māter,* mother.]

matroclinic, *mat-rō-klin′ik,* **matroclinous,** *-klī′nǝs, adjs.* inherited from the mother : more like the mother than the father.—*n.* **matrocli′ny.** [L. *māter* (or Doric Gr. *mātēr*), mother, and Gr. *klīnein,* to lean.]

matron, *mā′trǝn, n.* a married woman : an elderly lady of staid and sober habits : a woman in charge of nursing and domestic arrangements in a hospital, school, or other institution.—*ns.* **ma′tronage, ma′tronhood,** state of being a matron : a body of matrons.—*adj.* **ma′tronal,** pertaining or suitable to a matron : motherly : grave.—*v.t.* **ma′tronise,** to render matronly : to act as matron to : to chaperon.—*v.i.* to become a matron or matronly.—*adjs.* **ma′tron-like, ma′tronly,** like, becoming, or belonging to a matron : elderly : sedate.—*n.* **ma′tronship.** [Fr. *matrone*—L. *mātrōna*—*māter,* mother.]

matronymic. See **metronymic.**

matross, *mǝ-tros′, n.* (*obs.*) a gunner's assistant in artillery. [Du. *matroos,* app.—Fr. *matelot,* a sailor.]

matt, matte, *mat, adj.* Same as **mat** (2).

mattamore, *mat-ǝ-mōr′, n.* a subterranean chamber. [Fr. *matamore*—Ar. *matmūrah.*]

matte, *mat, n.* a product of the smelting of sulphide ores.—Also *regulus* and *coarse metal.* [Fr.]

matter, *mat′ǝr, n.* that which occupies space, and with which we become acquainted by our bodily senses : that out of which anything is made, material : subject or material of thought, speech, writing, dispute, &c. : substance (opp. to *form*) : (*Shak.*) good sense : anything engaging the attention : affair : subject : thing : that with which one has to do : cause or ground : thing of consequence : something that is amiss : that with which a court is concerned, something to be tried or proved : importance : an approximate amount : (*print.*) material for work, type set up, copy, &c. : that which may be sent by post (*postal matter*) : pus.—*v.i.* to be of importance : to signify : to form or discharge pus.—*v.t.* (*obs.*) to mind, concern oneself about.—*adjs.* **matt′erful,** full of matter, pithy ; **matt′erless** ; **matt′er-of-fact′,** adhering to literal, actual, or pedestrian fact : not fanciful : prosaic ; **matt′ery,** purulent : containing, discharging, or covered with pus.—**as a matter of fact,** really ; **for that matter,** as for that : indeed ; **matter of course,** a thing occurring in natural time and order, as to be expected ; **no matter,** it does not matter : it makes no difference. [O.Fr. *matiere*—L. *māteria,* matter.]

matting. See **mat.**

mattins. Same as **matins,** *pl.* of **matin.**

mattock, *mat′ǝk, n.* a kind of pickaxe for loosening the soil, with cutting end instead of a point. [O.E. *mattuc.*]

mattress, *mat′ris, n.* a bed made of a stuffed bag, or a substitute or supplementary structure of wire, hair, &c. : a mass of brushwood, &c., used to form a foundation for roads, &c., or for the walls of embankments, &c. [O.Fr. *materas* (Fr. *matelas*)— Ar. *matrah,* a place where anything is thrown.]

mature, *mǝ-tūr′, adj.* fully developed : perfected : ripe : well thought out : due : (*Milt.*) in due time : suppurating.—*v.t.* to bring to ripeness, full development, or perfection : to bring to a head : to cause to suppurate.—*v.i.* to come to or approach ripeness, full development, or perfection : to become due.—*adj.* **matur′able,** capable of being matured.—*v.t.* **maturate** (*mat′*), to make mature : (*med.*) to promote the suppuration of.—*v.i.* (*med.*) to suppurate perfectly.—*n.* **maturā′tion,** a bringing or a coming to maturity : the process of suppurating fully : the final stage in the production of a germ-cell, at which the reducing division occurs.—*adj.* **matur′ative** (or *mat′*), promoting ripening : promoting suppuration.—*n.* a medicine promoting suppuration.—*adv.* **mature′ly.** —*ns.* **mature′ness** ; **matur′ity,** ripeness : full development : the time of becoming due, as of a bill. [L. *mātūrus,* ripe.]

matutinal, *mat-ū-tī′nl* (or *mǝ-tūt′i-nǝl*), *adj.* pertaining to the morning : happening early in the day.—Also **matutine** (*mat′ū-tīn*). [L. *mātūtīnālis, mātūtīnus* ; see **matin.**]

maud, *mawd, n.* a Scottish shepherd's woollen plaid. [Origin unknown.]

maudlin, *mawd′lin, adj.* silly : sickly-sentimental : fuddled, half-drunk : (*obs.*) tearful.—*n.* **maud′linism,** the tearful stage of drunkenness. [M.E. *Maudelein,* through O.Fr. and L. from Gr. *Magdalēnē,* (woman) of Magdala, from the assumption that Mary Magdalene was the penitent woman of Luke vii. 38.]

maugre, maulgre, *maw′gǝr,* also *-gri, maw(l)-grē′, prep.* (*arch.*) in spite of : notwithstanding : (*Spens.,* with dative) a curse upon.—*adv.* in despite.—*n.* (*obs.*) ill-will : spite. [O.Fr. *malgré*—L. *male grātum*—*male,* badly, *grātum,* agreeable.]

maul, *mawl, n.* (*obs.*) a war-club or mace : a heavy wooden hammer or beetle, a mall : (*Rugby football*) a scrimmage : (*in goal*) a struggle for the ball when carried across the goal-line, but not yet touched down.—*v.t.* to beat with a maul or heavy stick : to handle roughly, batter, maltreat : (*U.S.*) to split with a maul.—*v.i.* to thrust forward in a close mass. [**mall.**]

maulstick, *mawl′stik*, *n.* a stick used by painters as a rest for the hand.—Also **mahl′stick.** [Du. *maalstok*—*malen*, to paint, *stock*, stick, assimilated to stick.]

maumet, mawmet. Same as **mammet.**

maun, *mawn*, *män*, *mun*, *v.t.* (*Scot.*) must.—**maunna** (*mawn′ä*, *-i*), must not. [See **mun.**]

maund, *mawnd*, *n.* (*Shak.*) a basket. [O.E. *mand.*]

maund, *mawnd*, *n.* a measure of weight in India, its value varying in different places from about 25 to about 85 pounds avoirdupois. [Hind. and Pers. *man.*]

maund, *mawnd*, *v.t.* and *v.i.* (*obs. slang*) to beg.— *n.* **maund′er,** a beggar.—*v.i.* to beg. [Poss. Fr. *mendier*, to beg—L. *mendicāre.*]

maunder, *mawn′dər*, *v.i.* to grumble : to mutter : to talk foolishly : to drivel.—*ns.* **maun′derer : maun′dering,** drivelling talk. [Origin unknown.]

maundy, *mawn′di*, *n.* the religious ceremony of washing the feet of the poor, in commemoration of Christ's washing the disciples' feet (John xiii.) —long practised by some monarchs.—**maundy money,** the dole given away on Maundy Thursday, the day before Good Friday, by the royal almoner, usually a penny for each year of the sovereign's age—the small silver coins specially coined since 1662. [Fr. *mandé*—L. *mandātum*, command (John xiii. 34).]

Maurist, *maw′rist*, *n.* a member of the reformed Benedictine Congregation of St *Maur*, settled from 1618 at the abbey of St *Maur*-sur-Loire, near Saumur, notable for its great services to learning.—Also *adj.*

Mauritius, *maw-rish′əs*, *adj.* of the island of *Mauritius* (named after Maurice (1567-1625) Prince of Orange).—**Mauritius hemp,** the fibre of an amaryllidaceous plant, *Furcraea gigantea.*

Mauser, *mow′zər*, *n.* a German magazine rifle, invented by Wilhelm *Mauser* (1834-82).

mausoleum, *maw-sō-lē′əm*, *n.* a magnificent tomb or monument.—*adj.* **mausole′an.** [L. *mausōlēum* — Gr. *Mausōleion*, the magnificent tomb of *Mausōlos* (d. 353 B.C.), satrap of Caria, erected by his widow Artemisia at Halicarnassus.]

mauther, mawther, *maw′dhər*, *n.* (*dial.*, esp. E. Anglia) a girl : a great awkward girl.—Also (esp. vocatively) **mawr, mor.** [Origin obscure.]

mauve, *mōv*, *mawv*, *n.* a purple aniline dye : its colour, that of mallow flowers.—*adj.* of the colour of mauve.—*n.* **mauv(e)′in(e),** mauve dye. [Fr., —L. *malva*, mallow.]

maverick, *mav′ər-ik*, *n.* (*U.S.*) a stray animal without an owner's brand, esp. a calf : anything dishonestly obtained.—*v.t.* to seize without legal claim. [From Samuel *Maverick*, a Texas cattle-raiser.]

mavis, *mā′vis*, *n.* the song-thrush. [Fr. *mauvis.*]

mavourneen, *mə-vōōr′nēn*, *n.* and *interj.* (Ir.) my dear one. [Ir. *mo mhurnín.*]

maw, *maw*, *n.* the stomach, esp. in the lower animals : the craw, in birds : the fourth stomach in ruminants : inward parts : (*fig.*) any insatiate gulf or receptacle.—*adj.* **maw′bound,** (of cattle) constipated by impaction of the rumen.—*n.* **maw′-worm,** a worm infesting the stomach or intestines. [O.E. *maga* ; Ger. *magen.*]

maw, *maw*, *n.* a mew or gull. [O.N. *már.*]

maw, *maw*, *n.* an old card-game. [Origin unknown.]

mawk, *mawk*, *n.* (now *dial.*) a maggot.—*adj.* **mawk′ish,** (*orig.*) maggoty : loathsome, disgusting : squeamish : insipid : sickly : sickly-sentimental, maudlin.— *adv.* **mawk′ishly.** — *n.* **mawk′ishness.** [O.N. *mathkr*, maggot.]

mawkin. Same as **malkin.**

mawmet, mawther. See **mammet, mauther.**

maw′seed, *n.* poppy seed as cage-bird food. [Ger. *mahsaat*—*mah*, poppy.]

max, *maks*, *n.* (*obs.*) gin. [Origin obscure.]

maxilla, *maks-il′ä*, *n.* a jawbone, esp. the upper : in arthropods an appendage close behind the

mouth, modified in connexion with feeding :— *pl.* **maxill′ae** (*-ē*).—*adj.* **maxill′ary** (or *maks′*), pertaining to a jaw or maxilla.—*n.* a bone forming the posterior part of the upper jaw.—*ns.* **maxill′-iped, -pede** (*-ped*, *-pēd*), in Crustacea, a jaw-foot, an appendage behind the mouth, adapted to help in passing food to the mouth ; **maxill′ūla**, in crustaceans, a maxilla of the first pair :—*pl.* **maxill′ūlae** (*-lē*). [L. *maxilla*, jawbone.]

maxim, *maks′im*, *n.* a general principle, serving as a rule or guide : a pithy saying : a proverb.—*ns.* **max′imist, max′im-mong′er.** [Fr. *maxime*— L. *maxima* (*sententia*, or some other word), greatest (opinion, &c.), fem., superl. of *magnus*, great.]

Maxim, *maks′im*, *n.* often put for **Max′im-gun′,** an automatic machine-gun invented by Hiram *Maxim* (1840-1916).

maximum, *maks′i-məm*, *adj.* greatest.—*n.* the greatest number, quantity, or degree : the highest point reached : (*math.*) the value of a variable when it ceases to increase and begins to decrease (*pl.* **max′ima**)—opp. to *minimum.*—*adj.* **max′imal,** of the highest or maximum value.—*n.* **max′imalist,** one who makes the fullest demands : a Bolshevik, one who demands the maximum programme.— *adv.* **max′imally.**—*v.t.* **max′imise,** to raise to the highest degree.—*v.i.* to give greatest scope to a doctrine. — **maximum and minimum thermometer,** a thermometer that shows the highest and lowest temperatures that have occurred since last adjustment. [L., superl. neut. of *magnus*, great.]

maxixe, *mä-shē′shä*, *n.* a Brazilian dance : a tune for it. [Port.]

maxwell, *maks′wəl*, *n.* a unit of magnetic flux—flux of magnetic induction per square centimetre in a magnetic field of the intensity of one gauss. [Named after James Clerk-*Maxwell* (1831-79), Scottish physicist.]

may, *mā*, *v.t.* expressing ability, permission, freedom, possibility, contingency, chance, competence, or wish, or softening a blunt question—used with *infin.* without *to* :—*infin.* and participles obsolete : *2nd pers. sing.* **mayst, mayest** ; *3rd* **may** ; *pa.t.* **might** (*mīt*), obs. **mought** (*mowt*) ; *2nd pers.* **mightest, mightst.**—*adv.* **may′be,** perhaps, possibly.—*n.* a possibility.—*adv.* **may′hap** (or *-hap′*), perhaps. [O.E. *mæg*, pr.t. (old pa.t.) of *magan*, to be able, pa.t. *mihte* ; cog. with Goth. *magan*, Ger. *mögen.*]

May, *mā*, *n.* (now) the fifth month of the year : the early or gay part of life : (**may**) may-blossom.— *v.i.* to gather may on Mayday : to participate in May sports.—*ns.* **May′-app′le,** Podophyllum or its egg-shaped fruit ; **may′-bee′tle, may′-bug,** the cockchafer ; **may′-bloom′, may′-bloss′om,** the hawthorn flower ; **May′day,** the first day of May, given to sports and to socialist and labour demonstrations.—Also *adj.*—*ns.* **May′-dew′,** the dew of May, esp. that of the morning of the first day of May, said to whiten linen, and beautify faces ; **may′-duke,** a variety of sour cherry ; **May′fair,** the aristocratic West End of London, once seat of a fair in May ; **may′flower,** the hawthorn or other flower that blooms in May ; **may′fly,** a short-lived plectopterous insect (Ephemera) that appears in May : the caddis-fly ; **May′-game,** sport appropriate to Mayday : frolic generally : **may′ing,** the observance of Mayday customs ; **May′-lā′dy,** the queen of the May ; **may′-lil′y,** the lily of the valley ; **May′-lord′,** a youth directing May-games : one enjoying transitory dignity.— *n.pl.* **May′-meet′ings,** meetings of various religious and philanthropic societies held in London in May.—*ns.* **May′-morn′, -morn′ing,** a morning in May : (*Shak.*) youthful freshness as of May **may′pole,** a pole erected for dancing round on Mayday ; **May′-queen′,** a young woman crowned with flowers as queen on Mayday ; **May′-time,** the season of May.—**May laws,** Prussian laws passed in three successive Mays (1873-75) restricting the power of the Church. [O.Fr. *Mai*—L. *Māius* (*mēnsis*), prob. (month) sacred to *Māia*, mother of Mercury.]

may, *mā*, *n.* a maid. [Prob. O.E. *mæg*, a kins-woman.]

maya, *mä′yä*, *n.* illusion. [Sans. *māyā.*]

Maya, *mä′yä*, *n.* one of an Indian people of Central America and Southern Mexico who developed a remarkable civilisation.—*adjs.* **Ma′ya**, **Ma′yan**. —*ns.* **Mayol′ogist**, **Mayol′ogy**.

mayhem, *mā′hem*, *mā′əm*, *n.* (*legal* and *U.S.*) maiming. [maim.]

mayonnaise, *mā-ə-nāz′*, or *mā′*, *n.* a sauce composed of the yolk of eggs, salad-oil, and vinegar or lemon-juice, seasoned: any cold dish of which it is an ingredient. [Fr.]

mayor, *mā′ər*, *mār*, *n.* the chief magistrate of a city or borough in England, Ireland, &c., whether man or woman.—*adj.* **may′oral**.—*ns.* **may′oralty**, **may′orship**, the office of a mayor; **may′oress**, a mayor's wife, or other lady who performs her social and ceremonial functions.—**Lord Mayor**, the chief magistrate of certain English, Welsh, Irish, and Australian cities and boroughs; **Mayor of the Palace**, in Merovingian France the king's major-domo or prime minister, the real ruler. [Fr. *maire*—L. *major*, comp. of *magnus*, great.]

mayster, *mās′ter*, **maysterdome**, &c., Spenserian forms of **master**, &c.

mayweed, *mā′wēd*, *n.* stinking camomile (*Anthemis Cotula*): corn feverfew (*Matricaria inodora*; scent-less mayweed): applied to various similar plants. [O.E. *mægtha*, mayweed, and **weed**.]

mazard, **mazzard**, *maz′ard*, *n.* (*Shak.*) a head or skull: a wild European cherry. [Prob. **mazer**.]

mazarine, *maz-ə-rēn′*, *n.* a rich blue colour: a blue gown or stuff.—Also *adj.*—*n.* **mazarinade′**, a satire or pamphlet against Cardinal *Mazarin* (1602-61).—**Mazarin(e) Bible**, the first printed Bible, printed by Gutenberg and Fust about 1450, of which the Cardinal had twenty-five copies; **mazarine hood**, a hood of a form said to have been worn by the Duchesse de *Mazarin*.

Mazdaism, *maz′dā-izm*, **Mazdeism**, *maz′dē-izm*, *ns.* the religion of the ancient Persians.—*adj.* **Mazdē′an**. [See **Ormuzd**.]

maze, *māz*, *n.* bewilderment: a labyrinth: a set of intricate windings.—*v.t.* to bewilder: to confuse.—*adj.* **maze′ful** (*Spens.*).—*n.* **maze′ment**. —*adv.* **maz′ily**.—*n.* **maz′iness**.—*adj.* **maz′y**. [Prob. from a lost O.E. word; the compound *āmasod*, amazed, occurs.]

maze, *māz*. Same as **mease** (of herrings).

mazer, *mā′zər*, *n.* (*Spens.*) a hard wood, probably maple: a cup of maple wood: a similar cup of other material. [O.Fr. *masere*, of Gmc. origin; cf. O.H.G. *masar*, O.N. *mösurr*, a maple-tree.]

mazurka, *mə-zōōr′kä*, or *-zur′*, *n.* a lively Polish dance: music for it, in triple time. [Pol., Masurian woman.]

mazut, **mazout**, *mə-zōōt′*, *n.* petroleum residue after distillation. [Russ. *mazut*, to daub, smear.]

me, *mē*, *mi*, *pers. pron.* the accusative and dative of **I**. [O.E. *mé.*]

me, an anglicised spelling of **mi**.

meacock, *mē′kok*, *adj.* (*Shak.*) timorous, effeminate, cowardly.—*n.* a milksop. [Origin unknown.]

mead, *mēd*, *n.* honey and water fermented and flavoured. [O.E. *meodu*; Ger. *met*, W. *medd*.]

mead, *mēd* (*poet.*), and **meadow**, *med′ō*, *ns.* a level tract producing grass to be mown down: a rich pasture-ground, esp. beside a stream.—*ns.* **mead′ow-brown′**, a butterfly of the Satyridae; **mead′ow-grass**, any grass of the genus Poa: (floating **meadow-grass**, manna-grass, flote-grass); **mead′ow-lark′**, (*U.S.*) a name for various species of birds of the genus Sturnella (family Icteridae); **mead′ow-rue′**, a genus (Thalictrum) of the buttercup family with rue-like leaves; **mead′ow-saff′ron**, Colchicum—also *autumn-crocus*, or *naked lady*; **mead′ow-sax′ifrage**, a saxifrage (*Saxifraga granulata*) that grows on banks and dry meadows: applied also to umbelliferous plants of the genera Seseli and Silaus.—*adj.* **mead′owy**. [O.E. *mǣd*, in oblique cases *mǣdwe—mǣwan*, to mow; Ger. *matte*.]

meadow-sweet, *med′ō-swēt*, *n.* the rosaceous plant queen of the meadows (*Spiraea Ulmaria*), a tall fragrant plant of watery meadows. [Earlier **mead-sweet**, which may be from **mead** (1) or from

mead (2), as the obs. **mead′wort** is in O.E. *meduwyrt.*]

meagre, *mē′gər*, *adj.* having little flesh: lean: poor: without richness or fertility: barren: scanty: without strength: jejune: maigre.—*n.* the maigre.—*adv.* **mea′grely**.—*n* **mea′greness**. [Fr. *maigre*—L. *macer*, *macra*, *-rum*, lean; cf. Ger. *mager*.]

meal, *mēl*, *n.* the food taken at one time: the *act* or occasion of taking food, as a breakfast, dinner, or supper.—*ns.* **meal′er**, one who takes his meals at a boarding-house, lodging elsewhere; **meal′-tide** (*arch.*; *Scot.* **meltith**, *mel′tith*, a meal), **meal′-time**, the time for a meal. [O.E. *mǣl*, time, portion of time; Du. *maal*, Ger. *mahl*.]

meal, *mēl*, *n.* grain ground to powder: other material in powder: a powdery surface-covering. —*v.t.* to cover with meal: to grind into meal.— *v.i.* to yield or be plentiful in meal.—*ns.* **meal′-ark**, (*Scot.*) a large chest for holding meal; **meal′iness**; **meal′-man**, or **meal′-monger**, one who deals in meal; **meal′-poke**, a beggar's meal-bag; **meal′-tree**, the wayfaring tree, from its mealy leaves and shoots; **meal′-worm**, the larva of a beetle (Tenebrio) abounding in granaries and flour-stores.—*adj.* **meal′y**, like meal: covered with meal or with something like meal: spotty: whitish.—*n.* **meal′y-bug**, a hothouse pest, a coccus insect with a white powdery appearance.— *adj.* **meal′y - mouthed** (*-mowdhd*), smooth-tongued: over-squeamish in choice of words.— *n.* **meal′y-mouth′edness**.—**Meal Monday**, the second Monday in February, an Edinburgh University (Arts) holiday, originally to allow the students to go home and replenish their stock of meal. [O.E. *melu*, *melo*; Ger. *mehl*, Du. *meel*, meal.]

meal, *mēl*, *v.t.* (*Shak.*, in *pa.p.* **meal′d**) to stain, spot. [O.E. *mǣlan*.]

mealie, *mēl′i*, *n.* (*S.Afr.*) an ear of maize: (esp. in *pl.*) maize. [S.Afr. Du. *milie*, millet.]

mean, *mēn*, *adj.* low in rank or birth: base: sordid: low in worth or estimation: of little value or importance: poor, humble: low: in-considerable: despicable: shabby: paltry: small-minded: ungenerous: stingy: (*U.S.*) out of sorts, uncomfortable. — *adj.* **mean′-born**.— *adv.* **mean′ly**.—*n.* **mean′ness**.—*adj.* **mean′-spir′ited**. —*n.* **mean′-spir′itedness**. [O.E. *gemǣne*; Ger. *gemein*; L. *commūnis*, common.]

mean, *mēn*, *adj.* intermediate: average: (*obs.*) moderate.—*n.* that which is between or inter-mediate: an average amount, or value: a middle state or position: an intermediate term in a progression: (*Spens.*) meantime: (*mus.*) a middle or intermediate part: an instrument or medium: (*obs.*) a mediator or intercessor:—*pl.* in form **means**, that by whose instrumentality anything is caused or brought to pass: (treated as *sing.* or *plur.*) way to an end: (treated as *pl.*) pecuniary resources, what is required for comfortable living. —*ns.* **mean′time**, **mean′while**, the intervening time.—*advs.* in the intervening time.—*n.* **mean′-tone**, (*mus.*) an interval of mean value between a major and a minor second, formerly used in a system of temperament.—**arithmetic(al) mean**, the sum of a number of quantities divided by their number; **by all means**, certainly; **by any means**, in any way; **by means**, (*Spens.*) because; **by no means**, certainly not; **geometric(al) mean**, the *n*th root of the product of *n* quantities; **golden mean**, the middle course between two extremes: a wise moderation; **harmonic mean**, the re-ciprocal of the arithmetical mean of the reciprocals of two quantities; **in the mean**, (*Spens.*) in the meantime; **means test**, the test of private re-sources, determining or limiting claim to a pension or allowance; **mean sun**, an imaginary sun moving uniformly in the equator, coinciding with the real sun at the equinoxes, its position giving **mean time**; **quadratic mean**, the square root of the arithmetical mean of the squares of the given quantities. [O.Fr. *meien* (Fr. *moyen*)—L. *mediānus—medius*, middle.]

mean, *mēn*, *v.t.* to have in mind as signification: to

intend, to purpose : to destine, design : to signify.
—*v.i.* to have in the mind : to have meaning or
disposition :—*pr.p.* **mean′ing ;** *pa.t.* and *pa.p.*
meant (*ment*) —*n.* **mean′ing,** that which is in
the mind or thoughts : signification : the sense
intended : purpose. — *adj.* significant. — *adjs.*
mean′ingful ; mean′ingless, senseless : expressionless : without significance.—*adv.* **mean′-
ingly,** significantly : intentionally. [O.E. *mǽnan ;*
Ger. *meinen,* to think.]

mean, meane, mein, mene, *mēn, v.t.* and *v.i.*
(*Shak.* and *Scot.*) to lament, to moan : to complain. [O.E. *mǽnan ;* cf. **moan.**]

meander, *mi-an′dər, n.* a sinuosity : a winding
course : a maze : an intricate fret pattern : perplexity.—*v.i.* to wind about : to be intricate : to
wander listlessly (with some reminiscence of
maunder).—*adjs.* **mean′dered,** formed into or
covered with mazy passages or patterns ; **mean′-
dering, mean′drian, mean′drous,** winding. [L.
Maeander—Gr. *Maiandros,* a winding river in
Asia Minor.]

meant, *ment, pa.t.* and *pa.p.* of **mean** (*v.t.*).

meare, *mēr,* Spenser's spelling of **mere** (2 and 3).
—**mear′d,** (*Spens.*) *pa.t.* of **mere** (3).

mease, *mēz,* maze, maize, maise, *māz, n.* (*local*)
a tale of five ' hundreds ' of herrings—varying
from 500 to 630. [O.Fr. *meise,* receptacle for
herrings ; O.N. *meiss,* box, basket ; O.H.G. *meisa.*]

mease, *mēz, v.t.* (*Scot.*) to assuage : to mitigate.
[O.Fr. *amesir*—L. *ad,* to, *mītis,* mild.]

measles, *mē′zlz, n.* (*pl.* in form, treated as *sing.*)
an infectious fever accompanied with eruptions
of small red spots upon the skin : a disease of
swine and cattle, caused by larval tapeworms :
(*obs.*) a blister or a disease of trees.—*n.* **mea′sle,**
a tapeworm larva.—*v.t.* to infect with measles.—*v.i.*
to take measles.—*adjs.* **mea′sled, mea′sly,** infected with measles : spotty : paltry, miserable.—
n. **meas′liness.**—German measles, a name
somewhat loosely used of a disease resembling
measles but mostly less prolonged and severe.
[M.E *maseles ;* cf. Du. *mazelen,* measles, O.H.G.
masala, blister ; Ger. *masern,* measles.]

measure, *mezh′ər, n.* ascertainment of extent by
comparison with a standard : a system of expressing the result of such ascertainment : amount
ascertained by comparison with a standard : that
by which extent is ascertained or expressed : size :
a standard or unit : a quantity by which another
can be divided without remainder : an instrument
for finding the extent of anything, esp. a graduated
rod or tape for length, or a vessel of known content
for capacity : the quantity contained in a vessel
of known capacity—often a bushel : adequacy or
due amount : some amount or degree, a portion :
proportion : moderation : restraint : (*Milt.*) limit :
extent : that which is meted out to one, treatment :
means to an end : an enactment or bill : rhythm :
a unit of verse—one foot or two feet : metre :
strict time : a bar of music : a strain : a dance,
esp. a slow and stately one : (*print.*) the width of a
page or column, usually in *ems :* (in *pl.,* geol.) a
series of beds or strata.—*v.t.* to ascertain or show
the dimensions or amount of : to mark out or lay
off : to mete out : to proportion : to pit : to
traverse : (*Spens.*) to sing or utter in measure.—
v.i. to be of the stated size : to take measurements.
—*adj.* **meas′urable,** that may be measured or
computed : moderate : in small quantity or
extent.—*n.* **meas′urableness.**—*adv.* **meas′ur-
ably.**—*adj.* **meas′ured,** determined by measure :
mensurable : rhythmical : with slow, heavy, steady
rhythm : considered : restrained.—*adv.* **meas′-
uredly.** — *adj.* **meas′ureless,** boundless. — *ns.*
meas′urement, the act of measuring : quantity
found by measuring (measurement goods,
light goods carried for charges according to bulk,
not weight) ; **meas′urer.**—*n.* and *adj.* **meas′ur-
ing.**—*ns.* **meas′uring-rod, -tape,** one for measuring with ; **meas′uring-worm,** a looper caterpillar.—**above,** or **beyond,** or (*arch.*) **out of,
measure,** to an exceedingly great degree ; **hard
measures,** harsh treatment ; **in a measure, in
some measure,** to some degree ; **measure one's**

length, to fall or be thrown down at full length ;
measure strength, to engage in a contest ;
measure swords, (*orig.*) to compare lengths of
swords before a duel : to fight ; **short measure,**
less than the due and professed amount ; **take
measures,** to adopt means to gain an end ; **take
one's measure,** to estimate one's character and
abilities ; **tread a measure,** to go through a
dance ; **within measure,** moderately ; **without
measure,** immoderately. [O.Fr. *mesure*—L.
mēnsūra, a measure—*mētīrī, mēnsum,* to measure.]

meat, *mēt, n.* anything eaten as food : (*obs.*) a meal :
(now chiefly *U.S.*) the edible part of anything :
the flesh of animals used as food—sometimes beef,
mutton, pork, veal, &c., as opposed to poultry,
fish, &c. : proleptically, game, destined prey :
(*fig.*) food for thought, substance, pith.—*ns.* **meat′-
eater,** one who eats butcher's meat ; **meat′-fly,**
a blowfly : a flesh-fly ; **meat′iness.**—*adj.* **meat′-
less,** foodless : without butcher's meat.—*ns.* **meat′-
man,** a seller of butcher's meat ; **meat′-mar′ket,**
a flesh-market ; **meat′-off′ering,** a Jewish sacrificial offering of fine flour or first-fruits with oil
and frankincense ; **meat′-pie′ ; meat′-safe,** a
receptacle for storing meat ; **meat′-sales′man,**
one who sells meat, esp. to the retail butchers ;
meat′screen, a metal screen behind roasting
meat, to throw back the fire's heat upon it ; **meat′-
tea′,** a high tea with meat ; **meat′-tub,** a pickling-
tub.—*adj.* **meat′y,** full of meat : fleshy : flesh-like
in taste or smell : pithy. [O.E. *mete.*]

meath, meathe, *mēdh, n.* a form of **mead,**
liquor.

meatus, *mi-ā′təs, n.* a passage or canal :—*pl.*
mea′tuses.—*adj.* **mea′tal.** [L. *meātus* (pl. *-ūs*)—
meāre, to go.]

meawes, a Spenserian spelling of (sea-)**mews.**

meazel. See **mesel.**

mebos, *mā′bos, n.* (*S.Afr.*) salted dried apricots.
[Perh. Japanese *umeboshi,* a kind of plum.]

Mecca, *mek′ä, n.* the birthplace of Mohammed, a
place of pilgrimage for Moslems : any outstanding
place reverenced or resorted to—e.g. St Andrews,
Mecca of golf.

mechanic, *mi-kan′ik, adj.* mechanical.—*n.* a handicraftsman : a skilled worker : an air-mechanic :
(*obs.*) a term of contempt for one of the lower
orders.—*adj.* **mechan′ical,** pertaining to machines :
dynamical : worked or done by machinery or by
mechanism : acting or done by physical not
chemical means : machine-like : of the nature of
a machine or mechanism : without intelligence or
conscious will : performed simply by force of
habit : reflex : skilled in mechanism : (*arch.*)
manual : manually employed : (*obs.*) technical :
mechanistic. — *n.* (*Shak.*) a mechanic. — *adv.*
mechan′ically. — *ns.* **mechanician** (*mek-an-
ish′ən*), a machine-maker : one skilled in the
structure of machines ; **mechan′ics** (treated as
sing.), dynamics, the science of the action of forces
on bodies, including kinetics and statics : the art
or science of machine construction.—*v.t.* **mech′-
anise,** to make mechanical : to adapt to mechanical
working.—*ns.* **mech′anism,** the construction of
a machine : arrangement and action by which a
result is produced : a philosophy that regards the
phenomena of life as explainable by mechanical
forces ; **mech′anist,** a mechanician : a believer
in philosophical mechanism.—*adj.* **mechanist′ic.**
—*adv.* **mechanist′ically.**—**mechanical powers,**
the elementary forms or parts of machines—three
primary, the lever, inclined plane, and pulley ; and
three *secondary,* the wheel-and-axle, the wedge,
and the screw ; **mechanical tissue,** any tissue
that gives a plant power of resisting stresses ;
mechanics' institute, an institution for the
education of mechanics, with lectures, library, &c.
[Gr. *mēchanikos*—*mēchanē,* a contrivance.]

Mechitharist. See **Mekhitarist.**

Mechlin, *mek′* or *mehh′lin, adj.* produced at *Mechlin*
or *Malines.*—*n.* lace made at Mechlin.

meconic, *mi-kon′ik, adj.* denoting an acid obtained
from poppies.—*ns.* **meconate** (*mek′an-āt,* or *mēk′*),
a salt of meconic acid ; **mec′onin,** a white, fusible,
neutral substance ($C_{10}H_{10}O_4$) existing in opium ;

mecō′nium, the first faeces of a new-born child, or of a newly emerged insect imago : opium ; **Meconops′is** (Gr. *opsis*, appearance), the Welsh poppy genus. [Gr. *mēkōn*, the poppy.]

Mecoptera, *mē-kop′tə-rä*, *n.pl.* an order of insects linking the Hymenoptera with the Trichoptera—the scorpion-flies. [Gr. *mēkos*, length, *pteron*, wing.]

medaewart, *med′ē-wärt*, *n.* meadow-sweet. [O.E. *meduwyrt* ; see **meadow-sweet**.]

medal, *med′l*, *n.* a piece of metal in the form of a coin bearing some device or inscription, struck or cast usually in commemoration of an event or as a reward of merit.—*v.t.* to decorate with a medal :—*pr.p.* med′alling ; *pa.t.* and *pa.p.* med′alled.—*n.* med′alet, a small medal, esp. the representation of saints, worn by Roman Catholics.—*adj.* **medallic** (*mi-dal′ik*).—*n.* **medallion** (*mi-dal′yən*), a large medal : a bas-relief of a round (sometimes a square) form : a round ornament, panel, tablet, or design of similar form.—*v.t.* to ornament with medallions : to make in the form of a medallion.—*n.* med′allist, one skilled in medals : a designer or maker of medals : one who has gained a medal.—**medal play**, golf scored by strokes for the round, not by holes. [Fr. *médaille*—It. *medaglia* ; through L.L. from L. *metallum*, metal.]

meddle, *med′l*, *v.t.* and *v.i.* (*arch.*) to mix.—*v.i.* to have to do (with *with*) : (*Shak.*) to engage in fight : to interfere unnecessarily, temerariously, or without being entitled.—*n.* medd′ler.—*adj* medd′lesome, given to meddling.—*n.* medd′lesomeness.—*n.* and *adj.* medd′ling. [O.Fr. *medler*, a variant of *mesler* (Fr. *mêler*)—L.L. *misculāre*—L. *miscēre*, to mix.]

Mede. See **Median** (2).

media, *mē′di-ä*, *n.* a voiced stop consonant, or letter representing it : the middle coat of a blood-vessel : a middle primary vein of an insect's wing. —See also **medium**. [L. *media* (*littera*, *tunica*, *vena*), middle (letter, coat, vein), fem. of *medius*, middle.]

mediaeval, *med-i-ē′vl*, *adj.* of the Middle Ages.— *ns.* mediae′valism, the spirit of the Middle Ages: devotion to mediaeval ideals ; mediae′valist, one versed in the history, art, &c., of the Middle Ages : one who follows mediaeval practices. — *adv.* mediae′vally.—Also **mediē′val**, &c. [L. *medius*, middle, *aevum*, age.]

medial, *mē′di-əl*, *adj.* intermediate : occurring within a word : median : pertaining to a mean or average.—*n.* (*phon.* ; *obs.*) a media.—*adv.* me′dially. [L.L. *mediālis*—L. *medius*, middle.]

median, *mē′di-ən*, *adj.* in the middle, running through the middle : situated in the straight line or plane (*median line*, *plane*) that divides anything longitudinally into symmetrical halves. — *n.* a straight line joining an angular point of a triangle with the middle point of the opposite side : a middle nervure of an insect's wing : in a series of values, the value middle in position (not usu. in magnitude). [L. *mediānus*—*medius*, middle.]

Median, *mē′di-ən*, *adj.* pertaining to ancient *Media*, its people, or their language (also *n.*)—*n.* **Mede**, one of an Indo-Germanic people and nation fused with the Persians about 500 B.C.—*adj.* **Me′dic**.— *v.i.* **Me′dise**, to become Median, or as the Medians : to favour the Persians (called Medes by the Greeks). —*v.t.* to make Median.—*n.* **Me′dism**, the adoption of Persian interests—to a Greek, treachery.—law **of the Medes and Persians**, the type of ' that which altereth not ' (Dan. vi. 12). [Gr. *Mēdos*, a Mede.]

mediant, *mē′di-ənt*, *n.* the third tone of a scale, about midway between tonic and dominant. [L.L. *mediāns*, -*āntis*, pr.p. of *mediāre*, to be in the middle.]

mediastinum, *mē-di-as-tī′nəm*, *n.* a membranous septum, or a cavity, between two principal portions of an organ, esp. the folds of the pleura and the space between the right and left lungs.—*adj.* **mediasti′nal**. [Neut. of L.L. *mediastinus*, median (in classical L. *mediastīnus* is a drudge)—*medius*.]

mediate ; *mē′di-it*, *adj.* middle : intervening : indirect : related or acting through something inter-

vening.—*v.i.* (-*āt*) to interpose between parties as a friend of each : to act as intermediary : to intercede : to be or act as a medium : to hold a mediate position.—*v.t.* to bring about, end, promote, obtain, or communicate by friendly intervention, or by intercession, or through an intermediary : to be the medium or intermediary of : to effect a relation between.—*n.* me′diacy, mediateness.—*adv.* me′diately.—*ns.* me′diateness, state of being mediate ; media′tion, the act of mediating or coming between : entreaty for another ; mediatīsa′tion.—*v.t.* me′diatise, to cause to act in a subordinate position or through an agent : to reduce from immediate to mediate vassal (of the empire) without loss of dignity : to annex, or to subordinate, as a smaller state to a larger neighbouring one.—*adj.* me′diative (-*ə-tiv*).—*n.* me′diātor, one who mediates between parties at strife :—*fem.* me′diātress, media′trix :—*pl.* mediātrices (-*trī′sēz*).—*adj.* mediātō′rial.—*adv.* mediātō′rially. — *n.* me′diatorship. — *adj.* me′diatory. [L.L. *mediāre*, -*ātum*, to be in the middle—L. *medius*.]

medic, *med′ik*, *adj.* (*poet.*) medical.—*n.* (*rare*) a physician : (*U.S. slang*) a medical student.—*n.* **medicas′ter**, a quack.—*adjs.* med′ico-chirur′gical, relating to both medicine and surgery ; med′ico-le′gal, relating to the application of medicine to questions of law. [L. *medicus*.]

medical, *med′i-kl*, *adj.* relating to the art of healing : relating to the art of the physician, distinguished from surgery.—*n.* (*coll.*) a student of medicine.—*adv.* med′ically. [L.L. *medicālis*—L. *medicus*, a physician—*medērī*, to heal.]

medicament, *med-ik′ə-mənt*, or *med′*, *n.* a substance used in curative treatment, esp. externally.—*v.t.* to treat with medicaments.—*adjs.* **medicamental** (-*ment′l*), **medicament′ary**.—*adv.* medicament′ally. [L. *medicāmentum*—*medicāre*.]

medicate, *med′i-kāt*, *v.t.* to treat with medicine : to impregnate with anything medicinal : to drug, doctor, tamper with.—*adj.* **med′icable**, that may be healed.—*adj.* med′icated.—*n.* medicā′tion.—*adj.* med′icative. [L. *medicāre*, -*ātum*, to heal—*medicus*.]

Medicean, *med-i-sē′ən*, *adj.* relating to the *Medici*, a distinguished Florentine family which attained to sovereign power in the 15th century.

medicine, *med′sin*, -*ən*, also (*esp. U.S.*) *med′i-sin*, -*sn*, *n.* any substance used (esp. internally) for the treatment or prevention of disease : a drug : the art or science of prevention and cure of disease : a charm : anything of magical power : (*Shak.*) a physician.—*v.t.* to treat or cure by medicine.— *adjs.* **medicinable** (*med′sin-ə-bl*), having a healing power ; **medicinal** (*med-is′i-nl*, sometimes *med-i-sī′nl* ; in *Shak.*, &c., *med′si-nl* ; *Milt.* med′′cinal), used in medicine : curative : relating to medicine : like medicine.—*adv.* medic′inally.—*ns.* med′-icine-ball, a heavy ball tossed and caught for exercise ; med′icine-bott′le ; med′icine-chest, a chest for keeping a selected set of medicines ; med′icine-dropp′er ; med′icine-man, among savages, a witch-doctor or magician ; med′iciner, (*arch.*) a physician. [L. *medicīna*—*medicus*.]

medick, *med′ik*, *n.* any species of Medicago, a genus distinguished from clover by its spiral or sickle-shaped pods and short racemes—including lucerne. [L. *mēdica*—Gr. *Mēdikē* (*poā*), Median (herb), i.e. lucerne.]

medico, *med′ik-ō*, *n.* (*slang*) a medical practitioner or student. [It. *medico*, or Sp. *médico*—L. *medicus*, a physician.]

medieval. Same as **mediaeval**.

medio-, *mē′di-ō-*, (in compounds) middle. [L. *medius*, middle.]

mediocre, *mē′di-ō-kər*, or -*ō′*, *adj.* of middling goodness (usu. disparagingly).—*n.* **mediocrity** (-*ok′*), a middling degree : a mediocre person. [Fr. *médiocre*—L. *mediocris*—*medius*, middle.]

Medise, Medism. See **Median** (2).

meditate, *med′i-tāt*, *v.i.* to consider thoughtfully (with *on*, *upon*)—*v.t.* to consider deeply, reflect upon : to revolve in the mind : to intend.—*adj.*

med′itated.—*n.* **medita′tion,** the act of meditating: deep thought: serious contemplation: a meditative discourse: a meditative treatment of a literary or musical theme.—*adj.* **med′itative.** —*adv.* **med′itatively.**—*n.* **med′itativeness.**— **meditate the muse** (Latinism, after Milton), to give one's mind to composing poetry. [L. *meditāri,* prob. cog. with L. *medēri,* to heal.]

mediterranean, *měd-i-tə-rā′ni-ən, adj.* situated in the middle of earth or land: land-locked: of the Mediterranean Sea (so called from being in the middle of the land of the Old World), or its shores. —**Mediterranean fever,** Malta or undulant fever; **Mediterranean race,** a long-headed dark race of white men, of medium stature, inhabiting south Europe and north Africa. [L. *mediterrāneus*— *medius,* middle, *terra,* earth.]

medium, *mē′di-əm, n.* the middle: the middle place or degree: a middle course: (*obs.*) a mean: any intervening means, instrument, or agency: instrumentality: a substance through which any effect is transmitted: that through which communication is maintained: a newspaper as a channel of information: an enveloping substance or element in which a thing exists or lives: environment: a vehicle for paint, &c.: a nutritive substance on which a culture (as of bacteria, tissue, &c.) may be fed: in spiritualism, the person through whom spirits are said to communicate with the material world: a person of supernormal sensibility:—*pl.* **me′dia,** or **me′diums.**—*adjs.* **me′dium,** intermediate: (*obs.*) mean, average: of a standard size of paper between demy and royal, now 18 in. by 23 in.; **mediumis′tic,** of or pertaining to spiritualistic mediums.—**circulating medium,** money passing from hand to hand, as coin, banknotes, &c. [L. *medium.*]

medius, *mē′di-əs, n.* the middle finger. [B. *medius,* middle.]

Medjidie, *me-jěd′i-e, n.* a Turkish order of knighthood founded by Sultan Abdu'l *Majid.*

medlar, *med′lər, n.* a small tree (*Mespilus,* or *Pyrus, germanica*) akin to the apple: its fruit. [O.Fr. *medler, mesler*—L. *mespilum*—Gr. *mespilon.*]

medle, an old spelling (*Shak.* and *Spens.*) of **meddle.**

medley, *med′li, n.* a mingled and confused mass: a miscellany: a song or piece of music made up of bits from various sources: a cloth woven from yarn of different colours: (*obs.*) a mêlée, fight. [O.Fr. *medler, mesler,* to mix.]

Médoc, *mā-dok′, n.* a French wine produced in the district of *Médoc,* department of Gironde.

medulla, *me-dul′ä, n.* the inner portion of an organ, hair, or tissue: bone-marrow: pith: a loose or spongy mass of hyphae.—*adjs.* **medull′ar, -y,** consisting of, or resembling, marrow or pith; **medull′ate,** having medulla; **med′ullated,** provided with a medullary sheath. — **medulla oblonga′ta,** that part of the brain that tapers off into the spinal cord; **medullary ray,** (*bot.*) a band of cells (appearing as a ray in cross-section) cutting radially through wood and bast; **medullary sheath,** (*bot.*) a thin layer surrounding the pith: (*anat.*) a whitish fatty membrane covering an axis-cylinder. [L. *medulla,* marrow.]

Medusa, *me-dū′zä, n.* one of the three Gorgons, whose head, with snakes for hair, turned beholders into stone, but was cut off by Perseus, and placed in Athena's aegis: medusa, a jellyfish: an individual of the free-swimming sexual generation of jellyfishes and Hydrozoa:—*pl.* medu′sae (-zē). —*adj.* medu′san.—*n.* a medusa.—*adjs.* medu′siform, like a jellyfish; medu′soid, like a medusa. —*n.* a sexual hydrozoan that remains attached to the parent hydroid colony. [L. *Medūsa*—Gr. *Medousa,* the Gorgon Medusa (lit. ruler).]

meed, *mēd, n.* wages: reward: what is bestowed for merit. [O.E. *méd*; Ger. *miete.*]

meek, *mēk, adj.* mild and gentle of temper: submissive.—*v.t.* **meek′en,** to render meek.—*v.i.* to become meek.—*adv.* **meek′ly.**—*n.* **meek′ness,** state or quality of being meek. [O.N. *mjúkr*; Du. *muik.*]

meer, *mēr, n.* an obsolete spelling of **mere.**—*adj.*

meer′ed, (*Shak.*) possibly, set up as a *mere* or division, dividing: according to some, sole. [mere (3) or mere (2).]

meerkat, *mēr′kat, n.* (*obs.*) a monkey: a South African carnivore (*Cynictis penicillata*) akin to the ichneumon: the suricate: a ground squirrel: a lemur. [Du. *meerkat,* monkey, as if overseas cat, from *meer,* sea, *kat,* cat, but perh. really an Eastern word; cf. Hind. *markat,* Sans. *markata,* ape.]

meerschaum, *mēr′shəm, n.* a fine light whitish clay, sepiolite—once supposed to be a petrified sea-scum: a tobacco-pipe made of it. [Ger.,— *meer,* sea, *schaum,* foam.]

meet, *mēt, adj.* fitting: qualified: (*Shak.*) even, quits.—*adv.* (*Shak.*) fittingly.—*adv.* **meet′ly.**—*n.* **meet′ness.** [Prob. from an O.E. (Anglian) form answering to W.S. *gemǣte*—*metan,* to measure.]

meet, *mēt, v.t.* to come face to face with: to come into the company of: to become acquainted with, be introduced to: to encounter in conflict: to find or experience: to refute: be suitable to: satisfy, as by payment: to receive, as a welcome: to cause to meet, bring into contact.—*v.i.* to come together from different points: to assemble: to have an encounter: to balance or come out correct: (*pa.t.* and *pa.p.* met).—*n.* a meeting, as of huntsmen: an assembly for racing.—*ns.* **meet′ing,** a coming face to face for friendly or hostile ends: an interview: an assembly: an organised assembly for transaction of business: an assembly for religious worship, esp. (in England) of Dissenters: a place of meeting: a junction; **meet′ing-house,** a house or building where people, esp. Dissenters, meet for public worship; **race′-meet′ing,** a stated occasion for horse-racing.—**give the** (or **a**) **meeting,** (*arch.*) appoint or come to a rendezvous, for a duel or other purpose; **meet half-way,** to make concessions in compromise; **meet in with, wi′** (*Scot.*), to meet with, come across; **meet the ear,** or **eye,** to be readily apparent; **meet with,** to come to or upon, esp. unexpectedly: to undergo, chance to experience: (*Bacon*) to obviate (as an objection); **well met,** an old complimentary greeting. [O.E. *métan,* to meet—*mót, gemót,* a meeting.]

mega-, *meg′ə-,* **megalo-,** *meg′ə-lō-,* in composition, big: in names of units, a million.—*adj.* **mega-cephalous** (-*sef′ə-ləs*; Gr. *kephalē,* head), large-headed.—*n.pl.* **Megacheiroptera** (-*kir-op′tər-ä*), the fruit-bats.—*ns.* **meg′acycle,** a million cycles; **megafar′ad,** a million farads; **meg′afog,** a fog-signal with megaphones pointing in several directions; **meg′alith** (Gr. *lithos,* stone), a huge stone, as in prehistoric monuments.—*adj.* **megalith′ic.** —*n.* **megaloma′nia,** the delusion that one is great or powerful: a mania, or passion, for big things.—*n.* and *adj.* **megaloma′niac.**—*n.* **meg′-alosaur** (Gr. *sauros,* a lizard), a gigantic Jurassic and Cretaceous dinosaur (Megalosaurus), carnivorous and partly bipedal.—*adj.* **megalosau′rian.**—*n.* **meg′aphone** (Gr. *phōnē,* voice), an appliance for talking at a distance by means of large funnels.—*v.t.* and *v.i.* to communicate by megaphone.—*ns.* **meg′apode** (Gr. *pous, podos,* foot), a mound-bird; **meg′aron** (Gr. *megaron*), the principal hall of an ancient Greek house; **meg′ascope** (Gr. *skopeein,* to view), an instrument for projecting an enlarged image.—*adj.* **mega-scopic** (-*skop′ik*), enlarged: visible to the naked eye.—*ns.* **megasporangium** (-*spor-an′ji-əm*), a sporangium producing only megaspores: — *pl.* **megasporan′gia**; **meg′aspore,** the larger of two forms of spore: a spore giving rise to a female gametophyte; **megasporophyll** (-*spor′ə-fil*), a sporophyll that carries or subtends only mega-sporangia; **Megathē′riu:n** (Gr. *thērion,* wild beast), a gigantic extinct S. American ground-sloth; **meg′ohm,** a million ohms. [Gr. *megas,* fem. *megalē,* neut. *mega,* big.]

Megaera, *mə-jē′rä, me-gī′rä, n.* one of the Furies. [L.,—Gr. *Megaira.*]

megilp, *mə-gilp′.* See **magilp.**

megrim, *mē′grim, n.* a pain affecting only one half of the head or face: vertigo: lowness of spirits:

a caprice. [Fr. *migraine*—Gr. *hĕmikrāntă*—*hēmi*, half, *krānion*, skull.]

megrim, *mē'grim, n.* the scald-fish.

meint. See ming.

meinie, mein(e)y, *mā'ni, n.* (*Shak.*) a retinue : a herd. [O.Fr. *mesnie*—L. *mānsiō, -ōnis*, a dwelling.]

meionite, *mī'ən-īt, n.* a scapolite with less sodium and silica than marialite. [Gr. *meiōn*, less, from its short vertical axis.]

meiosis, *mī-ō'.is, n.* (*rhet.*) understatement as a figure of speech : litotes : (*biol.*) cell-division with reduction of the number of chromosomes towards the development of a reproductive cell.—*adj.*

meiotic (*-ot'ik*). [Gr. *meiōsis*, diminution.]

meistersinger, *mīs'tər-zing-ər, -sing-ər, n.* one of the burgher poets and musicians of Germany in the 14th-16th centuries, the successors of the Minnesingers : — *pl.* **meistersinger, -s.** [Ger., master-singer.]

meith, *mēth, n.* (*Scot.*) a landmark : a boundary. [Prob. O.N. *mith*, a fishing-bank found by landmarks.]

Mejlis. Same as Majlis.

Mekhitarist, Mechitarist, *mehh-, mek-i-tär'ist, n.* an Armenian Uniat monk of a congregation founded by *Mekhitar* (1676-1749) at Constantinople in 1701, since 1717 with headquarters near Venice.—Also *adj.*

mekometer, *mē-kom'i-tər, n.* a form of rangefinder. [Gr. *mēkos*, length, *metron*, measure.]

melaconite, *mel-ak'ən-īt, n.* tenorite. [Gr. *melās*, black, *konis*, dust.]

melampode, *mel-am'pōd, mel', n.* (*Spens.*) the black hellebore. [Gr. *melampodion*.]

melanaemia, *mel-ən-ē'mi-ä, n.* presence of melanin in the blood. [Gr. *melās, -ănos*, black, *haima*, blood.]

melancholy, *mel'ən-kol-i, -kəl-i*, formerly *mel-ang'-kol-i, n.* (*obs.*) black bile, an excess thereof, or the mental condition or temperament supposed to result : (*obs.*) surliness : continued depression of spirits : dejection : melancholia : indulgence in thoughts of pleasing sadness : pensiveness.—*adj.* prone to, affected by, expressive of, or causing melancholy : depressed : pensive : deplorable.— *ns.* **melancho'lia,** a state of insanity characterised by dejection and misery ; **melancho'liac,** a sufferer from melancholia.—Also *adj.*—*adj.* **melancholic** (*-kol'ik*), affected with, or caused by, melancholy or melancholia : dejected : mournful. —*n.* a melancholiac.—*adj.* **melancho'lious.** [Gr. *melancholiă*—*melās, -ănos*, black, *cholē*, bile.]

Melanesian, *mel-ən-ēz'i-ən, -ēz'yən, -ēzh'(y)ən, adj.* pertaining to *Melanesia*, a group of islands lying N.E. of Australia, in which the dominant race is dark-skinned.—*n.* a native, or a language, of these islands. [Gr. *melās, -ănos*, black, *nēsos*, an island.]

mélange, *mā-län°zh', n.* a mixture : a medley. [Fr.]

melanic, *mi-lan'ik, adj.* black or dark in pigmentation.—*ns.* **melanin** (*mel'ə-nin*), dark pigment in skin, hair, &c.; **mel'anism,** more than normal development of dark colouring matter. — *adj.* **melanis'tic.**—*ns.* **mel'anite,** a black garnet ; **melano** (*mi-lä'nō, mel'ə-nō* ; on the analogy of *albino*), a person or animal abnormally dark ; **mel'anophore** (*-fōr*), a chromatophore containing melanin ; **melanō'sis,** an abnormal deposit of melanin : the associated condition of body.—*adjs.* **melanot'ic ; mel'anous,** dark-complexioned. —*n.* **melanū'ria,** the presence of a dark pigment in the urine.—*adj.* **melanū'ric.**—*n.* **melaphyre** (*mel'ə-fīr* ; after *porphyry*), orig. a dark porphyritic rock : applied very loosely to an altered basalt. [Gr. *melās, -ănos*, black.]

Melanochroi, *mel-ən-ō-krō'ī, n.pl.* a race or type of man with dark hair and pale skin — dark whites. — *adjs.* **melanochro'ic, melanochrous** (*-ok'rō-əs*). [Gr. *melās, -ănos*, black, and either *ōchros*, pale, or *chroä*, skin.]

melanterite, *mi-lan'tə-rīt, n.* native copperas. [Gr. *melantēriă*, a black pigment.]

Melastomaceae, *mel-ə-stō-mā's(h)i-ē, n.pl.* a tropical family of plants akin to the myrtles, very abundant in South America, characterised by the leaf-veins diverging from the base and meeting at the tip, named from the Old World genus **Melastoma** (*mi-las'tō-mä*). [Gr. *melās*, black, *stoma*, mouth, from the fruit of some staining the lips.]

meld, *meld, v.t.* and *v.i.* (*obs.* except in cards) to declare : to announce. [O.E. *meldan*, or Ger. *melden*.]

melder, *mel'dər, n.* (*Scot.*) the quantity of meal ground at one time. [O.N. *meldr*.]

mêlée, *mel'ā, n.* a fight in which the combatants are mingled together : a confused conflict : an affray. [Fr.,—*mêler*, to mix ; cf. **meddle, mell.**]

Melia, *mē'li-ä, n.* the nim tree genus, giving name to the family **Meliā'ceae** (mahogany, Cedrela, &c.).—*adj.* **meliā'ceous** (*-shəs*). [Gr. *meliä*, ash-tree (from a resemblance in leaves).]

Meliboean, *mel-i-bē'ən, adj.* in poetry, amoebean. [From *Meliboeus*, in Virgil's first eclogue.]

melic, *mel'ik, adj.* to be sung : lyric : strophic. [Gr. *melikos*—*melos*, song.]

melic, *mel'ik, n.* a grass (Melica) of the fescue tribe. —Also **mel'ic-grass'.** [Origin obscure.]

melilite, *mel'i-līt, n.* a tetragonal mineral, calcium aluminium magnesium silicate, often honey-yellow. [Gr. *meli*, honey, *lithos*, stone.]

melilot, *mel'i-lot, n.* a genus (Melilotus) of cloverlike plants with racemes of white or yellow flowers and a peculiar sweet odour. [Gr. *melilōtos*—*meli*, honey, *lōtos*, lotus.]

melinite, *mel'in-īt, n.* an explosive made from picric acid. [Fr. *mélinite*—Gr. *mēlinos*, quince yellow—*mēlon*, quince.]

meliorate, *mē'li-ə-rāt, v.t.* to make better.—*v.i.* to grow better.—*n.* **meliorā'tion.**—*adj.* **me'liorative,** tending towards improvement.—*ns.* **me'liorātor ;** **me'liorism,** the doctrine that the world is capable of improvement, as opposed to *optimism* and *pessimism* ; **me'liorist ; meliority** (*-or'i-ti*), betterness. [L.L. *meliōrāre, -ātum*—L. *melior*, better.]

meliphagous, *mel-if'ə-gəs, adj.* feeding upon honey. [Gr. *meli*, honey, *phagein* (aor.), to eat.]

mell, *mel, v.t.* and *v.i.* to mix, mingle.—*v.i.* to have to do (with *with*) : to have intercourse : to join in fight : to be concerned : to meddle. [O.F. *meller* ; cf. **meddle, medley.**]

mell, *mel, n.* a Northern form of **mall, maul.**

mellay, *mel'ā, n.* another form of **mêlée.**

melliferous, *mel-if'ə-rəs, adj.* honey-producing.— *ns.* **mellifica'tion,** honey-making ; **mellif'luence** (L. *fluĕre*, to flow), a flow of sweetness : a smooth sweet flow.—*adjs.* **mellif'luent, mellif'luous,**flowing with honey or sweetness : smooth.—*advs.* **mellif'luently, mellif'luously.**—*n.* **mell'ite,** honey stone.—*adjs.* **mellit'ic ; melliv'orous** (L. *vorāre*, to devour), eating honey. [L. *mel, mellis*, honey.]

mellow, *mel'ō, adj.* soft and ripe : well matured : soft to the touch, palate, ear, &c. : genial : half-tipsy.—*v.t.* to soften by ripeness or age : to mature. —*v.i.* to become soft : to be matured.—*adv.* **mell'owly.**—*n.* **mell'owness.**—*adj.* **mell'owy,** mellow. [Prob. O.E. *melu*, meal, influenced by *mearu*, soft, tender.]

melocoton, melocotoon, *mel-ō-kot-ōn', -ōōn', n.* (*obs.*) a large kind of peach.—Also **malakatoone'.**

melicott'on. [Sp. *melocotón*—It. *melocotogna*, quince, peach—L.L. *mēlum cotōneum*—Gr. *mēlon Kȳdōnion*, Cydonian (Cretan) apple, quince.]

melodrama, *mel'ō-drä-mä*, or *-drä', n.* (*obs.*) a play with musical accompaniment to the action and spoken dialogue, with or without songs : a kind of romantic and sensational drama, crude, sentimental, and conventional, with strict attention to poetic justice and happy endings—also **mel'o-drame** (*-dräm*). — *adj.* **melodramat'ic** (*-dra-mat'ik*), of the nature of melodrama : overstrained : sensational.—*n.* **melodramatist** (*-dram'ə-tist*), a writer of melodramas. [Gr. *melos*, a song, *drāma*, action.]

melody, *mel'ə-di, n.* an air or tune : music : an agreeable succession of single musical sounds, as distinguished from *harmony*.—*n.* **melodeon** (*mi-lō'di-ən*), a small reed organ : an improved accordion.—*adj.* **melodic** (*mi-lod'ik*).—*n.* **melod'ics,** the branch of music concerned with melody.—*adj.* **melō'dious,** full of melody : agreeable to the

ear.—*adv.* melo'diously.—*n.* melo'diousness.
—*v.t.* mel'odise, to make melodious: to reduce to the form of a melody.—*v.i.* to make melody: to perform a melody.—*n.* mel'odist. [Fr., through L.L.,—Gr. *melōidiā—melos*, a song, *ōidē*, a lay.]

melomania, *mel-ō-mā'ni-ä*, *n.* a craze for music.—*n.* meloma'niac.—*adj.* melomanic (-*man*'). [Gr. *melos*, song, *maniā*, madness.]

melon, *mel'ən*, *n.* a large sweet juicy gourd: the plant bearing it, musk-melon, water-melon, &c.: (*U.S.*) profits to be divided. [Fr.,—L. *mēlō*, -*ōnis*—Gr. *mēlon*, an apple.]

Melpomene, *mel-pom'i-nē*, *n.* the Muse of tragedy. [Gr. *Melpomēnē*, lit. songstress.]

melt, *melt*, *v.i.* to become liquid from the solid state, esp. by heat: to fuse: to dissolve: to stream with liquid: to lose distinct form: to blend: to shade off: to become imperceptible: to be dispersed or dissipated: to be softened emotionally.—*v.t.* to cause to melt in any sense (*pa.t.* melt'ed, *arch.* mōlt; *pa.p.* melt'ed, *arch.* mōlt'en, ymōlt'en, ymōlt').—*n.* the point of melting: molten material: quantity melted.—*n.* and *adj.* melt'ing.—*adv.* melt'ingly.—*ns.* melt'ingness; melt'ing-point, the temperature at which a given solid begins to become liquid; melt'ing-pot, a vessel for melting things in: (*fig.*) a state of dissolution preparatory to shaping anew.—*adj.* molt'en, melted: made of melted metal.—*adv.* molt'enly. [O.E. *meltan* (intrans. strong vb.), and *mæltan*, *meltan* (causative weak vb., W.S. *mieltan*); O.N. *melta*, to digest, to malt, Gr. *meldein*.]

meltith, *mel'tith*, *n.* (*Scot.*) a meal: a cow's yield at one milking. [meal-tide.]

melton, *mel'tən*, *n.* a strong cloth for overcoats. [*Melton* Mowbray.]

member, *mem'bər*, *n.* a distinct part of a whole, esp. a limb of an animal: a clause: one of a society: a representative in a legislative body.—*adj.* mem'-bered, having limbs.—*n.* mem'bership, the state of being a member or one of a society: the members of a body regarded as a whole.—*adj.* mem'-bral, pertaining to the limbs rather than the trunk.—member of parliament, a member of the House of Commons, M.P. [Fr. *membre*—L. *membrum*.]

membrane, *mem'brān*, -*brin*, *n.* a thin flexible solid sheet or film: a skin of parchment.—*adjs.* mem-branaceous (-*brə-nā'shəs*), membrān'eous (*rare*), mem'branous (-*brə-nəs*), like or of the nature of a membrane: (*bot.*) thin, translucent, and papery.—membrane bone, one formed directly from connective tissue without passing through a stage of cartilage. [L. *membrāna—membrum*.]

memento, *mi-men'tō*, *n.* something kept or given as a reminder: (*obs.*) a brown study:—*pl.* memen'tos or -toes. [L., imper. of *meminisse*, to remember.]

Memnon, *mem'non*, *n.* an Ethiopian king who fought for the Trojans: a statue of Amenoph III. at Thebes in Egypt, thought by the Greeks to be of Memnon and to give out a musical sound at sunrise in salutation of his mother Eos (the Dawn).—*adj.* Memnon'ian. [Gr. *Memnōn*.]

memo, *mem'ō*, *n.* a contraction for memorandum.

memoir, *mem'wär*, -*wor*, or -*oir*, *n.* (usu *pl.*) a written record set down as material for history or biography: a biographical sketch: a record of a study of some subject investigated by the writer: (in *pl.*) the transactions of a society.—*ns.* mem'oir-ism, the act or art of writing memoirs; mem'oir-ist, a writer of memoirs. [Fr. *mémoire*—L. *memoria*, memory—*memor*, mindful.]

memorandum, *mem-ə-ran'dəm*, *n.* something to be remembered: a note to assist the memory: (*law*) a brief note of some transaction: (*diplomacy*) a summary of the state of a question:—*pl.* memo-ran'dums, memoran'da. [L., a thing to be remembered, neut. gerundive of *memorāre*, to remember.]

memory, *mem'ə-ri*, *n.* the power of retaining and reproducing mental or sensory impressions: an impression so reproduced: a having or keeping in the mind: time within which past things can

be remembered: commemoration: a religious service in commemoration: remembrance.—*n.pl.* memorabil'ia (L.), things worth remembering: noteworthy points.—*adj.* mem'orable, deserving to be remembered: remarkable.—*adv.* mem'orably.—*adjs.* mem'orative, (*obs.*) pertaining to memory: aiding the memory; memō'rial, serving or intended to preserve the memory of anything: pertaining to memory: (*obs.*) remembered.—*n.* that which serves to keep in remembrance: a monument: a note to help the memory: a written statement of facts: a record: (*obs.*) memory: (in *pl.*) historical or biographical notices.—*v.t.* memō'rialise, to present a memorial to: to petition by a memorial.—*n.* memō'rialist, one who writes, signs, or presents a memorial.—*v.t.* mem'orise, to commit to memory: (*Shak.*) to cause to be remembered: to record, celebrate.—*adv.* memor'iter (L.), from memory: by heart.—Memorial Day, a day (esp. Decoration Day, 30th May) kept in honour of the men killed in the U.S. Civil War, 1861-65. [L. *memoria*, memory.]

Memphian, *mem-fi-ən*, *adj.* relating to *Memphis*, an ancient capital of Egypt.—Also Mem'phite (-*fīt*), Memphitic (-*fit'*).

mem-sahib, *mem'-sä-ib*, *n.* in India, a married European lady. [ma'am and sahib.]

men, plural of man.

menace, *men'əs*, -*is*, *n.* a threat or threatening: a show of an intention to do harm: a threatening danger.—*v.t.* to threaten.—*v.i.* to act in a threatening manner.—*adj.* men'acing.—*adv.* men'acingly. [Fr.,—L. *mināciae* (pl.), threats—*minae*, overhanging parts, threats.]

menage, obsolete form of manage.

ménage, *mā-näzh'*, *n.* a household: the management of a house: (*prov.*) benefit society: (*prov.*) an arrangement for selling on instalment. [Fr., through L.L.,—L. *mānsiō*, -*ōnis*, a dwelling.]

menagerie, *mi-naj'ə-ri*, *n.* a place for keeping wild animals, esp. for exhibition: a collection of such animals. [Fr. *ménagerie—ménage*.]

mend, *mend*, *v.t.* to remove a fault from: to repair: to make better: to correct: to improve: to improve upon: to supplement.—*v.i.* to grow better: to reform.—*n.* a repair: a repaired place: an act of mending: (in *pl.*; *arch.*) amends.—*ns.* mend'er; mend'ing, the act of repairing: a repair: things requiring to be mended.—mend one's pace, to go quicker; mend one's ways, to reform one's behaviour; on the mend, improving, recovering. [amend.]

mendacious, *men-dā'shəs*, *adj.* lying.—*adv.* menda'ciously.—*n.* mendacity (-*das'i-ti*), lying: a falsehood. [L. *mendāx*, -*ācis*, conn. with *mentīrī*, to lie.]

Mendelian, *men-dēl'i-ən*, *adj.* pertaining to the Austrian-German Gregor *Mendel* (1822-84), or his teaching on heredity.—*n.* a believer in Mendel's theory.—*n.* Men'delism (-*ə-lizm*).

mendicant, *men'di-kənt*, *adj.* begging.—*n.* a beggar: a begging friar.—*ns.* men'dicancy, mendicity (-*dis'i-ti*), the condition of a beggar: begging. [L. *mendīcāns*, -*āntis*, pr.p. of *mendīcāre*, to beg—*mendīcus*, a beggar.]

mends. See mend, amends.

mene, obs. form of mean.

Menevian, *men-ē'vi-ən*, *adj.* and *n.* (*geol.*) Middle Cambrian. [L.L. *Menevia*, St David's, in Pembrokeshire.]

meng, **menge**. Same as ming.

menhaden, *men-hā'dn*, *n.* an oily fish (*Brevoortia tyrannus*) of the herring family, found off the east coast of the United States. [From an Indian name.]

menhir, *men'hēr*, *n.* an ancient monumental standing stone. [Breton *men*, stone, *hir*, long.]

menial, *mē'ni-əl*, *adj.* of or pertaining to a train of servants or work of a humiliating or servile nature: servile.—*n.* a domestic servant: one performing servile work: a person of servile disposition. [A.Fr. *menial*; cf. meinie.]

meninx, *mē'ningks*, *n.* any of three membranes that envelop the brain and spinal cord:—*pl.* meninges (*men-in'jēz*).—*adj.* mening'eal,—*ns.*

meningitis (-*jī'*), inflammation of the meninges;
meningocele (*men-ing'gō-sēl*; Gr. *kēlē*, tumour),
protrusion of the meninges through the skull.
[Gr. *mēninx*, -*ingos*, a membrane.]

Menippean, *men-ip-ē'ən*, *adj.* pertaining to, or in
imitation or emulation of, the Greek satirist
Menippos (3rd cent. B.C.) of Gadara.

meniscus, *men-is'kəs*, *n.* a crescent-shaped figure:
a convexo-concave lens : a liquid surface curved
by capillarity :—*pl.* menisci (-*kī*; L. -*kē*).—*adj.*
menis'coid, (*bot.*) watchglass-shaped. [Gr. *mēnis-kos*, dim. of *mēnē*, the moon.]

Menispermum, *men-i-spər'məm*, *n.* the moonseed
genus, giving name to a family **Menispermā'ceae**
akin to the buttercup family. [Gr. *mēnē*, moon,
sperma, seed.]

Mennonite, *men'ən-īt*, *n.* one of a Protestant sect
combining some of the distinctive characteristics
of the Baptists and Friends. [From *Menno
Simons* (*d.* 1559), their chief founder.]

menology, *mē-nol'ə-ji*, *n.* a register or calendar of
Saints' days, esp. of the Greek Church. [Late Gr.
mēnologion—mēn, month, *logos*, account.]

menominee, *mi-nom'i-nē*, *n.* a whitefish of N.
American lakes. [From an Indian tribe.]

menopause, *men'ō-pawz*, *n.* the ending of menstruation, change of life. [Gr. *mēn*, month,
pausis, cessation.]

menopome, *men'ə-pōm*, *n.* the hell-bender—from
its persistent gill-aperture. [Gr. *menein*, to remain,
pōma, lid.]

mensal, *men'səl*, *adj.* monthly.—Also **men'sual**.
[L. *mēnsis*, month.]

mensal, *men'sal*, *adj.* belonging to the table. [L.
mēnsa, table.]

mense, *mens*, *n.* (*Scot.*) propriety : ornament :
credit.—*v.t.* to grace or set off something.—*adjs.*
mense'ful, decorous : respectable : gracious :
generous ; **mense'less**, graceless, uncivil. [O.N.
mennska, humanity ; cf. O.E. *mennisc*, humanity,
mennisc, human.]

menses, *men'sēz*, *n.pl.* the monthly discharge from
the uterus. [L. *mēnsēs*, pl. of *mēnsis*, month.]

Menshevik, *men-shev-ik'*, or *men'*, *n.* a moderate or
minority socialist in Russia—as opp. to *Bolshevik*:
a minimalist. [Russ., smaller.]

menstruum, *men'stroo-əm*, *n.* a solvent (from a
fancy of the alchemists):—*pl.* **men'strua**, the
menses.—*adj.* **men'strual**, monthly : pertaining
to the menses.—*v.i.* **men'struate**, to discharge
the menses. — *n.* **menstruā'tion**. — *adj.* **men'-
struous**. [L. neut. of *mēnstruus*, monthly—
mēnsis.]

mensur, *men-sōōr'*, *n.* a German students' duel, a
form of sport :—*pl.* **mensur'en**. [Ger., measurement (from the measured distance of the participants)—L. *mēnsūra*.]

mensurable, *men'sh(y)ər-ə-bl*, or -*sūr*-, *adj.* measurable : (*mus.*) having a fixed relative time-value for
each note.—*n.* **mensurabil'ity**.—*adj.* **mens'ural**,
pertaining to measure : (*mus.*) measurable.—*n.*
mensurā'tion, the act or art of finding by
measurement and calculation the length, area,
volume, &c., of bodies.—*adj.* **men'surātive**. [L.
mēnsūrāre, to measure.]

ment. See ming.

mental. See mentum.

mental, *men'tl*, *adj.* pertaining to the mind : done
in the mind, esp. in the mind alone, without outward expression : (*slang*) mentally unsound.—*ns.*
men'talism, process of mental action : idealism ;
men'talist ; **mentality** (-*tal'i-ti*), mind : mental
endowment : cast of mind : way of thinking ;
mentā'tion, mental activity.—*adv.* **men'tally.—
mental age**, the age in years, &c., at which an
average child would have reached the same stage
of mental development as the individual under
consideration. [Fr.,—L. *mēns*, *mentis*, the mind.]

menthol, *men'thol*, *n.* a camphor got from oil of
peppermint, used against neuralgia, &c.—*adj.*
men'tholated, containing menthol. [L. *mentha*,
mint.]

mention, *men'shən*, *n.* a brief notice : occurrence or
introduction of name or reference.—*v.t.* to notice
briefly : to remark : to name.—*adj.* **men'tionable**,

fit to be mentioned : worth mentioning.—**honourable mention**, an award of distinction not entitling to a prize ; **not to mention**, to say nothing
of — a parenthetical rhetorical pretence of refraining from saying all one might say. [L.
mentiō, -*ōnis*.]

mentonnière, *men-ton-i-er'*, *n.* a piece of armour
for the chin and throat. [Fr.,—*menton*, chin—L.
mentum.]

mentor, *men'tor*, -*tər*, *n.* a wise counsellor.—*adj.*
mentorial (-*tō'ri-əl*). [Gr. *Mentōr*, the tutor by
whom (or Athena in his form) Telemachus was
guided.]

mentum, *men'təm*, *n.* the chin : the central part
of the labium in insects.—*adj.* **men'tal**, (*anat.*)
pertaining to the chin. [L. *mentum*, the chin.]

menu, *men'ū*, *mə-nū*, *n.* a bill of fare. [Fr.,—L.
minūtus, small.]

mepacrine, *mep'ə-krēn*, *n.* a bitter yellow powder
derived from acridine dye compounds, used against
malaria—also *atabrin*, *atebrin*.

Mephistopheles, *mef-is-tof'i-lēz*, *n.* the devil in the
Faust story. — Also **Mephistoph'ilis**, **Mephos-
toph'ilus**, &c.: abbrev. **Mephis'tō**. — *adjs.*
Mephistophelē'an, **Mephistophē'lian**, **Meph-
istophelic** (-*fel'*), cynical, scoffing, malicious.
[Ety. unknown ; prob. influenced by Gr. *mē*, not,
phōs, *phōtos*, light, *philos*, loving.]

mephitis, *me-fī'tis*, *n.* a poisonous exhalation : a
foul stink.—*adjs.* **mephitic** (-*fit'*), -**al**.—*n.* **meph'-
itism** (-*it-izm*), mephitic poisoning. [L. *mephitis*.]

mercantile, *mər'kən-til*, *adj.* pertaining to merchants : having to do with trade : commercial :
mercenary.—*ns.* **mer'cantilism** ; **mer'cantilist.
—mercantile agency**, a means of getting information about the circumstances of merchants
for those who sell to them ; **mercantile law**, the
law relating to the dealings of merchants with
each other ; **mercantile marine**, the ships and
crews of any country employed in commerce ;
mercantile system, (*pol. econ.*) the system of
encouraging exportation and restricting importation, so that more may be received than is paid
away. [Fr.,—It. *mercantile*—L. *mercārī* ; cf.
merchant.]

mercaptan, *mər-kap'tan*, *n.* a substance analogous
to an alcohol, with sulphur instead of oxygen.—
n. **mercap'tide**, a compound in which a metal
takes the place of a hydrogen atom of a mercaptan. [L. *mercūrium captāns*, laying hold of
mercury, from the readiness with which it forms
mercury mercaptide.]

mercat, *mer'kət*, a Scottish form of market.

Mercator, *mər-kā'tar*, *mer-kā'tor*, *n.* a Latin translation of the name of the Flemish-born German
cartographer Gerhard Kremer (lit. shopkeeper ;
1512-94).—**Mercator's projection**, a representation of the surface of the globe in which the
meridians are parallel straight lines, the parallels
straight lines at right angles to these, their distances
such that everywhere degrees of latitude and
longitude have the same ratio to each other as on
the globe itself.

mercenary, *mər'sin-ər-i*, *adj.* hired for money :
actuated by the hope of reward : too strongly
influenced by desire of gain : sold or done for
money.—*n.* one who is hired : a soldier hired into
foreign service.—*adv.* **mer'cenarily**. [L. *mer-
cēnārius—mercēs*, hire.]

mercer, *mər'sər*, *n.* a dealer in textiles, esp. the
more costly : a dealer in small wares.—*n.* **mer'cery**,
the trade of a mercer : the goods of a mercer.
[Fr. *mercier*.]

mercerise, *mər'sər-īz*, *v.t.* to treat (cotton) so as to
make it appear like silk.—*ns.* **mercerīsā'tion** ;
mer'ceriser. [From John *Mercer* (1791-1866),
the inventor of the process.]

merchant, *mər'chənt*, *n.* a trader, esp. wholesale :
(*Scot.* and *U.S.*) a shopkeeper : (*obs.*) a supercargo : a merchantman : (*slang*) a fellow, esp. one
who specialises in some specified way.—*adj.*
commercial.—*v.i.* to trade.—*v.t.* to trade in.—
n. **mer'chandise** (-*dīz*), goods bought and sold
for gain : (*B.* and *Shak.*) trade : dealing.—*v.t.*
(*Shak.*) to make merchandise of, trade in.—*v.i.* to

trade.—*adj.* **mer'chantable**, fit or ready for sale: marketable.—*adj.* and *adv.* **mer'chantlike**, (*Shak.*) like a merchant.—*ns.* **mer'chantman**, a trading-ship: (*B.*) a merchant:—*pl.* **mer'chantmen**; **mer'chantry**, the business of a merchant: merchants collectively. — **merchant prince**, a merchant of great wealth, power, and consequence; **merchant service**, mercantile marine; **merchant ship**, a ship that carries merchandise; **merchant tailor**, a tailor who supplies the cloth for the clothes which he makes. [Fr. *marchand*.]

merchet, *mer'chit*, *n.* (*hist.*) a fine paid to a lord for the marriage of a daughter. [A.Fr. *merchet*; see **market**.]

Mercury, *mər'kū-ri*, *n.* the Roman god of merchandise, theft, and eloquence, messenger of the gods, identified with the Greek Hermes: the planet nearest the sun: **mercury**, a silvery metallic element (Hg; atomic number 80) liquid at ordinary temperatures, also called *quicksilver*: the column of mercury in a thermometer or barometer: a plant (dog's mercury, Mercurialis) of the spurge family: the plant Good King Henry: a preparation of mercury: a messenger: a title for a newspaper: (*obs.*) mercurial character.—*adj.* **Mercu'rial**, of or pertaining to Mercury the god, or the planet: (also **mercurial**) having the qualities attributed to persons born under the planet.—*n.* one born under the planet.—*adj.* **mercu'rial**, active: sprightly: often changing: containing mercury: of or like mercury or quicksilver: caused by quicksilver.—*n.* a drug containing mercury: (*obs.*) the plant mercury.—*v.t.* **mercu'rialise**, (*med.*) to affect with mercury: to expose to the vapour of mercury.—*ns.* **mercu'rialism**, a morbid condition due to mercury; **mercu'rialist**, a believer in the medical use of mercury: a mercurial person.—*adv.* **mercu'rially**.—*adjs.* **mercu'ric**, containing bivalent mercury; **mer'curous**, containing univalent mercury. [L. *Mercūrius*, prob. *merx, mercis,* merchandise.]

mercy, *mər'si*, *n.* forbearance towards one who is in one's power: an act of such forbearance: a good thing regarded as derived from God: a happy chance: a forgiving disposition: clemency.—*interj.* expressing thanks (now *obs.*) or surprise (for *God have mercy*).—Also **mercy on us**.—*adjs.* **mer'ciable**, (*Spens.*) merciful; **mer'ciful**, full of, or exercising, mercy.—*adv.* **mer'cifully**.—*n.* **mer'cifulness**.—*v.t.* **mer'cify** (*Spens.*, in *pa.p.* **mer'cifide**), to deal mercifully with, to pity.—*adj.* **mer'ciless**, without mercy: unfeeling: cruel.—*adv.* **mer'cilessly**.—*ns.* **mer'cilessness**; **mer'cy-seat**, the seat or place of mercy: the covering of the Jewish Ark of the Covenant: the throne of God.—**at the mercy of**, wholly in the power of; **for mercy!** (*obs.*), **for mercy's sake!** an earnest conjuration in the form of an appeal to pity; **sisters of mercy**, members of female religious communities who tend the sick, &c. [Fr. *merci*, grace—L. *mercēs*, -*ēdis*, pay, later favour.]

mere, *mēr*, *n.* a pool or lake.—Also (*obs.*) **meer**.—*n.* **mere'swine**, a porpoise: a dolphin. [O.E. *mere*, sea, lake, pool; Ger. and Du. *meer*, L. *mare*, the sea.]

mere, *mēr*, *adj.* unmixed: pure: only what is said and nothing else, nothing more, nothing better: sheer: absolute.—*adv.* (*obs.*) absolutely. — *adj.* **meered**, (*Shak.*) perh. entire. — *adv.* **mere'ly**, purely: entirely: simply: only: solely: without being more or better. [L. *merus*, unmixed.]

mere, *mēr*, *n.* a boundary.—*v.t.* to bound: to mark off.—*ns.* **meres'man**, a man appointed to ascertain boundaries; **mere'stone**, a boundary stone. [O.E. *gemǣre*.]

mere, **meri**, *mer'i*, *n.* a war-club: a greenstone trinket in the form of a war-club. [Maori.]

merel, **merell**. Same as **meril**.

meretricious, *mer-i-trish'əs*, *adj.* of the nature of harlotry: characteristic or worthy of a harlot: flashy: gaudy.—*adv.* **meretric'iously**.—*n.* **meretric'iousness**. [L. *meretrix*, -*īcis*, a harlot— *merēre*, to earn.]

merganser, *mər-gan'sər*, *n.* any bird of the genus Mergus (goosander, smew, &c.). [L. *mergus*, a diving bird, *ānser*, a goose.]

merge, *mərj*, *v.t.* (*arch.*) to dip or plunge: to cause to be swallowed up or absorbed in something greater or superior: to cause to coalesce, combine, or amalgamate.—*v.i.* to be swallowed up, or lost: to coalesce: to lose identity in something else: to combine or amalgamate.—*n.* **mer'ger**, (*law*) a sinking of an estate, title, &c., in one of larger extent or of higher value: a combine or absorption. [L. *mergĕre, mersum.*]

mericarp, *mer'i-kärp*, *n.* a separating one-seeded part of a schizocarp, esp. half of a cremocarp. [Gr. *meros*, a part, *karpos*, fruit.]

meridian, *me-rid'i-ən*, *adj.* of or at midday: on the meridian: pertaining to a meridian or the sun or other body on the meridian: at culmination or highest point.—*n.* midday: a midday dram or nap: a great circle through the poles of the earth, the heavens, or any spherical body or figure, or its representation on a map: in particular, that cutting the observer's horizon at the north and south points, which the sun crosses at local noon: culmination or highest point, as of success, splendour, power, &c.—*v.i.* to reach the meridian.—*adj.* **merid'ional**, pertaining to the meridian: in the direction of a meridian: midday: culminating: southern: characteristic of the south.—*n.* a southerner, esp. in France.—*n.* **meridional'ity**.—*adv.* **merid'ionally**.—**magnetic meridian** (see **magnetic**); **meridian altitude**, arc of a meridian between a heavenly body and the horizon; **meridian circle**, a telescope mounted to revolve in the plane of the meridian; **meridian passage**, the transit or passage of a heavenly body across the observer's meridian; **prime (or first) meridian**, the meridian from which longitudes are measured east or west, specif. that through Greenwich. [L. *merīdiānus, merīdiōnālis—merīdiēs* (for *medīdiēs*), midday—*medius*, middle, *diēs*, day.]

meril, **merel**, **merelle**, *mer'əl*, *n.* a counter used in the game of merils: (in *pl.*) a rustic game played by two persons with counters on a figure marked on the ground, a board, &c., consisting of three squares, one within another, the object to get three counters in a row at the intersection of the lines joining the corners and the mid-points of the sides. — Also **marls**, **marr'els**, **mor'als**, **morr'is**, **mir'acles**—fivepenny morris, the game as played with five pieces each; **ninepenny morris**, **nine men's morris**, with nine: (*Shak.*) the figure cut in the ground for the game. [O.Fr. *merel*, counter.]

merimake, *mer'i-māk*, *n.* (*Spens.*) merrymaking: sport.

meringue, *mə-rang'*, *n.* a crisp cake or covering made of a mixture of sugar and white of eggs. [Fr.; origin unknown.]

merino, *mə-rē'nō*, *n.* a sheep of a fine-woolled Spanish breed: a fine dress fabric, originally of merino wool: a fine woollen yarn, or knitted goods, now mixed with cotton: waste from fine worsted clothes: (*pl.* **merinos**).—*adj.* belonging to the merino sheep or its wool: made of merino. [Sp., a merino sheep, also a governor—L. *mājōrīnus*, greater, also (L.L.) a head-man—L. *mājor*, greater.]

merism, *mer'izm*, *n.* (*biol.*) repetition of parts.—*adj.* **merist'ic**. [Gr. *meros*, part.]

meristem, *mer'is-tem*, *n.* the formative tissue of plants, distinguished from the permanent tissues by the power its cells have of dividing and forming new cells.—*adj.* **meristematic** (-*sti-mat'ik*). [Gr. *meristos*, divisible, *merizein*, to divide—*meros*, a part.]

merit, *mer'it*, *n.* excellence that deserves honour or reward: worth: value: desert: that which one deserves: (in *pl.*, esp. in *law*) the intrinsic right or wrong.—*v.t.* to earn: to have a right to claim as a reward: to deserve.—*v.i.* to deserve: (*obs.*) to acquire merit.—*adj.* **meritō'rious**, possessing merit or desert: deserving of reward, honour, or praise.—*adv.* **meritō'riously**.—*n.* **meritō'riousness**.—**order of merit**, arrangement in which the best is placed first, the next best second, and so on: a strictly limited British order (O.M.),

Neutral vowels in unaccented syllables : *el'ə-mənt, in'fənt, ran'dəm*

instituted in 1902, for eminence in any field. [L.
meritum—merēre, -ītum, to obtain as a lot, to
deserve.]

merk, *merk, n.* the old Scots mark or 13s. 4d. Scots,
13⅓d. sterling. [**mark** (2).]

merle, *mərl, n.* the blackbird. [Fr.,—L. *merula*.]

merlin, *mər'lin, n.* a species of small falcon. [A.Fr.
merilun—O.Fr. *esmerillon*.]

merling, *mər'ling, n. (obs.)* the whiting. [O.Fr.
merlanke—L. *merula*, a sea-carp.]

merlon, *mər'lən, n. (fort.)* the part of a parapet
between embrasures. [Fr. *merlon*—It. *merlone*—
merlo, battlement.]

mermaid, *mər'mād, n.* a sea-woman, a woman to
the waist, with fish's tail.—*ns.* **mer'maid'en;
mer'man; mer'child; mer'folk; mer'-
people; mer'maid's-glove'**, the largest kind of
British sponge; **mer'maid's-purse'**, a sea-barrow.
[O.E. *mere*, lake, sea, *mægden*, maid.]

meroblastic, *mer-ō-blast'ik, adj. (zool.)* undergoing
or involving cleavage in part of the ovum only, as
where there is much yolk.—*adv.* **meroblast'ically.** [Gr. *meros*, part, *blastos*, a shoot, bud.]

merogenesis, *mer-ō-jen'i-sis, n. (biol.)* segmentation.—*adj.* **merogenetic** (*-ji-net'ik*). [Gr. *meros*,
part, *genesis*, production.]

merogony, *mer-og'ə-ni, n.* production of an embryo
from a fertilised fragment of an ovum without
a nucleus. [Gr. *meros*, part, *gonē*, birth.]

meroistic, *mer-ō-ist'ik, adj. (entom.)* of an ovary,
producing yolk-forming cells as well as ova. [Gr.
meros, part, *ōion*, egg.]

merome, *mer'ōm, n.* a merosome. [Gr. *meros*,
part.]

Merops, *mer'ops, n.* the bee-eater genus.—*n.*
merop'idan, a bird of the bee-eater family
.(**Merop'idae**). [Gr. *merops*, bee-eater.]

merosome, *mer'ō-sōm, n.* one of the serial segments
of which a body is composed, as the ring of a
worm, a metamere, a somite. [Gr. *meros*, part,
sōma, body.]

Merovingian, *mer-ō-vin'ji-ən, adj.* pertaining to the
first dynasty of Frankish kings in Gaul, founded
by Clovis.—*n.* a member of this family. [L.
Merovingi—Merovaeus or *Merovech*, king of the
Salian Franks (448-457), grandfather of Clovis.]

merry, *mer'i, adj. (obs.)* pleasant: sportive: cheerful: noisily gay: causing laughter: lively.—*adv.*
merr'ily.—*ns.* **merr'iment**, gaiety with laughter
and noise: mirth: hilarity; **merr'iness; merr'y-
an'drew**, a quack's zany: a buffoon: one who
makes sport for others; **merr'y-go-round**, a
revolving ring of hobby-horses, &c.; **merr'y-
make**, a merrymaking.—*v.i.* to make merry.—
ns. **merr'ymaker; merr'ymaking**, a merry
entertainment: a festival; **merr'yman**, a zany:
a jester: (in *pl.*; **merry men**) followers, in arms
or in outlawry; **merr'y-night'**, a village festival;
merr'ythought, a fowl's furcula or wishbone, in
playful divination pulled apart, the longer part
indicating the first to be married or fulfilment of a
wish.—**make merry**, to hold festival: to indulge
in enjoyment: to turn to ridicule (with *with* or
over); **merry dancers**, the aurora; **merry
England**, (*orig.*) pleasant England; **the merry
monarch**, Charles II. [O.E. *myr(i)ge*.]

merry, *mer'i, n.* a gean. [Fr. *merise*.]

mersion, *mər'shən, n.* dipping. [L. *mersiō, -ōnis*;
cf. **merge**.]

Merulius, *mə-rōō'li-əs, n.* the dry-rot fungus genus.

merycism, *mer'i-sizm, n.* rumination, a disease
symptom in man. [Gr. *mērȳkismos*.]

mesa, *mā'sä, n.* a table-shaped hill. [Sp.,—L.
mēnsa, table.]

mesail, mezail, *mes', mez'āl, n.* a vizor, esp. one
made in two parts. [Fr. *mézail*.]

mesaraic, *mes-ə-rā'ik, adj.* mesenteric. [Gr. *mesa-
raikos—mesos*, middle, *araiā*, flank, belly.]

mesaticephalic, *mes-ə-ti-sef-al'ik*, **mesaticeph-
alous**, *-sef'ə-ləs, adjs.* intermediate between dolicho-
cephalic and brachycephalic.—*n.* **mesaticeph'aly.**
[Gr. *mesatos*, midmost, *kephalē*, head.]

mescal, *mes-käl', n.* the peyote cactus, chewed or
drunk in infusion as an intoxicant in Mexico: an
intoxicant distilled from Agave.—*n.* **mescal'ism**,

addiction to mescal. [Sp. *mescal, mezcal*—Nahuatl
mexcalli.]

mesdames. See **madam.**

mese, *mes'ē, n. (Gr. mus.)* the middle string of the
lyre: its note: the keynote. [Gr. *mesē (chordē)*,
middle (string).]

meseems, *mi-sēmz', v.impers.* it seems to me (*poet.*):
—*pa.t.* **meseemed'.** [me (dat.) and **seem.**]

mesel, meazel, *mēz'l, n. (obs.)* a leper: (*Shak.*)
leprosy.—*adj.* leprous.—*adj.* **mes'eled.** [O.Fr.
mesel—L. *misellus*, dim. of *miser*, wretched.]

Mesembrianthemum, conventionally **Mesem-
bryanthemum**, *mi-zem-bri-an'thi-məm, n.* a genus
of succulent plants (family Aizoaceae) mostly
South African (Hottentot fig, ice-plant). [Gr.
mesēmbriā, midday—*mesos*, middle, *hēmerā*, day,
anthemon, a flower: some are open only about midday.]

mesencephalon, *mes-en-sef'ə-lon, n.* the mid-
brain.—*adj.* **mesencephalic** (*-si-fal'ik*). [Gr.
mesos, middle, and **encephalon.**]

mesentery, *mes'ən-tər-i*, or *mez', n.* a fold of the
peritoneum, keeping the intestines in place: in
coelenterates a vertical inward fold of the body-
wall.—*adjs.* **mesenteral** (*-tē'ri-əl*), **mesenteric**
(*-ter'ik*).—*n.* **mesenteron** (*-en'tər-on*), the mid-
gut. [Gr. *mesos*, middle, *enteron*, intestines.]

mesh, *mesh, n.* the opening between the threads of
a net: the threads and knots bounding the opening:
network: engagement of geared wheels or the
like.—*v.t.* to catch in a net: to provide or make
with meshes.—*v.i.* to become engaged, as gear-
teeth: to become entangled.—*ns.* **mesh'ing,
mesh'-work**, a network, web.—*adj.* **mesh'y**,
formed like network. [Perh. M.Du. *maesche*;
cf. O.E. *max*, net; Ger. *masche*.]

mesial, *mē'zi-əl, adj.* middle: in or towards the
median plane or line—also **me'sian.**—*adv.* **me'sially.** [Gr. *mesos*, middle.]

mesmerise, *mez'mər-īz, v.t.* to hypnotise: loosely,
to fascinate, dominate the will or fix the attention
of.—*adjs.* **mesmeric** (*-mer'ik*), **-al.**—*ns.* **mes-
merisā'tion; mes'meriser, mes'merist; mes'-
merism**, hypnotism as expounded, with some
fanciful notions, from 1775 by Friedrich Anton or
Franz *Mesmer*, a German physician (1734-1815):
hypnotic influence.

mesne, *mēn, adj. (law)* intermediate. [Law Fr.
mesne, middle; cf. **mean** (2).]

meso-, *mes'ō-*, in composition, middle.—*n.* **mes'o-
blast** (Gr. *blastos* shoot), the middle germinal
layer.—*adj.* **mesoblas'tic.**—*n.* **mes'ocarp** (Gr.
karpos, fruit), the middle layer of a pericarp.—
adjs. **mesocephalic** (*-si-fal'ik*), **mesocephalous**
(*-sef'ə-ləs*; Gr. *kephalē*, head), between dolicho-
cephalic and brachycephalic.—*ns.* **mesoceph'-
alism, mesoceph'aly; mes'oderm** (Gr. *derma*,
skin), mesoblast or tissues derived from it; **meso-
gloea** (*-glē'ä*; Gr. *gloiā*, glue), in coelenterates and
sponges, a structureless gelatinous layer between
ectoderm and endoderm; **mes'olite** (Gr. *lithos*,
stone), a zeolite intermediate in composition
between natrolite and scolecite.—*adj.* **Mesolith'ic**,
intermediate between Palaeolithic and Neolithic.—
ns. **mes'ophyll** (Gr. *phyllon*, leaf), the spongy
tissue within a leaf; **mes'ophyte** (*-fīt*; Gr.
phyton, plant), a plant intermediate between a
xerophyte and a hydrophyte.—*adjs.* **mesophytic**
(*-fit'ik*); **mesothoracic** (*-thō-ras'ik*).—*n.* **meso-
tho'rax**, the middle one of the three segments of
an insect's thorax.—*n.pl.* **Mesozo'a** (Gr. *zōion*,
animal), minute animals once thought intermediate
between Protozoa and Metazoa, prob. Metazoa
reduced by parasitism.—*adj.* **Mesozo'ic** (Gr. *zōē*,
life), of the Secondary geological period, including
the Triassic, Jurassic, and Cretaceous systems.
[Gr. *mesos*, middle.]

meson, *mēz'on, mes'on, n.* a particle (of several kinds)
equal in charge to an electron or positron, but with
a much greater mass, though less in mass than a
neutron or proton.—Also (after *electron*) **mes'-
otron.** [Gr. *meson*, neut. of *mesos*, middle.]

mesprise, mesprize, Spenserian forms of **misprise** (1 and 2).

mesquite, *mes-kēt', mes'kēt, n.* a leguminous tree or

fāte, fär, àsk; mē, hər (her); *mīne; mōte; mūte; mōōn; dhen* (then)

shrub (Prosopis) of America, with nutritious pods. [Mex. Sp. *mezquite*.]

mess, *mes, n.* a dish of food : a course : a meal : (*arch.*) a set of usually four persons served together at a banquet : (*Shak.*) a set of four : a number of persons who take their meals together, esp. in the fighting services : (*dial.*) a cow's yield at one milking : (*U.S.*) a quantity : (*U.S.*) a take or haul of fish : a dish of soft, pulpy or liquid stuff : liquid, pulpy or smeary dirt : a mixture disagreeable to the sight or taste : a medley : disorder : confusion : embarrassment : a bungle.—*v.t.* to supply with a mess : to make a mess of : to muddle : to befoul.—*v.i.* to eat of a mess : to eat at a common table : to belong to a mess : to make a mess : (*coll.*) to potter (often with *about*).—*ns.* **mess′iness ; mess′mate,** a member of the same mess : a commensal ; **mess′-room ; mess′-tin,** a soldier's utensil serving as plate, cup, and cooking-vessel ; **mess′-up′,** a mess, muddle, bungle, or confusion. —*adj.* **mess′y,** confused, untidy : involving mess : bungling.—**mess of pottage,** a material advantage accepted in exchange for something of higher worth, as by Esau (Gen. xxv. 29 ff.); **mess or mell,** (*Scot.*) to associate, have to do. [O.Fr. *mes* (Fr. *mets*), a dish—L. *mittĕre, missum,* to send, in L.L. to place.]

mess, *mes, n.* obs. form of **mass** (2 and 3).

message, *mes′ij, n.* any communication sent from one person to another : an errand : an official communication of a president, governor, &c., to a legislature or council : the teaching that a poet, sage, prophet, has to communicate to the world : domestic shopping, a journey for the purpose, or the goods bought.—*v.t.* to send as a message : to transmit as by signalling.—*v.i.* (*Dickens*) to carry a message.—*ns.* **mess′age-boy, -girl,** errand-boy or girl ; **mess′enger** (*-ən-jər*), one who carries messages or a message : a forerunner : a light scudding cloud preceding a storm : a small object sent along a line, as a paper up a kite string : the secretary-bird : a rope or chain connecting a cable with the capstan for heaving up the anchor : (*Scots law*) an officer who executes the summonses of the Court of Session, called a **mess′enger-at-arms ; mess′-enger-wire,** a wire supporting an overhead cable.—**king's, or queen's, messenger,** an officer who carries official despatches. [Fr.,—L.L. *mis-sāticum*—L. *mittĕre, missum,* to send.]

messan, *mes′an, n.* (*Scot.*) a lap-dog : a cur. [Perh. Gael. *measan.*]

Messiah, *ma-sī′ä, n.* the expected deliverer of the Jews : by Christians, applied to Jesus : a hoped-for deliverer, saviour, or champion generally— also **Messi′as.**—*n.* **Messi′ahship.**—*adj.* **Messianic** (*mes-i-an′ik*).—*ns.* **Messi′anism,** belief in a Messiah ; **Messi′anist.** [Gr. *Messiās*—Aram. *m'shīhă,* Heb. *māshīah,* anointed—*māshah,* to anoint.]

Messidor, *mes-i-dor′, n.* the tenth month of the French revolutionary calendar, about June 19th-July 18th. [Fr.,—L. *messis,* harvest, Gr. *dōron,* a gift.]

messieurs, *mes-yə ;* contracted and anglicised as **Messrs** (*mes′ərz*), *pl.* of **monsieur.**

messuage, *mes′wij, n.* (*law*) a dwelling and offices with the adjoining lands appropriated to the household : a mansion-house and grounds. [A.Fr. ; poss. orig. a misreading of *mesnage* ; cf. **ménage.**]

mestee, *mes-tē′,* **mustee,** *mus-tē′, n.* the offspring of a white and a quadroon.—*n.* **mestizo** (*mes-tē′zō ;* Sp. *-thō*), a half-caste, esp. of Spanish and American Indian parentage :—*pl.* **mesti′zos ;** *fem.* **mesti′za,** *pl.* **mesti′zas.** [Sp. *mestizo*—a L.L. derivative of L. *mixtus,* mixed.]

met, *pa.t.* and *pa.p.* of **meet.**

meta-, *met′ə-,* **met-ə′-,** with a following *h,* **meth-.** See *Prefixes.*—In *chem.* meta- indicates a derivative or polymer, or an acid or hydroxide derived from the ortho- form by loss of water molecules, or a benzene substitution product in which the substituted atoms or groups are attached to two carbon atoms which are themselves separated by one carbon atom (in this sense commonly represented by *m*).—*ns.* **met′a-acid ; metal′dehyde,** a poly-

mer or acetaldehyde ; **met′a-compound.** [Gr. *meta,* among, with, beside, after.]

metabasis, *met-ab′ə-sis, n.* a transition.—*adj.* **metabatic** (*met-ə-bat′ik*). [Gr. *metabasis — bainein,* to go.]

metabolism, *met-ab′əl-izm, n.* the sum-total of chemical changes of living matter : metamorphosis. —*n.pl.* **metab′ola,** insects that undergo metamorphosis.—*adj.* **metabolic** (*-bol′ik*), exhibiting or relating to metabolism.—*v.t.* **metab′olise.** [Gr. *metabolē,* change.]

metacarpus, *met-ə-kär′pəs, n.* the part of the hand (or its bones) between the wrist and the fingers, or the corresponding part, e.g. the foreleg of a horse between ' knee ' and fetlock.—*adj.* **metacarp′al.** [Gr. *karpos,* wrist.]

metacentre, *met′ə-sen-tər, n.* the point of intersection of a vertical line through the centre of gravity of a body floating in equilibrium and that through the centre of gravity of the displaced liquid when the body is slightly displaced.—*adj.* **metacen′tric.** [Gr. *kentron,* point.]

metachronism, *met-ak′ron-izm, n.* the error of dating an event too late. [Gr. *chronos,* time.]

metachrosis, *met-ə-krō′sis, n.* ability to change colour in animals. [Gr. *chrōsis,* colouring.]

metage, *mēt′ij, n.* official weighing of coal, grain, &c. : charge for such weighing. [**mete.**]

metagenesis, *met-ə-jen′i-sis, n.* (*biol.*) alternation of generations.—*adj.* **metagenetic** (*-ji-net′ik*). [Gr. *genesis,* generation.]

metagnathous, *met-ag′nə-thəs, adj.* of birds, having crossed mandibles : of insects, having biting jaws in the larvae, sucking in the adult state. [Gr. *gnathos,* jaw.]

metagrobolise, *met-ə-grob′əl-īz,* **metagrabolise,** *grab′, v.t.* to mystify : to puzzle out. [Obs. Fr. *metagraboulizer* (Rabelais).]

métairie, *mā′ter-ē, n.* a piece of land cultivated for a share of the produce. [Fr. ; see **métayer.**]

metal, *met′l, n.* an opaque elementary substance, possessing a peculiar lustre, fusibility, conductivity for heat and electricity, readiness to form positive ions, &c., such as gold, &c. : an alloy : that which behaves chemically like a true metal : courage or spirit (now spelt *mettle*) : intrinsic quality : guns of a ship-of-war : (*her.*) or or argent as a tincture : molten material for glass-making : (*mining*) country-rock : broken stones used for macadamised roads or as ballast for railways : (*pl.*) the rails of a railroad.—*adj.* made of metal.—*v.t.* to furnish or cover with metal.—*adjs.* **met′alled,** covered with metal, as a road ; **metallic** (*mi-tal′ik*), pertaining to, or like, a metal : consisting of metal. —*adv.* **metall′ically.**—*adjs.* **metallif′erous,** bearing or yielding metal ; **met′alline,** of, like, consisting of, or mixed with, metal.—*ns.* **met′alling,** road-metal, broken stones ; **metallisā′tion.**—*v.t.* **met′allise,** to make metallic.—*ns.* **met′allist,** a worker in metals ; **metallog′rapher.** — *adj.* **metallograph′ic.**—*ns.* **metallog′raphy,** the study of the structure and constitution of metals ; **met′-alloid,** a non-metal : an element resembling a metal in some respects, as selenium, tellurium.— *adjs.* **met′alloid, metalloid′al,** pertaining to, or of the nature of, the metalloids ; **met′ally,** suggestive of metal.—*ns.* **met′al-work, -er, -ing.** [O.Fr.,—L. *metallum*—Gr. *metallon,* a mine.]

metalepsis, *met-ə-lep′sis, n.* (*rhet.*) metonymy, esp. of a double, complicated, or indirect kind.—*adjs.* **metalep′tic, -al.** [Gr. *metalēpsis,* substitution.]

metallurgy, *met′əl-ər-ji,* or *-al′, n.* art and science applied to metals, including extraction from ores, refining, alloying, shaping, treating, and the study of structure, constitution, and properties.—*adjs.* **metallur′gic, -al,** pertaining to metallurgy.—*n.* **met′allurgist** (or *-al′*). [Gr. *metallourgeein,* to mine—*metallon,* a mine, *ergon,* work.]

metamerism, *met-am′ər-izm, n.* (*chem.*) a particular form of isomerism in which different groups are attached to the same central atom : (*zool.*) segmentation of the body along the primary axis, producing a series of homologous parts.—*ns.* **met′amer,** (*chem.*) a compound metameric with another ; **met′amere** (*-mēr ;* *zool.*), a segment, merome, or somite.—*adj.* **metameric** (*-mer'ik*). [Gr. *meros*, a part.]

metamorphosis, *met-ə-mor'fəs-is*, sometimes *-fōs'is*, *n.* change of shape, transformation: (*folklore*) transformation of a human being to a beast, stone, tree, &c.: the marked change which some living beings undergo in the course of growth, as caterpillar to butterfly, tadpole to frog: — *pl.* **metamor'phoses** (*-sēz*, or *-fō'sēz*).—*adj.* **metamor'phic**, showing or relating to change of form: (*geol.*) formed by alteration of existing rocks by heat, pressure, or other processes in the earth's crust.—*ns.* **metamor'phism**, transformation of rocks in the earth's crust (*contact metamorphism*, by contact with or neighbourhood of igneous material; *regional*, owing to general conditions over a wide region); **metamor'phist**, one who believes that Christ's body merged into the Deity at the Ascension.—*v.t.* **metamor'phose** (*-fōz, -fōs*), to transform: to subject to metamorphism or metamorphosis: to develop in another form. [Gr. *metamorphōsis—morphē*, form.]

metaphase, *met'ə-fāz*, *n.* the stage of mitosis at which the chromosomes form the equatorial plate. [Gr. *meta*, after, and **phase**.]

metaphor, *met'ə-fər*, *n.* a figure of speech by which a thing is spoken of as being that which it only resembles, as when a ferocious man is called a tiger. — *adjs.* **metaphoric** (*-for'ik*), **-al**. — *adv.* **metaphor'ically**. — *n.* **met'aphorist**. — mixed **metaphor**, an expression in which two or more metaphors are confused, as *to take arms against a sea of troubles*. [Gr. *metaphorā—pherein*, to carry.]

metaphosphoric, *met-ə-fos-for'ik*, *adj.* applied to an acid (HPO₃) containing a molecule less of water than orthophosphoric acid.—*n.* **metaphos'phate**, a salt of metaphosphoric acid. [See **meta-**.]

metaphrase, *met'ə-frāz*, *n.* a turning of prose into verse or verse into prose: a rendering in a different style or form: an altered wording: a word for word translation—also **metaphrasis** (*-af'rə-sis*).— *n.* **met'aphrast** (*-frast*), one who produces a metaphrase.—*adj.* **metaphrast'ic.** [Gr. *metaphrasis—phrasis*, a speaking.]

metaphysics, *met-ə-fiz'iks*, *n.* (treated as *sing.*) the science which investigates the first principles of nature and thought: ontology or the science of being: loosely and vaguely applied to anything abstruse, abstract, philosophical, subtle, transcendental, occult, supernatural, magical.—*n.* **metaphys'ic**, metaphysics: philosophical groundwork. —*adj.* metaphysical.—*adj.* **metaphys'ical**, pertaining to metaphysics: abstract: beyond nature or the physical: supernatural: fanciful: addicted to far-fetched conceits (applied by Johnson to Donne, Cowley, and others).—*adv.* **metaphys'ically.**— *n.* **metaphysician** (*-ish'ən*), one versed in metaphysics. [Originally applied to those writings of Aristotle which in the accepted order came after (Gr. *meta*) those dealing with natural science (*ia physika—physis*, nature).]

metaplasia, *met-ə-plā'si-ä*, *n.* tissue transformation, as of cartilage into bone. — *ns.* **metaplasis** (*-ap'lə-sis*), metaplasia: period of maturity in the life-cycle; **met'aplasm** (*-plazm*), cell-contents other than protoplasm: change in a word by addition, dropping, or exchange of parts.—*adj.* **metaplast'ic.** [Gr. *metaplasis, metaplasmos*, a moulding afresh—*plassein*, to form.]

metapsychics, *met-ə-sī'kiks*, *n.* (treated as *sing.*) the study of psychic phenomena beyond the limits of ordinary or orthodox psychology—'psychical research.' — *adjs.* **metapsych'ic**, **-al.** [From **psychic**, on the analogy of **metaphysics**.]

metasilicic, *met-ə-sil-is'ik*, *adj.* applied to an acid (H₂SiO₃) containing a molecule less of water than orthosilicic acid.—*n.* **metasil'icate** (*-i-kāt*), a salt of metasilicic acid. [See **meta-**.]

metasomatism, *met-ə-sō'mə-tizm*, *n.* (*geol.*) metamorphism by chemical changes in minerals.—*adj.* **metasomatic** (*-at'ik*). [Gr. *sōma, -atos*, body.]

metastable, *met'ə-stā-bl*, *adj.* in a condition resembling stability.—*n.* **metastability** (*-stə-bil'i-ti*). [Gr. *meta*, beside, and **stable**.]

metastasis, *met-as'tə-sis*, *n.* removal from one place

to another: transition: transformation: paramorphic change in rocks: metabolism: — *pl.* **metas'tasēs**.—*v.i.* **metas'tasise**, to pass to another part of the body, as a tumour.—*adj.* **metastatic** (*-stat'ik*). [Gr. *metastasis*, change of place —*stasis*, a standing.]

metatarsus, *met-ə-tär'səs*, *n.* that part of the foot, or its bones, between the tarsus and the toes.— *adj.* **metatar'sal.** [Gr. *tarsos*, the flat of the foot.]

Metatheria, *met-ə-thē'ri-ä*, *n.pl.* the marsupials. [Gr. *thērion*, a wild beast.]

metathesis, *met-ath'ə-sis*, *n.* transposition or exchange of places, esp. between the sounds or letters of a word :—*pl.* **metath'esēs.**—*adjs.* **metathetic** (*met-ə-thet'ik*), **-al.** [Gr.,—*metatithenai*, to transpose—*tithenai*, to place.]

metathorax, *met-ə-thō'raks*, *n.* the third and last segment of an insect's thorax.—*adj.* **metathoracic** (*-ras'ik*). [See **thorax**.]

métayer, *mā-te'yä*, *n.* a farmer who pays, instead of money rent, a fixed proportion of the crops.—*n.* **métayage** (*-yäzh'*), this system. [Fr.,—L.L. *medietārius*—L. *medietās*, half—*medius*, middle.]

Metazoa, *met-ə-zō'ä*, *n.pl.* many-celled animals— opp. to single-celled *Protozoa* :—*sing.* **metazo'on.** — *adjs.* **metazo'an, metazo'ic.** [Gr. *zōion*, animal.]

mete, *mēt*, *v.t.* to measure: to apportion (*pa.t.* **mēt'ed**, in Spens. **mott**).—*n.* measure.—*ns.* **mete'stick, mete'wand, mete'yard**, a measuring-rod. [O.E. *metan*; Ger. *messen*.]

mete, *mēt*, *n.* a boundary or limit. [L. *mēta*, a goal or boundary.]

metempiric, **-al**, *met-em-pir'ik*, *-əl*, *adjs.* beyond the scope of experience.—*ns.* **metempir'icism** (*-i-sizm*); **metempir'icist.**

metempsychosis, *met-emp-si-kō'sis*, *n.* the passing of the soul after death into some other body :—*pl.* **metempsychō'sēs.** [Gr. *metempsychōsis—en*, in, *psychē*, soul.]

meteor, *mē'tyər, mē'ti-ər, n.* (*orig.*, now *rarely*) any atmospheric phenomenon: a luminous appearance: one of numberless small bodies travelling through space, revealed to observation when they enter the earth's atmosphere as aerolites, fire-balls, or shooting-stars: anything brilliant or dazzling but short-lived.—*adj.* **meteoric** (*mē-ti-or'ik*), above the earth's surface: atmospheric: influenced by weather: of or pertaining to meteors in any sense: of the nature of a meteor: transiently flashing like a meteor.—*ns.* **me'teorist**, one versed in meteors; **me'teorite**, a fallen meteor: a meteor.—*adj.* **meteorit'ic, me'teorital** (*-it-l*).—*ns.* **me'teorogram**, a meteorograph record; **me'teorograph**, an instrument by which several meteorological elements are recorded in combination; **me'teoroid**, a meteor that has not reached the earth's atmosphere; **me'teorolite** (Gr. *lithos*, stone), a meteoric stone.—*adjs.* **meteorolog'ic, -al.**—*ns.* **meteorol'-ogist; meteorol'ogy**, study of weather and climate. —*adj.* **me'teorous** (or, usu. in poetry, *mē-tē'ər-əs*), like a meteor, meteoric.—**meteor crater**, a crater formed by the fall of a meteor; **meteoric iron**, iron as found in meteorites; **meteoric showers**, showers of meteors; **meteoric stones**, aerolites. [Gr. *ta meteōra*, things on high—*meta* and the root of *aeirein*, to lift.]

meter, *mē'tər, n.* a measurer: an apparatus for measuring, esp. quantity of a fluid, or of electricity, used: a gauge or indicator.—*v.t.* to measure by a meter. [**meter** (1).]

meter, American spelling of **metre** (1 and 2).

meth-, **meth-**. See **meta-**.

methane, *meth'ān, n.* marsh-gas (CH₄), the simplest hydrocarbon, found wherever the decomposition of vegetable matter is taking place under water, also in coal-mines, forming when mixed with air the deadly fire-damp. [**methyl**.]

metheglin, *meth-eg'lin, n.* a Welsh fermented liquor made from honey. [W. *meddyglyn—meddyg*, medicinal (—L. *medicus*, physician), *llyn*, liquor.]

methinks, *mi-thingks'*, **methink'eth, methink'**, *v.impers.* it seems to me: I think :—*pa.t.* **methought** (*mi-thawt'*). [O.E. *mē thyncth*, it seems to me; *thyncan*, to seem, has been confused with *thencan*, to think ; cf. Ger. *dünken*, to seem, *denken*, to think.]

method, *meth'ad*, *n.* the mode or rule of accomplishing an end : orderly procedure : manner : orderly arrangement : classification : system, rule : manner of performance : an instruction-book systematically arranged.—*adjs.* **methodic** (*mi-thod'ik*), **-al**, arranged with method : disposed in a just and natural manner : observing method : formal.—*adv.* **method'ically.**—*v.t.* **meth'odise**, to reduce to method : to dispose in due order.—*ns.* **Meth'odism**, the principles and practice of the Methodists ; **meth'odist**, one who observes method : **Methodist**, a follower of the Wesleys—a name given first to a group of students at Oxford ' for the regularity of their lives as well as studies.' —*adjs.* **Methodist'ic**, **-al**, resembling the Methodists, esp. as viewed by opponents : strict in religious matters.—*adv.* **Methodist'ically.**—*ns.* **methodol'ogy**, the science of method in scientific procedure ; **Meth'ody**, a disrespectful nickname for a Methodist. [Gr. *methodos*—*meta*, *hodos*, a way.]

methomania, *meth-ō-mā'ni-ä*, *n.* an intermittent morbid craving for alcohol. [Gr. *methē*, strong drink, *maniā*, madness.]

methought. See **methinks**.

Methuselah, *mi-th(y)ōō'za-lä*, *n.* a patriarch said to have lived 969 years (Gen. v. 27) : any very aged person.

methyl, *meth'il*, *n.* (*chem.*) the radical (CH_3) of wood (or methyl) alcohol ($CH_3 \cdot OH$).—*n.* **methylamine** (*-a-mēn'*), an inflammable gas ($CH_3 \cdot NH_2$) got from herring brine.—*v.t.* **meth'ylate**, to mix or impregnate with methyl alcohol : to introduce the radical CH_3 into. — *ns.* **methylā'tion** ; **meth'ylene**, the hypothetical compound CH_2.—*adj.* **methyl'ic.**—**methylated spirit**, alcohol made unpalatable with methyl alcohol, and usually other things ; **methyl-propyl ether**, an inhalation anaesthetic. [Gr. *meta*, *hylē*, wood.]

methysis, *meth'i-sis*, *n.* (*path.*) drunkenness.—*adj.* **methys'tic**, intoxicating. [Gr.]

metic, *met'ik*, *n.* a resident alien. [Gr. *metoikos*—*meta*, indicating change, and *oikos*, a house.]

meticulous, *me-tik'ū-ləs*, *adj.* timid : (popularly) overcareful, scrupulously careful. — *adv.* **metic'ulously.**—*n.* **metic'ulousness.** [L. *meticulōsus*, frightened—*metus*, fear.]

métier, *mā-tyā*, *n.* one's calling or business : that in which one is specially skilled. [Fr.,—L. *ministerium.*]

métif, *mā-tēf*, *n.* the offspring of a white and a quadroon.—*n.* **métis** (*mā-tēs*), an American half-breed, esp. one of French and Indian descent. [Fr. ; cf. *mestizo*.]

Metis, *mē'tis*, *n.* a Greek personification of prudence. [Gr. *mētis*.]

Metonic, *mi-ton'ik*, *adj.* pertaining to the Athenian astronomer *Mētōn* or his cycle (433 B.C.) of 19 years after which the moon's phases recur on the same days of the year.

metonym, *met'a-nim*, *n.* a word used in a transferred sense.—*adjs.* **metonym'ic**, **-al**.—*adv.* **metonym'ically.**—*n.* **metonymy** (*mi-ton'i-mi*), a trope in which the name of one thing is put for that of another related to it, the effect for the cause, &c., as ' the bottle ' for ' drink.' [Gr. *metōnymiā*—*meta*, and *onyma*=*onoma*, a name.]

metope, *met'o-pē*, also *met'ōp*, *n.* (*archit.*) the slab, plain or sculptured, between the triglyphs of a Doric frieze. [Gr. *metŏpē*—*meta* and *ŏpē*, an opening for a beam-end.]

metope, *met'ōp*, *n.* the face, forehead, frontal surface generally.—*adj.* **metopic** (*mit-op'ik*).—*ns.* **metopism** (*met'a-pizm*), the condition of having a persistent metopic or frontal suture ; **metoposcopy** (*met-a-pos'ka-pi* ; Gr. *skopeein*, to look), the study of character from the physiognomy.—*adjs.* **metoposcop'ic**, **-al**.—*n.* **metopos'copist.** [Gr. *metōpon*, forehead, lit. between the eyes—*meta*, and *ŏps*, eye.]

metre, *mē'tər*, *n.* that regulated succession of certain groups of syllables (long and short, stressed and unstressed) in which poetry is usually written : verse, or poetry generally : a scheme of versifica-

tion, the character of a stanza as consisting of a given number of lines composed of feet of a given number, arrangement, and kind : musical time.—*v.t.* and *v.i.* to versify.—*adjs.* **metred** (*mē'tərd*), rhythmical ; **metric** (*met'rik*), **-al**, pertaining to metre : in metre : consisting of verses.—*adv.* **met'rically.**—*n.* **metrician** (*me-trish'ən*), a metricist.—*v.t.* **met'ricise** (*-sīz*), to analyse the metre of. —*ns.* **met'ricist** (*-sist*), one skilled in metres : one who writes in metre ; **met'ric(s)**, the art or science of versification ; **metrificā'tion**, metrical structure : the act of making verses ; **met'rifier**, a versifier ; **met'rist**, one skilled in the use of metres : a student of metre ; **metromā'nia**, a mania for writing verses.—**common metre**, a quatrain in eights and sixes, of four and of three iambic feet alternately—also **service metre**, from its use in the metrical psalms, &c., and **ballad metre**, from its use in old ballads ; **long metre**, an octosyllabic quatrain, the four lines with four feet each ; **short metre**, the quatrain in sixes, with the third line octosyllabic. [O.E. *mēter* and O.Fr. *metre*, both — L. *metrum* — Gr. *metron*, measurement, metre ; and partly directly.]

metre, *mē'tər*, *n.* the fundamental unit of length in the metric system—intended to be one ten-millionth of a quadrant of a meridian, actually the length of a platino-iridium bar in Paris, 39·370147 inches : by British Act of Parliament (1897) legally 39·370113 inches.—*adj.* **metric** (*met'rik*).—**metric system**, a decimal system of weights and measures founded on the metre. [Fr. *mètre*—Gr. *metron*, measure.]

metric, *met'rik*, *adj.* quantitative.—*adj.* **met'rical**, pertaining to measurement.—*n.pl.* **met'rics**, the theory of measurement.—*n.* **metrol'ogy**, the science of weights and measures. [Gr. *metron*, measure.]

metronome, *met'ra-nōm*, *n.* an instrument with an inverted pendulum that can be set to beat so many times a minute, and so give the right speed of performance for a piece of music.—*adj.* **metronomic** (*-nom'ik*). [Gr. *metron*, measure, *nomos*, law.]

metronymic, *met-ra-nim'ik*, *adj.* derived from the name of one's mother or other female ancestor : indicating the mother : using such a system of naming.—*n.* an appellation so derived (cf. *patronymic*).—Also **matronymic** (prob.—L. *māter*), though Doric Greek is *mātēr*. [Gr. *mētēr*, *-tros*, mother, *onyma*=*onoma*, name.]

metropolis, *mi-trop'a-lis*, *n.* the capital of a country, county, &c. : the chief cathedral city, as Canterbury of England : the mother-city of an ancient Greek colony : a chief centre, seat or focus : (*biol.*) the main habitat :—*pl.* **metrop'olises**.—*adj.* **metropolitan** (*met-ra-pol'i-tan*), of a metropolis : of the mother-church.—*n.* the bishop of a metropolis, presiding over the other bishops of a province : an archbishop. — *n.* **metropol'itanate**. — *adj.* **metropolit'ical.** [Gr. *mētropolis*—*mētēr*, mother, *polis*, a city.]

metrostyle, *met'ra-stīl*, *n.* a device for regulating speed in a player-piano. [Gr. *metron*, measure, *stylos*, a pillar.]

mettle, *met'l*, *n.* temperament : ardent temperament : spirit : sprightliness : courage.—*adj.* (*Scot.*) mettlesome.—*adjs.* **mett'led**, **mett'lesome**, high-spirited : ardent.—*n.* **mett'lesomeness.**—**put on his mettle**, to rouse a person up to putting forth his best efforts. [metal.]

meu, *mū*, *n.* baldmoney or spignel. [L. *mēum*—Gr. *mēon*.]

meuse, muse, mews, *mūs*, *mūz*, *n.* a way of escape through a hedge, &c.—*v.i.* to pass through a meuse. [O.Fr. *muce*, a place for hiding things.]

meuse. See **mew** (3).

mev, *mev*, *n.* a million electron-volts. [From the initials of these words.]

meve, *mēv*, an obs. form of **move** (*vb.*).

mew, *mū*, *n.* a gull. [O.E. *mǣw* ; Du. *meeuw*, O.N. *mār*, Ger. *möwe*.]

mew, *mū*, *v.i.* to cry as a cat.—*n.* the cry of a cat.—*interj.* expressing derision. [Imit.]

mew, *mū*, *v.t.* to shed, moult, or cast : to change,

as the covering or dress: to confine, as in a cage.
—*v.i.* to cast the antlers or feathers: to moult.—
n. process of moulting: a cage for hawks, esp.
while mewing: a coop: a place of confinement:
a retreat: a hiding-place. — *n.* **mews, meuse**
(*mūz, mūs*; orig. *pl.* of mew, now commonly as
sing. with new *pl.* **mews′es**), a street or yard of
stabling (often converted into dwelling-houses or
garages)—from the king's mews at Charing Cross
when hawks were succeeded by horses. [O.Fr.
muer—L. *mūtāre*, to change.]

mewl, *mūl, v.i.* and *v.t.* to mew, squall. [Imit.]

Mexican, *meks′i-kən, adj.* of Mexico and its people.
—*n.* a native or citizen of Mexico: an Aztec: the
Nahuatl language: a Mexican dollar: a coarse
cotton cloth.—**Mexican hog**, the peccary; **Mexican tea**, a kind of goosefoot, used as an anthelmintic. [Sp. *Mexicano*, now *Mejicano.*]

meynt. See ming.

mezereon, *me-zē′ri-on, n.* a European shrub
(*Daphne Mezereum*) whose flowers appear in early
spring: its extremely acrid bark used in medicine.
[Ar. and Pers. *māzaryūn.*]

mezzanine, *mez′ə-nēn, n.* (*archit.*) an entresol: a
small low window: a room below the stage.—
Also *adj.* [Fr., — It. *mezzanino — mezzano* — L.
mediānus—medius, middle.]

mezzo-forte, *med′zō-for′tā, adj.* and *adv.* rather
loud. [It.]

mezzo-rilievo, *med′zō-ril-yā′vō, n.* a degree of
relief in figures half-way between high and low
relief. [It.]

mezzo-soprano, *med′zō-so-prä′nō, n.* a voice between soprano and contralto: low soprano: a
part for such a voice: a person possessing it.
[It. *mezzo*, middle, and *soprano.*]

mezzotint, *med′zō-tint*, **mezzotinto**, *-tint′ō, n.* a
method of copperplate engraving giving an even
gradation of tones by roughening a plate and
removing the bur for lights: an impression from
a plate so produced. [It. *mezzotinto—mezzo*,
middle, half, *tinto*, tint—L. *tingĕre, tinctum*, to
dye.]

mho, *mō, n.* a unit of electric conductance, that of a
body with a resistance of one ohm. [**ohm** spelt
backwards.]

mhorr, *mawr, n.* a West African gazelle. [Ar.]

mi, *mē, n.* the third note of the scale in sol-fa
notation—also anglicised in spelling as **me**. [See
Aretinian.]

miaow, *mi-ow′, myow′.* Same as **mew**.

miarolitic, *mī-ə-rə-lit′ik, adj.* (*geol.*) having irregular
cavities into which the constituent minerals of the
rock project with perfectly terminated crystals.
[It. *miarolo*, local name of a granite.]

miasma, *mi-* or *mī-az′mä, n.* an unwholesome
exhalation—also **mī′asm** :—*pl.* **mias′mata, mias′-
mas**, **mi′asms.**—*adjs.* **mias′mal**, **miasmat′ic,
mias′matous**, **mias′mic**, **mias′mous.** [Gr.
miasma, -atos, pollution—*miainein*, to stain, pollute.]

miaul, *mi-awl′, mi-owl′, v.i.* to cry as a cat.—*n.* a
mew. [Fr. *miauler*; imit.]

mica, *mī′kä, n.* a rock-forming mineral (muscovite,
biotite, lepidolite, &c.) with perfect basal cleavage,
the laminae flexible and elastic, and generally
transparent, silicate of aluminium with magnesium,
iron, or an alkali metal, used as an electric insulator
and as a substitute for glass :—*pl.* **mi′cas.**—*adj.*
micaceous (*-kā′shəs*).—*ns.* **mi′ca-schist′, -slate′**,
a metamorphic rock consisting of alternate folia of
mica and quartz.—*v.t.* **mi′cate**, to furnish with
mica. [L. *mīca*, a crumb; use probably influenced
by association with *mīcāre*, to glitter.]

Micawberish, *mi-kaw′bər-ish, adj.* like Wilkins
Micawber in Dickens's *David Copperfield*, jaunty and
improvident, always 'waiting for something to
turn up.'—*n.* **Micaw′berism.**

mice, *mīs*, plural of mouse.

micella, *mi-sel′ä*, **micelle**, *mi-sel′, ns.* a group of
molecular chains, a structural unit found in colloids:
a hypothetical unit of living matter.—*adj.* **micell′ar.**
[Dim. of L. *mica*, crumb, grain.]

Michaelmas, *mik′əl-məs, n.* the festival of St.
Michael, celebrated Sept. 29: a quarterly rent-
day in England.—*n.* **Mich′aelmas-dai′sy**, a wild

aster: any of several garden plants of the genus
Aster with clusters of small purple flowers.
[**mass** (2).]

miche, *mich, v.i.* (*dial.*) to mouch, skulk, slink: to
loaf: to play truant.—*v.t.* to pilfer.—*n.* **mich′er**,
—*n.* and *adj.* **mich′ing.** [Poss. O.Fr. *muchier*, to
hide; cf. **mooch.**]

mickle, *mik′l, adj.* (*arch.*) much: great.—*n.* a great
quantity.—*adv.* much.—*Scot.* **muck′le.**—**many
a little** (or **pickle**) **makes a mickle** (often
absurdly **many a mickle makes a muckle**),
every little helps. [O.E. *micel, mycel.*]

micky, *mik′i, n.* an Irishman: (*Austr.*) a wild
young bull. [**Michael.**]

mico, *mē′kō, n.* a marmoset, esp. the black-tailed.
[Port.,—Carib *meku*, monkey.]

micro-, *mī′krō-, -krə-, -krō′*, in composition, little,
abnormally small, on a microscopic scale, with
minute quantity, microscopic: in units, a millionth
part.—*n.* **microanal′ysis**, chemical analysis of
minute quantities.—*adj.* **microanalyt′ical.**—*ns.*
microbal′ance, a balance for measuring small
weights or forces; **microchem′istry**, chemistry
under the microscope.—*adj.* **microchem′ical.**—
ns. **microcopy′ing**, copying on microfilm; **micro-
detec′tion**; **microdetect′or**, an instrument for
detecting minute amounts or changes; **microdis-
sec′tion**, dissection under the microscope; **mi′cro-
film**, a photographic film for preserving a microscopic record of a document, which can be enlarged
in projection; **micro-or′ganism**, a microscopic
(or ultra-microscopic) organism; **microstruc′-
ture**, structure, especially of metals and alloys, as
revealed by the microscope; **mi′crowave**, in
wireless communication, one of very short wave-
length, variously understood as less than 10 metres,
less than one metre, or less than 20 centimetres.
[Gr. *mikros*, little.]

microbar, *mī′krə-bär, n.* one millionth of a bar (of
pressure).

microbe, *mī′krōb, n.* a microscopic organism, esp.
a disease-causing bacterium.—*adjs.* **micrō′bial,
micrō′bian, micrō′bic.** [Fr.,—Gr. *mikros* and
bios, life.]

microcephalous, *mī-krō-sef′ə-ləs, adj.* abnormally
small-headed.—Also **microcephalic** (*-si-fal′ik*).—
ns. **microceph′al**, an abnormally small-headed
person; **microceph′aly**, abnormal smallness of
head. [Gr. *kephalē*, head.]

Microcheiroptera, *mī-krō-kī-rop′tə-rä, n.pl.* bats
other than fruit-bats. [**Cheiroptera.**]

microcline, *mī′krə-klīn, n.* an anorthic potash-
felspar with cleavage-angle differing very slightly
from a right angle. [Gr. *klīnein*, to slant.]

micrococcus, *mī-krō-kok′əs, n.* a rounded bacillus:
—*pl.* **micrococci** (*-kok′sī*).—*adj.* **micrococc′al.**
[Gr. *kokkos*, a grain.]

microcosm, *mī′krə-kozm, n.* a little universe or
world: (often applied to) man, who was regarded
by ancient philosophers as a model or epitome of
the universe.—*adjs.* **micros′mic, -al**, pertaining
to the microcosm.—*n.* **microcosmog′raphy.**—
microcosmic salt, sodium ammonium hydrogen
phosphate, used as a blowpipe flux (originally got
from human urine). [Gr. *kosmos*, world.]

microcrystalline, *mī-krə-kris′təl-īn, -in, adj.* having
a crystalline structure visible only under the
microscope.

microcyte, *mī-krə-sīt, n.* a small red blood corpuscle. [Gr. *kytos*, a container (used as if = cell).]

microfarad, *mī-krə-far′ad, n.* one millionth of a
farad.—*n.* **mi′cromicrofarad**, one millionth of a
microfarad.

microfelsitic, *mī-krə-fel-sit′ik, adj.* of the crypto-
crystalline texture of a quartz-felsite groundmass.

microgamete, *mī-krə-gam-ēt′*, or *-gam′, n.* a male
gamete.

microgram, *mī′krə-gram, n.* one millionth of a
gram.

microgranite, *mī-krə-gran′it, n.* a completely but
minutely crystalline rock of the composition of
granite.—*adj.* **microgranit′ic.**

micrograph, *mī′krə-gräf, n.* a pantograph instrument for minute writing or drawing: a minute
picture: a delineation of a microscopic object.—

n. **micrographer** (*mī-krog'rə-fər*), one who draws or describes microscopic objects.—*adj.* **micrographic** (*mī-krə-graf'ik*), pertaining to micrography: minutely written or delineated: (*geol.*) showing intergrowth of crystalline constituents on a microscopic scale.—*n.* **microg'raphy**, the description of microscopic objects. [Gr. *graphein*, to write.]

microhenry, *mī-krə-hen'ri*, *n.* one millionth of a henry.

microhm, *mīk'rōm*, *n.* one millionth of an ohm.

Microlepidoptera, *mī-krō-lep-id-op'tər-ä*, *n.pl.* small moths of various kinds.

microlite, *mī'krə-līt*, *n.* a mineral composed of calcium, tantalum, and oxygen, occurring in very small crystals: an incipient crystal, detected under the microscope by polarised light.—*n.* **mi'crolith**, a microlite: a very small stone implement of the Stone Age. — *adjs.* **microlith'ic**; **microlitic** (*-lit'ik*). [Gr. *lithos*, a stone.]

micrology, *mī-krol'ə-ji*, *n.* the study of microscopic objects: study or discussion of trivialities.—*adjs.* **micrologic** (*-loj'*), **-al**.—*adv.* **microlog'ically**.— *n.* **microl'ogist**. [Gr. *logos*, discourse.]

microlux, *mī'krə-luks*, *n.* one millionth of a lux.

micrometer, *mī-krom'i-tər*, *n.* an instrument for measuring minute distances or angles. — *adjs.* **micrometric** (*mī-krə-met'rik*), **-al**.—*n.* **microm'etry**, measuring with a micrometer. [Gr. *metron*, measure.]

micromillimetre, *mī-krə-mil'i-mēt-ər*, *n.* one millionth of a millimetre: (*bot.*) one thousandth of a millimetre, or one micron.

micron, mikron, *mī-kron*, *n.* one millionth of a metre (denoted by μ). [Gr. *mīkron*, neut. of *mīkros*, little.]

Micronesian, *mī-krə-nē'zh(y)ən*, *-zyən*, *-zi-ən*, *adj.* pertaining to *Micronesia*, a group of small islands in the Pacific, north of New Guinea.—*n.* a native of the group. [Gr. *nēsos*, an island.]

micronutrient, *mī-krə-nū'tri-ənt*, *n.* a nutritive substance required in minute quantities by a plant. —Also *adj.*

micropegmatite, *mī-krə-peg'mə-tīt*, *n.* a micrographic intergrowth of quartz and felspar.—*adj.* **micropegmatitic** (*-tit'ik*). [pegmatite.]

microphone, *mī'krə-fōn*, *n.* an instrument for intensifying sounds: a sensitive instrument (pop. contracted **mike**, *mīk*), similar to a telephone transmitter, for picking up sound-waves to be broadcast or amplified and translating them, e.g. by means of a diaphragm and carbon granules, into a fluctuating electric current.—*adj.* **microphonic** (*-fon'ik*). [Gr. *phōnē*, voice.]

microphotograph, *mī-krə-fōt'ə-gráf*, *n.* strictly, a photograph reduced to microscopic size: loosely, a photomicrograph, or photograph of an object as magnified by the microscope.—*n.* **microphotographer** (*-og'rə-fər*). — *adj.* **microphotographic** (*-ə-graf'ik*).—*n.* **microphotog'raphy**.

microphyllous, *mī-krō-fil'əs*, *adj.* (*bot.*) small-leaved. [Gr. *phyllon*, leaf.]

micropsia, *mī-krop'si-ä*, *n.* a condition in which objects look smaller than usual. [Gr. *opsis*, appearance.]

micropterous, *mī-krop'tər-əs*, *adj.* with reduced fins or hind-wings. [Gr. *pteron*, wing.]

micropyle, *mī'krə-pīl*, *n.* (*bot.*) the orifice in the coats of the ovule leading to the apex of the nucellus, through which the pollen-tube commonly enters: (*zool.*) an opening by which a spermatozoon may enter an ovum.—*adj.* **micropy'lar**. [Gr. *pylē*, gate.]

microscope, *mī'krə-skōp*, *n.* an instrument for magnifying minute objects.—*adjs.* **microscopic** (*-skop'ik*), **-al**, pertaining to a microscope or to microscopy: magnifying: able to see minute objects: invisible or hardly visible without the aid of a microscope: minute.—*adv.* **microscop'ically**.—*ns.* **microscopist** (*mī-kros'kop-ist*, *mī-krə-skō'pist*); **micros'copy**.—compound, **simple microscope**, microscopes with respectively two and a single lens; **electron, proton, ultra-violet microscope**, one using a beam of electrons, protons, or ultra-violet rays. [Gr.*skopeein*, to look at.]

microsecond, *mī'krə-sek-ənd*, *n.* one millionth of a second.

microseism, *mī'krə-sīzm*, *n.* a slight earth-movement detectable only instrumentally.—*adjs.* **microseis'mic**, **-al**.—*ns.* **microseis'mograph**, an instrument for recording microseisms and distant earthquakes; **microseismom'eter**, an instrument for measuring microseisms; **microseismom'etry**. [Gr. *seismos*, earthquake.]

microsome, *mī'krə-sōm*, *n.* a minute granule or drop in cytoplasm. [Gr. *sōma*, body.]

microspore, *mī'krə-spōr*, *n.* the smaller of two forms of spore: a spore giving rise to a male gametophyte.—*ns.* **microsporangium** (*-spor-an'-ji-əm*), a sporangium producing only microspores: — *pl.* **microsporan'gia**; **microsporophyll** (*-spor'ə-fil*), a sporophyll that carries or subtends only microsporangia. [Gr. *sporos*, *sporā*, seed.]

microtome, *mī'krə-tōm*, *n.* an instrument for cutting thin sections of objects for microscopic examination.—*adjs.* **microtomic**, **-al** (*-tom'ik*, *-əl*).—*ns.* **microtomist** (*-krot'ə-mist*); **microt'omy**. [Gr. *tomē*, a cut.]

microtone, *mī'krə-tōn*, *n.* (*mus.*) an interval less than a semitone.—*n.* **microtonal'ity**.

microwatt, *mī'krə-wot*, *n.* one millionth of a watt.

micturition, *mik-tū-rish'ən*, *n.* the frequent desire to pass urine: (improperly) the act of urinating. —*n.* **mic'tion**, (*obs.*) voiding urine.—*v.i.* **mic'turate** (irregularly formed), to urinate. [L. *micturīre*, *-itum*, desiderative of *mingĕre*, *mi(n)ctum*, to pass urine, *mi(n)ctiō*, *-ōnis*, urination.]

mid-, *mid-*, in composition, the middle part of: of or in the middle of. [From **mid**, adj.: not always hyphened.]

mid, *mid*, *adj.* **middle**: situated between extremes: (*phon.*) uttered with the tongue in a position between high and low.—*n.* **middle.**—*ns.* **mid-age'**, (*Shak.*) middle age; **mid-air'**, a region somewhat above the ground: the midst of a course through the air; **mid'brain**, the part of the brain derived from the second brain vesicle of the embryo; **mid'day**, noon.—*adj.* of, at, or pertaining to noon. —*adj.* **midd'est**, (*Spens.*) middle: middlemost.— *n.* **midst.**—*ns.* **mid'-gut**, that part of the alimentary canal formed from the original gastrula cavity and lined with endoderm: also, the small intestine; **mid'-heav'en**, the middle of the sky or of heaven: the meridian; **mid'-hour**, the middle time: an intervening hour.—*adj.* **mid'land**, in the middle of, or surrounded by, land: distant from the coast: inland.—*n.* the interior of a country: (*pl.*) esp. (**Midlands**) the central parts of England.—*n.* **mid'-leg'**, the middle of the leg.—*adv.* as high or deep as the middle of the leg.—*n.* **mid'-Lent'**, the middle of Lent: the fourth Sunday in Lent.—*adj.* **mid'most**, middlemost.—*n.* the very middle.—*adv.* in the very middle.—*prep.* in the very middle of.—*n.* **mid'night**, the middle of the night: twelve o'clock at night: pitch darkness.—*adj.* of or at midnight: dark as midnight.— *ns.* **mid'noon'**, noon; **mid'-off'**, (*cricket*) a fieldsman on the *off* side nearly in line with the bowler: his position; **mid-on'**, a fieldsman on the *on* side nearly in line with the bowler: his position; **mid'rib**, the rib along the middle of a leaf; **mid'-sea'**, the open sea; **mid'-seas'on** (also *adj.*).— *adj.* **mid'ship**, in the middle of a ship.—*n.* **mid'-shipman**, once the title of a young officer (orig. quartered *amidships*) entering the navy—now a junior ranking below a sub-lieutenant, but above a naval cadet—abbrev. (by landsmen) **mid, midd'y**, jocularly **mid'shipmite**.—*adv.* **mid'ships**, amidships.—*ns.* **mid-sky'**, the middle of the sky; **midstream'**, the middle of the stream.—*adv.* in the middle of the stream.—*ns.* **mid'summer** (also *-sum'*), the middle of summer: the summer solstice, about the 21st of June; **Mid'summer-day**, the 24th of June.—*adj.* **mid-Victo'rian**, of or characteristic of the middle part of Queen Victoria's reign.—*n.* **mid'way**, the middle of the way or distance: a middle course: a central avenue in an American fair or exhibition.—*adj.* in the middle of the way or distance.—*adv.* **half-way.**—*prep.* half-way along or across.—*n.* **Mid'-week, Wednes-**

day (cf. Ger. *Mittwoch*).—*adj.* **mid'-week**, in the middle of the week.—*ns.* **Mid'west**, Middle West; **mid'-wick'et**, mid-off or mid-on; **mid-win'ter**, the middle of winter: the winter solstice (21st or 22nd December); or the time near it.— *adj.* **mid'-year**, in the middle of the (academic) year.—**midnight sun**, the sun visible at midnight in the polar regions; **midsummer madness**, madness attributed to the hot sun of midsummer, or the culmination of madness; **midsummer moon**, a season when madness was supposed to be rife. [O.E. *midd*; cf. Ger. *mitte*, L. *medius*, Gr. *mesos*.]

'mid, mid, for amid.

Midas, *mī'das*, *n.* a king of Phrygia whose touch turned all to gold, and on whom Apollo bestowed ass's ears: a genus of marmosets.—**Midas's ear**, a shell of the genus Auricula.

midden, *mid'ən*, *n.* a dunghill: a refuse-heap: (*ant.*) a kitchen-midden.—*ns.* **midd'en-cock'**; **midd'enstead**, a place where dung is heaped up. [Scand., as Dan. *mödding—mög*, dung; cf. **muck**.]

middle, *mid'l*, *adj.* equally distant (in measurement or in number of steps) from the extremes: intermediate: intervening: (*gram.*) intermediate between active and passive, reflexive or expressing an action in some way affecting the agent: Middle (of languages), between Old and Modern (as *Middle English, Middle High German*).—*n.* **middle**, the middle point, part, or position: midst: central portion, waist: (*gram.*) middle voice: (*log.*) middle term: a middle article.—*adjs.* **middle-aged** (-*ājd'*), of or about the middle period of life, between youth and old age, variously reckoned to suit the reckoner; **midd'le-class**, pertaining to, or included in, the middle class.—*ns.* **midd'le-earth'**, the earth, considered as placed between the upper and lower regions; **midd'leman**, one who occupies a middle position: a dealer who intervenes between producer and consumer: a go-between or agent: in Ireland, one who rents land in large tracts, and lets it in small portions.— *adjs.* **midd'lemost**, nearest the middle; **midd'le-sized**, of middle or average size.—*ns.* **midd'le-stitch'ing**, monk's-seam; **midd'le-weight**, a boxer (11 st. 6 lb. or under) or jockey of intermediate weight; **midd'le-world**, middle-earth.—**Middle Ages**, the time between the downfall of the Western Roman empire and the Revival of Learning and the Reformation (5th-15th cent.); **middle article**, a newspaper article of literary or general rather than topical interest, placed between the leading articles and other matter; **middle C**, the C in the middle of the piano keyboard: the first line below the treble or above the bass stave; **middle class**, that part of the people which comes between the aristocracy and the working-class; **middle distance** (same as **middle ground**); **Middle East**, the countries of Asia west of India (or of China); **Middle English** (see **English**); **middle ground**, the part of a picture between the foreground and background; **Middle Kingdom**, China; **middle passage**, the voyage across the Atlantic from Africa to the West Indies, which was a time of horror on board a slave-ship; **Middle States**, New York, New Jersey, Pennsylvania, Delaware; **middle term**, (*log.*) that term of a syllogism which appears in both premises but not in the conclusion; **middle watch**, that from midnight to 4 a.m.; **Middle West**, the Mississippi basin as far south as Kansas, Missouri, and the Ohio River. [O.E. *middel* (adj.); Du. *middel*, Ger. *mittel*; see **mid**.]

middling, *mid'ling*, *adj.* (*obs.*) intermediate: (*coll.*) moderate: indifferent: mediocre: fairly good.— *adv.* (*coll.*) fairly: fairly well.—*n.* (usu. in *pl.*) goods of a middle quality: the coarser part of ground wheat: partially concentrated ore. [Orig. Scots—mid and suff. -*ling*.]

Midgard, *mid'gärd*, *n.* (*Scand. myth.*) the abode of men, middle-earth. [O.N. *mithgarthr*=mid-yard.]

midge, *mij*, *n.* a small gnat-like fly, esp. of the family Chironomidae: a very small person.—*n.* **midg'et**, something very small of its kind: a very small person. [O.E. *mycg, mycge*; Ger. *mücke*.]

Midi, *mē-dē*, *n.* the south (of France).—*n.* **midinette** (*-net*), a Paris work-girl (noticeable at lunch-hour). [Fr. *midi*, midday; *midinette* is said to be from *midi* and *dinette*, lunch.]

midland, midmost, midnight, &c. See **mid**.

Midrash, *mid'rash*, *n.* the Hebrew exposition of the Old Testament—its two divisions, *Haggada* and *Halakha*:—*pl.* **Midrashim** (*mid-rä'shēm*), commentaries to individual books or sections of the Old Testament. [Heb., exposition.]

midriff, *mid'rif*, *n.* the diaphragm. [O.E. *mid*, middle, *hrif*, belly.]

midst, *midst*, *n.* middle.—*adv.* in the middle.— *prep.* (also **'midst** as if for **amidst**) amidst. [M.E. *middes*, from gen. of **mid**, with excrescent *t* (cf. **whilst**); perh. partly a superl.]

midwife, *mid'wīf*, *n.* a woman who assists others in childbirth:—*pl.* **midwives** (*mid'wīvz*).—*n.* **mid'-wifery** (-*wif-(ə-)ri*, -*if-ri*, -*wif'ri*), art or practice of a midwife: assistance at childbirth: obstetrics. [O.E. *mid*, with (Ger. *mit*, Gr. *meta*), *wif*, woman.]

mien, *mēn*, *n.* air or look: manner: bearing: expression of face. [Perh. **demean**, influenced by Fr. *mine*, of unknown origin.]

mieve, *mēv*, *v.t.* (*Spens.*). Same as **move**.

miff, *mif*, *n.* (*coll.*) a slight feeling or fit of resentment.—*v.t.* to put out of humour.—*v.i.* to take offence: to wither away.—*adj.* **miff'y**, ready to take offence or to wither away: touchy.—Also (*obs.*) **mift'y**. [Cf. Ger. *muffen*, to sulk.]

might, *mīt*, *pa.t.* of **may** (1).—*n.* **might'-have-been**, one who, or that which, might have been, or might have come to something.

might, *mīt*, *n.* power: ability: strength: energy or intensity of purpose or feeling.—*adj.* **might'ful**, (*Shak.*) mighty: powerful.—*adv.* **night'ily**.—*n.* **might'iness**, state of being mighty: power: greatness: great amount: a title of dignity: excellency.—*adj.* **might'y**, having greater power: strong: valiant: very great: important: exhibiting might: wonderful.—*adv.* (now *coll.*, usu. with a tinge of irony) very.—**might and main**, utmost strength. [O.E. *miht, meaht*; Ger. *macht*; cf. **may** (1).]

mignonette, *min-yə-net'*, *n.* a sweet-scented Reseda: a fine kind of lace. [Fr. *mignonette*, fem. dim. of *mignon*, daintily small, a darling.]

migraine, *mē-gren*, *n.* Same as **megrim** (1).

migrate, *mī'grāt*, *v.i.* to pass from one place to another: to change one's abode to another country, college, &c.: to change habitat periodically: to move (as parasites, phagocytes, &c.) to another part of the body: to pass in a stream (as ions, particles).—*n.* **mi'grant**, a person or animal that migrates or is migrating.—Also *adj.*—*adj.* **mi'-gratory** (-*grə-tə-ri*), migrating or accustomed to migrate: wandering.—*ns.* **migra'tion**, a change of abode: a removal from one country or climate to another, esp. in a body: a number removing together; **migra'tionist**, one who emigrates: one who explains facts by a theory of migration; **mi'grator**. [L. *migrāre*, -*ātum*; cf. *meāre*, to go.]

mihrab, *mē-räb'*, *n.* a niche or slab in a mosque marking the direction of Mecca. [Ar. *mihrāb*.]

mikado, *mi-kä'dō*, *n.* a title given by foreigners to the Emperor of Japan. [Jap., exalted gate.]

mike, *mīk*, *n.* a contraction of **microphone** and **microscope**.

mil, *mil*, *n.* a unit (*$\frac{1}{1000}$* in.) in measuring the diameter of wire: a proposed coin=£$\frac{1}{1000}$: in pharmacy, a millilitre. [L. *mille*, a thousand.]

milady, miladi, *mi-lā'di*, *n.* a French-English term for an English lady of quality. [Fr. modification of **my lady**.]

milch, *milch, milsh*, *adj.* giving milk.—*n.* **milch'-cow**, a cow yielding milk or kept for milking: (*fig.*) a ready source of gain or money. [O.E. *milce* (found in the compound *thri-milce*, May, when cows can be milked thrice a day); cf. **milk**.]

mild, *mīld*, *adj.* gentle in temper and disposition: not sharp or bitter: acting gently: gently and pleasantly affecting the senses: soft: calm.—*v.t.* **mild'en**, to render mild.—*v.i.* to become mild.— *adv.* **mild'ly**.—*n.* **mild'ness**.—*adj.* **mild'-spok'en**, having a mild manner of speech.—

mild ale, formerly, new ale, without the taste that comes from keeping: now ale with less hop flavouring than pale ale; **mild steel**, steel with little carbon. [O.E. *milde*, mild; cf. Ger. *mild*, O.N. *mildr*, gracious, &c.]

mildew, *mil'dū*, *n.* (*obs.*) honey-dew: a disease on plants, caused by the growth of minute fungi (Erysiphe, Oidium, &c.): a similar appearance on other things or of another kind: a fungus causing the disease.—*v.t.* to taint with mildew.—*adj.* **mil'-dewy.** [O.E. *meledéaw*, *mildéaw*, from a lost word for honey and *déaw*, dew; influenced by *melu*, meal.]

mile, *mīl*, *n.* a Roman unit of length, 1000 (double) paces (*mille passūs* or *passuum*; about 1611 English yards): applied to various later units, now in Britain and U.S. to one of 1760 yards or 5280 feet —*statute mile* (**geographical** or **nautical mile**, one minute of longitude measured along the equator—6082·66 feet: in British practice, *Admiralty measured mile*, 6080: in some countries 6076·0: in U.S. 6080·2; **German mile**, sometimes about 4⅔ statute miles; **Irish mile**, 2240 yards; **Scots mile**, (*obs.*) about 1976 yards).—*ns.* **mil'age**, **mile'age**, length in miles: (*U.S.*) travelling allowance at so much a mile; **mile'-castle**, a castellum placed at intervals along a Roman wall; **mil'er**, runner of a mile race; **mile'stone**, a stone or mark showing distance in miles: a stage or reckoning point. [O.E. *mīl*—L. *mīlia*, pl. of *mīlle* (*passuum*), a thousand (paces).]

Milesian, *mi-lē'z(y)ən*, *-zh(y)ən*, or *mī-*, *adj.* of *Miletus*, an Ionian Greek city of Asia Minor.—*n.* a native or citizen of Miletus.—**Milesian tales**, witty voluptuous tales, from a lost book so called by Aristides ' of Miletus ' (2nd cent. B.C.). [Gr. *Milēsios—Milētos*.]

Milesian, *mi-lē'sh(y)ən*, *-zh(y)ən*, or *mī-*, *adj.* of *Milesius* or *Miledh*, a mythical king of Spain, or his sons and their followers who seized Ireland: Irish.—*n.* (usu. jocular) an Irishman.

milfoil, *mil'foil*, *n.* yarrow or other species of Achillea: extended to other plants with finely divided leaves, as **wat'er-mil'foil** (Myriophyllum, family Haloragidaceae). [O.Fr.,—L. *mīllefolium*—*mīlle*, a thousand, *folium*, a leaf.]

miliary, *mil'i-ər-i*, *adj.* like a millet-seed: characterised by an eruption like millet-seeds. [L. *miliārius—milium*, millet.]

milieu, *mēl'yə*, *n.* environment, setting, medium, element. [Fr., middle.]

militant, *mil'itənt*, *adj.* fighting: engaged in warfare: actively contending: combative: using violence: militaristic.—*n.* one who takes active part in a struggle: one who seeks to advance a cause by violence.—*n.* **mil'itancy.**—*adv.* **mil'itantly.**—*adj.* **mil'itar**, (*obs.*) military.—*n.* **militarisā'tion.**—*v.t.* **mil'itarise**, to reduce or convert to a military model or method: to make militaristic: to subject to military domination.—*n.* **mil'itarism**, an excess of the military spirit: domination by an army, or military class or ideals: belief in such domination: tendency to overvalue military power or to view things from the soldier's point of view; **mil'itarist**, (*Shak.*) a soldier: a student of military science: one imbued with militarism.—*adjs.* **militarist'ic**; **mil'itary**, pertaining to soldiers, armies, or warfare: warlike.—*n.* soldiery: the army: (*obs.*) a soldier.—*v.i.* **mil'itate**, to serve as a soldier: to contend: to have weight, tell (esp. with *against*).—**church militant** (see **church**); **military band**, a band of brasses, wood-winds, and percussion; **military cross**, a decoration (M.C.) awarded since 1914 to army officers (below major) and warrant officers. [L. *miles*, *-itis*, a soldier, *militāris*, military, *militāre*, *-ātum*, to serve as a soldier.]

militia, *mi-lish'ä*, *n.* a body of men enrolled and drilled as soldiers, but only liable to home service (transformed in 1908 into the Special Reserve; again called militia, 1921): (*U.S.*) the National Guard and its reserve: a general levy: a territorial force: troops of the second line. — *n.* **milit'iaman.** [L. *mīlitia*, military service or force—*miles*, a soldier.]

milk, *milk*, *n.* a white liquid secreted by female mammals for the nourishment of their young: a milklike juice or preparation: lactation.—*v.t.* to squeeze or draw milk from: to supply with milk: to extract money, &c., from: to extract: to manipulate as if milking a cow.—*v.i.* to yield milk.—*adj.* **milk'-and-wa'ter**, insipid: wishy-washy.—*ns.* **milk'-bar**, a shop where milk, milk-shakes, and the like are sold for drinking on the spot; **milk'-choc'olate**, eating chocolate made from cocoa, cocoa-butter, sugar, and condensed or dried milk; **milk'-cow**, a milch-cow.—*adj.* **milk'en**, (*rare*) of or like milk.—*ns.* **milk'-denti'tion**, the first set of teeth; **milk'en-way**, (*Bacon*) the Milky Way; **milk'er**, one who milks: a machine for milking cows: a cow that gives milk; **milk'-fe'ver**, a fever accompanying the secretion of milk shortly after childbirth: in cows, a congestion of the brain (without fever) after calving; **milk'-gland**, a mammary gland; **milk'-house**, a place where milk is kept.—*adv.* **milk'ily.**—*ns.* **milk'iness**, cloudiness: mildness; **milk'ing**, the act or art of obtaining milk, literally or figuratively: the amount of milk drawn at one time; **milk'ing-stool**, a stool on which the milker sits; **milk'ing-time**; **milk'ing-tube**, a perforated tube inserted in a cow's teat; **milk'-kin'ship**, the bond arising from fostering; **milk'-leg**, white-leg.—*adjs.* **milk'less**; **milk'like**; **milk'-liv'ered**, (*Shak.*) white-livered.—*ns.* **milk'-loaf'**, a loaf of a sweetish kind of bread; **milk'maid**, a woman who milks; **milk'man**, a man who sells or delivers milk; **milk'-mō'lar**, a grinding milk-tooth, shed and superseded by a premolar; **milk'-porr'idge**, porridge made with milk instead of water; **milk'-pudd'ing**, sago, rice, or the like, baked with milk; **milk'-punch'**, a drink made of milk, rum or whisky, sugar, and nutmeg; **milk'-shake'**, milk shaken up with a flavouring; **milk'-sop**, a piece of bread sopped or soaked in milk: a soft, unadventurous, effeminate fellow; **milk'-su'gar**, lactose; **milk'-this'tle**, lady's thistle (Silybum Marianum), with white-veined leaves; **milk'-tooth**, one of the first or deciduous set of teeth; **milk'-tree**, a tree yielding a milklike nourishing juice, as the cow-tree of Venezuela, the massaranduba of Pará; **milk'-vetch**, a plant of the genus Astragalus, cultivated as fodder and supposed to increase yield of milk; **milk'-walk**, a milkman's round.—*adj.* **milk'-warm**, warm as new milk.—*n.* **milk'-weed**, a plant of the genus Asclepias, from its milky juice.—*adj.* **milk'-white**.—*ns.* **milk'wood**, any of various trees with latex; **milk'wort**, a plant (Polygala) supposed by some to promote production of milk (sea'-milkwort, Glaux).—*adj.* **milk'y**, made of, full of, like, or yielding milk: clouded: soft: gentle.—**milk and honey**, abundance, plenty: luxury; **milk of human kindness**, (*Shak.*) compassionate nature; **milk of lime, of magnesia**, a suspension of calcium hydroxide, magnesium hydroxide, in water; **milk of sulphur**, precipitated sulphur; **Milky Way**, the Galaxy. [O.E. (Mercian) *milc* (W.S. *meolc*), milk; Ger. *milch*, milk; L. *mulgēre*, Gr. *amelgein*, to milk.]

mill, *mil*, *n.* a machine for grinding by crushing between hard, rough surfaces, or for more or less similar operations: a building or factory where corn is ground, or manufacture of some kind is carried on, as spinning and weaving, paper-making, sawing of timber: (*Scot.*) a snuff-box (commonly **mull**), orig. one with grinding apparatus: (*slang*) a contest at boxing.—*v.t.* to grind: to press, stamp, roll, cut into bars, full, furrow the edges of, or otherwise treat in a mill: to froth up: (*slang*) to beat severely with the fists: to revolve in the mind. —*v.i.* to move round in a curve: to practise the business of a mill°r: (*slang*) to box.—*ns.* **mill'-board**, stout pasteboard, used esp. in binding books; **mill'dam**, the dam of a mill-pond: a mill-pond: (*Scot.*) a mill-race or tail-race; **mill'er**, one who owns or works a mill; **mill'er's-thumb'**, the bull-head.—*adj.* **milled**, prepared by a grinding-mill or a coining-press: transversely grooved on the edge (as a coin or screw-head): treated by machinery, esp. smoothed by calendering rollers in a paper-mill.—*ns.* **mill'-eye'**, the opening by which meal comes from a mill; **mill'-girl**; **mill'-hand'**, a factory worker; **mill'-horse**, a horse that turns a mill; **mill'ing**, the business of a miller: the act of passing anything through a mill: the act of fulling cloth: the process of turning and ridging the edge of a screw-head or coin: a gruelling; **milloc'racy**, (*obs.*) a governing class of mill-owners, or their rule; **mill'ocrat**; **mill'-owner**; **mill'pond**, a pond to hold water for driving a mill (proverbially smooth): (*jocularly*) the Atlantic Ocean; **mill'race**, the current of water that turns a mill-wheel, or the channel in which it runs; **mill'-six'pence**, (*Shak.*) a milled sixpence; **mill'stone**, one of the two stones used in a mill for grinding corn: (*fig.*) a very heavy burden; **mill'-stone-grit'**, a hard, gritty sandstone suitable for millstones: **Millstone Grit**, a series of grits, sandstones, shales, &c., underlying the British Coal Measures; **mill'-stream**, the stream of water that turns a mill-wheel; **mill'-tail**, a tail-race; **mill'-tooth**, a molar; **mill'-wheel**, a water-wheel used for driving a mill; **mill'-work**, the machinery of a mill: the planning and putting up of machinery in mills; **mill'wright**, a wright or mechanic who builds and repairs mills.—**gastric mill**, in Malacostraca, a digestive organ, sometimes known as the stomach, provided with muscles and ossicles for trituration of food; **go, put, through the mill**, to undergo, subject to, probationary hardships, suffering or experience, or severe handling; **miller's dog**, the tope (shark); **see through a millstone**, to see far into or through difficult questions. [O.E. *myln*—L.L. *molīna*—L. *mola*, a mill—*molĕre*, to grind.]

mill, *mil*, *n.* (*U.S.*) the thousandth part of a dollar (not coined): a mil. [L. *mīlle*, a thousand.]

mill, *mil*, *v.t.* and *v.i.* (*slang*) to rob: to steal.

millefiori, *mil-i-fi-ō'ri*, *n.* ornamental glass made by fusing coloured rods together.—*n.* **millefleurs** (*mēl-flər*), a perfume prepared from many kinds of flowers. [It. and Fr., thousand flowers—L. *mīlle*, *flōs*, *flōris*.]

millenary, *mil'in-ər-i* (also -*ēn'*, or -*en'*), *n.* a thousand: a thousand years: a thousandth anniversary: (*hist.*) a signatory of the Millenary Petition: a believer in the millennium.—*adj.* consisting of a thousand, or a thousand years: pertaining to the millennium or to belief in it.—*adj.* **millenā'rian**, pertaining to the millennium.—*n.* a believer in the millennium.—*ns.* **millenā'rianism**, **mill'enārism**.— **Millenary Petition**, a petition of Puritan tendency, signed by nearly a thousand clergymen, presented to James I. in 1603. [L. *mīllēnārius*, of a thousand—*mīlle*.]

millennium, *mil-en'i-əm*, *n.* a thousand years: the thousand years after the second coming of Christ: (*usu.* ironical) a coming golden age:—*pl.* **mill-enn'ia**.—*adj.* **millenn'ial**.—*ns.* **millenn'ialist**, a believer in the millennium; **millenn'ianism**, **millenn'iarism**. [L. *mīlle*, a thousand, *annus*, a year.]

millepede. See **millipede**.

millepore, *mil'i-pōr*, *n.* a hydrozoan coral with many pores or polyp-cells. [L. *mīlle*, a thousand, *porus*—Gr. *poros*, a passage.]

Millerian, *mil-ēr'i-ən*, *adj.* pertaining to W. H. *Miller* (1801-80), mineralogist, or to the crystallographic notation used by him, by which a plane is represented by indices which are the reciprocals of its intercepts on the axes (expressed as fractions of the parameters).—*n.* **mill'erite**, native nickel sulphide, crystallising in needles, named in his honour.

millesimal, *mil-es'im-əl*, *adj.* thousandth: consisting of thousandth parts.—*adv.* **milles'imally**. [L. *mīllēsimus*—*mīlle*, a thousand.]

millet, *mil'it*, *n.* a food-grain (*Panicum miliaceum*): extended to other species and genera (*Setaria*, *Panicum*, &c.).—*ns.* **mill'et-grass**, a tall panicled woodland grass (*Milium effusum*); **mill'et-seed'**.—*adj.* of the size or appearance of seeds of millet: miliary. [Fr. *millet*—L. *milium*.]

milli-, *mil'i-*, in composition, in names of units, a

thousandth part.—*ns.* **mill'iampere**, **mill'iare** (-*är*), **mill'ibar**, **mill'icurie**, **mill'igram**, **mill'i-litre**, **mill'ilux**, **mill'imetre**, **mill'imicron**, a thousandth part of an *ampere*, *are*, *bar*, &c. [L. *mīlle*, a thousand.]

milliard, *mil'yärd*, *n.* a thousand millions. [Fr.,—L. *mīlle*, a thousand.]

milliary, *mil'i-ər-i*, *adj.* pertaining to a Roman mile.—*n.* a Roman milestone. [L. *mīlliārius*, -*a*, -*um*.]

milliner, *mil'in-ər*, *n.* orig. a dealer in goods made in *Milan*—'fancy goods': one who makes or sells women's headgear, trimmings, &c.—*ns.* **horse'-mill'iner** (see **horse**); **mill'inery**, the articles made or sold by milliners: the industry of making them. [*Milaner*, a trader in Milan wares, esp. silks and ribbons.]

million, *mil'yən*, *n.* a thousand thousands (1,000,000): a very great number: a million pounds, dollars, &c.: (in *pl.*) a small Barbadian fish, the guppy (Lebistes), that multiplies very rapidly and feeds on mosquito larvae.—Also *adj.* (commonly preceded by *a*).—*n.* **millionaire** (-*är*'), a man worth a million pounds, dollars, &c. (more or less):—*jocular fem.* **millionair'ess**, **millionheir'ess**.—*adj.* **mill'ionary**, pertaining to, or consisting of, millions.—*adj.* and *adv.* **mill'ionfold** (usu. preceded by *a* or a numeral).—*adj.* and *n.* **mill'ionth**, the ten hundred thousandth.—**the million**, the great body of the people generally. [Fr.,—L.L. *mīlliō*, -*ōnis*—L. *mīlle*, a thousand.]

millipede, **millepede**, *mil'i-pēd*, *n.* any myriapod of the class Chilognatha, vegetarian cylindrical animals with many joints, most of which bear two pairs of legs: (*rarely*) a woodlouse.—Also **mill'iped**, **mill'eped** (-*ped*). [L. *mīllepeda*, a woodlouse—*mīlle*, a thousand, *pēs*, *pedis*, a foot.]

mill-mountain, *mil'mownt'ən*, *n.* purging flax. [Origin unknown.]

milor, **milord**, *mi-lor(d)'*, *n.* a rich Englishman. [Fr. modification of **my lord**.]

milreis, *mil'rās*, *n.* 1000 reis: a Port. coin superseded by the escudo: a coin of Brazil (now cruzeiro). [Port., thousand reis.]

milsey, *mil'si*, *n.* (*Scot.*) a milk-strainer. [**milk**, and either **sye** or **sile**.]

milt, *milt*, *n.* (*anat.*) the spleen: the soft roe of male fishes.—*v.t.* (of fishes) to impregnate.—*n.* **milt'er**, a male fish. [O.E. *milte*, spleen.]

Miltonic, *mil-ton'ik*, *adj.* relating to *Milton* (1608-1674), or to his poetry, or in his manner.—*adj.* **Miltonian** (-*tōn'i-ən*).—*n.* **Mil'tonism** (-*tən-izm*).

Milvus, *mil'vəs*, *n.* the kite genus.—*adj.* **mil'vine**. [L. *milvus*, a kite.]

mim, *mim*, *adj.* (*Scot.* and *prov.*) demure, prim.—*adj.* **mim'-mou'd'** (-*mōōd*; Scots form of **mouthed**). [Imit.]

mimbar, *mim'bär*, *n.* a mosque pulpit. [Ar. *minbar*.]

mime, *mīm*, *n.* an ancient farcical play of real life, with mimicry (esp. in its Latin form): an actor in such a farce: a mimic: a buffoon.—*v.t.* and *v.i.* to act as a mime: to act with mimicry: to mimic.—*ns.* **mīm'er**; **mimesis** (*mim-* or *mīm-ē'sis*), imitation or representation in art: the rhetorical use of a person's supposed or imaginable words: (*med.*) simulation of one disease by another: (*biol.*) mimicry; **mime'ster**.—*adjs.* **mimet'ic, -al** (*mim-* or *mīm-*), imitative: mimic: pertaining to or showing mimicry or miming.—*adv.* **mimet'ically**.—*ns.* **mimetite** (*mim'*, *mīm'*), a mineral, lead arsenate and chloride (from its resemblance to pyromorphite); **mimic** (*mim'ik*), a mime-actor: one who imitates, esp. one who performs in ludicrous imitation of others' speech and gestures: an unsuccessful imitator or imitation: a plant or animal exemplifying mimicry.—*adj.* (*obs.*) miming: imitative: mock or sham.—*v.t.* to imitate, esp. in ridicule or so as to incur ridicule: to ape: to produce an imitation of: to resemble deceptively:—*pr.p.* **mim'icking**; *pa.t.* and *pa.p.* **mim'icked**.—*adj.* (*obs.*) **mimical** (*mim'*).—*ns.* **mim'icker**; **mimicry** (*mim'*), act of mimicking: (*biol.*) an advantageous superficial resemblance to some other species or object; **mimog'rapher**, a writer of mimes; **mimog'-**

raphy; **Mīmus**, the mocking-bird genus. [Gr. *mīmos*, a mime, *mīmēsis*, imitation, *mīmētēs*, an imitator.]

mimic, mimmick. See also **minnick.**

Mimosa, *mim-ō′zä, n.* the sensitive plant genus: popularly extended to *Acacia* and other genera of the **Mimosā′ceae,** a regular-flowered family of Leguminosae. [Gr. *mīmos*, a mimic.]

Mimulus, *mim′ū-ləs, n.* the musk and monkey-flower genus of the figwort family. [Gr. *mīmos*, a mime, with L. dim. suffix *-ulus*, from the grinning corolla.]

mina, *mī′nä, n.* a Greek weight, or sum of money, 100 drachmas : (*B.*) a weight of money valued at fifty shekels.—Also **maneh** (*mä′ne*; Heb.). [L. *mīna*—Gr. *mnā*; cf. Heb. *mäneh*.]

mina. Same as **myna.**

minacious, *min-ā′shəs, adj.* threatening.—*n.* **minacity** (*-as′*). [L. *mināx, -ācis*—*minārī,* to threaten.]

minar, *min-är′, n.* a tower.—*n.* **min′aret,** a mosque tower, from which the call to prayer is given. [Ar. *manār, manārat,* lighthouse—*nār,* fire.]

minatory, *min′ə-tə-ri* (or *mīn′*), *adj.* threatening. [L. *minārī, -ātus,* to threaten.]

minauderie, *mēn-ō′də-rē, n.* a display of affectation. [Fr.]

mince, *mins, v.t.* to cut into small pieces : to chop fine : to diminish or suppress a part of in speaking : to pronounce affectedly.—*v.i.* to walk with affected nicety : to speak affectedly (*pr.p.* **minc′ing**; *pa.t.* and *pa.p.* **minced,** *minst*).—*n.* minced meat : mincemeat. — *ns.* **mince′meat,** meat chopped small—hence anything thoroughly broken or cut to pieces : a chopped mixture of raisins, peel, and other ingredients ; **mince-pie′,** a pie made with mincemeat or with minced meat ; **minc′er,** one who minces : a machine for mincing. —*adj.* **minc′ing,** not speaking fully out : speaking or walking with affected nicety.—Also *n.*—*adv.* **minc′ingly.—mince matters,** to speak of things with affected delicacy, or to soften an account unduly ; **minced collops** (see **collops**). [O.Fr. *mincier, minchier*—L. *minūtus*; cf. **minute.**]

mind, *mīnd, n.* memory : commemoration : (*obs.*) record, mention : thought : judgment : opinion : (*Shak., Milt.*) purpose : inclination : attention : direction of the will : state of thought and feeling : wits, right senses, sanity : consciousness : intellect : that which thinks, knows, feels, and wills : soul : personality : a thinking or directing person.—*v.t.* (*arch.* and *Scot.*) to remind : (*Spens.*) to bring to mind : (now chiefly *Scot.*) to remember : (*refl. arch.*) to remember (with *of*) : to attend to : to tend, have care or oversight of : to be careful about : to beware of : (*Shak.*) to purpose : to have a mind to : to value : to apply oneself to : to be troubled by, object to, dislike : (*obs.* or *dial.*) to notice.—*v.i.* (*dial.*) to remember (with *of*) : to attend : to care : to look out, take heed.—*ns.* **mind′-cure, mind′-healing,** cure or healing of a diseased mind, or of bodily ailment through the mind or by the supposed influence of a mind ; **mind′-curer, -healer.**—*adj.* **mind′ed,** willing : inclined : disposed : determined : (in composition) having a mind of such-and-such a kind or inclined towards this or that.—*ns.* **mind′edness,** (in composition) inclination ; **mind′er,** one who minds, esp. a machine : a child left to be minded.—*adj.* **mind′ful,** bearing in mind : taking thought or care : attentive : observant : having memory : (*obs.*) inclined.—*adv.* **mind′fully.**—*n.* **mind′fulness.**—*adj.* **mind′less,** without mind : stupid : disregardful : unmindful.—*adv.* **mind′lessly.**—*ns.* **mind′lessness ; mind′-reading,** thought-reading.—**absence of mind,** inattention to what is going on owing to absorption of the mind in other things ; **bear in mind,** to remember : to keep in one's memory and attention ; **break one's mind,** (*obs.*) to make known, confide, or divulge one's thoughts ; **change one's mind,** to come to a new resolution or opinion ; **do, or would, you mind?** please do : do you object? **have a (good, great) mind,** to wish or to be inclined strongly ; **have half a mind,** to be somewhat inclined ; **if you don't mind,** if you have no objection ; **in two**

minds, wavering ; make up one's mind, to come to a decision ; mind one's p's and q's, to be watchfully accurate and punctilious ; **mind's eye,** visual imagination, mental view, contemplation ; **mind your eye,** (*slang*) look out ; **mind your own business,** this is none of your affair ; **month's mind,** commemoration by masses one month after death or burial : strong desire or inclination ; **never mind,** do not concern yourself : it does not matter : you are not to be told ; **of one (or a) mind,** agreed ; **of two minds,** uncertain what to think or do ; **on one's mind,** weighing upon one's spirit ; **out of mind,** forgotten : out of one's thoughts ; **out of one's mind,** mad ; **piece of one's mind** (see **piece**) ; **presence of mind,** a state of calmness in which all the powers of the mind are on the alert and ready for action ; **put in mind,** to remind ; **set one's mind on,** to fix a settled desire upon ; **speak one's mind,** to say plainly what one thinks ; **time out of mind,** from time immemorial ; **to my mind,** to my thinking, in my opinion : to my liking ; **year's mind,** a commemorative service on the anniversary of a death or burial. [O.E. *gemynd*—*munan,* to think ; Dan. *minde,* memorial, L. *mēns,* the mind.]

Mindel, *min′dl, n.* (*geol.*) the second glaciation in the Alpine region.—*adjs.* **Min′del, Mindelian** (*-dē′li-ən*). [*Mindel,* a tributary of the Danube, in Bavaria.]

Mindererus, *min-dər-ē′rəs, n.* Latinised name of the German physician R. M. *Minderer* (*c.* 1570-1621).—**Mindererus spirit,** ammonium acetate solution, a diaphoretic.

mine, *mīn, pron.,* genitive of **I,** used predicatively or absolutely, belonging to me : my people : that which belongs to me : (adjectivally, esp. before a vowel or *h* or after its noun ; *arch.*) my. [O.E. *mīn.*]

mine, *mīn, n.* a place from which minerals are dug —not usually including building-stone, and legally distinguished from a quarry by being artificially lighted : (*arch.*) a cavity in the earth : a burrowing animal's gallery, as an insect's in a leaf : (*mil.*) an excavation dug under a position to give secret ingress, to subvert it, or to blow it up : an explosive charge therefor : a submerged or floating charge of explosives in a metal case to destroy ships : a land-mine : a rich source.—*v.t.* to excavate, tunnel, make passages in or under : to obtain by excavation : to work as a mine : to bring down or blow up by a mine : to beset with mines : to lay mines in or under.—*v.i.* to dig or work a mine or mines : to tunnel : to burrow : to lay mines : (*fig.*) to proceed secretly and insidiously.—*ns.* **mine′-captain,** overseer of a mine ; **mine′-field,** an area beset with mines ; **mine′-layer,** a ship for laying mines ; **mine′-owner ; mi′ner,** one who works in a mine : a soldier who lays mines : an insect or other animal that makes galleries in the earth, leaves, &c ; **mine′-sweeper,** a vessel for removing mines ; **mine′-thrower** (a transl. of Ger. **minenwerfer,** *mē′nən-ver-fər,* in soldiers' slang **minnie,** *min′i*), a trench-mortar ; **mine′-worker,** a miner.—*n.* and *adj.* **min′ing.**—*adj.* **min′y,** pertaining to mines : like a mine.—**miner's anaemia,** ankylostomiasis ; **miner's inch,** the amount of water that will flow in twenty-four hours through an opening of one square inch at a pressure of six inches of water ; **miner's lamp,** a lamp carried by a miner, commonly on his cap ; **miner's phthisis,** phthisis caused by breathing dusty air in mines ; **miner's worm,** the hook-worm that causes ankylostomiasis. [Fr. *mine* (noun), *miner* (verb), of doubtful origin.]

mine, *mīn, n.* (Shak., *Merry Wives,* I. iii. at end) perhaps for mind (disposition), or **mien.**

mineral, *min′ər-l, n.* a substance produced by processes of inorganic nature : a substance got by mining : ore : a substance neither animal nor vegetable : (*Shak.*) a mine : (*Shak.*) a poison : a mineral water (in a wide sense).—*adj.* relating to minerals : having the nature of minerals : impregnated with minerals, as water : of inorganic substance or nature.—*n.* **mineralisā′tion.**—*v.t.*

min'eralise, to make into a mineral: to give the properties of a mineral to: to impregnate with mineral water.—*v.i.* to go looking for and examining minerals.—*ns.* **mineralis'er**, one who, or that which, mineralises: an element that combines with a metal to form an ore, as sulphur: a gas or vapour that promotes the crystallising out of minerals from an igneous magma; **min'eralist**, one versed in or employed about minerals.—*adj.* **mineralog'ical**, pertaining to mineralogy.—*adv.* **mineralog'ically.**—*v.i.* **mineralogise** (-*al'*), to collect or study minerals.—*ns.* **mineral'ogist**, one versed in mineralogy; **mineral'ogy**, the science of minerals.—**mineral alkali**, (*obs.*) sodium carbonate; **mineral caoutchouc**, elaterite; **mineral coal**, coal in the ordinary sense, distinguished from charcoal; **mineral jelly**, a soft yellow substance resembling soft soap, got from the less volatile residue of petroleum; **mineral kingdom**, that department of nature which comprises substances that are neither animal nor vegetable; **mineral oil**, any oil of mineral origin; **mineral pitch**, natural asphalt; **mineral spring**, well, a spring of mineral water; **mineral tallow**, a soft yellowish natural hydrocarbon; **mineral tar**, pissasphalt; **mineral water**, spring water impregnated with minerals: an artificial imitation thereof: (loosely) an effervescent non-alcoholic beverage; **mineral wax**, ozokerite; **mineral wool**, a mass of fibres got by blowing steam through liquid slag. [Fr. *minéral*—*miner*, to mine; cf. **mine** (2).]

Minerva, *min-ǝr'vä*, *n.* the Roman goddess of wisdom, identified with the Greek Athena.—**Minerva Press**, a London printing-house that issued sentimental novels about 1800. [L., prob. from root of *mēns*, the mind.]

minette, *min-et'*, *n.* an intrusive rock of orthoclase and biotite in a close-grained ground-mass. [Fr.]

ming, **mingt**, **meng**, **meng**, **menge**, **menj**, *v.t.* and *v.i.* (*arch.*) to mix: to unite, couple: to work up: —*pa.t.* and *pa.p.* **minged**, **menged**, older forms **meint**, **meynt** (*ment*, *mänt*), **ment**. [O.E. *mengan*; Ger. *mengen*.]

Ming, *ming*, *n.* a Chinese dynasty (1368-1643).—*adj.* of the dynasty, its time, or esp. its pottery and other art.

mingle, *ming'gl*, *v.t.* and *v.i.* to mix.—*n.* a mixture: a medley.—*n.* **ming'le-mang'le**, a medley, jumble.—*adj.* jumbled.—*v.t.* to confuse, jumble together.—*ns.* **ming'lement**; **ming'ler**; **ming'ling.**—*adv.* **ming'lingly.** [Freq. of **ming**.]

mingy, *min'ji*, *adj.* (*coll.*) niggardly. [Perh. a portmanteau-word from **mangy** or **mean** and **stingy**.]

miniate. See **minium.**

miniature, *min'yǝ-tūr*, -*tyǝr*, or *min'i-(ǝ-)*, *n.* (*obs.*) rubrication: manuscript illumination: a painting on a very small scale, on ivory, vellum, &c.: the art of painting in this manner: a small or reduced copy of anything: a chess problem with few pieces or moves.—*adj.* on a small scale: minute.—*v.t.* to represent on a small scale.—*n.* **min'iaturist**, one who paints miniatures. [It. *miniatura*—L. *minium*, red lead; meaning affected by association with L. *minor*, *minimus*, &c., and their derivatives.]

minibus, *min'i-bǝs*, *n.* (*obs.*) a light passenger vehicle. [L. *minor*, less, *minimus*, least, and *omnibus*.]

Minié, *min'i-ā*, *adj.* invented by C. É. *Minié* (1814-1879)—applied to a bullet and a rifle adapted to it.

minify, *min'i-fī*, *v.t.* to diminish, in appearance or reality.—*n.* **minifica'tion.** [Ill-formed (after **magnify**) from L. *minor*, less.]

minikin, *min'i-kin*, *n.* a little darling: a diminutive or undersized person or thing: a small sort of pin: the treble string of a lute.—*adj.* diminutive: dainty: affected: mincing. [Obs. Du. *minneken*, dim. of *minne*, love; cf. **minnesinger**.]

minim, *min'im*, *n.* a least part: (*mus.*) a note (formerly the shortest) equal to two crotchets: (apothecaries' measure) one-sixtieth of a fluid drachm: (apothecaries' weight) a grain: a short down-stroke in handwriting: (*Milt.*) a diminutive creature: a friar, sister, or lay member of any of

three orders founded by St Francis of Paula (1416-1507)—so called as if humbler than even the Friars Minor.—*adj.* extremely minute.—*adj.* **min'imal**, of least, or least possible, size, amount, or degree: of the nature of a minimum.—*ns.* **min'imalist**, a Menshevik; **minimisā'tion.**—*v.t.* **min'imise**, to reduce to the smallest possible amount: to make as light as possible: to estimate at the lowest possible: (loosely) to lessen, diminish: (loosely) to belittle.—*ns.* **min'imism**, inclination to reduce a dogma to the least possible; **min'imist**; **min'imum**, the least quantity or degree, or the smallest possible: the lowest point or value reached: (*math.*) a value of a variable at which it ceases to diminish and begins to increase—opp. of *maximum*: (*pl.* **min'ima**).—*adj.* smallest or smallest possible.—*n.* **min'imus**, (*Shak.*) a being of the smallest size: in boys' schools, youngest of the surname.—**minimising glass**, a diminishing glass; **minim rest**, a rest of the duration of a minim; **minimum wage**, the lowest wage permitted by law or regulation for certain work: a fixed bottom limit to workers' wages in various industries. [L. *minimus*, -*a*, -*um*, smallest.]

miniment, *min'i-mǝnt*, *n.* obsolete form of **muniment.**

minion, *min'yǝn*, *n.* a darling, a favourite, esp. of a prince: a flatterer: a servile dependent: (*print.*) a small kind of type, about 10½ lines to the inch, between nonpareil and brevier. [Fr. *mignon*, *mignonne*.]

minish, *min'ish*, *v.t.* (*Spens.*) to make little or less: to diminish. [Fr. *menuiser*, to cut small, said of a carpenter—L. *minūtia*, smallness.]

minister, *min'is-tǝr*, *n.* (*arch.*) a servant: one who administers or proffers, in service or kindness: one who serves at the altar: a clergyman (not now usually, as in *Pr.Bk.*, of the Church of England): the head, or assistant to the head, of several religious orders: one transacting business for another: the responsible head of a department of state affairs: the representative of a government at a foreign court.—*v.i.* to give attentive service: to perform duties: to supply or do things needful: to conduce.—*v.t.* to furnish.—*adj.* **ministē'rial**, pertaining to a minister or ministry (in any sense): on the government side: administrative: executive: instrumental: conducive.—*n.* **ministē'rialist**, a supporter of the government in office.—*adv.* **ministē'rially.**—*adj.* **min'istering**, attending and serving.—*n.* **ministē'rium**, the body of the ordained Lutheran ministers in a district.—*adj.* **min'istrant**, administering: attendant.—*n.* **ministrā'tion**, the act of ministering or performing service: office or service of a minister.—*adj.* **min'istrative** (-*trǝ-tiv*, or -*trā-tiv*), serving to aid or assist: ministering.—*ns.* **min'istress**, a female who ministers; **min'istry**, act of ministering: service: office or duties of a minister: the clergy: the clerical profession: the body of ministers who manage the business of the country: a department of government, or the building it occupies: term of office as minister. [L. *minister—minor*, less.]

minium, *min'i-ǝm*, *n.* vermilion: red lead: its colour.—*adj.* **min'iate**, of the colour of minium.—*v.t.* to paint with minium: to illuminate.—*n* **miniā'tion.** [L. *minium*, red-lead, also cinnabar.]

miniver, **minever**, *min'i-vǝr*, *n.* white fur, orig. a mixed or variegated fur: the ermine in winter coat. [O.Fr. *menu*, small—L. *minūtus*, and *vair*, fur—L. *varius*, particoloured.]

minivet, *min'i-vet*, *n.* a brightly coloured shrike-like bird (*Pericrotocus* of several species) of India, &c. [Etymology unknown.]

mink, *mingk*, *n.* a small animal (of several species) of the weasel kind: its fur. [Perh. from Sw. *mänk*.]

minnesinger, *min'i-sing-ǝr*, Ger. -*zing-ǝr*, *n.* one of a 12th-13th cent. school of German amatory lyric poets, mostly of noble birth. [Ger. *minne*, love, *singer*, singer.]

minnick, *min'ik*, **minnock**, -*ǝk*, **mimmick**, *mim'*, *n.* (*dial.*) an affected person.—*v.i.* to be over-dainty in eating: to behave with affected primness.—**In**

Shak. *Mid. N.D.*, III. ii. 19 by some amended to *mimic*.

minnie, *min'i, n.* (*Scot.*; *hypocoristic*) mother.

minnie, *min'i, n.* (*army slang*) a trench-mortar or its bomb. [Ger. *minenwerfer*, mine-thrower—*mine*, mine, *werfer*, thrower.]

minnow, *min'ō, n.* a very small fresh-water fish (*Phoxinus phoxinus*) close akin to chub and dace: loosely extended to other small fish. [Prob. an O.E. form related to extant *myne*.]

mino, *mē'nō, n.* a raincoat of hemp, &c. [Jap.]

Minoan, *min-ō'ən, mīn-, adj.* pertaining to prehistoric Crete and its culture.—*n.* a prehistoric Cretan. [Gr. *Mīnōs*, a legendary king of Crete.]

minor, *mī'nor, adj.* lesser: inferior in importance, degree, bulk, &c.: inconsiderable: lower: (*mus.*) smaller (than major) by a semitone: in boys' schools, junior: Franciscan.—*n.* a person under age (21 years): (*log.*) the minor term, or minor premise: anything that is minor opposed to major.—*ns.* **minoritaire** (*mē-nor-ē-ter'*; Fr.), a member of a minority section of a party, esp. of socialists; **mī'norite,** a Franciscan friar (*fem.* **mī'noress**).—*adj.* Franciscan.—*n.* **minority** (*min-* or *mīn-or'i-ti*), the condition or fact of being little or less: the state or time of being under age (also **mī'norship**): the smaller number: less than half: the party of smaller numbers: the number by which it falls short of the other party—opp. to majority.—*adj.* of the minority.—**minor axis,** in conics, that perpendicular to the major axis; **minor canon** (see **canon**); **minor key, mode, scale,** one with its third a minor third above the tonic; **minor planet,** a small planet, any one of many hundreds with orbits between those of Mars and Jupiter; **minor poet,** a genuine but not great poet; **minor premise,** (*log.*) that in which the minor term occurs; **minor prophets,** the twelve from Hosea to Malachi in the Old Testament; **minor suit,** in bridge, clubs or diamonds; **minor term,** (*log.*) the term which is the subject of the conclusion; **minor third,** (*mus.*) an interval of three semitones; **minor tone,** an interval with a vibration ratio of $\frac{9}{10}$. [L. *minor*, less; cf. **minus**.]

Minorca, *min-or'ka, n.* a black variety of laying poultry of Mediterranean family. [From the island of *Minorca,* Sp. *Menorca*.]

Minotaur, *min'* or *mīn'ə-tawr, n.* the bull-headed monster in the Cretan Labyrinth, offspring of Pasiphae, wife of Minos. [Gr. *Mīnōtauros—Mīnōs*, Minos, *tauros,* bull.]

minster, *min'stər, n.* (*obs.*) a monastery: an abbey church or priory church: often applied to a cathedral or other great church without any monastic connexion. [O.E. *mynster—*L. *monastērium,* a monastery.]

minstrel, *min'strəl, n.* orig. a professional entertainer: a musician: now generally a mediaeval harper who sang or recited his own or others' poems: (*poet.*) a poet: a singer of nigger songs, with blacked face.—*n.* **min'strelsy** (*-si*), the art or occupation of a minstrel: music: a company or body of minstrels: a collection of songs. [O.Fr. *menestrel—*L.L. *ministeriālis—*L. *minister,* attendant.]

mint, *mint, n.* a place where money is coined, esp. legally: a source or place of fabrication: a vast sum of money.—*v.t.* to coin: to invent: to stamp.—*adj.* in mint condition.—*ns.* **mint'age,** coining: coinage: stamp: duty for coining; **mint'er;** **mint'-man,** one skilled in coining or coinage; **mint'-mark,** a mark showing where a coin was minted; **mint'-master,** the master of a mint: one who invents.—**mint condition,** state, the condition of a new-minted coin. [O.E. *mynet,* money—L. *monēta* ; see **money**.]

mint, *mint, n.* any plant of the aromatic labiate genus Mentha, as spearmint, peppermint, pennyroyal: (*U.S.*) any labiate.—*ns.* **mint'-ju'lep,** a spirituous drink flavoured with mint; **mint'-sauce,** chopped spearmint or other mint mixed with vinegar and sugar, used as a sauce for roast lamb: punningly, money.—*adj.* **mint'y.** [O.E. *minte—*L. *mentha—*Gr. *minthē, mintha.*]

mint, *mint, v.t.* and *v.i.* (*Scot.*) to purpose: to attempt: to aim: to threaten by movement: to venture: to aspire (with *at*): to hint.—*n.* attempt: aim: threatening gesture: an incipient movement. [O.E. *myntan,* to mean.]

minuend, *min'ū-end, n.* the number from which another is to be subtracted. [L. *minuendus* (*numerus*)—*minuĕre,* to lessen.]

minuet, *min-ū-et', n.* a slow, graceful dance in triple measure, invented in Poitou about the middle of the 17th century: the music for such a dance: a sonata movement in the same form. [Fr. *menuet —menu,* small—L. *minūtus,* small.]

minus, *mī'nəs, prep.* (*math.*) diminished by: (*coll.*) deficient in respect of, deprived of, without.—*adj.* negative.—*n.* a deficiency or subtraction: a negative quantity or term: the sign (also **minus sign**) of subtraction or negativity (−) opposed to *plus.*—**minus strain,** (*bot.*) one of two strains in heterothallism. [L. *minus,* neut. of *minor,* less.]

minuscule, *min', mīn'us-kūl,* or *-us', n.* a small cursive script, originated by the monks in the 7th–9th centuries: a manuscript written in it: (*print.*) a lower-case letter: opposed to *majuscule.*—Also *adj.*—*adj.* **minus'cular.** [L. (*littera*) *minuscula,* smallish (letter).]

minute, *min-ūt',* or *mīn-ūt', adj.* extremely small: having regard to the very small: exact.—*adv.* **minute'ly.**—*n.* **minute'ness.** [L. *minūtus,* pa.p. of *minuĕre,* to lessen.]

minute, *min'it, n.* the sixtieth part of an hour: the sixtieth part of a degree: an indefinitely small space of time: a particular moment: a brief jotting or note: (in *pl.*) a brief summary of the proceedings of a meeting: a minute's walk, or distance traversed in a minute.—*v.t.* to make a brief jotting or note of: to record in the minutes. —*ns.* **min'ute-bell,** a bell sounded every minute, in mourning; **min'ute-book,** a book of minutes or short notes; **min'ute-drop,** a drop falling at a minute's interval; **min'ute-glass,** a sand-glass that runs for a minute; **min'ute-gun,** a gun discharged every minute, as a signal of distress or mourning; **min'ute-hand,** the hand that indicates the minutes on a clock or watch; **min'ute-jack,** (*Shak.*) time-server, or a flighty, unstable person. —*adj.* **minutely** (*min'it-li*; Shak.), happening once a minute.—*ns.* **min'ute-man,** a man ready to turn out at a minute's warning, as in the American war of independence; **min'ute-watch,** a watch that marks minutes; **min'ute-while,** (*Shak.*) a minute's time. [Same word as foregoing.]

minutia, *mi-nū'shi-ā. n.* a minute particular or detail: — *pl.* **minū'tiae** (*-ē*). — *adj.* **minū'tiose** (*-shi-ōs*). [L. *minūtia,* smallness.]

minx, *mingks, n.* a pert young girl: a jade: a she-puppy. [Poss. from **minikin**; or L.Ger. *minsk, minske,* a wench, jade, cognate with Ger. *mensch,* man, human being.]

Miocene, *mī'ō-sēn, adj.* (*geol.*) of the Tertiary period preceding the Pliocene and having a smaller proportion of molluscan fossils of species now living. —*n.* the Miocene system, period, or strata. [Gr. *meiōn,* smaller, *kainos,* recent.]

miosis, *mī-ō'sis, n.* Same as **meiosis.**

mir, *mēr, n.* a Russian village community. [Russ.]

Mira, *mī'rā, n.* a variable star in the constellation Cetus. [L. *mīra* (fem.), wonderful.]

mirable, *mīr'ə-bl, adj.* (Shak.) wonderful.—*n.* **Mirabilis** (*mir-* or *mīr-ab'il-is*), the marvel of Peru genus: **mirabilis,** short for aqua mirabilis. [L. *mīrābilis,* wonderful.]

miracle, *mir'ə-kl, n.* a supernatural event: hyperbolically, a marvel, a wonder: a miracle-play.— *ns.* **mir'acle-mong'er,** one who pretends to work miracles; **mir'acle-play,** a mediaeval form of drama founded on Old or New Testament history, or the legends of the saints.—*adj.* **miraculous** (*-ak'ū-ləs*), of the nature of a miracle: done by supernatural power: very wonderful: able to perform miracles. — *adv.* **mirac'ulously.** — *n.* **mirac'ulousness.** [Fr.,—L. *mīrāculum—mīrārī, -ātus,* to wonder at.]

mirador, *mir-ə-dōr', n.* a belvedere or watch-tower. [Sp.]

mirage, *mi-räzh'*, *n.* an appearance of objects raised or depressed, erect or inverted, single or double, owing to the varying refractive index of layers of hot and cold air, the sky often simulating the appearance of water. [Fr. *mirer*, to look at— L. *mīrārī*, to wonder at.]

mirbane, *mər'bān*, *n.* apparently a meaningless name.—**essence**, or **oil**, of mirbane, nitrobenzene, as used in perfumery. [Origin unknown.]

mire, *mīr*, *n.* deep mud.—*v.t.* to plunge and fix in mire: to soil with mud.—*v.i.* to sink in mud.— *ns.* **mire'-drum**, the bittern; **mire'-snipe**, the common snipe; **mir'iness**.—*adj.* **mir'y**, consisting of mire: covered with mire. [O.N. *mýrr*, bog.]

mirific, **-al**, *mīr-if'ik*, *-əl*, *adjs.* wonder-working: marvellous.—*adv.* **mirif'ically**. [L. *mīrificus*— *mīrus*, wonderful, *facĕre*, to do.]

miriti, *mi-ri-tē'*, *mir'i-ti*, *n.* any palm of the genus Mauritia. [Tupí.]

mirk, **mirksome**. See **murk**.

mirligoes, *mir'li-gōz*, *n.pl.* (*Scot.*) dizziness.

mirliton, *mər'li-tən*, *mēr-lē-ton⁹*, *n.* a toy reed-pipe. [Fr.]

mirly. See **marl** (4).

mirror, *mir'ər*, *n.* a looking-glass: a reflecting surface: (*fig.*) a faithful representation: an example, good or bad.—*v.t.* to reflect an image of, as in a mirror: to furnish with a mirror.—*pr.p.* **mirr'oring**; *pa.p.* **mirr'ored**.—*n.* **mirr'or-im'age**, an image with right and left reversed as in a mirror. —*adj.* and *adv.* **mirr'orwise**, with interchange of left and right.—*ns.* **mirr'or-writer**, one who writes mirrorwise; **mirr'or-writing**, writing which is like ordinary writing as seen in a mirror. [O.Fr. *mireor*, *mirour*—L. *mīrārī*, *-ātus*, to wonder at.]

mirth, *mərth*, *n.* merriness: pleasure: delight: noisy gaiety: jollity: laughter.—*adj.* **mirth'-ful**, full of mirth: causing mirth: merry: jovial. — *adv.* **mirth'fully**. — *n.* **mirth'fulness**. — *adj.* **mirth'less**.—*n.* **mirth'lessness**. [O.E. *myrgth* —*myrige*, merry.]

Mirza, *mir'zä*, *mēr'zä*, *n.* as a Persian title (after a name) Prince; (before) official or learned man. [Pers. *mīrzā*, *mīrzā*.]

mis-. See, under *Prefixes*, **mis-** (1), or for words taken over from French, **mis-** (2).

mis, *mis*, *v.i.* (*Spens.*) to do amiss, fail. [**miss**.]

misacceptation, *mis-ak-sep-tā'shən*, *n.* understanding in a wrong sense.

misadventure, *mis-əd-vent'ūr*, *-yər*, *n.* ill-luck: mishap: accidental killing.—*adj.* **misadvent'-ured**, (*Shak.*) unfortunate; **misadvent'urous**.— *n.* **misadvent'urer**.

misadvertence, *mis-əd-vərt'əns*, *n.* inadvertence.

misadvise, *mis-əd-vīz'*, *v.t.* to advise ill.—*adj.* **misadvised'**. — *adv.* **misadvi'sedly**. — *n.* **misadvis'edness**.

misaim, *mis-ām'*, *v.t.* to aim ill.

misallege, *mis-ə-lej'*, *v.t.* to allege wrongly.

misalliance, *mis-ə-lī'əns*, *n.* an unsuitable alliance, esp. marriage with one of a lower rank—the Fr. *mésalliance*.—*adj.* **misallied'**.

misallotment, *mis-ə-lot'mənt*, *n.* a wrong allotment.

misanthrope, *mis'ən-thrōp*, *n.* a hater of mankind: one who distrusts everyone else — also **misan'-thropist** (*mis-an'throp-ist*).—*adjs.* **misanthropic**, **-al** (*mis-an-throp'ik*, *-əl*), hating or distrusting mankind.—*adv.* **misanthrop'ically**.—*ns.* **misan'-thropos**, (*Shak.*) a misanthrope; **misan'thropy**, hatred or distrust of mankind. [Gr. *mīsanthrōpos* —*mīseein*, to hate, *anthrōpos*, a man.]

misapply, *mis-ə-plī'*, *v.t.* to apply wrongly: to use for a wrong purpose.—*n.* **misapplica'tion** (*-ap-*).

misappreciate, *mis-ə-prē'shi-āt*, *v.t.* to fail to appreciate rightly or fully.—*n.* **misapprecia'tion**. —*adj.* **misapprec'iative**.

misapprehend, *mis-ap-ri-hend'*, *v.t.* to apprehend wrongly: to take or understand in a wrong sense. —*n.* **misapprehen'sion**.—*adj.* **misapprehen'-sive**.—*adv.* **misapprehen'sively**, by or with misapprehension or mistake.—*n.* **misapprehen'-siveness**.

misappropriate, *mis-ə-prō'pri-āt*, *v.t.* to put to a

wrong use: to take dishonestly for oneself.—*n.* **misappropria'tion**.

misarrange, *mis-ə-rānj'*, *v.t.* to arrange wrongly: to put in wrong order.—*n.* **misarrange'ment**.

misarray, *mis-ə-rā'*, *n.* want of proper order.

misassign, *mis-ə-sīn'*, *v.t.* to assign wrongly.

misaunter, *mis-awn'tər*, *n.* (*obs.*) misadventure. [**aunter**.]

misavised, *mis-ə-vīz'id*, *adj.* (*Spens.*) ill-advised.

misbecome, *mis-bi-kum'*, *v.t.* to be unbecoming or unsuitable to.—*adj.* **misbecom'ing**.—*n.* **misbecom'ingness**.

misbegot, **misbegotten**, *mis-bi-got'*, *-got'n*, *adj.* (*Shak.*) unlawfully begotten: monstrous.

misbehave, *mis-bi-hāv'*, *v.t.* (*refl.*) and *v.i.* to behave ill or improperly.—*adj.* **misbehaved'**, (*Shak.*) badly behaved: ill-bred.—*n.* **misbehav'iour**.

misbelieve, *mis-bi-lēv'*, *v.t.* to believe wrongly or falsely.—*ns.* **misbelief'** (or *mis'*), belief in false doctrine; **misbeliev'er**.—*adj.* **misbeliev'ing**.

misbeseem, *mis-bi-sēm'*, *v.t.* to suit ill.

misbestow, *mis-bi-stō'*, *v.t.* to bestow improperly, or on the wrong person.—*n.* **misbestow'al**.

misborn, *mis'bawrn*, or *mis-bawrn'*, *-born*, *adj.* abortive: deformed from birth: base-born. — *n.* **misbirth'**, an abortion.

miscalculate, *mis-kal'kū-lāt*, *v.t.* and *v.i.* to calculate wrongly.—*n.* **miscalcula'tion**.

miscall, *mis-kawl'*, *v.t.* to call by a wrong name: (*Spens.*; now mainly *Scots*—also **misca'**) to call by an ill name: to abuse or revile.

miscarriage, *mis-kar'ij*, *n.* an act or instance of miscarrying: failure: failure to reach the intended result or destination: ill-conduct: the act of bringing forth young prematurely, esp. accidentally, and esp. in the earlier stages.—*v.i.* **miscarr'y**, to be unsuccessful: to fail of the intended effect: to bring forth before the proper time: to be born prematurely.—*v.t.* (*obs.*) to lead astray.—**miscarriage of justice**, failure of the courts to do justice.

miscast, *mis-kâst'*, *v.t.* and *v.i.* to cast (in any sense) amiss or blameworthily.

miscegenation, *mis-i-jin-ā'shən*, *n.* mixing of race: interbreeding, intermarriage, or sexual intercourse between different races, esp. whites and coloured peoples.—*v.i.* **misc'egenate**, to practise miscegenation.—*v.t.* to produce by miscegenation.— —*adj.* mixed in race.—*ns.* **miscegena'tionist**, **misc'egenator**, **miscegenist** (*mis-ej'in-ist*), one who favours or practises miscegenation; **miscegen** (*mis'i-jən*), **misc'egene** (*-jēn*), **misc'egine** (*-jin*, *-jīn*), an individual of mixed race. [L. *miscēre*, to mix, *genus*, race.]

miscellaneous, *mis-əl-ān'i-əs*, *adj.* mixed or mingled: consisting of several kinds.—*adj.* **miscellanarian** (*-ən-ā'ri-ən*).—*n.* a writer of miscellanies.—*adv.* **miscellān'eously**.—*ns.* **miscellān'eousness**; **miscellanist** (*mis-el'ən-ist*, or *mis'əl-*), a writer of miscellanies; **miscellany** (*mis-el'*, or *mis'əl-*), a mixture of various kinds: a collection of writings on different subjects.—*n.pl.* **miscellā'nea** (L. *neut. pl.*), a miscellany. [L. *miscellāneus*—*miscēre*, to mix.]

mischallenge, *mis-chal'ənj*, *n.* (*Spens.*) a wrongful challenge.

mischance, *mis-châns'*, *n.* ill-luck: mishap.—*v.i.* to chance wrongly: to come to ill-luck.—*adjs.* **mischance'ful**; **mischan'cy** (chiefly *Scot.*), unlucky: dangerous.

mischanter, **mishanter**, *mi-shân'tər*, *n.* (*Scot.*) an unlucky chance, misfortune. [**aunter**; perh. influenced by obs. *mischant*, *meschant*—O.Fr. *mescheant* (Fr. *méchant*), unlucky, wicked.]

mischarge, *mis-chärj'*, *v.t.* to charge wrongly.— *n.* a mistake in charging.

mischief, *mis'chif*, *n.* an ill consequence: evil: injury: damage, hurt: the troublesome fact: a source of harm: petty misdeeds or annoyance: pestering playfulness: a mischievous person: (*coll.*) the devil.—*n.* **mis'chief-maker**, one who stirs up strife.—*n.* and *adj.* **mis'chief-making**.— *adj.* **mischievous** (*mis'chiv-əs*; *Spens.* usu. *-chēv'*), causing mischief: injurious: prone to mischief.

—*adv.* **mis′chievously.**—*n.* **mis′chievousness**. [O.Fr. *meschef*, from *mes-* (see pfx. **mis-** (2)), *chef*— L. *caput*, the head.]

miscible, *mis′si-bl*, *adj.* that may be mixed.—*n.* **miscibil′ity.** [L. *miscēre*, to mix.]

miscolour, *mis-kul′ər*, *v.t.* to colour falsely: to give a wrong meaning to: to misrepresent.

miscomprehend, *mis-kom-pri-hend′*, *v.t.* to misunderstand.—*n.* **miscomprehen′sion.**

miscompute, *mis-kəm-pūt′*, *v.t.* to reckon wrongly. —*n.* **miscomputā′tion** (*-kom-*), *n.* wrong computation: false reckoning.

misconceit, *mis-kən-sēt′*, *n.* (*Spens.*) misconception. —*v.t.* to have wrong conception of.

misconceive, *mis-kən-sēv′*, *v.t.* and *v.i.* to conceive wrongly: to mistake: (*obs.*) to suspect.—*n.* **misconcep′tion.**

misconduct, *mis-kon′dukt*, *n.* bad conduct: wrong management: adultery.—*v.t.* **misconduct** (*-kən-dukt′*).

misconjecture, *mis-kən-jekt′yər*, *n.* a wrong conjecture or guess.—*v.t.* or *v.i.* to guess or conjecture wrongly.

misconster, *mis-kon′stər*, *obs.* form of **misconstrue.**

misconstruction, *mis-kən-struk′shən*, *n.* wrong construction, construing, or interpretation: faulty construction.—*v.t.* **misconstruct′.**

misconstrue, *mis-kon′strōō*, or *-kən-strōō′*, *v.t.* to construe or to interpret wrongly.

miscontent, *mis-kən-tent′*, *n.*, *adj.*, and *v.t.* (*arch.*) discontent.—*adj.* **miscontent′ed.**—*n.* **miscontent′ment.**

miscopy, *mis-kop′i*, *v.t.* to copy wrongly or imperfectly.—*n.* an error in copying.

miscorrect, *mis-kər-ekt′*, *v.t.* to alter or mark wrongly in would-be correction.—*n.* **miscorrec′tion.**

miscounsel, *mis-kown′sl*, *v.t.* to advise wrongly.

miscount, *mis-kownt′*, *v.t.* to count wrongly: to misjudge.—*n.* a wrong counting.

miscreant, *mis′kri-ənt*, *n.* orig. a misbeliever, a heretic or infidel: a vile wretch, a detestable scoundrel.—*adj.* unbelieving.—*n.* **mis′creance, mis′creaunce** (*Spens.*), false religious belief. [O.Fr. *mescreant*—*mes-* (see pfx. **mis-** (2)), L. *crēdēns, -entis*, pr.p. of *crēdere*, to believe.]

miscreate, -d, *mis-krē-āt′, -id*, *adjs.* created amiss: deformed.—*v.t.* **miscreā′tion.**—*adj.* **miscreā′tive**, inclining towards wrong creation.—*n.* **miscreā′tor.**

miscredit, *mis-kred′it*, *v.t.* to disbelieve.

miscreed, *mis-krēd′*, *n.* a false creed.

miscue, *mis-kū′*, *n.* at billiards, a stroke spoiled by the slipping off of the cue.

misdate, *mis-dāt′*, *v.t.* to date wrongly.—*n.* a wrong date.

misdeal, *mis-dēl′*, *n.* a wrong deal, as at cards.— *v.t.* and *v.i.* to deal wrongly: to divide improperly: —*pa.t.* and *pa.p.* **misdealt** (*-delt′*).

misdeed, *mis-dēd′*, *n.* an evil deed.

misdeem, *mis-dēm′*, *v.t.* and *v.i.* to think ill (of): to think or judge wrongly (of): to suspect:—*pa.p.* **misdeemed′**, (*Spens.*) **misdempt′.**—*adjs.* **misdeem′ful**; **misdeem′ing**, misjudging: suspicious: (*Spens.*) deceiving.—*n.* misjudgment: suspicion.

misdemean, *mis-di-mēn′*, *v.t.* (*refl.*) and *v.i.* to misbehave.—*ns.* **misdemean′ant**, one who commits a misdemeanour or petty crime; **misdemean′our**, bad conduct: a misdeed: a legal offence of less gravity than a felony.

misdesert, *mis-di-zərt′*, *n.* (*Spens.*) ill-desert.

misdevotion, *mis-di-vō′shən*, *n.* ill-directed devotion.

misdid. See **misdo.**

misdiet, *mis-dī′ət*, *n.* (*Spens.*) improper feeding.

misdight, *mis-dīt*, *adj.* (*Spens.*) ill-arranged: in sorry plight.

misdirect, *mis-di-rekt′*, *v.t.* to direct wrongly.—*n.* **misdirec′tion.**

misdo, *mis-dōō′*, *v.t.* to do wrongly or badly: (*obs.*) to injure: (*obs.*) to kill.—*v.i.* to act amiss:—*pa.t.* **misdid′**; *pa.p.* **misdone′**; old *infin.* (*Spens.*) **misdonne′.**—*ns.* **misdo′er**; **misdo′ing.**

misdoubt, *mis-dowt′*, *v.t.* to have a doubt, suspicion, or foreboding of or about: to suspect.

—*n.* suspicion: hesitation: misgiving.—*adj.* **misdoubt′ful.**

misdraw, *mis-draw′*, *v.t.* to draw or draft badly.— *n.* **misdraw′ing.**

misdread, *mis-dred′*, *n.* (*Shak.*) dread of evil to come.

mise, *mēz*, *mīz*, *n.* (*obs.*) expenditure, outlay: in Wales and the county palatine of Chester, a payment to a new king, prince, Lord of the Marches, or earl, to secure certain privileges: the issue in a writ of right: (*hist.*) the adjustment of a dispute by agreement: a stake in gambling: the lay-out of cards. [O.Fr. *mise*, placing or setting—L. *mittēre, missum*.]

misease, *mis-ēz′*, *n.* distress: uneasiness.

miseducation, *mis-ed-ū-kā′shən*, *n.* improper or hurtful education: education that leaves one worse than before.

misemploy, *mis-im-ploi′*, *v.t.* to employ wrongly or amiss: to misuse.—*n.* **misemploy′ment.**

misentreat, *mis-in-trēt′*, *v.t.* to ill-treat.

misentry, *mis-en′tri*, *n.* a wrong entry.

miser, *mī′zər*, *n.* (*Spens., Shak.*) a wretch: one who lives miserably in order to hoard wealth: a niggard. —*adj.* like a miser.—*n.* **mi′serliness.**—*adj.* **mi′serly.** [L. *miser*, wretched.]

miser, *mīz′ər*, *n.* a well-boring instrument. [Origin doubtful.]

miserable, *miz′ə-rə-bl*, *adj.* wretched: exceedingly unhappy: causing misery: extremely poor or mean: contemptible.—*n.* a wretch: very weak tea.—*n.* **mis′erableness.**—*adv.* **mis′erably.** [Fr. *misérable*—L. *miserābilis*—*miser*.]

misère, *mē-zer′*, *miz-ār′*, *n.* in card games, an undertaking to take no tricks. [Fr. *misère*, misery.]

Miserere, *miz-e-rē′ri* (L. *mis-e-rā′re*), *n.* (*R.C.*) the 50th Psalm of the Vulgate (51st in A.V.)—from its first word: a musical setting of it: **miserere**, a misericord in a church stall. [L., 2nd pers. sing. imper. of *miserērī*, to have mercy, to pity—*miser*, wretched.]

misericord, misericorde, *miz-er′i-kord*, or *miz′ər-*, or *-kord′*, *n.* (*obs.*) mercy, forgiveness, pity: a relaxation of monastic rule: a room in a monastery where some relaxation of rule was allowed: a bracket on a turn-up seat in a choir-stall, allowing the infirm some support when standing: a narrow-bladed dagger for killing a wounded foe. [O.Fr. *misericorde*—L. *misericordia*—*misericors, -cordis*, tender-hearted.]

misery, *miz′ər-i*, *n.* wretchedness: extreme pain: miserable conditions: (*cards*) misère: (*Shak.*) avarice. [O.Fr.,—L. *miseria*.]

misesteem, *mis-es-tēm′*, *n.* disrespect.—*v.t.* to value wrongly.—*v.t.* mises′timate, to estimate wrongly.

misfaith, *mis-fāth′*, *n.* distrust.

misfall, *mis-fawl′*, *v.t.* (*obs.*) to befall unluckily:— *pa.t.* **misfell′**; *pa.p.* **misfall′en** (*Spens.* **misfalne′**).

misfare, *mis-fār′*, *n.* (*Spens.*) misfortune.—*v.i.* to fare ill.—*n.* **misfar′ing**, (*Spens.*) wrong-doing.

misfeasance, *mis-fēz′əns*, *n.* (*law*) the doing of a lawful act in a wrongful manner, as distinguished from *malfeasance*.—*n.* **misfeas′or.** [O.Fr. *mis-faisance*—pfx. *mes-* (see **mis-** (2)), *faisance*—*faire* —L. *facere*, to do.]

misfeature, *mis-fēt′yər*, *n.* ill feature, trait, or aspect: deformity. —*adjs.* **misfeat′ured**, ill-featured; **misfeat′uring**, distorting the features.

misfeign, *mis-fān′*, *v.i.* to feign with bad design.

misfire, *mis-fīr′*, *v.i.* to fail to go off, explode, or ignite, at all or at the right time.—*n.* such a failure.

misfit, *mis-fit′*, *n.* a bad fit: a thing that fits badly. —*v.t.* and *v.i.* to fit badly.

misform, *mis-form′*, *v.t.* to form or shape badly or improperly.—*n.* **misformā′tion.**

misfortune, *mis-for′tūn*, *n.* ill-fortune: an evil accident: calamity: (*coll.*) an illegitimate child, or the having of one.—*adj.* **misfor′tuned**, unfortunate.

misgive, *mis-giv′*, *v.t.* to suggest apprehensions to, fill with forebodings: to give amiss:—*v.i.* to have apprehensive forebodings: (*Scot.*) to fail:—*pa.t.* **misgave′**; *pa.p.* **misgiv′en.**—*n.* **misgiv′ing**, mistrust: a feeling that all is not well.

Neutral vowels in unaccented syllables : *el′ə-mənt*, *in′fənt*, *ran′dəm*

misgo, *mis-gō'*, *v.i.* (*obs.* or *dial.*) to go astray or amiss :—*pa.t.* wanting (**miswent'**, supplied from **miswend**) ; *pa.p.* **misgone** (*mis-gon'* ; *obs.*, now illit., **miswent'**).

misgotten, *mis-got'n*, *adj.* (*Spens.*) ill-gotten : **misbegotten**.

misgovern, *mis-guv'ərn*, *v.t.* to govern badly or unjustly.—*ns.* **misgov'ernaunce**, (*Spens.*) **mismanagement** ; **misgov'ernment**.

misgraff, *mis-gräf* (*Shak.*), **misgraft**, *mis-gräft'*, *v.t.* to graft unsuitably.

misgrowth, *mis-grōth'*, *n.* an irregular growth : an excrescence : a sport of nature.

misguggle, *mis-gug'l*, **mishguggle**, *mish-*, *v.t.* (*Scot.*) to bungle, mar.

misguide, *mis-gīd'*, *v.t.* to guide wrongly : to lead into error : (*Scot.*) to ill-treat.—*n.* (*obs.*) misbehaviour.—*n.* **misguid'ance.**—*adj.* **misguid'ed**, erring : misdirected : ill-judged.— *adv.* **misguid'edly.**

mishallowed, *mis-hal'ōd*, *adj.* consecrated to evil.

mishandle, *mis-han'dl*, *v.t.* to handle amiss or unskilfully : to maltreat.

mishanter. Same as **mischanter**.

mishap, *mis-hap'*, *n.* ill chance : unlucky accident : misfortune.—*v.i.* to happen unfortunately.—*v.i.* **mishapp'en**, (*Spens.*) to happen ill.

mishapt (*Spens.*), for **misshaped**.

mishear, *mis-hēr'*, *v.t.* and *v.i.* to hear wrongly.

mishit, *mis-hit'*, *v.t.* to hit faultily.—*n.* a faulty hit.

mishmash, *mish'mash*, *n.* a hotch-potch, medley.

mishmee, **mishmi**, *mish'mē*, *n.* the bitter tonic rootstock of an Assamese gold-thread (*Coptis Teeta*). [Said to be Assamese *mishmītīta*.]

Mishnah, **Mishna**, *mish'nä*, *n.* the Jewish oral law, finally redacted 220 A.D. :—*pl.* **Mish'nōth.**— *adjs.* **Mishnā'ic**, **Mish'nic.** [Heb. *mishnāh*— *shānāh*, to repeat, teach, learn.]

misimprove, *mis-im-prōōv'*, *v.t.* to turn to bad use : to make worse by would-be improvement.—*n.* **misimprove'ment.**

misinform, *mis-in-form'*, *v.t.* to inform or tell incorrectly.—*ns.* **misinform'ant**; **misinformā'tion**; **misinform'er.**

misinstruct, *mis-in-strukt'*, *v.t.* to instruct amiss.— *n.* **misinstruc'tion**, wrong instruction.

misintelligence, *mis-in-tel'i-jəns*, *n.* wrong or false information : misunderstanding : want of intelligence.

misintend, *mis-in-tend'*, *v.t.* to intend or aim in malice.

misinterpret, *mis-in-tər'prit*, *v.t.* to interpret wrongly : to explain wrongly.—*ns.* **misinterpretā'tion**; **misinter'preter.**

misjoin, *mis-join'*, *v.t.* to join improperly or unfitly. —*n.* **misjoin'der**, (*law*) an incorrect union of parties or of causes of actions in a suit.

misjudge, *mis-juj'*, *v.t.* and *v.i.* to judge wrongly.— *n.* **misjudg'ment**—also **misjudge'ment.**

misken, *mis-ken'*, *v.t.* (*Scot.*) tc be, or to appear, ignorant of : to fail or refuse to recognise.

misknow, *mis-nō'*, *v.t.* to misapprehend.—*n.* **misknowledge** (*mis-nol'ij*).

mislay, *mis-lā'*, *v.t.* to place amiss : to lay in a place not remembered : to lose :—*pa.t.* and *pa.p.* **mislaid'.**

mislead, *mis-lēd'*, *v.t.* to draw into error : to cause to mistake :—*pa.t.* and *pa.p.* **misled'.**—*n.* **mislead'er.**—*adj.* **mislead'ing**, deceptive.—*adv.* **mislead'ingly.**

misleared, *mis-lērd'*, *adj.* (*Scot.*) mistaught : unmannerly : ill-conditioned.

misleeke, *mis-lēk'*, *v.i.* (*Spens.*) for **mislike.**

misletoe. See **mistletoe.**

mislight, *mis-līt'*, *v.t.* to lead astray by a light.

mislike, *mis-līk'*, *v.t.* to dislike : to displease.—*v.i.* to disapprove.—*n.* dislike : disapprobation.

mislippen, *mis-lip'n*, *v.t.* (*Scot.*) to distrust : to suspect : to disappoint, deceive : to neglect, overlook.

mislive, *mis-liv'*, *v.i.* to live a bad life.

misluck, *mis-luk'*, *n.* ill-luck.—*v.i.* to meet with bad luck, to fail.

mismake, *mis-māk'*, *v.t.* to make amiss, shape ill.— *pa.p.* and *adj.* **mismade'.**

mismanage, *mis-man'ij*, *v.t.* to conduct badly : to conduct carelessly.—*n.* **misman'agement.**

mismanners, *mis-man'ərz*, *n.pl.* bad manners.

mismarry, *mis-mar'i*, *v.t.* and *v.i.* to marry unsuitably.—*n.* **mismarr'iage.**

mismatch, *mis-mach'*, *v.t.* to match unsuitably.— *n.* a bad match.—*n.* **mismatch'ment.**

mismate, *mis-māt'*, *v.t.* and *v.i.* to mate unsuitably.—*adj.* **mismat'ed.**

mismeasure, *mis-mezh'ər*, *v.t.* to measure wrongly. —*n.* **mismeas'urement.**

mismetre, *mis-mēt'ər*, *v.t.* to spoil the metre of.

misname, *mis-nām'*, *v.t.* to call by an unsuitable or wrong name.

misnomer, *mis-nō'mər*, *n.* a misnaming : a wrong or unsuitable name.—*v.t.* to misname. [O.Fr. from Fr. *mes-* (see pfx. **mis-** (2)) and *nommer*— L. *nōmināre*, to name.]

misobserve, *mis-ob-zərv'*, *v.t.* and *v.i.* to fail to observe : to observe amiss or incorrectly.

misocapnic, *mis-ō-kap'nik*, or *mīs-*, *adj.* hating smoke, esp. that of tobacco. [Gr. *mīseein*, to hate, *kapnos*, smoke.]

misoclere, *mis'ō-klēr*, or *mīs-*, *adj.* (*Fuller*) hating the clergy. [Gr. *mīseein*, to hate, *klēros*, clergy.]

misogamist, *mis-og'ə-mist*, or *mīs-*, *n.* a hater of marriage.—*n.* **misog'amy.** [Gr. *mīseein*, to hate, *gamos*, marriage.]

misogynist, *mis-oj'i-nist*, or *mīs-*, or *-og'*, *n.* a woman-hater.—*adjs.* **misogynist'ical**, **misog'ynous.** — *n.* **misog'yny.** [Gr. *mīseein*, to hate, *gynē*, a woman.]

misology, *mis-*, *mīs-ol'ə-ji*, *n.* hatred of reason, reasoning, or knowledge.—*n.* **misol'ogist.** [Gr. *mīseein*, to hate, *logos*, reason.]

misoneism, *mis-ō-nē'izm*, or *mīs-*, *n.* hatred of novelty.—*n.* **misonē'ist**—*adj.* **misonēist'ic.** [Gr. *mīseein*, to hate, *neos*, new.]

misorder, *mis-or'dər*, *n.* and *v.t.* disorder.

mispersuasion, *mis-pər-swā'zhən*, *n.* a wrong persuasion or notion : a false opinion.

mispickel, *mis'pik-əl*, *n.* arsenical pyrites, a mineral composed of iron, arsenic, and sulphur. [Ger.]

misplace, *mis-plās'*, *v.t.* to put in a wrong place : to set on an improper object.—*n.* **misplace'ment.**

misplay, *mis-plā'*, *n.* a wrong play.

misplead, *mis-plēd'*, *v.t.* and *v.i.* to plead wrongly. —*n.* **misplead'ing**, an error in pleading.

misplease, *mis-plēz'*, *v.t.* to displease.

mispoint, *mis-point'*, *v.t.* to punctuate wrongly.

mispraise, *mis-prāz'*, *v.t.* to praise amiss : to dispraise.

misprint, *mis-print'*, *v.t.* to print wrong.—*v.i.* to make foot; rints in unusual positions.—*n.* (*mis'-print*, *mis'print'*) a mistake in printing.

misprise, **misprize**, *mis-prīz'*, *v.t.* to scorn : to slight : to undervalue.—*n.* (*Spens.*) **mesprise**, **mesprize**, **misprize**) scorn : slighting : failure to value. [O.Fr. *mespriser*—pfx. *mes-* (see pfx. **mis-** (2)), L.L. *pretiāre*—L. *pretium*, price.]

misprise, **mis** ize, *mis-prīz'*, *v.t.* to mistake.— *n.* (*Spens.* **mesprize**) error.— *adj.* **misprised'**, mistaken. [O.Fr. *mespris*, pa.p. of *mesprendre*, to commit an offence ; cf. **misprision** (1).]

misprision, *mis-prizh'ən*, *n.* mistake : (*law*) criminal oversight or neglect in respect to the crime of another : any serious offence, failure of duty—*positive* or *negative*, according as it is maladministration or mere neglect.—**misprision of heresy, treason, &c.,** knowledge of and failure to give information about heresy treason, &c. [O.Fr. *mes-* (see pfx. **mis-** (2)), L.L. *prēnsiō*, *-ōnis*—L. *praehendere*, to take.]

misprision, *mis-prizh'ən*, *n.* failure to appreciate. [**misprise** (1), after the model of **misprision** (1).]

mispronounce, *mis-prə-nowns'*, *v.t.* to pronounce incorrectly. — *n.* **mispronunciation** (*-mun-si-ā'-shən*), wrong or improper pronunciation.

misproportion, *mis-prə-pōr'shən*, *n.* lack of due proportion.—*adj.* **mispropor'tioned.**

misproud, *mis-prowd'*, *adj.* unduly proud.

mispunctuate, *mis-pungk'tū-āt*, *v.t.* and *v.i.* to punctuate wrongly.—*n.* **mispunctuā'tion.**

misquote, *mis-kwōt'*, *v.t.* to quote wrongly.—*n.* **misquotā'tion.**

misrate, *mis-rāt'*, *v.t.* to value wrongly.

misread, *mis-rēd'*, *v.t.* to read wrongly.—*n.* **mis'-read'ing.**

misreckon, *mis-rek'n*, *v.t.* and *v.i.* to reckon or compute wrongly.—*n.* **misreck'oning.**

misregard, *mis-ri-gärd'*, *n.* (*Spens.*) inattention.

misrelate, *mis-ri-lāt'*, *v.t.* to relate incorrectly.—*n.* **misrelā'tion.**—**misrelated participle**, a participle which the grammatical structure of the sentence insists on attaching to a word it is not intended to qualify.

misremember, *mis-ri-mem'bər*, *v.t.* and *v.i.* to remember wrongly or imperfectly: (*dial.*) to forget.

misreport, *mis-ri-pōrt'*, *v.t.* to report falsely, misleadingly, or wrongly: (*Shak.*) to speak ill of.—*n.* false reporting or report: (*obs.*) ill repute.

misrepresent, *mis-rep-ri-zent'*, *v.t.* to represent falsely: to give a misleading interpretation to the words or deeds of: to be an unrepresentative representative of.—*n.* **misrepresentā'tion.**

misrule, *mis-rōōl'*, *n.* disorder: bad or disorderly government.—*v.t.* and *v.i.* to govern badly.—**Lord of Misrule**, a leader of Christmas revels.

Miss, *mis*, *n.* a title prefixed to the name of an unmarried (formerly, and now *dial.* and *U.S. illit.*, also a married) woman or girl (at first less respectful than *Mrs*): (*obs.*; without the name) an eldest daughter, young lady of the house: vocatively used alone in displeasure, real or assumed, otherwise *vulg.* (esp. in addressing a waitress): **miss**, a schoolgirl, or girl or woman with the faults attributed to schoolgirls: (in shops) one between a child and a woman: (*obs.*) a kept mistress:—*pl.* **miss'es**—either 'the Miss Hepburns' or 'the Misses Hepburn' may be said, but the latter is more formal.—*n.* **miss'hood.**—*adj.* **miss'ish**, schoolgirlish: having the faults attributed to schoolgirls — sentimental, insipid, namby-pamby, squeamish, silly, &c.—*ns.* **miss'ish-ness**; **miss'y**, (usu. subservient) the little girl.—*adj.* missish.—**Miss Nancy**, a very effeminate man. [Shortened form of **mistress**.]

miss, *mis*, *v.t.* (or *v.i.*, *arch.*, with *of*) to fail to hit, reach, find, meet, touch, catch, get, have, take advantage of, observe, see: to avoid or escape from danger of doing so: to fail: to omit: to discover the absence of: to feel the want of: to leave out: (*Shak.*) to do without.—*v.i.* to fail to hit or obtain: to fail: (*obs.*) to go wrong: to miss fire.—*n.* the fact or condition or an act or occasion of missing: failure to hit the mark: loss: feeling of loss or absence: (*Shak.*) wrong-doing.—*adj.* **miss'ing**, not to be found: not in the expected place: wanting: (*mil.*) of unascertained fate.—*adv.* **miss'ingly**, (*Shak.*) with sense of loss.—**give a miss**, in billiards, to allow an opponent to score by intentionally missing: to leave out, omit, avoid anything; **miss fire**, to fail to go off or explode (cf. **misfire**); **miss one's tip**, (*slang*) to fail in one's plan or attempt; **miss stays**, (*naut.*) to fail in going about from one tack to another; **miss the bus** (or **boat**), to lose one's opportunity. [O.E. *missan*; Du. *missen*, to miss.]

missal, *mis'l*, *n.* a book containing the complete service for mass throughout the year. [L.L. *missāle*, from *missa*, mass.]

missay, *mis-sā'*, *v.t.* and *v.i.* to say or speak amiss, wrongly, falsely, or in vain: to slander: to revile:—*pa.t.* and *pa.p.* **missaid** (*-sed'*).—*n.* **missay'ing.**

missee, *mis-sē'*, *v.t.* and *v.i.* to see wrongly.

misseem, *mis-sēm'*, *v.t.* (*Spens.*) to misbecome.—*adj.* **misseem'ing**, unbecoming.—*n.* false appearance.

missel, *mis'l*, *miz'l*, *n.* (*obs.*) mistletoe: the missel-thrush.—*n.* **miss'el-thrush**, a large thrush fond of mistletoe berries.—Also **miss'el-bird.** [O.E. *mistel*, *mistil*, mistletoe.]

missel-tree, *mis'l-trē*, *n.* a melastomaceous tree (*Bellucia Aubletii*) of northern South America, with edible berries.

missend, *mis-send'*, *v.t.* to send by mistake: to send to the wrong person or place:—*pa.t.* and *pa.p.* **missent'.**

misset, *mis-set'*, *v.t.* to set or place wrongly or unfitly: (*Scot.*) to put out of humour.

misshape, *mis-shāp'*, *v.t.* to shape ill: to deform.—*n.* deformity.—*adjs.* **misshap'en**, **misshaped'** (*Spens.* mishapt), ill-shaped.—*n.* **misshap'en-ness.**

missheathed, *mis-shēdh'id*, *adj.* (*Shak.*) wrongly sheathed.

missile, *mis'īl*, *mis'l*, *adj.* capable of being thrown or projected: pertaining to a missile.—*n.* a weapon or object for throwing by hand or shooting from a bow, gun, or other instrument. [L. *missilis*—*mittēre*, *missum*, to throw.]

missing. See **miss** (*vb.*).

mission, *mish'ən*, *n.* an act of sending, esp. to perform some function: the errand or purpose for which one is sent: that for which one has been or seems to have been sent into the world, vocation: a sending out of persons on a political or diplomatic errand, for the spread of a religion, or for kindred purpose: an organisation that sends out missionaries: its activities: a station or establishment of missionaries: any particular field of missionary enterprise: the body of persons sent on a mission: an embassy: a settlement for religious, charitable, medical, or philanthropic work in a district: a religious organisation or district not fully developed as a parish: a series of special religious services conducted by a missioner.—*adj.* of a mission or missions, esp. characteristic of the old Spanish missions in California.—*v.t.* (*rare*) to commission.—*v.t.* and *v.i.* **miss'ionarise**, to act as missionary (to, among, or in).—*n.* **miss'ionary**, one sent upon a mission, esp. religious.—*adj.* pertaining to missions.—*ns.* **miss'ionary-bish'op**, one having jurisdiction in an unconverted country, or in districts not yet formed into dioceses; **miss'ioner**, one who conducts a series of special mission services.—*v.t.* and *v.i.* **miss'ionise**, to do missionary work (upon, in, among).—**mission architecture**, the style of the old Spanish missions in California, &c. [L. *missiō*, *-ōnis*—*mittēre*, to send.]

missis, **missus**, *mis'is*, *-iz*, *n.* (*vulg. coll.*)—otherwise always written **Mrs**) mistress of the house: wife. [mistress.]

missive, *mis'iv*, *adj.* sent: (*obs.*) missile.—*n.* that which is sent, as a letter: (*Shak.*) messenger: (*obs.*) a missile: (*pl.*, Scots law) letters sent between two parties in which one makes an offer and the other accepts it.—**letter missive**, a missive, esp. from a sovereign or authority to a particular person or body, as one giving *congé d'élire*. [L.L. *missivus*—L. *mittēre*, *missum*.]

misspeak, *mis-spēk'*, *v.t.* and *v.i.* to speak wrongly.

misspell, *mis-spel'*, *v.t.* and *v.i.* to spell wrongly:—*pa.t.* and *pa.p.* **misspelt'**, **misspelled.**—*n.* **misspell'ing**, a wrong spelling.

misspend, *mis-spend'*, *v.t.* to spend ill: to waste or squander:—*pa.t.* and *pa.p.* **misspent'.**

misstate, *mis-stāt'*, *v.t.* to state wrongly or falsely.—*n.* **misstate'ment.**

misstep, *mis-step'*, *v.i.* to make a false step: to make a mistake.—*n.* a mistake in conduct, &c.

missuit, *mis-s(y)ōōt'*, *v.t.* to be unbecoming to.

missummation, *mis-sum-ā'shən*, *n.* wrong addition.

mist, *mist*, *n.* watery vapour seen in the atmosphere: cloud in contact with the ground: thin fog: rain in very fine drops: a suspension of liquid in a gas: a dimness or dim appearance: anything that dims or darkens the sight or the judgment.—*v.t.* to obscure or veil with mist or as with mist.—*v.i.* to become misty or veiled.—*n.* **mist'-flower**, a North American hemp-agrimony, with clusters of blue or violet flowers.—*adj.* **mist'ful**, misty.—*adv.* **mist'ily.**—*ns.* **mist'iness**; **mist'ing**, mist.—*adj.* misty: hazy: dimming.—*adj.* **mist'y**, full of, covered with, obscured by, mist: like mist: dim: obscure: clouded: vague: not perspicuous.—**Scotch mist**, a thick wetting mist: a drizzle. [O.E. *mist*, darkness, dimness; Ice. *mistr*, Du. *mist*.]

mistake, *mis-tāk'*, *v.t.* (*obs.*) to remove wrongfully: (*Spens.*; app.) to take or come upon to his loss: to understand wrongly: to ake for another thing or person : to be wrong about : to think wrongly : (*Spens.*) to believe wrongly to be.—*v.i.* to err in opinion or judgment : to do amiss : (*pa.t.* mis**took** ; *pa.p.* mistak′en, also mista′en′).—*n.* a taking or understanding wrongly : an error : (*mis*′) a faulty shot in cinematography.—*adjs.* mistak′able ; mistak′en, understood wrongly : guilty of or under a mistake : erroneous : incorrect : ill-judged.—*adv.* mistak′enly.—*ns.* mistak′enness ; mistak′ing (*Shak.*) a mistake.—**and no mistake**, (*coll.*) assuredly ; **be mistaken**, to make or have made a mistake : to be misunderstood ; **mistake one's man**, think too lightly of the man one has to deal with ; **mistake one's way**, take the wrong road. [M.E. *mistaken*—O.N. *mistaka*, to take wrongly—*mis*-, wrongly, *taka*, to take.]

misteach, *mis-tēch′*, *v.t.* to teach wrongly :—*pa.t.* and *pa.p.* **mistaught** (*mis-tawt′*).

mistell, *mis-tel′*, *v.t.* to count, narrate, or inform, wrongly :—*pa.t.* and *pa.p.* **mistold′**.

mistemper, *mis-tem′pər*, *n.* and *v.t.* (*obs.*) disorder. —*adj.* mistem′pered, (*Shak.*) tempered or mixed ill : (*Shak.*) tempered for an evil purpose.

mister, *mis′tər*, *n.* (*obs.*) craft, trade, profession : (*Spens.*) manner, kind (without *of*—what mister man orig.=man of what class, hence what kind of man) : (*Scot.*) need, necessity.—*v.i.* (*Spens.*) to be necessary : to have need.—*v.t.* to need.—*n.* mis′tery (see **mystery** (2)). [O.Fr. *mestier* (Fr. *métier*), trade—L. *ministerium*, service.]

Mister, *mis′tər*, *n.* a title prefixed to a man's name, and to certain designations (as Mr Justice, Mr Speaker), written **Mr**: (*vulg.*) sir.—*v.t.* mis′ter, to address as ' mister.' [**master**.]

misterm, *mis-tərm′*, *v.t.* to name wrongly or unsuitably.

mistery. Same as **mystery** (2).

misthink, *mis-thingk′*, *v.t.* (*Shak.*) to think ill of : to think wrongly.—*v.i.* to have wicked or mistaken thoughts :—*pa.t.* and *pa.p.* **misthought** (*mis-thawt′*).—*n.* misthought′, a wrong notion.

mistico, *mis′ti-kō*, *n.* a small Mediterranean coaster, between a xebec and a felucca. [Sp. *místico*, prob. from Ar.]

mistigris, *mis′ti-gris*, *n.* a variation of poker in which a joker or blank card can be given any value : the card so used.

mistime, *mis-tīm′*, *v.t.* to time wrongly.—*adj.* mistimed′, unseasonable.

mistitle, *mis-tī′tl*, *v.t.* to call by an unsuitable title.

mistle. Same as **mizzle** or **missel**.

mistletoe, *miz′l-tō*, or *mis′*, *n.* a hemiparasitic evergreen shrubby plant (*Viscum album*) with white viscous fruits, growing on the apple, apricot, &c. (very rarely on the oak) : extended to other species of its genus or family (Loranthaceae). [O.E. *misteltán*—*mistel*, *mistil*, mistletoe, *tán*, twig ; see **missel**.]

mistook, *mis-took′*, *pa.t.* of **mistake**.

mistral, *mis′träl*, *n.* a violent cold dry north-west wind in southern France. [Fr.,—Prov. *mistral*— L. *magistrālis*, masterful, *magister*, master.]

mistranslate, *mis-trăns-lāt′*, *v.t.* and *v.i.* to translate incorrectly.—*n.* mistranslā′tion.

mistrayned, *mis-trānd′*, *pa.p.* (*Spens.*) drawn away, misled.

mistreading, *mis-trēd′ing*, *n.* (*Shak.*) a false step, misdeed.

mistreat, *mis-trēt′*, *v.t.* to treat ill.—*n.* mistreat′ment.

mistress, *mis′tris*, *n.* (*fem.* of **master**) a woman employer of servants or head of a house or family : a woman (or anything personified as a woman) having power of ownership : a woman teacher, esp. in a school : a woman well skilled in anything : a woman loved and courted : a concubine : vocatively (*arch.* and *dial.*) madam : (*Shak.*) the jack at bowls : **Mistress** (*mis′iz* ; now usu. written **Mrs** ; *fem.* of **Mister, Mr**), a title prefixed to the name, once of any woman or girl, now ordinarily of a married woman, sometimes also prefixed to a designation. —*adj.* principal : leading : ruling.—*v.t.* to make a mistress of, pay court to as a mistress : to address as mistress : to become or be mistress of or over : (with *it*) to play the mistress.—*adjs.* mis′tressless ;

mis′tressly.—*n.* mis′tress-ship. [O.Fr. *maistresse* (Fr. *maîtresse*)—L.L. *magistrissa*, fem. from L. *magister*, master.]

mistrial, *mis-trī′əl*, *n.* a trial void because of error : (*U.S.*) an inconclusive trial.

mistrust, *mis-trust′*, *n.* distrust.—*v.t.* to distrust : to suspect.—*v.i.* to have suspicion.—*adj.* mistrust′ful.—*adv.* mistrust′fully.—*n.* mistrust′fulness.—*adv.* mistrust′ingly.—*adj.* mistrust′less.

mistryst, *mis-trist′*, *v.t.* (*Scot.*) to disappoint by not keeping an engagement.—*adj.* mistryst′ed, disturbed, put out.

mistune, *mis-tūn′*, *v.t.* to tune wrongly or falsely : to put out of tune.

misunderstand, *mis-un-dər-stand′*, *v.t.* to take in a wrong sense :—*pa.t.* and *pa.p.* **misunderstood′**. —*n.* **misunderstand′ing**, a mistake as to meaning : a slight disagreement.

misuse, *mis-ūs′*, *n.* improper use : application to a bad purpose : (*Shak.*) evil usage or behaviour. —*v.t.* misuse (*mis-ūz′*), to use for a wrong purpose or in a wrong way : to treat ill : (*Shak.*) to speak ill of : (*Shak.*) to deceive :—*pa.t.* (*Spens.*) misust (*-ūst′*).—*n.* misus′age, (*Spens.*) misconduct, evil practice : ill-usage : wrong use.

misventure, *mis-vent′yər*, *n.* a misadventure.—*adj.* misvent′urous.

miswandred, *mis-won′dərd*, *adj.* (*Spens.*) strayed over.

misween, *mis-wēn′*, *v.t.* and *v.i.* to judge wrongly.

miswend, *mis-wend′*, *v.i.* (*Spens.*) to go astray or amiss : to come to grief, miscarry :—*pa.t.* and *pa.p.* miswent′ (see **misgo**).

misword, *mis-wurd′*, *n.* (*dial.*) an angry or harsh word.—*v.t.* to word incorrectly.—*n.* misword′ing.

misworship, *mis-wur′ship*, *v.t.* to worship wrongly. —*n.* worship of a wrong object.

miswrite, *mis-rit′*, *v.t.* to write incorrectly.

misyoke, *mis-yōk′*, *v.t.* to yoke or marry unsuitably.

mite, *mīt*, *n.* a very small acaridan arachnid.—*adj.* **mit′y**, infested with mites. [O.E. *mīte.*]

mite, *mīt*, *n.* orig. an old Flemish coin of very small value : (*B.*) used to translate the Gr. *lepton*, of which two made a *kodrantēs* or ' farthing ' (Mark xii. 42): vaguely, a very small amount : a small contribution proportionate to one's means : a minute portion or fragment : a jot : a diminutive person : a small child. [M.Du. *mîte* (Du. *mijt*) ; perh. ult. the same as the preceding.]

miter, American spelling of **mitre**.

Mithras, *mith′ras*, **Mithra**, *-rä*, *n.* the ancient Persian light-god, whose worship became popular in the Roman Empire.—*n.* **Mithraeum** (*-rē′əm*), a grotto sacred to Mithras :—*pl.* **Mithrae′a**.—*adj.* **Mithrā′ic**.—*ns.* **Mithrā′icism**, **Mith′raism** (*-rā-izm*) ; **Mith′raist**. [L. and Gr. *Mithrās*—O.Pers. *Mithra* ; Sans. *Mitra*.]

mithridate, *mith′ri-dāt*, *n.* an antidote to poison, *Mithridates* (better, *Mithradátēs*), king of Pontus (reigned *c.* 120-63 B.C.), having traditionally made himself proof against poisons.—*adj.* **Mithridatic**, **Mithradatic** (*-dat′ik*), pertaining to Mithridates, esp. of his wars against Rome.—*n.* **mith′ridatism** (*-dāt-izm*), acquired immunity to a poison.— **mithridate mustard**, field penny-cress (*Thlaspi arvense*) ; **mithridate pepperwort**, field cress (*Lepidium campestre*).

mitigate, *mit′i-gāt*, *v.t.* to mollify, appease : to make more easily borne : to lessen the severity, violence, or evil of : to temper.—*adjs.* **mit′igable** ; **mit′igant**, mitigating.—*n.* **mitigā′tion**.—*n.* and *adj.* **mit′igative**.—*n.* **mit′igator**.—*adj.* **mit′igatory**. [L. *mītigāre, -ātum*—*mītis*, mild.]

mitochondria, *mit-ō-kon′dri-ä*, *n.pl.* thread-like bodies in cytoplasm. [Gr. *mitos*, thread, *chondros*, granule.]

mitosis, *mi-*, *mī-tō′sis*, *n.* an elaborate process of cell-division involving the arrangement of protoplasmic fibres in definite figures—karyokinesis.— *adj.* **mitotic** (*-tot′ik*). [Gr. *mitos*, fibre.]

mitraille, *mē-trä′ē*, *n.* small shot or projectiles sent in a shower, esp. from a mitrailleuse.—*ns.* **mit-railleur** (*-yər′*), **mitrailleuse** (*-yəz′*), a machine-gun that discharges a stream of small missiles. [Fr.]

fāte, fär, ȧsk ; mē, hər (her) ; *mīne ; mōte ; mūte ; mōōn ; ᵭhen* (then)

mitre, *mī'tər, n.* a Greek (or later) woman's head-fillet: (*Pope,* following *Homer*) a girdle: an eastern hat or turban: a high head-dress, cleft above, worn by archbishops and bishops, and by some abbots: (*fig.*) episcopal dignity; a gasteropod of the genus Mitra or its conical shell (**mit're-shell**): a gusset in sewing, &c.—*v.t.* to adorn with a mitre.—*adjs.* **mi'tral,** of or like a mitre: of the mitral valve; **mit'riform** (*mit',* or *mit'*), mitre-shaped.—**mitral valve,** a mitre-shaped valve of the heart. [Fr.,—Gr. *mitrā,* fillet.]

mitre, *mī'tər, n.* a joint (also **mi'tre-joint**) in which each piece is cut at an angle of 45° to its side, giving a right angle between the pieces: sometimes applied to any joint where the plane of junction bisects the angle: an angle of 45°: a gusset, a tapered insertion.—*v.t.* to join with a mitre: (*needlework*) to turn a corner in, by cutting out a triangular piece and joining.—*v.i.* to meet in a mitre.—*n.* **mi'tre-wheel,** a bevel-wheel having its face inclined 45° to its axis. [Origin unknown.]

mitt, *mit, n.* a mitten: (*U.S. slang*) a hand. [Shortened form.]

mitten, *mit'n, n.* a kind of glove, without a separate cover for each finger: a glove for the hand and wrist, but not the fingers: a boxing-glove: (*slang*) dismissal.—*adj.* **mitt'ened,** covered with a mitten or mittens.—*n.* **mitt'en-crab,** the woolly-hand crab, a Chinese crab that has done much damage to river banks in Germany since 1912.—**frozen mitten,** a chilly reception, the cold shoulder. [O.Fr. *mitaine*; origin obscure.]

mittimus, *mit'i-məs, n.* (*law*) a warrant granted for sending to prison a person charged with a crime: a writ by which a record is transferred out of one court to another: (*coll.*) dismissal, discharge: a nickname for a magistrate. [L., we send—*mittĕre,* to send.]

miurus, *mī-ū'rəs, n.* a hexameter with short penultimate syllable. [Latinised from Gr. *meiouros,* curtailed—*meiōn,* less, *ourā,* a tail.]

mix, *miks, v.t.* to combine so that the parts of one thing or things of one set are diffused among those of another: to prepare or compound in like manner: to blend: to mingle: to join: (*cinematography*) to combine in one film: to confound: to associate: to interbreed, cross: to involve. —*v.i.* to become mixed: to be joined: to associate: to have intercourse.—*n.* a mixing: a mixture, esp. a standard mixture: a formula giving constituents and proportions: a jumble, a mess.—*adj.* **mixed** (*mikst*), mingled: promiscuous: of or for both **sexes**: miscellaneous: confused: not select: combining characters of two or more kinds: (*phon.*) between front and back.—*adv.* **mix'edly** (or *mikst'li*).—*ns.* **mixed'ness**; **mix'er,** one who mixes: that by which or in which things are mixed: one who is easily sociable in all sorts of company: one who mixes drinks; **mix-in',** (*U.S.*) a fight.—*adj.* **mixt** (same as **mixed**).—Also *pa.p.* and *pa.t.*—*ns.* **mix'ter-max'ter, mix'tie-max'tie, mix'ty-max'ty, mix'y-max'y** (all *Scot.*), a confused jumble.—*adjs.* and *advs.* in a confused jumble.—*ns.* **mixtion** (*miks'tyən*), a mixture of amber, mastic, and asphaltum used as a mordant for gold-leaf: (*obs.*) mixture; **mix'ture** (*-tyər*), act of mixing: state of being mixed: the product of mixing: (*chem.*) a product of mixing in which the ingredients retain their properties—distinguished from *compound*: in an organ, a compound-stop giving harmonics: (*motoring*) a mixture of petrol vapour and air; **mix'-up',** confusion: a confused jumble.—*adj.* **mix'y,** mixed.—**mixed chalice,** the chalice prepared for the eucharist, containing wine mixed with water; **mixed doubles,** tennis matches with a male and a female player as partners on each side; **mixed foursome,** a golf match with a male and a female player as partners on each side; **mixed marriage,** one between persons of different religions or races; **mixed metaphor** (see metaphor); **mixed train,** a railway train made up partly of passenger carriages and partly of goods wagons. [L. *miscēre, mixtus,*

to mix; exact relation to O.E. *miscian,* Ger. *mischen,* uncertain.]

mixen, *miks'n, n.* a dunghill. [O.E. *mixen*—*mix, meox,* dung.]

mixo-, *miks'ō-,* in composition, mixed.—*adjs.* **mixo-barbar'ic,** part barbaric, part Greek; **mixo-lyd'ian,** in ancient Greek music the same as hyperdorian: in old church music applied to an authentic mode extending from *g* to *g,* with *g* for its final; **mixotroph'ic,** (*biol.*) combining different modes of nutrition. [Gr. *mixis,* mixing, *misgein,* to mix.]

mizmaze, *miz'māz, n.* a labyrinth: bewilderment. [maze.]

mizzen, mizen, *miz'n, n.* in a three-masted vessel, the hindmost of the fore-and-aft sails: the spanker or driver.—*adj.* belonging to the mizzen: nearest the stern.—*ns.* **mizz'en-course**; **mizz'en-mast**: **mizz'en-sail.** [Fr. *misaine,* foresail, foremast—It. *mezzana,* mizzen-sail—L.L. *mediānus,* middle —L. *medius,* middle; the development of meaning is puzzling.]

mizzle, *miz'l, v.i.* to rain in small drops.—*n.* fine rain.—*n.* **mizz'ling.**—*adj.* **mizz'ly.** [Cf. L.Ger. *miseln,* mist.]

mizzle, *miz'l, v.i.* (*slang*) to decamp. [Origin obscure.]

mizzle, *miz'l, v.t.* to confuse. [Origin obscure.]

mizzonite, *miz'ən-īt, n.* a scapolite richer in sodium than meionite. [Gr. *meizōn,* greater, from its longer vertical axis.]

Mjöllnir, Mjölnir, *myəl'nir, n.* Thor's terrible hammer. [O.N.]

mna, mnā. See mina.

mneme, *nē'mē, n.* a memory-like capacity of living matter for after-effect of stimulation of the individual or an ancestor.—*adjs.* **mnē'mic,** pertaining to the mneme; **mnemonic** (*ni-mon'ik*), aiding the memory.—*n.* a verse or other device to help the memory: (in *pl.*) the art of assisting the memory.—*adj.* **mnemon'ical.**—*ns.* **mnē'monist,** a teacher or practitioner of mnemonics; **Mnemosyne** (*nē-mos'i-nē,* or *-moz'*), the Greek goddess of memory, mother of the Muses.—*adj.* **mnemotechnic** (*nē-mō-tek'nik*), mnemonic.—*ns.* **mnemotech'nics,** mnemonics; **mnemotech'nist.** [Gr. *mnēmē,* memory, *mnēmōn,* mindful, *Mnēmosynē,* Mnemosyne.]

mo, *mō, adv.* and *adj.* (*arch.*) more.—Also **moe**; (*Scot.*) **mae** (*mā*), more (in number, not quantity). [O.E. *mā* (adv.); cf. more, most.]

mo. See moment.

moa, *mō'ä, n.* a gigantic extinct bird (Dinornis) of New Zealand. [Maori.]

Moabite, *mō'ə-bīt, n.* one of the ancient people of Moab, living east of the lower Jordan and the Dead Sea.—*adj.* of or pertaining to Moab.—**Moabite stone,** a basalt slab found (1868) at Dibon in Moab, with a long inscription in Hebrew-Phoenician letters, about the revolt of Mesha, king of Moab, against Israel (9th cent. B.C.; 2 Kings iii.).

moan, *mōn, n.* lamentation: a lament: a complaint: (*naval slang*) a grumble: a low murmur of pain: a sound like a murmur of pain.—*v.t.* to lament: to bemoan: to utter with moans: (*obs.*) to condole with.—*v.i.* to make or utter a moan.— *adj.* **moan'ful,** expressing sorrow: lamentable.— *adv.* **moan'fully.** [Unrecorded O.E. *mán* (noun) answering to the verb *mǽnan.*]

moat, *mōt, n.* a deep trench round a castle or fortified place, sometimes filled with water: a mote-hill.—*v.t.* to surround with a moat.—*adj.* **moat'ed.** [O.Fr. *mote,* mound.]

mob, *mob, n.* the mobile or fickle common people: the vulgar: the rabble: a disorderly crowd: a riotous assembly: a gang: (*Austr.*) a crowd, mixed collection, large herd or flock.—*v.t.* to attack in a disorderly crowd: to crowd around with vexatious curiosity or attentions: to drive by mob action.—*v.t.* and *v.i.* to form into a mob: —*pr.p.* **mobb'ing**; *pa.t.* and *pa.p.* **mobbed.**—*adj.* **mobb'ish.**—*ns.* **mobile** (*mō'bi-li*; 17th cent.), the mob; **mob'-law,** lynch-law: the will of the mob; **moboc'racy,** (*slang*) rule or ascendency exercised by the mob; **mob'ocrat**.—*adj.* **mobo-crat'ic**.—*n.* **mobs'man**, a member of a mob: a swell-mobsman. [L. *mōbile* (*vulgus*), the fickle (multitude); *movēre*, to move.]

mob, *mob*, *n.* (*obs.*) a loose woman: a négligé dress: a mob-cap.—*v.t.* to muffle the head of.—*adj.* **mobbed**, in dishabille: muffled up.—*n.* **mob'-cap**, a woman's indoor morning cap with puffy crown, a broad band, and frills.—**mob it**, (*obs.*) to go unobtrusively to an unfashionable part of the theatre. [Perh. *Mab*, for *Mabel*; but cf. O.Du. *mop*; mod. Du. *mopmuts*, a woman's nightcap.]

mobby, mobbie, *mob'i*, *n.* a spirituous beverage made from sweet-potatoes: (*U.S.*) fruit-juice for brandy-making: brandy made therefrom. [Carib *mabi*.]

mobile, *mō'bil*, *-bēl*, *-bil*, *adj.* movable: easily, speedily moved: not fixed: changing rapidly: of a liquid, characterised by great fluidity.—*n.* (*obs.*) with *great*, *principal*, &c., translation of primum mobile: a moving or movable body of part.—*ns.* **mobile** (*mō'bi-li*; see **mob**, 1); **mobilisation** (*mō-* or *mo-bil-i-zā'shan*, or *-i-*).—*v.t.* **mō'bilise**, to make movable, mobile, or readily available: to put in readiness for service in war: to call into active service, as troops.—*v.i.* to make armed forces ready for war: to undergo mobilisation.—*n.* **mobility** (*mō-bil'i-ti*), quality of being mobile: (*slang*) the mob. [Fr.,—L. *mōbilis—movēre*, to move.]

moble, mobble, *mob'l*, *v.t.* to muffle, as in a mob.—*adj.* **mobled**, (*Shak.*) muffled: other suggestions are richly endowed (cf. Fr. *meuble*), set in motion, violently agitated (L. *mōbilis*), or that there is no meaning at all. [Freq. of **mob** (2).]

moccasin, mocassin, *mok'a-sin*, *n.* a North American Indian's shoe of deerskin or other soft leather: a lady's slipper more or less resembling it: a venomous North American pit-viper.—*n.* **mocc'asin-flow'er**, a lady's-slipper orchid. [Powhatan *mock'asin*; Narragansett *mokuss'in*.]

Mocha, *mō'kä*, *n.* a fine coffee.—**Mocha stone**, a moss agate or similar stone. [Both first brought from *Mocha*, on the Red Sea.]

mochell. Same as **muchel**.

mock, *mok*, *v.t.* to deride: to scoff at derisively: to make sport of: to mimic in ridicule: to simulate: (*fig.*) to defy, set at naught, tantalise, disappoint, deceive, befool, as if in mockery.—*v.i.* to jeer: to scoff: to speak or behave as one not in earnest.—*n.* ridicule: a bringing into ridicule: a scoff: a mockery: a thing mocked.—*adj.* sham: false: resembling, or accepted as a substitute for, the true or real.—*adj.* **mock'able**, worthy of derision.—*ns.* **mock'age** (*obs.*); **mock'er**; **mock'ery**, derision: ridicule: subject of ridicule: mimicry: imitation, esp. a contemptible or insulting imitation: false show: insulting or ludicrous futility.—*adj.* **mock'-hero'ic**, burlesquing the heroic style.—*n.* a mock-heroic composition: (in *pl.*) mock-heroic verses: sham heroic utterances or pose.—*adj.* **mock-hero'ical**.—*adv.* **mock'-hero'ically**.—*n.* and *adj.* **mock'ing**.—*n.* **mock'ing-bird**, an American bird (Mimus) of the thrush family, that mimics other birds' songs and other sounds.—*adv.* **mock'ingly**.—*n.* **mock'ing-thrush'**, a thrasher.—*adj.* **mock'-mod'est**.—*ns.* **mock'-mod'esty**, sham modesty; **mock'-or'ange**, a tall shrub (Philadelphus, commonly called syringa) of the saxifrage family with strong-scented flowers: (*U.S.*) a kind of cherry-laurel; **mock'-priv'et**, a shrub (Phillyrea) akin to privet.—**mock moon**, a paraselene, or bright spot in the moon's halo, 22° to right or left of the moon, due to refraction from ice crystals floating vertically; **mocks the pauses**, (Shak., *Ant. and Cleo.*, V. i. 2) perh. throws away the opportunities given by the pauses; **mock sun**, a parhelion, or spot in the sun's halo; **mock turtle soup**, an imitation of turtle soup, made of calf's head or veal. [O.Fr. *mocquer*; origin uncertain.]

mockado, *mok-ä'dō*, *n.* (*obs.*) an inferior cloth of Flemish origin: trumpery. [Prob. It. *mocaiardo*, haircloth.]

mocker-nut, *mok'ər-nut*, *n.* a kind of hickory-nut with kernel difficult to extract.

mocock, *mō-kok'*, **mocuck**, *mō-kuk'*, *n.* an American Indian birch-bark box or basket. [Of Algonquian origin.]

mod, *mōd*, *n.* a Highland literary and musical festival. [Gael. *mod*—O.N. *mót*; cf. **moot**.]

mode, *mōd*, *n.* way or manner of acting, doing, happening, or existing: kind: form: manifestation: state of being: that which exists only as a quality of substance: (*gram.*) a mood: (*log.*) character as necessary, contingent, possible or impossible: (*log.*) a mood: (*petr.*) actual percentage mineral composition: (*statistics*) the value of greatest frequency: modality: fashion: that which is fashionable: fashionableness: (*obs.*) a model of fashion: alamode, or a garment made of it: open-work between the solid parts of lace: (*mus.*) the method of dividing the octave according to the position of its steps and half-steps: in old music the method of time-division of notes (*perfect* into three *imperfect* into two; *major*, division of large into longs, *minor* of long into breves).—*adj.* **modal** (*mōd'l*), relating to mode.—*ns.* **mod'alism**, the doctrine first set forth by Sabellius that the Father, the Son, and the Holy Spirit are not three distinct personalities but only three different modes of manifestation; **mod'alist**, one who holds this theory.—*adj.* **modalist'ic**.—*n.* **modality** (*mōd-al'i-ti*), fact or condition of being modal: mode: (*law*) the quality of being limited by a condition.—*adv.* **mod'ally**.—*adj.* **modish** (*mōd'ish*), fashionable: affectedly, foolishly, or absurdly fashionable.—*adv.* **mod'ishly**.—*ns.* **mod'ishness**; **mod'ist**, a follower of the fashion; **modiste** (*mō-dēst'*; Fr.), a professedly fashionable dress-maker or milliner.—**Greek modes** consist each of two disjunct tetrachords with a whole tone (diazeuctic tone) between them, or two conjunct tetrachords with a whole tone above (where the prefix is *hyper-*) or below them (*hypo-*); **Gregorian, mediaeval**, or **ecclesiastical modes** have the same names but do not correspond (see **authentic, plagal**, and the names of the several modes); **major mode**, a modern mode, consisting of two steps, a half-step, three steps, and a half-step; **minor mode**, a modern mode, consisting of a step, a half-step, two steps, a half-step, and two steps. [L. *modus*; partly through Fr. *mode*.]

model, *mod'l*, *n.* (*obs.*) plan, design: a preliminary solid representation, generally small, or in plastic material, to be followed in construction: something to be copied: a pattern: an imitation of something on a smaller scale: a person or thing closely resembling another: one who poses for an artist: one who exhibits clothes for a shop by wearing them: a pattern of excellence: an article of standard design or a copy of one: structural type: (*obs.*) a medal: (*Shak.*) a close covering or mould.—*adj.* of the nature of a model: set up for imitation: completely suitable for imitation, exemplary.—*v.t.* to form after a model: to shape: to make a model or copy of: to form in some plastic material: of a mannequin, to display (a garment) by wearing it.—*v.i.* to practise modelling: —*pr.p.* **mod'elling**; *pa.t.* and *pa.p.* **mod'elled**.—*ns.* **mod'eller**; **mod'elling**, the act or art of making a model of something, a branch of sculpture: rendering of solid form. [O.Fr. *modelle*—It. *modello*, dim. of *modo*—L. *modus*, a measure.]

modena, *mod'i-nä*, *n.* a shade of crimson. [*Modena* in Italy.]

moderate, *mod'ə-rāt*, *v.t.* to keep within measure or bounds: to regulate: to reduce in intensity: to make temperate or reasonable: to pacify: to preside as moderator over or at: (*obs.*) to decide as an arbitrator.—*v.i.* to become less violent or intense: to preside or act as a moderator.—*adj.* (*-rit*) kept within measure or bounds: not excessive or extreme: temperate: of middle rate.—*n.* one whose views are far from extreme: one of a party in the Scottish Church in the 18th century and early 19th, broad in matters of doctrine and discipline, opposed to Evangelicalism and popular rights.—*adv.* **mod'erately**.—*ns.* **mod'erateness**;

modera′tion, act of moderating : state of being moderated or moderate : freedom from excess : self-restraint : (in *pl.*) the first public examination at Oxford for B.A. (*coll.* mods) : the process of slowing down neutrons in an atomic pile ; **mod′eratism**, moderate opinions in religion or politics ; **mod′erātor**, one who, or that which, moderates or restrains : a president or chairman, esp. in Presbyterian church courts : an officer at the universities of Oxford and Cambridge who superintends the examination for degrees : an oil-lamp with regulated flow of oil : the material in which neutrons are slowed down in an atomic pile :—*fem.* **mod′erātrix** ; **mod′erātorship.**—**moderate (in) a call**, of a presbytery, to act with the congregation in calling the minister it has chosen. [L. *moderārī, -ātus*—*modus*, a measure.]

moderato, mod-*a*-rä′tō, *adj.* and *adv.* at a moderate speed. [It.]

modern, mod′*a*rn, *adj.* of or characteristic of present or recent time : not ancient or mediaeval : in education, mainly or wholly concerned with subjects other than Greek and Latin : (*print.*) of a style of type with contrasting thick and thin strokes, serifs at right-angles, curves thickened in the centre : (*Shak.*) everyday, commonplace : **Modern**, of a language, of or near the form now spoken and written, distinguished from *Old* and *Middle.*—*n.* one living in modern times, esp. distinguished from the ancient Greeks and Romans : a modernist : a modern printing type.—*n.* **modernīsā′tion.**—*v.t.* **mod′ernise**, to adapt to the present time, conditions, needs, language, or spelling.—*v.i.* to adopt modern ways.—*ns.* **mod′erniser** ; **mod′ernism**, a modern usage, expression, or trait : modern spirit or character : a tendency to adjust Christian dogma to the results of science and criticism ; **mod′ernist**, an admirer of modern ideas, ways, literature, studies, &c. : one who favours modernism ; **modern′ity.**—*adv.* **mod′ernly.**—*n.* **mod′ernness.** [L.L. *modernus*—*modo*, just now, orig. abl. of *modus*.]

modest, mod′ist, *adj.* restrained by a sense of seemliness : unobtrusive : unpretentious : unassuming : diffident : decent : chaste : pure and delicate, as thoughts or language : not excessive or extreme : moderate.—*adv.* **mod′estly.**—*n.* **mod′esty**, the quality or fact of being modest : a slight covering for a low neck. [L. *modestus*—*modus*, a measure.]

modicum, mod′i-k*a*m, *n.* a small quantity : (*obs.*) a small person : (*obs.* ; disrespectfully) a woman :—*pl.* **modicums.** [L. neut. of *modicus*, moderate—*modus*.]

modify, mod′i-fī, *v.t.* to moderate : (*philos.*) to determine the mode of : to change the form or quality of : to alter slightly : to vary : to differentiate : (*gram.*) to limit or qualify the sense of (said of an adverb) : (*philol.*) to subject to umlaut : (*Scots law*) to assess, decree, or award (a payment) :—*pr.p.* **mod′ifying** ; *pa.t.* and *pa.p.* **mod′ified.**—*adj.* **mod′ifiable.**—*n.* **modification** (-*fi-kā′shon*), act of modifying or state of being modified : result of alteration or change : changed shape or condition : (*biol.*) a change due to environment, lasting only as long as the operative conditions.—*adjs.* **mod′ificātive, mod′ificātory**, tending to modify : causing change of form or condition.—*adj.* **mod′ified** (-*fīd*), altered by modification : (*biol.*) homologous but developed in a different direction.—*n.* **mod′ifier** (-*fī-ar*), one who modifies : a modifying agent : a diacritic indicating modification, esp. umlaut. [Fr. *modifier*—L. *modificāre, -ātum*—*modus*, a measure, *facĕre*, to make.]

modillion, mod-il′yon, *n.* (*archit.*) an ornamental bracket under a Corinthian or other cornice. [It. *modiglione*—L. *modulus*—*modus*, a measure.]

modiolus, mo-dī′*a*-l*a*s, *n.* the axis of the cochlea of the ear : **Modiolus** (also **Modiola**) the horse-mussel genus.—*adj.* **modī′olar.** [L. *mŏdĭŏlus*, nave of a wheel, water-wheel bucket, drinking-vessel, &c., dim. of *modus*.]

modish, modist, modiste. See **mode.**

modius, mō′di-*a*s, L. mod′i-oos, *n.* a Roman dry measure, about a peck : a cylindrical head-dress of the gods :—*pl.* **mō′dii** (-*ī*). [L. *mŏdius*.]

modulate, mod′ū-lāt, *v.t.* to regulate, adjust, temper : to inflect, to vary the pitch or frequency of : to vary the amplitude or other character of : to vary under control.—*v.i.* (*mus.*) to pass from one key into another.—*adj.* **mod′ular**, of or pertaining to mode or modulation, or to a module.—*ns.* **modulā′tion** ; **mod′ulātor**, one who, or that which, modulates : (*radio*) any device for effecting modulation : a chart used in the tonic sol-fa notation on which modulations are shown ; **mod′ule**, a small measure or quantity : (*archit.*) a measure, often the semidiameter of a column, for regulating proportions of other parts : (*Shak.*) a model, image ; **mod′ulus**, (*math.*) a constant multiplier or coefficient : the positive square root of the sum of the squares of the real and imaginary parts of a complex number : a quantity expressing the relation between a force and the effect produced :—*pl.* **moduli** (mod′ū-lī). [L. *modulārī, -ātus*, to regulate, *modulus*, dim. of *modus*, a measure.]

modus, mō′d*a*s, *n.* the way in which anything works : a fixed payment instead of tithes :—*pl.* **mō′dī.**—See *Foreign Words.* [L. *mŏdus*, manner.]

moe, mō (*Shak.*). See **mo, mow** (1).

moellon, mō′*a*-lon, *n.* rubble in mason-work. [Fr.]

Moeso-gothic, mē-sō-goth′ik, *adj.* relating to the *Goths* who settled in *Moesia.*—*n.* their language.

mofette, mō-fet′, *n.* an opening in the earth giving out carbon dioxide with some nitrogen and oxygen—the last stage of volcanic activity. [Fr.,—It. *mofeta*, perh. L. *mephītis*, foul exhalation.]

mofussil, mō-fus′l, *n.* in India, all outside the capital or great towns.—*adj.* provincial : rural. [Hind. *mufassil*—Ar. *mufassal*, distinct, separate, pa.p. of *fassala*, to separate.]

moggan, mog′*a*n, *n.* (*Scot.*) a footless stocking. [Origin unknown.]

Mogul, mō-gul′, *n.* a Mongol or Mongolian, esp. **one** of the followers of Baber, the conqueror of India (1483-1530) : a name applied to the best quality of playing-cards.—*adj.* pertaining to the Mogul Empire, architecture, &c.—**Great Mogul**, the title by which Europeans knew the Emperors of Delhi. [Pers. *Mughul*, properly a Mongol.]

mohair, mō′hār, *n.* the long, white, fine silken hair of the Angora goat : other hair as a substitute for it : cloth made of it. [Ar. *mukhayyar* ; influenced by **hair.**]

Mohammedan, mō-ham′i-d*a*n, **Mahommedan**, m*a*-hom′, **Mahometan**, m*a*-hom′it-*a*n, **Muhammadan, Muhammedan**, mōō-ham′ä-d*a*n, -i-d*a*n, *adj.* pertaining to Mohammed (formerly popularly rendered as Mahomet) or to his religion.—*n.* a follower of Mohammed : one who professes Mohammedanism.—*v.t.* and *v.i.* **Mohamm′edanise**, &c., to convert to, or conform to, Mohammedanism.—*ns.* **Mohamm′edanism, Mohamm′edism**, &c., the religion of Mohammed, contained in the Koran.—See also **Mahoun**, **mammet**. [Ar. *Muhammad*, the great prophet of Arabia (*c.* 570-632) ; lit. praised.]

Moharram, Muharram, Muharrem, mō-, mōō-hur′um, *n.* the first month of the Mohammedan year : a great fast in commemoration of Hasan and Hosain during its first ten days : a public procession during the fast. [Ar. *muharram*, sacred.]

Mohawk, mō′hawk, *n.* an Indian of an Iroquois tribe of New York State : a Mohock : a skating movement from the edge on one foot to the same edge on the other in the opposite direction. [From an Algonquian name.]

Mohican, mō-hē′k*a*n **Mohegan**, -g*a*n, *n.* an Indian of a former tribe in Connecticut.—Also *adj.* [From a native name.]

Mohock, mō′hok, *n.* an aristocratic ruffian of early 18th-century London. [**Mohawk.**]

mohr. Same as **mhorr.**

mohur, mō′hur, *n.* a former Persian and Indian gold coin, in India fifteen rupees. [Pers. *mohr.*]

moider, moi′d*a*r, **moither**, -*dh*ar, *v.t.* to confuse : to stupefy, overcome.—*v.i.* to work hard : to wander in mind. [Dialect word ; origin obscure.]

moidore, moi′dōr, *n.* a disused gold coin of Portugal.

[Port. *moeda d'ouro*, lit. money of gold—L. *monēta*, *dē*, *aurum*.]

moiety, *moi'ə-ti*, *n.* half: one of two parts or divisions: (*Shak.*) a small share. [O.Fr. *moite*—L. *medietās*, *-tātis*, middle point, later half—*medius*, middle.]

moil, *moil*, *v.t.* to wet: to bedaub: to defile.—*v.i.* to toil: to drudge.—*n.* a spot: a defilement: labour: trouble: turmoil.—*n.* **moil'er**. [O.Fr. *moillier* (Fr. *mouiller*), to wet—L. *mollis*, soft.]

moineau, *moi'nō*, *n.* a small flat bastion to protect a fortification while being erected. [Fr.]

Moira, *moi'rä*, *n.* a Fate (goddess). [Gr. *Moirǎ*.]

moire, *mwär*, also *mwawr*, *mōr*, *moir*, *n.* orig. watered mohair: now watered silk or other fabric with watered appearance.—*adj.* **moiré** (*mwär'ā*, *moi'ri*), watered.—*n.* a watered appearance: sometimes used in error for moire. [Fr., from English **mohair**.]

moist, *moist*, *adj.* damp: humid: rainy: watery: (*Shak.*) juicy.—*v.t.* (*Shak.*) to moisten.—*vs.t.* **moisten** (*mois'n*), to make moist: to wet slightly; **moist'ify**, (jocular) to make moist.—*adv.* **moist'ly**. —*ns.* **moist'ness**; **moist'ure**, moistness: that which makes slightly wet: liquid, esp. in small quantity.—*adj.* **moist'ureless**. [O.Fr. *moiste* (Fr. *moite*), perh.—L. *mustum*, juice of grapes, new wine, perh. L. *mūcidus*, mouldy.]

moither. See **moider**.

moke, *mōk*, *n.* (*slang*) a donkey: a variety performer on several instruments: (*U.S. slang*) a negro. [Origin unknown.]

molar, *mō'lər*, *adj.* used for grinding: pertaining to a grinding tooth.—*n.* a grinding tooth, or back tooth. [L. *molāris*—*mola*, a millstone—*molĕre*, to grind.]

molar, *mō'lər*, *adj.* of or pertaining to mass or masses, or to large masses. [L. *molēs*, mass.]

Molasse, *mō-läs'*, *n.* a series of Oligocene or Miocene sandstones and sandy marls in Switzerland, France, and Germany. [Fr.]

molasses, *mo-las'iz*, *n.sing.* a thick treacle that drains from sugar. [Port. *melaço* (Fr. *mélasse*)—L.L. *mellāceum*—*mel*, *mellis*, honey.]

mold. See **mould**, **mole** (1).

moldwarp. See **mouldwarp**.

mole, *mōl*, *n.* (*obs.* except in Scots form **mail** and in **iron-mould**) a spot, esp. one caused by iron on linen: a small spot or elevation on the skin, often coloured and hairy.—*Spens.* **mōld**. [O.E. *māl*.]

mole, *mōl*, *n.* a small insectivorous animal (Talpa) with very small eyes and soft fur, which burrows in the ground and casts up little heaps of mould: extended to kindred or similar animals: (*fig.*) one who works in darkness or underground: one who sees ill.—*ns.* **mole'cast**, a molehill; **mole'-catcher**, one whose business it is to catch moles; **mole'-crick'et**, a burrowing insect (Gryllotalpa) of the cricket family, with forelegs like a mole's.—*adj.* **mole'-eyed**, having eyes like those of a mole: seeing imperfectly.—*ns.* **mole'hill**, a little hill or heap of earth cast up by a mole; **mole'rat**, a name for several burrowing rodents (Spalax, Bathyergus, &c.); **mole'skin**, the skin of a mole: mole's fur: a superior kind of fustian, double-twilled, cropped before dyeing: (in *pl.*) clothes, esp. trousers, made of this fustian; **mole'-spade**, a small spade used by mole-catchers.—**make a mountain out of a molehill**, to magnify a trifling matter; **mole out**, to seek, or elicit, bit by bit, as if by burrowing. [M.E. *molle*, *mulle*; cf. Du. *mol*, L.G. *mol*, *mul*; according to some a shortened form of **mouldwarp**.]

mole, *mōl*, *n.* a massive breakwater: an ancient Roman mausoleum. [Fr. *môle*—L. *molēs*, mass.]

molecule, *mol'i-kūl*, or *mōl'*, *n.* the smallest particle of any substance that retains the properties of that substance: a gram-molecule.—*adj.* **molecular** (*mol-ek'ū-lər*).—*n.* **molecularity** (*mol-ek-ū-lar'i-ti*).—*adv.* **molec'ularly**—**molecular weight**, the weight of a molecule referred to that of oxygen as 16 (or of hydrogen as 1). [Fr. *molécule*, dim.—L. *mōlēs*, mass.]

molendinar, *mol-en'din-ər*, *adj.* (jocular) pertaining

to a mill or a miller.—*n.* a molar tooth.—*adj.* **molen'dinary**, (jocular) relating to a mill.—*n.* a mill. [L.L. *molendīnum*, a mill—L. *molĕre*, to grind.]

molest, *mə-*, *mō-lest'*, *v.t.* to vex: to interfere with in a troublesome or hostile way: to annoy.—*n.* annoyance.—*ns.* **molestā'tion** (*mo-*, *mō-*); **molest'er**.—*adj.* **molest'ful**. [Fr. *molester*—L. *molestāre*—*molestus*, troublesome.]

molimen, *mō-lī'mən*, *n.* a great effort, esp. of any periodic effort to discharge a natural function.—*adj.* **moliminous** (*-lim'in-əs*). [L. *mōlīmen*—*mōlīrī*, to toil—*mōlēs*, mass.]

moline, *mō'līn*, *-līn'*, *adj.* (*her.*) like a millstone rind—applied to a cross with each arm ending in two outward curving branches.—*n.* a moline cross. [L. *mola*, a mill.]

Molinism, *mol'in-izm*, *n.* the doctrine of the 16th-cent. Spanish Jesuit Luis *Molina*, reconciling predestination and free will by God's foreknowledge, the efficacy of grace depending on the co-operation of the will.—*n.* **Mol'inist**.

Molinism, *mol'in-izm*, *n.* the quietism of Miguel de *Molinos* (17th cent.).—*n.* **Mol'inist**.

Moll, *mol*, *n.* a familiar form of *Mary*: a concubine: a prostitute.

mollah, **molla**. See **mullah**.

mollie, *mol'i*, *n.* an abbreviation of **mallemaroking**.

mollify, *mol'i-fī*, *v.t.* to soften: to assuage: to cause to abate: to appease.—*v.i.* to become soft: to relax in severity or opposition:—*pr.p.* **moll'i-fying**; *pa.t.* and *pa.p.* **moll'ified**.—*ns.* **mollifica-tion** (*-fi-kā'shən*); **moll'ifier**. [Fr. *mollifier*—L. *mollificāre*—*mollis*, soft, *facĕre*, to make.]

mollities, *mol-ish'i-ēz*, *n.* (L.) softness, softening.—*adj.* **mollitious** (*-ish'əs*), luxurious. [L. *mollitiēs*—*mollis*, soft.]

mollusc, **mollusk**, *mol'əsk*, *n.* one of the **Moll-usca** (*-us'kä*), a large phylum of invertebrates, without segments or limbs, usually having a mantle or fold of skin that secretes a shell—lamelli-branchs, gasteropods, cephalopods, and some smaller groups: a person of inert habit.—*adjs.* **mollus'can**, **mollus'cous**, of or belonging to the Mollusca.—*n.* **mollus'coid**, a member of a now abandoned division of invertebrates the **Mollus-coid'ea**, Polyzoa and brachiopods.—*adj.* of the Molluscoidea: like a mollusc. [L. *molluscus*, softish—*mollis*, soft.]

Molly, *mol'i*, *n.* dim. of *Mary*: a milksop.—*n.* **moll'ycoddle**, an effeminate fellow.—*v.t.* to coddle.—**Molly Maguire**, an Irish Ribbonman (1843) dressing as a woman: a member of a Pennsylvanian secret society crushed in 1877.

mollymawk, *mol'i-mawk*. Same as **mallemuck**.

Moloch, *mō'lok*, *n.* a Semitic god to whom children were sacrificed (also **Mo'lech**): any cause to which dreadful sacrifice is made or destruction due: an exceedingly spiny harmless Australian lizard.—*v.t.* **mo'lochise**, to sacrifice as to Moloch. [Gr. and L. *Moloch*—Heb. *Mōlek*.]

Molossian, *mol-os'i-ən*, *adj.* of *Molossia* or *Molossis* in Epirus, famous in ancient times for its great dogs, a kind of mastiff.—*n.* **moloss'us**, a metrical foot of three long syllables:—*pl.* **moloss'ī**.

molt, **molten**. See **melt**.

molto, *mol'tō*, *adv.* (*mus.*) very: much. [It.]

moly, *mō'li*, *n.* a magic herb given by Hermes to Odysseus as a counter-charm against the spells of Circe: a species of wild onion, *Allium Moly*. [Gr. *mōly*.]

molybdenum, *mol-ib'din-əm* (also *mol-ib-dē'nəm*), *n.* silvery-white metal (Mo; atomic number 42).—*ns.* **molyb'date**, a salt of molybdic acid; **molyb-dēn'ite** (or *-ib'dən-īt*), a mineral, molybdenum disulphide.—*adj.* **molyb'dic**.—*n.* **molybdō'sis**, lead-poisoning.—**molybdic acid**, H_2MoO_4. [Latinised neuter—Gr. *molybdaina*, a lump of lead, a leadlike substance—*molybdos*, lead.]

mome, *mōm*, *n.* (*obs.*) a buffoon: a carper. [Momus.]

mome, *mōm*, *n.* (*Spens.*) a blockhead. [Origin obscure.]

moment, *mō'mənt*, *n.* a point of time: a time so short that it may be considered as a point: a

fāte, fär, ǎsk; mē, hər (her); *mīne; mōte; mūte; mōōn; dhen* (then)

very short time (abbrev. in slang, mo): a second: a precise instant : the present, or the right, instant : (*Shak.*) moving cause or motive: importance, consequence: (*math.* ; *obs.*) an infinitesimal change in a varying quantity : a stage or turning-point: an element or factor (as in *psychological moment*, rightly used) : a measure of turning effect—the *moment of a force* about a point is the product of the force and the perpendicular on its line of action from the point.—*adjs.* momentān′eous, momentary: instantaneous ; mo′mentany, (*Shak.*) momentary.—*adv.* mo′mentarily.—*n.* mo′mentariness.—*adj.* mo′mentary, lasting for a moment: short-lived.—*adv.* mo′mently, every moment: for a moment.—*adj.* occurring every moment : of a moment.—*adj.* momentous (-*ment′*), of great consequence. — *adv.* moment′ously. — *ns.* moment′ousness ; moment′um, the quantity of motion in a body measured by the product of mass and velocity : (*pop.*) force of motion gained in movement, impetus :—*pl.* moment′a. [L. *mōmentum*, for *movimentum*—*movēre*, to move.]

mommet. See mammet.

Momus, mō′məs, *n.* the god of ridicule. [Latinised from Gr. *Mōmos*, blame, reproach, personified.]

mona, mō′nä, *n.* a West African monkey, *Cercopithecus mona*. [It., Sp., or Port. *mona*, monkey.]

monachism, mon′ək-izm, *n.* monasticism.—*adjs.* mon′achal, mon′achist.—*n.* Mon′achus, the monk-seal genus. [Gr. *monachos*, solitary—*monos*, alone.]

monacid, mon-as′id, **monoacid,** mon-ō-as′id, *adj.* having one replaceable hydrogen atom : capable of replacing one hydrogen atom of an acid. [Gr. *monos*, alone, and **acid.**]

monact, mon′akt, *adj.* one-rayed.—*adjs.* monact′inal (-*i-nəl* or -*ī′nəl*), monact′ine (-*in*). [Gr. *monos*, alone, *aktīs*, -*īnos*, a ray.]

monad, mon′ad, *n.* the number one: a unit: an ultimate unit of being, material and psychical: a spirit : God : a hypothetical primitive living organism or unit of organic life : a flagellate of the genus Monas or akin to it : a univalent element, atom, or radical.—Also *adj.*—*adjs.* monad′ic, -al; monad′iform, like a monad.—*ns.* mon′adism, monadol′ogy, a theory or doctrine of monads, esp. Leibniz's ; mon′as, a monad : **Monas,** a genus of flagellates. [Gr. *monas*, -*ados*, a unit—*monos*, alone.]

monadelphous, mon-ə-del′fəs, *adj.* of stamens, united by the filaments in one bundle : of a flower or plant, having all the stamens so united.—*n.pl.* Monadel′phia, in Linnaeus's system, a class of plants with stamens united in one bundle. [Gr. *adelphos*, brother.]

monandrous, mon-an′drəs, *adj.* having or allowing one husband or male mate (at a time): (*bot.*) having one stamen or one antheridium.—*n.pl.* Monan′dria, in Linnaeus's system, a class of plants with one stamen.—*n.* monan′dry, the condition or practice of being monandrous. [Gr. *anēr*, *andros*, a man, male.]

monarch, mon′ərk, *n.* a sole hereditary head of a state, whether titular or ruling.—*adjs.* mon′archal (-*ärk′əl*), monarch′ial, monarch′ic, -al. —*ns.* Monarch′ian, a Christian who denied the personal independent subsistence of Christ—*dynamic*, when regarding the divinity of Christ as only a power (*dynamis*) communicated to him ; *modalistic*, when regarding Christ as the Father who had assumed flesh, a mere *modus* of the Godhead ; monarch′ianism.—*adj.* monarch-ianis′tic.—*v.t.* mon′archise, to rule over as a monarch : to convert into a monarchy.—*v.i.* (also *v.t.* with *it*) to play the monarch.—*ns.* mon′-archism, the principles of monarchy : love of monarchy: mon′archist, an advocate of monarchy: a believer in monarchy : a monarchian.—Also *adj.* —*adj.* monarchist′ic.—*ns.* Monarch′o, (*Shak.*) a foppish fantastic megalomaniac (from a crazy Italian about Elizabeth's court) ; mon′archy, a kind of government of which there is a monarch : a state with monarchical government: the territory of a monarch. [Gr. *monarchēs*—*monos*, alone, *archein*, to rule.]

monarch, mon′ärk, *adj.* (*bot.*) having one xylem strand. [Gr. *monos*, alone, *archē*, origin.]

monastery, mon′as-tar-i, -tri, *n.* a house for monks, or (*rarely*) nuns.—*adjs.* monastē′rial, monastic (-*as′tik*), -al, pertaining to monasteries, monks, and nuns : recluse : solitary.—*n.* monas′tic, a monk.—*adv.* monas′tically.—*n.* monas′ticism (-*sizm*), the corporate monastic life or system of living. [Late Gr. *monastērion*—*monastēs*, a monk —*monos*, alone.]

monatomic, mon-ə-tom′ik, *adj.* consisting of one atom : having one replaceable atom or group: univalent. [**atom.**]

monaul, monal, mon′awl, *n.* a magnificent Himalayan pheasant (Lophophorus). [Nepali *munāl*.]

monaxial, mon-aks′i-əl, *adj.* having only one axis. —*adj.* monax′on, monaxial.—*n.* a monaxonic sponge spicule.—*adj.* monaxon′ic.—*n.pl.* Monaxon′ida, an order of sponges with monaxon spicules only. [Gr. *axōn*, and L. *axis*, axle.]

monazite, mon′əz-īt, *n.* (*min.*) a phosphate of cerium, lanthanum, neodymium, praseodymium, and usually thorium, a source of thorium. [Gr. *monazein*, to be solitary—on account of its rarity.]

monchiquite, mon′shi-kīt, *n.* a fine-grained lamprophyric rock, composed of olivine and augite with little or no felspar, in an analcite ground-mass. [From the Serra de *Monchique*, in S.W. Portugal.]

Monday, mun′di, *n.* the second day of the week.— *adj.* Mon′dayish, having the feelings that succeed Sunday's activities or inactivities, with the prospect of the week's work.—**black Monday, Handsel Monday, Meal Monday, Plough Monday** (see **black,** &c.). [O.E. *mónandæg*, *mónan*, gen. of *móna*, moon, *dæg*, day.]

moner, mōn′ər, **moneron,** mon-ēr′on, *n.* Haeckel's hypothetical simplest protozoan :—*pl.* monēr′a. [Gr. *monērēs*, single.]

monergism, mon′ər-jizm, *n.* (*theol.*) the doctrine that regeneration is entirely the work of the Holy Spirit, the natural will being incapable of co-operation. [Gr. *monos*, alone, *ergon*, work.]

monetary, mon′ or mun′i-tər-i, *adj.* of or relating to money : consisting of money.—*n.* monetisā′-tion.—*v.t.* mon′etise, to give the character of money to, to coin as money. [L. *monēta* (see **money**).]

moneth, munth (*Spens.*). Same as **month.**

money, mun′i, *n.* coin: pieces of stamped metal used in commerce : any currency used in the same way: wealth :—*pl.* mon′eys, mon′ies, (*arch.* and *legal*) sums of money : money.—*ns.* money′-bag, a bag for or of money: (*pl.*) a rich man ; mon′ey-bill, a bill introduced into parliament or congress for raising revenue or otherwise dealing with money.—*adj.* mon′ey-bound, unable to move for want of money.—*ns.* money′-box, a box for collecting or saving money, usu. with a slit for insertion ; mon′ey-broker, one who carries out transactions in money for others ; mon′ey-changer, one who exchanges one currency for another.—*adj.* mon′eyed, mon′ied, having money: rich in money: consisting in money.—*ns.* mon′eyer, one who coins money legally : (*obs.*) a capitalist ; mon′ey-grubber, a sordid accumulator of wealth ; mon′ey-lender, a professional lender of money at interest ; mon′ey-lending.—*adj.* mon′eyless, having no money.— *ns.* mon′ey-maker, one who acquires riches: anything that brings profit ; mon′ey-making, act of gaining wealth.—*adj.* lucrative, profitable.— *ns.* mon′ey-mar′ket, the market or field for the investment of money; mon′ey-or′der, an order for money deposited at one post-office, and payable at another ; mon′ey-scriv′ener, one who does financial business for clients ; mon′ey-spi′der, a small spider supposed to bring luck; mon′ey-spinner, a money-spider: a successful speculator: anything that brings much money ; mon′ey's-worth, something as good as money : full value ; mon′ey-taker, one who receives payments of money, esp. at an entrance-door : one who can be bribed ; mon′eywort, a round-leaved loosestrife, creeping Jenny.—**hard money,** coin ; **in the money,** (*racing,* &c.) among the prize-winners;

money down, money paid on the spot ; money of account, a monetary unit (not represented by current coins) used in keeping accounts ; pot(s) of money, a large amount of money ; ready money, money paid for a thing at the time at which it is bought : money ready for immediate payment. [O.Fr. *moneie* (Fr. *monnaie*)—L. *monēta*, money, a mint, *Monēta* (the reminder) being a surname of Juno, in whose temple at Rome money was coined.]

mong, *mung*, *n.* (now *dial.*) a mixture : a crowd.— *n.* **mong'corn**, **mung'corn**, maslin. [O.E. *gemang*.]

'mong, **'mongst**, aphetic for **among**, **amongst**.

monger, *mung'gər*, *n.* (chiefly in composition) a dealer, esp. in a petty or discreditable way : a trafficker.—*ns.* **mong'ering**, **mong'ery**. [O.E. *mangere*—L. *mangō*, *-ōnis*, a furbisher, slave-dealer —Gr. *manganeuein*, to use trickery.]

Mongol, *mong'gol*, *n.* a member of Genghis Khan's clan, or of the various populations under him : one of the people of Mongolia : their language : a member of a broad-headed, yellow-skinned, straight-haired, small-nosed human race, often with an epicanthic fold of skin (otherwise called Tungus) : a Mongoloid idiot.—*adj.* of the Mongols, Mongolia, or Mongolian.—*adj.* **Mongolian** (*mong-gō'li-ən*), of Mongolia, the Mongols, or their language.—*n.* the language of Mongolia.—*adj.* **Mongolic** (*-gol'ik*), Mongolian : of Mongolian type : of the division of the Ural-Altaic languages to which Mongolian, Buriat, and Kalmuck belong. —*v.t.* **Mong'olise**, to make Mongolian. — *n.* **Mong'olism**, a condition of mental deficiency combined with a Mongol-like appearance.—*adj.* **Mong'oloid**, of Mongolian race or type : affected with Mongolism.—*n.* a person of Mongolian type : a Mongolian idiot.—**Mongoloid eye**, an eye with an epicanthic fold. [Said to be from Mongol *mong*, brave.]

mongoose, *mung'*, *mong'gōōs*, *n.* an Indian animal of the civet family, a great slayer of snakes and rats : any other species of the genus (Herpestes), including the ichneumon : a Madagascan lemur :— *pl.* **mong'ooses**.—Also **mung'oose**, **mangouste'** (Fr.). [Marathi *mangūs*.]

mongrel, *mung'grəl*, *n.* an animal, esp. a dog, of a mixed breed (usu. in contempt) : a person, thing, or word of mixed or indefinite origin or nature : that which is neither one thing nor another.— *adj.* mixed in breed : ill-defined.—*v.t.* **mong'relise**.—*n.* **mong'relism**.—*adj.* **mong'relly**. [Prob. from root of O.E. *mengan*, to mix.]

monial, *mōn'i-əl*, *n.* a mullion. [O.Fr., of unknown origin.]

monied, **monies**. See **money**.

moniliform, *mon-il'i-form*, *adj.* like a string of beads. [L. *monile*, a necklace, *forma*, form.]

moniment, *mon'i-ment*, *n.* (*Spens.*). Same as **monument**.

moniplies, *mun'*, *mon'i-plīz*. See **manyplies**.

monism, *mon'izm*, *n.* a philosophical theory that all being may ultimately be referred to one category ; thus *idealism*, *pantheism*, *materialism* are monisms—as opposed to the dualism of matter and spirit.—*n.* **mon'ist**.—*adjs.* **monist'ic**, **-al**. [Gr. *monos*, alone.]

monition, *mon-ish'ən*, *n.* a reminding or admonishing : warning : notice : (*law*) a summons to appear and answer.—*adj.* **mon'itive**, conveying admonition.—*n.* **mon'itor**, one who admonishes : an adviser : an instructor : a senior pupil who assists in school discipline : (*obs.*) a back-board : apparatus for testing transmission in electrical communication : a person employed to monitor : a low ironclad with revolving gun-turrets (from an American ship so named, the first of its kind, 1862) : a genus (Varanus) of very large lizards of Africa, Asia, and Australia (from a fancy that they give warning of the presence of a crocodile) : a detector for radioactivity : (*fem.* **mon'itress**). — *v.t.* to act as monitor to : to check (as the body and clothing of persons working with radioactive materials) for radioactivity. — *v.i.* (*wireless*) to tap on to a communication circuit, usu. in order to ascertain that the transmission is that desired : to listen to foreign broadcasts in order to obtain news, code messages, &c.—*adj.* **monitō'rial**, relating to a monitor.—*adv.* **monitō'rially**.—*n.* **mon'itorship**.—*adj.* **mon'itory**, giving admonition or warning. [L. *monēre*, *-itum*, to remind.]

monk, *mungk*, *n.* formerly, a hermit : a man (other than a friar, but loosely often applied to a friar also) of a religious community living together under vows : a bullfinch : an inky blotch or over-inked place in print : formerly, touchwood for firing mines.—*ns.* **monk'ery** (contemptuous), monasticism : behaviour of monks : monks collectively ; **monk'-fish**, the angel-fish (shark) ; **monk'hood**, the state or character of a monk.—*adj.* **monk'ish** (depreciatory), pertaining to a monk : like a monk : monastic.—*ns.* **monk'-seal**, a seal (*Monachus albiventer*) of the Black Sea, Mediterranean, and N.W. Africa, dark grey above, light underneath ; **monks'hood**, wolfsbane, a poisonous ranunculaceous plant (Aconitum) with a large hoodlike posterior sepal ; **monk's'-rhu'barb**, patience-dock ; **monk's'-seam**, (*naut.*) a strong seam formed by overlapping two pieces and stitching on each side and down the middle—also *middle-stitching*. [O.E. *munuc*—L. *monachus*—Gr. *monachos*—*monos*, alone.]

monkey, *mungk'i*, *n.* any mammal of the Primates except man and (usually) the anthropoid apes : an ape : a name of contempt, esp. for a mischievous person, also of playful endearment : the falling weight of a pile-driver : a large hammer for driving bolts : (*slang*) 500 pounds, or dollars : (*slang*) anger : a liquor-vessel of various kinds : (*pl.* **monk'eys**).—*v.i.* to meddle with anything, to fool. —*v.t.* to imitate as a monkey does.—*ns.* **monk'ey-bag**, a small money-bag, hung round the neck ; **monk'ey-block**, a small swivel-block, used to guide running rigging ; **monk'ey-board**, a foot-board behind a vehicle ; **monk'ey-boat**, a narrow, half-decked river-boat ; **monk'ey-bread**, the baobab-tree or its fruit ; **monk'ey-en'gine**, a pile-driving engine ; **monk'ey-flow'er**, Mimulus ; **monk'ey-gaff**, a small gaff above the spanker-gaff for the flag ; **monk'ey-gland**, contemptuous name for an ape's testicle, grafted on man to effect rejuvenescence ; **monk'ey-grass**, a coarse fibre from the leaf-stalks of *Attalea funifera*, used for brooms, &c. ; **monk'ey-hammer**, a drop-press with a ram, which is raised and let drop freely. — *adj.* **monk'eyish**.—*ns.* **monk'eyism**, monkey-like behaviour ; **monk'ey-jacket**, a close-fitting jacket ; **monk'ey-jar**, a water-monkey ; **monk'ey-nut**, the pea-nut or ground-nut (Arachis) ; **monk'ey-pot**, the round-lidded outer shell of the sapucaia nut ; **monk'ey-pump**, a straw let through a gimlet-hole for sucking liquor from a cask ; **monk'ey-puzzle'**, the so-called Chile pine, *Araucaria imbricata*, with close-set prickly leaves ; **monk'ey-rail**, a light rail above the quarter-rail ; **monk'ey-rope**, a forest creeper or liana : a rope round a sailor's waist for working in a dangerous place ; **monk'ey-run**, a favourite place of parade and striking up of acquaintance ; **monk'ey-shine**, (*U.S. slang*) a monkeyish trick ; **monk'ey-tail**, a vertical scroll at the end of a hand-rail ; **monk'ey-trick** ; **monk'ey-wheel**, a tackle-block over which runs a hoisting-rope ; **monk'ey-wrench**, a screw-key with a movable jaw.—**have**, or **get**, **one's monkey up**, to be angry ; **suck the monkey**, to drink from a cask through an inserted tube : to drink rum, &c., from a coconut. [Origin doubtful.]

Mon-Khmer, *mōn'kmer'*, *adj.* of a group of Austro-asiatic languages that includes *Mon*, spoken in Pegu (Burma), and *Khmer* in Cambodia.

mono-, *mon'ō-*. See *Prefixes*.

monoacid. Same as **monacid**.

monobasic, *mon-ō-bā'sik*, *adj.* capable of reacting with one equivalent of an acid : (of an acid) having one replaceable hydrogen atom. [**base**.]

monoblepsis, *mon-ō-blep'sis*, *n.* a condition in which vision is more distinct when one eye only is used. [Gr. *monos*, single, *blepsis*, sight.]

monocardian, *mon-ō-kär'di-ən*, *adj.* having an undivided heart. [Gr. *kardiā*, heart.]

monocarpellary, *mon-ō-kär′pəl-ə-ri,* or *-pel′, adj.* of or with only one carpel.

monocarpic, *mon-ō-kärp′ik, adj.* fruiting once only. —*adj.* **monocarp′ous,** monocarpic: having only one ovary: producing one fruit. [Gr. *karpos,* fruit.]

monoceros, *mō-nos′ər-os, n.* a one-horned animal: the unicorn: (*Spens.*) perhaps the sword-fish, or the narwhal.—*adj.* **monoc′erous.** [Gr. *monokerōs* —*monos,* single, *keras,* a horn.]

monochasium, *mon-ō-kā′zi-əm, n.* a cymose inflorescence in which each axis in turn produces one branch:—*pl.* **monocha′sia.**—*adj.* **monocha′sial.** [Gr. *monos:* apparently on the analogy of *dichasium,* as if that were from Gr. *di-,* twice, and *chasis,* separation.]

monochlamydeous, *mon-ō-klə-mid′i-əs, adj.* (*bot.*) having a one-whorled perianth.—*n.pl.* **Monochlamyd′eae,** a division of the Archichlamydeae or Choripetalae, usually with perianth in one whorl. [Gr. *monos,* single, *chlamys,* a cloak.]

monochord, *mon′ō-kord, n.* an acoustical instrument with one string, sound-board and bridge: a similar instrument with more than one string and bridge: a clavichord: a tromba marina. [Gr. *monochordon*—*monos, chordē,* a gut-string.]

monochroic, *mon-ō-krō′ik, adj.* of one colour. [Gr. *monochroos*—*monos, chrōs,* colour.]

monochromatic, *mon-ō-krō-mat′ik, adj.* of one colour or wave-length only: completely colourblind: done in monochrome.—*ns.* **monochro′-masy,** complete colour-blindness; **monochro′-mat, -mate,** one who sees all colours as differing in brilliance only; **monochro′matism,** monochromatic vision; **mon′ochrome,** representation in one colour: a picture in one colour: monochromy; **monochro′mist,** one who practises monochrome; **mon′ochromy,** the art of monochrome. [Gr. *monochrōmatos*—*monos, chrōma, -atos,* colour.]

monocle, *mon′ə-kl, n.* a single eyeglass. [Fr. *monocle*—Gr. *monos,* L. *oculus,* eye.]

monocline, *mon′ō-kuin, n.* (*geol.*) a fold in strata followed by resumption of the original direction.— *adj.* **monoclin′al.** [Gr. *klīnein,* to cause to slope.]

monoclinic, *mon′ō-klin-ik, adj.* (*crystal.*) referable to three unequal axes, two intersecting each other obliquely and at right angles to the third. [Gr. *klīnein,* to incline.]

monoclinous, *mon′ō-klī-nəs,* or *-klī′, adj.* (*bot.*) hermaphrodite. [Gr. *monos, klīnē,* bed.]

mono-compound, *mon′ō-kom′pownd, n.* (*chem.*) a compound containing one atom or group of that which is indicated.

monocotyledon, *mon-ō-kot-i-lē′dən* (*botanists′ slang,* **mon′ocot**), *n.* a plant of the Monocotylē′dones (*-ēz*), or Monocot′ylae, one of the two great divisions of the Angiosperms, the embryos with one cotyledon, leaves commonly parallel-veined, the parts of the flower usually in threes, the vascular bundles scattered and (with exceptions) without cambium.—*adj.* **monocotylē′donous.**

monocracy, *mon-ok′rə-si, n.* government by one person.—*n.* **mon′ocrat** (*-ō-krat*).—*adj.* **monocrat′ic.** [Gr. *monos, kratos,* power.]

monocular, *mon-ok′ū-lər, adj.* one-eyed: of, for, or with one eye.—Also **monoc′ulous.** [Gr. *monos,* L. *oculus,* an eye.]

monocyclic, *mon-ō-sīk′lik, adj.* having one whorl or ring. [Gr. *monos, kyklos,* a wheel.]

monodactylous, *mon-ō-dak′ti-ləs, adj.* one-toed or one-fingered. [Gr. *monos, daktylos,* finger, toe.]

Monodelphia, *mon-ō-del′fi-ā, n.pl.* one of the three primary divisions of mammals, the placental mammals or Eutheria.—*adjs.* **monodel′phian, monodel′phic, monodel′phous.** [Gr. *monos, delphys,* womb.]

Monodon, *mon′ō-don, n.* the narwhal.—*adj.* **mon′o-dont,** one-tusked: of the monodon. [Gr. *monos, odous, odontos,* tooth, tusk.]

monodrama, *mon′ō-drä-mä, n.* a dramatic piece for a single performer.—*adj.* **monodramatic** (*-drə-mat′ik*).

monody, *mon′ə-di, n.* a mournful ode or poem in which a single mourner bewails: a song for one

voice: a manner of composition in which one part or voice carries the melody, the others accompanying.—*adjs.* **monodic** (*-od′*), **-al.**—*n.* **mon′-odist,** one who writes monodies. [Gr. *monōidiā*—*monos, ōidē,* song.]

monoecious, *mon-ē′shəs, adj.* having separate male and female flowers on the same plant.—*n.pl.* **Monoe′cia,** in the Linnaean system, a class so characterised.—*n.* **monoecism** (*-ē′sizm*). [Gr. *oikos,* a house.]

monogamy, *mon-og′ə-mi, n.* the rule, custom, or condition of marriage to one wife or husband at a time, or (now rarely) in life.—*adjs.* **monogamic** (*mon-ō-gam′ik*), **monogamous** (*-og′əm-*).— *n.* **monog′amist.** [Gr. *monos, gamos,* marriage.]

monogenesis, *mon-ō-jen′i-sis, n.* development of offspring from a parent like itself: asexual reproduction: community of origin.—*adj.* **monogenet′ic.**—*ns.* **monogenism** (*-oj′ən-izm*), the doctrine of the common descent of all living things, or of any particular group (esp. mankind) from one ancestor or pair; **monog′enist.**—*adjs.* **monogenist′ic; monog′enous.**—*n.* **monog′eny,** descent from one common ancestor or pair: asexual reproduction. [Gr. *monos, genesis,* generation.]

monoglot, *mon′ō-glot, n.* one who knows only one language.—Also *adj.* [Gr. *monos, glōtta,* tongue.]

monogony, *mon-og′ən-i, n.* asexual reproduction. [Gr. *monos, gonos,* begetting.]

monogram, *mon′ə-gram, n.* a figure consisting of several letters interwoven or written into one.— *adj.* **monogrammatic** (*-grə-mat′ik*). [Gr. *monos, gramma, grammatos,* a letter.]

monograph, *mon′ə-gräf, n.* a treatise written on one particular subject or any branch of it: a systematic account.—*v.t.* to write a monograph upon.—*ns.* **monographer** (*mon-og′rə-fər*), **monog′-raphist,** a writer of monographs.—*adjs.* **monographic** (*-graf′*), **-al,** pertaining to a monograph or a monogram: drawn in lines without colours.— *n.* **monog′raphy,** (*rare*) a monograph. [Gr. *monos, graphein,* to write.]

monogyny, *mon-oj′i-ni,* or *-og′, n.* the custom, practice, or condition of having only one wife: marriage with one wife: the habit of mating with one female.—*n.pl.* **Monogynia** (*mon-ō-jin′i-ā*), in various Linnaean classes of plants an order having one style.—*adjs.* **monogyn′ian; monog′ynous,** having one wife: practising monogyny: mating with one female: having one style: monogynian. [Gr. *monos, gynē,* woman.]

monohybrid, *mon-ō-hī′brid, n.* a cross between parents differing in one heritable character. [Gr. *monos* and **hybrid.**]

monohydric, *mon-ō-hī′drik, adj.* containing one hydroxyl group.

monolatry, *mō-nol′ə-tri, n.* the worship of one god without excluding belief in others.—*n.* **monol′ater.** —*adj.* **monol′atrous.** [Gr. *monos, latreiā,* worship.]

monolith, *mon′ō-lith, n.* a pillar, or column, of a single stone.—*adj.* **monolith′ic.** [Gr. *monos, lithos,* a stone.]

monologue, *mon′ə-log, n.* a composition put into the mouth of one person, or intended to be spoken by one person: a harangue that engrosses conversation.—*adjs.* **monologic** (*-loj′*), **-al.**—*v.i.* **monologise** (*mon-ol′ə-jīz*), to indulge in this.— Also **monologuise** (*-gīz*).—*ns.* **monol′ogist,** one who talks in monologue (also **mon′ologuist**); **monol′ogy,** the habit of doing so. [Gr. *monos, logos,* speech.]

monomachy, *mon-om′ə-ki, n.* single combat: a duel.—Also **monomā′chia.** [Gr. *monos,* alone, *machē,* a fight.]

monomania, *mon-ō-mā′ni-ā, n.* madness confined to one subject: an unreasonable interest in any particular thing.—*n.* **monomā′niac,** one affected with monomania.—*adjs.* **monomā′niac, monomaniacal** (*-mə-nī′ə-kl*). [Gr. *monos, maniā,* madness.]

monomer, *mon′, mōn′ə-mər, n.* the simplest of any series of compounds having the same empirical formula—opp. to **polymer.** [Gr. *monos,* and suff. *-mer.*]

Neutral vowels in unaccented syllables : *el′ə-mənt, in′fənt, ran′dəm*

monometallic, *mon-ō-mi-tal'ik, adj.* involving or using but one metal as a standard of currency.— *ns.* **monometallism** (*-met'əl-izm*); **monomet'-allist.** [Gr. *monos,* and **metal.**]

monomial, *mon-om'i-tər, adj.* (*pros.*) consisting of one measure.—*n.* a verse of one measure.

monomial, *mon-ō'mi-əl, n.* an algebraic expression of one term only : a name consisting of one word. —Also *adj.* [Ill-formed from Gr. *monos,* alone, L. *nōmen,* name.]

monomorphic, *mon-ō-mor'fik, adj.* existing in one form only.—*adj.* **monomor'phous.** [Gr. *monos, morphē,* form.]

monomyarian, *mon-ō-mī-ā'ri-ən, adj.* having one adductor muscle. [Gr. *monos, mȳs, myos,* muscle.]

monopetalous, *mon-ō-pet'ə-ləs, adj.* (*bot.*) having petals united.

monophagous, *mon-of'ə-gəs, adj.* having only one kind of food.—*n.* **monoph'agy** (*-ji*), feeding on one food : eating alone. [Gr. *monos, phagein* (aor.), to eat.]

monophobia, *mon-ō-fō'bi-ä, n.* morbid dread of being alone. [Gr. *monos,* alone, *phobos,* fear.]

monophthong, *mon'of-thong, n.* a simple vowel-sound.—*adj.* **monophthongal** (*-thong'gal*).—*v.t.* **mon'ophthongise** (*-gīz*), to turn into a monophthong. [Gr. *monophthongos—monos, phthongos,* sound, vowel.]

monophyletic, *mon-ō-fi-let'ik, or -fī-, adj.* derived from a single stock. [Gr. *monos, phyletikos,* pertaining to a tribesman—*phȳlē,* tube.]

monophyodont, *mon-ō-fī'ō-dont, adj.* having only one set of teeth.—*n.* an animal with but one set of teeth. [Gr. *monophyēs,* of simple nature, *odous, odontos,* tooth.]

Monophysite, *mō-nof'i-zīt, -sīt, n.* one who holds that Christ had but one composite nature.—*adj.* **monophysitic** (*-sit'ik, -zit'ik*).—*n.* **monoph'ysitism.** [Gr. *monos, physis,* nature.]

monoplane, *mon'ə-plān, n.* an aeroplane or glider with one set of planes or wings. [Gr. *monos,* and **plane.**]

monoplegia, *mon-ō-plē'ji-ä, n.* paralysis limited to a single part. [Gr. *monos, plēgē,* stroke.]

monopode, *mon'ə-pōd, n.* a one-footed man, table, &c.—*adj.* one-footed.—*adj.* **monopo'dial,** pertaining to or of the nature of a monopodium.— *adv.* **monopo'dially.**—*n.* **monopo'dium,** (*bot.*) an axis that continues to grow without being supplanted, as in the sympodium, by a lateral branch. [L. *monopodius, -um*—Gr. *monos,* and *pous, podos,* foot.]

monopoly, *mon-op'ə-li, n.* sole power, or privilege, of dealing in anything : exclusive command or possession : that of which one has such a sole power, privilege, command, or possession.—*v.t.* **monop'olise,** to have a monopoly of : to keep to oneself : to engross. — *ns.* **monop'oliser, monop'elist.**—*adj.* **monopolis'tic.** [L. *mono-pōlium*—Gr. *monopōlion—monos,* alone, *pōleein,* to sell.]

monoprionidian, *mon-ō-prī-ə-nid'i-ən, adj.* serrated on one side (of graptolites). [Gr. *monos, prīon,* a saw.]

monopteros, *mon-op'tər-os,* **monopteron,** *-on, n.* a circular Greek temple with one ring of columns.— *adj.* **monop'teral.** [Gr. *monos, pteron,* a wing.]

monoptote, *mon'op-tōt, n.* a word with but one case-form. [Gr. *monoptōtos—monos, ptōtos,* fallen ; cf. *ptōsis,* case. (see **case**).]

monorail, *mon'ō-rāl, n.* a railway with carriages running astride of one rail.—Also *adj.* [Gr. *monos,* alone, and **rail.**]

monorchid, *mon-or'kid, adj.* having only one testicle.—*n.* **monorch'ism.** [Faultily formed from Gr. *monorchis—monos, orchis, -eōs,* testicle.]

monorhine, *m n'ō-rīn, adj.* having one nostril.— Also **monorhin'al.** [Gr. *monos, rhīs, rhīnos,* nose.]

monorhyme, *mon'ə-rīm, n.* a series or tirade of lines al. rhyming together. — Also *adj.* — *adj.* **mon'orhymed** [Gr. *monos,* and **rhyme.**]

monosacchəride, *mon-ō-sak'ə-rīd, n.* a simple sugar tha. cannot be hydrolysed.

monosepalous, *mon-ō-sep'ə-ləs, adj.* (*bot.*) having the sepals all united. [Gr. *monos,* and **sepal.**]

monostich, *mon'ə-stik, n.* a poem of one line.— *adj.* **monostichous** (*-os'tik-əs*), in one line : in one row. [Gr. *monos, stichos,* row, line.]

monostrophic, *mon-ə-strof'ik, adj.* not divided into strophe, antistrophe, and epode : having the same strophic or stanzaic structure throughout.— *n.pl.* **monostroph'ics,** monostrophic verses. [Gr. *monostrophikos—monos, strophē,* a strophe.]

monostyle, *mon'ō-stīl, adj.* (*archit.*) consisting of a single shaft.—*adj.* **monostyl'ar.** [Gr. *monos, stȳlos,* a pillar.]

monosy, *mon'os-i, n.* (*biol.*) separation of parts normally fused.—Also **monō'sis.** [Gr. *monōsis* solitariness—*monos.*]

monosyllable, *mon-ə-sil'ə-bl, n.* a word of one syllable.—*adj.* **monosyllabic** (*-ab'ik*).—*n.* **monosyll'abism.**

monosymmetric, -al, *mon-ō-sim-et'rik, -əl, adjs.* having only one plane of symmetry.

monotelephone, *mon-ō-tel'i-fōn, n.* a telephone that transmits sounds of one pitch only.

monothalamous, *mon-ō-thal'ə-məs, adj.* single-chambered : with but one cavity : (of fruit) formed from a single flower.—Also **monothalamic** (*-am'ik*). [Gr. *monos, thalamos,* a chamber.]

monothecal, *mon-ō-thē'kl, adj.* having only one theca.—Also **monothe'cous.** [Gr. *thēkē,* case.]

monotheism, *mon'ō-thē-izm, n.* the belief in only one God.—*n.* **mon'otheist.**—*adjs.* **monotheist'ic, -al.** [Gr. *monos,* alone, *theos,* God.]

Monotheletism, *mon-ō-thel'i-tizm, n.* the doctrine that Christ had but one will—opp. to **Ditheletism.** —Also **Monothelism** (*mon-oth'əl-izm*), **Monothel'itism.**—*ns.* **Monoth'elēte, Monoth'elite.**— *adjs.* **Monothelēt'ic, -al.** [Gr. *monos,* alone, *thelētos,* a willer—*thelein,* to will.]

monotint, *mon'ə-tint, n.* drawing or painting in a single tint. [Gr. *monos,* and **tint.**]

monotocous, *mon-ot'ə-kəs, adj.* producing single offspring at a time : fruiting once only. [Gr. *monos, tokos,* birth, offspring.]

monotone, *mon'ə-tōn, n.* a single, unvaried tone or utterance : a succession of sounds having the same pitch : continued or extended sameness : sameness in colour.—*adj.* in monotone.—*v.t.* and *v.i.* to sing, declaim, speak, utter, in monotone.— *adjs.* **monotonic** (*-ton'ik*), in monotone ; **monotonous** (*mon-ot'ə-nəs*), uttered in one unvaried tone : marked by dull uniformity.—*adv.* **monot'onously.**—*ns.* **monot'onousness ; monot'ony,** dull uniformity of tone or sound : want of modulation in speaking or reading : (*fig.*) irksome sameness or want of variety. [Gr. *monos, tonos,* a tone.]

Monotremata, *mon-ō-trē'mə-tä, n.pl.* the lowest order of Mammalia, having a single opening for the genital and digestive organs.—*adj.* **monotre'-matous**—also **mon'otreme.**—*n.* **mon'otreme,** a member of the Monotremata. [Gr. *monos, trēma, -atos,* a hole.]

monotroch, *mon-ō-trok, n.* (*Scott, facet.*) a wheelbarrow. [Gr. *monos, trochos,* wheel.]

Monotropa, *mon-ot'rə-pä, n.* a genus akin to wintergreen — the bird's-nest and Indian-pipe, nourished by a fungal mycorrhiza in humus. [Gr. *monotropos,* solitary—*monos, tropos,* turn.]

monotype, *mon'ə-tīp, n.* a sole type, a species forming a genus by itself : a machine that casts and sets type, letter by letter.—Also *adj.*—*adj.* **monotypic** (*-tip'ik*). [Gr. *monos, typos,* impression.]

monovalent, *mon-ov'əl-ənt, mon-ō-vā'lənt, adj.* univalent. [Gr. *monos,* and **valent.**]

monoxide, *mo-nok'sīd, n.* an oxide with one oxygen atom in the molecule. [Gr. *monos.*]

monoxylon, *mon-oks'i-lon, n.* a canoe made from one log.—*adj.* **monox'ylous** [Gr.—*monos, xylon,* wood.]

monozygotic, *mon-ō-zī-got'ik, adj.* developed from one zygote. [Gr. *monos,* and **zygote.**]

Monroeism, *mon-rō'izm, n.* (or **Monroe doctrine**) President Monroe's principle (1823) of the non-intervention of Europe in the affairs of the American continents (existing colonies apart).

Monseigneur, *mon'-sen-yər, n.* my lord : **a title in**

France given to a person of high birth or rank, esp. to bishops, &c. (written *Mgr.*) : the Dauphin :— *pl.* Messeigneurs (*me-sen-yạr*).—*n.* Monsignor (*mon-sēn'yạr*; It. *mon-sin-yōr'*; It. from Fr.), Monsignore (*-yō'rā*), conferred on prelates and on dignitaries of the papal household—also *pl.* Monsigno'ri (*-rē*).—*n.* Monsieur (*mạs-yạ*), sir : a title of courtesy in France = *Mr* in English (printed *M.* or in full) : the eldest brother of the king of France : a Frenchman generally—arch. and illiterate or grotesque, moun'seer (or *-sēr'*) : a French gentleman :—*pl.* Messieurs (Fr. *mes-yạ*, written *MM.*; Eng. *mes'ərz*, written Messrs). -Monsieur de Paris, the public executioner. [Fr. *mon seigneur, sieur*, my lord—L. *meum seniōrem* (accus.), my elder.]

monsoon, *mon-soōn'*, *n.* a periodical wind of the Indian Ocean, S.W. from April to October, and N.E. the rest of the year : a similar wind elsewhere : in N. and W. India, the rains accompanying the S.W. monsoon.—*adj.* monsoon'al.— break of the monsoon, the first onset of the monsoon rain. [Port. *monção*—Malay *mūsim*—Ar. *mausim*, a time, a season.]

monster, *mon'stạr*, *n.* anything out of the usual course of nature : a prodigy : a fabulous animal : an abnormally formed animal or plant : a grotesque animal : a gigantic animal : anything gigantic : anything horrible from ugliness or wickedness.— *adj.* gigantic, huge.—*n.* monstrosity (*-stros'i-ti*; *obs.* monstruos'ity), the state or fact of being monstrous : marked abnormality : an abnormally formed animal, plant, part, or object : anything outrageously constructed.—*adj.* mon'strous (*obs.* mon'struous), out of the common course of nature : enormous : wonderful : horrible : outrageous : preposterous.—*adv.* (*arch.*) exceedingly. —*adv.* mon'strously.—*n.* mon'strousness. [Fr. *monstre*—L. *mōnstrum*, an omen, a monster— *monēre*, to warn.]

monstrance, *mon'strạns*, *n.* the receptacle in which the consecrated host is exposed in R.C. churches for the adoration of the people. [O.Fr., — L. *mōnstrāre*, to show.]

montage, *mon̄'-täzh'*, *n.* selection and piecing together of material for a cinematograph film with a view to effect. [Fr.,—*monter*, to mount.]

Montagnard, *mon̄'-tä-nyär*, *n.* one of the Mountain or the extreme democratic wing of the French Legislative Assembly (1st Oct. 1791 to 21st Sept. 1792), so called because sitting on the topmost benches. [Fr., mountaineer.]

montane, *mon'tān*, *adj.* mountainous : mountain-dwelling. [L. *montānus*—*mōns, montis*, a mountain.]

Montanism, *mon'tan-izm*, *n.* a 2nd-century heresy founded by the prophet and ' Paraclete ' *Montānus* of Phrygia—an ascetic reaction in favour of the old discipline and severity.—*n.* and *adj.* Mon'- tanist.—*adj.* Montanist'ic.

montant, *mont'ạnt*, *n.* a vertical member in panelling or framing : (*Shak.*) in fencing, apparently an upward blow (also, as if Sp., montant'o). [Fr.,— *monter*, to rise.]

montaria, *mont-ä-rē'ä*, *n.* in Brazil, a light canoe made of one log. [Port.]

Montbretia, *mon(t)-brēsh'yä*, *n.* a plant (Tritonia) of the iris family bearing bright orange-coloured flowers. [After a French botanist, Coquebert de *Montbret* (1780-1801).]

mont-de-piété, *mon̄'-dạ-pyä-tā* (Fr.), monte di pietà (*mon'tä dē pyä-tä'* (It.), *n.* a state pawnshop. [Fund (lit. mound) of pity or piety.]

monte, *mon'tā, -ti*, *n.* a shrubby tract, a forest : a Spanish-American gambling card-game.—three-card monte, a Mexican three-card trick. [Sp., mountain, scrub, cards remaining after a deal— L. *mōns, montis*, a mountain.]

monteith, *mạn-*, *mon-tēth'*, *n.* a large 17th- or 18th-century bowl, usually of silver, fluted and scalloped, for cooling punch-glasses (said to be named from 'a fantastical Scot ' who wore his cloak so scalloped) : a cotton handkerchief with white spots on a coloured ground (from Glasgow manufacturers).

montem, *mon'tem*, *n.* a former custom of Eton boys to go every third Whit-Tuesday to a hillock on the Bath road and exact ' salt-money ' from passers-by, for the university expenses of the senior scholar or school captain. [L. *ad montem*, to the hill.]

montero, *mon-tā'rō*, *n.* a huntsman : a Spanish horseman's helmet-like cap with a flap.—Also monte'ro-cap'. [Sp. *montero*, a huntsman—*monte* —L. *mōns, montis*, a mountain.]

Montessorian, *mon-tes-ōr'i-ạn*, *adj.* pertaining to Dr Maria *Montessori* or her method (*c.* 1900) of education, insisting on spontaneity and freedom from restraint.

montgolfier, *mon(t)-gol'fi-ạr*, *n.* a fire-balloon. [From the brothers Joseph Michel and Jacques Étienne *Montgolfier*, of Annonay, who sent up the first in 1783.]

month, *munth*, *n.* the moon's period : one of the twelve conventional divisions of the year, or its length—a *calendar* month.—*n.* month'ling, a month-old child.—*adj.* month'ly, performed in a month : done, recurring, or appearing once a month.—*n.* a monthly publication : a monthly rose : (*pl.*) the menses.—*adv.* once a month : in every month.—anomalistic month, the interval between the moon's perigee passages = 27·5545 days ; lunar month, a month reckoned by the moon : a synodic month ; monthly nurse, a nurse who attends a woman in the first month after childbirth ; monthly rose, a rose supposed to bloom every month ; month of Sundays, a tediously long time ; month's mind (see mind) ; sidereal, or stellar, month, the time in which the moon passes round the ecliptic to the same point among the stars = 27·3217 days ; solar month, one-twelfth of a solar year ; synodic month, the period of the moon's phases = 29·5306 days ; tropical, or periodic, month, from the moon's passing the equinox till she again reaches it = 27·3216 days. [O.E. *mónath*—*móna*, moon.]

monticellite, *mon-ti-sel'īt*, *n.* an orthorhombic calcium magnesium silicate. [After the Italian mineralogist Teodoro *Monticelli* (1759-1845).]

monticolous, *mon-tik'ə-lạs*, *adj.* mountain-dwelling. [L. *monticola*, a mountain-dweller—*mōns, montis,* mountain, *colĕre*, to inhabit.]

monticulus, *mon-tik'ū-lạs*, *n.* a little elevation— also mon'ticle and mon'ticule.—*adjs.* montic'- ulate, montic'ulous, having small projections. [L. *monticulus*, dim. of *mōns* mountain.]

montre, *mon̄'tr'*, *n.* the visible pipes of an organ, usually the open diapason. [Fr., sample, show.]

monture, *mon'tūr*, *mon̄'-tūr*, *n.* a mounting, setting, frame. [Fr.]

monument, *mon'ū-mṇt* (*obs.* amd *Scot.* mon'i- ment), *n.* anything that preserves the memory of a person or an event, a building, pillar, tomb, tablet, statue, &c. : any structure, natural or artificial, considered as an object of beauty or of interest as a relic of the past : a historic document or record (sometimes confused with muniment) : a relic, indication, or trace : a notable or enduring example : (*Spens.*) a warning token or admonition : (*Shak.*) a prodigy.—*v.t.* to commemorate by or on a monument.—*adj.* monumental (*-ment'ạl*), of or relating to or of the nature of a monument, tomb, memento, or token : memorial : massive and lasting : vast : impressive : amazing.—*adv.* monument'ally. [L. *monumentum, monimentum* — *monēre*, to remind.]

mony, *mun'i*, a Scots form of many.

monyplies, *mun'i-plīz*. See manyplies.

monzonite, *mon'zon-īt*, *n.* a coarse-grained intermediate igneous rock. [Monte *Monzoni* in the Dolomite Mountains.]

moo, *moō, v.i.* to low.—*n.* a cow's low. [Imit.]

mooch, mouch, *mōōch, v.i.* to play truant : to go blackberrying : to slouch about : to skulk : to loiter : to sponge.—*v.t.* to pilfer.—*n.* the act of mooching.—*n.* mooch'er, mouch'er. [Perh. O.Fr. *muchier*, to hide; cf. **miche**.]

mood, *mōōd*, *n.* (*gram.*) a form of the verb to express the mode or manner of an action or of a state of being: (*log.*) the form of the syllogism as determined by the quantity and quality of its three constituent propositions : in mediaeval music, mode in the sense of relative time value. [**mode.**]

Neutral vowels in unaccented syllables : *el'ə-mṇt, in'fṇnt, ran'dəm*

mood, *mōōd*, *n.* temporary state of the emotions: anger, heat of temper. — *adv.* **mood'ily.** — *n.* **moodi'ness,** sullenness.—*adjs.* **mood'y,** indulging in moods: sullen: (*obs.*) angry; **mood'y-mad',** (*Shak.*) mad with anger. [O.E. *mōd*, mind; cf. Ger. *mut*, courage.]

mooi, *mō'i*, *adj.* (*S.Afr.*) fine—a general word of commendation. [Du.]

mooktar. See **mukhtar.**

mool, *mōōl*, a Scots form of **mould.**

moola(h). See **mulla(h).**

moon, *mōōn*, *n.* the earth's satellite: a satellite: a month: anything in the shape of a moon or crescent: (*fort.*) a crescent-shaped outwork.—*v.t.* to adorn with moons or crescents.—*v.i.* to wander about or gaze vacantly at anything.—*n.* **moon'-beam,** a beam of light from the moon.—*adj.* **moon'-blind,** affected with moon-eye: blinded by the moon: night-blind: dim-sighted, purblind.—*ns.* **moon'-bow,** a rainbow cast by the moon; **moon'calf,** a false conception or fleshy mass formed in the womb: a monster: a deformed creature: a dolt.—*adj.* **mooned,** marked with the figure of a moon.—*ns.* **moon'er,** one who moons about; **moon'-eye,** a disease affecting horses' eyes: an American fresh-water shad-like fish; **moon'face,** a full, round face—a point of beauty in the East.—*adj.* **moon'-faced.**—*ns.* **moon'-fish,** the opah or other silvery disk-shaped fish; **moon'-flower,** the ox-eye daisy; **moon'-glade,** the track of moonlight on water; **moon'-god, -goddess,** a god or goddess representing or associated with the moon.—*adj.* **moon'ish,** like the moon: variable: inconstant.—*n.* **moon'-knife,** a leather-worker's crescent-shaped knife. — *adj.* **moon'less,** destitute of moonlight.—*n.* **moon'-light,** the light of the moon—sunlight reflected from the moon's surface: smuggled spirit.—*adj.* lighted by the moon: occurring in moonlight.—*ns.* **moon'lighter,** in Ireland, one who committed agrarian outrages by night about 1880; a moonshiner; **moon'lighting.**—*adjs.* **moon'lit,** lit or illumined by the moon; **moon'-loved,** loved by the moon. — *n.* **moon'-mad'ness,** lunacy, once thought to be connected with the moon's changes. —*adj.* (*Scott*) **moon'-raised,** excited or maddened by the moon.—*ns.* **moon'-raker,** a moon-sail: a Wiltshireman (from a Gotham story); **moon'-raking,** the following of crazy fancies; **moon'-rise,** the rising of the moon; **moon'-sail,** a small sail, sometimes carried above the skyscraper; **moon'seed,** a plant (Menispermum) with lunate seeds; **moon'set,** the setting of the moon; **moon'shine,** the shining of the moon: (*fig.*) show without reality: (*Shak.*) a month: smuggled spirits.—*adj.* lighted by the moon: made of moonshine, bodiless. — *n.* **moon'shiner,** a smuggler or illicit distiller of spirits.—*adj.* **moon'-shiny,** lighted by the moon: visionary, unreal.—*n.* **moon'-stone,** an opalescent orthoclase felspar, perh. sometimes selenite.—*adj.* **moon'struck** (also **moon'-stricken**), affected by the moon, lunatic, crazed.—*n.* **moon'wort,** a eusporangiate fern (*Botrychium Lunaria*) with lunate pinnae, or other of the genus: the plant honesty (from its silvery septum).—*adj.* **moon'y,** of or relating to the moon: moon-like: crescent-shaped: bearing a crescent: round and shining: moonlit: inclined to moon: fatuous: (*slang*) tipsy.—*n.* a noodle.—**eggs in moonshine,** an old dish, fried eggs with onions and various flavourings; **moonlight flitting,** a removal by night, with rent unpaid. [O.E. *mōna*; cf. Ger. *mond*, L. *mēnsis*, Gr. *mēn*.]

moonshee. Same as **munshi.**

Moon-type, *mōōn'-tīp*, *n.* a system of embossed lettering for the blind, invented by Dr William Moon (1847).

moop. Same as **moup.**

moor, *mōōr*, *n.* a wide tract of untilled ground, often covered with heath, and having a poor, peaty soil: a heath: (*Scot.*) **muir** (*mər, mōr, mūr*). —*ns.* **moor'-band,** a hard ferruginous layer formed under moorland soil (also **moor'-band pan, moor'-pan**); **moor'-buzz'ard,** the marsh-harrier; **moor'cock, moor'fowl,** the red grouse or heath-

cock; **moor'hen,** the water-hen: the female moorfowl; **moor'-ill,** (*Scot.*) a cattle disease of moorland districts, marked by haemoglobin in the urine.—*adjs.* **moor'ish, moor'y,** resembling a moor: sterile: marshy: boggy.—*n.* **moor'-land,** a tract of moor: moorish country.—*adj.* ot moorland.—*ns.* **moor'log,** a deposit of decayed woody material under a marsh, &c.; **moor'man,** a dweller in moors; **moor'-pout, muir'-pout, -poot** (-*powt*, -*pōōt*), a young grouse. [O.E. *mór.*]

moor, *mōōr*, *v.t.* to fasten by cable or anchor.—*v.i.* to make fast a ship, boat, &c.: to be made fast.—*ns.* **moor'age,** condition of being moored: act of mooring: a due paid for mooring: a place for mooring; **moor'ing,** act of mooring: that which serves to moor or confine a ship: in *pl.* the place or condition of a ship thus moored; **moor'ing-mast.** [Prob. from an unrecorded O.E. word answering to M.Du. *māren.*]

Moor, *mōōr*, *n.* a Mauretanian: a member of the mixed Arab and Berber people of Morocco and the Barbary coast: one of the Arab and Berber conquerors and occupants of Spain from 711 to 1492: in some countries, a Mohammedan: a dark-coloured person generally, a negro:—*fem.* **Moor'ess.**—*n.* **Moor'ery,** a Moorish quarter.—*adj.* **Moor'ish.** [Fr. *More, Maure*—L. *Maurus*, doubtfully connected with Byzantine Gr. *mauros*, black.]

moorva. Same as **murva.**

moose, *mōōs*, *n.* the American elk: a member of an American secret fraternity:—*pl.* **moose.**—*n.* **moose'-yard,** an area where the moose tread down the snow and spend the winter. [Algonquian *mus, moos.*]

moot, *mōōt*, *n.* orig. a meeting: (*hist.*) a deliberative or administrative assembly or court: its meeting-place: discussion: a law students' discussion of a hypothetical case.—*v.t.* to argue, dispute: to propose for discussion.—*v.i.* to dispute, plead.—*adj.* debatable.—*adj.* **moot'able,** debatable.—*ns.* **moot'er** or **moot'-court,** a meeting for discussion of hypothetical cases; **moot'-hall, -house,** a town-hall or council chamber: a hall for moot-courts; **moot'-hill,** a hill of meeting on which the moot was held (often confused with **mote-hill**); **moot'ing; moot'man,** a law-student who argues in moots.—**moot case,** a hypothetical case for discussion; **moot point,** an undecided or disputed point. [O.E. (*ge*)*mót* (n.), *mótian* (vb.), akin to *métan*, to meet.]

moove, an old spelling of **move.**

mop, *mop*, *n.* a bunch of rags, yarn, or the like, on the end of a stick, for washing, removing dust, soaking up liquid, &c.: any similar instrument, as for cleansing a wound, polishing, &c.: a thick outstanding head of hair: an act of mopping: (*prov.*) a hiring-fair (probably from the custom of carrying a badge of occupation).—*v.t.* to wipe, dab, soak up, or remove with a mop or as if with a mop: to clear away or dispose of as residue:—*pr.p.* **mopp'ing;** *pa.t.* and *pa.p.* **mopped.**—*adj.* **mop'-head'ed,** having a shaggy, unkempt head of hair.—*ns.* **mopp'er; mopp'et,** a rag-doll: a little woolly dog: a doll-like woman: a term of endearment or contempt, esp. for a girl or child.—*adj.* **mopp'y,** (*slang*) drunk.—*ns.* **mop'stick,** the handle of a mop: a hand-rail nearly circular in section: (also **map'stick**) a rod for raising a piano damper; **mop'sy,** a dowdy: a slattern: a term of endearment; **mop'-up',** an action of mopping up.—**mops and brooms,** half-drunk: out of sorts; **mop up,** to clear away or clean up with a mop: to clear away, dispose of, what is left of the enemy. [Possibly from O.Fr. *mappe*—L. *mappa*, a napkin; or possibly from the name Mabel.]

mop, *mop*, *n.* a grimace.—*v.i.* to grimace. [Cf. Du. *moppen*, to pout.]

mope, *mōp*, *v.i.* to go aimlessly and listlessly: to yield to low spirits.—*v.t.* to make spiritless.—*n.* a listless person: (esp. in *pl.*) moping.—*adv.* **mop'ingly.**—*adj.* **mop'ish,** dull: spiritless.—*adv.* **mop'ishly.**—*ns.* **mop'ishness; mop'us,** one who mopes.—*adj.* **mop'y.** [Origin obscure.]

mopoke, *mō'pōk, n.* an Australian frogmouth : a New Zealand owl : a silly.—Also **mope'-hawk, more'-pork.** [From the cry of the owl and of a kindred Australian species, mistakenly attributed to the frogmouth.]

mopus, *mop'əs,* **mawpus,** *maw'pəs, n. (slang)* a small coin.

moquette, *mō-ket', n.* a carpet material with a loose velvety pile—the back thick canvas, &c. [Fr.]

mora, *mō'rä, n. (law)* delay, esp. unjustifiable : *(pros.)* the duration of a short syllable or half that of a long. [L., delay.]

mora, morra, *mor'ä, n.* the game of guessing how many fingers are held up. [It. *mora.*]

moraceous. See under **morus.**

moraine, *mo-rān', n.* a continuous marginal line of débris borne on or left by a glacier : a garden imitation of this.—*adj.* **morain'ic.** [Fr.]

moral, *mor'əl, adj.* of or relating to character or conduct considered as good or evil : ethical : conformed to or directed towards right, virtuous : esp. virtuous in matters of sex : capable of knowing right and wrong : subject to the moral law : supported by evidence of reason or probability—opp. to *demonstrative* : (*Shak.*) moralising.—*n.* in *pl.* writings on ethics : the doctrine or practice of the duties of life : moral philosophy or ethics : principles and conduct, esp. sexual : in *sing.* the practical lesson that can be drawn from anything : an exposition of such lesson by way of conclusion : a symbol : (sometimes *mor-äl'*, after Ger. *moral* or Fr. *morale*) morality : (*slang*) a certainty : (*slang*) an exact counterpart : (usu. *mil.*) ; spelt **morale** to look French and suggest the Fr. pron. *mor-äl'*—the French word in this sense is *moral*) condition with respect to discipline and confidence, pride, fixity of purpose, faith in the cause fought for, &c.—*v.t.* and *v.i.* to moralise.—*ns.* **morale,** *mor-äl'* (Fr. *morale*), morality : (*mil.*) see above (**moral**) ; **moralisa'tion,** act of moralising, explanation in a moral sense.—*v.t.* **mor'alise,** to apply to a moral purpose : to explain in a moral sense : to make moral : to furnish with matter of morality.—*v.i.* to speak or write on moral subjects : to make moral reflections.—*ns.* **mor'aliser ; mor'alism,** a moral maxim : moral counsel : morality as distinct from religion ; **mor'alist,** one who teaches morals, or who practises moral duties : a moral as distinguished from a religious man : one who prides himself on his morality.—*adj.* **moralist'ic.**—*n.* **morality** (*mor-al'i-ti*), quality of being moral : that which renders an action right or wrong : the practice of moral duties apart from religion : virtue : the doctrine of actions as right or wrong : ethics : a mediaeval allegorical drama in which virtues and vices appear as characters (also **moral'ity-play**).—*n.* **mor'aller,** (*Shak.*) a moralist.—*adv.* **mor'ally,** in a moral manner : in respect of morals : to all intents and purposes, practically.—**moral agent,** one who acts under a knowledge of right and wrong ; **moral certainty,** a likelihood great enough to be acted on, although not capable of being certainly proved ; **moral courage,** power of facing disapprobation and ridicule ; **moral defeat,** a success so qualified as to count as a defeat, or to point towards defeat ; **moral faculty,** moral sense ; **moral law,** a law or rules for life and conduct, founded on what is right and wrong : the law of conscience : that part of the Old Testament which relates to moral principles, esp. the ten commandments ; **moral philosophy,** the philosophy or science of right and wrong, and duty, ethics ; **moral sense,** that power of the mind which knows or judges actions to be right or wrong, and determines conduct accordingly : tropological interpretation of the Bible, the finding of a secondary meaning relating to conduct ; **moral support,** the help afforded by approbation ; **moral theology,** ethics treated with reference to a divine source ; **moral victory,** a defeat in appearance, but in some important sense a real victory. [L. *morālis*—*mōs, mōris,* manner, custom, (esp. in *pl.*) morals.]

morall, *n.* (Shak., Mids. N. Dr.) amended by editors to **mural,** but poss. a misprint for **wall.**

morass, *mo-ras', n.* a tract of soft, wet ground : a marsh.—*adj.* **morass'y.**—**morass ore,** bog-iron ore. [Du. *moeras*—O.Fr. *maresc,* influenced by Du. *moer,* moor.]

morat, *mō'rat, n.* a drink made of honey and mulberry juice. [L.L. *mōrātum*—*mōrum,* mulberry.]

moratorium, *mor-ə-tō'ri-əm, n.* an emergency measure authorising the suspension of payments of debts for a given time : the period thus declared : —*pl.* **morator'ia, morator'iums.**—*adj.* **moratory** (*mor'ə-tə-ri*), delaying : deferring. [Neut. of L.L. *morātōrius,* adj. from *mora,* delay.]

Moravian, *mo-rä'vi-ən, adj.* pertaining to *Moravia* or the Moravians.—*n.* one of the people of Moravia : one of the *Unitas Fratrum* or *United Brethren,* a small body of Protestants of extraordinary missionary energy, founded in the 15th century.—*n.* **Mora'vianism.** [L. *Moravia,* Moravia—*Morava,* the river March.]

Moravian, *mo-rä'vi-ən, adj.* of the old province or the modern county of *Moray.*—*n.* a Moray man. [L.L. *Moravia,* Moray.]

moray, murray, murrey, murry, *mō'rä, mō-rä', mur'i, mur-ä', n.* an eel of the family Muraenidae. [Port. *moreia*—L. *mūraena*—Gr. *(s)mўraina,* fem. of *(s)mўros,* eel.]

morbid, *mor'bid, adj.* sickly : unwholesome : inclined to dwell on unwholesome or horrible thoughts : relating to, or of the nature of, disease. —*n.* **morbid'ity,** sickliness : unwholesomeness : ratio of sickness.—*adv.* **mor'bidly.**—*n.* **mor'bidness.** [L. *morbidus*—*morbus,* disease.]

morbidezza, *mor-bi-det'sä, n.* that quality of flesh-painting which gives the impression of life. [It.]

morbilli, *mor-bil'i, n.pl.* measles.—*adjs.* **morbill'-iform, morbill'ous.** [L.L. dim. of L. *morbus,* disease.]

morbus, *mor'bəs, n.* disease (Lat., used in phrases). —*adjs.* **morbif'erous,** disease-bringing ; **morbif'ic,** disease-causing.—**morbus gallicus,** the French disease, syphilis. [L.]

morceau, *mor'sō', n.* a piece of music : a short literary composition :—*pl.* **morceaux** (*-sō'*).— **morceau de salon** (*də-sä-lon⁰ ; mus.*), a drawing-room piece. [Fr. ; see **morsel.**]

mordacious, *mor-dä'shəs, adj.* given to biting : biting in quality (*lit.* or *fig.*).—*adv.* **mordä'ciously.** —*ns.* **mordacity** (*-das'i-ti*), **mordancy** (*mor'-dən-si*).—*adj.* **mor'dant,** biting : incisive : serving to fix dyes, paints, gold-leaf.—*n.* a corroding substance : any substance that combines with and fixes a dyestuff in material that cannot be dyed direct : a substance used to cause paint or gold-leaf to adhere.—*v.t.* to treat with a mordant. —*adv.* **mor'dantly.** [L. *mordēre,* to bite.]

mordent, *mor'dənt, n.* (*mus.*) a grace in which the principal note is preceded in performance by itself and the note below (twice in the double mordent) : the character indicating it : sometimes extended to other graces.—**inverted mordent,** the pralltriller. [Ger.,—It. *mordente.*]

more, *mōr, adj.* (serving as *comp.* of **many** and **much**) in greater number or quantity : (now *rare*) greater in size or importance : additional : other besides.—*adv.* to a greater degree : rather : again : longer : further : moreover.—*n.* a greater thing : something further or in addition :—*superl., adj.,* and *adv.* **most** (*mōst*).—*adj.* **mo'rish, more'-ish,** such that one wants more.—**any more,** anything additional : further ; **more and more,** continually increasing ; **more by token,** in proof of this, besides ; **more or less,** about : in round numbers ; **no more,** nothing in addition : never again : no longer in existence : dead. [O.E. *māra,* greater ; as an adv. **more** has superseded **mo.**]

more, *mōr, n.* a root : a stump : (*Spens.*) a plant. [O.E. *moru, more,* carrot, parsnip ; Ger. *möhre.*]

moreen, *mo-rēn', n.* a stout corded stuff, woollen, cotton, or both, often watered. [Poss. conn. with **moire.**]

morel, *mor-el', n.* any edible discomycete fungus of the genus Morchella. [Fr. *morille ;* cf. O.H.G. *morhila* (Ger. *morchel*), a mushroom ; **more** (2).]

morel, *mor-el', n.* a nightshade, esp. black night-

shade: (*obs.*; also *mor'əl*) a dark-coloured horse.—
adj. blackish. [L.L. *morellus*, blackish, perh.—L.
mōrum, a mulberry, perh. Late Gr. *mauros*, black.]
morel, *mor-əl'*, *mor'əl*, **morell'o,** *-ō*, *n.* a dark-red
cherry, much used in cooking and for cherry
brandy. [Possibly—It. *morello*, dark-coloured (see
preceding); possibly—Flem. *marelle*—It. *amarella*,
a dim. from L. *amārus*, bitter.]
morendo, *mo-ren'dō*, *adj.* and *adv.* (*mus.*) dying
away, in speed and tone. [It., dying.]
moreover, *mōr-ō'vər*, *adv.* more over or beyond
what has been said: further: besides: also.
[more, over.]
morepork. See mopoke.
Moresco, *mor-es'kō*, *n.* a Moorish dance or morris-
dance (It. *Moresca*): a Moor or Morisco.—*adj.*
Moorish. [It., Moorish.]
Moresque, *mor-esk'*, *adj.* in the Moorish manner.—
n. an arabesque. [Fr.,—It. *Moresco.*]
Moreton Bay, *mōr'tən bā*, the first settlement in
Queensland.—**Moreton Bay chestnut,** an Australian papilionaceous tree (*Castanospermum aus-
trale*): its chestnut-flavoured seed.
morganatic, *mor-gən-at'ik*, *adj.* of, by, or of the
nature of a left-handed marriage, that is, a marriage
(in some countries) between persons of unequal
rank (latterly only where one is of a reigning or
mediatised house), the marriage being valid, the
children legitimate, but unable to inherit the higher
rank, the wife (if the lower-born) not being granted
the husband's title.—*adv.* **morganat'ically.** [L.L.
morganātica, a gift from a bridegroom to his bride;
cf. Ger. *morgengabe*, O.E. *morgengifu*, a morning gift.]
morgay, *mor'gā*, *n.* the small spotted dogfish or
bounce. [Cornish and Welsh *morgi*—*mōr*, sea,
ci, dog.]
morgen, *mor'gən*, *n.* a unit of land-measurement—
in Holland, S. Africa, and parts of the U.S.A., a
little over two acres; in Norway, Denmark, and
Prussia, about two-thirds of an acre. [Du. and
Ger.; perh. *morgen*, morning, hence a morning's
ploughing.]
morgenstern, *mor'gən-stərn, -shtern, n.* a morning-
star (weapon). [Ger.]
Morglay, *mor'glā*, *n.* Sir Bevis of Hampton's sword:
hence, a sword. [Cf. claymore.]
morgue, *morg*, *n.* a place where dead bodies are
laid out for identification: a place, as in a newspaper office, where miscellaneous material for
reference is kept. [Fr.]
morgue, *morg*, *n.* hauteur. [Fr.]
moria, *mō'ri-ä*, *n.* folly. [Gr. *mōriā*.]
moribund, *mor'i-bund*, *adj.* about to die: in a
dying state. [L. *moribundus*—*morī*, to die.]
moriche, *mor-ē'chä*, *n.* the miriti palm. [Carib.]
morigeration, *mō-rij-ə-rā'shən*, *n.* deferential behaviour.—*adjs.* **morig'erate, morig'erous.** [L.
mōrigerātiō, -ōnis—*mōs, mōris*, custom, humour,
gerĕre, to bear.]
Moringa, *mor-ing'gä*, *n.* the horse-radish tree genus,
constituting a family **Moringā'ceae,** apparently
linking the poppies with the Leguminosae. [Perh.
Sinh. *murungā*.]
morion, morrion, *mor'* or *mōr'i-ən, n.* an open
helmet, without visor or beaver. [Fr., prob. from
Sp. *morrión*—*morra*, crown of the head.]
morion, *mor'i-ən, n.* black quartz. [Fr.]
Morisco, *mo-ris'kō, n.* a Moor, esp. a Christianised
Moor in Spain after the fall of Granada in 1492:
(*obs.*) the Moorish language: morisco, a morris-
dance or dancer: an arabesque.—*adj.* Moorish.—
(*obs.*) Morisk'.
Morisonian, *mor-i-sō'ni-ən, n.* a member of the
Evangelical Union, formed in 1843 by the Rev.
James Morison (1816-93), after his separation from
the United Secession Church—incorporated with
the Congregational Union of Scotland in 1896.—
n. Moriso'nianism.
morkin, *mor'kin, n.* a beast that has died by accident.
—*n.* **mor'ling, mort'ling,** a sheep dead of disease:
its wool. [A.Fr. *mortekine*—L. *morticīna* (fem. adj.),
carrion—*mors*, death.]
mormaor, *mor-mä'ər, n.* (*hist.*) a high steward.
[Gael. *mormaer*, now *mòrmhaor*—*mòr*, great, *maor*,
steward.]

Mormon, *mor'mən, n.* one of a religious sect in
Utah, U.S., openly polygamous till 1890, calling
itself *The Church of Jesus Christ of Latter-day
Saints*, founded in 1830 by Joseph Smith, whose
supplement to the Bible, the *Book of Mormon*, was
given out as translated from the golden plates of
one *Mormon.*—*ns.* **Mor'monism**; **Mor'monite.**
Mormops, *mor'mops, n.* a genus of repulsive-
looking American leaf-nosed bats. [Gr. *mormō*,
a bugbear, *ōps*, face.]
morn, *morn, n.* the first part of the day: morning.
— **the morn,** (*Scot.*) tomorrow; **the morn's
morn** or **morning,** tomorrow morning; **the
morn's nicht,** tomorrow night. [M.E. *morwen*—
O.E. *morgen*; Ger. *morgen*.]
morne, *morn, n.* the blunt head of a jousting-lance.
— *adjs.* **morné** (*mor-nā'*), of a lion rampant,
without teeth or claws; **morned,** (*her.*) blunted.
[Fr. *morner* (pa.p. *morné*), to blunt.]
morne, *morn, adj.* dismal, gloomy, sombre. [Fr.]
morning, *morn'ing, n.* the first part of the day:
the early part of anything: an early dram: a
slight repast before recognised breakfast.—*adj.* of
the morning: taking place or being in the morning.
—*ns.* **morn'ing-dress,** dress such as is usually
worn in the morning, as opposed to *evening-dress*;
morn'ing-gift, a gift made by the husband to the
wife on the morning after marriage; **morn'ing-
glo'ry,** an American Ipomoea or Convolvulus,
with showy purple, pink, or white flowers;
morn'ing-gown, a gown for wearing in the
morning; **morn'ing-land,** the east; **morn'ing-
prayer,** prayer in the morning: matins; **morn'-
ing-room,** a sitting-room for use in the morning.—
adv. **morn'ings,** (now *rare* or *dial.*) in the morning.
—*ns.* **morn'ing-sick'ness,** nausea and vomiting
in the morning, common in the early stages of
pregnancy; **morn'ing-star,** a planet, esp. Venus,
when it rises before the sun: a precursor: a
mediaeval weapon, a spiky ball attached directly
or by a chain to a handle; **morn'ing-tide,** the
morning time: early part; **morn'ing-watch,** the
watch between 4 and 8 a.m. [Contr. of M.E.
morwening; cf. **morn.**]
morocco, *mə-rok'ō, n.* a fine goat-skin leather
tanned with sumac, first brought from *Morocco*:
a sheep-skin leather imitation of it: a very strong
ale, anciently brewed in Westmorland.—*adj.* consisting of morocco.—**French morocco,** an inferior
kind of Levant morocco, with small grain; **Levant
morocco,** a fine quality of morocco, with large
grain; **Persian morocco,** a morocco finished on
the grain side.
moron, *mōr'on, n.* a somewhat feeble-minded
person: one who remains throughout life at the
mental age of eight to twelve.—Also *adj.* [Gr.
mōros, foolish.]
morose, *mə-rōs', adj.* sour-tempered: gloomy:
severe.—*adv.* **morose'ly.**—*ns.* **morose'ness**; (*obs.*)
morosity (*-os'i-ti*). [L. *mōrōsus*, peevish—*mōs,
mōris*, manner.]
Morpheus, *mor'fūs, n.* Greek god of dreams, son
of Hypnos (sleep).—*adjs.* **morphē'an** (also *mor'*),
morphet'ic (irreg. formed). [Gr. *Morpheus*, lit.
moulder, shaper—*morphē*, shape.]
morphew, *mor'fū, n.* a skin eruption. [It. *morfea*.]
morphia, *mor'fi-ä, n.* morphine.—*ns.* **mor'phine**
(*-fēn*), the principal alkaloid in opium, used as a
hypnotic; **mor'phinism,** the effect of morphine
on the system: the habit of taking morphine;
morphinoma'nia; **morphinoma'niac.** [Gr.
Morpheus, god of dreams.]
morphic, *mor'fik, adj.* relating to form, morphological.—*ns.* **morphallax'is,** regeneration in a
changed form (Gr. *allaxis*, change); **morphogenesis** (*-fə-jen'i-sis*), the origin and development
of a part, organ, or organism.—*adj.* **morpho-
genet'ic.**—*ns.* **morphogeny** (*-foj'i-ni*), morphogenesis; **morphographer** (*-fog'rə-fər*), morpho-
phog'raphy, descriptive morphology.—*adjs.* **mor-
pholog'ic, -al.**—*ns.* **morphol'ogist**; **morphol'-
ogy,** the science of form, esp. that of the outer
form, inner structure, and development of living
organisms and their parts: also of the external
form of rocks and land-features: also of the forms

of words ; **morphō′sis**, morphogenesis. — *adjs.* **morphŏt′ic**, pertaining to morphosis ; **morphotrop′ic.**—*n.* **morphot′ropy**, the effect on crystalline form of the addition or substitution of an element or radical. [Gr. *morphē*, form.]

Morpho, *mor′fō, n.* a tropical American genus of brilliant and gigantic butterflies, often bright blue. [Gr. *Morphō*, a name of Aphrodite.]

morrhua, *mor′ōō-ä, n.* an old generic, now specific, name of the cod (*Gadus morrhua*). [L.L. *morrua*.]

morris, morrice, *mor′is,* **morr′is-dance,** *ns.* a dance, according to some of Moorish origin, which came to be associated with May games, with (latterly) Maid Marian, Robin Hood, the hobby-horse, and other characters, who had bells attached to their dress : a tune for the dance.—*v.i.* **morr′is,** to perform by dancing.—*ns.* **morr′is-dancer ; morr′is-pike,** (*Shak.*) a Moorish pike. [**Moorish.**]

morris. See **meril** (for **nine men's morris**, &c.).

Morris-tube, *mor′is-tūb, n.* a small-bore rifle-barrel inserted in the breech of a larger for short-range practice. [R. *Morris* (*d.* 1891), the inventor.]

morrow, *mor′ō, n.* the day following the present : tomorrow : the next following day : the time immediately after any event. [M.E. *morwe* for *morwen* ; cf. **morn.**]

morse, *mors, n.* the walrus. [Lappish *morsa*, or Finn. *mursu*.]

morse, *mors, n.* the fastening of a cope. [L. *morsus*, a bite, catch.]

Morse, *mors, n.* signalling by a code in which each letter is represented by a combination of dashes and dots or their equivalents, invented by Sam. F. B. *Morse* (1791-1872).—Also *adj.*

morsel, *mor′sal, n.* a bite or mouthful : a small piece of food : a choice piece of food, a dainty : a small piece of anything : a small person.—*v.t.* to divide into morsels : to apportion in small parcels. [O.Fr. *morsel* (Fr. *morceau*, It. *morsello*), dim. from L. *morsus*—*mordēre, morsum,* to bite.]

morsing-horn, *mor′sing-horn, n.* the small horn that used to hold the fine powder used for priming. [Fr. *amorcer*, to prime (a gun).]

morsure, *mors′ūr, n.* a bite.—*adj.* **mors′al.** [L. *morsus*, bite.]

mort, *mort, n.* (*obs.*) a flourish sounded at the death of a buck, &c., in hunting : a sheep that has died a natural death : a dead body.—*ns.* **mort′-bell**, a funeral bell : **mort′cloth**, a pall ; **mort′-head**, a death's-head ; **mort′-safe**, a heavy grating used to guard a corpse against resurrectionists ; **mort′-stone**, a wayside stone on which the bearers lay the bier for a rest. [Fr. *mort*, death, dead.]

mort, *mort, n.* (*dial.*) a great deal. [Origin obscure.]

mort, *mort, n.* (*cant*) a woman : a loose woman. [Origin obscure.]

mortal, *mor′tl, adj.* liable to death : causing death : deadly : fatal : punishable with death : involving the penalty of spiritual death, as opposed to *venial* : to the death : implacable : human : (*coll.*) very great : (*coll.*) tediously long : (*coll.*) without exception : (*Scot. coll.*) very drunk.—*n.* a human being.—*adv.* (*dial.* or *coll.*) extremely : confoundedly.—*v.t.* **mor′talise**, to make mortal.—*n.* **mortality** (*-tal′i-ti*), condition of being mortal : death : frequency or number of deaths, esp. in proportion to population : the human race, nature, or estate.—*adv.* **mor′tally.**—*adj.* **mor′tal-star′ing**, (*Shak.*) deadly-visaged.—**bills of mortality** (see **bill**). [L. *mortālis*—*morī*, to die.]

mortar, *mor′tər, n.* a vessel in which substances are pounded with a pestle : a short piece of artillery for throwing a heavy shell, a bomb, a life-line, &c. : a cement of lime, sand, and water.—*v.t.* to join or plaster with mortar.—*n.* **mor′tar-board**, a square board with a handle beneath for holding mortar : a square-topped college cap. [O.E. *mortere*—L. *mortārium*, a mortar, matter pounded.]

mortgage, *mor′gij, n.* a conditional conveyance of, or lien upon, land or other property as security for the performance of some condition, as the payment of money, becoming void on the performance of the condition : the act of conveying, or the deed effecting it.—*v.t.* to pledge as security for a debt.—*ns.* **mortgagee**, one to whom a

mortgage is made or given ; **mort′gagor** (*-jər*), one who mortgages his property.—Also (sometimes) **mort′gager.** [O.Fr.,—*mort*, dead, *gage*, a pledge.]

mortice. See **mortise.**

mortician, *mor-tish′an, n.* (*U.S. vulg.*) an undertaker. [L. *mors, mortis*, death.]

mortiferous, *mor-tif′ər-əs, adj.* death-bringing : fatal.—*n.* **mortif′erousness.** [L. *mors, mortis,* death, *ferre*, to bring.]

mortify, *mor′ti-fī, v.t.* (*obs.*) to kill : to destroy the vital functions of : to deaden : to subdue by severities and penance : to vex in a humiliating way : (*Scots law*) to dispose of by mortification. —*v.i.* to lose vitality : to gangrene : to be subdued : to practise asceticism :—*pr.p.* **mor′-tifying ;** *pa.t.* and *pa.p.* **mor′tified.**—*adj.* **mortif′ic**, death-bringing : deadly.—*n.* **mortification** (*mor-ti-fi-kā′shən*), act of mortifying or state of being mortified : the death of part of the body : a bringing under of the passions and appetites by a severe or strict manner of living : humiliation : chagrin : that which mortifies or vexes : (*Scots law*) a bequest to some charitable institution.—*adj.* **mort′ified.**—*n.* **mor′tifier.**—*adj.* and *n.* **mor′tifying.** [Fr. *mortifier*—L.L. *mortificāre*, to cause death to—*mors, mortis,* death, *facēre*, to make.]

mortise, *mor′tis, n.* a hole made to receive a tenon—also **mor′tice.**—*v.t.* to cut a mortise in : to join by a mortise and tenon. [Fr. *mortaise* ; ety. unknown.]

mortmain, *mort′mān, n.* the transfer of property to a corporation, which is said to be a dead hand, or one that can never part with it again.—**statutes of mortmain**, acts of parliament restricting or forbidding the giving of property to religious houses. [Fr. *morte* (fem.), dead, *main*—L. *manus*, hand.]

mortuary, *mort′ū-ər-i, adj.* connected with death or burial.—*n.* a place for the temporary reception of the dead : a payment to the parish priest on the death of a parishioner or to a bishop or archdeacon on the death of a priest. [L. *mortuārius*—*mortuus*, dead, *morī*, to die.]

morula, *mor′ū-lä, n.* a solid spherical mass of cells resulting from the cleavage of an ovum : framboesia.—*adj.* **mor′ular.** [L. *mōrum*, a mulberry.]

Morus, *mō′rəs, n.* the mulberry genus, giving name to the family **Morā′ceae**, including fig, breadfruit, Ceará rubber.—*adj.* **morā′ceous.** [L. *mōrus*, a mulberry tree ; cf. Gr. *mŏrĕā*.]

mosaic, *mō-zā′ik, n.* the fitting together in a design of small pieces of coloured marble, glass, &c. : a piece of work of this kind : anything of similar appearance, or composed by the piecing together of different things : a leaf-mosaic : leaf-mosaic disease (or **mosaic disease**) : a hybrid with the parental characters side by side and not blended. —*adj.* relating to, or composed of, mosaic.—*adv.* **mosa′ically.**—*n.* **mosā′icist** (*-i-sist*), a worker in mosaic.—**mosaic gold**, an alloy of copper and zinc, ormolu, a stannic sulphide. [Fr. *mosaïque*—L.L. *mosaicum, mūsaicum*—*mūsa*—Gr. *mousa*, a muse ; cf. L.L. *mūsaeum* or *mūsīvum* (*opus*), mosaic (work).]

Mosaic, *mō-zā′ik, adj.* pertaining to *Moses*, the great Jewish lawgiver.—*n.* **Mō′saism.**—**Mosaic Law**, the law of the Jews given by Moses at Mount Sinai.

Mosasauros, *mō-sə-saw′rəs, n.* a gigantic Cretaceous fossil pythonomorph reptile. [L. *Mosa*, the Maas, near which the first was found, Gr. *sauros*, a lizard.]

moschatel, *mos-kə-tel′, n.* a small plant (*Adoxa Moschatellina*), constituting in itself the Adoxaceae, by some included in the honeysuckle family, with pale-green flowers and a supposed musky smell. [Fr. *moscatelle*—It. *moschatella*—*moscato*, musk.]

moschiferous, *mos-kif′ər-əs, adj.* producing musk. [L.L. *moschus*, Gr. *moschos*, musk, L. *ferre*, to bring.]

mose, *mōz, v.i.* only in Shak., *Taming of the Shrew,* III. ii. 51—**to mose in the chine**, to have glanders. [Supposed to be for *mourn in the chine*,

---

Neutral vowels in unaccented syllables : *el′ə-mənt, in′fənt, ran′dəm*

perh.—Fr. *morve d'eschine*, glanders, running from the spine: the morbid matter of glanders was thought to come from the spine. Another suggestion is that *mose* is for *pose*, catarrh, turned into a verb.]

Moselle, *mo-zel'*, *n.* white wine from the district of the river *Moselle*, with an aromatic flavour.

mosey, *mō'zi*, *v.i.* (*Amer. slang*) to move along gently: to jog: to make off: to hurry. [Perh. for **vamose**.]

Moslem, *moz'lem*, *n.* a Mussulman or Mohammedan.—*adj.* of or belonging to the Mohammedans.—Also **Mus'lim**.—*n.* **Mos'lemism**. [Ar. *muslim*, pl. *muslimīn—salama*, to submit (to God); cf. **Mussulman, Islam**.]

moslings, *moz'lingz*, *n.pl.* the thin shavings taken off by the currier in dressing skins. [Perh. **morsellings**.]

mosque, *mosk*, *n.* a Mohammedan place of worship. [Fr. *mosquée*—It. *moschea*—Ar. *masjid* (in N. Africa pron. *masgid*)—*sajada* (*sagada*), to pray.]

mosquito, *mos-kē'tō*, *n.* a gnat:—*pl.* **mosqui'to(e)s**.—**mosquito canopy, curtain, net**, an arrangement of netting to keep out mosquitoes. [Sp. dim. of *mosca*, a fly—L. *musca*.]

moss, *mos*, *n.* (now chiefly *Scots*) a bog: boggy ground or soil: any of the Musci, a class of Bryophytes, small plants with simply constructed leaves, and no woody material, attached by rhizoids, the zygote growing into a small spore-bearing capsule that grows parasitically on the parent plant: a mass of such plants: a moss-like growth, covering, or excrescence: loosely extended to plants of similar appearance to true mosses: a moss-rose.—*v.t.* to cover with moss: to clear of moss.—*v.i.* to gather moss.—*ns.* **moss'-ag'ate**, chalcedony with moss-like inclusions of chlorite, manganese oxide, &c.; **moss'-back**, a person of antiquated views; **moss-bluiter** (*-blüt'ər*, *-blit'ər*; *Scot.*), the bittern; **moss'-cheep'er**, (*Scot.*) the titlark; **moss'-crop**, (*Scot.*) cottongrass; **moss'-flow**, (*Scot.*) a watery bog.—*adj.* **moss'-grown**, covered with moss.—*ns.* **moss'-hag', -hagg'**, (*Scot.*) a pit or slough in a bog; **moss'iness**; **moss'-land**, wet, peaty land; **'moss'-litt'er**, a loose mass of lumps of peaty material; **moss'-plant**, a plant of moss: the sexual generation in the life-history of a moss, on which the asexual generation is parasitic; **moss'-rose**, a variety of rose having a moss-like growth on and below the calyx; **moss'-troop'er**, one of the freebooters that used to infest the mosses of the Border.— *n.* and *adj.* **moss'-troop'ing**. — *adj.* **moss'y**, overgrown or abounding with moss: like moss: boggy.—**club-moss** (see **lycopod**); **Iceland moss** (see **Iceland**). [O.E. *mós*, bog; Du. *mos*, Ger. *moos*, moss, bog.]

mossbunker, *mos'bung-kər*, *n.* the menhaden. [Du. *mars-banker*, the scad or horse-mackerel.]

most, *mōst*, *adj.* (*superl.* of **more**) greatest: in greatest quantity or number.—*adv.* in the highest degree: (*U.S.* and *dial.*) almost (perhaps aphetic).—*n.* the greatest number or quantity.—*advs.* **most'ly**, for the most part; **most'what**, (*Spens.*) for the most part, mostly.—**at (the) most**, at the utmost computation; **for the most part**, chiefly: in the main; **make the most of** (see **make**). [The Northumbrian form *mást* (*Scot.* **maist**) may have occurred in O.E. beside the ordinary form *mǽst*; or the vowel may come from analogy with the comparative; cf. Ger. *meist*.]

mot, *mot*, *n.* (*obs.*) a motto: a hunter's horn-call: (*mō*; Fr.) a pithy or witty saying. [Fr.,—L. *muttum*, a murmur.]

mote, *mōt*, *v.t.* (*arch.* in both senses) may: must:— 3rd pers. sing. pres. tense **mote**; *pa.t.* (*Spens.*) **mote, mot** (*mot*), in *pl.* **mot'en** (but see also **must**).—so **mote I thee**, so may I prosper. [O.E. *mōt*, may, pa.t. *móste*; confused with **mought** (*q.v.*) Ger. *muss*, must.]

mote, *mōt*, *n.* a particle of dust: a speck: a seed or other foreign particle in wool or cotton (Yorkshire **moit**): a stain or blemish: anything very small. — *adjs.* **mōt'ed, mote'y** (*Scot.* **motty, mot'i**), containing motes. [O.E. *mot*; Du. *mot*.]

mote, *mōt*, *n.* (*arch.*) a mound, esp. with a castle: a tumulus.—*n.* **mote'-hill**. [O.Fr. *mote* (Fr. *motte*); often confused with **moot, moot-hill**.]

motet, motett, *mō-tet'*, *n.* a polyphonic choral composition, usually unaccompanied, with biblical or similar prose text: loosely, an anthem or church cantata.—*n.* **motett'ist**. [Fr. *motet*, dim. of *mot*; cf. **mot**.]

moth, *moth*, sometimes *mawth*, *n.* the cloth-eating larva of the clothes-moth: the perfect insect of the same kind: any member of the Heterocera, a popular and unscientific division of the Lepidoptera, broadly distinguished from butterflies by duller colouring, thicker body, antennae not clubbed, wings not tilted over the back in rest, and by the habit of flying by night: that which eats away gradually and silently: (*obs.*) various kinds of insect vermin: (*fig.*) a fragile, frivolous creature, readily dazzled into destruction: a light aeroplane: —*pl.* **moths** (*moths, mawths, mawdhz*).—*n.* **moth'-ball**, a ball of naphthalene or other substance for keeping away clothes-moths.—*v.t.* **moth'-eat** (back formation), to prey upon, as a moth eats a garment.—*adjs.* **moth'-eaten**, eaten or cut by moths; **mothed** (*motht*), moth-eaten.—*ns.* **moth'-flower**, a flower pollinated by moths; **moth'-hunter**, a goatsucker.—*adj.* **moth'y**, full of moths: motheaten. [O.E. *moththe, mohthe*; Ger. *motte*.]

mother, *mudh'ər*, *n.* a female parent, esp. a woman: a matron: that which has produced anything: the female head of a religious house or other establishment: a familiar term of address to, or prefix to the name of, an old woman: extended to an ancestress, a step-mother, mother-in-law, foster-mother: an apparatus for chicken-rearing: (*obs.*) the womb: (*obs.*) hysteria.—*adj.* received by birth, as it were from one's mother: being a mother: acting the part of a mother: originating: used to produce others from.—*v.t.* to give birth to: to acknowledge, to adopt, to treat (especially irksomely), as a son or daughter: to foster: to attribute the maternity or authorship of (with *on* or *upon*): to find a mother for.—*ns.* **moth'er-cell**, (*biol.*) a cell that gives rise to others by division; **moth'er-church**, the church from which others have sprung: a principal church; **moth'er-cit'y**, one from which another was founded as a colony; **moth'er-coun'try, -land**, the country of one's birth: the country from which a colony has gone out; **moth'ercraft**, the knowledge and skill expected of a mother; **moth'erhood**, state of being a mother; **moth'ering**, a rural English custom of visiting the mother church or one's parents on Mid-Lent Sunday (**Mothering Sunday**); **moth'er-in-law**, the mother of one's husband or wife: (*obs.*) a step-mother:—*pl.* **mothers-in-law**.—*adj.* **moth'erless**, without a mother.—*ns.* **moth'erliness**; **moth'er-liq'uor, moth'er-lye**, mother-water.—*adj.* **moth'erly**, pertaining to, or becoming, a mother: like a mother. — *adj.* **moth'er-na'ked**, naked as at birth. — *ns.* **moth'er-of-mill'ions**, ivy-leaved toadflax; **moth'er-of-pearl**, the nacreous internal layer of the shells in some molluscs (also *adj.*); **moth'er-right**, succession in the female line: matriarchy; **moth'er-ship**, a ship having charge of torpedoboats or small craft; **moth'er's-mark, moth'er-spot**, a birth-mark; **moth'er-tongue**, native language: a language from which another has its origin; **moth'er-wa'ter**, the residual liquid remaining after others have been crystallised or precipitated; **moth'er-wit**, native wit: common sense; **moth'erwort**, a labiate (*Leonurus Cardiaca*) or other plant supposed to help womb disease.—**every mother's son**, every man without exception; **fits of the mother**, (*obs.*) hysteria; **Mother Carey's chicken**, the storm petrel, or similar bird; **Mother Hubbard**, a woman's loose flowing gown, like that proper to the nursery heroine; **mothers' meeting**, a periodical meeting of mothers connected with a church. [O.E. *mōdor*; Du. *moeder*, O.N. *móthir*, Ger. *mutter*, Ir. and Gael. *mathair*, L. *māter*, Gr. *mētēr*, Sans. *mátá, mátri*.]

mother, *mudh'ər*, *n.* dregs: scum: a slimy mass of bacteria that oxidises alcohol into acetic acid

fāte, fär, ȧsk; mē, hər (her); *mīne; mōte; mūte; mōōn; dhen* (then)

(in full, **mother of vinegar**).—*v.i.* to become mothery.—*adj.* **moth'ery**, like or containing mother. [Poss. the same as the foregoing; or poss.—Du. *modder*, mud; cf. **mud**.]

motif, *mō-tēf'*, *n.* a theme or subject: an element in a composition, esp. a dominant element: (*mus.*) a figure, subject, or leitmotif: an ornament added to a woman's garment, often symbolic. [Fr. *motif*; see **motive**.]

motile, *mō'til*, *adj.* capable of moving spontaneously as a whole: characterised by motion: imagining most readily in terms of muscular action.—*n.* one whose imagery naturally takes the form of feelings of action.—*n.* **motility** (*-til'i-ti*). [L. *mōtus*, movement.]

motion, *mō'shən*, *n.* the act, state, manner, of changing place: a single movement: change of posture: power of moving or of being moved: agitation: a natural impulse: a working in the mind: a feeling: an emotion: a prompting: an instigation: a formal proposal put before a meeting: an application to a court, during a case before it, for an order or rule that something be done, esp. something incidental to the progress of the cause rather than its issue: evacuation of the intestine: a piece of mechanism: (*mus.*) progression of a part: (*obs.*) a puppet show: (*Shak.*) a puppet: (in *pl.*) faeces.—*v.t.* to direct or indicate by a gesture: to move, propose: (*obs.*) to make a movement indicating as one's intention: to give motion to.—*v.i.* to offer a proposal.—*adj.* **mō'tional.**—*n.* **mō'tionist**, one who is skilled in motions.—*adj.* **mō'tionless**, without motion.—*ns.* **mō'tion-man**, (*obs.*) a puppet-showman; **mō'tion-pic'ture**, a cinematograph film.—**angular motion**, change of angle between a standard direction and a line joining the moving object and a fixed point; **laws of motion**, Newton's three laws: (1) Every body continues in its state of rest, or of uniform motion in a straight line, except so far as it may be compelled by force to change that state; (2) Change of motion is proportional to force applied, and takes place in the direction of the straight line in which the force acts; (3) To every action there is always an equal and contrary reaction. [Fr. *motion*—L. *mōtiō*, *-ōnis*—*movēre*, *mōtum*, to move.]

motive, *mō-tiv*, *adj.* causing motion: having power to cause motion: concerned with the initiation of action: (*obs.*) moving.—*n.* an incitement of the will: a consideration or emotion that excites to action: a motif: (*Shak.*) a moving part of the body.—*v.t.* to motivate.—*v.t.* **mo'tivāte**, to provide with a motive: to induce.—*n.* **motivā'tion.** —*adj.* **mo'tiveless**;—*ns.* **mo'tivelessness**; **mo'tive-power**, the energy or source of the energy by which anything is operated; **motiv'ity**, power of moving or of producing motion. [L.L. *mōtīvus*—L. *movēre*, *mōtum*, to move.]

motley, *mot'li*, *adj.* particoloured: variegated: made of, or dressed in, motley: jester-like: heterogeneous.—*n.* (*obs.*) a cloth of mixed colours: a particoloured garb, such as a jester wore: a patchwork: (*Shak.*) a jester.—*adj.* **mot'ley-mind'ed**, (*Shak.*) having a mind of heterogeneous and inconsistent contents. [Origin obscure.]

motmot, *mot'mot*, *n.* a tropical American bird (*Momotus*), akin to rollers and kingfishers, that nibbles its tail-feathers into racquet-shape. [Said to be Mexican name.]

motor, *mō'tər*, *n.* a mover: that which gives motion: a machine whereby some source of energy is used to give motion or perform work, esp. an internal-combustion engine or a machine for converting electrical into mechanical energy: a motor-car: a muscle, or a nerve, concerned in bodily movement.—*adj.* giving or transmitting motion: driven by a motor: of, for, with, relating to, motor vehicles: concerned with the transmission of impulses: initiating bodily movement: pertaining to muscular movement or the sense of muscular movement.—*v.t.* and *v.i.* to convey, traverse, or travel by a motor vehicle.—*ns.* **mo'tor-ban'dit**, a robber who uses a motor-car; **mo'tor-bi'cycle**, **-boat**, **-bus** **-car**, **-coach**, **-cy'cle**,

-launch, **-lorr'y**, **-ship**, one driven by a motor; **mo'tor-cy'cling**; **mo'tor-cy'clist.**—*adjs.* **mo'tor-driven**, driven by a motor; **motō'rial**, motory: motor.—*n.* **motorisā'tion.**—*v.t.* **mo'torise**, to furnish with, or adapt to the use of, a motor or motors: to interpret or imagine in terms of motor sensation.—*ns.* **mo'torist**, one who drives a motor-car, esp. for pleasure; **motō'rium**, that part of the nervous system concerned in movement; **mo'tor-jet**, a reciprocating engine with a fan for jet-propulsion; **mo'torman**, a man who controls a motor, esp. that of a tram-car; **mo'tor-trac'tion**, the conveyance of loads, including passengers, by motor vehicles; **mo'tor-trac'tor**, an internal-combustion engine for hauling loads, esp. for drawing agricultural implements.—*adj.* **mo'tory**, causing, conveying, imparting motion: motor. [L. *mōtor*—*movēre*, to move.]

mott, *mot* (*Spens.*), *pa.t.* of **mete**.

mottle, *mot'l*, *v.t.* to variegate blotchily.—*n.* a blotched appearance, condition, or surface: yarns of two colours folded together.—*adjs.* **mott'led**; **mott'le-faced.** — *n.* **mott'ling.** [Prob. from **motley**.]

motto, *mot'ō*, *n.* a short sentence or phrase adopted as representative of a person, family, &c., or accompanying a coat of arms: a passage prefixed to a book or chapter shadowing forth its matter: a scrap of verse or prose enclosed in a cracker or accompanying a sweetmeat:—*pl.* **mott'oes** (*-ōz*). —*adj.* **mott'o'd**, **mott'oed**. [It.,—L. *muttum*, a murmur.]

motty. See **mote** (2).

motuca, *mō-tōō'kä*, **mutuca**, *mōō-tōō'kä*, *n.* a large Brazilian biting fly of the Tabanidae. [Tupí *mutuca* (Port. *motuca*).]

mou', **mou**, *mōō*, *n.* a Scots form of **mouth**.

mouch, **moucher**. Same as **mooch**, &c.

moucharaby, *mōō-shar'ə-bi*, *n.* a balcony enclosed with lattice-work. [Fr.,—Ar. *mashrabiyyah*.]

mouchard, *mōō'shär'*, *n.* a police spy. [Fr.]

mouchoir, *mōō-shwär'*, *n.* a pocket-handkerchief. [Fr.]

moudi(e)wart, **-wort**, Scots forms of **mouldwarp**.

moue, *mōō*, *n.* a grimace of discontent, pout. [Fr.]

moufflon, **mouflon**, **muflon**, *mōōf'lon*, *n.* a wild sheep of the mountains of Corsica, &c.: extended to large big-horned wild sheep of other kinds:— *pl.* **moufflon**. [Fr. *mouflon*—L.L. *mufrō*, *-ōnis*.]

mought, *mōt*, *mowt* (*Spens. mawt*), (*obs.* and *dial.*) *pa.t.* of **may**. See also **mote** (1).

mouillé, *mōō-yā*, *adj.* (of *l* and *n*) sounded in a liquid manner, palatalised—as *ll* in '*mouillé*, *gl* in '*seraglio*,' *ñ* in '*Señor*.' [Fr., moistened.]

moujik, *mōō-zhik'*, *mōō'zhik*, *n.* Same as **muzhik**.

mould, *mōld*, *n.* loose or crumbling earth: earth, considered as the material of which the body is formed or to which it turns: the earth of the grave: (*obs.* or *arch.*) the ground, the land, the world: (in *pl.*) clods, esp. in allusion to the grave (*Scot.* **mouls**, **mools**, *mōōlz*): soil rich in decayed matter.—*v.t.* to cover with soil.—*v.i.* (*obs.*) to moulder.—*n.* **mould'-board**, the curved plate in a plough which turns over the soil.—*v.i.* **mould'er**, to crumble to mould: to turn to dust: to waste away gradually. — *v.t.* to turn to dust.—*adj.* **mould'(e)y**, like, or of the nature of, mould. [O.E. *molde*; Ger. dialect *molt*, *molten*, Goth. *mulda*.]

mould, *mōld*, *n.* a woolly or fluffy growth on bread, cheese, or other vegetable or animal matter: any one of various small fungi (Mucor, Penicillium, &c.) of different classes, forming such growths.— *v.i.* to become mouldy.—*v.t.* to cause or allow to become mouldy.—*n.* **mould'iness.**—*adj.* **mould'y**, overgrown with mould: like mould: stale: musty. [M.E. *mowle*; cf. O.N. *mygla*.]

mould, *mōld*, *n.* a templet: a hollow form in which a cast is made: a formed surface from which an impression is taken: the foundation upon which certain manufactured articles are built up: a thing formed in a mould, esp. a jelly or blanc-mange: nature: form: model: a pattern: that which is or may be moulded: (*archit.*) a set of mouldings. — *v.t.* to knead: (*obs.*) to mix: to shape: to model: to form in a mould.—*adj.*

mould'able.—*ns.* **mould'-candle,** a candle made in a mould, not dipped; **mould'er**; **mould'-fac'ing,** a fine powder or wash applied to the face of a mould to ensure a smooth casting; **mould'ing,** the process of shaping, esp. any soft substance: anything formed by or in a mould: an ornamental edging or band projecting from a wall or other surface, as a fillet, astragal, bead, &c.: a strip of wood that can be applied for the purpose; **mould'ing-board,** a baker's board for kneading dough; **mould'-loft,** a room in which the several parts of a ship's hull are laid off to full size from the construction drawings. [O.Fr. *modle, molle* (Fr. *moule*)—L. *modulus,* a measure.]

mouldwarp, *mōld′wawrp, n.* a mole: (*Scot.*) **mowdiwort,** *mow′di-wurt.* [O.E. *molde,* mould, **earth,** *tworpan,* to throw; cf. O.H.G. *multwurf* (Ger. *maulwurf*), Dan. *muldvarp.*]

moulin, *mōō-lan², n.* a shaft in a glacier worn by water running down a crack.—*n.* **moulinet** (*mōō-li-net′,* or *mōō′*), a machine for bending a crossbow. [Fr. *moulin,* mill, and dim. *moulinet*—L.L. *molinum.*]

moult, *mōlt, v.i.* to cast feathers or other covering: to fall off, be shed.—*v.t.* to shed.—*n.* the act, process, condition, or time of moulting.—*adj.* **moult'en,** (*Shak.*) having moulted.—*n.* **moult'ing.** [O.E. (*bi*)*mūtian,* to exchange—L. *mūtāre*; the *l,* first a freak of spelling, afterwards sounded.]

mound, *mownd, n.* (*obs.*) a boundary-fence or hedge: a bank of earth or stone raised as a protection: a hillock: a heap.—*v.t.* (*obs.*) to enclose with a fence or an embankment: to fortify with an embankment: to heap in a mound.—*ns.* **mound'-bird,** a megapode, or bird of the Australian family Megapodidae, gallinaceous birds that build large mounds as incubators; **mound'-builder,** one of the Indians who in early times built great mounds in the eastern United States: a mound-bird. [Origin obscure; O.E. *mund* means guardianship.]

mound, *mownd, n.* a king's orb. [Fr. *monde*—L. *mundus,* the world.]

mounseer, *mown′sēr,* or *sēr′, n.* (*arch., illit.,* or *derisive*) for *monsieur,* a Frenchman.

mount, *mownt, n.* (*arch.* except **Mount,** as prefix to a name) a mountain: a small hill or mound, natural or artificial: a fleshy protuberance on the hand. [O.E. *munt* and O.Fr. *mont,* both—L. *mōns, montis,* mountain.]

mount, *mownt, v.i.* to go up: to climb: to get upon horseback, bicycle, or the like: to extend upward: to extend backward in time: to rise in level or amount: (*obs.*) to amount.—*v.t.* to climb, ascend: to get up on: to cover or copulate with: to cause to rise, to lift, raise, erect: to place upon anything high: to put on horseback, or the like: to furnish with an animal, bicycle, &c., to ride on: to fix in a setting, on a support, stand, or mount: to furnish with accessories: to put in position and state of readiness for use or exhibition: to stage: to be armed with: to carry, wear, or put on.—*n.* a rise: an act of mounting: manner of mounting: a step to mount by: a signal for mounting: a riding animal or cycle: that upon which a thing is placed or in which it is set for fixing, strengthening, embellishing, esp. the card surrounding a picture, or the slide, cover-glass, &c., used in mounting an object for the microscope.—*adj.* **mount'ed,** on horseback: furnished with horses: set on high: (*her.*) raised on steps, generally three, as a cross: set up: set.—*ns.* **mount'er**; **mount'ing**; **mount'ing-block,** a block or stone to enable one to mount a horse; **mount'y, mount'ie,** (*coll.*) a Canadian mounted policeman.— **mount guard** (see **guard**). [Fr. *monter,* to go up—L. *mōns, montis,* mountain.]

mountain, *mownt′in, n.* a high hill: a wine made from mountain grapes: in Ireland, wild pasture land: **Mountain,** the extreme party in the French Revolution (see also **Montagnard**).—*adj.* of or relating to a mountain: growing, dwelling, or found on or among mountains.—*ns.* **mount'ain-ash′,** the rowan-tree; **mount'ain-beav'er,** the sewellel or Haplodon; **mount'ain-blue′,** blue carbonate of copper; **mount'ain-bram'ble,** the cloudberry; **mount'ain-cat′,** a catamount, a wild-cat; **mount'ain-chain′,** a number of mountains connected together in one line; **mount'ain-cork′,** **mount'ain-leath'er,** a matted mass of a fibrous amphibole, cork-like or leathery; **mount'ain-dew′,** whisky.—*adj.* **mount'ained.**— *n.* **mountaineer′,** an inhabitant of mountain country: a climber of mountains: a member of the Mountain.—*v.i.* to climb mountains.—*ns.* **mountaineer′ing,** mountain climbing; **mount'ain-flax,** amianthus; **mount'ain-everlast'ing,** the cat's-foot (*Antennaria dioica*), a small woolly composite plant of the hills and seashore; **mount'ain-hare′,** a smaller species of hare, grey in summer, usually white in winter.—*adv.* and *adj.* **mount'ain-high′, mount'ains-high′,** high as a mountain (hyperbolically).—*ns.* **mount'ain-lau'rel,** kalmia; **mount'ain-li′on,** the puma; **mountain-marr′ow,** lithomarge; **mount'ain-meal,** bergmehl.—*adj.* **mount'ainous,** full of, characterised by, mountains: large as a mountain: huge.—*ns.* **mount'ain-rail'way,** a light narrow-gauge railway for mountainous regions, usually a rack-railway; **mount'ain-sheep′,** the bighorn of the Rocky Mountains; **mount'ain-sick'ness,** sickness brought on by breathing rare-fied air; **mount'ain-side,** the slope of a mountain; **mount'ain-soap′,** a greasy kind of halloysite; **mount'ain-tall′ow,** hatchettite; **mount'ain-tea′,** the American evergreen *Gaultheria procumbens*; **mount'ain-top**; **mount'ain-wood′,** a fibrous wood-like asbestos.—**Mountain Limestone,** the lowest division of the Carboniferous in England, the Carboniferous Limestone; **Old Man of the Mountain,** a popular name for the chief of the *Hashshāshīn* (see **assassin**). [O.Fr. *montaigne*—L. *mōns, montis,* mountain. In some compounds *mountain* is used like Ger. *berg,* as if=mine.]

mountant, *mownt′ənt, n.* an adhesive paste for mounting photographs, &c.—*adj.* (*Shak.*) rising on high. [Fr. *montant,* pr.p. of *monter,* to mount.]

mountebank, *mown′ti-bangk, n.* a quack who harangues and plays the fool: a buffoon: a charlatan.—*v.t.* to win, effect, render, by mountebankery.—*v.i.* (or *v.t.* with *it*) to play the mountebank.—*ns.* **moun'tebankery, moun'tebanking, moun'tebankism.** [It. *montimbanco, montambanco*—*montare,* to mount, *in,* on, *banco,* bench.]

mountenance, mountenaunce, *mownt′ən-əns, -ăns, n.* (*Spens.*) amount: distance. [App. O.Fr. *montance,* assimilated to **maintenance**; cf. **mount, mountant.**]

moup, moop, *mōōp, v.t.* (*Scot.*) to nibble: to mumble.—*v.i.* to consort. [Origin obscure.]

mourn, *mōrn, v.i.* to grieve: to be sorrowful: to wear mourning: to murmur as in grief.—*v.t.* to grieve for: to utter in a sorrowful manner.—*n.* **mourn'er,** one who mourns: one who attends a funeral, especially a relative of the deceased: a person hired to lament or weep for the dead: (*U.S.*) a penitent at a revival meeting. — *adj.* **mourn'ful,** causing, suggesting, or expressing sorrow: feeling grief.—*adv.* **mourn'fully.**—*n.* **mourn'fulness.** — *adj.* **mourn'ing,** grieving: lamenting.—*n.* the act of expressing grief: the dress of mourners, or other tokens of mourning—also (*Scot.*) in *pl.*—*ns.* **mourn'ing-bord'er,** a black margin used on notepaper, &c., by those in mourning: (*coll.*) a dirty edge on a finger-nail; **mourn'ing-bride′,** the sweet scabious (*Scabiosa atropurpurea*); **mourn'ing-cloak′,** an undertaker's cloak, formerly worn at a funeral; **mourn'-ing-coach′,** a closed carriage for carrying mourners to a funeral; **mourn'ing-dove′,** an American pigeon with plaintive note.—*adv.* **mourn'ingly.**—*ns.* **mourn'ing-piece,** a picture intended to be a memorial of the dead; **mourn'ing-ring′,** a ring worn in memory of a dead person; **mourn'ing-stuff,** a lustreless black dress fabric, as crape, cashmere, &c., for making mourning clothes.— **half-mourning** (see **half**); **in mourning,** wearing black (in China white) in token of mourning: of a ship, painted blue: (*slang*) with eyes blackened. [O.E. *murnan*; O.H.G. *mornēn,* to grieve.]

mournival, *mōr′ni-val, n.* in gleek, a set of four aces, kings, &c. [Fr. *mornifle.*]

mouse, *mows, n.* a little rodent animal (*Mus*) found

in houses and in the fields : extended to various voles and other animals more or less like the mouse, the *flitter*-mouse, *shrew*-mouse : (*obs.*) a term of endearment : (*obs.*) a muscle : (*dial.*) part of a hind-leg of beef, next the round (also **mouse'-butt'ock** and **mouse'-piece**) : a match for firing a cannon or mine : (*naut.*) a knot or knob to prevent slipping : (*slang*) a black eye, or discoloured swelling : — *pl.* **mice** (*mīs*). — *v.i.* (*mowz*) to hunt for mice or as if for mice : to prowl. — *v.t.* to treat or to tear as a cat does a mouse : to paw or handle amorously : (*naut.*) to secure with a mouse. — *n.* **mouse'-colour,** the grey colour of a mouse. — *adjs.* **mouse'-colour, -ed.** — *n.* **mouse'-deer,** a chevrotain. — *adj.* **mouse'-dun,** mouse-coloured. — *ns.* **mouse'-ear,** a name of several plants with soft leaves shaped like a mouse's ear, esp. **forget-me-not** : (**mouse'-ear chick'-weed,** any plant of the genus Cerastium, akin to chickweed) ; **mouse'-hole,** a hole made or used by mice : a small hole or opening ; **mouse'-hunt,** (*Shak.*) a mouser ; **mouse'kin, mous'ie,** a young or little mouse ; **mouser** (*mowz'er*), a cat good at catching mice : a prying person ; **mousery** (*mows'ər-i*), a resort of mice ; **mouse'-sight,** myopia ; **mouse'-tail,** a small ranunculaceous plant (Myosurus) with a spike of seed-vessels very like the tail of a mouse ; **mouse'-trap,** a trap for mice. — *n.* and *adj.* **mousing** (*mowz'ing*). — *v.t.* **mousle** (*mowz'l*), to pull about roughly or disrespectfully. — *adj.* **mousy** (*mows'i*), like a mouse in colour or smell : abounding with mice. [O.E. *mūs,* pl. *mȳs* ; Ger. *maus,* L. *mūs,* Gr. *mȳs,* mouse, muscle.]

mousmee, mousmé, *mōōs'mā, n.* a Japanese girl, esp. a waitress. [Jap. *musume.*]

mousquetaire, *mōōs-kə-ter', n.* a musketeer : a woman's cloak trimmed with ribbons, with large buttons, fashionable about 1855 : a broad turn-over linen collar worn a few years earlier. — **mousquetaire glove,** a woman's glove, long-armed, loose at top, without slit lengthwise. [Fr.]

mousse, *mōōs, n.* an ice or other dish made from whipped cream. [Fr., moss.]

mousseline, *mōōs-lēn', n.* fine French muslin : a very thin glass-ware : a claret-glass made of it. — **mousseline-de-laine** (*-də-len'*), an all-wool muslin. [Fr.]

moust. See **must** (5).

moustache, mustache, *məs-, mus-, mōōs-tâsh', n.* the hair upon the upper lip — also **mustachio** (*-tä'shō*). — Also in *pl.* — *n.* **moustache'-cup,** a cup with the top partly covered to keep the moustache from being wet. — *adjs.* **moustached', mustach'ioed ; moustach'ial.** — **old moustache,** an old soldier. [Fr. *moustache*—It. *mostaccio*—Doric Gr. *mystax, -akos,* the upper lip, moustache.]

Mousterian, *mōōs-tē'ri-ən, adj.* of an early Palaeolithic culture between Acheulean and Aurignacian. [Le *Moustier,* a cave on the Vézère which has yielded implements of this age.]

moutan, *mōō'tan, n.* a tree-paeony. [Chin.]

mouter, *mōōt'ər,* a Scots form of **multure.**

mouth, *mowth, n.* the opening in the head of an animal by which it eats and utters sound : opening or entrance, as of a bottle, river, &c. : a consumer of food : a speaker : a spokesman : cry, voice, utterance : a wry face, a grimace (*pl.* **mouths,** *mowdhz*). — *v.t.* (*mowdh*) to utter : to utter with exaggerated, affectedly pompous, or self-conscious action of the mouth : to declaim or spout : to take in the mouth : to feel, mumble, or mangle with the mouth : to train to the bit. — *v.i.* to declaim, rant (also *v.t.* with *it*) : (*Shak.*) to apply mouths : to grimace : to debouch. — *adj.* **mouth-able** (*mowdh'ə-bl*), lending itself to elocutionary utterance. — *ns.* **mouth-breather** (*mouth'-brē-dhər*), one who habitually breathes through the mouth ; **mouth'-breeder,** a cichlid fish that carries its young in its mouth for protection. — *adj.* **mouthed** (*mowdhd*), having a mouth. — *n.* **mouther** (*mowdh'-ər*), one who mouths. — *adj.* **mouth-filling** (*mowth'*), full-sounding. — *ns.* **mouth'-friend,** (*Shak.*) one who only professes friendship ; **mouth'ful** (*-fəl*), as much as fills the mouth : a small quantity : a

big word : (*slang*) a momentous utterance : — *pl.* **mouth'fuls ; mouth'-hon'our,** (*Shak.*) insincere civility expressed. — *adjs.* **mouth'less ; mouth'-made,** (*Shak.*) insincere. — *ns.* **mouth'-organ,** a small musical instrument encasing metallic reeds, played by the mouth — a harmonicon or harmonica : Pan-pipes ; **mouth'piece,** the piece of a musical instrument, tobacco-pipe, mask, &c., held to or in the mouth : a cigarette-holder : a spokesman. — *adj.* **mouthy** (*mowdh'i*), ranting : affectedly over-emphatic. — **by word of mouth,** by means of spoken words ; **down in the mouth,** out of spirits : despondent ; **hand to mouth** (see **hand**) ; **make a poor mouth,** to profess poverty ; **stop the mouth of,** to silence. [O.E. *mūth* ; Ger. *mund,* Du. *mond.*]

move, *mōōv, v.t.* to cause to change place or posture : to set in motion : to impel : to excite to action : to persuade : to instigate : to arouse : to provoke : (*obs.*) to provoke to anger : to touch the feelings of : to propose formally before a meeting : to recommend. — *v.i.* to go from one place to another : to change place or posture : to walk, to carry oneself : to change residence : to make a motion as in an assembly : to bow or salute on meeting : to begin to act : to take action : to go about one's activities, live one's life, pass one's time : (in chess, draughts, &c.) to transfer a man in one's turn to another square : (*pr.p.* **mov'ing** ; *pa.t.* and *pa.p.* **moved**). — *n.* an act of moving : a beginning of movement : a proceeding or step : play in turn, as at chess : turn to play (in chess, draughts, &c.) : advantage depending on whose turn it is to play : the manner in which a chess-man, or the like, can be moved. — *adj.* **movable** (*mōōv'ə-bl*), (*obs.*) mobile : changeable : not fixed : (*Scots law*) other than heritable. — Also (esp. *law*) **move'able.** — *n.* (esp. in *pl.*) a portable piece of furniture : a piece of movable or moveable property. — *ns.* **mov'ableness** (**move'ableness**), **movabil'ity.** — *adv.* **mov'ably** (**move'ably**). — *adj.* **move'less,** motionless : immovable. — *adv.* **move'-lessly.** — *ns.* **move'lessness ; move'ment,** act or manner of moving : change of position : activity : impulse : motion of the mind, emotion : the moving parts in a mechanism, esp. the wheelwork of a clock or watch : melodic progression : accentual character : tempo or pace : a main division of an extended musical composition, with its own more or less independent structure : the suggestion of motion conveyed by a work of art : a general tendency or current of thought, opinion, taste or action, whether organised and consciously propagated or a mere drift ; **mov'er ; mov'ie, mov'y,** (*U.S. slang* : esp. in *pl.*) a moving picture : a cinematograph film. — Also *adj.* — *adj.* **mov'ing,** causing motion : changing position : affecting the feelings : pathetic. — *adv.* **mov'ingly.** — **get a move on,** hurry up : make progress ; **know a move or two,** to be sharp or knowing ; **movable feast,** a church feast whose date depends on that of Easter, as Shrove-Tuesday, Good-Friday, &c. ; **moving pictures,** the cinematograph ; **move on,** a policeman's warning to those who obstruct traffic by standing still ; **on the move,** changing or about to change one's place. [A.Fr. *mover,* O.Fr. *movoir* (Fr. *mouvoir*)—L. *movēre,* to move. The obsolete **meve, mieve,** represent those forms in Fr. with accented root-syllable, as *meuvent* (3rd pl.).]

mow, *mow,* also *mō, n.* a wry face. — *v.i.* to make grimaces. — **nae mows** (*nā mowz, Scot.*), no laughing matter. [O.Fr. *moue, moe* (Fr. *moue*), or M.Du. *mouwe,* both meaning grimace.]

mow, *mow, n.* a pile of hay, corn in sheaves, pease, &c., esp. in a barn : a place for such a heap in a barn. — *v.t.* to heap in a mow : — *pr.p.* **mow'ing ;** *pa.t.* and *pa.p.* **mowed** (*mowd*). — *v.i.* **mow'-burn,** to heat and ferment in the mow. — *adj.* **mow'burnt.** [O.E. *mūga,* heap ; O.N. *mūgi,* swath, crowd, mob.]

mow, *mō, v.t.* to cut down, or cut the grass upon, with a scythe or a grass-cutting machine : to cut down in great numbers : — *pr.p.* **mow'ing ;** *pa.t.* **mowed** (*mōd*) ; *pa.p.* **mowed** or **mown**

(*mōn*).—*adjs.* **mowed, mown.**—*ns.* **mow′er,** one who mows grass, &c.: a machine with revolving blades for mowing grass; **mow′ing,** the act of cutting: land from which grass is cut; **mow′ing-machine.** [O.E. *māwan*; Ger. *mähen*; L. *metĕre*, to reap.]

mowa, *mow′ä,* **mowra,** *mow′rä.* Same as **mahwa.**

mowdi(e)wart, -wort, Scots forms of **mouldwarp.**

moxa, *mok′sä, n.* a cauterising cone of the leaf-down of a wormwood (*Artemisia Moxa*), or sun-flower pith, cotton-wool, or other material.—*n.* **moxibustion** (-*bust′yən*; modelled on *combustion*), cauterisation by moxa. [Jap. *mogusa.*]

moy, *moi, n.* (*Shak.*) supposed by Pistol (misunderstanding a Frenchman's *moi*, me) to be the name of a coin, or possibly a measure (Fr. *muid*—L. *modius*) of corn.

moyity, moyle, (*Spens.*) for **moiety, moil.**

moyl, moyle, *moil, n.* (*obs.*) a mule. [O.Fr. *mul, mule.*]

Mozarab, *mō-zar′ab, n.* a privileged Christian Spaniard under Moorish rule.—*adj.* **Mozar′abic.** [Sp. *Mozárabe*—Ar. *musta′rib*, would-be Arab.]

moze, *mōz, v.t.* to gig, raise a nap on. [Origin obscure.]

mozetta, *mō-tset′tä, n.* a short cape to which a hood may be attached, worn by popes, cardinals, bishops, abbots. [It., dim. from *mozzo*, docked.]

mpret, *bret, n.* a former title of the ruler of Albania. [Albanian,—L. *imperātor*, emperor.]

M-roof. See under **M.**

Mr, Mrs. See **Mister, Mistress.**

MS. See **manuscript.**

mu, *mū, mōō, mü, n.* the Greek letter M *μ*, equivalent to M: as a numeral, *μ′*=40, *͵μ*=40,000: used as a symbol for *micron*. [Gr. *mȳ*.]

much, *much* (*comp.* **more**; *superl.* **most**), *adj.* in great quantity: (*obs.*) great: (*Shak.*) many.—*adv.* in a great degree: to a great extent: in nearly the same way: by far: in old ironical use, like the modern slang not much, I don't think.—*n.* a great deal: anything of importance or worth.—Also in unshortened form (*arch.*) **much′el,** *adj., adv.,* and *n.* (*Spens.*) **much′ell, moch′ell;** Northern form **mick′le, muck′le).**—*adv.* (*arch.* and *jocular*) **much′ly.**—*n.* **much′ness,** greatness: magnitude.—**make much of** (see **make**): **much about it,** something like what it usually is; **much of a muchness,** just about the same value or amount; **too much for,** more than a match for. [M.E. *muche, muchel*—O.E. *micel, mycel.*]

mucic, mucid, mucilage. See under **mucus.**

muck, *muk, n.* dung: manure: wet or clinging filth: anything contemptible or worthless, esp. gold (in the poets): rubbishy reading matter: a mess.—*v.t.* to clear of muck: to manure with muck: to befoul: to make a mess of (often with *up*).—*v.i.* to potter (usu. with *about*).—*n.* **muck′er,** one who mucks: a money-grubber: a mess: a heavy fall in, or owing to, the mire, or in general: a mishap, disaster.—*v.t.* to hoard: to squander: to vitiate.—*v.i.* to come to grief: to make a muddle of anything.—*ns.* **muck′-heap,** a dung-hill; **muck′iness; muck′-midd′en; muck′-rake,** a rake for scraping filth.—*v.i.* (*U.S.*) to seek out and expose scandals or supposed scandals, whether for worthy or unworthy motives.—*ns.* **muck′-raker, muck′-raking; muck′-sweat,** profuse sweat; **muck′-worm,** a worm or grub that lives in muck: one who acquires money by mean devices: a miser.—*adj.* **muck′y,** nasty, filthy: of the nature of muck: like muck. [Prob. Scand.; cf. O.N. *myki*, Dan. *mög*, dung.]

muck. See **amok.**

muckender, *muk′ən-dər, n.* (*obs.*) a handkerchief: a table-napkin. [Apparently from some Languedocian dialect; cf. Fr. *mouchoir*, Sp. *mocador*.]

Mucker, *mook′ər, n.* a nickname for a member of a Königsberg sect (1835) of dualistic theosophists: **mucker** (*muk′ər*; *U.S.*), a fanatical reformer: a hypocrite: a young townsman, not a student: a boorish person. [Ger.]

muckle, *muk′l,* a Scottish form of **mickle.**

muckluck, mukluk, mucluc, *muk′luk, n.* an Eskimo sealskin boot. [Eskimo.]

mucro, *mū′krō, n.* a short stiff sharp point forming an abrupt end.—*adjs.* **mu′cronate, -d** (-*krən-āt, -id*). [L. *mūcrō, -ōnis*, a sharp point.]

mucus, *mū′kəs, n.* the slimy fluid secreted by the mucous membrane of the nose or other parts.—*n.* **mu′cate,** a salt of mucic acid.—*adjs.* **mucedinous** (-*sed′*, -*sēd′*), mouldy, mildewy; **mu′cic** (-*sik*), applied to an acid got by oxidation of gums; **mu′cid,** mouldy, musty; **muciferous** (-*sif′*), secreting or conveying mucus.—*n.* **mu′cigen** (-*si-jen*), a substance secreted by the cells of mucous membrane, converted into mucin.—*n.* **mu′cilage** (-*si-lij*), a gluey mixture of carbohydrates in plants: any sticky substance: (*U.S.*) gum used as an adhesive.—*adj.* **mucilaginous** (-*laj′*).—*ns.* **mucilag′inousness;** **mu′cin,** any one of a class of albuminous substances in mucus.—*adjs.* **mucoid** (*mū′koid*), like mucus; **muco-pū′rulent,** of mucous and pus.—*ns.* **Mu′cor,** a genus of Zygomycete fungi including some of the commonest moulds, giving name to order or family **Mūcorā′les** or **Mūcorin′eae; mucos′ity.**—*aajs.* **mu′cous,** like mucus: slimy: viscous: producing mucus; **mu′culent,** like mucus.—**mucous membrane,** a lining of various tubular cavities of the body, with glands secreting mucus. [L. *mūcus,* nose mucus; cf. *mungĕre*, to wipe away.]

mud, *mud, n.* wet soft earth: a mixture of earthy or clayey particles with water.—*v.t.* to bury in mud: to clog with mud: to plaster with mud: to befoul: to make turbid: to supply with mud.—*v.i.* to hide in the mud.—*ns.* **mud′-bath,** a bath in mud, esp. as a remedy; **mud′-boat,** a board or sled for conveyance over mud-flats or swamps: a boat for carrying away dredged mud; **mud′-cat,** (*U.S.*) a name given to several species of catfish; **mud′-clerk,** (*U.S.*) an assistant purser; **mud′-cone,** a cone formed by a mud-volcano.—*adv.* **mudd′ily.**—*n.* **mudd′iness.**—*adj.* **mudd′y,** foul with mud: containing mud: covered with mud: of the nature of mud: like mud: mud-coloured: confused: stupid.—*v.t.* and *v.i.* to make or become muddy:—*pr.p.* **muddy′-ing;** *pa.t.* and *pa.p.* **mudd′ied.**—*adjs.* **muddy′-head′ed; mudd′y-mett′led,** (*Shak.*) spiritless.—*ns.* **mud′-fish,** a fish that burrows in mud, esp. a lung-fish; **mud′-flat,** a muddy stretch submerged at high water; **mud′-guard,** a screen to catch mud-splashes from a wheel; **mud′-hole,** a hole with mud in it: an opening for removing sediment from a boiler, &c.; **mud′-hook,** (*slang*) an anchor; **mud′-lark,** a name for various birds that frequent mud: one who picks up a living along the banks of tidal rivers: a street-arab.—*v.i.* to work or play in mud.—*ns.* **mud′-la′va,** a stream of mud from a volcano; **mud′-lump′,** an upstanding area of mud, often exhaling gases, as in the Mississippi delta; **mud′-minn′ow,** a small fish (Umbra) akin to the pikes; **mud′-pie′,** a moulded mass of mud made by children in play; **mud′-pupp′y,** (*U.S.*) the axolotl: a hellbender; **mud′scow,** a flat mud-boat; **mud′-skipper,** a goby that can skip about on bare mud; **mud′-slinger; mud′-slinging,** vilification; **mud′stone,** an argillaceous rock not distinctly fissile; **mud′-volca′no,** a vent that emits mud; **mud′wort,** a small mud-growing scrophulaceous plant (*Limosella aquatica*). [Cf. Old Low Ger. *mudde*, Du. *modder*.]

muddle, *mud′l, v.t.* to render muddy: to confuse: to bungle: to mix.—*v.i.* to wallow, dabble, or grub in mud: to potter about: to blunder.—*n.* confusion, mess: mental confusion, bewilderment.—*n.* **mudd′lehead,** a blockhead.— *adj.* **muddlehead′ed.**—*adv.* **muddlehead′edly.**—*n.* **muddlehead′edness.**—**muddle away,** to squander or fritter away confusedly; **muddle through,** to get through difficulties blunderingly. [Freq. of **mud.**]

mudir, *mōō-dēr′, n.* a local governor.—*n.* **mudir′ieh; mudir′ia,** a mudir's province or office. [Ar. *mudīr.*]

muezzin, *mōō-ez′in, n.* the Mohammedan official who calls to prayer.—Also **muedd′in.** [Ar. *mu′adhdhin.*]

fāte, fär, ȧsk; mē, hər (her); *mīne; mōte; mūte; mōōn; dhen* (then)

muff, *muf*, *n.* a cylinder of fur or the like for keeping the hands warm : a similar contrivance for the feet, ear, &c. : (*obs.*) a mitt.—*n.* **muffettee'**, (*obs.*) a muffler : a woollen cuff. [Prob. from Du. *mof* ; cf. Ger. *muff*, a muff.]

muff, *muf*, *n.* one who is awkward or unskilful, esp. in sport : a bungler : an unpractical person : one who wants savoir-faire : a failure, esp. to hold a ball.—*v.t.* to perform awkwardly : to bungle : to miss.—*v.i.* to act clumsily, esp. in letting a ball slip out of the hands. [Origin unknown.]

muffin, *muf'in*, *n.* a soft, porous cake, eaten hot with butter : a small plate : one who dangles after a young woman : a poor ball-player.—*ns.* **muff'in-bell'**, a bell rung by a muffin-man ; **muff'in-cap**, a round flat cap for men ; **muffineer'**, a dish for keeping muffins hot : a castor for sprinkling salt or sugar on muffins ; **muff'in-fight'**, **-worr'y**, (*coll.*) a tea-party ; **muff'in-man**, one who goes round selling muffins. [Origin unknown.]

muffle, *muf'l*, *n.* the thick naked upper lip and nose, as of a ruminant. [Fr. *mufle*.]

muffle, *muf'l*, *v.t.* to envelop, for warmth, concealment, stifling of sound, &c. : to blindfold : to deaden or dull the sound of.—*n.* (*obs.*) a boxing-glove : a means of muffling : a receptacle, oven, or compartment in which things can be heated in a furnace without contact with the fuel and its products : a muffled state : a muffled sound.—*adj.* **muff'led**.—*n.* **muff'ler**, a scarf for the throat : any means of muffling : one who muffles. [App. Fr. *mouffle*, mitten.]

mufti, *muf'ti*, *n.* an expounder of Mohammedan law : the civilian dress of one who wears a uniform when on duty : plain clothes : a civilian. [Ar. *mufti*.]

mug, *mug*, *n.* a cup with more or less vertical sides : its contents.—*ns.* **mug'ful** (*-fŏl*)—*pl.* **mug'fuls** ; **mugg'er**, a hawker of earthenware ; **mug'-house**, an alehouse ; **mug'-hunter**, (*games*) a pot-hunter. [Origin unknown ; cf. Norw. *mugga*, Sw. *mugg*.]

mug, *mug*, *n.* the face : the mouth.—*v.i.* (*theat.*) to grimace. [Poss. from the grotesque face on a drinking-mug.]

mug, *mug*, *n.* (*coll.*) a simpleton : an easy dupe. [Origin unknown.]

mug, *mug*, *n.* (*coll.*) a sap or swot : an exam.—*v.t.* and *v.i.* to study hard : to swot up. [Origin unknown.]

mug, *mug*, *n.* a woolly-faced sheep.—*ns.* **mug'-ewe**, **-lamb**, **-sheep**.

mugearite, *mŏŏ-gēr'īt*, *n.* a dark finely crystalline basic igneous rock composed mainly of oligoclase, orthoclase, and olivine, with iron oxides, developed at *Mugeary* in Skye.

mugger, *mug'ər*, *n.* a broad-snouted Indian crocodile. [Hind. *magar*.]

muggins, *mug'inz*, *n.* a children's card-game : a form of dominoes : a simpleton. [Ety. dub.]

Muggletonian, *mug-l-tŏ'ni-ən*, *n.* a member of a sect founded by John Reeve and Lodowick *Muggleton* (1609-98), who claimed to be the two witnesses of Rev. xi. 3-6.

muggy, *mug'i*, *adj.* foggy : close and damp, as weather : wet or mouldy, as straw.—Also **mugg'ish**. [Perh. O.N. *mugga*, mist.]

mugwort, *mug'wurt*, *n.* a common British wormwood. [O.E. *mucgwyrt*, lit. midge-wort.]

mugwump, *mug'wump*, *n.* an Indian chief : a person of great importance, or one who thinks himself so : one who dissociates himself from political parties, a snug Independent. [Algonkin *mugquomp*, a great man.]

Muhammedan, Muharram. See **Mohammedan, Moharram.**

muid, *mü-ē*, *n.* an old French measure of capacity : a hogshead : a dry measure for corn, &c. : (*S.Afr.* ; *mā'id*) a sack of 3 bushels. [Fr.,—L. *modius* ; cf. Du. *mud*.]

muil. See **mule** (2).

muir. See **moor** (1).

muist. See **must** (5).

mujik. Same as **muzhik.**

mukhtar, *mŏŏk'tär*, *n.* an Indian lawyer. [Ar. *mukhtār*, chosen.]

mulatto, *mü-lat'ō*, *n.* the offspring of a black and a white (*pl.* **mulatt'os**) :—*fem.* **mulatt'a, mulatt'ress.** [Sp. *mulato*, dim. of *mulo*, mule ; Fr. *mulâtre*.]

mulberry, *mul'bər-i*, *n.* the edible multiple fruit of any tree of the genus Morus (family Moraceae) : the tree bearing it, with leaves on which silkworms feed : extended to various fruits or plants more or less similar superficially or really : the colour of the fruit, a dark purple : a prefabricated harbour, used in invasion of Europe in 1944 (orig. a codeword).—*adj.* mulberry-coloured.—*adj.* **mulberry-faced**, having a face blotched with purple.—*n.* **mul'berry-fig**, the true sycamore (sycomore), a fig-tree with leaves like those of mulberry. [Prob. O.H.G. *mulberi* (Mod. Ger. *maulbeere*)—L. *mōrum* ; cf. **morus, berry.**]

mulch, also **mulsh**, *mulsh*, *n.* loose material, strawy dung, &c., laid down to protect the roots of plants.—*v.t.* to cover with mulch.—*adj.* soft. [Cf. Ger. dial. *molsch*, soft, beginning to decay ; O.E. *melsc*.]

Mulciber, *mul'si-bər*, *n.* Vulcan.—*adj.* **Mulcibē'rian.** [L.]

mulct, *mulkt*, *n.* a fine : a penalty.—*v.t.* to fine (*in* a fine ; or without *in*) : to deprive (with *of*) :—*pa.p.* **mulct'ed, mulct.** [L. *mulcta*, a fine.]

mule, *mūl*, *n.* the offspring of the ass and horse (esp. he-ass and mare) : a hybrid : a cross between a canary and another finch : a cotton-spinning machine : an obstinate person.—*adj.* hybrid.—*ns.* **mule'-deer**, a long-eared deer, black-tail of N. America ; **muleteer** (*mūl-i-tēr'*), a mule-driver.—*adj.* **mul'ish**, like a mule : obstinate.—*adv.* **mul'ishly.**—*n.* **mul'ishness.** [O.E. *mūl*—L. *mūlus* was superseded by O.Fr. *mul* (masc. ; in Mod. Fr. the dim. *mulet* is used), *mule* (fem.)—L. *mūlus, mūla.*]

mule, *mūl* (Scot. **muil**, *məl*), *n.* a loose slipper. [Fr. *mule.*]

muley, mulley, mooly, *mŏŏl'i, mūl'i*, *adj.* hornless. —*n.* a hornless cow : any cow. [Gael. *maol* or W. *moel*, bald.]

mulga, *mul'gä*, *n.* an Australian acacia. [Native word.]

muliebrity, *mū-li-eb'ri-ti*, *n.* womanhood. [L. *muliebritās, -tātis—mulier*, a woman.]

mull, *mul*, *n.* a muddle.—*v.t.* to bungle. [Origin obscure.]

mull, *mul*, *n.* a promontory. [Prob. Gael. *maol* or O.N. *múli*, snout ; cf. Ger. *maul.*]

mull, *mul*, *n.* (*Scot.*) a snuff-box. [See **mill** (1).]

mull, *mul*, *n.* a soft muslin.—Also **mul'mul(l).** [Hind. *malmal.*]

mull, *mul*, *v.i.* (*U.S.*) to cogitate, ponder, turn over in the mind. [Origin obscure.]

mull, *mul*, *v.t.* to crumble. [Cf. O.E. *myl*, dust.]

mull, *mul*, *v.t.* to warm, spice, and sweeten (wine, ale, &c.).—*adj.* **mulled.**—*n.* **mull'er.** [Origin obscure.]

mull, *mul*, *v.t.* (*Shak.*) to dull, stupefy. [Origin obscure ; perh. from the mulling of wine.]

mullah, moolah, mollah, *mul'ä, mŏŏl'ä, mol'ä, n.* a Mohammedan learned in theology and law : a Moslem schoolmaster or teacher : a fanatical preacher of war on the infidel. [Pers., Turk., and Hind. *mullā*—Ar. *maulā.*]

mullein, *mul'in*, *n.* a tall, stiff, yellow-flowered woolly plant (Verbascum) of the Scrophulariaceae —popularly known as *hag-taper*, *Adam's flannel*, *Aaron's rod*, *shepherd's club*. [A.Fr. *moleine.*]

muller, *mul'ər*, *n.* a pulverising tool. [Perh. O.Fr. *moloir—moldre* (Fr. *moudre*), to grind.]

mullet, *mul'it*, *n.* a fish of the genus Mugil, palatable, nearly cylindrical : another fish (Mullus), slightly compressed—**red mullet.** [O.Fr. *mulet*, dim.—L. *mullus*, red mullet.]

mullet, *mul'it*, *n.* (*her.*) a five-pointed star—cadency mark of a son. [O.Fr. *molette*, rowel of a spur—L. *mola*, a millstone.]

mulligatawny, *mul-i-ga-taw'ni*, *n.* an East Indian curry-soup. [Tamil *milagu-tannīr*, pepper-water.]

mulligrubs, *mul'i-grubz*, *n.pl.* (*coll.*) colic : sulkiness.

Neutral vowels in unaccented syllables : *el'ə-mənt, in'fənt, ran'dəm*

mullion, *mul'yən*, *n.* an upright division between the lights of windows, &c.—*adj.* **mull'ioned.** [Apparently from **monial.**]

mullock, *mul'ək*, *n.* rubbish, esp. mining refuse. [From obs. or dial. *mull*, dust; cf. O.E. *myl*.]

mulsh. Same as **mulch.**

mult-, multi-, in composition, much, many.— *adjs.* **multang'ular,** having many angles ; **multan'imous** (L. *animus*, mind), having a many-sided mind ; **mult(i)artic'ulate,** many-jointed. — *n.* **multeity** (*mul-tē'i-ti*; cf. **haecceity**), manifoldness, very great numerousness.—*adjs.* **multicam'erate** (L. *camera*, chamber), having many chambers or cells ; **multicap'itate** (L. *caput, -itis*, head), many-headed ; **multicau'line** (L. *caulis*, stem), having many stems ; **multicell'ular,** having or made up of many cells ; **multicen'tral,** having or proceeding from many centres ; **multicipital** (*mul-ti-sip'i-təl* ; L. *caput, -itis*, head), having many heads, multicapitate. — *n.* **multicolour** (*mul'ti-kul-ər*), diversity or plurality of colour.— *adj.* many - coloured. — *adjs.* **mul'ticoloured ;** **multicos'tate** (L. *costa*, rib), many-ribbed ; **multicus'pid,** having more than two cusps.—*n.* a multicuspid tooth.—*adj.* **multicus'pidate.**—*n.* **mul'ticycle,** (*obs.*) a velocipede with more than three wheels : one intended to carry several men. —*adjs.* **multiden'tate** (L. *dēns, dentis*, tooth), many-toothed ; **multidentic'ulate,** having many denticulations or fine teeth ; **multidigitate** (*-dij'i-tāt* ; L. *digitus*, finger), many-fingered ; **multidimen'sional,** (*math.*) of more than three dimensions ; **mul'tifaced,** many-faced ; **multifarious** (*mul-ti-fā'ri-əs* ; L. *multifārius*, poss. from *fārī*, to speak), having great diversity : made up of many parts : manifold : (*bot.*) in many rows or ranks.— *adv.* **multifā'riously.**—*n.* **multifā'riousness,** the state of being multifarious : multiplied variety : (*law*) the fault of improperly joining in one bill distinct and independent matters, and thereby confounding them.—*adjs.* **mul'tifid,** also **multif'idous,** cleft into many lobes ; **multiflo'rous,** many-flowered ; **mul'tifoil,** having more than five foils or arcuate divisions.—*n.* multifoil ornament.—*adjs.* **multifo'liate** (L. *folium*, leaf), with many leaves ; **multifo'liolate,** with many leaflets ; **mul'tiform,** having many forms, polymorphic.— *n.* that which is multiform.—*n.* **multiform'ity.**— *adjs.* **multiju'gate, multiju'gous** (L. *jugum*, yoke), consisting of many pairs of leaflets ; **multilat'eral** (L. *latus, lateris*, side), many-sided : with several parties or participants ; **multilineal** (*-lin'*), **multilin'ear,** having many lines ; **multilingual** (*-ling'gwəl*; L. *lingua*, tongue), in many languages ; **multilo'bate, mul'tilobed,** many-lobed ; **multilobular** (*-lob'ū-lər*), **multilob'ulate,** having many lobules ; **multilocular** (*-lok'ū-lər*), **multiloc'ulate,** many-chambered. — *n.* **multil'oquence,** much speaking.—*adjs.* **multil'oquent, multil'oquous.**—*ns.* **multil'oquy ; multimillionaire',** one who is a millionaire several times over.—*adj.* **multino'mial,** (*alg.*) consisting of more than two terms : relating to multinomials.—*n.* a multinomial expression. — *adjs.* **multinu'clear, multinū'cleate, -d,** having several nuclei ; **multinū'cleolate,** having several nucleoli.—*ns.* **multipara** (*mul-tip'ə-rä* ; L. *parĕre*, to bring forth), a woman who has given birth to a child for the second or later time, or is about to do so—opp. to **primapara ; multiparity** (*-par'i-ti*), condition of being a multipara : condition of being multiparous.—*adj.* **multip'arous,** pertaining to a multipara : (*zool.*) producing more than one at a birth (opp. to *uniparous*). — (*bot.*) giving rise to several lateral axes ; **multipar'tite** (L. *partītus*, divided), divided into many parts : much cut up into segments.—*ns.* **mul'tiped** (L. *pēs, pedis*, foot), a many-footed animal : (*obs.* ; also **multipode,** *-pēd*) a woodlouse ; **mul'tiplane,** an aeroplane with more than two sets of supporting planes. [L. *multus*, much.]

multiple, *mul'ti-pl, adj.* consisting of many elements or components, esp. of the same kind : manifold : compound : multiplied or repeated : (*teleg.*) allowing many messages to be sent over the same wire.—*n.* a quantity which contains another an exact number of times.—*adv.* **multiply** (*mul'ti-pli*).—**common multiple,** a number or quantity that can be divided by each of several others without a remainder ; **least common multiple,** the smallest number that forms a common multiple ; **multiple fruit,** a single fruit formed from several flowers in combination, as a pineapple, fig, mulberry ; **multiple shop, store,** one of many shops belonging to the same firm, often dispersed about the country. [Fr.,—L.L. *multiplus*—root of L. *plēre*, to fill.]

multiplepoinding, *mul-ti-pl-pind'ing, n.* (*Scots law*) a process by which a person who has funds claimed by more than one, in order not to have to pay more than once, brings them all into court that one of them may establish his right.

multiplex, *mul'ti-pleks, adj.* multiple. [L. *multiplex—plicāre*, to fold.]

multiply, *mul'ti-pli, v.t.* to increase the number of : to accumulate : (*obs.*) to magnify : to reproduce : (*math.*) to obtain the product of.—*v.i.* to become more numerous : to be augmented : to reproduce : to perform the mathematical process of multiplication :—*pr.p.* **mul'tiplying ;** *pa.t.* and *pa.p.* **mul'tiplied.**—*adjs.* **mul'tipliable, mul'tiplicable** (or *-plik'*).—*n.* **mul'tiplicand** (or *-kand'*), a quantity to be multiplied by another.—*adj.* **mul'tiplicate** (or *-tip'*), consisting of more than one : in many folds.—*n.* the condition of being in many copies : one of these copies.—*n.* **multiplica'tion,** the act of multiplying or increasing in number : (*bot.*) increase of number of parts by branching : the rule or operation by which quantities are multiplied.—*adj.* **mult'iplicātive** (or *-plik'ə-tiv*), tending or having power to multiply : (*gram.*) indicating how many times.—*ns.* **mul'tiplicātor,** (*math.*) a multiplier ; **multiplicity** (*-plis'i-ti*), the state of being manifold : a great number ; **mul'tiplier,** one who multiplies : a quantity by which another is multiplied : a device or instrument for intensifying some effect : a geared fishing-reel for drawing in the line quickly.—**multiplication table,** a tabular arrangement giving the products of pairs of numbers usually up to 12 ; **multiplying glass,** (*obs.*) a magnifying glass : a faceted glass for multiplying reflexions ; **multiply words,** to say much : to be wordy. [Fr. *multiplier*—L. *multiplicāre—plicāre*, to fold.]

multiply, *mul'ti-pli.* See under **multiple.**

multi-ply, *mul'ti-plī', n.* ply-wood of more than three thicknesses.

multi- (*continued*). — *adjs.* **multipo'lar,** having several poles or axons ; **multip'otent** (L. *potēns, -entis,* powerful ; *Shak.*), having power to do many things.—*n.* **multipres'ence,** the power of being in many places at once.—*adjs.* **multipres'ent ; multiram'ified** (L. *rāmus*, branch, *facĕre*, to make), having many branches.—*n.* **multiscience** (*mul-tish'əns ;* L. *scientia*, knowledge), knowledge of many things.—*adjs.* **multisep'tate,** having many septa ; **multisē'rial, multisē'riate,** in many rows ; **multisonant** (*mul-tis'ən-ənt* ; L. *sonāns, -āntis,* pr.p. of *sonāre*, to sound), having many sounds : sounding much ; **multispi'ral,** having many coils ; **multisulc'ate** (L. *sulcus*, furrow), having many furrows ; **multituber'culate, -d,** having many tubercles, as teeth.

multitude, *mul'ti-tūd, n.* the state of being many : a great number of individuals : a crowd : the mob. —*adjs.* **multitud'inary** (*rare*) ; **multitud'inous.** —*adv.* **multitud'inously.**—*n.* **multitud'inousness.** [L. *multitūdō, -inis—multus.*]

multi- (*continued*).—*ns.* **multiv'alence** (or *-vā'*), **multiv'alency** (or *-vā'* ; *chem.*), having a valency greater than one ; **multiv'ious** (L. *via*, way), going many ways ; **multiv'ocal** (L. *vōx, vōcis*, voice), of many meanings.—*n.* a word of many meanings. [L. *multus*, much.]

multivoltine, *mul-ti-vol'tīn, adj.* having several annual broods—of silkworm moths. [L. *multus*, much, It. *volta*, a turn, winding.]

multum, *mul'təm, n.* an adulterant in brewing. [Prob. neut. of L. *multus*, much.]

fāte, fär, ȧsk ; mē, hėr (her) ; *mīne ; mōte ; mūte ; mōōn ; dhen* (then)

multungulate, *mul-tung'gū-lāt, adj.* having the hoof divided into more than two parts. — *n.* a multungulate mammal. [L. *multus, ungula,* hoof.]

multure, *mul'tyər,* (*Scot.*) **mouter** (*mōōt'ər*), *n.* a fee, generally in kind, for grinding grain : the right to such a fee.—*v.t.* and *v.i.* to take multure (for).— *n.* **mul'turer** (**mou'terer**), one who receives multures : a miller : one who pays multures. [O.F. *molture, moulture*—L. *molitūra,* a grinding.]

mum, *mum, adj.* silent.—*n.* silence.—*interj.* not a word.—*v.i.* to act in dumb show : to act in a mummers' play : to masquerade :—*pr.p.* **mumm'-ing**; *pa.t.* and *pa.p.* **mummed.**—*n.* and *interj.* **mum'-bud'get,** mum.—*n.* **mum'chance',** a silent game with cards or dice : a fool.—*adj.* silent.—*ns.* **mumm'er,** an actor in a folk-play, usu. at Christmas : a masquerader : an actor ; **mumm'ery,** mumming : great show without reality : foolish ceremonial ; **mumm'ing.**—**mum's the word,** not a word. [An inarticulate sound with closing of the lips ; partly O.Fr. *momer,* to mum, *momeur,* mummer ; cf. Du. *mommen,* to mask.]

mum, *mum, n.* a wheatmalt beer, sometimes with oat and bean meal. [Ger. *mumme.*]

mum, mum, mummy, *mum'i, ns.* childish words for mother. [Cf. **mamma.**]

mum, *mum.* See **ma'am.**

mumble, *mum'bl, v.t.* and *v.i.* to say, utter, or speak indistinctly, softly, or perfunctorily : to mouth with the lips, or as with toothless gums.— *ns.* **mum'blement,** (*Carlyle*) mumbling speech ; **mum'ble-news,** (*Shak.*) a tale-bearer ; **mum'-bler.**—*n.* and *adj.* **mum'bling.**—*adv.* **mum'-blingly.** [Frequentative from **mum.**]

Mumbo-jumbo, *mum'bō-jum'bō, n.* a god or bug-bear of West Africa : **mumbo-jumbo,** any object of foolish worship or fear : mummery or hocus-pocus. [Said to be Mandingo.]

mummock, *mum'ək.* Same as **mammock.**

mummy, *mum'i, n.* an embalmed or otherwise pre-served dead body : the substance of such a body, formerly used medicinally : dead flesh : anything pounded to a formless mass : a bituminous drug or pigment.—*v.t.* to mummify :—*pr.p.* **mumm'y-ing**; *pa.t.* and *pa.p.* **mumm'ied.**—*ns.* **mumm'ia,** mummy as a drug ; **mummifica'tion.**—*adj.* **mumm'iform.**—*v.t.* **mumm'ify,** to make into a mummy :—*pr.p.* **mumm'ifying**; *pa.t.* and *pa.p.* **mumm'ified.**—*ns.* **mumm'y-case**; **mumm'y-cloth,** cloth for wrapping a mummy : a similar fabric used as a basis for embroidery : a fabric like crape with cotton or silk warp and woollen weft ; **mumm'y-wheat,** a variety of wheat alleged (in-credibly) to descend from grains found in Egyptian mummy-cases. [O.Fr. *mumie*—L.L. *mumia*—Ar. and Pers. *mūmiyā*—Pers. *mūm,* wax.]

mump, *mump, v.t.* to mumble or mutter : to mumble or munch : to get by, or visit for the purpose of, begging or sponging : (*obs.*) to cheat.— *v.i.* to mumble : to sponge : to sulk : to mope : to grimace : to play the beggar.—*ns.* **mump'er,** one who mumps : (*old cant*) a beggar ; **mump'-ing-day,** St Thomas's Day, 21st Dec., when the poor used to go around begging corn, money, &c. —*adj.* **mump'ish,** having mumps : dull : sullen. — *adv.* **mump'ishly.** — *n.* **mump'ishness.** — *n.* (*orig. pl.*) **mumps,** an infectious inflammation of the parotid gland : gloomy silence. [Cf. **mum** and Du. *mompen,* to cheat.]

mumpsimus, *mump'si-məs, n.* an error cherished after exposure : an antiquated person. [An ignorant priest's blunder (in an old story) for L. *sūmpsimus,* we have received, in the mass.]

mun, *mun, v.t.* (*dial.*) must—used in pres. indic. only ; *3rd pers.* **mun.**—Also **maun, man.** [O.N. *mon, mun,* or *man* (inf. *monu, munu*), a preterite-present verb.]

mun, *mun, n.* a provincial form of **man.**

munch, *mun(t)sh, v.t.* and *v.i.* to chew with marked action of the jaws.—*n.* **munch'er.** [Prob. imit.]

Munda, *moon'dä, n.* any member of a group of peoples of eastern India, or speaker of their group of languages (also called Kolarian), a division of the Austroasiatic family.—Also *adj.*

mundane, *mun'dān, adj.* worldly : earthly : cosmic. —*adv.* **mun'danely.**—*n.* **mundanity** (*-dan'i-ti*). [L. *mundānus*—*mundus,* the world.]

mundic, *mun'dik, n.* iron pyrites. [From Cornish.]

mundify, *mun'di-fi, v.t.* to cleanse, purify.—*n.* **mundifica tion.**—*adj.* **mundif'icative.** [L.L. *mundificāre*—L. *mundus,* clean, *facĕre,* to make.]

mundungus, *mun-dung'gəs, n.* (*arch.*) a rank-smelling tobacco. [Sp. *mondongo,* black pudding.]

mungo, *mung'gō, n.* the waste produced in a woollen-mill from hard spun or felted cloth, or from tearing up old clothes, used in making cheap cloth. [Origin obscure.]

mungoose. Same as **mongoose.**

municipal, *mū-nis'i-pl, adj.* pertaining to home affairs : pertaining to the government of a borough. —*n.* **municipalisā'tion.**—*v.t.* **munic'ipalise,** to erect into a municipality : to bring under municipal control or ownership.—*ns.* **munic'ipalism,** concern for the interests of one's municipality : belief in municipal control ; **municipality** (*-pal'i-ti*), a self-governing town : a district governed like a city : in France, a division of the country.—*adv.* **munic'ipally.** [L. *mūnicipālis*—*mūniceps, -ipis,* an inhabitant of a *mūnicipium,* a free town—*mūnia,* official duties, *capĕre,* to take.]

munificence, *mū-nif'i-səns, n.* magnificent liber-ality in giving : bountifulness.—*adj.* **munif'icent.** —*adv.* **munif'icently.** [L. *mūnificentia*—*mūnus,* a present, *facĕre,* to make.]

munify, *mū'ni-fi, v.t.* to fortify.—*n.* **munifience** (*-nif'i-əns* ; *Spens.*), defence, fortification. [Irregu-larly formed from L. *mūnīre,* to fortify, *facĕre,* to make.]

muniment, *mū'ni-mənt, n.* a means of defence : a record fortifying or making good a claim : (in *pl.*) furnishings, equipment, things provided.—*v.t.* **munite',** (*Bacon*) to fortify, strengthen. — *ns.* **munition** (*-nish'ən* ; commonly in *pl.*), fortifica-tion : defence : material used in war : military stores ; **munitioneer', munit'ion-work'er,** a worker engaged in making munitions :—*fem.* (*vulg.*) **munitionette'.** [L. *mūnīre, -ītum,* to fortify ; *mūnīmentum,* fortification, later, title-deeds— *moenia,* walls.]

munnion, *mun'yən.* Same as **mullion.**

munshi, moonshee, *mōōn'shē, n.* (*India*) a secre-tary : an interpreter : a language teacher. [Hind. *munshī*—Ar. *munshi'.*]

muntin, munting, *munt'in(g), n.* the vertical framing piece between door panels. [montant.]

muntjak, muntjac, *munt'jak, n.* a name for a group of small deer of the Oriental region. [From the Malay name.]

muqaddam, mokaddam, mocuddum, *mōō-kud'-um, mō-, n.* a head-man. [Ar.]

muraena, murena, *mū-rē'nä, n.* a favourite food-fish of the Romans, a moray : **Muraena,** the moray genus, giving name to a family of eels, **Murae'nidae.** [L. *mūraena*—Gr. *mўraina.*]

mural, *mū'ral, adj.* of, on, attached to, or of the nature of, a wall.—*n.* (*obs.*) a wall (in *Shak.* only a conjectural emendation ; see **moral**) : (*U.S.*) mural decoration.—**mural circle,** a large graduated circle, fixed to a wall, for measuring arcs of the meridian ; **mural crown,** an embattled crown given among the ancient Romans to him who first mounted the wall of a besieged city ; **mural painting,** a painting executed, especially in dis-temper colours, upon the wall of a building. [L. *mūrālis*—*mūrus,* a wall.]

murder, *mur'dər, n.* the act of putting a person to death intentionally and unlawfully : excessive or reprehensible slaughter not legally murder : (hyperbolically) torture, excessive toil or hardship. —*v.t.* to kill (ordinarily a person) unlawfully with malice aforethought : to slaughter : (hyper-bolically) to torture : to mangle in performance. —Also (now only *dial.*) **murther** (*-dhər*).—*n.* **mur'derer** (*obs.* or *dial.* **mur'therer**), one who murders, or is guilty of murder : (*obs.*) a small cannon (also **mur'dering-piece**) :—*fem.* **mur'der-ess.**—*adj.* **mur'derous.**—*adv.* **mur'derously.**— **murder will out,** murder cannot remain hidden : the truth will come to light. [O.E. *morthor*—

morth, death; Ger. *mord*, Goth. *maurthr*; cf. L. *mors, mortis*, death.]

mure, *mūr, n. (Shak.)* a wall.—*v.t.* to wall in or up: to confine: to close.—*n.* **mur'age**, a tax for the building or upkeep of town-walls.—*adj.* **mur'-iform**, (*bot.*) with cells arranged like bricks in a wall. [Fr. *mur* and L. *mūrus*, a wall.]

Murex, *mū'reks, n.* a genus of gasteropod molluscs, some of which yielded the Tyrian purple dye:—*pl.* **mu'rexes**, **mu'rices** (*-ri-sēz*). [L. *mūrex, -icis.*]

murgeon, *mur'jan, n. (Scot.)* a grimace.—*v.t.* and *v.i.* to mock with grimaces. [Origin obscure.]

muriate, *mūr'i-āt, n.* (*arch.* and *popular*) a chloride. —*adjs.* **mur'iāted**, impregnated or combined with chlorine or a chloride; **muriatic** (*-at'ik*), briny: hydrochloric. [L. *muria*, brine.]

muricate, *mūr'i-kāt, adj.* (*bot.*) rough or warty with short sharp points.—Also **mur'icated**. [L. *mūricātus—mūrex, -icis*, a murex, a sharp stone.]

Muridae, *mū'ri-dē, n.pl.* the mouse family. [L. *mūs, mūris*, a mouse.]

murine, *mūr'īn, -in, adj.* mouselike: of the mouse family or subfamily.—*n.* a murine animal. [L. *mūrīnus—mūs, mūris*, mouse.]

murk, mirk, *murk, mərk, (Scot.) mirk,'n.* darkness.— *adj.* dark: gloomy: obscure.—*adv.* **murk'ily.**—*n.* **murk'iness.**—*adj.* **murk'ish.**—*adjs.* **mirk'-some**; **murk'y, mirk'y**, dark: obscure: gloomy. [O.E. *mirce* (n. and adj.), O.N. *myrkr*, Dan. and Sw. *mörk*; the forms with *i* are chiefly due to Spenserian and Scottish influence.]

murken, *mur'kən, adj.* (*Austr. slang*) out of season (applied to game in the close time).

murl, *murl, v.t.* and *v.i.* (*Scot.*) to crumble.—*adj.* **murl'y.** [Origin obscure.]

murlain, murlan, murlin, *mur'lən, n.* (*Scot.*) a round, narrow-mouthed basket. [Gael. *mùrlan.*]

murmur, *mur'mər, n.* a low, indistinct sound, like that of running water: a rustling sound from the heart, lungs, &c.: a glide-vowel: a muttered or subdued grumble or complaint: (*Shak.*) rumour. —*v.i.* to utter a murmur: to grumble.—*v.t.* to say or utter in a murmur.—*ns.* **murmurā'tion**, murmuring: a doubtful word for a flock of starlings; **mur'murer.**—*n.* and *adj.* **mur'muring.** —*adv.* **mur'muringly.**—*adj.* **mur'murous.**—*adv.* **mur'murously.** [Fr. *murmure*—L. *murmur*; cf. Gr. *mormýrein*, to surge.]

murphy, *mur'fi, n.* (*coll.*) a potato:—*pl.* **mur'phies.** [From the common Irish name *Murphy*.]

murra, *mur'ä, n.* an unknown precious material for vases, &c., first brought to Rome by Pompey (61 B.C.) from the East, conjectured to be agate.— *adjs.* **murrhine, murrine** (*mur'īn, -in*), **myrr-hine** (*mir'īn, -in*). [L. *murra*; Gr. *morria* (pl.).]

murrain, *mur'in, -ən, n.* (*obs.*) a pestilence: now only a cattle-plague, esp. foot-and-mouth disease. —*adj.* affected with murrain: confounded.—*adv.* confoundedly. — Also **murr'en** (*Shak., Milt.*), **murr'ion** (*Shak.*), **murr'in** (*Spens.*).—*adj.* **murr'-ained.** [O.Fr. *morine*, pestilence, carcass.]

murram, *mur'əm.* Same as **marram.**

murre, *mur, n.* a guillemot: a razorbill. — *n.* **murrelet** (*mur'lit*), a name for various small birds akin to the guillemot. [Origin obscure.]

murrey, *mur'i, n.* and *adj.* mulberry-colour, dark purplish red. [O.Fr. *moré*—L. *mōrum*, mulberry.]

murr(h)ine. See **murra.**

murry. Same as **moray** (q.v.).

murther, murtherer. Same as **murder, mur-derer.**

murva, moorva, *mōōr'vä, n.* bowstring hemp. [Sans. *mūrvā*.]

Musa, *mū'zä, n.* the banana genus, giving name to a family **Musā'ceae** of (mostly) gigantic treelike herbs.—*adj.* **musā'ceous.** [Latinised from Ar. *mauz.*]

musang, *m(y)ōō-sang', n.* a paradoxure, or kindred animal. [Malay *mūsang.*]

Musca, *mus'kä, n.* the house-fly genus:—*pl.* **muscae**, *mus'ē.* — *n.* **muscatō'rium**, (*Eastern Church*) a flabellum.—*adj.* **muscid** (*mus'id*), of the house-fly family **Muscidae** (*mus'i-dē*).—*n.* a member of the family.—**muscae volitantes** (L.,

fluttering flies), ocular spectra like floating black spots before the eyes. [L. *musca*, a fly.]

muscadel, *mus-kə-del', or mus'.* Same as **mus-catel.**

muscadin, *müs-kä-danə, n. (hist.)* a fop or dandy: a middle-class moderate revolutionary. [Fr.]

muscadine, *mus'kə-dīn, -din, n.* (*arch.*) muscatel (wine, grape, or pear). [Perh. Prov. *muscat*, fem. *muscade.*]

muscardine, *mus'kär-din, -dēn, -dīn, n.* a silkworm disease caused by a fungus (Botrytis). [Fr.]

muscat, *mus'kat, n.* muscatel wine: a musky grape or its vine. [Prov. *muscat.*]

muscatel, *mus-kə-tel', or mus', n.* a rich spicy wine, of various kinds: a grape of musky smell or taste: the vine producing it: a raisin from the muscatel grape: a variety of pear.—Also **mus-cadel.** [O.Fr. *muscatel, muscadel*—Prov. *muscat*, musky.]

Muschelkalk, *moosh'əl-kälk, n.* the middle member of the Trias in Germany, largely shelly limestone —wanting in Britain. [Ger. *muschel*, shell, *kalk*, lime.]

Musci, *mus'ī, n.pl.* mosses, one of the two great divisions of the Bryophytes, the other being the Hepaticae or liverworts.—*n.* **muscology** (*-kol'ə-ji*), bryology.—*adjs.* **mus'coid** (*-koid*), **mus'cose**, moss-like. [L. *muscus*, moss.]

muscle, *mus'l, n.* a contractile structure by which bodily movement is effected: the tissue of which it is composed, flesh: bodily strength.—*v.i.* (*U.S.*) to make one's way, thrust.—*adjs.* **musc'le-bound**, having the muscles stiff and enlarged by over-exercise; **muscled** (*mus'ld*), having muscles.—*ns.* **musc'le-reading**, the interpretation of slight involuntary muscular movements; **musc'ling**, the delineation of muscles, as in a picture. [Fr. *muscle*, or directly—L. *mūsculus*, dim. of *mūs*, a mouse, a muscle.]

muscovado, *mus-kō-vä'dō, n.* unrefined sugar, after evaporating the cane-juice and draining off the molasses. [Sp. *mascabado.*]

Muscovy, *mus'kə-vi, n.* (*hist.*) the old principality of Moscow: extended to Russia in general.— *ns.* and *adjs.* **Muscovian** (*-kō'vi-ən*), Muscovite; **Mus'covite**, of Muscovy: Russian: a Russian: **muscovite**, (*min.*) common white mica, first got in Russia, a silicate of aluminium and potassium: its thin transparent plates, still used as ,glass— also **Muscovy glass.**—*adj.* **Muscovitic** (*-vit'ik*). —*n.* **mus'covy-duck** (see **musk**). [*Moscovia*, Latinised from Russ. *Moskva*, Moscow.]

muscular, *mus'kū-lər, adj.* pertaining to a muscle: consisting of muscles: having strong muscles: brawny: strong: vigorous. — *n.* **muscularity** (*-lar'i-ti*). — *adv.* **mus'cularly.** — *ns.* **musculā'-tion**, muscular action: musculature; **mus'culā-ture**, provision, disposition, and system of muscles. —*adj.* **mus'culous**, (*obs.*) muscular.—**muscular Christianity**, a vigorous combination of Christian living with devotion to athletic enjoyments asso-ciated with Charles Kingsley (who repudiated the name). [L. *mūsculus*; see **muscle.**]

muse, *mūz, v.i.* to study in silence: to be absent-minded: to meditate.—*v.t.* to meditate on: (*Shak.*) to wonder at: to say musingly.—*n.* deep thought: contemplation: a state or fit of absence of mind.—*adjs.* **mused**, bemused, muzzy, fuddled; **muse'ful**, meditative. — *adv.* **muse'fully.** — *n.* **mus'er.**—*n.* and *adj.* **mus'ing.**—*adv.* **mus'ingly.** [Fr. *muser*, to loiter, in O.Fr. to muse; perh. orig. to hold the muzzle (O.Fr. *muse*) in the air, as a dog that has lost the scent; perh. influenced by next word.]

Muse, *mūz, n.* one of the nine goddesses of the liberal arts—daughters of Zeus and Mnemosyne (**Calliope**, of epic poetry; **Clio**, of history; **Erato**, of love poetry; **Euterpe**, of lyric poetry; **Melpomene**, of tragedy; **Polyhymnia**, of lyric poetry and eloquence; **Terpsichore**, of dancing; **Thalia**, of comedy; **Urania**, of astronomy): an inspiring goddess more vaguely imagined: poetic character: poetry or art: (*Milt.*) an inspired poet. [Fr.,—L. *Mūsa*—Gr. *Mousa.*]

muset. Same as **musit.**]

musette, *mū-zet'*, *n.* an old French bagpipe: a simple pastoral melody or gavotte trio for, or in imitation of, the bagpipe. [Fr., dim. of *muse*, a bagpipe.]

museum, *mū-zē'əm*, *n.* orig. a temple, home, or resort of the Muses: a place of study: a resort of the learned: an institution or repository for the collection, exhibition, and study of objects of artistic, scientific, historic, or educational interest: (*U.S.*) an art gallery: a collection of curiosities: —*pl.* muse'ums.—*n.* muse'um-piece, a fine specimen, suitable for exhibit in a museum, or unsuitable for anything else. [L. *mūsēum*—Gr. *mouseion*; see Muse (2).]

mush, *mush*, *n.* meal boiled in water, esp. Indian meal: anything pulpy: sloppy sentimentality: rubbish: background of noise from a wireless receiver.—*v.t.* to reduce to mush: (*prov.*) to crush the spirit of, wear out.—*adv.* mush'ily.—*n.* mush'iness.—*adj.* mush'y. [Prob. mash.]

mush, *mush*, *v.t.* (*Scot.*) to notch or scallop the edges of. [Perh. Fr. *moucher*, to trim.]

mush, *mush*, *v.i.* (*Canada*) to travel on foot with dogs over snow.—*n.* a journey of this kind.—*n.* mush'er. [Prob. Fr. *marcher*, to walk.]

musha, *mush'ä*, *interj.* (*Irish*) expressing surprise. [Ir. *maiseadh*.]

mushroom, *mush'room*, *n.* an edible fungus (*Agaricus*, or *Psalliota*, *campestris*, or kindred species) of toadstool form: any edible fungus: any fungus of umbrella shape whether edible or not: any fungus: an object shaped like a mushroom: a hat with drooping brim: (*slang*) an umbrella: (*fig.*) anything of rapid growth and decay: (*fig.*) one who rises suddenly from a low condition: an upstart.—*adj.* of or like a mushroom.—*v.i.* to expand like a mushroom cap: to gather mushrooms.—*ns.* mush'room-anch'or, an anchor with mushroom-shaped head; mush'-roomer. [O.Fr. *mousseron*, perh. *mousse*, moss, which may be of Germanic origin.]

music, *mū'zik*, *n.* the art of expression in sound, in melody, and harmony, including both composition and execution: sometimes specially of instrumental performance to the exclusion of singing: the science underlying it: (*obs.*) a musical composition: the performance of musical compositions: compositions collectively: a connected series of sweet sounds: melody or harmony: pleasing sound: sound of definite pitch, not mere noise: (*arch.*) a band of musicians: (*obs.* or *dial.*) musical instruments: written or printed representation of tones, expression, &c., or of what is to be played or sung: sheets or books of parts or scores collectively: harmonious character: (*U.S.*) fun.—*adj.* of or for music.—*v.i.* to perform music:—*pr.p.* mu'sicking.—*adj.* mu'sical, pertaining to, of, with, or producing music: pleasing to the ear: of definite pitch (unlike mere noise): melodious: having skill in, or aptitude or taste for, music.—*n.* a musical person, party, or performance.—*n.* musicality (-*al'i-ti*).—*adv.* mu'sically.—*ns.* mu'sicalness; mu'sic-box, (*obs.*) a barrel-organ: a musical box: (jocularly) a piano; mu'sic-case, -fō'lio, a roll, portfolio, &c., for carrying sheet music; mu'sic-demy', a size of writing-paper, 20¾ in. × 14⅞ in.; mu'sic-dra'ma, that form of opera introduced by Wagner in which the relations of music and drama are reformed; mu'sic-hall, orig. and still sometimes a concert-hall, usu. now a hall for variety entertainments; mu'sic-holder, a music-case: a clip, rack, or desk for holding music during performance; mu'sic-house, a concert-hall: a firm dealing in music or musical instruments; musician (*mū-zish'ən*), one skilled in music: a performer or composer of music, esp. professional—(*obs.* or *dial.*) musi'cianer, mu'sicker.—*adj.* musi'cianly, characteristic of, or becoming, a musician.—*ns.* musi'cianship; mu'sic-master, -mistress, -teacher, a teacher of music.—*adj.* musicolog'ical.—*ns.* musicol'-ogist; musicol'ogy, scientific study of music; mu'sic-paper, paper ruled for writing music; mu'sic-pen, a five-channelled pen for drawing the stave; mu'sic-rack, a rack attached to a musical instrument for holding the player's music; mu'sic-roll', a case for carrying music rolled up: a roll of perforated paper for mechanical piano-playing; mu'sic-room, a room in which music is performed: (*obs.*) a room beside the stage in which the musicians were stationed; mu'sic-seller, a dealer in printed music; mu'sic-shell, a volute shell with markings like music; mu'sic-stand, a light adjustable desk for holding music during performance; mu'sic-stool, a piano-stool.—face the music (see face); musical box, a toy that plays tunes automatically, by projections from a revolving barrel twitching a comb; musical chairs, the game of prancing round a diminishing row of chairs and securing one when the music stops; musical comedy, a light dramatic entertainment with sentimental songs and situations held together by a minimum of plot; musical director, the conductor of an orchestra (in a theatre, &c.); musical flame, a flame that gives a musical tone when surrounded by an open tube; musical glasses (see harmonica); musical sand, sand of nearly uniform size of grain that gives out a definite note when walked on; music of the spheres (see spheres); rough music, uproar: charivari. [Fr. *musique*—L. *mūsica*—Gr. *mousikē* (*technē*), musical (art)—*Mousa*, a Muse.]

musimon, *mūs'* or *mus'-i-mon*, **musmon**, *mus'mon*, *n.* the moufflon. [L. *mus(i)mō, -ōnis*.]

musit, *mū'zit*, *n.* (*Shak.*) a gap in a fence or thicket through which an animal passes. [meuse (1).]

musive, *mū'siv*, *adj.* Same as mosaic (1).

musk, *musk*, *n.* a strong-smelling substance, used in perfumery, got chiefly from the male musk-deer: the odour thereof: the musk-deer: a species of Mimulus, said once to have smelt of musk.—*adj.*, or prefix to the names of many animals and plants, supposed to smell of musk.—*v.t.* to perfume with musk.—*ns.* musk'-bag, -cod, -pod, -pouch, -sac, a musk-gland; musk'-bag, -ball, a bag, ball, containing musk, as a perfuming sachet; musk'-beet'le, a longicorn beetle that smells of attar of roses; musk'-cat, a musk-yielding animal, usu. the musk-deer, prob. confused with the civet-cat: a scented effeminate dandy: a courtesan; musk'-ca'vy, the hog-rat; musk'-deer, a hornless deer (*Moschus moschiferus*) of Asia, chief source of musk; musk'-duck (also by confusion muscovy-duck), a large musky-smelling South American duck (*Cairina moschata*).—*adj.* musked (*muskt*), smelling or tasting like musk.—*n.* musk'-gland, a skin-pit in some animals producing musk.—*adv.* musk'ily.—*ns.* musk'iness; musk'-mall'ow, a species of mallow with faint odour of musk; musk'-mel'on, the common melon (apparently transferred from a musky-scented kind); musk'-ox, a long-haired ruminant (*Ovibos moschatus*) of northern Canada, exhaling a strong musky smell; musk'-pear, a fragrant variety of pear; musk'-plant, *Mimulus moschatus*; musk'-plum, a fragrant kind of plum; musk'-rat, the musquash: a musk-shrew: its skin; musk'-rose, a fragrant species of rose; musk'-sheep, the musk-ox; musk'-shrew, the desman: a musky-smelling Indian shrew; musk'-thist'le, a thistle (*Carduus nutans*) with large drooping scented heads.—*adj.* musk'y, having the odour of musk. [Fr. *musc*—L. *muscus*, Gr. *moschos*, prob.—Pers. *mushk*, perh.—Sans. *mushka*, a testicle (for which the gland has been mistaken).]

muskeg, *mus-keg'*, *n.* (*Canada*) swamp, bog, marsh. [Cree Indian word.]

musket, *mus'kit*, *n.* a male sparrow-hawk: a military hand firearm, esp. of an old-fashioned smooth-bore kind.—*n.* musketeer', a soldier armed with a musket; musketoon', musquetoon', a short musket: a soldier armed with one.—*adj.* mus'ket-proof, capable of resisting the force of a musket-ball.—*ns.* mus'ket-rest, a forked support for the heavy sixteenth-century musket; mus'ketry, muskets collectively: practice with, or the art of using, small-arms: fire of muskets: a body of troops armed with muskets; mus'ket-shot, shot for or from a musket: the discharge of a musket:

the range of a musket. [O.Fr. *mousquet*, musket, formerly a hawk—It. *moschetto*, perh.—L. *musca*, a fly.]

Muslim, *muz´*, *mus´lim*, *n.* and *adj.* Same as Moslem.

muslin, *muz´lin*, *n.* a fine soft cotton fabric, gauzy in appearance, but woven plain: (*U.S.*) cotton cloth for shorts, &c.: (*slang*) womankind: (*naut.*) (*slang*) sails, canvas: a collector's name for several different moths. — *adj.* made of muslin.— *adj.* **mus´lined,** clothed with muslin.—*ns.* **muslinet´,** a coarse kind of muslin; **mus´lin-kale,** (*Scot.*) thin broth made without meat. [Fr. *mousseline*—It. *mussolino*, from It. *Mussolo*, the town of Mosul in Mesopotamia.]

musquash, *mus´kwosh*, *n.* a large aquatic American animal akin to the voles, very destructive to dams and waterways (also *musk-rat*): its fur. [From an Amer. Ind. word.]

musrol, *muz´rōl*, *n.* (*obs.*) the nose-band of a bridle. [Fr. *muserolle*—It. *museruola*—*muso*, muzzle.]

muss, musse, *mus*, *n.* (*Shak.*) a scramble: disturbance: confusion, disorder: (*U.S.*) confused conflict: a mess.—*v.t.* and *v.i.* to disarrange: to mess.—*n.* **muss´iness.**—*adj.* **muss´y,** disordered. [Perh. different words; cf. **mess.**]

mussel, *mus´l* (formerly also **muscle, muskle,** *mus´l, mus´kl*), *n.* a marine lamellibranch shellfish of the family Mytilidae: a freshwater lamellibranch of the Unionidae: the shell of any of these: a mussel-plum.—*adj.* **mussel´led,** poisoned by eating infected mussels.—*ns.* **muss´el-plum,** a dark purple plum not unlike a mussel-shell; **muss´el-scalp´** (*Scot.* **-scaup**), a bed of mussels; **musse´l-shell´**. [O.E. *mús(c)le* ; cf. Ger. *muschel,* Fr. *moule*; all from L. *músculus*, dim. of *mús*, mouse.]

mussitation, *mus-i-tā´shən*, *n.* low muttering: speaking movement without sound.—*v.t.* **muss´itate,** to mutter. [L. *mussitāre*, freq. of *mussāre*, to mutter.]

Mussulman, Musulman, *mus´l-mən*, *-män´*, *n.* a Mohammedan :—*pl.* **Muss´ulmans**; blunderingly or facetiously **Mussulmen.**—Similarly **Muss´ul-woman.** [Pers. *musulmān*—Ar. *muslim, moslim,* Moslem.]

must, *must*, *v.t.* am, is, are obliged physically or morally: cannot but: insist upon (with *inf.* without *to*):—used only in the present (orig. past) indic. :—*3rd pers. sing.* **must.** [Orig. p.a.t. of *mote*—O.E. *móste,* p.a.t. of *mót*; cf. Ger. *müssen.*]

must, *must*, *n.* new wine: unfermented, or only partially fermented, grape-juice or other juice or pulp for fermentation: process of fermentation.—*adj.* **must´y.** [O.E. *must*—L. *mustum* (*vīnum*), new (wine).]

must, *must*, *n.* mustiness: mould. [App. back formation—**musty.**]

must, *must*, *n.* dangerous frenzy in some male animals, as elephants.—*adj.* in such a state.—*adj.* **must´y.** [Pers. and Hind. *mast,* intoxicated.]

must, muist, moust, *müst, moost,* *n.* (*obs. Scot.*) musk: hair-powder. — *v.t.* to powder. [O.Fr. *must,* a form of *musc*; see **musk.**]

mustache, mustachio. Same as **moustache.**

mustang, *mus´tang,* *n.* the feralised horse of the American prairies. [Sp. *mestengo,* now *mesteño,* belonging to the *mesta* or graziers' union, combined with *mostrenco,* homeless, stray.]

mustard, *mus´tərd,* *n.* the powdered seeds of various species of the Sinapis section of the genus Brassica: a pungent condiment made from it: the plant yielding it.—*ns.* **mus´tard-gas,** the vapour from a poisonous blistering liquid, (CH₂Cl·CH₂)₂S, got from ethelene and sulphur chloride; **mus´tard-oil,** a volatile oil got from black mustard seeds; **mus´tard-plas´ter,** a plaster made from black and white mustard flour, deprived of their fixed oil; **mus´tard-tree,** a name given to a shrub *Salvadora persica* (family Salvadoraceae, prob. akin to Oleaceae) on the theory that it is the plant referred to in the N.T., which others think is only black mustard grown tall, as it does in Palestine.— **black mustard,** *Brassica nigra*; **French mustard,** mustard prepared for table by adding salt, sugar,

vinegar, &c.; **garlic-mustard, hedge-mustard** (see **garlic, hedge**); **mustard and cress,** a salad of seedlings of white mustard and garden cress; **Sarep´ta mustard,** *Brassica juncea*; **white mustard,** *Brassica alba*; **wild mustard,** charlock. [O.Fr. *mo*(*u*)*sturde* (Fr. *moutarde*)—L. *mustum,* must (because the condiment was prepared with must).]

mustee. Same as **mestee.**

Mustela, *mus-tē´lä,* *n.* the marten genus, giving name to the family **Muste´lidae** (otters, badgers, and weasels) and the subfamily **Musteli´nae** (weasels and martens).—*adj.* and *n.* **mus´teline** (*-tal-īn*). [L. *mustēla,* weasel.]

muster, *mus´tər,* *n.* (*obs.*) a display, demonstration: (*arch.*) an example: a commercial sample: an assembling or calling together, esp. of troops, as for inspection, verification, &c.: inspection: an assembly: a register: (*Austr.*) a round-up: (perh. orig. a misunderstanding) a company of peacocks. —*v.t.* and *v.i.* (*obs.*) to show forth: to assemble: to enroll: to number.—*v.t.* to summon up (often with *up*).—*v.i.* to pass muster.—*ns.* **mus´terbook,** (*Shak.*) a book in which military forces or a ship's crew are registered; **mus´ter-file,** (*Shak.*) a muster-roll; **mus´ter-master,** one who has charge of the muster-roll; **mus´ter-party,** (*Austr.*) a rounding-up party; **mus´ter-roll,** a register of the officers and men in each company, troop, regiment, ship's crew, &c.: (*naut.*) roll-call.— **muster in,** (*U.S.*) to enroll, receive as recruits; **muster out,** (*U.S.*) to discharge from service; **pass muster,** to bear examination, be well enough. [O.Fr. *mostre, moustre, monstre*—L. *mōnstrum*—*monēre,* to warn.]

musty. See **must** (2 and 4).

musty, *must´i,* *adj.* mouldy: spoiled by damp: stale in smell or taste: deteriorated from disuse.

Musulman. Same as **Mussulman.**

mutable, *mū´ta-bl,* *adj.* that may be changed: subject to change: variable: inconstant, fickle.— *ns.* **mutabil´ity, mu´tableness.**—*adv.* **mu´tably.** —*n.* **mu´tagen,** (*biol.*) a substance that produces mutations.—*adj.* **mutagen´ic.**—*ns.* **mutan´dum,** something to be altered :—*pl.* **mutan´da**; **mu´tant,** a form arising by mutation.—*v.t.* and *v.i.* **mūtate´,** to cause or undergo mutation.—*ns.* **mutā´tion,** change: umlaut: in Celtic languages a change of initial consonant depending on the preceding word: in old music a change of syllable for the same note in passing to another hexachord: (*biol.*) discontinuous variation or sudden inheritable divergence from ancestral type; **mutā´tionist,** a believer in evolution by mutation.—*adjs.* **mu´tative, mu´tatory,** changing: mutable.—**mutation stop,** an organ-stop whose tones differ from those the keys indicate by an interval other than a whole number of octaves. [L. *mūtāre, -ātum,* to change —*movēre mōtum,* to move.]

mutch, *much, n.* (*Scot.*) a woman's close cap. [M.Du. *mutse*; Du. *muts,* Ger. *mütze.*]

mutchkin, *much´kin, n.* a Scottish liquid measure, three-fourths of an imperial, one-fourth of a Scottish pint. [Obsolete Du. *mudseken.*]

mute, *mūt, adj.* dumb: silent: (*law*) refusing to plead: without vocal utterance: unpronounced or faintly pronounced: pronounced by stoppage of the breath-passage.—*n.* a dumb person: a silent person: (*law*) one who refuses to plead: a funeral attendant: a dumb servant in an Eastern house: an actor with no words to speak: a stop-consonant: a clip, pad, or other device for subduing the sound of a musical instrument.—*v.t.* to deaden the sound of with a mute: to silence.— *adv.* **mute´ly.**—*ns.* **mute´ness**; **mut´ism,** dumbness.—**mute of malice,** (*law*) refusing to plead; **mute swan,** the common swan. [L. *mūtus.*]

mute, *mūt, v.i.* to dung, as birds.—*n.* birds' dung: an act of muting. [O.Fr. *mutir, esmeutir*; prob. Germanic; cf. **smelt.**]

mutessarif, *mōō-tes-ä´rif, n.* the head of a Turkish sanjak.—*n.* **mutessa´rifat,** his office or jurisdiction. [Turk. *mutesarif*—Ar. *mutasarrif.*]

muticous, *mūt´i-kəs, adj.* awnless: spineless: pointless. [L. *muticus,* awnless.]

mutilate, *mū′ti-lāt*, *v.t.* to maim: to remove a material part of: to deform by slitting, boring, or removing a part.—*adj.* mutilated.—*ns.* **mutilā′-tion**; **mu′tilātor**. [L. *mutilāre*, *-ātus*—*mutilus*.]

mutine, *mū′tin*, *n.* (*obs.*) mutiny: (*Shak.*) a mutineer, rebel.—*v.i.* (*Shak.*, *Milt.*) to mutiny, rebel.—*n.* **mutineer′**, one who mutinies.—*v.i.* to mutiny.—*adj.* **mu′tinous**, disposed to mutiny: unsubmissive: of the nature of, or expressing, mutiny.—*adv.* **mu′tinously.**—*n.* **mu′tinousness.** —*n.* **mu′tiny**, insurrection against constituted authority, esp. naval or military: revolt, tumult, strife.—*v.i.* to rise against authority, esp. in military or naval service:—*pr.p.* **mu′tinying**; *past.* and *pa.p.* **mu′tinied.**—**Mutiny Act**, an act passed by the British parliament from year to year, to regulate the government of the army, from 1689 down to 1879, when it was superseded. [Fr. *mutin*, *mutine*, *mōtum*, to move.]

mutoscope, *mū′tō-skōp*, *n.* an early form of cinematograph. [L. *mūtāre*, to change, Gr. *skopeein*, to look at.]

mutt, *mut*, *n.* (*slang*, orig. *U.S.*) a blockhead. [Perh. for **mutton-head.**]

mutter, *mut′ər*, *v.i.* to utter words in a low, indistinct voice: to murmur, esp. in hostility, grumbling, mutiny, or menace: to sound with a low rumbling. —*v.t.* to utter indistinctly.—*n.* (*Milt.*) a murmuring: indistinct utterance: low rumbling: subdued grumbling.—*ns.* **mutterā′tion**, (*Richardson*) complaining; **mutt′erer.**—*n.* and *adj.* **mutt′ering.**—*adv.* **mutt′eringly.** [Prob. imit., like prov. Ger. *muttern*; L. *muttīre.*]

mutton, *mut′n*, *n.* (*obs.* or *jocular*) a sheep: sheep's flesh as food: (*old slang*) woman as food for lust, hence illicit commerce.—*ns.* **mutt′on-bird**, an Australasian short-tailed shearwater whose flesh is said to taste like mutton; **mutt′on-chop.**—*adj.* shaped like a mutton-chop (of whiskers).—*ns.* **mutt′on-cut′let**; **mutt′on-fist**, a coarse, big hand: a printer's index-hand; **mutt′on-ham**, a salted leg of mutton; **mutt′on-head**, a heavy, stupid person.—*adj.* **mutt′on-head′ed**, stupid.—*ns.* **mutt′on-su′et**, the fat about the kidneys and loins of sheep; **mutt′on-thump′er**, a clumsy bookbinder.—*adj.* **mutt′ony.** — **laced mutton**, (*Shak.*) a loose woman; **return to our muttons**, (*coll.*) return to the subject of discussion—a playful translation of the judge's 'Revenons à nos moutons' in the old French farce of *Maître Pathelin*, in which the witnesses wander from the matter in dispute, some sheep. [O.Fr. *moton* (Fr. *mouton*), a sheep—L.L. *multō*, *-ōnis*; perh. of Celt. origin.]

mutual, *mū′tū-əl*, *adj.* interchanged: reciprocal: given and received: (*Shak.*; now regarded as incorrect) common, joint, shared by two or more.—*n.* **mutualisā′tion.**—*v.t.* **mu′tualise**, to put upon a mutual footing.—*ns.* **mu′tualism**, symbiosis, association benefiting both; **mutuality** (*-al′i-ti*). —*adv.* **mu′tually.**—**mutual-admiration society**, a group of persons supposed, generally satirically or humorously, to overestimate one another's and their own merits; **mutual friend**, (*Dickens*) a common friend; **mutual-improvement society**, a society whose members meet to hear lectures, read essays, hold debates, &c., in order to stimulate each other to improve in knowledge and in public speaking; **mutual insurance**, the system of a company in which the policy-holders are the shareholders; **mutual wall**, a wall equally belonging to each of two houses. [Fr. *mutuel*—L. *mūtuus*—*mūtāre*, to change.]

mutule, *mūt′ūl*, *n.* a kind of square, flat bracket, in Doric architecture, above each triglyph and each metope, with guttae. [L. *mūtulus*, a mutule, modillion.]

mutuum, *mū′tū-əm*, *n.* a bailment consisting of a loan of goods for consumption, as corn, coal, &c., to be returned in goods of the same amount. [L. neut. of *mūtuus*, lent.]

mux, *muks*, *v.t.* (*U.S.* and *dial.*) to spoil, botch.—*n.* a mess. [Origin obscure.]

muzhik, **moujik**, *mōō-zhik′*, *mōō′zhik*, *n.* a Russian peasant. [Russ. *muzhik′*.]

muzzle, *muz′l*, *n.* the projecting jaws and nose of an animal: a strap or a cage for the mouth to prevent biting: the extreme end of a gun, &c.—*v.t.* to put a muzzle on: to keep from hurting: to gag or silence.—*v.t.* and *v.i.* to touch, thrust, or investigate with the muzzle.—*ns.* **muzz′le-bag**, a canvas bag fixed to the muzzle of a gun at sea, to keep out water; **muzz′le-load′er**, a firearm loaded through the muzzle—opp. to *breech-loader.* — *adj.* **muzz′le - load′ing.** — *ns.* **muzz′ler**, one who muzzles: a blow on the mouth: a muzzle-loader: a direct head-wind; **muzz′le-veloc′ity**, the velocity of a projectile the moment it leaves the muzzle of a gun. [O.Fr. *musel* (Fr. *museau*)—L.L. *mūsellum*, dim. of *mūsum* or *mūsus*, beak.]

muzzy, *muz′i*, *adj.* dazed, bewildered: tipsy: blurred: hazy.—*adv.* **muzz′ily.** — *n.* **muzz′i-ness.** [Origin unknown.]

mvule, *mvōō′le*, *n.* a huge tropical African timber tree (*Chlorophora excelsa*) of the mulberry family.

my, *mī* (sometimes *mi*), *poss. adj.* or *gen.* of *pron.* I, of or belonging to me.—*interj.* expressing surprise (perh. for **my word**, or **my God**). [*mine*—O.E. *mīn* (gen.), of me.]

Mya, *mī′ä*, *n.* a genus of lamellibranch molluscs, the gapers, including the American soft or long clam. [Gr. *mȳs* or *myax*, a mussel.]

myalgia, *mī-al′ji-ä*, *n.* pain in muscle.—*adj.* **myal′gic.** [Gr. *mȳs*, muscle, *algos*, pain.]

myalism, *mī′əl-izm*, *n.* West Indian negro witchcraft.—*adj.* **my′al.** [Prob. of West African origin.]

myall, *mī′awl*, *n.* a wild Australian black.—*adj.* wild. [Australian *mail*, the blacks.]

myall, *mī′awl*, *n.* an Australian acacia of various species with hard, scented wood: their wood. [Australian *maiäl*.]

mycelium, *mī-sē′li-əm*, *n.* the white thread-like mass of hyphae forming the thallus of a fungus:—*pl.* **myce′lia.**—*adj.* **myce′lial.** [Gr. *mȳkēs*, a mushroom.]

Mycenaean, *mī-sē-nē′ən*, *adj.* of the ancient citystate of *Mycēnae* (Gr. *Mykēnai*) in Argolis, Agamemnon's kingdom, or its culture culminating in the Bronze Age.

Mycetes, *mī-sē′tēz*, *n.* the howler genus of South American monkeys. [Gr. *mykētēs*, bellower.]

mycetes, *mī-sē′tēz*, *n.pl.* (*rare* except in composition) fungi.—*ns.* **mycetol′ogy**, mycology; **mycetō′ma**, Madura foot, a disease of foot and leg in India, caused by a fungus.—*n.pl.* **Mycetozō′a**, the Myxomycetes or slime-fungi (when regarded as animals).—*n.* and *adj.* **mycetozō′an.**—*n.* **mycodomatium** (*mī-kō-dō′mä-shyəm*), a fungusgall:—*pl.* **mycodomā′tia.**—*adjs.* **mycologic** (*mī-kə-loj′ik*), **-al.**—*ns.* **mycologist** (*-kol′*); **mycol′ogy**, the study of fungi; **mycophagist** (*mī-kof′ə-jist*; Gr. *phagein*, to eat), a toadstool-eater; **mycoph′agy**; **mycorrhiza**, **mycorhiza** (*mī-kō-rī′zä*; Gr. *rhiza*, root), a fungal mycelium investing or penetrating the underground parts of a higher plant and supplying it with material from humus instead of root-hairs.—*adj.* **mycor(r)hī′zal.** —*n.* **mycosis** (*-kō′sis*), a disease due to growth of a fungus.—*adj.* **mycotic** (*-kot′ik*). [Gr. *mȳkēs*, *-ētos*, pl. *mȳkētēs*, a mushroom.]

mydriasis, *mi-drī′ə-sis*, *n.* morbid dilatation of the pupil of the eye.—*adj.* **mydriatic** (*mid-ri-at′ik*).—*n.* a drug causing this. [Gr. *mydriāsis*.]

myelitis, *mī-e-lī′tis*, *n.* inflammation of the spinal cord, or sometimes of the bone-marrow.—*n.* **my′elin**, the substance forming the medullary sheath of nerve-fibres.—*adj.* **my′eloid**, like, pertaining to, or of the nature of, marrow.—*n.* **my′elon**, the spinal cord. [Gr. *myelos*, marrow.]

mygale, *mig′ə-lē*, *n.* an American bird-catching spider. [Gr. *mȳgalē*, a field-mouse, a shrew—*mȳs*, mouse, *galeē*, weasel.]

myiasis, *mī′i-ə-sis*, *mī-ī-ā′sis*, *n.* disease caused by presence of flies or their larvae. [Gr. *myïa*, fly.]

Mylodon, *mī′lə-don*, *n.* a genus of gigantic Pleistocene ground-sloths.—*adj.* **my′lodont.** [Gr. *mylē*, a mill, *odous*, *odontos*, a tooth.]

mylohyoid, *mī-lō-hī′oid*, *adj.* pertaining to or near

the jaw-bone and the hyoid bone.—*n*. a muscle so placed. [Gr. *mylē*, a mill.]

mylonite, *mī′lən-īt*, *n*. a hard compact often streaky granular rock produced by crushing.—*adj*. **my-lonitic** (-*it′ik*).—*n*. **mylonītisā′tion**.—*v.t*. **my′-lonītise**, to turn into mylonite. [Gr. *mylōn*, a mill.]

myna, mynah, mina, *mī′nä*, *n*. a common black brown and white Indian bird of the starling family: applied also to several allied kinds. [Hind. *mainā*.]

mynheer, *min-hār′*, Du. *mən-ār′*, *n*. my lord: Dutch for *Mr* or *sir*: a Dutchman. [Du. *mijn*, my, *heer*, lord.]

myo-, *mī′ō-*, *mī-o′-*, in composition, muscle.—*n*. **my′oblast**, a cell producing muscle-tissue.—*adj*. **myoblast′ic**.—*ns*. **myocardī′tis**, inflammation of the myocardium; **myocar′dium**, the muscular substance of the heart; **my′ogram**, a myographic record; **my′ograph**, an instrument for recording muscular contractions.—*adjs*. **myograph′ic, -al**.—*ns*.**myog′raphist**; **myog′raphy**.—*adjs*.**my′oid**, like muscle; **myolog′ical**. — *ns*. **myol′ogist**; **myol′ogy**, the study of muscles; **myō′ma**, a tumour composed of muscular tissue; **my′osin**, a globulin of muscle whose formation is the cause of rigor mortis; **myosī′tis** (irregularly formed), inflammation of a muscle. [Gr. *mȳs, mȳos*, muscle.]

myomancy, *mī′ō-man-si*, *n*. divination from the movements of mice.—*adj*. **myoman′tic**. [Gr. *mȳs*, a mouse, *manteiā*, divination.]

myopia, *mī-ō′pi-ä*, *n*. shortness of sight.—*adj*. **myopic** (-*op′*), short-sighted.—*n*. a short-sighted person.—*ns*. **my′ops** (-*ops*), **my′ope** (-*ōp*), a short-sighted person. [Gr. *myōps*, short-sighted—*mȳein*, to shut, *ōps*, the eye.]

myosis, *mī-ō′sis*, *n*. abnormal contraction of the pupil of the eye.—*adjs*. **myosit′ic**; **myotic** (-*ot′*).—Also *n*. [Gr. *mȳein*, to close, blink.]

Myosotis, *mī-os-ō′tis*, *n*. the forget-me-not genus of the borage family. [Gr. *myosōtis*, Asperugo, pellitory—*mȳs, mȳos*, a mouse, *ous, ōtos*, an ear.]

myrbane. Same as **mirbane**.

myriad, *mir′i-əd*, *n*. any immense number.—*adj*. numberless.—*adj*. and *n*. (or *adv*.) **myr′iadfold**. —*n*. and *adj*. **myr′iadth**. [Gr. *mȳrias, -ados*, ten thousand.]

myriapod, *mir′i-ə-pod*, *n*. a member of the Myria-poda.—*n.pl*. **Myriapoda** (-*ap′ə-dä*), a class of Arthropoda with many legs, centipedes and millipedes.—Also **myriopod**, &c. [Gr. *mȳriopous, -podos*, many-footed—*mȳrios*, numberless, *pous, podos*, a foot.]

Myrica, *mi-rī′kä*, *n*. (orig.) the tamarisk: the sweet-gale or bog-myrtle genus, constituting the family **Myricā′ceae**. [Gr. *myrīkē* (*myrīkē*), tamarisk.]

myringa, *mir-ing′gä*, *n*. the ear-drum.—*ns*. **myr-ingitis** (-*in-ji′tis*), inflammation of the ear-drum; **myringoscope** (-*ing′gə-skōp*), an instrument for viewing the ear-drum. [L.L. *miringa*—Gr. *mēninx*, membrane.]

myriorama, *mir-i-ō-rä′mä*, *n*. a picture composed of interchangeable parts that can be variously combined. [Gr. *mȳrios*, numberless, *horāma*, a view.]

myrioscope, *mir′i-ə-skōp*, *n*. a variety of kaleido-scope. [Gr. *mȳrios*, numberless, *skopeein*, to view.]

Myristica, *mir-* or *mīr-is′ti-kä*, *n*. the nutmeg genus, giving name to the family **Myristicā′ceae**. —*adj*. **myris′tic**.—**myristic acid**, a fatty acid ($C_{13}H_{27}$·COOH) got from nutmegs. [Gr. *mȳri-zein*, to anoint.]

myrmecoid, *mər′mik-oid*, *adj*. ant-like. — *adjs*. **myrmecoph′agous**, feeding on ants : of the ant-bear genus **Myrmecoph′aga**; **myrmecoph′-ilous**, having a symbiotic relation with ants.—*n*. **myrmecoph′ily**. [Gr. *myrmēx, -ēkos*, ant.]

Myrmidon, *mər′mi-dən*, *n*. one of a tribe of warriors who accompanied Achilles to Troy : **myrmidon**, one of a ruffianly band under a daring leader : one who carries out another's orders without fear or pity.—*adj*. **myrmidō′nian**.—**myrmidons of the law**, policemen, bailiffs, &c. [Gr. *Myr-midōnes* (pl.).]

myrobalan, *mī-rob′ə-lən*, or *mi-*, *n*. the astringent fruit of certain Indian mountain species of Ter-minalia (Combretaceae) : a variety of plum.— **emblic myrobalan** (see **emblic**). [Gr. *mȳro-balanos*, bito—*myron*, an unguent, *balanos*, an acorn.]

myrrh, *mər*, *n*. a bitter, aromatic, transparent gum, exuded from the bark of Commiphora : sweet cicely.—*adj*. **myrrh′ic**.—*n*. **myrrh′ol**, the volatile oil of myrrh. [O.E. *myrra*—L. *myrrha*—Gr. *myrrā*; an Eastern word; cf. Ar. *murr*.]

myrrhine. See under **murra**.

myrtle, *mər′tl*, *n*. an evergreen shrub (Myrtus) with beautiful and fragrant leaves : extended to various other plants, some near akin, others not, e.g. a kind of beech in Australia (see also under **bog, wax**).—*n*. **myr′tle-wax**, wax from the candle-berry. [O.Fr. *myrtil*, dim. of *myrte*—L. *myrtus*—Gr. *myrtos*.]

Myrtus, *mər′təs*, the myrtle genus, giving name to the family **Myrtā′ceae**.—*adj*. **myrtā′ceous**. [L., —Gr. *myrtos*.]

myself, *mī-self′*, or *mi-self′*, *pron*. I or me, in person (used for emphasis, almost always in apposition) : me (reflexively). [**me, self**.]

mysophobia, *mī-sō-fō′bi-ä*, *n*. morbid fear of con-tamination. [Gr. *mȳsos*, defilement, *phobos*, fear.]

mystagogue, *mis′tə-gog*, *-gōg*, *n*. an initiator into religious mysteries — also **mystagō′gus**. — *adj*. **mystagog′ic** (-*goj′*, -*gog′*).—*n*. **mys′tagogy** (-*goj′-, -gog-*). [Gr. *mystēs*, one initiated, *agōgos*, a leader.]

mystery, *mis′tər-i*, *n*. a secret doctrine: (usu. in *pl*.) in ancient religions, rites known only to the initiated, as the Eleusinian mysteries : (*pl*.) the secrets of freemasonry, &c. : anything very obscure : that which is beyond human knowledge to ex-plain : anything artfully made difficult : a sacra-ment : a miracle play (also **mys′tery-play**). —*adj*. **mystē′rious**, containing mystery : having an air of mystery : obscure : secret : incompre-hensible.—*adv*. **mystē′riously**.—*n*. **mystē′rious-ness**.—**mys′tery-man**, a conjurer : a medicine-man ; **mys′tery-mong′er**, a dealer in mysteries ; **mys′tery-ship′**, a Q-boat. [L. *mystērium*—Gr. *mystērion*—*mystēs*, one initiated—*mȳeein*, to initiate —*mȳein*, to close the eyes.]

mystery, mistery, *mis′tər-i*, *n*. (*obs*.) office, service, duty : (*arch*.) craft, art, trade : (*Shak*.) skill : (*hist*.) a trade guild. [L.L. *misterium*—L. *mini-stērium*—*minister*, servant ; confused with *mystē-rium* and prob. with **maistry, mastery**.]

mystic, -al, *mis′tik, -əl*, *adjs*. relating to mystery, the mysteries, or mysticism : mysterious : sacredly obscure or secret : involving a sacred or a secret meaning hidden from the eyes of the ordinary person, only revealed to a spiritually enlightened mind : allegorical.—*n*. **mys′tic**, one who seeks or attains direct intercourse with God in elevated religious feeling or ecstasy.—*adv*. **mys′tically**.— *ns*. **mys′ticalness** ; **mys′ticism** (-*sizm*), the habit or tendency of religious thought and feeling of those who seek direct communion with God or the divine : fogginess and unreality of thought (with suggestion of **mist**) ; **mystificā′tion** ; **mys′tifier**, one who or that which mystifies : a hoaxer. — *v.t*. **mys′tify**, to make mysterious, obscure, or secret : to involve in mystery : to bewilder : to puzzle : to hoax :—*pr.p*. **mys′tify-ing** ; *pa.t*. and *pa.p*. **mys′tified**.—**mystic recita-tion**, the recitation of parts of the Greek liturgy in an inaudible voice. [L. *mysticus*—Gr. *mystikos* —*mystēs*, an initiate ; cf. **mystery**.]

mystique, *mēs-tēk*, *n*. incommunicable spirit, gift, or quality : secret (of an art) as known to its inspired practitioners. [Fr.]

myth, *mith* or (old-fashioned) *mīth*, *n*. an ancient traditional story of gods or heroes, esp. one offering an explanation of some fact or phenomenon : a story with a veiled meaning : mythical matter : a figment.—*adjs*. **myth′ic, -al**, relating to myths : fabulous : untrue. — *adv*. **myth′ically**. — *v.t*. **myth′icise** (-*i-sīz*), to make the subject of myth : to explain as myth.—*ns*. **myth′icism** (-*sizm*), theory that explains miraculous stories as myth ; **myth′iciser, myth′icist**.—*v.t*. **myth′ise**, to mythicise.—*ns.* **myth′ism,** mythicism ; **myth′-ist,** a maker of myths : a mythicist ; **mytho-gen′esis,** the production or origination of myths ; **mythog′rapher,** a writer or narrator of myths ; **mythog′raphy,** representation of myths in graphic or plastic art, art-mythology ; **mythol′oger, mytholō′gian,** a mythologist.—*adjs.* **mythol-og′ic, -al,** relating to mythology, fabulous.—*adv.* **mytholog′ically.**—*v.t.* **mythol′ogise,** to inter-pret or explain the mythological character of : to render mythical.—*ns.* **mythol′ogiser ; mythol′-ogist ; mythol′ogy,** a body of myths : the scientific study of myths : (*obs.*) symbolical meaning.—*adjs.* **mythopoeic** (*mith-ō-pē′ik* ; Gr. *poieein,* to make), **mythopoetic** (*-pō-et′ik*), myth-making. — *ns.* **mythopoe′ist,** a myth-maker ; **mythopŏ′et,** a myth-maker : a writer of poems on mythical subjects ; **mythus** (*mīth′əs* ; L.), **mythos** (*mīth′os* ; Gr.), myth.—**mythical theory,** the theory of D. F. Strauss (1808-74) and his school, that the Gospels are mainly a collection of myths, developed during the first two centuries, from the imagination of the followers of Jesus ; **comparative mythology,** the science that in-vestigates myths and seeks to relate those of different peoples. [Gr. *mȳthos,* talk, story, myth.]

Mytilus, *mit′i-ləs, n.* the common mussel genus.—*adjs.* **mytil′iform, myt′iloid.** [L. *mȳtilus, mītulus, mūtulus.*]

myxoedema, *mik-sē-dē′mä, n.* a diseased condition due to deficiency of thyroid secretion, character-ised by loss of hair, increased thickness and dryness of the skin, increase in weight, slowing of mental processes, and diminution of metabolism. [Gr. *myxa,* mucus, *oidēma,* swelling.]

myxoma, *mik-sō′mä, n.* a tumour of jelly-like substance :—*pl.* **myxō′mata.**—*adj.* **myxō′mat-ous.**—*n.* **myxomato′sis,** a contagious filterable-virus disease of rabbits. [Gr. *myxa,* mucus.]

Myxomycetes, *mik-sō-mī-sē′tēz, n.pl.* slime-fungi, a class of very simple plants, by some reckoned animals (Mycetozoa), forming in the vegetative stage naked masses of protoplasm with many nuclei, creeping on wet soil, on rotten wood, &c.—*n.sing.* **myxomycete** (*-sēt′*). [Gr. *myxa,* mucus, *mykētēs,* pl. of *mykēs,* a mushroom.]

Myxophyceae, *mik-sō-fish′i-ē, n.pl.* the Cyanophy-ceae. [Gr. *myxa,* slime, *phȳkos,* seaweed.]

Neutral vowels in unaccented syllables : *el′ə-mənt, in′fənt, ran′dəm*

N

N, n, *en, n.* the fourteenth letter of our alphabet, thirteenth of the Greek, representing a point nasal consonant sound, or along with *g* or before *g* or *k* a back nasal : anything having the shape of the letter : (*math.*) an indefinite number, esp. in a series : as a mediaeval numeral, N=90, and N̄=90,000 : (*print.*) a unit of measurement (en) =half an em.—**to the nᵗʰ (nth),** to any power : hence (*coll.*) unlimited.

na, *nä, adv.* a Scottish form of **no** (1) : (*ni, nä,* enclitically ; *Scot.*) not.

Naafi, *nä′fi, n.* an organisation for providing canteens for service-men and women : one of the canteens. [From the initials of *N*avy, *A*rmy, and *A*ir-*F*orce *I*nstitute.]

naam, nam, *näm, n.* (*hist.* ; *law*) distraint. [O.E. *nám,* related to *niman,* to take.]

naartje, *när′chi, n.* (*S.Afr.*) a small sweet orange like the mandarin. [Prob. conn. with **orange.**]

nab, *nab, v.t.* to seize :—*pr.p.* **nabb′ing** ; *pa.t.* and *pa.p.* **nabbed.**—*n.* **nabb′er.** [Origin obscure ; cf. **nap.**]

nab, *nab, n.* a hill-top : a promontory : a projection : the keeper of a door-lock. [O.N. *nabbr* or *nabbi.*]

nab, *nab, n.* (*obs. slang*) the head : a hat.

Nabataean, *nab-ə-tē′ən,* **Nabathaean,** *-thē′, n.* and *adj.* (one) of an ancient powerful Arab people about Petra. [Gr. *Nabat*(*h*)*aios.*]

nabk, *nabk, nubk, n.* the Christ's-thorn (*Zizyphus Spina-Christi*). [Ar. *nebq.*]

nabob, *nä′bob, n.* (*obs.*) a nawab : a European who has enriched himself in the East : any man of great wealth. [Hind. *nawwāb* ; see **nawab.**]

nabs, *nabz, n.* (*slang*) a personage, in such phrases as **his nabs,** himself. [Cf. **nob** (2), **nib** (2).]

nacarat, *nak′ə-rat, n.* a bright orange-red : a fabric so coloured. [Fr.]

nacelle, *nä-sel′, n.* (*obs.*) a little boat : a car or chamber on an aircraft. [Fr.,—L.L. *nāvicella,* dim. of L. *nāvis,* ship.]

nache, *näch, n.* the rump. [See **aitchbone.**]

nachschlag, *nähh′shlähh, n.* (*mus.*) a grace-note whose time is taken off the preceding note. [Ger., —*nach,* after, *schlag,* stroke.]

nachtmaal, *nähht′mäl, n.* Dutch Reformed Church Sacrament, Lord's Supper. [Du., night-meal.]

nacket, *nak′it,* **nocket,** *nok′it, n.* a snack, light lunch.

nacre, *nä′kər, n.* mother-of-pearl or a shellfish yielding it.—*adj.* **nä′creous.** — Also **nä′crous.** [Fr. ; prob. of Eastern origin.]

nadir, *nä′dēr, -dər, n.* the point of the heavens diametrically opposite to the zenith : the lowest point of anything. [Fr.,—Ar. *nadīr* (*nazīr*), opposite to.]

nae, *nä, adj.* a Scots form of **no** (2) : also for **no** (1), esp. with a comparative.—*ns.* **nae′body,** nobody ; **nae′thing,** nothing.

naevus, *nē′vəs,* L. *nī′voos, n.* a birth-mark : a pigmented spot or an overgrowth of small blood-vessels in the skin—*obs.* **naeve** :—*pl.* **naevi** (*nē′vī* ; L. *nī′vē*).—*adj.* **nae′void.** [L.]

nag, *nag, n.* a horse, esp. a small one : a riding-horse, or an inferior horse : (*Shak.*) a jade. [M.E. *nagge* ; origin obscure ; cf. M.Du. *negge, negghe* (mod. Du. *neg, negge*).]

nag, *nag, v.t.* or *v.i.* (with *at*) to worry or annoy continually : to find fault with constantly :—*pr.p.* **nagg′ing** ; *pa.t.* and *pa.p.* **nagged.**—*n.* **nagg′er.** [Cf. Norw. *nage,* to grow, rankle, Sw. *nagga,* to gnaw.]

naga, *nä′gä, n.* (*Ind.*) a snake, esp. the cobra : (*Hind. myth.*) a divine snake. [Sans. *nāga.*]

nagana, *nä-gä′nä, n.* a disease of horses and cattle caused by a trypanosome transmitted by tsetse-flies. [Zulu *nakane.*]

nagari. See **devanagari.**

Nahuatl, *nä′wät-l, n.* the language of the Aztecs.—Also *adj.*

naiad, *nī′ad, n.* a river nymph or spring nymph :—*pl.* **nai′adēs, nai′ads.**—*n.* **Nai′as,** a genus of water-plants, giving name to a family **Naiadā′ceae** akin to or including the pondweeds. [Gr. *nāias, -ados,* pl. *-adēs,* from *naein,* to flow.]

naiant, *nä′ənt, adj.* (*her.*) swimming horizontally. [Prob. from an A.Fr. form of O.Fr. *noiant,* pr.p.—L. *natāre,* to swim.]

naïf, *nä-ēf′,* **naïve,** *nä-ēv′, adj.* with natural or unaffected simplicity, esp. in thought, manners, or speech : artless : ingenuous.—*adv.* **naïve′ly.**—*ns.* **naïveté** (*nä-ēv′tä*), **naïvety** (*nä-ēv′ti*), natural simplicity and unreservedness of thought, manner, or speech. [Fr. *naïf,* fem. *naïve*—L. *nātīvus,* native—*nāscī, nātus,* to be born.]

naik, *nä′ik, n.* a lord or governor : a corporal of Indian infantry. [Urdu *nā′ik*—Sans. *nāyaka,* leader.]

nail, *näl, n.* a horny plate at the end of a finger or toe, usu. distinguished from a claw as being flattened : a claw : a small spike, usu. of metal, and with a head, used for fastening wood, &c. : a nail-shaped excrescence, esp. one at the tip of a bird's bill : a measure of length (2¼ inches).—*v.t.* to fasten, pierce, or stud with nails : (*fig.*) to fix : pin down, hold fast : (*slang*) to catch or secure.—*ns.* **nail′-bed,** that portion of the true skin on which a nail rests ; **nail′-brush,** a brush for cleaning the nails.—*adj.* **nailed,** having nails : fastened with nails.—*ns.* **nail′er,** a maker of nails ; **nail′ery,** a place where nails are made ; **nail′-head,** the head of a nail : an ornament shaped like it.—*adj.* **nail′-head′ed.**—*ns.* **nail′-head-spar′,** calcite crystallised in a scalenohedron terminated by a rhombohedron ; **nail′-hole,** a hole made by or for a nail : a notch for opening a pocket-knife ; **nail′ing,** nail making : fastening with nails ; **nail′-rod,** a strip of iron to be made into nails : iron in that form : (*Austr.*) strong coarse tobacco : a stick of liquorice.—**hit the nail on the head,** to touch the exact point ; **nail a lie to the counter,** expose it and put it out of currency, from the old custom of shopkeepers nailing counterfeit coins ; **on the nail,** on the spot. [O.E. *nægel* ; Ger. *nagel.*]

nain, *nän, adj.* (*Scot.*) own.—*n.* **nainsel′, nainsell′,** own self : a Highlander (from the Highlander's traditional habit of referring to himself as *her nainsel*). [Shortened from **mine ain,** my own.]

nainsook, *nän′sook, n.* a kind of muslin like jaconet. [Hind. *nainsukh*—*nain,* eye, *sukh,* pleasure.]

Nair, *nä′ir, n.* a people of Malabar.—Also *adj.*, esp. of a form of polyandry practised by them and of their family system and mother-right.

naissant, *näs′ənt, adj.* nascent : (*her.*) rising or coming forth. [Fr., pr.p. of *naître*—L. *nāscī, nātus,* to be born.]

naïve. See **naïf.**

Naja, *nä′jä, -yä, n.* the cobra genus.—Also **Naia.** [App. Linnaeus's misreading of *naga,* or of Sinh. *naiä, nayä.*]

naked, *nä′kid, adj.* without clothes : uncovered : bare : exposed : open to view : unconcealed : undisguised : evident : unarmed : defenceless : unprovided : without ornament : simple : artless : without the usual covering.—*adv.* **na′kedly.**—*n.* **na′kedness.**—**naked bed,** (*obs.*) a bed in which one is (*orig.*) entirely naked, (later) without ordinary day clothes ; **naked eye,** the eye unassisted by glasses of any kind ; **naked lady,** the meadow-saffron. [O.E. *nacod* ; Ger. *nackt.*]

fāte, fär, ȧsk ; mē, hər (her) ; *mīne ; mōte ; mūte ; mōōn ; dhen* (then)

naker, *nā'kər, n.* a kettledrum. [O.Fr. *nacre*— Ar. *naqāra.*]

nam, *pa.t.* of **nim.** See also **naam.**

namby-pamby, *nam'bi-pam'bi, adj.* feebly wishy-washy: prettily or sentimentally childish.—*n.* namby-pamby writing or talk: a namby-pamby person.—*adj.* **nam'by-pam'bical.**—*n.pl.* **nam'by-pam'bies.**—*n.* **nam'by-pam'biness.**—*adj.* **nam'-by-pam'byish.**—*n.* **nam'by-pam'byism.** [Nick-name given by Carey or by Swift to *Ambrose Philips* (1674-1749), whose simple odes to children were so judged by 18th-century Tories.]

name, *nām, n.* that by which a person or a thing is known or called: a designation: reputation: fame: a celebrity: family or clan: fictitiousness without reality: authority: behalf: assumed character of another.—*v.t.* to give a name to: to mention the name of: to designate: to speak of or to call by name: to state or specify: to utter (with cognate object): to mention for a post or office: to nominate: to mention formally by name in the House of Commons as guilty of disorderly conduct.—*adj.* **nam'able, name'able,** capable, or worthy, of being named.—*n.* **name'-child,** a person called after one.—*adj.* **named.**—*n.* **name'-day,** the day of the saint of one's name: in the Stock Exchange, the day when a ticket bearing the buyer's name and other particulars is given to the seller: the day on which a name is bestowed. —*adj.* **name'less,** without a name: anonymous: undistinguished: indescribable: unspeakable.— *adv.* **name'lessly.** — *n.* **name'lessness.** — *adv.* **name'ly,** (*obs.*) especially: by name: that is to say.—*ns.* **name'-part,** the part that gives title to a play, title-rôle; **name'-plate,** an attached plate bearing the name of occupant, owner, manu-facturer, &c.; **nam'er; name'sake,** one bearing the same name as another; **name'-son,** a male name-child.—*adj.* **name'worthy,** worth naming: distinguished.—*n.* **nām'ing.**—**call names,** to be-stow abuse upon; **in name,** fictitiously, as an empty title; **in name of,** on behalf of: by the authority of; **name after a person** (*U.S.* **name for**), to give the same name to in honour of a person; **name the day,** to fix a day, esp. for a marriage; **proper name,** a name given to a particular person, place, or thing; **take a name in vain,** to use a name lightly or profanely. [O.E. *nama*; Ger. *name*; L. *nōmen.*]

Nancy, *nan'si, n.* an effeminate young man—also **Nance, Nan'cy-boy, Miss Nan'cy.**—Also *adj.* [From the girl's name.]

Nancy-pretty, *nan'si-prit'i, n.* the plant *Saxifraga umbrosa,* London pride. [Prob. for none so pretty.]

nandine, *nan'din, n.* a West African palm-civet. [Prob. a native name.]

nandu, nandoo, *nan'dōō, n.* the ¬hea. [Tupí *nandú.*]

nanism, *nān'* or *nan'izm, n.* condition of being dwarfed.—*n.* **nanisā'tion,** artificial dwarfing. [Gr. *nānos, nannos,* dwarf.]

nankeen, *nan-kēn', n.* a buff-coloured cotton cloth first made at *Nanking* in China: (*pl.*) clothes, esp. breeches, made of nankeen.—Also **nankin'.**

nanny, *nan'i, n.* a she-goat (also **nann'y-goat**): a children's nurse, esp. one trained to take care of children. [From the woman's name.]

Nantz, *nants, n.* (*arch.*) brandy. [*Nantes* in France.]

naos, *nā'os, n.* a temple: the inner cell of a temple. [Gr. *nāos,* temple.]

nap, *nap, v.i.* to take a short or casual sleep (*pr.p.* **napp'ing**; *pa.p.* **napped**).—*n.* a short or casual sleep.—**catch napping,** to detect in error that might have been avoided: to take off one's guard. [O.E. *hnappian.*]

nap, *nap, n.* a woolly surface on cloth, now (dis-tinguished from *pile*) such a surface raised by a finishing process, not made in the weaving: the woolly surface removed in the process: a cloth with such a surface: a downy covering or surface on anything.—*v.t.* to raise a nap on: to remove nap from.—*adj.* **nap'less,** without nap, threadbare. —*n.* **napp'iness.**—*adj.* **napp'y,** downy: shaggy. [M.E. *noppe*; app.—M.Du. or M.L.G. *noppe.*]

nap, nap, *n.* the card-game *Napoleon*: in that game, a call of five: the winning of five tricks: a racing tip that professes to be a certainty—one that one may ' go nap ' on.—*v.t.* to name (a particular horse) as certain to win.—**go nap,** to undertake to win all five tricks: to risk all.

nap, *nap, v.t.* to seize: to steal. [Cf. Sw. *nappa,* Dan. and Norw. *nappe,* to catch, snatch; relation to **nab** uncertain.]

napalm, *nā'pälm, n.* a petroleum jelly, highly in-flammable, used in bombs.

nape, *nāp, n.* the back of the neck. [Origin obscure.]

napery, *nāp'ə-ri, n.* (*arch.* and *Scot.*) linen, esp. for the table. [O.Fr. *naperie*—L.L. *napāria*—*napa,* a cloth—L. *mappa,* a napkin.]

naphtha, *naf'thä* (sometimes *nap'thä*), *n.* rock-oil: a vague name for the liquid inflammable dis-tillates from coal-tar, wood, &c., esp. the lighter and more volatile.—*n.* **naph'thalene,** an ill-smelling hydrocarbon ($C_{10}H_8$) got by distillation of coal-tar, crystallising in plates, used for killing moths, &c.—*adj.* **naphthal'ic** (*naf-thal'ik*), per-taining to, or derived from, naphthalene.—*v.t.* **naph'thalise,** to treat with naphtha.—*ns.* **naph'-thol,** a hydroxyl derivative of naphthalene ($C_{10}H_7OH$), of two kinds; **naphthyl'amine** (or *-mēn'*), an amino-derivative of naphthalene ($C_{10}H_7NH_2$), of two kinds, used in dyeing. [Gr. *naphtha.*]

Napierian, Naperian, *nā-pē'ri-ən, adj.* pertaining to John *Napier* of Merchiston (1550-1617), or to his system of logarithms: now applied to natural logarithms, logarithms to the base *e,* the limit of $\left(1 + \dfrac{1}{m}\right)^m$ when *m* approaches infinity, Napier's own base being a quantity depending on e^{-1}.—**Napier's bones,** or **rods,** an invention of Napier's for multi-plying and dividing mechanically by means of rods.

napiform, *nāp'i-form, adj.* turnip-shaped. [L. *nāpus,* a turnip.]

napkin, *nap'kin, n.* a small square of linen, paper, &c., used at table or otherwise: (*Scot.*) a hand-kerchief.—*n.* **nap'kin-ring,** a ring in which a table-napkin is rolled. [Dim. of Fr. *nappe*— L. *mappa.*]

Naples-yellow, *nā'plz-yel'ō, n.* a light-yellow pig-ment, lead antimoniate, originally an Italian secret.

napoleon, *nə-pōl'yen,* or *-i-ən, n.* a twenty-franc gold coin issued by *Napoleon*: a French modifica-tion of the game of euchre, each player receiving five cards and playing for himself (commonly **nap**): a kind of rich iced cake.—*adj.* **Napoleonic** (*-i-on'ik*), relating to *Napoleon* I. or III., the Great or the Little.—*ns.* **Napol'eonism**; **Napol'eonist**; **napol'eonite,** an orbicular diorite found in Corsica, Napoleon's native island.

napoo, *nä-pōō', adj.* and *interj.* (*slang* of 1914 war) no more: used up: good for nothing: dead.— *v.t.* to kill. [Fr. *il n'y en a plus,* there is no more.]

nappe, *nap, n.* (*geol.*) a sheet of rock brought far forward by recumbent folding or thrusting. [Fr. *nappe,* table-cloth—L. *mappa.*]

napper, *nap'ər, n.* (*slang*) the head.

nappy, *nap'i, adj.* (of liquor) having a head: heady, strong: tipsy.—*n.* strong ale. [Perh. from **nappy,** shaggy; see **nap** (2).]

napron, *nā'prən, n.* earlier form (*Spens.*) of **apron.**

Narcissus, *när-sis'əs, n.* the daffodil genus of the Amaryllis family: esp. *N. poeticus* (the poet's narcissus) (*pl.* **narciss'uses** or **Narciss'ī**): in Greek myth., a youth who pined away for love of his own image, and was transformed into the flower.—*n.* **narciss'ism,** sensual gratification found in one's own body, whether as a normal stage of development or a pathological condition. [L.,— Gr. *Narkissos*; the connexion with *narkē,* numb-ness, seems to be fanciful.]

narco-analysis. See **narcotic.**

narcolepsy, *när'kō-lep-si, n.* a condition marked by short attacks of irresistible drowsiness. [Gr. *narkē,* numbness, and *lēpsis,* seizure.]

narcotic, *när-kot'ik, adj.* producing torpor, sleep, or deadness.—*n.* a medicine producing sleep or

Neutral vowels in unaccented syllables: *el'ə-mənt, in'fənt, ran'dəm*

stupor. — *ns.* **nar′co-analysis,** hypno-analysis when narcotics are used in producing the hypnotic state; **narcosis** (-*kō′sis*), the stupefying effect of a narcotic: — *pl.* **narco′ses** (-*sēz*). — *adv.* **narcot′ically.**—*n.* **nar′cotine** (-*kɔ-tēn*), one of the alkaloids in opium.—*v.t.* **nar′cotise,** to subject to the influence of a narcotic.—*n.* **nar′cotism,** the influence of narcotics. [Gr. *narkōtikos*—*narkē,* numbness, torpor.]

nard, *närd, n.* spikenard: an inappropriate name for matweed (*Nardus stricta*).—*v.t.* to anoint with nard. [L. *nardus*—Gr. *nardos.*]

nardoo, *när-dŏŏ′, n.* an Australian Marsilea: its sporocarps, eaten by the natives. [Native word.]

nare, *när, n.* (*arch.*) a nostril, esp. a hawk's.—*n.pl.* **när′ēs** (L.), nostrils.—*adjs.* **när′ial, när′ine** (-*īn*). —*n.* **när′icorn,** a horny termination of a bird's nostril. [L. *nāris,* pl. -*ēs,* nostril.]

narghile, *när′gil-i, n.* a hookah.—Also **nargile(h), narg(h)il(l)y.** [Pers. *nārgīleh*—*nārgīl,* a coconut (from which it used to be made).]

nark, *närk, n.* (*slang*) an informer: a police spy (*copper's nark*): one who curries favour, a pick-thank: a spoil-sport.—*v.t.* and *v.i.* to watch: to spy: to annoy: to tease.—**nark at,** to fret with persistent criticism. [Romany *nāk,* nose.]

narras, naras, *nar′ɔs, n.* the edible melon-like fruit of a South-west African long-rooted thorny cucurbitaceous shrub (*Acanthosicyos horrida*). [Hottentot *qnaras.*]

narrate, *nɔ-* or *na-rāt′, v.t.* to tell (of a series of events).—*v.i.* to recount or relate events.—*adj.* **narrāt′able.**—*n.* **narrā′tion,** act of telling: that which is told: an orderly account of a series of events. — *adj.* **narrative** (*nar′ɔ-tiv*), narrating: giving an account of any occurrence: inclined to narration: story-telling.—*n.* that which is narrated: a continued account of any series of occurrences: story.—*adv.* **narr′atively.**—*n.* **narrā′tor.** —*adj.* **narr′atory,** like narrative: consisting of narrative. [L. *narrāre,* -*ātum,* prob.—*gnārus,* knowing.]

narre, *när, adv.* (*Spens.*) an old compar. of **nigh.**

narrow, *nar′ō, adj.* of little breadth: of small extent from side to side: closely confining: limited: contracted in mind: bigoted: not liberal: parsimonious: with little to spare: close: strict, precise: detailed: keen.—*n.* a narrow part or place: (usu. in *pl.*) a narrow passage, channel, or strait.—*adv.* **narrowly.**—*v.t.* to make narrow: to contract or confine.—*v.i.* to become narrow: to reduce the number of stitches in knitting.—*adj.* **narr′ow-gauge,** of a railway, less than 4 ft. 8½ in. in gauge.—*n.* **narr′owing,** the act of making less in breadth: the state of being contracted: the part of anything which is made narrower.—Also *adj.*—*adv.* **narr′owly.**—*adj.* **narr′ow-mind′ed,** of a narrow or illiberal mind.—*ns.* **narr′ow-mind′edness; narr′owness.**—**narrow seas,** the seas between Great Britain and the Continent. [O.E. *nearu.*]

narrow. See **nary.**

Narthex, *när′theks, n.* a former genus of umbelliferous plants, now included in Ferula: **narthex,** a western portico or vestibule in an early Christian or Oriental church or basilica, to which women and catechumens were admitted. [Gr. *narthēx,* giant fennel, a cane or stalk, a casket, a narthex.]

narwhal, *när′wɔl, n.* a kind of whale (Monodon) with one large projecting tusk (occasionally two tusks) in the male. [Dan. *narhval*; O.N. *nāhvalr* may be from *nár,* corpse, *hvalr,* whale, from its pallid colour.]

nary, *när′i* (*U.S.* and *prov.*) for **ne′er a,** never a, not one.—Also **narrow (a),** *nar′ō.*

nas, *näz,,obs.* for **ne has** (*Spens.*) and for **ne was.**

nasal, *nä′zl, adj.* belonging to the nose: affected by, or sounded through, the nose.—*n.* a sound uttered through the nose: a letter representing such a sound: a paired bone that forms the bridge of the nose: the nose-piece in a helmet.—*ns.* **Nasalis** (*naz-ā′lis*), the proboscis monkey genus; **nasalisation** (*nä-zɔ-lī-zā′shɔn*).—*v.i.* **na′salise,** to render nasal, as a sound.—*n.* **nasality** (*nä-zal′i-ti*).—*adv.* **na′sally.**—*n.* **nasion** (*nä′zi-on*),

the median point of the nasofrontal suture. [L. *nāsus,* the nose.]

nasard, *naz′ärd, n.* an organ mutation-stop. [Fr.]

nascent, *näs′ɔnt, nas′ɔnt, adj.* coming into being.— *ns.* **nasc′ence** (*rare*), **nasc′ency.** [L. *nāscēns,* -*entis,* pr.p. of *nāscī, nātus,* to be born.]

naseberry, *näz′bɔr-i, -ber′i, n.* the sapodilla plum: the tree bearing it.—Also **neesberry** (*nēz′*), **nisberry** (*niz′*). [Sp. *néspera, nispero,* medlar tree— L. *mespilus,* medlar; cf. **medlar.**]

nashgab, *näsh′gäb, n.* (*Scot.*) prattle: chatter: a pert chatterer.—Also **gab′nash.**

Nasik, *nä′sik, n.* a town of Bombay.—Also *adj.,* esp. of an elaborate form of magic square devised there.

naso-, *nä′zō-,* in composition, nose: of the nose (and something else), as *adjs.* **nasofront′al,** pertaining to the nose and the frontal bone; **nasolac′rymal,** pertaining to the nose and tears, as the duct that carries tears from the eye and the nose. [L. *nāsus,* nose.]

nastic, *näs′tik, adj.* (of plant movements) not related to the direction of the stimulus. [Gr. *nastos,* close-pressed.]

Nasturtium, *nas-tur′shɔm, n.* the water-cress genus of Cruciferae: **nasturtium** (in popular use), the Indian cress (*Tropaeolum majus*), a garden climber. [L. *nāsus,* nose, *torquēre,* to twist (from its pungency).]

nasty, *näs′ti, adj.* disgustingly foul: nauseous: filthy: obscene: threatening: threatening danger: spiteful: ill-natured: difficult to deal with: awkward: unpleasant: objectionable. — *adv.* **nas′tily.**—*n.* **nas′tiness.** [Perh. for earlier *nasky* (cf. Sw. dial. *naskug, nasket*); or perh. connected with Du. *nestig,* dirty.]

nasute, *nä′zūt,* -*sūt,* or -*zūt′,* -*sūt′, adj.* keen-scented: critically discriminating: beaked.—*n.* a beaked soldier white-ant. [L. *nāsūtus*—*nāsus,* nose.]

natal, *nä′tɔl, adj.* pertaining to the **nates.**

natal, *nä′tl, adj.* of or connected with birth: native.—*adj.* **natalitial** (*nat-* or *nät-ɔ-lish′l*), pertaining to a birthday.—*n.* **natality** (*nɔ-, na-tal′i-ti*), birth: birth-rate. [L. *nātālis*—*nāscī, nātus,* to be born.]

natant, *nät-ɔnt, adj.* floating: swimming.—*n.* **natation** (*nat-* or *nät-ā′shɔn*), swimming. — *adjs.* **nätatō′rial, nä′tatory,** pertaining to swimming: having the habit of swimming: adapted or used for swimming.—*n.* **nätatō′rium** (*U.S.*), a swimming-pool. [L. *natāns,* -*āntis,* pr.p. of *natāre,* freq. of *nāre,* to swim.]

natch, *nach, n.* (*prov.*) the rump. [See **aitchbone.**]

nates, *nä′tēz, n.pl.* (L.) the buttocks.—*adjs.* **nä′tal; nä′tiform.** [L. *natis,* pl. -*ēs.*]

nathemore, *nä-thɔ-mōr′,* **nathemo,** -*mō′, advs.* (*Spens.*) not or never the more. [O.E. *nā thý má,* never the more (cf. following).]

nathless, natheless, nathelesse, naythles, *näth′, näth′, nädh′* or *nädh′(ɔ)-les,* or (as *Spens.*) -*les′, adv.* and *prep.* (*arch.*) notwithstanding. [O.E. *nā,* never, *thý,* by that (instrum. case), *læs,* less.]

nation, *nä′shɔn, n.* a body of people marked off by common descent, language, culture, or historical tradition: the people of a state: an American Indian tribe: a set of people, animals, &c.: a great number: an old division of students in universities: (in *pl.*) the heathen or Gentiles.— *adj.* **national** (*nash′nɔl,* -*ɔ-nɔl*), pertaining to a nation or nations: belonging or peculiar to, characteristic of, or controlled by a nation: public: general: attached to one's own country.—*n.* (usu. in *pl.*) a member or fellow-member of a nation.— *n.* **nationalīsā′tion.**—*v.t.* **nat′ionalise,** to make national: to make the property of the nation: to bring under national management: to naturalise: to make a nation of.—*ns.* **nat′ionalism; nat′ionalist,** one who favours or strives after the unity, independence, interests, or domination of a nation: a member of a political party specially so called, e.g. the Irish Nationalist party who aimed at Home Rule: an advocate of nationalisation.—*adj.* **nationalist′ic.**—*n.* **nationality** (-*al′it-i*), membership of, fact or state of belonging to, a particular nation: nationhood: a group or set having the character of a nation: national character.—*adv.* **nat'ionally.**—*n.* **nationhood** (*nā'*), state or fact of being a nation.—*adjs.* **nationless** (*nā'*), without nationality or nations; **nationwide,** covering the whole nation.—**national air, anthem,** an official song or hymn of a nation, sung or played on ceremonial occasions; **national church,** a church established by law in a country; **National Convention,** the sovereign assembly in France from Sept. 21, 1792, to Oct. 26, 1795; **national debt,** money borrowed by the government of a country and not yet paid back; **National Guard,** a force which took part in the French Revolution, first formed in 1789: (*U.S.*) organised militia of individual States; **national park,** an area owned by or for the nation, set apart for preservation and enjoyment of the beautiful or interesting; **national school,** in England, a school connected with the National Society, established in 1811, to promote elementary education; **National Socialist party,** an extrem nationalistic fascist party in Germany, led by Adolf Hitler. [L. *nātiō, -ōnis—nāscī, nātus,* to be born.]

nation, *nā'shon, n., adj., adv., interj.* (*U.S.*) for damnation.

native, *nā'tiv, adj.* belonging naturally: innate: inherent: natural: in a natural state: unsophisticated: occurring in a natural station: occurring naturally as a mineral (not manufactured), or naturally uncombined (as an element): belonging by birth: having a right by birth: born or originating in the place: being the place of birth or origin: belonging to the people originally or at the time of discovery inhabiting the country, esp. when they are coloured or uncivilised: connected by birth: (*obs.*) born a thrall: applied to Australian plants and animals to which the name of an already known different kind has been transferred: (of an oyster) raised in a (British) artificial bed.—*n.* one born in any place: one whose birth is the matter under consideration: a member of a native race: (*coll.* and vaguely) a coloured person: a white born in Australia: an indigenous species, variety, or breed, or an individual of it: a native oyster: (*obs.*) a born thrall.—*adj.* **na'tive-born,** born in the country: (*Scot.*) having a status by virtue of birth.—*adv.* **na'tively.**—*ns.* **na'tiveness; na'tivism,** the belief that the mind possesses some ideas or forms of thought that are inborn and not derived from sensation: the disposition to favour the natives of a country in preference to immigrants; **na'tivist.** — *adj.* **nativis'tic.** — *n.* **nativity** (*na-tiv'i-ti*), state or fact of being born: time, place, and manner of birth: nationality by birth: fact or status of being native: the birth of Christ, hence the festival commemorating it—Christmas, or a picture representing it: a horoscope: (*obs.*) bondage by birth.—**go native,** to associate oneself with and adopt the ways of the natives; **native bear,** the koala; **native rock,** unquarried rock. [L. *nātīvus—nāscī, nātus,* to be born.]

natrolite, *nāt'* or *nat'rə-līt, n.* a common fibrous zeolite, hydrated sodium aluminium silicate. [natron, and Gr. *lithos,* stone.]

natron, *nā'tron, n.* a hydrated carbonate of sodium found on some lake-borders.—*n.* **na'trium,** chemists' Latin for sodium. [Ar. *natrūn*—Gr. *nitron.*]

natter, *nat'ər, v.i.* (*N. of England*) to be peevish. —*adjs.* **natt'ered, natt'ery,** peevish. [Origin obscure.]

natterjack, *nat'ər-jak, n.* a toad with a yellow stripe down the back. [Origin unknown.]

natty, *nat'i, adj.* dapper: spruce.—*adv.* **natt'ily.**— *n.* **natt'iness.** [Possibly connected with neat.]

natural, *nat'ū-rol, adj.* pertaining to, produced by, or according to nature: furnished by or based on nature: not miraculous: not the work of man: not interfered with by man: inborn: having the feelings that may be expected to come by nature, kindly: normal: happening in the usual course: spontaneous: not far-fetched: not acquired: without affectation: not fictitious: physical: life-like, like nature: related by actual birth (not adoption, &c.): hence (now rarely) legitimate:

(now usually) illegitimate: natural-born, or having the status of the natural-born: in a state of nature, unregenerate: (*mus.*) according to the usual diatonic scale, not sharp or flat.—*n.* an idiot: (*mus.*) a tone that is neither sharp nor flat: a character (♮) cancelling a preceding sharp or flat: a white key in keyboard musical instruments.—*adj.* **nat'ural-born,** native.—*n.* **naturalisā'tion.**—*v.t.* **nat'uralise,** to make natural or easy: to adapt to a different climate or to different conditions of life: to grant the privileges of natural-born citizens to: to adopt into the language: to admit among accepted institutions, usages, &c.: to explain naturalistically.—*v.i.* to acquire citizenship in another country: to study natural history in the field.—*ns.* **nat'uralism,** following of nature: a close following of nature without idealisation: the theory that this should be the aim of literature, esp. the form of realism advocated or practised by Émile Zola: a world-view that rejects the supernatural: the belief that natural religion is of itself sufficient: deism; **nat'uralist,** one who studies nature, more particularly zoology and botany, esp. zoology, and esp. in the field: a dealer in live animals and articles of use and interest to students of nature, often a bird-stuffer: a believer in naturalism.—*adj.* **naturalist'ic,** pertaining to, or in accordance with, nature, natural history, or naturalism.—*adv.* **nat'urally,** in a natural manner: by nature: according to nature or one's own nature: in a life-like manner: normally: in the ordinary course: of course.—*n.* **nat'uralness.**— **natural death,** death owing to disease or old age, not violence or accident; **natural gas,** gases issuing from the earth, whether from natural fissures or bored wells; **natural history,** originally the description of all that is in nature, now used of the sciences that deal with the earth and its productions—botany, zoology, and mineralogy, esp. field zoology; **natural law,** a law of nature: the sense of right and wrong which arises from the constitution of the mind of man, as distinguished from the results of revelation or legislation; **natural logarithm,** one to the base *e*; **natural magic** (see magic); **natural numbers,** the whole numbers 1, 2, 3, and upwards; **natural order,** in botany, a category now usually called a family; **natural philosophy,** the science of the physical properties of bodies: physics, or physics and dynamics; **natural scale,** a scale of music written without sharps or flats; **natural science,** the science of nature, as distinguished from mental and moral science and from mathematics; **natural selection,** evolution by the survival of the fittest with inheritance of their fitness by next generation; **natural system,** a classification of plants and animals according to presumed relationship by descent, distinguished in botany from the artificial system of Linnaeus; **natural theology,** or **natural religion,** religion derived from reason without revelation. [L. *nātūrālis—nātūra,* nature.]

nature, *nā'tyor, n.* the power that creates and regulates the world: the power of growth: the established order of things: the cosmos: the external world, esp. as untouched by man: the qualities of anything which make it what it is: essence: being: constitution: kind or order: naturalness: normal feeling: kindliness: conformity to truth, or reality: inborn mind, character, instinct, or disposition: vital power, as of man or animal: course of life: nakedness: a primitive undomesticated condition: the strength or substance of anything.—*n.* **na'ture-cure,** treatment of disease by trusting mainly to nature.—*adj.* **na'tured,** having a certain temper or disposition (esp. in compounds, as *good-natured*).—*ns.* **na'ture-god',** a deity personifying some force of physical nature; **na'ture-knowl'edge, na'ture-study,** a branch of school work intended to cultivate the powers of seeing and enjoying nature by the observation of natural objects—e.g. plants, animals, &c.; **na'ture-myth',** a myth symbolising natural phenomena; **na'ture-print'ing,** printing from plates that have been impressed with some natural object; **na'ture-wor'ship, na'turism,** worship of

Neutral vowels in unaccented syllables: *el'ə-mənt, in'fənt, ran'dəm*

the powers of nature.—*adj.* **na′turing,** creative.—
n. **na′turist.**—*adj.* **naturist′ic.**—debt of nature,
death; **ease,** or **relieve, nature,** to evacuate the
bowels. [Fr.,—L. *nātūra*—*nāscī, nātus,* to be born.]

naught, *nawt, n.* nothing: a nought (q.v.): (*obs.*)
wickedness, evil.—*adj.* (*arch.*) good for nothing:
worthless: bad: immoral: hurtful: foiled:
ruined.—*adv.* ill: not at all.—**be naught,** (*obs.*)
keep out of the way: efface yourself: go to the
mischief; **come to naught,** to come to nothing,
to fail; **set at naught,** to treat as of no account,
to despise.—Also **nought.** [O.E. *náht, náwiht*—
ná, never, *wiht,* whit.]

naughty, *nawt′i, adj.* (*obs.*) worthless: (*Shak.*)
wicked: bad: ill-behaved: verging on the indecorous: now chiefly applied to children, or used
playfully in feigned censure. — *adv.* **naught′ily.**
—*n.* **naught′iness**—**naughty pack,** (*obs.*) a
person, esp. a woman, of loose life. a ' bad lot.'
[naught.]

naumachy, *naw′ma-ki,* **naumachia,** *naw-mā′ki-ä,
ns.* a sea-fight, esp. one got up as a spectacle among
the Romans: a place for the purpose. [Gr.
naumachiä—*naus,* a ship, *machē,* a fight.]

naunt, *nänt, n.* (*arch.*) aunt. [For **mine aunt.**]

nauplius, *naw′pli-əs, n.* a larval form in many
Crustacea, with one eye and three pairs of appendages :—*pl.* **nau′plii.**—*adjs.* **nau′pliiform, nau′-
plioid.** [L., a kind of shell-fish—Gr. *Nauplios,* a
son of Poseidon, *naus,* a ship, *pleein,* to sail.]

nausea, *naw′si-ä, -shi-ä, -shyä, n.*(*orig.*) sea-sickness:
a feeling of inclination to vomit: sickening disgust
or loathing.—*adj.* **nau′seant,** producing nausea.—
n. a substance having this quality.—*v.i.* **nau′seate,**
to feel nausea or disgust.—*v.t.* to loathe: to strike
with disgust.—*adjs.* **nau′seative,** causing nausea
or loathing; **nau′seous** (*-shəs, -shyəs, -shi-əs,
-si-əs*), producing nausea: disgusting: loathsome.
—*adv.* **nau′seously.**—*n.* **nau′seousness.** [L.,—
Gr. *nausiä,* sea-sickness—*naus,* a ship.]

nautch, *nawch,* **nach, natch, nāch, n.** in India, a
performance of professional dancing women known
as **nautch′-girls.** [Hind. *nāch,* dance.]

nautic, *nawt′ik* (*rare*), **-al,** *-əl, adjs.* of or pertaining
to ships, to sailors, or to navigation.—*adv.* **nau′tic-
ally.**—**Nautical Almanac,** a periodical book of
astronomical tables specially useful to sailors;
nautical mile (see **mile**). [L. *nauticus*—Gr.
nautikos—*nautēs,* sailor, *naus,* a ship.]

nautilus, *naw′ti-ləs, n.* a tetrabranchiate cephalopod
(*pearly nautilus*) of southern seas, with a chambered
external shell: a Mediterranean dibranchiate
cephalopod (*paper nautilus,* or argonaut) wrongly
believed by Aristotle to use its arms as sails :—*pl.*
nau′tiluses, or **nau′tili.** [L.,—Gr. *nautilos,* a
sailor, a paper nautilus—*naus,* ship.]

naval, *nā′vl, adj.* pertaining to war-ships or a
navy: (*obs.*) nautical.—*n.* **nav′alism,** cult of
naval supremacy or sea-power.—**Naval Brigade,**
a body of seamen organised to serve on land;
naval crown, a garland awarded to a Roman who
had distinguished himself in a sea-fight; **naval
officer,** an officer in the navy: (*U.S.*) a custom-
house officer of high rank. [L. *nāvālis*—*nāvis,*
a ship.]

navarch, *nāv′ärk, n.* an admiral.—*n.* **nav′archy,**
the office of navarch: a fleet. [Gr. *nauarchos*—
naus, ship, *archē,* rule.]

nave, *nāv, n.* the middle or main body of a basilica,
rising above the aisles: the main part of a church,
generally west of the crossing, including or excluding its aisles. [L. *nāvis,* a ship.]

nave, *nāv, n.* the hub or central part of a wheel,
through which the axle passes: (*Shak.*) the navel.
[O.E. *nafu;* cf. Du. *naaf,* Ger. *nabe.*]

navel, *nā′vl, n.* the umbilicus or depression in the
centre of the abdomen: a central point: (*her.*)
nombril.—*ns.* **na′vel-or′ange,** a variety of orange
with a navel-like depression, and a smaller orange
enclosed; **na′vel-string,** the umbilical cord;
na′velwort, pennywort (Cotyledon). [O.E. *nafela,*
dim. of *nafu,* nave of a wheel.]

navew, *nā′vū, n.* a rape or coleseed with carrot-
shaped root: a wild Swedish turnip. [Fr. *naveau,*
dim.—L. *nāpus.*]

navicert, *nav′* or *nāv′i-sərt, n.* a certificate granted
by a belligerent to a neutral ship testifying that
she carries no contraband of war. [**navigational
certificate.**]

navicula, *nav-ik′ū-lä, n.* an incense-boat: **Navicula,** a genus of diatoms.—*adj.* **navic′ular,** boat-
shaped: pertaining to the navicular bone.—*n.* the
navicular bone.—**navicular bone,** the scaphoid
bone; **navicular disease,** inflammation of the
navicular bone in horses. [L. *nāvicula,* dim. of
nāvis, a ship.]

navigate, *nav′i-gāt, v.i.* to conduct or manage a
ship, aircraft, &c., in sailing or flying: to find
one's way and keep one's course, esp. by water
or air: to sail or fly.—*v.t.* to conduct on a voyage:
to sail or fly over, on, or through.—*n.* **navigability**
(*-gə-bil′i-ti*).— *adj.* **nav′igable,** that may be
passed by ships, &c.: dirigible.—*ns.* **nav′igable-
ness; naviga′tion,** the act, science, or art of
conducting ships or aircraft, esp. the finding of
position and determination of course by astronomical observations and mathematical computations:
travel or traffic by water or air: (*arch.*) a voyage:
shipping generally: a navigable route: a canal or
artificial waterway; **nav′igātor,** one who navigates
or sails: one who directs the course of a ship, &c.:
an explorer by sea: a navvy: an instrumental or
other aid to navigation. [L. *nāvigāre, -ātum*—
nāvis, a ship, *agĕre,* to drive.]

navvy, *nav′i, n.* a labourer—originally a labourer
on a navigation or canal: a machine for digging
out earth, &c.—called also *French navvy.*—*v.i.* to
work as a navvy, or like a navvy.—*v.t.* to excavate:
—*pr.p.* **navv′ying;** *pa.t.* and *pa.p.* **navv′ied.**
[navigator.]

navy, *nā′vi, n.* a fleet of ships: the whole of a
nation's ships-of-war: the officers and men belonging to a nation's warships.—*adj.* of, used by,
such as is supplied to, the navy.—*n.* and *adj.* **na′vy-
blue′,** dark blue as in naval dress; **na′vy-list′,**
a list of officers and ships of a navy; **na′vy-yard,**
(*U.S.*) a government dockyard. [O.Fr. *navie*—
L. *nāvis,* a ship.]

nawab, *nə-wäb′, -wawb′, n.* a deputy or viceroy in
the Mogul empire: a Mohammedan prince or
noble: a title bestowed by the Indian government:
(*rarely*) a nabob. [Hind. *nawwāb*—Ar. *nawwāb,*
respectful pl. of *nā′ib,* deputy.]

nay, *nā, adv.* no: not only so, but: yet more: in
point of fact.—*n.* a denial: a vote against.—*n.*
nay′-say, a refusal.—*v.t.* to refuse: to deny.—
n. **nay′ward,** (*Shak.*) the negative side. [M.E.
nay, nai—O.N. *nei;* Dan. *nei;* cog. with **no.**]

nayword, *nā′wurd, n.* (*Shak.*) a catchword or watch-
word: a proverbial reproach, a byword (*Shak.*
ayword). [Origin obscure.]

Nazarene, *naz′ə-rēn, n.* an inhabitant of Nazareth,
in Galilee: a follower of Jesus of Nazareth, originally used of Christians in contempt: an early
Jewish Christian.—Also **Nazarē′an, Naz′arite.**

Nazarite, *naz′ə-rīt, n.* a Jewish ascetic under a vow
(see Numb. vi.)—also **Naz′irite.**—*adj.* **Nazaritic**
(*-it′ik*).—*n.* **Naz′aritism** (*-īt-izm*). [Heb. *nāzar,*
to consecrate.]

naze, *nāz, n.* a headland or cape. [O.E. *næs;* cf.
ness.]

Nazi, *nä′tsē, n.* and *adj.* for Ger. *National-sozialist,*
National Socialist, Hitlerite.—*ns.* **Naz′ism, Naz′i-
ism.** [Ger.]

nazir, *nā′zir, n.* an Indian court official who serves
summonses, &c.: an official of various kinds.
[Ar. *nāzir,* overseer.]

ne, *nē, ni, adv.* (*obs.*) not.—*conj.* (*obs.*) nor. [O.E.
ne.]

neafe, neaffe (*Shak.*). See **nieve.**

neal, *nēl, v.t.* and *v.i.* an aphetic form of **anneal.**

Neanderthal, *ni-an′dər-täl, adj.* of a Palaeolithic
species of man whose remains were first found in
1857 in a cave in the *Neanderthal,* a valley between
Düsseldorf and Elberfeld.—*n.* **Nean′derthaler.**—
adj. **Nean′derthaloid.**

neap, *nēp, adj.* of tides, of smallest range.—*n.* a
neap-tide.—*v.i.* to tend towards the neap.—*adj.*
neaped, left aground between spring tides.—*n.*
neap′-tide, neap tide, a tide of minimum ampli-

tude, occurring when the sun and moon are working against each other. [O.E. *nép*, app. meaning helpless; *népflód*, neap-tide.]

Neapolitan, *nē-ə-pol'i-tən, adj.* of the city or the former kingdom of Naples.—*n.* a native, citizen, or inhabitant of Naples.—**Neapolitan ice,** a combination of two different ices; **Neapolitan sixth,** a chord of the subdominant with its minor third and minor sixth; **Neapolitan violet,** a scented double variety of sweet violet. [L. *Neāpolitānus* —Gr. *Neápolis,* new town—*neos, -ā, -on,* new, *polis,* city.]

near, *nēr, adv.* (orig. compar. of **nigh**) nigher, more closely, to or at a shorter distance: (now as positive) to or at no great distance: close: closely: nearly: almost: narrowly: (new double *compar.* **near′er;** *superl.* **near′est**).—*prep.* close to (in all degrees of comparison).—*adj.* nigh: not far away in place or time: close in kin, friendship, imitation, approximation, or in any relation: close, narrow, so as barely to escape: short, as a road: stingy: of horses, vehicles, &c., left, left-hand (*compar.* **near′er;** *superl.* **near′est**).—*v.t.* and *v.i.* to approach: to come nearer.—*adjs.* **near′-begaun, near′-gaun,** (*Scot.*) niggardly; **near′-by,** neighbouring.—*adv.* (usu. **near-by′**) close at hand.— *adj.* **near′-hand,** (*Scot.*) near.—*adv.* nearly.—*adj.* **near′-legged,** (*Shak.*) walking so that the legs interfere.—*adv.* **near′ly,** at or within a short distance: closely: intimately: scrutinisingly, parsimoniously: almost: approximately but rather less.—*n.* **near′ness.**—*adj.* **near′-sight′ed,** shortsighted.—*n.* **near′-sight′edness.**—**Near East,** the countries of south-eastern Europe, as distinguished from the Middle East (Asia Minor to India) and the Far East or eastern Asia; **near miss,** (*lit.* and *fig.*) a miss that is almost a hit; **near point,** the nearest point the eye can focus. [O.E. *néar,* compar. of *néah,* nigh (adv.), and O.N. *nær,* compar. (but also used as pos.) of *ná,* nigh; cf. Ger. *näher.*]

near-, *nēr-,* in composition, almost, as *adj.* **near′-white′:** a substitute closely resembling, as *ns.* **near′-beer′, near′-silk′.**

Nearctic, *nē-ärk'tik, adj.* of the New World part of the Holarctic region. [Gr. *neos,* new, *arktikos,* northern—*arktos,* bear, the Great Bear.]

neat, *nēt,* an ox, cow, bull, &c.—*pl.* neat.—*ns.* **neat′-cattle;** neat′-herd; neat′-house; neat′-stall.—**neat's-foot oil,** an oil obtained from the feet of oxen; **neat's leather,** leather made of the hides of neat. [O.E. *néat,* cattle, a beast— *néotan, níotan,* to use; cf. Scot. **nowt** from O.N. *naut.*]

neat, *nēt, adj.* (*obs.*) clean: unmixed: undiluted: undiminished, net: (*Spens.*) clear, shining: elegant: trim: tidy: finished, adroit: deft: well and concisely put.—*adv.* neatly.—*adj.* **neat′-hand′ed,** dexterous.—*adv.* **neat′ly.**—*n.* **neat′ness.** [Fr. *net*—L. *nitidus,* shining—*nitēre,* to shine.]

neath, 'neath, *nēth, prep.* (*dial.* and *poet.*) beneath. [Aphetic for **aneath,** or for **beneath.**]

neb, *neb, n.* a beak or bill: (*obs.*) the mouth: the nose: a nib: the sharp point of anything.—*v.i.* to bill.—*v.t.* to put a neb on.—*adj.* **nebbed** (*nebd*), having a neb. [O.E. *nebb,* beak, face; cog. with Du. *neb,* beak.]

nebbuk, nebek, nebeck, *neb'ək.* Same as **nabk.**

nebel, *nē'bəl, n.* a Hebrew instrument, apparently a harp. [Heb. *nēbel.*]

neb-neb, *neb'-neb, n.* bablah pods. [Prob. an African word.]

nebris, *neb'ris, n.* a fawn-skin worn by Bacchus and his votaries. [Gr. *nebris.*]

nebula, *neb'ū-lä, n.* a little cloudiness: a slight opacity of the cornea: a liquid for spraying: a faint, misty appearance in the heavens produced either by a group of stars too distant to be seen singly, or by diffused gaseous matter:—*pl.* **neb′-ulae** (*-lē*).—*adjs.* **neb′ular,** pertaining to nebulae: like or of the nature of a nebula; **neb′ulé** (*-lā*), **neb′uly,** (*her.*) wavy.—*ns.* **nebule** (*neb'ūl*), a wavy moulding; **nebulisā′tion.**—*v.t.* **neb′ulise,** to reduce to spray.—*ns.* **nebulis′er,** a spraying

apparatus, an atomiser; **nebu′lium,** an element formerly assumed in order to explain two green lines in the spectra of gaseous nebulae—lines now known to be due to doubly ionised oxygen; **nebulos′ity.**—*adj.* **neb′ulous,** misty, hazy, vague: clouded: cloudlike: like, of the nature of, or surrounded by, a nebula.—*adv.* **neb′ulously.**— *n.* **neb′ulousness.**—**nebular hypothesis,** the theory of Laplace that the solar system was formed by the contraction and breaking up of a rotating nebula. [L. *nebula,* mist; cf. Gr. *nephelē,* cloud, mist.]

necessary, *nes'is-ə-ri, adj.* that must be: that cannot be otherwise: unavoidable: indispensable: under compulsion: not free.—*n.* that which cannot be left out or done without (food, &c.)—used chiefly in *pl.:* a privy: (*coll.*) money.—*n.* and *adj.* **necessā′rian.**—*n.* **necessā′rianism,** the doctrine that the will is not free, but subject to causes without, which determine its action.—*adv.* **nec′essarily.**—*n.* **nec′essariness.**—**necessary truths,** such as cannot but be true. [L. *necessārius.*]

necessity, *ni-ses'i-ti, n.* a state or quality of being necessary: that which is necessary or unavoidable: unavoidable compulsion: great need: poverty. —*n.* and *adj.* **necessitā′rian.**—*n.* **necessitā′rian-ism,** necessarianism.—*v.t.* **necess′itate,** to make necessary: to render unavoidable: to compel.— *n.* **necessitā′tion.**—*adjs.* **necess′itied,** (*Shak.*) subject by need; **necess′itous,** in necessity: very poor: destitute. — *adv.* **necess′itously.** — *n.* **necess′itousness.**—**natural necessity,** the condition of being necessary according to the laws of nature; **logical** or **mathematical,** according to those of human intelligence; **moral,** according to those of moral law; **of necessity,** necessarily; **works of necessity,** work so necessary as to be allowable on the Sabbath. [L. *necessitās, -ātis.*]

neck, *nek, n.* the part connecting head and trunk: (*fig.*) often in allusion to the halter or the yoke: the flesh of that part regarded as food: anything resembling that part: the part connecting head and body of anything, e.g. a violin: the plain lower part of the capital of a column: any narrow connecting part, e.g. an isthmus: anything narrow and throatlike, as the upper part of a bottle: a plug of igneous or fragmental rock filling a volcanic vent: a col: the part of a garment on or nearest the neck: a neck's length.—*v.t.* to strike, pull, or chop the neck of, esp. so as to kill: to catch or fasten by the neck: to embrace: to make a neck on: (*slang*) to drink.—*v.i.* (*slang*) to embrace.— *ns.* **neck′atee,** (*obs.*) a neckerchief; **neck′-band,** the part of a shirt, &c., encircling the neck: a band worn on the neck; **neck′beef,** the coarse flesh of the neck of cattle: inferior stuff; **neck′-bone,** a cervical vertebra; **neck′cloth,** a piece of folded cloth worn round the neck by men as a band or cravat, the ends hanging down often of lace.— *adj.* **necked,** having a neck.—*ns.* **neck′erchief,** a kerchief for the neck; **neck′gear,** apparel for the neck; **neck′-herr′ing,** (*obs.*) a heavy blow on the neck; **neck′ing,** the neck of a column: a neck-moulding; **neck′lace** (*-lis, -ləs*), a lace, chain, or string of beads or precious stones worn on the neck; **neck′let,** a simple form of necklace: a pendant strung for the neck: a small boa or fur for the neck; **neck′line,** the boundary-line of a garment at the neck; **neck′-moulding,** a moulding where the capital of a column joins the shaft; **neck′-piece,** a piece forming, covering, or bordering a neck; **neck′-sweet′bread,** the thymus gland of veal or lamb; **neck′tie,** a scarf or band tied round the neck; **neck′verse,** the test of ability to read for those who claimed benefit of clergy, usually Psalm li. 1, success giving the privilege of being branded on the hand instead of hanging; **neck′wear,** apparel for the neck; **neck′weed,** (*old slang*) hemp, source of the hangman's rope: (*U.S.*) a kind of speedwell, from its reputed medicinal virtue.—**get it in the neck,** to be severely dealt with, hard hit; **harden the neck,** to grow more obstinate; **neck and crop,** completely: bodily: in a heap: summarily and unceremoniously; **neck and neck,** exactly equal: side by side ; **neck or nothing**, risking everything ; **talk through (the back of) one's neck**, to talk wildly or absurdly wide of the truth : **tread on the neck of**, to oppress or tyrannise over. [O.E. *hnecca* ; Ger. *nacken*.]

necro-, *nek'rō-*, *-ro'*, in composition, dead : dead body.—*ns.* **necrōbiō′sis**, degeneration of living tissue ; **necrog′rapher**, an obituary writer ; **necrol′ater** ; **necrol′atry**, worship of, or morbid or sentimental reverence for, the dead, or dead bodies. — *adjs.* **necrōlog′ic**, **-al.** — *ns.* **necrol′- ogist** ; **necrol′ogy**, an obituary list ; **nec′rō- mancer**, a sorcerer ; **nec′rōmancy**, the art of revealing future events by calling up and question- ing the spirits of the dead : enchantment.—*adjs.* **necrōman′tic**, **-al.**—*adv.* **necrōman′tically.**— *adj.* **necroph′agous**, feeding on carrion.—*ns.* **necroph′ilism**, **necroph′ily**, a morbid liking for dead bodies.—*adj.* **necroph′ilous.**—*n.* **necrō- phō′bia**, a morbid horror of corpses. — *adj.* **necroph′orous**, carrying away and burying dead bodies, as burying beetles.—*ns.* **necrop′olis**, a cemetery ; **nec′ropsy** (or *-rop′*), a post-mortem examination. — *adjs.* **necrōscop′ic**, **-al.** — *n.* **necros′copy**, a post-mortem examination, autopsy. —*v.t.* and *v.i.* **necrose** (*nek-rōs′*), to affect with or undergo necrosis.—*n.* **necrō′sis**, death of part of the living body.—*adj.* **necrot′ic.**—*v.t.* and *v.i.* **nec′rōtise**, to necrose. [Gr. *nekros*, dead body, dead.]

nectar, *nek′tər*, *n.* the name given by Homer, Hesiod, Pindar, &c., to the beverage of the gods, giving life and beauty : a delicious beverage : the honey of the glands of plants.—*adjs.* **nectā′real**, **nectā′rean**, **nectā′reous**, **nec′tarous**, of or like nectar ; **nec′tared**, imbued with nectar : mingled, filled, or abounding with nectar.—*ns.* **nectā′reous- ness** ; **nec′tar-guide′**, a marking that guides insects to the nectary of a flower.—*adjs.* **nectā′rial**, of the nature of a nectary ; **nectarif′erous**, pro- ducing nectar ; **nec′tarine** (*-in*), sweet as nectar. —*n.* (*-ēn*, *-in*), a variety of peach with a smooth fruit.—*n.* **nec′tary**, a glandular organ that secretes nectar. [Gr. *nektar* ; ety. dub.]

nectocalyx, *nek-tō-kā′liks*, *n.* a hydrozoan swim- ming-bell :—*pl.* **nectocā′lyces** (*-li-sēz*). [Gr. *nēktos*, swimming, *kalyx*, shell, flower-cup.]

neddy, *ned′i*, *n.* a donkey. [From *Edward*.]

née, *nā.* See *Foreign Words*.

need, *nēd*, *n.* want of something which one cannot well do without : necessity : a state that requires relief : want of the means of living.—*v.t.* to have occasion for : to want : to require.—*v.i.* to be necessary.—*ns.* **need′-be**, a necessity ; **need- cess′ity**, a dialect or illiterate combination of **need** and **necessity** ; **need′er** ; **need′-fire**, fire produced by friction, to which a certain virtue is superstitiously attached : a beacon.—*adj.* **need′- ful**, full of need : having need : needy : necessary : requisite.—*adv.* **need′fully.**—*n.* **need′fulness.**— *adv.* **need′ily.**—*n.* **need′iness.**—*adj.* **need′less**, (*Shak.*) having no need : not needed : unnecessary. — *adv.* **need′lessly.** — *n.* **need′lessness.** — *adv.* **need′ly**, (*Shak.*) necessarily. — *n.* **need′ment**, (*Spens.*) something needed.—*adv.* **needs**, of neces- sity : indispensably.—*adj.* **need′y**, very poor : (*Shak.*) necessary.—*n.* **need′y-hood** (*Herrick*).— **the needful**, (*slang*) ready money. [O.E. *nēd*, *nied*, *nýd*, Du. *nood*, Ger. *noth*.]

needle, *nēd′l*, *n.* a small, sharp instrument for sewing : any similar slender, pointed instrument, as for knitting, etching, gramophone working, dissection, or hooked, as for crochet : the suspended magnet of a compass or galvanometer : a pointer on a dial : the pointed end of a hypodermic syringe : anything sharp and pointed : a pinnacle of rock : **an obelisk** : a long slender crystal : a strong beam passed through a wall as a temporary support : **a** long, narrow, stiff leaf : (*fig.*) irritation.—*adj.* (of **a** contest) intensely keen and acutely critical.—*v.t.* to sew : to pierce : to penetrate : to thread : to pass through : to underpin with needles : to irritate.—*v.i.* to pass out and in : to sew.—*ns.* **need′le-bath**, a shower-bath with very fine strong jets ; **need′le-book**, a needle-case in book form ;

need′le-case, a case for holding needles ; **need′le- craft**, the art of needlework ; **need′le-fish**, a pipe- fish : a garpike ; **need′leful**, as much thread as will serve conveniently for one threading of a needle ; **need′le-furze′**, the petty whin ; **needl′e- gun**, a gun in which the cartridge is exploded by the impact of a spike ; **need′le-paper**, black paper used for wrapping needles ; **need′le-point**, the point of a needle : a very sharp point : point-lace made with a needle. — *adj.* **need′le-point′ed**, pointed like a needle, round in section : without a barb, as a fish-hook.—*ns.* **need′ler**, a needle- maker ; **need′le-tin**, cassiterite in slender crystals ; **need′lewoman**, a woman who does needlework : a seamstress ; **need′lework**, work done with a needle : the business of a seamstress.—*adj.* **need′ly**, like needles.—**get the needle**, to be irritated ; **look for a needle in a haystack**, bottle of hay, to engage in a hopeless search. [O.E. *nǣdl* ; Ger. *nadel* ; cog. with Ger. *nähen*, to sew ; L. *nēre*, to spin.]

neeld, *nēld*, **neele**, *nēl*, obsolete forms of **needle**.

neem. Same as **nim** (3).

neep, *nēp*, *n.* (*Scot.*) a turnip. [O.E. *nǣp*—L. *nāpus*.]

ne'er, *nār*, *adv.* contr. of **never**.—*adj.* and *n.* **ne'er′-do-well** (*Scot.* *-weel*), good-for-nothing.

neesberry. Same as **naseberry**.

neeze, **neese**, *nēz*, *v.i.* and *n.* sneeze. [Cf. O.N. *hnjósa*, and **sneeze**.]

nef, *nef*, *n.* (*obs.*) a church nave : a mediaeval, usually shiplike, piece of plate for the great man's napkin, table utensils, &c. [Fr. *nef*, ship—L. *nāvis*.]

nefandous, *ni-fan′dos*, *adj.* abominable. [L. *ne- fandus*, unspeakable—*ne-*, not, *fandus*, to be spoken —*fārī*, to speak.]

nefarious, *ni-fā′ri-əs*, *adj.* extremely wicked : villainous. — *adv.* **nefā′riously.** — *n.* **nefā′rious- ness.**—*adj.* **nefast** (*ni-fāst′*), abominable. [L. *nefārius*, *nefāstus*—*nefās*, wrong, crime—*ne-*, not, *fās*, divine law, prob. from *fārī*, to speak.]

negate, *ni-gāt′*, *v.t.* to deny : to imply the non- existence of.—*ns.* **negation** (*-gā′shən*), act of saying no : denial : (*log.*) a negative proposition : the absence of certain qualities in anything : a thing characterised by the mere absence of qualities : a mere nothing ; **negā′tionist**, one who merely denies, without offering any positive assertion.— *adj.* **negative** (*neg′ə-tiv*), denying : expressing denial, refusal, or prohibition—opp. to *affirmative* : (*log.*) denying the connexion between a subject and a predicate : lacking positive quality : failing to affirm : opposite, contrary to, neutralising, that which is regarded as positive : (*math.*) less than nothing : reckoned or measured in the opposite direction to that chosen as positive : (*elect.*) at relatively lower potential : of, having, or producing negative electricity (see below) : (*opt.*, *phot.*) having dark for light and light for dark : in complementary colours : (*chem.*) acid : (*opt.*) laevorotatory : having the index of refraction for the extraordinary ray less than for the ordinary in double refraction : (*biol.*) in a direction away from the source of stimulus. —*n.* a word or statement by which something is denied : a word or grammatical form that expresses denial : a negative proposition or term : the right or act of saying no, or of refusing assent : the side of a question or the decision which denies what is affirmed : an image in which the lights and shades are reversed : a photographic plate bearing such an image : a negative quantity.—*v.t.* to prove the contrary of : to reject by vote : to veto : to reject by veto : to deny : to neutralise. —*adv.* **neg′atively.**—*ns.* **neg′ativeness** ; **neg′- ativism**, the doctrine or attitude of a negationist : a tendency to do the opposite of what one is asked to do ; **negativ′ity**, the fact of being negative.— *adj.* **neg′atory**, expressing denial. — **negative angle**, one generated by a straight line moving clockwise ; **negative electricity**, electricity arising from the excess of electrons, such as is developed in resinous bodies by rubbing with flannel, opposite to that obtained by rubbing glass ; **negative pole**, that pole of a magnet which turns to the south when the magnet swings freely ; **negative sign**, the sign (−, read *minus*) of subtraction. [L. *negāre*, *-ātum*, to deny.]

neglect, *ni-glekt'*, *v.t.* to treat carelessly : to pass by without notice : to omit by carelessness : to fail to bestow due care upon.—*n.* disregard : slight : omission : uncared-for state.—*adj.* **neglect'able**, (*rare*) negligible.—*ns.* **neglect'edness** ; **neglect'er**.—*adj.* **neglect'ful**, careless : accustomed to omit or neglect things : slighting.—*adv.* **neglect'fully**.—*n.* **neglect'fulness**.—*adv.* **neglect'ingly**, carelessly : heedlessly.—*n.* **neglection** (*-glek'shan*, *Shak.*), negligence.—*adj.* **neglect'ive**, (now *rare*) neglectful. [L. *neglegĕre*, *neglectum*—*neg-* or *nec-*, not, *legĕre*, to gather.]

négligé, *nā'glē-zhā*, *n.* easy undress.—*adj.* carelessly or unceremoniously dressed : careless.—*n.* **negligee** (*neg-li-jē'*), a plain, loose gown : a necklace, usually of red coral. [Fr., neglected.]

negligence, *neg'li-jəns*, *n.* fact or quality of being negligent : want of proper care : habitual neglect : a single act of carelessness or neglect, a slight : carelessness about dress, manner, &c. : omission of duty, esp. such care for the interests of others as the law may require.—*adj.* **neg'ligent**, neglecting : careless : inattentive : disregarding ceremony or fashion.—*adv.* **neg'ligently**.—*n.* **negligibil'ity**.—*adj.* **neg'ligible** (sometimes **neg'ligeable**), such as may be ignored.—*adv.* **neg'ligibly**. [L. *negligentia* for *neglegentia*—*neglegēre*, to neglect.]

negotiate, *ni-gō'shi-āt*, *v.i.* to carry on business : to bargain : to hold intercourse for the purpose of mutual arrangement.—*v.t.* to arrange for by agreement : to manage : to transfer or exchange for value : (*coll.* or *slang*) to cope with or tackle successfully.—*n.* **negotiabil'ity**.—*adj.* **nego'tiable**.—*ns.* **negotia'tion** ; **nego'tiator**—*jem.* **nego'tiatress** (*-shyā-*), **negotiatrix** (*ni-gō'shyā-triks*, or *ni-gō-shi-ā'triks*). [L. *negōtiārī*, *-ātus*—*negōtium*, business—*neg-*, not, *ōtium*, leisure.]

Negrillo, *ni-gril'ō*, *n.* a pygmy of equatorial Africa : —*pl.* **Negrill'os**. [Sp., dim. of *negro*, black.]

Negrito, *ni-grē'tō*, *n.* a pygmy of the Malayan region : —*pl.* **Negri'tos**. [Sp., dim. of *negro*, black.]

negro, *nē'grō*, *n.* one of the black-skinned woolly-haired African race of mankind : sometimes limited so as to exclude the Bantu, or extended to include other African races or other black races (*pl.* **ne'groes**).—*adj.* of or pertaining to the race of black men.—*ns.* **ne'gress**, a negro woman or girl ; **ne'gro-corn** (*W. Indies*), durra ; **ne'grohead**, tobacco soaked in molasses and pressed into cakes, so called from its blackness : an inferior rubber.—*adj.* **ne'groid**, of negro type : like a negro.—*n.* one who is of negro type : one who is a negro in a broad sense only.—*adj.* **negroid'al**.—*ns.* **ne'grō-ism**, any peculiarity of speech among negroes, esp. in the southern U.S. : devotion to the cause of the negroes ; **ne'grophil**, **ne'grophile**, a friend of the negro, and a supporter of his cause ; **negrophil'ism** (*ni-grof'*) ; **negroph'ilist** ; **ne'grophobe**, one who dislikes negroes ; **negropho'bia**. [Sp. *negro*—L. *niger*, *nigra*, *nigrum*, black.]

negus, *nē'gəs*, *n.* port or sherry with hot water, sweetened and spiced. [Said to be from Colonel *Negus*, its first maker, in Queen Anne's time.]

negus, *nē'gəs*, *n.* the king of Abyssinia. [Amharic.]

neif. See **nieve**.

neigh, *nā*, *v.i.* to utter the cry of a horse.—*n.* the cry of a horse. [O.E. *hnǣgan*.]

neighbour, *nā'bər*, *n.* a person who dwells near another : a person or thing that is near another : (*Scot.*) one of a pair.—*adj.* (*arch.* and *U.S.*) neighbouring.—*v.t.* and *v.i.* to live or be near.—*n.* **neigh'bourhood**, state of being neighbours, kindly feeling : a set of neighbours : a district, esp. with reference to its inhabitants : a district : a region lying near : a near position : nearness.—*adj.* **neigh'bouring**, being near : adjoining.—*n.* **neigh'bourliness**.—*adjs.* **neigh'bourly**, like or becoming a neighbour : friendly : social : (also *adv.*) ; **neigh'bour-stained**, (*Shak.*) stained with neighbours' blood.—**good neighbours**, the fairies ; **in the neighbourhood of**, (esp. *U.S.*) somewhere about. [O.E. *néahgebúr*—*néah*, near, *gebúr* or *búr*, a farmer.]

neist, *nēst*, a dialectic form of **nighest**, **next**.

neither, *nī'dhər*, or *nē'dhər*, *adj.* and *pron.* not either.—*conj.* not either : and not : nor yet.—*adv.* not at all : in no case. [O.E. *nǣther*, *nāwther*, abbrev. of *náhwæther*—*ná*, never, *hwæther*, whether ; the vowel assimilated to **either**.]

neive. Same as **nieve**.

nek, *nek*, *n.* (*S.Afr.*) a col. [Du., neck.]

nekton, *nek'ton*, *n.* the assemblage of actively swimming organisms in a sea, lake, &c. [Gr. *nēkton* (neut.), swimming.]

nelis, **nelies**, *nel'is*, *n.* a winter pear :—*pl.* **nel'is**, **nel'ies**. [Fr. *nélis*.]

nelly, *nel'i*, *n.* a large petrel. [Perh. the woman's name.]

nelson, *nel'sən*, *n.* a wrestling hold in which the arm is passed under the opponent's, and the hand placed on the back of his neck.

Nelumbium, *ni-lum'bi-əm*, **Nelumbo**, *-bō*, *ns.* a genus of water-lilies including the Egyptian bean of Pythagoras, and the sacred lotus. [Sinh. *nelumbu*.]

Nemathelminthes, *nem-ə-thel-min'thēz*, *n.pl.* according to some, a group including nematodes, Nematomorpha, and Acanthocephala. — *n.sing.* **nemathel'minth**.—*adj.* **nemathelmin'thic**. [Gr. *nēma*, *-atos*, a thread, *helmins*, *-minthos*, worm.]

nematocyst, *nem'ət-ō-sist*, or *-at'*, *n.* a stinging organ in jellyfishes, &c., a sac from which a stinging thread can be everted. [Gr. *nēma*, *-atos*, a thread, *kystis*, a bladder.]

nematode, *nem'ə-tōd*, *n.* a round-worm or thread-worm.—Also *adj.*—*ns.pl.* **Nematō'da**, **Nema-toid'ea**, the nematodes.—*adj.* **nem'atoid**. [Gr. *nēma*, *-atos*, thread, *eidos*, form.]

Nematomorpha, *nem-ət-ō-mor'fä*, *n.pl.* the hair-worms. [Gr. *nēma*, *-atos*, thread, *morphē*, form.]

nematophore, *nem'-ət-ō-fōr*, *n.* a mouthless type of hydrozoan polyp that engulfs food by pseudo-podia. [Gr. *nēma*, *-atos*, thread, *phoros*, carrying.]

Nemean, *nem-ē'ən*, *nem'i-ən*, *nēm'i-ən*, *adj.* of *Nemea* (Gr. *Nēmeä*), a valley of Argolis, famous for its games held in the second and fourth years of each Olympiad, and for the lion slain by Herakles.

Nemertea, *nem-ər-tin'i-ä*, *n.pl.* a phylum of worm-like animals, mostly marine, ciliated, often brightly coloured, with protrusile proboscis.—Also **Nemer'tea**.—*ns.* and *adjs.* **nemer'tean**, **nemer'-tine**, **nemer'tian**. [Gr. *Nēmertēs*, one of the nereids.]

Nemesia, *nem-ē'zh(y)ä*, *sh(y)ä*, *-si-ä*, *n.* a S. African genus of the figwort family, including some brightly coloured garden flowers. [Gr. *nemesion*, a kind of catchfly.]

Nemesis, *nem'i-sis*, *n.* (*myth.*) the Greek goddess of retribution : **nemesis**, retributive justice. [Gr. *nemesis*, retribution—*nemein*, to deal out, dispense.]

Nemophila, *nem-of'i-lä*, *n.* a N. American genus of Hydrophyllaceae, favourite garden annuals, esp. one with blue, white-centred flowers. [Gr. *nemos*, a glade, wooded pasture, *phileein*, to love.]

nemoral, *nem'ə-rəl*, *adj.* of a wood or grove.—*adj.* **nem'orous**, wooded. [L. *nemus*, *-ŏris*, a grove.]

nempt, *nemt*, (*Spens.*) named, called :—*pa.p.* of obs. **nemn**, to name. [O.E. *nemnan*.]

nenuphar, *nen'ū-fär*, *n.* a water-lily, esp. the common white or yellow : **Nenuphar**, a synonym of **Nuphar**. [L.L. *nenuphar*—Ar. and Pers. *nīnūfar*, *nīlūfar*—Sans. *nīlôtpala*—*nīl*, blue, *utpala*, lotus.]

neo-, *nē'ō-*, in composition, new, young. [Gr. *neos*.]

Neo-Catholic, *nē-ō-kath'ə-lik*, *adj.* and *n.* of, or a member of, the school of, liberal Catholicism that followed Lamennais, Lacordaire, and Montalembert about 1830 : Anglo-Catholic with extreme leanings towards Rome.

Neo-Christian, *nē-ō-kris'tyən*, *adj.* and *n.* of, or a believer in, a liberalised and rationalised Christianity.—*n.* **Neo-Christian'ity**.

neo-classic, *-al*, *nē-ō-klas'ik*, *-əl*, *adjs.* belonging to a revival of classicism, or classicism as understood by those who would revive it, e.g. in the 18th century.—*ns.* **neo-class'icism** (*-i-sizm*) ; **neo-class'icist**.

Neocomian, *nē-ō-kō′mi-ən*, *adj.* and *n.* (*geol.*) Lower Cretaceous. [L. *Neocōmium*, Neuchâtel— Gr. *neos*, new, *kōmē*, a village.]

Neo-Darwinism, *nē′ō-där′win-izm*, *n.* a later development of Darwinism, laying greater stress upon natural selection and denying the inheritance of acquired characters.—*ns.* and *adjs.* **Neo-Dar′win′ian**; **Neo-Dar′winist**.

neodymium, *nē-ō-dim′i-əm*, *n.* a metal (Nd; at. numb. 60), the chief component of the once-supposed element *didymium*. [Gr. *neos*, new.]

Neogaea, *nē-ō-jē′ä*, *n.* (*biol.*) the Neotropical region.—*adj.* **Neogae′an**. [Gr. *gaia*, earth.]

Neogene, *nē′ō-jēn*, *n.* and *adj.* (*geol.*) Miocene and Pliocene. [Gr. *neogenēs*, new-born.]

Neo-Gothic, *nē-ō-goth′ik*, *n.* and *adj.* (*archit.*) revived Gothic of the 19th century.

neogrammarian, *nē-ō-grə-mā′ri-ən*, *n.* a philologist of the 19th-century German school that introduced scientific exactitude into the study of sound change —a young grammarian (Ger. *junggrammatiker*).

Neohellenism, *nē-ō-hel′ən-izm*, *n.* the modern Hellenism inspired by the ancient: the devotion to ancient Greek ideals in literature and art, esp. in the Italian Renaissance.

Neo-Kantianism, *nē-ō-kan′ti-ən-izm*, *n.* the philosophy of *Kant* as taught by his successors.—*n.* and *adj.* **Neo-Kan′tian**.

Neo-Lamarckism, *nē-ō-lä-märk′izm*, *n.* a modern adaptation of Lamarckism.—*n.* and *adj.* **Ne′o-Lamarck′ian**.

Neo-Latin, *nē-ō-lat′in*, *n.* and *adj.* Romance, i.e. Italian, Rhaeto-Romanic, French, Provençal, Spanish, Portuguese, and Rumanian.

Neolithic, *nē-ō-lith′ik*, *adj.* of the later or more advanced Stone Age—opp. to *Palaeolithic*.—*n.* **ne′olith**, a Neolithic artifact. [Gr. *lithos*, a stone.]

neology, *nē-ol′ə-ji*, *n.* the introduction of new words, or new senses of old words: a neologism: (*theol.*) new doctrines, esp. German rationalism.— *n.* **neolō′gian**.—*adjs.* **neologic** (-*loj′*), **-al**.—*adv.* **neolog′ically**.—*v.i.* **neol′ogise**, to introduce new words or doctrines.— *ns.* **neol′ogism**, a new word, phrase, or doctrine: the use of old words in a new sense; **neol′ogist**.—*adjs.* **neologis′tic**, **-al**. [Gr. *logos*, word.]

Neo-Malthusianism, *nē-ō-mal-thūz′i-ən-izm*, *n.* doctrine of birth-control. [Gr. *neos*, new. **Malthusian**.]

neon, *nē′on*, *n.* a gas (Ne; at. numb. 10) found in the atmosphere by Sir Wm. Ramsay (1852-1916). —**neon lamp**, an electric discharge lamp containing neon, giving a red glow, used for advertising signs. [Neuter of Gr. *neos*, new.]

neonomianism, *nē-ō-nō′mi-ən-izm*, *n.* the doctrine that the gospel is a new law, and that faith has abrogated the old moral obedience.—*n.* **neonō′mian**. [Gr. *nomos*, law.]

neo-paganism, *nē-ō-pā′gən-izm*, *n.* a revival of paganism, or its spirit.—*n.* and *adj.* **neo-pa′gan**.— *v.t.* and *v.i.* **neo-pa′ganise**.

neophobia, *nē-ō-fō′bi-ä*, *n.* dread of novelty. [Gr. *phobos*, fear.]

neophyte, *nē′ō-fīt*, *n.* a new convert: one newly baptised: a newly ordained priest: a novice in a religious order: a tiro or beginner.—*adj.* **neophytic** (-*fit′ik*). [Gr. *neophytos*, newly planted— *phyein*, to produce.]

neoplasm, *nē′ō-plazm*, *n.* a morbid new growth or formation of tissue.—*adj.* **neoplas′tic**. [Gr. *plasma*, form, mould.]

Neoplatonism, *nē-ō-plā′tə-nizm*, *n.* a combination of Platonism with Oriental elements, developed by Plotinus, Porphyry, Proclus, &c.— *adj.* **Neo-platonic** (-*plə-ton′ik*).—*n.* **neopla′tonist**.

Neopythagoreanism, *nē-ō-pith-ag-ər-ē′ən-izm*, *n.* a revived Pythagoreanism of Alexandria beginning in the first century B.C.—*n.* and *adj.* **Neopythagorē′an**.

neoteny, *nē-ot′ən-i*, **neoteinia**, *nē-ō-tī′ni-ä*, *ns.* prolonged retention of larval or immature character or characters.—*adjs.* **neotenic** (*nē-ō-ten′ik*), **-tein′ic**. [Gr. *teinein*, to stretch.]

neoteric, **-al**, *nē-ō-ter′ik*, **-əl**, *adjs.* of recent origin, modern. — *adv.* **neoter′ically**. — *v.i.* **neoterise**, (*ni-ot′ə-rīz*).—*ns.* **neot′erism**, the introduction of new things, esp. new words; **neot′erist**. [Gr. *neōterikos*—*neōteros*, comp. of *neos*, new.]

Neotropical, *nē-ō-trop′ki-əl*, *adj.* (*biol.*) of tropical America.

neovitalism, *nē-ō-vī′tə-lizm*, *n.* the theory or belief that a complete causal explanation of vital phenomena cannot be reached without invoking some extra-material concept.—*n.* **neovi′talist**. [**vitalism**.]

Neozoic, *nē-ō-zō′ik*, *adj.* later than Palaeozoic: later than Mesozoic. [Gr. *zōikos*, of animals.]

nep, *nep*, **nip**, *nip*, *n.* catmint. [L. *nepeta*.]

nepenthe, *ni-pen′thē*, *n.* (*poet.*) a sorrow-lulling drink or drug: the plant yielding it.—*adj.* **nepen′thean**.—*n.* **Nepen′thes** (-*thēz*), nepenthe: the pitcher-plant genus, constituting a family **Nepenthā′ceae** akin to the Sarracenias and sundews. [Gr. *nepenthēs*, -*es*—pfx. *nē-*, not, *penthos*, grief.]

nephalism, *nef′ə-lizm*, *n.* total abstinence from alcoholic drinks.—*n.* **neph′alist**. [Gr. *nēphalios*, sober; *nēphein*, to be sober.]

nepheline, *nef′ə-lēn*, *n.* a rock-forming mineral, silicate of sodium, potassium, and aluminium, colourless, usually crystallising in hexagonal prisms. —Also **neph′elite**.—*ns.* **neph′eline-bas′alt**, a basalt with nepheline instead of (or in addition to) felspar; **neph′elinite**, a basalt-like rock compound of nepheline and pyroxene, with no felspar or olivine. [Gr. *nephelē*, a cloud (from the effect of acid).]

nephelometer, *nef-ə-lom′i-tər*, *n.* an instrument for measuring cloudiness, esp. in liquids.—*adj.* **nephelomet′ric**. [Gr. *nephelē*, cloud, *metron*, measure.]

nephew, *nev′ū*, or *nef′ū*, *n.* the son of a brother or sister: extended to a like relation by marriage: (*obs.*) a grandson or descendant: (*euphemistically*) a pope's or priest's son:—*fem.* **niece**. [O.Fr. *neveu*—L. *nepōs*, *nepōtis*, grandson; cf. O.E. *nefa*, Ger. *neffe*, nephew.]

nephology, *nef-ol′ə-ji*, *n.* the study of clouds.— *adjs.* **nephologic** (-*ə-loj′*), **-al**.—*n.* **nephol′ogist**. [Gr. *nephos*, cloud, *logos*, discourse.]

nephro-, *nef′rō-*, **nephr-**, in composition, kidney.— *ns.* **nephralgia** (*nef-ral′ji-ä*), **nephral′gy**, pain in the kidneys; **nephrec′tomy**, surgical removal of a kidney.—*adj.* **neph′ric**.—*ns.* **nephrid′ium**, in invertebrates and lower chordates, an organ serving the function of a kidney; **neph′rite**, the mineral jade, in the narrower sense—an old charm against kidney disease; **nephrit′ic**, a medicine for the kidneys.—*adjs.* **nephrit′ic**, **-al**, pertaining to the kidneys, or nephritis, or jade.—*ns.* **nephri′tis**, inflammation of the kidneys.— *adj.* **neph′roid**, kidney-shaped.—*ns.* **neph′ropexy** (Gr. *pēxis*, fixing), fixation of a floating kidney; **nephropto′sis** (Gr. *ptōsis*, fall), floating kidney; **nephrot′omy**, incision into the kidney. [Gr. *nephros*, a kidney.]

nepotism, *nep′o-tizm*, *n.* undue patronage to one's relations, esp. by a pope.—*adj.* **nepot′ic**.—*n.* **nep′otist**. [L. *nepōs*, *nepōtis*, a grandson.]

Neptune, *nep′tūn*, *n.* the Roman sea-god, identified with the Greek Poseidon: a remote planet of the solar system, discovered in 1846.—*adj.* **Neptū′nian**, pertaining to Neptune or to the sea: (*geol.*) formed by water.—*n.* an inhabitant of Neptune: a Neptunist.—*ns.* **Nep′tunist**, a believer in the origin of rocks generally as chemical precipitates from the sea—opp. to *Plutonist* or *Vulcanist*; **neptū′nium**, an element (Np; at. numb. 93) named as next after uranium, as Neptune is next after Uranus. [L. *Neptūnus*.]

nereid, *nē′rē-id*, *n.* (*Gr. myth.*) a sea-nymph, or daughter of the sea-god *Nereus*: a marine polychaete worm (Nereis, or kindred genus) superficially like a long myriapod. [Gr. *nērēis* or *nērēis* —*Nēreus*.]

Nerine, *ni-rī′nē*, *n.* a South African amaryllid genus, with scarlet or rose-coloured flowers, including the Guernsey lily. [L. *nērīnē*, a nereid.]

Nerita, *ni-rī′tä*, *n.* a round-shelled genus of gasteropods of warm seas.—*n.* **nerite** (*nē′rīt*), a sea-snail of the genus Nerita or its family Nerit′idae.— *adj.* **neritic** (*nē-rit′ik*), belonging to the shallow waters near land.—*n.* **Neritina** (*ner-it-ī′nä*), a brackish and fresh-water genus akin to Nerita, [Gr. *nērеitēs*, *nērītēs*, a sea-snail (of various kinds).]

Nerium, *nē′ri-əm*, *n.* the oleander genus. [Latinised from Gr. *nērion*.]

nerka, *nər′kä*, *n.* the sockeye salmon. [Origin unknown.]

Nernst, *nărnst*, *adj.* invented by or due to the German chemist and physicist Walter *Nernst* (1864-1942): applied esp. to an electric lamp with a filament or rod of rare-earth oxides whose conductivity is greatly increased by heating.

nero-antico, *nā-rō-an-tē′kō*, *n.* a deep-black marble found in Roman ruins. [It., black ancient.]

neroli, *ner′ə-lē*, *n.* an oil distilled from orange flowers. [Said to be named from its discoverer, an Italian princess.]

Neronian, *nē-rō′ni-ən*, *adj.* pertaining to Nero, Roman emperor from 54 to 68 A.D.: excessively cruel and tyrannical.—*adj.* **Neronic** (*-ron′ik*). [L. *Nērō*, *-ōnis*.]

nerve, *nərv*, *n.* (now chiefly *fig.*) a sinew: a bowstring: bodily strength: (*anat.*) a cord that conveys impulses between the brain or other centre and some part of the body: (*bot.*) a leaf-vein or rib: a nervure in an insect's wing: a vault rib: self-possession: cool courage: (*slang*) impudent assurance: (in *pl.*) nervousness.—*v.t.* to give strength, resolution, or courage to.—*adj.* **nerv′al**, of the nerves.—*ns.* **nerva′tion**, **nerv′ature**, disposition of nerves, esp. in leaves; **nerve′-cell**, any cell forming part of the nervous system; **nerve′-cen′tre**, an aggregation of nerve-cells from which nerves branch out.—*adj.* **nerved**, furnished with nerves.—*ns.* **nerve′-end**, **-end′ing**, the free end of a nerve, generally with accessory parts forming an end-organ; **nerve′-fi′bre**, an axon.—*adj.* **nerve′less**, without nerves or nervures: without strength: inert: slack, flabby: unnerved.—*ns.* **nerve′lessness**; **nerve′let**, a little nerve: a tendril; **nerv′er**, one who, or that which, nerves.—*adjs.* **nerve′-rack′ing**, distressfully straining the nerves; **nerv′ine** (*-ēn*, *-īn*), acting on the nerves: quieting nervous excitement.—*n.* a medicine that soothes nervous excitement.—*n.* **nervi′ness**.—*adj.* **nerv′ous**, having nerve: sinewy: strong, vigorous, showing strength and vigour: pertaining to the nerves: having the nerves easily excited or weak, agitated and apprehensive: shy: in a jumpy state.—*adv.* **nerv′ously**.—*n.* **nerv′ousness**.—*adj.* **nerv′ular**.—*ns.* **nerv′üle**, a small branch of a nervure; **nervūrā′tion**; **nerv′ure**, a leaf-vein: a chitinous strut or rib supporting and strengthening an insect's wing: a rib of a groined vault.—*adj.* **nerv′y**, nervous: cool: calling for nerve: jumpily excited or excitable.—**get on one's nerves**, to become oppressively irritating; **nervous system**, the brain, spinal cord, and nerves collectively. [L. *nervus*, sinew; cf. Gr. *neuron*.]

nescience, *nesh′(y)əns*, *nēsh′(y)əns*, *nes′yəns*, *n.* want of knowledge.—*adj.* **nesc′ient**. [L. *nescientia*—*nescīre*, to be ignorant—*ne-*, not, *scīre*, to know.]

nesh, *nesh*, *adj.* (*prov.*) soft, crumbly: tender.—*n.* **nesh′ness**. [O.E. *hnesce*.]

Nesiot, **Nēsīōt**, *nē′si-ōt*, *n.* (*anthrop.*) an Indonesian. [Gr. *nēsiōtēs*, an islander—*nēsos*, an island.]

Neskhi, **Neski**, *nes′ki*, *n.* cursive handwriting. [Ar. *naskhī*.]

ness, *nes*, *n.* a headland. [O.E. *næs*, *næss*.]

nest, *nest*, *n.* a structure prepared for egg-laying, brooding, and nursing, or as a shelter: a place of retreat, resort, residence, or lodgment: a den: a comfortable residence: a place where anything teems, prevails, or is fostered: the occupants of a nest, as a brood, a swarm, a gang: a set of things (as boxes, tables) fitting one within another: an accumulation: a tangled mass.—*v.i.* to build or occupy a nest: to go bird's-nesting.—*v.t.* and *v.i.* to lodge, settle.—*ns.* **nest′-egg**, an egg, real or sham, left or put in a nest to encourage laying: something laid up as the beginning of an accumulation; **nest′ing-box**, a box set up for birds to nest in; **nest′ing-place**.—**feather one's nest** (see **feather**). [O.E. *nest*; Ger. *nest*, L. *nīdus*.]

nestle, *nes′l*, *v.i.* to nest: to lie or press close or snug as in a nest: to settle comfortably or half hidden.—*v.t.* to cherish, as a bird does her young: to thrust close: to provide a nesting-place.—*n.* **nestling** (*nes′ling*), a young bird in the nest—also *adj.* [O.E. *nestlian*—*nest.*]

Nestor, *nes′tor*, *-tər*, *n.* an old king of Pylos, a Greek hero at Troy, remarkable for eloquence, wisdom, and long life: an old counsellor: an old man: the kea parrot genus. [Gr. *Nestōr.*]

Nestorian, *nes-tō′ri-ən*, *adj.* pertaining to Nestorius, patriarch of Constantinople (428-31), or to his teaching, that the divinity and humanity of Christ were not united in a single self-conscious personality.—*n.* a follower of Nestorius.—*n.* **Nestō′rianism**.

net, *net*, *n.* an open fabric, knotted into meshes: a piece of bag, or a screen or structure, of such fabric used for catching fish, butterflies, &c., carrying parcels, stopping balls, retaining back-hair, excluding pests: a network: machine-made lace of various kinds: a snare: a difficulty: (*lawn-tennis*) a let.—*adj.* of or like net or network.—*v.t.* to form into network: to mark or cover with network: to set with nets: to fish with nets: to form by making network: to take with a net: to capture: to send into the net.—*v.i.* to form network:—*pr.p.* **nett′ing**; *pa.t.* and *pa.p.* **nett′ed**.—*ns.* **net′ball**, a game in which a ball is thrown into a net hung from a pole; **net′-cord**, a string supporting a lawn-tennis net; **net′-fish**, any fish, like the herring, usually caught in nets—opp. to *trawl-fish* and *line-fish*; **net′-fish′ery**, a place for net-fishing: the business of net-fishing; **net′-fishing**, fishing with nets; **net′-ful**, enough to fill a net; **net′-play**, play near the net; **net′-player**; **net′-prac′tice**, cricket practice with nets:—*adj.* **nett′ed**, made into a net: reticulated: caught in a net: covered with a net.—*ns.* **nett′ing**, act or process of forming network: a piece of network: any network of ropes or wire; **nett′ing-need′le**, a kind of shuttle used in netting.—*adjs.* **nett′y**, like a net; **net′-veined**, having veins that branch and meet in a network; **net′-winged**, having net-veined wings.—*n.* **net′work**, any structure in the form of a net: a system of lines, e.g. railway lines, resembling a net.—**dance in a net**, to act in imagined concealment. [O.E. *net*, *nett*; Du. *net*, Ger. *netz.*]

net, **nett**, *net*, *adj.* (*obs.*) clean: (*obs.*) bright: (*obs.*) clear of all else: (*rare*) neat, trim: clear of all charges or deductions—opp. to *gross*: lowest, subject to no further deductions.—*v.t.* to gain or produce as clear profit:—*pr.p.* **nett′ing**; *pa.t.* and *pa.p.* **nett′ed**. [neat.]

nete, *nē′tē*, *n.* (*Gr. mus.*) the highest string or note of the lyre. [Gr. *nētē* or *neatē* (*chordē*), lit. lowest (string).]

nethelesse, *nedh′(ə-)les*, *adv.* (*Spens.*). Same as **nathless**.

nether, *nedh′ər*, *adj.* lower.—*n.* **Neth′erlander**, an inhabitant of the *Netherlands* or Low Countries, now Holland, formerly also Belgium. — *adj.* **Neth′erlandish**, Dutch. — *n.pl.* **neth′erlings**, (*Dickens*) stockings.—*adjs.* **neth′ermore**, (*rare*) lower; **neth′ermost**, lowest.—*n.* **neth′erstock**, a stocking.—*advs.* **neth′erward**, **-s**, downwards. [O.E. *neothera*, adj.—*nither*, adv., from the root *ni-*, down; Ger. *nieder*, low.]

Nethinim, *neth′in-im*, *n.pl.* the old Jewish temple servants. [Heb. *nĕthīnīm.*]

netsuke, *net′soo-kā*, *n.* a small Japanese button ornament. [Jap.]

nettle, *net′l*, *n.* a common weed (Urtica) with stinging hairs.—*v.t.* to sting: to sting with annoyance.—*ns.* **nett′le-cell**, a nematocyst; **nett′le-cloth**, cloth of nettle-fibre: thick japanned cotton; **nett′le-fish**, a jelly-fish; **nett′lerash**, a rash of red or white wheals with irritation like nettle-stings; **nett′le-tree**, a tree (Celtis) of the elm family, with nettle-shaped leaves, edible drupes, and wood good for turning: a tropical and Australian genus (Laportea) of the nettle family, with virulently stinging leaves.—**dead-nettle**, **hemp-nettle** (see **dead**, **hemp**). [O.E. *netele*; Ger. *nessel.*]

Neutral vowels in unaccented syllables : *el′ə-mənt*, *in′fənt*, *ran′dəm*

nettle. Same as **knittle.**

neuk, *nŏk, nūk,* a Scots form of **nook.**

neume, *nūm, n.* in mediaeval music, a succession of notes sung to one syllable : a sign giving a rough indication of rise or fall of pitch. [O.Fr.,—Gr. *pneuma,* breath.]

neur-, *nūr-,* **neuro-,** *nū′rō-,* in composition, nerve. —*adj.* **neu′ral,** of, or relating to, nerves : dorsal (opp. to *haemal*).—*n.* **neural′gia** (*nū-ral′jă, -jyă ;* Gr. *algos,* pain), paroxysmal intermittent pain along the course of a nerve : pain of a purely nervous character.—*adj.* **neural′gic.**—*ns.* **neurasthenia** (*nū-ras-thē′ni-ä ;* Gr. *astheneia,* weakness), nervous debility ; **neurasthē′niac,** one suffering from neurasthenia.—*adj.* **neurasthenic** (*-then′ik,* or *-thēn′ik*).—Also *n.* a neurastheniac.—*ns.* **neurā′-tion,** nervation ; **neurilemm′a, neurolemm′a** (Gr. *eilēma,* covering), the external sheath of a nerve-fibre ; **neuril′ity,** the essential character of nerve ; **neur′ine** (*-ēn, -in, -īn*), a very poisonous ptomaine formed in putrefying flesh.—*adj.* **neur′itic** (*-it′ik*), relating to, of the nature of, or having neuritis.—*n.* one suffering from neuritis.—*ns.* **neuri′tis,** inflammation of a nerve ; **neurog′lia** (Gr. *gliă,* glue), the supporting tissue of the brain and spinal cord, &c. ; **neurohypnol′ogy, neurypnol′ogy,** old names for the science of hypnotism. —*adj.* **neurolog′ical.**—*ns.* **neurol′ogist ;** **neurol′ogy,** the study of the nerves ; **neu′ron, neu′rone,** a nerve-cell with its processes ; **neur′opath** (*-păth ;* Gr. *pathos,* suffering), one whose nervous system is diseased or abnormal.—*adjs.* **neuropathic** (*-path′*), **-al.**—*ns.* **neuropathist** (*nū-rop′ə-thist*), a specialist in nervous diseases ; **neuropathol′ogy,** the pathology of the nervous system ; **neurop′athy,** nervous disease generally.—*n.pl.* **Neurop′tera** (Gr. *pteron,* wing), an order of insects which have generally four net-veined wings —ant-lions, lace-wings, &c.—*adj.* and *n.* **neurop′-teran.**—*adj.* **neurop′terous.**—*ns.* **neurop′terist,** a student of the Neuroptera ; **neurō′sis,** nervous activity, distinguished from or associated with mental : nervous disease : functional derangement through disordered nervous system, esp. without lesion of parts :—*pl.* **neurōses** (*-sēz*).—*adj.* **neurotic** (*-rot′ik*), of the nature of, characterised by, or affected by, neurosis.—*n.* a person with neurosis or disordered nerves : a medicine for nerve diseases.—*n.* **neurot′icism** (*-sizm*).—*adj.* **neurotrop′ic,** having a special affinity for nerve cells. —**neural arch,** the arch of a vertebra protecting the spinal cord. [Gr. *neuron,* a nerve.]

neuter, *nū′tər, adj.* neither one thing nor another : neutral : (*gram.*) neither masculine nor feminine : neither active nor passive : neither transitive nor intransitive : sexless : apparently sexless : sexually undeveloped : castrated : without functional, or any, androecium or gynaeceum.—*n.* a neutral : a neuter word, plant, or animal : esp. a worker bee, ant, &c. : a castrated cat.—*v.t.* to castrate. [L. *neuter,* neither—*ne,* not, *uter,* either.]

neutral, *nū′trəl, adj.* indifferent : taking no part on either side : not siding with either party : pertaining to neither party : not involved in a war or dispute : belonging to neither, esp. of two adjoining countries : of no decided character : having no decided colour : indistinct in sound : with no noticeable smell : belonging to neither of two opposites, as acid and alkaline, electrically positive and negative : neuter : without transmission of motion.—*n.* a person or nation that takes no part in a contest : a citizen or ship of a neutral state : an electric conductor ordinarily at zero potential : a position of gear in which no power is transmitted : a neuter.—*n.* **neutralisā′tion.**—*v.t.* **neu′tralise,** to declare neutral : to make inert : to render of no effect : to counteract. — *ns.* **neu′traliser ; neu′tralist,** one who takes or favours a neutral position ; **neutrality** (*-tral′i-ti*), fact or state of being neutral : those who are neutral.—*adv.* **neu′trally.** [L. *neutrālis—neuter,* neither.]

neutron, *nū′tron, n.* (*phys.*) an uncharged particle of about the same mass as the proton.—*ns.* **neutrett′o,** a name suggested for a neutral meson ; **neutrino**

(*-trē′nō*), an uncharged particle with the same mass as an electron. [L. *neuter,* neither.]

névé, *nā-vā, n.* firn. [Fr.,—L. *nix, nivis,* snow.]

nevel, *nev′əl, v.t.* (*Scot.*) to pound with the nieves. [**nieve.**]

never, *nev′ər, adv.* not ever : at no time : in no degree : not.—*adjs.* **nev′er-end′ing ; nev′er-fad′ing ; nev′er-fail′ing.**—*advs.* **nev′ermore,** at no future time ; **nevertheless′,** notwithstanding : in spite of that ; **nevermore′,** (*obs.*) none the more.—*n.* **nev′er-was′,** one who never was of any account.—**never so,** (*arch.*) ever so. [O.E. *nǣfre* —*ne,* not, *ǣfre,* ever.]

new, *nū, adj.* lately made or produced : young : fresh : not much used : having lately happened or begun to be : recent, modern : not before seen or known : only lately discovered or experienced : other than the former or preceding, different : additional : strange, unaccustomed : lately begun : beginning afresh : renewed : reformed or regenerated : restored or resumed : not of an ancient family : fresh from anything : uncultivated or only recently cultivated.—*n.* that which is new : a new thing : newness.—*adv.* (often joined by hyphen to its adj.) newly ; **anew.** —*v.t.* (*arch.*) to renew.—*v.i.* (*arch.*) to be renewed. —*adjs.* **new′-blown,** just come into bloom ; **new′-born,** newly born ; **new′come,** recently arrived.— *n.* **new′comer,** one who has lately come.—*v.t.* **new′-create,** (*Shak.*) to create anew.—*adjs.* **new′-fallen,** newly fallen ; **new′-fash′ioned,** made in a new way or fashion : lately come into fashion ; **new′-fledged,** having just got feathers ; **new′-found,** newly discovered or devised ; **new′ish,** somewhat new : nearly new ; **new′-laid,** newly laid.—*adv.* **new′ly,** very lately : (*rare*) afresh : (*rare*) in a new way.—*adjs.* **new′-made,** recently made ; **new′-marr′ied,** newly married.—*v.t.* **new′-mod′el,** to model or form anew.—*n.* the Parliamentary army as remodelled by Cromwell (1645). —*adj.* **new′-mown,** newly mown.—*n.* **new′ness.** —*adjs.* **new′-old′,** old but renewed : at once new and old ; **new′-risen,** having newly risen ; **new′-sad,** (*Shak.*) recently made sad.—**new birth** (see regeneration) ; **new chum,** a new arrival from the old country in Australia ; **New Church, New Jerusalem Church,** the Swedenborgian Church ; **New Englander,** a native or citizen of any of the New England states ; **New Jersey tea,** red-root ; **New Jerusalem,** the heavenly city ; **New Learning,** the new studies of the Renaissance ; **New Light,** a member of a relatively more advanced religious school—applied esp. to the party within the 18th-century Scottish Secession Church which adopted Voluntary views of the relations of Church and State, also sometimes to the Socinianising party in the Church of Scotland in the 18th century, &c. ; **new moon,** the moment when the moon is directly in line between the earth and sun, and therefore invisible : the time when the waxing moon becomes visible ; **new poor,** those who have come to think themselves poor by loss of advantages ; **New Red Sandstone,** (*geol.*) an old name for the Permian and Trias ; **new rich,** the recently enriched : parvenus ; **New Style** (see style) ; **new woman,** a name applied, esp. by scoffers, in the late 19th century to such women as actively sought freedom and equality with men ; **New World,** North and South America ; **New Year,** the first few days, **New Year's Day,** the first day, of the year ; **of new,** (*arch.*) anew : of late. [O.E. *nīwe, nēowe ;* Ger. *neu,* Ir. *nuadh,* L. *novus,* Gr. *neos.*]

newel, *nū′əl, n.* the upright column about which the steps of a circular staircase wind : an upright post at the end or corner of a stair handrail.— *adj.* **new′elled.** [O.Fr. *nual* (Fr. *noyau*), fruit-stone—L.L. *nucālis,* nutlike—L. *nux, nucis,* a nut.]

newell, *nū′əl, n.* (*Spens.*) a new thing. [A combination of *novel* and *new.*]

newfangled, *nū-fang′gld,* earlier **newfangle, -gl,** *adj.* unduly fond of new things : newly but superfluously devised.—*adv.* **newfang′ledly.**—*n.* **new′-fang′ledness, newfang′leness.** [M.E. *newe-*

fangel—newe (O.E. *niwe*), new, *fangel*, ready to catch—*fang*-, the stem of O.E. *fón*, to take.]

Newfoundland, *nū-fownd'land*, *adj.* of *Newfoundland* (*nū'fand-land'*).—*n.* a very large, intelligent breed of dog from Newfoundland, originally black, a strong swimmer.

Newgate, *nū-gāt*, *n.* a famous prison in London, originally housed in the *new gate* of the city, the latest building demolished in 1902-3.—Newgate Calendar, a record of Newgate prisoners, with their crimes ; Newgate frill, or fringe, a beard under the chin and jaw.

newmarket, *nū-mär'kit*, or *nū'*, *n.* a card game in which the stakes go to those who succeed in playing out cards whose duplicates lie on the table : a close-fitting coat, originally a riding-coat, for men or women. [*Newmarket*, the racing town.]

news, *nūz*, *n.* (orig. *pl.*) tidings : a report of a recent event : something one had not heard before : matter suitable for newspaper readers : news-paper : newsprint.—*v.t.* to report.—*ns.* news'-agent, one who deals in newspapers ; news'boy, a boy who delivers or sells newspapers ; news'-dealer, (*U.S.*) a news-agent ; news'-hawk, (*U.S.*) a newsboy ; news'iness ; news'letter, a written or printed letter containing news sent by an agent to his subscribers—the predecessor of the news-paper ; news'man, a bringer, collector, or writer of news : a seller of newspapers ; news'monger, one who deals in news : one who spends much time in hearing and telling news ; news'paper, a paper published periodically for circulating news, &c. ; news'paperdom ; news'paperism ; news'-paper-man', a journalist.—*adj.* news'papery.—*ns.* news'-print, paper for printing newspapers ; news'-reel, a cinematograph reel imparting news ; news'room, a reading-room with newspapers : (*U.S.*) the news department of a newspaper ; news'-sheet, a printed sheet of news, an early form of newspaper ; news'-stand, (*U.S.*) a stall for the sale of newspapers ; news'-val'ue, value as news from the journalist's point of view ; news'-vendor, a seller of newspapers ; news'-writer, a reporter or writer of news.—*adj.* news'y, gossipy.—*n.* (*U.S.*) a newsboy. [Late M.E. *newes*, an imit. of Fr. *nouvelles*.]

newt, *nūt*, *n.* a tailed amphibian (Triturus, Molge, or Triton) of the salamander family. [Formed with initial *n*, borrowed from the article *an*, from *ewt*, a form of *evet* or *eft*—O.E. *efeta, efete*.]

Newtonian, *nū-tō'ni-ən*, *adj.* relating to, according to, formed, or discovered by Sir Isaac *Newton* (1642-1726-7)—also Newtonic (*-ton'ik*).—New-tonian telescope, a form of reflecting telescope.

next, *nekst*, *adj.* (*superl.* of *nigh*) nearest in place, in kinship or other relation : nearest following (or preceding if explicitly stated) in time or order.—*adv.* nearest : immediately after : on the first occasion that follows : in the next place.—*prep.* nearest to.—*adj.* next'-door, dwelling in or occupying the next house, shop, &c. : at or in the next house : neighbouring.—*adv.* next-door'.—*adv.* next'ly (*rare*).—*n.* next'ness.—next best, biggest, &c., next in order after the best, biggest, &c. ; next door to (see door) ; next Saturday, &c., (on) the first Saturday after the present day : in Scotland often (on) the Saturday of next week ; next to, (*U.S.*) up to : thoroughly acquainted with ; next to nothing, almost nothing at all. [O.E. *nēhst* (*niehst*), superl. of *nēh* (*nēah*), near ; Ger. *nächst*.]

nexus, *nek'səs*, *n.* a bond : a linked group. [L. *nexus*, pl. *-ūs*—*nectĕre*, to bind.]

nib, *nib*, *n.* something small and pointed : a pen-point : a bird's bill : a peak : a projecting point or spike : a timber carriage pole : a handle on a scythe's shaft : (in *pl.*) crushed cocoa-beans : included particles in varnish, wool, &c.—*v.t.* to furnish with a nib : to point : to reduce to nibs.—*adj.* nibbed, having a nib. [neb.]

nib, *nib*, *n.* (*slang*) a person of the upper classes : a person of importance or appearance of import-ance.—his nibs, himself : his mightiness. [Cf. nabs, nob.]

nibble, *nib'l*, *v.t.* to bite gently or by small bites :

to eat by little at a time.—*v.i.* to bite gently : to show signs of accepting, as an offer, or of yielding, as to temptation (with *at*) : to find fault.—*n.* act of nibbling : a little bit.—*ns.* nibb'ler ; nibb'ling. —*adv.* nibb'lingly. [Origin obscure ; cf. L.G. *nibbelen*, Du. *knibbelen*.]

Nibelung, *nē'bəl-ŏŏng*, *n.* one of a supernatural race in German mythology, guardians of a treasure wrested from them by Siegfried, the hero of the *Nibelungenlied*, an epic of *c.* 1190-1210 :—*pl.* Ni'belungen. [Ger.]

niblick, *nib'lik*, *n.* a golf-club with a heavy head with wide face, used for lofting.

niccolite, *nik'əl'it*, *n.* a hexagonal mineral, nickel arsenide, also called kupfernickel, copper-nickel. [See nickel.]

nice, *nīs*, *adj.* (obs.) foolishly simple : (*Shak.*) wanton : (*Milt.*) coy : over-particular : hard to please : fastidious : forming or observing very small differences : calling for very fine discrimina-tion : done with great care and exactness, accurate : critical, hazardous : easily injured : delicate : dainty : agreeable : delightful : used in vague commendation by those who are not nice.—*adv.* nice'ly.—*ns.* nice'ness, quality of being nice : exactness : scrupulousness : pleasantness ; nicety (*nīs'i-ti*), quality of being nice : delicate manage-ment : exactness of treatment : degree of precision : fineness of perception or feeling : critical subtlety : a matter of delicate discrimination or adjustment : a refinement : (*Spens., Shak.*) coyness : fastidious-ness : a delicacy.—nice and, used almost adverb-ially—commendably, pleasantly ; to a nicety, with great exactness. [O.Fr. *nice*, foolish, simple —L. *nescius*, ignorant—*ne*, not, *scire*, to know.]

Nicene, *nī'sēn*, *adj.* pertaining to the town of *Nicaea*, in Bithynia, where an oecumenical council in 325 dealt with the Arian controversy, and another in 787 condemned the Iconoclasts.—*n.* and *adj.* Nicaean, (*nī-sē'ən*).—Nicene Creed, the creed based on the results of the first Nicene Council.

niche, *nich*, *n.* a recess in a wall : a suitable or actual place or condition in life or public estima-tion or the system of nature.—*v.t.* to place in a niche.—*adj.* niched, placed in a niche. [Fr.,—It. *nicchia*, niche, of doubtful origin.]

nick, *nik*, *n.* a notch : a score for keeping an account : a cut : a fraudulent dint in the bottom of a beer-can : the precise point aimed at : the precise moment of time : the last, critical, moment before it is too late : at hazard, a throw answer-ing to a main : a critical point : (*slang*) a prison or police-office : (*slang*) a policeman.—*v.t.* to notch : to cut in notches (as the hair of a fool) : to cut off : to debar, do (one out of something) : to mark by cutting, carve out : to cut : to snip : to score, as on a tally : to tally with : to hit with precision : to hit off : to catch in the nick of time : (*slang*) to catch : (*slang*) to arrest : to steal : to rob : to cheat at hazard, to defeat by throwing a nick : to throw the nick of.—*ns.* nick'er, one who, or that which, nicks : in the early 18th century, a brawler who broke windows with coppers ; nick'-stick, a tally.—out of all nick, (*Shak.*) out of all reckoning, exceedingly. [Possibly connected with nock, notch.]

Nick, *nik*, *n.* the devil, esp. Old Nick.—Also (*Scot.*) Nickie-ben'. [Apparently for *Nicholas*.]

nick, *nik*, *v.t.* (arch.) to deny (in the phrase *to nick with nay*). [Origin unknown ; possibly O.E. *ne ic*, not I.]

nickel, *nik'l*, *n.* a white magnetic metal (Ni ; at. numb. 28), very malleable and ductile, largely used in alloys : (*U.S.*) a 5-cent piece (of copper and nickel).—*adj.* of nickel.—*v.t.* to plate with nickel :—*pr.p.* nick'elling ; *pa.t.* and *pa.p.* nick'-elled.—*n.* nick'el-bloom, earthy annabergite.—*adjs.* nick'elic, of bivalent nickel ; nickelif'erous, containing nickel.—*n.* nick'eline, (obs.) nic-colite.—*v.t.* nick'elise, to plate with nickel.—*n.* nick'el-o'chre, earthy annabergite.—*adj.* nick'elous, of trivalent nickel.—*ns.* nick'el-plat'ing, the plating of metals with nickel ; nick'el-sil'ver, German silver ; nick'el-steel', a steel containing some nickel. [Ger. *kupfer-nickel*, niccolite—*kupfer*, copper, *nickel*, a mischievous sprite, goblin, because the ore looked like copper-ore but yielded no copper.]

nicker, *nik'ər*, *v.i.* (*Scot.*) to neigh: to snigger.—*n.* a neigh: a snigger: a loud laugh.—Also **nicher** (*nihh'ər*).

nicker, *nik'ər*, *n.* a water-monster or water-demon. [O.E. *nicor*.]

nicker, *nik'ər*, *n.* a clay marble (also **knicker**): the round seed of a Caesalpinia (or Guilandina), used for playing marbles (also **nick'ar**). [Cf. Du. *knikker*, North Ger. *knicker*.]

nicknack, &c. Same as **knick-knack**, &c.

nickname, *nik'nām*, *n.* a name given in contempt or sportive familiarity.—*v.t.* to give a nickname to. [M.E. *neke-name*, for *eke-name*, with *n* from the indefinite article; see **an**, **eke**, **name**.]

nicol, *nik'l*, *n.* a crystal of calcium carbonate so cut and cemented as to transmit only the extraordinary ray, used for polarising light.—Also **Nicol's prism**. [From William *Nicol* (*c.* 1768-1851) of Edinburgh, its inventor.]

nicotian, *ni-kō'sh(y)ən*, *adj.* of tobacco.—*n.* a tobacco smoker.—*n.* **Nicotiana** (-*shi-ā'nä*), the tobacco genus of Solanaceae.—*n.pl.* (-*ā'nä*, -*ā'nä*) the literature of tobacco.—*ns.* **nicotinamide** (-*tin'*), a member of the vitamin B₂ complex; **nicotine** (*nik'ə-tēn*), a poisonous alkaloid (C₁₀H₁₄N₂) got from tobacco leaves.—*adj.* **nicotinic** (-*tin'ik*).—*n.* **nic'otinism**, a morbid state induced by excessive misuse of tobacco.—**nicotinic acid**, a white crystalline substance, a member of the vitamin B₂ complex, deficiency of which is connected with the development of pellagra. [Jean *Nicot*, who introduced tobacco into France (1560).]

nictate, *nik'tāt*, *v.i.* to wink—also **nic'titate**.—*ns.* **nicta'tion**, **nicti'tion**.—**nictitating membrane**, the third eyelid, developed in birds, &c., a thin movable membrane that passes over the eye. [L. *nictāre*, -*ātum* and its L.L. freq. *nictitāre*, -*ātum*, to wink.]

nid, *nid*, **nide**, *nīd*, *n.* a pheasant's nest or brood. [L. *nīdus*, nest.]

niddering, **nidderling**, **nidering**, **niderling**, **niding**. See **nithing**.

niddle-noddle, *nid'l-nod'l*, *adj.* and *adv.* with nodding head.—*v.i.* to noddle the head: to waggle.—*v.t.* and *v.i.* **nid'-nod'**, to keep nodding. [**nod**.]

nidget, *nij'it*, *n.* (now *slang*) an idiot. [**idiot**, with *n* from the indefinite article.]

nidicolous, *nid-ik'ə-ləs*, *adj.* (of young birds) staying long in the nest. [L. *nīdus*, a nest, *colĕre*, to inhabit.]

nidifugous, *nid-if'ū-gəs*, *adj.* (of young birds) leaving the nest soon after hatching. [L. *nīdus*, nest, *fugĕre*, to flee.]

nidify, *nid'i-fi*, *v.i.* to build a nest.—Also **nidificate** (*nid'i-fi-kāt*).—*n.* **nidificā'tion**. [L. *nīdus*, nest, *facĕre*, to make.]

nidor, *nī'dor*, *n.* a strong smell or fume, esp. of animal substances cooking or burning.—*adv.* **nī'dorous**. [L. *nīdor*, -*ōris*.]

nidus, *nī'dəs*, *n.* a nest or breeding-place: a place where anything is originated, harboured, developed, or fostered: a place of lodgment or deposit: a point of infection: a nerve-centre:—*pl.* **nī'di**.—*adjs.* **nī'dal**, pertaining to a nest or nidus; **nidamen'tal**.—*ns.* **nidament'um**, an egg-capsule; **nidā'tion**, renewal of the lining of the uterus.—*adj.* **nidulā'tion** (nid-), nest-building. [L. *nīdus*, a nest.]

nie, an obsolete spelling of **nigh**.

niece, *nēs*, *n.* (*orig.*) a granddaughter: a female descendant: (now) a brother's or sister's daughter: extended to a like relation by marriage: (*euphemistically*) a pope's or priest's daughter:—*masc.* **nephew**. [O.Fr.,—L.L. *neptia*—L. *neptis*.]

niello, *ni-el'ō*, *n.* a method of ornamenting metal by engraving, and filling up the lines with a black composition: a work so produced: an impression taken from the engraved surface before filling up: the compound used in niello-work: (*pl.* **niell'i**, -*ē*, **niell'os**).—*v.t.* to decorate with niello:—*pr.p.* **niell'oing**; *pa.t.* and *pa.p.* **niell'oed**.—*adj.*

nielláted (*nē'*).—*n.* **niell'ist**. [It. *niello*—L.L. *nigellum*, a black enamel—L. *nigellus*, dim. of *niger*, black.]

Niersteiner, *nēr's(h)tīn-ər*, *n.* a Rhine wine, named from *Nierstein*, near Mainz.

Nietzschean, *nēch'i-ən*, *adj.* of Friedrich *Nietzsche* (1844-1900) or his philosophy.—*n.* a follower of Nietzsche.—*n.* **Nietzsch'eanism**.

nieve, **neive**, *nēv*, **neif**, **nief** (*Shak.* **neafe**, **neaffe**), *nēf*, *n.* the fist.—*ns.* **nieve'ful**, a closed handful; **nie'vie-(nie'vie-)nick-nack'**, a Scottish children's pastime, a mode of assigning by lot, by guessing which hand contains something, the holder repeating a rhyme. [M.E. *nefe*—O.N. *hnefi*, *neif*; cf. Sw. *näfve*, fist.]

nife, *nī'fi*, *n.* the earth's hypothetical core of nickel and iron. [Chemical symbols *Ni* and *Fe*.]

niff, *nif*, *n.* (*dial.* or *slang*) a stink.—*adj.* **niff'y**.

niffer, *nif'ər*, *v.t.* (*Scot.*) to barter.—*v.i.* to haggle.—*n.* an exchange: hazard. [Possibly **nieve**.]

niffnaff, *nif-naf'*, *n.* a trifle: a diminutive person.—*v.i.* to trifle.—*adjs.* **niff-naff'y**, **niff'y-naff'y**, fastidious.

Niflheim, *niv'l-hām*, *n.* (*Scand. myth.*) a region of mist, ruled over by Hel. [O.N. *Niflheimr*—*nifl*, mist, *heimr*, home.]

nifty, *nif'ti*, *adj.* (*slang*; chiefly *U.S.*) fine: spruce: smart.—*n.* **nift'iness**.

Nigella, *nī-jel'ä*, *n.* a genus of ranunculaceous plants, with finely dissected leaves, and whitish, blue, or yellow flowers, often almost concealed by their leafy involucres.—*Nigella damascena* is called love-in-a-mist, devil-in-a-bush, and ragged lady. [Fem. of L. *nigellus*, blackish—*niger*, black, from the black seeds.]

niger, *nī'jər*, *n.* (*obs.*) a negro.—*n.* **ni'ger-oil**, an oil got from the black seeds (**ni'ger-seeds**) of an East African compositous plant, *Guizotia abyssinica*, cultivated also in India. [L. *niger*, black.]

niggard, *nig'ərd*, *n.* one who grudges to spend or give away: a false bottom or side in a fire-grate.—*adj.* niggardly.—*v.t.* and *v.i.* (*Shak.*) to treat or behave as a niggard.—*ns.* **nig'ardise** (-*īz*; *arch.*), **nigg'ardliness**, meanness, stinginess.—*adj.* **nigg'ardly**, stingy.—*adv.* stingily: grudgingly. [Origin obscure.]

nigger, *nig'ər*, *n.* (derogatorily) a negro, or a member of any very dark-skinned race: a black insect larva of various kinds.—*adj.* negro: blackish brown.—*v.t.* to exhaust by overcropping: to char: to blacken.—*ns.* **nigg'erdom**, niggers collectively; **nigg'er-head**, a nodule, boulder, or boss of dark-coloured rock: an American river-mussel (Quadrula), a source of mother-of-pearl: negrohead tobacco: (*U.S.*) a tussock in a swamp.—*adj.* **nigg'erish**.—*ns.* **nigg'erism**, an idiom or expression characteristic of niggers: African blood; **nigg'erling**, a little nigger.—*adj.* **nigg'ery**.—**nigger in the wood-pile**, a hidden motive; **work like a nigger**, to toil hard like a slave. [Fr. *nègre*—Sp. *negro*; see **negro**.]

niggle, *nig'l*, *v.i.* to trifle, potter: to busy oneself with petty scrupulosity: to move in a fidgety or ineffective way.—*v.t.* to work, make, perform, with excessive detail: to befool.—*n.* small cramped handwriting.—*ns.* **nigg'ler**; **nigg'ling**, fussiness, finicking work: petty elaboration.—*adj.* overelaborate: petty: fussy: cramped.—*adj.* **nigg'ly**. [Cf. Norw. *nigle*.]

nigh, *nī*, *adj.* near.—*adv.* nearly.—*prep.* near to.—*v.t.* and *v.i.* to approach, draw near: (*obs.*) to touch.—*adv.* and *prep.* **nigh'-hand**, near hand: almost, nearly.—*adv.* **nigh'ly**, almost: closely: (*Spens.*) sparingly.—*n.* **nigh'ness**. [O.E. *néah*, *néh*; Du. *na*, Ger. *nahe*.]

night, *nīt*, *n.* the end of the day: the time from sunset to sunrise: the dark part of the twenty-four-hour day: darkness: (*fig.*) obscurity, ignorance, evil, affliction, or sorrow: death: the experience of a night: a night set apart for some purpose, esp. receiving visitors.—*adj.* belonging to night: occurring or done in the night: working or on duty by night.—*ns.* **night'-attire'**, garments worn in bed; **night'-bell**, a door-bell for use at night; **night'-bird**, a bird that flies or that sings at

fāte, fär, âsk; mē, hər (her); mīne; mōte; mūte; mōōn; dhen (then) night : a person who is active or about at night ; **night'-blind'ness**, inability to see in a dim light, nyctalopia ; **night'-brawl'er**, one who raises disturbances in the night ; **night'cap**, a cap worn at night in bed : a dram taken before going to bed ; **night'-cart**, a cart used to remove the contents of privies before daylight ; **night'-cellar**, a disreputable resort or tavern, open by night ; **night'-chair**, a night-stool ; **night'-churr**, the goatsucker, so called from its cry.—*n.pl.* **night'-clothes**, garments worn in bed.—*ns.* **night'-cloud**, stratus ; **night'-club**, a club open between nightfall and morning for amusement or dissipation ; **night'-crow**, (*Shak.*) an undefined bird of ill omen that cries in the night ; **night'-dog**, (*Shak.*) a dog that hunts in the night ; **night'dress**, attire for the night, esp. a night-gown.—*adj.* **night'ed**, benighted : (*Shak.*) darkened, clouded. — *n.* **night'fall**, the fall or beginning of the night : the close of the day : evening.—*adj.* **night'faring**, travelling by night.— *ns.* **night'fire**, a fire burning in the night : a Will-o'-the-wisp ; **night'-fish'ery**, a mode or place of fishing by night ; **night'-flower**, a flower that opens by night.—*adj.* **night'-flower'ing.**— *n.* **night'-fly**, a moth or fly that flies at night. —*adj.* **night'-fly'ing**, flying by night (also *n.*).—*ns.* **night'-foe**, one who makes his attack by night ; **night'-foss'icker**, one who robs a digging by night.—*adj.* **night'-foun'dered**, lost in the night.— *ns.* **night'-fowl**, a night-bird ; **night'-gear**, nightclothes ; **night'-glass**, a spy-glass with concentrating lenses for use at night ; **night'-gown**, a long loose robe for sleeping in, for men or women : (*obs.*) a dressing-gown ; **night'-hag**, a witch supposed to be abroad at night ; **night'-hawk**, a goatsucker : a prowler by night ; **night'-her'on**, a heron of nocturnal habit, of various kinds ; **night'-house**, a tavern open during the night ; **night'-hunter**, one who hunts, poaches, or prowls about the streets for prey by night ; **night'jar**, a goatsucker ; **night'-latch**, a door-lock worked by a key without and a knob within.—*adj.* **night'less**, having no night.—*ns.* **night'-light**, a bedroom lamp or candle that gives a subdued light all night : the faint light of the night : the light of phosphorescent sea-animals ; **night'-line**, a fishing-line set overnight.—*adj.* and *adv.* **night'long**, lasting all night. —*adj.* **night'ly**, done or happening by night or every night : (*Shak.*) dark as night.—*adv.* by night : every night.—*ns.* **night'-man**, a night watchman, worker, or scavenger ; **night'-owl**, an exclusively nocturnal owl : one who sits up very late ; **night'-pal'sy**, a numbness of the legs, incidental to women ; **night'piece**, a picture or literary or musical description of a night-scene : a painting to be seen best by artificial light ; **night'-por'ter**, a porter in attendance during the night ; **night'-rail**, a loose wrap or dressing-jacket ; **night'-rav'en**, (*Shak.*) a bird that cries at night, supposed to be of ill-omen ; **night'-rest**, the repose of the night ; **night'-robe**, a night-gown : a dressing-gown ; **night'-rule**, (*Shak.*) a revel at night.— *adv.* (*orig. gen. of n.*) **nights**, (*arch.* and *dial.*) by night.—*ns.* **night'-school**, a school held at night, esp. for those at work during the day ; **night'-sea'son**, the night-time ; **night'-shift**, a gang or group of workers that takes its turn by night : the time it is on duty : (*arch.*) a night-dress ; **night'-shirt**, a man's shirt for sleeping in ; **night'-shriek**, a cry in the night ; **night'-side**, the dark, mysterious, or gloomy side of anything ; **night'-sight**, power of vision by night ; **night'-soil**, the contents of privies, cesspools, &c., generally carried away at night ; **night'-spell**, a charm against harm by night ; **night'-steed**, one of the horses in the chariot of Night ; **night'-stick**, an American policeman's truncheon ; **night'-stool**, a close-stool for use in a bedroom ; **night'-ta'per**, a night-light burning slowly.—*n.pl.* **night'-terr'ors**, the sudden starting from sleep in fright.—*ns.* **night'-tide**, night-time : a flood-tide in the night ; **night'-time**, the time when it is night.—*adjs.* **night'-tripp'ing**, (*Shak.*) tripping about in the night ; **night'-wak'ing**, watching in the night.—*ns.* **night'-walk**, a walk in the night ; **night'-walk'er**, a

somnambulist : one who walks about at night, usu. for bad purposes, esp. a prostitute.—*n.* and *adj.* **night'-wan'derer**, one who wanders by night. —*adjs.* **night'-wan'dering** ; **night'-war'bling**, singing in the night ; **night'ward**, occurring towards night.—*ns.* **night'-watch**, a watch or guard at night : one who is on watch by night : time of watch in the night ; **night'-watch'man** ; **night'-work**, work done at night ; **night'-work'er** ; **night'y**, (*childish*) a night-gown.—**night air**, a peculiarly unwholesome gas imagined by some to circulate by night ; **night out**, a domestic servant's (or other's) night of freedom to be absent : a night away from home, work, and restrictions ; **of a night, of nights**, in the course of a night : some time at night. [O.E. *niht* ; Ger. *nacht*, L. *nox* ; Gr. *nyx*.]

nightingale, *nīt'ing-gāl*, *n.* a small bird of the thrush family celebrated for the rich love-song of the male heard chiefly at night. [O.E. *nihtegale* —*niht*, night, *galan*, to sing ; Ger. *nachtigall*.]

nightingale, *nīt'ing-gāl*, *n.* a flannel scarf with sleeves, worn by invalids sitting up in bed. [Florence *Nightingale* (1820-1910), Crimean hospital nurse.]

nightmare, *nīt'mār*, *n.* a dreadful dream accompanied with pressure on the breast and a feeling of powerlessness to move or speak—personified as an incubus or evil-spirit : (*fig.*) a horrifying experience.—*adjs.* **night'marish**, (*rare*) **night'mary**. [O.E. *niht*, night, *mara*, a nightmare ; cf. O.H.G. *mara*, incubus, O.N. *mara*, nightmare.]

nightshade, *nit'shād*, *n.* a name given to various plants, chiefly of the Solanaceae and chiefly poisonous or narcotic.—**deadly nightshade**, belladonna ; **woody nightshade**, bittersweet ; **black nightshade**, *Solanum nigrum* ; see also **enchanter**. [O.E. *nihtscada*, app.—*niht*, night, *scada*, shade.]

nigrescence, *nī-* or *ni-gres'ens*, *n.* blackness : dark colouring or pigmentation : blackening.—*adjs.* **nigres'cent**, growing black or dark : blackish ; **nigricant** (*nig'ri-kənt*), black : blackish. — *v.t.* **nig'rify**, to blacken.—*n.* **nig'ritude**, blackness. [L. *niger*, black.]

Nigritian, *ni-grish'ən*, *adj.* of *Nigritia*, or Sudan, esp. Western Sudan, the home of the negroes in the narrow sense.—*n.* a true negro. [L. *niger*, black.]

nigromancy, *nig'rə-man-si*, *n.* an old form of **necromancy**, the black art. [From association with L. *niger*, black.]

nigrosine, *nig'rō-sēn*, -*sin*, *n.* a blackish coal-tar colour dye. [L. *niger*, black.]

nihil, *nī'hil*, *n.* nothing.—*ns.* **ni'hilism** (*-hil-* or -*il-izm*), belief in nothing : denial of all reality, or of all objective growth of truth : extreme scepticism : nothingness : (*hist.*) in tsarist Russia a terrorist movement aiming at the overturn of all the existing institutions of society in order to build it up anew on different principles ; **ni'hilist**.—*adj.* **nihilist'ic.**—*n.* **nihility** (*-hil'*), nothingness : a mere nothing. [L. *nihil*, nothing.]

Nike, *nī'kē*, *n.* the Greek goddess of victory. [Gr. *nīkē*, victory.]

nil, *nil*, *n.* nothing : zero. [L. *nīl*, *nīhil*, nothing.]

nilgai, *nēl'* or *nil'gī*, **nilgau**, **nylghau**, -*gow*, -*gaw*, *n.* a large Indian antelope, the male slaty-grey, the female tawny. [Pers. and Hind. *nīl*, blue, Hind. *gāī*, Pers. *gāw*, cow.]

nill, *n'ill*, *nil*, *v.t.* (*Spens.*) will not : refuse :—*pa.t.* **nould**, **n'ould** (*nood*), also **nilled**.—**will'y nill'y**, will he, nill he, whether he will or not. [O.E. *nylle*—*ne*, not, *villan*, to wish.]

Nilometer, *nī-lom'i-tər*, *n.* a gauge for measuring the height of the Nile. [Gr. *neilometrion*.]

Nilot, *nīl'ot*, **Nilote**, -*ōt*, *n.* an inhabitant of the banks of the Upper Nile : a Hamitised negro of the Upper Nile.—*adj.* **Nilotic** (*-ot'ik*), of the Nile. [Gr. *Neilōtēs.*]

nim, *nim*, *v.t.* (*obs.*) to take : (now *slang*) to steal, pilfer :—*pa.t.* (*obs.*) **nam**, (now) **nimmed**.—*n.* **nim'mer**. [O.E. *niman*, to take.]

nim, *nim*, *n.* an old and widespread game, perh. orig. Chinese, in which two players take alternately from heaps or rows of objects (now usu. matches).

---

nim, *nĕm*, *n*. margosa, a species of Melia, yielding **nim′-oil**.—Also **neem**. [Hind. *nīm*.]

nimble, *nim′bl*, *adj*. light and quick in motion: active: swift.—*adjs*. **nim′ble-fing′ered**, skilful with the fingers: thievish; **nimbl′e-foot′ed**, swift of foot.—*ns*. **nim′bleness**, **nim′blesse** (*Spens*.), quickness of motion either in body or mind.—*adj*. **nim′ble-witt′ed**, quick-witted.—*adv*. **nim′bly**. [App. O.E. *nǣmel*, *numol*—*niman*, to take; cf. Ger. *nehmen*.]

nimbus, *nim′bəs*, *n*. a cloud or luminous mist investing a god or goddess: a halo: a rain-cloud:—*pl*. **nim′bī**, **nim′buses**.—*adjs*. **nimbed** (*nimd*); **nim′bused**. [L.]

nimiety, *ni-mī′i-ti*, *n*. excess.— *adj*. **nimious** (*nim′i-əs*; Scots law), excessive. [L. *nimis*, too much.]

niminy-piminy, *nim′i-ni-pim′i-ni*, *adj*. affectedly fine or delicate.—*n*. affected delicacy. [Imit.]

Nimrod, *nim′rod*, *n*. any great hunter. [From the son of Cush, Gen. x. 8-10.]

nincompoop, *nin*(*g*)*′kəm-pōōp*, *n*. a simpleton: a booby — earlier **nic′ompoop**, **nick′umpoop** — shortened to **nin′com**, **nin′cum**. [Origin unknown; not from L. *nōn compos* (*mentis*), not in possession of his wits.]

nine, *nīn*, *n*. the cardinal number next above eight: a symbol representing it (9, ix., &c.): a set of that number of things or persons (as a baseball team): a shoe or other article of a size denoted by 9: a card with nine pips: a score of nine points, tricks, &c.: the ninth hour after midday or midnight.—*adj*. of the number nine.—*n*. **nine′-eyes**, a lamprey (from its seven pairs of gill-pouches): a butterfly (from its spots).—*adj*. and *adv*. **nine′fold**, in nine divisions: nine times as much.—*adjs*. **nine′-foot**, **-inch**, **-mile**, &c., measuring 9 feet, &c.; **nine′-hole**, having nine holes.—*ns*. **nine′holes**, a game in which a ball is to be bowled into nine holes in the ground or a board: (*U.S*.) a difficulty, fix; **nine′pence**, the value of nine pennies: a coin of that value: a high standard of niceness, nimbleness, &c.—*adj*. **nine′penny**, costing, offered at, or worth ninepence.—*n*. a ninepence.—*n*. **nine′-pin**, a bottle-shaped pin set up with eight others for the game of nine′pins, a form of skittles—*n*. and *adj*. **nine′-score**, nine times twenty.—*adj*. **ninth** (*nīnth*), the last of nine: next after the eighth: equal to one of nine equal parts.—*n*. a ninth part: (*mus*.) an octave and a second: a tone at that interval.—*adv*. **nīnth′ly**, in the ninth place.—**nine days′ wonder** (see **wonder**); **ninepenny marl** or **morris**, **nine men′s morris** (see **meril**); **nine points of the law**, worth nine-tenths of all the points that could be raised (proverbially of possession); **nine worthies** (see **worth**); **the Nine**, the nine Muses; **to the nines**, to perfection, fully, elaborately. [O.E. *nigon*, Du. *negen*, L. *novem*, Gr. *ennea*, Sans. *nāvan*.]

nineteen, *nīn-tēn′*, or *nīn′tēn*, *n*. and *adj*. nine and ten.—*n*. and *adj*. **nine′teenth** (or *-tēnth′*).—*adv*. **nineteenth′ly**.—**nineteenth hole**, a golf clubhouse; **nineteen to the dozen**, with great volubility. [O.E. *nigonténe* (*-tiene*); see **nine**, **ten**.]

ninety, *nīn′ti*, *n*. and *adj*. nine times ten:—*pl*. **nine′ties**, the numbers ninety to ninety-nine: the years so numbered in a life or a century.—*adj*. **nine′tieth**, last of ninety: equal to one of ninety equal parts.—*n*. a ninetieth part. [O.E. *nigontig* (*hundnigontig*).]

ninny, *nin′i*, *n*. a simpleton.—Also **ninn′y-hammer**. [Possibly from **innocent**; poss.—It. *ninno*, child; Sp. *niño*.]

ninon, *nē-non°*, *n*. a silk voile or other thin fabric. [Fr. *Ninon*, a woman's name.]

Niobe, *nī′ō-bē*, *n*. a daughter of Tantalus, turned into stone as she wept for her children, slain by Artemis and Apollo.—*adj*. **Niobe′an**. [Gr. *Niobē*.]

niobium, *nī-ō′bi-əm*, *n*. a rare metal (Nb; at. numb. 41) discovered in the mineral tantalite—sometimes called *columbium*. [See **Niobe**.]

nip, *nip*, *n*. a small quantity of spirits—also **nipp′er** (*U.S*.).—*v.i.* to take a dram.—*n*. **nipp′erkin**, a small measure of liquor. [Origin obscure.]

nip, *nip*, *v.t*. to pinch: to press between two surfaces: to remove or sever by pinching or biting: to check the growth or vigour of: to give a smarting or tingling feeling to: to concern closely and painfully: to reprehend sharply: to snatch: (*slang*) to steal: (*slang*) to arrest.—*v.i.* to pinch: to smart: to go nimbly: (*pr.p.* **nipp′ing**; *pa.t.* and *pa.p.* **nipped**, *nipt*).—*n*. an act or experience of nipping: the pinch of cold: a nipping quality: (*Scot*.) pungency or bite: a sharp reprehension: (*min*.) a more or less gradual thinning out of a stratum: (*naut*.) a short turn in a rope, the part of a rope at the place bound by the seizing or caught by jambing: a small piece, such as might be nipped off: (*old slang*) a cut-purse.—*ns*. **nip′-cheese**, a stingy fellow: (*naut*.) a purser; **nipp′er**, one who, or that which, nips: a chela or great claw, as of a crab: a horse's incisor, esp. of the middle four: (*slang*) a pickpocket or cut-purse: a boy assistant to a costermonger, carter, &c.: a little boy: (in *pl*.) small pincers: various pincer-like tools: handcuffs.—*v.t*. to seize (two ropes) together.—*adv*. **nipp′ingly**.—*adj*. **nipp′y**, pungent, biting: (*slang*) nimble: niggardly.—**nip and tuck**, (*U.S*.) full speed: neck and neck; **nip in**, to cut in; **nip in the bud**, to cut off in the earliest stage. [Prob. related to Du. *nijpen*, to pinch.]

nip. See **nep**.

Nip. See **Nippon**.

Nipa, *nē′pä*, *nī′pä*, *n*. a low-growing East Indian palm of brackish water (*Nipa fruticans*): an alcoholic drink made from it. [Malay *nīpah*.]

nipperkin. See **nip** (1).

nippety-tipperty, *nip′ər-ti-tip′ər-ti*, *adj*. (*Scot*.) finical: mincing: fiddle-faddle.

nipple, *nip′l*, *n*. the pap of the breast: a teat: a small projection with an orifice.—*v.t*. to furnish with a nipple.—*ns*. **nipp′le-shield**, a defence for the nipple worn by nursing women; **nipp′le-wort**, a tall composite weed (*Lapsana communis*) with small yellow heads, once esteemed as a cure for sore nipples. [A dim. of *neb* or *nib*.]

Nippon, *nip-on′*, *n*. Japanese name of Japan.—*n*. and *adj*. **Nipp′onese**.—*n*. (*slang*) a Japanese.

nipter, *nip′tər*, *n*. the ecclesiastical ceremony of washing the feet—the same as *maundy*. [Gr. *niptēr*, a basin—*niptein*, to wash.]

nirl, *nirl*, *n*. (*Scot*.) a lump: a crumb: a stunted person.—*v.t*. to stunt: to shrink or shrivel: to pinch with cold.—*adjs*. **nirled**, **nirl′it**; **nirl′y**, **nirl′ie**, knotty: stumpy: stunted: niggardly. [Perh. **knurl**; or perh. related to mod. Ice. *nyrfill*, niggard.]

nirvana, *nir-vä′nä*, *n*. the cessation of individual existence—the state to which a Buddhist aspires as the best attainable. [Sans. *nirvāna*, a blowing out.]

nis, **n′is**, **nys**, *nis*, *niz*, (*Spens*.) a contraction for *ne is*, is not.

nis, *nis*, *n*. in Scandinavian folklore, a brownie or friendly goblin. [Dan. and Sw. *nisse*.]

Nisan, *nī′san*, *nē-sän′*, *n*. the name given after the Captivity to the Jewish month Abib. [Heb. *Nīsān*.]

nisberry. Same as **naseberry**.

nisi, *nī′sī*, *adj*. to take effect unless, after a time, some condition referred to be fulfilled.—See also *Foreign Words and Phrases*. [The L. conj. *nisi*, unless.]

Nissen, *nis′ən*, *adj*. designed by Col. P. N. *Nissen* (1871-1930), applied to a cylindrical corrugated-iron hut.

nisus, *nī′səs*, *n*. effort: striving: impulse. [L. *nīsus*, pl. *-ūs*.]

nit, *nit*, *n*. the egg of a louse or other vermin: a young louse: a term of contempt.—*n*. **nit′-grass**, a rare grass (*Gastridium*) with nit-like flowers.—*adj*. **nitt′y**, full of nits. [O.E. *hnitu*; Ger. *niss*.]

nithing, *nī′dhing*, *n*. (*hist*.) an infamous person: an abject coward: a traitor.—*adj*. cowardly: dastardly: niggardly—wrongly **nid(d)ering**, **nid-(d)erling** (*nid′*), **nid′ing**. [O.N. *nīthingr* (in O.E. as *nīthing*)—*nīth*, contumely; Ger. *neiding*.]

Nithsdale, *niths′dāl*, *n*. an 18th-century woman's riding-hood. [From the Countess of *Nithsdale*, who contrived her husband's escape from the Tower in her clothes in 1716.]

nitid, *nit'id, adj.* shining: gay. [L. *nitidus—nitēre*, to shine.]

niton, *ni'ton, n.* a former name for radon. [L. *nitēre*, to shine.]

nitre, *ni'tər, n.* (*obs.*) sodium carbonate: (now) potassium nitrate or saltpetre (**cubic nitre** is sodium nitrate, or Chile saltpetre): (*obs.*) a supposed nitrous substance in the air, &c.—*n.* **ni'trate**, a salt of nitric acid: a fertiliser—natural (potassium or sodium) or synthetic (calcium) nitrate.—*v.t.* to treat with nitric acid or a nitrate: to convert into a nitrate or nitro-compound.—*ns.* **nitra'tine** (*ni'tra-tin*), sodium nitrate as a mineral; **nitra'tion.**—*adj.* **ni'tric.**—*n.* **ni'tride**, a compound of nitrogen with another element.—*v.t.* to turn into a nitride: to case-harden by heating in ammonia gas.—*ns.* **ni'triding**; **ni'trile** (*-tril, -trēl, tril*), any of a group of organic cyanides (general formula R·C:N); **nitrifica'tion**, treatment with nitric acid: conversion into nitrates, esp. by bacteria through the intermediate condition of nitrites.—*v.t.* and *v.i.* **ni'trify**, to subject to or suffer nitrification:—*pr.p.* **ni'trifying**; *pa.t.* and *pa.p.* **ni'trified.**—*n.* **ni'trite**, a salt of nitrous acid.—*n.* **nitro-an'iline**, **nitran'iline**, any nitro-derivative of aniline.—*n.pl.* **ni'trobactē'ria**, bacteria that convert ammonium compounds into nitrites, and (esp.) those that convert nitrites into nitrates.—*ns.* **nitroben'zene**, a yellow oily liquid ($C_6H_5NO_2$) got from benzene and nitric and concentrated sulphuric acid; **nitrocell'ulose**, cellulose nitrate; **ni'tro-com'pound**, **ni'tro-deriv'ative**, a compound in which one or more hydrogens of an aromatic or aliphatic compound are replaced by nitro-groups; **nitroglyc'erine**, a powerfully explosive compound produced by the action of nitric and sulphuric acids on glycerine; **ni'tro-group**, the radical NO_2; **nitrom'eter**, an apparatus for estimating nitrogen or some of its compounds; **nitrosā'tion**, conversion of ammonium salts into nitrites; **ni'tro-silk**, an artificial silk in which fibres of cellulose nitrate are made and then turned into cellulose; **nitrō'sō-group**, the group NO; **nitrotoluene**, a nitro-derivative of toluene.—*adj.* **ni'trous.**—*n.* **nitrox'yl**, the group NO_2.—*adj.* **ni'try** (*obs.*), applied to the air, as supposed to contain nitre (see above).—*n.* **ni'tryl**, nitroxyl.—**nitric acid**, HNO_3; **nitric anhydride**, N_2O_5; **nitric oxide**, NO; **nitrous acid**, HNO_2; **nitrous anhydride**, N_2O_3; **nitrous oxide**, N_2O. [Fr.,—L. *nitrum*—Gr. *nitron*, sodium carbonate: prob. of Eastern origin; cf. Egyptian *ntr(j)*, Heb. *nether*, Ar. *nitrún*.]

Nitrian, *nit'ri-ən, adj.* belonging to *Nitriae* (Nitriai), a region of ancient Egypt west of the Nile delta, including the Natron lakes and a great assemblage of hermit settlements. [Gr. *nitriā*, a soda pit—*nitron*, soda.]

nitrogen, *ni'trō-jən, n.* a gas (N; at. numb. 7) forming nearly four-fifths of common air, a necessary constituent of every organised body, so called from its being an essential constituent of nitre.—*n.* **ni'trogen-fixā'tion**, the bringing of free nitrogen into combination.—*v.t.* **nitrogenise** (*-troj'*), to combine or supply with nitrogen.—**nitrogen cycle**, the sum total of the transformations undergone by nitrogen and nitrogenous compounds in nature—from free nitrogen back to free nitrogen. [Gr. *nitron*, sodium carbonate (but taken as if meaning nitre), and the root of *gennaein*, to generate.]

nitwit, *nit'wit, n.* (*slang*) a blockhead.—*adj.* **nit'-witted.**

nival, *ni'vəl, adj.* growing among snow.—*adj.* **niveous** (*niv'i-əs*), snowy, white.—*n.* **Nivôse** (*nē-vōz*), the 4th month of the French revolutionary calendar, about Dec. 21-Jan. 19. [L. *nix, nivis*, snow.]

nix, *niks, n.* (*Gmc. myth.*) a water-spirit, mostly malignant:—*fem.* **nix'ie**, **nix'y.** [Ger. *nix*, fem. *nixe*; cf. **nicker.**]

nix, *niks, n.* (*slang*) nothing: short for 'nothing doing, you'll get no support from me': (*U.S.*)

postal matter addressed amiss, usually in *pl.*—*n.* **nix-nie** (*niks'nē*; *S.Afr.*), nothing at all.—**nix my dolly**, (*obs. slang*) never mind. [Colloquial Ger. and Du. for Ger. *nichts*, nothing.]

nix, *niks, interj.* a cry to give warning of an approaching policeman, master, &c.

nizam, *ni-zäm', or nī-zam', n.* the title of the prince of Haidarabad in India: a Turkish soldier. [Hind. *nizām*, regulator.]

no, *nō, adv.* not so: not: (with *compar.*) in no degree, not at all.—*n.* a denial: a refusal: a vote or voter for the negative:—*pl.* **noes.**—**no more**, destroyed: dead: never again. [O.E. *ná—ne*, not, *á*, ever; cf. **nay.**]

no, *nō, adj.* not any: not one: by no means properly called.—*adj.* **no-account'**, (*U.S.*) worthless: insignificant.—*ns.* **no'-ball'**, (*cricket*) a ball bowled in such a way that it is disallowed by rules; **no'-man**, one ready to say 'no'; **no'-meaning**, want of meaning: something said that is deficient in meaning; **no-side'**, the termination of a game at Rugby football; **no'-trump'**, **no'-trumps'**, (*bridge*) a call for the playing of a hand without any trump suit.—*adj.* **no'-trump'.**—*n.* **no-trump'er**, a no-trump call: a hand suitable for a no-trump call: one addicted to calling no-trumps.—*advs.* **no'way**, **no'ways**, **no'wise**, in no way, manner, or degree.—**no doubt**, surely; **no end**, **no go** (see **end**, **go**); **no joke**, not a trifling matter; **no one**, nobody; **no time**, a very short time. [O.E. *nán*, none. See **none.**]

no, *nō, adv.* (*mod. Scot.*) not. [Perh. from *nocht*; see **not**, **nought.**]

no, *nō, n.* the Japanese drama developed out of a religious dance. [Jap. *nō.*]

Noachian, *nō-ā'ki-ən, adj.* pertaining to the patriarch *Noah*, or to his time—also **Noachic** (*-ak', -āk'*).—**Noah's ark**, a child's toy in imitation of the Ark with its occupants.

nob, *nob, n.* the head: the knave of the turn-up suit in cribbage.—**one for his nob**, a point scored for holding the nob: a blow on the head. [Perh. **knob.**]

nob, *nob, n.* a superior person.—*adv.* **nobb'ily.**—*n.* **nobb'iness.**—*adj.* **nobb'y**, smart. [Origin obscure; cf. **nabs**, **nib** (2).]

nobble, *nob'l, v.t.* (*slang*) to get hold of, esp. dishonestly: to win over, as by bribery: to swindle: to injure, destroy the chances of, as a racer.—*n.* **nobb'ler**, a finishing-stroke: a thimble-rigger's confederate: a dram of spirits. [Possibly **nab.**]

nobbut, *nob'ət, adv.* (*dial.*) only.—*prep.* except.—*conj.* except that. [**no**, **but.**]

nobility, *nō-bil'i-ti, n.* the quality of being noble: high rank: dignity: excellence: greatness of mind or character: descent from noble ancestors: nobles as a body.—*adj.* **nobil'iary**, of nobility.—*v.t.* **nobil'itate**, to ennoble.—*n.* **nobilitā'tion.** [See next word.]

noble, *nō'bl, adj.* illustrious: high in rank or character: of high birth: impressive: stately: generous: excellent.—*n.* a person of exalted rank: a peer: an obsolete gold coin=6s. 8d. sterling.—*n.* **no'ble-man**, a man who is noble or of rank: a peer:—*pl.* **no'blemen**; *fem.* **no'blewoman.**—*adj.* **no'ble-mind'ed.**—*ns.* **no'ble-mind'edness**; **no'ble-ness.**—*adv.* **no'bly.**—**most noble**, the style of a duke; **noble art**, boxing; **noble metal**, one that does not readily tarnish on exposure to air, as gold, silver, platinum—opposed to *base metal*; **noble opal**, precious opal, a translucent or semi-transparent bluish or yellowish white variety with brilliant play of colours. [Fr. *noble*—L. (g)*nōbilis*—(g)*nōscĕre*, to know.]

noblesse, *nō-bles', n.* nobility: nobleness: a body of nobility.—(*Spens.*) **no'blesse**, **no'bilesse.** [Fr.]

nobody, *nō'bə-di, n.* no person: no one: a person of no account. [**no**, **body.**]

nocake, *nō'kāk, n.* meal made of parched Indian corn. [Amer. Ind. word *nookik*, &c.]

nocent, *nō'sənt, adj.* (*rare*) hurtful: guilty.—*n.* (*obs.*) one who is hurtful or guilty.—*adv.* **nō'cently.** [L. *nocēns, -ēntis, pr.p. of nocēre*, to hurt.]

nock, *nok, n.* a notch, or a part carrying a notch, esp. on an arrow or a bow: the forward upper end of a sail that sets with a boom. [Origin obscure; appar. not the same as **notch**.]

noctambulation, *nok-tam-bū-lā'shən*, *n.* sleep-walking.—*ns.* **noctam'bulism**; **noctam'bulist**. [L. *nox, noctis*, night, *ambulāre*, *-ātum*, to walk.]

Noctilio, *nok-til'i-ō*, *n.* a South American genus, the hare-lipped bat. [L. *nox, noctis*, night, and the ending of *vespertiliō*, bat.]

Noctiluca, *nok-ti-l(y)ōō'kă*, *n.* a phosphorescent marine flagellate infusorian, abundant around the British coasts.—*adjs.* **noctilu'cent** (-*sənt*), **noctilu'cous** (-*kəs*), phosphorescent: shining in the dark. [L. *noctilūca*, the moon, a lantern—*nox, noctis*, night, *lūcēre*, to shine.]

noctivagant, *nok-tiv'ə-gənt*, *adj.* wandering in the night.—*n.* **noctivagā'tion**.—*adj.* **noctiv'agous**. [L. *nox, noctis*, night, *vagārī*, to wander.]

Noctua, *nok'tū-ă*, *n.* a generic name sometimes used as a general name for any member of the **Noctū'-idae**, a large family (or group of families) of mostly nocturnal, strong-bodied moths, the owlet-moths. —*n.* **noc'tuid**. [L. *noctŭa*, an owl—*nox*, night.]

noctuary, *nok'tū-ə-ri*, *n.* a record of the events or thoughts of night. [L. *nox, noctis*, night, on the analogy of **diary**.]

noctule, *nok'tūl*, *n.* the great bat, the largest British species. [Fr.,—It. *nottola*, L. *nox, noctis*, night.]

nocturn, *nok'tərn*, *n.* any one of the three sections of the office of Matins: (*obs.*) a daily portion of the psalter used at nocturns.—*adj.* **noctur'nal**, belonging to night: happening, done, or active by night.—*n.* an astronomical instrument for finding the hour by night: a person, animal, or spirit active by night.—*adv.* **noctur'nally**.—*n.* **nocturne** (*nok'turn* or *-turn'*), a dreamy or pensive piece, generally for the piano, esp. associated with the name of its inventor John Field (1782-1837) and Chopin, who developed it: (*paint.*) a moonlight or night scene. [L. *nocturnus—nox*, night.]

nocuous, *nok'ū-əs*, *adj.* hurtful.—*adv.* **noc'uously**. —*n.* **noc'uousness**. [L. *nocuus—nocēre*, to hurt.]

nod, *nod*, *v.i.* to give a quick forward motion of the head, esp. in assent, salutation, or command: to let the head drop in weariness: to lean over as if about to fall: to bend or curve downward, or hang from a curved support: (*fig.*) to commit a lapse.—*v.t.* to incline: to signify or direct by a nod: (*pr.p.* **nodd'ing**; *pa.t.* and *pa.p.* **nodd'ed**).— *n.* a quick bending forward of the head: a slight bow: a movement of the head as a gesture of assent or command.—*n.* **nodd'er**.—*n.* and *adj.* **nodd'ing**.—*v.t.* and *v.i.* **nodd'le**, to nod slightly: to keep nodding.—*n.* **nodd'y**, an inverted pendulum with a spring, used to test oscillation.—**a nodding acquaintance**, a slight acquaintance, as with a person one nods but does not speak to; **Land of Nod**, sleep (in punning allusion to the biblical land, Gen. iv. 16); **on the nod**, (*slang*) on tick. [M.E. *nodde*, not known in O.E.]

noddle, *nod'l*, *n.* (*obs.*) the back of the head: (*dial.*) the nape of the neck: (now jocular) the head. [Origin obscure.]

noddy, *nod'i*, *n.* a noodle: an oceanic bird (Anous) akin to the terns, unaccustomed to man and therefore easily taken and deemed stupid: an old game like cribbage: the knave in this and other games: an old form of cab with a door at the back. [Origin obscure: connexion doubtful.]

node, *nōd*, *n.* a knot: a knob or lump: a swelling: a place, often swollen, where a leaf is attached to a stem: a point of intersection of two great circles of the celestial sphere, esp. the orbit of a planet or the moon and the ecliptic: (*geom.*) a point at which a curve cuts itself, and through which more than one tangent to the curve can be drawn: a similar point on a surface, where there is more than one tangent-plane: a point of minimum displacement in a system of stationary waves: a meeting-place of lines, roads, or parts: (*fig.*) a complication in a story.—*adj.* **nōd'al**, of a node or nodes.—*v.t.* **nōd'alise**, to make nodal.—*n.* **nōdal'ity**, knottedness: state of being nodal.— *adj.* **nōd'āted**, knotted.—*n.* **nōdā'tion**, knottiness: a knotty place.—*adj.* **nodical** (*nōd'* or *nod'*), pertaining to the nodes: from a node round to the

same node again; **nodose** (*nŏd-ōs', nŏd'ōs*), having nodes, knots or swellings: knotty.—*n.* **nodosity** (*nō-dos'i-ti*), knottiness: a knotty swelling.—*adjs.* **nŏd'ous**, knotty; **nodular** (*nod'ū-lər*), of or like a nodule: in the form of nodules: having nodules or little knots; **nŏd'ulāted**, having nodules.—*ns.* **nŏdūlā'tion**; **nŏd'ūle**, a little rounded lump: a swelling on a root inhabited by symbiotic bacteria. —*adjs.* **nŏd'ūled**; **nŏd'ūlose**, **nŏd'ūlous**.—*n.* **nŏd'us** (L.), a knotty point, difficulty, complication: a swelling at the junction of nervures in an insect's wing:—*pl.* **nŏd'ī** (*-ī*). [L. *nōdus*; dim. *nōdulus*.]

Noël. See **Nowel**.

noesis, *nō-ē'sis*, *n.* the activity of the intellect.—*adj.* **noemat'ical**.—*adv.* **noemat'ically**.—*adj.* **noetic** (*nō-et'ic*), purely intellectual. [Gr. *noēsis—noein*, to perceive, think.]

Noetian, *nō-ē'sh(y)ən*, a Patripassian or follower of *Noëtus* of Smyrna (3rd cent.).—Also *adj.*—*n.* **Noe'tianism**.

nog, *nog*, *n.* (*obs.*) Norwich strong ale: egg-nog or similar drink. [Origin unknown.]

nog, *nog*, *n.* a stump or snag: a wooden peg, pin, or cog: a brick-sized piece of wood inserted in a wall to receive nails. — *n.* **nogg'ing**, a brick filling between timbers in a partition. [Origin unknown.]

noggin, *nog'in*, *n.* a small mug or wooden cup: its contents, a dram of about a gill. [Origin unknown; Ir. *noigin*, Gael. *noigean*, are believed to be from English.]

nohow, *nō'how*, *adv.* not in any way, not at all: in no definable way: (*coll.*—also **no'howish**) out of sorts.

noils, *noilz*, *n.pl.* short pieces of wool or other fibre separated from the longer fibres by combing.— Also *sing.* **noil**, the wool so separated. [Origin unknown.]

noint, **'noint**, an aphetic form of **anoint**.

noise, *noiz*, *n.* sound of any kind: an unmusical sound: an over-loud or disturbing sound: din: frequent or public talk: rumour: (*Shak.*) report: a band of musicians.—*v.t.* to spread by rumour.— *v.i.* to talk or call out loud.—*adjs.* **noise'ful**; **noise'less**.—*adv.* **noise'lessly**.—*n.* **noise'less-ness.**—*adv.* **nois'ily**.—*n.* **nois'iness**.—*adj.* **nois'y**, making a loud noise or sound: attended with noise: clamorous: turbulent.—**a big noise**, (*orig. U.S.*) a person of great importance; **make a noise in the world**, to achieve great notoriety. [Fr. *noise*, quarrel; perh. from L. *nausea*, disgust; but possibly from L. *noxia*, hurt—*nocēre*, to hurt.]

noisette, *nwä-zet'*, *n.* a hybrid between China and moss rose. [From Philippe *Noisette*, its first grower.]

noisette, *nwä-zet'*, *n.* a small choice piece of meat specially cooked: a nutlike sweet. [Fr., hazel-nut.]

noisome, *noi'səm*, *adj.* injurious to health: disgusting to sight or smell.—*adv.* **noi'somely**.—*n.* **noi'someness**. [noy.]

noli-me-tangere, *nō-lī-mē-tan'jə-ri*, *n.* a warning against touching: lupus or other disease of the face: a species of balsam, *Impatiens noli-(me-) tangere*, that ejects its ripe seeds at a light touch.— *adj.* warning off. [L. *nōlī* (infin. of *nōlle*), be unwilling, do not, *mē*, me, *tangĕre*, to touch.]

nolition, *nō-lish'ən*, *n.* unwillingness: absence of willingness. [L. *nōlle*, to be unwilling.]

noll, **noul**, **nowl** (*Spens.* **noule**, *Shak.* **nole**), *nōl*, *n.* the top of the head. [O.E. *hnoll*.]

nomad, **nomade**, *nom'ad, -əd*, also *nōm'*, *n.* one of a wandering pastoral community: a rover.— Also *adj.*—*adj.* **nomadic** (*nōm-* or *nom-ad'ik*).— *adv.* **nomad'ically**.—*n.* **nomadisā'tion**.—*v.i.* **nom'adise, to** lead a nomadic or vagabond life.— *v.t.* to make nomadic, transform to nomadism.—*n.* **nom'adism**. [Gr. *nomas, nomados—nomos*, pasture—*nemein*, to drive to pasture.]

no-man's-land, *nō'manz-land*, *n.* a waste region to which no one has a recognised claim: a debatable land, esp. between entrenched hostile forces.

nombril, *nom'bril*, *n.* (*her.*) a point a little below the centre of a shield. [Fr., navel.]

nom-de-plume, *non'-də-plōōm', -plüm'*, or **nom-,**

n. a pen-name, pseudonym. [Would-be Fr.—Fr. *nom*, name, *de*, of, *plume*, pen.]

nome, *nōm*, *n.* a province or department, esp. in ancient Egypt or modern Greece.—*ns.* **nomarch** (*nom'ärk*), the governor of a nome; **nom'archy**, a nome of modern Greece; **nom'os** (Gr.), a nome. [Gr. *nomos.*]

nomen, *nō'men*, *n.* a name, esp. of the *gens* or clan, a Roman's second name, as Gaius *Julius* Caesar. [L. *nōmen.*]

nomenclator, *nō'mən-klā-tər*, *n.* one who bestows names, or draws up a classified scheme of names: one who announces or tells the names of persons, esp. (*hist.*) in canvassing for a Roman election: (*obs.*) a book containing a list of words, a vocabulary.—*adjs.* **no'menclātive**, **nomenclatorial** (*nō-men-klə-tō'ri-əl*), **nomenclā'tural**.—*n.* **nō'menclāture** (or *nō-men'kle-tyər*), a system of names: terminology: a list of names: (*obs.*) a vocabulary: mode of naming: (now considered loose) a name. [L. *nōmenclātor—nōmen*, a name, *calāre* to call.]

nomic, *nom'ik*, *adj.* customary: conventional, esp. of spelling. [Gr. *nomikos—nomos*, custom.]

nominal, *nom'in-əl*, *adj.* pertaining to, or of the nature of, a name or noun: of names: by name: only in name: so-called, but not in reality: inconsiderable, hardly more than a matter of form: (*rare*) nominalistic.—*ns.* **nom'inalism**, the doctrine that general terms have no corresponding reality either in or out of the mind, being mere words; **nom'inalist**.—*adj.* **nominalist'ic**.—*adv.* **nom'inally**, by name: as a noun: in name only. [L. *nōminālis—nōmen*, *-ĭnis*, a name.]

nominate, *nom'in-āt*, *v.t.* to name: to mention by name: to appoint: to propose formally for election.—*adj.* (chiefly *Scots law*) nominated: elect.—*adj.* **nom'inable**, namable: fit to be named.—*adv.* **nom'inately**, by name.—*n.* **nominā'tion**, the act or power of nominating: state of being nominated: naming.—*adj.* **nominatival** (*nom-in-ə-tī'vl*, or *nom-nə-*).—*adv.* **nominatī'vally**. —*adj.* **nominative** (*nom'in-ə-tiv*, *nom'nə-tiv*; *gram.*), naming the subject: in the case in which the subject is expressed: (also *nom'in-ā-tiv*) nominated, appointed by nomination.—*n.* the nominative case: a word in the nominative case.—*adv.* **nom'inatively**.—*n.* **nom'inātor**, one who nominates.—**nominative absolute**, a nominative combined with a participle, but not connected with a finite verb or governed by any other word. [L. *nōmināre*, *-ātum*, to name—*nōmen.*]

nominee, *nom-in-ē'*, *n.* one who is nominated by another: one on whose life an annuity or lease depends: one to whom the holder of a copyhold estate surrenders his interest. [L. *nōmināre*, *-ātum*, to nominate, with *-ee* as if from Fr.]

nomism, *nōm'izm*, *nom'izm*, *n.* religious legalism: the view that moral conduct consists in the observance of a law.—*adj.* **nomist'ic** (*nom-*), based on law, or on a sacred book. [Gr. *nomisma*, established custom, *nomos*, a law.]

nomocracy, *nom-ok'rə-si*, or *nōm-*, *n.* government according to a code of laws. [Gr. *nomos*, law, *kratos*, power.]

nomogeny, *nom-* or *nōm-oj'ə-ni*, *n.* the origination of life according to natural law, not miracle—opp. to *thaumatogeny*. [Gr. *nomos*, law, and the root *gen-*, as in *genesis*, origination.]

nomography, *nom-* or *nōm-og'rə-fi*, *n.* the art of drawing up laws.—*n.* **nomog'rapher**. [Gr. *nomos*, law, *graphein*, to write.]

nomology, *nom-* or *nōm-ol'ə-ji*, *n.* the science of law: the science of the laws of the mind.—*adj.* **nomological** (*-ə-loj'*).—*n.* **nomol'ogist**. [Gr. *nomos*, law, *logos*, discourse.]

nomothete, *nom'ō-thēt*, or (Gr.) **nomothetes** (*nom-oth'i-tēz*), *n.* a lawgiver: a legislator: in ancient Athens, one of a body charged with revision of the laws.—*adj.* **nomothetic** (*-thet'ik*). [Gr. *nomothetēs—nomos*, law, and the root *the-*, as in *tithenai*, to set.]

non, *non*, a Latin word used as a prefix, not—as in *ns.* **non-abil'ity**, incapacity: inability: **non-accept'ance**, want of acceptance: refusal to accept; **non-ac'cess**, (*law*) want of opportunity

for marital commerce; **non-admiss'ion**, refusal of admission: failure to be admitted; **non-aggress'ion**, abstention from aggression.—*adj.* **non-alcohol'ic**, not alcoholic: not containing alcohol.—*ns.* **non-appear'ance**, failure or neglect to appear, esp. in a court of law; **non-arri'val**, failure to arrive; **non-attend'ance**, a failure to attend: absence; **non-atten'tion**, inattention; **non-Chris'tian**, other than Christian (also *adj.*); **non'-claim**, a failure to make claim within the time limited by law.—*adj.* **non-colle'giate**, not belonging to a college (also *n.*).—*ns.* **non-com'**, (*coll.*) a non-commissioned officer; **non-com'-batant**, any one connected with an army who is there for some other purpose than that of fighting, as a surgeon, a chaplain: a civilian in time of war. — *adjs.* **non-commiss'ioned**, not having a commission, as an officer in the army below the rank of commissioned officer; **non-committ'al**, not committing one or refraining from committing oneself, to any particular opinion or course of conduct: free from any declared preference or pledge: implying nothing, one way or the other.— *n.* a non-committal state or utterance.—*ns.* **non-commun'icant**, one who does not take communion on any particular occasion or in general, esp. formerly according to the rites of the Church of England: one who has not yet communicated; **non-commun'ion**; **non-compear'ance**, (*Scots law*) failure to appear in a court of law; **non-compli'ance**, neglect or failure of compliance.— *adj.* **non-comply'ing**.—*ns.* **non-compound'er**, one who does not compound or make composition: (*hist.*) a Jacobite who would restore James II. unconditionally; **non-con'**, (*coll.*) a Nonconformist (also *adj.*); **non-concurr'ence**, refusal to concur. —*adj.* **non-conduct'ing**, not readily conducting, esp. heat or electricity.—*n.* **non-conduct'or**, a substance or object that does not readily conduct heat or electricity.—*adj.* **nonconform'ing**, not conforming, esp. to an established church.—*n.* **nonconform'ist**, one who does not conform: esp. one who refused to conform or subscribe to the Act of Uniformity in 1662: usu. applied in England (**Nonconformist**) to a Protestant separated from the Church of England (also *adj.*).—*n.* **nonconform'ity**, want of conformity, esp. to the established church; **non'-content**, one not content: in House of Lords, one giving a negative vote.— *adjs.* **non-conten'tious**, not subject to contention; **non-contrib'utory**, not based on contributions. —*ns.* **non-cooperā'tion**, failure or refusal to co-operate, esp. (in India before 1947) with the government; **non-deliv'ery**, failure or neglect to deliver: the fact of not having been delivered.—*adj.* **non-effect'ive**, having no effect: not efficient or serviceable: unfitted or unavailable for service: relating to those so unfitted or unavailable.—*n.* a member of a force who is unfitted or unavailable for active service.—*adj.* **non-effic'ient**, not up to the standard required for service.—*n.* a soldier who has not yet undergone the full number of drills.— *n.* **non-e'go**, in metaphysics, the not-I, the object as opposed to the subject, whatever is not the conscious self.—*adj.* **non-elect'**, not elect.—*n.* **non-elec'tion**, state of not being elect: fact of not having elected or been elected.—*adjs.* **non-elec'tive**, not chosen by election; **non-elec'tric**, (*obs.*) conducting electricity.—*n.* a conductor.—*ns.* **non-elec'trolyte**, a substance, such as sugar, that gives a non-conducting solution; **non-en'try**, (*Scots law*, *hist.*) a vassal's heir's failure to renew investiture: a casualty that was due to the superior on such failure.—*adj.* **non-essen'tial**, not essential: not absolutely required.—*n.* something that is not essential, or is not of extreme importance.—*adj.* **non-Euclid'ean**, not according to Euclid's axioms and postulates.—*n.* **non-exist'ence**, the condition of not being: a thing that has no existence. — *adjs.* **non-exist'ent**; **non-ferr'ous**, containing no iron: other than iron: relating to metals other than iron; **non-flamm'able**, not capable of supporting flame though combustible; **non-for'feiting**, of a life insurance policy, not forfeited by reason of non-

Neutral vowels in unaccented **syllables**: *el'ə-mənt*, *in'fənt*, *ran'dəm*

payment.—*ns.* **non-fulfil′ment**, the fact of not fulfilling or not being fulfilled; **non-gre′mial**, a non-resident member, esp. of Cambridge University.—*adj.* applied to the examinations afterwards called local.—*ns.* **non-interven′tion**, a policy of systematic abstention from interference in the affairs of other nations; **non-intru′sion**, in Scottish Church history, the principle that a patron should not force an unacceptable minister on an unwilling congregation; **non-intru′sionist**. —*adj.* **non-iss′uable**, not capable of being issued: not admitting of issue being taken on it.—*n.* **non-join′der**, omission to join all the parties to an action or suit.—*adj.* **noniur′ing**, not swearing allegiance.—*n.* **Nonjur′or**, one of the clergy in England and Scotland who would not swear allegiance to William and Mary in 1689, holding themselves still bound by the oath they had taken to the deposed king, James II.—*adj.* **non-marr′ying**, not readily disposed to marry.—*ns.* **non′-mem′ber**, one who is not a member; **non′-met′al**, an element that is not a metal.—*adj.* **non-metall′ic**, not metallic: not of metal or like metal; **non-mor′al**, unconcerned with morality: involving no moral considerations; **non-nat′ural**, not natural: forced or strained.—*n.* in old medicine (usu. in *pl.*) anything not considered of the essence of man, but necessary to his well-being, as air, food, sleep, rest, &c.—*n.* **non-observ′ance**, neglect or failure to observe: disregard.—*adj.* **non-par′ty**, independent of party politics.—*ns.* **non-pay′ment**; **non-perform′ance**, neglect or failure to perform.—*adj.* **non-prior′ity**, without privilege of priority.—*n.* **non-produc′tion**.—*adj.* **non-profess′ional**, not professional or of a profession: not done in professional capacity.—*n.* **non-profi′cient**, one who has made no progress in the art or study in which he is engaged.—*adjs.* **non-provi′ded**, (of an elementary school or education in England and Wales) maintained but not provided by the local education authority, and managed by a committee in which the trustees form the majority; **non-quo′ta**, not included in a quota.—*n.* **non-regard′ance**, (*Shak.*) want of due regard.—*adj.* **non-representa′tional**, not aiming at the depicting of objects.—*n.* **non-res′idence**, fact of not residing at a place, esp. where one's official or social duties require one to reside or where one is entitled to reside.—*adj.* and *n.* **non-res′ident.**—*n.* **non-resist′ance**, the principle of not resisting violence by force, or of not resisting authority: passive submission.—*adjs.* **non-resist′ant**, **non-resist′ing** (of air-ships) having a balloon or gasbag with no internal framework to brace it, and no rigid keel; **non-skid′**, **non-slip′**, designed to reduce chance of slipping to a minimum. —*n.* **non-smo′ker**, one who does not smoke: a railway compartment in which smoking is supposed to be forbidden.—*adjs.* **non-smo′king**; **non-soci′ety**, not belonging to a society, esp. not a member of a trade union: employing men who are not members of a trade union; **non′-stop**, uninterrupted, without any stop or halt.—*n.* **non′-term**, (*obs.*) a vacation between terms: a time of inactivity.—*adj.* **non-u′nion**, not attached to a trade union: employing, or produced by, non-union workers.—*ns.* **non-u′nionist**; **non-u′sager**, a Nonjuror who rejected the usages; **non-u′ser**, (*law*) omission to take advantage of a right.—*adjs.* **non-util′ity**, not of the special kind made or sold for utility's sake; **non-vi′able**, not viable. [L. *nōn*, not.]

nonage, *non′ij*, *nōn′ij*, *n.* legal infancy, minority: time of immaturity generally.—*adj.* **non′aged**. [O.Fr. *nonage*—pfx. *non-* (L. *nōn*) and *age*, age.]

nonagenarian, *nōn-* or *non-ə-ji-nā′ri-ən*, *n.* one who is ninety years old or between ninety and a hundred.—*adj.* of that age. [L. *nōnāgēnārius*, relating to ninety—*nōnāgintā*, ninety.]

nonagesimal, *nōn-* or *non-ə-jes′i-məl*, *adj.* ninetieth. —*n.* a point of the ecliptic 90 degrees from its intersection by the horizon. [L. *nōnāgēsimus*—*nōnāgintā*, ninety.]

nonane, *nōn′ān*, *n.* a hydrocarbon (C₉H₂₀), ninth in the methane series. [L. *nōnus*, ninth.]

nonary, *nōn′ə-ri*, *adj.* based on nine. [L. *nōnārius*.]

nonce, *nons*, *n.* (almost confined to the phrase *for the nonce*, which in M.E. is sometimes a mere tag for rhyme's sake) the particular or express purpose (*Shak.*): the occasion: the moment, time being. —*n.* **nonce′-word**, a word coined for use at the moment. [From *for the nones*, i.e. *for then ones*, for the once, *then* being the dative (O.E. *tham*) of *the* and *ones* the genitive (O.E. *ānes*) of one substituted for the dative.]

nonchalance, *non′sha-ləns*, *n.* unconcern: coolness: indifference. —*adj.* **non′chalant.** —*adv.* **non′-chalantly.** [Fr.,—*non*, not, *chaloir*, to matter, interest—L. *calēre*, to be warm.]

non-come, *non′kum′*, *-kom′*, *n.* (*Shak.*) one of Dogberry's blundering words, perh. a confusion of *non-plus* and *non compos mentis.*

nondescript, *non′di-skript*, *adj.* not yet described: not easily classified: neither one thing nor another.—*n.* a person or thing not yet, or not easily, described or classed. [L. *nōn*, not, *dēscrībĕre*, -*scrīptum*, to describe.]

none, *nun*, *pron.* (*pl.* or *sing.*) not one: no person or persons: not the thing in question: not any: no portion or amount.—*adj.* (separated from the noun; otherwise *arch.*; formerly esp. before a vowel or *h*) no.—*adv.* in no degree: by no means: not at all.—*n.* **none′-so-prett′y**, **Nan′cy-prett′y**, London Pride (*Saxifraga umbrosa*).—*adj.* **none′-spar′ing**, (*Shak.*) all-destroying.—*adv.* **none′-the-less′** (or **none the less**), nevertheless. [O.E. *nān*—*ne*, not, *ān*, one.]

nonentity, *non-en′ti-ti*, *n.* the state of not being: a thing not existing: a person or thing of no importance. [L. *nōn*, not, *entitās* (see **entity**).]

Nones, *nōnz*, *n.pl.* in the Roman calendar, the ninth day before the Ides (both days included)—the 7th of March, May, July, and October, and the 5th of the other months: a church office originally for the ninth hour, or three o'clock, afterwards earlier. [L. *nōnae*—*nōnus*, ninth.]

non(e)such, *non′-*, *nun′such*, *n.* a unique, unparalleled, or extraordinary thing: black medick. [**none**, **such**.]

nonet, **nonette**, *nō-net′*, *n.* (*mus.*) a composition for nine performers.—Also **nonet′to**. [It. *nonetto*.]

non-feasance, *non-fē′zəns*, *n.* omission of something which ought to be done. [Pfx. *non-*, not, O.Fr. *faisance*, doing—*faire*—L. *facĕre*, to do.]

nonillion, *nō-nil′yən*, *n.* a million raised to the ninth power: (*U.S.*, as in France) one thousand raised to the tenth power.—*adj.* **nonill′ionth**. [L. *nōnus*, ninth, in imitation of **million**, **billion**.]

nonny, *non′i*, *n.* a meaningless word in old ballad refrain, &c., usually 'hey, nonny,' 'hey nonny nonny,' or 'hey nonny no'—once a cover for obscenity.

nonpareil, *non-pə-rel′*, *non′pə-rel*, *n.* a person or thing without equal: a fine variety of apple: a kind of comfit: a six-point printing-type.—*adj.* unequalled: matchless. [Fr. *non*, not, *pareil*, from a L.L. dim. of L. *pār*, equal.]

nonplus, *non′plus*, *n.* a state in which no more can be done or said: great difficulty.—*v.t.* to perplex completely, to puzzle:—*pr.p.* **non′plussing**; *pa.t.* and *pa.p.* **non′plussed**. [L. *nōn*, not, *plūs*, more.]

nonsense, *non′səns*, *n.* that which has no sense: language without meaning: absurdity: trifling: foolery: humbug: trivial things: that which is manifestly false.—Also *interj.*—*adj.* **nonsensical** (*-sens′*), without sense: absurd.—*ns.* **nonsensi-cality** (*non-sens-i-kal′i-ti*), **nonsens′icalness.**—*adv.* **nonsens′ically.** [Pfx. *non-* and **sense**.]

non-sequitur, *non-sek′wi-tər*, *n.* (the drawing of) a conclusion that does not follow logically from the premises. [L. *nōn*, not, and *sequitur*, follows, 3rd sing. pres. ind. of *sequī*, to follow.]

non-suit, *non′sūt*, *-sōot*, *n.* in England, the stopping of a suit by voluntary withdrawal of the plaintiff, or by the judge, when the plaintiff has failed to make out cause of action or to bring evidence.— *v.t.* to subject to a nonsuit. [A.Fr. *no(u)nsute*, does not pursue.]

nonuplet, *non′ūp-let*, *n.* a group of nine: esp. a group of nine notes played in the time of six or eight. [L. *nōnus*, ninth, on the analogy of *duplus*, *quadruplus*, &c.]

noodle, *nōōd′l*, *n.* a simpleton: a blockhead.—*n.* **nood′ledom.** [Cf. **noddy.**]

noodle, *nōōd′l*, *n.* a flat macaroni, usually made with eggs. [Ger. *nudel.*]

nook, *nook*, *n.* a corner: a narrow place formed by an angle: a recess: a secluded retreat.—*adjs.* **nook′-shott′en,** shot out into nooks and corners; **nook′y.** [M.E. *nok*, *noke*; prob. Scand.; Gael. and Ir. *niuc* is prob. from the Northern form **neuk.**]

noology, *nō-ol′ə-ji*, *n.* the science of the intellect.—*n.* **nōom′etry,** mind-measurement. [Gr. *noos*, the mind, *logos*, discourse, *metron*, measure.]

noon, *nōōn*, *n.* the ninth hour of the day in Roman and ecclesiastical reckoning, three o'clock p.m.: afterwards (when the church service called *Nones* was shifted to midday) midday: middle: greatest height.—*adj.* belonging to midday: meridional.—*v.i.* to rest at noon.—*n.* **noon′day,** midday: the time of greatest prosperity.—*adj.* pertaining to midday: meridional.—*ns.* **noon′ing,** (esp. *U.S.*) a repast or rest about noon; **noon′tide,** the time of noon, midday.—*adj.* pertaining to noon: meridional. [O.E. *nón*—L. *nōna* (*hōra*), the ninth (hour).]

no-one, *nō′wun*, *n.* and *pron.* nobody.—Also **no one.**

noop, *noop*, *n.* (*Scott*) a knob, tip (of the elbow). [Cf. **knop.**]

noose, *nōōs*, also *nōōz*, *n.* a loop with running knot which ties the firmer the closer it is drawn: a snare or bond generally, esp. hanging or marriage.—*v.t.* to tie or catch in a noose. [Perh. O.Fr. *nous*, pl. of *nou* (Fr. *nœud*)—L. *nōdus*, knot.]

nopal, *nō′pāl*, *pəl*, *n.* a Central American cactus (Nopalea) used for rearing cochineal insects. [Sp. *nopal*—Mex. *nopalli*.]

nope, *nōp*, *adv.* an emphatic, originally American, form of **no,** pronounced with a snap of the mouth.

nor, *nor*, *conj.* and not: neither—used esp. in introducing the second part of a negative proposition—correlative to *neither*. [App. from *nother*, a form of **neither.**]

nor, *nor*, *conj.* (*Scot.* and *dial.*) than. [Origin obscure.]

nor′, *nor*, a shortened form of **north.**

Norbertine, *nor′bərt-īn*, *-in*, *n.* and *adj.* Premonstratensian. [From *Norbert*, the founder (1119).]

Nordic, *nor′dik*, *adj.* of a tall, blond, dolichocephalic type of (generally Germanic) peoples in N.W. Europe: loosely used by Nazis.—Also *n.* [Fr. *nord*, north.]

Norfolk, *nor′fək*, *adj.* belonging to the English county of *Norfolk*.—**Norfolk capon,** a red herring; **Norfolk dumpling or turkey,** a native or inhabitant of Norfolk; **Norfolk Island pine,** a lofty Araucaria of Norfolk Island (in the Pacific, named after the ducal family of *Norfolk*); **Norfolk jacket,** a loose pleated coat with a waistband. [O.E. *northfolc*, north folk.]

noria, *nō′ri-ä*, *n.* an endless chain of buckets on a wheel for water-raising. [Sp. *noria*—Ar. *nā′ūrah*.]

norimon, *nor′i-mon*, *n.* a Japanese palankin. [Jap. *nori*, to ride, *mono*, thing.]

norite, *nō′rīt*, *n.* a gabbro with a rhombic pyroxene. [Norway.]

norland, norlan′, *nor′lən(d)*, *n.* (*Scot.* and *poet.*) the north country.—*adj.* belonging to or coming from the north. [**north, land.**]

norm, *norm*, *n.* a rule: a pattern: an authoritative standard: a type: the ordinary or most frequent value or state.—*n.* **nor′ma,** a rule: a standard: a square for measuring right angles.—*adj.* **nor′mal,** according to rule: not deviating from the standard: ordinary: well adjusted: functioning regularly: (*chem.*) having an unbranched chain of carbon atoms: (of a solution) having one gramme-molecule of the dissolved substance to a litre: (*geom.*) perpendicular.—*n.* a perpendicular: a normal instance or specimen.—*ns.* **nor′malcy,** (esp. *U.S.*) normality (an ill-formed word); **normalisā′tion,** **normal′ity.**—*v.t.* and *v.i.* **nor′malise.**—*adv.* **nor′mally.**—*adj.* **nor′mative,** establishing a standard. —**normal school,** a training-college for teachers in the practice of their profession. [L. *norma*, a rule.]

Norman, *nor′mən*, *n.* a native or inhabitant of Normandy: one of that Scandinavian people which settled in northern France about the beginning of the 10th century, founded the Duchy of Normandy, and conquered England in 1066: (*pl.* **Nor′mans**): the Norman-French dialect.—*adj.* pertaining to the Normans or to Normandy.—*n.* and *adj.* **Nor′man-French′,** French as spoken by the Normans.—*v.t.* **Nor′manise,** to give a Norman character to.—*n.* **Nor′manism.**—**Norman architecture,** a massive Romanesque style, prevalent in Normandy (10th-11th cent.) and England (11th-12th), the churches with semicircular apse and a great tower, deeply recessed doorways, small, round-headed windows, zigzag, billet, nailhead, and other characteristic ornaments; **Norman Conquest,** the conquest of England by Duke William of Normandy (1066); **Norman cross,** an elaborate memorial cross like a Gothic turret with niches for figures and pinnacles. [O.Fr. *Normanz*, *Normans*, nom. sing. and accus. pl. of *Normant*, Northman, from Scand.]

norman, *nor′mən*, *n.* (*naut.*) a bar inserted in a windlass to fasten or veer a rope or cable on. [Origin obscure.]

Norn, *norn*, *n.* (*Scand. myth.*) one of the three Fates —Urd, Verdande, and Skuld.—Also (Latinised) **Norn′a.** [O.N. *norn.*]

Norn, *norn*, *n.* the old Norse dialect of Orkney and Shetland.—Also *adj.* [O.N. *norrœna.*]

Norroy, *nor′oi*, *n.* (*her.*) an English king-of-arms whose jurisdiction lies north of the Trent. [O.Fr. *nord*, north, *roy*, king.]

Norse, *nors*, *adj.* Norwegian: ancient Scandinavian. —*n.* the Norwegian language: the language of the ancient Scandinavians—also **Old Norse.**—*n.* **Norse′man,** a Scandinavian or Northman. [Perh. Du. *noor(d)sch*; cf. Ice. *Norskr*; Norw. *Norsk.*]

north, *north*, *adv.* in the direction of, or towards, that point of the horizon or that pole of the earth or heavens which is opposite the sun at noon in Europe or elsewhere on the same side of the equator, or towards the sun in the other hemisphere: in the slightly different direction (*magnetic north*) in which a magnetic needle points.—*n.* the point of the horizon in that direction: the region lying in that direction: the part placed relatively in that direction: the north wind.—*adj.* lying towards the north: forming the part, or that one of two, that is towards the north: blowing from the north: (of a pole of a magnet, usually) north-seeking.—*v.i.* to turn or move towards the north.—*adjs.* **north′-bound,** bound for the north: travelling northwards; **north′-country,** belonging to the northern part of the country, esp. of England.—*n.* **north-coun′tryman.**—*adj.* and *adv.* **north-east′, nor′-east′** (also *north′, nor′*), midway between north and east.—*n.* the direction midway between north and east: the region lying in that direction: the wind blowing from that direction.—*n.* **north-east′er, nor′-east′er,** a strong wind from the north-east.—*adj.* and *adv.* **north-east′erly,** towards or from the north-east.—*adj.* **north′-east′ern,** belonging to the north-east: being in the north-east, or in that direction.—*adj.* and *adv.* **north-east′ward,** toward the north-east.—*n.* the region to the north-east.—*adj.* and *adv.* **north-east′wardly.**—*adv.* **north-east′wards.**—*n.* **norther** (*north′ər*), a wind or gale from the north, esp. applied to a cold wind that blows in winter over Texas and the Gulf of Mexico.—*v.i.* **norther** (*nordh′ər*), shift or veer to north.—*n.* **north′erliness** (*dh*).—*adj.* **north′erly** (*dh*), being toward the north: blowing from the north.—*adv.* toward or from the north.—*adj.* **north′ern** (*dh*), pertaining to the north: being in the north or in the direction toward it: proceeding from the north. —*n.* a native of the north: a north wind.—*n.* **north′erner** (*dh*), a native of, or resident in, the north, esp. of the northern United States.—*v.t.* **north′ernise** (*dh*), to give a northern character to. —*n.* **north′ernism** (*dh*), a northern idiom.—*adjs.* **north′ermost** (*obs.*), **north′ernmost, north′most** (*th*), most northerly.—*ns.* **north′ing** (*th*), motion, distance, or tendency northward: distance of a heavenly body from the equator northward: difference of latitude made by a ship in sailing: deviation towards the north; **north′land** (also *adj.*), land, or lands, of the north; **North′man**, an ancient Scandinavian.—*ns.*, *adjs.*, and *advs.* **north-north-east′**; **north-north-west′**, (in) a direction midway between north and north-east or north-west. — *adjs.* **north-pōl′ar**; **north′-seeking**, turning towards the earth's magnetic north pole.—*n.* **Northum′brian**, a native of the modern *Northumberland*, or of the old kingdom of *Northumbria* (O.E. *Northhymbre, Northhymbra-land*) stretching from the Humber to the Forth: the dialect of Old English spoken in Northumbria, later Northern English (including Scots).—*adj.* of Northumberland or Northumbria.—*adj.*, *adv.*, and *n.* **north′ward**, **nor′ward**, **norward** (*north′-ward, nor′ward, nor′əd*).—*adj.* and *adv.* **north′-wardly.** — *adv.* **north′wards.** — *adj.* and *adv.* **north-west′**, **nor′-west′** (also *north′, nor′*), midway between north and west.—*n.* the direction midway between north and west: the region lying in that direction: the wind blowing from that direction.—*n.* **north-**, **nor′-west′er**, a strong north-west wind. — *adjs.* and *advs.* **north′-west′erly**, toward or from the north-west; **north′-west′ern**, belonging to the north-west: being in the north-west or in that direction.—*adj.*, *adv.*, and *n.* **north-west′ward.**—*adj.* and *adv.* **north-west′wardly.**—*adv.* **north-west′wards.**—**North-east Passage**, a passage for ships along the north coasts of Europe and Asia to the Pacific, first made by Baron Nordenskiöld in 1878-79; **northern fern**, the hard fern (Lomaria); **northern lights**, the aurora borealis; **north pole**, the end of the earth's axis in the Arctic regions: its projection on the celestial sphere: (usually) that pole of a magnet which when free points to the earth's north magnetic pole (logically the other end); **North Star**, a star very near the north pole of the heavens, the Pole Star; **north water**, the space of open sea left by the winter pack of ice moving southward; **North-west Passage**, a sea-way from the Atlantic into the Pacific north of North America, first made (partly on the ice) by Sir Robert McClure, 1850-54. [O.E. *north*; cf. Ger. *nord*.]

norward, &c. Same as **northward**, &c.

Norway, *nor′wā*, *adj.* Norwegian.—*n.* (*obs.*) a Norwegian:—*pl.* (*Spens.*) **Norueyses.**—**Norway haddock**, the rose-fish or bergylt; **Norway pine**, the red pine, *Pinus resinosa*: its wood; **Norway rat**, the brown rat; **Norway spruce**, *Picea excelsa*.

Norwegian, *nor-wē′j(y)ən*, *adj.* of Norway, its people, or its language.—*n.* a native or citizen of Norway: the language of Norway: a kind of fishing-boat on the Great Lakes of America.—*adj.* (*Shak.*) **Norweyan** (-*wā′ən*), Norwegian.—**Norwegian oven**, **nest**, a hay-box. [L.L. *Norvegia*, Norway—O.N. *Norvegr* (O.E. *Northweg*)—O.N. *northr*, north, *vegr*, way.]

nose, *nōz*, *n.* the projecting part of the face used in breathing, smelling, and to some extent in speaking: the power of smelling: (*fig.*) flair, a faculty for tracking out, detecting, or recognising: a projecting fore-part of anything: a projection: a beak: a nozzle: the projecting edge of a step, a moulding, or a mullion: the withered remains of the flower on a gooseberry, apple, &c., opposite the stalk: the connecting part of a pair of spectacles: (*slang*) an informer.—*v.t.* to smell: to examine by smelling or as if by smelling: to track out, detect, or recognise: to touch, press, or rub with the nose: to thrust the nose into: to make (way) by feeling or pushing with the nose: to come or be face to face with: to oppose rudely face to face: to furnish with a nose: to remove the nose from (a gooseberry, &c.): to sound through the nose.—*v.i.* to sniff: to pry: to nuzzle: to move nose-first: to taper away in a noselike form.—*ns.* **nose′bag**, a bag for food, hung on a horse's nose: a picnicker's bag; **nose′-band**, the part of the bridle coming over the nose, attached to the cheek-straps; **nose′-bleed**, bleeding at the nose: (*obs.* or *U.S.*) yarrow or

other plant; **nose′-bleeding**.—*adj.* **nosed**, having a nose—esp. in composition, as bottle-*nosed*, long-*nosed*, &c.—*n.* **nose′-dive**, a headlong plunge.—*v.i.* to plunge nose-first.—*n.* **nose′-flute**, a flute blown by the nose; **nose′-herb**, (*Shak.*) a herb valued for its smell.—*adjs.* **nose′-led**, led by the nose, ruled and befooled completely; **nose′less**.—*n.* **nose′-leaf**, a membranous appendage on some bats' snouts:—*n.pl.* **nose′-nippers**, pince-nez. — *ns.* **nose′-painting**, colouring of the nose by drinking; **nose′-piece**, a nozzle: the end of a microscope tube carrying the objective: a nose-band: the nasal in armour; **nos′er**, a blow on the nose: a bloody nose: a severe rebuff: a strong head-wind: a prying person; **nose′-rag**, (*slang*) a handkerchief; **nose′-ring**, an ornament worn in the septum of the nose or in either of its wings: a ring in the septum of the nose for controlling a bull, swine, &c.—*adj.* **nos′ey**, **nos′y**, long-nosed: large-nosed: prying: ill-smelling: fragrant: sensitive to smells: nasal in sound.—*n.* a nickname for a nosey person.—*n.* **nos′ing**, the projecting rounded edge of the step of a stair or of a moulding.—**cut off one's nose to spite one's face**, to injure oneself rather than fail to injure another; **follow one's nose**, to go straight forward; **lead by the nose** (see lead); **make a long nose**, to put one's thumb to one's nose in defiance or derision; **nose to the grindstone** (see grindstone); **Nosey Parker**, a prying person; **put one's nose out of joint** (see joint); **snap off one's nose**, to speak snappily; **through the nose**, exorbitantly; **thrust one's nose into**, to meddle officiously with; **turn up one's nose at**, to refuse or receive contemptuously; **under one's very nose**, in full view: close at hand. [O.E. *nosu*; Ger. *nase*, L. *nāsus*.]

nosean, *nōz′i-ən*, *n.* a cubic mineral, aluminium sodium silicate and sulphate.—Also **nos′elite**. [Named after the German mineralogist K. W. *Nose* (*d.* 1835).]

nosegay, *nōz′gā*, *n.* a bunch of fragrant flowers: a posy or bouquet. [**nose, gay.**]

nosocomial, *nos-ō-kō′mi-əl*, *adj.* relating to a hospital. [Gr. *nosokomeion*, hospital—*nosos*, sickness, *komeein*, to tend.]

nosography, *nos-og′rə-fi*, *n.* the description of diseases.—*n.* **nosog′rapher.**—*adj.* **nosographic** (*nos-ə-graf′ik*). [Gr. *nosos*, disease, *graphein*, to write.]

nosology, *nos-ol′ə-ji*, *n.* the science of diseases: the branch of medicine which treats of the classification of diseases.—*adj.* **nosological** (-*ə-loj′*).—*n.* **nosol′ogist.** [Gr. *nosos*, disease, *logos*, discourse.]

nosophobia, *nos-ə-fō′bi-ə*, *n.* morbid dread of disease. [Gr. *nosos*, a disease, *phobos*, fear.]

nostalgia, *nos-tal′ji-ə*, *n.* home-sickness: sentimental longing for past times.—*adj.* **nostal′gic.** [Gr. *nostos*, a return, *algos*, pain.]

Nostoc, *nos′tok*, *n.* a genus of blue-green Algae, beaded filaments forming gelatinous colonies on damp earth, &c., once thought derived from fallen stars. [Appar. coined by Paracelsus.]

nostology, *nos-tol′ə-ji*, *n.* the study of senility or return to childish characteristics.—*adjs.* **nostologic** (-*ə-loj′*), **-al.** [Gr. *nostos*, return, *logos*, discourse.]

Nostradamus, *nos-trə-dā′məs*, *n.* one who professes to foretell the future.—*adj.* **nostradamic** (-*dam′ik*). [From the French astrologer (1503-1566).]

nostril, *nos′tril*, *n.* one of the openings of the nose. [M.E. *nosethirl*—O.E. *nosthyr(e)l*—*nosu*, nose, *thyrel*, opening; cf. **drill**, to pierce, and **thrill**.]

nostrum, *nos′trəm*, *n.* any secret, quack, or patent medicine: any favourite remedy or scheme. [L. *nostrum* (neut.), our own—*nōs*, we.]

not, *not*, *adv.* a word expressing denial, negation, or refusal.—*ns.* **not′-being**, the state or fact of not existing; **not′-I**, that which is not the conscious ego.—*adj.* and *adv.* **not-out′**, (*cricket*) still in: at the end of the innings without having been put out. [Same as **naught**, **nought**.]

not, **nott**, *not*, *adj.* with close-cut hair: polled.—*adjs.* **not′-head′ed**; **not′-pat′ed** (*Shak.*). [O.E. *hnot*.]

notable, *nō'tə-bl, adj.* worthy of being known or noted : remarkable : memorable : distinguished : noticeable : considerable : (now *rare*, sometimes with the old pronunciation *not'*) housewifely : capable, clever, industrious.—*n.* a person or thing worthy of note, esp. in *pl.* for persons of distinction and political importance in France in pre-Revolution times.—*n.pl.* **notabil'ia** (L.), things worthy of notice : noteworthy sayings.—*ns.* **notabil'ity,** the fact of being notable : a notable person or thing ; **no'tableness.**—*adv.* **no'tably.** [L. *notābilis*—*notāre,* to mark.]

notaeum, *nō-tē'əm, n.* the upper surface of a bird's trunk—opp. to *gastraeum.* [Latinised from Gr. *nōtaion* (neut.), adj.—*nōtos* or *nōton,* the back.]

notandum, *nō-tan'dəm, n.* something to be specially noted or observed :—*pl.* **notan'da.** [L., ger. of *notāre,* to note.]

notary, *nō'tə-ri, n.* an officer authorised to certify deeds, contracts, copies of documents, affidavits, &c. (generally **notary public**): anciently one who took notes or memoranda of others' acts.—*adj.* **notā'rial.**—*adv.* **notā'rially.**—*apostolical* **notary,** the official who despatches the orders of the pope : **ecclesiastical notary,** in the early church, a secretary who recorded the proceedings of councils, &c. [L. *notārius.*]

notation, *nō-tā'shən, n.* a system of signs or symbols : (*rare*) annotation. [L. *notātiō, -ōnis*—*notāre, -ātum,* to mark.]

notch, *noch, n.* a nick : an indentation : a narrow pass.—*v.t.* to make a nick in : to cut unevenly (as hair): to form, fix, or remove by nicking : to record by a notch : to score.—*n.* **notch'-board,** a board that receives the ends of the steps of a staircase.—*adj.* **notched,** nicked.—*n.* **notch'ing,** a method of joining timbers, by fitting into a groove or grooves. [Supposed to be from Fr. *oche* (now *hoche*) with *n* from the indefinite article ; not conn. with **nock.**]

notchel, nochel, *noch'l, n.* (*prov.*) notice that one will not be responsible for another's debts.—*v.t.* to repudiate the debts of. [Origin unknown.]

note, *nōt, n.* a significant or distinguishing mark : a characteristic : that by which a person or thing is known : a mark or sign calling attention : a written or printed symbol other than a letter : a stigma or mark of censure : an observation or remark : a comment attached to a text, explanatory, illustrative, critical, or recording textual variants : a jotting set down provisionally for use afterwards : an impression : a short statement or record : (*obs.*) a bill or account : a memorandum : a short informal letter : a diplomatic paper : a small size of paper used for writing : (*mus.*) a mark representing a sound (**whole note,** a semibreve): a key of a piano or other instrument : the sound or tone represented by the printed or written note : the song, cry, or utterance of a bird or other animal : (*obs.*) a tune : (*poet.*) music : a paper acknowledging a debt and promising payment, as a bank-note, a note of hand or promissory note : (*obs.*) a voucher or receipt : notice : attention : cognisance : distinction : reputation : eminence : importance : consequence : notability : (*Shak.*) intimation.—*v.t.* to make a note of : to notice : to attend to : to indicate : to mark : (*obs.*) to stigmatise : to mention : to record in writing or in musical notation : to add musical notation to : to set to music : to annotate : to denote.—*adj.* **nōt'al.**—*ns.* **note'book,** a book for keeping notes or memoranda : a bill-book ; **note'-case,** a pocket-book for bank-notes.—*adj.* **nōt'ed,** marked : well known : celebrated : eminent : notorious.—*adv.* **not'edly.** —*n.* **nōt'edness.**—*adj.* **note'less,** not attracting notice : unmusical.—*ns.* **note'let,** a short annotation or letter ; **note'-paper,** writing-paper intended for letters ; **nōt'er,** one who notes or observes : one who makes notes, an annotator ; **note'-shav'er,** (*U.S.*) one who discounts bills at an exorbitant rate : a usurer ; **note'worthiness.**—*adj.* **note'worthy,** worthy of note or of notice.—**note a bill,** to record a refusal of acceptance, as a ground of protest. [Fr.,—L. *nota,* a mark.]

note, n'ote, no'te, *nōt, v.t.* (*Spens.*) wot not :

(wrongly ; *Spens.*) could not. [O.E. *nát,* for *ne wát ;* see **ne, wot.**]

nothing, *nuth'ing, n.* no thing : the non-existent : zero number or quantity : the figure representing it, a nought : a thing or person of no significance or value : an empty or trivial utterance : a low condition : a trifle : no difficulty or trouble.— *adv.* in no degree : not at all.—*ns.* **nothingā'rian,** one who has no particular belief, esp. in religion ; **nothingā'rianism ; noth'ing-gift,** (*Shak.*) a gift of no value ; **nothi'ngism,** nothingness : triviality ; **noth'ingness,** non-existence : state of being nothing : worthlessness : insignificance : vacuity : a thing of no value.—**come to nothing,** to have little or no result : to turn out a failure ; **make nothing of** (see make); **next to nothing,** almost nothing. [no, thing.]

Nothofagus, *noth-ō-fā'gəs, n.* a genus of timber-trees of the southern hemisphere, close allied to beech. [Gr. *nothos,* spurious, L. *fāgus,* beech.]

notice, *nō'tis, n.* intimation : announcement : information : warning : a writing, placard, board, &c., conveying an intimation or warning : time allowed for preparation : cognisance : observation : heed : mention : a short book-review : civility or respectful treatment : (*obs.*) a notion.—*v.t.* to mark or observe : to regard or attend to : to mention : to make observations upon : to write or publish a notice of : to show sign of recognition of : to treat with civility.—*adj.* **no'ticeable,** that can be noticed : worthy of notice : likely to be noticed.—*adv.* **no'ticeably.**—*n.* **no'tice-board,** a board for fixing a notice on.—**give notice,** to warn beforehand : to inform : to intimate, esp. the termination of an agreement. [Fr. *notifier*— L. *nōtitia*—*nōscĕre, nōtum,* to get to know.]

notify, *nō'ti-fī, v.t.* to make known : to declare : to give notice or information of :—*pr.p.* **no'tifying ;** *pa.t.* and *pa.p.* **no'tified.**—*adj.* **no'tifiable,** that must be made known : (of diseases) that must be reported to public health authorities.—*n.* **notification** (*-fi-kā'shən*), the act of notifying : the notice given : the paper containing the notice. [Fr. *notifier*—L. *nōtificāre, -ātum*—*nōtus,* known, *facĕre,* to make.]

notion, *nō'shən, n.* a concept in the mind of the various marks or qualities of an object : an idea : an opinion, esp. one not very well founded : a caprice or whim : a liking or fancy : (*Shak., Milt.*) a mind : any small article ingeniously devised or invented, usually in *pl.*—*adj.* **no'tional,** of the nature of a notion : ideal : fanciful.—*n.* **no'tionalist,** a theorist.—*adv.* **no'tionally,** in notion or mental apprehension : in idea, not in reality.—*n.* **no'tionist,** one who holds ungrounded opinions. [Fr.,—L. *nōtiō, -ōnis*—*nōscĕre, nōtum,* to get to know.]

notitia, *nō-tish'i-ä, n.* a roll, list, register : a catalogue of public functionaries, with their districts : a list of episcopal sees. [L. *nōtitia ;* cf. **notice.**]

notochord, *nō'tō-kord, n.* a simple cellular rod, foreshadowing the spinal column, persisting throughout life in many lower vertebrates, as the amphioxus, &c.—*adj.* **notochord'al.** [Gr. *nōtos,* back, *chordē,* a string.]

Notodonta, *nō-tō-dont'ä, n.* a genus of moths whose larvae have toothlike humps, giving name to the family **Notodont'idae.**—*n.* **notodont'id,** a member of the family. [Gr. *nōtos,* back, *odous, odontos,* tooth.]

Notogaea, *nō-tō-jē'ä, n.* a zoological realm including Australia, the islands north of it, New Zealand, and Polynesia.—*adjs.* **Notogae'an, Notogae'ic.** [Gr. *nōtos,* south, *gaia,* land.]

notonectal, *nō-tō-nek'təl, adj.* swimming on the back, as certain insects : of the water-boatman genus (**Notonec'ta**) or family (**Notonec'tidae**) of hemipterous insects. [Gr. *nōtos,* back, *nēktēs,* a swimmer.]

notorious, *nō-tō'ri-əs, adj.* publicly known (now only in a bad sense): infamous.—*n.* **notori'ety,** state of being notorious : publicity : public exposure.—*adv.* **noto'riously.**—*n.* **noto'riousness.** [L.L. *nōtōrius*—*nōtus,* known.]

Notornis, *no-tor'nis, n.* a genus of flightless rails

(long thought extinct) in New Zealand and Norfolk Island. [Gr. *notos*, south, *ornis*, a bird.]

Notoryctes, *nō-tō-rik'tēs*, *n.* a blind burrowing marsupial of South Australia, the marsupial mole. [Gr. *notos*, south, *oryktēs*, digger.]

Nototherium, *nō-tō-thē'ri-əm*, *n.* a genus of Tertiary Australian fossil marsupials. [Gr. *notos*, south, *thērion*, a wild beast.]

Nototrema, *nō-tō-trē'mä*, *n.* the pouch-toad, a South American genus of tree frogs, with a brood-pouch on the female's back. [Gr. *nōtos*, the back, *trēma*, a hole.]

notour, *nō'tər*, *adj.* (*Scot.*; now only legal) well known, notorious. [L.L. *nōtōrius*.]

nott. Same as **not** (2).

notum, *nō'təm*, *n.* the dorsal aspect of the thorax in insects. [Latinised from Gr. *nōton*, back.]

Notus, *nō'təs*, *n.* the south or south-west wind. [L. *nōtus*—Gr. *nōtos*.]

notwithstanding, *not-with-stand'ing*, or *-widh-*, *prep.* in spite of.—*conj.* in spite of the fact that, although.—*adv.* nevertheless, however, yet. [Orig. a participial phrase in nominative absolute=L. *non obstante*.]

nougat, *nōō'gä*, *n.* a confection made of a sweet paste filled with chopped almonds or pistachio-nuts. [Fr. (cf. Sp. *nogado*, an almond-cake),—L. *nux, nucis*, a nut.]

nought, *nawt*, *n.* not anything: nothing: the figure o.—*adv.* in no degree.—**noughts and crosses**, a game in which one seeks to make three noughts, the other three crosses, in a row in the spaces of crossed parallel lines; **set at nought**, to despise, disregard, flout. [Same as **naught**.]

noul, **noule**, *nōl*, *n.* (*Spens.*). Same as **noll**.

nould, **noulde**, **n'ould**, (*Spens.*) *pa.t.* of **nill**.

noumenon, *nōō'* or *now'mi-non*, *n.* an unknown and unknowable substance or thing as it is in itself:—*pl.* **nou'mena**.—*adj.* **nou'menal**. [Gr. *nooumenon* (contraction for *noeomenon*), neuter of *pr.p.* pass. of *noeein*, to think—*noos* (*nous*), the mind.]

noun, *nown*, *n.* (*gram.*) a word used as a name: formerly including the adjective.—*adj.* **noun'al**.—**noun clause**, a clause equivalent to a noun. [A.Fr. *noun* (O.Fr. *non*; Fr. *nom*)—L. *nōmen*, name.]

nouns, *nownz*, *n.pl.* (*obs.*) used as a minced oath, in full *odds nouns*, for (*God's*) wounds.

noup, *nōōp*, *noop*, *n.* (*obs. Shetland*; *Scott*) a crag: a steep headland. [O.N. *gnúpr*.]

nourice, *nur'is*, *n.* (*obs.*) a nurse.—*n.* **nour'ice-fee'**, payment for a nurse. [O.Fr. *nurice*; see **nurse**.]

nourish, *nur'ish*, *v.t.* (*obs.*) to suckle: to feed: to furnish with food: to support: to help forward the growth of in any way: to allow to grow: to bring up: (*fig.*) to cherish: to educate.—*adj.* **nour'ishable**.—*n.* **nour'isher**.—*adj.* **nour'ishing**, affording nourishment or much nourishment.—*n.* **nour'ishment**, the act of nourishing: the state of being nourished: that which nourishes: nutriment. [O.Fr. *norir, nourir*, *-iss-* (Fr. *nourrir*)—L. *nūtrīre*, to feed.]

nouriture, **nourriture**, *nur'i-tyər*, *n.* nourishment: food: (*obs.*) bringing up, nurture. [See **nurture**.]

noursle, *nurs'l*, *v.t.* (*Spens.*) to bring up: to foster.—Also **nousle**, **nousell**, **nuzzle**. [A form of **nuzzle** influenced by **nurse**.]

nous, *nōōs*, *nows*, *n.* intellect: talent: (*slang*; *nows*) common-sense. [Gr. *nous*, contracted from *noos*.]

nova, *nō'vä*, *n.* a star that suddenly flares up with explosive violence:—*pl.* **no'vae** (*-vē*). [L. *nōva* (*stella*), new (star); fem. of *novus*, new.]

novaculite, *nō-vak'ū-līt*, *n.* a hone-stone, a very hard fine-grained silicious rock, sometimes containing minute garnets. [L. *novācula*, razor.]

novalia, *nō-vā'li-ä*, *n.pl.* (*Scots law*) waste lands newly reclaimed. [L. *novālia*.]

Novatian, *nō-vā'sh(y)ən*, *adj.* of or pertaining to the antipope *Novatianus* (251), or his party or sect, who favoured severity against the lapsed.—*ns.* **Nova'tianism**; **Nova'tianist**.

novation, *nō-vā'shən*, *n.* the substitution of a new obligation for the one existing: innovation. [L. *novātiō, -ōnis—novus*, new.]

novel, *nov'l*, *nuv'l*, *adj.* (*obs.*) new: new and strange:

of a new kind: felt to be new.—*n.* (earlier *no-vel'*; *obs.*) that which is new: (*obs.*) a piece of news: a new constitution or decree of Justinian or other Roman emperor, supplementary to the Codex: a fictitious prose narrative or tale presenting a picture of real life, esp. of the emotional crises in the life-history of the men and women portrayed.—*ns.* **nov'eldom**, the world of fiction; **novelette'**, a short novel, esp. one that is feeble, trite, and sentimental: Schumann's name for a short piano piece in free form.—*adj.* **novelett'ish**.—*n.* **novelett'ist**.—*v.t.* **nov'elise**, to make new or novel: to turn into a novel or novels.—*v.i.* to innovate: to write as a novelist.—*n.* **novelisā'tion**.—*adj.* **nov'elish**, savouring of a novel.—*ns.* **nov'elism**, (*obs.*) innovation, novelty: favouring of innovation: novel-writing; **nov'elist**, (*obs.*) an innovator: (*obs.*) a news-monger or news-writer: a novel-writer.—*adj.* **novelist'ic**.—*ns.* **novella** (*-el'ä*; L.), a Roman emperor's novel or decree:—*pl.* **novell'ae** (*-ē*): (It. *-el'lä*), a tale, short story:—*pl.* **novel'le** (*-lā*); **nov'elty**, newness: unusual appearance: anything new, strange, or different from what was known or usual before:—*pl.* **nov'elties**. [Partly through O.Fr. *novelle* (Fr. *nouvelle*), partly through It. *novella*, partly direct, from L. *novellus*, fem. *novella—novus*, new.]

November, *nō-vem'bər*, *n.* the eleventh month, ninth of the Roman year. [L. *November—novem*, nine.]

novena, *nō-vē'nä*, *n.* a devotion lasting nine days, to obtain a particular request, through the intercession of the Virgin or some saint. [L. *novēnus*, nine each, *novem*, nine.]

novenary, *nov'ə-nə-ri* (or *-ē'nər-i*), *adj.* pertaining to the number nine.—*n.* a set of nine things. [L. *novēnārius—novem*, nine.]

novennial, *nō-ven'yəl*, *adj.* recurring every ninth year. [L. *novennis—novem*, nine, *annus*, a year.]

novercal, *nō-vər'kl*, *adj.* pertaining to or befitting a stepmother. [L. *novercālis — noverca*, a stepmother.]

noverint, *nov'e-rint*, *n.* a writ—beginning with the words *noverint universi*, let all men know. [L. *nōverint*, 3rd pers. pl. perf. subj. of *nōscěre*, to get to know.]

Novial, *nō'vi-əl*, *nō-vi-äl'*, *n.* an artificial language devised by Otto Jespersen (1860-1943). [L. *novus*, new, and the initials of *international auxiliary language*.]

novice, *nov'is*, *n.* one new in anything: a beginner: a new convert or church member: an inmate of a religious house who has not yet taken the vows: a competitor that has not yet won a recognised prize. — *ns.* **nov'icehood**; **nov'iceship**; **noviciate**, **novitiate** (*-ish'i-āt*), the state of being a novice: the period of being a novice: a novice. [Fr.,—L. *novicius—novus*, new.]

novity, *nov'i-ti*, *n.* (*obs.*) innovation: newness. [L. *novitās, -ātis—novus*, new.]

Novocaine, *nō'vō-kān*, *n.* a local anaesthetic less toxic than cocaine. [Trade-mark name; L. *novus*, new, and **cocaine**.]

novum, *nō'vəm*, *n.* (*Shak.*) a game at dice in which the chief throws were nine and five. [Poss. L. *novem*, nine.]

now, *now*, *adv.* at the present time, or the time in question, or a very little before or after: as things are: used with the feeling of time lost or nearly lost in remonstrance, admonition, or taking up a new point.—*adj.* present.—*n.* the present time or the time in question.—*conj.* at this time when and because it is the fact: since at this time.—*interj.* expressing admonition, warning or (when repeated) reassurance.—**now and then**, or **again**, sometimes: from time to time; **now . . . now**, at one time . . . at another time; **now of late**, (*arch.*) lately; **the now**, (*Scot.*) at present: presently: very lately. [O.E. *nū*; Ger. *nun*, L. *nunc*, Gr. *nūn*.]

nowadays, *now'ə-dāz*, *adv.* in these times.—*Spens.* **now a** (or of) **dayes**. [now and days, O.E. *dæges*, gen. of *dæg*, day, to which the prep. a (O.E. *on*, which governed the dative) was later added.]

noway, **noways**, **nowise**. See **no**.

nowed, *nowd*, *adj.* (*her.*) knotted. [Fr. *noué*.]

Nowel, **Noël**, *nō-el'*, *n.* (*obs.* except in Christmas carols) Christmas. [O.Fr. (Fr. *noël*; cf. Sp. *natal*, It. *natale*),—L. *nātālis*, belonging to a birthday.]

nowhere, *nō'hwār*, *adv.* in or to no place: out of the running.—*n.* a non-existent place.—*adv.* **nō'-whither**, to no place: in no direction.—**nowhere near**, not nearly. [no, where, whither.]

nowl, *nōl*, *n.* (*Shak.*). Same as **noll**.

nown, *nōn*, *adj.* (*obs.*) own. [Orig. by wrong division of **mine own, thine own**.]

nowt, nout, *nowt*, *n.* (*Scot.*) cattle.—*n.* **nowt'-herd**. [O.N. *naut*; cognate with **neat** (1), O.E. *néat*.]

nowy, *nō'i*, *now'i*, *adj.* (*her.*) having a convex curvature near the middle. [O.Fr. *noé* (Fr. *noué*) —L. *nōdātus*, knotted.]

noxious, *nok'shəs*, *adj.* hurtful.—*adj.* **noxal** (*noks'l*), relating to wrongful injury.—*adv.* **nox'iously**.—*n.* **nox'iousness**. [L. *noxius*—*noxa*, hurt—*nocēre*, to hurt.]

noy, *noi*, *v.t.* (*Spens.*) to vex, hurt, annoy.—*n.* (*obs.* or *dial.*) vexation, hurt, trouble.—*ns.* **noy'ance** (*Spens.*, *Shak.*) annoyance; **noyes** (*noiz*; *Spens.*), noise (see **noise**). — *adjs.* **noy'ous**, (*Spens.*) vexatious: grievous: injurious; **noy'some**, noisome: hurtful. [Aphetic forms of **annoy**, &c.; see also **noisome**.]

noyade, *nwä-yäd'*, *n.* wholesale drowning, as by Carrier at Nantes, 1793-94. [Fr.,—*noyer*, to drown.]

noyau, *nwä-yō'*, *n.* a liqueur flavoured with bitter almonds or peach-kernels. [Fr., fruit-stone—L. *nucālis*, nutlike—*nux*, *nucis*, a nut.]

nozzle, *noz'l*, *n.* a little nose: the snout: a projection: an outlet tube, or spout: an open end of a tube. [Dim. of **nose**.]

nu, *nū*, *nü*, *n.* the thirteenth letter (N, *v*) of the Greek alphabet, answering to N: as a numeral *v'* = 50, *,v* = 50,000. [Gr. *nỹ*.]

nuance, *nū-äns̄'s*, *nwän̄'s*, *nū-äns'*, *n.* a delicate degree or shade of difference. [Fr.,—L. *nūbēs*, a cloud.]

nub, nubble, nubbly, nubby. See **knub**, &c.

nub, *nub*, *n.* (*obs. slang*) the gallows.—*v.t.* to hang. —*ns.* **nubb'ing-cheat**, the gallows; **nubb'ing-cove**, a hangman.

nub, *nub*, *n.* (*U.S.*) the point or gist. [Prob. **knub**.]

nubecula, *nū-bek'ū-lä*, *n.* a cloudiness:—*pl.* **nūbec'ulae** (*-lē*). [L. *nūbēcula*, dim. of *nūbēs*, cloud.]

nubile, *nū'bil*, *-bīl*, *adj.* marriageable (esp. of a woman).—*n.* **nubility** (*-bil'i-ti*). [L. *nūbilis*—*nūbĕre*, to veil oneself, hence to marry.]

nubilous, *nū'bi-ləs*, *adj.* cloudy.—*n.* **nu'bia**, a fleecy head-wrap formerly worn by women.—*adjs.* **nubif'erous**, cloud-bringing; **nu'biform**, cloudlike; **nubigenous** (*-bij'i-nəs*), cloud-born. [L. *nūbēs*, a cloud.]

nucellus, *nū-sel'əs*, *n.* the mass of tissue within the integuments of the ovule, containing the embryo-sac.—*adj.* **nucell'ar**. [A modern dim. from L. *nux*, *nucis*, nut; L. has *nucella*, a little nut.]

nucha, *nū'kä*, *n.* the nape of the neck.—*adj.* **nū'chal**. [L.L. *nucha*—Ar. *nukhā'*, spinal marrow.]

nuciferous, *nū-sif'ər-əs*, *adj.* nut-bearing. [L. *nux*, *nucis*, nut, *ferre*, to bear.]

nucivorous, *nū-siv'ə-rəs*, *adj.* nut-eating. [L. *nux*, *nucis*, nut, *vorāre*, to devour.]

nucleus, *nū'kli-əs*, *n.* a central mass or kernel: that around which something may grow: a core of flint from which pieces have been flaked off: the densest part of a comet's head or a nebula: (*obs.*) a nut kernel: (*obs.*) a nucellus: (*biol.*) a rounded body in the protoplasm of a cell, the centre of its life: (*phys.*) the massive part of an atom, distinguished from the outlying electrons: a stable group of atoms to which other atoms may be attached so as to form series of compounds: —*pl.* **nuclei** (*nū'kli-ī*).—*adjs.* **nū'cleal** (*-kli-əl*; *rare*), **nu'clear** (*-kli-ər*), **nu'cleary**, of, or of the nature of, a nucleus.—*v.t.* and *v.i.* **nu'cleate** (*-kli-āt*), to form into, or group around, a nucleus. —*adjs.* **nu'cleate**, **-d**, having a nucleus.—*n.* **nu'clein** (*-kli-in*), a colourless amorphous substance of varying composition, got from cell-nuclei.—*adjs.* **nuclē'olar**, of, or of the nature of, a nucleolus; **nu'cleolate**, **-d**, having a nucleus or a nucleolus: (of a spore) containing one or more conspicuous oil-drops.—*ns.* **nu'cleole**, a

nucleolus; **nuclē'olus**, a body observed within a cell-nucleus:—*pl.* **nuclē'oli** (*-lī*); **nu'cleon**, a general name for a neutron or a proton; **nu'cleo-pro'tein**, any of a group of compounds containing a protein molecule combined with a nuclein—important constituents of the nuclei of living cells. —**nuclear energy**, a more exact term for *atomic energy*, energy released or absorbed during reactions taking place in atomic nuclei; **nuclear** (or **atomic**) **fuel**, material, as uranium or plutonium, consumed to produce atomic energy; **nuclear physics**, the science of forces and transformations within the nucleus of the atom; **nuclear reactor**, an assembly of uranium, with moderator, in which a nuclear chain reaction can develop; **nucleic acid**, any of the complex acid components of nucleo-proteins. [L. *nucleus*—*nux*, *nucis*, a nut.]

nucule, *nūk'ūl*, *n.* a nutlet. [L. *nucula*, dim. of *nux*, *nucis*, a nut.]

nude, *nūd*, *adj.* naked: bare: undraped: (*law*) without consideration.—*n.* a nude figure or figures: undraped condition.—*n.* **nudā'tion**, act of making bare. — *adv.* **nude'ly**. — *n.* **nude'ness**. — *adjs.* **nu'dibranch** (*-brangk*), having naked gills (also *n.*): belonging to the **Nudibranchiā'ta**, shell-less marine gasteropods with gills exposed on the back and sides of the body; **nudicau'date**, having a hairless tail, as a rat; **nu'dicaul, -ous**, having a leafless stem.—*ns.* **nu'dism**; **nu'dist**, one who goes naked, or approves of going naked.—Also *adj.*—*n.* **nu'dity**, the state of being nude: a nude figure:—*pl.* **nu'dities**, naked parts usually covered. [L. *nūdus*, naked.]

nudge, *nuj*, *n.* a gentle poke, as with the elbow. [Origin obscure; perh. connected with Norw. *nugge*, to rub, or with **knock, knuckle**.]

nugatory, *nū'gə-tə-ri*, *adj.* trifling: worthless: inoperative: unavailing: futile.—*n.* **nu'gatori-ness**. [L. *nūgātōrius*—*nūgae*, trifles, trumpery.]

nugget, *nug'it*, *n.* a lump, esp. of gold. [Origin unknown; there is a Sw. dialect word *nug*, a lump, block.]

nuisance, *nū'səns*, *n.* (*obs.*) hurt or injury: that which annoys or hurts, esp. if there be some legal remedy: that which is offensive to the senses: a person or thing that is troublesome or obtrusive. —*n.* **nui'sancer**. [Fr.,—L. *nocēre*, to hurt.]

null, *nul*, *adj.* of no legal force: void: invalid: empty of significance: amounting to nothing.— *n.* (*obs.*) something of no value or meaning, a cipher or nought.—*v.t.* to annul, nullify: (*obs.*) to wipe out.—*ns.* **null'ity**, the state of being null or void: nothingness: want of existence, force, or efficacy; **null'ness**—**decree of nullity**, a decree that a marriage has never existed. [L. *nūllus*, not any, from *ne*, not, *ūllus*, any.]

null, *nul*, *n.* a knurl: a kink.—*v.i.* to kink.—*n.* **null'ing**, knurling. [**knurl**.]

nulla(h), *nul'ä*, *n.* a ravine: a water-course, not necessarily a dry one. [Hind. *nālā*.]

nulla-nulla, *nul'ä-nul'ä*, *n.* an Australian black's hard-wood club.—Also **null'a**. [Native word.]

nullifidian, *nul-i-fid'i-ən*, *adj.* having no faith, esp. religious.—*n.* one who has no faith. [L. *nūllus*, none, *fidēs*, faith.]

nullify, *nul'i-fī*, *v.t.* to make null: to annul: to render void or of no force:—*pr.p.* **null'ifying**; *pa.t.* and *pa.p.* **null'ified**.—*n.* **nullification** (*-fi-kā'shən*), a rendering void or of none effect, esp. (*U.S.*) of a contract by one of the parties, or of a law by one legislature which has been passed by another; **null'ifier** (*-fī-ər*). [Late L. *nūllificāre* —*nūllus*, none, *facĕre*, to make.]

nullipara, *nul-ip'ə-rä*, *n.* a woman who has never given birth to a child, esp. if not a virgin.—*adj.* **nullip'arous**.—*n.* **nulliparity** (*-i-par'i-ti*). [L. *nūllus*, none, *parĕre*, to bring forth.]

nullipore, *nul'i-pōr*, *n.* a coralline seaweed. [L. *nūllus*, none, *porus*, a passage, pore.]

numb, *num*, *adj.* having diminished power of sensation or motion: powerless to feel or act: stupefied: (*Shak.*) causing or (*Milt.*) of the nature of numbness.—*v.t.* to make numb: to deaden:— *pr.p.* **numbing** (*num'ing*); *pa.t.* and *pa.p.* **numbed** (*numd*). [O.E. *numen*, pa.p. of *niman*, to take.]

number, *num'bǝr*, *n*. that by which single things are counted or reckoned : quantity reckoned in units : a particular value or sum of single things or units : a representation in arithmetical symbols of such a value or sum : a full complement : a specified or recognised set, class, or group : (*obs.*) the multitude : some or many of the persons or things in question (often in *pl.*) : more than one : numerousness : (in *pl.*) numerical superiority : numerability : a numerical indication of a thing's place in a series, or one assigned to it for reference, as in a catalogue : a label or other object bearing such an indication : a person or thing marked or designated in such a way : an item : an issue of a periodical or serial publication : an integral portion of an opera or other composition : arithmetical faculty : (in *pl.*) rhythm, verses, music : (*gram.*) the property in words of expressing singular, (in some languages, as Greek) dual, and plural : **Numbers**, the fourth book of the Old Testament, in which an account of a census is given.—*v.t.* to count : (*Milt.*) to count out in payment : to apportion : to have lived through : to reckon as one : to mark with a number or assign a number to : to amount to.—*v.i.* to be reckoned in the number : to be of like number. — *n.* **num'berer.** — *adj.* **num'berless**, without number : more than can be counted.— **have**, or **get**, **one's number**, to size him up ; **his number is up**, he is doomed, has not long to live ; **number of the beast** (see **Apocalypse**) ; **number one**, he or that whose number is one, the first in the numbered series : (*slang*) self : oneself : (*naut. slang*) lieutenant, first officer (under the rank of commander). [Fr. *nombre*—L. *numerus*.]

numbles, *num'ble-pie'*. See **umbles**, **humble-pie**.

numerable, *nū'mǝr-ǝ-bl*, *adj*. that may be numbered or counted.—*n.* **numerabil'ity**.—*adv.* **nu'merably**.—*adj.* **nu'meral**, pertaining to, consisting of, or expressing number.—*n.* a figure or mark used to express a number, as I, 2, I., V., *a'*, *β'*, &c. : (*gram.*) a word used to denote a number : (in *pl.*) a badge indicating regiment, year of curriculum, &c.—*adv.* (*rare*) **nu'merally**, according to number.—*adj.* **nu'merary**, belonging to a certain number : contained within or counting as one of a body or a number—opp. to *supernumerary*.— *v.t.* **nu'merate**, to read off as numbers (from figures) : (*orig.*) to enumerate, to number.—*ns.* **numera'tion**, act of numbering : the art of reading figures and expressing the value in numbers : **nu'merator**, one who numbers : the upper number of a vulgar fraction, which expresses the number of fractional parts taken.—*adjs.* **numeric** (*-mer'ik*), **-al**, belonging to, expressed in, or consisting in, number : in number independently of sign : (*obs.* ; often with *same*) identical.—*adv.* **numer'ically**.—*n.* **numeros'ity**, numerousness : condition in respect of number : harmonious flow.—*adj.* **nu'merous**, great in number or quantity : many : consisting of or pertaining to a large number : rhythmical.—*adv.* **nu'merously**.—*n.* **nu'merousness**. [L. *numerus*, number.]

numinous, *nū'min-ǝs*, *adj*. pertaining to a divinity : suffused with feeling of a divinity.—*n.* **nu'minousness**. [L. *nūmen, -inis*, divinity.]

numismatic, *nū-miz-mat'ik*, *adj*. pertaining to money, coins, or medals.—*n.sing.* **numismat'ics**, the study of coins and medals.—*ns.* **numis'matist** ; **numismatol'ogist** ; **numismatol'ogy**. [L. *numisma*—Gr. *nomisma*, current coin—*nomizein*, to use commonly—*nomos*, custom.]

nummary, *num'ǝ-ri*, *adj*. relating to coins or money. —*adjs.* **numm'ular**, coin-shaped ; **numm'ulary**, **nummary** ; **numm'ulated**, coin-shaped. — *n.* **nummula'tion**, arrangement of blood-corpuscles in rouleaux.—*adj.* **numm'uline**, coin-shaped : nummulitic.—*n.* **numm'ulite**, a large coin-shaped fossil foraminifer, forming limestones.—*adj.* **nummulitic** (*-lit'ik*), pertaining to, composed of, or containing, nummulites. [L. *nummus*, a coin.]

numskull, *num'skul*, *n*. a blockhead.—*adj.* **num'skulled**. [numb, skull.]

nun, *nun*, *n*. a woman who, under a vow, has secluded herself in a religious house, to give her time to devotion : a kind of pigeon with feathers on its head like a nun's hood : a blue tit : a male smew : a tussock moth (*Psilurea monacha*), a pest in pine-forests.—*ns.* **nun'hood**, the condition of a nun ; **nunn'ery**, a house for nuns : nunship.— *adj.* **nunn'ish**.—*ns.* **nunn'ishness** ; **nun'ship**, the condition of a nun ; **nun's'-fidd'le**, a tromba marina ; **nun's'-flesh'**, an ascetic temperament ; **nun's'-veil'ing**, a woollen cloth, soft and thin, used by women for veils and dresses. [O.E. *nunne*—L.L. *nunna, nonna*, a nun, an old maiden lady, orig. mother ; cf. Gr. *nannē*, aunt, Sans. *nanā*, a child's word for mother.]

nun, *nun*, *n*. (*obs.*) a spinning top.—*n.* **nun'-buoy**, a buoy that tapers conically each way.

nunatak, *nōō'nä-täk*, *n*. a point of rock appearing above the surface of land-ice :—*pl.* **nu'nataks**, or (Sw.) **nu'natakkr**. [Eskimo.]

nunc dimittis, *nungk di-mit'tis*, *n*. the song of Simeon (Luke ii. 29-32) in the R.C. Breviary and the Anglican evening service. [From the opening words, *nunc dimittis*, now lettest thou depart.]

nuncheon, *nun'shǝn*, *n*. a light meal : a lunch. [M.E. *noneschenche*, noon-drink—O.E. *nón*, noon, *scenc*, drink ; cf. **noon**, **skink**.]

nuncio, *nun'shi-ō*, *n*. a messenger : one who brings tidings : an ambassador from the pope to an emperor or a king.—*n.* **nun'ciature**, a nuncio's office or term of office. [It. (now *nunzio*),—L. *nūntius*, a messenger, conjectured to be a contr. of *noventius* ; cf. *novus*, new.]

nuncle, *nung'kl*, *n*. (*Shak.*) a contr. of **mine uncle**.

nuncupate, *nung'kū-pāt*, *v.t.* to utter as a vow : to declare orally.—*n.* **nuncupā'tion**.—*adjs.* **nunc'ūpātive** (of a will), oral : designative ; **nunc'ūpatory** (*-pǝ-tǝ-ri* ; *obs.*), nuncupative : dedicatory. [L. *nuncupāre*, to call by name—prob. from *nōmen*, name, *capĕre*, to take.]

nundine, *nun'dīn*, *-din*, *n*. the ancient Roman market-day, every eighth day (ninth by Roman reckoning, counting both days).—*adj.* **nun'dinal** (*-din-*), pertaining to a fair or market. [L. *nūndinae*, market-day—*novem*, nine, *diēs*, a day.]

nunnation, *nun-ā'shǝn*, *n*. the addition of a final *n* in the declension of nouns. [As if L. *nunnātiō*— Ar. *nūn*, the letter n.]

Nuphar, *nū'fär*, *n*. the yellow water-lily genus. [Pers. *nūfar*, reduced form of *nīnūfar* ; see **Nenuphar**.]

nuptial, *nup'shǝl*, *adj*. pertaining to marriage : (*zool.*) pertaining to mating.—*n.* (usu. in *pl.*) marriage : wedding ceremony. — *n.* **nuptiality** (*-shi-al'i-ti*), nuptial character or quality : marriage-rate : (in *pl.*) wedding ceremonies and festivities. [L. *nuptiālis*—*nuptiae*, marriage—*nubĕre, nuptum*, to marry.]

nur, **nurr**. See **knurr**.

nuraghe, *nōō-rä'gä*, **nurhag**, *nōō-räg'*, *n*. a broch-like Sardinian round tower, probably of the Bronze Age :—*pl.* **nuraghi** (*-gē*), **nurhags**. [Sardinian dialect.]

nurl, See **knurl**.

nurse, *nurs*, *n*. one who suckles a child : one who tends a child : one who has the care of the sick, feeble, or injured, or who is trained for the purpose : one set apart to guide an incompetent officer or other : a worker bee, ant, &c., that tends the young : a budding form in tunicates : one who or that which feeds, rears, tends, saves, fosters, or develops anything, or preserves it in any desired condition : (*hort.*) a shrub or tree that protects a young plant : the state of being nursed (in the phrases *at nurse*, *out to nurse*).— *v.t.* to suckle : to tend, as an infant or a sick person : to bring up : to cherish : to manage with care and economy : to play skilfully, manipulate carefully, keep watchfully in touch with, in order to obtain or preserve the desired condition : to hold or carry as a nurse does a child.—*n.* **nurse'-child**, a child in care of a nurse : a foster-child.— *adj.* **nurse'like**.—*ns.* **nurse'maid**, a maid-servant who takes care of children ; **nurs'er** ; **nurs'ery**, (*Shak.*) nursing : place for nursing : an apartment for children : a place where young animals are reared, or where the growth of anything is promoted: a piece of ground where plants are reared for sale or transplanting: a race for two-year-old horses; **nurs'ery-gov'erness,** a governess for children who still require a nurse's care; **nurs'erymaid,** a maid employed in keeping a nursery: a nursemaid; **nurs'eryman,** a man who owns or works a nursery: one who is employed in cultivating plants, &c., for sale.—*v.t.* and *v.i.* **nurse'-tend,** to attend as a sick-nurse. — *ns.* **nurse'-tender; nurse'-tending; nurs'ing-fa'ther,** (*B.*) a foster-father; **nurs(e)'ling,** that which is nursed or fostered: an infant.—**nursery rhyme,** a traditional rhyme known to children; **nursery school,** a school for very young children (aged two to five); **nursing home,** a private hospital; **put (out) to nurse,** to commit to a nurse, usu. away from home; to put (an estate) under trustees. [O.Fr. *norrice* (Fr. *nourrice*)—L. *nūtrix, -īcis*—*nūtrīre,* to nourish.]

nurse, *nurs, n.* a shark: a dogfish. [Earlier *nuss,* perh. for (*an*) *huss, husk,* a dogfish.]

nursle, *nurs'l,* a mistaken form of **nousle, nuzzle.**

nurture, *nurt'yor, n.* upbringing: rearing: training: whatever is derived from the individual's experience, training, environment, distinguished from *nature,* or what is inherited: food.—*v.t.* to nourish: to bring up: to educate.—*adj.* **nurt'ural.** —*n.* **nurt'urer.** [O.Fr. *noriture* (Fr. *nourriture*) —L.L. *nūtrītūra*—L. *nūtrīre,* to nourish.]

nut, *nut, n.* popularly, any fruit with seed in a hard shell: (*bot.*) a hard dry indehiscent fruit formed from a syncarpous gynaeceum: often the hazel-nut, sometimes the walnut: (*slang*) the head: a hard-headed person, one difficult to deal with, a tough: a young blood (also **knut,** pron. *knut*): a small block, usu. of metal, for screwing on the end of a bolt: (*mus.*) the ridge at the top of the finger-board on a fiddle, &c.: (*mus.*) the mechanism for tightening or slackening a bow: a small lump of coal: a small biscuit or round cake: a coconut-shell drinking-cup: (in *pl., slang*) a source of joy. —*v.t.* to look for and gather nuts:—*pr.p.* **nutt'ing;** *pa.t.* and *pa.p.* **nutt'ed.**—*n.* **nutā'rian,** one who thinks nuts the best kind of food.—*adj.* **nut'-brown,** brown, like a ripe hazel-nut.—*ns.* **nut'-butt'er,** a butter-substitute made from nuts; **nut'cracker,** a bird (Nucifraga) of the crow family: (usu. in *pl.*) an instrument for cracking nuts.—*adj.* like a pair of nutcrackers, as toothless jaws.—*ns.* **nut'-gall,** a nut-like gall, produced by a gall-wasp, chiefly on the oak; **nut'-grass,** American sedges of various kinds, esp. one with edible tuberous root; **nut'hatch,** a bird (Sitta) that hacks nuts and seeks insects on trees like a creeper — also **nut'jobber, nut'pecker; nut'-hook,** a stick with a hook for pulling down nut-bearing boughs: a bailiff: a thief who uses a hook; **nut'let,** a one-seeded portion of a fruit that divides as it matures, as in labiates: the stone of a drupe; **nut'meal,** meal made from nuts; **nut'-oil,** an oil got from walnuts or other nuts; **nut'-pine,** the stone-pine or other species with large edible seeds.—*adj.* **nuts,** (*slang*) crazy.— *ns.* **nut'shell,** the hard covering of a nut; **nutt'er,** one who gathers nuts: nut-butter; **nutt'iness;** **nutt'ing,** the gathering of nuts; **nut'-tree,** any tree bearing nuts, esp. the hazel.—*adj.* **nutt'y,** abounding in nuts: having the flavour of nuts: foolishly amorous: mentally unhinged.—*ns.* **nut'-wee'vil,** a weevil (Balaninus) whose larvae live on hazel-nuts; **nut'-wrench,** an instrument for turning nuts on screws.—a (**hard**) **nut to crack,** a difficult problem; **be nuts on,** (*slang*) to be very fond of; **in a nutshell,** in small compass; **not for nuts,** not on any account. [O.E. *hnutu;* O.N. *hnot,* Du. *noot,* Ger. *nuss.*]

nutant, *nū'tont, adj.* nodding: drooping.—*v.i.* **nu'tate,** to nod: to droop: to perform a nutation. —*n.* **nutā'tion,** a nodding: (*astron.*) a fluctuation in the precessional movement of the earth's pole about the pole of the ecliptic; (*bot.*) the sweeping out of a curve by the tip of a growing axis.—*adj.* **nutā'tional.** [L. *nūtāre,* to nod.]

nutmeg, *nut'meg, n.* the aromatic kernel of an East Indian tree (Myristica), much used as a seasoning

in cookery. — *adjs.* **nut'megged; nut'meggy.** [M.E. *notemuge*—**nut** and inferred O.Fr. *mugue,* musk—L. *muscus,* musk.]

nutria, *nū'tri-ä, n.* the coypu: its fur. [Sp. *nutria,* otter—L. *lutra.*]

nutrient, *nū'tri-ont, adj.* feeding: nourishing.—*n.* **nu'triment,** that which nourishes: food.—*adj.* **nutrimental** (-*ment'l*).—*n.* **nutri'tion,** act or process of nourishing: food.—*adjs.* **nutri'tional;** **nutri'tious,** nourishing.—*adv.* **nutri'tiously.**—*n.* **nutri'tiousness.** — *adj.* **nu'tritive,** nourishing: concerned in nutrition.—*adv.* **nu'tritively.** [L. *nūtrīre,* to nourish.]

nux vomica, *nuks vom'ik-ä, n.* a seed that yields strychnine: the East Indian tree (*Strychnos Nux-vomica*; family Loganiaceae) that produces it. [L. *nux,* a nut, *vomĕre,* to vomit.]

nuzzer, *nuz'or, n.* a present to a superior. [Hind. *nazr,* gift.]

nuzzle, nousle, *nuz'l, v.t.* and *v.i.* to poke, press, burrow, root, rub, sniff, caress, or investigate with the nose.—*v.t.* to thrust in (the nose or head). —*v.i.* to snuggle: to go with the nose toward the ground. [Freq. vb. from **nose.**]

nuzzle, *nuz'l, v.t.* to train: to bring up: to foster. [Origin obscure; confused with **nurse;** see **noursle.**]

ny, an obs. spelling of **nigh.**

nyanza, *nyan'zä,* also *ni-* or *nĭ-an'zä, n.* a lake (esp. in African proper names). [Bantu.]

nyas, *nī'as, n.* an old form of **eyas** (q.v.).

nychthemeron, *nik-thē'mə-ron, n.* a complete day of 24 hours, a night and a day.—*adj.* **nychthē'-meral.** [Gr. *nychthēmeron—nyx, nyktos,* night, *hēmerā,* day.]

Nyctaginaceae, *nik-tə-jin-ā'si-ē, n.pl.* a family of plants, mainly tropical American, akin to the goosefoots and the pinks, including the marvel of Peru. [Gr. *nyx,* night.]

nyctalopia, *nik-tə-lō'pi-ä, n.* properly, night-blindness, abnormal difficulty in seeing in a faint light: by confusion sometimes, day-blindness. — *adj.* **nyctalōp'ic.**—*n.* **nyc'talops** (-*lops*), one affected with nyctalopia:—*pl.* **nyctalō'pes.** [Gr. *nyktalōps,* night-blind, day-blind—*nyx, nyktos,* night, *alaos,* blind, *ōps,* eye, face.]

nyctinasty, *nik'ti-nas-ti, n.* sleep-movement in plants, joint effect of changes in light and temperature.—*adj.* **nyctinas'tic.** [Gr. *nyx, nyktos,* night, *nastos,* pressed.]

nyctitropism, *nik-tit'ro-pizm, n.* the assumption by plants of certain positions at night.—*adj.* **nycti-tropic** (-*trop'*) [Gr. *nyx, nyktos, tropos,* turning.]

nye, an obs. spelling of **nigh.**

nylghau, nilgau. See **nilgai.**

nylon, *nī'lon, n.* a synthetic polymeric amide that can be formed into filaments: a stocking made of it.

nymph, *nimf, n.* (*myth.*) one of the beautiful Greek goddesses who inhabited mountains, rivers, trees, &c.: a young and beautiful maiden (often ironical): (*obs.*) an insect pupa: an immature insect, similar to the adult but with wings and sex-organs un-developed.—*n.pl.* **nymphae** (-*ē*), the labia minora. —*ns.* **Nymphaea** (-*ē'ä*), the white water-lily genus, giving name to a family of dicotyledons **Nymph-aeā'ceae,** akin to the buttercup family; **nymph-ae'um,** a temple, sanctuary, or grotto of the nymphs.—*adj.* **nymph'al.**—*n.* **nymph'alid,** a butterfly of the **Nymphalid'eae,** a family with reduced fore-legs and short hairy shins.—*adjs.* **nymphē'an; nymph'ic, -al; nymph'ish; nymph'-like; nymph'ly.**—*ns.* **nymph'olepsy,** a species of ecstasy or frenzy said to have seized those who had seen a nymph: a yearning for the unattainable; **nymph'olept,** a person so affected. — *adj.* **nympholept'ic.** — *n.* **nymphomā'nia,** morbid and uncontrollable sexual desire in women. —*n.* and *adj.* **nymphomā'niac.** [L. *nympha*—Gr. *nymphē,* a bride, a nymph.]

nys, *nis, niz* (*Spens.*) is not. [**ne,** is.]

nystagmus, *nis-tag'mas, n.* a spasmodic, lateral, oscillatory movement of the eyes, found in miners, &c.—*adjs.* **nystag'mic; nystag'moid.** [Latinised from Gr. *nystagmos—nystazein,* to nap.]

O

O, o, ō, n. the fifteenth letter of our alphabet, derived from Greek omicron, with four chief sounds in English, as in *note, not, son, do* : anything round or nearly so : a spangle : esp. in telephone jargon, nought or nothing :—*pl.* Oes, O's *(ōz)* : as a mediaeval Roman numeral, O=11, Ō=11,000 : *(chem.)* prefixed *o-* stands for *ortho-*.

O, oh, *ō, interj.* used in addressing or apostrophising, marking the occurrence of a thought, reception of information, or expressing wonder, admiration, disapprobation, surprise, protest, pain, or other emotion. The form O is chiefly used in verse (*O for, O that*).—**Fifteen O's,** fifteen meditations on Christ's Passion, each beginning with O, composed by St Bridget ; **O's of Advent,** seven anthems each beginning with O, sung on the days before Christmas Eve.

o', *o, ō, ə,* a worn-down form of **of** and of **on.**

O', *ō, prefix,* in Irish patronymics, descendant of. [Ir. *ó, ua*—O.Ir. *an,* descendant.]

oaf, *ōf, n.* a changeling : a dolt : an idiot : a lout :—*pl.* **oafs,** *(rarely)* **oaves.**—*adj.* **oaf'ish,** idiotic, doltish : lubberly : loutish. [O.N. *álfr,* elf ; cf. **elf, ouphe.**]

oak, *ōk, n.* a genus (Quercus) of trees of the beech family : its timber valued in shipbuilding, &c. : extended to various other trees, as **poison-oak, she-oak** (qq.v.).—*adj.* of oak.—*ns.* **oak'-apple,** a gall caused by an insect on an oak leaf ; **oak'-egg'er,** an egger moth whose caterpillars feed on oak.—*adj.* **oak'en,** of oak.—*ns.* **oak'enshaw,** a little oak-wood ; **oak'-fern,** a fern (*Phegopteris Dryopteris*) of the polypody family (a translation of Gr. *dryopteris,* a name transferred by Linnaeus to this species from some ferns growing on oak-trees) ; **oak'-gall,** a gall produced on the oak ; **oak'-leather,** a fungus mycelium in the fissures of old oaks ; **oak'ling,** a young oak ; **oak'-lump,** the lichen lungwort ; **oak'-mast,** acorns collectively ; **oak'-nut,** a gall on the oak ; **oak'-tree ;** **oak'-wood.**—*adj.* **oak'y,** like oak, firm : abounding in oaks.—**Oak-apple Day,** the 29th of May, the anniversary of the Restoration in 1660, when country boys used to wear oak-apples in commemoration of Charles II. lurking in the branches of an oak (the **Royal Oak**) from Cromwell's troopers after Worcester ; **sport one's oak** (*university slang*), to keep one's outer door shut when one does not want visitors ; **The Oaks,** a great English race (founded 1779) for three-year-old fillies—so named from an estate near Epsom. [O.E. *āc* ; O.N. *eik,* Ger. *eiche.*]

oaker (*Spens.*). Same as **ochre.**

oakum, *ōk'əm, n.* old (usu. tarred) ropes untwisted and teased out for caulking the seams of ships. [O.E. *ācumba* (*ǣcumbe*) from *ā-,* away from, and the root of *cemban,* to comb.]

oar, *ōr, n.* a light bladed pole for propelling a boat : a stirring-pole : a swimming organ : an oarsman. —*v.t.* to impel as by rowing.—*v.i.* to row.—*n.* **oar'age,** oars collectively : rowing movement.— *adj.* **oared,** furnished with oars.—*ns.* **oar'-fish,** a ribbon-fish (Regalecus) ; **oar'-lap,** a rabbit with its ears standing out at right angles to the head.— *adjs.* **oar'-foot'ed,** having swimming feet ; **oar'-less.**—*ns.* **oar'-lock** (*rare*), a rowlock ; **oars'man,** a rower : one skilled in rowing ; **oars'manship,** skill in rowing ; **oar'weed** (same as **oreweed**).— *adj.* **oar'y,** having the form or use of oars.—**lie or rest on one's oars,** to abstain from rowing without removing the oars from the rowlocks : to rest, take things easily : to cease from work ; **put in one's oar,** to interpose when not asked. [O.E. *ār.*]

oasis, *ō-ā'sis,* sometimes *ō'ə-sis, n.* a fertile spot or tract in a sandy desert : any place of rest or pleasure in the midst of toil and gloom :—*pl.* **oases** *(-sēz).* [Gr. *oasis,* an Egyptian word ; cf. Coptic *ouahe.*]

oast, *ōst, n.* a kiln to dry hops or malt.—*n.* **oast'-house.** [O.E. *āst.*]

oat, *ōt* (oftener in *pl.* **oats,** *ōts), n.* a well-known genus (Avena) of grasses, esp. *A. sativa,* whose seeds are much used as food : its seeds : a musical pipe of oat-straw : a shepherd's pipe, pastoral song generally.—*n.* **oatcake',** (in Scotland) a thin broad, hard dry cake of oatmeal : (in parts of England) a cake like pancake.—*adj.* **oat'en,** consisting of an oat stem or straw : made of oatmeal. —*ns.* **oat'-grass,** a grass of Avena or kindred genus used more as fodder than for the seed ; **oat'-meal,** meal made of oats.—**feel one's oats,** to be frisky or assertive ; **sow one's wild oats,** to indulge in youthful dissipation or excesses ; **wild oats,** a wild species of oat (*A. fatua*). [O.E. *āte,* pl. *ātan.*]

oath, *ōth, n.* a solemn appeal to a god or something holy or reverenced as witness or sanction of the truth of a statement : the form of words used : a more or less similar expression used lightly, exclamatorily, decoratively, or in imprecation : a swear-word : a curse :—*pl.* **oaths** *(ōdhz).*—*adj.* **oath'able** (*Shak.*), capable of taking an oath.—*n.* **oath'-breaking** (*Shak.*), perjury.—**on, under, upon oath,** sworn to speak the truth : attested by oath ; **take an oath,** to have an oath administered to one. [O.E. *áth* ; Ger. *eid,* O.N. *eithr.*]

ob, *ob, n.* an objection (in the phrase *ob and sol,* objection and solution).—*n.* **ob-and-soll'er,** a disputant. [From the marginal note *ob* in old books of controversial divinity.]

obang, *ō'bang, n.* an old Japanese oblong gold coin. [Jap. *ōban.*]

obbligato, *ob-(b)li-gä'tō, adj.* that cannot be done without.—*n.* a musical accompaniment of independent importance, esp. that of a single instrument to a vocal piece. [It.]

obcompressed, *ob'kəm-prest, adj.* (*bot.*) flattened from front to back.

obconic, -al, *ob-kon'ik, -əl, adjs.* (*bot.*) conical, attached by the point.

obcordate, *ob-kor'dāt, adj.* (*bot.*) inversely heart-shaped, as a leaf.

obdiplostemonous, *ob-dip-lō-stē'mən-əs, adj.* (*bot.*) having two whorls of stamens, the outer opposite the petals.

obdurate, *ob'dū-rāt,* sometimes (as *Shak., Milt.*) *-dū', adj.* hardened in heart or in feelings : difficult to influence, esp. in a moral sense : stubborn : hard.—*v.t.* and *v.i.* to make or become obdurate.— *n.* **ob'dūracy** (or *ob-dū'rə-si*), state of being obdurate : invincible hardness of heart.—*adv.* **ob'dūrately** (or *dū').—ns.* **ob'dūrateness** (or *-dū'),* **obdūrā'tion.**—*v.t.* and *v.i.* **obdūre',** to obdurate. [L. *obdūrāre, -ātum—ob-,* intens., against, *dūrāre,* to harden—*dūrus,* hard.]

obeah. See **obi.**

obedience, *ō-bē'dyəns, -di-əns, n.* the act of doing what one is told : the state of being obedient : willingness to obey commands : dutifulness : the collective body of persons subject to any particular authority : a written instruction from the superior of an order to those under him : any official position under an abbot's jurisdiction : (*arch.*) an obeisance.—*adjs.* **obē'dient,** obeying : ready to obey ; **obediential** (*ō-bē-di-en'shl*), pertaining to, of the nature of, obedience. — *n.* **obēdientiary** (*-en'sha-ri*), one subject to obedience : one charged with an obedience in a monastery.—*adv.* **obē'diently.**—**canonical obedience,** the obedience, as regulated by the canons, of an ecclesiastic to another of higher rank ; **passive obedience,** unresisting and unquestioning obedience to authority, like that taught by some Anglican divines as due even to faithless and worthless kings like Charles II. and James II. [L. *obēdientia*; see **obey**.]

obeisance, *ō-bā'səns*, *n*. (*obs*.) obedience: a bow or act of reverence: an expression of respect.— *adj*. **obei'sant**. [Fr. *obéissance—obéir—*L. *oboedīre*, to obey.]

obelus, *ob'i-ləs*, *n*. a sign (— or ÷) used in ancient manuscripts to mark suspected, corrupt, or spurious words and passages: (*print*.) a dagger-sign (†) used esp. in referring to footnotes (**double obelus**, ‡):—*pl*. **ob'eli** (*-lī*).—*n*. **obelion** (*ō-bē'li-on*), a point in the sagittal suture of the skull between the two parietal foramina.—*adjs*. **obelisc'al**, of, or of the nature of, an obelisk: **obelisc'oid**, of the form of an obelisk: **obeliscal**.—*v.t*. **ob'elise**, to mark with an obelus: to condemn as spurious, doubtful, corrupt, &c.—*n*. **ob'elisk**, a tall, four-sided, tapering pillar, usually of one stone, topped with a pyramid: an obelus. [L. *obelus*—Gr. *obelos* (dim. *obeliskos*), a spit.]

Oberon, *ō'bə-rən*, *n*. king of the fairies, husband of Titania. [O.Fr. *Auberon*; prob. Frankish.]

obese, *ō-bēs'*, *adj*. abnormally fat.—*ns*. **obese'ness**, **obesity** (*-bēs'*, *-bes'*). [L. *obēsus—ob-*, completely, *edēre*, *ēsum*, to eat.]

obey, *ō-bā'*, *v.i*. to render obedience: to do what one is told: to be governed or controlled.—*v.t*. to do as told by: to comply with: to be controlled by.—*n*. **obey'er**. [Fr. *obéir—*L. *oboedīre—ob-*, towards, *audīre*, to hear.]

obfuscate, *ob-fus'kāt*, *v.t*. to darken: to obscure.— *n*. **obfusca'tion**. [L. *obfuscāre*, *-ātum—ob-*, intens., *fuscus*, dark.]

obi, *ō'bi*, **obeah** (*obs*. **obia**), *ō'bi-ä*, *n*. witchcraft and poisoning practised by negroes of the West Indies, Guiana, &c.: a fetish or charm.—*v.t*. to bewitch.—*ns*. **o'beahism**, **o'beism**; **o'bi-man**; **o'bi-woman**. [Of W. African origin.]

obi, *ō'bi*, *n*. a broad, gaily embroidered sash worn by Japanese women and children. [Jap. *obi*.]

obit, *ob'it* or *ō'bit*, *n*. (*obs*.) death: date of death: funeral ceremonies: office for a dead person: a death anniversary: an anniversary or other commemoration of a death.—*adjs*. **ob'ital**, **obit'ual**, pertaining to obits.—*n*. **obit'uarist**, a writer of obituaries.—*adj*. **obit'uary**, relating to or recording the death of a person or persons.—*n*. a register of deaths (*orig*.) in a monastery: an account of a deceased person, or a notice of his death: a collection of death-notices: in a newspaper often extended to include notices of births and marriages, &c. [L.L. *obitus—obīre*, *-ītum*, to go to meet, travel over, die—*ob*, in the way of, *īre*, to go.]

object, *ob'jikt*, *n*. a thing presented or capable of being presented to the senses: a thing observed: a material thing: that which is thought of, regarded as being outside, different from, or independent of, the mind (opposed to *subject*): that upon which attention, interest, or some emotion is fixed: an oddity or deplorable spectacle: that towards which action or desire is directed, an end: (*gram*.) part of a sentence denoting that upon which the action of a transitive verb is directed, or standing in an analogous relation to a preposition: (*obs*.) interposition: (*Shak*.) presentation to view or to the mind.—*v.t*. object (*-jekt'*), (*arch*.) to put in front or in the way of anything or anybody: (*arch*.) to present to sense or mind: (*arch*.) to present, bring forward, or adduce: to offer in opposition: to bring as an accusation: (*obs*.) to impute.—*v.i*. to be opposed: to refuse assent.— *adj*. (*obs*.) opposed, interposed, exposed.—*ns*. **ob'ject-ball**, a ball that a player aims at striking with his own ball; **ob'ject-find'er**, a device in microscopes for locating an object in the field before examination by a higher power; **ob'ject-glass**, in an optical instrument, the lens or combination of lenses at the end next the object; **objectifica'tion** (*-jekt-*).—*v.t*. **object'ify**, to make objective.—*n*. **objec'tion**, act of objecting: anything said or done in opposition: inclination to object, dislike, unwillingness.—*adj*. **objec'tionable**, that may be objected to: requiring to be

disapproved of: distasteful.—*adv*. **objec'tionably**. —*v.t*. **object'ivate**, to render objective.—*n*. **objectivā'tion**.—*adj*. **object'ive** (also *ob'*), relating to or constituting an object: (*scholastic philos*., *obs*.) existing or considered only in relation to mind, subjective: (*mod. philos*.) of the nature of, or belonging to, that which is presented to consciousness (opposed to *subjective*), exterior to the mind, self-existent, regarding or setting forth what is external, actual, practical, uncoloured by one's own sensations or emotions: (*gram*.) denoting the object: in the relation of object (to a verb or preposition): objecting: (of lenses) nearest the object.—*n*. (*-jekt'*) the case of the grammatical object: a word in that case: an object-glass: the point to which the operations (esp. of an army) are directed.—*adv*. **object'ively**.—*n*. **object'iveness**.—*v.t*. **object'ivise**, to objectify.—*ns*. **object'ivism**, a tendency to lay stress on what is objective: a theory that gives priority to the objective: **object'ivist**.—*adj*. **objectivist'ic**.—*n*. **objectiv'ity**.—*adj*. **object'less**, having no object: purposeless.—*ns*. **ob'ject-less'on**, a lesson in which a material object is before the class: a warning or instructive experience; **object'or**; **object-soul**, a vital principle attributed by the primitive mind to inanimate objects.—**money**, **salary**, &c., **no object**, not being a thing aimed at; **distance**, **expense**, &c., **no object**, not being reckoned worthy of consideration (perh. by confusion with the foregoing). [L. *objectus*, pa.p. of *ob*(*j*)*icĕre*, or partly the noun *objectus*, *-ūs* (found in the abl.), or the freq. vb. *objectāre—ob*, in the way of, *jacĕre*, to throw.]

objure, *ob-jōōr'*, *v.i*. to swear.—*v.t*. to bind by oath: to charge or entreat solemnly.—*n*. **objurā'tion**, act of binding by oath: a solemn charge. [L. *objūrāre*, to bind by oath—*ob-*, down, *jūrāre*, to swear.]

objurgate, *ob'jər-gāt*, or *-jur'*, *v.t*. and *v.i*. to chide. —*n*. **objurgā'tion**.—*adjs*. **objur'gative**, **objur'gatory**. [L. *objurgāre*, *-ātum*, to rebuke—*ob-*, intens., *jurgāre*, to chide.]

oblanceolate, *ob-lan'si-ō-lāt*, *adj*. (*bot*.) like a lance-head reversed, as a leaf—about three times as long as broad, tapering more gently towards base than apex. [Pfx. *ob-*, and **lanceolate**.]

oblast, *ob'läst*, *n*. a province or district. [Russ.]

oblate, *ob'lāt*, *ob-lāt'*, *adj*. dedicated: offered up.— *n*. a dedicated person, esp. one dedicated to monastic life but not professed, or to a religious life.—*n*. **oblā'tion**, act of offering: a sacrifice: anything offered in worship, esp. a eucharistic offering: an offering generally. [L. *oblātus*, offered up, used as pa.p. of *offerre*; see **offer**.]

oblate, *ob'lāt*, *ob-lāt'*, *ō-blāt'*, *adj*. flattened at opposite sides or poles, as a spheroid—shaped like an orange.—*n*. **oblate'ness**. [Formed on the analogy of **prolate**, with the pfx. *ob-*.]

oblige, *ō-blīj'*, *ə-blīj'*, formerly *-blēj'*, *v.t*. to bind morally or legally: to constrain: to bind by some favour rendered, hence to do a favour to.—*v.i*. (*coll*.) to do something as a favour.—*n*. **obligant** (*ob'li-gənt*; *Scots law*), one who binds himself to another to pay or to perform something.—*v.t*. **ob'ligate** (*-li-gāt*), (*U.S. and arch*.) to constrain: to bind by contract or duty: (*arch. or prov*.) to bind by gratitude.—*adj*. (*bot*.) by necessity, without option. —*n*. **obligation** (*ob-li-gā'shən*), act of obliging: a moral or legal bond, tie, or binding power: that to which one is bound: a debt of gratitude: a favour: (*law*) a bond containing a penalty in case of failure.—*adv*. **obligatorily** (*ob'lig-ə-tər-i-li* or *o-blig'*).—*n*. **ob'ligatoriness** (or *o-blig'*).—*adj*. **ob'ligatory** (or *o-blig'*), binding: imposing duty: imposed as an obligation: obligate.—*ns*. **obligee** (*ob-li-jē'*), (*law*) the person to whom another is bound by obligation: one who is under an obligation for a favour; **oblige'ment**, a favour conferred.—*adj*. **oblig'ing**, disposed to confer favours: ready to do a good turn: courteous.—*adv*. **oblig'ingly**.— *ns*. **oblig'ingness**; **obligor** (*ob'li-gor*), (*law*) the person who binds himself to another. [Fr. *obliger* —L. *obligāre*, *-ātum—ob-*, down, *ligāre*, to bind.]

oblique, *ō-blēk'*, *ə-blēk'*, *adj*. slanting: neither perpendicular nor parallel: not at right angles: not parallel to an axis : not straightforward : indirect : underhand : (*geom.*) not a right angle : having the axis not perpendicular to the plane of the base : skew : (*bot.*) asymmetrical about the midrib : (*crystal.*) monoclinic.—*n.* an oblique line, figure, muscle, &c. : an oblique movement or advance, esp. one about 45° from the original direction.— *v.i.* to deviate from a direct line or from the perpendicular, to slant : to advance obliquely by facing half right or left and then advancing.—*v.t.* to turn aslant.—*ns.* **obliquation** (*ob-li-kwā'shən*), **obliqueness** (*-blēk'*), **obliquity** (*ob-lik'wi-ti*), state of being oblique : a slanting direction : error or wrong : irregularity.—*adv.* **oblique'ly.**—*adjs.* **obliquid** (*ob-lik'wid*; *Spens.*), oblique ; **obliq'uitous.**—**oblique case,** any case other than nominative and vocative (see **case**) ; **oblique motion,** (*mus.*) upward or downward motion of one part while another remains stationary ; **oblique narration** or **speech,** indirect speech (see **indirect**) ; **obliquity of the ecliptic,** the angle between the plane of the earth's orbit and that of the earth's equator. [L. *oblīquus* —*ob-*, intens., and the root of *līquis*, slanting.]

obliterate, *ō-blit'ə-rāt*, *v.t.* to blot out, so as not to be readily or clearly readable : to efface : (*med.* and *biol.*) to close up and do away with (as a tubular element).—*adj.* **oblit'erated,** effaced : without defined margins.—*n.* **oblitera'tion.**—*adj.* **oblit'erative.** [L. *oblitterāre,* -*ātum*—*ob-*, over, *littera* (*litera*), a letter.]

oblivion, *ō-bliv'i-ən*, *n.* forgetfulness : a state of having forgotten : amnesty : a state of being forgotten.—*adj.* **obliv'ious,** forgetful : prone to forget : causing, or associated with, forgetfulness : (*coll.*) raptly or absent-mindedly unaware : ignoring : (*rare*) forgotten.—*adv.* **obliv'iously.**—*ns.* **obliv'iousness ; obliviscence** (*ob-li-vis'əns*), forgetfulness : forgetting. [L. *oblīviō,* -*ōnis*, from the root of *oblīvīscī,* to forget.]

oblong, *ob'long*, *adj.* long in one way : longer than broad.—*n.* a rectangle longer than broad : any oblong figure, whether angular or rounded : (*bot.*) nearly elliptical, with sides nearly parallel, ends blunted, two to four times as long as broad. [L. *oblongus*—*ob-* (force obscure), and *longus*, long.]

obloquy, *ob'lə-kwi*, *n.* reproachful language : censure : calumny : disgrace. [L. *obloquium*—*ob*, against, *loquī*, to speak.]

obmutescent, *ob-mū-tes'ənt*, *adj.* speechless : persistently silent.—*n.* **obmutesc'ence.** [L. *obmūtēscēns,* -*entis*, pr.p. of *obmūtēscēre*, to become dumb —*ob-*, intens., *mūtus*, dumb.]

obnoxious, *ob-nok'shəs*, *adj.* liable (to hurt, punishment, or censure) : (*obs.*) subject to the authority : exposed : objectionable : offensive : (*erron.*) noxious, hurtful.—*adv.* **obnox'iously.**—*n.* **obnox'iousness.** [L. *obnoxius*—*ob*, exposed to, *noxa*, hurt.]

obnubilation, *ob-nū-bi-lā'shən*, *n.* clouding : darkening.—*v.t.* **obnū'bilate.** [L. *obnūbilāre*, to cloud over—L. *ob-*, over, *nūbilus*, cloudy.]

oboe, *ō'bō*, *ō'boi*, *ō'bō-ā*, *n.* a double-reed treble wood-wind instrument : an organ stop of similar tone.—*n.* **o'böist,** a player on the oboe.—**oboe d'amore** (*ō'bō-ā dä-mō'rä*; It., oboe of love), an old oboe a minor third lower ; **oboe di caccia** (*dē-kät'chä*; of the chase), an obsolete alto or tenor oboe. [It. *oboe*—Fr. *hautbois*; see **hautbois.**]

obol, *ob'ol*, *n.* in ancient Greece, the sixth part of a drachma in weight, or in money (about 1½d.).— *adj.* **ob'olary,** extremely poor.—*n.* **ob'olus** (L.), an obol : in the Middle Ages applied to various small coins, as the English halfpenny :—*pl.* **ob'oli** (*-ī*). [Gr. *obolos.*]

obovate, *ob-ō'vāt*, *adj.* (*bot.*) egg-shaped in outline, with the narrow end next the base.—*adv.* **obō'vately.**—*adj.* **obō'void,** solidly obovate. [Pfx. *ob-*, with conventional sense of reversed, and **ovate.**]

obreption, *ob-rep'shən*, *n.* (*obs.*) surprising by stealth : (*law*) obtaining or seeking to obtain a gift, &c., by false statement—different both in sense and in etymology from *subreption.*—*adj.* **obreptitious** (*-tish'əs*). [L. *obreptiō,* -*ōnis*—*ob*, in the way of, *rēpere*, to creep.]

obscene, *ob-sēn'*, *adj.* foul : filthy : indecent : disgusting : ill-omened.—*adv.* **obscene'ly.**—*ns.* **obscene'ness, obscenity** (*-sen'* or *-sēn'*). [L. *ob-scēnus.*]

obscure, *ob-skūr'*, *adj.* dark : not distinct : not easily understood : not clear, legible, or perspicuous : unknown : hidden : inconspicuous : lowly : unknown to fame : living or enveloped in darkness. —*n.* darkness : an obscure place : indistinctness. —*v.t.* to darken : to dim : to hide : to make less plain : to render doubtful.—*v.i.* to hide : to darken.—*ns.* **ob'scūrant** (*-ant*, or *ob-skūr'ənt*), one who labours to prevent enlightenment or reform ; **obscūrant'ism** (or *-skūr'*), opposition to inquiry or reform ; **obscūrant'ist** (or *-skūr*), an obscurant. —*adj.* pertaining to obscurantism.—*n.* **obscūrā'tion,** the act of obscuring or state of being obscured. —*adv.* **obscūre'ly.**—*ns.* **obscūre'ment ; obscūre'ness ; obscūr'er ; obscūr'ity,** state or quality of being obscure : darkness : an obscure place, point, or condition. [Fr. *obscur*—L. *obscūrus*—*ob-*, over, and the root seen in L. *scūtum,* shield, Gr. *skeuē,* covering.]

obsecrate, *ob'si-krāt*, *v.t.* to beseech : to implore.— *n.* **obsecrā'tion,** supplication : one of the clauses in the Litany beginning with *by.* [L. *obsecrāre,* -*ātum*, to entreat ; *ob*, before, *sacrāre*—*sacer,* sacred.]

obsequent, *ob'si-kwənt*, *adj.* flowing in a contrary direction to the original slope of the land, parallel to the *consequent* and perpendicular to the *subsequent* streams. [L. *ob*, face to face with, *sequēns,* -*entis*, pr.p. of *sequī*, to follow.]

obsequies, *ob'si-kwiz*, *n.pl.* funeral rites and solemnities :—*sing.* (*rare*) **ob'sequy** (*Milt.* obsequie). —*adjs.* **obsequial** (*-sē'kwi-əl*), **obse'quious** (*Shak.* ; see also next word). [L.L. *obsequiae,* a confusion of L. *exsequiae,* funeral rites, and *obsequium* ; see next word.]

obsequious, *ob-sē'kwi-əs*, *adj.* (*orig.*) compliant, obedient, dutiful : (now) compliant to excess : fawning.—*adv.* **obsē'quiously.**—*n.* **obsē'quiousness.** [L. *obsequiōsus,* compliant, *obsequium,* compliance—*ob-*, towards, *sequī*, to follow.]

observe, *ob-zərv'*, *v.t.* to keep in view : to watch : to subject to systematic watching : to regard attentively : to direct watchful and critical attention to with a view to ascertaining a fact : to ascertain by such attention : to notice : to attend to : to remark in words : to comply with : to act according to : to heed and to carry out in practice : to keep with ceremony : to celebrate : to keep (as silence) : (*Shak.*) to be deferential to, to humour.—*v.i.* to take observations : to make remarks.—*n.* (*Scot.*) a remark.—*adj.* **observ'able,** discernible, perceptible : worthy of note : notable : to be observed.— *n.* **observ'ableness.**—*adv.* **observ'ably.**—*ns.* **observ'ance,** the keeping of, or acting according to, a law, duty, custom, ceremony : the keeping with ceremony or according to custom : a custom observed or to be observed : a rule of religious life : an order or company accepting it (esp. the Observants), or their house : a deferential act or treatment : (*Shak.*) watchful heed : (now *rare*) observation ; **observ'ancy,** observance : observation : a house of Observants.—*adj.* **observ'ant,** observing : having powers of observing and noting : taking notice : keeping an observance : carefully attentive.—*n.* (*Shak.*) an obsequious attendant : one strict to comply with a custom, &c.—*ns.* **Observ'ant** or **Observ'antine** (*-ən-tin,* -*tēn*), a Franciscan friar of stricter rule.—*adv.* **observ'antly.**—*n.* **observā'tion,** act of observing : habit, practice, or faculty of seeing and noting : attention : the act of recognising and noting phenomena as they occur in nature, as distinguished from *experiment* : a reading of an instrument : the result of such observing : watching : (now *rare*) observance : that which is observed : a remark : the fact of being observed.— *adj.* **observā'tional,** consisting of, or containing, observations or remarks : derived from observation, as distinguished from *experiment.*—*adv.* **observā'tionally.**—*adj.* **observ'ative,** observant : observational.—*ns.* **ob'servātor** (now *rare* or *obs.*), one who observes in any sense : a remarker ; **ob-**

serv'atory, a building or station for making astronomical and physical observations : a viewpoint : a spying place ; **observ'er,** one who observes in any sense : one whose function it is to take observations : an airman who accompanies a pilot to observe : an air-force officer of like rank with an army lieutenant or a naval sub-lieutenant : one deputed to watch proceedings.—*adj.* **observ'ing,** habitually taking notice : attentive.—*adv.* **observ'ingly.—observation car,** a railway carriage designed to allow passengers to view scenery. [Fr. *observer*—L. *observāre, -ātum*—*ob*, towards, *servāre,* to keep.]

obsess, *ob-ses', v.t.* (*obs.*) to besiege : to beset : to occupy the thoughts of obstinately and persistently. —*n.* **obsession** (*-sesh'ǝn*), (*obs.*) a siege : persistent attack, esp. of an evil spirit : the state of being so molested from without—opp. to *possession,* or control by an evil spirit from within : morbid persistence of an idea in the mind, against one's will : a fixed idea.—*adj.* **obsess'ional.**—*n.* **obsess'ionist,** one who is obsessed by a fixed idea.—*adj.* **obsess'ive,** relating to obsession : obsessing. [L. *obsidēre, obsessum,* to besiege.]

obsidian, *ob-sid'i-ǝn, n.* a vitreous acid volcanic rock resembling bottle-glass. [From *obsidiānus,* a false reading of L. *obsiānus* (*lapis*), a stone found by one *Obsius* (wrongly *Obsidius*) in Ethiopia, according to Pliny.]

obsidional, *ob-sid'i-ǝn-ǝl, adj.* pertaining to a siege. —Also **obsid'ionary.** [L. *obsidiō, -ōnis,* a siege ; see **obsess.**]

obsign, *ob-sīn',* **obsignate,** *ob-sig'nāt, vs.t.* to seal, confirm.—*n.* **obsigna'tion** (*-sig-*).—*adj.* **obsig'natory.** [L. *obsignāre,* to seal up—*ob-,* over, *signāre,* to mark, seal.]

obsolescent, *ob-sǝ-les'ǝnt, adj.* going out of use : in course of disappearance : tending to become obsolete.—*v.i.* **obsolesce** (*-les'*), to be in process of going out of use.—*n.* **obsolesc'ence.**—*adj.* **ob'solete** (*-lēt*), gone out of use : antiquated : no longer functional or fully developed.—*adv.* **ob'soletely.**—*ns.* **ob'soleteness ; obsolē'tion** (*rare*) ; **ob'soletism.** [L. *obsolēscĕre, obsolētum,* perh. from pfx. *obs-* and the root of *alēre,* to nourish.]

obstacle, *ob'stǝ-kl, n.* anything that stands in the way of or hinders advance.—*adj.* (*Shak.*) stubborn. —**obstacle race,** a race in which obstacles have to be passed. [Fr.,—L. *obstāculum*—*ob,* in the way of, *stāre,* to stand.]

obstetric, -al, *ob-stet'rik, -ǝl, adjs.* pertaining to midwifery.—*ns.* **obstetrician** (*ob-sti-trish'ǝn*), one skilled in practising, or qualified to practise, obstetrics ; **obstet'rics,** midwifery. [L. *obstetrīcius* (the *-īc-* confused with the suffix *-ic*)—*obstetrīx, -īcis,* a midwife—*ob,* before, *stāre,* to stand.]

obstinate, *ob'sti-nāt, adj.* blindly or excessively firm : unyielding : stubborn : not easily subdued or remedied.—*n.* **ob'stinacy** (*-nǝ-si*), **ob'stinateness.**—*adv.* **ob'stinately.** [L. *obstināre, -ātum*—*ob,* in the way of, *stanāre* (found in compounds), a form of *stāre,* to stand.]

obstipation, *ob-sti-pā'shǝn, n.* extreme constipation. [L. *ob,* against, *stīpāre, -ātum,* to press.]

obstreperous, *ob-strep'ǝ-rǝs, adj.* making a loud noise : clamorous : noisy : unruly.—*v.t.* **obstrep'erate** (*Sterne*).—*adv.* **obstrep'erously.**—*n.* **obstrep'erousness.** [L. *obstreperus*—*ob,* before, against, *strepĕre,* to make a noise.]

obstriction, *ob-strik'shǝn, n.* obligation. [L. *ob-stringĕre, obstrictum,* to bind up.]

obstropalous, obstropulous, *ob-strop'ǝ-lǝs, -ū-lǝs,* vulgar forms of **obstreperous.**

obstruct, *ob-strukt', v.t.* to block up : to hinder from passing or progressing : to shut off : to hamper.—*v.i.* to be an obstruction : to practise obstruction.—*ns.* **obstruc'ter** (*rare*) ; **obstruc'tion,** act of obstructing : a state of being obstructed : that which hinders progress or action : an obstacle : opposition by dilatory tactics, as in a legislative assembly ; **obstruc'tionist,** a politician who practises obstruction.—*adj.* **obstruct'ive,** tending to obstruct : hindering.—*n.* a hindrance : a hinderer of progress.—*adv.* **obstruct'ively.**—*n.* **obstruct'or.** —*adj.* **obstruent** (*ob'stroo-ǝnt*), obstructing : block-

ing up.—*n.* anything that obstructs, esp. in the passages of the body. [L. *obstruĕre, obstructum*—*ob,* in the way of, *struĕre, structum,* to pile up, build.]

obtain, *ob-tān', v.t.* to get : to procure by effort : to gain : (*arch.*) to reach : (*obs.*) to hold, occupy. —*v.i.* to be established : to continue in use : to hold good : to prevail : (*rare*) to succeed : (*obs.*) to attain.—*adj.* **obtain'able.**—*ns.* **obtain'er ; obtain'ment ; obtention** (*-ten'shǝn*), getting. [Fr. *obtenir*—L. *obtinēre,* to occupy—*ob,* against, *tenēre,* to hold.]

obtect, *ob-tekt',* **obtect'ed,** *adjs.* having wings and legs immovably pressed against the body in a hard chitinous case, as many insect pupae. [L. *obtegĕre, obtectum,* to cover over—*ob-,* over, *tegĕre,* to cover.]

obtemper, *ob-tem'pǝr, v.t.* to yield obedience to.— Also *v.i.* (with *to, unto*).—Also **obtem'perate.** [L. *obtemperāre, -ātum*—*ob,* before, *temperāre,* to restrain oneself.]

obtend, *ob-tend', v.t.* (*obs.*) to hold out in opposition : to put forward, allege. [L. *obtendĕre,* to stretch before—*ob,* in front of, *tendĕre,* to stretch.]

obtest, *ob-test', v.t.* to call to witness : to adjure.— *v.i.* to protest.—*n.* **obtestā'tion.** [L. *obtestārī,* to call as a witness—*ob,* before, *testis,* a witness.]

obtrude, *ob-trōōd', v.t.* to thrust forward, or upon one, unduly or unwelcomely.—*v.i.* to thrust oneself forward.—*ns.* **obtrud'er ; obtrud'ing ; obtrusion** (*-trōō'zhǝn*), an unwanted thrusting in or forward, or upon one.—*adj.* **obtrusive** (*-trōō'siv*), disposed to thrust oneself in or forward : unduly prominent or projecting.—*adv.* **obtru'sively.**—*n.* **obtru'siveness.** [L. *obtrūdĕre*—*ob,* against, *trūdĕre, trūsum,* to thrust.]

obtruncate, *ob-trung'kāt, v.t.* to cut or lop off the head of. [L. *obtruncāre, -ātum,* to cut in pieces, mutilate—*ob-,* intens., *truncāre,* cut off.]

obtund, *ob-tund', v.t.* to blunt or dull : to deaden.— *adj.* **obtund'ent,** dulling.—*n.* an application to deaden irritation. [L. *obtundĕre,* to strike upon— *ob,* against, *tundĕre,* to thump.]

obturate, *ob'tū-rāt, v.t.* to stop up.—*ns.* **obturā'tion,** stopping up : in gunnery, stopping of a hole to prevent the escape of gas ; **ob'turator,** a structure or device that closes a cavity : (*anat.*) the structures closing a large opening in the hip-bone. [L. *obtūrāre, -ātum,* to stop up ; etymology obscure.]

obtuse, *ob-tūs', adj.* blunt : not pointed : (*bot.*) blunt or rounded at the tip : (*geom.*) greater than a right angle : dull : dull-witted : insensitive.— *adjs.* **obtuse'-ang'led, -ang'ular,** having an angle greater than a right angle.—*adv.* **obtuse'ly.**—*ns.* **obtuse'ness, obtus'ity.** [L. *obtūsus*—pa.p. of *obtundĕre ;* cf. **obtund.**]

obumbrate, *ob-um'brāt, v.t.* to overshadow.—*n.* **obumbrā'tion.** [L. *obumbrāre, -ātum*—*ob,* in the way of, *umbra,* shadow.]

obvention, *ob-ven'shǝn, n.* (*obs.*) any incidental occurrence, or advantage, esp. a fee. [L. *obvenīre, -ventum,* to come to meet, come by chance—*ob,* face to face with, *venīre,* to come.]

obverse, *ob'vǝrs, ob-vǝrs', adj.* turned towards one : complemental, constituting the opposite aspect of the same fact : (*bot.*) having the base narrower than the apex : (*log.*) got by obversion.—*n.* **obverse** (*ob'vǝrs*), the side of a coin containing the head, or principal symbol : the face or side of anything normally presented to view : a counterpart or opposite aspect : (*log.*) a proposition obtained from another by obversion.—*adv.* **obverse'ly.**—*n.* **obver'sion,** the act of turning a thing toward one : (*log.*) a species of immediate inference where the contradictory of the original predicate is predicated of the original subject, the quality of the proposition being changed—e.g. to infer from All A is B that No A is not B—also called *permutation* and *equipollence.*—*v.t.* **obvert',** to turn in the direction of, or face to face with, something : to infer the obverse of. [L. *obversus,* turned against, or towards —*ob-,* towards, *vertĕre,* to turn.]

obviate, *ob'vi-āt, v.t.* (*obs.*) to meet on the way : to prevent or dispose of in advance : to forestall. [L. *obviāre, -ātum*—*ob,* in the way of, *viāre, viātum,* to go—*via,* a way.]

Neutral vowels in unaccented syllables : *el'ǝ-mǝnt, in'fǝnt, ran'dǝm*

obvious, *ob'vi-əs, adj.* meeting one in the way: easily discovered or understood: clearly or plainly evident.—*adv.* **ob'viously.**—*n.* **ob'viousness.** [L. *obvius*—*ob, via;* see foregoing.]

obvolute, -d, *ob'və-l(y)ōōt,* or *-vo-, -id, adjs.* (*bot.*) arranged so that each leaf of a pair is conduplicate and enfolds one-half of the other.—*adj.* **obvolvent** (*-vol'vənt*), enwrapping: (*entom.*) curved downward or inward. [L. *obvolūtus,* pa.p., and *obvolvēns, -entis,* pr.p., of *obvolvĕre,* to enwrap—*ob-,* over, *volvĕre, volūtum,* to roll.]

oca, *ō'kä, n.* a South American wood-sorrel with edible tubers. [Sp., from Quechua.]

ocarina, *ok-ə-rē'nä, n.* a fluty-toned bird-shaped musical toy, orig. of terra-cotta. [It., dim. of *oca,* a goose.]

Occamism, *ok'əm-izm, n.* the doctrine of the nominalist schoolman, William of *Occam* or *Ockham* (*c.* 1270-*c.* 1349).—*n.* **Occ'amist.**—**Occam's razor**, the principle that entities are not to be multiplied beyond necessity.

occamy, *ok'ə-mi, n.* a silvery alloy. [**alchemy.**]

occasion, *o-kā'zhən, n.* a case of something happening: a juncture: (*Shak.*) the course of events: a suitable juncture: a special time or season: a chance of bringing about something desired: opportunity: an event which, although not the cause, determines the time at which another happens: a reason, pretext, or excuse: requirement: need: (usu. in *pl.*) business: (in *pl.; obs.*) necessary bodily functions: a special ceremony, celebration, or event: (*Scot.* formerly) communion service: (*Shak.*) doing, occasioning, matter of responsibility.—*v.t.* to give occasion or rise to: to cause: (*obs.*) to accustom.—*adj.* **occā'sional,** falling in the way or happening: occurring now and then: resulting from accident: produced on or for some special event or for special occasions: constituting the occasion.—*ns.* **occā'sionalism,** the Cartesian explanation of the apparent interaction of mind and matter by the direct intervention of God on the occasion of certain changes occurring in one or the other; **occā'sionalist; occāsional'ity.—*adv.* occā'sionally,** (*obs.*) casually: on or for an occasion: now and then.—*n.* **occā'sioner.—occasional cause,** the event which in the Cartesian philosophy is only the occasion, not the true cause: that by which the efficient cause comes into operation; **occasional conformist** (*hist.*), a Dissenter who qualified for office by conforming to the Church of England upon occasion; **occasional table,** a small portable ornamental table; **occasioned by** (*obs.*), owing to; **on occasion,** in case of need: as opportunity offers: from time to time; **take occasion,** to take advantage of an opportunity. [L. *occāsiō, -ōnis,* opportunity—*ob,* in the way of, *cadĕre, cāsum,* to fall.]

Occident, occident, *ok'si-dənt, n.* the quarter of the sky where the heavenly bodies set: the west—opp. to *Orient.—adj.* **Occidental, occidental** (*-dənt'l*), western: characteristic of the West (esp. Europe, America, the Western United States): relatively less precious, as a gem (because the best stones were presumed to come from the East).—*n.* a westerner: a language invented by Edgar de Wahl (1922).—*v.t.* **occiden'talise,** to cause to conform to western ideas or customs.—*ns.* **Occiden'talism,** the culture and ways of Occidental peoples; **Occiden'talist,** a student of Occidental languages: an Oriental who favours western ideas, customs, &c.,—*adv.* **occiden'tally.—occidental topaz,** a semiprecious yellow quartz; **occidental turquoise,** odontolite. [L. *occidēns, -entis,* setting, pr.p. of *occidĕre—ob,* towards, down, *cadĕre,* to fall.]

occiput, *ok'si-put, n.* the back of the head or skull.—*adj.* **occip'ital,** pertaining to the back of the head.—*n.* the occipital bone, the bone at the back of the skull.—*adv.* **occip'itally.** [L. *occiput—ob,* over against, *caput,* head.]

occlude, *o-klōōd', v.t.* to shut in or out: to cut or shut off: to stop (as a passage, cavity, or opening): to bring together (as the teeth or eyelids): to absorb or retain (as a gas by a metal or other solid).—*v.i.* to bite or close together (as the teeth).—*adj.*

occlu'dent, serving to occlude: occluding.—*n.* that which occludes.—*adj.* **occlu'sal** (*-səl*), pertaining to occlusion of teeth.—*n.* **occlu'sion** (*-zhən*), a closing of an opening, passage, or cavity: the act of occluding or absorbing: the bite or mode of meeting of the teeth.—*adj.* **occlu'sive** (*-siv*), serving to close: characterised by occlusion.—*n.* (*phon.*) a sound produced by closing the breath passage.—*n.* **occlu'sor,** that which closes, esp. a muscle for closing an opening. [L. *occlūdĕre, -clūsum—ob,* in the way of, *claudĕre,* to shut.]

occult, *ok-ult', ok'ult, adj.* hidden: (of a line, now *rare*) faint, or dotted, or to be rubbed out later: secret: esoteric: unknown: (*obs.*) not discovered without test or experiment: beyond the range of sense: transcending the bounds of natural knowledge: mysterious: magical: supernatural.—*v.t.* **occult** (*ok-ult'*), to hide: to hide by interposing.—*v.i.* to become temporarily invisible (as a lighthouse light).—*n.* **occulta'tion,** a concealing, esp. of one of the heavenly bodies by another: state of being hid.—*adj.* **occult'ed.**—*ns.* **occult'ism,** the doctrine or study of things hidden or mysterious—theosophy, &c.; **occult'ist,** one who believes in occult things.—*adv.* **occult'ly.**—*n.* **occult'ness.—occult sciences,** alchemy, astrology, magic, palmistry, &c. [L. *occultus,* pa.p. of *occulĕre,* to hide—*ob-,* over, and the root of *cēlāre,* to hide.]

occupy, *ok'ū-pī, v.t.* (*obs.*) to take possession of: to capture: to hold or have in possession: to take up, as a space, time, &c.: to tenant: to busy: (*B.*) to lay out in trade: (*obs.*) to cohabit with.—*v.i.* (*obs.*) to hold possession: (*obs.*) to trade: (*obs.*) to cohabit:—*pr.p.* **occ'upying;** *pa.t.* and *pa.p.* **occ'upied.**—*ns.* **occ'upance** (*rare*), **occ'upancy,** the act or fact of occupying, or of taking or holding possession: possession: the time during which one occupies; **occ'upant,** one who takes or has possession.—*v.t.* **occ'upāte** (*obs.*), to occupy.—*adj.* (*obs.*) occupied.—*n.* **occupā'tion,** the act of occupying: possession: state of being employed or occupied: that which occupies or takes up one's attention: habitual employment, profession, craft, or trade.—*adj.* occupational.—*adjs.* **occupā'tional,** connected with habitual occupation; **occ'upātive,** held by tenure based on occupation.—*n.* **occ'upier** (*-pī-ər*), one who occupies: an occupant: (*obs.*) one who practises: (*obs.*) a dealer.—**occupational disease,** a disease common among workers engaged in a particular occupation because encouraged by the conditions of that occupation; **occupational therapy,** treatment of a disease (incl. a mental disease) or an injury by a regulated course of suitable work. [Fr. *occuper*—L. *occupāre, -ātum—ob-,* to, on, *capĕre,* to take; the *-y* is unexplained.]

occur, *o-kur', v.i.* (*obs.*) to meet: to be presented, come into mind: to be: to be found: to happen: (of festivals) to fall on the same day:—*pr.p.* **occurr'ing;** *pa.p.* **occurred'.**—*n.* **occurr'ence,** the act or fact of occurring: anything that happens: an event, esp. one unlooked for or unplanned.—*adj.* **occurr'ent,** occurring: happening: turning up: to be found: incidental.—*n.* (*obs.*) one who or that which meets or comes in contact: (*arch.*) an occurrence, an item of news. [L. *occurrĕre—ob,* in the way of, *currĕre,* to run.]

ocean, *ō'shən, n.* the vast expanse of salt water that covers the greater part of the surface of the globe: any one of its great divisions (Atlantic, Pacific, Indian, Arctic, Antarctic; also Southern, German): (*fig.*) any immense expanse or vast quantity.—*adj.* pertaining to the great sea.—*ns.* **o'cean-bā'sin,** the depression in which the waters of an ocean are contained; **o'cean-grey'hound,** a very fast steamer.—*adjs.* **Oceanian** (*ō-shi-ā'ni-ən*), pertaining to *Oceania,* which includes Polynesia, Micronesia, Melanesia, with or without Australasia; **oceanic** (*ō-shi-an'ik*), pertaining to the ocean: found or formed in the ocean or high seas, pelagic: wide like the ocean.—*ns.* **oceanid** (*ō-sē'an-id*), a daughter of Oceanus: an ocean nymph:—*pl.* **oceanides** (*ō-sē-an'id-ēz*); **oceanographer** (*ō-si-ən-og'rə-fər,* or *ō-shən-,* or *ō-shi-ən-*).—*adj.* **oceanographic** (*ō-si-an-ō-graf'ik,* or *ō-shən-,* or *ō-shi-an-*).—*ns.* **oceanog'raphy,** the scientific description of the ocean; **oceanol′ogy; o′cean-stream′** (*Milt.*), the river Oceanus (Okeanos), supposed to encircle the land of the world.—**oceanic islands**, islands far from the mainland. [O.Fr. *occean*—L. *Ŏcĕănus* —Gr. *Ōkĕănos*, the river, or its god.]

ocellus, ō-sel′əs, *n.* a simple eye or eye-spot, distinguished from a compound eye, in insects and other lower animals: an eyelike or ringed spot of colour :—*pl.* **ocell′ī.**—*adjs.* **ocell′ar**, of, or of the nature of, an ocellus or ocelli; **ocell′ate** (or *os′əl-āt*), **-d**, eyelike and ringed : having an eyelike spot or spots.—*n.* **ocellation** (*os-ə-lā′shən*). [L. *ŏcellus*, dim. of *oculus*, an eye.]

ocelot, ō′- or o′si-lot, *n.* an American cat (*Felis pardalis*), like a small leopard.—*adj.* **o′celoid.** [Mex. *ocelotl*, jaguar.]

och, ohh, *interj.* (*Scot.*) expressing impatience, or contemptuous dismissal—pshaw, tut : (in *Ireland* and part of *Scotland*) expressing regret.

ochidore, ok′i-dōr, *n.* Kingsley's name (not otherwise known) for a shore-crab.

ochlocracy, ok-lok′rə-si, *n.* mob-rule.—*n.* **och′lo-crat** (-lō-krat). — *adjs.* **ochlocrat′ic, -al.** — *adv.* **ochlocrat′ically.** [Gr. *ochlokratiā* — *ochlos*, a crowd, *kratos*, power.]

ochone. See ohone.

Ochotona, ok-ō-tō′nä, *n.* the pika genus. [Mongol *ochodona.*]

ochre, ō′kər, *n.* a native pigment composed of fine clay and an iron oxide (limonite in yellow ochre, haematite in red): a paint manufactured from it, used for colouring walls, &c.: an earthy metallic oxide of various kinds: (*slang*) money, esp. gold. —*v.t.* to mark or colour with ochre.—*adjs.* **ochrā′-ceous, ochreous** (ō′kri-əs), **ochroid, o′chrous** (sometimes **o′cherous**), **o′chry** (also **o′chrey, o′chery**), consisting of, containing, or resembling ochre; **ochroleu′cous** (Gr. *leukos*, white), yellow-ish white. [Fr. *ocre*—L. *ōchra*—Gr. *ōchrā*—*ōchros*, pale yellow.]

o′clock. See clock.

ocrea (commonly **ochrea**), ok′ri-ä, *n.* (*bot.*) a sheath formed of two stipules united round a stem :—*pl.* oc(h)′reae (-ē).—*adj.* oc(h)′reate. [L. *ocrea*, a legging.]

oct-, octa-. See octo-.

octachord, ok′tə-kord, *n.* an eight-stringed instrument : a diatonic series of eight tones.—*adj.* **octachord′al.** [Gr. *oktachordos*—*chordē*, a gut string.]

octad, ok′tad, *n.* a set of eight things.—*adj.* **octad′ic.** [Gr. *oktas, -ados.*]

octagon, ok′tə-gon, *n.* a plane figure of eight sides and eight angles.—Also *adj.*—*adj.* **octagonal** (-*tag′ən-əl*).—*adv.* **octag′onally.** [Gr. *oktagōnos*, eight-angled—*gōniā*, an angle.]

octahedron, ok-tə-hē′dron, *n.* a solid bounded by eight plane faces :—*pl.* **octahē′drons, octahē′dra.** —*adj.* **octahē′dral.**—*n.* **octahē′drite**, anatase, crystallising in square bipyramids. [Gr. *oktaĕdron* —*hedrā*, a base.]

octamerous, ok-tam′ər-əs, *adj.* having parts in eights. [Gr. *meros*, part.]

octameter, ok-tam′i-tər, *n.* a line of eight feet or measures. [Gr. *metron*, measure.]

octandrous, ok-tan′drəs, *adj.* (*bot.*) having eight stamens.—*n.pl.* **Octan′dria**, a Linnaean class of plants with eight stamens.—*adj.* **octan′drian.** [Gr. *oktō*, eight, *anēr, andros*, a man (male).]

octane, ok′tān, *n.* any of a group of eighteen isomeric hydrocarbons (C_8H_{18}), eighth in the methane series. — **octane number**, the percentage by volume of so-called iso-octane in a mixture with normal heptane which has the same knocking characteristics as the motor fuel under test. [Gr. *oktō*, eight.]

octangular, ok-tang′gū-lər, *adj.* having eight angles.

octant, ok′tənt, *n.* an arc of one-eighth of the circumference of a circle : a sector of one-eighth of a circle : an angle-measuring instrument with such an arc : a division of space or of a solid figure or body divided into eight by three planes, usu. at right angles : (*astron.*) a position 45° distant from another position, esp. of the moon from conjunction or opposition.—*adj.* **octantal** (-*tant′əl*). [L. *octāns, -antis*, an eighth.]

octapla, ok′tə-plä, *n.* (treated as *sing.*) a book of eight (esp. Biblical) parallel texts. [Gr. *oktaplā* (contracted pl.), eightfold.]

octaploid, ok′tə-ploid, *adj.* eightfold : (*biol.*) having eight times the basic number of chromosomes.— *n.* a cell, organism, or form with eight sets of chromosomes.—*n.* **oc′taploidy**, the condition of being octaploid.—Also **oc′toploid**, &c. [Gr. *oktaploos*, eightfold, *eidos*, form.]

octapody, ok-tap′ə-di, *n.* (*pros.*) a line of eight feet. —*adj.* **octapodic** (*ok-tə-pod′ik*).—*n.* **octastich** (*ok′tə-stik*), a strophe of eight lines—also **octastichon** (*ok-tas′ti-kon*).—*adj.* **octas′tichous**, (*bot.*) in eight rows.—*adj.* **octastroph′ic**, consisting of eight strophes. [Gr. *pous, podos*, foot, *stichos*, row, line, *strophē*, strophe.]

octaroon. Same as **octoroon.**

octastyle, ok′tə-stīl, *adj.* (*archit.*) having eight columns at the end.—*n.* a building or portico so designed.—Also **oc′tostyle.** [Gr. *oktastȳlos*— *stȳlos*, a column.]

octave, ok′tiv, *-tāv, n.* a set of eight : the last day of eight beginning with a church festival : the eight days from a festival to its octave : (*mus.*) an eighth, or an interval of twelve semitones : a note or sound an eighth above (or below) another : the range of notes or keys from any one to its octave : an organ stop sounding an octave higher than the keys indicate : a cask containing the eighth part of a pipe of wine : an eight-lined stanza : the first eight lines of a sonnet.—*adj.* consisting of eight (esp. lines) : in octaves : sounding an octave higher.—*adj.* **octāv′al**, pertaining to an octave : based on the number eight.—*n.* **oc′tave-flute′**, the piccolo, an octave above the ordinary flute.— **great octave**, the bass octave, conventionally represented by capital letters, from C, on the second line below the bass stave, up; **small octave**, the tenor octave, from the second space in the bass. [Fr.,—L. *octāvus*, eighth—*octō.*]

octavo, ok-tā′vō, *adj.* having eight leaves to the sheet : (conventionally) of a size so obtained, whether so folded or not.—*n.* a book printed on sheets so folded : (conventionally) a book of such a size : contracted 8vo—usually meaning a medium octavo about 6 × 9½ inches :—*pl.* **octā′vos.** [L. *in octāvō*, in the eighth—*octāvus*, eighth.]

octennial, ok-ten′yəl, *-i-əl, adj.* happening every eighth year : lasting eight years.—*adv.* **octenn′-ially.** [L. *octennium*, ten years—*annus*, year.]

octet, octett, octette, ok-tet′, *n.* a group of eight (lines of verse, electrons, musicians, &c.) : a composition for eight musicians.

octillion, ok-til′yən, *n.* a million raised to the eighth power, expressed by a unit with forty-eight ciphers : (*U.S.*, as in France) one thousand raised to the ninth power, i.e. a unit with twenty-seven ciphers. [Modelled on **million**—L. *octō*, eight.]

octingenary, ok-tin-jē′nə-ri, *n.* an eight-hundredth anniversary.—Also **octingentenary** (-*jen-tē′*). [L. *octingēnārius*, 800 each.]

octo-, oct′tō, in composition, eight.—Also **oct-, oc′ta-** (in some words from Greek). [Gr. *oktō* and L. *octō.*]

October, ok-tō′bər, *n.* the tenth month, eighth in the Roman calendar : strong ale brewed in that month.—*n.* **Octo′brist**, a member of a Russian moderate liberal party who made the tsar's manifesto of October 1905 their basis. [L. *octōber*—*octō.*]

octocentenary, ok-tō-sen′tin-ə-ri, or *-sin-tēn′*, or *-sin-ten′, n.* an eight-hundredth anniversary.

octodecimo, ok-tō-des′i-mō, *adj.* having eighteen leaves to the sheet : contracted **18mo**, often read **eighteenmo.**—*n.* a book with sheets so folded. [L. *octodecim*, eighteen ; cf. **octavo.**]

octofid, ok′tō-fid, *adj.* (*bot.*) cleft into eight segments. [L. *octō*, and the root of *findĕre*, to cleave.]

octogenarian, ok-tō-ji-nā′ri-ən, *n.* one who is eighty years old, or between eighty and ninety.—Also *adj.*—*adj.* **octogenary** (*ok-tō-jē′nəri, ok-toj′i-nə-ri*). [L. *octōgēnārius*, pertaining to eighty.]

octogynous, ok-toj′i-nəs, *adj.* (*bot.*) having eight pistils or styles.—*n.pl.* **Octogyn′ia**, in various Linnaean classes, an order with eight pistils. [Gr. *oktō*, eight, *gynē*, wife.]

Neutral vowels in unaccented syllables : *el′ə-mənt, in′fənt, ran′dəm*

octohedron. Same as **octahedron.**

octonary, *ok'tə-nə-ri, adj.* based on the number eight.—*n.* a set of eight.—*adj.* **octonarian** (*ok-tō-nā'ri-ən*), having eight feet.—*n.* a line of eight feet. [L. *octōnārius.*]

octonocular, *ok-tō-nok'ū-lər, adj.* having eight eyes. [L. *octōnī,* eight at a time, *oculus,* eye.]

octopetalous, *ok-tō-pet'ə-ləs, adj.* having eight petals.

octoploid. Same as **octaploid.**

octopod, *ok'tō-pod, adj.* eight-footed or eight-armed. —*n.* an octopus or other member of the **Octopoda** (*-top'*), an order of dibranchiate cephalopods.— *adj.* **octop'odous.** [See next.]

octopus, *ok'tō-pəs,* or *ok-tō'pəs, n.* a genus (*Octo'pus*) of eight-armed cephalopods : any eight-armed cephalopod :—*pl.* **oc'topuses,** sometimes **octop'odēs** (octopi is wrong). [Gr. *oktapous—oktō,* eight, *pous, podos,* foot.]

octoroon, octaroon, *ok-tə-rōōn', n.* the offspring of a quadroon and a white : one who has one-eighth negro blood. [Modelled on **quadroon**—L. *octō,* eight.]

octosepalous, *ok-tō-sep'ə-ləs, adj.* having eight sepals.

octostichous, octostyle. Same as **octastichous, octastyle.**

octosyllabic, *ok'tō-sil-ab'ik, adj.* consisting of eight syllables : a line of eight syllables.—*n.* **octosyllable** (*-sil'ə-bl*), a word of eight syllables.

octroi, *ok-trwä, n.* (*obs.*) a commercial privilege, as of exclusive trade : a toll or tax levied at the gates of a city on articles brought in : the place where or officials to whom it is paid. [Fr.,—*octroyer,* to grant, from some such L.L. form as *auctōrizāre,* to authorise—L. *auctor,* author.]

octuor, *ok-tū-or, n.* an octet. [Modelled on L. *quatuor,* four, from *octō.*]

octuple, *ok'tū-pl, adj.* eightfold.—*v.t.* or *v.i.* to multiply by eight.—*n.* **oc'tūplet** (*mus.*), a group of eight notes to be played in the time of six. [L. *octuplus* ; cf. **duple, double.**]

ocular, *ok'ū-lər, adj.* pertaining to the eye or to vision : formed in, addressed to, or known by, the eye : received by actual sight : eyelike.—*n.* an eyepiece : (*facet.*) an eye.—*adv.* **oc'ularly.**—*adjs.* **oc'ulate, -d,** having eyes, or spots like eyes.— *n.* **oc'ulist,** one skilled in diseases of the eye. [L. *oculus,* the eye.]

od, *od* or *ōd, n.* Reichenbach's arbitrary name for a force supposed by him to manifest itself in light, magnetism, chemical action, hypnotism, &c.—*adj.* **o'dic.**—*ns.* **od'-force,** od ; **o'dism,** belief in od ; **od'yl(e)** (Gr. *hȳlē,* matter), od ; **od'ylism.**

od, odd, *od, n.* and *interj.* a minced form of **god.**— **od's-bobs,** God's body ; **od's-bodikins,** God's body ; **od's-life,** God's life ; **od's-nouns** (*nownz'*), God's wounds ; **od's-pit'ikins** (*Shak.*), God's pity ; **odzooks'** (same as **gadzooks**).—These are often written without an apostrophe.

odal, odaller. See **udal, udaller.**

odalisque, odalisk, *ō'də-lisk,* **odalique,** *-lik, n.* a female slave in a harem. [Fr.,—Turk. *ōdaliq— ōdah,* a chamber.]

odd, *od, adj.* unpaired : (*Spens.*) not matching : left over : additional : extra : not one of a complete set : one in excess of half the number : left over after a round number has been taken : additional in lower denominations or lower powers of ten : not exactly divisible by two (opp. to *even*) : strange : queer : casual : out-of-the-way : standing apart : (*Shak.*) at variance.—*adv.* (*Shak.*) oddly. —*n.* (*golf*) one stroke above the like : a stroke allowed in handicap : (*whist*) one trick above book : —in *pl.* **odds** (*odz,* sometimes treated as *sing.*), inequality : difference : difference in favour of one against another : more than an even wager : the amount or proportion by which the bet of one exceeds that of another : the chances or probability : advantage : dispute : scraps : miscellaneous pieces, as in the phrase **odds and ends** (perh. orig. meaning points and ends).—*ns.* **odd'-come-short,** a short remnant : (in *pl.*) odds and ends ; **odd'-come-short'ly,** an early day, any time.— *adj.* or *n.* **odd-e'ven** (*Shak.*) apparently, neither one thing nor another, as the time about midnight. —*n.* **odd'fellow,** a member of a secret benevolent society called Oddfellows.— *adj.* **odd'ish.** — *n.* **odd'ity,** the state of being odd or singular : strangeness : a singular person or thing.—*adjs.* **odd'-like** (*Scot.*), odd : odd-looking ; **odd'-look'-ing.**—*adv.* **odd'ly.**—*ns.* **odd'-man,** one employed to do such odd jobs as come up : an umpire : one who has a casting vote ; **odd'-man-out',** the singling out or elimination of one from a number for any purpose : a man who is left out when numbers are made up ; **odd'ment,** something remaining over : one of a broken set—often used in the plural ; **odd'ness** ; **odds'man** (*Scot.*), an umpire or arbiter.—**at odds,** at variance ; **make no odds,** to make no significant difference. [O.N. *oddi,* point, a triangle, odd number ; cf. O.N. *oddr,* O.E. *ord,* point.]

odd. See **od** (2).

ode, *ōd, n.* (*orig.*) a poem intended to be sung : an elaborate lyric, often of some length, generally addressed to somebody or something.—*adj.* **o'dic.** —*n.* **o'dist,** a writer of odes. [Fr. *ode*—Gr. *ōidē,* contr. from *aoidē—aeidein,* to sing.]

odeum, *ō-dē'əm, n.* in ancient Greece a theatre for musical contests, &c. : a concert-hall. — Also **odē'on.** [L. *ōdēum*—Gr. *ōideion.*]

Odin, *ō'din, n.* Woden. [O.N. *Othenn.*]

odium, *ō'di-əm, n.* hatred : offensiveness : blame : reproach attaching : quality of provoking hate.— *adj.* **o'dious,** hateful : offensive : repulsive : causing hatred.—*adv.* **o'diously.**—*n.* **o'diousness.** [L. *ōdium.*]

odometer. See **hodometer.**

Odonata, *ō-don-ā'tä, n.pl.* (*zool.*) the dragonfly order. [Ionic Gr. *odōn,* a tooth.]

odont-, odonto-, *od-ont'-, od'ont-, -ō-, -o'-,* in composition, tooth.—*ns.* **odontalgia** (*-al'ji-ä* ; Gr. *algos,* pain), **odontal'gy,** toothache.—*adjs.* **odontal'gic** ; **odon'tic,** dental.—*ns.* **odont'ist** (*facet.*) a dentist ; **odont'oblast** (Gr. *blastos,* a shoot), a dentine-forming cell ; **odon'tocete** (*-sēt* ; Gr. *kētos,* whale), a toothed whale.—*adj.* **odontogenic** (*-jen'ik*).— *ns.* **odontogeny** (*-oj'i-ni*), the origin and development of teeth ; **Odontoglos'sum** (Gr. *glōssa,* tongue), a tropical American genus of orchids ; **odont'ograph,** an instrument for obtaining approximate curves for gear-teeth ; **odontog'raphy,** description of teeth.—*adj.* **odont'oid,** toothlike.—*n.* **odont'olite** (Gr. *lithos,* stone), bone turquoise or occidental turquoise, a fossil bone or tooth coloured blue with phosphate of iron.—*adjs.* **odontolog'ic, -al.**—*ns.* **odontol'ogist** ; **odontol'ogy,** the science of the teeth ; **odonto'ma,** a tumour arising in connexion with the teeth.—*adjs.* **odonto'matous,** pertaining to odontoma ; **odontophoral** (*-tof'ə-ral* ; Gr. *phoros,* bearing), **odontoph'oran.**—*n.* **odon'tophore** (*-to-fōr*), the rasping apparatus in molluscs —the radula, its support, or the whole apparatus. —*adj.* **odontoph'orous.**—*n.* **Odontoph'orus,** a genus of American quails.—*n.pl.* **odontornithes** (*-or-nī'thēz,* or *-or'ni-thēz* ; Gr. *ornis, ornithos,* bird), fossil birds with teeth (not a natural class).—*adj.* **odontostom'atous** (Gr. *stoma, -atos,* mouth), having biting or toothed jaws. [Gr. *odous, odontos,* a tooth.]

odour, *ō'dər, n.* smell : (*fig.*) savour : repute.— *adjs.* **o'dorant, o'dorate, odorif'erous,** emitting a (usually pleasant) smell.—*adv.* **odorif'erously.** —*n.* **odorif'erousness.**—*adj.* **o'dorous** (sometimes formerly *ōd-ō'rəs*), emitting an odour or scent : sweet-smelling : fragrant.—*adv.* **o'dorously.**—*n.* **o'dorousness.**—*adjs.* **o'doured** ; **o'dourless.**— **in bad odour,** in bad repute ; **the odour of sanctity,** a fragrance after death alleged to be evidence of saintship : facetiously applied to the living who have denied themselves the sensual indulgence of washing. [A.Fr. *odour*—L. *odor, -ōris.*]

odso, *od'sō, interj.* expressing surprise. [For **gadso.**]

odyl(e). See **od** (1).

Odyssey, *od'is-i, n.* a Greek epic poem, ascribed to Homer, describing the ten years' wanderings of *Odysseus* (Ulysses) on his way home from the

Trojan war to Ithaca: a long wandering or tale of wandering.—*adj.* **Odyssē'an.** [Gr. *Odysseia.*]

oe. Same as **oy.**

oecist, *ē'cist,* **oikist,** *oi'kist, n.* (*hist.*) the founder of a colony. [Gr. *oikistēs—oikos,* a house.]

oecology, oecolog'ical, oeconomy, oecumenic, -al, &c. See **ecology, economy, ecumenic.**

oedema, *ē-dē'mā, n.* dropsy: pathological accumulation of fluid in tissue spaces: (*bot.*) an unhealthy mass of swollen parenchyma.—*adj.* **oede'matous.** [Gr. *oidēma, -atos,* swelling.]

Oedipus, *ē'di-pəs, n.* a king of Thebes who solved the Sphinx's riddle and unwittingly killed his father and married his mother.—*adj.* (*irreg.*) **Oedipē'an.—Oedipus complex** (*psych.*), a boy's unconscious rivalry and hostility towards his father. [Gr. *Oidipous,* lit. Swell-foot.]

œil-de-bœuf, *ə'ē-də-bəf, n.* a little round window: an octagonal vestibule at the court of Versailles, hence one elsewhere:—*pl.* **œils-de-bœuf** (*ə'ē-*). [Fr., ox-eye.]

œillade, *ə'ē-yâd,* formerly *āl'yad, il'yad, il'i-ad* (*Shak.* **illiad, eliad**), *n.* (*Shak.*) a glance or wink: an ogle. [Fr. *œillade—œil,* eye.]

oen-, *ēn-,* **oeno-,** *ēn'ō-, ēn-o'-,* in composition, wine.—Also **oin-, oino-.**—*adjs.* **oenan'thic** (Gr. *anthos,* flower), having or imparting the characteristic odour of wine; **oenolog'ical.**—*ns.* **oenol'ogist; oenol'ogy,** the science of wines; **oe'nomancy,** divination from the appearance of wine poured out in libations; **oenomā'nia, dipsomania; oen'-omel** (Gr. *meli,* honey), wine mixed with honey; **oenom'eter,** a hydrometer for measuring the alcoholic strength of wines; **oen'ophil, oenoph'-ilist,** a lover of wine. [Gr. *oinos,* wine.]

Oenothera, *ē-nō-thē'rā,* by some *ē-noth'ə-rā, n.* the evening primrose genus of Onagraceae. [Gr. *oinothēras,* perh. a wrong reading for *onothēras,* a plant whose roots smelt of wine, perh. oleander.]

o'er, *ōr* (*Scot. owr*; also **owre, ower**), a shortened form of **over.** For compounds, see **over-.**

o'ercome, *owr'kum, n.* (*Scot.*) the burden of a song: overplus.—*ns.* **o'er'lay,** a large cravat; **o'erword,** a refrain: a catchword.

oerlikon, *ər'li-kon, n.* an anti-aircraft gun of Swiss origin. [Oerlikon, near Zürich.]

oersted, *ər'sted, n.* a unit of magnetising force. [Named in honour of Hans Christian *Oersted* (1777-1851), Danish physicist.]

oes, *ōz,* a plural of **o.**

oesophagus, esophagus, *ē-sof'ə-gəs, n.* the gullet.—*adj.* **oesophageal** (*-faj'i-əl*). [Gr. *oisophagos,* gullet; origin unknown; app. connected with *phagein,* to eat.]

oestrus, *ēs'trəs, n.* a gadfly or bot: a vehement stimulus or frenzy: heat or sexual impulse, esp. in female mammals.—Also **oes'trum.**—*adjs.* **oes'-tral, oes'trous.** [L. *oestrus—*Gr. *oistros.*]

of, *ov, uv, əv, prep.* from: from among: out from: belonging to: among: proceeding or derived from: made from, having for material: having, or characterised by: in the manner that characterises: with respect to: owing to: with: over: concerning: during: by: on: in: specified as: constituted by: (*U.S.*) short of, to (of the time): measuring: aged: owning.—**of new** (*Spens.*), anew; **of purpose** (*B.*), intentionally. [O.E. *of;* Du. *af,* Ger. *ab,* L. *ab,* Gr. *apo.*]

off, *of, awf, adv.* away: in or to a position that is not on something: in motion: out of continuity: out of connexion, supply, activity, operation, or validity: to a finish, up: no longer available: in deterioration or diminution: into freedom.—*adj.* most distant: on the opposite or farther side: on the side of a cricket-field: (*cricket*) on the side opposite that on which the batsman stands (normally the bowler's left): (of a horse or vehicle) right: out of condition or form: not devoted to the particular or usual activity (as *off day, off season*).—*prep.* from: away from: removed from: opening out of: in or to a position or condition that is not on: disengaged from: disinclined to: out to sea from: from a dish of.—*n.* the off side.—*v.t.* to put off: to take off.—*v.i.* (or *v.t.* with *it*) to go off: (with *with, coll.*) to take off.—*interj.* away! depart!

—*adj.* and *adv.* **off'-and-on',** occasional(ly): intermittent(ly).—*ns.* **off'-break,** (*cricket*) of a ball on pitching, deviation towards the stumps from the off side: a delivery with such a deviation; **off'-chance,** a remote chance.—*adjs.* **off'-colour, -ed,** unsatisfactory in colour (as a diamond) and so inferior: (*S.Afr.*) half-caste, not pure white.—*ns.* **off'-come,** (*Scot.*) a subterfuge: a pretext: manner of coming off, issue, success; **off'-drive,** (*cricket*) a drive to the off side.—*adv.* **offhand',** extempore: at once: without hesitating.—*adjs.* **off'hand,** without study: impromptu: free and easy: ungraciously curt or summary; **off'-hand'ed.**—*adv.* **offhand'edly.**—*ns.* **offhand'ed-ness; off'ing,** the region some distance off-shore: a place or time some way off (**in the offing, in sight,** at hand).—*adj.* **off'ish,** aloof in manner.—*n.* **off'-li'cence,** a licence to sell alcoholic liquors for consumption off the premises only.—*v.t.* and *v.i.* **off'-load,** (*S.Afr.*) to unload.—*ns.* **off'-print,** a reprint of a single article from a periodical; **off'-put,** (*Scot.*) act of putting off (in any sense); **off'-putt'er.**—*n.* and *adj.* **off'-putt'ing.**—*n.* **off'-reck'oning** (usu. in *pl.*), a deduction: (*obs.*) an account between army officers and governments concerning men's clothes, &c.—*v.t.* and *v.i.* **off'saddle,** to unsaddle.—*ns.* **off'scouring** (usu. in *pl.*), matter scoured off: refuse: anything vile or despised; **off'scum,** scum, refuse; **off'set,** a thing set off against another as equivalent or compensation: a lateral shoot that strikes root and forms a new plant: a mountain spur: a side branch of anything: a sudden change of direction in a pipe: a reduction of thickness or the (usually sloping) ledge formed where part of a wall, buttress, bank, &c., is set back from the general face: (*U.S.*) a hillside terrace: a smudge on a newly printed sheet from another laid on it: offset printing (see below): in surveying, a perpendicular from the main line to an outlying point.—*v.t.* (*of-set', of'set*) to set off against something as an equivalent or compensation.—*v.i.* to branch off: (*of'set*) to make an effort.—*v.t.* **off-shake',** to shake off (*pa.p. Spens.* **off-shakt'**).—*n.* **off'shoot,** a branch or derivative of anything.—*adv.* **off-shore',** and *adj.* **off'-shore,** away from the shore: at some distance from the shore.—*n.* **off'side,** the far side: a horse's right (far from a man leading): (*cricket*) see **off** *adj.*: (*football,* &c.) the field between the ball and the opponents' goal.—*adj.* and *adv.* on the offside: between the ball, or the last player who had it, and the opponents' goal:—*n.pl.* **off'-sorts,** wool set aside in sorting, or unsuitable for a given purpose.—*n.* **off'spring,** a child, or children: progeny: issue: (*obs.*) ancestry: (*obs.*) source.—*adv.* and *adj.* **off'-stage',** not on the stage as visible to the spectators.—*n.* **off'take,** the act of taking off in any sense: take-off: that which is taken off: a channel, passage, or pipe for removing a fluid.—**be off,** to go away quickly; **come off, go off, show off, take off,** &c. (see **come, go, show, take,** &c.); **from off,** from a position on; **ill off,** poor or ill provided; **off one's feed,** without appetite; **off one's head,** crazy; **offset printing,** a method of printing lithographs, &c., by taking an impression first on a rubber cylinder and from the rubber to paper; **off with,** take off at once; **tell off,** to count: to assign, as for a special duty: to chide; **well off,** rich, well provided: fortunate. [Same as **of.**]

offal, *of'l, n.* waste or rejected parts, esp. of a carcase: a part cut off in dressing a carcase: anything unfit for use: refuse: anything worthless. [**off, fall.**]

offend, *o-fend', v.t.* to displease: to make angry: to do harm to: to hurt the feelings of: to affront: (*B.*) to cause to stumble or sin: to transgress.—*v.i.* to sin: to cause anger: (*B.*) to be made to stumble or sin.—*n.* **offence',** (*B.*) a stumbling: any cause of anger or displeasure: an injury: a transgression, an infraction of law: a crime: a sin: affront: assault.—*adjs.* **offence'ful,** (*Shak.*) giving offence or displeasure: injurious; **offence'-less,** (*Milt.*) unoffending: innocent.—*ns.* **of-fend'er:**—*fem.* (*Shak.*) **offend'ress: offense'** (chiefly *U.S.*), same as **offence.**—*adj.* **offens'ive,** causing offence, displeasure, or injury: used in

attack: making the first attack.—*n.* the act or course of action of the attacking party: the posture of one who attacks.—*adv.* offens'ively.—*n.* offens'iveness.—give offence, to cause displeasure; take offence, to feel displeasure, be offended. [L. *offendĕre, offēnsum—ob*, against, *fendĕre, fēnsum*, to strike (found in compounds).]

offer, *of'ər, v.t.* to present, esp. as an act of devotion, homage, charity, &c.: express willingness: to hold out for acceptance or rejection: to lay before one: to present to the mind: to attempt: to make a show of attempting, make as if: propose to give, pay, sell, or perform.—*v.i.* to present itself: to be at hand: to incline: to make an offer (*pr.p.* off'er-ing; *pa.t.* and *pa.p.* off'ered).—*n.* act of offering: state of being offered: first advance: that which is offered: proposal made: an attempt, essay: a knob on an antler.—*adj.* off'erable, that may be offered.—*ns.* off'erer: off'ering, act of making an offer: that which is offered: a gift: (*B.*) that which is offered on an altar: a sacrifice: (*pl.*) in Church of England, certain dues payable at Easter: off'ertory, act of offering: the thing offered: the verses or the anthem said or sung while the offerings of the congregation are being made: the money collected at a religious service: anciently a linen or silken cloth used in various ceremonies connected with the administration of the eucharist. [L. *offerre—ob*, towards, *ferre*, to bring.]

office, *of'is, n.* an act of kindness or attention: a service: (with *ill*, &c.) a disservice: a function or duty: settled duty or employment: a position imposing certain duties or giving a right to exercise an employment: possession of a post in the government: business: act of worship: order or form of a religious service, either public or private: that which a thing is designed or fitted to do: a place where business is carried on: a body or staff occupying such a place: a state department: the building in which it is housed: a latrine: (*slang*) a hint: (*pl.*) the apartments of a house or the subsidiary buildings in which the domestics discharge their duties.—*ns.* off'ice-bearer, one who holds office: one who has an appointed duty to perform in connexion with some company, society, church, &c.; off'ice-book, a book of forms of service; off'ice-boy, a boy employed to do minor jobs in an office (*fem.* off'ice-girl); off'ice-holder, one who holds a government office: (*U.S.*) a civil servant; off'ice-hunter, a self-seeking candidate for public employment; off'icer, one who holds an office: a person who performs some public duty: a person holding a commission in an army, navy, or air-force: one who holds a similar post in any force or body organised on a similar plan: a policeman: (*U.S.*) a waiter or hotel servant.—*v.t.* to furnish with officers: to command, as officers.—*n.* off'ice-seeker, a candidate for office.—*adj.* official (*of-ish'əl*), pertaining to an office: depending on the proper office or authority: done by authority: issued or authorised by a public authority or office: recognised in the pharmacopoeia (cf. **officinal**).—*n.* one who holds an office: a subordinate public officer: the deputy of a bishop, &c.—*ns.* offic'ialdom, officials as a body: the world of officials: officialism; officialese', stilted, wordy. and stereotyped English alleged to be characteristic of official letters and documents; offic'ialism, official position: excessive devotion to official routine and detail: the self-importance of a Jack-in-office; officiality (*of-ish-i-al'i-ti*), officialty (*of-ish'əl-ti*; *rare*), the charge, office, or jurisdiction of an official: the official headquarters of an ecclesiastical or other deliberative and governing body: officialism.—*adv.* officially (*of-ish'ə-li*).—*n.* officiant (*of-ish'i-ənt*), one who officiates at a religious service, one who administers a sacrament.—*v.i.* offic'iate, to perform the duties of an office.—*n.* offic'iātor. [Fr.,—L. *officium*, a favour, duty, service.]

officinal, *of-is'in-əl, adj.* belonging to, or used in, a shop: used in medicine: recognised in the pharmacopoeia (now *official*): sold by druggists. [L.L. *officīnālis—*L. *officīna*, a workshop, later a monastic store-room—*opus*, work, *facĕre*, to do.]

officious, *of-ish'əs, adj.* (*obs.*) obliging: (*Shak.*) dutiful: too forward in offering unwelcome or unwanted services: intermeddling: in diplomacy, informal, not official.—*adv.* offic'iously.—*n.* offic'iousness. [L. *officiōsus—officium*.]

offset, offside, offspring, &c. See under **off**.

oft, *oft*, often, *of'n, advs.* frequently: many times.—*adj.* oft'en (*B.*), frequent.—*n.* oft'enness, frequency. — *advs.* oft'times, oft'entimes, many times: frequently. [O.E. *oft*; Ger. *oft*, Goth. *ufta*.]

ogam, ogham, *og'əm, ō'əm, n.* an ancient Celtic alphabet of straight lines meeting or crossing the edge of a stone: any of its twenty characters.—*adjs.* og(h)am'ic (or *og', ō'*), og'mic. [O.Ir. *ogam*, mod. Ir. *ogham*.]

ogdoad, *og'dō-ad, n.* a set of eight. [Gr. *ogdoas, -ados—oktō*, eight.]

ogee, *ō'jē, ō-jē', n.* a moulding S-shaped in section: an S-shaped curve.—*adj.* having S-shaped curves.—*adj.* ogee'd. [Fr. *ogive*; see **ogive**.]

ogive, *ō'jiv, ō-jīv', n.* (*archit.*) a diagonal rib of a vault: a pointed arch or window.—*adj.* ogi'val. [Fr.; origin doubtful, poss.—Ar. *auj*, summit.]

ogle, *ō'gl, v.t.* to look at fondly with side glances.—*v.i.* to cast amorous glances.—*ns.* o'gle; o'gler; o'gling. [Cf. L.G. *oegeln*, freq. of *oegen*, to look at; Ger. *äugeln*, to leer, *auge*, eye.]

Ogpu, *og'pŏŏ, og-pŏŏ', n.* Russian secret police of 1922-34. [From the initials of *Obedinennoe Gossudarstvennoe Politicheskoe Upravlenie*, Unified State Political Directorate.]

ogre, *ō'gər, n.* a man-eating monster or giant of fairy tales:—*fem.* o'gress.—*adj.* o'gr(e)ish. [Fr. *ogre*, prob. invented by Perrault.]

Ogygian, *ō-gij'i-ən, ō-jij'i-ən, adj.* pertaining to the mythical Attic king *Ōgўgēs*: prehistoric, primaeval: of Circe's island, *Ogўgiā*.

oh, *ō, interj.* denoting surprise, pain, sorrow, &c. [See **o**.]

ohm, *ōm, n.* the unit of electrical resistance—that in common use being the **international ohm**, the resistance offered, at the temperature of melting ice, to an unvarying electric current by a column of mercury 14·4521 grams in mass, of uniform cross-sectional area, and 106·300 centimetres in length.—*adj.* ohm'ic.—*n.* ohmmeter (*ōm'mēt'ər*), an instrument for measuring electrical resistance.—**Ohm's law**, that strength of electric current is directly proportional to electromotive force and inversely to resistance. [Georg Simon *Ohm*, German electrician, 1787-1854.]

oho, *ō-hō', interj.* expressing triumphant surprise or gratification.

ohone, ochone, *ō-hōn', interj.* (*Ir.* and *Highland*) of lamentation. [Ir. and Gael. *ochoin*.]

oidium, *ō-id'i-əm, n.* the conidial stage of the vine-mildew and other fungi. [Gr. *ōion*, an egg, with dim. suffix *-idion* Latinised.]

oil, *oil, n.* the juice from the fruit of the olive-tree: any greasy liquid: (in *pl.*) oil-paints or painting: (in *pl.*) oilskins.—*v.t.* to smear, lubricate, or anoint with oil.—*v.i.* to take oil aboard as fuel.—*ns.* oil'-bath, a receptacle containing lubricating oil through which part of a machine passes; oil'-beetle, a beetle (Meloe and kindred) that emits a yellowish oily liquid from the legs when disturbed; oil'-belt, a belt of country yielding mineral oil; oil'-bird, the guacharo; oil'-burner, a ship that uses oil as fuel: a lamp-burner for use with oil; oil'cake, a cattle-food made of the residue of oil-seeds when most of the oil has been pressed out; oil'can, a can for carrying oil or for applying lubricating oil; oil'cloth, a canvas coated with linseed-oil paint; oil'-colour, a colouring substance mixed with oil.—*adj.* oiled, smeared, treated, lubricated, or impregnated with oil: preserved in oil: (*slang*) tipsy.—*ns.* oil'-engine, an internal-combustion engine burning vapour from oil; oil'er, one who, or that which, oils: an oil-can: (*coll.*) a coat of oilskin: a ship driven by oil: a ship that carries oil; oil'ery, the commodities, business, or establishment of an oil-man: oil'-field, a district that produces mineral oil; oil'-gas, illuminating gas or heating gas made by destructive distillation of oil; **oil'-gland,** the uropygial gland in birds, forming a secretion used in preening the feathers.—*adv.* **oil'ily.**—*ns.* **oil'-iness; oil'-man,** one who deals in oils; **oil'-mill,** a grinding-mill for expressing oil from seeds, &c.; **oil'nut,** the North American butter-nut, the buffalo-nut, or other oil-yielding nut; **oil'-paint'ing,** a picture painted in oil-colours: the art of painting in oil-colours; **oil'-palm,** a palm (*Elaeis guineensis*) whose fruit-pulp yields palm-oil; **oil'-press,** a machine for expressing oils from seeds or pulp; **oil'-seed,** any seed that yields oil; **oil'-shale,** a shale containing diffused hydrocarbons in a state suitable for distillation into mineral oils; **oil'-silk,** a transparent silk fabric impregnated with oxidised oil; **oil'skin,** cloth made waterproof by means of oil: a garment made of oilskin; **oil'stone,** a whetstone used with oil; **oil'-tanker,** a vessel constructed for carrying oil in bulk; **oil'-well,** a boring made for petroleum.—*adj.* **oil'y,** consisting of, containing, or having the qualities of oil: greasy: unctuous.—**oil one's palm,** to bribe him; **strike oil** (see **strike**). [O.Fr. *oile* (Fr. *huile*)—L. *oleum*—Gr. *elaion*—*elaiā,* olive-tree, olive.]

oillet, *oi'lit, n.* an obs. form of **eyelet.**

oino-, *oi-nō-,* in composition, an occasional variant in words beginning **oeno-.**

ointment, *oint'mənt, n.* anything used in anointing: (*med.*) any greasy substance applied to diseased or wounded parts: an unguent.—*v.t.* **oint** (*Dryden*), to anoint. [Fr. *oint,* pa.p. of *oindre*—L. *unguĕre,* to anoint.]

okapi, *ō-kä′pē, n.* a giraffe-like animal of the Semliki forests of Central Africa:—*pl.* **oka′pis.** [Native name.]

okay, *ō-kā′, adj.* (*slang*). See **O.K.** in List of Abbreviations.—*v.t.* to mark or pass as right.

oke, *ōk, n.* a Turkish weight of about 2¾ lb. avoir-dupois. [Turk. *ōqah,* appar. through Gr. from L. *uncia,* ounce.]

okra, *ok′rä, ōk′rä, n. Hibiscus esculentus,* gumbo. [From a W. African name.]

old, *ōld, adj.* advanced in years: having been long or relatively long in existence, use, or possession: of a specified (or to be specified) age: of long standing: worn or worn out: out of date: super-seded or abandoned: former: old-fashioned: antique: ancient: early: belonging to later life: belonging to former times: (of a language) of the earliest or earliest known stage: long practised or experienced: having the characteristics of age: familiar, accustomed: (*coll.*) in good plenty (esp. in *high old*): (*coll.*) a general word of familiar or affectionate approbation or contempt (often *good old*): reckoned according to Old Style (see below):—*comp.* **old′er, old′er** (q.v.); *superl.* **old′est, eld′est.**—*adv.* (*Shak.*) of old.—*n.* an old person: olden times, eld.—*n.* **old-clothes′man,** one who buys cast-off garments.—*v.t.* and *v.i.* **old′en,** to age.—*adj.* old, ancient.—*adj.* **old-fash′ioned,** of a fashion like that used long ago: out of date: cling-ing to old things and old styles: with manners like those of a grown-up person (said of a child).—*n.* **old-fash′ionedness.**—*adjs.* **old-fō′g(e)yish,** like an old fogey; **old-gen′tlemanly,** characteristic of an old gentleman; **old′ish,** somewhat old.—*ns.* **old-maid′hood, old-maid′ism.** — *adj.* **old-maid′ish,** like the conventional old maid, prim.—*n.* **old′ness.**—*adj.* **old′-school,** of the old school.—*n.* **old′ster** (*coll.*), a man getting old: a mid-shipman of four years' standing, a master's mate.—*adj.* **old′-time,** of or pertaining to times long gone by: of long standing: old-fashioned.—*ns.* **old′-tim′er,** one who has long been where he is; **old′-wife,** the hareld: a fish of various kinds—sea-bream, file-fish, &c.—*adjs.* **old-wom′anish,** like an old woman; **old′-world,** belonging to earlier times, antiquated, old-fashioned.—**old age,** the later part of life (**old′-age pension,** a pension for one who has reached old age, esp. under a national system instituted in 1908); **old bachelor,** somewhat elderly or confirmed bachelor; **old boy,** (*coll.*) one's father, husband, &c.: an old or oldish man, esp. one in authority, or one who has some

air of youthfulness: a former pupil:—*fem.* **old girl;** **Old Catholic,** a member of a body that broke away from the Roman Catholic Church on the question of papal infallibility; **old country,** the mother-country; **Old Dominion,** Virginia; **Old English** (see **English**): the form of black-letter used by 16th-century English printers; **old face,** the early roman type such as Caslon used; **Old Glory,** the Stars and Stripes; **old gold,** a dull gold colour like tarnished gold, used in textile fabrics; **old hand,** an experienced performer: an old convict; **Old Harry, Nick, One,** &c., the devil; **Old Hundred** (**Old Hundredth**), a famous tune set in England about the middle of the 16th century to Kethe's version of the 100th Psalm, marked 'Old Hundredth' in Tate and Brady (1696); **Old Light,** a member of a relatively less advanced religious school—applied esp. to the party in the Scottish Secession Church who continued to hold unchanged the principle of connexion between Church and State; **old maid,** a spinster, esp. one who is likely to remain a spinster: a woman, or more often a man, of the character supposed to be common among spinsters—fussy, prim, conven-tional, over-cautious, methodical: a simple game played by passing and matching cards: also the player left with the odd card; **old man,** unregen-erate human nature: an adult male kangaroo: (*coll.*) one's husband, father, or employer: the captain of a merchant ship: a familiar friendly or encouraging term of address: southernwood; **Old Red Sandstone,** the lacustrine or continental equivalent of the (marine) Devonian, so called in contradistinction to the New Red Sandstone (Per-mian and Trias); **old salt,** an experienced sailor; **old school,** those whose ways or thoughts are such as prevailed in the past; **old school tie,** the emblem of minor (esp. upper-class) loyalties; **old soldier** (see **soldier**); **old song,** a mere trifle, a very small price; **old squaw** (*U.S.*), the hareld; **old story,** something one has heard before: something that happened long ago, or has happened often; **Old Style** (see **style**): a type-face in imitation of old face; **Old Testament** (see **Testament**); **Old Tom,** a kind of sweetened gin; **old wife,** an old woman: one who has the character ascribed to old women: (*Scot.*) a chimney-cap for curing smoking; **old woman,** (*coll.*) one's wife or mother: an old-womanish person; **Old World,** the Eastern hemisphere.—**of old,** long ago: in or of ancient times: formerly. [O.E. *ald* (W.S. *eald*); Du. *oud,* Ger. *alt.*]

Olea, *ō′li-ä, n.* the olive genus, giving name to the family **Olea′ceae,** including ash, privet, and jasmine.—*adj.* **olea′ceous.** [L. *olea,* olive.]

oleaginous, *ō-li-aj′in-əs, adj.* oily.—*n.* **oleag′in-ousness.** [L. *oleāginus*—*oleum,* oil.]

oleander, *ō-li-an′dər, n.* an evergreen shrub (*Nerium Oleander*) of the Apocynaceae, with lance-shaped leathery leaves and beautiful red or white flowers, the rose-bay or rose-laurel. [L.L. *oleander;* deri-vation from *rhododendron,* influenced by *laurus* and *olea,* has been conjectured.]

oleaster, *ō-li-as′tər, n.* properly the true wild olive: extended to the so-called wild olive, Elaeagnus. [L. *oleaster*—*olea,* an olive-tree—Gr. *elaiā.*]

oleate, *ō′li-āt, n.* a salt of oleic acid.—*adj.* **olefiant** (*ō-li-fī′ant* or *ō-lē′fi-ənt*), oil-forming (in **olefiant gas,** ethylene).—*n.* **o′lefine** (*-fin, -fēn*), any hydro-carbon of the ethylene series.—*adjs.* **ole′ic** (or *ō′li-ik*), pertaining to or got from oil (as in **oleic acid,** $C_{18}H_{84}O_2$); **oleif′erous,** producing oil, as seeds.—*ns.* **olein** (*ō′li-in*), a glycerine ester of oleic acid; **oleo** (*ō′li-ō*), a contraction for oleograph or for oleomargarine; **o′leograph,** a print in oil-colours to imitate an oil-painting; **oleog′raphy;** **oleo-mar′garine,** margarine; **oleo-res′in,** a solution of a resin in an oil. [L. *oleum,* oil.]

olecranon, *ō-li-krā′non, n.* a process forming the upper part of the ulna.—*adj.* **olecra′nal.** [Gr. *ōlekrānon*—*ōlenē,* elbow, *krānion,* head.]

olent, *ō′lənt, adj.* having a smell. [L. *olēns, -ēntis,* pr.p. of *olēre,* to smell.]

Olenus, *ō′len-əs, n.* a typically Upper Cambrian genus of trilobites.—*n.* **Olenell′us,** a similar

Lower Cambrian genus. [Gr. *Ōlenos*, who was turned to stone.]

oleraceous, *ol-ər-ā'shəs*, *adj.* of the nature of a pot-herb, for kitchen use. [L. *(h)oleráceus—(h)olus*, *(h)oleris*, a pot-herb, vegetable.]

olfactory, *ol-fak'tə-ri*, *adj.* pertaining to, or used in, smelling.—*v.t.* **olfact'** *(facet.).*—*adj.* **olfact'ible.** —*n.* **olfac'tion.**—*adj.* **olfac'tive.** [L. *olfacēre*, to smell—*olēre*, to smell, *facēre*, to make.]

olibanum, *ol-ib'ə-nəm*, *n.* a gum-resin flowing from incisions in species of Boswellia in Somaliland and southern Arabia. [L.L., prob.—Gr. *libanos*, frank-incense.]

olid, *ol'id*, *adj.* rank-smelling. [L. *olidus—olēre*, to smell.]

olig-, oligo-, *ol'ig-, -ō-*, or *-o'-*, in composition, little, few.—*ns.* **oligaemia** *(ol-i-jē'mi-ä, -gē'mi-ä)*, ab-normal deficiency of blood; **ol'igarch** *(-ärk* ; Gr. *archē*, rule), a member of an oligarchy.—*adjs.* **oligarch'al, oligarch'ic, -ical.**—*ns.* **ol'igarchy** *(-är-ki)*, government by a small exclusive class : a state so governed : a small body of men who have the supreme power of a state in their hands ; **oligist** *(ol'i-jist* ; Fr. *fer oligiste—fer*, iron, Gr. *oligistos*, superl. of *oligos*, little ; as containing less iron than magnetite), crystallised haematite.—*adj.* **Oligocene** *(ol'i-gō-sēn)* (geol. ; Gr. *kainos*, new ; as having few fossil molluscs of living species), between Eocene and Miocene.—*n.* the Oligocene system, period, or strata.—*n.* **oligochaete** *(ol'i-gō-kēt* ; Gr. *chaitē*, bristle), any worm of the Oligo-chae'ta, chaetopods in which the locomotor organs are reduced to bristles—earth-worms, &c.—*adj.* **oligochrome** *(ol'i-gō-krōm* ; Gr. *chrōma*, colour), painted in few colours.—Also *n.*—*ns.* **oligoclase** *(ol'i-gō-klās, -klāz* ; Gr. *klāsis*, cleavage, because thought to have a less perfect cleavage than albite), a soda-lime triclinic felspar ; **oligocythaemia** *(ol-i-gō-sī-thē'mi-ä* ; Gr. *kytos*, a vessel, *haima*, blood), defect of red cells in the blood.—*adj.* **oligom'erous** (Gr. *meros*, a part), having few parts : having fewer members than the other whorls of a flower. [Gr. *oligos*, little, few.]

olio, *ō'li-ō*, *n.* a savoury dish of different sorts of meat and vegetables : a mixture : a medley : a miscellany : a variety entertainment :—*pl.* **olios.** [Sp. *olla*—L. *ōlla*, a pot ; cf. **olla.**]

oliphant, *ol'i-fənt*, *n.* an obsolete form of **elephant** : an ancient ivory hunting-horn.

olitory, *ol'i-tə-ri*, *adj.* pertaining to kitchen veget-ables.—*n.* a kitchen-garden : a pot-herb. [L. *(h)olitor*, gardener—*(h)olus*, *(h)oleris*, a pot-herb, vegetable.]

olive, *ol'iv*, *n.* a tree *(Olea europaea)* cultivated round the Mediterranean for its oily fruit : ex-tended to many more or less similar trees : the fruit of the olive-tree : peace, of which the olive was the emblem : a colour like the unripe olive : a person of olive-coloured complexion : an olive-shaped or oval object of various kinds : **a gasteropod** mollusc (Oliva) of warm seas with olive-shaped shell : a rolled lump of seasoned meat (usu. in *pl.*). —*adj.* of a brownish-green colour like the olive. —*adjs.* **oliva'ceous**, olive-coloured : olive-green ; **ol'ivary**, olive-shaped.—*ns.* **olivenite** *(ō-liv'ə-nīt*, or *ol'iv-)*, a mineral, hydrated copper arsenate, often olive-coloured ; **ol'ive-oil**, oil pressed from the fruit of the olive ; **ol'ive-shell**, the shell of the mollusc Oliva ; **ol'ivet**, an olive-shaped button : an oval mock-pearl for trade with savages ; **ol'ive-yard**, a piece of ground on which olives are grown ; **olivine** *(ol'iv-ēn)*, an orthorhombic rock-forming mineral, silicate of iron and magnesium, often olive-green, often altered to serpentine ; **ol'ivine-rock'**, dunite.—**olive branch**, a symbol of peace : a child (Ps. cxxviii. 3 ; *Pr. Bk.*) ; **olive drab**, the dull dark yellowish green of American uniforms. [Fr.,—L. *olīva*.]

Oliver, *ol'i-vər*, *n.* the comrade-in-arms of Roland (q.v.).

Oliver. See Bath.

oliver, *ol'i-vər*, *n.* a forge-hammer worked by foot. [Origin unknown.]

Oliverian, *ol-i-vē'ri-ən*, *n.* an adherent of the great Protector, *Oliver* Cromwell (1599-1658).

Olivetan, *ol-iv-ē'tən*, *n.* one of an order of Bene-dictine monks founded in 1313, the original house at Monte *Oliveto*, near Siena.

olla, (Lat.) *ol'ä*, (Sp.) *ōl'yä*, *n.* a jar or urn : an olio. —*n.* **olla-podrida** *(ōl'yä po-drē'dä* ; Sp., rotten pot), a Spanish mixed stew or hash of meat and vegetables : any incongruous mixture or mis-cellaneous collection. [L. *ōlla* and Sp. *olla*, pot, Sp. *podrida*—L. *putrida* (fem.).]

ollav, ollamh, *ol'äv*, *n.* a doctor or master among the ancient Irish. [Ir. *ollamh*.]

ology, *ol'ə'ji*, *n.* a science whose name ends in -ology : any science.

olpe, *ol'pē*, *n.* a Greek jug. [Gr. *olpē*.]

olykoek, olycook, *ol'i-kōōk*, *n.* (*U.S.*) a kind of doughnut. [Du. *oliekoek*, lit. oil-cake.]

Olympus, *ol-im'pəs*, *n.* the name of several moun-tains, esp. of one in Thessaly, abode of the greater Greek gods : heaven.—*ns.* **Olym'pia**, a district in Elis, also the city of Pisa in it, where the Olympic games in honour of Olympian Zeus were celebrated ; **Olym'piad**, in ancient Greece, a period of four years, being the interval from one celebration of the Olympic games to another, used in reckoning time (the traditional date of the first Olympiad is 776 B.C.) : a celebration of the Olympic games ; **Olym'pian**, a dweller on Olympus, any of the greater gods, esp. Zeus : a godlike person : a competitor in the Olympic games.—*adj.* of Olym-pus : godlike : (now *rare*) of Olympia.—*adj.* **Olym'pic**, of Olympia : (now *rare*) of Olympus.— *n.pl.* **Olym'pics**, the Olympic games.—**Olympic games**, the ancient games celebrated every four years at Olympia : quadrennial international ath-letic contests, held at various centres since 1896. [Gr. *Olympos.*]

omadhaun, *om'ə-dawn*, *n.* a fool. [Ir. *amadan*.]

omasum, *ō-mā'səm*, *n.* a ruminant's third stomach, the psalterium or manyplies.—*adj.* **omā'sal.** [L. *omāsum*, ox tripe ; a Gallic word.]

ombre, *om'bər, -brä, um'bər*, *n.* a game played with a pack of forty cards, usually by three persons, one against the others : the solo player. [Sp. *hombre*— L. *homō, -inis*, a man.]

ombrometer, *om-brom'i-tər*, *n.* a rain-gauge.—*n.* **om'brophil, -phile** *(-fil)*, a plant tolerant of much rain.—*adj.* **ombroph'ilous.**—*n.* **om'brophobe**, a plant intolerant of much rain.—*adj.* **ombroph'-obous.** [Gr. *ombros*, a rain-storm, *metron*, measure, *phileein*, to love, *phobeein*, to fear.]

ombú, *om-bōō'*, *n.* a South American tree, a species of Phytolacca, that grows isolated in the pampas : —*pl.* **ombús.**

omega, *ō'meg-ä*, *n.* the last letter of the Greek alphabet—long o (Ω, ω) : the conclusion : as a numeral ω'=800, ͵ω=800,000. [Late Gr. *ō mega*, great O ; opposed to omicron ; the earlier Gr. name of the letter was *ō*.]

omelet, omelette, *om'lit, -let*, *n.* a pancake made of eggs, beaten up, and fried in a pan (with or without cheese, herbs, ham, jam, or other addition). [Fr. *omelette*, earlier *amelette*, apparently by change of suffix and metathesis from *alemelle (l'alemelle* for *la lemelle)*, a thin plate—L. *lāmella, lāmina*, a thin plate.]

omen, *ō'men*, *n.* a sign of some future event, either good or evil : threatening or prognosticating charac-ter : *(Shak.)* an event prognosticated.—*v.t.* to portend. —*adj.* **o'mened**, affording or attended by omens, esp. in composition, as ill-*omened*. [L. *ōmen, -inis*.]

omentum, *ō-men'təm*, *n.* a fold of peritoneum pro-ceeding from one of the abdominal viscera to another :—*pl.* **omen'ta.**—*adj.* **omen'tal.**—*great* omentum, the epiploon. [L. *ōmentum.*]

omer, *ō'mər*, *n.* a Hebrew dry measure containing about half a gallon, ¹⁄₁₀ ephah. [Heb. *'ōmer*.]

omicron, *ō-mī'kron, o-mē'kron*, *n.* the fifteenth letter of the Greek alphabet—short o (O, o) : as a numeral o'=70, ͵o=70,000. [Late Gr. *o micron*, little O ; opposed to omega ; the earlier Greek name of the letter was *ou*.]

ominous, *om'* or *ōm'in-əs*, *adj.* pertaining to, or containing, an omen : portending evil : inaus-picious.—*adv.* **om'inously.**—*n.* **om'inousness** [See omen.]

omit, *ō-mit'*, *v.t.* to leave out : to fail, fail to perform : (*Shak.*) to disregard : (*Shak.*) to leave off, let go :—*pr.p.* **omitt'ing** ; *pa.t.* and *pa.p.* **omitt'ed.**—*adj.* **omiss'ible**, that may be omitted. —*n.* **omission** (*-mish'n*), act of omitting : a thing omitted.—*adj.* **omiss'ive**, omitting, of the nature of omission. — *ns.* **omitt'ance**, (*Shak.*) omission ; **omitt'er.** [L. *omittĕre, omissum—ob-*, in front, *mittĕre, missum*, to send.]

omlah, *om'lä*, *n.* a staff of officials in India. [Ar. *'umalā.*]

ommateum, *om-ə-tē'əm*, *n.* a compound eye :—*pl.* **ommate'a.**—*ns.* **ommatid'ium**, a simple element of a compound eye :—*pl.* **ommatid'ia** ; **ommatophore** (*-at'ō-fōr*), an eye-stalk, as in snails. [Gr. *omma, -atos*, an eye.]

omneity, *om-nē'i-ti*, **omniety**, *om-nī'i-ti*, *ns.* allness, the condition of being all. [L. *omnis*, all.]

omni-, *om'ni-*, in composition, all.—*n.pl.* **omniana** (*-ā'nä, -ä'nä*), ana about all sorts of things.—*n.* **omnibenev'olence**, universal benevolence.—*adj.* **omnibenev'olent.**—*n.* **omnicom'petence**, legal competence in all matters.—*adjs.* **omnicom'petent** ; **omnidirec'tional**, acting in all directions ; **omnifa'rious**, of all kinds ; **omnif'erous**, bearing or producing all kinds ; **omnif'ic**, all-creating ; **om'niform**, of, or capable of, every form.—*n.* **omniform'ity.**—*v.t.* **om'nify** (*rare*), to make universal.—*adj.* **omnigenous** (*-nij'i-nəs*), of all kinds.—*n.* **omnipar'ity**, general equality.—*adjs.* **omnip'arous**, producing all things ; **omnipā'tient**, enduring all things.—*ns.* **omnip'otence**, **omnip'otency**, unlimited power.—*adj.* **omnip'otent**, all-powerful. — *adv.* **omnip'otently.** — *n.* **omnipres'ence**, quality of being present everywhere at the same time.—*adj.* **omnipres'ent.**— *n.* **omniscience** (*om-nish'əns, -yəns*), knowledge of all things.—*adj.* **omnisc'ient**, all-knowing.—*adv.* **omnisc'iently.**—*adj.* **omniv'orous**, all-devouring : (*zool.*) feeding on both animal and vegetable food. [L. *omnis*, all.]

omnibus, *om'ni-bəs*, *n.* a large road-vehicle carrying a considerable number of passengers of the general public, or hotel guests (now almost always shortened to **bus**): an omnibus box : an omnibus book : a waiter's or waitress's assistant (*pl.* **om'nibuses**) —*adj.* widely comprehensive : of miscellaneous contents.—**omnibus book**, a large cheap volume very comprehensive in its sweep ; **omnibus box**, a theatre box for many persons ; **omnibus clause**, one that covers many different cases ; **omnibus train**, one that stops at every station. [Lit. for all, dative pl. of L. *omnis*.]

omnium, *om'ni-əm*, *n.* a Stock Exchange term for the aggregate value of the different stocks in which a loan is funded.—*n.* **om'nium-gath'erum** (*coll.*, *sham Latin*), a miscellaneous collection. [L., of all ; gen. pl. of *omnis*, all.]

omohyoid, *ō-mō-hī'oid*, *adj.* pertaining to shoulder-blade and hyoid.—*n.* the muscle joining these. [Gr. *ōmos*, shoulder.]

omophagia, *ō-mō-fāj'-yä, -i-ä*, *n.* the eating of raw flesh, esp. as a religious observance.—Also **omophagy** (*ō-mof'ə-ji*). — *adjs.* **omophagic** (*-faj'ik*), **omophagous** (*-mof'ə-gəs*). [Gr. *ōmophagiä—ōmos*, raw, *phagein*, to eat.]

omophorion, *ō-mō-fō'ri-on*, *n.* an Eastern bishop's vestment like the pallium. [Gr. *ōmophōrion—ōmos*, shoulder, *pherein*, to carry.]

omoplate, *ō'mō-plāt*, *n.* the shoulder-blade or scapula.—*n.* **omoplatoscopy** (*-plə-tos'kə-pi*), divination by observing the cracks in a burning shoulder-blade. [Gr. *ōmoplatē—ōmos*, shoulder, *platē*, blade, *skopeein*, to look.]

omphacite, *om'fə-sīt*, *n.* a grass-green pyroxene. [Gr. *omphax, -akos*, an unripe grape.]

omphalos, *om'fə-los*, *n.* the navel : a boss : a stone at Delphi held to mark the centre of the world : a centre.—*adjs.* **omphalic** (*-fal'ik*) ; **om'phaloid**, navel-like.—*n.* **om'phalomancy**, divination of the number of future children from the knots in the navel-string. [Gr. *omphalos*, navel.]

omrah, *om'rä*, *n.* a Mohammedan lord. [Urdu *umarā*, orig. pl. of Ar. *amīr*.]

on, *on*, *prep.* in contact with the upper, supporting, outer, or presented surface of : to a position in contact with such a surface of : in or to a position or state of being supported by : having for basis, principle, or condition : subject to : in a condition or process of : towards or to : directed towards : in the direction of : against : applied to : with action applied to : with inclination towards : close to, beside : exactly or very nearly at : at the time, date, or occasion of : very little short of : just after : concerning, about : with respect to : by (in oaths and adjurations) : at the risk of : assigned to : in addition to : (*obs.*) in : (*Shak., Milt.*, of gaining, taking) from : (*obs.* or *dial.*) of : (*Scot.*, of marriage) to : (*Scot.*, of waiting) for : (*U.S.*) against : (*coll.*) at the expense of, to the disadvantage of : (*coll.*) cognisant of, enlightened about.—*adv.* in or into a position on something : towards something : in advance : (*slang*) on the way to being drunk : forward : in continuance : in, or into, or allowing connexion, supply, activity, operation, or validity : in progress : on the stage, the table, the fire, the programme, the menu, or anything else : not off.— *interj.* forward ! proceed !—*adj.* (*cricket*) on the side on which the batsman stands (normally the bowler's right) : in a condition expressed by the adverb on : agreed upon : willing to participate.— *n.* the on side.—*v.i.* (*coll.*) to go on : (with *with*, *coll.*) to put on.—*n.* **on'-licence**, a licence to sell alcoholic liquors for consumption on the premises. —*adj.* and *adv.* **on'side**, not offside.—**on to**, to a position on (also **on'to**): forward to. [O.E. *on* ; Du. *aan* ; O.N. *ā* ; Ger. *an* ; Gr. *ana*.]

on-, *on-*, a dial. form of the prefix **un-**.

onager, *on'ə-jər*, *n.* the wild ass of Central Asia : an ancient military engine for throwing great stones. [L.,—Gr. *onagros—onos*, an ass, *agrios*, wild— *agros*, a field.]

Onagra, *on'ə-grä*, *n.* (*bot.*) an old name for Oenothera, giving name to the family **Onagrā'ceae.**— *adj.* **onagrā'ceous.** [Gr. *onagrä*, the plant also known as *oinothēras* ; see Oenothera.]

onanism, *ō'nən-izm*, *n.* self-pollution.—*n.* **o'nanist.** —*adj.* **onanist'ic.** [See Gen. xxxviii. 9.]

once, *wuns*, *adv.* a single time : on one occasion : at a former time : at some time in the future : (*obs.*) firstly : (*obs.*) in short : at any time.—*n.* one time.—*adj.* former.—*conj.* when once : as soon as. —*adj.* **once-accent'ed**, marked with one accent— applied to the octave beginning with middle C. —*ns.* **once-o'ver**, a single comprehensive survey ; **onc'er** (*eccles. slang*), one who goes to church once on Sunday.—**at once**, without delay : alike : at the same time ; **for once**, on one occasion only ; **once and again**, more than once : now and then ; **once (and) for all**, once only and not again ; **once in a way**, while, occasionally : rarely ; **once or twice**, a few times ; **once upon a time**, at a certain time in the past—the usual formula for beginning a fairy-tale. [O.E. *ānes*, orig. gen. of *ān*, one, used as adv.]

Oncidium, *on-sid'i-əm*, *n.* a tropical American genus of orchids. [Gr. *onkos*, a hook.]

oncology, *ong-kol'ə-ji*, *n.* the study of tumours.— *ns.* **oncom'eter**, an instrument for measuring variations in bulk of bodily organs ; **oncot'omy**, incision into a tumour. [Gr. *onkos*, bulk, mass, tumour.]

oncome, *on'kum, -kəm*, *n.* (*Scot.*) coming on : a sudden fall of rain or snow : the beginning of attack by some insidious disease.—*n.* **on'coming**, approach.—*adj.* advancing : approaching. [**on**, **come**.]

Oncorhynchus, *ong-kō-ringk'əs*, *n.* a North Pacific genus of salmon. [Gr. *onkos*, hook, *rhynchos*, beak.]

oncost, *on'kost*, *n.* overhead expenses : an oncost-man.—*adj.* paid by time : causing oncost.—*n.* **on'costman**, a mine-worker paid by the day. [**on**, **cost**.]

ondatra, *on-dat'rä*, *n.* the musquash. [Huron Indian.]

ondine. Same as **undine**.

onding, *on'ding*, *n.* (*Scot.*) onset, esp. a sudden fall of rain or snow. [**on**, **ding**.]

one, *wun*, *adj.* single : of unit number : undivided : the same : a certain : a single but not specified :

first.—*n.* the number unity: a symbol representing it: an individual thing or person: a thing bearing or distinguished by the number one.—*pron.* somebody: anybody.—*n.* one'-and-thir'ty, an old card-game like vingt-un, in which it was sought to make the pips add up to 31 and no more.—*adjs.* one'-eyed, having but one eye; one'fold, simple, single-minded; one'-hand'ed, with, by, or for one hand; one'-horse, drawn by a single horse: petty, mean, inferior; one'-ide'a'd, entirely possessed by one idea; one'-legged; one'-man, of, for, or done by one man.—*n.* one'ness, singleness: uniqueness: identity: unity.—*adj.* one'-piece, made in one piece.—*n.* oner (*wun'er*), slang), a person or thing unique or outstanding in any way: an expert: a heavy blow: a big lie.— Also one'-er, wunn'er.—*pron.* oneself', one's self, the emphatic and reflexive form of one.— *adj.* one'-sid'ed, limited to one side: partial: developed on one side only: turned to one side.— *adv.* one'-sid'edly.—*ns.* one'-sid'edness; one'-step, dance of U.S. origin danced to quick march time.—*v.i.* to dance a one-step.—*adjs.* one'-time, at one time: former; one'-to-one', corresponding each one uniquely to one; one'-way, proceeding, or permitting or set apart for traffic, in one direction only.—all one, just the same: of no consequence; at one, of one mind; one another, each other; one by one, singly in order; one day, on a certain day: at an indefinite time. [O.E. *án*; O.N. *einn*, Ger. *ein*; L. *ūnus*; Gr. *oinē*, ace.]

oneiric, *ō-nī'rik, adj.* belonging to dreams.—*n.* oneirocrit'ic, an interpreter of dreams.—*adj.* oneirocrit'ical.—*ns.* oneirocrit'icism; oneiro-dynia (*-ō-din'i-ā*), troubled sleep: nightmare; oneirology (*on-ī-rol'ə-ji*), the study of dreams; oneir'omancy, divination by dreams; oneiros'copist, an interpreter of dreams; oneiros'copy. —Also oni'ric, &c. [Gr. *oneiros*, a dream, *kritikos*, judging, *odynē*, pain, *logos*, discourse, *manteiā*, divination, *skopiā*, watching.]

onely, a Spenserian spelling of only.

onerous, *on'ə-rəs, adj.* burdensome: oppressive.— *adv.* on'erously.—*n.* on'erousness. [L. *onerōsus* —*onus*, a burden.]

oneyre, oneyer, *wun'yər, n.* (1 *Hen. IV.*, II. i.) probably the same as oner. [See one.]

onfall, *on'fawl, n.* an attack, onslaught, esp. (*Scot.*) of illness: (*Scot.*) a fall of rain or snow. [on, fall.]

ongoing, *on'gō-ing, n.* a going on: course of conduct: event: (*pl.*) proceedings, behaviour, esp. misbehaviour. [on, go.]

onion, *un'yən, n.* a pungent edible bulb of the lily family: the plant yielding it (*Allium cepa*): applied also to some kindred species: a flaming rocket used against aircraft: (*slang*) the head.—*v.t.* to apply an onion to: to produce by means of an onion.—*adj.* on'ion-eyed, (*Shak.*) having the eyes full of tears.—*n.* on'ion-skin, a very thin variety of paper.—*adj.* on'iony. [Fr. *oignon*—L. *ūniō*, *-ōnis*, union, a large pearl, an onion; see union.]

Oniscus, *on-is'kəs, n.* a genus of woodlice.—*adj.* onis'coid, of the family of Oniscus: like a woodlouse. [Gr. *oniskos*, dim. of *onos*, an ass.]

on-licence. See under on.

onlooker, *on'look-ər, n.* a looker on, observer.—*adj.* on'looking.

only, *ōn'li, adj.* single in number: without others of the kind: without others worthy to be counted. —*adv.* not more, other, or otherwise than: alone: merely: barely: just: (*obs.*) pre-eminently: (*rare*) singly.—*conj.* but: except that.—*prep.* (*dial.*) except. [O.E. *ánlic* (adj.)—*án*, one, *-lic*, like.]

onocentaur, *on-ō-sen'tawr, n.* a kind of centaur: half-man, half-ass. [Gr. *onos*, ass.]

onomastic, *on-ō-mas'tik, adj.* pertaining to a name, esp. pertaining to the signature to a paper written in another hand.—*n.* onomas'ticon, a dictionary of proper names. [Gr. *onomastikos, -on—onoma*, a name.]

onomatopoeia, *on-ō-mat-ō-pē'yä, n.* the formation of a word in imitation of the sound of the thing meant: a word so formed: (*rhet.*) the use of words whose sounds help to suggest the meaning—also onomatopoesis (*-pō-ē'sis*), or onomatopoiesis

(*-poi-ē'sis*).—*adjs.* onomatopoeic (*-pē'ik*), ono-matopoetic (*-pō-et'ik*). [Gr. *onomatopoiiā*, *-poiēsis—onoma, -atos*, a name, *poieein*, to make.]

onrush, *on'rush, n.* a rushing onward. [on, rush.]

onset, *on'set, n.* violent attack: assault: storming: beginning, outset.—*ns.* on'setter (*arch.*), an assailant; on'setting, incitement. [on, set.]

onshore, *on'shōr, adj.* toward the land.—*adv.* on'-shore'. [on, shore.]

onslaught, *on'slawt, n.* an attack or onset: assault. [Prob. Du. *aanslag* or Ger. *anschlag*, refashioned as Eng.]

onst, *wunst, adv.* a vulgar form of once.

onstead, *on'sted, n.* (*Scot.*) a farmstead: a farmhouse with its offices: the offices alone. [on, stead.]

onto, *on'too, prep.* to a place or position on.—Also on to.

ontogenesis, *on-tō-jen'i-sis, n.* the history of the individual development of an organised being as distinguished from *phylogenesis.*—Also ontogeny (*on-toj'i-ni*).—*adjs.* ontogenet'ic, ontogen'ic.—*adv.* ontogenet'ically. [Gr. *ōn, ontos*, pr.p. of *einai*, to be, *genesis*, generation.]

ontology, *on-tol'ə-ji, n.* the science that treats of the principles of pure being: that part of metaphysics which treats of the nature and essence of things.—*adjs.* ontologic (*-tə-loj'ik*), -al.—*adv.* ontolog'ically.—*n.* ontol'ogist. [Gr. *ōn, ontos*, pr.p. of *einai*, to be, *logos*, discourse.]

onus, *ō'nəs, n.* burden: responsibility. [L. *ŏnus, -eris.*]

onward, *on'wərd, adj.* going on: advancing: advanced.—*adv.* (also on'wards) toward a place or time in advance or in front: forward: in continuation of forward movement.—*adv.* on'wardly (*rare*). [on, and suff. -ward.]

onyx, *on'iks, n.* (*min.*) an agate formed of alternate flat layers of chalcedony, white or yellow and black, brown or red, used for making cameos: onychite, onyx-marble: a finger-nail-like opacity in the cornea of the eye.—*ns.* onycha (*on'i-kä*), an ingredient in ancient Jewish incense: the nail-like operculum of a mollusc; onych'ia, inflammation of the nail-bed; on'ychite, onyx-marble; onychi'tis, inflammation of the soft parts about the nail; onych'ium, a pulvillus in insects; onychocrypto'sis, ingrowing toe-nail; on'ychomancy, divination by the finger-nails; onychophagist (*-kof'ə-jist*), a nail-biter; onychoph'agy.—*n.pl.* Onychoph'ora, the Prototracheata, the class to which Peripatus belongs.—*n.* on'yx-mar'ble, a banded travertine or stalagmite, also called oriental alabaster. [Gr. *onyx, onychos*, nail, claw, onyx.]

oo', *ōō*, a Scots form of wool.

oo, *ōō*, a Scots form of we.—*gen.* oor.

oodles, *ōō'dlz, n.pl.* (*U.S.*) abundance. — Also ood'lins. [Perh. huddle.]

oof, *ōōf, n.* (*slang*) money—orig. oof'tish. [Yiddish —Ger. *auf* (dem) *tische*, on the table.]

oogamy, *ō-og'ə-mi, n.* union of unlike gametes.— *adj.* oog'amous. [Gr. *ōion*, egg, *gamos*, marriage.]

oogenesis, *ō-ō-jen'i-sis, n.* the genesis and development of the ovum—also oogeny (*ō-oj'i-ni*).—*adj.* oogenet'ic. [Gr. *ōion*, egg, *genesis*, formation.]

oogonium, *ō-ō-gō'ni-əm, n.* the female reproduction organ in seaweeds and fungi:—*pl.* oogo'nia.— *adj.* oogo'nial. [Gr. *ōion*, egg, *gonos*, offspring.]

ooidal, *ō-oi'dəl, adj.* egg-shaped. [Gr. *ōioeidēs—ōion* and *eidos*, form.]

oolakan, oulakan, *ōō'lə-kən.* Same as eulachon.

oolite, *ō'ə-līt, n.* (*geol.*) a kind of limestone composed of grains like the eggs or roe of a fish: Oolite, stratigraphically the upper part of the Jurassic in Britain, consisting largely of oolites.—*adj.* oolitic (*ō-ə-lit'ik*). [Gr. *ōion*, an egg, *lithos*, a stone.]

oology, *ō-ol'ə-ji, n.* the science or study of birds' eggs.—*n.* ool'ogist. [Gr. *ōion*, an egg, *logos*, discourse.]

oolong, oulong, *ōō'long, n.* a variety of black tea with the flavour of green. [Chin. *wu-lung*, black dragon.]

oom, *ōōm, n.* (*S.Afr.*) uncle. [Du.]

oomiak. Same as umiak.

oon, *ōn, n.* a Scots form of oven.

oons, *ōōnz, interj.* (*arch.*) a minced oath, for God's *wounds*.

oont, *ōōnt, n.* (*Anglo-Ind.*) a camel. [Hind. *ūnt.*]

oop. See **oup**.

oophoron, *ō-of'ər-on, n.* (*zool.*) an ovary.—*ns.* **oophorec'tomy**, (*surg.*) removal of an ovary; **oophori'tis**, inflammation of the ovary. [Gr. *ōiophoros*, *-on*, egg-bearing.]

oophyte, *ō'ə-fīt, n.* in ferns and mosses, the gametophyte. [Gr. *ōion*, egg, *phyton*, plant.]

oorial. Same as **urial**.

oorie. Same as **ourie**.

oosphere, *ō'ə-sfēr, n.* an unfertilised ovum. [Gr. *ōion*, egg, *sphairā*, sphere.]

oospore, *ō'ə-spōr, n.* a zygote, esp. a resting zygote. [Gr. *ōion*, egg, *sporos*, seed.]

ooze, *ōōz, n.* (*obs.*) sap: the liquor of a tan vat: gentle flow, as of water through sand or earth: slimy mud: a fine-grained, soft, deep-sea deposit, composed of shells and fragments of foraminifera, diatoms, and other organisms.—*v.i.* to flow gently: to percolate, as a liquid through pores or small openings: to leak.—*v.t.* to exude.—*adv.* **ooz'ily**.—*n.* **oozi'ness**.—*adj.* **ooz'y**, resembling ooze: slimy: oozing. [Partly O.E. *wós*, juice, partly O.E. *wáse*, mud.]

ooze, *ōōz, n.* (*Scot.*) fluff: nap.—*adj.* **ooz'y**. [Prob. pl. of **oo'**.]

op. See **opus**.

opacity, opacous. See under **opaque**.

opah, *ō'pä, n.* the kingfish (Lampris), a large seafish with laterally flattened body, constituting a family of uncertain affinities. [West African origin.]

opal, *ō'pl, n.* amorphous silica with some water, usually milky white with fine play of colour, in some varieties precious: opal-glass: the colouring of opal.—*adj.* of opal: like opal.—*adj.* **o'paled**.—*n.* **opalesc'ence**, a milky iridescence.—*adj.* **opalesc'ent**.—*n.* **o'pal-glass'**, white or opalescent glass.—*adj.* **o'paline** (*-ēn, -īn*), relating to, like, or of opal.—*n.* opal-glass: a photographic print fixed on plate-glass. — *adj.* **o'palised**, converted into opal: opalescent. [L. *opalus*; Gr. *opallios*, perh.—Sans. *upala*, gem.]

opaque, *ō-pāk', adj.* shady: dark: dull: that cannot be seen through: impervious to light or to radiation of some particular kind: (*fig.*) obscure, hard to understand: impervious to sense: doltish.—*v.t.* to make opaque.—*n.* **opacity** (*ō-pas'i-ti*), opaqueness. — *adj.* **opacous** (*ō-pā'kas*). — *adv.* **opaque'ly**.—*n.* **opaque'ness**, quality of being opaque: want of transparency. [L. *opācus.*]

ope, *ōp, adj., v.t.*, and *v.i.* (*poet.*) a shortened form of **open**.

opeidoscope, *op-ī'də-skōp, n.* an instrument for illustrating sound by means of light. [Gr. *ops* (found in the oblique cases), voice, *eidos*, form, *skopeein*, to look at.]

open, *ō'pn, adj.* not shut: allowing passage out or in: exposing the interior: unobstructed: free: unenclosed: exposed: uncovered: liable: generally accessible: available: ready to receive or transact business with members of the public: public: free to be discussed: obvious: unconcealed: undisguised: unfolded, spread out, expanded: unrestricted: not finally decided, concluded, settled, or assigned: not dense in distribution or texture: widely spaced: loose: much interrupted by spaces or holes: (*naut.*) showing a visible space between: clear: unfrozen: not frosty: not hazy: free from trees: frank: unreserved: (*mus.*) unstopped: without use of valve, crook, or key: (of an organ pipe) not closed at the top: (of a vowel sound) low, with wide aperture for the breath: (of a consonant) without stopping of the breath stream: (of a syllable) ending with a vowel.—*v.t.* to make open: to make as an opening: to make an opening in: to clear: to expose to view: to expound: to declare open: to begin.—*v.i.* to become open: to have an opening, aperture, or passage: to serve as passage: to begin to appear: to begin: to give tongue: to speak out.—*n.* a clear space: public view: open market: an opening.—*adjs.* **o'penable**; **o'pen-**

air', outdoor; **o'pen-armed'**, cordially welcoming.—*n.* **o'pen-cast**, in mining, an excavation open overhead.—Also *adj.* and *adv.*—*adj.* **o'pen-chain'**, (*chem.*) with atoms linked together as a chain with loose ends. — *n.* **o'pener**. — *adjs.* **o'pen-eyed**, (*Shak.*) watchful: astonished: fully aware of what is involved; **o'pen-field**, having the arable land in unenclosed strips held by different cultivators; **o'pen-hand'ed**, with an open hand: generous: liberal.—*n.* **o'pen-hand'edness**.—*adj.* **o'pen-heart'ed**, with an open heart: frank: generous.—*n.* **o'pen-heart'edness**.—*adj.* **o'pen-hearth**, making use of, or having, a shallow hearth of reverberating type.—*n.* **o'pening**, an open place: a breach: an aperture: a gap: a street or road breaking the line of another: a beginning: a preliminary statement of a case in court: the initial moves, or mode of beginning, in a game: (*U.S.*) a shopkeeper's first display of a new season's goods: the two pages exposed together when a book is opened: opportunity.—*adv.* **o'penly**.—*adj.* **o'pen-mind'ed**, free from prejudice: ready to receive and consider new ideas.—*n.* **o'pen-mind'edness**.—*adj.* **o'pen-mouthed**, gaping: expectant: greedy: clamorous.—*ns.* **o'penness**; **o'pen-ses'ame**, a spell or other means of making barriers fly open—from the story of Ali Baba and the Forty Thieves in the *Arabian Nights*; **o'pen-stitch** (*Scot.* **o'pen-steek**), a kind of open-work stitching; **o'pen-work**, any work showing openings through it.—*adj.* **open-cast**.—**open access**, public access to the shelves of a library; **open aestivation**, aestivation without overlap or meeting of the edges of the perianth leaves; **open book**, anything that can be read or interpreted without difficulty; **open bundle**, a vascular bundle with cambium; **open circuit**, a broken circuit; **open diapason**, one of the chief foundation stops of an organ; **open door**, free and equal opportunity of trading for all; **open fire**, an exposed fire on a domestic hearth: to begin to shoot; **open harmony**, chords not in close position; **open house**, hospitality to all comers; **open letter**, a letter addressed to a person but intended for public reading; **open note**, a note produced by an unstopped string, open pipe, or without crook, &c.: (*U.S.*) a printed or written note without a solid black head—a semibreve or minim; **open out**, to make or become more widely open: to expand: to disclose: to unpack: to develop: to bring into view: to open the throttle, accelerate; **open question**, a matter undecided; **open score**, one with a separate stave for each part; **open sea**, unenclosed sea, clear of headlands; **open secret**, a matter known to many but not explicitly divulged; **open shop**, a factory not confined to union labour; **open town**, one without troops or military installations, and hence, according to international law, immune from attack of any kind; **open up**, to open thoroughly or more thoroughly: to lay open: to disclose: to make available for traffic, colonisation, or the like; **open verdict**, a verdict that a crime has been committed without specifying the criminal. [O.E. *open*; cf. Du. *open*, O.N. *opinn*, Ger. *offen*; prob. related to **up**.]

opera, *op'ə-rä, n.* musical drama (**comic opera**— which may end tragically—admits spoken dialogue; **grand opera** does not): an opera-house.—*adj.* used in or for an opera.—*ns.* **op'era-cloak**, an elegant cloak for evening wear, esp. in the auditorium of a theatre; **op'era-danc'er**, one who dances in ballets introduced into operas; **op'era-glass**, a small binocular telescope for use in the theatre; **op'era-hat**, a collapsible tall hat; **op'era-house**, a theatre for opera; **op'era-sing'er**.—*adj.* **operatic** (*-at'ik*), pertaining to or resembling opera.—*adv.* **operat'ically**. [It.,—L. *opera*; cf. **operate**.]

opera, *op'ə-rä, pl.* of **opus**.

opera-bouffe, *op'ə-rä-bōōf, n.* a funny or farcical opera. [Fr. *opéra-bouffe*.—It. *opera-buffa*; cf. **buffoon**.]

operate, *op'ə-rāt, v.i.* to work: to exert strength: to produce any effect: to exert moral power:

(*U.S.*) to be in activity, act, carry on business : (*med.*) to take effect upon the human system : (*surg.*) to perform some unusual act upon the body with the hand or an instrument.—*v.t.* to effect : to produce by agency : to work : (*U.S.*) to conduct, run, carry on.—*adjs.* **op'erable**, admitting of an operation ; **op'erant**, operative : active : effective. —*n.* an operator.—*adj.* **op'erāting**.—*n.* **operā'tion**, act or process of operating : that which is done or carried out : agency : influence : method of working : action or movements : surgical performance.— *adjs.* **operā'tional**, relating to operations ; **op'erative**, having the power of operating or acting : exerting force : producing effects : efficacious.—*n.* a workman in a manufactory : a labourer.—*adv.* **op'eratively**.—*ns.* **op'erativeness** ; **op'erātor**, one who, or that which, operates : one charged with the operation of a machine, instrument, or apparatus : one who deals in stocks : (*U.S.*) a mineowner : (*math.*) a symbol, signifying an operation to be performed.—**operating table, theatre**, one set apart for use in surgical operations ; **operational research**, systematic investigation to discover how a weapon, tactic, or strategy can be altered to give better results ; **operative words**, the words in a deed legally effecting the transaction (e.g. *devise and bequeath* in a will) : (*loosely*) the most significant words. [L. *operārī, -ātus—opera*, work, closely connected with *opus, operis*, work.]

operculum, *ō-pər'kū-ləm, n.* (*bot.*) a cover or lid : (*zool.*) the plate over the entrance of a shell : the gill-cover of fishes :—*pl.* oper'cula.—*adjs.* **oper'cular**, belonging to the operculum ; **oper'culate, -d**, having an operculum. [L. *operculum—operīre*, to cover.]

operetta, *op-ə-ret'ä, n.* a short, light musical drama. —*n.* **operett'ist**, a composer of operettas. [It., dim. of *opera*.]

operose, *op'ə-rōs, adj.* laborious : tedious.—*adv.* **op'erosely**.—*ns.* **op'eroseness, operosity** (*-os'i-ti*). [L. *operōsus—opus, operis*, work.]

ophi-, ophio-, *of'i- -ō-*, or *-o'-*, in composition, snake.—*ns.* **ophical'cite**, a marble containing green serpentine ; **oph'icleide** (*-klīd* ; Fr. *ophicléide*— Gr. *kleis, kleidos*, key), a keyed wind-instrument developed from the serpent, a bass or alto key-bugle.—*n.pl.* **Ophid'ia** (Gr. *ophidion*, dim.), the snakes as an order or suborder of reptiles.—*n.* and *adj.* **ophid'ian**.—*ns.* **ophidiā'rium**, a snake-house ; **Ophioglossa'cum** (Gr. *glōssa*, tongue), the adder's-tongue genus, giving name to the **Ophioglossā'ceae**, a family of eusporangiate ferns ; **ophiol'ater**, a snake-worshipper ; **ophiol'atry** (Gr. *latreiā*, worship), snake-worship.—*adjs.* **ophiol'atrous** ; **ophiolog'ic, -al**.—*ns.* **ophiol'ogist** ; **ophiol'ogy**, the study of snakes ; **oph'iomorph** (Gr. *morphē*, form), a caecilian amphibian.—*adjs.* **ophiomorph'ic, -ous**, snakelike ; **ophioph'agous** (Gr. *phagein*, to eat), snake-eating.—*ns.* **ophioph'ilist**, a snake-lover ; **Oph'ism** ; **oph'ite**, a name given to various rocks mottled with green : (*anc.*) serpentine-rock : (later) a kind of diabase : **Ophite**, one of a Gnostic sect that reverenced snakes.—*adj.* **ophitic** (*of-it'ik*), pertaining to ophite : having pyroxene crystals enclosing felspar laths : **Ophitic**, of the Ophites.—*ns.* **Oph'itism** ; **Ophiura** (*-ōō'rä, -ū'rä* ; Gr. *ourā*, tail), a genus of brittle-stars.— *ns.* and *adjs.* **ophiu'ran** ; **ophiu'rid** ; **ophiu'roid**. —*ns.pl.* **Ophiu'rida, Ophiuroid'ea**, the brittle-stars, a class of echinoderms like starfish with long snaky sharply differentiated arms. [Gr. *ophis*, snake.]

ophthalm-, -of-thalm'-, of'-, in composition, eye.—*n.* **ophthalm'ia**, inflammation of the eye, esp. of the conjunctiva. — *adj.* **ophthal'mic**, pertaining to the eye.—*ns.* **ophthal'mist**, an ophthalmologist ; **ophthalmī'tis**, ophthalmia.—*adj.* **ophthalmolog'ical**.—*ns.* **ophthalmol'ogist** ; **ophthalmol'ogy**, the science of the eye, its structure, functions, and diseases ; **ophthalmom'eter**, an instrument for eye-measurements ; **ophthalmom'etry** ; **ophthalmoplegia** (*-plē'jyä* ; Gr. *plēgē*, a stroke), paralysis of one or more of the muscles of the eye ; **ophthal'moscope**, an instrument for examining the interior of the eye.—*adjs.* **ophthalmoscop'ic, -al**.—*adv.*

ophthalmoscop'ically. — *n.* **ophthalmos'copy,** examination of the interior of the eye with the ophthalmoscope. [Gr. *ophthalmos*, eye.]

opiate, *ō'pi-āt, n.* a drug containing opium to induce sleep : that which dulls sensation, physical or mental.—*adj.* inducing sleep.—*v.t.* to treat with opium : to dull.—*adj.* **o'piated**. [opium.]

opificer, *op-if'i-sər, n.* an artificer. [L. *opifex, -icis —opus*, work, *facēre*, to make.]

opine, *ō-pīn', v.t.* to suppose : to form or express as an opinion.—*adj.* **opin'able**, capable of being thought. [Fr. *opiner*—L. *opīnārī*, to think.]

opinicus, *o-pin'i-kəs, n.* (*her.*) a half-lion, half-dragon. [Origin unknown.]

opinion, *ō-pin'yən, n.* what seems to one to be probably true : judgment : estimation : favourable estimation : (*Shak.*) self-confidence : (*Shak.*) arrogance : (*Shak.*) reputation.—*adjs.* **opin'ionāted, opin'ionātive, opin'ioned**, unduly attached to one's own opinions : stubborn.—*advs.* **opin'ionately** (*obs.*), **opin'ionātively**.—*ns.* **opin'ionātiveness** ; **opin'ionist**, one who holds or gives an opinion, or (*obs.*) an unusual or heterodox opinion. [L. *opīniō, -ōnis*.]

opisometer, *op-i-som'i-tər, n.* a map-measuring instrument with a wheel that traces a line on the map and then runs backward along the scale. [Gr. *opisō*, backward, *metron*, measure.]

opisth-, opistho-, in composition, behind.—*n.* and *adj.* **opisthobranch** (*ō-pis'thō-brangk* ; Gr. *branchia*, gills).—*n.pl.* **Opisthobranch'ia**, an order of gasteropods having the gills behind the heart.— *adj.* **opisthocoelian** (*-sē'li-ən* ; Gr. *koilos*, hollow), hollow or concave behind, as a vertebra.—Also **opisthocoe'lous**.—*n.* **opisthodomos** (*op-is-thod'o-mos*), a rear-chamber in a Greek temple.—*adjs.* **opisthogloss'al** (Gr. *glōssa*, tongue), having the tongue attached in front, free behind, as in frogs ; **opisthog'nathous** (Gr. *gnathos*, jaw), having retreating jaws.—*n.* **opis'thograph**, a manuscript or slab inscribed on the back as well as the front.— *adj.* **opisthograph'ic**.—*n.* **opisthog'raphy**. [Gr. *opisthen*, behind.]

opium, *ō'pi-əm, n.* the dried narcotic juice of the white poppy.—*ns.* **o'pium-den'**, a resort of opium-smokers ; **o'pium-eat'er, -smoker**, one who makes a habitual use of opium. [L. *ōpium*— Gr. *opion*, dim. from *opos*, sap.]

opobalsam, *op-ō-bawl'səm, n.* balm of Gilead. [Gr. *opobalsamon—opos*, juice, *balsamon*, balsam-tree.]

opodeldoc, *op-ō-del'dok, n.* a name given by Paracelsus to various local applications : soap-liniment. [Derivation unknown, apparently Gr. *opos*, juice.]

opopanax, *ō-pop'ə-naks, n.* a gum-resin formerly used in medicine, got from the roots of a Persian (and S. European) species of parsnip : a perfume got from Commiphora. [Gr. *opos*, juice, *panax*, a panacea.]

oporice, *ō-por'i-sē, n.* a medicine prepared from quinces, pomegranates, &c. [Gr. *opōrikē—opōrā*, late summer, summer fruits.]

opossum, *ō-pos'əm, n.* any member of the American genus Didelphys, or family Didelphyidae, small marsupials, often pouchless, mainly arboreal, with prehensile tail : in Australia, a phalanger : opossum-fur.—Also (*U.S.*) **possum, 'possum.—to play possum**, to feign death. [American Indian.]

opotherapy, *op-ō-ther'ə-pi, n.* treatment by administration of extracts of animal organs, especially of ductless glands. [Gr. *opos*, juice, and **therapy**.]

oppidan, *op'i-dən, n.* a townsman : in university towns one who is not a member of the university, or a student not resident in a college : at Eton (formerly elsewhere) a schoolboy who is not a foundationer or colleger.—*adj.* urban. [L. *oppidānus—oppidum*, town.]

oppignorate, oppignerate, *op-ig'nə-rāt, v.t.* to pawn. — *n.* **oppignorā'tion**. [L. *oppignorāre, oppignerāre—ob*, against, *pignus, -oris, -eris*, a pledge.]

oppilate, *op'il-āt, v.t.* to block up, stop up.—*n.* **oppilā'tion**.—*adj.* **opp'ilātive**. [L. *oppilāre, -ātum —ob*, in the way, *pilāre*, to ram down.]

opponent, *o-pō'nənt, adj.* opposing : placed opposite or in front.—*n.* an opposer.—*n.* **oppo'nency**. [L.

oppōnēns, -entis, pr.p. of *oppōnĕre—ob,* in the way of, *pōnĕre,* to place.]

opportune, *op'ər-tūn,* or *-tūn'* (*Shak.* op-or'tūn), *adj.* occurring at a fitting time : conveniently presented : timely : convenient : suitable : opportunist.—*adv.* **opportune'ly** (or *op'*).—*ns.* **opportune'ness** (or *op'*); **opportun'ism** (or *op'*), practice of regulating actions by favourable opportunities rather than consistent principles; **opportun'ist** (or *op'*), a politician who waits for events before declaring his opinions, or shapes his policy to circumstances of the moment : a person without settled principles.—Also *adj.*—*n.* **opportun'ity,** (*rare*) opportuneness : (*obs.*) fitness : an occasion offering a possibility. [Fr. *opportun*—L. *opportūnus—ob,* before, *portus, -ūs,* a harbour.]

oppose, *o-pōz',* *v.t.* to place in front or in the way (with *to*): to place or apply face to face or front to front : to set in contrast or balance : to set in contention : to place as an obstacle : to face : to resist : to contend with.—*v.i.* to make objection.— *n.* **opposabil'ity.**—*adjs.* **oppos'able,** that may be opposed : capable of being applied by the front surface (as a thumb); **oppose'less,** (*Shak.*) not to be opposed, irresistible.—*n.* **oppos'er.** [Fr. *opposer* —L. *ob,* against, Fr. *poser,* to place—L. *pausāre,* to rest, stop; see **pose.**]

opposite, *op'ə-zit, adj.* placed over against : standing in front : face to face : facing on the other side : (*bot.*) of foliage leaves, in pairs at each node, with the stem between : of floral parts, on the same radius : directly contrary : diametrically opposed : opposed : corresponding.—*adv.* in or to an opposite position or positions.—*prep.* opposite to.—*n.* that which is opposed or contrary : an opponent : (*Milt.*) opposition.—*adv.* **opp'ositely.** —*n.* **opp'ositeness.**—*adj.* **oppositive** (*-poz'*), characterised by opposing : adversative : inclined to oppose.—**be opposite with** (*Shak.*), to be perverse and contradictory in dealing with; **opposite number,** one who has a corresponding place in another set : one who is allotted to another as partner, opponent, &c. [Fr.,—L. *oppositus—ob,* against, *pōnĕre,* to place.]

opposition, *op-ə-zish'ən, n.* the act of opposing or of setting opposite : the state of being opposed or placed opposite : opposed or opposite position : an opposite : contrast : contradistinction : resistance : (*logic*) a difference of quantity or quality between two propositions having the same subject and predicate : a body of opposers : the party that opposes the ministry or existing administration : (*astron.*) the situation of a heavenly body, as seen from the earth, when it is directly opposite to another, esp. the sun.—*adj.* of the parliamentary opposition.—*adj.* **opposi'tional.**—*n.* **opposi'tionist,** a member of the opposition. [L. *oppositiō, -ōnis;* cf. **opposite.**]

oppress, *o-pres', v.t.* to press against or upon : (*obs.*) to crush : (*obs.*) to smother : to overwhelm : (*obs.*) to take by surprise : to distress : to lie heavy upon : to treat with tyrannical cruelty or injustice : to load with heavy burdens : (*obs.*) to ravish.— *n.* **oppression** (*o-presh'ən*), act of oppressing : tyranny : feeling of distress or of being weighed down : dullness of spirits : (*Shak.*) pressure.— *adj.* **oppress'ive,** tending to oppress : overburdensome : tyrannical : heavy : overpowering.—*adv.* **oppress'ively.**—*ns.* **oppress'iveness; oppress'or.** [Fr. *oppresser*—L.L. *oppressāre,* freq. of L. *opprimĕre, oppressum—ob,* against, *premĕre,* to press.]

opprobrium, *o-prō'bri-əm, n.* disgrace, reproach, or imputation of shameful conduct : infamy : anything that brings such reproach.—*adj.* **opprobrious,** expressive of opprobrium or disgrace : reproachful : infamous.—*adv.* **oppro'briously.**— *n.* **oppro'briousness.** [L. *opprobrium—ob,* against, *probrum,* reproach.]

oppugn, *o-pūn', v.t.* to assail, esp. by argument : to oppose : to call in question.—*n.* **oppugnancy** (*o-pug'nən-si*), (*Shak.*) antagonism.—*adj.* **oppug'nant,** opposing : hostile.—*n.* an opponent.—*n.* **oppugner** (*o-pūn'ər*). [L. *oppugnāre,* to attack— *ob,* against, *pugna,* a fight.]

opsimath, *op'si-math, n.* one who learns late in life.

—*n.* **opsim'athy,** learning obtained late in life. [Gr. *opsimathēs—opse,* late, *mathē,* learning.]

opsiometer, *op-si-om'i-tər, n.* an optometer. [Gr. *opsis,* sight, *metron,* measure.]

opsonium, *op-sō'ni-əm, n.* anything eaten with bread as a relish, esp. fish.—*ns.* **opsomā'nia,** any morbid love for some special kind of food ; **opso-mā'niac.**—*adj.* **opsonic** (*op-son'ik*), relating to opsonin.—*n.* **op'sonin,** a constituent of blood-serum which makes bacteria more readily consumed by phagocytes. [Latinised from Gr. *opsōnion—opson,* cooked food, relish.]

opt, *opt, v.i.* to make a choice, esp. of nationality when territory is transferred.—*n.* **opt'ant,** one who opts : one who has exercised a power of choosing, esp. his nationality.—*adj.* **optative** (*opt'ə-tiv,* or *op-tā'tiv*), expressing desire or wish.—*n.* (*gram.*) a mood of the verb expressing wish.—*adv.* **op'tatively.** [L. *optāre, -ātum,* to choose, wish.]

optic, -al, *op'tik, -əl, adjs.* relating to sight, or to the eye, or to optics.—*n.* **op'tic,** (now mainly *facet.*) an eye : (*obs.*) a lens, telescope, or microscope.— *adv.* **op'tically.**—*ns.* **optician** (*op-tish'ən*), formerly one skilled in optics : one who makes or sells optical instruments ; **op'tics** (treated as *sing.*), the science of light ; **optol'ogist,** an optician ; **optol'ogy ; optom'eter,** an instrument for sight-testing ; **optom'etrist,** a sight-tester ; **optom'etry ; op'tophone,** an instrument that translates printed characters into arbitrary sounds, and so enables the blind to read ordinary type.—**optic axis,** the axis of the eye—a line through the middle of the pupil and the centre of the eye : in a doubly refracting crystal, a direction in which no double refraction occurs ; **optic lobe,** part of the mid-brain concerned with sight. [Gr. *optikos,* optic, *optos,* seen.]

optimate, *op'ti-māt, n.* (*rare* in *sing.*) a member of the aristocracy :—*pl.* (L.) **optimā'tēs.** [L. *optimās, -ātis—optimus,* best.]

optime, *op'ti-mi, n.* formerly, in the university of Cambridge, one of those in the second or third rank of mathematical honours (*senior* or *junior optime*), next to the wranglers. [L. *optimē* (adv.), very well, best.]

optimism, *op'ti-mizm, n.* Leibniz's doctrine that the world is the best of all possible worlds : a belief that everything is ordered for the best : (*loosely*) a disposition to take a bright, hopeful view of things : (*vulg.*) hopefulness, hope—opp. to *pessimism.*—*v.i.* **op'timise,** to take the most hopeful view of anything.—*v.t.* to make the most or best of.—*n.* **op'timist,** one who believes in optimism : (*commonly*) a sanguine person.—*adj.* **optimist'ic.** —*adv.* **optimist'ically.** [L. *optimus,* best.]

optimum, *op'ti-məm, n.* that point at which any condition is most favourable :—*pl.* **op'tima.**—Also *adj.* [L., neut. of *optimus,* best.]

option, *op'shən, n.* act of choosing : power or right of choosing : a thing that may be chosen : an alternative for choice : a power (as of buying at a fixed price) that may be exercised at will within a time-limit : wish.—*adj.* **op'tional,** left to choice : not compulsory : leaving to choice.—*adv.* **op'tionally.** —**local option** (see **local**). [L. *optiō, -ōnis optāre,* to choose.]

opto-. See optic.

opulent, *op'ū-lənt, adj.* wealthy : loaded with wealth : luxuriant : over-enriched.—*n.* **op'ulence,** riches : abounding riches.—*adv.* **op'ulently.** [L. *opulentus.*]

opulus, *op'ū-ləs, n.* the guelder rose. [L. *opulus,* a kind of maple.]

Opuntia, *ō-pun'shi-ä, n.* the prickly-pear genus of the cactus family. [L. *Opūntia* (*herba,* plant), of *Opūs* (Gr. *Opous*), a town of Locris where Pliny said it grew.]

opus, *op'əs,* or *ō'pəs, n.* a work, a musical composition—esp. one numbered in order of publication, as opus 6 (*op.* 6) :—*pl.* (not much used) **opera** (*op'ə-rä*). [L. *ŏpus, -eris,* work.]

opuscule, *o-pus'kūl, n.* a little work.—Also **opuscle** (*o-pus'l*), **opus'culum** :—*pl.* **-la.** [L. dim. of *opus.*]

or, *or, conj.* (or *adv.*) and *prep.* before (in time).

or ever, or e'er, or (by confusion) **or ere,** before

ever, before even. [O.E. (Northumbrian) and O.N. *ár*, early, with the sense of O.E. *ǽr*, ere ; see **ere**.]

or, *or*, *conj.* marking an alternative. [M.E. *other*.]

or, *or*, *n.* (*her.*) the tincture gold or yellow, indicated in engraving and chiselling by dots. [Fr.,—L. *aurum*, gold.]

orach, **orache**, *or'ich*, *n.* a genus (Atriplex) of the goosefoot family, sometimes used like spinach. [Fr. *arroche*—L. *atriplex*—Gr. *atraphaxys* ; origin unknown.]

oracle, *or'ə-kl*, *n.* a medium or agency of divine revelation : a response by or on behalf of a god : the place where such responses are given : the Jewish sanctuary : the word of God : a person with the repute or air of infallibility or great wisdom : an infallible indication : a wise or seeming-wise or mysterious utterance.—*v.i.* to utter as an oracle.—*v.i.* to speak as an oracle.—*adj.* **oracular** (*or-ak'ū-lər*), of the nature of an oracle : like an oracle : seeming to claim the authority of an oracle : delivering oracles : equivocal : ambiguous : obscure—also **orac'ulous** (now *rare*).—*ns.* **oracularity** (*-lar'i-ti*), **orac'ularness**, **orac'ulousness**.—*advs.* **orac'ularly**, **orac'ulously.—work the oracle**, to achieve the desired result by manipulation, intrigue, wire-pulling, favour, &c. : to raise money. [L. *ōrāculum*—*ōrāre*, to speak.]

oragious, *ō-rā'jəs*, *adj.* stormy. [Fr. *orageux*.]

oral, *ō'rl*, *adj.* relating to the mouth : near the mouth : uttered by the mouth : spoken, not written.—*n.* an oral examination.—*adv.* **o'rally.** [L. *ōs*, *ōris*, the mouth.]

orang. See **orang-utan.**

orange, *or'inj*, *-inzh*, *n.* a delightful gold-coloured fruit with a thick skin, within which are usually from eight to ten juicy divisions : the tree (*Citrus Aurantium*, of the Rutaceae) on which it grows : extended to various unrelated but superficially similar fruits and plants : a colour between red and yellow. —*adj.* pertaining to an orange : orange-coloured. —*ns.* **orangeade** (*-jād'*, *-zhād'*), a drink made with orange juice ; **or'ange-bloss'om**, the white blossom of the orange-tree, worn by brides : that of the mock-orange, similarly used.—*adj.* **or'ange-col'oured.—*ns.* **or'ange-flower**, orange-blossom (**orange-flower water**, a solution of oil of neroli) ; **or'ange-grass'**, a small American St John's-wort ; **or'ange-lil'y**, a garden lily with large orange flowers ; **or'ange-peel**, the rind of an orange, often candied ; **or'ange-root**, golden-seal ; **or'angery** (*-ri*, *-ər-i*), a house or other place for growing orange-trees ; **or'ange-squeez'er**, an instrument for squeezing out the juice of oranges ; **or'ange-stick**, a stick of orange-wood, used in the care of the nails.—*adj.* and *n.* **or'ange-taw'ny** (*Shak.*).—*ns.* **or'ange-tip'**, a butterfly (Euchloe or kindred) with an orange patch near the tip of the fore-wing ; **or'ange-tree** ; **or'ange-wife** (*Shak.*), a woman who sells oranges ; **or'ange-wood.** [Fr., ult. from Ar. *nāranj* ; cf. L.L. *arangia*, *aurantia*, *narancum* ; It. *arancia*, earlier *narancia* ; Sp. *naranja* ; the loss of the *n* may be due to confusion with the indef. art. (*una*, *une*), the vowel changes to confusion with L. *aurum*, Fr. *or*, gold.]

Orange, *or'inj*, *-inzh*, *adj.* relating to the family of the princes of *Orange*, a former principality from the 11th century, passing by an heiress to the house of Nassau in 1531, the territory ceded to France in 1713 : favouring the cause of the Prince of Orange in Holland or in Great Britain and Ireland : of or favouring the Orangemen : extreme Protestant Irish Conservative.—*ns.* **Or'angism (Or'angeism)** ; **Or'angeman**, a member of a society revived and organised in Ireland in 1795 to uphold Orange principles.

orang-utan, *ō-rang'-ōō-tan'*, strictly *ō'rang-ōō'tan*, also (old-fashioned) **orang-outang**, *ō-rang'-ōō-tang'*, formerly **oran(g)-outang**, *ō'ran(g)-ōō'tang*, *n.* an anthropoid ape, found only in the forests of Sumatra and Borneo, reddish-brown, arboreal in habit : (erroneously) a chimpanzee.—Also **orang'**. [Malay *ō'rang ū'tan*, man of the woods (said not to be applied by the Malays to the ape)—*ōrang*, man, *ūtan*, wood, wild.]

orant, *ō'rənt*, *n.* a worshipping figure in ancient

Greek and early Christian art. [L. *ōrāns*, *-antis*, pr.p. of *ōrāre*, to pray.]

orarian, *ō-rā'ri-ən*, *adj.* coastal.—*n.* a coast-dweller. [L. *ōrārius*—*ōra*, shore.]

orarium, *ō-rā'ri-əm*, *n.* (*ant.*) a handkerchief : (*obs.*) a stole : a scarf attached to a bishop's staff.—*n.* **ora'rion**, a Greek Church deacon's stole. [L. *ōrārium*—*ōs*, *ōris*, mouth.]

orarium, *ō-rā'ri'-əm*, *n.* a book of private devotions. [L. *ōrāre*, to pray.]

oration, *ō-rā'shən*, *n.* a formal speech : a harangue. —*v.i.* **orate'** (*facet.*), to harangue, hold forth. [L. *ōrātiō*, *-ōnis*—*ōrāre*, to pray.]

orator, *or'ə-tər*, *n.* (*obs.*) a spokesman : (*obs.*) a petitioner : a public speaker : a man of eloquence : —*fem.* **or'atress**, **oratrix** (*or-ā'triks*, or *or'ə-triks*). —*adjs.* **oratorial** (*or-ə-tō'ri-əl*), of an orator, oratory, or an oratory ; **orato'rian**, of an oratory.— *n.* a priest of an oratory : **Oratōrian**, a member of an Oratory.—*adj.* **oratorical** (*-tor'*), characteristic of an orator : addicted to oratory : rhetorical : relating to or savouring of oratory.—*adv.* **orator'ically.—*n.* **or'atory**, the art of the orator : rhetoric : rhetorical utterances or expression : a place for private prayer : a lectern for praying at : (*obs.*) a place of public speaking : **Oratory**, one of various congregations in the R.C. Church, esp. the Fathers of the Oratory, established by St Philip Neri (1515-95) : a church of the Oratorians. [L. *ōrātor*, *-ōris*—*ōrāre*, to pray.]

oratorio, *or-ə-tō'ri-ō*, *n.* a story, usually Biblical, set to music, with soloists, chorus, and full orchestra, scenery, costumes, and acting, however, being now dispensed with : the form of such composition :—*pl.* **orato'rios.**—*adj.* **orato'rial.** [It. *oratorio*—L. *ōrātōrium*, an oratory, because they developed out of the singing at devotional meetings in church oratories.]

orb, *orb*, *n.* a circle : a sphere : anything round : a celestial body : an eyeball : the mound or globe of a king's regalia : the space within which the astrological influence of a planet operates : a sphere carrying a planet in its revolution : a cycle of time : an orbit : a world.—*v.t.* to surround : to form into an orb.—*adjs.* **orbed**, in the form of an orb : circular ; **orbic'ular**, approximately circular or spherical : round : (*petr.*) having the component minerals crystallised in spheroidal aggregates.—*n.* **orbicula'ris**, a muscle surrounding an opening :— *pl.* **orbicula'rēs.**—*adv.* **orbic'ularly.**—*adj.* **orb'y**, orbed. [L. *orbis*, circle.]

orb, *orb*, *adj.* (*obs.*) bereaved, esp. of children.—*n.* (*archit.* ; *obs.*) an obscure term generally understood to mean a blind window or blank panel.— *n.* **orb'ity** (*obs.*), bereavement, esp. of children. [L. *orbus*, bereft.]

Orbilius, *or-bil'i-əs*, *n.* a flogging schoolmaster (from Horace's teacher).

orbit, *or'bit*, *n.* the path in which a heavenly body moves round another, or an electron round the nucleus of an atom (also **or'bital**), or the like : regular course or beat : (*loosely*) an orb : the hollow in which the eyeball rests—also **or'bita** : the skin round a bird's eye.—*adj.* **or'bital.** [L. *orbita*, a wheel-track—*orbis*, a ring, wheel.]

orc, *ork*, *n.* a fierce sea-monster : a killer-whale : an ogre.—*n.* **Or'ca**, the killer-whale genus. [L. *orca*.]

Orcadian, *or'kā'di-ən*, *adj.* of Orkney.—*n.* an inhabitant or a native of Orkney. [L. *Orcadēs*—Gr. *Orkadēs*, Orkney (Islands).]

orchard, *or'chərd*, *n.* an enclosed garden of fruit-trees.—*ns.* **or'chard-grass**, (*U.S.*) cock's-foot grass ; **or'chard-house**, a glass house for cultivating fruits without artificial heat ; **or'charding** ; **or'chardist**, **or'chardman**, one who grows and sells orchard fruits. [O.E. *ort-geard*, prob. L. *hortus*, garden, and O.E. *geard* ; see **yard.** Some connect the first part with O.E. *wyrt* ; see **wort.**]

orchat, *or'chat*, *n.* (*obs.*) a form of **orchard.** [Partly *dial.*, partly due to confusion with Gr. *orchatos*, a row of trees.]

orchel, **orchella.** See **archil.**

orchestra, *or'kis-trä*, former *-kes'*, *n.* in the Greek theatre, the place in front of the stage where the chorus danced: now the part of a theatre or concert-room in which the instrumental musicians are placed: a large company of musicians (strings, woodwinds, brasses, and percussion) playing together under a conductor: loosely applied to a small group, as in a restaurant.—*ns.* orchē'sis, the art of dancing or rhythmical movement of the body; orchesog'raphy, notation of dancing.—*adj.* chestic (-*kes'tik*), relating to dancing.—*n.* (*pl.* in form) orches'tics, the art of dancing.—*adj.* orchestral (-*kes'*), of or for an orchestra.—*n.* orches'tralist, an orchestral composer.—*v.t.* or'chestrate, to dispose among the instruments of an orchestra. —*ns.* orchestrā'tion, instrumentation; or'chestrātor, one who orchestrates or is skilled in orchestration.—*adj.* orches'tric, orchestic: orchestral. —*ns.* orchestrina (-*trē'nä*), orches'trion, names given to various keyboard or barrel-organ instruments designed to imitate an orchestra.—orchestra stalls, theatre seats just behind the orchestra. [Gr. *orchēstra*—*orcheesthai*, to dance.]

orchid, or'kid, *n.* any plant, or flower, of the Orchidā'ceae or Orchid'eae, a family of monocotyledons, including many tropical epiphytes, with highly specialised, often showy, flowers, the upper petal (by twisting actually the lower) serving as a landing-place for insects (*labellum*), the one fertile stamen (or two) united with the gynaeceum as a *column*, the pollen in masses.—*adjs.* orchidā'ceous, orchid'eous.—*ns.* or'chid-house; or'chidist, a fancier or grower of orchids; orchidol'ogist; orchidol'ogy, the knowledge of orchids; orchidomā'nia, a craze for orchids; orchidomā'niac; Or'chis, a genus of orchids, including several of the best-known British species: loosely applied to other genera. [Gr. *orchis*, -*ios* or -*eōs*, a testicle (from the appearance of the root-tubers in Orchis and others); the *d* is a blunder, as if the genitive were *orchidos*.]

orchil, orchilla. See archil.

orchitis, or-kī'tis, *n.* inflammation of a testicle.— *adj.* orchitic (-*kit'ik*). [Gr. *orchis*, -*ios* or -*eōs*, testicle.]

orcinol, or'sin-ol, *n.* a dihydric phenol got from archil and other lichens.—Also or'cin, or'cine.— *n.* orcein (or'si-in), a purple dye-stuff got from orcinol. [See archil.]

ord, ord, *n.* (*obs.*) a point: a beginning. [O.E. *ord*; cf. odd.]

ordain, or-dān', *v.t.* to arrange: to establish: to decree: to destine: to order: to assign, set apart: to appoint: to set apart for an office: to invest with ministerial functions: to admit to holy orders.—*adj.* ordain'able.—*ns.* ordain'er; ordain'ment. [O.Fr. *ordener* (Fr. *ordonner*)—L. *ordināre*, -*ātum*—*ordō*, -*inis*, order.]

ordeal, or'dēl, less justifiably or-dēl' or or-dē'əl, *n.* an ancient form of referring a disputed question to the judgment of God, by lot, fire, water, &c.: any severe trial or examination.—Latinised as ordalium (or-dā'li-əm).—*adj.* ordā'lian.—ordeal bean, the Calabar bean. [O.E. *ordēl*, *orddl* (W.S. would be *ordǣl*)—pfx or-, out, *dǣl*, deal, share; cf. Du. *oordeel*, Ger. *urteil*.]

order, or'dər, *n.* arrangement: sequence: disposition: due arrangement: due condition: condition of normal or due functioning: regular or suitable arrangement: method: system: tidiness: restrained or undisturbed condition: a form of procedure or ceremony: the accepted mode of proceeding at a meeting: a practice: grade, degree, rank, or position, esp. in a hierarchy: degree of a curve or equation: command: a written instruction to pay money: a customer's instruction to supply goods or perform work: a pass for admission or other privilege: a class of society: a body of persons of the same rank, profession, &c.: a fraternity, esp. religious or knightly: a body modelled on a knightly order to which members are admitted as an honour: the insignia thereof: (*biol.*) a group above a family but below a class: (*archit.*) one of the different ways in which the column and its entablature with their various parts are moulded and related to each other: one of the successively recessed arches of an archway: due action towards

some end, esp. in old phrase 'to take order': the position of a weapon with butt on ground, muzzle close to the right side: (*U.S.*) a portion or helping: (*pl.*), the several degrees or grades of the Christian ministry.—*v.t.* to arrange: to set in order: to put in the position of order: to regulate: (*Shak.*) to conduct: to command: to give an order for: (*U.S.*) to order to be.—*v.i.* to give command.— *interj.* used in calling for order or to order.—*ns.* or'der-book, a book for entering the orders of customers, the special orders of a commanding officer, or the motions to be put to the House of Commons; or'derer; or'dering, arrangement: management: the act or ceremony of ordaining, as priests or deacons.—*adj.* or'derless, without order: disorderly.—*n.* or'derliness.—*adj.* or'derly, in good order: regular: well regulated: of good behaviour: quiet: being on duty.—*adv.* regularly: methodically.—*n.* a non-commissioned officer who carries official messages for his superior officer, formerly the first sergeant of a company: a hospital attendant: a street cleaner.—full orders, priesthood; holy orders, an institution, in the Roman and Greek Churches a sacrament, by which one is specially set apart for the service of religion; in order, with the purpose (with *to*): in accordance with the rules of procedure at meetings: (*U.S.*) appropriate, suitable, likely; in short order, (*U.S.*) promptly; minor orders, in the Roman Catholic Church those of acolyte, exorcist, reader, doorkeeper, in the Eastern Churches, reader; money order (see money); order in council, an order by the sovereign with advice of the Privy Council; orderly bin, a street receptacle for refuse; orderly officer, the officer on duty for the day; orderly room, a room for regimental, company, &c., business; order of battle, arrangement of troops or ships in preparation for a fight; order of the day, business set down for the day: a proclamation by a dictator or military commander; postal order (see post); sailing orders, written instructions given to the commander of a vessel before sailing; sealed orders, instructions not to be opened until a specified time; standing orders or rules, regulations for procedure adopted by a legislative assembly; take order, to take measures; take orders, to be ordained; to order, according to, and in fulfilment of, an order. [Fr. *ordre*—L. *ordō*, -*inis*.]

ordinal, or'din-əl, *adj.* indicating order of sequence: relating to an order.—*n.* an ordinal numeral (first, second, third, &c.—distinguished from *cardinal*): (*obs.*) a book of rules: a service-book: a book of forms of consecration and ordination. [L.L. *ordinālis*—L. *ordō*, -*inis*, order.]

ordinance, or'din-əns, *n.* that which is ordained by authority, fate, &c.: regulation: (*U.S.*) a bye-law: artistic arrangement: planning: (*obs.*) preparation: (*obs.*) equipment: (*obs.*) ordnance: decree: a religious practice enjoined by authority, esp. a sacrament: (*Shak.*) social class or order.— *n.* or'dinand, a candidate for ordination.—*adj.* or'dinant, (*Shak.*) ordaining.—*n.* one who ordains. —*n.* or'dinate, a straight line parallel to an axis cutting off an abscissa: the *y*-co-ordinate in analytical geometry.—*v.t.* to ordain: to co-ordinate or order.—*adv.* ord'inately, in an ordered manner: restrainedly: with moderation.—*n.* ordinā'tion, the act of ordaining: admission to the Christian ministry by the laying on of hands of a bishop or a presbytery: established order. [L. *ordināre*, -*ātum*—*ordō*, order.]

ordinary, ord'(i-)nə-ri, *Scot.* ordinar, ord'nər, *adj.* according to the common order: usual: of the usual kind: customary: of common rank: plain: undistinguished: commonplace: (*coll.*) plain-looking: (of a judge or jurisdiction) by virtue of office, not by deputation: (of a judge in Scotland) of the Outer House of the Court of Session (Lord Ordinary).— *n.* a judge of ecclesiastical or other causes who acts in his own right, as a bishop or his deputy: (*hist.*) a chaplain who attended those condemned to death, esp. the chaplain of Newgate Prison: something settled or customary: (*obs.*) usual fare: a meal provided at a fixed charge: a place where such a meal is provided : (*obs.*) the company partaking of it : the common run, mass, or course : a high bicycle : (*her.*) one of a class of armorial charges, figures of simple or geometrical form, conventional in character : a reference-book of heraldic charges.—*adv.* or′dinarily.—in ordinary, in regular and customary attendance ; ordinary of the mass, the established sequence or fixed order for saying mass. [L. *ordinārius—ordō, -inis*, order.]

ordnance, *ord′nans, n.* (*orig.*) any arrangement, disposition, or equipment : munitions : great guns, artillery : a department concerned with supply and maintenance of artillery.—Ordnance datum, the standard sea-level of the Ordnance Survey, now mean sea-level at Newlyn, Cornwall ; Ordnance Survey, a preparation of official maps of Great Britain and Ireland, carried out by the Royal Engineers—once under the Master-general of the Ordnance. [ordinance.]

ordonnance, *or′də-nəns, n.* co-ordination, esp. the proper disposition of figures in a picture, parts of a building, &c. [Fr. ; cf. ordinance.]

Ordovician, *or-dō-vish′(y)ən, adj.* and *n.* Lapworth's word for Lower Silurian. [L. *Ordovicēs*, a British tribe of N. Wales.]

ordure, *ord′yər, n.* dirt : dung : excrement : (*fig.*) anything unclean.—*adj.* or′durous. [Fr.,—O.Fr. *ord*, foul—L. *horridus*, rough.]

ore, *ōr, n.* a mineral from which a metal (or less strictly, some other constituent) can be profitably extracted : (still sometimes) metal mixed with rock : (*poet.*) precious metal. [O.E. *ār*, brass, influenced by *ōra*, unwrought metal ; cf. L. *aes, aeris*, bronze.]

ore, *or, n.* (*local*) seaweed : tangle (Laminaria).—Also ore′weed, oar′weed. [O.E. *wār*.]

ore, o′re, *ōr,* old spellings of o′er for over.—For compounds see over-.—ore-wrought, -raught (*Shak.*), for over-reached in the sense of overtook ; ore-rested (*Shak.*), for overwrested.

öre, *ə′re, n.* a coin and money of account in Norway, Sweden, and Denmark. See krone.

oread, *ō′ri-ad, ō′ri-ad, n.* (*myth.*) a mountain nymph : —*pl.* o′reads, or orē′adēs. [L. *ōrĕas, -adis*—Gr. *oreias, oreiados—oros*, a mountain.]

oreide. See oroide.

oreography, oreology. See orography, orology.

orexis, *or-ek′sis, n.* appetite.—*adj.* orec′tic. [Gr. *orexis.*]

orfe, *orf, n.* a golden-yellow semi-domesticated variety of id. [Ger. *orfe*—Gr. *orphōs*, the great sea-perch.]

organ, *or′gən, n.* an instrument or means by which anything is done : a part of a body fitted for carrying on a natural or vital operation : a region of the brain fancied to be concerned with some mental or moral quality : a bump marking its position and development : a means of communicating information or opinions : (*obs.*) a musical instrument in general : a keyboard wind instrument consisting of a collection of pipes made to sound by means of compressed air : a system of pipes in such an organ, having an individual keyboard, a partial organ : a musical instrument in some way similar to a pipe-organ, as a pipeless organ : a barrel-organ. —*ns.* or′gan-builder, one who constructs organs ; organelle′, a specialised part of a cell serving as an organ ; or′gan-gallery, a gallery where an organ is placed ; or′gan-grinder, one who plays a hand-organ by a crank ; or′gan-harmō′-nium, a large harmonium.—*adjs.* organic (*or-gan′ik*), -al, pertaining to, derived from, like, of the nature of, an organ (in any sense) : of an organism, organum, or organisation : organised : inherent in organisation : structural : (*philol.*) belonging to the etymological structure of a word : instrumental : mechanical : (*chem.*) containing or combined with carbon : concerned with carbon compounds.—*adv.* organ′ically.—*ns.* organicism (*or-gan′i-sizm*), the conception of nature, life, or society as an organism : the theory that all disease is due to an organic lesion ; organ′icist ; organis-abil′ity.—*adj.* organis′able.—*n.* organisā′tion, the act of organising : the state of being organised : the manner in which anything is organised : an

organised system, body, or society : (*U.S.*) a party machine : the singing of the organum.—*v.t.* or′ganise, to supply with organs : to form into an organic whole : to co-ordinate and prepare for activity : to arrange.—*v.i.* to become organic : to be active in organisation.—*adj.* or′ganised, having or consisting of parts acting in co-ordination : having the nature of a unified whole : organic.—*ns.* or′ganiser, one who organises : part of an embryo that influences the development of the rest ; or′ganism, organic structure, or that which has it : that which acts as a unified whole : a living animal or vegetable.—*adj.* organis′mal. —*ns.* or′ganist, one who plays on an organ ; organity (*-gan′*), an organised whole ; or′gan-loft, the loft where an organ stands ; organogeny (*or-gən-oj′i-ni*), organogen′esis, the development of living organs ; organograph′y, a description of the organs of plants or animals.—*adj.* organometall′ic, consisting of a metal and an organic radical.—*ns.* or′ganon (Gr.), a method of investigation :—*pl.* or′gana ; organother′apy, treatment of disease by administration of animal organs or extracts of them, especially of ductless gland extracts ; or′gan-pipe, one of the sounding pipes of a pipe-organ (organ-pipe coral, a coral, Tubipora, with tubes arranged like organ-pipes) ; or′gan-point, a pedal-point ; or′gan-screen, an ornamental stone or wood screen on which an organ is placed ; or′-ganum (L.), an organon : in mediaeval music, a part in parallel motion to the canto fermo usually a fourth or fifth below or above :—*pl.* or′gana.— organic chemistry, the chemistry of carbon compounds ; organic disease, a disease accompanied by changes in the structures involved ; organic sensation, sensation from internal organs, as hunger ; organic vein (*obs.*), the jugular vein. [L. *organum*—Gr. *organon—ergon*, work.]

organdie, *or′gən-di, n.* fine muslin : book muslin. [Fr. *organdi*.]

organzine, *or′gən-zēn, n.* a silk yarn of two or more threads thrown together with a slight twist. [Fr. *organsin*—It. *organzino*, poss.—Urgenj, Turkestan.]

orgasm, *or′gazm, n.* immoderate excitement : culmination of sexual excitement : turgescence of any organ.—*adj.* orgas′tic. [Gr. *orgasmos*, swelling.]

orgeat, *or′ji-at, -zhat, or-zhä′, n.* a syrup made from almonds, sugar, &c., formerly from barley. [Fr. *orge*—L. *hordeum*, barley.]

orgue, *org, n.* (*obs.*) a row of stakes let down like a portcullis : (*obs.*) a weapon with several barrels in a row. [Fr., organ.]

orgulous, *or′gū-ləs,* orgillous, *or′gi-ləs, adj.* (*Shak.*) haughty. [O.Fr. *orguillus* ; cf. Fr. *orgueil*, It. *orgoglio*, pride ; prob. of Germanic origin.]

orgy, *or′ji, n.* usu. in *pl.* or′gies, a secret rite, as in the worship of Bacchus : esp. a frantic unrestrained celebration : a celebration in general : a riotous, licentious, or drunken revel.—Also (properly *pl.*) or′gia.—*n.* or′giast, one who takes part in orgies.—*adjs.* orgias′tic, or′gic. [Fr. *orgies*—L.—Gr. *orgia* (pl.).]

oribi, *or′i-bi, n.* a small South African antelope, the pale-buck. [Cape Du. app. from some native language.]

orichalc, *or′i-kalk, n.* (*Spens.* oricalche) a gold-coloured alloy : brass.—*adj.* orichalceous (*-kal′si-əs*). [Gr. *oreichalkos—oros*, a mountain, *chalkos*, copper ; sense influenced by association with L. *aurum*, gold.]

oriel, *ō′ri-əl, n.* a small room or recess with a polygonal window, built out from a wall, resting on the ground or (esp.) supported on brackets or corbels : the window of an oriel (in full o′riel-win′dow).—*adj.* o′rielled. [O.Fr. *oriol*, porch, recess, gallery.]

orient, *ō′ri-ənt, adj.* rising, as the sun : eastern : bright or pure in colour.—*n.* the part where the sun rises : sunrise : purity of lustre in a pearl : an orient pearl : Orient, the East : the countries of the East.—*v.t.* o′rient (or *-ent′*), to set so as to face the east : to build (lengthwise) east and west : to place in a definite relation to the points of the compass or other fixed or known directions : to determine the position of, relatively to fixed or known directions.—*n.* o'riency, orient quality.—*adj.* **oriental, Oriental,** (*-ent'al*), eastern: pertaining to, in, or from the east: orient.—*n.* a native of the east: an Asiatic.—*v.t.* **orient'alise.**—*ns.* **Orient'alism,** an eastern expression, custom, &c.: scholarship in eastern languages; **Orient'alist,** one versed in eastern languages: an oriental; **orientality** (*-al'i-ti*).—*adv.* **orient'ally.**—*v.t.* **o'rientāte,** to orient.—*v.i.* to face the east: to be oriented.—*ns.* **orientā'tion,** the act of orienting or orientating: the state of being oriented: determination or consciousness of relative direction: assumption of definite direction in response to stimulus; **o'rientātor,** an instrument for orientating.—**oriental alabaster,** onyx-marble; **oriental amethyst, emerald, topaz,** varieties or corundum resembling amethyst, emerald, topaz; **oriental ruby,** the true ruby, a variety of corundum; **oriental turquoise,** true turquoise; **Oriental Region,** Southern Asia and its islands from the Persian Gulf to Wallace's Line; **orientation table,** an indicator of tabular form for showing the direction of various objects —mountains and the like. [L. *oriēns, -entis,* pr.p. of *orīrī,* to rise.]

orifice, *or'i-fis, n.* a mouth-like opening, esp. small.—*n.* **or'ifex,** (*Shak.*) an orifice.—*adj.* **orificial** (*-fish'al*). [Fr.,—L. *ōrificium—ōs, ōris,* mouth, *facĕre,* to make.]

Oriflamme, *or'i-flam, n.* a little banner of red silk split into many points, borne on a gilt staff—the ancient royal standard of France. [Fr.,—L.L. *auriflamma—*L. *aurum,* gold, *flamma,* a flame.]

Origanum, *or-ig'a-nam, n.* the marjoram genus of labiates.—*n.* **or'igan(e)** (*-gan*), marjoram. [L. *orīganum—*Gr. *orīganon.*]

Origenist, *or'i-jin-ist, n.* a follower of *Origen* (*c.* 185-254 A.D.) in his allegorical method of scriptural interpretation, or his theology, esp. his heresies—the subordination though eternal generation of the Logos, pre-existence of all men, and universal restoration, even of the Devil.—*n.* Or'igenism.—*adj.* Origenist'ic.

origin, *or'i-jin, n.* the rising or first existence of anything: that from which anything first proceeds: (*math.*) the fixed starting-point or point from which measurement is made: source: derivation.—*adj.* **orig'inal,** pertaining to the origin or beginning: existing from or at the beginning: being such from the beginning: innate: standing in relation of source: not derived, copied, imitated, or translated from anything else: originative: novel: originating or having the power to originate in oneself: creative: independent in invention: odd in character.—*n.* origin: that which is not itself, or of which something else is, a copy, imitation, or translation: a real person, place, &c., serving as model for one in fiction: an inhabitant, member, &c., from the beginning: a person of marked individuality or oddity: (in *pl., Milt.*) original elements.—*n.* **original'ity.**—*adv.* **orig'inally.**—*v.t.* **orig'inate,** to give origin to: to bring into existence.—*v.i.* to have origin: to begin.—*n.* **originā'tion.**—*adj.* **orig'inātive,** having power to originate or bring into existence: originating.—*n.* **orig'inātor.—original sin,** innate depravity and corruption held to be transmitted to Adam's descendants in consequence of his sin. [L. *orīgō, -inis—orīrī,* to rise.]

orillion, *o-ril'yon, n.* a semicircular projection at the shoulder of a bastion intended to cover the guns and defenders on the flank. [Fr. *orillon—oreille,* an ear—L. *auricula,* dim. of *auris,* ear.]

oriole, *ōr'i-ōl, n.* a golden yellow bird (*Oriolus galbula,* the **golden oriole**) with black wings, or other member of the genus or of the Old World family **Oriol'idae,** related to the crows: in America applied to birds of the Icteridae (see **baltimore**). [O.Fr. *oriol—*L. *aureolus,* dim. of *aureus,* golden—*aurum,* gold.]

Orion, *ō-rī'an, n.* (*astron.*) a constellation containing seven very bright stars, three of which form Orion's belt. [Gr. *Orīōn,* a giant hunter slain by Artemis.]

orison, *or'i-zan, n.* a prayer. [O.Fr. *orison* (Fr. *oraison*)—L. *ōrātiō, -ōnis—ōrāre,* to pray.]

Oriya, *ō-rē'ya, n.* the language of Orissa in India, closely akin to Bengali: a member of the people speaking it.—Also *adj.*

orle, *orl, n.* (*her.*) a border within a shield at a short distance from the edge: a number of small charges set as a border. [O.Fr., border, from a dim. formed from L. *ōra,* border.]

orleans, *or'li-anz, n.* a fabric of cotton warp and worsted weft.—*n.* **Or'leanist,** a supporter of the family of the Duke of Orleans, brother of Louis XIV., as claimants to the throne of France.—Also *adj.*—*n.* Or'leanism. [*Orléans,* in France.]

orlop, *or'lop, n.* the lowest deck in a ship, a covering to the hold. [Du. *overloop,* covering—*overloopen,* to run over.]

ormer, *or'mar, n.* an ear-shell or sea-ear (Haliotis). [Channel Island Fr. *ormer* (Fr. *ormier*) for *oreille de mer,* sea-ear.]

ormolu, *or'mo-lōō, n.* an alloy of copper, zinc, and sometimes tin: gilt or bronzed metallic ware: gold-leaf prepared for gilding bronze, &c. [Fr. *or—*L. *aurum,* gold, and Fr. *moulu,* pa.p. of *moudre,* to grind—L. *molĕre,* to grind.]

Ormuzd, Ormazd, *or'muzd, n.* the chief god of the ancient Persians: the creator and lord of the whole universe: (later) the good principle, as opposed to *Ahriman,* the bad. [Pers. *Ahura-Mazdāh,* the Living God or Lord (*ahu,* the living, life, or spirit, root *ah,* to be), the Great Creator (*maz, dā,* Sans. *mahā, dhā*), or the Wise One.]

ornament, *or'na-mant, n.* anything meant to add grace or beauty or bring credit: additional beauty: a mark of honour: (usu. in *pl., Pr. Bk.*) articles used in the services of the church.—*v.t.* (*or-na-ment', or'na-ment*) to adorn: to furnish with ornaments.—*adj.* **ornament'al,** serving to adorn or beautify.—*n.* a plant grown for ornament or beauty.—*adv.* **ornament'ally.**—*ns.* **ornamentā'tion,** act or art of ornamenting: ornamental work; **ornament'er; ornament'ist.** [Fr. *ornement—*L. *ornāmentum—ornāre,* to adorn.]

ornate, *or-nāt', or'nāt, adj.* decorated: much or elaborately ornamented.—*adv.* **ornate'ly** (or *or'*).—*n.* **ornate'ness.** [L. *ornāre, -ātus,* to adorn.]

ornery, *or'na-ri, adj.* an American vulgarism for **ordinary.**

ornis, *or'nis, n.* the birds collectively of a region, its avifauna.—*adj.* **ornithic** (*or-nith'ik*), relating to birds.—*ns.* **ornithichnite** (*or-nith-ik'nīt*; Gr. *ichnos,* track), a fossil footprint of a bird.—*n.pl.* **Ornithodel'phia** (Gr. *delphys,* womb), the Prototheria or Monotremata—from the ornithic character of the urogenital organs.—*adjs.* **ornithodel'phian** (also *n.*), **ornithodel'phic, ornithodel'phous.**—*n.* Ornithogaea (*or-nī-thō-jē'a*; Gr. *gaia,* land), the New Zealand biological region.—*adjs.* **ornithoid** (*or'nith-oid*; Gr. *eidos,* form), bird-like; **ornitholog'ical.**—*adv.* **ornitholog'ically.**—*ns.* **ornithol'ogist; ornithol'ogy,** the study of birds; **ornithomancy** (*or-nī'thō-man-si, or'nith-ō-man-si*; Gr. *manteiā,* divination), divination by means of birds, by observing their flight, &c.—*adj.* **ornithoman'tic.**—*n.* **ornithomorph** (*or-nī'thō-morf, or'nith-ō-morf*), a figure or design in the form of a bird.—*adjs.* **ornithomorph'ic; ornithoph'ilous** (Gr. *phileein,* to love), bird-pollinated.—*ns.* **ornithoph'ily; ornithopter** (*or-nith-op'tar*; Gr. *pteron,* wing), a flying-machine with flapping wings; **Ornithorhynchus** (*or-nith-ō-ring'kos*; Gr. *rhynchos,* snout), the duck-bill; **ornithosaur** (*or-nī'thō-sawr*; Gr. *sauros,* lizard), a pterodactyl; **ornithoscopy** (*or-nith-os'ko-pi*; Gr. *skopeein,* to view), augury by observation of birds. [Gr. *ornis, ornīthos,* a bird.]

Orobanche, *or-ō-bang'kē, n.* the broom-rape genus of dicotyledons, giving name to the family **Orobanchā'ceae,** root-parasites without green leaves.—*adj.* **orobanchā'ceous.** [Gr. *orobanchē,* dodder, also broom-rape—*orobos,* bitter vetch, *anchein,* to strangle.]

orogenesis, *or-ō-jen'i-sis, n.* mountain-building.—*adjs.* **orogenet'ic, orogen'ic.** [Gr. *oros,* mountain, *genesis,* production.]

orography, *or-og'ra-fi, n.* the description of mountains—also **oreography** (*or-i-og'*).—*adjs.* **or(e)o**

graphic (-graf′ik), **-al**. [Gr. *oros*, *-eos*, mountain, *graphein*, to write.]

oroide, ō′rō-īd, *n.* an alloy of copper and zinc or tin, &c., imitating gold.—*n.* **o′rëide**, a similar or identical alloy. [Fr. or—L. *aurum*, gold, Gr. *eidos*, form.]

orology, *or-ol′ə-ji*, **oreology** (*or-i-ol′*), *ns.* the scientific study of mountains.—*adjs.* **or(e)olog′ical.**—*ns.* **or(e)ol′ogist**. [Gr. *oros*, *-eos*, mountain, *logos*, discourse.]

oropesa, *or-o-pē′zä*, *-pā′sä*, *n.* a fish-shaped float used in marine mine-sweeping to support the sweeping wire. [From the name of a trawler.]

orotund, ō′rō-tund, *adj.* full and round in utterance : pompously mouthed or mouthing.—Also **o′roro-tund.**—*ns.* **o(ro)rotund′ity**. [L. *ōs*, *ōris*, mouth, *rotundus*, round ; from Horace, *Ars Poetica*, 323.]

orphan, *or′fən*, *n.* one bereft of father or mother, or (usually) of both.—Also *adj.*—*v.t.* to make an orphan.—*ns.* **or′phanage**, the state of being an orphan : a house for orphans ; **or′phan-asy′lum** ; **or′phanhood**, or **or′phanism**. [Gr. *orphanos*, akin to L. *orbus*, bereaved.]

orpharion, *or-fā-rī′on*, *or-fā′ri-on*, *n.* a large lute-like instrument with six to nine pairs of metal strings. — Also **orpheō′reon**. [*Orpheus*, *Ariōn*, mythical musicians.]

Orpheus, *or′fūs*, *n.* a mythical Thracian musician and poet who could move inanimate objects by the music of his lyre, founder or interpreter of the ancient mysteries.—*adjs.* **Orphē′an**, pertaining to Orpheus ; **Or′phic**, pertaining to the mysteries associated with Orpheus : esoteric.—*n.* **Or′phism**, the system taught in the Orphic mysteries.—**Orpheus harmonica**, the panharmonicon.

orphrey, *or′fri*, *n.* gold or other rich embroidery, esp. bordering a vestment. [O.Fr. *orfreis*—L. *auriphrygium*, Phrygian gold.]

orpiment, *or′pi-mənt*, *n.* a yellow mineral, arsenic trisulphide, used as a pigment. [O.Fr.,—L. *auripigmentum*—*aurum*, gold, *pigmentum*, paint.]

orpine, **orpin**, *or′pin*, *n.* a purple-flowered, broad-leaved stonecrop. [Fr. *orpin*.]

Orpington, *or′ping-tən*, *n.* a breed of poultry (white, black, or buff) of general utility. [*Orpington* in W. Kent, where it took rise.]

orra, *or′ä*, *-ə*, *adj.* (*Scot.*) odd : not matched : left over : occasional, casual : supernumerary : worthless.—**orra man**, a farm-worker kept to do any odd job that may occur. [Origin unknown.]

orrery, *or′ər-i*, *n.* a clockwork model of the solar system. [From Charles Boyle, fourth Earl of *Orrery* (1676-1731), for whom one was made.]

orris, *or′is*, *n.* the Florentine or other iris : its dried rootstock (**orr′is-root′**), smelling of violets, used in perfumery. [Perh. **iris**.]

orris, *or′is*, *n.* a peculiar kind of gold or silver lace : upholsterers' galloon and gimp. [Perh. O.Fr. *orfreis* ; see **orphrey**.]

orseille, *or-sāl′*, same as **archil**, **orchil.**—*adj.* **orsell′ic**. [Fr.]

ort, *ort*, *n.* a fragment, esp. one left from a meal—usually *pl.* [Cf. Low Ger. *ort*, refuse of fodder.]

orthian, *orth′i-ən*, *adj.* high-pitched. [Gr. *orthios*.]

ortho-, *or′thō-*, *or-tho′-*, in composition, straight : upright : perpendicular : right : genuine : (*chem.*) derived from an acid anhydride by combination with the largest number of water molecules (distinguished from *meta-*) : (*organic chem.*) having substituted atoms or groups attached to two adjacent carbon atoms of the benzene ring (distinguished from *meta-* and *para-*)—in this sense commonly represented by *o-*.—*n.* and *adj.* **or′tho**, a contraction for **orthochromatic (plate)**.—*ns.* **orthoax′is**, (*crystal.*) the orthodiagonal ; **orthobō′rate**, a salt of **orthobō′ric acid**, boric acid ; **or′thocentre**, the point of intersection of the altitudes of a triangle ; **Orthoceras** (*or-thos′ə-ras* ; Gr. *keras*, horn), a genus of fossil cephalopods with straight shell.—*adj.* **orthochromat′ic** (Gr. *chrōma*, colour), correct in rendering the relation of colours, without the usual photographic modifications.— *ns.* **or′thoclase** (-klās, -klāz ; Gr. *klasis*, fracture), common or potash felspar, monoclinic, with cleavages at right angles ; **or′tho - compound** ; **orthodiag′onal**,

in a monoclinic crystal, that lateral axis which is perpendicular to the vertical axis ; **orthodontia** (-don′shi-ä ; Gr. *odous*, *odontos*, tooth), rectification of abnormalities in the teeth.—Also **orthodont′ics.**—*adj.* **orthodont′ic.**—*n.* **orthodont′ist**. —*adj.* **or′thodox** (Gr. *doxa*, opinion), sound in doctrine : believing, or according to, the received or established doctrines or opinions, esp. in religion : Orthodox, of the Eastern Church.—*n.* **or′thodoxy.**—*adj.* **orthodrom′ic** (Gr. *dromos*, a course, run).—*n.* **orthod′romy**, great-circle sailing. —Also **orthodrom′ics.**—*adjs.* **orthoepic** (or-thō-ep′ik ; Gr. *epos*, a word), **orthoep′ical.**—*ns.* **orthō′epist** ; **orthō′epy**, correct pronunciation ; **orthogen′esis** (Gr. *genesis*, generation), the evolution of organisms systematically in definite directions and not accidentally in many directions : determinate variation. — *adjs.* **orthogenet′ic** ; **orthognath′ic**, **orthog′nathous** (Gr. *gnathos*, jaw), having a lower jaw that neither protrudes nor recedes. — *n.* **orthog′nathism.**—*adj.* **orthog′onal** (Gr. *gōniā*, angle), right-angled (**orthogonal projection**, projection by lines perpendicular to the plane of projection).—*adv.* **orthog′onally.**—*ns.* **or′thograph**, a drawing in orthographic projections, esp. of the elevation of a building ; **orthog′rapher**, one skilled in orthography : a speller.—*adjs.* **orthograph′ic**, **-al**, pertaining or according to spelling : spelt correctly : in perspective projection, having the point of sight at infinity.—*adv.* **orthograph′ically.**—*ns.* **orthog′raphist**, an orthographer ; **orthog′raphy** (Gr. *orthographiā*, spelling, elevation—*graphein*, to write), the art or practice of spelling words correctly : spelling : orthographic projection : (Shak., *Much Ado*), apparently for orthographer ; **orthopaedia** (-pē-di′ä ; Gr. *pais*, *paidos*, a child), the art or process of curing deformities arising from disease or injury of bones, esp. in childhood—also **or′thopaedy**, **or′thopēdy**. —*adjs.* **orthopae′dic**, **-al**, **orthopē′dic**, **-al.**—*ns.* **orthopae′dics**, **orthopē′dics**, orthopaedic surgery ; **orthopae′dist**, **orthopē′dist** ; **orthophos′phate**, an ordinary phosphate.—*adj.* **orthophosphor′ic.**—*n.* **orthophyre** (or′thō-fīr ; *orthoclase* porphyry), a fine-grained syenitic rock with orthoclase crystals. —*adj.* **orthophyric** (-fir′ik).—*ns.* **orthopin′akoid**, in monoclinic crystals, a form consisting of two faces parallel to the orthodiagonal and the vertical axis ; **orthopnoea** (or-thop-nē′ä ; Gr. *orthopnoia*—*pneein*, to breathe), a condition in which one can only breathe when upright ; **or′thoprism**, in monoclinic crystals, a form parallel to the orthodiagonal.—*n.pl.* **Orthop′tera** (Gr. *pteron*, wing), the cockroach order of insects with firm fore-wings serving as covers to the fan-wise folded hind-wings.—*n.* and *adj.* **orthop′teran.**—*ns.* **orthop′-terist**, **orthopterol′ogist**, a student of the Orthoptera ; **orthopterol′ogy**. — *adjs.* **orthop′teroid** ; **orthop′terous**, pertaining to the Orthoptera ; **orthop′tic** (Gr. *optikos*, optic), relating to normal vision without a squint.—*n.* **orthop′tist**, a curer of squinting.—*adjs.* **orthorhom′bic** (Gr. *rhombos*, rhomb ; *crystal.*), referable to three unequal axes at right angles to each other ; **orthoscop′ic** (Gr. *skopeein*, to look at), having or giving correct vision, true proportion, or a flat field of view.—*n.* **orthosil′icate**, a salt of **orthosilicic** (-sil-is′ik) **acid**, H_4SiO_4.—*adjs.* **orthostat′ic** (Gr. *orthostatos*—*statos*, standing), standing erect : connected with the erect posture ; **orthos′tichous** (Gr. *stichos*, a row), arranged in vertical rows.—*ns.* **orthos′tichy**, a straight row, as of leaves vertically over one another on an axis ; **orthotonē′sis** (Gr. *tonos*, accent), accentuation of a proclitic or enclitic—opp. to *enclisis.* — *adjs.* **orthoton′ic**, taking an accent in certain positions but not in others—also **or′thotone** ; **orthotrop′ic** (Gr. *tropos*, a turn), manifesting orthotropism.—*n.* **orthot′ropism**, growth in the direct line of stimulus, esp. of gravity.—*adj.* **orthot′ropous**, (of an ovule) straight, having the nucellus in direct continuation of the funicle. [Gr. *orthos*, straight, upright, right.]

orthros, *or′thros*, *n.* one of the Greek canonical hours, corresponding to the Western lauds. [Gr. *orthros*, dawn.]

ortolan, *or'tō-lən*, *n.* a kind of bunting, common in Europe, and considered a great table delicacy. [Fr.,—It. *ortolano*—L. *hortulānus*, belonging to gardens—*hortulus*, dim. of *hortus*, a garden.]

orval, *or'vəl*, *n.* (*obs.*) clary. [Cf. Fr. *orvale*.]

Orvieto, *or-vyā'tō*, *n.* a white wine from *Orvieto* in Italy.—*n.* **Orvietan** (*or-vi-ē'tən*), a supposed antidote to poison ascribed to an Orvieto man.

oryctology, *or-ik-tol'ə-ji*, *n.* (*obs.*) mineralogy: palaeontology. [Gr. *oryktos*, dug, quarried.]

Oryx, *or'iks*, *n.* an African genus of antelopes. [Gr. *oryx*, *-ygos*, a pick-axe, an oryx antelope.]

Oryza, *ō-ri'zā*, *n.* a tropical genus of grasses, including rice. [Gr. *oryza*.]

Osage, *ō-sāj'*, *n.* an Indian of a tribe living in Oklahoma, &c.—*adj.* **O'sage.—O'sage orange**, a hedge-tree (*Maclura*) of the mulberry family, first found in the Osage country: its orange-like inedible fruit.

Oscan, *os'kən*, *n.* one of an ancient Italic people in southern Italy: their language akin to Latin.—also *adj.*

Oscar, *os'kər*, *n.* a gold-plated statuette awarded by the American Academy of Motion Picture Arts and Sciences to a film writer, actor, director, &c., for the year's best performance in his particular line. [Name fortuitously given.]

oscheal, *os'ki-əl*, *adj.* pertaining to the scrotum. [Gr. *oscheon*, scrotum.]

oscillate, *os'il-lāt*, *v.i.* to swing to and fro like a pendulum: to vibrate: to radiate electromagnetic waves: to vary between certain limits: to fluctuate.—*v.t.* to cause to swing or vibrate.—*adj.* **osc'illating.**—*n.* **oscilla'tion.**—*adj.* **osc'illative**, having a tendency to vibrate: vibratory.—*n.* **osc'illātor**, one who oscillates: apparatus for producing oscillations.—*adj.* **oscillatory** (*os'il-ə-tə-ri*), swinging: moving as a pendulum does: vibratory.—*ns.* **osc'illogram**, a record made by an oscillograph; **osc'illograph**, an apparatus for producing a curve representing a wave-form. [L. *ōscillāre*, *-ātum*, to swing.]

Oscines, *os'i-nēz*, *n.pl.* the song-birds, forming the main body of the Passeriformes.—*adj.* **osc'inine** or (faultily formed) **osc'ine.** [L. *oscen*, *oscinis*, a singing-bird.]

oscitancy, *os'i-tən-si*, *n.* yawning: sleepiness: stupidity.—*adj.* **osc'itant.**—*adv.* **osc'itantly.**—*v.i.* **osc'itate**, to yawn.—*n.* **oscita'tion**, yawning: sleepiness. [L. *ōscitāre*, to yawn.]

osculant, *os'kū-lənt*, *adj.* kissing: adhering closely: (*biol.*) intermediate between two genera, species, &c., linking.—*adj.* **os'cular**, pertaining to the mouth or osculum, or to kissing: osculating.—*v.t.* **os'culāte** to kiss: (*math.*) to have three or more coincident points in common with.—*v.i.* to be in close contact: to form a connecting-link.—*n.* **oscula'tion.**—*adj.* **os'culatory**, of or pertaining to kissing or osculation.—*n.* a carved tablet kissed by the priest and (now rarely) by the people at mass.—*ns.* **os'cule**, a little mouth: a small mouthlike aperture; **os'culum**, an exhalant aperture in a sponge: a sucker on a tapeworm's head. [L. *ōsculārī*, *-ātus*—*ōsculum*, a little mouth, a kiss, dim. of *ōs*, mouth.]

oshac, *ō'shak*, *n.* the ammoniac plant. [Ar. *ushshaq*.]

osier, *ōzh'(y)ər*, *ōz'i-ər*, *ōz'yər*, *n.* any willow whose twigs are used in making baskets, esp. *Salix viminalis.*—*adj.* made of or like osiers.—*n.* **o'sierbed**, a place where osiers grow.—*adj.* **o'siered**, covered or fringed with osiers: twisted like osiers.—*n.* **o'siery**, osier-work. [Fr. *osier* of unknown origin; there is a L.L. *ausāria* or *osāria*, willow-bed.]

Osiris, *ō-sī'ris*, *n.* the greatest of Egyptian gods, son of Seb and Nut, or Heaven and Earth, husband of Isis, father of Horus.—*adj.* **Osī'rian.** [Gr. *Osīris.*]

Osmanli, *os-man'li*, *adj.* of the dynasty of *Osmān*, who founded the Turkish empire in Asia, and reigned 1288-1326: of the Turkish empire: of the western branch of the Turks or their language.—*n.* a member of the dynasty: a Turk of Turkey. [Cf. **Ottoman**.]

osmeterium, *os-mē-tē'ri-əm*, or *oz-*, *n.* a forked

process behind the head of certain caterpillars, giving out a foul smell:—*pl.* **osmetē'ria.** [Gr. *osmē*, smell, stink, and suff. *-tērion*, denoting instrument.]

osmidrosis, *os-mi-drō'sis*, or *oz-*, *n.* the secretion of ill-smelling sweat. [Gr. *osmē*, smell, *hidrōs*, sweat.]

osmium, *ōs'mi-əm*, *n.* a grey-coloured metal (atomic number 76), the heaviest substance known, whose tetroxide has a disagreeable smell.—*ns.* **os'mate**, **os'miate**, a salt of the hypothetical osmic acid.—*adjs.* **os'mic**, containing osmium in higher valency; **os'mious**, **os'mous**, containing osmium in lower valency.—*n.* **osmirid'ium**, iridosmine.—**osmic acid**, strictly, a supposed acid H_2OsO_4: usually, osmium tetroxide, an ill-smelling substance used as a stain for fats in microscope work. [Gr. *osmē*, smell.]

osmosis, *os-mō'sis*, or *oz-*, *n.* diffusion of liquids through a porous septum.—Also **os'mose.**—*n.* **osmom'eter**, an apparatus for measuring osmotic pressure.—*adj.* **osmotic** (*-mot'ik*).—*adv.* **osmot'ically.** [Gr. *ōsmos*=*ōthismos*, impulse—*ōtheein*, to push.]

Osmunda, *os-mun'dä*, *n.* a genus including the royal fern, giving name to a family **Osmundā'ceae.** [Origin unknown.]

osnaburg, *oz'nə-burg*, *n.* a coarse linen, originally brought from *Osnabrück* in Germany: a coarse cotton.—Also *adj.*

osprey, *os'pri*, *-prā*, *n.* a bird of prey (*Pandion haliaetus*) that feeds on fish: an egret or other plume used in millinery, not from the osprey. [Supposed to be from L. *ossifraga*, misapplied; see **ossifrage**.]

osseous, *os'i-əs*, *adj.* bony: composed of, or like, bone: of the nature or structure of bone.—*ns.* **ossā'rium**, an ossuary; **ossein** (*os'i-in*), the organic basis of bone; **osselet** (*os'ə-let*, *os'let*), a hard substance growing on the inside of a horse's knee; **oss'icle**, a little bone or bone-like plate.—*adjs.* **ossic'ular**; **ossif'erous**, yielding or containing bones; **ossif'ic.**—*n.* **ossificā'tion**, the process or state of being changed into a bony substance.—*v.t.* **oss'ify**, to make into bone or into a bone-like substance.—*v.i.* to become bone:—*pr.p.* **oss'ifying**; *pa.t.* and *pa.p.* **oss'ified.**—*adj.* **ossiv'orous**, feeding on or consuming bones. [L. *os*, *ossis*, bone.]

osseter, *os-et'ər*, *n.* a species of sturgeon. [Russ. *osetr.*]

Ossian, *os(h)'i-ən*, *n.* a legendary Gaelic poet whose poems James Macpherson professed to translate.—*adjs.* **Ossianesque** (*-esk'*), in the manner of Macpherson's Ossian; **Ossianic** (*-an'ik*), relating to Ossian or to Macpherson's publications. [Gael. *Oisīn.*]

ossifrage, *os'i-frāj*, *n.* the lämmergeier: the osprey: (*U.S.*) the bald eagle.—*n.* **ossifraga** (*os-if'rə-gä*), the giant fulmar. [L. *ossifraga*, prob. the lämmergeier—*os*, *ossis*, bone, and the root of *frangēre*, to break.]

ossuary, *os'ū-ə-ri*, *n.* a bone-house or charnelhouse: a bone-urn. [L. *ossuārium*—*os*, bone.]

ostensible, *os-tens'i-bl*, *adj.* (*obs.*) that may be shown: outwardly showing or professed.—*n.* **ostensibil'ity.**—*adv.* **ostens'ibly.**—*adj.* **ostens'ive**, showing: exhibiting. — *adv.* **ostens'ively.** — *n.* **osten'sory**, a monstrance; **ostent'**, (*Shak.*) appearance, manner: portent; **ostenta'tion** (*-tən-*), act of showing: display to draw attention or admiration: boasting.—*adj.* **ostentā'tious**, given to show: fond of self-display: showy.—*adv.* **ostentā'tiously.**—*n.* **ostentā'tiousness.** [L. *ostendēre*, *ostēnsum* (*ostentum*), to show, and its freq. *ostentāre* —pfx. *obs-*, in front, *tendēre*, to stretch.]

osteo-, *os'ti-ō-*, *os-ti-o'-*, **oste-**, *os'ti-*, in composition, bone.—*adj.* **osteal** (*os'ti-əl*), relating to bone: sounding like bone on percussion.—*ns.* **osteitis** (*os-ti-ī'tis*), inflammation of a bone; **osteoarthrī'tis**, a form of arthritis in which the cartilages of the joint and the bone adjacent are worn away; **os'teoblast** (Gr. *blastos*, a shoot), a boneforming cell; **osteoclasis** (*os-ti-ok'lə-sis*; Gr. *klasis*, fracture), fracture of a bone for correction of a deformity: absorption and destruction of bone

Neutral vowels in unaccented syllables: *el'ə-mənt*, *in'fənt*, *ran'dəm*

25

tissue by osteoclasts ; **os'teoclast,** a surgical instrument for fracturing bone : a bone-destroying cell ; **osteocoll'a** (Gr. *kolla*, glue), a calcareous incrustation on roots, &c., once thought to unite bones ; **os'teoderm** (Gr. *derma*, skin), a bony dermal plate.—*adjs.* **osteoderm'al, osteoderm'atous, osteoderm'ic, osteoderm'ous.** — *ns.* **osteogen'esis, osteog'eny,** formation of bone : ossification.—*adjs.* **osteogenet'ic, osteogen'ic, osteog'enous.** —*n.pl.* **Osteoglossidae** (*-glos'i-dē*; Gr. *glōssa*, tongue), a family of bony fishes, including the arapaima.—*n.* **osteog'raphy,** description of bones.—*adj.* **ost'eoid,** bone-like.—*n.* **Osteol'epis** (Gr. *lepis*, scale), an Old Red Sandstone fossil fish with bone-like scales.—*adj.* **osteolog'ical.**—*ns.* **osteol'ogist ; osteol'ogy,** the study of bones, part of anatomy ; **osteomalacia** (*-ma-lā'shi-ä* ; Gr. *malakos*, soft), softening of bones by absorption of their calcium salts, attributed to deficiency of vitamin D ; **os'teopath** (*-pāth*), **osteop'athist** (*-a-thist*), a practitioner of osteopathy.—*adj.* **osteopathic** (*ost-i-ō-path'ik*).—*ns.* **osteop'athy,** a system of healing or treatment consisting largely of massage and manipulation ; **os'teophyte** (*-fīt* ; Gr. *phyton*, plant), an abnormal bony outgrowth.—*adjs.* **osteophytic** (*-fit'ik*) ; **osteoplast'ic.**—*ns.* **os'teoplasty,** a plastic operation by which a loss of bone is remedied ; **os'teotome** (Gr. *tomos*, cutting ; *surg.*), an instrument for cutting bones ; **osteot'omy,** the surgical cutting of a bone. [Gr. *osteon*, bone.]

ostinato, *os-tin-ä'tō, n.* (*mus.*) a ground-bass. [It. ; see **obstinate.**]

ostium, *os'ti-əm, n.* the mouth of a river : a mouth-like opening :—*pl.* **os'tia.**—*adj.* **os'tial.**—*n.* **os'tiary,** a doorkeeper : in the Roman Catholic Church, a member of the lowest of the minor orders : (*obs.*) a river-mouth.—*adjs.* **os'tiate,** having an ostium or ostia ; **os'tiolate,** having an opening.—*n.* **os'tiole,** a small opening. [L. *ostium.*]

ostler, hostler, *os'lər,* one who attends to horses at an inn :—*fem.* **ost'leress.** [**hosteler.**]

Ostmen, *ōst'men, n.pl.* the Danish settlers in Ireland. [O.N. *Austmenn,* Eastmen.]

ostrakon, ostracon, *os'trə-kon, n.* a potsherd or tile, esp. one used in ostracism in Greece or for writing on in ancient Egypt :—*pl.* **os'traka, -ca.** —*adjs.* **ostracean** (*os-trā'shən*), **ostrā'ceous,** of the nature of an oyster.—*n.* **Ostracion** (*os-trā'shi-on*), the coffer-fish genus.—*v.t.* **os'tracise** (*-sīz*), in ancient Greece, to banish by the vote of the people written on potsherds : to exclude from society.—*ns.* **os'tracism** (*-sizm*), banishment by ostracising : expulsion from society ; **os'tracod,** a member of the **Ostraco'da,** a class of minute crustacea with bivalve shells ; **os'tracoderm** (Gr. *derma*, skin), any member (as Cephalaspis) of a group of Silurian and Old Red Sandstone fishes or fish-like animals, generally cased in bony armour, with undeveloped lower jaw, with flippers but not ordinary paired fins. [Gr. *ostrakon,* a shell, tile, potsherd.]

Ostrea, *os'tri-ä, n.* the oyster genus.—*adj.* **osteā'ceous.** — *ns.* **ostreicul'ture** (*os-trē-i-*), oyster-culture ; **ostreicul'turist.** [L. *ostrea*—Gr. *ostreon,* oyster.]

ostreger, *os'tri-jər.* Same as **austringer.**

ostreophagous (*os-tri-of'ə-gəs, adj.* oyster-eating. —*ns.* **os'treophage** (*-fāj*), an oyster-eater ; **ostreoph'agy** (*-ə-ji*), oyster-eating. [Gr. *ostreon,* oyster, *phagein,* to eat.]

ostrich, *os'trich, -trij, n.* the largest living bird (Struthio), found in Africa, remarkable for its speed in running, and prized for its feathers.—*ns.* **os'trich-egg' ; os'trich-farm' ; os'trich-feath'er.**—*adj.* and *adv.* **os'trich-like,** usu. in reference to the supposed habit of hiding its head in danger. [O.Fr. *ostruche* (Fr. *autruche*)—L. *avis,* bird, L.L. *struthiō*—Gr. *strouthiōn,* an ostrich, *strouthos,* a bird.]

Ostrogoth, *os'trō-goth, n.* an eastern Goth—one of the tribe of east Goths who established their power in Italy in 493, and were overthrown in 555.—*adj.* **Os'trogothic.**

Ostyak, Ostiak, *os'ti-ak, n.* a member of a Ugrian people of Siberia : their language.—Also *adj.*

otalgia, *ō-tal'ji-ä, n.* earache—also **otal'gy.** [Gr. *ous, ōtos,* ear, *algē,* pain.]

otary, *ō'ta-ri, n.* a sea-lion or sea-bear, a seal with external ears :—*pl.* **o'taries.**—*adj.* **ot'arine.** [Gr. *ōtaros,* large-eared—*ous, ōtos,* ear.]

other, *udh'ər, adj.* (*orig.*) one of two : second : alternate : different : different from or not the same as the one in question (often with *than*) : not the same : remaining : additional : (*Spens.,* appar.) left.—*pron.* (or *n.*) other one : another : (*arch.* and *Scot.*) each other.—*adv.* otherwise.—*adj.* **oth'erguess** (see **othergates**).—*n.* **oth'erness.**—*advs.* **oth'erwhere,** elsewhere ; **oth'erwhile, oth'erwhiles,** at other times : sometimes ; **oth'erwise,** in another way or manner : by other causes : in other respects : under other conditions. —*conj.* else : under other conditions.—*n.* **oth'erworld,** a world other than, better than, or beyond this.—Also *adj.*—*adj.* **oth'erworld'ish.**—*n.* **otherworld'liness.**—*adj.* **otherworld'ly.**—**every other,** each alternate ; **rather . . . than otherwise,** rather than not ; **the other day,** on some day not long past, quite recently. [O.E. *ōther* ; cf. Ger. *ander,* L. *alter.*]

othergates, *udh'ər-gātz, adv.* (*obs.*) in another way.—*adj.* of another kind.—Also **oth'erguess** (in *Fielding, Goldsmith,* &c., **another guess**). [**other,** and gen. of **gate** (way).]

otic, *ō'tik, adj.* of or pertaining to the ear.—*ns.* **oti'tis,** inflammation of the ear ; **otocyst** (*ō'tō-sist*), an auditory or equilibristic vesicle ; **ot'olith** (Gr. *lithos,* stone), a calcareous concretion in the ear of various animals : an ear-bone ; **otol'ogist ; otol'ogy,** knowledge of the ear ; **otorrhoea** (*ō-tō-rē'ä* ; Gr. *rhoiā,* flow), a discharge from the ear ; **otosclero'sis,** formation of spongy bone in the capsule of the labyrinth ; **o'toscope,** an instrument for examining the ear. [Gr. *ous, ōtos,* ear.]

otiose, *ō'shi-ōs, adj.* unoccupied : indolent : inactive : functionless : futile : superfluous.—*n.* **otiosity** (*-os'i-ti*), ease, idleness. [L. *ōtiōsus*—*ōtium,* leisure.]

ottava, *ot-tä'vä, n.* an octave.—*n.* **ottavino** (*-vē'nō*), the piccolo.—**ottava rima** (*rē'mä*), an Italian stanza consisting of eight hendecasyllabic lines, rhyming *a b a b a b c c.* [It. ; cf. **octave.**]

otter, *ot'ər, n.* an aquatic fish-eating carnivore (*Lutra vulgaris*) of the weasel family : its brown short fur : a board travelling edge-up, manipulated on the principle of the kite, to carry the end of a fishing-line in a lake, or to keep open the mouth of a trawl (also **ott'er-board**) : a paravane.—*v.t.* or *v.i.* to fish with an otter-board.—*ns.* **otter'hound,** a dog of a breed used in otter-hunting ; **ott'er-hunting ; ott'er-shrew',** a large otter-like aquatic West African insectivore (*Potamogale velox*) ; **ott'er-trawl',** a trawl fitted with otter-boards ; **ott'er-trawl'ing.** [O.E. *otor,* akin to **water.**]

otto, *ot'ō,* **ottar,** *ot'ar, n.* See **attar.**

Ottoman, *ot-ō-mən, adj.* pertaining to the Turkish Empire, founded by 'Othmān or Osmān : Osmanli.—*n.* a Turk of Turkey : a cushioned seat for several persons sitting with their backs to one another : a low, stuffed seat without a back : a variety of corded silk.—*n.* **Ott'amite, Ott'omite,** a Turk.

ottrelite, *ot'ri-līt, n.* a mineral like chlorite but harder.—*n.* **ott'relite-slate,** a clay slate with minute plates of ottrelite. [*Ottrez* in the Ardennes, and Gr. *lithos,* stone.]

ou, ow, *ōō, interj.* (*Scot.*) expressing concession.—**ou ay,** why yes : O yes.

ouabain, wabain, *wä-bä'in, n.* a poisonous alkaloid got from apocynaceous roots and wood (Acokanthera, Strophanthus, &c.). [French spelling—Somali *wabayo,* a tree that yields it.]

oubit, *ōō'bit.* See **woubit.**

oubliette, *ōō-bli-et', n.* a dungeon with no opening but at the top : a secret pit in the floor of a dungeon into which a victim could be precipitated. [Fr.,—*oublier,* to forget—L. *oblīvīscī.*]

ouch, *owch, n.* a brooch : a clasped ornament : the socket of a precious stone. [O.Fr. *nouche.*]

ouch, *owch, interj.* expressing pain. [Ger. *autsch.*]

fāte, fär, ȧsk ; mē, hər (her) ; *mīne ; mōte, mūte, mōōn ; dhen* (then)

Oudenarde, ōō′də-närd, *n.* a tapestry representing foliage, &c., once made at *Oudenarde* in Belgium.

ought, *awt, n.* a variant of **aught**: also a vulgar corr. of **naught.**—*adv.* (*Scot.*) **oughtlings** (*ohh′-linz*), at all.

ought, *awt, pa.t.* of **owe**: now *obs.* or *dial.* except as an auxiliary verb (with time expressed by tense of the principal verb) should : is or was proper or necessary.—*n.* **ought′ness,** rightness.

ouglie, oughly, old spellings of **ugly.**—*adj.* **ough′ly-headed** (*Milt.*).

ouija, wē′jə, *n.* a board with an alphabet, used with a planchette. [Fr. *oui,* Ger. *ja,* yes.]

ouistiti, a French spelling of **wistiti.**

ouk, oulk, *n.* Scots forms of **week.**

oulakan, oulachon, ōō′lə-kən. See **eulachon.**

oulong. Same as **oolong.**

ounce, *owns, n.* the twelfth part of a pound troy =480 grains : $\frac{1}{16}$ of a pound avoirdupois=437½ troy grains : (*fig.*) a minute quantity.—**fluid ounce,** an avoirdupois ounce of distilled water at 62° Fahr. : (*U.S.*) ½ gill. [O.Fr. *unce*—L. *uncia,* the twelfth part; cf. **inch.**]

ounce, *owns, n.* originally, and still sometimes, a lynx : now generally the snow leopard (*Felis uncia*) of Central Asia : the jaguar : the cheetah : sometimes vaguely any moderate-sized wild beast of the cat tribe. [Fr. *once,* perh. for *lonce* (as if *l'once*)—Gr. *lynx.*]

oundy, *own′di, adj.* wavy : (*her.*) undé. [Fr. *ondé* ; cf. **undate.**]

oup, oop, *ōōp, v.t.* (*Scot.*) to bind round with thread or cord : to join. [Appar. **whip.**]

ouphe, ouph, *owf, ōōf, n.* (*Shak.*). Same as **oaf.**

our, *owr, pron.* (*gen.*) or *poss. adj.* pertaining or belonging to us—when used absolutely, **ours** (*owrz*), *prov.* **ourn** (*owrn*).—*reflex.* and *emphatic* **ourself′,** myself (regally or editorially) :—*pl.* **ourselves** (*-selvz′*). [O.E. *ūre,* gen. of *wē,* we.]

ourali, ōō-rä′lē, **ourari,** ōō-rä′rē. See **wourali.**

ourang-outang. Same as **orang-utan.**

ourebi. Same as **oribi.**

ourie, oorie, owrie, ōō′ri, *adj.* (*Scot.*) dingy : shabby : dreary : drooping : chill : inclined to shiver or shudder.

ourology, ouroscopy, &c. See **urology, &c.,** at **urine.**

ousel. See **ouzel.**

oust, *owst, v.t.* to eject or expel.—*n.* **oust′er** (*law*), ejection : dispossession. [A.Fr. *ouster* (O.Fr. *oster* ; Fr. *ôter*), to remove ; of obscure origin.]

out, *owt, adv.* (shading into *adj.* predicatively), not within : forth : abroad : to, towards, or at the exterior or a position away from the inside or inner part or from anything thought of as enclosing, hiding, or obscuring : from among others : from the mass : beyond bounds : away from the original or normal position or state : at or towards the far end, or a remote position : seawards : away from home or a building : in or into the open air : in or into a state of exclusion : not in office : not in use or fashion : no longer in the game : no longer in as batsman, dismissed : not batting : out of the contest and unable to resume in time : in the condition of having won : away from the mark : at fault : in error : not in form or good condition : at a loss : in or into a disconcerted, perplexed, or disturbed state : not in harmony or amity : in distribution : in or into the hands of others or the public : on loan : to or at an end : in an exhausted or extinguished state : completely : thoroughly : subjected to loss : in or to the field : in quest of or expressly aiming at something : in rebellion : on strike : in an exposed state : no longer in concealment or obscurity : in or into the open : before the public : in or into society : on domestic service : in existence : at full length : in an expanded state : in bloom : in extension : loudly and clearly : forcibly : unreservedly.—*adj.* external : outlying : remote : played away from home : outwards : not batting : exceeding the usual : in any condition expressed by the adverb **out.**—*n.* one who is out : that which is outside : a projection or outward bend (as in *outs and ins*) : an omission in setting type : (*dial.*) a paying out, esp. in *pl.*

rates and taxes, &c. : (*dial.*) an outing : (*U.S.*) a disadvantage, drawback : (*U.S.*) permission to go out : (*U.S.*) a way out.—*prep.* (now usu. *from out*) forth from : (now *rare*) outside of : along in an outward direction : (*U.S.*) without, short of.—*v.t.* to put out : to knock out.—*v.i.* to go out : (with *with*) to fetch out, to utter.—*interj.* alas : away, begone : you are, he is, out : shame (usu. *out upon*).—**at outs,** (*U.S.*) at odds ; **from out,** out from ; **murder will out** (see **murder**) ; **out and about,** able to go out, convalescent ; **out and away,** by far : beyond competition ; **out at elbow, heel, knee,** showing or threatening to show through the elbow, heel, knee, of a garment ; **out for,** abroad in quest of : expressly aiming at : dismissed from batting with a score of ; **out of,** from within : from among : not in : not within : excluded from : from (as source, material, motive, condition, possession, language, &c.) : born of : beyond the bounds, range, or scope of : deviating from, in disagreement with : away or distant from : without, destitute or denuded of ; **out of character,** not in keeping with character ; **out of course,** out of order ; **out of doors,** in or into the open air ; **out of favour,** disliked ; **out of hand,** instantly : beyond control ; **out of it,** excluded from participation : without a chance ; **out of joint,** not in proper connexion : disjointed, dislocated ; **out of one's mind,** mad ; **out of print,** no longer to be had from the publisher ; **out of temper,** cross, annoyed ; **out of the common,** unusual ; **out of the wood** (see **halloo**) ; **out of time,** too soon or too late : not keeping time in music ; **out of tune,** not true in pitch ; **outs and ins** (see **ins and outs**) ; **out to out,** in measurement from outside to outside : overall ; **out upon,** shame on ; **out with,** away with : not friendly with : to utter, ejaculate, divulge : to bring out, whip out.—See also **catch, date, fashion, knock, place, pocket, question, sight, sort, use, way, work, &c.** [O.E. *ūte, ūt* ; Goth. *ut,* Ger. *aus,* Sans. *ud.*]

out-, *owt-,* in composition.—*adj.* **out′-and-out,** thorough-going : thorough-paced : utter : absolute : unqualified.—*adv.* **out-and-out′,** finally and completely : definitely : unreservedly.—*n.* **out-and-out′er,** any person or thing that is a complete or extreme type : a thorough-going partisan : a great lie.—*v.t.* **out-ask′,** to proclaim the banns of for the last time.—*adj.* and *adv.* **out′-back** (*Austr.*), in, to, or of the back-country.—*n.* the back-country.—*n.* **out-back′er,** one from the back-country.—*vs.t.* **outbal′ance,** to outweigh ; **outbar′,** to bar out ; **outbar′gain,** to get the better of in a bargain ; **outbid′,** to make a higher bid than ; **outblust′er,** to exceed in blustering : to get the better of by bluster : to deprive by bluster. —*adj.* **out′board,** outside of a ship or boat : having engines outside the boat.—*adv.* outside of, or towards the outside of.—*adj.* **out′bound,** bound for a distant port.—*n.pl.* **out′bounds,** (*Spens.*) boundaries.—*vs.t.* **outbrag′,** to surpass in bragging or boasting : to surpass in beauty or splendour ; **outbrave′,** (*Shak.*) to excel in boldness or splendour : to outface.—*n.* **out′break,** a breaking out : a disturbance.—*v.i.* **outbreak′,** to burst forth.— *v.t.* and *v.i.* **outbreathe** (*owt-brēdh′*), to breathe out.—*adjs.* **outbreath′d,** (*-bretht′* ; *Shak.*) out of breath ; **out′bred.**—*ns.* **outbreed′ing,** breeding from parents not close akin : exogamy ; **out′-building,** a building separate from, but used in connexion with, a dwelling-house or a main building : an outhouse.—*v.t.* **outburn′,** to exceed in burning.—*v.i.* to burn away.—*n.* **out′burst,** a bursting out : an explosion.—*v.i.* **outburst′,** to burst out.—*adv.* **outby, outbye** (*owt-bī′,* ōōt-bī′ ; *Scot.*) out of doors : a little way off : outwards : (*min.*) towards the shaft.—*adj.* **out′by(e),** outdoor : outlying.—*ns.* **out′cast,** one who is cast out of society or home : anything rejected, eliminated, or cast out : (*Scot.*) a quarrel : an explosion.—*n.* **out′caste,** one who is of no caste or has lost caste.—*vs.t.* **outcaste′,** to put out of caste ; **outclass′,** to surpass so far as to seem in a different class.—*adj.* **outclassed′.** —*n.* **out′come,** the issue : consequence : result. —*v.t.* **outcraft′y,** (*Shak.*) to exceed in craft.—*n.*

out′crop, the cropping out of a rock.—*v.i.* (-*krop′*) to crop out.—*n.* **out′cry**, a loud cry of protest, distress, &c.: a confused noise: a public auction.—*v.t.* **outcry′**, to outdo in crying.—*v.i.* to cry out.—*adj.* **outdacious** (*owt-dā′shos*), an illiterate perversion of audacious.—*vs.t.* **outdance′**, to outdo in dancing; **outdare′**, to surpass in daring: to defy; **outdate′**, to put out of date.—*adj.* **outdāt′ed**.—*vs.t.* **outdis′tance**, to leave far behind: to outstrip; **outdo′**, to surpass: excel.—*adj.* **out′-door**, outside the door or the house: in or for the open air.—*adv.* **outdoors′**, out of the house: abroad (**outdoor relief**, help given to a pauper not living in the workhouse).—*vs.t.* **outdrive′**, to drive faster or farther than; **outdure′**, to outlast; **outdwell′**, (*Shak.*) to stay beyond.—*n.* **out′-dweller**, one who dwells elsewhere, esp. one who owns land in a parish but lives outside it.—*adj.* **out′ed**, ejected.—*n.* **out′-edge**, the furthest bound.—*adj.* **out′er** (O.E. *úterra*, comp.), more out or without: external—opp. to *inner* (**outer bar**, the junior barristers who plead outside the bar in court, as distinguished from King's Counsel and others who plead within the bar).—*n.* the outermost ring of a target, a shot striking it: in an electrical distribution system either of the conductors whose potential is above or below the earth's.—*adjs.* **out′ermost**, **out′most** (-*mast*, -*mōst*; O.E. *útemest*, superl.), most or farthest out: most distant.—*v.t.* **outface′**, to stare down: to bear down or maintain by bravery or impudence: to confront boldly: to maintain boldly or impudently to the face of.—*ns.* **outfall** (*owt′-fawl*), the outlet of a river, drain, &c.: a sortie: (*prov.*) a quarrel; **out′fangthief** (O.E. *útfangene-théof*—*út*, out, the root of *fón*, to take, *théof*, thief), the right of judging and fining thieves taken outside of one's own jurisdiction; **out′field**, (*Scot.*) arable land continually cropped without being manured—opp. to *infield*: any open field at a distance from the farm-steading: any undefined district or sphere: at cricket and baseball, the outer part of the field: the players who occupy it; **out′fielder**, one of such players.—*v.t.* **outfight′**, to surpass or defeat in fighting.—*n.* **out′-fit**, the act of fitting out for any enterprise: complete equipment: expenses for fitting out: (*U.S.*) a company travelling together for any purpose, esp. in charge of cattle: any set of persons, a gang.—*v.t.* to fit out, equip.—*v.i.* to get an outfit.—*ns.* **out′fitter**, one who furnishes outfits: one who deals in clothing, haberdashery, sporting equipment, &c.; **out′fitting**.—*vs.t.* **outflank′**, to extend beyond or pass round the flank of: to circumvent; **outflash′**, to surpass in flashing.—*v.i.* to flash out.—*ns.* **out′fling**, a sharp retort or gibe; **out′flow**, a flowing out: an outward current: outfall: amount that flows out.—*v.i.* **outflow′**, to flow out.—*n.* **out′flowing**.—*adj.* **outflow′ing** (or *owt′*).—*n.* **out′flush**, a sudden glow.—*vs.t.* **outflush′**, to flush more brightly than; **outfly′**, to surpass in flying: to fly faster than: to escape by swiftness of flight.—*v.i.* to fly out.—*vs.t.* **outfoot′**, to outstrip: to outsail; **outfrown′**, (*Shak.*) to frown down.—*n.* **out′gate**, (*Spens.* and *Northern*) an outlet: an exit.—*vs.t.* **outgen′eral**, to get the better of by generalship: to prove a better general than; **outgive′**, to surpass in liberality.—*v.i.* to give out, come to an end.—*n.* **out′giving**, a disbursement: an utterance: (*U.S.*) a declaration of policy.—*vs.t.* **outglare′**, to glare more than: to be more glaring than; **outgo′**, to outstrip: to surpass: to pass or live through: (*obs.*) to overreach.—*v.i.* to go out: to come to an end:—*pa.t.* **outwent′**; *pa.p.* **outgone′**.—*ns.* **out′go**, that which goes out: expenditure—opp. to *income*; **out′goer**, one who is going out or departing; **out′going**, act or state of going out: extreme limit: expenditure.—*adj.* departing—opp. to *incoming*, as a tenant.—*v.t.* **outgrow′**, to surpass in growth: to grow out of, grow too big for: to eliminate or become free from in course of growth.—*ns.* **out′growth**, that which grows out from anything: an excrescence: a product; **out′guard**, a guard at a distance or at the farthest distance

from the main body.—*v.i.* **outgush′**, to issue with force.—*ns.* **out′gush**, a gushing out; **out′haul**, a rope for hauling out the clew of a sail.—Also **out′hauler**.

outher, *ow′dhor*, *aw′dhor*, an old form, now *dial.*, of either.

out- (continued).—*vs.t.* **out-Her′od**, to overact the part of (*Herod*) in violence (*Hamlet*, III. ii.): to outdo, esp. in what is bad; **outhire′** (*Spens.* **outhyre**), to give out as if on hire.—*ns.* **out′house**, a separate building subsidiary to a main building; **out′ing**, ejection: distance out: an outdoor excursion or airing.—*v.t.* **outjest′**, (*Shak.*) to overcome by jesting: to excel in jesting.—*ns.* **out′jet**, **out′jut**, a projection.—*ns.* and *adjs.* **outjett′ing**, **outjutt′ing**.—*n.* **out′land**, a foreign land: land granted to tenants: an outlying land or territory.—*adj.* foreign: outlying.—*n.* **out′lander**, a foreigner: an uitlander.—*adj.* **outland′ish**, (*arch.*) foreign: queer, bizarre: out-of-the-way.—*adv.* **outland′ishly**.—*n.* **outland′ishness**; **out′lash**, a sudden burst or stroke.—*vs.t.* **outlast′**, to last longer than; **outlaunch′** (*Spens.* **outlaunce**), to launch forth.—*n.* **out′law** (O.E. *útlaga*—O.N. *útlági*—*út*, out, *lög*, law), one deprived of the protection of the law: (loosely) a bandit: an outcast: (*U.S.*) an unmanageable animal.—*v.t.* to place beyond the law: to deprive of the benefit of the law: to ban.—*ns.* **out′lawry**, the act of putting a man out of the protection of the law: state of being an outlaw; **out′lay**, that which is laid out: expenditure.—*v.t.* **outlay′**, to lay out in view: to expend: to surpass in laying.—*n.* **out′leap**, an act of leaping out: an excursion: an outburst.—*v.t.* **outleap′**, to leap beyond or over: to surpass in leaping.—*v.i.* to leap out.—*v.t.* **outlearn′**, (*Spens.*) to elicit: to surpass: to excel in learning: to get beyond the study of.—*adj.* **outler** (*ōōt′lor*; *poss.* =**outlier**; *Burns*), not housed.—*n.* a beast that is not housed: one who is out of office.—*n.* **out′let**, the place or means by which anything is let out: the passage outward, vent.—*v.t.* **outlie′**, to surpass in telling lies.—*v.i.* **outlie′**, to lie in the open: to camp: to lie stretched out.—*v.t.* to lie beyond.—*ns.* **out′lier**, one who lies in the open: one who lodges or lies apart from others or from a place with which he is connected: an outsider: a detached portion of anything lying some way off or out: (*geol.*) an isolated remnant of rock surrounded by older rocks; **out′line**, the outer line: the line by which any figure or object as seen is bounded: a sketch showing only the main lines: representation by such lines: a general statement without details: a statement of the main principles: a set-line in fishing.—*v.t.* to draw the exterior line of: to delineate or sketch.—*adj.* **outlinear** (*owt-lin′i-or*), like an outline.—*v.t.* **outlive** (*-liv′*), to live longer than: to survive: to live through: to live down.—*ns.* **outlodg′ing**, a lodging beyond bounds; **out′look**, a vigilant watch: a place for looking out from: a view, prospect: a prospect for the future: mental point of view.—*v.t.* **outlook′**, (*Shak. owt′*) to face courageously.—*v.i.* to look out.—*v.t.* **outlus′tre**, (*Shak.*) to outshine.—*adj.* **out′lying**, lying out or beyond: lodging apart: remote: on the exterior or frontier: detached.—*vs.t.* **outman′**, to outdo in manliness: to outnumber in men; **outmanoeu′vre**, to surpass in or by manoeuvring; **outman′tle**, to excel in dress or ornament; **outmarch′**, to march faster than: to leave behind by marching; **outmatch′**, to be more than a match for; **outmeas′ure**, to exceed in extent; **outmode′**, to put out of fashion.—*adjs.* **outmod′ed**; **out′most** (same as **outermost**).—*vs.t.* **outmove′**, to move faster than: to get the better by moving; **outname′**, to surpass in notoriety.—*n.* **out′ness**, state of being out: externality to the perceiving mind, objectiveness. — *vs.t.* **outnight′**, (*Shak.*, *Merch. of Ven.*, V. i) to surpass in mentioning nights; **outnum′ber**, to exceed in number.—*adjs.* **out-of-date′**, not abreast of the times: obsolete; **out-of-door(s)′**, in or for the open air: outdoor: outside of parliament.—*n.* **out-of-doors′**, the open air.—(*adv.* see **out of doors**).—*adj.* **out-of-the-way′**, uncommon: singular: secluded: remote

—*n.* **out-of-work′**, an unemployed person.—*adv.* and *prep.* **out-o′ver, out-owre** (*ōōt-owr′* ; *Scot.*), out over: over.—*vs.t.* **outpace′**, to walk faster than: to outstrip ; **out-par′amour,** (*Shak.*) to exceed in addiction to mistresses.—*ns.* **out′parish,** a parish associated with a town but beyond the boundary : an outlying parish ; **out′part,** a part remote from the centre.—*v.t.* **outpass′ion,** to go beyond in passionateness.—*n.* **out′-patient,** a hospital patient who is not an inmate.—*v.i.* **outpeep′,** to peep out. —*v.t.* **outpeer′,** (*Shak.*) to surpass or excel.—*n.* **out′-pension,** a pension granted to one who is not resident in an institution.—*v.t.* to grant an out-pension to.—*n.* **out′-pensioner,** a non-resident pensioner.—*v.t.* **outpoint′,** to score more points than.—*ns.* **out′port,** a port out of or remote from the chief port : a port away from the town or cus-toms area : a place of export ; **out′-porter,** a porter who carries luggage to and from, and not merely in, the place where he is employed ; **out′-post,** a post or station beyond the main body or in the wilds : its occupants : a remote settlement. —*v.t.* **outpour′,** to pour out : to send out in a stream.—*v.i.* to flow out in a stream.—*ns.* **out′-pour ; outpour′er ; out′pouring,** a pouring out : a passionate or fluent utterance.—*vs.t.* **outpower′,** to surpass in power ; **outpray′,** to exceed in earnest-ness or length of prayer : to overcome in or by prayer ; **outprize′,** (*Shak.*) to exceed in estima-tion.—*n.* **out′put,** quantity produced or turned out.—*n.pl.* **out′quarters,** quarters situated away from headquarters.

outrage, *owt′rij, -rāj, n.* (*Spens.*) excess, undue divergence from a mean : (*Shak.*) violence beyond measure : (*Spens.*) clamour : gross or violent injury : an act of wanton mischief : an atrocious act : gross offence to moral feelings : violation : rape.—*v.t.* to treat with excessive abuse : to shock grossly : to injure by violence, esp. to violate, to ravish.—*adj.* **outrageous** (*owt-rā′jəs*), violent : furious : turbulent : atrocious : monstrous : im-moderate.—*adv.* **outrā′geously.**—*ns.* **outrā′geous-ness ; outrance** (*ōō-tränᵉs′*), the utmost ex-tremity : the bitter end (**à outrance,** to the bitter end of a combat—erroneously in Eng. use, à l'ou-trance).—*adj.* **outré** (*ōō-trā*), beyond what is cus-tomary or proper : extravagant : overstrained.— *ns.* **outrecuidance** (*ōōt-ər-kwē′dans ; ōōt-r′-kwē′-dänᵉs ; obs.* Scott), presumption, overweening ; **outremer** (*ōō-tr′-mer′*), the region beyond sea : overseas. [Fr. *outre*—L. *ultrā,* beyond ; O.Fr. *cuider,* to think, plume oneself—L. *cōgitāre,* Fr. *mer*—L. *mare,* sea ; **outrage** (O.Fr. *ultrage*) is not connected with **out** and **rage,** but influenced by them.]

out- (continued).—*vs.t.* **outrank′,** to rank above ; **outreach′,** to reach or extend beyond : to over-reach : to stretch forth ; **outred′, outredd′en,** to surpass in redness ; **outreign′,** to reign longer than : (*Spens.* **outraigne**) to reign to the end of.— *n.* **outrelief′,** outdoor relief.—*v.t.* **outride′,** to ride beyond : to ride faster than : to ride safely through (a storm).—*ns.* **out′rider,** one who rides abroad : a servant on horseback who attends a carriage ; **out′rigger,** a projecting spar for extending sails or any part of the rigging : a projecting contrivance ending in a float fixed to the side of a canoe against capsizing : an iron bracket fixed to the outside of a boat carrying a rowlock at its extremity to in-crease the leverage of the oar : a light racing-boat with projecting rowlocks : a projecting beam for carrying a suspended scaffold in building : a pro-jecting frame to support the controlling planes of an aeroplane : an extension from the splinter-bar of a carriage to take another horse.—*adj.* **out′right,** out-and-out : unqualified : unmitigated : down-right : direct.—*adv.* **outright′,** directly : straight ahead : unreservedly : undisguisedly : at once and completely.—*vs.t.* **outri′val,** to surpass, excel ; **outroar′,** (*Shak.*) to exceed in roaring.—*n.* **out′-roar,** an uproar.—*v.t.* **outroot′,** to root out.—*ns.* **outrope** (*owt′rōp*), **out′roop** (-*rōōp* ; Du. *uitroep*) —*uit,* out, *roepen,* to cry ; *obs.*), an auction sale ; **out′roper, out′rooper,** (*obs.*) an auctioneer : formerly, the Common Crier of the City of London.

—*v.t.* **outrun′,** to go beyond in running : to exceed : to get the better of or to escape by run-ning (**outrun, or overrun, the constable,** to run into debt : to live beyond one's means).—*n.* **out′-runner.**—*v.i.* **outrush′,** to rush out.—*n.* **out′-rush,** a rushing out.—*vs.t.* **outsail′,** to leave behind in sailing : to sail beyond ; **outscold′,** (*Shak.*) to exceed in scolding ; **outscorn′,** (*Shak.*) to face out with scorn ; **outsell′,** to fetch a higher price than : to exceed in value : to surpass in the number or amount of sales.—*ns.* **out′-sentry,** a sentry placed at a distance ; **out′set,** a setting out : beginning : an outward current ; **out′setting ; out′settle-ment,** an outlying settlement.—*v.i.* **outshine′,** to shine out or forth.—*v.t.* to excel in shining : to be brighter than.—*n.* **out′shot,** (*Scot.*) a projection in a building.—*adj.* projecting.—*n.* **outside** (*owt′-sīd′, owt′sīd, owt-sīd′*), the outer side : the farthest limit : the outer surface : the exterior : an outside passenger : the outer part : (in *pl.*) the top and bottom quires of a ream of paper.—*adj.* on or from the outside : carried on the outside : exterior : superficial : external : extreme : beyond the limit : not enjoying membership.—*adv.* **outside′** (some-times *owt′*), on or to the outside : not within.— *prep.* **out′side′,** outside of : (*dial.*) except, apart from (**get outside of,** (*U.S.*) to comprehend : (*slang*) to eat or drink ; **outside chance,** a remote chance ; **outside country,** districts beyond the area of settlements in Australia ; **outside edge** (see **edge**) ; **outside in,** turned so that outside and inside change places : intimately (of knowing anything) ; **outside left, right,** in some games, a forward player on the extreme left, right ; **outside of,** in or to a position external to : (*U.S.*) apart from, except).—*ns.* **out′side-car,** an Irish jaunting-car in which the passengers sit back to back ; **outsid′er,** one who is not a member of a particular company, profession, &c., a stranger, a layman : one not considered fit to associate with : one who is not an inmate : one who is not participating : a race-horse not included among the favourites in the betting : one whose place in a game, at work, &c., is on the outside : (in *pl.*) a pair of nippers for turning a key in a keyhole from the outside ; **out′sight,** power of seeing external things : (*owt′sīt, ōōt′sihht* ; *Scot.*) outdoor pos-sessions. — Also *adj.* — *v.t.* **outsit′,** to sit beyond the time of : to sit longer than.—*adj.* **out′-size,** over normal size.—*n.* an exceptionally large size : anything, esp. a garment, of exceptionally large size.—*adj.* **out′sized.**—*n.* **out′skirt,** (usu. in *pl.*) the border.—*vs.t.* **outsleep′,** to sleep longer than : to sleep through : to sleep to or beyond the time of ; **outsmart′** (*coll.* ; *orig. U.S.*), to show more cleverness or cunning than, to outwit ; **outsoar′,** to soar beyond.—*n.* **out′sole,** the outer sole of a boot or shoe which rests on the ground.—*v.t.* and *v.i.* **out′span** (or -*span′* ; Du. *uitspannen*), to un-yoke or unharness from a vehicle.—*n.* (*owt′*) a stopping-place.—*v.t.* **outspeak′,** to say aloud : to speak more, louder, or longer than.—*v.i.* to speak boldly, to speak up.—*n.* **outspeckle** (*ōōt-spek′l* ; *Scot.*), a laughing-stock.—*adjs.* **outspent′,** thoroughly tired out ; **outspō′ken,** frank or bold of speech : uttered with boldness.—*n.* **outspō′kenness.**—*v.t.* **outsport′,** (*Shak.*) to sport beyond the limits of.— *v.t.* and *v.i.* **outspread′,** to spread out or over.— *adj.* **out′spread** (or *owt-spred′*), spread out.—*n.* an expanse.—*adj.* **outspread′ing,** *v.i.* **outspring′,** to spring out.—*n.* **out′spring,** outcome.—*v.t.* **out′-stand,** to withstand : to stand or endure through or beyond.—*v.i.* to stand out or project : to stand out (to sea) : to stand over, remain.—*adj.* **out′-stand′ing,** prominent : unsettled : unpaid : still to be attended to or done.—*adv.* **outstand′ingly.** —*vs.t.* **outstare′,** (*Shak.*) to stare down : to face the stare of unabashed : to gaze at without being blinded ; **outstay′,** to stay beyond or throughout : to stay longer than : to endure longer than ; **out′-step,** to step beyond, overstep ; **outstrain′,** to stretch out ; **outstretch′,** to stretch out : to reach forth : to spread out : to stretch to the end of : to stretch beyond ; **outstrike** (*owt-strīk′,* or *owt′*), to outdo in striking ; **outstrip′,** to outrun : to leave behind : to surpass ; **outstrip'**, to outdo in denuding oneself ; **outsum'**, to outnumber ; **outswear'**, to exceed in swearing : to overcome by swearing ; **outsweet'en**, to excel in sweetness.—*ns.* **out'swing**, an outward swing or swerve ; **out'swinger**, a ball bowled to swerve outwards.—*vs.t.* **outswell'**, (*Shak.*) to swell more than : to overflow ; **outtake'**, (*obs.*) to take out : to except.—*prep.* (*orig. pa.p.*) **outtäk'en**.—*vs.t.* **outtalk'**, to talk down : to outdo in talk ; **outtell'**, to tell forth : to tell to the end : to tell or count beyond ; **outtongue'**, (*Shak.*) to speak louder than ; **outtop'**, to reach higher than : to excel ; **outtrav'el**, to go faster or farther than : to go beyond ; **outval'ue**, exceed in value ; **outven'om**, (*Shak.*) to exceed in poisonousness ; **outvie'**, to compete with and surpass ; **outvill'ain**, (*Shak.*) to exceed in villainy ; **outvoice'**, (*Shak.*) to exceed in clamour or noise : to drown the voice of ; **out-vote'**, to defeat by a greater number of votes.—*n.* **out'voter**, a voter not resident in the constituency. —*v.t.* **outwalk'**, to walk farther, longer, or faster than : to walk beyond.—*n.* **out'wall**, the outside wall of a building : (*Shak.*) external appearance.— *adv.* **out'ward**, toward the outside : on the outside : outer : external : exterior : appearing externally : apparent : formal : not inherent, adventitious : (*theol.*) worldly, carnal : (*dial.*) dissolute.—*adv.* toward the exterior : away from port : to a foreign port : superficially.—*n.* (*Shak.*) external appearance : the outside.—*adj.* **out'wardbound**, bound outwards or to a foreign port.—*adv.* **out'wardly**, in an outward manner : externally : in appearance.—*n.* **out'wardness**, externality : objectivity.—*adv.* **out'wards**, in an outward direction.—*adj.* **out'ward-saint'ed**, appearing outwardly to be a saint.—*vs.t.* **outwatch'**, to watch longer than : to watch throughout the time of ; **outwear'**, to wear out : to spend, live through : to outlive, outgrow : to outlast ; **outwea'ry**, to weary out completely ; **outweed'**, (*Spens.*) to root out ; **outweep'**, to weep out, shed wholly : to surpass in weeping ; **outweigh'**, to exceed in weight or importance.—*v.t.* and *v.i.* **outwell'**, to pour or well out.—*v.t.* **outwent'**, used as *pa.t.* of **outgo**.—*v.i.* **outwick'**, in curling, to strike the outside of another stone and so send it within a circle.—*vs.t.* **outwin'**, (*Spens.*) to get out of ; **outwind** (*-wīnd'*), to unwind, extricate ; **outwing'**, to outstrip in flying : to fly beyond : to outflank ; **outwit'**, to surpass in wit or ingenuity : to defeat by superior ingenuity :— *pr.p.* **outwitt'ing** ; *pa.t.* and *pa.p.* **outwitt'ed**.— *prep.* **outwith** (*owt'with, ōōt'with* ; *Scot.*), outside of.—*adv.* outwards.—*n.* **out'work**, a work outside the principal wall or line of fortification : outdoor work, field-work : work done away from the shop or factory.—*v.t.* **outwork'**, (*Shak.*) to surpass in work : to work out or bring to an end : to finish :— *pa.t.* and *pa.p.* **outwrought'**, **outworked'**.—*n.* **out'worker**, one who works out of doors, or who takes away work to do at home.—*adj.* **outworn'** (or *owt'*), worn out : obsolete.—*vs.t.* **outworth'**, (*Shak.*) to exceed in value ; **outwrest'**, (*Spens.*) to extort.

ouvirandra, *ōō-vi-ran'drä, n.* the lattice-leaf of Madagascar. [From the Malagasy name.]

ouzel, ousel, *ōō'zl* (*Shak.* **woo'sel, woo'sell**), *n.* (*arch.*) a blackbird : (*Shak.*) apparently, a dark-complexioned person.—*ns.* **ou'zel-cock** ; **ring'-ou'zel**, a blackish thrush with a broad white band on the throat ; **wa'ter-ou'zel**, the dipper. [O.E. *ósle* ; cog. with Ger. *amsel.*]

ouzo, *ōō'zō, n.* an aniseed liqueur.

ova, *ō'vä, pl.* of **o'vum**.—*adj.* **o'val**, strictly, egg-shaped, like an egg in the round or in projection, rounded, longer than broad, broadest near one end : (loosely) elliptical or ellipsoidal, or nearly : (*bot.*) rounded at both ends, about twice as long as broad, broadest in the middle : (*obs.*) pertaining to eggs.—*n.* an oval figure or thing, e.g. an oval field.—*adv.* **o'vally**. [L. *ōvum*, egg ; *ōvālis* is modern Latin.]

ovary, *ō'va-ri, n.* the female genital gland : (*bot.*) the part of the gynaeceum that contains the ovules. —*adj.* **ovā'rian**, of or pertaining to the ovary.—*ns.* **ovā'riōle**, one of the egg-tubes forming an insect's

ovary ; **ovāriot'omist** ; **ovāriot'omy** (*surg.* ; Gr. *tomē*, a cut), the cutting of an ovary : usu. the removal of ovaries because of a tumour.—*adj.* (*rare*) **ovā'rious**, consisting of eggs.—*n.* **ovarī'tis**, inflammation of the ovary, oophoritis. [L.L. *ōvāria—ōvum*, egg.]

ovate, *ō'vät, adj.* egg-shaped : (*bot.*) shaped in outline like an egg, broadest below the middle.

ovate, *ov'ät, n.* an Eisteddfodic graduate neither a bard nor a druid. [W. *ofydd*, a philosopher, or lord ; fancifully identified with the unrelated Celtic word preserved in Gr. as *ouāteis* (pl.), Gaulish soothsayers.]

ovation, *ō-vā'shən, n.* in ancient Rome, a lesser triumph : an outburst of popular applause, an enthusiastic reception : rejoicing. — *v.t.* **ovate'**, (facetious back-formation) to receive with an ovation.—*n.* **ova'tor**. [L. *ŏvātiō, -ōnis—ŏvāre*, to exult.]

oven, *uv'n, n.* an arched cavity or closed chamber for baking, heating, or drying : a small furnace.— *ns.* **ov'en-bird**, a name for various birds that build oven-shaped nests, esp. the South American Furnarius ; **ov'en-tit**, the willow-warbler ; **ov'en-wood**, brushwood. [O.E. *ofen* ; Ger. *ofen.*]

over, *ō'vər, ō'er*, formerly *ore, ō're, ōr, prep.* above in place, rank, power, authority, contention, preference, value, quantity, number, &c. : in excess of : above and from one side of to the other : down from or beyond the edge of : from side to side or end to end of : along : throughout the extent of : until after : across : on or to the other side of : on, on to, about, or across the surface of, or all or much of : in discussion, contemplation, study of, or occupation with : concerning : on account of : in a sunk, submerged, or buried state beyond the level of.—*adv.* on the top : above : across : to or on the other side : from one person, party, condition, time, &c., to another : to sleep : outwards so as to overhang or fall : away from an upright position : through, from beginning to end, esp. in a cursory or exploratory way : throughout : into a reversed position : across the margin : again, in repetition : too much : in excess : left remaining : at an end.—*adj.* (usu. treated as a prefix) upper or superior : surplus : excessive.—*n.* (*cricket*) the series of balls (as *six-ball, eight-ball, over*), or the play, between changes in bowling from one end to the other : anything that is over : a surplus copy, &c. : an excess, overplus.—*v.t.* to go, leap, or vault over.—**all over**, at an end : everywhere : at the most characteristic : covered with, besmeared or bespattered with ; **over again**, afresh, anew ; **over against**, opposite ; **over and above**, in addition to : besides ; **over and over (again)**, many times : repeatedly ; **over head and ears**, completely submerged ; **over seas**, to foreign lands. [O.E. *ofer* ; Ger. *über*, L. *super*, Gr. *hyper* ; cf. **up**.]

over-, *ō'vər-*, in composition, above : excessive.— *v.i.* **overabound'**, to abound greatly or too much.— *adj.* **overabound'ing**.—*n.* **overabun'dance**.—*v.t.* **overact'**, to act with exaggeration, to overdo the performance of.—*v.i.* to act more than necessary. —*adj.* **o'ver-age**, above the limiting age : too old. —*adv.* **overall'**, **over-all'**, (*Spens.*) everywhere : above all : altogether : over the whole.—*adj.* **o'verall**, including everything : everything being reckoned : all-round.—*n.* **o'verall**, a protective garment worn over ordinary clothes for dirty work or weather : (*pl.*) trousers or leggings or combined shirt and trousers of this kind : cavalryman's trousers.—*adj.* **o'veralled**.—*n.* **over-anxi'ety**.— *adj.* **over-anx'ious**, too anxious.—*adv.* **over-anx'iously**.—*v.t.* **overarch'**, to arch over : to form above into an arch.—*v.i.* to hang over like an arch.—*n.* an overhead arch.—*adj.* and *adv.* **o'ver-arm**, with the arm raised above the shoulder.— *vs.t.* **overawe'**, to daunt by fear or by superior influence ; **overbal'ance**, to exceed in weight, value, or importance : to cause to lose (one's) balance.—*v.i.* to lose (one's) balance.—*n.* excess of weight or value.—*v.t.* **overbear'**, to bear down or overpower : to overwhelm : to overthrow.—*v.i.* to be too productive.—*adj.* **overbear'ing**, inclined to domineer, esp. in manner or conduct: haughty and dogmatical: imperious.—*adv.* **overbear'ingly.** —*n.* **overbear'ingness.**—*v.t.* and *v.i.* **overbeat'**, to beat down.—*v.t.* **overbid'**, to outbid: to make a bid that is greater than or counts above: to bid more than the value of.—*v.i.* to bid too high. —*n.* a higher bid: an unduly high bid. —*ns.* **overbidd'er**; **overbidd'ing.** —*v.i.* **overblow'**, to blow over or to be past its violence: to blow with too much violence: (*mus.*) to produce a harmonic instead of the fundamental tone, by excess of wind-pressure.—*v.t.* to blow away: to blow across: to overturn by blowing: (*mus.*) to blow with such force as to sound a harmonic instead of the fundamental.—*v.t.* **overblow'**, to cover with blossoms—*adjs.* **overblown'**, blown over or past, at an end: burnt by an excessive blast, in the Bessemer steel process: inflated to excess; **overblown'**, more than full-blown.—*adv.* **overboard'**, over the board or side: from on board: out of a ship.—*v.i.* **overboil'**, to boil over (the edge of a vessel).—*v.t.* and *v.i.* to boil too much. —*adj.* **overbold'**, excessively bold.—*adv.* **over-bold'ly.**—*v.t.* **overbound'**, to bound over.—*n.* **o'verbridge**, a bridge over a road or railway, &c., distinguished from one that carries it.—*vs.t.* **over-bridge'**, to bridge over; **overbrim'**, to fill to overflowing.—*v.i.* to be so full as to overflow.—*adj.* **overbrimmed'**, having a very wide brim.—*vs.t.* **overbrow'**, to overhang like a brow; **overbuild'**, to cover with buildings: to build above: to build in excess: to build too much upon or in; **over-bulk'**, (*Shak.*) to oppress by bulk, or to dwarf by greater bulk; **overburd'en**, **overburth'en**, to burden overmuch.—*n.* (*ō'*), an excessive burden: alluvial soil, &c., overlying a bed of clay or other substance to be dug, mined, or quarried.—*adj.* **overbur'densome.**—*v.t.* **overburn'**, to burn too much.—*v.i.* to be too zealous.—*adj.* **overbus'y**, too busy: officious.—*v.t.* to busy too much.—*v.t.* **overbuy'**, (*Shak.*) to buy too dear: to buy dearer than: (*refl.*) to put in the position of having bought too much: to buy too much of.—*v.i.* to buy too much:—*pa.t.* and *pa.p.* **overbought'.**—*adv.* **overby'**, a little way over—mainly in Scots forms, **owerby**, **o'erby** (*owr-bī'*).—*vs.t.* **overcall'**, (*bridge*) to outbid: to bid above: to bid too high on: to rank as a higher bid than; **overcan'opy**, to cover as with a canopy:—*pa.p.* **over-can'opied** (*Shak.*). **over-cann'oped**).—*n.* **overcapitalisā'tion.**—*v.t.* **overcap'italise**, to fix the capital to be invested in, or the capital value of, too high.—*adj.* **overcare'ful**, too careful.—*vs.t.* **overcarr'y**, to carry too far; **overcast'**, to overthrow: to cast as a covering: to cast a covering over: (*Spens.*) to shade: to throw stitches over the edge of: to cover with oversewn stitches: (*Scot.*) to recover, get over: (*arch.*) to seem too high, overestimate.—*v.i.* to grow dull or cloudy.—*adj.* clouded over.—*n.* a cloudy covering. —*n.* **overcast'ing**, the action of the verb overcast: in bookbinding, a method of oversewing single leaves in hem-stitch style to give the pliability of folded double leaves.—*vs.t.* **overcatch'**, (*arch.*) to over-take (*pa.p.* **overcaught'**, *Spens.*); **overcharge'**, to load with too great a charge: to overdo: to exaggerate: to charge too great a price.—*ns.* **o'ver-charge**, an excessive load or burden: too great a charge, as of gunpowder or of price; **o'vercheck**, a large prominent check-pattern combined with a smaller: a cloth so checked.—*adj.* **overclad'**, wearing too much clothing.—*v.t.* **overcloud'**, to cover over with clouds: to cause gloom or sorrow to.—*v.i.* to cloud over, become clouded over.—*v.t.* **overcloy'**, to surfeit.—*ns.* **o'vercoat**, an outdoor coat worn over all else, a topcoat; **o'vercoating**, cloth for overcoats.—*vs.t.* **overcol'our**, to colour too strongly: to exaggerate: to spread colour over; **overcome'**, (*arch.*) to cover, overspread: to come over: to get the better of: to conquer or subdue: to surmount.—*v.i.* to be victorious.—*n.* (*Scot.*) **o'ercome**, **owrecome** (*owr'kəm*), a cross-ing over: a surplus, excess: a fit or sudden access of illness: a refrain, by-word, or recurring theme. —*v.t.* **overcom'pensate**, to allow too much in compensation of.—*n.* **overcompensā'tion.**—*adj.*

overcompens'atory.—*n.* **over-con'fidence**, ex-cessive confidence.—*adj.* **over-con'fident.**—*vs.t.* **overcool'**, to cool too much; **overcorrect'**, to apply so great a correction to as to deviate in the opposite way: (*opt.*) to correct beyond achromat-ism, so that the red rays come to a focus nearer the lens than the violet.—*n.* **overcorrec'tion.**— *vs.t.* **overcount'**, to outnumber: to reckon too high: to overreach; **overcov'er**, to cover com-pletely. — *n.* **overcredu'lity.** — *adj.* **overcred'-ulous**, too ready to believe.—*vs.t.* **o'vercrop**, to take too much out by cultivation; **overcrow'**, *Spens.* **overcraw'**, *Shak.* **orecrowe'**, to crow over: to triumph over.—*v.t.* and *v.i.* **overcrowd'**, to fill or crowd to excess.—*n.* **overcrowd'ing.**—*adjs.* **over-dar'ing**, foolhardy; **overdat'ed**, out of date; **over-deter'mined**, having more than the necessary determining data or factors.—*v.t.* **over-devel'op**, to develop too much.—*n.* **over-devel'opment.**— *adj.* **overdight** (*-dīt'*, *Spens.*), dight or covered over: overspread.—*v.t.* **overdo'**, to do overmuch: to overact: to exaggerate: to carry too far: to harass, to fatigue: to cook too much or more than usual: to excel.—*n.* **overdo'er.**—*adj.* **overdone'.** —*ns.* **overdōs'age**; **o'verdose**, an excessive dose. —*v.t.* **overdose'**, to dose overmuch: to administer in excess.—*ns.* **o'verdraft**, the act or advantage of overdrawing: the excess of the amount drawn over the sum against which it is drawn; **o'verdraught** (*-dräft*), a current of air passing above or from above. —*v.t.* **overdraw'**, to exaggerate in drawing: to exaggerate: to draw beyond one's credit.—*v.t.* and *v.i.* **overdress'**, to dress too ostentatiously or elaborately.—*n.* **o'verdress**, an outer dress.—*v.t.* **overdrive'**, to drive too hard: to outdrive.—*adjs.* **overdrowsed'** (*Wordsworth* **o'er-drows'ed**), over-come by drowsiness; **overdue'** (or *ō'*), behind time for arrival: unpaid at the right time.—*vs.t.* **overdust'**, to sprinkle over or cover with dust; **overdye'**, to dye too deeply: to dye over with another colour.—*adj.* **overear'nest**, too earnest: cross.—*v.t.* **overeat'**, to surfeit with eating (gener-ally reflexive): (*Shak.*) perhaps, to nibble all over, perhaps, to surfeit on.—*v.i.* to eat too much.—*v.t.* **overes'timate**, to estimate too highly.—*n.* an exces-sive estimate.—*ns.* **overestimā'tion**; **overexcit-abil'ity.**—*adj.* **overexcit'able.**—*v.t.* **overexcite'**, to excite unduly or injuriously.—*n.* **overexcite'-ment.**—*v.t.* **overexert'**, to exert too much.—*n.* **overexer'tion.**—*v.t.* **overexpose'**, to expose too much, esp. (*phot.*) to light.—*n.* **overexpos'ure.**— *adj.* **over-ex'quisite**, (*Milt.*) excessively curious in detail of imagination.—*v.t.* **overeye'**, to survey, look upon: to watch.—*n.* **o'verfall**, a rippling or race of water: a sudden increase of depth: a place or structure for overflow of surplus waters: (*obs.*) a waterfall.—*v.t.* **overfall'**, to fall on or over: to assail.—*v.i.* to fall over.—*adv.* **overfar'**, too far: (*Shak.*) too too great an extent.—*vs.t.* and *vs.i.* **over-feed'**, to feed to excess (*pa.p.* and *pa.t.* **overfed'**); **overfill'**, to fill to overflowing.—*adj.* **overfine'**, too fine.—*n.* **overfine'ness.**—*vs.t.* **overfire'**, to fire too much; **overfish'**, to fish to excess; **over'-flour'ish**, to cover with blossom, or with flourishes or ornament; **overflow'**, to flow over: to flow over the surface of: to flood: to flow over and beyond: to pour forth: to cause to run over: (*fig.*) to cover, as with numbers.—*v.i.* to flow over the brim, bank, or boundary, escape by flowing out: to run over, shed liquid contents by reason of fulness or high level: to pass out in part, as under pressure: (*fig.*) to abound:—*pa.t.* **overflowed'**; *pa.p.* **overflowed'**, formerly and still sometimes **overflown'.**—*n.* **o'verflow**, a flowing over: that which flows over: a pipe or channel for spare water, &c.: an inundation: superabundance (**overflow meeting**, a supplementary meeting of those unable to find room in the main meeting).— *adj.* **overflow'ing**, flowing over: running over: overfull: over-abounding: exuberant.—*n.* over-flow: that which overflows: condition in which overflow occurs. — *adv.* **overflow'ingly.** — *v.t.* **overflush'**, to flush over.—*adj.* too flush.—*n.* **o'verflush**, superfluity.—*v.t.* **overfly'**, to out-soar: to fly over. — *n.* **o'verfold**, (*geol.*) a fold tilted over so that both limbs dip the same way, one upside down. — *v.t.* **overfold'**, to fold over: to thrust into an overfold. — *adj.* **overfond'**, (*obs.*) foolish to excess: too affectionate.—*adv.* **overfond'ly.**—*n.* **overfond'ness.** —*adj.* **overfor'ward**, too forward.—*n.* **overfor'-wardness.**—*adj.* **overfree'**, too free: unduly free. — *n.* **overfree'dom.** — *adv.* **overfree'ly.** — *v.t.* **overfreight'**, to overload.—*pa.p.* or *adj.* **overfraught'.**—*n.* **o'verfreight**, an excessive load.— *adj.* **overfull'**, (*Shak.*) too full.—*n.* **overful(l)ness.** —*vs.t.* **overgall'**, to blister or inflame all over, or greatly; **overgang'** (*Scot.* **o'ergang**, *owr-gang'*), to dominate: to overspread: to exceed; **overget'**, (*obs.*) to overtake: to get over, recover from: to overcome, possess the mind of; **overgive'**, (*Spens.*) to give over or up; **overglance'**, to look hastily over; **overglaze'**, to glaze over: to cover speciously.—*n.* **o'verglaze**, an additional glaze given to porcelain, &c.—*adj.* applied to, or suitable for painting on, a glazed surface.—*vs.t.* **overgloom'**, to cover with gloom: to scowl over; **overgo'**, to exceed: to surpass: to overpower: to go over: to pass over, traverse: to spread over: to pass over, forbear to speak of.—*v.i.* to go over: to pass on.—*n.* **overgo'ing**, passing over: crossing, traversing: transgression.—*v.t.* **overgorge'**, (*Shak.*) to gorge to excess.—*v.t.* and *v.i.* **overgrain'**, to grain over (a surface already grained).— *n.* **overgrain'er**, a brush for overgraining.—*v.t.* **overgrass'**, to grass over, conceal with grass.—*adjs.* **o'vergreat**, too great; **overgreed'y**, too greedy.— *v.t.* **overgreen'**, to cover with green or verdure: (*fig.*, *Shak.*) conceal.—*adj.* **overground'**, above ground.—*v.t.* **overgrow'**, to grow beyond: to grow more than: to grow too great for: to rise above: to cover with growth.—*v.i.* to grow beyond the normal or suitable size.—*adj.* **overgrown** (*ō'vər-grōn*, or *-grōn'*), grown beyond the natural size: covered over with a growth.—*n.* **o'vergrowth**, excessive or abnormally great growth: excess or superfluity resulting from growth: that which grows over and covers anything: (*crystal.*) growth of a crystal around another.—*v.t.* **overhaile'**, **overhale'**, (*Spens.*) to draw over: (*obs.*) to overtake, overpower: to examine.—*n.* **o'verhair**, the long hair overlying the fur of many animals.—*adv.* **overhand'** (or *ō'*), with hand above the object: palm-downwards: with hand or arm raised above the shoulders or (in swimming) coming out of the water over the head: (*min.*) from below: (*needle-work*) with stitches passing through in one direction and back round the edges.—*adj.* **o'verhand**, done or performed overhand (**overhand knot**, the simplest of all knots, tied by passing the end over the standing part and through the bight).—*v.t.* to sew overhand.—*adj.* and *adv.* **overhand'ed**, with hand above: with too many hands.—*adj.* **overhand'led**, (*Shak.*) handled or discussed too much. —*v.t.* **overhang'**, to hang over: to project over: to impend over: to cover with hangings.—*v.i.* to hang over, lean out beyond the vertical.—*n.* **o'verhang**, a projecting part: degree of projection. —*adj.* **overhapp'y**, excessively or too happy.—*n.* **overhaste'**, excessive haste.—*adv.* **overhas'tily.** *n.* **overhas'tiness.**—*adj.* **overhas'ty.**—*v.t.* **overhaul'**, to haul or draw over: to turn over for examination: to examine: (*naut.*) to overtake or gain upon.—*n.* **o'verhaul**, a hauling over: examination, esp. with a view to repair.—*adv.* **overhead'**, above one's head: aloft: in the zenith: in complete submergence: (now *Scot.*) taking one with another, in the lump, on the average, apiece.—*adj.* **o'verhead**, above one's head: well above ground level: all-round, general, average.—*n.* (often in *pl.*; also **overhead costs, charges**) the general expenses of a business—as distinct from the direct cost of producing an article: that which is overhead.—*vs.t.* **overhear'**, to hear without being meant to hear: to hear by accident: (*Shak.*) to hear over again or in turn; **overheat'**, to heat to excess.—*v.i.* to become too hot.—*n.* **o'verheat**, too great heat.—*vs.t.* **overhent'**, (*Spens.*) to overtake (*pa.t.* and *pa.p.* **overhent'**); **overhold'**, (*Shak.*) to overvalue.—*adj.* **overhung'**, overhanging: sus-

pended from above: covered over, adorned with hangings.—*v.t.* **overindulge'**, to indulge to excess. —*n.* **overindulg'ence.**—*adj.* **overindulg'ent.**— *v.t.* **overinform'**, to animate too much.—*n.* **overinsur'ance.**—*vs.t.* **overinsure'**, to insure for more than the real value; **overiss'ue**, to issue in excess, as bank-notes or bills of exchange.—*n.* **o'verissue**, excessive issue.—*v.t.* **overjoy'**, to fill with great joy: to transport with delight or gladness.—*n.* **o'verjoy**, joy to excess: transport.— *vs.t.* **overjump'**, to jump beyond: to pass by: to ignore: to jump too far for or over; **overkeep'**, to keep too long; **overkest'**, (*Spens.*) for **overcast** (*pa.t.* and *pa.p.*).—*adj.* **overkind'**, too kind.—*ns.* **overkind'ness**; **o'verking**, a king holding sovereignty over inferior kings.—*adj.* **o'verknee**, reaching above the knee.—*vs.t.* **overla'bour**, to labour excessively over: to be too nice with: to overwork; **overlade'**, to overburden:—*pa.p.* **overla'den**; **overlaid'**, *pa.t.* of **overlay**; **overlain**, *pa.p.* of **overlie.**—*adj.* **o'verland**, passing entirely or principally by land.—*adv.* **overland'** (or *ō'*), by or over land.—*v.t.* and *v.i.* (*Austr.*) to drive (flocks or herds) a long distance across country: to journey across country, esp. a long way.—*n.* **o'verlander** (or *-land'*).—*v.t.* **overlap'**, to extend over and beyond the edge of: to reach from beyond across the edge and partly rest on: to coincide in part with: to ripple over.—*n.* **o'verlap**, an overlapping part: (*geol.*) a disposition of strata where the upper beds extend beyond the boundary of the lower beds of the same series.—*vs.t.* **overlard'**, to smear over as with lard: to overload with fulsomeness; **overlaunch'**, (in shipbuilding) to unite by long splices or scarfs; **overlay'**, to cover by laying or spreading something over: (*Milt.*) to span: (*print.*) to put an overlay or overlays on: to cover to excess, encumber: (*rare*) to lay or place as a covering: (by confusion) to overlie:—*pa.t.* and *pa.p.* **overlaid'.** —*ns.* **o'verlay**, a piece of paper pasted on the impression-surface of a printing-press, so as to increase the impression in a place where it is too faint: a covering: (*Scot.*) a cravat: **overlay'ing**, a superficial covering: that which overlays: plating.—*adv.* **overleaf'**, on the other side of the leaf of a book.—*v.t.* **overleap'** (*Scot.* **overloup'**), to leap over: to pass over without notice (**overleap oneself**, to leap too far).—*n.* **o'verleather**, (*Shak.*) the upper part of a shoe.—*vs.t.* **overleaven'**, to leaven too much; **overlie'**, to lie above or upon: to smother by lying on:—*pr.p.* **overly'ing**; *pa.t.* **overlay'**; *pa.p.* **overlain'.**—*n.* **o'verlier** (or *-lī'*).— *v.t.* **overlive** (*-liv'*), to survive: to outlive: (*refl.*) to outlive the appropriate date of, or usefulness of.— *v.i.* to survive: to live too long: to live too fast, or so as prematurely to exhaust the fund of life: to live on too high a standard of luxury.—*v.t.* **overload'**, to load or fill overmuch.—*n.* (*ō'*) an excessive load.—*adj.* and *adv.* **overlong'**, too long. —*v.t.* **overlook'**, to look over: to see from a higher position: to view carefully: to oversee, superintend: to fail to notice or take into account: to pass by without cognisance or punishment: to slight: to bewitch by looking upon with the evil eye.—*ns.* **overlook'er**; **o'verlord**, a lord over other lords: a feudal superior.—*v.t.* **overlord'.**— *n.* **o'verlordship.**—*adj.* **overlust'y**, (*Shak.*) too lusty.—*adv.* **o'verly** (*-li*; *coll.*), excessively, too: (*obs.*) superciliously: (*Scot.*) casually.—*adj.* (*obs.*) supercilious, superior: (*Scot.*) casual.—*adj.* **overly'ing**, lying on the top.—*n.* **o'verman**, an overseer in mining, the man in charge of work below ground: superman.—*v.t.* **overman'**, to furnish with too many men.—*n.* **o'vermantel**, an ornamental structure, often with a mirror, set on a mantel-shelf.—*vs.t.* **overmast'**, to furnish with a mast or masts too long or too heavy; **overmas'ter**, to gain or have the mastery of: to overpower: to dominate; **overmatch'**, to be more than a match for: to defeat, overcome.—*n.* **o'vermatch**, one who is more than a match: (*obs.*) an overmatching. —*n.* **overmeas'ure** (or *ō'*), something given over the due measure.—*v.t.* (*-mezh'*) to measure above the true value.—*adj.* **overmerr'y**, extremely merry.— *v.t.* **overmount'**, to rise above: to excel in mounting.—*v.i.* to mount too high.—*adj.* and *adv.* **o'vermuch** (or -*much'*), too much.—*v.i.* **overmul'tiply**, to become too numerous.—*n.* **overmultiplica'tion.**—*vs.t.* **overmult'itude**, (*Milt.*) to outnumber ; **overname'**, (*Shak.*) to name over.—*adj.* **overneat'**, unnecessarily neat.—*v.t.* **overnet'**, to cover with a net : to overfish with nets.—*adj.* **overnice'**, too fastidious.—*adv.* **overnice'ly.**—*n.* **overnice'ness.**—*n.* **o'vernight**, (*Shak.* ; now chiefly *U.S.*) the evening just past.—*adv.* **overnight'**, all night : during the night : in the course of the night : on the evening of the day just past.—*adj.* done or occurring overnight : for the time from afternoon till next morning.—*vs.t.* **overoff'ice** (*Shak.* **o're-office**), apparently, to lord it over by virtue of office, or perhaps to exercise one's office over ; **overpaint'**, to put too much paint on : to depict with exaggeration ; **overpart'**, to assign too difficult a part to ; **overpass'**, to pass over : to pass by without notice : to exceed.—*v.i.* to pass over : to elapse.—*adj.* **overpast'**, over : at an end.—*v.t.* **overpay'**, to pay too much : to be more than an ample reward for.—*n.* **overpay'ment.**—*vs.t.* **overpeer'** (partly from **peer** (1), partly **peer** (2) ; *Shak.*), to peer over or down upon : to look down on : to tower over : to excel ; **overpeo'ple**, to fill with too many inhabitants ; **overperch'** (*Shak.* **ore-pearch'**), to fly up and perch on, fly over ; **overpersuade'**, to persuade against one's inclination ; **overpic'ture**, to surpass pictorially : to cover with pictures ; **overpitch'**, to pitch too far, or beyond the best distance.—*adjs.* **overpitched'**, steeply pitched, as a roof ; **overplaced'** (*Spens.* **overplast**, -*plâst'*), placed above.—*n.* **o'verplus**, that which is more than enough : surplus.—*adj.* surplus.— *vs.t.* **overply'**, to ply beyond strength ; **overpoise'**, to outweigh.—*ns.* **o'verpoise**, a weight sufficient to weigh another down ; **overpopula'tion**, excessive population.—*vs.t.* **overpop'ulate**, to people in excessive numbers ; **overpost'**, to hasten over quickly ; **overpower'**, to overcome, reduce to helplessness, by force : to subdue : to overwhelm : to furnish with too much power.—*adj.* **overpower'ing**, excessive in degree or amount : irresistible.—*adv.* **overpower'ingly.**—*v.t.* **overpraise'**, to praise too much.—*ns.* **overpraise'** (or **ō'**) ; **overprais'ing**, excessive praise.—*v.t.* **overpress'**, to oppress : to burden too heavily : to press unduly : to put too much pressure on.—*n.* **overpress'ure**, excessive pressure, esp. of work. —*v.t.* **overprint'**, to print too strongly or dark : to print too many copies of : to print (esp. a postage stamp) over already printed matter.—*n.* **o'verprint**, an offprint : that which is printed over an already printed surface, as on a postage stamp. —*v.t.* **overprize'**, to value too highly : (*obs.*) to surpass in value.—*v.t.* and *v.i.* **overproduce'.**—*n.* **overproduc'tion**, excessive production : production in excess of the demand.—*adjs.* **overproof'** (or **ō'**), containing more alcohol than does proof-spirit ; **overproud'**, too proud.—*vs.t.* **overrack'**, to overstrain ; **overrake'**, to sweep over.—*adjs.* **overrank'**, too rank or luxurious ; **overrash'**, too rash.—*adv.* **overrash'ly.**—*n.* **overrash'ness.**— *v.t.* **overrate'**, to rate or value too high.—*n.* **o'verrate**, an excessive estimate or rate.—*v.t.* **overreach'**, to reach or extend beyond : to overtake : to outwit or get the better of : (*refl.*) to defeat by one's own oversubtlety or by attempting too much. —*v.i.* to strike the hindfoot against the forefoot, as a horse :—*pa.t.* and *pa.p.* **overreached'** ; *arch.* **overraught'.**—*n.* **o'verreach**, the act of over-reaching : the injury thereby done.—*v.t.* **overread** (-*rēd'*), to read over.—*adj.* **overread** (-*red'*), having read too much.—*v.t.* and *v.i.* **overreck'on**, to compute too highly.—*vs.t.* **overred'**, (*Shak.*) to cover with a red colour ; **overrefine'**, to refine too much.—*n.* **overrefine'ment.**—*vs.t.* **overren'**, an arch. form of **overrun** ; **override'**, to injure or exhaust by too much riding : to ride over : to trample down on horseback : to slide or mount on the top or back of : to pass over : to overlap : to set aside : to be valid against : (*obs.*) to outride, overtake.—*adj.* **overripe'**, too ripe : more than ripe.—*v.t.* and *v.i.* **overrip'en.**—*n.* **overripe'ness.**

—*v.t.* **overroast'**, to roast too much.—*v.t.* and *v.i.* **overruff'**, to trump with a higher trump.—*n.* **o'verruff**, an act of overruffing.—*v.t.* **overrule'**, (*obs.*) to rule over : to modify or to set aside by greater power : to prevail over the will of, against a previous decision : to impose an overriding decision upon : to prevail over and set aside : (*law*) to annul, declare invalid : to rule against : to disallow.—*v.i.* to prevail.—*n.* **overrul'er.**—*v.t.* **overrun'**, to run over, across, through, all about : to run over, crush underfoot or under wheel : to spread over : to flow over : to grow over : to infest, swarm over : to infect widely : to spread over and take possession of : to run beyond : to exceed the limit of : to carry beyond a limit : to carry over into another line or page : to adjust the type of by overrunning : to outdo in running : to escape from by running faster : (*refl.*) to injure or exhaust by too much running.—*v.i.* to run over, overflow : to run beyond a limit :—*pr.p.* **overrunn'ing** ; *pa.t.* **overran'** ; *pa.p.* **overrun' (overrun the constable**, see **outrun**).—*ns.* **o'verrun**, an overrunning of type ; **overrunn'er.**—*v.i.* **oversail'** (Fr. *saillir*, to project), to project.—*n.* **o'versail**, projection.—*v.t.* **overscore'**, to score or draw lines across : to obliterate in this way.—*adj.* **overscru'pulous**, scrupulous to excess.—*n.* **overscru'pulousness.**—*adjs.* **overscutched** (-*skucht'*, -*skuch'id* ; *Scott*), worn out (after Shak., 2 *Hen. IV.*, III. ii., where **overschutch** is variously conjectured to mean overworn in service or whipped at the cart's tail) ; **o'versea**, **o'verseas**, across, beyond, or from beyond the sea.—*adv.* **oversea(s)'**, in or to lands beyond the sea : abroad.—*n.* **overseas'**, foreign lands.—*v.t.* **oversee'**, to see or look over : to superintend : to overlook, disregard : to see without being meant to see.—*adj.* **overseen'**, mistaken, ill-advised : drunk : versed.—*n.* **o'verseer** (-*sēr*, -*sē-ər*), one who oversees : a superintendent : an officer with care of the poor, and other duties : the manager of a plantation of slaves : (*obs.*) a critic or editor.—*vs.t.* and *vs.i.* **oversell'**, to sell too dear : to sell more of than is available ; **overset'**, (*obs.*) to oppress, press hard : to upset : to disorder.—*v.t.* **o'versew** (or -*sō'*), to sew together overhand.—*adj.* **oversexed'**, having sexual characteristics over-developed.—*vs.t.* **overshade'**, to throw a shade or shadow over : to darken ; **overshad'ow**, to throw a shadow over : to cast into the shade by surpassing, to outshine : to darken : to shelter or protect ; **overshine'**, (*Shak.*) to shine over or upon, illumine : (*Shak.*) to outshine.—*n.* **o'vershoe**, a shoe, esp. of waterproof, worn over another. —*advs.* **over-shoe'**, **over-shoes'**, deep enough to cover the shoes.—*v.t.* **overshoot'**, to shoot over or beyond, as a mark : to pass beyond, exceed, fail to stop at : to shoot, dart, or fly across overhead : to surpass in shooting : to injure or exhaust by too much shooting : to shoot with colour over the surface of (**overshoot oneself**, to venture too far, to overreach oneself).—Also *v.i.*—*adj.* **overshot'**, shot over : too much shot over : surpassed : overdone : in error by overshooting the mark : (*obs. slang*) drunk.—*adj.* **o'vershot**, having the upper jaw protruding beyond the lower : fed from above, as a water-wheel.—*v.t.* **overshower'**, to shower over.—*adj.* **o'verside**, acting or done over the side.—*adv.* **overside'**, over the side.—*prep.* (*Spens.* **over side**) over the side of.—*n.* **o'versight**, superintendence : a failure to notice : mistake : omission.—*v.t.* **oversize'**, to cover with size.—*n.* **o'versize**, a large or larger size.—*adj.* **o'versized** (or -*sizd'*).—*v.t.* **overskip'**, to skip, leap, or pass over : to overlook : to omit.—*ns.* **o'verskirt**, an outer skirt ; **overslaugh** (*ō'vər-slaw*) Du. *overslaan*, to miss, skip over ; *mil.*), exemption from duty in turn when employed on something else : (*U.S.*) a sand-bar.—*v.t.* **overslaugh'**, to remit or pass over by overslaugh : (*U.S.*) to pass over in favour of another : to hinder ; **oversleep'**, to indulge in sleeping too long : to sleep beyond.— *v.i.* to sleep too long.—*v.t.* **overslip'**, to slip by : to escape the notice of : to slip unnoticed from : to let slip.—*v.i.* to slip by : to make a slip, commit inadvertently.—*ns.* **o'verslip**, an inadvertency : a

Neutral vowels in unaccented syllables : *el'ə-mənt, in'fənt, ran'dəm*

close-fitting under-bodice ; **o′versman**, an over-seer : (*Scot.*) an umpire ; **o′versoul**, the divine principle forming the spiritual unity of all being.—*vs.t.* **oversow′**, to sow after something has been already sown : to sow over ; **overspend′**, to spend beyond : to exhaust or cripple by spending.—*v.i.* to spend too much.—*adj.* **overspent′**, excessively fatigued.—*ns.* **o′verspill**, that which is spilt over : population leaving a district, or displaced by changes in housing, &c. ; **o′verspin**, the spinning of a flying ball in the same direction as if it were rolling on the ground.—*vs.t.* **overspread′**, to spread over : to scatter over : to extend over : to be spread over ; **overstain′**, to stain all over ; **overstand′**, to outstay (*Shak.* **ore-stare′**), to outstare ; **overstate′**, to state too strongly : to exaggerate.—*n.* **ovetstate′ment.**—*vs.t.* **overstay′**, ro stay beyond ; **overstep′**, to step beyond : to exceed : to transgress.—*n.* **o′verstep**, (*geol.*) the transgression of an overlapping stratum over the edges of underlying unconformable strata. —*vs.t.* **overstink′**, to stink more than (*pa.t.* **overstunk′** ; *Shak.* **ore-stunck′**), **overstock′**, to stock overmuch.—*n.* **o′verstock**, excessive stock.—*v.t.* and *v.i.* **overstrain′**, to strain too much : to strain beyond the elastic limit.—*n.* **o′verstrain**, too great strain.—*adj.* **overstrained′**, strained to excess : exaggerated.—*vs.t.* **overstretch′**, to stretch to excess : to exaggerate ; **overstrew′**, to scatter over ; **overstride′**, to stride across : to stand astride of ; **overstrike′**, to strike with a downward blow (*pa.t.* **overstruck′** ; *Spens.* **overstrooke′**).— *adjs.* **overstrong′**, too strong ; **overstrung′**, too highly strung : (of a piano) having two sets of strings crossing obliquely to save space.—*v.t.* and *v.i.* **overstud′y**, to study too much.—*n.* **o′verstud′y.**—*v.t.* **oversubscribe′**, to subscribe for beyond what is offered.—*n.* **oversubscrip′tion.**— *adj.* **oversubt′le.**—*n.* **oversubt′lety**, excessive subtlety.—*v.t.* **oversupply′**, to supply too much of.—*n.* **o′versupply**, an excessive supply.—*vs.t.* **oversway′**, to overrule : to bear down ; **overswear′**, to swear anew.—*v.t.* and *v.i.* **overswell′**, to overflow.—*v.t.* **overswim′**, to swim across.
overt, *ō′vιrt, adj.* open to view : public : apparent. —*adv.* **o′vertly.**—**market overt**, open or public market ; **overt act**, something actually done in execution of an intent. [Fr. *ouvert,* pa.p. of *ouvrir,* to open.]
over- (continued).—*v.t.* **overtake′**, to come up with : to catch up with : to catch : to come upon : to take by surprise.—*adj.* **overta′ken**, fuddled.— *vs.t.* **overtalk′**, to talk over ; **overtask′**, to task overmuch : to impose too heavy a task on ; **overtax′**, to tax overmuch : to require too much of. — *adj.* **overte′dious**, (*Shak.*) too tedious.— *v.i.* **overteem′**, to teem, breed, or produce in excess.—*v.t.* to exhaust or wear out by breeding. —*v.t.* **overthrow′**, to throw over, overturn, upset : to ruin, subvert : to defeat utterly : to throw too far or too strongly.—*v.i.* (*obs.*) to be overturned : to throw too far.—*ns.* **o′verthrow**, act of overthrowing or state of being overthrown : (*cricket*) a ball missed at the wicket and returned from the field : a run scored in consequence ; **overthrow′er**, **o′verthrust** (**overthrust fault**), a reversed fault or thrust where older rocks are pushed up bodily upon the back of younger.—*v.t.* **overthwart′**, to lie athwart : to cross.—*adj.* opposite, transverse : contrary, perverse.—*adv.* crosswise : opposite.— *prep.* across, on the other side of.—*n.* **o′vertime**, time employed in working beyond the regular hours : work done in such time : pay for such work.—*adj.* and *adv.* during, for, or concerning such time.—*v.t.* **overtime′**, to time too long (esp. of a photographic exposure).—*adj.* and *adv.* **overtime′ly**, (*obs.*) too early, untimely.—*n.* **o′vertimer**, one who works overtime.—*v.t.* **overtoil′**, to overwork.—*n.* **o′vertone**, a harmonic or upper partial.—*v.t.* **overtop′**, to rise over the top of : to be higher than : to surpass : to exceed.—*v.i.* to rise too high.—*v.t.* **overtower′**, to tower above.— *v.i.* to soar too high.—*v.i.* **overtrade′**, to trade overmuch or beyond capital : to buy in more than can be sold or paid for.—*v.t.* to involve in trade

in such a way.—*n.* **overtrad′ing**, the buying of a greater amount of goods than one can sell or pay for.—*v.t.* **overtrain′**, to train so far as to do harm : to train too high.—*n.* **o′vertrick**, (*bridge*) a trick in excess of those contracted for.—*vs.t.* **overtrip′**, to trip nimbly over ; **overtrump′**, to trump with a higher card than one already played.—*v.i.* **overtrust′**, to trust too much.—*n.* **o′vertrust.**
overture, *ō′vιr-tūr, n.* (*obs.*) an opening, aperture : (*Shak.*) an opening up, disclosure : (*Spens.*) an open place : an opening of negotiations : an offer or proposal : an opening or opportunity : an opening or beginning : an instrumental prelude to an opera, oratorio, &c., or an independent composition in similar form (sonata form) : the method in Presbyterian usage of beginning legislation and maturing opinion by sending some proposition from the inferior courts to the General Assembly, and *vice versa* : also the proposal so sent.—*v.t.* to lay a proposal before : to put forward as an overture. [O.Fr. *overture* (Fr. *ouverture*), opening.]
over- (continued).—**overturn′**, *v.t.* to throw down or over : to upset : to subvert.—*ns.* **o′verturn**, an overturning : a turn-over ; **overturn′er** ; **overvalua′tion** ; **o′vervalue**.—*vs.t.* **overval′ue**, to set too high a value on ; **overveil′**, to veil over or cover.—*n.* **o′verview**, (*Shak.*) an inspection.—*adj.* **overvi′olent**, too violent.—*n.* **o′verwash**, a washing over : (*geol.*) material carried by glacier-streams over a frontal moraine.—Also *adj.*—*vs.t.* **overwatch′**, tc watch over : to watch through : to overcome with long watching ; **overwear′**, to wear out : to outwear, outlive :—*pa.t.* **overwore′** ; *pa.p.* and *adj.* **overworn′**.—*v.t.* **overwea′ry**, to overcome with weariness, weary out.—*adj.* excessively weary.—*v.t.* **overweath′er**, (*Shak.*) to batter by violence of weather.—*v.i.* **overween′**, to expect too much : to be presumptuous or arrogant : to think too highly, esp. of oneself.—*adj.* and *n.* **overween′ing.**—*v.t.* **overweigh′**, to be heavier than : to outweigh : to weigh down.—*n.* **o′verweight**, weight beyond what is required or what is allowed : preponderance.—*adj.* **overweight′**, above the weight required.—*vs.t.* **overweight′**, to weigh down : to put too heavy a burden on ; **overwent′** (see **overgo**) ; **overwhelm′**, to overspread and crush by something heavy or strong : to flow over and bear down : to reduce to helplessness : to overpower : to ply overpoweringly : (*obs.*) to overhang.—*n.* and *adj.* **overwhel′ming.**—*adv.* **overwhel′mingly.**— *vs.t.* **overwind** (*-wīnd′*), to wind too far :—*pa.t.* and *pa.p.* **overwound** ; **overwing′**, (*obs.*) to outflank : to fly over.—*v.i.* **overwin′ter**, to pass the winter.— *adj.* **overwise′**, wise overmuch : affectedly wise : wise in one's own estimation.—*adv.* **overwise′ly.** —*n.* **o′verword**, **o′erword** (*ōr′, Scot. owr′* ; also **owre′word**), the burden of a song : a habitual saying.—*v.t.* and *v.i.* **overwork′**, to work over-much.—*n.* **o′verwork**, additional work : **o′ver-work′**, excess of work.—*adj.* **overworn′** (or *ō′*), worn out : subdued by toil : spoiled by use : threadbare : trite : exhausted of meaning or freshness by excessive use : out of date : spent or past. — *vs.t.* **overwrest′**, overstrain ; **overwrest′le**, (*Spens.*) to overcome by wrestling ; **overwrite′**, to cover over with writing or other writing : to superscribe : to exhaust by writing too much : to write too much about : to write in a laboured manner.—*v.i.* to write too much or too artificially. —*adj.* **overwrought′** (and *pa.p.* of **overwork**), worked too hard : too highly excited : with highly strained nerves : worked or embellished all over : overdone.—*v.t.* **overyear′** (*obs.*), to keep into a second, or later, year.—*adj.* (*prov.*) kept over from one year to the next.—*adv.* (*prov.*) till next year.
ovibos, *ōv′i-bos, ov′i-bōs, n.* the musk-ox.—*adj.* **ovibō′vine**. [L. *ōvis*, sheep, *bōs, bovis*, ox.]
ovicide, *ō′vi-sīd, n.* (jocular) sheep-killing. [L. *ōvis*, sheep, *caedĕre*, to kill.]
Ovidian, *ō-vid′i-ιn, o*r *o-, adj.* of, like, or relating to the Latin poet *Ovid* (43 B.C.-17 A.D.).
oviduct, *ō′vi-dukt, n.* (*zool.*) the tube by which the egg escapes from the ovary.—*adj.* **ovidū′cal.** [L. *ōvum*, egg, *ducĕre, ductum,* to convey.]

oviferous, ō-vif′ə-rəs, *adj.* egg-carrying. [L. *ōvum*, egg, *ferre*, to bear.]

oviform, ō′vi-form, *adj.* egg-shaped. [L. *ōvum*, egg, *forma*, form.]

oviform, ov′i-form, ō′vi-form, *adj.* like a sheep: ovine. [L. *ōvis*, sheep, *forma*, form.]

ovigerous, ōv-ij′ə-rəs, *adj.* egg-carrying. [L. *ōvum*, an egg, *gerĕre*, to carry.]

ovine, ō′vīn, *adj.* of sheep: sheep-like. [L. *ovīnus* —*ŏvis*, sheep.]

oviparous, ō-vip′ə-rəs, *adj.* egg-laying.—*n.* **ovipar′ity** (-*par′i-ti*).—*adv.* **ovip′arously**. [L. *ōvum*, egg, *parĕre*, to bring forth.]

ovipositor, ō-vi-poz′i-tər, *n.* an egg-laying organ.— *v.i.* **ovipos′it**, to deposit eggs with an ovipositor.— *n.* **oviposition** (-pə-zish′ən). [L. *ōvum*, egg, *positor* —*pōnĕre*, to place.]

ovisac, ōv′i-sak, *n.* a brood-pouch : an egg-capsule. [L. *ōvum*, an egg, and **sac**.]

ovist, ō′vist, *n.* a believer in the doctrine that the ovum contains all future generations in germ. [L. *ōvum*, egg.]

ovoid, ō′void, *adj.* egg-shaped and solid in form (sometimes also of a plane figure) : (*bot.*) egg-shaped and attached by the broad end.—*n.* an egg-shaped figure or body.—*adj.* **ovoid′al**, ovoid. [L. *ōvum*, egg, Gr. *eidos*, form.]

ovolo, ō′vō-lō, *n.* (*archit.*) a moulding with the rounded part composed of a quarter of a circle, or of an arc of an ellipse with the curve greatest at the top. [It.,—L. *ōvum*, an egg.]

ovoviviparous, ō-vō-vi-vip′ə-rəs, or -vī-, *adj.* producing eggs which are hatched in the body of the parent. [L. *ōvum*, an egg, *vīvus*, living, *parĕre*, to bring forth.]

ovule, ōv′ūl, *n.* in flowering plants, the body which on fertilisation becomes the seed, answering to the megasporangium and consisting of the nucellus and its integuments with the embryo-sac (megaspore) : an undeveloped seed.—*adj.* **ōv′ular**.—*n.* **ōvulā′tion**, the formation of ova : the escape of the ovum in mammals.—*adj.* **ōvulif′erous**, carrying ovules. [Dim. from L. *ōvum*, egg.]

ovum, ō′vəm, *n.* an egg: (*biol.*) the egg-cell, or female gamete :—*pl.* o′va. [L. *ōvum*, egg.]

ow. Same as **ou**.

owche, owch, *n.* Same as **ouch**.

owe, ō, *v.t.* (*obs.* or *dial.*) to own : to be indebted for : to be under an obligation to repay or render : to feel as a debt or as due : to have to thank : to concede or be bound to concede as a handicap.— *v.i.* to be in debt :—*pa.t.* and *pa.p.* owed.—The old *pa.t.* **ought** and *pa.p.* **own**, now differently used, are given separately ; see also **owing**. [O.E. *āgan*, to own, possess, pres. indic. *āh*, preterite *āhte*, pa.p. *dgen* ; O.N. *eiga*, O.H.G. *eigan*, to possess.]

owelty, ō′el-ti, *n.* (*law*) equality. [A.Fr. *owelté*—L. *aequālitās*, -ātis.]

Owenite, ō′in-īt, *n.* a disciple of Robert *Owen* (1771-1858), who proposed to establish society on a basis of socialistic co-operation.—*adj.* **Owenian** (ō-ēn′i-ən).—*ns.* **Ow′enism** ; **Ow′enist**.

ower, owre, owr, Scots forms of **over**. For compounds see the forms in **over-**.

owing, ō′ing, *adj.* due : to be paid : imputable.— **owing to**, because of : in consequence of.

owl, owl, *n.* any member of the Striges, nocturnal predaceous birds with large broad heads, flat faces, large eyes surrounded by disks of feathers, short hooked beaks, silent flight, and howling or hooting cry : one who sits up at night : one who sees ill or shuns light : a solemn person : a wiseacre : a dullard : an owl-like breed of pigeon.—*v.i.* to behave like an owl.—*v.t.* (*obs.*) to smuggle (esp. wool or sheep from England to France).—*ns.* **owl′-car** (*U.S.*), a night tramcar ; **owl′er** (*obs.*), a smuggler (esp. of wool or sheep) ; **owl′ery**, an abode of owls : (*Carlyle*) owlishness ; **owl′et**, an owl : a young owl : a moth of the Noctuidae.— *adj.* **owl′-eyed**, having blinking eyes like an owl.— *n.* **Owl′-glass, Owle′-glass, Howle′glass, Owl′-spiegle**, *Tyll Eulenspiegel*, a mischievous clown hero of a folk-tale popular in Germany from the 16th century at least.—*adj.* **owl′ish**, like an owl : solemn : blinking : stupid : dull-looking.—*ns.*

owl′ishness ; **owl′-light**, dusk ; **owl′-moth, a** gigantic South American moth of the Noctuidae ; **owl′-parr′ot**, the kakapo ; **owl′-train** (*U.S.*), a night train.—*adj.* **owl′y**, owlish. [O.E. *ūle* ; Ger. *eule*, L. *ulula* ; imit.]

own, ōn, *v.t.* to possess, have belonging to one : to acknowledge as one's own : (*obs.*) to claim as one's own : to confess : to allow to be true : to admit, concede : to acknowledge, recognise.—*v.i.* to confess (with *to*).—*ns.* **own′er**, possessor, proprietor : (*slang*) captain of a warship ; **own′er-dri′ver**, one who drives his own car.—*adj.* **own′er-less**.—*n.* **own′ership**.—**own up**, to confess freely. [O.E. *āgnian—āgen*, one's own ; cf. **own** (adj.).]

own, ōn, *adj.* belonging to oneself : often used with reflexive force, *my own, his own*, &c., serving instead of a genitive to *myself, himself*, &c., or transferring the sense of *self* to the subject : sometimes used as an endearment.—**get one's own back**, retaliate, get even ; **hold one's own** (see **hold**) ; **on one's own**, on one's own account : on one's own initiative : by one's own efforts or resources : independently : set up in independence. [O.E. *āgen*, pa.p. of *āgan*, to possess ; cf. **owe**.]

owre, ower, o′er, owr, Scots forms of **over**. For compounds see **over-**.

owre, owr, *n.* (*Spens.*). Same as **ore** (1).

owrie. See **ourie**.

owsen, ow′sən, *n.pl.* Scots form of **oxen**. See **ox**.

ox, oks, *n.* a general name for male or female of common domestic cattle (bull and cow), esp. a castrated male of the species : extended to kindred animals :—*pl.* **ox′en**, used for both male and female. —*ns.* **ox′-ant′elope**, any antelope of the hartebeest group ; **ox′-bird**, the dunlin : the ox-pecker : an African weaver-bird : applied also to various other birds ; **ox′-bot**, a warble-fly larva infesting cattle ; **ox′-bow** (-bō), a collar for a yoked ox : a river-bend returning almost upon itself (forming an *ox-bow lake* when the neck is pierced and the bend cut off) ; **ox′er**, an oxfence ; **ox′eye**, a name for various birds, esp. the great titmouse : a wild chrysanthemum with yellow disk and white (*oxeye daisy*) or yellow ray (*yellow oxeye*, or corn marigold) : an elliptical dormer window.—*adj.* **ox′-eyed**, having large, ox-like eyes.—*ns.* **ox′fence**, a fence for confining cattle : a hedge with a rail ; **ox′gang, ox′gate, ox′land,** a bovate or one-eighth of a carucate or plough-land, the share attributed to each ox in a team of eight (averaging about 13 acres) ; **ox′head,** the head of an ox : a blockhead ; **ox′-pecker,** an African genus (Buphaga) of birds akin to starlings, that eat the parasites on cattle—also *beefeater* ; **ox′-tail**, the tail of an ox, esp. as used for making soup ; **ox′-tongue**, the tongue of an ox, used as food : a yellow-flowered milky-juiced composite (*Picris echioides*) ; **ox′-war′ble,** a swelling on the back of an ox : the fly whose larva produces it.—**have the black ox tread on one's foot**, to experience sorrow or misfortune. [O.E. *oxa*, pl. *oxan* ; Ger. *ochse*, Goth. *auhsa*, Sans. *ukshán*.]

Oxalis, oks′ə-lis, *n.* the wood-sorrel genus, giving name to the family **Oxalidā′ceae**, close akin to the Geranium family.—*adj.* **oxalic** (-*al′ik*), applied to an acid ($C_2H_2O_4$) obtained from wood-sorrel.— *n.* **ox′alate**, a salt of oxalic acid. [Gr. *oxalis*— *oxys*, sharp, acid.]

Oxford, oks′fərd, *adj.* belonging to the city, county, or university of Oxford.—*n.* **Oxfordian** (-*ford′-i-ən*), a division of the Middle Jurassic.—Also *adj.* —**Oxford bags**, very wide trousers ; **Oxford blue,** a dark blue ; **Oxford clay**, a dark blue or grey clay of the Oxfordian formation ; **Oxford English, a** form of standard English in which certain tendencies are (sometimes affectedly) exaggerated, widely believed to be spoken at Oxford ; **Oxford groups**, informal circles of followers of Dr Frank Buchman, who exchange religious experiences, and seek divine guidance individually (**the Oxford group**, his followers as a body) ; **Oxford movement**, the Tractarian movement. [O.E. *Oxnaford*, lit. oxen's ford.]

oxide, oks′īd, *n.* a compound of oxygen and some other element or radical.—*v.t.* **ox′idate** (-*id-āt*), to

oxidise.—*ns.* **ox′idase,** any of a group of enzymes that promote oxidation in plant and animal cells; **oxidā′tion,** oxidising. — *adj.* **oxidīs′able.** — *v.t.* and *v.i.* **ox′idise,** to combine with oxygen: to deprive (an atom or ion) of, or (*v.i.*) to lose, electrons.—*n.* **oxidīs′er,** an oxidising agent. [Fr. *oxide,* formed from *oxygène,* oxygen.]

oxlip, *oks′lip, n.* originally a hybrid between primrose and cowslip: now, a species of Primula (*P. elatior*) like a large pale cowslip.—Also (*Shak.*) **ox′slip.** [O.E. *oxanslyppe*—*oxan,* gen. of *oxa,* ox, *slyppe,* a slimy dropping; cf. **cowslip.**]

Oxonian, *oks-ō′ni-ən, adj.* of or pertaining to *Oxford* or to its university.—*n.* an inhabitant, native, student, or graduate of Oxford: a kind of shoe. [L. *Oxonia,* Oxford—O.E. *Oxnaford.*]

oxonium, *oks-ō′ni-əm, n.* a univalent basic radical, H₃O, in which oxygen is tetravalent, forming organic derivatives, **oxonium salts.** [*ox*ygen and amm*onium.*]

oxter, *oks′tər, n.* (*Scot.*) the armpit.—*v.t.* to take under the arm: to support by taking the arm. [O.E. *oxta.*]

oxy-, *oks′-i-,* in composition, sharp: pointed: acid: oxygen.—*adj.* **ox′y-acet′ylene,** involving, using, or by means of, a mixture of oxygen and acetylene. — *ns.* **ox′y-a′cid, ox′y-com′pound, ox′y-salt,** &c., an acid, compound, salt, &c., containing oxygen: one in which an atom of hydrogen is replaced by a hydroxyl-group; **ox′y-bro′mide, -chlo′ride, -flu′oride, -hal′ide, -i′odide,** a compound of an element or radical with oxygen and a halogen (bromine, &c.); **ox′yhaemoglo′bin,** a loose compound of oxygen and haemoglobin.—*adj.* **ox′y-hy′drogen,** involving or using a mixture of oxygen and hydrogen.—**ox′y-cal′cium light,** limelight. [Gr. *oxys,* sharp.]

oxygen, *oks′i-jən, n.* a gas (atomic number 8) without taste, colour, or smell, forming part of the air, water, &c., and supporting life and combustion.— —*v.t.* **ox′ygenāte** (or *oks-ij′*), to oxidise: to impregnate or treat with oxygen.—*n.* **oxygenā′tion.**— *v.t.* **ox′ygenise,** to oxygenate.—*adj.* **oxyg′enous.** [Gr. *oxys,* sharp, acid, and the root of *gennaein,* to generate, from the old belief that all acids contained oxygen.]

oxymel, *oks′i-mel, n.* a mixture of vinegar and honey. [Gr. *oxymeli*—*oxys,* sour, *meli,* honey.]

oxymoron, *ok-si-mō′ron, n.* a figure of speech, by means of which contradictory terms are combined, so as to form an expressive phrase or epithet, as *cruel kindness, falsely true,* &c. [Gr. neut. of

oxymōros, lit. pointedly foolish—*oxys,* sharp, *mōros,* foolish.]

oxyrhynchus, *ok-si-ring′kəs, n.* an Egyptian fish, sacred to the goddess Hathor, represented on coins and sculptures. [Gr. *oxyrrynchos*—*oxys,* sharp, *rhynchos,* a snout.]

oxytone, *oks′i-tōn, adj.* having the acute accent on the last syllable—*n.* a word so accented. [Gr. *oxys,* sharp, *tonos,* tone.]

oy, oye, oe, *oi, ō-i, ō, n.* (*Scot.*) a grandchild. [Gael. *ogha, odha.*]

oyer, *oi′ər, n.* a hearing in a law-court, an assize.— **oyer and terminer,** a royal commission conferring power to hear and determine criminal causes. [A.Fr. *oyer* (Fr. *ouïr*)—L. *audīre,* to hear.]

oyez, oyes, *ō-yes′, ō′yes, interj.* the call of a public crier, or officer of a law-court, for attention before making a proclamation.—*n.* (*oiz; Shak.*) a proclamation. [O.Fr. *oyez,* imper. of *oir* (Fr. *ouïr*), to hear.]

oyster, *ois′tər, n.* a well-known bivalve shellfish (Ostrea) used as food.—*ns.* **oys′ter-bank, -bed, -farm, -field, -park,** a place where oysters breed or are bred; **oys′ter-catcher,** the sea pie—a black and white wading bird with red bill and feet, feeding on limpets and mussels (not oysters); **oys′ter-fish′ery,** the business of catching oysters; **oys′ter-knife,** a knife for opening oysters; **oys′ter-patt′y,** a small pie or pasty made from oysters; **oys′ter-plant,** salsify: a seaside boraginaceous plant, *Mertensia maritima*—both supposed to taste like oysters; **oys′ter-shell,** the shell of an oyster.— *n.pl.* **oys′ter-tongs,** a tool for gathering oysters.— *ns.* **oys′ter-wench, -wife, -woman,** a woman who vends oysters. [O.Fr. *oistre* (Fr. *huître*)— L. *ostrea*—Gr. *ostreon,* an oyster—*osteon,* a bone.]

oystrige, *oi′strij, n.* (*Spens.*) for **ostrich.**

ozaena, *ō-zē′nä, n.* a fetid discharge from the nostrils. [Gr. *ozaina,* a fetid polypus of the nose— *ozein,* to smell.]

ozokerite, *ō-zō′kər-īt, -kēr′īt,* **ozocerite,** *ō-zos′ər-īt, ō-zō-sēr′īt, n.* a waxy natural paraffin. [Gr. *ozein,* to smell, *kēros,* wax.]

ozone, *ō′zōn, n.* an allotropic form (O₃) of oxygen, a powerful oxidising agent with a peculiar smell: an imagined constituent in the air of any place that one wishes to commend.—*n.* **ozonā′tion,** ozonisation.—*adj.* **ozonif′erous,** bringing or producing ozone.—*n.* **ozonīsā′tion.**—*v.t.* **o′zonise,** to turn into ozone: to charge or treat with ozone. —*n.* **ozonīs′er,** an apparatus for turning oxygen into ozone. [Gr. *ozōn, -on,* pr.p. of *ozein,* to smell.]

fāte, fär, ásk; mē, hər (her); *mīne; mōte; mūte; mōon; dhen* (then)

P

P, p, *pē, n.* the sixteenth letter of our alphabet, and of the Greek (see **pi**), representing a voiceless labial_stop: in mediaeval Roman notation, P = 400, P̄ = 400,000: in *chem.* p- is an abbreviation for para-.—**mind one's p's and q's,** to be watchfully careful in language and behaviour.

pa, *pä, n.* a childish or vulgar word for father. [papa.]

pa, pah, *pä, n.* a Maori fort. [Maori.]

pabouche, *pä-bōōsh', n.* a slipper. [See **baboosh**.]

pabulum, *pab'ū-lǝm, n.* food of any kind, espec. that of lower animals and of plants: provender: fuel: nourishment for the mind.—*adjs.* **pab'ūlar, pab'ūlous.** [L. *pābulum*—*pāscĕre*, to feed.]

paca, *pä'kä, n.* the so-called spotted cavy of South America, akin to the agouti. [Sp. and Port.,—Tupí, *paca*.]

pacable, *pāk'ǝ-bl, pak', adj.* capable of being appeased: willing to forgive.—*n.* **pacation** (*pǝ-kä'shǝn*). [L. *pācāre*, to appease—*pāx, pācis,* peace.]

pace, *pās, n.* a stride: a step: the space between the feet in walking, about 30 inches, or (among the Romans) the space between two successive positions of the same foot, over 58 inches: gait: rate of walking, running, &c. (of a man or beast): rate of speed in movement or work, often applied to fast living: a mode of stepping in horses in which the legs on the same side are lifted together: amble: a step of a stair, or the like: (*obs.*) a pass or passage.—*v.t.* to traverse with measured steps: to measure by steps: to train to perform paces: to set the pace for: to perform as a pace or paces.—*v.i.* to walk: to walk slowly and with measured tread: to amble.—*adj.* **paced,** having a certain pace or gait.—*ns.* **pace'-maker,** one who sets the pace, as in a race, or fig.; **pac'er,** one who paces: a horse whose usual gait is a pace.—**go the pace,** to go at a great speed: to live a fast life; **keep,** or **hold, pace with,** to go as fast as: to keep up with; **make, set the pace,** to regulate the speed for others by example; **put one through one's paces,** to set him to show what he can do. [Fr. *pas*—L. *passus,* a step—*pandĕre, passum,* to stretch.]

pace, *pā'sē, prep.* with or by the leave of (expressing disagreement courteously). [L., abl. of *pāx,* peace.]

Pace, *pās,* a Scots form of **Pasch.**

pacha, pachalic. See **pasha, pashalik.**

pachisi, *pä-chē'sē, -zē, n.* an Indian game like backgammon or ludo. [Hind. *pachīsī,* of twenty-five—the highest throw.]

pachy-, *pak'i-,* in combination, thick.—*adjs.* **pachycarp'ous,** having a thick pericarp; **pachydac'tyl, -ous** (Gr. *daktylos,* digit), having thick digits.—*n.* **pach'yderm** (Gr. *derma,* skin), any animal of the Pachydermata: an insensitive person.—*adj.* **pachyderm'al.**—*n.pl.* **Pachyderm'ata,** in old classification, those ungulates that do not ruminate—elephant, horse, pig, &c.—*adj.* **pachyder'matous,** thick-skinned: of the pachyderms: insensitive.—*n.* **pachyderm'ia,** abnormal thickness of skin or mucous membrane.—*adjs.* **pachyderm'ic, pachyderm'ous.**—*n.* **pachym'eter,** an instrument for measuring small thicknesses. [Gr. *pachys,* thick.]

pacify, *pas'i-fī, v.t.* to appease: to calm: to bring peace to.—*adjs.* **pac'ifiable; pacif'ic,** peacemaking: appeasing: inclining towards peace: peaceful: mild: tranquil: applied (**Pacific**) to the ocean between Asia and America, so called by its discoverer Magellan because he sailed peacefully over it after weathering Cape Horn: of the Pacific Ocean: pacifical.—*n.* the Pacific Ocean.—*adj.* **pacif'ical,** pacific (rare except in phrase *Letters pacifical,* letters recommending the bearer as one in peace and fellowship with the Church—also *Letters of peace, Pacificae*).—*adv.* **pacif'ically.**—*v.t.* **pacif'icāte,** to give peace to.—*ns.* **pacificā'tion,** peace-making: conciliation: appeasement: a peace treaty; **pacif'icātor,** a peacemaker.—*adj.* **pacif'icatory** (*-ǝ-tǝ-ri*), tending to make peace.—*ns.* **pacif'icism** (*-sizm*), the beliefs and principles of pacificists; **pacif'icist** (*-sist*), one who is opposed to war, or believes all war to be wrong; **pacif'er; pac'ifism, pac'ifist,** ill-formed but generally preferred forms of **pacificism, pacificist.** [Partly through Fr. *pacifier*—L. *pācificus,* pacific—*pācificāre*—*pāx, pācis,* peace, *facĕre,* to make.]

pack, *pak, n.* a bundle, esp. one made to be carried on the back by a pedlar or pack-animal: a collection, stock, or store: a bundle of some particular kind or quantity, as of wool, 240 lb.: the quantity packed at a time or in a season: a complete set of cards: a number of animals herding together or kept together for hunting: (*Scot.*) a shepherd's own sheep grazing along with his employer's as part payment: the forwards in a Rugby football team: a group of wolf-cubs in the Boy Scout movement: a worthless, disreputable or otherwise objectionable set of persons: a gang, as of thieves: a mass of pack-ice: a sheet for folding round the body to allay inflammation, fever, &c.: the use or application of such a sheet: a built support for a mine-roof: packing material: a cosmetic paste: a number of photographic plates or films exposed together: act of packing or condition of being packed: mode of packing: (*obs.*) a person of worthless or bad character.—*v.t.* to make into a bundled pack: to place compactly in a box, bag, or the like: to press together closely: to compress: to fill tightly or compactly: to fill with anything: to cram: to crowd: to envelop: to surround closely: to fill the spaces surrounding: (*U.S.*; of food) to prepare for preservation, transport and marketing: to assort or assemble (as a pack of cards or a jury) for some unjust object: to send away, dismiss: to form into a pack: to load with a pack: to carry in packs: (*U.S.*) to carry: (*Shak.*) to bring into a plot.—*v.i.* to form into a pack: to settle or be driven into a firm mass: to form a scrum: to admit of being put into compact shape: to put one's belongings together in boxes, bags, &c., as for a journey (often with *up*): to travel with a pack: to take oneself off, to depart in haste: (*Shak.*) to plot, intrigue, arrange privately.—*ns.* **pack'age,** the act, manner, or privilege of packing: a bundle, packet, or parcel: a case or other receptacle for packing goods in; **pack'-an'imal,** a beast used to carry goods on its back; **pack'-cinch** (*-sinsh*), a wide girth for a pack-animal; **pack'-cloth,** a cloth in which goods are enclosed: packsheet; **pack'-drill,** a military punishment of marching about laden with full equipment; **pack'er,** one who packs: one who packs goods for sending out: (*U.S.*) an employer or employee in the business of preparing and preserving food: (*Austr.*) a pack-animal: (*U.S.*) one who transports goods by means of pack-animals: a machine or device for packing; **pack'et,** a small package: a carton: a ship or vessel employed in carrying packets of letters, passengers, &c.: a vessel plying regularly between one port and another (also **pack'et-boat, pack'et-ship,** &c.): (*coll.*) a large amount of money: a small group: a cluster of bacteria: (*fig.*) used as equivalent to a quantum.—*v.t.* to parcel up.—*ns.* **pack'et-note,** a size of notepaper 5½ by 9 inches; **pack'-horse,** a horse used to carry goods on its back: a drudge; **pack'-ice,** a mass of large pieces of floating ice driven together by winds and currents; **pack'ing,** the act of putting into packs or of tying up for carriage or storing: material for packing: anything used to fill an empty space, or to make a joint close; **pack'ing-box, -case,** a box or framework for packing goods in; **pack'ing-need'le,** a strong needle for sewing up packages; **pack'ing-paper,** a strong and thick kind of wrapping-paper; **pack'ing-press,** a press for squeezing goods into small compass for packing; **pack'ing-sheet,** or **pack'sheet,** coarse cloth for packing goods; **pack'-load,** the load an animal can carry; **pack'man,** a pedlar or a man who carries a pack; **pack'-mule,** a mule used for carrying burdens; **pack'-saddle,** a saddle for packs; **pack'staff,** a staff for supporting a pedlar's pack when he rests; **pack'-thread,** a coarse thread used to sew up packages; **pack'-train,** a train of loaded pack-animals; **pack'-twine,** thin twine for tying up parcels; **pack'way,** a narrow path fit for pack-horses.—**pack a jury, meeting,** &c., to fill up with persons of a particular kind for one's own purposes; **send one packing,** to dismiss summarily. [M.E. *packe, pakke,* app.—M. Flem. *pac* or Du. or L. Ger. *pak.*]

pack, *pak, adj.* (*Scot.*) intimate, confidential. [Origin unknown.]

packfong, an incorrect form of **paktong.**

paco, *pä'kō, n.* alpaca:—*pl.* **pa'cos.** [Sp.,—Quechua *paco.*]

pact, *pakt, n.* that which is agreed on: an agreement, esp. informal or not legally enforceable.—*n.* **pac'tion,** (chiefly *Scot.*) a pact.—*v.t.* to agree.—*adj.* **pac'tional.** [L. *pactum—pacīscĕre, pactum,* to contract.]

pad, *pad, n.* a path: a thief on the high-road (usually *footpad*): (abbrev. from **pad'-horse**) a horse for riding on the road: an easy-paced horse.—*v.i.* to walk on foot: to trudge along: to walk with dull-sounding tread: to rob on foot:—*pr.p.* **padd'ing;** *pa.t.* and *pa.p.* **padd'ed.**—*ns.* **padd'ing-ken,** a thieves' lodging-house; **pad'-nag,** an ambling nag.—**pad the hoof,** (*slang*) to walk, trudge; **stand pad,** to beg by the roadside. [Du. *pad,* a path.]

pad, *pad, n.* anything stuffed with a soft material, to prevent friction, pressure, or injury, for inking, for filling out, &c.: a soft saddle: a cushion: a number of sheets of paper or other soft material fastened together in a block: a leg-guard for cricketers, &c.: the fleshy, thick-skinned under-surface of the foot of many animals, as the fox: the foot of a beast, esp. of chase: its footprint: (*U.S.*) a water-lily leaf: (usu. in *pl.*) thick watered ribbon for watch-guards.—*v.t.* to stuff, cover, or fill out with anything soft: to furnish with padding: to track by footprints: to impregnate, as with a mordant:—*pr.p.* **padd'ing;** *pa.p.* **padd'ed.**—*ns.* **pad'-cloth,** a cloth covering a horse's loins; **padd'er,** one who pads, or cushions; **padd'ing,** stuffing: matter of less value introduced into a book or article in order to make it of the length desired: the process of mordanting a fabric; **pad'-el'ephant,** a working elephant wearing a pad but no howdah; **pad'-saddle,** a treeless, padded saddle; **pad'-tree,** the wooden or metal frame to which harness-pads are attached.—**padded cell,** a room with padded walls in a lunatic asylum. [Origin obscure: possibly connected with **pod.**]

pad. Same as **ped.**

padang, *pad'ang, n.* a field. [Malay.]

padauk, padouk, *pä-dowk', n.* a Burmese timber tree of the red sandalwood genus. [Burmese.]

paddle, *pad'l, v.i.* to wade about or dabble in liquid or semi-liquid: to walk unsteadily or with short steps: to play or toy with the fingers: (*obs.*) to trifle. — *v.t.* to toy with or finger. — *n.* **padd'ler,** one who paddles: (in *pl.*) a protective garment for children paddling. [Cf. **pad** (1), and L. Ger. *paddeln,* to tramp about.]

paddle, padle, paidle, *päd'l, pād'l, n.* (*Scot.*) the lumpsucker.—Also **cock'-paid'le** (*masc.*), **hen'-paid'le** (*fem.*). [Origin unknown.]

paddle, *pad'l, n.* a small, long-handled spade: a short, broad, spoon-shaped oar, used for moving canoes: the blade of an oar: one of the boards of a paddle-wheel or water-wheel: a swimming animal's flipper: a paddle-shaped instrument for stirring, beating, &c.—*v.i.* to use a paddle, progress by use of paddles: to row gently: to swim about like a duck.—*v.t.* to propel by paddle: to slap.—*ns.* **padd'le-boat,** a paddle-steamer; **padd'le-board,** one of the boards of a paddle-wheel; **padd'le-box,** the covering of a paddle-wheel; **padd'ler,** one who paddles; **padd'le-shaft,** the axle on which paddle-wheels turn; **padd'le-staff,** a small spade or paddle; **padd'le-steam'er,** a steamer propelled by paddle-wheels; **padd'le-wheel,** the wheel of a steam-vessel, which by turning in the water causes it to move; **padd'le-wood,** the light, strong wood of a Guiana tree (*Aspidosperma*) of the dogbane family; **padd'ling,** a flock of wild duck on water. [Origin obscure.]

paddock, *pad'ək, n.* (*arch.* and *Scot.*) a toad or frog.—*n.* **padd'ock-stool,** a toadstool. [Dim. from late O.E. *pade, padde,* toad; O.N. *padda.*]

paddock, *pad'ək, n.* a small field under pasture, usu. near a house or stable: a small field in which horses are kept before a race: (*Austr.*) a field. [Apparently from earlier *parrock*—O.E. *pearroc,* park.]

paddy, *pad'i, n.* growing rice: rice in the husk.—*ns.* **padd'y-bird,** the Java sparrow or rice-bird; **padd'y-field.** [Malay *pādī,* rice in the straw.]

Paddy, *pad'i, n.* a familiar name for an Irishman, from St *Patrick*: (*coll.*) a rage.—*ns.* **Padd'yism,** a hibernicism; **padd'y-whack,** (*slang*) an Irishman, esp. a big one: a rage: a nurse's word for a slap.

padella, *pa-del'ä, n.* a shallow dish of fat with a wick used in illuminations. [It., a frying-pan—L. *patella.*]

pademelon, paddymelon, padymelon, *pad'i-mel-ən, n.* a small wallaby (*Macropus thetidis*). [From a native Australian name.]

paderero, *pad-ə-rā'rō.* Same as **pederero.**

padishah, *pä'di-shä, n.* chief ruler: great king, a title of the Shah of Persia, and Sultan of Turkey, the Great Mogul, or the (British) Emperor of India. [Pers. *pād,* master, *shāh,* king.]

padlock, *pad'lok, n.* a movable lock with a link turning on a hinge or pivot at one end, catching the bolt at the other. [Possibly prov. Eng. *pad,* a basket, and **lock.**]

padma, *päd'mä, n.* the sacred lotus. [Sans.]

padre, *pä'drā, n.* (*slang*) father, a title given to priests: an army chaplain: a parson.—*n.* **padrō'ne,** a shipmaster: an innkeeper: an employer: one who jobs out hand-organs, or who gets children to beg for him:—*pl.* **padrō'ni** (*-nē*). [Port. (also Sp. and Ital.) *padre,* It. *padrone*—L. *pater,* a father, *patrōnus,* a patron.]

Paduan, *pad'ū-ən, adj.* of *Padua.*—*n.* a native of Padua: a counterfeit Roman bronze coin made at Padua in the 16th century: the pavan.

paduasoy, *pad'ū-ə-soi, pä'də-soi, n.* a corded silk used in the 18th century: a garment made of it. [Fr. *pou-de-soie—pou, pout, poult* (of unknown origin), *de soie,* of silk; apparently influenced by *Padua.*]

Paean, *pē'ən, n.* the Homeric physician of the gods: later, an epithet of Apollo: **paean,** a lyric to Apollo or Artemis (or some other god): a song of thanksgiving or triumph: exultation.—*n.* **pae'on,** a foot of four syllables, any one long, three short.—*adj.* **paeon'ic** (*-on'ik*). [L. *Paeān, paeōn*—Gr. *Paiān.* -*ānos, paiōn,* -*ōnos.*]

paed-, *pēd-,* **paid-,** *pīd-,* **paedo-,** *pē'dō-,* **paido-,** *pī'dō-,* in composition, child, boy.—*adj.* **paeda-gog'ic** (see **pedagogic**).—*ns.* **paed'agogue** (see **pedagogue**); **paed'erast** (Gr. *erastēs,* lover), one who practises paederasty.—*adj.* **paederast'ic.**—*ns.* **paed'erasty,** unnatural commerce of a male with a male, esp. a boy; **paedeut'ic, paideut'ic, -s,** educational method or theory.—*adj.* **paediat'ric** (Gr. *iātrikos,* medical), relating to the medical treatment of children.—*ns.* **paediat'ric, -s,** the treatment of children's diseases; **paediatrician**

(-ə-trish'ən), paedī'atrist; paedī'atry; paedo-bap'tism, infant baptism; **paedobap'tist; pae-dogen'esis**, reproduction by an animal in the larval state.—*adj.* **paedogenet'ic**.—*ns.* **paedo-morph'ism** (Gr. *morphē*, form), retention of juvenile characters in the mature stage; **paed'o-tribe** (-*trīb*; Gr. *paidotribēs*), a gymnastic teacher; **paedot'rophy** (Gr. *tropheiā*, nursing), the art of rearing children. [Gr. *pais, paidos*, boy, child; *paideutēs*, teacher.]

paenula, *pē'nū-lä, n.* a Roman travelling cloak: a chasuble, esp. in its older form. [L. *paenula.*]

paeony, peony, *pē'ə-ni, n.* any plant of the genus Paeonia, of the buttercup family, with large showy crimson or white globular flowers: its flower.—Also (formerly) **pī'on(e)y**. [O.E. *peonie* and O.Fr. (Northern) *pione* (Fr. *pivoine*)—L. *paeōnia*—Gr. *paiōniā*—*Paiōn, Paiān*, physician of the gods (see **Paean**), from its use in medicine.]

pagan, *pā'gən, n.* a heathen: one who is not a Christian, Jew, or Mohammedan.—Also *adj.*—*v.t.* **pā'ganise**, to render pagan or heathen: to convert to paganism.—*adj.* **pā'ganish**, heathenish.—*n.* **pā'ganism**, heathenism: the beliefs and practices of the heathen. [L. *pāgānus*, rustic, peasant, also civilian (because the Christians reckoned themselves soldiers of Christ)—*pāgus*, a district.]

page, *pāj, n.* a boy attendant: a boy in buttons: (*hist.*) a youth training for knighthood, receiving education and performing services at court or in a nobleman's household: a contrivance for holding up a long skirt in walking.—*v.t.* to attend as a page: to seek or summon by sending a page around.—*n.* **page'hood**, condition of a page. [Fr. *page*; of obscure origin.]

page, *pāj, n.* one side of a leaf of a book, &c.— 4 pages in a folio sheet, 8 in a quarto, 16 in an octavo, 24 in a duodecimo, 36 in an octodecimo: the type, illustrations, &c., arranged for printing one side of a leaf: rhetorically, writings, literature: an incident, episode, or whatever may be imagined as matter to fill a page.—*v.t.* to number the pages of.—*n.* **page'-proof**, a proof of matter made up into pages.—*adj.* **paginal** (*paj'*).—*v.t.* **paginate** (*paj'*), to mark with consecutive numbers, to page.—*ns.* **pagina'tion**, the act of paging a book: the figures and marks that indicate the numbers of pages; **pā'ging**, the marking or numbering of the pages of a book. [Fr.,—L. *pāgina.*]

pageant, *paj'ənt*, or *pāj'-, n.* (*arch.*) a dramatic performance, scene, or part: (*obs.*) a movable stage or carriage for acting on: (*obs.*) a stage machine: a spectacle, esp. one carried around in procession: a series of tableaux or dramatic scenes connected with local history or other topical matter, performed either on a fixed spot or in procession: a piece of empty show.—*adj.* of the nature of a puppet: specious.—*n.* **page'antry**, splendid display: pompous spectacle: a fleeting show. [Origin obscure; Anglo-L. *pāgina* may be the classical word transferred from page to scene in a MS.; or *pāgina*, in the sense of slab, may have come to mean boarding, framework.]

pagoda, *pə-gō'dä*, **pagod**, *pag'od*, formerly also *pə-god'*, *n.* an Eastern temple, esp. in the form of a many-storied tapering tower, each story with a projecting roof: an ornamental building in imitation of this: an idol: a demigod: a former Indian coin, bearing the figure of a pagoda.—*ns.* **pago'da-sleeve**, a funnel-shaped outer sleeve turned back to show lining and inner sleeve; **pago'da-tree'**, a name for various erect trees of pagoda-like form: a fabulous Indian tree that dropped pagodas when shaken. [Port. *pagode*—Pers. *but-kadah*, idol-house, or some other Eastern word.]

pagri, *pug'rē, n.* a turban: a light scarf worn round the hat to keep off the sun.—Also **puggaree, puggree, puggery**. [Hind. *pagrī.*]

pah, *pä, interj.* an exclamation of disgust.

pah. See **pa** (2).

Pahlavi. Same as **Pehlevi.**

paid, *pād, pa.t.* and *pa.p.* of **pay**.—*adj.* (*obs.*) satisfied: (*Shak.*) drunk: hired.—**put paid**, to settle, finish.

paid-. See **paed-.**

paidle. See **paddle** (2).

paigle, pagle, *pā'gl, n.* the cowslip. [Origin unknown.]

paik, *pāk, v.t.* (*Scot.*) to thump, drub.—*n.* a blow: (in *pl.*, with *his*, &c.) a drubbing. [Origin unknown.]

pail, *pāl, n.* an open cylindrical or conical vessel with a hooped handle, for holding or carrying liquids: a pailful: (*U.S.*) a workman's dinner-can.—*n.* **pail'ful**, as much as fills a pail. [O.E. *pægel*, a gill measure, apparently combined with or influenced by O.Fr. *paele*, a pan—L. *patella*, a pan, dim. of *patera—patēre*, to be open.]

paillasse. Same as **palliasse.**

paillette, *pal-yet', n.* a spangle, esp. one used in enamel-painting.—*n.* **paillon** (*pal'yən, pä-yon'*), a piece of foil, to show through enamel, &c. [Fr.]

pain, *pān, n.* penalty: suffering: bodily suffering: anguish: (now only in *pl.*) great care or trouble taken in doing anything: (in *pl.*) the throes of childbirth.—*v.t.* to cause suffering to: (*arch.*; esp. *refl.*) to put to trouble.—*adjs.* **pained**, showing or expressing pain: suffering pain: distressed; **pain'ful**, full of pain: causing pain: requiring labour, pain, or care: (*arch.*) laborious, painstaking: distressing.—*adv.* **pain'fully**.—*ns.* **pain'-fulness; pain'-killer**, anything that does away with pain: a nostrum claiming to end pain.—*adj.* **pain'less**, without pain.—*adv.* **pain'lessly**.—*ns.* **pain'lessness; pains'taker**, one who takes pains or care: a careful worker.—*adj.* **pains'-taking**, taking pains or care.—*n.* careful diligence.—**be at pains, take pains**, to put oneself to trouble, be assiduously careful; **for one's pains**, as reward or result of trouble taken (commonly ironical); **under** or **on pain of**, under liability to the penalty of. [Fr. *peine*—L. *poena*, satisfaction—Gr. *poinē*, penalty.]

painim, *pā'nim*. See **paynim.**

paint, *pānt, v.t.* to cover over with colouring matter: to represent in a coloured picture: to produce as a coloured picture: to apply with a brush: to apply anything to, with a brush: (*fig.*) to describe or present as if in paint: to colour: to adorn, diversify: to represent speciously or deceptively.—*v.i.* to practise painting: to lay colours on the face: (*slang*) to tipple.—*n.* a colouring substance spread or for spreading on the surface: a cake of such matter.—*adj.* **paint'able**, suitable for painting.—*ns.* **paint'-box**, a box in which different paints are kept in compartments; **paint'-bridge**, a platform used by theatrical scene-painters; **paint'-brush**, a brush for putting on paint: the painted-cup (see below).—*adj.* **paint'ed**, covered with paint: ornamented with coloured figures: marked with bright colours: feigned.—*ns.* **paint'ed-cloth'**, a hanging of cloth painted with figures, a substitute for tapestry, formerly common in taverns; **paint'ed-cup'**, a scrophulariaceous plant (Castilleja) with brightly coloured upper leaves; **paint'ed-grass'**, striped canary-grass, gardener's garters; **paint'ed-la'dy**, the thistle-butterfly, orange-red spotted with white and black: the painted-cup: a party-coloured pink, sweetpea, gladiolus, &c.; **paint'ed-snipe'**, a genus (Rhynchaea) of birds akin to the snipes, the hen brightly coloured; **paint'er**, one who paints: an artist in painting: one whose occupation is painting: a house-decorator: a vivid describer; **paint'er's-col'ic**, lead-colic; **paint'er-stain'er**, a member of the London livery company of painters; **paint'iness; paint'ing**, the act or employment of laying on colours: the act of representing objects by colours: a painted picture: vivid description in words; **paint'ure**, (*Dryden*) the art of painting: a picture.—*adj.* **paint'y**, overloaded with paint, with the colours too glaringly used: smeared with paint.—**paint the lily**, to attempt to beautify that which is already beautiful; **paint the town red**, to break out in a boisterous spree. [O.Fr. *peint*, pa.p. of *peindre*, to paint—L. *pingĕre*, to paint.]

painter, *pānt'ər*, *n.* a rope for fastening a boat.—**cut the painter**, to sever ties; **lazy painter**, a small painter for use in fine weather only. [Origin obscure.]

painter, *pānt'ər*, *n.* (*U.S.*) the cougar. [**panther.**]

paiock(e), **pajock(e)**, *pā'jok? pā'ok? n.* an obscure word in Shakespeare (*Hamlet* III. ii.) conjectured to mean peacock (possibly a misprint for *pacock*; possibly =*pea-jock*).

pair, *pār*, *n.* two things equal, or suited to each other, or growing, grouped or used together: a set of two equal or like things forming one instrument, garment, &c., as a pair of scissors, tongs, trousers: a set of like things generally: (*obs.*) a pack (of cards): a flight of stairs: a couple: husband and wife: two persons betrothed to or in love with each other: a male and a female animal mated together: two persons or things associated together: two horses harnessed together: two cards of like designation: two voters on opposite sides who have an agreement to abstain from voting.—*v.t.* to couple: to sort out in pairs.—*v.i.* to be joined in couples: to be a counterpart or counterparts: to mate.—*adjs.* **paired**, arranged in pairs: set by twos of a like kind: mated; **pair'-horse**, for a pair of horses.—*ns.* **pair'ing**; **pair'ing-time**, the time when birds go together in pairs; **pair'-oar**, a boat rowed by two.—Also *adj.*—*n.* **pair'-roy'al**, three cards of the same denomination, esp. in cribbage and in the obs. post and pair: a throw of three dice all falling alike: a set of three (also **pairi'al**, **pri'al**).—*adv.* **pair'wise**, in pairs.—**pair of colours**, two flags carried by a regiment, one the national ensign, the other the flag of the regiment: hence an ensigncy; **pair off**, to arrange, set against each other, or set aside in pairs: to become associated in pairs. [Fr. *paire*, a couple—L. *paria*, neut. pl. of *pār*, afterwards regarded as a fem. sing., equal.]

pair, **paire**, *pār* (*obs.*), aphetic forms of **appair**.

pais, *pā*, *n.* the people from whom a jury is drawn. [O.Fr.]

paitrick, *pā'trik*, *n.* a Scots form of **partridge**.

pajamas. See **pyjamas**.

pajock(e). See **paiock(e)**.

pakeha, *pā'kā-hä*, *n.* a white man. [Maori.]

Pakhtu. See **Pushtu**.

pakka, *puk'ā*. Same as **pucka**.

paktong, *pak'tong*, *n.* nickel-silver.—Also (erroneously) **pack'fong**, **pak'fong**. [Chin. *peh*, white, *t'ung*, copper.]

pal, *pal*, *n.* (*slang*) a partner, mate: chum.—*v.i.* to associate as a pal:—*pr.p.* **pall'ing**; *pa.t.* and *pa.p.* **palled** (*pald*).—*adj.* **pally** (*pal'i*). [Gypsy.]

palabra, *pä-lä'brä*, *n.* a word: talk.—**pocas** (*pō'käs*) **palabras**, few words. [Sp.]

palace, *pal'is*, *n.* the house of a king or a queen: a very large and splendid house: a bishop's official residence: a large public building: a large and usually showy place of entertainment or refreshment.—*n.* **pal'ace-car**, a sumptuously furnished railway-car.—**palais de danse** (*pä-le də dän⁵*; Fr.), a dance-hall. [Fr. *palais*—L. *Palātium*, the Roman emperor's residence on the *Palatine* Hill at Rome.]

paladin, *pal'ə-din*, *n.* one of the twelve peers of Charlemagne's household: a knight-errant, or paragon of knighthood. [Fr.,—It. *paladino*—L. *palātinus*, belonging to the palace (cf. **palatine**.]

palae-, **palaeo-**, *pal'i-*, *-ō-*, also *pāl'-*, in composition, old.—*adj.* **Palaeanthrop'ic** (Gr. *anthrōpos*, man), of the earliest types of man.—*n.* **Palaeanthropus** (*-thrō'*), an extinct genus of man, including the Neanderthal and Heidelberg races.—*adj.* **Palaearc'tic**, of the Old World part of the Holarctic region.—*ns.* **palaeethnol'ogy**, the science of early man; **palaeichthyol'ogy**, the study of fossil fishes.—*adj.* **palaeobotan'ical**.—*ns.* **palaeobot'anist**; **palaeobot'any**, the study of fossil plants.—*adj.* **palaeocrys'tic** (Gr. *krystallos*, ice), consisting of ancient ice.—*n.* **palaeogaea** (*-jē'ä*; Gr. *gaia*, earth), the Old World as a biological region.—*n.* and *adj.* **Palaeogene** (*-jēn*; Gr. *palai(o)genēs*, born long ago), early Tertiary-Eocene and Oligocene.—*n.* **palaeog'rapher** (Gr.

graphein, to write), one skilled in palaeography.—*adjs.* **palaeograph'ic**, **-al**.—*ns.* **palaeog'raphist**; **palaeog'raphy**, ancient modes of writing: study of ancient modes of hand-writing; **pal'aeolith** (Gr. *lithos*, stone), a Palaeolithic artefact.—*adj.* **Palaeolith'ic**, of the earlier or ruder Stone Age.—*n.* **palaeomag'netism**, a study of the magnetism of ancient rocks and fossils, and of bricks, pottery, &c., made in past ages.—*adj.* **palaeontolog'ical**.—*ns.* **palaeontol'ogist**; **palaeontol'ogy** (Gr. *onta*, neut. pl. of pr.p. of *einai*, to be, *logos*, discourse), the study of fossils; **palaeophytol'ogy**, palaeobotany; **Palaeothē'rium** (Gr. *thērion*, a wild beast—*thēr*), an odd-toed Eocene fossil ungulate with tapir-like snout; **pal'aeotype**, A. J. Ellis's phonetic adaptation of ordinary alphabetical type.—*adjs.* **palaeotypic** (*-tip'ik*); **Palaeozo'ic** (Gr. *zōē*, life), of the division of the fossiliferous rocks, from Cambrian to Permian; **palaeozoolog'ical.**—*ns.* **palaeozool'ogist**; **palaeozool'ogy**, the study of fossil animals. [Gr. *palaios*, old.]

palaestra, *pal-ēs'trā*, *-es'*, *n.* (*ant.*) a wrestling school: a gymnasium: wrestling: a training-ground.—*adjs.* **palaes'tral**, **palaes'tric**, **-al**. [L. *palaestra*—Gr. *palaistrā*—*palaiein*, to wrestle.]

palafitte, *pal'ə-fit*, *n.* a prehistoric lake-dwelling. [It. *palafitta*—*palo* (—L. *pālus*), a stake, *fitto*, pa.p. of *figgere* (—L. *figĕre*), to fix.]

palagonite, *pal-ag'ə-nīt*, *n.* an altered basic vitreous lava.—*n.* **palag'onite-tuff**, a tuff composed of fragments of palagonite. [*Palagonia*, in Sicily.]

palama, *pal'ə-mā*, *n.* the webbing of a water-bird's foot :—*pl.* **pal'amae** (*-mē*).—*adj.* **pal'amate.** [Latinised from Gr. *palamē*, palm.]

palampore, **palempore**, *pal'əm-pōr*, *n.* a flowered chintz bedcover common in the East. [Origin doubtful.]

palanquin, **palankeen**, *pal-ən-kēn'*, *n.* a light litter for one, a box borne on poles on men's shoulders. [Port. *palanquim*; cf. Hind. *palang*, a bed—Sans. *palyanka*, a bed.]

palas, *pal-äs'*, *-äsh*, *n.* the dhak tree. [Hind. *palāś*.]

palate, *pal'it*, *-ət*, *n.* the roof of the mouth, consisting of the *hard palate* in front and the *soft palate* behind: the prominent part of the lower lip that closes the tube of a personate corolla: taste: relish: mental liking.—*v.t.* to taste: to relish.—*adj.* **pal'atable**, pleasant to the taste: acceptable.—*ns.* **palatabil'ity**, **pal'atableness**.—*adv.* **pal'atably**.—*adj.* **pal'atal**, pertaining to the palate: uttered by bringing the tongue to or near the hard palate.—*n.* a sound so produced.—*v.t.* **pal'atalise**, to make palatal.—*adj.* **pal'atine**, pertaining to the palate.—*n.* a paired bone forming part of the roof of the mouth.—**cleft palate**, a congenital defect of the palate, leaving a longitudinal fissure in the roof of the mouth. [L. *palātum*.]

palatial, *pə-lā'shl*, *adj.* of or like a palace. [See **palace**.]

palatine, *pal'ə-tīn*, *adj.* of the Palatine Hill or the palace of emperors there: of a palace: having royal privileges or jurisdiction: of a count or earl palatine (see below).—*ns.* **Palatine**, one of the seven hills of Rome: **palatine**, an officer of the palace: a noble invested with royal privileges and jurisdiction: a subject of a palatinate: a fur tippet (from the Princess Palatine of 1676); **pal'atinate** (or *pə-lat'*), office or rank of a palatine: province of a palatine, esp. an electorate of the ancient German Empire: at Durham University, a light purple blazer.—*adj.* at Durham, light purple or lilac.—**count, earl**, &c., **palatine**, a feudal lord with supreme judicial authority over a province; **county palatine**, the province of such a lord. [L. *palātīnus*; cf. **palace**.]

palaver, *pə-lä'vər*, *n.* a conference, esp. with African or other natives: a talk or discussion: idle copious talk: talk intended to deceive.—*v.i.* to hold a palaver: to prate.—*v.t.* to flatter.—*n.* **palav'erer**. [Port. *palavra*, word—L. *parabola*, a parable, later a word, speech—Gr. *parabolē*; cf. **parable**, **parabola**.]

palay, *pa-lā'*, *pä-lī'*, *-lā'*, *n.* the ivory-tree, a small S. Indian tree (Wrightia) of the dogbane family, with hard white wood. [Tamil.]

fāte, fär; ǎsk; mē, hər (her); mīne; mōte; mūte; mōōn; dhen (then)

pale, *pāl*, *n*. a stake of wood driven into the ground for fencing: anything that encloses or fences in: a limit: (*fig.*) the limit of what can be accepted as decent or tolerable: an enclosure: a marked-off district: (*her.*) a broad stripe from top to bottom of a shield.—*v.t.* to enclose with stakes: to fence: (*Shak.*) to encircle, crown.—*adv.* pale′-wise, (*her.*) vertically, like a pale.—*n.* palifica′tion (*pal-*, *pāl-*), act of strengthening by stakes.—*adj.* pāl′iform.—*n.* pāl′ing, the act of fencing: wood or stakes for fencing: a fence of stakes connected by horizontal pieces: an upright stake or board in a fence.—*adj.* pāl′y, (*her.*) divided by vertical lines.—**English Pale**, the district in Ireland within which alone the English had power for centuries after the invasion in 1172; **Jewish Pale**, that part of S.W. Russia in which alone Jews were formerly allowed to live. [Fr. *pal*—L. *pālus*, a stake.]

pale, *pāl*, *adj*. whitish: not ruddy or fresh: wan: of a faint lustre, dim: wanting in colour.—*v.t.* to make pale.—*v.i.* to turn pale.—*n.* paleness.—*ns.* pale′-ale, a light-coloured pleasant bitter ale; pale′buck, an antelope, the oribi.—*adjs.* pale′-dead, (*Shak.*) lustreless; pale′-eyed, (*Milt.*) dim-eyed.—*n.* pale′-face, (attributed to American Indians) a white person.—*adj.* pale′-heart′ed, (*Shak.*) dispirited.—*adv.* pale′ly.—*n.* pale′ness. —*adjs.* pale′-vis′aged (*Shak.*); pāl′ish, somewhat pale; pāl′y, pale: palish. [O.Fr. *palle*, pale (Fr. *pâle*)—L. *pallidus*, pale.]

pale, *pāl*, *n*. a baker's peel: a cheese-scoop.—*v.t.* to test by inserting a cheese-pale. [L. *pāla*, spade.]

palea, *pā′li-ä*, *n*. the membranous inner bract (*inferior palea*) or bracteole (*superior palea*) of an individual grass-flower, above the glumes: a scale on a fern-leaf or stem: a scale on the receptacle of some composite plants:—*pl.* pā′leae (*-ē*).—*n.* pale (*pāl*), a grass palea.—*adj.* paleā′ceous, chaffy.—*n.* palet (*pāl′it*), a palea. [L. *pālea*, chaff.]

paleobotany, &c. See palaeobotany, &c.

Palestinian, *pal-is-tin′i-ən*, *adj*. pertaining to *Palestine* (Gr. *Palaistīnē*), or to Israel.—Also *n.*—**Palestine soup**, artichoke soup, by a quibble on *Jerusalem* (see artichoke). [Cf. **Philistine**.]

palestra. Same as palaestra.

paletot, *pal′tō*, *n*. a loose overcoat. [Fr.]

palette, *pal′it*, *-et*, *n*. a little board with a thumb-hole on which a painter mixes his colours: the assortment or range of colours used by a particular artist or for any particular picture: a plate against which one leans in working a drill: a small plate covering a joint in armour, esp. at the armpit.—*n.* pal′ette-knife, a thin round-ended knife for mixing colours. [Fr.,—It. *paletta*—*pala*, spade—L. *pāla*, a spade.]

palfrey, *pawl′fri*, *n*. a saddle-horse, esp. for a lady. —*n.* palfrenier (*pal-frə-nēr′*), a groom.—*adj.* palfreyed (*pawl′*), riding on, or supplied with, a palfrey. [O.Fr. *palefrei*—L.L. *paraverēdus*, prob. from Gr. *para*, beside, L.L. *verēdus*, a post-horse, app. a Celtic word; confused with L. *frēnum*, a bridle.]

Pali, *pä′lē*, *n*. the sacred language of the Buddhists of India, &c., close akin to Sanskrit. [Sans. *pāli*, canon.]

Palilia, *pə-lil′i-ä*, *n.pl.* (*or sing.*) the festival of Pales (L. *Palēs*), Roman goddess of flocks, held on 21st April, traditional date of the founding of Rome.

palillogy, *pal-il′ə-ji*, *n*. a repetition of a word or phrase. [Gr. *palillogiā*—*palin*, again, *logos*, word, speech.]

palimpsest, *pal′imp-sest*, *n*. a manuscript in which old writing has been rubbed out to make room for new: a monumental brass turned over for a new inscription. [Gr. *palimpsēston*—*palin*, again, *psāein* (contracted *psēn*), to rub.]

palindrome, *pal′in-drōm*, *n*. a word, verse, or sentence that reads alike backward and forward, as Adam's first words to Eve: ' Madam, I'm Adam.'—*adjs.* palindromic (*-drom′*, *-drōm′*), -al.—*n.* pal′indromist (or *pə-lin′*), an inventor of

palindromes. [Gr. *palindromos*, running back—*palin*, back, *dromos*, a running.]

paling. See under pale.

palingenesis, *pal-in-jen′i-sis*, *n*. a new birth: re-incarnation: a second creation: regeneration: unmodified inheritance of ancestral characters: the new-formation of a rock by refusion.—Also palingenē′sia, palingen′esy.—*n.* palingen′esist. —*adj.* palingenet′ical.—*adv.* palingenet′ically. [Gr. *palin*, again, *genesis*, birth.]

palinode, *pal′i-nōd*, *n*. a poem of retractation: a recantation.—Also (*obs.*) pal′inody. [Gr. *palin-ōidiā*—*palin*, back, *ōidē*, song.]

palisade, *pal-i-sād′*, *n*. a fence of stakes: (*mil.*) a stake so used.—*v.t.* to surround or defend with a palisade. — Also palisā′do:—*pl.* palisā′does.—**palisade tissue**, a tissue occurring in leaves, composed of cells placed closely together with their long axes perpendicular to the surface. [Fr. *palissade* and Sp. *palizada*—L. *pālus*, a stake.]

palisander, *pal-i-san′dər*, *n*. jacaranda or other rose-wood. [Fr. *palissandre*, from a name used in Guiana.]

palki, **palkee**, *pāl′kē*, *n*. a palanquin. [Hind. *pālkī*.]

pall, *pawl*, *n*. (*arch.*) a rich cloth: a covering of rich cloth: a corporal: a frontal: a chalice-cover: a cloth spread over a coffin or tomb: a cloak, mantle, outer garment: a pallium: (*her.*) a bearing representing a pallium: (*fig.*) a curtain, covering, or cloak, as of smoke, darkness.—*v.t.* to cover with, or as with, a pall.—*n.* pall′-bearer, one of the mourners at a funeral who used to hold up the corners of the pall. [O.E. *pæll*, a rich robe—L. *pallium*; see pallium.]

pall, *pawl*, *v.i.* (*obs.*) to lose strength: to become vapid, insipid, or wearisome: to lose relish.—*v.t.* (*obs.*) to daunt: (*obs.*) to weaken: (*obs.*) to pale: to make vapid: to cloy. [Prob. from **appal**.]

palla, *pal′ä*, *n*. a Roman woman's mantle:—*pl.* pall′ae (*-ē*). [L. *palla*.]

Palladian, *pə-lā′di-ən*, *adj*. relating to **Pallas**, wisdom, or learning.

Palladian, *pə-lā′di-ən*, *adj*. in the style of architecture introduced by Andrea *Palladio* (1518-80), modelled on Vitruvius, its faults a superfluity of pilasters and columns, broken entablatures, and inappropriate ornament.—*n.* Pallā′dianism.

Palladium, *pə-lā′di-əm*, *n*. a statue of *Pallas* on whose preservation the safety of Troy depended: anything of like virtue: a safeguard. [L.,—Gr. *palladion*—*Pallas*, *Pallados*, Pallas.]

palladium, *pə-lā′di-əm*, *n*. a metallic element (at. numb. 46) resembling platinum, remarkable for its power of occluding hydrogen.—*adjs.* palladic (*-lad′*), pallā′dious, containing palladium in smaller or greater proportion respectively. [Named by its discoverer Wollaston (1803) after the newly discovered minor planet *Pallas*.]

pallah, *pal′ä*, *n*. the impala. [Sechuana *phala*.]

Pallas, *pal′as*, *n*. the Greek goddess Athēnē (also **Pall′as Athē′nē**): a minor planet discovered by Olbers in 1802.

pallescent, *pa-les′ənt*, *adj*. turning pale.—*n.* pallesc′ence. [L. *pallēscēns*, *-entis*, pr.p. of *pallēscĕre*, to turn pale.]

pallet, *pal′it*, *n*. a palette: a flat wooden tool with a handle, as that used for shaping pottery: a flat brush for spreading gold-leaf: a tool for lettering book-bindings: one of the points moved by the pendulum of a clock which check the motion of the escape or balance wheel: a disk of a chain-pump: a valve of an organ wind-chest, regulated from the keyboard: a board for carrying newly moulded bricks: a piece of wood built into a wall for the nailing on of joiner-work. [palette.]

pallet, *pal′it*, *n*. a mattress, or couch, properly a mattress of straw: a small or mean bed. [Prov. Fr. *paillet*, dim. of Fr. *paille*, straw—L. *palea*, chaff.]

palliasse, *pal-i-as′*, *pal-yas′*, *n*. a straw mattress: an under-mattress.—Also **paillasse′**. [Fr. *paillasse*—*paille*, straw—L. *palea*.]

palliate, *pal′i-āt*, *v.t.* to cloak: to disguise: to excuse, extenuate: to soften by pleading something in favour: to mitigate: to alleviate.—*adj.* (see under **pallium**).—*n.* **pallia′tion**, act of palliating: extenuation: mitigation: alleviation.—*adj.* **pall′iative** (*-ə-tiv*), serving to extenuate: mitigating: alleviating. — *n.* that which lessens pain, &c., or gives temporary relief.—*adj.* **pall′iatory**. [L. *palliāre, -ātum*, to cloak—*pallium*, a cloak.]

pallid, *pal′id, adj.* pale, wan.—*ns.* **pallid′ity**, **pall′idness.**—*adv.* **pall′idly.** [L. *pallidus*, pale.]

pallium, *pal′i-əm, n.* a large, square mantle, worn by learned Romans in imitation of the Greeks—the himation: a white woollen vestment like a double Y, embroidered with crosses, worn by the Pope, and conferred by him upon archbishops: (*zool.*) the mantle in molluscs, brachiopods, and birds:—*pl.* **pall′ia.** — *adj.* (*zool.*) **pall′ial.** — *n.* **pall′iament**, (*Shak.*) a Roman consular candidate's robe.—*adj.* **pall′iate**, having a pallium. [L. *pallium.*]

pall-mall, *pel′-mel′, n.* an old game, in which a ball was driven through an iron ring with a mallet: an alley for the game (hence the street in London). [Obs. Fr. *pale-maille*—*palmaille*—It. *pallamaglio*—*palla*, ball (cf. O.H.G. *pallā*), and *maglio*—L. *malleus*, a hammer; cf. **ball**; **pallone**.]

pallone, *päl-lō′nā, n.* an Italian game in which a ball is struck with a gauntlet or armguard. [It., augmentative of *palla*, ball.]

pallor, *pal′ər, n.* paleness. [L. *pallēre*, to be pale.]

palm, *päm, n.* the inner surface of the hand between wrist and fingers: the corresponding part of the fore-foot or of a glove: (*rare*) the sole of the foot: a handsbreadth (3 inches, or 4 inches): the length of the hand from wrist to finger-tip: a sailmaker's instrument used instead of a thimble: a flat expansion, as of an antler, or the inner surface of an anchor fluke: an act of palming: an old game (also **palm′-play**) in which a ball was struck with the palm.—*v.t.* to touch, or stroke with the palm: to hold or conceal in the palm: (esp. with *off*, and *on*, or *upon*) to impose, pass off: to bribe.—*adj.* **palmar** (*pal′mər*), relating to the palm; **palmate** (*pal′*), **-d**, hand-shaped: (*bot.*) having lobes radiating from one centre: (*zool.*) web-footed.—*adv.* **pal′mately.**—*adj.* **palmatifid** (*pal-mat′i-fid*; *bot.*), shaped like the hand, with the divisions extending about half-way down.—*n.* **palma′tion**, palmate formation: a palmate structure or one of its parts or divisions.—*adjs.* **palmatipart′ite**, palmately divided rather more than half-way; **palmatisect** (*pal-mat′i-sekt*), deeply cut in a palmate manner; **palmed** (*pämd*), having a palm: held or concealed in the palm.—*ns.* **palm′ful**, as much as the palm will hold; **palm′-grease′, -oil′**, a bribe; **palmiped** (*pal′mi-ped*), **palmipede** (*-pēd*), a web-footed bird.—*adj.* web-footed.—*ns.* **palmist** (*päm′ist*), one who tells fortune from the lines on the palm; **palm′istry**; **palmy** (*päm′i*), *Scot.*), a stroke of the tawse on the palm. [L. *palma*; cf. Gr. *palamē*; O.E. *folm.*]

palm, *päm, n.* any tree or shrub of the **Palmae** (*pal′mē*), a large tropical and sub-tropical family of monocotyledons, sometimes climbers but usually branchless trees with a crown of pinnate or fan-shaped leaves: a leaf of this tree borne in token of rejoicing or of victory: emblematically, pre-eminence, the prize: a branch of willow or other substitute in symbolic or ceremonial use.—*adjs.* **palmaceous** (*pal-mā′shəs*), of the palm family; **palmarian** (*pal-mā′ri-ən*); **palmary** (*pal′mər-i*), worthy of the palm: pre-eminent.—*ns.* **palm′-branch′**, a palm-leaf; **palm′-butt′er**, palm-oil in a solid state; **palm′-cabb′age**, the bud of the cabbage-palm; **palm′-cat′, palm′-civ′et**, the paradoxure; **palmette** (*pal-met′*; Fr.), an ancient architectural ornament like a palm-leaf; **palmetto** (*pal-*), a name for several kinds of palm, notably Sabal and the only European palm Chamaerops; **palm′-hon′ey**, evaporated coquito-palm sap; **palm′house**, a glass house for palms and other tropical plants; **palmiet** (*pal-mēt′*), a South African aloe-like riverside plant of the rush family

(*Prionum Palmita*); **palmifica′tion** (*pal-*), artificial fertilisation of dates by hanging a wild male flower-cluster on a cultivated female tree; **palmitate** (*pal′*), a salt of **palmit′ic acid**, a fatty acid ($C_{15}H_{31}$·COOH) got from palm-oil, &c.; **palmitin** (*pal′*), a white fat abundant in palm-oil: a glycerine ester of palmitic acid; **palm′-ker′nel**, the kernel of the oil-palm, yielding **palm-kernel oil**; **palm′-oil**, an oil or fat obtained from the pulp of the fruit of palms, esp. of the oil-palm; **palm′-su′gar**, jaggery; **Palm′-Sun′day**, the Sunday before Easter, in commemoration of the strewing of palm-branches when Christ entered Jerusalem; **palm′-tree**; **palm′-wine**, fermented palm sap.—*adj.* **palm′y**, bearing palms: flourishing: palm-like.—**pal′ma Chris′ti**, the castor-oil plant. [O.E. *palm, palma, palme*, also directly L. *palma*, palm-tree, from the shape of its leaves; see preceding.]

palmer, *päm′ər, n.* a pilgrim carrying a palm-leaf in token of having been in the Holy Land: a palmer-worm: a bristly artificial fly.—*n.* **palm′er-worm′**, a hairy caterpillar of various kinds, originally one of wandering habits. [palm (2).]

Palmerin, *pal′mər-in, n.* a knightly champion. [From *Palmerín*, a Spanish (or Portuguese) romance hero found as a child among *palm*-trees.]

palmyra, *pal-mī′rä, n.* an African and Asiatic palm (*Borassus flabellifer*) yielding toddy, jaggery, and **palmy′ra-nuts.**—*n.* **palmy′ra-wood**, properly the wood of the palmyra palm: any palm timber. [Port. *palmeira*, palm-tree, confused with *Palmyra* in Syria.]

palolo, *pä-lō′lō, n.* an edible sea-worm that burrows in coral-reefs, remarkable for its breeding swarms at a certain phase of the moon, the head remaining behind to regenerate. [Samoan.]

palp, *palp, n.* a jointed sense-organ attached in pairs to the mouth-parts of insects and crustaceans—also **pal′pus** :—*pl.* **pal′pī.**—*adj.* **pal′pal.** [L.L. *palpus*, a feeler (L. a stroking)—L. *palpāre*, to stroke.]

palp, *palp, v.t.* to feel, examine, or explore by touch: to speak fair.—*n.* **palpabil′ity.**—*adjs.* **palp′able**, that can be touched or felt: tangible: perceptible: easily found out, as lies, &c.: obvious, gross; **palp′able-gross′** (*Shak.*).—*n.* **pal′pableness.**—*adv.* **palp′ably.**—*v.t.* **palp′āte**, to examine by touch.—*n.* **palpā′tion**, the act of examining by means of touch. [L. *palpāre, -ātum*, to touch softly, stroke, caress, flatter.]

palpebral, *palp′i-brəl, adj.* of or pertaining to the eyelid. [L. *palpebra*, the eyelid.]

palpitate, *pal′pi-tāt, v.i.* to throb: to beat rapidly: to pulsate: to quiver.—*v.t.* to cause to throb.—*adj.* **pal′pitant**, palpitating.—*n.* **palpitā′tion**, act of palpitating: painful awareness of heart-beat. [L. *palpitāre, -ātum*, freq. of *palpāre*; cf. **palp**.]

palsgrave, *pawlz′grāv, n.* a count palatine :—*fem.* **palsgravine** (*pawlz′grə-vēn*). [Du. *paltsgrave* (now *paltsgraaf*) ; cf. Ger. *pfalzgraf*; see **palace**, **graf**.]

palstave, *pawl′stäv*, **palstaff**, *-stäf, n.* a Bronze Age axe, the flanges of the head joined by a cross ridge to engage the ends of the prongs of the kneed shaft. [Du. *paalstav*—O.N. *pálstafr*.]

palsy, *pawl′zi, n.* loss of control or of feeling, more or less complete, in the muscles of the body: paralysis.—*v.t.* to affect with palsy: to deprive of action or energy: to paralyse.—*adj.* **pal′sied.** [From **paralysis**.]

palter, *pawl′tər, v.i.* to trifle in talk: to use trickery: to dodge: to shuffle: to equivocate.—*n.* **pal′terer.** [Poss. conn. with **paltry**.]

paltry, *pawl′tri, adj.* mean: trashy: trumpery: not worth considering.—*adv.* **pal′trily.**—*n.* **pal′triness.** [Cf. Dan. *pialter*, rags, L.G. *paltrig*, ragged.]

paludal, *pal-*(*y*)*ōō′dl*, also *pal′, adj.* pertaining to marshes: marshy: malarial.—*adjs.* **palu′dic**, of marshes; **paludic′olous** (L. *colĕre*, to inhabit), marsh-dwelling: growing in marshes; **palu′dinal**, **pal′udine**, **palu′dinous**, of marshes: marshy.—*n.* **pal′udism**, malaria.—*adjs.* **pal′udose**, **pal′udous**, of marshes: marshy: inhabiting marshes: malarial.—*n.* **Pal′udrine**, a synthetic anti-malarial drug (trade-mark name).—*adjs.* **palustral** (*-us'trl*), **palus'trian, palus'trine** (*-trīn*), of marshes : inhabiting marshes. [L. *palūs, palūdis,* a marsh ; *palūster, -tris,* marshy.]

paludament, *pə-l(y)ōō'də-mənt, n.* a Roman general's or high military officer's cloak.—Also **paludament'um.** [L. *palūdāmentum.*]

paly. See under **pale** (1 and 2).

pam, *pam, n.* the knave of clubs, highest card in loo : a game like nap, in which it is highest card. [Said to be from the Fr. *Pamphile*—Gr. *Pamphilos,* lit. beloved of all.]

Pamaquine, *pam'ə-kwin, n.* an anti-malarial drug, a derivative of *quinoline.* [Trade-mark name.]

pampa, *pam'pä* (usu. in *pl.* **pampas**), *n.* a vast treeless plain in southern S. America.—*n.* **pam'pasgrass,** a tall, ornamental, reed-like grass (Gynerium, or Cortaderia) with large thick silvery panicles.—*adj.* **pampē'an.**—*n.* **pampero** (*păm-pā'rō*), a violent S.W. wind and from the Pampas. [Sp.,—Quechua *pampa, bamba,* plain.]

pampelmoose, *pam'pl-mōōs,, n.* See **pompelmoose.**

pamper, *pam'pər, v.t.* to feed with fine food : to gratify to the full : to over-indulge.—*ns.* **pam'peredness ; pam'perer.** [A freq. from (*obs.*) *pamp, pomp ;* cf. Ger. dial. *pampen,* to cram.]

pamphlet, *pam'flit, n.* a small book stitched but not bound : a separately published tractate, usu. controversial, on some subject of the day.—*n.* **pamphleteer',** a writer of pamphlets.—*v.i.* to write pamphlets.—*n.* and *adj.* **pamphleteer'ing.** [Anglo-L. *panfletus,* possibly from a Latin erotic poem *Pamphilus* (—Gr. *Pamphilos,* beloved of all) very popular in the Middle Ages.]

pan, *pan, n.* a broad, shallow vessel for use in the home or in arts or manufactures : anything of like shape, as the upper part of the skull (*brainpan*), the patella (*knee-pan*): a hollow in the ground, a basin, in which water collects in the rainy season, leaving a salt deposit on evaporation : a salt-pan : a salt-work : the part of a firelock that holds the priming : a hard layer (*hard-pan*) in or under the soil : a small ice-floe : a panful. —*v.t.* to wash in a gold-miner's pan : to obtain by evaporating in a pan : to yield : to obtain : to cook and serve in a pan.—*v.i.* to wash earth for gold : (usu. with *out*) to yield gold : (with *out*) to result, turn out : (with *out*) to come to an end, be exhausted : to cake : to enlarge in speech.— *n.* **pan'cake,** a thin cake of eggs, flour, sugar, and milk, fried in a pan : an aeroplane descent or landing with wings nearly horizontal.—*v.i.* to descend or alight so.—*ns.* **pan'-drop',** (*Scot.*) a hard ellipsoidal peppermint sweet ; **pan'ful,** as much as a pan will hold :—*pl.* **pan'fuls ; pan'han'dle,** a strip of territory stretching out from the main body like the handle of a pan.—*v.i.* (*U.S.*) to beg.—*ns.* **pan'-hand'ler ; pan'-loaf',** (*Scot.*) a loaf of a particular shape, made in a pan ; **pann'ikel** (see **pannicle**) ; **pann'ikin,** a small metal cup : a little pan or saucer : enough to fill a cup ; **pann'ing,** washing for gold : the gold so got.—**flash in the pan,** a mere flash in the pan of a flint-lock without discharge : a fitful show of beginning without accomplishing anything ; **pancake bell,** a church-bell rung on Shrove Tuesday, taken as the signal for pancake-making ; **pancake ice,** polar sea ice in thin flat slabs, found as winter draws near ; **Pancake Tuesday,** Shrove Tuesday. [O.E. *panne ;* a word common to the West Germanic languages, possibly an early borrowing from L. *patina.*]

Pan, *pan, n.* the Greek god of pastures, flocks, and woods, worshipped in Arcadia, and fond of music —with goat's legs and feet, and sometimes horns and ears : later (from association with *păn,* the whole) connected with pantheistic thought.—*n.* **Pan'-pipes, Pan's'-pipes,** the syrinx, a musical instrument attributed to Pan, made of reeds of different lengths, fastened in a row. [Gr. *Pān.*]

pan, *pän,* **pawn,** *pawn, n.* betel leaf : betel. [Hind. *pān.*]

pan-, pant-, panto-, in composition, all. [Gr. *pās, pāsa, pān,* gen. *pantos, pāsēs.*]

panacea, *pan-ə-sē'ä, n.* a universal medicine : a healing plant vaguely indicated (*Spens.* **panachaea,** *-kē'ä*). [Gr. *panakeia*—*akos,* cure.]

panache, *pa-näsh', n.* a plume : (*fig.*) knightly splendour : swagger. [Fr.,—It. *pennacchio*—*penna,* feather.]

panada, *pä-nä'dä, n.* a dish made of boiling bread to a pulp in water, and flavouring : a thick binding sauce of breadcrumbs or flour. [Sp.,—*pan*—L. *pānis,* bread.]

Panaesthesia, *pan-ēs-thē'zi-ä, -zyä,* or *-es-, n.* totality of perception : general awareness.—*n.* **panaesthetism** (*-ēs'* or *es'thi-tizm*). [Gr. *aisthēsis,* perception.]

Panagia. Same as **Panhagia.**

panama, *pan-ə-mä', n.* a republic, town, and isthmus of Central America : **panama (hat),** a hand-plaited hat made, not in Panama but in Ecuador, of plaited strips of the leaves of a South American cyclanthaceous plant (*Carludovica palmata*): an imitation thereof.—Also *adj.*—*n.* and *adj.* **Panamanian** (*-mä'ni-ən*). [Sp. *Panamá.*]

Pan-American, *pan-ə-mer'i-kən, adj.* including all America or Americans, North and South.—*n.* **Pan-Amer'icanism.**

Pan-Anglican, *pan-ang'gli-kən, adj.* representing or including all who hold the doctrines and polity of the Anglican Church.

panaritium, *pan-ə-rish'i-əm, n.* a whitlow. [L.L. *panāricium* for *parōnychium*—Gr. *parōnychiā*—*para,* beside, *onyx, -ychos,* nail.]

panarthritis, *pan-är-thrī'tis, n.* inflammation involving all the structures of a joint.

panary, *pan'ə-ri, adj.* of or pertaining to bread.—*n.* a bread store. [L. *pānārius*—*pānis,* bread.]

Panathenaea, *pan-ath-i-nē'ä, n.pl.* the chief national festival of ancient Athens—the lesser held annually, the greater every fourth year.— *adjs.* **Panathenae'an, Panathenā'ic.** [Gr. *Panathēnaia.*]

Panax, *pan'aks,* or *pān', n.* a genus of the aralia family. [Gr. *panax,* a name for various healing plants ; see **panacea.**]

pancake, pan-loaf, &c. See **pan.**

pan-handle. See **pan.**

pance. See **pansy.**

Panchatantra, *pun-chä-tunt'rä, n.* the oldest extant Sanskrit collection of beast-fables, in five books. [Sans., five books.]

pancheon, panchion, *pan'shən, n.* a coarse earthenware pan. [App. conn. with **pan** ; perh. influenced by **puncheon.**]

panchromatic, *pan-krō-mat'ik, adj.* equally or suitably sensitive to all colours : rendering all colours in due intensity.—*n.* **panchro'matism.** [Gr. *chrōma, -atos,* colour.]

pancratium, *pan-krā'shi-əm, n.* a combination of boxing and wrestling.—*adj.* **pancrā'tian.**—*n.* **pancrā'tiast** (*-shi-ast*), a competitor or victor in the pancratium.— *adj.* **pancratic** (*-krat'ik*), of the pancratium : excelling all round in athletics or accomplishments : of a lens, adjustable to different degrees of magnification.—*n.* **pan'cratist.** [Gr. *pankration*—*kratos,* strength.]

pancreas, *pan(g)'kri-as, n.* the sweetbread, a large gland discharging into the duodenum and containing islands of endocrine gland tissue.—*adj.* **pancreat'ic.**—*ns.* **pan'creatin,** the pancreatic juice ; **pancreatīt'is,** inflammation of the pancreas. [Gr. *pās, pān,* all, *kreas, -atos,* flesh.]

pand, *pand, n.* (*Scot.*) the valance of a bed. [Cf. O.Fr. *pandre,* to hang.]

panda, *pan'dä, n.* a remarkable raccoon-like animal (*Ailurus fulgens*) of the Himalaya.—**giant panda,** a larger beast (*Ailuropus melanoleucus*) of Tibet, apparently linking the panda with the bears. [Said to be its name in Nepal.]

Pandanus, *pan-dä'nəs, n.* the screw-pine, the typical genus of the **Pandanā'ceae,** a family of trees and bushes akin to the bulrushes and bur-reeds.—*adj.* **pandanā'ceous.** [Malay *pandan.*]

pandar. See **pander.**

pandation, *pan-dä'shən, n.* warping. [L. *pandātiō, -ōnis*—*pandāre, -ātum,* to bend.]

Pandean, *pan-dē'ən, adj.* of the god Pan : of Pan-

Neutral vowels in unaccented syllables : *el'ə-mənt, in'fənt, ran'dəm*

pipes.—**Pandean pipes**, **Pan-pipes**. [Irregularly formed from *Pān*.]

pandect, *pan′dekt*, *n.* a treatise covering the whole of any subject: (in *pl.*, **Pandects**) the digest of Roman law made by command of the Emperor Justinian in the 6th century.—*n.* **pandect′ist**. [L. *pandecta*—Gr. *pandektēs*—*pās, pān*, all, *dechesthai*, to receive.]

pandemic, *pan-dem′ik*, *adj.* incident to a whole people, epidemic over a wide area.—*n.* a pandemic disease.—*n.* **pandemia** (-*dē′mi-ä*), a widespread epidemic.—*adj.* **pande′mian**, vulgar: sensual. [Gr. *pandēmios*—*dēmos*, people.]

Pandemonium, *pan-di-mō′ni-əm*, *n.* the great hall of evil spirits, described in *Paradise Lost*, I. 710 ff.: **pandemonium**, any very disorderly or noisy place or assembly: tumultuous uproar.—*adjs.* **Pandemō′niac**, **Pandemoni′acal**, **Pandemō′-nian**, **Pandemonic** (-*mon′ik*). [Gr. *pās, pān*, all, *daimōn*, a spirit.]

pander, *pan′dər*, *n.* one who procures for another the means of gratifying his base passions: a pimp.—*v.t.* to play the pander for.—*v.i.* to act as a pander: to minister to the passions.—*ns.* **pan′deress**, a procuress; **pan′derism**, the employment or practices of a pander.—*adjs.* **pan′derly**, (*Shak.*) acting as a pander; **pan′derous**.—Also **pan′dar**, &c. [*Pandarus*, in the story of Troilus and Cressida as told by Boccaccio (*Filostrato*), Chaucer, and Shakespeare.]

pandermite, *pan-dər′mīt*, *n.* a hydrogen calcium borate found massive at *Panderma* on the Sea of Marmora.

pandiculation, *pan-dik-ū-lā′shən*, *n.* the act of stretching and yawning. [L. *pandiculārī*, *-ātus*, to stretch oneself.]

Pandion, *pan-dī′on*, *n.* the osprey genus. [Gr. *Pandiōn*, father of Procne and Philomela.]

pandit. Same as **pundit**.

Pandora, *pan-dō′rä*, *n.* the first woman, made for Zeus in order to punish man for the theft by Prometheus of heavenly fire, given a box from which escaped and spread all the ills of human life. [Gr. *pās, pān*, all, *dōron*, a gift.]

pandora, *pan-dō′rä*, **pandore**, *pan-dōr′*, *n.* an ancient Eastern musical instrument like a long-necked lute with (commonly) three strings: a bandore.—*n.* **pandū′ra**, a pandora: a Neapolitan instrument like a mandoline with eight metal wires, played with a quill.—*adjs.* **pan′dūrate**, **-d**, **pandū′riform**, fiddle-shaped. [Gr. *pandoura*, a 3-stringed instrument, fancifully connected with *Pān*, but probably an Eastern word; cf. **bandore**, **banjo**, **mandoline**.]

pandore, *pan′dōr*, *n.* an esteemed variety of oysters formerly got at Prestonpans on the Firth of Forth. [Said to be from the *doors* of the salt-*pans*, where they were found.]

pandour, *pan′dŏŏr*, *n.* an 18th-century Croatian foot-soldier in the Austrian service: a robber.—Also **pan′door**. [Fr.,—Serbo-Croat *pàndūr*—L.L. *banderius*, follower of a banner.]

pandowdy, *pan-dow′di*, *n.* (*U.S.*) a kind of apple pie or pudding. [Origin unknown.]

pandy, *pan′di*, *n.* a stroke on the palm as a school punishment.—*v.t.* to slap. [L. *pande*, hold out, imper. of *pandēre*.]

pandy, *pan′di*, *n.* (*coll., obs.*) an insurgent sepoy in the Indian Mutiny. [Said to be from *Pande*, a common surname.]

pane, *pān*, *n.* (*obs.*) a piece of cloth: a piece of cloth pieced together with others, or separated from others by slashing: a rectangular compartment: a panel: a slab of window glass: a flat side or face: a length of wall: the side of a quadrangle: a rectangular piece of ground.—*v.t.* to insert panes or panels in.—*adj.* **paned** (*pānd*), composed of panes or small squares: variegated. [Fr. *pan*—L. *pannus*, a cloth, a rag.]

pane. Same as **pean** (1, 2), **peen**.

panegoism, *pan-eg′ō-izm*, *n.* solipsism. [Gr. *egō*, I.]

panegyric, *pan-i-jir′ik*, *n.* a eulogy: laudation.—*adjs.* **panegyr′ic**, **-al**.—*adv.* **panegyr′ically**.—*n.* **panegyr′icon**, in the Greek Church, a collection of sermons for festivals.—*v.t.* **pan′egyrise** (or

-ej′ər-), to write or pronounce a panegyric on: to praise highly.—*ns.* **pan′egyrist** (or *-jir′*, or *-ej′ər-*); **pan′egyry**, a great assembly: a religious festival. [Gr. *panēgyrikos*, fit for a national festival—*pās, pān*, all, *agyris* (*agorā*), an assembly.]

paneity, *pa-nē′i-ti*, *n.* the state of being bread. [L. *pānis*, bread.]

panel, *pan′l*, *n.* (*obs.*) a cloth under a saddle: a crude form of saddle: a rectangular piece of any material: a compartment: a bordered rectangular area: a thin flat piece sunk below the general surface of a door, shutter, wainscot, or the like, often with a raised border: a compartment or hurdle of a fence: a strip of material inserted in a dress: a slip of parchment: such a slip containing a list of names, esp. of jurors: a jury: a list of doctors available for the purpose of national health insurance: such a doctor's list of patients: (*Scots law*) an accused person or persons (in *sing.*): a thin board on which a picture is painted: a large long photograph.—*v.t.* to furnish with a pane or panels: (*Scots law*) to put on trial:—*pr.p.* **pan′elling**; *pa.t.* and *pa.p.* **pan′elled**.—*n.* **pan′elling**, panel-work.—**panel doctor**, a doctor who is on the panel or has a panel; **panel saw**, a saw for cutting very thin wood; **panel working**, a method of working a coal-mine by dividing it into compartments. [O.Fr.,—L.L. *pannellus*—L. *pannus*, a cloth.]

pang, *pang*, *n.* a violent but not long-continued pain: a painful emotion.—*v.t.* to inflict a pang on.—*adjs.* **pang′ing**, (*Shak.*) painful; **pang′less**. [Possibly a form of **prong**.]

pang, *pāng*, *v.t.* (*Scot.*) to stuff, cram.—*adj.* stuffed, crammed, crowded: tight.—*adj.* **pang′-full′**, **-fu′′**, filled full. [Origin unknown.]

pangamy, *pan(g)′gə-mi*, *n.* random mating.—*adj.* **pangamic** (*pan-gam′ik*). [Gr. *gamos*, marriage.]

pangenesis, *pan-jen′i-sis*, *n.* Darwin's theory that every cell of the body contributes gemmules to the germ-cells and so shares in the transmission of inherited characters.—*n.* **pan′gen**, **-gene** (-*jēn*), a hypothetical unit of living matter.—*adj.* **pangenet′ic**. [Gr. *genesis*, production.]

Pan-German, *pan-jər′mən*, *adj.* pertaining to or including all Germans.—*n.* **Pan-Ger′manism**, a movement for a Greater Germany or union of all German peoples.

pangolin, *pang-gō′lin*, *n.* the scaly ant-eater, an edentate (Manis) of Asia and Africa. [Malay *peng-gōling*, roller, from its habit of rolling up.]

pangrammatist, *pan-gram′ə-tist*, *n.* one who contrives verses or sentences containing all the letters of the alphabet. [Gr. *gramma*, *-atos*, letter.]

Panhagia, **Panagia**, *pan-(h)ä-gi-ä*, *adj.* all-holy, an epithet of the Virgin in the Eastern Church: a cut loaf elevated in her honour: a medallion of the Virgin worn by bishops. [Gr. *hagios*, holy.]

panharmonicon, *pan-här-mon′i-kon*, *n.* a mechanical musical instrument mimicking an orchestra.

panhellenic, *pan-hel-ēn′ik*, or *-en′*, *adj.* pertaining to all Greece: including all Greeks.—*ns.* **panhellē′nion**, or (L.) **panhellē′nium**, a council representing all the sections of the Greeks; **panhell′enism** (-*ən-izm*), a movement or aspiration for Greek union; **panhell′enist**. [Gr. *Hellēnikos*, Greek—*Hellas*, Greece.]

panic, *pan′ik*, *n.* frantic or sudden fright: contagious fear: great terror without any visible ground or foundation: a state of terror about investments, impelling men to rush and sell what they possess.—*adj.* relating or due to the god Pan: of the nature of a panic: inspired by panic.—*v.t.* to throw into a panic.—*v.i.* to be struck by panic:—*pr.p.* **pan′icking**; *pa.t.* and *pa.p.* **pan′-icked**.—*n.* **pan′ic-bolt**, an easily moved bolt for emergency exits.—*adj.* **pan′icky**, inclined to, affected by, resulting from, or of the nature of, panic.—*n.* **pan′ic-mong′er**, one who creates or fosters panics.—*adjs.* **pan′ic-strick′en**, **-struck**, struck with a panic or sudden fear. [Gr. *pānikos*, belonging to Pan; *pānikon* (*deima*), panic (fear), fear associated with the god Pan.]

panic, *pan′ik*, *n.* any grass of the genus Panicum or of various closely related genera (also **pan′ic-**

grass'): the edible grain of some species.—Also **pan'ick, pann'ick.**—*n.* pan'icle, a raceme whose branches are themselves racemes: (loosely) a lax irregular inflorescence.—*adjs.* **pan'icled, panic'-ūlate, -d,** furnished with, arranged in, or like panicles.—*adv.* panic'ūlately.—*n.* **Pan'icum,** a large genus of grasses having the one- or two-flowered spikelets in spikes, racemes, or panicles —including several of the millets. [L. *pānicum*, Italian millet.]

panification, *pan-i-fi-kā'shən, n.* conversion into bread. [L. *pānis*, bread, *facĕre*, to make.]

panim, a Miltonic spelling of **paynim.**

Panionic, *pan-ī-on'ik, adj.* of or including all Ionians.

panisk, panisc, *pan'isk, n.* an inferior god, attendant on Pan. [Gr. *Pāniskos*, dim. of *Pān.*]

panislam, *pan-iz'lăm, n.* the whole Mohammedan world: panislamism.—*adj.* **panislam'ic.**—*ns.* **panis'lamism,** an aspiration or movement for the union of all Mohammedans; **panis'lamist.**

Panjabi. Same as **Punjabi.**

panjandrum, *pan-jan'drəm, n.* an imaginary figure of great power and importance, a burlesque potentate, from the Grand Panjandrum in a string of nonsense made up by Samuel Foote.—Also **panjan'darum.**

panlogism, *pan'lō-jizm, n.* the theory that the universe is an outward manifestation of the Logos.

panmixia, *pan-mik'si-ä, n.* (*biol.*) cessation of natural selection, as on a useless organ. [Gr. *mixis*, mixing.]

pannage, *pan'ij, n.* food picked up by swine in the woods, mast: the right to pasture swine in a forest. [O.Fr. *pasnage* — L.L. *pastiōnăticum* — *pascĕre*, *pastum*, to feed.]

pannelled, *pan'ld, v.t.* (*p.a.t.*) conjectured to be a misprint for *spanielled*, i.e. followed or fawned on as by a spaniel (Shak., *Ant. and Cle.*, IV. xii. 26).

pannicle, *pan'i-kl*, **panniculus,** *pə-nik'ū-ləs, n.* a thin, sheet-like investment. [L. *panniculus*, dim. of *pannus*, a cloth.]

pannier, *pan'yər*, or *pan'i-ər, n.* a provision-basket: a basket carried on the back: one of a pair of baskets slung over a pack-animal's back: (*archit.*) a sculptured basket: a contrivance for puffing out a woman's dress at the hips: the part so puffed out: a piece of basket-work for protecting archers, or, when filled with gravel or sand, for forming and protecting dikes, embankments, &c.: (*mil.*) a covered basket of medicines and surgical instruments, hence (blunderingly) an ambulance. —*adj.* **pann'iered.** [Fr. *panier*—L. *pānārium*, a bread-basket—*pānis*, bread.]

pannikell, *pan'i-kel, n.* (*Spens.*) the skull. [pan-nicle.]

pannikin. See **pan.**

pannose, *pan'ōs adj.* (*bot.*) like felt. [L. *pannōsus*—*pannus*, cloth.]

panocha, *pä-nō'chä, n.* a Mexican coarse sugar. [Sp.]

panoistic, *pan-ō-is'tik, adj.* (*entom.*) of an ovary, producing ova only, not yolk-forming cells—opp. to *meroistic*. [Gr. *ōion*, an egg.]

panomphaean, *pan-om-fē'ən, adj.* all-oracular, an epithet of Zeus: applied (after Rabelais) to the word drink. [Gr. *omphē*, a divine voice.]

panophobia, *pan-ō-fō'bi-ä, n.* a form of melancholia marked by groundless fears: erroneously used for **pantophobia.** [Gr. *Pān*, the god who inspired fears, *phobos*, fear.]

panophthalmitis, *pan-of-thal-mī'tis, n.* inflammation of the whole eye. [Gr. *ophthalmos*, eye.]

panoply, *pan'ə-pli, n.* complete armour: a full suit of armour: full or brilliant covering or array.— *adj.* **pan'oplied,** in panoply. [Gr. *panopliā*, full armour of a hoplite—*hopla* (pl.), arms.]

panopticon, *pan-op'ti-kon, n.* a prison in which all prisoners can be watched from one point: an exhibition room. [Gr. *optikon* (neut. adj.), for seeing.]

panorama, *pan-ə-rä'mä, n.* a wide or complete view: a picture disposed around the interior of a room, viewed from within in all directions:

a picture unrolled and made to pass before the spectator.—*adj.* **panoramic** (*-ram'ik*). [Gr. *horā-ma*, a view, from *horaein*, to see.]

panpharmacon, *pan-fär'mə-kon, n.* a universal remedy. [Gr. *pharmakon*, a drug.]

Pan-Presbyterian, *pan-prez-bi-tē'ri-ən, adj.* of, including, or representing all Presbyterians.

panpsychism, *pan-sik'izm, n.* the theory that all nature has a psychic side.—*n.* **panpsych'ist.**—*adj.* **panpsychist'ic.**

pansexualism, *pan-seks'ū-əl-izm, n.* the view that all mental activity is derived from sexual instinct. —*adj.* **pansex'ual.**—*n.* **pansex'ualist.**

Pan-Slav, *pan'-släv', adj.* of, including, or representing all Slavs.—*adj.* **Pan-Slav'ic.**—*ns.* **Pan'-Slav'ism,** a movement for the union of all Slav peoples; **Pan-Slav'ist.**—*adj.* **Pan-Slavon'ic.**

pansophy, *pan'sə-fi, n.* universal knowledge.—*adjs.* **pansophic** (*-sof'ik*), **-al.**—*ns.* **pan'sophism; pan'-sophist.** [Gr. *sophiā*, wisdom.]

panspermatism, *pan-spər'mə-tizm*, **panspermism,** *-mizm*, **panspermy,** *-mi, ns.* the doctrine of the widespread diffusion of germs, accounting for apparent spontaneous generation—*adjs.* **pan-spermat'ic, pansper'mic.**—*ns.* **pansper'matist, pansper'mist.** [Gr. *sperma*, *-atos*, seed.]

pansy, *pan'zi, n.* a name for various species of violet, esp. the heart's-ease (*Viola tricolor*) and garden kinds derived from it, as well as other species with up-turned side petals and large leafy stipules: a soft bluish-purple: an effeminate or namby-pamby man: a male homosexual.—Also (*obs.*: *Spens.*, &c.) **pance, paunce, pawnce** (*päns, pawns*).—*adj.* bluish-purple: effeminate.—*adj.* **pan'sied.** [Fr. *pensée*—*penser*, to think—L. *pēn-sāre*, to weigh.]

pant-. See **pan-.**

pant, *pant, v.i.* to gasp for breath: to run gasping: to throb: to wish ardently, to long, to yearn: to bulge and shrink successively, as ships' hulls, &c. —*v.t.* to gasp out.—*n.* **pant,** a gasping breath: a throb.—*n.* and *adj.* **pant'ing.**—*adv.* **pant'ingly.** [Apparently related to O.Fr. *pantoisier*, to pant.]

pant, *pănt, n.* (*Northern*) a public fountain: a puddle by a midden. [Origin obscure.]

pantable, *pan'tə-bl.* Same as **pantofle.**

pantagamy, *pan-tag'ə-mi, n.* a word that ought to mean universal bachelorhood, applied with unconscious irony to the universal marriage of the Perfectionists, in which every man in the community is the husband of every woman. [Gr. *gamos*, marriage, *agamiā*, bachelorhood.]

pantagraph. See **pantograph.**

Pantagruelism, *pan-tə-grōō'əl-izm, -tag'roo-, n.* the theories and practice of *Pantagruel* as described by Rabelais (*d.* 1553)—burlesque ironical buffoonery as a cover for serious satire.—*adj.* and *n.* **Panta-gruelian** (*-el'i-ən*).—*ns.* **Pantagruel'ion,** a magic herb, hemp; **Pantagru'elist** (or *-tag'roo-*).

pantaleon, *pan-tal'i-on, n.* a very large dulcimer invented about 1700 by *Pantaleon* Hebenstreit.

pantalets, *pan-tə-lets', n.pl.* long frilled drawers, worn by women and children in the first half of the 19th century: a detachable ruffle for these, or one simulating these: extended to various trouser-like garments worn by women.—Also **pantalettes.**—*adj.* **pantalett'ed.** [Dim. of **pan-taloons.**]

Pantaloon, *pan-tə-lōōn',* or *pan', n.* a character in Italian comedy, and afterwards in pantomime, a lean old man (originally a Venetian) more or less a dotard: **pantaloon,** (*Shak.*) a feeble old man: (in *pl.*) various kinds of trousers worn by or suggesting the stage pantaloon, as wide breeches of the Restoration, later combined breeches and stockings, later 18th-century trousers fastened below the calf or under the shoe, or (esp. in *U.S.*) trousers generally.—*n.* **pan'talon,** a garment in a quadrille.—*adj.* **pantalooned'.**—*n.* **pantaloon'-ery,** buffoonery. [Fr. *pantalon*—It. *pantalone*, from St *Pantaleone*, a favourite saint of the Venetians.]

pantechnicon, *pan-tek'ni-kon, n.* (*orig.*) a building in London intended for the sale of all kinds of artistic work, turned into a furniture-store: a furniture-van (in full **pantech′nicon-van′**). [Gr. *technē*, art.]

panter. See pantler.

pantheism, *pan′thē-izm*, *n.* the doctrine that identifies God with the universe: (*rare*) the worship of all gods.—*n.* **pan′theist**.—*adjs.* **panthēist′ic, -al**. —*ns.* **panthēol′ogist; panthēol′ogy**, a synthesis of all religions and the knowledge of all gods; **Pantheon** (*pan-thē′on, pan′thi-on*), a temple of all the gods, esp. the rotunda erected by Hadrian at Rome (on the site of Agrippa's of 27 B.C.), now the church of Santa Maria Rotonda, a burial-place of great Italians: a building serving as a general burial-place or memorial of the great dead, as Sainte Geneviève at Paris: an 18th-century place of amusement in London (Oxford Street): all the gods collectively: a complete mythology. [Gr. *theos*, a god, *pantheion*, a Pantheon.]

panther, *pan′thər*, *n.* a leopard, esp. a large one, formerly believed to be a different species: (*U.S.*) a puma—*fem.* **pan′theress**.—*adjs.* **pan′therine** (*-īn*), **pan′therish**. [Gr. *panthēr*.]

pantile, *pan′tīl*, *n.* a roofing tile whose cross-section forms an ogee curve: a tile concave or convex in cross-section: (*obs.*) a flat paving tile.—*adj.* (*obs. slang*) dissenting—chapels being often roofed with these.—*adj.* **pan′tiled**.—*n.* **pan′tiling**. [**pan, tile**.]

pantine, *pan′tēn*, *n.* (*obs.*) a pasteboard jumping-jack, fashionable in the 18th century. [Fr. *pantine*, afterwards *pantin*.]

pantisocracy, *pant-is-ok′rə-si*, or *-īs-*, *n.* a community (planned by Coleridge, Southey, and Lovell) in which all should have equal power.— *n.* **pantis′ocrat**.—*adj.* **pantisocrat′ic**. [Gr. *pās, pantos*, all, *isos*, equal, *krateein*, to rule.]

pantler, *pant′lər*, *n.* (*Shak.*) the officer in a great family who had charge of the bread and other provisions.—Also **pant′er**. [Fr. *panetier*—L. *pānis*, bread.]

pantofle, pantoffle, pantoufle, *pan′tof-l, -tof′l, tōōf′l*, *n.* a slipper: a high chopin: an overshoe.— Also **pantable** (*pan′tə-bl*).—**on one's pantables**, on one's dignity, high horse, lofty in manner. [Fr. *pantoufle*.]

pantograph, *pan′tə-gräf*, *n.* a jointed framework of rods for copying drawings, plans, &c., on the same, or a different, scale: a similar framework for other purposes, as for collecting a current from an overhead wire.—*n.* **pantographer** (*-tog′rə-fər*).—*adjs.* **pantographic** (*-tō-graf′ik*), **-al**.—*n.* **pantog′raphy**. —Also (*faulty*) **pan′tagraph, &c.** [Gr. *graphein*, to write.]

pantomime, *pan′tə-mīm*, *n.* (*hist.*) a Roman actor in dumb show: a play or an entertainment in dumb show: a theatrical entertainment, usually about Christmas, developed out of this, no longer in dumb show, with showy scenery, topical allusions, songs of the day, buffoonery and dancing strung loosely upon a nursery story, formerly ending with a transformation scene and a harlequinade: dumb show.—*adj.* of pantomime: pantomimic. —*adjs.* **pantomimic** (*-mim′ik*), **-al**.—*adv.* **pantomim′ically**.—*n.* **pan′tomimist**, an actor in or writer of pantomime. [L. *pantomīmus*—Gr. *pantomīmos*, imitator of all—*mīmos*, an imitator.]

panton, *pan′tən*, *n.* (*Scot.*) a slipper.—*n.* **pan′tonshoe′**, a horse-shoe for curing a narrow and hoofbound heel. [App. conn. with **pantofle**.]

pantophagy, *pan-tof′ə-ji*, *n.* omnivorousness.—*n.* **pantoph′agist**.—*adj.* **pantoph′agous** (*-gəs*). [Gr. *phagein*, to eat.]

pantophobia, *pan-tə-fō′bi-ä*, *n.* morbid fear of everything: (by confusion with **panophobia**) causeless fear. [Gr. *pās, pantos*, all, *phobos*, fear.]

pantopragmatic, *pan-tə-prag-mat′ik*, *adj.* meddling in everybody's business.—*n.* a universal busybody. —*n.* (treated as *sing.*) **pantopragmat′ics**, the science of universal benevolent interference. [From Peacock's imaginary society (*Gryll Grange*)—Gr. *pās, pantos*, all, *pragmata* (pl.), business.]

pantoscope, *pan′tə-skōp*, *n.* a panoramic camera: a very wide-angled photographic lens.—*adj.* **pantoscopic** (*-skop′ik*), giving a wide range of vision: bifocal. [Gr. *skopeein*, to look at.]

pantothenic, *pan-tō-then′ik*, *adj.* lit. from all quarters: applied to an acid, a member of the vitamin B_2 complex, so ubiquitous that the effects of its deficiency in man are not known. [Gr. *pantothen*, from everywhere.]

pantoun, *pan-tōōn′*, properly **pantun**, *pan-tōōn′*, *n.* a verse-form orig. Malay, quatrains rhyming *ab ab, b c b c*, &c., returning to rhyme *a* at the end. [Malay.]

pantry, *pan′tri*, *n.* a room or closet for provisions and table furnishings, or where plate, knives, &c., are cleaned.—*ns.* **pan′trymaid; pan′tryman**. [Fr. *paneterie*—L.L. *pānitāria*—L. *pānis*, bread.]

pants, *pants*, *n.pl.* (chiefly *U.S.*) trousers: (*vulg.*) drawers.—*n.pl.* **pant′ies**, (*vulg.*) very short drawers for children and women. [**pantaloons**.]

paolo, *pä′ō-lō*, *n.* an obsolete papal silver coin, worth about fivepence:—*pl.* **pa′oli** (*-lē*). [It. *Paolo*, Paul, i.e. Pope Paul V.]

pap, *pap*, *n.* soft food for infants, as of bread boiled with milk (often *fig.*): mash: pulp.—*v.t.* to feed with pap.—*ns.* **pap′-boat**, a boat-shaped vessel for pap; **pap′meat**, soft food for infants.—*adj.* **papp′y**.—*n.* **pap′spoon**. [Imit.]

pap, *pap*, *n.* a nipple: in place-names, a round conical hill. [App. Scand.]

papa, *pə-pä′* (*U.S. pä′pə*), *n.* (old-fashioned hypocoristic and genteel) father: (*pä′pä*; *obs.*) a pope: a priest of the Greek Church. [Partly through Fr. *papa*, partly directly from L.L. *pāpa*, Gr. hypocoristic *papās, pappās*, father.]

papacy, *pä′pə-si*, *n.* the office of pope: a pope's tenure of office: papal government. [L.L. *pāpātia* —*pāpa*, pope.]

papain, *pə-pä′in*, *n.* a digestive enzyme in the juice of papaw (Carica) fruits and leaves. [Sp. *papaya*, papaw.]

papal, *pä′pl*, *adj.* of the pope or the papacy.—*v.t.* and *v.i.* **pa′palise**, to render or become papal or papalist.—*ns.* **pa′palism**, the papal system; **pa′palist**, a supporter of the pope and of the papal system.—*adv.* **pa′pally**—**papal cross**, a cross with three cross-bars. [L.L. *pāpālis*—*pāpa*, pope.]

papaprelatist, *pä-pə-prel′ə-tist*, *n.* (*Scott*) a supporter of popish prelates.

Papaver, *pə-pä′vər*, *n.* the poppy genus, giving name to the family **Papaverā′ceae**.—*adj.* **papaveraceous** (*pə-pav′*, or *-pāv-ə-rā′shəs*) of the poppy family.—*n.* **papaverine** (*pə-pav′ə-rēn, -rīn*, or *-pāv′*), an alkaloid got from poppy juice.—*adj.* **papaverous** (*-pav′* or *-pāv′*), resembling or having the qualities of the poppy. [L. *papāver*, the poppy.]

papaw, *pə-paw′, paw′paw*, *n.* the tree *Carica papaya*, or its fruit, native to South America, but common in the tropics, the trunk, leaves, and fruit yielding papain, the leaves forming a powerful anthelmintic: the tree *Asimina triloba* (of the custard-apple family), or its fruit, native to the U.S.A.—Also **paw′paw, papaya** (*pə-pä′yä*). [Sp. *papayo* (tree), *papaya* (fruit), app. from Carib.]

pape, *päp*, *n.* a Scots form of pope.—*adj.* **pāp′ish**, popish.—*n.* (*dial.* and *illit.*, by confusion with papist) a papist.—*n.* **pāp′isher**.

paper, *pä′pər*, *n.* a material made in thin sheets as an aqueous deposit from linen rags, esparto, wood-pulp, or other form of cellulose, used for writing and printing, wrapping and other purposes: sometimes extended to similar materials not so made, as papyrus, rice-paper, to the substance of which some wasps build their nests, to cardboard, and even to tin-foil ('silver paper'): a piece of paper: a written or printed document or instrument, note, receipt, bill, bond, deed, &c.: a newspaper: an essay or literary contribution, esp. one read before a society: a set of examination questions: free passes of admission to a theatre, &c., also the persons so admitted: paper-money: paper-hangings for walls: a wrapping of paper: a quantity of anything wrapped in or attached to a paper.—*adj.* consisting or made of paper: papery: on paper.—*v.t.* to cover with paper: to fold in paper: to treat in any way by means of paper, as to sand-paper, &c.: to paste end-papers and fly-leaves to.—*ns.* **pa′per-back**, a book with paper cover; **pa′per-birch′,** an American birch with papery bark; **pa′per-case,** a box for writing materials, &c.; **pa′per-chase,** the game of hare and hounds, in which some runners (*hares*) set off across country strewing paper by which others (*hounds*) track them; **pa′per-cigar′,** (*obs.*) a cigarette; **pa′per-clip,** a clip of bent wire or the like, for holding papers together: a letter-clip; **pa′per-cloth,** a fabric prepared in the Pacific islands from the inner bark of the paper-mulberry; **pa′per-coal,** a lignite that splits into thin layers; **pa′per-cred′it,** credit given to a person because he shows that money is owing to him; **pa′per-cutter,** a paper-knife: a machine for cutting paper in sheets, for trimming the edges of books, &c.; **pa′per-day,** one of certain days in each term for hearing causes down in the paper or roll of business; **pa′per-enam′el,** an enamel for cards and fine note-paper.—*adj.* **pa′per-faced,** (*Shak.*) having a thin face like a sheet of paper: faced with paper.—*ns.* **pa′per-fastener,** a button with two blades that can be forced through papers and bent back; **pa′per-feeder,** an apparatus for delivering sheets of paper to a printing-press, &c.; **pa′per-file,** an appliance for filing papers; **pa′per-folder** (see **folder**); **pa′per-gauge,** a rule for measuring the type-face of matter to be printed, and the width of the margin; **pa′per-hanger,** one who papers walls.—*n.pl.* **pa′per-hangings,** paper for covering walls.—*ns.* **pa′pering,** the operation of covering with paper: the paper so used; **pa′per-knife,** a thin, flat blade for cutting open the leaves of books and other folded papers; **pa′per-maker,** a manufacturer of paper; **pa′per-making; pa′per-mar′bler,** one engaged in marbling paper; **pa′per-mill,** a mill where paper is made; **pa′per-mon′ey,** pieces of paper stamped or marked by government or by a bank, as representing a certain value of money, which pass from hand to hand instead of the coin itself; **pa′per-mul′berry,** a tree (*Broussonetia papyrifera*) of Eastern Asia and Polynesia, of the mulberry family, whose inner bark yields tapa cloth and paper-making material; **pa′per-mus′lin,** a glazed muslin; **pa′per-nau′tilus,** the argonaut (see **nautilus**); **pa′per-off′ice,** an office where state-papers are kept; **pa′per-pulp,** pulpy material for making paper; **paper-reed,** the papyrus; **pa′per-rul′er,** one who, or an instrument which, makes straight lines on paper; **pa′per-sail′or,** an argonaut; **pa′per-stain′er,** one who prepares paper-hangings: a poor author, scribbler; **pa′per-wash′ing,** (*phot.*) water in which prints have been washed; **pa′per-weight,** a small weight for keeping loose papers from being displaced.—*adj.* **pa′pery,** like paper.—**on paper,** planned, decreed, existing theoretically only. [A.Fr. *papir,* O.Fr. (Fr.) *papier*—L. *papȳrus* —Gr. *papyros,* papyrus.]

papeterie, *pap-ə-trē′,* n. a stationery-case. [Fr., stationery, paper-trade.]

Paphian, *pā′fi-ən,* adj. pertaining to *Paphos* in Cyprus, sacred to Aphrodite: lascivious.—*n.* a native of Paphos: a votary of Aphrodite: a whore.

papier-mâché, *pap′yā-mā′shā,* n. a material consisting of paper-pulp or of sheets of paper pasted together, treated so as to resemble varnished or lacquered wood or plaster.—*adj.* of papier-mâché. [Would-be French,—Fr. *papier* (see **paper**), *mâché,* chewed—L. *masticātus.*]

Papilio, *pə-pil′i-ō′,* n. the swallow-tailed butterfly genus, giving name to the family **Papilionidae** (*-on′i-dē*), in which all six legs are fully developed in both sexes.—*adj.* papilionā′ceous, of butter-flies: butterfly-like: of a form of corolla some-what butterfly-like, with a large posterior petal (*vexillum*), two side petals or wings (*alae*), and two anterior petals forming a keel (*carina*): of the **Papilionā′ceae,** a family of Leguminosae characterised by such a corolla, including pea, bean, clover, gorse, laburnum, &c. [L. *pāpiliō,* *-ōnis,* butterfly.]

papilla, *pə-pil′ä,* n. a small nipple-like protuber-ance: a minute elevation on the skin, esp. of the finger-tips and upper surface of the tongue, in

which a nerve ends: a protuberance at the base of a hair, feather, tooth, &c.: a minute conical protuberance as on the surface of a petal:—*pl.* **papill′ae** (*-ē*).—*adjs.* **papill′ar, papill′ary,** like, of the nature of, or having papillae; **papill′ate, -d, papillif′erous** (*pap-*), having papillae; **papill′iform,** in the form of a papilla.—*ns.* **papilli′tis,** inflammation of the head of the optic nerve; **papillō′ma,** a tumour formed by hypertrophy of a papilla or papillae, as a wart, &c.—*adjs.* **papillom′atous; pap′illōse,** full of papillae, warty—also **papill′ous; papill′ūlate,** finely papillose.—*n.* **papill′ūle,** a very small papilla. [L., dim. of *papula.*]

papillote, *pap′il-ōt,* n. a curl-paper. [Fr., app.— *papillon,* butterfly—L. *pāpiliō,* *-ōnis.*]

papish. See **pape.**

papist, *pā′pist,* n. an adherent of the pope: a name slightingly given to a Roman Catholic.—*n.* **pā′pism,** popery.—*adjs.* **pāpist′ic, -al,** pertaining to popery, or to the Church of Rome, its doctrines, &c.— *adv.* **pāpist′ically.**—*n.* **pā′pistry,** popery. [L.L. *pāpa,* pope.]

papoose, *pə-pōōs′,* n. a North American Indian child. [Narraganset *papoos.*]

pappus, *pap′əs,* n. (*bot.*) a ring or parachute of fine hair or down, representing the calyx limb, which grows above the seed and helps in wind-dis-semination in composites and some other plants: the downy beginnings of a beard.—*adjs.* **papp′ōse** (or *-ōs′*), **papp′ous.** [L. *pappus*—Gr. *pappos,* a grandfather, down, a pappus.]

paprika, *pap′ri-kä,* n. Hungarian red pepper, a species of Capsicum. [Hung.]

Papuan, *pap′ū-ən,* adj. pertaining to *Papua* or New Guinea.—*n.* a member of the black, dolicho-cephalic, frizzly-haired race inhabiting Papua, &c. [Malay *papuwa,* frizzled.]

papula, *pap′ū-lä,* **papule,** *pap′ūl,* ns. a pimple: a papilla:—*pl.* **pap′ūlae** (*-lē*), **pap′ules.**—*adj.* **pap′ūlar.**—*n.* **papūlā′tion,** the development of papules.—*adjs.* **pap′ūlose, pap′ūlous.** [L. *papula,* a pimple.]

papyrus, *pə-pī′rəs,* n. the paper-reed (*Cyperus Papyrus,* or kindred species), a tall plant of the sedge family, once common in Egypt: its pith cut in thin strips and pressed together as a writing material of the ancients: a manuscript on papyrus:—*pl.* **papy′ri** (*-rī*).—*adj.* **papyraceous** (*pap-i-rā′shəs*), papery.—*ns.* **papyrologist** (*pap-i-rol′ə-jist*); **papyrol′ogy,** the study of ancient papyri. [L. *papyrus*—Gr. *papyros;* probably Egyptian.]

par, *pär,* n. state of equality: equal value: norm or standard: state or value of bills, shares, &c., when they sell at exactly the price marked on them—i.e. without *premium* or *discount*: equality of condition: (*golf*) the number of strokes that should be taken for a hole or a round by perfect play, two putts being allowed on each green.— **above par,** at a premium, or at more than the nominal value; **at par,** at exactly the nominal value; **below par,** at a discount, or at less than the nominal value: out of sorts; **nominal par,** the value with which a bill or share is marked, or by which it is known; **par of exchange,** the value of currency of one country expressed in that of another; **par value,** value at par. [L. *pär,* equal.]

par, *pär,* n. Same as **parr.**

par, *pär,* n. a colloquial abbreviation of **paragraph.**

para, *pä′rä,* n. a small Turkish coin: the 40th part of a piastre: in Yugoslavia the 100th part of a dinar. [Turk. *pārah.*]

Pará, *pä-rä′,* n. a city, state, and estuary of Brazil. —**pará grass,** piassava; **pará nut,** Brazil nut; **pará rubber,** that got from *Hevea brasiliensis.*

para-, in composition, beside: faulty: disordered: abnormal: false: (*organic chem.*) having substituted atoms or groups attached to two opposite carbon atoms of the benzene ring—commonly represented by *p-.*—*n.* **pa′ra-compound.** [Gr. *para,* beside.]

parabaptism, *par-ə-bap′tizm,* n. uncanonical bap-tism.

parabasis, *pə-rab′ə-sis,* n. part of the Old Comedy

of Greece in which the chorus came forward and addressed the audience on behalf of the poet. [Gr., a going aside—*basis*, a going.]

parabema, *par-ə-bē'mə*, *n.* in Byzantine architecture, either the chapel of the prothesis or the diaconicon, when walled off from the bema :—*pl.* **parabe'mata**.—*adj.* **parabemat'ic.** [See bema.]

parable, *par'ə-bl*, *n.* a similitude : a fable or story of something which might have happened, told to illustrate some truth, or to make some duty clear : (*arch.*) a proverb : (*arch.*) discourse.—*v.t.* to represent by a parable.—*ns.* **parabola** (*pə-rab'ə-lä*), a curve, one of the conic sections, the intersection of a cone and a plane parallel to its side, or the locus of a point equidistant from a fixed point (the *focus*) and a fixed straight line (the *directrix*)—its equation with vertex as origin $y^2 = 4ax$: generalised to include any curve whose equation is $y^n = px^m$: —*pl.* **parab'olas**; **parab'ole** (*-lē*), in rhetoric, a similitude, simile, or metaphor.—*adjs.* **parabol'ic** (*par-ə-bol'ik*), **-al**, of or like a parable or a parabola or a parabole : expressed by a parable : belonging to, or of the form of, a parabola.—*adv.* **parabol'ically.**—*v.t.* **parab'olise**, to set forth by parable : to treat as a parable.—*ns.* **parab'olist**; **parab'oloid**, a surface or solid generated by the rotation of a parabola about its axis.—*adjs.* **parab'oloid, -al.** [Gr. *parabolē*, a placing alongside, comparison, parabola, &c.—*ballein*, to throw.]

parablepsis, *par-ə-blep'sis*, *n.* false vision : oversight.—Also **par'ablepsy.**—*adj.* **parablep'tic.** [Gr., looking askant—*blepein*, to see.]

parabolanus, *par-ə-bō-lā'nəs*, *n.* in the early Eastern Church, a layman who tended the sick. [Gr. *parabolos*, venturesome, exposing oneself.]

Paracelsian, *par-ə-sel'si-ən*, *adj.* of or relating to the famous German Swiss philosopher and physician, *Paracelsus* (1493-1541), or resembling his theories or practice. The name was coined for himself by Theophrastus Bombastus von Hohenheim, and apparently implied a claim to be greater than Celsus.

paracentesis, *par-ə-sen-tē'sis*, *n.* (*surg.*) tapping. [Gr. *parakentēsis*—*kenteein*, to pierce.]

parachronism, *par-ak'rən-izm*, *n.* an error in dating, esp. when anything is represented as later than it really was. [Gr. *chronos*, time.]

parachute, *par'ə-shōōt*, *n.* an apparatus like an umbrella for descending safely from a height : any structure serving a like purpose, as a pappus, a patagium.—*v.i.* to descend by parachute.—*n.pl.* **par'achute-troops'.**—*n.* **par'achutist.** [Fr. *parachute*—It. *para*, imper. of *parare*, to ward—L. *parāre*, to prepare, and Fr. *chute*, fall.]

paraclete, *par'ə-klēt*, *n.* an advocate or legal helper, or intercessor—applied to the Holy Ghost (John xiv. 26). [Gr. *paraklētos*—*parakaleein*, to call in, also to comfort—*kaleein*, to call.]

paracme, *pər-ak'mē*, *n.* the stage of decline or senescence after the culmination of development. [Gr. *akmē*, a point.]

paracrostic, *par-ə-kros'tik*, *n.* a poem whose initial letters reproduce its first verse.

paracusis, *par-ə-kū'sis*, *n.* disordered hearing. [Gr. *para*, beside, *akousis*, hearing.]

paracyanogen, *par-ə-sī-an'ə-jən*, *n.* a polymer of cyanogen.

parade, *pə-rād'*, *n.* show : display : ostentation : an assembling in order for exercise, inspection, &c. : a procession : ground for parade of troops : a public promenade : (*fencing*) a parry.—*v.t.* to show off : to thrust upon notice : to lead about and expose to public attention : to traverse in parade : to marshal in military order.—*v.i.* to march up and down as if for show : to pass in military order : to march in procession : to show off.—*n.* **parade'-ground.** [Fr.,—Sp. *parada*—*parar*, to halt—L. *parāre*, -*ātum*, to prepare.]

paradigm, *par'ə-dim*, *n.* an example, exemplar : (*gram.*) an example of the inflection of a word.—*adjs.* **paradigmatic** (*-dig-mat'ik*), **-al**.—*adv.* **paradigmat'ically.** [Fr. *paradigme*—Gr. *paradeigma*—*paradeiknynai*, to exhibit side by side—*deiknynai*, to show.]

paradise, *par'ə-dīs*, *n.* a park or pleasure-ground

esp. in ancient Persia : the garden of Eden : heaven : the abode (intermediate or final) of the blessed dead : any place of bliss : a garden : a parvis : a small private apartment.—*adjs.* **paradisaic** (*par-ə-dis-ā'ik*), **-al**, **paradisial** (*-dī'səl*), **paradisean** (*-dis-i-ən*), **paradisiac** (*dis'i-ak*, *diz'i-ak*), **paradisiacal** (*-dis-ī'ə-kl*), **paradisial** (*-dis'-diz'*), **paradisian** (*-dis'-, -diz'*), **paradisic** (*-dis'-, -diz'*).—*n.* **par'adise-fish**, a Chinese fresh-water fish (Macropodus), often kept in aquaria for its beauty of form and colouring. — **bird of paradise**, any bird of the family **Paradise'idae**, inhabitants chiefly of New Guinea, close akin to the crows but extremely gorgeous in plumage. [Gr. *paradeisos*, a park—O.Pers. *pairidaēza*, park.]

parados, *par'ə-dos*, *n.* earthworks protecting against a rear attack. [Pfx. *para-* as in **parachute**, and Fr. *dos*—L. *dorsum*, back.]

paradox, *par'ə-doks*, *n.* that which is contrary to received opinion : that which is apparently absurd but is or may be really true : a self-contradictory statement : paradoxical character.—*adj.* **paradox'al.**—*n.* **par'adoxer.**—*adj.* **paradox'ical.**—*adv.* **paradox'ically.**—*ns.* **paradox'icalness**; **Paradox'ides** (*-i-dēz*), a typically Middle Cambrian genus of trilobites, some very large (2 feet).—*adj.* **paradoxid'ian.**—*ns.* **par'adoxist**; **paradoxol'ogy**, utterance or maintaining of paradoxes ; **par'adoxy**, the quality of being paradoxical. [Gr. *paradoxos*, -*on*, contrary to opinion—*doxa*, opinion.]

paradoxure, *par-ə-dok'sūr*, *n.* a civet-like carnivore of Southern Asia and Malaysia, the palm-cat of India.—*adj.* **paradoxū'rine.** [Gr. *paradoxos*, paradoxical, *ourā*, tail.]

paraenesis, *parenesis*, *par-ēn'i-sis*, or -*en'*, *n.* exhortation.—*adjs.* **paraenetic** (*-net'ik*), **-al.** [Gr. *parainesis*—*aineein*, to commend.]

paraesthesia, *par-ēs-thē'si-ä*, or -*es-*, *n.* abnormal sensation. [Gr. *para*, beyond, *aisthēsis*, sensation.]

paraffin, *par'ə-fin*, *n.* originally, paraffin-wax—so named by its discoverer, Reichenbach, from its having little chemical affinity for other bodies : generalised to mean any saturated hydrocarbon of the methane series, gaseous, liquid, or solid, the general formula being C_nH_{2n+2} : paraffin-oil.—Also **par'affine.**—*v.t.* to treat with paraffin.—*ns.* **par'affin-oil'**, any of the mineral burning oils associated with the manufacture of paraffin, mixtures of liquid paraffin and other hydrocarbons ; **par'affin-scale'**, unrefined solid paraffin ; **par'affin-wax'**, a white transparent crystalline substance got by distillation of shale, coal, tar, wood, &c., a mixture of solid paraffins.—*adjs.* **paraffin'ic**, **par'affinoid**, **par'affiny. — liquid paraffin**, a liquid form of petrolatum, used as a mild laxative. [L. *parum*, little, *affīnis*, having affinity.]

paraffle, **parafle**, *pə-rä'fl*, *n.* (*Scot.*) pretentious display. [Cf. **paraph**.]

parage, *par'ij*, *n.* (*obs.*) lineage : high birth or rank : (*feudal law*) equality among persons of whom one does homage for all, the others holding of him. [Fr.]

paraglossa, *par-ə-glos'ä*, *n.* either of two appendages of the ligula in insects :—*pl.* **paragloss'ae** (*-ē*).—*adjs.* **paragloss'al**; **paragloss'ate.** [Gr. *glōssa*, tongue.]

paragnathous, *pər-ag'nə-thəs*, *adj.* having equal mandibles.—*n.* **parag'nathism.** [Gr. *para*, beside, *gnathos*, jaw.]

paragnosis, *par-ə-gnō'sis*, *n.* (*psych.*) wrong perception or understanding of sense-impressions. [Gr. *gnōsis*, knowing.]

paragoge, *par-ə-gō'jē*, -*gē*, *n.* an addition to the end of a word, as *t* in *against, amidst, amongst, whilst, d* in *drownd* (illiterate for *drown*).—*adjs.* **paragogic** (*-goj'ik*, -*gog'ik*), **-al.**—**paragogic future**, the cohortative tense in Hebrew—a lengthened form of the imperfect or future, usually confined to the first person, giving the sense of 'let me' or 'let us.' [Gr. *paragōgē*, a leading part, addition—*agein*, to lead.]

paragon, *par'ə-gon*, -*gən*, *n.* a model of perfection or supreme excellence : match, equal : (*Spens.*) mate : (*arch.*) rival : (*Spens.*) comparison : (*Spens.*)

emulation, competition: a diamond of 600 carats or more: (*obs.*) a black marble: (*obs.*) a camlet used for upholstering and dress: 20-point printing-type, intermediate between great-primer and double-pica.—*v.t.* to compare: to match: (*Shak.*) to surpass: (*Shak.*) to hold up as a paragon. [O.Fr. *paragon*—It. *paragone*, touchstone; origin obscure.]

paragonite, *par'ə-gən-it*, or *par-ag'*, *n.* a soda-mica, once mistaken for talc. [Gr. *paragōn*, misleading —*agein*, to lead.]

paragram, *par'ə-gram*, *n.* a play upon words by change of initial (or other) letter. — *n.* **paragramm'atist**, a punster. [Gr. (*skōmmata*) *para gramma*, (jokes) by letter.]

paragraph, *par'ə-gräf*, *n.* a sign (in ancient MSS. a short horizontal line, in the Middle Ages ⟨, now ¶, ℙ) marking off a section of a book, &c.: a distinct part of a discourse or writing marked by such a sign or now usually by indenting: a short passage, or a collection of sentences, with unity of purpose: a short separate item of news or comment in a newspaper.—*v.t.* to form into paragraphs: to write or publish paragraphs about.— *ns.* **par'agrapher**, **par'agraphist**, one who writes paragraphs, esp. for newspapers. — *adjs.* **paragraphic** (*-graf'*), **-al**. — *adv.* **paragraph'ically**. [Gr. *paragraphos*, written alongside—*graphein*, to write.]

paragraphia, *parə-graf'i-ä*, *n.* writing of wrong words and letters, owing to disease or injury.— *adj.* **paragraphic** (*-graf'ik*). [Gr. *para-*, indicating faultiness, *graphein*, to write.]

Paraguay, *par-ə-gwī'*, *-gwä'*, *n.* a country and river of South America.—**Paraguay tea**, maté.

paraheliotropic, *par-ə-hē-li-ō-trop'ik*, *adj.* (*bot.*) turning edgewise to the light.—*n.* **paraheliotropism** (*-ot'rə-pizm*). [Gr. *para*, beside, *hēlios*, sun, *tropos*, a turn—*trepein*, to turn.]

parakeet, **parrakeet**, *par'ə-kēt*, *n.* a small long-tailed parrot of various kinds.—Also **paroquet**, **parroquet** (*-ket*), **paraquito** (*pä-rä-kē'tō*). [Sp. *periquito*, It. *parrocchetto*, or O.Fr. *paroquet* (Fr. *perroquet*); the origin and relations of these are not determined.]

paraldehyde, *par-al'di-hīd*, *n.* a polymer, ($C_2H_4O)_3$, of acetaldehyde, used to induce sleep.

paraleipsis, **paralipsis**, *par-ə-līp'sis*, *-lip'*, *n.* (*rhet.*) a figure by which one fixes attention on a subject by pretending to neglect it, as ' I will not speak of his generosity,' &c.—*n.* **paral(e)ipom'enon**, a thing left out, added in supplement :—*pl.* **paral(e)ipom'ena**, esp. (in the Septuagint, &c.) the Books of Chronicles. [Gr. *paraleipsis*, *paraleipomenon* (neut. pr. part. pass.)—*paraleipein*, to leave aside—*leipein*, to leave.]

parallax, *par'ə-laks*, *n.* an apparent change in the position of an object caused by change of position in the observer: (*astron.*) the apparent change (measured angularly) in the position of a heavenly body when viewed from different points—when viewed from opposite points on the earth's surface this change is called the *daily* or *diurnal* or *geocentric parallax*; when viewed from opposite points of the earth's orbit, the *annual* or *heliocentric parallax*.—*adjs.* **parallac'tic**, **-al**. [Gr. *parallaxis*—*para*, beside, *allassein*, to change—*allos*, another.]

parallel, *par'ə-lel*, *adj.* extended in the same direction and equidistant in all parts: analogous, corresponding: alongside in time: (*mus.*) having a constant interval (major and minor being reckoned alike).—*n.* a parallel line: a line of latitude: an analogue, or like, or equal: an analogy: a tracing or statement of resemblances: a besieger's trench parallel to the outline of the place besieged: a printer's reference mark of two vertical lines: parallel arrangement.—*v.t.* to place so as to be parallel: to conform: to represent as parallel: to liken in detail: to find a parallel to: to match: to be or run parallel to.—*v.i.* to be or run parallel :— *pr.p.* **par'alleling**; *pa.t.* and *pa.p.* **par'alleled.**— *v.t.* **par'allelise**, to furnish a parallel to.—*ns.* **par'allelism**, state or fact of being parallel: resemblance in corresponding details: a balanced construction of a verse or sentence, where one

part repeats the form or meaning of the other: comparison: development along parallel lines: the theory or belief (in full **psychophysical parallelism**) that mind and matter do not interact but correspond; **par'allelist**, one who draws a parallel or comparison: a believer in psychophysical parallelism. — *adj.* **parallelis'tic**. — *adv.* **par'allelly**.—*adj.* **parallel-veined**, (*bot.*) having the main veins running side by side. — *adv.* **par'allelwise.**—**in parallel**, of electrical apparatus, so arranged that terminals of like polarity are connected together; **parallel bars**, a pair of fixed bars used in gymnastics; **parallel motion**, a name given to any linkage by which circular motion may be changed into straight-line motion; **parallel ruler** or **rulers**, rulers joined by two pivoted strips, for ruling parallel lines. [Gr. *parallēlos*, as if *par' allēloin*, beside each other.]

parallelepiped, *par-ə-lel-ep'i-ped* (or *-lel'*, or *-ə-pī'*), *n.* a solid figure bounded by six parallelograms, opposite pairs being identical and parallel.—Also **parallelepip'edon** (*pl.* **-a**), improperly **parallelopī'ped**, **parallelopī'pedon**. [Gr. *parallēlepipedon* —*parallēlos*, *epipedon*, a plane surface—*epi*, on, *pedon*, ground.]

parallelogram, *par-ə-lel'ō-gram*, *n.* a plane four-sided figure, the opposite sides of which are parallel and equal. — *adjs.* **parallelogrammat'ic**, **-al**, **parallelogramm'ic**, **-al**. — **parallelogram of forces**, a figure in which the direction and amount of two component forces are represented by two sides of a parallelogram, those of their resultant by the diagonal. [Gr. *parallēlogrammon* —*grammē*, a line.]

paralogism, *pə-ral'-ə-jizm*, *n.* false reasoning—also **paral'ogy**.—*v.i.* **paral'ogise** (*-jiz*), to reason falsely. [Gr. *paralogismos*—*logismos*—*logos*, reason.]

paralysis, *pə-ral'i-sis*, *n.* palsy, a loss of power of motion, or sensation, in any part of the body: deprivation of power of action.—*v.t.* **paralyse** (*par'ə-līz*), to afflict with paralysis: to deprive of power of action.—*n.* **paralys'er**—*adj.* **paralytic** (*par-ə-lit'ik*), of or pertaining to paralysis: afflicted with or inclined to paralysis.—*n.* one who is affected with paralysis. [Gr. *paralysis*, secret undoing, paralysis—*lyein*, to loosen.]

paramagnetic, *par-ə-mag-net'ik*, *adj.* magnetic in the ordinary sense—said of bodies that when freely suspended between the poles of a magnet place themselves parallel to the lines of force— opp. to *diamagnetic*.—*n.* **paramag'netism.**

paramastoid, *par-ə-mas'toid*, *adj.* situated near the mastoid, paroccipital.—*n.* a paramastoid process.

paramatta, **parramatta**, *par-ə-mat'ä*, *n.* a fabric like merino made of worsted and cotton. [App. from *Parramatta* in New South Wales.]

Paramecium, *par-ə-mē's(h)i-əm*, *n.* the slipper-animalcule, a slipper - shaped infusorian:—*pl.* **paramē'cia**. — Often misspelt **paramoecium**, **paramaecium**. [Gr. *paramēkēs*, long-shaped— *para*, alongside, *mēkos*, length.]

parament, *par'ə-mənt*, *n.* (*obs.*) a rich decoration, hanging, or robe. [L. *parāre*, to prepare.]

paramese, *pa-ram'i-sē*, *n.* (*Gr. mus.*) the string or tone next above the mese. [Gr. *paramesē*.]

parameter, *pə-ram'i-tər*, *n.* (*math.*) a line or quantity which serves to determine a point, line, figure, or quantity in a class of such things: a constant quantity in the equation of a curve: in conic sections, a third proportional to any diameter and its conjugate diameter: the latus rectum of a parabola: (*crystal.*) the intercept upon an axis of a crystal face chosen for purpose of reference (the *parametral plane*). — *adjs.* **param'etral**, **parametric** (*par-ə-met'rik*), **-al**. [Gr. *para*, beside, *metron*, measure.]

paramilitary, *par-ə-mil'i-tər-i*, *adj.* on military lines and intended to supplement the strictly military.

paramnesia, *par-am-nē'si-ä*, *n.* false memory. [Gr. *para*, and the root of *mimnēskein*, to remind.]

paramo, *pä'rä-mō*, *n.* a bare wind-swept elevated plain in South America:—*pl.* **par'amos**. [Sp. *páramo*.]

paramorph, *par'ə-morf*, *n.* (*min.*) a pseudomorph formed by a change in molecular structure without change of chemical composition. — *adj.* **para-morph'ic.**—*n.* **paramorph'ism.** [Gr. *morphē*, form.]

paramount, *par'ə-mownt, adj.* superior to all others : supreme :—opp. to *paravail.*—*n.* supreme chief : a superior. — *n.* **par'amount(t)cy.** — *adv.* **par'a-mountly.** [O.Fr. *paramont, par* (L. *per*) *à mont* (L. *ad montem*) ; see **amount.**]

paramour, *par'ə-mōōr, adv.* (*obs.*) by the way of love, as a lover, for love's sake, out of kindness.— *n.* a lover of either sex, formerly in an innocent, now usually in the illicit sense. [Fr. *par amour*, by or with love—L. *per amōrem.*]

paranephros, *par-ə-nef'ros, n.* the suprarenal gland, near the kidney.—*adj.* **paraneph'ric.** [Gr. *nephros*, kidney.]

paranete, *par-a-nē'tē, n.* (*Gr. mus.*) the string or tone next below the nete. [Gr. *paranētē.*]

parang, *pär'ang, n.* a heavy Malay knife. [Malay.]

paranitroaniline, *par-ə-nī-trō-an'i-lēn, n.* a nitro-derivative of aniline, used in dyeing.

paranoia, *par-ə-noi'ä, n.* a form of insanity charac-terised by fixed delusions, esp. of grandeur, pride, persecution.—Also (*rarely*) **paranoea** (*-nē'ä*).— *adj.* **paranoi'ac,** of paranoia.—*n.* a victim of paranoia.—Also **paranoe'ic, paranoic** (*-nō'ik*).— *adjs.* **par'anoid, paranoid'al,** resembling paranoia. [Gr. *paranoiä*—*noos,* mind.]

paranormal, *par-ə-nor'məl, adj.* abnormal, esp. psychologically.

paranthelion, *par-an-thē'li-on, n.* a diffuse whitish image of the sun, having the same altitude, at an angular distance of 90° to 140° :—*pl.* **paran-the'lia.** [Gr. *para,* beside, *anti,* against, *hēlios,* the sun.]

paranymph, *par'ə-nimf, n.* (*ant.* ; *Milt.*) a friend who went with the bridegroom to fetch the bride, a groomsman or bridesmaid : one who counten-ances and supports another. [Gr. *paranymphos*—*para,* beside, *nymphē,* a bride.]

parapet, *par'ə-pit, n.* a bank or wall to protect soldiers from the fire of an enemy in front : a low wall along the side of a bridge, edge of a roof, &c.—*adj.* **par'apeted,** having a parapet. [It. *parapetto,* from pfx. *para-* (see **parachute**) and It. *petto*—L. *pectus,* the breast.]

paraph, *par'af, n.* a mark or flourish under one's signature.—*v.t.* to append a paraph to, to sign with initials. [Fr. *paraphe* ; cf. **paragraph.**]

paraphasia, *par-ə-fā'zh(y)ä, n.* a form of aphasia in which one word is substituted for another.—*adj.* **paraphasic** (*-fā'zik, -sik*).

paraphernalia, *par-ə-fər-nāl'i-ä, n.pl.* formerly, property other than dower that remained under a married woman's own control, esp. articles of jewellery, dress, personal belongings : ornaments of dress of any kind : trappings : equipment : miscellaneous accessories. [Late L. *paraphernālia* —*parapherna*—Gr., from *para,* beyond, *phernē,* a dowry—*pherein,* to bring.]

paraphimosis, *par-ə-fi-mō'sis, n.* strangulation of the glans penis by constriction of the prepuce. [See **phimosis.**]

paraphonia, *par-ə-fō'ni-ä, n.* in Byzantine music, a melodic progression by fourths and fifths : a morbid change of voice : an alteration of the voice, as at puberty.—*adj.* **paraphonic** (*-fon'ik*). [Gr. *phōnē,* voice.]

paraphrase, *par'ə-frāz, n.* expression of the same thing in other words : an exercise in such ex-pression : a verse rendering of a biblical passage for church singing, esp. in the Church of Scotland. —*v.t.* to express in other words.—*v.i.* to make a paraphrase.— *ns.* **par'aphraser, par'aphrast** (*-frast*), one who paraphrases.— *adjs.* **para-phrast'ic, -al.** — *adv.* **paraphrast'ically.** [Gr. *paraphrasis*—*phrasis,* a speaking—*phrazein,* to speak.]

paraphysis, *pə-raf'i-sis, n.* a sterile filament among spore-bearing structures in lower plants :—*pl.* **paraphyses** (*-sēz*). [Gr., a side-growth—*physis,* growth.]

parapineal, *par-ə-pin'i-əl, adj.* beside the pineal gland—applied to the pineal eye.

paraplegia, *par-ə-plē'j(y)ä, n.* paralysis of the lower

part of the body.—*adjs.* **paraplectic** (*-plekt'ik*), **paraplegic** (*-plēj'* or *-plej'*). [Ionic Gr. *paraplēgiē,* a stroke on the side—*plēgē,* a blow.]

parapodium, *par-ə-pō'di-əm, n.* one of the jointless lateral appendages of polychaet worms, &c. : a swimming organ in some molluscs, a lateral expansion of the foot :—*pl.* **parapō'dia.**—*adj.* **parapō'dial.** [Gr. *pous, podos,* a foot.]

parapophysis, *par-ə-pof'i-sis, n.* a ventral trans-verse process of a vertebra :—*pl.* **parapoph'yses** (*-sēz*).— *adj.* **parapophysial** (*par-ap-ō-fiz'i-əl*). [apophysis.]

parapsychism, *par-ə-sī'kizm, n.* panpsychistic parallelism. — *adjs.* **parapsy'chic, -al ; para-psycholog'ical.**—*ns.* **parapsychol'ogist ; para-psychol'ogy,** psychical research : the study of phenomena such as telepathy and clairvoyance which seem to suggest that the mind can gain knowledge by means other than the normal per-ceptual processes ; **parapsychō'sis,** an abnormal psychosis.

paraquadrate, *par-ə-kwod'rāt, n.* the squamosal.

paraquito, *par-ə-kē'tō.* See **parakeet.**

para-red, *par'ə-red', n.* an azo-dye for cottons, derived from paranitroaniline.

pararosaniline, *par-ə-roz-an'i-lēn, n.* a base enter-ing into various dyestuffs, such as magenta.

pararthria, *par-är'thri-ä, n.* disordered articulation of speech. [Gr. *para,* beside, *arthron,* a joint.]

parasang, *par'ə-sang, n.* an old Persian measure of length, reckoned at 30 stadia, or between 3 and 4 miles. [Gr. *parasangēs,* from O.Pers. (mod. Pers. *farsang*).]

parascenium, *par-ə-sē'ni-əm, n.* in the Greek theatre, a wing, side-scene :—*pl.* **parascē'nia.** [Gr. *paraskēnion*—*skēnē,* tent, stage.]

parasceve, *par'ə-sēv, par-ə-sē'vē, n.* (*obs.*) prepara-tion : the eve of the Jewish Sabbath, Friday, the day of preparation : Good Friday. [L.L. *parascēvē* —Gr. *paraskeuē,* preparation—*para,* beside, *skeuē,* equipment.]

paraselene, *par-ə-se-lē'nē, n.* a mock moon :—*pl.* **paraselē'nae** (*-nē*). [Gr. *para,* beside, *selēnē,* moon.]

parasite, *par'ə-sīt, n.* a hanger-on or sycophant who frequents another's table : one who lives at the expense of society or of others and con-tributes nothing : an organism that lives in or on another organism and derives subsistence from it without rendering it any service in return : in literary but not scientific use extended to an epiphyte.—*adjs.* **parasitic** (*-sit'ik*), **-al,** of, of the nature of, caused by, or like a parasite : fawning : sycophantic : living on other plants or animals.— *adv.* **parasit'ically.**—*ns.* **parasit'icalness ; para-siticide** (*-sit'i-sīd*), that which destroys parasites ; **par'asitism** (*-sīt-izm*).—*adj.* **par'asitoid** (*-sīt-*), parasitic in one phase of the life-history, thereafter independent.—Also *n.*—*ns.* **parasitol'ogist ; para-sitol'ogy ; parasitō'sis,** infestation with parasites. [Gr. *parasītos*—*sītos,* corn, bread, food.]

parasol, *par'ə-sol,* or *-sol', n.* a sunshade : an aeroplane with its wings overhead. [Fr.,—It. *parasole*—pfx. *para-* (as in **parachute**), and *sole*— L. *sōl, sōlis,* the sun.]

parasphenoid, *par-ə-sfē'noid, adj.* alongside the sphenoid bone.—*n.* a bone of the skull, part of the cranial floor.

parastichy, *par-as'ti-ki, n.* (*bot.*) a secondary spiral joining leaf-bases on an axis, visible where the leaves are crowded together, e.g. the scales of a pine-cone. [Gr. *para,* beside, *stichos,* a row.]

parasympathetic, *par-ə-sim-pə-thet'ik, adj.* See under **sympathy.**

parasynthesis, *par-ə-sin'thi-sis, n.* derivation of words from compounds, as *come-at-able,* where *come* and *at* are first compounded and then the derivative suffix *-able* added. — *adj.* **parasyn-thetic** (*-thet'ik*).—*n.* **parasyn'theton,** a word so formed :—*pl.* **parasyn'theta.** [Gr.]

parataxis, *par-ə-tak'sis, n.* (*gram.*) the arrangement of clauses or propositions without connectives.— *adjs.* **paratac'tic, -al.**—*adv.* **paratac'tically.** [Gr., —*taxis,* arrangement.]

parathesis, *pə-rath'i-sis, n.* (*gram.*) apposition :

fāte, fär, ȧsk ; mē, hɜr (her) ; *mīne ; mōte ; mūte ; mōōn ; dhen* (then)

(*philol.*) compounding of words without change, as L. *rēspūblica* from *rēs* and *pūblica*. [Gr., placing alongside.]

parathyroid, *par-ə-thī'roid*, *adj.* beside the thyroid. —*n.* any of a number of small ductless glands apparently concerned with calcium metabolism.

paratonic, *par-ə-ton'ik*, *adj.* (*bot.*) induced by external stimulus. [Gr. *para*, beside, *tonos*, a stretching.]

paratroops, *par'ə-trŏŏps*, *n.pl.* troops carried by air, to be dropped by *parachute*.—*n.* par'atrooper.

paratyphoid, *par-ə-tī'foid*, *n.* a disease (of various types) resembling typhoid.—Also *adj.*

paravail, *par-ə-vāl'*, *adj.* inferior: lowest, said of a feudal tenant: of least account—opp. to *paramount*. [O.Fr. *par aval*, below—L. *per*, through, *ad*, to, *vallem*, accus. of *vallis*, valley.]

paravane, *par'ə-vān*, *n.* a fish-shaped device, with fins or vanes, towed from the bow, for deflecting mines along a wire and severing their moorings— sometimes called an ' otter ': an explosive device of similar design for attacking submerged sub- marines. [*parachute*, and **vane**.]

paravant, paravaunt, *par-ə-vänt'*, *-vawnt'*, *adv.* (*Spens.*) in front, first, beforehand, pre-eminently. [O.Fr. *paravant—par*, through, *avant*, before— L. *ab*, from, *ante*, before.]

Parazoa, *par-ə-zō'ä*, *n.pl.* a division of the animal kingdom, the sponges, co-ordinate with *Protozoa* and *Metazoa*. [Gr. *zōion*, animal.]

parboil, *pär'boil*, *v.t.* (*orig.*) to boil thoroughly: (now, by confusion) to boil slightly. [Fr. *parboillir* —L.L. *perbullīre*, to boil thoroughly; influenced by confusion with **part**.]

parbreak, *pär'brāk*, *n.* (*arch.*) a vomit.—*v.t.* and *v.i.* (*pär* or *-brāk'* ; *obs.*) to vomit :—*pa.p.* par'- breaked. [M.E. *brake*, to vomit ; cf. Du. *braken* ; the pfx. may be Fr. *par-*.]

parbuckle, *pär'buk-l*, *n.* a purchase made by making fast a rope in the middle and passing the ends under and then over a heavy object to be rolled up or down : a sling made by passing both ends of a rope through its bight.—*v.t.* to hoist or lower by a parbuckle. [Earlier *parbunkel*, *parbuncle* ; origin unknown.]

Parca, *pär'kä*, *n.* a Fate, any one of the Roman goddesses Nona, Decuma, and Morta, identified with the Greek Moirai :—*pl.* **Par'cae** (*-sē*). [L., prob. conn. with *parĕre*, to produce, not *parcĕre*, to spare.]

parcel, *pär'sl*, *n.* a little part : a portion : a quantity : a group : a set : a pack (depreciatively): a lot : an item : (*coll.*) a sum of money lost or won : a package, esp. one wrapped in paper and tied with string.—*adv.* (*arch.*) partly.—*adj.* (*arch.*) in part.—*v.t.* to divide into portions : to make up into parcels or a parcel : (*Shak.*) possibly, to make up into a total, complete, round off, or to add up or detail, item by item (*Antony and Cleopatra*, V. ii.) : (*naut.*) to cover with tarred canvas :— *pr.p.* par'celling ; *pa.t.* and *pa.p.* par'celled.— *n.* par'cel-bawd, (*Shak.*) one partly a bawd.— *adj.* par'cel-gilt', partially gilded.—*adv.* par'cel- wise, by parcels, piecemeal.—**parcel(s) post**, that department of the post-office which takes charge of the forwarding and delivery of parcels. [Fr. *parcelle* (It. *particella*)—L. *particula*, dim. of *pars*, *partis*, a part.]

parcener, *pär'sən-ər*, *n.* a co-heir.—*n.* par'cenary (*-ə-ri*), co-heirship. [A.Fr. *parcener*—L.L. *partiōn- ārius—pars*, part.]

parch, *pärch*, *v.t.* to make hot and very dry : to roast slightly : to scorch.—*v.i.* to be scorched : to become very dry.—*adj.* parched.—*adv.* parch'- edly.—*n.* parch'edness. [Origin unknown.]

parchment, *pärch'mənt*, *n.* the skin of a sheep, goat, or other animal prepared for writing on, &c. : a piece of this material : a manuscript written on it : a parchment-like membrane or skin.— *adj.* of parchment.—*v.t.* parch'mentise, to make like parchment, esp. by treating with sulphuric acid. — *adj.* parch'menty, like parchment. — **parchment paper, or vegetable parchment**, unsized paper made tough and transparent by dipping in sulphuric acid ; **virgin parchment**,

a fine kind of parchment made from the skins of new-born lambs or kids. [Fr. *parchemin*—L. *pergamēna* (*charta*), Pergamene (paper)—from Gr. *Pergamos*, Bergamo, in Asia Minor.]

parcimony, an obsolescent spelling of **parsimony**.

parclose, *pär'klōz*, *n.* a screen or railing in a church enclosing an altar or tomb, or separating a chapel or other portion from the main body of the church. [O.Fr. *pa.p.* (fem.) of *parclore*—L. *per*, through, *claudĕre*, *clausum*, to close.]

pard, *pärd*, *n.* the leopard.—*ns.* **pard'al** (*-əl*), **pard'ale** (*-əl*, *-äl* ; *Spens.*), **pard'alis**, a pard : a small pard once supposed a different species.— *adjs.* **pard'ed**, spotted ; **pard'ine** (*-īn*). [L. *pardus* (masc.), *pardalis* (fem.)—Gr. *pardos*, *pardalis* ; prob. of Eastern origin.]

pard, *pärd*, **pard'ner**, *-nər*, *ns.* (*U.S.*) slang forms of **partner**.

pardi, pardie, pardy. See **perdie**.

pardon, *pär'dn*, *v.t.* to forgive : to allow to go unpunished : to excuse : to tolerate : to grant in remission, refrain from exacting or taking : to grant remission of sentence to (even if the condemned has been found innocent).—*v.i.* to forgive : to grant pardon.—*n.* forgiveness, either of an offender or of his offence : remission of a penalty or punishment : forbearance : a warrant declaring a pardon : a papal indulgence : a festival at which indulgences are granted.—*adj.* par'don- able, that may be pardoned : excusable.—*n.* par'donableness.—*adv.* par'donably.—*n.* par'- doner, one who pardons : a licensed seller of papal indulgences.—*n.* and *adj.* par'doning.— *adj.* par'donless, unpardonable.—**pardon ?** I beg your pardon : what did you say ? **pardon me**, excuse me—used in apology and to soften a contradiction. [Fr. *pardonner*—L.L. *perdōnāre*— L. *per*, through, away, *dōnāre*, to give.]

pare, *pär*, *v.t.* to cut or shave off the outer surface or edge of : to trim : to remove by slicing or shaving : to diminish by littles.—*n.* **pār'er**. [Fr. *parer*—L. *parāre*, to prepare.]

paregoric, *par-i-gor'ik*, *adj.* soothing, lessening pain.—*n.* a medicine that soothes pain.—**pare- goric elixir**, an alcoholic solution of opium, benzoic acid, camphor, and oil of anise. [Gr. *parēgorikos—parēgoreein*, to exhort, comfort—*para*, and *agorā*, marketplace.]

pareira, *pə-rā'rä*, *n.* (*orig.*) a tropical menisper- maceous climbing plant (*Cissampelos Pareira*) or its root (now called **false pareira**): a South American plant of the same family (*Chondroden- dron tomentosum* : **pareira brava**, *brä'vä*, i.e. wild) : a tonic diuretic drug derived from its root.—**white pareira** (*Abuta rufescens*), another South American plant of the same family. [Port. *parreira*, wall- climber.]

parella, *pə-rel'ä*, *n.* a crustaceous lichen (*Lecanora Parella*) yielding archil : extended to others of like use.—Also **parelle'**. [Fr. *parelle*.]

parencephalon, *par-en-sef'ə-lon*, *n.* a cerebral hemi- sphere. [Gr. *para*, beside, *enkephalon*, brain.]

parenchyma, *pə-reng'ki-mä*, *n.* the ordinary soft thin-walled tissue of plants, not differentiated into conducting or mechanical tissue : soft spongy in- determinate tissue in animals.—*adj.* **parenchym'- atous**. [Gr. *para*, beside, *enchyma*, infusion, in- pouring.]

parenesis. See **paraenesis**.

parent, *pā'rənt*, *n.* one who begets or brings forth : a father or a mother : one who, or that which, produces : that from which anything springs or branches : an author : a cause : (as a Gallicism) a relative.—*n.* **pā'rentage**, descent from parents : extraction : rank or character derived from one's parents or ancestors : relation of parents to their children : state or fact of being a parent : (*Spens.*) parents collectively (or parent).—*adj.* **parental** (*pə-rent'əl*).—*adv.* **parent'ally**.—*n.* **pā'renthood**, state of being a parent : duty or feelings of a parent.—*adj.* **pā'rentless**, without a parent. [Fr. *parent*, kinsman—L. *parēns*, *-entis*, old pr.p. of *parĕre*, to bring forth.]

parenteral, *par-en'tər-əl*, *adj.* not intestinal : not by way of the alimentary tract (said of the administration of a drug).—*adv.* **paren'terally.** [Gr. *para*, beside, and *enteral*.]

parenthesis, *pə-ren'thi-sis, n.* a word or passage inserted in a sentence which is grammatically complete without it : (usu. in *pl.*) a round bracket ( ) used to mark off a parenthesis :—*pl.* **paren'-theses** (*-sēz*).—*v.i.* parenth'esise.—*adjs.* **paren-thetic** (*par-ən-thet'ik*), **-al.**—*adv.* **parenthet'ic-ally.** [Gr.,—*para*, beside, *en*, in, *thesis*, a placing.]

Pareoean, *par-ē-ē'ən, adj.* of a human race in-habiting South China, Burma, &c.—otherwise called Southern Mongoloid.—Also *n.* [Gr. *para*, beside, *eōs*, dawn.]

parergon, *pär-ər'gon, n.* a by-work, any work sub-sidiary to another :—*pl.* **parer'ga.** [Gr.,—*para*, beside, *ergon*, work.]

paresis, *par'i-sis, n.* a diminished activity of function —a partial form of paralysis.—*adj.* **paretic** (*-et'ik*). [Gr.,—*parienai*, to relax.]

parfait, *pär-fe', n.* a kind of frozen dessert containing whipped cream and eggs. [Fr., lit. perfect.]

parfleche, *pär-flesh', n.* a dried skin, usu. of buffalo : an article made of it. [App. Canadian Fr.]

pargana, pergunnah, *pər-gun'ä, n.* a division of a zillah in India. [Hind. and Pers. *parganah*.]

pargasite, *pär'gə-sīt, n.* a green amphibole. [*Pargas* in Finland.]

parget, *pär'jit, v.t.* to plaster over : to cover with ornamental plaster-work : to decorate the surface of : to bedaub : (*pr.p.* **par'geting**; *pa.t.* and *pa.p.* **par'geted**).—*n.* plaster spread over a surface : cow-dung plaster for chimney flues : ornamental work in plaster : surface decoration.—*v.t.* **parge**, to plaster.—*ns.* **par'geter**; **par'geting, parge'-work.**—The irregular forms **par'getting,** &c., are used by some. [App. O.Fr. *parjeter*, to throw all over.]

parhelion, *pär-hē'li-ən, n.* a mock-sun :—*pl.* **par-hē'lia.**—*adjs.* **parhelic** (*-hē'lik, -hel'ik*), **parheli-acal** (*-hē-lī'ə-kl*). [Irregularly—Gr. *parēlion*—*para*, beside, *hēlios*, sun.]

parhypate, *pär-hip'ə-tē, n.* ⟨Gr. *mus.*⟩ the lowest note but one in a tetrachord—next above the hypate. [Gr. *para*, beside ; see **hypate.**]

pariah, *pär'i-ä,* or *pär', n.* a member of a caste in Southern India lower than the four Brahminical castes : one of low or no caste : a social outcast : an ownerless cur of Eastern towns (in full **pariah dog**), a pye-dog. [Tamil *paraiyar*.]

parial. Same as **pairial**; see under **pair.**

Parian, *pā'ri-ən, adj.* of the island of *Paros*, in the Aegean Sea.—*n.* a native or inhabitant of Paros : a fine porcelain like marble.—**Parian marble,** a fine white marble found in Paros.

parietal, *pə-rī'i-tl, adj.* of a wall or walls : of, attached to, or having connexion with the side, or the inside of the wall, of a cavity, esp. a plant ovary : pertaining to or near the parietal bone : (*U.S.*) residing, or relating to residence, within the walls of a college.—*n.* a bone (**parietal bone**), forming with its fellow part of the sides and top of the skull, between the frontal and the occipital. [L. *parietālis*—*pariēs, parietis*, a wall.]

pari-mutuel, *pär-ē-mü-tü-el, n.* a betting-machine which automatically pools stakes and distributes winnings—a totalisator. [Fr., mutual bet.]

paring, *pār'ing, n.* act of trimming or cutting off : that which is pared off : the cutting off of the surface of grass land for tillage. [**pare.**]

paripinnate, *par-i-pin'āt, adj.* (*bot.*) pinnate without a terminal leaflet. [L. *pār*, equal.]

Paris, *par'is, n.* the capital of France.—*adj.* of, originating in, Paris.—*adj.* **Parisian** (*pə-riz'yən, -zhyən, -zhən*), of or pertaining to Paris.—*n.* a native or resident of Paris :—*Fr. fem.* **Parisienne** (*pä-rē-zyen', -zē-en'*).—**Paris doll,** a small figure dressed in the latest fashions, sent out by Paris modistes; **Paris green,** copper arsenite and acetate, a pigment and insecticide. [L. *Parisiī*, the Gallic tribe of the Paris district.]

parish, *par'ish, n.* a district having its own church and minister or priest of the Established Church : a civil district, a division of a county for ad-ministrative and local government purposes : in Louisiana a county : a district assigned by a church to a minister or priest : the people of a parish : (*U.S.*) a congregation or a denomination.—*adj.* belonging or relating to a parish : employed or supported by the parish : for the use of the parish. —*ns.* **par'ishen** (see **parochin**); **parishioner** (*pə-rish'ə-nər*), one who belongs to or is connected with a parish : a member of a parish church.— **on the parish,** in receipt of poor-relief; **parish church,** the church of the establishment for a parish; **parish clerk,** the clerk or recording officer of a parish : the one who leads the responses in the service of the Church of England; **parish council,** a body elected to manage the affairs of a parish; **parish councillor**; **parish minister, priest,** a minister or priest who has charge of a parish; **parish pump,** the symbol of petty local interests; **parish register,** a book in which the births, baptisms, marriages, and deaths of a parish are registered; **parish top,** a spinning-top for-merly kept for the amusement of the parish [A.Fr. *paroche* (Fr. *paroisse*)—L. *parochia*—Gr. *paroikiä*, an ecclesiastical district—*para*, beside, *oikos*, a dwelling ; altered by confusion with Gr. *parochos*, a purveyor.]

parisyllabic, *par-i-si-läb'ik, adj.* having the same number of syllables. [L. *pār*, equal.]

paritor, *par'i-tər, n.* (*Shak.*) aphetic for **apparitor.**

parity, *par'i-ti, n.* equality in status : parallelism : equivalence : a standard equivalence in currency. [Fr. *parité*—L. *paritās*—*pār*, equal.]

parity, *par'i-ti, n.* the condition or fact of having borne children. [L. *parēre*, to bring forth.]

park, *pärk, n.* an enclosed piece of land for beasts of the chase : a tract of land surrounding a mansion kept as a pleasure-ground : hence often part of the name of a house, street, or district : a piece of ground for public recreation : a piece of country kept in its natural condition as a nature-reserve or the like : (*Scot.*) a paddock, grass field : (*Ireland*) a field : (*U.S.*) a level valley among mountains : (*mil.*) a place occupied by artillery, wagons, &c. : a piece of ground where motor-cars or other vehicles may be left untended : an enclosed basin for oyster-culture.—*v.t.* to enclose in a park : to make a park of : to bring together in a body, as artillery : to place and leave in a parking-place : (*coll.*) to deposit and leave.—*v.i.* to use a car park or parking-place.—*ns.* **park'er,** (*obs.*) a park-keeper; **park'ing,** the action of the verb park : (*U.S.*) a turf strip, sometimes with trees, along the middle of a street; **park'ing-place.**—*adj.* **park'ish.**—*ns.* **park'keeper,** a park-officer; **park'land, -s,** park-like grassland dotted with trees.—*adjs.* **park'like**; **park'ly.**—*n.* **park'-off'icer,** the keeper of a park. —*advs.* **park'ward, -s.**—*n.* **park'way,** a broad road adorned with turf and trees, often connecting the parks of a town. [O.Fr. *parc*, of Gmc. origin; cf. O.E. *pearruc, pearroc*.]

parka, *pärk'ä, n.* (*Canada* and *Alaska*) a fur shirt with a hood or similar garment.—Also **parkee, parki** (*pärk'ē*). [Aleutian Eskimo word.]

parkin, *pär'kin,* **perkin,** *pər'kin, n.* (*Northern*) a biscuit of oatmeal and treacle. [Ety. unknown.]

parkleaves, *pärk'lēvz, n.* tutsan. [App. **park, leaf.**]

parlando, *pär-län'dō, adj.* and *adv.* (*mus.*) in de-clamatory style : in recitative. [It., speaking ; cf. next word.]

parle, *pärl, v.i.* (*arch.*) to talk : to confer : to parley.— *n.* talk : speech : parleying.—*n.* **par'lance,** speak-ing : conversation : diction, phraseology, jargon, mode of speech.—*v.i.* **par'ley,** to speak with an-other : to confer : to treat with an enemy.—*n.* talk : a conference with an enemy : a conference. —*n.* **parleyvoo',** (*slang*) French : a Frenchman.— *v.i.* to speak French. [Fr. *parler*, to speak (*parlez-vous?* do you speak ?)—L.L. *parlāre—parabolāre*— Gr. *parabolē*, a parable, word.]

parliament, *pär'lə-mənt, n.* a meeting for delibera-tion : a legislative body : in France, down to the Revolution, one of certain superior and final courts of judicature, in which also the edicts of the king were registered before becoming law : ginger-bread in the form of rectangular biscuits (also

fāte, fär, åsk; mē, hər (her); *mīne; mōte; mūte; mōōn; dhen* (then)

par′liament-cake; *Scot.* par′ley, par′ly).—*n.*
parliamentā′rian, an adherent of Parliament in
opposition to Charles I.: one skilled in the ways
of parliament.—*adj.* on the side of parliament.—
adv. parliamentarily (-*ment′ər-i-li*).—*n.* parlia-
ment′arism, the principles of parliamentary
government: the parliamentary system.—*adj.* par-
liament′ary, pertaining to parliament: enacted,
enjoined, or done by parliament: according to
the rules and practices of legislative bodies: (of
language) civil, decorous: for Parliament against
the Royalists. — *ns.* par′liament-heel′, a slight
careening of a ship; par′liament-hinge′, a hinge
that allows a door to be laid back along the wall;
par′liament-house, a building where parliament
sits or has sat; parliamenting (-*ment′ing*), acting
as member of parliament: debating; par′liament-
man′, a member of parliament: a parliamentarian.
—act of parliament, a statute that has passed
through both the House of Commons and the
House of Lords, and received the formal royal
assent; parliamentary agent, a person employed
by private persons or societies for drafting bills or
managing business to be brought before parliament; parliamentary burgh (see burgh);
parliamentary train, a railway train which, by
act of parliament (1844), ran daily with sufficient
accommodation for passengers at a penny a mile.
[Fr. *parlement—parler*, to speak.]

parlour, *pär′lər, n.* a room where conversation is
allowed in a monastery or nunnery: a private
room for conversation or conference in a public
building, office, &c.: a more or less private room
in an inn or tavern: a simple unpretentious
drawing-room or dining-room, or a smaller room
of similar kind: a family sitting-room or living-
room: (*U.S.*) a shop fitted like a room, or a room
attached to a shop, esp. for personal offices to
customers.—*adj.* used in or suitable for a parlour.
—*ns.* par′lour-board′er, a ~upil at a boarding-
school who enjoys particular privileges; par′lour-
car, (*U.S.*) a luxuriously fitted railway saloon
carriage; par′lour-maid, a maid-servant who
waits at table. [A.Fr. *parlur* (Fr. *parloir*)—*parler*,
to speak.]

parlous, *pär′ləs, adj.* (*arch.* and *facet.*) a form of
perilous.

parmacitie, *pär-məs-it′i, n.* (*Shak.*) for spermaceti.

Parmesan, *pär-mi-zan′,* or *pär′, adj.* pertaining
to *Parma.*—*n.* Parmesan cheese.—Parma violet,
Neapolitan violet.

Parnassus, *pär-na əs, n.* a mountain in Greece,
sacred to Apollo and the Muses: a collection of
poems.—*adj.* Parnass′ian, of Parnassus: of the
Muses: of a school of French poetry supposed to
believe in art for art's sake (from the collections
published as *Le Parnasse contemporain,* 1866-76).
—*n.* a poet: a member of the Parnassian school.
—*n.* Parnass′ianism.—grass of Parnassus, a
white-flowered plant of wet moors (*Parnassia
palustris*) of the saxifrage family.

Parnellism, *pär′nəl-izm, n.* the principles and policy
of Charles Stewart *Parnell* (1846-91) to promote
Home Rule for Ireland.—*n.* Par′nellite, a follower
of Parnell, esp. after the Irish party split.—Also
adj.

paroccipital, *par-ok-sip′i-tl, adj.* near the occiput.

parochial, *pə-rō′ki-əl, adj.* of or relating to a
parish: restricted or confined within narrow limits
—of sentiments, tastes, &c.: (*U.S.*) denomina-
tional.—*v.t.* paro′chialise, to make parochial: to
form into parishes: to do parish work.—*ns.*
paro′chialism, a system of local government
which makes the parish the unit: provincialism,
narrowness of view; parōchiality (-*al′*). — *adv.*
parō′chially.— parochial board, (formerly, in
Scotland) a board charged with poor-relief. [L.
parochiālis—parochia: see parish.]

parochin(e), parischan(e), parishen, *pä′rish-in,
n.* (*Scot.*) parish.

parody, *par′ə-di, n.* a burlesque imitation.—*v.t.* to
make a parody of:—*pr.p.* par′odying; *pa.t.* and
pa.p. par′odied.—*n.* par′odist. [Gr. *parōidiā—
para,* beside, *ōidē,* an ode.]

paroemia, *pə-rē′mi-ä, n.* a proverb, adage.—*adj.*

paroe′miac.—*n.* (*Gr. pros.*) the anapaestic dimeter
catalectic.—*adj.* paroe′mial.—*ns.* paroemiog′-
rapher, a writer or collector of proverbs; paroe-
miog′raphy, the study of pro-
verbs. [Gr. *paroimiā,* a proverb—*paroimos,* by
the road—*oimos,* road.]

parole, *pə-rōl′, n.* word of mouth: (*mil.*) word of
honour (esp. by a prisoner of war, to fulfil certain
conditions): the condition of having given one's
word of honour, or privilege of having it accepted:
(*U.S.*) conditional release of a prisoner: officers'
daily password in a camp or garrison.—*adj.* pertaining to parole: (usu. parol, *pär′ol*) given by
word of mouth — *pp.* to *documentary,* as *parol*
evidence.—*v.t.* parole, to put on parole: (*U.S.*)
to release on parole.—*v.i.* to give parole. [Fr.
parole, word—L. *parabola,* a parable, saying—
Gr.; see parable.]

paronomasia, *par-on-o-mā′syä, -zyä, -zh(y)ä, n.*
a play upon words—also paronom′asy (-*ə-si,
-ə-zi*).—*adjs.* paronomastic (-*mas′tik*), -al.—*n.*
paronym (*par′o-nim*), a word from the same root,
or having the same sound, as another.—*adj.*
paron′ymous.—*n.* paron′ymy. [Gr. *para,* beside, *onoma, onyma,* name.]

paronychia, *par-o-nik′i-ä, n.* a whitlow: Paronychia, the whitlow-wort genus of plants.—*adj.*
paronych′ial. [Gr. *para,* beside, *onyx, onychos,*
nail.]

paroquet. See parakeet.

parotid, *pə-rot′id, -rōt′, adj.* near the ear.—*n.* the parotid gland, a salivary gland in front of the ear—also
parō′tis.—*ns.* parotidi′tis, paroti′tis, inflammation
of the parotid gland, as in mumps. [Gr. *parōtis,
-idos—para,* beside, *ous, ōtos,* ear.]

parousia, *pə-rōō′zi-ä,* or -*row′, n.* (*theol.*) the second
coming of Christ. [Gr., *parousiā,* presence, arrival.]

paroxysm, *par′oks-izm, n.* a fit of acute pain: a
fit of passion, laughter, coughing, &c.: any sudden
violent action.—*adj.* paroxys′mal. [Gr. *paroxys-
mos—para,* beyond, *oxys,* sharp.]

paroxytone, *par-ok′si-tōn, adj.* having the acute
accent on the last syllable but one.—*n.* a word so
accented. [Gr. *paroxytonos—para,* beside, *oxys,*
acute, *tonos,* tone.]

parpen, *pär′pən, n.* a stone passing through a wall
from face to face: a wall of such stones: a partition: a bridge parapet.—Also par′pane, par′pend,
par′pent, par′point, per′pend, per′pent.—*ns.*
par′pen-stone; par′pen-wall. [O.Fr. *parpain.*]

parquet, *pär′kā, -kit, pär-kā′, -ket′, n.* a floor-
covering of wooden blocks fitted in a pattern:
(*U.S.*) the stalls of a theatre (parquet circle, that
part of the floor behind these).—*adj.* of parquetry.—
v.t. to cover or floor with parquetry:—*pa.p.*
par′queted, parquett′ed.—*n.* par′quetry (-*ki-tri*),
flooring in parquet. [Fr. *parquet,* dim. of *parc,* an
enclosure.]

parr, *pär, n.* a young salmon.

parrakeet. See parakeet.

parrel, parral, *par′əl, n.* a band by which a yard
is fastened to a mast.—parrel truck, a wooden
ball strung on a parrel. [Cf. O.Fr. *parail,* rigging.]

parrhesia, *pa-rē′syä, -zyä, n.* boldness of speech.
[Gr. *parrēsiā—para,* beside, beyond, *rhēsis,*
speech.]

parricide, *par′i-sīd, n.* the murder of a parent or
near relative, or the murder of anyone to whom
reverence is considered to be due: one who
commits such a crime.—*adj.* parricid′al. [Fr.,—
L. *parricīdium, pāricīdium* (the offence), *parricīda,
pāricīda* (the offender)—*caedĕre,* to slay; the connexion with *pater,* father, is apparently fanciful.]

parritch, *pär′ich, n.* Scots form of porridge.

parroquet. See parakeet.

parrot, *par′ət, n.* one of a family of tropical and
subtropical birds with brilliant plumage, hooked
bill, and zygodactyl feet, good imitators of human
speech: an unthinking repeater of the words of
others.—*v.t.* to repeat by rote: to teach to repeat
by rote.—*v.i.* to talk like a parrot (also *v.t.* with
it):—*pa.p.* parr′oted.—*ns.* parr′ot-beak, -bill,
-jaw, the New Zealand glory-pea, from the form
of its flowers; parr′ot-coal, (*Scot.*) cannel coal
(possibly from chattering as it burns); parr′ot-

cry', a catch-phrase senselessly repeated from mouth to mouth; **parr'ot-disease'**, psittacosis; **parr'oter ; parr'ot-fish,** a name applied to various fishes, esp. of the wrasse family and the kindred Scaridae, from their colours or their powerful jaws ; **parr'otry,** unintelligent imitation ; **parr'ot-wrasse,** a parrot-fish, esp. that of the Mediterranean (*Scarus cretensis*), prized by the ancients.— *adj.* **parr'oty,** like a parrot or parrot-coal. [Possibly Fr. *Perrot,* dim. of *Pierre,* Peter.]

parry, par'i, *v.t.* to ward or keep off : to turn aside : to avert: (*pr.p.* **parr'ying**), *pa.t.* and *pa.p.* **parr'ied**).—*n.* a turning aside of a blow or a thrust or of an attack of any kind, e.g. an argument or a jibe. [Perh. from Fr. *parez,* imper. of *parer*— L. *parāre,* to prepare, in L.L. to keep off.]

parse, pärz, also **pärs,** *v.t.* (*gram.*) to describe fully from point of view of classification, inflexion, and syntax (of a word) : to analyse (of a sentence).— *ns.* **pars'er ; pars'ing.** [L. *pars* (*oratiŏnis*), a part (of speech).]

parsec, pär'sek or **pär-sek',** *n.* the distance (about 19 billion miles) at which half the major axis of the earth's orbit subtends an angle of one second, a unit for measurement of distances of stars. [**parallax,** **second**.]

Parsee, Parsi, pär'sē, or **-sē',** *n.* a descendant of the Zoroastrians who emigrated from Persia to India in the 8th century.—*n.* **Par'seeism, Par'siism** (or *-sē'*), **Par'sism,** their religion. [Pers. *Pārsī—Pārs,* Persia.]

parsimony, pär'si-mən-i, *n.* sparingness in the spending of money : praiseworthy economy in use of means to an end : avoidance of excess : frugality : niggardliness. — *adj.* **parsimonious** (*-mō'ni-əs*).—*adv.* **parsimo'niously.**—*n.* **parsimo'niousness.**—**law of parsimony,** the principle of Occam's razor (see **Occamism**). [L. *parsimōnia—parcĕre, parsus,* to spare.]

parsley, pärs'li, *n.* a bright-green umbelliferous herb (*Carum Petroselinum*) with finely divided, strongly scented leaves, used in cookery.— **parsley fern,** a fern (*Cryptogramme crispa*) with bright green crisped leaves not unlike parsley. [O.E. *petersilie,* modified by Fr. *persil,* both— L. *petroselīnum*—Gr. *petroselīnon—petros,* a rock, *selīnon,* parsley.]

parsley-piert, pärs'li-pērt, parsley-pert, -pərt, *n.* a dwarf species of lady's-mantle (*Alchemilla arvensis*), a weed of dry waste ground. [Prob. Fr. *perce-pierre,* lit. pierce-stone.]

parsnip, parsnep, pärs'nip, *n.* an umbelliferous plant (*Pastinaca sativa* or *Peucedanum sativum*), or its edible carrot-like root. [L. *pastināca—pastinum,* a dibble ; prob. affected by **neep**.]

parson, pär'sn, *n.* the priest or incumbent of a parish : a rector : any minister of religion : one who is licensed to preach.—*ns.* **par'sonage,** the residence appropriated to a parson : (*orig.*) the house, lands, tithes, &c., set apart for the support of the minister of a parish ; (*Scott*) tithes; **par'son-bird,** a New Zealand honey-bird of glossy blue-black plumage with tufts of white at the neck, the tui.—*adjs.* **parsonic** (*-son'ik*), **-al, par'sonish.** —**parson's nose,** the rump of a fowl. [O.Fr. *persone*—L. *persōna,* a person, prob. in legal sense, or a mouthpiece.]

part, pärt, *n.* something less than the whole : a portion : that which along with others makes up, has made up, or may at some time make up, a whole : a constituent : a member or organ : an equal quantity : share : region : direction, hand, or side : participation : concern : interest : side or party : character taken by an actor in a play : words and actions of a character in a play or in real life : a voice or instrument in concerted music : that which is performed by such a voice or instrument : a copy of the music for it : a constituent melody or succession of notes or harmony : a section of a work in literature in music : a separately published portion or number : an inflected form of a verb : a quantity which taken a certain number of times (when unspecified, less than the whole) will equal a larger quantity: (in *pl.*) intellectual qualities, talents, or conduct.—*adj.* in

part : partial.—*adv.* in part : partly.—*v.t.* to divide : to separate : to break : to put or keep asunder : to set in different directions : to distribute : to share : (*Shak.*) to leave, quit.—*v.i.* to become divided or separated : to separate : to go different ways : to depart : to come or burst apart : to relinquish (with *with*) : (*B.*) to share. —*adj.* **part'ed,** divided : separated : sundered : departed : assigned a part : (*Shak.*) endowed with parts or abilities : (*bot.*) deeply cleft, as a leaf.— *n.* **part'er.**—*adj.* **part'ible,** that may be parted : separable.—*ns.* **partibil'ity ; part'ing,** the action of the verb to part : a place of separation or division : a dividing line : leave-taking.—*adj.* separating : dividing : departing : leave-taking : of or at leave-taking.—*n.* **part'ing-cup',** a two-handled drinking-cup.—*adv.* **part'ly,** in part : in some degree.—*ns.* **part'-own'er,** a joint owner ; **part'-pay'ment,** payment in part ; **part'-singing ; part'-song,** a melody with parts in harmony, usu. unaccompanied.—*adj.* **part'-time,** for part of working time only.—*ns.* **part'-tim'er ; part'-writing,** composition of music in parts.—**for my part,** as far as concerns me ; **for the most part,** commonly ; **in bad,** or **ill, part,** unfavourably ; **in good part,** favourably : without taking offence ; **in great part,** to a great extent ; **in part,** partly : so far as is concerned : not wholly but to some extent ; **on the part of,** so far as concerns : as done or performed by : in the actions of : on the side of ; **part and parcel,** essentially a part ; **part company,** to separate ; **parting of the ways,** a point at which a fateful decision must be made ; **part of speech,** one of the various classes of words ; **take part in,** to share or to assist in ; **take part with,** to take the side of. [O.E. and Fr. *part*—L. *pars, partis.*]

partake, pär-tāk', pər-tāk', v.i. to take or have a part or share (usu. with *of* or *in*) : to take some, esp. of food or drink : to have something of the nature or properties : (*Shak.*) to make common cause.—*v.t.* to have a part in : to share : to have a share in the knowledge of : (*Shak.*) to give a share of : (*Spens.*) to inform :—*pr.p.* **partā'king ;** *pa.t.* **partook' ;** *pa.p.* **partā'ken.**—*ns.* **partā'ker ; partā'king.** [Back-formation from **partaker**— **part, taker.**]

partan, pär'tn, *n.* (*Scot.*) the edible crab. [Gael.]

parterre, pär-ter', *n.* an arrangement of flower-beds : (esp. *U.S.*) the pit of a theatre, esp. the part under the galleries. [Fr.,—L. *per,* along, *terra,* the ground.]

parthenogenesis, pär-thi-nō-jen'i-sis, *n.* reproduction by means of an unfertilised ovum.—*adj.* **parthenogenetic** (*-ji-net'ik*). [Gr. *parthenos,* a virgin, *genesis,* production.]

Parthenon, pär'thi-non, *n.* the temple of Athēnē *Parthĕnos,* on the Acropolis at Athens. [Gr. *Parthenōn—parthenos,* a virgin.]

Parthian, pär'thi-ən, *adj.* of *Parthia.*—*n.* a native of Parthia.—**a Parthian shot,** a parting shot, from the Parthian habit of turning round in the saddle to discharge an arrow at a pursuer.

parti, pär'tē', *n.* a marriageable person considered as a match or catch. [Fr.]

partial, pär'shl, *adj.* relating to a part only : not total or entire : inclined to favour one person or party : having a preference or fondness (with *to*) : (*Shak.*) of partiality : component : (*bot.*) subordinate.—*n.* a partial tone, one of the single-frequency tones which go together to form a sound actually heard.—*ns.* **par'tialism ; par'tialist,** one who is biased : one who sees or knows only part : (*theol.*) a particularist ; **partiality** (*-shi-al'i-ti*).— *v.t.* **par'tialize,** (*Shak.*) to bias.—*adv.* **par'tially.** [Fr.,—L.L. *partiālis*—L. *pars, partis.*]

participate, pär-tis'i-pāt, *v.i.* to partake : to have a share.—*v.t.* to receive a part or share of.—*adjs.* **partic'ipable,** capable of being participated in or shared ; **partic'ipant,** participating : sharing.— *n.* a partaker.—*adv.* **partic'ipantly.**—*n.* **participa'tion.**—*adj.* **partic'ipative,** capable of participating.—*n.* **partic'ipator.** [L. *participāre,* *-ātum—pars, partis,* part, *capĕre,* to take.]

participle, pär'ti-sip-l, *n.* a word combining the

functions of adjective and verb.—**present participle, past** or **perfect participle,** referring respectively to an action roughly contemporaneous or past; the present participle is active, the past usually passive.—*adj.* **particip′ial.**—*adv.* **particip′ially.** [O.Fr. (Fr. *participe*),—L. *participium*—*pars, partis,* a part, *capēre,* to take.]

particle, *pär′ti-kl, n.* a little part: a very small portion: a clause of a document: a minute piece of matter: a little hard piece: (*mech.*) a material point: a smallest amount: a short, usu. indeclinable word, as a preposition, a conjunction, an interjection: a prefix or suffix: (*R.C. Church*) a crumb of consecrated bread or a portion used in the communion of the laity.—*adj.* **particular** (*pər-tik′ū-lər*), relating to a part: (*log.*) predicating of part of the class denoted by the subject: pertaining to a single person or thing: individual: special: worthy of special attention: detailed: (*obs.*) markedly and discriminatingly or intimately attentive towards a person: noteworthy: definite: concerned with or marking things single or distinct: minutely attentive and careful: fastidious in taste: particularist.—*n.* a distinct or minute part: a single point: a single instance: a detail: an item: (*Shak.*) personal relation: (*coll.*) a favourite: (*coll.*) a favourite drink (esp. *London particular,* a Madeira wine for the London market, hence a London fog).—*n.* **particularisā′tion.**—*v.t.* **partic′ularise,** to render particular: to mention the particulars of: to enumerate in detail: to mention as a particular or particulars.—*v.i.* to mention or attend to minute details.—*ns.* **partic′ularism,** attention to one's own interest or party: a minute description: the doctrine that salvation is offered only to particular individuals, the elect, and not to the race: attention to the interest of a federal state before that of the confederation: policy of allowing much freedom in this way.—*n.* and *adj.* **partic′ularist.**—*adj.* **particularist′ic.**—*n.* **particularity** (*-lar′i-ti*), quality of being particular: minuteness of detail: a single instance or case: a detail: peculiarity: (*obs.*) marked attention to a person.—*adv.* **partic′ularly,** in a particular manner: individually: severally: in detail: in the manner of a particular proposition: intimately: notably: in a very high degree.—*n.* **partic′ularness.**—*adj.* **partic′ulate,** having the form of or relating to particles.—**in particular,** especially: in detail: severally. [L. *particula,* dim. of *pars, partis,* a part.]

parti-coated, parti-coloured. See under **party.**

partisan, partizan, *pär-ti-zan′, pär′ti-zan, n.* an adherent, esp. a blind or unreasoning adherent, of a party or a faction: a light irregular soldier who scours the country and forays: in the Second World War, a member of Marshal Tito's resistance party in Yugoslavia.—Also *adj.*—*n.* **par′tisanship** (or -*zan′*). [Fr. *partisan,* from a dialect form of It. *partigiano*—*parte* (L. *pars, partis*), part.]

partisan, *pär′ti-zan, n.* a kind of halberd or long-handled weapon, common in the Middle Ages: a man armed with one. [Fr. *partizane* (now *pertuisane*)—It. *partesana,* of doubtful origin.]

partite, *pär′tīt, adj.* divided: cut nearly to the base.—*n.* **partition** (*-tish′ən*), *n.* act of dividing: state of being divided: a separate part: that which divides: a wall between rooms: a barrier, septum or dissepiment: (*mus.*) score.—*v.t.* to divide into shares: to divide into parts by walls, septa, or the like.—*ns.* **parti′tioner,** one who partitions property: **parti′tionist,** one who favours partition: **parti′tionment; parti′tion-wall,** an internal wall.—*adj.* **par′titive,** parting: dividing: distributive: (*gram.*) indicating that a part is meant.—*n.* a partitive word.—*adv.* **par′titively.**—*ns.* **partitur** (*-tōōr′; Ger.*), **partitura** (*-tōō′rä; It.*), score in music. [L. *partītus,* pa.p. of *partīrī* or *partīre,* to divide—*pars, partis,* part.]

Partlet, *pärt′lit, n.* a proper name for a hen, from Chaucer's *Pertelote* in the Nun's Priest's Tale: sometimes applied to a woman. [O.Fr. *Pertelote,* a woman's name.]

partlet, *pärt′lit, n.* (*obs.*) a neck-covering: a ruff: a kind of shirt. [App. O.Fr. *patelette,* a band.]

partner, *pärt′nər, n.* a sharer: an associate: one engaged with another in business: one who plays on the same side with another in a game: one who dances or goes in to dinner with another: a husband or wife: an associate in commensalism or symbiosis.—*v.t.* (*Shak.*) to join as a partner: to be the partner of.—*n.* **part′nership,** state of being a partner: a contract between persons engaged in any business. [Prob. a form of **parcener.**]

partridge, *pär′trij, n.* any member of a genus (*Perdix*) of game-birds of the pheasant family: extended to many other birds, esp. (in North America) the Virginian quail and the ruffed grouse, and (in South America) the tinamous.—*ns.* **par′tridge-berry,** a North American trailing plant of the madder family (*Mitchella repens*) or its fruit: applied also to the checker-berry; **par′tridge-wood,** a hard variegated tropical American cabinet-maker's wood (Andira) of the Papilionaceae: oak or other wood speckled owing to attack by a fungus. [Fr. *perdrix*—L. *perdix*—Gr. *perdix.*]

parture, *pärt′yər, n.* (*Spens.*) departure. [Prob. **part.**]

parturient, *pär-tū′ri-ənt, adj.* bringing, or about to bring, forth: of parturition.—*n.* **parturi′tion,** act of bringing forth. [L. *parturīre,* desiderative from *parĕre,* to bring forth.]

party, *par′ti, n.* (*obs.*) a part: a side in a battle, game, lawsuit, or other contest: a body of persons united in favour of a political or other cause: the spirit of faction: a small body of persons associated together in any occupation or amusement: a detachment: a company: a meeting or entertainment of guests: (*obs.*) a game: one concerned in any affair: a person who enters into a contract, e.g. of marriage: a possible match, in marriage: (*vulg.*) a person.—*adj.* pertaining to party: (*her.*) parted or divided.—*adjs.* **par′ti-coat′ed, par′ty-coat′ed,** having on a coat of various colours; **par′ti-col′oured, par′ty-col′oured,** variegated.—*ns.* **par′ty-call,** a call upon one's host or hostess after a party; **par′ty-cap′ital,** advantage or credit to one's party derived from some contingency; **par′ty-gov′ernment,** government by the prevailing political party; **par′tyism,** devotion to party; **par′ty-ju′ry,** a jury half of natives and half of aliens; **par′ty-line′,** a telephone exchange line used by a set of subscribers: a boundary between properties: the policy rigidly laid down by the party leaders; **par′ty-man′,** a partisan; **par′ty-pol′itics,** politics viewed from a party stand-point, or arranged to suit the views or interests of a party; **par′ty-spir′it,** the unreasonable spirit of a party-man.—*adj.* **par′ty-spir′ited.**—*ns.* **par′ty-ver′dict,** a joint verdict; **par′ty-wall,** a wall between two adjoining properties or houses. [Fr. *partie,* fem. (and also *parti,* masc.), pa.p. of *partir*—L. *partīre, partīrī,* to divide—*pars,* a part.]

parure, *pā-rür′, n.* a set of ornaments, &c. [Fr.]

parvanimity, *pär-və-nim′i-ti, n.* littleness of mind. [L. *parvus,* little, *animus,* mind.]

parvenu, *pär′və-nū, -nū, n.* an upstart: one newly risen into wealth, notice, or power, esp. if vulgar or exhibiting an inferiority complex.—Also *adj.* [Fr., pa.p. of *parvenir*—L. *pervenīre,* to arrive.]

parvis, parvise, *pär′vis, n.* an enclosed space, or sometimes a portico, before a church: (*erroneously*) a room over a church porch. [O.Fr. *parevis*; see **paradise.**]

pas, *pä, n.* a step: a dance—**have the pas of one,** to take precedence of him. [Fr.,—L. *passus*; cf. **pace.**]

Pasch, *päsk, Scot.* **Pace,** *päs, n.* the Passover: (*arch.*) Easter.—*adj.* **pasch′al.**—*ns.* **pasch′al-can′dle,** a large candle blessed and placed on the altar on the day before Easter; **pasch′al-flow′er** (see **pasque-flower**); **pasch′al-lamb,** the lamb slain and eaten at the Passover; **pasch′-egg** (*Scot.* **pace′-egg**), an Easter-egg.—**Pasch of the Cross,** Good-Friday. [L. *pascha*—Gr. *pascha*—Heb. *pesach,* the Passover—*pāsach,* to pass over.]

pasear, *pä-sā-är′, v.i.* (*U.S. slang*) to take a walk.—*n.* a walk.—*n.* **paseo** (*pä-sā′ō*), a walk: a street or promenade. [Sp.]

pash, *pash*, *v.t.* (*Shak.*) to strike, to dash, to crush.— *v.i.* to dash.—*n.* a blow. [Perh. imit.]

pash, *pash*, *n.* (*Shak.*) the head.

pash, *pash*, *n.* a slang abbreviation of **passion**.

pasha, *pä′shä*, *pä-shä′*, *n.* a Turkish title (abolished 1934) given to governors and high military and naval officers.—Also **pacha**.—*n.* **pash′alik** (or *pä-shä′lik*), the jurisdiction of a pasha. — Also **pachalic**. [Turk. *päshä*; cf. **bashaw**.]

Pashto, Pashtu. See **Pushtu**.

pasigraphy, *pə-sig′rə-fi*, *n.* a system of ideographic writing. — *adjs.* **pasigraphic** (*pas-i-graf′ik*), **-al**. [Gr. *päsi* (dat. pl.), to or for all, *graphein*, to write.]

paspy, *päs′pi*. Same as **passepied**.

pasque-flower, *päsk′flowr*, *n.* a species of anemone (*Anemone Pulsatilla*): extended to some other species. [Fr. *passefleur*, apparently—*passer*, to surpass, modified after *pasch*, as flowering about Easter.]

Pasquil, *pas′kwil*, **Pasquin**, *pas′kwin*, *n.* nickname (perh. after somebody who lived near) of an ancient statue dug up in Rome in 1501, to which it became customary to attach lampoons and satires: an imaginary lampooner or satirist: a lampoon or satire.—*v.t.* and *v.i.* to lampoon or satirise.—*ns.* **pas′quilant, pas′quiler, pasquinā′der**, a lampooner; **pasquinäde′**, a lampoon.— *v.t.* to lampoon. [It. *Pasquino*, *Pasquillo*.]

pass, *päs*, *v.i.* to proceed: to go or be transferred from one place to another: to make one's way: to reach, extend, or have a course: to undergo change from one state to another: to be transmitted: to change ownership: to change: (*obs.*) to *shade off: to be astir: to circulate: to be accepted or reputed or known: to go by: to go unheeded or neglected: to elapse, to go away: to disappear, come to an end, fade out: to die: to go or get through an obstacle, difficulty, test, ordeal, examination, &c.: to get through an examination without honours: to be approved: to meet with acceptance: to be sanctioned: to be made law: to be talented: to come through: to be voided: to happen: to be communicated or transacted: to sit or serve (upon a jury): to adjudicate: to be pronounced: (*obs.*) to care, reck (with of or for): (*obs.*) to surpass or beat everything: to exceed bounds: to perform a pass (see noun below): (*cards*) to abstain from making a call or declaration. —*v.t.* to go or get by, over, beyond, through, &c.: to undergo, experience: to undergo successfully: to spend (as time): to omit: to disregard: to exceed: to surpass: to cause or allow to pass: to transfer, transmit: to hand: to utter: to circulate: to pledge (as one's word): to emit: to perform a pass with or upon: to perform as a pass: (*obs.*) to esteem: (*pa.t.* and *pa.p.* passed, *päst*, rarely past).—*n.* a way by which one may pass or cross: a narrow passage, esp. over a range of mountains: a narrow defile: an act of passing: the passing of an examination, esp. without honours: (*obs.*) currency: (*Shak.*) reputation: event, issue, fulfilment, consummation: state or condition: a predicament, critical position: a passport: a written permission to go somewhere: a free ticket: (*fencing*) a thrust: (*football*) transference of the ball to another member of the team: transference in a juggling trick: a movement of the hand over anything, as by a mesmerist: (*Shak.*, *Measure for Measure*) perhaps trick, perhaps conduct.—*adj.* **pass′able**, that may be passed, travelled over, or navigated: that may bear inspection: that may be accepted or allowed to pass: tolerable.— *n.* **pass′ableness**.—*adv.* **pass′ably**.—*ns.* **pass′-book**, a book that passes between a trader and his customer, in which credit purchases are entered: a bank-book; **pass′-check**, a pass-out ticket; **pass′er**; **pass′er-by**, one who passes by or near: —*pl.* **pass′ers-by**.—*n.* and *adj.* **pass′ing** (seebelow). —*n.* **pass′key**, a key enabling one to enter a house: a key for opening several locks.—*adj.* **pass′less**, having no pass: impassable.—*n.* **pass′man**, one who gains a degree without honours.—*adj.* **pass′-out**, entitling one who goes out to return.—*n.* **pass′word**, (*mil.*) a secret word by which a friend may pass or enter a camp, &c.—**bring to pass**,

bring about, cause to happen; **come to pass**, to happen (apparently originally a noun in these expressions); **make a pass at**, (*slang*) to aim a short blow at, especially ineffectually: (*slang*) to make an unwelcome amorous advance to; **pass away**, to come to an end, go off: to die: to elapse; **pass off**, to impose fraudulently, to palm off: to take its course satisfactorily: to disappear gradually; **pass on**, to go forward: to proceed: to die: to transmit, hand on; **pass on**, or **upon**, to give judgment or sentence upon: to practise artfully or impose upon: to palm off; **pass out**, to distribute: to die: (*slang*) to faint, become unconscious or dead drunk: to go off; **pass over**, to overlook, to ignore; **pass the time of day**, to exchange any ordinary greeting of civility; **pass through**, to undergo, experience; **pass up**, (*U.S.*) to renounce, to have nothing to do with. [Fr. *pas*, step, and *passer*, to pass—L. *passus*, a step.]

passacaglia, *päs-sä-käl′yä*, *n.* (*mus.*) a slow solemn old Spanish dance-form, slower than the chaconne, in triple time, usually on a ground-bass. [Italianised from Sp. *pasacalle*—*pasar*, to pass, *calle*, street, appar. because often played in the streets.]

passade, *pä-säd′*, *n.* the motion of a horse to and fro over the same ground.—*n.* **passado** (*pä-sä′dō*; *Shak.*), in fencing, a thrust with one foot advanced. [Fr. *passade*, Sp. *pasada*—L. *passus*, step.]

passage, *pas′ij*, *n.* act of passing: transit: crossing: migration: transition: a journey (now only by water or air, or *fig.*): right of conveyance: possibility of passing: lapse, course: transmission: evacuation of the bowels: the passing of a bill: a means or way of passing: an alley: a corridor or lobby: a navigable channel or route: a crossing-place, ford, ferry, bridge, or mountain-pass: that which passes: (*Shak.*) traffic: an occurrence, incident, episode: transaction, inter-change of communication or intercourse, dealings together: a continuous but indefinite portion of a book, piece of music, &c., of moderate length: a run, figure, or phrase in music: an old dicing game, the object to throw doublets above (passing) ten, with three dice.—*v.i.* to make or perform a passage.—*ns.* **pass′age-boat**, a boat plying regularly for passengers; **pass′age-money**, fare; **pass′ageway**, a way of access: a corridor: an alley.—**bird of passage**, a migratory bird: (*fig.*) a transient visitor; **passage beds**, (*geol.*) transitional strata; **passage of arms**, any feat of arms: an encounter, esp. in words. [Fr. *passage*—L. *passus*, step.]

passage, *pas′ij*, *v.i.* to go sideways.—*v.t.* to cause (a horse) to go sideways. [Fr. *passager*—*passéger*— It. *passeggiare*, to walk—L. *passus*, step.]

passamezzo. See **passy-measure**.

passant, *pas′ənt*, *adj.* (*her.*) walking towards the dexter side, with dexter fore-paw raised. [Fr.]

passement, passment, *pas′mənt*, **passament**, *-ə-mənt*, *n.* decorative trimming.—*v.t.* to adorn with passement.—*n.* **passementerie** (*päs-mänᵉ-t(ə)-rē*; Fr.). [Fr.]

passenger, *pas′in-jər*, *n.* one who passes: one who travels in a public conveyance: (*fig.*) one carried along by others' efforts.—*adj.* of or for passengers.— *n.* **pass′enger-pig′eon**, an extinct North American pigeon that flew in vast numbers in search of food. [O.Fr. *passagier* (Fr. *passager*), with inserted *n*, as in *messenger*, *nightingale*.]

passe-partout, *päs-pär-tōō′*, *n.* a means of passing anywhere: a master-key: a card or the like cut as a mount for a picture: a kind of simple picture-frame, usually of pasteboard, the picture being fixed by strips pasted over the edges: adhesive tape or paper. [Fr., a master-key, from *passer*, to pass, *par*, over, *tout*, all.]

passepied, *päs′pyä*, *n.* a dance or dance-tune like the minuet, but quicker. [Fr., lit. pass-foot.]

Passeres, *pas′ə-rēz*, *n.pl.* an old order of birds (also called Insessores) comprising more than half of all the birds.—*n.pl.* **Passerifor′mes**, the huge order of perching birds (sparrow-like in form) including amongst others all British songsters.—*adj.* **pass′erine** (*-īn*). [L. *passer*, a sparrow.]

passible, *pas'i-bl, adj.* susceptible of suffering, or of impressions from external agents.—*ns.* **passibil'ity, pass'ibleness.**—*adv.* **pass'ibly.** [L. *passibilis*—*patī, passus,* to suffer.]

Passiflora, *pas-i-flō'rä, n.* the passion-flower genus, giving name to the family **Passiflorā'ceae.** [L. *passiō,* passion, *flōs, flōris,* flower.]

passing, *päs'ing, adj.* going by, through, or away: transient, fleeting: happening now: incidental: casual: (*arch.*) surpassing.—*adv.* (*arch.*) exceedingly: very.—*n.* the action of the verb to pass: a place of passing: a coming to an end: death: gold or silver thread with a silk core.—*ns.* **pass'ing-bell,** a bell tolled immediately after a death, originally to invite prayers for the soul passing into eternity; **pass'ing-note** (*mus.*), a note or tone effecting a smooth passage, but forming no essential part of the harmony: one forming an unprepared discord in an unaccented place in the measure. [pass.]

passion, *pash'n, n.* the sufferings (esp. on the Cross) and death of Christ: martyrdom: suffering: a painful bodily ailment (as *iliac passion*): fact, condition, or manner of being acted upon: passivity: a passive quality: strong feeling or agitation of mind, esp. rage, often sorrow: a fit of such feeling, esp. rage: an expression or outburst of such feeling: ardent love: sexual desire: an enthusiastic interest or direction of the mind: the object of such a feeling.—*v.i.* to imbue with passion.—*v.i.* to exhibit passion.—*adj.* **pass'ional.**—*ns.* **pass'ional, pass'ionary,** a book of the sufferings of saints and martyrs.—*adj.* **pass'ionate,** moved by passion: showing strong and warm feeling: easily moved to passion: intense, fervid: (*Shak.*) compassionate: (*Spens.*) moving to compassion.—*v.t.* to express with passion: to imbue with passion: to impassion.—*adv.* **pass'ionately.** —*n.* **pass'ionateness.**—*adj.* **pass'ioned,** moved by passion: expressing passion: expressed with passion.—*ns.* **pass'ion-flower,** any flower or plant of the genus Passiflora, consisting mostly of climbers of tropical and warm temperate America, from a fancied resemblance of parts of the flower to the crown of thorns, nails, and other emblems of Christ's Passion: the plant itself; **pass'ion-fruit,** the granadilla: any edible passion-flower fruit; **Pass'ionist,** a member of a Roman Catholic congregation devoted to the commemoration of the Passion of Christ by missions, &c.—*adj.* **pass'ionless,** free from passion: not easily excited to anger.—*ns.* **Pass'ion-mū'sic,** music to which words describing the sufferings and death of Christ are set; **Pass'ion-play,** a religious drama representing the sufferings and death of Christ; **Pass'ion-Sun'day,** the fifth Sunday in Lent; **Pass'iontide,** the two weeks preceding Easter; **Pass'ion-week,** Holy-week: the week before Holy-week. [O.Fr. *passiun* and L. *passiō, -ōnis*—*patī, passus,* to suffer.]

passive, *pas'iv, adj.* (*obs.*) suffering: acted upon: not acting: inert: owing to outside causes: not actively resisting: bearing no interest: (*Scots law*) under a liability: (*gram.*) expressing the suffering of an action by the person or thing represented by the subject of the verb.—*n.* the passive voice: a passive verb: a passive person.—*adv.* **pass'ively.**—*ns.* **pass'iveness, passiv'ity.**—**passive obedience,** absolute submission to the ruling power: obedience to the 'divine right of kings'; **passive resistance,** deliberate refusal (from scruples of conscience) to do what law or regulation orders, and submission to the consequent penalties; **passive resister.** [L. *passivus*—*patī, passus,* suffer.]

passman. See pass.

Passover, *päs'ō-vər, n.* annual feast of the Jews, to commemorate the destroying angel passing over the houses of the Israelites when he slew the firstborn of the Egyptians.—*adj.* pertaining to the Passover.

passport, *päs'pōrt, n.* authorisation to leave a port either to put to sea or to proceed inland: a permit for entering a country: (*fig.*) that which gives privilege of entry to anything. [Fr. *passeport*; cf. pass, port.]

passus, *pas'us, n.* a section, canto, or fytte. [L *passus,* plur. *-ūs,* a step.]

passy-measure, passemeasure, *pas'i-mezh'ər, n.* an old dance, a pavan in quicker time, called also **passamezzo** (*päs-sä-med'zō*), **passy measures pavan** (in *Shak.* app. misprinted *panin*). [It. *passemezzo.*]

past, *päst, adj.* bygone: elapsed: ended: in time that has already passed: (*gram.*) expressing action or being in time that has passed, preterite: immediately preceding the present: having served a term of office.—*n.* time that has passed: things that have already happened: bygone career, esp. if marked by tragedy or scandal: the past tense: a verb or verbal form in the past tense.—*prep.* after: after the time of: beyond, in place, &c.: beyond the possibility of.—*adv.* by: (*Scot.*) aside in store.—*v.t.* and *v.i.* an unusual pa.p. of pass.—*n.* **past'master,** one who has held the office of master (as among freemasons): hence, a thorough proficient (distinguished from **passed master;** see **master**). [An old pa.p. of pass.]

pastance, *pas'təns, n.* (*arch.*) pastime. [App. Fr. *passe-temps.*]

paste, *pāst, n.* a soft plastic mass: dough for piecrust, &c.: a doughy sweetmeat: a smooth preparation of food of various kinds suitable for spreading on bread: a cement made of flour, water, &c.: material for making pottery: (*fig.*) the basis of a man's character: a fine kind of glass for making artificial gems.—*adj.* of paste.— *v.t.* to fasten or cover with paste.—*n.* **paste'-board,** a stiff board made of sheets of paper pasted together: (*slang*) a visiting-card, playing-card, or ticket.—*adj.* of pasteboard: sham: trumpery.—*ns.* **paste'-eel',** a nematoid worm found in paste; **paste'-grain,** an imitation of moroccoleather, used in binding books and in making fancy goods; **pāst'er,** one who pastes: a slip of gummed paper; **pāst'iness.**—*adjs.* **pāst'y,** like paste; **past'y-faced',** pale and dull of complexion. [O.Fr. *paste* (Fr. *pâte*)—L.L. *pasta*—Gr. *pasta,* barley porridge (neut. pl. of *pastos,* sprinkled, salted)—*passein,* to sprinkle.]

pastel, *pas'tal, -tel, n.* chalk mixed with other materials and coloured for crayons: a drawing made with pastels: the process or art of drawing with pastels: woad.—*adj.* in pastel: (of colour) soft, quiet.—*n.* **pastellist** (*pas',* or *-tel'*). [Fr. *pastel*—It. *pastello*—L. *pasta,* paste.]

pastern, *pas'tarn, n.* (*obs.*) a hobble for a horse: the part of a horse's foot from the fetlock to the hoof, where the shackle is fastened. [O.Fr. *pasturon* (Fr. *paturon*)—O.Fr. *pasture,* pasture, a tether for a horse; cf. pester.]

Pasteurian, *päs-tər'i-ən, adj.* relating to Louis Pasteur (1822-95) or his methods.—*n.* **pasteurīsā'-tion,** sterilisation of milk, &c., by heating.—*v.t.* **pas'teurise.**—*ns.* **pasteuris'er,** an apparatus for sterilising milk, &c.; **pas'teurism,** Pasteur's method of inoculation with the attenuated virus of certain diseases, esp. hydrophobia.

pastiche, *päs-tēsh', n.* a jumble: a pot-pourri: a composition (in literature, music, or painting) made up of bits of other works or imitations of another's style.—Also **pasticcio** (*päs-tit'chō*; *pl.* **pasticci,** *-chē*). [Fr. (from It.) and It.—It. *pasta,* paste; see paste.]

pastil, *pas'til, n.* Same as pastel or pastille.

pastille, *pas-tēl', n.* a small cone of charcoal and aromatic substances, burned as incense, or for fumigation or fragrance: a small aromatic confection: a paper tube containing a firework which causes a small wheel to rotate: (*art*) the same as pastel. [Fr.,—L. *pastillus,* a little loaf.]

pastime, *päs'tīm, n.* that which serves to pass away the time: recreation. [pass, time.]

pastor, *päs'tər, n.* one who has care of a flock or of a congregation: a shepherd: a clergyman: in the Catholic Apostolic Church, a minister of the lowest grade: the rose-coloured starling (*Pastor roseus*), from its following sheep for the sake of parasites.—*adj.* **pas'toral,** relating to shepherds or to shepherd life: of the nature of pastureland: of or pertaining to the pastor of a church :

addressed to the clergy of a diocese by their bishop.—*n.* a poem, play, romance, opera, piece of music, or picture depicting the life of (usually idealised or conventionalised) shepherds: such writing as a genre: a pastoral letter: a book on the care of souls: a pastoral staff.—*ns.* **pastorale** (*pás-to-rä'lä*; It.), a pastoral composition in music: a pastoral, rustic, or idyllic opera or cantata; **pas'toralism**, pastoral character, fashion, cult, mode of writing; **pas'toralist.**—*adv.* **pas'torally.** —*n.* **pas'torate**, the office of a pastor: a pastor's tenure of office: a body of pastors.—*adj.* **pas'torly**, becoming a pastor.—*n.* **pas'torship.**—**pastoral address, or letter**, a letter or an address by a pastor to his people, or by a bishop to his clergy; **pastoral charge**, position of a pastor: the church, &c., over which a pastor is placed: an address to a newly ordained minister; **pastoral epistles**, those in the New Testament to Timothy and Titus; **pastoral staff**, a crosier: a tall staff forming part of a bishop's insignia, headed like a shepherd's crook; **pastoral theology**, that part of theology which treats of the duties of pastors in relation to the cure of souls. [L. *pástor*—*páscĕre*, *pástum*, to feed.]

pastourelle, *pás-tōō-rel'*, *n.* a mediaeval poetic genre, esp. Provençal and French, a dialogue between a knight and a shepherdess, or the like: a movement in a quadrille. [Fr., little shepherdess.]

pastry, *pās'tri*, *n.* articles made of paste or dough collectively: crust of pies, tarts, &c.: a small cake: (*Shak.*) a place where pastry is made: (*obs.*) the art or practice of making pastry.—*n.* **pās'trycook**, a maker or seller of pastry. [paste.]

pasture, *pást'yor*, *n.* (*arch.*) feeding: (*Spens.*) food: grazing: growing grass for grazing: grazing land: a grazing ground, piece of grazing land.—*v.i.* to graze.—*v.t.* to put to graze: to graze on.— *adj.* **past'urable**, fit for pasture.—*n.* **past'urage**, the business of feeding or grazing cattle: pastureland: grass for feeding: right of pasture.—*adj.* **past'ural**, of pasture.—*n.* **past'ure-land**, land suitable for pasture.—*adj.* **past'ureless**. [O.Fr. *pasture* (Fr. *pâture*)—L. *pástūra*—*páscĕre*, *pástum*, to feed.]

pasty, *pās'ti*, *adj.* See under **paste**.

pasty, *pás'ti*, *n.* a meat-pie baked without a dish. [O.Fr. *pastée*—L. *pasta*; see **paste**.]

pat, *pat*, *n.* a gentle stroke with a flat surface, as the palm of the hand: such a stroke as a caress or mark of approbation: a sound as of such a stroke: a small lump, esp. of butter, such as might be moulded by patting.—*v.t.* to strike (now only to strike gently) with the palm of the hand or other flat surface.—*v.i.* to tap: to make the sound of pats, as with the feet: (*pr.p.* **patt'ing**; *pa.t.* and *pa.p.* **patt'ed**).—*adv.* and *adj.* hitting the mark to a nicety: at the right time or place: exactly to the purpose: with or ready for fluent or glib repetition: (*U.S.*; of a hand in poker) not likely to be improved by drawing.—*n.* **pat'- ball**, rounders: gentle hitting in other games.— *adv.* **pat'ly** (*rare*), fitly, conveniently: glibly, fluently.—*n.* **pat'ness.**—**pat on the back**, a mark of encouragement or approbation; **stand pat**, (*U.S.*) in poker, to decide to play one's hand as it is: to refuse to change. [Prob. imit.]

Pat, *pat*, *n.* a nickname for an Irishman. [Patrick.]

patagium, *pat-ə-jī'əm*, *n.* a bat's wing-membrane: the parachute of a flying-squirrel, &c.: the fold of integument between the upper arm and the forearm of a bird: a paired scale on a moth's pronotum:—*pl.* **patagi'a.**—*adj.* **patagial** (*pə-tā'ji-əl*). [L. *patagium*—Gr. *patageion*, an edging.]

Patagonian, *pat-ə-gō'ni-ən*, *n.* an Indian of Patagonia: a giant.—*adj.* of Patagonia: gigantic. [Sp. *patagón*, big foot: the tallness of the Patagonians was grossly exaggerated by travellers.]

patamar, *pat'ə-mär*, *n.* a vessel on the Bombay coast with arched keel and great stem and stern rake. [Port.,—Konkani *pātamāri*.]

Patarin, -ine, Paterine, *pat'ər-in*, *-ēn*, *n.* (*hist.*) orig., an adherent of a popular party in Milan opposed to marriage of priests (11th century): later a nickname for Manichaeans, Cathari, and

other heretics. [Said to be from *Pattaria*, **a** district in Milan.]

Patavinity, *pat-ə-vin'i-ti*, *n.* the diction of the people of Padua, esp. Livy: provincialism generally. [L. *patavīnitās*—*Patavium*, Padua.]

patch, *pach*, *n.* a piece put on or to be put on to mend a defect: a piece of plaster for a cut or sore: a pad for a hurt eye: a small piece of ground: a plot: (*print.*) an overlay to obtain a stronger impression: a small piece of black silk, &c., stuck by ladies on the face, to bring out the complexion by contrast or as a political party badge—common in the 17th and 18th centuries: a smallish area differing in colour or otherwise from its surroundings: a plot of ground: a scrap or fragment: a scrap pieced together with others. —*v.t.* to mend with a patch: to put a patch on: to apply as a patch: to join in patchwork: mend or construct hastily, clumsily, or temporarily (commonly with *up*): to construct as a patchwork: to mark with patches.—*adj.* **patch'able.**—*n.* **patch'- box**, a fancy box for holding the patches worn on the face, generally having a mirror inside the lid.— *adj.* **patched**—*n.* **patch'er**—*adv.* **patch'ily.**—*n.* and *adj.* **patch'ing.**—*ns.* **patch-up'**, a provisional repairing; **patch'work**, work formed of patches or pieces sewed together: an incongruous combination: work patched up or clumsily executed: a surface diversified in patches.—*adj.* **patch'y**, covered with patches: diversified in patches: inharmonious, incongruous.—**not a patch on**, not fit to be compared with. [M.E. *pacche*; origin unknown; poss. conn. with **piece**.]

patch, *pach*, *n.* (*arch.*) a fool or jester: a booby: (*dial.*) an ill-natured person.—*ns.* **patch'cocke**, **patchocke**, (*Spens.*) perhaps a clown (reading and meaning doubtful; cf. **paiock**); **patch'ery**, (*Shak.*) knavery. [Perh. from preceding, from the patched coat; nickname of Cardinal Wolsey's fool, Sexton; perh. It. *pazzo*, fool.]

patchouli, patchouly, *pach'ōō-lē*, also *pə-chōō'lē*, *n.* a labiate shrub (*Pogostemon Patchouly*) of S.E. Asia: a perfume got from its dried branches. [Tamil *patch*, green, *ilai*, leaf.]

pate, *pāt*, *n.* the crown of the head: the head.— *adj.* **pāt'ed**, having a pate. [Origin unknown.]

patella, *pə-tel'ä*, *n.* (*ant.*) a little pan: the knee-pan: (*bot.*) a saucer-like apothecium: **Patella**, the limpet genus:—*pl.* **patell'ae** (*-ē*).—*adjs.* **patell'ar**, of the kneecap: **patell'ate** (or *pat'*), saucer-shaped: limpet-shaped; **patell'iform.**— **patellar reflex**, the knee-jerk. [L., dim. of *patina*, a pan.]

paten, *pat'ən*, *n.* a plate: a communion plate: **a** chalice-cover: a metal disk. [O.Fr. *patene*—L. *patena*, *patina*, a plate—Gr. *patanē*.]

patent, *pā'tənt*, or (esp. in *letters-patent* and *Patent Office*, and in U.S.) *pat'ənt*, *adj.* lying open: conspicuous, obvious, evident: generally accessible: protected by a patent: (*bot.*) spreading: expanding: (*slang*) ingenious.—*n.* an official document, open, and having the Great Seal of the government attached to it, conferring an exclusive right or privilege, as a title of nobility, or the sole right for a term of years to the proceeds of an invention: something invented and protected by a patent: **a** privilege: a certificate.—*v.t.* to secure a patent for.—*n.* **pā'tency**, openness: obviousness.—*adj.* **pā'tentable.**—*ns.* **pātentee'**, one who holds a patent, or to whom a patent is granted; **pā'tent-leath'er**, finely varnished leather.—*adv.* **pā'tently**, openly, obviously.—*ns.* **pā'tentor**, one who grants a patent; **pā'tent-right**, the exclusive right reserved by letters-patent.—*n.pl.* **pā'tent-rolls**, the register of letters-patent issued in England.— **nothing patent**, (*slang*) not very good; **patent medicine**, strictly, a medicine protected by **a** patent: (loosely) any proprietary medicine, esp. one liable to stamp duty, as made by secret process or for other reason; **Patent Office**, an office for the granting of patents for inventions; **patent outside, or inside**, a newspaper printed on the outside or inside only, sold to a publisher who fills the other side with his own material, **a** local news, &c.; **patent still**, a still performing several operations at once, and producing a purer spirit than a pot-still. [L. *patēns*, *-ēntis*, pr.p. of *patēre*, to lie open.]

pater, *pā'tər*, *n.* (*slang*) father. [L. *păter*.]

patera, *pat'ə-rä*, *n.* a round flat dish, esp. for receiving a sacrificial libation among the Romans : (*archit.*) a round flat ornament in bas-relief in friezes, &c.—often applied loosely to rosettes and other flat ornaments :—*pl.* **pat'erae** (*-rē*). [L.,— *patēre*, to lie open.]

patercove, *pat'ər-kōv*, *n.* Same as **patrico**.

paterero, *pat-ə-rā'rō*, *n.* :—*pl.* **patere'roes** (*-rōz*). Same as **pederero**.

paterfamilias, *pā-tər-fə-mil'i-as*, or *pat'ər-*, *n.* the father or head of a family or household :—*pl.* (strictly) **patresfamil'ias**. [L. *păter*, a father : *familiās*, old gen. of *familia*, a household.]

paternal, *pə-tər'n(ə)l*, *adj.* of a father : on the father's side : derived or inherited from the father : fatherly : showing the disposition or manner of a father.—*n.* **pater'nalism**, a system or tendency in which provident fostering care is apt to pass into unwelcome interference.—*adv.* **pater'nally**. —*n.* **pater'nity**, state or fact of being a father : fatherhood : the relation of a father to his children : origin on the father's side : origination or authorship. [L. *pater* (Gr. *patēr*), a father.]

paternoster, *pat-ər-nos'tər*, or *pāt'*, *n.* the Lord's Prayer : a muttered formula or spell : a harangue : a large bead in a rosary, at which, in telling, the Lord's Prayer is repeated : a rosary : anything strung like a rosary, esp. a fishing-line with hooks at intervals : (*archit.*) an ornament shaped like beads, used in astragals, &c. [L. *Pater noster*, ' Our Father,' the first words of the Lord's Prayer.]

path, *päth*, *n.* a way trodden out by the feet : a way for foot-passengers : course, route, line along which anything moves : course of action or conduct (*pl.* **paths**, *pädhz*).—*v.i.* (*Shaks.*) to go.— *n.* **path'finder**, one who explores the route, a pioneer.—*adj.* **path'less**, without a path : untrodden.—*n.* **path'way**, a path. [O.E. *pæth*; Ger. *pfad*.]

Pathan, *pə-tän'*, *put-(h)än'*, *n.* an Afghan proper : one of Afghan race settled in India.—Also *adj.*

pathos, *pā'thos*, *n.* the quality that raises pity.— *adj.* **pathetic** (*pə-thet'ik*), (*obs.*) relating to or affecting the passions or their expressions : affecting the emotions of pity, grief, sorrow : touching : (*anat.*) applied to the superior oblique muscle, which turns the eyeball upwards, and to the trochlear nerve connecting with it.—*n.* that which is pathetic : the style or manner fitted to excite emotion : (in *pl.*) attempts at pathetic expression. —*adj.* **pathet'ical**. — *adv.* **pathet'ically**.— *adj.* **pathic** (*path'ik*), passive.—*n.* a passive subject : a catamite.—*ns.* **pathogen** (*path'o-jen*), an organism or substance that causes disease ; **pathogen'esis**, **pathogeny** (*pə-thoj'ə-ni*), mode of production or development of disease.—*adjs.* **pathogenetic** (*path-ō-ji-net'ik*), **pathogenic** (*-jen'ik*), **pathog'enous**, producing disease ; **pathognomon'ic** (Gr. *gnōmōn*, a judge, index), indicative of a particular disease.—*n.* **pathog'nomy**.—*adjs.* **patholog'ic**, **-al**, relating to pathology in either sense.—*adv.* **patholog'ically**.—*ns.* **pathol'ogist** ; **pathol'ogy**, the study of diseases : the study of emotions or passions ; **pathopho'bia** (Gr. *phobos*, fear), morbid fear of disease.—**pathetic fallacy**, the reading of one's own emotion into external nature. [Gr. *pathos*, experience, suffering, feeling, pathos.]

'atible, *pat'i-bl*, *adj.* capable of suffering or being acted on : passible—*pati*, to suffer.]

'atibulary, *pə-tib'ū-lə-ri*, *adj.* of or pertaining to a gibbet or gallows. [L. *patibulum*, a gibbet.]

'atience, *pā'shəns*, *n.* quality of being able calmly to endure suffering, toil, delay, vexation, or the like : sufferance : a card-game of various kinds, generally for one person, the object to fit the cards as they turn up into some scheme : a species of dock (also **pa'tience-dock'** ; *Rumex Patientia*) used like spinach, or other species of dock : also applied to bistort.—*adj.* **pā'tient**, sustaining pain, delay, &c., without repining : not easily provoked :

persevering in long-continued or minute work : expecting with calmness : long-suffering : enduring : susceptible (of an interpretation).—*n.* one who bears or suffers : a person under medical or surgical treatment : a physician's client.—*v.t.* (*Shak.*) to make patient.—*adv.* **pā'tiently**. [Fr.,— L. *patientia*—*patī*, to bear.]

patin, **patine**. Obs. forms of **paten**.

patina, *pat'i-nä*, *n.* a shallow Roman pan : a eucharistic paten : a film of basic copper carbonate that forms on exposed surfaces of copper or bronze : a similar film of oxide, &c., on other metals : a film or surface appearance that develops on other substances (wood, flint, &c.) on long exposure or burial.—*adj.* **pat'inâted**.—*n.* **patinā'tion**.—*adj.* **pat'ined**. [L. *patina*, a dish, a kind of cake.]

patio, *pä'ti-ō*, *-tyō*, *n.* a courtyard. [Sp.]

patois, *pät'wä*, *n.* a vulgar or provincial dialect :— *pl.* **patois** (*-wäz*). [Fr. ; origin unknown.]

patonce, *pə-tons'*, *adj.* (*her.*) of a cross, having four arms expanding in curves from the centre, with floriated ends. [Origin unknown.]

patriarch, *pā'tri-ärk*, *n.* one who governs his family by paternal right : (*B.*) one of the early heads of families from Adam downwards to Abraham, Jacob, and his sons : a bishop ranking above primates and metropolitans : the head of certain Eastern Churches : a father or founder : a venerable old man : an oldest inhabitant : an old leader of a flock : the most imposing and greatest of its kind.—*adj.* **patriarch'al**, belonging or subject to a patriarch : like a patriarch : of the nature of a patriarch.—*ns.* **patriarch'alism**, the condition of tribal government by a patriarch : **pa'triarchate**, the province, dignity, office, term, or residence of a church patriarch : patriarchy ; **pa'triarchism**, government by a patriarch ; **pa'triarchy**, a community of related families under the authority of a patriarch : the patriarchal system.—**patriarchal cross**, a cross with two horizontal bars. [Gr. *patriarchēs*—*patriā*, family—*patēr*, father, *archē*, rule.]

patrician, *pə-trish'ən*, *n.* a member or descendant by blood or adoption of one of the original families of citizens forming the Roman people— opp. to *plebeian* : a nobleman of a new order nominated by the emperor in the later Roman Empire : an imperial Roman provincial administrator in Italy or Africa : a hereditary noble : an aristocrat. — Also *adj.* — *adj.* **patri'cianly**. — *n.* **patriciate** (*pə-trish'i-āt*), the position of a patrician : the patrician order. [L. *patrīcius*—*pater*, *patris*, a father.]

patricide, *pat'ri-sīd*, *n.* the murder of one's own father : one who murders his father.—*adj.* **patrici'dal**. [Doubtful L. *patricīda*, as if from *pater*, *patris*, father, *caedēre*, to kill ; prob. an error for *parricīda* ; see **parricide**.]

patrick, *pat'rik*, *n.* a 17th-century Irish halfpenny. —*adj.* **Patrician** (*pə-trish'ən*), of St Patrick.— **St Patrick's cabbage**, a saxifrage, London pride ; **St Patrick's cross**, a red saltire on a white ground, representing Ireland. [St *Patrick* (L. *Patrīcius*), 5th-century christianiser of Ireland.]

patrico, *pat'ri-kō*, *n.* (*slang*) a hedge-priest.— Also **pat'ercove**. [First part unexplained ; see **cove** (2).]

patrilineal, *pat-ri-lin'i-əl*, **patrilinear**, *-ər*, *adjs.* reckoned through the father or through males alone. [L. *pater*, *patris*, father, *linea*, line.]

patrilocal, *pat-ri-lō'kl*, *adj.* (of a form of marriage) in which the wife goes to live with the husband's group. [L. *pater*, *patris*, father, *locālis*—*locus*, place.]

patrimony, *pat'ri-mən-i*, *n.* an inheritance from a father or from ancestors : a church estate or revenue — *adj.* **patrimonial** (*-mō'ni-əl*).—*adv.* **patrimō'nially**. [L. *patrimōnium*, a paternal estate—*pater*, *patris*, a father.]

patriot, *pā'tri-ət*, sometimes *pat'*, *n.* one who truly, or ostentatiously and injudiciously, loves and serves his fatherland.—*adj.* devoted to one's country.— *adj.* **patriotic** (*pat-ri-ot'ik*, or *pāt'-*), like a patriot : actuated by a love of one's country : directed to the public welfare.—*adv.* **patriot'ically**.—*n.* **pā'-**

triotism (or *pat'*). [Gr. *patriōtēs*, fellow-countrymen—*patrios*—*patēr*, a father.]

Patripassian, *pat-ri-pas'i-ən*, *n.* a member of one of the earliest classes of anti-Trinitarian sectaries (2nd century), who denied the distinction of three persons in one God, maintaining that the sufferings of the Son could be predicated of the Father.—Also *adj.*—*n.* **Patripass'ianism.** [L. *pater, patris,* father, *patī, passus,* to suffer.]

patristic, -al, *pə-tris'tik, -əl, adjs.* pertaining to the fathers of the Christian Church.—*n.* **patris'ticism** (-*sizm*), mode of thought, &c., of the fathers.—*n.pl.* **patris'tics,** the knowledge of the fathers as a subject of study—sometimes **patrol'ogy.** [Gr. *patēr, pat(e)ros,* a father.]

patrol, *pə-trōl',* *v.i.* to go the rounds for purpose of watching, repressing, protecting, inspecting, &c.: to be on duty on a beat.—*v.t.* to go the rounds of: to perambulate: (*pr.p.* **patrōll'ing;** *pa.t.* and *pa.p.* **patrōlled').**—*n.* the act or service of going the rounds: perambulation: a body of men who go the rounds: a small reconnoitring party: a small group of boy scouts or girl guides. —*ns.* **patrŏll'er;** **patrol'-leader,** a boy scout or girl guide at the head of a patrol: **patrol'man,** (*U.S.*) a policeman on duty on a beat; **patrol'wagon,** (*U.S.*) a prison-van. [O.Fr. *patrouille,* a patrol, *patrouiller,* to patrol, orig. to paddle in the mud.]

patron, *pā'trən,* *n.* in ancient Rome, the former master of a freed slave, retaining certain rights: a Roman patrician who gave countenance and legal aid to his client in return for services: formerly, one who accepted a dedication and gave the author a present: a protector: one who countenances or encourages: a customer: a habitual attender: an upholder: one who has the right to appoint to any office, esp. to a living in the church: a guardian saint: captain of a Mediterranean vessel: a slave-owner: (*obs.*) a pattern:—*fem.* **pā'troness.**—*n.* **patronage** (*pat'*), support given by a patron: (*Spens.*) protection: guardianship of saints: the right of bestowing offices, privileges, or church benefices: habitual commercial dealings.—*v.t.* (*Shak.*) to countenance. —*adj.* **patronal** (*pāt', pat'rən-l, pə-trō'nl*).—*v.t.* **patronise** (*pat'*), to act as a patron toward: to give countenance or encouragement to: to assume the condescending air of a patron toward.—*n.* **pat'roniser.**—*adj.* **pat'ronising.**—*adv.* **pat'ronisingly.**—*adj.* **pā'tronless.**—**patron saint,** a saint regarded as a protector. [L. *patrōnus*—*pater, patris,* a father.]

patronymic, *pat-rə-nim'ik, adj.* derived from the name of a father or an ancestor.—*n.* a name so derived. [Gr. *patrōnymikos*—*patēr,* a father, *onyma* (*onoma*), a name.]

patroon, *pə-trōōn',* *n.* captain of a ship: coxswain of a longboat: holder of a grant of land under the old Dutch government of New York or New Jersey.—*n.* **patroon'ship.** [Fr. *patron,* Sp. *patrón,* and Du. *patroon*; cf. **patron.**]

patte, *pât,* *n.* a narrow band keeping a belt or sash in its place. [Fr.]

patté, pattée, *pa-tā', pat'i, adj.* (*her.*; of a cross) spreading towards the ends, or having the ends expanded in three clawlike divisions. [Fr., pawed.]

patten, *pat'n, n.* (*obs.*) a wooden shoe: a wooden sole mounted on an iron ring to raise the shoe above the mud: the base of a pillar.—*v.i.* to go on pattens.—*adj.* **patt'ened,** with pattens. [O.Fr. *patin,* clog (now skate), perh.—*patte,* paw.]

patten. An old form (*Shak.*) of **paten.**

patter, *pat'ər, v.i.* to pat or strike often, as hailstones: to make the sound of a succession of light pats: to run with short quick steps.—*n.* the sound of pattering. [Freq. of **pat.**]

patter, *pat'ər, v.i.* to repeat the Lord's Prayer: to gabble prayers: to talk rapidly and glibly, in the manner of a conjurer or comic singer.—*v.t.* to repeat hurriedly, to gabble.—*n.* glib talk, chatter: the cant of a class.—*ns.* **patt'erer,** one who sells articles on the street by speechifying: **patt'ersong,** a comic song in which a great many words are sung or spoken very rapidly.—**patter flash,** to talk the jargon of thieves. [**paternoster.**]

pattern, *pat'ərn, n.* a person or thing to be copied: a model: a model of an object to be cast, from which a mould is prepared: a sample: a typical example: a decorative design: a particular disposition of forms and colours: a design or figure repeated indefinitely: the distribution of shot on a target.—*v.t.* (*Shak.*) to make or be a pattern for: (*Shak.*) to match, parallel: to take as a pattern: to fashion after a pattern: to make a pattern upon.—*ns.* **patt'ern-maker,** one who makes the patterns for moulders in foundry-work; **patt'ern-shop,** the place in which patterns for a factory are prepared; **patt'ern-wheel,** the count-wheel in a clock. [Fr. *patron,* patron, pattern; cf. **patron.**]

pattle, *pât'l,* **pettle,** *pet'l, n.* (*Scot.*) a small long-handled spade for cleaning a plough. [Origin obscure; cf. **paddle.**]

patty, *pat'i, n.* a little pie.—*n.* **patt'y-pan,** a pan for baking patties. [Fr. *pâté*; cf. **pasty.**]

patulous, *pat'ū-ləs, adj.* spreading.—*n.* **pat'ulin,** a drug got from the mould *Penicillium patulum.* [L. *patulus*—*patēre,* to lie open.]

paucity, *paw'sit-i, n.* fewness: smallness of quantity. [L. *paucitās, -ātis*—*paucus,* few.]

paughty, *pawhh'ti, adj.* (*Scot.*) haughty. [Origin unknown.]

paul. Same as **pawl.**

paul, *pawl, n.* a paolo.—*ns.* **Paul'ian, Paul'ianist,** a follower of Paul of Samosata, a third-century Monarchian Unitarian of Antioch.—Also *adjs.*—*n.* **Paulician** (-*ish'ən*), a member of a seventh-century sect in Armenia and later in Thrace, with Marcionite and Adoptianist affinities (perh. from Paul of Samosata, or the apostle, or one of their founders).—Also *adj.*—*adj.* **Paul'ine** (-*īn*), of the apostle Paul.—*n.* a member of any religious order named after him: a scholar of St Paul's School, London.—*adj.* **Paulinian** (-*in'i-ən*), Pauline.—*ns.* **Paul'inism,** the teaching or theology of Paul; **Paul'inist.**—*adj.* **Paulinist'ic.**—**Paul Jones** (*jōnz*), a dance in the course of which each man seizes another partner—perh. from the Scottish-American seaman Paul Jones (1747-92), who excelled in the capture of prizes; **Paul Pry** (*prī*), one who pries into other people's business—from a character in John Poole's play (1825) so named; **Paul's'-man,** formerly, a lounger in the middle aisle of St Paul's, London. [L. *Paulus, Paullus,* a Roman cognomen, meaning 'little.']

pauldron, *pawl'drən,* **pouldron,** *pōl', n.* a separable shoulder-plate in armour. [O.Fr. *espalleron*—*espalle,* the shoulder.]

paulo-post-future, *paw'lō-pōst-fū'tyər, adj.* and *n.* future perfect: future immediately after the present. [L. *paulō,* a little, *post,* after, *futūrum,* future.]

Paulownia, *pawl-ō'ni-ä, n.* a Chinese and Japanese genus of trees of the figwort family, with showy flowers. [Named after the Russian princess Anna *Pavlovna.*]

paunce. See **pansy.**

paunch, *pawn(t)sh, n.* the belly: a protuberant belly: the first and largest stomach of a ruminant: (*naut.*) a rope mat to prevent chafing.—*v.t.* to eviscerate.—*adj.* **paunch'y,** big-bellied. [O.Fr. *panche* (Fr. *panse*)—L. *pantex, panticis.*]

pauper, *paw'pər, n.* a destitute person: one not required to pay costs in a law suit: one supported by charity or by some public provision:—*fem.* **pau'peress.**—*n.* **pauperisā'tion.**—*v.t.* **pau'perise,** to reduce to pauperism: to accustom to expect or depend on support from without.—*n.* **pau'perism,** state of being a pauper. [L., poor.]

pause, *pawz, n.* intermission: a temporary stop: cessation caused by doubt: hesitation: a mark for suspending the voice: (*mus.*) a continuance of a note or rest beyond its time, or a mark indicating this.—*v.i.* (*Shak.* v.t. reflex.) to make a pause.—*v.t.* to cause to stop.—*adjs.* **paus'al;** **pause'ful;**—*adv.* **pause'fully.**—*adj.* **pause'less.** —*adv.* **pause'lessly.**—*n.* **paus'er.**—*n.* and *adj.* **paus'ing;** —*adv.* **paus'ingly.**—**give pause,** cause to hesitate. [Fr.,—L. *pausa*—Gr. *pausis,* from *pauein,* to cause to cease.]

pavan, *pav'ən,* *n.* (*Shak.*) a slow dance, muc

practised in Spain: music for it, in 4-4 time.—
Also **pav′ane**, **pav′en**, **pav′in**. [Fr. *pavane*, or
Sp. or It. *pavana*—L. *pāvō, -ōnis*, peacock;
prob. not for It. *Padovana*, pertaining to *Padua*.]

pave, *pāv*, *v.t.* to cover with slabs or other close-set
pieces, so as to form a level surface for walking
on: to cover with anything close-set: to be such
a covering for.—*n.* (*U.S.*) pavement.—*n.* **pā′vage**,
a charge, or right to levy a charge, for paving
streets.—*adj.* **paved**.—*n.* **pave′ment**, a paved
surface, or that with which it is paved: a footpath by the side of a road (sometimes even when
unpaved): (*U.S.*) a roadway: a floor-like surface:
an underlying bed, esp. of fireclay under coal.—
v.t. to pave: to be a pavement for.—*adj.* **pā′ved**,
paved.—*n.* and *adj.* **pā′ving**.—*ns.* **pa′ving-stone**;
pā′viour, one who lays pavement or rams sets:
a paving-stone.—Also **pā′ver**, **pā′vior**.—**on the
pavement**, without a lodging; **pavement artist**,
one who seeks a living by drawing coloured pictures
on the pavement; **pavement epithelium**, epithelium in the form of a layer of flat cells; **pavement
light**, a window of glass blocks in the pavement
to light a cellar; **pave the way for**, to prepare
the way for: make easier: help to bring on. [Fr.
paver, prob. a back-formation from *pavement*—
L. *pavīmentum*—*pavīre*, to beat hard; cog. with
Gr. *paiein*, to beat.]

pavid, *pav′id*, *adj.* timid. [L. *pavidus*.]

pavilion, *pə-vil′yən*, *n.* a tent, esp. a large or
luxurious one: a tent-like covering: (*obs.*) a
canopy: a light building for players and spectators
of a game: an ornamental or showy building for
pleasure purposes: a projecting section of a
building, usually with a tent-like roof and much
decorated: a hospital block: an exhibition building: an ornamental building often turreted or
domed: the bell of a horn: the outer ear: (*obs.*) a
flag or ensign.—*v.t.* to furnish with pavilions: to
cover, as with a tent.—*n.* **pavil′ion-roof**, a tent-
like roof.—**Chinese pavilion**, a set of bells hanging
from a frame on a pole. [Fr. *pavillon*—L. *pāpiliō,
-ōnis*, a butterfly, a tent.]

pavis, **pavise**, *pav′is*, *n.* a shield for the whole
body. [O.Fr. *pavais*—It. *pavese*, prob. from *Pavia*
in Italy.]

Pavo, *pā′vō*, *n.* the peacock genus.—*n.* **pavone**
(*pə-vōn′*; *Spens.*), a peacock.—*adjs.* **pavō′nian**,
pavonine (*pav′ən-īn*). [L. *pāvō, -ōnis*, peacock.]

paw, *paw*, *n.* a clawed foot: (jocularly or contemptuously) a hand, or hand-writing.—*v.i.* to
draw the forefoot along the ground: to strike the
ground with the forefoot: to strike out with the
paw: to feel about or over anything, esp. offensively.—*v.t.* to scrape, feel, handle, or strike with
the forefoot or hand: to handle grossly, coarsely,
or clumsily. [O.Fr. *poe*, *powe*, prob. Gmc.; cf.
Du. *poot*, Ger. *pfote*.]

paw, *paw*, *interj.* (*obs.*) pah.—*adj.* (also **paw′paw**)
foul: obscene.

pawk, *pawk*, *n.* (*Scot.*) a trick.—*adv.* **pawk′ily**.—*n.*
pawk′iness.—*adj.* **pawk′y**, drily or slyly humorous. [Origin unknown.]

pawl, *pawl*, *n.* a catch engaging with the teeth of
a ratchet wheel to prevent backward movement.
[Origin obscure; poss. conn. with Du. or Fr. *pal*,
L. *pālus*, stake.]

pawn, *pawn*, *n.* something deposited as security
for repayment or performance: state of being
pledged (as *in* or *at pawn*).—*v.t.* to give in pledge:
to pledge.—*ns.* **pawn′broker**, a broker who lends
money on pawns; **pawn′broking**; **pawnee′**,
one who takes anything in pawn; **pawn′er**, one
who gives a pawn or pledge as security for money
borrowed; **pawn′shop**, a shop of a pawnbroker;
pawn′ticket, a ticket marked with the name of
the article, the amount advanced, &c., delivered
to the pawner of anything. [O.Fr. *pan*; cf. Du.
pand; connexion with L. *pannus*, cloth, very
doubtful.]

awn, *pawn*, *n.* a small piece in chess of lowest
rank and range: (*fig.*) a humble tool or lightly
valued agent. [O.Fr. *paon*, a foot-soldier—L.L.
pedō, -ōnis, a flat-footed person, a walker—L. *pēs,
pedis*, the foot.]

pawn, *pawn*, *n.* a gallery or covered walk. [Cf.
Du. *pand*.]

pawn, **pown**, **powin**, *pown*, *n.* (chiefly *Scot.*) **a**
peacock. [O.Fr. *poun*, Fr. *paon*—L. *pāvō, -ōnis*.]

pawnce. See **pansy**.

Pawnee, *paw′nē*, or *-nē′*, *n.* one of a tribe of Indians in
Nebraska, &c., afterwards in Oklahoma.—Also *adj.*

pawnee, *paw′nē*. See under **brandy**.

pawnee. See under **pawn** (1).

pawpaw. See **paw**, **papaw**.

pax, *paks*, *n.* the kiss of peace: an osculatory.—
interj. truce. — *n.* **pax′-board**, **pax′-brede** (i.e.
board), an osculatory. [L. *pāx*, peace.]

paxiuba, *päsh-ē-ōō′bä*, *n.* a Brazilian palm (*Iriartea
exorrhiza*) with stilt-roots. [Port., from Tupí.]

paxwax, *paks′waks*, *n.* the strong tendon in an
animal's neck. [Orig. *fax-wax*—O.E. (Anglian)
fæx (W.S. *feax*), hair, *weaxan*, to grow.]

pay, *pā*, *v.t.* (*obs.*) to satisfy, gratify: to give what
is due (in satisfaction of a debt, in exchange, in
compensation, in remuneration, &c.) to: to **give**
in satisfaction of a debt, in exchange, compensation,
remuneration, &c.: to settle, discharge, as a claim,
bill, debt, duty: to hand over money, &c., for: to
be or yield satisfactory remuneration or compensation for, or enough to discharge: to yield:
to be profitable to: to render: (*Shak.* and *dial.*)
to thrash: (*naut.*) of a rope, to allow or cause to
run out.—*v.i.* to hand over money or other equivalent, compensation, &c.: to afford an equivalent
or means of making payment: to be worth one's
trouble: to be profitable: to suffer or be punished:
to be the subject of payment of (*pr.p.* **pay′ing**;
pa.t. and *pa.p.* **paid**, (*obs.* except in the nautical
sense) **payed**, *pād*). — *n.* (*obs.*) satisfaction:
money given for service: salary, wages: receipt
of pay, service for pay, hire (esp. for an evil purpose): payment or time of payment: remunerative
yield of mineral.—*adj.* **paid** (see separate article).—
adj. **pay′able**, that may or should be paid: due:
profitable.—*ns.* **pay′-bill**, **-sheet**, a statement of
moneys to be paid to workmen, &c.; **pay′-box**,
pay′-desk, a box or desk at which a customer
pays; **pay′-day**, a regular day for payment, as of
wages; **pay′-dirt**, **-grav′el**, gravel or sand containing enough gold to be worth working; **payee′**,
one to whom money is paid; **pay′er**.—*n.* and
adj. **pay′ing**.—*ns.* **pay′-list**, **-roll**, a list of persons
entitled to pay, with the amounts due to each;
pay′-load, the part of an aeroplane's load for
which revenue is obtained; **pay′master**, the
master who pays: one who pays workmen, soldiers,
&c.; **pay′ment**, the act of paying: the discharge
of a debt by money or its equivalent in value:
that which is paid: recompense: reward: punishment; **pay′-office**, the place where payments are
made.—**pay back**, to pay in return (of a debt):
to give tit for tat; **pay down**, to pay in cash on
the spot; **pay for**, to make amends for: to
suffer for: to bear the expense of; **pay in**, to
contribute to a fund; **paying guest**, a boarder in
a private house; **Paymaster General**, the
minister at the head of a department of the
Treasury that makes payments on behalf of
government departments: (*U.S.*) in the navy, an
officer in charge of the Bureau dealing with payments, clothing, &c.: formerly also a similar officer
in the army; **pay off**, to pay in full and discharge: to take revenge upon: to requite: (*naut.*)
to fall away to leeward; **pay one's** or **its**, **way**,
to have, or bring, enough to pay expenses; **pay
out**, to cause to run out, as rope: to disburse:
to punish deservedly; **pay round**, to turn the
ship's head; **pay the piper**, to have all expenses
to pay; **pay through the nose**, to pay dearly;
pay up, to pay in full: to pay arrears: to accept
the necessity and pay. [Fr. *payer*—L. *pācāre*, to
appease; cf. *pāx*, peace.]

pay, *pā*, *v.t.* to smear with tar, &c.:—*pa.t.* and *pa.p.*
payed. [O.Fr. *peier*—L. *picāre*, to pitch.]

paynim, *pā′nim*, *n.* (*obs.*) heathendom: a heathen:
a non-Christian, esp. a Moslem.—Also *adj.*—Also
pai′nim, **pā′nim** (*Milt.*).—*n.* **pay′nimry**, heathendom. [O.Fr. *paienisme*, paganism—L. *pāgānismus*
—*pāgānus*, a pagan.]

paysagist, *pā'zə-jist*, *n.* a landscape-painter. [Fr. *paysagiste*.]

paysd, *pāzd*, (*Spens.*) for **peised, poised.**

pea, *pē*, *n.* a new singular formed from **pease** (q.v.), which was mistaken for a plural, with a new plural **peas**—the nutritious seed of the papilionaceous climbing plants *Pisum sativum* (garden pea) and *P. arvense* (field pea): the plant itself (also **pea'-plant**): extended to various similar seeds and plants (esp. of the genus Lathyrus), and to various small rounded objects, e.g. roe of salmon and some other fish, very small pieces of coal.— *ns.* **pea'berry**, a small round coffee seed, growing singly; **pea'-crab**, a little round crab (Pinnotheres) that lives symbiotically in lamellibranch shells.— *n. and adj.* **pea'-green** (or *-grēn'*), green like green peas.—*ns.* **pea'-iron**, limonite in little round nodules; **pea'nut**, monkey-nut or ground-nut (Arachis); **pea'-pod'**; **pea'-ri'fle**, a rifle throwing a very small bullet; **pea'cod, peas'cod** (see peasecod); **pea'shooter**, a small metal tube for blowing peas through; **pea'-soup** (see **pease-soup**); **pea-soup'er**, a fog like pea-soup.—*adj.* **pea-soup'y**.—*ns.* pea-stone, pisolite; **pea'-straw** (see **pease-straw**); **pea'-trainer**, an erection for pea-plants to climb on.—**Egyptian pea**, the chickpea; **peanut butter**, a paste made from ground roasted peanuts; **peanut oil**, oil expressed from peanuts; **split peas**, peas stripped of their membranous covering, dried and halved; **Sturt's desert pea**, a scarlet-flowered Australian glory-pea. [See **pease**.]

pea, *pē*, *n.* (*rare*) (*obs.*) a pea-fowl. [O.E. *péa* (*páwa*) —L. *pāvō*.]

peace, *pēs*, *n.* a state of quiet: freedom from disturbance: freedom from war: a treaty that ends a war: freedom from contention: freedom from disturbance: ease of mind or conscience: quiet: stillness: silence.—*v.i.* (*Shak.*) to be silent—passing in the *imper.* into *interj.* silence: be silent: hist.—*adj.* **peace'able**, disposed to peace: peaceful.—*n.* **peace'ableness**.—*adv.* **peace'ably**.—*n.* **peace'-breaker**, one who breaks or disturbs the peace.—*adj.* **peace'ful**, enjoying peace: tending towards or favouring peace: inclined to peace: belonging to time of peace: consistent with peace: tranquil: calm: serene.—*adv.* **peace'fully**.—*n.* **peace'fulness**.—*adj.* **peace'less**.—*ns.* **peace'lessness**; **peace'maker**, one who makes or produces peace: one who reconciles enemies: a revolver; **peace'making**; **peace'-monger**, a peacemaker from the point of view of those who think him a sentimental busybody; **peace'-off'ering**, among the Jews a thank-offering to God: a gift offered towards reconciliation, propitiation, or deprecation; **peace'-off'icer**, an officer whose duty it is to preserve the peace: a police-officer.—*adj.* **peace'-part'ed**, (*Shak.*) dismissed from the world in peace.—*ns.* **peace'-par'ty**, a political party advocating the making or the preservation of peace; **peace'-pipe**, the calumet; **peace'time**, time when there is no war.—*adj.* **peacetime**.—*n.* **peace'-warrant**, a warrant of arrest issued by a Justice of the Peace.—**at peace**, in a state of peace: not at war; **breach of the peace** (see **breach**); **hold one's peace**, remain silent; **in peace**, in enjoyment of peace; **keep the peace**, to refrain from disturbing the public peace; **kiss of peace** (see **kiss**); **peace establishment**, the reduced military strength maintained in time of peace; **peace of God**, the protection from acts of private warfare formerly offered by the Church to consecrated persons and places, and on Sundays and holy days; **letters of peace** (see **pacifical**); **make one's peace with**, to reconcile or to be reconciled with; **make peace**, to end a war; **the king's or queen's peace** (see **king**); **swear the peace**, to take oath before a magistrate that a certain person ought to be put under bond to keep the peace. [O.Fr. *pais* (Fr. *paix*)—L. *pāx, pācis*, peace.]

peach, *pēch*, *v.t.* (*Shak.*) to accuse, inform against, betray.—*v.i.* to betray one's accomplice: to become informer.—*n.* **peach'er**. [Aphetic form of **appeach**.]

peach, *pēch*, *n.* a sweet, juicy, velvety-skinned stone-fruit: the tree (*Prunus*, or *Amygdalus, persica*) bearing it, close akin to the almond: extended to other fruits and fruit-trees, as the quandong: (*U.S.*) peach-brandy: (*slang*) anything regarded as a very choice example of its kind, esp. a girl (in U.S. also **peacherino**, *-ə-rē'nō*): a yellow slightly tinged with red.—*adj.* of the peach: of the colour of a peach.—*ns.* **peach'-bloom'**, the powdery bloom on a peach: a similar appearance on the face, on pottery, &c.: a peach flower (also **peach'-bloss'om**): its pinkish colour: a moth with wings so coloured (*Thyatira batis*); **peach'-blow**, a pinkish glaze on porcelain, esp. Chinese porcelain.—Also *adjs.*—*n.* **peach'-brand'y**, a spirit distilled from the fermented juice of the peach.—*adj.* **peach'-coloured**, of the colour of a ripe peach (yellowish, tinged with red) or of peach-blossom (pink).— *ns.* **peach'-palm**, the pupunha, a South American palm (Bactris or Guilielma) with edible fruit like a peach in appearance; **peach'-stone**; **peach'-tree**; **peach'-water**, a flavouring extract from peach-leaves; **peach'-wood**, the wood of the peach-tree: Nicaragua wood (Caesalpinia).—*adj.* **peach'y**.—*n.* **peach'-yell'ows**, a virus disease that turns peach-leaves yellow and kills the tree. [O.Fr. *pesche* (Fr. *pêche*, It. *persica, pesca*)—L. *Persicum* (*mālum*), the Persian (apple). Its native country is unknown.]

peacock, *pē'kok*, *n.* a genus (Pavo) of large birds of the pheasant kind, consisting of the common peacock (*P. cristatus*) and the Javan (*P. muticus*), noted for gay plumage, esp. in the tail-coverts: the male of either species: a vainglorious person. —*v.t.* to make like a peacock.—*v.i.* to strut about or behave like a peacock.—*ns.* **pea'-chick**, a young pea-fowl; **pea'cock-blue'**, the blue of the peacock's neck.—Also *adj.*— *ns.* **pea'cock-butt'erfly**, a butterfly (*Vanessa Io*) with spots like those of the peacock's train; **pea'cock-copp'er**, copper pyrites, from the colours of its tarnish; **peacock'ery**, vainglorious ostentation; **pea'cock-fish**, a variegated Mediterranean wrasse; **pea'cock-flower**, a name for various species of Poinciana (flamboyant tree, Barbados pride).— *adjs.* **pea'cockish**; **pea'cock-like**.—*ns.* **pea'-cock-ore**, bornite: copper-pyrites; **pea'cock-pheas'ant**, an Asiatic genus (Polyplectron) akin to the peacocks and Argus pheasants; **pea'cock-stone**, a jeweller's name for the cartilaginous ligament of some molluscs; **pea'cock-throne'**, the throne of the kings of Delhi, carried off to Persia in 1739.—*adj.* **pea'cocky**.—*ns.* **pea'-fowl**, the peacock or peahen; **pea'hen**, the female of the peacock. [pea (2) and cock, &c.]

pea-crab. See under **pea** (1).

peag, *pēg*, **peak**, *pēk*, *n.* North American Indian shell-money. [Massachusetts *piak*.]

pea-jacket, *pē'-jak'it*, *n.* a sailor's coarse thick overcoat.—Also **pea'-coat**. [Du. *pie* (now *pij*), coat of coarse stuff, and **jacket, coat**.]

peak, *pēk*, *n.* a point: the pointed end or highest point of anything: the top of a mountain, esp. when sharp: a summit: a maximum point in a curve or the corresponding value in anything capable of being represented by a curve: a sharp projection: the projecting front of a cap or (formerly) of a widow's hood: a projecting point of hair on the forehead: a pointed beard: (*naut.*) the upper outer corner of a sail extended by a gaff or yard: the upper end of a gaff.—*adj.* maximum: of a maximum.—*v.i.* to rise in a peak. —*v.t.* (*naut.*) to tilt up.—*adj.* **peaked**, having a peak or peaks.—*n.* **peak'-load**, the maximum demand of electricity, or load on a power-station. —*adj.* **peak'y**, having a peak or peaks: like a peak. [Found from the 16th cent. (*peked* in the 15th); app. connected with **pike**.]

peak, *pēk*, *v.i.* (*Shak.*) to sneak or slink about: to mope: to droop, to look thin or sickly.—*adjs.* **peaked, peak'ing, peak'y**, having a pinched or sickly look, sharp-featured. [Origin unknown.]

peal, *pēl*, *n.* a loud sound: a number of loud sounds one after another: a set of bells tuned to each other: a chime or carillon: the changes rung upon a set of bells.—*v.i.* to resound in peals: (*Spens.*) to appeal.—*v.t.* to give forth in peals: (*Milt.*) to assail with din. [Apparently aphetic for appeal.]

peal, peel, *pēl, n.* (*local*) a grilse: a young sea-trout. [Origin unknown.]

pean, *pēn, n.* a heraldic fur, differing from ermine only in the ground being sable and the spots or. [Perhaps O.Fr. *pene, panne.*]

pean. Same as **peen** and **paean.**

peanut. See under **pea.**

pear, *pār, n.* an esteemed fruit a pome tapering towards the stalk and bulged at the end: the tree (*Pyrus communis*) bearing it, of the apple genus: extended to various fruits (**alligator-, anchovy-pear, prickly-pear,** &c.).—*ns.* **pear'-drop,** a pear-shaped pendant: a pear-shaped, pear-flavoured sweetmeat; **pear'monger,** a seller of pears; **pear'-push, -switch,** an electric push-button in a hanging pear-shaped bob; **pear'-tree.** [O.E. *pere, peru*—L.L. *pira*—L. *pirum* (wrongly *pyrum*), pear.]

pearce, peare, pearst, Spenserian spellings of **pierce, peer, pierced.**

pearl, *pərl, n.* a concretion of nacre formed in a pearl-oyster, pearl-mussel, or other shellfish, around a foreign body or otherwise, prized as a gem: nacre: a paragon or finest example: a lustrous globule: a granule: a tubercle of an antler burr: cataract of the eye: (*print.*) a five-point type (about 15 lines to the inch).—*adj.* of or like pearl: granulated.—*v.t.* to set or adorn with pearls or pearly drops: to make pearly: to make into small round grains.—*v.i.* to take a rounded form: to become like pearls: to fish for pearls.—*ns.* **pearl'-ash,** partly purified potassium carbonate; **pearl'-bar'ley** (see **barley**); **pearl'-butt'on,** a mother-of-pearl button; **pearl'-div'er,** one who dives for pearls.—*adj.* **pearled.**—*ns.* **pearl'er,** a pearl-fisher or his boat; **pearl'-essence,** a silvery preparation from fish scales used in making artificial pearls; **pearl'-eye,** cataract.—*adj.* **pearl'-eyed.**—*ns.* **pearl'-fisher,** one who fishes for pearls; **pearl'-fishery; pearl'-fishing; pearl'-gray, -grey',** a pale grey.—Also *adj.*—*n.* **pearl'iness.**—*n.* and *adj.* **pearl'ing.**—*ns.* **pearl'-ite,** a constituent of steel composed of alternate plates of ferrite and cementite; **pearl'-mill'et,** the bulrush millet or spiked millet (*Pennisetum typhoideum*), a grain much grown in India; **pearl'-muss'el,** a fresh-water mussel (*Unio margaritifera*) that yields pearls; **pearl'-oys'ter,** any oyster that produces pearls, esp. *Avicula* (or *Meleagrina*) *margaritifera*; **pearl'-pow'der,** a cosmetic of basic bismuth nitrate or of bismuth oxychloride; **pearl'-sā'go,** sago in round granules; **pearl'-tapiō'ca,** tapioca granulated and graded acc. to size: a potato-starch imitation; **pearl'-shell,** mother-of-pearl: a pearly or pearl-bearing shell; **pearl'-shell'er; pearl'-shell'ing; pearl'-spar,** a pearly-lustred pale dolomite; **pearl'-stone,** perlite; **pearl'-white,** a material made from fish-scales, used in making artificial pearls: basic nitrate of bismuth, used in medicine and as a cosmetic: bismuth trichloride, used as a pigment: lithopone: calcium sulphate; **pearl'wort,** a genus (Sagina) of small plants akin to chickweed.—*adj.* **pearl'y,** like pearl, nacreous: rich in pearls.—*n.* (in *pl.*, **pearl'ies**) pearl-buttons: coster-mongers' clothes covered with pearl-buttons.—**culture pearl,** a true pearl formed by artificial means, as by planting a piece of mother-of-pearl wrapped in oyster epidermis in the body of an oyster; **false pearl,** an imitation, as a glass bulb coated within with a preparation of fish scales; **pearl disease,** bovine tuberculosis; **pearly nautilus** (see **nautilus**). [Fr. *perle,* prob. either from L. *pirula,* a dim. of *pirum,* a pear, or from L. *pilula,* dim. of *pila,* a ball.]

earl, *pərl, n.* a small loop on the edge of lace, **ribbon,** &c.: in knitting, purl.—*v.t.* to purl.—*ns.* **pearl-edge,** an edging of small loops; **pearl'ing, pearl'in** (*Scot.*), lace of silk or of thread: (in *pl.*) edgings of such lace or clothes trimmed with it. [Cf. **purl.**]

pearmain, *pār'mān, n.* a variety of apple. [App. O.Fr. *parmain, permain.*]

peart, *pērt, adj.* lively: saucy: in good health and spirits.—*adv.* **peart'ly.** [pert.]

peasant, *pez'ənt, n.* a small farmer: a tiller of the soil: a countryman: a rustic: (*obs.*) a low-born or low fellow.—*adj.* of or relating to peasants, rustic, rural: rude.—*n.* **peas'antry,** the body of peasants: the condition or quality of a peasant.—**peasant proprietor,** a peasant who owns and works his own farm; **Peasants' Revolt,** Wat Tyler's rising of 1381; **Peasants' War,** a popular insurrection in Germany, in 1525. [O.Fr. *paisant* (Fr. *paysan*)—*pays*—assumed L. *pāgēnsis*—*pāgus,* a district.]

pease, *pēz, n.* orig., a pea or pea-plant (old *pl.* **peason,** *pēz'ən*): now almost wholly superseded by the new singular **pea** (q.v.) and plural **peas,** except in a collective sense.—*ns.* **pease'-bann'ock,** a bannock of pease-meal; **pease'-blossom; pease'-brose',** brose made of pease-meal; **pease'-cod, peas'cod,** the pod of the pea.—*adj.* **pease'cod-bell'ied,** of a doublet, peaked downwards in front.—*n.* **pease'cod-cuirass',** a cuirass shaped like the peasecod-bellied doublet; **pease'-meal, pease'-porr'idge, pease'-pudd'ing,** meal, porridge, or pudding made from pease; **pease'-soup, pea'-soup,** soup made from pease: a thick yellow heavy-smelling fog; **pease'-straw,** the stems and leaves of the pea-plant after the peas have been picked. [M.E. *pēse, pl. pēsen*—O.E. *pisa,* pl. *pisan*—L.L. *pisa,* L. *pisum*—Gr. *pison* or *pisos.*]

peaseweep, *pēz'wēp.* See **peewit**.

peat, *pēt, n.* a shaped block dug from a bog and dried or to be dried for fuel: the generally brown or nearly black altered vegetable matter (chiefly bog-moss) found in bogs, from which such blocks are cut.—*ns.* **peat'ary, peat'ery, pēt'ary, peat'-bank, -bed, -bog, -moor, -moss,** a region, bog moor, &c., covered with peat: a place from which peat is dug; **peat'-caster,** one who digs peats and throws them on the bank to dry; **peat'-casting; peat'-creel,** a basket for carrying peats; **peat'-hag, -hagg,** a hag in a peat-bog (see **hag** (3)); **peat'-hole; peat'man,** a carter or seller of peats; **peat'-reek',** the smoke of peat, imagined to add a special flavour to whisky: Highland whisky; **peat'-smoke'; peat'-spade,** a spade having a side wing at right angles for cutting peat in rectangular blocks; **peat'-stack',** a stack of peats, drying or stored.—*adj.* **peat'y,** like, of the nature of, abounding in, or composed of, peat. [From the 13th cent. in S.E. Scotland in Anglo-Latin as *peta,* a peat; possibly of British origin; cf. **piece.**]

peat, *pēt, n.* (*arch.*) an endearment applied to a woman or girl or friend or favourite: an advocate favoured by a judge.—*n.* **peat'ship** (*Scott*). [Origin obscure.]

peavey, peavy, *pē'vi, n.* (*U.S.*) a lumberman's spiked and hooked lever. [Joseph *Peavey,* its inventor.]

peaze. See **peise.**

peba, *pē'bä, n.* a South American armadillo. [Tupí.]

pebble, *peb'l, n.* a small roundish stone, esp. water-worn: transparent and colourless rock-crystal: a lens made of it: a semi-precious agate: a grained appearance on leather, as if pressed by pebbles: a large size of gunpowder.—*adj.* of pebble.—*v.t.* to stone or pelt: to impart pebble to (leather).—*adjs.* **pebb'led; pebb'ly,** full of pebbles.—*ns.* **pebb'le-pow'der,** gunpowder in large cubical grains; **pebb'le-stone,** a pebble; **pebb'le-ware,** a fine pottery of mixed coloured clays; **pebb'ling.** [O.E. *papol* (-*stán*), a pebble (-stone).]

pébrine, *pā-brēn', n.* a destructive protozoan disease of silk-worms. [Fr.]

pec, *pek, n.* a photoelectric cell. [From the initials.]

pecan, *pi-kan', n.* a North American hickory (also **pecan'-tree**): its nut (**pecan'-nut**). [Indian name; cf. Cree *pakan.*]

peccable, *pek'ə-bl, adj.* liable to sin.—*ns.* **peccabil'ity; pecc'ancy,** sinfulness: transgression.—

adj. **pecc'ant**, sinning: offending: morbid.—adv. **pecc'antly**. [L. peccāre, -ātum, to sin.]

peccadillo, pek-ə-dil'ō, n. a trifling fault:—pl. **peccadill'os** (or **peccadill'oes**). [Sp. pecadillo, dim. of pecado—L. peccātum, a sin.]

peccary, pek'ə-ri, n. either of two species of hog-like South American animals. [Carib pakira.]

pech, pegh, pehh, v.i. (Scot.) to pant.—n. a pant. [Imit.]

Pecht, Peght, pehht, n. (Scot.) a Pict. [O.E. (Anglian) Pehtas (W.S. Peohtas), Picts.]

peck, pek, n. a measure of capacity for dry goods, 2 gallons, or one-fourth of a bushel: a measuring vessel holding this quantity: an indefinitely great amount (as a peck of troubles). [M.E. pekke, pek. —O.Fr. pek, generally a horse's feed of oats; origin unknown.]

peck, pek, v.t. to strike or pick up with the point of the beak or other sharp instrument: to make, render, or cause to be by quick movement of the beak, &c.: to eat sparingly or with affectation of daintiness or (slang) eat in general: to kiss with dabbing movement.—v.i. to strike or feed with the beak or in similar manner: to cavil.— n. an act of pecking: a hole made by pecking: (slang) food.—ns. **peck'er**, that which pecks: a woodpecker: a kind of hoe: a part with an up-and-down movement in a telegraph instrument: (slang) spirit (as if orig. beak, nose, as in keep your pecker up); **peck'ing.**—adj. **peck'ish**, somewhat hungry. [App. a form of **pick** (1).]

peck, pek, v.t. (Shak. pecke) to pitch: to jerk.— v.i. to incline: to stumble, esp. of a horse by failing to put the foot down flat.—n. **peck'ing**, stone-throwing. [A form of **pitch** (2); cf. **pick** (2).]

Pecksniffian, pek-snif'i-ən, adj. like or of the hypocrite Pecksniff in Dickens's Martin Chuzzlewit.

Pecora, pek'ə-rä, n.pl. the Cotylophora, or ruminants other than camels and chevrotains. [L. pl. of pecus, -oris, cattle.]

pecten, pek'tən, n. a comb-like structure of various kinds, e.g. in a bird's or reptile's eye: the pubic bone: a tactile organ in scorpions: the scallop genus of molluscs, with ribbed shell:—pl. **pec'tines** (-tin-ēz).—adj. **pectinaceous** (-ā'shəs), like the scallops; **pec'tinal**, of a comb: comb-like: having bones like the teeth of a comb; **pec'tinate, -d**, toothed like a comb: having narrow parallel segments or lobes: like the teeth of a comb.—adv. **pec'tinately.**—n. **pectinā'tion**, the state of being pectinated: a comb-like structure. —adjs. **pectin'eal**, of the pubic bone: comb-like; **pec'tinibranchiate** (-brangk-i-āt), having comb-like gills. [L. pecten, -inis, a comb.]

pectic, pek'tik, adj. of, relating to, or derived from pectin.—ns. **pec'tin**, a mixture of carbohydrates found in the cell-walls of fruits, important for the setting of jellies; **pectisā'tion**.—v.t. and v.i. **pec'tise**, to congeal.—n. **pec'tōse**, a substance yield-ing pectin contained in the fleshy pulp of unripe fruit.—**pectic acid**, an insoluble substance (of various varieties) formed by hydrolysis of pectins. [Gr. pēktikos, congealing—pēgnynai, to fix.]

pectolite, pek'tə-līt, n. a zeolite-like monoclinic acid calcium sodium silicate. [Gr. pēktos, congealed, lithos, stone.]

pectoral, pek'tə-rəl, adj. of, for, on, or near the breast or chest: (fig.) coming from the heart or inward feeling.—n. armour for the breast of man or horse: an ornament worn on the breast, esp. the breastplate worn by the ancient Jewish high-priest, and the square of gold, embroidery, &c., formerly worn on the breast over the chasuble by bishops during mass: a chest-protector: a medicine for the chest: a pectoral cross: a pec-toral fin.—adv. **pec'torally.**—n. **pectoril'oquy** (L. loqui, to talk), the sound of the patient's voice heard through the stethoscope when applied to the chest in certain morbid conditions of the lungs.— **pectoral cross**, a gold cross worn on the breast by bishops, &c.; **pectoral fins**, the anterior paired fins of fishes; **pectoral girdle**, the shoulder-girdle, consisting of shoulder-blade, coracoid, and collar-bone; **pectoral theology**, the theology of

those who make much of experience and emotion as guides to a knowledge of divine truth. [L. pectorālis—pectus, pectoris, the breast.]

peculate, pek'ū-lāt, v.t. and v.i. to appropriate dis-honestly to one's own use, pilfer, embezzle.—ns. **pecula'tion**; **pec'ulātor**. [L. peculāri, -ātus— peculium, private property, akin to pecūnia, money.]

peculiar, pi-kū'lyər, adj. own: of one's own: be-longing exclusively: privately owned: appropri-ated: preserved: characteristic: special: very particular: odd, strange.—n. (obs.) private property or right: a parish or church exempt from the jurisdiction of the ordinary or bishop in whose diocese it is placed: anything exempt from ordinary jurisdiction: one of the Peculiar People: (print.) a type of unusual kind that has to be specially cast.—v.t. **pecu'liarise**, to set apart.— n. **peculiarity** (-li-ar'i-ti), quality of being peculiar or singular: that which is found in one and in no other: that which marks anything off from others: individuality: oddity. — adv. **pecu'liarly.** — n. **pecu'lium**, private property, esp. that given by a father to a son, &c.—**Peculiar People**, the people of Israel: an Evangelical denomination, founded in 1838, holding inspiration of Holy Scriptures, believers' baptism, Holy Communion, and Divine healing. [L. peculium, private property.]

pecuniary, pi-kū'nyə-ri, -ni-ə-ri, adj. relating to money: consisting of money.—adv. **pecu'niarily.** —adj. **pecu'nious** (rare), rich. [L. pecūnia, money, from the root that appears in L. pecudes (pl.), cattle, and fee.]

ped, ped, n. (prov.) a pannier or hamper.—Also **pad**. [Origin unknown.]

ped, ped, n. short for pedestrian.

pedagogue, ped'ə-gog, n. a teacher: a pedant.— v.t. to teach.—adjs. **pedagogic** (-gog', -goj'), **-al**. —adv. **pedagog'ically.**—ns. **pedagog'ics** (-gog', -goj'; treated as sing.), the science and principles of teaching; **ped'agoguery** (-gog-ə-ri), a school: schoolmastering: pedagoguishness. — adj. **ped'a-goguish**, like a pedagogue.—ns. **ped'agoguish-ness**; **ped'agog(u)ism** (-gizm, -jizm), spirit or system of pedagogy: teaching; **ped'agogy** (-gog-i, -goj-i), the science of teaching: instruction: train-ing. [Partly through Fr. and L. from Gr. paida-gōgos, a slave who led a boy to school—pais, paidos, boy, agōgos, leader—agein, to lead.]

pedal, ped'l (zool. also pē'dəl), adj. of the foot: of the feet of perpendiculars: of, with, or pertaining to a pedal or pedals.—n. (ped'l) a lever pressed by the foot: the lower and thicker part of a straw: a plait thereof: a pedal-point: a pedal-organ: a pedal-board.—v.i. to use a pedal or pedals: to advance by use of the pedals.—v.t. to drive by the pedals:—pr.p. **ped'alling**; pa.t. and pa.p. **ped'alled.**—ns. **ped'al-ac'tion**, the apparatus worked by the pedals of a musical instrument; **ped'al-board, ped'al-clavier'**, the keyboards of pedals of an organ or other instrument; **ped'al-bone**, a horse's coffin-bone; **pedalier** (-ēr'), a pedal-board attached to a piano for the bass strings; **ped'aller**, one who uses pedals; **ped'-alling**; **ped'al-organ**, the division of an organ played by means of pedals; **ped'al-point**, organ-point, a tone or tones (usu. tonic and dominant) sustained normally in the bass, while other parts move independently. [L. pedālis—pēs, pedis, foot.]

Pedaliaceae, pi-dā-li-ā'si-ē, n.pl. a family of tubi-floral dicotyledons akin to the bignonias. [Gr. pēdalion, a rudder, from the keeled fruit.]

pedant, ped'nt, n. (Shak.) a schoolmaster: one who is learned without being judicious, whose learning is indigested, or allowed to appear unseasonably: one who attaches too much importance to merely formal matters in scholarship.—adjs. **pedantic** (pid-ant'ik), **-al**, schoolmasterly: of the character or in the manner of a pedant.—adv. **pedant'ically** —v.t. **pedant'icise** (-i-sīz), to make pedantic, give pedantic form to.—n. **pedant'icism** (-i-sizm), a pedant's expression.—v.i. **pedant'ise**, to play the pedant.—v.t. to turn into a pedant.—ns. **ped'ant-ism**, pedantry: pedanticism; **pedantoc'racy**, government by pedants; **pedant'ocrat.**—adj. **pedantocrat'ic.**—n. **ped'antry**, the character of manner of a pedant: a pedantic expression: unduly rigorous formality. [It. *pedante* (perh. through Fr. *pédant*); connexion with **pedagogue** not clear.]

pedate, *ped'āt, adj.* footed: foot-like: (*bot.*) palmately lobed with the outer lobes deeply cut, or ternately branching with the outer branches forked. —*adv.* **ped'ately.**—*adj.* **pedatifid** (*pi-dat'i-fid*), divided in a pedate manner, but having the divisions connected at the base. [L. *pedātus*, footed—*pēs, pedis,* foot.]

pedder, *ped'ər,* **pether,** *pedh'ər, n.* (now *Scot.*) a pedlar.—*n.* **pedd'er-coffe** (prob. *kŏv*; *Scott* after *David Lyndsay*), see **cove.** [App.—**ped** (1).]

peddle, *ped'l, v.i.* to go about as a pedlar: to trifle. —*v.t.* to sell or offer as a pedlar.—*adj.* **pedd'ling,** unimportant.—*n.* the trade or tricks of a pedlar. [App. partly a back-formation from **pedlar,** partly from **piddle.**]

pederasty, &c. See **paed-, paedo-.**

pederero, *ped-ə-rā'rō, n.* an old gun for discharging stones, pieces of iron, &c., also for firing salutes.— Also **padere'ro, patere'ro, pedre'ro,** &c. [Sp. *pedrero*—L. *petra,* stone—Gr. *petrā.*]

pedesis, *ped-ē'sis, n.* Brownian movement.—*adj.* **pedetic** (*pi-det'ik*). [Gr. *pēdēsis,* jumping.]

pedestal, *ped'is-tl, n.* the support of a column, statue, vase, &c.: the fixed casting which holds the brasses in which a shaft turns, called also *axle-guard* or *pillow-block.* — *v.t.* to place on a pedestal.—*adj.* **ped'estalled.** [Fr. *piédestal*—It. *piedistallo,* for *piè di stallo,* foot of a stall—*piè,* foot (—L. *pēs, pedis*), *di,* of (L. *dē*), *stallo,* stall (see **stall**).]

pedestrian, *pi-des'tri-ən, adj.* on foot: of walking: not mounted on Pegasus, hence prosaic, uninspired: flat or commonplace.—*n.* a walker: one who practises feats of walking or running.—*v.i.* **pedes'trianise,** to walk. — *n.* **pedes'trianism,** walking, esp. as an exercise or athletic performance: pedestrian quality. [L. *pedester, -tris*—*pēs, pedis.*]

pedetentous, *ped-i-ten'təs, adj.* proceeding slowly. [L. *pedetentim, -temptim*—*pēs, pedis,* foot, *temptāre, -ātum,* to make trial of.]

pediatrics. See **paed-, paedo-.**

pedicel, *ped'i-sel, n.* the stalk of a single flower in an inflorescence: the stalk of a sedentary animal: the stalk of an animal organ, e.g. a crab's eye.— *n.* **pedicellā'ria,** a stalked (or sessile) bladed snapping forceps on the surface of a starfish or sea-urchin:—*pl.* **pedicellā'riae.**—*adj.* **pedicel'late** (or *-dis',* or *-sel'*), provided with a pedicel. [Botanists' dim. of L. *pēs, pedis,* the foot.]

pedicle, *ped'i-kl, n.* a little stalk.—*adjs.* **ped'icled; pedic'ŭlate,** stalked: belonging to the **Pediculā'ti,** the angler-fish order, whose pectoral fins have a wrist-like articulation: **pedic'ulated.** [L. *pediculus,* a little foot—*pēs, pedis,* foot.]

Pediculus, *pi-dik'ū-ləs, n.* the louse genus: a louse. —*adj.* **pedic'ular,** of lice: lousy.—*ns.* **Pediculā'ris,** the lousewort genus; **pediculā'tion, pediculō'sis,** lousiness.—*adj.* **pedic'ulous,** lousy. [L. *pēdiculus,* dim. of *pēdis,* a louse.]

pedicure, *ped'i-kūr, n.* the treatment of corns, bunions, or the like: one who treats the feet.— *v.t.* to apply foot-treatment to.—*n.* **ped'icurist.** [L. *pēs, pedis,* foot, *cūra, care.*]

pedigree, *ped'i-grē, n.* a line of ancestors: a scheme or record of ancestry: lineage: genealogy: distinguished and ancient lineage: derivation, descent: succession, series, set.—*adj.* of known descent.—*adj.* **ped'igreed,** having a pedigree. [App. Fr. *pied de grue,* crane's-foot, from the arrow-head figure in a stemma.]

pediment, *ped'i-mənt, n.* (*archit.*) a triangular structure crowning the front of a Greek building, less steeply sloped than a gable: in later architecture a similar structure, triangular, rounded, &c., over a portico, door, window, or niche.—*adjs.* **pedimental** (*-ment'l*); **ped'imented,** furnished with a pediment: like a pediment. [Earlier *periment,* prob. for **pyramid.**]

pedipalp, *ped'i-palp, n.* the second paired appendage in Arachnida (also **pedipalp'us**): a whip-scorpion. —*ns.pl.* **Pedipalp'ī, Pedipalp'ida,** the whip-

scorpions, an order of Arachnida with large pedipalps. [L. *pēs, pedis,* foot, *palpus,* stroking, in L.L. a feeler.]

pedlar, *ped'lər, n.* one who goes about with a pack of goods for sale (technically, one who carries it himself—distinguished from a *hawker,* who has a horse and cart, &c.): one who peddles.—*n.* **ped'lary,** the wares or occupation of a pedlar, [Prob. from **pedder,** with inserted *l,* as in **tinkler** from **tinker.**]

pedobaptism. See **paed-, paedo-.**

pedology, *ped-ol'ə-ji, n.* the study of soils.—*adj.* **pedological** (*-ə-loj'*).—*n.* **pedol'ogist.** [Gr. *pedion,* ground, *logos,* discourse.]

pedometer, *pid-om'i-tər, n.* an instrument for counting paces and so approximately measuring distance walked. [L. *pēs, pedis,* foot—Gr. *metron,* measure.]

pedotrophy. See **paed-, paedo-.**

pedrail, *ped'rāl, n.* a tractor with foot-like pieces on the circumference of its wheels: one of the pieces so used. [L. *pēs, pedis,* foot, and **rail.**]

pedrero, *ped-rā'rō.* Same as **pederero.**

peduncle, *pi-dung'kl, n.* the stalk of an inflorescence or of a solitary flower: the stalk by which a sedentary animal is attached: a narrow stalk-like connecting part: a tract of white fibres in the brain. — *adjs.* **pedun'cular, pedun'culate, -d.** [Botanists' L. *pedunculus*—L. *pēs, pedis,* the foot.]

peece, an obsolete spelling of **piece.**

peek, *pēk, n.* a peep.—*v.i.* to peep.—*n.* **peek'abo(o)',** a child's peeping game. [Origin obscure.]

peel, *pēl, v.t.* (*obs.*) to pill, pillage, plunder: to strip off the skin, bark, or other covering from: to strip off.—*v.i.* to come off as the skin: to lose the skin: (*coll.*) to undress.—*n.* rind, esp. that of oranges, lemons, &c., in the natural state or candied.—*n.* **peel-and-eat'**, (*Scot.*) potatoes served in their jackets.—Also *adj.*—*adj.* **peeled,** pillaged: bald: tonsured: stripped of skin, rind, or bark.— *ns.* **peel'er,** one who peels: a plunderer: a plant that impoverishes the soil: an instrument or machine for peeling or decorticating; **peel'ing,** the act of stripping: a piece, strip, or shred stripped off: (*print.*) the removing of the layers of a paper overlay, to get a lighter impression.— **pack and peel,** to have any dealings. [O.E. *pilian* —L. *pilāre,* to deprive of hair—*pilus,* a hair; perh. influenced by Fr. *peler,* to skin; cf. **pill** (2).]

peel, *pēl, n.* (*obs.*) a stake: (*hist.*) a palisaded enclosure: a peel-house.—*ns.* **peel'-house, peel'tower,** orig. a fortified dwelling-house, usually entered by ladder to the first floor, with vaulted ground floor for cattle, common on the Borders: now loosely used. [A.Fr. *pel*—L. *pālus,* stake.]

peel, *pēl, n.* a shovel, esp. a baker's wooden shovel: an instrument for hanging up paper to dry: (*U.S.*) the blade of an oar. [O.Fr. *pele*—L. *pāla,* a spade.]

peel. Same as **peal** (fish).

peeler, *pēl'ər, n.* a policeman, from Sir R. *Peel,* who established the Irish police (1812–18) and improved those in Britain (1828–30).—*n.* **Peel'ite,** a follower of Peel in the reform of the Corn-laws in 1846.

peen, pean, *pēn,* **pane,** *pān, n.* the end of a hammerhead opposite the hammering face.—*v.t.* to strike or work with a peen. [Origin uncertain; cf. Norw. *pen,* Ger. *pinne,* Fr. *panne.*]

peenge, *pēnj, pēnzh, v.i.* (*Scot.*) to whine like a peevish child. [Perh. based on **whinge.**]

peeoy, pioy, pioye, *pē-ō'i, n.* (*Scot.*) a home-made firework, a cone of damp gunpowder.

peep, *pēp, v.i.* to cheep like a chicken.—*n.* a high feeble sound.—*n.* **peep'er,** a young bird: (*U.S.*) a tree-frog. [Imit.; cf. pipe, L. *pīpāre,* Fr. *pépier,* Ger. *piepen, piepsen,* to cheep, Gr. *pīpos,* a young bird.]

peep, *pēp, v.i.* to look through a narrow opening: to look out from concealment: to look slyly, surreptitiously, or cautiously: to be just showing: to begin to appear.—*v.t.* to put forth from concealment as if to take a view: to direct as if to view.— *n.* a sly look: a beginning to appear: a speck of light or flame: a glimpse: a slit: (*slang*) an eye.—*ns.* **peep'er,** one that peeps: a prying person: (*slang*) the eye: (*slang*) a glass, for various purposes; **peep'-hole**, a hole through which one may look without being seen; **peep'-of-day'**, the first appearance of light in the morning; **peep'-show**, a small show viewed through a small hole, usually fitted with a magnifying-glass; **peep'-sight**, a back-sight with a small hole.—**peeping Tom**, a prying fellow, esp. one who peeps in at windows; **Peep-o'-day Boys**, an Ulster Protestant society (1780-95) opposed to the Catholic *Defenders*. [Origin obscure.]

peep, peepe, (*Shak.*) pēp, *n.* earlier forms of **pip** (3).

peer, pēr, *n.* an equal: a fellow: (*Spens.*) an antagonist: a nobleman of the rank of baron upward: a member of the House of Lords: one of Charlemagne's paladins: a member of any similar body:—*fem.* **peer'ess**.—*v.t.* peer, to equal: (*coll.*) to confer a peerage on.—*v.i.* to rank as equal.—*n.* **peer'age**, the rank or dignity of a peer: the body of peers: a book of the genealogy, &c., of the different peers.—*adj.* **peer'less**, unequalled: matchless.—*adv.* **peer'lessly**.—*n.* **peer'lessness**.—**House of Peers**, the House of Lords: **spiritual peer**, a bishop or archbishop qualified to sit in the House of Lords: **temporal peer**, any other member. [O.Fr. (Fr. *pair*)—L. *pār, paris*, equal.]

peer, pēr, *v.i.* to look narrowly or closely: to look with strain, or with half-closed eyes: to peep: to appear.—*v.t.* to protrude.—*adj.* **peer'y**, inclined to peer: prying: sly. [Origin unknown: perh. partly M.E. *piren* (cf. L.G. *piren*), influenced by *pere*, aphetic form of **appear**, partly from *pere* itself.]

peerie, peery, pēr'i, *n.* (*Scot.*) a pear-shaped wooden peg-top. [App. **pear**, pron. *pēr* in Scots.]

peesweep, peaseweep, pēz'wēp, *n.* (*Scot.*) the peewit. [Imit.]

peetweet, pēt'wēt, *n.* (*U.S.*) the spotted sandpiper. [Imit.]

peever, pē'vər, *n.* a tile, slab, or can-lid used in playing hop-scotch: (in *pl.*) hop-scotch.

peevish, pēv'ish, *adj.*: foolish: (*obs.*) vexatious: (*Shak.*) perverse: wayward: fretful.—*v.t.* peeve (back-formation), to irritate.—*v.i.* to be fretful: to show fretfulness.—*adv.* **peev'ishly**.—*n.* **peev'ishness**. [Origin unknown.]

peewit, pewit, pē'wit, also pū'it, *n.* the lapwing: its cry.—(*Scot.*) **pees'weep, pee'wee**. [Imit.]

peg, peg, *n.* a pin (esp. of wood): a fixture for hanging a hat or coat on: a pin for tuning a string: a small stake for securing tent-ropes, marking a position, boundary, claim, &c.: a pin for scoring as in cribbage: a pin in a cup to show how far down one may drink: hence a drink, esp. of brandy and soda: a degree or step: a wooden or other pin used in shoemaking: a turtle harpoon: a clothes-peg: a peg-top: a wooden leg: a leg: a poke or thrust: a theme.—*v.t.* to fasten, mark, score, furnish, pierce, or strike with a peg or pegs: to insert or fix like a peg: to score (as at cribbage): (*stock-exchange*) to keep from falling or rising by buying or selling at a fixed price: to stabilise: (*slang*) to drive.—*v.i.* to keep on working assiduously: to make one's way vigorously:—*pr.p.* **pegg'ing**; *pa.t.* and *pa.p.* **pegged**.—*n.* **peg'-box**, part of the head of a musical instrument in which the pegs are inserted.—*adj.* **pegged**.—*ns.* **pegg'-ing**; **peg'-leg**, a simple wooden leg: a man with a wooden leg; **peg'-tank'ard**, a drinking-vessel having each one's share marked off by a knob; **peg'-top**, a top with a metal point, spun by winding a string round it and suddenly throwing it: (in *pl.*) trousers narrowing at the ankles.—*adj.* shaped like a top.—**a peg too low**, tipsy: depressed; **peg away**, to work on assiduously; **peg out**, in croquet, to finish by driving the ball against the peg: in cribbage, to win by pegging the last hole before show of hands: to mark off with pegs: (*slang*) to become exhausted, be ruined, or die; **round peg in a square hole**, one who is unsuited to the particular position he occupies; **take down a peg**, to take down, to humble, to snub. [Cf. L.G. *pigge*, Du. dial. *peg*, Dan. *pig*.]

Pegasus, peg'ə-səs, *n.* the winged horse that sprang from Medusa's blood, by later writers associated with the Muses: hence, an embodiment of the power that raises a poet's imagination above the earth: a genus of small fishes superficially like sea-horses, of the coasts of Asia and Australia, with large, wing-like, pectoral fins: one of the constellations in the northern sky.—*adj.* **Pegasē'an**. [L. *Pēgasus*—Gr. *Pēgasos*.]

peggy, peg'i, *n.* a small warbler of various kinds— the white-throat, &c.: a washerwoman's dolly: a size of roofing slate, 10 by 14 in. [Hypocoristic from *Margaret*.]

pegh, Peght. See **pech, Pecht**.

pegmatite, peg'mə-tīt, *n.* graphic granite: a very coarsely crystallised granite, as in dykes and veins: any very coarse-grained igneous rock occurring in like manner.—*adj.* **pegmatitic** (*-tit'ik*). [Gr. *pēgma*, a bond, framework, from the root of *pēgnynai*, to fasten.]

Pehlevi, pā'le-vē, **Pahlavi**, pä'lä-vē, *n.* an ancient West Iranian idiom of the Sassanide period (3rd-7th cent. A.D.), largely mixed with Semitic words: the characters used in writing it.—Also *adj.* [Pers. *Pahlavi*, Parthian.]

peignoir, pen-wär, *n.* a woman's dressing-gown, esp. one worn when combing the hair: (loosely) a morning-gown. [Fr.,—*peigner*—L. *pectināre*, to comb.]

peinct, pānt, an obsolete spelling of **paint**.

peirastic, pī-ras'tik, *adj.* experimental: tentative. —*adv.* **peiras'tically**. [Gr. *peirastikos*—*peira*, a trial.]

peise, peize, pease, peaze, peyse, pāz, pēz, *n.* (*obs.*) weight: a weight: balance: (*Spens.*) a blow.—*v.t.* (*Spens., Shak.*) to balance: (*Spens.*) to poise: (*Shak.*) to put weights on, weigh down. —*v.i.* (*Spens.*) to press or settle downwards. [O.Fr. *peis*, weight, *peser*, to weigh; cf. **poise**.]

pejorate, pē'jər-āt, *v.t.* to make worse.—*n.* **pejorā'-tion**, a making or becoming worse: deterioration.—*adj.* **pē'jorative** (or *-jor'*), depreciating, disparaging.—*n.* a depreciating word or suffix.—*adv.* **pē'joratively**. [L. *pējor*, worse.]

pekan, pek'ən, *n.* the wood-shock, a large North American marten. [Canadian Fr. *pékan*—Algonquin *pékané*.]

Pekingese, Pekinese, pē-kin(g)-ēz', *adj.* of Peking, now Peiping, former capital of China.—*n.* a native or inhabitant of Peking: a dwarf pug-dog of a breed brought from Peking (also abbrev. **peke**).—**Peking man**, a fossil species of man (*Sinanthropus pekinensis*) first found (1929) S.W. of Peking.

pekoe, pek'ō, *n.* a scented black tea. [Chin. *pek-ho*, white down.]

pela, pā'lä, *n.* white wax from a scale-insect. [Chin. *peh-la*, white wax.]

pelage, pel'ij, *n.* a beast's coat of hair or wool. [Fr.]

Pelagian, pi-lā'ji-ən, *n.* a follower of *Pelagius*, a 5th-cent. British monk, who denied original sin.— Also *adj.*—*n.* **Pelā'gianism**.

pelagic, pi-laj'ik, *adj.* oceanic: of, inhabiting, or carried out in, the deep or open sea: living in the surface waters or middle depths of the sea: deposited under deep-water conditions. — *adj.* **pelagian**, pi-lā'ji-ən, pelagic.—*n.* a pelagic animal. [Gr. *pelagos*, sea.]

Pelargonium, pel-ər-gō'ni-əm, *n.* a vast genus of the geranium family, often cultivated under the name of geranium. [Gr. *pelargos*, stork, the beaked capsules resembling a stork's head.]

Pelasgic, pe-las'jik, *adj.* pertaining to the *Pelasgians* or *Pelasgi*, prehistoric inhabitants of Greece, of unknown affinities.—Also **Pelas'gian.**—**Pelasgian architecture**, cyclopean architecture.

Pele, pā'lā, *n.* the Hawaiian volcano goddess.— **Pele's hair**, volcanic glass drawn out into threads as it flies through the air.

pele, a Spenserian spelling of **peal**.

Pelecypoda, pel-e-sip'ə-dä, *n.pl.* the Lamellibranchs. [Gr. *pelekys*, axe, *pous, podos*, foot.]

pelerine, pel'ə-rin, *-rēn*, *n.* a woman's tippet or cape, esp. one with long ends coming down in front. [Fr. *pèlerine*, tippet, pilgrim (fem.); see **pilgrim**.]

pelf, pelf, *n.* riches (in a bad sense): money. [O.Fr. *pelfre*, booty; cf. **pilfer**.]

pelican, pel'i-kən, *n.* a large water-fowl, with enormous pouched bill, fabled in the Middle Ages to wound its breast and feed its young with its blood : an alembic with beaks that lead back to the body—used for continuous distillation : a dentist's beaked instrument : an old species of ordnance, or its shot.—*ns.* **pel'ican-fish**, a deep-sea fish (Eurypharynx) with enormous mouth and very little body ; **pel'ican-flower**, the goose-flower, an Aristolochia with a gigantic flower ; **pel'ican's-foot'**, a marine gasteropod mollusc (*Aporrhais pes-pelicani*) : its shell, with a lip like a webbed foot.—**pelican in her piety**, (*her.*) a pelican, with wings indorsed, feeding her young with her blood. [L.L. *pelicānus*—Gr. *pelekan*, *-ānos*, pelican ; cf. *pelekās*, *-āntos*, a woodpecker, and *pelekys*, an axe.]

pelisse, *pe-lēs'*, *n.* orig. a fur-lined or fur garment, esp. a military cloak : a lady's long mantle : a young child's out-of-door coat. [Fr.,—L.L. *pellicea* (*vestis*)—L. *pellis*, a skin.]

pelite, *pē'līt*, *n.* any rock derived from clay or mud. —*adj.* **pēlitic** (*-lit'ik*).—*ns.* **pē'loid**, any naturally produced medium used in medical practice as a cataplasm ; **pēlol'ogy** ; **pēlother'apy**, treatment by mud baths and the like. [Gr. *pēlos*, clay, mud.]

pell, *pel*, *n.* (*obs.*) a skin or film : a roll of parchment. [O.Fr. *pel* (Fr. *peau*)—L. *pellis*, a skin or hide.]

pellagra, *pel-ag'rä*, *-äg'rä*, *n.* a deadly deficiency disease marked by shrivelled skin, wasted body, and insanity.—*n.* **pellag'rin**, one afflicted with pellagra.—*adj.* **pellag'rous**, connected with, like, or afflicted with, pellagra. [Gr. *pella*, skin, *agrā*, seizure ; or It. *pelle agra*, rough skin.]

pellet, *pel'it*, *n.* a little ball : a small rounded boss : a small pill : a ball of shot : a mass of undigested refuse thrown up by a hawk or owl.—*v.t.* (*Shak.*) to form into pellets : to hit or pelt with pellets. [O.Fr. *pelote*—L. *pila*, a ball.]

pellicle, *pel'i-kl*, *n.* a thin skin or film : a film or scum on liquors.—*adj.* **pellic'ular**. [L. *pellicula*, dim. of *pellis*, skin.]

pellitory, *pel'i-tə-ri*, *n.* a plant (*Parietaria officinalis*) of the nettle family, growing on old walls (called *pellitory of the wall*), or other member of the genus. [L. (*herba*) *parietāria—parietārius—pariēs*, *parietis*, a wall.]

pellitory, *pel'i-tə-ri*, *n.* a North African and South European plant (*Anacyclus Pyrethrum*), known as *pellitory of Spain*, akin to camomile : extended to various similar plants, as yarrow, feverfew. [M.E. *peletre*—L. *pyrethrum*—Gr. *pyrethron*, pellitory of Spain ; see **pyrethrum**.]

pell-mell, *pel'-mel'*, *adv.* confusedly : promiscuously : headlong : helter-skelter : vehemently.—*adj.* confusedly mingled : promiscuous : indiscriminate : headlong. — *n.* disorder : confused mingling : a hand-to-hand fight. [O.Fr. *pesle-mesle* (Fr. *pêle-mêle*), *-mesle* being from O.Fr. *mesler* (Fr. *mêler*), to mix—L.L. *misculāre*—L. *miscēre* ; and *pesle*, a rhyming addition, perh. influenced by Fr. *pelle*, shovel.]

pellock, pellack, *pel'ək*, **pellach**, *pel'əhh*, *n.* (*Scot.*) a porpoise. [Origin unknown.]

pellucid, *pe-l(y)ōō'sid*, *adj.* perfectly clear : transparent.—*ns.* **pellucid'ity**, **pellu'cidness**.—*adv.* **pellu'cidly**. [L. *pellūcidus—per*, through, *lūcidus*, clear—*lūcēre*, to shine.]

pelma, *pel'mä*, *n.* the sole of the foot.—*adj.* **pelmatic** (*-mat'ik*).—*n.pl.* **Pelmatozo'a**, a division of the Echinodermata, typically stalked, including crinoids and the fossil blastoids and cystoids. [Gr. *pelma*, *-atos*, sole, stalk.]

pelmet, *pel'mit*, *n.* a fringe, valance, or other device hiding a curtain rod. [Perh. Fr. *palmette*.]

Pelopid, *pel'ō-pid*, a descendant of *Pelops*, son of Tantalus.

Peloponnesian, *pel-ō-pə-nē'-sh(y)ən*, *-zh(y)ən*, *-zyən*, *adj.* of the *Peloponnesus* or Peloponnese, the southern peninsula of Greece.—*n.* a native thereof. —**Peloponnesian War**, a war between Athens and Sparta, 431-404 B.C. [Gr. *Peloponnēsos*, Peloponnese—*Pelops* (see foregoing), *nēsos*, an island.]

peloria, *pi-lō'ri-ä*, *n.* regularity in a normally irregular flower.—Also **pelorism** (*pel'ər-izm*), **pel'ory**.—

adj. **pelor'ic** (*pi-lor'ik*), **pel'orised**. [Gr. *pelōr*, a monster.]

pelorus, *pel-ōr'əs*, *n.* a kind of compass. [Perh. *Pelorus*, Hannibal's pilot.]

pelota, *pel-ō'tä*, *n.* a ball-game resembling fives, of Basque origin. [Sp. *pelota*, ball.]

pelt, *pelt*, *n.* a raw hide : a hawk's prey when killed, especially when torn.—*ns.* **pelt'monger**, a dealer in skins ; **pelt'ry**, the skins of animals with the fur on them : furs. [App. a back-formation from **peltry**—O.Fr. *pelleterie*—L. *pellis*, a skin.]

pelt, *pelt*, *v.t.* to assail (formerly with repeated blows, now usu.) with showers of missiles, or of words, reproaches, pamphlets, &c. : to drive by showers of missiles : to shower.—*v.i.* to shower (blows or missiles) : to beat vigorously, as rain, hail : to speak angrily : to speed.—*n.* a blow : a pelting : a downpour, as of rain : a storm of rage : a rapid pace.—*n.* **pelt'er**, one who or that which pelts : a shower of missiles : a sharp storm of rain, of anger, &c.—*v.i.* to go full pelt : (*dial.*) to pelt.—*n.* and *adj.* **pelt'ing**—**full pelt**, at full speed. [Origin obscure.]

pelta, *pel'tä*, *n.* (*ant.*) a light buckler.—*n.* **peltast** (*pel't'ast*), a light-armed Greek soldier with a pelta. —*adj.* **pelt'ate**, (*bot.*) having the stalk attached not to the edge but near the middle of the under surface. [L.,—Gr. *peltē*.]

pelting, *pel'ting*, *adj.* (*Shak.*) paltry, contemptible.—*adv.* **pelt'ingly**. [App. conn. with **paltry**.]

Pelton-wheel, *pel'tn-hwēl'*, *n.* a water-wheel with specially shaped cups around the circumference within which jets impinge, invented by Lester Allen *Pelton*, American engineer (1829-1908).

pelvis, *pel'vis*, *n.* the bony cavity at the lower end of the trunk, of which the part above the plane through the promontory of the sacrum and the pubic symphysis is the *false pelvis*, the part below the *true pelvis* : the bony frame enclosing it : the cavity of the kidney : the basal part of a crinoid cup :—*pl.* **pel'ves** (*-vēz*).—*adjs.* **pel'vic** ; **pelvi'-form**, basin-shaped.—*ns.* **pelvim'eter**, an instrument for measuring the pelvis ; **pelvim'etry**.—**pelvic fin**, a fish's paired fin homologous with a mammal's hind-leg ; **pelvic girdle**, or **arch**, the posterior limb-girdle of vertebrates, with which the hind-limbs articulate, consisting of the haunch-bones (ilium, pubis and ischium united), which articulate with the sacrum. [L. *pelvis*, a basin.]

pembroke, *pem'brook*, *n.* (in full **pembroke table**) a small four-legged table with hinged flaps. [App. from *Pembroke* in Wales.]

pemmican, pemican, *pem'i-kən*, *n.* a North American Indian preparation of lean flesh-meat, dried, pounded, and mixed with fat and other ingredients : highly condensed information or reading-matter. [Cree *pimekan*.]

pemphigus, *pem'fi-gəs*, *n.* an affection of the skin with watery vesicles.—*adjs.* **pem'phigoid**, **pem'-phigous**. [False Latin—Gr. *pemphix*, *-igos*, blister.]

pen, *pen*, *n.* a small enclosure, esp. for animals : a West Indian farm or plantation : a dam or weir : animals kept in, and enough to fill, a pen.—*v.t.* to put or keep in a pen : to confine : to dam :—*pr.p.* **penn'ing** ; *pa.t.* and *pa.p.* **penned** or **pent**.—*n.* **pen'fold**, a fold for penning cattle or sheep : a pound.—**submarine pen**, a dock for a submarine, esp. if protected from attack from above by a deep covering of concrete. [O.E. *penn*, pen.]

pen, *pen*, *n.* a large feather : a flight-feather : a quill : a cuttle-bone : an instrument used for writing (with ink or otherwise), formerly made of a quill, but now of other materials : a nib : a nib with a holder : writing : literary style : an author. —*v.t.* to write, to commit to paper :—*pr.p.* **penn'-ing** ; *pa.t.* and *pa.p.* **penned**.—*n.* **pen'-and-ink'**, writing materials : a pen drawing.—*adj.* **writing** : written : executed with pen and ink, as a drawing. —*ns.* **pen'-case**, a receptacle for a pen or pens ; **pen'craft**, penmanship : the art of composition ; **pen'-driver**, a clerk ; **pen'-feather**, a quill feather : (*dial.*) an undeveloped feather.—*adj.* **pen'-feathered**.—*ns.* **pen'ful**, as much ink as a pen can take at a dip : as much as the reservoir of a fountain-pen can hold : what one can write with one dip of ink; **pen'-gun'**, (*Scot.*) a popgun made of a quill; **pen'holder**, a rod on which a nib may be fixed; **pen'knife**, orig. a knife for making or mending pens: a small pocket-knife; **pen'man**, one skilled in handwriting: a writer or author:—*fem.* **pen'woman**; **pen'manship**; **pen'-name**, a writer's assumed name.—*adj.* **penned**, written: quilled.—*ns.* **penn'er**, (*arch.*) a case for carrying pens; **pen'-nib**, a nib for a pen; **pen'-wiper**, a piece of cloth, leather, &c., for wiping ink from pens.—**talk like a pen-gun**, to chatter volubly. [O.Fr. *penne*—L. *penna*, a feather.]

pen, *pen*, *n.* a female swan. [Origin unknown.]

penal, *pē'nl*, *adj.* pertaining to, liable to, imposing, constituting, or used for, punishment.—*n.* **pēnal-isā'tion**.—*v.t.* **pē'nalise**, to make punishable: to put under a disadvantage.—*adv.* **pē'nally.**—**penal laws**, laws imposing penalties, esp. (*hist.*) in matters of religion; **penal servitude**, hard labour in a prison under different conditions from ordinary imprisonment, substituted in 1853 for transportation. [L. *poenālis*—*poena*—Gr. *poinē*, punishment.]

penalty, *pen'l-ti*, *n.* punishment: suffering or loss imposed for breach of a law: a fine or loss agreed upon in case of non-fulfilment of some undertaking: a fine: a disadvantage imposed upon a competitor for breach of a rule of the game, for want of success in attaining what is aimed at, as a handicap, or for any other reason arising out of the rules: a loss or suffering brought upon one by his own actions or condition: (*bridge*) a score for an opponent's failure to make his contract or for the bidder's success when the call is doubled. —**penalty goal**, one scored by a penalty kick; **penalty kick**, a free kick, or the privilege granted to a player to kick the ball as he pleases, because of some breach of the rules by the opposing side; **penalty line**, the boundary of the penalty area; **under**, or **on**, **penalty of**, with liability in case of infraction to the penalty of. [L.L. *poenālitās*, see foregoing.]

penance, *pen'ans*, *n.* (*obs.*) repentance: an act of mortification undertaken voluntarily or imposed by a priest to manifest sorrow for sin: (*R.C.* and *Orthodox*) the sacrament by which absolution is conveyed (involving contrition, confession, and satisfaction): expiation: (*Milt.*) punishment: hardship.—*v.t.* to impose penance on. [O.Fr.; cf. **penitence**.]

Penang-lawyer, *pē-nang'-law'yər*, *n.* a walking-stick made from the stem of a prickly dwarf palm (*Licuala acutifida*): misapplied to a Malacca cane. [*Penang*, its place of origin, and **lawyer**, if not from Malay *pinang līyar*, wild areca, or *pinang láyor*, fire-dried areca.]

penannular, *pen-an'ū-lər*, or *pēn-*, *adj.* in the form of an almost complete ring. [L. *paene*, almost, *annulāris*, annular.]

penates, *pe-nā'tēz*, *n.pl.* the household gods of a Roman family. [L. *penātēs*, prob. from the root found in *penus*, provisions, storeroom, *penes* in the house of, *penetrāre*, to penetrate.]

pence, *pens*, *n.* a plural of **penny.**

penchant, *pän'-shän'*, *n.* inclination: decided taste: bias. [Fr., pr.p. of *pencher*, to incline— assumed L.L. *pendicāre*—L. *pendēre*, to hang.]

pencil, *pen'sl*, *n.* a fine paint-brush: a small tuft of hairs: a writing or drawing instrument that leaves a streak of black-lead, chalk, slate, or other solid matter, esp. one of black-lead enclosed in wood and sharpened as required: a small stick of various materials shaped like a lead-pencil, for medical, cosmetic, or other purpose: the art of painting or drawing: (*geom.*) a system of straight lines meeting in a point: a set of rays of light diverging from or converging to a point: a narrow beam of light.—*v.t.* to paint, draw, write, or mark with a pencil: to apply a pencil to:—*pr.p.* **pen'-cilling**; *pa.t.* and *pa.p.* **pen'cilled.**—*ns.* **pen'cil-case**, a case for pencils: a metal case receiving a movable piece of black-lead or the like, used as a pencil; **pen'cil-ce'dar**, juniper of various kinds suitable for lead-pencils; **pen'cil-com'pass**, a compass having a pencil on one of its legs;

pen'cil-lead, graphite for pencils: a stick of it for a metal pencil-case.—*adj.* **pen'cilled**, painted, drawn, written or marked with a pencil: marked as if with a pencil: showing fine concentric streaking: having pencils of rays: radiated: tufted.—*ns.* **pen'ciller**; **pen'cilling**, the art or act of painting, writing, sketching, or marking with a pencil: marks made with a pencil: fine lines on flowers or feathers: a sketch: the marking of joints in brickwork with white paint; **pen'cil-ore**, radiating botryoidal graphite; **pen'cil-sharpener**, an instrument for sharpening lead-pencils by rotation against a blade; **pen'cil-sketch**; **pen'cil-stone**, a pyrophyllite used for making slate-pencils. [O.Fr. *pincel* (Fr. *pinceau*) —L. *pēnicillum*, a painter's brush, dim. of *pēnis*, a tail.]

pend, *pend*, *n.* (*Scot.*) a vaulted passage: a vaulted entrance to a passage-way. [L. *pendēre*, to hang.]

pend, *pend*, *v.i.* to hang, as in a balance, to impend. —*adj.* **pend'ing**, hanging: impending: remaining undecided: not terminated.—*prep.* during: until, awaiting. [Fr. *pendre* or L. *pendēre* to hang; sometimes aphetic for **append** or for **depend**.]

pend, an old spelling of **penned**, from **pen** (1) or **pen** (2).

pendant, sometimes **pendent**, *pen'dənt*, *n.* anything hanging, especially for ornament: a hanging ornament worn on the neck: the hanging (esp. decorated) end of a waist-belt: an earring: a lamp hanging from the roof: an ornament of wood or of stone hanging downwards from a roof: a pennant: a pendant-post: anything attached to another thing of the same kind, an appendix: a companion picture, poem, &c.—*ns.* **pen'dant-post**, a post placed against a wall, usu. resting on a corbel or capital, with a tie-beam or hammer-beam fixed to its upper end; **pen'dency**, undecided state: droop.—*adj.* **pen'dent**, sometimes **pen'dant**, hanging: dangling: drooping: over-hanging: not yet decided: grammatically incomplete, left in suspense.—*n.* **pendentive (-***dent'***)**, (*archit.*) a spherical triangle formed by a dome springing from a square base: part of a groined vault resting on one pier.—*adv.* **pen'dently.**—*ns.* **pen'dicle**, a pendant: a dependency or appendage: something attached to another, as a privilege, or a small piece of ground for cultivation; **pen'-dicler**, the tenant of a pendicle. [Fr. *pendant*, pr.p. of *pendre*, to hang—L. *pendēns*, *-entis*—pr.p. of *pendēre*, to hang.]

pendragon, *pen-drag'ən*, *n.* an ancient British supreme chief.—*n.* **pendrag'onship**. [W. *pen*, head, *dragon*, a dragon, dragon-standard.]

pendulum, *pen'dū-ləm*, *n.* theoretically, a heavy material point suspended by a weightless thread, free to swing without friction (*simple pendulum*): any weight so hung from a fixed point as to swing freely (*compound pendulum*): the swinging weight which regulates the movement of a clock: anything that swings or is free to swing to and fro:— *pl.* **pen'dulums.**—*adj.* **pen'dular**, relating to a pendulum.—*v.i.* **pen'dulate**, to swing, vibrate.— *adj.* **pen'duline**, building a pendulous nest.—*n.* **pendulos'ity.**—*adj.* **pen'dulous**, hanging loosely: swinging freely: drooping: dangling: overhanging: suspended from the top: floating in air or space.—*adv.* **pen'dulously.**—*n.* **pen'dulousness.** —**compensation pendulum**, a pendulum so constructed that its rod is not much altered in length by changes of temperature. [Neut. of L. *pendulus*, hanging—*pendēre*, to hang.]

Peneian, *pē-nē'yən*, *adj.* relating to the river *Pēneus* in the famous Vale of Tempe in Thessaly. [Gr. *Pēneios*, now Salambria.]

penelopise, *pi-nel'ə-pīz*, *v.i.* to act like Penelope, the wife of Ulysses, who undid at night the work she did by day, to gain time. [Gr. *Pēnelopē*.]

peneplain, *pē'ni-plān*, or *-plān'*, *n.* a land surface so worn down by denudation as to be almost a plain.—Also **pe'neplane**. [L. *paene*, almost, and **plain.**]

penetrate, *pen'i-trāt*, *v.t.* to thrust or force a way into the inside of: to pierce into or through: to permeate: to reach the mind or feelings of: (*fig.*)

to pierce with the eye or understanding, see into or through: to understand.—*v.i.* to make way or pass inwards.—*ns.* **pen'etrability** (-*trə-bil'i-ti*), **pen'etrableness**.—*adj.* **pen'etrable**.— *adv.* **pen'etrably**, so as to be penetrated.—*n.pl.* **penetrā'lia** (*pl.* of L. *penetral* or *penetrāle*), the inmost parts of a building: the most holy place in a temple: innermost mysteries.—*n.* **pen'etrancy**. —*adjs.* **pen'etrant**, penetrating; **pen'etrāting**, piercing: having keen and deep insight: sharp: keen: discerning.—*adv.* **pen'etrātingly**.—*n.* **penetrā'tion**, the act or power of penetrating or entering: acuteness: discernment: the space-penetrating power of a telescope.—*adj.* **pen'etrā-tive**, tending or able to penetrate: piercing: having keen and deep insight: reaching and affecting the mind.—*adv.* **pen'etrātively**.—*ns.* **pen'etrātiveness**; **pen'etrātor**. [L. *penetrāre*, *-ātum*—*penes*, in the house, possession, or power of; formed on the model of *intrāre*, to enter—*intus*, within; cf. **penates**.]

penfold. See **pen** (1), and cf. **pinfold**.

penguin, *peng'gwin*, *pen'*, *n.* a former name for the great auk: now any bird of the *Sphenisciformes*, flightless sea birds of the Southern Hemisphere, of peculiar structure: (*slang*) a training aeroplane that cannot fly: (*slang*) a member of the Women's Royal Air Force, ' flappers who did not fly.'—Also **pin'guin**.—*n.* **pen'guinery**, **pen'guinry**, a penguin rookery or breeding-place. [According to some, W. *pen*, head, *gwyn*, white, or the corresponding Breton words, though the great auk had a black head with two white patches: conjectures are *pin-wing*, and L. *pinguis*, fat.]

penguin. Same as **pinguin** (2).

peni, penie, Spenserian spellings of **penny**.

penicillate, *pen-i-sil'āt*, or *pen'*, *adj.* tufted: forming a tuft: brush-shaped.—*adj.* **penicill'iform**, paint-brush-shaped.—*ns.* **penicill'in**, a group of substances that stop the growth of bacteria, extracted from a mould, *Penicillium notatum*; **Penicill'ium**, a well-known genus of fungi (*Ascomycetes*; see *ascus*), including the common mould of jam, cheese, &c. (*P. glaucum*). [L. *pēnicillus*, paint-brush, dim. of *pēnis*, tail.]

peninsula, *pen-in'sū-lä*, *n.* a piece of land that is almost an island.—*adj.* **penin'sular**.—*n.* **penin-sular'ity**.—*v.t.* **penin'sulate**, to form into a peninsula.—**Peninsular War**, the war in Spain and Portugal carried on by Great Britain against Napoleon's marshals (1808-14); **The Peninsula**, Spain and Portugal. [L. *paenīnsula*—*paene*, almost, *īnsula*, an island.]

penis, *pē'nis*, *n.* the external male organ:—*pl.* **pē'nes** (*-nēz*).—*adj.* **pē'nial**. [L. *pēnis*, orig. a tail.]

penistone, *pen'i-stən*, *n.* a coarse frieze, formerly made at *Penistone* in Yorkshire.

penitent, *pen'i-tənt*, *adj.* suffering pain or sorrow for sin with will to amend: contrite: repentant: expressing sorrow for sin: undergoing penance: appropriate to penance.—*n.* one who sorrows for sin: one who has confessed sin, and is undergoing penance: a member of one of various orders devoted to penitential exercises and work among criminals, &c. — *ns.* **pen'itence**; **pen'itency** (*rare*).—*adj.* **penitential** (*-ten'shl*), of the nature of, pertaining to, or expressive of, penitence.—*n.* a book of rules relating to penance: a penitent: (in *pl.*) the behaviour or garb of a penitent: (*coll.*) black clothes.—*adv.* **peniten'tially**.—*adj.* **penitentiary** (*-ten'shə-ri*), relating to penance: penitential: penal and reformatory.—*n.* a penitent: an officer who deals with cases of penitence and penance: an office (under the *Grand Penitentiary*) at Rome dealing with cases of penance, dispensations, &c.: a book for guidance in imposing penances: (*obs.*) a place for the performance of penance: an asylum for prostitutes: a reformatory prison or house of correction: (*U.S.*) a prison. —*adv.* **pen'itently**.—**penitent form**, a seat for penitents at an evangelistic meeting; **penitential garment**, a rough garment worn for penance; **penitential psalms**, seven psalms suitable for being sung by penitents—the 6th, 32nd, 38th,

51st, 102nd, 130th, 143rd. [L. *paenitēns, -ēntis*, pr.p. of *paenitēre*, to cause to repent, to repent.]

penk. Same as **pink** (7).

penknife, penman. See under **pen**.

penna, *pen'ä*, *n.* a feather, esp. one of the large feathers of the wings or tail:—*pl.* **penn'ae** (*-ē*).— *adj.* **pennaceous** (*-ā'shəs*), featherlike.—*n.* **penne** (*pen; Spens.*), a pen: a pinion.—*adjs.* **penned**, feathered: quilled: winged; **penn'iform**, feather-shaped. [L. *penna*, feather, wing.]

pennal, *pen'əl*, *pen-äl'*, *n.* a freshman at a German university.—*n.* **penn'alism**, a system of fagging once in vogue at German universities. [Ger. *pennal*—L. *pennāle*, pen-case.]

pennant, *pen'ənt*, (*naut.*) *pen'ən*, *n.* (*naut.*) a dangling line with a block: a long narrow flag: a signalling flag: a pennon: (*U.S.*) a flag awarded for victory in a game.—**broad pennant**, a long swallow-tailed flag flown by a commodore. [A combination of **pendant** and **pennon**.]

Pennatula, *pen-at'ū-lä*, *n.* the typical genus of seapens.—*adj.* **pennatulā'ceous**. [Fem. of L. *pennātulus*, winged—*penna*.]

penneeck, penneech, *pen-ēk'*, *n.* (*Scott*) an old card-game with a new trump for every trick.

pennill, *pen'il*, *n.* a form of Welsh improvised verse: —*pl.* **pennill'ion**.—*n.* **pennill'ion-sing'ing**, a Welsh mode of singing in which the singer has to change words and measure according to the variations of his accompanist on the harp. [Welsh.]

pennine, *pen'īn*, *n.* a mineral of the chlorite group found in the *Pennine* Alps, a hydrous silicate of aluminium, magnesium, and iron.—Also **penn'in-ite** (*-in-īt*).

Pennisetum, *pen-i-sē'təm*, *n.* a genus, mainly African, of grasses with bristles around the spikelets, including bulrush millet or pearl millet. [L. *penna*, feather, *saeta*, bristle.]

pennon, *pen'ən*, *n.* a mediaeval knight-bachelor's ensign: a flag or streamer attached to a lance: a flag: a long narrow flag or streamer: (*Milt.*) a pinion or wing.—*n.* **penn'oncelle, pen'oncelle, penn'oncel, pen'oncel**, a small flag like a pennon. —*adj.* **penn'oned**, bearing a pennon. [O.Fr. *penon*, streamer, arrow-feather, prob.—L. *penna*, feather.]

penny, *pen'i*, *n.* a coin, originally silver, later copper, bronze since 1860, worth $\frac{1}{12}$ of a shilling, or four farthings: its value: applied to various more or less similar coins: (*U.S.*) a cent: a small sum: money in general: (*N.T.*) a denarius: pound, in *fourpenny, sixpenny, tenpenny* nails, four, six, ten *pound* weight to the thousand: (*pl.* **pennies**, *pen'iz*, as material objects; **pence**, *pens*, as units of value).—*adj.* sold for a penny: costing a penny.—*adjs.* **penn'ied**, possessed of a penny; **penn'iless**, without a penny: without money: poor.—*n.* **penn'ilessness**—*n.* and *v.i.* **penny-a-line'**.—*ns.* **penny-a-lin'er**, a hack-writer of the worst, or worst-paid, kind; **penny-a-lin'erism**, a hack-writer's expression; **penn'y-bank**, a savings-bank that takes pennies; **penn'y-cress**, a cruciferous plant of the genus Thlaspi, with round flat pods; **penn'y-dog'**, the tope or miller's dog, a kind of shark; **penn'y-dread'ful**, a blood-and-thunder tale or paper; **penn'y-far'thing**, a penny and a farthing: an old-fashioned ' ordinary ' bicycle, with a big wheel and a little; **penn'y-fee**, wages in money.—*adj.* **penny-in-the-slot**, worked by putting a penny in a slot.—*ns.* **penn'yland**, (*hist.*) land valued at a penny a year; **penn'y-piece**, a penny; **penn'y-pig**, (*Scot.*) a money-box, properly of earthenware (pig); **penn'y-post'**, a means of, or organisation for, carrying a letter for a penny; **penn'y-rent**, rent in money: income; **penn'y-stone, -stane** (*Scot.*), a round flat stone used as a quoit; **penn'ystone-cast'**, a stone's throw for such a stone; **penn'y-wedd'ing**, a wedding at which the guests contribute money to set up the bride and bridegroom; **penn'y-weight**, twenty-four grains of troy weight (the weight of a silver penny); **penn'y-whist'le**, a tin whistle or flageolet; **penn'y-wis'dom**, prudence in petty matters.—*adj.* **penn'y-wise**, saving small sums at the risk of larger: niggardly on improper occasions.—*ns.* **penn'y-wort,** a name given to various plants with round leaves, esp. Hydrocotyle (an umbelliferous marsh-plant) and navel-wort (Cotyledon); **penn'y-worth,** a penny's worth of anything: the amount that can be got for a penny: a good bargain—also **penn'orth** (*pen'ərth*; *coll.*). —**a pretty penny,** a considerable sum of money; **not a penny the worse,** never a whit the worse; **penny fee,** (*Scot.*) a small wage; **penny gaff,** (*slang*) a low-class theatre; **penny mail,** (*Scot.*) rent in money, not in kind: a small sum paid to the superior of land; **Peter's pence,** Rome-scot, a tax or tribute of a silver penny paid to the Pope in England perhaps from the time of Offa of Mercia, in Ireland from Henry II, abolished under Henry VIII: a similar tax elsewhere: a voluntary contribution to the Pope in modern times; **turn an honest penny,** to earn some money honestly. [O.E. *penig*, oldest form *pending*; cf. Ger. *pfennig*; Du. *penning*; O.N. *penningr*.]

pennyroyal, *pen-i-roi'əl, n.* a species of mint (*Mentha Pulegium*) once esteemed in medicine: (*U.S.*) a related plant, *Hedeoma pulegioides*. [M.E. *puliol real*—A.Fr. *puliol real*—L. *pūleium*, *pūlegium*, pennyroyal, and *regālis, -e*, royal.]

pennywinkle, *pen'-i-wingk-l.* See **periwinkle** (2).

penology, *pē-nol'ə-ji, n.* the study of punishment in its relation to crime: the management of prisons. —*adj.* **penological** (*-nə-loj'*).—*n.* **penologist** (*-nol'ə-jist*). [Gr. *poinē*, punishment, *logos*, discourse.]

pensil, *pen'sl, n.* a small pennon. [A.Fr. *pencel,* dim. of *penon*, pennon.]

pensile, *pen'sīl, -sil, adj.* hanging: suspended: overhanging: building a hanging nest. — *ns.* **pen'sileness, pensility** (*-sil'i-ti*). [L. *pēnsilis*—*pendēre,* hang.]

pension, *pen'shən, n.* (*obs.*) a periodical payment, as tribute, wages, &c.: an allowance of money as a bribe for future services, as a mark of favour, or in reward of one's own or another's merit: an allowance to one who has retired or has been disabled or reached old age or has been widowed or orphaned, &c.: (now pronounced as Fr., *pän²syon²*) a Continental boarding-house: board. —*v.t.* to grant a pension to.—*adjs.* **pen'sionable,** entitled, or entitling, to a pension; **pen'sionary,** receiving a pension: of the nature of a pension.— *n.* one who receives a pension: one whose interest is bought by a pension: (*hist.*) the syndic or legal adviser of a Dutch town.—*n.* **pen'sioner,** one who receives a pension: a dependent: (*obs.*) a gentleman-at-arms: one who pays out of his own income for his commons, chambers, &c., at Cambridge University = an Oxford *commoner*: (*obs.*) a boarder, esp. in a religious house.—**Grand Pensionary,** (*hist.*) the president of the States-general of Holland; **pension off,** to dismiss, or allow to retire, with a pension. [Fr.,—L. *pēnsiō, -ōnis*—*pendēre, pēnsum,* to weigh, pay.]

pensive, *pen'siv, adj.* meditative: expressing thoughtfulness with sadness. — *adj.* **pen'siv'd,** (*Shak.*) made pensive. — *adv.* **pen'sively.** — *n.* **pen'siveness.** [Fr. *pensif, -ive—penser*—L. *pēnsāre,* to weigh—*pendēre,* to weigh.]

penstock, *pen'stok, n.* a sluice. [**pen** (1), **stock.**]

pensum, *pen'səm, n.* a task: (*U.S.*) a school imposition. [L. *pēnsum.*]

pent, *pa.t.* and *pa.p.* of **pen,** to shut up.

pent, *pent, n.* a penthouse: a sloping or overhanging covering.—*n.* **pent'roof,** a roof that slopes one way only. [From **penthouse,** app. influenced by Fr. *pente,* slope.]

pent-, penta-, in composition, five.—*ns.* **pentachord** (*pen'tə-kord*; Gr. *chordē,* string), a musical instrument with five strings: a diatonic series of five notes; **pentacle** (*pen'tə-kl;* L.L. *pentaculum,* app.—Gr. *pente;* according to some O.Fr. *pentacol* —*pendre,* to hang, *à,* on, *col,* the neck), a pentagram or similar figure (sometimes a hexagram) or amulet used as a defence against demons; **Pentacrinus** (*-ak'rin-əs;* Gr. *krinon,* lily), a genus of fossil crinoids, in the form of a feathery five-rayed star on a long pentagonal stalk.—*adj.* **pentac'rinoid,** like, or akin to, *Pentacrinus.*—*n.* a young form of

some crinoids that resembles *Pentacrinus.*—*adj.* **pent'act** (Gr. *aktīs, aktīnos,* ray), five-rayed.—*n.* a five-rayed sponge spicule.—*adjs.* **pentactinal** (*-ak'tin-əl,* or *-ak-ti'nol*); **pentacy'clic** (Gr. *kyklos,* wheel), having five whorls.—*n.* **pent'ad** (Gr. *pentas, -ados*), a set of five things: a period of five years or five days: an atom, element, or radical with a combining power of five.—Also *adj.*—*adjs.* **pentad'ic;** **pentadac'tyl, pentadac'tyle** (*-til;* Gr. *daktylos,* finger, toe), having five digits.—*n.* a person with five fingers and five toes.—*adjs.* **pentadactyl'ic, pentadac'tylous.** — *ns.* **pentadac'tylism;** pentadac'tyly. — *adj.* **pentadel'-phous** (Gr. *adelphos,* brother), having five bundles of stamens: united in five bundles.—*n.* **pentagon** (*pen'tə-gon;* Gr. *pentagōnon—gōniā,* angle; *geom.*), a rectilineal plane figure having five angles and five sides: a fort with five bastions.—*adj.* **pentagonal** (*pen-tag'an-əl*).—*adv.* **pentag'onally.**—*ns.* **pen'tagram** (Gr. *pentagrammon—gramma,* a letter), a stellate pentagon or five-pointed star: a magic figure of that form; **pen'tagraph,** a wrong form of **pantograph.**—*n.pl.* **Pentagynia** (*-jin'i-ā;* Gr. *gynē,* a woman, in the sense of female; *obs.*), a Linnaean order of plants (in various classes) with five pistils.—*adjs.* **pentagyn'ian, pentagynous** (*-aj'*).—*ns.* **pental'pha** (Gr. *alpha,* the letter alpha), a pentacle; **Pentam'eron** (It. *Pentamerone*—Gr. *pente, hēmerā,* day), a famous collection of folktales in Neapolitan dialect by Giambattista Basile (*d.* 1632) supposed to be told during five days; **pentam'erism** (Gr. *meros,* part), condition of being pentamerous.—*adj.* **pentam'erous,** having five parts or members: having parts in fives.— *ns.* **pentam'ery; pentam'eter** (Gr. *pentametros—metron,* a measure), a verse of five measures or feet (**elegiac pentameter,** a verse of two penthemimers, the first admitting spondees instead of dactyls, the second dactyls only; **iambic pentameter,** a somewhat unsuitable name for the line used in the English heroic couplet and blank verse).—Also *adj.*—*n.pl.* (Gr.) **Pentan'dria** (Gr. *anēr, andros,* a man, a male), in Linnaeus's classification a class of plants with five stamens.—*adjs.* **pentan'drian, pentan'drous.** — *ns.* **pentane** (*pent'ān*), a hydrocarbon (C_5H_{12}), fifth member of the methane series; **pent'angle,** a pentacle: a pentagon.— *adjs.* **pentang'ular; pentaploid** (*pent'ə-ploid;* Gr. *pentaploos,* five-fold, *eidos,* form), five-fold: (*biol.*) having five times the haploid number of chromosomes.—*n.* a cell, organism, or form with five sets of chromosomes.—*n.* **pent'-aploidy,** the condition of having five sets of chromosomes.—*adj.* **pentapodic** (*pent-ə-pod'ik*).— *ns.* **pentapody** (*pen-tap'ə-di;* Gr. *pous, podos,* foot), a measure of five feet; **pentap'olis** (Gr. *polis,* a city), a group of five cities, esp. those of Cyrenaica — Cyrene, Berenice, Arsinoe, Ptolemais, and Apollonia.—*adjs.* **pentapolitan** (*pent-ā-pol'i-tən*); **pentarch** (*pent'ärk;* Gr. *archē,* beginning; of roots), having five vascular strands.—*ns.* **pent'arch** (Gr. *archē,* rule), a ruler or governor in a pentarchy; **pentarchy** (*pent'ärk-i*), government by five persons: a group of five kings, rulers, states, or governments; **pentastich** (*pent'ə-stik;* Gr. *stichos,* row, line), a group of five lines of verse:—*pl.* **pentastichs** (*-stiks*).—*adjs.* **pentastichous** (*pen-tas'ti-kəs*), five-ranked; **pen'tastyle** (Gr. *stylos,* a pillar), having five columns in front.—*n.* a building or portico with five columns.—*adj.* **pentasyllab'ic,** five-syllabled. — *n.* **Pentateuch** (*pent'ə-tūk;* Gr. *pentateuchos,* five-volumed— *teuchos,* a tool; later, a book), the first five books of the Old Testament.—*adj.* **pentateuch'al.**— *ns.* **pentath'lete,** a competitor in the pentathlon; **pentath'lon** (Gr. *pentathlon—athlon,* a prize), a contest in five exercises—wrestling, disk-throwing, spear-throwing, leaping, and running — also (Latinised) **pentath'lum.** — *adjs.* **pentatomic** (*pent-ə-tom'ik;* Gr. *atomos,* atom), having five atoms, esp. five atoms of replaceable hydrogen: pentavalent; **pentatonic** (*pent-ə-ton'ik;* Gr. *tonos,* tone), consisting of five tones or notes—applied esp. to a scale, a major scale with the fourth and seventh omitted; **pentavalent** (*pen-tav'ə-lənt,* *pen-tə-vā'lənt*), having a valency of five. [Gr. *pente*, five.]

penteconter, *pen-ti-kon'tər*, *n.* an ancient Greek ship with fifty oars. [Gr. *pentēkontērēs—pentē-konta*, fifty.]

Pentecost, *pent'i-kost*, *n.* a Jewish festival held on the fiftieth day after the Passover: the festival of Whitsuntide, seven weeks after Easter.—*adj.* **Pentecost'al**.—*n.pl.* offerings formerly made to the parish priest at Whitsuntide. [Gr. *pentēkostē* (*hēmerā*), fiftieth (day).]

Pentelic, **-an**, *pen-tel'ik*, *-ən*, *adjs.* of Mount *Pentel'icus* near Athens, famous for its marble.

penteteric, *pen-ti-ter'ik*, *adj.* occurring every fourth (by the old mode of reckoning, fifth) year. [Gr. *pentētērikos—etos*, a year.]

penthemimer, *pen-thi-mim'ər*, *n.* a metrical group of 2½ feet.—*adj.* **penthemim'eral**. [Gr. *pente*, five, *hēmi-*, half, *meros*, a part.]

penthia, *pen'thi-ä*, *n.* according to Spenser another name for the unidentified plant Astrophel.

penthouse, *pent'hows*, *n.* a shed or lean-to projecting from or adjoining a main building: a protection from the weather over a door or a window: any-thing of similar form, as an eyebrow:—*pl.* **pent'-houses** (*-how-ziz*).—*v.t.* to provide or cover with, or as with, a penthouse. [For **pentice**—Fr. *appentis*—L.L. *appendicium*, an appendage.]

pentice, pentise, *pen'tis*, *n.* See **penthouse**.

pentlandite, *pent'lənd-īt*, *n.* a native sulphide of iron and nickel. [Joseph Barclay *Pentland* (1797-1873), traveller in South America.]

pentode, *pent'ōd*, *n.* a thermionic tube with five electrodes. [Gr. *pente*, five, *hodos*, way.]

pentose, *pent'ōs*, *n.* a sugar (of various kinds) with five oxygen atoms.—*n.* **pent'osan** (*-san*), **pent'-osane** (*-sān*), a carbohydrate that yields pentose on hydrolysis. [Gr. *pente*, five.]

Pentothal, *pen'tō-thal*, *n.* registered trade-name for thiopentone, an intravenous anaesthetic, a sodium thiobarbiturate compound. — Also **pentothal sodium**.

pentroof. See **pent** (2).

Pentstemon, *pen(t)-stē'mən*, *n.* a mainly North American showy-flowered genus of Scrophulari-aceae, with a sterile fifth stamen. [Gr. *pente*, five, *stēmōn*, warp, as if stamen.]

pentylene, *pent'i-lēn*, *n.* an unsaturated hydro-carbon (C_5H_{10}) of the olefine series (in several isomers)—amylene.—Also **pent'ene**. [Gr. *pente*, five, *hylē*, matter.]

penult, *pi-nult'*, also *pē'nult*, **penult'ima**, *ns.* the syllable last but one.—*adj.* **penult'imate**, last but one.—*n.* the penult: the last but one. [L. *paenultima* (*syllaba*, &c.)—*paene*, almost, *ultimus*, last.]

penumbra, *pen-um'brä*, *n.* a partial or lighter shadow round the perfect or darker shadow of an eclipse: the less dark border of a sun-spot or any similar spot: the part of a picture where the light and shade blend into each other.—*adj.* **penum'bral**. [L. *paene*, almost, *umbra*, shade.]

penury, *pen'ū-ri*, *n.* want: great poverty.—*adj.* **penū'rious**, (*obs.*) in want: (*obs.*) scanty: niggardly: miserly.—*adv.* **penū'riously**. — *n.* **penū'riousness**. [L. *paenūria*.]

peon, *pē'on*, *n.* a day-labourer, esp. formerly in Spanish-speaking America, one working off a debt by bondage: in India (*pūn*) a foot-soldier, a messenger, a policeman.—*ns.* **pē'onage**, **pē'onism**, this kind of agricultural servitude. [Sp. *peón* and Port. *peão*—L.L. *pedō*, *-ōnis*—L. *pēs*, *pedis*, a foot.]

peony. Same as **paeony**.

people, *pē'pl*, *n.* a nation: a community: a body of persons held together by belief in common origin, speech, culture, political union, or other bond: a set of persons: transferred to a set of animals as if forming a nation—in these senses used as *sing.* with a *pl.* **peo'ples** (*B.* **peo'ple**): a body of persons linked by common leadership, headship, &c.: subjects: retainers: followers: employees: servants: congregation: attendants: near kindred: members of one's household: an-cestors and descendants: inhabitants of a place: transferred to animal inhabitants: the persons

associated with any business: laity: the mass of the nation: general population: populace: the citizens: voters: (approaching a *pron.*) they, one, folks—in these senses used as *pl.*—*v.t.* to stock with people or inhabitants: to inhabit: to occupy as if inhabiting. [O.Fr. *poeple*—L. *pŏpulus*.]

pep, *pep*, *n.* (*coll.*) vigour, go, spirit.—*v.t.* to put pep into (usu. with *up*).—*adjs.* **pep'ful**, **pepp'y**. [**pepper**.]

peperino, *pep-ə-rē'nō*, *n.* a dark tuff with many crystals and rock-fragments found in the Alban Hills. [It. *peperino*—L. *piper*, pepper.]

peplos, *pep'los*, *n.* an upper robe worn by women in ancient Greece.—*n.* **pep'lum** (L.), a peplos: an overskirt supposed to be like the peplos. [Gr. *peplos*.]

pepo, *pē'pō*, *n.* the type of fruit found in the melon and cucumber family, a large many-seeded berry formed from an inferior ovary, usually with hard epicarp. [L. *pēpō*, *-ōnis*—Gr. (*sikyos*) *pepōn*, (a melon eaten) ripe, distinguished from a cucumber eaten unripe.]

pepper, *pep'ər*, *n.* a pungent aromatic condiment consisting of the dried berries of the pepper plant, entire or powdered (*black pepper*), or with the outer parts removed (*white pepper*): any plant of the genus Piper, esp. *P. nigrum*, or of the family Piperaceae: a plant of the solanaceous genus Capsicum, or one of its pods (*red* or *Cayenne pepper*): extended to various similar condiments and the plants producing them.—*v.t.* to sprinkle or flavour with pepper: to sprinkle: to pelt with shot, &c.: to pelt thoroughly: to do for.—*v.i.* to pelt: to shower: to discharge shot, &c., in showers.—*adj.* **pepper-and-salt'**, mingled black and white.—*ns.* **pepp'er-box**, a box or bottle with a perforated top for sprinkling pepper: a turret or other object of similar shape; **pepp'er-cake**, a kind of spiced cake or gingerbread; **pepp'er-caster**, **-castor**, a pepper-box; **pepp'er-corn**, the dried berry of the pepper plant: some-thing of little value.—*adj.* like a peppercorn, as the little tight knots of hair on a Hottentot: trivial, nominal, as *peppercorn rent.*—*adj.* **pepp'ercorny**.—*ns.* **pepp'erer**, (*obs.*) a grocer: one who or that which peppers; **pepp'er-gin'gerbread**, (*Shak.*) hot-spiced gingerbread; **pepp'er-grass**, any cress of the genus Lepidium: pillwort (Pilularia); **pepp'eriness**; **pepp'ering**; **pepp'ermint**, an aromatic and pungent species of mint (*Mentha piperita*): a liquor distilled from it: a lozenge flavoured with it; **pepp'ermint-drop**, a confection so flavoured; **pepp'er-pot**, a West Indian dish of cassareep, flesh or dried fish, and vegetables, esp. green okra and chillies: a pepper-box; **pepp'erwort**, a cress of the genus Lepidium, esp. dittander (*L. latifolium*).—*adj.* **pepp'ery**, having the qualities of pepper: pungent: hot, choleric.—**Jamaica pepper**, allspice; **long pepper**, the fruit of *Piper longum*; **Negro pepper**, the produce of Xylopia (fam. Anonaceae), also called **Ethiopian pepper**. [O.E. *pipor*—L. *piper*—Gr. *peperi*—Sans. *pippalī*.]

Pepper's ghost, *pep'ərz gōst*, *n.* a phantom produced on the stage by a sheet of glass reflecting an actor on an understage. [John H. *Pepper* (1821-1900), improver and exhibitor of H. Dircks's invention.]

pepsin, *pep'sin*, *n.* any of a group of closely allied proteins, digestive enzymes of the gastric juice of vertebrates: (*med.*) a preparation containing pepsin from a pig's or other stomach.—*adj.* **pep'tic**, relating to or promoting digestion: having a good digestion: of or relating to pepsin or the digestive juices.—*n.* **pepticity** (*-tis'i-ti*), eupepsia.—*n. pl.* **pep'tics**, (*jocular*) the digestive organs.—*n.* **pep-tisa'tion**.—*v.t.* **pep'tise**, to bring into colloidal solution: to form into a sol from a gel.—*ns.* **pep'tōne**, a product of the action of enzymes on albuminous matter; **peptonīsā'tion**.—*v.t.* **pep'tonise**, to convert into peptones.—**peptic ulcer**, an ulcer of the stomach or duodenum, &c. [Gr. *pepsis*, digestion—*peptein*, to digest.]

Pepysian, *pep'si-ən*, *adj.* pertaining to Samuel *Pepys* (1633-1703), his inimitable diary, or the collections he bequeathed to Magdalene College, Cambridge.

Neutral vowels in unaccented syllables: *el'ə-mənt, in'fənt, ran'dəm*

per, *pər, prep.* for each, a : (chiefly commercial) by : (*her.*) in the manner or direction of.—**as per usual,** (*vulg.*) as usual. [L. and O.Fr. *per.*]

peracute, *per-ə-kūt', adj.* very sharp or violent.

peradventure, *per-əd-vent'yər, adv.* by adventure : by chance : perhaps.—*n.* uncertainty : question.

peraeon, peraeopod. See **pereion.**

perai, *pē-rī'.* See **piranha.**

perambulate, *pər-am'bū-lāt, v.t.* to walk through, about, around, up and down, or over : to pass through for the purpose of surveying : to beat the bounds of : to patrol : to wheel in a perambulator.—*v.i.* to walk about.—*ns.* **perambulā'tion,** act of perambulating : a survey or inspection by travelling through : beating the bounds : the district within which a person has the right of inspection ; **peram'bulātor,** one who perambulates : a wheel for measuring distances on roads : a light carriage for a child.—*adj.* **peram'bulatory.** [L. *perambulāre, -ātum*—*per,* through, *ambulāre,* to walk.]

percale, *per-käl', pər-kāl', n.* a closely woven French cambric.—*n.* **percaline** (*pər-kə-lēn',* or *pər'*), a glossy cotton cloth. [Fr. ; cf. Pers. *purgālah,* rag.]

percase, *pər-kās', adv.* (*obs.*) perchance : perhaps. [L. *per,* through, by, *cāsus,* a chance, a fall.]

perce, *pərs,* (*Spens.*) same as **pierce.**—Also (*infin.*) **percen.**—*adjs.* (*Spens.*) **perce'able,** pierceable ; **perce'ant,** (*Keats*) piercing.

perceive, *pər-sēv', v.t.* to become or be aware of through the senses : to get knowledge of by the mind : to see : to understand : to discern.—*adj.* **perceiv'able.**—*adv.* **perceiv'ably,** perceptibly.—*n.* **perceiv'er.**—*n.* and *adj.* **perceiv'ing.** [O.Fr. *percever* — L. *percipĕre perceptum* — pfx. *per-,* thoroughly, *capĕre,* to take.]

per cent (usu. written or printed with a point after it as if an abbreviation for *per centum,* but pronounced as a complete word, *pər-sent'*), *adv.* in the hundred : for each hundred or hundred pounds.—*n.* a percentage : (in *pl.,* in composition) securities yielding a specified percentage (as *three-percents*).—*n.* **percent'age,** rate per hundred : an allowance of so much for every hundred : a proportional part.—*adjs.* **percent'al, percen'tile.**—*n.* **percen'tile,** the value below which fall a specified percentage (as 25, 50, 75) of a large number of statistical units (e.g. scores in an examination) : percentile rank.—**percentile rank,** grading according to percentile group. [L. *per centum.*]

percept, *pər'sept, n.* an object perceived by the senses : the mental result of perceiving. — *n.* **perceptibil'ity.**—*adj.* **percep'tible,** that can be perceived : that may be known by the senses : discernible.—*adv.* **percep'tibly.**—*n.* **percep'tion,** act or power of perceiving : discernment : apprehension of any modification of consciousness : the combining of sensations into a recognition of an object : direct recognition : a percept : (*bot.*) reception of a stimulus.—*adjs.* **percep'tional ; percep'tive,** able or quick to perceive : discerning : active or instrumental in perceiving.—*ns.* **percep'tiveness ; perceptiv'ity.**—*adj.* **percep'tūal,** of the nature of, or relating to, perception. [L. *percipĕre, perceptum ;* see **perceive.**]

perch, *pərch, n.* a spiny-finned fresh-water fish of the genus Perca (*pər'kä*) : extended to various fishes of the same or kindred family, or other.—*n.pl.* **Percidae** (*pər'si-dē*), the perch family.—*adjs.* **per'ciform, per'cine** (*-sīn*), **per'coid** (*-koid*). [L. *perca* (partly through Fr. *perche*)—Gr. *perkē,* a perch, perh. conn. with *perknos,* dusky.]

perch, *pərch, n.* (*obs.* or *dial.* except in special uses) a pole : a pole serving as a navigation mark : a pole joining the fore and hind gear of some vehicles : a bar or frame for stretching cloth for examination : a bar for fixing leather for softening treatment : (*obs.*) a peg or bar for hanging things on : a rod for a bird to alight, sit, or roost on : anything serving the purpose for a bird, a person, or anything else : a high seat : a rod or pole, a measure of 5½ yards or (*square perch*) 30¼ square yards : a measure of stone-work, 24¾ or 25 cubic feet.—*v.i.* to alight, sit or roost on a perch : to be balanced on a high or narrow

footing : to settle.—*v.t.* to place, as on a perch : to stretch, examine, or treat on a perch.—*adj.* **perch'ed,** (*Milt.*) furnished with perches. — *ns.* **perch'er,** a bird that perches on trees ; **perch'ing,** examination of cloth on a perch : a process of leather-softening. — *adj.* with feet adapted for perching : insessorial.—**perched block,** a block of rock transported by land-ice and left aloft, often in an unstable position, when the ice retires ; **perching birds,** the Passeriformes. [Fr. *perche*— L. *pertica,* a rod.]

perchance, *pər-chäns', adv.* by chance : as it may happen : perhaps. [A.Fr. *par chance.*]

percheron, *per-shə-ronᵉ, pər'shə-ron, n.* a draught-horse of a breed originating in La *Perche* in southern Normandy.—Also *adj.* [Fr.]

perchloric, *pər-klō'rik, adj.* containing more oxygen than chloric acid—applied to an oily explosive acid, $HClO_4$.—*n.* **perchlō'rate,** a salt of perchloric acid.

percipient, *pər-sip'i-ənt, adj.* perceiving : having the faculty of perception.—*n.* one who perceives or can perceive : one who receives impressions telepathically or otherwise supersensibly.—*ns.* **percip'ience, percip'iency** (*rare*). [L. *percipiēns, -entis,* pr.p. of *percipĕre ;* cf. **perceive, percept.**]

percoct, *pər-kokt', adj.* well-cooked : overdone : hackneyed. [L. *percoctus, percoquĕre,* to cook thoroughly.]

percoid, *pər'koid.* See **perch** (1).

percolate, *pər'kō-lāt, v.t.* and *v.i.* to pass through pores or small openings : to filter.—*n.* a filtered liquid.—*ns.* **percolā'tion ; per'colātor,** an apparatus for percolating, esp. for making coffee. [L. *percōlāre, -ātum*—*per,* through, *cōlāre,* to strain.]

percurrent, *pər-kur'ənt, adj.* running through the whole length.—*adj.* **percur'sory,** cursory. [L. *percurrĕre,* to run through, *percursor,* one who runs through.]

percuss, *pər-kus', v.t.* to strike so as to shake : to tap for purposes of diagnosis.—*adj.* **percuss'ant,** (*her.*) bent round and striking the side, as a lion's tail—also **percussed'.**—*n.* **percussion** (*-kush'ən*), striking : impact : (*med.*) tapping directly or indirectly upon the body to find the condition of an organ by the sound : massage by tapping : (*mus.*) the striking or sounding of a discord, &c., as distinguished from preparation and resolution : collectively, instruments played by striking—drum, cymbals, triangle, &c. : a device for making an organ-pipe speak promptly by striking the reed.— *adj.* **percuss'ional.**—*ns.* **percuss'ion-bull'et,** a bullet that explodes on striking ; **percuss'ion-cap,** a metal case containing a fulminating substance which explodes when struck, formerly used for firing rifles, &c. ; **percuss'ion-fuse,** a fuse in a projectile that acts on striking ; **percuss'ion-hamm'er,** a small hammer for percussion in diagnosis ; **percuss'ion-lock,** a gun lock in which a hammer strikes a percussion-cap ; **percuss'ion-pow'der,** powder that explodes on being struck—fulminating powder.—*adj.* **percussive** (*-kus'*).—*adv.* **percuss'ively.**—*n.* **percuss'or,** a percussion-hammer—*adj.* **percutient** (*-kū'shyənt*), striking or having power to strike.—*n.* that which strikes or has power to strike.—**bulb of percussion** (see **bulb**). [L. *percussiō, -ōnis*—*percutĕre, percussum*— pfx. *per-,* thoroughly, *quatĕre,* to shake.]

percutaneous, *pər-kū-tā'ni-əs, adj.* done or applied through the skin.—*adv.* **percutā'neously.** [L. *per,* through, *cutis,* the skin.]

perdendo, *per-den'dō, adj.* and *adv.* (*mus.*) dying away in volume of tone and in speed.—Also **perden'dosi** (*-sē*). [It.]

perdie, perdy, *pər-dē', sometimes pər'dē, adv.* (*Spens., Shak.*) assuredly.—Also **pardie', pardy'.** [O.Fr. *par dé,* by God.]

perdition, *pər-dish'ən, n.* loss : ruin : utter loss or ruin : the utter loss of happiness in a future state : hell.—*adj.* **perdi'tionable.** [L. *perditiō, -ōnis perdĕre, perditum*—pfx. *per-,* entirely, *dăre,* to give, give up.]

perdu, perdue, *pər-dū', adj.* lost to view : concealed : in a post of extreme danger : on a forlorn hope or on a desperate enterprise : reckless.—*n.*

(*Shak.*) an outlying sentinel : one lying in concealment or ambush : one on a forlorn hope. [Fr., pa.p. of *perdre*, to lose—L. *perdĕre*, to destroy ; see preceding.]

perduellion, *pər-dū-el'yən*, *n.* treason. [L. *perduelliō*, *-ōnis*.]

perdurable, *pər-dūr'ə-bl* (Shak. *pər'*), *adj.* very durable, long continued : everlasting.—*n.* **perdurabil'ity**.—*adv.* **perdūr'ably** (Shak. *pər'*), very durably : everlastingly.—*ns.* **perdūr'ance** ; **perdūrā'tion**.—*v.i.* **perdūre'**, to endure. [L. *perdūrāre*—*per*, through, *dūrāre*, to last.]

peregal, *per'i-gl*, *adj.* (*obs.*) fully equal.—*n.* equal. [O.Fr. *paregal*—L. pfx. *per-*, thoroughly, *aequālis*, equal.]

peregrine, *per'i-grin*, *adj.* foreign : outlandish : making a pilgrimage or journey : applied to a species of falcon (*Falco peregrinus*) that was taken not from the nest but on passage.—*n.* an alien resident : a pilgrim or traveller in a foreign land : a peregrine falcon.—*v.i.* **per'egrinate**, to travel about : to live in a foreign country : to go on pilgrimage.—*v.t.* to traverse.—*adj.* foreign-looking. —*ns.* **peregrinā'tion**, travelling about : wandering : pilgrimage : a complete and systematic course or round : a sojourn abroad ; **per'egrinātor**, one who travels about ; **peregrin'ity**, foreignness : outlandishness. [L. *peregrīnus*, foreign—*peregre*, abroad—*per*, through, *ager*, field.]

pereion, *pə-rī'on*, *n.* the thorax in Crustacea :—*pl.* **pereï'a**.—*n.* **pereï'opod**, a crustacean's thoracic walking-leg.—Also in corrected form, **peraeon**, **peraeopod**. [Faultily formed from Gr. *peraioein*, to transport, to carry across.]

peremptory, *per'əm(p)-tə-ri*, or *pər-em(p)'*, *adj.* (*Rom. law*) precluding debate or dispute : final : admitting no refusal or denial : (*law*) definitely fixed : (*obs.*) utter : dogmatic : imperious : arrogantly commanding. — *adv.* **per'emptorily** (or *-emp'*).—*n.* **per'emptoriness** (or *-emp'*). [L. *peremptōrius*—*perimĕre*, *peremptum*, to destroy, prevent —pfx. *per-*, entirely, *emĕre*, to take, buy.]

perennial, *pər-en'yəl*, *adj.* lasting through the year : perpetual : never failing : growing constantly : (*bot.*) lasting more than two years : of insects, living more than one year.—*n.* a plant that lives more than two years.—*v.i.* **perenn'ate**, to live perennially : to survive from season to season, esp. through a period of inactivity.—*n.* **perennā'tion** (*per-*).—*adv.* **perenn'ially**. [L. *perennis*—*per*, through, *annus*, a year.]

perennibranchiate, *pər-en-i-brang'ki-āt*, *adj.* retaining the gills throughout life.—*adj.* and *n.* **perenn'ibranch** (*-brangk*).

perfay, *pər-fā'*, *interj.* (*arch.*) by my faith. [O.Fr. *par fei*.]

perfect, *pər'fekt*, *-fikt*, *adj.* done thoroughly or completely : completed : mature : complete : having all organs in a functional condition : having androecium and gynaeceum in the same flower : completely skilled or versed : thoroughly known or acquired : exact : exactly conforming to definition or theory : flawless : having every moral excellence : sheer, utter : (*Shak.*) completely contented : (*Shak.*) certain, completely assured : (*gram.*) expressing an act completed : (*mus.*) of the simpler kind of consonance : (*old music*) applied to time) triple.—*n.* the perfect tense : a verb in the perfect tense.—*v.t.* **perfect** (*pər-fekt'*, or *pər'*), to make perfect : to finish : to teach fully, to make fully skilled in anything : to print the second side of.—*ns.* **perfectā'tion** (*rare*) ; **perfect'er** (or *pər'*).—*n.pl.* **perfect'i** (*-ī*), a body of Catharists in the 12th and 13th centuries, of very strict lives.—*ns.* **perfectibil'ian**, a believer in the perfectibility of mankind ; **perfect'ibilism**, the belief that man is capable of becoming perfect or of progressing indefinitely towards perfection ; **perfect'ibilist** ; **perfectibil'ity**, capability of becoming perfect : perfectibilism.—*adj.* **perfect'ible**, capable of becoming perfect.—*ns.* **perfec'tion**, state of being perfect : a quality in perfect degree : the highest state or degree : an embodiment of the perfect : (loosely) a degree of excellence approaching the perfect.—*v.t.* **perfec'tionate**, to bring to

perfection.—*ns.* **perfec'tionism** ; **perfec'tionist**, one who claims to be perfect : one who aims at or calls for nothing short of perfection : one who holds some doctrine concerning perfection : one who thinks that moral perfection can be attained in this life : **Perfectionist**, one of the Bible Communists or Free-lovers, a small American sect founded by J. H. Noyes (1811-86), which settled at Oneida in 1848, holding that the gospel if accepted secures freedom from sin.—*adj.* **perfect'ive**, tending to make perfect.—*advs.* **perfect'ively** ; **per'fectly**.—*ns.* **per'fectness**, state or quality of being perfect : completeness ; **perfect'o** (*Sp.*), a large tapering cigar ; **perfect'or**, one who perfects : a machine for printing both sides at once.—**perfect cadence**, one passing from the chord of the dominant (or subdominant) to that of the tonic ; **perfect fifth**, the interval between two sounds whose vibration frequencies are as 2 to 3 ; **perfect fluid**, an ideal fluid, incompressible, of uniform density, offering no resistance to distorting forces ; **perfect fourth**, the interval between sounds whose vibration frequencies are as 3 to 4 ; **perfect insect**, the imago or completely developed form of an insect ; **perfect interval**, the fourth, fifth, or octave ; **perfect metals**, noble metals ; **perfect number**, a number equal to the sum of its aliquot parts, as $6 = 1 + 2 + 3$, $28 = 1 + 2 + 4 + 7 + 14$; **to perfection**, perfectly. [M.E. *parfit*—O.Fr. *parfit* ; later assimilated to L. *perfectus*, p.a.p of *perficĕre*—pfx. *per-*, thoroughly, *facĕre*, to do.]

perfervid, *pər-fər'vid*, *adj.* very fervid : ardent : eager.—*ns.* **perferv'idity** ; **perfer'vidness** ; **perfer'vor**, **-our**. [*Perfervidus*, a misreading or misquotation for L. *praefervidus*—*prae*, before, *fervidus*, fervid.]

perfet, *pər'fet*, *adj.* an older form (used by Milton) of **perfect**.

perficient, *pər-fish'ənt*, *adj.* effectual : actually achieving a result. [L. *perficiēns*, *-entis*, pr.p. of *perficĕre*, to complete—pfx. *per-*, thoroughly, *facĕre*, to do, make.]

perfidious, *pər-fid'i-əs*, *adj.* faithless : unfaithful : basely violating faith.—*adv.* **perfid'iously**.—*ns.* **perfid'iousness**, **per'fidy**. [L. *perfidiōsus*—*perfidia*, faithlessness—pfx. *per-*, implying destruction, *fidēs*, faith.]

perfoliate, *pər-fō'li-āt*, *adj.* (of a leaf) having the base joined around the stem, so as to appear pierced by the stem—orig. said of the stem passing through the leaf, or of the plant. [L. *per*, through, *folium*, a leaf.]

perforate, *pər'fə-rāt*, *v.t.* to bore through or into : to pierce or to make a hole through : to penetrate : to pass through by a hole.—*adj.* pierced by a hole or holes : having an aperture : (*bot.*) dotted with pellucid dots : pierced by rows of small holes for easy separation (as postage-stamps).—*adj.* **per'forable**.—*n.* **per'forans**, the long flexor muscle of the toes, or the deep flexor muscle of the fingers, whose tendons pass through those of the perforatus. —*adj.* **per'forant**, perforating.—*n.* **perforā'tion**, act of making a hole : formation of a hole or aperture : condition of being perforated : a hole through or into anything : a series, or one of a series, of small holes, as for ease in tearing paper.—*adj.* **per'forātive**, having power to pierce.—*ns.* **per'forātor**, one who bores : a boring instrument or organ ; **perforā'tus**, the short flexor of the toes or the superficial flexor of the fingers. [L. *perforāre*, *-ātum*—*per*, through, *forāre*, to bore.]

perforce, *pər-fōrs'*, *adv.* by force : of necessity. [O.Fr. *par force*.]

perform, *pər-form'*, *v.t.* to do : to carry out duly : to act in fulfilment of : to carry into effect : to fulfil : to bring about : to render : to execute : to go through duly : to act : to play in due form. —*v.i.* to do what is to be done : to execute a function : to act, behave : to act a part : to play or sing : to do feats, tricks, or other acts for exhibition.—*adj.* **perform'able**, capable of being performed : practicable.—*ns.* **perform'ance**, act of performing : a carrying out of something : something done : a piece of work : manner or success in working : execution, esp. as an exhibition or entertainment: an act or action; **perform'er**, one who performs: one who does or fulfils what is required of him: an executant: one who takes part in a performance or performances: one who does feats or tricks, esp. in exhibition.—*adj.* **perfor'ming**, that performs: trained to perform tricks.—*n.* performance.—**performing right**, the right to give a public performance of a piece of music or play. [A.Fr. *parfourmer*, app. an altered form of *parfourner*—O.Fr. *parfournir*, *par*—L. *per*, through, *fournir*, to furnish.]

perfume, *pər'fūm*, formerly and still sometimes *pər-fūm'*, *n.* sweet-smelling smoke or fumes from burning: any substance made or used for the sake of its smell: fragrance.—*v.t.* **perfume** (*pər-fūm'*, sometimes *pər'fūm*), to scent.—*adjs.* **per'fumed** (or *pər-fūmd'*); **per'fumeless** (or -*fūm'*).—*ns.* **perfu'mer**, one who fumigates: a maker or seller of perfumes; **perfu'mery**, perfumes in general: the art of preparing perfumes.—*adj.* **per'fumy**. [Fr. *parfum*—L. *per*, through, *fūmus*, smoke.]

perfunctory, *pər-fungk'tə-ri*, *adj.* done merely as a duty to be got through: done for form's sake, or in mere routine: acting without zeal or interest: merely formal: hasty and superficial.—*adv.* **perfunc'torily**.—*n.* **perfunc'toriness**.—[L. *perfunctōrius*—*perfunctus*, pa.p. of *perfungī*, to execute—pfx. *per*-, thoroughly, *fungī*, to do.]

perfuse, *pər-fūz'*, *v.t.* to pour or diffuse through or over: to force, as a liquid, through an organ or tissue.—*n.* **perfusion** (*-fū'zhən*).—*adj.* **perfusive** (*-fū'siv*). [L. *perfūsus*, poured over—*per*, through, *fundĕre*, *fūsus*, to pour.]

pergameneous, *pər-gə-mē'ni-əs*, *adj.* parchment-like. — *adj.* **pergamentaceous** (*-mən-tā'shəs*), parchment-like. [L. *pergamēna*; see **parchment**.]

pergola, *pər'gə-lä*, *n.* a structure with climbing plants along a walk. [It.,—L. *pergula*, a shed.]

pergunnah. See **pargana**.

perhaps, *pər-haps'*, *adv.* it may be: possibly: as it may happen. [From the pl. of **hap**, after the model of **peradventure, percase, perchance**.]

peri, *pē'ri*, *n.* a Persian fairy. [Pers. *parī* or *perī*, a fairy.]

peri-, *per'i-, pə-ri'-*, *pfx.* around. [Gr. *peri*, around.]

periagua, *per-i-ä'gwä*. See **piragua**.

periaktos, *per-i-ak'tos*, *n.* in the ancient Greek theatre a tall revolving prism at the side of the stage, giving change of scene. [Gr., revolving.]

perianth, *per'i-anth*, *n.* (*bot.*) calyx and corolla together, esp. when not clearly distinguishable.— Also *adj.* [Gr. *peri*, around, *anthos*, flower.]

periapt, *per'i-apt*, *n.* (*Shak.*) an amulet. [Gr. *periapton*, something hung round—*haptein*, to fasten.]

periblem, *per'i-blem*, *n.* (*bot.*) the layer of primary meristem from which the cortex is formed, covering the plerome. [Gr. *periblēma*, garment, mantle —*peri*, *ballein*, to throw.]

peribolos, *per-ib'o-los*, *n.* a precinct: its enclosing wall.—Also (Latinised) **perib'olus**. [Gr.,—*peri*, *ballein*, to throw.]

pericardium, *per-i-kär'di-əm*, *n.* (*anat.*) the sac round the heart.—*adjs.* **pericar'diac, pericar'dial, pericar'dian**.—*n.* **pericardi'tis**, inflammation of the pericardium. [Latinised from Gr. *perikardion*—*peri*, *kardiā*, heart.]

pericarp, *per'i-kärp*, *n.* (*bot.*) the wall of a fruit, derived from that of the ovary. [Gr. *perikarpion*—*peri*, *karpos*, fruit.]

pericentral, *per-i-sen'trəl*, *adj.* surrounding a centre or central body.—*adj.* **pericen'tric**. [Gr. *peri*, *kentron*, point, centre.]

perichaetium, *per-i-kē'shyəm*, *n.* a sheath or cluster of leaves around the archegonia (or the antheridia) in mosses and liverworts.—*adj.* **perichae'tial** (-*shl*). [Gr. *peri*, *chaitē*, flowing hair.]

perichondrium, *per-i-kon'dri-əm*, *n.* the fibrous investment of cartilage. [Gr. *peri*, *chondros*, cartilage.]

perichylous, *per-i-ki'ləs*, *adj.* (*bot.*) having water-storing tissue outside the green tissue. [Gr. *peri*, *chȳlos*, juice.]

periclase, *per'i-klāz*, -*klās*, *n.* native magnesia. [Gr. pfx. *peri*-, very, *klasis*, fracture (from its perfect cleavage).]

Periclean, *per-i-klē'ən*, *adj.* of *Pericles* (d. 429 B.C.) or the golden age of art and letters at Athens.

periclinal, *per-i-klī'nəl*, *adj.* (*geol.*) quaquaversal: (*bot.*) parallel to the outer surface.—*n.* **per'icline**, a variety of albite felspar of oblique appearance. [Gr. *periklīnēs*, sloping on all sides—*peri*, *klīnein*, to slope.]

periclitate, *per-ik'li-tāt*, *v.t.* to endanger. [L. *perīclitārī*, -*ātus*.]

pericope, *pər-ik'o-pē*, *n.* an extract, passage, esp. one selected for reading in church. [Gr. *perikopē* —*peri*, around, *koptein*, to cut.]

pericranium, *per-i-krā'ni-əm*, *n.* the membrane that surrounds the cranium: (loosely) skull or brain.—*adj.* **pericrā'nial**.—*n.* **per'icrāny**, (*obs.*) pericranium. [Latinised from Gr. *perikrānion*— *peri*, around, *krānion*, skull.]

periculous, *pər-ik'ū-ləs*, *adj.* (*obs.*) dangerous. [L. *periculum*, danger.]

pericycle, *per'i-sī-kl*, *n.* (*bot.*) the outermost layer or layers of the central cylinder.—*adj.* **pericy'clic**. [Gr. *perikyklos*, all round—*peri*, *kyklos*, a circle.]

periderm, *per'i-dərm*, *n.* the horny cuticular covering of a hydroid colony: the cork-cambium with the cork and other tissues derived from it, forming a protective outer covering in plants.—*adj.* **peridermal**. [Gr. *peri*, *derma*, skin.]

peridesmium, *per-i-des'mi-əm*, *n.* (*anat.*) the areolar tissue round a ligament. [Gr. *peri*, *desmos*, a band.]

peridinian, *per-i-din'i-ən*, *n.* a dinoflagellate.—*n.* **Peridin'ium**, a genus of dinoflagellates. [Gr. *peri*, *dīnos*, a whirl.]

peridium, *pər-id'i-əm*, *n.* the outer coat of a fungus fruit-body.—*adj.* **perid'ial**. [Latinised from Gr. *pēridion*, dim. of *pērā*, a wallet.]

peridot, *per'i-dot*, **peridote**, -*dōt*, *n.* olivine: a green olivine used in jewellery.—*adj.* **peridot'ic**.— *n.* **peridotite** (-*dō'tīt*), a coarse-grained igneous rock mainly composed of olivine, usually with other ferro-magnesian minerals but little or no felspar. [Fr. *pēridot*; origin unknown.]

peridrome, *per'i-drōm*, *n.* the space between cell and surrounding pillars in an ancient temple. [Gr. *peridromos*, running round—*peri*, *dromos*, a run.]

periegesis, *per-i-ē-jē'sis*, *n.* a description in manner of a tour: a progress or journey through. [Gr. *periēgēsis*—*peri*, *hēgeesthai*, to lead.]

perigastric, *per-i-gas'trik*, *adj.* surrounding the alimentary canal.—*n.* **perigastri'tis**, inflammation of the outer surface of the stomach. [Gr. *peri*, *gastēr*, belly.]

perigee, *per'i-jē*, *n.* (*astron.*) the point of the moon's orbit at which it is nearest the earth—opp. to *apogee*. — *adjs.* **perigē'al, perigē'an**. [Gr. *perigeion*, neut. of *perigeios*, round or near the earth— *peri*, *gē*, earth.]

perigenesis, *per-i-jen'i-sis*, *n.* reproduction (according to Haeckel's theory) by transmission not only of chemical material but of vibrations of plastidules. [Gr. *peri*, *genesis*, generation.]

perigone, *per'i-gōn*, *n.* (*bot.*) an undifferentiated perianth: a covering of the seed in sedges.—*adj.* **perigō'nial**.—*n.* **perigō'nium**, a cluster of leaves round moss antheridia. [Gr. *peri*, *gonē*, generative organ.]

perigynous, *pər-ij'i-nəs*, *adj.* (*bot.*) having the receptacle developed as a disk or open cup, with sepals, petals, and stamens borne on its margin, the carpels not embedded in it: of sepals, petals, or stamens, inserted on the receptacle in such a way—distinguished from *epigynous* and *hypogenous*.—*n.* **perig'yny**. [Gr. *peri*, *gynē*, woman (used for female).]

perihelion, *per-i-hē'li-ən*, *n.* the point of the orbit of a planet or a comet at which it is nearest to the sun—opp. to *aphelion*: (*fig.*) culmination.—Also *adj.* [Gr. *peri*, near, *hēlios*, the sun.]

perihepatic, *per-i-hi-pat'ik*, *adj.* surrounding the liver.—*n.* **perihepatitis** (-*hep-ə-tī'tis*), inflammation of the peritoneum covering the liver. [Gr. *peri*, *hēpar*, *hēpatos*, liver.]

peril, *per'il*, *n.* danger.—*v.t.* to expose to danger:— *pr.p.* **per'illing**; *pa.t.* and *pa.p.* **per'illed**.—*adj.* **per'ilous**, dangerous.—*adv.* **per'ilously**.—*n.* **per'ilousness**.—[Fr. *péril*—L. *periculum*.]

perilymph, *per'i-limf, n.* the fluid surrounding the membranous labyrinth of the ear. [Gr. *peri*, and **lymph.**]

perimeter, *par-im'i-tar, n.* (geom.) the circuit or boundary of any plane figure, or the sum of all its sides : an instrument for measuring the field of vision : the boundary of a camp or fortified position.—*adj.* **perimetric** (*per-i-met'rik*).—*n.* **perim'etry.** [Gr. *perimetros*—*peri, metron,* measure.]

perimorph, *per'i-morf, n.* a mineral enclosing another.—*adjs.* **perimorph'ic, perimorph'ous.** [Gr. *peri, morphē,* form.]

perinaeum, perineum, *per-i-nē'am, n.* the lower part of the body between the genital organs and the anus.—*adj.* **perinae'al, perinē'al.** [Latinised from Gr. *perinaion.*]

perineurium, *per-i-nū'ri-am, n.* the sheath of connective tissue about a bundle of nerve fibres.— *adj.* **perineu'ral.**—*n.* **perineuri'tis,** inflammation of the perineurium. [Gr. *peri, neuron,* nerve.]

period, *pē'ri-ad, n.* the time in which anything runs its course : an interval of time at the end of which events recur in the same order : the time required for a complete oscillation—reciprocal of the frequency : the time of a complete revolution of a heavenly body about its primary : the difference between two successive values of a variable for which a function has the same value : the recurring part of a circulating decimal : a set of figures (usu. three) in which a large number is marked off by commas : a series of chemical elements represented in a horizontal row of the periodic table : a stretch of time : a long stretch, an age : one of the main divisions of geological time : a stage or phase in history, in a man's life and development, in a disease, or in any course of events : a time : a division of the school day, the time of one lesson : the end of a course : a recurring time : catamenia : an end : a goal : a complete sentence, esp. one of elaborate construction : in music, a division analogous to a sentence : (in *pl.*) rounded rolling rhetoric : a mark (.) at the end of a sentence—a full stop : a rhythmical division in Greek verse.— *adj.* characteristic, representative, or imitative of a past period (of architecture, furniture-design, or the like).—*v.t.* (*Shak.*) to put an end to.—*adjs.* **periodic** (*pēr-i-od'ik*), relating to a period or periods : of revolution in an orbit : having a period : recurring regularly in the same order : (loosely) occurring from time to time : characterised by or constructed in periods : (*rare*) pertaining to periodicals ; **period'ical,** periodic : published in numbers at more or less regular intervals : of, for, or in such publications.—*n.* a magazine or other publication that appears at stated intervals (not usually including newspapers) : (*U.S.*) a recurring spree.—*n.* **period'icalist,** one who writes in a periodical.—*adv.* **period'ically,** at regular intervals : in a periodic manner : in a periodical publication : (loosely) from time to time.—*n.* **periodicity** (*-dis'*), the fact or character of being periodic : frequency.—**periodic function,** (*math.*) one whose values recur in a cycle as the variable increases ; **periodic table,** a table of chemical elements in order of atomic number arranged in horizontal series and vertical groups, showing how similar properties recur at regular intervals ; **periodic wind,** wind which blows at or for a certain period—e.g. a trade-wind, a monsoon, a land-breeze, a sea-breeze ; **the period,** the current age. [Fr. *période*—L. *periodus*—Gr. *periodos*—*peri,* around, *hodos,* a way.]

periodate, *par-ī'ō-dāt, n.* a salt of periodic acid.— **periodic acid** (*par-ī-od'ik*), an acid (HₕIO₆) containing more oxygen than iodic acid. [Pfx. *per-*, and **iodine.**]

Periophthalmus, *per-i-of-thal'mas, n.* a genus of fishes, allied to gobies, with protruding mobile eyes and pectoral fins used as legs. [Latinised from Gr. *peri,* around, *ophthalmos,* eye.]

periosteum, *per-i-os'ti-am, n.* a tough fibrous membrane covering the surface of bones.—Also **per'iost.** —*adjs.* **perios'teal ; periostit'ic.**—*n.* **periosti'tis,** inflammation of the periosteum. [Gr. *periosteon* (neut. adj.)—*peri, osteon,* a bone.]

periostracum, *per-i-os'tra-kam, n.* the horny outer layer of a mollusc's shell. [Latinised from Gr. *peri, ostrakon,* shell.]

periotic, *per-i-ō'tik, -ot'ik, adj.* around the inner ear. —*n.* a periotic bone. [Gr. *peri, ous, ōtos,* the ear.]

peripatetic, *per-i-pa-tet'ik, adj.* walking about : Aristotelian.—*n.* a pedestrian : an itinerant : an Aristotelian.—*adj.* **peripateti'cal.**—*n.* **peripatet'icism** (*-i-sizm*), the philosophy of Aristotle. [Gr. *peripatētikos*—*peripatos,* a walk—*peri,* about, *pateein,* to walk. Aristotle is said to have taught in the walks of the Lyceum at Athens.]

Peripatus, *per-ip'a-tas, n.* a genus of arthropods of the Onychophora, showing affinities with worms. [Gr. *peripatos,* a walking about ; cf. **peripatetic.**]

peripet(e)ia, *per-i-pe-tī'ä, n.* a sudden change of fortune, esp. in drama.—Also **perip'ety.** [Gr. *peripeteia*—*peri,* around, and *pet-* the root of *piptein,* to fall.]

periphery, *par-if'a-ri, n.* bounding line or surface : the outside of anything : a surrounding region.— *adjs.* **periph'eral, peripheric** (*per-i-fer'ik*), **-al.** [Gr. *periphereia*—*peri,* around, *pherein,* to carry.]

periphrasis, *par-if'ra-sis, n.* round-about expression (*pl.* **periph'rases,** *-sēz*).—*n.* **periphrase** (*per'i-frāz*), periphrasis (*pl.* **periphrās'es**).—*v.t.* to say with circumlocution.—*v.i.* to use circumlocution.—*adjs.* **periphrastic** (*per-i-fras'tik*), **-al.** —*adv.* **periphras'tically.** [Gr. *periphrasis*—*peri,* about, *phrasis,* speech.]

periplus, *per'i-plus, n.* a circumnavigation : a narrative of a coasting voyage. [Gr. *periploos,* contr. *-plous*—*peri, ploos, plous,* a voyage.]

periproct, *per'i-prokt, n.* (*zool.*) the region about the anus, esp. in a sea-urchin. [Gr. *peri, prōktos,* anus.]

peripteral, *par-ip'ta-ral, adj.* (*archit.*) having one row of columns all round. [Gr. *peripteros*—*peri,* about, *pteron,* a wing.]

periscian, *par-ish'i-an, n.* a dweller within the polar circle, whose shadow moves round in a complete circle on those days on which the sun does not set. —Also *adj.* [Gr. *peri,* around, *skiā,* a shadow.]

periscope, *per'i-skōp, n.* a tube with mirrors by which an observer in a trench, a submarine, &c., can see what is going on above.—*adj.* **periscopic** (*-skop'ik*). [Gr. *peri,* about, *skopeein,* to see.]

perish, *per'ish, v.i.* to pass away completely : to waste away : to decay : to lose life : to be destroyed: to be ruined or lost.—*v.t.* to destroy : to ruin : to cause to decay : to distress with cold, hunger, &c. —*n.* **perishabil'ity.**—*adj.* **per'ishable,** that may perish : subject to speedy decay.—*n.* that which is perishable : (in *pl.*) food or other stuff liable to rapid deterioration.—*n.* **per'ishableness.**— *adv.* **per'ishably.**—*adj.* **per'ished,** (*coll.* or *dial.*) distressed by cold, hunger, &c. : weakened or injured by age or exposure.—*n.* **per'isher,** (*slang*) a reprehensible and annoying person.—*adj.* **per'ishing,** (*coll.* or *dial.*) freezingly cold : vaguely used as a pejorative.—Also *adv.*—*adv.* **per'ishingly.** [O.Fr. *perir, pp. perissant*—L. *perīre, perītum,* to perish —pfx. *per-,* indicating destruction, *īre,* to go.]

perisperm, *per'i-sparm, n.* (*bot.*) nutritive tissue in a seed derived from the nucellus.—*adj.* **perisper'mic.** [Gr. *peri,* around, *sperma,* seed.]

perispomenon, *per-i-spō'man-on, adj.* having a circumflex accent on the last syllable.—*n.* a word so accented. [Gr. *perispōmenon* (contracted neut. pass. part.), drawn round, circumflexed—*peri, spaein,* to pull, pluck.]

perissodactyl, *par-is-ō-dak'til, adj.* having an odd number of toes.—*n.* an animal of the **Perissodac'tyla,** a division of ungulates with an odd number of toes on the hind-foot—horse, tapir, rhinoceros, and extinct kinds.—*adjs.* **perissodac'tylate, perissodactyl'ic, perissodac'tylous.** [Gr. *perissos,* odd, *daktylos,* a finger, toe.]

perissology, *per-is-ol'a-ji, n.* verbiage : pleonasm. [Gr. *perissologiā*—*perissos,* excessive, *logos,* speech.]

perissosyllabic, *par-is-ō-sil-ab'ik, adj.* having an additional syllable. [Gr. *perissosyllabos*—*perissos,* excessive, *syllabē,* syllable.]

peristalith, *par-is'ta-lith, n.* a stone-circle. [Irregularly formed from Gr. *peri,* around, *histanai,* to set up, *lithos,* a stone.]

peristaltic, *per-i-stalt'ik*, *adj.* forcing onward by waves of contraction, as the alimentary canal and other organs do their contents.—*n.* **peristal'sis.**—*adj.* **peristalt'ically**. [Gr. *peristaltikos—peristellein*, to wrap round—*peri*, around, *stellein*, to place.]

peristerite, *per-is'tər-īt*, *n.* an albite felspar with pigeon-like play of colour. [Gr. *peristerā*, pigeon.]

peristeronic, *per-is-tər-on'ik*, *adj.* of pigeons: pigeon-fancying. [Gr. *peristerōn*, *-ōnos*, pigeon-house.]

peristome, *per'i-stōm*, *n.* the area, or a structure, surrounding a mouth: the fringe of teeth around the mouth of a moss-capsule: the margin of a gasteropod shell.—*adjs.* **peristōm'al**, **peristomat'ic**, **peristōm'ial**. [Gr. *peri*, around, *stoma*, *-atos*, mouth.]

peristrephic, *per-i-stref'ik*, *adj.* moving round, revolving, rotatory. [Irregularly—Gr. *peristrephein*, to whirl—*peri*, round, *strephein*, to turn.]

peristyle, *per'i-stil*, *n.* a range of columns round a building or round a square: a court, square, &c., with columns all round.—*adj.* **peristy'lar**. [L. *peristȳl(i)um*—Gr. *peristȳlon*—*peri*, around, *stȳlos*, a column.]

perithecium, *per-i-thē's(h)i-əm*, *n.* a flask-shaped fruit-body in fungi:—*pl.* **-ia**. [Gr. *peri*, *thēkē*, case.]

peritonaeum, **peritoneum**, *per-i-tən-ē'əm*, *n.* a serous membrane enclosing the viscera in the abdominal and pelvic cavities.—*adjs.* **peritonae'al**, **peritonē'al**; **peritonitic** (*-it'ik*), of peritonitis: suffering from peritonitis.—*n.* **peritoni'tis**, inflammation of the peritonaeum. [Gr. *peritonaion*—*peri*, *teinein*, to stretch.]

perityphlitis, *per-i-tif-lī'tis*, *n.* inflammation of some part near the blind-gut. [Gr. *peri*, round, *typhlos*, blind.]

periwig, *per'i-wig*, *n.* a wig.—*v.t.* to dress with, or as with, a wig:—*pr.p.* **per'iwigging**; *pa.t.* and *pa.p.* **per'iwigged**.—*adj.* **per'iwig-pā'ted**, wearing a periwig. [Earlier *perwyke*, *perwig*, *perywig*, &c. —Fr. *perruque*; see **peruke**, **wig**.]

periwinkle, *per'i-wingk-l*, *n.* a creeping evergreen plant, growing in woods (*Vinca minor* and *V. major*; fam. Apocynaceae). [M.E. *peruenke*—O.E. *peruince*, from L. *pervinca*.]

periwinkle, *per'i-wingk-l*, *n.* an edible gasteropod (*Littorina littorea*) abundant between tide-marks, or other member of the genus: extended to other kinds. [O.E. (pl.) *pinewinclan* (or perh. *winewinclan*)—*wincle*, a whelk; cf. **pennywinkle**; prov. Eng., *pin-patch*.]

perjink, *par-jingk'*, *adj.* (*Scot.*) prim: finical.—Also **perjink'ety.**—*n.* **perjink'ity**, a nicety. [Origin unknown.]

perjure, *par'jər*, *v.t.* (*refl.*) to forswear oneself: to cause to swear falsely.—*v.i.* to swear falsely.—*n.* (*Shak.*) a perjured person.—*adj.* **per'jured**, having sworn falsely: being sworn falsely, as an oath.—*n.* **per'jurer.**—*adjs.* **perjurious** (*-jōō'ri-əs*), **per'jurous**, guilty of or involving perjury.—*n.* **per'jury**, false swearing: the breaking of an oath: (*law*) the crime committed by one who, when giving evidence on oath or affirmation as a witness in a court of justice, gives evidence which he knows to be false. [O.Fr. *parjurer*—L. *perjūrāre*—*per-*, *jūrāre*, to swear.]

perk, *pərk*, *v.i.* to bear oneself with self-confidence or self-assertion: to cock up: to stick out: to thrust forward (also *v.t.* with *it*): to move with pert briskness: to recover spirits or energy, esp. in sickness (with *up*): to sit upright: to cock or toss or hold up the head: to prank oneself up.—*v.t.* to prank or trim: to jerk up, cock up, prop up.— *adj.* brisk: self-confident in manner.—*adv.* **perk'ily.**—*n.* **perk'iness.**—*adj.* **perk'y**, self-assertive: cocky: pert: in good spirits. [Origin uncertain.]

perk, *pərk*, a Northern and East Anglian form of **perch**.

perkin. See **parkin**.

perlite, *pərl'īt*, *n.* any acid volcanic glass with perlitic structure: pearlite.—*adj.* **perlitic** (*-it'ik*), showing little concentric spheroidal or spiral cracks between rectilineal ones. [Fr. and Ger. *perle*, pearl.]

perlous, *pər'ləs*, *adj.* (*Spens.*). Same as **perilous**.

perlustrate, *pər-lus'trāt*, *v.t.* to traverse and inspect. —*n.* **perlustrā'tion**. [L. *perlustrāre*, *-ātum*.]

perm, *pərm*, *n.* (*coll.*) an abbreviation of **permutation**, and of **permanent wave**.—*v.t.* to impart a permanent wave to.

permanent, *pər'mə-nənt*, *adj.* remaining, or intended to remain, indefinitely.—*ns.* **per'manence**, fact or state of being permanent; **per'manency**, permanence: a thing that is permanent.—*adv.* **per'manently.**—**permanent magnet** (see **magnet**); **per'manent teeth**, the adult teeth, which come after the milk-teeth lost in childhood; **permanent wave**, an artificial wave in hair intended to last—familiarly contracted **perm**; **permanent way**, the finished road of a railway. [L. *permanēns*, *-entis*, pr.p. of *permanēre*—*per*, through, *manēre*, to continue.]

permanganic, *pər-mang-gan'ik*, *adj.* applied to an acid ($HMnO_4$) and its anhydride (Mn_2O_7) containing more oxygen than manganic acid and anhydride.—*n.* **permanganate** (*pər-mang'gə-nāt*), a salt of permanganic acid. [Pfx. *per-*, indicating excess (of oxygen), and **manganese**.]

permeate, *pər'mi-āt*, *v.t.* to pass through the pores of: to penetrate and fill the pores of: to pervade: to saturate.—*v.i.* to diffuse.—*n.* **permeabil'ity.**—*adj.* **per'meable.**—*adv.* **per'meably.**—*n.* **permea'tion.**—*adj.* **per'meative**, having power to permeate.—**magnetic permeability**, the ratio of flux-density to magnetising force. [L. *permeāre*—*per*, through, *meāre*, to pass.]

Permian, *pərm'i-ən*, *n.* (*geol.*) the uppermost Palaeozoic system.—*adj.* of that system.—*n.* and *adj.* **Permo-Carbonif'erous**, Upper Carboniferous and Lower Permian. [*Perm*, province in Russia, where it is widely developed.]

permit, *pər-mit'*, *v.t.* to allow: to indulge: to leave, refer, concede.—*v.i.* to allow:—*pr.p.* **permitt'ing**; *pa.t.* and *pa.p.* **permitt'ed.**—*n.* (*pər'mit*) permission, esp. in writing.—*n.* **permissibil'ity.**—*adj.* **permiss'ible**, that may be permitted: allowable. —*adv.* **permiss'ibly.**—*n.* **permission** (*-mish'ən*), act of permitting: leave.—*adj.* **permiss'ive**, granting permission or liberty: allowing: granted: not hindered.—*adv.* **permiss'ively.**—*ns.* **permiss'iveness**; **permitt'ance** (*rare*), permission; **permitt'er**; **permittiv'ity**, (*absolute permittivity*) the ratio of the electric displacement of a medium to the electric force producing it: (*relative permittivity*) the ratio of the electric flux-density produced in a medium to that which would be produced in a vacuum by the same electric force. [L. *permittěre*, *-missum*, to let pass through—*per*, through, *mittěre*, to send.]

permute, *pər-mūt'*, *v.t.* to interchange: to transmute: to subject to permutation.—*n.* **permūt-abil'ity.**—*adj.* **permūt'able**, interchangeable.—*v.t.* **per'mūtate**, to subject to permutation.—*n.* **permutā'tion**, (*obs.*) barter: transmutation: (*math.*) the arrangement of a set of things in every possible order: any one possible order or arrangement of a given number of things taken from a given number: (*logic*) immediate inference by obversion. [L. *permūtāre*, to change thoroughly—pfx. *per-*, *mūtāre*, to change.]

pern, *pərn*, *n.* a honey-buzzard (Pernis). [Cuvier's mistake for Gr. *pternis*, a kind of hawk.]

pernancy, *pər'nən-si*, *n.* (*law*) receiving. [A.Fr. *pernance* (O.Fr. *prenance*).]

pernicious, *pər-nish'əs*, *adj.* destructive: highly injurious: malevolent.—*adv.* **perni'ciously.**—*n.* **perni'ciousness**. [L. *perniciōsus*—pfx. *per-*, completely, *nex*, *necis*, death by violence.]

pernicious, *pər-nish'əs*, *adj.* (*Milt.*) swift, ready, prompt. [L. *pernix*, *-īcis*, nimble.]

pernickety, *pər-nik'i-ti*, *adj.* finical: exacting minute care.—*n.* **pernick'etiness**. [Scots; origin unknown.]

pernoctation, *pər-nok-tā'shən*, *n.* passing the night: a watch, vigil. [L. *per*, through, *nox*, *noctis*, night.]

perone, *per'o-nē*, *n.* the fibula.—*adj.* **peronē'al.**—*n.* **peronē'us**, one of several fibular muscles. [Gr. *peronē*.]

peroration, *per-ō-rā'shən*, *n.* the conclusion of a

speech: a rhetorical performance.—*v.i.* **per'orate**, to make a peroration: (*coll.*) to harangue. [L. *perōrātiō*, *-ōnis—per*, through, *ōrāre*, to speak—*ōs*, *ōris*, the mouth.]

peroxide, *pər-oks'īd*, *n.* an oxide with the highest proportion of oxygen: one that yields hydrogen peroxide on treatment with an acid: (*coll.*) hydrogen peroxide (H_2O_2).—*v.t.* to treat or bleach with hydrogen peroxide.—*n.* **peroxidā'tion** (*-id-*).—*v.t.* and *v.i.* **perox'idise**. [*per-*, indicating excess (of oxygen), and **oxide**.]

perpend, *pər-pend'*, *v.t.* to weigh in the mind, to consider carefully. [L. *perpendēre—*pfx. *per-*, thoroughly, *pendēre*, to weigh.]

perpend, *pər'pənd*, **perpent**, *-pənt*. Same as **parpen**.

perpendicular, *pər-pən-dik'ū-lər*, *adj.* erect: vertical: upright: in the direction of gravity or at right angles to the plane of the horizon: (*geom.*) at right angles to a given line or surface: in the Perpendicular style of architecture.—*n.* an instrument for determining the vertical line: a straight line or plane perpendicular to another line or surface: verticality or erectness: in a ship, a vertical line from each end of the water-line: (*slang*) a meal or entertainment at which the guests do not sit.—*n.* **perpendicularity** (*-lar'i-ti*), state of being perpendicular.—*adv.* **perpendic'ularly**. —**Perpendicular style**, a late English style of Gothic architecture (late 14th to mid-16th cent.) marked by vertical window-tracery, depressed or four-centre arch, fan-tracery vaulting, and panelled walls. [L. *perpendiculāris—perpendiculum*, a plumb-line—pfx. *per-*, completely, through, *pendēre*, to hang.]

perpetrate, *pər'pi-trāt*, *v.t.* to execute or commit (esp. an offence, a poem, or a pun).—*adj.* **per'petrable**.—*ns.* **perpetrā'tion**, **per'petrātor**. [L. *perpetrāre*, *-ātum—*pfx. *per-*, thoroughly, *patrāre*, to achieve.]

perpetual, *pər-pet'ū-əl*, *adj.* never ceasing: everlasting: not temporary: incessant: unintermitting: continuously blooming: perennial.—*adv.* **perpetually**. — *n.* a perennial: a continuously blooming hybrid rose.—*ns.* **perpet'ualism**; **perpet'ualist**, one who advocates the perpetual continuation of anything; **perpetuality** (*-al'i-ti*).—*adv.* **perpet'ually**.—*n.* **perpetual-mo'tionist**, a believer in the possibility of perpetual motion.— **perpetual curate**, formerly, in the Church of England, an incumbent of a parish who had no endowment of tithes—since 1868 called **vicar**; **perpetual motion**, a machine, or motion of a machine, that should do work indefinitely without receiving new energy from without; **perpetual screw**, an endless screw. [L. *perpetuālis—perpetuus*, continuous.]

perpetuate, *pər-pet'ū-āt*, *v.t.* to make perpetual: to cause to last for ever or for a very long time: to preserve from extinction or oblivion.—*adj.* **perpetuated**.—*adj.* **perpet'uable**.—*ns.* **perpet'uance**, **perpetuation**; **perpetuā'tion**, continuation or preservation for ever, or for a very long time: preservation from extinction or oblivion; **perpet'ūātor**. [L. *perpetuāre*, *-ātum—perpetuus*, perpetual.]

perpetuity, *pər-pi-tū'i-ti*, *n.* state of being perpetual: endless time: duration for an indefinite period: something lasting for ever: the sum paid for a perpetual annuity: the annuity itself: an arrangement whereby property is tied up, or rendered inalienable, for all time or for a very long time. [L. *perpetuitās*, *-ātis—perpetuus*, perpetual.]

perplex, *pər-pleks'*, *v.t.* to embarrass or puzzle with difficulties or intricacies: to bewilder: to tease with suspense or doubt: to complicate: to interweave: to tangle.—*n.* (*obs.*) a difficulty.—*adv.* **perplex'edly**.— *n.* **perplex'edness**. — *adj.* **perplex'ing**.—*adv.* **perplex'ingly**.—*n.* **perplex'ity**, state of being perplexed: confusion of mind arising from doubt, &c.: embarrassment: doubt: intricacy: tangle. [L. *perplexus*, entangled—*per-*, completely, *plexus*, involved, pa.p. of *plectēre*.]

perquisite, *pər'kwi-zit*, *n.* (*law*; *obs.*) property acquired otherwise than by inheritance: a casual profit: anything left over that a servant or other has by custom a right to keep: a tip expected upon some occasions: emoluments: something regarded as falling to one by right.—*ns.* **perquisition** (*-zish'ən*), a strict search: diligent inquiry; **perquis'itor**, the first purchaser of an estate. [L. *perquīsītum*, from *perquīrĕre*, to seek diligently— pfx. *per-*, thoroughly, *quaerĕre*, to ask.]

perradius, *pər-rā'di-əs*, *n.* any one of the primary radii of a coelenterate:—*pl.* **perradii** (*-ī*).—*adj.* **perra'dial**. [Mod. L.—pfx. *per-*, through, and *radius*.]

perrier, *per'i-ər*, *n.* (*obs.*) a machine or gun for discharging stones. [O.Fr.]

perron, *per'ən*, *per-on°*, *n.* a raised platform or terrace at an entrance door: an external flight of steps leading up to it. [Fr.,—L. *petra*, stone.]

perruque, **perruquier**. See **peruke**.

perry, *per'i*, *n.* a drink made from fermented pear juice. [O.Fr. *peré*—L.L. *pēra* (L. *pirum*), pear.]

persant, **persaunt** (*Spens.*). Same as **perceant**.

perscrutation, *pər-skroo-tā'shən*, *n.* a thorough search. [L. *per*, *scrūtārī*, to search carefully.]

perse, *pərs*, *adj.* dark blue, bluish-gray.—*n.* a darkblue colour: a cloth of such colour. [O.Fr. *pers*.]

perse, *pərs*, a Spenserian form of **pierce**:—*pa.p.* and *pa.t.* **perst**.

persecute, *pər'si-kūt*, *v.t.* to harass, afflict, hunt down, or put to death, esp. for religious or political opinions.—*n.* **persecū'tion**.—*adj.* **per'secūtive**. —*n.* **per'secūtor**.—*adj.* **per'secūtory**. [L. *persequī*, *persecūtus*—pfx. *per-*, thoroughly, *sequī*, to follow.]

perseity, *pər-sē'i-ti*, *n.* independent existence. [L. *per sē*, in itself.]

perseline, *pər'si-lēn*, *n.* a Spenserian form of purslane.

Perseus, *pər'sūs*, *n.* a fabled Greek hero, who slew the Gorgon Medusa, and rescued Andromeda from a sea-monster: a constellation in the northern sky.—*n.* **Per'seid** (*-si-id*), a meteor of a swarm whose radiant is in the constellation Perseus. [Gr. *Perseus*.]

persevere, *pər-si-vēr'*, formerly (*Shak.*) *pər-sev'ər*, *v.i.* (*obs.*) to continue: to continue steadfastly: to keep on striving.—*n.* **persevē'rance** (formerly *pər-sev'ər-əns*), act or state of persevering: continued application to anything which one has begun: a going on till success is met with.— *adj.* **persev'erant**, steadfast.—*v.i.* **persev'erate**, (*psych.*) to recur or tend to recur: to repeat the same actions or thoughts.—*ns.* **perseveration** (*pər-sev-ər-ā'shən*), meaningless repetition of an action, utterance, thought, &c.: tendency to experience difficulty in leaving one activity for another; **persev'erātor**.—*adj.* **persevē'ring**.— *adv.* **persevē'ringly**.—**perseverance of saints**, the Calvinistic doctrine that those who are effectually called by God cannot fall away so as to be finally lost. [Fr. *persévérer*—L. *persevērāre— persevērus*, very strict—pfx. *per-*, very, *sevērus*, strict.]

Persian, *pər'sh(y)ən*, *-zh(y)ən*, *adj.* of, from, or relating to *Persia*, its inhabitants, or language.—*n.* a native or citizen of Persia: the language of Persia: (*archit.*) a male figure serving as a column: a Persian cat.—*v.t.* and *v.i.* **Per'sianise**.— *adj.* **Persic** (*pər'sik*), Persian.—*n.* the Persian language.—*v.t.* and *v.i.* **Per'sicise** (*-sīz*), to turn Persian: to assimilate to what is Persian.—*ns.* **Per'sism**, a Persian idiom; **Per'sist**, one who has a scholarly knowledge of Persian and things Persian.—**Persian berry**, the fruit of several buckthorns; **Persian blinds** (see **persienne**); **Persian carpet**, a rich, soft carpet of the kind woven in Persia; **Persian cat**, a kind of cat with long, silky hair and bushy tail; **Persian powder**, an insect-powder made from Pyrethrum; **Persian wheel**, a large undershot wheel for raising water.

persicaria, *pər-si-kā'ri-ä*, *n.* a species of knot-grass with black-blotched leaves: extended to other species of Polygonum, by some made a separate genus. [L.L. *persicāria*, peach-tree, from the similarity in leaves.]

persico, **persicot**, *pər'si-kō*, *n.* a cordial flavoured with kernels of peaches and apricots. [Fr. *persico* (now *persicot*)—It. *persico*—L. *persicum*, a peach.]

persienne, *per-si-en'*, *n.* an Eastern cambric or muslin with coloured printed pattern: (in *pl.*) Persian blinds, outside shutters of thin movable slats in a frame. [Fr., Persian (fem.).]

persiflage, *per-si-fläzh'*, *n.* banter: flippancy.—*n.* **persifleur** (*-flər'*), a banterer. [Fr.,—*persifler*, to banter—L. *per*, through, Fr. *siffler*—L. *sībilāre*, to whistle, to hiss.]

persimmon, *pər-sim'ən*, *n.* a date-plum or date-plum tree. [From an Amer.-Indian word.]

persist, *pər-sist'*, *v.i.* to continue steadfastly or obstinately, esp. against opposition (often with *in*): to persevere: to insist: (*Milt.*) to continue to be, to remain: to continue to exist: to remain in the mind after the external cause is removed.— *v.t.* to assert or repeat insistently.—*ns.* **persis'-tence**, **persis'tency**, quality of being persistent: perseverance: obstinacy: duration, esp. of an effect after the exciting cause has been removed.— *adj.* **persis'tent**, persisting: pushing on, esp. against opposition: tenacious: fixed: constant or constantly repeated: (*zool.* and *bot.*) remaining after the usual time of falling off, withering, or disappearing: continuing to grow beyond the usual time.—*advs.* **persis'tently**; **persis'tingly**. —*adj.* **persis'tive**, (*Shak.*) persistent. [L. *per-sistĕre*—*per*, through, *sistĕre*, to cause to stand, to stand—*stāre*, to stand.]

person, *pėr'sn*, *n.* character represented, as on the stage: a capacity in which one is acting: a living soul or self-conscious being: a personality: a human being, sometimes used slightingly or patronisingly: an individual of a compound or colonial animal: the outward appearance, &c.: bodily form: human figure (often including clothes): bodily presence or action: (*obs.*) a personage: (*theol.*) a hypostasis of the Godhead: (*law*) a corporation regarded as having the rights and duties of a human person: (*gram.*) a form of inflexion or use of a word according as it, or its subject, represents the person, persons, thing, or things speaking (*first person*), spoken to (*second*), or spoken about (*third*).—*n.* **persona** (*pər-sō'nä*; L.), in psychology, the outermost part of the con-sciousness, what is in relation to the outside world, the expression of the personality.—*adj.* **per'son-able**, having a well-formed body or person: of good appearance.—*ns.* **per'sonableness**; **per'-sonage**, bodily frame or appearance: a person: an exalted or august person: a character in a play or story: (*Spens.*, &c.) recognised or imagined character or personality.—*adj.* **per'sonal**, of the nature of a person: or of relating to a person or personality: relating, referring, or pointing to a particular person or persons: aiming offensively at a particular person or persons: belonging or peculiar to a person: own: one's own: of private concern: relating to private concerns: bodily: in bodily presence: by one's own action: (*gram.*) indicating person: (*English law*) opposed to *real*, orig. not recoverable by a *real action* (for the resti-tution of the specific thing), but such as compen-sation might be claimed for: hence (now) passing at death not to the heir (as real property) but to the executor.—*n.pl.* **personalia** (*-ä'li-ä*; L.), notes, anecdotes, or particulars relating to persons. —*n.* **personalisa'tion**.—*v.t.* **per'sonalise**, to per-sonify.—*ns.* **per'sonalism**, the character of being personal: a theory or doctrine that attributes personality, or spiritual freedom and responsi-bility, as distinct from mere individuality, to human beings, esp. that enunciated by Emmanuel Mounier in 1936; **per'sonalist**, one who writes personal notes; **personal'ity**, fact or state of being a person or of being personal: existence as a person: individuality: distinctive or well-marked character: a person: direct reference to, or an utterance aimed at, a particular person or persons, esp. of a derog-atory nature: (*law; rare*) personalty: (*psych.*) the integrated organisation of all the psychological, intellectual, emotional, and physical character-istics of an individual, especially as they are pre-sented to other people.—*adv.* **per'sonally**, in a

personal or direct manner: in person: individu-ally: (*coll.*) for my part.—*n.* **per'sonalty**, (*law*) all the property which, when a man dies, goes to his executor or administrator, as distinguished from the realty, which goes to his heir-at-law.—*v.t.* **per'sonate**, to assume the likeness or character of: to play the part of: to mimic: to pass one-self off as: to represent in the form of a person: to symbolise.—*adj.* (*arch.*) feigned: mask-like: (*bot.*) of a lipped corolla, closed by an upward bulge of the lower lip.—*adj.* **per'sonāted**, feigned. —*ns.* **per'sonāting**; **personā'tion**.—*adj.* **per'-sonātive**, dramatic: presenting or presented through persons.—*n.* **per'sonātor**.—*v.t.* **per'son-ise**, to personify.—*n.* **personnel'** (Fr.), the persons employed in any service, as distinguished from the *matériel*.—**in person**, in actual bodily pre-sence: by one's own act, not by an agent or representative; **personal equation** (see equa-tion); **personal exception**, (*Scots law*) a ground of objection which applies to an individual and prevents him from doing something which, but for his conduct or situation, he might do; **per-sonal identity**, the continued sameness of the individual person, through all changes, as testified by consciousness; **personal rights**, rights which belong to the person as a living, reasonable being; **personal security**, security or pledge given by a person, as distinguished from the delivery of some object of value as security; **personal service**, the delivery of a message or an order into a person's hands, as distinguished from delivery in any other indirect way; **personal transaction**, something done by a person's own effort, not through the agency of another. [L. *persōna*, a player's mask, perh. from Etruscan *phersu*, masked figures, com-monly associated (in spite of difference of quantity) with *persōnāre*, -*ātum*—*per*, through, *sŏnāre*, to sound; cf. **parson**.]

personify, *pər-son'i-fī*, *v.t.* to represent as a person: to ascribe personality to: to be the embodiment of: (*rare*) to personate:—*pr.p.* **person'ifying**; *pa.t.* and *pa.p.* **person'ified**.—*ns.* **personificā'-tion**; **person'ifier**. [L. *persōna*, a person, *facĕre*, to make; see foregoing.]

perspective, *pər-spek'tiv*, formerly *pėr'*, *n.* (*obs.*) optics: (*obs.*) a telescope, microscope, or other optical instrument (also **perspective glass**): the art or science of drawing objects on a surface, so as to give the picture the same appearance to the eye as the objects themselves: appearance, or representation of appearance, of objects in space, with effect of distance, solidity, &c.: just pro-portion in all the parts: a picture in perspective: (*Shak.*) a picture or model that seems confused except when viewed in the right direction, or in some other way gives a fantastic effect: (*obs.*) a peep-show: a vista: a prospect of the future: (*obs.*) inspection.—*adj.* (*obs.*) optical: pertaining or according to perspective.—*adv.* **perspec'tively**. —**in perspective**, according to the laws of per-spective: in just proportion: (*obs.*) in prospect; **perspective plane**, the surface on which the picture of the objects to be represented in per-spective is drawn. [L. (*ars*) *perspectīva*, perspec-tive (art)—*perspicĕre*, *perspectum*—*per*, through, *specĕre*, to look.]

Perspex, *pėr'speks*, *n.* a proprietary thermoplastic resin of exceptional transparency and freedom from colour, used for windscreens, &c.

perspicacious, *pėr-spi-kā'shəs*, *adj.* (*arch.*) clear-sighted: clear-minded.—*adv.* **perspicā'ciously**. —*n.* **perspicacity** (-*kas'i-ti*). [L. *perspicāx*, -*ācis*; see perspective.]

perspicuous, *pėr-spik'ū-əs*, *adj.* lucid.—*n.* **per-spicū'ity**.—*adv.* **perspic'ūously**.—*n.* **perspic'-ūousness**. [L. *perspicuus*; see preceding.]

perspire, *pėr-spīr'*, *v.i.* to exude: to sweat.—*v.t.* to exhale.—*adj.* **perspīr'able**, capable of being per-spired or of perspiring.—*v.i.* **perspirate** (*pėr'spir-āt*; *rare*), to sweat.—*n.* **perspiration** (-*spir-ā'shən*), act of perspiring: sweat.—*adj.* **perspīr'atory**. [L. *perspīrāre*, -*ātum*—*per*, through, *spīrāre*, to breathe.]

perstringe, *pər-strinj'*, *v.t.* (*obs.*) to constrain: (*obs.*)

to touch on: (*obs.*) to dull: to censure. [L. *perstringĕre*—pfx. *per-*, thoroughly, *stringĕre*, to bind.]

persuade, *pər-swād'*, *v.t.* to induce by argument, advice, &c.: to bring to any particular opinion: to cause to believe: to convince: (*obs.*) to seek to induce: (*Shak.*) to urge.—*v.i.* (*obs.*) to plead: (*obs.*) to prevail: to use persuasive methods.— Also (*obs.*) **perswade'**. — *adj.* **persuad'able**. — *ns.* **persuad'er**; **persuasibility** (*-swās-i-bil'-i-ti*). —*adj.* **persuās'ible**, capable of being persuaded. —*n.* **persuasion** (*-swā'zhən*), act, process, method, art, or power of persuading: an inducement: state of being persuaded: settled opinion: a creed: a party adhering to a creed: (*facet.*) kind. —*adj.* **persuasive** (*-swās'*), having the power to persuade: influencing the mind or passions.—*n.* that which persuades or wins over.—*adv.* **persuā'sively**.—*n.* **persuā'siveness**.—*adj.* **persuās'ory**, persuasive. [L. *persuādēre*, *-suāsum*—pfx. *per-*, thoroughly, *suādēre*, to advise.]

persue, *pərs'ū*, *n.* (*Spens.*) a track of blood. [Fr. *percée*, act of piercing, confused with **pursue**.]

persue, an obsolete spelling of **pursue**.

persulphate, *pər-sul'fāt*, *n.* (*obs.*) that sulphate of a metal which contains the relatively greater quantity of oxygen or of the acid radical: a salt of **persulphuric** (*-fū'rik*) **acid** ($H_2S_2O_8$). [Pfx. *per-*, indicating excess, and **sulphate**.]

pert, *pərt*, *adj.* (*obs.*) open: unconcealed: brisk: (*Shak.*) perky: flourishing: (*obs.*) adroit: forward: saucy: impertinent: presumingly free in speech: (*obs.*) objectionable.—*n.* an impudent person.—*adv.* **pert'ly**.—*n.* **pert'ness**. [Aphetic for **apert**; see also **peart**.]

pertain, *pər-tān'*, *v.i.* to belong: to relate (with *to*). —*ns.* **per'tinence**, **per'tinency**, state of being pertinent: (*obs.*) an appurtenance.—*adj.* **per'tinent**, pertaining or related: to the point: fitted for the matter on hand: fitting or appropriate: suitable: apposite.—*n.* (chiefly *Scot.*) anything that goes along with an estate.—*adv.* **per'tinently**. [O.Fr. *partenir*—L. *pertinēre*—pfx. *per-*, thoroughly, *tenēre*, to hold.]

pertake, an old spelling (*Spens.*, *Shak.*) of **partake**.

perthite, *pərth'īt*, *n.* a parallel intergrowth of orthoclase and albite.—*adj.* **perthitic** (*-it'ik*). [*Perth*, Ontario, where it was first found.]

pertinacious, *pər-ti-nā'shəs*, *adj.* thoroughly tenacious: holding obstinately to an opinion or a purpose: obstinate: unyielding.—*adv.* **pertinā'ciously**. — *ns.* **pertinā'ciousness**; **pertinacity** (*-nas'i-ti*), quality of being pertinacious or unyielding: obstinacy: resoluteness. [L. *pertināx*, *-ācis*, holding fast—pfx. *per-*, thoroughly, *tenāx*, tenacious—*tenēre*, to hold.]

perttaunt like, an obscure phrase in Shakespeare (*Love's Labour's Lost*, V. ii.), possibly meaning like a *pair taunt* or *purtaunt'*, a double pair-royal or four cards of the same value. [**pair**, and Fr. *tant*, so much, i.e. counting as much again as a pairroyal in post and pair.]

perturb, *pər-turb'*, *v.t.* to disturb greatly: to agitate —also **per'turbate** (*-tər-bāt*).—*adj.* **perturb'able**. —*ns.* **pertur'bance**, perturbation; **perturb'ant**, anything that perturbs.—*adj.* **perturbing**.—*n.* **perturbā'tion**, act of perturbing or state of being perturbed: disquiet of mind: irregularity: (*astron.*) the disturbance produced in the simple elliptic motion of one heavenly body about another by the action of a third body, or by the non-sphericity of the principal body: a perturbing agent.—*adjs.* **perturbā'tional**; **pertur'bative**. — *n.* **per'turbātor**.—*adj.* and *n.* **pertur'batory**.—*adj.* **perturbed'**. — *adv.* **perturb'edly**.—*n.* **pertur'ber**. [L. *perturbāre*, *-ātum*—pfx. *per-*, thoroughly, *turbāre*, to disturb—*turba*, a crowd.]

pertuse, *pər-tūs'*, *adj.* punched: pierced: slit.— Also **pertūs'ate** (or *pər'*), **pertused** (*-tūst'*).—*n.* **pertusion** (*-tū'zhən*). [L. *pertundĕre*, *-tūsum*—*per*, through, *tundĕre*, to strike.]

pertussis, *pər-tus'is*, *n.* whooping-cough.—*adj.* **pertuss'al**. [Pfx. *per-*, indicating excess, L. *tussis*, cough.]

Peru, *pə-rōō'*, *n.* a country of S. America.—*adj.* **Peru'vian**, of Peru.—*n.* a native, inhabitant, or citizen of Peru.—**balsam of Peru, Peru balsam**, a fragrant acrid black viscid liquid, containing esters of benzoic and cinnamic acids, got from a tropical American papilionaceous tree *Myroxylon pereirae*; **marvel of Peru** (see **marvel**); **Peruvian bark**, cinchona bark. [Sp. *Perú*.]

peruke, *pər-ōōk'*, formerly *per'*, *n.* a wig.—Also (Fr.) **perruque**.—*n.* **perru'quier** (*per-ük-yā*; Fr.), a wigmaker. [Fr. *perruque*—It. *parrucca* (Sp. *peluca*); connexion with L. *pĭlus*, hair, very doubtful.]

peruse, *pər-ōōz'*, *v.t.* (*orig.*) to use up, wear out: (*Shak.*) to pass in scrutiny, one by one or piece by piece: to examine in detail: to revise: to read attentively or critically: (loosely) to read.—*ns.* **perus'al**, the act of perusing: careful examination: scrutiny: study: reading; **perus'er**. [L. pfx. *per-*, thoroughly, *ūtī*, *ūsus*, to use.]

pervade, *pər-vād'*, *v.t.* (*rare*) to pass through: to diffuse or extend through the whole of.—*n.* **pervasion** (*-vā'zhən*).—*adj.* **pervasive** (*-vā'siv*), tending or having power to pervade.—*adv.* **perva'sively**.—*n.* **perva'siveness**. [L. *pervādĕre*—*per*, through, *vādĕre*, to go.]

perverse, *pər-vərs'*, *adj.* turned aside from right or truth: obstinate in the wrong: capricious and unreasonable in opposition: froward: wrongheaded: wayward: (*Milt.*) adverse.—*adv.* **perverse'ly**.—*ns.* **perverse'ness**; **perversion** (*-ver'shən*), the act of perverting: condition of being perverted: the product of the process of perverting: a diverting from the true object: a turning from right or true: a distortion: a misapplication: a pathological deviation of sexual instinct: (*math.*) formation of a mirror-image: the mirror-image itself; **pervers'ity**, state or quality of being perverse.—*adj.* **pervers'ive**, tending to pervert.—*v.t.* **pervert'**, to turn wrong or from the right course: to wrest from the true meaning: to corrupt: to turn from truth or virtue: (*Shak.*) to divert, turn: (*math.*) to form a mirror-image of.—*v.i.* to go wrong or out of the right course.—*ns.* **per'vert**, one who has abandoned the doctrine assumed to be true: one whose sexual instinct is perverted; **pervert'er**.—*adj.* **pervert'ible**. [Partly through Fr.—L. *pervertĕre*, *perversum*—pfx. *per-*, thoroughly, wrongly, *vertĕre*, to turn.]

pervicacious, *pər-vi-kā'shəs*, *adj.* very obstinate.— *ns.* **pervicā'ciousness**, **pervicacity** (*-kas'i-ti*), **pervicacy** (*pər'vi-kə-si*; *obs.*). [L. *pervicāx*, *-ācis* —pfx. *per-*, thoroughly, *vincĕre*, to prevail.]

pervious, *pər'vi-əs*, *adj.* permeable: passable: penetrable: open.—*v.t.* **per'viate**, to make a way through.—*adv.* **per'viously**.—*n.* **per'viousness**. [L. *pervius*—*per*, through, *via*, a way.]

pesant, pesaunt, old spellings of **peasant**.

pesante, *pes-än'tā*, *adj.* (*mus.*) heavy: weighty.— Also *adv.* [It.]

peseta, *pe-sā'tä*, *n.* a Spanish franc. [Sp., dim. of *pesa*, weight.]

Peshito, Peshitto, *pe-shē(t)'tō*, **Peshitta**, *-tä*, *n.* a Syriac translation of the Bible.—Also *adj.* [Syriac *p'shī(t)tô*, *-tâ*, the simple.]

peshwa, *pāsh'wä*, *n.* the chief minister of the Mahrattas, later the real sovereign.—Also **peish'wa(h)**. [Pers. *pēshwā*, chief.]

pesky, *pes'ki*, *adj.* (*U.S. coll.*) annoying.—*adv.* **pes'kily**. [Perh. **pest**.]

peso, *pā'sō*, *n.* a Spanish five-peseta piece: a Mexican dollar: in S. and Central America a coin of various values. [Sp.,—L. *pēnsum*, weight.]

pessary, *pes'ə-ri*, *n.* a surgical plug, or medicated appliance, esp. one worn in the vagina. [Fr. *pessaire*—L.L. *pessārium*—Gr. *pessos*, a pebble, pessary.]

pessimism, *pes'i-mizm*, *n.* (*obs.*) the worst state: (*philos.*) the doctrine that the world is bad rather than good: a temper of mind that looks on the dark side of things: a depressing view of life: (loosely) despondency, hopelessness.—*n.* **pess'imist**, one who believes that everything is tending to the worst: one who looks too much on the

Neutral vowels in unaccented syllables: *el'ə-mənt*, *in'fənt*, *ran'dəm*

dark side of things—opp. to *optimist.—adjs.* **pessi-mis'tic, -al.** [L. *pessimus*, worst.]

pest, *pest, n.* any deadly epidemic disease : plague : anything destructive : any insect, fungus, or other organism that works destruction upon cultivated plants : a troublesome person or thing.—*adj.* **pest'ful,** pestilential.—*n.* **pest'house,** a hospital for plague or other infectious or contagious disease. —*adj.* **pestif'erous,** bringing plague or pestilence : pestilential : noxious : pestilent : annoying : plague-stricken.—*adv.* **pestif'erously.**—*n.* **pest'ilence,** any deadly epidemic disease : bubonic plague : anything that is hurtful to the morals.—*adjs.* **pest'-ilence-stricken ; pest'ilent,** deadly : producing pestilence : hurtful to health and life : pernicious : mischievous : vexatious ; **pestilential** (-*len'shl*), of the nature of pestilence : producing or infested with pestilence : destructive : baneful : detestable : pestering.—*advs.* **pestilen'tially, pest'ilently.**—*adj.* **pestolog'ical.**—*ns.* **pestol'ogist ; pestol'ogy,** the study of agricultural pests and methods of combating them. [Fr. *peste* and *pestilence*—L. *pestis, pestilentia.*]

Pestalozzian, *pes-tä-lot'sian, adj.* pertaining to Johann Heinrich *Pestalozzi* (1746-1827) or his educational reform.—*n.* a follower of Pestalozzi.

pester, *pes'tər, v.t.* (*obs.*) to clog : (*Milt.*) to huddle : to infest : to annoy persistently.—*n.* an annoyance.—*n.* **pes'terer.**—*adv.* **pes'teringly.**—*n.* **pes'-terment.**—*adj.* **pest'erous.** [App. from O.Fr. *empestrer* (Fr. *empêtrer*), to entangle—L. *in,* in, L.L. *pāstōrium,* a foot-shackle—L. *pāstus,* pa.p. of *pāscĕre,* to feed ; cf. **pastern** ; influenced by **pest.**]

pestle, *pes'l,* also *pest'l, n.* an instrument for pounding : (now *dial.*) a leg, esp. as food.—*v.t.* to pound. —*v.i.* to use a pestle. [O.Fr. *pestel*—L. *pistillum,* a pounder, *pīnsĕre, pistum,* to pound.]

pet, *pet, n.* a cherished tame animal : an indulged favourite : used as an endearment.—*adj.* kept as a pet : indulged : cherished : favourite.—*v.t.* to treat as a pet : to fondle : to pamper : to indulge. —*v.i.* (*U.S.*) to indulge in amorous caressing :— *pr.p.* **pett'ing ;** *pa.t.* and *pa.p.* **pett'ed.**—*adj.* **pett'ed.**—*ns.* **pett'er ; pett'ing.**—**pet aversion,** chief object of dislike ; **pet name,** a name used in familiar affection ; **petting party,** (*U.S.*) a gathering for the purpose of caressing as an organised sport. [Origin unknown ; not from Gael.]

pet, *pet, n.* a slighted and offended feeling : a slight or childish fit of aggrieved or resentful sulkiness : the sulks, huff.—*v.i.* to be peevish, to sulk.—*adj.* **pett'ed,** in a pet : apt to be in a pet.—*adv.* **pett'edly.**—*n.* **pett'edness.**—*adj.* **pett'ish,** peevish : sulky : inclined to sulk : of the nature of or expressive of sulkiness.—*adv.* **pett'ishly.**—*n.* **pett'-ishness.** [Origin unknown.]

petal, *pet'l, n.* a corolla leaf.—*adj.* **pet'aline** (-*īn*), of or like a petal.—*n.* **pet'alism,** a method of ostracism practised in ancient Syracuse, the name being written on an olive-leaf.—*adj.* **pet'alled,** having petals : also used in composition, as *white-petalled.*—*n.* **pet'alody** (Gr. *eidos,* form), transformation, esp. of stamens, into petals.—*adj.* **pet'-aloid,** having the appearance of a petal.—*n.* **petaloma'nia,** abnormal increase in number of petals. [Gr. *petalon,* a leaf.]

petara, *pi-tä'rä, n.* a travelling box or basket for clothes.—Also **pita'ra(h).** [Hind. *pitārāh, petārāh.*]

petard, *pe-tär(d)', a* case containing an explosive, used for blowing in doors, &c.—(*Shak.* **petar'**) : a moving firework.—**hoist with his own petard** (see **hoise**). [O.Fr.—*péter,* to crack or explode— L. *pēdĕre,* to break wind.]

petary, *pē'tər-i, n.* a peat-bog. [Mediaeval L. *petāria*—peat.]

petasus, *pet'ə-səs, n.* a low broad hat worn by Hermes. [Latinised from Gr. *petasos.*]

petaurist, *pe-taw'rist, n.* a flying-phalanger.—*adj.* **petau'rine.** [Gr. *petauristēs,* an acrobat.]

petchary, *pech'ə-ri, n.* the grey king-bird. [Imit.]

petechia, *pe-tē'ki-ä, n.* a small red or purple spot on the skin :—*pl.* **pete'chiae** (-*ē*).—*adj.* **petech'ial.** [Latinised from It. *petecchia.*]

peter, *pē'tər, v.i.* to dwindle away to nothing, be

dissipated or exhausted (with *out*). [Origin unknown ; orig. U.S. mining slang.]

peter, *pē'tər, n.* the Blue Peter (flag) : call for trumps.—*v.i.* to signal for trumps (by throwing a higher card than needful).—*ns.* **pe'ter-boat,** a kind of fishing-boat : a dredger's boat that goes equally well forward or astern ; **pe'ter-man,** a fisherman (in allusion to the apostle) ; **Peter-see-me',** a Spanish wine (from a grape introduced by Pedro *Ximenes*).—**Peter's pence** (see **penny**).

petersham, *pē'tər-shəm, n.* a heavy greatcoat designed by Lord *Petersham* : rough-napped cloth, generally dark blue, of which it was made : a heavy corded ribbon used for belts, hat-bands, &c.

petiole, *pet'i-ōl, n.* (*bot.*) a leaf-stalk : (*zool.*) a stalk-like structure, esp. that of the abdomen in wasps, &c.—*adjs.* **pet'iolar,** of, or of the nature of, a petiole ; **pet'iolate, -d, pet'ioled,** stalked.—*n.* **pet'iolule** (-*ol-ōōl*), the stalk of a leaflet in a compound leaf. [L. *petiolus,* a little foot, a petiole.]

petit, formerly *pet'it,* now *pet'i,* or as Fr. *pə-tē', adj.* a form of **petty,** small : insignificant (*obs.* except in legal and other French phrases) : in the Fr. *fem.* **petite** (*pə-tēt'*), applied to a woman, small-made (with a suggestion of neatness).—**petit four** (*pet'i fōōr*), a small very fancy biscuit ; **petit grain** (*pet'i grän*), dried unripe bitter oranges, or an oil distilled from them or their leaves and twigs ; **petit mal** (*pet'i mal*), a mild form of epilepsy without convulsions ; **petit point** (*pet'i point*), work in tent stitch. [Fr. *petit,* -*e.*]

petition, *pi-tish'ən, n.* a supplication : a prayer : a formal request to an authority : a written supplication signed by a number of persons : a written application to a court of law : the thing asked for : (*obs.*) a parliamentary bill : (*obs.*) an axiom or postulate.—*v.t.* to address a petition to : to ask for.—*adj.* **petit'ionary.**—*ns.* **petit'ioner,** one who petitions : (*hist.*) one of the party that petitioned Charles II. in 1680 to summon Parliament—opp. to *abhorrer* ; **petit'ioning ; petit'ionist.**—*adj.* **petitory** (*pet'i-tə-ri*), petitioning.—**Petition of Right,** a parliamentary declaration, in the form of a petition, of the rights of the people, assented to by Charles I. in 1628. [L. *petītiō, -ōnis*—*petĕre,* to ask.]

petitio principii, *pe-tish'i-ō prin-sip'i-ī,* L. *pe-tē'ti-ō prēng-kip'i-ē,* (*log.*) a begging of the question. [L. *petītiō prīncipiī.*]

Petrarchan, Petrarcan, *pi-trär'kən,* **Petrarchian** (-*ki-ən*), *adjs.* pertaining to the Italian poet Francesco *Petrarca* or *Petrarch* (1304-74).—*ns.* a follower or imitator of Petrarch.—*adj.* **Petrarch'al.** —*ns.* **Petrarch'ianism ; Petrarch'ianist.**—*v.i.* **Petrarchise** (*pē'trärk-īz*), to write in Petrarch's manner : to imitate Petrarch.—*ns.* **Petrarchism** (*pē'trärk-izm,* or *pi-trärk'izm*) ; **Pe'trarchist** (or -*trärk'*).—**Petrarch(i)an sonnet** (see **sonnet**).

petrary, *pet'rə-ri, n.* an engine for hurling stones. [L.L. *petrāria*—L. *petra*—Gr. *petrā,* rock.]

petre, (*coll.*) short for **saltpetre.**

petrel, *pet'rəl, n.* any bird of the genus Procellaria akin to the albatrosses and fulmars, esp. the **storm** (popularly **stormy**) **petrel,** or Mother Carey's chicken, a dusky sea-bird, rarely landing except to lay its eggs, the smallest web-footed bird known. [Fr. *pétrel*—L. *Petrus,* Peter, from its seeming to walk on the water ; see Matt. xiv. 29.]

Petri, or **petri, dish,** *pā'tri dish,* a shallow glass dish with an overlapping cover used for cultures of bacteria.—Also **Petri plate.** [R. J. *Petri,* German bacteriologist.]

petrify, *pet'ri-fī, v.t.* to turn into stone : (*geol.*) to fossilise by molecular replacement, preserving minute structure : (loosely) to encrust with stony matter : to make hard like a stone : to fix in amazement, horror, &c.—*v.i.* to become stone, or hard like stone :—*pr.p.* **pet'rifying ;** *pa.t.* and *pa.p.* **pet'rified.**—*n.* **petrifac'tion,** turning or being turned into stone : a petrified object : a fossil.— *adjs.* **petrifac'tive, petrif'ic,** petrifying.—*n.* **petrifica'tion,** petrifaction. [L. *petra*—Gr. *petrā,* rock, L. *facĕre, factum,* to make.]

Petrine, *pē'trīn, adj.* pertaining to, or written by,

the Apostle *Peter.—n.* Pē′trinism (*-trin-izm*), the Tübingen theory of F. C. Baur (1792-1860) and his school, of a doctrinal trend in primitive Christianity towards Judaism, ascribed to Peter and his party in opposition to *Paulinism.* [L. *Petrinus—Petrus,* Gr. *Petros,* Peter.]

pétrissage, *pā-trēs-äzh′, n.* massage by longitudinal rubbing and lateral squeezing. [Fr.,—*pétrir,* to knead.]

petroglyph, *pet′rō-glif, n.* a rock-carving, esp. prehistoric.—*adj.* petroglyph′ic. [Gr. *petrā,* a rock, *glyphein,* to carve.]

petrography, *pi-trog′rə-fi, n.* petrology.—*n.* petrog′-rapher.—*adjs.* petrographic (*pet-rō-graf′ik*), -al. —*adv.* petrograph′ically. [Gr. *petrā,* rock, *graphein,* to write.]

petrol, *pet′rol, -rəl, n.* formerly petroleum: now a mixture of light volatile hydrocarbons got by fractional distillation or cracking of petroleum, used for driving motor-cars, aeroplanes, &c.— *v.t.* to supply with petrol:—*pr.p.* pet′rolling; *pa.t.* and *pa.p.* pet′rolled.—*ns.* pet′rolage, treatment with petrol to stamp out mosquitoes; petrol-atum (*-ā′təm*), petroleum jelly.—*adj.* petroleous (*pi-trō′li-əs*), containing, or rich in, petroleum.— *ns.* petroleum (*pi-trō′li-əm*), a mixture of hydrocarbon oils got from oil-wells; pétroleur (*pā-trol-ər′*; *masc.*), pétroleuse (*-əz′*; *fem.*; *Fr.*), an incendiary who uses petroleum, as in Paris in 1871. —*adjs.* petrolic (*pi-trol′ik*), of petrol or petroleum; petrolif′erous (*pet-*), yielding petroleum.—pet′-roleum jelly, soft paraffin (*paraffinum molle*), the correct technical name for what is sometimes misnamed Vaseline. [L. *petra,* rock, *oleum,* oil.]

petrology, *pi-trol′ə-ji, n.* the science of the origin, chemical and mineral composition and structure, and alteration of rocks.—*adj.* petrological (*pet-rō-loj′*).—*adv.* petrolog′ically.—*n.* petrol′ogist. [Gr. *petrā,* rock, *logos,* discourse.]

petronel, *pet′rə-nel, n.* a large horse-pistol. [Fr. *petrinal—*L. *pectus, pectoris,* the chest (because held against the chest when used), or L. *petra,* stone (applied in sense of gun-flint).]

petronella, *pet-rən-el′ä, n.* a Scottish country-dance.

petrous, *pet′rəs, adj.* stony: petrosal.—*adj.* petrosal (*pi-trōs′əl*), relating to the stony part of the temporal bone.—*n.* the stony part of the temporal bone about the ear. [L. *petrōsus—petra—*Gr. *petrā,* rock.]

petted, pettish. See pet.

pettichaps, petty-chaps, *pet′i-chaps, n.* the garden or other warbler. [N. of England; app. petty and chap.]

petticoat, *pet′i-kōt, n.* (*orig.*) a short or small coat: a skirt, esp. an under-skirt, or a garment of which it forms part: any garment or drapery of similar form: a bell-shaped structure, as in telegraph insulators, &c.: (*coll.*) a woman.—*adj.* feminine: female: of women.—*n.pl.* pett′icoat-breech′es, loose short breeches worn by men in the 17th century. — *adj.* pett′icoated. — *n.pl.* pett′icoat-tails′, small cakes of shortbread. — petticoat government, domination by women. [petty, coat.]

pettifogger, *pet′i-fog-ər, n.* a paltry cavilling lawyer. —*v.i.* pett′ifog, to play the pettifogger.—*n.* pett′-ifoggery.—*n.* and *adj.* pett′ifogging. [petty; origin of second part obscure.]

pettitoes, *pet′i-tōz, n.pl.* pig's feet as food (formerly app. also other parts and of other animals): (*Shak.*) human feet. [Origin obscure, but early associated with petty and toe.]

pettle, *pet′l, v.t.* (*Scot.*) to indulge, pet. [Freq. of pet.]

pettle, *pet′l.* Same as pattle.

petty, *pet′i, adj.* small: of less importance: minor: trifling: lower in rank, power, &c.: inconsiderable, insignificant: contemptible: small-minded. —*n.* a junior schoolboy.—*adv.* pett′ily.—*n.* pett′-iness.—Petty Bag, a former office of the Court of Chancery: a clerk of that office; petty cash, miscellaneous small sums of money received or paid; petty larceny (see larceny); petty officer, a naval officer ranking with a non-commissioned officer in the army; Petty Sessions, a court in

which magistrates try trivial cases and refer others to a higher court; petty whin, a low spiny, papilionaceous shrub (*Genista anglica*) like a small whin. [Fr. *petit.*]

petulant, *pet′ū-lənt, adj.* orig. wanton, lascivious: showing peevish impatience, irritation, or caprice: forward, impudent in manner.—*ns.* pet′ulance, pet′ulancy. — *adv.* pet′ulantly. [L. *petulāns, -āntis—*assumed *petulāre,* dim. of *petēre,* to seek.]

Petunia, *pē-tū′ni-ä, n.* a South American genus of ornamental plants near akin to tobacco. [Tupí *petun,* tobacco.]

petuntze, *pe-toont′se, n.* a felspathic rock used in making Chinese porcelain. [Chin. *pai-tun-tse,* little white brick.]

pew, *pū, n.* an enclosed compartment or fixed bench in a church: formerly, a place for a preacher or reader: a box or stall in another building: (*slang*) a seat.—*ns.* pew′-chair, an additional seat hinged to the end of a pew; pew′-fellow, occupant of the same pew: companion; pew′-holder, one who rents a pew; pew′-opener, an attendant who shows strangers to pews; pew′-rent, rent paid for the use of a pew. [O.Fr. *puie,* raised place, balcony—L. *podia,* pl. of *podium—*Gr. *podion,* dim. of *pous, podos,* foot.]

pewit, *pē′wit, pū′it.* Same as peewit.

pewter, *pū′tər, n.* an alloy of three to nine parts of tin and one of lead: sometimes tin with a little copper and antimony: a vessel made of pewter, esp. a beer-tankard: (*slang*) prize-money.—*adj.* made of pewter.—*ns.* pew′terer, one who works in pewter; pew′ter-mill, a lapidary's pewter polishing-wheel for amethyst, agate, &c. [O.Fr. *peutre;* cf. It. *peltro,* L.G. *spialter,* Eng. spelter.]

peyote, *pā-yō′tä, n.* a Mexican intoxicant made from cactus tops. [Nahuatl word.]

pezant, an old spelling of peasant.

Peziza, *pe-zī′zä, n.* a genus of discomycete fungi with cup-like apothecia.—*adj.* pezi′zoid. [Gr. *pezis,* a puff-ball.]

pfennig, *pfen′ig, -ihh, n.* a German coin, the hundredth part of a mark.—Also (*obs.*) pfenn′ig.

phacoid, *fak′* or *fāk′oid,* phacoidal, *fə-koi′dl, adjs.* lentil-shaped, lens-shaped.—*ns.* phacolite (*fak′ə-līt*), a zeolite often lenticular in shape; phac′o-lith, a small lenticular igneous intrusion, shaped by folding in an anticline. [Gr. *phakos,* a lentil, *eidos,* form, *lithos,* stone.]

phaeic, *fē′ik, adj.* dusky.—*n.* phae′ism, duskiness, incomplete melanism (in butterflies). [Gr. *phaios,* dusky.]

phaenogam, *fē′nō-gam, n.* a spermatophyte or phanerogam.—*n.pl.* Phaenogamae (*fē-nog′ə-mē*). —*adjs.* phaenogamic (*-nō-gam′ik*), phaenoga-mous (*-nog′ə-məs*).—Also phe′nogam, &c. [Gr. *phainein,* to show, *gamos,* marriage.]

phaenology, phaenomenon. Same as phenology, phenomenon.

phaenotype, phenotype, *fē′nō-tip, n.* the characteristics manifested by a zygote irrespective of its constitution by genes—opp. to *genotype.—adj.* phaenotypic (*-tip′ik*). [Gr. *phainein,* to show, *typos,* stamp.]

Phaeophyceae, *fē-ō-fish′i-ē, n.pl.* the brown seaweeds, one of the main divisions of algae, in which the chlorophyll is masked by a brown pigment. [Gr. *phaios,* dusky, *phȳkos,* seaweed.]

Phaethon, *fā′i-thon, n.* the son of Helios, the Greek sun-god, who came to grief in driving his father's chariot: the tropic-bird genus (as seeking to keep to the sun's course).—*adj.* Phaethon′tic. [Gr. *Phaethōn, -ontos,* lit. shining; cf. *phaos, phōs,* light.]

phaeton, *fā′(i-)tn, n.* an open four-wheeled carriage for one or two horses. [From the foregoing.]

phagedaena, phagedena, *faj-* or *fag-i-dē′nä, n.* rapidly spreading destructive ulceration, once common in hospitals—hospital gangrene.—*adj.* phagedae′nic, phagedē′nic. [Gr. *phagedaina—phagein,* to eat.]

phagocyte, *fag′ō-sīt, n.* a white blood-corpuscle that engulfs bacteria and other harmful particles. —*adjs.* phagocytic (*-sit′*), -al.—*n.* phag′ocytism (*-sīt-*), the nature or function of a phagocyte.—*v.t.* phag′ocytose (*-sīt-ōs*), to subject to phagocytic action.—*n.* **phagocytō′sis**, destruction by phagocytes. [Gr. *phagein*, to eat, *kytos*, a vessel.]

phalange. See **phalanx.**

phalanger, *fal-an′jər*, *n.* any one of a group of small arboreal Australasian marsupials. [Gr. *phalangion*, spider's web, from their webbed toes.]

phalanstery, *fal′ən-stə-ri*, *n.* the dwelling of the phalange in the ideal social system of Fourier (1772-1837), a vast structure in the midst of a square league of cultivated land.—*adj.* **phalansterian** (-*stē′ri-ən*).—*ns.* **phalanstē′rianism**; **phal′ansterism**; **phal′ansterist**. [Fr. *phalanstère*, formed from Gr. *phalanx* on the model of *monastère*, monastery.]

phalanx, *fal′angks* (or *fāl′*), *n.* a solid formation of ancient Greek heavy-armed infantry: a solid body of men, &c.: a solid body of supporters or partisans: a Fourierist community: a bone of a digit: the part of a finger or toe answering to it: a joint of an insect's leg: a bundle of stamens:—*pl.* **phal′anxes** or (*biol.*) **phalanges** (*fal-an′jēz*).—*adj.* **phalangal** (*fal-ang′gl*), phalangeal.—*n.* **phalange** (*fal′anj*), a phalanx (in biological senses): (also *fal-ān′²zh*), a socialistic community in Fourier's scheme, consisting of 1800 persons living in a phalanstery: Primo de Rivera's Spanish fascist party:—*pl.* **phal′anges.**—*adj.* **phalan′geal.**—*ns.* **phalangid** (*fāl-an′jid*), a long-legged arachnid, a harvestman; **phalan′gist**, a Spanish fascist. [Gr. *phalanx*, *-angos*, a roller, phalanx, phalange, spider.]

phalarope, *fal′ə-rōp*, *n.* a wading bird (*Phalaropus*) with coot-like feet. [Gr. *phalaris*, a coot, *pous*, a foot.]

phallus, *fal′əs*, *n.* the penis: the symbol of generation in primitive religion: **Phallus**, the stinkhorn genus of fungi:—*pl.* **phall′ī**.—*adj.* **phall′ic.**—*ns.* **phall′icism** (-*sizm*), **phall′ism**, worship of the generative power of nature; **phall′in, phalloid′in**, two of the poisons occurring in the fungus *Amanita phalloides*—*adj.* **phall′oid**, like a phallus. [L.,—Gr. *phallos*.]

Phanariot, *fa-nar′i-ot*, *n.* one of the Greeks inhabiting the *Fanar* quarter of Constantinople, or of a Greek official class—in Turkish history mostly diplomatists, administrators, and bankers, also hospodars of Wallachia and Moldavia.—*adj.* **Phanar′iot.**—Also **Fanar′iot.** [Gr. *phānarion*, a lighthouse, from that on the Golden Horn.]

phanerogam, *fan′ər-ō-gam*, *n.* a spermatophyte.—*ns.pl.* **Phanerogamae** (-*og′ə-mē*), **Phanerogamia** (-*ō-gam′i-ä*).—*adjs.* **phanerogam′ic**, **phanerog′amous.** [Gr. *phaneros*, visible, *gamos*, marriage.]

phange, an old spelling (*Shak.*) of **fang.**

phantasm, *fan′tazm*, *n.* a vain, airy appearance: a fancied vision: an apparition: a spectre: a counterfeit: (*obs.*) an impostor.—Also **phantas′ma**:—*pl.* **phan′tasms, phantas′mata.**—*n.* **phan′tasim(e)**, (*Shak.*) a fantastic person.—*adjs.* **phantas′mal; phantasmā′lian** (*rare*).—*n.* **phantasmal′ity.**—*adv.* **phantas′mally.**—*adjs.* **phantas′mic, -al**; **phantasmogenet′ic**, begetting phantasms.—*adv.* **phantasmogenet′ically.** [Gr. *phantasma*—*phantazein*, to make visible—*phainein*, to bring to light—*phaein*, to shine.]

phantasmagoria, *fan-taz-mə-gō′ri-ə*, *n.* a fantastic series of illusive images or of real forms.—*adjs.* **phantasmagō′rial**, pertaining to or resembling a phantasmagoria; **phantasmagōr′ic, -al.** [A name given to a show in 1802 from Gr. *phantasma*, an appearance, and perh. *agorā*, an assembly.]

phantasy, phantastic, phantastry. Same as **fantasy, &c.**—*n.* **phantā′ciast**, one of those Docetae who believed Christ's body to have been a mere phantom.

phantom, *fan′təm* (*Spens.* **phantosme**, *fan-tōm′*), *n.* a deceitful appearance: an immaterial form: a visionary experience: a show without reality.—*adj.* illusive: unreal: spectral: imaginary: ghostly-looking: transparent and hardly visible.—*adjs.* **phantomat′ic, phan′tomish, phan′tomy**, relating to a phantom. [O.Fr. *fantosme*—Gr. *phantasma*.]

Pharaoh, *fā′rō*, *n.* a title of the kings of ancient Egypt: (*obs.*) faro.—*adj.* **pharaonic** (*fā-rā-on′ik*).—**Pharaoh's serpent**, the coiled ash of burning

mercuric thiocyanate. [L. and Gr. *pharaō*—Heb. *par′ōh*—Egypt. *pr-′o*, great house.]

phare, *fār*, *n.* a lighthouse. [Fr.; see **pharos.**]

Pharisee, *far′i-sē*, *n.* one of a religious school among the Jews, marked by their strict observance of the law and of religious ordinances: any one more careful of the outward forms than of the spirit of religion, a formalist.—*adjs.* **pharisā′ic, -al**, pertaining to, or like, the Pharisees: hypocritical.—*adv.* **pharisā′ically.** — *ns.* **pharisā′icalness**; **phar′isaism** (also **phar′iseeism**). [O.E. *phariseus*—L.L. *pharisaeus*—Gr. *pharisaios*—Heb.*pārūsh*, separated.]

pharmaceutic, -al, *fär-mə-sū′tik* (or *-kū′tik*), *-əl*, *adjs.* pertaining to the knowledge or art of preparing medicines.—*adv.* **pharmaceu′tically.**—*ns.* **pharmaceu′tics**, the science of preparing medicines; **pharmaceu′tist.** [Gr. *pharmakeutikos.*]

pharmacopoeia, *fär-mə-kə-pē′-(y)ä*, *n.* a book or list of drugs with directions for their preparation: a collection of drugs.—*adjs.* **pharmacopoe′ial, pharmacopoe′ian.** [Gr. *pharmakopoiiä*—*pharmakon*, a drug, *poieein*, to make.]

pharmacy, *fär′mə-si*, *n.* a department of the medical art which consists in the collecting, preparing, preserving, and dispensing of medicines: the art of preparing and mixing medicines: a druggist's shop: a dispensary.—*ns.* **phar′macist** (-*sist*), a druggist, one skilled in pharmacy: one legally qualified to sell drugs and poisons; **pharmacol′ogist**; **pharmacol′ogy**, the science of drugs; **pharmacop′olist** (Gr. *pōleein*, to sell), a dealer in drugs. [Gr. *pharmakeiä*, use of drugs, *pharmakon*, a drug.]

pharos, *fā′ros*, *n.* a lighthouse or beacon. [From the famous lighthouse on the island of *Pharos* in the Bay of Alexandria.]

pharynx, *far′ingks*, *n.* the cleft or cavity forming the upper part of the gullet, lying behind the nose, mouth, and larynx:—*pl.* **phar′ynges** (-*in-jēz*), **phar′ynxes.**—*adjs.* **pharyngal** (*fa-ring′gl*), **pharyngeal** (*fa-rin′ji-əl*); **pharyngitic** (*far-in-jit′ik*), pertaining to pharyngitis.—*n.* **pharyngitis** (*far-in-jī′tis*), inflammation of the mucous membrane of the pharynx.—*ns.* **pharyngoscope** (*fa-ring′gə-skōp*), an instrument for inspecting the pharynx; **pharyngoscopy** (*far-ing-gos′kə-pi*); **pharyngot′omy**, the operation of making an incision into the pharynx. [Gr. *pharynx*, *-ygos*, later *-yngos*.]

phase, *fāz*, *n.* the appearance at a given time of the illuminated surface exhibited by the moon or a planet—also **phasis** (*fā′sis*): aspect or appearance of anything at any stage: stage of advancement in a periodic change, measured from some standard point: (*chem.*) the sum of all those portions of a material system which are identical in chemical composition and physical state:—*pl.* **phases** (*fā′ziz*, *-sēz*).—*adjs.* **phased**, adjusted to be in the same phase at the same time; **phase′less**, unchanging; **phasic** (*fā′zik*, *-sik*).—**in, out of, phase**, in the same phase together, or in different phases. [Gr. *phasis*—*phaein*, to shine.]

phase. See **feeze.**

Phasma, *faz′mä*, *n.* the spectre-insect genus—*n.* **phas′mid**, a member of the **Phas′midae** (stick-insects, leaf-insects), the family of Orthoptera to which it belongs. [Gr. *phasma*, a spectre.]

pheasant, *fez′nt*, *n.* a richly-coloured gallinaceous bird (*Phasianus colchicus*), a half-wild game-bird in Britain: extended to others of the same or kindred genus (as *golden*, *silver*, *Argus*, *Amherst's* pheasant) and to other birds: (*U.S.*) the tufted grouse: (*S.Afr.*) a francolin: (*Austr.*) the lyre-bird: also the coucal (*swamp pheasant*): the flesh of the bird as food.—*ns.* **pheas′antry**, an enclosure for rearing pheasants; **pheas′ant's-eye**, a ranunculaceous plant (Adonis) with deep-red dark-centred flowers. [A.Fr. *fesant*—L. *phāsiānus*—Gr. *phāsiānos* (*ornis*, bird), from the river Phasis, in Colchis.]

pheazar, *fē′zər*, *n.* (*Shak.*) perh. one who feezes, perh. for vizier.

pheer, pheere. Same as **fere**, mate.

pheeze. Same as **feeze.**

phellem, *fel′əm*, *n.* (*bot.*) cork.—*ns.* **phell′oderm**

(Gr. *derma*, skin), a layer of secondary cortex formed by the phellogen on its inner side ; **phellogen** (*fel′ō-jen*), a layer of meristem that forms cork without, otherwise cork-cambium.—*adjs.* **phellogenetic** (*-ji-net′ik*) ; **phell′oid**, cork-like and formed like cork, but not, or very slightly, suberised.—*ns.* **phelloplas′tic**, a model in cork ; **phelloplas′tics**, the making of models in cork. [Gr. *phellos*, cork.]

phelonion, phaelonion, *fi-lō′ni-on, n.* an Eastern vestment like a chasuble. [Late Gr. *phailōnion, phēlōnion*, dim. of *phailonēs, phelonēs*, for *phainolēs* —L. *paenula*, a cloak.]

phen-. See also **phaen-, phoen-.**

phenacetin, *fin-as′i-tin, n.* an antipyretic drug, $C_{10}H_{13}NO_2$. [**acetic** and **phene**.]

phenacite, *fen′ə-sīt,* **phenakite,** *-kīt, n.* a mineral, beryllium silicate, sometimes deceptively like quartz.—*ns.* **phen′akism,** deceit ; **phenakist′oscope,** an instrument in which figures on a disk seen successively through a slit give the impression of motion. [Gr. *phenax* and *phenākistēs,* a deceiver ; *skopeein,* to look at.]

phene, *fēn, n.* an old name for benzene.—*n.* **phēn′ate,** a phenolate.—*adj.* **phēn′ic** (or *fen′*), of benzene or of phenyl. [Gr. *phainein,* to show, because obtained in the manufacture of illuminating gas.]

phengite, *fen′jīt, n.* a transparent stone used by the ancients for windows, prob. selenite : sometimes applied to kinds of mica.—Also **phengites** (*fen-ji′tēz*). [Gr. *phengitēs—phengos,* light.]

phenocryst, *fē′nō-krist, n.* a larger crystal in a porphyritic rock. [Gr. *phainein,* to show, and **crystal.**]

phenol, *fē′nol, n.* carbolic acid, a weak acid, C_6H_5OH, got as hygroscopic needles from coaltar, a powerful disinfectant : extended to the class of aromatic compounds with one or more hydroxyl groups directly attached to the benzene nucleus, weak acids with reactions of alcohols.— *n.* **phen′olate,** a salt of a phenol.—*adj.* **phenol′ic.** —*n.* **phenolphthalein** (*fē-nol-fthal′i-in,* or *-thal′*), a substance ($C_{20}H_{14}O_4$) got from phenol and phthalic anhydride, used as an indicator for weak acids.—**phenolic resins,** a group of plastics made from a phenol and an aldehyde. [See **phene**, **-ol** from **alcohol.**]

phenology, phaenology, *fē-nol′ə-ji, n.* the study of organisms as affected by climate, esp. dates of seasonal phenomena, as opening of flowers, arrival of migrants. — *adj.* **phenological** (*-ə-loj′*). — *n.* **phenol′ogist.** [Gr. *phainein,* to show, *logos,* discourse.]

phenomenon, now rarely **phaenomenon,** *fi-nom′-i-nən* or *-non, n.* anything directly apprehended by the senses or one of them : an event that may be observed : the appearance which anything makes to our consciousness, as distinguished from what it is in itself : (loosely) a remarkable or unusual person, thing, or appearance, a prodigy :—*pl.* **phenom′ena.**—*adj.* **phenom′enal,** pertaining to a phenomenon : of the nature of a phenomenon. —*v.t.* **phenom′enalise,** to represent as a phenomenon.—*ns.* **phenom′enalism,** the philosophical doctrine that the phenomenal and the real are identical—that phenomena are the only realities —also *externalism* ; **phenom′enalist.**—*adj.* **phenomenalist′ic.**—*n.* **phenomenality** (*-al′i-ti*), the character of being phenomenal.—*adv.* **phenom′enally.**—*v.t.* **phenom′enise,** to bring into the world of experience.—*ns.* **phenom′enism,** phenomenalism ; **phenom′enist.**—*adj.* **phenomenolog′ical.**—*n.* **phenomenol′ogy,** the science, or a description, of phenomena : the philosophy of Edmund Husserl (1859-1938)—opposed to positivism, and concerned with the experiences of the self. [Gr. *phainomenon,* pl. *-a,* neut. pr.p. pass. of *phainein,* to show.]

phenotype, *fen′ō-tīp, n.* one of a group of individuals all of which have a similar appearance regardless of their factorial constitution—opp. to *genotype* : a type determined by visible characteristics.—*adjs.* **phenotyp′ic(al)** (*-tip′*). [Gr. *phainein,* to show, and **type.**]

phenyl, *fē′nil, n.* an organic radical, C_6H_5, found in benzene, phenol, &c.—*adj.* **phenyl′ic.** [**phene,** and Gr. *hylē,* material.]

pheon, *fē′on, n.* (*her.*) the barbed head of a dart or arrow, esp. as a heraldic bearing. [Origin unknown.]

Pherecratic, *fer-e-krat′ik,* **Pherecrataean,** *-krə-tē′ən, adjs.* of the Greek poet *Pherecratēs.*—*n.* a metre used by him, spondee, dactyl, spondee, with variations.

phese. See **feeze.**

phew, *fū, interj.* an exclamation of petty vexation, unexpected difficulty, impatience, relief, contempt, &c. [A half-formed whistle.]

phi, *fī, fē, n.* the twenty-first letter (Φ, φ) of the Greek alphabet, orig. as aspirated *p* (as in *upheave*), now pronounced as *f* and transliterated *ph* : as a Greek numeral *φ′* = 500, *φ* = 500,000. [Gr. *phei.*]

phial, *fī′əl, n.* a vessel for liquids, esp. now a small medicine-bottle.—*v.t.* to put or keep in a phial :— *pr.p.* **phi′alling** ; *pa.t.* and *pa.p.* **phi′alled.**—*adj.* **phi′aliform,** saucer-shaped. [L. *phiala*— Gr. *phialē,* a broad shallow bowl.]

Phi Beta Kappa, *fī′* or *fē′, bē′* or *bā′tä kåp′ā,* the oldest of the American college Greek letter societies. [Gr. Φ.Β.Κ., the initial letters of its motto— *Philosophiā biou kybernētēs,* Philosophy is the guide of life.]

philabeg. See **filibeg.**

Philadelphian, *fil-ə-del′fi-ən, adj.* of the Pergamene city of Philadelphia or Philadelpheia (Ala-shehr) : of Philadelphia, Pennsylvania : of a mystic sect emphasising brotherly love, founded in London in 1652 under the influence of Boehme.—*n.* a native or inhabitant of Philadelphia : a member of the sect. [Gr. *philein,* to love, *adelphos,* a brother, *adelphē,* a sister.]

philamot. See **filemot.**

Philander, *fil-an′dər, n.* a conventional proper name for a lover : **philander,** a lover : a dangler after women : a male flirt : a philandering.—*v.i.* to make love : to flirt or coquet.—*n.* **philan′derer.** [Gr. *philandros,* fond of men or of a husband— *philein,* to love, *anēr, andros,* a man, husband : misapplied as if meaning a loving man.]

philanthropy, *fil-an′thrə-pi, n.* love of mankind, esp. as shown in services to general welfare.—*ns.* **philanthrope** (*fil′ən-thrōp*), **philan′thropist,** one who tries to benefit mankind.—*adjs.* **philanthropic** (*-throp′ik*), **-al,** doing good to others, benevolent.— *adv.* **philanthrop′ically.** [Gr. *philanthrōpiā— phileein,* to love, *anthrōpos,* a man.]

philately, *fil-at′i-li, n.* the study and collection of postage and revenue stamps and labels.—*adj.* **philatelic** (*fil-ə-tel′ik*). — *n.* **philat′elist.** [Fr. *philatélic,* invented in 1864—Gr. *phileein,* to love, *atelēs,* tax-free—*a-,* priv., *telos,* tax.]

philharmonic, *fil-är-mon′ik,* also *-här-, -ər-, adj.* loving music.—**philharmonic pitch,** a musical pitch slightly higher than French pitch (439 vibrations a second for A). [Gr. *phileein,* to love, *harmoniā,* harmony.]

philhellenic, *fil-hel-ēn′ik,* or *-en′ik, adj.* loving Greece : favouring the Greeks.—*ns.* **philhellene** (*-hel′ēn*), **philhellenist** (*-hel′in-ist*), a supporter of Greece, esp. in 1821-32 ; **philhell′enism.** [Gr. *phileein,* to love, *Hellēn,* a Greek.]

p(h)ilhorse, *fil′hors,* **pil′hors,** *n.* (*Shak.*). Same as **fillhorse** or **thillhorse.** [See **fill** (2), **thill.**]

philibeg. See **filibeg.**

Philippian, *fil-ip′i-ən, n.* a native of *Philippi* in Macedonia.—Also *adj.*

Philippic, *fil-ip′ik, n.* one of the three orations of Demosthenes against Philip of Macedon : any discourse full of invective.—*v.i.* **Phil′ippise,** to side with Philip : to utter an oracle inspired by Philip, or by bribery of the prevailing power. [Gr. *philippikos, philippizein—Philippos,* Philip.]

philippina, philippine. Same as **philopoena.**

Philistine, *fil′is-tīn* (*U.S. fil-is′tin*), *n.* one of the ancient inhabitants of south-west Palestine, enemies of the Israelites : a name applied by German students to persons not connected with the university (also **Philis′ter** ; *Ger.*) : (also **philistine**) a person of material outlook indifferent to culture :

(*slang*) an enemy: (*slang*) a bailiff.—*adjs.* **Phil-istē'an**, **Philis'tian** (both *Milt.*), **Phil'istine.**—*v.t.* **Phil'istinise** (*-tin-*).—*n.* **Phil'istinism.** [Gr. *Philistinos*—Heb. *P'lishtîm.*]

phillipsite, *fil'ips-īt*, *n.* a zeolite, hydrated silicate of potassium, calcium, and aluminium, often cross-shaped by twinning. [J. W. *Phillips*, mineralogist.]

Phillyrea, *fil-ir'i-ä*, *n.* the mock privet genus, Mediterranean shrubs akin to olive and privet. [Gr. *philyreā*, mock privet.]

philo-, **phil-**, in composition, loving: friend. [Gr. *phileein*, to love, *philos*, friend, loved.]

philogyny, *fil-oj'i-ni*, *n.* love of women.—*adj.* **philog'ynous.**—*n.* **philog'ynist.** [Gr. *gynē*, a woman.]

philology, *fil-ol'ə-ji*, *n.* the science of language: the study of etymology, grammar, rhetoric, and literary criticism: (*orig.*) the knowledge which enabled men to study and explain the languages of Greece and Rome.—*ns.* **philol'oger**, **philologian** (*-ə-lō'*), **philol'ogist**, **phil'ologue** (*-log*), one versed in philology.—*adjs.* **philologic** (*-ə-loj'ik*), **-al.**—*adv.* **philolog'ically.**—**comparative philology**, study of languages by comparing their history, forms, and relationships with each other. [Gr. *philologiā*—*logos*, word.]

philomath, *fil'ə-math*, *n.* a lover of learning.—*adjs.* **philomath'ic**, **-al.**—*n.* **philomathy** (*-om'ə-thi*), love of learning. [Gr. *philomathēs*, fond of learning—*math-*, root of *manthanein*, to learn.]

Philomel, *fil'ō-mel*, **Philomela**, *-mē'lä*, *n.* the nightingale personified.—Also (*obs.*) **Phil'omene** (*-mēn*). [Gr. *Philomēla*, daughter of Pandion, changed into a nightingale or swallow.]

philomot, *fil'ə-mot*, *n.* (*Addison*). Same as **filemot.**

philopoena, **philippina**, *fil-ip-ē'nä*, **philippine**, *fil'ip-ēn*, *n.* a game in which each of two persons eats a twin kernel of a nut, and one pays a forfeit to the other on certain conditions: the nut itself: the gift made as a forfeit. [Apparently from the Ger. formula of claiming the gift, *Guten Morgen, Vielliebchen*, Good morning, well-beloved, confused with Gr. *philos*, friend, *poinē*, penalty, and with Ger. *Philippchen*, little Philip.]

philoprogenitive, *fil-ō-prō-jen'i-tiv*, *adj.* having or relating to instinctive love of offspring: inclined to produce offspring.—*n.* **philoprogen'itiveness.** [Gr. *philo-*, L. *progeniēs*, progeny.]

philosopher, *fi-los'ə-fər*, *n.* a lover of wisdom: one versed in or devoted to philosophy: (formerly) a student of natural science or of the occult: (now mainly) a metaphysician: one who acts calmly and rationally in the affairs and changes of life.—*ns.* **philosophas'ter**, a superficial philosopher: one who poses as a philosopher; **phil'osophe** (*-sof*, *-zof*, or *zof'*), a philosopher: a thinker of the type of the French Encyclopaedists; **philos'-opheress**, **philos'ophess** (both *rare*).—*adjs.* **philosophic** (*-sof'* or *-zof'*), **-al**, pertaining or according to philosophy: skilled in or given to philosophy: becoming a philosopher: rational: calm.—*adv.* **philosoph'ically.**—*v.i.* **philos'ophise**, to reason like a philosopher: to form philosophical theories.—*ns.* **philos'ophiser**, a would-be philosopher; **philos'ophism**, would-be philosophy; **philos'-ophist.**—*adjs.* **philosophist'ic**, **-al.**—*n.* **philos'-ophy**, (*orig.*) pursuit of wisdom and knowledge: the science of being as being: the knowledge of the causes and laws of all things: the principles underlying any department of knowledge: reasoning: a particular philosophical system: calmness of temper.—**moral**, and **natural**, **philosophy** (see **moral**, **natural**); **philosopher's stone**, an imaginary stone or mineral compound, long sought after by alchemists as a means of transforming other metals into gold; **philosophical pitch**, a pitch used in acoustical calculations based on 512 vibrations for treble C. [Gr. *philosophos*—*phileein*, to love, *sophiā*, wisdom.]

philtre, **philter**, *fil'tər*, *n.* a drink, or (rarely) a spell, to excite love. [Fr. *philtre*—L. *philtrum*—Gr. *philtron*—*phileein*, to love, *-tron*, agent-suffix.]

phimosis, *fī-mō'sis*, *n.* narrowing of the preputial orifice. [Gr. *phīmōsis*, muzzling—*phīmos*, a muzzle.]

phinnock. Same as **finnock.**

phisnomy, *fiz'nə-mi*, *n.* an old form of **physiognomy**, the face.

phiz, *fiz*, **phizog**, *fiz-og'*, *ns.* (*slang*) the face. [**physiognomy**.]

phlebitis, *fli-bī'tis*, *n.* inflammation of a vein.—*n.* **phlebolite** (*fleb'ə-līt*; Gr. *lithos*, stone), a calcareous concretion found in a vein.—*v.t.* **phlebot'-omise** (Gr. *tomē*, a cut), to bleed.—*ns.* **phlebot'omist**, a blood-letter; **phlebot'omy**, blood-letting. [Gr. *phleps*, *phlebos*, a vein.]

Phlegethontic, *fleg-i-thon'tik*, *adj.* of or like the *Phlegethon*, a fiery river of Hades. [Gr. *phlegethōn*, *-ontos*, pr.p. of *phlegethein*—*phlegein*, to burn.]

phlegm, *flem*, *n.* the thick, slimy matter secreted in the throat, and discharged by coughing, regarded in old physiology as one (cold and moist) of the four humours or bodily fluids: the temperament supposed to be due to its predominance, sluggish indifference: calmness: one of the principles of old chemistry, a watery distilled liquid.—*adj.* **phlegmagogic** (*fleg-mə-gog'ik*, *-goj'ik*).—*ns.* **phleg'magogue** (*-gog*), a medicine expelling phlegm; **phlegmā'sia**, inflammation, esp. *Phlegmasia alba dolens*, white-leg.—*adjs.* **phlegmat'ic**, **-al**, abounding in or generating phlegm: cold and sluggish: not easily excited.—*adv.* **phlegmat'ically.**—*n.* **phleg'mon**, purulent inflammation.—*adjs.* **phlegmon'ic**, **phleg'monoid**, **phleg'monous**; **phlegmy** (*flem'i*). [By later return to Greek spelling, from M.E. *fleem*, *fleme*, *flemme*—O.Fr. *flemme*, *fleume*—L. *phlegma*—Gr. *phlegma*, *-atos*, flame, inflammation, phlegm (regarded as produced by heat), *phlegmasiā*, *phlegmonē*, inflammation—*phlegein*, to burn.]

Phleum, *flē'əm*, *n.* a small genus of grasses, timothy-grass. [Gr. *phleōs*, plume-grass.]

phloem, *flō'əm*, *n.* the bast or sieve-tube portion of a vascular bundle, by which elaborated food materials are transported in a plant. [Gr. *phloos*, bark.]

phlogiston, *flo-jis'ton*, *-gis'ton*, or *-tən*, *n.* an imaginary element, believed in the 18th century to separate from every combustible body in burning.—*adj.* **phlogis'tic**, (*chem.*) of, like, or containing phlogiston: combustible: (*med.*) inflammatory: fiery.—*v.t.* **phlogis'ticate**, to combine with phlogiston. [Gr. neut. of vbl. adj. *phlogistos*, burnt, inflammable—*phlogizein*, to set on fire.]

phlogopite, *flog'ə-pīt*, *n.* a magnesia mica, yellow or brown. [Gr. *phlogōpos*, fiery-looking—*phlox*, flame, *ōps*, face.]

Phlox, *floks*, *n.* a Siberian and American genus of Polemoniaceae, well-known garden plants. [Gr. *phlox*, flame, wallflower—*phlegein*, to burn.]

pho, **phoh.** Same as **foh.**

phobia, *fō'bi-ä*, **phobism**, *fō'bizm*, *ns.* a fear, aversion, or hatred, esp. morbid and irrational.—*n.* **phō'bist.** [Gr. *phobos*, fear.]

Phoca, *fō'kä*, *n.* the common seal genus: **phoca**, a seal: (*Spens.*) a scaly sea-monster:—*pl.* **pho'cas**, **pho'cae** (*-sē*).—*n.pl.* **Phocidae** (*fō'si-dē*), the true seals, with backward-turned hind-flippers and no external ear. [L. *phōca*—Gr. *phōkē*, a seal.]

Phocaena, *fō-sē'nä*, *n.* the porpoise genus. [Gr. *phōkaina.*]

Phoebus, *fē'bəs*, *n.* Apollo, the Greek sun-god: the sun.—*n.* **Phoebe** (*fē'bē*), his sister Artemis, the moon-goddess: the moon.—*adj.* **Phoebe'an.** [Latinised—Gr. *Phoibos*, *Phoibē*; *phoibos*, *-ē*, bright, *phaein*, to shine.]

Phoenician, *fi-nish'(y)ən*, *adj.* of Phoenicia, on the coast of Syria, its people, colonies (including Carthage), language, and arts.—*n.* one of the people of Phoenicia: their Semitic language. [Gr. *Phoinix*, *-ikos.*]

Phoenix, *fē'niks*, *n.* a fabulous Arabian bird, worshipped in ancient Egypt, the only individual of its kind, that burned itself every 500 years or so and rose rejuvenated from its ashes: hence anything that rises from its own or its predecessor's ashes: a paragon. [O.E. *fenix*, later assimilated to L. *phoenix*—Gr. *phoinix.*]

Pholas, *fō'las*, *n.* the piddock genus of rock-boring molluscs:—*pl.* **pholades** (*fō'lə-dēz*). [Gr. *phōlas*,

-*ados*, (adj.) lurking in a hole, (n.) the date-shell.

pholidosis, *fol-id-ō'sis*, *n.* arrangement of scales, as in fishes and reptiles. [Gr. *pholis, -idos,* scale.]

phon, *fon*, *n.* a unit of objective loudness.—*adj.* **phonal** (*fōn'əl*), vocal.—*v.i.* **phon'ate**, to produce vocal sound, to utter voice.—*n.* **phōnā'tion**, production of vocal sound.—*adj.* **phōn'atory.**— *n.* **phone** (*fōn*), an elementary speech sound: a telephone receiver: (also **'phone**; *coll.*) a telephone.—*v.t.* and *v.i.* (also **'phone**; *coll.*) to telephone.—*adj.* **phōn'ic** (or *fon'ik*), of sound, esp. vocal sound: voiced.—*n.* **phōn'ics** (or *fon'iks*), the science of sound, or of spoken sounds.—**phonic method,** a method of teaching reading through the phonetic value of letters and groups of letters. [Gr. *phōnē,* voice, sound; in part for **telephone.**]

phonautograph, *fōn-aw'tə-grāf, n.* an instrument for recording sound vibrations.—*adj.* **phonautographic** (*-graf'ik*).—*adv.* **phonautograph'ically.**

phoneme, *fōn'ēm, n.* a group or family of speech sounds felt in any one language to be merely variants of one sound.—*adj.* **phonemic** (*-nēm'* or *-nem'*).—*n.* **phonem'ics,** science of phonemic groups and contrasts. [Gr. *phōnēma,* a sound—*phōnē.*]

phonetic, *fō-net'ik, adj.* of, concerning, according to, or representing the sounds of spoken language. —Also **phonet'ical.**—*adv.* **phonet'ically,** according to pronunciation.—*n.* **phonetician** (*fō-ni-tish'ən*), one versed in phonetics.—*v.t.* **phonet'i-cise,** to make phonetic: to represent phonetically.—*ns.* **phonet'icism,** phonetic character or representation; **phonet'icist,** one who advocates phonetic spelling.—*n.* (*pl.* in form, treated as *sing.*) **phonet'ics,** that branch of linguistic science that deals with pronunciation.—*ns.* **pho'netism,** phonetic writing; **pho'netist,** a phonetician: an advocate or user of phonetic spelling.—**phonetic spelling,** the writing of a language by means of a separate symbol for every sound: often applied to a compromise, or a departure from conventional spelling more or less adapted as a guide to pronunciation. [Gr. *phōnētikos—phōnē,* voice.]

phoney, phony, *fō'ni, n.* and *adj.* (*U.S. slang*) counterfeit: unreal. [Origin unknown.]

phonocamptic, *fō-nə-kamp'tik, adj.* echoing: relating to echoes.—*n.* (treated as *sing.*) **phonocamp'tics,** the acoustics of echoes. [Gr. *phōnē,* voice, *kamptein,* to bend.]

phonogram, *fō'nə-gram, n.* a character representing a sound: a phonographic record.

phonograph, *fō'nə-grāf, n.* a character used to represent a sound: Edison's instrument for recording sounds on a cylinder and reproducing them: (*U.S.*) the ordinary word for any gramophone.—*ns.* **phonographer** (*fō-nog'rə-fər*), **phonog'raphist,** a writer of phonographic shorthand.—*adj.* **phonographic** (*fō-nə-graf'ik*), phonetic: of phonography: of or by means of the phonograph.—*adv.* **phonograph'ically.**—*n.* **phonog'raphy** (*fō-nog'rə-fi*), the art of representing each spoken sound by a distinct character: Pitman's phonetic shorthand: the use of the phonograph. [Gr. *phōnē,* voice, *graphein,* to write.]

phonolite, *fō'nə-līt, n.* clinkstone, a fine-grained intermediate igneous rock that rings under the hammer, composed of nepheline (or leucite), sanidine, and other minerals.—*adj.* **phonolitic** (*-lit'ik*). [Gr. *phōnē,* voice, sound, *lithos,* stone.]

phonology, *fō-nol'ə-ji, n.* phonetics: now generally the study of the system of sounds in a language and of the history of their changes.—*adj.* **phonolog'ical.**—*n.* **phonol'ogist.** [Gr. *phōnē,* voice, *logos,* discourse.]

phonophore, *fō'nə-fōr, n.* a sound-conducting apparatus, of various kinds: a device for telephoning and telegraphing simultaneously by the same wire (also **pho'nopore**). [Gr. *phōnē,* voice, *phoros,* carrying, *poros,* passage.]

phonotype, *fō'nə-tīp, n.* phonetic type.—*v.t.* to print phonetically.—*adj.* **pho'notypic** (*-tip'ik*), **-al.**—*ns.* **phō'notypist** (or *-tip'ist*); **pho'notypy** (*tip-i*). [Gr. *phōnē,* voice, sound, *typos,* impression.]

phony. See **phoney.**

phorminx, *for'mingks, n.* a kind of cithara. [Gr.]

Phormium, *for'mi-əm, n.* a New Zealand genus of the lily family—New Zealand flax or flax-lily. [Latinised—Gr. *phormion,* mat, faggot, kind of sage.]

phosgene, *fos'jēn, n.* a poisonous gas, carbonyl chloride (COCl₂) prepared from carbon monoxide and chlorine in sunlight. [Gr. *phōs,* light, and the root of *gignesthai,* to be produced.]

phosphene, *fos'fēn, n.* light seen when the eyeball is pressed. [Gr. *phōs,* light, *phainein,* to show.]

Phosphorus, *fos'far-əs, n.* the morning-star: **phosphorus,** a non-metallic element, of atomic number 15, a waxy, poisonous, and inflammable substance giving out light in the dark.—*n.* **phosphate** (*fos'fāt*), a salt of phosphoric acid.—*adj.* **phosphatic** (*fos-fat'ik*), of the nature of, or containing, a phosphate.—*ns.* **phosphaturia** (*fos-fat-ū'ri-ä*), excess of phosphates in the urine; **phos'phide** (*-fīd*), a compound of phosphorus and another element; **phos'phine** (*-fēn, -fīn*), phosphuretted hydrogen gas (PH₃): extended to substances analogous to amines with phosphorus instead of nitrogen; **phos'phite,** a salt of phosphorous acid; **phosphōn'ium,** the radical PH₄, analogous to ammonium; **Phos'phor,** the morning-star: **phosphor,** (*obs.*) phosphorus: a phosphorescent or fluorescent substance generally.—*v.t.* **phos'phorate,** to combine or impregnate with phosphorus: to make phosphorescent.—*n.* **phos'phor-bronze',** an alloy of copper, tin, and phosphorus.—*v.i.* **phosphoresce',** to shine in the dark like phosphorus. —*n.* **phosphoresc'ence.**—*adj.* **phosphoresc'ent.** —*n.* **phos'phoret** (or *-et'*; *obs.*), a phosphide.— *adjs.* **phos'phoretted** (or *-et'*) (see **phosphuretted**); **phosphoric** (*fos-for'ik*), of or like phosphorus: phosphorescent: (*chem.*) containing phosphorus in higher valency (**phosphoric acid,** any of the acids orthophosphoric, H₃PO₄, metaphosphoric, HPO₃, pyrophosphoric acid, H₄P₂O₇; **phosphoric anhydride,** P₂O₅).—*v.t.* **phos'phorise,** to combine or impregnate with phosphorus: to make phosphorescent.—*ns.* **phos'phorism,** (*obs.*) phosphorescence: poisoning by phosphorus; **phos'phorite,** impure massive apatite.—*adj.* **phos'phorous,** phosphorescent: (*chem.*) containing phosphorus in lower valency (**phosphorous acid,** H₃PO₃; **phosphorous anhydride,** P₂O₃).—*n.* **phosphuret** (*fos'-fūr-et* or *-et'*; *obs.*), a phosphide.—*adj.* **phos'phuretted** (or *-et'*), combined with phosphorus (**phosphuretted or phosphoretted hydrogen,** phosphine).—*n.* **phoss'y-jaw,** necrosis of the jawbone with fatty degeneration of the kidney, common among match-makers when yellow phosphorus was used. [L. *phōsphorus*—Gr. *phōsphoros,* light-bearer—*phōs,* light, *phoros,* bearing, from *pherein,* to bear.]

phot, *fot, fōt, n.* a unit of illumination, that of a point source of one standard candle on a surface everywhere one centimetre distant.—*adj.* **photic** (*fōt'ik*), of light.—*n.* (treated as *sing.*) **phot'ics,** the science of light, optics.—*n.* **phot'ism,** a sensation of light accompanying another sensation or thought. [Gr. *phōs, phōtos,* light.]

phot-, *fōt-,* **photo-,** *fō'tō-,* in composition, light: photographic.—*n., v.t., adj.* **pho'to,** a colloquial abbreviation of **photograph, -ic.**—*ns.* **pho'tocell,** a photoelectric cell; **photo-composi'tion,** (*print.*) setting of copy by projecting images of letters successively on a sensitive material; **photo-emiss'ion,** emission of electrons from the surface of a body on which light falls; **photo-engra'ving,** any process of engraving or of etching by the aid of photography; **photo-fin'ish,** a race finish in which a special type of photography is used to show the winner, &c.: a neck and neck finish of any contest.—*adj.* **photo-mechan'ical,** pertaining to mechanical printing from a photographically prepared plate.—*adv.* **photomechan'-ically.** — *ns.* **pho'to-process,** any process by which a matrix for printing is got by photographic means; **photo-recep'tor,** a nerve-ending receiving light-stimuli; **photo-relief',** a plate or image in relief got by photographic means.—*adj.* **photo-sens'itive,** affected by light, visible or invisible. [Gr. *phōs, phōtos,* light.]

photoconductivity, *fō-tō-kon-duk-tiv'i-ti, n.* property of varying conductivity under influence of light.

photoelectricity, *fō-tō-el-ik-tris'i-ti, n.* electricity, or a change of electric condition, produced by light or other electromagnetic radiation.—*adj.* **photoelectric** (*-i-lek'*), pertaining to photoelectricity, to photoelectrons, or to electric light.— *ns.* **photoelec'tron,** an electron ejected from a body by the incidence of ultra-violet rays or X-rays upon it; **photoelectron'ics,** the science dealing with the interactions of electricity and electromagnetic radiations, esp. those that involve free electrons.—**photoelectric cell,** any device in which incidence of light of suitable frequency causes an alteration in electrical state, esp. by photo-emission.

photogen, *fō'tō-jən, n.* a light-producing organ in animals : a light paraffin oil (also **photogene**).— *n.* **pho'togene** (*-jēn*), an after-image : a sensitive emulsion : (*obs.*) a photograph.—*adj.* **photogenic** (*-jen'*), producing light : produced by light : (*obs.*) photographic: having the quality of photographing well: (loosely) attractive, striking.—*n.* **photogeny** (*fō-toj'i-ni*; *obs.*), photography. [Root of Gr. *gignesthai*, to be produced.]

photogeology, *fō-tō-jē-ol'ə-ji, n.* (study of) geology by means of air photographs.

photoglyph, *fō'tō-glif, n.* a photographic engraving : a photogravure.—*adj.* **photoglyph'ic.**—*n.* **photoglyphy** (*fō-tog'li-fi*). [Gr. *glyphē,* carving.]

photography, *fō-tog'rə-fi, n.* the art or process of producing permanent and visible images by the action of light on chemically prepared surfaces.— *n.* **phot'ograph** (*-grāf*), an image so produced.— *v.t.* to make a picture of by means of photography.— *v.i.* to take photographs : to be capable of being photographed.—*n.* **photog'rapher.**—*adjs.* **photographic** (*-graf'ik*), **-al.**—*adv.* **photograph'ically.** —*n.* **photog'raphist.** [Gr. *graphein,* to draw.]

photogravure, *fō-tō-grə-vūr', n.* a method of photoengraving by the action of acids on a sensitised surface: a picture so produced. [Fr. *gravure,* engraving.]

photolithography, *fō-tō-li-thog'rə-fi, n.* a process of lithographic printing from a photograph.—*n.* and *v.t.* **photolith'ograph** (*-o-grāf*).—*n.* **photolithog'rapher.**—*adj.* **photolithographic** (*-graf'ik*).

photolysis, *fō-tol'i-sis, n.* (*chem.*) decomposition or dissociation under the influence of radiation : (*bot.*) the grouping of chloroplasts in relation to illumination.—*adj.* **photolytic** (*fō-tō-lit'ik*). [Gr. *lysis,* loosing—*lyein,* to loose.]

photometer, *fō-tom'i-tər, n.* an instrument for comparing intensity of light.—*adjs.* **photometric** (*fō-tō-met'rik*), **-al.**—*n.* **photom'etry.** [Gr. *metron,* measure.]

photomicrograph, *fō-tō-mī'krō-grāf, n.* an enlarged photograph of a microscopic object taken through a microscope.—*n.* **photomicrographer** (*-krog'rə-fər*).—*adj.* **photomicrographic** (*-krō-graf'ik*).— **photomicrog'raphy.** [Gr. *mikros,* little, *graphein,* to write.]

photon, *fō'ton, n.* a quantum of light. [Gr. *phōs, phōtos,* light.]

photonasty, *fō'tə-nas-ti, n.* (*biol.*) response to the stimulus of changed intensity of light without regard to direction.—*adj.* **photonas'tic.** [Gr. *nastos,* close-pressed.]

photoperiod, *fō-tō-pē'ri-əd, n.* the optimum length of day, as it affects the amount of light received by a plant, for that particular plant's normal growth and development.—*adj.* **photoperiod'ic.** —*n.* **photope'riodism,** the response of a plant to the relative lengths of day and night.

photophil, *fō'tə-fil, adj.* light-loving : turning towards the light.—*n.* an organism that seeks the light.—*adjs.* **photophil'ic, photophilous** (*-tof'*).— *n.* **photoph'ily.** [Gr. *phileein,* to love.]

photophobia, *fō-tō-fō'bi-ä, n.* a shrinking from light. —*n.* and *adj.* **pho'tophobe.**—*adj.* **photophobic** (*-fob'ik*). [Gr. *phobos,* fear.]

photophone, *fō'tō-fōn, n.* an apparatus for transmitting articulate speech to a distance along a beam of light.—*adj.* **photophonic** (*-fon'ik*).—*n.* **photophony** (*-tof'ə-ni*). [Gr. *phōnē,* voice.]

photophore, *fō'tō-fōr, n.* (*zool.*) a luminiferous organ. [Gr. *phoros,* bearing.]

photophoresis, *fō-tō-for-ē'sis, n.* migration of suspended particles under the influence of light. [Gr. *phorēsis,* transference.]

photopsia, *fōt-op'si-ä,* **photopsy,** *-si, n.* the appearance of flashes of light, owing to irritation of the retina. [Gr. *opsis,* appearance.]

photosphere, *fō'tō-sfēr, n.* the luminous envelope of the sun's globe, the source of light.—*adj.* **photospheric** (*-sfer'ik*). [Gr. *sphaira,* a sphere.]

Photostat, *fō'tō-stat, n.* a photographic apparatus for making facsimiles of MSS., drawings, &c., directly : a facsimile so made.—*v.t.* and *v.i.* to photograph by Photostat. [Gr. *statos,* set, placed ; trade-mark.]

photosynthesis, *fō-tō-sin'thi-sis, n.* (*bot.*) the building up of complex compounds by the chlorophyll apparatus of plants by means of the energy of light.—*adj.* **photosynthet'ic.**

phototaxis, *fō-tō-taks'is, n.* (*biol.*) a change of place under stimulus of light.—*adj.* **phototac'tic.** [Gr. *taxis,* arrangement.]

phototelegraph, *fō-tō-tel'i-grāf, n.* an instrument for transmitting drawings, photographs, &c., by telegraphy.

phototherapy, *fō-tō-ther'ə-pi,* **phototherapeutics,** *-pū'tiks, ns.* treatment of disease by light.—*adj.* **phototherapeut'ic.** [Gr. *therapeuein,* to tend.]

phototropism, *fōt-ot'rəp-izm, n.* (*bot.*) orientation in response to the stimulus of light : (*chem.*) reversible colour change on exposure to light.—*n.* **phototrope** (*fō'tō-trōp*), a substance that changes thus.—*adj.* **phototropic** (*fō-tō-trop'ik*).—*n.* **phototot'ropy,** change of colour due to wavelength of incident light. [Gr. *tropos,* turning.]

phototype, *fō'tō-tīp, n.* a printing block produced photographically.—*v.t.* to reproduce by phototype.—*adj.* **phototypic** (*-tip'ik*).—*n.* **phototypy** (*fō'tō-tī-pi* or *fō-tot'i-pi*). [Gr. *typos,* impression.]

photo-xylography, *fō-tō-zī-log'rə-fi, n.* woodengraving after a photographic impression on a wood-block. [Gr. *xylon,* wood, *graphein,* to write.]

photozincography, *fō-tō-zing-kog'rə-fi, n.* the process of engraving on zinc by taking an impression by photography and etching with acids.—*n.* **photozinc'ograph,** a picture so produced.

phrase, *frāz, n.* manner of expression in language : an expression : a group of words (sometimes as in *Shak.* a single word) generally not forming a clause but felt as expressing a single idea or constituting a single element in the sentence : a pithy expression : a catchword : an empty or high-sounding expression : (*Scot.*) fussy talk about one's feelings : (*mus.*) a short group of notes felt to form a unit.—*v.t.* to express in words : to style : (*Scot.*) to flatter, wheedle : (*mus.*) to mark, bring out, or give effect to the phrases of.—*n.* **phrase'-book,** a book containing or explaining phrases of a language.—*adj.* **phrase'less,** incapable of being described.—*ns.* **phrase'-man, phrase'-monger,** a user or maker of wordy or fine-sounding phrases ; **phraseogram** (*frā'zi-ō-gram*), a single sign, written without lifting the pen, for a whole phrase (esp. in shorthand) ; **phra'seograph,** a phrase that is so written. — *adjs.* **phraseolog'ic, -al.** — *adv.* **phraseolog'ically.**—*ns.* **phraseol'ogist,** a maker or a collector of phrases ; **phraseol'ogy,** style or manner of expression or arrangement of phrases : peculiarities of diction : a collection of phrases in a language ; **phra'ser,** a mere maker or repeater of empty phrases ; **phra'sing,** the wording of a speech or passage : (*mus.*) the grouping and accentuation of the sounds in performing a melody. —*adj.* **phra'sy,** inclining to emptiness and verbosity of phrase. [Gr. *phrasis—phrazein,* to speak.]

phratry, *frā'tri, n.* a social division of a people, often exogamous. [Gr. *phratriā* ; cf. L. *frāter,* Eng. **brother.**]

phrenesiac, *fri-nē'zi-ak, adj.* (*Scot.*) hypochondriac. —*n.* **phrenesis** (*fri-nē'sis*), phrenitis : delirium : frenzy.—*adj.* and *n.* **phrenetic, frenetic** (*fri-net'ik* ; formerly *fren'*), delirious : frantic : frenzied : mad : distracted.—*n.* ᴣ madman.—*adj.* **phrenet'ical, frenet'ical.**—*adv.* **phrenet'ically, frenet'ically.**—*adjs.* **phrenic** (*fren'ik*), of or near the midriff : (*obs.*) mental ; **phrenit'ic,** of or affected with phrenitis.—*n.* **phreni′tis,** inflammation of the brain: brain-fever.—*adjs.* **phrenolog′ic** (*fren-*), **-al.**—*adv.* **phrenolog′ically.**—*v.t.* **phrenol′ogise,** to examine phrenologically.—*ns.* **phrenol′ogist;** **phrenol′ogy,** a would-be science of mental faculties supposed to be located in various parts of the skull and investigable by feeling the bumps on the outside of the head.—**phrensical, phrensy, phrentick,** old forms of **frenzical, frenzy, frantic** (or **phrenetic**). [Gr. *phrēn, phrenos,* midriff, supposed seat of passions, mind, will.]

phrontistery, *fron′tis-tə-ri, n.* a thinking-place. [Gr. *phrontistērion—phrontistēs,* a thinker—*phron-eein,* to think; applied by Aristophanes to the school of Socrates.]

Phrygian, *frij′i-ən, adj.* pertaining to *Phrygia* in Asia Minor, or to its people.—*n.* a native of Phrygia: a Montanist: the language of the ancient Phrygians.—**Phrygian cap,** a conical cap with the top turned forward; **Phrygian mode,** in ancient Greek music, a mode of two tetrachords with a semitone in the middle of each and a whole tone between the tetrachords (as: *d e f g; a b c d*; but reckoned downwards by the Greeks): in old Church music, an authentic mode extending from *e* to *e,* with *e* as its final.

phthalic, (*f*)*thal′ik, adj.* applied to three acids, $C_6H_4(COOH)_2$, and an anhydride, derived from naphthalene.—*ns.* **phthal′ein** (*-i-in*), any one of a very important class of dye-yielding materials formed by the union of phenols with phthalic anhydride; **phthal′in,** a colourless crystalline compound obtained by reducing a phthalein. [naphthalene.]

phthiriasis, (*f*)*thī-rī′ə-sis, n.* infestation with lice. [Gr. *phtheiriāsis—phtheir,* a louse.]

phthisis, *thī′sis,* also *fthī′, tī′, n.* wasting disease: tuberculosis, esp. of the lungs.—*n.* **phthisic** (*tiz′ik,* sometimes *thī′sik, fthī′sik, tī′sik*), phthisis: vaguely, a lung or throat disease.—*adjs.* **phthisical** (*tiz′*), **phthis′icky.** [Gr. *phthisis—phthi(n)ein,* to waste away.]

phut, *fut, adv.* to grief, ruin, or collapse. [Hind. *phatnā,* to go.]

pH (-value) (*p* and H may also be written in various other styles), *pē-āch* (*val′ū*), *n.* a number used to express very small degrees of acidity or alkalinity in solutions—the logarithm to the base 10 of the reciprocal of the concentration of hydrogen ions in the solution.

phyco-, *fī-kō-,* in composition, seaweed.—*ns.* **phyco-cyan, phycocyanin** (*-sī′an, -ə-nin*; Gr. *kyaneos,* dark blue), a blue pigment in algae; **phyco-erythrin** (*-e-rith′rin*; Gr. *erythros,* red), a red pigment in algae.—*adj.* **phycolog′ical.**—*ns.* **phy-cologist** (*-kol′ə-jist*); **phycol′ogy,** the study of algae. — *n.pl.* **Phycomycetes** (*-mī-sē′tēz*; Gr. *mȳkētēs,* pl. of *mȳkēs,* a fungus), a class of fungi showing affinities with the green seaweeds.—*ns.* **phycophaein** (*-fē′in*; Gr. *phaios,* grey), a brown pigment in seaweeds; **phycoxan′thin** (Gr. *xanthos,* yellow), a yellow pigment in diatoms, brown sea-weeds, &c. [Gr. *phȳkos,* seaweed.]

phylactery, *fi-lak′tə-ri, n.* a charm or amulet: among the Jews, a slip of parchment inscribed with certain passages of Scripture, worn in a box on the left arm or forehead: a reminder: osten-tatious display of religious forms: a case for relics: in mediaeval art, a scroll at the mouth of a figure in a picture bearing the words he is sup-posed to speak.—*adjs.* **phylacteric** (*-ter′ik*), **-al.** [Gr. *phylaktērion—phylax,* a guard.]

phyle, *fī′lē, n.* a tribe or division of the people of a state in ancient Greece, at first on a kinship, later on a local, basis.—*ns.* **phylarch** (*fī′lärk*), the chief officer of a tribe: in Athens, the commander of the cavalry of a tribe; **phy′larchy,** the office of phylarch. [Gr. *phȳlē.*]

phyletic, *fī-let′ik, adj.* pertaining to a phylum: according to descent. [Gr. *phȳletikos—phȳlē.*]

phyllary, *fil′ə-ri, n.* an involucral bract. [Gr. *phyllarion,* dim. of *phyllon,* leaf.]

phyllite, *fil′īt, n.* a rock intermediate between clay-slate and mica-schist. [Gr. *phyllon,* a leaf.]

phylloclade, *fil′ō-klād, n.* a branch with the form

and functions of a leaf. [Gr. *phyllon,* leaf, *klados,* shoot.]

phyllode, *fil′ōd, n.* a petiole with the appearance and function of a leaf-blade.—*n.* **phyll′ody** (*-ō-di*), transformation of flower parts into leaves.—*adj.* **phyll′oid,** leaf-like. [Gr. *phyllon,* leaf, *eidos,* form.]

phyllomania, *fil-ō-mā′ni-ä, n.* abnormally excessive production of leaves. [Gr. *phyllon,* leaf, *maniā,* madness.]

phyllome, *fil′ōm, n.* any leaf or homologue of a leaf. [Gr. *phyllōma,* foliage.]

phyllophagous, *fi-lof′ə-gəs, adj.* leaf-eating. [Gr. *phyllon,* leaf, *phagein,* to eat.]

phyllopod, *fil′ō-pod, n.* a crustacean of the order **Phyllopoda** (*-op′ə-dä*), entomostraca with folia-ceous legs. [Gr. *phyllon,* leaf, *pous, podos,* foot.]

phylloquinone, *fil-ō-kwin′ōn,* or *-ōn′, n.* vitamin K_1. [Gr. *phyllon,* leaf, and **quinone.**]

phyllotaxis, *fil-ō-tak′sis, n.* the disposition of leaves on the stem.—Also **phyll′otaxy.**—*adjs.* **phyllo-tact′ic, -al.** [Gr. *phyllon,* a leaf, *taxis,* arrange-ment.]

Phylloxera, *fil-ok-sē′rä, n.* a genus of insects of a family akin to green-fly, very destructive to vines. [Gr. *phyllon,* a leaf, *xēros,* dry.]

phylogeny, *fī-loj′i-ni, n.* evolutionary pedigree or genealogical history—also **phylogenesis** (*fī-lō-jen′i-sis*).—*adj.* **phylogenet′ic.**—*adv.* **phylogenet′-ically.** [Gr. *phȳlon,* race, *genesis,* origin.]

phylum, *fī′ləm, n.* a main division of the animal or the vegetable kingdom:—*pl.* **phy′la.** [Gr. *phȳlon,* race.]

Physalia, *fī-sā′li-ä, n.* a genus of large oceanic colonial hydrozoa with a floating bladder—*Portu-guese man-of-war.*—*ns.* **Physalis** (*fis′* or *fīs′ə-lis*), the Cape gooseberry genus of Solanaceae, with persistent bladdery calyx; **Physeter** (*fī-sē′ter*), a sperm whale. [Gr. *phȳsallis,* a bladder, *phȳsētēr,* a blower, a whale, bellows—*phȳsaein,* to blow.]

physharmonica, *fis-här-mon′i-kä, n.* an early form of harmonium. [Gr. *phȳsa,* bellows, and **har-monica.**]

physic, *fiz′ik, n.* (*orig.*) natural philosophy, physics: the science, art, or practice of medicine: a medi-cine: anything healing or wholesome.—*adj.* (*obs.*) physical, natural: (*obs.*) medicinal.—*v.t.* to give medicine to: to heal:—*pr.p.* **phys′icking;** *pa.t.* and *pa.p.* **phys′icked.**—*adj.* **phys′ical,** pertaining to the world of matter and energy, or its study, natural philosophy: material: (*obs.*) materialistic: bodily: (*rare*) medical: (*obs.*) medicinal: (*Shak.*) wholesome. — *adv.* **phys′ically.** — *ns.* **physician** (*fi-zish′n*), one skilled in the use of physic or the art of healing: one legally qualified to practise medicine: one who makes use of medicines and treatment, distinguished from a surgeon who practises manual operations: a doctor: (*fig.*) a healer or healing influence; **physic′iancy,** post or office of physician; **physic′ianer,** (*rare*) a physician; **physic′ianship; phys′icism** (*-sizm*), belief in the material or physical as opposed to the spiritual; **phys′icist** (*-sist*), a student of nature: one versed in physics, a natural philosopher: one who believes the phenomena of life are purely physical. — *adj.* **phys′icky,** like medicine. — *n.* **phys′ic-nut,** the purgative seed of the tropical American *Jatropha Curcas,* a tree of the spurge family.—*n.* (treated as *sing.*) **phys′ics,** (*orig.*) natural science in general: (*now*) natural philosophy, the science of the properties (other than chemical) of matter and energy.—**physical astronomy,** the study of the physical condition and chemical composition of the heavenly bodies; **physical chemistry,** the study of the dependence of physical properties on chemical composition, and of the physical changes accompanying chemical reactions; **physical force,** force applied out-wardly to the body, as distinguished from per-suasion, &c.; **physical geography,** the study of the earth's natural features—its mountain-chains, ocean-currents, &c.; **physic garden,** (*orig.*) a garden of medicinal plants: a botanic garden. [Gr. *physikos,* natural—*physis,* nature.]

physiocracy, *fiz-i-ok′rə-si, n.* government, according to François Quesnay (1694-1774) and his followers, by a natural order inherent in society, land and its products the only true source of wealth, direct taxation of land the only proper source of revenue.—*n.* **phys′iocrat** (*-ō-krat*), one who maintains these opinions.—*adj.* **physiocrat′ic.** [Gr. *physis*, nature, *krateein*, to rule.]

physiognomy, *fiz-i-og′nə-mi* or *-on′ə-mi*, *n.* the art of judging character from appearance, esp. from the face: the face as an index of the mind: (*vulg.*) the face: the general appearance of anything: character, aspect.—*adjs.* **physiognomic** (*-nom′*), **-al.**—*adv.* **physiognom′ically.**—*n.* **physiog′-nomist.** [Gr. *physiognōmiā*, a shortened form of *physiognōmoniā—physis*, nature, *gnōmōn, -onos*, an interpreter.]

physiography, *fiz-i-og′rə-fi*, *n.* description of nature, descriptive science: physical geography.—*n.* **physiog′rapher.**—*adjs.* **physiographic** (*-ō-graf′ik*), **-al.** [Gr. *physis*, nature, *graphein*, to describe.]

physiolatry, *fiz-i-ol′ə-tri*, *n.* nature-worship.—*n.* **physiol′ater**, a nature-worshipper. [Gr. *physis*, nature, *latreiā*, worship.]

physiology, *fiz-i-ol′ə-ji*, *n.* the science of the processes of life in animals and plants.—*adjs.* **physiologic** (*-ə-loj′ik*), **-al.**—*adv.* **physiolog′ically.**—*ns.* **physiol′ogist**; **physiol′ogus**, a bestiary. [Gr. *physis*, nature, *logos*, discourse.]

physiotherapy, *fiz-i-ō-ther′ə-pi*, *n.* treatment of disease by natural remedies, as massage, fresh air, electricity.—Also **physiotherapeutics** (*-pūt′iks*).—*adj.* **physiotherapeut′ic.**—*n.* **physiother′apist.** [Gr. *therapeiā*, treatment.]

physique, *fiz-ēk′*, *n.* bodily type, build, or constitution. [Fr.]

physitheism, *fiz′i-thē-izm*, *n.* the ascription of physical form and attributes to deity: deification of powers of nature.—*adj.* **physitheis′tic.** [Gr. *physis*, nature, *theos*, god.]

phyto-, *fī′tō-*, in composition, plant.—*ns.* **phyto-benthos** (*-ben′thos*; Gr. *benthos*, depth), plants living at the bottom of water collectively; **phyto-gen′esis, phytogeny** (*-toj′i-ni*), evolution of plants.—*adjs.* **phytogenet′ic, -al**, relating to phyto-genesis; **phytogenic** (*-jen′ik*), of vegetable origin.—*n.* **phytogeog′rapher.**—*adj.* **phytogeograph′ic.**—*ns.* **phytogeog′raphy**, the geography of plant distribution; **phytog′rapher**, a descriptive botanist.—*adj.* **phytograph′ic.**—*ns.* **phytog′raphy**, descriptive botany; **Phytolacc′a** (see lac), the pokeweed genus, giving name to the family **Phyto-lacc′aceae**, allied to the pinks and the goosefoots.—*adj.* **phytolog′ical.**—*ns.* **phytol′ogist**, a botanist; **phytol′ogy**, botany.—*adj.* **phytopatholog′-ical.**—*ns.* **phytopathol′ogist; phytopathology** (Gr. *pathos*, suffering), the study of plant diseases.—*adjs.* **phytophagic** (*-faj′ik*), **phytophagous** (*-tof′ə-gəs*; Gr. *phagein*, to eat), plant-eating.—*ns.* **phytoplank′ton** (Gr. *plankton*, wandering), vegetable plankton; **phyto′sis**, presence of vegetable parasites or disease caused by them; **phytosterol** (*-tos′tə-rol*; formed on the model of *cholesterol*), a substance very like cholesterol got from plants; **phytot′omist; phytotomy** (*-tot′ə-mi*; Gr. *tomē*, a cut), plant anatomy. [Gr. *phyton*, plant.]

pi, *pī, pē, n.* the sixteenth letter (Π, π) of the Greek alphabet, answering to the Roman P: as a numeral π′ stands for 80, ⫫π for 80,000: (*math.*) a symbol for the ratio of the circumference of a circle to the diameter, approx. 3·14159. [Gr. *pei, pī.*]

pi (*print.*). Same as **pie.**

pi, *pī, adj.* (*slang*) an abbreviation of **pious**: religious: sanctimonious.—*n.* a pious, religious, or sanctimonious person or talk.—*n.* **pi′-jaw**, an admonition.

pia, *pē′ä, n.* a tropical monocotyledonous plant (Tacca: fam. Taccaceae) with a rhizome yielding E. India or Madagascar arrowroot. [Polynesian name.]

piacevole, *pyä-chā′vo-lā, adj.* (*mus.*) pleasant, playful. [It.]

piacular, *pī-ak′ū-lər, adj.* expiatory: requiring expiation: atrociously bad.—*n.* **piacularity** (*-lar′-i-ti*). [L. *piāculum*, sacrifice—*piāre*, to expiate—*pius*, pious.]

piaffe, *pi-af′, pyaf, v.i.* in horsemanship, to advance at a piaffer.—*n.* **piaff′er**, a gait in which the feet are lifted in the same succession as a trot, but more slowly.—Also *Spanish-twalk.* [Fr. *piaffer.*]

pia mater, *pī′ä mā′tər, n.* the vascular membrane investing the brain: (*Shak.*) the brain. [L. *pia māter*, tender mother, a mediaeval translation of Ar. *umm raqīqah*, thin mother.]

pianoforte, *pyä′nō-for-ti*, or *pē-ä′, generally shortened to* **piano** (*pyä′nō, pē-ä′nō*), *n.* a musical instrument with wires struck by hammers moved by keys:—*pl.* **pia′nofortes, pian′os.**—*ns.* **pia-nette** (*pē-ə-net′*), a small upright piano; **pianino** (*pyä-nē′nō, pē-ä-nē′nō*), (*orig.*) an upright piano: a small upright piano; **pi′anism**, the technique of the pianoforte.—*adj.* and *adv.* **pianissimo** (*pyä-nēs′si-mō, pē-ä-nis′i-mō*), very soft.—*n.* **pianist** (*pē′ə-nist*; also *pyan′, pē-an′ist*), one who plays the pianoforte, esp. expertly—also (Fr.) **pianiste** (*pē-ä-nēst′*), sometimes used as *fem.*—*adj.* **pianist′-ic.**—*adj.* and *adv.* **piano** (*pyä′nō, pē-ä′nō*), soft, softly.—*n.* a soft passage.—*ns.* **pia′no-accord′ion**, an elaborate accordion with a keyboard like a piano; **Pianola** (*pē-ə-nō′lä, pyan-*), a pneumatic contrivance for playing the piano by means of a perforated roll (registered trade-name); **pia′no-or′gan**, a piano like a barrel-organ, played by mechanical means; **pian′o-play′er**, a mechanical contrivance for playing the piano: a pianist; **pian′o-school′**, a school where piano-playing is taught: a method or book of instruction for the piano; **pian′o-stool**, a stool usually adjustable in height for a pianist; **pian′o-wire**, wire used for piano strings, and for deep-sea soundings, &c.—**player piano**, a piano with a piano-player. [It.—*piano*, soft—L. *plānus*, level, and *forte*, loud—L. *fortis*, strong.]

piarist, *pī′ə-rist, n.* one of a religious congregation for the education of the poor, founded in Rome in 1597 by Joseph Calasanza. [L. *patrēs scholārum piārum*, fathers of pious schools.]

piassava, *pē-äs-ä′vä*, **piassaba, -bä**, *n.* a coarse stiff fibre used for making brooms, &c., got from Brazilian palms, Attalea (coquilla) and Leopoldinia (chiquichiqui): the tree yielding it. [Port. from Tupí.]

piastre, *pi-as′tər, n.* a silver coin of varying value, used in Turkey (100 piastres = £T1) and elsewhere: the Spanish dollar. [Fr.,—It. *piastra*, a leaf of metal; see **plaster.**]

piazza, *pē-ät′sä*, also *pē-ad′zä, pē-az′ä, n.* a place or square surrounded by buildings: (erroneously) a walk under a roof supported by pillars: (*U.S.*) a veranda.—*adj.* **piazz′ian.** [It.,—L. *platea*—Gr. *plateia*, a street (fem. of *platys*, broad).]

pibroch, *pē′brohh, n.* a form of bagpipe music, variations on a theme. [Gael. *piobaireachd*, pipe-music—*piobair*, a piper—*piob*, from Eng. **pipe.**]

pica, *pī′kä, n.* a size of type, 12-point, giving about 6 lines to the inch: (**small pica**, 11-point). [Possibly used for printing *pies*; see **pie** (2).]

Pica, *pī′kä, n.* the magpie genus: **pica**, a craving for unsuitable food. [L. *pīca*, magpie.]

picador, *pik-ə-dōr′, n.* a mounted bull-fighter with a lance. [Sp.,—*pica*, a pike.]

picamar, *pik′ə-mär, n.* a bitter oily liquid got from tar. [L. *pix, picis*, pitch, *amārus*, bitter.]

picarian, *pik-ā′ri-ən, adj.* belonging to an obsolete order (**Pica′riae**) of birds including the wood-peckers.—*n.* any member of the order. [L. *pīcus*, woodpecker.]

picaroon, *pik-ə-rōōn′, n.* one who lives by his wits: a cheat: a pirate.—*adj.* **picaresque** (*-resk′*).—**picaresque novels**, the tales of Spanish rogue and vagabond life, much in vogue in the 17th century: novels of like type. [Sp. *picarón*, augmentative of *picaro*, rogue.]

picayune, *pik-ə-ūn′, n.* a small coin worth 6¼ cents, current in United States before 1857: a five-cent piece, or other small coin: anything of little or no value.—*adj.* petty.—*adj.* **picayun′ish.** [Prov. *picaioun*, an old Piedmontese copper coin.]

piccadill, *pik′ə-dil*, **pikadell, -del, piccadillo, -dil′ō**, **piccadilly, -i**, *n.* (*obs.*) a cut or vandyked edging, esp. to a woman's collar: a wide high collar of the early 17th century: a stiff support for a collar or ruff: (in the form **piccadilly**) a man's standing-up collar with the points turned over, first worn about 1870. [Cf. Sp. *picadillo*, a kind of hash.]

piccalilli, *pik'ə-lil-i*, *n.* a pickle of various vegetable substances with mustard and spices. [Ety. dub.]

piccaninny, pickaninny, *pik'ə-nin-i*, *n.* a little child: a negro child.—*adj.* very little. [Port. *pequenino*, dim. of *pequeno*, little, or possibly Sp. *pequeño niño*, little child.]

piccolo, *pik'ə-lō*, *n.* a small flute, an octave higher than the ordinary flute: an organ stop of similar tone:—*pl.* **picc'olos**. [It., little.]

pice, *pīs*, *n.sing.* and *pl.* a money of account and a copper coin, ¼ anna. [Hind. *paisā*.]

Picea, *pis'i-ä*, *pīs'i-ä*, *n.* the spruce genus of conifers. [L. *picea*, pitch-pine—*pix*, pitch.]

piceous, *pis'i-əs*, *pish'(i-)əs*, *adj.* like pitch: inflammable: black: reddish black.—*n.* **picene** (*pī'sēn*), a hydrocarbon (C₂₂H₁₄) got from tar. [L. *piceus—pix*, pitch.]

pichiciago, *pich-i-si-ä'gō*, or *-ä'gō*, *n.* a small burrowing South American armadillo. [Amer. Indian.]

pichurim, *pich'oo-rim*, *n.* a South American tree (*Nectandra puchury*) of the laurel family: its aromatic kernel (also **pichurim bean**). [Port. *pichurim*—Tupí *puchury*.]

picine. See Picus.

pick, *pik*, *n.* a tool for breaking ground, rock, &c., with head pointed at one end or both, and handle fitted to the middle: a pointed hammer: an instrument of various kinds for picking: an act, opportunity, or right of choice: a portion picked: the best or choicest: dirt on a printing type: (*Northern dial.*) a diamond in cards, also a spade.—*v.t.* to break up, dress, or remove with a pick: to make with a pick or by plucking: to poke or pluck at, as with a sharp instrument or the nails: to clear, to remove, or to gather, by single small acts: to detach, extract, or take separately and lift or remove: to pluck: to pull apart: to cull: to select, esp. one by one or bit by bit: to peck, bite, or nibble: to eat in small quantities or delicately: to open (as a lock) by a sharp instrument or other unapproved means: to rifle by stealth: to seek and find a pretext for (as a quarrel): (*U.S.*) to tidy up.—*v.i.* to use a pick: to eat by morsels: to pilfer.—*n.* **pick'-cheese**, the blue or the great titmouse: the fruit of the mallow.—*adj.* **picked** (*pikt*), selected, hence the choicest or best: (*Shak.*) exquisite, refined, punctilious: having spines or prickles, sharp-pointed.—*ns.* **pick'edness; pick'er**, one who picks or gathers up: a tool or machine for picking: one who removes defects from and finishes electrotype plates: a pilferer; **pick'ery**, (*Scots law*) pilfering; **pick'ing**, the action of the verb to pick: the quantity picked: that which is left to be picked: dabbing in stoneworking: the final finishing of woven fabrics by removing burs, &c.: removing defects from electrotype plates: (in *pl.*) odd gains or perquisites; **pick'lock**, an instrument for picking or opening locks; **pick'-me-up**, a stimulating drink; **pick'-pocket**, one who picks or steals from other people's pockets; **pick'-purse**, one who steals the purse or from the purse of another; **pick'-thank**, one who seeks to ingratiate himself by officious favours, or by tale-bearing; **pick'-tooth**, a toothpick; **pick'-up**, an act of picking up: reception: a recovery: a thing or person picked up: accelerating power: a device for picking up an electric current: a device enabling gramophone records to be reproduced electrically through a radio loudspeaker: a game, or a team, for which the captains pick their men alternately.—*adj.* for picking up: picked up.—**pick a hole in one's coat**, to find fault with one; **pick at**, to find fault with; **pick oakum**, to make oakum by untwisting old ropes; **pick off**, to select from a number and shoot: to detach and remove; **pick on**, (*U.S.*) to single out, esp. for anything unpleasant: to nag at: to carp at; **pick one's way**, to choose carefully where to put one's feet, as on dirty ground; **pick out**, to make out, distinguish: to pluck out: to select from a number: to mark with spots of colour,

&c.; **pick over**, to go over and select; **pick to pieces**, to pull asunder: to criticise adversely in detail; **pick up**, to lift from the ground, floor, &c.: to improve gradually: to gain strength bit by bit: to take into a vehicle, or into one's company: to scrape acquaintance informally with: to acquire as occasion offers: to gain: to come upon, make out, distinguish (as a signal, a track, a comet, &c.). [Ety. obscure; cf. peck, pike, pitch.]

pick, *pik*, a Northern form of **pitch** (1): also of **pitch** (2), esp. *v.i.* to throw the shuttle across the loom, and *n.* a throw of the shuttle, or a weft thread: also a form of **pique**.

pickaback, *pik'ə-bak*, *adv.* and *adj.* on the back like a pack.—*n.* a ride on one's back.—Also **pick'back**, **pick'apack**. [Connexion with pick (pitch), **pack**, and **back** obscure.]

pickaxe, *pik'aks*, *n.* a picking tool, with a point at one end of the head and a cutting blade at the other, used in digging. [M.E. *pikois*—O.Fr. *picois*, a mattock, *piquer*, to pierce, *pic*, a pick.]

pickeer, *pi-kēr'*, *v.i.* (*obs.*) to forage: to skirmish: to scout: (*obs.*) to flirt.—*n.* **pickeer'er**. [Ety. dub.]

pickelhaube, *pik-l-how'bə*, *n.* a German spiked helmet. [Ger.]

pickerel, *pik'ər-əl*, *n.* a young pike: (*U.S.*) a pike, esp. of smaller species.—*n.* **pick'erel-weed**, pondweed: (*U.S.*) Pontederia. [pike.]

picket, *pik'it*, *n.* a pointed stake or peg driven into the ground for fortification, tethering, military punishment, surveying, or other purpose: a surveyor's mark: a small outpost, patrol, or body of men set apart for some special duty: picketduty: a person or group set to watch and dissuade those who go to work during a strike: the old military punishment of standing on one foot on a pointed stake.—*v.t.* to tether to a stake: to strengthen or surround with pickets: to peg down: to subject to the picket: to post as a picket: to deal with as a picket or by means of pickets: to place pickets at or near.—*v.i.* to act as picket:—*pr.p.* **pick'eting**; *pa.t.* and *pa.p.* **pick'eted**.—Also **piquet, picquet**.—*ns.* **pick'etduty; pick'eter**, one who pickets in a labour dispute; **pick'et-fence**, (*U.S.*) a fence of pales; **pick'et-guard**, a guard kept in readiness in case of alarm. [Fr. *piquet*, dim. of *pic*, a pickaxe.]

pickle, *pik'l*, *n.* a liquid, esp. brine or vinegar, in which food is preserved: an article of food preserved in such liquid: (*pl.*) preserved onions, cucumber, &c., as a condiment: acid or other liquid used for cleansing or treatment in manufacture: a plight: (*coll.*) a troublesome child.—*v.t.* to preserve with salt, vinegar, &c.: to rub with salt or salt and vinegar, as an old naval punishment: to clean or treat with acid or other chemical.—*adj.* **pick'led**, treated with a pickle: (*slang*) drunk.—*ns.* **pick'le-herring**, a pickled herring: (*obs.*) a merry-andrew; **pick'ler**, one who pickles: a vessel for pickling: an article suitable, or grown, for pickling.—**have a rod in pickle**, to have a punishment ready. [M.E. *pekille, pykyl, pekkyll, pykulle*; cf. Du. *pekel*; Ger. *pökel*.]

pickle, *pik'l*, *n.* (*Scot.*) a small quantity: a grain of corn. [Origin unknown.]

pickle, *pik'l*, *v.t.* and *v.i.* to peck: to pick: to eat sparingly: to pilfer. [Dim. or freq. of **pick**.]

pickmaw, *pik'maw*, *n.* (*Scot.*) the black-headed gull. [Perh. pick (pitch), **maw** (mew).]

Pickwickian, *pik-wik'i-ən*, *adj.* relating to or resembling Mr *Pickwick*, the hero of Dickens's *Pickwick Papers.*—*n.* a member of the Pickwick Club.—**in a Pickwickian sense**, in a recondite or merely imaginary sense—a phrase by which a member of the Pickwick Club explained away unparliamentary language.

picnic, *pik'nik*, *n.* (*orig.*) a fashionable social entertainment, towards which each person contributed a share of the food: an open-air repast of a number of persons on a country excursion: an undertaking that is mere child's play, often ironically.—*adj.* of or for a picnic: picnicking.—*v.i.* to have a picnic—*pr.p.* **pic'nicking**; *pa.t.* and *pa.p.* **pic'nicked**.—*n.* **pic'nicker**.—*adj.* **pic'nicky**. [Fr. *piquenique*.]

picot, *pē-kō′*, *n.* a loop in an ornamental edging : a raised knot in embroidery.—*v.t.* to ornament with picots.—*adj.* **picoté** (*pē-kō-tā*). [Fr. *picot*, point, prick.]

picotee, *pik-ə-tē′*, *n.* a florists' variety of carnation, orig. speckled, now edged with a different colour. [Fr. *picoté*, pricked.]

picotite, *pik′ō-tīt*, *n.* a dark spinel containing iron, magnesium, and chromium. [From *Picot*, Baron de la Pérouse, who described it.]

picquet. See **picket, piquet.**

picra, *pik′rä*, *n.* short for hiera-picra.—*n.* **pic′rate**, a salt (highly explosive) of picric acid.—*adj.* **pic′ric** (**picric acid**, $C_6H_2(NO_2)_3 \cdot OH$, trinitrophenol, used as a yellow dye-stuff and as the basis of high explosives).—*ns.* **pic′rite**, a coarse-grained igneous rock composed mainly of olivine with ferro-magnesian minerals and usually some plagioclase ; **picrocar′mine**, a stain for microscope work made from carmine, ammonia, water, and picric acid ; **picrotox′in**, a bitter poisonous principle in the seeds of *Cocculus indicus*. [Gr. *pikros*, bitter.]

Pict, *pikt*, *n.* one of an ancient people of obscure affinities, in Britain, esp. north-eastern Scotland : in Scottish folklore, one of a dwarfish race of underground dwellers, to whom (with the Romans, the Druids, and Cromwell) ancient monuments are generally attributed : Steele's term for a painted woman.—*adj.* **Pict′ish.**—*n.* the (enigmatical) language of the Picts.—**Picts' house**, an earth-house. [L. *Pictī*, Picts ; possibly the same as *pictī*, pa.p. of *pingĕre*, to paint ; cf. **Pecht**.]

pictarnie, *pik-tär′ni*, *n.* (*Scott*) a tern. [Origin unknown.]

pictograph, *pik′tə-gräf*, *n.* a picture used as a symbol in picture-writing.—*n.* **pic′togram**, a pictograph : a graphic representation.—*adj.* **pictographic** (*-graf′ik*).—*adv.* **pictograph′ically.**—*n.* **pictography** (*pik-tog′rə-fi*), picture-writing. [L. *pictus*, painted—Gr. *graphein*, to write, *gramma*, a letter, figure.]

pictorial, *pik-tō′ri-əl*, *adj.* of a painter : of or relating to painting or drawing : of, by means of, like, or of the nature of a picture, or pictures.—*n.* a periodical in which pictures are prominent.—*adv.* **picto′rially.**—*adj.* **pictorical** (*-tor′i-kl*).—*adv.* **pictor′ically**, in the manner of a painter. [L. *pictor*, *-ōris*, painter—*pingĕre*, *pictum*, to paint.]

picture, *pik′tyər*, *n.* the art or act of painting : an imitative representation of an object on a surface : a portrait : a tableau : a visible or visual image : a person resembling another as closely as his portrait : an impressive sight, like a painting or worthy of being painted : a visible embodiment : a vivid verbal description : a cinematograph film : (in *pl.*) a cinematograph show, or the building in which it is given.—*v.t.* to depict, represent in a picture : to form a likeness of in the mind : to describe vividly in words.—*adj.* **pic′tural**, relating to, illustrated by, or consisting of pictures.—*ns.* **pic′tural**, (*Spens.*) a picture ; **pic′ture-book**, a book of pictures ; **pic′ture-card**, a court card ; **pic′ture-cord**, cord for hanging pictures ; **pic′ture-frame**, a frame for surrounding a picture ; **pic′ture-gallery**, a gallery, hall, or building where pictures are exhibited ; **pic′ture-goer**, one who goes much to the cinematograph ; **pic′ture-hat**, a lady's wide-brimmed hat, such as Gainsborough painted ; **pic′ture-house**, **-palace**, a building for cinematograph shows ; **pic′ture-restorer**, one who cleans and restores and sometimes ruins old pictures ; **pic′ture-rod**, **-rail**, **-mould′ing**, a rod, moulding, from which pictures may be hung ; **pic′ture-play**, a story told in motion pictures ; **pic′ture-wire**, wire for hanging pictures ; **pic′ture-writ′ing**, the use of pictures to express ideas or relate events.—**in the picture**, having a share of attention : adequately briefed ; **picture postcard**, a postcard bearing a picture, commonly a local view. [L. *pictūra*—*pingĕre*, *pictum*, to paint.]

picturesque, *pik-tyə-resk′*, *adj.* like a picture : such as would make a striking picture, implying some measure of beauty with much quaintness or immediate effectiveness : of language, vivid and colourful rather than precise : having taste or feeling for the picturesque.—*adv.* **picturesque′ly.**—*n.* **picturesque′ness.** [It. *pittoresco*—*pittura*, a picture—L. *pictūra*.]

picul, pecul, *pik′ul*, *n.* a Chinese weight, about $133\frac{1}{3}$ lb. [Malay *pikul*, a man's load.]

Picus, *pī′kəs*, *n.* an ancient Italian god, a son of Saturn, turned into a woodpecker by Circe : the woodpecker genus.—*adj.* **pī′sine** (*-sīn*). [L. *Picus*.]

piddle, *pid′l*, *v.i.* to deal in trifles : to trifle : to eat with little relish : to make water.—*n.* **pidd′ler**, a trifler.—*adj.* **pidd′ling**, trifling, paltry. [Origin obscure.]

piddock, *pid′ək*, *n.* the pholas. [Origin unknown.]

pidgin, *pij′in*, *n.* a Chinese corruption of **business** : affair.—Also **pig′eon.**—**pidgin English**, a jargon, mainly English in vocabulary with Chinese arrangement, used in communication between Chinese and foreigners : any similar jargon.

pi-dog, pie-dog. See **pye-dog.**

pie, *pī*, *n.* a magpie : a chatterer. [Fr.,—L. *pīca*.]

pie, pye, *pī*, *n.* a book of rules for determining the Church office for the day.—**by cock and pie**, (*Shak.*) a minced oath, app. by God and the pie. [L.L. *pīca*, possibly the same as L. *pīca*, magpie (from the black and white appearance of the page).]

pie, pi, *pī*, *n.* type confusedly mixed : a mixed state : confusion.—*v.t.* to reduce to pie :—*pr.p* **pie′ing, pye′ing** ; *pa.t.* and *pa.p.* **pied.** [Origin obscure ; perh. conn. with **pie** (4), or **pie** (2).]

pie, *pī*, *n.* a quantity of meat, fruit, or other food baked within or under a crust of prepared flour : (*coll.*) a welcome luxury, prize, or spoil.—*ns.* **pie′-counter**, (*U.S.*) a counter at which pies are sold : (*U.S.*) the source of patronage, bribes, spoils of office ; **pie′crust**, the paste covering or enclosing a pie ; **pie′-dish**, a deep dish in which pies are made ; **pie′man**, one who sells pies, esp. in the street ; **pie′-plant**, (*U.S.*) rhubarb ; **pie′-shop.**—**Périgord pie**, a pie of partridge flavoured with truffles (*Périgord*, now Dordogne, &c.) ; **piecrust table**, a Chippendale table with carved raised edge. [Origin unknown ; possibly from the bird, as a miscellaneous collector ; the Gael. *pighe* is from English.]

pie, *pī*, *n.* the smallest Indian copper coin, equal to $\frac{1}{3}$ of a pice, or $\frac{1}{12}$ of an anna. [Marathi *pā′ī*, a fourth.]

piebald, *pī′bawld*, *adj.* black and white in patches : (loosely) of other colours in patches : motley : heterogeneous.—*n.* a piebald horse or other animal. [pie (1), bald.]

piece, *pēs*, *n.* a part or portion of anything, esp. detached : a separate lump, mass, body, of any material, considered as an object (in Scots without *of* following) : a distance : a span of time : a single article : a definite quantity, as of cloth or paper : a literary, dramatic, musical, or artistic composition : a production, specimen of work : an example : an exemplification or embodiment : (*Scot.*) a little bread, buttered or not, esp. as a lunch : a gun : (*obs.*) a portion : (*obs.*) a wine-cup : a coin : a man in chess, draughts, or other game (in chess sometimes excluding pawns) : a person—now usually (disrespectfully) a woman.—*v.t.* to enlarge by adding a piece : to patch : to combine.—*n.pl.* **piece′-goods**, textile fabrics made in standard lengths.—*adj.* **piece′less**, not made of pieces.—*adv.* **piece′meal**, in pieces : to pieces : bit by bit.—*adj.* done bit by bit : fragmentary.—*n.* a small piece : bit by bit proceeding.—*v.t.* to dismember.—*v.t.* **piec′en**, (local) to join (esp. broken threads in spinning).—*ns.* **piec′ener, piec′er**, a boy or girl employed in a spinning-factory to join broken threads ; **piece′work**, work paid for by the piece or quantity, not by time.—**all to pieces**, into a state of disintegration or collapse : (*U.S.*) through and through, thoroughly ; **a piece**, each ; **a piece of**, an instance of : (*obs.*) a bit of, something of ; **a piece of one's mind**, a frank outspoken rating ; **in pieces**, in, or to, a broken-up state ; **of a piece**, as if of the same piece, the same in nature : homogeneous, uniform : in keeping, consistent (with *with*) ; **piece of eight**, a Spanish dollar worth eight reals, bearing the numeral 8 ; **piece of goods,** (*dial.*) a woman ; **piece of work,** a task : a fuss, ado ; **piece out,** to eke out ; **piece together,** to put together bit by bit ; **piece up,** to patch up : (*Shak.*) perh. to incorporate in one's own share ; **the piece,** (*Scot.*) apiece ; **to pieces,** into a state of disruption. [O.Fr. *piece*—L.L. *pecia*, *petium*, a fragment, a piece of land—thought to be of Celtic (Brythonic) origin ; cf. **patch**, **peat**, **petty**, and *Pit-* in place-names.]

pied, *pīd*, *adj.* variegated like a magpie : of various colours.—*n.* **pied′ness.** [pie (1).]

piedmont, *pēd′mənt*, *n.* (*U.S.*) a mountain-foot region.—Also *adj.* [*Piedmont* in Italy, lit. mountain-foot.]

piel′d, *pēld*, *adj.* (*Shak.*) tonsured. [See **peel**.]

piend, *pēnd*, *n.* a salient angle. [Origin unknown.]

piepowder, *pī′pow-dər*, *n.* (*obs.*) a wayfarer, itinerant.—**Court of Piepowder(s)**, an ancient court held in fairs and markets to administer justice in a rough-and-ready way to all comers—also *Court of Dusty Feet.* [O.Fr. *piedpoudreux*—*pied* (L. *pēs*, *pedis*), foot, *poudre* (L. *pulvis*), dust.]

pier, *pēr*, *n.* the mass of stone-work between the openings in the wall of a building : the support of an arch, bridge, &c. : a masonry support for a telescope or the like : a buttress : a gate-pillar : a mass of stone, iron-work, or wood-work projecting into the sea or other water, as a breakwater, landing-stage, or promenade : a jetty or a wharf.—*ns.* **pier′age**, toll paid for using a pier ; **pier′-glass**, (*orig.*) a mirror hung between windows : a tall mirror ; **pier′-head**, the seaward end of a pier ; **pier′-table**, a table fitted for the space between windows. [M.E. *pēr*, L.L. *pēra*; origin doubtful.]

pierce, *pērs*, *v.t.* to thrust or make a hole through : to enter, or force a way into : to touch or move deeply : to penetrate : to perforate : to make by perforating or penetrating.—*v.i.* to penetrate.—*n.* a perforation : a stab : a prick.—*adj.* **pierce′-able**, capable of being pierced.—*adj.* **pier′ced**, perforated : penetrated.—*n.* **pierc′er**, one who or that which pierces : any sharp instrument used for piercing : a sting : (*slang*) a keen eye.—*adj.* **pierc′ing**, penetrating : very acute : keen.—*adv.* **pierc′ingly.**—*n.* **pierc′ingness.** [O.Fr. *percer* ; of doubtful origin.]

Pierian, *pī-ē′ri-ən*, *adj.* of *Pieria*, in Thessaly, the country of the Muses : of the Muses.—*n.* **pierid** (*pī′ə-rid*), any butterfly of the Pieridae.—*n.pl.* **Pierides** (*pī-er′i-dēz*), the nine Muses :—*sing.* **Pi′eris.**—*n.* **Pi′eris,** the cabbage butterfly genus, typical of the family **Pier′idae** (*-dē*). [Gr. *pieriā*.]

Pierrot, *pē′ə-rō*, *pyer-ō*, *n.* a white-faced buffoon with loose long-sleeved garb : **pierrot**, a clown or comic singer at seaside resorts, &c. : an 18th-century women's low-cut basque, with sleeves :—*fem.* **Pierette′.** [Fr., dim. of *Pierre*, Peter.]

pierst, (*Spens.*) for **pierced** (*pa.t.* and *pa.p.*).

piert. Same as **peart.** See also **parsley-piert.**

piet. Same as **pyot.**

pietà, *pyā-tä′*, *n.* a representation of the Virgin with the dead Christ across her knees. [It.,—L. *pietās*, *-ātis*, pity.]

pietra-dura, *pyā′trä-dōō′rä*, *n.* inlaid work with hard stones—jasper, agate, &c. [It., hard stone.]

piety, *pī′i-ti*, *n.* (*obs.*) pity : the quality of being pious : dutifulness : devoutness : sense of duty towards parents, benefactors, &c. : duteous conduct.—*ns.* **pī′etism** ; **pī′etist**, one marked by strong devotional feeling : a name first applied to a sect of German religious reformers of deep devotional feeling (end of 17th century).—*adjs.* **pietist′ic, -al.** [O.Fr. *piete*—L. *pietās*, *-ātis.*]

piezo-, *pī′i-zō-*, *pī-ē′zō-*, in composition, pressure.—*adj.* **piezo,** short for **piezoelectric.**—*n.* **piezochem′istry,** the chemistry of substances under high pressure.—*adj.* **piezoelec′tric.**—*ns.* **piezoelectri′city,** electricity developed in certain crystals by mechanical strain, and the effect of an electric field in producing expansion and contraction along different axes ; **piezometer** (*-om′i-tər*), an instrument for measuring pressure or compressibility. [Gr. *piezein*, to press.]

piffero, *pif′e-rō*, *n.* a fife : an Italian bagpipe : **a rude oboe.**—*n.* **pifferaro** (*-ä′rō*), a piffero-player :—*pl.* **pifferari** (*-rē*). [It.,—O.H.G. *pfîfari*, piper.]

piffle, *pif′l*, *n.* nonsense : worthless talk.—*v.t.* to trifle : to act ineffectually. [Origin unknown.]

pig, *pig*, *n.* a swine : a young swine : swine's flesh as food, esp. that of the young animal : one who is like a pig, dirty, greedy, gluttonous, or cantankerous : an oblong mass of unforged metal, as first extracted from the ore : the mould into which it is run, esp. one of the branches, the main channel being the *sow* : (*slang*) a feast.—*v.i.* to bring forth pigs : to live, herd, huddle, sleep, or feed like pigs : to eat :—*pr.p.* **pigg′ing** ; *pa.t.* and *pa.p.* **pigged.**—*ns.* **pig′-bed,** a pig's sleeping place : a mould of sand in which a pig of iron is cast ; **pig′-deer,** the babiroussa.—*adjs.* **pig′-eyed,** having small dull eyes with heavy lids ; **pig′-faced.**—*ns.* **pig′-fish,** (*U.S.*) a name for the sailor's-choice and for various kinds of grunt : in Australia for various wrasses ; **pigg′ery,** a place where pigs are kept : piggishness.—*adj.* **pigg′ish,** like a pig : greedy : dirty : cantankerous.—*ns.* **pigg′ishness** ; **piggy,** **pigg′ie,** **pig′let,** **pig′ling,** a little pig.—*adj.* **pig′head′ed,** having a pig-like head : stupidly obstinate.—*adv.* **pig′head′edly.**—*ns.* **pig′head′edness** ; **pig′-herd** ; **pig′-iron,** iron in pigs or rough bars.—*v.i.* **pig′-jump,** to jump from all four legs without bringing them together.—*ns.* **pig′-lead,** lead in pigs ; **pig′-lily,** (*S.Afr.*) the lily of the Nile ; **pig′-nut,** the earth-nut (Conopodium) ; **pig′-rat,** the bandicoot rat ; **pig′sconce,** a pigheaded fellow : a blockhead ; **pig′skin,** the skin of a pig prepared as a strong leather : a saddle ; **pig′-sticker** ; **pig′-sticking,** boar-hunting with spears ; **pig′sty,** a pen for keeping pigs ; **pig′s-wash,** **pig′wash,** swill ; **pig′s-whis′per,** (*slang*) a low whisper : a very short space of time ; **pig′tail,** the tail of a pig : the hair of the head plaited behind in a queue : a roll of twisted tobacco ; **pig′weed,** goosefoot, amaranth, cow-parsnip, or other plant eaten by pigs ; **pig′-woman,** a woman who roasted pigs at fairs.—**a pig in a poke** (see **poke**). [M.E. *pigge* ; cf. Du. *bigge*, *big.*]

pig, *pig*, *n.* (*Scot.*) an earthenware crock, hot-water bottle, or other vessel : earthenware : a potsherd —*ns.* **pig′-man, -woman,** a dealer in pigs.—**pigs and whistles,** wrack and ruin. [Origin unknown.]

pigeon, *pij′ən*, *-in*, *n.* (*orig.*) a young dove : a dove : any bird of the dove family : extended to various other birds (e.g. the *Cape pigeon*) : a clay disk thrown from a trap and shot at as a substitute for a live pigeon : (*obs.*) a girl : (*slang*) one who is fleeced.—*v.t.* to gull.—*n.* **pig′eon-berry,** (*U.S.*) pokeweed or its fruit.—*adj.* **pig′eon-breast′ed,** having a narrow chest with breast-bone thrown forward.—*ns.* **pig′eon-flier, -flyer,** one who sends forth homing pigeons ; **pig′eon-flying.**— *adj.* **pig′eon-heart′ed,** timid.—*n.* **pig′eon-hole,** a niche for a pigeon's nest : a hole of similar appearance : a compartment for storing and classifying papers, &c. : a compartment of the mind or memory : (in *pl.*) the stocks : (in *pl.*) an old outdoor game like bagatelle.—*v.t.* to furnish with or make into pigeon-holes : to put into a pigeon-hole : to classify methodically : to lay aside and treat with neglect.—*n.* **pig′eon-house,** a dovecote. —*adj.* **pig′eon-liv′ered,** mild.—*ns.* **pig′eon-pea,** dal ; **pig′eon-post,** transmission of letters by pigeons ; **pig′eonry,** a place for keeping pigeons.— *adj.* **pig′eon-toed,** having all the toes at one level : in-toed.—*n.* **pig′eon-wing,** a caper in dancing. —**pigeon's milk,** partly digested food regurgitated by pigeons to feed their young : an imaginary liquid for which children are sent, as on 1st April. [O.Fr. *pijon*—L. *pīpiō*, *-ōnis*—*pīpīre*, to cheep.]

pigeon. Same as **pidgin.**

piggin, *pig′in*, *n.* a small pail or bowl of staves and hoops, one stave usually prolonged as a handle : a vessel of various other kinds. [Poss. from **pig** (2) ; the Celtic words seem to be from English.]

pight, *pīt*, an old *pa.t.* and *pa.p.* (*Spens.*) of **pitch** (2), pitched, set : also false archaism for present tense. —*adj.* (*Spens.*) well-knit : (*Shak.*) resolved.

Neutral vowels in unaccented syllables : *el′ə-mənt*, *in′fənt*, *ran′dəm*

pightle, *pī′tl, n.* a small enclosure: a croft. [Ety. dub.]

pigment, *pig′mənt, n.* paint: any substance used for colouring: that which gives colour to animal and vegetable tissues: (*Scott*) piment.—*adjs.* **pigmental** (-*men′tl*), **pig′mentary.** — *n.* **pigmenta′tion,** coloration or discoloration by pigments in the tissues. [L. *pīgmentum*—*pingĕre*, to paint.]

pigmy. Same as **pygmy.**

pignorate, pignerate, *pig′nər-āt, v.t.* to give or take in pledge or pawn.—*n.* **pignora′tion.** [L. *pignus*, -*eris* or -*oris*, a pledge.]

pigsney, pigsny, pigsnie, *pigz′ni, n.* (*arch.* or *dial.*) a term of endearment, esp. to a woman: sometimes used in contempt: (playfully): an eye. [**pig's eye,** with prosthetic *n* (from *an eye, mine eye*).]

pika, *pī′kä, n.* the tailless hare (Ochotona), a small rodent of mountain regions, akin to the rabbit. [Tungus *pūka.*]

pike, *pīk, n.* a sharp point: a weapon with a long shaft and a sharp head like a spear, formerly used by foot-soldiers: a spiked staff: a sharp-pointed hill or summit: a voracious fresh-water fish (*Esox lucius*) with pointed snout: extended to various other fishes: (*dial.*) a pick.—*v.t.* to kill or pierce with a pike: (*dial.*) to pick.—*adj.* **piked** (*pīkt, pīk′id*), spiked: ending in a point.—*ns.* **pike′-head,** the head of a pike or spear; **pike′man,** a man armed with a pike: one who wields a pick; **pike′-perch,** a percoid fish with pike-like jaws; **pik′er,** (*dial.*) one who picks: (*dial.*) a pilferer: (*U.S.*) one who bets, gambles, speculates, or does anything else in a very small way; **pike′staff,** the staff or shaft of a pike: a staff with a pike at the end.—**plain as a pikestaff** (orig. **packstaff**), perfectly plain or clear. [O.E. *pīc, pūic,* pick, spike; but partly from Fr. *pic* with the same meaning, and *pique* the weapon, and prob. partly from Scand. (Norw. dial. *pīk*) and from Sp. *pico,* peak; these may be related to L. *pīcus,* woodpecker, or to W. *pīg,* a point.]

pike, *pīk, v.i.* to speed.—*v.t.* to betake quickly. [Perh. orig. get a **pikestaff**; perh. Fr. *piquer,* to spur.]

pike, *pīk, n.* a turnpike: a toll: (*U.S.*) a main road. —*ns.* **pike′-keeper, pike′man,** a man in charge of a turnpike; **pi′ker,** a tramp. [Short for **turnpike.**]

pikelet, *pīk′lit, n.* (*local*) a tea-cake. [W. *bara pyglyd,* pitchy bread.]

pikul. Same as **picul.**

pilaster, *pi-las′tər, n.* a square column, partly built into, partly projecting from a wall.—*adj.* **pilas′tered.** [Fr. *pilastre*—It. *pilastro*—L. *pīla,* a pillar.]

pilau, *pi-low′, n.* a highly spiced Eastern dish of rice with a fowl, meat, or the like, boiled together or separately.—Also **pillau′, pilaw′, pilaff′, pilow′.** [Pers. *pilāw,* Turk. *pilāw, pilāf.*]

pilch, *pilch, n.* a fur cloak: a coarse leather or woollen cloak: a rug for a saddle: a light saddle: a flannel cloth for wrapping a child.—*n.* **pilch′er,** (*Shak.*) a scabbard. [O.E. *pyl(e)ce*—L.L. *pellicea* —L. *pellis,* skin.]

pilchard, *pil′chərd, n.* a sea-fish like the herring, but smaller, thicker, and rounder, common off Cornwall.—Earlier (*Shak.*) **pil′cher.** [Origin unknown: poss. Scand. (cf. Norw. *pilk,* artificial bait); Ir. *pilseir* is prob. from English.]

pilcorn, *pil′korn, n.* the naked oat, a variety in which the glume does not adhere to the grain. [For **pilled corn.**]

pilcrow, *pil′krō, n.* a paragraph-mark. [Origin obscure.]

pile, *pīl, n.* a set of things fitted or resting one over another, or in a more or less regular figure: a heap of combustibles for cremating a dead body, or for the burnt-offering, or for burning to death: a set of weights fitting one within another: a stack of arms: a heap of shot: a set of wrought-iron bars placed together for welding and rolling into one; a series of alternate plates of two metals for generating an electric current: a set of coins placed vertically one upon another: (*slang*) a great amount of money, a fortune: (*coll.*) a great accumulation, or number: a tall building: (*obs.*) the under iron for striking coins: (*obs.*) the reverse of a coin. —*v.t.* to lay in a pile or heap: to collect in a mass: to heap up: to load with heaps: to accumulate. —*v.i.* to come into piles: to accumulate: to go in crowds.—*n.* **pi′ler.**—**pile arms,** to prop three muskets, orig. with fixed bayonets, so that the butts remain firm, the muzzles close together pointing obliquely—also **stack arms; pile on the agony,** to overdo painful effects by accumulation, &c.; **pile up,** to run ashore: to crash. [Fr.,—L. *pīla,* a pillar.]

pile, *pīl, n.* an arrow-head: a Roman javelin: a large stake or cylinder driven into the earth to support foundations: (*her.*) an inverted pyramidal figure.—*v.t.* to drive piles into.—*ns.* **pile′-driver,** an engine for driving in piles: in games, a very heavy stroke, kick, &c.; **pile′-dwelling,** a dwelling built on piles, esp. a lake-dwelling; **pile′work,** work or foundations made of piles; **pile′-worm,** a ship-worm. [O.E. *pīl*—L. *pīlum,* a javelin.]

pile, *pīl, n.* a covering of hair, esp. soft, fine, or short hair: down: human body-hair: a single hair: a raised surface on cloth: now distinguished from *nap* as made not in finishing but in weaving, either by leaving loops (which may be cut) or by weaving two cloths face to face and cutting them apart.—*adjs.* **pilif′erous,** bearing hairs: ending in a hair-like point; **pil′iform,** hair-like. [L. *pilus,* a hair.]

pile, *pīl, n.* (usu. in *pl.*) a haemorrhoid.—*n.* **pile′-wort,** the lesser celandine (*Ranunculus Ficaria*), once thought a remedy for piles. [L. *pīla,* a ball.]

pileorhiza, *pī-li-ō-rī′zä, n.* (*bot.*) a root-cap. [L. *pileus,* -*um* (see next word), Gr. *rhiza,* root.]

pileum, *pī′li-əm, n.* the top of a bird's head:—*pl.* **pil′ea.**—*n.* **pi′leus,** a Roman felt cap: the expanded cap of a mushroom or toadstool, or other fungus:—*pl.* **pilei** (*pī′li-ī*).—*adjs.* **pi′leate, -d,** cap-shaped: capped: crested. [L. *pīleum, pileus,* for *pilleum, pilleus,* a felt cap; cf. Gr. *pilos,* felt.]

pilfer, *pil′fər, v.i.* and *v.t.* to steal in small quantities.—*ns.* **pil′ferage, pil′fering, pil′fery,** petty theft; **pil′ferer.**—*adv.* **pil′feringly.** [Prob. connected with **pelf.**]

pilgarlick, peelgarlic, *pil-,* *pēl-gär′lik, n.* a baldpate: a poor wretch: in whimsical self-pity, oneself.—*adj.* **pilgar′licky.** [**pill** (2), **peel,** and **garlic,** as like a pilled or peeled head of garlic.]

pilgrim, *pil′grim, n.* (*arch.* and *poet.*) a wanderer, wayfarer: one who travels to a distance to visit a holy place: allegorically or spiritually, one journeying through life as a stranger in this world: a Pilgrim Father: an original settler: newcomer. —*adj.* of or pertaining to a pilgrim: like a pilgrim: consisting of pilgrims. — *n.* **pil′grimage,** the journeying of a pilgrim: a journey to a shrine or other holy place or place venerated for its associations: the journey of life: a lifetime.— *adj.* visited by pilgrims.—*v.i.* to go on pilgrimage: to wander.—*ns.* **pil′grimager,** contemptuously, one who goes on pilgrimage; **pil′grim-bott′le,** a flat bottle with ears at the neck for a cord; **pil′grimer,** one who goes on pilgrimage.—*v.i.* (or *v.t.* with *it*) **pil′grimise,** to play the pilgrim.— **Pilgrim Fathers,** the Puritans who sailed for America in the *Mayflower,* and founded Plymouth in 1620; **pilgrim's shell,** a scallop-shell (called a cockle) used as a sign that one had visited the shrine of St James of Compostela; **pilgrim's sign,** a badge, often a leaden brooch, obtained at the shrine and worn on the hat by a pilgrim. [Assumed O.Fr. *pelegrin* (Fr. *pèlerin*)—L. *peregrīnus,* foreigner, stranger; see **peregrine.**]

pilhorse, *pil′hors,* or **philhorse,** *fil′* (*Shak.*). Same as **fillhorse** or **thillhorse.**

pili, *pē-lē′, n.* the nut (also **pili′-nut′**) of trees of the burseraceous genus Canarium. [Tagálog.]

pill, *pil, n.* a little ball of medicine: (*facet.*) a ball, e.g. a cannon-ball, tennis-ball, in *pl.* billiards: anything disagreeable that must be accepted: a tiresome person: (*slang;* also in *pl.*) a doctor.—*v.t.* to dose with pills : (*slang*) to blackball.—*ns.* **pill'-box,** a box for holding pills : a kind of one-horse carriage : (*mil. slang*) a small block-house ; **pill'-bug,** a wood-louse that rolls itself into a ball ; **pill'worm,** a millipede that curls up ; **pill'wort,** a water-fern (Pilularia) of lake-margins, with pill-like sporocarps. [L. *pīla,* perh. through O.Fr. *pile,* or from a syncopated form of the dim. *pilŭla.*]

pill, *pil, v.t.* and *v.i.* (*arch.*) to plunder : (*dial.*) to peel : (*obs.*) to make or become hairless.—*n.* (*Spens.*) husk, integument.—*n.* **pill'age,** act of plundering : plunder.—*v.t.* and *v.i.* to plunder.— *n.* **pill'ager.** [O.E. *pylian* and O.Fr. *peler,* both— L. *pilāre,* to deprive of hair ; cf. **peel.**]

pillar, *pil'ər, n.* (*archit.*) a detached support, not necessarily cylindrical or of classical proportions : a structure of like form erected as a monument, ornament, object of worship, &c. : a tall upright rock : a mass of coal or rock left in a mine to support the roof : anything in the form of a column : a supporting post : the post supporting a bicycle saddle : a cylinder holding the plates of a watch or clock in position : a pillar-box : one who, or anything that, sustains.—*ns.* **pill'ar-box,** a short hollow pillar for posting letters in ; **pill'arist, pill'ar-saint,** an ascetic living on the top of a pillar, a stylite ; **pill'ar-root,** a supporting root descending from a branch.—**from pillar to post,** from one state of difficulty to another : hither and thither. [O.Fr. *piler* (Fr. *pilier*)—L.L. *pilāre*— L. *pīla,* a pillar.]

pillau. See **pilau.**

pillicock, *pil'i-kok, n.* (allusively in *Shak.*) the penis : a term of endearment to a boy. [Cf. Norw. dial. *pill.*]

pillion, *pil'yən, n.* a pad or light saddle for a woman : a cushion behind a horseman for a second rider (usu. a woman) or a bag : the baggage-carrier of a motor-cycle, over the hind wheel, usable as an extra seat.—*adv.* on a pillion.—*v.t.* to seat on or furnish with a pillion.—*ns.* **pill'ionist, pill'ion-rider,** one who rides pillion ; **pill'ion-seat.** [Prob. Ir. *pillin,* Gael. *pillin, pillean,* a pad, a pack-saddle—*peall,* a skin or mat, L. *pellis,* skin.]

pilliwinks, *pil'i-wingks, n.pl.* an instrument of torture for crushing the fingers. [Origin unknown.]

pillory, *pil'ə-ri, n.* a wooden frame, supported by an upright pillar or post, with holes through which the head and hands were put as a punishment, abolished in England in 1837.—*v.t.* to set in the pillory : to hold up to ridicule :—*pr.p.* **pill'orying ;** *pa.t.* and *pa.p.* **pill'oried.**—Also **pill'orise.** [O.Fr. *pilori ;* Prov. *espitlori ;* poss. L.L. *speculātōrium,* a lookout—L. *speculāria,* window-panes—*specēre,* to look.]

pillow, *pil'ō, n.* a cushion for a sleeper's head : any object used for the purpose : a cushion for lace-making : a support for part of a structure.—*v.t.* to lay or rest for support : to serve as pillow for : to furnish or prop with pillows.—*v.i.* to rest the head.—*ns.* **pill'ow-bere, -beer, -case, -slip,** a cover for a pillow ; **pill'ow-cup,** a last cup before going to bed.—*adj.* **pill'owed,** supported by, or provided with, a pillow.—*ns.* **pill'ow-fight,** the sport of bethumping one another with pillows ; **pill'ow-lace,** lace worked with bobbins on a pillow ; **pill'ow-lava,** lava showing pillow-structure ; **pill'ow-structure,** in lavas, separation into pillow-shaped blocks.—*adj.* **pill'owy,** like a pillow : round and swelling : soft. [O.E. *pyle,* also *pylu*—L. *pulvīnus.*]

pillworm, pillwort. See **pill.**

Pilocarpus, *pī-lō-kär'pəs, n.* a genus of S. American rutaceous shrubs, including jaborandi.—*n.* **pilo-car'pine** (*-pēn*), an alkaloid ($C_{11}H_{16}O_2N_2$) got from jaborandi leaves. [Gr. *pilos,* felt, a felt cap, *karpos,* fruit.]

pilose, *pī'lōs, adj.* hairy : having scattered soft or moderately stiff hairs.—*adj.* **pī'lous,** hairy.—*n.* **pilosity** (*-los'i-ti*). [L. *pilōsus—pilus,* hair.]

pilot, *pī'lət, n.* (*arch.*) a steersman : one who conducts ships in and out of a harbour, along a dangerous coast, &c. : one who actually operates the flying controls of an aircraft : one who is qualified

to act as pilot : a guide : (*U.S.*) a cow-catcher. —*v.t.* to act as pilot to.—*ns.* **pi'lotage,** piloting : a pilot's fee ; **pi'lot-balloon',** a small balloon sent up to find how the wind blows ; **pi'lot-boat,** a boat used by pilots for meeting or leaving ships ; **pi'lot-burn'er, -jet, -light,** a small gas-burner kept alight to light another ; **pi'lot-cloth,** a coarse, stout cloth for overcoats ; **pi'lot-en'gine,** a locomotive sent before a train to clear its way, as a pilot ; **pi'lot-fish,** a carangoid fish that accompanies ships and sharks ; **pi'lot-flag, -jack,** the flag hoisted at the fore by a vessel needing a pilot ; **pi'lot-house,** a shelter for steering-gear and pilot —also *wheel-house* ; **pi'lot-jacket,** a pea-jacket.— *adj.* **pi'lotless,** without a pilot : not requiring a pilot, as an automatic aeroplane.—*ns.* **pi'lot-light,** a small electric light to show when the current is on ; **pi'lot-plant,** prototype machinery set up to begin a new process ; **pi'lot-whale,** the caa'ing-whale.—**pilot officer,** in the Air Force an officer ranking with an army second-lieutenant. [Fr. *pillotte,* now *pilote*—It. *pilota,* app. for earlier *pedota,* which may be—Gr. *pēdon,* oar, in pl. rudder.]

pilule, *pil'ūl, n.* a little pill.—Also **pil'ula.**—*adj.* **pil'ular.** [L. *pilŭla,* dim. of *pīla,* ball.]

pilum, *pī'ləm, n.* the heavy javelin used by Roman foot-soldiers :—*pl.* **pī'la.** [L. *pīlum.*]

pilus, *pī'ləs, n.* a hair :—*pl.* **pī'lī.** [L. *pĭlus.*]

piment, *pi-ment', n.* (*obs.*) spiced sweetened wine.— Also (*Scott*) **pigment** (*pig'mənt*).—*n.* **pimento** (*pi-ment'ō*), formerly Cayenne pepper : now all-spice or Jamaica pepper, the dried unripe fruits of a W. Indian tree (*Pimenta officinalis*) of the myrtle family : the tree itself : its wood. [O.Fr. *piment,* Sp. *pimienta,* and Port. *pimenta*—L. *pigmentum,* paint.]

pimp, *pimp, n.* one who procures gratifications for the lust of others : a pander.—*v.i.* to pander. [Origin obscure.]

pimpernel, *pim'pər-nel, n.* (*obs.*) burnet : (*obs.*) burnet-saxifrage (Pimpinella) : now, the poor man's weather-glass (*Anagallis arvensis*), a plant of the primrose family, with scarlet (or blue, &c.) flowers.—*n.* **Pimpinell'a,** the anise and burnet-saxifrage genus of umbelliferous plants.—**bastard pimpernel,** a small plant (*Centunculus minimus*) akin to the scarlet pimpernel ; **bog pimpernel,** *Anagallis tenella* ; **water pimpernel,** brookweed ; **yellow pimpernel,** the wood loosestrife (*Lysimachia nemorum*). [O.Fr. (and mod. Fr.) *pimprenelle,* and It. *pimpinella,* burnet ; origin doubtful.]

Pimpinella. See **pimpernel.**

pimping, *pimp'ing, adj.* petty : puny : paltry : sickly. [Origin obscure.]

pimple, *pim'pl, n.* a pustule : a small swelling, protuberance, or hill.—*adjs.* **pim'pled, pim'ply,** having pimples. [Origin unknown.]

pin, *pin, n.* a piece of wood or of metal used for fastening things together : a peg or nail : a sharp-pointed piece of wire with a rounded head for fastening clothes, &c. : an ornamental elaboration of this : a cylindrical part inserted into something, as the stem of a key, or part of a lock that a hollow-stemmed key fits : the projecting part of a dovetail joint : a peg aimed at in quoits : a peg in the centre of an archery target : the rod of a golf flag : a skittle or ninepin : a chess piece : a tuning peg in a stringed instrument : a measuring peg in a drinking-cup : a degree, stage, pitch : (*coll.*) a leg : a peak : the projecting bone of the hip : a hard spot or excrescence : a cask of 4½ gallons : short for clothes-pin, rolling-pin, tirling-pin, &c. : an act of pinning or state of being pinned : anything of little value.—*v.t.* to fasten with a pin : (*fig.*) to fix, to fasten, to enclose, to hold down : to make a small hole in : to insert chips of stone between the stones of :—*pr.p.* **pinn'ing ;** *pa.t.* and *pa.p.* **pinned.**—*ns.* **pin'-butt'ock,** (*Shak.*) a sharp, pointed buttock ; **pin'-case** (*obs.*) ; **pin'cushion,** a cushion for holding pins ; **pin'-dust,** brass filings, a product of pin-making.—*adj.* **pin'-eyed,** long-styled, with the stigma like a pin-head in the throat of the corolla (esp. of a *Primula*).—*n.* **pin'-feather,** a young,

---

Neutral vowels in unaccented syllables : *el'ə-mənt, in'fənt, ran'dəm*

unexpanded feather.—*adjs.* pin′-feathered; pin′-fire, discharged by a pin driven into the fulminate. —*ns.* pin′fish, a spiny fish of various kinds; pin′-head, the head of a pin; pin′hole, a hole for or made by a pin, or such as a pin might make; pin′-leg, (*Scot.*) a wooden leg; pin′-maker; pin′-making; pin′-man, a seller of pins; pin′-money, money allotted to a wife for private expenses, ostensibly to buy pins; pinn′er, one who pins: a pin-maker: a pinafore: a head-dress with lappets flying loose: one of these lappets; pinn′ing, a fastening: a chip of stone, &c., inserted in a joint of masonry; pin′point, the point of a pin: anything very sharp or minute. —*v.t.* to place, define, very exactly.—*ns.* pin′-prick, the prick of a pin; a petty act of irritation; pin′-stripe, a very narrow stripe in cloth; pin′-tail, a duck of the genus Dafila, with a pointed tail: a sand-grouse.—*adj.* pin′tailed, having a long, narrow tail.—*n.* pin′-tuck, a very narrow ornamental tuck.—*adj.* pin′-up, such as might have her portrait pinned up on a wall for admiration.—*n.* a girl of such a kind: a portrait so pinned up.—*n.* pin′-wheel, a wheel with pins at right angles to its plane, to lift the hammer of a striking clock: a paper toy windmill: a revolving firework.—a merry pin, a merry mood; pin and web, (*Shak.*) a disease of the eye, apparently cataract, characterised by a small excrescence like a pin-head, and a film (also web and pin); pinhole photography, the taking of photographs by the use of a pinhole instead of a lens; pin one (down) to, to keep him strictly to; pin one's faith on, to put entire trust in; pin on one's sleeve, to make entirely dependent on oneself, or at one's disposal; pins and needles, a tingling feeling as numbness passes off. [O.E. *pinn*, prob. —L. *pinna*, a feather, a pinnacle.]

piña, *pē′nyä*, *n.* (*obs.*) the pineapple: a fine cloth of pineapple leaf fibre (piña-cloth). [Sp., pine-cone, pineapple.]

pinacotheca, *pin-a-kō-thē′kä*, *n.* a picture-gallery. [Latinised from Gr. *pinakothēkē*—*pinax*, a tablet, picture, *thēkē*, repository.]

pinafore, *pin′a-fōr*, *n.* a loose covering over a dress, esp. a child's.—*adj.* pin′afored.—pinafore skirt, a skirt hung from the shoulders, or combined with a sleeveless bodice. [pin, afore.]

pinakoid, pinacoid, *pin′a-koid*, *n.* a crystal face, or a crystallographic form consisting of a pair of faces, parallel to two axes.—*adj.* pinakoid′al, pinacoid′al. [Gr. *pinax*, -*ākos*, slab, *eidos*, form.]

pinaster, *pī-* or *pi-nas′tər*, *n.* the cluster-pine. [L. *pīnāster*—*pīnus*, pine.]

pince-nez, *pangs′-nā*, *n.* a pair of eye-glasses with a spring for catching the nose:—*pl.* pince′-nez (-*nā*).—*adj.* pince′-nezed (-*nād*). [Fr., pinch nose.]

pincer, *pin′sər*, *n.* a grasping claw or forceps-like organ: (in *pl.*) a gripping tool with jaws and handles on a pivot, used for drawing out nails, squeezing, &c. (*fig.*; in *pl.*) a twofold advance that threatens to isolate part of an enemy's force. —*v.t.* to pinch with pincers.—*n.* pin′cer-move-ment. [O.Fr. *pincer*, to pinch.]

pinch, *pin*(*t*)*sh*, *v.t.* to compress a small part of between fingers and thumb or between any two surfaces, to nip: to squeeze: to crush: to nip off: (*obs.*) to bite: to bring or render by squeezing or nipping: to affect painfully or injuriously, as cold or hunger: to cause to show the effects of such pain or injury: to harass: to hamper: to restrict: to stint: (*obs.*) to find fault with: (*slang*) to purloin: (*slang*) to arrest: (*horse-racing*) to over-urge: (*U.S.*) to pluck, play pizzicato: to move along with a lever.—*v.i.* to nip or squeeze: to be painfully tight: to encroach: to carp: to live sparingly: (*mining*) to narrow, taper off.—*n.* an act or experience of pinching: a critical time of difficulty or hardship: an emergency: (*obs.*) a pleat: (*obs.*) an upward curl of a hat-brim: a place of narrowing, folding, difficulty, or steepness: a quantity taken up between the finger and thumb: an iron bar used as a lever.—*ns.* pinch′cock, a clamp that stops flow of liquid by pinching a

tube; pinch′commons, a niggard of food.—*adj.* pinched, having the appearance of being tightly squeezed: hard pressed by want or cold: narrowed: straitened.—*ns.* pinch′er, one who, or that which, pinches: (in *pl.*; *dial.*) pincers; pinch′fist, pinch′gut, pinch′penny, a niggard.—*v.i.* pinch′-hit, (*baseball*) to bat in place of another in an emergency: also *fig.*—*n.* pinch′-hitter.—*n.* and *adj.* pinch′ing.—*adv.* pinch′ingly.—at a pinch, in a case of necessity; know where the shoe pinches, to know by direct experience what the trouble or difficulty is. [O.Fr. *pincier*; prob. Gmc.]

pinchbeck, *pin*(*t*)*sh′bek*, *n.* a yellow alloy of copper, with much less zinc than ordinary brass, simulating gold, invented by Christopher *Pinchbeck* (*c.* 1670-1732), watchmaker.—*adj.* sham: in false taste.

pindari, pindaree, *pin-dä′rē*, *n.* a mercenary free-booter troublesome in India till 1817. [Hind. *pindārī*.]

Pindaric, *pin-dar′ik*, *adj.* after the manner or supposed manner of the Greek lyric poet *Pindar*.—*n.* a Pindaric ode: an irregular ode, according to the 17th-century conception of Pindar.—*v.t.* and *v.i.* Pin′darise (-*dər-īz*).—*ns.* Pin′darism, manner or supposed manner of Pindar: intoxication of style; Pin′darist. [Gr. *pindarikos*—*Pindaros*.]

pinder, *pin′dər*, *n.* one who impounds cattle.—Also pinn′er. [O.E. *pyndan*, to shut up—*pund*; cf. poind, pound (2).]

pine, *pīn*, *n.* any tree of the north temperate coniferous genus Pinus, with pairs or bundles of needle-leaves on short shoots and scale-leaves only on long shoots, represented in Britain by the Scots pine (*P. sylvestris*; often called *Scots fir*): extended to various more or less nearly allied trees and to some plants only superficially like: the timber of the pine: a pineapple plant or its fruit.—*adj.* of pines or pine-wood.—*ns.* pine′-apple, (*obs.*) a pine-cone: a large South American multiple fruit shaped like a pine-cone: the brome-liaceous plant (Ananas or Ananassa) bearing it: a finial shaped like a pine-cone or a pineapple: (*slang*) a bomb; pine′-barr′en, a level sandy tract growing pine-trees; pine′-beau′ty, -car′pet, kinds of moths whose larvae feed on pine-trees; pine′-beet′le, any beetle that attacks pine-trees, esp. the pine′-cha′fer (*Hylurgus piniperda*), which bores up through the leader; pine′-cone, the cone or strobilus of a pine-tree; pine′-finch, an American finch like the goldfinch: a large gros-beak of pine-forests; pine′-house, a house in which pineapples are grown; pine′-ker′nel, the edible seed of a pine-tree of various species; pine′-mar′ten, a British species of marten, *Mustela martes*, now rare, dark brown, with yellowish throat, and partly arboreal in habit; pine′-need′le, the acicular leaf of the pine-tree; pin′ery, a pine-house: a pine-forest; pine′-tree; pīnē′tum, a plantation of pine-trees: a collection of pine-trees for botanical or ornamental pur-poses:—*pl.* pīnē′ta; pine′-wood, a wood of pine-trees: pine timber; pine′-wool, a fibrous substance prepared from the leaves of the pine.—*adj.* pi′ny (wrongly piney), of, like, or abounding in pine-trees.—pine-tree money, silver money coined at Boston in the 17th century, bearing the figure of a pine-tree. [O.E. *pīn*—L. *pīnus*.]

pine, *pīn*, *n.* (*obs.*) punishment, torture: (*arch.*) suffering: (*Spens.*) want, starvation.—*v.t.* (*obs.*) to torment: to consume, cause to wear away: to starve: (*Milt.*) to grieve for.—*v.i.* to waste away, esp. under pain or mental distress: to languish with longing: to long: to repine. [O.E. *pīnian*, to torment—L. *poena*, punishment.]

pineal, *pin′i-əl*, or *pīn′*, *adj.* shaped like a pine-cone: connected with the pineal body.—pineal body, or gland, a small body at the end of an upgrowth from the optic thalami of the brain; pineal eye, a vestigial third eye in front of the pineal body, best developed in the New Zealand Sphenodon. [L. *pīnea*, a pine-cone—*pīnus*, pine.]

pinfold, *pin′fōld*, *n.* a pound or enclosure for cattle. —*v.t.* to impound. [O.E. *pundfald*, affected by *pyndan*; see pound, fold, pinder.]

ping, *ping*, *n.* a sharp ringing or whistling sound as

of a bullet.—*v.i.* to make such a sound.—*n.* **ping'-pong'**, a trade-name for table tennis. [Imit.]

pingle, *ping'(g)l*, (*Scot.* and *dial.*) *v.i.* to strive: to struggle with difficulties, exert oneself strongly: to work ineffectually: to trifle or dally, esp. with food.—*v.t.* to contend strongly with: to harass, worry: to eat with feeble appetite.—*n.* a strenuous contest or exertion.—*n.* **ping'ler.**—*adj.* **ping'ling.** [Cf. Sw. *pyngla*, to be busy in small matters, to work in a trifling way.]

pinguid, *ping'gwid*, *adj.* fat.—*v.t.* and *v.i.* **ping'uefy** (*-gwi-fī*), to fatten: to make or become greasy.—*ns.* **Pinguic'ula**, the butterwort genus; **pinguid'-ity, ping'uitude**, fatness. [L. *pinguis*, fat.]

pinguin. Same as penguin (1).

pinguin, *ping'gwin*, *n.* a West Indian plant, *Bromelia Pinguin*: its fruit.—Also **peng'uin.** [Perh. L. *pinguis*, fat; confused with **penguin**.]

pinion, *pin'yən*, *n.* a wing: the last joint of a wing: a flight feather, esp. the outermost.—*v.t.* to cut a pinion of: to confine the wings of: to confine by binding the arms. [O.Fr. *pignon*—L. *pinna* (*penna*), wing.]

pinion, *pin'yən*, *n.* a small wheel with teeth or 'leaves.' [Fr. *pignon*, pinion, in O.Fr. battle-ment—L. *pinna*, pinnacle.]

pink, *pingk*, *n.* a small sailing-ship, usu. with a narrow stern.—Also **pink'ie, pink'y.** [M.Du. *pin(c)ke*; Ger. *pinke*.]

pink, *pingk*, *v.t.* to stab or pierce, esp. with a sword or rapier: to decorate by cutting small holes or scallops.—*n.* a stab: an eyelet.—*adj.* **pinked**, pierced or worked with small holes.—*n.* **pink'ing-i'ron**, a tool for pinking or scalloping. [Cf. L.G. *pinken*, to peck.]

pink, *pingk*, *n.* any plant or flower of the caryophyl-laceous genus Dianthus, including carnation and sweet william: extended to some other plants, as **sea'-pink**, thrift, **Carolina pink** (see **Carolina**, **Spigelia**), **Indian pink** (see **Spigelia**, **pinkroot**): the colour of a wild pink, a light red: a scarlet hunting-coat or its colour: the person wearing it: one who is something of a socialist but hardly a red: the fine flower of excellence: the most perfect condition: the highest point, the extreme: (*obs.*) an exquisite.—*adj.* of the colour pink: slightly socialistic: (*obs.* and *U.S.*) exquisite, exclusively fashionable.—*v.t.* and *v.i.* to make or become pink.—*n.* **pink'-eye**, acute contagious conjunctivitis: an acute contagious infection in horses due to a filterable virus, the eye sometimes becoming somewhat red: a red discoloration in salt fish, &c.—*adj.* **pink'-eyed**, having pink eyes (see also pink (5)).—*ns.* **pink'iness**; **pink'ing**, the reddening of gem-stones by heat.—*adj.* **pink'ish**, somewhat pink.—*ns.* **pink'ishness**; **pink'ness**; **pink'root**, Indian pink, or other species of Spigelia: its root, a vermifuge.—*adj.* **pink'y**, inclining to pink.—**in the pink**, in perfect health or condition; **pink of perfection**, the acme. [Etymology doubtful.]

pink, *pingk*, *n.* a yellow lake.—**Dutch pink**, a yellow lake obtained from quercitron bark: (*slang*) blood. [Prob. different word from the preceding.]

pink, *pingk*, *v.i.* to wink: to blink: to peer: to peep.—*adj.* (*Shak.*) blinking.—*adjs.* **pink'-eyed**, having small or half-shut eyes (see also pink (3)); **pink'y**, winking. [Du. *pinken*, to wink.]

pink, *pingk*, *adj.* (*Shak.*) small.—*n.* (*Scot.*) anything small, as a peep of light.—*adj.* **pink'ie, pink'y**, (*Scot.*) small.—*n.* (*Scot.*) the little finger. [Du. *pink*, the little finger.]

pink, *pingk*, **penk**, *pengk*, *n.* a minnow: a samlet. [Cf. Ger. dial. *pinke*.]

pink, *pingk*, *n.* a tinkling sound: a chaffinch's note: a chaffinch.—*v.i.* to detonate or knock. [Imit.]

pinkie, pinky. See pink (1, 3, 5, 6).

pinna, *pin'ä*, *n.* a mollusc akin to the mussels, with triangular shell. [Gr.]

pinna, *pin'ä*, *n.* a leaflet of a pinnate leaf: any similar expansion: a wing, fin, feather, or similar expansion: the outer ear, esp. the upper part:—*pl.* **pinn'ae** (*-ē*).—*adjs.* **pinn'ate, -d**, shaped like a feather. having a row of leaflets on each side of the rhachis, or other expansions arranged in

like manner: furnished with wings or fins, or wing-like tufts.—*adv.* **pinn'ately.**—*adjs.* **pinn-atifid** (*pin-at'i-fid*), pinnately cut nearly or about half-way down; **pinnatipart'ite**, pinnately cut rather more than half-way; **pinnat'isect**, pinn-ately cut nearly to the midrib.—*n.* **pinn'iped** (*-i-ped*), **pinn'ipede** (*-pēd*; L. *pēs, pedis*, foot), a member of the **Pinnipe'dia** or paddle-footed Carnivora, seals, sea-lions, and walruses.—*adjs.* **pinn'ūlate, -d.**—*n.* **pinn'ūle**, a lobe of a leaflet of a pinnate leaf: a branchlet of a crinoid arm.—Also **pinn'ūla.** [L. *pinna*, a feather, dim. *pinnula.*]

pinnace, *pin'is, -əs, n.* a small vessel with oars and sails: a boat with eight oars: a man-of-war's tender boat: vaguely, a small boat: (*fig.*; *obs.*) a whore. [Fr. *pinasse.*]

pinnacle, *pin'ə-kl, n.* a slender turret or spiry structure in architecture: a high pointed rock or mountain like a spire: the highest point.—*v.t.* to be the pinnacle of: to set on a pinnacle: to raise as a pinnacle: to furnish with pinnacles.—*adj.* **pinn'acled.** [Fr. *pinacle*—L.L. *pinnāculum*, dim. from L. *pinna*, a feather.]

pinner, *pin'ər*. See pin, pinder.

pinnet, *pin'it, n.* (*Scott*) a pinnacle: (*Scot.*) a streamer. [Perh. **pennant**, associated with L. *pinna*, pinnacle.]

pinnock, *pin'ək, n.* the hedge-sparrow: the blue tit. [M.E. *pynnuc.*]

pinnoed, *pin'ōd, pa.p.* (*Spens.*) pinioned. [Perh. a misprint.]

pinny, pinnie, *pin'i, n.* short for **pinafore.**

pinnywinkle, pinniewinkle, *pin'i-wingk-l*, **pilnie-winks**, *pil'ni-wingks*, mistaken forms of **pilli-winks.**

pinochle, pinocle, *pin', pēn'ək-l, n.* a game like bezique: a declaration of queen of spades and knave of diamonds. [Origin unknown.]

pinole, *pē-nō'lā, n.* parched Indian corn or other seeds ground and eaten with milk: a mixture of vanilla and aromatic substances in chocolate. [Sp.,—Aztec *pinolli.*]

piñon, *pin-yon', pēn-yōn', n.* (*U.S.*) an edible pine-seed: the tree bearing it. [Sp.]

pint, *pīnt, n.* a measure of capacity=half a quart or 4 gills or about 568 cubic centimetres: (*U.S.*) 473 c.c. (liquid) or 551 c.c. (dry): (*med.*) about 20 fluid ounces: (*U.S.*) 16 U.S. fluid ounces.—*ns.* **pint'-pot**, a pot for holding a pint, esp. a pewter pot for beer: a seller or drinker of beer; **pint'-stoup**, a vessel for holding a Scots pint (about 3 imperial pints). [Fr. *pinte*; origin unknown.]

pintado, *pin-tä'dō, n.* a kind of petrel, the Cape pigeon: the guinea-fowl: chintz:—*pl.* **pinta'dos.** [Port., painted.]

pintail, pin-wheel. See pin.

pintle, *pin'tl, n.* (*arch.*) the penis: a bolt or pin, esp. one on which something turns. [O.E. *pintel.*]

pinto, *pin'tō, adj.* (*U.S.*) mottled: piebald.—*n.* a piebald horse. [Sp., painted.]

piny. See pine (1).

piny, *pī'ni, n.* (*obs.* or *dial.*). Same as **paeony.**

pioned, *pī'ən-id, adj.* (*Shak.*) perh. trenched (cf. **pioneer**): perh. overgrown with wild orchises, said to be called **pionies** at Stratford (**paeony**).

pioneer, *pī-ə-nēr', n.* a military artisan, employed in peace-time in painting and repairing barracks, and such work, in war in preparing the way for an army, and minor engineering works, as trench-ing: an excavator: a labourer: one who is among the first in new fields of enterprise, ex-ploration, colonisation, research, &c.—*v.t.* to act as pioneer to: to prepare as a pioneer.—*ns.* **pi'oner, py'oner** (*Shak.*), a military pioneer; an excavator; **pi'oning** (*Spens.*) **py'onings**, pioneer work: trenching. [O.Fr. *peonier* (Fr. *pionnier*)—*pion*, a foot-soldier—L.L. *pedō, pedōnis, a* foot-soldier—L. *pēs, pedis*, a foot. cf. **pawn, peon.**]

pioney, piony, *pī'ə-ni, n.* obs. forms of **paeony.** [See **pioned.**]

piou-piou, *pū-pū, n.* a French private soldier. [Fr. slang; perh. *pion*; see **peon.**]

pious, *pī'əs, adj.* dutiful: showing, having, or proceeding from piety: professing to be religious.—*adv.* **pi'ously.**—**pious fraud**, a deception practised with a good end in view: (*coll.*) a religious humbug; **pious opinion**, a belief widely held but not made a matter of faith. [L. *pius*.]

pioy, pioye. Same as **peeoy**.

pip, *pip, n.* roup in poultry, &c.: an ailment or distemper vaguely imagined: (*slang*) syphilis: (*coll.*) spleen, hump, disgust, offence.—*v.t.* to affect with the pip. [App.—M.Du. *pippe*—L.L. *pipita*—L. *pituita*, rheum.]

pip, *pip, n.* (*obs.*) a pippin: a small hard body (seed or fruitlet) in a fleshy fruit.—*adjs.* **pip′less**; **pipp′y.** [App. from **pippin.**]

pip, *pip,* earlier **peep, peepe** (*Shak.*), *pēp, n.* a spot on dice, cards, dominoes: a star as a mark of rank: a spot, speck: a blossom or corolla in a cluster, esp. of cowslips.—**a pip** (or **peepe**) **out**, two-and-thirty, one in excess of the total of pips aimed at in the old card-game of one-and-thirty, hence, having overshot one's mark: tipsy. [Origin unknown.]

pip, *pip, v.t.* (*slang*) to blackball: to pluck, plough, reject, or fail in an examination: to foil, thwart, get the better of: to hit with a bullet or the like: to wound: to kill.—*v.i.* to die (esp. with *out*):— *pr.p.* **pipp′ing**; *pa.t.* and *pa.p.* **pipped.** [Perh. from **pip** (2).]

pip, *pip, v.i.* to chirp, as a young bird. [Cf. **peep** (1).]

pipal, pipul, peepul, *pē′pul, -pəl, n.* the bo-tree. [Hind. *pīpal.*]

pipe, *pīp, n.* a musical wind instrument, or part of an instrument, consisting of or including a tube: any tube, or tubular part or thing, natural or artificial: a pipe-like volcanic vent, mass of ore, &c.: an entrance to a decoy: a tube with a bowl at one end for smoking: a fill of tobacco: the smoking of a fill of tobacco: the note of a bird: a voice, esp. a high voice: (usu. in *pl.*) the windpipe: a stick of wood or pipeclay for curling hair or a wig: a boatswain's whistle: (often in *pl.*) a bagpipe.— *v.i.* to play upon a pipe: to whistle, as the wind, or a boatswain: to speak or sing, esp. in a high voice: to peep or sing, as a bird: to weep: to become pipy.—*v.t.* to play on a pipe: to lead, call, or accompany with a pipe: to render, or cause to be, by playing a pipe: to propagate by piping: to ornament with piping: to supply with pipes: to convey by pipe.—*ns.* **pip′age,** conveyance or distribution by pipe; **pipe′-case,** a case for a tobacco-pipe; **pipe′clay,** a fine white, nearly pure, kaolin, free from iron, used for making tobacco-pipes and fine earthenware, and for whitening belts, &c.—*v.t.* to whiten with pipeclay.—*adj.* **piped**(*pīpt*), tubular or fistulous.—*ns.* **pipe′-dream,** a hope or fancy as futile and unreal as an opium-smoker's dream; **pipe′-dreamer**; **pipe′-fish,** a fish (of several species) of the sea-horse family, a long thin fish covered with hard plates, the jaws forming a long tube; **pipe′ful,** enough to fill a pipe; **pipe′-key,** a key with a hollow barrel; **pipe′-layer,** one who lays pipes for water, gas, &c.: (*U.S.*) a political wire-puller; **pipe′-laying.** —*adjs.* **pipe′less**; **pipe′like.**—*ns.* **pipe′-light, -er,** a spill of paper for lighting a pipe; **pipe′-line,** a long continuous line of piping to carry water from a reservoir, oil from an oil-field, &c.; **pipe′-major,** chief of a band of bagpipers; **Pipe′-off′ice,** formerly an office in the Court of Exchequer in which the clerk of the pipe made out crown-land leases; **pipe′-organ,** an organ with pipes; **pip′er,** a player on a pipe, esp. a bagpipe: a broken-winded horse: a young pigeon or other bird: a kind of gurnard: a pipe-smoker: a decoy dog: a kind of caddis-worm; **pipe′-rack,** a rack for tobacco-pipes; **pipe′-roll,** (*hist.*) a Great Roll of the Exchequer, containing yearly accounts of sheriffs, &c. (possibly from its pipelike form); **pipe′-stem,** the tube of a tobacco-pipe; **pipe′-stopp′le, -stapp′le,** (*Scot.*) a tobacco-pipe stem: anything very thin and brittle-looking; **pipe′-track,** the course of a pipe across country; **pipe′-tree,** (*obs.*) mock orange (*white pipe-tree*): the lilac (*blue pipe-tree*); **pipe′work,** a vein of ore in the form of a pipe: piping or pipes collectively, as in an organ; **pipe′wort,** a rare rush-like water-plant (*Eriocaulon septangulare*) of Ireland and the

Hebrides, only European representative of its family Eriocaulaceae; **pipe′-wrench,** a wrench that grips a pipe when turned one way.—*adj.* **pip′ing,** playing a pipe: sounding like a pipe: whistling: thin and high-pitched: characterised by pipe-playing (as opp. to martial music—*the piping times of peace*): hissing hot: very hot.—*n.* the action of the verb pipe in any sense: pipe-playing: a system of pipes: tubing: small cord used as trimming for clothes: strings and twists of sugar ornamenting a cake: a slip or cutting from a joint of a stem: hydraulicking.—*adj.* **pip′y,** pipe-like: having pipes: piping.—**drunk as a piper,** very drunk; **pay the piper,** bear the expense (and therefore call the tune, have control): to have to pay heavily; **pipe and tabor,** a small recorder, fingered by the left hand, and a small drum beaten by the same player with his right, formerly in use at rustic merry-makings, morris-dances, &c.; **pipe down,** to dismiss from muster, as a ship's company: to subside into silence; **pipeless organ,** a musical instrument, played like an organ, in which sounds, built up from whatever harmonics may be chosen, are produced by a loud-speaker; **pipe off,** to watch a house or person for purposes of theft; **pipe of peace** (see **calumet**); **pipe one's eye, tune one's pipes,** to weep; **piping crow,** an Australian bird (*Gymnorhina*) called a magpie, really akin to the shrikes; **piping hare,** a pika; **piping hot,** hissing hot, usu. hyperbolically. [O.E. *pīpe*—L. *pīpāre,* to cheep; cf. Du. *pijp,* Ger. *pfeife.*]

pipe, *pīp, n.* a cask or butt, of two hogsheads, varying according to the wine, ordinarily about 105 gallons.—*n.* **pipe′-wine,** (*Shak.*) wine from the cask, not bottled. [O.F. *pipe,* cask, tube; cf. preceding.]

pipemma *pip-em′ä, n.* (*mil. slang*) the letters PM: afternoon (*post meridiem*). [Signallers' or telephonists' names for the letters.]

Piper, *pip′ər, n.* the pepper genus, giving name to a family **Pipera′ceae** of dicotyledons.—*adjs.* **piperaceous** (*-ā′shəs*); **piperic** (*pip-er′ik*), applied to an acid ($C_{12}H_{10}O_4$) got from piperine.—*ns.* **piper′-idine,** a liquid base ($C_5H_{11}N$) got from piperine; **pip′erine,** an alkaloid ($C_{17}H_{19}O_3N$) found in pepper. [L. *piper,* pepper.]

pipette, *pip-et′, n.* a tube for transferring and measuring fluids. [Fr., dim. of *pipe,* pipe.]

pipi, *pē′pē, n.* a Brazilian Caesalpinia: its pods used in tanning. [Tupí *pipai.*]

piping. See under **pipe** (1).

pipistrelle, *pip-is-trel′, n.* a small reddish-brown bat, the commonest British bat. [Fr.,—It. *pipistrello,* a form of *vespertilio*—L. *vespertiliō,* bat—*vesper,* evening.]

pipit, *pip′it, n.* a lark-like genus (Anthus) of birds akin to wagtails, including the titlark. [Prob. imit.]

pipkin, *pip′kin, n.* a small pot, now only of earthenware: (*U.S.*) a piggin. [Poss. a dim. of **pipe.**]

pippin, *pip′in, n.* (*obs.*) a fruit pip: an apple of various varieties. [O.Fr. *pepin.*]

pipul. Same as **pipal.**

pipy. See under **pipe** (1).

piquant, *pē′kənt, adj.* stinging: pleasantly pungent: appetising: kindling keen interest.—*n.* **piq′uancy.** —*adv.* **piq′uantly.** [Fr., pr.p. of *piquer,* to prick.]

pique, *pēk, n.* animosity or ill-feeling: offence taken: a feeling of anger or vexation caused by wounded pride: resentment of a slight: dudgeon: (*obs.*) point or punctilio.—*v.t.* to wound the pride of: to nettle: to pride: to rouse, stir, provoke. [Fr. *pique,* a pike, pique, *piquer,* to prick; cf. **pike, prick.**]

pique, *pēk, n.* in piquet, the scoring of 30 points in one hand before the other side scores at all.— *v.t.* to score a pique against.—*v.i.* to score a pique. [Fr. *pic;* see **piquet.**]

pique, *pēk, n.* (*Browning*) for **peak** (1).

piqué, *pē-kā, n.* a stiff corded cotton fabric: inlaid work of gold or silver in point or strip (sometimes with mother-of-pearl) on tortoise-shell or ivory.—Also *adj.*—**piqué work,** inlaying in piqué needlework with a design made by stitching. [Fr. pr.p. of *piquer,* to prick.]

piquet. Same as **picket.**

piquet, *pi-ket'*, *n.* a game for two with 32 cards, with scoring for declarations and tricks. [Fr.; origin unknown.]

piragua, *pi-rä'gwä*, *n.* a South American dug-out canoe, or a craft with a single trunk as foundation, often a schooner-rigged barge.—Also **peria'gua**, or (*Fr.*) **pirogue** (*pi-rōg'*). [Sp. *piragua*—Carib *piraqua*.]

piranha, *pē-rän'yä*, **piraya,** *pē-rä'yä*, **perai, pirai,** *pē-rī'*, *ns.* a ferocious South American river-fish (Serrasalmo or Pygocentrus) of the Characinidae. [Port. from Tupí *piranya, piraya*.]

pirarucú, *pē-rä-rōō-kōō'*, *n.* the arapaima.

pirate, *pī-rät*, *n.* one who, without authority, attempts to capture ships at sea: a sea-robber: a pirates' ship: one who publishes without authority of the owner of the copyright: a private bus, or its driver, plying on the recognised route of others.—*v.t.* to rob as a pirate: to publish without permission.—*n.* **piracy** (*pī'rə-si*), the crime of a pirate: robbery on the high seas: unauthorised publication: infringement of copyright.—*adjs.* **piratic** (*pī-rat'ik*), **-al**, pertaining to a pirate: practising piracy.—*adv.* **pirat'ically.** [L. *pīrāta*—Gr. *peirātēs*—*peiraein*, to attempt.]

pirlicue, purlicue, *pir', pur'li-kū*, *n.* (*Scot.*) a peroration: a résumé in conclusion.—*v.t.* and *v.i.* to summarise in conclusion. [Origin unknown.]

pirn, *pərn*, (*Scot.*) *pirn*, *n.* a reel, bobbin, or spool. —**wind one a bonny pirn**, set a fine problem for him, involve him in difficulties. [Origin unknown.]

pirnie, *pir'ni*, *adj.* (*Scot.*) unevenly wrought: striped.—*n.* (*Scot.*) a striped woollen nightcap.— *adj.* **pirn'it,** (*Scot.*) interwoven with different colours: striped. [App. conn. with **pirn.**]

pirogue, *pi-rōg'.* See **piragua.**

pirouette, *pir-ōō-et'*, *n.* a spinning about on tiptoe. —*v.i.* to spin round on tiptoe.—*n.* **pirouett'er.** [Fr.]

pirrauru, *pi-row'roo*, *n.* among Australian blacks, a recognised supplementary husband or wife: the relation to such a person.—Also *adj.* [Native word.]

Pisces, *pis'ēz*, *n.pl.* (*zool.*) the class of fishes: (*astron.*) the Fishes, the twelfth sign of the zodiac, or the constellation that formerly coincided with it.—*ns.* **piscary** (*pisk'ə-ri*), right of fishing: a fishing pond; **pisca'tor,** an angler:—*fem.* **piscā'trix.**—*adjs.* **piscatorial** (*pis-kə-tō'ri-əl*), **piscatory** (*pis'kə-tə-ri*), relating to fishing: fishing; **piscicolous** (*pis-ik'ə-ləs*), parasitic within fishes; **piscicul'tural.**—*ns.* **pis'ciculture,** the rearing of fish by artificial methods; **pis'culturist; piscifau'na,** the assemblage of fishes in a region, formation, &c.—*adjs.* **pis'ciform,** having the form of a fish; **piscine** (*pis'īn*), of fishes: of the nature of a fish; **pisciv'orous,** feeding on fishes. [L. *piscis*, a fish; pl. *piscis, piscēs; piscātor,* fisher.]

piscina, *pis-ē'nä, pis-ī'nä*, *n.* a fish-pond: a swimming-pool (as in Roman baths): a basin and drain in old churches, usu. in a niche south of an altar, into which was emptied water used in washing the sacred vessels:—*pl.* **pisci'nas,** or **-ae.** —Also **piscine** (*pis'ēn*, or *-ēn'*). [L. *piscīna*—*piscis*, fish.]

pisé, *pē-zā'*, *n.* rammed earth or clay for walls or floors.—Also *adj.* [Fr.]

pish, *pish*, *interj.* expressing impatience.—*n.* an utterance of the exclamation.—*v.t.* to pooh-pooh. [Imit.]

pisiform, *pī'si-form, piz'i-form*, *adj.* pea-shaped.— *n.* a pea-shaped bone of the carpus. [L. *pisum*, pea, *forma*, shape.]

pismire, *pis'mīr*, *n.* an ant or emmet. [**piss**, from the strong smell of the ant-hill, M.E. *mire* (doubtful O.E. *míre*), ant.]

pisolite, *pī'sō-līt, piz'ō-līt*, *n.* a coarse oolite.—*adj.* **pisolitic** (*-lit'ik*). [Gr. *pisos*, pease, *lithos*, stone.]

piss, *pis*, *v.i.* to discharge urine.—*v.t.* to discharge as urine: to urinate on.—*n.* urine.—*ns.* **piss'abed,** (*prov.*) the dandelion; **piss'-pot,** a chamber-pot. [Fr. *pisser*.]

pissasphalt, *pis'as-falt*, *n.* a semi-liquid bitumen. [Gr. *pissa*, pitch, *asphaltos*, asphalt.]

pistachio, *pis-tä'(t)shi-ō, -(t)shyō,* or *pis-tä'*, *n.* the almond-flavoured fruit-kernel of a small western Asiatic tree (*Pistacia vera*) of the same genus of the cashew family as the mastic tree:—*pl.* **pistachios.** [Sp. *pistacho* and It. *pistacchio*—L.L. *pistāquium*— Gr. *pistákion*—Pers. *pistah*.]

pistareen, *pis-ta-rēn'*, *n.* an old Spanish two-real piece formerly current in the United States. [Prob. *peseta*.]

pistil, *pis'til*, *n.* (*bot.*) the ovary of a flower, with its style and stigma.—*adj.* **pis'tillate,** having a pistil but no (functional) stamens, female.—*n.* **pis'tillode,** an abortive pistil. [L. *pistillum*, a pestle.]

pistol, *pis'tl*, *n.* a small hand-gun, held in one hand when fired.—*v.t.* to shoot with a pistol:—*pr.p.* **pis'tolling;** *pa.t.* and *pa.p.* **pis'tolled.**—*ns.* **pistole** (*pis-tōl'*), an old Spanish gold coin=about 17s.: a 12-pound piece Scots=£1; **pistoleer',** one who carries or uses a pistol; **pis'tolet,** a pistol: a pistole: a gold coin of various kinds worth about 6s.; **pis'tol-shot.** [O.Fr. *pistole*, earlier *pistolet*—prob. from *Pistoia*, in Italy.]

piston, *pis'tən*, *n.* a cylindrical piece moving to and fro in a hollow cylinder, as in engines and pumps: a valve mechanism for altering the effective length of tube in brass musical instruments: a push-key for combining a number of organ stops.—*n.* **pis'ton-rod,** the rod to which the piston is fixed, and which moves up and down with it. [Fr.,— It. *pistone—pestare*, to pound—L. *pinsĕre, pistum*.]

pit, *pit*, *n.* a hole in the earth: a mine shaft: a mine, esp. a coal-mine: a place whence minerals are dug: (*arch.*) a prison, esp. a castle prison entered from above: a cavity in the ground or in a floor for any purpose, as reception of ashes, inspection of motor-cars, a bottom-sawyer: a hole for storing root-crops: a covered heap of potatoes, &c.: a grave, esp. one for many bodies: hell, or its lowest depths: a hole used as a trap for wild beasts: an enclosure for cock-fights or the like: the ground-floor of a theatre, or its occupants, or the part of the ground-floor behind the stalls: (*U.S.*) part of a corn exchange floor assigned to some particular business: a noisy card game mimicking a corn exchange: any hollow or depression, as the *pit of the stomach* below the breast-bone: an indentation left by smallpox: a minute depression in a surface: a hollow made by a rain-drop: (*bot.*) a thin place in a cell-wall, affording communication with another cell.—*v.t.* to mark with little hollows: to lay in a pit: to set to fight, as cocks in a cockpit: to match (with *against*).—*v.i.* to become marked with pits: (*med.*) to retain an impression for a time after pressing:—*pr.p.* **pitt'ing;** *pa.t.* and *pa.p.* **pitt'ed.** —*ns.* **pit'-brow,** the top of a shaft; **pit'-coal,** coal in the ordinary sense—not *charcoal*; **pit'-dwelling,** a primitive home made by roofing over a pit; **pit'fall,** a lightly covered hole as a trap: (*fig.*) a hidden danger; **pit'head,** the ground at the mouth of a pit, and the machinery, &c., on it; **pit'man,** a man who works in a coal-pit or a saw-pit, esp. at sinking, repair, and inspection of shafts and at pumping in a mine: (*U.S.*) a rod connecting a rotary with a reciprocating part; **pit'-pony,** a pony employed for haulage in a coal-mine; **pit'-prop,** timber used for support in the workings of a coal-mine; **pit'-saw,** a saw used in a saw-pit; **pit'-saw'yer,** a bottom-sawyer.— *adj.* **pitt'ed,** marked with small pits.—*ns.* **pitt'ing;** **pitt'ite,** one who frequents the pit of the theatre; **pit'-vill'age,** a group of miners' houses near a pit: a cluster of pit-dwellings; **pit'-vi'per,** any member of an American group of snakes, including the rattlesnake, with a pit between eye and nose. —**pit and gallows,** a feudal baron's right to drown female and hang male felons. [O.E. *pytt* —L. *puteus*, a well.]

pit, *pit*, *n.* (*U.S.*) a fruit-stone.—*v.t.* to remove the stone from. [App. Du. *pit*.]

pit, *pit*, *v.t.* (*Scot.*) to put:—*pa.t.* **pat, pât;** *pa.p.* **putten,** *put'n*, **pitt'en.** [See **put.**]

pita, *pē'tä*, *n.* the fibre of various species of Bromelia, Agave, &c.—Also **pi'ta-flax', -hemp'.** [Sp.,— Quichua *pita*, fine thread.]

Pitaka, *pit'ə-kə*, *n.* any one of the three divisions of the Buddhist canon. [Sans., basket.]

pitapat, *pit'ə-pat*, **pitty-pat**, *pit'i-pat*, **pit-pat**, *pit'pat'*, *adv.* with palpitation or pattering.—*adj.* fluttering: pattering.—*n.* a light, quick step: a succession of light taps: a patter.—*v.i.* to step or tread quickly: to patter: to palpitate. [Imit.]

pitara(h). See petara.

pitch, *pich*, *n.* the black shining residue of distillation of tar, &c.: extended to various bituminous and resinous substances, as *Burgundy pitch*.—*v.t.* to smear, cover, or caulk with pitch.—*adj.* **pitch'-black**, black as pitch.—*n.* **pitch'blende**, a black mineral of resinous lustre, fundamentally composed of uranium oxides, important as a source of radium.—*adj.* **pitch'-dark**, utterly dark.—*ns.* **pitch'iness**; **pitch'pine**, a name for several American pines that yield pitch and timber (*Pinus palustris*, *P. rigida*, &c.); **pitch'stone**, a volcanic glass of resinous lustre, usu. acid; **pitch'-tree**, a tree yielding pitch, turpentine, or resin, esp. silver fir, spruce, kauri pine, Amboyna pine.—*adj.* **pitch'y**, like or characteristic of pitch: smeared with pitch: abounding in pitch: black. [O.E. *pic*—L. *pix*, *picis*.]

pitch, *pich*, *v.t.* to thrust or fix in the ground: to set up: to establish: to set or plant firmly: to set in position: to lay out for sale: to set, cover, stud, or face: to pave with stones set on end or on edge: to make a foundation of stones for: (*obs.*) to set in array: to pit in opposition: (*obs.*) to determine or fix: to set in a key, to give this or that musical pitch, emotional tone, or degree of moral exaltation, &c.: to fling, throw, or toss, esp. in such a manner as to fall flat or in a definite position: (*golf*) to loft so as not to roll much on falling: (*baseball*) to deliver to the batsman by an overhand or underhand throw.—*v.i.* to settle: to alight: to fix the choice: to encamp: to plunge forward: to oscillate about a transverse axis: to slope down: to descend or fall away abruptly: to interlock (*pa.t.* and *pa.p.* **pitched**, *obs.* **pight**, q.v.).—*n.* act or manner of pitching: a throw or cast: degree, esp. of elevation or depression: the top, apex: height: a descent: slope: (*cricket*) ground between the wickets: a place set apart for playing or practising a game: the point where a ball alights: a station: the degree of acuteness of sound: a standard of acuteness for sounds (as **concert pitch**, **French pitch**): distance between successive points or things, as the centres of teeth in a wheel or a saw, the threads of a screw: (of a propeller) the angle between the chord of the blade and the plane of rotation: the distance a propeller would advance in one revolution.—*ns.* **pitch-and-toss'**, a game in which coins are thrown at a mark, the player who throws nearest having the right of tossing all, and keeping those that come down heads up; **pitch'er**, one who pitches: a paving-stone or sett: a baseball player who delivers the ball to the batsman: one who pitches a stall: a cutting or stake intended to take root; **pitch'-far'thing**, chuck-farthing; **pitch'fork**, a fork for pitching hay, &c.: a tuning-fork.—*v.t.* to lift with a pitchfork: to throw suddenly into any position.—*ns.* **pitch'ing**, the action of the verb to pitch: a facing of stone: a foundation of stone for a road surface: a cobble-stone surface of a road; **pitch'pipe**, a small pipe to pitch the voice or tune with.—**pitch and pay**, (*Shak.*) pay ready-money; **pitched battle**, a deliberate battle on chosen ground between duly arranged sides; **pitch in**, to set to work briskly; **pitch into**, to assail vigorously; **pitch (up)on**, to let one's choice fall upon. [App. conn. with **pick**, **pike**.]

pitcher, *pich'ər*, *n.* a vessel, usu. of earthenware, for holding or pouring liquids: (*Scot.*) a cylindrical tinned milk-can: (*U.S.*) a jug or ewer: a modified leaf or part of a leaf in the form of a pitcher, serving to catch insects.—*ns.* **pitch'erful**; **pitch'er-plant**, an insectivorous plant with pitchers, esp. Nepenthes, also Sarracenia, Darlingtonia, &c.— (**little**) **pitchers have** (**long**) **ears**, children tell tales: there may be listeners. [O.Fr. *picher*—

L.L. *picārium*, a goblet—Gr. *bīkos*, a wine-vessel.]

piteous, *pit'i-əs*, *adj.* (*arch.*) compassionate: fitted to excite pity: (*Milt.*) paltry.—*adv.* **pit'eously.**— *n.* **pit'eousness**. [O.Fr. *pitos*, *piteus*; cf. **pity**.]

pith, *pith*, *n.* the soft tissue within the ring of vascular bundles in the stems of dicotyledonous plants: similar material elsewhere, as the white inner skin of an orange: spinal marrow: innermost part: condensed substance, spirit, essence: mettle: live meaning: vigour: importance.— *v.t.* to remove the pith of: to sever, pierce, or destroy the marrow or central nervous system of. —*n.* **pith'-ball**, a pellet of pith.—*adv.* **pith'ily.** —*n.* **pith'iness**.—*adjs.* **pith'ful**; **pith'less**; **pith'-like**.—*ns.* **pith'-hat**, a sun-helmet of sola pith; **pith'-tree**, a tropical African papilionaceous tree (*Herminiera elaphroxylon*) whose very pith-like wood is used for floats, canoes, &c.—*adj.* **pith'y**, full of pith: forcible: strong: energetic: sententious and masterful. [O.E. *pitha*; Du. *pit*, marrow.]

Pithecanthropus, *pith-ē-kan-thrō'pəs*, *n.* a fossil ape-man discovered by Dr Eugene Dubois in Java in 1891-92. [Gr. *pithēkos*, ape, *anthrōpos*, man.]

pithecoid, *pith-ē'koid*, *adj.* ape-like. [Gr. *pithēkos*, ape, *eidos*, form.]

pithos, *pith'os*, *n.* a large Greek wine-jar. [Gr.]

pit-mirk, *pit'mirk*, *adj.* (*Scot.*) pitch-dark.

niton, *pē-ton'v*, *n.* iron peg or stanchion. [Fr.]

Pitta, *pit'ä*, *n.* a genus of birds, the so-called ant-thrushes of the Old World. [Telugu *pitta*.]

pittance, *pit'əns*, *n.* a special additional allowance of food or drink in a religious house, or a bequest to provide it: a dole: a very small portion or quantity: a miserable pay. [O.Fr. *pitance*—L. *pietās*, pity.]

pitter, *pit'ər*, *v.i.* to make a sound like a grasshopper.—*adv.* **pitt'er-patt'er**, with light pattering sound.—Also *n.* [Imit.]

pittie-ward, *pit'i-wərd*, *n.* an unexplained word in Shakespeare (*Merry Wives*, III. i.).

Pittite, *pit'īt*, *n.* a follower of William Pitt (1759-1806), statesman.—*n.* **Pitt'ism**.

pitty-pat. See pitapat.

pituita, *pit-ū-i'tä*, **pituite**, *pit'ū-īt*, *n.* phlegm.—*adj.* **pitū'itary**.—*n.* **pitū'itrin**, a hormone produced by the pituitary body.—**pituitary body**, a ductless gland at the base of the brain affecting growth, once thought to produce mucus. [L. *pituīta*.]

pity, *pit'i*, *n.* a feeling for the sufferings and misfortunes of others: a cause or source of pity or grief: an unfortunate chance: a matter for regret. —*v.t.* to feel pity for: to feel grief at: (*obs.*) to cause pity in:—*pr.p.* **pit'ying**; *pa.t.* and *pa.p.* **pit'ied**.—*adj.* **pit'iable**, to be pitied: miserable, contemptible.—*n.* **pit'iableness**.—*adv.* **pit'iably.** —*n.* **pit'ier**.—*adj.* **pit'iful**, feeling pity: compassionate: exciting pity: sad: despicable.— *advs.* **pit'iful** (*Shak.*), **pit'ifully**.—*n.* **pit'ifulness.** — *adj.* **pit'iless**, without pity: cruel.—*adv.* **pit'ilessly.**—*n.* **pit'ilessness**.—*adv.* **pit'yingly.**— **it pitieth me, you, them, &c.** (*Pr. Bk.*), it causeth pity in me, you, them, &c. [O.Fr. *pite* (Fr. *pitié*, It. *pietà*)—L. *pietās*, *pietātis*—*pius*, pious.]

pityriasis, *pit-i-ri'i-sis*, *n.* a branny scaliness of the skin.—*adj.* **pit'yroid**, bran-like. [Gr. *pityron*, bran.]

pium, *pi-ōōm'*, *n.* a small but very troublesome Brazilian biting fly. [Tupí.]

pivot, *piv'ət*, *n.* a pin on which anything turns: a soldier upon whom, or position on which, a body wheels: a centre-half in football: that on which anything depends or turns: a man of cardinal importance in an industry: a movement of the body as if on a pivot.—*adj.* of the nature of a pivot: cardinal: serving as a pivot.—*v.t.* to mount on a pivot.—*v.i.* to turn on or as if on a pivot.— *adj.* **piv'otal**.—*adv.* **piv'otally**.—*n.* **piv'ot-bridge**, a swing-bridge moving on a vertical pivot in the middle.—*adj.* **piv'oted**.—*ns.* **piv'oter**, one who makes and fits pivots: a golfer who turns his body; **piv'oting**, the pivot-work in machines; **piv'ot-man**, a man on whom a body of soldiers turns: a man of cardinal importance in industry, &c. [Fr. *pivot*, perh. related to It. *piva*, pipe, peg, pin.]

pix, *piks, n.* Same as **pyx.**

pixy, pixie, *pik′si,* **pisky,** *pis′ki, n. (S.W. England)* a small fairy.—*adjs.* **pix′ilated, pix′y-led,** bewildered.—*ns.* **pix′y-ring,** a fairy-ring; **pix′y-stool,** a toadstool or mushroom. [Origin obscure; cf. Sw. *pysk, pyske,* a small fairy.]

pize, *pīz, n.* a term of imprecation, pox, pest. [Origin unknown.]

pizzicato, *pit-si-kä′tō, adj. (mus.)* played by plucking the string, not with the bow—contradicted by *arco* or *col arco.*—*adv.* by plucking.—*n.* a tone so produced: a passage so played: the manner of playing by plucking. [It., twitched—*pizzicare,* to twitch.]

pizzle, *piz′l, n.* a penis: that of a bull used as an instrument of punishment. [L.G. *pesel* or Flem. *pezel.*]

placable, *plak′* or *plāk′ə-bl, adj.* that may be appeased: relenting: willing to forgive.—*ns.* **placabil′ity, plac′ableness.** — *adv.* **plac′ably.** — *v.t.* **placate** (*plə-kāt′, plā-kāt′, plak′, plāk′āt*), to conciliate.—*n.* **placā′tion,** propitiation.—*adj.* **placatory** (*plak′* or *plāk′ə-tə-ri*), conciliatory. [L. *plācāre,* to appease, akin to *placēre.*]

placard, *plak′ärd, n. (obs.)* an official permit or proclamation with a thin seal: a written or printed paper stuck upon a wall or otherwise displayed as an intimation: (*obs.*) a placcate or placket.—*v.t.* **placard** (*plak′ärd* or *plə-kärd′*), to publish or notify by placard: to post or set up as a placard: to put placards on or in. [O.Fr. *plackart, placard,* &c.—*plaquier,* to lay flat, plaster—M.Flem. *placken,* to plaster.]

placcate, *plak′āt, n.* See **placket.**

place, *plās, n.* an open space in a town, a marketplace or square: in street names, vaguely a row or group of houses, often short, secluded, or mean: a portion of space: a portion of the earth's surface, or any surface: a position in space, or on the earth's surface, or in any system, order, or arrangement: a building, room, piece of ground, &c., assigned to some purpose (as *place of business, entertainment, worship*): a particular locality: a town, village, &c.: a dwelling or home: a mansion with its grounds: (*obs.*) a battlefield: (*obs.*) a fortress, fortified town: a seat or accommodation in a theatre, train, at table, &c.: space occupied: room: the position held by anybody, employment, office, a situation, esp. under government or in domestic service: due or proper position or dignity: that which is incumbent on one: precedence: position in a series: high rank: position attained in a competition or assigned by criticism: position among the first three in a race: stead: (*obs.*) passage in a book: (*obs.*) a topic, matter of discourse: pitch reached by a bird of prey (*obs.* except in *pride of place*).—*v.t.* to put in any place: to assign to a place: to find a place for: to locate: to identify: to settle: to induct: to put in hand: to lend: to invest: to assign: to ascribe.—*adj.* **placed,** set in place or in a place: having a place: among the first three in a race: inducted to a charge.—*ns.* **place′-hunter,** one who covets and strives after a public post; **place′-kick,** in football, a kick made when the ball has been placed on the ground for that purpose.—*adj.* **place′less,** without place or office.—*ns.* **place′-man,** one who has a place or office under a government:—*pl.* **place′men; place′ment,** placing or setting: assigning to places; **place′-monger,** one who traffics in appointments to places; **place′-name,** a geographical proper name; **plac′er.**—**give place,** to make room: to be superseded; **have place,** to have existence; **in place, in position:** opportune; **out of place,** out of due position: inappropriate, unseasonable; **take place,** to come to pass: to take precedence. [Partly O.E. (Northumb.) *plæce,* market-place, but mainly Fr. *place,* both from L. *platea*—Gr. *plateia* (*hodos*), broad (street).]

placebo, *plə-sē′bō, n.* vespers for the dead: (*obs.*) a sycophant: a medicine given to humour or gratify a patient rather than to exercise any curative effect. [From the first words of the first antiphon of the office, *Placēbō Dominō,* I shall please the Lord.]

placenta, *plə-sen′tä, n.* the structure that unites the unborn mammal to the womb of its mother and establishes a nutritive connexion between them: (*bot.*) the part of the carpel that bears the ovules: a structure bearing sporangia:—*pl.* **placen′tae** (*-tē*).—*adj.* **placen′tal.**—*n.pl.* **Placentalia** (*plas-ən-tā′li-ä*), the Eutheria or placental mammals.—*n.* **placentā′tion,** the arrangement and mode of attachment of placentae or of placenta and fetus.—*adj.* **placent′iform,** cake-shaped. [L. *placenta,* a flat cake—Gr. *plakoeis* (contr. *plakous*) from *plax, plakos,* anything flat.]

placer, *plas′ər, pläs′ər, n.* a superficial deposit from which gold or other mineral can be washed. [Sp. *placer,* sandbank—*plaza,* place.]

placet, *plā′set* (L. *plā′ket*), *n.* a vote of assent in a governing body: permission given, esp. by a sovereign, to publish and carry out an ecclesiastical order, as a papal bull or edict. [L. *plăcet,* it pleases, 3rd sing. pres. indic. of *placēre,* to please.]

placid, *plas′id, adj.* calm.—*ns.* **placid′ity, plac′idness.**—*adv.* **plac′idly.** [L. *placidus*—*placēre,* to please.]

placitum, *plas′i-təm* (L. *plăk′i-toom*), *n.* a decision of a court or an assembly: a plea or pleading:—*pl.* **plac′ita.**—Also **plac′it** (wrongly **plac′et**).—*adj.* **plac′itory,** relating to pleas or pleading. [L., pa.p. neut. of *placēre,* to please.]

plack, *plak, n.* an old Scottish copper coin worth a third part of an English penny.—*adj.* **plack′less.** [Prob. Flem. *placke,* an old Flemish coin, orig. a flat disk.]

placket, *plak′it, n.* in armour, a breastplate or backplate, or a leather doublet with strips of steel (*obs.* **placc′ate**): an apron: a petticoat: a placket-hole: a pocket, esp. in skirt: a woman.—*Shak.* also **placc′at.**—*n.* **plack′et-hole,** a slit in a skirt. [Origin obscure; cf. **placard.**]

placoderm, *plak′ō-dərm, adj.* covered with bony plates, as some fossil fishes.—*n.* a fish so covered. [Gr. *plax, plakos,* anything flat, *derma,* skin.]

placoid, *plak′oid, adj.* plate-like: having placoid scales, irregular plates of hard bone, not imbricated, as sharks. [Gr. *plax, plakos,* anything flat and broad, *eidos,* form.]

plafond, *plä-fonÿ′, n.* a ceiling, esp. decorated: a soffit: a game like contract bridge. [Fr., ceiling, score above the line in bridge—*plat,* flat, *fond,* bottom.]

plagal, *plā′gl, adj.* of a Gregorian mode, having the final in the middle of the compass instead of at the bottom—opp. to *authentic.*—**plagal cadence,** one in which the subdominant chord precedes the tonic. [Gr. *plagios,* sidewise—*plagos,* a side.]

plagiary, *plā′ji-ə-ri, n.* one who steals the thoughts or writings of others and gives them out as his own: the crime of plagiarism.—*adj.* (*obs.*) practising or got by literary theft.—*v.t.* **pla′giarise,** to steal from the writings or ideas of another.—*ns.* **pla′giarism,** the act or practice of plagiarising; **pla′giarist,** a plagiary. [L. *plagiārius,* a kidnapper, plagiary—*plăga,* a net.]

plagioclase, *plā′ji-ō-klās, -klāz,* or *plaj′, n.* a felspar whose cleavages are not at right angles—albite, anorthite, or any mixture of them. [Gr. *plagios,* oblique, *klasis,* a fracture.]

plagiostome, *plā′ji-ō-stōm, n.* a plagiostomous fish, one of the **Plagiostomata** (*-stō′mə-tä*) or **Plagiostomi** (*-os′tə-mī*), the cross-mouthed fishes, sharks and rays, having the mouth as a transverse slit on the under side of the head.—*adjs.* **plagiostom′atous, plagios′tomous.** [Gr. *plagios,* crosswise, *stoma, -atos,* mouth.]

plagiotropism, *plā-ji-ot′rə-pizm, n.* orienting at right angles to the direction of stimulus.—*adj.* **plagiotropic** (*-ō-trop′ik*).—*adv.* **plagiotrop′ically.** —*adj.* **plagiotropous** (*-ot′rə-pəs*). [Gr. *plagios,* crosswise, *tropos,* a turning.]

plagium, *plā′ji-əm, n.* the crime of kidnapping. [L. *plăgium*—*plăga,* a net.]

plague, *plāg, n. (obs.)* a blow or wound: an affliction regarded as a sign of divine displeasure: a deadly epidemic or pestilence, esp. a fever caused by a bacillus (*B. pestis*) transmitted by rat-fleas from rats to man, characterised by buboes, or swellings of the lymphatic glands, by carbuncles and petechiae: murrain: any troublesome thing or person: (*coll.*) trouble.—*v.t.* (*rare*) to infest with disease: to pester or annoy.—*n.* **plague'-pit**, a common grave for plague victims.—*adj.* **plague'-some**.—*ns.* **plague'-sore**, an ulcer due to plague; **plague'-spot**, a spot on the skin indicating plague: a place where disease is constantly present.—*adj.* **plague'-stricken**.—*adv.* **plag'uily**, confoundedly.—*adj.* **plaguy** (*plā'gi*), of, or of the nature of, plague: vexatious: troublesome: confounded.—*adv.* (*Shak.*) confoundedly.—**plague on**, may a curse rest on; **what the** (*Shak.*) **a) plague,** what the devil. [O.Fr. *plague*—L. *plāga*, a blow; cf. Gr. *plēgē*.]

plaice, *plās*, *n.* a yellow-spotted flat-fish of the fam. Pleuronectidae (*Pleuronectes platessa*).—*n.* **plaice'-mouth,** a mouth placed awry.—*adj.* wry-mouthed. [O.Fr. *plaïs* (Fr. *plie*)—L.L. *platessa,* a flat-fish—perh. Gr. *platys*, flat.]

plaid, *plād* (by the English also *plad*), *n.* a long piece of woollen cloth, worn over the shoulder, usually in tartan as part of Highland dress, or checked as formerly worn by Lowland shepherds: cloth for it: a plaidman.—*adj.* like a plaid in pattern or colours.—*adj.* **plaid'ed,** wearing a plaid: made of plaid cloth.—*ns.* **plaid'ing,** a strong woollen twilled fabric; **plaid'man,** a Highlander; **plaid'-neuk'** (*-nɔk*), a pocket at the end of a plaid. [Perh. Gael. *plaide,* a blanket; but that may be from the Scots word.]

plain, *plān, v.t.* and *v.i.* to complain: to lament.—*n.* a complaint.—*n.* **plain'ant,** one who complains: a plaintiff.—*adj.* **plain'ful.**—*n.* **plain'ing,** (*Shak.*) complaint. [O.Fr. *plaigner* (Fr. *plaindre*)—L. *plangĕre*, to beat the breast, lament.]

plain, *plān, adj.* flat: level: even: unobstructed: without obscurity: clear: obvious: simple: downright, utter: not ornate: unembellished: unvariegated: uncoloured: unruled: without pattern, striation, markings, &c.: without gloss: uncurled: not twilled: not elaborate: without addition: not highly seasoned: deficient in beauty: (in meiosis) ugly: without subtlety: candid: outspoken: straightforward: undistinguished: ordinary: other than a court card: other than trumps.—*n.* an extent of level land: (*poetic*) the open country, esp. as a field of battle, or the scene of the activities of nymphs and swains or errant knights and distressed damsels.—*adv.* clearly: distinctly.—*v.t.* (*Shak.*) to make plain.—*n.* **plain'-chant,** plainsong.—*adj.* **plain'-clothes,** wearing ordinary clothes, not uniform, as a policeman on detective work.—*v.i.* **plain'-cook,** to cook ordinary dishes.—*v.t.* and *v.i.* **plain'-darn,** to darn with the ordinary cross pattern.—*n.* **plain'-deal'er,** one who is candid and outspoken.—*n.* and *adj.* **plain'-deal'ing.**—*adj.* **plain'-heart'ed,** having a plain or honest heart: sincere.—*n.* **plain'-heart'edness.**—*adj.* **plain'ish.**—*adv.* **plain'ly.**—*ns.* **plain'ness; plains'man,** a dweller in a plain; **plain'song,** unmeasured music sung in unison in ecclesiastical modes from early times, and still in use in R.C. and some Anglican churches: a simple melody: that to which a descant can be added.—*adj.* (*Shak.*) singing a simple theme.—*n.* **plain'-speaking,** straightforwardness or bluntness of speech.—*adj.* **plain'-spoken,** plain, rough, and sincere.—*n.pl.* **plain'stanes,** (*Scot.*) flagstones, pavement (also **plain'stones**).—*n.* **plain'work,** plain needlework, as distinguished from embroidery.—**plain as a pikestaff** (see pike); **plain sailing** (see plane). [Fr.,—L. *plānus*, plain.]

plaint, *plānt, n.* lamentation: complaint: a mournful song: a statement of grievance, esp. the exhibiting of an action in writing by a complainant in a court of law.—*adj.* **plaint'ful,** complaining.—*n.* **plaint'iff,** (*Eng. law*) one who commences a suit against another—opp. to *defendant*.—Also *adj.* (*Spens.*).—*adj.* **plaint'ive,** mournful.—*adv.* **plaint'ively.**—*n.* **plaint'iveness.**—*adj.* **plaint'less.** [O.Fr. *pleinte* (Fr. *plainte*)—L. *plangĕre, planctum,* to beat the breast, lament.]

plaister, *plās'tɔr, n.* an obsolete or Scots form of **plaster.**

plait, *plat, plāt, plēt, n.* a pleat or zigzag fold (usu. **pleat,** and pron. *plēt* even when spelt **plait**): a braid in which strands are passed over one another in turn: material so braided: a braided tress or queue (in these senses usu. *plat*, and sometimes spelt **plat**).—*v.t.* to pleat (usu. *plēt*): to braid or intertwine (usu. *plat*).—*adj.* **plait'ed.**—*ns.* **plait'er; plait'ing.** [O.Fr. *pleit, ploit* (Fr. *pli*)—L. *plicāre, -ĭtum, -ātum,* to fold.]

plan, *plan, n.* a figure or representation of anything projected on a plane or flat surface, esp. that of a building, floor, &c., as disposed on the ground: a large-scale detailed map of a small area: a scheme for accomplishing a purpose: a purposed method: a scheme drawn up beforehand: a scheme of arrangement: in the Methodist churches, a quarterly programme of services with preachers for each church in the circuit.—*v.t.* to make a plan of: to design: to lay plans for: to devise: (*U.S.*) to purpose.—*v.i.* to make plans:—*pr.p.* **plann'ing;** *pa.t.* and *pa.p.* **planned.**—*adj.* **plan'less.** — *n.* **plan'ner.** — **plan-position indicator** (abbrev. P.P.I.) (*radar*), an apparatus in which the position of reflecting objects is shown on the screen of a cathode-ray tube, as if on a plan. [Fr.,—L. *plānus,* flat.]

planarian, *plɔ-nā'ri-ɔn, adj.* and *n.* turbellarian. [L. *plānārius,* on level ground (taken as if meaning flat)—*plānus,* flat.]

planch, *plānsh, n.* (*obs.*) a plank: (*dial.*) a floor: a slab.—*v.t.* (*obs.*) to floor: to board.—*adj.* **planch'ed,** (*Shak.*) boarded.—*ns.* **planchet** (*plan'shit*), a blank to be stamped as a coin; **planchette** (*plän²-shet', plän-shet'*), a board mounted on two castors and a pencil-point, used as a medium for automatic writing and supposed spirit-messages. [Fr. *planche*—L. *planca.*]

plane, *plān, n.* any tree of the genus Platanus (see **platane**), esp. the oriental plane (*P. orientalis*) and the North American plane or buttonwood (*P. occidentalis*), trees with palmatifid leaves shedding their bark in thin slabs: in Scotland the great maple (*Acer Pseudoplatanus*).—*n.* **plane'-tree.** [Fr. *plane*—L. *platanus;* see **platane.**]

plane, *plān, n.* (*geom.*) a surface on which, if any two points be taken, the straight line joining them will lie entirely on the surface: any flat or level material surface: one of the thin horizontal structures used as wings and tail to sustain or control aeroplanes in flight: short for aeroplane or airplane (also '**plane**): an act of planing or soaring: in mines, a main road for transport of coal or other mineral: any grade of life or of development or level of thought or existence.—*adj.* having the character of a plane: pertaining to, lying in, or confined to a plane: level: smooth.—*v.t.* to make plane or smooth (see also **plane** (3)).—*v.i.* to travel by aeroplane: to soar: to volplane.—*adj.* **planar** (*plān'ɔr*).—*n.* **planation** (*plā-nā'shɔn*), making level.—*adj.* **plane'-pol'arised,** (of light) consisting of vibrations in one plane only.—*ns.* **planer** (*plān'ɔr*), one who levels or makes plane: a smoothing instrument (see also **plane** (3)): a wooden block beaten with a mallet to level a forme of type; **plane'-table,** an instrument used in field-mapping, with a sighting-telescope for observing objects, whose angles may be noted on a paper on the table of the instrument: an inclined table on which ore is dressed.—*v.t.* to survey with a plane-table.—*ns.* **planigraph** (*plan'i-gräf*), an instrument for reducing or enlarging drawings; **planimeter** (*plɔn-im'i-tɔr*), an instrument for measuring the area of a plane figure.—*adjs.* **planimetric** (*plān-, plan-i-met'rik*), **-al.**—*ns.* **planimetry** (*plɔn-im'i-tri*), the mensuration of plane surfaces; **planisphere** (*plan'*), a sphere projected on a plane.—*adjs.* **planispher'ic; plā'no-con'cave,** plane on one side and concave on the other; **plā'no-con'ical,** plane on one side and conical on the other; **plā'no-con'vex,** plane on one side and convex on the other.—*ns.* **planom'eter** (*plɔn-*), a plane surface used in machine-making as a gauge for plane surfaces; **Planor'bis,** a genus of pond-snails with flat spiral shell.—**plane (or plain) sailing,** the calculation of a ship's place in its course as if the earth were flat instead of spherical: easy work or going. [L. *plānum*, a flat surface, neut. of *plānus*, flat; cf. **plain**, and next word.]

plane, *plān*, *n.* a carpenter's tool for producing a smooth surface by paring off shavings: a tool or machine for smoothing other things.—*v.t.* to smooth or remove with a plane (see also **plane** (2)).—*ns.* **plā′ner**, one who uses a plane: a tool or machine for planing; **plān′ing-machine′**, a machine for planing wood or metals. [Fr. *plane* —L.L. *plāna*—*plānāre*, to smooth.]

planet, *plan′it*, *n.* in old astronomy, a heavenly body whose place among the fixed stars is not fixed (including sun and moon): a body (other than a comet or meteor) that revolves about the sun or other fixed star: a satellite of a planet (*secondary planet*): an astrological influence vaguely conceived.—*n.* **planetā′rium**, a machine showing the motions and orbits of the planets:—*pl.* **planetā′ria.**—*adjs.* **plan′etary**, pertaining to the planets or a planet, or this planet: consisting of, or produced by, planets: under the influence of a planet: erratic: revolving in an orbit; **planetic** (*plǝn-et′ik*), **-al.**—*n.* **plan′etoid**, a minor planet.—*adjs.* **planetoi′dal**; **plan′et-strick′en**, **plan′et-struck**, (*astrol.*) affected by the influence of the planets: blasted.—**inferior planets**, those within the earth's orbit (Mercury and Venus); **minor planets**, the numerous group of very small planets between the orbits of Mars and Jupiter; **superior planets**, those outside the earth's orbit. [Fr. *planète*—Gr. *planētēs*, wanderer—*planaein*, to make to wander.]

plangent, *plan′jǝnt*, *adj.* resounding: noisy: clangorous.—*n.* **plan′gency**. [L. *plangēns*, *-entis*, pr.p. of *plangĕre*, to beat.]

planish, *plan′ish*, *v.t.* to polish: to flatten.—*n.* **plan′isher**, a tool for planishing. [Obs. Fr. *planir*, *-issant*—*plan*, flat.]

plank, *plangk*, *n.* a long piece of timber, thicker than a board: (*U.S.*) a board on which shad or other food is roasted: one of the principles or aims that form the platform or programme of a party.—*v.t.* to cover with planks: to pay down or table: (*U.S.*) to roast on a plank.—*ns.* **plank′-bed**, a prison bed of wood without mattress; **plank′ing**, the act of laying planks: a series of planks: work made up of planks.—**walk the plank**, to walk (compulsorily) along a plank projecting over the ship's side into the sea. [L. *planca*, a board.]

plankton, *plangk′tǝn*, *n.* the drifting organisms in oceans, lakes, or rivers.—*adj.* (*irreg.*) **planktonic** (*-ton′ik*). [Neut. of Gr. *planktos*, *-ē*, *-on*, wandering.]

planoblast, *plan′ō-blast*, *n.* a free-swimming medusa. —*n.* **planogam′ete**, a motile gamete. [Gr. *plānos*, wandering.]

plano-concave, &c., **planometer**, **planorbis**. See **plane** (2).

plant, *plǎnt*, *n.* a vegetable organism, or part of one, ready for planting or lately planted: a slip, cutting, or scion: an offshoot: a young person: a sapling: a cudgel: any member of the vegetable kingdom, esp. (popularly) one of the smaller kinds: growth: amount planted: the sole of the foot: mode of planting oneself, stand: something deposited beforehand for a purpose: equipment, machinery, apparatus, for an industrial activity: (*U.S.*) a bedded oyster: (*slang*) a thief's hoard: (*slang*) a spy, detective, picket or cordon of detectives, or police trap: (*slang*) a deceptive trick, put-up job.—*v.t.* to put into the ground for growth: to introduce: to insert: to fix: to place firmly: to set in position: to station, post: to found: to settle: to locate: to place or deliver (as a blow, a dart): to leave in the lurch: (*slang*) to bury: (*slang*) to hide: to instil or implant: to furnish with plants: to colonise: to stock: to furnish or provide (with things disposed around): (*slang*) to salt (as a mine).—*v.i.* to plant trees, colonists, or anything else.—*n.* **plant′a**, the sole of the foot.—*adj.* **plant′able**.—*n.* **plant′age**, (*Shak.*) plants in general.—*adj.* **plant′ar**, of the sole of the foot.—*ns.* **plant′-associa′tion**, **plant′-forma′tion**,

an assemblage of plants growing together under like conditions, as in a salt-marsh, a pine-wood, &c.; **plantā′tion**, a place planted, esp. with trees: a colony: an estate used for growing cotton, rubber, tea, sugar, or other product of warm countries: (*Southern U.S.*) a large estate: act or process of introduction: (*Milt.*) the act of planting; **plant′er**, one who plants or introduces: the owner or manager of a plantation: a pioneer colonist: a settler: an instrument for planting; **plant′-house**, a structure for growing plants of warmer climates; **plant′ie-cruive** (*-krʒv′*; *Orkney* and *Shetland*), a kitchen garden, enclosure for cabbage.—*adj.* **plant′igrade**, walking on the soles of the feet.—*n.* an animal that walks so.—*n.* **plant′ing**, the act of setting in the ground for growth: the art of forming plantations of trees: (*Scot.*) a plantation.—*adjs.* **plant′less**, **plant′-like**. —*ns.* **plant′let**, **plant′ling**, a little plant; **plant′-lore**, folklore of plants: **plant′-louse**, an aphis or greenfly:—*pl.* **plant′-lice**; **plant′-pot**, a pot for growing a plant in; **plant′ule**, a plant embryo.—**plantation song**, a negro song, such as the blacks sang on American plantations; **plant out**, to transplant to open ground, from pot or frame: to dispose at intervals in planting. [O.E. *plante* (n.)—L. *planta*, shoot, slip, cutting, and O.E. *plantian* (vb.), and partly from or affected by Fr. *plante* and L. *planta*, plant, also (perh. a different word) sole.]

plantain, *plan′tān*, *n.* a roadside plant of genus **Plantā′go** (e.g. waybread, ribgrass; fam. **Plantaginā′ceae**) that presses its leaves flat on the ground. — *adj.* **plantaginaceous** (*plan-taj-i-nā′shǝs*). [L. *plantāgō*, *-inis*—*planta*, the sole of the foot.]

plantain, *plan′tān*, *n.* a musaceous plant: its fruit, a coarse banana: in India, a banana.—*n.* **plan′tain-eater**, an African bird (Musophaga) of a fam. Musophagidae akin to the cuckoos: extended to others of the family (touraco). [Origin doubtful.]

plantain, *plan′tān*, *n.* (*obs.*) a platane or plane-tree. [Obs. Fr. *plantain*—L. *platanus*.]

plantar, **plantigrade**. See **plant**.

planula, *plan′ū-lä*, *n.* a free-swimming two-layered, often flattened, larva of coelenterates, &c.—*adjs.* **plan′ular**; **plan′uliform**; **plan′uloid**. [Dim. of L. *plānus*, flat.]

planuria, *plan-ū′ri-ä*, *n.* the discharge of urine through an abnormal passage.—Also **plan′ury**. [Gr. *plǎnos*, wandering, *ouron*, urine.]

planxty, *plangks′ti*, *n.* an Irish dance or dance-tune, like a jig but slower. [Origin unknown; not native Irish.]

plap, *plap*, *n.* a flatter sound than a plop.—*v.i.* to make, or move with, such a sound. [Imit.]

plaque, *plǎk*, *n.* a plate, tablet, or slab hung on, applied to, or inserted in a surface as an ornament: a tablet worn as a badge of honour: (*med.*) a patch.—*n.* **plaquette′**, a small plaque. [Fr.; cf. **plack.**]

plash, *plash*, *v.t.* to interweave by partly cutting through, bending and twining the branches: to bend down: to break down: to make, mend, or treat, by cutting, bending, and interweaving stems and branches.—*n.* a plashed branch: a plashed place.—*n.* **plash′ing**. [O.Fr. *plassier*—L. *plectĕre*, to twist; cf. **pleach.**]

plash, *plash* (*Spens.* **plesh**, *plesh*), *n.* a shallow pool: a puddle.—*n.* **plash′et**, a puddle.—*adj.* **plash′y**. [O.E. *plæsc*.]

plash, *plash*, *n.* a dash of water: a splashing sound: (esp. *Scot.*) a sudden downpour.—*v.i.* to dabble in water: to splash.—*v.t.* to splash.—*adj.* **plash′y**. [Cf. M.L.G. *plaschen*, early Mod. Du. *plasschen*; perh. conn. with preceding.]

plasm, *plazm*, *n.* a mould or matrix: protoplasm: plasma.—*n.* **plas′ma**, plasm: a bright green chalcedony: protoplasm: the liquid part of blood, lymph, or milk.—*adjs.* **plasmat′ic**, **-al**, **plas′mic**, of plasma: protoplasmic.—*ns.* **plasmodesm** (*plaz′mō-dezm*; Gr. *desmos*, bond), a thread of protoplasm connecting cells; **plas′-modium**, a naked mass of protoplasm with many nuclei, as in slime-fungi:—*pl.* **plasmo′dia**;

---

plasmog′amy, fusion of cytoplasm only.—*v.t.* **plas′molyse** (-*līz*).—*n.* **plasmolysis** (-*mol′i-sis*; Gr. *lysis*, loosening), removal of water from a cell by osmosis, with resultant shrinking.—*adj.* **plasmolytic** (-*mō-lit′ik*).—*n.* **plasmosō′ma, plas′mosome** (Gr. *sōma*, body), a nucleolus. [Gr. *plasma, -atos*, a thing moulded—*plassein*, to mould.]

plast, plaste, *plāst*, (*Spens.*) *pa.t.* and *pa.p.* of **placed.**

plaster, *plås′tər, n.* a fabric coated with an adhesive substance for local application as a remedy, for protection of a cut, &c.: a pasty composition that sets hard, esp. a mixture of slaked lime, sand, and hair, used for coating walls and ceilings, &c.: calcium sulphate.—*adj.* made of plaster.— *v.t.* to apply plaster, or a plaster, to: to treat with plaster: to bedaub: to smear: to cover excessively, injudiciously, or meretriciously: to stick on or over: to reduce to plaster or a sticky mass: to shatter with shot: to smooth down: to smooth over: to treat with gypsum: to attach with plaster.—*adj.* **plas′tered,** daubed, treated, &c., with plaster: shattered: (*slang*) intoxicated.— *ns.* **plas′ter-board,** a building slab of plaster faced with paper or fibre; **plas′terer,** one who plasters, or one who works in plaster; **plas′tering; plas′ter-stone,** gypsum; **plas′ter-work.** — *adj.* **plas′tery,** like plaster: full of or covered with plaster.—**plaster cast,** a copy got by pouring a mixture of plaster of Paris and water into a mould formed from the object; **plaster of Paris,** gypsum (originally found near *Paris*) deprived by heat of part of its water of hydration. [O.E. *plaster* (in medical sense) and O.Fr. *plastre* (builder's plaster), both—L.L. *plastrum*—L. *emplastrum*—Gr. *emplastron* for *emplaston*—*en*, on, *plassein*, to mould, apply as a plaster.]

plastic, *plas′tik, adj.* having power to give form: shaping, formative: capable of being moulded: of or pertaining to moulding or modelling: modifiable: capable of permanent deformation without giving way: capable of, or pertaining to, metabolism and growth.—*n.* a substance that is, or can be made, capable of being moulded, or has set from a moulded substance, especially a synthetic resin: (*obs.*) a modeller or sculptor: the art of modelling or of sculpture (esp. in *pl.*): (in *pl.*, treated as *sing.*) plastic surgery.—*v.t.* **plas′ticise** (-*ti-sīz*), to make plastic.—*ns.* **plas′-ticine** (-*ti-sēn*; trade-mark name), a substitute for modelling clay; **plasticity** (-*tis′i-ti*), state or quality of being plastic.—**plastic arts,** the arts of shaping (in three dimensions), as sculpture, modelling; **plastic clay,** clay from which earthenware and bricks are made; **plastic force,** the force or power of growth in animals and plants; **plastic operation,** a surgical operation which restores a lost part, or repairs a deformed or disfigured part, of the body; **plastic surgery,** branch of surgery concerned with plastic operations. [Gr. *plastikos—plassein*, to mould.]

plastid, *plast′id, n.* (*obs.*) a living cell: a differentiated granule in protoplasm. — *n.* **plast′idule,** Haeckel's hypothetical unit of living protoplasm. [Gr. *plastis, -idos*, modeller (fem.).]

plastilina, *plås-ti-lē′nä, n.* a mixture of clay with oil, zinc oxide, wax, and sulphur for modelling. [It.]

plastogamy, *plast-og′ə-mi, n.* plasmogamy. [Gr. *plastos*, moulded, *gamos*, marriage.]

plastron, *plas′tron, n.* a breastplate worn under the hauberk: a fencer's wadded breast-shield: the under part of the shell of a tortoise or turtle, or other animal: the front of a dress-shirt: a separate ornamental front part of a woman's bodice. —*adj.* **plas′tral.** [Fr. *plastron*—It. *piastrone*— *piastra*, breastplate; cf. **piastre, plaster.**]

plat, *plat.* Same as **plait.**

plat, *plat, n.* a plot of ground: (*obs.* or *U.S.*) a diagram or a plan: (*obs.*) a scheme.—*v.t.* (now *U.S.*) to make a plan of, plot out. [**plot,** infl. by **plat,** 2].

plat, *plat, n.* (*obs.*) a flat thing: the flat, or flat part, or side: a mould-board: (esp. *U.S.*) a flat place or region. [App. Fr. *plat.*]

platane, platan, *plat′ən, n.* a plane-tree, any tree of the genus **Plat′anus** (see **plane** (1)), giving name to the family **Platanā′ceae,** akin to the witch-

hazel family.—*adj.* **platanā′ceous.** [L. *platanus* —Gr. *platanos—platys*, broad.]

platband, *plat′band, n.* a fascia or flat moulding projecting less than its own breadth: a lintel or flat arch: an edging of turf or flowers. [Fr. *platebande*, i.e. flat band.]

plate, *plāt, n.* a sheet, slab, or lamina of metal or other hard material, usually flat or flattish: metal in the form of sheets: a broad piece of armour: a scute or separate portion of an animal's shell: a broad thin piece of a structure or mechanism: a piece of metal, wood, &c., bearing or to bear an inscription to be affixed to anything: an engraved piece of metal for printing from: an impression printed from it, an engraving: a whole-page separately printed and inserted illustration in a book: a mould from type, &c., for printing from, as an electrotype or stereotype: part of a denture fitting the mouth and carrying the teeth: a film-coated sheet of glass or other material to photograph on: a plate - rail: a horizontal supporting timber in building: (*baseball*) a five-sided white slab at the home-base: a light racing horseshoe: a thermionic valve anode (orig. flat): (*hist.*) precious metal, esp. silver (Sp. *plata*, silver): (*Shak.*) a silver coin: wrought gold or silver: household utensils in gold or silver: table utensils generally: plated ware: a cup or other prize for a race or other contest: a race or contest for such a prize: a shallow dish: a plateful: a portion served on a plate: a church collection.—*v.t.* to overlay with metal: to armour with metal: to cover with a thin film of another metal: to make a printing plate of.—*n.* **plate′-arm′our,** protective armour of metal plates.— *adj.* **plā′ted,** covered with plates of metal: covered with a coating of another metal, esp. gold or silver: (*zool.*) armoured with hard scales or bone. —*ns.* **plate′-basket,** a basket for forks, spoons, &c.; **plate′-fleet,** (*hist.*) ships that carried American silver to Spain; **plate′ful,** as much as a plate will hold; **plate′-glass,** a fine kind of glass used for mirrors and shop-windows, orig. poured in a molten state on an iron plate; **plate′-layer,** one who lays, fixes, and attends to the rails of a railway; **plate′-leather,** a chamois leather for rubbing gold and silver; **plate′let,** a minute body in blood, concerned in clotting; **plate′man,** a man who has the care of silver-plate in a hotel, club, &c.; **plate′-mark,** a hall-mark; **plate′-powder,** a polishing powder for silver; **plate′-print′ing,** the process of printing from engraved plates; **plate′-proof,** a proof taken from a plate; **plā′ter;** **plate′-rack,** a frame for holding plates, &c., when not in use or when to drain after washing; **plate′-rail,** a flat rail with a flange; **plate′-room,** a room where silver-plated goods or printing plates are kept; **plate′-ship,** (*hist.*) a ship bringing silver to Spain from America; **plate′-warmer,** an apparatus for warming plates or keeping them warm; **plā′ting.**—*adj.* **plā′ty,** plate-like: separating into plates.—*ns.* **half′-plate,** in photography, a size of plate measuring 4½ by 6½ in. (4½ by 5½ in U.S.); **quar′ter-plate,** 3¼ by 4¼ in.; **whole′-plate,** 6½ by 8½ in. [O.Fr. *plate*, fem., and for the dish *plat*, masc., flat—Gr. *platys*, broad.]

plateasm, *plat′i-azm, n.* pronunciation with a wide mouth-opening, as in Doric Greek. [Gr. *plateiasmos—platys*, broad.]

plateau, *plā′tō, plä-tō′, n.* a tableland: an ornamented tray, plate, or plaque: a lady's flat-topped hat:—*pl.* **plateaux** (-*tōz*), also **plateaus.** [Fr.,— O.Fr. *platel*, dim. of *plat*.]

platen, *plat′n, n.* the work-table of a machine-tool: a flat part that in some printing-presses pushes the paper against the forme: the roller of a typewriter. [Fr. *platine—plat*, flat.]

plateresque, *plat-ə-resk′, adj.* (*archit.*) applied to a style resembling silversmith's work. [Sp. *plateresco* —*platero*, silversmith—*plata*, silver.]

platform, *plat′form, n.* (*obs.*) a plane figure or surface: (*obs.*) a ground-plan: (*Shak.*) a scheme, device, plan of action: a scheme of church government or of administrative policy: a party programme: a site: a basis: a raised level surface: a terrace: a plateau: a flooring: a raised floor for speakers, musicians, &c.: those who have seats on the platform at a meeting: (*fig.*) public speaking or discussion: a medium for discussion: a deck for temporary or special purpose: a position prepared for mounting a gun: a raised walk in a railway station giving access to trains: the flooring outside the entrance to a bus, tram-car, or sometimes a railway carriage. —*v.t.* to furnish with a platform: to sketch, plan: to place on, or as on a platform.—*v.i.* to speak or appear on a platform. [Fr. *plateforme*, lit. flat form.]

platinum, *plat'in-əm*, *n.* a noble metal (at. numb. 78), steel-grey, exceedingly valuable, malleable and ductile, very heavy and hard to fuse—older name **plat'ina.**—*adjs.* **plat'inum**, made of platinum; **platinic** (*plə-tin'ik*), of quadrivalent platinum; **platinif'erous**, platinum-bearing.—*v.t.* **plat'inise**, to coat with platinum.—*ns.* **plat'inoid**, one of the metals with which platinum is always found associated—*palladium, iridium,* &c.: an alloy of copper, zinc, nickel, and tungsten resembling platinum; **plat'inotype**, a method of photography by reducing a compound of platinum: a photograph so produced.—*adj.* **plat'inous**, of bivalent platinum.—**platinum black**, platinum in the form of a velvety black powder; **platinum lamp**, an electric lamp with a platinum filament. [Sp. *platina—plata*, silver.]

platitude, *plat'i-tūd*, *n.* flatness: a dull commonplace or truism: an empty remark made as if it were important.—*n.* **platitudina'rian**, one who indulges in platitudes.—*v.i.* **plat'itudinise.**—*adj.* **platitud'inous.** [Fr.,—*plat*, flat.]

Platonic, *plə-ton'ik*, *adj.* pertaining to *Plato*, the Greek philosopher (about 427-347 B.C.), or to his philosophy: of love, between soul and soul, without sensual desire (a Renaissance phrase): relating to or experiencing Platonic love.—*n.* a Platonist: a Platonic lover: (usu. in *pl.*) Platonic love.—*adj.* **Platon'ical** (*now rare*).—*adv.* **Platon'ically.**—*n.* **Platon'icism**, doctrine, practice, or profession of Platonic love: (*obs.*) Platonism.—*v.t.* **Platonise** (*plā'tən-īz*), to render Platonic.—*v.i.* to follow Plato.—*ns.* **Plā'tonism**, the philosophy of Plato: Platonicism; **Plā'tonist**, a follower of Plato. [Gr. *platōnikos—Platōn, -ōnos*, Plato.]

platoon, *plə-tōōn'*, *n.* orig. a small body of soldiers in a hollow square, or such a body firing together: a subdivision (¼) of a company: a squad: a volley. [Fr. *peloton*, ball, knot of men—L. *pila*, ball.]

Platt-Deutsch, *plät'-doich*, *n.* and *adj.* Low German. [Ger.]

platted, platting. Same as **plaited, plaiting.**

platter, *plat'ər*, *n.* a large flat plate or dish. [A.Fr. *plater—plat*, a plate.]

platy-, *plat'i-*, in composition, flat, broad. [Gr. *platys*, broad.]

platycephalous, *plat-i-sef'ə-ləs*, *adj.* having the vault of the skull flattened.—Also **platycephalic** (*-si-fal'ik*). [Gr. *kephalē*, head.]

Platyhelminthes, *plat-i-hel-min'thēz*, *n.pl.* the flatworms, a phylum including planarians, tape-worms, and flukes. [Gr. *helmins, -inthos*, intestinal worm.]

platypus, *plat'i-pəs, -poos*, *n.* the duck-bill:—*pl.* **plat'ypuses.** [Gr. *pous, podos*, a foot.]

platyrrhine, *plat'i-rin*, *adj.* broad-nosed: belonging to the division of the monkeys found in South America. — *n.* a New World monkey. [Gr. *platyrrīs, -īnos—rhīs, rhīnos*, nose.]

platysma, *plat-iz'mä*, *n.* a broad sheet of muscle in the neck. [Gr. *platysma*, a flat piece.]

plaudit, *plawd'it*, *n.* an act of applause: praise bestowed.—*adj.* **plaud'itory.** [Shortened from L. *plaudite*, applaud, an actor's call for applause at the end of a play, pl. imper. of *plaudēre, plausum*, to clap the hands.]

plausible, *plawz'i-bl*, *adj.* (*obs.*) that may be applauded: (*obs.*) acceptable: seemingly worthy of approval or praise: fair-showing: specious: ingratiating and fair-spoken. — *ns.* **plausibil'ity**, **plaus'ibleness.**—*adv.* **plaus'ibly**, in a plausible manner: (*Shak.*) with applause, by acclamation: (*obs.*) commendably, pleasantly. — *adj.* **plausive**

(*plaws'iv*), (*Shak.*) plausible: (*Shak.*) pleasing: applauding. [L. *plaudēre*, to clap the hands.]

plaustral, *plaw'strəl*, *adj.* (*jocose*) of a wagon. [L. *plaustrum*, a wagon.]

play, *plā*, *v.i.* (*obs.*) to operate: to move about irregularly, lightly, or freely: to have some freedom of movement: to flicker, flutter, shimmer, pass through rapid alternations: to move in, discharge, or direct a succession, stream, or shower (as of water, light, waves, missiles): to engage in pleasurable activity: to perform acts not part of the immediate business of life but in mimicry or rehearsal or in display: to amuse oneself: to sport: to make sport: to trifle: to behave without seriousness: to behave amorously or sexually: to take part in a game: to proceed with the game, perform one's part in turn: to send a ball or the like in the course of a game: (*arch.*) to contend with weapons: to wield a weapon: to gamble: (*Shak.*, now *Scot.*) to have a holiday: (*N. of England*) to be off work: to perform on a musical instrument: to give forth music: to come forth as music: to act a part.—*v.t.* to perform: to ply, wield: to cause or allow to play: to set in opposition, pit: to send, let off, or discharge in succession or in a stream or shower: to give a limited freedom of movement to: hence, to manage: to engage in a game or recreative mimicry: to proceed through as a game, part of a game, or an aggregate of games (as a stroke, trick, rubber, set): to stake or risk in play: to bring into operation in a game, as by striking (a ball), throwing on the table (a card), moving (a man): to compete against in a game: to compete for: to act as a play or as a part: to make believe in sport: to perform music on: to perform on a musical instrument: to lead, bring, send, render, or cause to be by playing: (*refl.*; *obs.* and *Scot.*) to amuse: (*pr.p.* **play'ing**; *pa.t.* and *pa.p.* **played**).—*n.* activity: operation: action of wielding: light fluctuating movement or change: limited freedom of movement: scope: recreative activity: display of animals in courtship: amusement: dalliance: (*Shak.*) a game: the playing of a game: manner of playing: procedure or policy in a game: (*Shak.* and *Scot.*) holiday: (*dial.*) a fair or festival: (*N. of England*) being off work: gambling: a drama or dramatic performance: (*fig.*) manner of dealing, as fair-play.—*adj.* **play'able**, capable (by nature or by the rules of the game) of being played, or of being played on.—*ns.* **play'-acting**, performance of plays: pretence; **play'-actor**, **play'-actress**, (usu. in contempt) a professional actor or actress; **play'-bill**, a bill announcing a play; **play'book**, a printed play or book of plays; **play'-box**, a box for toys and other valued possessions, esp. in a boarding-school; **play'boy**, a boy-actor: a lighthearted irresponsible person; **play'-day**, a holiday; **play'-debt**, a debt incurred in gambling.—*adj.* **played'-out**, exhausted: used up: no longer good for anything.—*ns.* **play'er**, one who plays: an actor: a trifler: an instrumental performer: a professional cricketer: a mechanism for playing a musical instrument; **play'er-pian'o**, a piano with player attached; **play'fellow**, a playmate.—*adj.* **play'ful**, sportive. — *adv.* **play'fully.** — *ns.* **play'fulness**; **play'-gōer**, one who habitually attends the theatre; **play'-gōing**; **play'ground**, a place for playing in, esp. one connected with a school: a holiday region; **play'house**, a theatre; **play'ing-card**, one of a pack used in playing games; **play'ing-field**, a public open space for games; **play'let**, a short play; **play'-mare**, (*Scot.*) a hobby-horse, as in the old morris-dance; **play'-mate**, a companion in play, esp. child's play; **play'-off**, a game to decide a tie; **play'-pen**, a fencing within which a young child may safely play; **play'-room**, a room for children to play in.—*adj.* **play'some**, playful.—*ns.* **play'-spell**, a time allowed for play; **play'thing**, a toy: a person or thing treated as a toy; **play'-time**, a time for play; **play'-way**, the educational use of play; **play'-world**, an imaginary world feigned in play; **play'wright**, **play'-writer**, a dramatist. —**bring, come, into play**, bring, come, into exercise, operation, use; **hold in play** (*arch.* hold play), to keep occupied, esp. to gain time or detain; **in, out of, play,** in, out of, such a position that it may be played; **make play,** to keep things going, push on with the game; **play at,** engage in the game of: make a pretence of: to practise without seriousness; **play fast and loose,** to act in a shifty, inconsistent, and reckless fashion; **play fine,** at billiards, to strike the object-ball near the edge—opp. **to play full,** to strike it nearer the middle than the edge; **play off,** to manipulate so as to counteract: (*golf*) to play from the tee: (*Shak.*) to toss off: to bring off (as a hoax); **play on,** to strike the ball on to one's own wicket: to direct one's efforts to the exciting of, work upon; **play the game,** to act strictly honourably; **play up,** to strike up, begin the music: to redouble one's efforts, play more vigorously: to show up well in a crisis or emergency: (*U.S.*) to give (esp. undue) prominence to, or to boost; **play upon,** to practise upon, work upon; **play upon words,** a pun or other manipulation or words depending on their sound; **play up to,** to act so as to afford opportunities to (another actor); **play with,** to play in company of, or as partner or opponent to: to dally with. [O.E. *pleg(i)an,* vb., *plega,* n.]

plea, *plē, n.* (*Scots law* and *hist.*) a lawsuit: a pleading: a prisoner's or defendant's answer to a charge or claim: (*Shak.*) a claim: an excuse: a pretext: urgent entreaty.—*v.t.* and *v.i.* to dispute in a law-court. [O.Fr. *plai, plaid, plait*—L.L. *placitum,* a decision—L. *placēre, -itum,* to please.]

pleach, *plēch, v.t.* to intertwine the branches of, as a hedge: (*Shak.*) to fold, as the arms: to plash. [From another form of O.Fr. *pless(i)er*—L. *plectēre,* to plait; Gr. *plekein.*]

plead, *plēd, v.i.* to carry on a plea or lawsuit: to argue in support of a cause against another: to put forward an allegation or answer in court: to implore.—*v.t.* to maintain by argument: to allege in pleading: to put forward as a plea: to offer in excuse: to sue for:—*pa.t.* and *pa.p.* **plead'ed,** also (*Spens.,* now *Scot., U.S.,* and *dial.*) **pled.**—*adj.* **plead'able,** capable of being pleaded.—*n.* **plead'er,** one who pleads: an advocate.—*adj.* **plead'ing,** imploring.—*n.* act of putting forward or conducting a plea: (in *pl.*) the statements of the two parties in a lawsuit: entreaty.—*adv.* **plead'ingly.**—**plead guilty, or not guilty,** to admit, or refuse to admit, guilt; **special pleading,** unfair or one-sided argument aiming rather at victory than at truth. [O.Fr. *plaidier*; cf. **plea.**]

please, *plēz, v.t.* to give pleasure to: to delight: to satisfy: to choose, to will.—*v.i.* to give pleasure: (formerly impers., the dative now the nominative) to like: to think fit: to choose.—*n.* **pleasance** (*plez'ans*; *arch.* and *poet.*), pleasure: enjoyment: pleasantness: (*obs.*) complaisance, pleasant behaviour: that which gives pleasure: a pleasure-ground or specialised part of a garden. — *adj.* **pleas'ant,** pleasing: agreeable: inoffensive: affable: good-humoured: cheerful: gay: facetious: tipsy. — *adv.* **pleas'antly.** — *ns.* **pleas'antness;** **pleas'antry,** (*obs.*) pleasantness, enjoyment: jocularity: a facetious utterance or trick:—*pl.* **pleas'antries.**—*adj.* **pleased** (*plēzd*), grateful: delighted. — *ns.* **pleaseman** (*plēz'man, -man*), (*Shak.*) an officious fellow, a pick-thank; **pleas'er.** —*adj.* and *n.* **pleas'ing.**—*adv.* **pleas'ingly.**—*n.* **pleas'ingness.**—*adj.* **pleasurable** (*plezh'a-bl*), able to give pleasure: delightful: gratifying: (*obs.*) pleasure-seeking.—*n.* **pleas'urableness.**—*adv.* **pleas'urably.**—*n.* **pleasure** (*plezh'ar*), agreeable emotions: gratification of the senses or of the mind: sensuality: dissipation: a source of gratification: what the will prefers: purpose: command: approbation.—*v.t.* (*arch.*) to give pleasure to.—*n.* **pleas'ure-boat,** a boat used for pleasure or amusement.— *adjs.* **pleas'ureful, pleas'ure-giving,** affording pleasure.— *ns.* **pleas'ure-ground,** ground laid out in an ornamental manner for pleasure; **pleas'ure-house,** a house to which one retires for recreation or pleasure. — *adj.* **pleas'ureless.** — *ns.* **pleas'urer;**

pleas'ure-seeker, one who seeks pleasure: a holiday-maker; **pleas'ure-seeking; pleas'ure-trip,** an excursion for pleasure.—**at pleasure,** when, if, or as one pleases; **if you please,** if you like: a polite formula of request or acceptance: (*ironically*) forsooth; **may it please you, so please you,** deferential or polite formulas of address or request; **please,** also **please to,** a polite formula equivalent to **if you please,** now felt as imperative, perh. orig. from the older **please it you, please it** (sometimes printed **pleaseth** in *Shak.*), **please you,** may it please you; **please yourself,** do as you like; **pleasure-pain principle,** principle dominating instinctual life in which activities are directed towards seeking pleasure and avoiding pain. [O.Fr. *plaisir* (Fr. *plaire*)—L. *placēre,* to please.]

pleat, *plēt.* Same as **plait.**

plebeian, *pli-bē'an* (in *Shak.* also **plebean,** *pleb'i-an*), *adj.* of the Roman plebs: of the common people: low-born: undistinguished: vulgar-looking: vulgar. —*n.* a member of the plebs of ancient Rome: a commoner: a member of a despised social class.— *v.t.* **plebei'anise.**—*ns.* **plebei'anism; plebifica'tion** (*pleb-i-*), the act of making plebeian.—*v.t.* **pleb'ify.** [L. *plēbēius*—*plēbs, plēbis.*]

plebiscite, *pleb'i-sit, -sīt, n.* (*Roman hist.*) a law enacted by the plebs assembled in the *Comitia tributa:* a direct vote of the whole nation or of the people of a district on a special point: an ascertainment of general opinion on any matter, as by inviting postcards. — *adj.* **plebisc'itary.** [Partly through Fr. *plébiscite*—L. *plēbiscītum*—*plēbs,* plebs, *scītum,* decree—*scīscere,* vote for.]

plebs, *plebz, n.* the less privileged originally of the two divisions of the Roman people. [L. *plēbs, plēbis.*]

Plecoptera, *plek-op'tar-ä, n.pl.* the stonefly order of insects, with hind-wings folded fanwise.—*adj.* **plecop'terous.** [Gr. *plekein,* plait, *pteron,* wing.]

Plectognathi, *plek-tog'na-thī, n.* an order of bony fishes including file-fishes, globe-fishes, coffer-fishes, sun-fishes.—*adjs.* **plectognathic** (*-to-gnath'-ik*), **plectog'nathous** (*-na-thas*). [Gr. *plektos,* plaited, *gnathos,* a jaw.]

Plectoptera, *plek-top'ta-rä, n.pl.* the mayfly order of insects, otherwise *Ephemerida.* [Gr. *plektos,* twisted, *pteron,* a wing.]

plectrum, *plek'tram, n.* the quill or other form of instrument for plucking the strings of the ancient Greek lyre or other musical instrument.—Also **plec'tre** (*-tar*), **plec'tron**:—*pl.* **plec'tra.** [L. *plēctrum*—Gr. *plēktron*—*plēssein,* to strike.]

pled, pled. See **plead.**

pledge, *plej, n.* something given as a security: a gage: a token or assuring sign: a child, as a token of love or binding obligation: (*obs.*) one who becomes surety for another: (*obs.*) a hostage: a solemn promise: a friendly sentiment expressed by drinking: a state of being given, or held, as a security.—*v.t.* to give as security: to bind by solemn promise: to vow: to give assurance of: to drink a toast in response to: to drink at the invitation of another: to drink to the health of.— *ns.* **pledgee',** the person to whom a thing is pledged; **pledger, pledgor** (*plej'ar*)—**take, or sign, the pledge,** to give a written promise to abstain from intoxicating liquor. [O.Fr. *plege* (Fr. *pleige*)—L.L. *plevium, plivium,* prob. Gmc.]

pledget, *plej'it, n.* a wad of lint, cotton, &c., as for a wound or sore: an oakum string used in caulking. [Origin unknown.]

Pleiad, *plī'ad, n.* any one of the seven daughters of Atlas and Pleione, changed into stars (one 'lost' or invisible): a brilliant group of seven, esp. seven Alexandrian tragic poets or (usu. as Fr., **Pléiade,** *plā-ē-äd*) the poets Ronsard, Du Bellay, Baif, Daurat, Jamin, Jodelle, Ponthus de Thiard. —*pl.* **Plei'ads, Pleiades** (*plī'a-dēz*), a group of six naked-eye and a multitude of telescopic stars in the shoulder of the constellation Taurus. [Gr. *pleias, plēias, -ados,* pl. *-adēs.*]

plein-air, *plen'-er', adj.* open-air: attaching importance to painting in the open-air.—*n.* **plein-air'ist,** a plein-air painter. [Fr. *en plein air,* in the open air.]

pleio-, plio-, *plī′ō-, plī-o′,* **pleo-,** *plē′ō-, plē-o′,* in composition, more. [Gr. *pleiōn* or *pleōn,* comp. of *polys,* many, much.]

Pleiocene. Same as **Pliocene.**

pleiochasium, *plī-ō-kā′zi-əm, n.* a cymose inflorescence in which each branch bears more than two lateral branches. [Gr. *chasis,* separation; but cf. **monochasium.**]

pleiomerous, *plī-om′ər-əs, adj.* having more than the normal number of parts.—*n.* **pleiom′ery,** the condition of having more than the normal number. [Gr. *meros,* part.]

Pleistocene, *plīs′tō-sēn, adj.* of the geological period following the Pliocene, having the greatest proportion of the fossil molluscs of living species.—*n.* the Pleistocene system, period, or strata. [Gr. *pleistos,* most (numerous), *kainos,* recent—from the proportion of living species of molluscs.]

plenary, *plē′nə-ri, adj.* full: entire: complete: (*law*) passing through all its stages—opp. to *summary*: having full powers.—*adv.* **ple′narily.**—*n.* **plē′narty,** the state of a benefice when occupied. —**plenary indulgence,** in the Roman Catholic Church, full or complete remission of temporal penalties to a repentant sinner; **plenary inspiration,** inspiration which excludes all mixture of error; **plenary powers,** full powers to carry out some business or negotiations. [L.L. *plēnārius*— L. *plēnus,* full—*plēre,* to fill.]

plenilune, *plen′, plēn′i-l(y)ōōn, n.* the full moon: time of full moon. — *adj.* **plenilu′nar.** [L. *plēnilūnium*—*plēnus,* full, *lūna,* moon.]

plenipotence, *plin-ip′ō-təns, n.* complete power— also **plenip′otency.**—*adjs.* **plenip′otent,** having full power; **plenipotential** (*plen-i-pō-ten′shal*); **plenipoten′tiary** (*-shə-ri, -shyə-ri*), having full powers.—*n.* a person invested with full powers, esp. a special ambassador or envoy to some foreign court.—Colloquially shortened to **plen′ipo.** [L. *plēnus,* full, *potentia,* power.]

plenish, *plen′ish, v.t.* to supply, stock: (*Scot.*) to provide, as a house or farm, with necessary furniture, implements, stock, &c. — *n.* **plen′ishing,** (*Scot.*) furniture. [O.Fr. *plenir, -iss-*— L. *plēnus,* full.]

plenitude, *plen′i-tūd, n.* fullness: completeness: plentifulness: repletion. — *adj.* **plenitud′inous.** [L. *plēnitūdō, -inis*—*plēnus,* full.]

plenty, *plen′ti, n.* a full supply: all that can be needed: abundance.—*adj.* (*Shak.*) plentiful: in abundance.—*adv.* (*coll.*) abundantly.—*adj.* **plenteous** (*plen′tyəs*), fully sufficient: abundant: fruitful: well provided: rich: giving plentifully.— *adv.* **plen′teously.** — *n.* **plen′teousness.** — *adj.* **plen′tiful,** copious: abundant: yielding abundance. — *adv.* **plen′tifully.** — *ns.* **plen′tifulness;** **plen′titude** (a mistake or misprint for **plenitude**). —**horn of plenty** (see **cornucopia**). [O.Fr. *plente* —L. *plēnitās, -ātis*—*plēnus,* full.]

plenum, *plē′nəm, n.* a space completely filled with matter: a full assembly.—*n.* **plē′nist,** one who believes all space to be a plenum. [L. *plēnum* (*spatium*), full (space).]

pleo-. See **pleio-.**

pleochroism, *plē-ok′rō-izm, n.* the property in some crystals of transmitting different colours in different directions.—*adj.* **pleochroic** (*plē-ō-krō′ik*). [Gr. *chroā,* colour.]

pleomorphic, *plē-ō-mor′fik, adj.* polymorphic.— Also **pleomor′phous.**—*n.* **pleomorph′ism.**

pleon, *plē′on, n.* the abdomen of a crustacean, bearing the swimming legs. — *n.* **ple′opod,** a swimming leg. [Gr. *pleōn,* swimming, pr.p. of *plēein.*]

pleonasm, *plē′ō-nazm, n.* redundancy, esp. of words: a redundant expression.—*ns.* **plē′onast,** one who is given to pleonasm; **ple′onaste** (Fr. *pléonaste*), a dark green to black magnesia-iron spinel (from its multitude of faces).—*adjs.* **pleonas′tic, -al.**—*adv.* **pleonas′tically.** [Gr. *pleonasmos*—*pleōn,* more.]

pleroma, *pli-rō′mä, n.* fullness: abundance: in Gnosticism, divine being, including all aeons which emanate from it.—*adj.* **pleromatic** (*-mat′ik*). [Gr. *plērōma*—*plērēs,* full.]

plerome, *plē′rōm, n.* (*bot.*) the central part of the apical meristem. [Gr. *plērōma,* filling.]

plerophory, *plē-rof′ə-ri, n.* full conviction.—Also **plerophō′ria.** [Gr. *plērŏphŏriā.*]

plesh, *plesh, n.* (*Spens.*) a plash, a pool. [**plash** (2).]

plesiosaur, *plē′si-ō-sawr, n.* a great Mesozoic fossil Sauropterygian reptile (Plesiosaurus or kindred genus) with long neck, short tail, and four flippers. —*adj.* **plesiosaur′ian.** [Gr. *plēsios,* near, *sauros,* lizard.]

plessor, plessimeter, &c. See **plexor,** &c.

plethora, *pleth′ər-ä,* sometimes *pli-thō′rä, n.* excessive fullness of blood: over-fullness in any way. — *adjs.* **plethoric** (*pli-thor′ik*; sometimes *pleth′ər-ik*), **plethor′ical.**—*adv.* **plethor′ically.** [Gr. *plēthōrā,* fullness—*pleos,* full.]

pleugh, *plōō, plōōhh, n.* Scots form of **plough.**— Also **pleuch.**

pleura, *plōō′rä, n.* a delicate serous membrane that covers the lung and lines the cavity of the chest: a side-piece: a pleuron:—*pl.* **pleu′rae** (*-rē*).—*adj.* **pleu′ral.**—*ns.* **pleurapoph′ysis,** a lateral process of a vertebra, with the morphological character of a rib: a rib:—*pl.* **pleurapoph′yses;** **pleurisy** (*plōō′ri-si*), inflammation of the pleura; **pleu′risy-root,** an American Asclepias (*A. tuberosa*) reputed as a diaphoretic and expectorant.—*adjs.* **pleurit′ic, -al,** of, affected with, or causing pleurisy.—*n.* a sufferer from pleurisy.—*ns.* **pleuri′tis,** pleurisy; **pleurodynia** (*plōō-rō-din′i-ä*; Gr. *odynē,* pain), neuralgia of the chest-wall; **pleu′ron,** the side-wall of a somite, esp. of an insect's thorax:—*pl.* **pleu′ra;** **pleuro-pneumō′nia,** pleurisy combined with pneumonia: a contagious disease of cattle, caused by a filterable virus, characterised by pleurisy and pneumonia. [Gr. *pleurā* and *pleuron,* rib, side.]

Pleuronectes, *plōō-rō-nek′tēz, n.* the plaice genus, giving name to the family **Pleuronec′tidae.** [Gr. *pleurā,* side, *nēktēs,* a swimmer.]

plexor, *pleks′ər,* **plessor,** *ples′ər, ns.* a percussion hammer.—*ns.* **plexim′eter, plessim′eter,** a small plate to receive the tap in examination by percussion.—*adjs.* **pleximet′ric, plessimet′ric.**—*ns.* **plexim′etry, plessim′etry.** [Gr. *plēxis,* a stroke, *plēssein,* to strike.]

plexus, *pleks′əs, n.* a network:—*pl.* **plex′uses,** or **plex′us** (L. *plexūs*).—*n.* **plex′ure,** an interweaving. [L. *plexus, -ūs,* a weaving.]

pliable, *plī′ə-bl, adj.* easily bent or folded: flexible: adaptable: easily persuaded: yielding to influence. —*ns.* **pliabil′ity, pli′ableness.**—*adv.* **pli′ably.**— *ns.* **pli′ancy, pli′antness.**—*adj.* **pli′ant,** bending easily: flexible: tractable: easily influenced: (*Shak.*) perh. suitable, perh. of compliant mood.— *adv.* **pli′antly.** [See **ply.**]

plica, *plī′kä, n.* a fold: plica Polonica:—*pl.* **pli′cae** (*-sē*).—*adjs.* **pli′cate** (or *-kāt′*), **-d,** folded fanwise, plaited.—*v.t.* **pli′cate** (also *plī-kāt′, plik-āt′*), to plait.—*adv.* **pli′cately.**—*ns.* **plicā′tion, plicature** (*plik′*), act of folding: state of being folded: a fold.—**plica Polonica,** a matted condition of the hair, with an adhesive secretion, a parasitic fungus, and vermin, formerly prevalent in Poland. [L. *plīca,* a fold.]

plied, plier, pliers, plies. See **ply.**

plight, *plīt, n.* (*obs.*) risk: pledge: engagement: promise.—*v.t.* to pledge:—*pa.p.* **plight′ed,** also **plight.**—*n.* **plight′er.**—*adj.* **plight′ful,** grievous. [O.E. *pliht,* risk; *pléon,* to risk; cf. Du. *pligt,* Ger. *pflicht,* an obligation.]

plight, *plīt, n.* (*Spens.*) a fold: a plait: mode of plaiting: condition, trim: evil state: good condition: mood: (*Spens.*) array.—*v.t.* to plait: to weave: to fold: to enfold:—*pa.p.* **plight′ed,** also (*Spens.*) **plight.** — *adj.* **plight′ed,** plaited: (*Shak.*) involved. [Assimilated in spelling to the foregoing, but derived from O.Fr. *plite*—L. *plicāre, plīcitum;* see **plait.**]

plim, *plim, v.t.* and *v.i.* (*prov.*) to swell. [Perh. conn. with **plump.**]

plimsoll, *plim′səl, -sol, n.* a rubber-soled canvas shoe.—**Plimsoll line or mark,** a ship's load-line or set of load-lines for different waters and conditions, required by the Merchant Shipping Act

(1876) passed at the instance of Samuel *Plimsoll* (1824-98).

plinth, *plinth, n.* the square block under the base of a column: a block serving as a pedestal: a flat-faced projecting band at the bottom of a wall: a similar projecting base in furniture. [L. *plinthus,* Gr. *plinthos,* a brick, squared stone, plinth.]

Pliocene, *plī'ō-sēn, adj.* (geol.) of the Tertiary period following the Miocene, and having a greater proportion of molluscan species now living.—*n.* the Pliocene system, period, or strata. [Gr. *pleiōn,* greater, more numerous, *kainos,* recent.]

Pliohippus, *plī-ō-hip'əs, n.* a Miocene and Pliocene genus of fossil horses. [Gr. *hippos,* horse.]

pliskie, *plis'ki, n.* (*Scot.*) condition or plight: a mischievous trick. [Origin unknown.]

plod, *plod, v.i.* to walk heavily and laboriously: to study or work on steadily and laboriously.—*v.t.* to traverse or make by slow and heavy walking (*pr.p.* **plodd'ing;** *pa.t.* and *pa.p.* **plodd'ed**).—*n.* a heavy walk: a thud.—*n.* **plodd'er,** one who plods on: a dull, heavy, laborious man: one who gets on more by unremitting toil than by inspiration. —*adj.* and *n.* **plodd'ing.**—*adv.* **plodd'ingly.** [Prob. imit.]

plod, *plod, v.t.* (*obs.*) to plot. [plot, by confusion with foregoing.]

plong, plonge, plongd, Spenserian spellings of **plunge, plunged.**

plop, *plop, n.* the sound of a small object falling vertically into water: the sound of the movement of small bodies of water: the sound of a cork coming out of a bottle, or of a bursting bubble.— *adv.* with a plop: plump.—*v.i.* to make the sound of a plop: to plump into water.—*v.t.* to set with a plop:—*pr.p.* **plopp'ing;** *pa.p.* **plopped.** [Imit.]

plosive, *plō'siv, -ziv, adj.* and *n.* (*phon.*) stop: implosive.

plot, *plot, n.* a small piece of ground: (*obs.*) a spot or small area on any surface: a ground-plan of a building, plan of a field, &c.: the story or scheme of connected events running through a play, novel, &c.: a secret scheme, usually in combination, to bring about something, often illegal or evil, a conspiracy: a stratagem or secret contrivance.— *v.t.* to lay out in plots, dispose: to make a plan of: to represent by a graph: to conspire or lay plans for.—*v.i.* to lay plots, conspire:—*pr.p.* **plott'ing;** *pa.p.* **plott'ed.**—*adjs.* **plot'ful; plot'-less; plot'-proof,** safe from any danger by plots.— *n.* **plott'er.**—*n.* and *adj.* **plott'ing.**—*adv.* **plott'-ingly.**—*n.* **plott'ing-paper,** paper ruled in squares for graph-drawing. [O.E. *plot,* a patch of ground; influenced by (or partly from) Fr. *complot,* a conspiracy; cf. **plat.**]

plot, *plot, plōt, v.t.* (*Scot.*) to dip or steep in very hot water: to scald and pluck: to fleece.—*n.*

plott'ie, plott'y, a spiced hot drink, as mulled wine. [Cf. Du. and Flem. *plooten,* to pluck.]

plotter, *plot'ər.* Same as **plouter.**

plough, *plow, n.* an instrument for turning up the soil in ridges and furrows: a joiner's plane for making grooves: (*fig.*) agriculture: a plough-team: ploughed land: **Plough,** seven stars of the Great Bear.—*v.t.* to turn up with the plough: to make furrows or ridges in: to make with a plough: to put or render with a plough: to tear, force, or cut a way through: to furrow: to wrinkle: (*university slang*) to reject in an examination: to fail in (a subject).—*v.i.* to work with a plough: to toil.—*adj.* **plough'able.**—*ns.* **plough'boy,** a boy who drives or guides horses in ploughing; **plough'er; plough'gate,** (*Scots hist.*) an undetermined or variable unit of land, by later writers taken as about 50 English acres, but earlier much more: a quantity of land of the extent of 100 acres Scots; **plough'ing; plough'-iron,** the coulter, the share, or other iron part of a plough; **plough'-jogger,** (*facet.*) a ploughman; **plough'land,** land suitable for tillage: (*hist.*) as much land as could be tilled with one plough (with a proportionate amount of pasture) —a carucate or eight oxgangs; **plough'man,** a man who ploughs:—*pl.* **plough'men; plough'-Mon'day,** an old ploughman's festival, the Mon-

day after Twelfth Day, supposed to mark the resumption of work after the holidays; **plough'-staff,** a tool for clearing a plough of earth, &c.; **plough'-stilt,** a plough-handle; **plough'-tail,** the end of a plough where the handles are: (*fig.*) farm-labour; **plough'-tree,** a plough-handle.— *adv.* and *adj.* **plough'wise,** as in ploughing.—*n.* **plough'wright,** one who makes and mends ploughs.—**plough a lonely furrow,** to be separated from one's former friends and associates and go one's own way; **plough in,** to cover with earth by ploughing; **plough the sands,** to work in vain or to no purpose; **put one's hand to the plough,** to begin an undertaking. [Late O.E. *plóh, plóg,* a ploughland; cf. O.N. *plógr.*]

ploughshare, *plow'shār, n.* the detachable part of a plough that cuts the under surface of the sod from the ground: a bird's pygostyle (also **plough-share bone).** [plough, and O.E. *scear,* plough-share—*scieran,* to shear, cut.]

plouter, plowter, *plow'tər, v.i.* (*Scot.*) to dabble in liquid: to potter.—*n.* a paddling or dabbling.— Also **plotter.** [Prob. imit.]

plover, *pluv'ər, n.* a general name for birds of the family (Charadriidae) to which the lapwing and dotterel belong: extended to some related birds: (*old slang*) a dupe: (*old slang*) a prostitute.—*adj.* **plov'ery,** abounding in plovers.—**plover's egg,** a lapwing's egg, or substitute. [Fr. *pluvier*—L. *pluvia,* rain; possibly from their restlessness before rain; cf. Ger. *regenpfeifer,* lit. rain-piper.]

plow, *plow* (chiefly American). Same as **plough.**

ploy, *ploi, n.* (*Scot.*) an employment, doings, affair, frolic, escapade, engagement for amusement. [Prob. **employ.**]

pluck, *pluk, v.t.* to pull off, out, or away: to pull forcibly: to snatch away: to rescue: to bring on or bring down: to pull: to tug: to twitch: to strip, as of feathers: to despoil, fleece: (*slang*) to fail, refuse a pass to, in an examination—from the custom of *plucking* (a piece of silk at the back of) *the proctor's gown,* in protest.—*v.i.* to make a pulling or snatching movement.—*n.* a single act of plucking: the heart, liver, and lungs of an animal—hence heart, courage, spirit. — *adj.* **plucked,** subjected to plucking: having pluck.— *n.* **pluck'er.**—*adv.* **pluck'ily.**—*n.* **pluck'iness.**— *adj.* **pluck'y,** having courageous spirit and pertinacity.—**pluck off,** (*Shak.*) to abate, come down the scale; **pluck up,** to pull out by the roots: to summon up, as courage: to gather strength or spirit. [O.E. *pluccian;* akin to Du. *plukken,* Ger. *pflücken.*]

pluff, *pluf, n.* (*Scot.*) a puff: a mild explosion: a shot: a powder-puff.—*v.t.* to puff: to shoot.— *v.i.* to go off with a puff: to rise, as a cake.—*adj.* (*dial.*) **pluff'y,** puffed up: fluffy. [Imit.]

plug, *plug, n.* a peg stopping, or for stopping, a hole: a bung: a stopper: filling for a tooth: volcanic rock stopping a vent: a fitting for a socket for giving electrical connexion: a piece of wood inserted in a wall to take nails: a fire-plug: a sparking-plug: (*slang*) a plug-hat: a blow or punch: a compressed cake of tobacco: a piece of it cut for chewing: a worn-out horse: a book that will not sell: anything worn-out or useless: a dogged plodding.—*v.t.* to stop with a plug or as a plug: to insert a plug in: to insert as a plug: (*slang*) to shoot: (*slang*) to punch with the fist: (*slang*) to force into familiarity by persistent repetition: to din into the ears of the public.— *v.i.* (*slang*) to go on doggedly:—*pr.p.* **plugg'ing;** *pa.t.* and *pa.p.* **plugged.**—*ns.* **plugg'er,** one who, or that which, plugs, esp. a dentist's instrument; **plugg'ing,** the act of stopping with a plug: the material of which a plug is made; **plug'-hat,** (*U.S.*) a top-hat; **plug'-ug'ly,** (*U.S.*) a street ruffian.—**plug in,** to complete an electric circuit by inserting a plug. [App. Du. *plug,* a bung, a peg; cf. Sw. *plugg,* a peg, Ger. *pflock.*]

plum, *plum, n.* a well-known stone-fruit: the tree producing it (*Prunus domestica* or kindred species) of the rose family: extended to various fruits and trees more or less similar (as *sapodilla plum, coco-plum, date-plum*): a raisin as a substitute for the true plum: a sugar-plum: a big stone embedded in concrete: something choice that may be extracted (sometimes in reminiscence of Jack Horner) or attained to, as one of the best passages in a book, one of the prizes of a career, or (*U.S.*) a government office as a reward of services, &c.: (formerly) a sum of £100,000: its possessor.—*ns.* **plum'-bloss'om**; **plum'-cake**, a cake containing raisins, currants, &c.—*n.* and *adj.* **plum'-colour**, dark purple. — *ns.* **plum'cot**, Luther Burbank's hybrid between *plum* and *apricot*; **plumdamas** (-*dä'mas*; *Scot.*), a damson; **plum'-duff**, a flour-pudding boiled with raisins.—*adj.* **plumm'y**, full of plums: plum-like: desirable.— *ns.* **plum'-porr'idge**, an antiquated dish, of porridge with plums, raisins, &c.; **plum'-pudd'ing**, a national English dish made of flour and suet, with raisins, currants, and various spices; **plum'-stone**; **plum'-tree**. [O.E. *plúme* —L. *prūnum*; cf. Gr. *prou(m)non*.]

plumage, *plōōm'ij*, *n.* a natural covering of feathers: feathers collectively.—*adj.* **plum'aged**. [Fr.,— *plume*—L. *plūma*, a feather, down.]

plumb, *plum*, *n.* a heavy mass, as of lead, hung on a string to show the vertical line, or for other purpose: verticality: a sounding lead, plummet. —*adj.* vertical: (*cricket*) level, true: sheer, thorough-going, out-and-out. — *adv.* vertically: precisely: (esp. *U.S.*) utterly.—*v.t.* to test by a plumb-line: to make vertical: to sound as by a plumb-line: to pierce the depth of, fathom, by eye or understanding: to weight with lead: to seal with lead: to do or furnish the plumber-work of.—*v.i.* to hang vertically: to work as a plumber.—*ns.* **plumbate** (*plum'bāt*), a salt of plumbic acid; **plumb'-bob**, a weight at the end of a plumb-line.—*adj.* **plumbeous** (*plum'bi-as*), leaden: lead-coloured: lead-glazed.—*ns.* **plumber** (*plum'ar*), orig. a worker in lead: now one who instals and mends pipes, cisterns, and other fittings for supply of water and gas and for household drainage; **plumb'er-work**; **plumb'ery**, plumber-work: a plumber's workshop.—*adjs.* **plumbic** (*plum'bik*), due to lead: of quadrivalent lead; **plumbiferous** (-*bif'*), yielding or containing lead. —*ns.* **plumbing** (*plum'ing*), the operation of making plumb: the craft of working in lead: the work of a plumber; **plum'bism** (-*bizm*), lead poisoning; **plum'bite** (-*bīt*), a salt of the weak acid lead hydroxide.—*adj.* **plumb'less**, incapable of being sounded. — *n.* **plumb'-line**, a line to which a bob is attached to show the vertical line: a vertical line: a plummet.—*adjs.* **plumbosol'vent** (better **plumbisol'vent**), able to dissolve lead; **plumbous** (*plum'bas*), of bivalent lead.—*n.* **plumb'-rule**, a board with a plumb-line and bob, for testing verticality.—**plumbic acid**, an acid of which lead dioxide is the anhydride. [Fr. *plomb* and its source, L. *plumbum*, lead.]

Plumbago, *plum-bā'gō*, *n.* a Mediterranean and tropical genus of ornamental plants (some cultivated) giving name to the **Plumbaginaceae** (-*baj-i-nā'si-ē*), a family of salt-steppe and seaside plants including sea-pink and sea-lavender, akin to the primrose family.—*adj.* **plumbaginaceous** (-*baj-i-nā'shas*). [L. *plumbāgō*, Pliny's translation of the Greek name *molybdaina*, lead, lead ore, the plant *Plumbago* (from its blue flowers).]

plumbago, *plum-bā'gō*, *n.* graphite.—*adj.* **plumbaginous** (-*baj'i-nas*). [L. *plumbāgō, -inis—plumbum*, lead.]

plumber. See under plumb.

plumber-block. See **plummer-block.**

plume, *plōōm*, *n.* a feather: a large showy feather: the vane of a feather: a bunch or tuft of feathers: a feather, or anything similar, used as an ornament, symbol, crest, &c.: a feather as a token of honour: (*obs.*) the plumule of a seed: any feathery structure.—*v.t.* to preen: (*fig.*) to pride, take credit to (with *on*): to adorn with plumes (*Milt.*) to set as a plume: to strip of feathers.—*n.* **plumassier** (*plōō-mā-sēr'*), a worker in feathers: a feather - seller. — *adj.* **plum'ate**, feathered: feathery.—*n.* **plume'-bird**, a long-tailed bird of paradise.—*adj.* **plumed**, feathered: adorned with

a plume: (*obs.*) plucked.—*n.* **plume'-grass**, a tall grass (*Erianthus*) akin to sugar-cane, with great silky panicles, grown for ornament.—*adj.* **plume'-less**.—*ns.* **plume'let**, a plumule: a little tuft; **plume'-moth**, any moth of the families Pterophoridae and Orneodidae, with deeply cleft wings. —*adj.* **plume'-pluckt**, (*Shak.*) stripped of plumes, humbled.—*n.* **plum'ery**, plumes collectively.— *adjs.* **plumigerous** (-*ij'a-ras*), plumaged; **plu'mi-ped**, having feathered feet.—*n.* **plu'mist**, a feather-dresser.—*adjs.* **plu'mose**, **plu'mous**, feathery: plume-like; **plu'my**, covered or adorned with down or plume: like a plume. [O.Fr.,—L. *plūma*, a small soft feather.]

plummer-block, *plum'ar-blok*, *n.* a metal frame or case for holding the end of a revolving shaft. [Origin unknown.]

plummet, *plum'it*, *n.* a leaden or other weight, esp. one on a plumb-line, a sounding-line, or a fishing-line: a plumb-rule. [O.Fr. *plomet*, dim. of *plomb*, lead; see plumb.]

plump, *plump*, *v.i.* to fall or drop into liquid, esp. vertically, passively, resoundingly, without much disturbance: to flop down: (esp. *Scot.*) to rain suddenly and heavily: to come suddenly or with a burst: to give all one's votes without distribution.—*v.t.* to plunge, souse: to fling down or let fall flat or heavily: to blurt: (*slang*) to strike or shoot.—*n.* the sound or act of plumping: (esp. *Scot.*) a sudden heavy fall of rain: (*slang*) a blow. —*adj.* and *adv.* with a plump: in a direct line: downright: in plain language: without hesitation, reserve, or qualification.—*n.* **plump'er**, a plump fall or blow: an undistributed vote that could have been divided: one who gives all his votes to one candidate or option: (*slang*) a downright lie: (*slang*) anything very big of its kind, a whacker.—*adv.* **plump'ly**. [L.G. *plumpen* or Du. *plompen*, to plump into water; prob. influenced by **plumb** and **plump** (2).]

plump, *plump*, *adj.* pleasantly fat and rounded: well filled out.—*v.t.* and *v.i.* to make or grow plump: to swell or round.—*v.i.* (*rare*) **plump'en.** —*n.* **plump'er**, a cork ball kept in the mouth, or other device to round the cheeks.—*adj.* **plump'ish.** — *n.* **plump'ness.** — *adj.* **plump'y**, **plump'ie** (*Shak.*), plump. [App. the same word as Du. *plomp*, blunt, L.G. *plump*.]

plump, *plump*, *n.* a cluster: a clump, as of trees, spearmen, waterfowl. [Origin unknown.]

plumula, *plōōm'ū-lä*, *n.* a plumule:—*pl.* **plum'ulae** (-*lē*).—*adjs.* **plumulā'ceous**, **plum'ular.**—*n.* **Plumulā'ria**, a genus of hydrozoa forming feathery colonies.—*n.* and *adj.* **plumulā'rian.**—*adj.* **plum'ulate**, downy.—*n.* **plum'ule**, a little feather or plume: a down feather: the embryo shoot in a seed: a scent-giving scale on the fore-wing of some male butterflies.—*adj.* **plum'ulose**. [L. *plūmula*, dim. of *plūma*, a feather, down-feather.]

plunder, *plun'dar*, *v.t.* to carry off the goods of by force: to pillage: to carry off as booty: to carry off booty from.—*v.i.* to pillage, carry off plunder.—*n.* pillage: booty: (*U.S.*) personal or household goods.—*ns.* **plun'derage**, the stealing of goods on board ship; **plun'derer.** — *adj.* **plun'derous.** [Ger. *plündern*, to pillage—*plunder*, household stuff, now trash.]

plunge, *plunj*, *plunzh*, *v.t.* to thrust or cast suddenly under the surface of a liquid, or into the midst of, the thick of, or the substance of anything: to immerse.—*v.i.* to fling oneself or rush impetuously, esp. into water, downhill, or into danger or discourse: to turn suddenly and steeply downward: to fire down upon an enemy from a height: to gamble or squander recklessly: to pitch as a ship: to pitch suddenly forward and throw up the hind-legs.—*n.* act of plunging.—*n.* **plung'er**, one who plunges: part of a mechanism with a plunging movement, as the solid piston of a force-pump: (*mil.*) a cavalry-man: a reckless gambler or squanderer.—*adj.* and *n.* **plung'ing.**—**plunge bath**, a bath large enough to immerse the whole body; **take the plunge**, to commit oneself definitely after hesitation. [O.Fr. *plonger*—L. *plumbum*, lead.]

plunk, *plungk*, *v.t.* to twang: to play in rough pizzicato: to put down, &c., in such a way that it makes a hollow or metallic sound.—*v.i.* to plump. —Also *n.* [Imit.]

pluperfect, *ploo-pər′fikt*, or *ploo′*, *adj.* (*gram.*) denoting that an action happened before some other past action referred to.—*n.* the pluperfect tense: a pluperfect verb or form. [L. *plûs quam perfectum* (*tempus*), more than perfect (tense).]

plural, *ploor′l*, *adj.* numbering more than one: more than onefold: (*gram.*) expressing more than one, or, where dual is recognised, more than two. —*n.* (*gram.*) the plural number: a plural word or form.—*n.* **pluralisā′tion**.—*v.t.* **plur′alise**, to make plural.—*v.i.* to hold two or more benefices or offices simultaneously.—*ns.* **plur′alism**, plurality: the holding by one person of more than one office at once, esp. ecclesiastical livings: a system allowing this: a philosophy that recognises more than one principle of being (opp. to *monism*) or more than two (opp. to *monism* and *dualism*); **plur′alist**, one who holds more than one office at one time: a believer in pluralism.—*adj.* **plural′ist′ic**.—*n.* **plurality** (*-al′i-ti*), the state or fact of being plural: numerousness: a plural number: the greater number, more than half: (*U.S.*) a majority over any other (distinguished from *majority*), which is used for an absolute majority or majority over all others combined): the holding of more than one benefice at one time: a living held by a pluralist.—*adv.* **plu′rally**.—**plural vote**, power of voting in more than one constituency, or more than once in one. [L. *plūrālis—plūs, plūris*, more.]

pluri-, *ploor′i-*, in composition, several: usu. more than two.—*adjs.* **plurilit′eral**, (*Heb. gram.*) containing more letters than three; **pluriloc′ular**, multilocular.—*ns.* **plurip′ara**, a multipara; **pluripres′ence**, presence in more places than one at the same time.—*adjs.* **plurise′rial, -iate**, in several rows. [L. *plûs, plûris*, more.]

plurisie, *ploor′i-si*, *n.* (*Shak.*) superabundance. [L. *plûs, plûris*, more; confused with **pleurisy**.]

plus, *plus*, *prep.* (*math.* and *coll.*) with the addition of.—*adj.* positive: additional: having an adverse handicap.—*n.* an addition: a surplus: a positive quality or term: the sign (also **plus sign**) of addition or positivity (+); opposed to *minus* (−). —**plus strain**, (*bot.*) one of the two strains in heterothallism. [L. *plûs*, more.]

plus-fours, *plus′-fōrz′*, *n.pl.* baggy knickerbockers or knickerbocker suit. [plus, four; from the four additional inches of cloth required.]

plush, *plush*, *n.* a fabric with a longer and more open pile than velvet: (in *pl.*) footman's breeches. —*adj.* of plush.—*adj.* **plush′y**. [Fr. *pluche* for *peluche—*L. *pila*, hair; cf. pile (3).]

pluteus, *ploo′ti-əs*, *n.* a sea-urchin or brittle-star larva, shaped like a many-legged easel.—*adj.* **plu′teal**. [L. *pluteus*, a shed, boarding, desk.]

Pluto, *ploo′tō*, *n.* the Greek god of the underworld: a planet beyond Neptune, discovered 1930.—*adjs.* **Pluto′nian**, of Pluto: of the underworld; **Plutonic** (*-ton′ik*), of Pluto: (*geol.*) hypogene, deep-seated, relating to, or formed under conditions of, subterranean heat: Plutonist. — *ns.* **Plutonism** (*ploo′tən-izm*); **Plu′tonist**, (*hist.* of *geol.*) a Vulcanist; **pluto′nium**, the element (Pu) of atomic number 94, named as next after neptunium (93), as the planet Pluto is beyond Neptune. [L. *Plûtō, -ōnis—*Gr. *Ploutōn, -ōnos*, Pluto.]

Plutus, *ploo′tas*, *n.* the Greek god of wealth.—*ns.* **plutocracy** (*ploo-tok′rə-si*), government by the wealthy: a ruling body or class of rich men; **plutocrat** (*ploo′tō-krat*), one who is powerful because of his wealth. — *adj.* **plutocrat′ic.** — *ns.* **plutol′atry** (Gr. *latreiā*, worship), worship of wealth; **plutol′ogist, pluton′omist**; **plutol′ogy, pluton′omy**, political economy. [L. *Plûtus*, Gr. *Ploutos* (Gr. *ploutos*, wealth).]

pluvial, *ploo′vi-əl*, *adj.* of or by rain: rainy.—*n.* (*hist.*) a rain-cloak: a cope or ceremonial mantle. —*n.* **pluviom′eter**, a rain-gauge.—*adjs.* **pluviomet′ric, -al**.—*n.* **Pluviôse** (*plü-vē-ōz′*; Fr.), the fifth month of the French Revolutionary calendar,

about 20th January to 18th February.—*adj.* **plu′vious**, rainy. [L. *pluvia*, rain.]

ply, *plī*, *n.* a fold: a layer or thickness: (*min.*) a layer of hard rock or of hard or soft in alternation: a bend: a bent or set: a strand: (*Scot.*) condition, esp. good condition:—*pl.* **plies**.—*v.t.* and *v.i.* to bend or fold:—*pr.p.* **ply′ing**; *pa.t.* and *pa.p.* **plied**; *3rd pers. sing.* **plies**.—*ns.* **pli′er**, one who plies: (in *pl.*) small pincers for bending or cutting wire, &c.; **ply′-wood**, boarding made of thin layers of wood glued together, the grain of each at right-angles to that of the next. [O.Fr. *pli*, a fold, *plier*, to fold—L. *plicāre*.]

ply, *plī*, *v.t.* to work at steadily: to use or wield diligently or vigorously: to keep supplying or assailing: to importune: to row or sail over habitually.—*v.i.* to work steadily: to make regular journeys over a route: to be in attendance for hire: to beat against the wind: to make one's way, direct one's course:—*pr.p.* **ply′ing**; *pa.t.* and *pa.p.* **plied**; *3rd pers. sing.* **plies**.—*n.* **pli′er**, one who plies: (*obs.*) a trader: (*obs.*) a tout. [Aphetic, from **apply**.]

Plymouth, *plim′əth*, *n.* a port in Devon: a port named after it in Massachusetts, with the supposed landing-place of the Pilgrims (Plymouth Rock). — *ns.* **Plym′outhism**; **Plym′outhist**, **Plym′outhite**, a Plymouth Brother.—**Plymouth Brethren**, a rigid religious sect, originating at Plymouth about 1830, out of a reaction against High Church principles and against a dead formalism associated with unevangelical doctrine; **Plymouth Rock**, an American breed of poultry: a nickname for a Plymouth Brother.

pneuma, *nū′mä*, *n.* breath: spirit, soul: a neume. —*n.* **pneumathode** (*nū′mä-thōd*; Gr. *hodos*, a way), a respiratory opening in plants.—*adjs.* **pneumatic** (*-mat′ik*), relating to air or gases: containing or inflated with air: worked or driven by air: spiritual; **pneumat′ical** (*rare*).—*adv.* **pneumat′ically**.—*ns.* **pneumaticity** (*nū-mo-tis′i-ti*), the condition of having air-spaces; **pneumat′ics** (treated as *sing.*), the science of the properties of gases: pneumatology.—*adj.* **pneumatol′ogical**.—*ns.* **pneumatol′ogist**; **pneumatol′ogy**, the theory of spiritual beings: psychology: (*theol.*) the doctrine of the Holy Spirit: pneumatics; **pneumatol′ysis** (Gr. *lysis*, solution), the destructive action of hot vapours of a magma of igneous rock.—*adj.* **pneumatolyt′ic**.—*ns.* **pneumatom′eter**, an instrument for measuring the quantity of air breathed or the force of breathing; **pneu′matophore** (or *-mat′*), an upward-growing respiratory root in swamp plants.—**pneumatic trough**, a vessel with a perforated shelf for filling gas-jars over a liquid. [Gr. *pneuma, -atos*, breath—*pneein*.]

pneumonia, *nū-mō′ni-ä*, *n.* inflammation of the lung. — *n.* **pneumoconiosis** (*nū-mō-kō-ni-ō′sis*; Gr. *konia*, dust), **pneumokonio′sis, pneumonokonio′sis**, any of various diseases caused by habitually inhaling mineral or metallic dust, as in coal-mining.—*adj.* **pneumogas′tric** (Gr. *gastēr*, belly), pertaining to the lungs and stomach.—*n.* vagus.—*n.* **pneumonec′tomy**, surgical removal of lung tissue.—*adj.* **pneumonic** (*-mon′*), pertaining to the lungs.—*n.* a medicine for lung diseases.—*n.* **pneumoni′tis**, pneumonia.—**pneumonia blouse**, a low-necked blouse, once an object of dread. [Gr. *pneumōn, -ōnos*, lung—*pneein*, to breathe.]

Pnyx, (*p*)*niks*, *n.* the meeting-place of the ancient Athenian assembly. [Gr. *pnyx*, gen. *pyknos*, perh. cog. with *pyknos*, crowded.]

Poa, *pō′ä*, *n.* a large genus of grasses, meadowgrass. [Gr. *pŏä*, grass.]

poach, *pōch*, *v.t.* to cook without the shell in boiling water.—*n.* **poach′er**, one who poaches eggs: a vessel with hollows for poaching eggs in. [App. Fr. *pocher*, to pocket—*poche*, pouch, the white forming a pocket about the yolk.]

poach, *pōch*, *v.i.* to intrude on another's preserves in order to pursue or kill game, or upon another's fishing to catch fish: to encroach, esp. on a partner's place or part in a game: to seek an unfair advantage: (*Shak.*, *potche*) to thrust: to trample in mud: to become trampled and muddy.

—*v.t.* to take illegally on another's ground or in another's fishing : to seek or take game or fish illegally on : to take in unfair encroachment : to poke or thrust : to stir up : to trample into holes and mud.—*ns.* **poach'er ; poach'iness ; poach'ing.**—*adj.* **poach'y,** spongy and sodden. [A form of **poke** (3), or from O.Fr. *pocher,* to poke.]

poake, a Shakespearian spelling of **poke** (pocket).

pochard, pockard, poker, *pōk', pok', pōch', poch'-ər(d), n.* a red-headed diving-duck (*Nyroca ferina*), esp. the male, the female being the dunbird. [Origin obscure.]

pochay, *pō'shā,* **po'chaise,** -*shāz.* See **post-chaise.**

pochette, *posh-et', n.* a small bag, esp. one carried by women : a pocket note-case or wallet. [Fr., dim. of *poche,* pocket.]

pock, *pok, n.* a small elevation of the skin containing pus, as in smallpox.—*adj.* **pocked.**—*ns.* **pock'mark, pock'pit,** the mark, pit, or scar left by a pock.—*adjs.* **pock'marked, pock'pitted ; pock'y,** marked with pustules : infected with pox : (*obs.*) confounded. [O.E. *poc,* a pustule ; Ger. *pocke,* Du. *pok* ; see **pox.**]

pock, *pok, n.* a Scots form of **poke,** bag.—*ns.* **pockman'tie, pockmank'y,** corrupt forms of **portmanteau,** influenced by **pock ; pock-pudding** (*pok'-pud'n*), a bag-pudding : a Scottish contemptuous name for a mere Englishman.

pocket, *pok'it, n.* a little pouch or bag, esp. one attached to a garment or a billiard-table or the cover of a book : a cavity : a rock cavity filled with ore, veinstone, &c. : a portion of the atmosphere differing in pressure or other condition from its surroundings : the innermost compartment of a pound-net : stock of money : a bag of wool, &c., containing about 168 lb.—*adj.* for the pocket : of a small size.—*v.t.* to put in one's pocket or a pocket : to appropriate : to take stealthily : to conceal : to enclose : to hem in : (*billiards*) to play into a pocket.—*v.i.* to form a pocket : (*U.S.*) to pucker :—*pr.p.* **pock'eting ;** *pa.t.* and *pa.p.* **pock'eted.**—*ns.* **pock'et-book,** a note-book : a wallet for papers or money carried in the pocket : a small book for the pocket ; **pock'etbor'ough** (see **borough**) ; **pock'et-comb,** a haircomb for the pocket ; **pock'etful,** as much as a pocket will hold :—*pl.* **pock'etfuls ; pock'et-glass,** a small looking-glass for the pocket ; **pock'et-gopher,** any American burrowing rodent of the family Geomyidae, with outward-opening cheek-pouches ; **pock'et-handk'erchief,** a handkerchief for the pocket ; **pock'et-hole,** the opening in a garment giving access to a pocket ; **pock'et-knife,** a knife with one or more blades folding into the handle for the pocket.—*adj.* **pock'etless.** —*ns.* **pock'et-money,** money carried for occasional expenses : an allowance, esp. to a boy or girl ; **pock'et-picking,** act or practice of picking the pocket ; **pock'et-piece,** a coin carried to bring luck ; **pock'et-pis'tol,** a pistol for the pocket : a small travelling flask for liquor.—*adj.* **pock'etsized,** small enough for the pocket.—**in,** or **out of,** pocket, with, or without, money : the richer, or the poorer, by a transaction ; **pick a person's pocket,** to steal from his pocket ; **pocket an insult, affront,** &c., to submit to or put up with it without protest. [A.Fr. *pokete* (Fr. *pochette,* dim. of *poche,* pouch).]

pococurante, *pō-kō-kōō-rän'tä, -kū-ran'ti, adj.* uninterested : indifferent : nonchalant.—*n.* a habitually uninterested person.—*ns.* **pococurantism** (-*kū-rant'izm*) ; **pococuran'tist.** [It. *poco,* little, *curante,* pr.p. of *curare,* to care—L. *cūrāre.*]

poculiform, *pok'ū-li-form, adj.* cup-shaped. [L. *pōculum,* cup.]

pod, *pod, n.* the fruit, or its shell, in pease, beans, and other leguminous plants—the legume : sometimes extended to the siliqua : a silk cocoon : a musk-bag : a paunch.—*v.t.* to shell or hull.—*v.i.* to form pods : to fill as pods :—*pr.p.* **podd'ing ;** *pa.t.* and *pa.p.* **podd'ed.**—*adj.* **podd'y,** corpulent. [Origin unknown.]

pod, *pod, n.* a school, esp. of whales or seals. [Origin unknown.]

podagra, *pod-ag'rä,* also *pod', n.* gout, properly in

the feet.—*adjs.* **podag'ral, podag'ric, -al, podag'rous,** gouty. [Gr. *podagrā—pous, podos,* foot, *agrā,* a catching.]

podal, *pō'dal, adj.* of the feet.—*adj.* **podalic** (*pod-al'ik*), of the feet. [Gr. *pous, podos,* foot.]

Podargus, *pō-där'gəs, n.* the typical frogmouth genus of birds. [Gr. *pous, podos,* foot, *ārgos,* inactive—*a-,* neg., *ergon,* work.]

podestà, *pod-est-tä', n.* (*hist.*) a governor, chief magistrate, or judge in an Italian town. [It. *podestà—L. potestās, -ātis,* power.]

podex, *pō'deks, n.* the rump : the anal region. [L. *pōdex.*]

podge, *poj,* **pudge,** *puj, n.* a squat or thick-set person or thing.—*n.* **podg'iness, pudg'iness.**— *adj.* **podg'y, pudg'y.** [Origin obscure.]

podiatry, *pod-ī'ə-tri, n.* treatment of disorders of the foot.—*n.* **podi'atrist.** [Gr. *pous, podos,* foot, *iātros, iătros,* physician.]

podium, *pō'di-əm, n.* a continuous pedestal, a stylobate : (*anat.*) a foot or hand : a tube-foot :— *pl.* **po'dia.**—*adj.* **pō'dial.**—*n.* **podite** (*pod'īt),* a walking leg of a crustacean. [Latinised from Gr. *pōdion,* dim. of *pous, podos,* foot.]

podley, *pod'li, n.* (*Scot.*) a young coalfish. [**pollack.**]

Podocarpus, *pod-ō-kär'pəs, n.* an eastern and southern genus of trees of the yew family. [Gr. *pous, podos,* foot, *karpos,* fruit.]

Podogona, *pod-og'ə-nä, n.pl.* the Ricinulei. [Gr. *pous, podos,* foot, *gonos,* reproductive organ ; see **Ricinulei.**]

podophthalmous, *pod-of-thal'məs, adj.* having eyes on stalks, as many higher crustaceans. [Gr. *pous, podos,* foot, *ophthalmos,* eye.]

Podophyllum, *pod-ō-fil'əm, pod'of'i-ləm, n.* a genus of the barberry family.—*n.* **podophyll'in,** a cathartic resin got from its rhizome. [Gr. *pous, podos,* foot, *phyllon,* leaf.]

Podostemon, *pod-ō-stē'mon, n.* the typical genus of a family of dicotyledons, **Podostemaceae** (-*mā'si-ē),* growing in tropical waterfalls, the vegetative parts more like a thallus than an ordinary flowering plant. [Gr. *pous, podos,* foot, *stēmōn,* warp (as if stamen), from the stalk on which the stamens stand.]

Podsnappery, *pod-snap'ər-i, n.* British Philistinism as exemplified in Mr *Podsnap* in Dickens's *Our Mutual Friend.*

podsol, podzol, *pod-zol', n.* a bleached sand soil, poor in humus. [Russ. *pod,* under, *zol,* ash.]

Podura, *pod-ū'rä, n.* a genus of spring-tails. [Gr. *pous, podos,* foot, *ourā,* tail.]

poe-bird, poy-bird, *pō'i-bərd, n.* the New Zealand parson-bird or tui. [Captain Cook's name, from Tahitian *poe,* pearl beads, taken by him to mean earrings, on account of the side-tufts of the bird's neck.]

poem, *pō'im, -em, n.* a composition in verse : a composition of high beauty of thought or language and artistic form, typically, but not necessarily in verse : (*fig.*) anything supremely harmonious and satisfying.—*adj.* **poemat'ic.** [Fr. *poème—L. poēma—Gr. poiēma, poieein,* to make.]

poenology. See **penology.**

poesy, *pō'i-zi, n.* poetry collectively or in the abstract : (*obs.*) a poem : (*obs.*) a motto or posy.— *v.i.* (*Keats*) to utter poetry. [Fr. *poésie—L. poēsis* —Gr *poiēsis—poieein,* to make.]

poet, *pō'it, -et, n.* the author of a poem or (formerly) of any work of literary art : a verse-writer : one skilled in making poetry : one with a poetical imagination :—*fem.* **pō'etess.**—*ns.* **pōetas'ter,** a petty poet : a writer of contemptible verses ; **pōetas'tering, pōetas't(e)ry.**—*adjs.* **poetic** (*pō-et'ik),* **-al,** of the nature or having the character of poetry : pertaining or suitable to a poet or to poetry : expressed in poetry : in the language of poetry : imaginative.—*n.* **poet'ic** (often *pl.* in form, treated as *sing.*), the branch of criticism that relates to poetry.—*adv.* **poet'ically.**—*n.* **poet'icule,** a petty poet.—*v.i.* **pō'etise,** to write as a poet or like a poet.—*v.t.* to make poetical : to record or celebrate in poetry.—*ns.* **pō'et-lau'reate** (see **laureate**) ; **pō'etresse,** (*Spens.*) a poetess ; **pō'etry,** the art of the poet : the essential quality of a

Neutral vowels in unaccented syllables : el'ə-mənt, in'fənt, ran'dəm

poem: poetical composition or writings collectively (rarely in *pl.*): poetical quality; **pō′et-ship.**—**poetic justice**, ideal administration of reward and punishment; **poetic licence**, a departing from strict fact or rule by a poet for the sake of effect. [Fr. *poète*—L. *poēta*—Gr. *poiētēs*—*poieein*, to make.]

poffle, *pof′l*, *n*. (*Scot*.) a pendicle. [Origin obscure.]

pogge, *pog*, *n.* the armed bullhead (*Agonus cataphractus*), a fish covered with bony plates. [Origin unknown.]

pogrom, *pog-rom′*, *n.* an organised massacre, esp. of Russian Jews. [Russ., destruction, devastation.]

poh, *pō*, *interj.* expressing impatient contempt. [Cf. **pooh.**]

poi, *pō′ē*, *n.* a Hawaiian dish, a paste of fermented taro root. [Hawaiian.]

poignado, poinado, *poi-nä′dō*, obsolete forms of **poniard.**

poignant, *poin′ənt*, *adj.* stinging, pricking: sharp: acutely painful: penetrating: pungent: piquant. — *n.* **poign′ancy.** — *adv.* **poign′antly.** [O.Fr. *poignant*, pr.p. of *poindre*—L. *pungĕre*, to sting.]

poikilitic, *poi-kil-it′ik*, *adj.* mottled: (*petr.*) having small crystals of one mineral irregularly scattered in larger crystals of another.—*n.* **poi′kilocyte** (*-ō-sīt*), an irregular red blood corpuscle.—*adjs.* **poikilotherm′al, poikilotherm′ic,** having variable blood-temperature—'cold-blooded.'—*n.* **poikilotherm′y,** cold-bloodedness. [Gr. *poikilos*, variegated.]

Poinciana, *poin-si-ä′nä*, *n.* a tropical genus of the Caesalpinia family—flamboyant tree, &c. [After De *Poinci*, a French West Indian governor.]

poind, *pēnd*, *pind*, *v.t.* (*Scot.*) to distrain: to impound.—*ns.* **poind′er; poind′ing.** [O.E. *pyndan*, to impound; cf. **pound** (2).]

poinsettia, *poin-set′i-ä*, *n.* a Mexican spurge, *Euphorbia pulcherrima*, with big scarlet leaves (hence also called *Mexican flame-leaf*). [From Joel Roberts *Poinsett* (1779-1851), American Minister to Mexico.]

point, *point*, *n.* a dot: a small mark used in Semitic alphabets to indicate a vowel, to differentiate a consonant, or for other purpose: a dot separating the integral and fractional parts of a decimal: a mark of punctuation: (*geom.*) that which has position but no magnitude: (*Shak.*) a whit (as in *no point*): a place or station, considered in relation to position only: a place in a scale, course, or cycle (as *boiling point, dead points*): a moment of time, without duration: a precise moment: a state: a juncture: a critical moment: the verge: a culmination: a conclusion: (*obs.*) resolution: (*obs.*) condition, case, plight (as in *in good point*): (*her.*) any one of nine fixed positions on a shield: (*obs.*) the entry, or the first notes, of a subject, as in a fugue (formerly marked by a dot): (*arch.*) a short strain or phrase of music, a call (as in a *point of war*): a unit in scoring, judging, or measurement: a character taken into account in judging: a distinctive mark or characteristic: a unit of measurement of type, approximately *¹⁄₇₂* inch: one of thirty-two divisions of the compass, or the angle between two successive divisions (⅛ of a right angle): a unit in rationing by coupon: in piquet, the strongest suit held and called, or the score for holding it: a particular: a head, clause, or item: a position forming a main element in the structure of an argument or discourse: a matter in debate, under attention, or to be taken into account: that which is relevant: that upon which one insists or takes a stand: the precise matter: the essential matter: that without which a story, joke, &c., is meaningless or ineffective: a clearly defined aim, object, or reason: a particular imparted as a hint: lace made with a needle (also **point′-lace**): (loosely) lace: (*obs.*) a piece of point-lace: a sharp end: a tip, or free end: a thing, part, or mark with a sharp end: a piercing weapon or tool: an etching-needle: the sharp end of a sword: sword-fighting: a tine: a spike: a tapering piece in electrical apparatus, as the end of a lightning-conductor: a cape or headland: (*boxing*) the tip of the chin: a horse's extremity:

a tagged lace formerly used for fastening clothes: (*U.S.*) a nib: a movable rail for passing vehicles from one track to another: a tapering division of a backgammon board: (*cricket*) a fielder or his position, on the off-side straight out from and near the batsman (as if at the point of the bat): the leading party of an advanced guard: a position at the head of a herd: a socket for making connexion with electric wiring: pointedness: pungency: sting: act or position of pointing: the vertical rising of a hawk, indicating the position of the prey: (*obs.*) a feat.—*adj.* (*phon.*) articulated with the tip of the tongue.—*v.t.* to insert points in: to mark with points: to mark off in groups of syllables for singing: to sharpen: to give point to: to prick in or turn over with the point of a spade: to show the position or direction of or draw attention to (now usu. with *out*): to place in a certain direction, direct (with *at*): to indicate: to insert white hairs in (a fur): to rake out old mortar from and insert new in the joints of: to ration by points.—*v.i.* to have or take a position in a direction (with *at, to, toward,* &c.): to indicate a direction or position by extending a finger, a stick, &c.: to indicate the position of game by an attitude: to hint: to aim.—*n.* **point′-duty,** the duty of a policeman stationed at a particular point to regulate traffic.—*adj.* **point′ed,** having a sharp point: sharp: (*archit.*) Gothic: keen: telling: epigrammatic: precise: explicit: aimed at particular persons: having marked personal application. — *adv.* **point′edly.** — *ns.* **point′edness; point′er,** one who points, in any sense: a rod for pointing to a blackboard, map, screen, &c.: an index-hand: (*U.S.*) a hint, tip, suggestion: a tool for clearing out old mortar from joints: a breed of dogs that point on discovering game: (in *pl.*) two stars of the Great Bear nearly in a straight line with the Pole Star; **point′ing; point′ing-stock,** a thing to be pointed at, a laughing-stock; **point′-lace** (see above).—*adj.* **point′less.**—*ns.* **points′man,** one on point-duty: one in charge of rail points; **point′-source,** a source of radiation that is, or is considered as, a mathematical point.—*adj.* **point′-to-point,** from one fixed point to another: across country.—*n.* a cross-country race, a steeplechase.—**at (a) point, points, all points,** (*Shak.,* &c.) in readiness: resolved: completely: in all respects; **at the point of,** on the verge of; **cardinal point** (see **cardinal**); **carry one's point,** to gain what one contends for; **dead points** (see **dead**); **from point to point,** from one particular to another; **give points to,** to give odds to: to give an advantageous hint on any subject; **in point,** apposite; **in point of,** in the matter of; **in point of fact,** as a matter of fact; **make a point of,** to treat as essential, make a special object of; **on the point of,** close upon: very near; **point for point,** exactly in all particulars; **point of honour** (see **honour**); **point of order,** a question raised in a deliberative society, whether proceedings are according to the rules; **point of view,** the position from which one looks at anything, literally or figuratively; **points of the compass** (see above); **potatoes and point,** a feigned Irish dish, potatoes alone, with a herring, &c., to point at; **put upon points,** to ration by points; **stand upon points,** to be punctilious; **stretch** (or **strain**) **a point,** to go further (esp. in concession) than strict rule allows; **to the point,** apposite; **to point,** (*Spens., Shak.*) to the smallest detail. [Partly Fr. *point,* point, dot, stitch, lace, partly Fr. *pointe,* sharp point, pungency—L. *punctum* and L.L. *puncta,* respectively—L. *pungĕre, punctum,* to prick.]

point, *point*, *v.t.* to appoint, determine, fix. [Aphetic for **appoint.**]

point-blank, *point′-blangk′*, *adj.* aimed directly at the mark without allowing for the downward curve of the trajectory: permitting such an aim: direct: straightforward: blunt.—*adv.* with point-blank aim: directly: bluntly: flat.—*n.* a point-blank shot or range: (*Shak.*) reach (of jurisdiction). [App. from **point** (vb.), and **blank** (of the target).]

point-device, point-devise, *point′-di-vīs′, n.* (*obs.*)

the point of perfection (in the phrase *at point device*).—*adj.* (*arch.*) fastidiously exact, esp. in dress.—*adv.* with exactitude: down to the smallest detail. [Lit. to the point arranged, or arranged to the point—O.Fr. *devis*, devised.]

pointel, *poin′tl, n.* a sharp instrument, esp. a style: (*obs.*) a pistil. [O.Fr.]

pointillism, *pwan′til-izm,* **pointillisme** (Fr., *pwanᵍ-tē-yēzm*), *n.* in painting, the use of separate dots of pure colour instead of mixed pigments.—*n.* **poin′tillist, pointilliste** (-*yĕst*). [Fr. *pointill-isme—pointille*, dim. of *point*, point.]

poise, *poiz, v.t.* to weigh: to hold so as to get some notion of the weight: to ponder, weigh in the mind: to weight, weigh down: to make stable, ballast: to balance: to counterbalance: to carry or hold in equilibrium.—*v.i.* to hang in suspense: to hover.—*n.* weight: balance: equilibrium: (*obs.*) a weight, as of a clock: bias: (*Spens.*) momentum: (*Shak.*) impact: carriage or balance of body: dignity and assurance of manner: suspense.—*n.* **pois′er.** [O.Fr. *poiser* (Fr. *peser*)—L. *pēnsāre*, freq. of *pendĕre*, to weigh, and O.Fr. *pois*—L. *pēnsum*, weight.]

poison, *poi′zn, n.* any substance which, taken into or formed in the body, destroys life or impairs health: any malignant influence: (*chem.*) a substance that inhibits the activity of a catalyst.—*v.t.* to administer poison to: to injure or kill with poison: to put poison on or in: to taint: to mar: to embitter: to corrupt.—*adj.* poisonous.—*adj.* **poi′sonable.**—*ns.* **poi′soner; poi′son-fang,** one of two large tubular teeth in the upper jaw of venomous snakes, through which poison passes from glands at their roots when the animal bites; **poi′son-gas,** any injurious gas used in warfare; **poi′son-gland,** a gland that secretes poison; **poi′son-ivy, poi′son-oak, poi′son-sumac(h),** names for various North American sumacs with ulcerating juice; **poi′son-nut,** nux vomica.—*adj.* **poi′sonous,** having the quality or effect of poison: noxious: (*coll.*) offensive.—*adv.* **poi′sonously.**—*n.* **poi′sonousness.** [O.Fr. *puison,* poison—L. *pōtiō, -ōnis,* a draught; cf. *potion.*]

poitrel, *poi′tral, n.* armour for a horse's breast. [O.Fr. *poitral*—L. *pectorāle,* a breast-plate—*pectus,* the breast.]

pokal, *pō-käl′, n.* an ornamental drinking-vessel. [Ger.,—It. *boccale*—Gr. *baukălis,* a vessel for cooling wine, &c.]

poke, *pōk, n.* (now chiefly *dial.*; *Scot.* **pock** (2)) a bag: a pouch: a pokeful.—*n.* **poke′ful,** as much as a poke will hold.—**a pig in a poke,** a blind bargain, as of a pig bought without being seen. [M.E. *poke*; affinities uncertain.]

poke, *pōk, n.* a projecting brim or front of a bonnet: a poke-bonnet.—*n.* **poke′-bonnet,** a bonnet with a projecting front, as worn by Salvationist women and field-workers.—*adj.* **poked.** [Perh. from foregoing, or from following word.]

poke, *pōk, v.t.* to thrust or push the end of anything against or into: to thrust forward or endwise: to make, put, render, or achieve by thrusting or groping: to stir up, incite: (*obs.*) to dress with a poking-stick: (*coll.*) to seclude or confine in a poky place.—*v.i.* to thrust, make thrusts: to feel about, grope: (*cricket*) to bat gently and cautiously: to potter: to stoop: to pry about: to live a dull or secluded life.—*n.* an act of poking.—*n.* **pō′ker,** one who pokes: a rod for poking or stirring a fire: an instrument for doing pokerwork: a stiff person: (*facet.*) a mace or macebearer: a poking-stick.—*adj.* **pō′kerish,** like a poker: stiff.—*adv.* **pō′kerishly.**—*n.* **pō′ker-work,** work done by burning a design into wood with a heated point.—*adj.* **pō′king,** pottering: petty: confined: stuffy: shabby.—*n.* **pō′king-stick,** a small rod formerly used for adjusting the plaits of ruffs.—*adj.* **pō′ky,** poking.—**by the holy poker,** a facetious oath of unknown meaning, perhaps belonging to **poker** (1) below; **poke fun at,** to banter; **poke one's head,** to stoop, hold the head forward; **poke one's nose,** to pry; **red-hot poker,** Kniphofia or Tritoma. [M.E. *pōken*; app. of L.G. origin.]

poke, *pōk, n.* a name for various American species of Phytolacca (also **poke′weed, poke′berry**): American or white hellebore (**Indian poke**). [Of American Indian origin.]

poker, *pō′kər, n.* a bugbear.—*adj.* **pō′kerish,** causing terror: uncanny.—**Old Poker,** the devil. [Cf. Dan. *pokker,* Sw. *pocker.*]

poker, *pō′kər, n.* a round game at cards, first played in America about 1835.—*n.* **po′ker-face,** an inscrutable face, useful to a poker-player: its possessor.—*adj.* **po′ker-faced.** [Ety. uncertain; poss. from German.]

Polabian, *pō-lä′bi-ən, n.* a member of a former West Slavonic people occupying the basin of the lower Elbe: their extinct language.—Also *adj.* [Slav. *po,* beside, *Labe,* the Elbe.]

polacca, *po-lak′ä, n.* a three-masted Mediterranean vessel, with fore and main masts each in one piece (also **polacre,** *po-lä′kər*): a polonaise, or composition in the manner of a polonaise. [It. *polacca, polacra,* Polish (fem.); Fr. *polacre*: application to the vessel not explained.]

Polack, *pōl′ak, n.* (*Shak.*) a Pole.—*adj.* Polish. [Pol. *Polak*; Ger. *Polack.*]

Poland, *pō′lənd, n.* a country of Europe.—*adj.* of Poland, Polish.—*n.* **Po′lander,** (*obs.*) a Pole.

polar, *pō′lar, adj.* of, or pertaining to, a pole (see **pole** (1)) or poles: belonging to the neighbourhood of a pole: referred to a pole: of the nature of, or analogous to, a pole: axial, cardinal: having polarity: directly opposed.—*n.* (*geom.*) the locus of the harmonic conjugate of a fixed point or pole with respect to the points in which a transversal through it cuts a circle or other conic.—*n.* **polarim′eter,** an instrument for measuring the rotation of the plane of polarisation of light.—*adj.* **polarimetric** (*pō-lar-i-met′rik*).—*ns.* **polarimetry** (*pō-lər-im′i-tri*); **Polaris** (*pō-lä′ris*), the Pole Star; **polarisation** (*pō-lər-ī-zā′shən*), the act of polarising: the state of being polarised: development of poles: (loosely) polarity: the effect of deposition of products of electrolysis upon electrodes, resulting in an opposing electromotive force: the restriction (according to the wave theory) of the vibrations of light to one plane; **polariscope** (*pō-lar′i-skōp*), an instrument for showing phenomena of polarised light.—*v.t.* **polarise** (*pō′lar-iz*), to subject to polarisation: to give polarity to: (*fig.*) to develop new qualities or meanings in.—*v.i.* to acquire polarity.—*adj.* **po′larised.**—*ns.* **po′lariser,** a device for polarising light; **polarity** (*pō-lar′i-ti*), state of having two opposite poles: the condition of having properties different or opposite in opposite directions or at opposite ends: the tendency to develop differently in different directions along an axis, as a plant towards base and apex, some animals towards head and tail: particular relation to this or that pole or opposed property rather than the other: (*fig.*) directedness: opposedness or doubleness of aspect or tendency; **po′laroid,** a manufactured material used for polarising light (registered tradename).—**polar bear,** a large white bear found in the Arctic regions; **polar circle,** the Arctic or the Antarctic Circle; **polar co-ordinates,** co-ordinates defining a point by means of a radius vector and the angle which it makes with a fixed line through the origin; **polar distance,** angular distance from the pole; **polar equation,** an equation in terms of polar co-ordinates; **polar forces,** forces that act in pairs and in different directions, as in magnetism; **polar lights,** the aurora borealis or australis. [L. *polāris—polus*: see **pole** (1).]

polder, *pōl′dər, n.* piece of low-lying reclaimed land: first stage in its reclamation.—Also *v.t.* [Du.]

pole, *pōl, n.* the end of an axis, esp. of the earth, the celestial sphere, or any rotating sphere: (of a great or small circle) the point where a perpendicular from the centre of a sphere cuts the surface of the sphere: (of a crystal face) the point where the normal from the origin cuts the sphere of projection: the end of an elongated body: a differentiated end: either of the two points of a body in which the attractive or repulsive energy is concentrated, as in a magnet: an electric terminal or electrode: (*geom.*) a fixed point: a point from which a pencil of rays radiates: a fixed point defining a polar: (*fig.*) an opposite extreme: (*poet.*, after Greek use) the heavens.—**poles apart, asunder,** widely separated, very different; **Pole Star,** Polaris, a star near the N. pole of the heavens: a guide or director. [L. *polus*—Gr. *polos,* pivot, axis, firmament.]

pole, *pōl, n.* a long rounded shaft, rod, or post, usu. of wood: a small tree: a single shaft to which a pair of horses may be yoked: a measuring rod of definite length: hence a measure of length, 5¼ yards, of area, 30¼ square yards: position next the inner boundary-fence in a race-course: the tail of certain animals.—*v.t.* to propel, push, strike, or stir with a pole: to furnish with poles.—*v.i.* to use a pole.—*adj.* **pole′-clipt,** (*Shak.*) hedged in with poles.—*n.* **pōl′ing,** supplying, propelling, or stirring with a pole or poles: poles collectively.—**under bare poles,** with all sails furled; **up the pole,** in a predicament: drunk: crazed: in favour. [O.E. *pál* (Ger. *pfahl*)—L. *pālus,* a stake.]

Pole, *pōl, n.* a native or citizen of Poland: a member of the people inhabiting Poland and speaking Polish.

pole-axe, -ax, *pōl′aks, n.* a battle-axe, originally short-handled: a long-handled axe or halbert: a sailor's short-handled axe for cutting away rigging: a butcher's axe with a hammer-faced back. [Orig. *pollax,* from **poll,** head, and **axe,** confused with **pole** (2).]

polecat, *pōl′kat, n.* a large relative of the weasel, which emits a stink—called also *fitchet* and *foumart:* (*Shak.*) a prostitute. [M.E. *polcat;* poss. Fr. *poule,* hen, and **cat.**]

polemarch, *pol′i-märk, n.* a title of several officials in ancient Greek states, orig. a military commander. [Gr. *polemarchos*—*polemos,* war, *archē,* rule.]

polemic, *po-lem′ik, adj.* given to disputing: controversial.—*n.* a controversialist: a controversy: a controversial writing or argument: (in *pl.,* esp. *theol.*) the practice or art of controversy.—*adj.* **polem′ical.**—*adv.* **polem′ically.** [Gr. *polemikos*—*polemos,* war.]

Polemonium, *pol-i-mō-ni′əm, n.* the Jacob's ladder genus of plants, giving name to the **Polemoniā′-ceae,** the phlox family.—*adj.* **polemoniā′ceous.** [Gr. *polemōnion,* St John's wort, or other plant.]

polenta, *po-len′tä, n.* an Italian porridge of maize, barley, chestnut, or other meal. [It.,—L. *polenta,* peeled barley.]

poley, *pō′li, adj.* (*Austr.*) hornless. [**poll** (1).]

polianite, *pō′li-ən-īt, n.* a steel-grey mineral, manganese dioxide. [Gr. *poliainesthai,* to grow grey—*polios,* hoary.]

Polianthes, *pol-i-an′thēz, n.* the tuberose genus of the amaryllis family. [Gr. *polios,* hoary, *anthos,* a flower.]

police, *pol-ēs′, n.* the system of regulations for the preservation of order and enforcement of law: the internal government of a state: a body of men employed to maintain order, &c.: its members collectively.—*adj.* of the police.—*v.t.* to control as police: to furnish with police: to guard or to put or keep in order.—*ns.* **police′-burgh′** (see **burgh**); **police′-con′stable,** a policeman of ordinary rank; **police′-court,** a court for trying small offences brought before it by the police; **police′-dog′,** a dog trained to help the police; **police′-force,** a separately organised body of police; **police′-inspect′or,** a superior officer of police who has charge of a department, next in rank to a superintendent; **police′-judge′,** **police′-mag′istrate,** one who presides in a police-court; **police′man,** a member of a police-force; **police′-manure′,** (*Scot.*) street sweepings used as manure; **police′-off′ice, -stā′tion,** the headquarters of the police of a district, used also as a temporary place of confinement; **police′-off′icer,** an ordinary policeman; **police′-state′,** a country in which secret police are employed to detect and stamp out any opposition to the government in

power; **police′-trap,** a strategic means whereby the police keep motor traffic under scrutiny and detect offenders against the law: a concealed and concerted timing arrangement to enforce a speed limit; **police′woman,** a woman member of a police-force. [Fr.,—L. *polītīa*—Gr. *polīteiā*—*polītēs,* a citizen—*polis,* a city.]

policy, *pol′i-si, n.* (*obs.*) a constitution: the art of government: statecraft: a course of action: a system of administration guided more by interest than by principle: dexterity of management: prudence: cunning: in Scotland (sometimes in *pl.*), the pleasure-grounds around a mansion. [O.Fr. *policie* (Fr. *police*)—L. *polītīa*—Gr. *polīteiā* (see **police**); in Scots perh. influenced by L. *polītus,* embellished.]

policy, *pol′i-si, n.* a writing containing a contract of insurance: (*U.S.*) a kind of gambling by betting on the numbers to be drawn in a lottery.—*ns.* **pol′icy-holder,** one who holds a contract of insurance; **pol′icy-shop,** a place where policy is played. [Fr. *police,* policy, app.—L.L. *apodissa,* a receipt—Gr. *apodeixis,* proof.]

poliomyelitis, *pol-i-ō-mī-ə-lī′tis, n.* inflammation of the grey matter of the spinal cord: infantile paralysis. [Gr. *polios,* grey, *myelos,* marrow.]

Polish, *pō′lish, adj.* of Poland, or its people or its language.—*n.* the Slavonic language of the *Poles.*

polish, *pol′ish, v.t.* to make smooth and glossy by rubbing: to bring to a finished state: to impart culture and refinement to.—*v.i.* to take a polish.—*n.* an act of polishing: gloss: refinement of manners: a substance applied to produce a polish.—*adjs.* **pol′ishable;** **pol′ished.**—*ns.* **pol′isher;** **pol′ishing-paste;** **pol′ishing-pow′der.** — *n.pl.* **pol′ishings,** particles removed by polishing.—*ns.* **polishing′-slate,** a diatomaceous slaty stone used for polishing glass, marble, and metals; **pol′ishment.**—**polish off,** (*slang*) to finish off: to dispose of finally. [O.Fr. *polir, polissant*—L. *polīre,* to polish.]

polite, *po-līt′, adj.* (*obs.*) glossy, polished: refined: of courteous manners.—*adv.* **polite′ly.** — *ns.* **polite′ness;** **politesse** (*pol-ē-tes′;* Fr.), superficial politeness.—**polite literature,** belles-lettres—poetry, essays, standard novels, &c., as distinguished from scientific treatises and the like. [L. *polītus,* pa.p. of *polīre,* to polish.]

politic, *pol′i-tik, adj.* (*rare*) political: (*obs.*) constitutional: in accordance with good policy: acting or proceeding from motives of policy: prudent: discreet: astutely contriving or intriguing.—*adj.* **polit′ical,** pertaining to policy or government: pertaining to parties differing in their views of government: (*obs.*) politic.—*adv.* **polit′ically.**—*ns.* **politicas′ter,** (*Milt.*) a petty politician; **politician** (*-tish′ən*), one versed in the science of government: one engaged in political life or statesmanship: one interested in party politics: a politic person: (*U.S.*) one who makes a profession or a game of politics, an intriguer.—*adj.* (*Milt.*) politic.—*v.t.* **polit′icise** (*-i-sīz*), to make political.—*v.i.* to play the politician: to discuss politics.—*adv.* **pol′iticly.**—*adj.* **politi′co-econom′ic,** of political economy.—*n.* (*pl.* in form, treated as *sing.*) **pol′itics,** the art or science of government: the management of a political party: political affairs or opinions: (*U.S.*) manoeuvring and intriguing.—*n.* **pol′itique** (*pol-ē-tēk;* Fr.), in French history, one of a moderate party between Huguenots and Catholics: a religious indifferentist: a temporiser.—**political economy,** the science of the production, distribution, and consumption of wealth; **political geography,** that part of geography which deals with the division of the earth for purposes of government, as states, colonies, counties, and the work of man, as towns, canals, &c.; **political science,** the science or study of government, as to its principles, aims, methods, &c.; **political verse,** Byzantine and modern Greek accentual verse, esp. iambic verse of fifteen syllables. [Gr. *politikos*—*politēs,* a citizen.]

polity, *pol′i-ti, n.* political organisation: form of political organisation, constitution: a body of people organised under a system of government. [Gr. *politeiā*.]

polka, *pōl'kā, n.* a Bohemian dance or its tune, in 2-4 time with accent on the third quaver, invented about 1830: applied to various things fashionable at the same time, esp. a woman's jacket.—*v.i.* **polk,** to dance a polka. [Perh. Czech *pulka*, half, from the half-step prevalent in it; or from Polish *polka*, a Polish woman.]

poll, *pōl, n.* the head: the hair of the head: the head and shoulders of a ling: the blunt end of the head of a hammer, miner's pick, &c.: a head as a unit in numbering, an individual: (*Shak.*) number of individuals: a register, esp. of voters: a voting: an aggregate of votes: a polled animal.—*adj.* polled: cut evenly (as in deed poll, opp. to *indenture*).—*v.t.* to cut off the hair, horns, top (of a tree), edge (of a deed) of: (*arch.*) to practise extortion upon: to receive or take the votes of: to receive, take, or cast (as a vote).—*v.i.* (*arch.*) to practise extortion: to vote.—*n.* **poll'-axe** (see **pole-axe).**—*adj.* polled, shorn: pollarded: deprived of horns: hornless.—*ns.* **poll'er; poll'ing-booth,** the place where people vote; **poll'-money, poll'-tax,** a tax of so much a head—i.e. on each person alike.—**at the head of the poll,** having the greatest number of votes at an election. [Cf. obs. Du. and L.G. *polle,* top of the head.]

Poll, poll, *pol, n.* a parrot.—*n.* **poll'-parrot.**—*v.t.* and *v.i.* to parrot. [*Poll*, a common name for a parrot; see **Molly.**]

poll, *pol, n.* (*Cambridge*) the mass of students who do not seek or obtain honours: a pass-degree.— *ns.* **poll'-degree'; poll'man.** [Said to be from Gr. *hoi polloi,* the many.]

pollack, *pol'ək, n.* a common fish of the cod family, with long narrow jaw and no barbel: extended to the coalfish.—Also **poll'ock.** [Etymology obscure; connexion with Gael. *pollag* doubtful.]

pollan, *pol'ən, n.* an Irish whitefish, esp. that (*Coregonus pollan*) found in Lough Neagh. [Perh. Ir. *poll,* lake; cf. **powan.**]

pollard, *pol'ərd, n.* a tree having the whole crown cut off, leaving it to send out new branches from the top of the stem: a hornless animal of horned kind: finer bran: flour or meal containing it: (*obs.*) a base foreign coin bearing a head.—*adj.* pollarded: awnless: bald.—*v.t.* to make a pollard of. [**poll** (1).]

poll-axe. Same as **pole-axe.**

pollen, *pol'ən, n.* the fertilising powder formed in the anthers of flowers.—*v.t.* to cover with pollen. —*ns.* **poll'en-basket,** a hollow in a bee's hind-leg in which pollen is carried; **poll'en-grain,** a grain of pollen, the microspore in flowering plants; **poll'en-sac,** a cavity in an anther in which pollen is formed, the microsporangium of flowering plants; **poll'en-tube,** an outgrowth from a pollen-grain by which the gametes are conveyed to the ovule.—*v.t.* **poll'inate,** to convey pollen to.— *ns.* **pollina'tion; poll'inium,** an agglutinated mass of pollen-grains:—*pl.* **pollin'ia.** [L. *pollen,* *-inis,* fine flour.]

pollent, *pol'ənt, adj.* strong. [L. *pollēns, -entis,* pr.p. of *pollēre,* to be strong.]

pollex, *pol'eks, n.* the thumb or its analogue:—*pl.* **pollices** (*pol'i-sēz*). [L. *pollex, -icis.*]

pollicie, pollicy (*Spens.*). Same as **policy.**

pollicitation, *pol-is-i-tā'shən, n.* a promise: a promise not yet accepted. [L. *pollicitātiō, -ōnis.*]

pollusion, *pol-(y)ŏŏ'zhən, n.* (*Love's Labour's Lost,* IV. iii.) Goodman Dull's blunder for **allusion.**

pollute, *pol-(y)ŏŏt', v.t.* to defile: to contaminate: to profane.—*adj.* defiled.—*adj.* **pollut'ed.** — *adv.* **pollut'edly.** — *ns.* **pollut'edness; pollut'er; pollution** (*pol-ōō'shən, -yōō'*). [L. *polluĕre, polluĭtus—pol-,* a form of *prō* or *per, luĕre,* to wash.]

Pollux, *pol'uks, n.* (*myth.*) the twin brother of Castor: a star in the constellation of the Twins. [L. for Gr. *Polydeukēs.*]

Polly, *pol'i, n.* a form of **Molly:** a parrot. [Cf. **Poll** (2).]

polly, *pol'i, n.* a slang abbreviation for **Apollinaris** (water).

pollywog, polliwog, *pol'i-twog,* **pollywig, polliwig,** *-wig, n.* a tadpole.—Also **porwigg'le.** [M.E. *pollwyggle*—**poll** (1), **wiggle.**]

polo, *pō'lō, n.* a game like hockey on horseback— of Oriental origin: a similar aquatic (*water polo*) or skating (*rink polo*) game.—*n.* **po'loist.** [Balti *polo,* polo ball; Tibetan *pulu.*]

polo, *pō'lō, n.* a Spanish gypsy dance. [Sp., an Andalusian popular song.]

polonaise, *pol-ə-nāz, n.* a woman's bodice and skirt in one piece, showing an under-skirt: a similar child's garment once worn in Scotland: a Polish national dance or promenade of slow movement in 3-4 time: a musical form in the same rhythm. [Fr., Polish (fem.).]

Polonia, *pol-ō'ni-ä, n.* mediaeval Latin name for Poland.—*adj.* and *n.* **Polo'nian.**—*n.* **Polonisation** (*pō-lən-ī-zā'shən*).—*v.t.* and *v.i.* **po'lonise,** to make or become Polish.—*ns.* **po'lonism,** a Polish idiom or charactertisic; **polonium** (*pol-ō'ni-əm*), a radioactive element (at. numb. 84) discovered by Mme Curie (a Pole); **polo'ny, -ie,** (*Scot.*) a child's polonaise.

polony, *po-lō'ni, n.* a dry sausage of partly cooked meat. [Prob. *Bologna,* in Italy; perh. *Polonia.*]

polt, *pōlt, n.* (now *dial.*) a hard blow: (*obs.*) a club. —*v.t.* (*dial.*) to beat.—*n.* **polt'foot,** a club-foot. —*adj.* club-footed. — *adj.* **polt'-footed.** [Origin obscure.]

poltergeist, *pol'tər-gīst, n.* a mysterious invisible agency asserted to throw things about: a noisy ghost. [Ger. *poltern,* to make a racket, *geist,* ghost.]

poltroon, *pol-trōōn'* (*Shak.* **poul'troone**), *n.* a dastard.—*adj.* and.—*n.* **poltroon'ery,** want of spirit. [Fr. *poltron*—It. *poltrone—poltro,* lazy.]

polverine, *pol'vər-ēn, n.* (*obs.*) glass-makers' potash. [It. *polverino*—L. *pulvis, pulvĕris,* dust.]

poly-, *pol'i-, pol-i'-,* in composition, many: several: much: denoting a polymer, as *polyethylene* (see below).—*adjs.* **polyacid** (*-as'id*), having several replaceable hydrogen atoms: capable of replacing several hydrogen atoms of an acid; **pol'yact** (Gr. *aktīs, -īnos,* ray), **polyacti'nal** (or *-akt'in-əl*), **polyact'ine,** many-rayed.—*n.pl.* **Polyadel'phia** (Gr. *adelphos,* brother), in Linnaeus's system a class of plants with three or more bundles of stamens.— *adj.* **polyadel'phous,** (of stamens) united in several bundles: having the stamens so united.—*n.pl.* **Polyan'dria** (Gr. *anēr, andros,* man, male), in Linnaeus's system a class of plants with many stamens inserted in the receptacle.—*adj.* **polyan'-drous,** having or allowing several husbands or male mates (at a time): (*bot.*) having a large and indefinite number of stamens or of antheridia.— *ns.* **pol'yandry** (or *-an'*), the condition or practice of being polyandrous: the social usage of some peoples in certain stages of civilisation in which a woman normally has several husbands; **polyan'-thus** (Gr. *anthos,* flower), a many-flowered supposed hybrid between cowslip and primrose:—*pl.* **polyan'thuses.**—*adj.* **pol'yarch** (Gr. *archē,* origin), having many xylem strands.—*n.* **pol'yarchy** (*-ärk-i*; Gr. *archein,* to rule), government by many persons.—*adjs.* **polyatom'ic,** (*chem.*) having many atoms, or replaceable atoms or groups: multivalent; **polyax'ial** (L. *axis*), **polyax'on** (Gr. *axōn,* axis), having many axes or several axis-cylinders.—*n.* a monaxonic sponge spicule.—*adjs.* **polyaxon'ic; polybas'ic,** capable of reacting with several equivalents of an acid: (of acids) having several replaceable hydrogen atoms; **polycarp'ic** (Gr. *karpos,* fruit), fruiting many times, or year after year; **polycarp'ous,** polycarpic: having an apocarpous gynaeceum.—*n.pl.* **Polychaeta** (*-kē'tä*; Gr. *chaitē,* bristle), a class of marine Chaetopods with numerous bristles.— *ns.* **polychaete,** any worm of the Polychaeta; **pol'ychrest** (*-krest*; Gr. *polychrēstos—chrēstos,* useful), a thing, esp. a medicine, useful in several ways.—*adj.* **polychroic** (*-krō'ik*), pleochroic.—*n.* **pol'ychroism.**—*adj.* **pol'ychrome** (*-krōm*; Gr. *chrōma,* colour), many-coloured.—*n.* a work of art (esp. a statue) in several colours: varied colouring. —*adjs.* **polychromat'ic, polychrom'ic.**—*n.* **pol'y-**

Neutral vowels in unaccented syllables : *el'ə-mənt, in'fənt, ran'dəm*

chromy, the art of decorating in many colours. —*adjs.* **polycotyle'donous**, with more than two cotyledons; **polycrot'ic** (Gr. *krotos*, a beat), of the pulse, having several beats to each heart-beat. —*n.* **polyc'rotism.**—*adj.* **polycyclic** (-*sī'klik*; Gr. *kyklos*, wheel), having many circles, rings, whorls, turns, or circuits.—*n.* **polycythaemia** (-*sī-thē'mi-ä*; Gr. *kytos*, a vessel, as if cell, *haima*, blood), excess of red blood-corpuscles. — *adj.* **polydac'tyl**, having more than the normal number of fingers or toes.—Also *n.*—*ns.* **polydac'tylism**, **-dac'tyly.**—*adj.* **polydac'tylous.**—*n.* **polydip'sia** (Gr. *dipsa*, thirst), excessive thirst.—*adjs.* **polyem'bryonate**; **polyembryonic** (-*on'ik*).—*ns.* **polyembryony** (-*em'bri-ɔn-i*), formation of more than one embryo from one ovule or from one fertilised ovum; **polyeth'ylene**, **polythene'**, a generic name for certain thermoplastics, polymers of ethylene; **Polygala** (*pol-ig'ɔ-lä*; Gr. *polygalon*, milkwort—*gala*, milk), the milkwort genus, giving name to the fam. **Polygalä'ceae.**—*adj.* **polygalaceous** (-*lä'shɔs*).—*n.pl.* **Polygamia** (*pol-i-gä'mi-ä*; Gr. *gamos*, marriage), in Linnaeus's classification, a class having male, female, and hermaphrodite flowers.—*adj.* **polygamic** (-*gam'ik*). —*n.* **polygamist** (*pol-ig'*).—*adj.* **polyg'amous.**—*ns.* **polygamy** (*pol-ig'ɔ-mi*), the rule, custom, or condition of marriage to more than one person at a time, or (now rarely) in life: sometimes used for **polygyny**: (*zool.*) mating with more than one in the same breeding season: (*bot.*) occurrence of male, female, and hermaphrodite flowers on the same or on different plants; **polygen'esis**, multiple origin, esp. of mankind.—*adjs.* **polygenet'ic**, of polygenesis: springing from several sources: of dyes, giving different colours with different mordants; **polygen'ic**, polygenetic: forming more than one compound with a univalent element. —*ns.* **polyg'enism**, belief in multiple origin, esp. of mankind; **polyg'enist.**—*adj.* **polyg'enous**, of multiple origin or composition.—*ns.* **polyg'eny**, polygenesis; **polyhalite** (-*hal'īt*; Gr. *hals*, salt), a triclinic mineral, sulphate of magnesium, potassium, and calcium.—*adj.* **pol'yglot** (Gr. *polyglōttos*—*glōtta*, tongue), in, of, speaking, or writing many languages.—*n.* one who speaks or writes many languages: a collection of versions in different languages of the same work, esp. a Bible.—Also **pol'yglott.**—*adjs.* **polyglott'al**, **polyglott'ic**, **polyglott'ous.**—*n.* **pol'ygon** (-*gon*, -*gɔn*; Gr. *gōniä*, angle), a plane figure bounded by straight lines, esp. more than four.—*adj.* **polyg'onal** (**polygonal numbers**, figurate numbers).—*adv.* **polyg'onally.** —*ns.* **Polygon'atum** (Gr. *polygonäton*—*gony*, -*atos*, knee), the Solomon's seal genus of the lily family; **Polyg'onum** (Gr. *polygonon*), the knot-grass genus, with swollen joints and sheathing stipules, of the dock family **Polygonä'ceae.**—*adj.* **polygonä'ceous.**—*ns.* **polyg'ony**, (*Spens.*) bistort; **pol'ygraph**, a copying, multiplying, or tracing apparatus: a copy. — *adj.* **polygraph'ic.** — *n.* **polygraphy** (*pol-ig'rɔ-fi*), voluminous writing.—*n.pl.* **Polygynia** (-*jin'*; Gr. *gynē*, woman, female), in various Linnaean classes of plants, an order with more than twelve styles.—*adjs.* **polygyn'ian**, of the Polygynia; **polygynous** (-*lij'* or -*lig'i-nɔs*), having several wives: mating with several females: having several styles: polygynian.—*n.* **polygyny** (-*lij'* or -*lig'*), the custom, practice, or condition of having a plurality of wives: the habit of mating with more than one female.—*adjs.* **polyhedral** (-*hed'*, -*hēd'*), **polyhed'ric.**—*ns.* **polyhed'ron** (Gr. *hedrä*, seat), a solid figure or body bounded by plane faces (esp. more than six); **polyhis'tor** (Gr. *polyistōr*—*histōreein*, to inquire, learn), a person of great and varied learning; **polyhistorian** (-*tō'ri-ɔn*).—*adj.* **polyhistoric** (-*tor'ik*).—*ns.* **polyhis'tory** (-*tɔr-i*); **polyhy'brid**, a cross between parents differing in several heritable characters.— *adj.* **polyhy'dric**, having several hydroxyl groups. —*ns.* **Polyhymnia** (*pol-i-him'ni-ä*), **Polymnia** (*pol-im'ni-ä*; Gr. *Polymnia* for *Polyumnia*—*hymnos*, hymn, ode), the muse of the sublime lyric; **polymas'tia**, **polymast'ism**, **pol'ymasty** (Gr. *mastos*, breast), the presence of supernumerary breasts or

nipples.—*adj.* **polymas'tic.**—*n.* **pol'ymath** (Gr. *polymathēs*—the root of *manthanein*, to learn), one who knows many arts and sciences.—*adj.* **polymath'ic.**—*ns.* **polym'athy**, much and varied learning; **pol'ymer** (Gr. *meros*, part; *chem.*), one of a series of substances alike in percentage composition, but differing in molecular weight, especially one of those of higher molecular weight as produced by polymerisation. — *adj.* **polymeric** (-*mer'ik*), of, in a relation of, or manifesting polymerism.—*ns.* **pol'ymeride**, a polymer; **polymerisä'tion.**—*v.t.* **polym'erise**, to combine to form a more complex molecule having the same empirical formula as the simpler ones combined: to render polymerous.—*v.i.* to change into a polymer.—*n.* **polym'erism.**—*adj.* **polym'erous**, having many parts: (*bot.*) having many parts in a whorl.—*ns.* **polym'ery**, condition of being polymerous; **pol'ymorph** (Gr. *polymorphos*, many-formed—*morphē*, form), any one of several forms in which the same thing may occur: an organism occurring in several forms: a substance crystallising in several systems.—*adj.* **polymorph'ic.**—*n.* **polymorph'ism.**—*adjs.* **polymorph'ous**; **Polynē'sian** (Gr. *nēsos* an island), of Polynesia, its prevailing race of brown men, or their languages (a division of the Austronesian).— *n.* a native of Polynesia: a member of the brown race of Polynesia.—*adj.* and *n.* **polynō'mial**, multinomial.—*ns.* **polynō'mialism**; **polyonym**(*pol'i-ɔ-nim*; Gr. *onyma*, a form of *onoma*, name), a name consisting of several words.—*adjs.* **polyonym'ic**, of more than two words; **polyon'ymous**, ha ing many names.—*ns.* **polyon'ymy**, multiplicity of names for the same thing; **polyp**, **polype** (*pol'ip*; L. *polypus*, -*ī*, adopted, and transformed to 2nd declension, from Gr. *polypous*, -*odos*—*polys*, many, *pous*, foot; see **polypus**), orig. (*obs.*) an octopus or cuttlefish: later extended to other animals with many arms or tentacles, esp. coelenterates and Polyzoa: an individual of a colonial animal: (*rare*) a polypus:—*pl.* **pol'yps**, **polypes** (*pol'ips*), **polypi** (*pol'i-pī*; L.); **pol'ypary**, the common investing structure of a colony of polyps; **polypep'tide**, a substance in which several molecules of an amino-acid are condensed.—*adjs.* **polypet'alous**, with free petals; **polyphagous** (*pō-lif'ɔ-gɔs*; Gr. *phagein* (aorist), to eat), eating many different kinds of food: eating much.—*n.* **polyph'agy** (-*ji*), the character of being polyphagous.—*adjs.* **pol'yphase**, having several alternating electric currents of like frequency but differing in phase; **Polyphē'mian**, **Polyphē'mic.** — *n.* **Polyphē'mus** (Gr. *Polyphēmos*), the Cyclops blinded by Odysseus.—*adjs.* **polyphloisbic** (*pol-i-flois'bik*; Gr. *polyphloisbos*—*phloisbos*, din), **poluphloisboiotic** (*pol-ōō-flois-boi-ot'ik*), **polyphloesboean** (*pol-i-flēs-bē'ɔn*, the *oi* and *oe* from the genitive ending in Homer's phrase *polyphloisboio thalassēs*, of the much-roaring sea), loud-roaring; **poluphloisboiotatot'ic** (*Thackeray*; as if from a Gr. superl. in -*otatos*).—*n.* **polyphone** (*pol'i-fōn*; Gr. *phōnē*, a voice), a symbol with more than one phonetic value. — *adj.* **polyphonic** (-*fon'ik*), many-voiced: of polyphones: of polyphony.—*ns.* **pol'yphonist**, a contrapuntist; **polyph'ony**, composition of music in parts each with an independent melody of its own.—*adjs.* **polyphyletic** (*pol-i-fil-et'ik*, or -*fīl-*; Gr. *phyletikos*, pertaining to a tribesman—*phylē*, a tribe), of multiple origin: descended by convergent lines from several ancestral groups; **polyphyllous** (*pol-i-fil'ɔs*; Gr. *phyllon*, leaf), having the perianth leaves free.—*ns.* **pol'ypide**, **pol'ypite**, a polyp of a colonial animal; **polyp'idom**, a polypary (Gr. *domos*, house). — *adjs.* **pol'ypine**; **pol'ypoid**; **pol'ypous.**— *n.pl.* **Polyplacoph'ora** (Gr. *plax*, *plakos*, a plate, slab), an order of molluscs, bilaterally symmetrical, with shell composed of eight transverse dorsal plates—the chitons, &c.—*adj.* **polyploid** (*pol'i-ploid*; on the analogy of *haploid*, *diploid*), having more than twice the normal haploid number of chromosomes.—*ns.* **pol'yploidy**, the polyploid condition; **polypod** (*pol'i-pod*), an animal with many feet: polypody; **Polypodium** (-*pō'di-ɔm*; Gr. *podion*, dim. of *pous*, a foot), the typical genus of Polypodiä´ceae, the family with stalked sporangia and vertical annulus to which most ferns belong—so named from the many-footed appearance of the rhizome; **polypody** (*pol'i-pod-i*), any fern of the genus Polypodium, esp. *P. vulgare.—adj.* **pol'ypoid**, like polypus.—*ns.* **Polyporus** (*pō-lip'ə-rəs*; Gr. *poros*, a pore), a large genus of pore-bearing fungi, often forming hoof-like and bracket-like growths on trees; **polypō'sis**, presence or development of polypi.—*adj.* **pol'ypous**, of the nature of a polyp.—*ns.* **polyprō'todont** (Gr. *prōtos*, first, *odous, odontos*, tooth), any member of the **Polyprotodont'ia**, che suborder of marsupials, including opossums, dasyures, &c., with many small incisors; **Polyp'terus** (Gr. *pteron*, a fin), an African genus of Crossopterygian fisher fishes, with the dorsal fin represented by detached rays; **polypus** (*pol'i-pəs*; Gr. *polypous, -odos*), a pedunculated tumour growing from mucous membrane:—*pl.* (L.) **pol'ypī**.—*adjs.* **polysep'alous**, having the sepals separate from each other; **polysty'lar**, **pol'ystyle** (Gr. *stylos*, column), having many columns; **polysyllabic** (*-ab'ik*), **-al.**—*adv.* **polysyllab'ically.**—*ns.* **polysyllab'icism**, **polysyll'abism**; **polysyll'able**, a word of many or of more than three syllables; **polysyndeton** (*pol-i-sin'de-ton*; Gr. *syndeton*, a conjunction—*syn*, together, *deein*, to bind; *rhet.*), figurative repetition of connectives or conjunctions; **polysynthesis** (*-sin'thi-sis*).—*adjs.* **polysynthet'ic**, **-al**, made up of many separate elements: (*crystal.*) built up of a number of small crystals in parallel growth: (*philol.*) combining many simple words of a sentence in one, as in the native languages of America—also called *incorporating.—adv.* **polysynthet'ically.**—*ns.* **polysynthet'icism** (*-i-sizm*), **polysyn'thetism**, the character of being polysynthetic.—*adj.* **polytechnic** (*-tek'nik*; Gr. *technikos—technē*, art), of many arts or technical subjects.—*n.* a school where such subjects are taught.—*adjs.* **polytech'nical**; **polythalamous** (*-thal'ə-məs*; Gr. *thalamos*, a chamber), having several cells or chambers.—*ns.* **polytheism** (*pol'i-thē-izm*; Gr. *theos*, a god), the doctrine of a plurality of gods; **pol'ytheist.**—*adjs.* **polytheist'ic**, **-al.**—*adv.* **polytheist'ically.**—*adj.* **polytocous** (*pol-it'ə-kəs*; Gr. *tokos*, birth), producing many or several at a birth or in a clutch.—*n.* **Polytrichum** (*pol-it'ri-kəm*; Gr. *thrix, trichos*, hair), a genus of tall hairy-capped mosses.—*adjs.* **polytypic** (*-tip'ik*), having many types and representatives; **polyvalent** (*pol-iv'ə-lənt, pol-i-vā'lənt*), multivalent.—*n.pl.* **Polyzō'a** (Gr. *zōion*, an animal), a phylum of aquatic animals, almost all colonial, with cup-shaped body, U-shaped food-canal, and a wreath of tentacles about the mouth:—*sing.* **polyzo'on.**—*n.* and *adj.* **polyzo'an.**—*adj.* **polyzoarial** (*-ā'ri-əl*).—*ns.* **polyzoä'rium**; **polyzō'ary**, a polyzoan colony, or its supporting skeleton.—*adjs.* **polyzō'ic**, having many zooids: pertaining to the Polyzoa; **polyzo'nal** (Gr. *zōnē*, belt), composed of many zones or belts; **polyzō'oid**, like, or of the nature of, a Polyzoon. [Gr. *polys, poleia, poly*, much.]

pom, *pom*, *n.* (*coll.*) short for Pomeranian dog.

pomace, *pum'is*, *n.* crushed apples for cider-making, or the residue after pressing: anything crushed to pulp, esp. after oil has been expressed.—*n.* **pom'ace-fly**, a fruit-fly (Drosophila). [App. L.L. *pōmācium*, cider—L. *pōmum*, apple, &c.]

pomade, *pom-äd'*, *n.* ointment for the hair—Latinised as **pomā'tum.**—*v.t.* to anoint with pomade. [Fr. *pommade*—It. *pomada, pomata*, lip-salve—L. *pōmum*, an apple.]

Pomak, *pō-mäk'*, *n.* a Mahommedan Bulgarian.

pomander, *pom'* or *pōm'ən-dər*, or *-an'dər*, *n.* (*Shak.*) a ball of perfumes, or a perforated globe or box in which courtiers, &c., used to carry it. [O.Fr. *pomme d'ambre*, apple of amber.]

pomato, *pom-ä'tō*, *-ä'tō*, *n.* a tomato grafted on a potato. [Portmanteau-word.]

pome, *pōm*, *n.* (*rare*) an apple : a fruit constructed like an apple, the enlarged fleshy receptacle enclosing a core formed from the carpels : a king's globe or mound : a priest's' hand-warming ball of hot water.—*adj.* **pomaceous** (*-ā'shəs*), relating to, consisting of, or resembling apples : of the apple family or the apple section of the rose family.—*ns.* **pome'-cit'ron**, the citron; **pome'roy**, **pomroy** (*pom', pum'roi*), an old variety of apple; **pome'-water**, **pom'water**, (*Shak.*) a sweet juicy apple; **pom'iculture**, fruit-growing : pomology.—*adjs.* **pomif'erous**, bearing apples, pomes, or fruit generally; **pomolog'ical.** — *ns.* **pomol'ogist**; **pomol'ogy**, the study of fruit-growing. [L. *pōmum*, a fruit, an apple.]

pomegranate, *pom'gran-it*, formerly *pom-, pumgran'it*, *n.* an Oriental fruit much cultivated in warm countries, with a thick leathery rind and numerous seeds with pulpy edible seed-coats : the tree (*Punica Granatum*; fam. Punicaceae) bearing it. [O.Fr. *pome grenate*—L. *pōmum*, an apple, *grānātum*, having many grains.]

pomelo, *pum'*, or *pom'il-ō*, *n.* the shaddock : the grape fruit—cf. **pompelmoose.** [Origin obscure.]

Pomeranian, *pom-i-rā'ni-ən*, *adj.* of *Pomerania.—n.* a native of Pomerania : a spitz or Pomeranian dog, a cross from the Eskimo dog, with a sharp-pointed face and an abundant white, creamy, or black coat.

Pomfret, *pum'frit*, **Pontefract**, *pon'ti-frakt*, *n.* a town in Yorkshire.—*n.* **Pomfret-** (*pum', pom'*), **Pon'tefract-cake**, a round flat liquorice sweetmeat made there. [A.Fr. *Pontfret*, L. *pōns, pontis*, bridge, *fractus*, broken.]

pommel, *pum'l*, *n.* (*obs.*) a knob : a ball-shaped finial : a knob on a sword-hilt : the high part of a saddle-bow : a heavy-headed ramming tool.—*v.t.* (usu. spelt **pummel**, q.v.).—*adjs.* **pomm'-elled**, having a pommel—in heraldry also **pommelé** (*pom'*), **pomm'etty.** [O.Fr. *pomel* (Fr. *pommeau*)—L. *pōmum*, an apple.]

pommy, *pom'i*, *n.* (*Austr.*) an immigrant from the British Isles. [From **pomegranate.**]

pomoerium, *pō-mē'ri-əm*, *n.* an open space around a town, within and without the walls. [L. *pōmoerium*, app. for *postmoerium—post* and *moiros*, old form of *mūrus*, wall.]

Pomona, *pō-mō'nä*, *n.* the Roman goddess of fruits. [L. *Pōmōna—pōmum*, fruit, apple.]

pomp, *pomp*, *n.* a procession : great show or display : ceremony : ostentation : vain show : worldly vanity : consequential bearing.—*n.* **pomposity** (*-os'i-ti*), solemn affectation of dignity : a ridiculously pompous action, expression, or person.—*adj.* **pomp'ous**, (*arch.*) stately : solemnly consequential.—*adv.* **pomp'ously.**—*n.* **pomp'ousness.** [Fr. *pompe*—L. *pompa*—Gr. *pompē*, a sending, escort, procession—*pempein*, to send.]

pompadour, *pom'pə-dōōr*, *n.* a fashion of dressing women's hair by rolling it back from the forehead over a cushion : a corsage with low square neck : a pattern for silk, with pink, blue, and gold leaves and flowers : a pink colour.—*adj.* in the fashion of Mme de Pompadour's time, or one associated with her. [Marquise de *Pompadour*, 1721-64.]

pompano, *pomp'ə-nō*, *n.* a general name for Carangoid fishes, esp. American food-fishes of the genus Trachynotus. [Sp. *pámpano*, a fish of another family.]

Pompeian, *pom-pē'ən*, *adj.* pertaining to *Pompeii*, a city buried by an eruption of Mount Vesuvius in 79 A.D., excavated since 1755.—*n.* **Pompei'an red'**, a red colour like that on the walls of Pompeian houses.

pompelmoose, *pom'pəl-mōōs*, *n.* the shaddock, esp. the grape-fruit.—Also **pam'pelmoose, -mouse**, **pom'pelmous(e)**, **pum'ple-nose**, **pom'pelo**, **pom'elo.** [Du. *pompelmoes*; origin obscure.]

pompey, *pom'pi*, *v.t.* (*Dickens*) to pamper (q.v.).

pompholyx, *pom'fō-liks*, *n.* a vesicular eruption chiefly on the palms and soles : impure zinc oxide.—*adj.* **pomphol'ygous.** [Gr. *pompholyx, -ygos*, bubble, slag—*pomphos*, a blister.]

pompier-ladder, *pom'pi-ər-lad'ər*, or (Fr.) *pon'-pyä'*, *n.* a fireman's ladder, a pole with cross-bars and hook. [Fr. *pompier*, fireman—*pompe*, pump.]

pompion, *pump'i-ən.* See **pumpkin.**

pompom, *pom'pom*, *n.* (*coll.*) a machine-gun. [Imit.]

pompon, *pom'pon*, also formerly **pompoon**, *pom-*

pŏŏn', *n.* a jewelled hair ornament on a pin : a fluffy or woolly ball, tuft, or tassel worn on a shoe, hat, &c. [Fr. *pompon*.]

'pon, *pon*, aphetic for **upon**.

ponceau, *ponͤ͡-sō'*, *n.* and *adj.* poppy colour.—*n.* a red dye :—*pl.* **ponceaux** (*-sōz'*). [Fr.]

ponceau, *ponͤ͡-sō'*, *n.* a small bridge or culvert. [Fr.]

poncho, *pon'chō*, *n.* a South American cloak, a blanket with a hole for the head : a cyclist's waterproof cape of like form :—*pl.* **pon'chos**. [Sp. from Araucanian.]

pond, *pond*, *n.* a small, usually artificial, lake : the stretch of water between locks in a canal : (*facet.*) the Atlantic.—*v.t.* to make into a pond.—*v.i.* to collect into a pond.—*ns.* **pond'age**, the capacity of a pond ; **pond'-life'**, animal life in ponds ; **pond'-lily**, a water-lily ; **pond'-master**, the man in charge of a swimming-pond ; **pond'-snail**, a pond-dwelling snail, esp. Limnaea ; **pond'weed**, any plant of the genus Potamogeton (**Canadian pondweed**, Anacharis). [M.E. *ponde* ; cf. **pound** (2).]

ponder, *pon'dər*, *v.t.* to weigh, now only in the mind : to think over : to consider.—*v.i.* to think (often with *on* and *over*).—*n.* **ponderabil'ity.**—*adjs.* **pon'derable**, that may be weighed : having sensible weight ; **pon'deral**, pertaining to weight: ascertained by weight.—*ns.* **pon'derance, pon'derancy**, weight.—*v.t.* and *v.i.* **pon'derate**, to weigh : to ponder.—*ns.* **pondera'tion**, weighing ; **pon'derer.**—*adv.* **pon'deringly.**—*ns.* **pon'derment** ; **ponderosity** (*-os'i-ti*).—*adj.* **pon'derous**, heavy : weighty : massive : unwieldy : lumbering : solemnly laboured.—*adv.* **pon'derously.**—*n.* **pon'derousness.** [L. *ponderāre*, and *pondus*, *pondĕris*, a weight.]

pone, *pōn*, *n.* (*U.S.*) maize bread : a maize loaf or cake. [Algonkin *pone*.]

pone, *pō'ni*, *pōn*, *n.* (*cards*) the player who cuts. [L. *pŏnĕ*, imper. of *pŏnĕre*, to place.]

ponent, *pō'nənt*, *adj.* (*Milt.*) western. [It. *ponente*, setting (of the sun)—L. *pŏnēns*, *-entis*, pr.p. of *pŏnĕre*, to put.]

ponerology, *pon-ə-rol'ə-ji*, *n.* (*theol.*) the doctrine of wickedness. [Gr. *ponēros*, bad, *logos*, discourse.]

pong, *pong*, *v.i.* (*slang*) to gag.

pongee, *pun-*, *pon-jē'*, *n.* a soft silk, made from cocoons of a wild silkworm : a fine cotton. [Perh. Chin. *pun-chī*, own loom.]

pongo, *pong'gō*, *n.* an anthropoid ape, orig. prob. the gorilla, but transferred to the orang-utan : a monkey. [Congo *mpongi*.]

poniard, *pon'yərd*, *n.* a small dagger.—*v.t.* to stab with a poniard. [Fr. *poignard*—*poing*—L. *pugnus*, fist.]

pons, *ponz*, *n.* (*anat.*) a connecting part, esp. the *pons Varolii*, a mass of fibres joining the hemispheres of the brain :—*pl.* **pon'tēs.**—*adjs.* **pon'tal**, **pon'tic**, **pon'tile**, relating to the pons of the brain. [L. *pōns*, *pontis*, a bridge.]

pontage, *pont'ij*, *n.* a toll paid on bridges : a tax for repairing bridges. [L.L. *pontāgium*—L. *pōns*, *pontis*, a bridge.]

Pontederia, *pont-e-dē'ri-ä*, *n.* an American genus of monocotyledonous water- or bog-plants, called pickerel-weed, giving name to a family **Pontederiā'ceae.** [After Giulio *Pontedera* (1688-1757), Italian botanist.]

pontianac, pontianak, *pont-i-ä'nak*, *n.* jelutong. [*Pontianak*, in Borneo.]

Pontic, *pon'tik*, *adj.* of the ancient kingdom and Roman province of *Pontus*, or of the *Pontus* Euxinus or Black Sea. [Gr. *Pontikos*—*pontos*, sea.]

pontifex, *pon'ti-feks*, *n.* in ancient Rome a member of a college of priests that had control of matters of religion, their chief being *Pontifex Maximus* : a pontiff : a bridge-builder :—*pl.* **pontifices** (*-tif'i-sēz*, *-kās*).—*n.* **pon'tiff**, a pontifex : a high-priest : (*R.C.*) a bishop, esp. the pope or *sovereign pontiff* : an oracular person.—*adjs.* **pontif'ic, -al**, of or belonging to a pontiff : splendid : pompously dogmatic.—*ns.* **pontif'ical**, an office-book for bishops ; **pontifical'ity.** — *adv.* **pontif'ically.**—*n.pl.* **pontif'icals**, the dress of a priest, bishop, or

pope.—*n.* **pontif'icate**, the dignity of a pontiff or high-priest : the office and dignity or reign of a pope.—*v.i.* to perform the duties of a pontiff : to play the pontiff.—*n.* **pon'tifice** (*-fis* ; *Milt.*), bridge-work, a bridge.—*v.i.* **pon'tify**, to play the pontiff.—**pontifical mass**, mass celebrated by a bishop while wearing his full vestments. [L. *pontifex*, *pontificis* (partly through Fr. *pontife*), which was supposed to be from *pōns*, *pontis*, a bridge, *facĕre*, to make, but is probably from an Oscan and Umbrian word *puntis*, propitiatory offering.]

pontil. See **punty.**

pontlevis, *pont-lev'is*, *ponͤ͡-lə-vē'*, *n.* a drawbridge. [Fr.]

pontoon, *pon-tōōn'*, *n.* a flat-bottomed boat, a ferry-boat, barge, or lighter : such a boat, or a float, used to support a bridge : a bridge of boats : a low vessel carrying plant, materials, and men for work at sea or on rivers : the floating gate of a dock : a boat-like float of an aeroplane : a float.—Also **ponton** (*pon'ton*, *pon'tōōn'*).—*v.t.* to cross by pontoon.—*ns.* **pontoneer'**, **pontonier'**, **pontonnier'**, a builder of pontoon-bridges ; **pontoon'-bridge**, a platform or roadway supported upon pontoons. [Fr. *ponton*—L. *pontō*, *-ōnis*, a punt, pontoon—*pōns*, a bridge.]

pontoon, *pon-tōōn'*, *n.* a card game of chance. [vingt-et-un (q.v.).]

pony, formerly also **poney**, *pō'ni*, *n.* a small horse—one less than 13 (or 14) hands high : (*slang*) £25 : (*U.S. slang*) a crib : (*U.S. slang*) a key : a small glass, esp. of beer.—*v.t.* and *v.i.* (*U.S. slang*) to pay or settle (with *up*) : to prepare or translate by help of a crib.—*ns.* **po'ny-carr'iage** ; **po'ny-en'gine**, a shunting engine ; **po'ny-skin**, the skin of a foal, esp. from the Kirghiz Steppes, used as a fur.—**Jerusalem pony**, an ass. [Scots **powney**, **powny**, prob.—*poulenet*, dim. of *poulain*—L.L. *pullānus*, a foal—L. *pullus*, a young animal.]

pood, *pōōd*, *n.* a Russian weight, *c.* 36 lb. avoirdupois. [Russ. *pud*.]

poodle, *pōōd'l*, *n.* a small curly-haired pet dog (sometimes grotesquely clipped in places).—*ns.* **pood'le-dog**, a poodle : an assiduous follower ; **pood'le-faker**, (*Anglo-Indian slang*) a man who seeks women's society. [Ger. *pudel* ; L.G. *pudeln*, to paddle, splash.]

pooh, *pōō*, *poo*, *interj.* of disdain.—*v.t.* **pooh-pooh'**, to make light of. [Imit.]

pooja, poojah. Same as **puja.**

pook, pouk, *pook*, *v.t.* (*Scot.*) to pluck : to pinch :—*pa.t.* and *pa.p.* **pook'it, pouk'it.** [Origin unknown.]

pool, *pōōl*, *n.* a small body of still water : a temporary or casual collection of water or other liquid : a puddle : a deep part of a stream. [O.E. *pól* ; Du. *poel*, Ger. *pfuhl* ; relation to Ir. and Gael. *poll*, W. *pwll*, undetermined.]

pool, *pōōl*, *n.* the stakes in certain games : the collective stakes of a number of persons who combine in a betting arrangement : an organised arrangement for betting in this way : a group of persons so combining : a game, or a set of players, at quadrille, &c. : a game or contest of various kinds in which the winner receives the pool : a game played on a billiard-table, each player trying to pocket the others' balls in rotation : a common stock or fund : a combination of interest : a combine : an arrangement for eliminating competition.—*v.t.* to put into a common fund or stock.—*v.i.* to form a pool. [Fr. *poule*, a hen, also stakes (possibly through an intermediate sense of plunder), but associated in English with **pool** (1).]

poon, *pōōn*, *n.* an Indian tree, *Calophyllum Inophyllum*, or other species of the genus (family Guttiferae).—*ns.* **poon'-oil**, an oil expressed from its seeds ; **poon'-wood.** [Sinh. *pūna*.]

poonac, *pōō'nak*, *n.* coconut oilcake. [Sinh. *punakku*.]

poop, *pōōp*, *n.* the after part of a ship : a high deck at the stern.—*v.t.* to break over the stern of : to ship over the stern.—*adj.* **pooped**, having a poop. [Fr. *poupe*—L. *puppis*, the poop.]

poop, poupe, *pōōp*, *v.t.* (*obs.*) to befool : to cozen :

to undo : to do for :—*pa.p.* in *Shak.* **poupt.** [Cf. Du. *poep,* clown.]

poor, *poor, adj.* possessing little or nothing : without means : needy : deficient : lacking : unproductive : scanty : mere : inferior : sorry : spiritless : in sorry condition : (in modest or ironical self-depreciation) humble : unfortunate, to be pitied (esp. of the dead).—*ns.* **poor'-box,** a money-box for gifts for the poor ; **poor'house** (*Scot.* **poor's-house, puir's'-house, -hoose),** a house established at the public expense for sheltering the poor—a workhouse.—*adj.* **poor'ish.**—*ns.* **poor-John',** (*Shak.*) salt hake ; **poor'-law** (often in *pl.*), the law or laws relating to the support of the poor. —Also *adj.*—*adv.* **poor'ly,** in a poor manner : badly : inadequately : in a small way : meanly.— *adj.* in ill-health.—*ns.* **poor'ness ; poor'-rate,** a rate or tax for the support of the poor ; **poor's'-box,** a poor-box.—*adj.* **poor'-spir'ited,** lacking in spirit. — *ns.* **poor'-spir'itedness ; poor's'-roll,** (*Scots law*) the list of poor litigants allowed to sue *in formā pauperis.*—**poor man of mutton,** (*Scot.*) cold mutton broiled, esp. the shoulder ; **poor man's weather-glass,** the pimpernel, reputed to close its flowers before rain ; **poor white,** a member of a class of poor, improvident, and incompetent white folks in the Southern States of America, and by extension elsewhere, called by the negroes *poor white trash.* [O.Fr. *poure, povre* (Fr. *pauvre*) —L. *pauper,* poor.]

poort, *port, poort, n.* (*S.Afr.*) a mountain pass. [Du.,—L. *porta,* gate.]

poortith, *poor'tith, n.* (*Scot.*) poverty. [O.Fr. *pouerteit, poverteit*—L. *paupertās, -ātis.*]

poorwill, *poor'wil, n.* a Western North American night-jar (Phalaenoptilus), smaller than the whip-poorwill. [From its note.]

pop, *pop, n.* a mild explosive sound, as of drawing a cork : a shot : (*slang*) a pistol : (*slang*) ginger-beer or other effervescing drink : (*slang*) pawn, or an act of pawning.—*v.i.* to make a pop : to shoot : to burst with a pop : to protrude : to come, go, slip, or pass, suddenly, unexpectedly, or unobtrusively : to pitch or alight : (*slang*) to propose marriage.—*v.t.* to cause to make a pop or to burst with a pop : to shoot : to thrust or put suddenly : (*slang*) to pawn : (*pr.p.* **popp'ing ;** *pa.t.* and *pa.p.* **popped**).—*adv.* with a pop : suddenly.—*ns.* **pop'-corn,** maize burst open and swelled by heating : a kind of maize suitable for this ; **pop'-eye,** a prominent or protruding eye.—*adj.* **pop'-eyed.**— *ns.* **pop'-gun,** a tube for shooting pellets by compressed air : a contemptible gun ; **popp'er,** one who pops : anything that makes a pop : a utensil for popping corn ; **popp'ing-crease** (see **crease**) ; **pop'-shop,** (*slang*) a pawnshop ; **pop'-visit,** a visit at an odd time, casual visit ; **pop'-weed,** bladderwort.—**pop off,** to make off : to die : to fall asleep ; **pop the question,** to make an offer of marriage. [Imit.]

pop. See **poppa, poppet, poppycock, popular.**

pope, *pōp, n.* the bishop of Rome, head of the R.C. Church : formerly applied also to the patriarch of Alexandria and other bishops : any spiritual head : a person wielding, assuming, or thought to assume authority like that of the pope : the ruff (fish).—*ns.* **pope'dom,** office, dignity, or jurisdiction of the pope : a pope's tenure of office ; **pope'hood, pope'ship,** the condition of being pope ; **pope'ling,** a little pope ; **pop'ery,** a hostile term for Roman Catholicism or whatever seems to savour of it.—*adj.* **pop'ish,** (*hostile*) relating to the pope or to popery.—*adv.* **pop'ishly.**—**Pope Joan,** a mythical female pope : an old card-game like newmarket ; **pope's eye,** the gland surrounded with fat in the middle of the thigh of an ox or a sheep ; **pope's head,** a long-handled brush ; **pope's knights,** Roman Catholic priests, formerly called Sir ; **pope's nose,** the fleshy part of a cooked bird's tail. [O.E. *pápa*—L.L. *pápa* —Gr. *pappas* (late Gr. *papās*), hypocoristic for father.]

pope, *pōp, n.* a parish priest in the Greek Orthodox Church. [Russ. *pop*—Late Gr. *papās* ; cf. preceding.]

Popian, *pōp'i-ən, adj.* pertaining to Alexander *Pope,* the poet (1688-1744).

popinjay, *pop'in-jā, n.* a parrot : a figure of a parrot set up to be shot at : a fop or coxcomb. [O.Fr. *papegai* ; cf. L.L. *papagallus* ; Late Gr. *papagallus* (also *papagas*), a parrot ; prob. Eastern ; influenced by **jay.**]

popjoy, *pop'joi, v.i.* to amuse oneself. [Poss. connected with **popinjay.**]

poplar, *pop'lər, n.* a genus (Populus) of trees of the willow family, including aspen, white poplar, black poplar (with its variety Lombardy poplar), cottonwood, &c. : (*U.S.*) the tulip-tree. [O.Fr. *poplier* —L. *pōpulus,* poplar-tree.]

poplin, *pop'lin, n.* a corded fabric with silk warp and worsted weft : an imitation in cotton or other material.—*n.* **poplinette',** an imitation poplin. [Fr. *popeline*—It. *papalina,* papal, from the papal town of Avignon, where it was made.]

popliteal, *pop-lit'i-əl,* often *pop-lit-ē'əl, adj.* of the back of the knee.—Also **poplit'ic.** [L. *poples, -itis.*]

poppa, popper, *pop'ə(r), n.* (*vulg., U.S.*) for papa.— Abbrev. **pop, pops.**

poppering, *pop'ər-ing,* **poperin, -in,** *n.* a variety of pear.—Also **poppering pear** (*Shak.* **pop'rin**). [*Poperinghe* in Belgium.]

poppet, *pop'it, n.* a puppet : (*obs.*) a doll : a darling (abbrev. **pop**) : a timber support used in launching a ship : a lathe-head : a valve that lifts bodily (also **popp'et-valve.** [An earlier form of **puppet.**]

popple, *pop'l, v.i.* to flow tumblingly : to heave choppily : to bob up and down : to make the sound of rippling or bubbling, or of repeated shots.—*n.* a poppling movement or sound.—*adj.* **popp'ly.** [Imit. ; or a freq. of **pop.**]

poppy, *pop'i, n.* a cornfield plant (of several species) or its large scarlet flowers : any other species of the genus Papaver, as the opium poppy, or of the kindred genera Glaucium (horned poppy), Meconopsis (Welsh poppy), &c. : extended to various unrelated plants.—*adj.* **popp'ied,** covered or filled with poppies : soporific : affected by opium.—*ns.* **popp'y-head,** the capsule of the poppy : a carved ornament in wood, often finishing the end of a pew ; **popp'y-oil,** a fixed oil from the seeds of the opium-poppy ; **popp'y-seed ; popp'y-water,** a soporific drink made from poppies.—**Poppy Day,** the anniversary of the armistice of 1918, 11th November, when artificial poppies are sold in commemoration of Flanders, where poppies abound. [O.E. *popig*—L. *papāver,* poppy.]

poppycock, *pop'i-kok, n.* (*U.S. slang*) balderdash. —Abbrev. **pop.**

populace, *pop'ū-ləs, n.* the common people : those who are not distinguished by rank, education, office, &c. [Fr.,—It. *popolazzo*—L. *pōpulus,* people.]

popular, *pop'ū-lər, adj.* of the people : pleasing to, enjoying the favour of, or prevailing among, the people : liked by one's associates : suited to the understanding or the means of ordinary people : (*obs.*) seeking the favour of the common people : democratic : (*obs.*) plebeian : (*obs.*) vulgar.—*n.* a popular or moderate-priced concert (abbrev. **pop**). —*n.* **popularisā'tion.**—*v.t.* **pop'ularise,** to make popular : to democratise : to present in a manner suited to ordinary people : to spread among the people.—*ns.* **pop'ulariser ; popularity** (-*lar'i-ti*), fact or state of being popular : seeking to gain favour with the people.—*adv.* **pop'ularly.**—*v.t.* **pop'ulate,** to people : to furnish with inhabitants : (*obs.*) to devastate.—*v.i.* to multiply by propagation. —*adj.* inhabited, peopled.—*ns.* **popula'tion,** act of populating : number of the inhabitants ; **pop'-ulism ; pop'ulist,** in U.S. a member of the People's Party, founded in 1891, advocating public ownership of public services, graduated income-tax, &c., or of a similar party elsewhere.—*adj.* **pop'ulous,** full of people : numerously inhabited : (*Shak.*) numerous : (*rare*) popular—*adv.* **pop'ulously.**— *n.* **pop'ulousness.**—**popular front,** an alliance of the more progressive or leftward political parties in the state. [L. *pōpulus,* the people.]

poral, *pō'rəl.* See **pore.**

porbeagle, *por'bē-gl, n.* a harmless North Atlantic and Mediterranean shark. [From Cornish dialect ; origin unknown.]

porcelain, *pors'lin, -lən, n.* a fine earthenware, white, thin, semi-transparent, first made in China : china-ware.—*adj.* of porcelain.—*ns.* **por'celain-cement'**, cement for mending china ; **por'celain-clay**, kaolin.—*v.t.* **porcellanise** (*por-sel'ən-īz*), **porc'elainise**, to bake into porcelain or porcel-lanite.—*n.* **porcell'anite**, a jasper-like shale highly indurated by contact metamorphism.—*adj.* **porcell'anous** (or *por'*), like porcelain—also **porcellā'neous**, **porc'elainous**, **porcelaineous** (*por-sə-lā'ni-əs*). [O.Fr. *porcelaine* — It. *porcellana*, cowrie.]

porch, *pōrch, n.* a building forming an enclosure or protection for a doorway : a portico or colonnade : (*U.S.*) a veranda : the Stoic school of philosophy, from the Painted Porch in the Agora of Athens where Zeno taught. [O.Fr. *porche*—L. *porticus*—*porta*, a gate.]

porcine, *por'sin, adj.* of pigs : swinish. [L. *porcīnus*—*porcus*, a swine.]

porcpisce, *por'pis, n.* (*Spens.*). Same as **porpoise**.

porcupine, *por'kū-pīn, n.* a large spiny rodent of various kinds.—*ns.* **por'cupine-grass**, a coarse, hard, spiny, tussocky grass (Triodia) that covers vast areas in Australia, commonly called spinifex ; **por'cupine-wood**, the wood of the coconut palm, from its spine-like markings. [O.Fr. *porc espin*—L. *porcus*, a pig, *spīna*, a spine.]

pore, *pōr, n.* a minute passage or interstice, esp. the opening of a sweat-gland.—*adj.* **por'al**, of or per-taining to pores.—*n.* **por'iness**.—*adj.* **porose** (-ōs', or *pōr'ōs*).—*n.* **porosity** (-os'i-ti).—*adj.* **por'ous**.—*n.* **por'ousness**.—*adj.* **por'y**.—**porous alloys**, alloys obtained by taking the constituents in powder form and pressing them together ; **porous plaster**, a plaster for the body, with holes to pre-vent wrinkling. [Fr.,—L. *porus*—Gr. *poros*, a passage.]

pore, *pōr, v.i.* to gaze with close and steady atten-tion (usu. with *over* or *upon*) : to ponder.—*n.* **por'er**. [Origin obscure.]

porgy, porgie, *por'gi, n.* a name given to many fishes, chiefly American species of sea-bream. [Partly Sp. and Port. *pargo*, app.—L. *pargus*, a kind of fish ; partly from American Indian names.]

Porifera, *por-if'ə-rä, n.pl.* a phylum of animals, the sponges :—*sing.* **por'ifer**.—*adjs.* **porif'eral**, **porif'-eran**, of the Porifera ; **porif'erous**, having pores. [L. *porus*, a pore, *ferre*, to bear.]

porism, *pōr'izm, por'izm, n.* in ancient Greek geometry a corollary : also a kind of proposition intermediate between a problem and a theorem, according to some a proposition affirming the possibility of finding such conditions as will render a certain problem capable of innumerable solutions. —*adjs.* **porismat'ic** (*por-*), **-al** ; **poris'tic, -al**. [Gr. *porisma*, a corollary, porism—*poros*, a way.]

pork, *pawrk, pork, n.* (*obs.*) a swine : swine's flesh as food.—*ns.* **pork'-butch'er**, one who kills pigs or sells pork ; **pork'-chop'**, a slice from a pig's rib ; **pork'er**, a young hog : a pig fed for pork ; **pork'-ling**, a young pig ; **pork'-pie'**, a pie made of minced pork.—*adj.* **pork'y**, pig-like : fat.—**pork-pie hat**, a hat somewhat like a circular pie, worn by men and women about 1850. [Fr. *porc*—L. *porcus*, a hog.]

pornocracy, *por-nok'rə-si, n.* the influence of courte-zans—esp. over the papal court in the earlier half of the 10th century. [Gr. *pornē*, a whore, *kratos*, rule.]

pornography, *por-nog'rə-fi, n.* description or por-trayal of prostitutes and prostitution : obscene writing, painting, and the like.—*n.* **pornog'rapher**. —*adj.* **pornographic** (*por-nō-graf'ik*). [Gr. *pornē*, a whore, *graphein*, to write, draw.]

porogamy, *por-* or *pōr-og'ə-mi, n.* entry of the pollen-tube through the micropyle—opp. to *chal-azogamy.* — *adj.* **porogamic** (-ō-gam'ik). [Gr. *poros*, a pore, *gamos*, marriage.]

poroscope, *por', or pōr'ō-skōp, n.* an instrument for investigating porosity or for examining pores or finger-prints.—*adj.* **poroscopic** (-skop'ik).—*n.* **por-**

oscopy (-os'kə-pi). [Gr. *poros*, pore, *skopeein*, to look at.]

porosis, *pō-rō'sis, n.* formation of callus, the knitting together of broken bones. [Gr. *pōrōsis*—*pōros*, callus.]

porpentine, *por'pən-tīn, n.* (*Shak.*). Same as **porcu-pine**.

porpess, porpesse, *por'pəs, n.* Same as **porpoise**.

Porphyra, *por'fir-ä, n.* a genus of seaweeds, with flat translucent red or purple fronds, purple laver. [Gr. *porphȳrä*, purple (dye).]

Porphyrio, *por-fir'i-ō, n.* the purple coot genus. [Gr. *porphyriōn*, purple coot.]

Porphyrogenite, *por-fir-oj'ən-īt, n.* a Byzantine emperor's son born in the purple or porphyry room assigned to empresses : hence, a prince born after his father's accession : one born in the purple.—*ns.* **Porphyrogenitism** (-ō-jen'it-izm), the Byzantine principle of the first son born after his father's accession succeeding to the throne ; **Por-phyrogen'iture**. [L. *porphyrogenitus* for Gr. *por-phyrogennētos—porphyros*, purple, *gennētos*, born.]

porphyry, *por'fir-i, n.* a very hard, variegated rock, of a purple and white colour, used in sculpture (*porfido rosso antico*), often used vaguely : (*geol.*) loosely, an igneous rock with large crystals in a fine-grained ground-mass.—*n.* **por'phyrite**, an old-fashioned name for an altered andesite or fine-grained diorite : porphyry.—*adjs.* **porphyr-itic** (-it'ik), like, or of the nature of, porphyry : having large crystals scattered among small or in a fine-grained or glassy ground-mass ; **por'phyrous**, purple. [Gr. *porphyrītēs—porphyros*, purple.]

porpoise, *por'pəs, n.* a short-snouted genus (Pho-caena) of the dolphin family, 4 to 8 feet long, gregarious, affording oil and leather : extended to similar forms.—Formerly also **por'pess, porc'-pisce**.—*v.i.* to move like a porpoise. [O.Fr. *porpeis*—L. *porcus*, a hog, *piscis*, a fish.]

porporate, *por'por-āt, adj.* (*Browning*) clad in purple. [It. *porporato*—L. *purpurātus*.]

porraceous, *por-ā'shəs, adj.* leek-green. [L. *por-rāceus—porrum*, a leek.]

porrect, *por-ekt', v.t.* to stretch forth : to present, hold out for acceptance.—*adj.* extended forward. —*n.* **porrec'tion**. [L. *porrigĕre, porrectum*, to stretch out.]

porridge, *por'ij, n.* a kind of pudding usually made by slowly stirring oatmeal in boiling water (in Scot-land often treated as a *pl.*) : (*obs.*) pottage.—*n.* **porr'idge-stick**, a stick for stirring porridge. [pottage, altered by influence of obs. or dial. *porray*, vegetable soup.—O.Fr. *porée*—L.L. *porrāta* —L. *porrum*, leek.]

porrigo, *por-ī'gō, n.* scalp disease of various kinds. —*adj.* **porriginous** (-ij'). [L. *porrīgō, -inis*, dand-ruff.]

porringer, porrenger, *por'in-jər, n.* a small dish for soup, porridge, &c. : (*Shak.*) a head-dress shaped like such a dish. [See **porridge, pottage** : for inserted *n* cf. **passenger, messenger**.]

port, *pōrt, n.* the larboard or left side of a ship.—*adj.* left.—*v.t.* and *v.i.* to turn left. (In helm orders, formerly, **port the helm**, meant turn the tiller to port, or the upper part of the wheel to starboard, and so the rudder, and the ship, to starboard ; since 1933 **port** means turn the ship to port.) [Ety. doubtful.]

port, *pōrt, n.* an instrumental tune : a bagpipe com-position. [Gael.]

port, *pōrt, n.* bearing : demeanour : carriage of the body : imposing bearing : style of living : (*obs.*) a retinue : the position of a ported weapon.—*v.t.* (*obs.*) to carry or convey : (*mil.*) to hold in a slant-ing direction upward across the body.—*n.* **port-abil'ity**.—*adj.* **port'able**, easily or conveniently carried or moved about : (*Shak.*) endurable.—*n.* a portable article.—*ns.* **port'age**, act of carrying : carriage : price of carriage : a space, track, or journey, over which goods and boats have to be carried or dragged overland : (*Shak.*) a sailor's private venture in a voyage ; **port'ance**, (*Spens.* ; *Shak.*) carriage, bearing.—*adjs.* **port'ate**, (*her.*) in a position as if being carried ; **port'atile**, port-able ; **port'ative**, easily carried.—*n.* (*obs.*) a portable organ (often *pair of portatives*).—*ns*. **port'-cray'on** (Fr. *porte-crayon*), a handle for holding a crayon; **porte-bonheur** (*port'-bon-ər'*, Fr.), a charm carried for luck; **porte'-monnaie** (*-mon-e'*; Fr.), a purse or pocket-book; **port'-fire**, a slow-match or match-cord. [Fr. *port*, *porter*—L. *portāre*, to carry.]

port, *pōrt*, *n*. a harbour: a town with a harbour.—*n*. **port'-ad'miral**, the admiral commanding at a naval port.—*n.pl*. **port'-charges**, harbour dues.—**port of call**, a port where vessels can call for stores or repairs; **port of entry**, a port where merchandise is allowed by law to enter. [O.E. *port*—L. *portus*, *-ūs*, akin to *porta*, a gate.]

port, *pōrt*, *n*. (*obs*.) a gate or gateway: (now chiefly *Scot*.) a town gate, or its former position: an opening in the side of a ship: a porthole or its cover: a passage-way for a ball or curling-stone: an outlet or inlet for a fluid: part of a bit curved for the tongue.—*n*. **port'age**, (*Shak*.) an opening. [Fr. *porte* (perh. also O.E. *port*)—L. *porta*, gate.]

port, *pōrt*, *n*. a fortified wine (dark-red or tawny, sometimes white) of the Douro valley, shipped from *Oporto*, Portugal.—Also **port'-wine'**.—*adjs*. **port-win'y**, **port'y**.

port, *pōrt*, *n*. (*hist*.) a town with market privileges: a borough.—*ns*. **port'man**, (*hist*.) a burgess, esp. one chosen to administer town affairs; **port'reeve** (O.E. *portgeréfa*), a mayor or principal magistrate. [Connexion with **port** (4) and **port** (5) obscure.]

porta, *pōr'tä*, *n*. (*zool*.) a gate-like structure, esp. the transverse fissure of the liver.—*adj*. **por'tal.—portal system**, the portal vein with its tributaries, &c.; **portal vein**, the vein that conveys to the liver the venous blood from intestines, spleen, and stomach. [L. *porta*, gate.]

Portague. See under **Portuguese**.

portal, *pōrt'əl*, *n*. a gate or doorway, esp. a great or magnificent one: any entrance: (*archit*.) the arch over a gate: the lesser of two gates. [O.Fr. *portal*—L.L. *portāle*—L. *porta*, a gate.]

portamento, *pōr-tä-men'tō*, *n*. (*mus*.) a continuous glide from one tone to another: sometimes applied to an execution between staccato and legato.—Also *adj*. and *adv*. [It.]

portas. See **portesse**.

portcullis, *pōrt-kul'is*, *n*. a grating that can be let down to close a gateway: (*her*.) a lattice: one of the pursuivants of the English College of Heralds: an Elizabethan silver halfpenny with a portcullis on the reverse.—*v.t*. to obstruct, as with a portcullis. [O.Fr. *porte coletce*, sliding gate.]

Porte, *pōrt*, *n*. (*hist*.) the Turkish imperial government, so called from the Sublime Porte or High Gate, the chief office of the Ottoman government at Constantinople.—**porte-cochère** (*port-kosh-er'*; Fr.), a house entrance admitting a carriage. [Fr. *porte*—L. *porta*, gate.]

portend, *pōr-tend'*, *v.t*. to betoken: presage.—*n*. **portent** (*pōr'tənt*), that which portends or fore-shows: foreshadowing import: an evil omen: a prodigy, marvel.—*adj*. **portentous** (*-tent'*), ominous: prodigious, extraordinary: impressive, solemn.—*adv*. **portent'ously**. [L. *portendĕre*, *portentum—por-*, equivalent to *prō* or *per*, *tendĕre*, to stretch.]

porter, *pōrt'ər*, *n*. a door-keeper or gate-keeper: one who waits at the door to receive messages:—*fem*. **port'eress**, **port'ress**.—*n*. **port'erage**, the office or duty of a porter.—**porter's lodge**, a house or an apartment near a gate for the use of the porter. [O.Fr. *portier*—L.L. *portārius*—L. *porta*, a gate.]

porter, *pōrt'ər*, *n*. one who carries burdens for hire: a dark-brown malt liquor, prob. because a favourite drink with London porters.—*ns*. **port'erage**, carriage: charge made by a porter for carrying goods; **porter'-house**, a house where porter is sold: a chop-house; **port'erhouse-steak**, (*U.S.*) a choice cut of beef-steak next to the sirloin.—*adv*. **port'erly**, like a porter: coarse. [O.Fr. *porteour* (Fr. *porteur*) —L. *portātor*, *-ōris—portāre*, to carry.]

portesse, *pōrt'əs*, *-es*, *n*. (*Spens*.) a portable breviary.—Also **port'ess**, **port'as**, **port'hors**, **port'house**, **portous**, **port'hos**, **porteous** (*pōr'tyəs*).—**porteous roll**, (*Scots law*) a list of persons to be tried. [O.Fr.

portehors (L.L. *porteforium*)—L. *portāre*, to carry, *foris*, out of doors.]

portfolio, *pōrt-fō'li-ō*, *n*. a case or pair of boards for loose papers, drawings, &c.: a collection of such papers: the office of a minister of state:—*pl*. **portfo'lios**. [It. *portafogli(o)*—L. *portāre*, to carry, *folium*, a leaf.]

porthole, *pōrt'hōl*, *n*. a hole or opening in a ship's side for light and air, or (formerly) for pointing a gun through. [**port** (5), **hole**.]

portico, *pōr'ti-kō*, *n*. (*archit*.) a range of columns along the front or side of a building: a colonnade: (*philos*.) the Painted Porch:—*pl*. **por'ticos**, **por'ticoes**.—*adj*. **por'ticoed**, furnished with a portico. [It.,—L. *porticus*, a porch.]

portière, *por-tyer'*, *n*. a curtain hung over the door or doorway of a room. [Fr.]

portion, *pōr'shən*, *n*. a part: an allotted part: an amount of food served to one person: destiny: the part of an estate descending to an heir: a dowry.—*v.t*. to divide into portions: to allot as a share: to furnish with a portion.—*adj*. **por'-tioned**.—*ns*. **por'tioner**, (*Scots law*) the holder of a small feu originally part of a greater: a portionist of a benefice (**heir'-por'tioner**, see **heir**); **por'-tionist**, a postmaster of Merton College: one of two or more incumbents sharing a benefice.—*adj*. **por'tionless**, having no portion, dowry, or property. [O.Fr.,—L. *portiō*, *-ōnis*.]

Portland, *pōrt'lənd*, *adj*. belonging to or associated with the Isle of Portland, a peninsula of Dorset.—*n*. **Portlandian** (*-land'i-ən*), a group of sands and limestones, the middle group of the Upper or Portland Oolite.—Also *adj*.—**Portland arrow-root**, **Portland sago**, a farina prepared in the Isle of Portland from wake-robin tubers; **Portland cement**, a cement made by burning a mixture of clay and chalk of the colour of Portland stone; **Portland stone**, an oolitic building-stone quarried in the Isle of Portland.

portlast, *pōrt'last*, *n*. (*obs. naut*.) probably the gunwale.—Also **portoise** (*pōrt'iz*) and wrongly **port'-land**.—**yards down a portlast**, with yards down on or near the deck. [Origin unknown.]

portly, *pōrt'li*, *adj*. having a dignified port or mien: corpulent.—*n*. **port'liness**. [**port** (3).]

portman. See **port** (7).

portmanteau, *pōrt-man'tō*, *n*. large travelling-bag that folds back flat from the middle: (*rare*) a rack for hanging clothes: Lewis Carroll's term for a word into which are packed the sense (and sound) of two words (also **portman'teau-word**—e.g. *slithy* for *lithe* and *slimy*):—*pl*. **portman'-teaus**, or **portman'teaux** (*-tōz*).—Also (*both obs.*) **portman'tle**, **portman'tūa**. [Fr.,—*porter*, to carry, *manteau*, a cloak.]

portoise. See **portlast**.

portrait, *pōr'trit*, *n*. the likeness of a real person: a vivid description in words: (*rare*) portraiture.—*v.t*. (*obs*.) to portray.—*ns*. **por'trait-bust**; **por'-trait-gall'ery**; **por'traitist**, **por'trait-painter**; **por'trait-paint'ing**; **por'traiture**, a likeness: art or act of making portraits: a collection of pictures —*v.t*. **portray** (*pōr-trā'*), to paint or draw the likeness of: to describe in words: (*obs*.) to adorn with portraiture or representations.—*ns*. **portray'al**, the act of portraying: a representation; **por-tray'er**. [O.Fr. *po(u)rtrait*, *po(u)rtraire*—L. *prō-trahĕre*, *-tractum*; see **protract**.]

portreeve. See **port** (7).

Portuguese, *pōr-tū-gēz'*, or *pōr'*, *adj*. of Portugal, its people, and its language.—*n*. a native or citizen of Portugal: the language of Portugal:—*pl*. **Portuguese** (whence the vulgar *sing*. **Portug(u)ee'**).—*n*. **portague**, **portigue** (*pōrt'ə-gū*), an old Portuguese gold coin, worth about £4.—**Portuguese man-of-war**, Physalia.

Portulaca, *pōr-tū-lā'ka*, *n*. the purslane genus, giving name to the family Portulacā'ceae, mostly succulent herbs of dry places, akin to the Caryophyllaceae. [L. *portulāca*, purslane.]

pos, *poz*, *adj*. (*slang*) an abbreviation of **positive**.

posada, *pō-sä'dä*, *n*. an inn. [Sp.,—*posar*, to lodge.]

posaune, *pō-zow'nə*, *n*. the trombone. [Ger.]

pose, *pōz*, *n*. an attitude: an assumed attitude: an

affectation of a mental attitude: in dominoes, the right to begin the game: (*Scot.*) a secret hoard.—*v.i.* to assume or maintain a pose: to attitudinise.—*v.t.* to put in a suitable attitude: to posit: to assert: to claim: to propound.—*ns.* pos'er, one who poses; poseur (*pōz-ər'*; Fr.), an attitudiniser:—*fem.* poseuse (-*əz'*). [Fr. *poser*, to place—L.L. *pausāre*, to cease—L. *pausa*, pause—Gr. *pausis*. Between Fr. *poser* and L. *pōnĕre, positum*, there has been confusion, which has influenced the derivatives of both words.]

pose, *pōz, v.t.* to puzzle: to perplex by questions: to bring to a stand.—*ns.* pos'er, one who, or that which, poses: a difficult question; pos'ing.—*adv.* pos'ingly. [Aphetic for oppose, or appose, which was confused with it.]

posé, *pō-zā', adj.* (*her.*) standing still. [Fr. pa.p. of *poser*; see pose (1).]

Poseidon, *pos-ī'don, -dōn, n.* the Greek sea-god, identified with Neptune by the Romans.—*adj.* Poseidōn'ian. [Gr. *Poseidōn, -ōnos.*]

posh, *posh, adj.* (*slang*) spruced up, smart: superb. —*v.t.* and *v.i.* to trim up, to polish.

poshteen. See posteen.

posit, *poz'it, v.t.* to set in place, dispose: to postulate, assume as true, definitely or for argument's sake:—*pr.p.* pos'iting; *pa.t.* and *pa.p.* pos'ited. [L. *pōnĕre, positum*, to lay down.]

position, *poz-ish'ən, n.* situation: place occupied: attitude, disposition, arrangement: state of affairs: a proposition or thesis: the ground taken in argument or in a dispute: principle laid down: place in society: high standing: a post or appointment: occurrence in an open or closed syllable: situation of the left hand in playing the violin, &c.: method of finding the value of an unknown quantity by assuming one or more values.—*adj.* of or defining position.—*v.t.* to set in place: to determine the position of, locate.—*adjs.* posi'tional; posi'tioned, placed.—position ratio, a ratio determining the position of a point in a range or of a ray in a pencil—that of the distances from two fixed points in the range, or of the sines of the angular distances from two fixed rays. [Fr.,—L. *positiō, -ōnis—pōnĕre, positum*, to place.]

positive, *poz'i-tiv, adj.* definitely, formally, or explicitly laid down: express: beyond possibility of doubt: absolute: (*gram.*) expressing a quality simply without comparison: downright, out-and-out: fully convinced: over-confident in opinion: matter-of-fact: concrete: material: actual: characterised by the presence of some quality, not merely absence of its opposite: of a bacteriological test, confirming the presence of the suspected organism, &c.: (*math.*) greater than zero, or conventionally regarded as greater than zero, indicating such a quantity: in the direction of increase, actual or conventional: (*biol.*) in a direction toward the source of stimulus: (*phot., opt.*) having the lights and shades not reversed: (*elect.*) having a relatively high potential: of, having, or producing positive electricity (see below): (*opt.*) dextrorotatory: having a greater index of refraction for the extraordinary than for the ordinary ray in double refraction: (*chem.*) basic.—*n.* that which is positive: reality: a positive quantity: the positive degree, or an adjective or adverb in it: an image in which lights and shades or colours, or both, are unchanged: a photographic plate with the lights and shades of the original: a positive organ (see below).—*adv.* pos'itively.— *ns.* pos'itiveness, state or quality of being positive: certainty: confidence; pos'itivism, actual or absolute knowledge: certainty: assurance: positive philosophy (see below); pos'itivist, a believer in positivism.—*adj.* positivist'ic.—*n.* posi-tiv'ity.—positive angle, one generated by a straight line moving counter-clockwise; positive electricity, such as is developed in glass by rubbing with silk, arising from deficiency of electrons; positive organ, a small supplementary church organ, originally portable and placed upon a stand; positive philosophy, the philosophical system originated by Comte (1798-1857)—its foundation the doctrine that man can have no knowledge of

anything but phenomena, and that the knowledge of phenomena is relative, not absolute: also 20th-century developments of this (logical positivism) much concerned with determining whether or not statements are meaningful; positive pole, of a magnet, that end (or pole) which turns to the north when the magnet swings freely; positive rays, canal-rays, a stream of positively electrified particles towards the cathode of a vacuum-tube (positive-ray analysis, the detection of gases, and determination of their molecular weights, by measuring the parabolas produced upon a photographic plate by positive rays deflected in two directions at right angles to each other by a magnetic and an electric field); positive sign, the sign (+ read *plus*) of addition. [L. *positīvus*, fixed by agreement—*pōnĕre, positum*, to place.]

positron, *poz'i-tron, n.* a particle differing from the electron in having a positive charge: a *positive electron.*—Also pos'iton.

posnet, *pos'nit, n.* a small cooking-pot with feet and handle. [O.Fr *pocenet.*]

posology, *pos-ol'ə-ji, n.* the science of quantity: the science of dosage.—*adj.* posological (-*ə-loj'i-kl*). [Gr. *posos*, how much, *logos*, discourse.]

poss, *adj.* a slang abbreviation of possible.

posse, *pos'i, n.* power: possibility: a force or body (of constables).—in posse, in potentiality; posse comitatus, force of the county, men called out by the sheriff to aid in enforcing the law. [L. *posse*, to be able, *comitātūs*, of the county.]

possess, *poz-es', v.t.* (*obs.*) to inhabit, occupy: to have or hold as owner, or as if owner: to have: to seize: to obtain: (*Spens.*) to attain: to maintain: to control: to be master of: to occupy and dominate the mind of: to put in possession (with *of*, formerly *in*): to inform, acquaint: to imbue: to impress with the notion or feeling: (*obs.*) to prepossess.—*adj.* possessed', in possession: self-possessed: dominated by a spirit that has entered one, or other irresistible influence.— *n.* possession (*poz-esh'ən*), act, state, or fact of possessing or being possessed: a thing possessed: a subject foreign territory.—*adjs.* possess'ionary; possess'ionate, holding or allowed to hold possessions (opp. to *mendicant*).—*n.* a possessionate monk.—*adjs.* possess'ioned; possess'ive, pertaining to or denoting possession: genitive: showing a desire to treat as a possession.—*n.* (*gram.*) a possessive adjective or pronoun: the possessive case or a word in it.—*adv.* possess'-ively. — *ns.* possess'or; possess'orship. — *adj.* possess'ory.—what possesses him, &c.? what malign influence causes him, &c. (to act so foolishly)?; writ of possession, a process directing a sheriff to put a person in possession of property recovered in ejectment. [O.Fr. *possesser* —L. *possidēre, possessum.*]

posset, *pos'it, n.* a dietetic drink, milk curdled as with wine, ale, or vinegar.—*v.t.* (*Shak.*) to curdle. —*v.i.* to make a posset.—posset cup, a large cup or covered bowl for posset. [M.E. *poschote, possot*; origin unknown.]

possible, *pos'i-bl, adj.* that may be or happen: that may be done: not contrary to the nature of things: contingent: potential: practicable: such as one may tolerate, accept, or get on with.—*n.* a possibility: that which or one who is possible: the highest possible score: (*Gallicism*) one's best: (*slang*; in *pl.*) necessaries.—*ns.* poss'ibilism, the policy of confining efforts to what is immediately possible or practicable; poss'ibilist; possibil'ity, state of being possible: that which is possible: a contingency. — *adv.* poss'ibly. [L. *possibilis* — *posse*, to be able.]

possum, 'possum, *pos'əm, n.* a colloquial aphetic form of opossum.—play possum, to feign death: to dissemble.

post, *pōst, n.* a stout, stiff stake or pillar of timber or other material, usually fixed in an upright position: an upright member of a frame: a winning-post, starting-post, &c.: the pin of a lock: a solid thickish stratum: a pillar of coal left in a mine as a support: (*Shak.*) a tavern doorpost, on which a score was chalked.—*v.t.* to stick up on a post, hence on a board, door, wall, hoarding, &c.: to announce, advertise, or denounce by placard: to placard as having failed in an examination, or failed to be classed: to announce as overdue: to affix a bill or bills to.— *n.* post′er, a bill-sticker: a large printed bill or placard for posting.—*v.t.* to stick bills on: to advertise or publish by posters.—*n.* post′-mill, a windmill pivoted on a post.—between you and me and the (bed-, lamp-, &c.) post, in confidence; from pillar to post (see pillar); poster colours, matt water-colours for designing posters and other reproduction work; sheriff's post, (*hist*) a post at a sheriff's door. [O.E. *post*— L. *postis*, a doorpost—*pōnĕre*, to place.]

post, *pōst, n.* a fixed place or station, esp. a place where a soldier or body of soldiers is stationed: a fixed place or stage on a road, for forwarding letters and change of horses: a body of men stationed at a post: a trading station: an office, employment, or appointment: a messenger carrying letters by stages or otherwise: (*obs.* or *dial.*) a postman: a public letter-carrier: an established system of conveying letters: (*Shak.*) a posthorse: a mail-coach: (*obs.*) a packet-boat: a despatch, delivery, or batch of letters: a post-office, or post-office letter-box: (*Shak.*) haste: a size of writing-paper, double that of common note-paper (originally with water-mark, a post-horn): full rank as naval captain (see post-captain below): a bugle-call (*first* or *last*) summoning soldiers to their quarters or (*last post*) performed at a military funeral: a name often given to a newspaper: a stake in a game: a good or winning hand, as in the old card-game of post and pair, in which the players vied on the goodness of their hands, a pair-royal being best.—*v.t.* to station: to entrust to the post-office for transmission: (*Shak.*) to shift, transfer to another (as blame; with *over* or *off*): (*book-k.*) to transfer to another book, or enter in a book, or carry to an account: to supply with necessary information: to appoint to a post: to raise to the rank of captain: to stake.—*v.i.* to travel with posthorses, or with speed: to move up and down in the saddle, in time with the horse's movements.—*adv.* with posthorses: with speed.— *ns.* post′age, money paid for conveyance by post: (*obs.*) travel with posthorses; post′age-stamp, an embossed or printed stamp or an adhesive label to show that the postal charge has been paid. —*adj.* post′al, of or pertaining to the mail-service. —*n.* (*U.S.*; in full post′al-card) a postcard issued by the post-office with printed stamp.—*ns.* post′-bag, a mail-bag: letters received, collectively; post′boy, a boy that rides posthorses or who carries letters: a postilion; postcard, a card on which a message may be sent by post: (*U.S.*) such a card not issued by the post-office.—*v.t.* to send a postcard to.—*n.* post′-chaise (popularly po′′-chay, po′chay, po′chaise), a carriage, usually four-wheeled, for two or four passengers with a postilion, used in travelling with posthorses.—*v.i.* to travel by post-chaise.—*ns.* post′-day, the day on which the post or mail arrives or departs; post′er, (*Shak.*) one who travels post: a post-horse: one who posts a letter.—*adj.* and *adv.* post′-free, without charge for postage: with postage prepaid.—*n.* post′haste′ (from the old direction on letters, *haste, post, haste*), haste in travelling like that of a post.—*adj.* speedy: immediate.—*adv.* with utmost haste or speed.—*ns.* post′-horn, a postman's horn: a long straight brass horn blown by a coach guard; post′horse, a horse kept for posting; post′house, a house where horses are kept for posting: a post-office. —*n.* and *adj.* post′ing.—*ns.* post′-letter, a letter in the custody of the post-office; post′-man, a post or courier: a letter-carrier: post′-mark, the mark stamped upon a letter at a post-office defacing the postage-stamp or showing the date and place of expedition or of arrival; post′master, the manager or superintendent of a post-office: one who supplies posthorses (see also separate article below); Post′master-Gen′eral,

the minister at the head of the post-office department; post′mastership; post′mistress; post′-office, an office for receiving and transmitting letters by post, and other business: Post Office, a department of the government which has charge of the conveyance of letters.—*adj.* post′-paid, having the postage prepaid.—*ns.* post′-road, a road with stations for posthorses; post′-time, the time for the despatch or for the delivery of letters; post′-town, post-village, a town, village, with a post-office; post′woman, a female letter-carrier. —general post, a game in which the players change places simultaneously; postal order, an order issued by the postmaster authorising the holder to receive at a post-office payment of the sum printed on it; postal tube, a cylinder for sending rolled-up papers by post; postal union, an association of the chief countries of the world for international postal purposes; post-man's knock, a parlour kissing-game; post-office box, a box in the post-office into which are put the letters addressed to a particular person or firm; post-office savings-bank, a branch of the post-office in which money may be deposited at a fixed rate of interest. [Fr. *poste*—It. *posta* and *posto*—L. *pōnĕre, positum,* to place.]

post-, *pōst-, pfx.* after: behind—as *post-canonical, post-classical, post-embryonic, post-primary, post-Reformation, post-war,* &c.—*adj.* post-bell′um, after the war.—*n.* post-commun′ion, the part of the eucharistic office after the act of communion. —*adj.* succeeding communion.—*v.t.* post′date′, to date after the real time: to mark with a date (as for payment) later than the time of signing.—*adj.* post-dilu′vial, after the Flood: (*obs. geol.*) after the diluvial period.—*n.* and *adj.* post-dilu′vian. —*n.* post′-entry, an additional entry of merchandise at a custom-house.—*adjs.* post′-exil′ian, post-exil′ic, after the time of the Babylonian captivity of the Jews.—*ns.* post′-exist′ence, existence in a subsequent life; post′fix, a suffix.— *v.t.* postfix′, to add as a suffix.—*adjs.* post-glā′cial, after the glacial epoch; post-grad′uate, belonging to study pursued after graduation.—*n.* post-impress′ionism, a movement in painting that came after Impressionism, aiming at the expression of the spiritual significance of things rather than mere representation.—*n.* and *adj.* post-impress′ionist.—*n.* post′lude, a concluding movement or voluntary.—*adj.* post-merid′ian, coming after the sun has crossed the meridian: in the afternoon.—*n.* post-millenā′rian, a believer in post-millennialism.—*adj.* post-millenn′ial.—*n.* post-millenn′ialism, the doctrine that the Second Advent will follow the millennium.—*adjs.* post-nas′al, behind the nose; post-na′tal, after birth. —*n.pl.* post-nā′tī (see ante-nati).—*adjs.* post-Ni′cene, after the Nicene council; post-nup′tial, after marriage.—*n.* postscē′nium, the part of the stage behind the scenery.—*adj.* Post-Ter′tiary, later than Tertiary—Pleistocene and Recent.— Also *n.* [L. *post,* after, behind.]

post-captain, *pōst′kap′tin, n.* formerly, a naval officer *pos/ed* to the rank of captain, a full captain distinguished from a commander, called captain by courtesy. [post (2).]

posteen, *pos-tēn′, n.* an Afghan greatcoat, generally of sheepskin with the fleece on.—Also (erron.) poshteen′. [Pers. *postī,* leather.]

poste restante, *pōst res-tän°t, n.* a department of a post-office where letters are kept till called for. [Fr., remaining post.]

posterior, *pos-tē′ri-ər, adj.* coming after: later: hinder: (*bot.*) on the side next the axis.—*n.* (usu. *pl.*) descendants, posterity: (commonly in *pl.*) hinder parts, buttocks: (in *pl.* ; *Shak.*) latter part. —*n.* posteriority (*pos-tē-ri-or′i-ti*).—*adv.* pos-tē′riorly.—*n.* posterity (-*ter′i-ti*), those coming after: succeeding generations: a race of descendants. [L. *postērior,* comp. of *posterus,* coming after—*post,* after.]

postern, *pōst′ərn, n.* a back door or gate: a small private door: a sally-port.—*adj.* back: private. [O.Fr. *posterne, posterle*—L. *posterula,* a dim. from *posterus.*]

Neutral vowels in unaccented syllables : *el′ə-mənt, in′fənt, ran′dəm*

posthumous, *post'ū-məs*, *adj.* after death: born after the father's death: published after the author's or composer's death.—*adv.* **post'humously.** [L. *posthumus, postumus,* superl. of *posterus,* coming after—*post,* after; the *h* inserted from false association with *humāre,* to bury.]

postiche, *pos-tēsh'*, *adj.* superfluously and inappropriately superadded to a finished work: counterfeit.—*n.* a counterfeit substitute, esp. a bunch of false hair: sham. [Fr., — It. *posticio* — L. *postīcus,* hinder.]

posticous, *pos-tī'kəs, adj.* (*bot.*) posterior: (*bot.*) outward, extrorse. [L. *postīcus,* hinder—*post.*]

postil, *pos'til, n.* a marginal note, esp. in the Bible: a commentary: a homily: a book of homilies.— *v.t.* and *v.i.* to gloss.—*v.t.* and *v.i.* **pos'tillate.**—*ns.* **postillā'tion**; **pos'tillātor**; **pos'tiller.** [O.Fr. *postille* (It. *postilla*)—L.L. *postilla,* possibly— L. *post illa* (*verba*), after those (words).]

postilion, postillion, *pos-* or *pōs-til'yən, n.* a postboy: one who guides posthorses, or horses in any carriage, riding on one of them.—**Also postill'ion.** [Fr. *postillon*— It. *postiglione—posta,* post.]

postliminary, *pōst-lim'in-ə-ri, adj.* subsequent: sometimes used in error for **postliminiary** (see next word).—**Also postlim'inous** (erron. **postlimin'ious**). [On the analogy of **preliminary.**]

postliminy, *pōst-lim'i-ni, n.* the right of a returned exile, prisoner, &c., to resume his former status; the right by which persons or things taken in war are restored to their former status.—*adj.* **postlimin'iary.** [L. *postlīminium,* lit. return behind the threshold—*līmen, -inis,* threshold.]

postmaster, *pōst'-mās-tər, n.* a portioner, or scholar on the foundation of Merton College, Oxford. [Origin unknown.] See also under **post** (2).

post-mortem, *pōst'-mor'təm, adj.* after death.—*n.* a post-mortem examination, autopsy: discussion of a game or hand after play. [L. *post mortem* (accus. of *mors, mortis,* death).]

post-obit, *pōst-ob'it, -ōb'it, adj.* taking effect after someone's death.—*n.* a borrower's bond securing payment on the death of someone from whom he has expectations. [L. *post obitum* (accus. of *obitus, -ūs,* death), after the death.]

postpone, *pōs*(*t*)*-pōn', v.t.* to put off to a future time: to defer: to delay: to subordinate.—*ns.* **postpone'ment, postpōn'ence** (*rare*); **postpōn'er; postposition** (*pōst-poz-ish'ən*), placing, or position, after: a word or particle placed after a word, usu. with the force of a preposition.—*adjs.* **postposi'tional; postpositive** (*-poz'*). [L. *postpōnĕre, -positum—post,* after, *pōnĕre,* to put.]

post-prandial, *pōst-pran'di-əl adj.* after-dinner. [L. *post,* after, *prandium,* a repast.]

postscript, *pō*(*st*)*'skript, n.* a part added to a letter after the signature: an addition to a book after it is finished. [L. *post,* after, *scrīptum,* written, pa.p. of *scrībĕre,* to write.]

postulate, *pos'tū-lāt, v.t.* to claim: to take for granted, assume: (*geom.*) to assume as a possible or legitimate operation without preliminary construction: to nominate, subject to sanction of ecclesiastical authority.—*v.i.* to make demands.— *n.* a stipulation: an assumption: a fundamental principle: a position assumed as self-evident: (*geom.*) an operation whose possibility is assumed: a necessary condition: (*Scot. hist.*) a person nominated to a benefice by the king, pending the pope's consent.—*ns.* **pos'tulant,** a petitioner: a candidate, esp. for holy orders, or admission to a religious community; **postulā'tion.**—*adj.* **pos'-tulatory,** supplicatory: assuming or assumed as a postulate.—*n.* **postulā'tum,** a postulate. [L. *postulāre, -ātum,* to demand—*poscĕre,* to ask urgently.]

posture, *pos'tyər, n.* relative disposition of parts, esp. of the body: carriage, attitude, pose: state of affairs: disposition of mind.—*v.t.* to place in a particular manner.—*v.i.* to assume a posture: to pose: to attitudinise.—*adj.* **pos'tural.**—*ns.* **pos'turemaker, pos'ture-master,** one who teaches or practises artificial postures of the body: a contortionist; **pos'turer, pos'turist,** an acrobat. [Fr., —L. *positūra—pōnĕre, positum,* to place.]

posy, *pō'zi, n.* a motto, as on a ring: a bunch of flowers. [**poesy.**]

pot, *pot, n.* a deep or deepish vessel for manufacturing, cooking or preserving purposes, or for growing plants, or holding jam, &c., or holding or pouring liquids: the contents or capacity thereof: (*billiards*) a pocket, or a stroke in which the object ball enters a pocket: earthenware: (*coll.*) a cup or other prize: a large sum of money: a heavily backed horse: an important person (usu. *big pot*): a pot-shot: a simple helmet: a wicker trap for lobsters, &c.: a size of paper (also **pott**) about 12 in. by 15 in. (from its original water-mark).—*v.t.* to put up in pots for preserving: to put in pots: to cook in a pot: to plant in a pot: to drain, as sugar: to shoot for the pot, by a pot-shot, or generally, to bag, win, secure: to pocket (as a billiard-ball): to epitomise, esp. in travesty.—*v.i.* (*Shak.*) to tipple: to have a pot-shot:—*pr.p.* **pott'ing;** *pa.p.* **pott'ed.**—*ns.* **pot'-ale,** refuse from a grain distillery; **pot'-bar'ley,** barley whose outer husk has been removed by mill-stones.—*adj.* **pot'-bellied.**—*ns.* **pot'-bell'y,** a protuberant belly; **pot'-boiler,** a work in art or literature produced merely to secure the necessaries of life: a producer of such works; **pot'-boiling.** —*adj.* **pot'-bound,** having roots compressed in a mass without room for growth.—*ns.* **pot'-boy,** a boy in a public-house who carries pots of ale to customers; **pot'-companion,** a comrade in drinking; **pot'ful,** as much as a pot will hold:—*pl.* **pot'fuls; pot'-gun,** a mortar: a pop-gun; **pot'-hanger,** a device for hanging a pot or a pothook on; **pot'-hat,** a bowler hat: formerly, a top-hat; **pot'-head,** a stupid person; **pot'-herb,** a vegetable (esp.) for flavouring—e.g. parsley; **pot'-hole,** a pot-shaped hole: a hole in rock ground by revolving stones in an eddying current; **pot'-holing,** spelaeology: exploring caves; **pot'hook,** a hook for hanging a pot over a fire: a hooked stroke in writing; **pot'house,** an alehouse; **pot'-hunter,** one who hunts for the sake of getting food: one who shoots for the sake of a bag or competes for the sake of prizes; **pot'-hunting; pot'-lid,** the cover of a pot: (*Scot.* **pat'-lid'**) a curling-stone played exactly on to the tee; **pot'-liquor,** a thin broth in which meat has been boiled; **pot'-luck',** what may happen to be in the pot for a meal without special preparation for guests; **pot'-man,** a pot-companion: a pot-boy; **pot'-metal,** an alloy of copper and lead: scraps of old iron pots, &c.; **pot'-plant,** a plant grown in a pot; **pot'-roast,** braised meat.—*v.t.* to braise.—*ns.* **pot'-shop,** a small public-house; **pot'-shot,** a shot within easy range: a casual or random shot. —*adj.* **pot'sick,** sickly from growing in a pot.—*ns.* **pot'-stick,** a stick for stirring what is being cooked in a pot; **pot'-still,** a still in which heat is applied directly to the pot containing the wash (opp. to *patent still*).—*adj.* made in a pot-still.—*n. pot'stone,* impure talc or steatite, a massive finely felted aggregate of talc, usually with mica and chlorite, such as has been cut into pots.—*adjs.* **pot'-val'iant; pot'-val'orous,** brave owing to drink.—*ns.* **pot'-val'our; pot'-wall'oper** (see **pot-waller**).—**go to pot,** to go to ruin: go to pieces (orig. in allusion to the cooking-pot, not the melting-pot); **keep the pot (a-)boiling,** to procure the necessaries of life: to keep going briskly without stop. [Late O.E. *pott;* cf. Ger. *pott;* Sw. *potta;* Dan. *potte;* Fr. *pot;* origin unknown.]

potable, *pō'tə-bl, adj.* fit to drink.—*n.* (*rare*) a beverage. [L. *pōtābilis—pōtāre,* to drink.]

potamic, *pot-am'ik, adj.* of rivers.—*adj.* **potamological** (*pot-ə-mə-loj'i-kl*). — *ns.* **potamologist** (*-mol'ə-jist*); **potamol'ogy,** the scientific study of rivers. [Gr. *potamos,* a river.]

Potamogeton, *pot-am-ō-jē'ton, -gē'ton, n.* the pondweed genus of water-plants with floating and submerged leaves, giving name to a family of monocotyledons, **Potamogetonā'ceae.** [Gr. *potamogeitōn,* pondweed — *potamos,* river, *geitōn,* neighbour.]

potash, *pot'ash, n.* a powerful alkali, potassium carbonate, originally got in a crude state by lixiviating wood *ash* and evaporating in *pots*—hence **pot-ashes, pot-ash**: potassium hydroxide (*caustic potash*): sometimes the monoxide or (vaguely) other compound of potassium: potash-water.—*adj.* containing, or rich in, potassium.—*v.t.* to treat with potash.—*n.* **pot′ash-wa′ter,** an aerated water containing potassium bicarbonate.—Also **potass′-wa′ter.**—*ns.* **potass** (*pot-as′, pot′as*; now *rare*), potash; **potass′a** (now *rare*), potassium monoxide, or sometimes hydroxide.—*adj.* **potass′ic,** of potassium.—*n.* **potass′ium,** an alkali metal (symbol K, for *kalium*; at. numb. 19), discovered by Davy in 1807 in potash. [Eng. **pot, ash,** or the corresponding Du. *pot-asschen.*]

potation, *pō-tā′shən, n.* drinking: a draught: liquor. [L. *pōtātiō, -ōnis—pōtāre, -ātum,* to drink.]

potato, *pə-* or *pō-tā′tō, n.* originally the sweet-potato, plant or tuber (see under **sweet**): now usually a South American plant, *Solanum tuberosum,* widely grown in temperate regions, or its tuber:—*pl.* **potā′toes.**—*ns.* **potā′to-app′le,** the fruit of the potato; **potā′to-bō′gle,** (*Scot.*) a scarecrow.—*n.pl.* **potā′to-chips′,** long pieces of potato fried in fat.—*ns.* **potā′to-disease′, -rot,** a destructive disease of the potato caused by a parasitic fungus, *Phytophthora infestans*; **potā′to-fing′er,** (*Shak.*) a fat finger; **potā′to-pit,** a clamp of potatoes; **potā′to-spir′it,** alcohol made from potatoes; **potā′to-trap′,** (*slang*) the mouth.—**small potatoes,** (*U.S.*) anything of no great worth; **the (clean) potato,** the right thing. [Sp. *patata*—Haitian *batata,* sweet-potato.]

potch, potche. Same as **poach** (2) in sense of thrust or trample.—*n.* **potch′er,** a machine for breaking and bleaching pulp in paper-making.

pote, *pōt, v.t.* and *v.i.* (*obs.* except *dial.*) to poke, thrust, esp. with the foot: (*obs.*) to crimp with a poting-stick.—*n.* **pot′ing-stick,** a poking-stick for ruffs, &c. [O.E. *potian.*]

poteen, potheen, *po-tyēn′, -chēn′, -tēn′, n.* Irish whisky illicitly distilled. [Ir. *poitín,* dim. of *pota,* pot, from Eng. **pot** or Fr. *pot.*]

potent, *pō′tənt, adj.* powerful: mighty: strongly influential: cogent: (*her.*) formed of or terminating in crutch-heads.—*n.* (*Shak.*) a prince, potentate: a support: (*obs.*) a crutch.—*n.* **pō′tence,** power: (*obs.*) a gibbet: a structure shaped like a gibbet: in watchmaking, a bracket for supporting the lower pivot: a revolving ladder in a dovecot: a right-angled military formation.—*adj.* **pō′tencé** (*-sā*), in heraldry, potent.—*n.* (*her.*) a marking of the shape of T.—*ns.* **pō′tency,** power: potentiality: a wielder of power: (*geom.*; of a point with respect to a circle) the rectangle between the segments into which a chord of the circle is divided at the point; **pō′tentate,** one who possesses power: a prince.—*adj.* **pōtential** (*-ten′shl*), powerful, efficacious: latent: existing in possibility, not in reality: (*gram.*) expressing power, possibility, liberty, or obligation.—*n.* anything that may be possible: a possibility: the potential mood, or a verb in it: of a point in a field of force, the work done in bringing a unit (of mass, electricity, &c.) from infinity to that point.—*n.* **pōtentiality** (*pō-ten-shi-al′i-ti*).—*adv.* **pōten′tially.**—*n.* **pōtentiary** (*-ten′shi-ə-ri*; *rare*), a person invested with power or influence.—*v.t.* **pōten′tiate,** to give power to.—*n.* **pō′tentiom′eter,** an instrument for measuring difference of electric potential.—*adv.* **pō′tently.**—**potential energy,** the power of doing work possessed by a body in virtue of its position. [L. *potēns, -entis,* pr.p. of *posse,* to be able—*potis,* able, *esse,* to be.]

Potentilla, *pō-tən-til′ä, n.* a genus of the rose family, including silverweed and barren strawberry, differing from Fragaria (strawberry) in having a dry receptacle. [L.L., dim. of L. *potēns,* powerful, from its once esteemed medicinal virtues.]

pothecary, *poth′i-kə-ri, n.* an aphetic form of **apothecary.**—Also **poticary** (*pot′*).

other, *podh′ər,* now often *podh′ər,* **pudder,** *pud′ər, n.* a choking smoke or dust: fuss: commotion: turmoil.—*v.t.* to fluster, to perplex.—*v.i.* to make a pother.—*adj.* **poth′ery.** [Origin unknown; app. not conn. with **powder.**]

potiche, *po-tēsh′, n.* an Oriental vase.—*n.* **potichomā′nia,** a craze for imitating Oriental porcelain by lining glass vessels with paper designs, &c. [Fr. *potiche, potichomanie.*]

potin, *po-anɡ′, n.* an old compound of copper, zinc, lead, and tin. [Fr.]

potion, *pō′shən, n.* a draught: a dose of liquid medicine or poison. [Fr.,—L. *pōtiō, -ōnis—pōtāre,* to drink.]

potlatch, *pot′lach, n.* in north-west U.S., an Indian winter festival, or the gift-giving at that time: (*coll.*) any feast or gift. [Chinook.]

potoroo, *pot-ō-rōō′, n.* the marsupial kangaroo-rat. [Native Australian name.]

pot-pourri, *pō-pōō-rē′, n.* orig. a mixed stew, an olla podrida: a mixture of sweet-scented materials, chiefly dried petals: a selection of tunes strung together: a literary production composed of unconnected parts. [Fr. *pot,* pot, *pourri,* rotten, pa.p. of *pourrir*—L. *putrēre,* to rot.]

potsherd, *pot′shərd, n.* a piece of broken pottery—(*obs.*) **pot′-shard, pot′-share** (*Spens.*). [**pot, shard** (2).]

pott (paper), **potted, potting.** See **pot.**

pottage, *pot′ij, n.* (*arch.*) vegetables boiled with or without meat: a thick soup: soup: (*obs.*) oatmeal porridge. [Fr. *potage*—*pot,* jug, pot.]

potter, *pot′ər, n.* one who makes articles of baked clay, esp. earthenware vessels.—*n.* **pott′ery,** articles of baked clay collectively, esp. earthenware vessels: a place where such goods are manufactured: the art of the potter. [**pot.**]

potter, *pot′ər, v.i.* to busy oneself in a desultory way: to dawdle.—*n.* **pottering:** diffuse talk.—*n.* **pott′erer.**—*n.* and *adj.* **pott′ering.**—*adv.* **pott′eringly.** [**pote.**]

pottingar, *pot′in-gər, n.* an old Scottish form of **apothecary.**

pottinger, *pot′in-jər, n.* a maker of *pottage.* [For *n* cf. **messenger, passenger,** &c.]

pottle, *pot′l, n.* (*arch.*) half a gallon, or thereby: a chip basket for strawberries.—*adjs.* **pott′le-bod′ied,** having a body shaped like a pottle; **pott′le-deep,** to the bottom of the pottle-pot.—*n.* **pott′le-pot,** (*Shak.*) a half-gallon drinking-vessel. [O.Fr. *potel,* dim. of *pot,* pot.]

potto, *pot′ō, n.* a West African genus (Perodicticus) of lemurs: also applied to the kinkajou. [Said to be a West African name.]

potty, *pot′i, adj.* (*coll.*) trifling: petty: crazy: dotty. [Origin obscure.]

pot-waller, *pot′-wol′ər, n.* in certain English boroughs, before the Reform Bill of 1832, one who satisfied the test as a voter by boiling his pot on his own fireplace within the borough—sometimes in the open air before witnesses to establish a bogus claim.—Variously altered popularly to **pot′-wabb′ler, -wobb′ler, -wall′oner, -wall′oper.**—*adj.* **pot′-wall′oping.** [**pot,** and O.E. *w(e)allan,* to boil.]

pouch, *powch* (*Scot. pōōch*), *n.* a poke, pocket, or bag: any pocket-like structure, as a kangaroo's marsupium, a monkey's cheek-pouch, &c.—*v.t.* to pocket: to form into a pouch: to tip.—*v.i.* to form a pouch: to be like a pouch.—*adj.* **pouched,** having a pouch.—*n.* **pouch′ful:**—*pl.* **pouch′fuls.**—*adj.* **pouch′y,** baggy.—**pouched mouse,** a small marsupial, Phascologale: an American jumping rodent (Dipodomys) with cheek-pouches opening outwards; **pouched rat,** a pocket gopher. [O.N. Fr. *pouche* (O.Fr. *poche*); cf. **poke.**]

pouder, poudre, obsolete spellings of **powder.**

pouf, pouffe, *pōōf, n.* a puffed mode of hair-dressing: a pad worn in the hair by women in the 18th century: in dressmaking, material gathered up into a bunch: a soft ottoman or large hassock.—*adj.* **poufed.** [Fr. *pouf.*]

pouk. See **pook.**

pouke. See **puck.**

poulaine, *pōō-lān′, n.* a long, pointed shoe-toe. [O.Fr. (*à la*) *Poulaine,* (in the fashion of) Poland.]

poulard, *pōō-lärd′, n.* a fattened or spayed hen. [Fr. *poularde*—*poule,* hen.]

poulder, pouldre, obsolete spellings of **powder.**

pouldron, *pōl′drən.* Same as **pauldron.**

poule, *pōōl, n.* a movement in a quadrille. [Fr.]

poulp, poulpe, *pōōlp, n.* the octopus. [Fr. *poulpe*—L. *pŏlypus*—Doric Gr. *pṓlypos = polypous*; see **polyp.**]

poult, *pōlt, n.* a chicken: the young of the common domestic fowl or of other farmyard or game bird. —*ns.* **poult′er** (*Shak.*), **poult′erer,** one who deals in dead fowls and game; **poult′ry,** domestic or farmyard fowls collectively; **poult′ry-farm, -yard,** a farm, yard, where poultry are confined and bred.—**poulters′ measure,** a rhymed couplet in which the first line has twelve, the second fourteen, syllables—from the varying number of eggs formerly sold by poulterers as a dozen. [Fr. *poulet,* dim. of *poule*—L.L. *pulla,* hen, fem. of L. *pullus,* young animal.]

poult-foot. Same as **polt-foot.**

poultice, *pōl′tis, n.* a soft composition applied in a cloth to sores.—*v.t.* to put a poultice upon. [L. *pultēs,* pl. of *puls, pultis* (Gr. *poltos*), porridge.]

pounce, *powns, n.* a hawk's (or other) claw, esp. the innermost, or any but the hind-claw: (now *dial.*) a punch: (*obs.*) a puncture: a sudden spring or swoop with attempt to seize.—*v.t.* to emboss by blows on the other side: (*obs.*) to puncture, pink: to ornament with small holes: to seize with the claws.—*v.i.* to make a pounce: to dart: to fix suddenly upon anything.—*adj.* **pounced,** furnished with claws. [Derived in some way from L. *punctiō, -ōnis*—*pungĕre, punctum,* to prick; cf. **puncheon** (1).]

pounce, *powns, n.* sandarach, cuttle-bone, or other fine powder for preparing a writing surface or absorbing ink: coloured powder dusted through perforations to mark a pattern.—*v.t.* to prepare with pounce: to trace, transfer, or mark with pounce: (*obs.*) to powder or sprinkle.—*n.* **pounce′-box,** a box with a perforated lid for sprinkling pounce. [Fr. *ponce,* pumice—L. *pūmex, pūmicis.*]

pouncet-box, *pown′sit-boks, n.* (*Shak.*) a pomander (also shortened to **poun′cet**): sometimes used for **pounce-box** (see above). [Prob. for *pounced-box,* i.e. perforated box; see **pounce** (1).]

pounching (*Spens.*). Same as **punching.**

pound, *pownd, n.* a unit of weight of varying value, long used in western and central Europe, more or less answering to the Roman *libra,* whose symbol *lb.* is used for pound: in avoirdupois weight, 16 ounces avoirdupois, or 7000 grains, or about 453·592 grammes: in troy weight, 12 ounces troy, or 5760 grains, or about 373·242 grammes: (*Shak.*) a pound-weight: (*Spens.*) the balance: a unit of money, originally the value of a pound-weight of silver: 20 shillings (the pound sterling, written *£,* for *libra*). (The *pound Scots* was, at the Union, worth 1s. 8d.; the *Egyptian pound* (*£E.*), the *Turkish pound* (*£T.*), &c., are each 100 piastres; the *Peruvian pound* 10 soles):— *pl.* formerly **pound,** now **pounds** (except *coll.* and in compounds and certain phrases).—*v.t.* (*slang*) to bet on as almost a certainty.—*ns.* **pound′age,** a charge or tax made on each pound: a commission, or a share in profits, of so much a pound; **pound′al,** the foot-pound-second unit of force; **pound′-cake,** a sweet cake containing proportionally about a pound of each chief ingredient; **pound′-day,** a day on which gifts of one pound weight of various goods are invited for charity; **pound′er,** a specimen weighing a pound: in composition, anything weighing, or worth, or carrying, or one who has, receives, or pays, so many pounds. —*adj.* **pound′-fool′ish,** neglecting the care of large sums in attending to little ones.—*n.* **pound′-weight,** as much as weighs a pound: a weight of one pound used in weighing. [O.E. *pund*— L. (*libra*) *pondō,* (pound) by weight, *pondō,* by weight—*pendĕre,* to weigh.]

pound, *pownd, n.* an enclosure in which strayed animals are confined, or distrained goods kept: any confined place: (now *Scot.* and *dial.*) a pond: a level part of a canal between two locks: the last compartment of a pound-net.—*v.t.* to put in a pound: to enclose, confine.—*ns.* **pound′age; pound′-keeper, pound′-master; pound′-net,** an arrange-

ment of nets for trapping fish. [O.E. *pund* (in compounds), enclosure.]

pound, *pownd, v.t.* to beat into fine pieces: to bruise: to bray with a pestle: to bethump: (*Spens.*) to lay on, shower.—*v.i.* to beat: to thump: to beat the ground: to make one's way heavily: to struggle on.—*n.* the act or sound of pounding.—*n.* **pound′er.** [O.E. *púnian,* to beat; *-d* excrescent, as in **sound** (3), **bound** (4).]

poupt, *pōōpt* (*Shak.; pa.p.*). See **poop** (2).

pour, *pōr, v.t.* to cause or allow to flow in a stream: to send forth or emit in a stream or like a stream: (*Spens.*) to send downstream: (*obs.*) to spread out: (*Scot.*) to drain (as cooked potatoes).—*v.i.* to stream: to rain heavily: to pour out tea, coffee, &c.: to allow liquid contents to run out duly.— *n.* a pouring: an amount poured at a time.—*ns.* **pour′er: pourie** (*pōōr′i; Scot.*), a vessel with a spout: a cream-jug: an oiling-can.—*n.* and *adj.* **pour′ing.**—**it never rains but it pours,** things never happen singly; **pouring wet,** raining hard. [M.E. *pouren;* origin obscure.]

pourboire, *pōōr-bwär, n.* a tip. [Fr.,—*pour,* for, *boire,* to drink.]

pourparler, *pōōr-pär′lā, n.* (usu. in *pl.*) an informal preliminary conference. [Fr.]

pourpoint, *pōōr′point, n.* a mediaeval quilted doublet. [Fr.]

poursew, poursue, poursuit(t), in *Spens.* for **pursue, pursuit.**

pourtray, an old-fashioned spelling of **portray**:— *pa.p.* in *Spens.* **pour′trahed** (3 syllables), **pour′trayd, purtraid, purtrayd.**—*n.* **pour′traict,** an obsolete spelling of **portrait.**

pousse, *pōōs, n.* (*Spens.*) pease. [**pulse** (2).]

pousse-café, *pōōs-kä-fā, n.* a cordial, liqueur, or combination of several in layers, served after coffee. [Fr., push-coffee.]

poussette, *pōōs-et′, n.* an act of dancing round each other in the manner of two couples in a country-dance.—*v.i.* to perform a poussette. [Fr., dim. of *pousse,* push.]

pout, *powt, v.i.* to push out the lips, in sullen displeasure or otherwise: to protrude.—*v.t.* to protrude.—*n.* a protrusion, esp. of the lips.—*ns.* **pout′er,** one who pouts: a variety of pigeon having its breast inflated; **pout′ing.**—*adv.* **pout′ingly.** [M.E. *powte,* of doubtful origin.]

pout, *powt, n.* a fish, the bib—also **whit′ing-pout.** —*ns.* **eel′-pout** (see **eel**); **horn′-pout, horned-pout,** an American (Amiurid) cat-fish; **pout′ing,** the whiting-pout. [O.E. (*æle-*)*pūte,* (eel-)*pout*— perh. conn. with foregoing with reference to the bib's inflatable membrane on the head.]

pout, poot, *pōōt, n.* a Scots form of **poult.**—*v.i.* to shoot at young partridges or young grouse.

pouther, *pōō′dhar,* a Scots form of **powder.**

poverty, *pov′ar-ti, n.* the state of being poor: necessity: want: lack: deficiency: (*obs.*) a band of pipers.—*adj.* **pov′erty-strick′en,** suffering from poverty. [O.Fr. *poverte* (Fr. *pauvreté*)—L. *paupertās, -ātis*—*pauper,* poor.]

pow, *pow, n.* (*Scot.*) head, poll: a head of hair. [**poll** (1).]

powan, *pow′an, pō′an, n.* a species of whitefish (*Coregonus*) found in Loch Lomond and Loch Eck. [Scots form of **pollan.**]

powder, *pow′dar, n.* dust: any solid in fine particles: gunpowder: hair-powder: face-powder: a medicine in the form of powder.—*v.t.* to reduce to powder: to sprinkle, daub, or cover with powder: to salt by sprinkling: to sprinkle.— *v.i.* to crumble into powder: to use powder for the hair or face.—*ns.* **pow′der-box,** a box for face-powder, hair-powder, &c.; **pow′der-clos′et, pow′dering-clos′et,** a small room in which hair was powdered; **pow′der-down,** a kind of down on some birds that readily disintegrates in powder. —*adj.* **pow′dered,** reduced to powder: sprinkled, or daubed, or dusted with powder: salted.—*ns.* **pow′der-flask, pow′der-horn,** a flask (originally a horn) for carrying gunpowder; **pow′dering-gown,** a loose dressing-gown worn while the hair was being powdered; **pow′dering-tub,** a vessel in which meat is salted: (*obs.*) a tub for treatment of venereal disease by sweating; **pow'der-mag'azine**, a place where gunpowder is stored; **pow'der-met'allurgy**, the science and art of preparing metals for use by reducing them, as a stage in the process, to powder form; **pow'der-mill**, a mill in which gunpowder is made; **pow'der-monk'ey**, a boy employed to carry powder to the gunners on a ship-of-war; **pow'der-puff**, a soft, downy ball for dusting powder on the skin; **pow'der-room**, a ship's powder-magazine: a room for powdering the hair (also **pow'dering-room**).—*adj.* **pow'dery**, of the nature of powder: like powder: covered with powder: dusty: friable. [O.Fr. *poudre*—L. *pulvis, pulveris*, dust.]

powellise, *pow'əl-īz, v.t.* (of timber) to season and preserve by boiling in a saccharine solution. [W. *Powell*, the inventor.]

powellite, *pow'əl-īt, n.* a mineral, calcium molybdate. [After John Wesley *Powell* (1834–1902), American geologist, &c.]

power, *pow'ər, powr, n.* ability to do anything—physical, mental, spiritual, legal, &c.: capacity for producing an effect: strength: energy: faculty of the mind: moving force of anything: right to command, authority: rule: influence: control: governing office: permission to act: a paper giving authority to act: potentiality: a wielder of authority, strong influence, or rule: that in which such authority or influence resides: a spiritual agent: a being of the sixth order of the celestial hierarchy: a state influential in international affairs: (*arch.*) an armed force: (now *dial.* or *coll.*) a great deal or great many: (*B.*) a mark of subjection: the sound-value of a letter: (*mech.*) rate of doing work: energy, or supply of energy, available for doing work: an instrument serving a means of applying energy (see **mechanical**): (*math.*) the product of a number of equal factors, generalised to include negative and fractional numbers: the potency of a point with respect to a circle: (*opt.*) magnifying strength, or a lens possessing it.—*adj.* concerned with power: worked by mechanical power, by any form of energy but that of muscle.—*v.t.* to equip with mechanical energy.—*adjs.* **pow'ered**, having power; **pow'erful**, having great power: mighty: forcible: efficacious: intense: impressive, esp. in a disagreeable way or in doubtful taste: (*vulg.*) very great.—*adv.* (*vulg.*) exceedingly.—*adv.* **pow'erfully**;—*ns.* **pow'erfulness**; **pow'er-house, -station**, a place where mechanical power (esp. electric) is generated; **pow'er-lathe, -loom, -press**, a lathe, loom, press, worked by mechanical power, as water, steam, electricity.—*adj.* **pow'erless**, without power: weak: impotent: helpless.— *adv.* **pow'erlessly**.—*ns.* **pow'erlessness**; **pow'er-plant**, an industrial plant for generating power: the assemblage of parts generating motive power in a motor-car, aeroplane, &c.; **pow'er-politics**, international politics in which the course taken by states depends upon their knowledge that they can back their decisions with force or other compulsive action.—**in one's power**, at one's mercy: within the limits of what one can do; **in power**, in office: (*Spens.*) in potentiality; **the powers that be**, the existing ruling authorities (from Rom. xiii. 1). [O.Fr. *poer* (Fr. *pouvoir*)—L.L. *potēre* (for L. *posse*), to be able.]

powin, pown. See pawn (4).

pownd, powre, Spenserian spellings of **pound** (3), **pour**.

powney, pownie, powny, *pow'ni*. See pony.

powsowdy, *pow-sow'di, n.* (*Scot.*) any mixture of heterogeneous kinds of food.—Also **pousow'die**. [Origin unknown.]

powter, *pow'tər, v.i.* (*Scot.*) to poke: to rummage. —*v.t.* to poke: to get by groping. [Origin obscure.]

powwaw, *pow-waw', interj.* (*Shak.*) pooh.

powwow, *pow'wow*, **pawaw**, *pä-waw', n.* an American Indian conjuror: a rite, often with feasting: a conference.—*v.i.* **powwow'**, to hold a powwow: to confer. [Algonkin *powwaw, powah*.]

pox, *poks, n.* (*pl.* of pock) pustules: (as *sing.*) an eruptive disease, esp. smallpox or syphilis: sheep-pox.—*v.t.* to infect with pox.—*interj.* plague.

poynant, *poin'ənt, adj.* (*Spens.*, &c.). Same as **poignant**.

poynt, poyse, poyson, old spellings of **point, poise, poison**.

poz, pozz, pos, *poz, adj.* an old slang abbreviation of **positive**.

pozzolana, *pot-sō-lä'nä*, **pozzuolana**, *-swō-, n.* a volcanic dust first found at *Pozzuoli*, near Naples, which forms with mortar a cement that will set in air or water.—*adj.* **pozzola'nic**.

praam. Same as pram (1).

prabble, *prab'l, n.* (*Shak.*) Welsh pronunciation of **brabble**.

practic (old spellings **practick, practique**), *prak'tik, adj.* relating to or of the nature of practice or action: (*obs.*) practising: (*obs.*) practice: (*Spens.*) skilled: (*Spens.*) cunning.—*n.* practice as opposed to theory: (esp. in *pl.*) practices, doings: practical experience: (esp. *Scots law*) legal usage or case-law: a practical man.—*n.* **practicabil'ity**.—*adj.* **prac'ticable**, that may be practised, carried out, accomplished, used, or followed: passable, as a road.—*n.* **prac'ticableness**.— *adv.* **prac'ticably**.— *adj.* **prac'tical**, in, relating to, concerned with, well adapted to, or inclining to look to, actual practice, actual conditions, results, or utility: practised: practising, actually engaged in doing something: efficient in action: workable: virtual.—*n.* a practical man: a practical examination. — *ns.* **prac'ticalism**, devotion to what is practical; **prac'ticalist**; **practical'ity**.—*adv.* **prac'tically**, in a practical way: by a practical method: to all intents and purposes: very nearly, as good as.—*ns.* **prac'ticalness**; **prac'tice** (-*tis*), action, performance: actual doing: proceeding: habitual action: custom: legal procedure: repeated performance as a means of acquiring skill, esp. in playing a musical instrument: form so acquired: the exercise of a profession: a professional man's business, as a field of activity or a property: (*arch.*) negotiation: scheming: plotting: trickery: working upon the feelings: (*arith.*) a compendious way of multiplying quantities involving several units, by means of aliquot parts; **practician** (-*tish'ən*), a practiser or practitioner: a practical man; **prac'tisant**, an agent or fellow in conspiracy.—*v.t.* **practise** (*prak'tis*, formerly -*tiz'*; *U.S.* practice), to put into practice: to perform: to carry out: to do habitually: to exercise, as a profession: to exercise oneself in, or on, or in the performance of, in order to acquire or maintain skill: to train by practice: to put to use: (*obs.*) to frequent: (*obs.*) to compass: (*Milt.*) to contrive: (*Shak.*) to plot. —*v.i.* to act habitually: to be in practice (esp. medical or legal): to exercise oneself in any art, esp. instrumental music: to proceed, esp. to seek to injure, by underhand means: to tamper, work (with *upon, on*): to scheme: to have dealings: to use artifices: to work by artifice (on the feelings).—*adj.* **prac'tised**, skilled through practice.—*n.* **prac'tiser**.—*adj.* **prac'tising**, actually engaged in professional employment.—*n.* **practitioner** (-*tish'ən-ər*; irreg. from *practician*), one who is in practice, esp. in medicine: one who practises.—*adj.* **prac'tive**, practical.—**general practitioner**, one who practises medicine and surgery without specialising; **practical joke**, a joke that consists in action, not words, usually an annoying trick; **practical politics**, proposals or measures that may be carried out at once or in the near future. [Obs. Fr. *practique*—L. *practicus* —Gr. *prāktikos*, fit for action—*prāssein*, to do.]

prad, *prad, n.* (*slang*) a horse. [Du. *paard*—L.L. *paraverēdus*; see palfrey.]

prae-. See pre-.

praecoces, praecocial. See under **precocious**.

praedial, predial, *prē'di-əl, adj.* pertaining to, connected with, or derived from, the land: landed: rural: agrarian: attached to the land.—*n.* a praedial slave. [L.L. *praediālis*—*praedium*, an estate.]

praemunire, *prē-mū-nī'ri, n.* a writ issued under statutes of Richard II. and others, summoning a person accused of suing in a foreign court

Neutral vowels in unaccented syllables : *el'ə-mənt, in'fənt, ran'dəm*

for matters cognisable by the law of England, used especially against papal claims, and later extended to various offences: an offence that could be so dealt with: the penalty for such an offence: a predicament or scrape. [From the words of the writ, *praemūnīre faciās*, cause to warn, or see that thou warn, the word *praemūnīre*, properly to fortify in front, defend, being confused with *praemonēre*, to forewarn.]

praenomen, *prē-nō'mən* (L. *prī-nō'men*), *n.* the name prefixed to the family name in ancient Rome, as *Gaius* in Gaius Julius Caesar: the generic name of a plant or animal. [L. *praenōmen—nōmen*, name.]

praeses. Same as **preses.**

praeter-. See **preter-.**

praetor, *prē'tər*, *-tor* (L. *prī'tor*), *n.* a magistrate of ancient Rome next in rank to the consuls.—*adj.* **praetorian** (*-tō'ri-ən*).—*n.* a former praetor or man of like rank: a member of the emperor's bodyguard.—*ns.* **praeto'rium**, a general's tent: a governor's residence: a court or headquarters; **prae'torship**—**praetorian gate**, the gate of a Roman camp in front of the general's tent, and nearest to the enemy; **praetorian guard**, the bodyguard of the Roman Emperor. [L. *praetor*, for *praeitor—prae*, before, *īre*, *itum*, to go.]

pragmatic, *prag-mat'ik*, *adj.* relating to affairs of state: relating to, or of the nature of, pragmatism: pragmatical.—*n.* an edict: a man of business: a busybody: an opinionative person.—*adj.* **pragmat'ical**, active: practical: matter of fact: interfering with the affairs of others: officious: meddlesome: self-important: opinionative: pragmatic.—*n.* **pragmat'icality**—*adv.* **pragmat'ically**.—*n.* **pragmat'icalness**—*v.t.* **prag'matise**, to interpret or represent as real: to rationalise.—*ns.* **pragmatis'er**; **prag'matism**, pragmatical quality: matter-of-factness: a treatment of history with an eye to cause and effect and practical lessons: (*phil.*) humanism or practicalism, a philosophy, or philosophic method, that makes practical consequences the test of truth; **prag'matist**, a pragmatic person: a believer in pragmatism.—**pragmatic sanction**, a special decree issued by a sovereign, such as that of the Emperor Charles VI. settling his dominions upon Maria Theresa. [Gr. *prāgma*, *-atos*, deed—*prāssein*, to do.]

prahu, *prā'(h)ōō.* Same as **prau.**

Prairial, *pre-ri-äl'* (Fr. *pre-ryâl'*), *n.* the ninth month of the French revolutionary calendar, about 20th May to 18th June. [Fr.,—*prairie*, meadow.]

prairie, *prā'ri*, *n.* a treeless plain, flat or rolling, naturally grass-covered.—*adj.* **prai'ried.**—*ns.* **prai'rie-chick'en, -hen,** an American genus (Cupidonia or Tympanuchus) of grouse: the sharp-tailed grouse (Pedioecetes) of the western United States; **prai'rie-dog**, a gregarious burrowing and barking North American marmot (Cynomys); **prai'rie-oy'ster**, (*U.S.*) a raw egg with condiments; **prai'rie-schoon'er**, an emigrants' long covered wagon; **prai'rie-tur'nip**, breadroot; **prai'rie-wolf**, the coyote.—**prairie value**, the value of land in its natural state before it has been improved by man. [Fr.,—L. *prātum*, a meadow.]

praise, *prāz*, *v.t.* (*Shak.*) to assign a value to, appraise: to speak highly of: to commend: to extol: to glorify, as in worship.—*n.* commendation: glorifying: the musical part of worship: that for which praise is due: (*Scot.*, in ejaculatory expressions) Goa.—*adjs.* **praise'ul**; **praise'less.**—*n.* **prais'er.**—*adv.* **praise'worthily.**—*n.* **praise'worthiness.**—*adj.* **praise'worthy**, worthy of praise: commendable.—*n.* and *adj.* **prais'ing.**—*adv.* **prais'ingly.** [O.Fr. *preiser*—L.L. *preciāre* for L. *pretiāre*, to prize—*pretium*, price.]

Prâkrit, *prā'krit*, *n.* a collective name for languages or dialects in an immediate relation to Sanskrit. —*adj.* **Prâkrit'ic.** [Sans. *prākrita*, the natural—*prakriti*, nature.]

praline, *prā'lĕn*, *n.* an almond or nut kernel with a brown coating of sugar.—Also **prawlin** (*praw'lin*). [Fr. *praline*, from Marshal Duplessis-*Praslin*, whose cook invented it.]

pralltriller, *präl'tril-ər*, *n.* an inverted mordent, a grace in which the principal note is preceded in performance by itself and the note above. [Ger.]

pram, **praam**, *präm*, *n.* a flat-bottomed Dutch or Baltic lighter: a barge fitted as a floating battery. [Du. *praam.*]

pram, *pram*, *n.* a slightly vulgar abbreviation of **perambulator**: a milkman's hand-cart.

prance, *prāns*, *v.i.* to bound from the hind legs: to go with a capering or dancing movement: to move with exaggerated action and ostentation: to swagger: to ride a prancing horse.—*v.t.* to cause to prance.—*n.* an act of prancing: swagger. —*n.* **pranc'er.**—*adj.* and *n.* **pranc'ing.**—*adv.* **pranc'ingly.** [M.E. *praunce*; origin unknown.]

prandial, *pran'di-əl*, *adj.* (*facet.*) relating to dinner. [L. *prandium*, a morning or midday meal.]

prang, *prang*, *n.* (*R.A.F. slang*) a crash: a bombing-attack.—*v.t.* to crash or smash: to bomb heavily.

prank, *prangk*, *n.* (*obs.*) an evil deed: a malicious or mischievous trick: a trick: a practical joke: a frolic.—*v.i.* to play pranks.—*adjs.* **prank'ful**, **prank'ish**, **prank'some**, **prank'y.** [Origin unknown.]

prank, *prangk*, *v.t.* to dress or adorn showily: to bespangle: to set in adornment.—*v.i.* (also *v.t.* with *it*) to make great show.—*n.* and *adj.* **prank'ing.**—*adv.* **prank'ingly.** [Akin to Du. *pronken*, Ger. *prunken*, to show off; cf. **prink.**]

prank, **pranck**, **prancke**, *prangk*, *v.t.* (*obs.*) to pleat, fold: to set in order. [Origin unknown.]

prank, *prangk*, *n.* (*rare*) prancing.—*v.i.* (and *v.t.* with *it*) to prance.—*v.i.* **prank'le**, to prance lightly. [Poss. conn. with **prance.**]

prase, *prāz*, *n.* a leek-green quartz. [Gr. *prason*, leek.]

praseodymium, *prāz-ī-ō-dim'i-əm*, *n.* a metal (Pr; at. numb. 59) with green salts, separated from the once-supposed element didymium. [Gr. *prasios*, leek-green—*prason*, leek, and **didymium.**]

prat, *prat*, *n.* (*old cant*) the buttock.—*v.t.* (*Shak.*, punningly) to beat. [Origin unknown.]

prate, *prāt*, *v.i.* to talk foolishly (or, formerly, boastfully or insolently): to tattle: to be loquacious.—*v.t.* to utter pratingly: to blab.—*n.* foolish or superfluous talk.—*n.* **pra'ter.**—*n.* and *adj.* **pra'ting.**—*adv.* **pra'tingly.** [Cf. L.G. *praten*, Dan. *prate*, Du. *praaten*.]

pratie, **praty**, *prā'ti*, *n.* an Anglo-Irish form of potato.

pratincole, *prat'ing-kōl*, *n.* a bird akin to the plovers, with swallow-like wings and tail. [L. *prātum*, meadow, *incola*, an inhabitant.]

pratique, *prat'ik*, *-ēk'*, *n.* permission to hold intercourse or to trade after quarantine or on showing a clean bill of health. [Fr.]

prattle, *prat'l*, *v.i.* to talk much and idly: to utter child's talk.—*v.t.* to utter in a prattling way.—*n.* empty talk.—*ns.* **prattl'ebox**, a prattler; **prattle'ment**, prattle; **pratt'ler**, one who prattles: a child. [Dim. and freq. of **prate.**]

prau, **prahu**, *prā'ōō*, **proa**, *prō'ā*, *n.* a Malay boat or ship, esp. a vessel with sails and oars, with both ends alike, and a flat side kept to leeward. [Malay *prāū.*]

praunce, Spenser's form of **prance.**

pravity, *prav'i-ti*, *n.* wickedness. [L. *prāvitās-ātis*.]

prawle, *prawl*, *n.* Shakespeare's Welsh form of **brawl.**

prawn, *prawn*, *n.* a small edible shrimp-like crustacean (*Palaemon serratus* or kindred species).—*v.i.* to fish for prawns. [M.E. *prayne*, *prane*; origin unknown.]

praxinoscope, *praks'in-ō-skōp*, *n.* an optical toy giving effect of motion by reflexion of successive pictures in a rotating box. [Irregularly, from Gr. *prāxis*, doing, *skopeein*, to look.]

praxis, *praks'is*, *n.* practice: an example or collection of examples for exercise: a model example. [Gr. *prāxis—prāssein*, to do.]

pray, *prā*, *v.i.* to ask earnestly: to entreat: to express one's desires to, or commune with, a god or some spiritual power.—*v.t.* to ask earnest and reverently, as in worship: to supplicate:

present as a prayer : to render, get, put, or cause to be, by praying :—*pr.p.* **pray'ing** ; *pa.t.* and *pa.p.* **prayed.**—*ns.* **pray'er,** one who prays : (*prăr, prā'ər*) the act of praying : entreaty : a petition to, or communing with, a god or spiritual power : the wish put forward or the words used : a form used or intended for use in praying : public or (in *pl.*) family worship : a petition to a public body, e.g. a legislature : the thing prayed for ; **pray'er-bead',** a jequirity bean ; **pray'er-book,** a book containing prayers or forms of devotion, esp. the Book of Common Prayer of the Church of England.—*adj.* **prayerful** (*prăr'fool*), given to prayer : in a spirit or mental attitude of prayer. — *adv.* **prayer'fully.** — *n.* **prayer'fulness.**—*adj.* **prayer'less,** without or not using prayer. — *adv.* **prayer'lessly.** — *ns.* **prayer'lessness** ; **prayer'-meet'ing,** a shorter and simpler form of public religious service, in which laymen often take part ; **prayer'-monger,** one who prays mechanically ; **prayer'-rug,** a small carpet on which a Moslem kneels at prayer ; **prayer'-wheel,** a drum wrapped with strips of paper inscribed with prayers deemed by Lamaists to be proffered when the drum is turned.—*n.* and *adj.* **pray'ing.** —*adv.* **pray'ingly**—pray, I pray you, I ask you ; **pray in aid,** (*law* ; *Shak.*) to call in, or call for, help ; **praying insect,** the mantis. [O.Fr. *preier* (Fr. *prier*), to pray, and O.Fr. *preiere,* prayer (—L.L. *precāria*) — L. *precārī* — *prex, precis,* a prayer.]

pray, Spenser's usual spelling of **prey.**

pre-, prae-, *prē-, pri-, pfx.* (1) in front, anterior, in front of, the anterior part of, as **predent'ate,** having teeth in the forepart of the jaw only ; **prēscū'tum,** in insects, a tergal plate in front of the scutum ; **prēster'num,** the anterior part of the sternum ; (2) before in time, beforehand, in advance, as **prēannounce'** ; **prē-con'quest** ; **prēdelin'eate** ; **prē-eter'nity,** an eternity of past time ; **prēling'ual,** before the use of language ; **prē'-print,** part of a publication printed in advance ; **prēver'nal,** flowering before spring ; **prē'-war,** before whichever war is in people's minds ; **prē'-warn',** to warn, or give warning of, beforehand ; (3) surpassingly, as **prēful'gent,** extremely bright ; **prēpunc'tual,** more than punctual : coming before time. [L. *prae,* in front of.]

preace, *prēs* (*Spens.*). Same as **press.**

preach, *prēch, v.i.* to deliver a sermon : to discourse earnestly : to give advice in an offensive, tedious, or obtrusive manner.—*v.t.* to set forth in religious discourses : to deliver, as a sermon : to proclaim or teach publicly : to render or put by preaching. —*n.* (*coll.*) a sermon.—*ns.* **preach'er,** one who discourses publicly on religious matter : a minister or clergyman : an assiduous inculcator or advocate ; **preach'ership.**—*v.i.* **preach'ify,** to preach tediously : to sermonise : to weary with feigned advice. — *adv.* **preach'ily.** — *ns.* **preach'iness** ; **preach'ing** ; **preach'ing-cross,** a cross in an open place at which monks, &c., preached ; **preach'ing-fri'ar,** a Dominican ; **preach'ing-house,** a Methodist church ; **preach'ment,** a sermon, in contempt : a sermon-like discourse : sermonising. — *adj.* **preach'y,** given to tedious moralising : savouring of preaching. — **preach down, up,** to decry, extol ; **preaching with a view,** preaching as a candidate in a vacant pastoral charge ; **the Preacher,** the author or spokesman of the Book of Ecclesiastes : the book itself. [Fr. *prêcher*—L. *praedicāre, -ātum,* to proclaim.]

preacquaint, *prē-ə-kwānt', v.t.* to inform beforehand.—*n.* **preacquaint'ance.**

pre-Adamite, *prē-ad'ə-mīt, n.* one who lived, or a descendant of those who lived, or a believer in the existence of a human race, before *Adam.* —*adjs.* **pre-Ad'amite** ; **preadamic** (*-a-dam'ik*), **-al,** existing before Adam ; **preadamit'ic, -al.**

preadaptation, *prē-ad-ap-tā'shən, n.* adaptation preceding change of condition.

preadmonish, *prē-ad-mon'ish, v.t.* to forewarn.— *n.* **preadmoni'tion.**

preamble, *prē-am'bl, n.* preface : introduction, esp. that of an Act of Parliament, giving its reasons

and purpose : (*Milt.* **praeamble**) a prelude.— *adjs.* **pream'būlary, pream'būlatory.**—*v.i.* **pream'būlate,** (*obs.*) to go first : to make a preamble. [Fr. *préambule*—L. *prae, ambulāre,* to go.]

preappoint, *prē-ə-point', v.t.* to appoint beforehand.

prearrange, *prē-ə-rānj', v.t.* to arrange beforehand. —*n.* **prearrange'ment.**

prease, preasse (*Spens.*). Same as **press.**

preassurance, *prē-ə-shoor'əns, n.* assurance given or felt beforehand.

preaudience, *prē-aw'di-əns, n.* right to be heard before another : precedence at the bar among lawyers.

prebend, *preb'ənd, n.* the share of the revenues of a cathedral or collegiate church allowed to a clergyman who officiates in it at stated times.—*adj.* **prebendal** (*pri-bend'l*).—*n.* **preb'endary,** a resident clergyman who enjoys a prebend, a canon : the honorary holder of a disendowed prebendal stall. [L.L. *praebenda,* an allowance—L. *praebēre,* to allow, grant.]

Pre-Cambrian, *prē-kam'bri-ən, adj.* and *n.* (geol.) Archaean, including all before the Cambrian.

precarious, *pri-kā'ri-əs, adj.* depending upon the will of another : depending on chance : insecure : uncertain : dangerous, risky : (*obs.*) supplicating. —*adv.* **precā'riously.**—*n.* **precā'riousness.** [L. *precārius*—*precārī,* to pray.]

precast, *prē-käst, adj.* of concrete blocks, &c., cast before putting in position.

precatory, *prek'ə-tə-ri, adj.* of the nature of, or expressing, a wish, request, or recommendation.— *adj.* **prec'ative,** supplicatory : (*gram.*) expressing entreaty. [L. *precārī,* to pray.]

precaution, *pri-kaw'shən, n.* a caution or care beforehand : a measure taken beforehand.—*v.t.* to forewarn.—*adjs.* **precau'tional, precau'tionary, precau'tious.**

precede, *prē-sēd', v.t.* to go before in position, time, rank, or importance : to cause to be preceded.— *v.i.* to be before in time or place.—*ns.* **precedence** (*pri-sē'dəns* ; also *prēs', pres'i-dəns*), the act of going before in time : the right of going before : priority : the state of being before in rank : the place of honour : the foremost place in ceremony —also **precedency** (*pri-sē'dən-si* ; *prēs', pres'*) ; **precedent** (*pres'i-dənt* ; also *prēs'*), that which precedes : (*Shak.*) the original of a copy : (*Shak.*) a token : (*obs.*) a model : a past instance that may serve as an example : a previous judicial decision or proceeding.—*adj.* (*pri-sē'dənt*) preceding.—*adjs.* **precedented** (*pres'i-dent-id*), having a precedent : warranted by an example ; **precedential** (*pres-i-den'shl*), of the nature of a precedent.—*adv.* **prece'dently.**—*adj.* **prece'ding,** going before in time, rank, &c. : antecedent : previous : foregoing : immediately before.—**take precedence of,** to precede in ceremonial order. [Fr. *précéder*—L. *praecēdĕre, -cessum,*—*prae, cēdĕre,* to go.]

precedence, *pri-sēz',* a Scots form of **precise.**

precentor, *pri-* or *prē-sen'tər* (Scot. *pri-zen'tər*), *n.* the leader of the singing of a church choir or congregation : in some English cathedrals a member of the chapter who deputes this duty to a succentor :—*fem.* **precen'tress, precen'trix.**— *n.* **precen'torship.** [L.L. *praecentor, -ōris*—L. *prae, canĕre,* to sing.]

precept, *prē-sept, n.* rule of action : a commandment : principle, or maxim : (*law*) the written warrant of a magistrate : a mandate.—*adjs.* **preceptial** (*pri-sep'shi* ; *Shak.*), consisting of precepts ; **precep'tive,** containing or giving precepts : directing in moral conduct : didactic.—*n.* **precep'tor,** one who delivers precepts : a teacher : an instructor : (*U.S.*) a tutor : the head of a school : the head of a preceptory of Knights Templars :— *fem.* **precep'tress.**—*adjs.* **precepto'rial** (*prē-*) ; **precep'tory** (*pri-*), giving precepts.—*n.* a community of Knights Templars (occasionally extended to a commandery of the Hospitallers) : its estate or buildings. [L. *praeceptum,* pa.p. neut. of *praecipĕre,* to take beforehand—*prae, capĕre,* to take.]

precession, *pri-sesh'ən, n.* the act of going before : a moving forward : the precession of the equinoxes (see below) or the analogous phenomenon in spinning-tops and the like.—*adj.* **precess'ional.** —**precession of the equinoxes,** a slow westward motion of the equinoctial points along the ecliptic, caused by the greater attraction of the sun and moon on the excess of matter at the equator, such that the times at which the sun crosses the equator come at shorter intervals than they would otherwise do. [L.L. *praecessiō, -ōnis—praecēdĕre*; see **precede.**]

prechristian, *prē-krist'yən, adj.* belonging to times before the Christian era or before the prevalence of Christianity.

precinct, *prē'singkt, n.* a space, esp. an enclosed space, around a building or other object (also in *pl.*): a district or division within certain boundaries: a district of jurisdiction or authority: (*U.S.*) a division for police or electoral purposes. [L.L. *praecinctum,* pa.p. neut. of *praecingĕre—prae, cingĕre,* to gird.]

precious, *presh'əs, adj.* of great price or worth: cherished: very highly esteemed: (often in irony, arrant, worthless, ' fine '): affecting an overrefined choiceness.—*adv.* (*Shak.*) preciously: (*coll.*) extremely, confoundedly.—*n.* used as a term of endearment.—*n.* **preciosity** (*presh-i-os'i-ty,* or *pres-*), fastidious overrefinement.—*adv.* **prec'iously.**—*n.* **prec'iousness.**—**precious metals,** gold, silver (sometimes mercury, platinum, and others of high price); **precious stone,** a stone of value and beauty for ornamentation: a gem or jewel. [O.Fr. *precios* (Fr. *précieux*)—L. *pretiōsus—pretium,* price.]

precipice, *pres'i-pis, n.* (*obs.*) a headlong fall: a high vertical or nearly vertical cliff: (*Shak.*) **prec'epit.**—*adj.* **prec'ipiced.**—*n.* **precipitabil'ity** (*pri-*).—*adj.* **precip'itable,** (*chem.*) that may be precipitated. — *ns.* **precip'itance, precip'itancy,** quality of being precipitate: headlong fall: headlong haste or rashness: impulsively hasty action. —*adj.* **precip'itant,** falling headlong: rushing down with too great velocity: impulsively hasty. —*n.* anything that brings down a precipitate.— *adv.* **precip'itantly.**—*v.t.* **precip'itate,** to hurl headlong: to force into hasty action: to bring on suddenly or prematurely: to bring down from a state of solution or suspension.—*v.i.* (*Shak.*) to fall headlong: to rush in haste: to come out of solution or suspension: to condense and fall, as rain, hail, &c.—*adj.* (*-āt* or *-it*) falling, hurled, or rushing headlong: sudden and hasty: without deliberation: rash.—*n.* (*-āt, -it*) a substance separated from solution or suspension, usually falling to the bottom: moisture deposited as rain, snow, &c.—*adv.* **precip'itately.**—*n.* **precipitā'tion,** act of precipitating: headlong fall or rush: (*Shak.*) sheer drop: impulsive action: great hurry: rash haste: impulsiveness: rain, hail, and snow (sometimes also dew): amount of rainfall, &c.: the formation or coming down of a precipitate: separation of suspended matter: a precipitate.—*adj.* **precip'itative.**—*ns.* **precipitā'tor,** one who precipitates: a precipitating agent: an apparatus or tank for precipitation; **precip'itin,** an antibody which in contact with an antigen produces a precipitate in the blood.— *adj.* **precip'itous,** like a precipice: sheer: (*rare*) precipitate. — *adv.* **precip'itously.** — *n.* **precip'itousness.** [L. *praeceps, praecipitis,* headlong, *praecipitium,* precipice, *praecipitāre, -ātum,* to precipitate—*prae, caput, -itis,* head.]

précis, *prā'sē, n.* an abstract:—*pl.* **précis** (*-sēz*). [Fr.]

precise, *pri-sīs', adj.* definite: exact: accurate: free from vagueness: very, identical: scrupulously exact: scrupulous in religion: puritanical: over-exact: prim: formal.—*adv.* **precise'ly.**— *ns.* **precise'ness; precisian** (*pri-sizh'ən*), an over-precise person: a formalist: formerly, in hostility, a Puritan; **precis'ianism; preci'sianist,** a precisian; **preci'sion,** quality of being precise: exactness: minute accuracy: (*obs.*) mental separation (partly in confusion with **prescission**): (*obs.*) a precise definition.—*adj.* for work of minute accuracy.—*n.* **precis'ionist,** one who insists on precision: a purist.—*adj.* **precisive**

(*pri-sī'siv*), cutting off: pertaining to precision. [Fr. *précis, -e*—L. *praecīsus,* pa.p. of *praecīdĕre— prae, caedĕre,* to cut.]

preclassical, *prē-klas'i-kl, adj.* of, or characteristic of, a time before the classical age.

preclude, *pri-klood', v.t.* to close beforehand: to shut out beforehand: to hinder by anticipation: to prevent.—*n.* **preclusion** (*pri-kloo'zhən*).—*adj.* **preclusive** (*-kloo'siv*), tending to preclude: hindering beforehand.—*adv.* **preclu'sively.** [L. *praeclūdĕre, -clūsum—claudĕre,* to shut.]

precocious, *pri-kō'shəs, adj.* early in reaching some stage of development, as flowering, fruiting, ripening, mental maturity: precocial: flowering before leaves appear: showing early development. —*n.pl.* **praecoces** (*prē'kō-sēz;* L. *prī'ko-kās*), praecocial birds (opp. to *altrices*).—*adj.* **precocial, praecocial** (*pri-kō'shl*), hatched with a complete covering of down, able to leave the nest at once and seek food: premature: forward.—*adv.* **precō'ciously.** — *ns.* **precō'ciousness, precocity** (*pri-kos'i-ti*), state or quality of being precocious: early development or too early ripeness of the mind. [L. *praecox, -ōcis—prae, coquĕre,* to cook, ripen.]

precognition, *prē-kog-nish'ən, n.* foreknowledge: (*Scots law*) a preliminary examination of witnesses as to whether there is ground for prosecution: evidence so obtained.—*adj.* **precog'nitive** (*pri-*). —*v.t.* **precognosce** (*prē-kog-nos'*), to take a precognition of.

precompose, *prē-kəm-pōz', v.t.* to compose beforehand.

preconceive, *prē-kən-sēv', v.t.* to conceive or form a notion of before having actual knowledge.—*ns.* **preconceit',** a preconceived notion; **preconcep'tion,** act of preconceiving: previous opinion formed without actual knowledge.

preconcert, *prē-kən-sərt', v.t.* to settle beforehand. —*n.* **preconcert** (*-kon'*), a previous arrangement. —*adv.* **preconcert'edly.**—*n.* **preconcert'edness.**

precondemn, *prē-kən-dem', v.t.* to condemn beforehand.

precondition, *prē-kən-dish'ən, n.* a condition that must be satisfied beforehand.

preconise, *prē'kən-īz, v.t.* to proclaim: to summon publicly: (of the pope) to proclaim and ratify the election of as bishop.—*n.* **preconisation** (*prēkən-ī-zā'shən,* or *-kon-i-*). [L. *praecō, -ōnis,* a crier, a herald.]

preconscious, *prē-kon'shəs, adj.* pertaining to a state prior to consciousness.

preconsume, *prē-kən-sūm', v.t.* to consume beforehand.

precontract, *prē-kən-trakt', v.t.* to contract beforehand: to betroth previously.—*n.* **precontract** (*-kon'*), a previous contract or betrothal.

precordial, praecordial, *prē-kor'di-əl, adj.* in front of the heart. [L. *cor, cordis,* heart.]

precurrer, *prē-kur'ər, n.* (*Shak.*) a forerunner.—*n.* **precurse** (*pri-kurs'; Shak.*), a prognostication.— *adj.* **precur'sive.**—*n.* **precur'sor,** a forerunner: a predecessor: an indication of the approach of an event.—*adj.* **precur'sory.** [L. *praecurrĕre, -cursum —currĕre,* to run.]

predacious, *pri-dā'shəs, adj.* living by prey: predatory.—*n.* **predā'tion.**—*adj.* **predative** (*pred'*). —*n.* **pred'ator.**—*adv.* **pred'atorily.**—*n.* **pred'atoriness.**—*adj.* **pred'atory,** plundering: of, relating to, or characterised by plundering: living by plunder: (*obs.*) deleterious. [L. *praeda,* booty.]

predate, *prē-dāt', v.t.* to date before the true date: to antedate: to be earlier than.

predecease, *prē-di-sēs', n.* death before another's death, or before some other time.—*v.t.* to die before.—*adj.* **predeceased',** deceased at an earlier time.

predecessor, *prē-di-ses'ər, n.* one who has been before another in anything: a thing that has been supplanted or succeeded: an ancestor. [L. *praedēcessor—dēcessor,* a retiring officer—*dē,* away *cēdĕre,* to go, depart.]

predefine, *prē-di-fīn', v.t.* to define, determine designate, beforehand. — *n.* **predefinition** (*prē def-i-nish'ən*).

predella, *pri-del'ä*, *n.* the platform or uppermost step on which an altar stands: a retable: a painting or sculpture, on the face of either of these: a painting in a compartment along the bottom of an altarpiece or other picture. [It., prob.—O.H.G. *pret*, board.]

predesign, *prē-di-zīn'*, *v.t.* to design beforehand.— *v.t.* **predesignate** (*prē-dez'ig-nāt*, or *-des'*), to specify beforehand.—*adj.* designated in advance: (*log.*) having the quantification of the predicate distinctly expressed (*Sir W. Hamilton*).—*n.* **predesigna'tion**.—*adj.* **predes'ignatory**.

predestine, *prē-* or *pri-des'tin*, *v.t.* to destine or decree beforehand: to foreordain.—*adj.* **predestina'rian**, believing in, or pertaining to, the doctrine of predestination.—*n.* one who holds the doctrine of predestination.—*n.* **predestina'rianism**.—*v.t.* **predes'tinate**, to determine beforehand: to preordain by an unchangeable purpose. —*adj.* foreordained: fated.—*n.* **predestina'tion**, act of predestinating: (*theol.*) God's decree fixing unalterably from all eternity whatever is to happen, esp. the eternal happiness or misery of men: fixed fate.—*adj.* **predes'tinative**.—*ns.* **predes'tinātor**, one who predestinates or foreordains: (*obs.*) a predestinarian; **predes'tiny**, irrevocably fixed fate.

predetermine, *prē-di-tər'min*, *v.t.* to determine or settle beforehand.—*adjs.* **predeter'minable**; **predeter'minate**, determined beforehand.—*ns.* **predetermina'tion**; **predeter'minism**, determinism.

predevote, *prē-di-vōt'*, *adj.* foreordained.

predial. Same as **praedial**.

predicable, *pred'i-kə-bl*, *adj.* that may be predicated or affirmed of something: attributable.—*n.* anything that can be predicated of another, or esp. of many others: one of the five attributes— genus, species, difference, property, and accident. —*n.* **predicabil'ity**.

predicament, *pri-dik'ə-mənt*, *n.* (*log.*) one of the classes or categories which include all predicables: condition: an unfortunate or trying position.— *adj.* **predicamental** (*-ment'l*). [L.L. *praedicāmentum*, something predicated or asserted.]

predicant, *pred'i-kənt*, *adj.* predicating: preaching. —*n.* one who affirms anything: a preacher: a preaching-friar or Dominican: a predikant. [L. *praedicāns, -āntis*, pr.p. of *praedicāre*; see next.]

predicate, *pred'i-kāt*, *v.t.* (*rare*) to preach: to affirm: to assert: (*log.*) to state as a property or attribute of the subject: (*U.S.*) to base on certain grounds: sometimes used wrongly for **predict**.— *n.* (*log.*) that which is predicated of the subject: (*gram.*) the word or words by which something is said about something.—*n.* **predica'tion**.—*adj.* **predicative** (*pri-dik'ə-tiv*, or *pred'i-kā-tiv*), expressing predication or affirmation: affirming: asserting.—*adv.* **predicatively**.—*adj.* **pred'icatory**, affirmative. [L. *praedicāre, -ātum*, to proclaim—*prae*, forth, *dīcāre*, (orig.) to proclaim.]

predict, *pri-dikt'*, *v.t.* to foretell.—*adj.* **predic'table**. —*n.* **predic'tion** (*-shən*).—*adj.* **predic'tive**, foretelling: prophetic.—*n.* **predic'tor**. [L. *praedictus*, pa.p. of *praedicĕre—dīcĕre*, to say.]

predigest, *prē-di-jest'* or *-dī-*, *v.t.* to digest artificially before introducing into the body.—*n.* **predigestion** (*-jest'yən*), digestion beforehand: (*obs.*) hasty digestion.

predikant, *prā-di-känt'*, *n.* a Dutch Reformed preacher, esp. in South Africa. [Du.,—L. *praedicāns, -āntis*; see **predicant, preach**.]

predilection, *prē-di-lek'shən*, *pred-i-*, *n.* favourable prepossession of mind: preference.—*adjs.* **predilect'**, **-ed**, chosen: favoured: preferred. [L. *prae, dīligĕre, dīlectum*, to love—*dī-, dis-*, apart, *legĕre*, to choose.]

predispose, *prē-dis-pōz'*, *v.t.* to dispose or incline beforehand: to render favourable: to render liable. — *adj.* **predispō'sing**.—*n.* **predisposition** (*-pəz-ish'ən*).—*adj.* **predisposi'tional**.

predominate, *pri-dom'in-āt*, *v.t.* (*Shak.*) to prevail over.—*v.i.* to be dominant: to surpass in strength or authority: to prevail: to be most numerous or abounding: to have a commanding position.—

ns. **predom'inance, predom'inancy**.—*adj.* **predom'inant**, ruling: having superior power: ascendant: preponderating: prevailing: commanding in position or effect.—*adv.* **predom'inantly**.—*n.* **predomina'tion**.

predoom, *prē-dōōm'*, *v.t.* to condemn in advance: to foreordain.

Pre-Dravidian, *prē-drə-vid'i-ən*, *adj.* of a dark woolly-haired, broad-nosed race of man, including Sakai, Veddas, and Australian blacks.—Also *n.*

predy, pronunciation unknown, *adj.* (*obs. naut.*) cleared for action.—*v.t.* make ready. [Origin unknown; poss. from make the ship *ready*.]

pree, *prē*, *v.t.* (*Scot.*) to make a trial of, esp. by tasting or by kissing. [**prieve**.]

pre-elect, *prē-i-lekt'*, *v.t.* to choose beforehand.— *n.* **pre-elec'tion**, (*obs.*) preference: election in anticipation.—*adj.* before election.

pre-eminent, *prē-em'in-ənt*, *adj.* eminent above others: surpassing others in good or bad qualities: outstanding: extreme.—*n.* **prē-em'inence**.—*adv.* **prē-em'inently**.

pre-employ, *prē-im-ploi'*, *v.t.* to employ beforehand.

pre-emption, *prē-em*(*p*)*'shən*, *n.* act or right of purchasing in preference to others: a piece of land so obtained: a belligerent's right to seize neutral contraband at a fixed price: seizure.— *v.t.* **pre-empt** (*prē-empt'*, *-emt'*), to secure as first-comer: (*U.S.*) to secure by pre-emption: to take possession of.—*v.i.* (*bridge*) to make a pre-emptive bid.—*adjs.* **prē-empt'ible**; **prē-emptive**. —*n.* **prē-empt'or**.—**pre-emptive bid**, (*bridge*) an unusually high bid intended to deter others from bidding. [L. *prae, emptiō, -ōnis*, a buying—*emĕre*, to buy.]

preen, *prēn*, *v.t.* to compose and arrange as birds do their feathers: to trim: to plume or pride (oneself).—**preen gland**, the uropygial gland that secretes oil used in preening the feathers. [App. **prune** (2) assimilated to the following word.]

preen, *prēn*, *n.* (*Scot.*) a pin.—*v.t.* to pin. [O.E. *prēon*, pin, brooch.]

pre-engage, *prē-in-gāj'*, *v.t.* to engage beforehand. —*n.* **prē-engage'ment**.

pre-establish, *prē-is-tab'lish*, *v.t.* to establish beforehand. — **pre-established harmony** (see **harmony**).

preeve, *prēv*, *n.* and *v.t.* obs. form of **proof** and **prove**.

pre-exilic, *prē-eg-zil'ik*, *adj.* before the exile—of O.T. writings prior to the Jewish exile (*c.* 586-538 B.C.).—Also **pre-exil'ian**.

pre-exist, *prē-ig-zist'*, *v.i.* to exist beforehand, esp. in a former life.—*v.t.* to exist before.—*n.* **prē-exist'ence**, previous existence, esp. of the soul, before the generation of the body with which it is united in this world.—*adj.* **prē-exist'ent**.

prefabricate, *prē-fab'ri-kāt*, *v.t.* to make standardised parts of beforehand, for assembling later.— *n.* **prefab'**, (*slang*) a prefabricated house.—*adj.* **prefab'ricated**, composed of such parts.—*n.* **prefabrica'tion**.

preface, *pref'is*, *n.* something said by way of introduction or preliminary explanation: a statement, usually explanatory, placed at the beginning of a book, not regarded as forming (like the introduction) part of the composition: the ascription of glory, &c., in the liturgy of consecration of the eucharist: anything preliminary or immediately antecedent.—*v.t.* to say by way of preface: to introduce by a preface: to precede: to front.— *v.i.* to make preliminary remarks.—*adjs.* **prefacial** (*pri-fā'shl*; *rare*); **prefatorial** (*pref-ə-tō'ri-əl*), serving as a preface or introduction.—*advs.* **pre-fato'rially, prefatorily** (*pref'ə-tər-i-li*).—*adj.* **pref'atory**, pertaining to a preface: serving as an introduction: introductory. [Fr. *préface*—L.L. *prēfātia* for L. *praefātiō—prae, fārī, fātus*, to speak.]

prefard, *pri-färd'*, a Spenserian form of **preferred** (*pa.t.* and *pa.p.*).

prefect, praefect, *prē-fekt*, *n.* one placed in authority over others: a commander: a school pupil with some measure of authority over others: in France, the administrative head of a department.— *adj.* **prēfectō'rial**. — *n.* **prē'fectship**. — *adj.* **pre-**

fect′ural (*pri-*).—*n.* prē′fecture, the office, term of office, or district of a prefect : the house or office occupied by a prefect. [O.Fr. *prefect* (Fr. *préfet*) and L. *praefectus*, pa.p. of *praeficĕre—prae*, *facĕre*, to make.]

prefer, *pri-fər′*, *v.t.* (*obs.*) to set in front : (*arch.*) to put forward, offer, submit, present, for acceptance or consideration : to promote : to advance : to hold in higher estimation : to choose or select before others : to like better (with *to*, or *rather than* ; not with *than* alone) :—*pr.p.* preferring (*pri-fər′ing*) ; *pa.t.* and *pa.p.* preferred (*pri-fərd′*). —*n.* preferabil′ity (*pref-*).—*adj.* pref′erable (*obs.* preferr′able, *pri-fer′*), to be preferred : having priority.—*adv.* pref′erably, by choice : in preference.—*n.* pref′erence, the act of choosing, favouring, or liking one above another : estimation above another : the state of being preferred : that which is preferred : priority : an advantage given to one over another : a card game resembling auction bridge.—*adj.* preferential (*pref-ər-en′shl*), having, giving, or allowing a preference.—*ns.* preferen′tialism ; preferen′tialist, one who favours a preferential tariff.—*adv.* preferen′tially.—*ns.* prefer′ment, advancement : promotion : superior place, esp. in the Church ; preferr′er.—preference shares, or stock, shares or stock on which the dividends must be paid before those on other kinds ; preferential tariff, one by which lower customs duties are imposed on goods from certain countries than from others. [Fr. *préférer*—L. *praeferre—ferre*, to bear.]

prefigure, *prē-fig′ər*, *v.t.* to imagine beforehand : to foreshadow by a type.—*adj.* prefig′urate (*-ū-rāt*), prefigured.—*v.t.* to prefigure.—*n.* prefigūrā′tion. —*adj.* prefig′ūrātive.—*n.* prefig′urement (*-ər-mənt*).

prefix, *prē-fiks′*, *v.t.* to put before, or at the beginning : to fix beforehand.—*ns.* prē′fix, a particle or word put before, and usually joined to, a word to affect its meaning : a title placed before a name, as *Mr*, *Sir* ; prefixion (*-fik′shən*), prefix′ture. [L. *praefigĕre*, *-fixum—figĕre*, to fix.]

prefloration, *prē-flō-rā′shən*, *n.* (*bot.*) aestivation. [L. *flōs*, *flōris*, flower.]

prefoliation, *prē-fō-li-ā′shən*, *n.* (*bot.*) vernation. [L. *folium*, leaf.]

preform, *prē-form′*, *v.t.* (*Shak.*) to form beforehand : to determine the shape of beforehand.—*ns.* prē-formā′tion ; prēformā′tionism ; prēformā′-tionist, a believer in the now exploded theory that the plant or animal (and therefore all its descendants) was already preformed in the germ (the ovum according to the ovists, the sperm according to the animalculists) and had only to be unfolded without formation of any new parts. —*adj.* prēfor′mative.

prefrontal, *prē-front′əl*, *-frunt′l*, *adj.* in front of, or in the fore-part of, the frontal bone, lobe, scale, &c.—*n.* a bone or scale so situated.

pre-glacial, *prē-glā′shl*, *adj.* earlier than the glacial period.

pregnable, *preg′nə-bl*, *adj.* that may be taken by assault or force : vulnerable. [Fr. *prenable—prendre*, to take—L. *praehendĕre*.]

pregnant, *preg′nənt*, *adj.* with child or young : impregnated : fertile : teeming : fruitful : fruitful in results : momentous : significant : threatening : freighted : swelling : full of thoughts, ready-witted, inventive : full of promise : (*Shak.*) disposed, ready, apt, ready to act : full of meaning : pithy and to the purpose : conveying a compressed meaning beyond what the grammatical construction can strictly carry : weighty : cogent : obvious : clear.—*ns.* preg′nance (*obs.*), preg′-nancy.—*adv.* preg′nantly. [L. *praegnāns*, *-āntis*, from earlier *praegnās*, *-ātis*, app.—*prae* and the root of *gnāscī*, to be born ; but in some meanings from or confused with O.Fr. *preignant*, pr.p. of *preindre*—L. *premĕre*, to press.]

pregustation, *prē-gus-tā′shən*, *n.* a foretaste.

prehallux, *prē-hal′uks*, *n.* a rudimentary innermost toe.

preheminence, an obsolete spelling of pre-eminence.

prehend, *pri-hend′*, *v.t.* (*rare*) to seize.—*adjs.* prehen′sible, (*rare*) capable of being grasped ; prehen′sile (*-sīl*), capable of grasping – also prehen′sive, prehensō′rial (*prē-*), prehen′sory (*pri-*). — *ns.* prehensility (*prē-hen-sil′i-ti*) ; prehension (*pri-hen′shən*) ; prehen′sor, one who seizes. [L. *praehendĕre*, *-hēnsum*, to seize.]

prehistoric, -al, *prē-his-tor′ik*, *-əl*, *adjs.* of a time before extant historical records.—*n.* prēhistō′rian. —*adv.* prēhistor′ically.—*n.* prēhis′tory.

prehnite, *prān′īt*, *n.* a zeolite-like mineral, an acid calcium aluminium silicate, usu. a pale green. [Named after Col. van *Prehn*, who brought it from South Africa in the 18th century.]

prehuman, *prē-hū′mən*, *adj.* at a stage of development before full humanity has been developed : earlier than the appearance of man.

preif, preife, *prēf*, *obs.* forms of proof.

prejink, *pri-jingk′*. Same as perjink.

prejudge, *prē-juj′*, *v.t.* to judge or decide upon before hearing the whole case : to condemn unheard.—*n.* prejudg′ment (*rarely* prejudge′ment). —*adj.* prejudicant (*prē-jōōd′i-kənt*).—*v.t.* pre-jud′icāte, to judge beforehand.—*v.i.* to form an opinion beforehand. — *n.* prejudicā′tion. — *adj.* prejud′icātive.

prejudice, *prej′oo-dis*, *n.* a judgment or opinion formed beforehand or without due examination : (*obs.*) a prejudgment : (*Spens.* prejudize) prognostication : prepossession in favour of or (usu.) against anything : bias : injury or hurt : disadvantage.—*v.t.* to fill with prejudice : to prepossess : to bias the mind of : to injure or hurt : (*obs.*) to prejudge, esp. unfavourably. — *adjs.* prej′udiced, having prejudice : biased ; prejudicial (*-dish′l*), injurious : detrimental : (*obs.*) prejudiced : (*prē-joo-*) relating to matters to be decided before a case comes into court.—*adv.* prejudic′ially.—without prejudice, a phrase used to require an understanding that nothing said at this stage is to detract from one's claims if the negotiation fails. [Fr. *préjudice*, wrong, and L. *praejūdicium—jūdicium*, judgment.]

prelate, *prel′it*, *n.* an ecclesiastic of high rank : a chief priest : (*U.S.*) a clergyman :—*fem.* prel′atess.—*ns.* prelacy (*prel′ə-si*), the office of a prelate : the order of bishops or the bishops collectively : church government by prelates : episcopacy ; prel′ateship.—*adjs.* prelatial (*pri-lā′shəl*), of a prelate ; prelatic (*pri-lat′ik*), -al, pertaining to prelates or prelacy : (in hostility) episcopal or episcopalian.—*adv.* prelat′ically.— *v.t.* and *v.i.* prel′atise, to make or to become prelatical.—*adj.* prel′atish (*Milt.*).—*ns.* prel′atism, (usu. hostile) episcopacy or episcopalianism : domination by prelates ; prel′atist, an upholder of prelacy ; prel′ature, prel′aty (*Milt.*), prelacy. [Fr. *prélat*—L. *praelātus—prae*, *lātus*, borne.]

prelect, *pri-lekt′*, *v.i.* to lecture.—*ns.* prelec′tion ; prelec′tor, a public reader or lecturer. [L. *prae-legĕre*, *-lectum—prae*, *legĕre*, to read.]

prelibation, *prē-lī-bā′shən*, *n.* a foretaste : an offering of first-fruits. [L. *praelībātiō*, *-ōnis—prae*, *lībāre*, to taste.]

preliminary, *pri-lim′in-ə-ri*, *adj.* introductory : preparatory : preceding or preparing for the main matter.—*n.* that which precedes : introduction (often in *pl.*, prelim′inaries) : a preliminary or entrance examination (in student slang shortened to prelim′) : (in *pl.*) preliminary pages—titles, preface, contents, introduction, &c. (in printers' slang prelims′).—*adv.* prelim′inarily. [L. *prae*, *līmen*, *-inis*, threshold.]

prelude, *prel′ūd*, *n.* a preliminary performance or action : an event preceding and leading up to another of greater importance : (*mus.*) a preliminary strain, passage, or flourish, often improvised : an introduction or first movement of a suite : a movement preceding a fugue : an overture : an introductory voluntary : a short independent composition such as might be the introduction to another, or developed out of the prelude in the literal sense.—*v.t.* (*prel′ūd*, formerly and still by some *pri-lūd′*, *-lōōd′*) to precede as a prelude, serve as prelude to : to introduce with

a prelude: to perform as a prelude.—*v.i.* to furnish a prelude: to perform a prelude: to serve as a prelude.—Also (*ns.*) **preludio** (*pre-lōō′di-ō*; It.), **praeludium** (*prī-lōō′di-ōōm*; L.), **prelu′sion** (*-zhən*).—*adjs.* **preludial** and **preludious** (*pri-lōō′*, or *-lū′*; both *rare*); **prelusive** (*-lōō′* or *-lū′siv*), of the nature of a prelude: introductory. —*advs.* **prelu′sively**; **prelu′sorily**.—*adj.* **prelu′sory** (*-sə-ri*), introductory. [Fr. *prélude*—L.L. *praelūdium*—L. *lūdĕre*, to play.]

premandibular, *prē-man-dib′ū-lər*, *adj.* in front of the lower jaw.—*n.* a bone so placed in fishes, &c.

premature, *prem′ə-tūr*, *prēm′*, or *-tūr′*, *adj.* ripe before the time: unduly early.—*adv.* **prema′turely** (or *prem′*, *prēm′*).—*ns.* **premature′ness** (or *prem′*; *rare*); **prematur′ity.** [L. *praemātūrus*—*prae*, *mātūrus*, ripe.]

premaxilla, *prē-maks-il′ä*, *n.* a bone in front of the maxilla.—*adj.* **premaxill′ary** (or *-maks′*).—*n.* the premaxilla.

premeditate, *prē-med′i-tāt*, *v.t.* to meditate upon beforehand: to design previously.—*v.i.* to deliberate beforehand.—*adv.* **premed′itatedly.**—*n.* **premedita′tion.**—*adj.* **premed′itative.** [L. *prae-meditārī*, *-ātus*—*prae*, *meditārī*, to meditate.]

premier, *prem′i-ər*, *-yər*, by some *prēm′i-ər*, formerly also *pri-mēr′*, *adj.* prime or first: chief: (*her.*) most ancient.—*n.* the first or chief: the prime minister: (*U.S.*) the Secretary of State.—*n.* **première** (*prəm-yer′*; Fr., *fem.*), a leading actress, dancer, &c.: first performance of a play—also *adj.*—*n.* **prem′iership.** [Fr.,—L. *prīmārius*, of the first rank—*prīmus*, first.]

premillenarian, *prē-mil-ən-ā′ri-ən*, *n.* a believer in the premillennial coming of Christ.—Also *adj.*—*n.* **premillena′rianism.**

premillennial, *prē-mil-en′yəl*, *adj.* before the millennium.—*ns.* **premillenn′ialism**, premillenarianism; **premillenn′ialist.**

premise, **premiss**, *prem′is*, *n.* (*log.*) a proposition stated or assumed for after-reasoning, esp. one of the two propositions in a syllogism from which the conclusion is drawn: (in the form **premise** only, usu. in *pl.*, **prem′ises**) the matter set forth at the beginning of a deed: the beginning of a deed setting forth its subject-matter: the aforesaid, hence, a building and its adjuncts, esp. a publichouse: a presupposition: (*Shak.*) a condition stipulated beforehand: (*Shak.*) antecedent happenings or circumstances.—*v.t.* **premise** (*pri-mīz′*, also *prem′is*), to mention or state first, or by way of introduction: to prefix: to state or assume as a premiss: (*med.*) to perform or administer beforehand.—*adj.* **premi′sed**, (*Shak.*) sent before due time. [Fr. *prémisse* and L. (*sententia*, &c.) *praemissa*, (a sentence, &c.) put before—*mittĕre*, *missum*, to send.]

premium, *prē′mi-əm*, *n.* a reward: a prize: a bounty: payment made for insurance: a fee for admission as a pupil for a profession: excess over original price or par—opp. to *discount*: anything offered as an incentive:—*pl.* **pre′miums.—at a premium**, above par. [L. *praemium*—*prae*, above, *emĕre*, to buy.]

premolar, *prē-mō′lər*, *adj.* in front of the true molar teeth.—*n.* a tooth between the canine and the molars (called molar or milk-molar in the milk dentition).

premonish, *prē-mon′ish*, *v.t.* to admonish or warn beforehand.—*n.* **premonition** (*prē-mən-ish′ən*), a forewarning: a feeling that something is going to happen.—*adjs.* **premonitive** (*pri-mon′*), **premon′itory**, giving warning or notice beforehand. —*n.* **premon′itor**, one who, or that which, gives warning beforehand.—*adv.* **premon′itorily.** [On the model of **admonish**—L. *praemonēre*—*monēre*, to warn.]

Premonstratensian, *pri-mon-strə-ten′sh(y)ən, -si-ən*, *adj.* of an order of canons regular, the Norbertines or White Canons, founded by St Norbert, in 1119, at *Prémontré*, near Laon, or of a corresponding order of nuns.—*n.* a member of the order.—Also (*n.* and *adj.*) **premon′strant.** [L. *prātum mōnstrātum*, the meadow pointed out, or (*locus*) *praemōnstrātus*, (the place) foreshown (in a vision), i.e. *Prémontré*.]

premorse, *pri-mors′*, *adj.* ending abruptly, as if bitten off. [L. *praemorsus*, bitten in front—*prae*, *mordēre*, *morsus*, to bite.]

premosaic, *prē-mō-zā′ik*, *adj.* before the time of Moses.

premotion, *prē-mō′shən*, *n.* an (esp. divine) impulse determining the will.—*v.t.* **premove′.**—*n.* **premove′ment.**

prenasal, *prē-nā′zl*, *adj.* in front of the nose.—*n.* a bone at the tip of the nose, as in pigs.

prenatal, *prē-nā′tl*, *adj.* before birth.

prenominate, *pri-nom′in-āt*, *adj.* (*Shak.*) forenamed.—*v.t.* (*Shak.*) to name or state beforehand.

prenotion, *prē-nō′shən*, *n.* preconception.

prent, *prent* (*Scot.*). Same as **print**.

prentice, **'prentice**, *pren′tis*, aphetic for **apprentice.**—*n.* **pren′ticeship**, **'pren′ticeship.**

prenzie, app. *adj.* in *Shak.* (*Measure for Measure*, III. i. 92, 95) conjectured to mean primsie: according to others princely: or connected with **prone** (homily): or Fr. *prenez garde*: or a misprint.

preoccupy, *prē-ok′ū-pī*, *v.t.* to occupy, fill, or (*obs.*) wear beforehand or before others: to take or have possession of to the exclusion of others or other things: to fill the mind of: to prejudice.—*ns.* **prēoc′cupancy**, occupying before others: condition of being preoccupied; **prēocc′upant**, a prior occupant.—*v.t.* **prēocc′upate**, to preoccupy: to anticipate.—*n.* **prēoccupā′tion.**—*adj.* **prēocc′upied**, already occupied: lost in thought, abstracted.

preoption, *prē-op′shən*, *n.* first choice.

preoral, *prē-ō′rəl*, *adj.* in front of the mouth.—*adv.* **preō′rally.**

preordain, *prē-or-dān′*, *v.t.* to ordain, appoint, or determine beforehand. — *n.* **preordain′ment.** — *v.t.* **preor′der**, to arrange or ordain beforehand. *ns.* **preor′dinance**, a rule previously established: that which is ordained beforehand; **preordinā′tion**, preordaining.

prep, *prep*, *adj.* (*coll.* contr. for) *prep*aratory.—*n.* school slang for *prep*aration, preparation of lessons: a preparatory school: a pupil in a preparatory school.

prepaid. See **prepay.**

prepare, *pri-pār′*, *v.t.* to make ready or fit: to bring into a suitable state: to dispose: to adapt: to train, as for an examination: to get up, learn: (*arch.*) to provide, furnish: to subject to a process for bringing into a required state: to make, produce: to cook and dress: to lead up to.—*v.i.* to make oneself ready: to make preparation.—*n.* (*Shak.*) preparation. — *n.* **preparation** (*prep-ə-rā′shən*), the act of preparing: preliminary arrangement: course of being prepared: preliminary study of prescribed classwork: readiness: that which is prepared or made up, as a medicine: an anatomical or other specimen prepared for study or preservation: the day before the Sabbath or other Jewish feast-day: devotional exercises introducing an office: (*mus.*) the previous introduction, as an integral part of a chord, of a note continued into a succeeding dissonance.—*adj.* **preparative** (*pri-par′ə-tiv*), serving to prepare: preliminary.—*n.* that which prepares the way: preparation.—*adv.* **prepar′atively.**—*n.* **prepar′ator.**—*adv.* **prepar′atorily.**—*adj.* **prepar′atory**, preparing: previous: introductory. — *adv.* preparatorily. — *adj.* **prepared** (*pri-pārd′*), made ready, fit, or suitable: ready.—*adv.* **prepa′redly.**—*ns.* **prepa′redness**; **prepā′rer.**—**preparatory school**, one which prepares pupils for a public or other higher school. [Fr. *préparer*—L. *praeparāre*—*prae*, *parāre*, to make ready.]

prepay, *prē′pā′*, *v.t.* to pay before or in advance.— *adj.* **pre′paid′.**—*adj.* **prepay′able.**—*n.* **prepay′ment.**

prepense, *pri-pens′*, *adj.* premeditated: intentional, chiefly in the phrase 'malice prepense' = malice aforethought or intentional.—*v.t.* (*Spens.*) to consider. — *adv.* **prepense′ly.** — *adj.* **prepens′ive** (*Fielding*). [O.Fr. *purpense*.]

prepollence, *pri-pol′əns*, *n.* predominance.—*n.* **prepoll′ency.**—*adj.* **prepoll′ent.** [L.L. *praepollentia* —*prae*, *pollēre*, to be strong.]

Neutral vowels in unaccented syllables : *el′ə-mənt, in′fənt, ran′dəm*

prepollex, *prē-pol'eks*, *n.* in some animals, a rudimentary innermost finger.

preponderate, *pri-pon'dər-āt*, *v.i.* to weigh more: to turn the balance: to prevail or exceed in number, quantity, importance, influence, or force.— *v.t.* to outweigh (*lit.* or *fig.*).—*ns.* **prepon'derance**, **prepon'derancy**. — *adj.* **prepon'derant**. — *advs.* **prepon'derantly**, **preponderā'tingly**. [L. *praeponderāre*, *-ātum* — *prae*, *ponderāre*, *-ātum*, to weigh—*pondus*, a weight.]

preponderate, *pri-pon'də-rāt*, *v.t.* and *v.i.* (*Fielding*) to ponder beforehand.

preposition, *prep-ə-zish'ən*, *n.* a word placed usually before a noun or its equivalent to mark some relation : (*obs.*) a prefix : (*prē-*) position in front. —*adj.* **preposi'tional** (*prep-*).—*adv.* **preposi'tionally.**—*adj.* **prepositive** (*pri-poz'i-tiv*), put before : prefixed.—*n.* **praepost'or**, **prepos'itor**, a school prefect (for L. *praepositus*). [L. *praepositiō*, *-ōnis* —*praepōnĕre*, *-positum*—*prae*, *pōnere*, to place.]

prepossess, *pre-poz-es'*, *v.t.* to possess beforehand: to take beforehand : to fill beforehand, as the mind with some opinion or feeling : to preoccupy : to bias or prejudice, esp. favourably.—*adjs.* **prepossessed'**, biased, prejudiced ; **prepossess'ing**, tending to prepossess : making a favourable impression.— *adv.* **prepossess'ingly**. — *n.* **prepossession** (*-esh'ən*), previous possession : preoccupation : bias, usually favourable.

preposterous, *pri-pos'tə-rəs*, *adj.* (*rare, lit.*) inverted, having or putting the last first : contrary to the order of nature or reason : utterly absurd.—*adv.* **prepos'terously**. — *n.* **prepos'terousness**. [L. *praeposterus*—*prae*, before, *posterus*, after—*post*, after.]

prepotent, *prē-pō'tənt*, *adj.* powerful in a very high degree : prevailing over others or another in taking effect : having power to transmit to offspring more characteristics than the other parent : taking precedence in effect.—*ns.* **prepo'tence**, **prepo'tency.**

prepuce, *prē'pūs*, *n.* the loose skin of the penis, the foreskin.—*adj.* **preputial** (*pri-pū'shyəl*, *-shəl*). [L. *praepūtium.*]

Pre-Raphaelite, Praeraphaelite, *prē-raf'ā-əl-īt*, *n.* one who would return to the spirit and manner of painters before the time of *Raphael* (1483-1520) : a member of a group (the Pre-Raphaelite Brotherhood, or ' P.R.B.', 1848) of painters and others (D. G. Rossetti, W. Holman Hunt, J. E. Millais, &c.) who practised or advocated a truthful, almost rigid, adherence to natural forms and effects. — Also *adj.* — *ns.* **Pre-Raph'aelism**, **Pre-Raph'aelitism**. — *adjs.* **Pre-Raphaelist'ic**, **Pre-Raphaelitist'ic** ; **Pre-Raphaelit'ish.**

pre-Reformation, *prē-ref-ər-mā'shən*, *adj.* before the Reformation : dating from before the Reformation.

prerelease, *prē-ri-lēs'*, *n.* release of a cinematograph film before the normal date : exhibition of a film so released.—Also *adj.*

prerequisite, *prē-rek'wi-zit*, *n.* a condition or requirement that must previously be satisfied.—*adj.* required as a condition of something else.

prerogative, *pri-rog'ə-tiv*, *n.* a peculiar privilege shared by no other : a right arising out of one's rank, position, or nature : (*rare*) the right of voting first. — *adj.* arising out of, or held by, prerogative : voting first. — *adj.* **prerog'atived**, (*Shak.*) having a prerogative. — *adv.* **prerog'atively.**—Prerogative Court, formerly a court having jurisdiction over testamentary matters ; **royal prerogative**, the rights which a sovereign has by right of office, which are different in different countries. [L. *praerogātīvus*, asked first for his vote—*prae, rogāre*, *-ātum*, to ask.]

prerosion, *prē-rō'zhən*, *n.* corrosion of a crystal by a solvent forming new faces (*prerosion faces*) on the corners and edges. [L. *praerōdĕre*, *-rōsum*, to gnaw at the tip—*rōdĕre*, to gnaw.]

prerupt, *prē-rupt'*, *adj.* broken off : abrupt. [L. *praeruptus*—*prae, rumpĕre*, to break.]

presage, *pres'ij*, formerly also *pri-sāj'*, *n.* a prognostic : an omen : an indication of the future : a foreboding : a presentiment. — *v.t.* **presage** (*pri-sāj'*), to portend : to forebode : to warn of

as something to come : to forecast : (*Spens.*) to point out, reveal : to have a presentiment of.— *v.i.* to have or utter a presage.—*adj.* **presage'ful.** —*ns.* **presage'ment** (*obs.*) ; **presag'er**. [L. *praesāgium*, a foreboding—*prae, sāgus*, prophetic.]

presanctify, *prē-sangk'tifī*, *v.t.* to consecrate beforehand.—*n.* **presanctificā'tion.**

presbyopia, *prez-bi-ō'piä*, *n.* difficulty in accommodating the eye to near vision, a defect increasing with age—also **pres'byopy.**—*n.* **pres'byope**, one so affected.—*adj.* **presbyopic** (*-op'ik*). [Gr. *presbys*, old, *ōps, ōpos*, the eye.]

presbyte, *prez'bīt*, *n.* etymologically an old man, but used for one who is presbyopic. [Gr. *presbytēs*, an old man.]

presbyter, *prez'bi-tər*, *n.* an elder : a minister or priest in rank between a bishop and a deacon : a member of a presbytery : (*obs.*) a Presbyterian. —*adj.* **presbyt'eral**, of a presbyter or presbyters. *n.* **presbyt'erate**, the office of presbyter : a body of presbyters : the order of presbyters. — *adj.* **presbyterial** (*-tē'ri-əl*), of a presbytery : of church government by elders. — *adv.* **presbytē'rially.**—*adj.* **Presbytē'rian**, pertaining to, or maintaining the system of church government by presbyters : of a church so governed.— *n.* a member of such a church : an upholder of the Presbyterian system.—*v.t.* and *v.i.* **Presbytē'rianise**, to make or become Presbyterian : to move towards Presbyterianism.—*ns.* **Presbytē'rianism**, the form of church government by presbyters ; **pres'bytership** ; **pres'bytery**, a church court ranking next above the kirk-session, consisting of the ministers and one ruling elder from each church within a certain district : the district so represented : the Presbyterian system : part of a church reserved for the officiating priests, the eastern extremity : (*R.C.*) a priest's house.— **Reformed Presbyterian Church**, the Cameronians ; **United Presbyterian Church**, a religious body formed by the union of the Secession and Relief Churches in 1847, included in the United Free Church from 1900, and (except a minority) in the Church of Scotland from 1929. [Gr. *presbyteros*, comp. of *presbys*, old.]

prescience, *prē'sh(y)əns, -shi-əns*, also *pre'*, *n.* foreknowledge : foresight. — *adj.* **pre'scient**. — *adv.* **pre'sciently**. [L. *praesciēns, -entis*, pr.p. of *praescīre—prae, scīre*, to know.]

prescientific, *prē-sī-ən-tif'ik*, *adj.* before the scientific age, before knowledge was systematised.

prescind, *pri-sind'*, *v.t.* to cut off, cut short, separate : to abstract.—*v.i.* to withdraw the attention (*from*).—*adj.* **prescind'ent**.—*n.* **prescission** (*prisish'ən*).

prescious, *prē'shyəs*, *adj.* prescient. [L. *praescius —praescīre* ; cf. **prescience**.]

prescribe, *pri-skrīb'*, *v.t.* to lay down as a rule or direction : to give as an order : to appoint : (*med.*) to give directions for, as a remedy : to limit, set bounds to : to claim by prescription.—*v.i.* to lay down rules : (*med.*) to give or make out a prescription : to make a claim on account of long possession : to become of no force through time.— *ns.* **prescrib'er** ; **prescript** (*prē'skript* ; formerly *-skript'*), an ordinance or rule : a remedy or treatment prescribed.—*adj.* (*prē'* or *-skript'*) prescribed. —*n.* **prescriptibil'ity** (*pri-*).—*adj.* **prescrip'tible**, subject to prescription : invalidated by lapse of time.—*n.* **prescrip'tion**, act of prescribing or directing : (*med.*) a written direction for the preparation of a medicine : a recipe : (*law*) custom continued until it becomes a right or has the force of law : (*law*) limitation of time within which action may be taken.—*adj.* **prescrip'tive**, prescribing, laying down rules : consisting in, or acquired by, custom or long-continued use : customary. [L. *praescrībĕre, -scrīptum*, to write before, lay down in advance, demur to—*prae, scrībĕre*, to write.]

presence, *prez'əns*, *n.* fact or state of being present —opp. to *absence* : immediate neighbourhood : a presence-chamber or other place where a great personage is : an assembly, esp. of great persons : a present personality : impression made by one's bearing, esp. imposing bearing : something felt or imagined to be present.—*n.* **pres′ence-chamber**, the room in which a great personage receives company.—**presence of mind**, power of keeping one's wits about one : coolness and readiness in emergency, danger, or surprise ; **real presence**, the true and substantial presence, according to the belief of Roman Catholics, of the body and blood of Christ in the eucharist. [O.Fr.,—L. *praesentia* ; see following words.]

present, *prez′ənt, adj.* in the place in question or implied—opp. to *absent* : at hand : ready : found or existing in the thing in question : before the mind : attentive, watchful, not absent-minded : now under view or consideration : now existing : not past or future : (*gram.*) denoting time just now, or making a general statement : in or of the present tense : immediate. — *n.* that which is present : the present time : the present tense : a verb in the present tense : present business or occasion : present document or (in *pl.*) writings.— *adjs.* **pres′ent-day′**, belonging to or found in the present time, contemporary ; **presential** (*pri-zen′shl*), relating to presence : having or implying actual presence : present : as if present : formed from the present tense.—*n.* **presentiality** (*-shi-al′i-ti*). — *advs.* **presen′tially**; **pres′ently**, (*obs.* or *Scot.*) at present, now : (*obs.*) for the time being : (*obs.*) at once : before long : directly, immediately, necessarily. — *n.* **pres′entness**. — **at present**, at the present time, now ; **for the present**, for the moment : now for the time being. [O.Fr.,—L. *praesēns, -sentis,* present.]

present, *prez′ənt, n.* a gift. [O.Fr. *present,* orig. presence, hence gift (from the phrase *mettre en present à,* put into the presence of, hence offer as a gift to).]

present, *pri-zent′, v.t.* to set before one, introduce into presence or to notice, cognisance, or acquaintance : to introduce at court : to introduce to the public, as on the stage : to put on the stage : to exhibit to view : to have as a characteristic : to put forward : to proffer : to make a gift of : to appoint to a benefice : to nominate to a foundation : to put forward or bring up for examination, trial, dedication, a degree, consideration, &c. : to deliver : to bestow something upon, endow (with *with*) : to represent, depict, or symbolise : (*arch.*) to represent the character of, act, personate : to point, direct, aim, turn in some direction : to apply : (*obs.*) to offer the greetings of, 'remember' : (*mil.*) to hold vertically in front of the body in salute to a superior : (*refl.*) to come into presence, attend, appear : (*refl.*) to offer (occur).—*v.i.* to make presentation to a living : to offer : (*obstetrics*) to be directed, to be in position for coming first.— *n.* the position of a weapon in presenting arms or in aiming.—*n.* **presentabil′ity**.—*adj.* **present′able**, capable of being presented : fit to be presented : fit to be seen : passable.—*adv.* **present′ably**. — *n.* **presentation** (*prez-ən-tā′shən*), act of presenting : mode of presenting : right of presenting : that which is presented : immediate cognition : a setting forth, as of a truth : representation.—*adj.* that has been presented : of or for presentation. — *adj.* **presenta′tional**. — *ns.* **presenta′tionism**, the doctrine of immediate cognition of objects ; **presenta′tionist**.—*adj.* **presentative** (*pri-zent′ə-tiv*), subject to right of presentation : presenting to the mind (esp. that which is not imitative) : pertaining to immediate cognition.—*ns.* **presentee** (*prez-ən-tē′*), one who is presented to a benefice ; **presenter** (*pri-zent′ər*). —*adj.* **present′ive**, presenting a conception to the mind, not a mere relation.—*ns.* **present′iveness**; **present′ment**, act of presenting : a statement : a jury's statement to a court of matters within its knowledge : a representation : an image, delineation, picture : a presentation to consciousness.—**present arms**, to bring the weapon to a vertical position in front of the body. [O.Fr. *presenter*—L. *praesentāre—praesēns,* present (in place or time).]

presentient, *prē-sen′sh(y)ənt, adj.* having a presentiment.—*n.* **prēsen′sion**.

presentiment, *pri-zent′i-mənt,* sometimes *-sent′, n.* a foreboding, esp. of evil.—*adj.* **presentimental** (*-ment′l*).

preserve, *pri-zərv′, v.t.* to keep safe from harm or loss : to keep alive : to keep in existence : to retain : to maintain, keep up : to guard against shooting or fishing by unauthorised persons : to keep sound : to keep from or guard against decay : to pickle, season, or otherwise treat for keeping.—*v.i.* to preserve game, fish, ground, or water, &c.—*n.* preserved fruit or jam (often in *pl.*) : a place or water where shooting or fishing is preserved : anything regarded as closed or forbidden to outsiders : (in *pl.*) spectacles to protect the eyes from dust or strong light.—*n.* **preservabil′ity**.—*adj.* **preser′vable**.—*n.* **preservā′tion** (*prez-*).—*adj.* **preser′vative**, serving to preserve. —*n.* a preserving agent : a safeguard : a prophylactic. — *adj.* and *n.* **preser′vatory**. — *n.* **preserv′er**. [Fr. *préserver*—L. *prae, servāre,* to keep.]

preses, praeses, *prē′siz, n.* (chiefly *Scot.*) a president or chairman. [L. *praeses, -idis* ; cf. next word.]

preside, *pri-zīd′, v.i.* to be in the chair : to be at the head : to superintend : to be guardian or tutelary god : to be at the organ or piano (orig. as a kind of conductor).—*v.t.* (*rare*) to be at the head of.—*ns.* **presidency** (*prez′i-dən-si*), the office of a president, or his dignity, term of office, jurisdiction, or residence : (*hist.*) each of three main divisions of India : a Mormon governing council ; **pres′ident**, one who is chosen to preside over the meetings of a society, conference, &c. : the elected head of a republic : the head of a board, council, or department of government : the title of the head of certain colleges, universities, and other institutions : (*hist.*) a colonial or state governor : (*U.S.*) the chairman of a company, a bank governor, or head of an organisation generally. — *adj.* (*Milt.*) presiding, superintending. — *n.* **pres′identess**.—*adj.* **presidential** (*-den′shl*), presiding : of a president or presidency.—*n.* **pres′identship**.—**Lord President**, the presiding judge of the Court of Session ; **Lord President of the Council**, a member of the House of Lords who presides over the privy council ; **presiding officer**, a person in charge of a polling-place. [Fr. *présider* —L. *praesidēre—prae, sedēre,* to sit.]

president, (*Spens., Shak., Milt.*) for **precedent**.

presidial, *pri-sid′i-əl, adj.* pertaining to a garrison, a presidio, or a president : (*Fr. hist.*) provincial.— *adj.* **presid′iary**, garrisoning : of a garrison.—*ns.* **presid′io**, (*Sp. Amer.,* &c.) a military post : a penal settlement ; **presid′ium**, a standing committee in the Soviet system. [L. *praesidium,* a garrison—*praesidēre,* to preside.]

presignify, *prē-sig′ni-fī, v.t.* to intimate beforehand. —*n.* **prēsignificā′tion**.

press, *pres,* formerly also **prease, prease, preasse,** &c., *prēs, v.t.* to exert a pushing force upon : to squeeze : to compress : to clasp : to thrust onwards or downwards : to squeeze out : to imprint, stamp, print : to flatten, condense, dry, shape, or smooth by weight or other squeezing force : to put to death by application of heavy weights : to bear heavily on : to harass : to beset : to urge strongly : to invite with persistent warmth : to offer urgently or abundantly (with *upon*) : to throng, crowd : to present to the mind with earnestness : to lay stress upon : to hurry on with great speed.—*v.i.* to exert pressure : to push with force : to crowd : to go forward with violence : to be urgent in application, entreaty, or effort : to strive : to strain : (*golf*) to strive to do too much, to the loss of ease and effectiveness.—*n.* an act of pressing : pressure : crowd : crowding : thick of a fight : stress : urgency : a cupboard or shelved closet or recess : a bookcase : an apparatus for pressing : a printing-machine : printing : a printing organisation : often extended to a publishing house : printing activities : newspapers and periodicals collectively : the journalistic profession : a common name for a newspaper : reception by newspapers and periodicals generally. —*ns.* **press′-agent**, one who arranges for newspaper advertising and publicity, esp. for an actor or theatre; **press'-bed,** a bed enclosed in a cupboard, or folding up into it; **press'-book,** a book printed at a private press; **press'-box,** an erection provided for the use of reporters at sports, shows, &c.; **press'-cutt'ing,** a paragraph or article cut out of a newspaper or magazine; **pressed'-day,** the third day of a three days' visit; **press'er; press'fat,** (*B.*) the vat for collecting the liquor from an olive or wine press; **press'ful; press'-gall'ery,** a reporters' gallery; **press'ing.**—*adj.* urgent: importunate: crowding.—*adv.* **press'ingly.** — *ns.* **pression** (*presh'ən*; *rare*), pressure: impress; **press'man,** one who works a printing-press: a journalist or reporter; **press'mark,** a mark upon a book to show its place in a library; **press'-proof,** the last proof before printing; **press'-room,** a room where printing-presses are worked: a room for the use of journalists; **pressure** (*presh'ər*), act of pressing or squeezing: the state of being pressed: (*Shak.*) impression, stamp: constraining force or influence: that which presses or afflicts: urgency: strong demand: a force directed towards the thing it acts upon, measured as so much weight upon a unit of area: difference of electric potential.—*adj.* **press'urised,** (of an aeroplane, &c.) fitted with a device that maintains nearly normal atmospheric pressure.—*n.* **press'-work,** the operation of a printing-press: journalistic work.—**at press, in the press,** in course of printing: about to be published; **go to press,** to begin to print or to be printed; **liberty of the press,** the right of publishing books, &c., without submitting them to a government authority for permission; **press of sail,** as much sail as can be carried; **pressure cooker,** an autoclave, esp. one for domestic use; **the press,** printed matter generally, esp. newspapers. [Fr. *presser*—L. *pressāre*—*premēre*, *pressum*, to press.]

press, *pres*, *v.t.* to carry off and force into service, esp. in the navy: to requisition: to turn to use in an unsuitable or provisional way.—*n.* **impress'ment:** authority for impressing.—*ns.* **press'-gang,** a gang or body of sailors under an officer empowered to impress men into the navy; **press'-money,** earnest-money. [prest.]

pressure. See press (1).

prest, *prest*, *adj.* (*Spens.*, *Shak.*) ready. [O.Fr. *prest*—L. *praestō*, at hand.]

prest, *prest*, *v.t.* (*obs.*) to lend: to pay in advance: to engage by paying earnest: to enlist: to impress for service.—*n.* (*obs.*) a loan: payment in advance: enlistment-money.—*n.* **presta'tion,** payment or service required by custom or promise. [O.Fr. *prester*—L. *praestāre*, to offer, discharge.]

Prester John, *pres'tər jon*, *n.* the mythical mediaeval Christian priest-king of a vast empire in Central Asia (and later in Ethiopia). [O.Fr. *prestre* (Fr. *prêtre*), priest.]

presternum, *prē-stər'nəm*, *n.* the anterior part of the sternum.

prestidigitation, *pres-ti-dij-i-tā'shən*, *n.* sleight-of-hand.—*n.* **prestidig'itātor.** [Fr. *prestidigitateur*—*preste*, nimble, L. *digitus*, finger.]

prestige, *pres-tēzh'*, *n.* (*orig.*) a conjuring trick, illusion: glamour: standing or ascendancy in men's minds owing to associations, station, success, &c.—*adj.* consisting in, or for the sake of, prestige.—*n.* **prestigiator** (*pres-tij'i-ā-tər*), a conjurer.—*adj.* **prestigious** (-*tij'əs*), juggling: deceitful. [Fr.,—L. *praestigium*, delusion—*praestringēre*, to dazzle, blind; see prestriction.]

presto, *pres'tō*, *adj.* (*mus.*) very quick.—*n.* a presto movement or passage.—*adv.* quickly, quicker than *allegro*.—*adv.* or *interj.* (as in conjuring tricks) at once.—*adv.*, *n.*, and *adj.* (*superl.*) **prestis'simo.** [It.,—L. *praestō*, at hand.]

pre-stressed, *prē'-strest'*, *adj.* (of concrete) strengthened with stretched piano wires instead of large steel bars as in reinforced concrete.

prestriction, *pri-strik'shən*, *n.* blindness: blind-folding. [L. *praestrictiō*, -*ōnis*—*praestringēre*, to draw tight.]

presume, *pri-zūm'*, *v.t.* to take as true without examination or proof: to take for granted: to assume provisionally: to take upon oneself, esp. with over-boldness.—*v.i.* to venture beyond what one has ground for: to act forwardly or without proper right: to rely, count (with *on, upon*), esp. unduly.—*adj.* **presūm'able,** that may be presumed or supposed to be true.—*adv.* **presūm'ably.**—*n.* **presūm'er.**—*adj.* **presūm'ing,** venturing without permission: unreasonably bold. — *adv.* **presūm'ingly.**—*n.* **presumption** (-*zum'shən*, -*zump'shən*), act of presuming: supposition: strong probability: that which is taken for granted: confidence grounded on something not proved: conduct going beyond proper bounds: (*law*) an assumption of a fact from known facts: an assumption made failing proof to the contrary. —*adj.* **presumptive** (-*zump'*, -*zum'tiv*), (*obs.*) presuming: grounded on probable evidence: giving grounds for presuming (see heir for **heir-presumptive**). — *adv.* **presump'tively.** — *adj.* **presumptuous** (-*zump'tū-əs*, or -*zum'*), presuming.— *adv.* **presump'tuously.**—*n.* **presump'tuousness.** [L. *praesūmĕre*, -*sūmptum*—*prae*, *sūmĕre*, to take—*sub*, under, *emĕre*, to buy.]

presuppose, *prē-sə-pōz'*, *v.t.* to assume or take for granted: to involve as a necessary antecedent.—*n.* **presupposition** (*prē-sup-ə-zish'ən*).

presurmise, *prē-sər-mīz'*, *n.* (*Shak.*) a surmise previously formed.

pretend, *pri-tend'*, *v.t.* (*Spens.*) to stretch forth, or in front: (*obs.*) to offer: to profess, now only falsely: to feign: (*obs.*) to claim: (*obs.*) to allege: to allege falsely: to make believe: (*obs.*) to purpose: to venture, attempt, undertake: (*obs.*) to indicate.—*v.i.* (*obs.*) to reach or go forward: (*obs.*) to be a claimant: to aspire: to be a suitor: to make a claim: to feign: to make believe.—*n.* **pretence'** (in American spelling **pretense'**), an act of pretending: something pretended: an allegation: an aim, purpose: the thing aimed at: appearance or show to hide reality: false show: a false allegation: a sham: pretentiousness: a pretext: claim.—*adj.* **pretence'less,** without a pretext.—*n.* **pretend'ant** (or -ent), a claimant: a suitor: a pretender.— *adj.* **pretend'ded.** — *adv.* **preten'dedly.**—*ns.* **preten'der,** a claimant, esp. to a throne: a candidate: (*obs.*) a suitor: one who pretends; **preten'dership.**—*adv.* **preten'dingly.** — *n.* **preten'sion,** pretence: show: pretext: claim: aspiration, esp. to marriage: pretentiousness.—*adj.* **preten'tious** (-*shəs*), overassuming: seeming to claim much, or too much. —*adv.* **preten'tiously.**—*n.* **preten'tiousness.** [L. *praetendĕre*—*prae*, *tendĕre*, *tentum*, *tēnsum*, to stretch.]

preter-, praeter-, *prē'tər-*, *pfx.* beyond. [L. *praeter*.]

preterhuman, *prē-tər-hū'mən*, *adj.* more than human.

preterite, *pret'ə-rit*, *adj.* past.—*n.* the past tense: a word in the past tense: a form of the past tense. —*ns.* **pret'erist,** one who holds the prophecies of the Apocalypse already fulfilled; **pret'eriteness; preterition** (*prē-tə-rish'ən*), the act of passing over: omission of mention in a will: (*rhet.*) paraleipsis: the doctrine that God passes over the non-elect in electing to eternal life.—*adjs.* **preteritive** (*pri-ter'i-tiv*), used only in the preterite; **preter'ito-pres'ent, -presen'tial, pret'erite-pres'ent,** having an original preterite still preterite in form but present in meaning. [L. *praeteritus*—*īre*, *ītum*, to go.]

pretermit, *prē-tər-mit'*, *v.t.* to pass by: to omit: to leave undone: to desist from for a time:—*pr.p.* **pretermitt'ing;** *pa.t.* and *pa.p.* **pretermitt'ed.**—*n.* **pretermission** (-*mish'ən*). [L. *praetermittĕre*, -*missum*—*mittĕre*, to send.]

preternatural, *prē-tər-nat'yə-rəl*, *adj.* out of the ordinary course of nature: abnormal: supernatural.—*n.* **preternat'uralism,** belief in the preternatural: preternatural character or event.— *adv.* **preternat'urally.**—*n.* **preternat'uralness.**

preterperfect, *prē-tər-pər'fikt*, *adj.* (old gram.) perfect.

preterpluperfect, *prē-tər-plōō-pər'fikt*, *adj.* (*gram.*) pluperfect: (*facet.*) beyond the more than perfect.

pretext, *prē'tekst*, *n.* an ostensible motive or reason, put forward as excuse or to conceal the true one. [L. *praetextus*, *-ūs*, pretext, outward show, *praetextum*, pretext—*praetexĕre*, *-textum*, to weave in front, border—*texĕre*, to weave.]

pretty, *prit'i*, *adj.* (*orig.*) tricky: ingenious: (esp. ironically) fine: commendable: neat: (*arch.* or *Scot.*) stalwart: pleasing in a moderate way but not deeply: having some superficial attractiveness but not striking beauty: beautiful without dignity: insipidly graceful: considerable.—*n.* a pretty thing or person: a knick-knack: the fairway of a golf-course: the fluted part of a glass.—*adv.* fairly: (*coll.* or *illit.*) prettily.—*n.* **prettifica'-tion.**—*v.t.* **prett'ify**, to trick out in an excessively ornamental or namby-pamby way.—*adv.* **prett'ily**, in a pretty manner: pleasingly: elegantly: neatly.—*n.* **prett'iness**, the quality of being pretty: an instance of the quality: a prettyism. —*adj.* **prett'yish**, somewhat pretty.—*ns.* **prett'y-ism**, trivial daintiness of style or an instance of it; **pretty-prett'iness**; **pretty-pretty**, (*coll.*) a knick-knack.—*adj.* namby-pamby.—*adj.* **pretty-spoken**, speaking or spoken prettily.—**a pretty penny**, a good large sum; **only pretty Fanny's way**, only what must be expected and accepted of the person (*T. Parnell*); **pretty much**, very nearly; **sitting pretty**, in an advantageous position. [O.E. *prættig*, tricky—*prætt*, trickery. The origin of the word is unknown.]

prevail, *pri-vāl'*, *v.i.* (*obs.*) to gain strength: to gain the victory: to succeed: to have the upper hand: to urge successfully (with *on* or *upon*): to be usual or most usual: to hold good, be in use, be customary.—*v.t.* (*obs.*) avail: (*obs.*) to persuade.—*adj.* **prevail'ing**, having great power: controlling: bringing about results: very general or common.—*adv.* **prevail'ingly.**—*ns.* **prevail'-ment**, (*Shak.*) power of overcoming; **prevalence** (*prev'ə-ləns*), **prev'alency**, the state of being prevalent or wide-spread: superior strength or influence: preponderance: effective influence.— *adj.* **prev'alent**, prevailing: having great power: victorious: wide-spread: most common.—*adv.* **prev'alently.** [L. *praevalēre*—*prae*, *valēre*, to be powerful.]

prevaricate, *pri-var'i-kāt*, *v.i.* (*obs.*) to deviate: to shift about from side to side: to evade the truth: to quibble: (*obs.*) to undertake a thing with the purpose of defeating or destroying it: (*law*) to betray a client by collusion with his opponent.— *v.t.* (*obs.*) to pervert, transgress.—*ns.* **prevarica'-tion**; **prevar'icator**, one who prevaricates: formerly in Cambridge University a satirical orator at Commencement. [L. *praevāricārī*, *-ātus*, to walk straddlingly or crookedly, to act collusively— *prae*, *vāricus*, straddling—*vārus*, bent.]

prevent, *pri-vent'*, *v.t.* (*obs.*) to precede: (*obs.*) to be, go, or act earlier than: (*obs.*) to go faster than: to anticipate, forestall: to satisfy in advance: to meet or provide for in advance: to balk: to preclude: to stop, keep, or hinder effectually: to keep from coming to pass.—*n.* **prevenancy** (*prev'ən-ən-si*, *rare*), courteous anticipation of others' wishes.—*v.t.* **prevene** (*pri-vēn'*; *rare*), to precede: (*obs.*) to anticipate.—*n.* **preve'nience.**— *adj.* **preve'nient**, antecedent: predisposing: preventive.—*n.* **preventabil'ity.**—*adj.* **preven'table** (also **-ible**).—*ns.* **preven'ter**, one who, or that which, prevents or hinders: (*naut.*) a supplementary rope or part; **preven'tion**, act of preventing: anticipation or forethought: obstruction.—*adjs.* **preven'tive** (also, irregularly, **preven'tative**), tending to prevent or hinder: prophylactic: concerned with the prevention of smuggling.—*ns.* that which prevents: a prophylactic.—*adv.* **preven't-ively.** — *n.* **preven'tiveness.** [L. *praevenīre*, *-ventum*—*venīre*, to come.]

previous, *prē'vi-əs*, *adj.* going before in time: former: (*facet.*) premature.—*adv.* previously (usu. with *to*).—*adv.* **prē'viously.**—*n.* **prē'viousness.** —**previous examination**, the Little-go at Cambridge; **previous question**, in parliament, a motion 'that the question be not now put.' If the decision be 'ay,' the debate is ended without a vote on the main issue. In public meetings **the** carrying of the 'previous question' means that the meeting passes on to the next business. [L. *praevius*—*prae*, *via*, a way.]

previse, *prē-vīz'*, *v.t.* (*rare*) to foresee: to forewarn.—*n.* **prevision** (*-vizh'ən*), foresight: foreknowledge.—*v.t.* to endow with prevision.—*adj.* **provisional** (*-vizh'ən-əl*). [L. *praevidēre*, *-vīsum* —*prae*, *vidēre*, to see.]

prewyn, a Shakespearian form of **prune** (fruit).

prex, *preks*, *n.* in U.S. college slang the president of a college.—Also **prex'y.**

prey, *prā*, *n.* booty, plunder: (*B.*) that which is preserved from loss in battle, as one's own life: an animal that is, or may be, killed and eaten by another: a victim: depredation: (*Spens.*, *Shak.*) the act of seizing.—*v.i.* (commonly with *on* or *upon*) to make depredations: to take plunder: to seek, kill, and feed: to live (*on*) as a victim: to waste, eat away, distress.—*v.t.* (*Spens.*) to plunder.—*adj.* **prey'ful**, (*Shak.*) bent upon prey. —**beast**, **bird**, **of prey**, one that devours other animals, esp. higher animals—applied usually to the Carnivora and Falconiformes. [O.Fr. *preie* (Fr. *proie*)—L. *praeda*, booty.]

prial, *prī'əl.* Same as **pair-royal.**

Priapus, *prī-ā'pəs*, *n.* an ancient deity personifying male generative power, guardian of gardens.— *adjs.* **Priapean** (*prī-ə-pē'ən*), **Priapic** (*-ap'ik*).— *n.* **pri'apism**, persistent erection of the penis. [Latinised from Gr. *Priāpos.*]

pribble, *prib'l*, *n.* a modification of **prabble**, usu. coupled with it.—Also **pribb'le-prabb'le.**

price, *prīs* (also sometimes in Spens. **prise**, *prīs*, *prīz*), *n.* the amount, usually in money, for which a thing is sold or offered: that which one forgoes or suffers for the sake of or in gaining something: money offered for capture or killing of anybody: that for which one can be bribed: betting odds: (*arch.*) value: (also **prize**; *Spens.*, *Shak.*) valuation.—*v.t.* to fix, state, or mark the price of: (*coll.*) to ask the price of: (*Spens.*) to pay the price of: (*Shak.*) to prize, value.—*ns.* **price'-curr'ent** (often in *pl.*, **pric'es-curr'ent**), a list of prevailing prices at any time: a list of the prices paid for any class of goods, &c.; **price'-cutting**, lowering of prices to secure custom.—*adjs.* **priced**, having a price assigned: valued at such-and-such a price; **price'less**, beyond price, invaluable: (*slang*) supremely and delectably absurd.—*ns.* **price'lessness**; **price'-list**, a list of prices of goods offered for sale.—**above**, **beyond price**, so valuable that no price can or would be enough; **at a price**, at a somewhat high price; **in great price**, in high estimation; **of price**, of great value; **price of money**, the rate of discount in lending or borrowing capital; **price on one's head**, a reward offered for one's capture or slaughter; **what price**—?, what about (this or that) now?: what do you think of?; **without price**, priceless: without anything to pay. [O.Fr. *pris* (Fr. *prix*)—L. *pretium*, price; cf. **praise**, **prize**.]

prick, *prik*, *n.* anything sharp and piercing, as a thorn, spine, goad: the act, experience, or stimulus of piercing or puncturing: a puncture: a mark or wound made by puncturing: (*obs.*) a note in written music: (*Shak.*) a graduation on a dial: (*obs.*) a dot: a point of space or time: (*Shak.*) an hour-point on a clock: (*Spens.*) point, pitch: the centre of an archery target: a mark or target: a hare's footprint:—*v.t.* to pierce slightly with a fine point: to give a feeling as of pricking: to make by puncturing: to urge with, or as with, a spur or goad: to write out in musical notation: to indicate with a prick or dot, to tick off, hence select: to trace with pricks: to pin: to pick with a point: to insert in small holes: to stick, stick over: to erect, cock, stick up: (*fig.*) to incite: to deck out: to pain.—*v.i.* to pierce, make punctures: to seek insensitive spots by sticking pins in a suspected witch: to have a sensation of puncture or prickling: to begin to turn sour: to stand erect: to ride with spurs, or quickly.—*adj.* **prick'-eared**, having erect or noticeable ears.—*ns.* **prick'er**, a piercing instrument : a witch-finder : a light-horseman : a priming wire ; **prick'ing** ; **prickle** (*prik'l*), a little prick : a sharp point growing from the epidermis of a plant or from the skin of an animal.—*v.t.* and *v.i.* to prick slightly.—*v.i.* to have a prickly feeling. — *ns.* **prick'le-back**, the stickle-back ; **prick'liness**. — *n.* and *adj.* **prick'ling**. — *adj.* **prick'ly**, full of prickles : tingling as if prickled. —*ns.* **prick'ly-ash**, the toothache-tree (Xanthoxylum) ; **prick'ly-heat**, a skin disease, inflammation of the sweat-glands with intense irritation ; **prick'ly-pear**, a cactaceous genus (Opuntia) with clusters of prickles : its pear-shaped fruit ; **prick'-me-dain'ty**, (*Scot.*) an affected person.—*adj.* overprecise.—*ns.* **prick'-song**, (*Shak.*) written music : descant ; **prick'-spur**, a spur with one point ; **prick'-the-gar'ter**, fast-and-loose ; **prick'-(the)-louse**, (*Scot.*) a tailor.—**prick up one's ears**, begin to listen intently. [O.E. *prica*, point ; cf. Du. *prik*.]

pricket, *prik'it*, *n.* (*Shak.*) a fallow deer buck in his second year, with straight unbranched antlers : a spike serving as a candlestick. [**prick.**]

pride, *prīd*, *n.* state or feeling of being proud : too great self-esteem : haughtiness : a proper sense of what is becoming to oneself and scorn of what is unworthy : a feeling of pleasure on account of something worthily done or anything connected with oneself : that of which one is proud : splendour : magnificence : beauty displayed : ostentation : a peacock's attitude of display : exuberance : prime : high spirit, mettle : (*Shak.*) sexual excitement in a female animal : a company of lions.—*v.t.* to make proud : (*refl.*) to take pride to.—*adj.* **pride'ful**.—*adv.* **pride'fully**.—*n.* **pride'-fulness**.—*adj.* **pride'less**.—**pride of place**, culmination of an eagle's or hawk's flight : distinction of holding the highest position (see **place**) ; **take a pride in**, make a thing an object in which one's pride is concerned. [O.E. *prýde*, *prýte—prúd*, *prút*, proud.]

pridian, *prid'i-ən*, *adj.* pertaining to yesterday. [L. *prīdiānus—pridiē*—stem of *prius*, before, *diēs*, day.]

pried, prier, pries. See **pry.**

prie-dieu, *prē'dyə'*, *n.* a praying-desk or chair for praying on. [Fr., pray-God.]

prief, priefe, *prēf*, *n.* (Spens. ; *Scot.*). See **proof.** —*v.t.* **prieve.** See **prove.**

priest, *prēst*, *n.* an official conductor of religious rites : a mediator between a god and worshippers (*fem.* **priest'ess**) : a minister above a deacon and below a bishop : a clergyman : a club or mallet for killing fish.—*ns.* **priest'craft**, priestly policy, trickery, or deception ; **priest'hood**, the office or character of a priest : the priestly order ; **priest'-king**, a king with priestly functions.— *adjs.* **priest'-like** ; **priest'ly**, pertaining to or like a priest.—*ns.* **priest'liness** ; **priest'ling**, a contemptible priest.—*adjs.* **priest'-rid** , **-ridden**, dominated by priests, — *n.* **priest'ship**. — **high priest**, a chief priest ; **priest's hole**, a secret room for a priest in time of persecution or repression. [O.E. *préost*—L. *presbyter*—Gr. *presbyteros*, an elder.]

prig, *prig*, *n.* (rogues' cant ; *obs.*) a tinker : (*slang*) Shak.) a thief.—*v.t.* to filch.—*ns.* **prigg'er**, a thief ; **prigg'ing** ; **prigg'ism.** [Origin unknown.]

prig, *prig*, *v.i.* (*Scot.*) to entreat : to importune : to haggle.—**prig down**, to seek to beat down (a price or the seller). [Origin unknown.]

prig, *prig*, *n.* (*obs.*) a coxcomb : a precisian : a person of precise morals without a sense of proportion. — *n.* **prigg'ery** — *adj.* **prigg'ish.** — *adv.* **prigg'ishly.**—*ns.* **prigg'ishness, prigg'ism.** [Origin unknown.]

prim, *prim*, *adj.* exact and precise : stiffly formal. —*v.t.* to deck with great nicety : to form, set, or purse into primness.—*v.i.* to look prim : to prim the mouth :—*pr.p.* **primm'ing** ; *pa.t.* and *pa.p.* **primmed.**—*adv.* **prim'ly.**—*n.* **prim'ness.** [Late 17th-cent. cant.]

prima. See **primo.**

primacy, *prī'mə-si*, *n.* the position of first : the chief place : the office or dignity of a primate.

prima donna, *prē'mä don'(n)ä*, *n.* the leading lady in opera :—*pl.* **pri'ma donn'as, prime donne** (*prē'mä don'nā*). [It.,—L. *prima domina*.]

primaeval. Same as **primeval.**

primage, *prīm'ij*, *n.* a payment, in addition to freight, made by shippers for loading, originally a gratuity to captain and crew, afterwards made to owners. [Anglo-L. *primāgium*.]

primary, *prī'mə-ri*, *adj.* first : original : of the first order (e.g. in a system of successive branchings) : first - formed : primitive : chief : elementary : fundamental : belonging to the first stages of education, elementary : of a feather, growing on the manus : (*U.S.*) relating to primaries : **Primary**, (*geol.*) Palaeozoic (but orig. applied to rocks supposed to be older than any fossiliferous strata). —*n.* that which is highest in rank or importance, a planet in relation to its satellites : a primary coil : a primary feather : a substance obtained directly, by extraction and purification, from natural, or crude technical, raw material—cf. intermediate : (*American politics*) a meeting of the voters of a political party in an electoral division to nominate candidates, or to elect delegates to a nominating convention representing a larger area : an election (also **primary election**) by local members of a party of candidates to be nominated for election, or of delegates to nominate them. — *adv.* **pri'marily.** — *n.* **pri'mariness.** — **primary assembly**, in U.S. politics, a primary ; **primary battery, cell**, one producing an electric current by irreversible chemical action ; **primary coil**, one carrying an inducing current ; **primary colours**, those from which all others can be derived—physiologically red, green, violet, or blue, for pigments red, yellow, blue : also red, orange, yellow, green, blue, indigo, and violet ; **primary planet**, a planet distinguished from a satellite. [L. *primārius—primus*, first.]

primate, *prī'māt*, *-mit*, *n.* one who is first : (*R.C. Church*) a bishop or archbishop to whose see was formerly annexed the dignity of vicar of the holy see : (*Ch. of Eng.*) an archbishop over a province : (*zool.*) a member of the order Primates. —*adj.* **prima'tal.**—*n.pl.* **Primates** (*prī-mā'tēz*), the highest order of mammals, including lemurs, monkeys, anthropoid apes, and man.—*n.* **pri'mateship.**—*adjs.* **prima'tial** (*-shl*), **primatic** (*-mat'ik*), **-al.** [L.L. *primās, -ātis*—L. *primus*, first.]

prime, *prīm*, *adj.* first in order of time, rank, or importance : primary : chief : main : of the highest quality : original : (*Shak.*) in sexual excitement : (*arith.*) divisible by no whole number except unity and itself : having no common integral factor but unity.—*n.* the first of the lesser hours of the Roman breviary : the time of this office, about six in the morning, or sometimes sunrise : the time from the beginning of the artificial day to terce (about nine) : the beginning : the spring : the world's youth : (*obs.*) the new moon, or its first appearance : the best part : the height of perfection : full health and strength : a prime number : a first subdivision or a symbol marking it (′) : a fundamental tone : an old card-game, probably the same as primero : (*fencing*) the first guard against sword-thrusts, also the first and simplest thrust.—*adj.* **prī'mal**, first : original : chief.—*n.* **primal'ity.**—*adv.* **prime'ly.**—*n.* **prime'ness.** — *adj.* **prim'y**, (*Shak.*) in prime, blooming.—**prime cost** (see **cost**) ; **prime meridian**, that chosen as zero for reference ; **prime minister**, the chief minister of state ; **prime mover**, in mediaeval astronomy, the primum mobile : a natural source of energy : a machine that transforms energy from such a source into motive power ; **prime number**, one divisible only by itself or unity ; **prime vertical**, a great celestial circle passing through the east and west points of the horizon, and cutting the meridian at right angles at the zenith. [L. *primus*, first ; partly through O.E. *prīm*—L. *prīma* (*hōra*), first (hour).]

prime, *prīm*, *v.t.* to charge, fill : to supply with powder or other means of igniting the charge (of a firearm) : to lay a train to : to bring into activity or working order by a preliminary charge (as a man by giving him liquor, a pump by pouring in water, an internal-combustion engine by injecting gas or oil): to post up, coach, cram beforehand with information or instructions: to prepare for painting by laying on a first coat of paint or oil, &c.: (*obs.*) to make up with cosmetics.—*v.i.* to prime a gun: (of a boiler) to send water with the steam into the cylinder: (of the tides) to recur at progressively shorter intervals.—*ns.* **prī′mer,** one who primes: a priming-wire: a detonator; **prī′ming,** the action of the verb in any sense: the progressive shortening of the interval between tides as spring tide approaches: a detonating charge that fires a propellant charge: a tube for priming an internal-combustion engine: a priming-wire: a first coat of paint; **prī′ming-iron, -wire,** a wire passed through the touch-hole of a cannon to clear it and pierce the cartridge; **prī′ming-pow′der,** detonating powder: a train of powder. [Etymology obscure.]

primer, *prī′mər,* or *prim′ər, n.* a small book of hours or prayer book for laymen, used also for teaching reading: a first reading-book: an elementary introduction to any subject: (*prim′ər*) printing type of two sizes, **long primer** (10-point) and **great primer** (18-point). [L. *prīmārius,* primary.]

primero, *pri-mā′rō, n.* an old card-game. [Sp. *primera.*]

primeval, primaeval, *prī-mē′vl, adj.* belonging to the first ages. [L. *primaevus—prīmus,* first, *aevum,* an age.]

primigenial, *prī-mi-jē′ni-əl, adj.* first made: original: primal—wrongly **primoge′nial.** [L. *primigenius—prīmus,* first, *genus,* kind.]

primigravida, *prī-mi-grav′i-dä, n.* a woman pregnant for the first time:—*pl.* **primigrav′idae** (-*dē*). [L. fem. adjs. *prīma,* first, *gravida,* pregnant.]

primine, *prī′min, n.* the outer (rarely the inner or first formed) coat of an ovule. [L. *prīmus,* first.]

primipara, *prī-mip′ə-rä, n.* a woman who has given birth to a child for the first time only, or is about to do so.—*adj.* **primip′arous.** [L. *prīma* (fem.), first, *parĕre,* to bring forth.]

primitiae, *pri-mish′i-ē, n.pl.* first-fruits: the first year's revenue of a benefice—also **primi′tias** (*Spens.*).—*adj.* **primitial** (-*mish′l*), of first-fruits: (loosely) primeval, original. [L. *prīmitiae—prīmus,* first.]

primitive, *prim′i-tiv, adj.* belonging to the beginning, or to the first times: original: ancient: antiquated, old-fashioned: crude: not derivative: fundamental: (*biol.*) first-formed, of early origin: (*old geol.*) of the earliest formation.—*n.* that from which other things are derived: a rootword: a Primitive Methodist: a painter or picture of pre-Renaissance date or manner.—*adv.* **prim′itively.** — *ns.* **prim′itiveness; prim′itivism,** approbation of primitive ways, primitive Christianity, primitive art, &c.: Primitive Methodism. —**Primitive Methodist,** a member of a religious body (Primitive Methodist Connexion) founded in 1810, united with the Wesleyan Methodists and United Methodists in 1932. [L. *prīmitīvus,* an extension of *prīmus.*]

primo, *prē′mō, n.* (*mus.*) the first or principal part. —*adj.* first:—*fem.* **prī′ma.** [It.,—L. *prīmus.*]

primogenit, *prī-mō-jen′it, adj.* and *n.* (*obs.*) first-born. — *adjs.* **primogen′ital; primogen′itary; primogen′itive.—n.** (*Shak.*) primogeniture.—*ns.* **primogen′itor,** earliest ancestor: forefather:—*fem.* **primogen′itrix; primogen′iture,** the state or fact of being first-born: inheritance by or of the first-born child or (*male primogeniture*) son; **primogen′itureship** (*rare*). [L. *prīmōgenitus—prīmō,* first (adv.), *genitus,* born, *genitor,* begetter.]

primordial, *prī-mor′di-əl, adj.* existing from the beginning: original: rudimentary: first-formed. —*n.* first principle or element.—*ns.* **primor′dialism; primordiality** (-*al′i-ti*).—*adv.* **primor′dially.—n.** **primor′dium,** the primitive source: the first discernible rudiment. [L. *prīmordium—prīmus,* first, *ordīrī,* to begin.]

primrose, *prim′rōz, n.* a plant (*Primula vulgaris*), or its flower, common in spring in woods and meadows: extended to others of the genus Primula: formerly some other (and brighter) flower: (*her.*) a conventionalised flower, sometimes four-petalled: (*Spens.*) the choicest.—*adj.* pale yellow, like a primrose.—*v.i.* to go gathering primroses.—*adjs.* **prim′rosed; prim′rosy.—evening primrose** (see **evening**); **Primrose League,** an association for Conservative propaganda—formed in 1883 in memory of Lord Beaconsfield, named from his supposed favourite flower; **primrose path, way** (both *Shak.*), the life of pleasure; **primrose peerless,** the two-flowered daffodil. [O.Fr. *primerose,* as if—L. *prima rosa;* perh. really through M.E. and O.Fr. *primerole*—L.L. *prīmula—prīmus,* first.]

primsie, *prim′zi, adj.* (*Scot.*) prim, demure. [prim.]

Primula, *prim′ū-lä, n.* the primrose genus, giving name to the dicotyledonous family **Primulā′ceae,** including pimpernel, water-violet, cyclamen, &c. —*adj.* **primulā′ceous.—n.** **prim′uline** (-*lēn*), a yellow dye got from coal-tar. [L.L. *prīmula*— L. *prīmus,* first.]

primum mobile, *prī′məm mōb′* or *mob′i-lē* (L. *prē′moom mō′bi-lä*), in mediaeval astronomy the outermost of the revolving spheres of the universe, carrying the others round in 24 hours: any great source of motion. [L. *prīmum mōbile.*]

primus, *prī′məs* (L. *prē′moos*), *n.* the presiding bishop in the Scottish Episcopal Church, without metropolitan authority.—*adj.* (in boys' schools) senior. [L. *prīmus,* first.]

primy. See under **prime** (1).

prince, *prins, n.* one of the highest rank: (*obs.* or *arch.*) a king or queen: a sovereign (of some small countries): a male member of a royal or imperial family: a title of nobility, as formerly in Germany (*Fürst*): a chief: anybody or anything that is first in merit or demerit, or most outstanding.—*v.t.* (with *it*) to play the prince.—*ns.* **prince′-bish′op,** a bishop ranking as prince or having the power of prince of his diocese; **prince′-con′sort,** a prince who is husband of a reigning queen; **prince′dom,** a principality: the estate, jurisdiction, sovereignty, or rank of a prince; **prince′hood,** rank or quality of a prince; **prince′-impē′rial,** the eldest son of an emperor; **prince′-kin,** a little or young prince; **prince′let, prince′ling,** a petty prince.—*adj.* **prince′like,** like a prince: becoming a prince.—*n.* **prince′liness.—** *adj.* **prince′ly,** of a prince or princess: of the rank of prince: princelike: becoming a prince: magnificent: sumptuous: lavish. — Also *adv.* — *n.* **prin′cess** (or -*ses′*), *fem.* of **prince:** a prince's wife (of recognised rank): a size of roofing slate, 24 by 14 inches: a woman's garment with skirt and bodice in one piece (in this sense also (*Fr.*) **princesse** (*prin′,* or -*ses′*)).—*adv.* **prin′cessly,** like a princess. — *n.* **prin′cess-roy′al,** the eldest daughter of a sovereign.—*adj.* **prin′cified,** ridiculously dignified.—**prince of darkness, prince of this world,** Satan; **Prince of Peace,** Christ: the Messiah; **Prince of Wales,** the eldest son of the English sovereign; **Prince Rupert's drops** (see **drop**); **prince's feather,** a tall showy Amaranthus with spikes of rose-coloured flowers: London pride: applied also to various other plants; **prince's metal,** a gold-like alloy of copper and zinc, with more zinc than in brass, attributed to Prince Rupert. [Fr.,—L. *prīnceps—prīmus,* first, *capĕre,* to take.]

principal, *prin′si-pl, adj.* taking the first place: highest in rank, character, or importance: chief: of the nature of principal or a principal.—*n.* a principal person: the head of a college or university, or sometimes of a school: one who takes a leading part: money on which interest is paid: a main beam, rafter, girder, or timber: a roof-truss: the structural framework of a roof: (*law*) the person who commits a crime, or one who aids and abets him in doing it: a person for whom another becomes surety: a person who, being *sui juris,* employs another to do an act which he is competent himself to do: one who fights a duel: (*mus.*) an organ-stop like the open diapason but an octave higher.—*n.* **principality** (-*pal′i-ti*), status, dignity, or power of a prince: condition of being a prince: the territory of a prince or the country that gives him title: a member of one of the orders of angels.—*adv.* **prin'cipally.**—*ns.* **prin'cipalness,** the state of being principal or chief; **prin'cipalship,** position of a principal. —**the Principality,** Wales. [L. *prīncipālis*—*prīnceps, -ipis,* chief.]

principate, *prin'si-pāt, n.* princehood: principality: the Roman empire in its earlier form in which something of republican theory survived. [L. *prīncipātus*—the emperor's title *prīnceps* (*cīvitātis*), chief (of the city or state).]

principium, *prin-sip'i-əm* (L. *pring-kip'i-oom*), *n.* the general's quarters in a Roman camp: a beginning: a first principle: an element:—*pl.* **princip'ia.**—*adj.* **princip'ial,** elementary. [L. *prīncipium.*]

principle, *prin'si-pl, n.* (*obs.*) a beginning: a source, root, origin: that which is fundamental: essential nature: theoretical basis: a faculty of the mind: a source of action: a fundamental truth on which others are founded or from which they spring: a law or doctrine from which others are derived: a settled rule of action: consistent regulation of behaviour according to moral law: a component: (*chem.*) a constituent part from which some quality is derived: (*Milt.*) a motive appliance or force.—*v.t.* to establish in principles: to impress with a doctrine.—*adj.* **prin'cipled,** holding certain principles: having, or behaving in accordance with, good principles: invoking or founded on a principle.—**first principles,** fundamental principles, not deduced from others; **in principle,** so far as general character or theory is concerned, without respect to details or particular application; **on principle,** on grounds of principle: for the sake of obeying or asserting a principle; **principle of contradiction,** the logical principle that a thing cannot both be and not be; **principle of excluded middle,** (*log.*) the principle that a thing must be either one thing or its contradictory; **principle of sufficient reason** (see **reason**). [L. *prīncipium,* beginning—*prīnceps.*]

princox, *prin(g)'koks, n.* (*Shak.*) a conceited fellow: a coxcomb: a jocular, grotesque, or ironical endearment.—Also **prin'cock** (-*kok*). [Origin obscure.]

prink, *pringk, v.t.* and *v.i.* to deck up, smarten. [App. conn. with **prank** (2).]

print, *print, n.* an impression: a mould or stamp: a moulded pat of butter: (*arch.*) exactitude of plaiting, crimping, or setting (a ruff, hair, &c.): (*arch.*) exactitude: printed state: printed characters or lettering: an edition: a printed copy: a printed picture: an engraving: a newspaper: a positive photograph made from a negative (or negative from positive): a printed cloth, esp. calico stamped with figures: (*archit.*) a plastercast in low relief.—*adj.* (*obs.*) printed: of printed cotton.—*v.t.* to press in: to impress: to mark by pressure: to impress on paper, &c., by means of types, plates, or blocks: to produce or reproduce by such means: to cause to be so printed: to stamp a pattern on or transfer it to: (*phot.*) to produce as a positive picture from a negative, or as a negative from a positive: to write in imitation of type: (*Shak.*) to express in writing: (*Milt.*) to designate in print.—*v.i.* to practise the art of printing: to publish a book: to yield an impression, or give a positive, &c.—*adj.* **print'able,** capable of being printed: fit to print.—*ns.* **print'er,** one who, or that which, prints: one who is employed in printing books, &c.: a device for printing, as telegraph messages, photographs, &c.: a cotton cloth made for printing; **print'ing,** act, art, or business of the printer: the whole number of copies printed at one time, an impression; **print'ing-house,** a building where printing is carried on: a printing-office; **print'ing-ink,** ink used in printing; **print'ing-machine,** a printing-press worked by power; **print'ing-office,** an establishment where books, &c., are printed; **print'ing-paper,** a paper suitable for printing purposes; **print'ing-press,** a machine by which impressions are taken in ink upon paper from types, plates, &c.—*adj.* **print'less,** receiving or

leaving no impression.—*ns.* **print'-seller,** one who sells prints or engravings; **print'-shop,** a printseller's shop; **print'-works,** an establishment where cloth is printed.—**in print,** (*obs.*) in exact order, formally set, crimped, or plaited: existing in printed form: printed and still to be had (opp. to *out of print*); **printer's devil** (see **devil**); **printer's ink,** printing-ink; **printer's mark,** an engraved device used by printers as a trademark. [M.E. *print, prente,* &c.—O.Fr. *preinte, priente*—*preindre, priembre*—L. *premère,* to press.]

prior, *prī'ər, adj.* previous.—*adv.* previously (with *to*).—*n.* the officer next under the abbot in an abbey (*claustral prior*): the head of a priory of monks (*conventual prior*) or of a house of canons regular or of friars: in Italy formerly a magistrate:—*fem.* **pri'oress.**—*ns.* **pri'orate,** rank or term of office of a prior or prioress: a priory; **priority** (*prī-or'i-ti*), state of being first in time, place, or rank: preference: the privilege of preferential treatment. — *adj.* having, entitling to, or allowed to those who have, priority.—*ns.* **pri'orship;** **pri'ory,** a convent of either sex subject to an abbey.—**grand priory,** a province of the Knights of St John, under a *grand prior.* [L. *prior, -ōris,* former.]

prisage, *prī'zij, n.* the former right of the English kings to two tuns of wine from every ship importing twenty tuns or more. [O.Fr. *prise,* taking.]

Priscianist, *prish'(y)ən-ist, n.* a grammarian.—**break Priscian's head,** to commit false grammar. [*Priscianus,* Latin grammarian (fl. *c.* 500 A.D.).]

prise, priser. See **price, prize.**

prism, *prizm, n.* (*geom.*) a solid whose ends are similar, equal, and parallel polygons, and whose sides are parallelograms: an object of that shape, esp. a triangular prism of glass or the like for resolving light into separate colours: (*crystal.*) a crystal form of three or more faces parallel to an axis: (loosely) prismatic colours or spectrum. —*adjs.* **prismat'ic, -al,** resembling or pertaining to a prism: built up of prisms: separated or formed by a prism.—*adv.* **prismat'ically.**—*n.* **pris'moid,** a figure like a prism, but with similar unequal ends.—*adjs.* **pris'moidal; pris'my,** prismatic in colour.—**prismatic colours,** the seven colours into which a ray of white light is refracted by a prism—red, orange, yellow, green, blue, indigo, and violet; **prismatic compass,** a surveying instrument which by means of a prism enables the compass-reading to be taken as the object is sighted; **prismatic powder,** pebblepowder. [Gr. *prisma, -atos,* a piece sawn off, sawdust, a prism—*priein,* to saw.]

prison, *priz'n, n.* a building for the confinement of criminals or others: a jail: any place of confinement: confinement.—*v.t.* to shut in prison: to enclose: to restrain.—*n.pl.* **pris'on-bars',** the bars of a prison window, door, &c.: whatever confines or restrains: prisoners'-base.—*ns.* **pris'on-breaker,** one who escapes out of prison; **pris'on-breaking; pris'on-crop,** hair cut very short; **pris'on-door'; pris'oner,** one under arrest or confined in prison: a captive, esp. in war; **pris'oners'-** (or **prisoner's-**) **base,** a game in which those caught are held as prisoners (app. for *prison-bars*); **pris'on-house,** a prison or prison building; **pris'onment,** (*Shak.*) imprisonment, confinement.—*adj.* **pris'onous** (*Dickens*). — *ns.* **pris'on-ship'; pris'on-van,** a closed conveyance for carrying prisoners. [O.Fr. *prisun*—L. *prēnsiō, -ōnis,* for *praehēnsiō,* seizure—*praehendĕre, -hēnsum,* to seize.]

pristine, *pris'tīn, adj.* original: former: belonging to the earliest time. [L. *prīstinus;* cf. *priscus,* antique, *prior,* former.]

prithee, prythee, *pridh'ē, -i, interj.* for (I) pray thee.

prittle-prattle, *prit'l-prat'l, n.* empty talk. [**prattle.**]

privacy, *priv'ə-si,* or *priv' n.* seclusion: a place of seclusion: retreat: retirement: avoidance of notice or display: secrecy: a private matter. [**private.**]

privado, *pri-vä'dō, n.* (*obs.*) a private friend, esp. of a prince. [Sp.,—L. *prīvātus,* private.]

privat dozent, *prē-vät' dō-tsent', n.* in German universities, a recognised teacher not a member of the salaried staff. [Ger.,—L. *prīvātus*, private, *docēns, -entis*, teaching, *docēre*, to teach.]

private, *prī'vit*, *adj*. apart from the state: not invested with public office: (of a member of parliament) not in the ministry: (of a soldier) not an officer or non-commissioned officer: peculiar to oneself: belonging to, or concerning, an individual person or company: own: relating to personal affairs: in an unofficial capacity: not public: not open to the public: not made known generally: confidential: retired from observation: alone: (*obs.*) privy.—*n.* privacy: (*Shak., Milt.*) a private person: (in *pl.*) private parts: a common soldier: (*Shak.*) a secret message.— *adv.* **prī'vately.**—*n.* **prī'vateness** (*rare*).—**private act**, **bill**, one that deals with the concerns of private persons; **private hotel**, a term of uncertain meaning popularly understood to imply that the proprietors do not bind themselves to receive chance travellers; **private judgment**, freedom to judge for oneself, untrammelled by the interpretation of the church; **private law**, that part of law which deals with the rights and duties of persons as individuals; **private parts**, the external sexual organs; **private school**, a school run independently by an individual or a group, especially for profit; **private wrong**, an injury done to an individual in his private capacity. [L. *prīvātus*, pa.p. of *prīvāre*, to deprive, to separate.]

privateer, *prī-va-tēr'*, *n.* a private vessel commissioned to seize and plunder an enemy's ships: the commander or one of the crew of a privateer.— *v.i.* to cruise in a privateer.—*ns.* **privateer'ing**; **privateers'man.** [*privateer.*]

privation, *prī-vā'shon*, *n.* state of being deprived of something, esp. of what is necessary for comfort: (*log.*) absence of any quality. — *adj.* **privative** (*priv'a-tiv*), causing privation: consisting in the absence or removal of something: expressing absence or negation.—*n.* that which is privative or depends on the absence of something else: (*log.*) a term denoting the absence of a quality: (*gram.*) a privative prefix, affix, or word.—*adv.* **priv'atively.** [L. *prīvātiō, -ōnis, prīvātivus— prīvāre*, to deprive.]

privet, *priv'it*, *n.* a half-evergreen European shrub (*Ligustrum vulgare*) of the olive family, used for hedges. [Origin unknown.]

privilege, *priv'i-lij*, *n.* an advantage granted to or enjoyed by an individual, or a few: freedom from burdens borne by others: a happy advantage: prerogative: a sacred and vital civil right: (*Shak.*) advantage yielded: (*Shak.*) right of sanctuary.— *v.t.* to grant a privilege to: to exempt: to authorise, license.—*adj.* **priv'ileged.**—**breach of privilege**, any interference with or slight done to the rights or privileges of a legislative body; **privilege of parliament**, special rights or privileges enjoyed by members of parliament, as freedom of speech, and freedom from arrest except on a criminal charge; **question of privilege**, any question arising out of the rights of an assembly or of its members; **writ of privilege**, an order for the release of a privileged person from custody. [Fr. *privilège*—L. *privilēgium—prīvus*, private, *lex, lēgis*, a law.]

privy, *priv'i*, *adj.* (*obs.*) familiar, intimate: private: pertaining to one person: for private uses: secret: appropriated to retirement: sharing the knowledge of something secret.—*n.* (*law*) a person having an interest in an action, contract, conveyance, &c.: a latrine.—*adv.* **priv'ily**, privately: secretly.— *ns.* **priv'ity**, (*arch.*) privacy: (*arch.*) secrecy: something kept private: (*Spens.*) innermost thoughts, private counsels: knowledge, shared with another, of something private or confidential: knowledge implying concurrence: any legally recognised relation between different interests; **priv'y-cham'ber**, private apartment in a royal residence; **priv'y-coun'cil**, originally the private council of a sovereign to advise in the administration of government—its functions are now mainly formal or performed by committees, &c.; **priv'y-coun'cillor**; **priv'y-purse**, an allowance for the

private or personal use of the sovereign; **priv'y-seal**, the seal used by or for the sovereign in subordinate matters, or those not to pass the great seal.—**gentlemen of the privy-chamber**, officials in the royal household in attendance at court. [Fr. *privé*—L. *prīvātus*, private.]

prize, **prise**, *prīz*, *v.t.* to force (esp. up or open) with a lever. [Fr. *prise*, hold, grip; see **prize** (2).]

prize (*Spens., Shak.* **prise**), *prīz*, *n.* (*obs.*) seizure: that which is taken by force, or in war, esp. a ship.—*v.t.* to make a prize of.—*ns.* **prize'-court**, a court for judging regarding prizes made on the high seas; **prize'-crew**, a crew put aboard a prize to bring her to port; **prize'-money**, share of the money or proceeds from any prizes taken from an enemy. [Fr. *prise*, capture, thing captured—L. *praehēnsa—praehendere*, to seize.]

prize (*Spens., Shak.* **prise**), *prīz*, *n.* a reward or symbol of success offered or won in competition by contest or chance, or granted in recognition of excellence: anything well worth striving for: a highly valued acquisition: (*Shak.*) privilege or advantage: (*Spens.*) esteem: (*Shak.*) valuation, appraisal.—*adj.* awarded, or worthy of, a prize.— *v.t.* to set a price on: to value: to value highly: (*Spens.* **pryse**) to pay for.—*adj.* **priz'able**, valuable.—*ns.* **prize'-list**, a list of winners; **prize'-man**, a winner of a prize, esp. an academic prize; **priz'er**, (*rare*) an appraiser; **prize'-winner.** [A differentiated form of **price** and **praise**—O.Fr. *pris* (n.), *prisier* (vb.)—L. *pretium*, price.]

prize (*Spens.* **prise**), *prīz*, *n.* (*obs.*) an athletic contest: a match.—*ns.* **prize'-fight**, a public boxing-match for money; **prize'-fighter**, orig. one who fights for a prize: now, a professional pugilist; **prize'-fighting**; **priz'er**, a contestant in a prize or match; **prize'-ring**, a ring for prize-fighting: the practice itself.—**play one's** (or a) **prize**, engage in a match: sustain one's part. [Possibly from the foregoing.]

pro-, *prō-*, *Gr. pfx.* before (in time or place): in front: the front part: primitive. [Gr. prep. *pró*, before; cf. L. *prō*, Eng. **for**, **fore**.]

pro-, *prō-*, *L. pfx.* before (in place or time): forward, forth: instead of: (in new formations) in favour of—as **pro'-Boer**; **pro'-Ger'man**; **pro'-ne'gro**; **pro'-sla'very.** [L. prep. *prō*, earlier *prōd*, in comp. sometimes *prō-*; cf. preceding.]

pro, *prō*, *n.* a *coll.* contraction of **professional** (golfer, cricketer, actor, &c.) and of **probationary** (nurse):—*pl.* **pros** (*prōz*).

pro, *prō*, *n.* one who favours or votes for some proposal: a reason or argument in favour :—*pl.* **pros** (*prōz*).—*adv.* **pro and con** (L. *prō et contrā*), for and against.—*v.t. and v.i.* to consider or discuss for and against :—*pr.p.* **pro'ing and conn'ing**, **pro-and-conn'ing**; *pa.p.* **pro'd and conned**, **con'd**, **pro-and-conned'**.—*n.pl.* **pros and cons**, reasons or arguments for and against. [L. *prō*, for.]

proa, *prō'ä*. See **prau**.

proairesis, *prō-ā'ri-sis*, or *-ī'*, *n.* the act of choosing. [Gr. *proairesis*.]

probable, *prob'a-bl*, *adj.* (*orig.*, now *rare*) that can be proved: having more evidence for than against: giving ground for belief: likely: colourable, plausible.—*n.* probable opinion: one that has a good chance, or is likely to turn out or become the thing in question.—*ns.* **probabil'iorism**, the doctrine that in case of doubt one is bound to choose the more probable opinion; **probabil'iorist**; **prob'abilism**, the doctrine that of two opinions, both reasonable, one may follow one's own inclination, as a doubtful law cannot impose a certain obligation; **prob'abilist**; **probabil'ity**, quality of being probable: appearance of truth: that which is probable: chance or likelihood of something happening :—*pl.* **probabil'ities.**—*adv.* **prob'ably.**—**probable error**, a quantity assumed as the value of an error, such that the chances of the real error being greater are equal to those of it being less; **probable evidence**, evidence not conclusive, but admitting of some degree of force. [Fr.,—L. *probābilis—probāre, -ātum*, to prove.]

proball, *prō'bl*, *adj.* (*Shak.*) supposed to mean plausible. [App. a contracted form of **probable**.]

probang, *prō'bang*, *n*. an instrument for pushing obstructions down the oesophagus. [Called *provang* by its inventor, the Welsh judge, Walter Rumsey (1584-1660); origin unknown; prob. influenced by **probe**.]

probate, *prō'bāt*, *-bit*, *n*. the proof before a competent court that a written paper purporting to be the will of a person who has died is indeed his lawful act: the official copy of a will, with the certificate of its having been proved.—*adj.* relating to the establishment of wills and testaments. —*n.* **probation** (*prə-*, *prō-bā'shən*), testing: proof: a preliminary time or condition appointed to allow fitness or unfitness to appear: noviciate: suspension of sentence with liberty on good behaviour under supervision, esp. allowed to a first-offender: time of trial: moral trial.—*adjs.* **probā'tional**, relating to, or serving the purpose of, probation or trial; **probā'tionary**, probational: on probation.—*n.* a probationer.—*ns.* **probā'tioner**, one who is on probation or trial: an offender under probation: a novice: (esp. *Scot.*) one licensed to preach, but not ordained to a pastorate: **probā'tionership.**—*adjs.* **probative** (*prō'bə-tiv*), testing: affording proof; **prōbatory**, testing.— **Probate Court**, a court created in 1858 to exercise jurisdiction in matters touching the succession to personal estate in England; **probate duty**, a tax on property passing by will; **probation officer**, one appointed to advise and supervise offenders under probation. [L. *probāre*, *-ātum*, to test, prove.]

probe, *prōb*, *n*. an instrument for exploring a wound, locating a bullet, and the like: an act of probing: an exploratory bore: a prod: an investigation.— *v.t.* to examine with or as with a probe: to examine searchingly.—*v.t.* and *v.i.* to pierce.—*n.pl.* **probe'-sciss'ors**, scissors used to open wounds, the blade having a button at the end. [L. *proba*, proof, later examination—*probāre*, to prove.]

probity, *prob'i-ti*, or *prōb'*, *n*. uprightness: moral integrity. [L. *probitās*, *-ātis—probus*, good.]

problem, *prob'ləm*, *n*. a matter difficult of settlement or solution: a question or puzzle propounded for solution: (*chess*) the question how to win in so many moves beginning with a hypothetical situation: (*geom.*) a proposition in which something is required to be constructed, not merely proved as in a theorem: a source of perplexity.— *adjs.* **problemat'ic**, **-al**, of the nature of a problem: questionable: doubtful.—*adv.* **problemat'ically.** —**problem child**, one whose character presents an exceptionally difficult problem to parents, teachers, &c.; **problem novel**, **play**, one presenting or expounding a problem, social, moral, &c. [Gr. *problēma*, *-atos—pro*, before, *ballein*, to throw.]

proboscis, *prə-*, *prō-bos'is*, *n*. a trunk or long snout: a trunk-like process, as the suctorial mouth-parts of some insects: (*facet.*) a nose:—*pl.* **probosc'ises**, **probosc'ides** (*-i-dēz*).—*n.pl.* **Proboscid'ea**, the elephant order of mammals.—*adj.* and *n.* **proboscid'ean.—proboscis monkey**, a very long-nosed Bornean monkey (*Nasalis larvatus*). [L.,— Gr. *proboskis*, a trunk—*pro*, expressing motive, *boskein*, to feed.]

probouleutic, *prō-bōō-lū'tik*, *adj.* for preliminary deliberation. [Gr. *probouleusis*, preliminary deliberation.]

procacity, *prə-kas'i-ti*, *n*. petulance.—*adj.* **procacious** (*-kā'shəs*). [L. *procācitās*, *-ātis—procāx*, forward, insolent, shameless—*procāre*, to demand.]

procathedral, *prō-kə-thē'drəl*, *n*. a church used temporarily as a cathedral.

proceed, *prə-*, *prō-sēd'*, *v.i.* to go on: to continue: to advance: to pass on: to begin and go on: to act according to a method: to go from point to point: to advance to a higher degree (as *to proceed M.A.*) or more developed state: to prosper: to come forth: to result: to be descended: to take measures or action: to take legal action: to prosecute: (*Shak.*) to go on, be transacted, happen. —*v.t.* to say in continuation.—*n.* **prō'ceed** (usu. in *pl.*), outcome: money got from anything.— *adj.* **procedural** (*-sēd'yə-rəl*). — *ns.* **procē'dure**,

mode of proceeding: method of conducting business, esp. in a law case or a meeting: course of action: a step taken or an act performed; **proceed'er**; **proceed'ing**, a going forward: progress: advancement: course of conduct: (*Shak.*) perh. advantage: step: operation: transaction: (in *pl.*) a record of the transactions of a society. [Fr. *procéder*—L. *prōcēdĕre—prō*, before, *cēdĕre*, *cessum*, to go.]

proceleusmatic, *pros-e-lūs-mat'ik*, *adj.* inciting, encouraging.—*n.* in ancient prosody, a foot of four short syllables. [Gr. *prokeleusmatikos—pro*, before, *keleuein*, to urge, order.]

Procellaria, *pros-e-lā'ri-ä*, *n*. the petrel genus.— *adj.* **procella'rian.** [L. *procella*, a storm.]

procephalic, *prō-si-fal'ik*, *adj.* of the forepart of the head. [Gr. *pro*, before, *kephalē*, head.]

procerebrum, *prō-ser'i-brəm*, *n*. the fore-brain: the prosencephalon.—*adj.* **procer'ebral.** [L. *prō*, before, *cerebrum*, brain.]

procerity, *prō-ser'i-ti*, *n*. tallness. [L. *prōcēritās*, *-ātis—prōcērus*, tall.]

process, *prō'ses*, sometimes *pros'* (*Milt. prō-ses'*), *n*. a state of being in progress or being carried on: course: (*Shak.*) a narrative: a series of actions or events: a sequence of operations or changes undergone: (*print.*) a photo-process: (*law*) a writ by which a person or matter is brought into court: an action, suit, or the proceedings in it as a whole: progression: proceeding: (*Shak.*) an edict: (*biol.*) a projecting part, esp. on a bone.— *v.t.* to serve a summons on: to sue or prosecute: to subject to a special process: to produce or print photomechanically.—*adj.* produced by a special process, as synthetically, photomechanically, &c.—*ns.* **pro'cess-block**, a photomechanically made block for printing a picture; **pro'cess-server**, (*Shak.*) a bailiff. [Fr. *procès*—L. *prōcessus*, *-ūs*, advance; cf. **proceed**.]

procession, *prə-*, *prō-sesh'ən*, *n*. the act of proceeding: a train of persons, or of boats, shadows, &c., moving forward together as in ceremony, display, demonstration, &c.: the movement of such a train: a litany sung in procession.—*v.i.* to go in procession.—*v.t.* to go through or around in procession: to celebrate by a procession.—*v.i.* **process** (*prō-ses'*; back-formation), to go in processions.—*adj.* **process'ional.**—*n.* a book of litanies hymns, &c., for processions: a hymn sung in procession.—*n.* **process'ionalist.**—*adj.* **process'-ionary.**—*ns.* **process'ioner**, (*U.S.*) a county officer who determines boundaries; **process'ioning**, going in procession: (*U.S.*) perambulation of boundaries.—**processionary moth**, a European moth (*Cnethocampa processionea*) whose caterpillars go out seeking food in great processions; **Procession of the Holy Ghost**, (*theol.*) the emanation of the Holy Spirit from the Father (*single procession*), or from the Father and Son (*double procession*). [L. *prōcessiō*, *-ōnis*; cf. **proceed**.]

prochronism, *prō'kron-izm*, *n*. a dating of an event before the right time—opp. to *metachronism*. [Gr. *pro*, before, *chronos*, time.]

procidence, *pros'*, *prōs'i-dəns*, *n*. prolapse.—*adj.* **proc'ident**. [L. *prōcidentia—prō*, forward, *cadĕre*, to fall.]

procinct, *prō-singkt'*, *n*. (*Milt.*) preparedness. [L. *prōcinctus*, *-ūs—prō*, beforehand, *cingĕre*, *cinctum*, to gird.]

proclaim, *prə-*, *prō-klām'*, *v.t.* to cry aloud: to publish abroad: to announce officially: to denounce: to announce the accession of: to place under restrictions by proclamation.—*n.* **proclaim'**, proclamation: proclaiming.—*ns.* **proclaim'ant**; **proclaim'er**; **proclamation** (*prok-lə-mā'shən*), the act of proclaiming: that which is proclaimed: official notice given to the public: proscription.— *adj.* **proclamatory** (*-klam'ət-ər-i*). [Fr. *proclamer* —L. *prōclāmāre*, *prōclāmāre—prō*, out, *clāmāre*, to cry.]

proclitic, *prō-klit'ik*, *adj.* so closely attached to the following word as to have no accent.—*n.* a proclitic word. [A modern coinage on the analogy of **enclitic**—Gr. *pro*, forward, *klīnein*, lean.]

proclivity, *prə-*, *prō-kliv'i-ti*, *n*. inclination: pro-

pensity.—*adj.* **proclive** (-*klīv'*; *arch.*), inclined: prone: headlong. [L. *prŏclīvis—prō*, forward, *clīvus*, a slope.]

procoelous, *prō-sē'ləs, adj.* cupped in front. [Gr. *pro*, before, *koilos*, hollow.]

proconsul, *prō-kon'sl, n.* a Roman magistrate with almost consular authority outside the city, orig. one whose consulate had expired, often governor of a province: sometimes applied to a colonial or dominion governor.—*adj.* **procon'sular** (-*sū-lər*). —*ns.* **procon'sulate** (-*sū-lit*, -*lāt*), **procon'sulship** (-*sl-ship*), the office, or term of office, of a proconsul. [L. *prŏcōnsul*.]

procrastinate, *prō-kras'ti-nāt, v.t.* (*rare*) to put off till some future time: to defer.—*v.i.* to defer action. — *n.* **procrastinā'tion,** act or habit of putting off, dilatoriness.—*adjs.* **procras'tinātive, procras'tināting, procras'tinātory.** — *ns.* **procras'tinātiveness; procras'tinātor.** [L. *procrāstināre, -ātum—prō*, onward, *crāstīnus*, of to-morrow—*crās*, tomorrow.]

procreate, *prō'kri-āt, v.t.* to engender: to beget: to generate.—*v.i.* to produce offspring.—*n.* **prō'creant** (-*kri-ənt*), a generator.—*adj.* generating: connected with or useful in reproduction.—*n.* **prōcreā'tion.** — *adj.* **prō'creātive,** having the power to procreate: generative: productive.— *ns.* **prō'creātiveness; prō'creātor,** a parent. [L. *prŏcreăre, -ătum—prō*, forth, *creăre*, to produce.]

Procrustean, *prō-krus'ti-ən, adj.* violently making conformable to a standard—from *Procrustes* (Gr. *Prŏkroustēs*), a fabulous Greek robber, who stretched or cut his captives' legs to make them fit a bed. [Gr. *prokrouein*, to lengthen out.]

procrypsis, *prō-krip'sis, n.* (*biol.*) protective coloration.—*adj.* **procryp'tic.** — *adv.* **procryp'tically.** [Gr. *pro*, before, *krypsis*, hiding, *kryptein*, to hide.]

proctal, *prok'tl, adj.* anal.—*ns.* **proctalgia** (-*al'ji-ä*), neuralgic pain in the rectum; **procti'tis,** inflammation of the rectum.—*adj.* **proctodae'al** (-*to-dē'əl*).—*n.* **proctodae'um,** the posterior part of the alimentary canal, formed by invagination of ectoderm. [Gr. *prŏktos*, anus, *algos*, pain, *hodaios*, on the way.]

proctor, *prok'tər, n.* a procurator or manager for another: an attorney in the spiritual courts: a representative of the clergy in Convocation: an official in the English universities whose functions include enforcement of university regulations.— *n.* **proc'torage.**—*adj.* **proctō'rial.**—*adv.* **proctō'rially.**—*v.t.* **proc'torise,** to exercise the power of a proctor against.—*n.* **proc'torship.**—**king's proctor,** an official who intervenes in divorce cases in England if collusion or fraud is suspected. [procurator.]

procumbent, *prō-kum'bənt, adj.* lying or leaning forward: prone: prostrate: (*bot.*) lying on the ground. [L. *prŏcumbēns, -entis*, pr.p. of *prŏcumbĕre—prō*, forward, *cumbĕre*, to lie down.]

procurator, *prok'ū-rā-tər, n.* a financial agent in a Roman imperial province, sometimes administrator of part of it: one who manages affairs for another: one authorised to act for another: an agent in a law court.—*n.* **proc'urator-fis'cal** (see **fiscal**).—*adj.* **procuratorial** (-*rə-tō'ri-əl*).—*ns.* **proc'uratorship; proc'uratory** (-*rə-tər-i*), authorisation to act for another. [L. *prŏcūrātor, -ōris*; see next word.]

procure, *prə-, prō-kūr', v.t.* to contrive to obtain or bring about: to bring upon one: to induce: (*Shak.*) to induce to come, bring: (*Spens.*) to urge earnestly: to obtain for another's immoral purposes.—*v.i.* to pander, pimp.—*adj.* **procur'able,** to be had.—*ns.* **procuracy** (*prok'ū-rə-si*), office of a procurator; **procurā'tion,** management of another's affairs: the instrument giving power to do so: a sum paid by incumbents to the bishop or archdeacon on visitations: procuring; **procure'ment,** the act of procuring in any sense; **procur'er,** one who procures: a pander:—*fem.* **procur'ess,** a bawd. [Fr. *procurer*—L. *prŏcūrāre*, to manage—*prō*, for, *cūrāre, -ātum*, to care for.]

Procyon, *prō'si-on, n.* a first-magnitude star in the constellation of the Lesser Dog: the raccoon genus, giving name to the family **Procyon'idae**

(raccoons, **coatis,** &c.). [Gr. *Prŏkyōn*, the star Procyon, rising before the Dogstar—*pro*, before, *kyōn*, a dog.]

prod, *prod, v.t.* to prick: to poke, as with the end of a stick (*pr.p.* **prodd'ing;** *pa.t.* and *pa.p.* **prodd'ed).**—*n.* an act of prodding: a sharp instrument, as a goad, an awl, a skewer. [Origin unknown; O.E. *prodbor* seems to mean auger.]

prodigal, *prod'i-gl, adj.* wasteful of one's means: squandering: lavish.—*n.* a waster: a spendthrift. —*adv.* (*Shak.*) prodigally.—*v.t.* **prod'igalise,** to spend lavishly, waste.—*n.* **prodigality** (-*gal'i-ti*), state or quality of being prodigal: extravagance: profusion: great liberality. — *adv.* **prod'igally,** wastefully. [Obs. Fr.,—L. *prŏdigus—prōdigĕre,* to squander—pfx. *prōd-* (early form of *prō-*), away, forth, *agĕre*, to drive.]

prodigy, *prod'i-ji, n.* a portent: any person or thing that causes great wonder: a wonder: a monster: a child of precocious genius or virtuosity.—*n.* **prodigios'ity.**—*adj.* **prodig'ious,** like a prodigy: astonishing: more than usually large in size or degree: monstrous.—*adv.* **prodig'iously.**—*n.* **prodig'iousness.** [L. *prōdigium,* a prophetic sign—pfx. *prōd-* (earlier form of *prō-*), in advance, prob. the root of *ad-agium* (see **adage**).]

proditor, *prod'i-tər, n.* a traitor.—*adjs.* **proditō'rious, prod'itory.** [L. *prōditor, -ōris—prōdĕre, -itum,* to betray—*prō*, forth, *dăre*, to give.]

prodromus, *prod'rom-əs, n.* an introductory treatise: a premonitory event: a sign of approaching disease:—*pl.* **prod'romi** (-*ī*).—Also **prodrome** (*prod'rōm*).—*adjs.* **prod'romal, prodrom'ic.** [Latinised from Gr. *prodromos,* forerunner—*pro,* before, *dromos,* a run.]

produce, *prə-, prō-dūs', v.t.* to bring forward or out: to extend: to bring into being: to bring forth: to yield: to bring about: to make: to put on the stage: to prepare for exhibition to the public.— *v.i.* to yield: to create value. — *ns.* **produce** (*prod'ūs*), that which is produced: product: proceeds: crops: yield, esp. of fields and gardens; **produce'ment,** (*Milt.*) product; **producer,** one who produces, esp. commodities, or a play or similar exhibition: one who exercises general control over, but does not actually make, a motion picture (cf. **director**): a furnace in which a mixed combustible gas is produced by passing air and steam through incandescent coke; **produ'cer-gas,** gas made in a producer, chiefly a mixture of hydrogen and carbon-monoxide diluted with nitrogen; **producibil'ity.**—*adj.* **produc'ible,** that may be produced: that may be generated or made: that may be exhibited.—*ns.* **product** (*prod'əkt, -ukt*), a thing produced: a result: a work: offspring: a quantity got by multiplying; **productibil'ity** (*prə-dukt-*), capability of being produced.—*adj.* **product'ile,** capable of being drawn out in length. —*n.* **produc'tion,** act of producing: that which is produced: fruit: product: a work, esp. of art: putting upon the stage: bringing out: (*pol. econ.*) creation of values: extension: in Scots law, a document produced in court.—*adjs.* **produc'tional; produc'tive,** having the power to produce: generative: that produces: producing richly: fertile: efficient.—*adv.* **produc'tively.**— *ns.* **produc'tiveness, productiv'ity** (*prod-, prōd-*). —**producer(s') goods,** goods, such as raw materials and tools, used in the production of consumer(s') goods. [L. *prōdūcĕre, -ductum—prō*, forward, *dūcĕre*, to lead.]

proem, *prō'em, n.* an introduction: a prelude: a preface.—*adj.* **proemial** (*prō-ē'mi-əl*). [Fr. *proème* —L. *prooemium*—Gr. *prooimion*—*pro*, before, *oimē*, a song, *oimos*, a way.]

proembryo, *prō-em'bri-ō, n.* (*bot.*) a group of cells formed in the dividing zygote, from which part the embryo arises.

proenzyme, *prō-en'zīm, n.* an enzyme in an inactive form which can be activated—often by another enzyme.

prof, *prof, n.* a familiar abbreviation of **professor.**

proface, *prō-fās', interj.* (*Shak.*) may it profit you! —a phrase of welcome. [O.Fr. *prou*, profit, *fasse*, 3rd pers. sing. pres. subj. of *faire*, to do.]

profane, *prə-, prō-fān′, adj.* not sacred : secular : showing contempt of sacred things : uninitiated : unhallowed : ritually unclean or forbidden.—*v.t.* to treat with contempt or insult in spite of the holiness attributed : to desecrate : to violate : to put to an unworthy use.—*n.* **profanation** (*prof-ə-nā′shən*).—*adj.* **profanatory** (*prō-fan′ə-tər-i*).—*adv.* **profane′ly**.—*ns.* **profane′ness** ; **profān′er** ; **profanity** (*-fan′*), irreverence : that which is profane : profane language or conduct. [L. *profānus*, outside the temple, not sacred, unholy—*prō*, before, *fānum*, a temple.]

profectitious, *prō-fek-tish′əs, adj.* derived from a parent or ancestor. [L.L. *profectīcius*—L. *prōficīscī, profectus,* to proceed.]

profess, *prə-, prō-fes′, v.t.* to make open declaration of : to declare in strong terms : to claim (often insincerely) to have a feeling of : to pretend to : to claim to be expert in : to be professor of : (*R.C.*) to receive into a religious order by profession.— *v.i.* to enter publicly into a religious state : (*Shak.*) to pretend friendship : to be a professor.—*adj.* **professed**, openly declared : avowed : acknowledged : having made profession.—*adv.* **profess′-edly**.—*adj.* **profess′ing**, avowed : pretending, soi-disant.—*n.* **profession** (*-fesh′ən*), the act of professing : open declaration : avowal : religious belief : pretence : an employment not mechanical and requiring some degree of learning : calling or known employment : the collective body of persons engaged in any profession : entrance into a religious order : the vow then taken.—*adj.* **profess′ional**, pertaining to a profession : engaged in a profession or in the profession in question : competing for money prizes or against those who sometimes do so : undertaken as a means of subsistence, as opp. to *amateur.*—*n.* one who makes his living by an art, or makes it his career—opp. to *amateur, dilettante* : one who engages in sport for livelihood or gain or against those who do so (with various rules of interpretation for each sport)—opp. to *amateur* : (in full *professional examination*) any one of the successive examinations towards a degree in medicine (in Scottish universities).—*v.t.* **profess′ionalise,** to give a professional character to : to give over to professionals.—*n.* **profess′ionalism,** the status of professional : the outlook, aim, or restriction of the mere professional : the predominance of professionals in sport.—*adv.* **profess′ionally.**—*ns.* **professor** (*prə-fes′ər*), one who professes : one who openly declares belief in certain doctrines : a teacher of the highest grade in a university or college (prefixed to the name) : assumed often by mountebanks, quacks, dancing-masters, &c. : *fem.* (*rare*) **profess′oress** ; **profess′orate,** professorate. — *adj.* **professorial** (*prof-es-ō′ri-el*).— *adv.* **professō′rially.**—*ns.* **professō′riate,** the office or chair of a professor : his period of office : body of professors ; **profess′orship.** [L. *professus,* perf.p. of *profitērī*—*prō,* publicly, *fatērī,* to confess.]

proffer, *prof′ər, v.t.* to offer for acceptance, to tender, present : to offer to undertake : (*pr.p.* **proff′ering** ; *pa.t.* and *pa.p.* **proff′ered**).—*n.* an offer, tender : an incipient act.—*n.* **proff′erer.** [A.Fr. *proffrir*— L. *prō,* forward, *offerre* ; see **offer.**]

proficient, *prə-, prō-fish′ənt, adj.* competent : well-skilled : thoroughly qualified.—*n.* (*Shak.*) one who is making progress in learning : an adept : an expert.—*ns.* **profic′ience** (now *rare* or *obs.*) ; **profic′iency.**—*adv.* **profic′iently.** [L. *prōficiēns, -entis,* pr.p. of *prōficĕre,* to make progress.]

profile, *prō′fīl, -fēl, -fil, n.* an outline : a head or portrait in a side-view : the side-face : the outline of any object without foreshortening : a drawing of a vertical section of country, in an engineering work, &c. : a graph.—*v.t.* to draw in profile : to make an outline of : to show in profile : to give a profile to : to shape the outline of.—*ns.* **prō′filer** ; **prō′filist,** one who draws profiles. [It. *profilo*—L. *prō,* before, *filum,* a thread.]

profit, *prof′it, n.* gain : the gain resulting from the employment of capital : the excess of selling price over first cost : advantage : addition to good or value : benefit : improvement.—*v.t.* to benefit

or to be of advantage to.—*v.i.* to gain advantage : to receive profit : (*Shak.*) to make progress, to improve : to be of advantage.—*adj.* **prof′itable,** yielding or bringing profit or gain : lucrative : productive. — *n.* **prof′itableness.** — *adv.* **prof′itably.**—*n.* **profiteer′,** one who takes advantage of an emergency to make exorbitant profits.—*v.i.* to act as a profiteer.—*ns.* **profiteer′ing ; prof′iter ; prof′iting.**—*adj.* **prof′itless,** without profit.—*adv.* **prof′itlessly.**—*n.* **prof′it-shar′ing,** a voluntary agreement under which the employee receives a share, fixed beforehand, in the profits of a business. [Fr.,—L. *prōfectus,* progress—*prōficĕre, prōfectum,* to make progress.]

profligate, *prof′li-gāt, -git, adj.* (*obs.*) overthrown, defeated : abandoned to vice : without virtue or decency : dissolute : prodigal.—*n.* one leading a profligate life : one shamelessly vicious : an abandoned person.—*n.* **prof′ligacy** (*-gə-si*), state or quality of being profligate : a vicious course of life.—*adv.* **prof′ligately.** [L. *prōfligātus,* pa.p. of *prōfligāre*—*prō,* forward, *flīgĕre,* to dash.]

profluent, *prō′floo-ənt, adj.* (*Milt.*) flowing forth.— *n.* **prō′fluence.** [L. *prō,* forth, *fluĕre,* to flow.]

profound, *prə-, prō-fownd′, adj.* deep : deep-seated : far below the surface : intense : abstruse : intellectually deep : penetrating deeply into knowledge.—*n.* the sea or ocean : an abyss, great depth.—*adv.* **profound′ly.**—*ns.* **profound′ness, profundity** (*-fund′*), state or quality of being profound : depth of place, of knowledge, &c. : that which is profound. [Fr. *profond*—L. *profundus*—*pro,* forward, *fundus,* bottom.]

profulgent, *prə-, prō-ful′jent, adj.* shining forth, radiant. [L. *prō,* forth, *fulgēns, -entis,* pr.p. of *fulgēre,* to shine.]

profuse, *prə-, prō-fūs′, adj.* liberal to excess : lavish : extravagant : over-abounding.—*adv.* **profūse′ly.** —*ns.* **profūse′ness ; profuser** (*-fūz′ər* ; *Herrick*), a prodigal, spendthrift ; **profusion** (*-fū′zhən*), state of being profuse : extravagance : prodigality. [L. *prōfūsus,* pa.p. of *prōfundĕre*—*prō,* forth, *fundĕre,* to pour.]

prog, *prog, v.t.* to pierce : to prick : to poke.—*v.i.* to poke about for anything : to forage for food : to beg.—*n.* a pointed instrument : a thrust : provisions, esp. for a journey. [Origin unknown ; perh. several distinct words.]

prog, *prog, n.* university slang for **proctor.**—*v.t.* to proctorise.—*n.* **progg′ins,** a proctor.

progenitor, *prō-jen′i-tər, n.* a forefather : an ancestor : a parent : the founder of a family :—*fem.* **progen′itress, progen′itrix.** — *adj.* **progenitō′-rial.**—*ns.* **progen′itorship ; progen′iture,** a begetting ; **progeny** (*proj′ə-ni*), offspring : descendants : race : (*Shak.*) lineage. [L. *prōgenitor, prōgeniēs*—*prōgignĕre*—*prō,* before, *gignĕre, genitum,* to beget.]

proglottis, *prō-glot′is, n.* a detachable tapeworm joint :—*pl.* **proglott′idēs.** [Gr. *pro,* before, *glōttis, -idos,* a pipe mouthpiece.]

prognathous, *prog′nə-thəs,* also **prog-** or **prŏg-nā′thəs,** *adj.* with projecting jaw—also **prognathic** (*prog-, prŏg-nath′ik*).—*n.* **prog′nathism** (or *-nath′-, -nāth′*). [Gr. *pro,* forward, *gnathos,* a jaw.]

Progne, *prog′nē, n.* a personification of the swallow, sometimes of the nightingale. [L. *Prognē*—Gr. *Proknē,* Philomela's sister, transformed into a swallow, or a nightingale.]

prognosis, *prog-nō′sis, n.* forecasting, or forecast esp. of the course of a disease :—*pl.* **prognos′es** (*-ēz*).—*n.* **prognostic** (*prog-, prag-nost′ik*), a fore-telling : an indication of something to come : a presage : a symptom on which prognosis can be based.—*adj.* indicating what is to happen by signs or symptoms : of prognosis.—*v.t.* **prognos′ticate** to foretell : to indicate as to come.—*n.* **prog-nostica′tion.**—*adj.* **prognos′ticative.**—*n.* **prog-nost′icator,** a predictor, esp. a weather prophet. [Gr. *prognōsis*—*pro,* before, *gignōskein,* to know.]

programme, program, *prō′gram, n.* (*Scot.,* obs.) a public notice : a paper, booklet, or the like giving a scheme of proceedings arranged for an entertainment, conference, course of study, &c. with relevant details : the items of such a scheme

collectively: a plan of things to be done.—*v.t.*
to provide with, enter in, &c., a programme.—*adj.*
programmatic (*-grə-mat'ik*), of a programme:
of, or of the nature of, programme music.—
programme music, music that seeks to depict
a scene or tell a story. [Gr. *programma*, proclamation—*pro*, forth, *gramma*, a letter.]
progress, *prō'gres*, sometimes *pro'*, *n.* forward movement: advance: continuation: advance to some-
thing better or higher in development: gain in
proficiency: course: passage from place to place:
a procession: a journey of state: a circuit.—*v.i.*
progress' (formerly, as *Shak.*, *prō'*), to go forward:
to make progress: to go on, continue: to go in
progress, travel in state.—*v.t.* (*obs.*) to traverse.—
n. **progression** (*prə-*, *prō-gresh'ən*), motion onward: act or state of moving onward: progress:
movement by successive stages: (*mus.*) a regular
succession of chords: movements of the parts in
harmony: (*math.*) change from term to term
according to some law: a series of terms so related
(see **arithmetic, geometry, harmony**).—*adjs.*
progress'ional; progress'ionary. — *ns.* **progress'ionism,** sympathy with or advocacy of
progress: belief that social or other evolution is
towards higher or better things; **progress'ionist,**
a believer in progressionism: a progressive: one
who favours progress or reform; **progress'ism**
(or *prō'*, *pro'*), progressionism; **progress'ist** (or
prō', *pro'*), one who advocates a progressive policy:
a progressionist: **progress'ive,** forward-moving:
making progress: of the nature of progress: advancing by successive stages: (in games, e.g. **progressive whist**) played by several sets of players,
some of whom move round from table to table after
each hand, according to rule: advancing towards
better and better or higher and higher: in favour
of progress—applied to various parties in municipal and national politics more or less favouring
reform: of such a party.—*n.* one who favours
progress or reform: a member of a party called
progressive.—*adv.* **progress'ively.**—*n.* **progress'-
iveness.**—**in progress,** going on: in course of
publication. [Fr. *progresse* (now *progrès*)—L. *prō-
gressus*, *-ūs*—*prō*, forward, *gradī*, to step.]
progymnasium, *prō-jim-nā'zi-əm*, or (*Ger.*) *prō-
gim-nä'zi-oom*, *n.* in Germany, a classical school
in which the higher classes are wanting.
prohibit, *prə-*, *prō-hib'it*, *v.t.* to forbid: to prevent.
—*ns.* **prohib'iter,** or; **prohibition** (*prō-hi-
bi'shən* or *prō-i-*), the act of prohibiting, forbidding,
or interdicting: an interdict: the forbidding by
law of the manufacture and sale of alcoholic drinks.
— *adj.* **prohibi'tionary.** — *ns.* **prohibi'tionism;
prohibi'tionist,** one who favours prohibition, esp.
of the manufacture and sale of alcoholic drinks.—
adj. **prohibitive** (*-hib'*), tending to make impossible
or preclude.—*adv.* **prohib'itively.**—*adj.* **prohib'-
itory,** that prohibits or forbids: forbidding. [L.
prohibēre, *prohibitum*—*prō*, before, *habēre*, to have.]
proin, proine, proign, *proin*, obsolete forms of
prune (to preen, to lop).
project, *proj'ekt*, *n.* (*Shak.*) a notion: (*obs.*) speculative imagination: a projection: a scheme of
something to be done: a proposal for an undertaking: an undertaking.—*v.t.* **project** (*prə-*, *prō-
jekt'*), to throw out or forward: to throw, propel:
to cause to jut out, stretch out: to scheme, plan,
devise: (*Shak.*) to set forth, set before the mind:
to cast (as a light, a shadow, an image) upon a
surface or into space: to throw an image of: to
show outlined against a background: (*geom.*) to
derive a new figure from, so that each point corresponds to a point of the original figure according
to some rule, esp. by a system of parallel, converging, or diverging rays through the original
points meeting a surface: to externalise: to make
objective.—*v.i.* to jut out: (*alchemy*) to throw powder
of projection upon the metal to be transmuted.—
adj. **projec'tile,** caused by projection: impelling:
capable of being thrown or thrust forth.—*n.* **projectile** (*proj'ik-tīl*, or *prə-*, *prō-jek'tīl*), a body projected by force: a missile, esp. one discharged
by a gun.—*n.* and *adj.* **projec'ting.**—*n.* **projec'tion**
(*-shən*), an act or method of projecting: the fact

or state of being projected: planning: that which
is projected: a jutting out: that which juts out:
the standing out of a figure: (*geom.*) a figure got
by projecting another: a method of representing
geographical detail upon a plane: a projected
image: (*alchemy*) the throwing in of powdered
philosopher's stone, to effect transmutation, hence
transmutation itself in general.—*adjs.* **projec'-
tional; projec'tive,** projecting: of projection:
derivable by projection: unchanged by projection.
—*ns.* **projectivity** (*proj-ek-tiv'i-ti*); **project'ment**
(*rare*), design; **projec'tor,** one who projects enterprises: a promoter of speculative schemes for
money-making: an apparatus for projecting, esp.
an image or a beam of light: a straight line joining
a point with its projection; **projec'ture,** a jutting
out.—**projecting powder,** (*alchemy*) the philosopher's stone in powder. [L. *prōicĕre*, *prōjectum*—
prō, forth, *jacĕre*, to throw.]
proke, *prōk*, *v.t.* and *v.i.* (*dial.*) to poke.—*n.* **prōk'er,**
a poker. [Origin obscure.]
prolapse, *prō-laps'*, or *prō'laps*, *n.* (*med.*) a falling
down, or out of place.—Also **prolap'sus.**—*v.i.*
prolapse', to slip out of place. [L. *prōlābī*, *prō-
lāpsus*, to slip forward—*prō*, forward, *lābī*, to slip.]
prolate, *prō'lāt*, *adj.* drawn out along the polar
diameter, as a spheroid: widespread.—*v.t.* **prolate'**, (*obs.*) to lengthen out in utterance.—*adv.*
pro'lately.—*ns.* **pro'lateness** (or *-lāt'*); **prolation** (*prō-lā'shən*), utterance: (*mediaeval mus.*) the
time-ratio of semibreve to minim (in *great* or *perfect
prolation*, three minims to a semibreve; *lesser* or
imperfect, two).—*adj.* **prolative** (*prō-lā'tiv*, *prō'la-
tiv*; *gram.*), completing the predicate. [L. *prōlātus*,
produced — *prō*, forward, *lātus*, used as perf.p. of
ferre, to carry.]
proleg, *prō'leg*, *n.* an insect larva's abdominal leg,
distinguished from a thoracic or 'true' leg. [L.
pfx. *prō*, and **leg.**]
prolegomena, *prō-leg-om'in-ä*, *n.pl.* an introduction, esp. to a treatise:—*sing.* **prolegom'enon.**—
adjs. **prolegom'enary, prolegom'enous.** [Gr.
prōlegomenon, pl. *-a*, pass. part. neut. of *prolegein*—
pro, before, *legein*, to say.]
prolepsis, *prō-lep'sis*, or *-lēp'*, *n.* anticipation: the
rhetorical figure of anticipation, use of a word not
literally applicable till a later time: a figure by
which objections are anticipated and answered:—
pl. **prolep'sēs.**—*adjs.* **prolep'tic, -al.**—*adv.* **prolep'tically.** [Gr. *prōlēpsis*—*pro*, before, *lambanein*,
to take.]
proletarian, *prō-li-tā'ri-ən*, *adj.* of the poorest
labouring class: having little or no property.—
n. a member of the poorest class: (*bot.*) a plant
without reserves of food.—*ns.* **proletā'rianism,**
the condition of the poorest classes; **proletā'riat**
(*-ət*), **-ate,** the proletarian class: the wage-earning
class, esp. those without capital.—*n.* and *adj.*
pro'letary (*-ər-i*), proletarian. [L. *prōlētārius*, (in
ancient Rome) a citizen of the sixth and lowest
class, who served the state not with his property
but with his *prōlēs*, offspring.]
proliferate, *prō-lif'ə-rāt*, *v.i.* to grow by multiplication of parts (cells, buds, shoots, &c.): to reproduce by proliferation: to reproduce abundantly.
—*v.t.* to produce by proliferation.—*n.* **prolifera'-
tion,** growth and extension by multiplication of
cells: production of vegetative shoots from a
reproductive structure: repeated production of
new parts: production of shoots that may become
new plants: production of abnormal or supernumerary parts: a structure formed by proliferat-
ing. — *adjs.* **prolif'erative, prolif'erous.** — *adv.*
prolif'erously. [L. *prōlēs,* progeny, *ferre*, to
bear.]
prolific, *prə-*, *prō-lif'ik*, *adj.* reproductive: fertilising: fertile: producing much offspring: fruitful:
abounding.—*n.* **prolif'icacy** (*-ə-si*).—*adj.* **prolif'-
ical** (*rare* or *obs.*).—*adv.* **prolif'ically.**—*ns.* **pro-
lifica'tion,** the generation of young: (*bot.*) development of a shoot by continued growth of a
flower; **prolificity** (*-is'i-ti*), **prolif'icness.** [L.
prōlēs, offspring, *facĕre,* to make.]
prolix, *prō'liks,* or *-liks'*, *adj.* long and wordy: long-
winded: dwelling too long on particulars: (*obs.* or

rare) long.—*adj.* **prolixious** (*prō-lik'shəs*; *Shak.*), dilatory.—*n.* **prolix'ity.**—*adv.* **prolix'ly** (or *prō'*). —*n.* **prolix'ness** (or *prō'*). [L. *prōlixus*—*prō*, forward, *liquī*, to flow.]

proll, prole, proul, *prōl*, **proler,** *prōl'ər*, earlier forms of **prowl, prowler.**

prolocutor, *prō-lok'ū-tər*, *n.* a spokesman: a chairman, esp. of the lower house of Convocation:—*fem.* **prolocu'utrix.**—*ns.* **prolocu'tion** (*prō-* or *pro-*), an introductory speech or saying; **prōloc'utorship.** [L. *prōlocūtor*—*prōloquī*, -*locūtus*, to speak out—pfx. *prō-*, *loquī*, to speak.]

prologue, *prō'log*, *n.* in a Greek play, the part before the entry of the chorus: an introduction to a poem, &c.: a speech before a play: the speaker of a prologue: an introductory event or action.—*v.t.* (*prō'log* or *pro-lōg'*), to introduce: to preface.—*v.i.* **pro'logise** (-*gīz*, -*jīz*), to speak a prologue—also **pro'loguise.** [Fr.,—L. *prologus*—Gr. *prologos*—*pro*, before, *logos*, speech.]

prolong, *prə-*, *prō-long'*, *v.t.* to lengthen out: (*Spens., Shak.*) to postpone.—*v.i.* to lengthen out. *adj.* **prolongable** (*prō-long'ə-bl*).—*v.t.* **prolongate** (*prō'long-gāt*), to lengthen. — *ns.* **prolongation** (-*long-gā'shən*), lengthening out: a piece added in continuation: continuation; **prolonger** (-*long'ər*). [L. *prōlongāre*—*prō*, forward, *longus*, long.]

prolonge, *prō-lonj'*, *n.* a rope for a gun-carriage. [Fr.]

prolusion, *prō-l(y)ōō'zhən*, *n.* a preliminary performance, activity, or display: an essay preparatory to a more solid treatise.—*adj.* **prolu'sory** (-*sə-ri*). [L. *prōlūsiō*, -*ōnis*—*prō*, before, *lūdĕre*, *lūsum*, to play.]

prom, *prom*, *n.* an abbreviation of **promenade**: a promenade concert.

promachos, *prom'ə-kos*, Gr. -*hhos*, *n.* a champion or defender: a tutelary god. [Gr.]

promenade, *prom-i-näd'* or -*nād'*, *n.* a walk, ride, or drive for pleasure, show, or gentle exercise: a processional dance: (*U.S.*) a school or college dance: a place where people walk to and fro: a paved terrace on a sea-front: an esplanade.—*v.i.* to walk, ride, or drive about in promenade.—*v.t.* to lead about and exhibit: to go in promenade about or through.—*n.* **promenader** (-*äd'ər*).—**promenade concert,** one in which the audience can move about; **promenade deck,** a deck on which passengers walk about. [Fr.,—*promener*, to lead about (*se promener*, to take a walk)—L. *prōmināre*, to drive forwards—*prō*, forward, *mināre*, to threaten.]

Promethean, *prō-mē'thi-ən*, -*thyən*, *adj.* pertaining to *Prometheus* (-*thūs*) who stole fire from heaven, for which Zeus chained him to a rock, to be tortured by a vulture.—*n.* a glass tube containing sulphuric acid and an inflammable mixture brought together by pressing—an early kind of match.—*n.* **prome'thium** (formerly **prome'theum**), element 61 (symbol Pm). [Gr. *Promētheus*.]

prominent, *prom'i-nənt*, *adj.* standing out: projecting: most easily seen: catching the eye or attention: in the public eye.—*ns.* **prom'inence**, state or quality of being prominent: a prominent point or thing: a projection; **prom'inency**, a prominence.—*adv.* **prom'inently.**—**solar prominence**, a great tongue of incandescent gas shooting out from the sun. [L. *prōminēns*, -*entis*, pr.p. of *prōminēre*, to jut forth—*prō*, forth, *minae*, projections, threats.]

promiscuous, *prō-mis'kū-əs*, *adj.* confusedly or indiscriminately mixed: collected together without order: indiscriminate: haphazard: belonging to a mixed set: (*old slang*) far from choice: (*coll.*) casual, accidental.—*n.* **promiscu'ity** (*prom-*), mixture without order or distinction: promiscuous sexual intercourse.—*adv.* **promis'cuously.** [L. *prōmiscuus*—*prō*, inten., *miscēre*, to mix.]

promise, *prom'is*, *n.* an engagement to do or keep from doing something: expectation, or that which raises expectation: a ground for hope of future excellence: (*rare*) fulfilment of what is promised. —*v.t.* to engage by promise: to betroth: to encourage to expect: to afford reason to expect: to assure: to engage to bestow.—*v.i.* to make a

promise or promises: to afford hopes or expectations: (*rare*) to stand sponsor.—*ns.* **prom'ise-breach**, (*Shak.*) violation of promise; **prom'ise-breaker** (*Shak.*). — *adj.* **prom'ise-crammed**, (*Shak.*) fed to repletion with empty promises.—*n.* **promisee'**, the person to whom a promise is made. —*adj.* **prom'iseful.**—*n.* **prom'ise-keeping.**—*adj.* **prom'iseless.**—*n.* **prom'iser.**—*adj.* **prom'ising**, affording ground for hope or expectation: likely to turn out well.—*adv.* **prom'isingly.**—*n.* **prom'isor** (*law*).—*adj.* **promiss'ive** (*prə-*), conveying a promise: of the nature of a promise.—*n.* **promiss'or**, (*Rom. law*) the maker of a promise.—*adv.* **prom'issorily.**—*adj.* **prom'issory**, containing a promise of some engagement to be fulfilled.—**be promised**, (*rare*) to have an engagement: **breach of promise** (see **breach**); **promised land**, the land promised by God to Abraham and his seed: Canaan: heaven; **promissory note**, a written promise to pay a sum of money on some future day or on demand; **the Promise**, the assurance of God to Abraham that his descendants should become the chosen people. [L. *prōmissum*, neut. pa.p. of *promittĕre*, to send forward—*prō*, forward, *mittĕre*, to send.]

promontory, *prom'ən-tər-i*, -*tri*, *n.* a headland or high cape: (*anat.*) a projection, ridge, or eminence.—*adj.* standing out like a promontory. [L.L. *prōmontōrium* (L. *prōmuntŭrium*), assimilated to *mōns*, mountain.]

promote, *prə-*, *prō-mōt'*, *v.t.* to help forward: to further: to further the progress of: to raise to a higher grade: to take steps for the passage or formation of: to set in motion (as the office of a judge in a criminal suit).—*ns.* **promo'ter**, one who promotes: one who takes part in the setting up of companies: a promotor: (*obs.*) a professional informer: a substance that increases the efficiency of a catalyst; **promotion** (-*mō'shən*), the act of promoting: advancement in rank or in honour: encouragement: preferment.—*adj.* **promo'tive.** —*n.* **promo'tor**, one who presents candidates for graduation in Scottish universities.—**be on one's promotion**, to have right or hope of promotion: to be on good behaviour with a view to chances of promotion. [L. *prōmovēre*, -*mōtum*—*prō*, forward, *movēre*, to move.]

prompt, *prom(p)t*, *adj.* ready in action: performed at once: paid or due at once: ready for delivery: (*Shak.*) readily inclined.—*adv.* promptly, punctually, to the minute.—*v.t.* to incite: to instigate: to move to action: to supply forgotten words to: to help with words or facts when one is at a loss: to suggest to the mind.—*n.* a time limit for payment: an act of prompting: words furnished by the prompter.—*ns.* **prompt'-book, -copy,** a copy of a play for the prompter's use; **prompt'-box,** a box for the prompter in a theatre; **prompt'er**, one who prompts, esp. actors; **prompt'ing; prompt'itude**, promptness: readiness: quickness of decision and action.—*adv.* **prompt'ly.**—*ns.* **prompt'ness; prompt'-note,** a note of reminder of time-limit of payment; **prompt'-side**, the side of the stage where the prompter is—usually to the actor's left in Britain, to his right in U.S.A.; **prompt'ūary**, a repository: a reference book of facts; **prompt'ure**, (*Shak.*) suggestion: instigation. [L. *prōmptus*—*prōmĕre*, to bring forward.]

promulgate, *prom'əl-gāt* (U.S. *prə-mul'*), *v.t.* to proclaim, publish abroad: to make widely known: to put in execution by proclamation (as a law)—(*arch.*) **promulge** (*prō-mulj'*).—*ns.* **promulga'tion; prom'ulgator.** [L. *prōmulgāre*, -*ātum*.]

promuscis, *prō-mus'is*, *n.* a proboscis, esp. of Hemiptera.—*adj.* **promusc'idate**, like or having a promuscis. [L. *prōmuscis*, -*idis*, a popular perversion of *proboscis*.]

promycelium, *prō-mī-sē'li-əm*, *n.* a short germtube put out by some fungal spores, producing spores of different types. [Gr. *pro*, for, and **mycelium**.]

pronaos, *prō-nā'os*, *n.* the vestibule in front of a temple:—*pl.* **prona'oi.** [Gr. *prŏnāos*—*pro*, before, *nāos*, a temple.]

prone, *prōn, adj.* with the face, ventral surface, or palm of the hand downward: prostrate: directed downward: (loosely) lying or laid flat: descending steeply: disposed, inclined, naturally tending: willing: (*Shak.*) ready, eager: (*Shak., Meas. for Meas.*) perhaps passive, or with downcast eyes, or fervent.—*v.t.* **prōn′ate,** (of the hand) to turn palm downward or backward with radius and ulna crossed—opp. to *supinate.*—*ns.* **prōnā′tion,** the act of pronating; **prōnā′tor,** the muscle of the forearm that pronates the hand.—*adv.* **prone′ly.**—*n.* **prone′ness.** [L. *prōnus.*]

prone, *prōn, n.* (*obs.*) a place in a church where intimations are given out: hence, a homily. [Fr. *prône.*]

prong, *prong, n.* (now chiefly *dial.*) a fork of any kind: a tine, tooth, or spike of a fork or forked object: a tine, spur, or projection, as on an antler: (*U.S.*) a fork of a stream or inlet.—*v.t.* to stab with a prong: to furnish with prongs.—*n.* **prong′buck,** the pronghorn (properly the male).—*adj.* **pronged,** having prongs.—*ns.* **prong′-hoe,** a hoe with prongs; **prong′horn,** an American antelope-like ruminant (*Antilocapra americana*), only representative of the family *Antilocapridae,* with deciduous horns pronged in front.—*adj.* **prong′-horned.** [M.E. *prange*; origin obscure.]

pronominal. See **pronoun.**

pronotum, *prō-nō′təm, n.* the back of an insect's prothorax:—*pl.* **pronō′ta.**—*adj.* **pronō′tal.** [Gr. *pro,* before, *nōton,* back.]

pronoun, *prō′nown, n.* a word used instead of a noun, i.e. to indicate without naming.—*adj.* **pronominal** (*prə-, prō-nom′in-əl*), belonging to, or of the nature of, a pronoun.—*adv.* **pronom′inally.**

pronounce, *prə-, prō-nowns′, v.t.* to proclaim: to utter formally: to utter rhetorically: to declare: to utter: to articulate.—*v.i.* to pass judgment: to articulate one's words.—*n.* (*Milt.*) pronouncement.—*adjs.* **pronounce′able,** capable of being pronounced; **pronounced′,** marked with emphasis: marked.—*adv.* **pronoun′cedly.**—*ns.* **pronounce′-ment,** a confident or authoritative assertion or declaration; **pronoun′cer.**—*n.* and *adj.* **pronoun′cing.** [Fr. *prononcer*—L. *prōnuntiāre*—*prō,* forth, *nūntiāre,* to announce—*nūntius,* a messenger.]

pronto, *pron′tō, adv.* (*U.S. slang*) promptly, quickly. [Sp. *pronto*—L. *prōmptus,* at hand.]

Prontosil, *pron′tō-sil, n.* trade-mark name for some of the sulphonamide drugs.

pronunciamento, *prō-nun-si-ə-men′tō, n.* a manifesto: a formal proclamation. [Sp. *pronunciamiento.*]

pronunciation, *prō-nūn-si-ā′shən, n.* mode of pronouncing: articulation. [L. *prōnuntiātiō, -ōnis*; cf. **pronounce.**]

proo, *pruh, prōō, interj.* (*Scot.*) a call to a cow to come near.

prooemium, *prō-ē′mi-əm, n.* same as **proem.**—Also **prooe′mion.**

proof, *prōōf, n.* that which proves or establishes the truth of anything: the fact, act, or process of proving or showing to be true: demonstration: evidence that convinces the mind and goes toward determining the decision of a court: an instrument of evidence in documentary form: (*Scots law*) the taking of evidence by a judge upon an issue framed in pleading: (*Scots law*) a trial before a judge without a jury: (*arith.*) a checking operation: a test: (*obs.*) experience: (*obs.*) issue, outcome, upshot: a test: testing, esp. of guns: ability to stand a test: invulnerability: impenetrability: armour of proof: a standard strength of spirit (alcohol and water of relative density 12/13 at 51° F.—i.e. 49·28 per cent. of alcohol): (*print.*) an impression taken for correction: an early impression of an engraving: (*phot.*) the first print from a negative: (*pl.* **proofs**).—*adj.* impervious: invulnerable: of standard strength (of alcohol).—*v.t.* to make impervious, esp. to water: to take a proof of: to test.—*n.* **proof′-charge,** a charge used to test the strength of a gun.—*v.t.* **proof′-correct,** to correct in proof.—*ns.* **proof′-correct′-ing;** **proof′-correction;** **proof′-house,** a house fitted up for proving firearms; **proof′ing,**

the process of making waterproof, gasproof, &c.: material used for the purpose.—*adj.* **proof′less,** wanting proof or evidence.—*ns.* **proof′-mark,** a mark stamped on a gun to show that it has stood the test; **proof′-puller,** one who pulls proofs.—*v.t.* and *v.i.* **proof′-read,** to read and correct in proof.—*ns.* **proof′-reader,** one who reads printed proofs to discover and correct errors; **proof′-reading;** **proof′-sheet,** an impression taken on a slip of paper for correction before printing finally; **proof′-spirit,** a standard mixture of alcohol and water; **proof′-text,** a passage of the Bible adduced in proof of a doctrine.—**armour of proof,** armour that has been tested, or can be confidently relied upon; **artist's proof,** a first impression from an engraved plate or block; **burden of proof** (see **burden**); **over, under proof,** containing in 100 volumes enough alcohol for so many volumes more, or less, than 100; **proof before letters,** one taken before the title is engraved on the plate. [O.Fr. *prove* (Fr. *preuve*)—L. *probāre,* to prove.]

prootic, *prō-ot′ik, adj.* in front of the ear.—*n.* an anterior bone of the auditory capsule. [Gr. *pro,* before, *ous, ōtos,* ear.]

prop, *prop, n.* a rigid support: a supplementary support: a stay: a strut: a timber supporting a mine-roof: a supporter, upholder: (*slang*) a leg: a boxer's extended arm: (*Austr.*) an act of propping in a horse.—*v.t.* to hold up by means of something placed under or against: to support or to sustain: (*slang*) to hit straight or knock down.—*v.i.* (*Austr.*) to stop suddenly (of a horse): —*pr.p.* **propp′ing;** *pa.t.* and *pa.p.* **propped.**—*n.* **prop′-root,** a root growing down from a trunk or branch, serving to prop up a tree. [M.E. *proppe*; cf. Du. *proppe,* vine-prop, support.]

prop, *prop, n.* (*slang*) a tie-pin: a brooch. [Du. *prop.*]

prop, *prop, n.* a coll. or slang abbreviation of (aircraft) **propeller,** (theatrical) **property,** (geometrical) **proposition.**—*n.* **props,** property-man.

propaedeutic, *prō-pē-dū′tik, n.* (often in *pl.*) a preliminary study.—*adjs.* **propaedeut′ic, -al.** [Gr. *propaideuein,* to teach beforehand—*pro,* before, *paideuein,* to teach.]

propagate, *prop′ə-gāt, v.t.* to increase by natural process: to multiply: to pass on: to transmit: to spread from one to another: (*obs.*) to increase.—*v.i.* to multiply: to breed.—*adj.* **prop′agable.**—*ns.* **propagan′da,** a congregation of the Roman Catholic Church, founded 1622, charged with the spreading of Catholicism (*dē propāgandā fidē,* 'concerning the faith to be propagated'—not a plural but ablative singular): any association, activity, plan, &c., for the spread of opinions and principles, esp. to effect change or reform; **propagand′ism,** practice of propagating tenets or principles: zeal in spreading one's opinions: proselytism; **propagand′ist**—also *adj.*—*n.* **propagā′tion.**—*adj.* **prop′agative.**—*n.* **prop′agator.**—*v.t.* **propage** (*prō-pāj′; Congreve*), to beget, propagate. [L. *prōpāgāre, -ātum,* conn. with *prōpāgō,* a layer.]

propale, *prō-pāl′, v.t.* to disclose.—*v.i.* (*Scott*) to make a display. [L.L. *prōpalāre*—*prōpalam,* openly —*prō,* forth, *palam,* openly.]

propane, *prō′pān, n.* a hydrocarbon (C_3H_8), third member of the methane series. [**propionic.**]

proparoxytone, *prō-par-ok′si-tōn, adj.* having the acute accent on the third last syllable.—*n.* a word thus accented. [Gr. *proparoxytonos*; see **paroxytone.**]

propel, *prə-, prō-pel′, v.t.* to drive forward:—*pr.p.* **propell′ing;** *pa.t.* and *pa.p.* **propelled′.**—*n.* **propell′ant,** that which propels: an explosive for propelling projectiles.—*adj.* **propell′ent,** driving.—*n.* a driving agent: a motive.—*ns.* **propell′er,** one who, or that which, propels: driving mechanism: a shaft with spiral blades (*screw-propeller*) for driving a ship, aeroplane, &c.: a screw-steamer: a helical blower (*air-propeller, propeller fan*): a spinning-bait; **propell′er-blade;** **propell′er-shaft,** the shaft of a propeller: the driving shaft between gear-box and rear axle in a motor vehicle; **propel′-ment,** propulsion: propelling mechanism. [L. *prōpellĕre*—*prō,* forward, *pellĕre,* to drive.]

Neutral vowels in unaccented syllables: *el′ə-mənt, in′fənt, ran′dəm*

propend, *prə-*, *prō-pend'*, *v.i.* (*Shak.*) to incline.— *adj.* **propend'ent**; **propense** (*-pens'*), inclined: sometimes used in the sense of prepense.—*adv.* **propense'ly.**—*ns.* **propense'ness**, **propen'sion** (*Shak.*), **propens'ity**, inclination of mind: favourable inclination: tendency to good or evil: disposition: tendency to move in a certain direction. —*adj.* **propen'sive.** [L. *prōpendēre*, *-pēnsum*, to hang forward—*prō*, *pendēre*.]

propene. Same as **propylene.**

proper, *prop'ər*, *adj.* own: appropriate: peculiar: confined to one: (*her.*) in natural colouring: strict: strictly applicable: strictly so-called: (now *coll.* or *slang*) thorough, out-and-out: befitting: decorous, seemly: conforming strictly to convention: goodly: belonging to only one: comely: in liturgics, used only on a particular day or festival. —*n.* a service, psalm, &c., set apart for a particular day or occasion.—*adv.* (*coll.*) very, exceedingly.— *adj.* **prop'er-false'**, (*Shak.*) handsome and deceitful.—*adv.* **prop'erly**, in a proper manner: strictly: (*coll.*) entirely, extremely. — *n.* **prop'erness.** — **proper chant**, (*obs.*) the key of C major; **proper fraction**, a fraction that is less than 1 in value; **proper motion**, a star's apparent motion relatively to the celestial sphere, due partly to its own movement (peculiar motion), partly to that of the solar system (parallactic motion). [Fr. *propre*—L. *prōprius*, *prōprius*, own.]

properispomenon, *prō-per-i-spŏm'e-non*, *n.* a word with the circumflex accent on the penult.—Also *adj.* [Gr. *prŏperispŏmenon*, pass. part. neut. of *properispaein*, to circumflex on the penult—*pro*, before, *peri*, round, *spaein*, to draw.]

property, *prop'ər-ti*, *n.* that which is proper to any person or thing: a quality that is always present: a characteristic: (*Shak.*) an essential detail: any quality: (*obs.*) propriety, fitness: that which is one's own: the condition of being one's own: a piece of land owned by somebody: right of possessing, employing, &c.: ownership: an article required on the stage: a mere tool or cat's-paw: (*Shak.*) individuality, personal identity.—*v.t.* (*Shak.*) to treat as a property: to appropriate.—*adj.* of the nature of a stage property.—*adj.* **prop'ertied**, (*Shak.*) imbued with properties: possessed of property.—*ns.* **prop'erty-man**, **-mas'ter**, one who has charge of stage properties; **prop'erty-room**, the room in which stage properties are kept; **prop'erty-tax**, a tax levied on property, at the rate of so much per cent. on its value.—**property qualification**, a qualification (as for office, voting) depending on possession of so much property. [O.Fr. *properte*; see **propriety**.]

prophase, *prō'fāz*, *n.* a preliminary stage of mitosis, preceding the formation of the equatorial plate. [Gr. *pro*, before, and **phase**.]

prophecy, *prof'i-si*, *n.* inspired or prophetic utterance: prediction: (*obs.*) public interpretation of Scripture, or preaching. [O.Fr. *prophecie*—L. *prophētīa*—Gr. *prophēteiā*—*prophētēs*, prophet.]

prophesy, *prof'i-sī*, *v.i.* to utter prophecies: to speak prophetically: (*obs.*) to expound the Scriptures: (*obs.*) to preach: to foretell the future.— *v.t.* to foretell:—*pa.t.* and *pa.p.* **proph'esīed.**— *ns.* **proph'esier**; **proph'esying.** [A variant of **prophecy**.]

prophet, *prof'it*, *n.* a spokesman of deity: one who proclaims a divine message: an inspired teacher, preacher, or poet: the spokesman of a group, movement, or doctrine: a minister of the second order of the Catholic Apostolic Church: a foreteller, whether claiming to be inspired or no: a tipster:—*fem.* **proph'etess.**—*ns.* **proph'ethood**, **proph'etship.**—*adjs.* **prophetic** (*prə-fet'ik*), **-al.**— *adv.* **prophet'ically.**—*n.* **proph'etism.**—*former prophets*, Joshua, Judges, Samuel, and Kings; *latter prophets*, the prophets properly so called; *major prophets*, the prophets whose books come before that of Hosea; *minor prophets*, the prophets from Hosea to Malachi; *school of the prophets*, a school among the ancient Jews for training young men as teachers of the people; *the Prophet*, Mahommed; *the prophets*, one of the three divisions into which the ancient Jews divided their Scriptures—consisting of the *former* and the *latter* prophets (see above). [Fr. *prophète* —L. *prophēta*—Gr. *prophētēs*—*pro*, for, *phanai*, to speak.]

prophylactic, *prof-i-lak'tik*, *adj.* guarding against disease.—*n.* a preventive of disease.—*n.* **prophylax'is** (not a Greek word), preventive treatment. [Gr. *prophylaktikos*—*pro*, before, *phylax*, a guard.]

prophyll, *prō'fil*, *n.* (*bot.*) a bracteole. [Gr. *pro*, before, *phyllon*, leaf.]

propine, *prə-pīn'*, *v.t.* (chiefly *Scot.*, *arch.*) to pledge in drinking: to present, offer.—*n.* a tip: a gift. [L. *propīnāre*—Gr. *propīnein*, to drink first—*pro*, before, *pīnein*, to drink.]

propinquity, *prə-ping'kwi-ti*, *n.* nearness. [L. *propinquitās*, *-ātis*—*propinquus*, near—*prope*, near.]

propionic, *prō-pi-on'ik*, *acid*, one of the fatty acids, $C_2H_5 \cdot COOH$; the first of the series that yields derivatives of a fatty character. [Gr. *pro*, before, *pīŏn*, *-on*, fat.]

propitiate, *prə-pish'i-āt*, *v.t.* to render favourable: to appease.—*adj.* **propi'tiable.**—*n.* **propitiā'tion**, act of propitiating: atonement: atoning sacrifice.—*adj.* **propi'tiātive.**—*n.* **propi'tiātor.**—*adv.* **propi'tiatorily** (*-ə-tər-i-li*).—*adj.* **propi'tiatory**, propitiating: expiatory.—*n.* the Jewish mercyseat: (*arch.*) a propitiation.—*adj.* **propitious** (*-pish'əs*), favourable: disposed to be gracious: of good omen.—*adv.* **propi'tiously.**—*n.* **propi'tiousness.** [L. *propitiāre*, *-ātum*, to make favourable—*propitius*, well-disposed.]

propodeon, *prō-pod'i-on*, *n.* in some Hymenoptera, the first abdominal segment, fused with the thorax and so in front of the waist.—Wrongly Latinised as **propod'eum.** [Gr. *pro*, before, *podeōn*, *-ōnos*, a weaskin neck.]

propolis, *prop'ə-lis*, *n.* bee-glue, a brown sticky resinous substance gathered by bees from trees and used by them as cement and varnish. [Gr. *propolis*.]

propone, *prə-pōn'*, *v.t.* (now *Scot.*) to put forward, propose, propound: to put before a court.—*adj.* **propōn'ent**, bringing forward, proposing: bringing an action.—*n.* a propounder or proposer: (*U.S.*) a favourer, advocate. [L. *prōpōnēre*—*prō*, forward, *pōnēre*, to place.]

proportion, *prə-pōr'shən*, *n.* the relation of one thing to another in magnitude: fitness of parts to each other: due relation: relation of rhythm or of harmony: (*Shak.*) adjustment in due ratio: ratio: (*math.*) the identity or equality of ratios: the rule of three: equal or just share: relative share, portion, inheritance, contribution, quota, fortune: (*coll.*) a part or portion: (*pl.*) dimensions: (*obs.*) form, figure.—*v.t.* to adjust or fashion in due proportion: to regulate the proportions of: (*Shak.*) to be in due proportion to: to divide proportionally.—*adj.* **propor'tionable**, that may be proportioned: having a due or definite relation. —*n.* **propor'tionableness.**—*adv.* **propor'tionably.** —*adj.* **propor'tional**, relating to proportion: in proportion: (*math.*) having the same or a constant ratio: proportionate, in suitable proportion.—*n.* (*math.*) a number or quantity in a proportion.—*n.* **proportional'ity.**—*adv.* **propor'tionally.**—*adj.* **propor'tionate**, in fit proportion: proportional.— *v.t.* to adjust in proportion. — *adv.* **propor'tionately.** — *n.* **propor'tionateness.** — *adj.* **propor'tioned.**—*n.* **propor'tioning**, adjustment of proportions.—*adj.* **propor'tionless**, ill-proportioned.—*n.* **propor'tionment.**—**proportional representation**, a system intended to give parties in an elected body a representation as nearly as possible proportional to their voting strength: often loosely applied to the system of transferred vote. [L. *prōportiō*, *-ōnis*—*prō*, in comparison with, *portiō*, part, share.]

propose, *prə-pōz*, *v.t.* (*obs.*) to put forward or exhibit: to put before one's own or another's mind: to propound: (*Shak.*) to face: (*Shak.*) to imagine, suppose: to offer for consideration or acceptance: (*Shak.*) to formulate as something to be exacted: to proffer: to offer: to suggest or lay before one as something to be done: to purpose or intend: to move formally: to nominate: to invite the company to drink (a health):

to enunciate.—*v.i.* to form or put forward an intention or design: to offer, especially marriage: (*Shak.*) to converse.—*n.* (*obs.*) a proposal: (*Shak.*) talk, discourse.—*adj.* **propōs'able.**—*ns.* **propōs'al,** an act of proposing: an offer, esp. of marriage: (*U.S.*) a tender: anything proposed: a plan; **propōs'er.** [Fr. *proposer*—pfx. *pro-*, *poser*, to place; see **pose.**]

proposition, *prop-ə-zish'ən, n.* an act of propounding or (more rarely) proposing: the thing propounded or proposed: (*Shak.*) an offer: (*Shak.*) a question propounded: a statement of a judgment: (*log.*) a form of statement in which a predicate is affirmed or denied of a subject: a premiss, esp. a major premiss: (*math.*) a statement of a problem or theorem for (or with) solution or demonstration: (*mus.*) enunciation of a subject in a fugue: (*slang*, orig. *U.S.*) any situation, thing, or person considered as something to cope with, as an enterprise, job, opponent, &c.—*adj.* **proposi'tional.** [L. *prōpositiō, -ōnis*—*prō*, before; see **position.**]

propound, *prə-pownd', v.t.* to offer for consideration: to set forth as aim or reward: (*Spens.*) to purpose: (*law*) to produce for probate.—*n.* **propound'er.** [**propone.**]

propraetor, *prō-prē'tər, -tor* (L. *prō-prī'tor*), *n.* a magistrate of ancient Rome, who, after acting as praetor in Rome, was appointed to the government of a province.—*adjs.* **propraetorial** (*-tō'ri-əl*), **propraeto'rian.** [L. *prōpraetor*—*prō praetōre*, for the praetor.]

proprietor, *prō-prī'ə-tər, n.* an owner:—*fem.* **proprī'etress, proprī'etrix** (sham Latin).—*n.* **proprī'etary,** an owner: a body of owners: ownership.—*adj.* of the nature of property: legally made only by a person or body of persons having special rights: owning property.—*adj.* **proprietorial** (*-tō'ri-əl*).—*adv.* **proprieto'rially.**—*n.* **propri'etorship.** [L.L. *proprietārius*—*proprius*, own; **proprietor** has been formed irregularly; it is not a Latin word.]

propriety, *prō-prī'ə-ti, n.* (*obs.*) ownership: rightness, as in the use of words: appropriateness: seemliness: decency: conformity with good manners: conformity with convention in language and conduct: (*obs.*) a character, quality, or property: (*Shak.*) particular nature, individuality. [Fr. *propriété*—L. *proprietās, -ātis*—*proprius*, own.]

proprioceptive, *prō-pri-ō-sep'tiv, adj.* of, pertaining to, or made active by, stimuli arising from movement in the tissues.—*n.* **propriocep'tor,** a sensory nerve-ending receptive of such stimuli.— **proprioceptive sense,** the sense of muscular position. [L. *proprius*, own, after **receptive.**]

proproctor, *prō-prok'tər, n.* a proctor's substitute or assistant.

proptosis, *prop-tō'sis, n.* forward displacement, esp. of the eye. [Gr. *proptōsis*—*pro*, forward, *ptōsis*, fall.]

propugnation, *prō-pug-nā'shən, n.* (*Shak.*) defence. [L., *prō*, for, *pugnāre*, to fight.]

propulsion, *prə-pul'shən, n.* driving forward.—*adjs.* **propul'sive, propul'sory.** [L. *prōpellēre, prōpulsum*, to push forward; see **propel.**]

propyl, *prō'pil, n.* the alcohol radical C_3H_7.—*ns.* **pro'pylamine,** an amine of propyl; **pro'pylene,** **propene.**—*adj.* **propyl'ic.** [**propionic** and Gr. *hȳlē*, matter.]

propylaeum, *prop-i-lē'əm, propylon, prop'i-lon, ns.* a gateway of architectural importance, leading into a temple, &c.:—*pl.* **propylae'a, prop'yla.**—*ns.* **prop'ylite,** an andesite altered by solfataric action, orig. applied to andesites of the beginning (or gateway) of the Tertiary time; **propylitisā'tion.**—*v.t.* **prop'ylitise.** [Gr. *propylaion* (used in pl., *-a*) and *propylon*—*pro*, before, *pylē*, a gate.]

prore, *prōr, n.* (*poet.*) a prow: a ship. [Obs. Fr.,— L. *prōra*, prow—Gr. *prōirā*.]

prorector, *prō-rek'tər, n.* a university or college rector's substitute or assistant.

prorogue, *prə-, prō-rōg', v.t.* (*obs.*) to prolong: (*Shak.*) to postpone: (*Shak.*) perh., to keep from exertion: to discontinue the meetings of for a time

without dissolving.—*v.t.* **prō'rogāte,** to prorogue. —*n.* **prōrogā'tion.** [L. *prōrogāre, -ātum*—*prō*, forward, *rogāre*, to ask.]

prosaic, -al, *prō-zā'ik, -əl, adjs.* like prose: unpoetical: matter-of-fact: commonplace: dull: (*rare*) in or relating to prose.—*adv.* **prosā'ically.** —*ns.* **prosā'icalness; prosā'icism** (*-sizm*), prosaism; **prosā'icness,** quality of being prosaic; **prō'sāism,** a prose idiom: a prosaic phrase: prosaic character; **prō'sāist,** a writer of prose: a commonplace person. [L. *prōsa*, prose.]

proscenium, *prō-sē'ni-əm, n.* the front part of the stage: the curtain and its framework. [Latinised from Gr. *proskēnion*—*pro*, before, *skēnē*, stage.]

proscribe, *prō-skrib', v.t.* to put on the list of those who may be put to death: to outlaw: to ostracise: to prohibit: to denounce.—*ns.* **prōscrib'er; prō'script,** one who is proscribed; **prōscrip'tion.** —*adj.* **prōscrip'tive.**—*adv.* **prōscrip'tively.** [L. *prōscribēre*—*prō-*, before, publicly, *scribēre, scriptum*, to write.]

prose, *prōz, n.* the direct, straightforward arrangement of words, free from poetical measures: ordinary spoken and written language: all writings not in verse: a composition in prose, esp. as an exercise in Latin or Greek: a piece of prosing: a familiar or gossipy talk: prosaic character: a prosy talker.—*adj.* of or in prose: not poetical: plain: dull.—*v.i.* to write prose: to speak or write tediously.—*v.t.* to compose in prose: to turn into prose.—*ns.* **prose'man,** a prose-writer; **prose'-poem,** a prose work or passage having some of the characteristics of poetry; **prō'ser; prose'-writer.**—*adv.* **prō'sily.**—*ns.* **prō'siness; prō'sing,** speaking or writing in a dull or prosy way.—*adj.* **prō'sy,** dull, tedious, humdrum. [Fr., —L. *prōsa*—*prorsus*, straightforward—*prō*, forward, *vertēre, versum*, to turn.]

prosector, *prō-sekt'ər, n.* one who dissects a body for the illustration of anatomical lectures: the official anatomist of a zoological society.—*adj.* **prosectō'rial.**—*n.* **prosec'torship.** [L.L. *prōsector*—*prō-secāre, -sectum*, to cut up—*prō-*, away, *secāre*, to cut.]

prosecute, *pros'i-kūt, v.t.* to follow onwards or pursue, in order to reach or accomplish: to engage in, practise: to follow up: (*obs.*) to pursue, chase: to pursue by law: to bring before a court.—*v.i.* to carry on a legal prosecution.—*adj.* **pros'ecūtable.**—*ns.* **prosecū'tion,** the act of prosecuting in any sense: the prosecuting party in legal proceedings; **pros'ecūtor,** one who prosecutes or pursues any plan or business: one who carries on a civil or criminal suit:—*fem.* **pros'ecūtrix** (modern L.): —*pl.* **pros'ecūtrixes, prosecutrices** (*-kū-tri'sēz, -kū'tri-sēz*).—**public prosecutor,** one appointed to conduct criminal prosecutions in the public interest. [L. *prōsequī, -secūtus*—*prō*, onwards, *sequī*, to follow.]

proselyte, *pros'i-līt, n.* one who has come over from one religion or opinion to another: a convert, esp. from paganism to Judaism.—*v.t.* and *v.i.* (*U.S.*) to proselytise.—*v.t.* **pros'elytise,** to convert.—*v.i.* to make proselytes.—*ns.* **pros'elytiser; pros'elytism,** being, becoming, or making a convert: conversion.—**proselyte of the gate,** a heathen allowed to live in Palestine on making certain concessions to Judaism. [Gr. *prosēlytos*, a newcomer, resident foreigner—*pros*, to, and the stem *elyth-*, used to form aorists for *erchesthai*, to go.]

prosencephalon, *pros-en-sef'ə-lon, n.* the fore-brain, comprising the cerebral hemispheres and olfactory processes.—*adj.* **prosencephalic** (*-si-fal'ik*). [Gr. *pros*, to, used as if for *pro*, before, *enkephalon*, brain—*en*, in, *kephalē*, head.]

prosenchyma, *pros-eng'ki-mä, n.* a plant-tissue of long cells with pointed ends—conducting or supporting tissue.—*adj.* **prosenchymatous** (*-kim'ə-tas*). [Gr. *pros*, to, *enchyma*, an infusion, in-pouring.]

proseuche (*-cha*), *pros-ū'kē* (*-kä*), *n.* a place of prayer, oratory:—*pl.* (L.) **proseu'chae** (*-kē*). [Gr. *proseuchē*, prayer, place of prayer—*pros*, to, *euchē*, prayer.]

prosilient, *prō-sil'i-ənt, adj.* outstanding.—*n.* **pro-sil'iency.** [L. *prōsiliēns, -entis,* pr.p. of *prosilīre,* to leap forward—*prō-,* forward, *salīre,* to leap.]

prosit, *prō'sit, interj.* good luck to you, a salutation in drinking healths customary among German students. [L. *prōsit,* used as 3rd pers. sing. pres. subj. of L. *prōdesse,* to be of use—*prō*(d)-, for, *esse,* to be.]

proslambanomenos, *pros-lam-ban-om'e-nos, n.* (*anc. Gr. mus.*) an additional note at the bottom of the scale. [Gr., pr.p. pass. of *proslambanein,* to take in addition—pfx. *pros-, lambanein,* to take.]

prosody, *pros'ə-di, n.* the study of versification.—*adjs.* **prosodial** (*pros-, prəs-ō'di-əl*), **prosodic** (*-od'ik*), **-al.**—*ns.* **proso'dian, pros'odist,** one skilled in prosody.—*adv.* **prosod'ically.** [L. *prosōdia,* Gr. *prosōidiā—pros,* to, *ōidē,* a song.]

prosopopoeia, *pros-ō-pō-pē'yä, n.* personification. [Gr. *prosōpopoiiā—prosōpon,* face, person, *poieein,* to make.]

prospect, *pros'pekt, n.* outlook : direction of facing : (*Milt.*) a look-out or view-point : a wide view : view, sight, field of view : a scene : a pictorial representation, view : (*Shak.*) position for being observed : a survey or mental view : outlook upon the probable future : expectation : chance of success : (*Russ. prospekt'*) a wide street : (*obs.*) a prospect-glass : (*U.S.*) a probable customer : (*mining*) a place thought likely to yield a valuable mineral : a sample, or a test or the yield of a test of a sample from such a place : a probable source of profit.—*v.i.* **prospect',** to look around : (*prəs-pekt'* ; *U.S. pros'*) to make a search, esp. for chances of mining : to promise or yield results to the prospector.—*v.t.* (*-pekt'*) to face, view : (*-pekt'* ; *U.S. pros'*) to explore, search, survey, or test for profitable minerals.—*ns.* **pros'pect-glass,** a telescope or field-glass ; **prospect'ing** (*U.S. pros'*), searching a district for minerals with a view to further operations ; **prospec'tion,** looking to the future : foresight.—*adj.* **prospec'tive,** probable or expected future : looking forward : yielding distant views : looking to the future.—*n.* prospect. —*n.* **prospect'ive-glass,** a prospect-glass : a scrying crystal.—*adv.* **prospec'tively.**—*n.* **pro-spec'tiveness** ; **prospec'tor** (*U.S. pros'*), one who prospects for minerals ; **prospec'tus,** the outline of any plan submitted for public approval, particularly of a literary work or of a joint-stock concern : an account of the organisation of a school :—*pl.* **prospec'tuses.** [L. *prōspectus, -ūs—prōspicēre, prospectum—prō-,* forward, *specĕre,* to look.]

prosper, *pros'pər, v.i.* to thrive : to get on : to experience favourable circumstances : to flourish : to turn out well.—*v.t.* to cause to prosper.—*n.* **prosperity** (*-per'i-ti*), the state of being prosperous : success : good fortune.—*adj.* **pros'perous,** thriving : successful. — *adv.* **pros'perously.** — *n.* **pros'perousness.** [L. *prosper, prosperus.*]

prostate, *pros'tāt, n.* a gland in males at the neck of the bladder.—Also **prostate gland.**—*adj.* **pros-tatic** (*pros-tat'ik*).—*ns.* **pros'tatism** (*-tat-izm*), a morbid condition associated with enlargement of the prostate ; **prostati'tis,** inflammation of the prostate gland. [Gr. *prostatēs,* one who stands in front, the prostate—*pro,* before, *sta,* root of *histanai,* to set up.]

prosthesis, *pros'thə-sis, n.* addition as a prefix : the fitting of artificial parts to the body.—*adj.* **prosthetic** (*-thet'ik*). [Gr. *prosthesis,* adj. *pros-thetikos—pros,* to, *thesis,* putting.]

prostitute, *pros'ti-tūt, v.t.* to devote to, or offer or sell for, evil or base use : to hire out for indiscriminate sexual intercourse : to devote to such intercourse as a religious act : to degrade by publicity or commonness.—*adj.* openly devoted to lewdness : given over (to evil) : basely venal : (*obs.*) hackneyed, debased by commonness.—*n.* a common harlot or whore : a base hireling.—*ns.* **prostitu'tion,** the act or practice of prostituting : lewdness for hire : devotion to base purposes ; **pros'titutor.** [L. *prōstituĕre, -ūtum,* to set up for sale—*prō,* before, *statuĕre,* to place.]

prostomium, *prō-stō'mi-əm, n.* part of a worm's head in front of the mouth.—*adj.* **prosto'mial.** [Gr. *pro,* before, *stoma,* mouth.]

prostrate, *pros'trāt, adj.* prone : lying or bent with face on the ground : (loosely) lying at length : (*bot.*) procumbent, trailing : lying at mercy : reduced to helplessness : completely exhausted.—*v.t.* **prostrate'** (or *pros'*), to throw forwards on the ground : to lay flat : to overthrow : to reduce to impotence or exhaustion : to bend in humble reverence.—*n.* **prostrā'tion.** [L. *prōstrātus,* pa.p. of *prōsternĕre—prō,* forwards, *sternĕre,* to spread.]

prostyle, *prō'stīl, n.* (*Gr. archit.*) a front portico of not more than four columns, without *antae* : a building with such a portico and no other.—*adj.* having a prostyle. [Gr. *prostylon—pro,* before, *stylos,* a column.]

prosy. See **prose.**

prosyllogism, *prō-sil'ə-jizm, n.* a syllogism whose conclusion becomes the major premise of another. [Gr. *pro,* before, *syllogismos,* syllogism.]

protactinium, *prōt-ak-tin'i-əm, n.* radioactive element (at. numb. 91) that yields actinium on disintegration. [Gr. *prōtos,* first, and **actinium.**]

protagonist, *prō-tag'ən-ist, n.* the chief actor, character, or combatant. [Gr. *prōtos,* first, *agōnistēs,* a combatant, actor.]

protandry, *prōt-an'dri, n.* in hermaphrodite organisms, ripening and shedding of the male elements before the female is ready to receive them : in flowers, opening of the anthers before the stigmas can receive pollen — opp. to *protogyny.* — *adj.* **protan'drous.** [Gr. *prōtos,* first, *anēr, andros,* man, male.]

protasis, *prot'ə-sis, n.* the conditional clause of a conditional sentence—opp. to *apodosis* : the first part of a dramatic composition.—*adj.* **protatic** (*prə-tat'ik*). [Gr. *protasis,* proposition, premise, protasis—*pro,* before, *tasis,* a stretching, *teinein,* to stretch.]

Protea, *prō'ti-ä, n.* a large South African genus of shrubs or small trees, of the mainly Australian family **Protea'ceae,** with big cone-shaped heads of flowers : a plant of the genus.—*adj.* **protea'ceous.** [Proteus ; from the varied character of the family.]

Protean, protean, *prō'ti-ən, prō-tē'ən, adj.* readily assuming different shapes : variable : inconstant. [Proteus.]

protect, *prə-, prō-tekt', v.t.* to shield from danger, injury, change, capture, loss : to defend : to strengthen : to seek to foster by import duties : (*Shak.*) to act as regent for : to screen off, prevent danger from.—*adjs.* **protect'ed** ; **protect'ing.**—*adv.* **protect'ingly.**—*ns.* **protec'tion,** act of protecting : state of being protected : defence : that which protects : guard : a writing guaranteeing against molestation or interference : a fostering of home produce and manufactures by import duties : patronage : concubinage : control of a country's foreign relations, and sometimes internal affairs, without annexation ; **protec'tionism** ; **pro-tec'tionist,** one who favours the protection of trade by duties on imports — also *adj.*—*adj.* **protec'tive,** affording protection : intended to protect : defensive : sheltering. — *n.* that which protects. — *adv.* **protec'tively.** — *ns.* **protec'tive-ness** ; **protec'tor,** one who protects from injury or oppression : a protective device : a means of protection : a guard : a guardian : a regent : the head of the state during the Commonwealth (*Lord Protector*) :—*fem.* **protec'tress, protec'trix.** —*adj.* **protec'toral,** of a protector or a regent.—*n.* **protec'torāte,** the position, office, term of office, or government of a protector : (*hist.*) the Commonwealth period : guardianship : authority over a vassal state : relation assumed by a state over a territory which it administers without annexation and without admitting the inhabitants to citizenship.—*adjs.* **protectō'rial** (*prō-*) ; **pro-tec'torless.**—*ns.* **protec'torship** ; **protec'tory,** an institution for destitute or delinquent children. —**protective coloration,** likeness in the colour of animals to their natural surroundings tending to prevent them from being seen by their enemies. [L. *prōtegĕre, -tēctum—prō-,* in front, *tegĕre,* to cover.]

protégé, *prō'*, or *pro'tā-zhā*, *n.* one under the protection or patronage of another : a pupil : a ward : —*fem.* protégée (*-zhā*). [Fr.,—pa.p. of *protéger*, to protect—L. *prōtegĕre*.]

protein, *prō'tē-in*, *n.* any member of a group of complex nitrogenous substances that play an important part in the bodies of plants and animals, compounds of carbon, hydrogen, oxygen, nitrogen, usually sulphur, often phosphorus, &c., easily hydrolysed into mixtures of amino-acids. — *ns.* pro'tease (*-tē-ās, -āz*), any enzyme that splits up proteins ; pro'teid (*-tē-id*), an abandoned name for protein, still in popular use ; proteolysis (*-ol'i-sis*), splitting of proteins by enzymes.—*v.t.* pro'teolyse (*-ō-līz*).—*adj.* proteolytic (*-ō-lit'ik*). [Gr. *prōteios*, primary—*prōtos*, first.]

protend, *prō-tend'*, *v.t.* to stretch forth : to hold out.—*ns.* protense', (*Spens.*) extension in time ; proten'sion, duration ; proten'sity.—*adj.* proten'sive. [L. *prōtendĕre*, *-tentus* (*-tēnsus*)—*prō-*, forward, *tendĕre*, to stretch.]

proterandry, *prot-ər-an'dri*, or *prōt-*, *n.* protandry. —*adj.* proteran'drous. [Gr. *proteros*, earlier, *anēr*, *andros*, man, male.]

proterogyny, *prot-*, *prōt'ər-oj'i-ni*, or *-og'*, *n.* proterogyny.— *adj.* proterog'ynous. [Gr. *proteros*, earlier, *gynē*, woman, female.]

Proterozoic, *prot-ər-ō-zō'ik*, or *prōt-*, *n.* and *adj.* (*orig.*) Lower Palaeozoic (Cambrian to Silurian) : Pre-Cambrian : Upper Pre-Cambrian. [Gr. *proteros*, earlier, *zōē*, life.]

protervity, *prō-tər'vi-ti*, *n.* peevishness : perversity : wantonness. [L. *prōtervus*, *prōtervus*.]

protest, *prə-*, *prō-test'*, *v.i.* to express or record dissent or objection : to make solemn affirmation, professions, or avowal.—*v.t.* to make a solemn declaration of : to declare : to note, as a bill of exchange, on account of non-acceptance or non-payment : (*Shak.*) to proclaim : (*Shak.*) to vow : (*Milt.*) to call to witness : (*U.S.*) to make a protest against.—*ns.* prō'test, an affirmation or avowal : a declaration of objection or dissent : the noting by a notary-public of an unpaid or unaccepted bill : a written declaration, usually by the master of a ship, stating the circumstances attending loss or injury of ship or cargo, &c. ; Protestant (*prot'is-tənt*), one of those who, in 1529, protested against an edict of Charles V. and the Diet of Spires denouncing the Reformation : a member, adherent, or sharer of the beliefs of one of those churches founded by the Reformers (formerly by some confined to Anglicans or Lutherans, now disavowed by some Anglicans) : prot'estant, (*Herrick*) an avowed lover : (sometimes *prō-tes'tənt*) one who protests.—*adj.* Protestant (*prot'*), of Protestants, or Protestantism : protestant (*prot'is-*, or *prō-tes'tənt*), protesting : one who protests.—*v.t.* Prot'estantise.—*ns.* Prot'estantism, the Protestant religion : state of being a Protestant ; protestation (*prō-tes-tā'shan*), an avowal : an asseveration : a declaration in pleading : (*rare*) a protest ; protest'er, -or, one who protests, esp. (*Scot. hist.*) a Remonstrant or opponent of the Resolutioners.—*adv.* protest'ingly. [Fr. *protester*—L. *prōtestārī*, *-ātus*, to bear witness in public—*prō*, before, *testārī*—*testis*, a witness.]

Proteus, *prō'tūs*, *n.* an ancient Greek sea-god who assumed many shapes to evade having to foretell the future : a European genus of cave-dwelling tailed amphibians with persistent gills. [Gr. *Prōteus.*]

Protevangelium, *prot-ev-an-jel'i-əm*, *n.* the promise to Eve : a gospel attributed to James the Less : an inferred source of the canonical gospels. [Gr. *prōtos*, first, L. *evangelium*—Gr. *euangelion*, gospel.]

prothalamion, *prō-thə-lā'mi-on*, *n.* a poem celebrating a coming marriage. [App. coined by Spenser from Gr. *pro*, before, *thalamos*, a bridechamber.]

prothallus,] *prō-thal'əs*, prothallium, *-i-um*, *ns.* the gametophyte or sexual generation in ferns and their allies, a small plate of tissue derived from a spore and bearing antheridia and archegonia : the homologous stage in gymnosperms : — *pl.*

prothall'i, prothall'ia.—*adjs.* prothall'ial, prothall'oid. [Gr. *pro*, before, *thallos*, a young shoot.]

prothesis, *proth'i-sis*, *n.* in the Greek Church the preliminary oblation of the eucharistic elements before the liturgy : the table used : the chapel or northern apse where it stands : (*gram.*) development of an inorganic initial sound.—*adj.* prothetic (*prə-*, *prō-thet'ik*). [Gr. *prothesis*—*pro*, before, and the root of *tithenai*, to place.]

prothonotary, protonotary, *prō-t(h)on'at-ə-ri*, *prōt(h)ō-nō'tə-ri*, *n.* a chief notary or clerk : a chief secretary of the chancery at Rome : a chief clerk or registrar of a court.—*adj.* prot(h)onotā'rial.— *n.* prot(h)onotā'riat, the college constituted by the twelve apostolical prothonotaries in Rome. [L.L. *prōt(h)onotārius*—Gr. *prōtos*, first, L. *notārius*, a clerk.]

prothorax, *prō-thō'raks*, *n.* the anterior segment of the thorax of insects.—*adj.* prothoracic (*-ras'*).

prothyl(e). See protyle.

Protista, *prō-tis'tä*, *n.pl.* a large group of unicellular organisms on the border-line between plants and animals : a proposed term for a biological kingdom including Protozoa and Protophyta :—*sing.* pro'tist. —*adj.* protist'ic.—*ns.* protistol'ogist ; protistol'ogy. [Gr. *prōtistos*, very first—*prōtos*, first.]

protium, *prō'ti-əm*, *-shi-əm*, *n.* ordinary hydrogen of atomic weight 1, distinguished from deuterium. [Gr. *prōtos*, first.]

proto-, *prō'tō-*, prot-, *prōt-*, in composition, first : first of a series : first-formed : primitive : ancestral. [Gr. *prōtos*, first.]

protoactinium, *prō-tō-ak-tin'i-əm*, *n.* a former variant of protactinium.

Protococcus, *prō-tō-kok'əs*, *n.* an abandoned genus of rounded unicellular algae, one of which renamed *Pleurococcus vulgaris* forms a green film common on trees, &c.—*adj.* protococc'al.—*n.pl.* Protococcales (*-ā'lēz*), the order of green algae to which it belongs. [Gr. *kokkos*, a berry.]

protocol, *prō'tō-kol*, *n.* an original note, minute, or draft of an instrument or transaction : a draft treaty : an official or formal account or record : (*U.S.*) a record of transfer of lands : an official formula : a body of diplomatic etiquette. — *v.i.* to issue, form protocols.—*v.t.* to make a protocol of :—*pr.p.* pro'tocolling ; *pa.t.* and *pa.p.* pro'tocolled.—Also prō'tocolise.—*n.* pro'tocolist, a registrar or clerk. [Fr. *protocole*—L.L. *prōtocollum*—Late Gr. *prōtokollon*, a glued-on descriptive first leaf of a MS.—Gr. *prōtos*, first, *kolla*, glue.]

protogine, *prō'tō-jin*, *-jēn*, *n.* a gneissose granite of the Alps with sericite. [Gr. *prōtos*, first, *ginesthai*, to come into being (as once thought to be the first-formed granite).]

protogyny, *prōt-oj'i-ni*, or *-og'*, *n.* in hermaphrodite organisms, ripening of the female germ-cells before the male : in flowers, ripening of stigmas before stamens.—*adj.* protog'ynous. [Gr. *prōtos*, *gynē*, woman, female.]

proto-historic, *prō-tō-his-tor'ik*, *adj.* belonging to the earliest age of history, just after the prehistoric. —*n.* proto-his'tory.

protomartyr, *prō'tō-mär-tər*, *n.* the first martyr in any cause, esp. St Stephen. [Late Gr. *prōtomartyr.*]

proton, *prō'ton*, *n.* a particle with charge equal and opposite (positive) to that of an electron but much greater mass.—*adj.* protonic (*-ton'ik*). [Gr., neut. of *prōtos*, first.]

protonema, *prō-tə-nē'mä*, *n.* a branched filament produced by germination of a moss spore, giving rise to moss-plants from buds. [Gr. *prōtos*, *nēma*, thread.]

protonotary. Same as prothonotary.

Protophyta, *prō-tof'i-tä*, *n.pl.* the unicellular plants : —*sing.* protophyte (*prō'tə-fīt*).—*adj.* protophytic (*-fit'ik*). [Gr. *prōtos*, first, *phyton*, a plant.]

protoplasm, *prō'tə-plazm*, *n.* living matter, the physical basis of life. — *adj.* protoplasm'ic. — *n.* prō'toplast, he who, or that which, was first formed : an original : the first parent : (*biol.*) an energid.—*adj.* protoplast'ic. [Gr. *prōtos*, first, *plasma*, form—*plassein*, to form.]

protospatharius, *prō-tə-spā-thā'ri-əs*, *n.* captain of

the guards at Byzantium.—Also (*Fr.*) **protospat(h)aire** (*-thär'*, *-tār'*). [Gr. *prōtos*, first, *spathārios*, a guardsman—*spathē*, a blade.]

Prototheria, *prō-tə-thē'ri-ä*, *n.pl.* the monotremes. [Gr. *prōtos*, first, *thēr*, wild beast.]

Prototracheata, *prō-tə-trak-i-ā'tä*, *n.pl.* a class of primitive tracheate arthropods to which Peripatus belongs. [Gr. *prōtos*, first; see **trachea**.]

prototype, *prō'tə-tīp*, *n.* the first or original type or model from which anything is copied: an exemplar: a pattern: an ancestral form.—*adjs.* **pro'totypal**, **prototypical** (*-tip'*). [Fr., — Gr. *prōtos*, first, *typos*, a type.]

protoxide, *prō-tok'sīd*, *n.* that oxide of a series which has the smallest number of oxygen atoms.

Protozoa, *prō-tō-zō'ä*, *n.pl.* the lowest and simplest of animals, unicellular forms or colonies multiplying by fission:—*sing.* **protozō'on**.—*n.* and *adj.* **protozō'an**.—*adjs.* **protozō'ic**, pertaining to the Protozoa: (*obs. geol.*) containing remains of the earliest life of the globe (variously applied); **protozoolog'ical**.—*ns.* **protozool'ogist**; **protozool'ogy**. [Gr. *prōtos*, first, *zōion*, an animal.]

protract, *prō-trakt'*, *v.t.* to draw out or lengthen in time: to prolong. to put off in time: to lengthen out: to protrude: to draw to scale.—*adj.* **protrac'ted**, drawn out in time: prolonged: postponed: lengthened out: drawn to scale.—*adv.* **protrac'tedly**.—*adj.* **protrac'tile**, susceptible of being thrust out.—*n.* **protrac'tion** (*-shən*), act of protracting or prolonging: the delaying of the termination of a thing: the plotting or laying down of the dimensions of anything on paper: a plan drawn to scale.—*adj.* **protrac'tive**, drawing out in time: prolonging: delaying.—*n.* **protrac'tor**, one who, or that which, protracts: an instrument for laying down angles on paper: a muscle whose contraction draws a part forward or away from the body. [L. *prōtrahĕre*, -*tractum*—*prō*, forth, *trahĕre*, to draw.]

protreptic, *prō-trep'tik*, *adj.* hortative.—*n.* an exhortation.—*adj.* **protrep'tical**. [Gr. *protreptikos* —*pro*, forward, *trepein*, to turn, direct.]

protrude, *prō-trōōd'*, *v.t.* to thrust or push out or forward: to obtrude.—*v.i.* to stick out, project.— *adjs.* **protrud'able**, **protru'sible** (*-trōōs'i-bl*), **protru'sile** (*-sīl*), able to be protruded.—*n.* **protru'sion** (*-zhən*), the act of protruding: the state of being protruded: that which protrudes.—*adj.* **protru'sive**, thrusting or impelling forward: protruding.—*adv.* **protru'sively**.—*n.* **protru'siveness**. [L. *prōtrūdĕre*, -*trūsum*—*prō*, forward, *trūdĕre*, to thrust.]

protuberance, *prō-tūb'ər-əns*, *n.* a bulging out: a swelling.—*adj.* **protū'berant**.—*adv.* **protū'berantly**.—*v.i.* **protū'berate**, to bulge out.—*n.* **protūberā'tion**. [L. *prōtūberāre*, -*ātum*—*prō*, forward, *tūber*, a swelling.]

protyle, **prothyle**, *prō't(h)īl*, **prothyl**, *prō'thil*, *n.* a hypothetical primitive matter from which the chemical elements have been thought to be formed. [Gr. *prōtos*, first, *hȳlē*, matter.]

proud, *prowd*, *adj.* having excessive self-esteem: arrogant: haughty: having a proper sense of self-respect: having an exulting sense of credit due to or reflected upon oneself: having a glowing feeling of gratification: giving reason for pride or boasting: manifesting pride: having an appearance of pride, vigour, boldness, and freedom: stately: mettlesome: swelling: sexually excited (esp. of some female animals).—*n.* **proud'-flesh**, a growth or excrescence of flesh in a wound.—*adjs.* **proud'-heart'ed**, (*Shak.*) having a proud spirit; **proud'ish**, somewhat proud.—*adv.* **proud'ly**.—*adj.* **proud'-mind'ed**, (*Shak.*) proud in mind.— *n.* **proud'ness**, (*rare*) pride.—*adjs.* **proud'-pied**, (*Shak.*) gorgeously variegated; **proud'-stom'ached**, of haughty spirit, arrogant.—**do one proud**, (*coll.*) to treat one sumptuously. [O.E. *prúd*, *prút*, proud; perh. from a L.L. word connected with L. *prōdesse*, to be of advantage.]

proustite, *prōōs'tīt*, *n.* a red silver ore, sulphide of arsenic and silver. [J. L. *Proust* (1754-1826), French chemist, who distinguished it from pyrargyrite.]

provand, **provend**, *prov'ənd*, **proviant**, *prov'i-ənt*, *n.* an allowance of food: (*Shak.*) provender: provisions: fodder. — *adj.* **prov'ant**, issued to soldiers, hence inferior. [M.L.G. *provande*, Du. *provande*, *proviand*, Ger. *proviant*, app. — L.L. *provenda* for L. *praebenda*—*praebēre*, to allow.]

prove, *prōōv*, *v.t.* to test, experience, suffer: to test the genuineness of: to ascertain: to establish or ascertain as truth by argument or otherwise: to demonstrate: (*arith.*) to check by the opposite operation: to obtain probate of.—*v.i.* to make trial: to turn out: to be shown afterwards: (*arch.*) to become: (*obs.*) to turn out well :—*pa.p.* **proved**.—Also (*obs.*) **preve** (with *pa.p.* surviving, esp. in *Scots law*, **proven**), **pree** (*Scot.*).—*adj.* **prov'able** (also **prove'able**).—*adv.* **prov(e)'ably**.—*n.* **prov'er**.—**proving ground**, a place for testing scientifically: also *fig.*; **the exception proves the rule**, the making of an exception proves that the rule holds good otherwise. [O.Fr. *prover*—L. *probāre*—*probus*, excellent; partly perh.—O.E. *prófian*, to assume to be—L. *probāre*; but the forms **preve**, &c., represent the O.Fr. vowel corresponding to a stressed vowel in L., as 3rd pers. sing. *prueve*.]

proveditor, *prō-ved'i-tər*, **provedor(e)**, **providor**, *prov-i-dōr'*, *n.* a high official, governor, inspector, commissioner: a purveyor. [It. *provveditore*, Port. *provedor*, Sp. *proveedor*.]

proven, *prōōv'n*, *prōōv'n* (esp. *Scots law*), *pa.p.* of **preve** (see **prove**), and *adj.*, proved.—**not proven**, a verdict declaring that guilt has been neither proved nor disproved.

provenance, *prov'i-nəns*, *n.* source. [Fr.,—L. *prō-*, forth, *venīre*, to come.]

Provençal, *prov-än^g-säl'*, *adj.* of or pertaining to *Provence*, in France, or to its inhabitants or language.—*n.* a native or the language of Provence, *langue d'oc*. [L. *prōvinciālis*—*prōvincia*, province.]

provender, *prov'in-dər*, *-ən-dər*, *n.* food: dry food for beasts, as hay or corn: esp. a mixture of meal and cut straw or hay.—*v.t.* and *v.i.* to feed. [O.Fr. *provendre* for *provende*—L.L. *provenda*; see **provand**.]

provenience, *prō-vē'ni-əns*, *n.* provenance. [L. *prōvenīre*; see **provenance**.]

proverb, *prov'ərb*, *n.* a short familiar sentence expressing a supposed truth or moral lesson: a byword: (*B.*) a saying that requires explanation: (*pl.* **Proverbs**) a book of maxims in the Old Testament: a dramatic composition in which a proverb gives name and character to the plot.— *v.t.* to speak of proverbially: make a byword of: to provide with a proverb.—*adj.* **prover'bial** (*prə-vər'bi-əl*), like or of the nature of a proverb: expressed or mentioned in a proverb: notorious. —*v.t.* **prover'bialise**, to speak in proverbs.—*ns.* **prover'bialism**, a saying in the form of, or like, a proverb; **prover'bialist**.—*adv.* **prover'bially**. [Fr. *proverbe* — L. *prōverbium* — *prō-*, publicly, *verbum*, a word.]

provide, *prə-*, *prō-vīd'*, *v.t.* to make ready beforehand: to prepare for future use: to supply: to appoint or give a right to a benefice, esp. before it is actually vacant: to stipulate.—*v.i.* to procure supplies, means, or whatever may be desirable, make provision: to take measures.—*adj.* **provī'dable**.—*pa.p.* or *conj.* **provi'ded**, (often with *that*) on condition: upon these terms: with the understanding.—*n.* **provi'der**.—**provided school**, in England and Wales, a school maintained by, and under the management of, the local authority. [L. *prōvidēre*—*prō*, before, *vidēre*, to see.]

providence, *prov'i-dəns*, *n.* foresight: prudent management and thrift: timely preparation: (*theol.*) the foresight and benevolent care of God: God, considered in this relation (usu. with capital): an ordering or intervention by God for this purpose: an occurrence attributed to God's ordering or intervention: (*U.S.*) a disaster.—*adjs.* **prov'ident**, seeing beforehand, and providing for the future: prudent: thrifty: frugal; **providential** (*-den'shl*), affected by, or proceeding from, divine providence: (*rare*) provident.—*advs.* **providen'-**

tially; **prov′idently.** [L. *prŏvidēns, -ēntis,* pr.p. of *prŏvidēre—prŏ,* before, *vidēre,* to see.]

province, *prov′ins, n.* a portion of an empire or a state marked off for purposes of government or in some way historically distinct: the district over which an archbishop has jurisdiction: a territorial division of the Jesuits, Templars, and other orders: a faunal or floral area: a region: vaguely, a field of duty, activity, or knowledge: a department: (in *pl.,* esp. *theat.* and *journalism*) all parts of the country but the capital.—*adj.* **provincial** (*prə-vin′shl*), relating to a province: belonging to a province or the provinces: local: showing the habits and manners of a province: unpolished: narrow.—*n.* an inhabitant of a province or country district: (*R.C.*) the superintendent of the heads of the religious houses in a province.—*v.t.* **provin′cialise,** to render provincial.—*ns.* **provincialism,** a manner, a mode of speech, or a turn of thought peculiar to a province or a country district: a local expression: **provinciality** (*-shi-al′i-ti*).—*adv.* **provin′cially.** [Fr.,—L. *prŏvincia,* an official charge, hence a province.]

provincial-rose, *prə-vin′shl-rōs′, n.* the cabbage-rose, cultivated at *Provins* in Seine-et-Marne, France: (*Shak.*) a shoe rosette.

provine, *prə-vīn′, v.t.* and *v.i.* to propagate by layering. [Fr. *provigner* — O.Fr. *provain* — L. *prŏpāgŏ, -inis,* a slip, layer.]

provision, *prə-vizh′ən, n.* act of providing: that which is provided or prepared: measures taken beforehand: a clause in a law or a deed: a stipulation: a rule for guidance: an appointment by the pope to a benefice not yet vacant: preparation: previous agreement: a store or stock: (commonly in *pl.*) store of food: food.—*v.t.* to supply with provisions or food.—*adj.* **provi′sional,** provided for the occasion: temporary: containing a provision.—*adv.* **provi′sionally.**—*adj.* **provi′sionary,** (*rare*) provisional.—*n.* **provi′sion-merchant,** a general dealer in articles of food.— **provisional judgment,** a judgment given as far as the available evidence admits, but subject to correction under more light; **provisional order,** an order granted by a secretary of state, which, when confirmed by the legislature, has the force of an act of parliament; **provisional remedy,** a means of detaining in safety a person or property until a decision upon some point in which they are concerned be come to. [Fr.,—L. *prŏvīsiŏ, -ōnis—prŏvidēre;* see **provide.**]

proviso, *prə-, prō-vī′zō, n.* a provision or condition in a deed or other writing: the clause containing it: any condition:—*pl.* **provisos** (*-zōz*).—*adv.* **provi′sorily** (*-zə-ri-li*).—*adj.* **provi′sory,** containing a proviso or condition: conditional: making provision for the time: temporary. [From the L. law phrase *prŏvīsŏ quod,* it being provided that.]

provisor, *prə-, prō-vī′zər, n.* one who provides: a purveyor: a person to whom the pope has granted the right to the next vacancy in a benefice. —**Statute of Provisors,** an act of the English parliament passed in 1351 to prevent the pope from exercising the power of creating provisors. [L. *prŏvīsor, -ōris,* provider.]

provitamin, *prō-vīt′ə-min, n.* a substance not a vitamin that is readily transformed into a vitamin within an organism. [L. *prō,* before, and **vitamin.**]

provoke, *prə-vōk′, v.t.* to call forth: to summon: (*obs.*) to call out, challenge: excite or call into action, stimulate: to incite, bring about: to excite with anger: to annoy, exasperate.—*v.i.* (*Dryden*) to appeal.—*adj.* **provocable** (*prov′ək-ə-bl*).—*ns.* **prov′ocant; provoca′tion,** act of provoking: that which provokes: any cause of danger.—*adj.* **provocative** (*-vok′*), tending to provoke or excite. —*n.* anything that stirs up or provokes.—*ns.* **provoc′ativeness; prov′ocātor.**—*adjs.* **provoc′atory; provōk′able.**—*ns.* **provoke′ment** (*Spens.*); **provōk′er.** — *adj.* **provōk′ing,** irritating. — *adv.* **provōk′ingly.** [L. *prŏvocāre, -ātum—prō-,* forth, *vocāre,* to call.]

provost, *prov′əst, n.* the dignitary set over a cathedral or collegiate church: in certain colleges, the head: (*Scotland*) the chief magistrate of a burgh,

answering to mayor in England: (*Shak.*) an officer who arrests and keeps in custody.—*ns.* **prov′ost-mar′shal** (*army, prə-vō′*), the head of military police, an officer with special powers for enforcing discipline and securing prisoners till brought to trial: (*navy*) an officer (master-at-arms) having charge of prisoners; **prov′ostry,** the office or authority of a provost; **prov′ostship,** the office of a provost.—**Lord Provost,** the chief magistrate of Edinburgh, Glasgow, Perth, Aberdeen, or Dundee; **Lady Provost,** the wife (or other female relative) of a Lord Provost as supporting him in certain of his official duties. [O.E. *profast* (*prafost*), O.Fr. *provost* (Fr. *prévôt*)—L.L. *prōpositus—prō-* for *prae,* at the head, *positus,* set.]

prow, *prow,* formerly sometimes *prō, n.* the forepart of a ship: the nose of an aeroplane: **a** projecting front part: (*poet.*) a ship. [Fr. *proue,* or Port., Span., or Genoese *proa*—L. *prōra*—Gr. *prōïra.*]

prow, *prow, adj.* (*arch.*) valiant:—*superl.* **prow′est.** —*n.* **prow′ess,** bravery: valour: daring: accomplishment.—*adj.* **prow′essed.** [O.Fr. *prou* (Fr. *preux*); conn. with L. *prōd-* in *prōdesse.*]

prowl, *prowl,* earlier *prōl, v.i.* to keep moving about as if in search of something: to rove in search of prey or plunder.—*n.* (*coll.*) the act of prowling: a roving for prey.—*n.* **prowl′er.**—*n.* and *adj.* **prowl′ing.**—*adv.* **prowl′ingly.** [M.E. *prollen;* origin unknown.]

proximate, *proks′i-mit, -māt, adj.* nearest or next: without anything between, as a cause and its effect: near and immediate.—*adj.* **prox′imal,** at the near, inner, or attached end (opp. to *distal*).—*advs.* **prox′imally; prox′imately. —** *n.* **proxim′ity,** immediate nearness in time, place, relationship, &c.—*adv.* **prox′imo,** next month—often written **prox.** (for L. *proximō mēnse*)—**proximate cause,** a cause which immediately precedes the effect; **proximate object,** immediate object. [L. *proximus,* next, superl. from *propior* (comp.)—*prope,* near.]

proxy, *prok′si, n.* the agency of one who acts for another: one who acts or votes for another: the writing by which he is authorised to do so: a substitute.—*adj.* **prox′y-wedd′ed,** (*Tenn.*) wedded by proxy. [procuracy.]

proyn, proyne, *proin,* obsolete forms of **prune** (to preen, to lop).

prozymite, *proz′i-mīt, n.* one who uses leavened bread in the eucharist—opp. to *azymite.* [Gr. *prozymia,* ferments.]

Pruce, *proōs, n.* (*obs.*) Prussia.—*adj.* (*obs.*) Prussian. [A.Fr. *Prus, Pruz,* &c.]

prude, *proōd, n.* a woman of priggish or affected modesty: one who pretends extreme propriety. —Also *adj.* (*rare*).—*n.* **pru′dery,** manners of a prude. — *adj.* **pru′dish.** — *adv.* **pru′dishly.** — *n.* **pru′dishness.** [O.Fr. *prode,* fem. of *prou, prod,* excellent; cf. **prow** (2), **proud.**]

prudent, *proō′dənt, adj.* cautious and wise in conduct: discreet: characterised by, behaving with, showing, having, or dictated by forethought.— *n.* **pru′dence,** quality of being prudent: wisdom applied to practice: attention to self-interest: caution.—*adj.* **prudential** (*-den′shl*), having regard to considerations of prudence: relating to prudence: prudent: (*U.S.*) concerned with administration.—*n.* a matter or consideration of prudence (generally *pl.*): a prudent maxim.— *ns.* **pruden′tialism,** a system based on prudence alone; **pruden′tialist; prudentiality** (*-den-shi-al′i-ti*).—*advs.* **pruden′tially; pru′dently.** [L. *prūdēns, prūdentis,* contr. of *prŏvidēns,* pr.p. of *prŏvidēre,* to foresee.]

prud′homme, *prü-dom′, n.* (*hist.*) a discreet man: a skilled workman: in France, a member of a board for settling labour disputes. [O.Fr. *prud* or *prod* (nom. *pros*), good, *homme,* man.]

pruh. Same as **proo.**

pruina, *proō-i′nä, n.* (*bot.*) a powdery bloom or waxy secretion.—*adj.* **pruinose** (*proō′i-nōs*), covered with pruina: having a frosted look. [L. *pruīna,* hoarfrost.]

pruines, a Shakespearian spelling of **prunes** (fruit).

Neutral vowels in unaccented syllables: *el′ə-mənt, in′fənt, ran′dəm*

prune, *proo̅n*, *v.t.* to trim by lopping off superfluous parts : to divest of anything superfluous : to remove by pruning. — Formerly also **proin(e)**, **proyn(e)**. — *ns.* **pru′ner** ; **pru′ning**, the act of pruning or trimming ; **pru′ning-bill**, **-hook**, a hooked bill for pruning with ; **pru′ning-knife**, a large knife with a slightly hooked point for pruning. — *n.pl.* **pru′ning-shears**, shears for pruning shrubs, &c. [O.Fr. *proignier* ; origin unknown.]

prune, *proo̅n*, *v.t.* to preen.—Formerly also **proin.** [Origin obscure.]

prune, *proo̅n*, *n.* (*obs.*) a plum : a dried plum : (*U.S.*) a plum suitable for drying : the dark purple colour of prune-juice.—Obsolete forms **pruine**, **prewyn** (*Shak.*).—*adj.* of the colour of prune-juice.—**prunes and prism**, part of a formula for setting the lips ' serviceable in the formation of a demeanour ' (Dickens, *Little Dorrit*). [Fr.—L. *prūna*, pl. of *prūnum* (taken for a *sing.*) ; cf. Gr. *prou(m)non*, plum.]

prunella, *proo̅-nel′ä*, *n.* sore throat : quinsy. [Latinised from Ger. *bräune*, quinsy (from the brownness of the tongue), or L.L. *brūnus*—general Germanic *brûn*, brown.]

Prunella, *proo̅-nel′ä*, *n.* the self-heal genus of labiate plants, once reputed to cure *prunella* (see preceding).—Also **Brunella.**

prunella, *proo̅-nel′ä*, *n.* a strong silk or woollen stuff, formerly used for academic and clerical gowns and women's shoes—also **prunelle′**, **prunell′o**.—*adj.* of prunella. [App. Fr. *prunelle*, sloe, dim. of *prune*, plum.]

prunello, *proo̅-nel′ō*, *n.* a little prune : a kind of dried plum :—*pl.* **prunell′os.** [Obs. It. *prunella*, dim. of *pruna* (now *prugna*), plum.]

prunt, *prunt*, *n.* a moulded glass ornament or glass : a tool for making it.—*adj.* **prunt′ed.**

prurient, *proo̅′ri-ənt*, *adj.* itching : uneasily or morbidly interested, curious, or craving : dallying with lascivious thoughts : (*bot.*) causing itching. —*ns.* **pru′rience**, **pru′riency.**—*adv.* **pru′riently.** [L. *prūriens*, *-entis*, pr.p. of *prūrīre*, to itch.]

prurigo, *proo̅-rī′gō*, *n.* an eruption on the skin, causing great itching.—*adj.* **pruriginous** (*-rij′i-nəs*). —*n.* **pruri′tus**, itching. [L. *prūrīgo*, *-inis*, *prūrītus*, *-ūs*—*prūrīre*, to itch.]

Prussian, *prush′ən*, *adj.* of or pertaining to *Prussia*. —*n.* an inhabitant, native, or citizen of Prussia.— *v.t.* and *v.i.* **Pruss′ianise**, to make or become Prussian.—*ns.* **Prussianis′er** ; **Pruss′ianism**, spirit of Prussian nationality : often used for arrogant militarism ; **prussiate** (*prus′* or *prush′i-āt*), a cyanide : a ferricyanide : a ferrocyanide.—*adj.* **pruss′ic** (also sometimes *proo̅s′*), pertaining to Prussian blue.—*n.* **Prussifica′tion.**—*v.t.* **Pruss′ify**, to Prussianise, assimilate to the Prussian.—**Old Prussian**, the extinct Baltic language of the former inhabitants of East and West Prussia ; **Prussian** (or **prussian**) **blue**, ferric ferrocyanide, discovered in Berlin ; **prussic acid**, hydrocyanic acid, a deadly poison, first obtained from Prussian blue.

pry, *prī*, *v.i.* to peer or peep into that which is closed : to examine things with impertinent curiosity (*pr.p.* **prying** ; *pa.t.* and *pa.p.* **pried** ; *3rd pers. sing. pr.t.* **pries**).—*n.* (*rare*) a prying : one who pries — cf. *Paul Pry*, in John Poole's (1792-1879) comedy so called, first produced in 1825.—*n.* **pri′er**, one who pries—also **pry′er.**— *n.* and *adj.* **pry′ing.**—*adv.* **pry′ingly.**—**pry out**, to investigate or find out by prying. [M.E. *prien* ; origin unknown.]

pry, *prī*, *v.t.* a form of **prize**, to lever ; to extract.

prys, **pryse**, old spellings of **price**, **prize.**

pryse, *prīz*, *n.* (*Scott*) a horn-blast at the taking or killing of a deer. [O.Fr. *pris*, taken ; cf. **prize** (2).]

prytaneum, *prit-an-ē′əm*, *n.* the town-hall of an ancient Greek city. [Latinised from Gr. *prytaneion* —*prytanis*, a presiding magistrate.]

pr′ythee, **prythee**, *pridh′ē*. Same as **prithee.**

psalm, *säm*, *n.* a devotional song or hymn, esp. one of those included in the Old Testament **Book of Psalms.**—*ns.* **psalm′-book**, a book containing psalms for purposes of worship ; **psalmist**

(*säm′ist*), a composer of psalms, esp. (**Psalmist**) David.—*adjs.* **psalmodic** (*sal-mod′ik*), **-al**, pertaining to psalmody.—*v.i.* **psalmodise** (*sal′*, *säm′*), to practise psalmody.—*ns.* **psalmodist** (*sal′*, *säm′ə-dist*), a singer of psalms ; **psalmody** (*sal′*, or *säm′* ; Gr. *psalmōidiä*, singing to the harp), the singing of psalms, esp. in public worship : psalms collectively ; **psalm′-tune**. [O.E. (*p*)*salm*, (*p*)*sealm* —L.L. *psalmus*—Gr. *psalmos*, music of or to a stringed instrument—*psallein*, to pluck.]

Psalter, *sawl′tər*, *n.* the Book of Psalms, esp. when separately printed.—*adj.* **psalterian** (*sawl-tē′ri-ən*), pertaining to a psalter : like a psaltery. — *ns.* **psal′tery**, an ancient and mediaeval stringed instrument like the zither, played by plucking ; **Psaltery**, (*rare*) the Psalter ; **psal′tress**, a woman who plays upon the psaltery. [O.E. *saltere*—L. *psaltērium*—Gr. *psaltērion*, a psaltery.]

psalterium, *sawl-tē′ri-əm*, *n.* the third division of a ruminant's stomach, the omasum or manyplies. [From the appearance of its lamellae, like a stringed instrument ; see the foregoing.]

psammite, *sam′īt*, *n.* any rock composed of sand-grains. — *adj.* **psammitic** (*-it′ik*). — *n.* **psamm′-ophil(e)**, a sand-loving plant. — *adj.* **psamm′oph′ilous.** — *n.* **psamm′ophyte** (*ō-fīt*), a plant that grows only on sand.—*adj.* **psammophytic** (*-fit′ik*). [Gr. *psammos*, sand.]

psellism, (*p*)*sel′izm*, *n.* a defect in articulation— also **psellis′mus.** [Gr. *psellismos*—*psellos*, stammering.]

psephism, (*p*)*sē′fizm*, *n.* a decree of the Athenian assembly (from the voting with pebbles).—*n.* **pse′phite**, a rock composed of pebbles, a conglomerate. [Gr. *psēphos*, a pebble.]

pseud-, (*p*)*sūd-*, **pseudo-**, *sū′dō-*, in composition, sham, false, spurious : deceptively resembling : isomerous with : temporary, provisional.—As a separate word, *adj.* **pseu′do**, false, sham.—*n.* (*obs.*) a pretender. — *ns.* **pseudaesthe′sia**, imaginary feeling, as in an amputated limb ; **pseudax′is**, a sympodium ; **pseudepig′rapha** (*pl.*), books ascribed to Old Testament characters, but not judged genuine by scholars.—*adjs.* **pseudepigraph′ic**, **-al**.—*ns.* **pseudepig′raphy**, the ascription to books of false names of authors ; **pseudimä′go**, a subimago ; **pseudo-ac′id**, a compound not an acid but isomeric with and transformable into an acid.—*adj.* **pseu′do-archā′ic**, sham-antique : artificially archaistic : blunderingly imitative of the old.—*ns.* **pseudo-ar′chäism** ; **pseu′dobulb**, a swollen stem internode in some orchids ; **pseu′do-carp**, a fruit formed from other parts in addition to the gynaeceum ; **pseudo-Christian′ity** ; **pseudo-class′icism.** — *adj.* and *n.* **pseudo-Goth′ic**, sham or would-be Gothic.—*ns.* **pseu′dograph**, a writing falsely ascribed ; **pseudog′raphy**, unsatisfactory spelling ; **pseudol′ogy**, the science of lying ; **pseu′do-mar′tyr**, a false martyr ; **pseudomem′brane**, a false membrane ; **pseu′domorph**, a portion of a mineral showing the outward form of another which it has replaced by molecular substitution or otherwise ; **pseu′donym**, a fictitious name assumed, as by an author.—*adj.* **pseudonym′ity.** — *adj.* **pseudon′ymous.** — *adv.* **pseudon′ymously**—*ns.* **pseudopo′dium**, a temporary process sent out by the protoplasm of a unicellular organism or phagocyte, for locomotion or feeding :—*pl.* **pseudopo′dia** ; **pseu′doscope**, a kind of stereoscope that interchanges convex and concave in appearance ; **pseu′do-solu′tion**, a colloidal suspension ; **pseu′dosymm′etry** (*crystal.*) a deceptively near approach to a higher degree of symmetry, as in **pseu′docu′bic** degree of symmetry ; **pseu′dohexag′onal** crystals, simulating cubic or hexagonal symmetry. [Gr. *pseudēs*, false.]

pshaw, *shaw*, *psha*, *interj.* expressing contempt or impatience.—*v.i.* to say ' pshaw.'—*v.t.* to say ' pshaw ' at. [Spontaneous expression.]

psi, *psī*, *psē*, *n.* the twenty-third letter (Ψ, ψ) of the Greek alphabet, equivalent to *ps* : as a Greek numeral ψ′=700, ͵ψ=700,000.—*n.* **psi′-phenom′enon**, the phenomena of parapsychology. [Gr. *psei.*]

psilanthropism, (*p*)*sī-lan′thrə-pizm*, *n.* the doctrine that Christ was a mere man.—*adj.* **psilanthrop-**

(-*throp'*). — *ns.* **psilan'thropist**; **psilan'thropy.** [Gr. *psilos*, bare, *anthrōpos*, man.]

psilomelane, (*p*)*sī-lom'ə-lān*, *n.* an oxide of manganese, usually with barium, &c., occurring in smooth black botryoidal masses. [Gr. *psilos*, bare, *melas*, *-anos*, black.]

Psilophyton, (*p*)*sī-lō-fī'ton*, *n.* a very simple Devonian fossil pteridophyte, giving name to the order **Psilophytales** (*-fī-tā'lēz*), early land-plants. [Gr. *psilos*, bare, *phyton*, plant.]

psilosis, (*p*)*sī-lō'sis*, *n.* loss of hair: sprue (from loss of epithelium): (*Gr. gram.*) deaspiration. [Gr. *psilōsis—psilos*, bare.]

Psilotum, (*p*)*sī-lō'təm*, *n.* a genus of rootless pteridophytes giving name to the order **Psilotā'-ceae.** [Gr. *psilōton*, the name of some plant— *psilos*, bare (because of the almost leafless stem).]

Psittacus, (*p*)*sit'ä-kəs*, *n.* the grey parrot genus.— *adj.* **psitt'acine** (*-sīn*), of parrots.—*n.* **psittacosis** (*-kō'sis*), a contagious disease of parrots and other birds, communicable to man. [Gr. *psittakos*, parrot.]

psoas, (*p*)*sō'as*, *n.* a muscle of the loins and pelvis: the tenderloin. [Gr. (pl.) *psoai*, the accus. *psoās*, being mistaken for a nom. sing.]

Psocoptera, (*p*)*sō-kop'tər-ä*, *n.pl.* an order of insects consisting of the book-lice and their kindred. [*Psocus*, a genus included in the order, Gr. *pteron*, wing.]

psora, (*p*)*sō'rä*, *n.* scabies, itch.—*n.* **psōrī'asis**, a skin disease in which red scaly papules and patches appear.—*adjs.* **psōrīat'ic**; **psō'ric.** [Gr. *psōrā*, *psōriāsis*, itch.]

psyche, *sī'kē*, *n.* the soul, spirit, mind: the principle of mental and emotional life, conscious and unconscious: a butterfly: a cheval-glass: **Psyche**, in late Greek mythology the personification of the soul, depicted as a young woman with butterfly's wings, the beloved of Eros: a genus of bombycid moths (the females wingless, sometimes legless): one of the minor planets.— *v.t.* **psych, psyche** (*sīk*; *slang*), to subject to psycho-analysis.—*ns.* **psych'agogue** (*-ə-gog*; Gr. *agōgos*, guide), conductor of souls to the underworld (a title of Hermes): a caller-up of spirits: one who guides the mind: a means of restoring consciousness; **psychasthē'nia** (etymologically *-the-nī'ä*; Gr. *asthĕneia*, weakness), a severe functional mental disorder, characterised by fixed ideas, ruminative states, and hypochondriacal conditions; **psychi'ater** (Gr. *iātros*, *iātros*, physician), a psychiatrist.—*adj.* **psychīat'rical.**—*ns.* **psychi'-atrist**, one who treats diseases of the mind; **psychi'atry.**—*adjs.* **psych'ic, -al**, pertaining to the psyche, soul, or mind: spiritual: spiritualistic: beyond, or apparently beyond, the physical: sensitive to or in touch with that which has not yet been explained physically.—*n.* **psych'ic**, that which is of the mind or psyche: a spiritualistic medium.— *adv.* **psych'ically.** — *ns.* **psy'chics** (treated as *sing.*), the science of psychology: psychical research; **psy'chism**, the doctrine of a universal soul; **psy'chist**, a psychologist: one interested in psychical research.—*v.t.* **psycho-an'alyse**, to subject to psycho-analysis.— *ns.* **psycho-anal'ysis**, a method of investigation and psychotherapy whereby nervous diseases or mental ailments are traced to forgotten hidden concepts in the patient's mind and treated by bringing these to light; **psycho-an'alyst.**—*adjs.* **psycho-analyt'ic, -al.**—*n.* **psychogen'esis**, origin or development of the mind: origination in the mind. —*adjs.* **psychogenet'ic, -al.**—*ns.* **psychog'ony**, origin or development of the mind or soul; **psych'ogram**, a supposed spirit-writing; **psych'o-graph**, an instrument by which it is got.—*adjs.* **psychograph'ic, -al.**—*ns.* **psychog'raphy**, spirit-writing: psychological biography or delineation; **psych'oid**, the regulative principle directing the behaviour of a developing organism; **psychokin-ē'sis**, movement by psychic agency.—*adjs.* **psycholog'ic, -al.**—*adv.* **psycholog'ically.**—*v.i.* **psy-chol'ogise.**—*ns.* **psychol'ogist**; **psychol'ogy**, the science of mind; **psychom'etry**, measurement of mental phenomena: an occult power of divining the secret properties of things by mere contact.— *adjs.* **psychomet'ric, -al**; **psy'chomōtor**, pertaining to such mental action as induces muscular contraction.—*ns.* **psychoneurō'sis**, mental disease without apparent anatomical lesion: functional disorder of the mind in one who is legally sane and shows insight into his condition; **psycho-pannychism** (*-pan'ik-izm*; Gr. *pannychos*, all night long—*pās*, *pāsa*, *pān*, all, *nychios*, nightly), sleep of the soul from death to resurrection; **psychopann'ychist**; **psy'chopath** (*-path*), one who shows a pathological degree of congenital emotional instability without organic mental disorder; **psychop'athist**, an alienist; **psychop'-athy**, derangement of mental functions. — *adj.* **psychophys'ical.**—*ns.* **psychophys'icist**; **psy-chophys'ics**, the study of the relation or correspondence of the mental and physical; **psycho-physiol'ogy**, experimental or physiological psychology; **psy'chopomp** (Gr. *pompos*, guide), a conductor of souls to the other world; **psychō'sis**, mental condition: grave mental disorder:—*pl.* **psychō'sēs.**—*adj.* **psychosomat'ic** (Gr. *sōma*, body), of mind and body as a unit: concerned with physical diseases having emotional origin.—*ns.* **psy-chotherapeut'ics, -ther'apy**, treatment of disease by hypnosis, psycho-analysis and similar means; **psychother'apist.**—*adj.* **psychot'ic**, pertaining to psychosis.—**psychical research**, investigation of phenomena apparently implying a connexion with another world; **psychic force**, a power not physical or mechanical, supposed to cause certain so-called spiritualistic phenomena; **psychological moment**, properly the psychological element or factor, misunderstood by a French translator from German and applied to the moment of time when the mind could best be worked upon: hence now often the very moment, the nick of time. [Gr. *psychē*, soul, butterfly, *Psychē*, Psyche.]

psychrometer, *sī-krom'i-tər*, *n.* originally a thermometer: now a wet-and-dry-bulb hygrometer. —*adjs.* **psychrometric** (*sī-krō-met'rik*), **-al**.—*n.* **psychrom'etry.** [Gr. *psychros*, cold, *metron*, a measure.]

ptarmic, (*p*)*tär'mik*, *n.* a substance that causes sneezing. [Gr. *ptarmos*, a sneeze.]

ptarmigan, *tär'mi-gən*, *n.* a mountain-dwelling grouse, white in winter: extended to other species of Lagopus, as willow-grouse. [Gael. *tàrmachan*.]

Pterichthys, (*p*)*tər-ik'this*, *n.* a genus of Old Red Sandstone ostracoderms, with wing-like appendages. [Gr. *pteron*, wing, *ichthys*, fish.]

pteridophyte, *ter'id-ō-fīt*, *n.* a vascular cryptogam or a member of the **Pteridophyta** (*-of'i-tä*), one of the main divisions of the vegetable kingdom— ferns, lycopods, horsetails. [Gr. *pteris*, *-idos*, a fern, *phyton*, a plant.]

pteridosperm, *ter'id-ō-spərm*, *n.* a fossil plant of a group resembling ferns, but having seeds. [Gr. *pteris*, *-idos*, fern, *sperma*, seed.]

pterin, (*p*)*ter'in*, *n.* any of a group of substances occurring as pigments in butterfly wings, important in biochemistry.—**pteroic** ((*p*)*ter-ō'ik*) **acid**, the original folic acid found in spinach; **pteroyl-glutamic** ((*p*)*ter'ō-il-gloo-tam'ik*) **acid**, the folic acid that is therapeutically active in pernicious anaemia. [Gr. *pteron*, a wing.]

pterion, (*p*)*ter'*, or (*p*)*tĕr'i-on*, *n.* in craniometry, the suture where the frontal, squamosal, and parietal bones meet the wing of the sphenoid:—*pl.* **pter'ia.** [Gr. dim. of *pteron*, wing.]

Pteris, (*p*)*ter'is*, (*p*)*tē'ris*, *n.* a genus of ferns with spore-clusters continuous along the pinnule margin, usually taken to include bracken, which some separate as **Pterid'ium.** — *ns.* **pteridol'ogist**; **pteridol'ogy**, the science of ferns; **pterido-mā'nia**, a passion for ferns; **pteridoph'ilist**, a fern-lover. [Gr. *pteris*, *-idos*, or *-eōs*, male-fern— *pteron*, a feather.]

pterodactyl, pterodactyle, *ter-ə-dak'til*, *n.* a fossil (Jurassic and Cretaceous) flying reptile with large and bird-like skull, long jaws, and a flying-membrane attached to the long fifth finger. [Gr. *pteron*, wing, *daktylos*, finger.]

pteropod, (*p*)ter′ə-pod, *n.* any member of the **Pteropoda** (-op′ə-dä), a group of gasteropods that swim by wing-like expansions of the foot.— **pteropod ooze**, a deep-sea deposit composed largely of pteropod shells. [Gr. *pteron*, wing, *pous*, *podos*, foot.]

pterosaur, (*p*)ter′ə-sawr, *n.* a member of the **Pterosaur′ia**, the pterodactyls.—*n.* and *adj.* **pterosaur′ian**. [Gr. *pteron*, wing, *sauros*, lizard.]

pterygium, (*p*)tər-ij′i-əm, *n.* a vertebrate limb: a wing-like growth:—*pl.* **pteryg′ia**.—*adj.* **pteryg′ial**. —*n.* a bone in a fin. [Latinised from Gr. *pterygion*, dim. of *pteryx*, -*ygos*, wing.]

pterygoid, (*p*)ter′i-goid, *adj.* wing-like: of or near the pterygoid.—*n.* (in full, **pterygoid bone, plate, process**) in various vertebrates a paired bone of the upper jaw behind the palatines, known in human anatomy as the pterygoid plates of the sphenoid bone. [Gr. *pteryx*, -*ygos*, wing.]

Pterygotus, (*p*)ter-i-gō′təs, *n.* a genus of Eurypterids named from the broad swimming paddles. [Latinised from Gr. *pterygōtos*, winged.]

pteryla, (*p*)ter′i-lä, *n.* a patch of contour feathers in birds:—*pl.* **pter′ylae** (-lē).—*adjs.* **pterylograph′ic, -al.** — *adv.* **pterylograph′ically.** — *ns.* **pterylog′raphy**; **pterylō′sis**, arrangement of pterylae. [Gr. *pteron*, feather, *hȳlē*, forest.]

ptilosis, til-ō′sis, *n.* plumage or mode of feathering. [Gr. *ptilōsis*—*ptilon*, a down feather.]

ptisan, tiz′n, tiz-an′, *n.* a medicinal drink made from barley: a decoction.—Also **tisane.** [Gr. *ptisanē*, peeled barley, barley-gruel—*ptissein*, to winnow.]

ptochocracy, (*p*)tō-kok′rə-si, *n.* the rule of beggars or paupers—wholesale pauperisation. [Gr. *ptōchos*, a beggar, *kratos*, power.]

Ptolemaic, tol-i-mā′ik, *adj.* pertaining to the *Ptolemies*, Greek kings of Egypt (from Alexander's general to Caesar's son), or to *Ptolemy* the astronomer (fl. A.D. 150)—also **Ptolemaean** (-mē′ən).— *n.* **Ptolemā′ist**, a believer in the **Ptolemaic system**, Ptolemy's form of the ancient Greek planetary theory, according to which the heavenly bodies revolved about the earth in motions compounded of eccentric circles and epicycles.

ptomaine, tō′mā-in, -ēn, -in (these now rare), tō′mān, tō-mān′ (these orig. illiterate, now established), *n.* a loosely used name for amino-compounds, some poisonous, formed from putrefying animal tissues — *putrescine, cadaverine, neurine, choline,* &c. [It. *ptomaina*—Gr. *ptōma*, a corpse.]

ptosis, (*p*)tō′sis, *n.* downward displacement: drooping of the upper eyelid. [Gr. *ptōsis*—*piptein*, to fall.]

ptyalin, (*p*)tī′ə-lin, *n.* a ferment in saliva that turns starch into sugar. — *adj.* **ptyalagogic** (-ə-goj′ik, -gog′ik).—*n.* **ptyalagogue** (-al′ə-gog), a sialagogue. — *v.t.* **pty′alise**, to induce ptyalism in. — *n.* **pty′alism**, excessive flow of saliva. [Gr. *ptyalon*, spittle—*ptyein*, to spit.]

ptyxis, (*p*)tiks′is, *n.* the folding of each individual leaf in the bud—distinguished from *vernation*, the arrangement of the whole. [Gr. *ptyxis*.]

pub, *pub*, *n.* (*slang*) short for **public-house**.—*n.* **pub′-crawl**, a progression from pub to pub.— Also *v.i.*

puberty, pū′bər-ti, *n.* the beginning of sexual maturity.—*adjs.* **pū′beral**; **pūberulent** (-ber′ū-lənt), **pūber′ūlous**, feebly or minutely pubescent. —*ns.* **pū′bes** (-bēz), the lower part of the hypogastric region: the hair growing thereon at puberty; **pūbescence** (-es′əns), puberty: a soft downy covering, esp. in plants, of adpressed hairs. —*adjs.* **pūbes′cent**; **pū′bic**, of the pubes or the pubis.—*n.* **pū′bis** (for L. *os pūbis*, bone of the pubes), a bone of the pelvis which in man forms the anterior portion of the *os innominatum* :— *pl.* **pū′bises** (**pu′bes** is a blunder).—As a prefix **pū′biō-** (wrongly **pū′bo-**). [L. *pūber* and *pūbes*, -*eris*, grown-up, downy, and *pūbes*, -*is*, grown-up youth, the pubes.]

public, pub′lik, *adj.* of or belonging to the people: pertaining to a community or a nation: general: common to, shared in by, or open to all: generally known: in open view, unconcealed, not private: engaged in, or concerning, the affairs of the community: (now *rare* except in the phrase *public spirit*) devoted or directed to the general good: international: open to members of a university as a whole, not confined to a college: of a public-house.—*n.* the people: the general body of mankind: the people, indefinitely: public view or a public place, society, or the open: a public-house, tavern.—*ns.* **pub′lican**, the keeper of an inn or public-house: (*Roman hist.*) a taxfarmer: a tax-collector; **publicā′tion**, the act of publishing or making public: a proclamation: the act of sending out for sale, as a book: that which is published as a book, &c.; **public′-house′**, (*obs.*) a house open to the public: one chiefly used for selling alcoholic liquors to be consumed on the premises: an inn or tavern.— *v.t.* **pub′licise** (-sīz), to give publicity to: to advertise.—*ns.* **pub′licist** (-sist), one who writes on or is skilled in public law, or on current political topics: (esp. *U.S.*) an advertising agent; **publicity** (-lis′i-ti), the state of being public or open to the knowledge of all: notoriety: (chiefly *U.S.*) advertising. — *adv.* **pub′licly.** — *ns.* **pub′licness** (*rare*).—*adjs.* **pub′lic-school**; **pub′lic-spir′ited**, having a spirit actuated by regard to the public interest: with a regard to the public interest.— *adv.* **pub′lic-spir′itedly.**—**in public**, in open view: among people: in society; **public funds**, government funded debt; **public holiday**, a general holiday; **public lands**, lands belonging to government, esp. such as are open to sale, grant, &c.; **public law**, international law; **public orator**, an officer of English universities who is the voice of the Senate upon all public occasions; **public prosecutor**, an official whose function is to prosecute persons charged with offences; **public relations**, (used adjectivally) directing relations with the public, e.g. by promoting knowledge through advertisement; **public school**, a school under the control of a publicly elected body: an endowed classical school for providing a liberal education for such as can afford it— Eton, Harrow, Rugby, Winchester, Westminster, Shrewsbury, Charterhouse, St Paul's, Merchant Taylors', &c.; **public trustee**, an official who acts as trustee or executor if required; **public woman**, a prostitute. [L. *pūblicus*—*pop*(*u*)*lus*, the people.]

publish, pub′lish, *v.t.* to make public: to divulge: to announce: to proclaim: to send forth to the public: to put forth and offer for sale: to put into circulation: of an author, to get published. —*v.i.* to publish a work, newspaper, &c.—*adj.* **pub′lishable.**—*ns.* **pub′lisher**, one who makes public: one who publishes books: one who attends to the issuing and distributing of a newspaper: (*U.S.*) a newspaper proprietor; **pub′lishment**, publication, esp. (*U.S.*) of banns. [Fr. *publier*— L. *pūblicāre*, with -*ish* on the model of other verbs.]

Puccinia, puk-sin′i-ä, *n.* a genus of rust-fungi, including the wheat-rust, parasitic in alternate generations on barberry and wheat or other grass. —*adj.* **pucciniā′ceous.** [Named after Tomaso Puccini, Italian anatomist.]

puccoon, puk-ōōn′, *n.* bloodroot: extended to species of gromwell and other American plants yielding pigments. [Virginian Indian name.]

puce, pūs, *n.* and *adj.* brownish-purple. [Fr. *puce*— L. *pūlex*, -*icis*, a flea.]

pucelle, pū-sel′, *n.* (*obs.*) a maid, virgin, esp. the Maid of Orleans, Jeanne d'Arc (1412-31): (*obs.*; also **puzzle**, *puz′l*) a dirty drab, a slut.—*n.* **pū′celage**, virginity. [Fr.,—L.L. *pūlicella*; origin doubtful.]

puck, *puk*, **pouke**, *pook*, *n.* a goblin or mischievous sprite; **Puck**, Robin Goodfellow, a merry fairy in *Midsummer Night's Dream*, &c. (**Puck-hairy** in Ben Jonson's *Sad Shepherd*).—*adj.* **puck′ish.** [O.E. *pūca*; cf. O.N. *pūki*, Ir. *puca*, W. *pwca*.]

puck, *puk*, *n.* a rubber disk used instead of a ball in ice-hockey.

pucka, pukka, pakka, puk′ä, *adj.* (*Anglo-Ind.*) outand-out good: thorough: complete: solidly built: settled: durable: permanent: full-weight: straight forward: real: genuine: sure. [Hind. *pakkā*, cooked, ripe.]

pucker, *puk′ər*, *v.t.* and *v.i.* to cockle, wrinkle.—*n.* a corrugation or wrinkle: a group of wrinkles, esp. irregular ones: (*coll.*) agitation, confusion.—*adj.* **puck′ery**, astringent: tending to wrinkle. [Cf. **poke**, a bag.]

puckfist, *puk′fist*, *-fīst*, *n.* a puff-ball: (*arch.*) a braggart: (*obs.*) a niggard. [App. **puck**, and the root of O.E. *fisting*, breaking of wind.]

pud, *pud*, *n.* (*coll.*) a paw, fist, hand. [Cf. **pad** (2), or Du. *poot*, paw.]

pud, *pood*. Same as **pood**.

pudder, *pud′ər*. Same as **pother**.

pudding, *pood′ing*, *n.* a skin or gut filled with seasoned minced meat and other materials (as blood, oatmeal), a kind of sausage: (*Shak.*) stuffing for a cooked carcase: (usu. in *pl.*) entrails: a soft kind of dessert food, usually farinaceous, commonly with sugar, milk, eggs, &c.: a pad of rope, &c., used as a fender on the bow of a boat or elsewhere (also **pudd′ening**): (*fig.*) material gain: a fat, dull, or heavy-witted person.—Also (now *vulg.* or *dial.*) **pudden** (*pood′n*, *pud′n*).—*n.* **pudd′ing-bag**, a bag for cooking a pudding in: a piece of good fortune.—*adjs.* **pudd′ing-faced**, having a fat, round, smooth face; **pudd′ing-head′ed**, (*coll.*) stupid.—*ns.* **pudd′ing-pie**, a pudding with meat baked in it: applied to various kinds of pastry; **pudd′ing-pipe**, the long pulpy pod of the purging-cassia tree; **pudd′ing-sleeve**, a large loose sleeve gathered in near the wrist; **pudd′ing-stone**, conglomerate; **pudd′ing-time**, dinner-time: (*obs.*) the right moment. — *adj.* **pudd′ingy** (*-ing-i*). [M.E. *poding*; origin unknown; relation to L.G. *pudde-wurst*, black pudding, and Fr. *boudin*, obscure.]

puddle, *pud′l*, *n.* a small muddy pool: a mixture of clay and sand: a muddle: a muddler.—*v.t.* to make muddy: to work into puddle, to stir and knead: to cover with puddle: to make watertight by means of clay: to convert from pig-iron into wrought-iron by stirring in a molten state.—*v.i.* to make a dirty stir.—*ns.* **pudd′ler**, **pudd′ling**.—*adj.* **pudd′ly**, full of puddles. [App. dim. of O.E. *pudd*, ditch.]

puddock, *pud′ək*, *n.* Same as **paddock** (1).

pudency, *pū′dəns-i*, *n.* (*Shak.*) shamefacedness, modesty.—*adjs.* **pudendal** (*-den′*), pertaining to the pudenda; **puden′dous**, shameful. — *n.* **puden′dum**, and *pl.* **puden′da**, the external genital organs.—*adjs.* **pu′dent**, modest; **pu′dibund**, shamefaced: prudish.—*n.* **pudibund′ity**.—*adj.* **pu′dic**, (*obs.*) modest: pudendal. — *ns.* **pudicity** (*-dis′i-ti*), modesty; **pu′dor**, (*obs.*) sense of shame. [L. *pudēre*, to make (or be) ashamed, *pudendum*, something to be ashamed of, *pudīcus*, *pudibundus*.]

pudge, *puj*, **pudgy**, *puj′i*, **puds(e)y**, *pud′zi*. Same as **podge**, **podgy**.

pueblo, *pweb′lō*, *n.* a town or settlement (in Spanish-speaking countries): a communal habitation of the Indians of New Mexico, &c.: an Indian of the pueblos. [Sp., town—L. *populus*, a people.]

puer, *pūr*, *n.* and *v.t.* Same as **pure** (in tanning).

puerile, *pū′ər-il*, *adj.* (*rare*) pertaining to children: childish: trifling: silly.—*n.* **puerility** (*-il′i-ti*), quality of being puerile: that which is puerile: a childish expression: an instance of childishness or foolish triviality. [L. *puerīlis*—*puer*, a boy.]

puerperal, *pū-ər′pər-əl*, *adj.* relating to childbirth.—*adv.* **puer′perally**.—*n.* **pūerpē′rium**, the time from onset of labour to return to normal state.—**puerperal fever**, fever occurring in connexion with childbirth: now confined to morbid conditions owing to introduction of organisms into the genital tract; **puerperal insanity**, insanity occurring in connexion with childbirth. [L. *puerpera*, a woman in labour—*puer*, a child, *parĕre*, to bear.]

puff, *puf*, *v.i.* to blow in whiffs: to breathe out vehemently or pantingly: (*obs.*) to snort scornfully: to emit puffs: to issue in puffs: to make the sound of a puff: to go with puffs: to swell up. —*v.t.* to drive with a puff: to blow: to emit in

puffs: to play (as a wind instrument) or smoke (as a pipe) with puffs: to inflate or swell: to elate unduly: to extol, esp. in disingenuous advertisement: to put out of breath.—*n.* a sudden, forcible breath, blast, or emission: a gust or whiff: a cloud or portion of vapour, dust, air, &c., emitted at once: a sound of puffing: a downy pad for powdering: anything light and porous, or swollen and light: a biscuit or cake of puff-paste or the like: a part of a fabric gathered up so as to be left full in the middle: ostentation: laudation intended or serving as advertisement.—*ns.* **puff′-adder**, a thick, venomous African snake (*Bitis arietans* or kindred species) that distends its body when irritated; **puff′-ball**, a gasteromycete fungus (Lycoperdon, &c.) with ball-shaped fructification filled when ripe with a snuff-like mass of spores; **puff′-bird**, any bird of a South American family akin to barbets, with the habit of puffing out the head-feathers; **puff′-box**, a box for toilet powder and puff.—*adj.* **puffed**, distended: inflated: gathered up into rounded ridges, as a sleeve: out of breath.—*ns.* **puff′er**, one who puffs: a steam-engine: a steamboat: one employed to bid at an auction to incite others and run up prices; **puff′ery**, advertisement disguised as honest praise: puffs collectively.—*adv.* **puff′ily**.—*ns.* **puff′iness**; **puff′ing**.—*adv.* **puff′ingly**.—*ns.* **puff′-paste**, a flour paste in thin layers: pastry made thereof (**puff′-pastry**); **puff′-puff**, a child's word for a railway engine or train.—*adj.* **puff′y**, puffed out with air or any soft matter: tumid: bombastic: coming in puffs: puffing: short-winded.—**puffed out**, quite out of breath; **puffed up**, swollen with pride, presumption, or the like. [O.E. *pyffan*, or kindred form; cf. Ger. *puffen*, &c.]

puffin, *puf′in*, *n.* a sea-bird (Fratercula) of the auk family, with brightly coloured parrot-like beak. [Origin obscure: connexion with **puff** is conjectured.]

pug, *pug*, *n.* (*obs.*) a goblin, a puck (in Ben Jonson **Pug**, an inferior devil): a term of endearment: (*obs.*) a harlot: (*slang*) an upper servant: a monkey: a fox: a pug-dog: a pug-nose: a pug-moth: a pug-engine.—*ns.* **pug′-dog**, a small short-haired dog with wrinkled face, upturned nose, and short curled tail; **pug′-engine**, a shunting engine. — *adjs.* **pug′-faced**, monkey-faced; **pugg′ish**, **pugg′y**, like a monkey or a pug-dog: snub-nosed. — *ns.* **pugg′y**, a term of endearment: (*Scot.*) a monkey: a fox; **pug′-moth**, a name for the smaller moths of the geometrid fam. Larentidae; **pug′-nose**, a short, thick nose with the tip turned up.—*adj.* **pug′-nosed**. [Connexion with **puck** (1) is conjectured.]

pug, *pug*, *n.* clay ground and worked with water.—*v.t.* to grind with water and make plastic: to line or pack with pugging.—*ns.* **pugg′ing**, beating or punching: the working of clay for making bricks, in a pug-mill: clay, sawdust, plaster, &c., put between floors to deaden sound; **pug′-mill**, a machine for mixing and tempering clay. [Origin unknown.]

pug, *pug*, *n.* (Anglo-Ind.) a beast's foot-print.—*v.t.* to track. [Hind. *pag*.]

puggaree. Same as **pagri**.

pugging, *pug′ing*, *adj.* (*Shak.*) thieving.—*v.t.* and *v.i.* **pug**, (*dial.*) to tug. [Origin unknown.]

pugh, an old spelling of **pooh**.

pugil, *pū′jil*, *n.* (orig.) a small handful, (now) as much as the thumb and two fingers can lift, a pinch. [L. *pugillus*.]

pugil, *pū′jil*, *n.* (*obs.*) a boxer.—*ns.* **pu′gilism**, the art or practice of boxing: prize-fighting; **pu′gilist**.—*adjs.* **pugilist′ic**, *-al*.—*adv.* **pugilist′ically**. [L. *pugil*, a boxer.]

pugnacious, *pug-nā′shəs*, *adj.* given to fighting: combative: quarrelsome.—*adv.* **pugnā′ciously**.—*n.* **pugnacity** (*-nas′i-ti*), inclination to fight: fondness for fighting: quarrelsomeness. [L. *pugnāx*, *-ācis*—*pugnāre*, to fight.]

puh, a Shakespearian spelling of **pooh**.

puir, *pər*, *pār*, *adj.* Scots form of **poor**.

puisne (*Shak.* **puisny**), *pū′ni*, *adj.* an obsolete form of puny, surviving as applied to certain judges—junior: (*Shak.*) petty, insignificant.—*n.* a puisne judge. [O.Fr. (Fr. *puîné*), from *puis*—L. *posteā*, after, *né*—L. *nātus*, born.]

puissant, puissaunt, *pwis'ənt,* sometimes *pū'is-ənt,* *-awnt', -ânt', pū-is'ənt,adj.* powerful.—*n.* **puissance** *-aunce* (*-əns, -awns', -âns'*), power.—*adv.* **puissantly** (*-ənt-li*). [Fr. *puissant,* app. formed as a pr.p. from a vulgar L. substitute for L. *potēns, -entis*; see potent.]

puja, *pōō'jä, n.* worship: reverential observance: a festival. [Sans. *pūjā,* worship.]

puke, *pūk, v.t.* and *v.i.* vomit.—*v.t.* to cause to vomit.—*n.* vomit: an emetic.—*n.* **pū'ker,** an emetic. [Poss. connected with Flem. *spukken,* Ger. *spucken.*]

puke, *pūk, n.* (*obs.*) a fine woollen cloth: a colour between russet or purple and black.—*adj.* (*Shak.*) made of puke: of the colour puke. [M.Du. *puuc,* the best woollen cloth.]

pukka. Same as pucka.

pulchritude, *pul'kri-tūd, n.* beauty.—*adj.* **pulchritud'inous.** [L. *pulchritūdō, -inis*—*pulcher,* beautiful.]

puldron. Same as pauldron.

pule, *pūl, v.t.* and *v.i.* to pipe: to whimper or whine.—*n.* pū'ler.—*n.* and *adj.* **pū'ling.**—*adv.* **pū'lingly.**—*adj.* **pū'ly,** whining: sickly. [Imit.: cf. Fr. *piauler.*]

Pulex, *pū'leks, n.* the flea genus, giving name to the family **Pulicidae** (*-lis'i-dē*). [L. *pūlex, -icis.*]

pulka, *pul'kä, n.* a Laplander's boat-shaped sledge.—Also **pulk, pulk'ha.** [Finnish *pulkka,* Lappish *pulkke, bulkke.*]

pull, *pool, v.t.* to pluck: to remove by plucking: to extract: to pick, cull, gather by hand: to strip, deprive of feathers, hair, &c.: to draw: to move, or try or tend to move, towards oneself or in the direction so thought of: to render, or bring to be, by pulling: to row: to transport by rowing: to stretch: to hold back (esp. a horse to prevent his winning): to take as an impression or proof, orig. by pulling the bar of a hand-press: (*cricket and golf*) to strike to the left (or right for the left-handed): to bring down: to take a draught of: (*U.S.*) to draw or fire (a weapon): (*slang*) to snatch, steal: (*slang*) to arrest: (*slang*) to raid.—*v.i.* to give a pull: to perform the action of pulling anything: to tear, pluck: to drag, draw: to strain at the bit: to exert oneself: to go with a pulling movement: to row: to suck: to strike the ball to the left, &c.—*n.* an act, bout, or spell of pulling: a pulling force: a row: a stiff ascent: a draught of liquor: (*print.*) a proof, single impression: advantage: an apparatus for pulling: the quantity pulled at one time.—*ns.* **pull'-back,** a hindrance: a drawback: a device for making a skirt hang close and straight in front; **pull'er.**—*adj.* **pull'-on,** requiring only to be pulled on, without fastening.—*n.* a pull-on garment of any kind.—*ns.* **pull'over,** a jersey, a jumper, a body garment put on over the head; **pull'-through,** a cord with rag for cleaning a rifle barrel; **pull'-up',** an act of pulling up: a sudden stoppage: a suitable place (esp. for carters) for pulling up.—**pull a face,** to grimace; **pull apart,** to bring asunder by pulling; **pull caps,** to scuffle; **pull devil pull baker,** do your best, both sides; **pull down,** to take down or apart: to demolish: to bring down: to reduce in health or vigour; **pull for,** to row for; **pull off,** to carry through successfully; **pull oneself together,** to collect one's faculties; **pull one's leg** (see leg); **pull one's weight,** to pull with full effect to one's weight in rowing: to do one's full share of work, co-operate wholeheartedly; **pull round,** to bring, or come, back to good health or condition or to consciousness; **pull the long bow,** to lie or boast beyond measure; **pull through,** to bring or get to the end of something difficult or dangerous with some success; **pull up,** to pull out of the ground: to tighten the reins: to bring to a stop: to halt: to take to task: to gain ground; **pull up stakes,** to prepare to leave a place. [O.E. *pullian,* to pluck, draw.]

pullet, *pool'it, n.* a young hen, esp. from first laying to first moult.—*n.* **pull'et-sperm',** (*Shak.,* derisively) eggs (lit. the chalaza, once believed to be the male element in the egg). [Fr. *poulette,* dim. of *poule,* a hen—L.L. *pulla,* a hen, fem. of L. *pullus,* a young animal.]

pulley, *pool'i, n.* a wheel turning about an axis, and receiving a rope, chain, or band on its rim, used for raising weights, changing direction of pull, transmission of power, &c.: a block: a combination of pulleys or blocks:—*pl.* **pull'eys.** [M.E. *poley, puly*—O.Fr. *polie* (Fr. *poulie*)—L.L. *polegia,* supposed to be from a dim. of Gr. *polos,* axle; but prob. influenced by association with L. *pullus,* a young animal, Gr. *pōlos,* a foal.]

Pullman, *pool'mən, n.* a railway saloon or sleeping-car, first made by George M. *Pullman* (1831-97) in America.—In full **Pullman car.**

pullulate, *pul'ū-lāt, v.i.* to sprout: to sprout abundantly: to teem: to increase vegetatively. — *n.* **pullulā'tion.** [L. *pullulāre, -ātum*—*pullulus,* a young animal, sprout—*pullus.*]

pulmo, *pul'mō, n.* lung:—*pl.* **pulmo'nes** (*-nēz*).—*n.* **pul'mobranch** (*-brangk*), a lung-book. — *adj.* **pulmobranch'iate.**—*n.* **Pulmonaria**(*-mə-nā'ri-ä*), the lungwort genus of the borage family.—*adj.* **pul'monary** (*-mən-ər-i*), of the lungs or respiratory cavity: of the nature of lungs: having lungs: diseased or weak in the lungs.—*n.pl.* **Pulmonā'ta,** an air-breathing order of Gasteropoda.—*n.* **pul'monate,** a member of the Pulmonata.—*adj.* having lungs, lung-sacs, or lung-books, or similar organs.—*adj.* **pulmonic** (*-mon'ik*), of the lungs.—*n.* a medicine for disease of the lungs.—*n.* **Pul'motor,** a registered trade-mark for an apparatus for forcing air and/or oxygen into and out of the lungs. [L. *pulmō, -ōnis,* lung.]

pulp, *pulp, n.* any soft fleshy part of an animal, e.g. the tissue in the cavity of a tooth: the soft part of plants, esp. of fruits: any soft structureless mass: the soft mass obtained from the breaking and grinding of rags, wood, &c., before it is hardened into paper: crushed ore.—*v.t.* to reduce to pulp: to make pulpy: to deprive of pulp.—*v.i.* to become pulp or like pulp.—*ns.* **pulp'board,** cardboard made directly from a layer of pulp; **pulp'-cav'ity,** the hollow of a tooth containing pulp; **pulp'-en'gine,** a machine for making pulp for paper; **pulp'er,** a machine for reducing various materials to pulp.—*v.t.* **pulp'ify.**—*adv.* **pulp'ily.**—*ns.* **pulp'iness**; **pulp'mill,** a machine or factory for pulping wood, roots, or other material.—*adj.* **pulp'ous.**—*ns.* **pulp'stone,** a grindstone for pulping wood; **pulp'wood,** wood suitable for paper-making: a board of compressed wood-pulp and adhesive.—*adj.* **pulp'y.** [L. *pulpa,* flesh, pulp.]

pulpit, *pool'pit, n.* a raised structure for preaching from: an auctioneer's desk or the like: preachers or preaching collectively: (*obs.*) a platform.—*adj.* belonging to the pulpit.—*adj.* **pul'pited.**—*ns.* **pulpiteer', pul'piter,** one who speaks from a pulpit: a preacher; **pul'pitry,** sermonising; **pul'pitum,** a rood-screen. [L. *pulpitum,* a stage.]

pulque, *pool'kā, n.* a fermented drink made in Mexico from agave sap. [Sp. *Amer.*]

pulsate, *pul'sāt,* or *-sāt', v.i.* to beat, throb: to vibrate: to thrill with life or emotion.—*n.* **pulsatance** (*pul'sə-tans, pul-sā'tans*), frequency multiplied by *2π.*—*adj.* **pul'satile** (*-sə-til*), capable of pulsating: pulsatory: rhythmical: (*mus.*) played by percussion.—*ns.* **Pulsatill'a,** pasque-flower (because beaten by the wind); **pulsā'tion,** a beating or throbbing: a motion of the heart or pulse: any measured beat: vibration. — *adj.* **pulsative** (*pul'sə-tiv* or *-sāt'*).—*n.* **pulsā'tor** (or *pul'sə-tər*), a machine, or part of a machine, that pulsates or imparts pulsation, as for separating diamonds from earth, for regulating the rhythmical suction of a milking machine, for pumping.—*adj.* **pulsatory** (*pul'sə-tər-i,* or *-sā'*), beating or throbbing.—**pulsating current,** an electric current that changes periodically in intensity but not in direction. [L. *pulsāre, -ātum,* to beat, freq. of *pellēre, pulsum,* to drive.]

pulse, *puls*, *n.* a beating or throbbing: a measured beat or throb: a vibration: a single beat or impulse: (*radio*) a signal of very short duration: the beating of the heart and the arteries: (*fig.*) a thrill.—*v.i.* to beat, as the heart: to throb: to pulsate. — *v.t.* to drive by pulsation. — *adj.* **pulse′less.**—*ns.* **pulse′lessness**; **pulse′-rate**, the number of beats of a pulse per minute; **pulse′-wave**, the expansion of the artery, moving from point to point, like a wave, as each beat of the heart sends the blood to the extremities; **puls′idge** (Mistress Quickly in 2 *Henry IV.*), pulse.—*adj.* **pulsif′ic**, producing a single pulse.—*ns.* **pulsim′-eter**, an instrument for measuring the strength or quickness of the pulse; **pul′sojet**, in jet-propulsion, an intermittent jet; **pulsom′eter**, a pulsimeter: a pump that draws in water by condensation of steam in two chambers alternately.—**feel one's pulse**, to test or measure the heart-beat, usu. by holding the patient's wrist: to explore a person's feelings or inclinations in a tentative way. [L. *pulsus—pellĕre, pulsum*; partly O.Fr. *pouls, pous*, remodelled on Latin.]

pulse, *puls*, *n.* seeds of leguminous plants as food collectively—beans, pease, lentils, &c.: the plants yielding them.—*adj.* **pultā′ceous**, macerated and softened. [L. *puls, pultis*, porridge; cf. Gr. *poltos*, and **poultice**.]

pultun, pultan, pulton, pultoon, *pul′tun, -tən, -toon*, *n.* (*Ind.*) an infantry regiment. [Hind. *pultan*—Eng. **battalion**.]

pulu, *poo̅′loo̅*, *n.* a silky fibre from the Hawaiian tree-fern leaf-bases. [Hawaiian.]

pulver, *pul′vər*, *v.t.* (*obs.*) to reduce to powder.—*adj.* **pul′verable** (*rare*).—*ns.* **pulverā′tion** (*rare*), pulverisation; **pul′verine**, barilla ash. — *adj.* **pul′verisable** (or *-īz′*).—*n.* **pulverisā′tion.**—*v.t.* **pul′verise**, to reduce to dust or fine powder.— *v.i.* to fall down into dust or powder.—*n.* **pul′-veriser**, one who pulverises: a machine for pulverising or for spraying.—*adj.* **pul′verous**, dusty or powdery.—*n.* **pulverulence** (*-ver′ū-ləns*). —*adj.* **pulver′ūlent**, consisting of fine powder: powdery: dusty-looking: readily crumbling.— **Pulver Wednesday, pulvering day** (*obs.*), Ash Wednesday. [L. *pulvis, pulveris*, powder.]

pulvil, *pul′vil*, *n.* perfumed powder: extended to snuff and other powders.—Also **pulvil′io, pul-vill′io, pulville′.**—*v.t.* **pul′vil**, to powder or scent with pulvil:—*pa.p.* **pul′villed.**—*adj.* **pul′vilised.** [It. *polviglio—polve*, powder—L. *pulvis*.]

pulvinus, *pul-vī′nəs*, *n.* a cushion-like swelling, esp. one at the base of a leaf or leaflet, by whose changes of turgidity movements are effected:— *pl.* **pulvi′ni** (*-nī*).—*adjs.* **pulvill′ar**, of a pulvillus: cushion-like; **pulvill′iform**—*n.* **pulvill′us**, a little cushion or pad: a pad between the claws of an insect's foot:—*pl.* **pulvill′i** (*-ī*).—*adj.* **pulvinar** (*-vī′nər*), cushion-like: of a pulvinus.—*n.* (*-när*) a Roman cushioned seat: a small pillow or pad: a knob on the optic thalamus.—*adjs.* **pul′vinate** (*-vin-āt*), **-d**, cushion-like: pillowy: bulging.—*n.* **pul′vinule**, the pulvinus of a leaflet. [L. *pulvīnus*, cushion, pillow; dim. *pulvillus*; *pulvīnar*, a cushioned couch.]

pulwar, *pul′wär*, *n.* a light keelless boat used on the Ganges. [Hind. *palwār*.]

pulza-oil, *pool′zä-oil*, *n.* an oil obtained from physic-nut seeds. [Origin unknown.]

puma, *pū′mä*, *n.* the cougar (*Felis concolor*), a large reddish-brown American cat:—*pl.* **pu′mas.** [Peruv. *puma*.]

pumelo. Same as **pomelo.**

pumice, *pum′is*, sometimes *pū′mis*, *n.* an acid glassy lava so full of gas-cavities as to float in water: a frothy portion of any lava: a piece of such lava used for smoothing or cleaning.—*v.t.* to smooth or clean with pumice-stone—also **pumicate** (*pū′mi-kāt*; *rare*). — *adj.* **pumiceous** (*-mish′əs*). — *ns.* **pum′ice-stone; pum′ie** (stone), **pum′y** (stone), (*Spens.*) a pebble, stone. [O.E. *pumic* (*-stán*), pumice (-stone); reintroduced—O.Fr. *pomis*; both —L. *pūmex, -icis*.]

pummel, *pum′l*, *n.* a less usual spelling of **pommel.** —*v.t.* (the usual spelling) to beat, pound, bethump,

esp. with the fists:—*pr.p.* **pumm′elling**; *pa.t.* and *pa.p.* **pumm′elled.** [**pommel.**]

pump, *pump*, *n.* a machine for raising fluids or for compressing, rarefying, or transferring gases: a stroke of a pump: an act of pumping.—*v.t.* to raise, force, compress, exhaust, empty, remove, or inflate with a pump: to discharge by persistent effort: to move in the manner of a pump: to subject to, or elicit by, persistent questioning: (*obs.*) to pump water on: to put out of breath (esp. in *pass.*; often with *out*). — *v.i.* to work a pump: to work like a pump: to move up and down like a pump-handle: to spurt.—*ns.* **pump′er; pump′-gun**, a gun whose chamber is fed by a pump-like movement; **pump′-hand′le**, the lever that works a pump; **pump′-head, -hood**, a frame covering the upper wheel of a chain-pump, serving to guide the water into the discharge-spout; **pump′-room**, the apartment at a mineral spring in which the waters are drunk; **pump′-water**, water from a pump; **pump′-well**, a well from which water is got by pumping: the compartment in which a pump works. [Ety. dub.]

pump, *pump*, *n.* a light dancing-shoe without fastening.—*adj.* **pumped**, wearing pumps. [Origin unknown.]

pumpernickel, *poomp′ər-nik-l*, *n.* rye bread, much used in Westphalia. [Ger. The Ger. word means a rackety goblin, a coarse lout, rye-bread (poss. from its giving forth a sound like *pump* when struck).]

pumpkin, *pum(p)′kin*, in U.S. often *pung′kin*, *n.* a plant (*Cucurbita Pepo*) of the gourd family, or its fruit.—Also **pump′ion.** [O.Fr. *pompon*—L. *pepŏ* —Gr. *pepŏn*, ripe; see **pepo.**]

pumy. See **pumice.**

pun, *pun*, *v.t.* (*Shak.*) to pound: to ram: to consolidate by ramming:—*pr.p.* **punn′ing**; *pa.t.* and *pa.p.* **punned.**—*n.* **punn′er**, a tool for punning, a ram. [See **pound** (3).]

pun, *pun*, *v.i.* to play upon words alike or nearly alike in sound but different in meaning (*pr.p.* **punn′ing**; *pa.t.* and *pa.p.* **punned**).—*n.* a play upon words.—*ns.* **punn′ing; pun′ster**, a maker of puns. [A late-17th-century word; origin unknown; It. *puntiglio*, fine point, has been conjectured.]

punalua, *poo-nä-loo̅′ä*, *n.* a system of group-marriage, sisters (by blood or tribal reckoning) having their husbands in common, or brothers their wives, or both. — *adj.* **punalu′an.** [Hawaiian.]

punce, *puns*, *n.* (*Austr.*) an effeminate man.

Punch, *pun(t)sh*, *n.* a hook-nosed hunchback, chief character in the street puppet-show 'Punch and Judy': the chief illustrated English comic paper (1841). [Shortened from **Punchinello.**]

punch, *pun(t)sh*, *adj.* (*prov.*) short and thick.—*n.* a thick-set short man: a short-legged, round-bodied horse, long bred in Suffolk.—*adj.* **punch′y.** [Poss. shortened from **puncheon**, or from **Punchinello**, or a variant of **bunch.**]

punch, *pun(t)sh* (*obs.* poonsh), *n.* a drink ordinarily of spirit, water, sugar, lemon-juice, and spice (with variations).—*ns.* **punch′-bowl**, a large bowl for making punch in; **punch′-ladle**, a ladle for filling glasses from a punch-bowl. [Traditionally from the five original ingredients, from Hind. *pānch*, five—Sans. *panchan*; but the vowel presents a difficulty.]

punch, *pun(t)sh*, *v.t.* to prod: to poke: (*U.S.*) to drive (cattle): to strike with a forward thrust, as of the fist: to thump: (*Northern*) to kick: to stamp, pierce, perforate, indent, by a forward thrust of a tool or part of a machine: to make, obtain, or remove by such a thrust: to press in vigorously the keys or button of: to record by pressing a key.—*v.i.* to perform an act of punching: to clock (*in* or *out*).—*n.* a vigorous thrust or forward blow: striking power: effective forcefulness: a tool or machine for punching: a die: a prop for a mine roof.—*ns.* **punch′-ball**, a suspended ball used for boxing practice; **punch′er**, one who punches: an instrument for punching: (*U.S.*) a cow-puncher, drover: (*Austr.*) the driver of a team ; **punch'-prop**, in mines, a short piece of wood used as a prop.—*adj.* **punch'-drunk**, stupefied by blows. [**pounce**; or from **puncheon** (1); possibly in some senses for **punish**.]

puncheon, *pun'(t)shn, n.* (*obs.*) a dagger : a tool for piercing, or for stamping : a short supporting post : a split trunk with one face smoothed for flooring, &c. [O.Fr. *poinson*—L. *pungĕre, punctum, to prick*.]

puncheon, *pun'(t)shn, n.* a cask : a liquid measure of from 70 to 120 gallons. [O.Fr. *poinson*, a cask ; origin obscure.]

Punchinello, *pun(t)sh-i-nel'ō, n.* a hook-nosed character in an Italian puppet-show : a buffoon, any grotesque personage. [It. *Pulcinella*, a Neapolitan buffoon, of doubtful origin.]

punctate, -d, *pungk'tāt, -id, adjs.* dotted : pitted.—*ns.* **puncta'tion**; **puncta'tor**, one who marks with dots—esp. applied to the Massoretes who invented the Hebrew vowel-points. [L. *punctum*, a point, *puncture*—*pungĕre, punctum*, to prick.]

punctilio, *pungk-til'i-ō, -yō, n.* a nice point in behaviour or ceremony : a point about which one is scrupulous : nicety in forms : exact observance of forms :—*pl.* **punctilios**.—*adj.* **puncti'lious**, attentive to punctilio : scrupulous and exact.—*adv.* **puncti'liously**. — *n.* **puncti'liousness**. [It. *puntiglio* and Sp. *puntillo*, dims. of *punto*—L. *punctum*, a point.]

puncto, *pungk'tō* (*Shak.*). Same as **punto**.

punctual, *pungk'tū-əl, adj.* of the nature of a point : pertaining to a point, or points : of punctuation : observant of nice points : punctilious : exact in keeping time and appointments : done at the exact time : up to time.—*ns.* **punc'tualist**, an authority on or observer of punctilios ; **punctuality** (-*al'i-ti*).—*adv.* **punc'tually**. [L.L. *punctuālis*—*punctum*, a point.]

punctuate, *pungk'tū-āt, v.t.* to mark with points : to mark off with the usual stops, points of interrogation, and the like : to intersperse : to emphasise.—*n.* **punctua'tion**, the act or art of dividing sentences by points or marks.—*adj.* **punc'tuative**.—*n.* **punc'tuator**. [L.L. *punctuāre, -ātum*, to prick—L. *punctum*.]

punctum, *pungk'təm, n.* (*anat.*) a point, dot : a minute aperture :—*pl.* **punc'ta**.—*adjs.* **punc'tulate, -d**, minutely dotted or pitted.—*ns.* **punctula'tion** ; **punc'tule**, a minute dot, pit, or aperture.—**punctum caecum** (*sē'kəm*; L. *poongk'toom kī'koom*, blind spot), the point of the retina from which the optic nerve fibres radiate. [L. *punctum*—*pungĕre, punctum*, to prick.]

puncture, *pungk'tyər, n.* a pricking : a small hole made with a sharp point : perforation of a pneumatic tire.—*v.t.* and *v.i.* to make or get a puncture.—*adj.* **punc'tured**, perforated : pierced : marked with little holes : consisting of little holes.—*n.* **punctura'tion**. [L. *punctūra*—*pungĕre*, to prick.]

pundigrion, *pun-dig'ri-on, n.* (*obs.*) a pun. [Origin unknown ; It. *puntiglio* is only a conjecture.]

pundit, pandit, *pun'dit, n.* one who is learned in the language, science, laws, and religion of India : any learned man : an Indian surveyor sent secretly into forbidden lands.—*n.* **pun'ditry**. [Hind. *pandit*—Sans. *pandita*.]

pundonor, *poon-dō-nōr', n.* point of honour :—*pl.* **pundonor'es** (-*ās*). [Sp.,—*punto de honor*.]

pungent, *pun'jənt, adj.* sharp : (*bot.*) ending in a hard sharp point : pricking or acrid to taste or smell : keenly touching the mind : painful : keen : sarcastic.—*ns.* **pun'gency** (*Crabbe*, **pun'gence**).—*adv.* **pun'gently**. [L. *pungēns, -entis*, pr.p. of *pungĕre*, to prick.]

Punic, *pū'nik, adj.* of ancient Carthage : Carthaginian : faithless, treacherous, deceitful (as the Romans alleged the Carthaginians to be) : (*obs.*)—**purple**.—*n.* the Semitic language of ancient Carthage.—*n.* **Pu'nica**, the pomegranate genus, constituting the family **Punica'ceae** (akin to the myrtle and loosestrife families).—*adj.* **punica'ceous**.—**Punic apple**, (*obs.*) the pomegranate; **Punic faith**, treachery. [L. *Pūnicus*—*Poenī*, the Carthaginians.]

punily. See **puny**.

punish, *pun'ish, v.t.* to cause to suffer for an offence : to cause one to suffer for : (*coll.*) to handle or beat severely, maul : (*coll.*) to consume a large quantity of.—*v.i.* to inflict punishment.—*n.* **punishabil'ity**.—*adj.* **pun'ishable**.—*ns.* **pun'isher**; **pun'ishment**, act or method of punishing : penalty imposed for an offence : (*coll.*) severe handling. [Fr. *punir, punissant*—L. *pūnīre*, to punish—*poena*, penalty.]

punition, *pū-nish'ən, n.* punishment.—*adjs.* **pu'nitive** (-*ni-tiv*), concerned with, inflicting, or intended to inflict, punishment ; **pu'nitory**. [L. *pūnīre*, to punish.]

Punjabi, Punja(u)bee, Panjabi, *pun-jä'bē, n.* a native or inhabitant of the *Punjab* in India and Pakistan : the language of the Punjab.—*adj.* of the Punjab. [Hind. *Panjābī*.]

punk, *pungk, n.* (*arch.*) a prostitute, strumpet. [Origin unknown.]

punk, *pungk, n.* (*U.S.*) touchwood : tinder : a preparation of amadou used as tinder : anything worthless : balderdash.—*adj.* rotten : worthless, miserable. [Poss. **spunk**; or poss. of American Indian origin.]

punka, punkah, *pung'kä, n.* a fan : a palm-leaf fan : a large mechanical fan for cooling a room. [Hind. *pankhā*, a fan.]

punnet, *pun'it, n.* a small shallow chip-basket, as for strawberries. [Origin unknown.]

punning, punster. See **pun**.

punt, *punt, n.* a flat-bottomed boat with square ends.—*v.t.* to propel by pushing a pole against the bottom : to transport by punt.—*v.i.* to go in a punt : to go shooting in a punt : to pole a punt or boat.—*ns.* **punt'er**; **punt'-fishing**, fishing from a punt ; **punt'-gun**, a heavy gun of large bore used for shooting water-fowl from a punt ; **punt'-pole**, a pole for propelling a punt ; **punts'-man**, a sportsman who uses a punt. [O.E. *punt*—L. *pontō, -ōnis*, punt, pontoon ; cf. **pontoon**.]

punt, *punt, v.i.* to stake against the bank : to back a horse.—*n.* **punt'er**, one who punts : a professional gambler. [Fr. *ponter*.]

punt, *punt, n.* the act of kicking a dropped football before it touches the ground.—*v.t.* to kick in this manner : to knock. [Origin obscure.]

punto, *pun'tō*, also **puncto**, *pungk'tō, n.* (*obs.*) a moment : (*obs.*) a point, punctilio : (*Shak.* **punc'to**) a pass or thrust in fencing.—**punto dritt'o**, a direct or straight hit ; **punto rever'so** (It. *riverso*), a back-handed stroke. [Sp. and It. *punto*—L. *punctum*, a point.]

punty, puntee, pontie, ponty, *pun'ti*, **pontil**, *pon'til, n.* an iron rod used in holding and manipulating glass-ware during the process of making. [Prob. Fr. *pontil*, app.—It. *pontello, puntello*, dim. of *punto*, point.]

puny, *pū'ni, adj.* (*obs.*) puisne : (*Shak.*) inexperienced : stunted : feeble :—*comp.* **pū'nier**; *superl.* **pū'niest**.—*adv.* **pū'nily**.—*n.* **pū'niness**. [**puisne**.]

pup, *pup, n.* a shortened form of **puppy**.—*v.t.* and *v.i.* to whelp :—*pr.p.* **pupp'ing**; *pa.t.* and *pa.p.* **pupped**.—**in pup**, (of a bitch) pregnant ; **sell a pup**, inveigle one into a specious bad bargain : to swindle.

pupa, *pū'pä, n.* an insect in the usually passive stage between larva and imago : an intermediate stage of development in some other invertebrates :—*pl.* **pupae** (*pū'pē*).—*n.* **pu'pa-case**, a puparium.—*adjs.* **pū'pal**, of a pupa ; **pūpā'rial**.—*n.* **pūpā'rium**, the last larval skin separated but retained as a hard protective covering for the pupa : sometimes, the covering and the pupa.—*v.i.* **pū'pate**, to become a pupa.—*n.* **pūpā'tion**.—*adjs.* **pūpig'erous** (-*pig'ə-rəs*), having a puparium ; **pūpip'arous**, having pupae developed within the body of the mother. [L. *pūpa*, a girl, a doll.]

pupil, *pū'pl, -pil, n.* (Rom. and *Scots law*) a boy up to the age of 14, or a girl up to 12 : a ward : one who is being taught : one who is being or has been taught by a particular teacher.—*adj.* under age.—*ns.* **pu'pillage**, state of being a pupil : the time during which one is a pupil (in *Shak.*, &c., sometimes taken as two words, **pupil age**); **pupillar'ity**, the state or time of being legally a

pupil.—*adjs.* **pu′pillary,** pertaining to a pupil or ward, or one under academic discipline. (These words are sometimes spelt with one *l*.)—**pupil teacher,** a pupil who does some teaching as part of his training for later entry into the profession. [Fr. *pupille*—L. *pūpillus, pūpilla,* dims. of *pūpus,* boy, *pūpa,* girl.]

pupil, *pū′pl, -pil, n.* the apple of the eye: the round opening in the eye through which the light passes: a central spot, esp. within a spot.—*n.* **pupilabil′ity,** an intentionally unintelligible word in *Tristram Shandy* (IV. i.).—*adjs.* **pu′pillary; pu′pillate,** (*zool.*) having a central spot of another colour. (These words sometimes with one *l.*) [L. *pūpilla,* pupil of the eye, orig. the same as the preceding, from the small image to be seen in the eye.]

puppet, *pup′it, n.* a doll or image moved by wires or hands in a show: a marionette: one who acts just as another tells him.—*adj.* behaving like a puppet: actuated by others.—*ns.* **pupp′etry,** play of, or with, puppets: puppets collectively: puppet-like action: puppet-shows: anything like or associated with puppets: (*obs.*) dress of puppets; **pupp′et-play,** a drama performed by puppets; **pupp′et-show,** an exhibition of puppets: a puppet-play; **pupp′et-valve** (see **poppet**). [Earlier *poppet*; cf. O.Fr. *poupette,* dim. from L. *pūpa.*]

puppy, *pup′i, n.* (*dial.*) a puppet: (*obs.*) a lap-dog, toy-dog: a young dog: a whelp: a young seal: a conceited young man.—*v.t.* and *v.i.* to pup.—*ns.* **pupp′y-dog; pupp′ydom.**—*adj.* **pupp′y-head′ed,** (*Shak.*) having the mind of a puppy.—*n.* **pupp′y-hood.**—*adj.* **pupp′yish.**—*n.* **pupp′yism,** conceit in men. [App. Fr. *poupée,* a doll or puppet—L. *pūpa.*]

pupunha, *pōō-pōōn′ya, n.* the peach-palm: its fruit. [Port. from Tupí.]

pur. See **purr.**

pur, *pur, n.* (*obs.*) the knave in the game of post and pair.

Purana, *pōō-rä′na, n.* any one of a class of sacred books in Sanskrit literature, cosmogonical, legendary, religious, &c.—*adj.* **Puranic** (*-răn′ik*). [Sans. *purāna—purā,* of old.]

Purbeck, *pur′bek, adj.* of the Isle (really peninsula) of *Purbeck,* in Dorset.—*n.* and *adj.* **Purbeck′ian,** (*geol.*) Jurassic of the uppermost stage.—**Purbeck marble, stone,** a fresh-water shelly limestone much quarried in the Isle.

purblind, *pur′blīnd, adj.* (*orig.* apparently) wholly blind: nearly blind: dim-sighted, esp. spiritually. —*adv.* **pur′blindly.**—*n.* **pur′blindness.** [**pure** (or perh. O.Fr. intens. pfx. *pur-*), and **blind.**]

purchase, *pur′chas, v.t.* (*obs.*) to seek to bring about: (*obs.*) to bring about: to acquire: (*law*) to get in any way other than by inheritance: to buy: to obtain by labour, danger, &c.: (*Shak.*) to be amends for (with *out*): to raise or move by a mechanical power.—*v.i.* (*Shak.*) to strive: to make purchases: to accumulate possessions.—*n.* act of purchasing: (*obs.*) seizure: that which is purchased: acquisition: prize, booty: (*obs.*) whatever one can do for oneself by shifts: annual rent: bargain: (*obs.*) price: worth: any mechanical advantage in raising or moving bodies or apparatus: advantageous hold, or means of exerting force advantageously. — *adj.* **pur′chasable.** — *n.* **pur′chaser.**—**purchase money,** the money paid, or to be paid, for anything; **purchase system,** the system by which, before 1871, commissions in the British army could be bought: (**so many**) **years′ purchase,** a price paid for a house, an estate, &c., equal to the amount of so many years′ rent or income: probability of lasting so long. [O.Fr. *porchacier* (Fr. *pourchasser*), to seek eagerly, pursue—*pur* (L. *prō*), for, *chacier, chasser,* to chase.]

purdah, *pur′dä, n.* a curtain, esp. for screening women′s apartments: seclusion of women. [Urdu and Pers. *pardah.*]

purdonium, *purdō′ni-əm, n.* a kind of coal-scuttle introduced by one *Purdon.*

pure, *pūr, adj.* clean: unsoiled: unmixed: not adulterated: free from guilt or defilement: chaste: **free** from bad taste, meretriciousness, solecism,

barbarism: modest: mere: that and that only: utter, sheer: practising as a surgeon but not as a physician, or as a physician but not a surgeon: non-empirical, involving an exercise of mind alone, without admixture of the results of experience: (*obs.*) excellent, fine: (*biol.*) homozygous, breeding true: (*law*) unconditional: free from ritual uncleanness.—*n.* purity: dog′s dung or similar substance used by tanners (also **puer**).—*adv.* purely: without admixture: (*obs.*) utterly, thoroughly.—*v.t.* to cleanse, refine: to treat with pure (also **puer**).—*adjs.* **pure′-blood, -ed, pure′-bred,** of unmixed race.—*adv.* **pure′ly,** chastely: unmixedly: unconditionally: wholly, entirely: (*dial.*) wonderfully, very much.—*n.* **pure′ness.**—**pure mathematics,** mathematics treated without application to observed facts of nature or to practical life; **pure reason,** reason alone, without any mixture of sensibility; **pure science,** science considered apart from practical applications. [Fr. *pur*—L. *pūrus,* pure.]

purée, *pū′rā, pū-rā, n.* food material reduced to pulp and passed through a sieve: a soup without solid pieces. [Fr.]

purfle, *pur′fl, v.t.* to ornament the edge of, as with embroidery or inlay.—*n.* a decorated border: (*obs.*) a profile.—*n.* **pur′fling,** a purfle, esp. around the edges of a fiddle. [O.Fr. *pourfiler*—L. *prō,* before, *filum,* a thread.]

purfled, *pur′fld, adj.* (*Scot.*) short-winded.—*adj.* **pur′fly** (*Carlyle*).

purge, *purj, v.t.* to purify: to remove impurities from: to clear of undesirable elements or persons: to remove as an impurity: to clarify: to clear from accusation: to expiate: to evacuate, as the bowels.—*v.i.* to become pure by clarifying: to evacuate the bowels: to have frequent evacuations: to take a purgative.—*n.* act of purging: an expulsion or massacre of those who are not trusted: a purgative.—*n.* **purgation** (*pur-gā′shən*), a purging: a clearing away of impurities: (*law*) the act of clearing from suspicion or imputation of guilt, a cleansing.—*adj.* **purgative** (*purg′a-tiv*), cleansing: having the power of evacuating the intestines.—*n.* a medicine that evacuates.—*adv.* **pur′gatively.**—*adjs.* **purgato′rial, purgato′rian,** pertaining to purgatory; **pur′gatory,** purging or cleansing: expiatory.—*n.* (*R.C.*) a place or state in which souls are after death purified from venial sins: any kind or state of suffering for a time: (*coll.*) intense discomfort: (*U.S.*) a ravine: (*U.S.*) a swamp.—*n.* **purger** (*purj′ər*).—*n.* and *adj.* **purging** (*purj′*).—**purging cassia, flax** (see **cassia, flax**). [Fr. *purger*—L. *pūrgāre, -ātum*—earlier *pūrigāre*—*pūrus,* pure.]

purify, *pū′ri-fī, v.t.* to make pure: to cleanse from foreign or hurtful matter: to free from guilt, from ritual uncleanness or from improprieties or barbarisms in language.—*v.i.* to become pure:—*pr.p.* **pu′rifying;** *pa.t.* and *pa.p.* **pu′rified.**—*n.* **purifica′tion.**—*adj.* **pu′rificative.**—*n.* **pu′rificātor.**—*adj.* **pu′rificātory,** tending to purify or cleanse.—*n.* **pu′rifier.**—**Purification of the Blessed Virgin Mary,** a feast observed in the R.C. Church on 2nd February, in commemoration of the purification of the Virgin Mary according to the Jewish ceremonial (Lev. xii. 1-4) forty days after the birth of Christ. [Fr. *purifier*—L. *pūrificāre*—*pūrus,* pure, *facĕre,* to make.]

purim, *pū′rim, pōōr-ēm′, n.* the feast of lots held about 1st of March, in which the Jews commemorated their deliverance from the plot of Haman, as related in Esther. [Heb. *pūrīm* (sing. *pūr*), lots; origin unknown.]

purin, purine, *pūr′in, -ēn, n.* a white crystalline substance, $C_5H_4N_4$, which with oxygen forms uric acid ($C_5H_4N_4O_3$), and is the nucleus of many other derivatives. [Contracted from L. *pūrum ūricum* (*acidum*), pure uric (acid).]

purism, *pūr′izm, n.* fastidious, esp. over-fastidious, insistence upon purity of language in vocabulary or idiom.—*n.* **pūr′ist.**—*adj.* **pūris′tic.** [L. *pūrus,* pure.]

Puritan, *pūr′i-tən, n.* one who in the time of Elizabeth and the Stuarts wished to carry the reformation of the Church of England further by purifying it of ceremony: an opponent of the Church of England on account of its retention of much of the ritual and belief of the Roman Catholics: an opponent of the Royalists in the 17th century: any person of like views or in sympathy with the historical Puritans: a person strictly moral in conduct, or (*slightingly*) professing a too-strict morality: an advocate of purity in any sense.—*adj.* pertaining to the Puritans.—*adjs.* pūritanic (*-tan'ik*), **-al.**—*adv.* pūritan'ically.—*v.t.* and *v.i.* pūr'itanise.—*n.* pūr'itanism. [L. *pūrus*, pure.]

purity, pūr'i-ti, *n.* condition of being pure: freedom from mixture of any kind, sin, defilement, or ritual uncleanness: chastity: sincerity: freedom from foreign or improper idioms or words. [L. *pūritās, -ātis—pūrus.*]

purl, purl, *v.i.* to flow with a murmuring sound: to flow in eddies: to curl or swirl.—*n.* (*obs.*) a trickling rill: a movement or murmuring as of a stream among stones: an eddy or ripple (also **pirl**).—*n.* and *adj.* purl'ing. [Cf. Norw. *purla*, to babble, Sw. dial. *porla*, to purl, ripple.]

purl, purl, *v.i.* to spin round: to capsize: to go head over heels: to fall headlong or heavily.—*v.t.* to throw headlong.—*n.* a heavy or headlong fall: an upset.—*n.* purl'er, a headlong or heavy fall or throw. [Perh. conn. with **purl** (1).]

purl, purl, *v.t.* to embroider or edge with gold or silver thread: to fringe with a waved edging, as lace: to knit with inverted stitches.—*n.* twisted gold or silver wire: (also **pearl**) a loop or twist, esp. on an edge: a succession of such loops, or a lace or braid having them: a fold, pleat, or frilling: knitting with inverted stitches (also **pearl**).—*adj.* (also **pearl**) with inverted stitches. [Origin unknown: perh. different words; cf. **pearl** (2).]

purl, purl, *n.* formerly, ale with wormwood: ale warmed and spiced. [Origin unknown.]

purler, purl'ər, *n.* (*Austr.*) something extremely good.

purlicue. Same as **pirlicue.**

purlieu, pur'lū, *n.* borders or outskirts: (*orig.*) a tract wrongly added to a royal forest, but disafforested by a new perambulation. [A.Fr. *puralee*, land severed by perambulation—O.Fr. *pur* (=L. *prō*), *allee*, going; infl. by Fr. *lieu*, place.]

purlin, purline, pur'lin, *n.* a piece of timber stretching across the principal rafters to support the common or subsidiary rafters. [Origin obscure.]

purloin, pər-loin', *v.t.* to filch, steal.—*v.i.* to practise theft.—*n.* purloin'er. [A.Fr. *purloigner*, to remove to a distance—*pur*- (L. *prō*), for, *loin* (L. *longē*), far.]

purpie, purp'y, pur'pi, *n.* (*obs.* Scot.) purslane.—*n.* wa'ter-pur'pie, brooklime. [O.Fr. *parpié*—L.L. *pullī pēs*, colt's foot, purslane.]

purple, pur'pl, *n.* (*hist.*) crimson: the Tyrian crimson dye, got in ancient times from various shellfish (Murex, Purpura, Buccinum, &c.): the animal yielding it: a crimson cloth or garment anciently worn by kings and emperors: the dignity of king or emperor: cardinalate, so called from the red hat and robes: now, any mixture of blue and red: a purple pigment: a purple-red pigment in the rods of the mammalian eye and in parts of other eyes (**visual purple**): a purple flower (see **long-purples**): (in *pl.*) purpura: (in *pl.*) swine-fever: (in *pl.*) ear-cockle.—*adj.* of the colour purple, mixed red and blue: blood-red: bloody.—*v.t.* to make purple.—*v.i.* to become purple.—*adjs.* pur'ple-born, porphyrogenite; pur'ple-coloured.—*n.* pur'ple-finch, an American finch with red head and breast in the cock; pur'ple-fish, a shellfish yielding purple dye; pur'ple-heart, -wood, the purple-coloured wood of species of Copaifera (fam. Caesalpiniaceae).—*adjs.* pu'rple-hued; pur'ple-in-grain, fast dyed in grain; pur'plish, pur'ply, somewhat purple.—**born in the purple**, born in the purple chamber (see **porphyrogenite**): hence, of exalted birth; **purple emperor**, one of the largest of British butterflies, and one of the most richly coloured (*Apatura iris*); **purple of Cassius**, a red or purple pigment discovered by Andreas Cassius (*c.* 1683), made from

stannous, stannic, and gold chlorides in solution; **purple patch**, a passage of fine, or (often) overornate, writing. [O.E. (Northumb.) *purpl(e)*, purple (adj.).—*purpur* (n.)—L. *purpura*—Gr. *porphȳrā*, purple-fish.]

purport, pur'pərt, -pōrt, formerly also *pur-pōrt'*, *n.* meaning conveyed: substance, gist, tenor: (*Spens.*) outward appearance, guise, as conveying an impression: (*rare*) purpose.—*v.t.* purport' (also *pur'*), to give out as its meaning: to convey to the mind: to seem to mean—often with an infinitive phrase as its object: (*rare*) to purpose.—*adj.* pur'portless. [O.Fr., from *pur* (Fr. *pour*)—L. *prō*, for, *porter*—L. *portāre*, to carry.]

purpose, pur'pəs, *n.* idea or aim kept before the mind as the end of effort: power of seeking the end desired: act or fact of purposing: an end desired: a useful function: (*Shak.*) intention of going: (*Shak.*) purport: (*Spens.*) conversation, conversational speech: (in *pl.*) a sort of conversational game.—*v.t.* to intend.—*v.i.* (*Spens.*) to discourse.—*adjs.* pur'posed, intentional: intended: purposeful; pur'poseful, directed towards a purpose: actuated by purpose.—*adv.* pur'posefully.—*n.* pur'posefulness.—*adj.* pur'poseless, without purpose: aimless: having no purpose in mind.—*adv.* pur'poselessly.—*n.* pur'poselessness.—*adj.* pur'pose-like, (*Scot.*) efficient-looking: purposed.—*adv.* pur'posely, intentionally.—*adj.* pur'posive, directed towards an end.—*n.* pur'posiveness.—**on** (*arch.* of) **purpose, of set purpose**, with design, intentionally; **to good** (or **some**) **purpose**, with good effect; **to the purpose**, to the point, or material to the question. [O.Fr. *pourpos, propos*—L. *prōpositum*, a thing intended—*prō*, forward, *pōnēre, positum*, to place; cf. **propose**.]

purpresture, pur-pres'tyər, *n.* encroachment upon public property. [O.Fr. *purpresture*—*pour*, for (L. *prō*), *prendre*—L. *praehendēre*, to take.]

Purpura, pur'pū-rä, *n.* a genus of marine gasteropods yielding purple dye: **purpura**, purples, an eruption of small purple spots, caused by extravasation of blood.—*n.* and *adj.* pur'pure, purple.—*adjs.* purpū'real, purple; purpū'ric, relating to purpura.—*n.* pur'purin, a purple colouring-matter got from madder. [L. *purpura*—Gr. *porphȳrā*.]

purr, pur, pur, *v.i.* to utter a low, murmuring sound, as a cat when pleased.—*v.t.* to say or utter with or by purring.—*ns.* purr; purr'ing.—*adv.* purr'ingly. [Imit.]

purse, purs, *n.* a small bag for carrying money: a sum of money in a purse: a sum given as a present or offered as a prize: funds: a live coal flying out of the fire, as an omen: a purse-like receptacle or cavity.—*v.t.* to put into a purse or one's own purse, to pocket: to contract as the mouth of a purse: to draw into folds or wrinkles.—*v.i.* to pucker: (*obs.*) to take purses.—*ns.* purse'-bearer, one who has charge of another's money: a treasurer: one who carries in a bag the Great Seal for the Lord Chancellor, or the royal commission for the Lord High Commissioner; purse'ful, as much as a purse can hold: enough to fill a purse; purse'-net, a net that closes like a purse; purse'-pride.—*adj.* purse'-proud, proud of one's wealth: insolent from wealth.—*ns.* purs'er, formerly a naval paymaster: an officer in charge of cabins, stewards, &c.; purs'ership; purse'-seine, a seine that can be drawn into the shape of a bag; purse'-snatcher; purse'-snatching. — *n.pl.* purse'-strings, the strings fastening a purse (usu. *fig.*).—*n.* purse'-tak'ing, robbing.—**privy purse**, an allowance for a sovereign's private expenses; **public purse**, the nation's finances. [O.E. *purs*, app.—L.L. *bursa*—Gr. *byrsa*, a hide.]

pursew, Spenser's usual spelling of **pursue.**

purslane, purs'lin, *n.* a pot and salad herb (*Portulaca oleracea*) of the Portulacaceae: any member of the genus or the family.—**sea purslane**, a fleshy seaside sandwort (*Arenaria*, or *Honckenya peploides*): orache of various species; **water purslane**, a small-flowered prostrate lythraceous plant of wet places (*Peplis Portula*).—Also **purslain.** [O.Fr. *porcelaine*—L. *porcilāca, portulāca*; see **Portulaca.**]

pursue, pər-s(y)ōō', v.t. to harass, persecute, persist in opposing or seeking to injure: (Scots law) to prosecute or sue: to follow in order to overtake and capture or kill: to chase: to hunt: to follow with haste: to follow up: to follow the course of: to be engaged in: to carry on: to seek to obtain or attain: to proceed in accordance with: to proceed with.—v.i. to follow: to go on or continue: to act as a prosecutor at law.—adj. pursu'able.—ns. pursu'al, pursu'ance, pursuit: carrying out or following out.—adj. pursu'ant, pursuing: in pursuance (with to; approaching an adv.).—adv. pursu'antly.—n. pursu'er, one who pursues: (Scots law) a plaintiff.—n. and adj. pursu'ing.—adv. pursu'ingly. [A.Fr. pursuer, pursiver—popular L. forms pro-, per-sequĕre, -īre, for L. prōsequī, persequī—prō- (the prefixes being confused), and sequī, to follow.]

pursuit, pər-s(y)ōōt', n. the act of pursuing: endeavour to attain: occupation: employment: that which is pursued. [A.Fr. purseute, fem. pa.p.; see pursue.]

pursuivant, pur's(w)i-vənt, n. an attendant or follower: a state messenger with power to execute warrants: an officer ranking below a herald. [Fr. poursuivant, pr.p. of poursuivre, to pursue.]

pursy, purs'i, adj. puffy: fat and short: short-winded.—n. purs'iness. [O.Fr. poulsif, broken-winded—poulser (Fr. pousser)—L. pulsāre, to drive.]

pursy, purs'i, adj. pursed up: puckered. [purse.]

purtenance, pur'tən-əns, n. that which pertains or belongs: (B.) the inwards of an animal. [Earlier form of pertinence.]

purulent, pū'r(y)oo-lənt, adj. consisting of, of the nature of, forming, full of, characterised by, or like pus.—ns. pū'rulence, pū'rulency.—adv. pū'rulently. [L. pūrulentus—pūs, pūris, pus.]

purvey, pur-vā', v.t. to provide, furnish: to supply.—v.i. to furnish provisions or meals as one's business.—ns. purvey'ance, the act of purveying: (Spens.) preparation in advance: (Spens.) furnishings, equipment: a procuring of victuals: that which is supplied: the former royal prerogative of pre-emption of necessaries; purvey'or, one whose business is to provide victuals or meals: an officer who formerly exacted provisions for the use of the king's household. [A.Fr. purveier (Fr. pourvoir)—L. prōvidēre; see provide.]

purview, pur'vū, n. the body or enacting part of a statute distinguished from the preamble: enactment: scope: range: field of activity or view: competence. [A.Fr. purveu, provided, pa.p. of purveier; see purvey.]

pus, pus, n. a thick yellowish fluid formed by suppuration, consisting of serum, white blood cells, bacteria, and débris of tissue. [L. pūs, pūris; cf. Gr. pyon.]

Puseyism, pū'zi-izm, n. the High Church and Catholic principles of Dr E. B. Pusey (1800-1882), and other Oxford divines, as set forth in 'Tracts for the Times.'—adjs. Pūseyist'ic, -al.—n. Pū'seyite.

push, poosh, v.t. to thrust or press against: to drive by pressure: to press or drive forward: to urge: to press hard: to put forth: to advance, carry to a further point: to promote, or seek to promote, vigorously and persistently: to make efforts to promote the sale of: to effect by thrusting forward.—v.i. to make a thrust: (B.) to butt: to exert pressure: to make an effort: to press forward: to make one's way by exertion: to reach forth: to be urgent and persistent: to play a push-stroke.—n. a thrust: an impulse: pressure: a help to advancement: enterprising or aggressive pertinacity: an effort: an onset: an offensive: a push-stroke: (Austr. slang) a gang of convicts: a gang of roughs: a company: (coll.) dismissal.—ns. push'-ball, a game in which an enormous ball is pushed; push'-bicycle (coll. -bike), -cycle, one propelled by foot; push'-button, a knob which when pressed puts on or cuts off an electric current, as for bells, &c.; push'-cart, (U.S.) a street vender's barrow; push'-chair, a folding-chair with wheels, for a child; push'er, one who pushes:

a machine or part that pushes: an air-screw placed behind: an aeroplane so propelled: a child's table implement, or a finger of bread, used for pushing food on to a fork: a self-assertive person: one who assiduously seeks social advancement.—adj. push'ful, energetically or aggressively enterprising.—adv. push'fully.—n. push'fulness.—adj. push'ing, pressing forward in business: enterprising: self-assertive. — adv. push'ingly. — ns. push'-off', an act of pushing off a boat: a send-off; push'-pin, (Shak.) a children's game in which pins are pushed one across another; push'-stroke, a push instead of an ordinary hit or stroke at a ball: in billiards one in which the cue is still or again in contact with the cue-ball when the cue-ball touches the object-ball.—at a push, when circumstances urgently require; push off, of a rower or a boat, to leave the bank, shore, &c.; push one's fortune, to busy oneself in seeking a fortune; push out, to row or be rowed out towards open water; push the bottle, to take one's liquor and pass the bottle round. [Fr. pousser—L. pulsāre, freq. of pellĕre, pulsum, to beat.]

push, poosh, interj. (Shak.) pish.—n. (Shak.) an exclamation of 'push.' [pish.]

Pushtu, Pashtu, Pushtoo, push'tōō, **Pushto, Pashto**, -tō, **Pakhtu**, puhh'tōō, **Pakhto**, -tō, n. the language of the Afghans proper. [Afghan Pashtō, Pakhtō.]

pusillanimous, pū-si-lan'i-məs, adj. wanting firmness of mind: mean-spirited: cowardly.—adv. pusillan'imously.—n. pusillanim'ity. [L. pusillanimis—pusillus, very little, animus, mind.]

pusle, an old spelling of puzzle.

puss, poos, n. a familiar name for a cat: a hare, in sportsmen's language: a playfully pejorative name for a child or a girl: a puss-moth.—ns. puss'-gen'tleman, a dandy; puss'-moth, a thick-bodied hairy notodontid moth (Dicranura, or Cerura, vinula) whose caterpillar feeds on willow or poplar leaves; puss'y, a dim. of puss: anything soft and furry: a willow catkin—also puss'y-cat; Puss'yfoot, U.S. nickname of William E. Johnson (1862-1945), from his stealthy ways as a revenue officer: hence, from his prohibitionist campaigns, a prohibitionist. — v.i. to go stealthily: to act timidly or cautiously.—ns. puss'yfooter; puss'y-will'ow, a common American willow, Salix discolor, or other species with silky spring catkins.—puss in the corner, a children's game in which the places are continually being changed, while the player who is out tries to secure one of them. [Cf. Du. poes, puss; Ir. and Gael. pus, a cat.]

pussel, pus'l, puz'l, n. (Shak.) a dirty drab. [pucelle.]

pustule, pus'tūl, n. a pimple containing pus: pimple-like or warty spot or elevation.—adjs. pus'tular, pus'tulous.—v.t. and v.i. pus'tulate.—n. pustulā'tion. [L. pustula.]

put, poot, v.t. to push or thrust: to cast, throw, hurl (esp. by a thrusting movement of the hand from the shoulder): to push: to drive: to impel: to convey, transport: to force, constrain: to incite: to place, or cause to be, in such and such a position, state, predicament, relation, &c.: to set: to place, lay, deposit: to apply: to append, affix: to connect: to add: to commit: to assign: to assign or suggest a course of action to (with on, as a diet, a study, a track; or to, as a task): to subject: to reduce: to convert: to render: to express: to assert, have: to propound: to submit to a vote: to impose: to impute: to call upon, oblige, stake, venture, invest: to repose (as trust, confidence).—v.i. (arch. or Northern) to thrust: (naut.) to proceed, make one's way: (U.S.) to set out, esp. hurriedly: (U.S.) to flow (pr.p. putting (poot'); pa.t. and pa.p. put).—n. a push or thrust: a cast, throw, esp. of a heavy stone from the shoulder: (stock exchange) an option of selling within a certain time certain securities or commodities, at a stipulated price.—ns. put'-and-take, a gambling game played with a top; put'-off, an excuse, a makeshift, evasion: a postponement; putter (poot'ər), one who puts: one who pushes or hauls trams in a coal-mine; putt'er-

Neutral vowels in unaccented syllables: el'ə-mənt, in'fənt, ran'dəm

on, (*Shak.*) an instigator; **putt′er-out,** (*obs.*) one who deposited money on going abroad, on condition of receiving a larger sum on his return, if he ever returned; **putt′ing,** the act or sport of hurling a heavy stone or weight from the hand by a sudden thrust from the shoulder; **putt′ing-stone,** a heavy stone used in the sport of putting the stone.—*adj.* **put-up′,** speciously preconcerted. —**put about,** to change the course, as of a ship: to publish, circulate: (*Scot.*) to distress; **put across,** to carry out successfully, bring off: to perform so as to carry the audience with one; **put an end,** or a stop, **to,** to cause to discontinue; **put away,** to renounce: to divorce: to kill: to stow away, pack up, set aside: to stow away in one's stomach; **put back,** to push backward: to delay: to repulse: to turn and sail back for port; **put by,** to set aside: to parry: to store up; **put case** (see **case**); **put down,** to crush, quell: to degrade: (*Shak.*) to confute: to enter, write down on paper: to reckon: to attribute: (*rare*) to give up: to surpass, outshine; **put for,** to make an attempt to gain; **put forth,** to extend: to propose: to publish: to exert: to display: to lend at interest: to set out from port: to produce, extrude; **put in,** to introduce: to insert: to lodge, deposit, hand in: to make a claim or application: to enter: to enter a harbour: to interpose: to perform towards completing a total: to spend, pass, fill up with some occupation: to appoint; **put in an appearance** (see **appearance**); **put in mind,** to remind; **put it past one,** judge it inconsistent with one's character; **put off,** to lay aside: (*arch.*) to take off: to lay aside the character of: to palm off: (*arch.*) to dismiss: to turn aside with evasions, excuses, or unsatisfying substitutes: to divert, turn aside from a purpose: to postpone: to idle away, spend in vain: to disconcert: to push from shore; **put on,** to don, clothe with: to assume, esp. deceptively: to superpose: to impose: to affix, attach, apply: to add (as weight, charges, &c.): to stake: to move forward: (*obs.*) to move faster: to set to work: to set in operation: to incite: to turn on the supply of: to score: to stage: (*pa.p.; Scot.*) clad (as *well put on,* or *putten on;* respectably dressed); **put out,** to expel: to dismiss from a game and innings: to send forth: to stretch forth: to extinguish: to place at interest: to expend: to publish: to disconcert: to put to inconvenience: to offend: to dislocate: to exert: to produce: to place with others or at a distance: to go out to sea, leave port: to remove bodily or blind (an eye); **put over,** (*Shak.*) to refer: to carry through successfully: to impress an audience, spectators, the public, favourably with: to impose, pass off; **put through,** to bring to an end: to accomplish: to put in telephonic communication; **put to,** to apply: to add to: to connect with: to harness: to shut: to set to; **put to death** (see **death**); **put to it,** to press hard: to distress; **put to rights** (see **rights**); **put to sea,** to begin a voyage; **put two and two together,** to draw a conclusion from various facts; **put up,** to start from cover, as a hare: to stow away, put aside: to parcel up: to sheathe: to compound: (*obs.*) to endure tamely: to accommodate with lodging: to take lodgings: to nominate or stand for election: to expose for sale: to present (as a good game, fight, or defence, a prayer): to preconcert; **put up to,** to incite to: to make conversant with, supply with useful information or tips about; **put upon,** to take undue advantage of: to impose upon; **put up with,** to endure; **stay put,** to remain passively in the position assigned. [Late O.E. *putian* (found in the verbal-noun *putung,* instigation); there were also *potian* and *pytan,* which may account for some of the dialect forms; cf. Dan. *putte,* Sw. *putta.*]

put, *put.* See **putt.**

putamen, *pū-tā′mən, n.* a fruit-stone: the membrane within an egg-shell: the lateral part of the lenticular nucleus of the cerebrum. [L. *putāmen,* clippings, waste, *putāre,* to prune.]

putative, *pū′ta-tiv, adj.* supposed: reputed: commonly supposed to be.—**putative marriage,** a marriage supposed invalid by canon law, but entered into in good faith by at least one of the parties. [L. *putātivus—putāre, -ātum,* to suppose.]

putchock, putchuk, pachak, puch-uk′, *n.* costusroot (so-called). [Hind. *pachak;* origin obscure.]

puteal, *pū′ti-əl, n.* a well-curb. [L. *pūteal, -ālis—puteus,* a well.]

puteli, *put′e-lē, n.* a flat-bottomed Ganges craft. [Hind. *patelī.*]

putid, *pū′tid, adj.* rotten: foul. [L. *pūtidus.*]

putlog, *put′log,* **putlock,** *-lok, n.* a cross-piece in a scaffolding, the inner end resting in a hole left in the wall. [Origin obscure; **putlock** seems to be the older form.]

putois, *pü-twä′, n.* a brush of polecat's hair, or substitute, for painting pottery. [Fr.]

putrefy, *pū′tri-fī, v.t.* to cause to rot: to corrupt.—*v.i.* to rot:—*pr.p.* pu′trefying; *pa.t.* and *pa.p.* pu′trefied.—*adj.* **putrefacient** (*-fā′shənt*), causing putrefaction.—*n.* **putrefaction** (*-fak′shən*), rotting.—*adjs.* **putrefac′tive; putrefi′able.**—*n.* **putrescence** (*-tres′əns*), incipient rottenness.—*adjs.* **putresc′ent; putresc′ible.**—*n.* **putresc′ine** (*-ēn, -in*), a substance, H₂N(CH₂)₄NH₂, formed in putrefaction of flesh.—*adj.* **pu′trid,** rotten: (*slang*) wretchedly bad.—*ns.* **putrid′ity, pu′tridness.**—**putrid fever,** typhus. [L. *putrefacĕre, putrēscĕre, putridus—puter, putris,* rotten.]

putsch, *pooch, n.* a sudden revolutionary outbreak. [Swiss Ger. dialect.]

putt, also **put,** *put, v.t.* (*Scot.*) to hurl in putting (as a weight, stone; see **put**): (*golf*) to strike in making a putt.—*v.i.* to make a putt or putts (*pr.p.* **putting,** *put′; pa.p.* and *pa.t.* **putted,** *put′*).—*n.* (*Scot.*) a throw or cast (see **put**): (*golf*) a delicate stroke such as is made with a putter on, or sometimes near, a putting-green, with the object of rolling the ball, if possible, into the hole. —*ns.* **putter** (*put′ər*), one who putts or can putt: a short stiff golf-club with upright striking-face, used in putting; **putt′ing,** (*Scot.*) the exercise of hurling a heavy weight (see **put**): the act or art of making a putt; **putt′ing-cleek,** a putter of cleek design, the blade long and narrow, running straight from the shaft; **putt′ing-green,** the turf, made firm and smooth for putting, round each of the holes of a golf-course: by the rules all within 20 yards of the hole, hazards excluded; **putt′ing-stone** (see **put**). [A Scottish form of **put.**]

putt, put, *put, n.* an old card-game like nap. [Perh. **put.**]

putt, put, *put, n.* a greenhorn: a bumpkin. [17th-century slang; origin unknown.]

puttee, puttie, *put′ē, -i, n.* a cloth strip wound round the leg, from ankle to knee, as a legging. [Hind. *patṭī.*]

puttock, *put′ək, n.* (*Shak.*) a kite: a buzzard: a kite-like person. [M.E. *puttok,* perh. conn. with O.E. *pyttel,* kite.]

putty, *put′i, n.* orig. putty-powder (*polishers'* or *jewellers' putty*): a cement of whiting and linseed-oil (*glaziers'* or *painters' putty*): a fine cement of slaked lime and water only (*plasterers' putty*): a yellowish grey colour.—*v.t.* to fix, coat, or fill with putty:—*pr.p.* putt′ying; *pa.t.* and *pa.p.* putt′ied. —*n.* **putt′ier,** a glazier.—*adjs.* **putt′y-coloured; putt′y-faced,** having a putty-coloured face.—*ns.* **putt′y-knife,** a blunt, flexible tool for laying on putty; **putt′y-pow′der,** stannic oxide (often with lead oxide) used for polishing glass. [Fr. *potée,* potful, putty-powder—*pot.*]

puture, *pū′tyər,* **pulture,** *pul′, n.* the claim of foresters, &c., to food for man, horse, and dog within the bounds of a forest. [A.Fr. *puture,* Old Northern Fr. *pulture*—L.L. *pu(l)tūra,* app.— L. *puls, pultis,* porridge.]

puy, *pwē, n.* a small volcanic cone, as in Auvergne. [Fr., hill—L. *podium,* a height; cf. **pew, podium.**]

puzel, puzzel. See **pucelle, pussel,** also **puzzle.**

puzzle, *puz′l, v.t.* to embarrass: to perplex: to bewilder: to afford difficulty of solution to: to set a problem that gives difficulty to: to entangle, complicate: to solve by systematic or assiduous thinking (with *out*).—*v.i.* to be bewildered: to labour at solution: to search about.—*n.* bewilderment: perplexity: anything that puzzles: a problem: a riddle or a toy designed to try ingenuity.—*ns.* puzz'ledom, bewilderment; puzz'le-head, one who is puzzle-headed.—*adj.* puzz'le-head'ed, having the head full of confused notions.—*ns.* puzz'le-head'edness; puzz'lement, the state of being puzzled; puzz'le-monkey, monkey-puzzle; puzz'le-peg, a piece of wood so secured under a dog's jaw as to keep his nose from the ground; puzz'ler.—*adj.* puzz'ling, posing: perplexing.—*adv.* puzz'lingly. [The suggested derivation from opposal or apposal is open to the objection that the verb is known earlier than the noun.]

puzzolana, *poot-sō-lä'nä*. Same as pozzolana.

pyaemia, *pī-ē'mi-ä, n.* infection of the blood with bacteria from a septic focus, with abscesses in different parts of the body.—Also pye'mia.—*adj.* pyae'mic. [Gr. *pyon*, pus, *haima*, blood.]

pycnic. Same as pyknic.

pycnidium, *pik-nid'i-əm, n.* in some fungi a receptacle like a perithecium, containing hyphae which produce conidia.—*n.* pycnid'iospore, a conidium produced in a pycnidium. [Gr. *pyknos*, thick, dense, dim. suff. *-idion* Latinised to *-idium*.]

pycnite, *pik'nīt, n.* a columnar variety of topaz. [Gr. *pyknos*, dense.]

pycno-, pykno-, *pik'nō-, pik-no'-,* in composition, dense, close.—*ns.* pycnoconid'ium, a pycnidiospore; pycnog'onid (Gr. *gony*, knee), a sea-spider.—*n.pl.* Pycnogon'ida, the sea-spiders, a class of marine arthropods with more leg than body.—*adj.* pycnog'onoid.—*ns.* pycnom'eter, pyknom'eter, an instrument for determining specific gravities; pyc'non, in Greek music, that part of the tetrachord (chromatic or enharmonic) where the smallest intervals fell: in mediaeval music, a semitone; pyc'nospore, a pycnidiospore.—*adj.* pycnostyle (Gr. *stylos*, column), with close-set columns, 1½ diameters apart.—*n.* a pycnostyle building. [Gr. *pyknos*, dense.]

pyebald. See piebald.

pye-dog, *pī'-dog, n.* an ownerless or pariah dog. [Anglo-Ind. *pye, paë*; Hind. *pāhī*, outsider.]

pyelitis, *pī-ə-lī'tis, n.* inflammation of the pelvis of the kidney.—*adj.* pyelitic (*-lit'ik*). [Gr. *pyelos*, a trough.]

pyemia. See pyaemia.

pyengadu, *pyeng-gä-dōō', n.* the ironwood (Xylia; Mimosaceae) of Burma, &c. [Burmese *pyeng-kadō*.]

pygal, *pī'gəl, adj.* belonging to the rump or posteriors of an animal.—*n.* the posterior median plate of a chelonian carapace. [Gr. *pȳgē*, rump.]

pygarg, *pī'gärg, n.* (*B.*) possibly the addax antelope. [Gr. *pȳgē*, rump, *argos*, white.]

pygidium, *pī-gid'i-əm,* or *-jid', n.* in insects, the tergum of the last abdominal somite: the tail-shield of a trilobite.—*adj.* pygid'ial. [Latinised from Gr. *pȳgidion*, dim. of *pȳgē*, rump.]

pygmy, pigmy, *pig'mi, n.* a member of the race of dwarfs said by the ancients to have warred with cranes, or of any of the actual dwarf human races, negritos, negrillos, and others: one of the ancient diminutive dwellers in underground houses, &c., in whom some scholars see the historical origins of the fairies and elves of folklore: an elf: (*obs.*) an anthropoid ape: a dwarf: any person, animal, or thing relatively diminutive or in some way insignificant.—*adj.* dwarfish: diminutive: of the pygmies.—*adj.* Chrysomaean, pyg-, pigmean (*-mē'ən*). [Gr. *pygmaios*, measuring a *pygmē* (13½ inches, distance from elbow to knuckles).]

pygostyle, *pī'gō-stīl, n.* the bone of a bird's tail. [Gr. *pȳgē*, rump, *stylos*, a column.]

pyjamas, *pə-, pi-,* or *pī-jä'məz, n.pl.* loose trousers tied round the waist, worn by Indians: (in European use) a sleeping-suit.—Also paja'mas.—*adj.* pyja'ma'd, pyja'maed, wearing pyjamas.—*ns.* pyja'ma-jacket, -trousers. [Pers. and Hind. *pāējāmah—pāē*, leg, *jāmah*, clothing.]

pyknic, *pik'nik, adj.* characterised by short squat stature, small hands and feet, relatively short limbs, domed abdomen, short neck, round face. [Gr. *pyknos*, thick.]

pyknometer. Same as pycnometer.

pylon, *pī'lon, n.* a gateway, gate-tower, gatehouse, or mass of building through which an entrance passes, esp. the gateway of an Egyptian temple: a guiding mark at an aerodrome: a structure for support of power-cables:—*pl.* py'lons. [Gr. *pylōn, -ōnos—pylē*, a gate.]

pylorus, *pī-* or *pī-lō'rəs, n.* the opening from the stomach to the intestines.—*adj.* pyloric (*-lor'ik*). [L.,—Gr. *pylōros*, gate-keeper, pylorus—*pylē*, an entrance, *ōrā*, care; cf. *ouros*, a guardian.]

pyne. Same as pine (2).

pyogenic, *pī-ə-jen'ik, adj.* pus-forming. — *adj.* py'oid, purulent.—*n.* pyorrhoea (*-rē'ä*; Gr. *rhoiä*, flow), discharge of pus: now, suppuration in the sockets of teeth. [Gr. *pyon*, pus.]

pyoning. See pioneer.

pyot, pyat, pyet, piet, *pī'ət, n.* (*Scot.*) a magpie.—*adj.* pied.—*adj.* pi'oted. [pie (1).]

pyracanth, *pī'ra-kanth,* pyracantha, *-kan'thä, n.* a thorny evergreen shrub near akin to hawthorn. [Gr. *pȳrakantha—pȳr*, fire, *akanthos*, thorn.]

pyralis, *pir'ə-lis, n.* (*obs.*) an insect feigned to live or breed in fire: Pyralis, a genus of moths, giving name to a heterogeneous family the Pyralidae (*pir-al'i-dē*).—*n.* pyr'alid, a member of the family. [Gr. *pȳrālis—pȳr*, fire.]

pyramid, *pir'ə-mid, n.* a solid figure on a triangular, square, or polygonal base, with triangular sides meeting in a point: any object or structure of that or similar form, esp. a great Egyptian monument: (*crystal.*) a crystal form of three or more faces each cutting three axes: (in *pl.*) a game played on a billiard-table in which the balls are arranged in pyramid shape:—*pl.* usu. pyr'amids, also pyramides (*pir-am'i-dēz*), and sometimes (*poet.*) pyram'id(e)s.—*adjs.* pyram'idal, pyramid'ic, -al, having the form of a pyramid.—*advs.* pyram'idally, pyramid'ically.—*ns.* pyramid'-ion, the small pyramidal apex of an obelisk; pyram'idist, one who studies the Egyptian Pyramids; pyr'amis, (*Shak.* &c.) a pyramid:—(*pl.*) pyram'ides, pyr'amises; pyram'idon, an organ-stop with pipes like inverted pyramids. [Gr. *pyramis, -idos*.]

pyrargyrite, *pīr-,* or *pir-är'jir-īt, n.* ruby-silver ore, sulphide of silver and antimony. [Gr. *pȳr*, fire, *argyros*, silver.]

pyre, *pir, n.* a pile of combustibles for burning a dead body.—*adj.* pyr'al. [L. *pyra*—Gr. *pȳrä—pȳr*, fire.]

pyrene, *pī'rēn, n.* a fruit-stone.—*ns.* pyrē'nocarp (Gr. *karpos*, fruit), a perithecium; pyrē'noid, a small round albuminous body concerned in starch-formation, found in the chloroplasts of some algae, &c.—*n.pl.* Pyrēnomycē'tēs (Gr. *mykēs*, fungus), a group of Ascomycetes whose characteristic fructification is the perithecium.—*adj.* pyrenomyce'tous. [Gr. *pȳrēn, -ēnos*, fruit-stone.]

pyrene, *pī'rēn, n.* a hydrocarbon ($C_{16}H_{10}$) got by dry distillation of coal. [Gr. *pȳr*, fire.]

Pyrenean, Pyrenaean, *pir-ə-nē'ən, adj.* of the Pyrenees, the mountains between France and Spain.—*n.* a native of the Pyrenees: (in *pl.; obs.*) the Pyrenees.—*n.* pyrenē'ite, a black garnet. [L. *Pȳrēnaeus*—Gr. *Pȳrēnaios*.]

Pyrethrum, *pī-rēth'rəm, pī-reth'rəm, pir-eth'rəm, n.* a former genus of composite plants now merged in Chrysanthemum, including feverfew: pyrethrum, still applied to various garden flowers, esp. varieties of *Chrysanthemum coccineum*: insect-powder of flower-heads of various species of pyrethrum: in pharmacy, the root of pellitory of Spain. [L.,—Gr. *pȳrēthron*, pellitory of Spain.]

pyretic, *pī-ret'ik, pir-et'ik, adj.* of, of the nature of, for the cure of, fever.—*ns.* pyretol'ogy, study of fevers; pyretother'apy, treatment by inducing high body temperature; pyrex'ia, fever. [Gr. *pȳretikos*, feverish—*pȳretos*, fever; and *pȳressein*, to be feverish—*pȳr*, fire.]

Pyrex, *pī'reks, n.* a registered trade-mark applied to glassware resistant to heat. [Gr. *pȳr*, fire, and L. *rēx*, king.]

pyrheliometer, *pir-hē-li-om'i-tər, n.* an instrument for measuring the heating effect of the sun's rays.

—*adj.* **pyrheliometric** (*-ō-met'rik*). [Gr. *pȳr*, fire, *hēlios*, sun, *metron*, measure.]

pyridine, *pir'*, or *pīr'i-dēn*, *-dīn*, *n.* a strong-smelling, colourless, strongly basic liquid, C_5H_5N, got in distillation of bone-oil, coal-tar, &c.—*n.* **pyridox'-in(e),** a pyridine derivative, a member of the vitamin B_2 complex. [Gr. *pȳr*, fire.]

pyriform, *pir'i-form, adj.* pear-shaped. [L. *pirum*, a pear, *forma*, form.]

pyrites, *pīr-*, *pir-ī'tēz, n.* a brassy yellow mineral, disulphide, crystallising in the cubic system, iron occurring in octahedra, pyritohedra, &c. (also called pyrite, *pī'rīt*, **iron pyri'tes**): extended to a large class of mineral sulphides and arsenides.— *adjs.* **pyritic** (*pir-*, *pīr-it'ik*), **-al; pyritif'erous.** —*v.t.* **pyr'itise,** to convert into, or replace by, pyrites.—*adj.* **pyritohē'dral.**—*n.* **pyritohē'dron,** a pentagonal dodecahedron:—*pl.* **pyritohē'dra.**— *adj.* **pyr'itous.**—**arsenical pyrites,** mispickel; **cockscomb pyrites, spear pyrites,** twinned forms of marcasite; **copper pyrites,** sulphide of copper and iron, chalcopyrite, a mineral much resembling iron pyrites; **magnetic pyrites,** pyrrhotite. [Gr. *pȳrītēs*, striking fire—*pȳr*, fire.]

pyrithiamine, *pi-ri-thī'ə-mēn, n.* an anti-vitamin causing thiamine (vitamin B_1) deficiency. [Gr. *pȳr*, fire, and **thiamine.**]

pyro-, *pī'rō-*, in composition, fire, heat, fever: (*chem.*) obtained by heating or as if by heating, or by removing (theoretically) a molecule of water. —*adjs.* **pyro-acet'ic, pyrophosphor'ic, pyro-sulphu'ric, pyrotartar'ic,** &c., related in this way to acetic, phosphoric, &c., acid.—*ns.* **pyro-phos'phate, pyrotar'trate,** &c., a salt of such an acid. [Gr. *pȳr*, in compounds *pȳr-*, fire.]

pyro, *pī'rō, n.* (*photog.*) a familiar abbreviation of **pyrogallol,** or **pyrogallic acid.**

pyroballogy, *pī-rō-bal'ə-ji, n.* (*Sterne*) the science of artillery. [Gr. *pȳr*, fire, *ballein*, to throw, *logos*, discourse.]

pyroclastic, *pī-rō-klas'tik, adj.* formed of fragments by igneous agency. [Gr. *pȳr*, *klastos*, broken.]

pyro-electric, *pī-rō-i-lek'trik, adj.* becoming positively and negatively electrified at opposite poles on heating or cooling: of pyro-electricity.—*n.* **pyro-electricity** (*-el-ik-tris'i-ti*), the property of being pyro-electric: the study of the phenomena shown by pyro-electric crystals.

pyrogallol, *pī-rō-gal'ol, n.* a phenol got by heating *gallic* acid—also called **pyrogall'ic acid.**

pyrogenic, *pī-rō-jen'ik,* **pyrogenetic,** *-jin-et'ik, adjs.* produced by, or producing, heat or fever.

pyrognostic, *pī-rog-nos'tik, adj.* pertaining to testing of minerals by flame. [Gr. *gnōstikos,* discriminating.]

pyrography, *pī-rog'rə-fi, n.* poker-work.—*n.* **pyrogravure'.**

Pyrola, *pir'ə-lä, n.* the wintergreen genus, giving name to the family **Pyrolä'ceae,** akin to the heaths. [Dim. of *pyrus,* a misspelling of L. *pirus,* a pear-tree.]

pyrolatry, *pī-rol'ə-tri, n.* fire-worship.—*n.* **pyrol'ater,** a fire-worshipper. [Gr. *latreiā,* worship.]

pyroligneous, *pī-rō-lig'ni-əs, adj.* got by distillation of wood.—**pyroligneous acid,** wood-vinegar, a mixture of acetic acid, methyl alcohol, &c.; **pyroligneous alcohol,** wood-spirit, methyl alcohol. [Gr. *pȳr,* and L. *ligneus—lignum,* wood.]

pyrolusite, *pī-rō-l(y)ōō'sīt, n.* native manganese dioxide. [Gr. *pȳr, lousis,* washing, from its use in decolorising molten glass.]

pyromancy, *pī'rō-man-si, n.* divination by fire.— *adj.* **pyromant'ic.** [Gr. *manteiā,* divination.]

pyromania, *pī-rō-mā'ni-ä, n.* an incendiary mania. —*n.* and *adj.* **pyromā'niac.**—*adj.* **pyromaniacal** (*-mə-nī'ə-kl*).

pyromeride, *pī-rom'ər-īd, n.* a nodular rhyolite. [Gr. *meros,* part, as if meaning only partly fusible.]

pyrometer, *pī-rom'i-tər, n.* an instrument for measuring high temperatures.—*adjs.* **pyrometric** (*pī-rō-met'rik*), **-al.**—*n.* **pyrom'etry.** [Gr. *metron,* measure.]

pyromorphite, *pī-rō-mor'fīt, n.* an ore (chloride and phosphate) of lead, so called because the blowpipe bead crystallises on cooling. [Gr. *morphē,* form.]

pyrope, *pī'rōp, n.* a fiery red gem-stone (also *poet.* **pyro'pus**): (*min.*) a red magnesia-alumina garnet, used in jewellery. [Gr. *pyrōpos,* fiery-eyed— *ōps, ōpos,* eye, face.]

pyrophone, *pī'rō-fōn, n.* an organ producing interference-tones by pairs of flames in tubes, invented by Eugène Kastner (1852-82). [Gr. *phōnē,* sound, voice.]

pyrophorus, *pī-rof'ə-rəs, n.* anything that takes fire on exposure to air: **Pyrophorus,** a genus of tropical American fireflies (elaterid beetles).—*adjs.* **pyrophoric** (*-rō-for'ik*), **pyroph'orous.** [Gr. *pȳro-phoros,* fire-bearer, *pȳr, pherein,* to carry.]

pyrophotograph, *pī-rō-fō'tə-gräf, n.* a burnt-in photograph, as on glass or porcelain.—*adj.* **pyrophotograph'ic.**—*n.* **pyrophotog'raphy.**

pyrophyllite, *pī-rō-fil'it, n.* a clay mineral that exfoliates before the blowpipe. [Gr. *pȳr, phyllon,* leaf.]

pyroscope, *pī'rō-skōp, n.* an instrument for measuring the intensity of radiant heat. [Gr. *skopeein,* to view.]

pyrosis, *pī-rō'sis, n.* water-brash. [Gr. *pȳrōsis— pȳr,* fire.]

Pyrosoma, *pī-rō-sō'mä, n.* a genus of compound tunicates, with brilliant phosphorescence. — *n.* **py'rosome.** [Gr. *sōma,* body.]

pyrotechnics, *pī-rō-tek'niks, n.* the art of making fireworks: display of fireworks: showy display in talk, music, &c.—*adjs.* **pyrotech'nic, -al.**—*adv.* **pyrotech'nically.**—*ns.* **pyrotech'nist,** a maker of fireworks: one skilled in, or given to, pyrotechnics; **py'rotechny,** pyrotechnics. [Gr. *technikos,* skilled—*technē,* art.]

pyroxene, *pī'rok-sēn,* a general name for a group of minerals distinguished from amphiboles by a cleavage angle about 87°, metasilicates of calcium, magnesium, aluminium, and other metals, usually green or black, very common in igneous rocks— augite, diopside, enstatite, &c.—*adj.* **pyroxenic** (*-sen'ik*).—*n.* **pyrox'enite** (*-ən-īt,* or *-ēn'īt*), a rock compound essentially of pyroxene. [Gr. *pȳr, xenos,* stranger (because Haüy thought that pyroxene crystals in lava had only been accidentally caught up).]

pyroxylic, *pī-rok-sil'ik, adj.* (*obs.*) pyroligneous.— *ns.* **pyroxyle** (*-rok'sil*), **pyrox'ylin, -e,** nitrated cotton. [Gr. *xylon,* wood.]

pyrrhic, *pir'ik, n.* an ancient Greek war-dance: a foot of two short syllables.—*adj.* pertaining to the dance or to the foot.—*n.* **pyrrhicist** (*pir'i-sist*), a pyrrhic dancer. [Gr. *pyrrichē* (*orchēsis*), pyrrhic dance, said to be from *Pyrrhichos,* the inventor.]

Pyrrhic, *pir'ik, adj.* of or pertaining to *Pyrrhus,* king of Epirus (318-272 B.C.).—**Pyrrhic victory,** a victory gained at too great a cost, in allusion to Pyrrhus's exclamation after his defeat of the Romans at Heraclea on the Siris (280), ' Another such victory and we are lost.'

Pyrrhonism, *pir-ən-izm, n.* the complete scepticism of *Pyrrhō* (Gr. *Pyrrōn*) of Elis (3rd cent. B.C.).— *adj.* and *n.* **Pyrrhonian** (*pir-ō'ni-ən*).—*adj.* **Pyrrhonic** (*-on'ik*).—*n.* **Pyrrh'onist.**

pyrrhotite, *pir'ō-tīt, n.* magnetic pyrites, an iron sulphide, often with nickel.—Also **pyrrh'otine** (*-tēn*). [Gr. *pyrrotēs,* redness—*pȳr,* fire.]

pyrrhous, *pir'əs, adj.* reddish. [Gr. *pyrros,* flame-coloured—*pȳr.*]

Pyrus, *pī'rəs, n.* the pear and apple genus of the rose family. [A misspelling of L. *pirus,* a pear-tree.]

Pythagorean, *pī-thag-ə-rē'ən, adj.* pertaining to *Pythagoras* (6th cent. B.C.), the celebrated Greek philosopher, or to his philosophy: transformed, as if by transmigration of the soul (taught by Pythagoras): vegetarian.—*n.* a follower of Pythagoras.—*ns.* **Pythagorē'anism, Pythag'orism,** his doctrines.—**Pythagorean letter,** or Samian letter, the Greek letter Υ, for Pythagoras (a Samian) a symbol of the parting of the ways for vice and virtue; **Pythagorean theorem,** that the square on the hypotenuse of a right-angled triangle is equal to the sum of the squares on the other two sides.

Pythia, *pith'i-ä, n.* the priestess who delivered the oracles of Pythian Apollo at Delphi.—*adj.* **Pyth'ian.**

of Delphi, the oracle there, the priestess, or the games held near.—*n.* a native or inhabitant of Delphi: the priestess of Apollo there: Apollo.—*adj.* **Pyth'ic,** Pythian: ecstatic.—**Pythian games,** one of the four national festivals of ancient Greece, in honour of Apollo, held every four years at Delphi; **Pythian verse,** the dactylic hexameter. [Gr. *Pȳthō,* old name of Delphi; see **python.**]

Pythium, *pith'i-əm, n.* a genus of fungi, cause of damping-off of seedlings. [Gr. *pȳthein,* to cause to rot.]

pythogenic, *pī-thō-jen'ik, adj.* produced by filth. [Gr. *pȳthein,* to rot, root of *gignesthai,* to become.]

Python, *pī'thən, n.* the great snake killed by Apollo at Delphi: **python,** a familiar or possessing spirit: one possessed by a spirit: an utterer of oracles: a large snake that crushes its victims, esp. and properly one of the Old World genus *Python,*

akin to the boas.—*n.* **Py'thoness,** the priestess of the oracle of Apollo at Delphi: **pythoness,** a witch.—*adj.* **pythonic** (*-thon'ik*). [Gr. *Pȳthōn,* the snake slain at *Pȳthō* (Delphi) by Apollo, according to legend from *pȳthein,* to rot, because it rotted.]

pyx, *piks, n.* a box: (*R.C.*) a vessel in which the host is kept after consecration, now usu. that in which it is carried to the sick: a box at the Mint in which sample coins are kept for testing.—*v.t.* to test the weight and fineness of, as the coin deposited in the pyx.—*ns.* **pyxid'ium,** (*bot.*) a capsule that opens by a transverse circular split: —*pl.* **pyxid'ia; pyx'is,** a little box or casket as for jewels, drugs, toilet materials, &c.—**trial of the pyx,** trial by weight and assay of gold and silver coins by a jury of goldsmiths. [L. *pyxis,* a box—Gr. *pyxis, -idos,* dim. *pyxidion—pyxos,* box-tree.]

Neutral vowels in unaccented syllables : *el'ə-mənt, in'fənt, ran'dəm*

Q

Q, q, *kū, n.* the seventeenth letter of our alphabet, derived from the abandoned Greek letter koppa (q.v.), and representing in English the same sound as *K*, but always in English followed by *u* (sounded as *w*, except in words from or modelled on French, Spanish, &c.), used, however, in transliterating Semitic *qōph*: Old English used *cw* instead of *qu*, and mediaeval Scots *quh* for *hw* (*wh*): as a mediaeval Roman numeral Q = 500, Q̄ = 500,000.—*n.* **Q'-boat,** a naval vessel disguised as a merchant ship or fishing-boat, to deceive and destroy submarines. [L. *cū*.]

qua, *kwā,* L. *kwā, adv.* in the capacity of. [L. *quā,* adverbial abl. fem. of *quī,* who.]

quack, *kwak, n.* the cry of a duck.—*v.i.* to make the sound of a quack.—*v.i.* **quack'le,** to quack. [Imit.]

quack, *kwak, n.* a shortened form of **quacksalver**: a charlatan.—Also *adj.*—*v.i.* to play the quack. —*v.t.* to puff, vend, or treat in the manner of a quack.—*ns.* **quack'ery,** the pretensions or practice of a quack, esp. in medicine; **quack'salver,** a boastful pretender to knowledge and skill (esp. in medicine) that he does not possess.—*adj.* **quack'salving.** [Du. *quacksalver* (now *kwak-zalver*), perh. one who quacks about his salves.]

quad, *kwod, n.* an abbreviation of **quadrangle, quadrat, quadruped** (i.e. horse), **quadruplet.**—*adj.* abbreviation for **quadruple.**—*v.t.* to fill with quadrats.

quadragenarian, *kwod-rǝ-ji-nā′ri-ǝn, n.* one who is forty years old.—Also *adj.* [L. *quadrāgēnārius*—*quadrāgēnī,* forty each.]

Quadragesima, *kwod-rǝ-jes′i-mā, n.* (*obs.*) the forty days of Lent: the first Sunday in Lent.—*adj.* **quadrages′imal,** of the number forty: of Lent. [L. *quadrāgēsimus, -a, -um,* fortieth—*quadrāgintā,* forty—*quattuor,* four.]

quadrangle, *kwod-rang′gl,* also *kwod′, n.* a plane figure with four angles (and therefore four sides): an object or space of that form: a court or open space, usually rectangular, enclosed by a building (as a college): sometimes the enclosing building. —*adj.* **quadrang′ular** (*-gū-lǝr*).—*adv.* **quadrang′ularly.**—**complete quadrangle,** a figure composed of four points joined by six straight lines or sides. [Fr.,—L. *quadrangulum*—*quattuor,* four, *angulus,* an angle.]

quadrans, *kwod′ranz,* L. *kwäd′räns, n.* a Roman copper coin, the fourth part of the as:—*pl.* **quadran′tēs.**—*n.* **quadrant** (*kwod′rǝnt*), the fourth part of a circle or its circumference, a sector or an arc of 90°: an area, object, street, of that form: an instrument with an arc of 90° for taking altitudes.—*adj.* **quadrantal** (*-rant′l*). [L. *quadrāns, -antis,* a fourth part—*quattuor,* four.]

quadrat, *kwod′rat, n.* a piece of type-metal lower than the letters, used in spacing between words and filling out blank lines (commonly **quad**)—distinguished as **em** (▮), **em** (▮), **two-em** (▮▮), and **three-em** (▮▮▮).—*adj.* **quad′rate** (*-r āt, -rit*), square: rectangular: squarish: squared: square, as a power or root: (*fig.*) balanced: conformable. —*n.* a square or quadrate figure or object: the quadrate bone, suspending the lower jaw in vertebrates other than mammals: (*obs.*) quartile.—*v.t.* and *v.i.* to square: to conform.—*adj.* **quadratic** (*-rat′ik*), of or like a quadrate: (*alg.*) involving the square but no higher power: (*crystal.*) tetragonal. —*n.* a quadratic equation.—*adj.* **quadrat′ical.**—*ns.* **quadrā′trix** a curve by which a curved figure (as the circle) may be squared; **quad′rature** (*-rǝ-tyǝr*), squareness: (*Milt.*) a square space: squaring: the finding of an equal square: an angular distance of 90°: the position of a heavenly body at such an angular distance, or the time of

its being there; **quadrā′tus,** the name of several quadrangular muscles.—**B quadrā′tum, quadrate B** (see **B**). [L. *quadrātus,* pa.p. of *quadrāre,* to square—*quattuor,* four.]

quadrennium. See **quadriennium.**

quadri-, *kwod′ri-,* in composition, four: square. [L. *quadri-*—*quattuor,* four.]

quadric, *kwod′rik, adj.* of the second degree. [L. *quadra,* a square.]

quadriceps, *kwod′ri-seps, n.* the great thigh muscle that extends the leg (from its four insertions).— *adj.* **quadricipital** (*-sip′i-tl*). [L. *caput, -itis,* head.]

quadricone, *kwod′ri-kōn, n.* a quadric cone, or cone having a conic as base.

quadriennium, *kwod-ri-en′i-ǝm, n.* four years:— *pl.* **quadrienn′ia.**—*adj.* **quadrienn′ial,** lasting four years: once in four years.—*n.* a quadriennial event.—*adv.* **quadrienn′ially.**—The forms **quadrenn′ium,** &c., are incorrect but not uncommon. [L. *quadriennium*—*annus,* year.]

quadrifarious, *kwod-ri-fā′ri-ǝs, adj.* fourfold: in four rows. [L. *quadrifārius;* cf. **multifarious.**]

quadrifid, *kwod′ri-fid, adj.* four-cleft. [L. *quadrifidus,* from the root of *findēre,* to cleave.]

quadrifoliate, *kwod-ri-fō′li-āt, adj.* four-leaved. [L. *folium,* a leaf.]

quadriform, *kwod-ri-form, adj.* fourfold: having four forms or aspects. [L. *forma,* form.]

quadriga, *kwod-ri′gä,* L. *kwäd-rē′gä, n.* in Greek and Roman times a two-wheeled car drawn by four horses abreast:—*pl.* **quadri′gae** (*-jē,* L. *-gī*). [L., a later singular from *quadrīgae,* a team of four, for *quadrijugae*—*jugum,* a yoke.]

quadrigeminal, *kwod-ri-jem′i-nl, adj.* having four similar parts.—Also **quadrigem′inate, quadrigem′inous.** [L. *geminī,* twins.]

quadrilateral, *kwod-ri-lat′ǝr-l, adj.* four-sided.— *n.* (*geom.*) a plane figure bounded by four straight lines: a group of four fortresses, esp. Mantua, Verona, Peschiera, and Legnago. — **complete quadrilateral,** a figure consisting of four straight lines intersecting in six points or vertices. [L. *quadrilaterus*—*latus, lateris,* a side.]

quadriliteral, *kwod-ri-lit′ǝr-l, adj.* of four letters.— *n.* a word or a root of four letters. [L. *litera,* a letter.]

quadrille, *kwa-dril′,* or *kǝ-, n.* one of four groups of horsemen (or others): a square dance for four couples or more, in five movements: music for such a dance.—*v.i.* to dance quadrilles.—*n.* **quadrill′er.** [Fr.,—Sp. *cuadrilla,* a troop, app.— *cuadra*—L. *quadra,* a square.]

quadrille, *kwa-dril′,* or *kǝ-, n.* a four-handed game with 40 cards, not unlike ombre.—*v.i.* to play quadrille. [Fr., perh.—Sp. *cuatrillo,* the game of quadrille, or *cuartillo,* fourth part.]

quadrillion, *kwod-, kwǝd-ril′yǝn, n.* a million raised to the fourth power, represented by a unit and 24 ciphers: (*U.S.* and *France*) a thousand to the fifth power, a unit with 15 ciphers.—*n.* and *adj.* **quadrill′ionth.** [Modelled on **million.**]

quadrilocular, *kwod-ri-lok′ū-lǝr, adj.* having four compartments. [L. *loculus,* dim. of *locus,* place.]

quadringenary, *kwod-rin-jē′nǝr-i, n.* a four-hundredth anniversary or its celebration. [L. *quadringēnārius,* of four hundred each.]

quadrinomial, *kwod-ri-nō′mi-ǝl, adj.* (*alg.*) of four terms.—*n.* an expression of four terms. [Irregularly from L. *nōmen, -inis,* a name.]

quadripartite, *kwod-ri-pär′tīt, adj.* in four parts: having four parties: (*bot.*) deeply cleft into four parts, as a leaf: (*archit.*) divided, as a vault, into four compartments.—*n.* **quadriparti′tion.** [L. *partīrī, -itum,* to divide.]

quadrireme, *kwod´ri-rēm, n.* a ship with four banks of oars. [L. *quadrirēmis—rēmus,* an oar.]

quadrisection, *kwod-ri-sek´shən, n.* division into four equal parts. [L. *sectiō, -ōnis,* cutting.]

quadrisyllable, *kwod-ri-sil´ə-bl, n.* a tetrasyllable. *—adj.* **quadrisyllab´ic.**

quadrivalent, *kwod-riv´ə-lənt,* or *-ä´lənt, adj.* having a valency of four.*—n.* **quadriv´alence** (or *-vä´*).

quadrivium, *kwod-riv´i-əm, n.* in mediaeval education, the four branches of mathematics (arithmetic, geometry, astronomy, music).—*adj.* **quadriv´ial.** [L., the place where four roads meet—*via,* a way.]

quadroon, *kwod-rōōn´, n.* the offspring of a mulatto and a white: extended to any analogous cross.— Also **quarteroon´.** [Sp. *cuarterón—cuarto,* a fourth.]

quadrumanous, *kwod-rōō´mən-əs, adj.* four-handed: of the obsolete order **Quadru´mana,** the Primates other than man:—*sing.* **quad´ruman, -mane** (*-man, -mān*). [L. *manus,* a hand.]

quadruped, *kwod´rōō-ped, n.* a four-footed animal: usu. a mammal, esp. a horse.—*adj.* four-footed.— *adj.* **quadrupedal** (*-rōō´-pi-dəl*). [L. *pēs, pedis,* a foot.]

quadruple, *kwod´rōō-pl,* also (esp. in Scotland) *-rōō´, adj.* fourfold: having four parts, members, or divisions.—*n.* four times as much: a coin worth four pistoles.—*v.t.* to increase fourfold: to equal four times.—*v.i.* to become four times as much.— *n.* **quad´ruplet** (or *-rōō´*), any combination of four things: a group of four notes performed in the time of three: a cycle for four riders: one of four born at a birth.—*adv.* **quad´ruply** (*-pli,* or *-rōō´pli*), in a fourfold manner.—**Quadruple Alliance,** a league formed in 1718 by Britain, France, Austria, and Holland against Spain. [Fr.,—L. *quadruplus,* from the root of *plēre,* to fill.]

quadruplex, *kwod´rōō-pleks, adj.* fourfold: of a telegraphic system, capable of sending four messages at once, two each way, over one wire.—*n.* an instrument of this kind.—*v.t.* to make quadruplex.—*adj.* **quadru´plicate,** fourfold.—*n.* one of four corresponding things: fourfoldness.—*v.t.* to make fourfold.—*ns.* **quadruplica´tion;** **quadruplicity** (*-plis´i-ti*); **quad´ruply** (*-plī; Scots law*), a reply to a triple. [L. *quadruplex, -icis,* fourfold—*plicāre, -ātum,* to fold.]

quaere. See **query.**

quaestor, *kwēs´tor, -tər,* L. *kwīs´tor, n.* an ancient Roman magistrate, in early times an investigator, prosecutor, or judge in murder cases, later a treasurer with various other functions: in the Middle Ages an officer (usu. **ques´tor**) who granted indulgences: a treasurer.—*n.* **quaes´tionary** (*-tyən-ə-ri; Scott*), a pardoner.—*adj.* **quaestorial** (*-tō´ri-əl*).—*n.* **quaes´torship.**—*adj.* **quaes´tuary,** money-making: gain-seeking.—*n.* a gain-seeker: a pardoner. [L. *quaestor, -ōris — quaerĕre, quaesītum,* to seek.]

quaff, *kwäf, v.t.* to drink or drain in large draughts. —*v.i.* to drink largely.—*n.* a draught.—*n.* **quaff´er.** [Origin obscure.]

quaff, *kwäf,* a variant of **quaich.**

quag, *kwag, n.* a boggy place, esp. one that quakes underfoot.—*n.* **quagg´iness.**—*adj.* **quagg´y.** [Cf. **quake.**]

quagga, *kwag´ä, n.* an extinct S. African wild ass (*Equus quagga*), less fully striped than the zebra. [Said to be Hottentot *quacha.*]

quagmire, *kwag´mīr, n.* wet boggy ground that yields or quakes under the feet.—*v.t.* to entangle, as in a quagmire.—*adj.* **quag´miry.** [App. **quag, mire.**]

quahog, quahaug, *kwaw´hog, -hawg, kwə-hog´, -hawg´, n.* an edible Venus mollusc (*Venus mercenaria*) of the N. American Atlantic coast—also known as round clam: also *Cyprina islandica* (*black quahog*). [Narraganset Ind. *poquauhock.*]

quaich, quaigh, *kwähh, n.* (*Scot.*) a drinking-cup, usually of staves and hoops. [Gael. *cuach,* a cup.]

quail, *kwāl, v.i.* to languish, decline: to flinch: to fail in spirit: (*Shak.*) to slacken.—*v.t.* (*obs.*) to subdue: to daunt.—*n.* **quail´ing** (*Shak.*). [M.E. *quayle;* origin obscure.]

quail, *kwāl, n.* a genus (Coturnix) of small birds of the partridge family: in America extended to various similar small game-birds, as the California quail (Lophortyx) and the bobwhite: (*Shak.*) a whore. — *n.* **quail´-pipe,** a whistle for alluring quails into a net (also **quail´-call**): (*obs.*) the throat. [O.Fr. *quaille;* prob. Gmc.]

quaint, *kwänt, adj.* (*Shak.*) skilful, esp. in use of language: (*obs.*) cunning: (*obs.*) ingenious: (*Spens., Milt.*) fine: (*obs.*) affectedly fanciful or elaborate: (*Spens.*) affectedly nice or prim: pleasantly odd: whimsical. — *adv.* **quaint´ly.** — *n.* **quaint´ness.** [O.Fr. *cointe*—L. *cognitus,* known; perh. confused with *comptus,* neat.]

quair, *kwār,* obs. form of **quire** (1).

quake, *kwāk, v.i.* to quiver or vibrate, as the earth or a quagmire: to tremble, esp. with cold or fear. —*v.t.* (*Shak.*) to cause to tremble: to shake by earthquake.—*n.* a tremor: an earthquake: a shudder.—*ns.* **quä´kiness; quä´king; quä´king-grass,** a moorland grass of the genus Briza, with pendulous panicled tremulous spikelets.— *adv.* **quä´kingly.**—*adj.* **quä´ky,** shaky. [O.E. *cwacian;* perh. allied to *quick.*]

Quaker, *kwä´ker, n.* one of the Society of Friends, founded by George Fox (1624-91): a dummy cannon.—*adj.* of the Quakers: (*U.S.*) of Philadelphia ('the Quaker city,' because founded by William Penn).—*n.* **Quä´ker-bird,** the sooty albatross.—*n.pl.* **Quä´ker-butt´ons,** the round seeds of nux vomica. — *ns.* **Quä´ker-colour,** drab; **Quä´kerdom; Quä´keress.**—*adjs.* **Quä´kerish, Quä´kerly,** like a Quaker. — *n.* **Quä´kerism.** [Nickname (not adopted by themselves, and earlier applied to another sect) given them by Justice Bennet at Derby, because Fox bade him and others *quake* at the word of the Lord.]

qualify, *kwol´i-fī, v.t.* to ascribe a quality to: to characterise: to add a quality to the connotation of: to render capable or suitable: to furnish with legal power: to limit by modifications: to moderate: to mitigate: to appease: to abate: to reduce the strength of: to vary: (*Scots law*) to prove, confirm.—*v.i.* to take the necessary steps to fit oneself for a certain position, activity, or practice:— *pr.p.* **qual´ifying;** *pa.p.* and *pa.t.* **qual´ified.**— *adj.* **qual´ifiable** (*-fī-ə-bl*).—*n.* **qualification** (*-fi-kā´shən*), qualifying: distinctive quality: modification: restriction: that which qualifies: a quality that fits a person for a place, &c.: (*obs.*) an accomplishment: a necessary condition: (*log.*) the attaching of quality, or the distinction of affirmative and negative, to a term.—*adj.* and *n.* **qual´ificative.**—*n.* **qual´ificâtor,** (*R.C.*) one who prepares ecclesiastical causes for trial.—*adj.* **qual´ificátory.**—*adj.* **qual´ified** (*-fīd*), fitted: competent: having the necessary qualification: modified: limited. — *adv.* **qual´ifiedly** (*-fīd-li*).—*n.* **qual´ifier** (*-fī-ər*).—*n.* and *adj.* **qual´ifying.** [Fr. *qualifier* or L.L. *quālificāre*—L. *quālis,* of what sort, *facĕre,* to make.]

quality, *kwol´i-ti, n.* that which makes a thing what it is: nature: character: kind: property: attribute: social status: high social status: persons of the upper class collectively: grade of goodness: excellence: profession, esp. (*Shak.*) the actor's profession: (*Shak.*) manner: skill, accomplishment: timbre, that character of a sound that depends on the overtones present, distinguished from loudness and pitch: (*log.*) the character of a proposition as affirmative or negative. — *adj.* (*vulg.*) of high grade of excellence.—*adj.* **qual´itative,** relating to, or concerned with, quality, esp. opp. to *quantitative.*—*adv.* **qual´itatively.**— *adj.* **qual´itied,** endowed with a quality or qualities. [O.Fr. *qualité*—L. *quālitās, -tātis—quālis,* of what kind.]

qualm, *kwäm,* also *kwawm, n.* an access of faintness or sickness: a sickly feeling: an uneasiness, as of conscience.—*adj.* **qualm´ish.**—*adv.* **qualm´ishly.** — *n.* **qualm´ishness.** — *adjs.* **qualm´less; qualm´y.** [Perh. O.E. *cwealm,* death, murder, torment, pain.]

quamash, *kwom´ash, kwə-mash´.* Same as **camass.**

quandary, *kwon-dā´ri,* also *kwon´də-ri, n.* a state of perplexity: dilemma: (*obs.*) a hard plight. [Ety. dub.]

quandong, *kwan'* or *kwon'dong, n.* a small Australian tree (*Fusanus acuminatus*) of the sandalwood family: its edible drupe (*native peach*) or edible kernel (**quan'dong-nut**).—Also **quan'dang, quan'tong.**

quannet, *kwon'it, n.* a file mounted like a plane. [Origin unknown.]

quant, *kwänt, kwont, n.* (*Kent, E. Angl.*) a punting or jumping pole, with a flat cap.—*v.t.* to punt. [Cf. **kent;** poss. conn. with L. *contus,* Gr. *kontos.*]

quantic, *kwon'tik, n.* (*math.*) a rational integral homogeneous function of two or more variables.— *adj.* **quan'tical.** [L. *quantus,* how great.]

quantify, *kwon'ti-fī, v.t.* to determine with respect to quantity: to fix or express the quantity of.— *n.* **quantification** (*-fi-kā'shon*).—**quantification of the predicate,** (*log.*) the attachment of a sign of quantity to the predicate. [L. *quantus,* how great, *facĕre,* to make.]

quantity, *kwon'ti-ti, n.* the amount of anything: bulk: size: a sum: a determinate amount: an amount, portion: a considerable amount: (*Shak.*) a fragment, scrap: a large portion: length or shortness of duration of a sound or syllable: (*log.*) extension: the character of a proposition as universal or particular: anything which can be increased, divided, or measured: (*Shak.*) proportion. —*adj.* **quan'titative** (less justifiably **quan'titive**), relating to, or concerned with, quantity, esp. opp. to *qualitative.*—*adv.* **quan'titatively.**—**quantity surveyor,** one who estimates quantities required, obtains materials, evaluates work done, &c. [O.Fr. *quantité*—L. *quantitās, -tātis—quantus,* how much.]

quantivalence, *kwon-tiv'ə-ləns,* or *-ti-vā'ləns, n.* valency. — *adj.* **quantiv'alent** (or *-vā'*). [L. *quantus,* how much—*valēns, -ēntis,* pr.p. of *valēre,* to be worth.]

quantum, *kwon'təm, n.* quantity: amount: (*phys.*) a naturally fixed minimum amount of some entity which is such that all other amounts of that entity occurring in physical processes in nature are integral multiples thereof:— *pl.* **quan'ta.**—*v.t.* **quan'tise,** to express in terms of quanta or in accordance with the quantum theory.—**quantum theory,** Planck's theory of the emission and absorption of energy not continuously but in finite steps. [L. *quantum,* neut. of *quantus,* how much.]

quaquaversal, *kwā-kwə-vər'sl, kwā-kwä-, adj.* (*geol.*) dipping outward in all directions from a centre: facing or bending all ways.—*adv.* **quaquaver'sally.** [L. *quāquā,* whithersoever, *vertĕre, versum,* to turn.]

quarantine, *kwor'ən-tēn, n.* forty days: a time (orig. for a ship forty days) of compulsory isolation or detention to prevent spread of contagion or infection: isolation or detention for such a purpose: the place where the time is spent.—*v.t.* to subject to quarantine.—**quarantine flag,** a yellow flag displayed by a ship in quarantine, with a black spot if there be contagious disease on board. [It. *quarantina—quaranta,* forty—L. *quadrāgintā.*]

quarrel, *kwor'l, n.* a square-headed arrow as for a cross-bow (*Spens.* **quar'le**): a diamond pane of glass: a square tile.—*n.* **quarr'el-pane.** [O.Fr. *quarrel* (Fr. *carreau*)—L.L. *quadrellus—quadrus,* a square.]

quarrel, *kwor'l, n.* (*obs.*) a complaint, charge: an objection: (*obs.*) an action at law: a ground of complaint or action: a cause contended for: an unfriendly contention or dispute: a breach of friendship: (*Shak.*) quarrelsomeness: (*Shak.,* possibly) a quarreller.—*v.i.* to cavil, find fault: to dispute violently: to fall out: to disagree violently. —*v.t.* (*obs.*) to call in question: (*obs.*) to object to: (now *Scot.*) to chide: to bring, render, by quarrelling:—*pr.p.* **quarr'elling;** *pa.t.* and *pa.p.* **quarr'elled.**—*n.* **quarr'eller.**—*n.* and *adj.* **quarr'elling.**—*adjs.* **quarr'ellous,** (*Shak.*) **quarrelsome:** **quarr'elsome,** disposed to quarrel.—*adv.* **quarr'elsomely.** —*n.* **quarr'elsomeness.**—**quarrel with one's bread and butter,** to act in a way prejudicial to one's means of subsistence; **take up a quarrel,** (*Shak.*) to settle a dispute. [O.Fr. *querele*—L. *querēla—querī, questus,* to complain.]

quarrender, quarender, *kwor'ən-dər,* **quarantine,**

quarenden, quarrington, *-ən-tin, -dən, -ing-tən, n.* (*S.W. England*) a kind of red apple. [Origin unknown.]

quarry, *kwor'i, n.* an open excavation for building-stone, slate, or other rock: a source of building-stone, &c.: a great mass of stone or rock: a source from which information can be extracted.—*v.t.* to dig from, or as from, a quarry: to cut into or cut away:—*pr.p.* **quarr'ying;** *pa.t.* and *pa.p.* **quarr'ied.** — *adj.* **quarr'iable.** — *ns.* **quarr'ier,** a quarryman; **quarr'yman,** one who works in a quarry; **quarr'ymaster,** the owner of a quarry; **quarr'y-sap, quarr'y-water,** the water in the pores of unquarried or newly quarried stone. [L.L. *quareia,* for *quadrāria*—L. *quadrāre,* to square.]

quarry, *kwor'i, n.* (*obs.*) a deer's entrails given to the dogs on a hide: a hawk's reward for a kill: a bird flown at by a hawk: a hunted animal: prey: a victim: a hunter's heap of dead game: (*Shak.*) a heap of corpses: (Shak., *Macbeth,* I. ii.) according to some, slaughter, or spoil; others would read **quarrel.** [O.Fr. *cuiree, curee,* said to be from *cuir*—L. *corium,* hide.]

quarry, *kwor'i, n.* a quarrel of glass: a square paving-tile or slab. [A form of **quarrel** (1); or perh. from O.Fr. *quarré*—L. *quadrātus,* squared.]

quart, quarte, *kärt, n.* a sequence of four cards: a position in fencing.—**quart and tierce,** practice between fencers. [Fr. *quarte.*]

quart, *kwawrt, n.* the fourth part of a gallon, or two pints: a vessel containing two pints: as much as will fill it: (*Spens.*) a quarter, region: (*mus.*) a fourth.—*ns.* **quarta'tion,** the mixing of gold with three parts of silver as a stage towards purification; **quart'-pot.** [Fr. *quart, -e*—L. *quārtus, -a, -um,* fourth—*quattuor,* four.]

quartan, *kwawr'tən, adj.* occurring every third (by Roman reckoning fourth) day, as a fever.—*n.* quartan malaria. [L. *quārtānus,* of the fourth.]

quarter, *kwawr'tər, n.* a fourth part: the fourth part of a cwt.=28 (*U.S.* 25) lb. avoirdupois: 8 bushels (perh. orig. a fourth of a ton of corn): the fourth part of an hour—of the year—of the moon's period (or the moon's position at the end of it)—of the world, &c.: a 25-cent piece: a limb with adjacent parts of the trunk, esp. of the dismembered body of one who has been executed, or of a beast's carcass: a haunch: (*her.*) one of the four parts of a quartered shield: an ordinary occupying one-fourth of the field: a quartering: a cardinal point, or any point, of the compass: the region about any point of the compass: hence a region generally, and also figuratively: a town district inhabited by a particular class: (*Shak.*) a part of an army, camp, &c.: lodging, as for soldiers, esp. in *pl.*: an assigned station: (*Shak.*) terms, relations, treatment, esp. favourable: mercy granted to an antagonist (perh. from sending to quarters): the part of a ship's side abaft the beam: a quarter-mile race.—*v.t.* to divide into four equal parts: to divide into parts or compartments: to station, lodge, or impose in quarters: (*her.*) to bear, place, or divide quarterly: to beat or range as for game.— *v.i.* to be stationed: to lodge: to range for game: to drive with wheels between the ruts, or horse astride of a rut: hence, to drive to the side of the road, or from side to side.—In composition, **quar'ter-,** *adjectivally,* one-fourth part (of); *adverbially,* to the extent of one-fourth.—*ns.* **quar'terage,** a quarterly payment: quarters, lodging; **quar'ter-blood,** offspring of a white and a half-breed.—*adj.* **quar'ter-bound,** having leather or cloth on the back only, not the corners.—*ns.* **quar'ter-boy, quar'ter-jack,** an automaton that strikes the quarter-hours.—*adj.* **quar'ter-bred,** having only one-fourth pure blood, as horses, cattle, &c.—*ns.* **quar'ter-day,** the first or last day of a quarter, on which rent or interest is paid; **quar'ter-deck,** the part of the deck of a ship abaft the mainmast—used by cabin passengers and by superior officers (and saluted on warships): **quar'ter-decker,** (*coll.*) a stickler for naval etiquette.—*adj.* **quar'tered.**—*ns.* **quar'ter-evil, -ill,** black-quarter; **quar'ter-gallery,** a projecting balcony on a ship's quarter; **quar'ter-guard,** a

fāte, fär, ȧsk; mē, hər (her); *mīne; mōte; mūte; mōōn; dhen* (then)

guard of a battalion in camp; **quar'ter-gunner**, (*U.S.*) a naval petty-officer, under the gunner; **quar'ter-horse**, (*U.S.*) a horse that can run a quarter of a mile or so at great speed.—*adj.* **quar'tering**, sailing nearly before the wind: striking on the quarter of a ship, as a wind.—*n.* assignment of quarters: (*archit.*) a series of small upright posts for forming partitions, lathed and plastered only, or boarded also: (*her.*) the division of a coat by horizontal and vertical lines: one of the divisions so formed: the marshalling of coats in these divisions, indicating family alliances: any one of the coats so marshalled.—*n.* **quar'ter-jack**, a quarter-boy: (*slang*) a quartermaster. — *adj.* **quar'terly**, relating to a quarter, esp. of a year: recurring, or published, once a quarter: (*her.*) divided into or marshalled in quarters.—*adv.* once a quarter: (*her.*) in quarters or quarterings.—*n.* a quarterly periodical.—*ns.* **quar'termaster**, an officer who finds quarters for soldiers, and attends to supplies: (*naut.*) a petty officer who attends to the helm, signals, &c. :—*fem.* **quar'termistress** (or **quartermaster**); **quar'termaster-gen'eral**, a staff-officer who deals with questions of transport, marches, quarters, fuel, clothing, &c.; **quar'termaster-ser'geant**, a non-commissioned officer who assists the quartermaster; **quar'ternote**, a crotchet: a quarter-tone; **quar'ter-plate** (see **plate**); **quar'ter-road**, a road divided into four strips by ruts and horse-track; **quar'terround**, a moulding whose section is about a quadrant, an *ovolo*; **quar'ter-seal**, the seal kept by the director of the Chancery of Scotland—the *testimonial* of the Great Seal; **quar'ter-sessions**, a court held quarterly by justices of the peace; **quar'ter-staff**, a long staff, or weapon of defence, grasped at a quarter of its length and at the middle: play with this weapon; **quar'ter-tone**, half a semitone; **quar'ter-wind**, a wind blowing on a ship's quarter.—**at close quarters**, in very near proximity: hand-to-hand; **keep a (bad) quarter**, (*obs.*) to make a disturbance; **keep good quarter**, (*Shak.*) keep good watch or good order. [O.Fr. *quarter*—L. *quārtārius*, a fourth part—*quārtus*, fourth.]

quartern, *kwor'to(r)n*, *n.* a quarter, esp. of a peck, a stone, a pound (weight), a pint, or a hundred.— *n.* **quar'tern-loaf**, a four-pound loaf, as if made from a quarter of a stone of flour. [A.Fr. *quartrun*, O.Fr. *quarteron*—*quart(e)*, fourth part.]

quarteroon. Same as **quadroon**.

quartet, **quartette**, **quartett**, *kwawr-tet'*, *n.* a set of four: a composition for four voices or instruments: a set of performers or instruments for such compositions.—Also (*It.*) **quartett'o**. [It. *quartetto*, dim. of *quarto*—L. *quārtus*, fourth.]

quartic, *kwawr'tik*, *adj.* (*math.*) of the fourth degree. —*n.* a function, curve, or surface of the fourth degree. [L. *quārtus*, fourth.]

quartile, *kwawr'til*, *n.* (*astrol.*) an aspect of planets when their longitudes differ by 90°: in frequency-distribution, a value such that a fourth, a half, or three-quarters of the numbers under consideration fall below it.—Also *adj.*—*n.* **quartile deviation**, the distance between the values below which the last fourth and above which the highest fourth fall.

quarto, *kwawr'tō*, *adj.* having the sheet folded into four leaves or eight pages (often written **4to**).— *n.* a book of sheets so folded, or of such a size :— *pl.* **quar'tos** (demy quarto, $8\frac{3}{4} \times 11\frac{1}{4}$ in.; medium quarto, $9\frac{1}{4} \times 11\frac{3}{4}$ in.; royal quarto, $10 \times 12\frac{1}{2}$ in.).— **small quarto**, a square octavo: a book having eight leaves to a sheet but the shape of a quarto. [L. (*in*) *quārtō*, (in) one-fourth.]

quartodeciman, *kwawr-tō-des'i-mən*, *n.* one who celebrated Easter on the 14th of Nisan without regard to the day of the week.—Also *adj.* [L.L. *quartodecimānus*—L. *quārtus decimus*, fourteenth.]

quartz, *kwawrts*, *n.* the commonest rock-forming mineral, composed of silica, occurring in hexagonal crystals (clear and colourless when pure) or crypto-crystalline.—*adj.* of quartz.—*adj.* **quartzif'erous**, quartz-bearing.—*ns.* **quartz'ite**, **quartz'-rock'**, a metamorphosed sandstone with the grains welded together.—*adj.* **quartzitic** (-*it'ik*), of or like

quartzite.—*n.* **quartz'-mill**, a mill or machine for crushing auriferous quartz.—*adj.* **quartz'ose**, of, like, or rich in quartz.—*ns.* **quartz-por'phyry**, an igneous rock with crystals of quartz and felspar in a compact or finely crystalline ground-mass of the same; **quartz'-schist'**, a schistose quartzite with mica.—*adj.* **quartz'y**.—**quartz glass**, fused quartz. [Ger. *quarz*.]

quash, *kwosh*, *v.t.* to crush: to subdue or extinguish suddenly and completely: to annul. [O.Fr. *quasser* (Fr. *casser*)—L. *quassāre*, intens. of *quatĕre*, to shake.]

Quashee, **Quashie**, *kwosh'i*, *n.* a West African negro name: **quash'ee, -ie**, a negro, esp. in the West Indies. [Ashanti name given to one born on Sunday.]

quasi, *kwā'sī*, L. *kwä'sē*, *adv.* as if, as it were.—In composition, **quasi-**, in a certain manner, sense, or degree: in appearance only, as **quasi-historical**. [L.]

Quasimodo, *kwas-i-mō'dō*, *n.* the first Sunday after Easter, Low Sunday. [From the first words of the introit for the day, 1 Peter, ii. 2; L. *quasi modo geniti infantes*, as new-born babes, &c.]

quassia, *kwosh'(y)ä*, *n.* a South American tree (*Quassia amara*; fam. Simarubaceae), whose bitter wood and bark are used as a tonic: now generally a West Indian tree of the same family (*Picraena excelsa*). [Named by Linnaeus from a negro *Quassi*, who discovered its value against fever.]

quat, *kwot*, *n.* a pimple: (*Shak.*) an insignificant person. [Origin unknown.]

quatch-buttock, *kwoch'-but'ək*, *n.* (*Shak.*) appar. a flat or squat buttock.

quatercentenary, *kwot-*, *kwat-ər-sen'tin-ər-i*, *-sin-ten'ər-i*, *-sin-tēn'ər-i*, *n.* a quadringenary or 400th anniversary, or its celebration. [L. *quater*, four times.]

quaternary, *kwo-tər'nər-i*, *adj.* consisting of four: by fours: in fours: of the fourth order: based on four: with four variables: **Quaternary**, (*geol.*) Post-Tertiary.—*n.* the number four: a set of four: **Quaternary**, the Post-Tertiary era or group of strata (Pleistocene and Recent).—*adj.* **quater'nate**, in sets of four.—*n.* **quater'nion**, a set or group of four: in mathematics, the operation of changing one vector into another, or the quotient of two vectors, depending on four geometrical elements and expressible by an algebraical quadrinomial: (in *pl.*) a calculus concerned with this, invented by Sir William Rowan Hamilton (1805-65).—*adj.* **quater'nion'd**, (*Milt.*) divided into groups of four.—*ns.* **quater'nionist**, a student of quaternions; **quatern'ity**, fourfoldness: a set of four: a fourfold godhead. [L. *quaternī*, four by four.]

quatorze, *kə-torz'*, *n.* the four aces, kings, queens, knaves, or tens in piquet, counting 14.—*n.* **quator-zain** (*kat'ər-zān*, *kät-or'zān*), a stanza or poem of fourteen lines. [Fr. *quatorze*, *quatorzaine*.]

quatrain, *kwot'rān*, *n.* a stanza of four lines usually rhyming alternately. [Fr.]

quatrefoil, *kat'ər-foil*, or *kat'rə-foil*, *n.* a four-petalled flower or leaf of four leaflets: (*archit.*) a piercing or ornament divided by cusps into four lobes.—Also **quat'refeuille** (*fə-ē*, *-fēl*). [O.Fr. *quatre*, four, *foil* (Fr. *feuille*), leaf.]

quattrocento, *kwät-rō-chen'tō*, *n.* the 15th century in Italian art and literature.—*ns.* **quattrocent'-ism**; **quattrocen'tist**. [It., four hundred.]

quaver, *kwā'vər*, *v.i.* to tremble, quiver: to speak or sing with tremulous uncertainty: to trill.—*v.t.* utter or sing tremulously.—*n.* a trembling, esp. of the voice: (*mus.*) half a crotchet.—*n.* **quā'verer**. —*n.* and *adj.* **quā'vering**.—*adv.* **quā'veringly**.— *adj.* **quā'very**. [Freq. from obs. or dial. *quave*, M.E. *cwavien*, to shake; akin to **quake**, **quiver**.]

quay, *kē*, *n.* a landing-place: a wharf for the loading or unloading of vessels.—*n.* **quay'age**, provision of quays: space of quays: payment for use of a quay.—*n.* and *adj.* **quay'side**.—Earlier forms **kay** (*kā*), **key**. [O.Fr. *kay*, *cay*, perh. Celtic: partly assimilated to mod. Fr. spelling *quai*.]

quayd, *kwād*, *adj.* or *pa.p.* (*Spens.*) daunted. [Perh. for **quelled**.]

queach, *kwēch, n. (obs.)* a thicket.—*adj.* **queach'y**, **queech'y**, forming a thicket: boggy: sickly. [Origin obscure.]

quean, *kwēn, n.* a saucy girl: a woman of worthless character: (*Scot.*) a girl—in N.E. Scotland **queyn** (*kwīn*), dim. **queyn'ie**, the ordinary words for a girl. [O.E. *cwene*, woman; cf. **queen** (O.E. *cwén*).]

queasy, **queazy**, *kwē'zi, adj.* unsettled: ticklish: uneasy: causing nausea: sick, squeamish: inclined to vomit: fastidious: nice.—*adv.* **quea'sily.** —*n.* **quea'siness.** [Poss. O.Fr. *coisier*, to hurt; poss. O.N. *kveisa*, a boil.]

quebracho, *kā-brä'chō, n.* the name of several South American trees yielding very hard wood (*white quebracho*, Aspidosperma; fam. Apocynaceae; *red quebracho*, Schinopsis; fam. Anacardiaceae): their wood or bark. [Sp.,—*quebrar*, to break, *hacha*, axe.]

Quechua, *kech'wä.* Same as **Quichua**.

queen, *kwēn, n.* the consort or wife of a king: a female monarch: a presiding goddess: a woman or (*fig.*) anything that is pre-eminent in excellence, beauty, &c.: a sexually functional female social insect: female cat: a playing-card bearing the figure of a queen, in value next below a king: in chess, a piece that can be moved any distance in any straight line: a size of roofing-slate, 3 feet by 2. —*v.t.* to make a queen of: to substitute a queen (or other piece) for: to rule as queen: to supply with a queen: (with *it*) to play the queen.—*ns.* **queen'-bee**; **queen'-con'sort**, the wife of a reigning king; **queen'craft**, craft or policy on the part of a queen; **queen'dom**, queenhood: the realm of a queen; **queen'-dow'ager**, a king's widow; **queen'hood**, the state of being a queen; **queen'ing**, an apple, of various varieties; **queen'-ite**, a queen's partisan; **queen'let**, a petty queen. —*adjs.* **queen'less**; **queen'-like**, like a queen.—*n.* **queen'liness.**—*adj.* **queen'ly**, becoming or suitable to a queen: like a queen.—*adv.* in the manner of a queen.—*ns.* **queen'-moth'er**, a queen-dowager that is mother of the reigning king or queen: a queen or queen-bee that is a mother; **queen'-of-the-mead'ow(s)**, the meadow-sweet; **queen'-post**, one of two upright posts in a trussed roof, resting upon the tie-beam, and supporting the principal rafters; **queen'-rē'gent**, a queen who reigns as regent; **queen'-reg'nant**, a queen reigning as monarch; **queen's'-arm**, a musket; **queen'ship**, the state, condition, or dignity of a queen; **queen'-stitch**, an embroidery pattern of square within square.—**Queen Anne's Bounty**, a fund for augmenting poorer livings of the Church of England, formed (1703) out of first-fruits and tenths; **Queen Anne's dead**, that is old news; **Queen Anne style**, (*archit.*) the simplified Renaissance manner of the early 18th century, or an imitation of it, plain and simple, with classic cornices and details; **Queen of Heaven**, Ashtoreth: (*R.C.*) the Virgin Mary; **Queen of the May**, May Queen; **Queen's tobacco pipe**, a kiln at London Docks for burning contraband goods (till 1891); **queen's ware**, cream-coloured Wedgwood ware; **queen's yellow**, basic mercuric sulphate.—For **Queen's Bench, Council**, &c., see **King's**. [O.E. *cwén*; Goth. *qēns*; O.N. *kvæn*; Gr. *gynē*; cf. **quean.**]

queene-apple, *kwēn'ap-l, n.* (*Spens.*) app. a quince. [See **quince.**]

Queensland-nut, *kwēnz'lənd-nut', n.* a proteaceous tree of *Queensland* and New South Wales: its edible nut.

queer, *kwēr, adj.* odd, singular, quaint: open to suspicion, dubious: counterfeit: having a sensation of coming sickness: (*dial.*) sick, ill.—*v.t.* (*slang*) to quiz: to cheat: to spoil.—*adj.* **queer'ish.** —*n.* **queer'ity.**—*adv.* **queer'ly.**—*n.* **queer'ness.** —**Queer Street**, the feigned abode of persons in debt or other difficulties; **queer the pitch**, (*showman's slang*) to make the place of performance unavailable: to spoil one's chances; **shove the queer**, (*slang*) to pass bad money. [Perh. Ger. *quer*, across; cf. **thwart.**]

queest, *kwēst.* Same as **cushat.** — Also **quest**, **quoist**, **quist.**

queez-maddam, *kwēz'-mad'əm, n.* (*Scott*) a French jargonelle pear. [Fr. *cuisse-madame.*]

queint, *kwānt, adj.* (*Spens.*). Same as **quaint.**

queint, *kwānt* (*Spens.*), *pa.p.* of **quench.**

quelch, *kwel(t)sh, v.i.* and *v.t.* to squelch. [Imit.]

quell, *kwel, v.t.* (*obs.*) to kill: to extinguish: to crush: subdue: (*Spens.*) to disconcert, to abash. —*v.i.* (*Spens.*) to die, perish: (*Spens.*) to subside, abate.—*ns.* **quell'er**, one who quells or crushes: a slayer. [O.E. *cwellan*, to kill, causal of *cwelan*, to die; cf. **quail** (vb.).]

queme, *kwēm, v.t.* (*Spens.*) to please, suit, fit. [O.E. *cwéman*; cf. Ger. *bequem*, fit.]

quench, *kwen(t)sh, v.t.* to put out: to put out the flame, light, or sight of: to stop (a discharge of electrically charged particles): to cool with liquid: to slake: to damp down: to put an end to: to put to silence: to destroy: to extinguish thirst, hope, &c., in.—*v.i.* to be extinguished: to die down: to lose zeal: (*Shak.*) to subside in passion, grow cold.— *n.* **quenching.**—*adj.* **quench'able.**—*n.* **quench'er**, one who, or that which, quenches: a draught or drink.—*n.* and *adj.* **quench'ing.**—*adj.* **quench'less**, not to be extinguished.—*adv.* **quench'lessly.** —**quenched spark**, an oscillatory spark discharge extinguished after the first few oscillations. [O.E. *cwencan*, found only in the compound *ácwencan*, to quench, causative of *cwincan* (*ácwincan*); cf. Old Fris. *kwinka*, to go out.]

quenelle, *kə-nel', n.* a forcemeat ball of chicken, veal, or the like. [Fr.]

quep, *kwep, interj.* (*Scott*) erroneously for **gup** (1).

Quercus, *kwər'kəs, n.* the oak genus of the beech family.—*ns.* **quercetum** (*kwər-sē'təm*), a collection of oak-trees; **quer'citron** (*-si-trən*), a North American oak, the dyer's oak or yellow-barked oak: its inner bark, yielding a yellow dye (from **citron**). [L. *quercus*, oak.]

querimony, *kwer'i-mən-i, n.* complaint.—*adj.* **querimonious** (*-mō'ni-əs*).—*adv.* **querimō'niously.** [L. *querimōnia*—*querī*, to complain.]

querist, *kwē'rist, n.* an inquirer. [L. *quaerĕre*, to seek, ask.]

quern, *kwərn, n.* a stone handmill.—*n.* **quern'-stone**. [O.E. *cweorn*; O.N. *kvern*, Goth. (*asilu-*) *qaírnus*, (ass-)mill.]

querulous, *kwer'ū-ləs*, also *-oo-, -ə-, adj.* complaining: peevish.—*adv.* **quer'ulously.**—*n.* **quer'ulousness.** [L.L. *querulōsus*—*querī*, to complain.]

query, *kwē'ri, n.* formerly often **quaere**, *kwē'ri, n.* an inquiry: the mark of interrogation (?).—*v.t.* to inquire into: to question: to doubt: to mark with a query.— *v.i.* to question:—*pa.t.* and *pa.p.* **que'ried.**—*n.* and *adj.* **que'rying.**—*adv.* **que'ryingly.** [L. *quaere*, imper. of *quaerĕre*, *quaesītum*, to inquire.]

quest, *kwest, n.* the act of seeking: search: pursuit: an adventure, expedition, or undertaking with the purpose of achieving or finding some definite object: a searching party: a jury of inquest: inquiry, investigation: (*R.C.*) a collection of alms or donations: a searching for game by dogs, or their outcry on finding it.—*v.i.* to go in search: to go begging: to give tongue.—*v.t.* to go in quest of or after.—*ns.* **quest'ant** (*Shak.*), **quest'er**, **quest'rist** (*Shak.*), one who goes on a quest.—*n.* and *adj.* **quest'ing.** [O.Fr. *queste* (Fr. *quête*)—L. (*rēs*) *quaesīta*, (a thing) sought—*quaerĕre*, *quaesītum*, to seek.]

quest. See **queest.**

question, *kwest'yən, n.* an inquiry: an interrogation: the putting of a problem: a demand for an answer: an interrogative sentence or other form of words in which it is put: a unit task in an examination: a problem: a subject of doubt or controversy: (*Shak.*) discussion, conversation: a subject of discussion, esp. the particular point actually before the house, meeting, or company: subjection to examination: (*hist.*) examination by torture: objection, demur: doubt: the measure to be voted upon: vaguely, a relevant matter. —*v.t.* to put questions to: to call to account: to examine by questions: to inquire: to inquire concerning: to throw doubt upon: to regard as doubtful: to challenge, take exception to.—*v.i.* to ask questions: to inquire: (*Shak.*) to discuss, converse.—*adj.* **quest′ionable,** that may be questioned: doubtful: uncertain: open to suspicion: (*Shak.*) such as questions may be put to, not unwilling to be conversed with.—*n.* **quest′ionableness.**—*adv.* **quest′ionably.**—*adj.* **quest′ionary,** asking questions: in the form of questions.—*n.* an asker of questions: a questionnaire: a questionnary (see **quaestor**).—*n.* and *adj.* **quest′ionbegg′ing** (see **beg**).—*n.* **quest′ioner.**—*n.* and *adj.* **quest′ioning.**—*adv.* **quest′ioningly.**—*n.* **quest′ionist,** a questioner, a doubter: formerly, an undergraduate in his last term before proceeding to a degree.—*adj.* **quest′ionless,** unquestioning: beyond question or doubt. — *adv.* certainly. — *ns.* **quest′ion-mark,** a point of interrogation; **quest′ion-mas′ter,** one who presides at a sitting for the putting of questions; **questionnaire** (*kes-tē-on-er′, kwes-tyən-ār′*), a series of questions: a prepared set of written questions, for purposes of compilation or comparison.—**in question,** under consideration; **make question,** demur; **out of question,** doubtless; **out of the question,** not to be thought of. [O.Fr.,—L. *quaestiō, -ōnis—quaerĕre, quaesītum,* to ask.]

questor. See **quaestor.**

quetzal, *ket-säl′, k(w)et′sal, n.* a golden green Central American bird (the *resplendent trogon*) with very long tail-feathers: the Guatemalan currency unit, or dollar. [Aztec *quetzalli.*]

queue, *kū, n.* a pendent braid of hair at the back of the head, a pigtail: a file of persons, &c., awaiting their turn: (*her.*) the tail of a beast.—*v.t.* to place or arrange in a queue: to track, dog.—*v.i.* to form, or take one's place in, a queue (usu. with *up*).—*adj.* **queued** (*kūd*), tailed: in a queue.—*n.* **queu′ing, queue′ing.** [Fr.,—L. *cauda,* a tail.]

quey, *kwui, kwā, n.* (*Scot.*) a heifer: a young cow that has not yet had a calf. [O.N. *kvíga*; Dan. *kvie.*]

quh-, *hw-,* older Scots spelling for **wh-.** [O.E. *hw-.*]

quibble, *kwib′l, n.* an evasive turning away from the point in question into matters irrelevant, merely verbal, or insignificant: a pun: a petty conceit.—*v.i.* to evade a question by a play upon words: to cavil: to trifle in argument: to pun.—*ns.* **quibb′ler**; (*obs.*) **quib′lin,** a quibble.—*n.* and *adj.* **quibb′ling.**—*adv.* **quibb′lingly.** [Perh. dim. of obs. *quib,* quibble, which may be—L. *quibus,* dat. or abl. pl. of *quī,* who, a word frequent in legal use; or a variant of **quip.**]

quich, *kwich, v.i.* (*Spens.*) to stir, to move.—Also (*obs.* or *dial.*) **quatch, quetch, quitch.** [O.E. *cweccan,* to shake, causative of *cwacian,* to quake.]

Quichua, *kēch′wä,* **Quechua,** *kech′wä, n.* a Peruvian Indian of the race that was dominant in the Inca empire: the language of the Quichua.—Also *adj.*—*adj.* **Quich′uan, Quech′uan.**—Also *n.* [Sp. *Quichua, Quechua.*]

quick, *kwik, adj.* living: alive: lively: swift: speedy: nimble: fresh: ready: sensitive: readily responsive: ready-witted: prompt in perception or learning: hasty: pregnant: at the stage of quickening: quickset: active: mobile: piercing. —*adv.* without delay: rapidly: soon.—*n.* the living: (*Spens.*) a living thing: a living plant, esp. hawthorn in a hedge (also collectively): the life: the living flesh: the sensitive parts, esp. under the nails: the tenderest feelings.—*adjs.* **quick′-an′swered** (*Shak.*) quick at answering: **quick′-born,** born alive; **quick′-change,** quick in making a change, esp. (of a performer) in appearance; **quick′-conceiv′ing,** quick at understanding.—*v.t.* **quick′en,** to give life to: to stimulate: to impart energy or liveliness to: to invigorate: to revive: to accelerate.—*v.i.* to become alive or lively: to revive: to be stimulated: to reach the stage in pregnancy when the mother becomes conscious of the movement of the child: to move faster.—*n.* **quick′ener.**—*n.* and *adj.* **quick′ening.** —*adjs.* **quick′-eyed,** having acute sight or lively eyes; **quick′-fire, -firing,** designed to allow a quick succession of shots.—*ns.* **quick′-firer**; **quick′-hedge,** a hedge of living plants; **quick′-**

lime, unslaked lime (CaO); **quick′-lunch,** a snack served promptly.—Also *adj.*—*adv.* **quick′ly.**—*ns.* **quick′match,** cotton thread impregnated with an inflammable mixture; **quick′ness**; **quick′sand,** a loose watery sand ready to swallow those who walk on it, boats, &c.: anything similarly treacherous.—*adjs.* **quick′-sandy**; **quick′-scent′ed, quick′-scent′ing,** having a keen scent; **quick′-selling**; **quick′set,** formed of living plants.—*n.* a living plant, slip, or cutting, esp. of hawthorn, or a series of them, set to grow for a hedge: a quickset hedge.—*adj.* **quick′-sight′ed,** having quick sight or discernment.—*ns.* **quick′-sight′edness**; **quick′-silver,** mercury.—*adj.* of mercury.—*v.t.* to overlay or to treat with quicksilver or amalgam.—*adj.* **quick′silvered.**—*n.* **quick′silvering,** the mercury on the back of a mirror.—*adjs.* **quick′silverish, quick′silvery.**—*n.* **quick′step,** a march step or tune in quick time.—*adv.* **quick′-stick, -s,** without delay. — *adj.* **quick′-tem′pered,** irascible. — *ns.* **quick′thorn,** hawthorn; **quick′-trick,** a card that should win a trick in the first or second round of the suit; **quick′-water,** a solution of nitrate of mercury.—*adj.* **quick′-witted,** having ready wit.—*n.* **quick′-witt′edness.** [O.E. *cwic*; O.N. *kvikr,* living.]

quick, *kwik, n.* couch-grass or its rootstocks.—Also **quick′en, quick′-grass.** [Northern form of **quitch.**]

quicken, *kwik′ən, n.* (*Northern*) the rowan.—Also **quick′beam** (*Southern*), **quick′en-tree, wick′en, wick′y.** [O.E. *cwicbéam, cwictréow,* aspen.]

quicken. See **quick** (1 and 2).

quid, *kwid, n.* that which a thing is, substance. [L., what.]

quid, *kwid, n.* something chewed or kept in the mouth, esp. a piece of tobacco. [**cud.**]

quid, *kwid, n.* (*slang*) a sovereign: formerly, a guinea:—*pl.* **quid**; or in sense of ready money, **quids.**—**quid′ let,** a sovereign.

quidam, *kwi′dam, n.* somebody: a certain person:—*pl.* **quidams.** [L. *quīdam.*]

quiddany, *kwid′ə-ni, n.* a confection of quince-juice and sugar. [L. *cotōnea,* quince—*cydōnia*; see **quince.**]

quiddity, *kwid′i-ti, n.* the whatness or essence of anything: any trifling nicety: a cavil: a captious question: quibble.—Also (contracted) **quidd′it.**—*adj.* **quidd′itative.** [Schoolman's L. *quidditās, -tātis.*]

quiddle, *kwid′l, v.i.* to trifle.—*ns.* **quidd′le,** a fastidious person; **quidd′ler.**

quidnunc, *kwid′nungk, n.* a newsmonger. [L. *quid nunc?*, what now?]

quiesce, *kwi-es′, v.i.* to quiet down: to become silent (as a Hebrew consonant).—*ns.* **quiesc′ence, quiesc′ency,** rest: inactivity: silence of a consonant.—*adj.* **quiesc′ent,** resting: not sounded: inactive: still.—*adv.* **quiesc′ently.** [L. *quiēscĕre,* to rest.]

quiet, *kwī′ət, adj.* at rest: calm: undisturbed: unaccompanied by disturbance: without loudness, gaudiness, ostentation, formality, or obtrusiveness of any kind: still: without bustle or restlessness: without much activity: peaceable: gentle: inoffensive.—*n.* rest: repose: calm: stillness: peace: freedom from noise or disturbance.—*v.t.* and *v.i.* to make or become quiet.—*v.t.* and *v.i.* **qui′eten,** to quiet.—*n.* and *adj.* **qui′etening.**—*n.* **qui′eter.**—*n.* and *adj.* **qui′eting.** —*ns.* **qui′etism,** mental tranquillity: the doctrine that religious perfection on earth consists in passive and uninterrupted contemplation of the Deity; **qui′etist.**—*adj.* **quietist′ic.**—*n.* and *adj.* **qui′etive,** sedative. — *adv.* **qui′etly.** — *n.* **qui′etness.** — *adj.* **qui′etsome,** (*Spens.*) undisturbed.—*n.* **qui′etude,** quietness.—**on the quiet** (or **Q.T.**; *slang*), clandestinely: unobtrusively. [L. *quiētus* (adj.), *quiēs, -ētis* (n.), *quiētāre* (vb.).]

quietus, *kwi-ē′tes,* L. *kwē-ā′toos, n.* an acquittance: discharge from office: discharge from life: extinction: putting to silence. [L. *quiētus est,* he is quiet.]

quight, *kwīt,* (*Spens.*). See **quit, quite.**

qui-hi, -hye, *kwī′-hī′, n.* an Anglo-Indian, esp. in

Bengal. [Hind. *koī hai*, the call for a servant, Is anyone there?—*koī*, anyone, *hai*, is.]

quill, *kwil*, *n.* (*obs.*) a reed, hollow stalk or internode, or the like: (*obs.*) a small tube: the hollow basal part of a feather: a large feather: a porcupine's spine: a goose or other feather used as a pen: hence a pen generally, or the profession of letters: a thing made from a quill feather, as a toothpick, an angler's float, a plectrum: a weaver's bobbin, of reed or other material. (*mach.*) a hollow shaft: a musical pipe made from a reed or the like: hence (Shak., *M.N.D.*, III. i. 134) throat, or perh. voice: a roll of curled bark, as cinnamon: (*obs.*) a cylindrical plait. — *v.t.* to goffer: to wind on a bobbin. — *ns.* **quill'-driver** (*used derogatorily*), a clerk: an assiduous writer; **quill'-driving.** — *adj.* **quilled**, furnished with, or formed into quills: tubular.—*ns.* **quill'-feather**, a large stiff wing or tail feather; **quill'ing**, a ribbon or strip gathered into flutings; **quill'man**, a clerk; **quill'-nib**, a quill-pen shortened for use with a holder; **quill'pen**; **quill'wort**, any plant of the genus Isoëtes (from the quill-like leaves). [Ety. obscure; cf. L.G. *quiele*, Ger. *kiel*.]

quill, *kwil*, *n.* (*Shak.*) a combination (in the phrase *in the quill*, in a body, in concert). [Fr. *cueille*.]

quillet, *kwil'it*, *n.* a subtlety in argument: a quibble. [Perh. L. *quidlibet*, what you will.]

quillon, *kē-yon²*, *n.* either arm of the cross-guard of a sword-handle. [Fr.]

quilt, *kwilt*, *n.* a bed-cover of two thicknesses with padding sewn in compartments: any material or piece of material so treated, esp. when worn under or instead of armour: a thick coverlet: a thick covering placed over beehive frames.—*v.t.* to pad, cover, or line with a quilt: to form into a quilt: to stitch in: to seam like a quilt: to cover with interlaced cord: to thrash. — *adj.* **quilt'ed.** — *ns.* **quilt'er**, a person or machine that makes quilting; **quilt'ing**, the act of making a quilt: that which is quilted: a cloth for making quilts: a cloth with a pattern like a quilt: a covering of rope-yarn: a thrashing with a rope's end; **quilt'ing-bee**, a gathering of women to help one in quilting a counterpane, combined with social amusement; **quilt'ing-cott'on**, cotton wadding; **quilt'ing-frame**, an adjustable frame for holding a fabric for quilting. [O.Fr. *cuilte* (Fr. *couette*)—L. *culcita*, a cushion.]

quin, *kwin*, *n.* short for **quintuplet**.

quina, kina, china, *kē'nä*, *n.* cinchona bark: any tree yielding it: quinine.—Also **quinaquina, kinakina, chinachina** (*kē-nä-kē'nä*), **quinquina** (*kin-* or *king-kē'nä*, *kwing-kwī'nä*).—*adj.* **quinic** (*kwin'ik*).—**quinic acid**, an acid got from cinchona bark. [Sp. *quina*, *quinaquina*—Quichua *kina*, *kina-kina*, *kinkina*, bark.]

quinary, *kwī'nər-i*, *adj.* fivefold: by fives: in fives: of the fifth order: based on five: with five variables.—*adj.* **qui'nate**, in sets of five: with five leaflets arising at one point. [L. *quīnī*, five by five.]

quince, *kwins*, *n.* a golden, globose or pear-shaped, fragrant, austere fruit, good for jellies, marmalade, &c., or the tree or shrub (*Cydonia oblonga*), akin to pear and apple, that bears it: extended to the near-allied *Japanese quince* (see **japonica**) and to the unrelated *Bengal quince*, the bael-fruit. [Orig. pl. of *quine*—O.Fr. *coin* (Fr. *coing*)—L. *cotōneum*—Gr. *kydōnion*—*Kydōniā*, in Crete.]

quincentenary, *kwin-sen'tin-ər-i*, *-sin-ten'ər-i*, or *-sin-tēn'ər-i*, *n.* and *adj.* quingentenary. [Irreg. formed—L. *quinque*, five, and **centenary**.]

quinche, *kwinsh*, *v.i.* (*Spens.*) to stir, move. [Origin doubtful.]

quincunx, *kwin'kungks*, *n.* an arrangement of five things at the corners and centre of a square, or of a great number of things (esp. trees) spaced in the same way.—*adj.* **quincuncial** (*-kun'shl*), of or in a quincunx: (*bot.*) of aestivation, having two leaves overlapping at each edge, two underlapping at each edge, and one overlapping and underlapping.—*adv.* **quincun'cially.** [L. *quincunx*—*quinque*, five, *uncia*, a twelfth part.]

quingentenary, *kwin-jen-tē'nər-i*, *-ten'ər-i*, or *-jen'-tən-ər-i*, *n.* a five-hundredth anniversary or its

celebration.—Also *adj.* [L. *quīngentī*, five hundred.]

quinine, *kwin-ēn'*, *kwin'ēn*, in U.S. *kwī'nīn*, *n.* a colourless, inodorous, very bitter alkaloid (C₂₀H₂₄O₂N₂·3H₂O), got from cinchona bark, or one of its salts, used against malaria and fevers. [See **quina**.]

quinnat, *kwin'ət*, *n.* the king-salmon. [From an Amer. Ind. name.]

quinoa, *kē'nō-ä*, *n.* a South American goosefoot, used like rice (seeds) or spinach (leaves). [Sp. *quinoa*—Quichua *kinua*.]

quinol, *kwin'ol*, *n.* a reducing agent and photographic developer, C₆H₄(OH)₂, got by reduction of quinone.—*ns.* **quin'oline** (*-ō-lēn*), a pungent, colourless liquid (C₉H₇N), first got from quinine; **quinone** (*kwin'ōn*, *kwin-ōn'*), a golden-yellow crystalline compound (C₆H₄O₂) usually prepared by oxidising aniline: a general name for a benzene derivative in which two oxygen atoms replace two hydrogen.—Also **kinone** (*kē'nōn*). [**quina**.]

quinqu-, quinque-, *kwin'kw(i)-*, in composition, five. [L. *quinque*, five.]

quinquagenarian, *kwin-kwə-ji-nā'ri-ən*, *n.* one who is fifty years old.—Also *adj.* [L. *quīnquāgēnārius*—*quīnquāgēnī*, fifty each.]

Quinquagesima, *kwin-kwə-jes'i-mä*, *n.* Shrove Sunday (also **Quinquagesima Sunday**)—apparently as fifty days before Easter Sunday (both counted).—*adj.* **quinquages'imal**, of the number fifty: of fifty days. [L. *quīnquāgēsimus*, *-a*, *-um*, fiftieth; cf. **quadragesima**, **sexagesima**, **septuagesima**.]

quinquecostate, *kwin-kwi-kos'tāt*, *adj.* five-ribbed. [L. *costa*, rib.]

quinquefarious, *kwin-kwi-fā'ri-əs*, *adj.* fivefold: in five rows. [Cf. **multifarious**.]

quinquefoliate, *kwin-kwi-fō'li-āt*, *adj.* with five leaflets. [L. *folium*, leaf.]

quinquennium, *kwin-kwen'i-əm*, *n.* a period of five years:—*pl.* **quinquenn'ia.**—Also (*irreg.*) **quinquenn'iad.**—*adj.* **quinquenn'ial**, occurring once in five years: lasting five years.—*n.* a fifth anniversary or its celebration.—*adv.* **quinquenn'ially.** [L. *annus*, year.]

quinquereme, *kwin'kwi-rēm*, *n.* an ancient ship with five sets of rowers. [L. *quīnquerēmis*—*rēmus*, an oar.]

quinquevalent, *kwin-kwev'ə-lənt* (or *-kwi-vā'*), having a valency of five.—*n.* **quinquev'alence** (or *-vā'*).

quinquina. See **quina**.

quinsy, *kwin'zi*, *n.* suppurative tonsillitis.—*ns.* **quin'sy-berry**, the black-currant; **quins'y-wort**, squinancy-wort. [L.L. *quinancia*—Gr. *kynanchē*; see **cynanche**.]

quint, *kwint*, *n.* (*mus.*) a fifth: an organ-stop a fifth above the foundation stops: the E string of a violin: (*kint*; old-fashioned *kent*) a sequence of five cards in piquet.—*ns.* **quint'-ma'jor**, ace to ten; **quint'-mi'nor**, knave to seven. [Fr. *quinte* —L. *quīntus*, *-a*, *-um*, fifth.]

quinta, *kin'tä*, *n.* a country house. [Sp. and Port.]

quintain, *kwin'tin*, *-tən*, *n.* a post for tilting at, often with a turning cross-piece to strike the unskilful tilter. [O.Fr. *quintaine*, thought to be—L. *quīntāna via*, the road adjoining the fifth maniple in a camp.]

quintal, *kwin'tl*, *n.* a hundredweight: 100 kilograms. [Fr. and Sp. *quintal*—Ar. *qintār*—L. *centum*, a hundred.]

quintan, *kwin'tən*, *adj.* occurring every fourth (by Roman reckoning fifth) day. [L. *quīntānus*, of the fifth.]

quintessence, *kwin-tes'əns*, or *kwin'*, *n.* orig. a fifth entity, in addition to the four elements: the pure concentrated essence of anything: the most essential part, form, or embodiment of anything.—*adj.* **quintessential** (*-ti-sen'shl*). — *v.t.* **quintessen'tialise.** [Fr.,—L. *quīnta essentia*, fifth essence.]

quintet, quintette, quintett, *kwin-tet'*, *n.* a composition for five voices or instruments: a set of performers or instruments for such compositions. —Also (*It.*) **quintet'to.** [It. *quintetto*, dim. of *quinto*—L. *quīntus*, fifth.]

quintic, *kwin'tik*, *adj.* of the fifth degree.

quintillion, *kwin-til'yən*, *n.* the fifth power of a

million, represented by a unit and thirty ciphers: (*U.S.* and *France*) the sixth power of one thousand —a unit with eighteen ciphers.—*n.* and *adj.* **quintill'ionth.**

quintroon, *kwin-trōōn', n.* the offspring of a white by an octoroon: one who is fifth (inclusive) in descent from a negro. [Sp. *quinterón*—L. *quīntus,* fifth.]

quintuple, *kwin'tū-pl, adj.* fivefold: having five parts, members, or divisions.—*n.* five times as much.—*v.t.* and *v.i.* to increase fivefold.—*n.* **quin'tūplet** (also *-tū'*), a set of five things: a group of five notes played in the time of four: one of five born at a birth. [L. *quintus,* fifth, on the model of **quadruple.**]

quintuplicate, *kwin-tū'pli-kāt, adj.* fivefold.—*n.* one of five corresponding things: fivefoldness.— *v.t.* to make fivefold.—*n.* **quintuplicā'tion.** [L. *quintuplex, -icis—quīntus,* fifth, *plicāre,* to fold.]

quinze, *kwinz, n.* a card game, like vingt-et-un, the object being to count as nearly to fifteen as possible without going above it. [Fr., fifteen.]

quip, *kwip, n.* a repartee: a gird: a gibe: a quibble: a fanciful jest or action: a knick-knack.—*v.i.* to utter quips.—*v.t.* to assail with quips.—*adj.* **quipp'ish.** [Perh. from obs. *quippy,* which may be—L. *quippe,* forsooth.]

quipu, *kē'pōō, n.* a mnemonic contrivance of knotted cords used by the ancient Peruvians—depending on order, colour, and kind.—Also **quip'o.** [Quichua *quipu,* knot.]

quire, *kwīr, n.* formerly, four sheets of paper or parchment folded together in eight leaves; now, the twentieth part of a ream, twenty-four sheets, each having a single fold: (*obs.*; also **quair,** *kwār*) a (quire-filling) book or poem.—*v.t.* to fold in quires. [O.Fr. *quaier* (Fr. *cahier*), prob. from L.L. *quaternum,* a set of four sheets—L. *quatuor,* four.]

quire, *kwīr, n.* obs. spelling of **choir.**—*n.* **quirister** (*kwir'*), chorister.

Quirinus, *kwi-rī'nəs,* L. *kwi-rē'noos, n.* an Italic god, afterwards identified with Romulus—*n.* **Quirinal** (*kwir'in-əl*), one of the hills of Rome: the Italian government (from the palace there).— *n.pl.* **Quirinalia** (*kwir-i-nā'li-ä*), a festival in honour of Quirinus, on Feb. 17. [L. *Quirīnus.*]

Quirites, *kwi-rī'tez,* L. *kwi-rē'tās, n.pl.* the citizens of ancient Rome in their civil capacity. [L. *Quirītēs,* orig. the Samnite people of *Cures* (united with the Romans).]

quirk, *kwərk, n.* a sudden turn, twist, jerk, or flourish: an artful evasion: a quibble: a quip: (*Shak.*) a trick, knack, way: (*archit.*) an acute sharp-edged groove alongside a moulding.—*v.i.* to turn sharply: to utter or execute quips: to move jerkily.—*v.t.* to assail with a quirk: to furnish with a quirk.—*n.* **quirk'iness.**—*adjs.* **quirk'ish: quirk'y.** [Origin unknown.]

quirt, *kwərt, n.* a Spanish-American braided hide riding-whip.—*v.t.* to strike with a quirt. [Mexican-Sp. *cuarta.*]

quisling, *kwiz'ling, n.* a native puppet prime minister set up by an occupying foreign power. [Vidkun *Quisling,* who played that part in Norway during German occupation (1940-45).]

quist, *kwist.* See **queest.**

quit, *kwit,* (*arch.*) **quite** (*Spens.* **quight, quyte),** *kwīt, v.t.* to pay: to repay: to absolve: to requite: **to release from obligation**: **to clear off**: **to discharge**: to remit: to free: to clear of blame, &c.: to acquit: to depart from: to cease to occupy: (*obs.* except *reflex.*) to rid: to let go: (*U.S.*) to leave off: (*reflex.*) to behave, acquit: to be worth.—*v.i.* to leave off: (*U.S.*) to depart.—*pr.p.* **quit'ing** (*arch.* **quīt'ing**); *pa.p.* **quitt'ed** (**quīt'ed,** quit).—*adj.* **quit,** set free: clear: quits: acquitted: released from obligation.—*n.* **quit'-claim,** a deed of release. —*v.t.* to relinquish claim or title to: to release, discharge.—*n.* **quit'-rent,** a rent in lieu of services. —*adj.* **quits,** even: neither owing nor owed.—*ns.* **quitt'al,** (*Shak.*) requital; **quitt'ance,** release: discharge: acquittance: requital.—*v.t.* (*obs.*) to repay.—*n.* **quitt'er,** (*U.S.*) a shirker: one who gives up easily.—**cry quits** (formerly **quittance),**

to declare oneself even with another, and so satisfied; **double or quits,** the alternative, left to chance, of doubling or cancelling payment; **quit scores,** to balance accounts. [O.Fr. *quiter* (Fr. *quitter*)—L.L. *quiētāre,* to pay—L. *quiētāre,* to make quiet—*quiētus,* quiet.]

qui tam, *kwī tam,* L. *kwē tăm, n.* an action by an informer partly on his own behalf, partly on the state's. [From the first words, L. *quī tam,* who as much (for the king as for himself).]

quitch, *kwich, n.* couch-grass.—Also **quitch'-grass.** [O.E. *cwice*; cf. **couch-grass, quick** (2).]

quitch. Same as **quich.**

quite. See **quit.**

quite (*Spens.* **quight),** *kwīt, adv.* completely: wholly: entirely: enough to justify the use of the word: (*coll.*; often **quite so**) exactly, indeed, yes. [quit.]

quitter, quittor, *kwit'ər, n.* pus: a fistulous sore on a horse's hoof. [Poss. O.Fr. *quiture,* cooking— L. *coctūra.*]

quiver, *kwiv'ər, adj.* (*Shak.*) nimble, active. [O.E. *cwifer,* found in the adverbial form *cwiferlice,* zealously.]

quiver, *kwiv'ər, n.* a case for arrows.—*adj.* **quiv'ered,** furnished with a quiver: sheathed, as in a quiver.—*n.* **quiv'erful,** (*fig.*) a large family (Psalms cxxvii. 5). [O.Fr. *cuivre*; prob. Gmc.; cf. O.H.G. *kohhar* (Ger. *kocher*), O.E. *cocer.*]

quiver, *kwiv'ər, v.i.* to shake with slight and tremulous motion: to tremble: to shiver.—*ns.* **quiv'er, quiv'ering.**—*adv.* **quiv'eringly.**—*adj.* **quiv'erish.** [Poss. conn. with **quiver** (1).]

qui vive, *kē vēv, n.* alert. [From the French sentry's challenge, lit. (long) live who ?—*qui,* who, vive, 3rd pers. sing. pres. subj. of *vivre,* to live—L. *vivĕre.*]

quixotic, *kwiks-ot'ik, adj.* like Don *Quixote,* the knight-errant in the great romance of Cervantes (1547-1616), extravagantly romantic.—*adv.* **quixot'ically.**—*ns.* **quix'otism, quix'otry.**

quiz, *kwiz, n.* an odd-looking person or (*Jane Austen*) thing: a monocle, often with a handle: a piece of banter or quiet mockery: a mocking look: a hoax: one who practises any of these: (*U.S.*) an oral examination: a sportive catechism or general-knowledge test: (*obs.*) a bandalore or yo-yo (*pl.* **quizz'es).**—*v.t.* to poke fun at: to eye with an air of mockery: to catechise, interrogate. —*v.i.* to practise derisive joking:—*pr.p.* **quizz'ing;** *pa.t.* and *pa.p.* **quizzed.**—*ns.* **quizz'er; quizz'ery.**—*adj.* **quizz'ical.**—*n.* **quizzical'ity.**— *adv.* **quizz'ically.**—*n.* **quizzifica'tion,** quizzing. —*v.t.* **quizz'ify,** to turn into a quiz.—*ns.* **quizz'iness,** oddness; **quizz'ing; quizz'ing-glass,** a monocle. [Origin obscure.]

quo', *kə, ko, v.t.* a Scots form of **quoth.**—**quod,** an obsolete form of **quoth,** used esp. at the end of a poem with the poet's name.

quod, *kwod, n.* (*slang*) prison.—*v.t.* to imprison. [Origin unknown.]

quodlibet, *kwod'li-bet, n.* a scholastic argument: a humorous medley of tunes.—*n.* **quodlibetā'rian,** one given to quodlibets.—*adjs.* **quodlibet'ic, -al.** [L., what you please—*quod,* what, *libet,* it pleases.]

quodlin, *kwod'lin,* an obsolete form of **codlin.**

quoif, *koif.* Same as **coif.**

quoin, *koin, n.* a wedge, esp. for locking type in a forme, or for raising a gun: a salient angle, esp. of a building: a corner-stone, esp. a dressed corner-stone: a keystone: a voussoir.—*v.t.* to wedge: to secure, or raise by wedging. [See **coin.**]

quoist, *kwoist.* See **queest.**

quoit, *koit* (*U.S. kwoit*), *n.* a heavy flat ring for throwing as near as possible to a hob or pin: a dolmen cover: a dolmen: (in *pl.,* treated as *sing.*) the game played with quoits.—*v.i.* to play at quoits. —*v.t.* to throw like a quoit.—*n.* **quoit'er.** [Origin obscure.]

quondam, *kwon'dam, adj.* former. [L., formerly.]

quooke, *kwook* (*Spens.*), *pa.t.* of **quake.**

quop, *kwop, v.i.* (*obs.* or *dial.*) to throb. [M.E. *quappe*; imit.]

quorum, *kwō'rəm, n.* orig. a number of specially named justices of the peace of whom some must be present before any business could be done:

(loosely) the whole body of justices: a minimum number of persons necessary for transaction of business in any body. [L. *quōrum*, of whom, from the wording of the commission, of whom we will that you, so-and-so, be one (two, &c.).]

quota, *kwō'tä*, *n.* a proportional share, a part assigned :—*pl.* quo'tas.—**quota immigrant**, any immigrant (to the U.S.A.) admitted as one of the yearly quota allowed to his country of origin, and not by the rules for non-quota immigrants. [L. *quota* (*pars*), the how-manieth (part)—*quotus*, of what number—*quot*, how many.]

quote, *kwōt*, old-fashioned *kōt* (*Shak.* **coat, coate, cote**), *v.t.* orig. to divide into chapters, verses, &c., number the chapters of, or mark with references: to refer to: to cite: to adduce as authority, illustration, or example: to give the actual words of : (*Shak.*) to examine as if looking up a reference: to record : to note, set down, mention, in writing or mentally : (*theat.*) to set down in the prompter's book as due to be called : to give the current price of: to enclose within quotation-marks.—*v.i.* to make quotations.—*n.* a quotation : a quotation-mark.—*adj.* **quo'table**, lending itself (or himself) to quotation: fit to quote.—*ns.* **quo'tableness, quōtabil'ity**.—*adv.* **quo'tably**.—*ns.* **quōtā'tion**, act of quoting: that which is

quoted : a price quoted : a quadrat for filling blanks in type (orig. those between marginal references) ; **quōtā'tion-mark**, one of the marks (*print.* quotes) used to note the beginning and the end of a quotation.—*adjs.* **quōtā'tious, quō'tative**, given to quoting. — *n.* **quō'ter**. — *adj.* **quote'worthy**. [L.L. *quotāre*, to divide into chapters and verses—L. *quotus*, of what number—*quot*, how many.]

quoth, *kwōth, kwəth, v.t.* (1st and 3rd pers. sing., past tense, of the otherwise obs. vb. **quethe**) said (followed by its subject).—*interj.* **quōtha**, forsooth, indeed (lit. quoth he ; see a, *pron.*). [O.E. *cwæth*, pret. of *cwethan*, to say ; cf. **bequeath**.]

quotidian, *kwot-id'i-ən*, *adj.* every-day: daily.—*n* a fever or ague that recurs daily. [L. *quotīdiānus* —*quotīdiē*, daily—*quot*, how many, *diēs*, day.]

quotient, *kwō'shənt*, *n.* (*math.*) the number of times one quantity is contained in another. [L. *quotiēns, quotiēs*, how often—*quot*, how many (with *t* from false appearance of being a participle).]

quotition, *kwō-tish'ən*, *n.* division regarded as repeated subtraction or measuring. [From L. *quot.*]

quo warranto, *kwō wo-ran'tō*, *n.* a writ calling upon one to show by what warrant he holds or claims a franchise or office. [L.L. *quō warrantō* (abl.), by what warrant.]

Qurân, *koo-rän'*, *n.* Same as **Koran**.

fāte, fär, ásk ; mē, hər (her) ; *mīne ; mōte ; mūte ; mōōn ; dhen* (then)

R

R, r, *är, n.* the eighteenth letter in our alphabet—the 'dog letter,' from the trilling (evanescent in Southern England) of the tip of the tongue: as a mediaeval numeral, R=80; R̄=80,000.—**R months,** the time when oysters are in season (from the spelling of the names of the months from September to April); **the three R's,** reading, writing, and arithmetic. [L. *er.*]

Ra, *rä, n.* the Egyptian sun-god.

rabanna, *rə-ban′ä, n.* a Madagascar raffia fabric. [Malagasy.]

rabat, rabatte, *rə-bat′, v.t.* (geom.) to rotate into coincidence with another plane.—*ns.* **rabatt′ing; rabat′ment, rabatte′ment.** [Fr. *rabattre,* to lower.]

rabato, *rə-bä′tō.* Same as **rebato.**—*n.* **rabatine** (*rab′ə-tēn; Scott*), a low collar.

rabbet, *rab′it, n.* a groove cut to receive an edge.—*v.t.* to groove: to join by a rabbet :—*pr.p.* **rabb′eting;** *pa.t.* and *pa.p.* **rabb′eted.**—*ns.* **rabb′eting-machine′, -plane, -saw; rabb′et-joint.** [Fr. *rabat—rabattre,* to beat back.]

rabbi (Rabbi when prefixed), *rab′i* or *rab′ī,* **rabbin,** *rab′in, n.* a Jewish expounder or doctor of the law :—*pl.* **rabb′is, rabb′ins.**—*n.* **rabb′inate,** the dignity or tenure of office of a rabbi: a body of rabbis.—*adjs.* **rabbin′ic, -al,** pertaining to the rabbis or to their opinions, learning, and language.—*n.* **Rabbin′ic,** late Hebrew.—*adv.* **rabbin′ically.**—*ns.* **rabb′inism,** the doctrine or teaching of the rabbis: a rabbinical peculiarity of expression: the late Jewish belief which esteemed the oral equally with the written law; **rabb′inist, rabb′inite,** one who adheres to the Talmud and traditions of the rabbis; **rabboni** (rab-ō′ni, -nī), my great master. [Heb. *rabbi,* my great one—*rabh,* great, master.]

rabbit, *rab′it, n.* the cony, a small burrowing animal of the hare family: its flesh (as food): its fur: a persistent but incurably inferior player at lawn-tennis or other game.—*v.i.* to hunt rabbits.—*ns.* **rabb′iter,** one who hunts rabbits; **rabb′it-fish,** the king of the herrings (Chimaera) or other fish fancied to resemble a rabbit; **rabb′it-hole,** a rabbit's burrow; **rabb′it-hutch,** a box for housing rabbits; **rabb′it-punch,** a blow on the back of the neck; **rabb′itry,** a place where rabbits are kept: the play of a rabbit in games; **rabb′it-squirrel,** a chincha; **rabb′it-sucker,** (*Shak.*) a sucking rabbit; **rabb′it-warren.**—*adj.* **rabb′ity.**—**Welsh rabbit,** melted cheese, with or without ale, &c., poured over hot toast—sometimes written ' Welsh rarebit ' by wiseacres. [M.E. *rabet;* poss. from O.N.Fr.]

rabbit, *rab′it, v.t.* confound (often in *od rabbit, d′rabbit,* or *drabbit,* for God rabbit). [Perh. a facetious substitution for **rat.**]

rabble, *rab′l, n.* a disorderly assemblage or crowd: a mob: the lowest class of people: a confused stream of words.—*adj.* of or like a rabble.—*v.t.* and *v.i.* to gabble.—*v.t.* to mob.—*ns.* **rabb′lement,** a rabble: tumult; **rabb′ling,** esp. (*Scot. hist.*) the mobbing and ousting of the Episcopal 'curates' at the Revolution.—**rabble rout,** (*obs.*) the mob, rabble. [Cf. Du. *rabbelen,* to gabble, L.G. *rabbeln.*]

rabble, *rab′l, n.* a puddling-iron.—*v.t.* to stir with a rabble.—*n.* **rabb′ler.** [Fr. *râble*—L. *rutābulum,* a poker.]

Rabelaisian, *rab-ə-lā′zi-ən, n.* a follower, admirer, or student of François *Rabelais* (d. 1553 or 1554).—*adj.* of or like Rabelais: extravagantly humorous: robustly outspoken: (loosely) coarsely indecent.—*n.* **Rabelais′ianism.**

rabi, *rub′ē, n.* the spring grain harvest in India. [Ar. *rabī′,* spring.]

abid, *rab′id, adj.* raging: fanatical: affected with

rabies.—*adj.* **rab′ic,** of rabies.—*adv.* **rab′idly.**—*ns.* **rabid′ity, rab′idness; rabies** (*rä′-* or *ra′bi-ēz*), the disease called hydrophobia, caused by a virus transmitted by the bite of an infected animal. [L. *rabidus* (adj.), *rabiēs* (n.)—*rabĕre,* to rave.]

raca, *rä′kä, adj.* (*B.*) worthless. [Chaldee *rēkä* (a term of reproach).]

rac(c)ahout, *räk′ə-hōōt, n.* acorn meal. [Fr.,—Ar. *rāqaut.*]

raccoon, racoon, *rə-kōōn′, n.* an American animal (*Procyon lotor,* or other species) related to the bears: its fur.—*ns.* **raccoon′-berry,** Podophyllum; **raccoon′-dog,** a raccoon-like wild dog (Nyctereutes) of Eastern Asia. [From an Amer. Ind. name.]

race, *räs, n.* the descendants of a common ancestor: esp. those who inherit a common set of characteristics : such a set of descendants, narrower than a species: a breed: (*obs.*) a stud or herd: ancestry, lineage, stock: the condition of belonging by descent to a particular group: inherited disposition: a class or group, defined otherwise than by descent: (*obs.*) a sex: peculiar flavour, as of wine, by which its origin may be recognised: raciness, piquancy.—*ns.* **race′-hat′red,** animosity accompanying difference of race; **race′-su′icide,** voluntary cessation of reproduction, leading to the extinction of the race.—*adj.* **racial** (*rä′shl, -shyəl, -shi-əl*), of, relating to, race or a race.—*ns.* **ra′cialism,** race hatred, rivalry, or feeling; **ra′cialist.**—*adv.* **racily** (*räs′i-li*).—*n.* **ra′ciness.**—*adj.* **ra′cy,** having a distinctive flavour imparted by the soil, as wine: exciting to the mind by strongly characteristic thought or language: spirited: pungent: zestful. [Fr.,—It. *razza,* of doubtful origin.]

race, *räs, n.* (arch. and *Scot.*) a run or onward rush: a fixed course, track, or path, over which anything runs: a channel bringing water to or from a wheel: a groove in which anything runs (as ball-bearings, a rope): a regular running over a fixed course, as of the sun: a rapid current: a competitive trial of speed in progression: (in *pl.*) a meeting for horse-racing: a competition in getting ahead of others figuratively: (*rare*) a running or racing place.—*v.i.* to run swiftly: to contend in speed: to run wildly (as an engine, a propeller) when resistance is removed.—*v.t.* to cause to race: to rush: to contend in a race with.—*ns.* **race′-ball,** a ball in connexion with a race-meeting; **race′-card,** a programme for a race-meeting; **race′course, -path, -track,** a course for running races over; **race′-cup,** a piece of plate forming a prize at a race; **race′-goer,** a habitual attender at race-meetings; **race′-going; race′-horse,** a horse bred for racing; **race′-meet′ing** (see **meeting**); **ra′cer,** one who or that which races; **race′-way,** a mill-race; **ra′cing; ra′cingbit,** a light jointed ring-bit. [O.N. *rás;* O.E. *rǽs.*]

race, *räs, n.* (*Shak.*) a rootstock of ginger. [O.Fr. *rais*—L. *rādix, -īcis,* a root.]

race, *räs,* also **ratch, rach,** *n.* a white streak down a beast's face. [Origin unknown.]

race, *räs, v.t.* to scratch: (*Spens.*) to raze: (*Spens.*) to erase: (*Shak.*) to slash.—*n.* a cut, slit, scratch. [An otherwise obs. form of **raze** or **rase.**]

race, *räs, v.t.* (*Spens.*) to tear away or off, pluck, snatch.—Also **rase** (*Shak.*). [O.Fr. *arrachier.*]

raceme, *ra-, rə-, rä-sēm′, ras′ēm, n.* an indefinite inflorescence in which stalked flowers are borne in acropetal succession on an unbranched main stalk: a similar group of sporangia.—*n.* **racemation** (*ras-i-mā′shən*), a gleaning or gathering of grapes: a residue: a cluster or bunch of grapes or of anything else.—*adjs.* **racemed′** (or *ras′, räs′*), in or having racemes; **racemic** (*ra-sē′mik, -sem′ik*), ap-

Neutral vowels in unaccented syllables : *el′ə-mənt, in′fənt, ran′dəm*

plied to an acid obtained from a certain kind of grape, an optically inactive form of tartaric acid: hence applied to similar compounds of dextro-rotatory and laevorotatory enantiomorphs.—*n.* **rac-emisation** (*ras-i-mī-zā′shən*), a changing into a racemic form.—*v.t.* and *v.i.* **rac′emise.**—*n.* **rac′-emism,** the quality of being racemic.—*adj.* **racemose** (*ras′i-mōs*), of the nature of or like a raceme: of, in, or having racemes: like a bunch of grapes. [L. *racēmus,* a bunch of grapes.]

rache, also **rach, ratch,** *rach, n.* a dog that hunts by scent. [O.E. *racc,* setter; O.N. *rakki.*]

rachis, sometimes **rhachis,** *rā′kis, n.* the spine: an axis, as of a feather, an inflorescence, a pinnate leaf.—*adjs.* **ra′chial;** less correctly **rachidial** (*rə-kid′*), **rachid′ian.**—*n.* **rachilla** (*rə-kil′ä*), the axis of a grass spikelet. [Gr. *rhachis, -ios,* or *-eōs,* spine.]

rachitis, *ra-, rə-kī′tis, n.* rickets.—*adj.* **rachitic** (*-kit′ik*). [Gr. *rhachītis,* inflammation of the spine: adopted by Dr Gleeson in 1650 in the belief that it was the etymon of **rickets.**]

racial, raciness, &c. See **race** (1).

rack, *rak, n.* an instrument for stretching, esp. an instrument of torture: hence (*fig.*) an extreme pain, anxiety, or doubt: stress, esp. of weather: a framework, grating, shelf, or the like, on or in which articles are disposed or set aside: a grating from which beasts may pull down fodder: (*Spens.*) a bar or framework as for chaining a prisoner: a bar with teeth to work into those of a wheel, pinion, or endless screw.—*v.t.* to stretch forcibly or excessively: to strain: to wrest, overstrain, distort: to torture: to practise rapacity upon: ({Spens.*) to extort: to put in a rack: to move or adjust by rack and pinion.—*n.* **rack′er.**—*n.* and *adj.* **rack′ing.**—*ns.* **rack′-rail,** a cogged rail; **rack′-rail′way,** a mountain railway with a rack in which a cog-wheel on the locomotive works; **rack′-rent,** a rent stretched to the utmost annual value of the thing rented, exorbitant rent.—*v.t.* to subject to such rents.—*ns.* **rack′-rent′er,** one who exacts or pays rack-rent; **rack′work,** mechanism with a rack.—**rack and manger,** all abundance freely supplied: waste and destruction (perh. from confusion with *rack and ruin*); **rack and pinion,** a means of turning rotatory into linear or linear into rotatory motion by a toothed wheel engaging in a rack; **rack one's brains,** strain one's memory, ingenuity, &c. [Prob. M.Du. *recke* (Du. *rek, rak*) or L.G. *reck, recke, rack*; cf. O.N. *rakkr,* straight, Ger. *rack,* rail, *recken,* to stretch; Eng. **reach.**]

rack, *rak, n.* same as **wrack,** destruction: (*Milt.*) a crash.—**rack and ruin,** a state of neglect and collapse. [**wrack** (1), or O.N. *rek,* wreckage.]

rack, *rak, n.* (*Shak.*) flying cloud: driving mist: a track: (*Scot.*) a shallow ford.—*v.i.* (*Shak.*) to drift, to drive. [App. O.N. *rek,* drifting wreckage, or some kindred form; cf. **wrack, wreck, wreak**; O.E. *wrecan,* to drive.]

rack, *rak, v.t.* to draw off from the lees. [Prov. *arracar*—*raca,* husks, dregs.]

rack, *rak, n.* (*prov.*) the neck and spine of a fore-quarter of a carcass: (*obs.*) a vertebra: a horse's bones.—*n.* **rack′abones,** (*U.S.*) a very thin horse, man, &c. [Perh. O.E. *hracca,* occiput.]

rack, *rak, n.* (now *U.S.*) a horse's gait at which the legs at the same side move nearly together.—*v.i.* to go in that gait.—*n.* **rack′er.** [Origin obscure.]

rack, *rak, n.* aphetic for **arrack.**—*n.* **rack′-punch.**

rack, *rak, n.* a young rabbit's skin. [Origin unknown.]

racket, *rak′it, n.* a bat with roughly elliptical head, usually of strung catgut, for playing tennis, badminton, &c.: a snowshoe of like design: (in *pl.*) a simplified derivative of the old game of tennis, played against an end-wall.—*v.t.* to strike with a racket.—*ns.* **rack′et-court, -ground;** **rack′et-press,** a press for keeping a racket in shape; **rack′et-tail,** a humming-bird with two long racket-shaped feathers.—*adj.* **rack′et-tailed.** [Fr. *raquette,* poss.—Ar. *rāhat,* the palm of the hand.]

racket, *rak′it, n.* din: clamour: hubbub: hurly-burly: fuss: noisy or hustling gaiety: dissipation: a noisy merry-making: a dodge: fraudulent, violent, or otherwise unscrupulous money-making activities: strain of excitement: responsibility: liability for expenses.—*v.i.* to make or engage in racket.—*v.t.* to disturb, stir, affect by racket:—*pr.p.* **rack′eting;** *pa.t.* and *pa.p.* **rack′-eted.**—*n.* **racketeer′,** one who extorts money or other advantage by threats or illegal interference.—*v.i.* to act as a racketeer.—*ns.* **racketeer′ing; rack′eter,** a noisy or gay person; **rack′etry.**—*adj.* **rack′ety,** noisy: energetically gay.—**stand the racket,** endure the strain: take the consequences or responsibility: pay expenses. [Prob. imit.]

racket(t), *rak′it, n.* an old instrument like the bassoon. [Origin doubtful.]

racloir, *rä-klwär, n.* a scraper. [Fr.]

raconteur, *ra-kon-tər′, rä-kōn²-tər′, n.* a teller of anecdotes:—*fem.* **raconteuse** (*-tзz′*). [Fr.]

racoon. See **raccoon.**

Racovian, *rə-kō′vi-ən, n.* a 17th-century Polish Socinian—their seminary being at *Raków.*—Also *adj.*

racquet. Same as **racket** (1).

racy. See **race** (1).

rad, *rad* (*Spens.*), *pa.t.* and *pa.p.* of **read,** and *pa.t.* of **ride.**

rad, *rad, adj.* (*Scot.*) afraid. [O.N. *hrǣddr.*]

rad, *rad, n.* short for **radical** (in politics).

radar, *rā′där, n.* radiolocation, the use of high-powered wireless pulses for locating objects or determining one's own position. [American code-word, from *radio* detection and ranging, appropriately a palindrome word.]

raddle, *rad′l, n.* a flexible rod or strip of wood used to make hurdles, fences, or (with plaster) walls, by weaving between uprights: a hurdle, door, fence, or the like so made: a hedge formed by interweaving the branches of trees: a wooden bar used in weaving.—*v.t.* to interweave: (*Northern*) to thrash. [A.Fr. *reidele,* rail.]

raddle, *rad′l, n.* reddle or ruddle (red ochre).—*v.t.* to colour or mark with red ochre: to rouge coarsely.—*adj.* **radd′led.**—*n.* **radd′leman.** [See **ruddle.**]

raddocke, *rad′ək* (*Shak.*). Same as **ruddock.**

rade, *rād.* Northern form of **rode.** [See **ride.**]

radial, *rā′di-əl, adj.* pertaining to a ray or radius: along, in the direction of, a radius or radii: having rays, spokes, or parts diverging from a centre: arranged like spokes or radii: near the radius of the arm.—*n.* a radiating part: a radial artery, nerve, engine, plate, &c.—*ns.* **radiale** (*-ā′li*; L. *rā-di-ā′lā*), a wrist-bone in line with the radius:—*pl.* **radia′lia; radialisation** (*rād-yəl-ī-zā′shən*).—*v.t.* **rā′dialise,** to arrange radially.—*n.* **rādiality** (*-al′*), radial symmetry.—*adv.* **rā′dially,** in the manner of radii or of rays.—**radial artery,** the smaller branch of the brachial artery at the elbow; **radial engine,** one with its cylinders radially arranged; **radial symmetry,** symmetry about several planes intersecting in a common axis; **radial velocity,** the component of velocity along the observer's line of sight. [L.L. *radiālis*—L. *radius.*]

radian, *rā′di-ən, n.* a unit of circular measure, the angle subtended at the centre of a circle by an arc equal to the radius, nearly 57°·3. [L. *radius.*]

radiant, *rā′di-ənt, rā′dyənt, adj.* emitting rays: issuing in rays: glowing: shining: beaming with happy emotion.—*n.* that which emits radiations: a point from which rays emanate: the centre from which meteoric showers seem to proceed: (*geom.*) a straight line from a point about which it is conceived to revolve.—*ns.* **rā′diance, rā′diancy.**—*adv.* **rā′diantly.** [L. *radiāns, -āntis,* pr.p. of *radiāre,* to radiate—*radius.*]

radiate, *rā′di-āt, v.i.* to emit rays: to shine: to issue in rays: to diverge from a point or points: to transmit wirelessly.—*v.t.* to send out in or by means of rays: to communicate by wireless: to broadcast.—*adj.* (*-it, -ət, -āt*) having rays: having ray-florets: spreading like a ray or rays: radial radially arranged: of the Radiata.—*n.* an animal of the Radiata.—*n.pl.* **Rādiā′ta,** in Cuvier's obsolete classification, the lowest subkingdom of animals, radially symmetrical—echinoderms, coel

enterates, polyzoans, &c.—*adj.* **rā′diated.**—*adv.*
rā′diately.—*n.* **rādiā′tion,** act of radiating: the
emission and diffusion of rays: that which is
radiated: energy transmitted in electromagnetic
waves: radial arrangement.—*adj.* **rā′diātive.**—*n.*
rā′diātor, that which radiates: apparatus for
radiating heat, as for warming a room, or cooling
an engine: a wireless transmitting aerial. [L.
radiāre, to shine, *radiātus,* rayed—*radius.*]
radical, *rad′i-kl, adj.* pertaining to, constituting,
proceeding from, or going to the root: fundamental: original: intrinsic: inherent: thorough:
primary: primitive: implanted by nature: not
derived: (*bot.*) proceeding from near the root:
(*politics,* commonly **Radical**) favouring thorough-
going but constitutional social and political reform,
advanced Liberal.—*n.* a root, in any sense: (*chem.*;
sometimes **rad′icle**) a group of atoms behaving
like a single atom and passing unchanged from one
compound to another—now usually confined
to electrically neutral entities as distinguished
from charged ion**s**: **Radical,** an advocate of
radical reform or member of the Radical party.—
v.t. and *v.i.* **rad′icalise,** to make or become radical.
—*ns.* **Rad′icalism,** the principles or spirit of a
Radical; **radicality** (-*kal′i-ti*).—*adv.* **rad′ically.**
—*n.* **rad′icalness.**—*adjs.* **rad′icant,** rooting from
the stem; **rad′icāte,** rooted: deeply rooted:
firmly established: fixed.—*v.t.* to root: to plant
or fix deeply and firmly.—*adj.* **rad′icāted,** rooted,
established.—*ns.* **radicā′tion,** rooting: implant-
ing: rootedness: general character of the root-
system; **rad′icel** (-*sel*), a rootlet.—*adjs.* **rad′-**
icellose; radicicolous (-*sik′ə-ləs*), inhabiting, or
parasitic on, roots; **radiciform** (*ra-dis′*), like a
root; **radiciv′orous,** root-eating.—*n.* **rad′icle,** a
little root: the part of a seed that becomes the
root: a rhizoid: (*chem.*) a radical.—*adj.* **radic′-**
ūlar, pertaining to a radicle, a rootlet, or the root
of a tooth, nerve, &c.—*n.* **rad′icūle.**—*adj.* **radic′-**
ulose, having many rootlets or rhizoids.—**radical**
axis, the locus of a point of equal potency with
respect to two circles. [L. *rādix, -īcis,* a root.]
radio-, *rā′di-ō-, -o′,* in composition, rays, radiation,
radium, radio: (*chem.*) a radioactive product or
isotope, as **radioactin′ium, rādiotho′rium,** both
isotopes of thorium; **rādioel′ement.**—*n.* **rā′dio,**
wireless communication: a wireless receiving or
transmitting set: a wireless message or broadcast.
—*adj.* of, for, transmitted or transmitting by,
wireless.—*v.t.* and *v.i.* to communicate by wireless.
—*adj.* **rādioact′ive.**—*ns.* **rādioactiv′ity,** spontaneous disintegration, first observed in certain heavy
elements (radium, actinium, uranium, thorium)
with emission of α-rays, β-rays, and γ-rays;
rādioaut′ograph, in tracer work, the representation of a treated specimen on a photographic
plate by means of radiations from the radioisotope
employed; **rādio-bea′con,** apparatus that transmits signals for direction-finding; **rādiochem′-**
istry, the chemistry of radioactivity; **rādio-**
communica′tion, wireless telegraphy or telephony; **rādio-com′pass,** a wireless direction-
finding instrument; **rādioel′ement,** a radio-
isotope.—*adj.* **rādiogenic** (-*jen′ik*), produced by
radioactive disintegration.—*ns.* **rādiogoniom′eter,**
a wireless direction-finder; **rā′diogram,** an X-ray
photograph: a wireless telegram: (for **rādio-**
gram′ophone) a combined wireless receiver and
gramophone; **rā′diograph** (-*gráf*), an instrument
for recording radiation: an X-ray photograph:
the wireless telegraph. — *adj.* **rādiographic**
(-*graf′ik*). — *ns.* **rādiography** (-*og′rə-fi*), X-ray
photography: radiotelegraphy: study of radioactivity; **rādiois′otope,** a radioactive isotope
of a stable element; **rādiolocā′tion,** position-
finding by wireless signals: radar, determination
of one's own position or that of an object, e.g. an
enemy aircraft, by reflection of wireless waves.—
adj. **rādiolog′ical.**—*ns.* **rādiol′ogist; rādiol′-**
ogy, the study of radioactivity and radiation or
their application to medicine; **rādiom′eter,** an
instrument that measures radiant energy by the
rotation of a vane with bright and black sides.—
adj. **rādiomet′ric.**—*n.* **rā′diophōne,** an instru-

ment for producing sound by radiant energy: a
wireless telephone.—*adj.* **rādiophonic** (-*fon′ik*).—
ns. **rādiophon′ics, rādiophony** (-*of′ə-ni*); **rādios′-**
copy, examination by X-rays; **rā′diotel′egram**,
-tel′egraph, -teleg′raphy, -tel′ephone, -teleph′-
ony, wireless telegraph, telephone, &c.; **rādio-**
therapeut′ics, -ther′apy, treatment of disease by
radiation, as by X-rays, &c.—**radio astronomy,**
astronomical study by means of radar: also study of
radio waves generated in space; **radio sonde** (Fr.
sonde, plummet, probe), apparatus for ascertaining
atmospheric conditions at great heights, consisting
of a hydrogen-filled balloon, radio transmitter(s),
&c. [L. *rādius,* a rod, spoke, radius, ray.]
Radiolaria, *rā-di-ō-lā′ri-ä, n.pl.* an order of marine
Protozoa with fine radial pseudopodia. — *adj.*
radiola′rian. — Also *n.* — **radiolarian ooze,** a
deep-sea deposit in which the siliceous skeletons
of Radiolaria predominate. [L.L. *radiolus,* dim.
of L. *rādius,* radius.]
radish, *rad′ish, n.* a cruciferous plant, *Raphanus*
sativus or other member of the genus: its pungent
root, eaten as a salad. [Fr. *radis*—Prov. *radit*z*
or It. *radice*—L. *rādix, -īcis,* a root.]
radium, *rā′di-əm, n.* a radioactive metallic element
(Ra; at. numb. 88) discovered by the Curies in 1898,
found in pitchblende and other minerals, remarkable for its active spontaneous disintegration.—
radium A, B, &c., successive products in the disintegration of radon; **radium emanation,** radon.
[L. *rādius,* a ray.]
radius, *rā′di-əs, n.* (*geom.*) a straight line from the
centre to the circumference of a circle or surface
of a sphere: a radiating line: anything placed
like a radius, as the spoke of a wheel, the movable
arm of a sextant: a radial plane of symmetry in a
coelenterate: a line from a fixed point (e.g. the
focus of a conic) to a point on a curve: the outer
bone (in supine position) of the forearm in man,
or its homologue in other animals: a barbule of a
feather: the third vein of an insect's wing: (*rare*)
a ray-flower or the ray-flowers of a head collectively: a distance from a centre, conceived as
limiting an area or range:—*pl.* **radii** (*rā′di-ī*); L.
rā′di-ē).—*adj.* **ra′dial** (q.v.).—**radius vector** (*pl.*
radii vectō′res), a straight line joining a fixed with
a variable point. [L. *rādius,* a rod, spoke, ray.]
radix, *rā′diks,* L. *rā′dēks, n.* (*obs.*) a root, root-
number, root-word: a source: a basis: the
quantity on which a system of numeration, or of
logarithms, &c., is based:—*pl.* **radices** (*rā′di-sez,*
L. *rā-dē′kās*). [L. *rādix, -īcis,* root.]
radome, *rā′dōm, n.* a protective covering for micro-
wave antennae.
radon, *rā′don, n.* a gaseous radioactive element (Rn;
at. numb. 86), the first disintegration product of
radium—radium emanation, formerly called niton.
[radium, and **-on,** as in *argon, xenon,* &c.]
radula, *rad′ū-lä, n.* a mollusc's tongue or rasping
ribbon.—*adjs.* **rad′ular; rad′ulāte; rad′ūli-**
form, rasp-like. [L. *rādula,* a scraper—*rādere.*]
Raetian. See **Rhaetian.**
Raf, *raf, n.* (*coll.*) the R.A.F. (Royal Air Force).
rafale, *rä-fäl′, n.* a burst of artillery in quick rounds.
[Fr., gust of wind.]
raff, *raf, n.* riff-raff: one of the riff-raff: a rakish,
flashy, or blackguardly fellow.—*adj.* **raffish.**—*adj.*
raff′ish, rakish: flashy. — *adv.* **raff′ishly.** — *n.*
raff′ishness. [Cf. **riff-raff.**]
raffia, *raf′i-ä, n.* the Raphia palm or its leaf-bast.
[**Raphia.**]
raffinose, *raf′i-nōs, n.* a trisaccharide sugar. [Fr.
raffiner, to refine.]
raffle, *raf′l, n.* an old dicing game, the stakes going
to the thrower of a pair-royal: a lottery for an
article.—*v.t.* to sell by raffle.—*v.t.* to engage in a
raffle.—*n.* **raff′ler.** [Fr. *rafle,* a pair-royal.]
raffle, *raf′l, n.* a rabble: riff-raff: lumber: rubbish:
a jumble: a tangle. [Cf. **raff.**]
raffle, *raf′l, n.* a.t. to notch: to crumple. [Ety. dub.]
Rafflesia, *raf-lē′zi-ä, n.* a genus (giving name to the
family **Rafflesiā′ceae,** akin to the birth-wort
family) of parasitic plants in Sumatra, Java, &c.,
one species having the largest known flowers, a
yard across, carrion-scented, the rest of the plant

reduced to threads within the tissues of its host-plant. [Named after Sir T. Stamford *Raffles* (1781-1826), British governor in Sumatra (1818), who sent it to Brown, the botanist.]

raft, *räft, n.* (*U.S.*) a crowd: a miscellaneous lot. [**raff.**]

raft, *räft, n.* a flat floating mass of logs or other material (ice, vegetation, &c.): a flat structure of logs, &c., for support or for conveyance on water: (*U.S.*) a dense mass of floating water-fowl: a wide layer of concrete to support a building on soft ground.—*v.t.* to transport on a raft: to form into a raft: to traverse by raft.—*v.i.* to manage a raft: to travel by raft: to form into a raft: to pile up by overriding, as ice.—*ns.* **raft'-bridge,** a raft used as a bridge: a bridge supported on rafts; **raft'er, raft'man,** a raftsman; **raft'-port,** in ships, a large port for timber; **raft'-rope,** a rope for towing blubber; **rafts'man,** one who works on a raft. [O.N. *raptr,* rafter.]

raft, *räft, obs. pa.t.* and *pa.p.* of **reave**: in Keats *pa.p.* of **rive.**

rafter, *räf'tər, n.* an inclined beam supporting a roof.—*v.t.* to furnish with rafters: to plough so that a strip is overturned upon unploughed ground.—*n.* **raft'er-bird,** the spotted fly-catcher. —*adj.* **raft'ered,** having (esp. visible) rafters. —*n.* **raft'ering.** [O.E. *ræfter,* a beam.]

rag, *rag, n.* a worn, torn, or waste scrap of cloth: a tatter: a shred, scrap, or smallest portion: (*old slang*) a farthing: a jagged projection: (contemptuously or playfully) a flag, sail, theatre curtain, garment, newspaper, or paper money: the pithy part of an orange, lemon, &c.: a worthless or beggarly person: (in *pl.*) tattered clothing. —*adj.* of,. for, or dealing in rags.—*v.t.* to tear to rags: to make ragged: to perform in ragtime.— *v.i.* to become ragged, to fray: (*U.S. slang*) to dress (*out*).—*ns.* **rag-and-bone'-man,** one who collects or traffics in rags, bones, or other rubbish; **rag-ba'by,** a rag-doll; **rag'-bag,** a bag for rags and abandoned garments: a slattern; **rag'bolt,** a bolt with barbs to prevent withdrawal; **rag'-book,** a child's book mounted on cloth; **rag'-bush,** a bush to which shreds of cloth are tied as offerings to the local spirit, esp. by a well; **rag'-doll',** a doll made of rags: a slattern; **rag'-dust,** finely divided rags, used for making flock-paper; **rag'-fair,** an old-clothes market: (*mil. slang*) a kit inspection.—*adj.* **ragg'ed,** shaggy: rough-edged: jagged: uneven in execution: (*her.*) raguly: torn or worn into rags: wearing ragged clothes.—*n.* **ragg'ed-la'dy,** *Nigella damascena.*— *adv.* **ragg'edly.**—*ns.* **ragg'edness; ragg'ed-Rob'in,** a campion (*Lychnis flos-cuculi*) with deep-cleft petals.—*adj.* **ragg'edy,** ragged-looking.—*n.* **ragg'ery,** rags or the ragged collectively: (*slang*) clothes, esp. women's: raggedness.—*adj.* **ragg'y,** rough: ragged: of the nature of a rag.—*ns.* **rag'-man,** a man who collects or deals in rags: the devil; **rag'-mon'ey,** (*slang*) paper money; **rag'-paper,** paper made from rags; **rag'-picker,** one who collects rags from bins, heaps, &c.; **rag'-tag,** the rabble (also **ragg'le-tagg'le**); **rag'time,** a highly syncopated form of music of American negro origin: a tune, song, or dance in ragtime; **rag'weed,** ragwort: (*U.S.*) any species of the composite genus Ambrosia; **rag'wheel,** a toothed wheel: a polishing-wheel made of cloth disks clamped together; **rag'-woman; rag'-wool,** shoddy; **rag'worm,** a nearly white burrowing marine worm (*Nephthys caeca*), used as bait by fishermen; **rag'wort,** a common coarse yellow-headed composite weed (*Senecio Jacobaea*) of pastures: any similar species of the genus with long rays (from the cut leaves).—**ragged school,** a voluntary school for destitute children; **ragged staff,** (*her.*) a stick with branch stubs; **rag-tag and bobtail,** riff-raff. [O.E. *ragg,* inferred from the adj. *raggig,* shaggy; O.N. *rögg,* shagginess, tuft.]

rag, ragg, *rag, n.* a rough hard stone of various kinds, esp. one breaking in slabs: a large rough slate (3 ft. by 2).—*ns.* **rag'stone; rag'work,** undressed masonry in slabs. [Poss. from foregoing.]

rag, *rag, v.t.* to rate: to banter: to assail or beset

with questions, chaff, horseplay.—*v.i.* to wrangle: to indulge in a rag (*pa.t.* and *pa.p.* **ragged,** *ragd*). —*n.* an outburst of organised horseplay, usually in defiance of authority.—*n.* **ragg'ing.**—*adj.* **ragg'y,** (*slang*) irritated.—**lose one's rag,** (*coll.*) to lose one's temper. [Perh. shortened from **bullyrag;** perh. from **rag** (1), as in **red rag.**]

ragamuffin, *rag'ə-muf-in,* or *-muf', n.* a ragged, disreputable boy or man: **Ragamuffin,** (*obs.*) the name of a devil. [Poss. **rag** (1).]

rag'd, ragde, *ragd,* (*Shak.*) for **ragged,** shaggy, jagged: perh. unruly: poss. also (*räjd*) for **raged,** irritated (as if *pa.p.* of *v.t.*).

rage, *räj, n.* madness: overmastering passion of any kind, as desire or (esp.) anger: inspired frenzy: ardour: a fit of any of these: a mania or craze for anything: vogue: a thing in vogue: violence, stormy or furious activity: (*Shak.*) a flood.— *v.i.* to behave or speak with passion, esp. with furious anger: to be violent: to storm: to be prevalent and violent: (*Scot.*) to scold (with *at* or *on*): (*Milt.*) to be violently bent on.—*v.t.* (see **rag'd**).—*adj.* **rage'ful.**—*n.* **rä'ger.**—*adj.* **rä'ging.** —*adv.* **rä'gingly.**—**all the rage,** quite the fashion. [Fr.,—L. *rabiēs—rabēre,* to rave.]

ragg, ragged, raggee. See **rag** (2), **rag** (1), **ragi.**

raggle, *rag'l, n.* (*Scot.*) a groove in masonry, esp. to receive the edge of a roof.—*v.t.* to make a raggle in. [Origin obscure.]

ragi, raggee, raggy, *rä'gē, rag'i, n.* a millet (*Eleusine coracana*) much grown in India, Africa, &c. [Hind. (and Sans.) *rāgī.*]

raglan, *rag'lən, n.* an overcoat with sleeve in one piece with the shoulder. [From Lord *Raglan* (1788-1855), commander in the Crimea.]

ragman, *rag'mən,* **ragment,** *rag'mənt, n.* (*obs.*) a catalogue: (*obs.*) a document with pendent seals: (*obs. Scot.*) a rigmarole.—**Ragman Rolls,** a collection of instruments by which the Scottish nobles, &c., subscribed allegiance to Edward I. [Origin obscure.]

ragman. See **rag** (1).

ragmatical, *rag-mat'i-kl, adj.* (*Fielding, Smollett*) app. riotous, disorderly. [Perh. from **rag** (1) after **pragmatical.**]

Ragnarök, *rag'na-rək, n.* (*Scand. myth.*) the coming mutual destruction of the gods and the powers of evil, and the end of this world, to be superseded by a better. [O.N. *ragna rök,* history or judgment of the gods (—*rögn, régin,* gods—*rök,* reason, judgment), sophisticated into *ragna rökr,* twilight of the gods (—*rökr,* darkness).]

ragout, *rä-gōō', n.* a highly seasoned stew of meat and vegetables.—*v.t.* to make ragout of. [Fr. *ragoût—ragoûter,* to restore the appetite.]

ragstone. See **rag** (2).

ragtime, ragweed, ragwort. See **rag** (1).

raguly, *rag'ū-li, adj.* (*her.*) with projections like oblique stubs of branches.—Also **rag'ūled.** [Origin obscure.]

rah, 'rah, *rä, raw, interj., n., v.i.* (*U.S.*) for **hurrah.**

Rahu, *rä'hōō, n.* (*Hindu myth.*) the demon that swallows the sun and moon at eclipses.

raid, *räd, n.* a sudden swift inroad, orig. by horsemen, for assault or seizure: an air attack: an invasion unauthorised by government: an incursion of police: an onset or onslaught for the purpose of obtaining or suppressing something.—*v.t.* to make a raid on.—*v.i.* to go on a raid.—*n.* **raid'er,** one who raids: a raiding aeroplane.—**raid the market,** to derange prices artificially for future gain. [Scots form of **road** (revived by Scott)— O.E. *rád,* riding.]

raik, *räk, n.* course, journey: range: pasture.— *v.i.* to go: to range. [O.N. *reik* (n.), *reika* (vb.) walk; coalescing later with **rake** (4).]

rail, *räl, n.* a bar extending horizontally or at a slope between supports or on the ground, often to form a support, a fence, a guard, a track for wheels: the railway as a means of travel or transport: a horizontal member in framing or panelling (as in a door): the capping part of bulwarks: (in *pl.*) a racecourse barrier: (in *pl.*) railway shares.—*v.t.* to enclose or separate with rails: to furnish with rails: to send by railway.—*v.i.* to travel by railway.

—*adj.* **rail'-borne,** carried by railway.—*ns.* **rail'-car,** (*U.S.*) a railway carriage: a self-propelled railway carriage; **rail'-fence,** (*U.S.*) a fence of wooden posts and rails; **rail'head,** the furthest point reached by a railway under construction: the end of railway transport; **rail'ing,** fencing: fencing materials: (often in *pl.*) a barrier or ornamental structure, usu. of upright iron rods secured by horizontal connexions.—*adj.* **rail'less.**—*ns.* **rail'man,** a railway employee; **rail'-mo'tor,** a self-propelled railway carriage; **rail'road,** (chiefly *U.S.* and *Canada*) a railway.—*v.t.* (*U.S.*) to push forward unduly.—*ns.* **rail'roader,** (*U.S.*) a railway worker or official; **rail'-splitter,** (*U.S.*) one who splits logs for fence-rails; **rail'way,** a track laid with rails for wheels to run on, esp. for locomotives with passenger and goods wagons : a system of such tracks with equipment and organisation.—Also *adj.*—*ns.* **rail'way-car** (*U.S.*), **rail'way-carr'iage,** a railway vehicle for passengers; **rail'way-cross'ing,** an intersection of railway lines or of road and railway, esp. without a bridge; **rail'way-stitch,** a name for various quickly worked stitches. [O.Fr. *reille*—L. *rēgula,* a ruler.]

rail, *rāl,'v.i.* to scoff : to use vigorously or mockingly reproachful language: to banter : to revile.—*v.t.* to bring or render by raillery.—*n.* (*Spens.* **rayle**) reviling.—*n.* **rail'er.**—*adj.* and *n.* **rail'ing.**—*adv.* **rail'ingly.**—*n.* **raillery** (*rāl'ər-i*; old-fashioned *ral'*), railing or mockery: banter: playful satire. [Fr. *railler.*]

rail, *rāl, n.* any bird of the genus Rallus, esp. the water-rail, or other member of the family Rallidae, esp. the corncrake or land-rail. [O.Fr. *rasle* (Fr. *râle*).]

rail (*Spens.* **rayle, raile**), *rāl, v.i.* (*arch.*) to flow, gush. [Origin obscure.]

rail, *rāl, n.* (*obs.* except in **night-rail**) a garment: a cloak: a neckerchief.—*n.* **raill'y,** (*Scott*) a jacket. [O.E. *hrægl.*]

raiment, *rā'mənt, n.* clothing. [**arrayment.**]

rain, *rān, n.* water from the clouds in drops : a shower : a fall of anything in the manner of rain: (in *pl.*) the rainy season.—*v.i.* to fall as or like rain : to send down rain.—*v.t.* to shower.—*ns.* **rain'band,** a dark band in the solar spectrum, due to water vapour in the earth's atmosphere; **rain'-bird,** a bird, as the green woodpecker and various kinds of cuckoo, supposed to foretell rain.—*adj.* **rain'-bound,** detained by rain.—*n.* **rain'bow,** the coloured bow caused by refraction and internal reflexion of light in raindrops : any similar array of colours : (*slang*) a much discoloured bruise: a rainbow-trout: a S. American humming-bird, the cock with rainbow-coloured head.—*adj.* of, or coloured like, the rainbow.—*n.* **rain'bow-chaser,** a visionary, one who tries to reach the end of the rainbow.—*adjs.* **rain'bow-coloured, rain'bowed, rain'bow-tint'ed.**—*n.* **rain'bow-trout,** a finely marked and coloured Californian trout (*Salmo irideus*).—*adj.* **rain'bowy.**—*ns.* **rain'-chamber,** a compartment for condensing noxious fumes by spray; **rain'-cloud,** nimbus, a dense dark sheet of cloud that may shed rain or snow; **rain'coat,** a light overcoat proof against moderate rain; **rain'-doctor,** a rain-maker; **rain'drop,** a drop of rain; **rain'fall,** a shower of rain : the amount (by depth of water) of rain that falls; **rain'-forest,** tropical forest with very heavy rainfall; **rain'-gauge,** an instrument for measuring rainfall; **rain'iness.**—*adj.* **rain'less.**—*ns.* **rain'-maker,** one who professes to bring rain; **rain'-plover,** the golden plover; **rain'-print,** a little pit made by a raindrop in clay, &c., sometimes preserved in rocks.—*adj.* **rain'proof,** more or less impervious to rain.—*v.t.* to make rainproof.—*n.* a rainproof overcoat.—*n.* **rain'storm.**—*adj.* **rain'tight,** rainproof.—*ns.* **rain'-tree,** a S. American tree (*Pithecolobium Saman*) of the mimosa family, under which there is a constant rain of juice ejected by Cicadas; **rain'-wash,** the washing away of earthy matter by rain: downward creep of superficial deposits soaked in rain : matter so transported; **rain'-water,** water that falls or has lately fallen as rain.—*adj.* **rain'y,** characterised by rain.—a

rainy day, (*fig.*) a possible future time of need; **rainbow dressing,** a gaudy display of flags on a ship; **right as rain,** perfectly in order. [O.E. *regn*; Du. and Ger. *regen,* O.N. *regn.*]

rain, raine (*Spens.*). Same as **reign.**

raise, *rāz, v.t.* to cause to rise : to make higher or greater : to lift : to exalt: to advance : to elevate : to set up or upright: to rouse: to stir up : to elate : to rear, grow, or breed: to produce : to give rise to : to build, erect : to bring into being: to bring to life: to utter : to establish: to institute: to bring forward into consideration or notice: to bring into relief : to intensify : to call up : (*naut.*) to cause to rise in view by approaching: to levy, get together, collect : to cause to swell : to extol : to remove, take off : to produce a nap on.—*n.* a rising road : (*coll.*) an increase.—*adj.* **rais'able.**—*ns.* **rais'er,** one who, or that which, raises a building, &c.: the riser of a step; **rais'ing; rais'ing-bee,** (*U.S.*) a gathering of neighbours to help in raising the frame of a house, &c.—**raise a siege,** to abandon, or put an end to, a siege; **raised beach,** (*geol.*) an old sea-margin above the present water-level; **raised pastry, pie,** pastry, pie, with the support of a dish at the sides; **raise money on,** to get money by pawning; **raise one's hat,** to take one's hat off in salutation; **raise the market** (**upon**), to bring about a rise in prices (to the disadvantage of); **raise the roof,** to make a prodigious din; **raise the wind,** to get together the necessary money by any shift. [M.E. *reisen*—O.N. *reisa,* causative of *risa,* to rise; cf. **rise, rear.**]

raise, *rāz, n.* (*N. of England*) a cairn. [O.N. *hreysi.*]

raisin, *rā'zn, n.* a dried grape. [Fr., grape—L. *racēmus,* a bunch of grapes.]

rait. Same as **ret.**

raiyat, raiyatwari. Same as **ryot, ryotwari.**

raj, *räj, n.* rule, sovereignty.—*n.* **ra'ja(h),** an Indian prince or king: a Malay chief.—*ns.* **ra'ja(h)ship; raj'pramukh** (*-mook*), head of a state or states union in the Democratic Republic of India; **Rajput, -poot** (*räj'pōōt*), a member of a race or class claiming descent from the original Hindu military and ruling caste. [Hind. *rāj, rājā, Rājpūt*—Sans. *rājan,* a king (cog. with L. *rēx*), *putra,* son.]

rake, *rāk, n.* a toothed bar on a handle, for scraping, gathering together, smoothing, &c.: a similar tool for various purposes, toothed, notched, or bladed : a wheeled field implement with long teeth for gathering hay, scraping up weeds, &c.: an extremely thin person or horse.—*v.t.* to scrape, smooth, clear, break up, draw, gather, remove, cover, uncover, search, ransack, with a rake or as if with a rake : to cover with ashes so as to keep smouldering : to pass over violently and swiftly : to enfilade : to afford or take a view all over or quite through.—*v.i.* to work with or as if with a rake : to search minutely.—*ns.* **rake'-off,** pecuniary share, esp. unearned or illicit ; **rā'ker,** one who rakes: a scavenger : a raking implement : in games, a long, fast, low-flying shot (perh. partly from **rake** (4)); **rake'shame,** (*Milt.*) a base, dissolute wretch.—*n.* and *adj.* **rā'king.**—**rake up,** to revive from oblivion (usu. something scandalous). [O.E. *raca*; Ger. *rechen,* rake; O.N. *reka,* shovel.]

rake, *rāk, n.* a debauched or dissolute person, esp. a man of fashion.—*v.i.* to lead a rake's life: to make a practice of lechery.—*n.* **rā'kery,** dissoluteness.—*adj.* **rā'kish.**—*adv.* **rā'kishly.**—*n.* **rā'kishness.** [**rakehell.**]

rake, *rāk, n.* inclination from the vertical or horizontal.—*v.i.* to incline.—*v.t.* to slope: to cut aslant.—*n.* **rā'ker,** a sloping shore, support.—*adj.* **rā'kish,** with raking masts: swift-looking: piratelike: dashing: jaunty.—*adv.* **rā'kishly.** [Ety. dub.]

rake, *rāk, v.i.* (now *dial.*) to proceed, esp. swiftly: to roam, range about: of a hawk, to fly wide: of a dog, to follow the scent wanderingly along the ground.—*n.* **rā'ker,** a very fast pace: a plunge in betting.—*adj.* **rā'king,** advancing swiftly. [O.E. *racian,* to go forward, hasten.]

rake, *rāk, n.* (*Northern*) a track, esp. up a hill or in a gully or a pasture : a pasture : a journey, esp. in fetching things : the amount carried at one journey, load, gang : an irregular, usu. vertical, vein of ore : a string, as of wagons.—*v.i.* to form into single file, as sheep. [O.N. *rāk*, stripe ; partly coalescing with **raik**.]

rakehell, *rāk'hel*, *n.* an utterly debauched person.— *adjs.* **rake'hell, -y.** [Prob. **rake** (1) and **hell** : such as might be found by raking out hell.]

raki, *rāk'ē*, *n.* a spirituous liquor used in the Levant and Greece.—Also **rak'ee.** [Turk. *rāqī.*]

rakshas, rakshasa, *rāk'shäs, -ä, n.* (*Hindu myth.*) an evil spirit. [Sans. *rakśas.*]

râle, *räl*, *n.* (*path.*) a sound from a diseased lung. [Fr.]

rallentando, *ral-ən-tan'dō*, *adj.* and *adv.* (*mus.*) becoming slower.—*n.* a slowing. [It., pr.p. of *rallentare*, to slacken.]

Rallus, *ral'əs*, *n.* the water-rail genus of birds, giving name to the family **Rall'idae**.—*adj.* **rall'ine** (*-īn*). [Latinised from Fr. *râle.*]

rally, *ral'i*, *v.t.* to reassemble : to gather to one's support : to bring together for united effort : to muster by an effort (as the faculties) : to pull together, revive.—*v.i.* to come together, esp. from dispersal, or for renewed effort, or in support of a leader, friend, or cause : to recover : to recover in some degree lost health, power, vigour, value, &c. : (*pr.p.* **rall'ying** ; *pa.p.* and *pa.t.* **rall'ied**).—*n.* a reassembly for renewed effort : a gathering for a common purpose : a mass-meeting : a pantomime mêlée : a temporary or partial recovery : a quick exchange of blows in boxing : a series of to and fro strokes in deciding a point, as in tennis.— *ns.* **rall'ier** ; **rall'ying-cry**, a slogan ; **rall'ying-point.** [O.Fr. *rallier*—pfx. *re-* and *allier* ; see **ally**.]

rally, *ral'i*, *v.t.* and *v.i.* to banter :—*pr.p.* **rall'ying** ; *pa.t.* and *pa.p.* **rall'ied.**—*n.* **rall'ier.**—*adv.* **rall'yingly.** [Fr. *railler* ; cf. **rail** (2).]

Ralph, *rālf, rāf, n.* the imp of mischief in a printing-house. [Personal name—O.E. *Rædwulf.*]

ram, *ram, n.* a male sheep, a tup : (*astron.*) Aries : a battering-ram : a ship's beak for striking an enemy ship : a warship with such a beak : a water-ram or hydraulic ram (see **hydraulic**) : the monkey of a pile-driver : the striking head of a steam-hammer : a piston applying pressure : a machine with such a piston : a rammer : an act of ramming.—*v.t.* to thrust roughly, stuff hard, cram : to block up : to beat hard, pun : to drive hard down : to strike, batter, pierce with a ram :—*pr.p.* **ramm'ing** ; *pa.t.* and *pa.p.* **rammed.**—*ns.* **ram'cat**, a he-cat ; **ram'-jet**, a continuous jet with compression by aerodynamic ram ; **ramm'er**, one who or that which rams : esp. a paviour's tool.—*adj.* **ramm'ish**, rank in smell or taste : strongly sexual.—*ns.* **ram'rod**, a rod for ramming down a charge or for cleaning a gun-barrel ; **ram's'-horn**, the horn of a ram : a trumpet, snuff-box, or other thing like or made of it.—Also *adj.* [O.E. *ram, rom* ; Ger. *ramm.*]

Ramadan, Ramadhan, *ram-ə-dän', n.* the Mohammedan month of fasting by day. [Ar. *Ramadān.*]

ramal, ramate, &c. See **ramus.**

Rāmāyana, *rä-mä'yä-nä, n.* the Sanskrit epic of *Rāma.*

ramble, *ram'bl, v.i.* to go as fancy leads : to wander : to walk for pleasure : to wander in mind or discourse : to be desultory, incoherent, or delirious : to straggle or trail, as a plant.—*n.* a roving about : an irregular excursion : rambling.—*n.* **ram'bler**, one who rambles : a trailing climbing plant, esp. a rose with small clustered flowers.—*n.* and *adj.* **ram'bling.**—*adv.* **ram'blingly.** [M.E. *romblen* ; app. conn. with **roam.**]

rambutan, *ram-bōō'tən, n.* a lofty Malayan tree (*Nephelium lappaceum*), akin to the longan : its hairy edible fruit. [Malay *rambūtan*—*rambut*, hair.]

rameal, rameous. See **ramus.**

ramekin, ramequin, ramakin, *ram'ə-kin, n.* a mixture of cheese, eggs, &c., baked in separate moulds, or served on toast. [Fr. *ramequin*—obs. Flem. *rammeken.*]

ramentum, *ra-ment'əm, n.* a chaffy scale, as on ferns :—*pl.* **rament'a.** [L. *rāmentum*, a scraping —*rādēre*, to scrape.]

ramfeezle, *ram-fē'zl, v.t.* (*Scot.*) to weary out.

ramgunshoch, *ram-gun'shohh, adj.* (*Scot.*) rough.

rami, ramie, ramee, *ram'ē, n.* rhea or China-grass (*Boehmeria nivea*), a plant of the nettle family, long cultivated in China : its fibre, used for cloth, bank-note paper, gas mantles, &c. : a garment thereof. [Malay *rami.*]

ramify, &c. See under **ramus.**

Ramil(l)ie(s), *ram'i-li(z), n.* a name for several articles and modes of dress in fashion after Marlborough's victory at *Ramillies* (1706)—esp. a form of cocked hat, and a wig with a long plaited tail.— Also *adj.*

Ramism, *rā'mizm, n.* the system of logic of Peter *Ramus* (1515-72).—*ns.* and *adjs.* **Rā'mean, Rā'mist.**

rammer, rammish. See **ram.**

ramose, ramous. See under **ramus.**

ramp, *ramp, v.i.* to climb : to grow rankly : to rear as if climbing : to slope from one level to another : to rage : to range about wildly.—*v.t.* to provide with a ramp : to bend into a ramp : to snatch : to rob : to hustle into paying a fictitious debt : to swindle.—*n.* a romp, tomboy : a disorderly or loose woman : an act of ramping : an inclined plane : the slope of a wall-top or the like between two levels : an upwardly concave bend in a handrail : a swindle : a stunt worked for private profit : a worked-up excitement or craze, esp. for some gain : an exploitation of a special situation to increase prices or the like.—*adj.* **rampā'cious**, (*Dickens*) rampageous.—*n.* **rampāge'** (*U.S.* also *ram'* ; *Scot.* **rampauge, -pawj'**), turbulently or aggressively excited behaviour or rushing about.— *v.i.* to storm : to rush about wildly.—*adj.* **rampā'geous.**—*ns.* **rampā'geousness** ; **rampall'ian**, (*Shak.*) a term of abuse ; **ramp'ancy.**—*adj.* **ramp'ant**, rearing : (*her.*) standing in profile, on the left hind-leg : high-spirited : fierce : unrestrained : unchecked in growth or prevalence : (of an arch) having springers on different levels.— *adv.* **ramp'antly.**—*ns.* **ramp'er**, one who ramps : esp. one who makes a disturbance to cover the activities of others : a rampsman ; **ramps'man**, (*slang*) one who ramps bookmakers. [Fr. *ramper*, to creep, to clamber.]

rampart, *ram'pärt, -part, n.* a flat-topped defensive mound : that which defends.—*v.t.* to fortify or surround with ramparts. [Fr. *rempart*—O.Fr. *rempar*—*remparer*, to defend—L. pfx. *re-*, *ante*, *parāre*, to prepare.]

rampick, *ram'pik*, **rampike, -pīk**, *n.* (*arch.* and *U.S.*) a dead tree, or one decayed at the top, broken off, or partly burned.—*adjs.* **ram'pick, -ed.** [Origin obscure.]

rampion, *ram'yən, -i-ən, n.* a bell-flower (*Campanula Rapunculus*) whose root is eaten as a salad : any species of the kindred genus Phyteuma. [Cf. It. *raponzolo*, Ger. *rapunzel*, Fr. *raiponce.*]

rampire, *ram'pīr, n. arch.* for **rampart.**—*adj.* **ram'pired.**

ramrod. See **ram.**

ramshackle, *ram'shak'l, adj.* tumble-down. [Ety. doubtful.]

ramson, *ram'zən, n.* (orig. pl. of the now *dial.* **rams** ; usu. in double pl. form **ramsons**) wild or broad-leaved garlic. [O.E. *hramsa, hramse, hramsan* (pl.).]

ramstam, *ram'stam', adj.* and *adv.* (*Scot.*) headlong. [Poss. **ram.**]

ramus, *rā'məs, n.* a branch of anything, esp. a nerve : a process of a bone : the mandible, or its ascending part : a feather barb :—*pl.* **rā'mi.**—*adjs.* **rā'mal**, **rā'meal**, **rā'meous**, **rā'mous**, of a branch ; **rā'mate, rā'mous**, ramose (*rə-mōs', rā'mōs*) branched. — *n.* **ramification** (*ram-i-fi-kā'shən*), branching : a branch, esp. a remote branch, offshoot, or link.—*v.t.* and *v.i.* **ram'ify**, to divide into branches :—*pr.p.* **ram'ifying** ; *pa.t.* and *pa.p.* **ram'ifīed.**—*adjs.* **ram'ūlar**, of a branch ; **ram'ūlose, ram'ūlous**, having ramuli.—*n.* **ram'ūlus**, a little branch :—*pl.* **ram'ūli.** [L. *rāmus*, a branch.]

ran, *pa.t.* of **run.**

Rana, *rā'nä, n.* the typical genus of frogs, giving name to the family Ranidae (*ran'i-dē*).—*adj.* **ranarian** (*rə-nā'ri-ən*), froggy.—*n.* **rana'rium**, a place where frogs are reared.—*adjs.* **raniform** (*ran'*), frog-like; **ranine** (*rā'nīn*), of the under side of the tongue (seat of ranula); **ranivorous** (*rə-niv'ər-əs*), frog-eating.—*n.* **ranula** (*ran'ū-lä*), a cyst in the gland under the tongue (poss. from a fancied resemblance to a little frog). [L. *rāna*, dim. *rānula*, a frog, ranula.]

rana, *rä'nä*, *n.* a Rajput prince. [Hind.]

rance, *räns*, *n.* a prop, shore: a bar.—*v.t.* to prop: to bar. [Fr. *ranche*.]

rancelman. See **ranzelman.**

ranch, *rän(t)sh*, *n.* a stock-farm, as in western N. America, with its buildings and persons employed. —*v.i.* to manage or work upon a ranch.—*ns.* **ranch'er, ranchero** (*rän-chā'rō*; Sp.), **ranch'-man**, one employed in ranching; **rancheria** (*rän-chä-rē'ä*), a herdsmen's hut or village: a settlement of Indians; **ranch'ing**; **rancho** (*rän'chō*), a rude hut, or group of huts, esp. for travellers: a ranch:—*pl.* **ran'chos.** [Sp. *rancho*, mess, mess-room.]

ranch, *rän(t)sh*, *v.t.* (*Dryden*) to tear. [Cf. **race** (5).]

rancid, *ran'sid*, *adj.* rank in smell or taste, as butter or oil that is going bad.—*ns.* **rancid'ity, ran'cid-ness.** [L. *rancidus*.]

rancour, *rang'kər*, *n.* harboured bitterness: deep-seated enmity: spite: virulence: (*Shak.*) sourness. — *adj.* **ran'corous.** — *adv.* **ran'corously.** [O.Fr.,—L. *rancor*, *-ōris*, an old grudge—*rancēre*, to be rancid.]

rand, *rand*, *n.* a border, margin: a strip, esp. of flesh or of leather: (*S.Afr.*; *ränt*) a ridge overlooking a valley.—**the Rand**, the Witwatersrand goldfield. [O.E. and Du. *rand*, border.]

rand, *rand*, *v.i.* an old form of **rant**.

randan, *ran-dan'*, *n.* a din, uproar: riotous conduct: spree.

randan, *ran-dan'*, *n.* a boat rowed by three, the second with two oars.—Also **randan gig.**

random, *ran'dəm*, *n.*, *adj.*, and *adv.* tandem with three horses.

randle-balk, *ran'dl-bawk*, **-perch,** **-pərch, -tree,** *-trē*, *ns.* (*Scot.* and *N. England*) a bar in a chimney for hanging pots: **randle-tree,** (*Scott*) applied to a tall, raw-boned woman.—Also **rann'le(l)-, rann'le-, ran'tle-.** [Cf. Norw. *randa-tre—rand*, space above a fireplace.]

random, *ran'dəm*, also formerly (*Spens., Shak.*) **randon, -dən,** *n.* (*obs.*) a rush, full speed: (*Spens.*) uncontrolled or unguarded state, freedom: haphazard: (*obs.*) elevation of a gun: irregular masonry.—*adj.* haphazard, chance: fired at an elevation: uncontrolled: irregular.—*advs.* **ran'domly, ran'domwise.** [O.Fr. *randon—randir*, to gallop.]

randy, randie, *ran'di*, *adj.* (*Scot.*) boisterous: aggressively or coarsely loud-spoken.—*n.* a violent beggar, esp. a woman: a coarse virago: a romping girl. [Poss. **rand** (2).]

ranee. See **rani.**

rang, *rang*, *pa.t.* of **ring.**

range, *rānj*, *v.t.* to set in a row or rows: to assign a place among others to (esp., *refl.*, to take sides): to classify: to arrange: to straighten, level: to traverse freely or in all directions: to sail along: to bring to bear.—*v.i.* to lie in a direction: to extend: to take or have a position in a line, or alongside: to take sides: to lie evenly: to move, have freedom of movement, occur, or vary, within limits: to rove at large: to beat about, as for game: to be inconstant: to have a range.—*n.* a row or rank: a system of points in a straight line: anything extending in line, as a chain of mountains, a row of connected buildings: (*Austr.*) a mountain: a stretch of open country, esp. one used for grazing: (*U.S.*) a north and south strip of townships six miles wide: line of lie: an act of ranging: scope, compass: movement, freedom of movement, or variation between limits: space or distance between limits: area, or distance within which anything moves, can move, occurs, is possible, acts efficiently, or varies: a place for practice in shooting: firing elevation of a gun: an enclosed kitchen fireplace fitted with appliances of various kinds.—*ns.* **range'finder,** an instrument for finding the

distance of an object; **ran'ger,** a rover: a dog that beats the ground: a forest or park officer: a member of a body of troops, usu. mounted and employed in policing an area: a member of a senior branch of the Girl Guide organisation: (in *pl.*) a name sometimes taken by football clubs; **rang'ership;** **rang'iness.**—*adj.* **ran'gy,** disposed or well able to roam: roomy: long-legged and thin: (*Austr.*) mountainous.—**to range oneself,** to side, take sides: (as a Gallicism) to settle down to reputable ways, esp. on marrying. [Fr. *ranger,* to range—*rang,* a rank.]

rani, ranee, *rän'ē,* *n. fem.* of **raja.** [Hind. *rānī—*Sans. *rājñī,* queen, fem. of *rājan.*]

Ranidae, &c. See **Rana.**

rank, *rangk,* *n.* a row: a row of soldiers standing side by side (opp. to *file*): any row thought of as so placed (e.g. of squares along the player's side of a chessboard): (in *pl.*) soldiers, esp. private soldiers—often (with *the*) private soldiers collectively: (in *pl.*) persons of ordinary grade: a row of cabs awaiting hire: a cabstand: a set of organ pipes: arrangement in line: order, grade, or degree: station: high standing.—*v.t.* to place in a line: to assign to a particular class or grade: to place on the list of claims against a bankrupt: (*U.S.*) to take rank over.—*v.i.* to have a place in a rank, grade, scale, or class: to move in rank: to be admitted as a claim against the property of a bankrupt.—*adj.* **ranked,** (*Shak.*) app. bordered with rows.—*n.* **rank'er,** one who serves or has served as a private soldier: an officer who has risen from the ranks.—**rank and file,** common soldiers: ordinary people; **take rank of,** to take precedence of. [O.Fr. *renc* (Fr. *rang*), perh.—O.H.G. *hring, hrinc,* ring.]

rank, *rangk, adj.* (*obs.*) strong, lusty, vigorous: (*obs.*) violent: growing high and luxuriantly: coarsely overgrown: (*Shak.*) swollen: (*law*) excessive: (*Spens.*) abounding: (*Spens.*) dense: out-and-out, arrant, utter: over-productive: offensively strong-scented or strong-tasted: gross: foul: (*Shak.*) lustful, in heat: grossly obvious: deep-cutting.—*adv.* (*Spens.*) violently: utterly.—*adv.* **rank'ly.**—*ns.* **rank'ness; rank'-rī'der,** a hard rider: a moss-trooper: a highwayman. — *adj.* **rank'-rī'ding.** [O.E. *ranc,* proud, strong.]

ranke, *rangk,* *n.* (*Shak., As You Like It,* III. ii.) app. a jog-trot (perh. a misprint for **rack** (6)): otherwise explained as a repetition of the same rhyme like a file of so many butterwomen.

rankle, *rangk'l, v.i.* to fester: to cause festering: to go on vexing, irritating, or embittering.—*v.t.* to cause to fester: to envenom: to embitter.—*n.* a rankling. [O.Fr. *rancler, raoncler—draoncler,* app.—L.L. *dra(cu)nculus,* an ulcer, dim. of L. *dracō—*Gr. *drakōn,* dragon.]

rannel(l)-, rannie-, &c. See **randle-.**

ransack, *ran'sak* (or *-sak'*), *v.t.* to search thoroughly: to plunder: to pillage.—*n.* eager search.—*n.* **ran'sacker.** [O.N. *rannsaka — rann,* house, *sækja,* to seek.]

ranselman. See **ranzelman.**

ransom, *ran'səm, n.* redemption from captivity: price of redemption: expiation: a huge sum: an extortionate price.—*v.t.* to pay, demand, or accept ransom for: to redeem: to expiate.—*adj.* **ran'somable.**—*n.* **ran'somer.**—*adj.* **ran'someless.**—**hold to ransom,** to retain until a ransom shall be paid: to hold up to gain a concession; **put to ransom,** to offer for release for ransom. [Fr. *rançon—*L. *redemptiō, -ōnis,* redemption.]

rant, *rant, v.i.* to declaim bombastically: to storm, scold: to sing, play, or make merry, noisily.—*v.t.* to utter declamatorily.—*n.* empty declamation: bombast: a tirade: (*Scot.*) a noisy frolic: a lively tune.—*ns.* **ran'ter,** one who rants: an extravagant preacher: a member of a Commonwealth anti-nomian sect: (as a byname) a Primitive Methodist: a roisterer: (*Scot.*) a noisy musician; **ran'terism.** —*adv.* **rant'ingly.** [Obs. Du. *ranten,* to rave; L.L. *randen,* Ger. *ranzen.*]

rantipole, *rant'i-pōl, n.* a wild reckless person.— Also *adj.* [Perh. **rant.**]

rantle-. See **randle-.**

ranula. See **Rana.**

Ranunculus, rə-nung'kū-ləs, n. the buttercup genus: —*pl.* **ranun'culī, ranun'culuses.**—*adj.* **ranun'culā'ceous,** of the buttercup family (**Ranunculā'-ceae**). [L. *rānunculus,* dim. of *rāna,* a frog.]

ranz-des-vaches, ron⁰(s)'-dā-väsh', n. a French Swiss herdsman's song or alpenhorn melody. [Swiss Fr.; *ranz,* of doubtful meaning, Fr. *des vaches,* of the cows.]

ranzelman, ran'zl-mən, **rancelman, ranselman,** -sl-, n. formerly in Orkney and Shetland a constable or searcher for stolen goods. [O.N. *reynsla,* searching.]

rap, rap, n. a sharp blow: the sound of a knock.—*v.t.* and *v.i.* to strike or knock sharply: (*obs. slang*) to swear or testify, esp. falsely: to communicate by raps.—*v.t.* (*U.S.*) to censure, reprove: to utter sharply.—*v.i.* to rattle, patter:—*pr.p.* **rapp'ing;** *pa.t.* and *pa.p.* **rapped.**—*n.* **rapp'er,** one who raps: a door-knocker: a great lie or oath: a spirit-rapper. [Imit.]

rap, rap, v.t. to snatch: to grab: (*Shak.*) to carry away in spirit or with joy:—*pr.p.* **rapp'ing;** *pa.p.* **rapped** or **rapt.** [Perh. partly akin to M.L.G. *rappen,* Sw. *rappa,* to snatch; mainly a backformation from **rapt.**]

rap, rap, n. an 18th-century Irish counterfeit halfpenny: as a type of worthlessness, a whit. [Origin obscure.]

rapacious, rə-pā'shəs, adj. grasping: greedy of gain: living by prey.—*adv.* **rapā'ciously.**—*ns.* **rapā'ciousness, rapacity** (-*pas*'). [L. *rapāx,* -*ācis*—*rapĕre,* to seize and carry off.]

rape, rāp, n. (*obs.*) rapine, plunder, seizure: carnal knowledge of a woman without her legal consent. —*v.t.* to seize and carry off: to commit rape upon: (*obs.*) to ravish or transport, as with delight.—*n.* **rā'per.**—*adj.* **rā'ping,** (*her.*) tearing prey: (*obs.*) ravishing, delighting. [Prob. L. *rapĕre,* to snatch, confused with **rap** (2).]

rape, rāp, n. a division of Sussex. [Origin obscure.]

rape, rāp, n. a plant (*Brassica Napus*) near akin to the turnip, cultivated for its herbage and oil-producing seeds: applied to various closely allied species or varieties.—*ns.* **rape'-cake,** refuse of rape-seed after the oil has been expressed; **rape'-oil; rape'-seed.** [L. *rāpa, rāpum,* a turnip.]

rape, rāp, n. refuse in wine-making. [Fr. *râpe.*]

Raphanus, raf'ə-nəs, n. the radish genus.—*n.* **raphania** (rə-fā'ni-ä), ergotism (attributed by Linnaeus to wild radish seeds). [Gr. *rhaphanis.*]

raphe, rā'fē, n. a seam-like junction: the ridge on the side of an anatropous ovule continuing the funicle to the chalaza. [Gr. *rhaphē,* a seam.]

Raphia, rā'fi-ä, raf'i-ä, n. a genus of handsome pinnately-leaved palms: **raphia,** raffia. [Malagasy.]

raphis, rhaphis, rā'fis, **raphide, rhaphide,** rā'fid, n. a needle-like crystal, usu. of calcium oxalate, occurring in plant cells:—*pl.* **r(h)aphides** (raf'i-dēz, rā'fīds). [Gr. *rhaphis,* -*idos,* a needle—*rhaptein,* to sew.]

rapid, rap'id, adj. swift: quickly accomplished: steeply-sloping: (*phot.*) requiring short exposure. —*n.* a very swift-flowing part of a river with steep descent and often broken water but no actual drop (usu. in *pl.*).—*n.* **rapidity** (rə-pid'i-ti).—*adv.* **rap'idly.**—*n.* **rap'idness** (*rare*). [L. *rapidus*—*rapĕre,* to seize.]

rapier, rā'pi-ər, n. a long slender sword, suitable for thrusting. [Fr. *rapière.*]

rapine, rap'in, -in, n. plundering: prey: (*Milt.*) ravishment, transport. [L. *rapīna*—*rapĕre,* to seize.]

raploch, rap'lohh, n. and adj. (*Scot.*) homespun.

rapparee, rap-ər-ē', n. a wild Irish plunderer. [Ir. *rapaire,* half-pike, robber.]

rappee, ra-pē', n. a coarse, strong-flavoured snuff. [Fr. *râpé,* rasped, grated—*râper,* to rasp.]

rappel, rä-, rə-pel', n. call to arms by beat of drum. [Fr.]

rapper, rapping. See **rap.**

Rappist, rap'ist, **Rappite,** -īt, ns. a Harmonist, follower of George *Rapp.*

rapport, ra-por', n. relation: connexion: sympathy: emotional bond: spiritualistic touch. [Fr.]

rapprochement, ra-prosh'män⁰, n. a drawing together: establishment or renewal of cordial relations. [Fr.]

rapscallion, rap-skal'yən, n. See **rascal.**

rapt, rapt, adj. snatched or carried away: abducted: carried out of this world: transported, enraptured, entranced: wholly engrossed. [L. *raptus,* pa.p. of *rapĕre,* to seize and carry off; but partly also pa.p. of **rap** (2).]

raptor, rap'tər, n. a ravisher: a plunderer: a bird of prey, member of the abandoned order **Raptores** (-tō'rēz). — *adjs.* **raptatō'rial, raptō'rial,** predatory: adapted to predatory life. [L. *raptor,* -*ōris,* a plunderer—*rapĕre,* to seize.]

rapture, rap'tyər, n. a seizing and carrying away: extreme delight: transport: ecstasy: a paroxysm. —*v.t.* to enrapture.—*adj.* **rap'tured.**—*adj.* **rap'tureless.**—*v.i.* **rap'turise,** to go into raptures.— *n.* **rap'turist.**—*adj.* **rap'turous.**—*adv.* **rap'turously.** [**rapt.**]

rare, rār, adj. thin: not dense: sparse: seldom met with: uncommon: excellent: especially good: extraordinary: (*coll.*) used as a mere intensive (esp. in **rare** and).—*ns.* **rare'bit,** a would-be correction of (*Welsh*) **rabbit**; **rarefac'tion** (rār-i-, rar-i-), rarefying.—*adjs.* **rarefac'tive, rar'efiable.**—*v.t.* and *v.i.* **rar'efy,** to make or become less dense:—*pr.p.* **rar'efying;** *pa.t.* and *pa.p.* **rar'efied.**—*adv.* **rare'ly,** seldom: choicely: remarkably well.—*ns.* **rare'ness; rarity** (rār' or rar'i-ti), state of being rare: thinness: something valued for its scarcity: uncommonness.—**rare earth,** an oxide of a rare-earth element, any of a group of metallic elements (some of them **rare**) closely similar in chemical properties and very difficult to separate: now more usu. a rare-earth element itself. [Fr.,—L. *rārus.*]

rare, rār, adj. See **rear** (3).

rare, rār, **rear, rēr,** adj. and adv. (*obs.*) early.—*adj.* **rare'ripe,** early ripe.—*adv.* **rear'ly.** [**rathe.**]

raree-show, rār'ē-shō, n. a show carried about in a box: a spectacle. [App. a Savoyard showman's pron. of **rare show.**]

ras, räs, n. a headland: an Abyssinian prince. [Ar. *ras, ra's,* head.]

rascal, räs'kl, n. (*obs.*) the rabble: (*obs.*) one of the rabble: a knave, rogue, scamp: (playfully) a fellow: (*Shak.*) a deer out of condition.—*adj.* of the rabble: knavish: wretched: out of condition. —*n.* and *adj.* **rascaille** (räs-kä'i; *Scott*), rabble.— *ns.* **ras'caldom,** the world or conduct of rascals; **ras'calism; rascality** (-*kal*'), the rabble: character or conduct of rascals; **rascallion** (-*kal'yən*), **rapscall'ion,** a rascal: a low, mean wretch.—*adjs.* **ras'cal-like, ras'cally** (*superl.,* **Shak., ras'-calliest**). [O.Fr. *rascaille* (Fr. *racaille*), scum of the people.]

rase, rāz. Same as **raze.** See also **race** (5 and 6), and **rise.**

rash, rash, adj. over-hasty: wanting in caution: (*Shak.*) operating suddenly: (*Shak.*) calling for haste.—*adv.* rashly.—*adv.* **rash'ly.**—*n.* **rash'ness.** [Cf. Dan. and Sw. *rask*; Du. and Ger. *rasch,* rapid.]

rash, rash, n. a slight eruption on the skin. [Perh. O.Fr. *rasche* (Fr. *rache*).]

rash, rash, v.t. (*obs.*) to tear, drag. [O.Fr. *arrachier,* to uproot; cf. **race** (6).]

rash, rash, v.t. (*Spens.*) to slash: (*Shak.*) to plunge or thrust in, stick. [Variant of **raze, rase, race.**]

rash, rash, v.i. (*obs.*) to dash, rush.—*v.t.* (*Shak.*) to stick, thrust forcibly. [Origin obscure.]

rash, räsh, n. a Scots form of **rush** (plant).

rasher, rash'ər, n. a thin slice of bacon. [Poss. from **rash** (4).]

Raskolnik, ras-kol'nik, n. in Russia, a dissenter from the Orthodox Church. [Russ.]

rasorial, ra-, rə-sō'ri-əl, adj. scraping the ground for food.—*n.pl.* **Rasō'res** (-rēz), an obsolete order, gallinaceous birds with or without the pigeons. [L. *rāsor,* -*ōris,* scraper.]

rasp, räsp, n. a coarse file: any similar surface: a mollusc's tongue: an insect's stridulating apparatus: a rasp at a door: a grating sound or feeling. —*v.t.* to grate as with a rasp: to grate upon: to

risp : to utter gratingly.—*v.i.* to have a grating effect : to scrape, as on a fiddle.—*ns.* **rasp′atory**, a surgeon's rasp ; **rasp′er**, one who, or that which, rasps : (*coll.*) a difficult fence ; **rasp′-house** (Du. *rasphuis*), a house of correction, where dye-wood was rasped ; **rasp′ing**, a filing.—*adj.* grating, harsh.— *adv.* **rasp′ingly**.—*adj.* **rasp′y**, rough. [O.Fr. *raspe* (Fr. *râpe*) ; perh. Gmc.]

rasp, *räsp*, *n.* (now *coll.* and *Scot.*) a raspberry.—*n.* **raspberry** (*räz′bər-i*), the fruit of *Rubus Idaeus* : the plant producing it : extended to some kindred species : (*slang*) a sign of disapproval, esp. a noise produced by blowing hard with the tongue between the lips.—*adj.* of, made with, or like raspberry. — *n.* **rasp′berry-bush.** — **raspberry jam tree**, an Australian acacia (from the smell of its wood). [Earlier *raspis* ; origin unknown.]

rasse, *ras′(ə)*, *n.* a small civet. [Jav. *rase*.]

rast, *räst* or *räst*, a Spenserian *pa.p.* of **race**=**raze**.

raster, *ras′tər*, *n.* (*television*) a complete set of lines appearing at the receiver as a rectangular patch of light. [Perh.—L. *rāstrum*, as next word.]

rastrum, *ras′trəm*, *n.* a music-pen. [L. *rāstrum*, rake.]

rasure, **razure**, *rā′zh(y)ər*, *n.* the act of scraping or shaving : erasure : obliteration. [L. *rāsūra.*]

rat, *rat*, *n.* any of the larger animals of the genus *Mus* (distinguished from *mouse*) : extended to various kindred or superficially similar animals : a renegade, turn-coat (from the rat's alleged desertion of a doomed ship) : a strike-breaker : a worker for less than recognised wages : a miserable or ill-looking specimen.—*v.i.* to hunt or catch rats : to desert or change sides for unworthy motives : (of a workman) to work as a rat :—*pr.p.* **ratt′-ing** ; *pa.t.* and *pa.p.* **ratt′ed.**—*ns.* **rat′-catcher**, a professional killer of rats : unconventional hunting garb ; **rat′-catching** ; **rat′-flea**, a flea that infests rats ; **rat′-hole** ; **rat′-hunting** ; **rat′-kangaroo′**, the potoroo, a marsupial kangaroo-rat ; **rat′-pit**, an enclosure where rats are worried by dogs ; **rat′-poison**, any poison for rats.—*adj.* **rat′proof.**—*interj.* **rats**, (*slang*) expressing contemptuous in-credulity.—*ns.* **rats′bane**, poison for rats, esp. white arsenic : a name for many poisonous plants ; **rat′s-tail**, **rat′-tail**, the tail of a rat : anything like a rat's tail : a thin coherent dangling lock of hair : an excrescence on a horse's leg.—*adj.* **rat′s-tail**, **rat′-tail**, **rat′-tailed**, having a tail like a rat : like a rat's tail : of a spoon, ridged along the back of the bowl.—*ns.* **rat′er**, a killer of rats, esp. a dog : one who rats ; **ratt′ery**, apostasy : a place where rats are kept or abound ; **ratt′ing**, apostasy : rat-hunting.—Also *adj.*—*adj.* **ratt′ish**, rat-like : rat-infested.—*n.* **rat′-trap**, a trap for catching rats : a toothed bicycle pedal.—Also *adj.* —*adj.* **ratt′y**, rat-like : rat-infested : wretched : (*slang*) angry, irritable.—**smell a rat**, to have a suspicion of something afoot. [O.E. *ræt* ; cf. Ger. *ratte.*]

rat, *rat*, *v.t.* (in imprecations) for **rot**. [Cf. **drat.**]

rata, *rä′tä*, *n.* a myrtaceous New Zealand tree (Metrosideros) with hard wood. [Maori.]

ratable, **rateable**, *rā′tə-bl*, *adj.* See **rate.**

ratafia, *rat-ə-fē′ä*, *n.* a flavouring essence made with the essential oil of almonds : a cordial or liqueur flavoured with fruit-kernels : an almond biscuit or cake. [Fr. ; origin unknown ; cf. **tafia.**]

ratan, *ra-tan′*, *n.* Same as **rattan.**

rataplan, *rat-ə-plan′*, *n.* a drumming sound. [Fr.]

rat-a-tat, *rat-ə-tat′.* Same as **rat-tat.**

ratch, *rach*, *n.* a ratchet : a ratchet-wheel.—*ns.* **ratch′et**, a click or pawl ; **ratch′et-wheel**, a wheel with inclined teeth with which a pawl engages. [Cf. Ger. *ratsche*, Fr. *rochet.*]

ratch. Same as **reach.**

ratch. Same as **race** (4).

rate, *rāt*, *n.* (*Shak.*) estimated amount or value : (*Shak.*) estimation : (*obs.*) a fixed quantity : price or cost : amount corresponding : ratio : esp. time-ratio, speed : amount determined according to a rule or basis : a standard : a class or rank, esp. of ships or of seamen : manner, mode : extent, degree : (often *pl.*) an amount levied by a local authority according to the assessed value of property : a clock's gain or loss in unit time.—*v.t.*

(*Shak.*) to allot : (*Shak.*) to calculate : to estimate : to value : to settle the relative rank, scale, or position of : to value for purpose of rate-paying.—*v.i.* to be placed in a certain class.—*n.* **rāt(e)abil′ity**, —*adj.* **rāt(e)′able.**—*adv.* **rāt(e)′ably.**—*ns.* **rāte′-cutting**, a lowering of charges to obtain traffic ; **rāte′payer**, one who pays a local rate ; **rāt′er**, one who makes an estimate : (in composition) a ship, &c., of a given rate (as *second-rater*) ; **rāt′ing**, a fixing of rates : classification according to grade : the class of any member of a crew : a sailor of such a class : the tonnage-class of a racing yacht. [O.Fr., —L.L. *rata* (*pars*), reckoned (part), rate—*pa.p.* of L. *rērī*, *rātus*, to think, judge.]

rate, *rāt*, *v.t.* to scold : to chide : to reprove : to drive by scolding.—*v.i.* to scold.—*n.* a reproof to a dog. [M.E. *raten* ; origin obscure.]

rate. Same as **ret.**

Ratel, *rä′təl*, *rä′təl*, *n.* a badger-like genus (Mellivora) of Africa and India, akin to the gluttons. [S.Afr. Du. *ratel*, app.—Du. *raat*, honeycomb.]

rath, *räth*, **rathe**, *rädh*, *adj.* (*arch.*) quick : eager : early :—*comp.* **rather** (*rädh′ər* ; *Spens.*), earlier ; *superl.* **rath′est**, (*obs.* or *dial.*) earliest.—*adv.* **rathe** (*rādh* ; *Milt.*), early :—*comp.* **rather** (see below) ; *superl.* (*obs.*) **rath′est.** [O.E. *hræd* (rarely *hræth*), quick, *hræthe*, *hrathe*, quickly ; O.N. *hrathr.*]

rath, *räth*, *n.* a prehistoric hill-fort. [Ir.]

rather, *rä′dhər*, *adv.* (*Shak.*) sooner, more quickly : more readily : more willingly : in preference : more than otherwise : more properly : somewhat, in some degree :—*irreg. superl.* **ra′therest** (*Shak.*). —*interj.* **ra′ther** (sometimes affectedly *rä-dhər′*), I should think so : yes, indeed.—*adv.* (*coll.*) **ra′therish.**—**the rather**, all the more. [Comp. of **rath** ; O.E. *hrathor.*]

ratheripe, *rädh′rīp*, **rathripe**, *räth′rīp*, *adj.* (*arch.* and *dial.*) early ripe.—*n.* an early-ripening variety. [**rath**(e), **ripe.**]

ratify, *rat′i-fī*, *v.t.* to approve and sanction : to give validity to :—*pr.p.* **rat′ifying** ; *pa.t.* and *pa.p.* **rat′ified.**—*ns.* **ratifica′tion** ; **rat′ifier.** [Fr. *ratifier* —L. *rātus*, pa.p. of *rērī* (see **rate** (1)), *facĕre*, to make.]

ratine, **ratteen**, *rat-ēn′*, *n.* a rough, open dress-fabric. [Fr. *ratine.*]

ratio, *rā′shi-ō*, *rā′shi-ō*, *rā′shō*, *rä′shi-ō*, *n.* the relation of one thing to another of which the quotient is the measure : quotient : proportion : (*rare*) a portion, allowance. —**compound**, **inverse**, **ratio** (see **compound**, **inverse**). [L. *rătiō*, -*ōnis*, reason—*rērī*, *rătus*, to think.]

ratiocinate, *rat-* or *rash-i-os′i-nāt*, *v.i.* to reason. —*n.* **ratiocina′tion.**—*adjs.* **ratioc′inative**, **ratioc′-inatory.** [L. *ratiōcinārī*, -*ātus.*]

ration, *ra′shən*, sometimes *rā′*, *n.* a fixed allowance or portion : (in *pl.*, *coll.*) food.—*v.t.* to put on an allowance : to supply with rations : to restrict the supply of to so much for each.—*ns.* **ra′tion-book**, **-card**, a book, card, of coupons or vouchers for rationed commodities ; **ra′tion-money**, money in lieu of rations. [Fr.,—L. *ratiō*, -*ōnis.*]

rational, *rash′ən-əl*, *adj.* of the reason : endowed with reason : agreeable to reason : sane : intelligent : judicious : commensurable with natural numbers.—*n.* a rational being or quantity : (in *pl.*) rational dress, i.e. knickerbockers instead of skirt. —*ns.* **rationale** (*rash-i-ō-nä′li*, -*yə-nä′li*), under-lying principle : a rational account : a theoretical explanation or solution ; **rationalisation** (*rash-nəl-ī-zā′shən*).—*v.t.* **rat′ionalise**, to make rational : to free from irrational quantities : to conform to reason : to reorganise scientifically : to interpret rationalistically : to substitute conscious reasoning for unconscious motivation in explaining.—*v.i.* to think, or argue, rationally or rationalistically : to employ reason, rationalism, or rationalisation.— *ns.* **rat′ionalism**, a system of belief regulated by reason, not authority : a disposition to apply to religious doctrines the same critical methods as to science and history, and to attribute all phenomena to natural rather than miraculous causes ; **rat′ion-alist.**—*adj.* **rationalist′ic.**—*adv* **rationalist′ic-ally.**—*n.* **rationality** (*rash-ən-al′i-ti*), quality of being rational : the possession or due exercise of reason : reasonableness. — *adv.* **rat′ionally. — rational horizon** (see horizon). [L. *rationālis, -e* —*ratiō.*]

rational, *rash′ən-əl, n.* the Jewish high-priest's breastplate : a bishop's vestment like the pallium. [L. * rationāle,* Vulgate translation of Gr. *logion,* oracle.]

ratite, *rat′īt, adj.* having a keel-less breastbone : of the Ratitae (*rā-tī′tē*), flightless birds—ostrich, rhea, emu, kiwi, &c. [L. *ratis,* raft.]

ratlin, rattlin, -line, -ling, *rat′lin, n.* one of the small lines forming steps of the rigging of ships. [Origin obscure.]

ratoon, *rat-, rət-ōōn′, n.* a new shoot from the ground after cropping, esp. of sugar-cane or cotton.—*v.i.* to send up ratoons.—*v.t.* to cut down so as to obtain ratoons.—*n.* **ratoon′er,** a plant that ratoons. [Sp. *retoño,* shoot.]

rat-rhyme, *rat′rīm, n.* (*Scot.*) a bit of doggerel : a screed.

rattan, ratan, *rā-tan′, n.* a climbing palm (Calamus or other) with very long thin stem : a cane made of it. [Malay *rōtan.*]

rattan, *rə-tan′, n.* the continuous beat of a drum.

rat-tat, *rat′-tat′, n.* a knocking sound. [Imit.]

ratteen. Same as ratine.

ratten, *rat′n, v.t.* to practise sabotage upon.

ratter, ratting, &c. See rat.

rattle, *rat′l, v.i.* to make a quick succession or alternation of short hard sounds : to move along rapidly with a rattle : to chatter briskly and emptily. —*v.t.* to cause to rattle : (*Shak.*) to assail with rattling : to utter glibly, as by rote : to perform or push through to completion in a rapid, perfunctory, or noisy manner : (*obs.*) to scold loudly : (*slang*) to fluster, disconcert, irritate.—*n.* an instrument or toy for rattling : a watchman's or merry-maker's instrument for making a whirring noise : (*old slang*) a dice-box : a plant whose seeds rattle in the capsule—applied to two scrophulaceous plants, *yellow-rattle* or cock's-comb (*Rhinanthus Crista-galli*) and *red-rattle* or marsh lousewort (*Pedicularis palustris*) : the rings of a rattlesnake's tail : a vivacious prattler : the sound of rattling : the crackling of paper : a sound in the throat of a dying person : racket.—*ns.* **ratt′lebag,** a rattle or rattling apparatus : (*Scot.*) one who causes commotion ; **ratt′le-brain, -head, -pate,** a shallow, voluble, volatile person.—*adjs.* **ratt′le-brained, -headed, -pated.**—*ns.* **ratt′ler,** a rattle : (*old slang*) a coach : (*coll.*) a rattlesnake : (*coll.*) a telling blow : (*coll.*) an excellent specimen of the kind ; **ratt′lesnake,** a venomous American pit-viper (Crotalus) with rattling horny rings on the tail ; **ratt′le-trap,** a contemptuous name for any apparatus, equipment, finery, bric-à-brac : a rickety vehicle : (*slang*) the mouth ; **ratt′ling.**—*adj.* making a rattle : smart, lively : (*coll.*) strikingly good. —Also *adv.* [M.E. *ratelen* ; cf. Ger. *rasseln,* Du. *ratelen,* to rattle ; connexion with O.E. plant names *hratele, hrætelwyrt* is questioned.]

rattling. Same as ratline.

ratton, *rat′n, n.* (now *Northern*) a rat. [Fr. *raton.*]

raucle, *rawk′l, adj.* (*Scot.*) rough : vigorous : hale.

raucous, *raw′kəs, adj.* hoarse.—*adv.* **rau′cously.** —*n.* **rau′cousness.**—*adj.* **raucid** (*raw′-sid* ; *Lamb*), raucous. [L. *raucus,* hoarse.]

raught, *rawt,* obs. *pa.t.* and *pa.p.* of reach (1 and 2) and reck.

raun (*Scott*). Same as **rawn.**

raunch, *rawnsh, v.t.* (*Spens.*). Same as race (6).

raunge, *rawnj,* an obs. form of range.

ravage, *rav′ij, v.t.* and *v.i.* to lay waste : to destroy : to pillage.—*n.* devastation : ruin.—*n.* **rav′ager.** [Fr. *ravager*—*ravir,* to carry off by force—L. *rapēre.*]

rave, *rāv, v.i.* to rage : to talk as if mad, delirious, or enraptured.—*v.t.* to utter wildly.—*n.* **rā′ver.**— *n.* and *adj.* **rā′ving.**—*adv.* **rā′vingly.** [Perh. O.Fr. *raver,* which may be—L. *rabēre,* to rave.]

rave, *rāv, n.* a side piece of a wagon. [Ety. obscure.]

rave, *rāv,* (*Scot.*) *pa.t.* of **rive.**

ravel, *rav′l, v.t.* to entangle : to disentangle, untwist, unweave, unravel (usu. with *out*).—*v.i.* to

become entangled : to be untwisted or unwoven : (*obs.*) to search (with *into*) : (*pr.p.* **rav′elling** ; *pa.t.* and *pa.p.* **rav′elled**).—*n.* a tangle : a broken thread.—*ns.* **rav′elling,** a ravelled out thread ; **rav′elment.** [App. Du. *ravelen.*]

ravel bread, *rav′l bred, n.* (*obs.* or *dial.*) wholemeal bread, intermediate between white and brown. —Also ravelled bread.

ravelin, *rav′lin, n.* a detached work with two embankments raised before the counterscarp. [Fr.]

raven, *rā′vn, n.* a large glossy black species of crow. —*adj.* black as a raven.—*ns.* **rā′ven('s)-bone,** the gristle on the spoon of the brisket, the raven's perquisite in the chase ; **rā′ven('s)-duck,** fine hempen sail-cloth. [O.E. *hræfn* ; O.N. *hrafn.*]

raven, *rav′in, n.* (see ravin).—*v.t.* to devour hungrily or greedily : to hunger intensely for.— *v.i.* to prey rapaciously : to be intensely hungry : to roam about hungrily after prey.—*adj.* **rav′enous,** plundering : rapacious : voracious : intensely hungry.—*adv.* **rav′enously.**—*n.* **rav′enousness.** [O.Fr. *ravine,* plunder—L. *rapīna,* plunder.]

ravin, also **raven, ravine,** *rav′in, n.* rapine : preying : (*Spens., Milt.*) prey.—*adj.* (*Shak.*) ravening. —*v.t.* and *v.i.* (see **raven,** *vb.*).—*adj.* **rav′in′d,** (*Shak.*) prob. sated, gorged. [Same as foregoing.]

ravine, *rə-vēn′, n.* a deep, narrow gorge.—*adj.* **ravined′,** scored with ravines : trenched. [Fr.,— L. *rapīna,* rapine, violence.]

ravish, *rav′ish, v.t.* to seize or carry away by violence : to abduct : to snatch away from sight or from the world : to rape : to enrapture.—*n.* **rav′isher.**—*adj.* **rav′ishing,** delighting to rapture : transporting. — *adv.* **rav′ishingly.** — *n.* **rav′ishment.** [Fr. *ravir, raviss-*—L. *rapēre,* to seize and carry off.]

raw, *raw, adj.* not altered from its natural state : not cooked or dressed : unwrought : not prepared or manufactured : not mixed : having the skin abraded or removed : showing through the skin : crude : untrained : out of condition : red and inflamed : immature : inexperienced : chilly and damp.—*n.* a skinned, sore, or sensitive place : the raw state : that which is raw.—*adjs.* **raw′bone** (*Spens.*), **raw′boned,** with little flesh on the bones : gaunt.—*n.* **raw′head (-and-bloody-bones),** a bugbear or pair of bugbears to frighten children. —*adj.* **raw′hide,** of untanned leather.—*n.* a rope or whip of untanned leather.—*adj.* **raw′ish.**—*adv.* **raw′ly.**—*n.* **raw′ness.**—a **raw deal,** harsh, inequitable treatment ; **raw material,** material (often in its natural state) that serves as the starting point of a manufacturing or technical process : (*fig.*) that out of which something is made, or makable, or may develop. [O.E. *hréaw* ; Du. *rauw,* O.N. *hrár,* Ger. *roh.*]

rawn, raun, *rawn, n.* (*Scot.*) fish-roe : a female fish. [Cf. Dan. *ravn,* roe.]

rax, *raks, v.t.* (*Scot.*) to stretch : to strain : to reach : to reach out, hand.—*v.i.* to stretch : to reach out. —*n.* a stretch : a strain. [O.E. *raxan.*]

ray, *rā, n.* (*obs.*) array.—*v.t.* to array : to dress : (*Shak.*) to defile, dirty. [array.]

ray, *rā, n.* a line along which light or other energy, or a stream of particles, is propagated : a narrow beam : a gleam of intellectual light : a look or glance : a radiating line or part : the radially extended fringing outer part of an inflorescence : a supporting spine in a fin.—*v.t.* to radiate : to furnish with rays.—*v.i.* to radiate.—*adj.* **rayed.**— *n.* **ray′-fungus,** a bacterium (Actinomyces) that forms radiating threads, some species pathogenic.— *adj.* **ray′less.** [O.Fr. *rais* (accus. *rai*)—L. *radius,* a rod.]

ray, *rā, n.* a skate, thornback, torpedo, or kindred elasmobranch fish. [Fr. *raie*—L. *raia.*]

ray. Same as re (1).

rayah, *rī′ä, n.* a non-Mohammedan subject of Turkey. [Ar. *ra′īyah*—*ra′ā,* to pasture.]

rayle, *rayne,* old spellings of rail, rain, reign.

rayon, *rā′ən, n.* (*Spens.*) a ray : artificial silk. [Fr. *rayon,* ray.]

raze, *rāz, n.* (*Shak.*). Same as race (3).

raze, *rāz, v.t.* to graze : to scrape : to erase : to slash, cut into ornamental devices : to lay level with the ground.—*adj.* **razed.** [Fr. *raser*—L. *rādĕre*, *rāsum*, to scrape.]

razee, *rä-zē′, n.* a ship cut down by reducing the number of decks. [Fr. *rasé*, cut down.]

razor, *rā′zor, n.* a keen-edged implement for shaving.—*adj.* **rā′zorable,** (*Shak.*) fit to be shaved.—*n.* **rā′zor-back,** a sharp ridge: a rorqual: a sharp-backed pig.—*adj.* sharply ridged.—*ns.* **rā′zor-bill,** a species of auk, with compressed bill; **rā′zor-blade; rā′zor-edge,** a very fine sharp edge, as that on which a balance swings: a critically balanced situation; **rā′zor-fish,** a lamellibranch mollusc (Solen), with shell like a razor handle; **rā′zor-shell,** its shell, or the animal itself; **rā′zor-strop.**—**Occam's razor** (see **Occamism**). [O.Fr. *rasour*; see **raze** (2).]

razure; Same as **rasure.**

razz, *raz, n.* raspberry in slang sense.—*v.t.* and *v.i.* to jeer (at).

razzia, *raz′yä, n.* a pillaging incursion. [Fr., Algerian Ar. *ghāzīah*.]

razzle-dazzle, *raz′l-daz′l, n.* (*slang*) a rowdy frolic or spree.—Also **razz′le.** [App. from **dazzle.**]

re, *rā, n.* (*mus.*) the second note of the scale in sol-fa notation—also anglicised in spelling as **ray.** [See **Aretinian.**]

re, *rē, prep.* (*commercial jargon*) concerning. [L. *in rē* (abl. of *rēs*, thing), in the matter.]

re, *rē, n.* See **ruff** (2).

re-, *rē-* (see *Prefixes*), again: back—used so freely, esp. with verbs, that it is impossible to give a full list; see also separate articles following.—*v.t.* **rēabsorb′.**—*n.* **rēabsorp′tion.**—*vs.t.* **rēaccus′-tom; rēacquire′; rēaddress′; rēadjust′.**—*ns.* **rēadjust′ment; rēadmiss′ion.** — *v.t.* **rē-admit′.**—*n.* **rēadmitt′ance.**—*v.t.* **rēadopt′.**—*n.* **rēadop′tion.**—*n., v.t.,* and *v.i.* **rēadvance′.**—*v.t.* and *v.i.***rēadvise′.**—*v.t.***rēaffirm′.**—*n.* **rēaffirmā′-tion.**—*v.t.* **rēaffor′est.**—*n.* **rēafforestā′tion.**—*v.t.* **rēallot′.**—*n.* **rēallot′ment.**—*vs.t.* **rē-al′ter; rē-amend′.**—*n.* **rē-amend′ment.**—*v.t.* **rē-annex′.**—*n.* **rē-annexa′tion.**—*v.t.* **rēappar′el.**—*v.i.* **rē-appear′.**—*ns.* **rēappear′ance; rēapplica′tion.** *v.i.* **rēapply′.**—*v.t.* **rēappoint′.**—*n.* **rēappoint′-ment.** — *v.t.* **rēappor′tion.**—*n.* **rēappor′tion-ment; rēapprais′al.**—*v.t.* **rēappraise′.**—*ns.* **rē-appraise′ment; rēapprais′er.**—*v.i.* **rēarise′.**—*v.t.* and *v.i.* **rēarm′.**—*n.* **rēarm′ament.**—*v.t.* **rēarrange′.**—*n.* **rēarrange′ment.**—*n.* and *v.i.* **rēarrest′.**—*v.t.* and *v.i.* **rēascend′.**—*ns.* **rēascen′-sion; rēascent′; rēassem′blage.**—*v.t.* and *v.i.* **rēassem′ble.**—*n.* **rēassemb′ly.**—*v.t.* **rēassert′.** —*n.* **rēasser′tion.**—*v.t.* **rēassess′.**—*n.* **rēassess′-ment.**—*v.t.* **rēassign′.**—*n.* **rēassign′ment.**—*v.t.* **rēassume′.**—*n.* **rēassump′tion.**—*vs.t.* and *vs.t.* **rēawake′; rēawak′en.**—*n.* **rēawak′ening.**—*v.t.* **rēbaptise′.**—*ns.* **rēbap′tism; rēbap′tist.**—*v.t.* **rēbind′:**—*pa.t.* and *pa.p.* **rēbound′.**—*vs.i.* **rē-bloom′; rēbloss′om.**—*v.t.* and *v.i.* **rēboil′.**—*p.adj.* **rēborn′.**—*vs.t.* **rēbrace′; rēbroad′cast.**—Also *n.*—*vs.t.* **rēbuild′; rēbur′y; rēcal′culate; rēcen′tre; rēcharge′; rēclose′; rēclothe′; rēcoin′.**—*ns.* **rēcoin′age; rēcolonisā′tion.**—*v.t.* **rēcol′onise.**—*n.* **rēcombina′tion.**—*v.t.* and *v.i.* **rēcombine′.**—*v.t.* and *v.i.* **rēcommence′.**—*n.* **rēcommence′ment.**—*n., v.t.,* and *v.i.* **rēcom-miss′ion.**—*v.t.* **rēcommit′,** to commit back: to commit again.—*ns.* **rēcommit′ment; rēcom-mitt′al.**—*vs.t.* **rēcompact′; rēcompose′.**—*ns.* **rēcomposi′tion; rēcondensā′tion.**—*v.t.* and *v.i.* **rēcondense′.**—*vs.t.* **rēconfirm′; rēcon′quer.**—*ns.* **rēcon′quest; rēconsecrā′tion.**—*v.t.* **rēcon′-secrate; rēconsid′er.**—*ns.* **rēconsiderā′tion; rēconsolidā′tion.**—*vs.t.* and *vs.i.* **rēconsol′idate; rēcross′.**—*v.t.* **rēcrystallisā′tion.**—*v.t.* and *v.i.* **rēcryst′allise.**—*vs.t.* **rēdec′orate; rēded′icate.** —*v.i.* and *v.t.* **rēdescend′.**—*v.t.* **rēdescribe′.**—*n.* **rēdetermina′tion.**—*vs.t.* **rēdeter′mine; rē-devel′op(e).**—*n.* **rēdevel′opment.**—*vs.t.* **rēdip′; rēdirect′; rēdiscov′er.**—*ns.* **rēdiscov′erer; rē-discov′ery; rēdissolu′tion.**—*vs.t.* **rēdissolve′; rēdistil′.**—*n.* **rēdistillā′tion.**—*v.t.* **rēdistrib′ute.** —*n.* **rēdistribu′tion.**—*v.t.* and *v.i.* **rēdivide′.**—*n.* **rēdivis′ion.**—*v.t.* and *v.i.* **rē′-do′:**—*pa.t.* **rē′-did′;** *pa.p.* **rē′-done′.**—*v.t.* and *v.i.* **rēdraw′.**—*vs.t.* **rēdrive′;**

rē-ed′it; rē-ed′ucate.—*n.* **rē-educā′tion.**—*v.t.* **re-elect′.**—*n.* **rē-elec′tion.**—*v.t.* **rē-el′evate.**—*ns.* **rē-elevā′tion; rē-eligibil′ity.**—*adj.* **rē-el′-igible.**—*v.i.* and *v.t.* **rē-embark′.**—*ns.* **rē-em-barkā′tion; rē-embod′iment.**—*v.t.* **rē-embod′y.** —*v.i.* **rē-emerge′.**—*n.* **rē-emer′gence.**—*v.t.* **rē-enact′.**—*n.* **rē-enact′ment.**—*vs.i.* **rē-encour′-age; rē-endow′.**—*n.* **rē-endow′ment.**—*v.t.* and *v.i.* **rē-engage′.**—*n.* **rē-engage′ment.**—*v.t.* and *v.i.* **rē-enlist′.**—*ns.* **rē-enlist′er; rē-enlist′ment.** — *v.t.* **rē-enter′.**—*n.* **rē-erec′tion.** — *v.t.* **rē-estab′lish.**—*ns.* **rē-estab′lishment; rē-examinā′tion.**—*v.t.* **rē-exam′ine.**—*n.* **rē-exist′.**—*n.* **rē-exist′ence.**—*v.t.* and *v.i.* **rē-expand′.**—*n.* **rē-expan′sion.**—*v.t.* **rē-export′.**—*ns.* **rē-ex′port; rē-exportā′tion.**—*vs.t.* **rēface′; rēfash′ion.**—*n.* **rēfash′ionment.**—*v.t.* **rēfledge′.**—*v.t.* and *v.i.* **rēfloat′.**—*vs.t.* **rēfoot′; rēform′ulate.**—*n.* **rēfortificā′tion.**—*vs.t.* **rēfort′ify; rēfound′.**—*ns.* **rēfoundā′tion; rēfound′er.**—*n.* and *v.t.* **rēfrac′-ture.**—*vs.t.* **rēframe′; rēfur′bish.**—*v.t.* and *v.i.* **rēfur′nish.**—*v.t.* **rēgive′.**—*n.* and *v.t.* **rēgrant′.**—*vs.t.* **rēgrind′; rēgroup′.**—*n.* **rēgrowth′.**—*v.t.* **rēhand′le.**—*n.* **rēhand′ling.**—*v.t.* **rēheat′.**—*n.* **rēheat′er.**—*vs.t.* **rēheel′; rē-ignite′; rēillume′;** **rēillum′ine; rēimpose′.**—*n.* **rēimposi′tion.**—*v.t.* and *adj.* **rēincar′nate.** — *ns.* **rēincarna′-tion; rēincarnā′tionism,** belief in reincarnation of the soul; **rēincarnā′tionist.** — *vs.t.* **rē-increase′; rēinfuse′; rēinhab′it; rēinsert′.** —*n.* **rēinser′tion.**—*vs.t.* **rēinspire′; rēinspir′it;** **rēinter′.**—*n.* **rēinter′ment; rēinter′pret.**—*n.* **rēinterpretā′tion.**—*v.t.* **rēinterr′ogate.**—*n.* **rēinterroga′tion.**—*v.t.* **rēintroduce′.**—*n.* **rēin-troduc′tion.**—*v.t.* **rēinvolve′.**—*adj.* **rēiss′uable.** —*v.t.* and *n.* **rēiss′ue.**—*v.t.* and *v.i.* **rēkin′dle.**—*v.t.* **rēlet′.**—*vs.t.* and *vs.i.* **rēlight′; rēload′.**—*n.* **rēmarr′iage.**—*v.t.* and *v.i.* **rēmarr′y.**—*vs.t.* **rēmod′el; rēmon′etise; rēmould′; rēname′;** **rēnum′ber.**—*n.* **rēoccupa′tion.**—*v.t.* **rēocc′upy.** —*v.t.* and *v.i.* **rēo′pen.**—*v.t.* **rēordain′.**—*n.* **rē-ordina′tion; rēorganisā′tion.**—*vs.t.* **rēor′gan-ise; rēpā′per; rēpeo′ple.**—*n.* **rēperus′al.**—*vs.t.* **rēperuse′; rēplant′.**—*n.* **rēplanta′tion.**—*v.t.* **rēplay′.**—*n.* (*rē′*).—*vs.t.* **rēpot′.**—*n.* **rēpott′ing.**—*v.t.* **rē′read′** (*-rēd*):—*pa.t.* and *pa.p.* **rē′read′** (*-red*).—*v.t.* and *v.i.* **rēreg′ister.**—*v.t.* and *n.* **rē′reseat′.**—*vs.t.* **rēseat′; rēsell′:**—*pa.t.* and *pa.p.* **rēsōld′.**—*v.t.* and *v.i.* **rēsett′le.**—*n.* **rēsett′lement.**—*v.t.* **rēshape′.**—*v.t.* and *n.* **rēship′.**—*n.* **rēship′-ment.**—*v.t.* and *n.* **rēshuff′le.**—*v.t.* and *v.i.* **rē-sign** (*rē′-sīn′*), to sign again.—*v.t.* **rēspell′.**—*v.t.* and *v.i.* **rēstart′.**—*n.* **rēstart′er.**—*v.t.* **rēstate′.**—*n.* **rēstate′ment.**—*vs.t.* **rēstock′; rētell′:**—*pa.t.* and *pa.p.* **rētold′.**—*n.* **rētell′er.**—*vs.t.* **rētie′; rē-transfer′.**—*n.* **rētrans′fer; rētri′al.**—*vs.t.* **rē-trim′; rēturf′; rēurge′; rēuse** (*-ūz′*).—*n.* (*-ūs′*).—*vs.t.* **rēutt′er; rēvac′cinate.**—*n.* **rēvaccinā′-tion.**—*v.t.* and *n.* **rēvamp′.**—*v.t.* and *v.i.* **rēvic-tual** (*rē-vit′l*):—*pr.p.* **revict′ualling;** *pa.t.* and *pa.p.* **revict′ualled.**—*v.t.* and *n.* **rēvis′it.**—*ns.* **rēvis′itant; rēvisitā′tion.**—*vs.t.* **rēwind′:**—*pa.t.* and *pa.p.* **rēwound′; rēwire′; rēword′.**—*v.t.* **rē-write′:**—*pa.t.* **rēwrote′;** *pa.p.* **rēwritt′en.**

reach, *rēch, v.t.* to stretch forth, hold out: to hand, pass: to deal, strike: to succeed in touching or getting: to arrive at: to extend to: to attain to: to get at: (*obs.*) to take, snatch, seize: (*obs.*) to stretch, lengthen out.—*v.i.* to stretch out the hand: to extend: to amount: to attain: to succeed in going or coming:—*pa.t.* and *pa.p.* **reached,** (*obs.*) **raught** (*rawt*).—*n.* act or power of reaching: extent of stretch: range, scope: (*obs.*) artifice: a stretch or portion between defined limits, as of a stream between bends: (*naut.*) the distance traversed between tacks: (*obs.*) a bay.—*adj.* **reach′-able.** — *n.* **reach′er.**—*p.adj.* **reach′ing.**—*adjs.* **reach′less,** unattainable; **reach′ - me - down,** ready-made.—*n.* (often in *pl.*) ready-made or second-hand attire: trousers. [O.E. *rǣcan* (pa.t. *rǣhte, rähte*; pa.p. *gerǣht*) Ger. *reichen*, to reach.]

reach. Same as **retch.**

react, re-act, *rē-akt′, rē′akt′, v.t.* to act anew.—*v.i.* **react** (*ri-akt′*), to return an impulse in the opposite direction: to act in return: to act with mutual effect : to act in resistance : to swing back in the opposite direction : to respond to a stimulus : to undergo chemical change produced by a reagent : (loosely) to act, behave.—*ns.* reac′tance, (*elect.*) the component of impedance due to inductance or capacitance ; reac′tant, (*chem.*) a substance taking part in a reaction ; reac′tion, action resisting other action : mutual action : an action or change in an opposite direction : backward tendency from revolution, reform, or progress : response to stimulus : the chemical action of a reagent : a transformation within the nucleus of an atom : acidity or alkalinity ; reac′tionarism ; reac′tionarist.— *adj.* reac′tionary, of or favouring reaction.—*n.* one who attempts to revert to past political conditions. —*ns.* reac′tionist ; reac′tion-time, the interval between stimulus and reaction.—*v.t.* reac′tivate, to restore to an activated state.—*n.* reactivā′tion. —*adj.* reac′tive.—*adv.* reac′tively.—*ns.* reac′- tiveness, reactivity (rē-ak-tiv′i-ti) ; reactor (ri-ak′tər).—(nuclear) reactor (see nucleus). [L.L. reagĕre, -āctum—agĕre, to do.]

read, rēd, *v.t.* (arch.) to advise (see rede) : to make out : to interpret : to expound : (*Spens.*) to make known : to declare : (*Spens.*) to name : to solve : to understand as by interpretation of signs : to collect the meaning of : to go over progressively with silent understanding of symbols or with utterance aloud of words or performance of notes : to accept or offer as that which the writer intended : to learn from written or printed matter : to find recorded : to observe the indication of : to register, indicate : to teach, lecture on : to study : to impute by inference (as to read a meaning into).—*v.i.* to perform the act of reading : to practise much reading : to study : to find mention : to give the reader an impression : to endure the test of reading : to deliver lectures : to have a certain wording : —*pa.t.* and *pa.p.* read (red).—*n.* read (rēd), a spell of reading : (*Scot.*) an opportunity of reading : (*Spens.*) counsel, a saying, an interpretation.—*adj.* read (red), versed in books : learned.—*ns.* readabil′ity (rēd-), read′ableness.—*adj.* read′able, interesting and attractively written : (*rare*) legible.—*adv.* read′ably.—*ns.* read′er, one who reads or reads much : one who reads prayers in church : a lecturer, esp. a higher grade of university lecturer : a proof-corrector : one who reads and reports on MSS. for a publisher : a reading-book : (*thieves′ cant*) a pocket-book ; read′ership.—*adj.* read′- ing, addicted to reading.—*n.* the action of the verb *read* : perusal : study of books : public or formal recital, esp. of a bill before Parliament : the actual word or words that may be read in a passage of a text : the indication that can be read off from an instrument : matter for reading : lettering : an interpretation : a performer's conception of the meaning, rendering —*ns.* read′ing-book, a book of exercises in reading ; read′ing-boy, (*print.*) a reader's assistant ; read′ing-desk, a desk for holding a book or paper while it is read : a lectern ; read′ing-lamp, a lamp for reading by ; read′ing- room, a room for consultation, study, or investigation of books in a library : a room with papers, periodicals, &c., resorted to for reading : a proofreaders' room.—first, second, and third reading, the three successive formal readings of a bill before parliament ; read between the lines, to detect a meaning not expressed ; read off, to take as a reading from an instrument ; read (oneself) in, (Church of England) to enter into possession of a benefice by reading the Thirty-nine Articles ; read up, to amass knowledge of by reading. [O.E. rǣdan, to discern, read—rǣd, counsel.]

read, rēd, *n.* a ruminant's fourth stomach, the abomasum. [O.E. rēad.]

ready, red′i, *adj.* prepared : (*obs.*) dressed, attired : willing : inclined : liable : dexterous : prompt : quick : handy : at hand : immediately available : direct.—*adv.* readily (now only in *compar.* and *superl.*, read′ier, read′iest).—*n.* the position of a firearm ready to be fired : (*coll.*) preparation : (*slang*) ready-money.—*v.t.* to make ready.—*adv.* read′ily. — *n.* read′iness. — *adj.* read′y-made, made before sale, not made to order.—*n.* a ready-

made article, esp. a garment.—*adjs.* read′y-money, paying, or for payment, in money on the spot ; read′y-moneyed, -monied, having, or of the nature of, ready money ; read′y-to-eat′ ; read′y- to-wear′ ; read′y-witted.—make ready, (*obs.*) to dress, put on one's clothes : to prepare (esp. a forme for printing) ; ready money, money ready at hand : cash ; ready reckoner, a book of tables giving the value of so many things at so much each, and interest on any sum of money from a day upwards. [O.E. (*ge*)*rǣde* ; cf. Ger. *bereit*.]

reaedify. Same as re-edify.

reagent, rē-ā′jənt, *n.* a substance with characteristic reactions, used as a chemical test.—*n.* reā′gency. [See react.]

reaggravation, rē-ag-rə-vā′shən, *n.* the last warning before excommunication. [aggravation.]

reak, reik, rēk, *n.* (*obs.*) a prank—usu. in *pl.* reaks, rex (reks), sometimes with an allusion to L. *rēx*, king. [Origin obscure.]

real, rē′əl, *adj.* actually existing : not counterfeit or assumed : true : genuine : sincere : authentic : (*law*) pertaining to things fixed, as lands or houses. —*adv.* (*coll.*, *U.S.*, *Scot.*) really, quite, veritably.— *n.* a real thing : that which is real : a realist.— *adj.* re′al-estate′, (*U.S.*) concerned with or dealing in property in land.—*adj.* realī′sable (or rē′).—*n.* realisā′tion (or -*li*-).—*v.t.* rē′alise, to make real, or as if real : to bring into being or act : to accomplish : to convert into real property or money : to obtain, as a possession : to feel strongly : to comprehend completely : to bring home to one's own experience.—*n.* rē′aliser.—*adj.* rē′alising.— *ns.* rē′alism, the mediaeval doctrine that general terms stand for real existences—opp. to nominalism : the doctrine that in external perception the objects immediately known are real existences : the tendency to look to, to accept, or to represent things as they really are (often in their most ignoble aspect) : literalness and precision of detail, with the effect of reality : the taking a practical view in human problems (often the short view) ; rē′alist.—*adj.* rēalist′ic, pertaining to the realists or to realism : life-like.—*adv.* rēalist′ically.—*n.* reality (ri-al′i-ti, or rē-), the state or fact of being real : that which is real and not imaginary : truth : verity : (*law*) the fixed, permanent nature of real property.—*adv.* rē′ally, in reality : actually : in truth.—*ns.* rē′al- ness ; rē′altor, (*U.S.*; irregularly formed) an agent for the buying and selling of landed property ; rē′alty, land, with houses, trees, minerals, &c., thereon : the ownership of, or property in, lands—also real estate.—real image, one through which rays actually pass, capable of being projected on a screen (opp. to virtual image) ; real presence (see presence) ; real school (Ger. realschule, rä-äl′shoo̅′lə), a German school teaching modern languages, science, and technical subjects but not classics—the highest grade being the real gymnasium (Ger. realgymnasium, rä′-äl′gim-nä′zi- oom), opp. to the gymnasium proper, or classica school. [L.L. reālis—L. rēs, a thing.]

real, rē′əl, *adj.* (*obs.*) royal.—*n.* re′alty, (*obs.* royalty.—real tennis, royal tennis, or tenni properly so called, not lawn-tennis. [O.Fr.,—L regālis, royal.]

real, rä-äl′, rē′əl, *n.* a quarter of a peseta : a forme Spanish coin, one-eighth of a dollar. See also reis [Sp.,—L. rēgālis, royal.]

realgar, ri-al′gär, -gər, *n.* a bright red monoclini mineral, arsenic monosulphide. [Mediaeval L.,- Ar. rahj-al-ghār, powder of the mine or cave.]

realign, rē-ə-līn′, *v.t.* to align afresh : to group o divide on a new basis.—*n.* realign′ment.

really, rē-ə-li′, *v.t.* (*obs.*) to rally : (*Spens.*) realli to form anew. [Fr. *réalier*=*rallier* ; see rally

realm, relm, earlier reame, rēm, *n.* a kingdom : domain, province, region.—*adj.* realm′less. [O.F realme—hypothetical L.L. regālimen—L. regāl royal.]

ream, rēm, *n.* 20 quires.—printer's ream, 5 sheets of paper. [Ar. rizmah, a bundle.]

ream, rēm, *n.* (*Scot.*) cream : froth.—*v.i.* to cream to froth : to overflow.—*v.t.* to skim.—*adjs.* ream ing, foaming : brimming ; ream′y. [O.E. réam

ream, *rēm*, *v.t.* to enlarge the bore of.—*ns.* **ream'er**; **ream'ing-bit.** [App. O.E. *rýman*, to open up, make room—*rúm*, room.]

reame, *rēm*, *n.* (*Spens.*, &c.). See **realm**.

reanimate, *rē-an'i-māt*, *v.t.* to restore to life: to infuse new life or spirit into.—*v.i.* to revive.—*n.* **reanimā'tion.**

reanswer, *rē-än'sər*, *v.t.* (*Shak.*) to be equivalent to.

reap, *rēp*, *v.t.* to cut down, as grain: to clear by cutting a crop: to derive as an advantage or reward. —*ns.* **reap'er**, one who reaps: a reaping-machine; **reap'ing-hook**, a sickle; **reap'ing-machine**, a machine for cutting grain; **reap'-silver**, money paid in commutation for service in reaping. [O.E. *rípan* or *ripan*.]

rear, *rēr*, *n.* the back or hindmost part or position, especially of an army or fleet: a position behind: (*slang*) a latrine.—*adj.* placed behind: hinder.— *v.t.* (*Bunyan*) to attack in the rear.—*ns.* **rear-ad'miral**, an officer next below a vice-admiral— orig. one in command of the rear; **rear'-arch**, **-dorse**, **-dos**, **-dorter** (see **rere-**); **rear'-guard** (O.Fr. *rereguarde*), the rear of an army: a body of troops protecting it; **rear'-lamp**, **-light**, a light carried at the back of a vehicle.—*adj.* **rear'most**, last of all.—*ns.* **rear'-rank**; **rear'view-mirror**, a mirror that shows what is behind a vehicle.—*adj.* **rear'ward**, **rere'ward**, in or toward the rear.— *adv.* backward: at the back.—*n.* (*arch.*) rear: rear-guard (partly from A.Fr. *rerewarde*).—**bring up the rear**, to come last. [Aphetic for **arrear**; also partly from O.Fr. *rere* (Fr. *arrière*).]

rear, *rēr*, *v.t.* to raise, cause or help to rise: to set up: (*Spens.*) to originate, to bring into being: to erect: to build up: to lift up or off: to hold up: to take up: (*Spens.*) to take away: to bring up: to breed and foster: to rouse: to stir up: to dislodge from covert.—*v.i.* to rise on the hind-legs.— *ns.* **rear'er**; **rear'horse**, a praying insect (from its attitude). [O.E. *ræran*, to raise, causative of *rísan*, to rise.]

rear, *rēr*, *adj.* (*obs.* or *dial.*; *U.S.* **rare**, *rār*) underdone.—*adjs.* **rear'-boiled**; **rear'-roast'ed**. [O.E. *hrér*.]

rear. Same as **rare** (3).

rearmouse. Same as **reremouse**.

reason, *rē'zn*, *n.* ground, support, or justification of an act or belief: a premise, esp. when placed after its conclusion: a motive or inducement: an underlying explanatory principle: a cause: the mind's power of drawing conclusions and determining right and truth: the exercise of this power: sanity: conformity to what is fairly to be expected or called for: moderation: fair treatment, e.g. satisfaction by a duel, or doing one's fair share in drinking: (*Shak.*) a remark, a sententious saying: (*Spens.*) proportion.—*v.i.* to exercise the faculty of reason: to deduce inferences from premises: to argue: to debate: (*Shak.*) to converse.—*v.t.* to examine or discuss: to debate: to think out: to set forth logically: to bring by reasoning.—*adj.* **rea'sonable**, endowed with reason: rational: acting according to reason: agreeable to reason: just: not excessive: moderate. — *adv.* (now *illit.*) reasonably. — *n.* **rea'sonableness.** — *adv.* **rea'sonably.**—*adj.* **rea'soned**, argued out.—*ns.* **rea'soner**; **rea'soning.**—*adj.* **rea'sonless.**—*by reason of**, on account of: in consequence of; **do one reason**, to give one the satisfaction of a duel: to [drink without shirking; **no reason but**, (*Shak.*) no reason for it being otherwise, hence, no possible alternative; **principle of sufficient reason**, that nothing happens without a sufficient reason why it should be as it is and not otherwise; **pure reason**, reason absolutely independent of experience. [Fr. *raison*—L. *ratiō*, *-ōnis*—*rērī*, *rătus*, to think.]

reassure, *rē-ə-shoōr'*, *v.t.* to assure anew: to reinsure: to give confidence to: to confirm.—*ns.* **reassur'ance**; **reassur'er**.—*adj.* **reassur'ing.**— *adv.* **reassur'ingly.**

east, **reest**, **reist**, *rēst*, *v.i.* to become rancid (esp. of bacon).—*n.* **reast'iness**, &c.—*adj.* **reast'y**, &c. [M.E. *rest*, *reest*, rancid.]

east. See **reest** (2).

---

reata, **riata**, *rē-ä'tä*, *n.* a lariat. [Sp.]

reate, *rēt*, *n.* water-crowfoot. [Origin obscure.]

Réaumur, *rā-ō-mür*, *adj.* of a thermometer or thermometer scale, having the freezing-point of water marked 0° and boiling-point 80°. [From the French physicist, R. A. F. de *Réaumur* (1683-1757), who introduced the scale.]

reave, also (orig. *Scot.*) **reive**, *v.t.* and *v.i.* to plunder: to rob:—*pa.t.* and *pa.p.* **reft** (*obs.* **raft**). —*n.* **reav'er**, **reiv'er**. [O.E. *réafian*, to rob; cf. Ger. *rauben*, to rob.]

reback, *rē-bak'*, *v.t.* to put a new back on.

rebarbative, *ri-bärb'ə-tiv*, *adj.* repellent. [Fr. *rébarbatif*—*barbe*, beard.]

rebate, *ri-bāt'*, *v.t.* to reduce: to abate: to dull: to blunt: (*her.*) to diminish by removal of a projection.—*n.* (or *rē'*) discount: repayment or drawback.—*n.* **rebāte'ment**, abatement: reduction: discount: (*B.*) a narrowing. [Fr. *rabattre*, to beat back—pfx. *re-* and *abattre*, to abate.]

rebate, *rab'it*. Same as **rabbet**.

rebato, *rə-bä'tō*, *n.* (*Shak.*) a stiff collar or support for a ruff.—Also **reba'ter**, **raba'to**. [Fr. *rabat*.]

Rebecca, *ri-bek'ä*, *n.* a leader of those who demolished toll-gates in the Rebecca riots in Wales from 1843.—*ns.* **Rebecc'aism**; **Rebecc'aite.** [In allusion to Gen. xxiv. 60.]

rebeck, **rebec**, *rē'bek*, *n.* an old Eastern instrument of the viol class, shaped like a mandoline. [O.Fr. *rebec*—Ar. *rebāb*, *rabāb* (change of ending unexplained).]

rebel, *reb'(ə)l*, *n.* one who rebels: one who resents and resists authority or grievous conditions.— *adj.* rebellious.—*v.i.* (*ri-bel'*) to renounce the authority of the laws and government, or to take up arms and openly oppose them: to oppose any authority: to revolt: to offer opposition: to feel repugnance:—*pr.p.* **rebell'ing**; *pa.t.* and *pa.p.* **rebelled'.**—*ns.* **reb'eldom**; **rebell'er** (now *rare*). —*adv.* **reb'el-like** (*Shak.*).—*n.* **rebell'ion** (*-yən*), act of rebelling: revolt.—*adj.* **rebell'ious**, engaged in rebellion: characteristic of a rebel or rebellion: inclined to rebel: refractory.—*adv.* **rebell'iously.**—*n.* **rebell'iousness.** [Fr. *rebelle* —L. *rebellis*, insurgent—pfx. *re-*, *bellum*, war.]

rebellow, *rē-bel'ō*, *v.i.* (*Spens.*) to bellow in return: to echo back a loud noise.

rebid, *rē-bid'*, *v.t.* and *v.i.* to bid again, esp. (*bridge*) on the same suit as a previous bid.—*n.* a renewed bid, esp. on one's former suit.

rebirth, *rē-børth'*, *n.* a new entrance into a living form: reincarnation: renewal of life.

rebite, *rē-bīt'*, *v.t.* to freshen by a new application of acid (to a plate).

reboant, *reb'ō-ənt*, *adj.* rebellowing: loudly resounding.—*n.* **reboā'tion.** [L. *reboāns*, *-āntis*, pr.p. of *reboāre*—*re-*, again, *boāre*, to cry aloud.]

rebound, *ri-bownd'*, *v.i.* to bound or start back from collision: to bound in response: to recoil: to reverberate: to re-echo.—*v.t.* to throw back: to re-echo.—*n.* act of rebounding: recoil. [Fr. *rebondir*; see **bound** (3).]

rebuff, *ri-buf'*, *n.* a beating back: sudden check: unexpected refusal: snub.—*v.t.* to beat back: to check: to repulse: to snub. [O.Fr. *rebuffe*— It. *ribuffo*, a reproof—It. *ri-* (=L. *re-*), back, *buffo*, puff.]

rebuke, *ri-būk'*, *v.t.* to check, restrain, beat back: to put to shame: to reprove sternly.—*n.* (*obs.*) a check: (*obs.*) a putting to shame: a reproach: stern reproof, reprimand.—*adjs.* **rebūk'able**; **rebūke'ful.**—*adv.* **rebūke'fully.**—*n.* **rebūk'er.**— *adv.* **rebūk'ingly.** [A.Fr. *rebuker* (O.Fr. *rebucher*) —pfx. *re-*, *bucher*, to strike.]

rebus, *rē'bəs*, *n.* an enigmatical representation of a name by pictures punningly representing parts of the word, as in a puzzle or a coat of arms:—*pl.* **re'buses.** [L. *rēbus*, by things, abl. pl. of *rēs*, thing.]

rebut, *ri-but'*, *v.t.* to drive back: to repel: to meet in argument or proof: to refute.—*v.i.* (*Spens.*) to recoil: (*law*) to return an answer:—*pr.p.* **rebutt'-ing**; *pa.t.* and *pa.p.* **rebutt'ed.**—*adj.* **rebutt'able.** —*ns.* **rebutt'al**; **rebutt'er.** [O.Fr. *reboter*, *rebouter*, *rebuter*, to repulse; see **butt**.]

Neutral vowels in unaccented syllables: *el'ə-mənt*, *in'fənt*, *ran'dəm*

recalcitrate, *ri-kal'si-trāt*, *v.t.* and *v.i.* to kick back.—*v.i.* to have repugnance: to be refractory. —*n.* **recal'citrance**, repugnance or opposition: refractoriness.— *adj.* **recal'citrant**, refractory: obstinate in opposition.—*n.* a recalcitrant person. —*n.* **recalcitrā'tion**. [L. *recalcitrāre*, to kick back—*calx, calcis*, the heel.]

recalesce, *rē-kal-es'*, *v.i.* to show anew a state of glowing heat.—*n.* **recales'cence**, (*phys.*) the renewed glowing of iron at a certain stage of cooling from white-heat. [L. *re-*, again, *calēscĕre*, to grow hot.]

recall (rarely **recal**), *ri-kawl'*, *v.t.* to call back: to command to return: to bring back as by a summons: to remove from office: to revoke: to call back to mind.—*n.* act, power, or possibility of recalling or of revoking: a signal or order to return: the calling back of a performer to the stage or platform by applause: a right of electors to dismiss an official by a vote.—*adj.* **recall'able**, capable of being recalled.—*n.* **recall(l)'ment**.

recant, *ri-kant'*, *v.t.* to retract.—*v.i.* to revoke a former declaration: to unsay what has been said, esp. to declare one's renunciation of one's former religious belief.—*ns.* **recantā'tion** (*rē-*); **recant'er** (*ri-*). [L. *recantāre*, to revoke—*cantāre*, to sing, to charm.]

recapitulate, *rē-kə-pit'ū-lāt*, *v.t.* to go over again the chief points of: to go through in one's own life-history the stages of.—*n.* **recapitulā'tion**, act of recapitulating: summing up: the final repetition of the subjects in sonata form after development.—*adjs.* **recapit'ūlātive**; **recapit'ūlatory**, repeating again: of the nature of a recapitulation. [L. *recapitulāre*, *-ātum—re-*, again, *capitulum*, heading, chapter—*caput*, head.]

recaption, *rē-kap'shən*, *n.* reprisal: (*law*) taking back by peaceable means of goods, wife, or children from one who has no right to detain them.

recapture, *rē-kap'tyər*, *v.t.* to capture back or retake, as a prize from a captor: to recover by effort.—*n.* act of retaking: recovery: a thing recaptured.—*ns.* **recap'tor**; **recap'turer**.

recast, *rē-kåst'*, *v.t.* to cast or mould anew: to reconstruct: to compute anew: (*pa.t.* and *pa.p.* **recast'**).—*n.* (*rē'kåst, rē-kåst'*) shaping anew: that which has been shaped anew.

recede, *ri-sēd'*, *v.i.* to go, draw, or fall back: to withdraw: to retreat: to bend or slope backward: to give up a claim.—*v.t.* **re-cede** (*rē'-sēd'*), to cede back.—*adj.* **reced'ing**, sloping backward. [L. *recēdĕre, recessum—re-*, back, *cēdĕre*, to go, yield.]

receipt, *ri-sēt'*, *n.* receiving: place of receiving: (*obs.*) capacity: a written acknowledgment of anything received: that which is received: a recipe, esp. in cookery: (*obs.*) anything prepared after a recipe.—*v.t.* to mark as paid. [O.Fr. *receite, recete* (Fr. *recette*)—L. *recepta*, fem. pa.p. of *recipĕre*, to receive, with *p* restored after L.]

receive, *ri-sēv'*, *v.t.* to take, get, or catch, usu. more or less passively: to have given or delivered to one: to experience: to take in or on: to admit: to accept: to meet or welcome on entrance: to harbour: to await in resistance: to experience, or learn of, and react towards: to accept as authority or as truth: to take into the body: to reset: to be acted upon by, and transform, electrical signals.—*v.i.* to be a recipient: to participate in communion: to receive signals: to hold a reception of visitors.—*ns.* **receivabil'ity**, **receiv'-ableness.**—*adj.* **receiv'able.**—*n.* **receiv'al** (*rare*). —*adj.* **received'**, generally accepted.—*ns.* **receiv'er**, one who receives: an officer who receives taxes: a person appointed by a court to manage property under litigation, receive money, &c.: one who receives stolen goods: (*chem.*) a vessel for receiving the products of distillation, or for containing gases: the glass vessel of an air-pump in which the vacuum is formed: an instrument by which electrical signals are transformed into suitable form: a receiving-set; **receiv'er-gen'eral**, an officer who receives revenues; **receiv'ership.**—*n.* and *adj.* **receiv'ing.**—*ns.* **receiv'ing-house**, a depot: a house where letters, &c., are left for transmission; **receiv'ing-office**,

a branch post-office for receipt of letters, &c.; **receiv'ing-order**, an order putting a receiver in temporary possession of a debtor's estate, pending bankruptcy proceedings; **receiv'ing-room**, a room where patients, inmates, &c., are received; **receiv'ing-set**, apparatus for receiving wireless communications; **receiv'ing-ship'**, a stationary ship for naval recruits.—**Received Standard English**, the dialect of the English public schools and of those who are in what is called society. [A.Fr. *receivre* (Fr. *recevoir*)—L. *recipĕre, receptum* —*re-*, back, *capĕre*, to take.]

recense, *ri-sens'*, *v.t.* to revise critically.—*n.* **recen'sion**, a critical revision of a text: a text established by critical revision: a review. [L. *recēnsiō, -ōnis—re-*, again, *cēnsēre*, to value.]

recent, *rē'sənt*, *adj.* of late origin or occurrence: fresh: modern: **Re'cent**, of the present geological period—Post-Glacial.—*n.* **rē'cency.**—*adv.* **rē'cently.**—*n.* **rē'centness**. [L. *recēns, recentis*.]

recept, *rē'sept*, *n.* an image or idea formed by repeated similar perceptions.— *n.* **receptacle** (*ri-sep'ta-kl*; also, as *Shak., res'ip-ta-kl*), that in which anything is or may be received or stored: the enlarged end of an axis bearing the parts of a flower or the crowded flowers of an inflorescence: in flowerless plants a structure bearing reproductive organs, spores, or gemmae.—*adj.* **receptacular** (*res-ip-tak'ū-lər*).—*n.* **reseptac'ulum**, a receptacle: —*pl.* **receptac'ula.**—*n.* **receptibil'ity** (*ri-*).—*adj.* **recept'ible**, capable of receiving.—*ns.* **reception** (*ri-sep'shən*), the act, fact, or manner of receiving or of being received: taking in: act or manner of taking up signals: a formal receiving, as of guests: treatment on coming: (*Milt.*) capacity for receiving; **recep'tionist**, one employed to receive callers, hotel-guests, patients, customers, or the like, and make arrangements; **recep'tion-order**, an order for the reception and detention of a person in a mental hospital; **recep'tion-room**, a room for formal receptions: any public room in a house.—*adj.* **recep'tive**, capable of receiving: quick to receive or take in esp. (*fig.*) ideas: pertaining to reception or receptors.—*ns.* **recep'-tiveness, receptivity** (*res-ep-tiv'i-ti*); **recep'tor**, a receiver: an organ adapted for reception of stimuli. [L. *recipĕre, receptum*, to receive.]

recess, *rē-ses'*, *n.* a going back or withdrawing: retirement: seclusion: remission of business: part of a room formed by a receding of the wall: a niche or alcove: an indentation: a retired spot: a nook: a sinus or depression.—*v.t.* to make a recess in: to put into a recess.—*v.i.* (*U.S.*) to adjourn.—*adj.* **recessed'**, having a recess.—*ns.* **recession** (*ri-sesh'ən*), act of receding: withdrawal: the state of being set back: (*U.S.*) a movement towards a slump: (*rē'sesh'ən*) a ceding back; **recessional** (*ri-sesh'ən-əl*), a hymn sung during recession or retirement of clergy and choir. —*adjs.* **recess'ional; recessive** (*-ses'*), tending to recede: (*Mendelism*) of an ancestral character, apparently suppressed in cross-bred offspring in favour of the alternative character in the other parent, though it may be transmitted to later generations: of accent, tending to move toward the beginning of the word.—*adv.* **recess'ively.**— *n.* **recess'iveness.**—**recessed** arch, one arch within another. [See **recede.**]

Rechabite, *rek'ə-bīt*, *n.* a descendant of Jonadab, son of *Rechab*, who did not drink wine or dwell in houses (Jer. xxxv. 6-7): a total abstainer from intoxicating drinks, esp. a member of the order so named: a tent-dweller.—*n.* **Rech'abitism**.

réchauffé, *rā-shō'fā*, *n.* a warmed-up dish: a fresh concoction of old material. [Fr.]

recheat, *ri-chēt'*, **rechate**, *ri-chāt'* (*Shak.*), *n.* a horn-call to assemble hounds.—*v.i.* to sound the recheat. [O.Fr. *racheter, rachater*, to reassemble.]

recherché, *rə-sher'shā*, *adj.* particularly choice: select: peculiar and refined: rare. [Fr.]

rechlesse, *rech'lis*, *adj.* (*Spens.*). Same as **reckless**.

rechristen, *rē-kris'n*, *v.t.* to name anew.

recidivism, *ri-sid'i-vizm*, *n.* the habit of relapsing into crime.—*n.* **recid'ivist**. [Fr. *récidivisme*—L. *recidīvus*, falling back.]

recipe, *res'i-pi*, *n.* directions for making something, esp. to be cooked : (now *rare*) a prescription :—*pl.* **rec'ipes**. [L. *recipe*, take, imper. of *recipĕre*.]

recipient, *ri-sip'i-ənt*, *adj.* receiving : receptive.— *n.* one who or that which receives.—*ns.* **recip'ience**, **recip'iency**, a reception : receptivity. [L. *recipiēns*, *-entis*, pr.p. of *recipĕre*, to receive.]

reciprocal, *ri-sip'rō-kl*, *adj.* acting in return : mutual : complementary : inverse : alternating : interchangeable : giving and receiving or given and received : (*gram.*) expressing mutuality : reflexive.—*n.* that which is reciprocal : (*math.*) the multiplier that gives unity.—*n.* **reciprocality** (*-kal'i-ti*).—*adv.* **recip'rocally.**—*n.* **recip'rocant**, a differential invariant.—*v.t.* **recip'rocate**, to give and receive mutually : to requite : to interchange : to alternate.—*v.i.* to move backward and forward : (*coll.*) to make a return or interchange.—*ns.* **recip'rocating-en'gine**, an engine in which the piston moves to and fro in a straight line ; **reciproca'tion.**—*adj.* **recip'rocative**, characterised by or inclined to reciprocation.—*ns.* **recip'rocator**, one who or that which reciprocates : a double-acting steam-engine ; **reciprocity** (*res-i-pros'i-ti*), mutual relation : concession of mutual privileges or advantages, esp. mutual tariff concessions. [L. *reciprocus*.]

recision, *ri-sizh'ən*, *n.* cutting back. [L. *recīsiō*, *-ōnis*—*recīdĕre*, to cut off.]

recite, *ri-sīt'*, *v.t.* to repeat from memory : to declaim : (*rare*) to read aloud : to narrate : to give the particulars of : (*U.S.*) to repeat to a teacher, be heard a lesson in.—*v.i.* to give a recitation : (*U.S.*) to repeat, or be heard, a lesson. —*ns.* **reci'tal**, act of reciting : setting forth : enumeration : narration : a public performance of music, usu. by one performer, or one composer, or of some particular character : (*law*) that part of a deed which recites the circumstances ; **recitation** (*res-i-tā'shən*), act of reciting : a piece for declaiming : (*U.S.*) the repeating or hearing of a prepared lesson : hence (*U.S.*) a lesson generally ; **recita'tionist**, a declaimer ; **recita'tion-room**, (*U.S.*) a class-room ; **recitative** (*-tə-tēv'*) or (*It.*) **recitativo** (*re-sit-ä-tē'vō*, or *rā-chē-tä-tē'vō*), a style of song resembling speech in its succession of tones and freedom from melodic form : a passage to be sung in this manner.—*adj.* in the style of recitative.—*ns.* **reciter** (*ri-sīt'ər*) ; **recit'ing-note**, the note on which, in a Gregorian chant, the greater part of a verse is sung. [L. *recitāre*—*citāre*, *-ātum*, to call.]

reck, *rek*, *v.t.* to care, desire : to regard : to concern.—*v.i.* (usu. with *of*) to care : to heed : to matter : (*pa.t.* and *pa.p.* **recked**, *obs.* or *arch.* **raught**, *rawt*).—*n.* care : heed.—*adj.* **reck'less**, careless : heedless of consequences : rash.—*adv.* **reck'lessly.** — *n.* **reck'lessness.** — **what reck** ? (*Scot.*) what does it matter ? [O.E. *reccan*, *rēcan* ; cf. O.H.G. *ruoh*, care, Ger. *ruchlos*, regardless.]

reckan, *rek'ən*, *adj.* or *pa.p.* (*Scott*, ostensibly Cumberland dial.) *pa.p.* **racked** or **ricked.**

reckling, *rek'ling*, *n.* the weakest, smallest, or youngest of a litter or family.—*adj.* puny. [Origin obscure.]

reckon, *rek'n*, *-ən*, *v.t.* to count : to place or class : to esteem : to estimate, judge : to think, believe : to think, suppose : to expect : to calculate : to charge to account.—*v.i.* to calculate : to judge : to go over or settle accounts (fol. by *with*) : to concern oneself (with *with*) : to count or rely (with *on* or *upon*).—*ns.* **reck'oner** ; **reck'oning**, counting : calculation, esp. of a ship's position : a tavern bill : settlement of accounts : judgment. [O.E. *gerecenian*, to explain ; Ger. *rechnen*.]

reclaim, *ri-klām'*, *v.t.* orig. to call back (as a hawk) : to win back : to win from evil, wildness, waste, submersion : (*rē-klām'*) to claim back.— *v.i.* (*ri-klām'*) to exclaim in protest : (*Scots law*) to appeal.—*n.* recall : possibility of reform.—*adj.* **reclaim'able.**—*adv.* **reclaim'ably.** [O.Fr. *reclamer*—L. *reclāmāre*.]

reclamation, *rek-lə-mā'shən*, *n.* act of reclaiming : state of being reclaimed. [L. *reclāmātiō*, *-ōnis*—*reclāmāre*—*clāmāre*, to cry out.]

réclame, *rā-kläm*, *n.* art or practice by which publicity or notoriety is secured : publicity. [Fr.]

recline, *ri-klīn'*, *v.t.* to lay on the back : to incline or bend (properly backwards).—*v.i.* to lean in a recumbent position, on back or side : (of the plane of a sun-dial) to make an angle with the vertical : to rely.—*adj.* or *adv.* (*Milt.*) recumbent. —*adj.* **reclinate** (*rek'li-nāt*), bent down or back. —*n.* **reclina'tion** (*rek-li-*), reclining : bending back : angle of a dial with the vertical.—*adj.* **reclined'**, recumbent : reclinate.—*n.* **recli'ner.**— *adj.* **recli'ning.**—*n.* **recli'ning-chair**, an invalid's chair. [L. *reclīnāre*, *-ātum*—*clīnāre*, to bend.]

recluse, *ri-klōōs'*, *adj.* enclosed, as an anchorite : secluded : retired : solitary.—*n.* a religious devotee who lives shut up in a cell : one who lives retired from the world.—*adv.* **recluse'ly.**—*ns.* **recluse'ness**, seclusion from society : retirement ; **reclusion** (*-klōō'zhən*), religious seclusion : the life of a recluse : seclusion in prison.—*adj.* **reclu'sive** (*-siv*), of seclusion.—*n.* **reclu'sory**, a recluse's cell. [L. *reclūsus*, pa.p. of *reclūdĕre*, to open, in later Latin, shut away—*re-*, back, away, *claudĕre*.]

recognise, *rek'og-nīz*, *v.t.* to know again : to identify as known or experienced before : to acknowledge : to show sign of knowing : to see the truth of : to acknowledge the status of.—*adj.* **recognis'able** (or *rek'*).—*adv.* **recognis'ably** (or *rek'*).—*ns.* **recognisance** (*ri-kog'ni-zəns*), a recognition : acknowledgment : (*arch.*) a token : (*ri-kon'i-zəns*) a legal obligation entered into before a magistrate to do, or not to do, some particular act : money pledged for the performance of such an obligation ; **recogniser** (*rek'og-nīz-ər*, or *-nīz'ər*) ; **recognition** (*rek-og-nish'ən*), act of recognising : state of being recognised : acknowledgment : acknowledgment of status : a sign, token, or indication of recognising : (*Scots law*) a return of the feu to the superior.—*adjs.* **recognitive** (*ri-kog'*), **recog'nitory**. [L. *recognōscĕre* and O.Fr. *reconoistre*, *reconoiss-* ; see **cognosce**, **cognition**.]

recoil, *ri-koil'* (*Spens.* **recoyle**, **recule**, **recuile**), *v.t.* (*obs.*) to beat back.—*v.i.* to retreat, fall back : (*obs.*) to retire : (*obs.*) to revert : to start back : to rebound : to stagger back : to kick, as a gun : to shrink : (*Shak.*) to degenerate.—*n.* retreat : a starting or springing back : rebound : the kick of a gun.—*n.* **recoil'er**. [Fr. *reculer*—*cul*—L. *cūlus*, the hinder parts.]

recollect, *rek-əl-ekt'*, *v.t.* to recall to memory : to remember, esp. by an effort : to absorb in mystical contemplation : (usu. *refl.*) to recall to the matter in hand, or to composure or resolution : (*rē'kəl-ekt'* ; *Shak.*) to gather : to collect over again.—*n.* (*rek'*) a Franciscan friar of a reformed branch, aiming at detachment from creatures and recollection in God.—Also (Fr.) **récollet** (*rā-kol-ā*). —*adj.* **recollect'ed.**—*adv.* **recollect'edly.**—*ns.* **recollect'edness** ; **recollec'tion** (*rek-*), act or power of recollecting : a memory, reminiscence : a thing remembered : mystical contemplation.— *adj.* **recollec'tive**—recollected terms, (*Shak.*) variously explained as known by heart, picked, studied, wanting spontaneity. [L. *recolligĕre*, to gather again or gather up—*colligĕre* ; see **collect**.]

recomfort, *ri-kum'fərt*, *v.t.* (*arch.*) to comfort : to console : to reinvigorate : to refresh.—*adj.* **recom'fortless**, (*Spens.*) comfortless.—*n.* **recom'-forture**, (*Shak.*) consolation.

recommend, *rek-ə-mend'*, *v.t.* to commend, commit, or consign : to commend or introduce as suitable for acceptance, favour, appointment, or choice : to make acceptable : to advise : (*Shak.*) to inform.—*adj.* **recommend'able.**—*adv.* **recommend'ably.** — *n.* **recommenda'tion.** — *adj.* **recommend'atory.**—*n.* **recommend'er.**

recompense, *rek'əm-pens*, *v.t.* to return an equivalent to or for : to repay.—*n.* (formerly **recompence**) return of an equivalent : that which is so returned : requital. [O.Fr. *recompenser*—L. *compēnsāre*, to compensate.]

reconcile, *rek'ən-sīl*, *v.t.* to restore or bring back to friendship or union : to bring to agreement or contentment : to pacify : to make or prove consistent : to admit or restore to membership of a church : to adjust or compose : (*Spens.*) to regain, conciliate.—*n.* rec′oncilability (or *-sĭl′*).—*adj.* rec′oncilable (or *-sĭl′*).—*n.* rec′oncilableness (or *-sĭl′*). — *adv.* rec′oncilably (or *-sĭl′*). — *ns.* rec′oncilement (or *-sĭl′*) ; rec′onciler ; reconcilia′tion (*-sil-*).—*adj.* reconciliatory (*-sil′i-ə-tər-i*). [L. *reconciliāre, -ātum—conciliāre*, to call together.]

recondite, *rek′ən-dīt, ri-kon′dīt, adj.* hidden : obscure : abstruse : profound. [L. *recondĕre, -itum*, to put away—*re-*, again, *condĕre*, to establish, store.]

recondition, *rē-kən-dish′ən, v.t.* to repair and refit : to restore to original or sound condition.

reconnaissance, *ri-kon′i-səns, n.* reconnoitring : a preliminary survey.—**reconnaissance in force**, an attack by a large body to discover the enemy's position and strength. [Fr.]

reconnoitre, *rek-ə-noi′tər, v.t.* to examine with a view to military operations or other purpose.—*v.i.* to make preliminary examination.—*n.* a reconnaissance.—*n.* reconnoi′trer. [Fr. *reconnoître* (now *reconnaître*)—L. *recognōscĕre*, to recognise.]

reconstitute, *rē-kon′sti-tūt, v.t.* to constitute anew : to restore the constitution of (esp. of dried foods). —*adj.* reconstit′uent (*-kən-*).—*n.* reconstitū′tion, constituting afresh : refounding : restoration to original condition : theoretical reconstruction on the spot of the supposed details of a crime.

reconstruct, *rē-kən-strukt′, v.t.* to construct again : to rebuild : to remodel : to restore in imagination or theory.—*n.* reconstruc′tion, the act of reconstructing : a thing reconstructed : reorganisation : a model representing a series of sections : a theoretical representation or view of something unknown : the upbuilding of moral and material public well-being after a great upheaval : (*U.S.*) the process of restoring the Seceding States to the rights and privileges of the Union after the Civil War. — *adjs.* reconstruc′tional ; reconstruc′-tionary. — *n.* reconstruc′tionist. — *adj.* reconstruc′tive.—*n.* reconstruc′tor.

reconvalescence, *ri-kon-vəl-es′əns, n.* recovery from illness.

reconvert, *rē-kən-vərt′, v.t.* to convert back to a former state, religion, &c.—*n.* reconver′sion.

reconvey, *rē-kən-vā′, v.t.* to transfer back to a former owner, as an estate.—*n.* reconvey′ance.

record, *ri-kord′, v.t.* (*obs.*) to get by heart : (*Spens.*) to go over in one's mind : (*Spens.*) to repeat from memory : to narrate, set forth : to sing in an undertone, practise quietly (esp. of birds) : to call to mind : to set down in writing or other permanent form : to trace a curve or other representation of (sometimes one capable of reproducing the original) : to perform before a recording instrument : to mark, indicate : to bear witness to : to register (as a vote or verdict) : to celebrate. —*v.i.* to sing, warble, esp. in quiet rehearsal : to make a record.—*n.* record (*rek′ord*, formerly *ri-kord′*), a register : a formal writing of any fact or proceeding : a book of such writings : past history : a witness, a memorial : memory, remembrance : anything entered in the rolls of a court, esp. the formal statements or pleadings of parties in a litigation : a curve or other representation of phenomena made by an instrument upon a surface : a plate or cylinder bearing such a representation and capable (as in the case of the gramophone) of reproducing the phenomena : a performance or occurrence not recorded to have been surpassed.—*adj.* not surpassed.—*adj.* record′able (*ri-*), able to be recorded : worthy of record.—*ns.* recordā′-tion (in *Shak.*, rek′), remembrance : commemoration : recording ; record′er (*ri-*), one who records or registers, esp. the rolls, &c., of a city : a judge of a city or borough court of quarter-sessions : one who performs before a recording instrument : a recording apparatus : an old form of fipple-flute, like a flageolet ; record′ership, the office of recorder, or the time of holding it.—*n.* and *adj.* record′ing.—**beat, or break, the record**, to outdo the highest achievement yet recorded ; **close the record**, an act of a Scottish judge after each party has said all he wishes to say by way of statement and answer ; **off the record**,

not for publication in the press, &c. ; **public records**, contemporary officially authenticated statements of acts and proceedings in public affairs, preserved in the public interest ; **recording angel**, an angel supposed to keep a book in which every misdeed is recorded against the doer ; **Record Office**, a place where public records are kept ; **trial by record**, a common law mode of trial when a disputed former decision of the court is settled by producing the record. [O.Fr. *recorder*—L. *recordārī*, to call to mind, get by heart.]

recount, *ri-kownt′, v.t.* to narrate the particulars of : to detail : **recount, re-count** (*rē-kownt′*), to count over again.—*n.* a second or new counting (as of votes).—*ns.* recount′al (*ri-*) ; recount′-ment, (*Shak.*) relation in detail, recital. [O.Fr. *reconter—conter*, to tell.]

recoup, *ri-kōōp′, v.t.* (*law*) to deduct or keep back (from what is claimed by a counterclaim) : to make good : to indemnify.—*n.* recoup′ment. [Fr. *recouper*, to cut back—*couper*, to cut.]

recoure, recower, *ri-kowr′, v.t.* (*Spens.*) a variant of **recover**. See also **recure**.

recourse, *ri-kōrs′, n.* a flowing back : withdrawal : recurrence : (*Shak.*) flow : return : freedom to return : access : resort : resort for aid or protection : right to payment, esp. by the drawer or indorser of a bill of exchange not met by the acceptor.—*v.i.* (*Spens.*) to return, go back, revert. [Fr. *recours*—L. *recursus—re-*, back, *currĕre, cursum*, to run.]

recover, re-cover, *rē-kuv′ər, v.t.* to cover again. [See **cover**.]

recover, *ri-kuv′ər, v.t.* to get or find again : to regain : to reclaim : to bring back : to retrieve : to cure : to revive : to restore : to rescue : to succeed in reaching : to attain : to obtain as compensation : to obtain for injury or debt.—*v.i.* to regain health or any former state : to get back into position : (*law*) to obtain a judgment.—*n.* (*obs.*) recovery : possibility of recovery : return to a former position, as in rowing or exercise with a weapon : the position so resumed.—*n.* recover-abil′ity.—*adj.* recov′erable.—*ns.* recov′erable-ness ; recoveree′, one against whom a judgment is obtained in common recovery ; recov′erer, one who recovers ; recov′eror, one who recovers a judgment in common recovery ; recov′ery, the act, fact, process, possibility, or power of recovering, or state of having recovered, in any sense : (*law*) a verdict giving right to the recovery of debts or costs.—**common recovery**, a former method of transferring an entailed estate by a legal fiction ; **recover the wind of,** (*Shak.*) to get to windward of (so as to drive a hare into a toil, or take the wind out of one's sails) : to gain an advantage over. [O.Fr. *recouvrer*—L. *recuperāre* ; see **recuperate**.]

recower. See **recoure**.

recreant, *rek′ri-ənt, adj.* surrendering : craven : false : apostate.—*n.* one who yields in combat : a craven : a mean-spirited wretch : an apostate : a renegade.—*ns.* rec′reance, rec′reancy.—*adv.* rec′reantly. [O.Fr., pr.p. of *recroire*, to yield in combat—L.L. *recrēdĕre*, to surrender—L. *crēdĕre*, to entrust.]

recreate, *rek′ri-āt, v.t.* to reinvigorate : to refresh : to indulge, gratify, or amuse by sport or pastime. —*v.i.* to take recreation.—*n.* recrea′tion, refreshment after toil, sorrow, &c. : pleasurable occupation of leisure time : an amusement or sport : a source of amusement : (*rē-*) a new creation.—*adjs.* recreā′-tional (rek-), rec′reative (and *rē-krē-ā′tiv*).

recrement, *rek′ri-mənt, n.* waste, dross : a secretion that is reabsorbed.—*adjs.* recremental (*-ment′l*), recrementitial (*-mən-tish′l*), recrementi′tious. [L. *recrēmentum*, dross—*cernĕre*, to sift.]

recriminate, *ri-krim′in-āt, v.i.* to charge an accuser. —*n.* recriminā′tion, act of accusing in return : counter-charge. — *adj.* recrim′inative. — *n.* recrim′inator.—*adj.* recrim′inatory. [L. *crim-inārī*, to accuse.]

recrudesce, *rē-krōō-des′, v.i.* to break out afresh. — *ns.* recrudesc′ence, recrudesc′ency. — *adj.* recrudesc′ent. [L. *recrūdēscĕre—crūdus*, raw.]

recruit, ri-krōōt′, *n.* (*obs.*) a reinforcement: a new supply (of men, money, health, &c.): renewal: restoration: a soldier or other newly enlisted.— *v.i.* to obtain fresh supplies: to recover in health, pocket, &c.: to enlist new soldiers.—*v.t.* to reinforce: to replenish: to restore: to reinvigorate: to enlist or raise.—*ns.* **recruit′al**, renewed supply: restoration; **recruit′er**.—*adj.* **recruit′ing.**—*ns.* **recruit′ing-ground**, a place where recruits may be obtained; **recruit′ment**, recruiting. [Obs. Fr. *recrute*, reinforcement, prov. pa.p. fem. of *recroître*—L. *recrēscĕre*, to grow again.]

rect-, *rekt-*, **recti-**, *rekt′i-*, in composition, right: straight.—**recta, rectal, rectally** (see **rectum**). [L. *rēctus*, straight, right.]

rectangle, rek′tang-gl, or *-tang′*, *n.* a four-sided plane figure with all its angles right angles.—**rec′tangled**, having a right angle; **rectang′ūlar**, of the form of a rectangle: at right angles: rightangled.—*n.* **rectangūlar′ity.**—*adv.* **rectang′ūlarly.**—**rectangular hyperbola**, one whose asymptotes are at right angles; **rectangular solid**, one whose axis is perpendicular to its base. [L.L. *rēct*(*i*)*angulum*—L. *angulus*, an angle.]

rectify, rek′ti-fī, *v.t.* to set right: to correct: to redress: to adjust: (*chem.*) to purify by distillation: (of an arc) to determine the length of: (of an alternating current) to change to direct: (*wireless*) to transpose to a suitable frequency:— *pr.p.* **rec′tifying**; *pa.t.* and *pa.p.* **rec′tified.**—*adj.* **rec′tifiable.**—*ns.* **rectifica′tion** (*-fī*); **rec′tifier**, one who rectifies (esp. alcohol): apparatus for rectifying (esp. spirit, an alternating current, or electromagnetic waves). [Fr. *rectifier*—L.L. *rēctificāre*—*facĕre*, to make.]

rectilineal, rek-ti-lin′i-əl, *adj.* rectilinear.—*adj.* **rectilin′ear** (*-i-ər*), in a straight line or lines: straight: bounded by straight lines.—*n.* **rectilinearity** (*-ar′i-ti*).—*adv.* **rectilin′early.** [L. *līnea*, a line.]

rection, rek′shən, *n.* (*gram.*) syntactical government. [L. *rēctiō*, *-ōnis*, government.]

rectipetality, rek-ti-pi-tal′i-ti, **rectipetaly**, *-pet′əl-i*, *ns.* (*bot.*) tendency to grow in a straight line. [L. *petĕre*, to seek.]

rectirostral, rek-ti-ros′trəl, *adj.* straight-billed. [L. *rōstrum*, a beak.]

rectiserial, rek-ti-sē′ri-əl, *adj.* in straight rows. [L. *seriēs*, a row.]

rectitis, rek-tī′tis, *n.* inflammation of the rectum. —*adj.* **rectitic** (*-tit′ik*).

rectitude, rek′ti-tūd, *n.* (*obs.*) straightness: rightness: uprightness: integrity. [Fr.,—L.L. *rēctitūdō*—L. *rēctus*, straight.]

recto, rek′tō, *n.* the right-hand page of an open book, the front page of a leaf—opp. to *verso*. [L. *rēctō* (*foliō*), on the right (leaf).]

rector, rek′tər, *n.* (*obs.*) a ruler, governor, or controller: in the Church of England, a clergyman of a parish where the tithes are not impropriate: an Episcopal clergyman with charge of a congregation in the United States or (since 1890) Scotland: the head-master of a superior public school in Scotland, Germany, &c.: the chief elective officer of many Scottish (*Lord Rector*) and foreign universities: a college head (as at Lincoln and Exeter Colleges, Oxford; Science and Technology, London): (R.C.) an ecclesiastic in charge of a congregation, an important mission, a college, or a religious house, esp. the head of a Jesuit seminary.—*adj.* **rec′toral**, of God as a ruler.—*ns.* **rec′torate**, a rector's office or term of office; **rec′toress**, **rec′tress**, a female rector: (*coll.*) a rector's wife. —*adj.* **rectorial** (*-tō′ri-əl*), of a rector.—*n.* an election of a Lord Rector.—*ns.* **rec′torship**; **rec′tory**, the province or residence of a rector.— **lay rector**, a layman who enjoys the great tithes of a parish; **Rector Magnificus**, the head of a German university. [L. *rēctor*, *-ōris*—*regĕre*, *rēctum*, to rule.]

rectrix, rek-triks, *n.* a female governor: a long tail-feather, used in steering:—*pl.* **rectrices** (rek-rī′sēz).—*adj.* **rectricial** (*-trish′l*). [L. *rēctrix*, *-īcis*, fem. of *rēctor*.]

rectum, rek′təm, *n.* the terminal part of the large

intestine:—*pl.* **rec′ta.**—*adj.* **rec′tal.**—*adv.* **rec′t-ally.**—In composition, **rec′to-.** [L. neut. of *rēctus*, straight.]

rectus, rek′təs, *n.* a straight muscle:—*pl.* **rec′tī.** [L.]

recuile, recule, ri-kūl′ (*Spens.*). Same as **recoil.**

recumbent, ri-kum′bənt, *adj.* reclining.—*ns.* **recum′bence, recum′bency.**—*adv.* **recum′bently.** [L. *recumbĕre*—*cubāre*, to lie down.]

recuperate, ri-kū′pər-āt, *v.t.* and *v.i.* to recover.— *adj.* **recu′perable**, recoverable.—*n.* **recuperā′tion.**—*adj.* **recu′perative** (*-ə-tiv*).—*n.* **recu′perātor**, an arrangement by which something lost is regained, as the heat of waste gases in a furnace.— *adj.* **recu′peratory.** [L. *recuperāre*, to recover.]

recur, ri-kur′, *v.i.* to revert: to have recourse: to come up or come round again, or at intervals: to occur again: to be repeated in cycles:—*pr.p.* **recurr′ing**; *pa.t.* and *pa.p.* **recurred′.**—*ns.* **recurr′ence, recurr′ency.**—*adj.* **recurr′ent**, returning at intervals: running back in the opposite direction or toward the place of origin.—*adv.* **recurr′ently.**—**recurring decimal**, a decimal fraction in which after a certain point one figure (*repeating decimal*) or a group of figures (*circulating*) is repeated to infinity. [L. *recurrĕre*—*currĕre*, to run.]

recure, ri-kūr′, *v.t.* (*Spens.*, *Shak.*, *Milt.*) to cure, remedy, heal, bring back to a better state: (*Spens.*) to recover, get back.—*v.i.* (*obs.*) to recover, get well.—*n.* (*obs.*) cure: (*obs.*) recovery.—*adj.* **recure′less**, incurable. [Partly L. *recūrāre*, to cure, partly for **recoure** (q.v.), a form of **recover**.]

recurve, ri-kurv′, *v.t.* and *v.i.* to bend back.—*adj.* **recurved′.**—*adj.* **recurviros′tral**, with up-bent bill. [L. *recurvāre*; *rōstrum*, beak.]

recuse, ri-kūz′, *v.t.* to reject, object to (e.g. a judge).—*ns.* **recusance** (*rek′ū-zəns* or *ri-kū′zəns*; *rare*), **recusancy** (*-i*); **recusant** (*rek′* or *ri-kū′*), one (esp. a Roman Catholic) who refused to attend the Church of England when it was legally compulsory: a dissenter: one who refuses, esp. to submit to authority.—*adj.* refusing or neglecting to attend the Church of England: refusing generally. —*n.* **recusā′tion**, (*law*) an objection or appeal. [L. *recūsāre*—*causa*, a cause.]

red, red, *adj.* (*comp.* **redd′er**; *superl.* **redd′est**) of a colour like blood: extended traditionally to mean golden, and by custom to other colours more or less near red: revolutionary, or supposedly revolutionary.—*n.* the colour of blood: a red pigment: red clothes: a revolutionary or one who favours sweeping changes, variously applied to radical, republican, anarchist, socialist, communist, &c.: a former squadron of the British fleet: a cent.—*ns.* **red′-belly**, char, or other redbellied fish: the slider, a terrapin; **red′-bidd′y**, a drink made of red wine and methylated spirit.— *adj.* **red′-blood′ed**, having red blood: abounding in vitality, and usually in crudity.—*ns.* **red′-book**, a book bound in red, esp. a court-guide, peerage, directory of persons in the service of the state, official regulations, or the like; **red′-box**, a minister's red-covered box for official papers; **red′breast**, the robin; **red′-bud**, the Judas-tree; **red′-cap**, (*local*) a goldfinch: a Scottish castle goblin (also **red′-cowl**): (*army slang*) a military policeman; **red′coat**, a British soldier; **red′-curr′ant**, the small red berry of a shrub of the gooseberry genus.—*adj.* **red′-currant.**—*n.* **red′-deer**, the common stag or hind, reddish-brown in summer.—*v.t.* **redd′en**, to make red.—*v.i.* to grow red: to blush.—*adj.* **redd′ish.**—*ns.* **redd′-ishness**; **red′dog**, the lowest grade of flour in high milling.—*adj.* **redd′y**, reddish.—*n.* **red′-eye**, the rudd.—*adj.* **red′-fig′ured**, (of Greek vases) having red (unpainted) figures on a blackglazed ground.—*ns.* **red flag** (see **flag**); **red′-gum**, a rash on the gums of teething infants: a Eucalyptus (of various kinds) with red gum.— *adj.* **red′-haired.**—*n.* **red′-hand**, the bloody hand (see **hand**).—*adj.* **red′-hand′ed**, in the very act, or immediately after, as if with bloody hands.— *ns.* **red′-hat**, a cardinal: (*army slang*) a staff officer; **red′-head**, a person with red hair.— *adj.* **red′-head′ed**, having a red head or red hair:

Neutral vowels in unaccented syllables : el′ə-mənt, in′fənt, ran′dəm

(*slang*) angrily excited.—*n.* **red'-heat**, the temperature at which a thing is red-hot.—*adjs.* **red'-heeled**; **red'-hot**, heated to redness; **red'-latt'ice**, (*Shak.*) savouring of the alehouse (whose lattice was conventionally painted red).—*n.* **red'-lead'**, an oxide of lead (Pb₃O₄) of a fine red colour, used in paint-making.—*adjs.* **red'-legged**; **red'-letter**, marked with red letters, as holidays or saints' days in the old calendars: deserving to be so marked.—*n.* **red light**, a rear-light: a danger-signal: (*U.S.*) a brothel.—*adjs.* **red-'light**, (*U.S.*) disreputable; **red'-looked**, (*Shak.*) having a red look.—*adv.* **red'ly.**—*adj.* **red'-mad'**, (*Scot.*) stark mad.—*ns.* **red'-man**, **red man**, a redskin, an American Indian: (*alchemy*) prob. red mercuric sulphide; **red'ness**; **red'-plague**, **-murrain**, (*Shak.*) bubonic plague; **red'poll**, a name for two birds (*lesser* and *mealy redpoll*) akin to the linnet: a beast of a red breed of polled cattle.—*adj.* **red'-polled**, having a red poll: red and polled.—*ns.* **Red'-root**, a genus (Ceanothus) of the buckthorn family—*New Jersey Tea*; **red rot**, a disease of oaks, &c., caused by Polyporus, the wood becoming brown and dry; **red'-san'ders**, a papilionaceous tree (*Pterocarpus santalinus*) of tropical Asia, with heavy dark-red heartwood, used as a dye, &c. (see also **sandalwood**); **red'-seed**, the food of mackerel, small floating crustaceans, &c.; **red'-shank**, a sandpiper with red legs: (in derision) a Highlander or an Irishman; **red'-shirt**, a follower of Garibaldi (1807-82), from his garb: a revolutionary or anarchist; **red'skin**, a Red Indian; **red'start** (O.E. *steort*, tail), a bird (Ruticilla or Phoenicurus) with a conspicuous chestnut-coloured tail: an American warbler, superficially similar; **red'streak**, an apple with streaked skin; **red'-tape'**, the tape used in government offices: rigid formality of intricate official routine.—*adj.* **red'-tape'.**—*ns.* **red-tap'ism**, **red-tap'ist**; **red'top**, (*U.S.*) a kind of bent grass (*Agrostis stolonifera*); **red'-water**, a cattle disease due to a protozoan parasite in the blood, transmitted by ticks; **red'wing**, a thrush with reddish sides below the wings; **red'wood**, Sequoia: a red dye-wood in general.—*adj.* **red-wood'**, **-wud'** (*Scot.*), stark mad.—**in the red**, overdrawn at the bank, in debt; **red admiral**, a common butterfly (*Vanessa Atalanta*) with reddish-banded wings; **red algae**, seaweeds, the Rhodophyceae or Florideae; **red cabbage**, a purplish cabbage used for pickling; **red cedar**, a name for various species of Cedrela and of juniper; **red cent**, a cent (formerly coined in copper); **red clay**, a clayey deposit of oceanic abysses, stained reddish or brown by manganese and iron oxides: cave-earth; **red cock**, a figurative name for an incendiary fire; **Red Crag**, a middle division of the English Pliocene; **Red Cross**, a red cross on a white ground, the old national flag of England (as in Spenser's Red'cross Knight, representing holiness and the Church of England): the Swiss flag with colours reversed, hence an organisation for tending sick and wounded in war, enjoying privileges under the Convention of Geneva (1864); **Red En'sign**, a red flag with the Union Jack in the canton, till 1864 the flag of the Red Squadron, now flown by British merchant ships; **red giant**, **dwarf**, a red star of high, low, luminosity; **red herring**, a herring cured and dried, of reddish appearance: a subject introduced to divert discussion, as a herring drawn across a track would throw hounds out; **red-hot po'ker**, the plant Tritoma or Kniphofia; **Red Indian**, an American Indian; **red pepper** (see **pepper**); **red rag**, (*slang*) the tongue: a cause of infuriation (as red is said to be to a bull); **red ratt'le**, lousewort; **red ribbon**, **riband**, the ribbon of the Order of the Bath; **red snow**, snow coloured by a microscopic red alga; **red spider**, a spinning mite that infests leaves; **Royal Red Cross**, a decoration for nurses, instituted 1883; **see red**, to grow furious: to thirst for blood. [O.E. *réad*; cf. Ger. *rot*, L. *ruber, rūfus*, Gr. *erythros*, Gael. *ruadh*.]

red. Same as **redd** (1 and 2).

redact, *ri-dakt'*, *v.t.* to edit, work into shape: to

frame.—*ns.* **redac'tion**; **redac'tor.**—*adj.* **redactō'rial** (*re-*, *rē-*). [L. *redigĕre, redāctum*, to bring back—pfx. *red-*, *agĕre*, to drive.]

redan, *ri-dan'*, *n.* (*fort.*) a field-work of two faces forming a salient. [O.Fr. *redan*—L. *re-*, *dēns, dentis*, a tooth.]

redargue, *ri-där'gū*, *v.t.* (*obs.* or *Scot.*) to refute: to confute. [L. *redarguĕre*—*red-*, *arguĕre*, argue.]

redd, **red**, *red*, *v.t.* (chiefly *Scot.*) to put in order, make tidy: to clear up: to disentangle: to comb: to separate in fighting.—*v.i.* to set things in order, tidy up (usu. with *up*): (*pr.p.* **redd'ing**; *pa.t.* and *pa.p.* **redd**, **red**).—*n.* an act of redding: refuse, rubbish.—*adj.* (*Scots law*) vacated.—*ns.* **redd'er**; **redd'ing**, **redd'ing-up'**; **redd'ing-comb**, **-kame**, a hair-comb; **redd'ing-straik**, a stroke received in trying to separate fighters. [Partly O.E. *hreddan*, to free, rescue (cf. Ger. *retten*, to rescue); prob. partly from or influenced by O.E. *rǽdan* (see **rede**, **read**); cf. also **rid**.]

redd, **red**, *red*, (*Spens.*) *pa.t.* and *pa.p.* of **read**: (*Scot.*) same as **rede** (*pres. tense*).

redd, *red*, *n.* (*Scot.*) fish or frog spawn: a spawning-place. [Origin obscure.]

reddendum, *ri-den'dom*, *n.* (*law*) a reserving clause in a lease:—*pl.* **redden'da.**—*n.* **redden'do,** (*Scots law*) service to be rendered or money to be paid by a vassal, or the clause in a charter specifying it. [L., to be rendered, gerundive of *reddĕre.*]

reddle, reddleman. See **ruddle**.

rede, *rēd*, *v.t.* an old spelling of **read**, retained as an archaism in the senses of to counsel or advise, expound, relate.—*n.* advice: resolution: saying, tale: interpretation.—*n.* **rede'craft**, logic.—*adj.* **rede'less**, without counsel or wisdom.

redeem, *ri-dēm'*, *v.t.* to buy back: to compound for: to recover or free by payment: to free oneself from, by fulfilment: to ransom: to rescue, deliver, free: to get back: to reclaim: to pay the penalty of: to atone for: to compensate for: (of time) to put to the best advantage.—*n.* **redeemabil'ity.**—*adj.* **redeem'able.**—*n.* **redeem'ableness.**—*adv.* **redeem'ably.**—*n.* **redeem'er.**—*adjs.* **redeem'ing**; **redeem'less**, not to be redeemed.—**the Redeemer**, the Saviour, Jesus Christ. [L. *redimĕre* (perh. through Fr. *rédimer*)—*red-*, back, *emĕre*, to buy.]

redeliver, *rē-di-liv'ǝr*, *v.t.* to restore: to free again: (*Shak.*) to report the words of.—*ns.* **redeliv'erance**; **redeliv'erer**; **redeliv'ery.**

redemption, *ri-dem(p)'shǝn*, *n.* act of redeeming: atonement.—*ns.* **redemp'tioner**, an emigrant who bound himself to service until his fare was made up; **Redemp'tionist**, a Trinitarian friar.—*adj.* **redemp'tive.**—*n.* **Redemp'torist**, a missionary priest of a congregation founded by Alfonso Liguori in 1732 for work among the people.—*adj.* **redemp'tory.** [L. *redimĕre, redemptum*; cf. **redeem**.]

redeploy, *rē-di-ploi'*, *v.t.* to rearrange so as to promote greater efficiency.—*n.* **redeploy'ment.**

redia, *rē'di-ä*, *n.* a form in the life-cycle of the trematodes:—*pl.* **rē'diae** (*-ē*). [Named after Francesco Redi (1626-98), Italian naturalist.]

redingote, *red'ing-gōt*, *n.* a long double-breasted (orig. man's, later woman's) overcoat. [Fr.,—Eng. **riding-coat**.]

redintegrate, *red-in'ti-grāt*, *v.t.* to restore to wholeness, to renew: to restore, re-establish.—*adj.* restored: renewed.—*n.* **redintegrā'tion.** [L. *redintegrāre, -ātum*—*red-*, again, *integrāre*, to make whole—*integer*.]

redisburse, *rē-dis-burs'*, *v.t.* to refund.

redolent, *red'ō-lǝnt*, *adj.* fragrant: smelling (with *of*): suggesting associations. — *ns.* **red'olence**, **red'olency.** — *adv.* **red'olently.** [L. *redolēns, -entis*—*red-*, again, *olēre*, to emit smell.]

redouble, *ri-dub'l*, *v.t.* and *v.i.* to double: to repeat: to re-echo: to increase: (*rē'dub'l*) to double after previous doubling.—*n.* (*rē'dub'l*) an act or fact of redoubling, as in bridge.—*n.* **redoub'lement** (*ri-*).

redoubt, *ri-dowt'*, *n.* (*fort.*) a field-work enclosed on all sides, its ditch not flanked from the parapet: an inner last retreat. [Fr. *redoute*—It. *ridotto-*

L. *reductus*, retired—*redūcĕre*; the *b* from confusion with next word.]

redoubt, ri-dowt', *v.t.* (*arch.*) to fear.—*adjs.* **redoubt'able**, formidable: valiant; **redoubt'ed**. [O.Fr. *redouter*, to fear greatly—L. *re-*, back, *dubitāre*, to doubt.]

redound, ri-downd', *v.i.* (*Spens.*) to overflow: (*Milt.*) to be in excess: (*Spens.*) to surge: (*Spens.*) to be filled: to flow back: to return: to rebound, be reflected or echoed: to turn, recoil, be reflected, as a consequence (to one's credit, discredit, advantage, &c.): to conduce: (*Spens.*) to rise one above another in receding series.—*v.t.* (*fig.*) to cast, reflect.—*n.* the coming back, as an effect or consequence, return.—*n.* and *adj.* **redound'ing**. [Fr. *rédonder*—L. *redundāre*—*red*-, back, *undāre*, to surge—*unda*, a wave.]

redowa, red'ō-vä, *n.* a Bohemian dance: music for it, usually in quick triple time. [Ger. or Fr.,—Czech *reydovák*.]

redraft, rē-dráft', *n.* a new draft or copy: a new bill of exchange which the holder of a protested bill draws on the drawer or endorsers, for the amount of the bill, with costs and charges.

redress, ri-dres', *v.t.* to set right: to readjust: (*Spens.*) to restore: to remedy: to compensate.—*n.* relief: reparation.—*v.t.* and *v.i.* **re-dress** (rē'dres'), to dress again: to dress in different clothes.—*n.* **redress'er** (ri-), one who redresses abuses or injuries.—*adj.* **redress'ive**, (*Thomson*) affording redress. [Fr. *redresser* (see **dress**); partly from pfx. *re-* and **dress**.]

redruthite, red'rooth-īt, *n.* copper glance, a mineral found at *Redruth* in Cornwall.

redshort, red'short, *adj.* brittle at red-heat.—Also **red'sear, -share, -shire.** [Sw. *rödskör*—*röd*, red, *skör*, brittle.]

reduce, ri-dūs', *v.t.* (now *rare*) to bring back: to restore to an old state: to bring into a new state: to change to another form: to express in other terms: to range in order or classification: to adapt, adjust: to translate: to put (as into writing, practice): to bring into a lower state: to lessen: to diminish in weight or girth: to weaken: (*mil.*) to degrade: to impoverish: to subdue: to subject to necessity: to drive into a condition: to break up, separate, disintegrate: (*mil., obs.*) to disband: to bring to the metallic state: to remove oxygen from, or affect in an analogous manner, as by combining with hydrogen, or removing any strongly electronegative atoms or groups: (*Scots law*) to annul.—*v.i.* to resolve itself: to slim, or lessen weight or girth.—*p.adj.* **reduced'**, in a state of reduction: weakened: impoverished: diminished: simplified in structure.—*ns.* **reduc'er**, one who reduces: a means of reducing: a joint-piece for connecting pipes of varying diameter; **reducibil'ity**.—*adj.* **reduc'ible**, that may be reduced.—*n.* **reduc'ibleness**.—*adj.* **reduc'ing**.—*n.* **reduction** (-*duk'shən*), act of reducing or state of being reduced: diminution: lowering of price: subjugation: (*arith.*) changing of numbers or quantities from one denomination to another.—*adj.* **reduc'tive**, (*arch.*) bringing back: reducing. —*adv.* **reduc'tively.**—**reduce to the ranks,** to degrade, for misconduct, to the condition of a private soldier; **reducing agent,** a substance with a strong affinity for oxygen, or the like, serving to remove it from others; **reducing flame,** a hot luminous blowpipe flame in which substances can be reduced; **reduction division,** (*biol.*) meiosis; **reduction works,** smelting works. [L. *redūcĕre*, *reductum*—*re*-, back, *dūcĕre*, to lead.]

reduit, rā-dwē, *n.* an inner fortified retreat for a garrison. [Fr. *réduit*.]

redundant, ri-dun'dənt, *adj.* (*Milt.*) surging: (*obs.*) overflowing: copious: over-copious: superfluous. — *ns.* **redun'dance**, **redun'dancy**. — *adv.* **redun'dantly.** [L. *redundāns*, -*āntis*, pr.p. of *redundāre*, to overflow.]

reduplicate, ri-dū'pli-kāt, *v.t.* to double: to repeat. —*v.i.* to double: (*gram.*) to exhibit reduplication. —*adj.* doubled: (*gram.*) showing reduplication: (*bot.*) in aestivation, valvate with edges turned outwards. — *n.* **reduplica'tion**, a folding or

doubling: (*gram.*) the doubling of the initial part, in inflection and word-formation, as in L. *fefelli*, perf. of *fallō*, Gr. *tetyphă*, perf. of *typtō.*—*adj.* **redū'plicătive.** [L. *reduplicāre*, -*ātum*—*duplicāre*, to double.]

ree, rē, see **ruff** (2).

reebok, rā'bok, *n.* a South African antelope. [Du.]

reech, rēch. Same as **reek.**—*adj.* **reech'y** (*Shak.*) rechie, reechie), smoky, grimy.

re-echo, rē-ek'ō, *v.t.* to echo back: to repeat as or like an echo.—*v.i.* to give back echoes: to resound.—*n.* a re-echoing.

reed, reede (*Spens.*). Same as **rede.**

reed, rēd, *n.* a tall stiff hard-culmed marsh or water grass of various kinds, esp. *Phragmites communis*: a thing made, or formerly made, of a reed or reeds—a pen, an arrow, a measuring rod, a music pipe, the vibrating tongue of an organ-pipe or wood-wind instrument (with or without the parts to which it is attached), a weaver's appliance for separating the warp threads and beating up the weft, thatching: a small reedlike moulding: a reed-instrument.—*adj.* (*Shak.*) reedlike.—*v.t.* to thatch.—*ns.* **reed'-band**, a band of reed-instruments; **reed'-bed**; **reed'-bird**, the bobolink; **reed'-bunt'ing**, the black-headed bunting; **reed'-drawing**, the combing out of rough straw by means of a frame.—*adjs.* **reed'ed**, covered with reeds: having reeds; **reed'en**, of reed.—*ns.* **reed'er**, a thatcher; **reed'-grass**, a reedlike grass of various kinds (as Phalaris, Arundo); **reed'iness**; **reed'ing**, the milling on the edge of a coin: a reed moulding; **reed'-instrument**, a wood-wind with reed—as clarinet, oboe, bassoon; **reed'-knife**, a tool for organ-tuning; **reed'ling**, the bearded titmouse; **reed'-mace**, cat's tail (Typha); **reed'-or'gan**, a keyboard instrument with free reeds, as the harmonium, the American organ; **reed'-pheas'ant**, the bearded titmouse; **reed'-pipe**, an organ-pipe whose tone is produced by the vibration of a reed, the pipe acting as resonator; **reed'-rond**, (*East Anglia*) a reed thicket; **reed'-sparr'ow**, the reed-bunting: the sedge-warbler; **reed'-stop**, a set of reed-pipes controlled by a single stop-knob; **reed'-war'bler**, a warbler that frequents marshy places and builds its nest on reeds—also called **reed'-wren**, the **reed'-thrush** being a larger species (greater reed-warbler).—*adj.* **reed'y**, abounding with reeds: resembling or sounding as a reed.—**free reed**, a reed vibrating in an opening without touching the sides. [O.E. *hréod*; cf. Du. and Ger. *riet*.]

re-edify, rē-ed'i-fī, *v.t.* to rebuild. — (*Spens.*) **reëd'ifye.**—*ns.* **re-edifica'tion**; **re-ed'ifier.** [L. *aedificāre*, to build.]

reef, rēf, *n.* a chain of rocks at or near the surface of water: a shoal or bank: (orig. *Austr.*) a gold-bearing lode or vein: (*S.Afr.*) the encasing rock of a diamond-mine, all ground in the mine other than diamondiferous.—*n.* **reef'-builder**, a coral-animal that forms reefs. [Du. *rif*—O.N. *rif*.]

reef, rēf, *n.* a portion of a sail that may be rolled or folded up.—*v.t.* to reduce the exposed surface of, as a sail: to gather up in a similar way.— *ns.* **reef'-band**, a strengthening strip across a sail; **reef'er**, one who reefs: (*slang*) a midshipman: a reefing-jacket; **reef'ing**; **reef'ing-jack'et**, a short thick double-breasted jacket; **reef'-knot**, a knot used in tying reef-points, an ordinary knot with one end brought through again alongside the former part, resulting in two loops passing symmetrically through each other; **reef'-point**, a short rope on a reef-band to secure a reefed sail. [O.N. *rif*.]

reek, rēk, *n.* smoke: vapour: fume.—*v.i.* to emit smoke, fumes, or (esp. evil) smell: to exhale. — *v.t.* to expose to smoke: to exhale.—*adj.* **reek'ing**. —*adj.* **reek'y** (*Scot.* reek'ie), smoky: smoked: (*Shak.*) foul.—**Auld Reekie,** Edinburgh. [O.E. *réc*; O.N. *reykr*, Ger. *rauch*, Du. *rook*, smoke; a Northern form; cf. **reech**.]

reel, rēl, *n.* a cylinder, drum, spool, bobbin, or frame on which thread, fishing-line, wire, cables, photographic film, or the like may be wound: a length of material so wound—for cinematograph

Neutral vowels in unaccented syllables : *el'ə-mənt*, *in'fənt*, *ran'dəm*

film 1000 feet : a sound like that of a fisherman's **reel** : (*Scot.*) a loud rattling : a din : a whirl : a **stagger** : a lively dance, esp. Highland or Irish : a tune for it, usu. in 4-4, sometimes in 6-8 time. —*v.t.* to wind on a reel : to take off by or from a reel : to draw by means of a reel : to utter fluently and unhesitatingly : (*Spens.*) to cause to whirl or roll : (*Shak.*) to stagger along : to dance reelingly. —*v.i.* to whirl : to seem to swirl or sway : to **totter** : to stagger : to waver : to be hurled : to make the sound of a fisherman's reel : (*Scot.*) to rattle : to dance the reel.—*n.* reel′er, one who reels : the grasshopper-warbler.—*n.* and *adj.* **reel′ing.**—*adv.* reel′ingly.—(right) off the reel, in uninterrupted course or succession : without stop or hesitation ; reel off, to give out with rapidity or fluency ; Virginia reel, an American country-dance. [O.E. *hréol*, but possibly partly of other origin ; Gael. *righil* (the dance) may be from English.]

re-enforce, *rē-in-fōrs′*, *v.t.* to strengthen : to reinforce : (*Shak.*) to reassemble, rally.—*n.* re-enforce′ment, reinforcement.

re-enter, *rē-en′tər*, *v.t.* and *v.i.* to enter again or anew : in engraving, to cut deeper.—*p.adj.* re-en′tering, entering again : pointing or turned inwards.—*n.* re-en′trance, the act or achievement of entering again : the fact of being re-entrant (in this sense also re-en′trancy).—*adj.* re-en′trant, pointing inwards (opp. to *salient*) : (*elect.*) returning upon itself at the ends.—*n.* a re-entering angle : a valley, depression, &c., running into a main feature : the concavity between two salients.—*n.* re-en′try, an entering again : resumption of possession : (*cards*) bringing one's hand in again.

reest, reasty. See reast (1).

reest, reist, reast, *rēst*, *v.t.* (*Scot.*) to cure with smoke.—*v.i.* to be smoke-dried. [Origin obscure.]

reest, reist, *rēst*, *v.i.* (*Scot.*) of a horse, suddenly to refuse to move, to baulk.—*n.* a sudden fit of stubbornness.—*adj.* reest′y. [Perh. rest, or arrest.]

reeve, *rēv*, *n.* (*hist.*) a high official, chief magistrate of a district : a bailiff or steward. [O.E. *geréfa* ; cf. grieve (*Scots*).]

reeve, *rēv*, *v.t.* to pass the end of a rope through : to pass through any hole, as the channel of a block : to thread one's way through : to fasten by reeving :—*pa.t.* and *pa.p.* reeved, rove. [Origin obscure.]

reeve, *rēv*, ree, *rē*, *n.* fem. of ruff (2). [Origin obscure.]

refection, *ri-fek′shən*, *n.* refreshment : a meal or repast.—*v.t.* refect (*-fekt′* ; back-formation), to refresh.—*v.i.* to take a repast.—*ns.* refec′tioner, refectorian (*rē-fek-tō′ri-ən*), the officer in charge of the refectory and its arrangements ; refectory (*ri-fek′tər-i* ; sometimes *ref′ik-*), a dining-hall, esp. monastic.—Refection Sunday, Refreshment Sunday. [L. *reficĕre, refectum—facĕre*, to make.]

refel, *ri-fel′*, *v.t.* to refute : to disprove : to confute : to repulse :—*pr.p.* refell′ing ; *pa.t.* and *pa.p.* refelled′. [L. *refellĕre—fallĕre*, to deceive.]

refer, *ri-fər′*, *v.t.* (*obs.*) to reproduce, represent : to assign : to impute : to attribute : to bring into relation : to deliver, commit, or submit : to hand over for consideration : to direct for information, confirmation, testimonials, or whatever is required : to direct the attention of : (*obs.*) to postpone : (*rare*) to recount : to direct to sit an examination again, fail.—*v.i.* to have relation or application, to relate : to direct the attention : to turn for information, confirmation, &c. : to turn, apply, or have recourse : to make mention or allusion (with to) :—*pr.p.* referr′ing ; *pa.t.* and *pa.p.* referred′.—*adj.* referable or *ref′ər-ə-bl* ; sometimes referr′ible, *ri-fer′i-bl*), that may be referred or assigned.—*n.* referee (*ref-ə-rē′*), one to whom anything is referred : an arbitrator, umpire, or judge.—*v.t.* to act as referee for.—*v.i.* to act as referee.—*ns.* ref′erence, the act of referring : a submitting for information or decision : (*law*) the act of submitting a dispute for investigation or decision : relation : allusion : (loosely) one who is referred to : (loosely) a testimonial : a direction to a book

or passage ; ref′erence-book, a book to be consulted on occasion, not for consecutive reading ; ref′erence-mark, a character, as *, †, or a cock-up figure, used to refer to notes ; referendary (*-end′ə-ri*), a referee : formerly a court official who was the medium of communication with the pope, emperor, &c. ; referen′dum, the principle or practice of submitting a question directly to the vote of the entire electorate.—*adj.* referential (*-en′shl*), containing a reference : pointing or referring to something else.—*adv.* referen′tially. —terms of reference, a guiding statement defining the scope of an investigation or similar piece of work : (loosely) the scope itself. [L. *referre*, to carry back—*ferre*, to carry.]

refigure, *rē-fig′ər*, *v.t.* (*Shak.*) to represent anew, reproduce : to restore to form : to calculate anew.

refill, *rē-fil′*, *v.t.* to fill again.—*n.* (*rē′* or *-fil′*) a fresh fill : a duplicate for refilling purposes.

refine, *ri-fīn′*, *v.t.* to purify : to clarify : to free from coarseness, vulgarity, crudity : to make more cultured.—*v.i.* to become more fine, pure, subtle, or cultured : to apply or affect subtlety or nicety : to improve by adding refinement or subtlety (with *on* or *upon*).—*adj.* refined′.—*adv.* refin′edly, in a refined manner : with affected elegance.—*ns.* refin′edness (*obs.*) ; refine′ment, act or practice of refining : state of being refined : culture in feelings, taste, and manners : an improvement : a subtlety : an excessive nicety ; refin′er ; refin′ery, a place for refining ; refin′ing. [L. re-, denoting change of state, and fine.]

refit, *rē-fit′*, *v.t.* to fit out afresh and repair.—*v.i.* to undergo refitting.—*ns.* refit′, refit′ment, refitt′ing. [fit (1).]

reflate, *rē-flāt′*, *v.t.* to inflate after deflation.—*n.* refla′tion.

reflect, *ri-flekt′*, *v.t.* to bend or send back or aside : to throw back after striking : to give an image of in the manner of a mirror : (*fig.*) to express, reproduce : (*fig.*) to cast, shed (as credit, discredit) : to consider meditatively.—*v.i.* to bend or turn back or aside : to be mirrored : (*Shak.*) to cast a light : to meditate : to cast reproach or censure (with *on* or *upon*) : to bring harmful results.—*adj.* reflect′ed, cast or thrown back : turned or folded back : mirrored.—*n.* reflect′er, (*Swift*) one who casts reflections.—*adj.* reflect′ing. —*adv.* reflect′ingly, meditatively : with implication of censure.—*n.* reflection, also (now chiefly in scientific use) reflexion (*ri-flek′shən*), a turning, bending, or folding aside, back, or downwards : folding upon itself : rebound : change of direction when a ray strikes upon a surface and is thrown back : reflected light, colour, heat, &c. : an image in a mirror : the action of the mind by which it is conscious of its own operations : attentive consideration : contemplation : a thought or utterance resulting from contemplation : censure or reproach.—*adjs.* reflec′tionless ; reflect′ive, reflecting : reflected : meditative.—*adv.* reflect′ively.—*ns.* reflect′iveness ; reflect′or, a reflecting surface, instrument, or body : a reflecting telescope ; reflet (*ra-flē′, -flā′* Fr.), an iridescent or metallic lustre.—*adj.* reflex (*rē′fleks*, formerly *ri-fleks′*), bent or turned back : reflected : reciprocal : turned back upon itself : involuntary, produced by or concerned with response from a nerve-centre to a stimulus from without : (*paint.*) illuminated by light from another part of the same picture : (*wireless*) using the same valve or valves for high- and low-frequency amplification. —*n.* reflection : reflected light : a reflected image : an expression, manifestation, outward representation : a reflex action : a reflex wireless set.—*v.t.* reflex′, to bend back : (*Shak.*) to project, direct. —*adj.* reflexed′, (*bot.*) bent abruptly backward or downward.—*n.* reflexibil′ity.—*adjs.* reflex′ible ; reflex′ive, (*gram.*) indicating that the action turns back upon the subject.—*advs.* reflex′ively ; reflex′ly (or *rē′*).—reflecting microscope, one using a system of mirrors instead of lenses ; reflecting telescope, one in which an image is produced by a concave mirror and magnified by an eyepiece ; reflex light, a lens with reflecting back, sending back a beam of red light when the headlight, e.g. of a motor-car, shines on it. [L. *reflectĕre*, *reflexum—flectĕre*, to bend.]

reflow', *rē-flō'*, *v.i.* to ebb: to flow again.—*ns.* **reflow'ing**, **reflow'ing**, ebb: reflux.

refluent, *ref'loo-ǝnt*, *adj.* flowing back: ebbing: tidal.—*ns.* **ref'luence**, **reflux** (*rē'fluks*), flowing back: ebb. [L. *refluēns*, *-entis*, pr.p. of *refluĕre—fluĕre*, *fluxum*, to flow; *fluxus*, *-ūs*, a flow.]

refocillate, *ri-fos'il-āt*, *v.t.* (*obs.*) to refresh, cherish.—*n.* **refocilla'tion**. [L. *refocillāre*, *-ātum*, to cherish—*focus*, a hearth.]

reform, *re-form*, *rē'form'*, *v.t.* and *v.i.* to form again or anew.—*v.t.* **reform'** (*ri-*), to transform: (*Milt.*) to restore, rebuild: to amend: to make better: to remove defects from: to redress: to bring to a better way of life: (*Spens.*) to chastise: (*Milt.*) to prune: (*mil. hist.*) to break up in reorganisation, hence to disband, dismiss.—*v.i.* to abandon evil ways.—*n.* amendment or transformation, esp. of a system or institution: a stricter offshoot or branch of a religious order: an extension or better distribution of parliamentary representation.—*adj.* **reform'able** (*ri-*).—*ns.* **reformabil'ity**; **re-formation** (*rē'-for-mā'shǝn*), the act of forming again: (*ref-ǝr-mā'shǝn*) the act of reforming: amendment: improvement: **Reformation**, the great religious revolution of the 16th century, which gave rise to the various evangelical or Protestant organisations of Christendom; **reforma'tionist**.—*adjs.* **reformative** (*ri-form'ǝ-tiv*), tending to produce reform; **refor'matory**, reforming: tending to produce reform.—*n.* an institution for reclaiming young delinquents.—*adj.* **re'formed'**, **re'-formed'**, formed again or anew: (*ri-formd'*) changed: amended: improved: **Reformed'**, Protestant, esp. Calvinistic in doctrine or polity.—*ns.* **reform'er**, one who reforms: one who advocates political reform: **Reform'er**, one of those who took part in the Reformation of the 16th century; **reform'ism**; **reform'ist**, a reformer: an advocate of reform, or of not very thorough-going reform.—**Reformed Presbyterian**, Cameronian. [L. *refōrmāre*, *-ātum—fōrmāre*, to shape—*fōrma*, form; partly from *re-* and **form**.]

reformado, *ref-or-mā'dō*, *-mä'dō*, *n.* (*hist.*) a disbanded or dismissed soldier: an officer whose company has been disbanded: an officer without a command: a volunteer serving as an officer.—Also **reformāde'** (*Bunyan*). [Sp. *reformado*, reformed.]

refract, *ri-frakt'*, *v.t.* to deflect on passage into another medium, as rays of light, sound, &c.: to produce by refraction.—*adj.* (*rare*) **refracted**.—*adjs.* **refract'able**, refrangible; **refrac'ted**, deflected on passage into another medium: (*bot.*) bent sharply back from the base; **refract'ing**.—*n.* **refrac'tion**.—*adj.* **refrac'tive**, refracting: of refraction.—*ns.* **refractivity** (*rē-frak-tiv'i-ti*); **rēfractom'eter**, an instrument for measuring refractive indices; **refrac'tor** (*ri-*), anything that refracts: a refracting telescope.—**angle of refraction**, the angle between a refracted ray and the normal to the bounding surface; **double refraction**, the separation of an incident ray of light into two refracted rays, polarised in perpendicular planes; **refractive index**, the ratio of the sine of the angle of incidence to that of the angle of refraction when a ray passes from one medium to another. [L. *refringĕre*, *refrāctum—frangĕre*, to break.]

refractory (formerly **refractary**), *ri-frak'tǝr-i*, *adj.* unruly: unmanageable: obstinate: perverse: resistant to ordinary treatment, stimulus, disease, &c.: esp. difficult of fusion: fire-resisting.—*n.* a substance that is able to resist high temperatures, &c., used in lining furnaces, &c.—*adv.* **refrac'torily**.—*n.* **refrac'toriness**. [L. *refrāctārius*, stubborn.]

refrain, *ri-frān'*, *n.* a burden, a line or phrase recurring, esp. at the end of a stanza: the music of such a burden. [O.Fr. *refrain—refraindre—*L. *refringĕre—frangĕre*, to break.]

refrain, *ri-frān'*, *v.t.* to curb: to restrain: (*Shak.*) to abstain from: (*obs.*) to keep away from.—*v.i.* to keep from action: to forbear: to abstain.

[O.Fr. *refrener—*L.L. *refrēnāre—re-*, back, *frēnum*, a bridle.]

refrangible, *ri-fran'ji-bl*, *adj.* that may be refracted.—*n.* **refrangibil'ity**. [See **refract**.]

refresh, *ri-fresh'*, *v.t.* to make fresh again: to freshen up: to give new vigour, life, liveliness, spirit, brightness, fresh appearance, coolness, moistness, &c., to.—*v.i.* to become fresh again: (*coll.*) to take refreshment, esp. drink.—*v.t.* **refresh'en**, to make fresh again.—*ns.* **refresh'ener**; **refresh'er**, one who, or that which, refreshes: (*coll.*) a cool drink: a fee paid to counsel for continuing his attention to a case, esp. when adjourned: (*coll.*) a douceur to encourage further exertions: a subsequent course of training or instruction to maintain or reattain the old standard (also *adj.*).—*adj.* **refresh'ful**, full of power to refresh: refreshing. — *adv.* **refresh'fully**. — *adj.* **refresh'ing**, pleasantly cooling, inspiriting, reviving, invigorating.—*adv.* **refresh'ingly**.—*ns.* **refresh'ment**, the act of refreshing: state of being refreshed: renewed strength or spirit: that which refreshes, as food or rest: (in *pl.*) drink or a light meal; **refresh'ment-room.**—**Refreshment**, or **Refection, Sunday**, the fourth Sunday in Lent, when the story of the loaves and fishes is read in English and R.C. churches.

refrigerant, *ri-frij'ǝ-rant*, *adj.* cooling: giving a feeling of coolness: refreshing.—*n.* a freezing or cooling agent: that which gives a cool feeling.—*v.t.* **refrig'erāte**, to freeze: to make cold: to make to feel cool: to expose to great cold, as for preservation of food.—*v.i.* to become cold.—*n.* **refrigera'tion**.—*adj.* **refrig'erative** (*-rǝ-tiv*), cooling.—*n.* **refrig'erator** (*-rā-tǝr*), an apparatus or chamber for producing and maintaining a low temperature.—*adj.* **refrig'eratory** (*-rǝ-tǝr-i*), cooling: refrigerative.—*n.* a refrigerator: a chamber in which ice is formed: a water-filled vessel for condensing in distillation. [L. *refrīgerāre*, *-ātum—re-*, denoting change of state, *frīgerāre—frīgus*, cold.]

refringe, *ri-frinj'*, *v.t.* (*obs.*) to refract.—*ns.* **fring'ency**, refractivity.—*adj.* **refring'ent**. [L. *refringĕre*; see **refract**.]

reft, *reft*, *pa.t.* and *pa.p.* of **reave**.

refuge, *ref'ūj*, *n.* shelter or protection from danger or trouble: an asylum or retreat: a street island for foot-passengers: recourse in difficulty.—*v.t.* and *v.i.* to shelter.—*n.* **refugee'**, one who flees for refuge to another country, esp. from religious persecution or political commotion: a fugitive.—**house of refuge**, a shelter of the destitute. [Fr.,—L. *refugium—fugĕre*, to flee.]

refulgent, *ri-ful'jǝnt*, *adj.* casting a flood of light: radiant: beaming.—*ns.* **reful'gence**, **reful'gency**. [L. *refulgēns*, *-ēntis*, pr.p. of *refulgēre—re-*, inten., *fulgēre*, to shine.]

refund, *ri-* or *rē-fund'*, *v.t.* (now *rare*) to pour back: to repay.—*v.i.* to restore what was taken.—*v.t.* (*rē-fund'*) to fund anew.—*ns.* **refund** (*rē'fund* or *ri-fund'*); **refund'er**; **refund'ment** (*ri-*). [L. *refundĕre—fundĕre*, to pour.]

refuse, *ri-fūz'*, *v.t.* to decline to take or accept: to renounce: to decline to give or grant: (of a horse) to decline to jump over: (*cards*) to fail to follow suit to: to decline to meet in battle: (*mil.*) to hold back from the regular alignment in action.—*v.i.* to make refusal.—*v.t.* **re-fuse** (*rē-fūz'*), to fuse again.—*adj.* **refus'able** (*ri-*).—*ns.* **refus'al**, the act of refusing: the option of taking or refusing: a thing refused; **refus'er**; **re-fusion** (*rē-fū'zhǝn*), a new or repeated fusion. [Fr. *refuser*—L. *refūsum*, pa.p. of *refundĕre—fundĕre*, to pour; cf. **refund**.]

refuse, *ref'ūs*, *adj.* rejected as worthless.—*n.* that which is rejected or left as worthless. [Fr. *refus*; see foregoing.]

refute, *ri-fūt'*, *v.t.* to disprove.—*adj.* **refutable** (*ref'ūt-ǝ-bl*, or *ri-fūt'*).—*adv.* **ref'utably** (or *ri-fūt'*).—*ns.* **refu'tal**; **refutā'tion** (*ref-*); **refu'ter**. [L. *refūtāre*; see **confute**.]

regain, *ri-* or *rē-gān'*, *v.t.* to gain back: to get back to.—*n.* recovery.—*adj.* **regain'able**.—*ns.* **regain'er**; **regain'ment**. [Fr. *regaigner* (now *regagner*).]

regal, $r\bar{e}'gl$, *adj.* royal: kingly.—*adj.* **regalian** (ri-$g\bar{a}'li$-∂n), regal.—*ns.* **regalism** ($r\bar{e}'g\partial l$-izm), royal supremacy, esp. in Church matters; **re'galist**; **regality** (ri-$gal'i$-ti), state of being regal: royalty: sovereignty: (*Scot.*) a territorial jurisdiction formerly conferred by the king.—*adv.* **re'gally**. [L. *rēgālis*—*rēx*, a king—*regĕre*, to rule.]

regal, $r\bar{e}'gl$, *n.* a small portable organ. [Fr. *régale*.]

regale, ri-$g\bar{a}l'$, *v.t.* to feast: to gratify.—*v.i.* to feast.—*n.* a feast: a choice dish.—*n.* **regale'ment**. [Fr. *régaler*—It. *regalare*, perh.—*gala*, a piece of finery.]

regalia, ri-$g\bar{a}'li$-$\ddot{a}$, L. $r\bar{a}$-$g\bar{a}'li$-$\ddot{a}$, *n.pl.* royal privileges or powers (*sing.* **rega'le**): the insignia of royalty—crown, sceptre, &c., esp. those used at a coronation: (loosely) insignia or special garb generally, as of the Freemasons. [L. *rēgālis*, royal, neut. sing. *-e*, pl. *-ia*.]

regalia, ri-$g\bar{a}'li$-$\ddot{a}$, *n.* a big cigar. [Sp. *regalía*, royal privilege.]

regard, ri-$g\ddot{a}rd'$, *v.t.* to look at: to observe: to heed: to look to: to esteem or consider: to esteem highly: to have kindly feelings for: to respect: to take into account: to have respect or relation to.—*v.i.* to look: to give heed.—*n.* (*orig.*) look: (*Shak.*) a thing seen: (*Shak.*) intention: attention with interest: observation: estimation: esteem: kindly, affectionate, or respectful inclination: care: consideration: a thing to be considered: repute: respect: relation: reference: (*pl.*) in messages of greeting, respectful good will.—*adjs.* **regard'able**, worthy of consideration; **regard'ant**, attentive: (*her.*) looking backward.—*n.* **regard'er**.—*adj.* **regard'ful**, heedful: respectful.—*adv.* **regard'fully**.—*n.* **regard'fulness**.—*prep.* **regard'ing**, concerning.—*adj.* **regard'less**, heedless: inconsiderate.—*adj.* and *adv.* (*U.S.* and *vulg.*) without regard to expense.—*adv.* **regard'lessly**.—*n.* **regard'lessness**.—**as regards**, with regard to; **in regard of**, in view of: with respect to: in comparison with; **in this regard**, in this respect. [Fr. *regarder*—*garder*, to keep, watch.]

regatta, ri-$gat'\ddot{a}$, *n.* a yacht or boat race-meeting. [It. (Venetian) *regata*.]

regelation, $r\bar{e}$-ji-$l\bar{a}'sh\partial n$, *n.* freezing together again (as of ice melted by pressure when the pressure is released).—*v.t.* and *v.i.* **rē'gelāte**. [L. *gelāre*, to freeze.]

regency, $r\bar{e}'j\partial n$-si, *n.* the office, term of office, jurisdiction, or dominion of a regent: a body entrusted with vicarious government: (*specif.*) in French history, the minority of Louis XV., 1715-23, when Philip of Orleans was regent: in English history, the years 1810-20, when the Prince of Wales (George IV.) was Prince Regent.—*adj.* of, or in the style prevailing during, the French (or English) regency.—*n.* **rē'gence**, (*obs.*) government.

regenerate, ri-$jen'\partial r$-$\bar{a}t$, *v.t.* to produce anew: (*theol.*) to renew spiritually: to put new life or energy into: to restore: to reform.—*v.i.* to undergo regeneration, to be regenerated.—*adj.* ($-it$, $-\bar{a}t$) regenerated, renewed: changed from a natural to a spiritual state. — *adj.* **regen'erable**. — *ns.* **regen'eracy** ($-\partial$-si); **regenera'tion**, renewal of lost parts: spiritual rebirth: reformation: recovery of waste heat or other energy that would have been lost.—*adj.* **regen'erative**.—*adv.* **regen'eratively**.—*n.* **regen'erātor**, one who, or that which, regenerates: a chamber in which waste heat is, by reversal of draught, alternately stored up and given out to the gas and air entering.—*adj.* **regen'eratory** ($-\partial$-$t\partial r$-i). [L. *regenerāre*, $-\bar{a}tum$, to bring forth again—*re*–, again, *generāre*, to generate.]

regent, $r\bar{e}'j\partial nt$, *adj.* ruling: invested with interim or vicarious sovereign authority.—*n.* a ruler: one invested with interim authority on behalf of another: formerly in Scotland and elsewhere, a professor: a master or doctor who takes part in the regular duties of instruction and government in some universities.—*ns.* **rē'gent-bird**, a bowerbird (Sericulus) named in honour of the Prince Regent; **rē'gentship** (*Shak.*). [L. *regēns*, $-entis$, pr.p. of *regĕre*, to rule.]

regest, ri-$jest'$, *n.* (*obs.*) a register. [See **register**.]

regicide, $rej'i$-$s\bar{i}d$, *n.* the killing or killer of a king.—*adj.* **regici'dal**. [L. *rēx*, *rēgis*, a king, on the analogy of **homicide**, **parricide**, &c.]

régie, $r\bar{a}$-$zh\bar{e}$, *n.* a system of government monopoly, esp. in tobacco: the department concerned: tobacco sold by it. [Fr.]

régime, $r\bar{a}$-$zh\bar{e}m'$, *n.* regimen: administration. —Also **regime**. [Fr.,—L. *regimen*.]

regimen, $rej'i$-men, *n.* government: system of government: (*med.*) course of treatment, as diet: grammatical government: prevailing system or set of conditions.—*adj.* **regim'inal**. [L. *regimen*, *-inis*—*regĕre*, to rule.]

regiment, $rej'm\partial nt$, $rej'i$-$m\partial nt$, *n.* government: control: rule: regimen: a region under government: (*usu.* *rej'm\partial nt*) a body of soldiers constituting the largest permanent unit, commanded by a colonel.—*v.t.* ($rej'i$-$ment$, $-ment'$) to form into a regiment or regiments: to systematise, classify: to organise: to subject to excessive control.—*adj.* **regimental** ($-i$-$ment'l$), of a regiment.—*n.* (*in pl.*) the uniform of a regiment.—*n.* **regimentation** ($-i$-men-$t\bar{a}'sh\partial n$). [L.L. *regimentum*—L. *regĕre*, to rule.]

reginal, ri-$j\bar{i}'nl$, *adj.* of a queen: siding with a queen. [L. *rēgīna*, queen.]

region, $r\bar{e}'j\partial n$, *n.* a tract of country: any area or district, esp. one characterised in some way: a realm: a portion or division, as of the body: a portion of space: (*Shak.*, *Milt.*) the atmosphere, or a division of it, esp. the upper air: (*obs.*) the heavens.—*adj.* (*Shak.*) of the air.—*adj.* **rē'gional**.—*ns.* **rē'gionalism**, regional patriotism or particularism; **rē'gionalist**.—*adv.* **rē'gionally**.—*adj.* **rē'gionary**. [A.Fr. *regiun*—L. *rēgiō*, *-ōnis*—*regĕre*, to rule.]

register, $rej'is$-$t\partial r$, *n.* a written record or official list, regularly kept: the book containing such a record: a recording or indicating apparatus: (now *rare* or *U.S.*) a registrar: apparatus for regulating a draught: a register-plate: an organ stop or stop-knob: the compass of a voice or instrument: the range of tones produced in a particular manner: (*print.*) exact adjustment of position, as of colours in a picture, or letterpress on opposite sides of a leaf: registration: an entry in a register: a certificate of registration.—*v.t.* to enter or cause to be entered in a register: to record: to indicate: to put on record: to express: to represent by bodily expression: to adjust in register.—*v.i.* to enter one's name (esp. as a hotel guest): to correspond in register: (*coll.*) to make an impression, reach the consciousness.—*adj.* **reg'istered**, recorded, entered, or enrolled, as a voter, a letter requiring special precautions for security, &c.: made with a register-plate.—*n.* **reg'ister-plate**, in rope-making, a disk with holes to give each yarn its position: a chimney damper.—*adj.* **reg'istrable**.—*ns.* **reg'istrar** ($-tr\ddot{a}r$, or $-tr\ddot{a}r'$), one who keeps a register or official record; **Reg'istrar-Gen'eral**, an officer having the superintendence of the registration of all births, deaths, and marriages; **reg'istrarship**, office of a registrar; **reg'istrary**, Cambridge University registrar; **registrā'tion**, the act or fact of registering: something registered: the act or art of combining stops in organ-playing; **reg'istry**, registration: an office or place where a register is kept: a register: an entry in a register. —**Lord Clerk-Register**, an officer of the General Register House with duties concerned with the election of Scottish representative peers, formerly custodian of records and registers; **parish register**, a book in which births, deaths, and marriages are inscribed; **Register House**, the building in Edinburgh where Scottish records are kept; **register office**, a record-office: an employment office; **registry office**, an office for putting domestic servants in touch with employers: (*coll.*) a registrar's office, where births, &c., are recorded and civil marriages are celebrated; **ship's register**, a document showing the ownership of a vessel. [O.Fr. *registre* or L.L. *registrum*, for L. pl. *regesta*, things recorded—*re*–, back, *gerĕre*, to carry.]

regius, $r\bar{e}'ji$-∂s, L. $r\bar{a}'gi$-oos, *adj.* royal, as **rē'gius profess'or**, one whose chair was founded by

Henry VIII., or, in Scotland, by the Crown; **rē′gium dō′num**, a former annual grant of public money to nonconformist ministers in England, Scotland, and esp. Ireland. [L. *rēgius—rēx*, king.]

reglet, *reg′lit*, *n.* a flat, narrow moulding: a fillet: (*print.*) a strip for spacing between lines. [Fr. *réglet*, dim. of *règle*—L. *rēgula*, a rule.]

regma, *reg′mä*, *n.* (*bot.*) a fruit that splits into dehiscent parts:—*pl.* **reg′mata.** [Gr. *rhēgma*, *-atos*, a breaking.]

regnal, *reg′nl*, *adj.* of a reign.—*adj.* **reg′nant**, reigning (often after the noun, as queen regnant, a reigning queen, not a *queen consort*): prevalent. [L. *rēgnālis—rēgnum*, a kingdom, *rēgnāns, -āntis*, pr.p. of *rēgnāre*, to reign.]

regorge, *ri-*, *rē-gorj′*, *v.t.* to disgorge, regurgitate: to swallow again: (*Milt.*) to gorge to repletion.—*v.i.* to gush back. [Pfx. *re-* in various senses; *gorge*; or Fr. *regorger*, to overflow, abound.]

regrate, *ri-grāt′*, *v.t.* (*hist.*) to buy and sell again in or near the same market, thus raising the price—once a criminal offence in England.—*ns.* **regrā′ter, -tor**, (*hist.*) one who regrates: (*S.W. England*) a middleman; **regrā′ting.** [O.Fr. *regrater*; of doubtful origin.]

regrede, *ri-grēd′*, *v.i.* to retrograde.—*n.* **regrē′-dience** (*Herrick*). [L. *regredī—re-*, *gradī*, to go.]

regreet, *ri-grēt′*, *v.t.* to greet in return: (*Shak.*) to greet again: (*Shak.*) to greet.—*v.i.* to exchange greetings.—*n.* a greeting in return: (*Shak.*) a greeting (mutual or simple).

regress, *rē′gres*, *n.* passage back: return: reversion: backward movement or extension: right or power of returning: re-entry.—*v.i.* (*ri-gres′*) to go back: to recede: to return to a former place or state: to revert: (*astron.*) to move from east to west.—*n.* **regression** (*ri-gresh′ən*), act of regressing: reversion: return towards the mean.—*adj.* **regressive** (*ri-gres′iv*), going back: returning.—*adv.* **regress′ively**, in a regressive manner: by return.—*ns.* **regress′iveness** (*ri-*); **regressiv′ity** (*rē-*). [L. *regressus, -ūs* (n.) and *-ī* (perf.p. of *regredī*); see **regrede**.]

regret, *ri-gret′*, *v.t.* to remember with sense of loss or of having done amiss: to wish otherwise: (*pr.p.* **regrett′ing**; *pa.t.* and *pa.p.* **regrett′ed**).—*n.* sorrowful wish that something had been otherwise: sorrowful feeling of loss: compunction: an intimation of regret or refusal.—*adj.* **regret′ful**, feeling regret.—*adv.* **regret′fully.**—*adj.* **regrett′able**, to be regretted.—*adv.* **regrett′ably.** [O.Fr. *regreter, regrater*; poss. conn. with **greet**.]

reguerdon, *ri-gər′dən*, *n.* (*Shak.*) reward.—*v.t.* (*Shak.*) to reward. [O.Fr. *reguerdon.*]

regula, *reg′ū-lä*, *n.* the rule of a religious order: (*archit.*) a fillet, esp. under the Doric taenia, below each triglyph:—*pl.* **reg′ulae** (*-lē*).—*adj.* **reg′ular** (*-lər*), subject to a monastic rule (opp. to *secular*): governed by or according to rule, law, order, habit, custom, established practice, mode prescribed, or the ordinary course of things: of a marriage, celebrated by a minister of religion after proclamation of banns: normal: habitual: constant: steady: uniform: periodical: duly qualified: (*gram.*) inflected in the usual way (esp. of weak verbs): symmetrical, esp. (*bot.*) radially symmetrical or actinomorphic: (*geom.*) having all the sides and angles equal or all faces equal, equilateral, and equiangular, the same number meeting at every corner: also (of a pyramid) having a regular polygon for base and the other faces similar and equal isosceles triangles: (*mil.*) permanent, professional, or standing (opp. to *militia*, *volunteer*, and *territorial*): (*coll.*) thorough, out-and-out, esp. (*U.S.*) in party politics: (*slang*) of the same way of thinking as the speaker, hence ready to help or abet him, loyal, swell: (*coll.*) veritable.—*n.* a member of a religious order who has taken the three ordinary vows: a soldier of the regular army: a regular customer.—*n.* **regularisā′tion.**—*v.t.* **reg′ularise**, to make regular.—*n.* **regularity** (*-lar′i-ti*), state, character, or fact of being regular.—*adv.* **reg′ularly.**—*v.t.* **reg′ulate**, to control: to adapt or adjust continuously: to adjust by rule.—*v.i.* to

make regulations.—*n.* **regulā′tion**, act of regulating: state of being regulated: a rule or order prescribed.—*adj.* prescribed by regulation.—*adj.* **reg′ulātive**, tending to regulate.—*n.* **reg′ulātor**, one who, or that which, regulates: a controlling device, esp. for the speed of a clock or watch.—*adj.* **reg′ulatory** (*-lə-tər-i*). [L. *rēgula*, a rule—*regĕre*, to rule.]

regulus, *reg′ū-ləs*, *n.* an impure metal, an intermediate product in smelting of ores: antimony: **Regulus**, a first-magnitude star in Leo: the goldcrest genus.—*adj.* **reg′uline**.—*v.t.* **reg′ulise**, to reduce to regulus. [L. *rēgulus*, dim. of *rēx*, a king.]

regur, regar, *rä′, rē′gur*, *n.* the rich black cotton soil of India, full of organic matter. [Hind. *regar*.]

regurgitate, *ri-*, *rē-gur′ji-tāt*, *v.t.* to cast out again: to pour back: to bring back into the mouth after swallowing. —*v.i.* to gush back. — *adj.* **regur′gitant**.—*n.* **regurgitā′tion**. [L.L. *regurgitāre, -ātum—re-*, back, *gurges, gurgitis*, a gulf.]

reh, *rä*, *n.* an efflorescence of sodium salts on the soil in India. [Hindustani.]

rehabilitate, *rē-(h)ə-bil′i-tāt*, *v.t.* to reinstate, restore to former privileges, rights, rank, &c.: to clear the character of: to bring back into good condition, working order, prosperity: to make fit, after disablement, for making a living or playing a part in the world.—*n.* **rehabilitā′tion**. [L.L. *rehabilitāre, -ātum*; see **habilitate**.]

rehash, *rē-hash′*, *n.* something made up of materials formerly used.—Also *v.t.*

rehear, *rē-hēr′*, *v.t.* to hear again: to try over again, as a lawsuit.—*n.* **rehear′ing.**

rehearse, *ri-hərs′*, *v.t.* to repeat, say over, or read aloud: to enumerate: to recount, narrate in order: to perform privately for practice or trial: to practise beforehand: to train by rehearsal.—*v.i.* to take part in rehearsal.—*ns.* **rehears′al**, the act of rehearsing: repetition: enumeration: narration: a performance for trial or practice; **rehears′er**; **rehears′ing**. [O.Fr. *rehercer, reherser—re-*, again, *hercer*, to harrow—*herce* (Fr. *herse*)—L. *hirpex, -icis*, a rake, a harrow.]

rehoboam, *rē-(h)ō-bō′əm*, *n.* (*slang*) a large liquor measure or vessel, two jeroboams. [*Rehoboam*, king of Israel.]

rehouse, *rē-howz′*, *v.t.* to provide with a new house or houses.—*n.* **rehous′ing**.

Reich, *rïhh*, *n.* Germany as an empire (First Reich), federal republic (Second Reich), or unitary republic (Third Reich). — *ns.* **Reichsbank** (*rïhhs′-bängk*), the German state bank; **Reichsland** (*-länt*), imperial territory (i.e. Alsace-Lorraine); **reichsmark** (*-märk*), the German monetary unit 1924-48 (about 1 shilling); **Reichsrat(h)** (*-rät*), the Parliament of the former Austrian Empire: a deliberative Council of the German Republic, representing the States (under the Weimar constitution); **Reichstag** (*-tähh*), the Parliament of the German Reich. [Ger., O.E. *rīce*, kingdom; cf. **bishopric.**]

reif, *rēf*, *n.* (*Scot.*) spoliation. [O.E. *rēaf*; cf. **reave.**]

reify, *rē′i-fī*, *v.t.* to think of as a material thing.—*n.* **reification** (*-fi-kā′shən*).

reign, *rān*, *n.* (*arch.*) kingdom: realm: domain: rule, actual or nominal, of a monarch: predominance: predominating influence: time of reigning.—*v.i.* to be a monarch: to be predominant: to prevail. [O.Fr. *regne*—L. *rēgnum—regĕre*, to rule.]

reik. Same as **reak.**

reimbattell′d, *rē-im-bat′ld*, *pa.p.* (*Milt.*) drawn up again in battle array.

reimburse, *rē-im-burs′*, *v.t.* to repay: to pay an equivalent to for loss or expense.—*n.* **reimburse′ment**. [L.L. *imbursāre—in*, in, *bursa*, purse.]

reim-kennar, *rïm′ken-ər*, *n.* an enchanter, enchantress. [App. invented by Scott—Ger. *reim*, rhyme, *kenner*, knower.]

rein, *rān*, *n.* the strap of a bridle or either half of it: (*fig.*) any means of curbing or governing.—*v.t.* (*Shak.*) to fasten or tie by the rein: to furnish with reins: to govern with the rein: to restrain

Neutral vowels in unaccented syllables: *el′ə-mənt, in′fənt, ran′dəm*

or control : to stop or check (with *in* or *up*).—
v.i. (*Shak.*) to answer : to stop or slow up.—*ns.*
rein′-arm, rein′-hand, normally the left (opp.
to *whip-hand*).—*adj.* rein′less, without rein or
restraint.—*n.* reins′man, a skilful driver.—draw
rein, to pull up, stop riding ; give rein (or
the reins) to, to allow free play to, apply no
check to ; take the reins, to take control. [O.Fr.
reine, resne, rene (Fr. *rêne*), perh. through (hypothetical) L.L. *retina*, from L. *retinēre*, to hold back.]
rein. See reindeer, reins.

reindeer, rān′dēr, *n.* a large heavy deer (Rangifer),
wild and domesticated, of northern regions,
antlered in both sexes, the American variety (or
species) called the caribou.—Also (*rare*) rein.—
Reindeer Age, (*archaeol.*) the Magdalenian ;
reindeer moss, a lichen (*Cladonia rangiferina*),
the winter food of the reindeer. [O.N. *hreinndȳri*,
or O.N. *hreinn* (O.E. *hrán*) and deer.]

reinette, rā-net′. Same as rennet (apple).

reinforce, rē-in-fōrs′, *v.t.* to enforce again : to
strengthen with new force or support : to
strengthen : to increase by addition.—*v.i.* (*Shak.*)
to get reinforcements.—*n.* reinforce′ment, act
of reinforcing : additional force or assistance, esp.
of troops (commonly in *pl.*).—reinforced concrete, concrete strengthened by embedded steel
bars.

reinform, rē-in-form′, *v.t.* to inform anew : to
give form to again : to reanimate.

reinfund, rē-in-fund′, *v.i.* to flow in again. [L.
fundĕre, to pour.]

reins, rānz, *n.pl.* (*rare* or *obs.* in *sing.*) the kidneys,
now esp. as formerly supposed seat of emotion :
the loins. [O.Fr. *reins*—L. *rēn*, pl. *rēnēs.*]

reinstall, rē-in-stawl′, *v.t.* to install again.—*n.*
reinstal′ment.

reinstate, rē-in-stāt′, *v.t.* to restore to or re-
establish in a former station or condition.—*ns.*
reinstāte′ment ; reinstā′tion (*rare*).

reinsure, rē-in-shōōr′, *v.t.* to insure against risk
undertaken by insurance.—*ns.* reinsur′ance ; re-
insur′er.

reintegrate, rē-in′ti-grāt, reintegrā′tion. Same
as redintegrate, &c.

reinvest, rē-in-vest′, *v.t.* to clothe again : to endow
again : to invest again.—*n.* reinvest′ment.

reinvigorate, rē-in-vig′ər-āt, *v.t.* to put new vigour
into.—*n.* reinvigorā′tion.

reird, rērd, raird, rārd, *n.* (*Scot.*) an uproar,
clamour, din. [O.E. *reord.*]

reis, rīs. Same as rice (2).

reis, rās, *n.pl.* (*sing.* real, rā-āl′) an obsolete Portuguese and Brazilian money of account, 1000 reis
making a *milreis.* [Port.]

reist. Same as reast, or as reest (2 or 3).

reiter, rī′tər, *n.* a German cavalry soldier. [Ger.]

reiterate, rē-it′ər-āt, *v.t.* to repeat : to repeat
again and again.—*n.* reit′erance.—*adjs.* reit′er-
ant, reiterating ; reit′erate, -d.—*adv.* reit′er-
atedly.—*n.* reiterā′tion, act of reiterating : the
printing of the second side of a sheet.—*adj.*
reit′erative.—*n.* a word expressing reiteration :
a word formed by reduplication, commonly with
a difference.

reive, reiver. Same as reave, reaver.

reject, ri-jekt′, *v.t.* to throw away : to discard : to
refuse to accept, admit, or accede to : to refuse :
to renounce.—*n.* (usu. rē′) one who or that which
is rejected.—*adjs.* rejec′table or -ible.—*n.pl.*
rejectamen′ta, refuse : excrement. — *ns.* re-
jec′tion ; reject′or (also -er). [L. *rejicĕre,*
rejectum—*re-*, back, *jacĕre*, to throw.]

rejoice, ri-jois′, *v.t.* to make joyful : to gladden :
(*Shak.*) to be joyful because of.—*v.i.* to feel joy :
to exult : to make merry.—*adj.* rejoice′ful.—*n.*
rejoice′ment, rejoicing ; rejoic′er ; rejoic′ing,
act of being joyful : expression, subject, or experience of joy : (in *pl.*) festivities, celebrations,
merry-makings.—*adv.* rejoic′ingly.—rejoice in,
often facetiously, to have. [O.Fr. *resjoir, resjoiss-*
(Fr. *réjouir*)—L. *re-, ex, gaudēre*, to rejoice.]

rejoin, ri-join′, *v.i.* (*law*) to reply to a charge or
pleading, esp. to a plaintiff's replication.—*v.t.* to
say in reply, retort.—*v.t.* and *v.i.* (ri- and rē-) to

join again.—*ns.* rejoin′der (ri- ; *law*), the defendant's answer to a plaintiff's replication : an answer
to a reply : an answer ; rejoin′dūre (reioyn′dure,
Shak.), a joining again.

rejourn, ri-jurn′, *v.t.* (*Shak.*) to postpone, defer.
[Cf. adjourn.]

rejuvenate, ri-jōō′vi-nāt, *v.t.* to make young again :
to restore to youthful condition or to activity :
(*geol.*) to restore (by uplift) to earlier condition of
active erosion.—*v.i.* to rejuvenesce.—*ns.* rejuvenā′-
tion ; reju′venator.—*v.i.* rejuvenesce (-*es*′), to
grow young again : to recover youthful character :
(*biol.*) to undergo change in cell-contents to a
different, usu. more active, character : to resume
growth.—*v.t.* to rejuvenate.—*n.* rejuvenesc′ence.
—*adj.* rejuvenesc′ent.—*v.t.* reju′venise, to rejuvenate. [L. *juvenis*, young, *juvenēscĕre*, to
become young.]

reke, rēk, *v.i.* (*Spens.*) to reck. [O.E. *rēcan.*]

relapse, ri-laps′, *v.i.* to slide, sink, or fall back,
esp. into evil : to return to a former state or
practice : to backslide : to fall away.—*n.* a falling
back into a former bad state : (*med.*) the return
of a disease after partial recovery.—*adj.* relapsed′,
having relapsed.—*n.* relap′ser.—*adj.* relap′sing.
—relapsing fever, an infectious disease characterised by recurrent attacks of fever with enlargement of the spleen, caused by a Spirochaete
transmitted by ticks and lice. [L. *relābī, relāpsus*
—*lābī*, to slide.]

relate, ri-lāt′, *v.t.* to recount, narrate, tell : (*Milt.*)
to give an account of : (*Spens.*) to bring back :
to refer, bring into connexion or relation.—*v.i.*
(*law*) to date back in application : to have reference
or relation : to connect : (*Shak.*) to discourse.—
adj. relā′ted, recounted : referred : connected :
allied by kindred or marriage.—*ns.* relā′tedness ;
relā′ter, one who relates ; relā′tion, act of relating : state or mode of being related : narrative
or recital : statement : (*law*) an information : way
in which one thing is connected with another :
(*philos.*) a quality that can be predicated, not
of a single thing, but only of two or more together :
respect, reference : a relative by birth or marriage :
(in *pl.*) mutual dealings.—*adj.* relā′tional, pertaining to, expressing, or of the nature of, relation.—
adv. relā′tionally.—*ns.* relā′tionism, (*philos.*) the
doctrine that relations have an objective existence :
the doctrine of relativity of knowledge ; relā′tion-
ist.—*adj.* relā′tionless, kinless : unrelated.—*n.*
relā′tionship, state or mode of being related :
relations.—*adjs.* relatival (rel-ə-tī′vl), pertaining
to relation, esp. grammatical relation ; rel′ative
(-ə-tiv), in or having relation : correlative : corresponding : (*mus.*) having the same key-signature :
relevant : comparative : not absolute or independent : relating, having reference : (*gram.*) referring to an antecedent.—*n.* that which is relative :
a relative word, esp. a relative pronoun : one who
is related by blood or marriage.—*adv.* rel′atively.
—*ns.* rel′ativeness ; rel′ativism, relationism : a
doctrine of relativity ; rel′ativist ; relativ′itist,
one who studies or accepts relativity ; relativ′ity,
state or fact of being relative : a principle which
asserts that all phenomena occurring in the physical
universe are so conditioned that it is impossible by
their means to detect absolute motion or position,
and asserts further that all physical laws are unchanged in form whatever be the system of axes to
which they are referred ; relator (ri-lā′tər), one
who relates : a narrator : (*law*) one who lays an
information before the Attorney-General, enabling
him to take action.—relative density, specific
gravity, the weight of a substance compared with
that of an equal volume of a standard substance
(e.g. hydrogen, water) under the same, or standard,
conditions ; relative humidity, ratio of the
amount of water vapour in the air to the amount
that would saturate it at the same temperature ;
relativity of knowledge, the doctrine that the
nature and extent of our knowledge is determined
not merely by the qualities of the objects known,
but necessarily by the conditions of our cognitive
powers. [L. *relātus, -a, -um*, used as pa.p. of
referre, to bring back—*re-, ferre.*]

relax, *ri-laks'*, *v.t.* and *v.i.* to loosen: to slacken: to make or become less close, tense, rigid, strict, or severe.—*n.* a relaxing.—*adj.* and *n.* relax'ant, laxative: (a substance) having the effect of relaxing.—*n.* relaxā'tion (*re-*, *rē-*), act of relaxing: state of being relaxed: (*law*) partial remission: (*Scots law*) release from outlawry: recreation.—*adjs.* relax'ative; relax'ing, enervating. [L. *relaxāre*, *-ātum—laxus*, loose.]

relay, *ri-lā'*, also *rē'lā*, *rē'lā'*, *n.* a fresh set of dogs in hunting: a supply of horses, &c., to relieve others on a journey: a station for either of these: a relieving shift of men: a supplementary store of anything: a relay-race, or one of its stages: any device by which a weak electric current or other small power is used to control a strong one. —*v.t.* to place in, relieve, control, supply, or transmit by relay: to broadcast anew.—*v.i.* to obtain a relay: to operate a relay:—*pa.t.* and *pa.p.* relayed.—*n.* re'lay-race', a race between teams, each man running part of the total distance. [O.Fr. *relais*, relay of horses or dogs; origin obscure.]

relay, *rē-lā'*, *v.t.* to lay again:—*pa.t.* and *pa.p.* rēlaid'.

release, *rē-lēs'*, *v.t.* to grant a new lease of.

release, *ri-lēs'*, *v.t.* to let loose: to set free: to let go: to relieve: to slacken: to undo: to remit: to relinquish: (*law*) to surrender, convey, give up a right to: to make available, authorise sale, publication, exhibition, &c., of.—*n.* a setting free: liberation: discharge or acquittance: remission: mode of releasing: the giving up of a claim, conveyance: a catch for holding and releasing: authorisation to make available on a certain date: a thing so made available.—*adj.* releas'able.—*ns.* releasee', one to whom an estate is released: release'ment, release; releas'er; releas'or (*law*). [O.Fr. *relaissier*—L. *relaxāre*, to relax.]

relegate, *rel'i-gāt*, *v.t.* to banish: to send away, to consign: to dismiss: to assign: to refer: (*football*) to remove to a lower class.—*adj.* rel'egable.—*n.* relegā'tion. [L. *relēgāre*, *-ātum—re-*, away, *lēgāre*, to send.]

relent, *ri-lent'*, *v.i.* (*obs.*) to melt: to soften or grow less severe: (*Spens.*, *Milt.*) to give way: (*Spens.*) to abate, slacken: (*Spens.*) to slacken pace.—*v.t.* (*obs.*) to melt: (*Spens.*, *Burns*) to soften, cause to relent: (*Spens.*) to relax, moderate: (*Spens.*) to slow down: (*Spens.*) to regret, repent. —*n.* relenting: (*Spens.*) slowing.—*n.* and *adj.* relent'ing.—*adj.* relent'less, unrelenting: inexorable: merciless, stern.—*adv.* relent'lessly. —*ns.* relent'lessness; relent'ment (*rare*). [L. *re-*, back, *lentus*, sticky, sluggish, pliant.]

relevant, *rel'i-vont*, *adj.* bearing upon, or applying to, the purpose: pertinent: related: sufficient legally. — *ns.* rel'evance, rel'evancy. — *adv.* rel'evantly. [L. *relevāns*, *-āntis*, pr.p. of *relevāre*, to raise up, relieve; from the notion of helping; cf. **relieve**.]

reliable, **&c.** See **rely**.

relic, *rel'ik*, *n.* that which is left after loss or decay of the rest: a corpse (gener. *pl.*): (*R.C.*) any personal memorial of a saint, held in reverence as an incentive to faith and piety: a souvenir: a memorial of antiquity or object of historic interest: a survival from the past.—Also (*obs.*) rel'ique.— *n.* rel'ic-monger, one who traffics in or collects relics. [Fr. *relique*—L. *reliquiae*; see **reliquiae**.]

relict, *rel'ikt*, *n.* (*obs.*) a relic: a survivor or surviving trace: (*arch.*) a widow.—*adj.* (*ri-likt'*) left behind: surviving: (*geol.*) formed by removal of surrounding materials. [L. *relictus*, *-a*, *-um*, left, pa.p. of *relinquěre*, to leave.]

relide, *ri-līd'*, *pa.p.* (*Spens.*) for **relied**, in the sense of rejoined.

relief, *ri-lēf'*, *n.* the lightening or removal of any burden, discomfort, evil, pressure, or stress: release from a post or duty: one who releases another by taking his place: that which relieves or mitigates: aid in danger, esp. deliverance from siege: assistance to the poor: fresh supply of provisions: (*hunting*; *obs.*) feeding or seeking

food: a certain fine paid to the overlord by a feudal tenant's heir on coming into possession: (*Scots law*) release from obligation, or right to reimbursement of expenses thereby incurred: anything that gives diversity: projection or standing out from the general surface, ground, or level: a sculpture or other work of art executed in relief: appearance of standing out solidly: distinctness by contrast, esp. in outline.—*adj.* relief'less.—

Relief Church, a body that left the Church of Scotland on account of the oppressive exercise of patronage, organised in 1761, united with the United Secession Church in 1847 to form the United Presbyterian Church; **relief map**, a map in which the form of the country is shown by elevations and depressions of the material used, or by the illusion of such elevations and depressions, or (loosely) by other means. [O.Fr. *relef—relever*; see **relieve**, also **rilievo**.]

relieve, *ri-lēv'*, *v.t.* (*Shak.*) to lift up: to bring, give, or afford relief to: to release: to release from duty by taking the place of: to ease: to mitigate: to raise the siege of: to set off by contrast: to break the sameness of: to bring into relief: (*obs.*) to feed.—*adj.* reliev'able.—*n.* reliev'er.—*adj.* reliev'ing.—relieving arch, an arch in a wall to relieve the part below it from a superincumbent weight; **relieving officer**, an official appointed to superintend the relief of the poor. [O.Fr. *relever*—L. *relevāre*, to lift, relieve—*levāre*, to raise—*levis*, light.]

relievo, *ri-lē'vō*, also (*It.*) **rilievo**, *rē-lyä'vō*, *n.* (in art) relief: a work in relief: appearance of relief. [It. *rilievo*.]

religion, *ri-lij'ən*, *n.* belief in, recognition of, or an awakened sense of, a higher unseen controlling power or powers, with the emotion and morality connected therewith: rites or worship: any system of such belief or worship: devoted fidelity: monastic life: a monastic order: (*obs.*) Protestantism.—*adj.* relig'ionary, (*rare*) religious.— *n.* a member of a religious order: (*obs.*) a Protestant. —*n.* relig'ioner, a member of an order: a Protestant.—*v.t.* relig'ionise, to imbue with religion. —*v.i.* to make profession of being religious.—*ns.* relig'ionism, religiosity: bigotry; relig'ionist, one attached to a religion: a bigot.—*adjs.* relig'ionless; religiose (*-lij'i-ōs*, or *-ōs'*), morbidly or sentimentally religious.—*n.* religiosity (*-i-os'iti*), spurious or sentimental religion: religious feeling. —*adj.* and *adv.* religioso (*-i-ō'sō*; It.; *mus.*), in a devotional manner.—*adj.* relig'ious (*-əs*), of, concerned with, devoted to, or imbued with, religion: scrupulous: (*R.C.*) bound to a monastic life: strict.—*n.* one bound by monastic vows.— Also (*Fr.*) religieux (*rə-lē-zhyə*), *fem.* religieuse (*-zhyəz*).—*adv.* relig'iously.—*n.* relig'iousness. [L. *religiō*, *-ōnis*, *n.*, *religiōsus*, adj., perh. conn. with *religāre*, to bind, perh. with *relegěre*, to read again.]

reline, *rē-līn'*, *v.t.* to mark with new lines: to renew the lining of.

relinquish, *ri-ling'kwish*, *v.t.* to give up: to let go. —*n.* relin'quishment. [O.Fr. *relinquir*, *relinquiss-* —L. *relinquěre*, *relictum—re-*, *linquěre*, to leave.]

relique, *rel'ik*, *ri-lēk'*, *n.* an old form of **relic**.— *ns.* reliquaire (*rel-i-kwār'*), rel'iquary (*-kwər-i*), a receptacle for relics.—*adj.* rel'iquary, of relics: residual. [Fr.]

reliquiae, *ri-lik'wi-ē* (L. *re-lik-wi-ī*), *n.pl.* remains. [L.,—*relinquěre*, to leave.]

relish, *rel'ish*, *n.* a flavour: characteristic flavour: enough to give a flavour: appetising flavour: zest-giving quality or power: an appetiser, condiment: zestful enjoyment: gusto: pleasureful inclination.—*v.t.* to like the taste of: to be pleased with: to enjoy: to appreciate discriminatingly: to give a relish to: (*obs.*) to taste, experience.—*v.i.* to savour, smack: to have an agreeable taste: to give pleasure.—*adj.* rel'ishable. [O.Fr. *reles*, *relais*, remainder—*relaisser*, to leave behind.]

relish, **rellish**, *rel'ish*, *n.* a musical ornament.— *v.t.* (*Shak.*) to warble. [Origin obscure.]

relive, *rē-liv'*, *v.t.* and *v.i.* to live again: (*rē-līv'*; *Spens.*) to revive.

reliver, *ri-liv'ər*, *v.t.* (*Shak.*) to deliver back.

relucent, *ri-l(y)ōō'sənt*, *adj.* reflecting: shining. [L. *relūcēns, -ēntis*, pr.p. of *relūcēre*, to shine back.]

reluct, *ri-lukt'*, *v.i.* to be unwilling (with *at*): to hold back.—*ns.* **reluc'tance**, (*Milt.*) opposition, resistance: unwillingness: **reluc'tancy**. — *adj.* **reluc'tant**, (*Milt.*) struggling: unwilling: resisting.—*adv.* **reluct'antly.**—*v.i.* **reluct'āte**, to be reluctant.—*n.* **relucta'tion** (*rel-*), repugnance. [L. *reluctārī*—*re-*, against, *luctārī*, to struggle.]

relume, *ri-lūm'*, *v.t.* to light anew: to rekindle: to light up again.—*v.t.* **relu'mine** (*-in*), to relume. [L. *relūmināre*—*lūmen, -inis*, light.]

rely, *ri-lī'*, *v.i.* (*obs.*) to rally: (*obs.*) to rest as on a support: to depend confidently:—*pr.p.* **rely'ing**; *pa.t.* and *pa.p.* **relied'.**—*n.* **reliabil'ity.**—*adj.* **reli'able**, to be relied on, trustworthy. — *n.* **reli'ableness.**—*adv.* **reli'ably.** (These four words are sometimes condemned as formed neither from a trans. verb nor from a noun.)—*n.* **reli'ance**, trust: that in which one trusts:—*adj.* **reli'ant.**—*n.* **reli'er** (*Shak.*).—**reliability test, trial,** a public test of the qualities of motor vehicles. [O.Fr. *relier*—L. *religāre*, to bind back.]

remain, *ri-mān'*, *v.i.* to stay or be left behind: to continue in the same place: (*Shak.*) to dwell, abide: to be left after or out of a greater number: to continue in one's possession, mind: to continue unchanged: to continue to be: to be still to be dealt with (often without subject *it*): (*Spens., Milt.*) to await.—*n.* (*Shak.*) stay, abode: esp. in *pl.* **remains'**, what is left: relics: a corpse: the literary productions of one dead.—*n.* **remain'der**, that which remains or is left behind after the removal of a part or after division: the residue, rest: (*Shak.*) balance of an account: an interest in an estate to come into effect after a certain other event happens: right of next succession to a post or title: residue of an edition when the sale of a book has fallen off.—*adj.* (*Shak.*) left over.—*v.t.* to make a remainder of.—*n.* **remain'derman**, one to whom a remainder is devised. [O.Fr. *remaindre*—L. *remanēre*—*re-*, back, *manēre*, to stay.]

remake, *rē-māk'*, *v.t.* to make anew.—*adj.* **rēmade'.**—*ns.* **rēmade'**, **rēmake'**, a thing (as a gutta golf-ball) made over again from the original materials.

remand, *ri-mand'*, *v.t.* to send back (esp. a prisoner into custody to await further evidence).—*n.* act of remanding: recommittal.—**remand home**, a place of detention for children and young persons on remand or awaiting trial: also for some undergoing punishment. [O.Fr. *remander*, or L.L. *remandāre*—*mandāre*, to order.]

remanent, *rem'ən-ənt*, *adj.* remaining.—*n.* a remainder: a remnant.—*ns.* **rem'anence, -cy**; **rem'anet**, a remainder: a postponed case or parliamentary bill. [L. *remanēns, -ēntis*, pr.p., and *remanet*, 3rd pers. sing. pres. indic. of *remanēre.*]

remanié, *rə-mä-nyā*, *n.* (*geol.*) a fossil or other relic of an older rock preserved as a fragment in a later deposit. [Fr. pa.p. of *remanier*, to rehandle.]

remark, *ri-märk'*, *v.t.* (*Milt.*) to mark out: to notice: to comment, utter as an observation, say incidentally or in comment: (*rē-märk*) to mark again.—*v.i.* (*ri-*) to comment, make an observation.—*n.* noteworthiness: observation: comment: (also as Fr., **remarque'**) a marginal drawing or other distinguishing mark on an engraving or etching indicating an early state of the plate: also a print or proof bearing this special remark.—*adj.* **remark'able**, noteworthy: unusual, singular, strange, distinguished.—*n.* a remarkable thing.—*n.* **remark'ableness.** — *adv.* **remark'ably.**—*adj.* **remarked'**, conspicuous: (also **remarqued'**) bearing a remark, as an etching.—*n.* **remark'er.** [O.Fr. *remarquer*—*re-*, inten., *marquer*, to mark.]

remblai, *rän³-ble*, *n.* earth used to form a rampart, embankment, &c.: stowage in a mine. [Fr.]

remble, *rem'(b)l*, *v.t.* (*N.E. England*) to remove, clear. [Origin obscure.]

Rembrandtesque, *rem-brän-tesk'*, or *-brən-*, *adj.* like the work of *Rembrandt* (1606-69), esp. in his contrast of high lights and deep shadows.—*adj.* **Rem'brandtish.**—*n.* **Rem'brandtism.**

remeasure, *rē-mezh'ər*, *v.t.* to measure anew: (*Spens.*) to retrace.—*n.* **remeas'urement.**

remedy, *rem'i-di*, *obs.* and *Scot.* **remede, remeid, remead** (*ri-mēd'*), *n.* any means of curing a disease, redressing, counteracting, or repairing any evil or loss: reparation: redress: range of tolerated variation in the weight of a coin.—*v.t.* to remove, counteract, or repair:—*pr.p.* **rem'edying**; *pa.t.* and *pa.p.* **rem'edied.**—*adj.* **remē'diable.** —*adv.* **remē'diably.**—*adj.* **remē'dial**, tending or intended to remedy.—*adv.* **remē'dially.**—*adjs.* **remē'diat(e)**, (*Shak.*) remedial; **rem'ediless** (formerly *-med'*), without remedy: incurable.—*adv.* **rem'edilessly** (*-med'*).—*n.* **rem'edilessness** (*-med'*).—**no remedy**, (*Shak.*) of necessity: **what remedy?**, (*obs.*) what help is there for it? [A.Fr. *remedie*, O.Fr. *remede*—L. *remedium.*]

remember, *ri-mem'bər*, *v.t.* to keep in or recall to memory or mind: (*obs.*) to mention, record: (*obs.*) to commemorate: (*Shak.*) to bear in mind as something to be mentioned: to bear in mind as one deserving of honour or gratitude, or as one to be rewarded, tipped, or prayed for: (*arch.* or *dial.*) to remind: (*Shak.*) to bethink: (*arch.*) to occur to: to recall to the memory of another (often as a greeting).—*v.i.* to have the power or perform the act of memory: (*Shak., Milt.*; now *Scot.* and *U.S.*) to have memory (with *of*).—*adj.* **remem'berable.** — *adv.* **remem'berably.** — *ns.* **remem'berer**; **remem'brance**, memory: that which serves to bring to or keep in mind: a reminder: a souvenir: a memorandum: a memorial: the reach of memory: (in *pl.*) a message of friendly greeting; **remem'brancer**, one who or that which reminds: a recorder: an officer of exchequer (**King's Remembrancer**).—**remember your courtesy**, (*obs.*) remember to put your hat on, which you have taken off in courtesy; **Remembrance Day**, Nov. 11th or preceding Sunday commemorating the fallen of the World Wars. [O.Fr. *remembrer*—L. *re-*, again, *memor*, mindful.]

remercy, *ri-mər'si*, *v.t.* (*Spens.*) to thank:—*pa.t.* (*Spens.*) **remer'cied.** [O.Fr. *remercier.*]

remerge, *rē-mərj'*, *v.t.* (*Tenn.*) to merge again.

remex, *rē'meks*, *n.* one of the large feathers of a bird's wing—primary or secondary:—*pl.* **remiges** (*rem'i-jēs*).—*v.i.* **remigate** (*rem'i-gāt*), to row.—*n.* **remiga'tion.** [L. *rēmex, -igis*, a rower—*rēmus*, oar, *agĕre*, to row.]

remigrate, *rem'i-grāt*, *v.i.* to change back: (also *rē-mī'*) to migrate again or back.—*n.* **remigrā'tion** (*rem-i-* or *rē-mī-*).

remind, *ri-mīnd'*, *v.t.* to put in mind.—*n.* **remind'er**, that which reminds.—*adj.* **remind'ful**, mindful: reminiscent, exciting memories. [Pfx. *re-*, and **mind.**]

reminiscence, *rem-i-nis'əns*, *n.* recollection: an account of something remembered: the recurrence to the mind of the past.—*v.i.* **reminisce** (*-nis'*; back-formation; *coll.*), to recount reminiscences. — *adj.* **reminisc'ent**, suggestive, remindful: addicted to reminiscences: pertaining to reminiscence.—Also *n.*—*adj.* **reminiscential** (*-sen'shl*), of, or of the nature of, reminiscence.—*adv.* **reminisc'ently.** [L. *reminīscēns, -entis*, pr.p. of *reminīscī*, to remember.]

remise, *ri-miz'*, *n.* (*law*) surrender of a claim: (*rə-mēz'*) an effective second thrust after the first has missed: a coach-house: a livery-carriage.—*v.t.* (*ri-miz'*) to surrender. [Fr. *remis, remise*—*remettre*—L. *remittĕre*, to send back, remit, relax.]

remiss, *ri-mis'*, *adj.* negligent: slack: lax: wanting in vigour.—*n.* **remissibil'ity.**—*adj.* **remiss'ible**, that may be remitted.—*n.* **remission** (*ri-mish'ən*), act of remitting: slackening: abatement: relinquishment of a claim: pardon: forgiveness.—*adj.* **remiss'ive**, remitting: forgiving.—*adv.* **remiss'ly.**—*n.* **remiss'ness.**—*adj.* **remiss'ory**, of remission. [L. *remittĕre, remissum*; see **remit.**]

remit, *ri-mit'*, *v.t.* to relax: to pardon: to refrain from exacting or inflicting: to give up: to desist from: to transfer: to transmit, as money, &c.: to put again in custody: to refer to another court, authority, &c.: to refer for information: to send or put back.—*v.i.* to abate: to relax: to de-

sist: (*pr.p.* **remitt'ing**; *pa.t.* and *pa.p.* **remitt'ed**).
—*n.* (*law*) reference of a case or matter to another.
—*ns.* **remit'ment**, remission: remitting: remittance; **remitt'al**, remission: reference to another court, &c.; **remitt'ance**, the sending of money, &c., to a distance: the sum or thing sent; **remitt'ance-man**, one dependent upon remittances from home; **remittee'**, the person to whom a remittance is sent.—*adj.* **remitt'ent**, remitting at intervals.—*adv.* **remitt'ently**.—*n.* **remitt'er**, one who makes a remittance.—**remittent fever**, a severe type of malaria in which the temperature falls slightly from time to time. [L. *remittĕre, remissum—re-*, back, *mittĕre*, to send.]

remnant, *rem'nənt, n.* a fragment or a small number surviving or remaining after destruction, defection, removal, sale, &c., of the greater part: esp. a remaining piece of cloth: a tag or quotation: a surviving trace: (*Scott*) trace of a fact.—*adj.* remenant, remainder. [**remanent**.]

remonstrance, *ri-mon'strans, n.* a strong or formal protest, expostulation.—*adj.* **remon'strant**, remonstrating: **Remonstrant**, Dutch Arminian.—*n.* one who remonstrates: (*Scot. hist.*) a Protester: a member of the Dutch Arminian party whose divergence from Calvinism was expressed in the articles in the Remonstrance of 1610.—*adv.* **remon'strantly**.—*v.i.* **remon'strāte**, to make a remonstrance.—*v.t.* to say or (*obs.*) state in remonstrance: (*obs.*) to demonstrate.—*adv.* **remon'stratingly**.—*n.* **remonstrā'tion** (*rem-ən-*).—*adjs.* **remon'strative**, remon'stratory (*-stra-tər-i*), expostulatory.—*n.* **remon'strator**.—**Grand Remonstrance**, a famous statement of abuses presented to Charles I. by the House of Commons in 1641. [L. *re-*, again, *mōnstrāre*, to point out.]

remontant, *ri-mon'tənt, adj.* blooming more than once in the same season.—*n.* a remontant plant, esp. a rose. [Fr.]

remora, *rem'o-rä, n.* the sucking-fish, formerly believed to stop ships by attaching its sucker: an obstacle. [L. *rĕmŏra*, delay, hindrance—*mora*, delay.]

remorse, *ri-mors', n.* the gnawing pain of conscience: compunction: (*Spens., Shak., Milt.*) pity, compassionate feeling: (*Shak.*) mitigation: (*Shak.*) probably, matter of conscience: (*Spens.*) bite.—*adj.* **remorse'ful**, penitent: compassionate.—*adv.* **remorse'fully**.—*n.* **remorse'fulness**.—*adj.* **remorse'less**, without remorse: cruel.—*adv.* **remorse'lessly**. — *n.* **remorse'lessness**. [O.Fr. *remors* (Fr. *remords*)—L.L. *remorsus—*L. *remordēre, remorsum*, to bite again—*re-*, again, *mordēre*, to bite.]

remote, *ri-mōt', adj.* far removed, in place, time, chain of causation or relation, resemblance or relevance: widely separated: very indirect.—*adv.* **remote'ly**.—*ns.* **remote'ness**; **remō'tion**, (*Shak.*) removal: remoteness. [L. *remōtus*, pa.p. of *removēre*; see **remove**.]

remoud, *ri-mōōd', pa.t.* (*Spens.*) for removed.

remount, *rē-mownt', v.t.* and *v.i.* to mount again. —*n.* a fresh horse, or supply of horses.

remove, *ri-mōōv', v.t.* to put or take away: to transfer: to withdraw: to displace: to succeed, as a dish on the table: to make away with.—*v.i.* to go away: to change abode.—*n.* removal: (*Shak.*) the raising of a siege: (*Shak.*) absence: step or degree of remoteness or indirectness: in some schools, an intermediate class: promotion: a dish removed to make way for another, or taking the place of one so removed.—*n.* **removabil'ity**. — *adj.* **remov'able**. — *adv.* **remov'ably**. — *n.* **remov'al**, the act of taking away: displacing: change of place: transference: going away: change of abode: a euphemism for murder.—*adj.* **removed'**, remote: distant by degrees, as in descent.—*ns.* **remov'edness**; **remov'er**, one who or that which removes: one who conveys furniture from house to house.—**removal terms**, (*Scot.*) 28th May and 28th November, called Whitsunday and Martinmas. [O.Fr. *remouvoir—*L. *removēre, remōtum—re-*, away, *movēre*, to move.]

remuda, *rä-mōō'dhä, ri-mü'dä, n.* a supply of remounts. [Sp., exchange.]

remunerate, *ri-mü'nə-rāt, v.t.* to recompense:

to pay for service rendered.—*adj.* **remü'nerable**. — *n.* **remünerā'tion**, recompense: reward: pay.—*adj.* **remü'nerative**, profitable.—*ns.* **remü'nerativeness**; remü'nerātor. — *adj.* **remü'neratory** (*-ə-tər-i*), giving a recompense. [L. *remunerāri* (late *-āre*), *-ātus—mūnus, -ēris*, a gift.]

remurmur, *ri-mur'mər, v.t.* and *v.i.* to echo, repeat, or resound in murmurs.

renaissance, *ri-nā'səns, n.* a new birth: **Renaissance**, the revival of arts and letters, the transition from the Middle Ages to the modern world.—*adj.* of the Renaissance. [Fr.; cf. **renascence**.]

renal, *rē'nl, adj.* of the kidneys. [L. *rēnālis—rēnēs* (sing. *rēn*, rare), the kidneys.]

renascent, *ri-nas'ənt,* also *-nās', adj.* coming into renewed life or vitality.—*n.* **renasc'ence**, being born anew: **Renascence, Renaissance**. [L. *renāscēns, -entis*, pr.p. of *renāscī—nāscī*, to be born.]

renay, reney, *ri-nā', reny, ri-nī', v.t.* (*obs.*) to renounce, abjure, forswear: to deny:—*pr.p.* **renay'ing, reny'ing**; *pa.p.* **renayed', renied'**. [O.Fr. *renaier, renier—*L. *renegāre.*]

rencounter, *ren-kownt'ər*, **rencontre**, *rän²-kon²-tr'* (Fr.), *n.* a chance meeting: an encounter: a casual combat: a collision.—*v.t.* to meet: to encounter. [Fr. *rencontre.*]

rend, *rend, v.t.* to tear asunder with force: to split: to tear away.—*v.i.* to become torn:—*pa.t.* and *pa.p.* **rent**. [O.E. *rendan,* to tear.]

render, *ren'dər, v.t.* to give up: to give back, return, give in return: to make up: to deliver: to hand over: to give: to surrender: to yield: to tender or submit: to show forth: to represent or reproduce, esp. artistically: to perform: to translate: to perform or pay as a duty or service: (*refl.*) to present or betake (with *at*): to cause to be: to melt: to extract, treat, or clarify by melting: to plaster with a first coat.—*n.* an act of rendering: that which is rendered.—*adj.* **ren'derable**.—*ns.* **ren'derer**; **ren'dering**; **rendi'tion**, surrender: (*U.S.*) rendering. [O.Fr. *rendre—*L.L. *rendĕre*, app. formed by influence of *prendĕre*, to take—L. *reddĕre—re-*, back, *dăre*, to give.]

rendezvous, *rän²'di-vōō, ron', n.* an appointed meeting-place: a meeting by appointment: a general resort:—*pl.* **rendezvous** (*-vōō*): (*obs.*) **rendezvous'es**.—*v.i.* to assemble at any appointed place. [Fr. *rendez-vous,* render yourselves—*rendre,* to render.]

renegade, *ren'i-gād,* **renegate**, *-gāt, n.* one faithless to principle or party: an apostate: a turncoat: esp. a Christian turned Mahommedan—also **renega'do**.—*v.i.* **ren'egade**, to turn renegade.—*adjs.* **ren'egade, -ate**, apostate.—*n.* **renegā'tion**.—*v.t.* **renegue, renege** (*ri-nēg'*), to renounce: to apostatise from.—*v.i.* to deny: to refuse: to revoke at cards.—Also **renig** (*-nig'; U.S.*), **renague** (*-nāg'; Ir.*).—*n.* **reneg'(u)er**. [L.L. *renegātus—*L. *re-*, inten., *negāre, -ātum,* to deny; partly through Sp. *renegado.*]

renew, *ri-nū', v.t.* to renovate: to transform to new life, revive: to begin again: to repeat: to make again: to invigorate: to substitute new for: to restore: to renovate: to regenerate.—*v.i.* to be made new: to begin again.—*adj.* **renew'able**.—*ns.* **renew'al**, renewing; **renew'edness**; **renew'er**; **renew'ing.**

renfierst, *ren-fērst', pa.p.* (*Spens.*) made fierce. [App. modelled on the next.]

renforce, *ren-fōrs', v.t.* (*obs.*) to reinforce: to force again.—*v.i.* to renew efforts:—(in *Spens. pa.t.* **renforst'**, *pa.p.* **renforst'**). [See **reinforce**.]

reniform, *ren'i-form, adj.* kidney-shaped. [L. *rēnēs* (sing. *rēn*), the kidneys, *forma,* form.]

renig. See **renegue** (under **renegade**).

renitent, *ri-nī'tənt, ren'i-tənt, adj.* resistant: reluctant: recalcitrant.—*n.* **reni'tency** (or *ren'*). [L. *renītēns, -entis,* pr.p. of *renītī,* to resist.]

renne, ren, *v.i.* (*Spens.*) to run.—Also *pa.p.—n.* **renn'ing**. [See **run**.]

rennet, *ren'it, n.* any means of curdling milk, esp. a preparation of calf's stomach.—*n.* **renn'et-bag**, the fourth stomach of a ruminant. [O.E. *rinnan,* to run; cf. **earn** (2), **yearn** (3).]

rennet, *ren'it*, *n.* a sweet kind of apple. [O.Fr. *reinette*, dim. of *reine*, queen—L. *rēgīna*, a queen; or *rainette*, dim. of *raine*, a frog—L. *rāna*.]

renounce, *ri-nowns'*, *v.t.* to disclaim: to disown: to reject publicly and finally: to recant: to abjure.—*v.i.* to fail to follow suit at cards.—*n.* a failure to follow suit. — *ns.* **renounce'ment**; **renoun'cer**. [O.Fr. *renuncer*—L. *renuntiāre—re-*, away, *nuntiāre*, *-ātum*, to announce.]

renovate, *ren'ō-vāt*, *v.t.* to renew or make new again: to make as if new: to regenerate.—*ns.* **renovā'tion**; **ren'ovātor**. [L. *re-*, again, *novāre*, *-ātum*, to make new—*novus*, new.]

renown, *ri-nown'*, *n.* fame.—*v.t.* to make famous: to celebrate.—*adj.* **renowned'**, famous.—*n.* **renown'er**, one who gives renown. [O.Fr. *renoun* (Fr. *renom*)—L. *re-*, again, *nōmen*, a name.]

rent, *rent*, *n.* an opening made by rending: a fissure.—*v.t.* and *v.i.* (*obs.* or *dial.*) to rend.—Also *pa.t.* and *pa.p.* of **rend**.

rent, *rent*, *n.* periodical payment for use of another's property, esp. houses and lands: revenue.—*v.t.* to hold or occupy by paying rent: to let or hire out for a rent: to charge with rent.—*v.i.* to be let at a rent.—*adj.* **rent'able**.—*ns.* **rent'al**, a rent-roll: rent: annual value: (*Scot.*) a kindly tenant's lease: (*U.S.*) the takings of a circulating library; **rent'aller**, (*Scot.*) a kindly tenant; **rent'-charge**, a periodical payment charged upon rent; **rent'-collector**; **rent'-day**; **rente** (*rän°t*; Fr.), annual income: (in *pl.*) French or other government securities or income from them; **rent'er**, a tenant who pays rent: one who lets out property: a farmer of tolls or taxes: a theatre shareholder.—*adj.* and *adv.* **rent'-free**, without payment of rent.—*ns.* **rentier** (*rän°-tyā*; Fr.), a fund-holder: one who has a fixed income from stocks and the like; **rent'-restric'tion**, restriction of landlord's right to raise rent; **rent'-roll**, a list of tenements and rents: total income from property.—**for rent**, (*U.S.*) to let. [Fr. *rente*—L. *reddita* (*pecūnia*), money paid—*reddĕre*, to pay; cf. **render**.]

renunciation, *ri-nun-si-ā'shon*, *n.* act of renouncing: self-resignation. — *adjs.* **renun'ciative** (*-sha-tiv*, *-sya-tiv*, *-si-ā-tiv*), **renun'ciatory** (*-sha-tər-i*, *-si-ə-tər-i*). [L. *renūntiāre*, proclaim; see **nuncio**.]

renverse, *ren-vərs'*, *v.t.* to reverse: to upset:—*pa.t.* and *pa.p.* **renversed'**, **renverst'** (*Spens.*). [Fr. *renverser*—pfx. *re-*, *enverser*.]

reny. See **renay**.

reorient, *rē-ō'ri-ənt*, *adj.* rising again.—*v.t.* (*-ent*) to orient again.—*n.* **rēorientā'tion**.

rep, *repp*, *rep*, *n.* a corded cloth.—Also **reps** (*reps*). —*adj.* **repped** (*rept*), transversely corded. [Fr. *reps*, perh.—Eng. **ribs**.]

rep, *rep*, *n.* a slang abbreviation of **repertory** (theatrical), **repetition** (school), **reputation** (*obs.* and *U.S.*), and perh. of **reprobate** (see **rip**).

repaid, *pa.t.* and *pa.p.* of **repay**.

repaint, *rē-pānt'*, *v.t.* to paint anew.—*n.* a repainted golf-ball.—*n.* **repaint'ing**.

repair, *ri-pār'*, *v.i.* to betake oneself: to go: to resort: (*Shak.*) to return.—*v.t.* (*Spens.*) to restore to its position: (*Spens.*) to withdraw.—*n.* resort: place of resort: concourse. [O.Fr. *repairer*, to return to a haunt—L.L. *repatriāre*, to return to one's country—L. *re-*, back, *patria*, native country.]

repair, *ri-pār'*, *v.t.* to mend: to make amends for: to make good: (*Shak.*) to restore, refresh, revivify. —*n.* restoration after injury or decay: supply of loss: sound condition: condition in respect of soundness.—*adj.* **repair'able**, capable of being mended (esp. of material things): falling to be repaired.—*ns.* **repair'er**; **repair'man**, one who does repairs; **repair'-shop**. — *n.* **reparability** (*rep-ər-ə-bil'i-ti*). — *adj.* **reparable** (*rep'ər-ə-bl*), capable of being made good or (*rare*) being mended: falling to be repaired.—*adv.* **rep'arably**. —*n.* **reparā'tion**, repair: supply of what is wasted: amends: compensation.—*adjs.* **reparative** (*ri-par'ə-tiv*); **repar'atory**. [O.Fr. *reparer* —L. *reparāre—parāre*, to prepare.]

repand, *ri-pand'*, *adj.* slightly wavy. [L. *repandus* —*re-*, back, *pandus*, bent.]

reparable, &c. See **repair** (2).

repartee, *rep-är-tē'*, *n.* a ready and witty retort: skill in making such retorts.—*v.t.* and *v.i.* to retort with ready wit. [O.Fr. *repartie—repartir—partir*, to set out—L. *partīrī*, to divide.]

repartition, *rep-ər-tish'ən*, *n.* distribution: (*rē-pär-*), a second partition: a division into smaller parts.—*v.t.* (*rē-pär-*) to partition anew.

repass, *rē-pás'*, *v.t.* and *v.i.* to pass again: to pass in the opposite direction.—*n.* **repassage** (*rē-pas'ij*).

repast, *ri-pást'*, *n.* a meal: (*Spens.*) refreshment of sleep.—*v.t.* and *v.i.* (*Shak.*) to feed.—*n.* **repas'ture**, (*Shak.*) food. [O.Fr. *repast* (Fr. *repas*) —L.L. *repastus*—L. *pascĕre*, *pastum*, to feed.]

repatriate, *rē-* or *ri-pāt'ri-āt*, or *-pat'*, *v.t.* to restore or send back to one's country.—*n.* a repatriated person.—*n.* **repatriā'tion**. [L.L. *repatriāre*, *-ātum*, to return to one's country—*patria*.]

repay, *rē-pā'*, *ri-pā'*, *v.t.* to pay back: to make return for: to recompense: to pay or give in return.—*v.i.* to make repayment:—*pr.p.* **repay'ing**; *pa.t.* and *pa.p.* **repaid'**.—*adj.* **repay'able**, that is to be repaid: due.—*n.* **repay'ment**.

repeal, *ri-pēl'*, *v.t.* to revoke: to annul: (*Spens.*, *Milt.*) to quash, repress, set aside: to abrogate: to recall from banishment.—*n.* abrogation: **Repeal**, (*hist.*) dissolution of the Union between Great Britain and Ireland, called for by O'Connell.—*adj.* **repeal'able**.—*n.* **repeal'er**, one who repeals: **Repealer**, an advocate of Repeal. [O.Fr. *rapeler* —pfx. *re-*, *appeler*, to appeal.]

repeat, *ri-pēt'*, *v.t.* to say, do, perform, go over, again: to iterate: to quote from memory: to say off: to recount: (*Milt.*) to celebrate: to say or do after another: to tell to others, divulge: to cause to recur: to reproduce: (*refl.*) to repeat the words or actions of: (*obs.*) to seek again: (*obs.*) to ask back.—*v.i.* to recur: to make repetition: to strike the last hour, quarter, &c., when required: to fire several shots without reloading: to rise so as to be tasted after swallowing: (*U.S.*) to vote (illegally) more than once.—*n.* a repetition: a retracing of one's course: (*mus.*) a passage repeated or marked for repetition: dots or other mark directing repetition: a unit of a repeated pattern: an order for more goods of the same kind.—*adj.* done or occurring as a repetition.—*adjs.* **repeat'able**, able to be done again: fit to be told to others; **repeat'ed**, done again: reiterated.—*adv.* **repeat'edly**, many times repeated: again and again.—*n.* **repeat'er**, one who, or that which, repeats, or does a thing that he or it has done before: a decimal fraction in which the same figure (or sometimes figures) is repeated to infinity: a watch or clock, or a firearm, that repeats: a ship that repeats an admiral's signals: (*teleg.*) an instrument for automatically retransmitting a message: a thermionic amplifier inserted in a telephone circuit (also **repeating coil**).—*n.* and *adj.* **repeat'ing**.—**repeat oneself**, to say again what one has said already. [Fr. *répéter*—L. *repetĕre*, *repetitum—re-*, again, *petĕre*, to seek.]

repel, *ri-pel'*, *v.t.* to drive off or back: to repulse: to reject: to hold off: to provoke aversion in: to repudiate:—*pr.p.* **repell'ing**; *pa.t* and *pa.p.* **repelled'**.—*ns.* **repell'ence**, **repell'ency**.—*adj.* **repell'ent**, driving back: able or tending to repel: distasteful.—*n.* that which repels.—*adv.* **repell'ently**.—*n.* **repell'er**.—*adj.* **repell'ing**.—*adv.* **repell'ingly**. [L. *repellĕre—pellĕre*, to drive.]

repent, *ri-pent'*, *v.i.* to regret, sorrow for, or wish to have been otherwise, what one has done or left undone (with *of*): to change from past evil: to feel contrition: (*Spens.*) to sorrow.—*v.t.* (*refl.* or *impers.*; *arch.*) to affect with contrition or with regret: to regret, be sorry for.—*n.* (*Spens.*) repentance.—*n.* **repent'ance**, act of repenting: penitent state of mind.—*adj.* **repent'ant**, experiencing or expressing repentance.—*n.* (*rare*) penitent.—*adv.* **repent'antly**.—*n.* **repent'er**.—*adv.* **repent'ingly**. [O.Fr. *repentir*—L. *paenitēr* to cause to repent.]

repent, *rē'pənt*, *adj.* (*bot.*) lying on the ground and rooting. [L. *repēns*, *-entis*, *pr.p.* of *repĕre*, to creep.]

repercuss, rē-pər-kus′, v.t. (obs.) to drive back, reflect, reverberate.—n. **repercussion** (-kush′ən), driving back: reverberation: echo: reflection: a return stroke, reaction, or consequence.—adj. **repercussive** (-kus′iv), driving back: reverberating: echoing: repeated. [L. repercutĕre, -cussum —re-, per, quatĕre, to strike.]

repertory, rep′ər-tər-i, n. a storehouse, repository: a stock of pieces that a person or company is prepared to perform.—n. **repertoire** (rep′ər-twär; Fr. répertoire), a performer's or company's repertory.—**repertory theatre**, a theatre with a repertoire of plays and a stock or permanent company. [L.L. repertōrium—L. reperīre, to find again— parĕre, to bring forth.]

répétiteur, rā-pā-tē-tər, n. a coach, tutor: one who rehearses opera singers, &c. [Fr.; cf. **repeat**.]

repetition, rep-i-tish′ən, n. act of repeating: recital from memory: a thing repeated: power of repeating a note promptly.—n. **rep′etend** (-tend, or -tend′), the recurring part of a decimal fraction: a recurring note, word, refrain, &c.—adj. (rep′) to be repeated.—adjs. **repeti′tional**, **repeti′tionary**, **repetitious** (-tish′əs), of the nature of, or characterised by, repetition; **repetitive** (ri-pet′i-tiv), iterative: overmuch given to repetition.—advs. **repeti′tiously**, **repet′itively**.—ns. **repeti′tiousness**, **repet′itiveness**. [L. repetĕre, -ītum, to seek again, repeat—petĕre, to seek; cf. **repeat**.]

repine, ri-pīn′, v.i. to fret (with at or against): to feel discontent: to murmur: to grudge.—n. (Shak.) a repining.—ns. **repīne′ment**; **repīn′er**. —n. and adj. **repīn′ing**, grumbling: grudging: fretting.—adv. **repīn′ingly**. [App. from **pine** (2).]

repique, ri-pēk′, n. at piquet, the winning of thirty points or more from combinations or in one's own hand, before play begins.—v.t. to score a repique against.—v.i. to score a repique. [Fr. repic.]

replace, ri- or rē-plās′, v.t. to put back: to provide a substitute for: to take the place of, supplant.— adj. **replace′able**.—ns. **replace′ment**, act of replacing: (crystal.) the occurrence of a face or faces in the position where the principal figure would have a corner or edge; **replac′er**, a substitute.— **replaceable hydrogen**, hydrogen atoms that can be replaced in an acid by metals to form salts. [**place**.]

replenish, ri-plen′ish, v.t. to fill again: to fill completely: to stock abundantly: to people.— adj. **replen′ished**, (Shak.) complete, consummate.—ns. **replen′isher**, one who replenishes: an apparatus for maintaining an electric charge; **replen′ishment**. [O.Fr. replenir, -iss-, from re- plein, full—L. re-, again, plēnus, full.]

replete, ri-plēt′, adj. full: completely filled: filled to satiety: abounding (with with).—v.t. to fill to repletion.—ns. **replete′ness**, **replē′tion**, superabundant fullness: surfeit: (med.) fullness of blood: plethora. [L. replētus, pa.p. of replēre— plēre, to fill.]

replevy, ri-plev′i, v.t. to bail: to recover, or restore to the owner, after distraint, upon pledge to try the right at law.—n. replevin.—adjs. **replev′iable**, **replev′isable** (-i-səb-l).—n. **replev′in**, replevying: a writ or action in such a case. [O.Fr. replevir—plevir, to pledge.]

replica, rep′li-kä, n. a duplicate, properly one by the original artist: a facsimile: (mus.) a repeat. [It.,—L. replicāre, to repeat.]

replicate, rep′li-kāt, v.t. to fold back: to repeat: to make a replica of: to reply.—n. (mus.) a tone one or more octaves from a given tone.—adj. folded back.—n. **replicā′tion**, a reply: the plaintiff's answer to the defendant's plea: doubling back: copy, reproduction: (Shak.) reverberation, echo. [L. replicāre, -ātum, to fold back—plicāre, to fold.]

replum, rep′ləm, rē′pləm, n. a partition in a fruit formed by ingrowth of the placentas, as in Cruciferae:—pl. **rep′la**. [L. replum, the upright in the frame of a folding door.]

reply, ri-plī′, v.t. to say in answer.—v.i. to answer: to respond in action, as by returning gun-fire: to echo: to answer a defendant's plea: (pr.p. **reply′ing**; pa.t. and pa.p. **replied**′).—n. an answer,

response: (Scots law) a replication: (mus.) the answer in a fugue.—n. **repli′er**. [O.Fr. replier— L. replicāre; see **replicate**.]

repone, ri-pōn′, v.t. (Scots law) to restore to office or status: to rehabilitate. [L. repōnĕre, to put back—pōnĕre, to put.]

report, ri-pōrt′, v.t. (Spens.) to convey: to bring back, as an answer, news, or account of anything: to give an account of, esp. a formal, official, or called-for account: to state in such an account: to relate: to circulate publicly: to transmit as having been said, done, or observed: to write down or take notes of, esp. for a newspaper: to lay a charge against: to echo back: (refl.) to make personal announcement of the presence and readiness of.—v.i. to make a statement: to write an account of occurrences: to make a formal report: to report oneself: to act as a reporter.— n. a statement of facts: a formal or official statement, as of results of an investigation or matter referred: a statement on a school pupil's work and behaviour or the like: an account of a matter of news, esp. the words of a speech: (Shak.) reporting, testimony: general talk: rumour: hearsay: (B.) repute: explosive noise.—adj. **report′-able**.—ns. **report′age**, journalistic reporting, style, or manner: gossip; **report′er**, one who reports, esp. for a newspaper.—n. and adj. **report′ing**.— adv. **report′ingly**, (Shak.) by common report.— adj. **reportō′rial** (rep-ər-, -or-). — **reported speech**, indirect speech; **reported verses** (Fr. vers rapportés), verses that combine a number of parallel sentences by collocation of corresponding parts, as Sidney's 'Virtue, beauty, and speech did strike, wound, charm, My heart, eyes, ears, with wonder, love, delight'; **report stage**, the stage at which a parliamentary bill as amended in committee is reported to the House, before the third reading. [O.Fr. reporter—L. reportāre—re-, back, portāre, to carry.]

repose, ri-pōz′, v.t. to lay at rest: to give rest to: (rare) to lay up, deposit: to place, set (as confidence): to place in trust.—v.i. to rest: to be still: to rely.—n. rest: quiet: stillness: calm: ease of manner: serenity: restful feeling or effect: (Milt.) a place of rest.—n. **repōs′al** (Shak. **re-pōs′all**, another reading **repōs′ure**), reposing.— adj. **repōsed′**, calm: settled.—adv. **repō′sedly**. —n. **repōs′edness**.—adj. **repōse′ful**.—adv. **repōse′fully**. [Fr. reposer—L.L. repausāre; confused with the following; cf. **pose**, **compose**, **expose**, &c.]

reposit, ri-poz′it, v.t. to lay up.—ns. **reposition** (rep-o-zish′ən), replacing: reinstatement: laying up; **repos′itor**, an instrument for replacing a displaced organ; **repos′itory**, a place or receptacle in which anything is laid up: a collection or museum: a mart, esp. for horses: an abode of souls: a storehouse, magazine, as of information: a place of accumulation: a confidant. [L. repōnĕre, repositum, to put back, lay aside—pōnĕre, to put; confused with foregoing.]

repossess, rē-poz-es′, v.t. to regain possession of: to put again in possession.—n. **repossession** (-esh′ən).

repost. Same as **riposte**.

repoussé, rə-pōō-sā, or -pōō′, adj. raised in relief by hammering from behind or within.—n. repoussé work.—n. **repoussage** (-sazh′). [Fr.]

repp. Same as **rep**.

reprehend, rep-ri-hend′, v.t. to find fault with: to reprove.—n. **reprehend′er**.—adj. **reprehen′sible**, blameworthy.—adv. **reprehen′sibly**.—n. **reprehen′sion**, reproof: censure.—adj. **reprehen′sive**, containing reproof: given in reproof.—adv. **reprehensively**.—adj. **reprehen′sory**. [L. repraehendĕre, -hēnsum—re-, intens., praehendĕre, to lay hold of.]

represent, rep-ri-zent′, v.t. to exhibit the image of: to use, or serve, as a symbol for: to stand for: to exhibit, depict, personate, show an image of, by imitative art: to act: to be a substitute, agent, deputy, member of parliament, or the like, for: to correspond or be in some way equivalent or analogous to: to serve as a sample of: to present

Neutral vowels in unaccented syllables: el′ə-mənt, in′fənt, ran′dəm

earnestly to mind : to give out, make to appear, allege : **re-present'** (*rē-*), to present again.—*adj.* **represent'able** (*rep-ri-*).—*ns.* **representa'men,** (*psych.*) the product of representation; **represent'ant,** a representative; **representation** (*-zən-tā'shən*), act, state, or fact of representing or being represented : that which represents : an image : picture : dramatic performance : a mental image : a presentation of a view of facts or arguments : a petition, remonstrance, expostulation : assumption of succession by an heir : a body of representatives : **re-presentation** (*rē-pres-ən-tā'shən*), renewed presentation.—*adj.* **representa'tional** (*rep-ri-zən-*).—*ns.* **representa'tionism,** the doctrine that in the perception of the external world the immediate object represents another object beyond the sphere of consciousness; **representa'tionist.**—*adj.* **representative** (*rep-ri-zent'ə-tiv*), representing : exhibiting a likeness : typical : pertaining to representation.—*n.* a sample : a typical example or embodiment : one who represents another or others, as a deputy, delegate, ambassador, member of parliament, agent, successor, heir : (*obs.*) a representative legislative body.—*adv.* **represent'atively.**—*ns.* **represent'ativeness ; represent'er ; represent'ment, rē-present'ment.**—**House of Representatives,** the lower branch of the United States Congress, consisting of members chosen biennially by the people : also of various State and other legislatures ; **representative peers,** Scottish and Irish peers chosen by their fellows to sit in the House of Lords. [L. *repraesentāre, -ātum—praesentāre,* to place before.]

repress, *ri-pres',* *v.t.* to restrain : to keep under : to put down : to banish to the unconscious : (*rē-*) to press again.—*adj.* **repress'ible.**—*adv.* **repress'ibly.** — *n.* **repression** (*-presh'ən*). — *adj.* **repress'ive.**—*adv.* **repress'ively.**—*n.* **repress'or.** [L. *reprimĕre, repressum—premĕre,* to press.]

reprieve, *ri-prēf',* *n.* (*Spens.*) reproach, insult, shame, reproof.—*v.t.* **reprieve** (*-prēv'*), to reprove. [See **reproof.**]

reprieve, *ri-prēv'* (*Shak.* **repreeve';** *Spens.* **reprive, repryve,** *-prīv'*), *v.t.* to delay the execution of : to give a respite to : to rescue, redeem.—*n.* a suspension of a criminal sentence : interval of ease or relief.—*n.* **repriev'al.** [Supposed to be from A.Fr. *repris,* pa.p. of *reprendre,* to take back (see **reprise**) ; the *v* app. by confusion, perh. with **reprieve,** reprove.]

reprimand, *rep'ri-månd, n.* a severe reproof.—*v.t.* (also *-månd'*) to reprove severely, esp. publicly or officially. [Fr. *réprimande—L. reprimĕre, repressum,* to press back—*premĕre,* to press.]

reprime, *ri-prīm, v.t.* (*rare*) to repress. [See **repress.**]

reprint, *rē-print', v.t.* to print again : to print a new impression of, esp. with little or no change. —*n.* **rē'print,** a later impression : printed matter used as copy.

reprise (*Spens.* **reprize**), *ri-prīz', v.t.* (*obs.*) to gain anew : (*obs.*) to recapture.—*n.* a yearly charge or deduction : (*Dryden*) reprisal : a renewed or alternating spell of action : (*mus.*) resumption of the first subject.—*n.* **repris'al,** seizure in retaliation : (*Shak.*) a prize : an act of retaliation : recapture : compensation. [Fr. *reprise—reprendre—L. repraehendĕre.*]

reproach, *ri-prōch', v.t.* to cast in one's teeth : to censure severely : to upbraid : to bring into discredit.—*n.* upbraiding : reproof : censure : disgrace : a source or matter of disgrace or shame.— *adj.* **reproach'able.**—*n.* **reproach'er.**—*adj.* **reproach'ful,** reproving : (*obs.*) deserving of reproach, disgraceful. — *adv.* **reproach'fully.** — *n.* **reproach'fulness.** — *adj.* **reproach'less,** irreproachable.—**the Reproaches,** antiphons chanted in R.C. churches on Good Friday, in which Christ reproaches the Jewish people. [Fr. *reprocher,* perh. from L. *prope,* near ; cf. **approach** ; or from *reprobāre* ; see **reprobate.**]

reprobate, *rep'rō-bāt, adj.* (*arch.*) failing to pass a test (esp. of silver) : base : rejected by God : given over to sin : depraved : unprincipled : condemnatory.—*n.* one rejected by God : an abandoned

or profligate person : one lost to shame : (often playfully) a scamp.—*v.t.* to reject : to disapprove : to censure : to disown.—*ns.* **rep'robacy** (*-bə-si*), state of being a reprobate ; **rep'robance,** (*Shak.*) reprobation ; **rep'robāter ; reproba'tion,** the act of reprobating : rejection : fore-ordination to eternal perdition : utter abandonment : severe censure or condemnation.—*adjs.* **rep'robātive, rep'robatory,** condemnatory.—*n.* **rep'robātor,** (*Scots law*) an action to prove a witness perjured or biased. [L. *reprobāre, -ātum,* to reprove, contrary of *approbāre—probāre,* to prove.]

reproduce, *rē-prō-dūs', v.t.* to produce a copy of : to form anew : to propagate : to reconstruct in imagination. — *n.* **reprodū'cer.** — *adj.* **reprodū'cible.**—*n.* **reproduction** (*-duk'shən*), the act of reproducing : the act of producing new organisms —the whole process whereby life is continued from generation to generation : regeneration : a copy, facsimile : a representation.—*adj.* **reproduc'tive.** — *adv.* **reproduc'tively.** — *ns.* **reproduc'tiveness, reproductiv'ity.**

reproof, *ri-prōōf', n.* a reproving : rebuke : censure : reprehension : (*Shak.*) shame, disgrace : (*obs.*) disproof : (*rē-*) a second or new proof.—*v.t.* (*rē-*) to make waterproof again.—*n.* **reproval** (*ri-prōō'vl*), reproof.—*v.t.* **reprove',** to rebuke : to censure : (*obs.*) to disprove or refute.—*ns.* **repro'ver ; repro'ving.**—*adv.* **repro'vingly.** [O.Fr. *reprover* (Fr. *réprouver*)—L. *reprobāre* ; see **reprobate.**]

repryve. See **reprieve.**

reps, reps. See **rep** (1).

reptile, *rep'til, adj.* creeping : like a reptile in nature.—*n.* any animal of the class **Reptilia** (*-til'i-ä*), vertebrates with scaly integument, cold blood, right and left aortic arch, partially divided heart, single occipital condyle, pulmonary respiration, and pentadactyl limbs (sometimes wanting) : a creeping thing : a base, malignant, abject, or treacherous person.—*adjs.* **reptilian** (*-til'i-ən*) ; **reptilif'erous,** bearing fossil reptiles ; **reptil'ious,** like a reptile. [L.L. *reptilis, -e—repĕre,* to creep.]

republic, *ri-pub'lik, n.* (*arch.*) the state : a form of government without a monarch, in which the supreme power is vested in the people and their elected representatives : a state or country so governed.—*adj.* **repub'lican,** of or favouring a republic : **Republican,** of the Republican party. —*n.* one who advocates a republican form of government : **Republican,** in U.S., orig. an Anti-Federal—now a member of the political party opposed to the *Democrats,* and favouring an extension of the powers of the national government. — *v.t.* **repub'licanise.** — *n.* **repub'licanism.** — **Republican era,** the era adopted by the French after the downfall of the monarchy, beginning with 22nd September 1792 ; **republic of letters,** the world of books and authors. [L. *rēspublica,* commonwealth—*rēs,* affair, *publica* (fem.), public.]

republish, *rē-pub'lish, v.t.* to publish again.—*ns.* **republica'tion ; repub'lisher.** [Pfx. *re-,* and **publish.**]

repudiate, *ri-pū'di-āt, v.t.* to divorce : to reject : to cast off : to disown : to refuse or cease to acknowledge : to disavow.—*adj.* **repū'diable.**— *ns.* **repūdia'tion ; repūdi'ationist,** one who favours repudiation of public debt.—*adj.* **repū'diative.**—*n.* **repū'diātor.** [L. *repudiāre, -ātum —repudium,* divorce—*re-,* away, and the root of *pudēre,* to be ashamed.]

repugn, *ri-pūn', v.t.* (*Shak.*) to fight against, to oppose : to be repugnant to.—*v.i.* to be repugnant. —*ns.* **repugnance** (*ri-pug'*), inconsistency : aversion ; **repug'nancy,** repugnance : (*Shak.*) opposition.—*adj.* **repug'nant,** inconsistent : incompatible : distasteful : disgusting : opposing : resisting. [L. *repugnāre—re-,* against, *pugnāre,* to fight.]

repulp, *rē-pulp', v.t.* to bring back to a state of pulp.

repulse, *ri-puls', v.t.* to drive back : to beat off : to rebuff.—*n.* a driving back : a beating off : a check : a refusal : a rebuff.—*n.* **repulsion** (*-pul'shən*), driving off : a repelling force, action, or influence.—*adj.* **repul'sive,** that repulses or drives off: repelling: cold, reserved, forbidding: causing aversion and disgust.—*adv.* repul'sively.—*n.* repul'siveness. [L. *repulsus*, pa.p. of *repellēre*—*re-*, back, *pellĕre*, to drive.]

repurchase, rē-pur'chās, *v.t.* to purchase or buy back or again.—*n.* the act of repurchasing: that which is repurchased.

repure, ri-pūr', *v.t.* to purify again: to refine thoroughly.

repute, ri-pūt', *v.t.* to account, deem.—Also (*arch.*) *v.i.* with *of.*—*n.* general opinion or impression: attributed character: widespread or high estimation: fame.—*adj.* reputable (*rep'ūt-ə-bl*), in good repute: respectable: honourable: consistent with reputation.—*adv.* rep'ūtably.—*n.* repūtā'tion (*rep-*), repute: estimation: character generally ascribed: good report: fame: good name.—*adj.* rep'ūtātive, reputed: putative.—*adv.* rep'ūtatively, by repute.—*adj.* reputed (*ri-pūt'id*), supposed, reckoned to be such: of repute.—*adv.* repūt'edly, in common repute or estimation.—*adj.* repute'less, (*Shak.*) without good repute.—*n.* reput'ing, (*Shak.*) pluming oneself.—reputed owner, a person who has to all appearance the title to the property; reputed pint, what is commonly called a pint, but not necessarily of legal standard. [L. *reputāre*, *-ātum*—*putāre*, to reckon.]

requere, ri-kwēr', *v.t.* (*Spens.*) to require.

request, ri-kwest', *n.* the asking of a favour: a petition: a favour asked for: the state of being sought after.—*v.t.* to ask as a favour: to ask politely: to ask for.—*n.* request'er.—Court of Requests, a former English court of equity, abolished 1641: a local small debt court, superseded by the County Court—called also *Court of Conscience*; request note, an application for a permit to remove excisable goods. [O.Fr. *requeste* (Fr. *requête*)—L. *requīsītum*, pa.p. of *reqīrēre*—*re-*, away, *quaerĕre*, to seek.]

requicken, rē-kwik'n, *v.t.* (*Shak.*) to give new life to.

requiem, rek'vi-em, *n.* a mass for the rest of the soul of the dead: music for it: any music of similar character: (*obs.*) rest. [L., accus. of *requiēs* (*re-*, inten., *quiēs*, rest): first word of the introit.]

requight, a Spenserian spelling of requite.

require, ri-kwīr', *v.t.* to ask: to demand: to exact: to direct: to call for: to request: to need: to necessitate.—*v.i.* to ask.—*adj.* requir'able.—*adj.* required', (*U.S.*) compulsory as part of a curriculum.—*ns.* require'ment, a need: a thing needed: a necessary condition: a demand; requir'er; requir'ing. [L. *requīrēre*; partly through O.Fr. *requerre*, later assimilated to L.]

requisite, rek'vi-zit, *adj.* required: needful: indispensable.—*n.* that which is required, necessary, or indispensable.—*ns.* req'uisiteness; requisi'tion, the act of requiring: a formal demand or request: a formal call for the doing of something that is due: a demand for the supply of anything for military purposes: a written order for the supply of materials: the state of being in use or service.—*v.t.* to demand a requisition from: to demand or take by requisition: to seize: to call in: to press into service.—*adj.* requisi'tionary.—*ns.* requisi'tionist, requis'itor, one who makes a requisition.—*adj.* requis'itory. [L. *requīsītus*, pa.p. of *requīrēre*; see require.]

requite, ri-kwīt', *v.t.* to repay: to bestow the like in return: to retaliate: to retaliate on: (*obs.*) to counterbalance:—*pa.t.* requit'ed (*Spens.* requit'); *pa.p.* requit'ed (*Shak.* requit', requitt'ed).—Also (*Spens.*) requight (*-kwīt'*).—*n.* requite', requital.—*v.t.* requit (*-kwit'*; *obs.*), to requite (*pa.p.*, *Shak.*, requitt'ed).—*n.* (*Burns*) requital.—*adj.* requi'table.—*n.* requi'tal, the act of requiting: payment in return: recompense: reward.—*adjs.* requite'ful; requite'less, without requital, free.—*ns.* requite'ment; requi'ter. [Pfx. *re-*, and quit.]

requoyle, a Shakespearian spelling of recoil.

rerail, rē-rāl', *v.t.* to replace on the rails.

rere-, rēr-, in composition the same as rear- (1).—*ns.* rere'-arch, rear'-arch, an arch supporting the inner part of a wall's thickness, as in a splayed

window; rere'brace (*-brās*; Fr. *bras*, arm), armour of the arm from shoulder to elbow; rere'dorse, -dosse, -dos (L. *dorsum*, Fr. *dos*, back), a screen or panelling behind an altar or seat: a choir-screen: the back of a fireplace; rere'dorter, a privy behind a monastic dormitory; rere'-supper, a late meal, after supper; rere'ward, rearward.

reremouse, rearmouse, rēr'mows, *n.* a bat:—*pl.* rere'-, rear'mice. [O.E. *hréremús*, app.—*hréran*, to move, *mús*, a mouse.]

resalute, rē-sə-l(y)ōōt', *v.t.* to salute anew or in return.

rescind, ri-sind', *v.t.* to cut away: to annul, abrogate.—*n.* rescission (*-sizh'ən*), abrogation: (*obs.*) cutting off.—*adj.* rescissory (*-sis'ər-i*), annulling. [L. *rescindĕre*, *rescissum*—*re-*, back, *scindĕre*, to cut.]

rescript, rē'skript, *n.* the official answer of a pope or an emperor to any legal question: an edict or decree: a rewriting. [L. *rescriptum*—*re-*, *scrībĕre*, *scriptum*, to write.]

rescue, res'kū, *v.t.* to free from danger, captivity, or evil plight: to deliver forcibly from legal custody: to recover by force: (*pr.p.* res'cuing; *pa.t.* and *pa.p.* res'cued).—*n.* the act of rescuing: deliverance from danger or evil: forcible recovery: forcible release from arrest or imprisonment: relief of a besieged place: (*arch.*) a rescuer or rescuing party: a person or thing rescued: (*bridge*) a bid (rescue bid) to bring one's partner out of a dangerous situation.—*adj.* res'cuable.—*n.* res'cuer. [O.Fr. *rescourre*—L. *re-*, *excutĕre*—*ex*, out, *quatĕre*, to shake. Spenser's *reskewes* may be the plural, or may be for obs. *rescous*—O.Fr. *rescous(s)e.*]

rescue-grass, res'kū-gräs, *n.* a S. American brome-grass. [Origin unknown.]

research, ri-sərch', *n.* a careful search: investigation: systematic investigation towards increasing the sum of knowledge.—*v.i.* to make researches: re-search (rē'), to search again.—*n.* research'er.—*adj.* research'ful. [Obs. Fr. *recerche* (mod. Fr. *recherche*); see search.]

réseau, rā-zō', *n.* a fine meshed ground for lacework: a network of lines for reference in star-photographs. [Fr., network.]

resect, ri-sekt', *v.t.* to cut away part of, esp. the end of a bone.—*n.* resection (*-sek'shən*). [L. *resecāre*, *-sectum*, to cut off—*secāre*, to cut.]

Reseda, ri-sē'dä, *n.* the mignonette genus, giving name to the family Reseda'ceae: reseda, a pale green colour (often as Fr. réséda, rā-zā-dä).—Also *adj.* [L. *reseda*, said to be from *resēdā morbis*, assuage diseases, first words of a charm used in applying it as a poultice.]

reseize, rē-sēz', *v.t.* (*Spens.*) to reinstate. [seise.]

resemble, ri-zem'bl, *v.t.* to be like: (*arch.*) to compare.—*v.i.* to be like.—*n.* resem'blance, likeness: appearance: an image.—*adj.* resem'blant.—*n.* resem'bler.—*adj.* resem'bling. [O.Fr. *resembler* (Fr. *ressembler*)—*re-*, again, *sembler*, to seem—L. *similāre*, to make like—*similis*, like.]

resent, ri-zent', *v.t.* to take ill: to consider as an injury or affront.—*v.i.* (*obs.*) to savour.—*n.* resent'er.—*adj.* resent'ful.—*advs.* resent'fully; resent'ingly.—*adj.* resent'ive.—*n.* resent'ment. [O.Fr. *ressentir*—L. *re-*, in return, *sentīre*, to feel.]

reserve, ri-zərv', *v.t.* to hold back: to save up, esp. for a future occasion or special purpose: to keep, retain: to preserve: to spare: to set apart: to book, engage.—*n.* the keeping of something reserved: state of being reserved: that which is reserved: a reservation: a reserved store or stock: a tract of land reserved for a special purpose: (*sport*) a substitute kept in readiness: (esp. in *pl.*) a military force kept out of action until occasion serves: (esp. in *pl.*) a force not usually serving but liable to be called up when required: part of assets kept readily available for ordinary demands: artistic restraint: restrained manner: reticence: aloofness: a secret: limitation, restriction: a mental reservation.—*adj.* kept in reserve: of the reserves.—*adj.* reserv'able.—*ns.* reservā'tion (*rez-*), the act of reserving or keeping back: the withholding from a statement of a word or clause

Neutral vowels in unaccented syllables: el'ə-mənt, in'fənt, ran'dəm

necessary to convey its real meaning: something withheld: safe keeping: a tract of public land reserved for some special purpose, as for Indians, schools, game, &c.: the pope's retention to himself of the right to nominate to a benefice: a limitation: the booking of a seat, room, passage, &c.: a booked seat, room, &c.; **reserv'atory** (*ri-zərv'ə-tər-i*; *obs.*), a receptacle: a reservoir.— *adj.* **reserved'**, reticent: uncommunicative: aloof in manner: booked.—*adv.* **reserv'edly.**—*ns.* **reservedness** (*ri-zərvd'nis*); **reserv'ist**, a member of a reserve force.—**mental reservation**, the holding back of some word or clause which is necessary to convey fully the meaning really intended by the speaker; **reservation of the sacrament**, the practice of reserving part of the consecrated bread of the eucharist for the communion of the sick; **reserved occupation**, employment of national importance that exempts from service in the armed forces; **without reserve**, a phrase implying that a property will be sold absolutely, neither the vendor nor anyone acting for him bidding in it. [O.Fr. *reserver*—L. *reservāre*—*re-*, back, *servāre*, to save.]

reservoir, *rez'ər-vwär, -vwawr, n.* a receptacle: a store: a receptacle for fluids, esp. a large basin, artificial lake, or tank for storing water.—*v.t.* to store. [Fr.]

reset, *rē-set'*, *v.t.* and *v.i.* to set again.—*adj.* **re-sett'able.**

reset, *ri-set'*, *v.t.* (*Scot.*) to harbour: to receive, knowing to be stolen.—Also *v.i.*—*n.* harbouring of a proscribed person: receiving of stolen goods.— *n.* **resett'er.** [O.Fr. *recet(t)er*—L. *receptāre*— *recipĕre*, to receive.]

resiant, *rez'i-ənt, -ant, adj.* and *n.* (*obs.* or *arch.*) resident.—*n.* **res'iance.** [O.Fr. *reseant*, pr.p. of *reseoir*—L. *residēre*.]

reside, *ri-zīd'*, *v.i.* to dwell permanently: to be in residence: to abide: to be vested: to inhere. —*ns.* **residence** (*rez'i-dəns*), act of dwelling in a place: the act of living in the place required by regulations or performance of functions: a stay in a place: a dwelling-place: a dwelling-house, esp. one of some pretensions: that in which anything permanently inheres or has its seat; **res'idency**, the official abode of a Resident: an administrative district under a Resident.—*adj.* **res'ident**, dwelling in a place for some time: residing on one's own estate, or the place of one's duties, or the place required by certain conditions: not migratory: seated: inherent.—*n.* one who resides: an animal that does not migrate: a public minister at a foreign court: a representative of a governor in a protected state: the governor of a Residency (esp. in the former Dutch East Indies). —*n.* **res'identer** (*Scot. -dent'*), an inhabitant.— *adjs.* **residential** (*-den'shl*), of, for, or connected with residence: suitable for or occupied by houses, esp. of a better kind; **residentiary** (*-den'shə-ri*), resident: officially bound to reside: pertaining to or involving official residence.—*n.* an inhabitant: one bound to reside, as a canon.—*ns.* **residen'tiaryship**; **res'identship**; **resi'der.** [L. *residēre* —*re-*, back, *sedēre*, to sit.]

residue, *rez'i-dū, n.* that which is left, remainder: what is left of an estate after payment of debts, charges, and legacies.—*adj.* **resid'ual**, remaining as residue or difference.—*n.* that which remains as a residue or as a difference.—*adjs.* **resid'uary**, of, or of the nature of, a residue, esp. of an estate; **resid'uous**, (*rare*) residual.—*n.* **resid'uum** (L.), a residue:—*pl.* **resid'ua.** [L. *residuum*—*residēre*, to remain behind.]

resign, *ri-zīn'*, *v.t.* to yield up: to submit calmly: to relinquish: to entrust.—*v.i.* to give up office, employment, &c.: (*rare*) to submit.—*n.* **resigna-tion** (*rez-ig-nā'shən*), act of giving up: state of being resigned or quietly submissive: (*Scots law*) the form by which a vassal returns the feu into the hands of a superior.—*adj.* **resigned** (*ri-zīnd'*), calmly submissive.—*adv.* **resignedly** (*ri-zīn'id-li*). —*ns.* **resign'edness**; **resign'er**; **resign'ment.** [O.Fr. *resigner*—L. *resignāre, -ātum*, to unseal, **annul**—*signāre*, to seal—*signum*, a mark.]

re-sign. See **re-.**

resile, *ri-zīl'*, *v.i.* to recoil: to rebound: to recover form and position elastically: (esp. *Scot.*) to draw back from a statement, agreement, course, to back out.—*ns.* **resilience** (*ri-zil'i-əns*), recoil: elasticity, physical or mental; **resil'iency**, elasticity.—*adj.* **resil'ient**, elastic, physically or in spirits. [L. *resilīre*, to leap back—*salīre*, to leap.]

resin, *rez'in, n.* rosin, a substance got by distillation of turpentine: any member of the class to which it belongs, compounds of carbon, hydrogen, and oxygen, formed as waste products of plants, or manufactured synthetically.—*v.t.* to rosin: to treat with resin: to remove resin from.—*ns.* **res'ināte**, a salt of any of the acids occurring in natural resins; **res'iner**, a resin gatherer.—*adj.* **resinif'erous**, yielding resin.—*n.* **resinifica'tion.** —*v.t.* and *v.i.* **res'inify**, to make or become a resin or resinous.—*v.t.* **res'inise**, to treat with resin.—*n.* **resino'sis**, abnormal flow of resin.— *adj.* **res'inous**, of, like, containing, of the nature of, resin: of the lustre of resin: (*elect., obs.*) negative (as produced by rubbing a resin).—*adv.* **res'inously.** [Fr. *résine*—L. *rēsīna*.]

resinata, *rez-i-nä'tä, n.* Greek white wine with resinous flavour. [L. *rēsīnāta* (fem.), resined.]

resipiscence, *res-i-pis'əns, n.* change to a better frame of mind.—Also **resipisc'ency.**—*adj.* **resipisc'ent.** [L. *resipīscentia*—*resipīscĕre*—*re-*, again, *sapĕre*, to be wise.]

resist, *ri-zist'*, *v.t.* to strive against: to oppose: to stand against: to withstand: to hinder the action of: to be little affected by: (*Shak.*) to be distasteful to.—*v.i.* to make opposition.—*n.* a coating applied as a protection against chemical action.—Also *adj.*—*ns.* **resis'tance**, act or power of resisting: opposition: the opposition of a body to the motion of another: that property of a substance in virtue of which the passage of an electric current through it is accompanied with a dissipation of energy: an electrical resistor; **resis'tance-box**, a box containing resistors; **resis'tance-coil**, a coil of wire used to offer resistance to the passage of electricity; **resis'tant**, one who, or that which, resists.—*adj.* **resis'tant** (less usu. **resis'tent**), making resistance: withstanding adverse conditions, as parasites, germs, antibiotics.— *ns.* **resis'ter**; **resistibil'ity.**—*adj.* **resis'tible.**— *advs.* **resis'tibly**; **resis'tingly.**—*adj.* **resis'tive.**— *adv.* **resis'tively.**—*n.* **resistiv'ity** (*rez-*).—*adj.* **resist'less**, irresistible: unresisting, unable to resist.— *adv.* **resist'lessly.**—*ns.* **resist'lessness**; **resist'or**, a piece of apparatus used to offer electric resistance. —**resistance (movement)**, a party continuing opposition to a foreign occupying power after the country has nominally capitulated. [L. *resistĕre*— *re-*, against, *sistĕre*, to make to stand.]

reskew, reskue (*Spens.*). Same as **rescue.**

resoluble, *rez'əl-ū-bl, adj.* that may be resolved, dissolved, analysed.—*adj.* **resolute** (*rez'əl-ūt, -ōōt*), having a fixed purpose: constant in pursuing a purpose: determined.—*n.* (*Shak.*) a determined person.—*adv.* **res'olutely.**—*ns.* **res'oluteness**; **resolution** (*rez-əl-ū'shən, -ōō'shən*), act of resolving: analysis: separation of components: melting: solution: state of being resolved: fixed determination: that which is resolved: removal of or freedom from doubt: (*mus.*) progression from discord to concord: a formal proposal put before a meeting, or its formal determination thereon: substitution of two short syllables for a long: the making visible of detail: the disappearance or dispersion of a tumour or inflammation: **re-solu'tion** (*rē-sol-*), renewed or repeated solution; **resolu'tioner** (*rez-əl-*), one who joins in or accepts a resolution: **Resolutioner**, (*Scot. hist.*) one who approved of the resolutions of 1650 admitting to civil and military office all persons except those excommunicate and hostile to the Covenant— opp. to the *Protesters.* — *adj.* **res'olutive.** — *n.* **resolvabil'ity.**—*adj.* **resolvable** (*ri-zolv'*).—*v.t.* **resolve'**, to separate into components: to make visible the details of: to analyse: to break up: to melt: to transform: to relax: to solve: to dissipate: to free from doubt or difficulty: to convince: to assure: to inform: to answer: to pass as a resolution: to determine: to disperse, as a tumour: (*mus.*) to make to pass into a concord.—*v.i.* to undergo resolution: to melt: to come to a determination (often with *on* to indicate the course chosen): (*Shak.*) to be convinced: (*Shak.*) to decide to go to a place (with *on*): (*Spens.*) to take counsel: (*law*) to lapse.—*n.* anything resolved or determined: resolution: fixed purpose.—*adj.* **resolved'**, fixed in purpose.—*adv.* **resolvedly** (*ri-zol'vid-li*), resolutely. — *n.* **resol'vedness**.—*adj.* **resol'vent**, having power to resolve.—*n.* that which causes or helps solution or resolution.—*n.* **resol'ver**. [L. *resolvĕre*, *resolūtum*—*re-*, inten., *solvĕre*, to loose.]

resonance, *rez'on-əns*, *n.* resounding: sonority: sympathetic vibration: the sound heard in auscultation: (*chem.*) a term used in valency theory to describe a condition, observed in certain compounds, when the bonds are neither single nor double.—*n.* **res'onance-box**, a chamber in a musical instrument for increasing its sonority by vibration in sympathy with the strings.—*adj.* **res'onant**, resounding, ringing: giving its characteristic vibration in sympathy with another body's vibration.—*adv.* **res'onantly**.—*v.i.* **res'onate**, to resound: to vibrate sympathetically.—*n.* **reson-ā'tor**, a resonating body or device, as for increasing sonority or for analysing sound. [L. *resonāre*, *-ātum—re-*, back, *sonāre*, to sound.]

resorb, *ri-sorb'*, *v.t.* to absorb back.—*adj.* **resorb'ent**. [L. *resorbēre*, to suck back.]

resorcin, *ri-zor'sin*, *n.* a colourless phenol, $C_6H_4(OH)_2$, used in dyeing, photography, and medicine.—Also **resor'cinol**. [**resin** and **orcin**.]

resorption, *ri-sorp'shən*, *n.* resorbing, esp. of a mineral by rock magma.—*adj.* **resorp'tive**. [See **resorb**.]

resort, *ri-zort'*, *v.i.* (*obs.*) to revert: to go: to betake oneself: to have recourse: to apply: to go or be habitually.—*n.* act of resorting: a place much frequented: a haunt: that which one has or may have recourse to: concourse: thronging: repair.—*n.* **resort'er**, a frequenter.—**in the last resort**, orig. (a Gallicism, *en dernier ressort*), without appeal: hence, as a last expedient. [O.Fr. *resortir* (Fr. *ressortir*), to rebound, retire—*sortir*, to go out; origin obscure.]

resound, *ri-zownd'*, *v.t.* to echo: to sound with reverberation: to sound or spread the praises of.—*v.i.* to echo: to re-echo, reverberate: to sound sonorously.—*adj.* **resound'ing**.—*adv.* **resound'ingly**. [Pfx. *re-*, and **sound**.]

resource, *ri-sōrs'*, *n.* a source or possibility of help: an expedient: (*pl.*) means of raising money: means of support: means of occupying or amusing oneself: resourcefulness. — *adj.* **resource'ful**, fertile in expedients: rich in resources.—*n.* **resource'fulness**. — *adj.* **resource'less**. [O.Fr. *ressource—resourdre—*L. *resurgĕre*, to rise again.]

respeak, *rē-spēk'*, *v.t.* (*Shak.*) to echo.

respect, *ri-spekt'*, *v.t.* to look to, regard, consider, take into account: to heed: to refer to, relate to, have reference to: to treat with undue discrimination: to feel or show esteem, deference, or honour to: to refrain from violating: (*obs.* and *her.*) to face, look at.—Also *v.i.*—*n.* (*Spens.*) heed: (*obs.*) an aspect: a particular: a relation: reference: regard: consideration: undue discrimination: deferential esteem: (often in *pl.*) a greeting or message of esteem. — *n.* **respectabil'ity**. — *adj.* **respec'table**, worthy of respect: considerable: passable: mediocre: (*obs.*) of good social standing: fairly well-to-do: decent and well-behaved: reputable: seemly: presentable: timidly or priggishly conventional.—*n.* **respec'tableness**.—*adv.* **respec'tably**.—*adj.* **respec'tant**, (*her.*) facing each other: looking back.—*n.* **respec'ter**.—*adj.* **respect'ful**, showing or feeling respect.—*adv.* **respect'fully**.—*n.* **respect'fulness**.—*prep.* **respect'ing**, concerning: considering.—*adj.* **respec'tive**, having respect: (*Shak.*) regardful, considerate: heedful: discriminating: (*obs.*) respectful: (*Shak.*) worthy of respect: relative: particular or several, relating to each distributively.—*adv.* **respec'tively**.

—*adj.* **respect'less**, regardless.—**respect of persons**, undue favour, as for wealth, &c.; **in respect of**, in the matter of: (*obs.*) because of: (*obs.*) in comparison with: **with respect to**, with regard to. [L. *respicĕre*, *respectum—re-*, back, *specĕre*, to look.]

respire, *ri-spīr'*, *v.i.* to breathe: to take breath.—*v.t.* to breathe: to exhale.—*adj.* **respirable** (*res'pər-ə-bl*, *ri-spīr'ə-bl*), fit for breathing.—*ns.* **respiration** (*res-pər-ā'shən*), breathing: the taking in of oxygen and giving out of carbon dioxide, with associated physiological processes: a breath: a breathing-space; **res'pirător**, an appliance worn on the mouth or nose to filter and warm the air breathed: a gas-mask.—*adj.* **respiratory** (*res'pər-ə-tər-i*, *ri-spī'rə-tər-i*), of or for, pertaining to, or serving for, respiration. [L. *respīrāre*, *-ātum—spīrāre*, to breathe.]

respite, *res'pīt*, *-pit*, *n.* temporary cessation: pause: interval of rest: (*law*) temporary suspension of the execution of a criminal.—*v.t.* to grant a respite to: to relieve by a pause: to delay: (*Shak.*) to prolong. [O.Fr. *respit* (Fr. *répit*)—L. *respectus*, respect.]

resplend, *ri-splend'*, *v.i.* to shine brilliantly: to radiate: to be gorgeously bright or splendid.—*ns.* **resplend'ence**, **resplend'ency**.—*adj.* **resplend'ent**.—*adv.* **resplend'ently**. [L. *resplendēre—re-*, inten., *splendēre*, to shine.]

respond, *ri-spond'*, *v.i.* to answer: to utter liturgical responses: to act in answer: to react.—*n.* a response to a versicle in liturgy: a half-pillar or half-pier attached to a wall to support an arch (answering to one at the other end of an arcade, &c.).—*ns.* **respond'ence**, response: correspondence, consequence; **respond'ency**, consequence. —*adj.* **respond'ent**, answering: corresponding: responsive.—*n.* one who answers: one who refutes objections: a defendant, esp. in a divorce suit.—*ns.* **respondentia** (*res-pon-den'shä*), a loan on a ship's cargo, payable only on safe arrival; **respond'er** (*ris-*); **respond'er**, an answer: an oracular answer: an answer made by the congregation to the priest during divine service: a responsory: a reaction, esp. sympathetic.—*adj.* **response'less**.—*n.* **responsibil'ity**, state of being responsible: a trust or charge for which one is responsible.—*adj.* **respon'sible**, liable to be called to account or render satisfaction: answerable: governed by a sense of responsibility: involving responsibility: capable of discharging duty: able to pay: respectable-looking.—*adv.* **respon'sibly**.—*n.pl.* **respon'sions** (*-shənz*), the first of the three examinations for the B.A. degree at Oxford, ' smalls.'—*adj.* **respon'sive**, ready to respond: answering: correspondent: with responses.—*adv.* **respon'sively**. — *n.* **respon'siveness**. — *adj.* **responso'rial** (*rē-*), responsive.—*n.* an office-book containing the responsories.—*adj.* **respon'sory**, making answer.—*n.* an anthem sung after a lesson: a liturgical response. [L. *respondēre*, *respōnsum—re-*, back, *spondēre*, to promise.]

ressaldar. Same as **risaldar**.

rest, *rest*, *n.* repose, refreshing inactivity: intermission of, or freedom from, motion or disturbance: tranquillity: (*Shak.*) invigoration by resting: a place for resting: a prop or support (e.g. for a musket, a billiard cue, a violinist's chin): motionlessness: a pause in speaking or reading: an interval of silence in music, or a mark indicating it.—*v.i.* to repose: to be at ease: to be still: to be supported: to lean: to put trust: to have foundation: to settle, alight: to remain.—*v.t.* to give rest to: to place or hold in support: to lean: to base.—*ns.* **rest'-cure**, treatment by repose; **rest'-day**, a day of rest: the first day of a three days' visit; **rest'er**.—*adj.* **rest'ful**, at rest: restgiving: tranquil.—*adv.* **rest'fully**.—*ns.* **rest'fulness**; **rest'-house**, a house of rest for travellers. —*n.* and *adj.* **rest'ing**.—*ns.* **rest'ing-place**, a place of rest: a stair-landing; **rest'ing-spore**, a spore that can germinate after a period of dormancy; **rest'ing-stage**, a state of suspended activity.—*adj.* **rest'less**, without rest: unresting: impatient of inactivity or of remaining still: uneasily active: uneasy: never-ceasing: giving or allowing no

rest.—*adv.* **rest'lessly.**—*ns.* **rest'lessness ; rest'-room.**—**at rest,** stationary : in repose : free from disquiet. [O.E. *rest, ræst ;* Ger. *rast,* Du. *rust ;* converging and merging in meaning with the following words.]

rest, *rest, n.* remainder : all others : reserve fund : (*tennis,* &c.) a rally : (*primero*) a stake whose loss ends the game.—*v.i.* to remain (see also preceding word).—**for the rest,** as regards other matters ; **set up one's rest,** (*arch.*) to make one's final stake : hence, to take a resolution : to take up abode. [Fr. *reste*—L. *restāre,* to remain—*re-,* back, *stāre,* to stand.]

rest, *rest, n.* a contrivance on a breastplate to prevent the spear from being driven back.—*v.t.* (*Shak.*) to arrest. [Aphetic for **arrest.**]

restaurant, *res'tə-rän[2], -rawn[2], n.* a place where meals may be had.—*ns.* **res'taurant-car,** a railway carriage in which meals are served ; **restaurateur** (*res-tō-rä-tər, res-tər-ə-tər'*), the keeper of a restaurant. [Fr.,—*restaurer,* to restore.]

restem, *rē-stem', v.t.* (*Shak.*) to force back against the current. [**stem.**]

rest-harrow, *rest'-har-ō, n.* a papilionaceous plant (*Ononis*) with long, tough, woody roots. [**rest** (3), and **harrow** (1).]

restiff, *res'tif,* an obsolete form of **restive.**

restiform, *res'ti-form, adj.* cord-like. [L. *restis,* a cord, *forma,* form.]

restitute, *res'ti-tūt, v.t.* to restore.—*v.i.* to make restitution.—*ns.* **restitū'tion ; restitū'tionism ;** restorationism ; **restitū'tionist.**—*adj.* **restitutive** (*ri-stit',* or *res'tit-*).—*n.* **res'titūtor.**—*adj.* **restit'ū-tory.** [L. *restituĕre, -ūtum*—*re-, statuĕre,* to make to stand.]

restive, *res'tiv, adj.* (*obs.*) inert : unwilling to go forward : obstinate, refractory : uneasy, as if ready to break from control. — *adv.* **res'tively. — *n.* res'tiveness.** [O.Fr. *restif*—L. *restāre,* to rest.]

restore, *ri-stōr', v.t.* to repair : to bring, put, or give back : to make good : to reinstate : to bring back to a (supposed) former state, or to a normal state : to reconstruct mentally, by inference or conjecture.—*n.* (*Spens.*) restitution.—*adj.* **restōr'-able.**—*ns.* **restōr'ableness ; restoration** (*res-tō-rā'shən,* or *-tə-, -to-*), act or process of restoring : a reinstatement of or in kingship (as the Restoration of the Stuarts, the Bourbons) : renovations and reconstruction (sometimes little differing from destruction) of a building, painting, &c. : a reconstructed thing or representation.—*adj.* **Restora'tion,** of the time of the Restoration of Charles II.—*ns.* **restorā'tionism** (*theol.*) receiving of a sinner to divine favour : the final recovery of all men ; **restorā'tionist,** one who holds the belief that after a purgation all wicked men and angels will be restored to the favour of God, a universalist.—*adj.* **restorative** (*ris-tor'ə-tiv*), tending to restore, esp. to strength and vigour.—*n.* a medicine that restores.—*adv.* **restor'atively.**—*n.* **restōr'er.** [O.Fr. *restorer*—L. *restaurāre, -ātum.*]

restrain, *ri-strān', v.t.* to hold back : to control : to subject to forcible repression : (*Shak.*) to tighten : (*Milt.*) to forbid.—*v.i.* (*rare*) to refrain.—*adjs.* **restrain'able ; restrained',** controlled : self-controlled : showing restraint : (*Shak.*) forbidden.—*adv.* **restrain'edly.**—*ns.* **restrain'edness ; restrain'er.**—*n.* and *adj.* **restrain'ing.**—*ns.* **restraint',** act of restraining : state of being restrained : a restraining influence : restriction : forcible control : artistic control or reticence : want of liberty : reserve.—**restraint of princes,** embargo. [O.Fr. *restraindre, restrai(g)n*— L. *restringĕre, restrictum*—*re-,* back, *stringĕre,* to draw tightly.]

restrict, *ri-strikt', v.t.* to limit.—*adj.* **restrict'ed.** —*adv.* **restrict'edly.**—*ns.* **restric'tion ; restric'-tionist,** one who favours restriction.—Also *adj.*— *adj.* **restric'tive,** restricting : tending to restrict : expressing restriction.—*adv.* **restric'tively.**—*v.t.* **restringe** (*ri-strinj'*), to restrict.—*n.* and *adj.* **re-strin'gent,** astringent. [L. *restringĕre, restrictum.*]

resty, *rest'i, adj.* restive : (*Shak.*) sluggish : (*Spens.*) inoperative, ineffectual. [**restive,** or partly **rest** (1).]

result, *ri-zult', v.i.* to issue (with *in*) : to follow as a consequence : (*obs.*) to rebound : to be the outcome : (*law*) to revert.—*n.* consequence : outcome : outcome aimed at : quantity obtained by calculation : (*obs.* and *U.S.*) decision, resolution, as of a council.—*adj.* **result'ant,** resulting : resulting from combination (as of tones sounded together).—*n.* a force compounded of two or more forces : a sum of vector quantities : a resultant tone : a result of combination.—*adjs.* **result'ative,** expressing result ; **result'ful ; result'ing ; result'-less.**—*n.* **result'lessness.** [L. *resultāre,* to leap back—*saltāre,* to leap.]

resume, *ri-zūm', -zōōm', v.t.* to take back : to assume again : to take up again : to begin again. —*v.i.* to take possession again : to begin again in continuation.—*adj.* **resum'able.**—*ns.* **résumé** (*rā-zü-mā, rez'ū-mā ;* Fr. *pa.p.*), a summary ; **resumption** (*ri-zump'shən,* or *zum'*), act of resuming.—*adj.* **resumptive** (-*zump', -zum'*).—*adv.* **resump'tively.** [L. *resūmĕre, -sūmptum*—*re-, sūmĕre,* to take.]

resupinate, *ri-s(y)ōō'pin-āt, adj.* (*bot.*) upside down by twisting.—*n.* **resupina'tion.**—*adj.* **resupine** (*rē-sū-pīn',* or -*sōō-*), lying on the back. [L. *resupināre, -ātum,* and *resupīnus*—*re-,* back, *supīnus,* bent backward.]

resurge, *ri-surj', v.i.* to rise again.—*n.* **resur'gence.** —*adj.* **resur'gent.**—*v.t.* **resurrect** (*rez-ər-ekt'*) : back-formation), to restore to life : to revive : to disinter.—*v.i.* to come to life again.—*n.* **re-surrection** (-*ek'shən*), a rising from the dead : resuscitation : revival : a thing resurrected : body-snatching. — *adjs.* **resurrec'tional ; resurrec'-tionary.**—*v.t.* **resurrec'tionise.**—*ns.* **resurrec'-tionism ; resurrec'tionist, resurrec'tion-man,** one who stole bodies from the grave for dissection ; **resurrec'tion-pie,** a dish compounded of remnants of former meals ; **resurrec'tion-plant,** a plant that curls in a ball in drought and spreads again in moisture, as rose of Jericho, some selaginellas.— *adj.* **resurrect'ive.**—*n.* **resurrect'or.** [L. *re-surgĕre, resurrēctum*—*re-, surgĕre,* to rise.]

resurvey, *rē-sur-vā', v.t.* to survey or examine again.—*n.* (-*sur'*) a new survey.

resuscitate, *ri-sus'i-tāt, v.t.* and *v.i.* to revive.— *adjs.* **resusc'itable ; resusc'itant.**—*n.* one who, or that which, resuscitates.—*n.* **resuscitā'tion.**—*adj.* **resusc'itātive,** tending to resuscitate : reviving : revivifying : reanimating.—*n.* **resusc'i-tātor.** [L. *resuscitāre, -ātum*—*re-, sus-, sub-,* from beneath, *citāre,* to put into quick motion—*ciēre,* to make to go.]

ret, *ret,* **rate, rait,** *rāt, v.t.* to expose to moisture. —*v.t.* and *v.i.* to soak : to soften, spoil, or rot by soaking or exposure to moisture : to rot :—*pr.p.* **rett'ing, rāt'ing, rait'ing ;** *pa.t.* and *pa.p.* **rett'ed, rāt'ed, rait'ed.**—*n.* **rett'ery,** a place where flax is retted. [App. akin to **rot.**]

retable, *ri-tā'bl, n.* a shelf behind an altar. [Fr. *rétable*—L.L. *retrōtabulum.*]

retail, *rē'tāl,* formerly (still by some) *ri-, rē-tāl', n.* sale to consumer, or in small quantities.—*adj.* in, of, engaged in, concerned with, such sale.— *adv.* by retail.—*v.t.* (*ri-, rē-tāl'*) to sell by retail : to repeat in detail : to put about, hand on by report.—*ns.* **retail'er ; retail'ment.** [O.Fr. *retail,* piece cut off—*tailler,* to cut.]

retain, *ri-tān', v.t.* to keep : to hold back : to continue to hold : to keep up : to employ or keep engaged, as by a fee paid : to keep in mind.— *adj.* **retain'able.**—*ns.* **retain'er,** one who or that which retains : a dependent, a person attached to a family without being a servant : authorisation : a retaining fee (**general,** to secure a priority of claim on a counsel's services ; **special,** for a particular case) ; **retain'ership ; retain'ment.**— **retaining fee,** the advance fee paid to a lawyer to defend a cause ; **retaining wall,** a wall to prevent a bank from slipping down. [Fr. *retenir* —L. *retinēre*—*re-,* back, *tenēre,* to hold.]

retake, *rē-tāk', v.t.* to take again : to take back : recapture : (*pa.t.* **retook' ;** *pa.p.* **retā'ken**).—*n.* a second or repeated photographing or photograph, esp. for a motion picture.—*ns.* **retāk'er ; retāk'ing,**

retaliate, ri-tal′i-āt, *v.t.* to requite: to inflict in return.—*v.i.* to return like for like (esp. in hostility). —*ns.* **retaliā′tion**, return of like for like: imposition of a tariff against countries that impose a tariff; **retaliā′tionist.**—*adj.* **retal′iātive.**—*n.* **retal′iātor.**—*adj.* **retal′iatory** (-āt-ər-i, -ət-ər-i). [L. *retāliāre*, *-ātum*—*re-*, *tāliō*, *-ōnis*, like for like— *tālis*, such.]

retama, re-tā′mä, *n.* a name for various desert switch-plants—papilionaceous and caesalpiniaceous —esp. species of Spartium, Cytisus, and Genista, with yellow or white flowers. [Sp.,—Ar. *retām* (pl.).]

retard, ri-tärd′, *v.t.* to slow: to keep back: to delay: to defer.—*v.i.* to slow down: to delay.— *n.* delay: lag.—*adj.* **retar′dant.**—*n.* **retardā′tion** (rē-), slowing: delay: lag.—*adjs.* **retardative** (ri-tärd′ə-tiv); **retar′datory.**—*ns.* **retar′der**; **retard′ment.** [L. *retardāre*, *-ātum*—*re-*, *tardāre*, to slow.]

retch, rēch, also *rech*, *v.i.* to strain as if to vomit. —*n.* an act of retching. [O.E. *hrǽcan*—*hrāca*, a hawking.]

retch, rech, **rech′less**, &c. Obs. forms of **reck**, &c.

retene, rē′tēn, ret′ēn, *n.* a hydrocarbon ($C_{18}H_{18}$) got from tar.—*ns.* **retinalite** (ret′, or ri-tin′), a resinous-lustred serpentine: **retinis′pora**, **retinos′pora**, a cypress or kindred conifer in a perpetuated juvenile form, once placed in a separate genus; **ret′inite**, (*obs.*) pitchstone: a variety of amber; **ret′inol**, an oil distilled from resin. [Gr. *rhētīnē*, pine resin.]

retention, ri-ten′shən, *n.* act or power of retaining: memory: custody: (*med.*) inability to void.— *adj.* **reten′tive**, retaining: tenacious: retaining moisture.—*adv.* **reten′tively.**—*ns.* **reten′tiveness**, **retentiv′ity** (rē-). [L. *retentiō*, *-ōnis*; O.Fr. *retentif*; see **retain.**]

retexture, rē-tekst′yər, *n.* weaving anew. [L. *retexĕre*, to weave anew, weave or unweave.]

retiarius, rē′shi-ā-ri-əs, L. rā-ti-ä′ri-oos, *n.* a gladiator armed with a net.—*adj.* **retiary** (rē′shi-ər-i), of nets: using a net as a weapon, as a gladiator or a spider. [L. *rētiārius*—*rēte*, net.]

reticent, ret′i-sənt, *adj.* reserved or sparing in communication.—*ns.* **ret′icence**, **ret′icency.** [L. *reticēns*, *-ēntis*, pr.p. of *reticēre*—*re-*, *tacēre*, to be silent.]

reticle, ret′i-kl, *n.* an attachment to an optical instrument consisting of a network of lines of reference.—*adj.* **reticular** (ri-tik′ū-lər), netted: netlike: reticulated: of the reticulum.—*adv.* **retic′ularly.**—*adj.* **retic′ulary.**—*v.t.* **retic′ulate**, to form into or mark with a network.—*v.i.* to form a network.—*adj.* netted: marked with network: net-veined.—*adj.* **retic′ulated**, reticulate: (of masonry) of lozenge-shaped stones, or of squares placed diamond-wise: of rusticated work with ridges of uniform width between irregular sinkings.—*adv.* **retic′ulately.**—*ns.* **reticulā′tion**, network: netlike structure; **reticule** (ret′i-kūl), a reticle: a small bag, orig. and properly of network, carried by ladies; **retic′ulum**, a network: the second stomach of a ruminant. [L. *rēticulum*, dim. of *rēte*, net.]

retiform, rē′ti-form, *adj.* having the form of a net. [L. *rēte*, net, *forma*, form.]

retina, ret′i-nä, *n.* the sensitive layer of the eye:— *pl.* **ret′inas**, **ret′inae** (-nē).—*adj.* **ret′inal.**—*ns.* **retinī′tis**, inflammation of the retina; **retinos′-copist**; **retinos′copy**, examination of the eye by observing a shadow on the retina; **retinula** (ri-tin′ū-lä), a cell playing the part of retina to an ommatidium:—*pl.* **retin′ulae** (-lē).—*adj.* **retin′ular.** [L.L. *rētina*, app.—L. *rēte*, net.]

retinaculum, ret-i-nak′ū-ləm, *n.* a connecting band: a means of retention: the apparatus that holds an insect's forewing and hindwing together: the sticky attachment of a pollen-mass, as in orchids:— *pl.* **retinac′ula.**—*adj.* **retinac′ūlar.** [L. *retināculum*, a holdfast—*retinēre*; see **retain, retention.**]

retinite, retinol, retinospora, &c. See under **retene.**

retinue, ret′i-nū, formerly ri-tin′ū, *n.* a body of retainers: a suite or train. [Fr. *retenue*, fem. pa.p. of *retenir*; see **retain.**]

retire, ri-tīr′, *v.i.* to withdraw: to retreat: to recede: to withdraw from society, office, public or active life, business, profession, &c.: to go into seclusion or to bed: (*obs.*) to return.—*v.t.* to withdraw: to draw back: to withdraw from currency: to cause to retire.—*n.* (now *rare*) retirement: (*obs.*) retreat: (*obs.*) a place of retirement: (*obs.*) return: a signal to retreat.—*ns.* **retī′racy**, (*U.S.*) seclusion: (*U.S.*) enough to retire on; **retī′ral**, giving up of office, business, &c.: withdrawal.—*adj.* **retired′**, withdrawn: reserved in manner: secluded, sequestered: withdrawn from business or profession: (*obs.*) recondite.—*adv.* **retired′ly** (or ri-tī′rid-li). — *ns.* **retired′ness** (or ri-tī′rid-nis); **retire′ment**, act of retiring: state of being or having retired: solitude: privacy: a time or place of seclusion.—*adj.* **retir′ing**, reserved: unobtrusive: retreating: modest: given to one who retires from a public office or service. —*adv.* **retir′ingly.**—*n.* **retir′ingness.**—**retired list**, a list of officers who are relieved from active service but receive a certain amount of pay (**retired pay**). [Fr. *retirer*—*re-*, back, *tirer*, to draw.]

retort, ri-tort′, *v.t.* to throw back: to return upon an assailant or opponent: to answer in retaliation: to answer sharply or wittily: (*Shak.*) to reject: to purify or treat in a retort.—*v.i.* to make a sharp reply.—*n.* retaliation: a ready and sharp or witty answer: the art or act of retorting: a vessel in which substances are placed for distillation, typically a flask with long bent-back neck.—*adj.* **retor′ted**, bent back: thrown back: turned back. —*ns.* **retor′ter**; **retortion** (-tor′shən); also **retor′sion**), retorting: bending, turning, or casting back: retaliation.—*adj.* **retor′tive.** [L. *retorquēre*, *retortum*—*re-*, back, *torquēre*, to twist.]

retouch, rē-tuch′, *v.t.* to touch again: to touch up, seek to improve by new touches.—*n.* an act of touching up, esp. of a photograph by pencil-work on the negative.—*n.* **retouch′er.**

retour, ri-tōōr′, *n.* a return: (*Scots law*) an extract from chancery of the service of an heir to his ancestor.—*v.t.* to return as heir: to return to chancery. [O.Fr. *retour*, return.]

retrace, ri-, or rē-trās′, *v.t.* to trace back: to go back upon: to run over with the eye or in the memory: (rē-) to renew the outline of.—*adj.* **retrace′able** (ri-).

retract, ri-trakt′, *v.t.* to draw back: to withdraw: to revoke: to unsay: (*chess*) to undo (the previous move): to pronounce with tongue drawn back.— *v.i.* to take back, or draw back from, what has been said or granted.—*adj.* **retrac′table.**—*n.* **retractā′tion** (rē-), revoking: recantation.—*adj.* **retrac′ted**, drawn in: turned back: cancelled: revoked: pronounced with tongue drawn in.— *adj.* **retrac′tile** (-*tīl*), that may be drawn back.— *ns.* **retractility** (rē-trak-til′i-ti); **retraction** (ri-trak′shən), drawing back: retractation.—*adj.* **retrac′tive**, tending to retract: (*chess*) involving the reversal of the previous move.—*adv.* **retrac′tively.** —*n.* **retrac′tor**, a device or instrument for holding parts back: a muscle that pulls in a part: a chess-problem that involves the reversal of the previous move. [Mainly from L. *retrahĕre*, *retractum*; partly from *retractāre*, *retractātum*—*re-*, back, *trahĕre*, to draw.]

retract, retrait, retraite, ri-trāt′, obs. forms of **retreat** (*n.* and *v.i.*).

retrait. See **retrate** (2).

retranslate, rē-träns-lāt′, or -*trəns-*, *v.t.* to translate anew: to translate back into the original language: to transfer back.—*n.* **retranslā′tion.**

retransmit, rē-träns-mit′, *v.t.* to transmit again: to transmit back: to transmit a stage further.—*n.* **retransmiss′ion.**

retrate, ri-trāt′, *n.* and *v.i.* (*Spens.*). Same as **retreat.**

retrate, retraitt, ri-trāt′, *n.* (*Spens.*) a portrait, portraiture. [It. *ritratto*.]

retread, rē-tred′, *v.t.* to tread again (*pa.t.* **retrod′**; *pa.p.* **retrodd′en**): to repair the tread of (a tire) (*pa.t.* and *pa.p.* **retread′ed**).

retreat, ri-trēt′, *n.* a withdrawal: an orderly withdrawal before an enemy, or from a position of danger or difficulty: a signal (by bugle or drum) for withdrawal or for retirement to quarters: (*Shak.*) recall of pursuers: retirement: seclusion: retirement for a time for religious meditation: a time of such retirement: place of privacy, seclusion, refuge, or quiet: an institution for treatment of the insane, drunkards, or others.—*v.i.* to draw back: to relinquish a position: to retire: to recede.—*v.t.* (*rare*) to withdraw. [O.Fr. *retret, -e,* pa.p. of *retraire*—L. *retrahĕre,* to draw back.]

retree, ri-trē′, *n.* slightly damaged paper. [Perh. Fr. *retret, retrait;* see preceding.]

retrench, ri-tren(t)sh′, *v.t.* to cut off, out, or down: to protect by a retrenchment.—*v.i.* to cut down expenses.—*n.* **retrench′ment,** an act or instance of retrenching: economy: (*fort.*) a work within another for prolonging defence. [O.Fr. *retrencher* (Fr. *retrancher*)—*re-,* off, *trencher,* to cut; see **trench.**]

retribute, ri-trib′ūt, ret′ri-būt, *v.t.* to give in return: to give in return for.—*v.i.* to make requital.—*n.* **retribution** (*ret-ri-bū′shən*), requital (now esp. of evil).—*adj.* **retrib′ūtive** (*ri-*), repaying: rewarding or punishing suitably.—*n.* **retrib′ūtor.**—*adj.* **retrib′ūtory.** [L. *retribuĕre, -ūtum,* to give back—*re-,* back, *tribuĕre,* to give.]

retrieve, ri-trēv′, *v.t.* to search for and fetch, as a dog does game: to recover: to rescue: to save: to make good.—*v.i.* to find and fetch in game.—*n.* retrieving.—*adj.* **retriev′able.**—*n.* **retriev′ableness.**—*adv.* **retriev′ably.**—*ns.* **retriev′al,** retrieving; **retrieve′ment** (*rare*); **retriev′er,** a dog trained to find and fetch game that has been shot: one of a breed suited to this task: one who retrieves.—*n.* and *adj.* **retriev′ing.** [O.Fr. *retroev-, retreuv-,* stressed stem of *retrover* (Fr. *retrouver*)—*re-,* again, *trouver,* to find.]

retro-, ret′rō-, rē′trō-, *pfx.* backwards: behind. [L. *retrō.*]

retroact, rē-trō-akt′, or ret′rō-, *v.i.* to act backward, or in return or opposition, or on something past or preceding.—*n.* **retroac′tion.**—*adj.* **retroac′tive,** applying to, affecting, things past: operating backward.—*adv.* **retroac′tively.**—*n.* **retroactiv′ity.** [L. *retroagĕre, -āctum—agĕre,* to do.]

retrobulbar, rē-trō-bul′bər, or ret-rō-, *adj.* behind the eyeball. [L. *bulbus,* onion.]

retrocede, ret-rō-, rē-trō-sēd′, *v.i.* to move back or (*med.*) inwards.—*v.t.* to cede back, grant back.—*adj.* **retroce′dent.**—*n.* **retrocession** (*-sesh′ən*).—*adj.* **retrocess′ive.** [L. *retrōcēdĕre, -cessum—cēdĕre,* to go, yield; partly from *retrō* and *cede,* or Fr. *céder.*]

retrochoir, rē′trō-kwīr, or ret′rō-, *n.* (*archit.*) an extension of a church behind the position of the high altar.

retroflex, ret′rō-fleks, or rē′trō-, *adj.* bent back.—Also **retroflect′ed, ret′roflexed.**—*n.* **retroflexion** (*-flek′shən*). [L. *flectĕre, flexum,* to bend.]

retrograde, ret′rō-grād (or rē′trō-), *adj.* moving or directed backward or (*astron.*) from east to west, relatively to the fixed stars: inverse: habitually walking or swimming backwards: degenerating: reverting: (*Shak.*) contrary.—*n.* one who goes back or degenerates: backward movement.—*v.i.* to go back or backwards.—*v.t.* to cause to go back.—*ns.* **retrogradation** (*-grə-dā′shən*); **ret′rogress** (*-gres*), backward movement: degeneration.—*v.i.* **retrogress′,** to retrograde. — *n.* **retrogression** (*-gresh′ən*), a going backward: a decline in quality or merit.—*adjs.* **retrogress′ional, retrogress′ive.**—*adv.* **retrogress′ively.** [L. *retrōgradus,* going backward, *retrōgressus,* retrogression—*retrō,* backward, *gradī, gressus,* to go.]

retromingent, ret-rō-, rē-trō-min′jənt, *adj.* urinating backward.—*n.* a retromingent animal.—*n.* **retromin′gency.**—*adv.* **retromin′gently.** [L. *mingĕre,* to urinate.]

retro-operative, ret-rō-, rē-trō-op′ər-ə-tiv, *adj.* retrospective in effect.

retropulsion, ret-rō-, rē-trō-pul′shən, *n.* pushing backwards: a tendency to walk backwards in the paralysed.—*adj.* **retropul′sive.**

retrorse, ri-trors′, *adj.* turned back or downward.—*adv.* **retrorse′ly.** [L. *retrōrsus—retrōversus.*]

retrospect, ret′rō-spekt (or rē′trō-), *n.* reference, regard: a backward view: a view or a looking back: a contemplation of the past.—*v.i.* to look back.—*v.t.* to look back on.—*n.* **retrospec′tion.**—*adj.* **retrospec′tive,** looking back: retroactive.—*adv.* **retrospec′tively.** [L. *specĕre, spectum,* to look.]

retroussé, rə-trōōs′ā, rə-troos-ā, *adj.* turned up (esp. of the nose).—*n.* **retroussage** (*-āzh′*), wiping aside of ink on an engraved plate to soften tones. [Fr. *retrousser* (pa.p. *retroussé*), to turn up.]

retrovert, ret-rō-, rē-trō-vərt′, rē′trō-vərt, *v.t.* to turn back.—*n.* **retrover′sion,** a turning or falling back: backward displacement. [L. *retrōvertĕre, -versum—vertĕre,* to turn.]

retry, rē-trī′, *v.t.* to try again (judicially):—*pr.p.* **retry′ing;** *pa.t.* and *pa.p.* **retried′.**—*n.* **rētri′al.**

retted, rettery, retting. See **ret.**

retund, ri-tund′, *v.t.* to blunt. [L. *retundĕre,* to beat back.]

return, ri-turn′, *v.i.* to come or go back: to revert: to recur: (*B.*) to turn away: (*archit.*) to continue with change of direction.—*v.t.* (*Shak.*) to turn round: to turn at an angle: (*Spens.*) to turn back: to give, put, cast, bring, or send back: to answer: to retort: to report officially: to report as appointed or elected: hence, to elect to parliament: to give in return: (in games) to lead back or hit back: to requite: to repay: to respond to with the like: to render: to yield: (*Shak.*) to come back over.—*n.* the act of returning: a recurrence: reversion: (*archit.,* &c.) continuation, or a continuing stretch, at an angle, esp. a right angle: that which comes in exchange: proceeds, profit, yield: recompense: requital: an answer: an answering performance: a thing returned, esp. an unsold newspaper: (*pl.*) a light-coloured mild tobacco (orig. refuse): (*law*) the rendering back of a writ by the sheriff, with his report: an official report: hence, election to parliament: a return ticket.—*adj.* returning: for return: in return: at right angles.—*adjs.* **return′able; return′less.**—**by return** (of post), by the next post leaving in the opposite direction; **return crease** (see **crease**); **returning officer,** the officer who presides at an election; **return match,** a second match played by the same set of players; **return shock,** an electric shock due to induction sometimes felt after a lightning-flash; **return ticket,** a ticket entitling a passenger to travel to a place and back to his starting-point. [Fr. *retourner* —*re-,* back, *tourner,* to turn.]

re-turn, rē′-turn′, *v.t.* and *v.i.* to turn again or back.

retuse, ri-tūs′, *adj.* with the tip blunt and broadly notched. [L. *retūsus—retundĕre,* to blunt.]

reunion, rē-ūn′yən, *n.* a union, or a meeting, after separation: a social gathering of friends or persons with something in common. [Fr. *réunion—re-,* again, *union,* union.]

reunite, rē-ū-nīt′, *v.t.* and *v.i.* to join after separation.

rev, rev, *n.* (*slang*) a revolution (in an internal-combustion engine).—*v.t.* to increase the speed of revolution in (often with *up*).—*v.i.* to revolve: to increase in speed of revolution:—*pr.p.* **revv′ing;** *pa.t.* and *pa.p.* **revved.** [revolution.]

revalenta, rev-ə-len′tä, *n.* lentil-meal. — Earlier **ervalen′ta.** [*Ervum Lens,* Linnaean name of the lentil, L. *ervum,* bitter vetch, *lēns, lentis,* lentil.]

revalorise, rē-val′ər-īz, *v.t.* to re-establish or restore the value of (esp. currency).—*ns.* **rēvalorisā′tion;** **rēvalūā′tion.**—*v.t.* **rēval′ue,** to make a new valuation of: to give a new value to.

reveal, ri-vēl′, *v.t.* to make known, as by divine agency or inspiration: to disclose: to divulge: to make visible: to allow to be seen.—*adj.* **reveal′able.**—*n.* **reveal′er.**—*n.* and *adj.* **reveal′ing.**—*n.* **reveal′ment,** revelation. [O.Fr. *reveler* (Fr. *révéler*)—L. *revēlāre—re-,* back, *vēlāre,* to veil—*vēlum,* a veil.]

reveal, ri-vēl′, *n.* the side surface of a recess, or of the opening for a doorway or window between the frame and the outer surface of the wall. [O.Fr. *revaler,* to lower.]

reveille, ri-vel′i, ri-val′i, ri-vāl′yi, (U.S.) rev-ə-lē′, *n.* the sound of the drum or bugle at daybreak to awaken soldiers : a summons to awake or get up. [Fr. *réveillez*, awake, imper. of *réveiller*—L. re-, *vigilāre*, to watch.]

revel, *rev'l*, *v.i.* to feast or make merry in a riotous or noisy manner : to take intense delight, to luxuriate (with *in*).—*v.t.* to spend in revelry : (*pr.p.* **rev'elling**; *pa.t.* and *pa.p.* **rev'elled**).—*n.* a riotous feast : merrymaking : a festival or (often in *pl.*) occasion of merrymaking, dancing, masking, &c. — *ns.* **rev'eller**; **rev'elling**; **rev'el-rout'**, boisterous revelry : a crowd of revellers ; **rev'elry**, revelling.—**Master of the Revels**, an official organiser of entertainments, esp. at court or in the Inns of Court. [O.Fr. *reveler*—L. *rebellāre*, to rebel.]

revelation, *rev-i-lā'shən*, *n.* the act or experience of revealing : that which is revealed : a disclosure : an enlightening experience : divine or supernatural communication : **Revelation (of St John)**, or, popularly, **Revelations**, the Apocalypse or last book of the New Testament.—*adj.* **revelā'tional**. —*n.* **revelā'tionist**, a believer in divine revelation : one who makes a revelation : the author of the Apocalypse or an apocalyptic book.—*adj.* **rev'elā-tive**.—*n.* **rev'elātor**.—*adj.* **rev'elatory**. [L. *revēlāre, -ātum* ; see **reveal**.]

revenant, *rəv-nän⁰*, *rev'ə-nənt*, *n.* one who returns after a long absence, esp. from the dead : a ghost. [Fr., pr.p. of *revenir*, to come back.]

revenge, *ri-venj'*, *-venzh'*, *v.t.* to inflict injury in retribution for : (esp. *refl.*) to avenge.—*v.i.* to take vengeance.—*n.* a malicious injuring in return for injury received : the passion for retaliation of evil : its satisfaction : in games, opportunity of retaliation in a return game : (*obs.*) punishment. —*adj.* **revenge'ful**, ready to seek revenge.—*adv.* **revenge'fully**.—*n.* **revenge'fulness**.—*adj.* **revenge'less**. — *ns.* **revenge'ment** (now *rare*); **reveng'er**.—*n.* and *adj.* **reveng'ing**. — *adv.* **reveng'ingly**.—*adj.* **reveng'ive** (*Shak.*). [O.Fr. *revenger, revencher* (Fr. *revancher*)—L. re-, *vindicāre*, to lay claim to.]

revenue, *rev'in-ū* (formerly also *ri-ven'ū*), *n.* receipts or return from any source : income : the income of a state : a government department concerned with it.—*n.* **rev'enue-cutt'er**, an armed vessel employed in preventing smuggling.—*adj.* **rev'-enued**.—**Inland Revenue**, revenue from stamps, excise, income-tax, &c. [Fr. *revenue*, pa.p. (fem.) of *revenir*, to return—L. *revenīre*—re-, back, *venīre*, to come.]

reverberate, *ri-vər'bər-āt*, *v.t.* to beat or send back : to reflect : to echo : to heat in a reverberatory furnace.—*v.i.* to recoil, rebound : to be reflected : to re-echo : to resound.—*adj.* reverberated : (*Shak.*) reverberating.—*v.t.* **reverb'** (after *Shak.*). — *adj.* **rever'berant**, reverberating. — *n.* **reverberā'tion**. — *adj.* **rever'berātive**. — *n.* **rever'berātor**.—*adj.* **rever'beratory** (*-ət-ər-i*, or *-āt-*).—**reverberatory furnace**, a furnace in which the flame is turned back over the substance to be heated. [L. *reverberāre, -ātum*—re-, back, *verberāre*, to beat—*verber*, a lash.]

revere, *ri-vēr'*, *v.t.* to regard with high respect : to venerate.—*adj.* **rever'able**.—*n.* **reverence** (*rev'ər-əns*), high respect : respectful awe : veneration : state of being held in high respect : a gesture or observance of respect.—*v.t.* to venerate. —*n.* **rev'erencer**.—*adj.* **rev'erend**, worthy of reverence : clerical : **Reverend** (usu. written **Rev.**), a title prefixed to a clergyman's name.—*n.* a clergyman.—*adjs.* **rev'erent**, feeling or showing reverence : **reverential** (*-en'shl*), proceeding from reverence : respectful : submissive.—*advs.* **reveren'tially**; **rev'erently**.—*n.* **reverer** (*ri-vēr'ər*). —**His, Your, Reverence**, (now Ir. or playful) a mode of referring to or addressing a clergyman ; **Most Reverend** is used of an archbishop, **Right Reverend**, a bishop, or Moderator or former Moderator of the Church of Scotland, **Very Reverend**, a dean, or (if a clergyman) a Scottish University principal ; **save** or **saving (your) reverence** (*obs.* contr. to **sir-reverence**), with all due respect to you—an apology for introducing an

unseemly word or subject. [O.Fr. *reverer* (Fr. *révérer*)—L. *reverērī*—re-, inten., *verērī*, feel awe.]

reverie, revery, *rev'ə-ri*, *n.* an undirected train of thoughts or fancies in meditation : mental abstraction : a piece of music expressing such a state of mind : a waking dream : a brown study.—*n.* **rev'erist**. [Fr. *rêverie*—*rêver*, to dream.]

revers, *ri-vēr'*, *n.* any part of a garment that is turned back, as a lapel : —*pl.* **revers** (*-vērz'*, *-verz'*). [Fr.,—L. *reversus*.]

reverse, *ri-vərs'*, *v.t.* (*Spens.*) to bring back : (*Spens.*) to turn aside : to turn the other way about, as upside down, outside in, &c. : to invert : to set moving backwards : to annul.—*v.i.* to move in the opposite direction : to set an engine moving backwards : (*Spens.*) to return.—*n.* the contrary, opposite : the back, esp. of a coin or medal (opp. to *obverse*) : a set-back, misfortune, defeat : a back-handed sword-stroke : an act of reversing. —*adj.* contrary, opposite : turned about : acting in the contrary direction : reversing : (*obs.*) back-handed : (*mil.*) of the rear.—*n.* **rever'sal**, act of reversing.—*adj.* **reversed'**.—*adv.* **rever'sedly**.— *adj.* **reverse'less**, unalterable.—*adv.* **reverse'ly**. —*ns.* **rever'ser**, one who, or that which, reverses : a reversing device : (*Scots law*) a borrower on wadset ; **rever'si** (*-sē*), a game in which a captured man is not removed from the board but turned upside down to show the captor's colour : reversis ; **reversibil'ity**. — *adj.* **rever'sible**. — *n.* a fabric having both sides well finished.—*n.* and *adj.* **rever'sing**.—*n.* **rever'sion** (*-shən*), the act or fact of reverting or of returning : that which reverts or returns : the return, or the future possession, of any property after some particular event : the right to succeed to possession or office : a sum payable upon death : that which is left over, remains : (*biol.*) return to ancestral type.—*adj.* **rever'sional**. — *adv.* **rever'sionally**. — *adj.* **rever'sionary**, relating to reversion : of reversion : of the nature of a reversion.—*n.* one who has a reversion.—*ns.* **rever'sioner**, a reversionary ; **rever'sis**, an old card-game in which the taker of fewest tricks won : **rever'so**, a verso : a back-handed sword-stroke. — **reverse the charges**, charge a telephone call to the one who receives it instead of to the caller ; **reversing layer**, a layer of the sun's chromosphere that reverses bright lines of the spectrum to dark absorption lines. [L. *reversāre*, to turn round : partly through Fr.]

revert, *ri-vərt'*, *v.t.* to turn back : to reverse.— *v.i.* to return : to fall back to a former state : to recur to a former subject : to return to the original owner or his heirs.—*adj.* **rever'ted**, reversed : turned backwards.—*adjs.* **rever'tible**; **revert'ive** (*Thomson*). [L. re-, *vertěre*, to turn.]

revest, *ri-vest'*, *v.t.* (*Spens.*) to clothe again : to vest again.—*v.i.* to vest again.—*ns.* **revest'iary**, **revest'ry**, a vestry. [O.Fr. *revestir*, or re-, *vestir* —L. *revestīre, vestīre*, to clothe again, to clothe.]

revet, *ri-vet'*, *v.t.* to face with masonry, &c. :— *pr.p.* **revett'ing**; *pa.t.* and *pa.p.* **revett'ed**.—*n.* **revet'ment**, a retaining wall, facing. [Fr. *revêtir*, to reclothe.]

revie, *rē-vī'*, *v.t.* formerly, in card-playing, to stake more on (than an opponent has proposed) : to bandy in emulation.—*v.i.* to stake higher : (*pr.p.* **rēvy'ing**; *pa.t.* and *pa.p.* **rēvied'**).—*n.* the response of venturing a higher stake. [Fr. *renvier* —L. re-, *invitāre*, to invite.]

review, *ri-vū'*, *n.* a viewing again (also **re-view**, *rē'-vū'*) : a looking back, retrospect : a reconsideration : a survey : a revision : a critical examination : a critique : a periodical with critiques of books, &c. : a display and inspection of troops or ships : (*law*) the judicial revision of a higher court.—*v.t.* to see, view, or examine again (also **rē-view'**) : to look back on or over : to survey : to examine critically : to write a critique on : to inspect, as troops : to revise.—*v.i.* to write reviews.— *adj.* **review'able**, capable of being reviewed.— *ns.* **review'al**, a review of a book : reviewing ; **review'-copy**, a copy of a book sent by the publisher to a periodical for review ; **review'er**, a writer of critiques : a writer in a review. [Partly pfx. *re-* and **view**; partly Fr. *revue*, pa.p. (fem.) of *revoir*—L. *revidēre*—*vidēre*, to see.]

revile, ri-vīl', *v.t.* to assail with bitter abuse.—*v.i.* to utter revilings.—*n.* revilement.—*ns.* **revile'-ment**, the act of reviling: a reviling speech; **revil'er**.—*n.* and *adj.* **revil'ing**.—*adv.* **revil'ingly**. [O.Fr. *reviler*—L. *re-*, *vilis*, worthless.]

revindicate, ri-vin'di-kāt, *v.t.* to reclaim: to claim and get back: to restore.—*n.* **revindicā'tion**.

revise, ri-vīz', *v.t.* to review and amend: to examine with a view to correction: to go over in renewed study, with a view to refreshing and repairing gaps in the memory.—*n.* review: a further proof-sheet in which previous corrections have been given effect to.—*adj.* **revis'able**, liable to revision.—*ns.* **revi'sal**, revision; **revi'ser** (also -or); **revision** (-*vizh'ən*), act or product of revising.—*adjs.* **revi'sional**, **revi'sionary**, pertaining to revision.—*ns.* **revi'sionism**; **revi'sionist**, an advocate of revision (e.g. of a treaty): an evolutionary Marxist: a reviser of the Bible.—*adj.* **revi'sory**. —**Revised Version**, an English translation of the Bible issued 1881-85 (Apocrypha 1895); **revising barrister**, till 1918, a barrister appointed to revise the parliamentary voters' roll. [Fr. *reviser* and L. *revisēre*—*re-*, back, *visēre*, inten. of *vidēre*, to see.]

revive, ri-vīv', *v.t.* and *v.i.* to bring back or come back to life, vigour, being, activity, consciousness, memory, good spirits, freshness, vogue, notice, currency, use, the stage, or the metallic state.— *n.* **revivabil'ity**.—*adj.* **revi'vable**.—*adv.* **revi'v-ably**.—*ns.* **revi'val**, act or fact of reviving: state of being revived: recovery from languor, neglect, depression, &c.: renewed performance, as of a play: renewed interest or attention: a time of extraordinary religious awakening or working up of excitement, esp. accompanied with extravagance: quickening: renewal: awakening; **revi'valism**; **revi'valist**, one who promotes religious, architectural, or other revival: an itinerant preacher. —*adj.* **revivalist'ic**.—*ns.* **revive'ment** (*rare*); **revi'ver**, one who, or that which, revives: a renovating preparation: (*slang*) a stimulant.—*n.* and *adj.* **revi'ving**.—*adv.* **revi'vingly**.—*n.* **revi'vor**, (*law*) the revival of a suit which was abated by the death of a party or other cause.— **Gothic Revival**, the resuscitation of Gothic architecture in (and before) the 19th century; **Romantic Revival** (see **romantic**); **Revival of Learning**, the Renaissance. [L. *revivēre*, to live again—*vivēre*, to live.]

revivify, ri-viv'i-fī, *v.t.* to restore to life: to put new life into: to reactivate.—*v.t.* and *v.i.* (*chem.*) to revive—*pr.p.* **reviv'ifying**; *pa.t.* and *pa.p.* **reviv'ified**.—*n.* **revivifica'tion**. [L.L. *revivificāre* —*re-*, *vivus*, alive, *facēre*, to make.]

reviviscent, rev-i-vis'ənt, **revivescent**, -*ves'ənt*, *adj.* reviving.—*ns.* **revivisc'ence**, **revivisc'ency** (also -**esc-**). [L. *revivīscēre*, -*ēscēre*.]

revoke, ri-vōk', *v.t.* (now *rare*) to recall, call back: (*Spens.*) to withdraw: (*Spens.*) to check: to annul: to retract.—*v.i.* to make revocations: to neglect to follow suit (at cards).—*n.* revocation, recall: act of revoking at cards.—*adj.* **revocable** (*rev'ō-kə-bl*).—*ns.* **rev'ocableness**, **revocabil'ity**.—*adv.* **rev'ocably**.—*n.* **revocā'tion**, recall: act of revoking. —*adj.* **rev'ocatory**.—*n.* **revoke'ment**, (*Shak.*) revocation. [L. *revocāre*—*vocāre*, to call.]

revolt, ri-vōlt', *v.i.* to renounce allegiance: to rise in opposition: to turn or rise in disgust, loathing, or repugnance.—*v.t.* (*Spens.*) to turn back: to cause to rise in revolt: to inspire revulsion or repugnance in.—*n.* a rebellion: insurrection: secession: (*Shak.*) revulsion: (*Shak.*) a rebel.—*adj.* **revolt'ed**, insurgent: shocked, outraged.—*n.* **revolt'er**.—*adj.* **revolt'ing**.—*adv.* **revolt'ingly**. [Fr. *révolter*—L. *re-*, *volutāre*, freq. of *volvēre*, *volutum*, to turn.]

revolution, rev-əl-ōō'shən, or -ū', *n.* act or condition of revolving: movement in an orbit, as distinguished from rotation: less commonly, rotation: a complete turn, through four right angles, in translation, rotation, winding, or angular movement: a cycle of phenomena or of time: re-

currence in cycles: (*obs.*) turning over in the mind: (*Shak.*) mutation: a great upheaval: a radical change, esp. in government: (*geol.*) a time of intensified change in the earth's features —*adjs.* **revolu'tional**, of revolution in movement; **revolu'tionary**, of, favouring, or of the nature of, revolution, esp. in government or conditions.— *n.* one who takes part in a revolution.—*n.* **revolu'tioner**, (*hist.*) a supporter of a revolution, esp. that of 1688.—*v.t.* **revolu'tionise**, to cause radical change in.—*ns.* **revolu'tionism**; **revolu'tionist**, one who favours revolution.—**the American Revolution**, the change from the condition of British colonies to national independence effected by the thirteen states of the American Union in 1776; **the French Revolution**, the overthrow of the old French monarchy and absolutism (1789); **the Revolution**, the expulsion of James II. from the British throne (1688-89), and the establishment of a really constitutional government under William III. and Mary. [L.L. *revolūtiō*, -*ōnis*.]

revolve, ri-volv', *v.t.* and *v.i.* (*obs.*) to roll back, return: to ponder: to move about a centre: to rotate.—*adj.* **revolute** (*rev'əl-ūt*, -*ōōt*), rolled backward.—*ns.* **revol'vency**, revolution: tendency to revolve; **revol'ver**, a revolving device of various kinds: a pistol with a rotating magazine.—*n.* and *adj.* **revol'ving**. [L. *revolvēre*, *revolūtum*—*volvēre*, to roll.]

revue, ri-vū', *n.* a loosely constructed theatrical show, more or less topical and musical. [Fr., review.]

revulsion, ri-vul'shən, *n.* (*med.*) diversion to another part, esp. by counter-irritation: withdrawal: disgust: a sudden change or reversal, esp. of feeling. —*adjs.* **revul'sionary**; **revul'sive** (-*siv*). [L. *revellēre*, *revulsum*, to pluck back — *vellēre*, to pluck.]

rew, rōō (*Spens.*). Same as **rue** (1 and 2) and **row** (1).

reward, ri-wawrd', *n.* that which is given in return for good (sometimes evil), or in recognition of merit, or for performance of a service.—*v.t.* to give or be a reward to or for: (*B.*) to give as a reward.—*adj.* **reward'able**, capable or worthy of being rewarded. — *ns.* **reward'ableness**; **reward'er**.—*adjs.* **reward'ful**, yielding reward; **reward'less**, unrewarded. [O.Fr. *rewarder*, *regarder*—*re-*, again, *warder*, *garder*, to guard; see **regard**, **guard**, **ward**.]

reword, rē-wurd', *v.t.* (*Shak.*) to repeat, re-echo: to word afresh, put into different words.

rewth, rōōth (*Spens.*). Same as **ruth**.

rex. See **reak**.

Reynard, **reynard**, rān' or ren'ärd, -ərd, *n.* a fox, from the name given to the fox in the famous beast epic of L.G. origin, *Reynard the Fox.*—in Spens. **Reyn'old**. [M.Du. *Reynaerd* — O.H.G. *Reginhart*, lit. strong in counsel.]

rhabdus, rab'dəs, *n.* a rodlike sponge spicule.— *adj.* **rhab'doid**, rodlike.—*n.* a rodlike body.—*ns.* **rhab'dolith** (Gr. *lithos*, stone), a calcareous rod in some Protozoa; **rhab'dom** (Gr. *rhabdōma*, bundle of rods), a fourfold rod in the compound eye of an arthropod; **rhab'domancy** (Gr. *manteiā*, divination), divination by rod; **rhab'domantist**; **rhabdomyō'ma**, a tumour of striped muscle.— *n.pl.* **Rhabdoph'ora**, the graptolites.—*n.* **rhab'do-sphere**, an aggregation of rhabdoliths in oceanic ooze. [Latinised from Gr. *rhabdos*, rod.]

rhachis, **rhachitis**. Same as **rachis**, **rachitis**.

Rhadamanthine, rad-ə-man'thīn, *adj.* rigorously just and severe, like *Rhadamanthus* (Gr. -*os*), a judge of the lower world.

Rhaetia, **Raetia**, rē'sh(y)ā, *n.* a province of the Roman Empire, roughly Grisons and Tirol, to which Vindelicia was added.—*adj.* and *n.* **R(h)ae'-tian**.—*adj.* **Rhaetic** (*rē'tik*; *geol.*), uppermost Trias or (acc. to others) lowest Jurassic.—Also *n.* —*n.* **Rhae'to-Roman'ic**, a general name for a group of Romance dialects spoken from south-eastern Switzerland to Friuli (Rumonsch, Ladino, Friulian).—Also *adj.*

Rhamnus, ram'nəs, *n.* the buckthorn genus,

fāte, fär, ȧsk; mē, hər (her); mīne; mōte; mūte; mōōn; dhen (then)

giving name to the family **Rhamnā′ceae.**—*adj.* **rhamnā′ceous.** [Latinised from Gr. *rhamnos.*]

rhamphoid, *ram′foid, adj.* hook-beak-shaped.— *ns.* **Rhamphast′os,** the typical genus of toucans; **Rhamphorhynchus** (*ram-fō-ring′kas*; Gr. *rhynchos,* snout), a genus of pterodactyls; **rhamphothē′ca** (Gr. *thēkē,* case), the horny sheath of a bird's bill. [Gr. *rhamphos,* a hooked beak.]

raphe, rhaphis. Same as **raphe, raphis.**

rhapontic, *rā-pon′tik, n.* ordinary kitchen-garden rhubarb. [L.L. *rhā ponticum,* Pontic rhubarb; see **rhubarb.**]

rhapsody, *raps′ə-di, n.* (*Gr. hist.*) an epic or instalment of an epic recited at one sitting: (*obs.*) a patching or stringing together of poems: any wild or unconnected composition: a rigmarole: an ecstatic or unrestrainedly enthusiastic utterance of feeling: an irregular emotional piece of music. —*n.* **rhapsode** (*raps′ōd*), a reciter of Homeric or other epics.—*adjs.* **rhapsodic** (*-od′ik*), of rhapsodes or rhapsodies: of the nature of rhapsody; **rhapsod′ical,** rhapsodic: unrestrainedly enthusiastic, rapt.—*adv.* **rhapsod′ically.**—*v.t.* **rhaps′odise** (*-ə-dīz*), to piece together: to recite in rhapsodies. —*v.i.* to write or utter rhapsodies.—*n.* **rhaps′odist,** a rhapsode: one who rhapsodises. [Gr. *rhapsōidiā,* an epic, a rigmarole—*rhaptein,* to sew, *ōidē,* a song.]

rhatany, *rat′ə-ni, n.* a South American caesalpiniaceous plant (species of Krameria): its astringent root. [Sp. *ratania*—Quichua *rataña.*]

rhea, *rē′ä, n.* ramie. [Assamese *rihā.*]

Rhea, *rē′ä, n.* the daughter of Uranus and Ge, wife and sister of Kronos: the fifth satellite of Saturn: **rhea,** the South American ostrich (Rhea). [Gr. *Rhēā.*]

rhematic, *rē-mat′ik, adj.* of words or verbs: word-making. [Gr. *rhēma, -atos,* word, verb.]

Rhemish, *rē′mish, adj.* of *Rheims* (Reims) in north-eastern France.—**Rhemish version,** the English translation of the New Testament by Roman Catholics of the English college there (1582).—*n.* **Rhē′mist,** a translator of the Rhemish version.

Rhenish, *ren′ish, adj.* of the river *Rhine.*—*n.* Rhine wine.—*n.* **rhenium** (*rē′ni-əm*), a chemical element (Re; at. numb. 75) discovered by X-ray spectroscopy in Germany in 1925. [L. *Rhēnus,* the Rhine.]

rheo-, *rē′ō-, rē-o′-,* in composition, current, flow. —*n.* **rhe′ochord, rhe′ocord,** a wire rheostat.— *adjs.* **rheolog′ic, -al.**—*ns.* **rheol′ogist; rheol′ogy,** the science of the deformation and flow of matter; **rheom′eter,** an instrument for measuring a current of fluid: (*obs.*) a galvanometer; **rhe′ostat,** an instrument for varying an electric resistance; **rheotax′is,** rheotropism; **rhe′otome,** (*elect.*) an interrupter; **rhe′otrope,** a commutator for reversing an electric current.—*adj.* **rheotrop′ic.** —*n.* **rheot′ropism,** (*biol.*) response to the stimulus of flowing water. [Gr. *rheos,* flow.]

rhesus, *rē′səs, n.* the bandar (*Macacus rhesus*), an Indian monkey.—Also **rhesus monkey.**—**Rhesus factor, Rh-factor,** any of a group of weakly antigenic agglutinogens in human red blood cells, inherited according to Mendelian laws, **Rh-positive** persons being those who react to sera containing appropriate agglutinins in the same way as rhesus monkeys, and **Rh-negative** those (a very much smaller number) who do not—important in blood transfusion and as explaining haemolytic disease of the newborn. [Gr. *Rhēsos,* a king of Thrace, arbitrarily appĺied.]

rhetor, *rē′tor, n.* (*Gr. hist.*) a teacher of rhetoric or professional orator.—*n.* **rhetoric** (*ret′ər-ik*), the theory and practice of eloquence, whether spoken or written, the whole art of using language so as to persuade others: the art of literary expression, esp. in prose: false, showy, artificial, or declamatory expression.—*adjs.* **rhetoric** (*ri-tor′ik*); **rhetor′ical,** pertaining to rhetoric: oratorical: inflated, over-decorated, or insincere in style.—*adv.* **rhetor′ically.**—*n.* **rhetorician** (*ret-ər-ish′ən*), one who teaches the art of rhetoric: an orator: a user of rhetorical language.—*v.i.* **rhetorise** (*rē′*), to play the orator.—*v.t.* to address rhetorically.—

rhetorical question, a question in form, for rhetorical effect, not calling for an answer. [Gr. *rhētōr.*]

rheum, *rōōm, n.* a mucous discharge, esp. from the nose: (*poet.*) tears: (*obs.*) cold in the head: (in *pl.*) rheumatic pains: (*obs.*) ill humour.—*adj.* **rheumatic** (*rōō-mat′ik*; *Shak. rōō′*), of the nature of, pertaining to, apt to cause, or affected with, rheumatism or (*obs.*) rheum.—*n.* one who suffers from rheumatism: (in *pl.*; *coll.*) rheumatic pains. —*adj.* **rheumat′ical.**—*adv.* **rheumat′ically.**— *adj.* **rheum′aticky.**—*n.* **rheumatism** (*rōō′mə-tizm*), a name used loosely for pain and stiffness in muscles and joints (*dial.* and *vulg.* **rheu′matiz, -tize, -tise, -teese**). — *adjs.* **rheumatis′mal; rheum′atoid,** resembling rheumatism; **rheumed; rheum′y.**—**rheumatic fever,** an acute disease characterised by fever, multiple arthritis, and liability of the heart to be inflamed; **rheumatoid arthritis,** a disease or diseases characterised by inflammation and swelling of joints, often chronic. [Gr. *rheuma, -atos,* flow—*rheein,* to flow.]

Rheum, *rē′əm, n.* the rhubarb genus. [Latinised from Gr. *rhēon.*]

rhexis, *reks′is, n.* rupture, esp. of a blood-vessel. [Gr. *rhēxis,* breach.]

rhime, an obs. spelling of **rhyme, rime.**

rhin-, *rin-,* **rhino-,** *rī′nō-,* *rī-no′-,* in composition, nose.—*adj.* **rhi′nal,** of the nose.—*n.* **rhinencephalon** (*rīn-en-sef′ə-lon*; Gr. *enkephalon,* brain), the olfactory lobe of the brain.—*adj.* **rhinencephalic** (*-al′ik*).—*ns.* **rhini′tis,** inflammation of the mucous membrane of the nose; **rhi′nō,** coll. abbreviation of rhinoceros:—*pl.* **rhi′nos; rhinoceros** (*rī-, ri-nos′*), *obs.* **rhinoc′erot** (*-ot*), **-ote** (*-ōt*) (Gr. *rhinokerōs, -ōtos*—*keras,* horn), a large ungulate of several species in Africa and southern Asia, constituting a family (**Rhinocerot′idae**), characterised by one or two horns on the nose:— *pl.* **rhinoc′eroses,** *obs.* **rhinocerotes** (*-ō′tēz*); **rhinoc′eros-bee′tle,** a large beetle (Oryctes or Dynastes) with a large up-curved horn on the head; **rhinoc′eros-bird,** a beef-eater that alights on the rhinoceros: a hornbill.—*adj.* **rhinocerotic** (*-ot′ik*).—*ns.* **rhīnolalia** (*-lā′li-ä*; Gr. *laliā,* talk), nasal speech; **rhi′nolith** (Gr. *lithos,* stone), a concretion in the nose.—*adj.* **rhīnolog′ical.**—*ns.* **rhīnol′ogist,** a nose specialist; **rhīnol′ogy,** study of the nose: nasal pathology; **rhīnopharyngitis** (*rī-nō-far-in-jī′tis*), inflammation of the nose and pharynx; **rhīnophy′ma** (Gr. *phȳma,* growth, tumour), overgrowth of skin and subcutaneous tissue of the nose.—*adj.* **rhīnoplas′tic.**—*ns.* **rhī′noplasty,** plastic surgery of the nose; **rhinorrhagia** (*rī-nō-rā′jyä*; Gr. *rhēgnynai,* to break), excessive nose-bleeding; **rhīnorrhoea** (*-rē′ä*; Gr. *rhoiā,* flow), excessive mucous discharge from the nose. —*adj.* **rhīnorrhoe′al.**—*ns.* **rhīnoscleroma** (*-sklē-rō′mä*), a disease with hard swelling in the nose, &c.; **rhi′noscope,** an instrument for examining the nose.—*adj.* **rhinoscop′ic.**—*ns.* **rhīnos′copy; rhīnothē′ca** (Gr. *thēkē,* case), the sheath of a bird's upper mandible. [Gr. *rhīs, rhīnos,* nose.]

Rhine, *rin, n.* a river of Europe.—*ns.* **Rhine′berry, Rhein′berry,** the buckthorn berry: the buckthorn; **Rhine′grave,** a count with possessions on the Rhine:—*fem.* **Rhine′gravine** (*-ēn*; Du. *Rijngrave,* now *-graaf;* fem. *Rijngravin*); **Rhine′stone,** a rock-crystal: a paste diamond; **Rhine′wine,** wine made from grapes grown in the Rhine valley. [Ger. *Rhein;* Du. *Rijn.*]

rhine, *rēn, n.* (Somerset, &c.) a ditch or water-course.

Rhineodon, *rī-nē′ō-don,* **Rhinodon,** *rī′nō-don, n.* a gigantic shark of the Indian Ocean. [Gr. *rhīnē,* a file, a shagreen shark, *odous, odontos,* tooth.]

rhino, *rī′nō, n* (*slang*) money.—*adj.* **rhinocerical** (*-ser′i-kl;* old slang), rich. [Connexion with **rhino,** rhinoceros obscure.]

rhipidate, *rip′i-dāt, adj.* fan-shaped.—*ns.* **rhipid′ion,** in the Greek Church, the eucharistic fan or flabellum; **rhipid′ium,** a fan-shaped cymose inflorescence.—*ns.pl.* **Rhipip′tera, Rhipidop′tera,** the Strepsiptera. [Gr. *rhīpis, rhīpidos,* a fan.]

rhiz-, *rīz-,* **rhizo-,** *rī′zō-,* *rī-zo′-,* in composition, root.—*adjs.* **rhīzan'thous,** seeming to flower from the root; **rhī'zic,** of the root of an equation.—*ns.* **rhī'zine** (*-zin*), a lichen rhizoid; **rhī'zocarp** (Gr. *karpos,* fruit), a water-fern or heterosporous fern : a plant with sporangia on rootlike processes : a perennial herb : a plant fruiting underground.—*adjs.* **rhīzocar'pic, rhīzocar'pous.**—*n.* **rhī'zocaul** (Gr. *kaulos,* stalk), the rootlike stalk of a hydrozoon colony.—*n.pl.* **Rhīzoceph'ala** (Gr. *kephalē,* head), an order of Cirripedes parasitic on crabs.—*adjs.* **rhīzogen'ic, rhīzogenet'ic,** producing roots.—*n.* **rhī'zoid,** a short hairlike organ in the lower plants, serving as a root.—*adjs.* **rhīzoi'dal; rhīzō'matous.**—*ns.* **rhī'zome** (Gr. *rhizōma,* a root-mass), a root-stock, an underground stem producing roots and leafy shoots; **rhī'zomorph** (Gr. *morphē,* form), a rootlike mass of fungal hyphae.—*adjs.* **rhīzoph'agous,** root-eating; **rhī-zoph'ilous,** growing on roots.—*ns.* **Rhīzoph'ora,** the mangrove genus, with great development of aerial roots, giving name to the family **Rhizophora'ceae; rhī'zophore,** a root-bearing structure, esp. in Selaginella; **rhī'zopod,** any member of the **Rhīzop'oda,** Protozoa with rootlike pseudopodia; **Rhī'zopus,** a genus of moulds. [Gr. *rhiza,* root.]

Rh-negative. See **rhesus.**

rho, *rō, n.* the seventeenth letter (P, ρ) of the Greek alphabet, answering to R : as a numeral ρ'=100, ,ρ=100,000. [Gr. *rhō.*]

rhod-, *rōd'-,* **rhodo-,** *rō'dō-,* in composition, rose : rose-coloured.—*ns.* **rhō'damine** (*-mēn*), a dyestuff, usually red, akin to fluorescein (see **amine**); **rhō'danate,** in dyeing, a thiocyanate.—*adj.* **rhōdan'ic,** thiocyanic.—*v.t.* **rhō'danise,** to electroplate with rhodium.—*adj.* **rhō'dic,** of rhodium in higher valency.—*ns.* **Rhodites** (*rō-dī'tēz*), a gall-fly that forms bedeguars on the wild-rose; **rhō'dium,** a metallic element (Rh; at. numb. 45) of the platinum group, resembling aluminium, forming rose-coloured salts; **rhō'diumwood,** the scented wood of Canary Island convolvulus, yielding **oil of rhodium**; **rhōdochrosite** (*-krō'sīt*; Gr. *rhodochrōs,* rose-coloured), manganese spar, a pink rhombohedral mineral, manganese carbonate; **rhōdodaph'ne** (or *rod-*; *Spens.*; Gr. *daphnē,* laurel), oleander; **Rhōdoden'dron** (or *rod-*; Gr. *dendron,* tree), a genus of trees and shrubs of the heath family, with leathery leaves and large showy slightly zygomorphic flowers, some species being called Alpine rose; **rhō'donite,** a rose-red anorthic pyroxene, manganese silicate; **rhō'dophane** (Gr. *phainein,* to show), a red pigment in the retinal cones of birds, &c.—*n.pl.* **Rhōdophyceae** (*-fish'i-ē*; Gr. *phȳkos,* seaweed), the Florideae or red seaweeds (including some forms that are neither red nor found in the sea), one of the main divisions of the algae, in which the chlorophyll is usually masked by a red pigment.—*n.* **rhōdop'sin** (Gr. *opsis,* sight), visual purple.—*adj.* **rhō'dous,** of rhodium in lower valency.—*n.* **Rhodymenia** (*rō-di-mē'ni-ä*; Gr. *hymēn,* a membrane), the dulse genus of red seaweeds. [Gr. *rhodon,* rose.]

Rhode Island, *rōd ī'lānd, n.* an island of the United States, named from a supposed resemblance to the island of *Rhodes* : the state of which it forms part.—**Rhode Island red,** an American breed of domestic fowl, good for general purposes.

Rhodes, *rōdz, n.* an island and ancient city-state of the Aegean.—*n.* and *adj.* **Rhō'dian.**—**Rhodian laws,** the earliest system of marine law; **Rhodian school,** a school of Hellenistic sculpture, of which the Laocoon is the greatest product. [Gr. *Rhodos.*]

Rhodesia, *rō-dē'zi-ä, -zhi-ä, -zh(y)ä, n.* a region of South Africa named after Cecil John *Rhodes.*—*adj.* and *n.* **Rhode'sian.**—**Rhodesian man,** an extinct race of man represented by a skull found at Broken Hill, Northern Rhodesia, in 1921.

rhodium. See **rhod-.**

rhodomontade. Same as **rodomontade.**

rhodora, *rō-dō'rä, n.* a handsome N. American species of Rhododendron, or separate kindred genus. [L. *rhodōra,* meadow-sweet, said to be a Gallic plant-name.]

Rhoeadales, *rē-ə-dā'lēz, n.pl.* an order or cohort of dicotyledons including poppies, Cruciferae, &c.—*n.* **rhoe'adine** (*-dēn*), an alkaloid found in poppies. [Gr. *rhoias, -ados,* corn-poppy.]

rhomb, *rom(b), n.* an equilateral parallelogram (usually excluding the square): a lozenge-shaped object : (*obs.*) anything that whirls, as (*Milt.*) the wheel of day and night : a magic wheel; (*crystal.*) a rhombohedron.—*ns.* **rhombencephalon** (*rom-bən-sef'ə-lon*; Gr. *enkephalon,* brain), the hind-brain; **rhombenporphyr** (*rom-bən-por'fēr*; Ger.), **rhomb'(en)-por'phyry,** an intermediate, moderately fine-grained igneous rock with felspar phenocrysts rhombic in section.—*adjs.* **rhombic** (*rom'bik*), shaped like a rhombus : (*crystal.*) orthorhombic; **rhombohē'dral,** of a rhombohedron : (*crystal.*) trigonal.—*n.* **rhombohē'dron,** a crystal form of six rhombi, in the trigonal or hexagonal system, a hemihedral form of the hexagonal pyramid :—*pl.* **rhombohē'dra** (Gr. *hedrä,* seat).—*adj.* **rhom'boid,** like a rhombus : (*bot.*) nearly square, with petiole at one of the acute angles.—*n.* a figure approaching a rhombus, a parallelogram, usu. one that is not a rhombus nor a rectangle.—*adj.* **rhomboid'al,** more or less like a rhomboid.—*ns.* **rhomboi'dēs,** a rhomboid; **rhom'bos,** a bull-roarer :—*pl.* **rhom'-boi; rhom'bus,** (*geom.*) a rhomb : an object shaped like a rhomb :—*pl.* **rhom'bī.** [Gr. *rhombos,* bull-roarer, magic wheel, rhombus.]

rhonchus, *rong'kəs, n.* a bronchial sound, heard in auscultation.—*adjs.* **rhonch'al, rhonch'ial,** of rhonchus : of snoring. [Latinised from Gr. *rhonchos,* wheezing.]

rhone. Same as **rone.**

rhopalic, *rō-pal'ik, adj.* of a verse, having each word a syllable longer than the one before.—*n.* **rho'palism.** [Gr. *rhopalikos,* club-like, *rhopalon,* a club.]

Rhopalocera, *rō-pəl-os'ə-rä, n.pl.* butterflies, distinguished from moths.—*adjs.* **rhopaloc'eral, rhopaloc'erous.** [Gr. *rhopalon,* a club, *keras,* a horn.]

rhotacise, *rō'tə-siz, v.t.* and *v.i.* to change to an *r*-sound (esp. from *z*).—*n.* **rho'tacism,** excessive, exceptional, or exceptionable sounding of *r* : burring : change or tendency to change to *r.* [Gr. *rhōtakizein—rhō,* the Greek R.]

Rh-positive. See **rhesus.**

rhubarb, *rōō'bärb, -bərb, n.* any species of the genus Rheum, of the dock family : the root-stock, or a cathartic got from it (chiefly from *R. officinale*) : the leaf-stalks (chiefly of *R. Rhaponticum*) cooked and used like fruit.—*adj.* **rhu'barby.**—**monk's rhubarb,** patience dock. [O.Fr. *reubarbe*—L.L. *rheubarbarum,* for *rhäbarbarum*—Gr. *rhä,* rhubarb—*Rhä,* the Volga, and L. *barbarum* (neut.)—Gr. *barbaron,* foreign; influenced by *rhēum,* Gr. *rhēon.*]

rhumb, *rum, n.* a loxodromic curve : any point of the compass.—*ns.* **rhumb'-line, -course, -sailing.** [Fr. *rumb,* or Sp. or Port. *rumbo*—L. *rhombus*; see **rhomb.**]

Rhus, *rus, n.* the sumach genus of the cashew-nut family. [L.,—Gr. *rhous.*]

rhy, (*Spens.*) for **rye.**

rhyme, rime, *rīm, n.* identity in sound from the last stressed vowel to the end, provided that the consonant or consonant group preceding be not the same : extended to other correspondences in sound, as head-rhyme or alliteration, to inexact correspondences, as eye-rhyme, and to variations not tolerated in modern English verse but received in French, as rich rhyme (where the preceding consonants are alike), identical rhyme (where like-sounding words of different meaning are used): a word or group of words agreeing in this way with another : versification, verses, a poem or a short piece of verse, in which this correspondence occurs at the ends of lines (or within the lines, in internal rhyme): a jingle.—*v.i.* to be in rhyme : to correspond in sound : to make or find a rhyme or rhymes : to harmonise : to chime : to make rhymes or verses.—*v.t.* to put into rhyme : to compose in rhyme : to use or treat as a rhyme.—*adjs.* **rhymed, rimed** (*rīmd*), in rhyme; **rhyme'less.** — *ns.* **rhyme'-letter,** the alliterating letter; **rhy'mer, ri'mer,** a user of rhyme : a poet : an inferior poet : a minstrel; **rhyme'-roy'al** (app. a commendatory name), a seven-line stanza borrowed by Chaucer, from the French—its formula, *a b a b b c c*; **rhyme'-ster**, a poetaster: a would-be poet; **rhyme'-word**, a word used as a rhyme; **rhy'mist**, a versifier.—**without rhyme or reason**, without either sound or sense; **rhyme to death**, to kill by incantations (as rats were supposed to be killed in Ireland): to pester with rhymes. [O.Fr. *rime*—L. *rhythmus*—Gr. *rhythmos*; see **rhythm**; associated and confused with O.E. *rīm*, number.]

rhynch-, *ringk-*, **rhyncho-,** *ringk'ō-*, *ringk-o'-,* in composition, snout.—*ns.pl.* **Rhynchobdell'ida** (Gr. *bdella*, leech), an order of leeches with proboscis but no jaw; **Rhynchocephalia** (*-si-fā'li-ā*; Gr. *kephalē*, head), a primitive order of reptiles extinct but for the New Zealand tuatara.—*n.* **rhynch'ocoel** (*-sēl*; Gr. *koilos*, hollow), the cavity in which the proboscis of a nemertine lies.—*adj.* **rhynch'odont** (Gr. *odous*, *odontos*, tooth), with toothed beak.—*n.* **Rhynchonell'a**, a genus of hinged brachiopods with prominent beak.—*n.pl.* **Rhynchoph'ora** (Gr. *pherein*, to bear), a group of beetles with snouts—the weevils.—*adj.* **rhynch-oph'orous**, of the Rhynchophora: snouted.—*n.pl.* **Rhyncho'ta**, the Hemiptera. [Gr. *rhynchos*, a snout.]

Rhyniaceae, *rī-ni-ā'si-ē, n.pl.* a family of very simple land plants (Psilophytales) found as Old Red Sandstone fossils at *Rhynie* in Aberdeenshire.

rhyolite, *rī'ō-līt, n.* an acid igneous rock with a glassy or cryptocrystalline groundmass and generally phenocrysts of quartz and alkali-felspar—called also *liparite.* — *adj.* **rhyolitic** (*-lit'ik*). [Irregularly—Gr. *rhyax, -akos,* a (lava) stream, *lithos,* a stone.]

rhyparography, *rip-ə-rog'rə-fi, n.* genre or still-life pictures, esp. of sordid subjects.—*n.* **rhyparog'-rapher**—*adj.* **rhyparographic** (*-graf'ik*). [Gr. *rhyparos,* dirty, *graphein,* to write.]

rhythm, *rim,* an obs. spelling of **rhyme.**

rhythm, *ridhm,* or *rithm, n.* regular recurrence, esp. of stresses or of long and short sounds: a pattern of recurrence. — *adjs.* **rhyth'mal**; **rhythmed** (*ridhmd*); **rhyth'mic, -al.**—*n.* **rhyth'mic** (also in *pl.*), the science or theory of rhythm.—*adv.* **rhyth'mically.**—*v.t.* **rhyth'mise**, to subject to rhythm.—*v.i.* to act in or observe rhythm.—*n.* **rhyth'mist**, one skilled in rhythm.—*adj.* **rhythm'-less.**—*ns.* **rhythmom'eter**, a kind of metronome; **rhythmopœia** (*-ō-pē'yä*; Gr. *poieein*, to make), the art of composing rhythmically; **rhyth'mus**, rhythm. [L. *rhythmus*—Gr. *rhythmos*—*rheein*, to flow; cf. **rhyme.**]

Rhytina, *ri-tī'nä, n.* a recently extinct genus of Sirenia—Steller's sea-cow. [Gr. *rhytis*, a wrinkle.]

Rhytisma, *rit-iz'mä, n.* a genus of fungi that cause black spots on maple leaves. [Gr. *rhytisma*, a patch or darn.]

rhyton, *rī'ton, n.* drinking-cup or horn (Greek, &c.) with a hole in the point to drink by:—*pl.* **rhy'ta.** [Gr. *rhyton,* neut. of *rhytos,* flowing.]

ria, *rē'ä, n.* (geol.) a normal drowned valley. [Sp. *ria*, river-mouth.]

rial. Same as **ryal.**

Rialto, *rē-al'tō, n.* a district and island of Venice, with a famous bridge over the Grand Canal. [It., contracted from *rialzato*, raised.]

riant, *rī'ənt, adj.* laughing: gay.—*n.* **rī'ancy.** [Fr., pr.p. of *rire*—L. *rīdēre*, to laugh.]

riata. See **reata.**

rib, *rib, n.* one of the bones that curve round and forward from the backbone: (*facet.*) a wife (from Gen. ii. 21-23): a piece of meat containing one or more ribs: a curved member of the side of a ship running from keel to deck: a strengthening bar: a rodlike structure supporting or strengthening a membrane, as one of the greater veins of a leaf, a nervure in an insect's wing, a member supporting the fabric of an aeroplane wing or of an umbrella: (*Scot.*) a bar of a grate: the shaft of a feather: one of the parallel supports of a bridge: the side of a fiddle: a framing timber: a purlin: a raised band: a prominence running in a line: a ridge: a ridge raised in weaving or knitting: a moulding or projecting band on a ceiling.—*v.t.* to furnish, form, cover, or enclose with ribs: to plough with spaces

between the furrows (**rib'-plough**):—*pr.p.* **ribb'-ing**; *pa.t.* and *pa.p.* **ribbed.**—*adj.* **ribbed**, having ribs: ridged.—*ns.* **ribb'ing**, an arrangement of ribs; **ribb'ing**, an arrangement of ribs; **rib'-bone**, a rib; **rib'-grass**, the ribwort plantain. — *adjs.* **rib'less**; **rib'like.** — *v.t.* **rib'-roast**, to beat soundly.—*ns.* **rib'-roaster**, (*coll.*) a severe blow on the ribs; **rib-roast'ing**; **rib'-vaulting**; **rib'work**; **rib'wort** (or **rib'wort plan'tain**), a common weed (*Plantago lanceolata*) with narrow strongly ribbed leaves and short brown heads.—**false rib**, one joined indirectly to the breast-bone or (**floating rib**) not at all; **true rib**, one joined directly by its cartilage. [O.E. *ribb*, rib, *ribbe*, ribwort; Ger. *rippe*, rib.]

ribald, *rib'əld, n.* (*obs.*) a menial of the lowest grade: a loose, low character: an obscene speaker or writer.—*adj.* low, base, mean: licentious: foul-mouthed: sometimes loosely, jeering, floutingly derisive.—Also **rib'aud,ryb'auld**(*Spens.*).—*n.* **rib'-aldry**, obscenity: filthiness: low and vulgar scurrility.—Also **rib'audry** (*obs.*).—*adj.* **rib'audred,** (Shak., *Ant. and Cleop.*) an obscure word, perh. for *ribaud-rid*, ridden by a ribald, or for *ribaldried*, composed of ribaldry. [O.Fr. *ribald*, *ribaut* (Fr. *ribaud*); origin doubtful.]

riband, ribband, *rib'ən*(*d*), spellings of **ribbon**, used also in derivatives and compounds, now rare except in heraldic and sporting use.

ribattuta, *rē-bät-tōō'tä, n.* (*mus.*) the slow beginning of a trill. [It.]

ribband. Same as **riband, ribbon.**

ribble-rabble, *rib'l-rab'l, n.* a mob: gabble. [**rabble.**]

ribbon, *rib'ən, n.* material woven in narrow bands or strips: a strip of such or other material: anything resembling such a strip, as a road, a stripe of colour: a torn strip, tatter, shred: a watch-spring: an endless saw: a mollusc's radula: a strip of inking cloth, as for a typewriter: (*her.*) a diminutive of the bend, one-eighth of its width: (in *pl.*) driving reins.—*adj.* made of ribbon: having bands of different colours.—*v.t.* to adorn with ribbons: to stripe: to streak. — *ns.* **ribb'on-building, -development**, building, growth of towns, in long strips along the main roads; **ribb'on-fish**, a long, slender, laterally compressed fish of the family Trachypteridae, esp. the oarfish; **ribb'on-grass**, gardener's garters, a striped canary-grass; **Ribb'-onism**, an Irish secret society movement, at its height about 1835-55, opp. to the Orangemen, named from its badge, a green ribbon; **Ribb'on-man**; **ribb'onry**, ribbons collectively; **ribb'on-seal**, a banded North Pacific seal; **ribb'on-weed**, sugar-wrack; **ribb'on-worm**, a nemertine.—*adj.* **ribb'ony.** [O.Fr. *riban*; origin obscure.]

Ribes, *rī'bēz, n.* the black and red currant genus of the saxifrage family (generally including gooseberry), in some classifications giving name to a separate family **Ribēsiā'ceae.** [L.L. *ribes*—Ar. *ribās*, sorrel.]

ribibe, *rib'ib, rib-ib', n.* (*obs.*) a rebeck: (*obs.*) an old crone.—*n.* **ribible** (*ri-bib'l, ri-bī'bl*), a rebeck. [Perh. M.E. *ribibe*, a rebeck; see **rebeck.**]

ribose, *rī'bōs, n.* a pentose, $C_5H_{10}O_5$.—*n.* **riboflavin** (*rī-bō-flā'vin*), member of vitamin B_2 complex, in yellowish-brown crystals, promoting growth in children. [From **arabinose** by transposition of letters; L. *flāvus*, yellow.]

ribston(e), *rib'stən, n.* (in full **Ribston pippin**) a fine variety of winter apple brought from Normandy to *Ribston Hall* in Yorkshire.

Ricardian, *ri-kär'di-ən, adj.* pertaining to David *Ricardo* (1772-1823), or his economic teaching.—*n.* a follower of Ricardo.

Riccia, *rik'si-ä, n.* a genus of liverworts. [From the Italian botanist P. Francisco *Ricci*.]

rice, *rīs, n.* a grass (*Oryza sativa*) much grown in the tropics: its grain, a valuable food.—*ns.* **rice'-beer**, a fermented drink made from rice; **rice'-bird**, the bobolink (as a feeder on true rice or so-called wild rice): the paddy bird or Java sparrow; **rice'-bis'cuit**, a sweet biscuit made of flour mixed with rice; **rice'-field**; **rice'-flour**; **rice'-glue**, a cement made by boiling rice-flour in soft water; **rice'-grain**, a marking like a grain of rice on the sun's photosphere : a decoration in pottery made by pressing rice or other seeds into the clay before firing ; **rice'-grass**, cord-grass ; **rice'-milk**, milk boiled and thickened with rice ; **rice'-paper**, sliced and flattened pith of a Formosan tree, *Fatsia* (*Aralia*) *papyrifera* (once thought to be made from rice) : a similar material made from other plants, or from linen trimmings ; **rice'-pol'ishings**, the parts rubbed off in milling rice ; **rice'-pudd'ing** ; **rice'-soup** ; **rice'-wa'ter**, an invalid's drink of water in which rice has been boiled : a cholera patient's evacuation, of similar appearance.—*adj.* **rice'y**, **ri'cy**.—Canada, Indian, water, or **wild rice**, Zizania. [O.Fr. *ris*—L. *oryza*—Gr. *oryza*, a word of Oriental origin.]

rice, *rīs*, *n.* (*obs.* except *dial.*) twigs or small branches collectively, brushwood : a twig or small branch. [O.E. *hrís* ; Ger. *reis*.]

ricercare, *rē-chẽr-kä'rā*, **ricercata**, *rē-chẽr-kä'tä*, *n.* a contrapuntal forerunner of the fugue : later, a very elaborate form of fugue. [It.]

rich, *rich*, *adj.* abounding in possessions : wealthy : fortunate in having any good thing : abundantly furnished : having any ingredient or quality in great abundance : productive : fertile : deep in colour : full-toned : full-flavoured : abounding in fat, sugar, fruit, or seasonings : full : splendid and costly : sumptuous : elaborately decorated : ample : pregnant with matter for laughter.—*v.t.* (*Shak.*) to enrich.—*v.i.* (*obs.*) to grow rich.—*v.t.* and *v.i.* **rich'en**, to make or become richer.—*adj.* **rich'- left**, (*Shak.*) left heir to much wealth.—*adv.* **rich'ly**.—*n.* **rich'ness**. [O.E. *ríce*, great, powerful ; Ger. *reich*, Du. *rijk*, Goth. *reiks* ; perh. reinforced by Fr. *riche*, rich.]

Richardia, *ri-chär'di-ä*, *n.* the calla-lily (Zantedeschia). [From the French botanists L. C. M. *Richard* (1754-1821) and his son.]

riches, *rich'iz*, *n.* (now usu. treated as *pl.*) wealth —(*Spens.*) **rich'esse**. [O.Fr. *richesse*—*riche*, rich.]

richt, *rihht*, Scots form of **right**.

Ricinulei, *ris-i-nū'li-ī*, *n.pl.* the Podogona, a rare order of blind arachnids with male organs on the third leg. [L. *rīcinus*, a tick.]

Ricinus, *ris'i-nəs*, *n.* a genus of one species (*Ricinus communis*, castor-oil plant) of the spurge family.— *adj.* **ricinolē'ic** (or *-ō'lē-ik*), pertaining to castor-oil, as **ricinoleic acid** ($C_{18}H_{34}O_3$), an oily acid got from castor-oil. [L. *ricinus*, the castor-oil plant.]

rick, *rik*, *n.* a stack : a heap.—*v.t.* to stack.—*ns.* **rick'-barton**, a stack-yard ; **rick'-burner**, an incendiary who fired stacks ; **rick'er**, an implement for shocking hay ; **rick'-lifter** ; **rick'stand**, a flooring for a stack ; **rick'stick**, a toothed stick for combing thatch on a stack ; **rick'yard**. [O.E. *hréac* ; O.N. *hraukr*.]

rick, *rik*, *v.t.* to sprain or strain.—*n.* a sprain or strain. [App. a variant of **wrick**.]

ricker, *rik'ər*, *n.* a spar or young tree-trunk. [Perh. Ger. *rick*, pole.]

rickets, *rik'its*, *n.sing.* a disease of children, characterised by softness of the bones caused by deficiency of vitamin D.—*adv.* **rick'etily**, shakily.— *n.* **rick'etiness**, unsteadiness.—*adj.* **rick'ety** (formerly, and still by some, **rick'etty**), affected with rickets : feeble, unstable : tottery, threatening to collapse. [First recorded in S.W. England in the 17th cent., perh. M.E. *wrikken*, to twist ; or Gr. *rhachitis* (see **rachitis**).]

Rickettsia, *rik-et'si-ä*, *n.* a minute micro-organism found in lice and ticks and in the blood and tissues of typhus and other patients :—*pl.* **Rickett'siae** (-*ē*). —Also **Rickettsia body**. [After Howard Taylor *Ricketts* (1871-1910), American pathologist.]

rickle, *rik'l*, *n.* (*Scot.*) a loose heap : a rickety or ramshackle structure or collection.—*adj.* **rick'ly**. [Poss. Scand. ; connexion with **rick** (1) very doubtful.]

rickshaw, *rik'shaw*, *n.* abbrev. of **jinrickshaw**.

ricochet, *rik-ō-shā'*, *-shet'*, or *rik'*, *n.* a glancing rebound or skip, as of a projectile flying low.—*v.i.* to glance : to skip along the ground :—*pr.p.* **ricocheting** (*-shā'ing*), **ricochetting** (*-shet'ing*) ; *pa.t.* and *pa.p.* **ricocheted** (*-shād'*), **ricochetted** (*-shet'id*). [Fr.]

rictus, *rik'təs*, *n.* the gape, esp. of a bird : the chink or aperture of a lipped corolla.—*adj.* **ric'tal**, of the gape : at the corners of the mouth. [L. *rictus*, -*ūs*.]

rid, *rid*, *v.t.* to free : to deliver : to clear : to disencumber : to expel : (*obs.*) to remove, as by banishment, or by murder, make away with :—*pr.p.* **ridd'ing** ; *pa.t.* and *pa.p.* **rid** or **ridd'ed**.—*n.* **ridd'ance**, clearance : removal : disencumberment : deliverance : a thing that one is well rid of. —**a good riddance**, a welcome relief ; **get rid of**, to disencumber oneself of ; **rid way**, (*Shak.*) to cover ground, make progress. [O.N. *rythja*, to clear ; with senses converging upon **redd** (1).]

rid, **ridden**. See **ride**.

riddle, *rid'l*, *n.* an obscure description of something which the hearer is asked to name : a puzzling question : anything puzzling.—*v.t.* to solve : to puzzle.—*v.i.* to make riddles : to speak obscurely. —*adj.* and *adv.* **riddl'e-like** (*Shak.*).—*ns.* **ridd'ler** ; **ridd'ling**, propounding of riddles : speaking in riddles.—*adj.* enigmatic : explaining riddles.—*adv.* **ridd'lingly**.—**ridd'le-me-ree'**, a fanciful modification of **riddle me a riddle**, or **riddle my riddle**, hence, *n.* a rigmarole. [O.E. *rǣdelse*—*rǣdan*, to guess, to read—*rǣd*, counsel ; cog. with Du. *raad*, Ger. *rath*.]

riddle, *rid'l*, *n.* a large coarse sieve.—*v.t.* to separate with a riddle : to make full of holes like a riddle, as with shot.—*v.i.* to use a riddle : to sift.—*ns.* **ridd'ler** ; **ridd'ling**.—*n.pl.* **ridd'lings**, the part, whether finer or coarser, rejected after riddling : refuse. [O.E. *hriddel*, earlier *hridder*.]

ride, *rīd*, *v.i.* to travel or be borne on the back of an animal, on a bicycle, or in a public vehicle, formerly, still sometimes, and commonly in U.S., in any vehicle or (*U.S.*) boat, also on a broomstick, the waves, the whirlwind, &c. : to float or seem to float buoyantly : to go on horseback on a raid, in procession, across a ford : to serve as a cavalryman : to lie at anchor : to sit or move as if on horseback : to turn, rest, or grate upon something : to work up out of position : to admit of riding : to weigh when mounted.—*v.t.* to traverse, trace, ford, or perform on horseback, on a bicycle, &c. : to sit on : to bestride : to sit on and control : to travel on : to control at will, or oppressively : to rest or turn on : to overlap : to mount upon : to sustain, come through, esp. while riding at anchor (usu. with *out*) : to give a ride to, or cause to ride : (*U.S.*) to convey by vehicle : (*pa.t.* **rōde**, *arch.* **rid**, *Scot.* **raid**, **rade** ; *pa.p.* **ridd'en**, *arch.* **rid**, **rode**).—*n.* a journey on horseback, on a bicycle, or in a vehicle : a spell of riding : a road for horse-riding, esp. one through a wood : an excise officer's district.—*adj.* **rī'dable**, **rīde'able**.—*n.* **rī'der**, one who rides or can ride : (*obs.*) a commercial traveller : a mosstrooper : an object that rests on or astride of another, as a piece of wire on a balance for fine weighing : an added clause or corollary : a proposition that a pupil or candidate is asked to deduce from another : a gold coin bearing a mounted figure (Du. and Flem. *rijder*).—*adjs.* **rī'dered** ; **rī'derless**.— *n.* **rī'ding**, the action of the verb ride : a track, esp. a woodland track, for riding on : an excise-officer's district : anchorage. — Also *adj.*—*n.* **rī'ding-boot**, a high boot worn in riding.—*n.pl.* **rī'ding-breeches**.—*ns.* **rī'ding-cloak** ; **rī'ding-coat**, a coat, esp. an overcoat, worn by riders ; **rī'ding-committ'ee**, a committee of ministers sent by the General Assembly to carry out an ordination or induction, where the local presbytery refused to act, under the 18th-cent. Moderate domination in Scotland ; **rī'ding-crop** ; **rī'ding-glove** ; **rī'ding-habit**, a dress for riding, esp. one with a long skirt for riding side-saddle ; **rī'ding-hood**, a hood formerly worn by women when riding ; **rī'ding-horse** ; **rī'ding-in'terest**, (*Scots law*) an interest depending on other interests ; **rī'ding-light**, a light hung out in the rigging at night when a vessel is riding at anchor ; **rī'ding-master**, a teacher of riding ; **rī'ding-rhyme**, the heroic couplet, perh. from Chaucer's use of it in the *Canterbury Tales* ; **rī'ding-robe**, a riding-habit ; **rī'ding-rod**, a light cane for equestrians ; **rī'ding-school** ; **rī'ding-skirt** ; **rī'ding-suit** ; **rī'ding-whip**. — **ride a**

hobby (see **hobby**); **to ride and tie,** to ride and go on foot alternately, each tying up the horse, or leaving the bicycle by the roadside, and walking on—also *n., adv., v.i.* **ride'-and-tie'**; **ride down,** to overtake by riding : to charge and overthrow or trample; **ride for a fall,** to court disaster; **ride out,** to keep afloat throughout (a storm) : to cut out from a herd by riding; **ride to hounds,** to take part in fox-hunting; **ride up,** to work up out of position; **riding the fair,** the ceremony of opening a fair by a procession. [O.E. *rídan*; Du. *rijden*, Ger. *reiten*.]

rident, *rī'dənt, adj.* laughing or beamingly smiling. [L. *rīdēns, -entis,* pr.p. of *rīdēre,* to laugh.]

ridge, *rij, n.* (*obs.*) the back : the earth thrown up by the plough between the furrows : a strip of arable land, usu. between furrows : a rib on a stocking, &c. : a long narrow top or crest : the horizontal line of a roof-top : a narrow elevation : a hill-range.—*v.t.* and *v.i.* to form into ridges : to wrinkle.—*n.* **ridge'-bone,** the spine.—*adj.* **ridged,** having ridges.—*ns.* **ridge'-piece, ridge'-pole,** the timber forming the ridge of a roof; **ridge'-rope,** the central rope of an awning; **ridge'-tile,** a tile that bestrides the ridge of a roof; **ridge'way,** a track along a hill-crest; **ridg'ing,** the forming of ridges : covering with ridge-tiles.—*adj.* **ridg'y,** having ridges. [O.E. *hrycg*; O.N. *hryggr,* Ger. *rücken,* back.]

ridgel, ridgil, *rij'əl, n.* a male animal with but one testicle in position or remaining.—Also **ridgling** (*rij'ling*), **rig** (*rig*).—Northern forms **rigg'ald, rig'ling, rig'lin** (*rig'*). [App. from preceding, from the undescended testicle near the back.]

ridicule, *rid'i-kūl, n.* (*rare*) absurdity : derision : mockery.—*v.t.* to laugh at : to expose to merriment : to deride : to mock.—*n.* **ridic'uler.**—*adj.* **ridic'ulous,** deserving or exciting ridicule : absurd.—*adv.* **ridic'ulously.**—*n.* **ridic'ulousness.** [L. *rīdiculus—rīdēre,* to laugh.]

ridicule, *rid'i-kūl, n.* for **reticule.**

Riding, *rī'ding, n.* one of the three divisions of Yorkshire : extended to divisions elsewhere. [For *thriding*—O.N. *thrithi,* third.]

riding. See **ride.**

ridotto, *ri-dot'ō, n.* a public dancing-party. [It.]

riebeckite, *rē'bek-īt, n.* a monoclinic amphibole, silicate of sodium and iron. [Named after the German traveller Emil *Riebeck* (1853-85).]

riem, *rēm, n.* a raw-hide thong. [Du.]

Riemannian, *rē-man'i-ən, adj.* pertaining to the German mathematician G. F. Bernhard *Riemann* (1826-66), or to his work or concepts.—**Riemannian geometry,** the non-Euclidean geometry of **Riemannian space** (*elliptic space*), space of more than three dimensions in which e.g. the sum of the angles of a triangle is more than two right angles.

rieve, riever. Same as **reave, reaver.**

rifacimento, *rē-fä-chi-men'tō, n.* a recasting of a literary or musical work :—*pl.* **rifacimen'ti** (*-tē*). [It.]

rife, *rif, adj.* prevalent : abounding : current.—Also *adv.*—*adv.* **rife'ly.**—*n.* **rife'ness.** [O.E. *rýfe,* rife; Du. *rijf,* O.N. *rífr.*]

riffle, *rif'l, n.* (*U.S.*) a shallow section in a river where the water flows swiftly.—*v.t.* to form a riffle : to handle with a light noise, as in turning pages : to shuffle by the method in which the corner of a card from one part of the pack falls alternately with that of a card in the other part of the pack.—Also *v.i.* [Cf. **ripple** (1).]

riff-raff, *rif'-raf, n.* the scum of the people : rubbish.—*adj.* rubbishy. [M.E. *rif* and *raf*—O.Fr. *rif et raf.*]

rifle, *rī'fl, v.t.* to plunder : to ransack : to disarray : (of a hawk) to seize only the feathers of : to injure.—*n.* **ri'fler.** [O.Fr. *rifler.*]

rifle, *rī'fl, v.t.* to groove spirally : (also *v.i.*) to shoot with a rifle.—*n.* a firearm with spirally grooved barrel.—*ns.* **ri'fle-bird, ri'fleman-bird,** an Australian bird of paradise : a New Zealand bushwren; **ri'fle-corps,** a body of soldiers armed with rifles; **ri'fle-green,** a dark green, the colour of a rifleman's uniform (also *adj.*); **ri'fle-grenade',** a grenade or bomb fired from a rifle; **ri'fleman,** a soldier armed with a rifle : a rifle-bird; **ri'fle-pit,** a pit to shelter riflemen; **ri'fle-range,** the range of a rifle : a place for rifle practice; **ri'fle-shot;** **ri'fling,** the spiral grooving of a gun-bore. [O.Fr. *rifler,* to scratch; cf. Ger. *riefeln,* and preceding word.]

rift, *rift, n.* a cleft : a fissure : a chink : (*Spens.*) a riven fragment.—*v.t.* and *v.i.* to cleave, split.—*n.* **rift'-vall'ey,** a valley formed by subsidence of a portion of the earth's crust between two faults. [Cf. Dan. and Norw. *rift,* a cleft.]

rifte, *rift,* (*Spens.*) *pa.p.* of **rive.**

rig, *rig, v.t.* (*naut.*) to fit with sails and tackling : to fit up or fit out : to equip : to set up, set in working order : (now *coll.*) to dress, clothe : (*pr.p.* **rigg'ing;** *pa.t.* and *pa.p.* **rigged**).—*n.* form and arrangement of masts, sails, and tackling : an outfit : garb : general appearance : (*U.S.*) a driving turnout : (*U.S.*) a well-boring plant.—*ns.* **rigg'er,** one who rigs ships : one who puts together and attends to the rigging of aircraft : in machinery, a narrow drum; **rigg'ing, tackle** : the system of cordage which supports a ship's masts and extends the sails : the system of wires and cords in an aircraft; **rigg'ing-loft,** a long workshop where rigging is fitted : the place in a theatre from which the scenery is manipulated; **rig'-out,** an outfit.—**rig out,** to furnish with complete dress, &c. [Origin obscure; perh. conn. with Norw. *rigga,* to bind.]

rig, *rig, n.* the Northern form of **ridge.**—*ns.* **rigg'ing,** the roof; **rigg'ing-tree,** a roof-tree.

rig, *rig, n.* a frolic, prank, trick.—*v.t.* to manipulate unscrupulously.—**run a rig,** to play a prank. [Origin obscure.]

rig, *rig, n.* a wanton.—*v.i.* to wanton : to romp.—*adj.* **rigg'ish,** (*Shak.*) wanton. [Origin obscure.]

rig, riggald, rigling. See **ridgel.**

rigadoon, *rig-ə-dōōn', n.* a lively jig-like dance for one couple, or its music. [Fr. *rigaudon.*]

Rigel, *rī'gəl, -jəl, n.* a first-magnitude star in the foot of Orion. [Ar. *rijl,* foot.]

right, *rīt, adj.* straight : direct : perpendicular : forming one-fourth of a revolution : with axis perpendicular to base : true : genuine : veritable : characteristic : truly judged or judging : appropriate : in accordance, or identical, with what is true and fitting : not mistaken : accurate : fit : sound : intended to be exposed (as a side, e.g. of cloth) : morally justifiable or incumbent : just : in accordance with what should be : equitable : justly to be preferred or commended : at or towards that side at which in a normal person is the better-developed hand (of a river, as referred to one going downstream; on the stage, from the point of view of an actor looking at the audience) : sitting at the president's right hand (in Continental assemblies) : hence, conservative or inclined towards conservatism.—*adv.* straight : straightway : quite : just, exactly : in a right manner : justly : correctly : (*arch.* and *dial.* or in special phrases) very : to or on the right side.—*n.* that which is right or correct : rightness : fair treatment : equity : truth : justice : just or legal claim : what one has a just claim to : due : (in *pl., arch.*) a stag's brow, bez, and trez antlers : (*Spens.*) territory : the right hand : the right side : a glove, shoe, &c., for the right hand, foot, &c. : the region on the right side : the right wing : the conservatives.—*v.t.* to set right : to set in order : to rectify : to redress : to vindicate : to do justice to : to avenge : to set right side up or erect.—*v.i.* to recover an erect position.—*interj.* expressing agreement, acquiescence, or readiness.—*adj.* **right'able,** capable of being righted.—*n.* **right'-about',** the directly opposite quarter (in drill or dismissal; also **right-about face**).—*adv.* to the right-about (face).—*v.i.* to turn right-about (face).—*adj.* **right'-and-left',** having a right and a left side, part, &c. : bilaterally symmetrical : on both sides : from both barrels.—*n.* a shot or a blow from each barrel or hand.—*adv.* on both sides : on all hands : towards one side, then the other : in all directions.—*adj.* **right-ang'led,** having a right angle, one equal to a fourth of a revolution; **right'-bank,** on the right bank.—*adj.* and *adv.* **right'-down,** out-and-out.—*adj.* **right'-drawn,** (*Shak.*) drawn

in a just cause.—*v.t.* **right'en**, to set right.—*n.*
right'er, one who sets right or redresses wrong.—
adj. **right'ful**, having a just claim: according to
justice: belonging by right.—*adv.* **right'fully.**—
ns. **right'fulness**, righteousness: justice.—*adj.*
right'-hand, at the right side: with thread or
strands turning to the right: chiefly relied on
(as *one's right-hand man*).—*adj.* **right'-hand'ed**,
using the right hand more easily than the left:
with or for the right hand: with rotation towards
the right, or clockwise.—*adv.* towards the right.—
ns. **right'-hand'edness**; **right'-hand'er**, a blow
with the right hand: a right-handed person.—*n.*
right'ing.—*adjs.* **right'less**, without rights; **right'-
lined**, rectilinear.—*adv.* **right'ly.**—*adj.* **right'-
mind'ed**, having a mind disposed towards what
is right, just, or according to good sense: sane.—
ns. **right'-mind'edness**; **right'ness.** — *interj.*
righto', **right-oh'**, (*coll.*) expressing acquiescence.
—*adj.* **right'-think'ing**, of approved opinions.—
n., adj., and *adv.* **right'ward.**—*adv.* **right'wards.**
—*n.* **right'-whale**, a whale of the typical genus
Balaena, esp. the Greenland whale.—*adj.* **right'-
wing**, of or on the right wing: pertaining to
the extreme political right.—*n.* **right'-wing'er**,
a player on the right wing: a member of the
right wing of a party.—**all right** (see **all**); **by
rights** (formerly **right**), rightfully: if all were
right; **do one right**, to do one justice: to keep
pace with in drinking: to drink the health of;
have a right, no right, to be entitled or not entitled: (*illit.* or *dial.*) to be under a moral obligation, no obligation; **have right**, (*arch.*) to be
right; **in one's own right**, by absolute and personal right, not through another; **in one's right
mind**, quite sane; **in right of**, by virtue of: by
title vested in; **in the right**, right: maintaining
a justifiable position; **put, set, to rights**, to set in
order; **right as a trivet, as rain** (see **trivet,
rain**); **right ascension** (see **ascension**); **right
away**, (chiefly *U.S.*) straightway: without delay;
right down, plainly; **Right Honourable**, a title
of distinction given to peers below the rank of
marquis, to privy-councillors, to present and past
cabinet ministers, to certain Lord Mayors and Lord
Provosts, &c.; **right off**, without delay; **right
out**, (*Shak.*) outright; **Right Reverend** (see
reverend); **right of entry**, a legal right to enter
a place; **right of way**, the right of the public to
pass over a piece of ground; **right-of-way**, a track
over which there is such a right: (*U.S.*) the strip of
land occupied by a railway-track, a road, &c.;
right the helm, to put it amidships, in a line with
the keel; **send**, &c., **to the right-about**, (*coll.*)
to dismiss summarily, or force to retreat. [O.E.
riht (n. and adj.), *rihte* (adv.), *rihten* (vb.); cf. Ger.
recht, L. *rēctus.*]

right, (*Shak.*, *Milt.*) for **rite**.

righteous, *rī′chəs, -tyəs, adj.* just, upright.—*adv.*
right'eously.—*n.* **right'eousness**, rectitude: a
righteous act. [O.E. *rihtwīs—riht*, right, *wīs*, wise,
prudent, or *wise*, wise, manner.]

rigid, *rij′id, adj.* stiff: unbending: unyielding:
rigorous: strict: of an airship, having a rigid
structure to maintain shape.—*n.* a rigid person or
airship.—*adv.* **rig'idly.**—*n.* **rig'idness.**—*n.*
rigid'ity.—*adv.* **rig'idly.**—*n.* **rig'idness.** [L. *rigidus—rigēre*, to be stiff.]

Rigil, *rij′il*, n. a first-magnitude double star in the
foot of the Centaur. [Cf. **Rigel.**]

rigmarole, *rig′mə-rōl*, n. a long rambling discourse.—*adj.* prolix and incoherent. [ragman
roll.]

rigol, rigoll, *rig′əl*, n. a gutter or water-channel: a
groove, esp. an encircling groove: (*Shak.*) a circlet.
[Fr. *rigole*, gutter, groove.]

rigor, *rī′gor* (L. *rig′or*), n. (*med.*) a sense of chilliness
with contraction of the skin, a preliminary symptom
of many diseases: (*bot.*) failure to react to stimulus,
under unfavourable conditions: (*zool.*) a rigid
irresponsive state caused by a sudden shock, as
when an animal is said to sham dead: (*rig′ər*) another, chiefly American, spelling of **rigour.**—*ns.*
rigorism (*rig′ər-izm*), extreme strictness: the doctrine that in doubtful cases the strict course should
be followed; **rig'orist.**—*adj.* **rig'orous**, rigidly

strict or scrupulous: exact: unsparing: severe:
(*Spens.*) harsh, violent.—*adv.* **rig'orously.**—*ns.*
rig'orousness; **rigour** (*rig′ər*), stiffness: hardness: rigor: severity: unswerving enforcement of
law, rule, or principle: strict exactitude: austerity:
extreme strictness: severity of weather or climate.
—**rigor mortis** (L.), stiffening of the body after
death. [L. *rigor—rigēre*, to be stiff.]

Rigsdag, *rigz′dag, rēgz′däg*, n. the parliament of
Denmark. [Dan.,—*rige*, kingdom, *dag*, day.]

Rigveda, *rig-vā′dä*, n. the first of the four Vedas.
[Sans. *ric*, a hymn, *veda*, knowledge.]

rigwiddie, rigwoodie, *rig-wid′i, -wəd′i, -wud′i*, or
rig′, n. (*Scot.*) a cart-horse's back-band.—*adj.* lean
and tough: stubborn: a vague word of reproach,
with a suggestion of the *widdy*, or halter. [**rig**,
widdy=withy.]

rile, *rīl*, **riley**, *rīl′i*, forms of **roil, roily.**

rilievo, *rēl-yā′vō*, n. (*sculp., archit.*) relief. [It.]

rill, *ril*, n. a very small brook: a runnel: a small
trench: (*astron.*) also **rille** from Ger. *rille*) a
narrow furrow on the moon.—*v.i.* to flow in a rill
or rills.—*ns.* **rill'et**, a little rill; **rill'mark**, (*geol.*)
a marking produced by water trickling down a
beach or bank. [Cf. Du. *ril*, Ger. (orig. L.G.) *rille*,
channel, furrow.]

rim, *rim*, n. the outermost circular part of a wheel,
not including the tire: an edge, border, brim, or
margin, esp. when raised or more or less circular:
an encircling band, mark, or line.—*v.t.* to form or
furnish a rim to:—*pr.p.* **rimm'ing**; *pa.t.* and
pa.p. **rimmed.**—*n.* **rim'-brake**, a brake acting on
the rim of a wheel.—*adjs.* **rim'less**; **rimmed.**
[O.E. *rima* (found in compounds).]

rim, *rim*, n. a membrane: the peritoneum. [O.E.
rēoma; cf. **riem.**]

rima, *rī′mä* (L. *rē′mä*), n. a chink: esp. the gap
between vocal cords and arytaenoid cartilages:—
pl. **rimae** (*rī′mē*, L. *rē′mī*).—*n.* **rime** (*rīm*: obs.),
a chink: a fissure.—*adjs.* **ri'mose** (or *ri-mōs′*),
ri'mous, full of chinks: covered with cracks. [L.
rīma.]

rime, *rīm*, n. hoar-frost or frozen dew.—*v.t.* to
cover with rime.—*adj.* **rī'my.** [O.E. *hrīm*; Du.
rijm, Ger. *reif.*]

rime, rimer, &c. Same as **ream** (3), **reamer,
rhyme, rhymer**, &c.

rin, *rin*, a Scots form of **run.**

rind, *rīnd*, n. bark: peel: crust: outside.—*v.t.* to
bark.—*adjs.* **rind'ed**; **rind'less**; **rind'y.** [O.E.
rinde; Du. and Ger. *rinde.*]

rind, rynd, *rīnd*, n. a fitting that supports an upper
millstone, cross-shaped with expanded ends. [Cf.
M.Du. *rijn*, M.L.G. *rīn.*]

rinderpest, *rin′dər-pest*, n. a malignant and contagious disease of cattle. [Ger., cattle-plague.]

rine, *rīn*, n. (*Spens.*, &c.). Same as **rind.**

rinforzando, *rin-for-tsän′dō*, *adj.* (*mus.*) with sudden
accent. [It., reinforcing.]

ring, *ring*, n. a circlet or small hoop, esp. one of
metal, worn on the finger, in the ear, nose, or elsewhere: any object, mark, arrangement, group, or
course of like form: an encircling band: a rim:
a short cylinder for holding a table-napkin: a link
of chain-mail: an encircling cut in bark: a zone
of wood added in a season's growth, as seen in
sections: a mark of fungus growth in turf (**fairy
ring**): a flat crowd of very small satellites encircling Saturn: an annulus: a segment of a
worm, caterpillar, &c.: a closed chain of atoms:
a circular ripple: a circular earthwork or rampart
an arena: a space set apart for boxing, wrestling
circus performance, riding display of animals, o
the like: an enclosure for bookmakers: pugilism
prize-fighters or bookmakers with their associate
collectively: a combination or clique, esp. organ
ised to control the market or for other self-seekin
purpose.—*v.t.* to encircle: to put a ring on or in
to put on in the manner of a ring: to cut a rin
in the bark of: to cut into rings: to go in rin
round: (*Austr.*) to excel, be the quickest shee
shearer in.—*v.i.* to move in rings: to gather or b
in a ring:—*pa.t.* and *pa.p.* **ringed**; former
sometimes, and still in sheep-shearing competition
rung.—*n.* **ring'-ar'mature**, one with a ring-shape

core.—*v.t.* **ring'-bark,** to strip a ring of bark from. —*ns.* **ring'bit,** a horse's bit with rings at the ends ; **ring'-bolt,** a bolt with a ring through a hole at one end ; **ring'bone,** a bony callus on a horse's pastern-bone : the condition caused by this ; **ring'-canal,** a circular canal within the rim of a jellyfish : a circular vessel of the water-vascular system of echinoderms ; **ring'-carrier,** (*Shak.*) a go-between ; **ring'-compound,** a chemical compound with a closed chain ; **ring'-cross,** a circle with crossed diameters ; **ring'-dance,** a round dance ; **ring'-dial,** a portable sundial ; **ring'-dott'erel,** the ringed plover ; **ring'dove,** the wood-pigeon, from the broken white ring or line on its neck ; **ring'-dropping,** a sharper's trick of pretending to find a dropped ring and selling it ; **ring'-dyke,** (*geol.*) a dyke with more or less circular outcrop.— *adj.* **ringed,** surrounded by, or marked with, a ring or rings : ring-shaped : composed of rings.—*ns.* **ringer** (ring'ər), one who rings : a throw of a quoit that encircles the pin : a quoit so thrown : a person or thing of the highest excellence : (*Austr.*) the quickest and most expert of a group of shearers ; **ring'-fence,** a fence continuously encircling an estate : a complete barrier.—*v.t.* to shut off completely.—*ns.* **ring'-finger,** the third finger, esp. of the left hand, on which the wedding-ring is worn ; **ring'-gauge,** a gauge in the form of a ring ; **ring'-ing** ; **ring'leader,** one who takes the lead in mischief.—*adj.* **ring'less.**—*n.* **ring'let,** a little ring : a fairy ring : a fairy dance in a ring : a long curl of hair.—*adj.* **ring'leted.** — *ns.* **ring'man,** (*obs.* or *dial.*) the third finger of the hand : a bookmaker ; **ring'-master,** one who has charge of performances in a circus-ring ; **ring'-money,** money in the form of rings.—*adj.* **ring'-necked** (*-nekt*), having the neck marked with a ring.—*ns.* **ring'-ou'zel,** **-ou'sel** (see ouzel) ; **ring'-plov'er,** a ring-necked plover of various kinds.—*adj.* **ring'-porous,** having annual rings marked by large pores.—*ns.* **ring'-road,** a road or boulevard encircling a town or its inner part ; **ring'-shake,** a defect in timber, separation along the annual rings ; **ring'side,** the side of the prize-ring ; **ring'sider,** one who attends prize-fights.—*adj.* **ring'-small,** small enough to pass through a ring of standard size.—*n.* stones of such a size.—*ns.* **ring'-snake,** a common English snake, the grass-snake (also **ringed snake**) : a harmless American snake with yellow collar ; **ring'-stand,** a stand for chemical vessels, with rings clamped to a vertical rod : a stand for finger-rings ; **ring'ster,** a member of a ring ; **ring'-stopper,** a rope for securing an anchor-ring to the cat-head. —*adjs.* **ring'-straked** (*B.*), **-streaked,** streaked in rings.—*n.* **ring'-tail,** (*naut.*) a studding-sail set upon the gaff of a fore-and-aft sail : a light sail set abaft and beyond the spanker : the female or young male of the hen-harrier, from a rust-coloured ring on the tail-feathers.—*adjs.* **ring'-tail, -tailed** (*-tāld*), having the tail marked with bars or rings of colour, as a lemur : having a tail curled at the end.—*ns.* **ring'-taw,** a game of marbles, with rings marked on the ground ; **ring'-time,** (*Shak.*) time for giving rings ; **ring'-walk,** an encircling walk ; **ring'-wall,** an enclosing wall ; **ring'-winding,** winding that threads a ring.—*adv.* **ring'wise.**—*ns.* **ring'-work,** work executed in rings ; **ring'worm,** a skin disease characterised by ring-shaped patches, caused by fungi.—**hold, keep, the ring,** to watch a fight and keep others from interfering ; **ride, or tilt, at the ring,** to practise the sport of riding rapidly and catching a hanging ring on a spear ; **ring the shed,** (*Austr.*) to win a sheep-shearing competition. [O.E. *hring* ; O.N. *hringr* ; Ger., Dan., and Sw. *ring*.]

ring, *ring,* *v.i.* to give a metallic or bell-like sound : to sound aloud and clearly : to give a characteristic or particular sound : to resound, re-echo : to be filled with sound, or a sensation like sound, or report, or renown : to cause a bell or bells to sound, esp. as a summons or signal.—*v.t.* to cause to give a metallic or bell-like sound : to sound in the manner of a bell : to summon, usher, announce by a bell or bells : to re-echo, resound, proclaim : (*pa.t.* **rang,** now rarely **rung,** *obs.* **rong** ; *pa.p.* **rung**).—

n. a sounding of a bell : the characteristic sound or tone, as of a bell or a metal, or of a voice : a ringing sound : a set of bells.—*n.* **ring'er.**—*n.* and *adj.* **ring'ing.**—*adv.* **ring'ingly.**—**ring down,** or **up (the curtain),** to give the signal for lowering or raising ; **ring in,** to ring more rapidly before stopping, as a final intimation to lingering church-goers ; **ring in, out,** to usher in, out (esp. the year) with bell-ringing ; **ring off,** to signal the ending of a telephone conversation ; **ring out,** to sound loudly, clearly, and suddenly ; **ring the bell,** to achieve a great success (from the bell of a shooting-gallery bull's-eye) : to fit in with or start a train of association ; **ring the bells backward,** to reverse the order of chimes ; **ring the changes,** to proceed through all the permutations in ringing a chime of bells : to do a limited number of things repeatedly in varying order ; **ring true,** to sound genuine (like a tested coin) ; **ring up,** to summon by bell, esp. to the telephone. [O.E. *hringan* ; O.N. *hringja* ; Ger. *ringen* ; Dan. *ringe*.]

ring, *ring, n.* and *v.i.* an obs. Scots form of **reign** :— *pa.t.* **rang.**

ringent, *rin'jənt, adj.* gaping. [L. *ringēns, -entis,* pr.p. of *ringī*.]

rink, *ringk, n.* a course for tilting or racing : a portion of a bowling-green, curling-pond, &c., allotted to one set of players : a division of a side playing on such a portion : a piece of ice prepared for skating : a building or floor for roller-skating or ice-skating.—*v.i.* to skate on a rink. [Orig. Scots ; origin obscure.]

rinse, *rins, v.t.* to wash lightly by pouring, shaking, or dipping.—Also *n.*—*ns.* **rins'er** ; **rins'ing.**—*n.pl.* **rins'ings,** liquid in which something has been rinsed. [O.Fr. *rinser* (Fr. *rincer*).]

rinthereout, *rin'dha-rōōt, n.* and *adj.* (*Scot.*) vagrant : vagabond. [**run thereout**.]

riot, *rī'ət, n.* wild revelry : debauchery : loose living : unrestrained squandering or indulgence : tumult : a disturbance of the peace by a crowd (legally three or more).—*v.i.* to take part or indulge in riot : to revel.—*ns.* **rī'oter** ; **rī'oting** ; **rī'otise, -ize** (*-īz* ; *Spens.*), riot, extravagance.—*adj.* **rī'otous.**—*adv.* **rī'otously.**—*ns.* **rī'otousness** ; **rī'otry.**—**Riot Act,** a statute designed to prevent riotous assemblies : a form of words read as a warning to rioters to disperse ; **read the riot act,** (*fig.*) to give vehement warning that something must cease ; **run riot,** to act or grow without restraint. [O.Fr. *riot, riotte*.]

rip, *rip, v.t.* to slash or tear open, apart, off, or out : to make by such an action : to reopen (with *up*) : to cleave or saw with the grain : to strip (as a roof) : to utter explosively (with *out*).—*v.i.* to part in rents : to break out violently : to rush, go forward unrestrainedly : (*pr.p.* **ripp'ing** ; *pa.t.* and *pa.p.* **ripped,** or **ript**).—*n.* a rent : an unchecked rush.—*ns.* **rip'-cord,** a cord for opening a balloon's gas-bag or enabling a parachute to open ; **ripp'er,** one who rips : a tool for ripping : (*slang*) a person or thing especially admirable.—*adj.* **ripp'ing,** (*slang*) excellent.—Also *adv.*—*adv.* **ripp'ingly.**—*ns.* **ripp'ing-saw,** **rip'-saw,** a saw for cutting along the grain. [Precise origin uncertain ; cf. Fris. *rippe,* Flem. *rippen,* Norw. *rippa*.]

rip, *rip, n.* (*dial.*) a wicker basket : (*dial.*) a coop.— *n.* **ripp'er, ripp'ier,** (*obs.*) one who carries fish inland to sell. [O.N. *hrip,* basket.]

rip, *rip, n.* an inferior horse : a disreputable person. [Poss. **rep**.]

rip, *rip, n.* a stretch of broken water : a disturbed state of the sea. [Perh. **rip** (1).]

rip, *ripp, rip, n.* (*Scot.*) a handful, esp. a plucked handful, of grass or corn. [Poss. **rip** (1) ; connexion with **reap** involves difficulty.]

riparian, *rī-pā'ri-ən, adj.* of or inhabiting a river-bank.—*n.* an owner of land bordering a river.—*adj.* **ripā'rial.** [L. *rīpārius—rīpa,* a river-bank.]

ripe, *rīp, adj.* ready for harvest : arrived at perfection : fit for use : fully developed : finished : ready : resembling ripe fruit : mature.—*v.t.* and *v.i.* to ripen.—*adv.* **ripe'ly.**—*v.t.* and *v.i.* **ri'pen,** to make or grow ripe or riper.—*n.* **ripe'ness.** [O.E. *rīpe,* ripe, *rīpian,* to ripen ; conn. with *rīp,* harvest, and perh. *reap* ; cf. Du. *rijp,* Ger. *reif*.]

Neutral vowels in unaccented syllables : *el'ə-mənt, in'fənt, ran'dəm*

ripe, rīp, *v.t.* and *v.i.* (*Scot.*) to grope, search, ransack.—*n.* rip′er. [O.E. *rȳpan*, to rob.]

ripidolite, rip-id′ō-līt, or rip-, *n.* clinochlore. [Gr. *rhīpis*, *-idos*, fan.]

ripieno, ri-pyā′nō, *adj.* (*mus.*) supplementary.—*n.* a supplementary instrument or performer :—*pl.* **ripie′ni** (-nē).—*n.* ripie′nist, a supplementary instrumentalist. [It.]

riposte, ri-pōst′, *n.* a quick return thrust after a parry : a repartee.—*v.t.* and *v.i.* to answer with a riposte. [Fr.,—It. *risposta*, reply.]

ripp, ripper, rippier, ripping. See **rip** (various).

ripple, rip′l, *n.* light fretting of the surface of a liquid : a little wave : a similar appearance in anything : a sound as of rippling water.—*v.t.* to ruffle the surface of : to mark with ripples.—*v.i.* to move or run in ripples : to sound like ripples.—*n.* **ripp′le-mark**, an undulatory ridging produced in sediments by waves, currents, and wind, often preserved in sedimentary rocks.—*adj.* **ripp′le-marked.**—*n.* ripp′let, a small ripple.—*n.* and *adj.* **ripp′ling.**—*adv.* ripp′lingly.—*adj.* ripp′ly. [Origin obscure.]

ripple, rip′l, *n.* a toothed implement for removing seeds, &c., from flax or hemp.—*v.t.* to clear of seeds by drawing through a ripple : to remove by a ripple.—*n.* ripp′ler. [Cf. L.G. and Du. *repel*, a ripple, hoe, Ger. *riffel*.]

Rippon, rip′ən, *n.* (*obs.* ; in full **Rippon spur**) a spur made at *Ripon*, once famous for the manufacture.

Ripstone pippin, (*Dickens*) for **Ribstone pippin.**

ript. Same as **ripped** (see **rip**, 1).

Ripuarian, rip-ū-ā′ri-ən, *adj.* applied to the Franks on the lower Rhine and their laws.—*n.* a Ripuarian Frank. [Generally said to be from L. *rīpa*, a riverbank.]

risaldar, ris-äl-där′, *n.* the commander of a troop of Indian cavalry. [Hind. *risāladdār*.]

rise, rīz, *v.i.* to get up : to become erect, stand up : to come back to life : to become hostile : to revolt : to close a session : to break up camp : to raise a siege : to move upward : to come up to the surface : to fly up from the ground : to come above the horizon : to grow upward : to advance in rank, fortune, &c. : to swell : to increase : to increase in price : to become more acute in pitch : to be excited : to be cheered : to come into view, notice, **or consciousness** : to spring up : to take origin : to have source : to come into being : to extend upward : to tower : to slope up : to come to hand, chance to come : to respond as to provocation, or to a situation calling forth one's powers : to excavate upward.—*v.t.* to cause to rise : (*U.S.*) to surmount : (*naut.*) to raise, view better by nearing : (*pa.t.* **rose**, rōz, *Scot.* **raise, rase,** rāz, *U.S. coll.* **riz** ; *pa.p.* **risen,** riz′n, *U.S. coll.* **riz**).—*n.* **rising** : ascent : a coming up to the surface, as of a fish : the sport of making a butt of one by deception : increase in height : vertical difference or amount of elevation or rising : increase of salary, price, &c. : an upward slope : a sharpening of pitch : origin : occasion : the riser of a step : a shaft excavated from below.—*ns.* **ris′er**, one who rises, esp. from bed : that which rises : the upright portion of a step ; **ris′ing**, the action or process of the verb in any sense : a revolt : a prominence : a swelling : a hill.—*adj.* and *pr.p.* ascending : increasing : coming above the horizon : advancing : growing up : approaching the age of : (*U.S.*) quite as much as.—**give rise to,** to cause, bring about ; **on the rise,** in process of rising, esp. in price ; **rise from the ranks,** to work one's way up from private soldier to commissioned officer : to become a self-made man ; **rise to the occasion,** to prove equal to an emergency ; **take a rise out of,** to lure into reacting to provocation, or (loosely) to make sport of ; **take rise,** to originate ; **the rise of,** (*U.S.*) more than. [O.E. *rīsan* ; O.N. *rīsa,* Goth. *reisan,* Ger. *reisen*.]

rishi, rish′i, *n.* a sage or poet. [Sans.]

risible, riz′i-bl, *adj.* able or inclined to laugh : of laughter : ludicrous.—*n.* risibil′ity, laughter : inclination to laugh : faculty of laughter. [L. *risibilis—rīdēre, rīsum,* to laugh.]

risk, also (*obs.*) **risque, risk,** *n.* hazard : chance of

loss or injury.—*v.t.* to expose to hazard : to venture, to take the chance of.—*n.* risk′er, one who risks.—*adj.* risk′ful.—*adv.* risk′ily.—*ns.* risk′iness ; risk′-money, allowance to a cashier to compensate for ordinary errors.—*adjs.* risk′y, dangerous : risqué (a Gallicism) ; risqué (rēs-kā ; Fr. *pa.p.*), audaciously bordering on the unseemly.—**run a risk,** to incur hazard. [Fr. *risque*—It. *risco* : origin uncertain.]

risoluto, rē-zō-lōō′tō, *adj.* and *adv.* with resolution. [It.]

risorgimento, ri-sor-ji-men′tō, *n.* a revival, rebirth : **Risorgimento,** the Renaissance : the liberation and unification of Italy in the 19th century. [It.,—L. *resurgĕre*.]

risotto, ri-zot′tō, *n.* a dish of rice cooked with onions and cheese, or with gravy, &c. [It.,—*riso,* rice.]

risp, risp, *v.t.* (*Scot.*) to rasp : to grate.—*v.i.* to make a grating sound : to tirl.—*n.* a rasp or coarse file : a baker's grater : a roughened bar, on which a ring is grated, used instead of a knocker or door-bell : a grating sound.—*n.pl.* risp′ings, portions risped off. [O.N. *rispa,* to scratch.]

risque, risqué. See **risk.**

Riss, ris, *n.* the third stage of glaciation in the Alps. —*adjs.* **Riss, Riss′ian.** [From a tributary of the Danube in Württemberg.]

rissole, ris′ōl, rēs-ōl′, *n.* a fried ball or cake of minced food. [Fr.]

risus, rī′səs (L. rē′sōōs), *n.* a laugh : a grin.—**risus sardon′icus,** a sardonic grin, or drawing back of the corners of the mouth by spasm of the muscles, as in tetanus. [L. *rīsus, -ūs,* laugh.]

rit, ritt, rit, *v.t.* (*Scot.*) to score : to scratch : to slit. —*n.* a scratch : a slit. [M.E. *ritten* ; cf. Ger. *ritzen*.]

ritardando, rē-tär-dän′dō, *adj.* and *adv.* with diminishing speed.—*n.* a ritardando passage : a slowing down. [It.]

rite, rīt, *n.* a ceremonial form or observance, esp. religious : a liturgy.—*adj.* rite′less. [L. *rītus*.]

ritornello, rit-or-nel′ō, *n.* a short instrumental passage in a vocal work, e.g. a prelude or refrain :— *pl.* **ritornelli** (-ē).—Also **ritornel′, -nell′, -nelle′, ritournelle′.** [It.]

ritter, rit′ər, *n.* a knight.—*n.* **ritt′-mas′ter,** a captain of cavalry. [Ger. *ritter, rittmeister*.]

ritual, rit′ū-əl, *adj.* relating to, or of the nature of, rites.—*n.* manner of performing divine service, or a book containing it : a body or code of ceremonies : performance of rites : ceremonial.—*ns.* **rit′ualism,** attachment of importance to ritual, esp. with the implication of undue importance ; **rit′ualist,** one skilled in or devoted to a ritual : one of the High Church party in the Church of England.—*adj.* ritualist′ic.—*adv.* ritualist′ically.—*v.i.* rit′ūalise, to practise or turn to ritualism.— *v.t.* to make ritualistic.—*adv.* rit′ually.—**ritual choir,** part of a church used as a choir. [L. *rītuālis—rītus* : see **rite.**]

riva, rīv′ä, rēv′ä, *n.* (*Shetland*) a cleft in rock. [O.N. *rifa.*]

rivage, riv′ij, rīv′ij, *n.* (*poet.*) a bank, shore. [Fr.,— L. *rīpa,* a bank.]

rival, rī′vl, *n.* one pursuing an object in competition with another : one who strives to equal or excel another : one for whom, or that for which, a claim to equality might be made : (*Shak.*) a partner, fellow.—*adj.* standing in competition : of like pretensions or comparable claims.—*v.t.* to stand in competition with : to try to gain the same object against : to try to equal or excel : to be worthy of comparison with :—*pr.p.* rī′valling ; *pa.t.* and *pa.p.* rī′valled.—*n.* rī′valess, a female rival.—*adj.* rī′val-hating (*Shak.*).—*v.i.* rī′valise, to enter into rivalry.—*n.* **rivality** (*-val′i-ti*), rivalry : (*Shak.*) equality.—*adj.* rī′valless.—*ns.* rī′valry, state of being a rival : competition : emulation : feeling of a rival ; rī′valship, emulation. [L. *rīvālis,* said to be from *rīvus,* river as one who draws water from the same river.]

rive, rīv, *v.t.* to tear asunder : to rend : to split : (*Shak.*) to discharge as if with rending : (*obs.*) to pierce : (*Scot.*) to plough up.—*v.i.* to tug, tear : to split :—*pa.t.* rīved—*Scot.* rave (rāv) ;

pa.p. **riven** (*riv'n*), **rived** (*rīvd*)—*Spens.* **rive** (*riv*)—*Keats* raft. [O.N. *rīfa*.]

rivel, *riv'l*, *v.t.* and *v.i.* to wrinkle.—*adj.* **riv'elled.** [O.E. *rifelede*, rivelled.]

river, *riv'ər*, *n.* a large stream of water flowing over the land: sometimes extended to a strait or inlet: (*arch.*) a place for hawking: a stream in general.—*adj.* of a river or rivers: dwelling or found in or near a river or rivers.—*adj.* **riv'erain** (*-ān*), of a river or its neighbourhood.—*n.* a riverside dweller.—*ns.* **riv'er-bank**; **riv'er-basin**, the whole region drained by a river with its affluents; **riv'er-bed**, the channel in which a river flows; **riv'er-bottom**, (*U.S.*) alluvial land along the margin of a river; **riv'er-craft**, small vessels that ply on rivers; **riv'er-dragon**, (*Milt.*, with ref. to Ezek. xxix. 3) Pharaoh: a crocodile; **riv'er-drift**, old alluvia of rivers; **ri'ver-driver**, (*U.S.*) one who conducts logs downstream.—*adj.* **riv'ered**, watered by rivers.—*ns.* **riv'eret**, (*arch.*) a small river; **riv'er-flat**, a piece of alluvial land by a river; **riv'er-front**, land, quays, buildings, &c., facing a river; **riv'er-god**, the tutelary deity of a river; **riv'er-head**, the source of a river; **riv'er-hog**, the capybara: an African wild pig; **riv'er-horse**, the hippopotamus: the kelpie: (*S.Afr.*) a pole bestridden by Kafirs in crossing rivers.—*adj.* **riv'erine** (*-īn*, *-ēn*), of, on, or dwelling in or near a river.—*n.* riv'er-jack (or river-jack viper), a West African viper.—*adjs.* **riv'erless**; **riv'erlike.**—*ns.* **riv'er-man**, one who makes his livelihood on or along a river; **riv'er-mouth**; **riv'er-mussel**, a fresh-water mussel; **riv'er-rat**, a thief who prowls about a river; **riv'er-sand**, sand from a river-bed; **riv'erscape**, a picture of river scenery; **riv'erside**, the bank or neighbourhood of a river.—*adj.* beside a river.—*ns.* **riv'er-terr'ace**, a terrace formed when a river eats away its old alluvium deposited when its flood-level was higher; **riv'er-tide**, the current of a river: the tide from the sea rising or ebbing in a river; **riv'er-wall**, a wall confining a river within bounds; **riv'er-wa'ter**; **riv'erway**, a river as a waterway; **riv'erweed**, Podostemon.—*adj.* **riv'ery**, of or like a river: well-rivered. [O.Fr. *rivere* (Fr. *rivière*)—L. *rīpārius*, adj.—*rīpa*, bank; cf. It. *riviera*.]

rivet, *riv'it*, *n.* bearded wheat. [Origin obscure.]

rivet, *riv'it*, *n.* a bolt fastened by hammering the end.—*v.t.* to fasten with rivets: to fix immovably: to clinch or hammer out the end of:—*pr.p.* **riv'eting**; *pa.t.* and *pa.p.* **riv'eted** (formerly often **riv'etting**, **riv'etted**).—*ns.* **riv'eter**, one who rivets: a machine for riveting; **riv'et-head**; **riv'et-hearth**, a forge for heating rivets; **riv'eting**. [O.Fr. *rivet—river*, to clinch; origin obscure.]

rivière, *rē-vyer*, *n.* a necklace of diamonds or other precious stones, usu. in several strings. [Fr., river.]

rivo, *rē'vō*, *rī'vō*, *interj.* (*Shak.*) a drinking-cry.

rivulet, *riv'ū-lit*, *n.* a small river. [L. *rīvulus*, dim. of *rīvus*, a stream, perh. through It. *rivoletto*—*rivolo—rivo*.]

rix-dollar, *riks'-dol-ər*, *n.* a silver coin, worth about 2s. 3d. to 4s. 6d., once current in various countries. [Obs. Du. *rijcksdaler* (Du. *rijksdaalder*)—Du. *rijk*, kingdom (cf. O.E. *rīce*), *daler*, dollar.]

'z, *riz*, (*U.S. dial.*) *pa.t.* and *pa.p.* of **rise.**

rizzer, rizzar, rizzor, *riz'ər*, *v.t.* (*Scot.*) to dry, esp. in the sun.—*n.* a rizzered haddock. [Cf. obs. Fr. *ressorer*, to dry.]

rizzer, rizzar, rizard, rizzart, *riz'ər(d)*, *-ərt*, *n.* (*Scot.*) a red currant. [Earlier *razour*; origin unknown.]

roach, *rōch*, *n.* a silvery fresh-water fish of the carp family: applied to various American fishes.—**as sound as a roach**, perfectly sound. [O.Fr. *roche*.]

roach, *rōch*, *n.* a concave curve in the foot of a square sail.—*v.t.* to arch: to cut short (as a horse's mane): to cut, or cut the hair or mane of, in an upright ridge. [Origin uncertain.]

road (*Shak.*, *Spens.*, &c., **rode**), *rōd*, *n.* (*Shak.*) a ride, horseback journey: (*Shak.*, *Spens.*) a raid, incursion: a track suitable for wheeled traffic, esp. for through communication (often in street-names):

a highway: a roadway: a way of approach: **course**: a mine-passage: (often in *pl.*) a roadstead: (*U.S.*) a railway: journeying: wayfaring, tour: (*coll.*) dismissal: (*Shak.*) a prostitute.—*ns.* **road'-agent**, (*U.S.*) a highwayman; **road'-bed**, the foundation of a railway track: the material laid down to form a road; **road'-book**, a guide-book to the roads of a district.—*adj.* **road'-borne**, carried by road.—*ns.* **road'-bridge**, a bridge carrying a road; **road'-craft**, knowledge and skill useful to wayfarers and drivers; **road'-end'**, the place where a road branches off from another; **road'-hog**, a swinishly selfish or boorishly reckless motorist or other user of the road.—Also *v.i.*—*adj.* **road'-hoggish.**—*ns.* **road'house**, a roadside public-house, refreshment-room, or inn, catering for motorists, cyclists, &c.; **road'-maker**; **road'-making**; **road'man**, one who keeps a road in repair: one who uses the roads, an itinerant; **road'-mender**; **road'-mending**; **road'-metal**, broken stones for roads; **road'-metalling**; **road'-roller**, a heavy roller used on roads; **road'-runner**, the chaparral cock; **road'-scraper**, an implement for clearing roads of loose material; **road'-sense**, aptitude for doing the right thing in driving; **road'side**, the border of a road: wayside.—*adj.* by the side of a road.—*ns.* **roads'man**, a driver: a roadman; **road'stead**, a place near a shore where ships may ride at anchor; **road'ster**, a horse, cycle, or car, suitable for ordinary use on the road: a coach-driver or other traveller by road; **road'-survey'or**, one who supervises roads; **road'way**, the way or part of a road or street used by horses and vehicles; **road'-worthiness.**—*adj.* **road'worthy**, fit for the road.—**in, out of, the** (or one's) **road**, (chiefly *Scot.*) in, out of, the way; **on the road**, travelling, esp. as a commercial traveller or a tramp: on the way to some place; **rule of the road** (see **rule**); **take the road**, to set off, depart; **take to the road**, to become a highwayman. [O.E. *rād*, a riding, raid; cf. **raid**, **ride**.]

roading. See **rode** (3).

roam, *rōm*, *v.i.* to rove about: to ramble.—*v.t.* to wander over: to range.—*n.* a wandering: a ramble.—*n.* **roam'er.** [M.E. *romen*; origin obscure.]

roan, *rōn*, *adj.* bay or dark, with spots of grey and white: of a mixed colour, with a decided shade of red.—*n.* a roan colour: a roan animal, esp. a horse. [O.Fr. *roan* (Fr. *rouan*).]

roan, *rōn*, *n.* grained sheepskin leather.—*adj.* of roan. [Poss. *Roan*, early form of *Rouen*.]

roan. Same as **rone.**

roar, *rōr*, *v.i.* to make a full, loud, hoarse, low-pitched sound, as a lion, fire, wind, the sea, cannon: to bellow: to bawl: to guffaw: to take in breath with a loud noise, as a diseased horse: (*obs.*) to behave in a riotous, bullying, noisy manner: to rush forward with loud noise from the engine.—*v.t.* to utter vociferously.—*n.* a sound of roaring.—*ns.* **roar'er**, one who roars: a horse that roars: (*obs.*) a roaring boy; **roar'ing**, the action of the verb in any sense: a disease of horses marked by roaring.—*adj.* uttering or emitting roars: riotous: proceeding with very great activity or success.—*adv.* **roar'ingly.**—**roaring boy**, (*obs.*) a boisterous bullying reveller, swaggerer, or brawler; **roaring forties**, the tract of stormy west winds south of 40° S. latitude (occasionally also in the Atlantic north of 40° N.); **the roaring game**, curling. [O.E. *rārian*; but partly from M.Du. *roer*, stir, disturbance.]

roast, *rōst*, *v.t.* to cook before a fire: to bake: to parch by heat: to heat strongly: to dissipate the volatile parts of (esp. sulphur) by heat: (*slang*) to banter.—*v.i.* to undergo roasting.—*adj.* roasted.—*n.* a joint, esp. of beef, roasted or to be roasted: an operation of roasting: (*slang*) banter.—*ns.* **roast'-beef**; **roas'ter**, apparatus for roasting: a pig, &c., suitable for roasting: a very hot day.—*n.* and *adj.* **roast'ing.**—*ns.* **roas'ting-jack**, an apparatus for turning a joint in roasting; **roast'-meat.**—**cry roast-meat**, to publish one's good luck foolishly; **roastbeef plant**, the fetid iris (from its smell); **rule the roast** (mistakenly **roost**), to lord it, predominate. [O.Fr. *rostir* (Fr. *rôtir*); of Gmc. origin.]

roate, an old spelling (*Shak.*) of **rote** (1).

rob, *rob*, *v.t.* to deprive wrongfully and forcibly: to steal from: to plunder: to deprive: to take as plunder: to carry off.—*v.i.* to commit robbery:—*pr.p.* **robb′ing**; *pa.t.* and *pa.p.* **robbed.**—*ns.* **robb′er**, one who robs; **robb′er-crab**, a large coconut-eating land-crab of the Indian Ocean: a hermit-crab; **robb′er-fly**, any fly of the Asilidae, large, bristly, insect-eating flies; **robb′ery**, theft from the person, aggravated by violence or intimidation: plundering.—**Robber Council** or **Synod**, a council held at Ephesus in 449, afterwards repudiated, which reinstated Eutyches (from the violence of its proceedings); **rob Peter to pay Paul**, to satisfy or benefit one by depriving another. [O.Fr. *rober*, of Gmc. origin; cf. **reave**, O.H.G. *roubōn*, Ger. *rauben*.]

rob, *rob*, *n.* a fruit syrup. [Ar. *robb*.]

robalo, *rob′a-lō*, *n.* an American pike-like fish (Centropomus), of a family akin to the sea-perches. [Sp. *róbalo*, bass.]

robe, *rōb*, *n.* a gown or loose outer garment: a gown or dress of office, dignity, or state: a rich dress: a woman's dress: (in *pl.*) clothes, garb: a dressed bison hide, or the like.—*v.t.* to dress: to invest in robes.—*v.i.* to assume official vestments.—*ns.* **robe-de-chambre** (*rob-da-shän²-br′*; Fr.), a dressing-gown; **robe′-maker**, a maker of official robes; **rob′ing**, the putting on of robes or clothes: apparel: a trimming on a robe; **rob′ing-room**, room in which official robes may be put on.—**Mistress of the robes**, the head of a department in a queen's household; **the robe**, or **the long robe**, the legal profession. [Fr. *robe*, orig. booty; cf. **rob**, **reave**, O.H.G. *raup* (Ger. *raub*), booty.]

robertsman *rob′ərdz-man*, *n.* (*obs.*) a stout robber.—Also **rob′ertsman.** [App. from **Robert**; allusion unknown.]

robin, *rob′in*, *n.* the redbreast or **rob′in-red′breast** (*Erithacus rubecula*), a widely-spread singing bird with reddish-orange breast: extended to other birds, as a red-breasted thrush of N. America (**American robin**).—*ns.* **Rob′in Good′fellow**, a tricky English domestic spirit or brownie—Puck; **Rob′in-run-(in)-the-hedge**, cleavers or goosegrass: ground-ivy: also various other hedgeside plants. [A familiar form of **Robert**; cf. *Jackdaw*, *Magpie*.]

robin, *rō′bin*, *n.* (*obs.*) trimming on a gown. [robing.]

Robinia, *ro-bin′i-ä*, *n.* the locust or false acacia genus of Papilionaceae. [From its introducer to cultivation, the Paris gardener Jean *Robin* (1550–1629).]

roble, *rō′blå*, *n.* a name for various species of oak, Nothofagus, and other trees. [Sp.,—L. *rōbur*, oak.]

robot, *rō′bot*, *n.* a mechanical man: a more than humanly efficient automaton: an automatic traffic signal. [Czech *robota*, statute labour; from Karel Čapek's play *R.U.R.* (1920).]

roburite, *rō′bər-īt*, *n.* a flameless explosive, chlorinated dinitro-benzene with ammonium nitrate. [L. *rōbur*, strength.]

robust, *rō-bust′*, *adj.* stout, strong, and sturdy: constitutionally healthy: vigorous: thick-set: over-hearty.—*adj.* **robust′ious** (-*yəs*), robust: (*Shak.*) violent: (*Milt.*) strong or rough.—*adv.* **robust′iously.**—*n.* **robust′iousness.**—*adv.* **robust′ly.**—*n.* **robust′ness.** [L. *rōbustus*—*rōbur*, strength, oak.]

roc, *rok*, *n.* a fabulous bird, able to carry off an elephant—also **rok**, **ruc**, **rukh** (*rōōk*). [Pers. *rukh*.]

rocaille, *rō-kā′i*, *n.* artificial rockwork or similar ornament: scroll ornament: rococo. [Fr.]

rocambole, *rok′əm-bōl*, *n.* a plant close akin to garlic. [Fr.]

Roccella, *rok-sel′ä*, *n.* a genus of lichens, yielding archil and litmus. [It. *orcella*, remodelled on *rocca*, rock; see **archil**.]

Rochelle, *rō-shel′*, properly **La Rochelle**, a town of France.—*ns.* **Rochelle′-pow′der**, seidlitz powder; **Rochelle′-salt**, sodium potassium tartrate, discovered in 1672 by Seignette, a *Rochelle* apothecary.

roche moutonnée, *rosh mōō-to-nā*, *n.* a smooth, rounded, hummocky rock-surface due to glaciation:—*pl.* **roches moutonnées** (same pron.). [Fr. *roche*, a rock, *moutonnée*, a kind of wig; applied by De Saussure.]

rochet, *roch′it*, *n.* (*obs.*) a mantle: a close-fitting surplice-like vestment proper to bishops and abbots. [O.Fr., of Gmc. origin; cf. Ger. *rock*, O.E. *rocc*.]

rock, *rok*, *n.* a large outstanding natural mass of stone: (*geol.*) a natural mass of one or more minerals, consolidated or loose: any variety or species of such an aggregate: (*U.S.*) a stone, pebble, lump of rock: a hard sweetmeat made in sticks: (*fig.*) a sure foundation or support, anything immovable, a danger or obstacle: for **rock-fish**, **rock-pigeon**, **Plymouth Rock fowl**: (*U.S. slang*) a coin.—*adj.* of rock: found on, in, or among rocks.—*v.t.* (*U.S. slang*) to stone: to clear of calcareous deposit.—*ns.* **rock′-al′um**, alum prepared from alunite; **rock′-badger**, the Cape hyrax; **rock′-basin**, a lacustrine hollow in rock, excavated by glacier-ice; **rock′-bird**, a puffin or other bird that nests or lives on rocks; **rock′-borer**, any mollusc or other animal that bores into rocks; **rock′-bottom**, bedrock: the very bottom, esp. of poverty or despair.—*adj.* the lowest possible.—*adj.* **rock′-bound**, hemmed in by rock.—*ns.* **rock′-brake**, parsley-fern; **rock′-breaker**, a machine for breaking stones; **rock′-butt′er**, a butter-like exudation from rocks containing alum; **rock′-cake**, a small hard bun with irregular top; **rock′-cod**, a cod found on rocky sea-bottoms: a name for various Australian and other fishes, mostly of the sea-bass family; **rock′-cook**, the small-mouthed wrasse; **rock′-cork**, mountain-cork; **rock′cress**, a cruciferous plant, Arabis; **rock′-crys′tal**, colourless quartz, esp. when well crystallised; **rock′-dove**, a pigeon that nests on rocks, source of the domestic varieties; **rock′-drill**, a tool for boring rock; **rock′er**, **rock′ier**, the rock-dove; **rock′ery**, a heap of rock fragments in a garden, for growing rock-plants; **rock′-fall**, a fall of rock: a mass of fallen rock; **rock′-fish**, any fish that haunts rocks or rocky bottoms: applied as a name to several such fishes, as wrasse, striped bass, black goby; **rock′-flour**, finely divided rock material, such as is found under glaciers.—*adj.* **rock′-forming**, occurring as a dominant constituent of rocks.—*ns.* **rock′-garden**, a garden of rockery, for rock-plants; **rock′-gua′no**, a rock phosphatised by percolations from guano.—*adj.* **rock′-hewn**, hewn out of rock.—*ns.* **rock′-hopper**, a crested penguin; **rock′iness**; **rock′-lark**, the rock-pipit; **rock′-leather**, mountain-leather; **rock′ling**, a small fish of the cod family with barbels on both jaws; **rock′-oil**, petroleum; **rock′-perch**, a scorpion-fish; **rock′-pigeon**, the rock-dove; **rock′-pipit**, a pipit inhabiting rocky coasts; **rock′-plant**, a plant adapted to growing on or among rocks; **rock′-rabb′it**, a hyrax; **rock′-rose**, a plant of either of the genera Cistus and Helianthemum of the family Cistaceae; **rock′-sal′mon**, **rock′-tur′bot**, wolf-fish disguised for the market; **rock′-salt**, salt as a mineral, halite; **rock′-scor′pion**, a person born in Gibraltar (also **rock′-liz′ard**); **rock′-snake**, a python: a krait; **rock′-sparrow**, a genus (Petronia) akin to the true sparrow; **rock′-tar′**, petroleum; **rock′-temple**, a temple hewn out of the solid rock; **rock′-tripe**, an edible arctic lichen of various kinds; **rock′-vi′olet**, a violet-scented alga growing on mountain rocks; **rock′water**, water issuing from a rock; **rock′weed**, bladderwrack or kindred sea-weed growing on rocks; **rock′-wood′**, a wood-like asbestos; **rock′work**, (*archit.*) masonry in imitation of rock: rockery: rock-climbing.—*adj.* **rock′y**, full of rocks: like rock.—**on the rocks**, penniless; **Rock English**, the Gibraltar dialect; **Rock fever**, undulant fever (from Gibraltar); **Rocky Mountain goat**, a white N. American animal intermediate between goat and antelope; **the Rock**, Gibraltar; **the Rockies**, the Rocky Mountains. [O.Fr. *roke*—L.L. *rocca*.]

rock, *rok*, *n.* a distaff.—*n.* **rock′ing**, (*Scot.*) an evening party, orig. for spinning. [M.E. *roc*; cf. M.Du. *rocke*; O.N. *rokkr*; Ger. *rocken*.]

rock, *rok*, *v.t.* and *v.i.* to sway to and fro, tilt from side to side.—*n.* a rocking movement.—*n.* **rock′er**, one who rocks: apparatus that rocks: a curved support on which anything rocks: a rocking-horse: (*U.S.*) a rocking-chair: a mining cradle: a skate with curved blade: a mezzotint engraver's tool for preparing a surface.—*adv.* rock'ily.—*n.* rock'iness.—*n.* and *adj.* rock'ing.—*ns.* rock'ing-chair, a chair mounted on rockers; rock'ing-horse, the figure of a horse mounted on rockers; rock'ing-stone, a logan, or finely poised boulder that can be made to rock; rock'ing-tool, an engraver's tool for roughing a plate; rock'-shaft, in engines, a shaft that oscillates instead of revolving.—*adj.* rock'y, disposed to rock: shaky: tipsy: (*slang*) unpleasant, unsatisfactory.—off one's rocker, out of one's right mind. [O.E. *roccian.*]

rockaway, *rok'ə-wā, n.* an American four-wheeled pleasure carriage, formerly made at *Rockaway*, New Jersey.

rocket, *rok'it, n.* a cylinder full of inflammable material, projected through the air for signalling, carrying a line to a ship in distress, or for firework display: apparatus for propulsion by a backward jet of gas.—*v.i.* to move like a rocket: to fly straight up rapidly when flushed.—*n.* rock'eter. [It. *rocchetta,* of Gmc. origin.]

rocket, *rok'it, n.* a cruciferous salad plant (*Eruca sativa*) of Mediterranean countries: extended to dame's violet (Hesperis) and other plants of the same family (sea'-rocket, Cakile; wall'-rocket, Diplotaxis; yell'ow-rocket, winter-cress, Barbarea) or of other families (blue'-rocket, monk's hood: larkspur; dy'er's-rocket, weld). [O.Fr. *roquette*—L. *ērūca.*]

rococo, *rō-kō'kō, rō-kō-kō', n.* a debased style of architecture, decoration, and furniture-making prevailing in Louis XV.'s time, marked by endless multiplication of ornamental details unrelated to structure, with rockwork, shells, scrolls, and unsymmetrical and broken curves, a lighter, freer, frivolous development of the baroque: any art showing the same spirit.—*adj.* in the style of rococo: florid and tasteless: grotesque: (*obs.*) old-fashioned and queer. [Fr., prob.—*rocaille,* rockwork.]

rocquet, *rok'it, n.* a rochet. [O.Fr., a Northern form of *rochet.*]

rod, *rod, n.* a long straight shoot: a slender stick: a slender bar of metal or other matter: a sceptre or similar emblem of authority: a stick or bunch of twigs as emblem or instrument of punishment: a stick or wand for magic, divination: a riding-crop: a slender pole or structure carrying a fishing-line: a measuring stick: a pole or perch (5½ yards, or 16½ feet): a square pole (272¼ sq. ft.): (of brickwork) 272 sq. ft. of standard thickness of 1½ bricks or 306 cubic ft.: (*B.*) race or tribe: a rod-shaped body of the retina sensitive to light.—*ns.* rod'-fisher; rod'-fishing.—*adjs.* rod'less; rod'like. —*ns.* rod'man, rods'man, one who holds, carries, or uses a rod, esp. an angler; rod'ster, an angler.— a rod in pickle, punishment in reserve; kiss the rod, accept punishment with submission; Napier's rods (see Napierian). [O.E. *rodd*; cf. O.N. *rudda,* club.]

rode, *rōd, pa.t.* of ride.

rode, *rōd, n.* (*Spens., Shak.*) an old spelling of road. —*n.* (*Shak.*) rode'way.

rode, *rōd, v.i.* to fly in the evening, esp. of woodcock.—*n.* rōd'ing, road'ing, a woodcock's evening flight. [Origin obscure.]

rodent, *rō'dənt, adj.* gnawing: of the Rodentia.—*n.* a member of the Rodentia.—*n.pl.* Rodentia (-*den'shä, -shyä*), an order of mammals with prominent incisor teeth and no canines, as squirrels, beavers, rats, rabbits. [L. *rōdēns, -entis,* pr.p. of *rōdĕre,* to gnaw.]

rodeo, *rō-dā'ō, n.* a place where cattle are assembled: a round-up of cattle: an exhibition of cowboy skill. [Sp.,—*rodar,* to go round—L. *rotāre,* to wheel.]

rodomontade, *rod-ō-mon-tād', n.* extravagant boasting, like that of *Rodomonte* in Ariosto's *Orlando Furioso.*—*v.i.* to bluster or brag.—*n.* rodomontā'der.

roe, *rō, n.* a mass of fish-eggs (also *hard roe*): sometimes milt (*soft roe*).—*adj.* roed, containing roe.— *n.* roe'stone, oolite. [M.E. *rowe*; cf. O.N. *hrogn,* M.H.G. *roge,* Ger. *rogen.*]

roe, *rō, n.* a small species of deer: sometimes applied to the female red deer.—*ns.* roe'-buck, the male roe; roe'buck-berry, roe'-blackberry, the stone-bramble; roe'-deer, a roe. [O.E. *rá, ráha*; Ger. *reh,* Du. *ree.*]

Roe (Richard). See Doe (John).

Roentgen. See Röntgen.

rogation, *rō-gā'shən, n.* an asking: supplication.— *adj.* rogatory (*rog'ə-tə-ri*).—letters rogatory (see letter); Rogation Days, the three days before Ascension Day, when supplications were recited in procession; Rogation flower, the milkwort, which was carried in Rogation Day processions; Rogation Sunday, that before Ascension Day; Rogation Week, the week in which the Rogation Days occur. [L. *rogātiō, -ōnis*—*rogāre,* to ask.]

Roger, *roj'ər, n.* a man's personal name: (*cant*) a goose.—Jolly Roger, the pirates' skull-and-crossbones flag; (Sir) Roger de Coverley (*də-kuv'ər-li*), an English country-dance (whence the name of the *Spectator* character). [Fr., of Gmc. origin, equivalent to O.E. *Hróthgár.*]

rogue, *rōg, n.* a vagrant: a rascal: a wag: a mischievous person (often playfully or affectionately): a plant that falls short of a standard, or is of a different type from the rest of the crop: a sport, or variation from type: a horse that shirks: a savage elephant or other animal cast out or withdrawn from its herd.—*v.i.* to play the rogue.—*v.t.* to cheat: to eliminate rogues from.—*ns.* rogue'-el'ephant; rogue'-money, a former assessment in Scotland for the expense of catching, prosecuting, and maintaining rogues; roguery (*rōg'ər-i*), knavish tricks: fraud: mischievousness: waggery; rogue'ship. —*adjs.* roguing (*rōg'ing*), roaming, or behaving like a rogue; roguish (*rōg'ish*), knavish: mischievous: waggish: villainous: confounded.— *adv.* rog'uishly.—*n.* rog'uishness.—*adj.* rog'uy (*obs.*).—rogues' gallery, a police collection of photographs of criminals; rogues' Latin, cant; rogues' march, derisive music played at a drumming-out. [Cant; origin unknown.]

roil, *roil* (also rile, *ril*), *v.t.* to make turbid: to annoy, irritate (now usu. rile).—*adj.* roil'y, turbid. [Origin doubtful.]

roin, roinish. Same as royne, roynish.

roister, royster, *rois'tər, n.* a blusterer: a noisy reveller.—*v.i.* to bluster, swagger: to revel noisily. —*v.i.* roist, royst (back-formation from the n.), to roister.—*n.* rois'terer, roys'terer.—*adj.* rois'-terous, roys'terous.—*adj.* rois'ting, roys'ting, blustering, boisterous: (*Shak.*) rousingly defiant. [O.Fr. *rustre,* a rough, rude fellow—O.Fr. *ruste*— L. *rusticus,* rustic.]

rok. Same as roc.

roke, *rōk. n.* vapour: steam: mist: small rain: smoke.—*v.t.* and *v.i.* to steam: to smoke.—*adj.* rōk'y. [Perh. Scand.]

rokelay, rocklay, *rok'(ə)-lā, n.* (*Scot.*) a woman's short cloak, worn in the 18th century. [Fr. *roquelaire*; see roquelaure.]

roker, *rōk'ər, n.* any ray other than skate, esp. the thornback. [Perh. Dan. *rokke,* Sw. *rocka,* ray.]

Roland, *rō'lənd, n.* a hero of the Charlemagne legend: hence a hero: a worthy match (with allusion to Oliver).—a Roland for an Oliver, tit for tat: as good as one got.

rôle, role, *rōl, n.* a part played by an actor or other: a function. [Fr.]

roll, *rōl, n.* a scroll: a sheet of paper, parchment, cloth, or other material bent spirally upon itself into a nearly cylindrical form: a document in such form: a register: a list, esp. of names: a spirally wound cake, or one of dough turned over to enclose other material: a small loaf: a revolving cylinder: a roller: a more or less cylindrical package, mass, or pad: a cylindrical moulding: a volute: a bookbinder's tool with a small wheel for impressing designs: a part turned over in a curve: an act of rolling: a swaying about an axis in the direction of motion: a continuous reverberatory or trilling sound: an undulation: a wavelike flow.—*v.i.* to move like a ball, a wheel, a wheeled vehicle, or a passenger in one: to perform revolutions: to sway on an axis in the direction of motion: to turn over or from side to side: to swagger: to wallow: to go with a roll : to move in, on, or like waves : to flow : to undulate : to wander : to sound with a roll : to use a roller : to curl.—*v.t.* to cause to roll : to turn on an axis : to move with a circular sweep (as the eyes) : to wrap round on itself : to enwrap : to curl : to wind : to drive forward : to move upon wheels : to press, flatten, spread out, thin, or smooth with a roller or between rollers : to round by attrition : to beat rapidly, as a drum : to rumble : to peal : to trill : to pour in waves : (*Scot.*, of a clock) to wind.—*adj.* **roll′-about′**, podgy. —*ns.* **roll′-call**, the calling of a list of names, to ascertain attendance ; **roll′-collar**, a collar of a garment turned back in a curve.—*adj.* **rolled.**— *ns.* **roll′er**, one who or that which rolls : a revolving or rolling cylinder : a contrivance including a heavy cylinder or cylinders for flattening roads or turf : a long, coiled-up bandage (**roll′er-band′age**) : a long heavy wave : a small solid wheel : a kind of tumbler pigeon : a bird (Coracias) of a family akin to the kingfishers, with a habit of flight like a tumbler pigeon (Ger. *roller*) : a kind of canary with a soft trilling song ; **roll′er-skate**, a skate with wheels instead of a blade.—Also *v.i.*— *ns.* **roll′er-skat′er**; **roll′er-skat′ing**; **roll′er-tow′el**, an endless towel on a roller.—*n.* and *adj.* **roll′ing.**—*ns.* **roll′ing-mill**, a factory or machine for rolling metal into various shapes between rolls ; **roll′ing-pin**, a cylinder for rolling dough ; **roll′ing-stock**, the stock or store of engines and vehicles that run upon a railway.—*adjs.* **roll′-top**, having a flexible cover of slats that rolls up ; **roll′-up**, suitable for rolling up.—**a rolling stone gathers no moss**, a rover does not grow rich ; **Master of the Rolls**, the head of the Record Office ; **rolled gold**, metal coated with gold and rolled very thin ; **roll up**, (*coll.*) to assemble, arrive. [O.Fr. *rolle* (n.), *roller* (vb.)—L. *rotula*, dim. of *rota*, a wheel.]

rollick, *rol′ik*, *n.* to behave in a careless, swaggering, frolicsome manner.—*adj.* **roll′icking**. [Origin unknown.]

rollock. See **rowlock**.

roly-poly, *rōl′i-pōl′i*, *n.* a pudding made of a sheet of paste, covered with jam or fruit, and rolled up : a round, podgy person : an old game in which balls are bowled into holes or thrown into hats placed on the ground.—*adj.* round, podgy. [Prob. **roll**.]

rom, rom, *n.* a gypsy man. [Romany, man, husband.]

romage, *rum′ij*, *n.* (*Shak.*) tumult. [**rummage**.]

Romaic, *rō-mā′ik*, *n.* and *adj.* modern Greek.—*n.* **romā′ika**, a modern Greek dance. [Mod. Gr. *Rhōmaikos*, Roman (i.e. of the Eastern Roman Empire)—*Rhōmē*, Rome.]

romal, *rō-mäl′*, **rumal**, *rōō-mäl′*, *n.* a handkerchief : a head-cloth. [Pers. *rūmāl—rū*, face, *māl*, wiping.]

Roman, *rō′mən*, *adj.* pertaining to Rome, esp. ancient Rome, its people, or the empire founded by them : pertaining to the Roman Catholic religion, papal : (of type) of the ordinary upright kind (indicated in proofs by *rom.*), as opp. to *italics* : (of numerals) written in letters (as IV, iv), opp. to *Arabic* : (of handwriting) round and bold : (of a nose) highbridged.—*n.* a native or citizen of Rome : a Roman Catholic : Roman letter or type.—*adj.* **Romanic** (*rō-man′ik*), of Roman or Latin origin : Romance. —*n.* the Romance language or languages collectively.—*n.* **Romanisation** (*rō-mə-nī-zā′shən*).— *v.t.* **Ro′manise**, to make Roman or Roman Catholic : to bring under Roman or Roman Catholic influence : to represent by the Roman alphabet.—*v.i.* to accept Roman or Roman Catholic ways, laws, doctrines, &c. : to become Roman Catholic.—*n.* **Romani′ser**.—*adj.* **Ro′manish**, (in hostility) Roman Catholic : savouring of Roman Catholicism.—*ns.* **Ro′manism**, Roman Catholicism ; **Ro′manist**, a Roman Catholic : one versed in Romance philology or Roman law or antiquities. —*adj.* Roman Catholic.—*adj.* **Romanist′ic.**—*in composition* **Romano-** (*rō-mā′nō*), Roman : Romanised : Roman and (as **Roma′no-Brit′ish**).— **Roman candle**, a firework discharging a succession of white or coloured stars ; **Roman Catholic**, recognising the spiritual supremacy of the Pope or Bishop of Rome : a member of the Roman Catholic Church ; **Roman Catholicism**, the doctrines and polity of the Roman Catholic Church collectively ; **Roman cement**, a hydraulic cement made from calcareous nodules from the London Clay ; **Roman Empire**, the ancient empire of Rome, divided in the 4th century into the Eastern and Western Empires (see also **Holy**) ; **Roman law**, the system of law developed by the ancient Romans—civil law ; **Roman nettle**, a nettle, rare in Britain, with female flowers in heads, traditionally introduced by the Romans ; **Roman snail**, the edible snail (*Helix pomatia*), much valued by the Romans. [L. *Rōmānus—Rōma*, Rome.]

Romance, *rō-mans′*, *n.* a general name for the vernaculars that developed out of popular Latin—French, Provençal, Italian, Spanish, Portuguese, Rumanian, Romansch, with their various dialects. —Also *adj.*—*n.* **romance′**, a tale of chivalry, orig. one in verse, written in one of these vernaculars : any fictitious and wonderful tale : a fictitious narrative in prose or verse which passes beyond the limits of ordinary life : a Spanish historical ballad : romantic fiction as a literary genre : a romantic occurrence or series of occurrences : a love affair, (journalistically) esp. any affair involving a marriage between different social classes : romantic atmosphere or feeling : a leaning towards the romantic : an imaginative lie : romanticism : (*mus.*) a composition of romantic character.—*v.i.* to write or tell romances : to talk extravagantly or with an infusion of fiction : to lie : to build castles in the air.—*n.* **roman′cer.**—*adj.* **roman′cical**, (*Lamb*) dealing with romance.—*n.* and *adj.* **roman′cing**. [O.Fr. *romanz*—(hypothetical) L.L. *rōmānicē* (adv.), in (popular) Roman language.]

Romanesque, *rō-mən-esk′*, *adj.* of the transition from Roman to Gothic architecture, characterised by round arches and vaults.—*n.* the Romanesque style, art, or architecture. [Fr.]

Romansch, Romansh, R(o)umansch, Rumonsch, *rō-, rōō-mänsh′*, *-monsh′*, *n.* and *adj.* Rhaeto-Romanic : sometimes confined to the Upper Rhine dialects. [Romansch.]

romantic, *rō-man′tik*, *adj.* pertaining to, of the nature of, inclining towards, or savouring of, romance : fictitious : extravagant, wild : fantastic. —*adj.* **roman′tical.**—*n.* **romantical′ity.**—*adv.* **roman′tically.**—*ns.* **roman′ticism** (*-sizm*), romantic quality, feeling, tendency, principles, or spirit ; **roman′ticist.**—**Romantic Revival**, the late eighteenth-century and early nineteenth-century revolt against classicism or neo-classicism to a more picturesque, original, free, and imaginative style in literature and art. [Fr. *romantique*—O.Fr. *romant*, romance.]

Romany, Rommany, *rom′ə-ni*, *n.* a gypsy (also **Rom′anes**, *-nes*) : the language of the gypsies.— *adj.* gypsy.—**Romany rye** (*rī*), a gentleman who affects the society of gypsies. [Gypsy *rom*, man.]

romaunt, *rō-mavnt′*, *n.* (*arch.*) a romance. [O.Fr. *romant* ; see **romance**.]

Rome, *rōm*, formerly *rōōm*, *n.* the capital of the Roman Empire, now of Italy : often used for the Roman Catholic Church or Roman Catholicism.— *ns.* **Rome′-penny, -scot**, (*obs.*) Peter's penny ; **Rome′-runner**, (*obs.*) a self-seeking cleric who had much resort to Rome.—*adj.* and *adv.* **Rome′ward** —*adv.* **Rome′wards.**—*n.* **Rōm′ic**, a phonetic notation devised by Henry Sweet, based upon the original Roman values of the letters.—*adj.* **Rōm′ish** (hostile) Roman Catholic : (*obs.*) Roman. [L *Rōma*.]

romp, *romp*, *v.i.* to frolic actively : to move along easily and quickly, esp. in winning a race.—*n.* one esp. a girl, who romps : a tomboy : a vigorous frolic : a swift easy run.—*n.* **romp′er**, one who romps : (usu. in *pl.*) a child's garb for play.—*adv.* **romp′ingly.**—*adj.* **romp′ish.**—*adv.* **romp′ishly** —*n.* **romp′ishness**. [ramp.]

roncador, *rong-kə-dōr′*, *n.* a name for various American fishes, esp. of the maigre family, from the sound they emit. [Sp., snorer.]

rondache, *ron-dâsh′*, *n.* a buckler. [Fr.]

ronde, *rond*, *n.* a script printing-type. [Fr., *round* (*fem.*).]

rondeau, *ron′dō, ronʹ-dō, n.* a form of poem characterised by closely-knit rhymes and a refrain, and, as defined in the 17th century, consisting of thirteen lines, divided into three unequal strophes, not including the burden (repeating the first few words) after the eighth and thirteenth lines—brought into vogue by Swinburne: (*mus.*) a rondo:—*pl.* **ron′-deaux** (*-dōz*).—*ns.* **ron′del**, a verse-form of thirteen or fourteen lines on two rhymes, the seventh and thirteenth being identical with the first, and the eighth and (if present) the fourteenth with the second; **rondino** (*-dē′nō*; It. dim.), a short rondo:—*pl.* **rondi′nos**; **ron′do** (It., from Fr.), a musical composition whose principal subject recurs in the same key in alternation with other subjects, often the last movement of a sonata:—*pl.* **ron′dos**; **rondolet′to**, a short rondo. [Fr. *rondeau*, earlier *rondel*—*rond*, round.]

rondure, *rond′yər*, a Shakespearian form of **roundure**. [Origin unknown.]

rone, roan, rhone, *rōn, n.* (*Scot.*) a roof-gutter. [Origin unknown.]

rong, *rong* (*Spens.*), *p.t.* of **ring**.

ronne, ronning (*Spens.*). Same as **run** (*infin.* and *pa.p.*), **running**.

ront, ronte (*Spens.*). Same as **runt**.

Röntgen, Roentgen, *rənt′yən, ront′, runt′*, also *-gen, adj.* of the German physicist Konrad von Röntgen (1845–1923), discoverer of the **Röntgen rays**, or X-rays (see **X**).—*v.t.* **Rönt′genise**, to treat by the Röntgen rays.—*ns.* **Röntgenog′raphy**, photography by these rays; **Röntgenol′ogy**, the study of the rays; **Röntgenos′copy**, observation by means of them; **Röntgenother′apy**, healing by means of them.

ronyon, runnion, *run′yən, n.* (*Shak.*) a term of reproach to a woman. [Some connect with Fr. *rogne*, mange.]

rood, *rōōd, n.* Christ's cross: a cross or crucifix, esp. at the entrance to a church chancel: (locally) a rod, pole, or perch, linear or square (with variations in value): the fourth part of an acre, or forty square poles.—*ns.* **rood′-beam**, a beam for supporting the rood; **Rood Day (Holy-rood Day, Rood-mas Day)**, the feast of the Exaltation (14th September) or of the Invention (3rd May) of the Cross; **rood′-loft**, a gallery over the rood-screen; **rood′-screen**, an ornamental partition separating choir from nave; **rood′-steeple, -tower**, that over the crossing of a church; **rood′-tree**, (*obs.*) Christ's cross. [O.E. *rōd*, gallows, cross.]

roof, *rōōf, n.* the top covering of a building or vehicle: a ceiling: the overhead surface, structure, or stratum of a vault, arch, cave, excavation, &c.: the upper covering of the mouth (the palate) or of any cavity: a dwelling: a culmination: a high or highest plateau (as *the roof of the world*, the Pamir): an upper limit: an aeroplane's ceiling or limiting height:—*pl.* **roofs**.—*v.t.* to cover with a roof: to shelter.—*n.* **roof′-board**, a board lying under slates or tiles.—*adj.* **roofed**.—*ns.* **roof′er**, one who makes or mends roofs: a roof-board; **roof′-garden**, a garden on a flat roof; **roof′-guard**, a device to prevent snow from sliding off a roof; **roof′ing**, covering with a roof: materials for a roof: the roof itself: shelter.—*adj.* for roofing.—*adjs.* **roof′less**; **roof′like**.—*ns.* **roof′-plate**, a wall-plate that receives the lower ends of the rafters of a roof; **roof′-tree**, the ridge-pole: the roof.—*adj.* **roof′y**, having a roof or roofs. [O.E. *hróf*; Du. *roef*.]

rooinek, *rō′i-nek, n.* a Boer nickname for an Englishman. [Cape Du., red neck—Du. *rood, nek*, from his complexion.]

rook, *rook, n.* a gregarious species of crow: a sharper: (*obs.*) a simpleton.—*v.t.* to fleece.—*n.* **rook′ery**, a breeding-place of rooks in a group of trees: a breeding-place of penguins, or seals, &c.: a crowded cluster of mean tenements: an evil resort: (*slang* or *dial.*) a disturbance.—*adjs.* **rook′ish**; **rook′y**, (*Shak.*) abounding in rooks: or poss. black, murky (see **roky**). [O.E. *hróc.*]

rook, *rook, n.* a castle in chess. [O.Fr. *roc*—Pers. *rukh*.]

rook, *rook* (*Shak.*). Same as **ruck** (2).

rookie, rooky, *rook′i, n.* (*slang*) a raw beginner: a callow recruit. [App. from **recruit**.]

room, *rōōm, room, n.* space: necessary or available space: space unoccupied: opportunity, scope, or occasion: stead: a particular place: (*obs.*) an assigned place, as in a theatre: (*B.*) a seat: appointment, office: (*obs.*) a holding of land: a compartment: a chamber: a cottage sitting-room: company in a room.—*v.t.* and *v.i.* (chiefly *U.S.*) to lodge: to share a room or rooms (with *with*). — *adj.* **roomed**, having rooms. — *ns.* **room′er**, (*U.S.*) a lodger, usu. taking meals elsewhere; **room′-fellow**, one who shares a room; **room′ful**, as much or as many as a room will hold:—*pl.* **room′fuls**. — *adv.* **room′ily**. — *ns.* **room′iness**; **room′ing-house**, (*U.S.*) a house with furnished rooms to let; **room′-mate**, (*U.S.*) a fellow-lodger. —*adjs.* **room′-ridden**, confined to one's room; **room′some**, roomy; **room′y**, having ample room: wide: spacious. [O.E. *rúm*; Ger. *raum*, Du. *ruim*.]

roon, *rən, n.* **rund**, *run*(*d*), *rən*(*d*), *n.* (*Scot.*) a list or selvage: a strip or thread of cloth.—Also (*Galt*) **royne** (*roin*).

roop, *rōōp, v.i.* (*Scot.*) to make a hoarse sound.—*n.* a hoarse sound: hoarseness.—*adjs.* **roop′it, roop′y**, (*Scot.*) hoarse. [Variant of **roup**.]

roose, *rōōz*, (*Scot.*) *rəz, v.t.* (*dial.*) to praise. [M.E. *rosen*—O.N. *hrósa*, to praise.]

roost, *rōōst, n.* a perch or place for a sleeping bird: a henhouse: a sleeping-place: bed: a set of fowls resting together: (*Scot.*) a loft or garret or its roof.—*v.i.* to settle or sleep on a roost or perch: to perch: to go to rest for the night.—*n.* **roost′er**, a domestic cock.—**come home to roost**, recoil upon oneself. [O.E. *hróst*; Du. *roest.*]

roost, *rōōst, n.* (*Orkney and Shetland*) a tidal race. [O.N. *röst.*]

root, *rōōt, n.* ordinarily and popularly, the underground part of a plant, esp. when edible: (*bot.*) that part of a higher plant which never bears leaves or reproductive organs, ordinarily underground and descending, and serving to absorb salts in solution, but often above-ground, often arising from other parts, often serving other functions, though morphologically comparable: the source, cause, basis, foundation, occasion of anything, as an ancestor, an element from which words are derived: an embedded or basal part, as of a tooth, a hair, a dam: a growing plant with its root: (*math.*) the factor of a quantity which, taken so many times, produces that quantity: any value of the unknown quantity for which an equation is true: (*mus.*) the fundamental note on which a chord is built.—*v.i.* to fix the root: to be firmly established: to develop a root.—*v.t.* to plant in the earth: to implant deeply: to fix by the root: to uproot (usu. with *up*): to remove entirely by uprooting, clear away, eradicate, extirpate (usu. with *out*).—*n.* **root′age**, the act of striking root: state of being rooted: roothold: root-system.—*adj.* and *adv.* **root′-and-branch′**, without leaving any part.—*n.* **root′-beer**, a drink made from roots of dandelion, sassafras, &c.—*adj.* **root′-bound**, (*Milt.*) rooted to the ground: potbound.—*ns.* **root′-cap**, a sheath of cells at the tip of a root; **root′-cause**, fundamental cause; **root′-climber**, a plant that climbs by means of roots, as ivy; **root′-crop**, a crop of esculent roots; **root′-eater**.—*adj.* **root′ed**, having roots: fixed by roots, or as by roots: firmly established.—*adv.* **root′edly**.—*ns.* **root′edness**; **root′-er**.—*adjs.* **root′-fallen**, fallen by roots giving way; **root′-fast**, firmly rooted.—*ns.* **root′-hair**, a fine tubular outgrowth from a cell by which a young root absorbs water; **root′hold**, maintenance of position by roots: a footing; **root′-house**, a summer-house built of roots: a storehouse for potatoes, &c.; **root′-knot**, an enlargement of a root caused by a nematode.—*adj.* **root′less**.—*ns.* **root′let**, a little root; **root′-par′asite**, a plant parasitic on a root; **root′-pressure**, an upward forcing of sap, shown by the bleeding of plants.—*v.t.* **root′-prune**, to prune the roots of.—*ns.* **root′-pruning**; **root′-rubb′er**, rubber got from the roots of certain African apocynaceous plants;

root'-sheath, the sheath of the root of an orchid, a hair, a feather, &c.; **root'-stock**, *(bot.)* rhizome, esp. if short, thick, and more or less erect: a source, ancestral form; **root'-sys'tem**; **root'-tu'bercle**, a swelling on a root, inhabited by symbiotic bacteria. —*adj.* **root'y**, abounding in, consisting of, or like roots: rank.—**strike**, **take**, **root**, to root, to become established. [Late O.E. *rót*—O.N. *rót*; Dan. *rod*; Goth. *waurts*, O.E. *wyrt*.]

root, earlier **wroot**, *rōōt*, *v.t.* to turn up with the snout.—*v.i.* to grub: to poke about: to rummage: *(U.S.)* to shout or applaud as a partisan—*n.* **root'er**.—*n.* and *adj.* **root'ing**.—*v.t.* and *v.i.* **root'le**, to grub. [O.E. *wrótan*—*wrót*, a snout; see also **rout** (3).]

rooty, *rōōt'i*, *n. (mil. slang)* bread. [Urdu *roti*, loaf.]

rope, *rōp*, *n.* a thick twisted cord, technically, one over an inch in thickness: a string of pearls, onions, &c.: a glutinous stringy formation: a local lineal measure, 20 feet.—*v.t.* to fasten, bind, enclose, mark off, or *(U.S.* and *Austr.)* catch with a rope: *(horse-racing)* to hold back to avoid winning.—*v.i.* to form into a rope.—*adj.* **roped** *(rōpt)*.—*ns.* **rope'-dance**, a tight-rope performance; **rope'-danc'er**; **rope'-drilling**, boring by a drill worked by a rope; **rope'-house**, a storehouse for ropes: a house where salt is crystallised from brine trickling along ropes; **rope'-ladder**, a ladder of ropes; **rope'-machine**; **rope'-maker**; **rope'-making**; **rō'per**, a rope-maker: one who ropes a horse: a decoy (also **ro'per-in').**—*adj.* **rope'-ripe**, deserving to be hanged.—*n.* **rōp'ery**, ropework: knavery.—*v.t.* **rope's-end'**, to beat with a rope's end.—*adj.* **rope'-soled**, having a sole of rope.—*ns.* **rope'-stitch**, work in stitches laid diagonally side by side; **rope'-trick**, a disappearing trick with a rope: *(Shak.)* poss. a rhetorical figure, or, acc. to some, a trick deserving the gallows; **rope'-walk**, a long narrow shed or alley for rope-spinning; **rope'-walker**, a tight-rope performer; **rope'way**, a means of transmission by ropes; **rope'work**, a rope-walk or rope factory: a system of ropes; **rope'-yarn**, yarn for making ropes, or got by untwisting ropes.—*adv.* **rōp'ily**.—*n.* **rōp'iness**.—*n.* and *adj.* **rōp'ing**.—*adj.* **rō'py**, stringy: glutinous: wrinkled like loops of rope: *(slang)* bad of its kind. —**give one rope** (to hang himself), to allow a person full scope to defeat his own ends; **know the ropes** (see **know**); **on the high ropes**, elated: arrogant; **rope in**, bring in, enlist (esp. one who has some reluctance); **rope's end**, the end of a rope used for flogging; **ropes of sand**, a bond with no cohesion. [O.E. *ráp*; O.N. *reip*, Ger. *reif*.]

Roquefort, *rok'for*, *n.* a cheese orig. made (of ewe's milk) at *Roquefort* in France.

roquelaure, *rok'∂-lōr*, *n.* a man's short cloak worn in the 18th and early 19th century. [Fr., after the Duc de *Roquelaure* (1656-1738).]

roquet, *rō'kā*, *n.* in croquet, a stroke by which the player's ball strikes an opponent's.—*v.t.* to strike by a roquet.—*v.i.* to play a roquet.—*n.* **roque** *(rōk)*, an American game, a modification of croquet. [Prob. formed from **croquet**.]

rore, *rōr*, an obs. spelling *(Shak.)* of **roar** (tumult).

roric, *rō'rik*, **rorid**, *rō'rid*, **roral**, *rō'rəl*, *adjs.* dewy. [L. *rōs*, *rōris*, dew.]

rorqual, *ror'kwəl*, *n.* any whale of the genus Balaenoptera (finback). [Fr.,—Norw. *röyrkval*, lit. red whale.]

rorty, *ror'ti*, *adj. (slang)* gay.—*ns.* **rort** *(Austr.)*, a racket; **ror'ter** *(Austr.)*, a spiv. [Ety. dub.]

Rosa, *rō'zä* (L. *ros'ā*), *n.* the rose genus, giving name to the family Rosā'ceae.—*n.* **rosace** *(rō-zäs'*, *-zäs'*; Fr.; *archit.)*, a rosette: a rose-window.—*adj.* **rosaceous** *(rō-zā'shəs)*, of the rose family: roselike.—*ns.* **rosā'rian**, a rose-fancier; **rosā'rium**, a rose-garden: a rosary *(rō'zər-i)*, a rose-garden or rose-bed (also **ro'sery**): *(obs.)* a chaplet: a series of prayers: a string of beads used by Roman Catholics as a guide to devotions.—*adj.* **ro'seate** *(-zi-it, -zi-āt)*, rosy: rose-scented: of roses: unduly favourable or sanguine. [L. *rōsa*, rose; *rosārium*, rose-garden; *rosaceus*, *roseus*, rosy.]

rosaker, *ros-ā'kər*, **resalgar**, *res-al'gər*, obs. variants of realgar.

rosalia, *rō-zā'lyä*, *n. (mus.)* a series of repetitions of the same passage, each a tone higher. [Said to be from an Italian folksong, *Rosalia cara mia*.]

rosaniline, *rō-zan'i-lin, -lēn, -lin*, *n.* a base derived from aniline, with red salts used in dyeing. [**rose**, **aniline**.]

rosary. See **Rosa**.

rosa-solis, *rō-zä-sō'lis*, *n. (obs.)* the sundew: a cordial, orig. flavoured with sundew juice, afterwards with various spices. [Orig. L. *rōs sōlis*, dew of the sun, altered to *rōsa*, rose.]

roscid, *ros'id*, *adj.* dewy. [L. *rōscidus*—*rōs*, dew.]

Roscius, *rosh'i-əs* (L. *rōs'ki-oos)*, *n.* a famous Roman actor *(d.* 62 B.C.): hence, a great actor.—*adj.* **Rosc'ian**. [L. *Rōscius*.]

rose, *pa.t.* of **rise**.

rose, *rōz*, *n.* the flower of any species of the genus Rosa: the shrub bearing it, generally prickly, with white, yellow, pink, or red flowers, numerous stamens and carpels, achenes enclosed in the receptacle: extended to various flowers or plants, some with little resemblance to the true rose (see, e.g., under **Christmas**, **guelder-**, **rose**, **rock)**: a paragon: a rosette, esp. on a shoe: a rose-cut stone: a rose-window: a perforated nozzle: the typical colour of the rose—pink or light crimson: the pink glow of the cheeks in health: erysipelas. —*adj.* of, for, or like the rose or roses: rose-coloured.—*v.t.* to make like a rose, in colour or scent.—*adj.* **roseal** *(rō'zi-əl)*, roselike.—*ns.* **rose'-apple**, an E. Indian tree of the clove genus: its edible fruit; **rose'-bay**, the oleander (**rose-bay laurel**, **rose-laurel)**: any rhododendron: a willow-herb (**rose-bay willow-herb)** common where woods have been felled; **rose'-beetle**, the rose-chafer: the rose-bug; **rose'-bowl**, an ornamental bowl for cut flowers; **rose'-bud**; **rose'-bug**, an American beetle that eats roses; **rose'-bush**; **rose'-camp'ion**, a garden species of campion *(Lychnis coronaria)*; **rose'-chafer**, a beetle *(Cetonia aurata)* that eats roses.—*adj.* **rose'-cheeked**.—*n.* **rose'-colour**, pink.—*adj.* **rose'-col'oured**, pink: seeing or representing things in too favourable a light.—*n.* **rose'-comb**, a fowl's low tubercled comb.—*adj.* **rose'-combed**.—*n.* **rose'-cross**, a cross within a circle: a Rosicrucian. —*adj.* **rose'-cut**, cut in nearly hemispherical form, with flat base and many small facets rising to a low point above.—*adj.* **rosed**, *(Shak.)* flushed: having a rose or roses.—*ns.* **rose'-di'amond**, a rose-cut diamond; **rose'-drop**, a rose-flavoured sweet: a red eruption on the nose; **rose'-el'der**, the guelder-rose; **rose'-en'gine**, an apparatus for engine-turning; **rose'-fish**, the bergylt; **rose'-garden**; **rose'-hip**, the fruit of the rose.—*adj.* **rose'-hued**.—*ns.* **rose'-knot**, a rosette of ribbon or the like; **rose'-lau'rel**, oleander; **rose'-leaf**, the leaf of a rose: usu. a rose-petal.—*adjs.* **rose'less**; **rose'like**; **rose'-lipped**, having red lips.—*ns.* **rose'-mallow**, hollyhock: hibiscus; **rose'-no'ble**, an old English gold coin with the figure of a rose.—*adj.* **rose'-pink**, rose-coloured: sentimental.—*n.* a pink colour: a pink pigment.—*ns.* **rose'-quartz**, a rose-coloured quartz; **rose'-rash**, roseola.—*adj.* **rose'-red**, red as a rose.—*ns.* **rose'-root**, a stonecrop *(Sedum roseum)* with rose-scented root; **rō'sery**, a rose-garden (cf. **rosary)**; **rose'-tō'paz**, a topaz coloured pink by heat; **rose'-tree**, a standard rose; **rose'-wa'ter**, water distilled from rose-leaves.—*adj.* sentimental: superfine.—*ns.* **rose'-win'dow**, a circular window with radiating compartments; **rose'wood**, the valuable heavy dark-coloured wood of many trees, notably Brazilian and Indian species of Dalbergia (Papilionaceae), said to smell of roses when fresh-cut; **rose'-wood-oil**, oil of rhodium *(cf.* **rose'zhar**; *Spens.* **rosiere**, *rō-zi-ār'*, *-ēr'*; Fr. *rosier)*, a rose tree or bush.—*adv.* **rō'sily**.—*n.* **rō'siness**.—*adj.* **rō'sy**, of or abounding in roses: roselike: rose-red: blooming: blushing: bright, hopeful, promising. —*n. (old slang)* wine.—*v.t.* and *v.i.* to redden.—*adjs.* **rō'sy-bos'omed**; **rō'sy-cheeked**; **rō'sy-col'oured**.—*n.* **rō'sy-drop**, rose-drop.—*adjs.* **rō'sy-fing'ered**, Homer's favourite epithet *(rhododaktylos)* of the dawn; **rō'sy-foot'ed.—rose of**

Jericho, a cruciferous plant (*Anastatica hierochuntica*) of N. Africa and Syria, that curls in a ball in drought ; **rose of Sharon**, (*Song of Solomon*) probably a narcissus : now applied to a species of hibiscus ; **rosy cross**, the emblem at the Rosicrucians ; **under the rose**, in confidence ; **Wars of the Roses**, a disastrous dynastic struggle in England (1455-85), between the Houses of Lancaster and York, from their emblems, the red and the white rose. [O.E. *róse*—L. *rŏsa*, prob.—Gr. *rhŏdeā*, a rose-bush, *rhodon*, rose.]

rosella, *rō-zel'ä*, *n.* a handsome Australian parrakeet, first observed at Rose Hill near Sydney. [For *rosehiller*.]

roselle, rozelle, *rō-zel'*, *n.* an East Indian hibiscus.

rosemary, *rōz'mə-ri*, *n.* a small fragrant pungent Mediterranean labiate shrub (Rosmarinus). [L. *rōs marīnus*, sea dew.]

roseola, *rō'zē'ə-lä*, *n.* rose-coloured rash : German measles. [Dim. from L. *roseus*, rosy.]

roset, rosit, rozet, rozit, *roz'it*, *n.* (*Scot.*) rosin.—*v.t.* to rosin.—*adj.* **ros'ety** (sometimes **ros'etty**), &c. [rosin.]

rosette, *rō-zet'*, *n.* a knot of radiating loops of ribbon or the like in concentric arrangement : a close radiating group of leaves, usu. pressed to the ground : (*archit.*) a rose-shaped ornament : any structure, arrangement, or figure of similar shape : a curve whose polar equation is $r = a \sin m\theta$: a disk, esp. of copper, formed by throwing water on molten metal.—*adj.* **rosett'ed**. [Fr., dim. of *rose*.]

Rosicrucian, *roz'* or *rōz'i-krōō'sh(y)ən*, *n.* a member of an alleged secret society whose members made great pretensions to knowledge of the secrets of Nature, transmutation of metals, elemental spirits, magical signatures, &c.—affirmed to have been founded (1459) by Christian *Rosenkreuz* : a member of one or other of various modern fraternities. —Also *adj.*—*n.* **Rosicru'cianism**. [Prob. a Latinisation of *Rosenkreuz*, rose cross, L. *rŏsa*, rose, *crux*, cross.]

rosin, *roz'in*, *n.* the residue of turpentine distillation. —*v.t.* to rub or cover with rosin.—*adj.* **ros'ined**. —*ns.* **ros'inate**, a resinate ; **ros'in-oil**, an oil distilled from rosin ; **ros'in-plant, -weed**, Silphium. —*adj.* **ros'iny**. [resin.]

Rosinante, Rozinante, *roz-in-an'ti*, *n.* Don Quixote's horse : a sorry nag. [Sp. *Rocinante*, explained as *rocin antes*, formerly a rouncy.]

rosmarine, *roz'mə-rīn*, *n.* (*Spens.*) a walrus, or a sea-monster supposed to lick dew off the rocks. [Dan. *rosmar*, walrus ; influenced by the following word.]

rosmarine, *roz'mə-rīn, -rēn*, *n.* (*Spens.*) rosemary. (*Jonson*) sea dew. [See **rosemary**.]

Rosminian, *ros-min'i-ən*, *adj.* of Antonio Rosmini-Serbati (1797-1855), his philosophy, or the Institute of Charity founded by him.—Also *n.*—*n.* **Rosmin'ianism**.

rosolio, rosoglio, *rō-zō'lyō*, *n.* a sweet cordial made with raisins (formerly, it is said, with sundew). [It. *rosolio*—L. *rōs sōlis*, dew of the sun.]

rost, an old spelling of **roast**.

rostellum, *ros-tel'əm*, *n.* a little beak : a beaklike outgrowth from an orchid column : the forepart of a tapeworm's head. [L. *rŏstellum*, dim. of *rŏstrum*, beak.]

roster, *rōs'tər* (or *ros'*), *n.* a list showing order of rotation, as for army duties : (*coll.*) any roll of names.—*v.t.* to put in a roster. [Du. *rooster*, orig. gridiron (from the ruled lines)—*roosten*, to roast.]

rostrum, *ros'trəm* (L. *rōs'troom*), *n.* a beak : (properly in *pl.*, **ros'tra**) a platform for public speaking (from the *Rostra* in the Roman forum, adorned with the beaks of captured ships).—*adjs.* **ros'tral**, of or like a rostrum ; **ros'trāte, -d**, beaked ; **rostrocarinate** (*ros-trō-kar'in-āt* ; L. *carīna*, keel), beaked and keeled.—*n.* a supposed flint implement with beak and keel. [L. *rōstrum*, beak—*rōdĕre*, *rōsum*, to gnaw.]

rosula, *roz'ū-lä*, *n.* a leaf-rosette.—*adj.* **ros'ūlate**, in a rosette. [L.L. dim. of L. *rŏsa*, rose.]

rot, *rot*, *v.i.* to putrefy : to decay : to become corrupt : to suffer from wasting disease, esp. in

prison, or sheep-rot : (*slang*) to talk nonsense, to chaff.—*v.t.* to cause to rot : (*slang*) to chaff : (*pr.p.* **rott'ing**; *pa.t.* and *pa.p.* **rott'ed**).—*n.* decay : putrefaction : corruption : collapse : applied to various diseases of sheep, timber, &c. : (*slang*) worthless or rotten stuff : (*slang*) bosh.—*interj.* expressing contemptuous disagreement.—*ns.* **rot'-grass**, soft grass, butterwort, pennywort, or other plant reputed to cause sheep-rot ; **rot'-gut**, bad liquor ; **rot'-stone**, rottenstone. [O.E. *rotian*, *pa.p. rotod*; cf. **rotten**.]

rota, *rō'tä*, *n.* a roster : a course, round, routine, cycle, of duty, &c. : the Roman Catholic supreme ecclesiastical tribunal : a round, a canon, a rondo, or other composition with much repetition.—*adj.* **rō'tal**.—*ns.* **rotam'eter**, an instrument for measuring curved lines by running a wheel along them ; **rō'taplane**, rotor-plane ; **Rōtā'rian**, a member of a Rotary Club.—Also *adj.*—*n.* **Rōtā'rianism**.—*adj.* **rotary** (*rō'tər-i*), turning like a wheel : of the nature of rotation : working by rotation of a part : **Rotary**, of an international system of clubs with a wheel as badge, each member being of a different occupation.—*n.* **rotary**, a rotary apparatus : **Rotary**, a Rotary Club : Rotarianism.—*adj.* **rōtāt'able**.—*v.t.* and *v.i.* **rō-tāte'**, to turn like a wheel : to put, take, go, or succeed in rotation.—*adj.* **rō'tate**, wheel-shaped— with united petals in a plane with almost no tube. —*n.* **rotā'tion**, a turning round like a wheel : succession in definite order, as of crops : recurrent order.—*adjs.* **rotā'tional** ; **rotative** (*rō'tə-tiv*).—*n.* **rotā'tor**.—*adj.* **rotatory** (*rō'tə-tər-i* ; *rō-tāt'ər-i*), rotary. [L. *rŏta*, a wheel, *rotāre, -ātum*, to turn.]

rotch, roch, *roch*, *n.* the little auk.—Also **rotch'ie**. [Cf. Du. *rotje*, petrel ; Fris. *rotgies*, pl. of *rotgoes*, brent-goose.]

rote, *rōt*, *n.* mechanical memory, repetition, or performance without regard to the meaning.—*v.t.* (*Shak.* **roate**) to fix by rote (according to others, to root) : to discourse by rote. [Origin obscure ; L. *rŏta*, a wheel, and O.Fr. *rote*, road, have been conjectured.]

rote, *rōt*, *n.* a mediaeval stringed instrument. [O.Fr. *rote*, a fiddle, prob. through Gmc. from Celt. ; W. *crwth*, Gael. *cruit*.]

rote, *rōt*, *n.* (now *U.S.*) the roar of surf. [Ety. obscure.]

rotenone, *rō'ti-nōn*, *n.* an insecticide prepared from derris and other plants. [Origin unknown.]

rother, *rodh'ər*, *n.* (*Shak.*, *emendation*) an ox, cow. —*n.* **roth'er-beast**. [O.E. *hrýther*, an ox, a cow ; cf. Ger. pl. *rinder*, horned cattle.]

rotifer, *rōt'if-ər*, *n.* a wheel-animalcule, or member of the **Rotif'era**, minute aquatic animals whose rings of waving cilia suggest a rotating wheel. [L. *rŏta*, a wheel, *ferre*, to carry.]

rotl, *rot'l*, *n.* a variable Levantine weight. [Ar. *ratl*.]

rotograph, *rō'tə-gräf*, *n.* a photograph as of a manuscript, made directly by throwing a reversed image on a roll of sensitive paper.—*v.t.* to photograph by this method. [L. *rota*, a wheel, Gr. *graphein*, to write.]

rotolo, *rō'tō-lō*, an Italian form of **rotl**.

rotor, *rō'tər*, *n.* a rotating part, esp. of a dynamo, motor, or turbine : a revolving cylinder for propulsion of a ship : a revolving aerofoil.—*ns.* **ro'tor-plane**, a helicopter or autogyro ; **ro'tor-ship**; **ro'tor-station**, an aerodrome designed specially for helicopters. [For **rotator**.]

rotten, *rot'n*, *adj.* putrefied : decaying : affected by rot : corrupt : unsound : disintegrating : (*slang*) deplorably bad : (*slang*) miserably out of sorts.— *adv.* **rott'enly**.—*ns.* **rott'enness** ; **rott'enstone**, a decomposed silicious limestone that has lost most of its calcareous matter, used for polishing metals.— *v.t.* to polish with rottenstone.—**rotten borough**, a borough that still (till 1832) sent members to parliament though it had few or no inhabitants. [O.N. *rotinn*; cf. **rot**.]

rotten, rotton, *rot'n*. Same as **ratton**.

rotter, *rot'ər*, *n.* a thoroughly depraved or worthless person. [**rot**.]

rotula, *rot'ū-lä*, *n.* the knee-pan : a radial piece of

Aristotle's lantern in sea-urchins. [L. *rotula*, dim. of *rota*, a wheel.]

rotund, *rō-tund'*, *adj.* round: rounded: nearly spherical: convexly protuberant.—*v.t.* to round.— *n.* **rotund'a**, a round (esp. domed) building or hall. —*adj.* **rotund'ate**, rounded off: orbicular.—*adv.* **rotund'ity**, roundness: a round mass.—*adv.* **rotund'ly**. [L. *rotundus—rota*, a wheel.]

roturier, *ro-tü-ryā*, *n.* a plebeian. [Fr., prob.—L.L. *ruptūra*, ground broken by the plough—L. *rumpĕre*, *ruptum*, to break.]

rouble. Same as **ruble**.

roucou, *rōo-kōo'*, *n.* annatto. [Fr.,—Tupí *urucú*.]

roué, *rōo'ā*, *n.* a profligate, rake, debauchee. [A name given by Philippe, Duke of Orléans, Regent of France 1715-23, to his dissolute companions.— Fr. *roué*, broken on the wheel—pa.p. of *rouer— roue*—L. *rota*, a wheel.]

Rouen cross, *rōo'än⁹ kros*, a cross in fretwork as a brooch or pendant. [*Rouen* in France.]

rouge, *rōozh*, *n.* a mixture of safflower and talc, or other powder used to redden the face: a polishing powder of hydrated ferric oxide.—*v.t.* to colour with rouge.—*v.i.* to use rouge: to blush.— **rouge-et-noir** (*rōozh-ā-nwär*), a gambling card-game played on a table with two red and two black diamond marks on which stakes are laid.—also *trente-et-quarante*.—**Rouge Croix** (*krwä*), **Rouge Dragon**, two of the pursuivants of the Heralds' College. [Fr. *rouge*—L. *rubeus*, red.]

rouge, *rōoj*, *n.* (*Eton*) a scrimmage: a touch-down in football. [Origin unknown.]

rough, *ruf*, *adj.* uneven: rugged: unshorn: un-shaven: unpolished: harsh: crude: unelabor-ated: without attention to minute correctness: unbroken (as a horse): coarse: rude: unrefined: ungentle: turbulent: aspirate: astringent.—*adv.* roughly: with roughness or risk of discomfort.— *n.* rough state: that which is rough: rough ground, esp. uncut grass, &c., beside a golf fairway: a piece inserted in a horse's shoe to keep him from slipping: a hooligan, a rowdy.—*v.t.* to make rough: to ruffle: to roughen the shoes of: to shape roughly: to treat roughly.—*n.* **rough'age**, refuse of grain or crops: bran, fibre, &c., in food: coarse food that promotes intestinal movement.—*adjs.* **rough'-and-read'y**, ready to hand or easily im-provised, and serving the purpose well enough: willing and moderately efficient; **rough'-and-tum'ble**, haphazard and scrambling.—Also *adv.*— *n.* a scuffle: haphazard struggling.—*v.t.* **rough'-cast**, to shape roughly: to cover with rough-cast. —*n.* plaster mixed with small stones, used to coat walls.—*adj.* coated with rough-cast.—*adj.* **rough'-coat'ed**.—*vs.t.* **rough'-draft**, **-draw**, to draft roughly; **rough'-dry**, to dry without smoothing; **rough'en**, to make rough.—*v.i.* to become rough. —*n.* **rough'er**, one who performs preliminary operations.—*adjs.* **rough'-foot'ed**, with feathered feet; **rough'-grained**, coarse-grained.— *vs.t.* **rough'-grind'**, to grind roughly; **rough'-hew'**, (*Shak.*) to hew to the first appearance of form.—*n.* **rough'-hew'er**.—*adj.* **rough'-hewn**.—*ns.* **rough'-hound**, a small species of dogfish; **rough'-house**, (*U.S.*; also **rough house**) a disturbance: a brawl. —*v.i.* to brawl: to make a disturbance.—*v.t.* to maltreat.—*n.* **rough'ie**, (*Scott*) a dry bough, esp. one used as a torch.—*adjs.* **rough'ish**; **rough'-legged**, with feathered or hairy legs.—*adv.* **rough'ly**.—*ns.* **rough'-neck**, (*U.S. slang*) an un-mannerly lout: a hooligan or tough; **rough'ness**, the quality of being rough: a rough place: (*U.S.*) **roughage**.—*adj.* **rough'-per'fect**, nearly perfect in the memorising of a part.—*n.* **rough'-rider**, a rider of untrained horses: a horse-breaker: an army riding-master's assistant: an irregular cavalry-man.—*adjs.* **rough'-shod**, provided with roughened horse-shoes; **rough'-spoken**, rough in speech.— *ns.* **rough'-string**, an intermediate support for the steps of a wooden stairway; **rough'-stuff**, coarse paint laid on after the priming, and before the finish: violent behaviour.—*adj.* **rough'-wrought**, shaped out or done roughly, or in a preliminary way.—*n.* **rough'y** (see **roughie**).—**cut up rough (see cut); ride rough-shod over**, to set at nought,

domineer over without consideration; **rough in**, to sketch in roughly; **rough it**, to take whatever hardships come; **rough on**, hard luck for: press-ing hard upon; **rough out**, to shape out roughly. [O.E. *rúh*, rough; Ger. *rauch, rauh*, Du. *ruig*.]

rought, *rawt*, an obs. pret. of **reck**.

roul, roule, obs. forms of roll.

roulade, *rōo-läd'*, *n.* (*mus.*) a melodic embellish-ment: a run. [Fr.,—*rouler*, to roll.]

rouleau, *rōo-lō'*, *n.* a roll or coil: a cylindrical pile or column of coins, blood corpuscles, or other disks:—*pl.* **rouleaus, rouleaux** (-*lōz'*). [Fr.]

roulette, *rōol-et'*, *n.* a little roller: a game of chance in which a ball rolls from a rotating disk into one or other of a set of compartments answering to those on which the players place their stakes: a tool with a toothed disk for engraving rows of dots, for perforating paper, &c.: a cylinder for curling hair or wigs: (*geom.*) the locus of a point carried by a curve rolling upon a fixed curve. [Fr.]

roum, *rōom*, an old spelling of **room**.—*n.* **roum'ing** (see **souming** and **rouming**).

Roumanian. See **Rumanian**.

Roumansch. See **Romansch**.

rounce, *rowns*, *n.* in a hand printing-press, the apparatus, or its handle, for moving the carriage. [Du. *ronse*.]

rounceval, *rown'si-vl*, *n.* (*obs.*) a giant: a great bouncing woman: a marrow-fat pea.—*adj.* gigantic. [Poss. *Roncesvalles*, in the Pyrenees.]

rouncy, *rown'si*, *n.* (*arch.*) a riding-horse: a nag. [O.Fr. *ronci*.]

round, *rownd*, *v.t.* (*arch.*) to whisper: to whisper to. —*v.i.* to whisper. [O.E. *rúnian*, to whisper; cf. **rune**.]

round, *rownd*, *adj.* having a curved outline or sur-face: approaching a circular, globular, or cylin-drical form: in a course returning upon itself: enveloping: with horizontal swing: plump: pro-nounced with lips contracted to a circle: smooth and full-sounding: sonorous: well finished-off: periodic, as a sentence: approximate, without regarding minor denominations: full: not in-considerable in amount: plain-spoken: candid: honest: unsparing: without mincing: vigorous: unqualified.—*adv.* about: on all sides: every way: in a ring: in a curve: in rotation: from one to another successively: indirectly: circuitously: to-wards the opposite quarter: (*Shak.*) roundly: (*U.S.*) in the neighbourhood.— *prep.* about: around: on every side of: all over: to every side of in succession: past, beyond.—*n.* a round thing or part: a ring, circumference, circle, or globe, esp. the earth or the sky: a ladder rung or similar rounded connecting part: a slice of toast: a cut of beef across the thigh-bone: a brewer's vessel for beer during fermentation: a projecting corner-turret (not necessarily round in shape): a carving in the round: a coil: a bend: a circuit: a course returning upon itself: a dance in a ring, or its tune: a canon sung in unison: a cycle or recurring series of events or doings: a complete revolution or rotation: an accustomed walk: a prescribed circuit: a complete series of holes in golf: scope: routine: a volley, as of firearms or applause: ammunition of one shot: a successive or simul-taneous action of each member of a company or player in a game: a portion dealt around to each: a bout, as in boxing: a defined stage in a competi-tion: roundness: (*sculp.*) the condition of being visible from all sides, not merely in relief.—*v.t.* to make round: to surround: to go round: **to turn round**: to finish off: to give finish to.—*v.i.* to become round: to go round: to go to the rounds.— *adj.* **round'about**, circuitous: indirect: cut evenly, without tails or train: plump.—*n.* a merry-go-round: a place where traffic circulates in one direc-tion: a devious way: a round earthwork: a round dance: (*U.S.*) a short jacket.—*v.i.* to go round and round.—*ns.* (jocular) **roundabouta'tion**, **round-aboutil'ity**. — *advs.* **roundabout'edly**, **round'-aboutly**.—*n.* **round'aboutness**.—*adjs.* **round'-arch**, **-ed**, having semicircular arches; **round'-arm**, with nearly horizontal swing of the arm; **round'-backed**; **round'-eared**; **round'ed**.—

ns. **round′edness**; **round′er**, one who or that which rounds: a thing that is round (see also **roundure**): one who goes the round: a complete circuit in rounders: (in *pl.*) a bat-and-ball game in which players run from station to station.—*adjs.* **round′-eyed**; **round′-faced**.—*ns.* **round′-fish**, any fish other than a flat fish: the carp: an American whitefish; **round′hand**, a style of penmanship in which the letters are well rounded and free; **Round′head**, a Puritan (from the close-cut hair). —*adj.* **round′-head′ed**, puritanical: having a round head, top, or end: brachycephalic.—*n.* **round′-house**, (*obs.*) a lock-up: a cabin on the after part of the quarter-deck: (*U.S.*) an engine-house with a turntable.—*n.* and *adj.* **round′ing**.— *adjs.* **round′ish**; **round′-leaved**.—*adv.* **round′ly**. —*n.* **round′-mouth**, a cyclostome.—*adj.* **round′-mouthed**.—*n.* **round′ness**.—*adjs.* **round′-nosed**; **round′-shoul′dered**, with shoulders bending forward from the back.—*n.* **rounds′man**, one who goes round, esp. one sent by a shopkeeper to take orders and deliver goods: (*U.S.*) a policeman who acts as inspector.—*adj.* **round′-ta′ble**, meeting on equal terms, like the inner circle of King Arthur's knights, who sat at a round table.—*n.* **round′-trip**, a trip to a place and back again.—*adj.* (*U.S.*) return. — *ns.* **round′-top**, a mast-head plat-form; **round′-up**, a driving together, as of all the cattle on a ranch, a set of persons wanted by the police, &c.—*adj.* **round′-winged**.—*n.* **round′-worm**, a threadworm or nematode, a member of the Nematoda, unsegmented animals with long rounded body, mostly parasitic.—**bring, come, round** (see **bring, come**); **in round numbers**, roughly, approximately; **in the round**, capable of being viewed from all sides, not merely in relief; **round about**, an emphatic form of round: the other way about: about; **round dance**, a dance in a ring: a dance in which couples revolve about each other; **round game**, a game, esp. a card-game, in which each plays for his own hand; **round off**, to finish off neatly; **round on**, to turn on, assail in speech; **round out**, to fill out to roundness; **round robin** (**Robin**), a paper with signatures in a circle, that no one may seem to be a ringleader; **round to**, to turn the head of a ship to the wind; **round tower**, a tall tapering tower of circular section, of early Christian origin, common in Ireland; **round up**, to ride round and collect: to gather in (wanted persons). [O.Fr. *rund* (Fr. *rond*)—L. *rotundus*—*rota*, a wheel.]

roundel, *rown′dl*, *n.* anything circular: a circle: a disk: a ladder rung: a ring-dance, a rondel: a round turret.—*ns.* **roun′delay**, a song with a re-frain: a dance in a ring; **roun′dle**, a roundel; **round′let** (*-lit*), a little circle or disk; **rown′dell**, (*Spens.*) a bubble. [O.Fr. *rondel, -le, rondelet*, dims. of *rond*, round.]

roundure, *rownd′yər* (*Shak.* **round′er**, **rond′ure**), *n.* roundness: a round form or space: a circle, circuit: a globe. [Fr. *rondeur*—*rond*, round.]

roup, *rowp*, *n.* (*Scot.*) sale by auction.—*v.t.* to sell by auction.—*n.* **rouping′-wife**, (*Scot.*) a woman who conducts or buys at auctions. [Scand.]

roup, *roōp*, *n.* an infectious disease of the respiratory passages of poultry: (*Scot.*) hoarseness.—*adjs.* **roup′it** (*Scot.*); **roup′y**. [Perh. imit.]

rouse, *rowz*, *v.t.* (*orig. refl.*) to shake the feathers of: to ruffle, set up: to start, as from cover or lair: to stir up: to awaken: to disturb: to excite: to put in action: to haul in (as a cable).—*v.i.* (*obs.*) to shake oneself: to rise from cover: (*Shak.*) to stand erect (of hair): to awake: to be excited to action.—*n.* (*obs.*) a shake of the feathers, body, &c.: reveille.—*adj.* **rous′ant**, (*her.*) rising as a bird.— *ns.* **rouse′about**, (*Austr.*) an odd man on a station; **rouse′ment**, (*U.S.*) religious excitement; **rous′er**, one who, or that which, rouses: anything astonish-ing.—*adj.* **rous′ing**, awakening: stirring: vigor-ously active: great: violent.—*adv.* **rous′ingly**.— *v.t.* **roust**, to stir up: to rout out.—*v.i.* to move energetically.—*ns.* **roust′about**, (*U.S.*) a wharf labourer: one who does odd jobs: (*U.S.* and *Austr.*) a rouseabout; **roust′er**, a roustabout.— **rouse on** (*Austr.*), to reprove. [Origin obscure.]

rouse, *rowz*, *n.* a carousal: a bumper. [Prob. aphetic for **carouse**; Dan. and Sw. *rus*, drunken-ness, has also been suggested.]

roussette, *roō-set′*, *n.* a fruit-bat: a dogfish. [Fr.]

rout, *rowt*, *n.* a tumultuous crowd: a rabble: a pack, herd, or flock: a large party: a fashionable evening assembly: a defeated body: an utter defeat: disorderly flight: disturbance: brawl: riot: clamour: a fuss.—*v.i.* to behave riotously.— *v.t.* to defeat utterly: to put to disorderly flight.— *ns.* **rout′-cake**, a rich sweet cake for receptions; **rout′ing**, going to receptions.—*adj.* **rout′ous**.— *adv.* **rout′ously**.—*n.* **rout′-seat**, a bench hired out for routs. [O.Fr. *route*, from the pa.p. of L. *rumpĕre, ruptum*, to break.]

rout, *rowt*, *v.i.* to snore. [O.E. *hrútan*.]

rout, *rowt*, *v.t.* to grub up, as a pig: to scoop out: to turn up: to turn out, fetch out: to rummage out: to bring to light.—*v.i.* to grub: to poke about.—*n.* **rout′er**. [An irreg. variant of **root** (2), **wroot**.]

route, *roōt* (formerly, and still in the army, *rowt*), *n.* a way, course that is or may be traversed: march-ing orders.—*ns.* **route′-march**, a long march of troops in training; **route′-step**, an order of march in which soldiers are not required to keep step. [Fr.,—L. *rupta* (*via*), broken (way); see **rout** (1).]

routh, **rowth**, *rowth, rowth, n.* (*Scot.*) abundance.—*adj.* plentiful.—*adj.* **routh′ie**. [Origin obscure.]

routine, *roō-tēn′*, *n.* regular, unvarying, or mechan-ical course of action or round.—*adj.* keeping an unvarying round: forming part of a routine.—*ns.* **routineer′**; **routi′nism**; **routi′nist**. [Fr.]

roux, *roō*, *n.* a thickening made of equal quantities of butter and flour cooked together. [Fr. (*beurre*) *roux*, brown (butter).]

rove, *rōv*, *v.t.* to wander over or through: to dis-charge at random.—*v.i.* to practise piracy: to aim, as in archery, at some casual mark: to wander about: to ramble: to change about inconstantly: to troll with live bait.—*n.* wandering: a mode of incomplete ploughing.—*n.* **rō′ver**, a pirate: a robber: a random or distant mark: an arrow for shooting at rovers: a wanderer: an inconstant person: a croquet ball or player ready to peg out: a member of a senior branch of the Boy Scout organisation (also **rover scout**).—*n.* and *adj.* **rō′ving**.—*adv.* **rō′vingly**.—**at rovers**, at a distant mark: at random: conjecturally. [Partly at least from Du. *rooven*, to rob, *roofer*, robber—*roof*, plunder; perh. partly from a Midland form of obs. Northern English *rave*, to wander.]

rove, *rōv*, *v.t.* to twist slightly in preparation for spinning.—*n.* a roved sliver.—*ns.* **rō′ver**, a machine for roving: one who attends it; **rō′ving**, the pro-cess of giving the first twist to yarn: rove. [Origin obscure.]

rove, *rōv*, *pa.t.* and *pa.p.* of **reeve**.

rove-beetle, *rōv′-bē′tl*, *n.* the devil's coach-horse, or other beetle of the family Staphylinidae. [Cf. Du. *roof-kever*, lit. reif chafer—*roof*, robbery.]

row, *rō*, *n.* a line or rank of persons or things, as seats, houses, turnips: a series in line: often in street-names, of a single or double line of houses.— *v.t.* (*rare*) to set in or with a row or rows.—**a hard row to hoe**, a destiny fraught with hardship. [O.E. *ráw*; Ger. *reihe*, Du. *rij*.]

row, *rō*, *v.t.* to propel with an oar: to transport by rowing: to achieve, render, perform, effect, com-pete in, by use of oars: to use, as an oar.—*v.i.* to work with the oar: to be moved by oars.—*n.* an act or spell of rowing: a journey in a rowing-boat. —*adj.* **row′able**, capable of being rowed or rowed on.—*ns.* **row′-barge**; **row′boat** (*U.S.*); **row′er**; **row′ing-boat**; **row′-port**, a small square hole for an oar in a vessel's side. [O.E. *rówan*.]

row, *row, n.* a noisy squabble: a brawl: a din, hubbub: a chiding or rating.—*v.t.* (*obs.*) to rag: to rate. — *v.i.* to make a disturbance. [A late 18th century word, poss. a back-formation from **rouse** (2).]

row, *row, n.* and *vb.* a Scots form of **roll**.

row, *row*, an obs. or dial. form of **rough**.

rowan, *row′ən*, also *rō′ən, n.* the mountain-ash (*Sorbus*, or *Pyrus, Aucuparia*), a tree of the rose

Neutral vowels in unaccented syllables: *el′ə-mənt, in′fənt, ran′dəm*

family with pinnate leaves : its small red berry-like fruit.—*ns.* row'an-berry ; row'an-tree. [Cf. Norw. *raun*, Sw. *rönn*.]

row-dow(-dow), *row'-dow'(-dow')*, *n.* the sound of a drum.—*n.* rowdedow', rowdydow', hubbub. —*adj.* row'dy-dow'dy, uproarious. [Echoic.]

rowdy, *row'di*, *n.* orig. a lawless American back-woodsman : a noisy, turbulent person.—Also *adj.* —*adv.* row'dily.—*n.* row'diness.—*adj.* row'-dyish.—*n.* row'dyism. [Origin unknown.]

rowdy, *row'di*, *n.* (*obs. slang*) money.

rowel, *row'əl*, *n.* a little spiked wheel on a spur : the rowel-head : a knob, ring, or disk on a horse's bit : a disk used as a seton for animals.—*v.t.* to prick with the rowel :—*pr.p.* row'elling ; *pa.t.* and *pa.p.* row'elled.—*ns.* row'el-head, the axis of a rowel ; row'el-spur, a spur with a rowel. [Fr. *rouelle*—L.L. *rotella*, dim. of L. *rota*, a wheel.]

rowen, *row'ən*, *n.* aftermath.—Also row'an, row'-ing, raw'ing, rawn (*rawn*). [From a Northern form of O.Fr. *regain*.]

rowlock, *rul'ək*, *n.* a contrivance serving as fulcrum for an oar.—Also roll'ock, rull'ock. [Prob. for oarlock—O.E. *árloc*.]

rowme, *rowm*, *n.* (*Spens.*) room : station. [room.]

rownd, an obs. spelling of round (1 and 2).

rowt. Same as rout (3).

rowth. Same as routh.

Roxburghe, *roks'bər-ə*, *n.* a style of binding for books, with cloth or paper sides, plain leather back, gilt top, other edges untrimmed, named from the Duke of *Roxburghe* (1740-1804), book-collector.

royal, *roi'əl*, *adj.* of a king or queen : kingly : being a king or queen : of a reigning family : founded, chartered, or patronised by a king or queen : magnificent : of more than common size or excellence : of writing-paper, 19 by 24 in., of printing-paper, 20 by 25 (royal octavo, a book size 6¼ by 10 in.).— *n.* a royal person : a gold coin of various kinds : a sail immediately above the topgallant sail : formerly a stag's second tine, now the third : a stag of twelve points.—*n.* roy'alet, a petty king.—*v.t.* roy'alise, (*Shak.*) to make royal or (*Milt.*) royalist : to fill with royal presence.—*v.i.* to play the king.—*ns.* roy'alism, attachment to monarchy ; roy'alist, an adherent of royalism : a cavalier during the English civil war : in American history, an adherent of the British government : in French history, a supporter of the Bourbons.—Also *adj.*—*adv.* roy'ally. —*n.* roy'alty, kingship : the character, state, or office of a king : kingliness : the person of the sovereign : members of royal families collectively or (*coll.*) one such member : a queen-bee, queen-termite, &c. : kingdom : royal authority : a right or prerogative granted by a king or queen, esp. a right over minerals : payment to an author, composer, &c., for every copy sold or every public performance : the area of a royal domain : a royal burgh.—royal blue, a bright, deep-coloured blue ; royal commission, a body of persons nominated by the Crown to inquire into and report on some matters ; royal fern (*Osmunda regalis*), the most striking of British ferns ; royal fish, a 'fish' that is the king's perquisite when cast ashore or caught near the land (whale, sturgeon, porpoise) ; royal jelly, the food of a developing queen-bee ; royal marriage, in bezique, king and queen of trumps ; royal mast, the fourth and highest part of the mast, commonly made in one piece with the top-gallant mast ; royal palm, a palm (*Oreodoxa regalis*) of the cabbage-palm genus ; royal road, a short and easy way of circumventing difficulties ; royal tennis, the old game of tennis, distinguished from lawn tennis ; the Royals, formerly the first regiment of foot in the British Army (the Royal Scots). [Fr.,—L. *rēgālis*, regal.]

royne, *roin*, *v.i.* (*Spens.*) to mutter, growl, roar. [Prob. conn. with groin (2).]

royne. See roon.

roynish, *roin'ish*, *adj.* (*Shak.*) scurvy, mangy : mean. [O.Fr. *roigne*, mange.]

royster, &c. Same as roister, &c.

rozelle. Same as roselle.

rozet, rozit. See roset.

rub, *rub*, *v.t.* to apply friction to : to move some-

thing with pressure along the surface of : to move with pressure along the surface of something : to clean, polish, or smooth by friction : to remove, erase, or obliterate by friction (usu. with *away*, *off*, *out*) : to grind, sharpen, chafe, treat, by friction : to cause to pass by friction (with *in*, *through*, &c.) : (*Shak.*) to impede : to irritate, fret : to take a rubbing of.—*v.i.* to apply, or move with, friction : to meet an impediment (esp. of a bowl) : to chafe : to grate : to fret : to make shift to get along somehow : to admit of being rubbed : (*pr.p.* rubb'ing ; *pa.t.* and *pa.p.* rubbed).—*n.* process or act of rubbing : (*bowls*) an impediment, or a meeting with an impediment : an inequality or uneven place : a difficulty : a hitch : an irritating experience.—*n.* rubb'er, one who, or that which, rubs or massages : an eraser : a thing for rubbing with, as a hard brush, a file, a whetstone, emery-cloth, a coarse towel, a polishing-pad : a rubbing part of a machine : a soft brick that can be cut and smoothed : an uneven place : a rub or impediment in bowls : a rebuff or irritating experience : caoutchouc, india-rubber, or a substitute : a piece of india-rubber, esp. for erasing, or as part of a brake : (*U.S.*) an overshoe of india-rubber : (*U.S.*) a rubber-neck : (*pl.*) a disease in sheep with great heat and itchiness.—*adj.* of, yielding, or concerned with, india-rubber.—*v.t.* to coat, cover, or furnish with rubber.—*v.i.* (*U.S.*) to rubber-neck.—*adj.* rubb'er-cored, of a golf-ball, having a tightly wound band of rubber enclosed in a gutta-percha cover.—*v.t.* rubb'erise, to treat or coat with rubber.—*n.* rubb'er-neck, (*U.S.*) one who cranes or twists his neck in curiosity.—*v.i.* (*U.S.*) to behave as a rubber-neck.—*ns.* rubb'er-solu'tion, a solution of rubber in naphtha or carbon disulphide, for repairing pneumatic tires ; rubb'er-stamp, an instrument for stamping by hand with ink, the characters being in flexible vulcanised rubber : (*fig.*) a conventional person, or one unquestioningly devoted to routine or officialdom.— *adj.* rubb'ery, resembling rubber in some quality.— *ns.* rubb'ing, application of friction : (*Shak.*) experience of rubs : an impression of an inscribed surface produced by rubbing heel-ball or plumbago upon paper laid over it ; rubb'ing-post, one for cattle to rub against ; rubb'ing-stone, a stone for smoothing ; rub'down, an act or experience of rubbing down ; rub'stone, a whetstone.—rub down, to rub from head to foot, as after exercise : to search by passing the hands over the body ; rub in, to force into the pores by friction : to be unpleasantly insistent in emphasising ; rub on (or of) the green, an accident to a golf-ball ; rub out, to erase ; rub shoulders, to come into social contact ; rub the wrong way, to irritate by tactless handling ; rub up, to polish : to freshen one's memory of. [Cf. L.G. *rubben*.]

rub. See rubber (2).

rub, *rub*, a Scots form of rob :—*pa.t.* rubb'it, rubb'et.

rub-a-dub(-dub), *rub'ə-dub(-dub')*, *n.* the sound of a drum. [Echoic.]

rubato, *rōō-bä'tō*, *adj.* and *adv.* (*mus.*) in modified or distorted rhythm. [It., pa.p. of *rubare*, to steal.]

rubber, rubberise, &c. See under rub (1).

rubber, *rub'ər*, *n.* formerly in bowls (also rubbers, *sing.* or *pl.*), now chiefly in bridge and whist, the winning of, or play for, the best of three games (sometimes five) : vaguely, a spell of card-playing : in bowls also a rub (see rub, 1).—Also rub. [Origin obscure.]

rubbish, *rub'ish*, *n.* fragments of ruinous buildings : waste matter : litter : trash : trumpery : nonsense. —*n.* rubb'ish-heap.—*adjs.* rubb'ishing ; rubb'-ishly (*rare*) ; rubb'ishy, worthless : paltry : trashy. [Origin obscure : app. conn. with rubble.]

rubble, *rub'l*, *n.* loose fragments of rock or ruined buildings : undressed irregular stones used in rough masonry and in filling in : masonry of such a kind.—*adj.* of rubble. — *ns.* rubb'le-stone ; rubb'le-work, coarse masonry.—*adj.* rubb'ly. [Origin obscure ; cf. rubbish.]

rubefy, *rōō'bi-fī*, *v.t.* to redden.—*adj.* rubefacient (*-fā'shənt*), reddening.—*n.* an external application that reddens the skin.—*n*. **rubefaction** (*-fak'shən*), reddening. [L. *rubefacĕre*—*rubeus*, red, *facĕre*, to make.]

rubella, *roo-bel'ä*, *n*. German measles, an infectious disease with pink rash, like measles but milder.— *ns*. **rubell'an** (or *roō'*), an altered biotite ; **rubell'- ite**, a red tourmaline ; **rubeola** (*-bē'o-lä*), measles : German measles. [Dims. from L. *rubeus*, red.]

Rubia, *roō'bi-ä*, *n*. the madder genus, giving name to the **Rubiä'ceae**, a family of sympetalous dicotyledons akin to the Caprifoliaceae.—*adj*. **rubiä'- ceous**. [L. *rubia*, madder—*rubeus*, reddish.]

rubicelle, *roō'bi-sel*, *n*. an orange-coloured spinel. [Fr., prob.—*rubis*, ruby.]

Rubicon, *roō'bi-kon*, *-kən*, *n*. a stream of Central Italy (perhaps the Fiumicino), separating Caesar's province of Gallia Cisalpina from Italia proper— its crossing by Caesar (B.C. 49) being thus a virtual declaration of war against the republic ; **rubicon**, in piquet, the winning of a game before one's opponent scores 100.—*v.t*. to defeat in this way. **—cross the Rubicon**, take a decisive, irrevocable step. [L. *Rubicō*, *-ōnis*.]

rubicund, *roō'bi-kund*, *-kənd*, *adj*. ruddy.—*n*. **rubi- cund'ity**. [L. *rubicundus*—*rubēre*, to be red.]

rubidium, *roō-bid'i-əm*, *n*. a soft silvery-white metallic element (Rb ; at. numb. 37). [L. *rubidus*, red (from two red lines in its spectrum).]

rubify, a less commendable spelling of **rubefy**.

rubiginous, *roō-bij'i-nəs*, *adj*. rusty-coloured.—Also **rubig'inose** (*-nōs*). [L. *rūbigō* or *rōbīgō*, *-inis*, rust.]

rubin, &c. See **ruby**.

ruble, rouble, *roō'bl*, *n*. the Russian monetary unit, 100 kopecks. [Russ. *rublʹ*, perh.—*rubitʹ*, to cut ; or Pers. *rūpīya*, a rupee.]

rubric, *roō'brik*, *n*. (*arch*.) red ochre : a heading, guiding rule, entry, liturgical direction, orig. one in red : a flourish after a signature : a thing definitely settled.—*adj*. in red : ruddy : (*obs*.) inscribed with book titles.—*adj*. **ru'brical**.—*adv*. **ru'brically**.—*v.t*. **ru'bricate**, to mark with red : to write or print in red : to make a red-letter saint : to furnish with rubrics : to regulate by rubric. **— ns**. **rubricā'tion** ; **rubricā'tor** ; **rubrician** (*-brish'ən*), one who follows, or is versed in, liturgical rubrics. [L. *rubrīca*, red ochre—*ruber*, red.]

Rubus, *roō'bəs*, *n*. the raspberry and bramble genus of the rose family. [L. *rubus*, a bramble-bush.]

ruby, *roō'bi*, *n*. a highly-prized stone, a pure transparent red corundum : extended to other stones, as varieties of spinel and garnet : redness : applied to various red things (lip, pimple, wine, glass, blood) : (*print*.) a type smaller than nonpareil and larger than pearl (5½ points).—*adj*. red as a ruby. —*v.t*. to redden :—*pr.p*. **ru'bying** ; *pa.t*. and *pa.p*. **ru'bied**.—*adj*. **ru'bied**, red as a ruby.—*n*. **ru'bin**, **ru'bine** (*-bin* ; *Spens*.), a ruby.—*adjs*. **rubin'eous** ; **ru'bious**, ruby, red, ruddy ; **ru'by-coloured** ; **ru'by-red'**.—*ns*. **ru'by-sil'ver**, proustite : pyrargyrite ; **ru'by-spinel'**, a ruby-red spinel (also *spinel-ruby*) ; **ru'by-tail**, a gold-wasp, or cuckoofly ; **ru'by-throat**, a humming-bird with a ruby gorget.—*adj*. **ru'by-throated**. [O.Fr. *rubi* and *rubin*—L. *rubeus*—*ruber*, red.]

ruc. Same as **roc**.

ruche, *roōsh*, *n*. a plaited frilling.—*v.t*. to trim with ruche.—*n*. **ruch'ing**. [Fr. ; prob. Celt.]

ruck, *ruk*, *n*. a wrinkle, fold, or crease.—*v.t*. and *v.i*. to wrinkle.—*n*. **ruck'le**, a pucker, crease.—*v.t*. and *v.i*. to pucker, crease. [O.N. *hrukka*, a wrinkle.]

ruck, *ruk*, *v.i*. to squat : to crouch down : to cower : to huddle.—*v.t*. (*Shak*. rook, rook, *refl*.) to set squatting. [Prob. Scand. ; cf. Norw. dial. *ruka*, to crouch.]

ruck, *ruk*, *n*. a heap, stack, or rick, as of fuel, hay, &c. : a multitude : the common run.—*v.t*. to heap. [Prob. Scand. ; Norw. *ruk*, a rick.]

ruckle, *ruk'l*, *n*. (*Scot*.) a rattle in the throat : a gurgle.—*v.i*. to rattle : to gurgle. [Cf. Norw. dial. *rukl*.]

rucksack, *rook'sak*, *-zäk*, *n*. a bag carried on the back by tourists. [Ger. dial. *ruck* (Ger. *rücken*), back, and Ger. *sack*, bag.]

ruckus, *ruk'əs*, *n*. (*U.S.*) a disturbance. [Perh. a combination of **ruction** and **rumpus**.]

ructation, *ruk-tā'shən*, *n*. (*obs*.) eructation. [L. *ructāre*, to belch.]

ruction, *ruk'shən*, *n*. (*slang*) a disturbance : a rumpus. [Poss. for **insurrection**.]

rud, *rud*, *n*. redness : flush : complexion : (*dial*.) ruddle.—*v.t*. (*Spens*.) to redden :—*pa.p*. **rudd'ed**. [O.E. *rudu*, redness, *rēodan*, to redden.]

rudas, *roō'dəs*, *n*. (*Scot*.) a foul-mouthed old woman : a randy, a hag.—*adj*. coarse. [Origin obscure.]

Rudbeckia, *rud-* or *rood-bek'i-ä*, *n*. a N. American genus of composites, of the sunflower sub-family. [In honour of the Swedish botanist Olaus *Rudbeck* (1630-1702).]

rudd, *rud*, *n*. the red-eye, a fish close akin to the roach. [Prob. O.E. *rudu*, redness.]

rudder, *rud'ər*, *n*. a steering apparatus : a flat structure hinged to the stem of a ship or boat for steering : a vertical control surface for steering an aeroplane to right or left.—*n*. **rudd'er-fish**, the pilot-fish, or other fish that accompanies ships.—*adj*. **rudd'erless**. [O.E. *rōthor*, oar ; Ger. *ruder*, oar.]

ruddle, *rud'l*, *n*. red ochre.—*v.t*. to mark with ruddle : to rouge coarsely.—Also **radd'le**, **redd'le**. —*n*. **rudd'leman**, one who digs or deals in ruddle. —Also **radd'leman**, **redd'leman**. [Cf. **rud**.]

ruddock, *rud'ək*, *n*. the redbreast : a gold coin : a kind of apple. [O.E. *rudduc* ; cf. **rud**.]

ruddy, *rud'i* (*comp*. **rudd'ier**, *superl*. **rudd'iest**), *adj*. red : reddish : of the colour of the skin in high health : rosy, glowing, bright : (euphemistically) bloody.—*v.t*. to make red :—*pr.p*. **rudd'ying** ; *pa.t*. and *pa.p*. **rudd'ied**.—*adv*. **rudd'ily**.—*n*. **rudd'iness**. [O.E. *rudig* ; cf. **rud**, **red**.]

rude, *roōd*, *adj*. uncultured : unskilled : discourteously unmannerly : ungentle : harsh : crude : undeveloped : unwrought : coarse : rugged : rough : roughly or unskilfully fashioned : violent : robust.—*adv*. (*rare*) rudely.—*adv*. **rude'ly**.—*ns*. **rude'ness** ; **rudesby** (*roōdz'bi* ; *Shak*.), an uncivil fellow.—*adj*. **rud'ish**. [L. *rudis*, rough.]

ruderal, *roō'dər-əl*, *adj*. (*bot*.) growing in waste places or among rubbish. [L. *rūdus*, *-eris*, rubbish.]

Rüdesheimer, Rudesheimer, *rü'*, *roō'dəs-hī-mər*, *n*. a white Rhine wine highly esteemed—named from *Rüdesheim*, opposite Bingen.

rudiment, *roōd'i-mənt*, *n*. (usu. in *pl*.) a first principle or element : anything in a rude or first state : an organ in the first discernible stage : often applied to an organ that never develops beyond an early stage.—*adj*. **rudimental** (*-ment'l*), rudimentary.— *adv*. **rudimen'tarily**.—*n*. **rudimen'tariness**.— *adj*. **rudimen'tary**, of rudiments : elementary : in an early or arrested stage of development. [L. *rudimentum*—*rudis*, rough, raw.]

rue, *roō*, *n*. a strong-smelling shrubby Mediterranean plant (*Ruta graveolens*), with pinnately divided leaves and greenish-yellow flowers, punningly (see next word) symbolic of repentance, compunction, or compassion : any other member of its genus : extended with qualification to other plants (see **goat's-rue**, **meadow-rue**, **wall-rue**). —*adj*. **rue'-leaved**. [Fr. *rue*—L. *rūta*—Peloponnesian Gr. *rhȳtē*.]

rue, *roō*, *n*. (*arch*.) repentance : regret : sorrow : pity.—*v.t*. (*arch*.) to affect with repentance, grieve : to be sorry for : to repent of : to wish not to have been or happened : to compassionate.—*v.i*. to feel remorse or regret : to take pity : to change one's mind, contemplate backing out :—*pr.p*. **rue'ing**, **ru'ing** ; *pa.t*. and *pa.p*. **rued**.—*n*. **rue'-bargain**, a forfeit for withdrawing from a bargain.—*adj*. **rue'ful**, sorrowful : piteous : deplorable : mournful : melancholy.—*adv*. **rue'fully**.—*ns*. **rue'fulness** ; **ru(e)'ing**, repentance.—**take the rue**, (*Scot*.) to change one's mind, esp. about an intended marriage. [O.E. *hrēow*, n., *hrēowan*, vb. ; cf. Ger. *reue*, O.H.G. *hriuwa*, mourning.]

ruelle, *rü-el'*, *n*. the space between a bed and the wall : a bed-chamber where great French ladies held receptions in the morning in the 17th and 18th centuries : a morning reception. [Fr., dim. of *rue*, street.]

Ruellia, *roō-el'i-ä*, *n*. a genus of the acanthus family. [Named after the French botanist Jean *Ruel* (1479-1537).]

rufescent, roo-fes'ẽnt, adj. inclining to redness. [L. rŭfescĕre, to turn reddish—rūfus, reddish.]

ruff, ruf, n. a frill, usu. starched and plaited, worn round the neck, esp. in the reigns of Elizabeth and James: a beast's or bird's collar of long hair or feathers: a ruffed breed of domestic pigeons.— v.t. to furnish with a ruff: (Spens.) to ruffle: (falconry) to strike without securing.—adj. **ruffed** (ruft), having a ruff. [Cf. **ruffle**.]

ruff, ruf, n. a kind of sandpiper, the male with an erectile ruff during the breeding season:—fem. **reeve, ree**. [Poss. **ruff** (1), but the fem. is a difficulty.]

ruff, ruf, n. an old card-game, slam, trump (also called **ruff and honours**): an act of trumping.— v.t. and v.i. to trump. [Perh. conn. with O.Fr. roffle, It. ronfa, a card-game.]

ruff, ruf, n. a low vibrating beat of a drum: (Scot.) applause, esp. with the feet.—v.t. and v.i. to beat or be beaten with a ruff: (Scot.) to applaud.—ns. **ruff'-a-duff'**, drumming; **ruff'le**, a ruff of drums. —v.i. to ruff. [Prob. imit.]

ruff, ruf, a variant of **rough**.

ruff, ruffe, ruf, n. the pope, a small fresh-water fish of the perch family, with one dorsal fin.—n. **ruff'in**, (Spens.) the ruff. [Perh. **rough**.]

ruff, ruffe, ruf, n. (obs.) pitch or height of exaltation: elation: excitement. [Cf. Sw. ruff, spirit.]

ruffian, ruf'i-ən, -yən, n. a brutal, violent person: a bully.—adj. brutal: ruffianly: violent.—v.i. to play the ruffian.—adj. **ruff'ianish**.—n. **ruff'ianism**. —adjs. **ruff'ian-like; ruff'ianly**. [O.Fr. ruffian (Fr. rufien); source obscure.]

ruffle, ruf'l, v.t. to make uneven, disturb the smoothness of: to set up (as feathers): to wrinkle: to disorder: to agitate: to turn the leaves of hastily: to disturb the equanimity of, irritate, discompose. —v.i. to wrinkle: to grow rough: to flutter.—n. a frill, esp. at the wrist or neck: a ruff: a rippled condition: annoyance: a quarrel: agitation.—adj. **ruff'led**, having a ruffle.—n. **ruff'ler**, an apparatus for making ruffles.—n. and adj. **ruff'ling**. [Cf. L.G. ruffelen.]

ruffle, ruf'l, v.i. to struggle: to bluster: to swagger. —v.t. to handle roughly or offensively: (Shak.) to snatch.—n. an encounter, a tumult: (Shak.) bustle. —n. **ruff'ler**, (obs.) a beggar posing as a maimed soldier: a swaggerer. [Origin obscure.]

ruffle. See ruff (4).

rufous, roo'fəs, adj. reddish or brownish-red. [L. rūfus, akin to ruber, red.]

rug, rug, n. (obs.) a coarse, rough woollen fabric: a thick, heavy floor-mat, esp. for the hearth: a thick covering or wrap, as for travelling.—adj. made of rug.—ns. **rugg'ing; rug'-gown**, a gown of rug: (obs.) a watchman.—adj. **rug'-head'ed**, (Shak.) shock-headed. [Cf. Norw. rugga, rogga, coarse coverlet, Sw. rugg, coarse hair.]

rug, rug, v.t. (Scot.) to pull roughly.—n. a tug: a haul, share.—n. **rugg'ing**. [Prob. Scand.]

rug, rug, adj. (old slang) secure: snug.

Rugby, rugby, rug'bi, n. a form of football which (unlike Association) permits carrying the ball:— (coll.) **rugg'er**. [From Rugby school.]

rugged, rug'id, adj. rough: uneven: shaggy: uncouth: toilsome: sturdy and rough: massively irregular: (U.S.) robust.—adv. **rugg'edly**.—n. **rugg'edness**.—adj.**rugg'y**, rough: uneven. [Prob. related to rug (1).]

rugose, roo'gōs, -gōs', adj. wrinkled: covered with sunken lines.—Also **ru'gous**.—adv. **ru'gosely** (or -gōs').—n. **rugosity** (-gos'i-ti).—adjs. **ru'gulose**, finely rugose. [L. rūgōsus—rūga, a wrinkle.]

ruin, roo'in, roo'in, n. downfall: collapse: overthrow: complete destruction: wreck: loss of fortune or means: bankruptcy: undoing: seduction or departure from chastity of life: downfallen, collapsed, wrecked, or irretrievably damaged state (often in pl.): cause of ruin: broken-down remains, esp. of a building (often in pl.): devastation: (slang) bad gin (blue ruin).—v.t. to reduce or bring to ruin.—v.i. to fall headlong: to go to ruin.—adj. **ru'inable**.—v.t. **ru'inate**, (Shak.) to ruin, to destroy: to demolish: to reduce to poverty: (Spens.; refl.) to fling headlong.—adj. (arch.) in

ruins: ruined.—n. **ruinā'tion**, act of ruining: state of being ruined.—adj. **ru'ined**.—n. **ru'iner**. —n. and adj. **ru'ining**.—adj. **ru'inous**, fallen to ruins: decayed: bringing ruin: (Milt.) as of crashing.—adv. **ru'inously**.—n. **ru'inousness**, the state or quality of being ruinous: mischievousness.—**ruin agate, marble**, one with markings like ruins. [L. ruīna—ruĕre, to tumble down.]

rukh. Same as **roc**.

rule, rool, n. a straight-edged strip used as a guide in drawing straight lines or as a measuring-rod, or means of mechanical calculation: a type-high strip of metal for printing straight lines: a straight line printed or drawn on paper, &c.: a dash: a straight-edge used for securing a flat surface in plaster or cement: (Milt.) a straight shaft of light: government: control: prevalence: that which is normal or usual: conformity to good or established usage: well-regulated condition: (obs.) conduct: (obs.) misrule: a principle: a standard: a code of regulations, as of a religious order: a regulation, whether imposed by authority or voluntarily adopted: an order of a court: a guiding principle: a method or process of achieving a result: a regulation that must not be transgressed: a maxim or formula that it is generally best, but not compulsory, to follow: (in pl.) an area around a prison in which privileged prisoners were allowed to live: the privilege of living there.—v.t. to draw with a ruler: to mark with (esp. parallel) straight lines: to govern: to control: to manage: to prevail upon: to determine or declare authoritatively to be: to determine, decree.—v.i. to exercise power (with over): to decide: to be prevalent: to stand or range in price.—adjs. **ru'lable**, governable: (U.S.) allowable; **rule'less** (Spens. ru'lesse), unruly, lawless: without rules; **rule-of-thumb'**, according to rule of thumb (see below).—n. **ru'ler**, a strip or roller for ruling lines: one who rules.—v.t. to strike with a ruler.—n. **ru'lership**. adj. **ru'ling**, predominant: prevailing: reigning. —n. a determination by a judge, esp. an oral decision: the act of making ruled lines.—adj. **ru'ly**, orderly in behaviour.—**as a rule**, usually; **be ruled**, take advice; **rule of faith**, in polemical theology, the authoritative sources of the doctrines of the faith; **rule of the road**, the regulations to be observed in traffic by land, water, or air—thus in Britain drivers, riders, and cyclists take the left side in meeting, and the right in overtaking; **rule of three**, the method of finding the fourth term of a proportion when three are given; **rule of thumb**, any rough-and-ready practical method, arbitrary or based on experience rather than principle; **rule out**, to exclude. [O.Fr. reule (Fr. règle)—L. rēgula—regĕre, to rule.]

rullion, rul'yən, n. (Scot.) a raw-hide shoe. [O.E. rifeling.]

rum, rum, n. a spirit distilled from fermented sugarcane juice or from molasses: (U.S.) intoxicating liquor generally.—ns. **rum'-bloss'om, -bud**, a pimple on the nose; **rum'bo**, rum-punch; **rum'-butt'er**, a mixture of butter and sugar with rum, &c.—adj. **rumm'y**.—ns. **rum'-punch'**, punch made with rum; **rum'-runn'er**, one who smuggles rum: **rum'-runn'ing**; **rum'-shop**; **rum'-shrub**, a liqueur of rum, sugar, lime or lemon juice. &c. [Perh. from **rumbullion**, or kindred form.]

rum, rum, adj. (obs. slang) good: (slang) queer, droll, odd.—n. a queer person.—advs. **rum'ly**; **rumm'ily**.—n. **rumm'iness**.—adjs. **rumm'ish**; **rumm'y**. [Cant.]

rumal. See **romal**.

Rumanian, Roumanian, roo-mā'ni-ən, **Ruman, Rouman**, roo'mân, adjs. pertaining to Rumania or its language.—n. a native or citizen of Rumania, or member of the same people: the (Romance) language of Rumania. [Rumanian Romănia—L. Rŏmânus, Roman.]

rumba, room'bä, rum'bä, n. a violent Cuban negro dance or a modification of it. [Sp.]

rumbelow, rum'bi-lō, n. a meaningless word, occurring as burden in old sea-songs.

rumble, rum'bl, v.i. to make a low heavy grumbling or rolling noise: to move with such a noise.—v.t.

to give forth, or to agitate or move, with such a sound. — *n.* a sound of rumbling: a seat for servants behind a carriage, or for extra passengers in a two-seater car.—*ns.* **rum′bler; rum′ble-tum′ble,** a rumble-seat: a lumbering vehicle: a tumbling motion.—*n.* and *adj.* **rum′bling.**—*adv.* **rum′blingly.** [Perh. L.G.; cf. Du. *rommelen,* Ger. *rummeln.*]

rumbullion, *rum-bul′yən, n.* (*obs.*) rum. [Origin obscure.]

rumbustical, *rum-bust′i-kl,* **rumbustious,** *-yəs, adjs.* (*coll.*) boisterous. [Prob. *robust.*]

rume, a Shakespearean spelling of *rheum.*

rumen, *rōō′men, n.* the paunch or first stomach of a ruminant.—*pl.* **ru′mina.** [L. *rūmen, -inis,* gullet.]

Rumex, *rōō′meks, n.* the dock and sorrel genus of Polygonaceae. [L. *rūmex, -icis,* a kind of dart, also sorrel (from its hastate leaves).]

rumfustian, *rum-fus′tyən, n.* a kind of negus.

rumgumption, *rum-gum(p)′shən, n.* (*Scot.*) common sense.—Also **rum(m)el-, rum(m)le-, rumble-gump′tion** (*rum′l-*).

ruminant, *rōō′min-ənt, n.* an animal that chews the cud.—*adj.* cud-chewing: meditative.—*n.pl.* **Ruminantia** (*-an′shyā, -shā*), the cud-chewing division of the even-toed ungulates.—*adv.* **ru′minantly.**—*v.i.* **ru′mināte,** to chew the cud: to regurgitate for chewing: to meditate.—*v.t.* to chew over again: to muse on.—*adj.* (*bot.*) mottled as if chewed.—*adv.* **ru′minātingly.**—*n.* **rumina′tion.** — *adj.* **ru′minative.** — *adv.* **ru′minatively.** — *n.* **ru′minātor.** [L. *rūminăre, -ātum—rūmen, -inis,* the gullet.]

rumkin, *rum′kin, n.* (*obs.*) a kind of drinking-vessel.

rumkin, *rum′kin, n.* a tailless fowl. [App. **rump.**]

rummage, *rum′ij, n.* (*orig.*) stowage of casks, &c., in a ship's hold: a thorough search, as by customs officers: an overhauling search: (*Shak.*) **romage**) commotion, upheaval.—*v.t.* to arrange, esp. (*orig.*) in a ship's hold: to ransack: to overhaul: to search: to stir.—*v.i.* to make a search.—*n.* **rumm′ager.**—**rummage sale,** a sale at which buyers are allowed to rummage among the goods: also a sale of odds and ends or undesired goods. [Fr. *arrumage* (now *arrimage*), stowage.]

rummer, *rum′ər, n.* a large drinking-glass. [Du. *roemer*; Ger. *römer.*]

rummy. See **rum** (1 and 2).

rummy, *rum′i, n.* a card-game in which cards are drawn from the stock and sequences, triplets, &c., are laid on the table.

Rumonsch. See **Romansch.**

rumour, *rōō′mər, n.* clamour: general talk, repute: hearsay: flying report: a current story.—*v.t.* to put about by report.—*adj.* **ru′morous,** resounding: full of rumours: of the nature of rumours: vaguely heard.—*n.* **ru′mourer.** [O.Fr.—L. *rūmor, -ōris,* a noise.]

rump, *rump, n.* the hinder part of an animal's body, the root of the tail with parts adjoining: in birds, the uropygium: contemptuously, a remnant.—*v.t.* to turn one's back upon: (*Scot.*) to clean out of money.—*ns.* **rump′-bone′,** the coccyx; **rump′-end; Rump′er,** a member or supporter of the Rump Parliament.—*adj.* **rump′-fed,** (*Shak.*) prob. with well-nourished rump.—*ns.* **rump′le,** (*Scot.*) a rump; **rump′le-bane′,** rump-bone.—*adj.* **rump′less.**—*ns.* **rump′-post,** the share bone or pygostyle of a bird; **rump′-steak,** steak cut from the thigh near the rump.—**the Rump,** the remnant of the Long Parliament, after Pride's expulsion (1648) of about a hundred Presbyterian royalist members. [Scand.; cf. Dan. *rumpe,* Sw. and Norw. *rumpa,* O.N. *rumpr,* Ger. *rumpf,* Du. *romp.*]

rumple, *rum′pl, n.* a fold or wrinkle.—*v.t.* to crush out of shape: to make uneven. [Du. *rompel*; cf. O.E. *hrimpan,* to wrinkle.]

rumpus, *rum′pəs, n.* an uproar: a disturbance.

rumti-iddity, rumpti-iddity, *rum(p)-ti-id′i-ti, interj.* a meaningless refrain.

run, *run,* formerly also **ren,** *ren*; *Scot.* **rin,** *rin, v.i.* to proceed by lifting one foot before the other in down: to go swiftly, at more than a walking pace: to hasten: to proceed quickly: to betake oneself: to flee: to progress, esp. smoothly and quickly:

to go about freely: to ride at a running pace: to roll: to revolve: to go with a gliding motion: to slip: to go on wheels: to travel, cover a distance: to make a short journey: to swim in shoals: to ascend a river for spawning: to ply: to have a definite sequence, as of notes, words: to proceed through a sequence of operations, work, or go, as a machine: to follow a course: to keep the stage without interruption: to flow: to spread, diffuse: to emit or transmit a flow: to melt: to fuse: (now *dial.*) to curdle: to have a course, stretch, or extent: to range: to average: to elapse: to tend: to come to be, become, pass: to be current: to be valid: to recur repeatedly or remain persistently (in the mind): to come undone, as by the dropping or breaking of a stitch: to compete in a race: (*U.S.*) to be a candidate.—*v.t.* to cause to run: to chase, hunt: to drive forward: to thrust: to pierce: to drive: to pass quickly: to range, run about or throughout: to hurry through: to enter, promote, put forward (as a horse, candidate, or protégé): to render, by running or otherwise: to conduct, manage: to follow: to traverse: to cause to extend, form in a line: to sew slightly: to shoot along or down: to perform, achieve, or score by running, or as if by running: to flee or desert from: to incur: to risk and pass the hazard of: to smuggle: to have or keep current or running: to compete with in a race: to press or put to it, in competition or difficulty: to coagulate: to fuse: to emit, discharge, flow with: (*pr.p.* **runn′ing**; *pa.t.* **ran**; *pa.p.* **run**).—*n.* an act, spell, or manner of running: a journey, trip: distance, time, or quantity run: a continuous stretch, spell, series, or period: a shoal, migration, or migrating body: a roulade: a spell of being in general demand: a rush for payment, as upon a bank: a unit of scoring in cricket: a batsman's passage from one popping-crease to the other: a circuit in baseball: flow or discharge: course: prevalence: the ordinary or average kind, the generality: a track: a path made by animals: (*U.S.*) a small stream: a range of feeding-ground: an enclosure for chickens, &c.: freedom of access to all parts: the playing of a salmon: general direction: a ladder in knitting. —*adj.* having been poured, smuggled, coagulated: having run.—*ns.* **run′about,** a gadabout: a vagabond: a small light vehicle or aeroplane; **run′-away,** a fugitive: a horse that bolts: a flight.— *adj.* fleeing: done by or in flight.—*adj.* **run′-down′,** in weakened health.—*n.* **run′let,** a runnel.—*adj.* **runn′able,** of a stag, fit for hunting.—*ns.* **runn′er,** one who, or that which, runs or can run: a fugitive: a racer: a messenger: an agent: a tout: an intelligencer: a rooting stem that runs along the ground: a rope to increase the power of a tackle: a smuggler: a Bow Street officer: a ring, loop, or the like, through which anything slides or runs: the part on which a sledge, a skate, or a drawer slides: the passage by which metal is poured into a mould: a strip of cloth as a table ornament: a revolving millstone: (*Scot.*) a slice across a carcase of beef below the breast: a climbing plant of the kidney-bean genus (*Phaseolus multiflorus*; **runner-bean, scarlet-runner**): a breed of domestic duck (**runner duck**): a vessel for conveying fish, oysters, &c.; **runn′er-up′,** a competitor (orig. a dog) that holds out to the last heat: the competitor next after the winner.—*adj.* **runn′ing,** racing: habitually going at a run: current: successive: continuous: flowing: discharging: easy: cursive: itinerant: done at or with a run: hasty.— *n.* action of the verb: the pace.—*ns.* **runn′ing-banq′uet,** a slight or hasty collation; **runn′ing-board,** a footboard along the side of a motor-car or (*U.S.*) locomotive; **runn′ing-gear,** the wheels and axles of a vehicle; **runn′ing-hand,** a style of rapid writing without lifting the pen; **runn′ing-knot,** a knot that will form a noose on pulling.—*adv.* **runn′ingly.**—*adj.* **runn′y,** inclined to run or liquefy.—*ns.* **run′-off′,** a race to decide a dead heat: (*vulg.*) urination; **run-on′,** in verse, carrying the sense on beyond the end of the line; **run′way,** a trail, track, or passageway: a path for aircraft to take off from.—**in the long run,** in the end or final result; **in, out of, the running,** competing with, without, a fair chance of success; **make, take up, the running,** to take the lead: to set the pace; **run across,** to come upon by accident; **run down,** to pursue to exhaustion or capture: to collide with and knock over or sink: to disparage: to become unwound or exhausted; **run hard,** to press hard behind; **run in,** to go in: to arrest and take to a lock-up: (print.) to insert a word, &c., without making a break or new paragraph: **run in** (new machinery) into good condition by preliminary working; **run in the blood,** family, to be a hereditary character; **run into debt,** to get into debt; **run it fine,** to allow very little margin, as of time; **running commentary,** a commentary accompanying a text: a broadcast description of a game or other event in progress; **running fight,** a fight between pursuer and pursued; **running fire,** (mil.) a rapid succession of firing; **running footman,** a servant who ran before or alongside a horseman or carriage; **running lights,** the lights shown by vessels between sunset and sunrise; **running ornament,** an ornament in which the design is continuous; **running rigging,** all the rigging except the shrouds, stays, and lower mast-head pendants; **running title,** the title of a book, &c., continued from page to page on the upper margin; **run off,** to cause to flow out: to take impressions of, to print: to repeat, recount; **run on,** (print.) to continue in the same line, and not in a new paragraph; **run out,** to run short: to terminate, expire, determine: to leak, let out liquid: to put out (a batsman running between the wickets and not yet in his ground): dismissed thus; **run over,** to overflow: to overthrow: to go over cursorily; **run short,** to come to be short, lacking, or exhausted; **run through,** to exhaust: to transfix: to read or perform quickly or cursorily but completely; **run together,** to mingle or blend; **run to seed,** to shoot up too rapidly in preparation for seeding, instead of producing the vegetative growth desired by the grower: to disappoint expectation of development: to become exhausted: to go to waste; **run up,** to make or mend hastily: to build hurriedly: to string up, hang: (golf) to send the ball rolling or flying low towards the hole: to incur increasingly. [O.E. rinnan, irnan, iernan, to run; causative rennan, to curdle; see also **earn** (2).]

runagate, run′ə-gāt, n. a vagabond: a renegade: an apostate: a fugitive. [renegade, influenced by run, agate (adv.).]

runch, runsh, n. (Scot.) charlock: wild radish. [Origin obscure.]

runcible, run′si-bl, adj. app. a nonsense-word of Edward Lear's, whose phrase runcible spoon has been applied to a broad-pronged pickle-fork.

runcinate, runs′in-āt, adj. (bot.) with backward-pointing lobes. [L. runcina, a plane, formerly misunderstood as a saw.]

rund, run(d), rən(d). Same as **roon.**

rundale, run′dāl, n. a system of holding land in single holdings made up of detached pieces: land or a share of it so held.—Also adj. [run, and the Northern form of dole (1).]

rundle, run′dl, n. a round, a ladder-rung: a ring, circle, disk, or ball.—adj. **run′dled.** [roundel.]

rundlet, rund′lit, **runlet,** run′lit, n. a small barrel. [Fr. rondelet.]

rune, rōōn, n. a letter of the futhork or ancient Germanic alphabet: a secret, a mystic symbol, sentence, spell, or song: a song or canto.—n. **rune′-craft,** knowledge of runes.—adj. **runed.**—n. **rune′-stave** (O.E. rúnstæf), a runic letter.—adj. **ru′nic,** of, pertaining to, written in, inscribed with runes: Scandinavian: Northern: (wrongly) in the manner of ancient Northumbrian and Celtic interlacing ornament. [O.E. and O.N. rún, mystery, rune; Goth. and O.H.G. rūna.]

rung, rung, n. a spoke: a cross-bar or rail: a ladder round or step: a ship's floor-timber: (Scot.) a cudgel. [O.E. hrung; Ger. runge.]

rung, rung. See **ring** (2).

rung, rung, adj. having a ring through the nose. [ring (1).]

runkle, rung′kl, n. a wrinkle, crease.—v.t. and v.i. to wrinkle: to crease. [Prob. Scand.; cf. ruck, ruckle.]

runlet. See run, rundlet.

runnel, run′l, n. a little brook. [O.E. rynel, dim. of ryne, a stream—rinnan, to run.]

runner, running. See run.

runnet. Dial. variant of rennet (1).

runnion. See ronyon.

runrig, run′rig, n. (Scot.) a form of land-tenure, the same as rundale.—Also adj. and adv. [run, rig.]

runt, runt, n. a small, stunted, or old ox or cow: anything undersized: a large breed of domestic pigeon: a dead tree-stump or trunk: a cabbage-stem: a vague term of reproach, esp. to the old, boorish, or curmudgeonly.—adjs. **runt′ed; runt′-ish; runt′y.** [Origin obscure.]

rupee, rōō-pē′, n. an Indian monetary unit and silver coin, fixed at 1s. 6d. in 1927. [Urdu rūpiyah—Sans. rūpya, silver.]

Rupert's-drop, rōō′pərts-drop′, n. a tailed bulb formed by dropping molten glass in water, bursting when the tail is broken—probably discovered by Prince Rupert (1619-82).

rupia, rōō′pi-ä, n. a skin ulcer covered by crusts of dried secretion and dead tissue. [Gr. rhypos, filth.]

rupicoline, roo-pik′ō-līn, **rupicolous, -ləs,** adjs. rock-dwelling. [L. rūpēs, a rock, colěre, to inhabit.]

rupture, rup′tyər, n. a breach, breaking, or bursting: the state of being broken: breach of harmony, relations, or negotiations: hernia, esp. abdominal.—v.t. and v.i. to break or burst.—n. **rup′turewort,** a caryophyllaceous plant (Herniaria), once thought to cure hernia. [L.L. ruptūra—L. rumpěre, ruptum, to break.]

rural, rōō′rl, adj. of the country.—n. (obs.) a country-dweller. — n. **ruralisa′tion.** — v.t. **ru′ralise,** to render rural.—v.i. to become rural: to rusticate.—ns. **ru′ralism; ru′ralist; rurality** (-al′i-ti).—adv. **ru′rally.**—n. **ru′ralness.**—adj. **ruridecanal** (rōō-ri-di-kā′nl; sometimes -dek′ən-l), of a rural dean(ery).—**rural dean** (see dean). [L. rūrālis—rūs, rūris, the country.]

Ruritania, rōō′r-i-tān′yä, n. a fictitious land of historical romance (in S.E. Europe) discovered by Anthony Hope.—n. and adj. **Rurita̅n′ian.**

Rusa, rōō′sä, n. the sambur genus of deer.—adj. **ru′sine** (-sīn). [Malay rūsa.]

rusa, roosa, rōō′sä, n. an Indian grass (**rusa grass,** Andropogon or Cymbopogon), from which an aromatic oil (**rusa oil**) is distilled. [Hind. rúsá.]

rusalka, rōō-sal′kä, n. a Russian water-nymph. [Russ.]

ruse, rōōz, n. a trick, stratagem, artifice. [O.Fr. ruse—ruser, reüser, to get out of the way, double on one's tracks; see **rush** (1).]

rush, rush, v.i. to move forward with haste, impetuosity, or rashness.—v.t. to force out of place: to hasten or hustle forward, or into any action: to move, transport, drive, push, in great haste: to capture, secure, surmount, pass, by a rush: (coll.) to defraud: (coll.) to overcharge.—n. a swift impetuous forward movement: a sudden simultaneous or general movement (as a **gold rush**): an onset: a stampede: a migratory movement or body: a run upon anything: rapidly increased activity: bustling activity: a sound of rushing.—n. **rush′er.—rush hours,** day's time of maximum activity or traffic. [A.Fr. russcher, O.Fr. reusser reüser, ruser (Fr. ruser); see **ruse.**]

rush, rush, n. any plant of the grass-like marsh-growing genus Juncus: a stalk or round stalk like leaf of such a plant: a rushlight, a rush wick a type of something of no value or importance: extended to various more or less similar plants (se **bulrush, club-rush, Dutch** or **scouring rush wood-rush**): (Shak.) a rush-ring.—adj. of rush or rushes.—v.t. to m⸱ke or strew with rushes.—v.⸱ to gather rushes.—n. **rush′-bearing,** a countr observance of carrying rushes to strew the church the day of the festival.—adj. **rush′-bottomed** having a seat made with rushes.—ns. **rush′-candle rush′light,** a candle or night-light having a wic of rush-pith: a small, feeble light.—adjs. **rush′e⸱** made of rushes; **rush′-grown.**—ns. **rush′-holde⸱**

a stand for a rushlight; **rush′iness.**—*adj.* **rush′-like.**—*n.* **rush′-ring,** a ring of plaited rush, sometimes formerly as an improvised wedding-ring.—*adjs.* **rush′y,** rush-like: abounding in, or made of, rushes; **rush′y-fringed.** [O.E. *risce*; Ger. *risch.*]

rusk, *rusk, n.* a small cake like a piece of very hard toast. [Sp. *rosca,* a roll; origin unknown.]

rusma, *ruz′mä, n.* a depilatory of lime and orpiment. [App. Turk. *khirisma*—Gr. *chrīsma,* ointment.]

russel, *rus′l, n.* a ribbed cotton and woollen material. —*n.* **russ′el-cord,** a kind of rep made of cotton and wool. [Poss. Flem. *Rijssel,* Lille.]

Russellite, *rus′əl-īt, n.* a member of the International Bible Students′ Association, or Jehovah′s Witnesses, a millenialist sect founded by the American Pastor C. T. *Russell* (1852-1916).—Also *adj.*

russet, *rus′it, n.* a coarse homespun cloth or dress: a reddish-brown colour: a reddish-brown variety of apple.—*adj.* made of russet: homespun, homely, rustic: reddish-brown: of brown leather.—*v.t.* and *v.i.* to make or become russet in colour.—*n.* **russ′eting,** a russet apple.—*adj.* **russ′ety.** [O.Fr. *rousset*—L. *russus,* red.]

Russian, *rush′(y)ən, adj.* of Russia or its people.— *n.* a native or citizen of Russia: the Slavonic language of most Russians.—*n.* and *adj.* **Russ** (*rus*), Russian. —*adj.* **Russia** (*rush′ä, -yä*), Russian.—*ns.* **russia, russia leather; Russianisā′tion.**—*v.t.* **Russ′ianise,** to give Russian characteristics to: to make Russian. —*ns.* **Russ′ianism; Russ′ianist; Russification** (*rus-i-fi-kā′shən*).— *v.t.* **Russ′ify,** to Russianise. —*adj.* **Russo-Byzan′tine,** Byzantine as developed in Russia.—*ns.* **Russ′ophil(e),** one who favours Russian policy (also *adj.*); **Russoph′ilism; Russoph′ilist; Russ′ophobe,** one who dreads or hates the Russians (also *adj.*); **Russoph′obist; Russophō′bia,** the dread of Russian policy.— **russia** (or **Russia**) **leather,** a fine brownish-red leather with a characteristic odour.

Russniak, *rus′ni-ak, n.* and *adj.* Ruthenian: Ukrainian or Little Russian. [Ruthenian *Rusnjak.*]

rust, *rust, n.* the reddish-brown coating on iron exposed to moisture: any similar coating or appearance: a plant-disease characterised by a rusty appearance, caused by various fungi of the Uredineae: a fungus causing such disease, notably *Puccinia graminis,* which attacks wheat: corrosion: injurious influence or consequence, esp. of mental inactivity or idleness: the colour of rust.—*v.i.* to become rusty: to affect with rust: to become dull or inefficient by inaction.—*v.t.* to make rusty: to impair| by time and inactivity.— *adjs.* **rust′-coloured; rust′ed.** — *n.* **rust′-fungus.**—*adv.* **rust′ily.**—*n.* **rust′iness.**—*n.* and *adj.* **rust′ing.**— *adjs.* **rust′less,** free from rust: proof against rust; **rust′-proof; rust′-resist′ant; rust′y,** covered with rust: impaired by inactivity, out of practice: dull: affected with rust-disease: rust-coloured: of a rusty black: time-worn: rough: raucous: obstinate: discoloured.—*n.* **rust′y-back,** the scale-fern.—*adj.* **rust′y-coloured.** [O.E. *rúst*; Ger. *rost.*]

rustic, *rus′tik, adj.* of, or characteristic of, the country or country-dwellers: country-dwelling: like countryfolk or their works: simple and plain: awkward: uncouth: unrefined: roughly made: made of rough branches: of masonry, with sunken or chamfered joints, sometimes with roughened face.—*n.* a peasant: a clown: a rough-surfaced brick or stone: rustic masonry.—*adj.* and (*rare*) *n.* **rus′tical.**—*adv.* **rus′tically.**—*v.t.* **rus′ticate,** to send into the country: to banish for a time from town or college: to build in rustic masonry.—*v.i.* to live in the country: to become rustic.—*n.* **rusticā′tion.**—*adj.* **rusticial** (-*tish′l*; *Scott,* as a false archaism).—*v.t.* and *v.i.* **rus′ticise** (-*ti-sīz*).— *ns.* **rusticity** (-*tis′i-ti*), rustic manner: simplicity: rudeness; **rus′tic-ware,** a terra-cotta of a light brown paste, having a brown glaze; **rus′tic-work,** rusticated masonry: summer-houses, &c., of rough branches. [L. *rūsticus*—*rūs,* the country.]

rustle, *rus′l, v.i.* to make a soft, whispering sound, as of dry leaves: to go about with such a sound:

(*U.S.*) to stir about, hustle: (*U.S.*) to steal cattle. —*v.t.* to cause to rustle: (*U.S.*) to get by rustling. —*n.* a quick succession of small sounds, as that of dry leaves: a rustling: (*U.S.*) bustle.—*n.* **rus′tler.** —*n.* and *adj.* **rus′tling.**—*adv.* **rus′tlingly.** [Imit.; cf. Flem. *ruysselen.*]

rustre, *rus′tər, n.* (*her.*) a lozenge pierced with a circular opening.—*adj.* **rus′tred.** [Fr.]

rusty. See **rust.**—Also a variant of **reasty** and of **reesty.**

rut, *rut, n.* a furrow made by wheels: a fixed course difficult to depart from.—*v.t.* to furrow with ruts :— *pr.p.* **rutt′ing;** *pa.t.* and *pa.p.* **rutt′ed.**—*adj.* **rutt′y.** [Origin obscure; prob. not Fr. *route.*]

rut, *rut, n.* sexual excitement in male deer: also in other animals.—*v.i.* to be in heat.—*v.t.* (*rare*) to copulate with.—*n.* **rut′-time.**—*n.* and *adj.* **rutt′ing.** —*adj.* **rutt′ish,** lustful. [O.Fr. *ruit, rut*—L. *rugītus*—*rugīre,* to roar.]

Ruta, *roō′tä, n.* the rue genus of dicotyledons, giving name to the family **Rutā′ceae,** which is usually made to include the orange, &c.—*adj.* **rutā′ceous.** [L. *rūta*; see **rue** (1).]

rutabaga, *roō-tə-bā′gä, n.* the Swedish turnip. [Sw. dial. *rotabagge.*]

ruth, *roōth, n.* pity: remorse: sorrow: matter for pity: (*obs.*) misfortune, calamity.—*adj.* **ruth′ful,** pitiful, sorrowful: piteous, causing pity.—*adv.* **ruth′fully.**—*adj.* **ruth′less,** pitiless: unsparing. —*adv.* **ruth′lessly.**—*n.* **ruth′lessness.** [M.E. *ruthe, reuth*; see **rue** (2); ending influenced by Scand., as O.N. *hryggth.*]

Ruthene, *roō-thēn′, n.* a member of a branch of the Little Russian division of the Slavs on both sides of the Carpathians: the language of the Ruthenes. —*n.* and *adj.* **Ruthēn′ian,** Ruthene.

ruthenium, *roō-thē′ni-əm, n.* a metallic element (Ru; at. numb. 44) of the platinum group, found in the Ural Mountains. [L.L. *Ruthenia,* Russia.]

rutilant, *roō′ti-lənt, adj.* shining: glowing ruddily. [L. *rutilāns, -āntis,* pr.p. of *rutilāre,* to be reddish.]

rutile, *roō′til, n.* a reddish-brown mineral of the tetragonal system, titanium oxide.—*adj.* **rutilated** (*roō′til-āt-id*), enclosing needles of rutile. [L. *rutilus,* reddish.]

rutter, *rut′ər, n.* (*obs.*) a mercenary horse-soldier. [M.Du. *rutter*—O.Fr. *routier.*]

ry-, in many words an old spelling of **ri-.**

ryal, rial, *rī′əl, adj.* and *n.* (*obs.*) royal.—esp. *n.* a coin of various kinds—an old English gold coin worth about ten shillings, a Spanish real, and others. [O.Fr. *rial,* royal.]

rybat, *rib′ət, n.* a dressed stone at the side of a door, window, &c. [Prob. conn. with **rebate** (2).]

rybaudrye, *rib′awd-ri, n.* (*Spens.*). Same as **ribaldry.**

rye, *rī, n.* a grass (Secale, esp. *S. cereale*) allied to wheat and barley: its grain, used for making bread: rye-grass: rye-whisky.—*adj.* of rye.—*ns.* **rye′-bread; rye′-coffee,** a coffee-substitute made from rye; **rye′-corn,** (*Austr.*) rye; **rye′-flour; rye′-grass,** a pasture and fodder grass (species of Lolium), with flat spikelets appressed edgewise in a two-rowed spike; **rye′-roll′,** a dark treacly cookie, not understood to be of rye.—*n.* and *adj.* **rye′-straw.**—*ns.* **rye′-whis′ky,** a spirituous beverage made chiefly from rye; **rye′-wolf** (Ger. *Roggenwolf*), an evil creature of German folklore lurking in the rye-fields. [O.E. *ryge*; O.N. *rugr,* Ger. *roggen* (also *rocken*).]

rye, *rī, n.* a gypsy word for gentleman. [Romany *rei, rai,* lord.]

ryepeck, rypeck, ripeck, *rī′pek, n.* (*prov.*) a pole used for mooring a punt. [Origin obscure.]

ryfe, *rīf, adj.* (*Spens.*). Same as **rife.**

ryke, *rīk,* a Scots form of **reach.**

rymme, an old spelling of **rim** (1 and 2).

rynd. Same as **rind** (2).

ryot, raiyat, *rī′ət, n.* an Indian peasant.—*n.* **ry′ot-wari, raiyatwari** (-*wä-rē*), a system of land-tenure by which each peasant holds directly of the state. [Hind. *raiyat, raiyatwārī*—Ar. *ra′īyah,* a subject.]

rype, *rü′pə,* n. a ptarmigan :—*pl.* **ry′per.** [Dan.]

rythme, *rīm,* an old spelling of **rhyme.**

ryve, an old spelling of **rive.**

S

S, s, *es*, *n.* the nineteenth letter in our alphabet, seventeenth in the Roman, its usual sound a voiceless open-blade consonant (sibilant), but often voiced, and sometimes a voiceless blade-point sound (represented usually by *sh*), or voiced (as in *pleasure*): any mark or object of the form of the letter: in chemistry, the symbol for sulphur: **as a** mediaeval Roman numeral, S=7 or 70; S̄= 70,000.—**collar of SS** (see **ess**).

's, *z*, a shortened form of **God's, has, is,** or (*Scot.*) **as, sal** (1).

sa', *sä*, *v.t.* an obs. contraction of **save.**

sab, *säb*, *n.* (*Scot.*) a form of **sob.**

Saba, *sä'bä*, *n.* Sheba, an ancient people of Yemen. —*n.* and *adj.* **Sabaean, Sabean** (*-bē'ən*).—Also applied by confusion to adherents of Sabaism and of Sabianism. [Gr. *Saba*—Ar. *Saba'*; Heb. *Shebā.*]

sabadilla, *sab-ə-dil'ä*, *n.* seeds of a liliaceous plant, Schoenocaulon, yielding veratrine.—Also **cebadill'a, cevadill'a.** [Sp. *cebadilla*, dim. of *cebada*, barley.]

Sabaism, *sä'bä-izm*, *n.* the worship of the host of heaven. [Heb. *tsäbä*, host.]

Sabal, *sä'bal*, *n.* an American genus of palms, the palmettos. [Origin unknown.]

Sabaoth, *sa-bä'oth*, *n.pl.* armies, used only in the Bible phrase, 'Lord of Sabaoth': (*sab'əth*; *Spens.*) erroneously for Sabbath. [Heb. *tsebäōth* (transliterated *sabaōth* in Gr.), pl. of *tsabä*, an army.]

sabaton, *sab'ə-ton*, *n.* armour for the foot, not necessarily broad-toed. [Prov. *sabató*; cf. **sabot,** Sp. *zapata.*]

Sabbath, *sab'əth*, *n.* among the Jews, Saturday, set apart for rest from work: among most Christians, Sunday: a sabbatical year of the Jews: a time of rest: (also **sabb'at**) a witches' midnight meeting. —*adj.* of or appropriate to the Sabbath.—*n.* **Sabbatā'rian,** one who observes Saturday as Sabbath: one who believes in or practises observance, or strict observance, of the Sabbath (Saturday or Sunday).—Also *adj.*—*ns.* **Sabbatā'rianism**; **Sabb'ath-breach**; **Sabb'ath-breaker.**—*ns.* and *adjs.* **Sabb'ath-breaking**; **Sabb'ath-day.**—*adjs.* **Sabb'athless**; **sabbatic** (*səb-at'ik*), **-al,** pertaining to, or resembling, the Sabbath: enjoying or bringing rest; **sabb'atine,** pertaining to Saturday.— *v.t.* **sabb'atise,** to observe as a Sabbath: *v.i.* to keep a Sabbath.—*n.* **sabb'atism,** sabbatical rest: observance of the Sabbath.—**Sabbathday's journey,** 2000 cubits, or about five furlongs, which a Jew was permitted to walk on the Sabbath (Josh. iii. 4); **Sabbath school,** a Sunday school; **sabbat'ical year,** every seventh year, in which the Israelites allowed their fields and vineyards to lie fallow: a professor's year off, for study, travel, &c. [Heb. *Shabbāth.*]

Sabella, *sä-bel'ä*, *n.* a genus of tube-building sea-worms. [L. *sabulum*, sand.]

Sabellian, *sə-bel'i-ən*, *n.* and *adj.* orig. Sabine: now generally used in a wide sense to include kindred peoples and languages. [L. *Sabellus*, poet. dim. of *Sabinus.*]

Sabellian, *sə-bel'i-ən*, *n.* a follower of *Sabellius* (3rd century).—Also *adj.*—*n.* **Sabell'ianism,** the teaching of Sabellius, that Father, Son, and Holy Ghost are one and the same person in different aspects.

saber, American spelling of **sabre.**

Sabian, *sä'bi-ən*, **Zabian,** *zä'*, **Tsabian,** *tsä'*, *n.* an adherent of a religion or a group of religions mentioned in the Koran as entitled to toleration, prob. akin to the Mandaeans: Mandaean: by confusion sometimes a Sabaean, sometimes an

adherent of Sabaism.—Also *adj.*—*n.* **Sā'bianism.** [Ar. *as*—*Sābi'ūn.*]

Sabine, *sab'īn*, *n.* one of an ancient people of central Italy, afterwards united with the Romans. —Also *adj.* [L. *Sabīnus.*]

sable, *sä'bl*, *n.* an arctic and subarctic marten: its lustrous dark brown fur: a paint-brush of its hair. —*adj.* of sable. [O.Fr.: prob. from Slav.]

sable, *sä'bl*, *n.* and *adj.* black (orig. *her.*, now chiefly *poet.*): dark.—*n.* a sable antelope: (in *pl.*) mourning garments.—*v.t.* to darken.—*adj.* **sa'ble-coloured.**—**sable antelope,** a large South African antelope (*Hippotragus niger*), black above, white below. [Fr. *sable*; poss. the same as the foregoing.]

sabot, *säb'ō*, *n.* a wooden shoe, as worn by the French peasantry: an attachment to guide a projectile through the bore.—*n.* **sabotage** (*-täzh'*), prosecution of a dispute by destruction.—*v.t.* and *v.i.* to destroy or damage in this way.—*ns.* **saboteur** (*-tər'*), one who sabotages; **sabotier** (*-tyä'*), a wearer of wooden shoes: a Waldensian. [Fr. *sabot.*]

sabre, *sä'bər*, *n.* a curved, cutting, cavalry sword: a soldier armed with a sabre.—*v.t.* to wound or kill with a sabre.—*ns.* **sä'bre-cut**; **sä'bre-rattling,** military bluster; **sä'bre-tooth** (in full **sabre-toothed tiger**), a Tertiary fossil carnivore (Machaerodus) with extremely long upper canine teeth; **sä'bre-wing,** a humming-bird of a group with bent outer primaries in the male. [Fr. *sabre*— Ger. *sabel* (now *säbel*): origin unknown.]

sabretache, *sab'ər-tash*, *n.* a flat bag slung from a cavalry officer's sword-belt. [Fr. *sabretache*— Ger. *säbeltasche*—*säbel*, sabre, *tasche*, pocket.]

sabulous, *sab'ū-ləs*, *adj.* sandy: gritty. [L. *sabulum*, sand.]

saburra, *sə-bur'ä*, *n.* a granular deposit, as in the stomach.—*adj.* **saburr'al.**—*n.* **saburrā'tion,** (*med.*) application of hot sand. [L. *saburra*, sand.]

sac, *sak*, *n.* (biol.) a pouch.—*adjs.* **sacc'ate,** pouched: pouch-like: gibbous: enclosed in a sac; **sacci-form** (*sak'si-form*), **sacc'ūlar,** sac-like; **sacc'ūl-ated,** formed in a series of sac-like expansions: enclosed.—*ns.* **sacculā'tion**; **sacc'ūle, sacc'ulus,** a small sac:—*pl.* **sacc'ules, sacc'ulī.** [L. *saccus*, a bag; see **sack** (1).]

sac, *sak*, *n.* (law) the privilege of a lord of manor of holding courts.—*adj.* **sac'less,** (*Scott*) unchallengeable, not to be molested (see **sackless**). See also **soc.** [O.E. *sacu*, strife.]

Saccharum, *sak'ä-rəm*, *n.* the sugar-cane genus of grasses.—*n.* **sacch'arate,** a salt of saccharic acid. —*adjs.* **sacch'arated,** sugared, sweetened; **saccharic** (*sak-ar'ik*), of sugar (**saccharic acid,** an acid, $H_2C_6H_8O_8$, got by oxidation of sugar).— *n.* **sacch'aride,** a carbohydrate: a compound with sugar.—*adj.* **saccharif'erous,** sugar yielding. —*v.t.* **sacchar'ify** (or *sak'*), to convert into sugar. —*ns.* **saccharim'eter,** a polarimeter or other instrument for testing sugars; **saccharim'etry;** **sacch'arin, -ine** (*-in, -ēn*), an intensely sweet, white crystalline solid ($C_5H_4COSO_2NH$) prepared from toluene.—*adj.* **sacch'arine** (*-in, -ēn*), of the nature of sugar: of, containing, or yielding sugar: sugary: of sickly sweetness.—*n.* **saccharinity** (*-in'i-ti*).—*adjs.* **sacch'aroid, -oid'al,** like loaf-sugar in texture.—*ns.* **saccharom'eter,** a hydro-meter or other instrument for measuring concentration of sugar solutions; **Saccharomyces** (*-ō-mī'sēz*; Gr. *mykēs*, fungus), the yeast genus of ascomycete fungi; **sacch'arose** (*-ōs*), any carbohydrate, esp. cane sugar. [L. *saccharum*—Gr. *sakcharon*, sugar, a word of Eastern origin; cf. **jaggery, sugar.**]

fāte, fär, ȧsk; mē, hər (her); *mīne; mōte; mūte; mōōn; dhen* (then)

saccos. See **sakkos.**

sacellum, *sə-sel'əm, n.* a god's unroofed sanctuary: a little chapel : a tomb or monument in the form of a chapel within a church :—*pl.* **sacell'a.** [L. dim. of *sacrum,* a holy place—*sacer,* consecrated.]

sacerdotal, *sas-ər-dō'tl, adj.* priestly : sacerdotalist. —*v.t.* **sacerdō'talise,** to render sacerdotal.—*ns.* **sacerdō'talism,** the spirit of the priesthood : devotion to priestly interests : priestcraft : the belief that the presbyter is a priest in the sense of offering a sacrifice in the eucharist : claim for, or attribution to, a priesthood, of special or supernatural powers ; **sacerdō'talist.**—*adv.* **sacerdō't- ally.** [L. *sacerdōs, -ōtis,* a priest—*sacer,* sacred, *dăre,* to give.]

sachem, *sā'chem, n.* a North American Indian chief : a Tammany leader.—*ns.* **sā'chemdom, sā'chemship.** [Algonquian.]

sachet, *sā'shā, n.* a bag of perfume. [Fr.]

sack, *sak, n.* a large bag of coarse material : a sackful : a varying measure of capacity : a woman's gown, loose at the back : a train hung from the shoulders of such a gown : a loose coat, hanging at the back : (*slang*) dismissal.—*v.t.* to put into a sack : (*slang*) to dismiss.—*ns.* **sack'cloth,** cloth for sacks : coarse cloth, formerly worn in mourning or penance ; **sack'-coat,** a man's short loose coat. —*adj.* **sack-doudling** (*-dood'lin ; Scott*), bagpiping (cf. **doodle,** and Ger. *dudelsack*).—*ns.* **sack'ful,** as much as a sack will hold :—*pl.* **sack'fuls ; sack'- ing,** sackcloth ; **sack'-race,** a race in which the runners are encased in sacks ; **sack'-tree,** the upas (from the use of its inner bark). [O.E. *sacc*— L. *saccus*—Gr. *sakkos* ; prob. Phoenician.]

sack, *sak, n.* the plundering or devastation of a town : pillage.—*v.t.* to plunder : to ravage.—*ns.* **sack'age, sack'ing,** sack. [Fr. *sac* ; according to some the same as the foregoing (putting in a bag).]

sack, *sak, n.* the old name of a Spanish wine, the favourite drink of Falstaff.—*n.* **sack'-poss'et,** posset made with sack.—**burnt sack,** mulled sack. [Fr. *sec*—L. *siccus,* dry.]

sackbut, *sak'but, n.* an old instrument with a slide like the trombone : (*B.*) a mistranslation of Aramaic *sabbekā,* the sambuca. [Fr. *saquebute,* perh. O.Fr. *saquier,* to draw out, and *bouter,* to push.]

sackless, *sak'lis, adj.* (*arch.* and *Scot.*) innocent : guileless : feeble : dispirited (see also under **sac**). [O.E. *sacléas—sacu* ; **sac, sake.**]

sacque, a sham-French spelling of **sack** (garment).

sacra, sacral. See **sacrum.**

sacrament, *sak'rə-mənt, n.* a religious rite variously regarded as a channel or as a sign of grace— amongst Protestants generally *Baptism* and the *Lord's Supper*—amongst Roman Catholics, also *Confirmation, Penance, Holy Orders, Matrimony,* and *Extreme Unction* : the Lord's Supper specially : a symbol of something spiritual or secret : a sign, token, or pledge of a covenant : a religious mystery : a Roman soldier's oath on enlistment : (*Rom. law*) a pledge deposited by each party to a suit : a solemn oath : an oath of purgation : materials used in a sacrament.—*v.t.* to bind by an oath.— *adj.* **sacramental** (*-ment'l*).—*ns.* **sacramen'tal- ism ; sacramen'talist.**—*adv.* **sacramen'tally.**— *n.* **sacramentā'rian,** one who holds a high or extreme view of the efficacy of the sacraments : (*obs.*) a denier of the real presence in the sacrament of the Lord's Supper.—Also *adj.*—*n.* **sacra- mentā'rianism.**—*adj.* **sacramen'tary,** pertaining to the sacrament or sacraments : sacramentarian.— *n.* a book containing all the prayers and ceremonies used at the celebration of the R.C. sacraments : one who denies the doctrine of the real presence.— *n.* **sac'rament-house,** an ambry for reservation of the sacrament.—**take the sacrament upon or to,** to take communion in confirmation of an oath. [L. *sacrāmentum,* an oath, pledge—*sacrāre,* to consecrate—*sacer,* sacred.]

sacrarium, *sā-krā'ri-əm* (L. *sā-krä'ri-oom*), *n.* (*Rom. ant.*) a place where the Penates or other holy things were kept : the presbytery of a church. [L. *sacrārium—sacer,* holy.]

sacred, *sā'krid, adj.* consecrated : devoted : set apart or dedicated, esp. to God : holy : proceeding from God : religious : entitled to veneration : not to be violated : accursed.—*adv.* **sa'credly.**— *n.* **sa'credness.**—**sacred ape,** the hanuman of India ; **sacred beetle,** an Egyptian scarab ; **sacred cat,** the house cat of Egypt, sacred to Pasht ; **sacred college,** the body of cardinals ; **sacred fish,** oxyrhyncus ; **Sacred Heart,** (*R.C.*) the physical heart of Christ, adored with special devotion since the 18th century. [Pa.p. of obs. *sacre*—O.Fr. *sacrer*—L. *sacrāre*—*sacer,* sacred.]

sacrifice, *sak'ri-fīs,* in the poets sometimes *-fīz, n.* the offering of a slaughtered animal on an altar to a god : any offering to a god : (*theol.*) Christ's offering of himself : (*R.C.*) the Mass : destruction, surrender, or forgoing of anything valued for the sake of anything else, esp. a higher consideration : loss by selling cheap : a victim offered in sacrifice. —*v.t.* to offer up in sacrifice : to make a sacrifice of : to give up for a higher good or for mere advantage : to make a victim of : to allow to come to destruction or evil.—*v.i.* to offer sacrifice.— *n.* **sac'rificer.**—*adj.* **sacrificial** (*-fish'l*).—*adv.* **sacrifi'cially.**—*v.t.* and *v.i.* **sac'rify,** (*obs.*) to sacrifice :—*pa.p.* (*Spens.*) **sac'rifide.**—**sacrifice hit,** in baseball, a hit to enable another player to score or to gain a base. [L. *sacrificium—sacer,* sacred, *facĕre,* to make.]

sacrilege, *sak'ri-lij, n.* a profanation of anything holy : the breaking into a place of worship and stealing therefrom.—*adj.* **sacrilegious** (*-lēj'əs,* often *-lij'*).—*adv.* **sacrilē'giously.**—*ns.* **sacrilē'gious- ness ; sacrilē'gist.** [Fr. *sacrilège*—L. *sacrilegium* —*sacer,* sacred, *legĕre,* to gather.]

sacring, *sā'kring, n.* (*arch.*) consecration.— *n.* **sa'cring-bell,** in R.C. churches, a small bell rung to call attention to the more solemn parts of the service of the Mass. [See **sacred.**]

sacrist, *sak'rist, sā'krist, n.* a sacristan : a person in a cathedral who copies out music for the choir and takes care of the books.—*ns.* **sacristan** (*sak'*), an officer in a church who has care of the sacred vessels and other movables : a sexton ; **sacristy** (*sak'*), an apartment in a church where the sacred utensils, vestments, &c., are kept : vestry. [L.L. *sacrista, sacristānus,* a sacristan, *sacristia,* a vestry —L. *sacer.*]

sacrosanct, *sak'rō-sang(k)t, adj.* inviolable.—*n.* **sacrosanc'tity.** [L. *sacrōsanctus—sacer,* sacred, *sanctus,* pa.p. of *sancīre,* to hallow.]

sacrum, *sā'krəm, n.* a triangular bone composed of fused vertebrae wedged between two innominate bones, so as to form the keystone of the pelvic arch :—*pl.* **sā'cra.**—*adj.* **sā'cral.**—**sā'crō-,** in composition, sacrum, e.g. *adjs.* **sācrocos'tal,** connected with the sacrum and having the character of a rib (also *n.*) ; **sācröil'iac,** pertaining to the sacrum and ilium. [L. (*os*) *sacrum,* holy (bone) : so called for unknown reason.]

sad, *sad* (*comp.* **sadd'er,** *superl.* **sadd'est**), *adj.* (*orig.*) sated : (*Spens., Milt.*) steadfast, constant : staid : sedate : serious : earnest : grave : soberminded : sorrowful : deplorable (often playfully) : heavy, stiff : doughy : sober, dark-coloured.— *v.t.* **sadd'en,** to make sad.—*v.i.* to grow sad.— *adjs.* **sad'-coloured ; sadd'ish ; sad'-eyed, -faced, -hearted** (all *Shak.*).—*n.* **sad'-iron,** a flat-iron.—*adv.* **sad'ly.**—*n.* **sad'ness.**—**in sober sadness,** in serious earnest. [O.E. *sæd,* sated ; cf. **Du.** *zat,* Ger. *satt* ; L. *sat, satis.*]

saddle, *sad'l, n.* a seat for a rider : a pad for the back of a draught animal : anything of like shape : a col : that part of the back on which the saddle is placed : a mark on that part : a butcher's cut, including a part of the backbone with the ribs : the hinder part of a cock's back : a worm's clitellum. —*v.t.* to put a saddle on : to encumber : to impose as a burden or encumbrance.—*adjs.* **sadd'leback, sadd'lebacked,** saddle-shaped : with a depression in the middle of the back : marked on the back : of a coping, sloping from the middle to each side.—*ns.* **sadd'leback,** a saddle-shaped hill, coping, animal, or object : the great black-backed gull : the hooded crow : the male harp-seal : a breed of goose : a breed of pig : a saddle-roof ;

sadd'le-bag, a bag carried at, or attached to, the saddle.—*adj.* upholstered in cloth in imitation of camels' saddle-bags.—*ns.* **sadd'le-bar**, a bar for sustaining stained glass in a window; **sadd'le-blanket**, a folded blanket used as a saddle-cloth; **sadd'le-bow** (-*bō*), the arched front of a saddle; **sadd'le-cloth**, a housing cloth placed under a saddle.—*adj.* **sadd'le-fast**, firmly seated in the saddle.—*ns.* **sadd'le-feather**, **-hackle**, one of the long, slender feathers drooping from a cock's saddle; **sadd'le-girth**, a band that holds the saddle in its place; **sadd'le-horse**, a riding horse; **sadd'le-lap**, the skirt of a saddle.—*adjs.* **sadd'le-less**; **sadd'le-nosed**, with nose sunken at the bridge.—*ns.* **sadd'le-pillar**, **-pin**, the support of a cycle saddle, which fits a socket in the frame; **sadd'ler**, a maker or seller of saddles: a soldier who has charge of cavalry saddles (also **sadd'ler-cor'poral**, **-ser'geant**): the harp-seal: (*U.S.*) a saddle-horse; **sadd'le-roof**, a tower roof with two gables; **sadd'le-room**, a room where saddles and harness are kept; **sadd'lery**, occupation of a saddler: his shop or stock-in-trade: a saddle-room.—*adjs.* **sadd'le-shaped**, arched: concave and convex in sections at right angles to each other; **sadd'le-sick**, **-sore**, chafed with riding.—*ns.* **sadd'le-spring**, a spring supporting a cycle-saddle; **sadd'le-tree**, the frame of a saddle.—**in the saddle**, in control; **put the saddle on the right horse**, to impute blame where it is deserved; **saddle up**, (*S.Afr.*) to saddle a horse: to mount. [O.E. *sadol*, *sadel*; cf. Du. *zadel*, Ger. *sattel*.]

Sadducee, *sad'ū-sē*, *n.* one of a Jewish sceptical school or party of aristocratic traditionists in New Testament times.—*adj.* **Sadducae'an**, **Sadducean** (-*sē'ən*).—*ns.* **Sadd'uceeism**, **Sadd'ucism**, scepticism. [Gr. *Saddoukaios*—Heb. *Tsadūqīm*.]

sadism, *sād'izm*, *n.* sexual perversion with passion for cruelty.—*n.* sad'ist.—*adj.* sadis'tic. [Comte (called Marquis) de *Sade* (1740-1814).]

sae, *sā*, *adv.* Scottish form of **so**.

saeculum, **seculum**, *sek'ūl-əm*, *n.* an astronomical or geological age. [L., a generation.]

safari, *sä-fä'rē*, *n.* an expedition or caravan, especially for hunting.—*v.i.* to go on safari. [Swahili.]

safe, *sāf*, *adj.* unharmed: free from danger: secure: sound: certain: sure: reliable: cautious. —*n.* a chest or closet, safe against fire, thieves, &c.: a ventilated box or cupboard for meat, &c. —*v.t.* (*obs.*) to make safe: (*Shak.*) to bring safely. —*prep.* (*Spens.*) save.—*n.* safe-con'duct, a permission to pass or travel with guarantee of freedom from molestation: a convoy.—*v.t.* (-*kon'*, or -*dukt'*) to convoy.—*ns.* safe'-deposit, a safe storage for valuables; safe'guard, keeping safe, protection: safety: a guard: a contrivance, condition, or provision to secure safety: a safe-conduct: (*obs.*) an overskirt for riding.—*v.t.* to protect.—*ns.* safe'guarding, protection, especially by import duties; safe'-keeping, keeping in safety: safe custody.—*adv.* safe'ly.—*ns.* safe'ness; safe'ty (in *Spens.* often *sāf'i-ti*), state or fact of being safe: close custody: a safeguard: a safety-bicycle; safe'ty-arch, an arch in the body of a wall to relieve the pressure; safe'ty-bicycle, a common low-wheeled bicycle; safe'ty-bolt, the safety-lock of a firearm; safe'ty-cage, a mine-cage with a catch to prevent a fall; safe'ty-catch, any catch to secure safety, as in a miners' cage or a gun; safe'ty-curtain, a fireproof theatre curtain; safe'ty-fuse, a slow-burning fuse that can be lighted at a safe distance: a fuse inserted for safety in an electric circuit; safe'ty-glass, a sandwich of plastic between sheets of glass: glass reinforced with wire, or toughened; safe'ty-lamp, a miners' lamp that will not ignite inflammable gases; safe'ty-light, a warning light: a light that will not readily cause a fire; safe'ty-lock, a lock that cannot be picked by ordinary means: in firearms, a device for preventing accidental discharge; safe'ty-match, a match that can be ignited only on a prepared surface; safe'ty-paper, paper difficult to imitate or tamper with without detection, as for bank-notes; safe'ty-

pin, a pin in the form of a clasp with a guard covering its point: a pin for locking a piece of machinery, a grenade, a mine, &c.; safe'ty-plug, a plug that melts when the temperature rises too high; safe'ty-razor, a razor with protected blade; safe'ty-rein, a rein for preventing a horse from running away; safe'ty-stop, a contrivance for preventing accidents in machinery; safe'ty-valve, a valve that opens when the pressure becomes too great: (*fig.*) any outlet that gives relief.—**err on the safe side**, to choose the safer alternative; **safe and sound**, secure and uninjured. [O.Fr. *sauf*—L. *salvus*.]

saffian, *saf'i-an*, *n.* leather tanned with sumach and dyed in bright colours. [Russ. *saf'yan*.]

safflower, *saf'lowr*, *n.* a thistle-like composite (*Carthamus tinctorius*) cultivated in India: its dried petals, used for making a red dye and rouge. [Cf. Du. *saffloer*, O.Fr. *saffleur*.]

saffron, *saf'rən*, *n.* a species of crocus: its dried stigmas, used as a dye and flavouring: its colour, orange-yellow.—*n.* saff'ron-cake, a cake flavoured with saffron.—*adj.* saff'roned, coloured or flavoured with saffron.—*adj.* saff'rony, coloured somewhat like saffron.—*n.* saf'ranin(e), a coal-tar dye, giving various colours.—**bastard saffron**, safflower; **meadow saffron**, Colchicum. [O.Fr. *safran*—Ar. *za'farān*.]

sag, *sag*, *v.i.* to bend, sink, or hang down, esp. in the middle: to yield or give way as from weight or pressure: to hang heavy: to droop: to drag oneself heavily along: to make leeway: (*pr.p.* **sagg'ing**; *pa.p.* and *pa.t.* sagged).—*n.* a droop.—*adj.* sagging.—*n.* and *adj.* sagg'ing. [Cf. Sw. *sacka*, to sink down; L.G. *sacken*, to sink.]

saga, *sä'gä*, *n.* a prose tale in the old literature of Iceland: a body of legend about some subject: a romantic tale.—*n.* sa'gaman, a narrator of sagas. [O.N. *saga*; cf. saw (3).]

sagacious, *sə-gā'shəs*, *adj.* keen in perception or thought: discerning and judicious: wise.—*adv.* sagā'ciously.—*ns.* sagā'ciousness, sagacity (-*gas'i-ti*). [L. *sagāx*, -*ācis*.]

sagamore, *sag'ə-mōr*, *n.* an American Indian chief. [Penobscot *sagamo*; cf. sachem.]

sagapenum, *sag-ə-pē'nəm*, *n.* a fetid gum-resin, from *Ferula persica*. [Gr. *sagapēnon*.]

sagathy, *sag'ə-thi*, *n.* a woollen stuff. [Origin unknown; cf. Fr. *sagatis*, Sp. *sagatí*.]

sage, *sāj*, *n.* a garden labiate plant (*Salvia officinalis*) used for stuffing for goose, &c.: any plant of the genus, as clary: extended to wood germander (*wood-sage*).—*ns.* sage'-apple, an edible gall formed on Mediterranean sage; sage'brush, a plant-formation of shrubby Artemisias, on dry American plains: any of the Artemisias forming it; sage'-cheese, a cheese flavoured and mottled with sage leaves; sage'-cock, **-grouse**, a large North American grouse that feeds on sagebrush; sage'-green, greyish green, as in sage leaves; sage'-rabbit, a small hare of the sagebrush; sage'-tea', an infusion of sage leaves, a domestic tonic; sage'-thrash'er, the mountain mocking-bird. [O.Fr. *sauge* (It. *salvia*)—L. *salvia*—*salvus*, safe.]

sage, *sāj*, *adj.* wise.—*n.* a man of great wisdom.—*adv.* sage'ly.—*n.* sage'ness.—**seven sages** (see seven). [Fr. *sage*—L. *sapĕre*, to be wise.]

sagene, *sə-jēn'*, *n.* a net.—*n.* sagenite (*saj'ən-īt*, *sə-jē'nīt*), rutile in a network of needles.—*adj.* sagenitic (*saj-ən-it'ik*). [Gr. *sagēnē*, drag-net.]

saggar, **saggard**, **sagger**, **seggar**, **sagg'ar**, *seg'ər*(d), *n.* a clay box in which pottery is packed for baking. [Perh. safeguard.]

sagged, **sagging**. See sag.

saginate, *saj'i-nāt*, *v.t.* to fatten.—*n.* saginā'tion. [L. *saginăre*, to fatten.]

sagitta, *sə-jit'ä*, *n.* a keystone: a versed sine: the middle stroke of the letter epsilon.—*adj.* sagittal (*saj'it-l*), arrow-shaped: like a sagitta: pertaining or parallel to the sagittal suture.—*adv.* sag'ittally. —*ns.* Sagitt[ä]'ria, the arrow-head genus; Sagit-tä'rius, the Archer, a constellation and a sign o[f] the zodiac; sag'ittary, a centaur: an archer.— *adj.* sag'ittate, shaped like an arrow-head wit[h] the barbs pointing backwards.—**sagittal suture**

that between the two parietal bones of the skull. [*L. sagitta*, an arrow.]

sago, *sā′gō, n.* a nutritive farinaceous substance produced from the pith of Metroxylon and other palms (Arenga, Caryota, Oreodoxa), and Cycads (Cycas).—*n.* **sa′go-palm.** [Malay *sāgū*.]

saguaro, *sä-(g)wä′rō, n.* the giant cactus. [From an American Indian language.]

saguin, sagoin, sagouin, *sag′win,* sag-oin′, *n.* a titi monkey. [Fr. *sago(u)in*—Port. *saguim*—Tupí *saguin*.]

sagum, *sā′gəm* (L. *säg′oom*), *n.* a Roman military cloak:—*pl.* **sa′ga.** [L. *sāgum*; prob. Gaulish.]

sahib, *sä′ib, n.* a term of respect given in India to persons of rank and to Europeans: Sir or Mr: a European: a gentleman. [Ar. *sāhib*, orig. friend.]

sai, *sä′i, n.* the capuchin monkey. [Tupí, monkey.]

saibling, *zīp′ling, n.* the char. [Ger. dial.]

saic, saick, saique, *sä-ēk′, sä′ik, n.* a Levantine vessel like a ketch. [Fr. *saïque*—Turk. *shāïqā*.]

saice. Same as **syce.**

said, *sed, pa.t.* and *pa.p.* of **say.**—*adj.* beforementioned.

saiga, *sī′gä, n.* a west Asian antelope. [Russ.]

saikless, *säk′lis, adj.* a Scots form of **sackless.**

sail, *sāl, n.* a sheet of canvas, framework of slats, or other structure, spread to catch the wind, so as to propel a ship, drive a windmill, &c.: a wing, esp. a hawk's: any sail-like organ or object: sails collectively: a ship or ships: a trip in a vessel: an act or distance of sailing: a number sailing or flying together: a condition of having sails set or filled.—*v.i.* to progress or travel by **sail:** to go by water: to set out on a voyage: to make excursions in sailing-craft: to glide or float smoothly along.—*v.t.* to navigate: to cause to sail, as a toy boat: to pass over or along in a ship: to fly through.—*adj.* **sail′able,** navigable.—*n.* **sail′-boat,** (*U.S.*) a sailing-boat.—*adjs.* **sail′-borne; sail′-broad,** (*Milt.*) broad or spreading like a sail. —*n.* **sail′-cloth,** a strong cloth for sails.—*adj.* **sailed,** having sails.—*ns.* **sail′er,** a boat or ship that can sail; **sail′-fish,** a fish that shows a large dorsal fin, esp. the basking shark or a kind of swordfish (Histiophorus); **sail′-fluke,** the whiff (from exposing its tail); **sail′-flying,** flying in a sailplane; **sail′ing,** travelling or journey by sails or on water: a ship's departure from port: act or mode of directing a ship's course.—Also *adj.* —*ns.* **sail′ing-boat,** a boat moved by sails; **sail′ing-master,** an officer in charge of navigation, esp. of a yacht (formerly in U.S. navy a warrant officer); **sail′ing-ship,** a ship driven by sails.— *adj.* **sail′less.**—*ns.* **sail′-loft,** a loft where sails are made; **sail′-maker; sail′or,** one who is employed in the management of a ship, esp. one who is not an officer: a mariner: a seaman: a navigator: one who is tolerant of the motion of a ship: (*coll.*) a sailor-hat; **sail′or-hat,** a lady's hat like a man's straw hat: a hat with a wide, upcurved brim; **sail′oring,** occupation as a sailor. —*adjs.* **sail′orless; sail′or-like; sail′orly.**—*ns.* **sail′or-man,** a seaman; **sail′plane,** a glider that can rise with an upward current; **sail′-room,** a room in a vessel where sails are stowed.—*adj.* **sail′y,** like a sail.—*n.* **sail′-yard,** the yard on which sails are extended.—**full sail,** with sails filled with the wind: with all sails set; **make sail,** to spread more canvas; **sail close to (or near) the wind** (see **wind**); **sailing orders,** instructions to the captain of a ship at setting forth on a voyage; **set sail,** to spread the sails: to set forth on a voyage; **shorten sail,** to reduce its extent; **strike sail,** to lower the sail or sails: (*Shak.*) to abate one's pretensions; **under sail,** having the sails spread: moved by sails. [O.E. *segel*; cf. Du. *zeil*, Ger. *segel*.]

sail, *sāl, v.t.* to project.—*n.* projection. [O.Fr. *saillir*, to jut—L. *salīre*, to leap.]

saimiri, *sī-mē′rē, n.* a squirrel-monkey. [Tupí *sai*, monkey, *miri*, little.]

sain, *sān, v.t.* (*arch.*) to make the sign of the cross over: (by association with L. *sānāre*) to heal. [O.E. *segnian*—L. *signāre*—*signum*, mark.]

saine, *sān,* a Spenserian form of the infin. and the

pres. indic. pl. of **say**: (*Shak.*) an editor's reading for **faine** (*Love's Lab. Lost*, III. i. 88) taken as a *pa.p.* of **say.**

sainfoin, *sān′foin, n.* a leguminous fodder-plant (*Onobrychis viciaefolia*).—Also **saint′foin.** [Fr. *sainfoin*, prob.—*sain*, wholesome, *foin*, hay—L. *sānum fēnum*.]

saint, *sānt,* when prefixed to a name *sint, sn*(*t*), *adj.* (or *n.* in apposition) holy.—*n.* a holy person: one eminent for virtue: (*B.*) an Israelite, a Christian, or one of the blessed dead: one canonised: an angel: a member of various religious bodies, esp. Puritans, as used of themselves or as a nickname: a sanctimonious person.—*v.i.* (or *v.t.* with *it*) to play the saint.—*v.t.* to make a saint of: to hail as saint.—*n.* **saint′dom.**—*adj.* **saint′ed,** made a saint, holy: sacred: gone to heaven: canonised. —*ns.* **saint′ess; saint′hood.** — *adj.* **saint′ish,** saintlike.—*n.* **saint′ism,** the character or quality of a saint: sanctimoniousness.—*adj.* **saint′like.**— *ns.* **saint′liness; saint′ling.**—*adj.* **saint′ly,** of, like, characteristic of, or befitting a saint.—*n.* **saint′ship.**—**saint's day,** a day set apart for the commemoration of a particular saint; **St Agnes's Eve,** 20th January; **St Agnes's flower,** the snowflake; **St Andrew's cross,** a cross in the form of the letter X: a white saltire on a blue field, as borne on the banner of Scotland; **St Andrew's Day,** 30th November; **St Anthony's fire,** erysipelas; **St Anthony's nut,** earthnut or pignut; **St Barbara's cress,** yellow rocket; **St Barnaby's thistle,** a knapweed flowering about the saint's day (11th June); **St Bernard's dog or (great) St Bernard,** a cross between a short-haired Newfoundland and mastiff, formerly kept at the hospice of the Great St Bernard (St Bernard's of Menthon) to rescue travellers lost in the snow; **St Crispin's Day,** a shoemakers' festival, 25th October; **St Cuthbert's beads,** enclinite joints; **St Dabeoc's heath,** a rare Irish heath; **St David's Day,** 1st March; **St Elmo's fire,** a corposant; **St George's cross,** a red cross on a white field; **St George's Day,** 23rd April; **St Hubert's disease,** hydrophobia; **St Ignatius's bean,** the poisonous seed of a plant (*Strychnos Ignatii*) akin to nux vomica; **St James's,** the British court; **St John's bread,** the carob bean; **St John's Day,** 27th December; **St Johnston's riband,** or tippet, the hangman's rope (St Johnstoun=Perth); **St John's wort,** any Hypericum; **St Julien,** an esteemed red Bordeaux wine from the Médoc region; **St Leger,** a horse-race run since 1776 at Doncaster, so called since 1778 from Col. *St Leger*; **St Luke's summer,** a spell of pleasant weather about the middle of October; **St Martin's evil,** drunkenness; **St Martin's summer,** a spell of mild, damp weather in late autumn; **St Nicholas's clerks,** thieves; **St Patrick's cabbage,** London pride; **St Patrick's Day,** 17th March; **St Peter's fish,** the dory; **St Peter's wort,** the square-stalked St John's wort: extended to several plants; **St Stephen's,** the Houses of Parliament; **St Swithin's Day,** 15th July; **St Valentine's Day,** 14th February (see **valentine**); **St Vitus's dance,** chorea. [Fr.,—L. *sanctus*, holy.]

Saint-Simonism, *sən*(*t*)-*, sin*(*t*)-*sī′mən-izm, n.* the socialistic system of the Comte de *Saint-Simon* (1760-1825).—*ns.* **Saint-Simō′nian** (also *adj.*); **Saint-Simō′nianism; Saint-Si′monist.**

sair, *sār,* Scots form of **sore, savour, serve.**

saist (*Spens., Milt.*). Same as **sayest** (see **say**).

saith, *seth,* (*arch.*) 3rd pers. sing. pres. indic. of **say.**

saith, saithe, *sāth, n.* (*Scot.*) the coalfish. [O.N. *seithr.*]

Saiva, Shaiva, *s*(*h*)*ī′va, n.* a votary of *Siva.*—*n.* **S(h)ai′vism.**

sajou, *sä-zhōō′, -jōō′, n.* a capuchin monkey. [Fr., —Tupí *sai*, monkey, and augmentative *-uassu*.]

sake, *sä′ki, n.* Japanese rice-beer: alcoholic liquor generally. [Jap.]

sake, *sāk, n.* cause: account: regard: advantage: behalf: purpose: aim, object.—**for any sake,** by all means: I beseech you; **for old sake's sake,** for the sake of old times, for auld langsyne. [O.E. *sacu,* strife, a lawsuit; Du. *zaak,* Ger. *sache;*

O.E. *sacan*, to strive, Goth. *sakan*; cf. **sac**, **sackless**, **seek**.]

saker, *sā′kər*, *n.* a species of falcon (*Falco sacer*) used in hawking, esp. the female: an obsolete small cannon.—*n.* **sa′keret**, the male saker. [Fr. *sacre*, prob.—Ar. *saqr*, confounded with L. *sacer* sacred.]

saki, *sä′ki*, -*kē*, *n.* a South American monkey of the genus Pithecia, with long bushy non-prehensile tail. [Fr., for Tupí *sai*, or *saguin*; cf. **sai**, **saguin**.]

sakieh, **sakiyeh**, **sakia**, *sä′ki-(y)ə*, *n.* an Eastern water-wheel. [Ar. *sāqiyah*.]

sakkos, *sak′os*, *n.* an Eastern bishop's vestment like an alb or a dalmatic. [Gr. *sakkos*, a bag.]

saksaul. Same as **saxaul.**

Sakti, **Shakti**, *s(h)äk′*, *shuk′tē*, *n.* (Hinduism) the female principle, esp. as personified in the wife of Siva or other god.—*ns.* S(h)ak′ta, a worshipper of the Sakti; **S(h)ak′tism.** [Sans. *shakti*, divine energy.]

sal, *säl*, a Northern form of **shall.**

sal. See **sial.**

sal, *säl*, *n.* a large gregarious tree (*Shorea robusta*; fam. Dipterocarpaceae) of north India with teak-like wood. [Hind. *sāl*.]

sal, *sal*, *n.* (*chem.* and *pharmacy*) a salt.—**sal alem′broth** (an alchemist's word of unknown origin), mercury ammonium chloride—also *salt of wisdom*; **sal ammoniac**, ammonium chloride; **sal prunella**, **prunelle**, saltpetre cast in cakes; **sal volatile** (*vol-at′i-li*), smelling-salts. [L. *sāl*.]

salaam, *sä-läm′*, *n.* a word and gesture of salutation in the East, chiefly among Moslems: obeisance: greeting.—*v.i.* to perform the salaam. [Ar. *salām*, peace; Heb. *shālōm*.]

salable, **salableness**, **salably.** See **sale.**

salacious, *sə-lā′shəs*, *adj.* lustful: lecherous.—*adv.* **salā′ciously.** — *ns.* **salā′ciousness**, **salacity** (-*las′i-ti*). [L. *salāx*, -*ācis*—*salīre*, to leap.]

salad, *sal′əd*, also (*arch.*) **sallad**, **sallet** (*sal′it*), *n.* a dish of uncooked herbs, generally mixed, with or without oil and vinegar or other dressing, sometimes including slices of egg, lobster, &c.: a plant grown for or used in salads: (*fig.*; *Shak.*) something savoury.—*ns.* **sal′ad-bowl**; **sal′ad-burnet**, the common burnet; **sal′ad-dressing**, **-oil**, sauce, olive-oil, used in dressing salads; **sal′ad-herb**, **-plant**; **sal′ading**, herbs for salads; **sal′ad-plate**—**salad days** (*Shak.*) the time when one is ' green in judgment, cold in blood ' (*Ant. and Cleop.* I. v. 74). [Fr. *salade*—L. *sāl*, salt.]

salade. Same as **sallet** (1).

salal, **sallal**, *sal′al*, *n.* a N.W. American ericaceous shrub (*Gaultheria Shallon*).—*n.* **sal(l)′al-berry**, its edible fruit. [Chinook jargon.]

salamander, *sal′ə-man-dər*, or -*man′*, *n.* a genus (Salamandra) of tailed amphibians, nearly related to the newts, harmless, but long dreaded as poisonous, once supposed able to live in fire or to put out fire: an elemental spirit believed by Paracelsists to live in fire: one who braves exposure to fire unscathed (physical, military, or amatory): a poker used red-hot for kindling fires: a hot metal plate for browning meat, &c.—*adjs.* **salaman′der-like** (also *adv.*); **salaman′drian**; **salaman′drine** (also *n.*). [Fr. *salamandre*—L. *salamandra*—Gr. *salamandrā*; prob. of Eastern origin.]

salami, *sa-lä′mi*, **salame**, -*mā*, *n.* a highly seasoned Italian sausage. [It.]

salmon. See **salmon** (2).

salangane, *sal′ang-gān*, *n.* a swiftlet (Collocalia) that builds edible nests. [Tagálog *salangan*.]

salary, *sal′ə-ri*, *n.* a periodical payment (usually at longer intervals than a week) for services other than mechanical.—*v.t.* to pay a salary to.—*n.* **salariat** (*sə-lā′ri-ət*), the salary-drawing class or body.—*adj.* **sal′aried.** [O.Fr. *salarie* (Fr. *salaire*)—L. *salārium*, salt-money, salt.]

salband, *säl′band*, *zäl′bänt*, *n.* (*geol.*) the crust of a dyke or vein. [Ger. *salband*, selvage—*selb*, self, *ende*, end.]

sale, *säl*, *n.* act of selling: the exchange of anything for money: power or opportunity of selling: demand: public offer of goods to be sold, esp. at reduced prices or by auction: the state of being offered to buyers.—*adj.* intended for selling: vendible.—*n.* **salabil′ity** (also **saleabil′ity**).—*adj.* **sal(e)′able**, that may be sold: in good demand. — *n.* **sal(e)′ableness.** — *adv.* **sal(e)′ably.** — *ns.* **sale′-cat′alogue**; **sale′-price**, price asked at a special sale; **sale′-room**, an auction-room; **sales′-clerk**, (*U.S.*) one who sells in a store or shop; **sales′man**, a man who sells goods, esp. in a shop: (*U.S.*) a commercial traveller or canvasser: —*fem.* **sales′woman**; **sales′manship**, the art of selling: skill in presenting wares in the most attractive light or in persuading purchasers to buy; **sale′work**, work or things (made) for sale: work carelessly done.—**forced sale**, a sale compelled by a creditor; **sale of work**, a sale of things made by members of a congregation or association to raise money. [Late O.E. *sala*, perh. —O.N. *sala*.]

sale, *säl*, *n.* sallow: (*Spens.*) wicker. [See **sallow** (1).]

salep, *sal′əp*, *n.* dried Orchis tubers: a food or drug prepared from them. [Turk. *sālep*, from Ar.]

saleratus, *sal-ə-rā′təs*, *n.* (*U.S.*) potassium or sodium bicarbonate, used in baking-powders. [L. *sāl aerātus*, aerated salt.]

Salesian, *səl-ē′shən*, *adj.* of St Francis of *Sales* or his order, the Visitants.—*n.* a follower of St Francis: a member of his order.

salewd, (*Spens.*) *pa.t.* of **salue.**

salfern, *sal′fərn*, *n.* gromwell (*Lithospermum arvense*).

Salian, *sā′li-ən*, *adj.* pertaining to a tribe of Franks on the lower Rhine.—*n.* one of this tribe.—*adj.* **Salic**, **Salique** (*sal′ik*).—**Salic law**, a law among the Salian Franks limiting the succession of certain lands to males—held later to apply to the succession to the crown of France. [L. *Salii*, Salians.]

Salian, *sā′li-ən*, *adj.* pertaining to the *Salii*, or priests of Mars in ancient Rome.

Salicaceae, *sal-i-kā′si-ē*, *n.pl.* a family of Archichlamydeae, willows and poplars.—*adj.* **salicā′ceous** (-*shəs*).—*ns.* **sal′icet** (-*set*), **salicional** (*səl-ish′ə-nəl*), an organ stop with a tone like that of willow pipes; **salicetum** (-*sē′təm*), a thicket or plantation of willows:—*pl.* **salicē′tums**, **salicē′ta**; **sal′icin** (-*sin*), a bitter crystalline glucoside ($C_{13}H_{18}O_7$) got from willow-bark, &c.; **salicylate** (*sə-lis′i-lāt*), a salt of salicylic acid.—*v.t.* to treat with salicylic acid.—*adj.* **salicylic** (*sal-i-sil′ik*; Gr. *hȳlē*, matter, material).—**salicylic acid**, an acid ($C_7H_6O_3$) originally prepared from salicin. [L. *salix*, *salicis*, a willow.]

Salicornia, *sal-i-kor′ni-ä*, *n.* the glasswort or marsh-samphire genus of the goosefoot family, small cactus-like salt-marsh plants. [Perh. L. *sāl*, salt, *cornū*, a horn.]

salient, *sā′li-ənt*, *adj.* leaping or springing: projecting outwards, as an angle: outstanding: prominent: striking.—*n.* an outward-pointing angle esp. of a fortification or line of defences.—*ns* **sā′lience**, the quality or condition of being salient: projection: (*Spens.*) **saliaunce**) onset; **sā′liency.**—*n.pl.* **Salientia** (-*en′shyä*), the frog and toad order of Amphibia. — *adv.* **sā′liently.** — **salient point**, first rudiment, esp. (formerly) of the heart. [L. *saliēns*, -*entis*, pr.p. of *salīre*, to leap.]

saliferous, *sa-lif′ər-əs*, *adj.* salt-bearing. [L. *sāl salis*, salt, *ferre*, to bear.]

salify, *sal′i-fī*, *v.t.* to combine or impregnate with or form into a salt:—*pr.p.* **sal′ifying**; *pa.t.* and *pa.p.* **sal′ified.**—*adj.* **sal′ifiable.**—*n.* **salifica′tion.** [Fr. *salifier*—L. *sāl*, *salis*, salt, *facĕre*, to make.]

saligot, *sal′i-got*, *n.* the water-chestnut. [Fr.]

salina, *sə-lē′na*, or -*lī′*, *n.* a salt lagoon, lake, marsh or spring: a salt-pan: a salt-work. [Sp.,—L. *salīna* (in pl. only)—*sāl*, salt.]

saline, *sā′līn*, or *sə-līn′*, *adj.* salt: salty: of the nature of a salt: abounding in salt: of the salts of alkali metals and magnesium: adapted to an environment with salt.—*n.* (*sə-līn′*, also *sā′līn*) a salina: a salt: crude potash: an effervescent aperient powder.—*ns.* **salinity** (*sə-lin′i-ti*), saltness; **salinometer** (*sal-i-nom′i-tər*), a hydrometer for measuring saltness of water. [L. *salīnus*, cf. *salina*.]

Salique. Same as **Salic** (see **Salian**).

saliva, *sə-lī'və*, *n.* spittle.—*adjs.* **sali'val** (*rare*); **salivary** (*sal'i-vər-i*), pertaining to, secreting, or conveying saliva.—*v.i.* **sal'ivate,** to produce or discharge saliva, esp. in excess.—*v.t.* to cause to secrete excess of saliva.—*n.* **salivā'tion,** flow of saliva, esp. in excess. [L. *saliva*.]

Salix, *sal'iks*, *sā'liks*, *n.* the willow genus. [L. *sălix, -icis.*]

sallal. See **salal**.

sallee, *sal'ē*, *n.* (*Austr.*) Acacia of various kinds: a species of Eucalyptus. [From a native word, or **sally**=**sallow**.]

sallee-man, *sal'ē-man*, *n.* a Moorish pirate: a hydrozoan with sail-like crest.—Also **sall'y-man.** —*n.* **sall'ee-rover.** [*Sallee*, on the coast of Morocco.]

sallenders, *sal'ən-dərz*, *n.* a skin disease affecting the hocks of horses. [Cf. Fr. *solandre.*]

sallet, *sal'it*, *n.* a light helmet (esp. 15th century) with neck-guard.—Also **salade** (*sä-läd'*). [Fr. *salade*; cf. It. *celata*; perh.—L. *galea caelāta,* engraved helmet.]

sallet. See **salad**.

sallow, *sal'ō*, *n.* a willow, esp. the broader-leaved kinds with comparatively brittle twigs—(*Scot.*) **sauch, saugh** (*sawhh*).—*ns.* **sall'ow-kitten,** a small puss-moth whose larva feeds on sallow; **sall'ow-thorn,** sea-buckthorn.—*adj.* **sall'owy,** abounding in sallows. [O.E. (Anglian) *salh*, late stem *salg-* (W.S. *sealh, séales*); cf. Ger. *sal(weide)*, L. *salix.*]

sallow, *sal'ō*, *adj.* of a pale yellowish colour.— *v.t.* to make sallow.—*adj.* **sall'owish,** somewhat sallow.—*n.* **sall'owness.**—*adj.* **sall'owy.** [O.E. *salo, salu*; cf. Du. *zaluw,* and O.H.G. *salo.*]

sally, *sal'i*, *n.* a leap: a swaying: an outrush: a sudden rushing forth of troops to attack besiegers: a going forth, excursion: outburst of fancy, wit, &c.: a projection: a running from side to side.— *v.i.* to rush out suddenly: to set forth, issue.— *v.t.* to sway by running from side to side (of a ship):—*pr.p.* **sall'ying;** *pa.t.* and *pa.p.* **sall'ied.** —*n.* **sall'yport,** a gateway for making a sally from a fortified place: a large port for the escape of the crew from a fire-ship. [Fr. *saillie—saillir* (It. *salire*)—L. *salīre*, to leap.]

sally, *sal'i*, *n.* the raising of a bell by pull of the rope: the woolly grip of a bell rope.—*v.t.* to bring into position of sally. [Perh. from preceding.]

sally, *sal'i*, a variant of **Sallee** and of **sallow** (willow).

Sally Lunn, *sal'i-lun'*, *n.* a sweet spongy tea-cake. [From a girl who sold them in the streets of Bath, *c.* 1797.]

salmagundi, *sal-mə-gun'di*, *n.* a dish of minced meat with eggs, anchovies, vinegar, pepper, &c.: a medley, miscellany.—Also **salmagun'dy.** [Fr. *salmigondis*; origin obscure.]

salmi, *sal'mē*, *n.* a ragout, esp. of game. [Fr.; perh. from preceding, or from It. *salame*, sausage.]

Salmo, *sal'mō*, *n.* the salmon and trout genus of fishes, giving name to the family **Salmonidae** (*sal-mon'i-dē*). —*n.* **sal'monid.** —*n.* and *adj.* **sal'monoid.** [L. *salmō, -ōnis*, salmon.]

salmon, *sam'ən*, *n.* a large, highly esteemed fish (*Salmo salar*), with silvery sides, that ascends rivers to spawn: extended to many closely allied fishes, and to some that resemble it superficially in some respects: the flesh of any of these as food: the colour of salmon flesh, a pinkish orange:—*pl.* **salmon**; or **salmons**, of kinds of salmon.— *adj.* salmon-coloured.— *ns.* **salm'on-berry,** a salmon-coloured American raspberry; **salm'on-coble,** a salmon-fisher's boat; **salm'on-colour,** an orange-pink. — *adj.* **salm'on-coloured.** — *ns.* **salm'on-disease,** a bacterial disease of salmon formerly attributed to a fungus (Saprolegnia); **salm'onet,** a samlet; **salm'on-fisher, -fishery, -fishing;** **salm'on-fly,** any artificial fly for taking salmon; **salm'on-fry'; salm'on-ladder,** a series of steps to permit a salmon to pass upstream; **salm'on-leap,** a waterfall ascended by salmon at

a leap; **salm'on-leister, -spear,** an instrument for spearing salmon; **salm'on-tackle,** rod, line, and fly for taking salmon; **salm'on-trout',** a fish (*Salmo trutta*) like the salmon, but smaller and thicker in proportion: in America applied to various kinds of trout.—**Burnett salmon,** the Australian lungfish (from the Burnett River). [O.Fr. *saumon*—L. *salmō, -ōnis*, from *salīre,* to leap.]

salmon, *sam'ən*, **salamon,** *sal'ə-mən*, *n.* supposed to mean the mass, as in the vagrants' inviolable oath *by* (*the*) *salmon.*

Salomonic. Same as **Solomonic.**

salon, *sal-on⁹*, *n.* a drawing-room: a reception-room: a periodic gathering of notable persons in the house of a society queen: **Salon**, a great annual exhibition of works by living artists in Paris. [Fr.]

saloon, *sə-lōōn'*, *n.* a spacious hall for receptions, for works of art, &c.: a large public room (for billiards, for dancing, for hairdressing, &c.): a large public cabin or dining-room for passengers: a saloon-carriage: a saloon-car: (*U.S.*) a drinking-bar.—*ns.* **saloon'-car',** a motor-car with enclosed body; **saloon'-carr'iage,** a railway carriage open from end to end; **saloon'-deck,** an upper deck reserved for saloon or first-class passengers; **saloon'ist, saloon'-keeper,** (*U.S.*) a publican; **saloon'-passenger,** a passenger entitled to use the principal cabin: a first-class passenger on board a ship; **saloon'-pistol, saloon'-rifle,** one for use in a shooting-gallery. [Fr. *salon.*]

saloop, *sə-lōōp'*, *n.* salep: a drink made from salep, later from sassafras. [**salep.**]

salop. Same as **salep.**—*adj.* **salop'ian** (*Lamb*).

Salop, *sal'əp*, *n.* Shropshire.—*adj.* **Salopian** (*-ō'pi-ən*), of Shropshire: of Shrewsbury School.—*n.* a native or inhabitant of Shropshire: one educated at Shrewsbury School. [A.Fr. *Sloppesberie*—O.E. *Scrobbesbyrig.*]

salp, *salp*, *n.* a free-swimming tunicate (Salpa).— *n.* and *adj.* **salp'ian.** [L. *salpa*—Gr. *salpē*, a kind of fish.]

salpinx, *sal'pingks*, *n.* an ancient Greek trumpet: the Eustachian tube: the Fallopian tube.—*adjs.* **salpingian** (*-pin'ji-ən*), of the salpinx; **salpin-git'ic,** of, of the nature of, salpingitis.—*n.* **salpin-gitis** (*-ji'tis*), inflammation of a Fallopian tube. [Gr. *salpinx, -ingos,* a trumpet.]

salse, *sals,* *n.* a mud volcano. [*Salsa*, name of one near Modena.]

salsify, salsafy, *sal'si-fi*, *n.* a purple-flowered species of goat's-beard, cultivated for its root, tasting like asparagus.—**black salsify,** scorzonera. [Fr. *salsifis,* prob.—It. *sassefrica.*]

Salsola, *sal'sō-lä*, *n.* the saltwort genus of the goosefoot family.—*adj.* **salsolā'ceous.** [Obs. It. dim. of *salso*—L. *salsus*, salt (*adj.*).]

salsuginous, *sal-sōō'ji-nəs*, *adj.* salty: growing in salty soil. [L. *salsūgō, -inis*, saltness.]

salt, *sawlt*, *n.* chloride of sodium, occurring naturally as a mineral (rock-salt) and in solution in sea-water, brine-springs, &c.: smack, savour: piquancy: wit and good sense: saving or pre-serving quality: a salt-marsh or salting: an influx of salt water: a sailor, esp. an old sailor: a salt-cellar: a compound in which metal atoms or electropositive radicals replace one or more of the replaceable hydrogen atoms of an acid—generalised to include the acid itself: (in *pl.*) smelling-salts: Epsom salt or other salt or mixture of salts used in medicine, esp. as a purgative: money collected at Montem.—*adj.* containing salt: tasting of salt: seasoned or cured with salt: overflowed with salt water: growing in salt soil: inhabiting salt water: pungent: (*coll.*) excessively costly.—*v.t.* to sprinkle, season, cure, impregnate with salt: to immunise (as by inoculation): to season: to acclimatise: (*slang*) to assign an excessive value to or in: (*mining slang*) to add gold, ore, &c., to, in order to give a false appearance of riches.— *ns.* **salt'-box,** a box for holding salt, esp. one with a clapper lid, once used as in burlesque music along with the marrow-bones, tongs, &c.; **salt'-bush,** any Australian shrubby plant of the goosefoot family.—*adj.* **salt'-butt'er**, (*Shak.*) fed on nothing better than salt butter, gross.—*ns.* **salt'-cake**, crude sodium sulphate; **salt'-cat**, a salt mixture given as a digestive to pigeons; **salt'-cote**, (*obs.*) a building where salt is made.—*adj.* **salt'ed.**—*ns.* **salt'er**, one who salts, or who makes or deals in salt: a drysalter; **salt'-fat** (erron. **salt'-foot**), a large saltcellar marking the class boundary at table: a pickling-tub; **salt'-glaze**, a glaze produced on pottery by volatalisation of common salt in the kiln; **salt'-horse'**, (*slang*) salt beef; **salt'iness**; **salt'ing**, the act of preserving, seasoning, &c., with salt: the celebration of the Eton Montem: a meadow flooded by the tides (suff. *-ing*, indicating a meadow in place-names). — *adj.* **salt'ish.** — *adv.* **salt'ishly.** — *ns.* **salt'ishness**; **salt'-junk'**, (*sailors' slang*) salt beef. —*adj.* **salt'less.**—*n.* **salt'-lick**, a place to which animals resort for salt.—*adv.* **salt'ly.**—*ns.* **salt'-marsh'**, land liable to be flooded with salt water; **salt'-mine**, a mine of rock-salt; **salt'-money**, an allowance for salt: money collected at Montem; **salt'ness**; **salt'-pan**, a large basin for obtaining salt by evaporation: a salt-work: a natural depression in which salt accumulates or has accumulated by evaporation; **salt'-pit**, a pit for obtaining salt by evaporation; **salt'-rheum**, **salt rheum**, (*Shak.*) a discharge of mucus from the nose: (*U.S.*) eczema; **salt'-spoon**, a small spoon for taking salt at table; **salt'-spring**, a brine spring.—*adj.* **salt'-water**, of salt water.—*ns.* **salt'-work(s)**, a place where salt is made; **salt'-wort**, a fleshy, prickly plant (*Salsola Kali*) of sandy sea-shores, of the goosefoot family, or other plant of the genus: sometimes applied to the glasswort (*Salicornia*).—*adj.* **salt'y**, saltish.—**above, below, the salt**, among those of high, or low, social class, the saltcellar marking the boundary when all dined together; **lay, put, cast salt on one's tail**, fi✻d or catch him, from the jocularly recommended method of catching a bird; **salt down**, to preserve with salt: hence, to lay by, store up; **salt of sorrel**, acid potassium oxalate, a solvent for ink-stains; **salt of tartar**, a commercial name for purified potassium carbonate; **salt of the earth**, the choice few of the highest excellence (Matt. v. 13); **salt of vitriol**, sulphate of zinc; **salt of wisdom**, sal alembroth; **salt of wormwood**, potassium carbonate; **salt out**, to obtain as a precipitate by adding a salt; **take with a grain of salt**, to believe with some reserve; **worth one's salt**, good for anything at all—worth the value of the salt one consumes. [O.E. (Anglian) *salt* (W.S. *sealt*); cf. Ger. *salz*, also L. *sāl*, Gr. *hals*.]

salt, *sawlt*, *n.* sexual desire, esp. in bitches.—*adj.* **in heat**: (*Shak.*) salacious. [L. *saltus*, *-ūs*, leap.]

saltant, *sal'tənt*, *sawl'tənt*, *adj.* leaping: dancing: (*her.*) salient.—*n.* (*biol.*) a changed form developed suddenly.—*v.i.* **sal'tate.**—*n.* **saltā'tion**, a leaping or jumping: spurting, pulsation: (*biol.*) an abrupt variation.—*adjs.* **saltatō'rial**, **saltatō'rious**; **sal'tatory**, leaping: dancing: having the power of, or used in, leaping or dancing: changing abruptly. [L. *saltāre*, *-ātum*, inten. of *salīre*, to leap.]

saltarello, *sal-tä-rel'ō*, *n.* a lively dance with skips, for two dancers: its music, in triple time. [It. *saltarello*, Sp. *saltarelo*—L. *saltāre*, to dance.]

saltcellar, *sawlt'sel-ər*, *n.* a table vessel for holding salt: a depression behind the collar-bone. [**salt**, and O.Fr. *saliere*—L.L. *salārium*—*sāl*, salt.]

saltern, *sawlt'ərn*, *n.* a salt-works. [O.E. *s(e)altern* —*s(e)alt*, salt, *ærn*, house.]

saltier. See **saltire**, **satyr**.

saltigrade, *sal'ti-grād*, *adj.* going by leaps.—*n.* a jumping spider. [L. *saltus*, *-ūs*, a leap, *gradī*, to go.]

saltimbanco, *sal-tim-bangk'ō*, *n.* (*obs.*) a mountebank, a quack. [It.]

saltire, **saltier**, *sal'*, *sawl'tīr*, *n.* (*her.*) an ordinary in the form of a St Andrew's cross.—*adj.* **sal'tier-wise**. [O.Fr. *saultoir*, *sautoir*—L.L. *saltātōrium*, a stirrup—L. *saltāre*, to leap.]

saltpetre, *sawlt-pē'tər*, *n.* potassium nitrate.—*ns.* **saltpē'treman**, (*hist.*) one authorised to search for saltpetre: one who prepares saltpetre; **saltpē'trepaper**, touch-paper.—**Chile or cubic saltpetre**,

sodium nitrate; **Norway saltpetre**, calcium nitrate.—(*U.S.*) **saltpeter**. [O.Fr. *salpetre*—L.L. *salpetra*, prob. for L. *sāl petrae*, salt of stone.]

saltus, *sal'tas*, *n.* a breach of continuity: a jump to conclusion. [L., a leap, pl. *saltūs*.]

salubrious, *sə-l(y)ōō'bri-əs*, *adj.* healthful, health-giving. — *adv.* **salu'briously.** — *ns.* **salu'briousness**, **salu'brity**. [L. *salūbris*—*salūs*, *salūtis*, health.]

salue, *sal-(y)ōō'*, or *sal'*, *v.t.* (*obs.*) to salute:— *pa.t.* (*Spens.*) **salewd'** (also **sal'ued**, which may be for **salve'd**, hailed with *salve*, the Latin greeting). [Fr. *saluer*—L. *salūtāre*.]

saluki, *sə-lōō'kē*, *-gē*, *n.* a silky-haired Persian or Arabian greyhound. [Ar. *seluqi*.]

salutary, *sal'ū-tər-i*, *adj.* promoting health or safety: wholesome.—*adv.* **sal'utarily.**—*n.* **sal'utariness**. [L. *salūtāris*—*salūs*, health.]

salute, *sal-(y)ōōt'*, *v.t.* to greet with words or (now esp.) with a gesture or with a kiss: to greet: to hail: to honour formally by a discharge of cannon, striking of colours, &c.: (*Shak.*) to affect, act upon.—*v.i.* to perform the act of saluting, esp. in the military manner.—*n.* act or position of saluting: greeting: a kiss: a complimentary discharge of cannon, dipping colours, presenting arms, &c.— *n.* **salutation** (*sal-ū-tā'shən*), act or words of greeting: a visit of ceremony: (*Shak.*) a quickening (of the blood), excitement: the Angelic Salutation (see **ave**). — *adj.* **salūtā'tional.** — *n.* **salutatorian** (*sə-lōō-tə-tō'ri-ən*), in American colleges, the graduand who pronounces the address of welcome.—*adv.* **salu'tatorily.**—*adj.* **salu'tatory**. —*n.* an audience chamber: an address of welcome, esp. in American colleges.—*n.* **salu'ter**, one who salutes: (*hist.*) in Spain, one who professed to work miracles in the name of St Catherine (Sp. *saludador*). [L. *salūtāre*, *-ātum* (vb.), and *salūs*, *salūtis* (n.), partly through Fr. *salut*.]

salutiferous, *sal-ū-tif'ər-əs*, *adj.* conducive to health or wellbeing. [L. *salūtifer*—*salūs*, *salūtis*, health, *ferre*, to bring.]

salvage, *sal'vij*, *n.* and *adj.* (*Spens.*, *Shak.*, &c.). Same as **savage**.

salvage, *sal'vij*, *n.* compensation made by the owner to persons, other than the ship's company, for preserving ship or cargo from danger of loss: rescue of property from fire or other peril: the raising of sunken or wrecked ships: saving of waste material for utilisation: anything saved in any of these ways.—*v.t.* to save from danger of loss or destruction: to recover or save as salvage. —*n.* **sal'vage-corps**, a body of men employed in salvage work. [L.L. *salvāgium*—*salvāre*, to save.]

salvarsan, *sal'vər-san*, *n.* a compound of arsenic, discovered by Paul Ehrlich (1854-1915) as a remedy for syphilis. [L. *salvus*, safe, whole, Ger. *arsen*, arsenic.]

salve, *salv*, *v.t.* to explain by hypothesis: to explain, clear up, harmonise: to save from objection: to vindicate: to preserve unhurt: to salvage. — *n.* **salvabil'ity**. — *adj.* **salv'able**. — *ns.* **salvā'tion**, act of saving: means of preservation from any serious evil: (*theol.*) the saving of man from the power and penalty of sin, the conferring of eternal happiness; **Salvā'tionism**; **Salvā'tionist**, a member of the Salvation Army; **sal'vatory**, a repository.—*adj.* saving.—**Salvation Army**, an organisation for the spread of religion among the masses, founded by Wm. Booth about 1865. [L.L. *salvāre*, to save; partly back-formation from **salvage**.]

salve, *säv*, also *salv*, *n.* an ointment: a remedy: anything to soothe the feelings or conscience.— *v.t.* to anoint: to smear: to heal: to soothe.— *n.* and *adj.* **salv'ing**. [O.E. *s(e)alf*, ointment; Ger. *salbe*, Du. *zalf*.]

salve, *sal'vi*, *interj.* hail.—*n.* a greeting: (*R.C.*) an antiphon beginning *Salve Regina*. [L. *salvē*, imper. of *salvēre*, to be well.]

salver, *sal'vər*, *n.* a tray on which anything is presented.—*adj.* **sal'ver-shaped**, of a corolla, having a long tube with limbs spread out flat. [Sp. *salva*, the precautionary tasting of food, as by a prince's taster, hence the tray on which it was presented to the prince—*salvar*, to save—L.L. *salvāre*.]

Salvia, *sal'vi-ä, n.* the sage genus. [L. *salvia*, sage.]

Salvinia, *sal-vin'i-ä, n.* a genus of water-ferns, giving name to a family **Salviniā'ceae.**—*adj.* **salvinia'ceous.** [Named after Antonio Maria *Salvini* (1653-1729), Italian Greek scholar.]

salvo, *sal'vō, n.* a saving clause: a reservation: a pretext: an expedient for saving appearances, avoiding offence, &c. [L. *salvō*, ablative of *salvus*, safe: (one's right, honour, &c.) being saved.]

salvo, *sal'vō, n.* a simultaneous discharge of artillery in salute or otherwise: a round of applause:—*pl.* **salvo(e)s** (*sal'vōz*). [It. *salva*, salute—L. *salvē*, hail.]

sal-volatile. See sal.

salvor, *sal'vər, n.* one who salvages.

sam, *sam, adv.* (*Spens.*) together. [O.E. *samen*.]

samara, *sam'ə-rä, sə-mä'rä, n.* a dry indehiscent, usually one-seeded fruit, with a wing. [L. *samara, samera*, elm seed.]

Samaritan, *sə-mar'i-tən, adj.* of *Samaria,* in Palestine.—*n.* a native of Samaria, an adherent of the religion of Samaria, slightly differing from Judaism: the Aramaic dialect of Samaria: one who charitably gives help in need (*good Samaritan*; Luke x. 30-37).—*n.* **Samar'itanism.**—**Samaritan Pentateuch,** a recension of the Hebrew Pentateuch accepted by the Samaritans as alone canonical. [L. *Samārītānus*.]

samarium, *sə-mā'ri-əm, n.* a metallic element (Sm; at. numb. 62) observed spectroscopically in samarskite.—*n.* **samarskite** (*sə-mär'skit*), a mineral containing uranium. [Named in honour of Col. *Samarski*.]

Samaveda, *sä-mä-vä'dä, n.* the name of one of the four Vedas. [Sans. *Sāmaveda*.]

sambar, sambur, *sam'bər, n.* a large Indian deer. [Hind. *sā*(*m*)*bar*.]

sambo, *sam'bō, n.* offspring of an American Indian or mulatto and a negro: **Sambo,** colloquially used as a proper name for a negro. [Sp. *zambo*, said to be from L. *scambus*—Gr. *skambos*, bow-legged: perh. partly Fulah *sambo*, uncle.]

Sam Browne, *sam-brown', n.* a military officer's belt with shoulder strap. [Invented by General Sir Samuel James *Browne* (1824-1901).]

sambuca, *sam-bū'ka, n.* an ancient musical instrument like a harp. [L. *sambūca*—Gr. *sambȳkē*, prob. an Asiatic word; cf. Aramaic *sabbekā*.]

sambur. Same as **sambar.**

same, *sām, adj.* identical (commonly with *as,* also with *with* or a relative): not different: unchanged: unvaried: mentioned before.—*pron.* (*vulg.*) the aforesaid, it, them, they, &c.—*n.* (*rare*) an identical thing.—*adj.* **same'ly,** unvaried.—*n.* **same'ness,** the being the same: tedious monotony.—**all the same,** for all that; **at the same time,** still, nevertheless; **the same,** the same thing or person: the aforesaid: in the same way. [O.E. *same* (only in phrase *swá same,* likewise); Goth. *sama*; L. *similis,* like, Gr. *homos*.]

samel, *sam'l, adj.* underburnt (as a brick). [App. O.E. pfx. *sam-,* half, *æled,* burned.]

samen, *sām'ən,* an obs. Scots form of **same.**

Samian, *sā'mi-ən, adj.* of the Greek island of *Samos.* —*n.* (also **Sā'miot, Sā'miote**) a native of Samos. —**Samian earth,** an argillaceous astringent earth; **Samian letter,** the Pythagorean letter; **Samian stone,** a goldsmiths' polishing stone; **Samian ware,** brick-red or black pottery, with lustrous glaze: a later imitation made in Roman Gaul, &c.

samiel, *sä'mi-əl, n.* the simoom. [Ar. *samm,* poison, Turk. *yel,* wind.]

samisen, *sam'i-sen, n.* a Japanese guitar. [Jap.]

samite, *sam'īt, n.* a kind of heavy silk stuff. [O.Fr. *samit*—L.L. *examitum*—Gr. *hexamiton*—*hex,* six, *mitos,* thread.]

samlet, *sam'lit, n.* a young salmon. [**salmon,** suff. -**let.**]

Sammy, *sam'i, n.* (slang) a noodle: (mil. slang; from *Uncle Sam*) an American expeditionary soldier. [**Samuel.**]

Samnite, *sam'nīt, n.* a member of an ancient

Sabine people of central Italy: their language: a Roman gladiator armed like a Samnite.—Also *adj.* [L. *Samnīs, -ītis*.]

samnitis, *sam-nī'tis, n.* (*Spens.*) a poisonous plant unknown.

samovar, *sam'ō-vär, -vär', n.* a Russian tea-urn heated by charcoal in a tube. [Russ. *samovar,* lit. self-boiler.]

Samoyed(e), *sam-ō-yed',* or *sam', n.* one of a Ugrian people of north-west Siberia: their Ural-Altaic language: a dog of a breed used by them.—Also *adj.* (*Milt.* **Sam'oed**)—*adj.* **Samoyed'ic.** [Russ. *Samoyed.*]

samp, *samp, n.* a coarsely ground maize: porridge made from it. [From an American Indian word.]

sampan, *sam'pan, n.* a Chinese boat.—Also **san'pan.** [Chin. *san,* three, *pan,* board.]

samphire, *sam'fīr,* **sampire,** *-pīr, n.* an umbelliferous plant (*Crithmum maritimum*) of sea-cliffs, whose fleshy leaves are used in pickles: extended to other plants used in the same way—to *Inula crithmoides,* a plant related to elecampane (*golden samphire*), to glasswort (*marsh samphire*), to saltwort (*prickly samphire*). [Fr. (*herbe de*) *Saint Pierre,* Saint Peter('s herb).]

sampi, *sam'pi, -pē, n.* supposed name of a Greek numerical character, Τ, ↑, or ϡ, representing 900 and perhaps originally the same as the letter san. [Gr. *sampī.*]

sample, *sam'pl, n.* a specimen, a small portion to show the quality of the whole: (*Spens., Shak.*) an example for imitation or (*obs.*) warning.—*adj.* serving as a sample.—*v.t.* (*obs.*) to match: to take, try, or offer a sample or samples of.—*ns.* **sam'pler; sam'pling.** [M.E. *essample*; see **example.**]

sampler, *sam'plər, n.* (*obs.*) an exemplar, type, pattern: a test-piece of embroidery formerly expected from a girl, commonly including an alphabet, with figures, often names, &c.—*ns.* **sam'pler-work, sam'plery.** [O.Fr. *essemplaire*—L. *exemplar*; see **exemplar.**]

samshoo, samshu, *sam'shoo, n.* Chinese rice spirit. [Pidgin; origin doubtful.]

Samson, *sam'sn, n.* an abnormally strong man (from the Hebrew champion of Judges xiii.-xvi.).—**Samson('s) post,** (*obs.*) a kind of mousetrap: a strong post in a ship.

samurai, *sam'ōō-rī, n.* (*Jap. hist.*) a military retainer of a daimio: a member of the military caste:—*pl.* **samurai.** [Jap.]

san, *san, n.* a discarded letter of the Greek alphabet, Ϻ, perh. originally the same as sampi. [Doric Gr. *san,* sigma.]

sanative, *san'ə-tiv, adj.* healing.—*n.* **sanatō'rium** (imitation Latin), a hospital, esp. for consumptives or convalescents: a health station.—*adj.* **san'atory,** healing: of healing. [L. *sānāre -ātum,* to heal.]

sanbenito, *san-be-nē'tō, n.* a garment worn by Inquisition victims at public recantation or execution:—*pl.* **sanbeni'tos.** [Sp. *San Benito,* St Benedict, from its resemblance to St Benedict's scapular.]

sancho, sanko, *sang'kō, n.* a West African guitar. [Ashanti *osanku.*]

sancho-pedro, *sang'kō-pē'drō, n.* a card game—the nine of trumps called **sancho,** the five **pedro.**

sanctify, *sang(k)'ti-fī, v.t.* to make, declare, regard as, or show to be sacred or holy: to set apart to sacred use: to free from sin or evil: to consecrate: to invest with a sacred character: to make efficient as the means of holiness: to sanction:—*pr.p.* **sanc'tifying;** *pa.t.* and *pa.p.* **sanc'tified.**—*n.* **sanctificā'tion.**—*adj.* **sanc'tified,** made holy: sanctimonious.—*adv.* **sanc'tifiedly** (*-fī-id-li*), sanctimoniously.—*n.* **sanc'tifier** (*-fī-ər*), one who sanctifies: the Holy Spirit.—*n.* and *adj.* **sanc'tifying.**—*adv.* **sanc'tifyingly.** [Fr. *sanctifier*—L. *sanctificāre*—*sanctus,* holy, *facĕre,* to make.]

sanctimony, *sang(k)'ti-mən-i, n.* (*obs.*) holiness: outward, affected, or simulated holiness.—*adj.* **sanctimonious** (*-mō'ni-əs*), (*obs.*) holy: simulating holiness.—*adv.* **sanctimō'niously.**—*n.* **sanctimō'niousness.** [L. *sanctimōnia*—*sanctus.*]

sanction, *sang(k)'shən*, *n.* (*ethics*) motive for obedience to any moral or religious law: (*law*) penalty or reward expressly attached to non-observance or observance of a law or treaty: act of ratifying, or giving authority: confirmation: support: permission, countenance.—*v.t.* to give validity to: to authorise: to countenance. [L. *sanctiō, -ōnis—sancīre, sanctum*, to ratify.]

sanctitude, *sang(k)'ti-tūd*, *n.* saintliness. [L. *sanctitūdō, -inis.*]

sanctity, *sang(k)'ti-ti*, *n.* quality of being sacred or holy: purity: godliness: inviolability: saintship: (in *pl.*) holy feelings, obligations, or objects.

sanctuary, *sang(k)'tū-ər-i*, *n.* a holy place: a place of worship: the most holy part of a temple, church, &c.: the sacrarium: the chancel: a place affording immunity from arrest: the privilege of refuge therein: a place of refuge: a private retreat: a nature, animal, or plant reserve.—*v.t.* **sanc'tuarise**, to afford sanctuary to. [L. *sanctuārium.*]

Sanctus, *sang(k)'təs*, *n.* the hymn *Holy, holy, holy*, from Isa. vi.: music for it.—*n.* **sanc'tum**, a sacred place: a private room.—**sanc'tum sanc-to'rum**, the Holy of Holies: any specially reserved retreat or room; **sanc'tus bell**, a bell rung at the Sanctus: the sacring bell. [L. *sanctus, -a, -um*, holy.]

sand, *sand*, *n.* a mass of rounded grains of rock, esp. quartz: (in *pl.*) a tract covered with this, as on a sea-beach or desert: (*rare*) a sand-grain: (in *pl.*) sandstones: (*fig.* in *pl.*) moments of time, from use in the hour-glass: (*U.S. slang*) firmness of character.—*adj.* of sand.—*v.t.* to sprinkle, cover, mix, or polish with sand.—*n.* **sand'bag**, a bag of sand or earth: an engraver's leather cushion.—*v.t.* to furnish with sandbags: to assail with a sandbag:—*pa.p.* **sand'bagged.**—*ns.* **sand'bagger**; **sand'-bank**, a bank of sand; **sand'-bath**, a bath in sand: a vessel for heating without direct exposure to the source of heat; **sand'-bed**, a layer of sand, esp. one used in founding or moulding: (*fig. Scot.*) a toper; **sand'-binder**, a plant whose roots or rootstocks fix shifting sands; **sand'-blast**, a sand-laden wind: sand driven by a blast of air or steam for glass-engraving, finishing metal surfaces, &c. — Also *v.t.* — *ns.* **sand'-blasting**; **sand'-box**, a box for sand for sprinkling, for golf tees, or other purpose: the explosive capsule of a tropical American tree (Hura) of the spurge family, formerly used to sprinkle sand on wet ink; **sand'-boy**, a young sand-hawker, proverbial for jollity; **sand'-break**, sandy ground diversifying the country; **sand'-bunker**; **sand'-castle**, a model of a castle made by children at play on the sands; **sand'-cherry**, an American dwarf cherry; **sand'-crack**, a crack in a hoof; **sand'-dance**, a dance performed on a sanded surface; **sand'-dart**, a British noctuid moth; **sand'-devil**, a small whirlwind; **sand'-dollar**, a flat sea-urchin; **sand'-dune**, a ridge of loose sand drifted by the wind.—*adj.* **sand'ed**, (*Shak.*) yellow: sprinkled, covered, or mixed with sand.—*ns.* **sand'-eel**, the launce; **sand'-flag**, a fissile sandstone; **sand'-flea**, the chigoe or jigger: a sand-hopper; **sand'-fly**, a small biting midge (Simulium): a moth-like midge (Phlebotomus) that transmits **sand-fly fever**, a fever due to a filter-passing infection; **sand'-glass**, a glass instrument for measuring time by the running out of sand; **sand'-grain**; **sand'-grass**, any grass that grows on sand; **sand'groper**, a West Australian (*orig.* a pioneer); **sand'-grouse**, any bird of the genera Pterocles and Syrrhaptes, with long pointed wings, once mistaken for grouse because of their feathered legs but now reckoned as a sub-order (Pterocletes) akin to pigeons; **sand'-heap**; **sand'-hill**, a hill of sand; **sand'-hog**, (*U.S. slang*) one who works in compressed air; **sand'-hole**; **sand'-hopper**, an amphipod crustacean (Talitrus, Orchestia, &c.) of the seashore (and also inland regions) that jumps by suddenly straightening its bent body; **sand'iness**, sandy quality, esp. in colour; **sand'-ing**; **sand'-lark**, a name applied to various smaller shore birds: a sandpiper; **sand'-launce**, **sand'ling**, the launce; **sand'-lizard**, an oviparous

lizard (*Lacerta agilis*) of Europe and S. England; **sand'man**, a fairy who throws sand into children's eyes towards bedtime; **sand'-martin**, a martin that nests in sandy banks; **sand'-mason**, a tube-worm that makes its tube of sand; **sand'-mole**, the Cape mole-rat; **sand'paper**, paper or cloth coated with sand.—*v.t.* to smooth or polish with sandpaper.—*ns.* **sand'-peep**, (*U.S.*) any small sand-piper; **sand'-pipe**, a tubular hollow in chalk, usually filled with clay, sand, &c., from above; **sand'piper**, the summer snipe or other bird of a group intermediate between plovers and snipe, haunting sandy shores and river banks and uttering a clear piping note; **sand'-pit**, a place from which sand is dug; **sand'-pride**, a small river lamprey; **sand'-pump**, a pump for raising wet sand or mud; **sand'-saucer**, an egg-mass of certain sea-snails; **sand'-screw**, a burrowing amphipod (from its wriggling movements); **sand'-shoe**, a shoe for walking or playing on the sands, usually with canvas upper and rubber sole; **sand'-skipper**, a sand-hopper; **sand'-snake**, a short-tailed, boa-like genus (Eryx) of Old World snakes; **sand'-spout**, a moving pillar of sand; **sand'-star**, an ophiurid, esp. of the short-armed kind, as Ophiura; **sand'stone**, a rock formed of compacted and more or less indurated sand (**Old Red Sandstone**; see **old**); **sand'-storm**, a storm of wind carrying along clouds of sand; **sand'-sucker**, the rough dab; **sand'-table**, a tray for moulding sand on or for demonstration of military tactics: an inclined trough for separating heavier particles from a flow of liquid, as in ore-dressing, paper-making (also **sand'-trap**); **sand'-thrower**, a tool for throwing sand on newly sized or painted surfaces; **sand'-wasp**, a solitary burrowing insect of several families akin to the true wasps; **sand'-worm**, the lugworm or other worm that lives on the sand; **sand'wort**, any species of Arenaria; **sand'wort-spurr'ey**, Spergularia.—*adjs.* **sand'y**, consisting of, covered with, containing, like, or (*Shak.*) measured by sand: loose: coloured like sand; **sand'yish**.—*n.* **sand'y-lav'erock**, (*Scot.*) a sand-lark. [O.E. *sand*; Du. *zand*, Ger. *sand*, O.N. *sandr*.]

sandal, *san'dl*, *n.* a sole bound to the foot by straps: an ornate shoe or slipper: a slipper-strap: a slight rubber overshoe.—*adj.* **san'dalled**, wearing or fastened with sandals.—*n.pl.* **sandal shoon**, (*arch.*) sandals. [L. *sandalium*—Gr. *sandalion*, dim. of *sandalon*.]

sandal, *san'dal*, *n.* a long narrow N. African boat. [Turk., Pers., and Ar.]

sandal, *san'dl*, **sandalwood**, *-wood*, *ns.* a compact and fine-grained very fragrant East Indian wood: the parasitic tree yielding it, *Santalum album* (**white sandalwood**), or other species: extended to other woods, as red-sanders, Barbados pride (Adenanthera), both called **red sandalwood**. [L.L. *santalum*—Gr. *sandanon.*]

sandarach, sandarac, *san'dər-ak*, *n.* realgar: the resin (in full **gum sandarach, sandarac resin**) of the Moroccan **sandarach tree** (*Callitris quadrivalvis*; Coniferae) powdered to form pounce and used in making varnish. [L. *sandaraca*—Gr. *sandarãkē, -chē.*]

sand-blind, *sand'blīnd*, *adj.* half-blind. [Prob. O.E. pfx. *sam-*, half, and **blind**, affected by **sand**.]

Sandemanian, *san-di-mā'ni-ən*, *n.* a Glassite, or follower of Robert *Sandeman* (1718-71).—Also *adj.*

sander, zander, *zan', san'dər*, *n.* a pike-perch. [Ger.]

sanderling, *san'dər-ling*, *n.* a sandpiper without a hind toe. [App. from **sand**.]

sanders, *san'dərz*, **sanderswood**, *-wood*, *ns.* sandal-wood, esp. red sandalwood (**red-sanders**; see **red**). [O.Fr. *sandre*, variant of *sandal*, *santal*, sandalwood.]

sandiver, *san'di-vər*, *n.* glass-gall. [O.Fr. *suin de verre*, lit. exudation of glass.]

sandwich, *san(d)'wij*, *-wich*, *n.* any sort of food between two slices of bread, said to be named from the fourth Earl of *Sandwich* (1718-92), who would not leave the gaming-table: anything in like arrangement.—*v.t.* to lay or place between two layers : to fit tight between two others or two of another kind : to intercalate.—*ns.* **sand'-wich-board;** **sand'wich-man,** a man who perambulates the streets between two advertising boards.

Sandy, *san'di, n. (coll.)* a Scot. [From *Alexander.*]

sane, *sān, adj. (rare)* sound, healthy : sound in mind : rational.—*adv.* **sane'ly.** [L. *sānus.*]

sang, *sang, pa.t.* of sing.—*n.* a Scots form of **song.**

sang, *sâng, n.* blood *(Scot.* in oaths ; *her. sän²)* : *(vet. sâng)* anthrax.—*ns.* **sang-de-boeuf** *(säṅ²-də-bəf′),* a deep red colour (lit. ox-blood) ; **sangfroid** *(-frwä′),* coolness, self-possession (lit. cold blood). [Fr., blood.]

sang, *sâng, n.* a Chinese organ played by mouth. [Chin. *shêng.*]

sangar, sungar, *sung'gər, n.* a stone breastwork. [Pushtu *sangar.*]

sangaree, *sang-gə-rē′, n.* a West Indian drink of wine, diluted, sweetened, spiced, &c. [Sp. *sangria.*]

sanglier, *sang'li-ər, n. (obs.* and *her.)* a wild boar. [Fr.,—L. *singulāris,* solitary.]

Sangraal, Sangrail, Sangreal, *san(g)-grāl′, san(g)′-grāl′, n.* the holy grail. [**saint, grail.**]

Sangrado, *sän(g)-grä′dō, n.* a blood-letter, from Dr *Sangrado* in *Gil Blas.* [Sp. *sangrador,* a blood-letter.]

sanguiferous, *sang-gwif′ər-əs, adj.* blood-carrying (L. *ferre,* to carry).—*n.* **sanguificā'tion,** blood-making.—*v.i.* **sang'uify** *(-fī),* to make blood.—*v.t.* to turn into blood.—*n.* **Sanguinaria** *(-gwinä′ri-ä),* blood-root.—*adv.* **sanguinarily** *(-gwin-ə-ri-li).*—*n.* **sang'uinariness.**—*adjs.* **sang'uinary,** bloody ; **sanguine** *(sang'gwin),* (rare) of blood : blood-red : bloody : of the complexion or temperament in which blood was supposed to predominate over the other humours : hence ardent, confident and inclined to hopefulness : abounding in blood : ruddy : florid : of a full habit.—*n.* a blood-red colour : a red chalk : a drawing in red chalks.—*v.t.* to colour blood-red : to stain with blood.—*adv.* **sang'uinely.**—*n.* **sang'uineness.**—*adj.* **sanguin'eous,** of or having blood : blood-red : bloody : sanguine : full-blooded.—*n.* **sanguin'ity,** sanguineness.—*adj.* **sanguin'olent,** bloody.—*n.* **Sanguisorb'a,** burnet (L. *sorbēre,* to absorb, from its supposed styptic property).—*adj.* **sangu(in)iv'orous,** feeding on blood (L. *vorāre,* to devour). [L. *sanguis, -inis,* blood ; adjs. *sanguineus, sanguinārius, sanguinolentus* ; partly through Fr. *sanguin.*]

Sanhedrim, Sanhedrin, *san'i-drim, -drin, n. (hist.)* a Jewish council or court, esp. the supreme council and court at Jerusalem : any similar assembly, a parliament.—*n.* **San'hedrist,** a member of the Sanhedrin. [Heb. *sanhedrīn*—Gr. *synedrion*—*syn,* together, *hedrā,* a seat.]

sanicle, *san'ik'l, n.* a woodland umbelliferous plant (in full **wood'-san'icle** : *Sanicula europaea)* with glossy leaves, head-like umbels, and hooked fruits : any plant of the genus : extended to various other plants. [O.Fr., perh. L. *sānāre,* to heal, from once-supposed power.]

sanidine, *san'i-dēn, n.* a clear glassy variety of potash felspar, usually tabular. [Gr. *sanis, sanidos,* a board.]

sanies, *sā'ni-ēz, n.* a thin discharge from wounds or sores.—*adj.* **sa'nious.** [L. *saniēs.*]

sanify, *san'i-fī, v.t.* to make healthy. [L. *sānus* sound, *facĕre,* to make.]

sanitary, *san'i-tər-i, adj.* pertaining to, or concerned with the promotion of health, esp. connected with drainage and sewage disposal : conducive to health.—*n.* **sanitā'rian,** one who favours or studies sanitary measures.—*adj.* concerned with sanitary matters or reforms.—*n.* **sanitā'rianism.**—*adv.* **san'itarily.**—*ns.* **san'itarist ; sanitā'rium** (sham Latin), a sanatorium :—*pl.* **-ia,** or **-iums ; san'itary-ware,** coarse-glazed earthenware for sewer-pipes.—*v.t.* **san'itate** (back-formation), to make sanitary : to furnish with sanitary appliances.—*ns.* **sanitā'tion,** measures for the promotion of health, esp. drainage and sewage disposal ; **sanitā'tionist.** [Fr. *sanitaire*—L. *sānitās,* health.]

sanity, *san'i-ti, n. (arch.)* health : soundness of mind. [L. *sānitās*—*sānus,* healthy.]

sanjak. *san'jak, n.* formerly, a subdivision of a Turkish vilayet or eyalet. [Turk. *sancak,* flag, sanjak.]

sank, *sangk, pa.t.* of **sink.**

Sankhya, *säng'kyä, n.* one of the six great systems of orthodox Hindu philosophy. [Sans. *samkhya.*]

sannup, *san'əp, n.* the husband of a squaw : a brave. [Amer. Ind. word.]

sans, *sanz, prep. (Shak.)* without : *(sän²)* in various French phrases, without. [Fr.]

sansa, *san'sä.* Same as **zanze.**

sansculotte, *sän²-kü-lot′, n.* in the French Revolution, the court party's nickname for a democrat (apparently as wearing long trousers instead of knee-breeches) : hence generally (usu. in hostility) a strong republican, democrat, or revolutionary : one whose breeches are wanting or defective.—*n.* **sansculotterie** *(-rē′* or *-ə-rē′).*—*adj.* **sansculott'ic.** —*ns.* **sansculott'ism ; sansculott'ist.** [Fr. *sans,* without, *culotte,* knee-breeches.]

sanserif, *san-ser'if, n.* a type without serifs.—Also *adj.*

Sansevieria, *san-sev-i-ēr'i-ä, n.* the bowstring-hemp genus of the lily family. [Named after the Neapolitan inventor Raimondo di Sangro, Prince of *San Severo* (1710-71).]

Sanskrit, or (old-fashioned) **Sanscrit,** *sans'krit, n.* the ancient Indo-Germanic literary language of India.—Also *adj.*—*n.* **Sans'kritist,** one skilled in Sanskrit. [Sans. *samskrita,* put together, perfected —*sam,* together, *krita,* done, perfected, from *kri,* cog. with L. *creāre,* to create.]

Santa Claus, *san'ta klawz′, n.* a fat rosy old fellow who brings children Christmas presents. [U.S. modification of Du. dial. *Sante Klaas,* St Nicholas.]

santal, *san'tal, n.* sandalwood.—*n.pl.* **Santalā'ceae,** the sandalwood family.—*adj.* **santalā'ceous.**—*ns.* **san'talin,** the colouring matter of red sandalwood ; **San'talum,** the sandalwood genus. [Gr. *santalon.*]

santir, *san-tēr′,* **santur, santour,** *-tōōr′, n.* an Eastern dulcimer. [Ar. *santīr,* Pers. and Turk. *sāntūr.*]

santon, *san'ton, n.* an Eastern dervish or saint. [Sp. *santōn*—*santo,* holy—L. *sanctus,* holy.]

santonica, *san-ton'i-kä, n.* the dried unexpanded flower-heads of a species of wormwood.—*n.* **san'tonin** *(-tən-),* an anthelmintic extracted from it. [Gr. *santonikon,* as found in the country of the *Santones* in Gaul.]

saouari. Same as **souari.**

sap, *sap, n.* vital juice : juice generally : sapwood : a saphead : a simpleton : a plodding student.—*v.i.* to play the part of a ninny : to be studious.—*v.t.* to drain or withdraw the sap from.—*adj.* **sap'ful,** full of sap.—*ns.* **sap'-green,** a green paint made from the juice of buckthorn berries : its colour (also *adj.*) ; **sap'head,** a silly fellow.—*adjs.* **sap'-headed ; sap'less.**—*ns.* **sap'lessness ; sap'ling,** a young tree (also *adj.*) : a young greyhound ; **sap'ling-cup,** a wooden ale-cup of staves and hoops ; **sapp'iness.**—*adj.* **sapp'y.**—*ns.* **sap'-rot,** dry-rot ; **sap'-wood,** alburnum. [O.E. *sæp ;* L.G. *sap,* juice, Ger. *saft.*]

sap, *sap, n.* sapping : a trench (usually covered or zigzag) by which approach is made towards a hostile position.—*v.t.* to undermine.—*v.i.* to make a sap : to proceed insidiously :—*pr.p.* **sapp'ing ;** *pa.p.* and *pa.t.* **sapped.**—*ns.* **sap'head,** the furthest point reached by a sap ; **sapp'er,** one who saps : a private in the Royal Engineers (formerly Royal Sappers and Miners). [It. *zappa* and Fr. *sappe* (now *sape)* ; cf. L.L. *sappa,* a pick.]

sapajou, *sap'ə-jōō, n.* a capuchin monkey : *(obs.)* a spider monkey. [Fr. from a Tupí name.]

sapan. Same as **sappan.**

sapego. See **serpigo.**

sapid, *sap'id, adj.* perceptible by taste : having a decided taste : well-tasted : savoury : grateful, relishing, exhilarating.—*n.* **sapid'ity.**—*adj.* **sap'idless,** *(Lamb)* insipid. [L. *sapidus*—*sapĕre,* to taste.]

sapience, *sā'pi-əns, n.* discernment : wisdom (often ironical) : judgment.—*adjs.* **sā'pient ; sāpiential** *(-en'shl).*—*adv.* **sā'piently** [L. *sapientia*—*sapĕre,* to be wise.]

Sapindus, *sə-pin'dəs, n.* the soapberry genus, giving

name to the **Sapindā′ceae**, a family akin to the maples and horse-chestnuts.—*adj.* **sapindā′ceous.** [L. *sāpō Indicus,* Indian soap.]

Sapium, sā′pi-əm, *n.* the tallow-tree genus of the spurge family.

sapi-utan, sä-pi-ōō′tän, *n.* the wild ox of Celebes.— Also **sap-i-ou′tan.** [Malay *sāpi,* cow, *ūtan,* wild, wood.]

sapling. See sap.

sapodilla, sap-ō-dil′ä, *n.* a large evergreen W. Indian sapotaceous tree, *Achras sapota* (naseberry): its edible fruit (**sapodilla plum**): its durable timber. [Sp. *zapotilla,* dim. of *zapota* (see Sapota).]

saponaceous, sap-ō-, or *sap-ə-nā′shəs, adj.* soapy: soap-like.—*n.* **Sapona′ria,** the soapwort genus.— *adj.* **saponifiable** (*sap-on′i-fī′ə-bl*).—*n.* **saponificā′-tion,** turning into or forming of soap: hydrolysis of esters.—*v.t.* **sapon′ify,** to convert into soap.— *v.i.* to become soap:—*pr.p.* **sapon′ifying;** *pa.t.* and *pa.p.* **sapon′ified.**—*ns.* **saponin** (*sap′ə-nin*), a glucoside from soapwort, &c., that gives a soapy froth; **sap′onite,** a soapy amorphous silicate of magnesium and aluminium found in cavities in serpentine. [L. *sāpō, -ōnis,* soap, prob. from Gmc.]

sapor, sā′por, *n.* taste.—*adj.* **sā′porous** (*-pər-əs*). [L. *sapor, -ōris.*]

Sapota, sə-pō′tä, *n.* a genus (by some included in Achras) giving name to the **Sapotaceae** (*sap-ō-tā′si-ē*), a tropical family mostly of trees, often abounding in milky juice (gutta-percha).—*adj.* **sapotā′ceous** (*-shəs*). [Sp. *zapote* — Nahuatl *tzapotl.*]

sappan, sapan, *sap′an,* -*ən, n.* brazilwood (*Caesalpinia Sappan*)—usu. **sap(p)′an-wood.** [Malay *sapang.*]

sapped, sapper, sapping. See sap (2).

sapperment, *sap-ər-ment′, interj.* a German oath. [Ger. *sakrament,* sacrament.]

sapphire, *saf′īr, n.* a brilliant precious variety of corundum, generally of a beautiful blue: the blue colour of a sapphire.—*adj.* of sapphire: deep pure blue.—*adj.* **sapph′ired,** coloured with sapphire blue.— *ns.* **sapph′ire-quartz,** a blue quartz; **sapph′ire-wing,** a blue-winged humming-bird.— *adj.* **sapph′irine** (*-ir-īn*), of, or like, sapphire.—*n.* a blue mineral, aluminium-magnesium silicate. [O.Fr. *safir*—L. *sapphīrus*—Gr. *sappheiros,* lapis lazuli.]

Sappho, *saf′ō, n.* a great Greek lyric poetess (*c.* 600 B.C.) of Lesbos: a kind of humming-bird. —*adj.* **Sapph′ic.**—*n.* usu. in *pl.* verses in a form said to have been invented by Sappho in stanzas of four lines each, three *Lesser Sapphics* thus: —∪∪ |—∪ |—∪∪ |—∪ |—∪, followed by an adonic, viz. |—∪∪ |—∪.—*n.* **Sapph′ism,** unnatural passion between women, of which she was accused. [Gr. *Sapphō.*]

sapples, *sap′lz, n.pl.* (*Scot.*) soap-suds.

sapraemia, *sap-rē′mi-ä, n.* presence of products of putrefactive bacteria in the blood.—*adj.* **saprae′-mic.** [Gr. *sapros,* rotten, *haima,* blood.]

saprobe, *sap′rōb, n.* an organism living in foul water. —*adj.* **saprobiotic** (*sap-rō-,* or *sap′rə-bī-ot′ic*), feeding on dead or decaying plants or animals. [Gr. *sapros,* rotten, *bios,* life.]

saprogenic, *sap-rō-jen′ik,* or *-rə-,* **saprogenous,** *sə-proj′i-nəs, adjs.* growing on decaying matter: causing, or caused by putrefaction. [Gr. *sapros,* rotten, and the root of *gignesthai,* to produce.]

Saprolegnia, *sap-rō-leg′ni-ä,* or *-rə-, n.* a genus of fungi, one species of which grows on diseased salmon and was formerly thought to be the cause of the disease. [Gr. *sapros,* rotten, *legnon,* border.]

saprophagous, *sap-rof′ə-gəs, adj.* feeding on decaying organic matter. [Gr. *sapros,* rotten, *phagein* (aor.), to eat.]

saprophyte, *sap′rō-fīt,* or *-rə-, n.* a plant that feeds upon decaying organic matter.—*adj.* **saprophytic** (*-fit′ik*).—*adv.* **saprophyt′ically.**—*n.* **sap′rophyt-ism.** [Gr. *sapros,* rotten, *phyton,* a plant.]

sapucaia, *sap-oo-kä′yä, n.* a Brazilian tree (Lecythis) whose urn-shaped fruit (monkey-pot) contains a number of finely-flavoured oval seeds or nuts.—*n.* **sapuca′ia-nut.** [Tupí.]

sar, sär. See sargus.

sar, sa′r, *sär,* a Scots form of savour (*n.* and *vb.*).

saraband, *sar′ə-band, n.* a slow Spanish dance, or dance-tune: a suite-movement in its rhythm, in 3-4 time strongly accented on the second beat (a dotted crotchet or minim). [Sp. *zarabanda.*]

Saracen, *sar′ə-sən, n.* a Syrian or Arab nomad: a Mohammedan: an opponent of the Crusaders: a Moor or Berber: (*obs.*) a non-Christian.—Also *adj.* —*adjs.* **Saracenic** (*-sen′ik*), **-al.**—*n.* **Sar′acenism.** —**Saracenic architecture,** a general name for Mohammedan architecture. [O.E. *Saracene* (pl.)— L. *Saracēnus*—late Gr. *Sarakēnos.*]

sarafan, *sar-ə-fan′,* or *sar′, n.* a Russian peasant woman's cloak. [Russ.]

sarangi, *sä′rung-gē, n.* an Indian fiddle. [Hind.,— Sans. *sārangī.*]

Sarapis. See Serapis.

Saratoga, *sar-ə-tō′gä, n.* (in full **Saratoga trunk**: *U.S.*) a large travelling trunk. [*Saratoga Springs,* resort in New York State.]

sarbacane, *sär′ba-kän, n.* a blow-gun. [Fr.]

sarcasm, *sär′kazm, n.* a bitter sneer: a satirical remark in scorn or contempt, often but not necessarily ironical: a jibe: the quality of such sayings. —*adjs.* **sarcas′tic, -al,** containing or inclined to sarcasm.—*adv.* **sarcas′tically.** [L. *sarcasmus*— Gr. *sarkasmos*—*sarkazein,* to tear flesh like dogs, to speak bitterly—*sarx, sarkos,* flesh.]

sarcenchyme, *sär-seng′kim, n.* a soft tissue of sponges with close-packed cells and reduced gelatinous matrix.—*adj.* **sarcenchymatous** (*-kim′ə-təs*). [Gr. *sarx, sarkos,* flesh, *enchyma,* an infusion.]

sarcenet. See sarsenet.

sarco-, *sär′kō,* *-ko′-,* in composition, flesh. [Gr. *sarx, sarkos,* flesh.]

sarcocarp, *sär′kō-kärp, n.* (*bot.*) the fleshy pericarp of a stone fruit. [Gr. *karpos,* fruit.]

sarcocolla, *sär-kō-kol′ä, n.* a Persian gum from Astragalus or other plants, reputed to heal wounds. [Gr. *sarkokolla*—*kolla,* glue.]

Sarcocystis, *sär-kō-sis′tis, n.* a genus of Sporozoa parasitic in muscles of mammals. [Gr. *kystis,* a bladder.]

sarcode, *sär′kōd, n.* protoplasm, esp. of Protozoa.— *n.* **Sarcodes,** *sär-kō′dēz,* the Californian snow-plant. — *adj.* **sarcodic** (*-kod′ik*), protoplasmic: flesh-like.—*n.pl.* **Sarcodina** (*-kō-dī′nä*), a class of Protozoa with pseudopodia.—*adj.* **sar′coid,** flesh-like. [Gr. *sarkōdēs, sarkoeidēs*—*eidos,* form.]

sarcolemma, *sär-kō-lem′ä, n.* the sheath of muscle fibre. [Gr. *lemma,* husk.]

sarcology, *sär-kol′ə-ji, n.* the anatomy of the fleshy parts. [Gr. *logos,* discourse.]

sarcoma, *sär-kō′mä, n.* a tumour derived from connective tissue: any fleshy excrescence: (*bot.*) a fleshy disk:—*pl.* **sarcō′mata.**—*adj.* **sarcō′matous.** [Gr. *sarkōma*—*sarx,* flesh.]

Sarcophaga, *sär-kof′ə-gä, n.* a genus of flesh-flies.— —*adjs.* **sarcoph′agal,** flesh-eating: pertaining to sarcophagi; **sarcoph′agous,** feeding on flesh.—*ns.* **sarcoph′agus,** a limestone used by the Greeks for coffins, thought to consume the flesh of corpses: a stone coffin, esp. one with carvings: a tomb or cenotaph of similar form:—*pl.* **sarcoph′agi** (*-jī, -gī*), **sarcoph′aguses; sarcoph′agy** (*-ji*), flesh-eating. [Latinised from Gr. *sarkophagos*—*phagein* (aor.), to eat.]

Sarcoptes, *sär-kop′tēz, n.* the itch-mite genus.—*adj.* **sarcop′tic.** [Irregularly, from Gr. *koptein,* to cut.]

sarcous, *sär′kəs, adj.* of flesh or muscle. [Gr. *sarx, sarkos,* flesh.]

sard, *särd, n.* a deep-red chalcedony.—Also **sard′ius.** [L. *sarda, sardius,* and Gr. *sardion,* also *sardios* (*lithos*), the Sardian (stone)—*Sardeis,* Sardis, in Lydia.]

Sard, *särd, n.* and *adj.* Sardinian. [L. *Sardus.*]

sardine, *sär′dēn, sär-dēn′,* a young pilchard, commonly tinned in oil: applied at various times and places to other fishes.—**packed like sardines,** crowded closely together. [Fr. *sardine*—It. *sardina* —L. *sardina;* Gr. *sardīnos,* or *-ē.*]

sardine, *sär′dīn, -dīn, n.* sard (stone).—Also *adj.* (Rev. iv. 3).—Also **sar′dius.** [Gr. *sardīnos* (*lithos*) —*sardios.*]

Sardinian, *sär-din′i-ən, -yən, adj.* of the island or former kingdom of *Sardinia* or of the inhabitants.— *n.* a native, citizen, or member of the people of Sardinia : their language or dialect of Italian.

sardonic, *sär-don′ik, adj.* forced, heartless, or bitter, said of a forced unmirthful laugh : sneering.— *adjs.* **sardó′nian** (*obs.*) ; **sardon′ical.**—*adv.* **sardon′ically.** [Fr. *sardonique*—L. *sardonius*—late Gr. *sardonios,* doubtfully referred to *sardonion,* a plant of Sardinia (Gr. *Sardō*) which was said to screw up the face of the eater.]

sardonyx, *sär′də-niks, n.* an onyx with layers of cornelian or sard. [Gr. *sardonyx*—*Sardios,* Sardian, *onyx,* a nail.]

sargasso, *sär-gas′ō, n.* gulf-weed (Sargassum) : a floating mass or expanse of it, as the **Sargasso Sea** in the North Atlantic. [Port. *sargaço.*]

Sargus, *sär′gas, n.* a genus of sea-breams, known also as **sar, sar′go** (Sp.). [Gr. *sargos.*]

sari, *sär′ē, n.* a Hindu woman's chief garment, a long cloth wrapped round the waist and passed over the shoulder and head.—Also **sar′ee.** [Hind. *sārī.*]

sark, *särk,* **serk,** *serk, n.* (*Scot.*) a shirt or chemise : a surplice.—*ns.* **sark′ful** ; **sark′ing,** a lining for a roof : material for shirts ; **sark′-tail′.** [O.E. *serc* ; O.N. *serkr.*]

Sarmatia, *sär-mā′shyä, -shi-ä, n.* anciently a region reaching from the Vistula and Danube to the Volga and Caucasus : (*poet.*) Poland.—*n.* and *adj.* **Sarmā′tian.**—*adj.* **Sarmatic** (*-mat′ik*).

sarment, *sär′mənt, n.* (*obs.*) a cut twig or cutting : a sarmentum : a long weak twig.—*adjs.* **sarmentaceous** (*-ā′shas*), **sar′mentose** (or *-ōs′*), **sarmentous** (*-ment′əs*), having sarmenta or runners : creeping.—*n.* **sarmentum** (*-ment′əm*), a runner :— *pl.* **sarment′a.** [L. *sarmentum,* a twig—*sarpĕre,* to prune.]

sarong, *sä′rong, n.* a Malay petticoat for man or woman : a cloth for making it. [Malay *sārung.*]

saros, *sä′ros, sā′ros, n.* a Babylonian cycle of 3600 years : now (from a misunderstanding) an astronomical cycle of 6585 days and 8 hours, after which relative positions of the sun and moon recur.—*adj.* **saronic** (*sə-ron′ik*). [Gr. *saros*—Babylonian *shāru,* 3600.]

Sarracenia, *sär-ə-sē′ni-ä, n.* the side-saddle flower, an American genus of insectivorous plants, with pitchers, giving name to the family **Sarraceniā′-ceae,** akin to the sundew family. [After Dr *Sarrazin,* who sent them to Europe from Quebec.]

sarrasin, sarrazin, *sär′ə-zin, n.* buckwheat. [Fr. (*blé*) *sarrasin,* Saracen (corn).]

sarrusophone, *sä-rus′ō-fōn, n.* a reed instrument of brass, devised by a French bandmaster, *Sarrus.* [Gr. *phōnē,* voice.]

sarsaparilla, *sär-sə-pə-ril′ä, n.* any tropical American Smilax : its dried root : a medicinal preparation from it : extended to various plants or roots of like use.—Shortened to **sar′sa, sar′za.** [Sp. *zarzaparilla—zarza,* bramble (from Basque), and a dim. of *parra,* vine.]

sarsen, *sär′sn, n.* a grey-wether.—Also **sars′den, sar′sen-stone, Sar′acen's-stone.** [App. forms of Saracen.]

sarsenet, sarcenet, sarsnet, *särs′nit, -net, n.* a thin tissue of fine silk.—*adj.* of sarsenet : (*Shak.*) mild. [A.Fr. *sarzinett,* prob. *Sarzin,* Saracen.]

sartor, *sär′tor, n.* (playfully) a tailor.—*adj.* **sartorial** (*-tō′ri-əl*).—*adv.* **sartō′rially.**—*adj.* (*rare*) **sartō′rian.**—*n.* **sartō′rius** (L. *adj.*), a thigh muscle that crosses the leg, as when a tailor sits. [L. *sartor,* a patcher.]

sarus, *sä′rəs, sā′rəs, n.* an Indian crane.—Also **sarus crane.** [Hind. *sāras.*]

sa sa, *sä sä′, interj.* of incitement : a fencer's exclamation on thrusting. [Fr. *ça ça,* there, there.]

sasarara. Same as **siserary.**

sash, *sash, n.* (orig. shash, *shash*) a turban cloth : a band or scarf, worn round the waist or over the shoulder.—*v.t.* to dress or adorn with a sash. [Ar. *shāsh.*]

sash, *sash, n.* a frame, esp. a sliding frame, for window panes.—*v.t.* to furnish with sashes.—*ns.* **sash′-door,** a door having panes of glass ; **sash′-frame,** the frame in which the sash of a window is suspended ; **sash′-tool,** a glazier's brush for removing oil : a house-painter's small brush ; **sash′-window,** a window with sash or sashes, opp. to *casement window.* [Fr. *châssis.*]

sasin, *sas′in, n.* the common Indian antelope. [Nepalese.]

sasine, *sä′sin, n.* (*Scots law*) the act of giving legal possession of feudal property, infeftment. [A variant of seisin, Law L. *sasina.*]

saskatoon, *sas-kə-tōōn′, n.* the shad-bush : its fruit. [Cree *misáskwatomin.*]

sass, *sas,* **sassy,** *sas′i.* Same as **sauce, saucy.**

sassaby, *sə-sä′bi, n.* the bastard hartebeest, a large S. African antelope. [Sechuana *tsessébe.*]

sassafras, *sas′ə-fras, n.* a tree (*Sassafras officinale*) of the laurel family common in N. America : the bark, esp. of its root, a powerful stimulant : an infusion of it : extended to various plants with similar properties.—**sassafras nut,** the pichurim bean ; **sassafras oil,** a volatile aromatic oil distilled from sassafras. [Sp. *sasafrás.*]

Sassanid, *sas′ə-nid, n.* one of the *Sassanidae,* the dynasty that ruled Persia from A.D. 226 to 641.— *adj.* **Sassā′nian.**

sassarara. Same as **siserary.**

sasse, *sas, n.* (*obs.*) a sluice or lock. [Du. *sas.*]

Sassenach, *sas′ə-nahh, n.* a Saxon : an Englishman : a Lowlander. [Gael. *Sasunnach.*]

sassolite, *sas′ə-līt, n.* native boric acid—first found near *Sasso* (province of Pisa).—Also **sass′olin.**

sastrugi. See **zastruga.**

sat, *sat, pa.t.* and *pa.p.* of **sit.**

Satan, *sā′tan* (old-fashioned *sat′ən*), *n.* the chief evil spirit or fallen angel : the Devil : a devil.— Also **Satanas** (*sat′an-as*), **Sathan** (*sā′than*), **Sathanas** (*sath′*).—*adjs.* **satanic** (*sə-tan′ik*), **-al.**—*adv.* **satan′ically.**—*ns.* **satan′icalness** ; **sā′tanism,** devilish disposition : Satan-worship : the characteristics of the Satanic school.—*n.* and *adj.* **Sā′tanist.**—*ns.* **satanity** (*sə-tan′*), devilishness ; **sātanol′ogy ; sātanoph′any** (Gr. *phainein,* to show), an appearance of Satan ; **sātanophō′bia** (Gr. *phobos,* fear), fear of the Devil.—**Satanic school,** Southey's name for Byron, Shelley, and other unorthodox revolutionaries ; **Satan monkey,** the black saki. [Gr. and L. *Satān, Satanās*—Heb. *sātān,* enemy—*sātan,* to be adverse.]

satara, *sä-tä′rä, sat′ə-rä, n.* a ribbed, hot-pressed and lustred woollen cloth. [*Sátára* in India.]

satchel, *sach′l, n.* a small bag, as for school-books. —*adj.* **satch′elled.** [O.Fr. *sachel*—L. *saccellus,* dim. of *saccus* ; see **sack, sac.**]

sate, *sāt, v.t.* to satisfy fully : to glut.—*adjs.* **sāt′ed ; sate′less,** insatiable.—*n.* **sat′edness.** [M.E. *sade* —O.E. *sadian,* to become satiated, *gesadian,* to satiate (cf. **sad**), remodelled after L. *sat,* enough ; or directly and originally—L. *satiāre, -ātum.*]

sate, *sat,* also (in rhyme) *sāt,* a poetical archaism for **sat,** *pa.t.* and *pa.p.* of **sit.**

satellite, *sat′ə-līt, n.* an attendant : an obsequious follower : a body revolving about a planet : a smaller companion to anything.—Also *adj.*—*n.* **satelles** (*sat-el′ēz* ; *obs.*), a satellite :—*pl.* **satell′-ites** (*-i-tēz* ; *Pope*).—*adj.* **satellitic** (*-lit′ik*).— **satellite town,** a garden city, limited in size, built near a great town to check overgrowth. [L. *satelles, satellitis,* an attendant.]

sati. Same as **suttee.**

satiate, *sä′shi-āt, v.t.* to gratify fully : to glut.—*adj.* glutted.—*n.* **sātiabil′ity.** — *adj.* **sā′tiable.** — *ns.* **sātiā′tion ; satiety** (*sə-tī′ə-tit*), state of being satiated : surfeit. [L. *satiāre, -ātum—satis,* enough.]

satin, *sat′in, n.* a closely woven silk with a lustrous and unbroken surface showing much of the warp. —*adj.* of, like, or (*obs.*) clad in satin.—*v.t.* to make satiny.—*ns.* **sat′in-bird,** or **satin bower-bird,** a satiny blue and black bower-bird ; **satinet′, satinette** (*Scott,* **satinett′a**), a thin satin : a modification of satin with a slightly different weave : a cloth with a cotton warp and a woollen weft ; **sat′in-fin′ish,** a satiny polish ; **sat′in-paper,** a fine, glossy writing-paper ; **sat′in-sheet′ing,** a twilled cotton and silk fabric with a satin surface ; **sat′in-spar,** a satiny fibrous calcite, or aragonite, or gypsum ; **sat′in-stitch,** an em-

---

broidery stitch, repeated in parallel lines, giving a satiny appearance; **sat′in-stone,** a fibrous gypsum; **sat′inwood,** a beautiful, smooth, satiny ornamental wood from India: the rutaceous tree (*Chloroxylon Swietenia*) yielding it: extended to several more or less similar woods and trees.—*adj.* **sat′iny,** like satin. [Fr. *satin,* app.—L.L. *sēta,* silk (L. *saita,* bristle).]

satire, *sat′īr, n.* a literary composition, orig. in verse, essentially a criticism of folly or vice, which it holds up to ridicule or scorn—its chief instruments, irony, sarcasm, invective, wit, and humour: satirical writing as a genre: its spirit: the use of, or inclination to use, its methods: satirical denunciation or ridicule: (*obs.* ; from confusion with **satyr**) a satirist.—*adjs.* **satiric** (*sa-tir′ik*), **-al,** pertaining to, or conveying, satire: sarcastic: abusive. —*adv.* **satir′ically.**—*n.* **satir′icalness,** the state or quality of being satirical.—*v.t.* **satirise** (*sat′ər-īz*), to make the object of satire: to censure severely.— *v.i.* to write satire.—*n.* **sat′irist,** a writer of satire. [L. *satira, satura* (*lanx*), full (dish), a medley.]

satisfy, *sat′is-fī, v.t.* to pay in full: to compensate or atone for: to give enough to: to be enough for: to supply fully: to fulfil the conditions of: to meet the requirements of: to content: to free from doubt: to convince.—*v.i.* to give content: to make payment or atonement:—*pr.p.* **sat′isfying;** *pa.t.* and *pa.p.* **sat′isfied.**—*n.* **satisfaction** (*-fak′shon*), act of satisfying: state of being satisfied, content: payment: quittance: gratification: comfort: that which satisfies: amends: atonement: reparation: satisfying of honour, as by a duel: conviction.—*adv.* **satisfac′torily.**—*n.* **satisfac′toriness.**—*adjs.* **satisfac′tory,** satisfying: giving contentment: such as might be wished: making amends or payment: atoning: convincing; **sat′isfiable; sat′isfied.**—*n.* **sat′isfier.**—*adj.* **sat′isfying.**—*adv.* **sat′isfyingly.**—**satisfaction theory** (of the Atonement), the ordinary theory of Catholic orthodoxy that Christ made satisfaction to Divine justice for the guilt of human sin by suffering as the human representative, and that thus Divine forgiveness was made possible. [O.Fr. *satisfier*— L. *satisfacĕre, satis,* enough, *facĕre,* to make.]

sative, *sā′tiv, adj.* (*obs.*) cultivated. [L. *sativus.*]

satrap, *sat′rap, -rap, sā′trap, n.* a viceroy or governor of an ancient Persian province: a provincial governor, esp. if powerful or ostentatiously rich: a tyrannical person.—*adjs.* **sat′rapal, satrap′ic, -al.**—*n.* **sat′rapy,** a satrap's province, office, or time of office. [Gr. *satrapēs,* from Old Pers. *khshathrapāvan-,* country-protector.]

Satsuma, *sat′soo-mä, n.* a province of S.W. Japan. —**Satsuma ware,** a yellowish pottery with gilding and enamel made there from end of 16th century.

saturate, *sat′ū-rāt, -yə-, v.t.* to interfuse: to soak: to imbue: to charge to the fullest extent possible: to satisfy all the valencies of: to cover (a target area) completely with bombs dropped simultaneously.—*adj.* saturated: deep in colour, free from white. — *adjs.* **sat′urable; sat′urated.**—*ns.* **satura′tion; sat′urātor.** [L. *saturāre, -ātum— satur,* full, akin to *satis,* enough.]

Saturday, *sat′ər-dā, n.* the seventh day of the week, dedicated by the Romans to Saturn, the Jewish Sabbath. [O.E. *Sæter-, Sætern(es)dæg,* Saturn's day.]

Saturn, *sat′ərn, n.* the ancient Roman God of agriculture: commonly used for the Greek Kronos, with whom he came to be identified: the second in size and sixth in distance from the sun of the major planets, believed by the astrologers to induce a cold, melancholy, gloomy temperament: (*alch.*) the metal lead.—*n.pl.* **Saturnā′lia,** the festival of Saturn in mid-December, when slaves and masters exchanged garb and parts: hence (often as *sing.* without capital) an orgy.—*adj.* **saturnā′lian,** of the Saturnalia: riotously merry.—*n.* **Satur′nia** (*sat-, sat-*), a genus of very large moths.—*adj.* **Satur′nian,** pertaining to Saturn, whose fabulous reign was called the golden age: happy: pure: simple: in the metre in which the oldest Latin poems were written: of the planet Saturn: of the genus Saturnia.—*n.* one born under Saturn, or of saturnine temperament: the son of Saturn (Jupiter or

Zeus): a fancied inhabitant of Saturn.—*adjs.* **satur′nic,** affected with lead-poisoning; **sat′urnine,** grave: gloomy: phlegmatic: caused or poisoned by lead.—*ns.* **sat′urnism,** lead-poisoning; **sat′urnist,** (*obs.*) a gloomy person.—**Saturn's tree,** an arborescent deposit of lead from a solution of a lead salt. [L. *Sāturnus—serēre, sătum,* to sow.]

satyr, *sat′ər, n.* a Greek wood-god, with tail and long ears, represented by the Romans as part goat: (*B.*) a desert demon: a very lecherous person: an orang-utan: any butterfly of the Satyridae: (formerly, by confusion) a satire or satirist.— Shakespeare's **saltiers** (*Wint. Tale,* IV. iv. 353) is perh. meant to mark a rustic confusion of satyr and saultier (jumper):—*fem.* **sat′yra, sat′yress.**— *n.* **sat′yral,** (*her.*) a monster compounded of man, lion, and antelope.—*adj.* **satyresque′.**—*n.* **satyrī′asis,** morbid and overpowering sexual desire in men, corresponding to nymphomania in women.— *adjs.* **satyric** (*sa-tir′ik*), **-al,** of satyrs: having a chorus of satyrs.—*n.pl.* **Satyridae** (*-tir′i-dē*), a family of butterflies (otherwise **Satyri′nae,** a subfamily of Nymphalidae) including meadow-browns, heaths, marbled whites, &c.—*n.* **sat′irisk,** a little satyr. [L. *satyrus*—Gr. *satyros.*]

sauba, *sä-ōō′bä, saw′bä, n.* a S. American leaf-carrying ant.—Also **saü′ba-ant.** [Tupí.]

sauce, *saws, n.* a dressing poured over food: (*fig.*) anything that gives relish: (*U.S.*) vegetables eaten with meat: (*U.S.*) stewed fruit: a solution of salt, &c., used in individual processes: (*obs.*) a pert or impudent person: (*coll.*) pert or impertinent language.—*v.t.* to add or give sauce to: to make piquant or pleasant: (*Shak.*) to rebuke: (*Shak.*) to make to pay dear: (*obs.*) to belabour.—*ns.* **sauce′-alone,** garlic-mustard; **sauce′-boat,** a vessel for sauce; **sauce′-box,** a saucy person; **sauce-crayon** (*sōs krā-yōn*; Fr.), a soft black pastel used for backgrounds; **sauce′man,** (*U.S.*) a vegetable seller; **sauce′pan,** a pan in which sauce or any small thing is boiled; **sauce′pan-fish,** the king-crab.—*adv.* **sauc′ily.**—*n.* **sauc′iness.**— *adj.* **sauc′y** (*comp.* **sauc′ier;** *superl.* **sauc′iest),** tasting of sauce: pert: piquantly audacious: smart and trim (as of a ship): disdainful: (*Shak.*) lascivious. [Fr. *sauce*—L. *salsa—sallēre, salsum,* to salt—*sāl,* salt.]

saucer, *saw′sər, n.* (*orig.*) a dish for salt or sauce: a shallow dish, esp. one placed under a tea or coffee cup: anything of like shape.—*n.* **sau′cer-eye,** a large round eye.—*adj.* **sau′cer-eyed.**—*n.* **sau′cerful:**—*pl.* **sau′cerfuls.** [O.Fr. *saussiere*—L.L. *salsārium*—L. *salsa,* sauce.]

sauch, saugh, *sawhh,* Scots form of **sallow** (willow).

saucisse, *sō-sēs′,* **saucisson,** *-ōn?, ns.* a tube of powder for firing a mine. [Fr., sausage.]

sauerkraut, *sow′, zow′ər-krowt, n.* a German dish of cabbage allowed to ferment with salt, &c. [Ger., sour cabbage.]

saufgard, *sawf-gärd′, n.* (*Spens.*). Same as **safe-guard.**

sauger, *saw′gər, n.* a small American pike-perch.

saul, a Scots form of **soul.**

saulge, *sawj. n.* (*Spens.*). Same as **sage** (plant).

saulie, *saw′li, n.* (*Scot.*) a hired mourner. [Ety. obscure.]

sault, *sawlt, n.* (*obs.*) a leap (also **salt**): in N. America (*sōō*) a waterfall or rapid. [Fr. *saut,* 17th-cent. *sault*—L. *saltus, -ūs,* leap.]

saunt, *sawnt,* a Scots form of **saint.**

saunter, *sawn′tər, v.i.* to wander about idly: to loiter: to lounge: to stroll: (*obs.*) to dawdle.— *n.* a sauntering: a sauntering gait: a leisurely stroll. — *ns.* **saun′terer; saun′tering.** — *adv.* **saun′teringly.** [Origin obscure.]

saurel, *sō-rel′, sawr′əl, n.* the horse-mackerel, scad. [Fr.]

Sauria, *saw′ri-ä, n.pl.* in old classifications an order of reptiles, the lizards with (at first) the crocodiles. —*adj.* **sau′rian.**—*n.* a member of the Sauria: a lizard-like fossil reptile.—*adjs.* **saurog′nathous,** having a lizard-like arrangement of the palate-bones (as woodpeckers, **Saurog′nathae;** Gr. *gnathos,* jaw); **saur′oid,** lizard-like.—*n.pl.* **Saurop′oda** (Gr. *pous, podos,* foot), a suborder of gigantic

herbivorous dinosaurs.—*adj.* **saurop′odous.**—*n.pl.*
Saurop′sida (Gr. *opsis*, -*eōs*, appearance), a main
division of the Vertebrata—birds and reptiles.—*n.*
and *adj.* **saurop′sidan.** — *n.pl.* **Sauroptery′gia**
(*saw-rop-tər-ij′i-ä*; Gr. *pterygion*, a fin), an order
of fossil reptiles, aquatic or amphibious, including
Plesiosaurus.—*adj.* **sauropteryg′ian.**—*n.pl.* **Saururae** (*saw-rōō′rē*; Gr. *ourā*, tail), an extinct
(Jurassic) subclass of birds, with teeth and jointed
tail—Archaeopteryx, &c. [Gr. *saurā*, *sauros*, a
lizard.]
saury, *saw′ri,* *n.* the skipper (Scombresox), a sharp-
beaked fish akin to the garfish. [Perh. Gr. *sauros*,
lizard.]
sausage, *sos′ij,* *n.* chopped meat seasoned and
stuffed in a tube of gut or the like: anything of
like shape, e.g. an observation balloon.—*ns.*
saus′age-bassoon′, the rackett; **saus′age-meat′,**
meat prepared for making sausages; **saus′age-
poi′soning,** botulism; **saus′age-roll′,** minced
meat cooked in a roll of pastry: a curl of hair of
similar shape. [Fr. *saucisse*—L.L. *salsīcia*—L.
salsus, salted.]
saussurite, *saw-sū′rīt,* *n.* a dull opaque mass of
zoisite, albite, &c., formed by the alteration of
felspar.—*adjs.* **saussuritic** (-*it′ik*); **saussu′rit-
ised.** [After the Swiss geologist H. B. de *Saussure*
(1740-99).]
saut, *sawt,* a Scottish form of **salt.**
sauté, *sō′tā,* *adj.* fried lightly and quickly.—Also
v.t. [Fr.]
Sauterne(s), *sō-tərn′,* -*tern′,* *n.* esteemed white wine
produced at *Sauternes* in the Gironde, France.
savage, *sav′ij,* also (*arch.*) **salvage,** *sal′vij,* *adj.* in
a state of nature: wild: uncivilised: ferocious:
furious.—*n.* (now *rare*) a wild beast: an enraged
horse or other animal: a human being in a wild
state: a brutal, fierce, or cruel person.—*v.t.* to
make savage: to assail savagely, esp. with teeth.—
v.i. to play the savage.—*n.* **sav′agedom,** a savage
state: savages collectively.—*adv.* **sav′agely.**—*ns.*
sav′ageness; **sav′agery** (-*ri*, also -*ər-i*), fierceness: ferocity: uncivilised condition: wildness:
wild growth of plants; **sav′agism.** [O.Fr. *salvage*—
L. *silvāticus*, pertaining to the woods—*silva*, a wood.]
savanna, savannah, *sə-van′ä,* *n.* a tract of level
land, covered with low vegetation, treeless, or
dotted with trees or patches of wood.—*ns.* **savann′a
flower,** a West Indian apocynaceous plant (Echiles);
savann′a-forest, parklands; **savann′a-sparr′ow,**
a N. American sparrow (Passerculus); **savann′a-
watt′le,** fiddlewood. [Sp. *zavana* (now *sabana*),
said to be from Carib: not from *sábana*, sheet.]
savant, *sä-vän°,* *sä′vän°,* *n.* a learned man. [Fr.
obs. pr.p. of *savoir*, to know.]
savate, *sä-vät,* *n.* boxing with the use of the feet.
[Fr.]
save, *sāv,* *v.t.* to bring safe out of evil: to rescue:
to bring or keep out of danger: to protect: to
prevent or avoid the loss, expenditure, or performance of, or the gain of by an opponent: to reserve:
to spare: to deliver from the power of sin and
from its consequences: to husband: to hoard: to
be in time for: to obviate, to prevent.—*v.i.* to act
as a saviour: to be economical.—*prep.* except.—
conj. (*Shak.*) were it not that: unless.—*n.* an act
of saving, esp. in games.—*adj.* **sav′able.**—*ns.*
sav′ableness; **save′-all,** a contrivance intended
to save anything from being wasted: a miser.—
adj. stingy.—*adj.* **saved.**—*v.t.* **save′gard** (*Spens.*)
to protect.—*n.* **sa′ver.**—*adj.* **sa′ving,** protecting:
preserving: redeeming: (*theol.*) securing salvation: frugal: making a reservation: directed
towards the avoidance of loss rather than the
making of profit.—*prep.* excepting.—*n.* the action
of the verb: that which is saved: (*pl.*) earnings.—
adv. **sa′vingly.**—*n.* **sa′vingness.**—save appearances, (*astron., Milt.*) to make hypothesis accord
with observation: to keep up an appearance of
wealth, comfort, consistency, harmony, propriety,
&c.; save one's face, save the mark (see face,
mark); save up, to accumulate for some purpose
by refraining from spending; save you, (*arch.*) a
greeting=God keep you; savings bank, a bank
established to encourage thrift by taking small

deposits, investing under regulations for safety,
and giving compound interest; savings certificate, a certificate of having invested a small sum in
government funds; saving game, a policy or
procedure aiming rather at avoiding loss than
making a profit. [Fr. *sauver*—L. *salvāre*—*salvus*,
safe.]
saveloy, *sav′ə-loi,* *n.* a highly seasoned sausage,
orig. of brains. [Fr. *cervelat*, *cervelas*, a saveloy—
It. *cervellata*—*cervello*, brain—L. *cerebellum*, dim.
of *cerebrum*, the brain.]
savin, savine, *sav′in,* *n.* a species of juniper (*Juniperus Sabina*) with very small imbricated leaves:
its tops yielding an irritant volatile oil, anthelmintic
and abortifacient: extended to Virginian juniper
(' red cedar ') and other plants. [O.Fr. *sabine*—
L. *sabīna* (*herba*), Sabine (herb).]
saviour, *sā′vyər,* *n.* one who saves from evil:
Saviour, a title applied by Christians to Jesus
Christ.
savoir-faire, *sav-wär-fer′,* *n.* the faculty of knowing
just what to do and how to do it: tact. [Fr.]
savoir-vivre, *sav-wär-vē′vr′,* *n.* good breeding:
knowledge of polite usages. [Fr.]
savory, *sā′vər-i,* *n.* a labiate flavouring herb (Satu-
reia, esp. *S. hortensis*, summer savory, or *S. montana*,
winter savory). [App.—L. *saturēia*.]
savour, also (*U.S.*) **savor,** *sā′vər,* *n.* taste: odour:
flavour: relish: (*B.*) repute.—*v.i.* to taste or smell
in a particular way: (*lit.* or *fig.*) to have a flavour:
to smack.—*v.t.* to flavour, season: to taste, smell:
to be conscious of: to relish: to perceive critically:
to taste with conscious direction of the attention.—
adjs. **sä′vorous,** pleasant to the taste; **sä′voured,**
having a savour.—*adv.* **sä′vourily.**—*n.* **sä′vouri-
ness.**—*adj.* **sä′vourless.**—*adv.* **sä′vourly,** (*obs.*)
relishingly: feelingly: understandingly. — *adj.*
sä′voury, of good savour or relish: fragrant:
having savour or relish: appetising: salty or
spiced (opp. to *sweet*): (*arch.*) savouring of edification or holiness.—*n.* a savoury course or dish.
[O.Fr. *sav*(*o*)*ur* (Fr. *saveur*)—L. *sapor*—*sapēre*, to
taste.]
Savoy, *sə-voi′,* *n.* a district, formerly of the kingdom
of Sardinia, now of S.E. France, giving name to a
former palace and sanctuary and to a theatre in
London: savoy, a winter cabbage with a large
close head and wrinkled leaves—originally from
Savoy.—*n.* **Savoyard** (*sav′oi-ärd*), a native or inhabitant of Savoy, or of the Savoy precinct in
London: a performer in the Gilbert and Sullivan
operas produced at the Savoy theatre.—Also *adj.*
[Fr. *Savoie*, *Savoyard*.]
savvy, savvey, savey, *sav′i,* *v.t.* and *v.i.* (*slang*) to
know: to understand.—*n.* general ability: com-
mon sense. [Sp. *sabe*—*saber*, to know—L. *sapēre*,
to be wise.]
saw, *saw,* *pa.t.* of **see.**
saw, *saw,* *n.* a toothed cutting instrument.—*v.t.* to
cut with, or as with, or as, a saw: to play harshly
and crudely (as a fiddler).—*v.i.* to use a saw: to
make to and fro movements, as if with a saw:—
pa.t. **sawed;** *pa.p.* **sawed** or (usu.) **sawn.**—*ns.*
saw′-bill, a merganser: a motmot; **saw′-blade;**
saw′bones, (*slang*) a surgeon; **saw′dust,** dust or
small particles of wood, &c., detached in sawing.—
v.t. to sprinkle with sawdust.—*adjs.* **saw′dusty;**
sawed.—*n.* **saw′-edge.**—*adj.* **saw′-edged,** serrated.—*ns.* **saw′er** (*rare*); **saw′-fish,** a ray (Pristis)
or (sometimes) a shark (Pristiophorus; **saw′-
shark**) with a flattened bony beak toothed on the
edges; **saw′-fly,** a hymenopterous insect of various
kinds with saw-like ovipositor; **saw′-frame,** the
frame in which a saw is set; **saw′-gate, -kerf,** the
gap made by a saw; **saw′-horse,** a trestle for supporting wood that is being sawn.—*n.* and *adj.*
saw′ing.—*n.* **saw′-mill,** a mill for sawing timber.
—*adj.* **sawn.**—*ns.* **saw′pit,** a pit in which one
sawyer stands while another stands above; **saw′-
set,** an instrument for turning saw-teeth to right
and left.—*n.pl.* **saw′-tones,** harsh notes.—*n.* **saw′-
tooth.**—Also *adj.*—*adj.* **saw′-toothed.**—*ns.* **saw′-
wort,** a name for various composites with serrate
leaves (Serratula, Saussurea, &c.); **saw′yer,** one
who saws timber, esp. at a sawpit: (*U.S.*) a

stranded tree that bobs in a river. [O.E. *saga*; Ger. *säge*.]

saw, *saw*, *n*. a saying: a proverb: (*Spens.*) a decree. [O.E. *sagu*, from the root of *secgan*, to say, tell.]

saw, *saw*, a Scots form of **sow** (*vb*.) and of **salve** (ointment).

sawder, *saw'dər*, *v.t.* to flatter, blarney.—*n.* (in phrase *soft sawder*) flattery. [Prob. **solder**.]

sawn, *sawn*, *pa.p.* of **saw**; also (*Northern*) of **sow**; (*Shak.*) perh. of **sow**, perh. of **see**.

Sawney, **Sawny**, *saw'ni*, *n.* an old nickname for a Scotsman. [For *Sandy*, from *Alexander*.]

sax, *saks*, *n.* a chopper for trimming slates. [O.E. *sæx* (W.S. *seax*), a knife.]

sax, a Scottish form of **six**.

saxatile, *sak'sə-til*, *adj.* rock-dwelling. [L. *saxātilis* —*saxum*, a rock.]

saxaul, **saksaul**, *sak'sawl*, *n.* a low, thick, grotesquely contorted tree (Haloxylon) of the goosefoot family, found on the salt steppes of Asia.

Saxe, *saks*, *adj.* made in, or characteristic of, Saxony (of china, &c.): of a deep shade of light blue (*Saxe blue*, also *Saxon* or *Saxony blue*).—*n.* Saxon blue, a dye colour: (*phot.*) an albuminised paper. [Fr. *Saxe*, Saxony.]

saxhorn, *saks'horn*, *n.* a brass wind-instrument having a long winding tube with bell opening, invented by Antoine or Adolphe *Sax* (1814–94).

saxicavous, *sak-sik'ə-vəs*, *adj.* rock-boring.—*n.* **Saxic'ava**, a genus of rock-boring lamellibranchs. [L. *saxum*, a rock, *cavāre*, to hollow.]

saxicolous, *sak-sik'ə-ləs*, *adj.* living or growing among rocks.—*n.* **Saxic'ola**, the wheatear genus. —*adj.* **saxic'oline**. [L. *saxum*, a rock, *colĕre*, to inhabit.]

saxifrage, *sak'si-frij*, -*frāj*, *n.* any species of the genus Saxifraga: extended to other plants (see burnet saxifrage, golden saxifrage).—*n.* **Saxifraga** (-*sif'rə-gä*), the London pride genus, giving name to the family **Saxifragā'ceae**, near akin to the rose family.—*adj.* **saxifragā'ceous**. [L. *saxifraga*—*saxum*, a stone, *frangĕre*, to break (from growing in clefts of rock, or, according to Pliny, from supposed efficacy in breaking up a calculus in the bladder).]

Saxon, *saks'ən*, *n.* one of a N. German people that conquered most of Britain in the 5th and 6th centuries (including or excluding the Angles and Jutes): the language of that people on the Continent (Old Saxon) or in Britain (Anglo-Saxon, Old English): an Englishman or Lowland Scotsman: one whose native language is English: the English language: a native, inhabitant, or citizen of Saxony in the later German sense (now in S. Germany).—*adj.* pertaining to the Saxons in any sense, their language, country, or architecture.—*n.* **Sax'ondom**, the Anglo-Saxon or English-speaking world.—*adj.* **Saxonic** (-*on'ik*).—*v.t.* and *v.i.* **Sax'onise**, to make or become Saxon.—*ns.* **Sax'onism**, a Saxon or English idiom: a preference for native English words, institutions, &c.; **Sax'onist**, a scholar in Old English; **sax'onite**, a hypersthene peridotite; **sax'ony**, a soft woollen yarn or cloth.— **Saxon architecture**, a style of building in England before the Norman Conquest, marked by the peculiar 'long and short' work of the quoins, the projecting fillets running up the face of the walls and interlacing like woodwork, and the balusterlike shafts between the openings of the upper windows resembling the turned woodwork of the period; **Saxon Shore** (L. *Litus Saxonicum*), in Roman times, the coast districts from Brighton to the Wash, peculiarly exposed to the attacks of the Saxons, or perh. already partly settled by them, and therefore placed under the authority of a special officer, the 'Count of the Saxon Shore.' [L. *Saxŏnēs* (pl.); of Ger. origin; cf. O.E. *Seaxe*; Ger. *Sachsen*; O.E. *seax*, O.H.G. *sahs*, knife, short sword; see **sax** (1).]

saxophone, *sak'sō-fōn*, *n.* a military and dance band instrument with reed, metal tube, and about twenty finger-keys.—*n.* **saxophonist** (-*sof'ən-ist*). [*Sax*, the inventor (see **saxhorn**), Gr. *phōnē*, the voice.]

say, *sā*, *v.t.* to utter or set forth, as words or in

words: to speak: to assert, affirm, state, declare: to tell: to go through in recitation or repetition.— *v.i.* to make a statement: to speak: to declare, set forth in answer to a question:—*2nd sing. pr. ind.* **sayst** (*sāst*), **sayest** (*sā'ist*); *3rd sing.* **says** (*sez*, *səz*), archaic **saith** (*seth*); *pr.p.* **say'ing**; *pa.p.* and *pa.t.* **said** (*sed*); *2nd sing.* **saidst** (*sedst*), also **said'est**.—*n.* something said: a remark: a speech: (*obs.*) a saw: what one wants to say: opportunity of speech: a voice, part, or influence in a decision. —*adj.* **say'able**.—*ns.* **say'er**; **say'ing**, something said: an expression: a maxim; **say'-so**, a dictum: authority: a rumour: hearsay.—**I say**, an exclamation calling attention or expressing surprise, protest, sudden joy, &c.; **it is said**, or **they say**, **it is commonly reputed**; **it says** (now almost illiterate), the text runs thus: **it is said**; **nothing to say for oneself**, no defence: no small-talk; **nothing to say to**, no dealings with; **not to say**, indeed one might go further and say; **say**, for example: suppose: (*U.S.*) I say: in 18th-cent. verse a common introduction to a rhetorical question; **says I, says you**, vivaciously (or naïvely) ungrammatical substitutes for said I, you; **sooth to say**, in truth: if the truth must be told; **that is to say**, in other words; **to say nothing of**, not to mention; **what do you say to?**, how about?: are you inclined towards? [O.E. *secgan* (*sægde*, *gesægd*); O.N. *segja*, Ger. *sagen*.]

say, *sā*, *n.*, *v.t.*, and *v.i.* (*obs.*; *Spens.*, *Shak.*) an aphetic form of **assay**.—*ns.* **say'er**; **say'-master**; **say'-piece**.

say, *sā*, *n.* a woollen stuff like serge.—*adj.* (*Shak.*) of **say**.—*n.* **say'on**, a mediaeval peasant's sleeveless jacket. [O.Fr. *saie*—L. *saga*, pl. of *sagum*, military cloak.]

sayne, *sān*, (*Spens.*) *inf.* and *pl.* of *pr.t.* of **say** (1).

sayyid, **sayid**, **said**, *sī'* or *sā'(y)id*, *sād*, *n.* a descendant of Mohammed's daughter Fatima. [Ar. *Sayyīd*.]

sazhen, *sä-zhen'*, *n.* a Russian measure, about 7 feet. [Russ.]

sbirro, *zbir'rō*, *n.* an Italian police officer:—*pl.* **sbirri** (-*rē*). [It.]

'sblood, *zblud*, **'sbodikins**, *zbod'i-kinz*, **'sbuddikins**, *zbud'*, **'zbud**, *zbud*, *interjs.* obsolete oaths. [God's blood, body.]

scab, *skab*, *n.* vaguely, a skin disease, esp. with scales or pustules, and esp. one caused by mites (as in *sheep scab*): a fungous disease of various kinds in potatoes, apples, &c.: a crust formed over a sore, or in any of these diseases: a scoundrel: a blackleg.—*v.i.* to develop a scab: to play the scab.— *adj.* **scabbed** (*skabd*, *skab'id*), affected or covered with scabs: diseased with scab: vile, worthless.— *ns.* **scabb'edness**; **scabb'iness**.—*adj.* **scabb'y**. [App. from an O.N. equivalent of O.E. *scæb*, *sceabb* (see **shabby**), influenced by association with L. *scabiēs*.]

scabbard, *skab'ərd*, *n.* a sheath, esp. for a sword.— *v.t.* to sheathe.—*n.* **scabb'ard-fish**, a long narrow fish (Lepidopus) of the hairtail family.—*adj.* **scabb'ardless**. [M.E. *scauberc*, app. — A.Fr. *escaubers* (pl.), prob. Gmc.]

scabble, *skab'l*. Same as **scapple**.

scabies, *skā'bi-ēz*, *n.* the itch. [L. *scăbiēs*—*scăbĕre*, to scratch.]

scabious, *skā'bi-əs*, *n.* any plant of the genus **Scabio'sa** of the teasel family, as the *Devil's-bit scabious*, long thought efficacious in scaly eruptions: a plant (*Jasione montana*; *sheep's*, or *sheep's-bit scabious*) of the bell-flower family, of similar appearance. [L. *scăbiōsus*—*scăbiēs*, the itch.]

scabrous, *skā'brəs*, *adj.* rough: rough with projecting points: scurfy: harsh: beset with difficulties: bordering on the indecent.—*adjs.* **scaberulous** (*skə-ber'ū-ləs*), **scā'brid**, somewhat scabrous. — *ns.* **scabridity** (*skə-brid'i-ti*), **scā'brousness**. [L. *scăbrōsus*, *scăbridus*—*scăber*, rough.]

scad, *skad*, *n.* a carangoid fish (*Caranx*, or *Trachurus*, *trachurus*) with armoured and keeled lateral line, superficially like a coarse mackerel, also called *horse-mackerel*. [App. Cornish dial.; perh. **shad**.]

scaff, *skäf*, *n.* (*Scot.*) food: riff-raff (also **scaff'-**

fāte, fär, äsk; mē, hər (her); mīne; mōte; mūte; mōōn; dhen (then) raff'). [Perh. Du. or Ger. *schaffen*, to procure food ; cf. **scoff** (2).]

scaffie, *skăf'i*, *n.* (*Scot. coll.*) short for **scavenger**.

scaffold, *skaf'ŏld*, *n.* a temporary erection for men at work on a building, and their tools and materials : a raised platform, as for performers, spectators, or executions : a raised framework, as for hunters, or among some primitive peoples for disposal of the dead : a framework : (*fig.*) capital punishment. —*v.t.* to furnish with a scaffold : to put on a scaffold : to sustain.—*ns.* **scaff'oldage** (*Shak.* **scaff'olage**), a scaffolding : the gallery of a theatre ; **scaff'older** ; **scaff'olding**, a framework for painters, builders, &c., at work : materials for scaffolds : (*fig.*) a frame, framework : the action of the verb. [O.Fr. *escadafault* (Fr. *échafaud*), of obscure origin ; cf. It. *catafalco*.]

scaglia, *skal'yä*, *n.* an Italian limestone, usu. reddish. —*n.* **scagliŏ'la**, an imitation stone of cement and chips.—Also *adj.* [It. *scaglia*, scale, dim. *scagliuola*.]

scaith. See skaith.

scala, *skā'lä* (L. *skä'lä*), *n.* a ladder-like structure, as any of the canals of the cochlea :—*pl.* **scalae** (*-lē* ; L. *-lī*).—*adj.* **scā'lable**, that can be climbed. —*ns.* **scalade** (*skə-lād'*), **scalado** (*-lä'dō, -lä'dō* ; It. *scalada*), an escalade.—*adj.* **scalar** (*skā'lər*), ladder-like : numerical : represented by a point in a scale : having magnitude only, not direction.— *n.* a scalar quantity.—*n.* **Scalaria** (*skə-lā'ri-ä*), the wentletrap genus.—*adj.* **scalariform** (*skə-lar'i-form*), ladder-like. [L. *scāla*, a ladder.]

scal(l)awag. Same as **scallywag**.

scald, *skawld*, *v.t.* to injure with hot liquid : to cook or heat short of boiling : to treat with very hot water : (now *dial.*) to burn, scorch.—*v.t.* to be scalded : to be hot enough to scald.—*n.* a burn caused by hot liquid.—*n.* **scald'er**.—*n.* and *adj.* **scald'ing**—**scaldings**, a cry of warning to get out of the way, as if of hot water. [O.Fr. *escalder* (Fr. *échauder*)—L.L. *excaldāre*, to bathe in warm water—*ex*, from, *calidus*, warm, hot.]

scald, scaldic. Same as **skald, skaldic**.

scald, *skawld*, *adj.* scabby : scurfy : paltry.—*n.* scurf on the head : a scurvy fellow.—*ns.* **scald'-berry**, the blackberry (from a belief that it causes scald-head) ; **scald'-crow** (*Ir.*), the hooded crow ; **scald'fish**, the smooth sole ; **scald'-head**, a diseased scalp : scalp disease of various kinds. [For **scalled**.]

scaldino, *skäl-dē'nō*, *n.* an Italian earthenware brazier :—*pl.* **scaldi'ni** (*-nē*). [It. *scaldare*, to warm.]

scale, scail, skāl. Same as **skail**.

scale, *skāl*, *n.* a ladder : (*Milt.*) a scaling ladder : (*obs.*) a flight of steps : a graduated series or order : a graduated measure : a system of definite tones used in music : a succession of these performed in ascending or descending order of pitch through one octave or more : compass or range of a voice or instrument : a numeral system : a system or scheme of relative values or correspondences : ratio of representation to object : relative extent.—*v.t.* to mount, as by a ladder : to climb : to change according to scale.—*v.i.* to mount.—*ns.* **scale'-stair'**(case), (*Scot.*) stairs in straight flights ; **scal'ing**, climbing : adjustment to or in a scale ; **scal'ing-ladder**, a ladder for escalade : a fireman's ladder.—**on a large, small, scale**, in a great, small, way ; **on the scale of**, in the ratio of ; **scale and platt**, (*Scot.*) stairs with straight flights and landings ; **to scale**, in proportion to actual dimensions. [L. *scāla*, a ladder—*scandĕre*, to mount.]

scale, *skāl*, *n.* a thin plate on a fish, reptile, &c. : a readily detached flake : a lamina : an overlapping plate in armour : a small, flat, detachable piece of cuticle : a reduced leaf or leaf-base, often membranous, or hard and woody : a small flat structure clothing a butterfly's or moth's wing : the waxy shield secreted by a scale-insect : an encrustation : a film, as on iron under the hammer : a side piece of a razor or clasp-knife handle.—*v.t.* to clear of scales : to peel off in thin layers.—*v.i.* to come off in thin layers or flakes.—*ns.* **scale'-arm'our**, armour of overlapping scales ; **scale'-board**, a

very thin slip of wood.—*adj.* **scaled**, having scales : cleared of scales.—*ns.* **scale'-fern**, a fern (*Ceterach officinarum*) whose back is densely covered with rusty-coloured scales ; **scale'-fish**, a dry-cured fish, as haddock, hake, pollack : a fish with scales ; **scale'-insect**, any insect of the homopterous family Coccidae, in which the sedentary female fixes on a plant and secretes a waxy shield ; **scale'-leaf**, a scale that is homologically a leaf.—*adjs.* **scale'less** ; **scale'like.**—*ns.* **scale'-moss**, a liverwort with small leaflike structures, as Jungermannia ; **scal'er**, one who scales fish, boilers, &c. : an instrument for scaling, as for removing tartar from the teeth ; **scale'-work**, imbricated ornament ; **scal'iness** ; **scal'ing**, formation, peeling off, shedding, removal, or arrangement of scales or scale : a scaled-off piece.—Also *adj.*—*adj.* **scal'y**, covered with scales : like scales : shabby : formed of scales : inclined to scale.—*ns.* **scal'y-bark**, hickory : hickory-nut ; **scal'y-leg**, a disease of legs and feet in poultry, caused by a mite. [M.E. *scāle*—O.Fr. *escale*, husk, chip of stone, of Gmc. origin ; cf. **scale** (4), **shale, shell**.]

scale, *skāl*, *n.* a balance pan : (usu. in *pl.*, by Shak. treated as *sing.*) a balance : (in *pl.*) Libra, a constellation and a sign of the zodiac.—*v.t.* to weigh : to weigh up.—*v.i.* to be weighed, as a jockey (often *scale in*).—*n.* **scale'-beam**, the beam of a balance. [A Northern form from O.N. *skál*, bowl, pan of balance ; cf. O.E. *scealu*, shell, cup, Du. *schaal*, Ger. *schale*, and preceding word.]

scale, *skāl*, *v.t.* (*Shak., Cor.* I. i. 97) variously explained as, to spread, disseminate (see **skail**), to lay bare, make clear (see **scale**, 3), or as a misprint for **stale.**

scalene, *skal-ēn'*, *adj.* (of a triangle) with three unequal sides : (of a cone or cylinder) with axis oblique to the base : (of a muscle) obliquely situated and unequal-sided, connecting ribs with neck. —*n.* **scalēnohē'dron**, (*crystal.*) a hemihedral form bounded in the hexagonal system by twelve, in the tetragonal by eight, faces, each a scalene triangle. [Gr. *skalēnos*, uneven, *hedrā*, seat.]

scall, *skawl*, *n.* (*B.*) scabbiness, esp. of the scalp.— *adj.* (*Shak.*) scurvy : mean.—*adj.* **scalled** (see **scald**). [O.N. *skalli*, bald head.]

scallion, *skal'yon*, *n.* the shallot : the leek : an onion with defective bulb. [O.N. Fr. *escalogne*— L. *Ascalōnia* (*cēpa*), Ascalon (onion).]

scallop, *skol'əp, skal'əp*, *n.* a bivalve (Pecten) having a sub-circular shell with sinuous radiating ridges and eared hinge-line : a valve of its shell : a dish or other object of like form : a shallow dish in which oysters, &c., are cooked, baked, and browned : a potato slice cooked in batter : one of a series of curves in the edge of anything.—*v.t.* to cut into scallops or curves : to cook in a scallop with crumbs of bread, &c.—*adj.* **scall'oped**, having the edge or border cut into scallops or curves.—*n.* **scall'op-shell**, the shell of a scallop, esp. that of a Mediterranean species, the badge of a pilgrim to the shrine of St James of Compostela. [O.Fr. *escalope* ; of Gmc. origin ; cf. Du. *schelp*, shell ; Ger. *schelfe*, husk.]

scallywag, scallawag, scalawag, *skal'i-wag, -ə-wag*, *n.* an undersized animal of little value : a good-for-nothing : (*U.S. hist.*) a Southerner who co-operated with the Republicans in the Reconstruction period. [Origin obscure ; association with *Scalloway* in Shetland, in allusion to its small cattle or ponies, is regarded as a joke.]

scalp, *skalp* (*Scot.* **scaup**, *skawp*), *n.* (*obs.*) the skull : the outer covering of the skull : the top or hairy part of the head : the skin on which the hair of the head grows : a piece of that skin torn off as a token of victory by the North American Indians : a bare rock or mountain-top : a bed of oysters or mussels.—*v.t.* to cut the scalp from : (*U.S.*) to buy cheap in order to sell below ordinary price : (*U.S.*) to destroy the political influence of.—*ns.* **scalp'er** ; **scalp'ing-knife**, a knife for scalping enemies ; **scalp'ing-tuft**, a scalp-lock.— *adj.* **scalp'less.**—*n.* **scalp'-lock**, a long tuft of hair left unshaven as a challenge. [M.E. *scalp* ; perh. Scand. ; cf. O.N. *skálpr*, sheath ; cf. **scallop**.]

Neutral vowels in unaccented syllables : *el'ə-mənt, in'fənt, ran'dəm*

scalp, *skalp*, *v.t.* and *v.i.* (*rare*) to scrape : to cut : to engrave.—*n.* **scalp'el**, a small knife for dissecting or operating.—*adj.* **scalpell'iform**, shaped like a scalpel.—*n.* **scalp'er**, a scalprum : an engraver's scauper.—*adj.* **scalp'riform**, chisel-shaped.—*n.* **scalp'rum**, a surgeon's rasping instrument. [L. *scalpĕre*, to scrape, cut, *scalper*, *scalprum*, dim. *scalpellum*, a knife.]

scamble, *skam'bl*, *v.i.* (*Shak.*) to scramble : to get along somehow : to shamble : to sprawl.—*v.t.* to get together : to remove piecemeal : to scatter as for a scramble : to squander.—*ns.* **scam'bler**, a mealtime parasite ; **scam'bling**, scrambling : a haphazard meal—also *adj.*—*n.pl.* **scam'bling-days**, days of makeshift meals in Lent.—*adv.* **scam'blingly**, strugglingly. [Origin obscure ; app. related to **shamble** and **scramble**.]

scamel, *skam'l*, *n.* (*Shak.*) alleged to be a Norfolk name for the bar-tailed godwit : or a misprint for **staniel**, **stannel**, or for **sea-mell**, an alleged variant of **sea-mew**.

scammony, *skam'on-i*, *n.* an Anatolian convolvulus : its dried root : a cathartic gum-resin obtained from its root or that of a substitute. [Gr. *skammōniā*.]

scamp, *skamp*, *v.i.* (*dial.*) to go about idly : (*obs.*) to take to the highway (as a robber).—*n.* (*obs.*) a highwayman : a rascal : a lively, tricky fellow.—*v.i.* **scamp'er**, (*obs.*) to decamp : to run or skip about briskly.—*n.* an act of scampering.—*adj.* **scamp'ish**, rascally. — *adv.* **scamp'ishly.** — *n.* **scamp'ishness.** [O.Fr. *escamper* or It. *scampare*, to decamp ; see **decamp**.]

scamp, *skamp*, *v.t.* to do, execute, perfunctorily or without thoroughness.—*ns.* **scamp'er** ; **scamp'-ing** ; **scamp'-work.** [Poss. O.N. *skemma*, to shorten ; cf. **skimp**, **scant**.]

scan, *skan*, *v.t.* to analyse metrically : to utter so as to bring out the metrical structure : to examine critically : (*obs.*) to judge : (*Shak.*) to interpret, read : to make out : to examine closely : to scrutinise : to examine all parts of in systematic order : (in television) to pass a beam over every part of in turn : (loosely) to cast an eye negligently over : (*Spens.*, in *pa.p.* **scand**) to climb, scale.—*v.i.* to agree with the rules of metre :—*pr.p.* **scann'ing** ; *pa.t.* and *pa.p.* **scanned** (*Spens.* **scand**).—*n.* a scanning.—*n.* **scann'er**, one who scans or can scan : a perforated disk (also **scann'ing-disk**) used in television.—*n.* and *adj.* **scann'ing.**—*n.* **scan'sion**, act, art, or mode of scanning verse : scanning in television. [L. *scandĕre*, *scānsum*, to climb.]

scand. See **scan.**

scandal, *skan'dl*, *n.* a stumbling-block to faith : anything that brings discredit upon religion : injury to reputation : something said which is injurious to reputation : a false imputation : malicious gossip : slander : opprobrious censure : a disgraceful fact, thing, or person : a shocked feeling.—*v.t.* to defame : (*obs.*) to disgrace : (*obs.*) to shock.—*ns.* **scan'dal-bearer**, a propagator of malicious gossip ; **scandalisā'tion.**—*v.t.* **scan'dalise**, to give scandal or offence to : to shock : to disgrace : to slander.—*v.i.* to talk scandal.—*adj.* **scan'dalled**, disgraceful : slandered.—*ns.* **scan'dal-monger**, one who deals in defamatory reports ; **scan'dal-mongering, -monging.**—*adj.* **scan'dalous**, giving scandal or offence : calling forth condemnation : openly vile : defamatory.—*adv.* **scan'dalously.**—*n.* **scan'dalousness.**—**scan'dalum magnā'tum**, speaking slanderously of high personages, abbrev. *scan. mag.* [L. *scandalum*—Gr. *skandalon*, a stumbling-block.]

scandent, *skan'dant*, *adj.* climbing. [L. *scandēns*, *-entis*.]

Scandinavian, *skan-di-nā'vi-ən*, *adj.* of, or characteristic of, *Scandinavia*, the peninsula divided into Norway and Sweden, but, in a historical sense, applying also to Denmark and Iceland : (*philol.*) North Germanic. — *n.* a native of Scandinavia : a member of the dominant Nordic race of Scandinavia.—*n.* and *adj.* **Scan'dian.**—*adj.* **Scan'dic.**—*n.* **scan'dium**, a metallic element (Sc ; at. numb. 21) discovered in 1879 in the Scandinavian mineral euxinite. [L. *Scandināvia*, *Scandia.*]

Scandix, *skan'diks*, *n.* the Venus's comb genus of umbelliferous plants. [Gr.]

scansion. See **scan.**

Scansores, *skan-sō'rēz*, *n.pl.* in old classifications an order of birds, climbers, with two toes before and two behind. — *adj.* **scansō'rial**, climbing : adapted for climbing. [L. *scandēre*, *scānsum*, to climb.]

scant, *skant*, *adj.* not full or plentiful : scarcely sufficient : deficient : short, poorly supplied : sparing.—*n.* scarcity.—*adv.* barely : scantily.—*v.t.* to stint : to restrict : to reduce : to dispense sparingly : to slight.—*adv.* **scant'ily.**—*ns.* **scant'iness** ; **scant'ity** (*rare*).—*adv.* **scant'ly.**—*ns.* **scant'ness** ; **scant'-o'-grace**, (*Scot.*) a good-for-nothing.—*adj.* **scant'y**, meagre : deficient : skimped : wanting in fulness : parsimonious. [O.N. *skamt*, neut. of *skammr*, short.]

scantle, *skan'tl*, *v.t.* to stint : to make scant : to shorten (sail).—*v.i.* to become scant.—*n.* (*Shak.* ; various reading for **cantle**) a portion.—*n.* **scant'-ling**, a small portion.—*adj.* petty. [Prob. **scant**, with senses merging in the following word.]

scantling, *skant'ling*, *n.* a measured size : a measurement : an allotted portion : dimensions of a cross-section : a sample or pattern : a gauge : a narrow piece of timber.—*n.* **scan'tle**, a gauge for slates.—*v.t.* to adjust to measure. [O.Fr. *escantillon*, *eschantillon*, of uncertain etymology ; with senses merging in foregoing word.]

scape, *skāp*, *n.* an escape : an escapade : a transgression : a slip.—*v.t.* and *v.i.* (also *'scape*) to escape.—*ns.* **scape'gallows**, one who deserves hanging ; **scape'grace**, a graceless, hare-brained fellow.—*adj.* **scape'less**, not to be escaped.—*ns.* **scape'ment**, escapement ; **scape'-wheel**, escapewheel. [**escape.**]

scape, *skāp*, *n.* (*bot.*) a peduncle rising from the ground, without foliage leaves : (*entom.*) the basal part of an antenna : the shaft or stem of a feather : (*archit.*) the shaft of a column.—*adjs.* **scape'less** ; **scapigerous** (*skə-pij'ər-əs*), having a scape. [L. *scāpus*, a shaft.]

scape, *skāp*, *n.* the cry of the snipe when flushed : the snipe itself. [Prob. imit.]

scape, *skāp*, *n.* a landscape or other picture of scenery (often in compounds). [**landscape.**]

scapegoat, *skāp'gōt*, *n.* a goat on which, once a year, the Jewish high-priest laid symbolically the sins of the people, and which was then allowed to escape into the wilderness (Levit. xvi.) : any animal used in like manner : one who is made to bear the misdeeds of another. [**escape** and **goat.**]

scaphocephalus, *skaf-ō-sef'ə-ləs*, *n.* boat-shaped head.—*adjs.* **scaphocephalic** (*-si-fal'ik*), **scapho-cephalous** (*-sef'ə-ləs*).—*n.* **scaphoceph'aly.** [Gr. *skaphē*, a boat, *kephalē*, a head.]

scaphoid, *skaf'oid*, *adj.* boat-shaped. [Gr. *skaphē*, a boat, *eidos*, form.]

Scaphopoda, *skaf-op'ə-dä*, *n.pl.* the tusk-shell class of molluscs, in which the foot is trilobed or has a terminal disk and the mantle forms a tube enclosed by the tubular univalve shell.—*n.* and *adj.* **scaph'opod.** [Gr. *skaphos*, a spade, *pous*, *podos*, a foot.]

scapolite, *skap'ō-līt*, *n.* a silicate of aluminium, calcium, and sodium with some chlorine, crystallising in the tetragonal system. [Gr. *skāpos*, a rod, *lithos*, a stone.]

scapple, *skap'l*, **scabble**, *skab'l*, *v.t.* to work without finishing, as stone before leaving the quarry. [O.Fr. *escapeler*, to dress timber.]

scapula, *skap'ū-lä*, *n.* the shoulder-blade.—*adj.* **scap'ular**, of the shoulder-blade or shoulder.—*n.* originally an ordinary working garb, now the mark of the monastic orders, a long strip of cloth with an opening for the head, worn hanging before and behind over the habit : two pieces of cloth tied together over the shoulders, worn by members of certain lay confraternities of the Roman Catholic Church : a supporting bandage worn over the shoulder : a shoulder feather.—*adj.* and *n.* **scap'ulary**, scapular.—*adj.* **scap'ūlated**, with noticeable scapular feathers.—*n.* **scap'ūlimancy** (Gr. *manteiā*, divination), divination by means of

shoulder-blades.—*adj.* **scapŭliman'tic.** [L. *scapulae*, the shoulder-blades.]

scapus, *skā'pəs* (L. *skā'poos*). Same as **scape** (2):— *pl.* **scapi** (*-pī*; L. *-pē*). [L.]

scar, *skär*, *n.* the mark left by a wound or sore: any mark or blemish: (*fig.*) any mark, trace, or result of injury, material or moral: a mark at a place of former attachment, as of a leaf or a muscle.—*v.t.* to mark with a scar.—*v.i.* to become scarred:— *pr.p.* **scarr'ing;** *pa.t.* and *pa.p.* **scarred.**—*adjs.* **scar'less,** without scars: unwounded; **scarred.** —*n.* and *adj.* **scarr'ing.**—*adj.* **scarr'y.** [O.Fr. *escare*—L. *eschara*—Gr. *eschara*, a hearth, brazier, burn, scar.]

scar, *skär*, **scaur,** *skawr*, *n.* a precipitous bare place on a hill-face: a cliff: a reef in the sea.—*adj.* **scarr'y.** [App. O.N. *sker*, *skera*, to cut.]

scar, *skär*, **scar'fish,** *n.* a parrot-wrasse.—*n.* **Scarus** (*skā'rəs*), the parrot-wrasse genus, giving name to the family **Scaridae** (*skar'i-dē*). [L. *scārus*—Gr. *skaros*.]

scar, scarre, *skär*, (*Shak.*, *Milt.*, *Scot.*) a form of **scare**:—*pa.t.* and *pa.p.* **scarred, scarr'd.**

scarab, *skar'əb*, *n.* a dung-beetle, esp. the sacred beetle of the ancient Egyptians (*Scarabaeus*, or *Ateuchus, sacer,* or kindred species): a gem cut in the form of a beetle: (*obs.*) a term of abuse.—*ns.* **scarabaeid** (*skar-ə-bē'id*), any beetle of the *Scarabaeidae*; **scarabae'ist,** one who studies dung-beetles; **scarabae'oid,** a gem more remotely resembling a beetle; **Scarabae'us,** the scarab genus, giving name to the **Scarabae'idae**, a large family of lamellicorn beetles, some of them of great size (chafers, dung-beetles): a scarab; **scar'abee,** a scarab; **scar'aboid,** a scarabaeoid. —*adj.* like a scarab. [L. *scarabaeus*; cf. Gr. *kārabos*.]

scaramouch, *skar'ə-mowch*, *n.* a bragging, cowardly buffoon. [Fr. *Scaramouche*—It. *Scaramuccia*, a stock character in Italian comedy.]

scarce, *skārs*, *adj.* by no means plentiful: not often found: hard to get: short in supply: short (with *of*): (*obs.*) sparing.—*adv.* **scarcely:** (*Milt.*) with difficulty: hardly ever.—*adv.* **scarce'ly,** only just: not quite: (*obs.*) scantily.—*ns.* **scarce'ness;** **scarc'ity,** state or fact of being scarce: shortness of supply, esp. of necessaries: dearth: want: deficiency: niggardliness.—**make oneself scarce,** to decamp. [O.N.Fr. *escars* (Fr. *échars*), niggardly, from a L.L. substitute for L. *excerptus*, pa.p. of *excerpĕre—ex,* out, *carpĕre,* to pick.]

scarcement, *skārs'mənt*, *n.* (*Scot.*) a ledge formed by the setting back of a wall, buttress, or bank. [Poss. from **scarce.**]

scare, *skār*, *v.t.* to startle, to affright: to drive or keep off by frightening.—*n.* a fright: a panic: a baseless public alarm. — *adj.* **frightened.** — *ns.* **scare'crow,** anything set up to scare birds: a vain cause of terror: a person meanly clad; **scare'-head, -heading, -line,** a newspaper heading designed to raise a scare; **scare'monger,** an alarmist; **scare'mongering;** **scar'er.** — *adj.* **scar'y,** frightening: timorous: fluttered.—**scare up,** (*U.S.* and *dial.*) to beat up: to hunt out: to produce quickly. [M.E. *skerre*—O.N. *skirra,* to avoid—*skiarr,* shy; vowel history obscure.]

scarf, *skärf*, *n.* a light, usually decorative piece of dress thrown loosely on the shoulders about the neck, or over the head, &c.: a military or official sash: a band worn about the neck with ends hanging in front, formerly the mark of a clergyman of some degree of dignity, esp. a nobleman's chaplain: hence, a chaplaincy: a crape streamer: a veil: a necktie: a muffler: a cravat: a sling: (*pl.* **scarfs, scarves**).—*v.t.* to cover, as if with a scarf: to wrap as a scarf.—*adj.* **scarfed,** decorated with pendants.—*ns.* **scarf'-pin,** an ornamental pin worn in a scarf: a tie-pin; **scarf'-ring,** an ornamental ring through which the ends of a scarf are drawn.—*adv.* **scarf'wise.** [Perh. O.N.Fr. *escarpe* (Fr. *écharpe*), sash, sling.]

scarf, *skärf*, *n.* a joint between pieces placed end to end, cut so as to fit with overlapping like a continuous piece: an end so prepared: a longitudinal cut in a whale's carcase.—*v.t.* to join with a scarf-

joint: to make a scarf in.—*ns.* **scarf'ing; scarf'-joint.** [Perh. Scand.]

scarfskin, *skärf'skin*, *n.* the surface skin. [Origin doubtful; perh. **scarf** (1); perh. related to **scurf.**]

scarify, *skar'i-fī*, *v.t.* to make a number of scratches or slight cuts in: to break up the surface of: to lacerate: to criticise severely:—*pr.p.* **scar'ifying;** *pa.t.* and *pa.p.* **scar'ified.**—*ns.* **scarification** (*-fi-kā'shən*); **scar'ificātor,** a surgical instrument for scarifying: a scarifier; **scar'ifier,** one who scarifies: an implement for breaking the surface of the soil or of a road. [L. *scarificāre, -ātum,* for L. *scarīfāre* — Gr. *skarīphaesthai* — *skarīphos,* an etching tool.]

scarious, *skā'ri-əs, adj.* (*bot.*) thin, dry, stiff, and membranous: (*zool.*) scaly, scurfy. [Origin unknown.]

scarlatina, *skär'lə-tē'nä, n.* scarlet-fever. [It. *scarlattina.*]

scarlet, *skär'lit, n.* orig. a fine cloth, not always red: a brilliant red: a brilliant red cloth, garment, or garb, or its wearer.—*adj.* of the colour called scarlet: dressed in scarlet.—*v.t.* to redden.—*ns.* **scar'let-bean,** the scarlet-runner; **scar'let-fē'ver,** an infectious fever, usually marked by a sore throat and a scarlet rash; **scar'let-hat,** a cardinal's hat; **scar'let-runn'er,** a scarlet-flowered climber (*Phaseolus multiflorus*) of the kidney-bean genus, with edible beans.—**scarlet geranium,** a scarlet-flowered pelargonium; **scarlet woman,** the woman referred to in Rev. xvii.—variously taken as pagan Rome, Papal Rome, or the world in its anti-Christian sense. [O.Fr. *escarlate* (Fr. *écarlate*), thought to be from Pers. *saqalāt,* scarlet cloth.]

scarmoge, *skär'məj, n.* (*Spens.*) same as **skirmish.**

scarp, *skärp, n.* (*her.*) a diminutive of the bend sinister, half its width. [O.Fr. *escarpe;* cf. **scarf** (1).]

scarp, *skärp, n.* an escarp: an escarpment.—*v.t.* to cut into a scarp.—*adj.* **scarped.**—*n.* **scarp'ing.** [It. *scarpa.*]

scarpines, *skär'pinz, n.pl.* an instrument of torture for the feet.—*n.* **scarpet'to,** a hemp-soled climbing-boot :—*pl.* **scarpet'ti** (*-tē*). [It. *scarpino scarpetto,* dims. of *scarpa,* shoe.]

scarre, *n.* (*Shak.*) a word of unknown meaning in *All's Well* (IV. ii. 38), probably a misprint, but never satisfactorily explained.

scarred, scarring, scarry. See **scar** (1 and 2).

scart, *skärt, v.t.* (*Scot.*) to scratch: to scrape.—*n.* a scratch: a dash or stroke of a pen.—*adj.* **scart'-free.** [See **scrat.**]

scart, scarth; Scarus; scarves; scary. See **skart;** **scart** (3); **scar** (3); **scarf;** **scare.**

scat, scatt, skat, *n.* (*hist.*) tribute: a tax; esp. udaller's land-tax. [O.N. *skattr;* cf. O.E. *sceatt,* money, Du. *schat,* Ger. *schatz.*]

scat, *skat, interj.* be off!—*v.t.* to scare away.

scat, *skat, n.* (*Western*) a blow: a spell: a sudden shower.—*adv.* in collapse: to bankruptcy.

scatch, *skach, n.* a stilt. [O.N.Fr. *escache* (Fr. *échasse*); cf. **skate.**]

scathe, *skādh* (*Spens.* also **scath, skath;** *Scot.* **skaith, scaith,** *skāth*), *n.* hurt: injury: damage.— *v.t.* to injure: to blast, scorch, wither: to scorch with invective.—*adj.* **scathe'ful,** hurtful.—*n.* **scathe'fulness.**—*adjs.* **scathe'less** (*Scot.* **skaith'-less, scaith'less**), without injury; **scath'ing.**— *adv.* **scath'ingly.** [O.N. *skathe;* cf. O.E. *sceatha,* an injurer; Ger. *schade,* injury.]

scatole. Same as **skatole.**

scatophagous, *skat-of'ə-gəs, adj.* dung-eating. [Gr. *skōr, skatos,* dung, *phagein* (2nd aor.), to eat.]

scatter, *skat'ər, v.t.* to disperse: to throw loosely about: to strew: to sprinkle: to dispel.—*v.i.* to disperse: to throw shot loosely.—*n.* scattering: a sprinkling.—*n.* **scatt'er-brain,** one incapable of sustained attention or thought.—*adjs.* **scatter'-brained;** **scatt'ered,** dispersed irregularly, widely, in all directions, or here and there: thrown about: (*Spens., Shak.*) casually dropped: distracted.— *adv.* **scatt'eredly** (*-ərd-li*).—*ns.* **scatt'erer;** **scatt'ergood,** a spendthrift; **scatt'er-gun,** a shot-gun; **scatt'ering,** dispersion: radiation afresh of wave-energy when a ray is incident on an obstacle or when it enters an irregularly ionised region: that which is scattered: a small proportion occurring sporadically.—*adj.* dispersing: sporadic: diversified. — *adv.* scatt′eringly. — *n.* scatt′erling, (*Spens.*) a vagrant.—*adj.* scatt′ery, dispersed: sparse: giving an effect of scattering. [Origin obscure; *scatered* occurs in the *O.E. Chronicle* (anno 1137); cf. shatter.]

scattermouch, *skat′ər-mowch, n.* (*sailors' slang*) any Latin or Levantine. [scaramouch influenced by scatter.]

scaturient, *skat-ū′ri-ənt, adj.* gushing. [L. *scatū-riēns, -entis—scatūrīre,* to gush out.]

scaud, *skawd,* a Scots form of scald.

scaup, *skawp, n.* (*Scot.*) a scalp: a scaup-duck.— *n.* scaup′-duck, a pochard that feeds on mussel-scaups. [scalp (1).]

scauper, *skaw′pər, n.* a tool with semicircular face, used by engravers. [scalper.]

scaur, *skawr,* a Scots form of scare.

scaur. Same as scar (2).

scaury, *skö′ri, n.* (*Orkney* and *Shetland*) a young gull. — Also (*Scott*) scou′rie, scow′rie. [O.N. *skári.*]

scavage, *skav′ij, n.* a toll formerly levied in boroughs on goods offered for sale by outsiders: (*obs.*) street refuse.—*n.* scav′ager, the officer who collected the toll, later charged with keeping the streets clean.— *v.t.* scav′enge (*-inj, -inzh*; back-formation), to cleanse.—*v.i.* to act as scavenger.—*n.* the sweeping out of waste gases from an internal-combustion engine.—*n.* scav′enger (*-jər*), one who cleans the streets: a person or apparatus that removes waste: an animal that feeds on garbage: one who deals or delights in filth.—*v.i.* to act as scavenger.—*ns.* scav′engering; scav′engery, street-cleaning; scav′enging, street-cleansing: scavenge. [A.Fr. *scavage,* inspection; prob. of Gmc. origin; cf. O.E. *sceáwian,* to inspect; see show.]

scavenger, *skav′in-jər, n.* a perversion of the name of *Skevington,* Lieutenant of the Tower under Henry VIII., inventor of an instrument of torture, the scavenger's, or Skevington's, daughter.

scaw. Same as skaw.

scazon, *skā′zon, n.* a choliamb. — *n.* and *adj.* scazontic (*ska-zon′tik*). [Gr. *skazōn,* limping.]

sceat, sceatt, *shāt, n.* (*hist.*) a small silver (or gold) coin of Old English times :—*pl.* sceatt′as. [O.E.]

scedule. See schedule.

scelerate, *sel′ər-āt, adj.* (*obs.*) wicked.—*n.* (also scelerat, after Fr. *scélérat*) a villain. [L. *scelerātus —scelus,* crime.]

scena, *shā′nä, n.* an operatic scene: an elaborate dramatic recitative followed by an aria :—*pl.* scene (*shā′nä*).—*ns.* scenario (*shā-nä′ri-ō*), a skeleton of a dramatic work, film, &c., scene by scene; scenary (*sē′nər-i*; *obs.*), disposition of scenes: scenery. [It.,—L. *scēna.*]

scend, 'scend. See send (*n.*).

scene, *sēn, n.* (*orig.*) the stage: (*obs.*) a stage performance: the place of action in a play (hence in a story, an actual occurrence, &c.): its representation on the stage: a painted slide, hanging, or other object, used for this purpose: a curtain, veil, or screen: a division of a play marked off by the fall of the curtain, by a change of place, or (in Latin, French, and some English plays) by the entry or exit of any important character; an episode: a dramatic or stagy incident, esp. an uncomfortable, untimely, or unseemly display of hot feelings: a landscape, picture of a place or action: a view, spectacle.—*v.t.* to set in a scene.—*ns.* scene′-dock, the space where scenery is stored; scene′-man, a scene-shifter; scene′-painter, one who paints scenery for theatres; scēn′ery, (*obs.*) dramatic action: theatrical slides, hangings, &c., collectively: prospects of beautiful, picturesque, or impressive country; scene′-shifter, one who sets and removes the scenery in a theatre.—*adjs.* scenic (*sē′nik, sen′ik*), pertaining to scenery: dramatic: theatrical; scēn′ical.—*adv.* scen′ically.—*adjs.* scēno-graph′ic, -al.— *adv.* scēnograph′ically. — *n.* scēnog′raphy, perspective drawing: scene-painting.—behind the scenes, at the back of the visible stage: outside the public view: in a posi-

tion to know what goes on: in private; scenic railway, a railway on a small scale, running through artificial representations of picturesque scenery. [L. *scēna*—Gr. *skēnē,* a tent, stage building.]

scent, earlier sent, *sent, v.t.* to track, find, or discern by smell, or as if by smell: to perfume.—*v.i.* to give forth a smell: to sniff: to smell.—*n.* odour: sense of smell: a substance used for the sake of its smell: trail by smell: paper strewn by the pursued in hare and hounds.—*ns.* scent′-bag, a scent-gland: a sachet: a bag of strong smelling stuff dragged over the ground for a drag-hunt; scent′-bottle, a small bottle for holding perfume; scent′-box.—*adjs.* scent′ed, having a smell, fragrant: impregnated or sprinkled with perfumery: endowed with a sense of smell; scent′ful, odoriferous: quick of scent.—*n.* scent′-gland, a gland that secretes a substance of distinctive smell, for recognition, attraction, or defence.—*n.* and *adj.* scent′-ing.—*adj.* scent′less, having no smell: affording, retaining, or carrying no scent.—*ns.* scent′-organ, a scent-gland: a smelling organ; scent′-scale, on male butterflies' wings, a scale that gives off a scent. [Fr. *sentir*—L. *sentīre,* to perceive.]

scepsis, skepsis, *skep′sis, n.* philosophic doubt. [Gr. ; see next.]

sceptic, sometimes (and in *U.S.*) skeptic, *skep′tik, adj.* pertaining to the philosophical school of Pyrrho and his successors, who asserted nothing positively and doubted the possibility of knowledge: (*rarely*) sceptical.—*n.* a sceptic philosopher: one who withholds belief from prevailing doctrines, esp. in religion: one who inclines to disbelieve: an inquirer who has not arrived at a conviction.— *adj.* scep′tical, of or inclined to scepticism: (now often) doubtful, or inclined towards incredulity.— *adv.* scep′tically.—*v.i.* scep′ticise, to act the sceptic.—*n.* scep′ticism, that condition in which the mind is before it has arrived at conclusive opinions: doubt: the doctrine that no facts can be certainly known: agnosticism: sceptical attitude towards Christianity: general disposition to doubt. [L. *scepticus*—Gr. *skeptikos,* thoughtful, *skeptesthai,* to consider.]

sceptre, *sep′tər, n.* a staff or baton borne as an emblem of kingship. — *adjs.* scep′tral, regal; scep′tred, bearing a sceptre: regal; scep′tre-less; scep′try (*Keats*) regal. [L. *sceptrum*— Gr. *skēptron,* a staff—*skēptein,* to prop, stay.]

scerne, *sərn, v.t.* (*Spens.*) to discern. [discern, or It. *scernere.*]

sceuophylax, *s(k)ū-of′i-laks, n.* (*Gr. Church*) a sacristan.—*n.* sceuophylacium (*-lā′si-əm*), a sacristy. [Gr. *skeuos,* a vessel, *phylax,* a watcher.]

schadenfreude, *shä′dən-froi-də, n.* pleasure in others' misfortunes. [Ger.,—*schade,* hurt, *freude,* joy.]

schalstein, *shäl′shtīn, n.* a slaty diabase tuff. [Ger. —*schale,* shell, scale, *stein,* stone.]

schappe, *shap′ə, n.* silk with gum, &c., partly removed by fermentation.—*v.t.* to subject to this process. [Ger.]

schedule, *shed′ūl* (*U.S.* sked′ūl), formerly (as *Shak.*)

scedule, *sed′ūl, n.* a slip or scroll with writing: list, inventory, or table: a supplementary, explanatory, or appended document: an appendix to a bill or act of parliament: a form for filling in particulars, or such a form filled in: (*U.S.*) time-table, plan, programme, or scheme.—*v.t.* to set as in a schedule: (*U.S.*) to plan, appoint, arrange.— *adj.* sched′uled, entered in a schedule (scheduled castes, the former untouchables): planned, appointed, arranged (to happen at a specified time). [O.Fr. *cedule* (Fr. *cédule*)—L.L. *sc(h)edula,* dim. of *scheda,* a strip of papyrus—Gr. *schedē.*]

scheelite, *shē′līt, n.* native calcium tungstate.—

Scheele's (*shā′ləz*) green, a poisonous yellowish green pigment, copper hydrogen arsenite. [From the Swedish chemist K. W. *Scheele* (1742-86), who investigated them.]

schellum. Same as skellum.

schelm, shelm (*S.Afr.* s′hhelm*), n.* a rascal. [Ger. and Du. ; cf. skellum.]

schema, *skē′mä, n.* a scheme, plan: a diagrammatic outline or synopsis: the image of the thing wi

scheme 987 scholastic

which the imagination aids the understanding in its procedure : (*Gr. Church*) the monastic habit :— *pl.* **schē′mata.**—*adjs.* **schematic** (*ski-mat′ik*), **-al.** —*adv.* **schemat′ically.**—*v.t.* **schē′matise,** to reduce to or represent by a scheme.—*ns.* **schē′matism,** form or outline of a thing : arrangement, disposition in a scheme : **schē′matist,** one who frames a scheme : (*obs.*) a projector. [Gr. *schēma, -atos,* form, from the reduced grade of the root of *echein,* to have (as in the fut. *schēsein*).]

scheme, *skēm, n.* (*obs.*) a rhetorical figure : a diagram of positions, esp. (*astrol.*) of planets : a diagram : a table : a system : a plan of purposed action for achieving an end : a plan for building operations of various kinds, or the buildings, &c., constructed, or the area covered (e.g. *housing scheme, irrigation scheme*) : a plan pursued secretly, insidiously, by intrigue, or for private ends : a project : a programme of action : (*obs.*) an escapade. —*v.t.* to plan : to reduce to a system : to lay schemes for.—*v.i.* to form a plan : to lay schemes : to indulge in an escapade.—*n.* **schē′mer.**—*n.* and *adj.* **schē′ming.** [schema.]

scherzo, *sker′tsō, n.* a lively busy movement in triple time, usually with a trio, now generally taking the place of the minuet in a sonata or a symphony. —*adj.* and *adv.* **scherzan′do,** with playfulness.— *n.* a scherzando passage or movement. [It.,—Gmc. ; cf. Ger. *scherz,* jest.]

schiavone, *skyä-vō′nā, n.* a 17th-century baskethilted broadsword used by the Doge's bodyguard of Slavs. [It. *Schiavoni,* Slavs.]

schiedam, *skē′dam,* or *-dam′, n.* Holland gin, chiefly made at Schiedam (*s′hhē-däm′*), near Rotterdam.

schiller, *shil′ər, n.* a peculiar bronze-like lustre in certain minerals, as hypersthene, due to diffraction caused by minute plates of haematite, &c., developed in separation planes.—*n.* **schillerisā′tion,** the development of such plates.—*v.t.* **schill′erise,** to impart a schiller to.—*n.* **schill′er-spar,** schillerised enstatite (bronzite). [Ger.]

schilling, *shil′ing, n.* an Austrian coin (in use after 1925) equal to one hundred groschen. [Ger. ; cf. **shilling.**]

schimmel, *shim′l, n.* a roan horse. [Ger. ; also Du.]

schindylesis, *skin-di-lē′sis, n.* an articulation formed by the fitting of one bone into a groove in another. —*adj.* **schindyletic** (*-let′ik*). [Gr. *schindylēsis,* cleaving.]

schipperke, *skip′ər-kə, -ki,* also *ship′,* or (Du.) *s′hhip′, n.* a small tailless breed of dogs, favourites of the Belgian bargees. [Du., little boatman.]

schism, *sizm, n.* a breach, esp. in the unity of a church : promotion of such a breach : a body so formed.—*ns.* **schisma** (*skiz′mä*), half the difference between twelve perfect fifths and seven octaves ; **schismatic** (*siz-mat′ik*), one who favours a schism or belongs to a schismatic body : (*R.C.*) a Catholic who avoided penalties by occasional conformity.— *adjs.* **schismat′ic, -al,** tending to, favouring, or of the nature of, a schism.—*adv.* **schismat′ically.**— *n.* **schismat′icalness.**—*v.i.* **schis′matise,** to practise schism : to make a schism.—*ns.* **schism′-house, -shop,** contemptuous Anglican terms for a nonconformist church.—**great,** or **Greek schism,** the separation of the Greek church from the Latin, finally completed in 1054 ; **Western schism,** the division in the Western church from 1378 to 1417, when there were antipopes under French influence at Avignon. [Gr. *schisma,* a split, rent, cleft, partly through O.Fr. (*s*)*cisme.*]

schist, *shist, n.* any crystalline foliated metamorphic rock not coarse and felspathic enough to be called gneiss, as mica-schist, hornblende-schist : sometimes extended (as in French) to shaly rocks.— *adj.* **schist′ose.**—*n.* **schistosity** (*-os′i-ti*).—*adj.* **schist′ous.** [Fr. *schiste*—Gr. *schistos,* split ; pron. due to German influence.]

schiz-, *skiz-,* **schizo-,** *skiz′ō-,* **skī-zo′-,** or *skiz-,* in composition, cleave, cloven. [Gr. *schizein,* to cleave.]

Schizaea, *skī-zē′ä, n.* a tropical genus of ferns, giving name to the fam. **Schizaeā′ceae,** with

sporangia splitting longitudinally by an apical annulus.—*adj.* **schizaeā′ceous.** [Gr. *schizein,* to split.]

Schizanthus, *skī-zan′thəs, n.* a showy Chilean genus of Solanaceae. [Gr. *anthos,* flower.]

schizocarp, *skī′zō-kärp, n.* a dry fruit that splits into several indehiscent one-seeded portions.—*adj.* **schizocar′pous.** [Gr. *karpos,* fruit.]

schizogenesis, *skī-zō-jen′i-sis, n.* reproduction by fission.—*adjs.* **schizogen′ic, schizogenetic** (*-ji-net′ik*), **schizogenous** (*-zoj′i-nəs*), reproducing, reproduced, or formed by fission or splitting ; **schizogonous** (*-zog′ən-əs*).— *n.* **schizog′ony,** schizogenesis, esp. in Protozoa. [Gr. *genesis, gonē,* generation.]

schizognathous, *skī-zog′nə-thəs, adj.* of some birds, having the bones of the palate separate. [Gr. *gnathos,* jaw.]

schizoid, *skī′zoid, adj.* showing qualities of a schizophrenic personality, such as asocial behaviour, introversion, tendency to phantasy, but without definite mental disorder.—*n.* a schizoid person. [Gr. *eidos,* form.]

Schizomycetes, *skī-zō-mī-sē′tēz, n.pl.* the bacteria : —*sing.* **schizomycete** (*-sēt′*). [Gr. *mykēs* (pl. *mykētēs*), a fungus.]

schizophrenia, *skī-zō-frē′ni-ä, n.* dementia praecox or kindred form of insanity, marked by introversion and loss of connexion between thoughts, feelings, and actions.—*adj.* **schizophrenic** (*-fren′ik*). [Gr. *phrēn,* mind.]

Schizophyta, *skī-zof′i-tä, n.pl.* plants that multiply only by fission—bacteria and blue-green algae. [Gr. *phyton,* plant.]

schizopod, *skī′zō-pod, adj.* having each leg divided into exopodite and endopodite.—*n.* a member of the **Schizopoda** (*-zop′-*), an order (according to some) of Malacostraca. — *adjs.* **schizop′odal, schizop′odous.** [Gr. *pous, podos,* foot.]

schizothymia, *skī-zō-thī′mi-ä, n.* manifestation of schizoid traits within normal limits.—*adj.* **schizothy′mic.** [Gr. *thymos,* mind, temper.]

schläger, *shlā′gər, n.* a German student's duelling-sword. [Ger.,—*schlagen,* to beat.]

schlich, *shlihh, n.* the finer portions of crushed ore, separated by water. [Ger.]

schlieren, *shlē′rən, n.pl.* streaks of different colour, structure, or composition in igneous rocks. [Ger.]

schmelz, *shmelts, n.* glass used in decorative work. [Ger. *schmelz,* enamel.]

schnapper, *shnap′ər.* Same as **snapper** (Australian fish). [Germanised.]

schnapps, schnaps, *shnäps, n.* Holland gin, Hollands. [Ger. *schnapps,* a dram.]

schnauzer, *shnowt′sər, n.* a German breed of terrier. [Ger.]

Schneiderian, *shnī-dē′ri-ən, adj.* pertaining to the German anatomist Konrad Victor *Schneider* (1614-1680).—**Schneiderian membrane,** the olfactory mucous membrane, studied by him.

schnitzel, *shnit′sl, n.* a veal cutlet. [Ger.]

scholar, *skol′ər, n.* a pupil : a disciple : a student : an educated person : one whose learning (esp. in Latin and Greek) is extensive and exact : a holder of a scholarship.—*adj.* **schol′ar-like,** like or befitting a scholar.—*n.* **schol′arliness.**—*adj.* **schol′arly,** of, natural to a scholar : having the learning of a scholar.—*adv.* (*Shak.*) as becomes a scholar.— *n.* **schol′arship,** scholarly learning : a foundation or grant for the maintenance of a pupil or student : the status and emoluments of such a pupil or student. [O.E. *scólere,* and (in part) O.Fr. *escoler,* both from L.L. *scholāris*—*schola* ; see **school** (1).]

scholarch, *skō′lärk, n.* the head of a school, esp. of philosophy. [Gr. *scholarchēs.*]

scholastic, *skol-, skol-as′tik, adj.* pertaining to schools or schoolmen : subtle : pedantic.—*n.* a schoolman : one who adheres to the method or subtleties of the schools of the Middle Ages : a Jesuit who has taken his first vows only.—*adj.* (*arch.*) **scholas′tical.**—*adv.* **scholas′tically.**—*n.* **scholas′ticism** (*-sizm*), the aims, methods, and products of thought which constituted the main endeavour of the intellectual life of the Middle Ages : the method or subtleties of the schools of philosophy: the collected body of doctrines of the schoolmen. [Gr. *scholastikos—scholē*; see **school** (1).]

scholion, *skŏ′li-on*, **scholium**, *-əm*, *n.* an explanatory note, such as certain ancient grammarians wrote on passages in manuscripts: an observation or note added to a mathematical proposition: often in *pl.* (Gr. and L.) **scho′lia.—** *n.* **scho′liast**, a writer of scholia: an annotator: a commentator.—*adj.* **scholias′tic**. [Gr. *scholion*, *scholiastēs—scholē*; see **school** (1).]

school, *skōol*, *n.* a place for instruction: an institution for education, esp. primary or secondary, or for teaching of special subjects: a division of such an institution: a building or room used for that purpose: the work of a school: the time given to it: the body of pupils of a school: the disciples of a particular teacher: those who hold a common doctrine or follow a common tradition: a method of instruction: an instruction book (now usu. in music): the body of instructors and students in a university, college, faculty, or department: a group of studies in which honours may be taken: (in *pl.*) academic institutions: (in *pl.*) an academic disputation: (in Oxford, in *pl.*) the B.A. examinations: a university building, now (Oxford) the examination hall.—*adj.* of school, schools, or the schools.—*v.t.* to educate in a school: to train: to instruct: to coach in a part to be played: to teach overbearingly: (*obs.*) to admonish: to discipline.—*ns.* **school′-bag**, a bag for carrying school-books; **school′-bell**, a bell to announce time for school; **school′-board**, formerly, an elected board of school managers for a parish, town, or district; **school′-book**, a book used in school; **school′boy**, a boy attending school.—Also *adj.*—*adjs.* **school′boy′ish**; **school′-bred′.**—*ns.* **school′-child**; **school′craft**, learning; **school′-dame**, mistress of a dame's school; **school′-day**, a day on which schools are open: (in *pl.*) time of being a school pupil; **school′-divine′**; **school′-divin′ity**, scholastic or seminary theology; **school′-doc′tor**, a schoolman: (*obs.*) a school-teacher: a physician appointed to examine or attend the pupils of a school or schools. —*adj.* **schooled**, trained: experienced. — *ns.* **school′ery**, (*Spens.*) something taught, precepts; **school′fellow**, one taught at the same school at the same time; **school′-friend**, one who is or has been a friend at school; **school′-friend′ship**; **school′girl**, a girl attending school.—*adj.* **school′-girlish**.—*n.* and *adj.* **school′-going**.—*ns.* **school′-house**, a building used as a school: a house provided for a school-teacher (**school house**, a headmaster's or headmistress's boarding-house: its boarders); **school′ing**, instruction or maintenance at school: tuition: training: discipline: school fees: reproof: reprimand; **school′-inspec′tor**, an official appointed to examine schools; **school′-ma′am**, (*U.S.*) a schoolmistress: (*coll.*) a prim pedantic woman; **school′-maid**, a schoolgirl; **school′man**, a philosopher or theologian of mediaeval scholasticism: (*U.S.*) a teacher; **school′master**, the master or one of the masters of a school: (*Shak.*) a tutor.—Also *v.t.* and *v.i.*—*n.* and *adj.* **school′mastering.**—*adjs.* **school′-masterish**; **school′masterly.** — *ns.* **school′-mastership**; **school′-mate**, school-friend: a schoolfellow; **school′-miss**, a raw or affected schoolgirl; **school′mistress**; **school′-point**, a point for scholastic disputation; **school′-room**, a school classroom: in a house, a room for receiving or preparing lessons in; **school′-ship**, a training-ship.—*adj.* **school′-taught**, taught at school or in the schools.—*ns.* **school′-teach′er**, one who teaches in a school; **school′-teach′ing**; **school′-term**, a word or term in use in the schools or among schoolmen: a division of the school year; **school′-tide**, school-days; **school′-time**, the time at which a school opens, or during which it remains open: school-days.—*adj.* **school′-trained**, trained at school.—*adj.* and *adv.* **school′ward.**—*adv.* **school′wards.**—*n.* **school′-work.**—**approved school**, a school, under the supervision of the Home Secretary, for juvenile delinquents or child-

ren in need of care; **the schoolmaster is abroad,** a phrase of Brougham's implying that education and intelligence are now widely spread. [O.E. *scól* —L. *schóla*—Gr. *scholē*, leisure, a school.]

school, *skōol*, *n.* a shoal of fish, whales, or other swimming animals: a flock, troop, assemblage, esp. of birds.—*v.i.* to gather or go in schools.—*adj.* (or in composition) going in schools.—*n.* and *adj.* **school′ing.**—*n.* **school′master**, the leader of a school, esp. of whales. [Du. *school*; cf. **shoal** (1).]

schoole (Shak., *Macb.* I. vii. 6). Same as **shoal** (2).

schooner, *skoon′ər*, *n.* a sharp-built, swift-sailing vessel, generally two-masted, fore-and-aft rigged, or with top and topgallant sails on the foremast: a covered emigrant-wagon (**prairie schooner**): a large beer-glass.—*adj.* **schoon′er-rigged.** [Early 18th-century (Massachusetts) *skooner*, *scooner*, said to be from a prov. Eng. word *scoon*, to skim.]

schorl, *shorl*, *n.* black tourmaline.—*adj.* **schorlā′-ceous.**—*n.* **schorl′-rock′**, a rock compound of schorl and quartz. [Ger. *schörl*.]

schottische, *sho-tēsh′*, *shot′ish*, *n.* a dance, or dance-tune like the polka. [Ger. (*der*) *schottische* (*tanz*), (the) Scottish (dance); pronunciation sham French.]

schout, *skout*, *n.* a municipal officer. [Du.]

schrecklich, *shrek′lihh*, *adj.* frightful.—*n.* **schrecklichkeit** (*-kīt*), frightfulness. [Ger.]

schuit, *skoit*, *n.* a Dutch flat-bottomed river-boat. [Du.]

schwa, *shvä*, *n.* an indistinct vowel sound shown in Hebrew by two dots (:)—transliterated *ĕ*, &c.: in phonetics, an unaccented neutral vowel (ə). [Ger., —Heb. *schĕwa*.]

schwärmerei, *shver′mər-ī*, *n.* sentimental enthusiasm, as of a schoolgirl. [Ger., swarming.]

Schwenkfelder, *shvengk′fel-dər*, *n.* a member of a religious sect, founded by Kaspar von *Schwenckfeld* (1490-1561).—Also **Schwenkfeld′ian.**

sci-, *sī-*, *skī-*. For various words see under **ski-**.

Sciaena, *sī-ē′nä*, *n.* the maigre genus of fishes, giving name to the fam. Sciae′nidae. — *adj.* **sciae′noid.** [Gr. *skiaina*, a kind of fish.]

sciatic, *sī-at′ik*, *adj.* of, or in the region of, the **hip.**— Also **sciat′ical.**—*n.* **sciat′ica**, neuritis of the great sciatic nerve which passes down the back of the thigh. [L.L. *sciaticus*, fem. *-a*—Gr. *ischion*, hip-joint.]

science, *sī′əns*, *n.* knowledge: knowledge ascertained by observation and experiment, critically tested, systematised and brought under general principles: a department or branch of such knowledge or study: (*obs.*) a skilled craft: (now usu. *jocular*) trained skill, esp. in boxing. — *adjs.* **sci′enced**, versed, learned; **sci′ent**, having science; **sciential** (*-en′shl*), of, having, or producing, science: scientific; **scientif′ic** (L. *facĕre*, to make), orig. (of a syllogism) demonstrative, producing knowledge: hence of, relating to, based on, devoted to, according to, used in, or versed in, science.—Also (*rare*) **scientif′ical.**—*adv.* **scientif′-ically.**—*ns.* **sci′entism**, the habit or manner of men of science; **sci′entist**, a man of science, esp. natural science.—*adj.* **scientis′tic.**—**the** (**noble**) **science**, the art of boxing. [L. *scientia—sciēns*, *-entis*, pr.p. of *scire*, to know.]

scilicet, *sī′li-set* (L. *skē′li-ket*), *adv.* to wit, namely. [L. *scilicet—scire licet*, it is permitted to know.]

Scilla, *sil′ä*, *n.* the squill genus of the lily family, including some bright blue spring flowers. [L.,— Gr. *skilla*, the officinal squill.]

scimitar, *sim′i-tər*, *n.* a short, single-edged, curved sword, broadest at the point end, used by the Turks and Persians. [Poss. through Fr. *cimeterre* or It. *scimitarra*—Pers. *shamshīr*; but doubtful.]

scincoid, *singk′oid*, *adj.* like a skink. [Gr. *skinkos*, a skink, *eidos*, form.]

scintilla, *sin-til′ä*, *n.* a spark.—*adj.* **scin′tillant**, sparkling.—*v.i.* **scin′tillate**, to sparkle, twinkle.— *v.t.* to emit in sparks: to sparkle with.—*n.* **scintillā′tion.** [L., a spark.]

scio-. For various words see **skio-**.

sciolism, *sī′ə-lizm*, *n.* superficial pretensions to knowledge.—*n.* **sci′olist**, a pretender to science.— *adjs.* **sciolis′tic**; **sci′olous.** [L. *sciolus*, dim. of *scius*, knowing—*scire*, to know.]

sciolto, *shol'tō*, *adj.* and *adv.* (*mus.*) free. [It.]
scion, *sī'ən*, *n.* a detached piece of a plant capable of propagating, esp. by grafting : a young member of a family : a descendant, offshoot. [O.Fr. *sion*, *cion* ; origin obscure.]
scire facias, *sī'ri fā'shi-as*, *n.* a writ requiring a person to appear and show cause why a record should not be enforced or annulled. [L. *scire facias*, make him to know.]
scirocco. See sirocco.
Scirpus, *sir'pəs*, *n.* the club-rush genus of the sedge family. [L., a rush.]
scirrhus, *skir'əs*, *sir'əs*, *n.* (*med.*) a hard swelling : a hard cancer.—*adj.* **scirr'hous**. [Latinised from Gr. *skirros*, *skīros*, a tumour.]
scissel, *sis'l*, *n.* metal clippings : scrap left when blanks have been cut out.—Also **sciss'il**. [O.Fr. *cisaille*—*ciseler*—*cisel*, a chisel ; for the spelling cf. scissors.]
scissile, *sis'īl*, *adj.* capable of being cut : readily splitting.—*ns.* **scission** (*sish'ən*, *sizh'ən*), cutting : division : splitting : schism ; **scissiparity** (*sis-i-par'i-ti* ; L. *parĕre*, to bring forth), reproduction by fission ; **scissure** (*sish'ər*), a cleft : a fissure : a rupture : a division : cutting. [L. *scissilis*, *scissiō*, *-ōnis*, *scissūra*—*scindĕre*, *scissum*, to cut, cleave.]
scissors, *siz'ərz*, *n.pl.* (rarely treated as *sing.*) a cutting instrument with two blades pivoted to close together and overlap—usu. smaller than shears : a position or movement like that of scissors.—*v.t.* **sciss'or**, to cut with scissors.—*ns.* **sciss'or-bill**, a skimmer ; **sciss'or-blade** ; **sciss'or-case** ; **sciss'or-cut** ; **sciss'orer**, a scissors-and-paste compiler ; **sciss'or-leg**, the deformity of crossed legs ; **sciss'ors-and-paste'**, literary or journalistic matter collected from various sources with little or no original writing.—Also *adj.* —*ns.* **sciss'or-tail**, an American fly-catcher ; **sciss'or-tooth**, a carnassial tooth.—*adv.* **sciss'or-wise**. [O.Fr. *cisoires*—L.L. *cīsōrium*, a cutting instrument—*caedĕre*, *caesum*, to cut ; the spelling *sc-* is due to erroneous association with *scindĕre*, *scissum* ; cf. foregoing.]
Scitamineae, *sit-ə-min'i-ē*, *n.pl.* an order or cohort of monocotyledons including the banana, ginger, Indian shot, and arrowroot families.—*adj.* **scitamin'eous**. [App.—L. *scītāmenta*, delicacies.]
Sciurus, *sī-ū'rəs*, *n.* the squirrel genus, giving name to the fam. **Sciu'ridae**.—*adjs.* **sciurine** (*sī-ūr'īn*, or *sī'*) ; **sciuroid** (*-ū'*).—*n.* **sciurop'terus** (Gr. *pteron*, wing), a genus of flying squirrels. [L. *sciūrus*—Gr. *skiouros*—*skiā*, shadow, *ourā*, tail.]
sclaff, *sklăf*, *n.* (*Scot.*) a light slap or its sound : (*golf*) a stroke in which the sole of the club scrapes the ground before striking the ball.—*v.t.* and *v.i.* to strike or play with a sclaff. [Imit.]
sclate, *sklāt*, a Scots form of slate.—*n.* **sclate'-stane'**, a piece of slate (such as money got from the Devil turned into).
sclaunder, **sclave**, **Sclave**, **Sclavonian**, &c., **sklawn'der**, &c., obsolete forms of slander, slave, Slav, Slavonian, &c.
sclera, *sklēr'ä*, *n.* the sclerotic.—*adj.* **scle'ral**.—*ns.* **sclere** (*sklēr*) a skeletal element : a sponge spicule ; **sclereid**, **-eide** (*sklēr'i-id* ; *bot.*), a thick-walled cell ; **sclerema** (*sklər-ē'mä*), hardening of (esp. subcutaneous) tissues ; **sclerenchyma** (*sklər-eng'ki-mä* ; Gr. *enchyma*, in-filling), plant tissue with thick, lignified cell-walls : hard skeletal tissue, as in corals.—*adj.* **sclerenchymatous** (*skler-eng-kim'ə-təs*).—*ns.* **scleri'asis**, hardening of tissue : a hard tumour : an induration ; **sclē'rite**, a hard skeletal plate or spicule ; **scleritis** (*sklər-ī'tis*), **sclerotitis**.—*adj.* **sclerocaulous** (*sklēr-ō-kaw'ləs*).—*ns.* **sclē'rocauly** (Gr. *kaulos*, stem), possession of a hard, dry stem ; **scleroderm** (*skler'*, *sklēr'*), a hard integument.—*adj.* **scleroder'matous**.—*n.* **scleroder'm(i)a**, hardness and rigidity of skin by substitution of fibrous tissue for subcutaneous fat. —*adjs.* **scleroder'mic**, **scleroder'mous**, hard-skinned : pertaining to a scleroderm or to sclerodermia.—*ns.* **scleroder'mite**, the integument of a segment in arthropods ; **scleroma** (*sklər-ō'mä*), hardening : morbid hardening : formation of nodules in the nose, &c. ; **sclerom'eter**, an instru-

ment for measuring the hardness of minerals ; **sclerophyll** (*skler'ō-fil*), a hard, stiff leaf.—*adj.* **sclerophyll'ous**.—*n.* **scler'ophylly**, possession of sclerophylls.—*v.t.* **sclerose** (*sklər-ōs'*), to harden : to affect with sclerosis.—*v.i.* to become sclerosed.— *n.* **sclerosis** (*sklər-ō'sis*), hardening : (*med.*) morbid hardening, as of arteries : (*bot.*) hardening of tissue by thickening or lignification.—*adj.* **sclerō'tal**, sclerotic.—*n.* a bony plate in the sclerotic of some animals.—*adj.* **sclerot'ic**, hard, firm, applied esp. to the outer membrane of the eye-ball : of sclerosis : sclerosed.—*n.* the outermost membrane of the eye-ball.—*ns.* **sclerotī'tis** (*skler-*, *sklēr-*), inflammation of the sclerotic ; **sclerotium** (*sklər-ō'shi-əm*), a hard, tuber-like body, the resting stage of many fungi :—*pl.* **sclero'tia**.—*adj.* **sclē'rous**, hard or indurated : ossified or bony. [Gr. *sklēros*, hard.]
sclim, **sklim**, **sklim**, a Scots form of climb.
scoff, *skof*, *n.* mockery : a jibe, jeer : an object of derision.—*v.i.* to jeer (with *at*).—*v.t.* (*Shak.*) to jeer at.—*n.* **scoff'er**.—*n.* and *adj.* **scoff'ing**.—*adv.* **scoff'ingly**. [Cf. obs. Dan. *skof*, jest, mockery, O.Fris. *schof*.]
scoff, **skoff**, *skof*, *v.t.* (*dial.* and *slang*) to devour : to plunder.—*v.i.* to feed.—*n.* food : a meal. [App. scaff, reinforced from S. Africa by Du. *schoft*, a meal.]
scog. See skug.
Scoggin, **Scogan**, *skog'ən*, *n.* a supposed fool of Edward IV., on whom the contents of a 16th-century jest-book were fathered : hence a buffoon.
scoinson, *skoin'sən*. Same as scuncheon.
scold, *skōld*, *n.* a rude clamorous woman or other : a scolding.—*v.i.* to brawl : to vituperate : to find fault vehemently or at some length.—*v.t.* to chide : to rebuke.—*n.* **scold'er**.—*n.* and *adj.* **scold'ing**. [App. O.N. *skáld*, poet (through an intermediate sense, lampooner).]
scolex, *skō'leks*, *n.* a tapeworm head :—*pl.* **scoleces** (*skō-lē'sēz* ; erroneously **scō'lices**).—*adjs.* **scō'lecid** (*-lə-sid*), **scōleciform** (*-les'i-form*), like a scolex.—*n.pl.* **Scōleciform'ia**, the lugworm order. —*n.* **scō'lecite** (*-sīt*), a lime zeolite that curls before the blowpipe. —*adj.* **scōlecoid** (*-lē'koid*), like a scolex. [Gr. *skolēx*, *-ēkos*, a worm.]
scoliosis, *skol-i-ō'sis*, *n.* lateral spinal curvature.— *adj.* **scoliotic** (*-ot'ik*). [Gr. *skoliōsis*, obliquity.]
scollop. Same as scallop.
Scolopax, *skol'ə-paks*, *n.* the woodcock genus, giving name to the fam. **Scolopacidae** (*-pas'i-dē*). —*adj.* **scolopaceous** (*-pā'shəs*). [Gr. *scolopax*, *-ākos*, a woodcock.]
Scolopendra, *skol-ə-pen'drä*, *n.* a genus of centipedes, some a foot long : **scolopendra**, (*Spens.*) a fabulous fish that voided the hook.—*adjs.* **scolopen'driform**, **scolopen'drine**.—*n.* **Scolopen'drium**, the hart's-tongue fern genus (from the appearance of the sori). [Gr. *skolopendra*, skolopendrion.]
Scolytus, *skol'i-təs*, *n.* typical genus of Scolytidae (*-it'i-dē*), a family of bark-beetles.—*adj.* **scol'ytoid**. [Gr. *skolyptein*, to strip.]
Scomber, *skom'bər*, *n.* the mackerel genus, giving name to the fam. **Scom'bridae** (*-bri-dē*).—*n.* **Scom'bresox** (L. *esox*, pike), the skipper genus, giving name to the **Scombresocidae** (*-sos'i-dē*).— *adj.* **scom'broid**, of or like the mackerel family. [L. *scomber*—Gr. *skombros*, a mackerel.]
scomfish, *skum'fish*, *v.t.* (*Scot.*) to stifle : to disgust. [From *discomfish*, a by-form of discomfit, from the stem appearing in the Fr. pr.p.]
sconce, *skons*, *n.* a small fort or earthwork : a shelter : a chimney-seat : a slab of floating ice.— *v.t.* to entrench : to screen.—**build a sconce**, to run up a score and have to keep away. [Du. *schans*.]
sconce, *skons*, *n.* the head : the crown of the head : brains, wits. [Origin obscure.]
sconce, *skons*, *n.* (*Oxford*) a fine (paid in ale or otherwise) : a two-handled mug used for the purpose (holding about a quart) : a forfeit.—*v.t.* to fine. [Origin obscure.]
sconce, *skons*, *n.* a candlestick or lantern with a handle : a bracket candlestick : a street wall-lamp.

[O.Fr. *esconse*—L.L. *absconsa*, a dark lantern—*abscondĕre*, to hide.]

sconcheon, scontion. Same as **scuncheon.**

scone, *skon*, by Southrons often pronounced *skōn, n.* (*Scot.*) a flattish, usually round or quadrant-shaped plain cake of dough without much butter, with or without currants, baked on a girdle or in an oven. [Perh. from Du. *schoon* (*brot*), fine (bread).]

scoog. See skug.

scoop, *skōōp, n.* a bailing-vessel: a concave shovel or lipped vessel for skimming or shovelling up loose material: an instrument for gouging out apple-cores, samples of cheese, &c.: anything of like shape: an act of scooping: a sweeping stroke: a scooped-out place: anything got by or as by scooping, a haul: the forestalling of other news-papers in obtaining a piece of news: an item of news so secured.—*v.t.* to bail out: to lift, obtain, remove, hollow, or make with, or as if with, a scoop: to secure in advance of or to the exclusion of others.—*adjs.* **scooped; scooped'-out.**—*ns.* **scoop'er,** one who scoops: an engraver's tool: the avocet; **scoop'ful:**—*pl.* **scoop'fuls; scoop'-ing; scoop'-net,** a long-handled dipping net: a net for scooping along the bottom. [Prob. partly M.L.G. or M.Du. *schôpe,* bailing-vessel, partly M.Du. *schoppe,* shovel.]

scoot, *skōōt, v.t.* and *v.i.* (*Scot.*) to squirt.—*v.i.* (*Scot.*) to slip suddenly: (*coll.*) to make off with celerity.—*n.* (*Scot.*) a squirt: an act of scooting.—*n.* **scoot'er,** one who scoots: a child's toy, a wheeled footboard with steering handle, propelled by kicking the ground: a development thereof driven by a motor (also *motor-scooter, auto-scooter*): a boat for sailing on ice and water: a swift motor-boat: (*U.S.*) a simple form of plough. [Prob. from O.N., akin to shoot.]

scoot, *skoot, n.* (*Scot.*) an insignificant person.

scopa, *skō'pä, n.* a bee's pollen-brush:—*pl.* **sco'pae** (*-pē*).—*adj.* **scō'pate,** tufted.—*n.* **scopula** (*skop'ū-lä*), a little tuft of hairs. [L. *scōpae,* twigs, a broom.]

scope, *skōp, n.* point aimed at: aim: range: field or opportunity of activity: room for action: spaciousness: length of cable at which a vessel rides at liberty. [It. *scopo*—Gr. *skopos,* aim—*skopeein,* to view.]

scope, *skōp, n.* short for **microscope, telescope, horoscope,** &c.

Scopelus, *skop'ə-ləs, n.* a genus of deep-water fishes with luminous spots, giving name to the fam. **Scopelidae** (*-el'i-dē*). [Gr. *skopelos,* a rock, thought by Cuvier to mean a kind of fish.]

scopolamine, *sko-pol'ə-mēn, n.* an alkaloid used as an anaesthetic, got from the genus Scopolia and other plants of the Solanaceae. [Named after *Scopoli* (1723-88), Italian naturalist; **amine.**]

Scops, *skops, n.* a genus of owls. [Gr. *skōps.*]

scorbutic, -al, *skor-bū'tik, adjs.* of, like, of the nature of, or affected with, scurvy. [L.L. *scor-būticus,* poss. from M.L.G. *schorbuk.*]

scorch, *skorch, v.t.* to burn slightly or superficially: to parch: to dry up, wither, or affect painfully or injuriously by heat or as if by heat: to wither with scorn, censure, &c.—*v.i.* to be burned on the surface: to be dried up: to cycle or drive furiously.—*n.* an act of scorching: an injury by scorching.—*adj.* **scorched.**—*n.* **scorch'er,** one who, that which, scorches: a day of scorching heat: anything stinging.—*n., adj.,* and *adv.* **scorch'ing.**—*adv.* **scorch'ingly.** — *n.* **scorch'ingness.** — **scorched earth,** country devastated before evacuation so as to be useless to an advancing enemy. [Perh. M.E. *skorken;* cf. O.N. *skorpna,* to shrivel; poss. affected by O.Fr. *escorcher,* to flay.]

scorch, *skorch, v.t.* (*Shak.; Scott*) to slash (in *Macbeth* Theobald conjecturally read *scotch'd* for *scorch'd*). [Perh. **score,** influenced by **scratch.**]

scordato, *skor-dä'tō, adj.* (*mus.*) put out of tune.—*n.* **scordatura** (*-too'rä*), a temporary departure from normal tuning. [It.]

score, *skōr, n.* a notch, gash, or scratch: an incised line: a boldly drawn line, as one marking a dele-tion: a line marking a boundary, starting-place, or defined position: an arrangement of music on a number of staves (perh. orig. with the bar divisions running continuously through-all): a composition so distributed: a notch in a tally: an account of charges incurred (as in a tavern) by tallies or (later) chalk marks or the like: a debt incurred: a reckoning, account, ground: (*Spens.*) total num-ber, tale: the total or record of points made in a game: an addition made thereto: a set of twenty (sometimes verging upon numeral *adj.*): twenty or twenty-one pounds: (*Shak.*) twenty paces: a fixed number (20 to 26) of tubs of coal.—*v.t.* to mark with or by scores: to record in or with a score: to make a score through as a mark of deletion (with *out*): to write in score: to distribute among the instruments of the orchestra: to make as a score: to add to a score: to achieve: to enumerate: to record: (*U.S.*) to rebuke.—*v.i.* (*obs.*) to keep or run up a score: to make a point: to achieve a success.—*ns.* **scor'er,** one who, or that which, scores: one who keeps the marks in a game; **scor'ing; score'-board, scor'ing-board,** a board on which the score is exhibited, as at cricket; **scor'ing-card,** a card for recording the score in a game.—**go off at score,** to make a spirited start; **pay off old scores,** to repay old grudges; **run up a score,** to run up a debt; **score off,** achieve a success against, get the better of. [Late O.E. *scoru.*—O.N. *skor. skora;* cf. O.E. *sceran* (pa.p. *scoren*), to shear.]

scoria, *skō'ri-ä, n.* dross or slag from metal-smelting: a piece of lava with steam-holes:—*pl.* **scō'riae** (*-ē*).—*adjs.* **scō'riac, scōriaceous** (*-ri-ā'shəs*).—*n.* **scōrifica'tion,** reduction to scoria: assaying by fusing with lead and borax; **scō'rifier,** a dish used in assaying.—*v.t.* **scō'rify,** to reduce to scoria.—*adj.* **scō'rious.** [L.,—Gr. *skōriä*—*skōr,* dung.]

scorn, *skorn, n.* hot or extreme contempt, usu. less self-conscious than disdain: an expression of contempt: the object of contempt.—*v.t.* to feel or express scorn for: to refuse with scorn: (*obs.*) to make a mock of.—*v.i.* (*obs.*) to scoff.—*n.* **scorn'er.**—*adj.* **scorn'ful.**—*adv.* **scorn'fully.**—*ns.* **scorn'-fulness; scorn'ing.**—**think scorn,** to disdain or think beneath one. [O.Fr. *escarn,* mockery; of Gmc. origin; cf. O.H.G. *skern,* mockery.]

scorodite, *skor'ō-dīt, n.* hydrous ferric arsenate. [Gr. *skorodon,* garlic, from the smell under the blowpipe.]

Scorpaena, *skor-pē'nä, n.* a genus of large-headed, spiny fishes giving name to the fam. **Scorpae'-nidae,** the scorpion-fishes or sea-scorpions. [Gr. *skorpaina,* a kind of fish.]

scorper, *skor'pər, n.* a gouging chisel. [For scauper.]

scorpioid, *skor'pi-oid, adj.* like a scorpion, or a scor-pion's curled tail.—**scorpioid cyme,** a uniparous cymose inflorescence in which the plane of each daughter axis is at right angles, to right and left alternately, with its parent axis, that of the whole coiled in bud—a cincinnus or cicinnus. [Gr. *skorpios,* scorpion, *eidos,* form.]

scorpion, *skor'pi-ən, n.* any member of the **Scor-pionid'ea,** or **Scorpionida** (*-on'i-dä*), an order of Arachnida with head and thorax united, pincers, four pairs of legs, and a segmented abdomen in-cluding a tail with a sting: (*B.*) a form of scourge: an old engine for hurling missiles: any person of virulent hatred or animosity: (*mil. slang*) a rock-scorpion (see **rock**): Scorpion, (*astron.*) the constellation or the sign Scorpio.—*ns.* **Scor'pio** (*-ō*), a genus of scorpions: a constellation and a sign of the zodiac; **scor'pion-fish,** any of the Scor-paenidae; **scor'pion-fly,** an insect of the Mecop-tera (from the male's upturned abdomen); **scor'-pion-grass,** forget-me-not. — *adj.* **scorpionic** (*-on'ik*).— *n.* **scor'pion-spider,** a whip-scorpion, [L. *scorpiō, -ōnis*—Gr. *skorpios.*]

scorse, *skors, v.t.* (*Spens.*) to chase. [It. *scorsa,* a run—*scorrere*—L. *excurrĕre.*]

scorse, *skors, n.* (*Spens.*) exchange.—*v.t.* (*Spens.*) and *v.i.* to exchange.—*n.* (*obs.*) one who barters. [Poss. from *horse-scorser* for **horse-courser.**]

scorzonera, *skor-zō-nē'rä, n.* a plant like dandelion, with edible root—*black salsify.* [It.]

scot, *skot, n.* a payment, esp. a customary tax: a

fāte, fär, ásk; mē, hər (her); *mīne; mōte; mūte; mōōn; dhen* (then)

share of a reckoning (also **shot**).—*adj.* **scot'-free'**, free from scot: untaxed: entirely free from expense, injury, &c.—**scot and lot**, an old legal phrase embracing all parochial assessments for the poor, the church, lighting, cleansing, and watching. [O.E. *scot, sceot*; but prob. partly from O.N. *skot*, and O.Fr. *escot*; see **shot**, **escot**.]

Scot, *skot, n.* (*hist.*) one of a Gaelic-speaking people of Ireland, afterwards also in Argyllshire: (now) a Scotsman or Scotswoman of any race or language.—*n.* **Scott'y**, a nickname for a Scotsman: (*coll.*) a Scotch terrier.—**Irish Scot**, (*obs.*) a Highlander. [O.E. *Scottas* (pl.)—L.L. *Scottus*.]

Scotch, *skoch, adj.* a form of **Scottish** or **Scots**, in common use even among Scottish dialect speakers, though disliked or resented by many Scotsmen: applied esp. to products or supposed products of Scotland: having the character popularly attributed to a Scotsman—an excessive leaning towards defence of oneself and one's property.—*n.* Scotch whisky, or a glass of it: the Scottish (Northern English) dialect: (as *pl.*) the Scots.—*adj.* and *n.pl.* (*U.S.*) **Scotch-Irish**, Irish of Scottish descent.—*ns.* **Scotch'man**, a Scotsman: (*S.Afr.*) a florin (from a tradition of a Scotsman who benefited from its resemblance to a half-crown); **Scotch'woman**; **Scotch'ness**; **Scotch'y**, a nickname for a Scotsman.—*adj.* having Scottish characteristics.—**Scotch and English**, prisoner's base; **Scotch attorney**, (*W. Indies*) a climber (Clusia) that strangles trees; **Scotch barley**, pot or hulled barley; **Scotch bluebell**, the harebell; **Scotch bonnet**, a round flat blue woollen cap with a tuft on the top: the fairy-ring mushroom; **Scotch broth**, broth made with pot-barley and plenty of various vegetables chopped small; **Scotch cart**, (*S.Afr.*) a strong, springless, two-wheeled uncovered farm cart with one shaft; **Scotch catch** or **snap**, a short accented note followed by a longer—not peculiar to Scottish music; **Scotch collops**, minced beef (sometimes called **scotched collops**); **Scotch curlies**, a variety of kale; **Scotch draper**, an itinerant dealer differing from a pedlar in not carrying his goods about with him; **Scotch egg**, a hard-boiled egg cut in two and enclosed in sausage-meat; **Scotch elm**, the wych elm (*Ulmus montana*): sometimes the common English elm (*U. campestris*); **Scotch fiddle**, the itch (from the movements of the fingers it excited); **Scotch fir**, Scots pine; **Scotch hand**, a wooden bat for manipulating butter; **Scotch kale**, a variety of kale; **Scotch mist**, a fine rain; **Scotch pebble**, an agate or similar stone; **Scotch rose**, the burnet rose (*Rosa spinosissima*); **Scotch terrier**, a rough-haired, prick-eared, strongly-built little dog; **Scotch thistle**, the cotton thistle, national emblem of Scotland (not native); **Scotch verdict**, not proven; **Scotch woodcock**, egg and anchovies on toast. [From **Scottish**.]

scotch, *skoch, v.t.* to gash: to score: (from Theobald's conjecture in *Macbeth*; see **scorch**, 2) to maim, cripple for the time without killing: to frustrate: to kill.—*n.* (*Shak.*) a gash: a score on the ground (as for hop-scotch). [Origin unknown.]

scotch, *skoch, n.* a strut, wedge, block, &c., to prevent turning or slipping, as of a wheel, gate, ladder.—*v.t.* to stop or block: to frustrate. [Perh. a form of **scatch**.]

scoter, *skō'tər, n.* a genus (Oedemia) of northern sea-ducks, usu. black or nearly.—Also **scoter duck**. [Origin obscure.]

Scotia, *skō'sh(y)ä, n.* (*poet.*) Scotland. — *adjs.* **Sco'tian** (*rare*); **Scotic** (*skot'ik*), of the ancient Scots of Ireland; **Scot'ican**, (*eccles.*) of Scotland.—For **Scotice, Scoticism, Scotish**, see **Scottice**, &c. [L.L. *Scōtia, Scōticus.*]

scotia, *skō'ti-ä, -shi-ä, n.* a hollow moulding, esp. at the base of a column. [Gr. *skōtiä—skotos*, darkness.]

Scotism, *skō'tizm, n.* the metaphysical system of Johannes Duns *Scotus* (*c.* 1265-1308), a native of Maxton in Roxburghshire (not Duns, Berwickshire, Dunstane, Northumberland, or Down, north Ireland), the great assailant of the method of Aquinas in seeking in speculation instead of in practice the foundation of Christian theology—his theological descendants were the Franciscans, in opposition to the Dominicans, who followed Aquinas.—*n.* **Scō'tist**, a follower of Duns Scotus.—*adj.* **Scotist'ic**.

Scotland, *skot'lənd, n.* (*hist.*) Ireland: now, the country forming the northern member of the United Kingdom.—**Scotland Yard**, former or (New Scotland Yard) present headquarters of the Metropolitan Police (said to be from a palace of the kings of Scotland on the old site): hence the London Criminal Investigation Department.

scotoma, *skot-ō'mä, n.* a blind spot due to disease of the retina or optic nerve:—*pl.* **scoto'mata.**—*n.* **scot'omy** (*obs.*). [Gr. *skotōma*, dizziness—*skotos*, darkness.]

Scots, *skots, adj.* Scottish (almost always used of money, measures, law, and preferably of language).—*n.* the dialect of Lowland Scotland, Northern English.—*ns.* **Scots'man**; **Scots'woman**.—**Scots Greys**, a famous regiment of dragoons, established in 1683; **Scots Guards**, a Scottish force which served the kings of France from 1418 to 1759, nominally to 1830: a well-known regiment of Guards in the British army, formerly Scots Fusilier Guards; **Scots pine**, the only native British pine, *Pinus sylvestris*; see also **mile, pint, pound**. [Shortened form of Scots *Scottis*, Scottish.]

Scot(t)ice, *skot'i-sē, adv.* in Scots.—*v.t.* **Scott'icise**, to render Scottish or into Scots.—*n.* **Scott'icism** (*obs.* **Scot'icism**), a Scottish idiom: Scottish feeling. [L.L. *Scott- Scōt-icē* (adv.), *-icus* (adj.).]

Scot(t)ify, *v.t.* to make Scottish:—*pr.p.* **Scot(t)'ifying**; *pa.t.* and *pa.p.* **Scot(t)'ified.**—*n.* **Scot(t)ificā'tion.** [Scot, and L. *facĕre*, to make.]

Scottish (*obs.* **Scotish**), *skot'ish, adj.* of Scotland, its people, or its English dialect.—*n.* (*rare*) Scots: (as *pl., rare*) the Scots.—*v.t.* (*rare*) to translate into Scots.—*ns.* **Scott'ishman**; **Scott'ishness** (both *rare*). [O.E. *Scottisc*, earlier *Scyttisc*.]

scoug. See **skug**.

scoundrel, *skown'drəl, n.* a low mean blackguard: a man without principle.—*ns.* **scoun'dreldom**, the world of scoundrels; **scoun'drelism.** — *adj.* **scoun'drelly.** [Origin unknown.]

scoup, scowp, *skowp, v.i.* (*Scot.*) to bound: to caper: to scamper. [Origin unknown.]

scour, *skowr, v.t.* to clean, polish, remove, or form by hard rubbing: to scrub: to cleanse: to free from grease, dirt, or gum: to flush or cleanse by a current: to purge, esp. drastically: to clear out: to rake with fire: (*fig.*) to punish.—*v.i.* to scrub or polish: to be scoured: (of cattle) to have diarrhoea.—*n.* the action, place, or means of scouring: diarrhoea in cattle: (*Scot.*) a swig of liquor.—*ns.* **scour'er**, one who scours: an instrument or container for scouring: a cathartic; **scour'ing**, scrubbing: vigorous cleansing: clearing: erosion: purging: (often in *pl.*) matter removed or accumulated by scouring: off-scouring.—Also *adj.*—*ns.* **scour'ing-rush**, (*U.S.*) Dutch rush; **scour'ing-stick**, a rod for scouring a gun. [Prob. M.Du. or M.L.G. *schüren*—O.Fr. *escurer*—L. *ex cūrāre*, take care of.]

scour, *skowr, v.i.* to rush or skurry along: to range about, esp. in quest or pursuit: to make off.—*v.t.* to range over or traverse swiftly, vigorously, riotously, or in search or pursuit: to molest as a scourer.—*n.* **scour'er** (*obs.* **scowr'er**; *hist.*), a member of a roistering band that scoured the streets, maltreating watchmen and others. [Poss. O.N. *skúr*, storm, shower; cf. **shower**.]

scourer, *skowr'ər, n.* a scout. [Aphetic; see **discoverer**.]

scourge, *skurj, n.* a whip: an instrument of divine punishment: a cause of widespread affliction.—*v.t.* to whip severely: to afflict.—*n.* **scourg'er.** [A.Fr. *escorge*—L. *excoriāre*—L. *excoriāre*, to flay—*corium*, leather (perh. as made of a strip of leather, perh. as a flaying instrument).]

scourse. See **scorse** (2).

scout, *skowt, n.* watch, spying: one (or *obs.*, a party) sent out to bring in information: a spy: a boy scout (see **boy**): an official who helps motorists on the roads: one who watches or attends at a little distance: a fielder, as in cricket: (*slang*) a person: a ship for reconnoitring: a small light aeroplane orig. intended for reconnaissance: a light armoured car for reconnaissance: a college servant at Oxford (perh. a different word; cf. Cambridge *gyp*, and Dublin *skip*).—*v.t.* to watch closely: to reconnoitre.—*v.i.* to act the scout.—*ns.* scout'craft, the knowledge and skill proper to a scout, esp. a boy scout; scout'er, a senior member of the boy scouts; scout'ing; scout'law, the code of rules of the boy scouts; scout'master, the leader of a band of scouts: an adult in charge of a troop of boy scouts. [O.Fr. *escoute*— *escouter*—L. *auscultāre*, to listen.]

scout, *skowt*, *v.t.* to mock, flout: to dismiss or reject with disdain. [Cf. O.N. *skúta*, a taunt.]

scout. Same as scoot.

scouth, scowth, *skōōth*, *skowth*, *n.* (*Scot.*) free range: scope: plenty.

scouther, scowder, *skow'd*(*h*)*ər*, *v.t.* (*Scot.*) to scorch, singe: to overheat: to toast slightly: to blight.—*n.* a scorch or burn.

scouther, scowther, *skōō'dhər*, *n.* (*Scot.*) a slight or flying shower.—*v.i.* to drizzle: to threaten rain or snow.—*n.* scou'thering, a sprinkle of snow.—*adj.* scou'thery.

scow, *skow*, *n.* a flat-bottomed boat. [Du. *schouw*.]

scowl, *skowl*, *v.i.* to contract the brows in a look of baleful malevolence: to look gloomy and threatening.—*v.t.* (*Milt.*) to give forth with a scowl.—*n.* a scowling look.—*adj.* scow'ling.—*adv.* scow'lingly. [Cf. Dan. *skule*, to scowl.]

scowp, scowther. See scoup, scouther.

scrab, *skrab*, *v.t.* to scratch.—*v.t.* and *v.i.* scrabb'le, to scratch: to scrape: to sprawl.—*v.i.* to scramble. —*n.* a scrawl. [Du. *schrabben*, to scratch, freq. *schrabbelen*; cf. scrape.]

scrae, *scrā*, *n.* (*Scott*). Same as scree.

scrag, *skrag*, *n.* a sheep's or (*slang*) human neck: the bony part of the neck: a lean person or animal. —*v.t.* to hang: to throttle: to wring the neck of: to tackle by the neck.—*n.* scrag'-end', the scrag of a neck.—*adj.* scragg'ed (or *skragd*), scraggy.— *n.* scragg'edness.—*adv.* scragg'ily.—*n.* scragg'iness.— *adj.* scragg'y, lean, skinny, and gaunt. [Prob. crag (2).]

scrag, *skrag*, *n.* a stump; a rough projection.—*adjs.* scragged, scragg'ling, scragg'ly, scragg'y, irregular, straggling. — *adv.* scragg'ily. — *ns.* scragg'iness; scrag'-whale, a whale with knobbed back. [Cf. scrog.]

scraich, scraigh, *skrāhh*, *v.i.* (*Scot.*) to screech: to make a scratchy sound.—*n.* a screech: a scratchy sound. [Cf. scraugh, skreigh.]

scram, *skram*, *v.i.* (*U.S. slang*; usu. in the *imper.*) to be off. [Perh. scramble.]

scram, *skram*, *adj.* (*S.W. England*) puny: withered. —*v.t.* to benumb: to paralyse. [Cf. scrimp.]

scramble, *skram'bl*, *v.i.* to make one's way with disorderly struggling haste: to get along somehow: to clamber: to wriggle irregularly: to sprawl: to dash or struggle for what one can get before others.—*v.t.* to throw down to be scrambled for: to put, make, get together, scramblingly: (of eggs) to beat up and heat to thickness with milk, butter, &c.: (of radiotelephone conversation) to make unintelligible by a device that alters frequencies. —*n.* act of scrambling: a disorderly performance: a dash or struggle for what can be had: a form of motor or motor-cycle trial.—*n.* scram'bler.—*adj.* scram'bling, confused and irregular.—*adv.* scram'blingly. [Cf. the dialect word *scramb*, to rake together with the hands.]

scran, *skran*, *n.* provisions: broken victuals.—bad scran to you, (*Ir.*) bad fare to you. [Ety. dub.]

scranch, *skran*(*t*)*sh*, *v.t.* to crunch. [Prob. imit.; cf. Du. *schransen*, to eat heartily.]

scrannel, *skran'l*, *adj.* thin: meagre: squeaking: (*Milt.*) grating, scratchy.—*adj.* scrann'y, lean: meagre.

scrap, *skrap*, *n.* a small fragment: a piece of leftover food: a remnant: a punched-out picture, cutting, or the like, intended or suited for preservation in a scrap-book: residue after extraction of oil from blubber, fish, &c.: metal clippings or other waste: anything discarded as worn-out, out of date, or useless.—*adj.* consisting of scrap.—*v.t.* to consign to the scrap-heap: to discard:—*pr.p.* scrapp'ing; *pa.p.* and *pa.t.* scrapped.—*ns.* scrap'-book, a blank book for pasting in scraps, cuttings, &c.; scrap'-heap, a place where old iron is collected: rubbish-heap; scrap'-iron, scrap'-metal, scraps of iron or other metal, of use only for remelting; scrap'-man.—*adv.* scrapp'ily.— *n.* scrapp'iness.—*adj.* scrapp'y, fragmentary: disconnected: made up of scraps. [O.N. *skrap*, scraps; cf. scrape.]

scrap, *skrap*, *n.* (*slang*) a fight: scrimmage.—Also *v.i.*

scrape, *skrāp*, *v.t.* to press a sharp edge over: to move gratingly over: to smooth, clean, clear, reduce in thickness, abrade, remove, form, collect, bring, render, by such an action: to get together by laborious effort: to erase: (contemptuously) to fiddle.—*v.i.* to graze: to scratch: to scratch the ground: to grate: to make a grating sound (as students with the feet, in disapprobation): to draw back the foot in making obeisance: to fiddle: to save penuriously: to get with difficulty (with *through, along, home*, &c.).—*n.* an act, process, or spell of scraping: a shave: a stroke of the bow: a grating sound: a stroke (of a pen): a scraped place in the ground: an abrasion: a mass of earth scraped up, as by a rabbit: a backward movement of one foot accompanying a bow: a scraping or thin layer: thin-spread butter: a predicament that threatens disgrace or friction with authority.—*ns.* scrape'-good, a miser; scrape'-gut, a fiddler; scrape'-penny, a miser; scrap'er, one who scrapes: a fiddler: a barber: a scraping instrument or machine, esp. for shoe-soles, hides, roads: an engraver's tool: a scratching bird; scrap'erboard, a clay-surface board on which drawings can be made by scraping tints off as well as applying them: such a drawing: this method; scrap'ing, the action of the verb: its sound: a piece scraped off.—scrape acquaintance with, to contrive somehow to get on terms of acquaintance. [O.E. *scrapian* or O.N. *skrapa*.]

scrat, *skrat*, *v.t.* and *v.i.* (*obs.* or *dial.*) to scratch. [M.E. *scratte*; origin doubtful.]

scratch, *skrach*, *v.t.* to draw a sharp point over the surface of: to hurt, mark, render, seek to allay discomfort in, by so doing: to dig or scrape with the claws: to write hurriedly: to erase or delete (usu. with *out*): to strike along a rough surface: to withdraw from a competition.—*v.i.* to use the nails or claws: to scrape: to make a grating or screechy noise: to retire from a contest or engagement: to get (along or through) somehow.—*n.* an act, mark, or sound of scratching: a slight wound: a scrawl: the line up to which boxers are led—hence test, trial, as in 'to come up to (the) scratch': the starting-point for a competitor without handicap: one who starts from scratch: a fluke, esp. in billiards: a scratch-wig: (in *pl.*) a disease in horses with the appearance of scratches on the pastern.—*adj.* improvised: casual: hastily or casually got together: without handicap.—*ns.* scratch'-back, a back-scratcher: a toy that makes a sound of tearing cloth; scratch'-brush, a wire brush; scratch'-coat, a first coat of plaster; scratch'er.—*adv.* scratch'ily.—*n.* scratch'iness. —*n.* and *adj.* scratch'ing.—*adv.* scratch'ingly. —*adj.* scratch'less.—*ns.* scratch'-wig, a wig that covers only part of the head; scratch'-work, sgraffito in plaster.—*adj.* scratch'y, like scratches: uneven: ready or likely to scratch: grating or screechy: itchy. [Poss. M.E. *cracchen*, to scratch, modified by scrat.]

Scratch, *skrach*, *n.* the Devil (usu. Old Scratch). [Cf. O.N. *skratte*, goblin, monster.]

scrattle, *skrat'l*, *v.i.* (*W. of England*) to keep scratching: to scuttle. [Freq. of scrat.]

scraugh, scrauch, *skrawhh*, *n.* (*Scot.*) a raucous squawk.—*v.i.* to make a scraugh. [Imit.]

scraw, *skraw*, *n.* a thin sod. [Ir. *sgrath*.]

scrawl, *skrawl*, *v.t.* and *v.i.* to mark or write irregularly or hastily: to scribble.—*n.* irregular, hasty, or bad writing: a broken branch of a tree: (*Lincoln-*

shire; *Tennyson*) a small crab.—*n.* **scrawl'er.**— *n.* and *adj.* **scrawl'ing.**—*adv.* **scrawl'ingly.**—*adj.* **scrawl'y.** [Perh. conn. with **crawl** or **sprawl**.]

scrawm, *skrawm, v.t.* (*prov.*) to scratch. [Prob. Du. *schrammen,* to graze.]

scrawny, *skraw'ni,* (*U.S.*). Same as **scranny.**

scray, scraye, *skrā, n.* the tern. [Cf. W. *ysgräell.*]

screak, *skrēk, v.t.* to screech: to creak.—*n.* a screech: a creak. [Cf. O.N. *skrækja.*]

scream, *skrēm, v.t.* and *v.i.* to cry out in a loud shrill voice, as in fear or pain: to laugh shrilly and uncontrolledly: to shriek.—*v.i.* (*coll.*: of colours) to be acutely inharmonious.—*n.* a shrill, sudden cry, as in fear or pain: a shriek: a loud whistling sound: (*coll.*) anything supposed to make one **scream** with laughter.—*n.* **scream'er,** one who screams: a large spur-winged S. American bird (Palamedea, *horned screamer*; Chauna, *crested screamer*) with loud harsh cry: a different S. American bird, the seriema (also called *crested screamer*): (*slang*) anything likely or intended to thrill with emotion, as a sensational headline: (*slang*) an exclamation mark.—*adj.* **scream'ing.**— *adv.* **scream'ingly.** — **screaming farce,** one highly ludicrous. [M.E. *scræmen.*]

scree, *skrē, n.* sloping mass of débris at the base of a cliff. [O.N. *skritha,* a landslip—*skritha,* to slide.]

screech, *skrēch, v.i.* to give forth a harsh, shrill, and sudden cry or noise.—*v.t.* to utter in such tones.— *n.* a harsh, shrill, and sudden cry: a strident creak: a screeching or screaming bird (as barn-owl, swift, missel-thrush).—*ns.* **screech'er,** one who screeches: the swift or other screeching bird; **screech'-hawk,** the nightjar; **screech'-martin,** the swift; **screech'-owl,** the barn-owl: a bringer of bad news; **screech'-thrush,** the missel-thrush: the fieldfare.—*adj.* **screech'y,** shrill and harsh, like a screech. [M.E. *scrichen*; cf. **scritch.**]

screed, *skrēd, n.* a shred: a strip: a border: a long effusion, spoken or written: (*obs.*) a drinking bout: a guide to the thickness of mortar required: (*Scot.*) a rent, a tear.—*v.t.* to repeat glibly.—*v.i.* to rend. [O.E. *scréade,* shred.]

screen, *skrēn, n.* a shield against danger, observation, wind, heat, light, or other outside influence: a piece of room furniture in the form of a folding framework or of a panel on a stand: (*Scot.*) a clothes-horse: a protection against wind on a vehicle: a large scarf: a sheltering row of trees: a body of troops or formation of ships intended as a cover: a wall masking a building: a partial partition cutting off part of a room, a church choir, or side chapel: a coarse sifting apparatus: a netruled plate for half-tone photography: a mosaic of primary colours for colour photography: a white sheet or the like on which images may be projected: hence, the cinematograph: (*cricket*) a white erection against which the batsman sees the bowler.—*v.t.* to shelter or conceal: to sift coarsely: to sort out by, or subject to, tests of ability, desirability, &c.: to project or exhibit on a screen or on the screen: to make a motion-picture of.—*v.i.* to show up on, or be suitable for, the screen.—*ns.* **screen'er;** **screen'ing.** — *n.pl.* **screen'ings,** material eliminated by sifting.—*n.* **screen'-wiper,** a contrivance for wiping the wind-screen of a car in rain. [App. related in some way to O.Fr. *escran* (Fr. *écran*), which may be—O.H.G. *skrim, skerm* (Ger. *schirm*).]

screeve, *skrēv, v.t.* and *v.i.* (*slang*) to write, esp. begging letters: to draw on the pavement.—*n.* a piece of writing: a begging letter.—*n.* **screev'er;** **screev'ing.** [Prob. It. *scrivere*—L. *scrībĕre,* to write.]

screw, *skrōō, n.* a cylinder with a helical groove or ridge, used as a fastening, as a mechanical power, and otherwise: anything of similar form: a screw-propeller or ship driven by one: a thumbscrew: a corkscrew: a twisted cone of paper, or portion of a commodity contained in it: a turn of the screw: (*fig.*) pressure: a twist: a spin imparted to a ball: (*slang*) a stingy fellow, an extortioner, a skinflint: a broken-winded horse: salary. —*v.t.* to fasten, tighten, compress, force, adjust,

extort by a screw, a screwing motion, or as if by a screw: to apply a screw to: to twist: to turn in the manner of a screw: to pucker.—*v.i.* to admit of screwing: to wind: to worm.—*n.* **screw'-bolt,** a bolt with a screw-thread.—*adj.* **screw'-down,** closed by screwing.—*n.* **screw'driver,** an instrument for turning and driving screws.—*adj.* **screwed,** (*slang*) tipsy.—*n.* **screw'er.**—*n.* and *adj.* **screw'ing.**—*ns.* **screw'-nail,** a nail made in the form of a screw; **screw'-pile,** a pile ending in a screw; **screw'-pine,** a plant of the genus Pandanus or its family—from the screw-like arrangement of the leaves; **screw'-plate,** a plate of steel with holes for cutting screw-threads; **screw'-press,** a press worked by a screw; **screw'-propell'er,** a propeller with helical blades; **screw'-steam'er,** a steamer driven by screw; **screw'-thread,** the ridge of a screw.—*adv.* **screw'-wise.**—*n.* **screw'-wrench,** a tool for gripping screw-heads.—*adj.* **screw'y,** exacting: close: worthless: tipsy.— **a screw loose,** something defective (esp. mentally); **put on, turn, the screw,** to apply pressure progressively: to exact payment. [Earlier *scrue*; app. O.Fr. *escroue,* of obscure origin; prob. conn. with L.G. *schrûve,* Ger. *schraube.*]

scribble, *skrib'l, v.t.* to scrawl: to write badly, carelessly, or worthlessly (in handwriting or substance). —*n.* careless writing: a scrawl.—*ns.* **scribb'lement;** **scribb'ler,** a petty author; **scribb'ling;** **scribb'ling-book, -paper.**—*adv.* **scribb'lingly.**— *adj.* **scribb'ly.** [A freq. of **scribe,** or L.L. *scribillāre*—L. *scrībĕre,* to write.]

scribble, *skrib'l, v.t.* to card roughly.—*ns.* **scribb'-ler,** a carding machine: one who tends it; **scribb'-ling.** [Prob. from L.G.]

scribe, *skrīb, n.* (*B.*) an expounder and teacher of the Mosaic and traditional law: a writer: a public or official writer: a clerk, amanuensis, secretary: a copyist: a penman: a pointed instrument to mark lines on wood, &c.—*v.t.* to mark, score: to fit by so marking: to incise: to write.—*v.i.* to play the scribe.—*adjs.* **scri'bable,** capable of being written upon; **scribā'cious,** given to writing.—*n.* **scribā'ciousness.**—*adj.* **scri'bal.**—*ns.* **scri'ber,** a scribing tool; **scri'bing; scri'bism.** [L. *scrība,* a scribe, and *scrībĕre,* to write.]

scriene (*Spens.*). Same as **screen.**

scrieve, *skrēv, v.i.* (*Scot.*) to glide swiftly along. [Prob. O.N. *skrefa*—*skref,* stride.]

scriggle, *skrig'l, v.i.* to writhe: to wriggle.—*n.* a wriggling.—*adj.* **scrigg'ly.** [Cf. **struggle.**]

scrike, *skrīk, v.i.* (*Spens.*) to shriek.—*n.* (*obs.*) a shriek. [Prob. Scand.]

scrim, *skrim, n.* cloth used in upholstery, &c. [Origin obscure.]

scrimmage, *skrim'ij,* **scrummage,** *skrum'ij, n.* a tussle: a scrum.—*v.i.* to take part in a scrimmage. —*n.* **scrimm'ager, scrumm'ager.** [See **skirmish.**]

scrimp, *skrimp, adj.* scanty: stinted.—*adv.* barely. —*v.t.* to stint: to keep short.—*v.i.* to be sparing or niggardly.—*adj.* **scrimped,** pinched.—*adv.* **scrimp'ily.**—*n.* **scrimp'iness.**—*adv.* **scrimp'ly,** sparingly: scarcely. — *n.* **scrimp'ness.** — *adj.* **scrimp'y,** scanty. [Cf. Sw. and Dan. *skrumpen,* shrivelled, O.E. *scrimman,* to shrink.]

scrimshank. Same as **skrimshank.**

scrimshaw, *skrim'shaw, n.* a sailor's spare-time handicraft, as engraving fanciful designs on shells, whales' teeth, &c.: anything so executed.—Also **scrim'shander, scrim'shandy.**—*v.t.* and *v.i.* to work or decorate in this way.—*n.* **scrim'shoner,** one who does scrimshaw. [Origin obscure.]

scrimure, *skrim'yər, n.* (*Shak.*) a fencer. [Fr. *escrimeur.*]

scrine, scryne, *skrīn, n.* (*Spens.*) a chest for records: a shrine. [O.Fr. *escrin*—L. *scrīnium,* a chest; cf. **shrine.**]

scrip, *skrip, n.* a writing: a scrap of paper or of writing: short for **subscription,** hence a preliminary certificate, as for shares allotted: share certificates, or shares or stock collectively: (*U.S. hist.*) paper money less than a dollar. [See **script, subscription**; but partly perh. from **scrap.**]

scrip, *skrip, n.* a small bag: a satchel: a pilgrim's

pouch.—*n.* **scripp'age,** (*Shak.*) contents of a scrip. [Cf. O.N. *skreppa,* a bag, and O.Fr. *escrep*(*p*)*e.*]

script, *skript, n.* a writing: (*law*) an original document: (*Shak.*) a list of actors and their parts: a text for broadcasting: handwriting, system or style of handwriting: handwriting in imitation of type: type in imitation of handwriting: (also '**script**) short for *manuscript* or *typescript.* [L. *scriptum—scrībĕre,* to write.]

scriptorium, *skrip-tō'ri-əm, n.* a writing-room, esp. in a monastery:—*pl.* **scripto'ria.**—*adjs.* **scripto'rial; scrip'tory** (-*tər-i*), by, in, or relating to writing. [L. *scriptōrium—scrībĕre.*]

scripture, *skrip'tyər, n.* handwriting: something written: (in *sing.* or *pl.*) sacred writings of a religion, esp. (**Scripture, -s**) the Bible: (*rare*) a biblical text.—Also *adj.*—*adj.* **scrip'tural,** of, in, warranted by Scripture: of writing.—*ns.* **scrip'turalism,** literal adherence to the Scriptures; **scrip'turalist,** a literalist in obedience to the letter of Scripture: (*obs.*) a student of Scripture.—*adv.* **scrip'turally.**—*ns.* **scrip'ture-read'er,** one who reads the Bible in cottages, barracks, &c.; **scrip'turism; scrip'turist,** one versed in Scripture: one who bases his belief on the Bible and the Bible alone. [L. *scriptūra—scrībĕre,* to write.]

scritch, *skrich, n.* a screech.—*v.t.* and *v.i.* to screech. —*n.* **scritch'-owl.** [See **screech.**]

scrive, *skrīv, v.t.* to describe: to scribe.—*n.* **scrive'-board, scrieve'-board,** a shipbuilder's drawing-board.

scrivener, *skriv'nər, n.* a scribe: a copyist: one who draws up contracts, &c.: one who lays out money at interest for others.—*ns.* **scriv'enership; scriv'ening,** writing.—**scrivener's palsy,** writer's cramp. [O.Fr. *escrivain* (Fr. *écrivain*)—L.L. *scribānus*—L. *scrība,* a scribe.]

scrobe, *skrōb, n.* a groove.—*adj.* **scrobic'ulate** (*skrob-*), pitted. [L. *scrobis,* a ditch.]

scroddled, *skrod'ld, adj.* (of pottery) made of clay scraps of different colours. [Cf. L.G. *schrodel,* scrap.]

scrofula, *skrof'ū-lä, n.* (*obs.*) tuberculosis, esp. of the lymphatic glands, called also king's evil.—*adj.* **scrof'ulous.** [L. *scrŏfulae—scrōfa,* a sow (supposed to be liable to it).]

scrog, *skrog, n.* (*Scot.*) a stunted bush or small tree: a crab-apple, fruit or tree: a bushy place: scrubby wood: a broken branch: (*her.*) a branch.—*ns.* **scrog'-apple; scrog'-bush** (**-buss**).—*adj.* **scrogg'ie, scrogg'y,** covered with scrogs: stunted. [Origin obscure.]

scroll, *skrōl, n.* a roll of paper, parchment, &c.: a ribbon-like strip, partly coiled or curved, often bearing a motto: a writing in the form of a roll: a rough draft: a schedule: a spiral ornament or part: (*U.S.*) a flourish to a signature representing a seal.—*v.t.* to set in a scroll: to draft.—*v.i.* to curl.—*adj.* **scrolled,** formed into a scroll: ornamented with scrolls.—*n.* **scroll'-saw,** a saw for cutting scrolls.—*adv.* **scroll'wise.**—*n.* **scroll'work,** ornament in scrolls. [Earlier **scrowl**(**e**), formed (perh. as dim.) from **scrow.**]

scrooge. See **scrouge.**

scroop, *skrōōp, n.* a scraping noise.—*v.i.* to make a scroop. [Imit.]

Scrophularia, *skrof-ū-lā'ri-ä, n.* the figwort genus, giving name to the **Scrophulariaceae** (-*lar-i-ā'si-ē*), a family of sympetalous dicotyledons with zygomorphic flowers, including foxglove, mullein, speedwell, eyebright.—*adj.* **scrophulariā'ceous.** [L. *scrŏfulae,* from its supposed curative virtue; see **scrofula.**]

scrotum, *skrō'təm, n.* the bag that contains the testicles.—*adj.* **scrō'tal.** [L. *scrŏtum.*]

scrouge, scrowdge, *skrowj,* **scrooge,** *skrōōj, v.t.* and *v.i.* to squeeze: to crowd.—*n.* **scroug'er,** (*U.S.*) a whopper: something large. [Cf. **scruze.**]

scrounge, *skrownj, v.t.* (*mil. slang*) to purloin: to 'pinch': to cadge.—*v.i.* to hunt around: to sponge.—*ns.* **scroung'er; scroung'ing.** [Origin doubtful.]

scrow, *skrō, n.* a scroll: a writing: a hide clipping. [A.Fr. *escrowe*; see **escroll, escrow, scroll.**]

scrowl, scrowle, *skrōl,* old spellings of **scroll.**

scroyle, *skroil, n.* (*Shak.*) a wretch. [Origin doubtful.]

scrub, *skrub, v.t.* to rub hard: to wash by hard rubbing with a stiff brush: (*gas-making*) to purify. —*v.i.* to use a scrubbing-brush: to drudge: to make a rapid to-and-fro movement as if with a scrubbing-brush: (*pr.p.* **scrubb'ing;** *pa.t.* and *pa.p.* **scrubbed**).—*n.* an act of scrubbing: a worn or short-bristled brush or broom: a drudge.—*ns.* **scrubb'er,** one who scrubs: apparatus for freeing gas from tar, ammonia, and sulphuretted hydrogen; **scrubb'ing; scrubb'ing-board,** a washing-board; **scrubb'ing-brush,** a brush with short stiff bristles for scrubbing floors, &c. [Perh. obs. Du. *schrubben,* or a corresponding lost O.E. word.]

scrub, *skrub, n.* a stunted tree: stunted trees and shrubs collectively: brushwood: country covered with bushes or low trees, esp. the Australian evergreen xerophytic dwarf forest or bush of Eucalyptus, Acacia, &c.: an undersized or inferior animal, esp. one of indefinite breed: an insignificant or mean person: anything small or mean.— *adj.* mean: insignificant: undersized: (of a team) improvised, hastily got together for the occasion: a player in a second or inferior team.—*adj.* **scrubb'ed,** (*Shak.*) stunted. — *ns.* **scrubb'er,** (*Austr.*) an animal that has run wild; **scrub'-bird,** an Australian bird (*Atrichornis*) akin to the lyre-bird.—*adj.* **scrubb'y,** stunted: covered with scrub: mean.—*ns.* **scrub'-rider,** one who looks for cattle that stray into the scrub; **scrub'-turkey,** a mound-bird; **scrub'-ty'phus,** a typhus-like disease transmitted by a mite. [A variant of **shrub.**]

scruff, *skruf, n.* the nape of the neck. [See **scuft.**]

scruff, *skruf,* **scruff'y.** Same as **scurf, scurfy.**

scrum, *skrum, n.* a scrimmage: (*Rugby football*) a closing-in of rival forwards round the ball on the ground, or in readiness for its being inserted (by the scrum-half) between the two compact pushing masses.—*n.* **scrum'-half,** (*Rugby football*) a half-back whose duty it is to put the ball into the scrum and secure it as soon as it emerges therefrom. [Abbreviation of **scrummage**; see **scrimmage, skirmish.**]

scrumptious, *skrump'shəs, adj.* (*slang*) delightful.— Also **scrumm'y.**

scrunch, *skrun*(*t*)*sh,* variant of **crunch.** — *adj.* **scrunch'y.**

scrunt, *skrunt, n.* (*Scot.*) anything stunted (as an apple, a tree) or worn: a niggard.—*adj.* **scrunt'y.**

scruple, *skrōō'pl, n.* a small weight—in apothecaries' weight, 20 grains: (*obs.*) a sexagesimal division, as a minute of time or arc: a very small quantity: a difficulty or consideration, usu. moral, obstructing action, esp. one turning on a fine point or one that is baseless: a doubt, disbelief, or difficulty.—*v.i.* to hesitate from a scruple.—*ns.* **scru'pler; scrupulosity** (-*pū-los'i-ti*).—*adj.* **scru'pulous,** directed by scruples: having scruples, doubts, or objections: conscientious: cautious: exact: captious.—*adv.* **scru'pulously.**—*n.* **scru'pulousness.** [L. *scrūpulus,* dim. of *scrūpus,* a sharp stone, anxiety.]

scrutiny, *skrōō'ti-ni, n.* a vote by poll: close, careful, or minute investigation or examination: a searching look: official examination of votes: (*hist.*) examination of the catechumens.—*adj.* **scru'table,** accessible to scrutiny.—*ns.* **scrutā'tor,** a close examiner: a scrutineer; **scrutineer',** one who makes a scrutiny, esp. of votes.—*v.t.* and *v.i.* **scru'tinise,** to examine closely.—*n.* **scru'tiniser.** —*adj.* **scru'tinising.**—*adv.* **scru'tinisingly.**—*adj.* **scru'tinous.**—*adv.* **scru'tinously.**—**scrutin-de-liste** (*skrü-tan°-də-lēst*; Fr.), a method of voting for the French Chamber of Deputies, in which the voter casts his ballot for any combination of the whole number of candidates for the department —opp. to **scrutin d'arrondissement** (*där-ōn°-dēs-män°*), in which method he votes only for his local candidates. [L. *scrūtinium,* and *scrūtārī,* to search even to the rags—*scrūta,* rags, trash.]

scruto, *skrōō'tō, n.* a kind of stage trap-door. [Origin obscure.]

scrutoire, *skroo-twär', -tōr', n.* (*obs.*). Same as **escritoire.**

scruze, *skrōōz*, *v.t.* (*Spens.*; now *dial.*) to squeeze. [Perh. **screw** combined with **squeeze**.]

scry, *skrī*, *v.t.* (*arch.* and *dial.*) to descry.—*v.i.* to practise crystal-gazing :—*pr.p.* **scry'ing**; *pa.t.* and *pa.p.* **scried**, (*Spens.*) **scryde**.—*ns.* **scry'er**; **scry'ing**. [Aphetic for **descry**.]

scryne (*Spens.*). Same as **scrine**.

scuchin, scuchion, Spenserian forms of **scutcheon**.

scud, *skud*, *v.i.* to sweep along easily and swiftly : to drive before the wind.—*v.t.* to traverse swiftly : (*pr.p.* **scudd'ing**; *pa.t.* and *pa.p.* **scudd'ed**).—*n.* act of scudding : driving cloud, shower or spray : a gust : (*school slang*) a swift runner.—*n.* **scudd'er**. — *v.i.* **scudd'le**, to scuttle. [Perh. Du. or L.G.]

scud, *skud*, *v.t.* (*Scot.*) to slap, spank.—*n.* (often in *pl.*) a slap : a spanking.

scuddaler, scudler. Same as **skudler**.

scudo, *skōō'dō*, *n.* an old Italian silver coin, usually worth about 4s. :—*pl.* **scu'di** (-*dē*). [It.,—L. *scūtum*, a shield.]

scuff, *skuf*, *n.* a form of **scruff** or **scuft**.

scuff, *skuf*, *v.t.* and *v.i.* to shuffle : to brush, graze, touch lightly : to abrade : to make or become shabby by wear.—*v.t.* to cuff.—*n.* (*Scot.*) a glancing touch or blow or its sound.—*adv.* with a scuff.— *v.i.* **scuff'le**, to struggle confusedly : to shuffle.— *v.t.* to hoe, scarify : to shuffle.—*n.* a confused struggle : a thrust-hoe: an agricultural scuffler.— *n.* **scuff'ler**, one who scuffles : an implement for scarifying the soil.—*adj.* **scuff'y**, (*Scot.*) shabby: rubbed, abraded : with the sound of a light rubbing. [Cf. Sw. *skuffa*, to shove; Du. *schof-felen*; shove, shovel, **shuffle**.]

scuft, *skuft*, *n.* (*prov.*) the nape of the neck.—Also **scuff, scruff**. [Poss. O.N. *skopt, skoft*, the hair.]

scug, scog, scoug, scoog, &c. See **skug**.

scul, scull, sculle, *skul, n.* (*Shak., Milt.*). See **school** (of fish).

sculduddery, sculduddry, *skul-dud'(ə-)ri, n.* (*Scot., facet.*) breach of chastity : bawdy talk or writing. —*adj.* bawdy.—*n.* **skulduggery** (-*dug'*; *U.S.*), underhand malpractices.

sculk, **scull**, obs. spellings of **skulk, skull**.

scull, *skul, n.* a short, light spoon-bladed oar for one hand : an oar used over the stern : (*obs.*) a sculling-boat : (*obs.*) a sculler : an act or spell of sculling.—*v.t.* to propel with sculls, or with one oar worked like a scull over the stern.—*v.i.* to use sculls.—*ns.* **scull'er**, one who sculls : a small boat pulled by one man with a pair of sculls; **scull'ing**; **scull'ing-boat**. [Origin obscure.]

scull, **skull**, *skul, n.* a shallow basket for fish, &c. [Poss. O.N. *skjóla*, pail.]

scullery, *skul'ər-i, n.* a room for rough kitchen work, as cleaning of utensils.—*n.* **scull'ery-maid**. [O.Fr. *escuelerie—escuelier*—L.L. *scutellārius*—L. *scutella*, a tray.]

scullion, *skul'yən, n.* a servant for drudgery.— *adj.* base. [Poss. O.Fr. *escouillon*, a dish-clout— L. *scōpa*, a broom; or from Fr. *souillon*, scullion, influenced by **scullery**.]

sculp, *skulp, v.t.* and *v.i.* (chiefly jocular) to carve : to engrave : to sculpture.—Also **sculpt**. [L. *sculpĕre*; partly a back-formation from **sculptor**, **sculpture**.]

sculpin, *skul'pin, n.* the dragonet : (*U.S.*) a marine Cottus or other large-headed, spiny, useless fish : (*slang*) a good-for-nothing person or animal. [Poss. **scorpaena**.]

sculptor, *skulp'tər, n.* an artist in carving : a statuary :— *fem.* **sculp'tress**. — *adj.* **sculp'tural** (-*tyər-əl*).—*adv.* **sculp'turally**.—*n.* **sculp'ture**, the act of carving, esp. in stone : extended to clay-modelling or moulding for casting : work, or a piece of work, in this kind : (*obs.*) engraving : shaping in relief : (*biol.*) spines, ridges, &c., standing out from the surface.—*v.t.* to carve : to represent in sculpture : to shape in relief : to mark with sculpturings. — *adjs.* **sculp'tured**, carved : engraved : (*bot., zool.*) having elevations on the surface ; **sculpturesque'**, statue-like.—*n.* **sculp'turing**. [L. *sculptor, -ōris, sculptūra*—*sculpĕre, sculptum*, to carve.]

scum, *skum, n.* foam or froth : matter coming to

or floating on the surface : (*fig.*) offscourings of the population.—*v.t.* to skim.—*v.i.* to form, throw up a scum :—*pr.p.* **scumm'ing**; *pa.t.* and *pa.p.* **scummed**.—*n.* **scumm'er**, a skimming instrument. — *n.pl.* **scumm'ings**, skimmings. — *adj.* **scumm'y**. [Cf. Dan. *skum*, Ger. *schaum*, foam.]

scumber, *skum'bər, v.t.* and *v.i.* to defecate (of dog or fox).—*n.* dung.—Also **skumm'er**. [Prob. O.Fr. *descumbrer*, to disencumber.]

scumble, *skum'bl, v.t.* to soften the effect of by a very thin coat of opaque or semi-opaque colour, or by light rubbing.—*n.* colour so laid : the effect so produced.—*n.* **scum'bling**. [Freq. of **scum**.]

scumfish. Same as **scomfish**.

scuncheon, sconcheon, scontion, *skun', skon'shən, n.* the inner part of a jamb. [O.Fr. *escoinson*.]

scunner, *skun'ər, v.i.* (*Scot.*) to take a loathing.— *v.t.* to excite a loathing in : to disgust, nauseate.— *n.* a loathing : an object, or a manifestation, of loathing. [Perh. M.E. *scurn*, to shrink; origin unknown.]

scup, *skup*, **scuppaug**, *skup'awg*, or -*awg'*, *ns.* the porgy. [Narragansett *mishcuppauog*.]

scupper, *skup'ər, n.* a hole to drain a ship's deck. [Origin disputed.]

scupper, *skup'ər, v.t.* (*slang*) to slaughter : to do for.

scuppernong, *skup'ər-nong, n.* a grape from the *Scuppernong* river, N. Carolina : wine from it.

scur, skur. Same as **skirr**.

scurf, *skurf, n.* a crust of branny scales : an incrustation.—*n.* **scurf'iness**.—*adj.* **scurf'y**. [O.E. *scurf, sceorf*.]

scurril(e), *skur'il, adj.* (*arch.*) like or worthy of a vulgar buffoon: indecently opprobrious or jocular. —*n.* **scurril'ity**.—*adj.* **scurr'ilous**, scurril.—*adv.* **scurr'ilously**.—*n.* **scurr'ilousness**. [L. *scurrīlis* —*scurra*, a buffoon.]

scurrior, scurrier, *skur'i-ər, n.* (*obs.*) a scout. [See **discoverer**.]

scurry, skurry, *skur'i, v.i.* to hurry briskly or flutteringly : to scuttle.—*n.* flurried haste : a flurry. [From **hurry-skurry**, reduplication of **hurry**; or back-formation of **scurrier**; or from **scour**.]

scurvy, *skur'vi, adj.* scurfy : shabby : vile, contemptible.—*n.* a disease marked by bleeding and sponginess of the gums, due to a lack of fresh vegetables and consequently of vitamin C.—*adv.* **scur'vily**, in a scurvy manner : meanly, basely.— *ns.* **scur'viness**; **scur'vy-grass**, a cruciferous plant (*Cochlearia officinalis*) used by sailors as an anti-scorbutic: ale medicated with it. [**scurf**; the application to the disease helped by similarity of sound; see **scorbutic**.]

scuse, 'scuse, *skūs, n.* and *skūz, v.t.* aphetic for **excuse**.

scut, *skut, n.* a short erect tail like a hare's : a hare. [Origin obscure.]

scutage, *skū'tij, n.* a tax on a knight's fee, esp. one in lieu of personal service. [L.L. *scūtāgium*— L. *scūtum*, shield.]

scutch, *skuch, v.t.* to dress (e.g. flax) by beating : to switch.—*n.* a swingle : a bricklayer's cutting tool.—*ns.* **scutch'er**, a person, tool, or part of a machine that scutches : the striking part of a threshing-mill; **scutch'ing**. [Prob. O.Fr. *escous-ser*, to shake off.]

scutcheon, *skuch'ən, n.* an aphetic form of **escutcheon**.

scute, *skūt, n.* a scutum : an écu : a dermal plate. —*adjs.* **scūt'al**; **scūt'ate**, protected by scutes: buckler-shaped; **scūt'iform**. — *ns.* **scūt'iger**, (*jocular*) a squire; **scūt'um**, (*hist.*) the oblong shield of Roman heavy-armed infantry : a scute: the second tergal plate of a segment of an insect's thorax :—*pl.* **scūt'a**. [L. *scūtum*, a shield.]

scutellum, *skūt-el'əm, n.* a scale of a bird's foot: the third tergal plate of a segment of an insect's thorax : a structure, supposed to be the cotyledon, by which a grass embryo absorbs the endosperm :— *pl.* **scūtell'a**.—*adjs.* **scūtell'ar**, of a scutellum; **scūt'ellate**.—*n.* **scūtellā'tion**, scale arrangement. [L. *scutella*, a tray, dim. of *scutra*, a platter, confused in scientific use with *scūtulum*, dim. of *scūtum*, a shield.]

scutter, *skut'ər, v.i.* to run hastily : to scurry.—*n.* a hasty run. [A variant of **scuttle** (3).]

scuttle, *skut'l, n.* a shallow basket : a vessel for holding coal.—*n.* **scutt'leful.** [O.E. *scutel*—L. *scutella,* a tray.]

scuttle, *skut'l, n.* an opening in a ship's deck or side : its lid : a shuttered hole in a wall, roof, &c. : its shutter or trap-door.—*v.t.* to make a hole in, esp. in order to sink.—*ns.* **scutt'le-butt**, **-cask**, a cask with a hole cut in it for drinking-water. [O.Fr. *escoutille,* hatchway.]

scuttle, *skut'l, v.i.* to dash with haste.—*n.* an act of scuttling.—*n.* **scutt'ler.** [**scuddle**.]

scybalum, *sib'ə-ləm, n.* a hard fecal mass in the intestine :—*pl.* **scyb'ala.**—*adj.* **scyb'alous.** [Latinised from Gr. *skybalon,* dung.]

scye, *sī, n.* an opening for insertion of a sleeve. [Origin obscure.]

Scylla, *sil'ä, n.* a six-headed monster who sat over a dangerous rock opposite Charybdis. [Gr. *Skylla.*]

scyphus, *sīf'əs, n.* (*ant.*) a large Greek drinking-cup : a cup-shaped structure :—*pl.* **scyph'ī.**—*n.* **scyphis'toma**, the segmenting polyp stage of a jellyfish (Gr. *stoma,* mouth). — *ns.pl.* **Scyphomedū'sae, Scyphozō'a**, the jellyfishes as a class. [Gr. *skyphos,* cup.]

scytale, *sit'ə-lē, n.* a Spartan secret writing on a strip wound about a stick, unreadable without a stick of like thickness. [Gr. *skytalē,* a staff.]

scythe, *sīdh, n.* an instrument with a large curved blade for mowing : a blade attached to a war-chariot wheel.—*v.t.* and *v.i.* to mow with a scythe. —*adj.* **scythed**, armed or cut with scythes.— *ns.* **scythe'man, scyth'er**, one who uses a scythe ; **scythe'-stone**, a whet for scythes. [O.E. *sīthe* ; cf. O.N. *sigthr,* Ger. *sense.*]

Scythian, *sith'i-ən, adj.* of *Scythia,* an ancient country N. and E. of the Black Sea, of its nomadic people or of their language.—*n.* a member of the people : the language of Scythia.—**Scythian lamb**, barometz.

'sdeath, *zdeth, interj.* (*obs.*) an exclamation of impatience—for *God's death.*

sdeigne, sdein, sdaine, sdayn, *zdān, v.t.* and *v.i.* (*Spens., Milt.*) to disdain.—*adj.* **sdeign'full.** —*adv.* **sdeign'fully.** [It. *sdegnare,* aphetic for *disdegnare* ; or Eng. **disdain.**]

sdrucciola, *zdrŏŏt'chō-lä, adj.* (of rhyme) triple. [It., slippery.]

sea, *sē, n.* the great mass of salt water covering the greater part of the earth's surface : the ocean : any great expanse of water : a great (esp. salt) lake—mainly in proper names : swell or roughness : a great wave : the tide : a wide expanse. —*adj.* **marine.**—*ns.* **sea'-ā'corn**, an acorn-shell ; **sea'-add'er**, a pipefish : a marine stickleback ; **sea'-air'**, the air at sea or by the sea ; **sea'-an'chor**, a floating anchor used in a gale ; **sea'-anem'one**, a solitary soft-bodied polyp of the Zoantharia ; **sea'-ape**, the sea-otter : the thresher shark : a manati ; **sea'-bank**, the seashore : an embankment to keep out the sea ; **sea'-bass** (-*bas*), a perch-like marine fish of various kinds, esp. of the Serranidae and the Sciaenidae ; **sea'-bat**, a name for various fishes with long or outspread fins ; **sea'-bā'ther** ; **sea'-bā'thing** ; **sea'-beach**, a shelf of sand, gravel, &c., bordering the sea ; **sea'-bean'**, the cacoon (Entada) or other foreign seed cast up by the sea : a mollusc's operculum, worn as an amulet ; **sea'-bear**, the polar bear : the fur-seal ; **sea'-beast** ; —*adjs.* **sea'-beat, -en**, lashed by the waves.—*ns.* **sea'-beet**, wild beet ; **sea'berry**, Halorhagis ; **sea'-bird**, any marine bird ; **sea'-bis'cuit**, ship-biscuit ; **sea'-blite**, a salt-marsh plant (*Suaeda maritima*) of the goose-foot family ; **sea'-blubb'er**, a jelly-fish.—*adj.* **sea'-blue**, blue like the sea.—*n.* **sea'board**, the country bordering the sea.—Also *adj.*—*n.* **sea'-boat**, a craft considered with reference to her behaviour in bad weather.—*adjs.* **sea'-born**, produced by the sea ; **sea'borne**, carried on the sea.—*ns.* **sea'-bottle**, a translucent inflated seaweed (Valonia) : bladderwrack ; **sea'-bott'om**, the floor of the sea ; **sea'-boy**, (*Shak.*) a sailor-boy ; **sea'-breach**, an

inroad of the sea ; **sea'-bream**, any fish of the Sparidae, a family of spiny-finned fishes, with teeth of the character of incisors and molars : any fish of the Bramidae, a family akin to the mackerels ; **sea'-breeze**, a breeze from the sea, esp. owing to convection in the daytime ; **sea'-buck'thorn**, a willow-like seaside shrub (*Hippophae rhamnoides*) of the family Eleagnaceae ; **sea'-bun**, a heart-urchin ; **sea'-bur'dock**, clotbur (Xanthium) ; **sea'-butt'erfly**, a pteropod ; **sea'-calf**, the common seal ; **sea'-cana'ry**, the white whale ; **sea'-cap**, (*Shak.*) a cap worn on shipboard ; **sea'-captain**, the captain of a merchant ship ; **sea'-card**, a compass card : a sea-chart ; **sea'-cat**, a cat-fish : a weaver-fish ; **sea'-change**, (*Shak.*) a change effected by the sea ; **sea'-chart**, a chart of the sea, its coasts, &c. ; **sea'-chest**, a seaman's trunk ; **sea'-cliff**, a cliff fronting or formed by the sea ; **sea'-coal**, (*arch.*) coal in the ordinary sense, not charcoal (possibly as first worked where exposed by the sea).—Also *adj.*—*ns.* **sea'coast**, the land adjacent to the sea ; **sea'-cob**, a seagull ; **sea'-cock**, a gurnard : a valve communicating with the sea through a vessel's hull : a bold mariner or sea rover ; **sea'-cole'wort**, sea-kale : wild cabbage ; **sea'-cook**, a ship's cook (by sailors supposed to disgrace his son) ; **sea'-cow**, the walrus : rhytina (Steller's sea-cow) or other sirenian : (*S.Afr.*) Du. *zeekoe*) the hippopotamus ; **sea'-craft**, skill in navigation : seamanship : sea-going craft ; **sea'-craw'fish, -cray'fish**, a spiny lobster ; **sea'-crow**, a name of many birds, as skua, chough, cormorant ; **sea'-cū'cumber**, a holothurian (as trepang, bêche-de-mer) ; **sea'-dace**, the bass ; **sea'-dev'il**, a devil dwelling in the sea : a devil-fish : the angler-fish ; **sea'-dog**, the seal : a dog-fish : an old sailor : a pirate : (*her.*) a beast like a talbot with dorsal fin and beaver's tail ; **sea'-dott'erel**, the turnstone ; **sea'-dove**, the little auk ; **sea'-drag'on**, the dragonet : the fish Pegasus : an Australian leafy sea-horse ; **sea'-drome**, a floating aerodrome ; **sea'-duck**, any duck of the pochard group ; **sea'-dust**, dust from distant land falling at sea ; **sea'-ea'gle**, erne or other Haliaetus : the eagle-ray ; **sea'-ear**, an earshell (Haliotis) ; **sea'-eel**, a conger ; **sea'-egg**, a sea-urchin ; **sea'-el'ephant**, the elephant-seal ; **sea'-fan**, an alcyonarian coral with fan-like skeleton ; **sea'fārer**, a traveller by sea, usu. a sailor ; **sea'fāring.**— Also *adj.*—*ns.* **sea'-feath'er**, a feathery alcyonarian, sea-pen ; **sea'-fight**, a battle between ships at sea ; **sea'-fir**, a sertularian colony ; **sea'-fire**, phosphorescence at sea ; **sea'-fish**, any salt-water or marine fish ; **sea'-fish'er** ; **sea'-fish'ing** ; **sea'-floor**, the bottom of the sea ; **sea'-foam**, the froth of the sea ; **sea'-fog**, a fog coming from the sea.—*n.pl.* **sea'-folk**, seafaring people.— *ns.* **sea'-food**, (*U.S.*) food got from the sea, esp. shellfish ; **sea'-fowl**, a sea-bird ; **sea'-fox**, the thresher, or fox-shark ; **sea'-front**, the side of the land, of a town, or of a building that looks towards the sea : a promenade with its buildings fronting the sea ; **sea'-froth**, the foam of the sea ; **sea'-fur'below**, a brown seaweed (Saccorhiza) with a bulb of tentacular outgrowths above the primary holdfast ; **sea'-gate**, a seaward gate of a tidal basin, &c. : an outlet to the sea ; **sea'-gill'iflower**, thrift ; **sea'-gin'ger**, millepore coral ; **sea'-gir'dle**, tangle, esp. *Laminaria digitata.*— *adj.* **sea'-girt**, surrounded by sea.—*ns.* **sea'-god**, -godd'ess, a god, goddess, ruling over or dwelling in the sea.—*adj.* **sea'-gōing**, sailing on the deep sea : suitable for deep-sea voyages.—*ns.* **sea'-gown**, (*Shak.*) a short-sleeved garment worn at sea ; **sea'-grape**, any plant of the genus Ephedra, or its fruit : seaside-grape : glasswort : gulf-weed : (in *pl.*) cuttlefish eggs in masses ; **sea'-grass**, a grass or grasslike plant growing by or in the sea—Enteromorpha, thrift, grasswrack, &c.—*n.* and *adj.* **sea'-green**, green like the sea.—Also **sea'-water-green** (*Shak.*).—*ns.* **sea'-gull**, a gull : (*N.Z.*) a dock-labourer not yet admitted to a union ; **sea'-haar**, (*Scot.* and *N.E. England*) a haar coming from the sea ; **sea'-hare**, a tectibranch gasteropod (Aplysia) with ear-like tentacles ; **sea'-**

hawk, a skua; **sea′-heath′**, a wiry heath-like pink-flowered plant (Frankenia) of salt-marshes and chalk-cliffs; **sea′-hedge′hog**, a sea-urchin: a globe-fish; **sea′-hog**, a porpoise; **sea′-holl′y**, eryngo; **sea′horse**, the fabulous hippocampus: Hippocampus or kindred fish: the walrus: (*obs.*) the hippopotamus; **sea′-hound**, a dogfish; **sea′-ice′**.—*adj.* **sea′-island**, (of cotton) of the kind grown on the islands off the coast of South Carolina.—*ns.* **sea′-jell′y**, a jellyfish; **sea′-kale**, a fleshy glaucous cruciferous seaside plant (*Crambe maritima*) cultivated for its blanched sprouts; **sea′-king**, a king of the merfolk: Poseidon or Neptune: a viking chief; **sea′-lane**, a navigable passage between islands, ships, icefloes, &c.; **sea′-lark**, a name for various shore-birds, as sandpipers: the rock-pipit; **sea′-lav′ender**, a plumbaginaceous genus (Statice) of salt-marsh plants; **sea′-law**, maritime law, esp. mediaeval customary law; **sea′-law′yer**, a captious sailor: a shark.—*n.pl.* **sea′-legs**, ability to walk on a ship's deck when it is pitching or rolling.—*ns.* **sea′-lem′on**, a doridoid; **sea′-len′til**, gulf-weed; **sea′-leop′ard**, a spotted seal of the southern seas: wolf-fish skin; **sea′-lett′er**, **-brief**, a document of description that used to be given to a ship at the port where she was fitted out; **sea′-lett′uce**, a seaweed (Ulva) with flat translucent green fronds —green laver; **sea′-lev′el**, the mean level of the surface of the sea.—*adj.* **sea′-like**, like the sea.—*adv.* in the manner of the sea.—*ns.* **sea′-lil′y**, a crinoid; **sea′-line**, a coast-line: a sea-horizon: a line for sounding or fishing in deep water; **sea′-lion**, a seal with external ears and with hind flippers turned forward (usu. excluding the sea-bears or fur-seals): (*her.*) a lion with the tail of a fish; **sea′-loach**, a rockling; **sea′-loch**, (*Scot.*) a lakelike arm of the sea; **sea′-long′worm**, a long nemertean (Lineus); **sea′-lord**, a naval member of the Board of Admiralty; **sea′-lungs**, a ctenophoran; **sea′-maid**, (*Shak.*) a mermaid: a sea-nymph; **sea′man**, a sailor: a man other than an officer or apprentice, employed aboard ship: a merman.—*adjs.* **sea′manlike**, showing good seamanship; **sea′manly**, characteristic of a seaman.—*ns.* **sea′manship**, the art of handling ships at sea; **sea′-marge**, the margin of the sea; **sea′mark**, a mark of tidal limit: any object serving as a guide to those at sea: a signal of danger; **sea′-mat**, hornwrack (Flustra), a common polyzoan like a flat horny seaweed; **sea′-maw**, (now *Scot.*) a sea-mew; **sea′-mew**, any gull; **sea′-mile**, a geographical or nautical mile; **sea′-milk′wort**, Glaux; **sea′-mon′ster**, any huge marine animal, esp. fabulous; **sea′-moss**, carrageen: seaweed: a polyzoan; **sea′-mouse**, an elliptical polychaet (Aphrodite) covered with iridescent silky hairs; **sea′-nett′le**, a jellyfish; **sea′-nymph**, a minor sea-goddess; **sea′-on′ion**, the officinal squill; **sea′-or′ach(e)**, any seaside species of orach; **sea′-or′ange**, a large globose orange-coloured holothurian; **sea′-ott′er**, a N. Pacific animal (Enhydris) akin to the true otters: its silvery brown fur, now very rare; **sea′-owl′**, the lumpsucker; **sea′-parr′ot**, a puffin; **sea′-pass**, a neutral ship's passport in wartime; **sea′-pass′age**, a journey by sea; **sea′-path′**, (*Milt.*) a way that a fish may take; **sea′-pay′**, pay for actual service on a ship in commission; **sea′-pen′**, a feather-like alcyonarium (Pennatula or kindred form): a squid's internal shell; **sea′-perch**, a bass or other fish of the Serranidae; **sea′-pie**, a sailor's dish made of salt-meat, vegetables, and dumplings baked: the oyster-catcher; **sea′-piece**, a picture representing a scene at sea; **sea′-pig**, a porpoise: a dolphin: a dugong; **sea′-pike′**, a pike-like marine fish of various kinds—robalo, belone, hake, &c.; **sea′-pink**, thrift; **sea′plane**, an aeroplane with floats instead of landing-wheels; **sea′plane-carr′ier**, a ship that carries seaplanes; **sea′-poach′er**, the pogge; **sea′-por′cupine**, the globe-fish (Diodon); **sea′port**, a port or harbour on the sea: a place with such a harbour; **sea′-power**, a nation strong **at sea**: naval strength; **sea′-purse**, a mermaid's

purse; **sea′-purs′lane** (see **purslane**); **sea′-quake**, a seismic disturbance at sea; **sea′-rān′ger**, in the Girl Guide organisation a ranger who trains specially in seamanship and the like; **sea′rat**, a pirate; **sea′-reed**, marram-grass; **sea′-risk**, hazard of injury or loss by sea; **sea′-road**, a route followed by ships; **sea′-robb′er**, a pirate; **sea′-rob′in**, an American fish (esp. Prionotus) of the gurnard family, with red or brown colouring; **sea′-rock′et**, a fleshy cruciferous seaside plant (Cakile); **sea′-room**, space to manoeuvre a ship without danger; **sea′-rose′mary**, (*U.S.*) sea-lavender; **sea′-rō′ver**, a pirate; **sea′-rō′ving**, piracy; **sea′-salt**, salt got from sea-water.—*adj.* salt as the sea.—*ns.* **sea′sand**, sands of the seashore; **sea′-sat′yre**, (*Spens.*) a sea-monster of some kind; **sea′scape**, a sea-piece; **sea′-scor′pion**, a scorpion-fish: a father-lasher (*Cottus scorpius*); **sea′-scout**, a member of an offshoot of the Boy Scouts trained in seamanship and the like; **sea′-scout′ing**; **sea′-ser′pent**, an enormous marine animal of serpent-like form, frequently seen and described by credulous sailors, imaginative landsmen, and common liars: a sea-snake; **sea′-ser′vice**, service on board ship; **sea′-shell′**, a marine shell; **sea′shore**, the land immediately adjacent to the sea: (*law*) the foreshore.—*adj.* **sea′-should′ring** (*Spens.*).—*n.* **sea′-shrub′**, a sea-fan.—*adj.* **sea′-sick′**, sick owing to the rolling of a vessel at sea: (*Shak.*) travel-worn. — *ns.* **seasick′ness**; **sea′side**, the neighbourhood of the sea.—Also *adj.*—*ns.* **sea′side-grape′**, the grape-tree (Coccoloba) or its fruit; **sea′-sleeve′**, a cuttle-fish; **sea′-slug**, a nudibranch: a holothurian; **sea′-snail**, any snail-like marine gasteropod: an unctuous fish (Liparis) akin to the lumpsucker; **sea′-snake**, a snake that lives in the sea, esp. of the very venomous family Hydrophidae of the Indian and Pacific oceans: the sea-serpent; **sea′-snipe**, a sandpiper: the snipe-fish; **sea′-sol′dier**, a marine; **sea′-sorr′ow**, (*Shak.*) afflictions at sea; **sea′-spī′der**, a pycnogonid; **sea′-squirt**, an ascidian; **sea′-star′**, a starfish; **sea′-stick**, a herring cured at sea; **sea′-stock**, fresh provisions for use at sea; **sea′-storm′**; **sea′-strand′**; **sea′-sur′geon**, a tropical genus (Acanthurus) of spiny-finned fishes with a lancet-like spine ensheathed on each side of the tail; **sea′-swall′ow**, a tern: the storm petrel: a flying-fish. — *adj.* (*Shak.*) **sea′-swall′ow′d**.—*ns.* **sea′-swine**, a porpoise: the ballan-wrasse; **sea′-tang**, **-tan′gle**, tangle; **sea′-term**, a nautical word.—*adj.* **sea(s)′-tost** (*Shak.*).—*ns.* **sea′-trout**, the salmon-trout (*Salmo trutta*), or its variety the bull-trout (var. *eriox*): extended to various other fishes in U.S. and Australia; **sea′-turn**, a gale from the sea; **sea′-tur′tle**, a marine turtle: a black guillemot; **sea′-ū′nicorn**, the narwhal; **sea′-ur′chin**, one of the Echinoidea, a class of Echinoderms with globular, ovoid, or heart-shaped, sometimes flattened body and shell of calcareous plates, without arms; **sea′-view′**, a view of the sea: a seascape; **sea′-wall′**, a wall to keep out the sea.—*adj.* **sea′-walled**, walled against or by the sea. —*adj.* and *adv.* **sea′ward**, towards the sea or the open sea.—*n.* the seaward side, direction, or position.—*adj.* and *adv.* **sea′wardly.**—*adv.* **sea′-wards.**—*ns.* **sea′-ware**, seaweed; **sea′-wa′ter**, water of or from the sea; **sea′-wave**; **sea′-way**, a way by sea: progress through the waves: a heavy sea; **sea′weed**, marine algae collectively: any marine alga; **sea′-whis′tle**, a seaweed (*Ascophyllum nodosum*) whose bladders can be made into whistles; **sea′-wife**, a kind of wrasse; **sea′-wind′**, a wind from the sea; **sea′-wing**, a sail; **sea′-wolf**, the wolf-fish: the bass: (*obs.*) the sea-elephant: a viking: a pirate; **sea′-woman**, a mermaid; **sea′-worm**, any marine worm.—*adj.* **sea′-worn**, worn by the sea or by seafaring.—*n.* **sea′worthiness.**—*adj.* **sea′worthy**, fit for sea: able to endure stormy weather.—*n.* **sea′-wrack**, coarse seaweeds of any kind: grass-wrack.—**all at sea**, out of one's reckoning: completely at a loss; **at full sea**, at full tide; **at**

Neutral vowels in unaccented syllables : *el′ə-mənt, in′fənt, ran′dəm*

sea, away from land: on the ocean: astray;
go to sea, to become a sailor; **heavy sea,** a sea
in which the waves run high; **molten sea,** the
great brazen laver of 1 Kings vii. 23-26; **short
sea,** a sea in which the waves are choppy, irregular,
and interrupted; **the four seas,** those bounding
Great Britain. [O.E. *sǽ*; Du. *zee*, Ger. *see*,
O.N. *sér*, Dan. *sö*.]

seacunny, *sē'kun-i, n.* a lascar steersman or quartermaster. [App. Pers. *sukkānī*—Ar. *sukkān*, rudder,
confused with *con* and **con.**]

seal, *sēl, n.* a piece of wax, lead or other material,
stamped with a device and attached as a means of
authentication or attestation: a wafer, circular
mark, or other substitute: a piece of wax, &c.,
stamped or not, used as a means of keeping closed
a letter, door, &c.: the design stamped: an
engraved stone or other stamp for impressing a
device, or a trinket of like form: a confirming
token: that which closes: an obligation to secrecy:
an impression: a device to prevent passage of a
gas: water in a gas-trap: an otter's (or other)
footprint.—*v.t.* to set a seal to: to stamp: to
fasten with a seal: to confirm: to ratify: to
close up: to enclose: to settle irrevocably: to
set apart.—*v.i.* to set one's seal to something.—
n. seal'-cyl'inder, a cylinder-seal.—*adj.* sealed.
—*ns.* seal'-engrav'ing, the art of engraving seals;
seal'er; seal'ing; seal'ing-day, (*Shak.*) a day
for sealing; **seal'ing-wax,** formerly beeswax, now
usually a composition of shellac, turpentine,
vermilion or other colouring matter, &c., for
sealing—also (*obs.*) **seal'-wax; seal'-pipe,** a dip-
pipe; **seal'-ring,** a signet-ring.—**Great Seal,** the
state seal of the United Kingdom; **Privy Seal,**
the seal appended to grants, and in Scotland
authenticating royal grants of personal rights;
sealed book, something beyond one's knowledge
or understanding; **set one's seal to,** to give one's
authority or assent to; **the seals,** symbolically
the office of Lord Chancellor or of Secretary of
State; **under seal,** authenticated; **under sealed
orders,** under orders only to be opened at sea.
[O.Fr. *seel*—L. *sigillum*, dim. of *signum*, a mark.]

seal, *sēl, n.* a member of the Pinnepedia, usually
excluding the walrus and often excluding the
otaries: sealskin.—*adj.* of seal or sealskin.—*v.i.*
to hunt seals.—*ns.* seal'er, a seal-fisher; seal'ery,
seal-fishery; seal'-fish'er, a hunter of seals: a
sealing ship; **seal'-fish'ing, seal'ing; seal'-
rook'ery,** a seals' breeding-place; **seal'skin,** the
prepared fur of the fur-seal, or an imitation (as of
rabbit-skin, or of mohair): a garment made of
this.—Also *adj.* [O.E. *seolh* (gen. *séoles*); O.N.
selr.]

seal. Same as **seel** (1).

seal, *sēl, v.t.* to tie up.—*n.* a rope or chain for
tying up an animal. [O.E. *sǽlan*—*sál*, rope.]

sealgh, sealch, *selhh, n.* (*Scot.*) a seal. [See **seal.**]

sealyham, *sēl'i-əm, n.* (in full **sealyham terrier**)
a long-bodied, short-legged, hard-coated terrier,
first bred at *Sealyham* in Pembrokeshire.

seam, seame, *sēm, n.* (*Shak.*) grease: hog's lard
(*Scot.* **saim,** *sām*).—*v.t.* to grease. [O.Fr. *saim*,
O.E. *seime*; cf. L. *sagīna*, stuffing, feasting.]

seam, *sēm, n.* a line of junction between edges sewn
together, or between other edges generally: the
turned-up edges of such a line on the wrong side
of the cloth: ornamentation of such a junction:
a suture: a crack: the mark of a cut: a wrinkle:
a stratum, esp. if thin or valuable: a piece of
sewing-work.—*v.t.* to join, furnish, or mark with
seams: to pick out the seams of.—*ns.* seam'er;
seam'iness; seam'ing-lace, a lace, braid, &c.,
to insert in or cover seams.—*adjs.* seam'less;
seam'-rent, rent along a seam.—*ns.* seam'-set,
a tool for flattening seams in metal, &c.; **seamster**
(*sem'*), **seam'stress** (see **sempster**); **seam'-
stressy,** (*Sterne*) sewing.—*adj.* seamy (*sēm'i*),
having a seam or seams.—*n.* seam'y-side, (*Shak.*)
the wrong side of a garment: hence the disreputable side or aspect. [O.E. *séam*—*síwian*, to
sew; Du. *zoom*, Ger. *saum.*]

seam, *sēm, n.* a pack-horse load (e.g. 8 bushels of
grain, 9 pecks of apples, 120 lb. of glass): a

cartload. [O.E. *séam*, a burden—L.L. *sauma*—
Gr. *sagma*, a pack-saddle.]

sean, *sēn.* Same as **seine.**

séance, *sā'än⁸s, n.* a sitting, esp. of psychical
researchers or of spiritualists. [Fr.,—L. *sedēre*,
to sit.]

seannachie, *sen'ə-hhē, n.* a Highland or Irish
genealogist and transmitter of family tradition.—
Also **seann'achy, senn'achie.** [Gael. *seana-
chaidh.*]

sear, *sēr, n.* the catch that holds a gun at cock or
half-cock.—**tickle(d) a th' sere,** (*Shak.*) ready to
go off. [Cf. O.Fr. *serre*—L. *sera*, a bar.]

sear, *sēr, adj.* (usu. **sere**) dry and withered:
(*Spens.* **seare**) burning.—*v.i.* (rarely **sere**) to
become sere.—*v.t.* to make sere: to dry up: to
scorch: to brand: to cauterise: to render callous
or insensible.—*n.* a mark of searing.—*adj.* **seared.**
—*n.* seared'ness.—*n.* and *adj.* sear'ing.—*ns.*
sear'ing-iron; sear'ness, sere'ness.—**the sere,**
the (so *Shak.*; not and) **yellow leaf,** the autumn
of life. [O.E. *séar,* dry, *séarian,* to dry up; L.G.
soor, Du. *zoor.*]

search, *sərs,* **search,** *sərch, v.t.* to sift.—*n.* a sieve.
[O.Fr. *saas*; *r* unexplained.]

search, *sərch, v.t.* to explore all over with a view
to finding something: to examine closely: to
examine for hidden articles by feeling all over:
to ransack: to scrutinise: to probe: to penetrate
all parts of: to put to the test: to seek out (usu.
with *out*).—*v.i.* to make a search.—*n.* the act
or power of searching: thorough examination:
quest: (*Shak.*) a search-party.—*adj.* search'able.
—*n.* search'er, one who searches: one appointed
to search, as a custom-house officer: an inspector
of various kinds: a probe.—*adj.* search'ing,
penetrating: thorough-going.—*adv.* search'ingly.
—*n.* search'ingness.—*adj.* search'less, unsearch-
able.—*ns.* search'light, a lamp and reflector
throwing a strong beam of light for picking out
objects by night: the light so projected; **search'-
par'ty,** a party sent out in search of somebody or
something; **search'-warr'ant,** a warrant authorising the searching of a house, &c.—**right of search,**
the right of a belligerent to search neutral ships
for contraband of war. [O.Fr. *cercher* (Fr. *chercher*)
L. *circāre*, to go about—*circus*, a circle.]

sease, seasd, seasure (*Spens., Milt.*). See under
seize.

season, *sē'zn, n.* one of the four divisions of the
year: the usual, natural, legal, or appropriate
time, or time of year for anything: any particular
time: time, esp. of some continuance, but not
long: (*coll.*) a season ticket: (*obs.*) seasoning.—
v.t. to mature: to temper: to bring into suitable
condition: to inure: to render savoury: to
flavour: to imbue: (*Shak.*) to preserve from
decay: (*Shak.*) to mature, confirm, imbue with
the flavour of.—*v.i.* to become seasoned.—*adj.*
sea'sonable, in due season: timely.—*n.* sea'sonableness.—*adv.* sea'sonably.—*adj.* sea'sonal,
according to season.—*adv.* sea'sonally.—*adj.*
sea'soned.—*ns.* sea'soner; sea'soning, the process or act by which anything is seasoned: the
process of acclimatisation: that which is added
to food to give relish: in diamond-cutting, the
charging of the laps or wheels with diamond-dust
and oil: the coating of dyed leather with liquid
albumen; **sea'soning-tub,** a trough in which
dough is set to rise.—*adj.* sea'sonless, without
difference of seasons.—**close season,** close time;
in season, ripe, fit and ready for use: allowed to
be killed: fit to be eaten; **in season and out of
season,** at all times; **out of season,** inopportune:
not in season; **season ticket,** a ticket valid any
number of times within a specified period. [O.Fr.
seson (Fr. *saison*)—L. *satiō, -ōnis,* a sowing.]

seat, *sēt, n.* anything used or intended for sitting
on: a chair, bench, saddle, &c.: part of a chair
on which the body rests: a sitting: a mode of
sitting: a place where one may sit, as in a theatre,
church, &c.: a right to sit: a constituency:
membership: that part of the body or of a garment
on which one sits: that on which anything rests:
site, situation: a place where anything is located,

settled, or established: post of authority: a throne: a capital city: station: abode: mansion: sitting-room.—*v.t.* to place on a seat: to cause to sit down: to place in any situation, site, &c.: to establish: to fix: to assign a seat to: to furnish with a seat or seats: to fit accurately: to make baggy by sitting.—*v.i.* (*Spens.*) to sit or lie down: to become baggy by sitting.—*adj.* seat´ed.— *ns.* -sea´ter, (in composition) a vehicle seated for so many; seat´ing, the taking, provision, or arrangement of seats: a supporting surface: material for seats.—*adj.* seat´less.—*ns.* seat´-rent, payment for a church sitting; seat´-stick, a walking-stick that can be made to serve as a seat. —lord of seat, a lord of Session; take a seat, to sit down. [O.N. *sæti*, seat; cf. O.E. *sæt*, ambush.]

se-baptist, *sē-bap´tist, n.* one who baptises himself. [L. *sē*, himself.]

Sebat. See Shebat.

sebesten, *si-bes´tən, n.* an Oriental boraginaceous tree (Cordia): its edible plum-like fruit. [Ar. *sabastān*.]

sebum, *sē´bəm, n.* the fatty secretion that lubricates the hair and skin.—*adjs.* sebaceous (*si-bā´shəs*), tallowy: of, like, of the nature of, or secreting sebum; sebacic (*si-bas´ik*), applied to an acid, (CH₂)₈(COOH)₂, got from fats.—*n.* sebate (*sē´bāt*), a salt of sebacic acid.—*adjs.* sebif´erous (*si-*), bearing fatty matter; sebif´ic, producing fatty matter.—*n.* seborrhoea (*seb-ə-rē´ä*), excessive discharge from the sebaceous glands.—*adj.* sebor-rhoe´ic. [L. *sēbum*, suet.]

sebundy, *si-bun´di, n.* Indian irregular soldiery or soldier. [Urdu *sibandī.*]

sec, *sek, adj.* dry, of wines. [Fr.]

secant, *sē´kant, sek´ənt, adj.* cutting.—*n.* a cutting line: (*trig.*) *orig.*, a straight line from the centre of a circle through one end of an arc to the tangent from the other end: *now*, as a function of an angle, the ratio of the hypotenuse to the base of a right-angled triangle formed by dropping a perpendicular from a point on one side of the angle to the other (negative if the base is the side produced)—in trigonometrical notation written sec. [L. *secāns*, -*āntis*, pr.p. of *secāre*, to cut.]

sécateur, *sek´ə-tər, n.* (usu. in *pl.*) pruning-shears. [Fr.]

secco, *sek´kō, n.* (*mus.*) unaccompanied: plain.— *n.* painting on dry plaster. [It., dry—L. *siccus.*]

secede, *si-sēd´, v.i.* to withdraw, esp. from a party, religious body, federation, or the like.—*ns.* secē´der, one who secedes: one of a body of Presbyterians (Secession Church; see presbyterian) w'.o seceded from the Church of Scotland about -733); secession (-*sesh´ən*), the act of seceding: a body of seceders.—Also *adj.*—*ns.* secess´ionism: secess´-ionist (*U.S.* slang also secesh´, secesh´er), one who favours or joins in secession.—Also *adjs.*— War of Secession, the American Civil War. [L. *sēcēdĕre*, *sēcessum*, *sē*-, apart, *cēdĕre*, to go.]

secern, *si-sərn´, v.t.* to separate: to discriminate: to secrete.—*n.* and *adj.* secern´ent.—*n.* secern´-ment. [L. *sēcernere*, *sēcrētum*, to separate.]

seckel, *sek´l, n.* a variety of pear. [Owner's name.]

seclude, *si-klōōd´, v.i.* to shut off, esp. from association or influence.—*adj.* seclud´ed, retired: withdrawn from observation or society.—*adv.* seclud´edly.—*ns.* seclusion (*si-klōō´zhən*), the act of secluding: the state of being secluded: retirement: privacy: solitude; seclu´sionist.—*adj.* seclu´sive (-*siv*), tending to or favouring seclusion. [L. *sēclūdĕre*, -*clūsum*,—*sē*-, apart, *claudĕre*, to shut.]

secodont, *sek´ə-dont, adj.* with cutting back teeth. —Also *n.* [L. *secāre*, to cut, Gr. *odous, odontos*, tooth.]

second, *sek´ənd, adj.* next after or below the first: other, alternate: additional: supplementary: another, as it were: inferior: (*gram.*) referring to the person or persons addressed: (*Shak.*) helpful, favouring.—*adv.* next after the first: in the second place.—*n.* one who, or that which, is second or of the second class: a place in the second class: one who attends another in a duel or a prize fight: a supporter: the 6oth part of a minute

of time, or of angular measurement: (*gram.*) the second person: (*mus.*) the interval between successive tones of the diatonic scale: (in *pl.*) goods of a second quality.—*v.t.* to follow: to act as second to: to back: to further: to assist: to encourage: to support after the mover of a nomination or resolution: (*mus.*) to sing second to: to follow up with another: (*mil.*; *si-kond´*, -*goond´*) to transfer temporarily to some special employment.—*n.* Sec´ond-ad´ventist, one who expects a second coming of Christ.—*adv.* sec´ond-arily. — *n.* sec´ondariness. — *adj.* sec´ondary, subordinate: subsidiary: of a second order: of a second stage: derivative: induced: of education, between primary and higher: of a feather, growing in the second joint of the wing: Secondary, (*geol.*) Mesozoic.—*n.* sec´ondary, a subordinate: a delegate or deputy: a satellite: that which is secondary, as a feather, coil, &c.—*ns.* and *adjs.* sec´ond-best, next to the best (come off second-best, to get the worst of a contest); sec´ond-class, of the class next to the first.—*ns.* sec´ond-day´, Monday; seconde (*si-kond´*, *sə-gon*³*d*; Fr. *fem.*), a position in parrying; sec´onder, one who seconds a motion or nomination: a supporter: a member of a second group.—*n.* and *adj.* sec´ond-floor (see floor).—*adj.* sec´ond-hand´, derived from another: not original: already used by a previous owner: dealing in second-hand goods.— *n.* (*sek´*) a hand that indicates seconds.—*adv.* indirectly, at second hand: after use by a previous owner.—*ns.* sec´ond-in-command´, the next under the commanding officer; sec´ond-lieuten´ant, an army officer of lowest commissioned rank— formerly ensign or cornet.—*adv.* sec´ondly, in the second place.—*ns.* sec´ond-mark, the character ″, used for seconds of arc or time or for inches; secondo (-*on´dō*; *It.*), the lower part in a duet. —*adj.* sec´ond-rate, inferior: mediocre.—*ns.* second-rāt´er; sec´onds-hand, a hand that marks seconds; sec´ond-sight´, a gift of prophetic vision attributed to certain persons, esp. Highlanders; sec´onds-pen´dulum, a pendulum that makes one swing a second.—at second hand, through an intermediate source, indirectly: by hearsay; Second Advent, Coming, a second coming of Christ; secondary alcohol, one containing the group CH·OH; secondary battery, cell, one in which the chemical action is reversible; secondary coil, one carrying an induced current; second ballot, a system of election whereby a second vote is taken, the candidate or candidates who received fewest votes in the first ballot being eliminated; second childhood, mental weakness in extreme old age; second cousin, one who has the same pair of great-grandparents, but different grandparents: (loosely) a first cousin's child, or a parent's first cousin (properly *first cousin once removed*); second nature, a deeply ingrained habit; second story, the first floor; second thoughts, reconsideration; second wind, recovery of breath in prolonged exertion. [Fr.,— L. *secundus—sequī, secūtus*, to follow.]

secret, *sē´krit, adj.* kept back from knowledge of others: guarded against discovery or observation: unrevealed: hidden: secluded: recondite, occult: preserving secrecy: admitted to confidence, privy. —*adv.* (*poet.*) secretly.—*n.* a fact, purpose, method, &c., that is kept undivulged: participation in knowledge of such a fact: (*obs.*) a nostrum: anything unrevealed or unknown: secrecy: (*obs.*) a secret or private place: a piece of armour hidden by clothes: the key or principle that explains or enables: an inaudible prayer, esp. in the Mass: (in *pl.*; *obs.*) external sex organs.— *n.* secrecy (*sē´kri-si*), the state or fact of being secret: concealment: seclusion: confidence: power or habit of keeping secrets: the keeping of secrets: a secret.—*n.pl.* secreta (*si-krē´tä*), products of secretion.—*ns.* se´cretage, treatment of furs with mercury before pelting; secretaire (*sek-ri-tār´*), a secret repository: a writing-desk, escritoire.—*adj.* secretarial (*sek-ri-tā´ri-əl*).—*ns.* secretār´iat(e) (-*ət*), secretaryship: a secretary's office: a body of secretaries; sec´retary (-*tər-i*), one employed to write or transact business for another or for a society, company, &c.: the minister at the head of certain departments of state: a secretaire: an old legal style of hand-writing (**secretary hand**): type in imitation of it (**secretary type**); **sec′retary-bird′**, a long-legged snake-eating African bird of prey (Ser-pentarius)—said to be named from the tufts of feathers at the back of its head like pens stuck behind the ear; **sec′retaryship**, the office, duties, or art of a secretary.—*v.t.* **secrete** (si-krēt′), to hide: to appropriate secretly: to form and separate by the activity of living matter.—*ns.* **secrē′tin**, a hormone that stimulates the pancreas; **secrē′tion**, the act of secreting: that which is secreted: a mass of mineral matter formed by inward growth in a cavity.—*adjs.* **secrē′tional**; **secrē′tive** (sometimes sē′kri-tiv), given to secrecy: very reticent: indicative of secrecy.—*adv.* **secrē′-tively.**—*n.* **secrē′tiveness.**—*adv.* **sē′cretly, in secret**: in concealment: inaudibly (of prayers).—*n.* **sē′cretness.**—*adj.* **secrē′tory**, secreting.—**in secret**, with precautions against being known: in confidence, as a secret: secretly; **in the secret**, admitted to, participating in, knowledge of the secret; **of secret**, (*Shak.*) of a secret character; **open secret** (see **open**); **secret agent**, one em-ployed in secret service; **Secretary of State**, a cabinet minister holding one of the more important portfolios (in *U.S.* the foreign secretary); **Secret Service**, a department of government service whose operations are not disclosed: its activities: espion-age. [L. *sēcernĕre*, *sēcrētum*—*sē-*, apart, *cernĕre*, to separate.]

sect, *sekt*, *n.* a body of followers: a school of opinion; esp. in religion or philosophy: a subdivision of one of the main religious divisions of mankind: an organised denomination, used esp. by members of the greater churches to express their disappro-bation of the lesser: a dissenting body: a party: a class of people: (now *illit.*) a sex.—*adjs.* **secta′rial**, distinctive of sect (esp. in India); **secta′rian**, of a sect or sectary: narrow, exclusive: denomina-tional.—*n.* (*hist.*) an Independent: one of a sect: one strongly imbued with the characteristics of a sect. — *v.t.* **secta′rianise.** — *ns.* **secta′rianism**; **sectary** (sekt′ər-i), a follower, a votary: one of a sect: a dissenter; **secta′tor**, (*rare*) an adherent of a school or party. [L. *secta*, a school or following —*sequi*, *secūtus*, to follow, influenced by *secāre*, to cut.]

sect, *sekt*, *n.* (*Shak.*) a cutting.—*adj.* **sectile** (sek′til), capable of being cut with a knife without breaking.—*ns.* **sectility** (-til′i-ti); **sec′tion** (-shən), act of cutting: a division: a portion: one of the parts into which anything may be considered as divided or of which it may be built up: the line of intersection of two surfaces: the surface formed when a solid is cut by a plane: (*geol.*) an exposure of rock in which the strata are cut across: a plan of anything represented as if cut by a plane or other surface: a thin slice for microscopic examin-ation: a one-mile square of American public lands: a subdivision of a company, platoon, battery, &c.: a number of men detailed for a special service: (*U.S.*) a district or region: a frame for a honey-comb: a section-mark.—*v.t.* to divide into sec-tions: to make a section of.—*adj.* **sec′tional**, of a section: in section: built up of sections.—*n.* **sec′tionalism**, class spirit.—*adv.* **sec′tionally.**—*n.* **sec′tion-cutter**, an instrument for making sec-tions for microscopic work.—*v.t.* **sec′tionise**, to section.—*ns.* **sec′tion-mark**, the sign §, used to mark the beginning of a section of a book or as a reference-mark; **sec′tor** (-tər), a plane figure bounded by two radii and an arc: an object of like shape: a length or section of a fortified line or army front: a mathematical instrument con-sisting of two graduated rules hinged together, originally with a graduated arc: a telescope turning about the centre of a graduated arc.—*adjs.* **sec′toral**, of a sector; **sectorial** (-tō′ri-əl), sectoral: adapted for cutting.—*n.* a carnassial tooth. [L. *secāre*, *sectum*, to cut.]

secular, sek′ū-lər, *adj.* pertaining to or coming or observed once in a lifetime, generation, century, age (*Rom. hist.* about 100 to 120 years): appre-ciable only in the course of ages: age-long: age-old: pertaining to the present world, or to things not spiritual: civil, not ecclesiastical: lay: not concerned with religion: not bound by monastic rules (opp. to *regular*): of the secular clergy.—*n.* a layman: an ecclesiastic (as a parish priest) not bound by monastic rules: (*U.S.*) a negro song other than a spiritual.—*n.* **secularisa′tion.**—*v.t.* **sec′-ularise**, to make secular.—*ns.* **sec′ularism**, the belief that the state, morals, education, &c., should be independent of religion: G. J. Holyoake's (1817-1906) system of social ethics.—*n.* and *adj.* **sec′ularist.**—*adj.* **secularist′ic.**—*n.* **secularity** (-lar′-).—*adv.* **sec′ularly.**—**secular arm**, the civil power; **secular games**, (*Rom. hist.*) games held at long intervals; **secular hymn**, a hymn for the secular games. [L. *saeculāris*—*saeculum*, a lifetime, generation.]

secund, sē′kund, also *sek′und*, *si-kund′*, *adj.* (*bot.*) all turned to the same side.—*ns.* **sec′undine** (-*in*, -*īn*), the afterbirth: the inner (rarely outer and second formed) coat of an ovule; **secundogeniture** (-*jen′*), inheritance of or by a second child or son. [L. *secundus*, following, second.]

secure, si-kūr′, *adj.* without care or anxiety: confi-dent: over-confident: free from danger: safe: assured: affording safety: stable: firmly fixed or held.—*adv.* (*poet.*) in security.—*v.t.* to make secure, safe, or certain: to make secure the pos-session of: to establish in security: (*obs.*) to prevent: to seize and guard: to get hold of: to contrive to get: (*obs.*) to plight or pledge: to guarantee: to fasten.—*v.i.* to make sure.—*adj.* **secūr′able.**—*n.* **secūr′ance** (*rare*).—*adv.* **secure′ly.** — *ns.* **secure′ment**; **secure′ness**; **secūr′er** (*obs.*) one who dwells in fancied security; **secūr′ity**, state, feeling, or means of being secure: protection from espionage: certainty: (*arch.*) carelessness: a pledge: a surety: a guarantee: a right conferred on a creditor to make him sure of recovery: (usu. in *pl.*) bonds or certificates in evidence of debt or property.—*adj.* for securing security. [L. *secūrus* —*sē-*, without, *cūra*, care.]

securiform, si-kū′ri-form, *adj.* axe-shaped. [L. *secūris*, axe—*secāre*, to cut, *forma*, form.]

sed, se′d, Miltonic spellings of said (*pa.t.* and *pa.p.*).

sedan, si-dan′, *n.* a covered chair for one, carried on two poles (also **sedan′-chair**): a litter: a palanquin: (*U.S.*) a closed motor-car in one com-partment. [App. not conn. with *Sedan* in France; poss. It. *sedere*, to sit.]

sedate, si-dāt′, *adj.* composed: staid. — *adv.* **sedāte′ly.**—*n.* **sedāte′ness.**—*adj.* **sedative** (sed′ə-tiv), calming: composing: allaying excitement or pain.—*n.* a sedative medicine or agent. [L. *sēdātus*, pa.p. of *sēdāre*, to still.]

sedent, sē′dənt, *adj.* seated.—*adv.* **sedentarily** (sed′ən-tər-i-li).—*n.* **sed′entariness.**—*adj.* **sed′-entary**, sitting much: requiring much sitting: inactive: stationary: not migratory: lying in wait, as a spider: (*zool.*) attached to a substratum. —**sedentary soil**, soil remaining where it was formed. [L. *sedēns, -ēntis* (pr.p.), and *sedentārius*—*sedēre*, to sit.]

sederunt, si-dē′runt, si-dā′rənt, L. sā-dā′roont, *n.* in Scotland a sitting, as of a court: a list of persons present.—**Acts of Sederunt**, ordinances of the Court of Session. [L. *sēdērunt*, there sat—*sedēre*, to sit.]

sedge, *sej*, *n.* any species of Carex or other plant of the Cyperaceae, a family distinguished from grasses by its solid triangular stems and leaf-sheaths without a slit: extended to iris and other plants.—*ns.* **sedge′-bird**, **sedge′-war′bler**, **sedge′-wren**, a common British warbler of watery places. —*adjs.* **sedged**, of sedge: bordered with sedge; **sedg′y**, of like, abounding with sedge. [O.E. *secg*; cf. L.G. *segge*.]

sedigitated, se-dij′i-tā-tid, *adj.* six-fingered. [L. *sēdigitus*—*sex*, six, *digitus*, finger.]

sedilia, si-dil′i-ä, *n.pl.* seats (usu. three, often in niches) for the officiating clergy, on the south side of the chancel :—*sing.* **sedile** (*si-dī'li* ; L. *se-dē'lā*). [L. *sedíle*, pl. *sedília*, seat.]

sediment, *sed'i-mənt*, *n.* what settles at the bottom of a liquid : dregs : a deposit.—*v.t.* to deposit as sediment : to cause or allow to deposit sediment.——*adj.* **sedimentary** (-*men'tər-i*).—*n.* **sedimentā'- tion**, deposition of sediment. — **sedimentary rocks**, those formed by accumulation and deposition of fragmentary materials or organic remains. [L. *sedimentum*—*sedēre*, to sit.]

sedition, *si-dish'ən*, *n.* insurrection : public tumult : vaguely, any offence against the state short of treason.—*n.* **sedi'tionary**, an inciter to sedition : inducement to attempt, otherwise than by lawful means, alteration in church or state.—*adj.* **sedi'- tious**. — *adv.* **sedi'tiously**. — *n.* **sedi'tiousness**. [O.Fr.,—L. *sēditiō*, -*ōnis*—*sēd-*, away, *īre*, *ītum*, to go.]

seduce, *si-dūs'*, *v.t.* to draw aside from party, belief, allegiance, service, duty, &c. : to lead astray : to entice : to corrupt : to induce to perform an act of unchastity with oneself.—*ns.* **sedūce'ment**, act of seducing or drawing aside : allurement ; **sedū'cer**.—*n.* and *adj.* **sedū'cing**.— *adv.* **sedū'cingly**.—*n.* **seduction** (*si-duk'shən*), act of seducing : allurement.—*adj.* **seduc'tive**, alluring.—*adv.* **seduc'tively**.—*ns.* **seduc'tiveness** ; **seduc'tor**, one who leads astray :—*fem.* **seduc'- tress**. [L. *sēdūcĕre*, *sēductum*—*sē-*, aside, *dūcĕre*, to lead.]

sedulous, *sed'ū-ləs*, *adj.* assiduous.—*ns.* **sedulity** (*si-dū'li-ti*) ; **sed'ulousness**.—*adv.* **sed'ulously**. [L. *sēdulus*—*sē dolō*, without deception, hence in earnest.]

Sedum, *sē'dəm*, *n.* the stone-crop genus of Crassulaceae. [L. *sēdum*, house-leek.]

see, *sē*, *n.* a seat, esp. of dignity or authority : a throne, esp. a bishop's : the office of bishop of a particular diocese : (wrongly according to some) a cathedral city, also a diocese.—**Holy See**, the papal court. [O.Fr. *se, siet*—L. *sēdēs*, -*is*—*sedēre*, to sit.]

see, *sē*, *v.t.* to perceive by the sense seated in the eye : to perceive mentally : to apprehend : to recognise : to understand : to learn : to be aware by reading : to look at : to judge, to deem : to refer to : to ascertain : to make sure : to make sure of having : to wait upon, escort : to call on : to receive as a visitor : to meet : to consult : to experience : to meet and accept by staking a similar sum : (*Shak.*) to spend on seeing (with *away*).—*v.i.* to have power of vision : to see things well enough : to look or inquire : to be attentive : to consider :—*pa.t.* **saw** (illit. **see, seed, seen**) ; *pa.p.* **seen**.—*imper.*, passing into *interj.*, **see**, look : **behold**.—*n.* (rare) an act of seeing.—*adj.* **see'able**. —*n.* **see'ing**, sight : vision : clear-sightedness : atmospheric conditions for good observation.—*adj.* having sight, or insight : observant : discerning.— *conj.* (also **seeing that**) since : in view of the fact. —*ns.* **see'ing-stone**, a scrying crystal ; **seer** (*sē'ər*), one who sees : (*sēr*) one who sees into the future.— **have seen one's best days**, to be now on the decline ; **let me see**, a phrase employed to express reflection ; **see about**, to consider : do whatever is to be done about : attend to ; **see off**, to accompany at one's departure ; **see out**, to conduct to the door : to see to the end : to outlast ; **see over**, to be conducted all through ; **see through**, to participate in to the end : to back up till difficulties end : to understand the hidden nature of ; **see to**, to look after : to make sure about ; **see what I can do**, do what I can ; **well** (ill) **seen**, well (ill) versed. [O.E. *séon* ; Ger. *sehen*, Du. *zien*.]

eecatchie, *sē'kach-i*, *n.pl.* male Aleutian furseals :—*sing.* **see'catch**. [Russ. *sekach*, prob. from Aleutian Indian.]

eed, *sēd*, *n.* that which is sown : (*bot.*) a multicellular structure by which flowering plants reproduce, consisting of embryo, stored food, and seedcoat, derived from the fertilised ovule : a small hard fruit or part in a fruit, a pip : a seed-like object or aggregate : semen : spawn : condition of having or proceeding to form seed : sown land : grass and clover grown from seed : first principle : germ : a crystal introduced to start crystallisation :

offspring, descendants, race : a small bubble in glass : (*slang*) a tournament player who has been seeded.—*v.i.* to produce seed : to run to seed.—*v.t.* to sow : to sprinkle, powder, dust : to remove seeds from : in lawn-tennis tournaments, &c., to arrange (the draw) so that the best players do not meet in the early rounds : to deal with (good players) in this way.—*ns.* **seed'bed**, a piece of ground for receiving seed ; **seed'box**, a plant capsule ; **seed'cake**, a cake with caraway seeds ; **seed'coat**, the covering derived from the ovule's integuments ; **seed'-coral**, coral in small irregular pieces ; **seed'-corn**, grain for sowing ; **seed'-drill**, a machine for sowing seeds in rows.—*adj.* **seed'ed**, cleaned of seeds : having seeds : bearing seed : full-grown : sown : (*her.*) showing seeds or carpels. —*ns.* **seed'er**, a seed-drill : an apparatus for removing seeds from fruit : a seed-fish ; **seed'- field**, a field in which seed is sown ; **seed'-fish**, a fish about to spawn.—*adv.* **seed'ily**.—*n.* **seed'- iness**.—*n.* and *adj.* **seed'ing**.—*ns.* **seed'-lac**, granular residues of lac after trituration ; **seed'- leaf**, a cotyledon, leaf contained in a seed.—*adjs.* **seed'less** ; **seed'-like**.—*ns.* **seed'ling**, a plant reared from the seed—also *adj.* ; **seed'lip**, a sower's basket (O.E. *sǽdléap*—*léap*, basket) ; **seed'- lobe**, a cotyledon ; **seed'ness**, (*Shak.*) sowing ; **seed'-oil**, oil expressed from seeds ; **seed'-oyster**, a very young oyster ; **seed'-pearl**, a very small pearl ; **seed'-plant**, a spermatophyte or flowering plant : a plant grown from or for seed ; **seed'-plot**, a piece of nursery ground, a hot-bed ; **seed'- potato**, a potato tuber for planting ; **seed'-shop** ; **seeds'man**, a dealer in seeds : a sower ; **seed'- stalk**, the funicle ; **seed'-time**, the season for sowing seeds ; **seed'-vessel**, a dry fruit : the ovary of a flower.—*adj.* **seed'y**, abounding with seed : having the flavour of seeds : not cleared of seeds : run to seed : worn out : out of sorts : shabby.—*n.* **seed'y-toe**, a disease of the horse's foot.—**run to seed** (see **run**). [O.E. *sǽd* ; cf. *sáwan*, to sow ; O.N. *sáth* ; Ger. *saat*.]

seek, *sēk*, *v.t.* to look for : to try to find, get, or achieve : to ask for : to aim at : to resort to, betake oneself to : to advance against : to try : to search, examine.—*v.i.* to make search : (*Milt.*) to resort :—*pa.t.* and *pa.p.* **sought** (*sawt*).—*ns.* **seek'er**, one who seeks : an inquirer : a dissector's probing instrument : a telescopic finder : **Seek'er**, a member of a 17th-century sect who sought for the true church ; **seek-no-fur'ther**, a reddish winter apple.—**seek after**, to go in quest of ; **seek for**, to look for ; **seek out**, to look for and find : to bring out from a hidden place ; **sought after**, in demand ; **to seek**, not to be found : wanting : at a loss to know : defective, faulty. [O.E. *sécan* (pa.t. *sóhte*, pa.p. *gesóht*) ; cf. Ger. *suchen*.]

seel, *sēl*, *v.t.* to sew up the eyelids of, as a hawk : to blindfold : to blind, hoodwink. [O.Fr. *siller*, *ciller*—*cil*—L. *cilium*, eyelid, eyelash.]

seel, **sele**, **seal** (*Scot.* **seil**), *sēl*, *n.* (*prov.*) happiness : good fortune : opportune time : season : time of day.—*adj.* **seel'y**, (*obs.*) fortunate, happy, good : (*Spens.*) simple, innocent : pitiful, wretched, trifling : (*obs.*) to be pitied, poor : foolish (see **silly**).—**pass the seel of the day**, to greet in passing. [O.E. *sǽl*, time, due time, happiness ; see **silly**.]

seel, *sēl*, *v.i.* to heel over suddenly.—*n.* a sudden heeling. [Origin obscure.]

seeld, *sēld*, **seel'ing**, Spenserian forms of **seld**, **ceiling**.

seely. See **seel** (2).

seem, *sēm*, *v.i.* to appear : to appear to oneself : to appear to be : (*Spens.*) to be befitting.—*v.t.* (*arch.*) to beseem, befit.—*ns.* **seem'er** ; **seem'ing**, appearance : semblance : a false appearance : way of thinking.—*adj.* apparent : ostensible.—*adv.* apparently : in appearance only (esp. in composition, as **seem'ing-sim'ple**, **seem'ing-vir'tuous**). —*adv.* **seem'ingly**, apparently : as it would appear.—*n.* **seem'ingness**.—*adj.* **seem(e)'less(e)**, (*Spens.*), unseemly : indecorous.—*ns.* **seem'li- he(a)d** (*Spens.* **seem'lyhed**), seemliness ; **seem'- liness**.—*adj.* **seem'ly** (*comp.* **seem'lier**, *superl.*

seem'liest), becoming: suitable: decent: handsome.—Also *adv.*—**it seems,** it appears: it would
seem; **it would seem,** it turns out: I have been
told; **meseems, meseemed, himseemed,** &c.,
it seems, seemed, to me, &c. [O.N. *sǣma,* to
beseem.]

seen, seer. See **see** (2).

seep, *sēp, v.i.* to ooze, percolate.—*n.* **seep'age.**—
adj. **seep'y.** [Cf. **sipe.**]

seer, *sēr, n.* an Indian weight of widely ranging
amount, officially about 2 lb. [Pers. *sīr.*]

seersucker, *sēr'suk-ər, n.* a thin Indian linen (or
cotton) striped or checked fabric. [Pers. *shīr o
shakkar,* lit. milk and sugar.]

seesaw, *sē'saw, sē'saw, n.* alternate up-and-down
motion: repeated alternation, as a cross-ruff at
cards, sing-song speech: a plank balanced so that
its ends may move up and down alternately: the
sport of rising and sinking on it.—*adj.* going like
a seesaw.—*adv.* in the manner of a seesaw.—
v.i. to play at seesaw: to move or go like a seesaw.
—*v.t.* to make to go up and down. [Prob. a
redup. of **saw,** from a sawyer's jingle—*See saw
sack a down.*]

seethe, *sēdh, v.t.* to boil: to soak to a condition as
if boiled.—*v.i.* to boil: (*lit.* or *fig.*) to surge:
(*pa.t.* **seethed** or **sod**; *pa.p.* **seethed** or **sodd'en**).
—*n.* surge.—*n.* **seeth'er.**—*n.* and *adj.* **seeth'ing.**
[O.E. *sēothan* (*pa.t. séath,* pl. *sudon*; *pa.p. soden*);
O.N. *sjótha,* Ger. *sieden.*]

seewing, a Spenserian spelling of **suing** (see **sue**).

seg, *seg, n.* (*obs.* or *dial.*). Same as **sedge.**

seggar. Same as **saggar.**

seg(h)ol, *se-gōl', n.* a vowel-point in Hebrew with
sound of *e* in *pen,* placed under a consonant,
thus ·.·.—*n.* **seg(h)'ōlate,** a disyllabic noun form
with tone-long vowel in the first and a short
seghol in the second syllable. [Heb.]

segment, *seg'mənt, n.* a part cut off: a portion:
part of a circle, ellipse, &c., cut off by a straight
line, or of a sphere, ellipsoid, &c., by a plane:
a section: one of a linear series of similar portions,
as of a vibrating string between nodes, a somite
or metamere of a jointed animal, **or a joint of an
appendage:** a lobe of a leaf-blade not separate
enough to be a leaflet.—*v.t.* and *v.i.* (also -**ment'**)
to divide into segments.—*adj.* **segmental** (-**ment'l**),
of a segment: by segments: forming or formed
of a segment, segments, arc, or arcs.—*adv.* **seg-
men'tally.**—*adjs.* **seg'mentary, seg'mentate.**—
n. **segmentā'tion.**—*adj.* **segment'ed** (or **seg'**).—
segmental arch, an arch forming an arc of a
circle whose centre is below the springing. [L.
segmentum—*secāre,* to cut.]

segno, *sā'nyō, n.* (*mus.*) a sign to mark the beginning
or end of repetitions—:§:. [It.,—L. *signum,* a
mark.]

sego, *sē'gō, n.* a showy liliaceous plant (*Calochortus*)
of western U.S. [Ute Indian name.]

segreant, *seg'ri-ənt, adj.* (*her.*) gener. understood to
mean with raised wings. [Earlier *sergreant,* origin
unknown.]

segregate, *seg'ri-gāt, v.t.* to set apart: to seclude:
to isolate: to group apart.—*v.i.* to separate out
in a group or groups or mass.—*adj.* set apart.—
n. that which is segregated.—*adj.* **seg'regable.**—
n. **segregā'tion,** act of segregating: state of being
segregated: (*Shak.*) dispersal: (*Mendelism*) separation of dominants and recessives in the second
generation of a cross: a segregated mass or group.
—*adj.* **seg'regative.** [L. *sēgregāre, -ātum*—*sē-,*
apart, *grex, gregis,* a flock.]

seguidilla, *seg-i-dēl'yä, n.* a Spanish dance: a
tune for it, in triple time. [Sp.,—L. *sequī,* to
follow.]

seiche, *sāsh, sesh, n.* a tide-like fluctuation in lakes.
[Swiss Fr.]

Seidlitz, *sed'lits, adj.* applied to an aperient powder
(or rather pair of powders), Rochelle salt and
sodium bicarbonate mixed together, and tartaric
acid—totally different from the mineral water of
Sedlitz in Bohemia.

seignior, *sā', sē'nyər,* **seigneur,** *sen'yər', n.* a title
of address: a feudal lord, lord of a manor.—*ns.*
seign'iorage, seign'orage, lordship: an overlord's royalty on minerals: a percentage on minted
bullion; **sei'gnioralty, seignory.**—*adjs.* **seigniō'-
rial, seigneu'rial, seignoral** (*sān', sen'*), **sign-
ō'rial** (*sin-*), manorial.—*ns.* **seign'iorship; seign'-
(i)ory,** feudal lordship: (*hist.*) the council of an
Italian city-state: (also **seigneurie,** *sen'yə-rē*) a
domain.—**Grand Seignior,** the Sultan of Turkey.
[Fr. *seigneur*—L. *senior, -ōris,* comp. of *senex,* old.
In L.L. *senior* is sometimes equivalent to *dominus,*
lord.]

seil. Same as **sile.**

seine, *sān,* or *sēn, n.* a large vertical fishing-net
whose ends are brought together and hauled.—
v.t. and *v.i.* to catch or fish with a seine.—
ns. **seine'-boat; seine'-fishing; seine'-net;
sein'er; seine'-shooting; sein'ing.** [O.E. *segne*
—L. *sagēna*—Gr. *sagēnē,* a fishing-net.]

seise, *sēz, v.t.* an old spelling of **seize,** still used
legally in the sense of to put in possession:—*pa.p.*
seis'ed, (*Spens.*) reached, attained.—*n.* **seis'in,**
possession (now, as freehold): an object handed
over as a token of possession: (*Scots law*) sasine.

seism, *sīzm, n.* an earthquake.—*adjs.* **seis'mal,
seis'mic.**—*ns.* **seismicity** (-*mis'i-ti*), liability to
or frequency of earthquakes; **seis'mism,** earthquake phenomena; **seis'mogram,** a seismograph
record; **seis'mograph,** an instrument for registering earthquakes; **seismog'rapher.**—*adjs.* **seismograph'ic, -al.**—*n.* **seismog'raphy,** the study of
earthquakes.—*adjs.* **seismolog'ic, -al.**—*ns.* **seismol'ogist; seismol'ogy,** the science of earthquakes; **seismom'eter,** an instrument for measuring earth-movements.—*adjs.* **seismomet'ric, -al.**
—*n.* **seismom'etry.**—*adj.* **seismonas'tic.**—*ns.*
seismonas'ty (Gr. *nastos,* pressed; *bot.*), response
to mechanical shock; **seis'moscope,** an instrument for detecting earthquakes.—*adj.* **seismo-
scop'ic.** [Gr. *seismos,* a shaking—*seiein,* to shake.]

seity, *sē'i-ti, n.* a self: selfhood. [L. *sē,* oneself.]

seize, formerly, and still in legal sense, sense
(*Spens., Shak., Milt.,* **sease, seaze, ceaze,** &c.),
sēz, v.t. to put in legal possession: to fix: to
take possession of: to grasp suddenly, eagerly, or
forcibly: to take by force: to take prisoner: to
apprehend: to lash or make fast: (*naut.* and
Spens.) to reach, attain.—*v.i.* to lay hold: to
clutch: (*Spens.*) to penetrate: to jam or weld
partially for want of lubrication.—*adj.* **seiz'able.**
—*ns.* **seiz'er; seiz'in** (see **seise**); **seiz'ing,** the
action of the verb: a cord to seize ropes with;
seizure (*sē'zhər*), act of seizing: capture: grasp:
thing seized: a sudden fit or attack of illness.
[O.Fr. *saisir*—L.L. *sacīre,* prob. Gmc.; cf. O.H.G.
sazzan, to set, Ger. *setzen,* Eng. *set.*]

sejant, *sē'jənt, adj.* (*her.*) sitting. [For *seiant,* Fr.
séant, pr.p. of *seoir*—L. *sedēre,* to sit.]

sekos, *sē'kos, n.* a sacred enclosure. [Gr. *sēkos.*]

sel, *sel, n.* (*Scot.*) self.

selachian, *si-lā'ki-ən, n.* any fish of the shark
class.—Also *adj.* [Gr. *selachos.*]

seladang, *se-lä'dang,* **sladang,** *slä'dang, n.* the
gaur. [Malay *seladang, saladang.*]

Selaginella, *sel-aj-i-nel'ä, n.* a genus of heterosporous club-mosses constituting the family
Selaginellā'ceae. [Dim. of L. *selāgō, -inis,* a
plant mentioned by Pliny.]

selah, *sē'lä, n.* in the psalms, a Hebrew word
probably meaning pause.

Selbornian, *sel-bor'ni-ən, adj.* of *Selborne* in Hampshire, or of Gilbert White (1720-84), author of
The Natural History of Selborne: (*geol.*) Gault
and Upper Greensand.—*n.* an admirer of Gilbert
White: the Gault and Upper Greensand.

selcouth, *sel'kōōth, adj.* (*Spens.*) strange. [O.E.
sel(d)cúth—*seldan,* seldom, *cúth,* known—*cunnan,*
to know.]

seld, *seld, adj.* (*Spens.*) rare, uncommon.—*adv.*
seldom, rarely.—*adjs.* **seld'seen,** rarely seen;
seld'shown, (*Shak.*) rarely shown. [See **seldom.**]

seldom, *sel'dəm, adv.* rarely.—*adj.* infrequent.—
sel'domness.— *adv.* **sel'dom-times.** [O.E.
seldum, altered (on the analogy of *whilum, whilom*)
from *seldan;* Ger. *selten.*]

sele. Same as **seel** (2).

select, *si-lekt', v.t.* to pick out from a number

preference: (*Austr.*) to free-select.—*adj.* picked out: choice: exclusive. — *adj.* **selec'ted.** — *n.* **selec'tion,** act of selecting: thing or collection of things selected: (*mus.*) a pot-pourri: a horse selected as likely to win a race: free-selection.— *adj.* **selec'tive,** having or exercising power of selection: able to discriminate, e.g. between different frequencies. — *adv.* **selec'tively.** — *ns.* **selectiv'ity** (*sel-*), ability to discriminate; **select'-man,** in New England towns, one of a board of officers chosen to manage local business; **select'-ness**; **select'or.**—**select committee,** a number of members of parliament chosen to report and advise on some matter. [L. *sēligĕre, sēlectum—sē-,* aside, *legĕre,* to choose.]

Selene, *se-lē'nē, n.* the Greek moon-goddess—Artemis, Phoebe.—*n.* **selenate** (*sel'i-nāt*), a salt of selenic acid.—*adj.* **selenic** (*si-lē'nik, -len'ik*), of the moon: of selenium in higher valency (**selenic acid,** H_2SeO_4).—*n.* **selenide** (*sel'i-nīd*), a compound of selenium with an element or radical.—*adj.* **selē'nious,** of selenium in lower valency (**selenious acid,** H_2SeO_3).—*n.* **selenite** (*sel'i-nīt*), a moon-dweller: gypsum, esp. in transparent crystals (anciently supposed to wax and wane with the moon): a salt of selenious acid.—*adj.* **selenitic** (*sel-i-nit'ik*).—*n.* **selenium** (*si-lē'*), a non-metallic element (Se; at. numb. 34) discovered by Berzelius in 1817 and named from its resemblance to tellurium.—*adj.* **selē'nodont** (Gr. *odous, odontos,* tooth), having crescentic ridges on the crowns of the molar teeth.—*ns.* **selē'nograph,** a delineation of the moon; **selenographer** (*sel-in-og'rə-fər*), a student of selenography.—*adjs.* **selenographic** (*si-lē-nə-graf'ik*), **-al.**—*n.* **selenography** (*sel-i-nog'rə-fi*), delineation or description of the moon: study of the moon's physical features.—*adj.* **selēnolog'ical.**—*ns.* **selenol'ogist,** a selenographer; **selenol'ogy,** scientific study of the moon.—**selenium cell,** a photo-electric cell depending on the fact that light increases the electric conductivity of selenium. [Gr. *selēnē,* moon.]

Seleucid, *se-lū'sid, n.* a member of the dynasty (**Seleu'cidae**) that ruled Syria from 312 to 65 B.C., beginning with Alexander's general, *Seleucus I.* (Nicator).—Also *adj.*—*adj.* **Seleu'cidan.**

self, *self, pron.* (*obs., commercial,* or *vulg.*) oneself, myself, himself, &c.—*n.* an identical person, personality, ego: a side of one's personality: identity: personality: what one is: self-interest: a self-coloured plant or animal: a thing (esp. a bow) made in one piece:—*pl.* **selves** (*selvz*); of things in one colour or one piece, **selfs.**—*adj.* (*arch.*) very, same, identical: (*arch.*) own: uniform in colour: made in one piece.—*v.t.* to fertilise by the same individual (self-fertilise), or by the same strain (inbreed).—**one self,** (*Shak.*) one and the same, one only; **one's self** (see **oneself**). [O.E. *self*; Du. *zelf*; Ger. *selbe,* Goth. *silba.*]

self-, *self-,* in composition, acting upon the agent: by, of, in, in relation to, &c., oneself or itself: automatic.—*ns.* **self'-aban'donment,** disregard of self; **self'-abase'ment**; **self'-abnegā'tion,** renunciation of one's own interest: self-denial.—*adj.* **self'-absorbed',** wrapped up in one's own thoughts or affairs.—*ns.* **self'-abuse',** (*Shak.*) self-deception: revilement of oneself: masturbation; **self'-abus'er**; **self'-accusā'tion.** — *adjs.* **self'-accus'atory**; **self'-act'ing,** automatic.—*ns.* **self'-ac'tion,** spontaneous or independent action; **self'-activ'ity,** an inherent power of acting.—*adj.* **self'-adjust'ing,** requiring no external adjustment.—*ns.* **self'-admiss'ion,** (*Shak.*) admission of self-will alone as motive; **self'-advert'isement**; **self'-advertis'er.**—*n.pl.* **self'-affairs',** (*Shak.*) one's own affairs.—*adj.* **self'-affec'ted,** (*Shak.*) affected well towards oneself.—*n.* **self'-affirma'tion,** assertion of the existence of the self.—*adj.* **self'-affright'ed,** (*Shak.*) frightened at oneself.—*n.* **self'-applause'.**—*adjs.* **self'-appoint'ed**; **self'-approv'ing**; **self'-assert'ing, self'-assert'ive,** given to asserting one's opinion or to putting oneself forward.—*n.* **self'-asser'tion.**—*adj.* **self'-assumed',** assumed by one's own act.—*ns.* **self'-**

assump'tion, conceit; **self'-assū'rance,** assured self-confidence. — *adjs.* **self'-assured'**; **self'-bal'anced,** balanced without outward help: stable; **self'-begot', self'-begot'en,** being its own parent, as the phoenix.—*n.* **self'-bind'er,** a reaping-machine with automatic binding apparatus: a portfolio that grips loose sheets.—*adjs.* **self'-blind'ed**; **self'-born',** born of itself, as the phoenix; **self'-borne',** (*Shak.*) perh. carried by and against itself, perh. native-born.—*ns.* **self'-boun'ty,** (*Shak.*) native goodness; **self'-breath',** (*Shak.*) one's own utterances.—*adj.* **self'-cen'tred,** fixed independently: centred in self.—*n.* **self'-char'ity,** (*Shak.*) love of oneself.—*adj.* **self'-clōs'ing,** shutting automatically.—*n.* **self'-cock'er,** a firearm in which the hammer is raised by pulling the trigger.—*adjs.* **self'-cock'ing**; **self'-collect'ed,** self-possessed.— *n.* **self'-colour,** uniform colour: natural colour.—*adj.* **self'-coloured.**—*ns.* **self'-command',** self-control; **self'-commun'ion,** communing with oneself, introspective meditation; **self'-compar'ison,** (*Shak.*) something to compare with oneself; **self'-complā'cence,** satisfaction with oneself, or with one's own performances. — *adj.* **self'-complā'cent.** — *n.* **self'-conceit',** an over-high opinion of oneself, one's own abilities, &c.: vanity.—*adj.* **self'-conceit'ed.** —*ns.* **self'-conceit'edness**; **self'-concentrā'tion,** concentration of one's thoughts upon oneself; **self'-condemnā'tion.**—*adjs.* **self'-condemned',** condemned by one's own actions or out of one's own mouth; **self'-condemn'ing.**—*n.* **self'-con'fidence,** confidence in, or reliance on, one's own powers: self-reliance.—*adj.* **self'-con'fident.**—*adv.* **self'-con'fidently.**—*adj.* **self'-confīd'ing,** relying on one's own powers.—*n.* **self'-congratulā'tion.**—*adjs.* **self'-con'jugate,** conjugate to itself; **self'-con'scious,** conscious of one's own mind and its acts and states: conscious of being observed by others.—*ns.* **self'-con'sciousness**; **self'-con'sequence,** self-importance.—*adjs.* **self'-con'sequent**; **self'-consid'ering,** considering in one's own mind, deliberating.—*n.* **self'-consist'ency,** consistency of each part with the rest: consistency with one's principles.—*adjs.* **self'-consis'tent**; **self'-con'stituted,** constituted by oneself; **self'-consūmed'**; **self'-consūm'ing,** consuming oneself, or itself; **self'-contain'ed,** wrapped up in oneself, reserved: of a house, not approached by an entrance common to others: complete in itself.—*ns.* **self'-contempt'**; **self'-content',** self-complacency; **self'-contradic'tion,** the act or fact of contradicting oneself: a statement whose terms are mutually contradictory.— *adj.* **self'-contradic'tory.** — *n.* **self'-control',** power of controlling oneself.—*adj.* **self'-convict'ed,** convicted by one's own acts or words.— *n.* **self'-convic'tion.**—*adj.* **self'-cov'ered,** (*Shak.*) perh. disguised by oneself, perh. clothed in one's native semblance.—*ns.* **self'-crit'icism,** critical examination and judgment of one's own works and thoughts; **self'-cult'ure,** development and education of one's personality by one's own efforts; **self'-dān'ger,** (*Shak.*) danger to oneself; **self'-deceit',** self-deception.—*adjs.* **self'-deceit'ful**; **self'-deceived'.** — *ns.* **self'-deceiv'er**; **self'-decep'tion,** deceiving oneself; **self'-defence',** defending one's own person, rights, &c. (**art of self-defence,** boxing); **self'-delight',** delight in one's own being or thoughts; **self'-delu'sion,** the delusion of oneself by oneself; **self'-deni'al,** forbearing to gratify one's own appetites or desires.—*adj.* **self'-deny'ing.**—*adv.* **self'-deny'ingly.**—*adj.* **self'-depraved',** depraved by one's own act.—*ns.* **self'-despair',** a despairing view of one's own nature, prospects, &c.; **selfe'-despight',** (*Spens.*) injury to oneself; **self'-destruc'tion,** the destruction of anything by itself: suicide.—*adj.* **self'-destruc'tive.** — *n.* **self'-determinā'tion,** determination without extraneous impulse: direction of the attention or will to an object: the power of a population to decide its own government and political relations or of an individual to live his own life.—*adjs.* **self'-deter'mined**; **self'-deter'mining.**—*n.* **self'-devō'ted.**—*n.* **self'-devō'-**

tion, self-sacrifice.—*adjs.* self'-direct'ed; self'-direct'ing.—*ns.* self'-direc'tion; self'-direct'or; self'-dis'cipline.—*adj.* self'-disliked' (*Spens.* selfe'-dislik'ed).—*n.* self'-dispar'agement.—*adj.* self'-displeased'.—*ns.* self'-dispraise'; self'-distrust'; self'-doubt'.—*adjs.* self'-draw'ing, (*Shak.*) of one's, its, own drawing, or drawn from itself; self'-driv'en; self'-ed'ucated, educated by one's own efforts.—*n.* self'-efface'ment, keeping oneself in the background out of sight: withdrawing from notice or rights.—*adjs.* self'-effac'ing; self'-elect'ed, elected by oneself or itself; self'-elect'ive, having the right to elect oneself or itself, as by co-option of new members.—*ns.* self'-elec'tion; self-end', (*obs.*) a private or selfish end.—*adj.* self'-endeared', -indeared', self-loving.—*ns.* self'-enjoy'ment, internal satisfaction; self'-esteem', good opinion of oneself: self-respect; self'-ev'idence.—*adj.* self'-ev'ident, evident without proof.—*ns.* self'-examina'tion, a scrutiny into one's own state, conduct, &c.; self'-exam'ple, one's own example.—*adj.* self'-excit'ing, itself supplying the exciting current.—*n.* self'-exist'ence.—*adjs.* self'-exist'ent, existing of or by oneself or itself, independent of any other cause; self'-explan'atory, obvious, bearing its meaning in its own face.—*ns.* self'-explica'tion, the power of explaining oneself; self'-express'ion, the giving of expression to one's personality, as in art.—*adjs.* self'-faced', undressed or unhewn, esp. of a stone showing a natural cleavage; self'-fed', fed by itself or automatically: fed upon itself.—*n.* self'-feed'er.—*adj.* self'-feed'ing.—*n.* self'-feel'ing, one's own experience.—*adj.* self'-fer'tile, fertile by its own pollen or sperm.—*ns.* self'-fertilisa'tion; self'-fertil'ity. — *adj.* self'-fig'ured, of one's own devising.—*n.* self'-fill'er, a fountain-pen that can be filled without a dropping-tube.—*adj.* self'-forget'ful, unselfishly forgetful of self.—*adv.* self'-forget'fully.—*adjs.* self'-glazed', glazed in one tint; self'-glo'rious, boastful; self'-gov'erning. —*n.* self'-gov'ernment, self-control: autonomy: government without outside interference: democracy. — *adjs.* self'-gra'cious, gracious towards oneself or spontaneously gracious; self'-harm'ing. —*ns.* self-heal', prunella; self'-heal'ing, spontaneous healing: healing oneself.—Also *adj.*—*ns.* self'-help', doing things for oneself without help of others; self'hood, personal identity: existence as a person: personality: selfishness; self'-humilia'tion; self'-iden'tity, identity of a thing with itself; self'-immola'tion, offering oneself up in sacrifice: suttee; self'-import'ance, an absurdly high sense of one's own importance: pomposity. — *adjs.* self'-import'ant; self'-imposed', taken voluntarily on oneself.—*n.* self'-impregna'tion, impregnation of a hermaphrodite by its own sperm.—*adj.* self'-incompat'ible, having reproductive organs that cannot function together.—*ns.* self'-induc'tance, the property of an electric circuit whereby self-induction occurs; self'-induc'tion, the property of an electric circuit by which it resists any change in the current flowing in it; self'-indul'gence, undue gratification of one's appetites or desires.—*adj.* self'-indul'gent.—*n.* self'-infec'tion, infection of the entire organism from a local lesion.—*adj.* self'-inflict'ed, inflicted by oneself on oneself.—*ns.* self'-insu'rance, laying aside a fund to cover losses; self'-in'terest, private interest: regard to oneself.—*adjs.* self'-in'terested; self'-invi'ted, invited by nobody but oneself; self'-involved', wrapped up in oneself or one's own thoughts: inwoven into itself; self'ish, chiefly or wholly regarding one's own self: void of regard to others. —*adv.* self'ishly.—*ns.* self'ishness; self'ism, concentration upon self: the selfish theory of morals—that man acts from the consideration of what will give him the most pleasure; self'ist.— *adj.* self'-killed'.—*n.* self'-kill'er.—*adj.* self'-know'ing.—*n.* self'-knowl'edge, knowledge of one's own nature.—*adjs.* self'-left', left to oneself; self'less, having no regard to self.—*ns.* self'lessness; self'-life', self-existence: life only for

oneself.—*adjs.* self'-light'ing, igniting automatically; self'-like, exactly similar; self'-lim'ited, (*path.*) running a definite course; self-lost', lost by one's own act.—*n.* self'-love', the love of oneself: tendency to seek one's own welfare or advantage: desire of happiness.—*adjs.* self'-lov'ing; self'-lum'inous, emitting a light of its own; self'-made', made by oneself: risen to a high position from poverty or obscurity by one's own exertions.—*ns.* self'-mas'tery, self-command: self-control; self'-mett'le, (*Shak.*) natural spirit. —*adj.* self'-misused', spoken ill of by oneself.— *n.* self'-mo'tion, spontaneous motion.—*adj.* self'-moved', moved spontaneously from within.—*ns.* self'-mur'der, suicide; self'-mur'derer.—*adj.* self'-mur'dering. — *ns.* self'-neglect', -ing (*Shak.*), neglect of oneself; self'ness, egotism: personality; self'-offence', one's own offence: failure in what is due to oneself.—*adj.* self'-o'pened, opened of its own accord.—*n.* self'-opin'ion, high, or unduly high opinion of oneself or of one's own opinion.—*adjs.* self'-opin'ionated, -opin'ionative, -opin'ioned, obstinately adhering to one's own opinion; self'-pi'ous, hypocritical. —*n.* self'-pit'y, pity for oneself.—*adjs.* self'-plant'ed, planted without man's agency; self'-pleas'ing; self'-poised', balanced without outside help.—*ns.* self'-pollina'tion, transfer of pollen to the stigma of the same flower (or sometimes the same plant or clone); self'-pollu'tion, masturbation; self'-por'trait, a portrait of oneself painted by oneself; self'-por'traiture.—*adj.* self'-possessed', having self-possession. — *ns.* self'-possess'ion, collectedness of mind: calmness; self-praise', the praise of oneself by oneself; self'-preserva'tion, care, action, or instinct for the preservation of one's own life.—*adjs.* self'-preser'vative, self'-preser'ving.—*ns.* self'-pride', self-esteem; self'-prof'it, private interest. —*adjs.* self'-prop'agating, propagating itself when left to itself; self'-propell'ing, carrying its own means of propulsion.—*ns.* self'-protec'tion, self-defence; self'-prun'ing, natural shedding of twigs. —*adjs.* self'-raised', raised by oneself: grown without cultivation; self'-rais'ing, (of flour) already mixed with something that causes it to rise (also self'-ris'ing).—*n.* self'-realisa'tion, the attainment of such development as one's mental and moral nature is capable of.—*adj.* self'-record'ing, recording its own readings. — *n.* self'-regard', self-interest: self-respect.—*adjs.* self'-regard'ing; self'-reg'istering, self-recording; self'-reg'ulating, regulating itself. — *n.* self'-reli'ance, healthy confidence in one's own abilities.—*adjs.* self'-reli'ant; self'-rely'ing.—*ns.* self'-renuncia'tion, self-abnegation; self'-repres'sion, restraint of expression of the self; self'-reproach', prickings of conscience; self'-reproof'; self'-reprov'ing, reproof of conscience; self'-repug'nance.—*adj.* self'-repug'nant, self-contradictory: inconsistent. — *ns.* self'-resem'blance, (*Spens.*) appearance of being what one really is; self'-respect', respect for oneself or one's own character. — *adjs.* self'-respect'ful; self'-respect'ing; self'-restrained', restrained by one's own will.— *ns.* self'-restraint', a refraining from excess: self-control; self'-rev'erence, great self-respect.— *adjs.* self'-rev'erent; self'-right'eous, righteous in one's own estimation: pharisaical.—*n.* self'-right'eousness.—*adjs.* self'-right'ing, righting itself when capsized; self'-rig'orous, rigorous towards oneself; self'-rolled' (*Milt.* self'-rowld'), coiled on itself.—*n.* self'-rule'.—*adj.* self'-rul'ing. —*n.* self'-sac'rifice, forgoing one's own good for the sake of others. — *adjs.* self'-sac'rificing; self'-same, the very same.—*ns.* self'-same'ness, identity; self'-satisfac'tion, satisfaction with oneself. — *adjs.* self'-sat'isfied; self'-sat'isfying, giving satisfaction to oneself.—*n.* self'-seek'er, one who looks mainly to his own interests.—*n.* and *adj.* self'-seek'ing.—*n.* self'-ser'vice, helping oneself, as in a restaurant.—Also *adj.*—*adjs.* self'-severe' (*Milt.*); self'-slain'.—*n.* self'-slaugh'ter, suicide. — *adj.* self'-slaugh'tered. — *ns.* self'-slay'er; self'-sov'ereignty, sovereignty over, or inherent in, oneself.—*adj.* **self'-sown'**, sown naturally without man's agency.—*n.* **self'-star'ter**, an automatic contrivance for starting a motor: a car fitted with one.—*adj.* **self'-ster'ile**, unable to fertilise itself.—*n.* **self'-steril'ity**.—*adjs.* **self'-styled'**, called by oneself: pretended; **self'-subdued'**, (*Shak.*) subdued by one's own power; **self'-substan'tial**, (*Shak.*) composed of one's own substance. —*n.* **self'-suffi'ciency**. —*adjs.* **self'-suffi'cient**, requiring nothing from without: excessively confident in oneself; **self'-suffic'ing**.—*ns.* **self'-sugges'tion**, autosuggestion; **self'-support**, support or maintenance without outside help: paying one's way.—*adjs.* **self'-support'ed**; **self'-support'ing**.—*n.* **self'-surren'der**, a yielding up of oneself or one's will.—*adjs.* **self'-surviv'ing**, remaining as a mere ruin of itself; **self'-sustained'**, sustained by one's own power; **self'-sustain'ing**. —*ns.* **self'-sustain'ment**; **self'-sus'tenance**, **self'-sustentā'tion**.—*adjs.* **self'-taught**; **self'-tempt'ed**; **self'-think'ing**, thinking for oneself; **self'-torment'ing**. — *n.* **self'-torment'or**. — *adj.* **self'-tor'turable** (*Shak.*).—*ns.* **self'-tor'ture**; **self'-trust'**, self-reliance: (*Shak.*) confidence in one's own faithfulness to oneself.—*adj.* **self'-unā'ble**, (*Shak.*) insufficient of one's own ability.—*ns.* **self'-vī'olence**, suicide; **self'-will'**, obstinacy.—*adjs.* **self'-willed'**; **self'-wind'ing**, (of a watch) wound by the wearer's spontaneous movements, or by opening and shutting the case: automatically wound by electricity.—*n.* **self'-wrong'**, (*Shak.*) wrong done to a person by himself. [O.E. *self*; Du. *zelf*, Ger. *selbe*, Goth. *silba*.]

-self, *self*, *pl.* **-selves**, *selvz*, a suff. forming reflexive and emphatic pronouns.—**be oneself**, **himself**, &c., to be in full possession of one's powers: to be (once more) at one's best: (*Scot.*) to be alone; **by oneself**, &c., alone.

selictar, *se-lik'tär*, *n.* a sword-bearer. [Turk. *silihdār*—Pers. *silahdār*—Ar. *silh*, weapon.]

Seljuk, *sel-jŏŏk'*, *n.* a member of any of the Turkish dynasties (11th-13th cent.) descended from *Seljūq* (grandfather of Togrul Beg): a Turk subject to the Seljuks.—*adjs.* **Seljuk'**, **Seljuk'ian**.

sell, **selle**, *sel*, *n.* (*arch.*) a seat: (*Spens.*) a saddle. [O.Fr. *selle*—L. *sella*—*sedēre*, to sit.]

sell, *sel*, *v.t.* to give or give up for money or other equivalent: to impose upon, trick: to promote the sale of: (*obs.*) to cry up: (*U.S.*) to make acceptable: (*U.S.*) to convince of the value of something.—*v.i.* to make sales: to be sold, to be in demand for sale: (*pa.t.* and *pa.p.* **sold**).—*n.* a deception.—*adj.* **sell'able**, that can be sold.—*ns.* **sell'er**, one who sells: that which has a sale; **sell'ing-plate**, **-race**, a race of which the winning horse must be put up for auction at a price previously fixed; **sell'ing-price**, the price at which a thing is sold.—**sell a bargain** (see **bargain**); **sell one's life dearly**, to do great injury to the enemy before one is killed; **sell out**, to dispose entirely of: to sell one's commission; **sell up**, to sell the goods of, for debt; **to sell**, for sale. [O.E. *sellan*, to give, hand over; O.N. *selja*, Goth. *saljan*.]

sell, *sel*, *n.* a Scots form of **self**:—*pl.* **sells**.

seltzer, *selt'sər*, *n.* a mineral water from Nieder-*Selters* in Prussia, or an imitation.—*n.* **selt'zogene**, a gazogene.

selvage, **selvedge**, *sel'vij*, *n.* a differently finished edging of cloth: a border.—*v.t.* to border. [**self**, **edge**.]

selves, *selvz*, *pl.* of **self**.

semantic, *si-man'tik*, *adj.* relating to meaning, esp. of words.—*n.* (in *sing.* or *pl.*) the science of the development of the meaning of words.—*ns.* **seman'tron**, a wooden or metal bar used instead of a bell in Orthodox churches and in mosques:—*pl.* **seman'tra**; **sem'aphore** (*-ə-fōr*), a signalling apparatus, an upright with arms that can be turned up or down—often the signaller's own body and arms, with flags.—*v.t.* and *v.i.* to signal thus.—*adj.* **semaphoric** (*-for'ik*).—*adv.* **semaphor'ically**.—*n.* **semasiology** (*si-mā-zi-ol'ə-ji*, or *-si-*), semantics.—*adj.* **sematic** (*si-mat'ik*; *biol.*), serving for recognition, attraction, or warning.

—*ns.* **semeiol'ogy** (*sem-ī-*, *sēm-ī-*), the study of symptoms; **semeion** (*sē-mī'on*), in ancient prosody, the unit of time: one of the two divisions of a foot: a mark of metrical or other division:—*pl.* **semei'a**.—*adj.* **semeiotic** (*sē-mī-ot'ik*), pertaining to symptoms.—*n.* (*pl.* in form) **semeiot'ics**, semeiology. [Gr. *sēma*, *-atos*, *sēmeion*, a sign, *sēmantron*, a seal (later a semantron), *sēmāsiā*, meaning, *sēmantikos*, significant.]

semble, *sem'bl*, *v.i.* (*obs.*) to seem: to feign.—*v.t.* (*obs.*) to pretend: to picture, image. — *adj.* **sem'blable**, (*Shak.*) resembling, similar, like.—*n.* (*Shak.*) like, fellow.—*adv.* **sem'blably**, (*Shak.*) in like manner.—*n.* **sem'blance**, likeness: appearance: outward show: apparition: image.—*adj.* **sem'blant**, resembling: seeming.—*n.* (*Spens.*) semblance: cheer, countenance, entertainment: demeanour.—*adj.* **sem'blative**, (*Shak.*) resembling or seeming: simulative. [Fr. *sembler*, to seem, to resemble—L. *simulāre*—*similis*, like.]

semble, *sem'bl*, *v.t.* to bring together, collect, esp. as some female moths do males by scent.—*n.* **sem'bling-box**, a collector's box enclosing a captive female. [Aphetic from **assemble**.]

semé, **semée**, *sem'ā*, *adj.* (*her.*) strewn or scattered over with small bearings, powdered. [Fr., pa.p. of *semer*—L. *sēmināre*, to sow.]

semen, *sē'men*, *n.* the liquid that carries spermatozoa. —For derivatives see **semin-** below. [L. *sēmen*, *-inis*, seed.]

semester, *si-mes'tər*, *n.* a university half-year course (German, &c.).—*adjs.* **semes'tral**, **semes'trial**, half-yearly. [L. *sēmēstris*—*sex*, six, *mēnsis*, a month.]

semi-, *sem'i-*, *pfx.* half: (loosely) nearly, partly, incompletely.—*ns.* **sem'i**, **sem'ie**, a semi-bajan; **sem'iangle**, a half-angle.—*adj.* **sem'i-ann'ual**, (chiefly *U.S.*) half-yearly.—*adv.* **sem'i-ann'ually**. —*adj.* **sem'i-ann'ular**, half-ring-shaped.—*n.* and *adj.* **sem'i-Ā'rian**, homoiousian. — *n.* **sem'i-Ā'rianism**. — *adjs.* **sem'i-attached'**, partially bound; **sem'i-automat'ic**, partly automatic but requiring some tending by hand.—*ns.* **sem'i-ax'is**, a half-axis; **sem'i-bā'jan**, (*hist.*, *Scot.univ.*) a second-year student.—*n.* and *adj.* **sem'i-barbā'rian**.—*ns.* **sem'i-bar'barism**; **sem'ibrēve**, half a breve (2 minims or 4 crochets); **sem'ibuil**, a pope's bull issued between election and coronation; **semicar'bazide**, a base ($H_2N \cdot CO \cdot NH \cdot NH_2$) reacting with aldehydes and ketones to form **semicar'bazones**.—*adj.* **sem'i-centenn'ial**, occurring at the completion of fifty years.—*n.* (*U.S.*) a jubilee.—*ns.* **sem'ichōr'us**, half of a chorus: a passage sung by it; **sem'icircle**, half a circle, bounded by the diameter and half the circumference. — *adjs.* **sem'icircled**; **semicir'cular** (**semicircular canals**, the curved tubes of the inner ear concerned with equilibrium).—*adv.* **semicir'cularly**. — *ns.* **sem'icirque**, a semicircular hollow: a semicircle; **sem'icolon**, the point (;) marking a division greater than the comma; **semicō'ma**, a condition approaching coma.—*adj.* **semico'matose**.—*ns.* **semiconduct-iv'ity**; **semiconduct'or**, formerly, any substance with electrical conductivity between that of metals and of non-conductors: now, any solid, non-conducting at low temperatures or in pure state, which is a conductor at higher temperatures or when very slightly impure.—*adj.* **sem'i-con'scious**.—*ns.* **semicyl'inder**, a longitudinal half-cylinder; **sem'idem'isem'iquaver**, half a demisemiquaver.—*adj.* **semidepō'nent**, passive in form in the perfect tenses only.—Also *n.*—*adj.* **sem'i-detached'**, partly separated: joined by a party wall to one other house only.—*n.* **sem'i-diam'eter**, half the diameter, esp. the angular diameter.—*adjs.* **semidiur'nal**, accomplished in twelve hours: pertaining to half the time or half the arc traversed between rising and setting; **semi-divine'**, half-divine: of, of the nature of, a demigod.—*n.* **sem'i-dome'**, half a dome, esp. as formed by a vertical section. — *adjs.* **semidomes'ticated**, partially domesticated: half-tame; **sem'i-doub'le**, having only the outermost stamens converted into petals.—*n.* a festival less solemn than a double.—*adj.* **sem'i-dry'ing**, of oils, thickening without completely drying on exposure.—*n.* sem'i-ellipse', half of an ellipse, bounded by a diameter, esp. the major axis.—*adjs.* sem'i-ellip'tical; semifi'nal, immediately before the final.—*n.* a last round but one.—*n.* semifi'nalist, a competitor in a semi-final.—*adj.* semiflu'id, nearly solid but able to flow to some extent.—Also *n.*—*adj.* semiglob'-ular.—*n.* semi-grand, a square piano with curtailed keyboard.—Also *adj.*—*n.* and *adj.* semi-im'becile.—*adj.* sem'i-independ'ent, not fully independent.—*ns.* semi-ju'bilee, the twenty-fifth anniversary; sem'i-lat'us rec'tum, half the latus rectum, terminated at the focus.—*adjs.* sem'i-liq'uid, half-liquid; semilu'cent, half-trans-parent; sem'i-lu'nar, -lu'nate, half-moon shaped. —*n.* semilune (-*lōōn*), a half-moon-shaped object, body, or structure.—*adj.* sem'imen'strual, half-monthly.—*n.* sem'i-met'al, (*obs.*) a metal that is not malleable.—*adj.* sem'i-month'ly, (chiefly *U.S.*) half-monthly.—*n.* a half-monthly periodical. —*adj.* sem'i-mute', with speech impaired by loss of hearing.—Also *n.*—*adjs.* sem'i-nūde', half-naked; semi-occā'sional, (*U.S.*) occurring now and then.—*adv.* semi-occā'sionally.—*adj.* sem'i-offic'ial, partly official.—*adv.* sem'i-offic'ially. —*n.* sem'i-ō'pal, a dull variety of opal.—*adjs.* sem'i-opaque', partly opaque; sem'iovip'arous, producing imperfectly developed young; semi-pal'mate, half-webbed: half web-footed.—*ns.* semipalmā'tion; semipar'asite, a partial para-site, feeding partly independently.—*adj.* semi-parasit'ic.—*n.* sem'iped, in verse, a half-foot. —*n.* and *adj.* Sem'i-Pelā'gian.—*n.* Sem'i-Pelā'gianism, the middle course between Augus-tinian predestination and Pelagian free-will.—*adj.* sem'ipellu'cid, imperfectly transparent.—*n.* semiperim'eter, half the perimeter.—*adj.* semi-per'meable, permeable by a solvent but not by the dissolved substance.—*ns.* sem'iplume, a feather with ordinary shaft but downy web; semipor'celain, a coarse ware resembling porce-lain.—*adj.* semi-pre'cious, valuable, but not valuable enough to be reckoned a gem-stone.— *n.* sem'iquāver, half a quaver.—*adj.* sem'i-rig'id, of an airship, having a flexible gasbag and stiffened keel.—*n.* sem'i-ring, a half-ring.—*adj.* sem'i-sag'ittate, shaped like half an arrowhead.—*n.* and *adj.* Sem'i-Sax'on, (*obs.*) Early Middle English (*c.* 1150-1250).—*adjs.* sem'i-skilled'; semiterete', half-cylindrical.—*n.* sem'itone, half a tone—one of the lesser intervals of the musical scale as from B to C.—*adj.* semiton'ic.—*n.* semitranspā'rency.— *adjs.* semitranspā'rent, imperfectly transparent; semi-trop'ical, sub-tropical; semi-tū'bular, like half of a tube divided longitudinally; sem'i-un'cial, inter-mediate between uncial and minuscule.—*n.* a semi-uncial letter.—*n.* sem'ivowel, a sound par-taking of the nature of both a vowel and a con-sonant: a letter representing it.—*adj.* sem'i-week'ly, issued or happening twice a week.—Also *n.* and *adv.* [L. *sēmi-*, half-; cf. Gr. *hēmi-*, O.E. *sam-*.]

seminal, *sem'in-l*, *adj.* pertaining to, or of the nature of, seed or of semen: generative.—*n.* seminality (-*al'i-ti*), the germinating principle: germ.—*adv.* sem'inally.—*v.t.* sem'ināte, to sow: to propagate.—*n.* seminā'tion, sowing: seed-dispersal: seeding.—*adj.* seminif'erous, seed-bearing: producing or conveying semen. [See semen.]

seminar, *sem-in-är'*, *n.* (*orig.* Ger.) a group of ad-vanced students working in a specific subject of study under a teacher.—*adjs.* seminarial (-*ä'ri-əl*); seminā'rian, of a seminary.—*n.* a student in a seminary, esp. of R.C. theology.—*ns.* sem'inarist (-*ər-ist*), a student in a seminary or in a seminar: a Roman Catholic priest educated in a foreign seminary: a teacher in a seminary; sem'inary (-*ə-ri*), a seed-plot: a breeding-place: a place of origin and fostering, nursery: formerly, a pretentious name for a school (esp. for young ladies): a college, esp. for R.C. (in *U.S.* also other) theology: a seminary priest.—*adj.* seminal: of a seminary: of a seminar. [L. *sēminārium*, a seed-plot—*sēmen*, seed.]

Seminole, *sem'i-nōl*, *n.* an American Indian of an offshoot of the Creeks, originally in Florida, now mostly in Oklahoma. [Creek *Simánole*, lit. run-away.]

semis, *sē'mis*, L. *sā'mis*, *n.* a bronze coin of the ancient Roman republic, half an as. [L. *sēmis*, *sēmissis*.]

semitar, semitaur, old spellings of scimitar.

Semite, *sem'* or *sēm'it*, *n.* a member of any of the peoples said (Gen. x.) to be descended from Shem, or speaking a Semitic language.—*adj.* Semitic (*sem-*, *sim-*, *səm-it'ik*).—*n.* any Semitic language: (in *pl.*) Semitic studies.—*n.* Semitīsā'tion.—*v.t.* Sem'itise, to render Semitic in language, religion, or otherwise.—*ns.* Sem'itism, a Semitic idiom or characteristic: Semitic ways of thought: the cause of the Semites, esp. the Jews; Sem'itist, a Semitic scholar.—Semitic languages, Assyrian, Aramaean, Hebrew, Phoenician, Arabic, Ethiopic, &c. [Gr. *Sēm*, Shem; applied by J. G. Eichhorn.]

semmit, *sem'it*, *n.* (*Scot.*) an undershirt.

Semnopithecus, *sem-nō-pith-ē'kəs*, *n.* the hanuman genus. [Gr. *semnos*, honoured, *pithēkos*, an ape.]

semolina, *sem-ə-lē'nä*, *n.* the particles of fine, hard wheat that do not pass into flour in milling. [It. *semolino*, dim. of *semola*, bran—L. *simila*, fine flour.]

sempiternal, *sem-pi-tər'nl*, *adj.* everlasting.—Also semp'itern.—*ns.* sempiter'nity; sempiter'num, (*obs.*) a durable woollen cloth. [L. *sempiternus*—*semper*, ever.]

semple, *sem'pl*, *adj.* a Scottish form of simple, esp. meaning not of gentle birth.

semplice, *sem'plē-che*, *adj.* (*mus.*) simple, without embellishments. [It.]

sempre, *sem'pre*, *adv.* (*mus.*) always, throughout. [It.,—L. *semper*, always.]

sempster, seamster, *sem'stər*, *n.* one who sews— orig. *fem.*, now only *masc.*:—*fem.* semp'stress, seam'stress.—*ns.* semp'stering, semp'stressing, semp'stress-ship. [O.E. *séamestre*; see seam.]

semsem, *sem'sem*, *n.* sesame. [Ar. *simsim.*]

semuncia, *si-mun'sh(y)ä*, *n.* a Roman half-ounce: a bronze coin, an as in its ultimate value.—*adj.* semun'cial. [L. *sēmuncia*—*sēmi-*, half, *uncia*, a twelfth.]

sen, *sen*, *n.* a Japanese copper coin, the hundredth part of a yen:—*pl.* sen. [Jap.]

senary, *sēn'*, *sen'ər-i*, *adj.* of, involving, based on, six.—*n.* a set of six: a senarius.—*n.* senarius (*se-nä'ri-əs*), a verse of six iambs or equivalents. [L. *sēnārius*—*sēnī*, six each—*sex*, six.]

senate, *sen'it*, *n.* the governing body of ancient Rome: a legislative or deliberative body, esp. the upper house of a national or state legislature: a body of venerable or distinguished persons: the governing body of certain British universities (in Scotland, Senā'tus Academ'icus).—*ns.* sen'ate-house, the meeting-place of a senate; senator (*sen'ə-tər*), a member of a senate (Senator of the College of Justice, a Lord of Session).—*adj.* senatorial (*sen-ə-tō'ri-əl*).— *adv.* senatō'rially, with senatorial dignity. — *n.* sen'atorship. — senā'tus consult' (L. *senātūs consultum*), a decree of the senate. [L. *senātus—senex, senis*, an old man.]

send, *send*, *v.t.* to cause, direct, or tell to go: to propel: to cause to be conveyed: to dispatch: to forward: to grant.—*v.i.* to dispatch a message or messenger: (*naut.*; sometimes scend, 'scend) to pitch into the trough of the sea: (*pa.t.* and *pa.p.* sent; *naut.* send'ed).—*n.* (*Scot.*) a messenger: (*Scot.*) one or more sent to fetch a bride: a message: an impetus or impulse: a plunge.— *ns.* send'er, one who sends: a transmitting instru-ment; send'ing, dispatching: pitching: trans-mission: that which is sent (esp. by a wizard); send'-off, a farewell demonstration.—send down, to rusticate or expel; send for, to require by message to come or be brought; send word, to send an intimation. [O.E. *sendan*; O.N. *senda* Goth. *sandjan*, Ger. *senden.*]

sendal, *sen'dəl*, *n.* a thin silk or linen. [O.Fr. *cendal*, prob.—Gr. *sindōn*; see sindon.]

Seneca, *sen'i-kä*, *n.* an Iroquois Indian of a tribe

in New York state, &c.—*adj.* **Sen′ecan.—Seneca oil,** crude petroleum, used by them.

Senecan, *sen′i-kən, adj.* of, in the manner of, Lucius Annaeus *Seneca,* Stoic philosopher and writer of declamatory tragedies (*c.* B.C. 4-A.D. 65).

Senecio, *se-nē′s*(*h*)*i-ō, n.* the groundsel and ragwort genus of composite plants. [L. *senex,* an old man, from the hoary pappus.]

senega, *sen′i-gä, n.* an American milkwort (*Polygala Senega*; **senega snakeroot**): its dried root, reputed by the *Seneca* Indians good for snake-bites.

senescent, *si-nes′ənt, adj.* verging on old age: ageing.—*n.* **senesc′ence.** [L. *senēscēns, -entis,* pr.p. of *senēscĕre,* to grow old—*senex,* old.]

seneschal, *sen′i-shl, n.* a steward: a major-demo. —*n.* **sen′eschalship.** [O.Fr. (Fr. *sénéchal*), of Gmc. origin, lit. old servant; cf. Goth. *sineigs,* old, *skalks,* O.E. *scealc,* servant.]

sengreen, *sen′grēn, n.* the house-leek. [O.E. *singréne,* evergreen, house-leek, periwinkle—pfx. *sin-,* one, always (cf. L. *semel,* once), *gréne,* green; cf. Ger. *sin*(*n*)*grüne,* periwinkle.]

Senhor, *se-nyōr′,* **Senhora,** *-ä,* **Senhorita,** *-ē′tä, ns.* the Portuguese forms corresponding to the Spanish **Señor, Señora, Señorita.**

senile, *sē′nīl, adj.* characteristic of or attendant on old age: showing the decay or imbecility of old age.—*n.* **senility** (*si-nil′i-ti*), old age: the imbecility of old age. [L. *senīlis—senex, senis,* old.]

senior, *sēn′yər, adj.* elder: older or higher in standing: more advanced: first.—*n.* one who is senior: (*U.S.*) a fourth-year student.—*n.* **seniority** (*sē-ni-or′i-ti*), state or fact of being senior: priority by age, time of service, or standing: a body of seniors or senior fellows.—**senior optime** (see **optime**); **senior service,** the navy. [L. *senior, -ōris,* comp. of *senex,* old.]

senna, *sen′ä, n.* a shrub (Cassia, of various species): its purgative dried leaflets.—**bladder senna,** a papilionaceous shrub (Colutea) with similar properties; **senna tea,** an infusion of senna. [Ar. *sanā.*]

sennachie. Same as **seannachie.**

sennet, *sen′it, n.* (*Shak.*) a trumpet or woodwind announcement of a stage entrance (or exit) in state. [App. a form of **signet.**]

sennight, *sen′it, n.* (*arch.*) a week. [**seven, night.**]

sennit, *sen′it,* **sinnet,** *sin′it, n.* a flat braid of rope yarn.

Senonian, *si-nō′ni-ən, n.* (*geol.*) a Cretaceous stage answering to the English Upper Chalk.—Also *adj.* [L *Senonēs,* a tribe of central Gaul.]

Señor, *se-nyōr′, n.* a gentleman: in address, sir: prefixed to a name, Mr :—*fem.* **Señora** (*se-nyō′rä*), a lady: madam: as a title, Mrs.—*n.* **Señorita** (*sen-yō-rē′tä*), a young lady: Miss. [Sp.,—L. *senior,* older.]

sens, *sens, adv.* (*Spens.*) since.

sensation, *sen-sā′shən, n.* awareness of a physical experience, without any element derived from previous experiences: awareness by the senses generally: an effect on the senses: power of sensing: an emotion or general feeling: a thrill a state, or matter, of general excited interest in the public, audience, &c.: melodramatic quality or method: (*slang*) enough to taste, as of liquor. —*adj.* **sensā′tional.—***ns.* **sensā′tionalism,** the doctrine that our ideas originate solely in sensation: a striving after wild excitement and melodramatic effects; **sensā′tionalist.—***adj.* **sensationalist′ic.** —*adv.* **sensā′tionally.—***ns.* **sensā′tionism;** **sen-sā′tionist, sensā′tion-monger,** a dealer in the sensational; **sense** (*sens*), faculty of receiving sensation, general or particular: immediate consciousness: inward feeling: impression: opinion: mental attitude: discernment: understanding: appreciation: feeling for what is appropriate: discerning feeling for things of some particular kind: (usu. in *pl.*) one's right wits: soundness of judgment: reasonableness: sensible or reasonable discourse: that which is reasonable: plain matter of fact: the realm of sensation and sensual appetite: (*Shak.*) a sense-organ: meaning: interpretation: purport: gist: (esp. in *geom.,* after Fr. *sens*)

direction.—*v.t.* to have a sensation, feeling, or appreciation of: to appreciate, grasp, comprehend. —*adjs.* **sensed,** endued with meaning; **sense′ful,** significant: full of good sense; **sense′less,** unconscious: deficient in good sense: meaningless.—*adv.* **sense′lessly.—***ns.* **sense′lessness;** **sense′-organ,** a structure specially adapted for the reception of stimuli, as eye, ear, nose; **sense′-percep′tion,** perception by the sense; **sensibil′ity,** sensitiveness: sensitivity: capacity of feeling or emotion: readiness and delicacy of emotional response: sentimentality: (often in *pl.*) feelings that can be hurt.—*adj.* **sen′sible,** perceptible by sense: perceptible: easily perceived: appreciable: having power of sensation: conscious: sensitive: (*obs.*) having sensibility: easily affected: delicate: cognisant: aware: emotionally conscious: having or marked by good sense, judicious.—*n.* an object of sense: that which is sensible.—*n.* **sen′sibleness.—***adv.* **sen′sibly,** in a sensible manner: to a sensible or perceptible degree: so far as the senses show.—*adj.* **sensile** (*sen′sīl*), sentient: capable of affecting the senses. —*ns.* **sen′sism,** sensationalism in philosophy; **sen′sist;** **sensitīsā′tion.** — *v.t.* **sen′sitise,** to render sensitive, or more sensitive, or sensitive in a high degree.—*adj.* **sen′sitised.—***n.* **sen′sitiser.** —*adj.* **sen′sitive,** having power of sensation: feeling readily, acutely, or painfully: capable of receiving stimuli: reacting to outside influence: ready and delicate in reaction: sensitised: (*phot.*) susceptible to the action of light: pertaining to, or depending on, sensation.—*n.* one who or that which is sensitive, or abnormally or excessively sensitive.—*adv.* **sen′sitively.—***ns.* **sen′sitiveness, sensitiv′ity; sensitom′eter,** an instrument for measuring sensitivity, as of photographic films.— *adj.* **senso′rial,** sensory.—*ns.* **senso′rium,** the seat of sensation in the brain: the brain: the mind: the nervous system; **sen′sory,** the sensorium.—*adj.* of the sensorium: of sensation.— *adj.* **sen′sual** (*-sū-əl, -shoo-əl*), of the senses, as distinct from the mind: not intellectual or spiritual: carnal: worldly: connected with gratification, esp. undue gratification of bodily sense: voluptuous: lewd.—*n.* **sensualīsā′tion.—***v.t.* **sen′sualise,** to make sensual: to debase by carnal gratification.—*ns.* **sen′sualism,** sensual indulgence: the doctrine that all our knowledge is derived originally from sensation: the regarding of the gratification of the senses as the highest end; **sen′sualist,** one given to sensualism or sensual indulgence: a debauchee: a believer in the doctrine of sensualism.—*adj.* **sensualist′ic.—***n.* **sensual′ity** (*Milt.* **sen′sualty**), indulgence in sensual pleasures: lewdness.—*adv.* **sen′sually.—***ns.* **sen′sualness;** **sen′suism,** (*philos.*) sensationalism; **sen′suist.—** *adj.* **sen′suous,** pertaining to sense (without implication of lasciviousness or grossness): connected with sensible objects: easily affected by the medium of the senses.—*adv.* **sen′suously.—***n.* **sen′suousness.** — **five senses,** sight, hearing, smell, taste, and touch; **bring one to his senses,** to make one recognise the facts: let him understand that he must mend his behaviour; **in a sense,** in a sense other than the obvious one: in a way: after a fashion; **in, out of, one's senses,** in or out of one's right wits, normal rational condition; **sensation novel,** one dealing in violent effects and strained emotion; **sensible horizon,** the visible horizon; **sensible note,** leading note; **sensitive flame,** a flame that rises or falls in response to sound; **sensitive plant,** a plant, esp. *Mimosa pudica,* that shows more than usual irritability when touched or shaken, by movements of leaves, &c. [L. *sēnsus—sentīre,* to feel.]

sent, an earlier spelling (*Spens., Shak., Milt.*) of **scent,** *n., v.t.,* and *v.i.,* smell: sense.

sent, *sent, pa.t.* and *pa.p.* of **send.**

sentence, *sen′təns, n.* opinion: a judgment, decision: determination of punishment pronounced by a court or a judge: a maxim: a number of words making a complete grammatical structure, generally begun with a capital letter and ended with a full-stop or its equivalent: sense: meaning: matter.—*v.t.* to pronounce judgment on: to condemn.—*n.* **sen'tencer.**—*adj.* **senten'tial** (*-ten'shl*).—*adv.* **senten'tially.**—*adj.* **senten'tious,** full of meaning: aphoristic, abounding (often superabounding) in maxims.—*adv.* **senten'tiously.**—*n.* **senten'tiousness.**—**Master of the Sentences,** Peter Lombard (12th cent.), from his collection of opinions from Augustine, &c. [Fr.,—L. *sententia* —*sentīre,* to feel.]

sentient, *sen'sh*(*y*)*ənt, adj.* conscious: capable of sensation: aware: responsive to stimulus.—*n.* that which is sentient: a sentient being or mind. —*ns.* **sen'tience, sen'tiency.** [L. *sentiēns, -entis,* pr.p. of *sentīre,* to feel.]

sentiment, *sen'ti-mənt, n.* a thought or body of thought tinged with emotion: opinion: judgment: a thought expressed in words: a maxim: a thought or wish propounded to be ratified by drinking: emotion: feeling bound up with some object or ideal: regard to ideal considerations: sensibility, refined feelings: consciously worked-up or partly insincere feeling: sentimentality. — *adj.* **sentimental** (*-men'tl*), pertaining to, given to, characterised by, indulging in, abounding in, expressive of, sentiment or sentimentality.—*v.i.* **sentimen'talise,** to behave sentimentally: to indulge in sentimentality.—*v.t.* to make sentimental: to treat sentimentally.—*ns.* **sentimen'talism, sentimentality** (*-man-tal'i-ti*), disposition to wallow in sentiment: self-conscious working up of feeling: affectation of fine feeling: sloppiness; **sentimen'talist,** one who affects, seeks to work up, or luxuriates in sentiment or fine feeling: one guided by mere sentiment: one who regards sentiment as more important than reason.—*adv.* **sentimen'tally.** [L.L. *sentimentum*—L. *sentīre,* to feel.]

sentinel, *sen'ti-nl, n.* one posted on guard, a sentry: guard.—*adj.* acting as a sentinel.—*v.t.* to watch over: to post as a sentinel: to furnish with sentinels.—*v.i.* to keep guard.—**sentinel crab,** a crab of the Indian Ocean with long eye-stalks. [Fr. *sentinelle*—It. *sentinella,* watch, sentinel.]

sentry, *sen'tri, n.* a sentinel: a soldier on guard: watch, guard.—*ns.* **sen'try-box,** a box to shelter a sentry; **sen'try-go,** a sentry's beat or duty: (*obs.*) a watch-tower. [Etymology obscure.]

Senussi, *sen-ōōs'ē, n.* a member of a Moslem sect or confraternity, chiefly in N.E. Africa, founded by Sidi Mohammed ben Ali es-Senussi (*d.* 1860; named from the *Senus* Mountains):—*pl.* **Senussi.** —Also **Senoussi.**

senvy, *sen'vi, n.* (*obs.*) mustard (plant or seed). [O.Fr. *senevé*—L. *sināpi*—Gr. *sināpi,* mustard.]

senza, *sen'tsä, prep.* (*mus.*) without. [It.]

sepad, *sə-pad', v.t.* to suppose: to warrant. [A ghost-word; from J. M. Barrie's mishearing of **I'se** (=I sal) **uphaud,** I shall uphold.]

sepal, *sep'l,* also *sēp'l, n.* a member of a flower calyx.—*adjs.* **sep'aline** (*-īn*), **sep'aloid, sep'alous.** —*n.* **sep'alody** (Gr. *eidos,* form), transformation of other members into sepals. [Fr. *sépale,* invented by N. J. de Necker (1790) from Gr. *skepē,* cover.]

separate, *sep'ə-rāt, v.t.* to divide: to part: to sunder: to sever: to disconnect: to disunite: to remove: to isolate: to keep apart: to seclude: to set apart for a purpose: to shut off from cohabitation, esp. by judicial decree: to remove cream from by a separator.—*v.i.* to part: to withdraw: to secede: to come out of combination or contact: to become disunited.—*adj.* (*sep'ə-rit, -rāt, sep'rit*) separated: divided: apart from another: distinct.—*n.* an off-print.—*n.* **separability** (*-ə-bil'i-ti*).—*adj.* **sep'arable,** that may be separated or disjoined.—*n.* **sep'arableness.**—*advs.* **sep'arably; sep'arately.**—*ns.* **sep'arateness; separā'tion,** act of separating or disjoining: state of being separate: disunion: chemical analysis: cessation of cohabitation by agreement or judicial decree, without a formal dissolution of the marriage tie; **separā'tionist,** one who favours separation, esp. political or ecclesiastical; **sep'aratism** (*-ə-tizm*); **sep'aratist,** one who withdraws or advocates separation, esp. from an established church, a dissenter: (*hist.*) an Independent: (by

Unionists) a Home Ruler: a believer in separate authorship of parts, esp. of the Homeric poems.— *adj.* **sep'arative** (*-ə-tiv*), tending to separate.— *ns.* **sep'arātor,** one who, or that which, separates: a machine for separating cream from milk by whirling; **separatory** (*sep'ər-ə-tər-i*), an instrument for separating.—*adj.* having the function of separating.—*ns.* **sep'arātrix,** a separating line; **separā'tum,** a separate off-print. — **separate maintenance,** a provision made by a husband for his separated wife; **separation allowance,** government allowance to a service-man's wife and dependents. [L. *sēparāre, -ātum—sē-,* aside, *parāre,* to put.]

Sephardim, *se-fär'dēm, n.pl.* the Spanish and Portuguese Jews.—*adj.* **Sephar'dic.** [Heb.]

sephen, *sef'en, n.* a sting-ray. [Ar. *safan,* shagreen.]

sepia, *sē'pi-ä, n.* a cuttlefish, esp. of Sepia or kindred genus: cuttlefish ink: a pigment made from it, or an artificial imitation: its colour, a fine brown: a sepia drawing.—*adj.* of the colour of sepia: done in sepia.—*ns.* **sē'piolite** (Gr. *lithos,* stone), meerschaum; **sē'piost, sēpiostaire'** (Fr. *sépiostaire*—Gr. *osteon,* bone), **sē'pium,** cuttlebone. [L.,—Gr. *sēpiā,* cuttlefish, *sēpion,* cuttlebone.]

sepiment, *sep'i-mənt, n.* a hedge, a fence. [L. *saepīmentum,* a hedge.]

sepoy, *sē'poi, n.* an Indian soldier in European service. [Urdu and Pers. *sipāhī,* horseman.]

seppuku, *sep-ōō'koo, n.* hara-kiri. [Jap.]

seps, *seps, n.* a very venomous snake known to the Greeks: **Seps,** a genus of almost legless skinks. [Gr. *sēps.*]

sepsis, *sep'sis, n.* putrefaction: invasion by pathogenic bacteria. [Gr. *sēpsis,* putrefaction.]

sept, *sept, n.* (*orig.* in Ireland) a division of a tribe.— *adj.* **sept'al.** [Prob. for *sect,* influenced by L. *saeptum*; see next.]

sept, *sept, n.* an enclosure: a fence.—*n.pl.* **sept'a** (see **septum** below).—*adjs.* **sept'al,** partitional: growing in hedges; **septā'rian.**—*n.* **septā'rium,** a nodule with a network of mineral-filled cracks:— *pl.* **septā'ria.** — *adj.* **sept'ate,** partitioned. — *n.* **septā'tion,** division by partitions.—*adjs.* **septicī'dal** (L. *caedĕre,* to cut), with splitting of septa, as when a fruit dehisces by separation of the carpels; **septif'erous,** having partitions; **sept'iform,** in the form of a partition; **septif'ragal** (root of L. *frangĕre,* to break), with separation of the outer walls of the carpels from the septa.— *n.* **sept'um,** (*biol.*) a partition:—*pl.* **sept'a.** [L. *saeptum* (used in pl.), a fence, enclosure—*saepīre,* to fence.]

sept-, septi-, septem-, in composition, seven. [L. *septem.*]

September, *səp-, sep-tem'bər, n.* the ninth, orig. seventh, month of the year.—*adj.* **Septem'berish.** —*ns.* **Septembriser** (*sep'təm-brī-zər*), a Septembrist: a partridge-shooter; **Septem'brist,** a participator in the September massacres in Paris, Sept. 2-7, 1792. [L. *September, -bris.*]

septemfid, *sep'təm-fid, adj.* seven-cleft. [Root of *findĕre,* to cleave.]

septemvir, *sep-tem'vir, n.* one of a board of seven :— *pl.* **septem'virī, -virs.**—*n.* **septem'virate,** the office of septemvir: a board of septemviri: a group of seven men. [L.,—*vir,* man.]

septenarius, *sep-ti-nā'ri-əs, n.* a seven-foot verse, esp. a trochaic tetrameter catalectic.—*adj.* **septenary** (*sep-tē'nə-ri,* or *sep'tə-nə-ri*), numbering or based on seven.—*n.* a seven, set of seven (esp. years): a septenarius. [L. *septēnārius,* of seven.]

septennium, *sep-ten'i-əm, n.* seven years :—*pl.* **septenn'ia.**—*n.* **septenn'ate,** a period of seven years.—*adj.* **septenn'ial.**—*adv.* **septenn'ially.**— **Septennial Act,** a statute of 1716, in force till 1911, limiting the duration of a parliament to seven years. [L. *septennis*—*annus,* a year.]

septentrion, *sep-ten'tri-ən, n.* (*Shak.*) the north :— *pl.* **septen'trions, septentriō'nēs,** the seven stars of the Plough: the Great Bear.—*adjs.* **septen'trion** (*Milt.*), **-al,** northern.—*adv.* **septen'trionally.** [L. *septentriōnēs,* i.e. *septem triōnēs,* the seven plough-oxen.]

septet, septette, septett, *sep-tet',* *n.* a composition for seven performers: a set of seven (esp. musicians). [Ger. *septett*—L. *septem.*]

sept-foil, *set'foil,* *n.* tormentil: a figure divided by seven cusps. [Fr. *sept,* seven, O.Fr. *foil*—L. *folium,* a leaf.]

septic, *sep'tik,* *adj.* putrefactive.—*n.* **septicaemia** (*sep-ti-sē'mi-ä*; Gr. *haima,* blood), presence of pathogenic bacteria in the blood.—*adv.* **sep'tically.** —*n.* **septicity** (*-tis'i-ti*).—**septic tank,** a tank in which sewage is decomposed by anaerobic bacteria. [Gr. *sēptikos*—*sēpein,* to putrefy.]

septilateral, *sep-ti-lat'ər-əl,* *adj.* seven-sided. [L. *latus, lateris,* a side.]

septillion, *sep-til'yən,* *n.* the seventh power of a million: (*U.S.,* as in *France*) the eighth power of a thousand. [Modelled on **million.**]

septimal, *sep'ti-ml,* *adj.* relating to, based on, seven.—*ns.* **septime** (*sep'tēm*), the seventh position in fencing; **sep'timole** (*-mōl*), a group of seven notes to be played in the time of four or six. [L. *septimus,* seventh—*septem,* seven.]

septleva, *set'lə-vä,* *n.* in basset, seven times as much added to the first stake. [Fr. *sept-et-le-va,* seven and the first stake.]

septuagenarian, *sep-tū-ə-ji-nā'ri-ən,* *n.* a person seventy years old, or between seventy and eighty. —*adj.* of that age.—*adj.* **septuagenary** (*-ə-jē'nər-i, -aj'in-ər-i*), consisting of or relating to seventy.— *n.* one seventy years old. [L. *septuāgēnārius*— *septuāgēnī,* seventy each.]

Septuagesima, *sep-tū-ə-jes'i-mä,* *n.* the third Sunday before Lent (also **Septuagesima Sunday**)— apparently in continuation of the sequence Quadragesima, Quinquagesima, &c. [L. *septuāgēsimus, -a, -um,* seventieth.]

Septuagint, *sep'tū-ə-jint,* *n.* the Greek Old Testament, traditionally attributed to 72 translators at Alexandria in the 3rd century—usually expressed by LXX.—*adj.* **Septuagin'tal.** [L *septuāgintā*— *septem,* seven.]

septum. See sept (2).

septuor, *sep'tū-or,* *n.* a septette. [Fr.,—L. *septem,* after *quatuor.*]

septuple, *sep'tū-pl,* *adj.* sevenfold.—*v.t.* to multiply sevenfold.—*n.* **sep'tuplet,** a septimole: one of seven at a birth. [L.L. *septuplus*—L. *septem,* seven; cf. **quadruple.**]

sepulchre, *sep'əl-kər,* *n.* a tomb: a recess, usually in the north chancel wall, or a structure placed in it, to receive the reserved sacrament and the crucifix from Maundy Thursday or Good Friday till Easter (**Easter sepulchre**): burial.—*v.t.* (formerly sometimes *si-pul'kər*) to entomb: to enclose as a tomb.—*adjs.* **sepulchral** (*si-pul'krəl*), of, of the nature of, a sepulchre: funeral: as if of or from a sepulchre: funereal, gloomy, dismal: hollow-toned; **sepul'chrous** (*rare*); **sepul'tural.** —*n.* **sep'ulture,** burial: a tomb or burial-place.— *v.t.* to entomb. [L. *sepulcrum, sepultūra*—*sepelīre, sepultum,* to bury.]

sequacious, *si-kwā'shəs,* *adj.* ready to follow a leader or authority: compliant: pliant: observing logical sequence or consistence: in long-drawn-out sequence or train.—*ns.* **sequā'ciousness, sequacity** (*si-kwas'i-ti*). [L. *sequāx, sequācis*— *sequī,* to follow.]

sequel, *sē'kwəl,* *n.* that which follows: (*obs.*) followers: (*obs.*) successors: consequences: up-shot: a resumption of a story already complete in itself: (*Shak.*) sequence: (*Scots law*) an allowance to mill servants in thirlage.—*n.* **sequela** (*si-kwē'lä*), morbid affection following a disease: often in *pl.* **sequē'lae** (*-lē*). [L. *sequēla*—*sequī,* to follow.]

sequence, *sē'kwəns,* *n.* state or fact of being sequent or consequent: succession: order of succession: a series of things following in order: a set of three or more cards consecutive in value: that which follows: consequence: (*mus.*) successive repetition in higher or lower parts of the scale or in higher or lower keys: in cinematography, a division of a film: in liturgics, a hymn in rhythmical prose, sung after the gradual and before the gospel.— *adj.* **sē'quent,** following: consequent: successive:

consecutive.—*n.* (*Shak.*) a follower: that which follows.—*adj.* **sequential** (*si-kwen'shl*).—*n.* **sequentiality** (*-shi-al'i-ti*).—*adv.* **sequen'tially.**— **sequence of tenses,** the relation of tense in subordinate clauses to that in the principal. [L. *sequēns, -entis,* pr.p. of *sequī,* to follow.]

sequester, *si-kwes'tər,* *v.t.* to set aside: to seclude: to set apart: to confiscate: to remove from one's possession until a dispute can be settled, creditors satisfied, or the like: to hold the income of for the benefit of the next incumbent: to sequester the estate or benefice of.—*v.i.* (*obs.*) to seclude oneself.—*n.* (*sek'wes-tər*; *Shak.*) seclusion.—*adj.* **seques'tered,** retired, secluded.—*v.t.* **sequestrate** (*sek', sēk',* or *si-kwes'*), to sequester: to make bankrupt.—*ns.* **sequestrā'tion** (*sek-, sēk-*), act of sequestering: (*Scots law*) bankruptcy; **seq'uestrātor.** [L.L. *sequestrāre, -ātum*—L. *sequester,* a depositary—*secus,* apart.]

sequin, *sē'kwin,* *n.* an old Italian gold coin worth about 9s. 4d.: a spangle. [Fr.,—It. *zecchino*— *zecca,* the mint; of Ar. origin.]

Sequoia, *si-kwoi'ä,* *n.* a genus of gigantic conifers, the Californian big tree or mammoth tree and the redwood—sometimes called Wellingtonia. [After the Cherokee chief *Sequoiah.*]

sérac, *sā-rak', sā'rak,* *n.* one of the cuboidal or pillar-like masses into which a glacier breaks on a steep incline. [Swiss Fr., originally a kind of cheese.]

seraglio, *se-rāl'yō,* *n.* women's quarters in a Mohammedan house or palace: a harem: a collection of wives or concubines: an enclosure: a Turkish palace, esp. that of the sultans at Constantinople. [It. *serraglio*—L. *sera,* a door-bar, confused with Turk. *saray, serāī,* a palace.]

serai, *se-rā'i,* *n.* a khan, caravanserai: (*erron.*) a seraglio, harem. [Turk. (orig. Pers.) *saray, serāī.*]

serail, *se-rāl',* *n.* seraglio. [Fr. *sérail.*]

serang, *se-rang',* *n.* a lascar boatswain. [Pers. *sarhang,* a commander.]

serape, *se-rä'pä,* *n.* a Mexican riding-blanket. [Sp. *sarape.*]

seraph, *ser'əf,* *n.* a six-winged celestial being (Isa. vi.): an angel of the highest of the nine orders: a person of angelic character or mien :— *pl.* **ser'aphs, ser'aphim,** formerly also **ser'aphin, ser'aphins, ser'aphims,** the plurals in -im and -in also occurring as *obs. sing.*—*adjs.* **seraphic** (*-af'*), **-al.**—*adv.* **seraph'ically.**—*n.* **ser'aphine** (*-ēn*), a keyboard reed instrument, precursor of the harmonium.—**Seraphic Doctor,** St Bonaventura: St Teresa; **Seraphic Father,** St Francis; **Seraphic order,** the Franciscans. [Heb. *Serāphīm* (pl.).]

Serapis, Sarapis, *sə-, se-rā'pis,* *n.* a god of the Greeks of Egypt, identified with Apis and Osiris. —*n.* **Serapeum** (*ser-ə-pē'əm*), a temple of Serapis. —*adj.* **Ser-, Sarapic** (*-ap'ik*). [Gr. *Sarāpis,* later (also L.) *Serāpis.*]

seraskier, *ser-as-kēr',* *n.* a Turkish commander-in-chief or war minister.—*n.* **seraskier'ate,** the office of seraskier. [Turk. pron. of Pers. *ser'asker*—*ser,* head, Ar. *'asker,* army.]

Serb, *sərb,* **Serbian,** *sər'bi-ən,* *ns.* a native or citizen of Serbia: a member of the people principally inhabiting Serbia: the South Slav language of Serbia.—*adj.* of Serbia, its people, or their language. —*ns.* and *adjs.* **Serbo-Cro'at, Serbo-Croā'tian.** [Serb. *Srb.*]

Serbonian, *sər-bō'ni-ən,* *adj.* like *Sirbōnis, Serbōnis,* a now dry lake in the N.E. corner of Egypt, 'Where armies whole have sunk' (*Paradise Lost,* II. 594).

serdab, *sər-däb',* *n.* an underground chamber: a secret chamber in an Egyptian tomb. [Pers. *sard,* cold, *āb,* water.]

sere. See **sear** (1 and 2), **cere.**

sere, *sēr,* *n.* (*obs.*) a claw. [O.Fr. *serre*—*serrer,* to hold.]

serein, *se-rän°',* *n.* fine rain from a cloudless sky. [Fr.,—L. *sērum,* evening, *sērus,* late.]

serenade, *ser-i-nād',* *n.* a composition like a symphony, usually slighter and in more movements: a performance in the open air by night, esp. at a lady's window: a piece suitable for such performance.—*v.t.* se'renade, to entertain with a serenade.—*v.i.* to perform a serenade.—*ns.* serenä'der; serenata (*-i-nä'tä*), a (symphonic) serenade: a pastoral cantata; ser'enate, (*Milt.*) a serenade. [Fr. *sérénade*, and It. *serenata*—L. *serēnus*, bright clear sky; meaning influenced by L. *sērus*, late.]

serendipity, ser-ən-dip'i-ti, *n.* the faculty of making happy chance finds. [*Serendip*, a former name for Ceylon. Horace Walpole coined the word (1754) from the title of the fairy-tale 'The Three Princes of Serendip,' whose heroes 'were always making discoveries, by accidents and sagacity, of things they were not in quest of.']

serene, sə-rēn', *adj.* calm: unclouded: unruffled: an adjunct to the titles of some princes (translating Ger. *Durchlaucht*).—*n.* calm brightness: serenity: serene sky or sea: pure air.—*v.t.* to tranquillise: to clear.—*adv.* serēne'ly, calmly, coolly.—*ns.* serēne'ness; serenity (*-ren'i-ti*).—all serene, (*slang*) everything as it should be: all right; drop serene, (*Milt.*) amaurosis. [L. *serēnus*, clear.]

serene, ser'ēn, sə-rēn', *n.* (*obs.*) a supposedly unwholesome night-dew: serein. [serein.]

serf, sərf, *n.* a person in modified slavery, esp. one attached to the soil: a villein:—*pl.* serfs.—*ns.* serf'age, serf'dom, serf'hood, serf'ship.—*adj.* serf'ish. [Fr.,—L. *servus*, a slave.]

serge, serj, *n.* a strong twilled fabric, now usually of worsted.—*adj.* of serge. [Fr.,—L. *sērica*, silk; see seric.]

sergeant, serjeant, sär'jənt, *n.* orig. a servant: (*obs.*) an officer who made arrests: (usu. with *g*) a non-commissioned officer next above a corporal: (with *g*) an officer of police: (usu. with *g*) alone or as a prefix, designating certain officials: (with *j*) formerly, a barrister of highest rank (in full serjeant-at-law). — *ns.* ser'gean(t)cy, ser'jean(t)cy, office or rank of sergeant, serjeant; ser'geant- (or ser'jeant-) at-arms, an officer of a legislative body or the Court of Chancery, for making arrests, &c.; ser'geant-drumm'er, drummajor; ser'geant-fish, a fish with stripes, esp. the cobia (Rhachicentron) of S.E. U.S., akin to the mackerels; ser'geant-mā'jor, formerly, an officer of rank varying from major to majorgeneral: now, the highest non-commissioned officer (regimental sergeant-major, a warrant officer on the staff of a battalion, regiment, &c.); ser'geantship, ser'jeantship; ser'geantry, serjeanty; ser'jeanty, a condition of tenure by service in person to the king (grand serjeanty) or rendering some small object (petty serjeanty). —Common Serjeant, in London, an assistant to the Recorder. [Fr. *sergent*—L. *serviēns*, *-entis*, pr.p. of *servīre*, to serve.]

serial, seriate, &c. See under series.

Seric, ser'ik, *adj.* Chinese: seric, silken.—*adj.* sericeous (sə-rish'əs), silky: covered with soft silky appressed hairs: with silky sheen.—*ns.* sericin (ser'i-sin), the gelatinous substance of silk; ser'icite, a silky soapy potash mica.—*adj.* sericitic (-sit'ik).—*ns.* sericitīsā'tion, conversion (esp. of orthoclase) into sericite; ser'iculture, silkworm breeding—also sericiculture (ser'i-si-kult-yər); ser(ic)icul'turist. [Gr. *sērikos*—*Sēr*, a Chinese, a silkworm (pl. *Sērēs*).]

sericon, ser'i-kon, *n.* conjectured to be a red (or black) tincture in alchemy.

seriema, ser-i-ē'mä, -ā'mä, *n.* the crested screamer. [Tupí.]

series, sē'ri-ēz, sē'rēz, *n.* a set of things in line or in succession, or so thought of: a set of things having something in common, esp. of books in similar form issued by the same house: a set of things differing progressively: a succession of quantities each derivable from its predecessor according to a law: a taxonomic group (of various rank): a geological formation: succession: sequence: linear or end-to-end arrangement:—*pl.* se'ries.—*adj.* se'rial, forming a series: in series: in a row: in instalments: of publication in instalments: of supernumerary buds, one above another.—*n.* a publication, esp. a story, in instal-

ments.—*v.t.* se'rialise, to arrange in series: to publish serially.—*ns.* se'rialist, a writer of serials; seriality (-al'i-ti).—*adv.* se'rially.—*adj.* se'riate, in rows.—*advs.* se'riately; seriā'tim, one after another.—arithmetical series, a series progressing by constant difference; geometrical series, a series progressing by constant ratio. [L. *seriēs*—*serēre*, *sertum*, to join.]

serif, ser'if, *n.* the short cross-line at the end of a stroke in a letter.—Also seriph and ceriph. [Origin obscure; poss. Du. *schreef*, stroke.]

serin, ser'in, *n.* a smaller species of canary.—*n.* serinette', a small barrel-organ for training songbirds. [Fr., canary.]

seringa, sə-ring'gä, *n.* a Brazilian rubber-tree (Hevea): mock-orange (Philadelphus). [Port.; see syringa.]

serious, sē'ri-əs, *adj.* grave: staid: earnest: disinclined to lightness: in earnest: not to be taken lightly: approaching the critical or dangerous: concerned with weighty matters: professedly religious.—*adjs.* se'rio-com'ic, -al, partly serious and partly comic.—*adv.* se'riously.—*n.* se'riousness. [L.L. *sēriōsus*—L. *sērius*.]

seriph. See serif.

serjeant. See sergeant.

serk. See sark.

serkali, ser-käl'ē, *n.* the Government: white rulers. [Swahili.]

sermon, sər'mən, *n.* a discourse, esp. one delivered, or intended to be delivered, from the pulpit, on a Biblical text: a harangue.—*v.t.* and *v.i.* to preach: to discourse.—*ns.* sermoneer', ser'moner (both *rare*), a preacher: a sermoniser; sermonet(te)', a little sermon.—*adjs.* sermonic (-mon'ik), -al.—*n.* ser'moning.—*v.i.* ser'monise, to compose sermons: to preach.—*v.t.* to preach to. —*n.* sermonīs'er.—*adj.* ser'monish. [L. *sermō*, *sermōnis*—*serēre*, to join.]

sero-, sē'rō-, in composition, serum.

seron, seroon, si-rōn', -ron', -rōōn', *n.* a crate or hamper: a bale wrapped in hide. [Sp. *serón*.]

serotine, ser'ō-tīn, -tin, *n.* a small reddish bat.—*adj.* late, in occurrence, development, flowering, &c.—*adj.* serotinous (si-rot'i-nəs). [L. *sērōtinus*—*sērus*, late.]

serous, &c. See serum.

serow, ser'ō, *n.* a Himalayan goat-antelope. [Lepcha *sa-ro*.]

serpent, sər'pənt, *n.* formerly, any reptile or creeping thing, esp. if venomous: now, a snake: a person treacherous or malicious: an obsolete crooked bass wind instrument of wood covered with leather: a twisting firework: Serpent, a northern constellation.—*adj.* serpentlike: serpent's.—*v.i.* to wind.—*ns.* ser'pent-eater, the secretary-bird: the markhor; ser'pent-god, -goddess, a deity in the form of a snake: a deified snake.—*adjs.* serpentiform (-pent'), snake-shaped; ser'pentine (-tin), snakelike: winding: tortuous.—*n.* a winding track: an old kind of cannon: a soft, usually green mineral, a hydrated magnesium silicate, occurring in winding veins and in masses, formed by alteration of olivine, &c.: a rock (in full ser'pentine-rock), commonly an altered peridotite, composed mainly of the mineral serpentine.—*v.t.* and *v.i.* to wind: to insinuate.—*adv.* ser'pentinely.—*adj.* serpentinic (-tin'ik).—*n.* and *adj.* ser'pentining.—*adv.* serpenti'ningly.—*n.* serpentinīsā'tion (-tin-īz-).—*v.t.* ser'pentinise, to convert into serpentine.—*v.i.* to wind.—*adj.* serpenti'nous, of serpentine: winding. — *v.i.* ser'pentise, to wind.—*v.t.* to make to wind.—*adj.* and *adv.* ser'pentlike.—*ns.* ser'pent-liz'ard, the lizard Seps; ser'pentry, serpents collectively; ser'pent-star, a brittle star; ser'pent-stone, an ammonite: a snake-stone; ser'pent-wor'ship.—serpentine verse, a line that begins and ends with the same word (from the figure of a snake with its tail in its mouth, common as a symbol of eternity); the old serpent, Satan. [L. *serpēns*, *-entis*, pr.p. of *serpĕre*, to creep; cf. Gr. *herpein*.]

serpigo, ser-pī'gō, *n.* (*Shak.* sapego, or suppeago) any spreading skin disease.—*adj.* serpiginous (-pij').[L.L. *serpīgō*—L. *serpĕre*, to creep.]

fāte, fär, ȧsk; mē, hər (her); mīne; mōte; mūte; mōōn; dhen (then)

erpula, *sər'pū-lä*, *n.* a polychaete worm (Serpula or kindred genus) with twisted calcareous tube:—*pl.* **ser'pulae** (*-lē*).—*n.* **ser'pulite**, a fossil resembling a worm-tube. [L., a snake—*serpĕre*, to creep.]

err, serre. See **serried**.

erra, *ser'ä*, *n.* a saw: anything sawlike (L.): a mountain-range (*Port.*):—*pl.* **serr'ae** (*-ē*, L.); **serr'as** (*Port.*). — *ns.* **serradill'a**, **serradell'a** (*Port.*), bird's-foot (Ornithopus); **serr'an**, a fish of the genus Serranus, or its family; **Serranus** (*sə-rā'nos*), the typical genus of **Serranidae** (*-ran'i-dē*), the sea-perch family, akin to the perches. — *ns.* and *adjs.* **serranid** (*ser'ən-id*); **serr'anoid**.—*n.* **Serrasal'mo** (L. *salmō*, salmon), the piranha genus of fishes.—*adj.* **serr'ate**, notched like a saw: (*bot.*) with sharp forward-pointing teeth.—*v.t.* to notch.—*n.* **serra'tion**, saw-edged condition: (usu. in *pl.*) a sawlike tooth.—*adjs.* **serratiros'tral** (L. *rōstrum*, beak), saw-billed; **serratulate** (*sər-at'ū-lāt*), minutely serrate.—*ns.* **serrature** (*ser'ə-tyər*), serration; **serrā'tus**, one of several muscles of the thorax.—*adjs.* **serricorn** (*ser'*; L. *cornū*, horn), having serrate antennae; **serr'ulate, -d**, finely serrate.—*n.* **serrulā'tion**. [L. and Port. (from L.) *serra*, a saw.]

erried, *ser'id*, *adj.* close-set.—*v.t.* **serr, serre** (*sər*), to press close: to close the ranks of.—*n.* **serrefile, serafile** (*ser'ə-fil*; see **file**), a file of officers or men detailed to ride in rear of the rear rank of a squadron when in line: a soldier so detailed.—*adj.* **serried** (*ser'id*).—*v.t.* and *v.i.* **serr'y**, to close together. [Fr. *serrer* or its pa.p. *serré*—L. *sera*, bar, lock.]

ertularia, *sər-tū-lā'ri-ä*, *n.* a common genus of hydroids with double row of sessile hydrothecae. —*n.* and *adj.* **sertulā'rian**. [L. *serta*, garlands.]

eruewe (i.e. **servewe**), Spenserian spelling of **surview**.

erum, *sē'rəm*, *n.* a watery liquid, esp. that which separates from coagulating blood:—*pl.* **sēr'a, sēr'ums**.—*ns.* **serol'ogy** (*sē-*, *si-*); **seros'ity** (*sē-*); **sēroth'erapy**, **sēr'um-ther'apy**, treatment or prevention of disease by injecting blood-serum containing the appropriate anti-bodies. — *adj.* **sē'rous**, pertaining to, like, of the nature of, serum.—**serous membrane**, a thin membrane, moist with serum, lining a cavity and enveloping the viscera within, e.g. the pericardium, the peritoneum. [L. *sĕrum*, whey.]

erval, *sər'vl*, *n.* a large, long-legged, short-tailed African cat or tiger-cat. [Port. (*lobo*) *cerval*, lit. deer-wolf, transferred from another animal.]

ervant, *sər'vənt*, *n.* one who is hired to perform service, especially personal or domestic service of a menial kind, or farm labour, for another or others: one who is in the service of the state, the public, a company, or other body: one who serves: a ministrant: formerly, a man conventionally accepted by a lady (called his *mistress*) as binding himself to devoted attendance: in formal epistolary use, formerly in greeting and leave-taking, now sometimes in colloquial jocularity, applied in seeming humility to oneself: a slave: (in *pl.*) formerly a designation conceded by a great personage to a company of actors, to evade legal difficulties.—*v.t.* to subject.—*ns.* **ser'vant-girl, -lass**.—*adj.* **ser'vantless**.—*ns.* **ser'vant-maid**, a female domestic servant; **ser'vant-man**, a male servant; **ser'vantry**, servants collectively; **ser'-vantship**, position or relation of a servant.—**servants' hall**, a servants' dining- and sitting-room. [Fr., pr.p. of *servir*—L. *servīre*, to serve.]

erve, *sĕrv*, *v.t.* to be a servant to: to be in the service of: to worship: to work for: to render service to: to perform service for or under: to perform the duties or do the work connected with: of a male animal, to cover: to attend as assistant: to be of use to or for: to avail: to suffice for: to satisfy: to further: to minister to: to attend to the requirements of: to supply: to furnish with materials: to help to food, &c.: to send or bring to table: to deal: (*Spens.*) to put into action, bring to bear: (*tennis*, &c.) to put into play by striking: to treat, behave towards:

to be opportune to: to conform one's conduct to: to undergo, work out, go through: to bind with cord, tape, &c.: (*law*) to deliver or present formally, or give effect to: (*Scots law*) to declare (heir).—*v.i.* to be a servant: to be in service or servitude: to render service: to be a member, or take part in the activities, of an armed force: to perform functions: to wait at table: to attend to customers: to act as server: to answer a purpose, be of use, do: to be opportune or favourable: to suffice.—*n.* service of a ball.—*ns.* **ser'ver**, one who serves, esp. at meals, mass, or tennis: a salver: a fork, spoon, or other instrument for distributing or helping at table; **serv'ery**, a room or rooms adjoining a dining-room, from which meals and liquors are served and in which utensils are kept.—*n.* and *adj.* **serv'ing**.—*ns.* **serv'ing-mall'et**, a mallet with grooved head used in serving ropes; **serv'ing-man**, (*arch.*) a man-servant.—**serve one a trick**, to play a trick on one; **serve one right**, to be no worse than one deserves; **serve one's time**, to pass through an apprenticeship; **serve out**, to deal or distribute: to punish: to retaliate on; **serve the (or one's) turn**, to suffice for one's immediate purpose or need; **serve time**, to undergo a term of imprisonment, &c.; **serve up**, to bring to table. [Fr. *servir*—L. *servīre*, to serve.]

Servian (*obs.*). Same as **Serbian**.

Servian, *sər'vi-ən*, *adj.* of *Servius* Tullius, legendary king of Rome.

service, *sər'vis*, *n.* condition or occupation of a servant or of one who serves: work: act or mode of serving: employ: employment as a soldier, sailor, or airman, or in any public organisation or department: the personnel so employed: the force, organisation, or body employing it (in the *pl.* usu. the fighting forces): that which is required of its members: that which is required of a feudal tenant: performance of a duty or function: actual participation in warfare: a warlike operation: a performance of religious worship: a liturgical form or office or a musical setting of it: a good turn, good offices, benefit to another: duty or homage ceremonially offered, as in health-drinking, correspondence, or greeting: use: hard usage: availability: disposal: supply, as of water, railway-trains: expediting: waiting at table: that which is served, a course: order of dishes: a set, as of dishes for a particular meal: supplementary activities for the advantage of customers: cost of interest and sinking-fund charges: cord or other material for serving a rope.—*adj.* of the army, navy, or air-force: for the use of servants.—*v.t.* to provide or perform service for (e.g. motor-cars).—*ns.* **serviceabil'ity**, **ser'viceableness**.—*adj.* **ser'viceable**, able or willing to serve: advantageous: useful: capable of rendering long service, durable.—*adv.* **ser'viceably**.—*ns.* **ser'vice-book**, a book of forms of religious service: a prayer-book; **ser'vice-court**, in lawn-tennis, the area outside of which a served ball must not fall; **ser'vice-flat**, a flat in which domestic service is provided and its cost is included in the rent.—*adj.* **ser'viceless**.—*ns.* **ser'vice-line**, the boundary of the service-court, 21 feet from the net; **ser'vice-man**, a member of a fighting service; **ser'vice-pipe, -wire**, a branch from a main to a building; **ser'vice-res'ervoir**, a reservoir for supplying water to a particular area; **ser'vice-room**, a room in a club or hotel where visitors' requirements are attended to.—**active service**, service of a soldier, &c., in the field (widely interpreted by the authorities); **at your service**, at your disposal: also a mere phrase of civility; **have seen service**, to have fought in war: to have been put to long or hard use. [Fr., —L. *servitium*.]

service, *sər'vis*, *n.* a tree (*Pyrus domestica*) very like the rowan.—*ns.* **ser'vice-berry**, its pear-shaped fruit: (*U.S.*) shadbush or its fruit; **ser'vice-tree**.—**wild service**, a tree of the same genus (*P. torminalis*) with sharp-lobed leaves. [O.E. *syrfe*—L. *sorbus*.]

servient, *sər'vi-ənt*, *adj.* subordinate: subject to a servitude or easement. [L. *serviēns, -entis*, pr.p. of *servīre*, to serve.]

serviette, *sər-vi-et',* n. (*vulg.* except in older Scottish use) a table-napkin. [Fr.]

servile, *sər'vīl, adj.* pertaining to slaves or servants : slavish : meanly submissive : cringing : controlled, subject : slavishly or unintelligently imitative : expressing mere grammatical relations.—*n.* a servile person.—*adv.* **ser'vilely.**—*ns.* **ser'vilism** (*-vil-izm*), systematic or habitual servility : servile spirit : a system based on slavery or advocacy of it ; **servility** (*-vil'i-ti* ; *obs.*), servitude : slavishness of manner or spirit : slavish deference. [L. *servīlis—servus,* a slave.]

Servite, *sər'vīt, n.* a member of the mendicant order of Servants of the Virgin, founded at Florence in 1233.

servitor, *sər'vi-tər, n.* one who serves : a servant : a man-servant : (*obs.*) one who serves in war : (*Scot., obs.*) an assistant, apprentice, lawyer's clerk, assistant schoolmaster, or the like : a follower or adherent : formerly, in Oxford, an undergraduate partly supported by the college, his duty to wait on the fellows and gentlemen commoners at table : in Edinburgh, a classroom janitor :—*fem.* **ser'vitress.**—*adj.* **servitō'rial.**—*n.* **ser'vitorship.** [L.L. *servītor, -ōris—*L. *servīre,* to serve.]

servitude, *sər'vi-tūd, n.* state of being a slave or (now *rare*) servant : slavery : subjection : compulsory labour : subjection to irksome conditions : a burden on property obliging the owner to allow another person or thing an easement. [L. *servitūdō.*]

servo(-)mechanism, *sər'vo-mek'an-izm, n.* any remote-control mechanism. [serve.]

sesame, *ses'ə-mi, n.* a plant (*Sesamum indicum*) of the Pedaliaceae, yielding gingili-oil.—*n.* **ses'ame-grass,** gama-grass.—*adj.* **ses'amoid,** shaped like a sesame seed.—*n.* a sesamoid bone, or small rounded bone in the substance of a tendon.—**open sesame** (see **open**). [Gr. *sēsamē,* a dish of sesame (Gr. *sēsamon*).]

sesqui-, *ses'kwi-, pfx.* in the ratio of one and a half to one, or one and an *n*th to one.—*adj.* **sesquialter** (*-al'tər ;* L. *alter,* second), as three to two.—*ns.* **sesquial'tera,** (*mus.*) a perfect fifth : three notes against two : an organ stop reinforcing harmonics ; **sesquicentenn'ial,** a hundred and fiftieth anniversary.—Also *adj.*—*n.* **sesquiox'ide,** an oxide with three atoms of oxygen to two.—*adjs.* **sesquip'edal, sesquipedā'lian** (L. *sēsquipedālis—pēs, pedis,* foot), a foot and a half long—usually (after Horace, *Ars Poetica,* 97) of polysyllabic vocables.—*ns.* **sesquipedā'lianism, sesquipedality** (*-pi-dal'i-ti*).—*adj.* **sesquip'licate** (L. *sēsquiplex, -plicis*), of, or as, the square roots of the cubes.—*ns.* **sesquisul'phide,** a compound with three atoms of sulphur to two ; **sesquiter'tia,** a perfect fourth : four notes against three. [L. *sēsqui—sēmisque—sēmis* (for *sēmi-as*), half a unit, *que,* and.]

sess, *ses, n.* Same as **cess.**

sessa, *ses'ä, sesey, ses'ē, interj.* or *interjs.* (*Shak.*) of disputed meaning.—Other readings are **caese, cease ; ceas, sese.** [Poss. reduplication of *sa* ; poss. Sp. *cesa,* or Fr. *cessez,* cease.]

sessile, *ses'il, adj.* stalkless : sedentary. — *adj.* **sess'ile-eyed.** [L. *sessilis,* low, squat—*sedēre, sessum,* to sit.]

session, *sesh'ən, n.* an act of sitting : a seated position : the enthronement of Christ at God's right hand : a sitting, series of sittings, or time of sitting, as of a court or public body : the time between the meeting and prorogation of Parliament : a school year (sometimes a school day) : in Scotland, &c., a division of the academic year (**winter session** of two terms, **summer session** of one) : the kirk-session : formerly, the Court of Session : (in *pl.*) quarter-sessions.—*adj.* **sess'ional.** —*adv.* **sess'ionally.**—*ns.* **sess'ion-clerk',** the official who records the transactions of a kirk-session ; **sess'ion-house,** a building where sessions are held (also **sess'ions-house**) : the room where a kirk-session meets.—**Court of Session,** the supreme civil court of Scotland. [Fr.,—L. *sessiō, sessiōnis—sedēre, sessum,* to sit.]

sesspool. Same as **cesspool.**

sesterce, *ses'tərs, n.* a Roman coin, the *sestertius* worth 2½ asses, later 4 asses.—*n.* **sester'tium** (*-shi-əm*), a money of account equal to 100 sesterces :—*pl.* **sester'tia.** [L. *sestertius,* two and a half—*sēmis,* half, *tertius,* third ; *sestertium,* prob. orig. gen. plur. for *mille sestertium,* a thousand sesterces.]

sestet, sestett, sestette, *ses-tet', n.* a group of six : the last six lines of a sonnet : a composition for six performers (also **sestet'to**). [It. *sestetto—sesto—*L. *sextus,* sixth.]

sestina, *ses-tē'nä, n.* an old verse-form of six six-lined stanzas having the same end-words in different orders, and a triplet introducing all of them.—Also **sestine** (*-tēn'*). [It.,—L. *sextus,* sixth.]

set, *set, v.t.* to seat : to place : to put : to fix : to put, place, or fix in position or required condition : to apply : to cause to be : to plant : to stake : to put on eggs : to put under a hen : to dispose, array, arrange : to put to catch the wind : to spread, lay, cover, as a table : to compose, as type : to put in type : to embed : to frame : to mount : to beset or bestow about : to stud, dot : sprinkle, variegate : to form or represent, as in jewels : (*Shak.*) to imprint : to make to become solid, coagulated, rigid, fixed, or motionless : to begin to form (as fruit or seed) : to regulate : to appoint : to ordain : to assign : to prescribe : to propound : to present for imitation : to put upon a course, start off : to incite, direct : (*Northern*) to escort : to put in opposition : to posit : to rate, value : to pitch, as a tune : to compose or fit music to : to sharpen, as a razor : to indicate by crouching : (*Scot.* and *local*) to lease or let to a tenant : (chiefly *Scot.*) to become : befit : conversely, to appear to advantage in.—*v.i.* (now *vulg.*) to sit : to hang in position : to be in session : to go down towards or below the horizon, to decline : to offer a stake : to become rigid, fixed, hard, solid, or permanent : to coagulate : of a bone, to knit : to settle down : to begin to develop, as fruit : to have or take a course or direction : to begin to go : to dance in a facing position : to acquire a set or bend : to point out game by crouching : to apply or betake oneself : (*pr.p.* **sett'ing** ; *pa.t.* and *pa.p.* **set**).—*adj.* in any of the senses of the participle : prescribed : deliberate, intentional : prearranged : formal : settled : fixed : rigid : determined : regular : established : ready : of mature habit or body.—*n.* a group of persons or things, esp. such as associate, occur, or are used together or have something in common : a clique : a coterie : complete series, collection, or complement : company performing a dance : a series of dance movements or figures : a complete apparatus, esp. for wireless receiving : an act, process, mode, or time of setting : a setting : an inclination : direction of flow : a dog's indication of game : (now *dial.*) bodily build : permanent effect of strain : hang of a garment : a young plant-slip for planting : **set scene:** (for the following senses, **set** or **sett**) the number of a weaver's reed, determining the number of threads to the inch : the texture resulting : a square or a pattern of tartan : paving-block of stone or wood : (*Scots*) a lease or letting : (*Cornwall,* &c.) a mining lease or area worked : a place with fixed fishing-nets : a too for setting in various senses : a badger's burrow : (*tennis*) a group of games in which the winning side wins six, with such additional games as may be required in the case of deuce : the constitution of a burgh.—*ns.* **set'-back,** a check, reverse, or relapse ; **set'-down,** an unexpected rebuff : snub : a rating ; **set'ness ; set'-off,** a claim set against another : a counterbalance : an ornament : a setting forth : (*archit., print.*) an offset ; **set'-out,** an outfit : preparations : a display of dishes, dress, &c. : a company, clique.—*adj.* **set'-stitch'd** (*Sterne*) perh. embroidered.—*ns.* **sett'er,** one who or that which sets : a dog that sets : a dog of breed derived from the spaniel and (probably) pointer : one who finds victims for thieves, &c.

a spy; sett′er-forth′; sett′er-off′; sett′er-on′; sett′er-out′; sett′er-up′; sett′ing, act of one who sets: direction of current: fixation: mounting: adaptation to music; sett′-to′, a bout: a hot contest:—*pl.* set′-tos′, set-to′s′; set-up′, bodily carriage and physique: (*U.S.*) configuration, arrangement, structure.—**dead set** (see **deadset**); **set about**, to begin, take in hand: to attack: to spread, as a rumour; **set against**, to assail: **set agoing**, to put in motion; **set apart**, to put aside, or out of consideration; **set aside**, to put away: to reject: to annul: to lay by; **set at naught** (see **naught**); **set by**, to lay up: to put aside: (*arch.*) to value or esteem, to care; **set down**, to lay on the ground: to put in writing: to appoint (*Shak.*, a time for): to judge, esteem: to snub: (*Shak.*) to pitch, encamp: to attribute, charge: to lay down authoritatively; **set eyes on**, to see, catch sight of; **set fair**, steadily fair; **set fire to**, to ignite; **set forth**, to exhibit, display: to expound, declare: to praise, recommend: to publish: to start on a journey; **set free**, to release, put at liberty; **set hand to**, to set to work on; **set in**, to begin: to become prevalent: to run landwards; **set in hand**, to undertake: to set someone about doing; **set little, much**, &c., **by**, to regard, esteem little, much, &c.; **set off**, to mark off, lay off: to start off: to send off: to show in relief or to advantage: to counterbalance: to make an offset, mark an opposite page; **set on**, to move on: to incite to attack: to instigate: bent upon; **set one′s face against** (see **face**); **set one′s hand to**, to sign; **set one′s heart on** (see **heart**); **set oneself**, to bend one′s energies; **set oneself against**, to discountenance, oppose; **set one′s teeth**, to clench the teeth, as in a strong resolution; **set on fire**, to ignite; **set on foot**, to set agoing, to start; **set out**, to mark off: to equip and send forth: to start, go forth: to begin with an intention: to adorn: to expound; **set piece**, a piece of theatrical scenery with a supporting framework, distinguished from a side-scene or drop-scene: a picture in fireworks: an elaborately prepared performance; **set sail** (see **sail**); **set speech**, a studied oration; **set square**, a right-angled triangular drawing instrument; **set terms**, deliberately picked, usually outspoken, language; **set to**, to affix: to apply oneself: (*Shak.*) to set, as a bone; **set up**, to erect: to put up: to exalt—jeeringly in Scots **set you** (**him**, &c.) up: to begin: to enable to begin: to place in view: to put in type: to begin a career: to make pretensions; **set upon**, (to) set on. [O.E. *settan*; cog. with Ger. *setzen*, O.N. *setja*, Goth. *satjan*; *settan* is the weak causative of *sittan*, to sit; the noun is from the verb, but may be partly from O.E. *set*, seat, partly from O.Fr. *sette*—L. *secta*, sect.]

seta, *sē′tä*, *n.* a bristle: a bristle-like structure: the stalk of a moss capsule:—*pl.* se′tae (*-tē*).— *adjs.* setaceous (*si-tā′shos*), setose (*sē′tōs, -tōs′*). [L. *saeta* (*sēta*), bristle.]

seton, *sē′tn*, *n.* a thread or the like passed through the skin as a counter-irritant and means of promoting drainage: an issue so obtained. [L.L. *sētō, -ōnis*, app.—L. *sēta, saeta*, bristle.]

settee, *se-tē′*, *n.* a long seat with a back. [Prob. **settle**.]

settee, *se-tē′*, *n.* a single-decked Mediterranean vessel with long prow and lateen sails. [Prob. It. *saettia*.]

setter, setting. See under **set**.

setter, *set′ər*, *v.t.* (chiefly *Northern*) to treat with a seton of setterwort root.—*n.* an issue so produced in cattle.—*n.* sett′erwort, stinking hellebore. [Perh. from M.L.G.]

settle, *set′l*, *n.* a long high-backed bench: (*B.*) a ledge.—*v.t.* to dispose in stability, rest, or comfort: to adjust: to lower: to compact, cause to subside: to regulate: to fix: to establish, set up, or install (e.g. in residence, business, marriage, a parish): to colonise: to make clear: to determine: to decide: to put beyond doubt or dispute: to restore to good order: to quiet: to compose: to secure by gift or legal act: to create successive interests in, use

or income going to one person while the corpus of the property remains another′s: to make final payment of: to dispose of, put out of action, stun, kill.—*v.i.* to alight: to come to rest: to subside: to sink to the bottom (or form a scum): to dispose oneself: to take up permanent abode: to become stable: to fix one′s habits (often with *down*): to grow calm or clear: to come to a decision or agreement: to adjust differences: to settle accounts.— *n.* sett′le-bed, a settle adaptable as a bed.—*adj.* sett′led.—*ns.* sett′ledness; sett′lement, act of settling: state of being settled: payment: arrangement: placing of a minister: a subsidence or sinking: a settled colony: a local community: an establishment of social workers aiming at benefit to the surrounding population: a settling of property, an instrument by which it is settled, or the property settled, esp. a marriage-settlement: residence in a parish or other claim for poor-relief in case of becoming destitute; sett′ler, one who settles: a colonist: a decisive blow, argument, &c.; sett′ling; sett′ling-day, a date fixed by the stock exchange for completion of transactions.—**settle in**, to prepare to remain indoors for the night. [O.E. *setl*, seat, *setlan*, to place; the vb. may be partly from, or influenced by, late O.E. *sehtlian*, to reconcile.]

setwall, *set′wol*, *n.* (*orig.*) zedoary: now, valerian.— Also **setuale** (*-ū-āl*; *Spens.*), cet′ywall, &c. [O.Fr. *citoual*—L.L. *zedoāria*—Ar. *zedwār*.]

seven, *sev′n*, *n.* the cardinal number next above six: a symbol representing it (7, vii., &c.): a set of that number of persons or things: a shoe or other article of a size denoted by that number: a card with seven pips: a score of seven points, tricks, &c.: the seventh hour after midday or midnight.—*adj.* of the number seven.—*n.* sev′en-a-side, a speedy form of Rugby football played by seven men on each side instead of fifteen (also sev′ens).—*adj.* sev′en-day, for seven days.—*adj.* and *adv.* sev′enfold, in seven divisions: seven times as much.—*adj.* sev′en-league, taking seven leagues at a stride, as the ogre′s boots acquired by Hop-o′-my-Thumb.—*n.* sev′enpence, the value of seven pennies.—*adj.* sev′en-penny, costing or worth sevenpence.—*n.* a sevenpenny book.—*n.* and *adj.* sev′en-score.—*adj.* sev′enth, last of seven: next after the sixth: equal to one of seven equal parts.—*n.* a seventh part: a tone or semitone less than an octave: a note at that interval.—*n.* and *adj.* sev′enth-day, Saturday.—*adj.* observing Saturday as Sabbath.—*adv.* sev′enthly, in the seventh place.—**Seven against Thebes**, the war of seven heroes to reinstate Polynices in Thebes against Eteocles; **Seven Champions of Christendom**, St George for England, St Andrew for Scotland, St Patrick for Ireland, St David for Wales, St Denis for France, St James for Spain, St Anthony for Italy; **seven deadly sins**, pride, covetousness, lust, anger, gluttony, envy, and sloth; **Seven Sages**, Solon of Athens, Thales of Miletus, Pittacus of Mitylene, Bias of Priene in Caria, Chilon of Sparta, Cleobulus tyrant of Lindus in Rhodes, and Periander tyrant of Corinth: an Eastern cycle of tales in which seven wise men contend in story-telling against a woman for the life of a belied prince; **Seven Seas**, the Arctic, Antarctic, North and South Atlantic, North and South Pacific, and Indian Oceans; **Seven Sleepers**, seven Christian youths at Ephesus said to have slept walled up in a cave *c.* 250 A.D. to 447; **Seven Stars**, the planets known to the ancients: the Plough: the Pleiades; **Seventh-day Adventists**, a sect that expect the second coming of Christ and observe Saturday as the Sabbath; **seventh heaven** (see **heaven**); **Seven Wonders of the World**, the Pyramids, the Hanging Gardens of Babylon, the Temple of Artemis at Ephesus, Phidias′s statue of Zeus at Athens, the Mausoleum at Halicarnassus, the Colossus of Rhodes, and the Pharos of Alexandria; **Seven Years′ War**, the struggle for Silesia between Frederick the Great and the Empress Maria Theresa (1756-63). [O.E. *seofon*; Du. *zeven*, Ger. *sieben*, Goth. *sibun*, Gr. *hepta*, L. *septem*.]

seventeen, *sev-n-tēn',* or *sev',* *n.* and *adj.* seven and ten.—*adj.* **sev'enteen-hund'er,** (*Burns*) woven with a reed of 1700 divisions (i.e. fine linen).—*adj.* and *n.* **sev'enteenth** (or *-tēnth').—adv.* **seventeenth'ly.** [O.E. *seofontiene—seofon, tien,* ten.]

seventy, *sev'n-ti,* *n.* and *adj.* seven times ten :—*pl.* **sev'enties,** the numbers seventy to seventy-nine : the years so numbered in a life or any century.— *adj.* **sev'entieth,** last of seventy : equal to one of seventy equal parts.—*n.* a seventieth part.—**the Seventy,** the Jewish Sanhedrim : the disciples sent out in Luke x. : the Septuagint translators— often LXX. [O.E. (*hund)seofontig.*]

sever, *sev'ər,* *v.t.* and *v.i.* to separate : to divide : to cleave.—*adj.* **sev'erable.**—*n.* **sev'erance.** [Fr. *sevrer,* to wean—L. *sēparāre,* to separate.]

several, *sev'ər-l,* *adj.* separate : private : belonging or pertaining distributively, not jointly : particular : distinct : different : various : sundry : more than one (usu. more than three), but not very many.— *n.* privately owned land, esp. enclosed pasture : private property : (*Shak.*) a detail, particular : (*Shak.*) an individual person.—*adj.* and *adv.* **sev'eralfold.** — *adv.* **sev'erally,** separately. — *n.* **sev'eralty,** separateness : individual ownership. —**in several,** separately, individually. [O.Fr.,— L. *sēparāre,* to separate.]

severe, *si-vēr',* *adj.* rigorous : very strict : unsparing : pressing hard : hard to endure : austerely restrained or simple.—*adv.* **severe'ly.**—*ns.* **severe'ness ; severity** (*si-ver'i-ti*). [L. *sevērus.*]

severy, *sev'ə-ri,* *n.* a compartment of vaulting. [O.Fr. *civoire*—L. *cibōrium ;* see **ciborium.**]

Sèvres, *sev'r',* *adj.* made at Sèvres, near Paris.—*n.* Sèvres porcelain.

sew, *sō,* *v.t.* to join, attach, enclose, or work upon with a needle and thread or with wire.—*v.i.* to ply the needle :—*pa.t.* **sewed** (*sōd*) ; *pa.p.* **sewn** (*sōn*) or **sewed.**—*ns.* **sew'er ; sew'ing ; sew'ing-machine.**—**sew up,** to enclose or close up by sewing : (*slang*) to complete satisfactorily : (*slang*) to tire out, bring to a standstill, nonplus, or make drunk. [O.E. *siwian, séowian ;* O.H.G. *siuwen,* Goth. *siujan.*]

sew (*Spens.*). Same as **sue.**

sew, *sū* (now *dial.*), *v.t.* to drain : *v.i.* to ooze : (*naut.*) to be aground.—*n.* **sew'age,** refuse carried off by sewers. [Perh. O.Fr. *essewer* (cf. **sewer,** 2) ; perh. partly from **sewer** (2), partly from O.E. *séon,* to strain, ooze.]

sewel. See **shewel.**

sewellel, *si-wel'əl,* *n.* an American rodent linking beavers and squirrels. [Chinook *shewallal,* a robe of its skin.]

sewer, *sū'ər,* *n.* an officer who superintends the service at table. [O.Fr. *asseour—asseoir,* to set down—L. *ad,* to, *sedēre,* to sit. Skeat makes it from *sew,* to set, serve, *sew,* pottage—*séaw,* juice.]

sewer, *s(y)ōō'ər,* old-fashioned *shōr,* *n.* a channel for receiving the discharge from house-drains and streets.—*v.t.* to provide with sewers.—*ns.* **sew'erage,** system or provision of sewers : sewage ; **sew'ering ; sew'er-gas,** the contaminated air of sewers ; **sew'er-rat,** the brown rat. [O.Fr. *seuviere,* a canal—L. *ex,* out, *aqua,* water.]

sewin, sewen, *sū'in,* *n.* a Welsh sea-trout grilse. [Origin unknown.]

sex, *seks,* *n.* that by which an animal or plant is male or female : the quality of being male or female : either of the divisions according to this, or its members collectively (*arch.,* **the sex,** the female sex, women) : the whole domain connected with this distinction : (by confusion) sect.—Also *adj.*—*v.t.* to ascertain the sex of.—*ns.* **sex'-appeal',** power of attracting, esp. of exciting desire in, the other sex ; **sex'-cell,** an egg-cell or sperm ; **sex'-chro'mosome,** a chromosome that determines sex ; **sex'-determina'tion,** the settling of what the sex of a new organism is to be.—*adj.* **sexed** (*sekst*), having sex : being male or female : having strongly developed sexual characters, feelings, or desires.—*n.* **sex'-in'tergrade,** an intersex.—*adj.* **sex'less,** of neither sex : without sex : without sexual feelings.—*n.* **sex'lessness.**—*adjs.* **sex'-**

lim'ited, developed only in one sex ; **sex' linked',** inherited along with sex, that is, by factor located in the sex-chromosome.—*n.* **sex' rever'sal,** change from male to female or femal to male in the life of the individual.—*adj.* **sex'ūal** of, by, having, characteristic of, sex, one sex o other, or organs of sex.—*v.t.* **sex'ūalise,** to attri bute sex to.—*ns.* **sex'ūalism,** emphasis on sex **sex'ūalist ; sexual'ity.**—*adv.* **sex'ūally.**—**sexua selection,** that province of natural selection i which preference for mates having certain char acters comes into play ; **sexual system,** th Linnaean system of plant classification according t sexual organisation. [L. *sexus, -ūs.*]

sex-, seks-, sexi-, -i-, in composition, six.—*adj* **sex'fid,** six-cleft.—*n.* **sex'foil,** a window, desigr &c., with six lobes or leaves.—*adjs.* **sex(i)va'len** (or *-iv'ə-lənt*), of valency six ; **sexloc'ūlar,** wit six compartments ; **sexpart'ite,** parted in si> [L. *sex,* six.]

sexagenarian, *sek-sə-ji-nā'ri-ən,* *n.* a person sixt years old, or between sixty and seventy.—*adj.* o that age.—*adj.* **sexagenary** (*sek-sə-jē'nər-i, -saj'in ər-i*), of, containing, based on, sixty : sexagenariar —*n.* a sexagesimal fraction : a sexagenarian. [L *sexāgēnārius,* pertaining to sixty—*sexāgintā,* sixty.]

Sexagesima, *sek-sə-jes'i-mä,* *n.* the second Sunda before Lent (also **Sexagesima Sunday**)—appar ently so named on the false analogy of Quadra gesima, &c.—*adj.* **sexages'imal,** pertaining tc based on, sixty.—*n.* a sexagesimal fraction.—*adu* **sexages'imally,** by sixtieths. [L. *sexāgēsimus, -c -um,* sixtieth.]

sexcentenary, *sek-sen'tin-ər-i,* or *-sin-tēn'ər-i -sin-ten',* *n.* a 600th anniversary.—Also *adj.*

sexennial, *sek-sen'yəl,* *adj.* lasting six years : recur ring every six years.—*adv.* **sexenn'ially.** [L. *se> six, annus,* year.]

sext, sekst, *n.* (*eccles.*) the office of the sixth hou said at midday, afterwards earlier : (*mus.*) a sixth an organ stop giving the twelfth and the tierce (sixth apart).—*adj.* **sex'tan,** recurring every fifth da (sixth by old reckoning). [L. *sextus,* sixth—*sex,* six.]

sextans, *seks'tanz,* *n.* a Roman bronze coin wort a sixth of an as.—*n.* **sex'tant** (*-tənt*), an instrumen with an arc of a sixth of a circle, for measurin angular distances.—*adj.* **sextantal** (*-tant'l*). [L *sextāns, -antis,* a sixth.]

sextet, sextett, sextette, *seks-tet',* *n.* altered form (partly through Ger.) of **sestet.**

sextile, *seks'tīl,* *n.* (*astrol.*) a position 60° apart (als **sextile aspect).** [L. *sextilis,* sixth.]

sextillion, *seks-til'yon,* *n.* the sixth power of million : (*U.S.* after the French) the sevent power of 1000. [For *sexillion,* after **billion,** &c.]

sextodecimo, *seks-tō-des'i-mō,* *n.* a book or a siz of book made by folding each sheet into sixteer leaves :—*pl.* **sextodec'imos.**—Also *adj.* [L. (*in sextō decimō,* (in) one-sixteenth.]

sextolet, *seks'tə-let,* *n.* a group of six notes performe in the time of four. [Ger. *sextole*—L. *sex.*]

sexton, *seks'tən,* *n.* an officer who rings a churcl bell, attends the clergyman, digs graves, &c. : burying-beetle (also **sex'ton-bee'tle).**—*ns.* **sex' toness ; sex'tonship.** [sacristan.]

sextuor, *seks'tū-or,* *n.* a sextet. [Fr.,—L. *sex,* afte *quatuor,* four.]

sextuple, *seks'tū-pl,* *adj.* sixfold.—*n.* six times a much.—*v.t.* and *v.i.* to increase or multiply sixfolc —*n.* **sex'tüplet,** (*mus.*) a sextolet : one of six born at a birth. [L.L. *sextuplus.*]

sey, *sī,* *n.* (*Scot.*) part of a carcase of beef includin the sirloin. [Origin obscure.]

seyen, seysure, Shakespearean spellings of **scion** seizure.

'sfoot, *sfoot, interj.* (*Shak.*) for God's foot.

sforzando, *sfor-tsän'dō,* **sforzato,** *sfor-tsä'tō, adjs* and *advs.* (*mus.*) forced, with sudden emphasis Abbrev. *sf.* and *sfz.,* or marked >, ∧.—Also *ns* [It., pr.p. and pa.p. of *sforzare,* to force—L. e> out, L.L. *fortia,* force.]

sgraffito, *zgräf-fē'tō,* *n.* a kind of decorative work i which different colours are got by removal of oute layers :—*pl.* **sgraffi'ti** (*-tē*). [It.,—L. *ex-,* and I graffito, q.v.]

shabble, *shab'l*, *n.* (*Scot.*) an old rusty sword. [Cf. It. *sciabola*, Pol. *szabla*, and **sabre**.]

shabby, *shab'i*, *adj.* dingy, threadbare, or worn, as clothes: having a look of poverty: mean in look or conduct: low: paltry.—*adv.* **shabb'ily.**—*n.* **shabb'iness.**—*adj.* **shabb'y-genteel'**, keeping up or affecting an appearance of gentility, though really very shabby. [Obs. or dial. *shab*, scab—O.E. *sceabb*.]

shabrack, *shab'rak*, *n.* a trooper's housing or saddle-cloth. [Ger. *schabracke*, prob.—Turk. *çáprãq*.]

shack, *shak*, *n.* a roughly built hut. [Amer.; origin obscure.]

shackle, *shak'l*, *n.* a prisoner's or slave's ankle-ring or wrist-ring, or the chain connecting a pair: a hobble: a staple-like link, closed with a pin: the curved movable part of a padlock: a coupling of various kinds: (in *pl.*) fetters, manacles: a hindrance.—*v.t.* to fetter: to couple: to hamper.—*ns.* **shack'le-bolt**, the pin of a shackle; **shack'le-bone**, (*Scot.*) the wrist. [O.E. *sceacul*.]

shad, *shad*, *n.* an anadromous fish akin to the herring: extended to various other fishes.—*adj.* **shad'-bell'ied**, flat-bellied—opp. to *pot-bellied*: of a coat, sloping away gradually in front.—*n.* **shad'bush**, the June-berry (Amelanchier), flowering at shad spawning-time. [O.E. *sceadd*.]

shaddock, *shad'ək*, *n.* an Oriental citrus fruit like a very large orange, the larger pear-shaped variety, distinguished from the finer grape-fruit: the tree that bears it. [Introduced to the W. Indies *c.* 1700 by Captain *Shaddock*.]

shade, *shād*, *n.* partial or relative darkness: interception of light: obscurity: a shadow: a momentary expression of face: a shady place: (in *pl.*) the abode of the dead, Hades: shelter from light or heat: that which casts a shadow: a screen: (*U.S.*) a window-blind: a cover to modify or direct light of a lamp: an inverted glass vessel formerly put over a clock or ornament: a projecting cover to protect the eyes from glare: an awning for a shop-window: (*obs.*) a lace head-covering: a variety or degree of colour: a hue mixed with black: the dark part of a picture: a very minute difference: the disembodied soul: a ghost.—*v.t.* to screen: to overshadow: to mark with gradations of colour or shadow: to soften down: to darken: (*Spens.*) to shadow forth: (*U.S.*) to lower very slightly, as a price.—*v.i.* to pass imperceptibly (*away, into*, &c.).—*adjs.* **shā'ded**; **shade'less**.—*ns.* **shade'-plant**, a plant adapted to light of low intensity; **shade'-tree**, a tree planted to give shade.—*adv.* **shā'dily.** —*ns.* **shā'diness**; **shā'ding**, making a shade: the marking of shadows or shadow-like appearance: the effect of light and shade: fine gradations: nuances: toning down: modification of sound by anything put on top of an organ-pipe: slight lowering of prices.—*adj.* **shā'dy**, having, or in, shade: sheltered from light or heat: (*coll.*) not fit to bear the light, disreputable. [O.E. *sceadu*; see **shadow**.]

shade, *shād*, *v.t.* (*Scot.*) to shed (the hair). [See **shed**.]

shadoof, shaduf, *shä-dōōf'*, *n.* a contrivance for raising water by a bucket on a counterpoised pivoted rod. [Egyptian Ar. *shãdûf*.]

shadow, *shad'ō*, *n.* shade cast by interception of light by an object: the dark figure so projected on a surface, mimicking the object: the dark part of a picture: a reflected image: a mere appearance: a ghost, spirit: an unreal thing: a representation: a person or thing wasted away almost to nothing: an inseparable companion: a spy or detective who follows one: shade: protective shade: darkness: gloom: affliction.—*adj.* unreal: feigned: existing only in skeleton.—*v.t.* to shade: to cloud or darken: to represent as by a shadow: to typify: to hide: to attend like a shadow, follow and watch: to shadowcast.—*v.i.* to cast a shadow: to darken.—*ns.* **shad'ow-box'ing**, sparring practice with an imaginary opponent; **shad'ow-cab'inet**, a body of opposition leaders meeting from time to time and ready to take office. —*v.t.* **shad'owcast**, in microscopy, to cast shadows of projecting parts of (a specimen) by exposing to

a stream of vapour of a heavy metal.—*ns.* **shad'ow-casting**; **shad'ower**; **shad'ow-fight**, a fight between or with shadows or imaginary foes; **shad'ow-fig'ure**, a silhouette; **shad'owiness**; **shad'ow-ing.**—*adj.* **shad'owless.**—*ns.* **shad'ow-pan'to-mime, -play**, one in which the spectators see only shadows on a screen.—*adj.* **shad'owy**, shady: like a shadow: symbolic: secluded: unsubstantial.—**shadow of death**, the darkness of death: threatening approach of death. [O.E. *sceadwe*, gen., dat., and accus. of *sceadu* (shade representing the nom.); cf. O.H.G. *scato*, Gr. *skotos*, darkness.]

Shafiite, *shaf'i-ït*, *n.* a member of one of the four principal sects of the Sunnites, or orthodox Muslims. [Ar. *Shãfi'ï*, the name of the founder.]

shaft, *shäft*, *n.* anything long and straight: a stem: an arrow: (esp. *fig.*) a missile: the main, upright, straight, or cylindrical part of anything: the part of a cross below the arms: the part of a column between the base and the capital: the rachis of a feather: the thill of a carriage on either side of the horse: a straight handle: a pole: a ray or beam of light: a rotating rod that transmits motion: a well-like excavation or passage.—*adj.* **shaft'ed.** —*ns.* **shaft'er, shaft'-horse**, a horse harnessed between shafts; **shaft'ing**, system of shafts.—*adj.* **shaft'less.**—**make a shaft or a bolt of it** (*Shak. on't*), to venture and take what comes of it—the shaft and the bolt being the arrows of the long-bow and the cross-bow respectively. [O.E. *sceaft*; perh. partly Ger. *schacht*, pit-shaft.]

shag, *shag*, *n.* a ragged mass of hair, or the like: a long coarse nap: a kind of tobacco cut into shreds: the green cormorant (app. from its crest), or other species.—*adj.* shaggy: shaggy-haired.—*v.t.* to make shaggy.—*v.i.* (*Spens.*) to hang in shaggy clusters.—*n.* **shag'-bark**, a kind of hickory tree.—*adjs.* shag'eared (**shagge-ear'd**, *Shak.*); **shagged** (*shag'id, shagd*), shaggy, rough: (*coll.*) tired out.—*n.* **shag'edness.**—*adv.* **shagg'ily.**—*n.* **shagg'iness.**—*adjs.* **shagg'y**, long, rough, and coarse: having long, rough, coarse hair, wool, vegetation, &c.: rugged; **shag'-haired**. [O.E. *sceacga*.]

shagreen, *shə-grēn'*, *n.* a granular leather made from horse's or ass's skin: the skin of shark, ray, &c., covered with small nodules—formerly **chagrin'.**—*adj.* (also **shagreened'**) of, or covered with, shagreen. [Fr. *chagrin*—Turk. *sagri*, horse's rump, shagreen.]

shagroon, *shə-grōōn'*, *n.* an original settler in New Zealand of other than English origin. [Perh. Ir. *seachrán*, wandering.]

shah, *shä*, *n.* the king of Persia. [Pers. *shäh*.]

shairn. See **sharn**.

Shaitan, *shï-tän'*, *n.* Satan: **shaitan**, an evil spirit: a devilish person: a dust storm. [Ar. *shaitãn*—Heb. (see **Satan**).]

shake, *shāk*, *v.t.* to move with quick, short, to-and-fro movements: to brandish: to make to tremble or to totter: to disturb the stability of: to cause to waver: to disturb: to put, send, render, cause to be, by shaking: to scatter or send down by shaking: to split: (*U.S.*) to get rid of, give up.— *v.i.* to be agitated: to tremble: to shiver: to shake hands: to trill: (*pa.t.* **shook**, *obs.* **shāked**, **shākt**; *pa.p.* **shāk'en**, *obs.* **shāked**, **shākt**, **shook**).—*n.* a shaking: a tremulous motion: a damaging or weakening blow: a shaken-up drink: a trillo, rapid alternation of two notes a tone or semitone apart, commonly ending with a turn: a fissure: (*coll.*) a moment.—*ns.* **shake'-bag**, a fighting-cock turned out of a bag: a large fighting-cock; **shake'down**, a temporary bed (orig. made by shaking down straw).—*adj.* **shāk'en.**—*ns.* **shāk'er**, one who shakes: a contrivance for shaking (e.g. drinks); **Shaker**, a name applied to members of various religious bodies, as the Quakers, the Believers in Christ's Second Appearing (founded in Manchester about 1750), the Children of God (founded about 1864); **shake'-rag**, (*obs.*) a ragged fellow; **shāk'erism**.—*adv.* **shāk'ily.**—*n.* **shāk'iness**.—*n.* and *adj.* **shāk'ing**.—*adj.* **shāk'y**, shaking or inclined to shake: loose: tremulous: precarious: uncertain: wavering: unsteady: full of cracks or clefts.—(no) **great shakes**, of (no) great account; **shake down** (*U.S. slang*), to cheat of one's money at one stroke : to extort protection money from ; **shake hands**, to salute by grasping the hand and moving it up and down ; **shake (off) the dust (of) from one's feet**, to renounce all intercourse ; **shake the head**, to turn the head from side to side in token of reluctance, disapproval, &c.; **shake up**, to rouse, mix, disturb, loosen by shaking : (*Shak.*) to upbraid. [O.E. *sc(e)acan.*]

Shakespearian, Shaksperian, Shakespearean, *shāk-spē′ri-ən, adj.* of or relating to *Shak(e)spe(a)re*, or his works.—*n.* a student of Shakespeare.—*n.* **Shak(e)spe(a)riana** (*-i-ä′nä*), items or lore relating to Shakespeare.

shako, *shak′ō, n.* a nearly cylindrical military cap. [Hung. *csákó*.]

shale, *shāl, n.* clay rock splitting readily into thin laminae along the bedding-planes.—*ns.* **shale′mine, -miner; shale′-oil**, oil distilled from oil-shale.—*adj.* **shā′ly**. [Ger. *schale*, lamina ; or from the following word.]

shale, *shāl, n.* (*Shak.*) a shell or husk.—*v.t.* to shell. [O.E. *sc(e)alu* ; cf. **scale**.]

shall, *shal, shəl, v.t.* originally expressing debt or moral obligation, now used with the infinitive of a verb (without *to*) to form (in sense) a future tense, expressing in the first person mere futurity (as **will** in the second and third), in the second and third implying also promise, command, decree, or control on the part of the speaker : must, will have to, is to, &c. (2nd and 3rd persons, and interrogatively 1st) : may be expected to, may chance to, may well (all persons) : may in future contingency, may come to (all persons) :—*inf.* obsolete ; no *participles* ; *2nd pers. sing.* (*arch.*) **shalt** ; 3rd, **shall** ; *pa.t.* **should** (*shood, shəd*) ; *2nd pers.* (*arch.*) **shouldest, shouldst**. [O.E. *sculan*, pr.t. *sceal, scealt, sceal* ; pa.t. *sceolde* ; cf. Ger. *soll*, Goth. *skal*, O.N. *skal*.]

shallon, *shal′ən, n.* salal.

shalloon, *shə-lōōn′, n.* a light woollen stuff for coatlinings, &c. [Perhaps made at *Châlons-sur-Marne*.]

shallop, *shal′əp, n.* formerly, a heavy fore-and-aft-rigged boat : a dinghy : a small or light boat. [Fr. *chaloupe* ; cf. **sloop**.]

shallot, shalot, *shə-lot′, eschalot, esh-ə-lot′*, or *esh′, n.* a garlic-flavoured species (*Allium ascalonicum*) of onion. [O.Fr. *eschalote*, variant of *escalogne* ; see **scallion**.]

shallow, *shal′ō, adj.* of no great depth, concavity, profundity, penetration : superficial.—*adv.* at or to no great depth.—*n.* a shallow place.—*v.t.* to make shallow.—*v.i.* to grow shallow.—*n.* and *adj.* **shall′owing.**—*adv.* **shall′owly,** (*Shak.*) simply, foolishly. — *n.* **shall′owness.** [M.E. *schalowe*, perh. related to **shoal**.]

shalm, *shäm.* Same as **shawm**.

shalt, *shalt*, 2nd pers. sing. of **shall**.

sham, *sham, n.* (*obs.*) a hoax : a counterfeit.—*adj.* pretended : false.—*v.t.* to pretend : to feign : (*obs.*) to impose upon.—*v.i.* to make false pretences : to pretend to be (as *to sham dead, sick*) :—*pr.p.* **shamm′ing** ; *pa.t.* and *pa.p.* **shammed.**—*n.* **shamm′er.**—**sham Abraham** (see **Abrahamman**). [First found as slang, late 17th cent.]

shama, *shä′mä, n.* an Indian song-bird of the thrush family. [Hind. *çāmā*.]

shaman, *shäm′an, -ən, n.* a wizard-priest, primarily of N. Asia : (*pl.* **sham′ans**).—Also *adj.*—*adj.* **shamanic** (*-an′*).—*ns.* **Sham′anism**, the religion of N. Asia, based essentially on magic and sorcery ; **sham′anist.** — *adj.* **shamanist′ic.** [Russ.,—Tungus.]

shamble, *sham′bl, v.i.* to walk with an awkward, unsteady gait.—*n.* a shambling gait.—*n.* and *adj.* **sham′bling.** [Poss. from next word, in allusion to trestle-like legs.]

shamble, *sham′bl, n.* a butcher's market stall : in *pl.* (sometimes treated as *sing.*), a flesh-market, hence, a slaughter-house : (*fig.*) a place of carnage. [O.E. *scamel* (Ger. *schemel*), stool—L.L. *scamellum*, dim. of *scamnum*, a bench.]

shame, *shām, n.* the humiliating feeling of having appeared to disadvantage in one's own eyes, or those of others, as by shortcoming, offence, or unseemly exposure, or a like feeling on behalf of anything one associates with oneself : susceptibility to such feeling : fear or scorn of incurring disgrace or dishonour : modesty : bashfulness : disgrace, ignominy : disgraceful wrong : cause or source of disgrace : a thing to be ashamed of : (*arch.*) those parts of the body that it is felt to be immodest to expose.—*v.t.* to make ashamed : to cover with reproach : to disgrace : to put to shame by greater excellence : to drive or compel by shame.—*v.i.* to be ashamed.—*adjs.* **shamed**, ashamed ; **shame′-faced** (orig. **shame′fast**, O.E. *scamfæst*), very modest or bashful : abashed.—*adv.* **shame′-facedly.** — *ns.* **shame′facedness, shame′fastness,** modesty.—*adj.* **shame′ful,** disgraceful.—*adv.* **shame′fully.** — *n.* **shame′fulness.** — *adj.* **shame′less,** immodest : done without shame.—*adv.* **shame′lessly.**—*n.* **shame′lessness.**—*adj.* **shame′-proof,** (*Shak.*) insensible to shame.—*n.* **shā′mer,** one who or that which makes ashamed.—*adj.* **shame′worthy.**—**for shame,** an interjectional phrase, you should be ashamed ; **put to shame,** to disgrace, esp. by excelling ; **tell the truth and shame the devil,** put the devil to disgraceful defeat by boldly telling the truth ; **think shame,** to be ashamed. [O.E. *sc(e)amu* ; Ger. *scham.*]

shammy, *sham′i, n.* (in full **shamm′y-leath′er**) a soft leather, originally made from chamois-skin, now usually from sheepskin, by working in oil : a piece of it.—Also *adj.*—*v.t.* **sham′oy** (or *-moi′*), to prepare thus. [**chamois.**]

shampoo, *sham-pōō′, v.t.* to massage : to wash and rub (the scalp and hair) : (*pa.t.* and *pa.p.* **shampooed′, shampoo′d**).—*n.* an act or process of shampooing : a preparation for the purpose :—*pl.* **shampoos′.**—*n.* **shampoo′er.** [Hind. *chāmpnā*, to squeeze.]

shamrock, *sham′rok, n.* the national emblem of Ireland, a trifoliate leaf or plant : in living popular tradition the lesser yellow trefoil : in the English poets often wood-sorrel : according to some white clover, hop-trefoil, black medick, or some other (or any) leaf or plant with three leaflets. [Ir. *seamróg*, Gael. *seamrag*, dim. of *seamar*, trefoil.]

Shan, *shän, n.* a member of a people akin to the Siamese, in China, Siam, Burma, and Assam : their language.—Also *adj.*

shand, shan, *shan(d), n.* (*cant*) base coin.

Shandean, *shan′di-ən, shan-dē′ən, adj.* characteristic of Tristram *Shandy* or the Shandy family, or their creator Laurence Sterne.—*n.* a person of Shandean character.

shandry, *shan′dri, n.* (*N. England*) a light cart on springs.—*n.* **shan′drydan,** a shandry : an old-fashioned chaise : a rickety vehicle. [Origin unknown.]

shandygaff, *shan′di-gaf, n.* a mixture of beer and ginger-beer or lemonade.—Also **shan′dy.** [Origin unknown.]

shanghai, *shang-hī′, v.t.* to drug or make drunk and ship as a sailor :—*pr.p.* **shanghai′ing** ; *pa.t.* and *pa.p.* **shanghaied′, shanghai′d′.** — *n.* **shanghai′er.** [*Shanghai* in China.]

shank, *shangk, n.* the leg from knee to foot : the lower part of the fore-leg : a shaft, stem, straight or long part : the part of a shoe connecting sole with heel : the leg of a stocking : a long-handled ladle for molten metal : an act of shanking a golf-ball : (*dial.*) the end, latter part.—*v.i.* to be affected with disease of the footstalk : to take to one's legs (also *v.t.* with *it*).—*v.t.* (*Scot.*) to dispatch unceremoniously : (*golf*) to strike with junction of the shaft.—*n.* **shank′-bone.**—*adj.* **shanked,** having a shank : affected with disease of the shank or footstalk.—**on Shanks's mare,** nag, pony, &c., on foot. [O.E. *sc(e)anca,* leg ; Du. *schonk,* L.G. *schanke.*]

shanny, *shan′i, n.* the smooth blenny. [Origin obscure.]

shan't (sometimes **sha′n't**), *shänt,* (*coll.*) a contraction of **shall not**.

fāte, fär, ȧsk ; mē, hėr (her) ; *mīne ; mōte ; mūte ; mōōn ; dhen* (then)

hantung, shan-tung', -toong', n. a plain rough cloth of wild silk. [*Shantung* province in China.]

hanty, shant'i, n. a roughly built hut. [App. Fr. *chantier*, a timber-yard (in Canada a woodcutters' headquarters).]

hanty, shant'i, n. a song with chorus, sung by sailors while heaving at the capstan, or the like—also **chanty, chantie, chantey** (shan'ti).—n. **shant'yman,** the solo-singer in shanties. [Said to be from Fr. *chanter* (imper.), sing.]

hape, shāp, v.t. to form: to fashion: to give form to: to body forth: to embody: to devise: (obs.) to purpose: to direct: to determine.—v.i. to take shape: to develop: to give promising signs: (*Shak.*) to conduce: to become fit: (pa.t. **shaped,** *Spens.* **shope,** shōp; pa.p. **shāped,** arch. **shāp'en**). —n. form: figure: disposition in space: guise: form or condition: that which has form or figure: an apparition: a pattern: (*cook.*) a mould: a jelly, pudding, &c., turned out of a mould.—adjs. **shāp'able, shape'able; shaped,** having a shape, or a definite, determinate, or adapted shape; **shape'less,** of ill-defined or unsatisfactory shape: (*Shak.*) purposeless.—ns. **shape'lessness; shape'-liness.**—adjs. **shape'ly,** well-proportioned; **shap'en,** fashioned: definitely shaped.—n. **shap'er.**—n. and adj. **shap'ing.**—**in any shape or form,** (often merely) at all; **in the shape of, in the guise of:** of the nature of; **shape one's course,** direct one's way; **take shape,** to assume a definite form or plan: to be embodied or worked out in practice. [O.E. *scieppan,* pa.t. *scóp,* pa.p. *scapen,* to create, form, with new present developed from the pa.p., influenced by the n. *gesceap,* creation, form; cf. O.N. *skapa,* Ger. *schaffen, schöpfen.*]

haps, shaps, n.pl. short for **chaparejos.**

hard, shärd, n. (*Shak.*) a piece of cow-dung.—n. **shard'-beetle,** a dor-beetle, laying its eggs under cow-dung.—adjs. **shard'-borne** (see separate article); **shard'ed,** (*Shak.*) sheltered under dung. [Cf. **sharn.**]

hard, shärd, **sherd,** shərd, n. (now *dial.*) a gap: (*Spens.*) a boundary water: a scrap, broken piece, esp. of pottery. [O.E. *sceard,* cleft, potsherd; cf. *sceran,* to cut; Ger. *scharte,* notch.]

hard, shärd. Same as **chard.**

hard, shärd, n. a beetle's wing-case. [From a misunderstanding of Shakespeare's **shard-borne.**]

hard, shar'd, shärd, (*Spens.*) pa.t. and pa.p. of **share** (1 and 2).

hard-borne, shärd'börn, -born, adj. (*Shak.*) born in dung: later used as meaning borne on elytra. [shard (1); cf. shard (4).]

hare, shār, n. a part allotted, contributed, owned, taken, or (*Spens.*) cut off: a division, section, portion: a fixed and indivisible section of the capital of a company.—v.t. to divide into shares: to apportion: to give or take a share of: to participate in: to have in common.—v.i. to have, receive, or give a share.—ns. **share'-cap'ital,** money derived from the sale of shares in a business, and used for carrying it on; **share'holder,** one who owns a share, esp. in a company; **share'man, shares'man,** a fisherman who shares profits with the owners; **share'-out,** a distribution in shares; **share'-pusher,** one who seeks to sell shares otherwise than through recognised channels; **shar'er.**—**shar'ing.**—**go shares,** to divide; **share and share alike,** in equal shares; **share bone,** pubis. [O.E. *scearu*; cf. **shear.**]

hare, shār, n. ploughshare or corresponding part of another implement.—v.t. to cut, cleave:—pa.t. and pa.p. **shared**; (*Spens.*) **shard** (shärd). [O.E. *scear*; cf. foregoing word, and **shear.**]

hark, shärk, n. a general name for elasmobranchs other than skates, rays, and chimaeras—voracious fishes, with fusiform body, lateral gill-slits, and mouth on the under side: sometimes confined to the larger kinds, excluding the dog-fishes: an extortioner: a swindler: a sharper: a sponging parasite: a person dangerous to sailors.—v.i. to play the shark: to sponge.—v.t. to get by sharking: to get together hastily, to pick up (with *up*).—ns. **shark'er; shark'ing; shark'-oil,** oil from shark's liver, used like cod-liver oil; **shark'skin.** [Origin doubtful; Ger. *schurke,* scoundrel, Austrian Ger. *schirk,* sturgeon, Fr. dial. *cherquier,* to seek, L. *carcharus,* dogfish—Gr. *karcharos,* jagged, have been suggested.]

sharn, shärn, n. (*dial.*) cow-dung.—adj. **sharn'y.**—**sharny peat,** a cake of cow-dung mixed with coal. [O.E. *scearn*; cf. O.N. *skarn.*]

sharp, shärp, adj. cutting: piercing: penetrating: acute: having a thin edge or fine point: affecting the senses as if pointed or cutting: severe: harsh: keen: eager: (*Shak.*) hungry: alive to one's own interests: barely honest: of keen or quick perception: alert: pungent, sarcastic: brisk: abrupt: sudden in onset: clear-cut: unblurred: well-defined: high in pitch, or **too** high: raised a semitone: (obs. phon.) voiceless.—adv. high or too high in pitch: punctually, precisely: sharply.—n. a note raised a semitone: the symbol for it: the key producing it: (*Milt.*) sharpness: a long slender needle: a small sword or duelling-sword: (in pl.) hard parts of wheat, middlings: (in pl.) sword-fighting in earnest.—v.t. and v.i. (obs. or dial.) to sharpen: to shark.—adjs. **sharp'-edged.**—v.t. and v.i. **sharp'en,** to make or become sharp in any sense. —ns. **sharp'ener; sharp'er,** a cheat.—adjs. **sharp'-eyed; sharp'-ground,** ground to a sharp edge.—n. and adj. **sharp'ing,** cheating.—adjs. **sharp'ish; sharp'-looking,** (*Shak.*) hungry-looking.—adv. **sharp'ly.**—n. **sharp'ness.**—adjs. **sharp'-nosed,** having a pointed nose: keen of scent; **sharp'-pointed; sharp'-set,** hungry: keen in appetite for anything, esp. food or sexual indulgence; **sharp'-shod,** (of a horse) having spikes in the shoes to prevent slipping.—ns. **sharp'-shooter,** a good marksman: a soldier set apart for work as a marksman; **sharp'-shooting.**—adjs. **sharp'-sight'ed,** having acute sight: shrewd; **sharp'-toothed; sharp'-vis'aged,** thin-faced; **sharp'-witt'ed.**—**look sharp,** be quick: hurry up; **sharp practices,** knavish ways, verging on dishonesty; **sharp's the word,** be brisk; **sharp-tailed grouse,** a grouse of western Canada and U.S. whose middle tail-feathers are longer than the rest. [O.E. *scearp*; O.N. *skarpr,* Ger. *scharf.*]

shaster, shas'tər, **shastra,** shäs'trä, n. a holy writing. [Hind. *çāstr,* Sans. *çāstra—çās,* to teach.]

shatter, shat'ər, v.t. (*Milt.*) to scatter: to dash to pieces: to wreck.—v.i. to break into fragments.—n. a fragment: impaired state.—n. **shatt'er-brain,** a scatter-brain.—adjs. **shatt'er-brained; shatt'er-proof,** proof against shattering; **shatt'ery,** brittle. [Perh. L.G.; cf. **scatter.**]

shauchle, shawhh'l, v.i. (*Scot.*) to shuffle.—v.t. to put out of shape or down-at-heel.—n. a shuffling gait: a down-at-heel shoe.—adj. **shauch'ly.**

shave, shāv, v.t. to scrape or pare off a superficial slice, hair (esp. of the face), or other surface material from: to tonsure: to remove by scraping or paring: to pare closely: to graze the surface of: to plunder, fleece.—v.i. to remove hair by a razor: to pass or escape with little margin: (pa.p. **shāved,** or arch. **shāv'en**).—n. the act or process of shaving: a paring: a narrow miss or escape: a paring or slicing tool.—ns. **shave'-grass,** Dutch rush; **shave'ling,** a tonsured cleric.—adj. **shā'ven,** shaved: tonsured: close-cut: smoothed.—ns. **shā'ver,** one who shaves: a barber: a sharp or extortionate dealer: (coll.) a chap, a youngster; **shā'vie,** (*Scot.*) a trick; **shā'ving,** the act of scraping or using a razor: a thin slice, esp. a curled piece of wood planed off; **shā'ving-brush,** a brush for lathering the face; **shā'ving-soap,** soap for lathering in preparation for shaving; **shā'ving-stick,** a cylindrical piece of shaving-soap. [O.E. *sc(e)afan*; Du. *schaven,* Ger. *schaben.*]

Shavian, shā'vi-ən, adj. pertaining to the dramatist George Bernard *Shaw* (1856-1950).—n. a follower or admirer of Shaw.

shaw, shaw, n. a small wood. [O.E. *sc(e)aga*; O.N. *skógr,* Dan. *skov.*]

shaw, shaw, v.t. and v.i. Scots form of **show.**—n. show, appearance: the above-ground parts of a potato plant, turnip, &c.

shawl, *shawl*, *n.* a loose covering for the shoulders, &c.—*v.t.* to wrap in a shawl.—*n.* **shawl'ing.**—*adj.* **shawl'less.**—*ns.* **shawl'-patt'ern,** a pattern like that of an Eastern shawl such as those woven in Kashmir; **shawl'-waist'coat,** a waistcoat with a large staring pattern like that of a shawl.—**Paisley shawl,** a shawl such as those made at Paisley, Scotland, in the style of Kashmir shawls—an ornamental device known as a cone being a feature of the pattern. [Pers. *shāl.*]

shawm, *shawm,* **shalm, shäm,** *n.* a musical instrument of the oboe class, having a double reed enclosed in a globular mouthpiece. [O.Fr. *chalemie, chalemel*—L. *calamus,* a reed.]

Shawnee, *shaw-nē',* *n.* an Indian of an Algonquin tribe now mostly in Oklahoma.—*n.* **shawnee'-wood,** a species of Catalpa. [Shawnee *Shawunogi.*]

shay, *n.* See **chaise.**

shaya, See **chay** (2).

shchi, shtchi, *shchē,* *n.* cabbage soup. [Russ.]

she, *shē* (or when unemphatic *shi*), *nom.* (irregularly or ungrammatically *accus.* or *dat.*) *fem. pron. of the 3rd pers.* the female (or thing spoken of as female) named before, indicated, or understood (*pl.* **they**).—*n.* (*nom., accus.,* and *dat.*) a female (*pl.* **shes**).—*adj.* female (esp. in composition, as **she'-ass', she'-bear', she'-dev'il**). [Prob. O.E. *séo,* fem. of the def. art., which in the 12th cent. came to be used instead of the pron. *héo.*]

shea, *shē, shē'ä,* *n.* an African tree (**shea'-tree,** Butyrospermum), whose seeds (**shea'-nuts**) yield **shea'-butt'er.** [Mungo Park's spelling of Mandingo *si.*]

sheading, *shē'ding,* *n.* one of the six divisions or districts of the Isle of Man. [**shedding.**]

sheaf, *shēf,* *n.* a bundle of things bound side by side, esp. stalks of corn : a bundle of (usually 24) arrows : —*pl.* **sheaves** (*shēvz*).—*v.s.t.* **sheaf, sheave,** to bind in sheaves.—*v.s.i.* to make sheaves.—*adj.* **sheaf'y,** perh., made of straw. [O.E. *scéaf*; cf. Ger. *schaub,* Du. *schoof.*]

sheal, sheel, shiel, *shēl,* **shill, shil,** *v.t.* (*Shak.*) to shell or husk.—*n.* **sheal'ing—(sheel'ing—,** &c.) **hill,** a hill where grain is winnowed by the wind. [Related to **shell, shale, scale.**]

sheal, shealing. Same as **shiel, shieling.**

shear, *shēr,* *v.t.* to cut, or clip, esp. with shears : to cut superfluous nap from : to achieve or make by cutting : to tonsure : (*Scot.*) to reap with a sickle : to subject to a shear.—*v.i.* to separate : to cut : to penetrate : to reap with a sickle : (*pa.t.* **sheared,** *arch.* and *poet.* **shore** ; *pa.p.* **shorn,** also, less commonly in ordinary senses, but always of deformation and usually of metal-cutting, **sheared**). —*n.* a shearing or clipping : a strain, stress, or deformation in which parallel planes remain parallel, but move parallel to themselves.—*ns.* **shear'er,** one who shears sheep : (*Scot.*) a reaper : **shear'-hog,** a sheep between first and second shearings ; **shear'-hulk, -leg** (see **sheer**) ; **shear'-ing ; shear'ling,** a shear-hog ; **shear'man,** one who shears superfluous nap from cloth.—*n.pl.* **shears,** (*orig.* and *Scot.*) scissors : now usu. a larger instrument of similar kind, with pivot or spring : applied by Spenser to wings (**winged sheares**) as instruments for cutting the air : a hoisting apparatus (see **sheers**).—*ns.* **shear'-steel,** steel suitable for making shears, &c. ; **shear'water,** a genus (Puffinus ; not the puffins, but akin to the petrels) of oceanic birds that skim the water. [O.E. *sceran* ; O.N. *skera,* to clip, Ger. *scheren,* to shave.]

'sheart, *särt, interj.* (*obs.*) for **God's heart.**

sheat-fish, *shēt'-fish,* **sheath-fish, shēth',** *n.* a gigantic fish (*Silurus glanis*) of European rivers : any kindred fish. [Ger. *scheidfisch.*]

sheath, *shēth,* *n.* a case for a sword or blade : a close-fitting (esp. tubular or long) covering : a clasping leaf-base : an insect's wing-case :—*pl.* **sheaths** (*shēdhz*).—*v.t.* **sheathe** (*shēdh*), to put into or cover with a sheath or casing.—*adj.* **sheathed** (*shēdhd*), having or enclosed in a sheath.—*ns.* **sheath'ing** (*-dh-*), that which sheathes : casing : covering of a ship's bottom ; **sheath'-knife,** a

knife encased in a sheath.—*adjs.* **sheath'less, sheath'-winged,** coleopterous ; **sheath'y** (*-th* or *-dh-*), sheath-like.—**sheathe the sword,** to en[d] war. [O.E. *scéath, scǽth* ; Ger. *scheide,* O.N. *skeithir.*]

sheave, *shēv,* *n.* a shive, slice, slab : a groove[d] wheel, pulley-wheel : a fragment : a speck, par[ticle] ticle of impurity, as in paper. [Related to **shive.**]

sheave, sheaves, &c. See **sheaf.**

Sheba, *shē'bä.* See **Saba.**

shebang, *shē-bang',* *n.* a room, house, shop, hut &c. : a vehicle : affair, matter, &c. [U.S. slang.]

Shebat, *shē'bät,* *n.* the fifth (ecclesiastically eleventh Jewish month, parts of January and February.— Also **Se'bat.** [Heb. *Sh'bāt.*]

shebeen, *shi-bēn',* *n.* an illicit liquor-shop.—*v.i.* t[o] keep a shebeen.—*ns.* **shebeen'er ; shebeen'ing** [Anglo-Ir.]

Shechinah, *shi-kī'nä,* *n.* Same as **Shekinah.**

shecklaton. See **checklaton.**

shed, *shed,* *v.t.* to part, separate : to cast off : t[o] drop : to emit : to pour forth : to cast, throw (a light) : to impart : to cause effusion of : (*dial.*) t[o] spill : (*Spens.*) to besprinkle.—*v.i.* to fall off (*Spens.*) to dispense : (*pr.p.* **shedd'ing** ; *pa.t.* an[d] *pa.p.* **shed**).—*n.* (*obs.* or *dial.*) a parting.—*adj* cast : spilt, emitted.—*ns.* **shedd'er,** one wh[o] sheds : a female salmon or the like after spawning **shedd'ing.** [O.E. *scádan, scéadan* (strong vb.) to separate ; Ger. *scheiden.*]

shed, *shed,* *n.* a structure, often open-fronted, fo[r] storing or shelter : an outhouse. [App. a varian[t] of **shade.**]

sheel, sheeling. See under **sheal, shieling.**

sheen, *shēn, adj.* (*poet.*) beautiful : bright : shining —*n.* shine : lustre : radiance : glistening attire.— *v.i.* (*obs.* except *Scot.*) to shine : to gleam : to hav[e] a lustre.—*adj.* **sheen'y,** lustrous : glistening [O.E. *scéne* (W.S. *scíene, scȳne*), beautiful ; D[u] *schoon,* Ger. *schön* : influenced by **shine.**]

sheeny, *shēn'i,* *n.* (*slang*) a Jew.—*adj.* Jewish.

sheep, *shēp,* *n.* a beardless woolly wild or domesti[c] animal (Ovis) of the goat family: sheepskin : [a] sheepish person : one who is like a sheep, as i[n] being a member of a flock (or congregation), i[n] following an example, in being at the mercy of th[e] wolf or the shearer, in tameness of spirit, &c.:— *pl.* **sheep.**—*n.* **sheep'-biter,** a dog that bites o[r] worries sheep : (*Shak.*) prob. an oppressive super[ior] visor.—*n.* and *adj.* **sheep'-biting,** hang-dog.—*n[s.]* **sheep'-cote,** an enclosure for sheep ; **sheep'-dip** a disinfectant vermin-killing preparation used i[n] washing sheep ; **sheep'-dog,** a dog trained t[o] watch sheep, or of a breed used for that purpose (*slang*) a chaperon.—*adj.* **sheep'-faced,** sheepis[h] bashful. — *ns.* **sheep'-farmer ; sheep'-fold sheep'-hook,** a shepherd's crook.—*adj.* **sheep'ish** like a sheep : awkwardly out of countenance.— *adv.* **sheep'ishly.**—*ns.* **sheep'ishness ; sheep' ked,** a wingless fly (Melophagus) that sucks sheep' blood ; **sheep'-louse,** a louse (Trichodectes) tha[t] infests sheep : (loosely) a sheep-ked :—*pl.* **sheep' lice ; sheep'-master,** owner of sheep ; **sheep' pen ; sheep'-plant,** vegetable sheep ; **sheep' pox,** a contagious eruptive disease of sheep, re sembling smallpox ; **sheep'-rot,** liver rot ; **sheep' run,** a tract of grazing country for sheep ; **sheep's' bit (or sheep's scabious),** a campanulaceous plan[t] (Jasione) with blue heads resembling scabious **sheep'-scab,** a mange in sheep transmitted b[y] mites ; **sheep'-scor'ing,** the counting of shee[p] (**sheep-scoring numerals,** numerals of Ol[d] Welsh origin, used by shepherds, knitters, and i[n] counting-out rhymes by children) ; **sheep's' eye,** a wishful amorous look ; **sheep's'-foot,** [a] printer's claw-hammer ; **sheep'-shank,** a sheep' leg : (*Scot.*) something of slender importance a nautical knot for shortening a rope ; **sheep's' head,** the head of a sheep, esp. as food (also *adj.*) a dolt : an American fish allied to the porgie **sheep'-shearer ; sheep'-shearing ; sheep' silver,** money paid in commutation of some righ[t] connected with sheep ; **sheep'skin,** the skin of [a] sheep : leather or parchment prepared from it **sheep'-stealer ; sheep'-stealing ; sheep'-tick**[,] strictly, a tick (Ixodes) that infests sheep : commonly, a sheep-ked ; **sheep'-track** ; **sheep'walk,** a range of pasture for sheep ; **sheep'-wash,** sheepdip.—*adjs.* **sheep'-whis'tling,** (*Shak.*) tending sheep ; **sheep'y,** (*rare*) sheeplike.—**black sheep,** the disreputable member of a family or group. [O.E. *scéap* ; Ger. *schaf.*]

heer, *shēr, adj.* (*arch.*) bright, clear : thin : pure : unmingled : mere, downright : plumb : unbroken : vertical or very nearly.—*adv.* clear : quite : plumb : vertically.—*n.* a very thin fabric.—*adv.* **sheer'ly.** [M.E. *schēre,* perh. from a lost O.E. equivalent of O.N. *skærr,* bright.]

heer, *shēr, v.i.* to deviate : to swerve.—*v.t.* to cause to deviate.—*n.* deviation : oblique position : fore-and-aft upward curve of a ship's deck or sides. —*ns.* **sheer'-hulk,** an old dismasted ship with a pair of sheers mounted on it : popularly, a mere hulk, as if from **sheer** (1) ; **sheer'-leg, shear'-leg,** one of the spars of sheers.—*n.pl.* **sheers, shears,** an apparatus for hoisting heavy weights, having legs or spars spread apart at their lower ends, and hoisting tackle at their joined tops.— **sheer off,** to move aside : to take oneself off. [Partly at least another spelling of **shear** ; perh. partly from the L.G. or Du. equivalent, *scheren,* to cut, withdraw.]

heet, *shēt, n.* a large wide expanse or thin piece : a large broad piece of cloth, esp. for a bed, a penitent, or a corpse : a large broad piece of paper : a section of a book printed upon one piece of paper, a signature : as much copy as will fill a sheet : a pamphlet, broadside, or newspaper : (*poet.*) a sail : (*geol.*) a sill (**intrusive sheet**) : sheet-rubber.—*adj.* in the form of a sheet : printed on a sheet.—*v.t.* to wrap or cover with, or as with, a sheet : to furnish with sheets : to form into sheets.—*v.i.* to form or run in a sheet.—*ns.* **sheet'-copper, -iron, -lead, -metal, -rubber, -tin, &c.,** copper, iron, &c., in thin sheets.—*adj.* **sheet'ed,** wrapped or covered with a sheet, esp. a winding-sheet : with a white band or belt, as a cow : spread as a sheet.—*ns.* **sheet'-glass,** a kind of crown-glass made in a cylinder and flattened out ; **sheet'ing,** cloth for sheets : protective boarding or metal covering : formation into sheets ; **sheet'-light'-ning,** diffused appearance of distant lightning.— *adj.* **sheet'y.** [O.E. *scéte* (W.S. *scíete*), *scéat* ; cf. next word.]

heet, *shēt, n.* a rope attached to the lower corner of a sail : (in *pl.*) the part of a boat between the thwarts and the stern or bow.—**a sheet,** or **three sheets, in the wind,** half-drunk, or drunk. [O.E. *scéata,* corner ; akin to foregoing.]

heet-anchor, *shēt'angk'ər, n.* an anchor for an emergency : chief support : last refuge. [Formerly *shut-, shot-, shoot-anchor* ; origin doubtful.]

heikh, sheik, *shāk, shēk, n.* an Arab chief : (*slang*) a girl's young man or ideal film hero : a Hindu convert to Islam. [Ar. *shaikh—shākha,* to be old.]

heiling. Same as **shieling.**

hekel, *shek'l, n.* a Jewish weight (about half an ounce) and coin (about 2s. 9d.) : (in *pl.* ; *slang*) money. [Hcb. *sheqel—shāqal,* to weigh.]

hekinah, Shechinah, *shi-kī'nä, n.* the divine presence. [Heb. *shekīnāh—shākan,* to dwell.]

heldrake. *shel'drāk, n.* a large duck (Tadorna) with free hind-toe.—Also **shell'drake, shiel'drake :**— *fem.* **sheld'duck, shel'duck, shell'duck, shiel'-duck.** [Prob. dial. *sheld* (cf. Du. *schillede*), variegation, and **drake.**]

helf, *shelf, n.* a board fixed on a wall, in a bookcase, &c., for laying things on : a shelfful : a terrace : a ledge : a shoal : a sandbank :—*pl.* **shelves,** (*shelvz*). —*v.t.* to shelve.—*ns.* **shelf'-cat'alogue,** a library catalogue arranged by shelves ; **shelf'ful,** enough to fill a shelf :—*pl.* **shelf'fuls** ; **shelf'-mark,** indication on a book of its place in a library ; **shelf'-room,** space or accommodation on shelves.—*adj.* **shelf'y.**—**on the shelf,** shelved : laid aside from employment or prospect of marriage. [O.E. *scylf,* shelf, ledge, pinnacle, or L.G. *schelf* ; perh. partly from some other source.]

hell, *shel, n.* a hard outer covering, esp. of a shell-fish, a tortoise, an egg, or a nut : a husk, pod, or rind : a shelled mollusc : an outer framework : a crust : a hollow sphere or the like : a mere outside, empty case, or lifeless relic : any frail structure : a frail boat : a light coffin : a conch trumpet : a lyre of tortoise shell : an explosive projectile shot from a cannon : a piece of quicklime : in some schools, an intermediate class (from one that met in an apse at Westminster).—*adj.* of, with, or like shell or shells.—*v.t.* to separate from the shell : to case : to throw shells at.—*v.i.* to peel, scale : to separate from the shell.—*n.* **shellac, shell-lac** (*shel-ak'* ; also *shel'ak*), lac in thin plates, got by melting seed-lac, straining, and dropping.—*v.t.* to coat with shellac :—*pr.p.* **shellack'ing ;** *pa.t.* and *pa.p.* **shellacked'.**—*ns.* **shell'back,** an old sailor ; **shell'bark,** a hickory with peeling bark.— *adj.* **shell'bound,** unable to escape from the shell. —*n.* **shell'crater,** a hole in the ground made by a bursting shell.—*adj.* **shelled,** having a shell : separated from the shell.—*ns.* **shell'-egg,** one in the shell, in its natural state ; **shell'er ; shell'fire,** bombardment with shells ; **shell'fish,** a shelled aquatic invertebrate, esp. a mollusc or crustacean, or such animals collectively ; **shell'ful ; shell'-heap,** a heap of shells : a kitchen midden ; **shell'-hole,** a shell-crater ; **shell'-ice,** ice no longer supported by water ; **shell'iness ; shell'ing ; shell'-jack'et,** tight, short undress military jacket.—*adjs.* **shell'-less ; shell'-like.**—*ns.* **shell'-lime,** lime made from sea-shells ; **shell'-lime'stone,** a limestone mainly consisting of shells ; **shell'-marl,** a white, earthy, lacustrine deposit ; **shell'-mon'ey,** wampum ; **shell'-mound,** a shell-heap ; **shell'-or'nament,** decoration in which a shell-form is prominent ; **shell'-parakeet, -parrot,** the budgerigar.—*adj.* **shell'-proof,** able to resist shells or bombs.—*ns.* **shell'-sand,** sand consisting in great part of calcareous organic remains ; **shell'shock,** mental disturbance caused by bursting of shells near at hand.—*adj.* **shell'shocked.**—*n.* **shell'-work,** work composed of or adorned with shells.— *adj.* **shell'y,** of or like shell or shells : abounding in shells : having a shell : testaceous.—*n.* **shell'y-coat,** (*Scot.*) a water goblin dressed in shells : a sheriff's messenger.—**shell out,** (*slang*) to pay up : to disburse. [O.E. *scell* (W.S. *sciell*) ; Du. *schel,* O.N. *skel.*]

Shelta, *shel'tä, n.* an Irish vagrants' secret jargon. [*Shelrū,* poss. a perversion of O.Irish *béulra,* language.]

shelter, *shel'tər, n.* a shielding or screening structure, esp. against weather : a place of refuge, retreat, or temporary lodging in distress : asylum : screening : protection.—*v.t.* to screen : to shield : to afford asylum or lodging to : to harbour.—*v.i.* to take shelter.—*adj.* **shel'tered.**—*n.* **shel'terer.**—*n.* and *adj.* **shel'tering.**—*adjs.* **shel'terless ; shel'tery,** affording shelter. [Doubtfully referred to obs. *sheltron,* which is—O.E. *scield-* (*sceld-*) *truma,* shield-troop, phalanx—*scield* (Anglian *sceld*), shield, *truma,* troop—*trum,* firm.]

sheltie, shelty, *shel'ti, n.* a Shetland pony. [Perh. O.N. *Hjalti,* Shetlander.]

shelve, *shelv, v.t.* to furnish with shelves : to place on a shelf : to put aside.—*v.i.* to slope, incline.— *n.* a ledge : a shelf.—*n.pl.* **shelves,** *pl.* of **shelf** and of **shelve.**—*n.* **shelv'ing,** provision of, or material for, shelves : shelves collectively : the act of putting upon a shelf or setting aside : a slope.— *adj.* shallowing : sloping.—*adj.* **shel'vy,** having sandbanks : overhanging. [See **shelf.**]

Shemite, &c. See **Semite, &c.**

shemozzle, *shi-moz'l, n.* (*slang*) a mess : a scrape : a rumpus.—Also **shlemozz'le.**—*v.i.* to make off. [Yiddish,—Ger. *schlimm,* bad, Heb. *mazzâl,* luck.]

shenanigan, *shi-nan'i-gən, n.* (*U.S. slang*) trickery : humbug.

shend, *shend, v.t.* (*obs.* or *poet.*) to put to shame : to disgrace : to reproach : to punish : to discomfit :— *pa.t.* and *pa.p.* **shent.** [O.E. *scendan,* to disgrace.]

she-oak, *shē'-ōk, n.* (*Austr.*) a casuarina tree. [**she,** in the sense of inferior, and **oak,** from the grain of its wood.]

Sheol, *shē'ōl, n.* the place of departed spirits. [Heb. *she'ōl.*]

shepherd, shep′ərd, n. one who tends sheep (fem. **shep′herdess**): a swain: a pastor.—v.t. to tend or guide as a shepherd: to watch over, protect the interests of, or one's own interests in.—v.i. to tend sheep.—adj. **shep′herdless**.—n. **shep′herdling**, a little shepherd.—**Shepherd kings**, the Hyksos; **shepherd's check**, tartan, a small black and white checked pattern; **shepherd's club**, the great mullein; **shepherd's cress**, a small cruciferous plant, Teesdalia; **shepherd's myrtle**, butcher's broom; **shepherd's needle**, Venus's comb; **shepherd's pie**, a dish of meat cooked with potatoes on the top; **shepherd's purse**, a cosmopolitan cruciferous weed with flat obcordate pods (Capsella bursa-pastoris); **shepherd's rod**, the small teasel; **the Good Shepherd**, Jesus Christ (John x. 11). [O.E. scéaphirde; see sheep, herd.]

sherardise, sher′ərd-īz, v.t. to coat with zinc by heating with zinc-dust in absence of air. [From Sherard Cowper-Coles, the inventor of the process.]

Sheraton, sher′ə-tən, n. a kind or style of furniture designed by Thomas Sheraton (1751-1806).

sherbet, shər′bət, n. a fruit-juice drink: a childish effervescent drink, or powder for making it: (U.S.) a kind of water-ice. [Turk. and Pers. sherbet, from Ar.; cf. **shrub** (2), **syrup**.]

sherd, shərd, n. See **shard**.

shere, a Spenserian spelling of **sheer** (bright).

sheriat, sher-ē′at, n. the body of Islamic religious law. [Turk. sheri′at, law.]

sherif, shereef, shə-rēf′, n. a descendant of Mohammed through his daughter Fatima: a prince, esp. the Sultan of Morocco: the chief magistrate of Mecca.—adj. **sherif′ian, shereef′ian**. [Ar. sharīf, noble, lofty.]

sheriff, sher′if, n. (hist.) the king's representative in a shire, with wide powers judicial and executive: now in England, the chief officer of the crown in the shire, his duties being chiefly ministerial rather than judicial: in Scotland, the chief judge of the county: in the United States, the chief executive officer of the county, his principal duties to maintain peace and order, attend courts, guard prisoners, serve processes, and execute judgments.—ns. **sher′iffalty, shrievalty**; **sher′iff-clerk′**, in Scotland, the registrar of the sheriff's court, who has charge of the records of the court:—pl. **sher′iff-clerks′**; **sher′iff-court′**, the sheriff's court: **sher′iff-dep′ute**, in Scotland, till the abolition of the heritable jurisdictions in 1748, a lawyer who acted as deputy for the sheriff: thereafter sometimes the sheriff himself:—pl. **sher′iff-dep′utes**; **sher′iffdom**, the office, term of office, or territory under the jurisdiction of a sheriff; **sher′iff-prin′cipal**, in Scotland, a sheriff properly so-called; **sher′iff-off′icer**, in Scotland, an officer connected with the sheriff-court, charged with arrests, serving of processes, &c.; **sher′iffship**, the office of sheriff; **sher′iff′s-post**, (hist.) a painted post for affixing proclamations, at a sheriff's door; **sher′iff-sub′stitute**, a Scottish acting-sheriff, appointed by the crown, resident in his judicial district:—pl. **sher′iffs-sub′stitute**.—**high sheriff**, an English sheriff proper: (U.S.) the chief executive officer of a district; **honorary sheriff-substitute**, one who may act in the absence of the sheriff-substitute; **under sheriff**, an English sheriff's deputy who performs the execution of writs. [O.E. scīrgerēfa—scīr, shire, gerēfa, reeve; cf. **reeve, grieve** (2), Ger. graf, count.]

sherris, sher′is, n. (Shak.). Same as **sherry**.—n. **sherr′is-sack′**.

sherry, sher′i, n. white wine grown in the neighbourhood of Jerez de la Frontera in Spain: a wine of like type.—n. **sherry-cob′ler**, a drink composed of sherry, lemon, sugar, ice, &c.—**sherry party**, a gathering at which sherry is drunk. [Xeres, earlier form of Jerez.]

shet, shet, obs. or dial. form of **shut**.

sheuch, sheugh, shōōhh, n. (Scot.) a ditch, drain.—v.t. to plant temporarily. [**sough** (2).]

sheva, shə-vä′, n. a Hebrew point (:) indicating absence of vowel or a neutral vowel. [Heb. shewā.]

shew, shō, formerly (as Milt.) shōō. Same as **show**:

—pa.p. **shewn** (shōn).—n. **shew′bread**, the twelve loaves offered weekly in the sanctuary by the Jews

shewel, shōō′əl, n. a scarecrow or mark to scare deer. [Connected with **shy**.]

Shiah, shē′ä, n. a Mohammedan sect, or a member of it, recognising Ali, Mohammed's son-in-law as his successor. [Ar. shī′a, sect.]

shibboleth, shib′ə-leth, n. (B.) the Gileadite test word for an Ephraimite, who could not pronounce sh (Judges xii. 5-6): any such test: a peculiarity of speech: the criterion or catchword of a group a cant phrase. [Heb. shibbō′leth, an ear of corn or a stream.]

shidder, shid′ər, n. (Spens.) a female animal. [she deer; cf. **hidder**.]

shied, shier, shies, shiest. See **shy** (1 and 2).

shiel. Same as **sheal**.

shiel, sheal, shēl, n. (Scot.) a hut: a shelter.—n. **shiel′ing, sheal′ing**, a shepherd's summer hut a summer grazing. [Prob. from a lost O.E. equivalent of O.N. skáli, hut.]

shield, shēld, n. a broad plate carried to ward of weapons, esp. one with a straight top and tapering curved sides: a protective plate, screen, pad, or other guard: a protection: a tubular structure pushed forward in tunnelling: a shield-shaped escutcheon used for displaying arms: a shield-shaped piece of plate as a prize: any shield-shaped design or object: (U.S.) a policeman's badge.—v.t. to protect by shelter: to ward off: (Shak.) to forfend.—ns. **shield′-bearer**; **shield′-bug**, a heteropterous insect with much developed scutellum (fam. Pentatomidae); **shiel′der**; **shield′-fern**, Aspidium; **shield′-hand**, the left hand.—adj **shield′less**.—ns. **shield′ling**, a protected person **shield′-maid, -maiden, -may**, an Amazon: a Valkyrie.—adj. **shield′-shaped**, usu., shaped like the conventional shield: sometimes, buckler-shaped: peltate.—n. **shield′wall**, a defence of interlocked shields.—**shield of brawn**, the thick skin of a pig's side, esp. when stuffed with meat [O.E. sceld (W.S. scield); Ger. schild, O.N. skjöldr protection.]

shift, shift, v.i. to manage, get on, do as one can to change: to change position: to fluctuate: to change one's clothes: to resort to expedients: to move: to go away.—v.t. to change: to change the clothes of: to change the position of: to remove to dislodge: to transfer: to evade, shun: to rid to quit: (slang) to swallow: to put off.—n. an expedient: an artifice: provision of clothes or (arch.) other things for use in rotation or substitution: hence, (arch.) a smock: a set of person taking turns with another set: time of working o such a set: a change: change of position: general or bodily displacement of a series (as of lines in the spectrum, consonant or vowe sounds, faulted strata): in violin-playing, any position of the left hand except that nearest the nut: a removal.—adj. **shift′ed**.—ns. **shift′er**, one who shifts, esp. a scene-shifter: one who resorts to shifts, tricks, evasions, or sophistry; **shift′iness shift′ing**.—adj. unstable: shifty.—n.pl. **shift′ing-boards**, partitioning to prevent shifting of cargo.—adv. **shift′ingly**.—n. **shift′-key**, a typewriter key used to bring a different set of letters (as capitals into play.—adj. **shift′less**, without a smock without resource or expedient: inefficient: feck less.—adv. **shift′lessly**.—n. **shift′lessness**.—adj **shift′y**, full of, or ready with, shifts or expedients evasive, tricky, suggesting trickery.—**make** (a **shift**, contrive to do somehow; **shift about**, to vacillate: to turn quite round to the opposite point; **shift for oneself**, to depend on one's own resources. [O.E. sciftan, to divide, allot O.N. skipta.]

Shiite. See **Shiah**.

shikar, shi-kär′, n. hunting, sport.—ns. **shikar′ee shikar′i**, a hunter. [Urdu, from Pers. shikār.]

shill, shilling. See **sheal**.

shillelah, shi-lā′lä, n. the conventional Irishman's oak or blackthorn cudgel. [Shillelagh, an oak-wood in County Wicklow.]

shilling, shil′ing, n. a coin or its value, 12 pence, or **(East Africa shilling)** Kenya, &c.) 100 cents.—

adj. costing or offered for a shilling : also in compounds, as **two'-shilling, three'-shilling,** &c.—*adj.* **shill'ingless.**—*n.* **shill'ingsworth.**—**shilling shocker,** a sensational story published at a shilling ; **take the shilling,** to enlist as a soldier by accepting the recruiting officer's shilling—discontinued since 1879. [O.E. *scilling* ; Ger. *schilling.*]

shilly-shally, *shil'i-shal'i, adv.* in silly hesitation.—*n.* vacillation : one who vacillates.—*v.i.* to vacillate.—*n.* **shill'y-shall'ier.** [A reduplication of **shall I ?**]

shilpit, *shil'pit, adj.* (*Scot.*) sickly-looking : washy. [Ety. dub.]

shimmer, *shim'ər, v.i.* to gleam tremulously, to glisten.—*ns.* **shimm'er, shimm'ering,** a tremulous gleam.—*adj.* **shimm'ery.** [O.E. *scimerian*—*scimian,* to shine ; Ger. *schimmern.*]

shimmy, *shim'i, n.* a shivering dance.—Also **shimm'y-shake.** [App. from **chemise.**]

shin, *shin, n.* the forepart of the leg below the knee : the lower part of a leg of beef.—*v.i.* to swarm, climb by gripping between the legs : to use one's legs, hasten along.—*v.t.* to climb by swarming : to kick on the shins.—*ns.* **shin'-barker,** a cur that barks at one's shins ; **shin'-bone,** the tibia ; **shin'-plas'ter,** (*U.S.*) a brown-paper patch for a sore on the shin : (*U.S.*) paper money of small value. [O.E. *scinu,* the shin (*scinbán,* shin-bone) ; Du. *scheen,* Ger. *schiene.*]

shindy, *shin'di, n.* (*slang*) a row, disturbance.—**kick up a shindy,** to make a disturbance. [Perh. **shinty.**]

shine, *shīn, v.i.* to give or reflect light : to beam with steady radiance : to glow : to be bright : to appear pre-eminent.—*v.t.* to cause to shine (*pa.t.* and *pa.p.* **shone,** *shon* ; *B.,* and in sense of polished, **shined**).—*adj.* (*Spens.*) **sheen.**—*n.* brightness : lustre : sunshine : a dash, brilliant appearance : an act or process of polishing : (*slang*) a tea-party or the like : (*slang*) a shindy.—*adj.* **shine'less.**—*n.* **shin'er,** one who or that which shines : (*slang*) a coin, esp. a sovereign : a small glittering fish of various kinds.—*adj.* **shin'ing.**—*adv.* **shin'ingly.**—*n.* **shin'ingness.**—*adj.* **shin'y,** clear, unclouded : glossy.—Also *adv.* (*Spens.*).—**take the shine out of,** (*slang*) to outshine, eclipse. [O.E. *scínan* ; Ger. *scheinen* ; in some senses perh. a different word ; cf. **shindy.**]

shingle, *shing'gl, n.* a wooden slab (or substitute) used like a roofing-slate (also collectively) : a board : (*U.S.*) a small sign-board or plate : a mode of hair-cutting showing the form of the head at the back (from the overlap of the hairs).—*v.t.* to cover with shingles : to cut in the manner of a shingle.—*adjs.* **shing'led ; shing'le-roofed.**—*ns.* **shing'ler ; shing'ling.** [L.L. *scindula,* a wooden tile—L. *scindĕre,* to split.]

shingle, *shing'gl, n.* coarse gravel : a large pebble : a bank or bed of large rounded stones.—*adj.* **shing'ly.** [Origin obscure.]

shingles, *shing'glz, n.pl.* the disease *Herpes zoster,* an eruption usually running along an intercostal nerve. [L. *cingulum,* a belt—*cingĕre,* to gird.]

shinne, *shin, n.* (*Shak.*) a form of **chin.**

shinny. Same as **shinty.**

Shinto, *shin'tō, n.* the Japanese nature and hero cult.—*ns.* **Shin'tōism ; Shin'tōist.** [Jap.,—Chin. *shin tao*—*shin,* god, *tao,* way, doctrine.]

shinty, *shin'ti,* **shinny,** *shin'i, n.* a game like hockey : the stick (also **shin'ty-stick**), or ball (or substitute) used therein. [Origin obscure.]

ship, *ship, n.* a large vessel, esp. a three-masted square-rigged sailing vessel : a racing-boat : sometimes any floating craft : an aircraft.—*v.t.* to put, receive, or take on board : to send or convey by ship : to engage for service on board : to fix in position.—*v.i.* to embark : to engage for service on shipboard :—*pr.p.* **shipp'ing ;** *pa.t.* and *pa.p.* **shipped.**—*ns.* **ship'-bis'cuit,** hard biscuit for use on shipboard ; **ship'board,** a ship's side, hence a ship ; **ship'-boy,** a boy that serves on a ship ; **ship'-breaker,** one who breaks up old ships ; **ship'-broker,** a broker for sale, insurance, &c., of ships ; **ship'builder ; ship'building ; ship'-canal',** a canal large enough for ships ; **ship'-**

cap'tain, one who commands a ship ; **ship('s)'-car'penter,** a carpenter employed on board ship or in a shipyard ; **ship'-chand'ler,** a dealer in supplies for ships ; **ship'-chand'lery ; ship'-fē'ver,** typhus ; **ship'ful ; ship'-hold'er,** a remora.—*adj.* **ship'less.**—*ns.* **ship'-lett'er,** a letter sent by a vessel which does not carry mails ; **ship'-load,** the actual or possible load of a ship ; **ship'-man,** (*arch.*) a sailor : a skipper : a pilot :—*pl.* **ship'men ; ship'-master,** the captain of a ship ; **ship'mate,** a fellow-sailor ; **ship'ment,** putting on board : a consignment by ship ; **ship'-money,** a tyrannical tax imposed by the king on seaports, revived without authorisation of parliament by Charles I. in 1634-37 ; **ship'-of-the-line',** before steam navigation, a man-of-war large enough to take a place in a line of battle ; **ship'-owner,** the owner of, or owner of a share in, a ship or ships.—*adj.* **shipped,** (*Shak.*) furnished with a ship or ships : embarked.—*ns.* **shipp'er,** one who sends goods by ship ; **shipp'ing,** ships collectively : accommodation on board ship : putting aboard ship : transport by ship : (*Shak.*) a voyage.—*n.pl.* **shipp'ing-art'icles,** articles of agreement between the captain and his crew.—*ns.* **ship'pound,** in the Baltic ports, twenty lispounds ; **ship'-rail'way,** a railway for carrying ships overland.—*adjs.* **ship'-rigged,** having three masts with square sails and spreading yards ; **ship'shape,** in a seamanlike condition : trim, neat, proper.—*ns.* **ship'-tire,** (*Shak.*) a shiplike head-dress ; **ship'-way,** a sliding-way for launching ships : a support for ships under examination or repair : a ship-canal ; **ship'-worm,** a wormlike lamellibranch mollusc (*Teredo,* &c.) that makes shell-lined tunnels in wood ; **ship'wreck,** the wreck or destruction (esp. by accident) of a ship : destruction, ruin, disaster : (*rare*) wreckage.—*v.t.* to wreck : to make to suffer wreck.—*v.i.* to suffer wreck.—*ns.* **ship'wright,** a wright or carpenter employed in shipbuilding ; **ship'yard,** a yard where ships are built or repaired.—**on shipboard,** upon or within a ship ; **ship a sea,** to have a wave come aboard ; **ship's husband** (see **husband**) ; **ship's papers,** documents that a ship is required to carry ; **ship the oars,** to put the oars in the rowlocks : to bring the oars into the boat ; **take ship,** or **shipping,** to embark. [O.E. *scip* ; Goth. *skip,* O.N. *skip,* Ger. *schiff.*]

shippen, shippon, *ship'n, n.* (*prov.*) cowhouse, cattle-shed. [O.E. *scypen* ; cf. **shop.**]

shippo, *ship'ō', n.* Japanese cloisonné ware. [Jap. *shippō,* seven precious things.]

shire, *shīr* (in composition *-shir, -shər*), *n.* a county : applied also to certain smaller districts, as Richmondshire and Hallamshire.—*ns.* **shire'-horse,** a large, strong draught-horse, once bred chiefly in the Midland shires ; **shire'man,** a sheriff ; **shire'-moot** (O.E. *scirgemót* ; *hist.*), the court of the shire ; **shire'-reeve** (see **sheriff**).—**the Shires** (often *shērz*), those English counties whose names end in shire, esp. (for hunting) Leicestershire, Rutlandshire, Northamptonshire, and part of Lincolnshire. [O.E. *scír,* office, authority.]

shirk, *shark, v.t.* to evade : to slink out of facing or shouldering.—*v.i.* to go or act evasively.—*n.* one who shirks.—*n.* **shirk'er.** [Cf. **shark.**]

Shirley poppy, *shər'li pop'i, n.* a variety of common poppy produced at *Shirley,* Croydon.

shirr, shir, *shər, n.* (*U.S.*) a puckering or gathering.—*v.t.* to pucker, make gathers in.—*adj.* **shirred.**—*n.* **shirr'ing.** [Origin unknown.]

shirra, *shir'ä, n.* a Scots form of **sheriff.**

shirt, *short, n.* a man's sleeved undergarment : a woman's blouse : a covering.—*v.t.* to put a shirt on.—*ns.* **shirt'-band,** the neckband of a shirt ; **shirt'-butt'on ; shirt'-frill',** a frill on the breast of the shirt ; **shirt'-front',** the breast of a shirt : a dickey ; **shirt'ing,** cloth for shirts.—*adj.* **shirt'less.**—*ns.* **shirt'-pin,** an ornamental pin fastening a shirt at the neck ; **shirt'-sleeve ; shirt'-stud ; shirt'-tail',** the flap at the back of a shirt ; **shirt'-waist,** (*U.S.*) a woman's blouse.—*adj.* **shirt'y,** (*slang*) ruffled in temper.—**Black Shirt,** a fascist ; **boiled shirt,** (*U.S.*) a white shirt (with starched front) ; **Brown Shirt,** a Nazi ; **in one's shirt,**

wearing nothing but a shirt, or nothing over the shirt; **in one's shirt sleeves,** with coat off; **keep one's shirt on,** keep calm; **put one's shirt on,** bet all one has on; **Red Shirt,** a follower of Garibaldi. [O.E. *scyrte*; cf. **short.**]

shittim, *shit'im, n.* in full **shitt'im wood** (*B.*), the wood of the **shitt'ah tree,** believed to be an acacia: applied also to various other trees. [Heb. *shittāh,* pl. *shittīm.*]

shivaree, *shiv-ə-rē', n.* a U.S. form of **charivari.**—*v.t.* (*U.S.*) to give a mock serenade to.

shive, *shiv, n.* (*Shak.* and *Scot.*) a slice, as of bread: a thin wide cork or bung. [M.E. *schive*; cf. O.N. *skífa*; Du. *schijf,* Ger. *scheibe.*]

shiver, *shiv'ər, n.* a splinter: a chip: a small fragment.—*v.t.* and *v.i.* to shatter.—*adj.* **shiv'ery,** brittle.—**shiver my timbers,** a stage sailor's oath. [Early M.E. *scifre*; cf. **shive, sheave**; Ger. *schiefer.*]

shiver, *shiv'ər, v.i.* to quiver: to make an involuntary muscular movement as with cold.—*v.t.* to cause to quiver.—*n.* a shivering movement or feeling.—*n.* and *adj.* **shiv'ering.**—*adv.* **shiv'eringly.**—*adj.* **shiv'ery,** inclined to shiver or to cause shivers.—**the shivers,** (*coll.*) a shivering fit: the ague: a thrill of horror or fear. [M.E. *chivere*; origin obscure.]

shoal, *shōl, n.* a multitude of fishes, &c., swimming together: a flock, swarm, great assemblage.—*v.i.* to gather or go in shoals, swarm.—*adv.* **shoal'wise,** in shoals. [O.E. *scolu,* troop; cf. **school** (2).]

shoal, *shōl, adj.* shallow.—*n.* a shallow.—*v.i.* to grow shallow: to come to shallow water.—*v.t.* to find to be shallowing: to make shallow.—*ns.* **shoal'ing; shoal'-mark,** an indication of shoalwater; **shoal'ness; shoal'-water.**—*adj.* **shoal'y,** full of shallows. [O.E. *sceald,* shallow.]

shock, *shok, n.* a violent impact, orig. of charging warriors: a dashing together: a shaking or unsettling blow: a sudden shaking or jarring as if by a blow: a blow to the emotions or its cause: a convulsive excitation of nerves, as by electricity: prostration of voluntary and involuntary functions caused by trauma, a surgical operation, or excessive sudden emotional disturbance: (*coll.*) a stroke of paralysis.—*v.t.* to meet or assail with a shock: to shake or impair by a shock: to give a shock to: to harrow or outrage the feelings of: to affect with abashed and horrified indignation.—*v.i.* to collide with violence.—*n.* **shock'-absorber,** a contri ance for damping shock, as in an aeroplane alighting or a car on a bad road.—*adj.* **shocked.**—*n.* **shock'er,** (*coll.*) a very sensational tale.—*adj.* **shock'ing,** giving a shock: revolting to the feelings, esp. to over-sensitive modesty: execrable: deplorably bad.—*adv.* (*coll.*) deplorably.—*adv.* **shock'ingly.**—*n.* **shock'ingness.**—*n.pl.* **shock'-troops,** troops trained or selected for attacks demanding exceptional physique and bravery.—**shock tactics,** (*orig.*) tactics of cavalry attacking in masses and depending for their effect on the force of impact: (*fig.*) any action that seeks to achieve its object by means of suddenness and force; **shock wave,** a wave of the same nature as a sound wave but of very great intensity, caused e.g. by an atomic explosion, or by a body moving with supersonic velocity. [App. Fr. *choc* (n.), *choquer* (vb.), or perh. directly from a Gmc. source; cf. Du. *schok.*]

shock, *shok. n.* a stook, or propped-up group of sheaves, commonly twelve: three score.—*v.t.* to set up in shocks.—*n.* **shock'er.** [M.E. *schokke*; the corresponding word in some Gmc. languages has come to mean sixty.]

shock, *shok, n.* a dog with long, shaggy hair: a mass of shaggy hair. — Also *adj.* — *ns.* **shock'-dog; shock'-head.**—*adjs.* **shock'-head, -ed.** [Cf. **shough.**]

shod. See shoe.

shoddy, *shod'i, n.* wool from shredded rags: cloth made of it, alone or mixed: anything inferior seeking to pass for better than it is.—*adj.* of shoddy: inferior and pretentious: cheap and nasty: sham. —*adv.* **shodd'ily.**—*n.* **shodd'iness.** [Origin unknown.]

shoe, *shōō, n.* a stiff outer covering for the foot, not

coming above the ankle (or **in** U.S. not much above): a rim of iron nailed to a hoof: anything in form, position, or use like a shoe, as in a metal tip or ferrule, a piece attached where there is friction, a drag for a wheel, the touching part of a brake, the block by which an electric tractor collects current: (*pl.* **shoes,** *shōōz*; also, *arch.* and *dial.,* **shoon,** *shōōn, Scot. shün, shin*).—*v.t.* to put shoes or a shoe on:—*pr.p.* **shoe'ing**; *pa.t.* and *pa.p.* **shod** (rarely **shoed**).—*adj.* **shod** (*shod*).—*ns.* **shoe'-bill,** the whalehead, a large African bird (Balaeniceps) with heavy bill; **shoe'black,** one who blacks shoes; **shoe'-brush; shoe'-buckle,** a buckle for the front of a shoe, as fastening or ornament; **shoe'horn, shoe'ing-horn,** an instrument for helping the heel into the shoe: any means of drawing on; **shoe'ing; shoe'ing-smith; shoe'-lace,** a string passed through eyelet holes to fasten a shoe; **shoe'-latchet,** a thong for fastening a shoe, sandal, &c.; **shoe'-leather,** leather for shoes: shoes or shoeing generally.—*adj.* **shoe'less.** —*ns.* **shoe'maker,** one who makes (now more often only sells or mends) shoes and boots; **shoe'making; shoe'-nail,** a nail for fastening a horseshoe: a nail for a shoe sole; **shoe'-peg,** a peg for fastening parts of a shoe together; **shoer** (*shōō'ər*), a horse-shoer; **shoe'-rose,** a rosette on a shoe; **shoe'-shop; shoe'string,** (*U.S.*) a shoe-lace: (*U.S.*) anything paltry: a minimum of capital; **shoe'-tie,** a shoe-lace, esp. an ornate one. —**another pair of shoes,** (*coll.*) quite a different matter; **be in, step into, one's, or a dead man's, shoes,** to be in, or succeed to, one's place; **die in one's shoes,** to die by violence, esp. by hanging; **shoestring fungus,** any fungus forming long rhizomorphs, esp. one that destroys trees. [O.E. *scóh* (pl. *scós*); Goth. *shóhs,* Ger. *schuh.*]

shog, *shog, v.i.* to shake: to sway: to jog: to move on, be gone.—*v.t.* to shake:—*pr.p.* **shogg'ing**; *pa.t.* and *pa.p.* **shogged.**—*n.* a jog, shock. [M.E. *shogge,* perh. related to **shock** and O.H.G. *scoc,* a swing.]

shogun, *shō'gōōn, n.* the commander-in-chief and real ruler of feudal Japan.—*adj.* **shō'gunal.**—*n.* **shō'gunate.** [Jap. *shōgun.*]

shola, *shō'lä, n.* (*India*) thicket. [Tamil *çolai.*]

shola. See sola.

shone, *shon, pa.t.* and *pa.p.* of shine.

shoo, *shōō, interj.* used to scare away fowls, &c. —*v.i.* to cry 'Shoo!'—*v.t.* to drive away by calling 'Shoo!' [Instinctive; cf. Ger. *schu,* Gr. *sou.*]

shook, *shook, pa.t.* of shake.

shool, *shōōl, v.i.* to saunter about, skulk: to beg: to sponge. [Perh. Ir.]

shool, *shōōl, shōl, Scot. shül, shil, n.* and *v.* a dialect form of shovel.

shoon, *shōōn,* an old *pl.* of shoe.

shoot, *shōōt, v.t.* to dart: to let fly with force: to discharge: to precipitate, launch forth: to tip out, dump: to cast: to send down a shoot: (*games*) to kick or hit at goal: to thrust forward: to slide along: to slide the bolt of: to put forth in growth: to crystallise: to pass rapidly through, under, or over: to hit, wound, or kill with a shot: to photograph, esp. for motion pictures: to variegate: to produce play of colour in (usu. in *pa.p.*).—*v.i.* to dart forth or forward: of a cricket ball, to start forward rapidly near the ground: to send darting pains: to sprout: to elongate rapidly: to jut out far or suddenly: to tower: to send forth a missile, &c.: to discharge a shot or weapon: to use a bow or gun in practice, competition, hunting, &c.: to crystallise: (*pa.t.* and *pa.p.* **shot**; see also **shotten**). —*n.* (*Shak.*) a shot: a shooting: a shooting match, party, expedition: a shooting pain: a movement of the shuttle: a weft thread: the shooting of a film: new growth: a sprout: the stem and leaf parts of a plant: a dump: a chute (see **chute**).—*adj.* **shoot'able,** that may be shot, or shot over.—*n.* **shoot'er; shoot'ing,** action of the verb in any sense: a twinge of quick pain: killing of game with firearms over a certain area: the right to do so: the district so limited: the planing of edges that are to be joined.—Also *adj.*—*ns.* **shoot'ing-**

board, a board for steadying a piece of wood for shooting; **shoot'ing-box, -lodge,** a small house in the country for use in the shooting season; **shoot'ing-gall'ery,** a long room used for practice or amusement with firearms; **shoot'ing-iron,** (*slang*) a revolver; **shoot'ing-jack'et,** a short coat for shooting in; **shoot'ing-range,** a place for shooting at targets; **shoot'ing-star,** a meteor; **shoot'ing-stick,** a printer's tool for driving quoins: a walking-stick with a head that opens out into a seat. [O.E. *scéotan*; Du. *schieten*, Ger. *schiessen*; in some senses merging with Fr. *chute*, fall.]

shop, *shop, n.* a building or room in which goods are sold: a place where mechanics work, or where any kind of industry is pursued: a place of employment or activity, esp. a theatre: talk about one's own business.—*v.i.* to visit shops, esp. for the purpose of buying.—*v.t.* (*slang*) to imprison, or cause to be imprisoned: to give employment to:—*pr.p.* **shopp'ing;** *pa.p.* **shopped.**—*ns.* **shop'-bell,** a bell that rings at the opening of a shop-door; **shop'board,** a counter: a bench on which tailors work; **shop'-boy, -girl,** a boy or girl employed in a shop; **shop'-door; shop'-front; shop'ful; shop'keeper,** one who keeps a shop of his own; **shop'keeping; shop'-lift'er; shop'-lift'ing,** stealing from a shop; **shop'man,** one who serves in a shop: (*rare*) a shopkeeper: (*U.S.*) a workshop man; **shopp'er; shopp'ing,** visiting shops to buy or see goods.—*adj.* for shopping.—*adj.* **shopp'y,** commercial: abounding in shops: given to talking shop: concerning one's own pursuit.—*n.* **shop'-sign,** indication of trade and occupier's name over a shop.—*adj.* **shop'-soiled,** somewhat tarnished by being exposed in a shop.—*ns.* **shop'-stew'ard,** a representative of factory or workshop hands elected from their own number; **shop'-walker,** one who walks about in a shop to see customers attended to; **shop'-window,** a window of a shop in which wares are displayed (also *fig.*); **shop'woman.**—*adj.* **shop'worn.**—**all over the shop,** dispersed all around. [O.E. *sceoppa,* a treasury, perh. booth.]

shope, *shōp, obs. pa.t.* (*Spens.*) of **shape.**

shore, *shōr, n.* the land bordering on the sea or a great sheet of water: the foreshore.—*v.t.* to set on shore.—*ns.* **shore'-boat,** a boat plying near or to the shore; **shore'-crab,** a crab (*Carcinus maenas*) very common between tidemarks; **shore'-due,** (*Scot.*) a harbour-due.—*adj.* **shore'going,** going, or for going, ashore: land-dwelling.—*n.* **shore'-leave,** leave of absence to go ashore.—*adj.* **shore'less,** having no shore, unlimited.—*ns.* **shore'-line,** the line of meeting of land and water: a rope connecting a net with the land; **shore'man,** a dweller on the shore: a landsman: (*U.S.* also **shores'man**) one who has a shoregoing job connected with fishery; **shore'-side,** the neighbourhood of the shore.—Also *adj.*—*adj.* and *adv.* **shore'ward.** — *adv.* **shore'wards.** — *n.* **shore'weed,** a plant (*Litorella lacustris*) of lake-margins of the plantain family.—**on shore,** on the land: ashore. [M.E. *schore*; cf. Du. *schoor, schor.*]

shore, *shōr, n.* a prop.—*v.t.* to prop (often with *up*). —*ns.* **shor'er; shor'ing,** propping: a set of props. [Cf. Du. *schoor,* O.N. *skortha.*]

shore, *shōr, v.t.* (*Scot.*) to warn, threaten: to offer. —*n.* threatening. [Origin obscure.]

shore, *shōr, n.* (*arch.* and *coll.*) a sewer—usu. (as *Shak.*) **common-shore.** [Perh. **sewer;** perh. **shore** (1).]

shore, *shōr, pa.t.,* **shorn,** *shorn, pa.p.* See **shear.**

short, *short, adj.* of little length, tallness, extent, or duration: in the early future (as *short day, date*): concise: curt: abrupt: snappish: crisp yet readily crumbling: brittle: on the hither side: failing to go far enough or reach the standard: deficient: lacking: scanty, in inadequate supply: in want, ill supplied: in default: unable to meet engagements: pertaining to the sale of what one cannot supply: (*pros.* of accentual verse, loosely) unaccented: (*coll.*) undiluted with water, neat: **short-woolled.**—*adv.* briefly: abruptly: without leaving a stump: on this or the near side.—*n.* that which is short: shortness, abbreviation, summary:

a short-circuit: (in *pl.,* formerly) small-clothes, (now) short trousers (as for football): (in *pl.*) the bran and coarse part of meal, in mixture.—*v.t.* and *v.i.* (*obs.*) to shorten: to short-circuit: (*Shak.*) to fall short of, or perh. make to fail.—*ns.* **short'age,** deficiency; **short'bread,** a brittle crumbling cake of flour and butter; **short'cake,** shortbread or other friable cake: (*U.S.*) a light cake, prepared in layers with fruit between, served with cream; **short'-cir'cuit,** (*elect.*) a new path of comparatively low resistance between two points of a circuit: a deviation of current by a path of low resistance.—*v.t.* to establish a short-circuit in: (*surg.*) to interconnect where there was obstruction between: (*fig.*) to provide with a short-cut.—*v.i.* to cut off current by a short-circuit: to save a roundabout passage.—*ns.pl.* **short'-clothes, short'-coats,** the shortened skirts of a child when the first long clothes are left off.—*v.t.* **short'-coat,** to put into short-coats.—*n.* **short'coming,** act of coming or falling short: neglect of, or failure in, duty: defect.—*adj.* **short'-cut,** cut short instead of in long shreds.—*n.* tobacco so cut: a shorter way than the usual.—*adj.* **short'-dāt'ed,** having little time to run from its date, as a bill. — *n.* **short'-divi'sion,** division without writing down the working out.—*v.t.* **short'en,** to make shorter: to make to seem short or to fall short: to draw in or back: to check: to make friable: to put in short-clothes.—*v.i.* to become shorter.—*ns.* **short'ener; short'ening,** making or becoming shorter: fat for making pastry short; **short'gown,** (*Scot.*) a woman's loose jacket; **short'hand,** a method of swift writing to keep pace with speaking: writing of such a kind.—Also *adj.*—*adj.* **short'-hand'ed,** short of workers: with short hands.—*n.* **short'horn,** one of a breed of cattle having very short horns—*Durham* or *Teeswater.*—*adj.* **short'ish.**—*n.* **short'-leg,** (*cricket*) the fielder or the field near the batsman on the leg side behind the wicket.—*adj.* **short'-lived** (or *-līvd*), living or lasting only for a short time.—*adv.* **short'ly,** soon: briefly: curtly: (*rare*) for a short time: a little: with shortness in that which is indicated. — *ns.* **short'ness; short'-rib,** a floating rib.—*adj.* **short'-sight'ed,** having clear sight only of near objects: lacking foresight. — *adv.* **short'-sight'edly.** — *ns.* **short'-sight'edness; short'-slip,** (*cricket*) the fielder, or the field, near the batsman on the off side behind the wicket.—*adjs.* **short'-spō'ken,** curt in speech; **short'-stā'ple,** having the fibre short.—*ns.* **short'-stop,** the player at baseball between the second and third base; **short'-sword,** a sword with a short blade.—*adjs.* **short'-tem'pered,** easily put into a rage; **short'-wind'ed,** soon becoming breathless.—**at short sight,** payable soon after being presented; **for short,** as an abbreviation; **in short,** in a few words; **make short work of,** to settle or dispose of promptly; **short of,** less than: without going so far as; **short sheep,** short-woolled sheep; **stop short,** to come to a sudden standstill; **take (up) short,** to take by surprise or at a disadvantage: to interrupt curtly; **the short and the long (of it;** *Shak.*), same as **the long and the short.** [O.E. *sc(e)ort*; cf. O.H.G. *scurz.*]

shot, *shot, pa.t.* and *pa.p.* of **shoot.**—*adj.* hit or killed by shooting: elongated by rapid growth: (*Spens.*) advanced (in years): with warp and weft of different colours: showing play of colours: (*local*) rid.—*n.* a rejected animal.

shot, *shot, n.* act of shooting: a blast: an explosive charge: a photographic exposure, esp. for motion pictures: a unit in fi'm-production: a stroke or the like in a game: an attempt: a spell: a turn: a guess: the casting of a net: a set of nets or length of net cast: an aggressive remark: an injection: a dram: a marksman: a projectile, esp. one that is solid and spherical, without bursting charge: a cannon-ball: a weight for putting: a bullet: a small pellet of which several are shot together: such pellets collectively: flight of a missile, or its distance: range, reach: a plot of land: (also **scot**) a payment, esp. of a tavern reckoning: a contribution.—*v.t.* to load with shot:—*pr.p.* **shott'ing;** *pa.t.* and *pa.p.* **shott'ed.**—*n.* **shot'-clog,**

(*arch.*) one who is good for nothing but paying the bill.—*adj.* shot'-free, scot-free : safe from shot.— *ns.* shot'-gun, a smooth-bore gun for small shot, a fowling-piece ; shot'-hole, a hole made by a shot or in timber by a boring insect, or in a leaf by a fungus : a hole in a wall for shooting from : a hole bored for a blast.—*adjs.* shot'proof, proof against shot ; shott'ed.—*ns.* shot'-tower, a tower where small shot is made by dropping molten lead into water ; shot'-window, (*obs.*) apparently a window with a hinged shutter : explained also as a projecting window.—a shot in the locker, something yet in reserve ; stand shot, to pay the bill. [O.E. *sc(e)ot, gesc(e)ot* ; cf. shoot.]

shotten, *shot'n*, (*obs.*) *pa.p.* of shoot.—*adj.* (*Shak.*) having ejected the spawn : in composition, dislocated, also shooting out.

shough (*Shak.* showghe), *shog, shok, shuf, n.* a shaggy kind of lap-dog. [Perh. shock.]

should, *shood, pa.t.* of shall. [O.E. *sceolde.*]

shoulder, *shōl'dər, n.* the part about the junction of the body with the fore-limb : the upper joint of a fore-leg cut for the table : part of a garment covering the shoulder : a coat-hanger : a bulge, protuberance, offshoot like the human shoulder : a curve like that between the shoulder and the neck or side.—*v.t.* to thrust with the shoulder : to take upon the shoulder or in a position of rest against the shoulder : to set shoulder to shoulder : to fashion with a shoulder or abutment.—*v.i.* to jostle.—*ns.* shoul'der-belt, a belt that passes across the shoulder ; shoulder'-blade, the broad, flat, blade-like bone (*scapula*) of the shoulder ; shoul'der-bone, shoulder-blade ; shoul'der-clapp'er, (*Shak.*) a bailiff.—*adj.* shoul'dered, having a shoulder or shoulders (shouldered arch, a lintel on corbels).—*n.* shoul'der-gir'dle, the pectoral girdle.—*adv.* shoul'der-height, as high as the shoulder.—*adj.* and *adv.* should'er-high', as high as the shoulder.—*n.* and *adj.* shoul'dering. —*ns.* shoul'der-joint ; shoul'der-knot, a knot worn as an ornament on the shoulder ; shoul'der-mark, (*U.S.*) a badge of naval rank worn on the shoulder ; shoul'der-note, a note at the upper outside corner of a page.—*adj.* shoul'der-shott'en, (*Shak.*) with dislocated or sprained shoulder.—*n.* shoul'der-slip, a sprain of the shoulder.—*adj.* shoul'der-slipped.—*n.* shoul'der-strap, a strap worn on or over the shoulder : (*U.S.*) a narrow strap of cloth edged with gold lace worn on the shoulder with uniform to indicate rank.—cold shoulder (see cold) ; put one's shoulder to the wheel, set to work in earnest, as if to get a coach out of the mire ; shoulder-of-mutton sail, a triangular sail. [O.E. *sculdor* ; Ger. *schulter,* Du. *schouder.*]

shout, *showt, n.* a loud cry : a call : (*slang*) a call for a round of drinks.—*v.i.* to utter a shout : (*slang*) to stand drinks all round.—*v.t.* to utter with a shout. —*n.* shout'er.—*n.* and *adj.* shout'ing.—*adv.* shout'ingly. [Ety. unknown.]

shouther, *shoo'dhər,* Scots form of shoulder.

shove, *shuv, v.t.* and *v.i.* to thrust : to push : to jostle.—*n.* a push, thrust.—*ns.* shove'-groat, shovel-board (also *adj.,* as in shove'-groat shilling, a smooth-worn shilling suitable for playing shovel-board) ; shove'-half'penny, a similar game ; shov'er, one who shoves : punningly, a chauffeur. [O.E. *scúfan* ; Du. *schuiven,* Ger. *schieben.*]

shovel, *shuv'l, n.* a broad spade-like tool : a scoop : a shovelful : a shovel-hat.—*v.t.* to move with, or as if with, a shovel : to gather in large quantities. —*v.i.* to use a shovel :—*pr.p.* shov'elling ; *pa.t.* and *pa.p.* shov'elled.—*ns.* shov'elful, as much as a shovel will hold :—*pl.* shov'elfuls ; shov'el-hat, a hat with a broad brim, turned up at the sides, and projecting in front—affected by Anglican clergy ; shov'el-head, a Mississippi sturgeon ; shov'eller, one who shovels : a duck (Spatula) with expanded bill. [O.E. *scofl,* from *scúfan,* to shove.]

shovel-board, *shuv'l-bōrd,* shuffle-board, *shuf', n.* an old game in which a coin or other disk was driven along a table by the hand : a modern development played in America : a deck game played with wooden disks and cues : a table for the game :

(*Shak.*) a shove-groat shilling. [App. shove and board, confused with shovel and shuffle.]

show (now rarely shew), *shō, v.t.* to present to view : to exhibit : to display : to set forth : to cause or allow to be seen or known : to prove : to manifest : to indicate : to usher or conduct (with *in, out, over, round, up,* &c.).—*v.i.* to appear : to come into sight : to be visible : (*pa.t.* showed, rarely shewed, *shōd* ; *pa.p.* shown, shewn, *shōn,* or showed, shewed).—*n.* act of showing : display : exhibition : a sight or spectacle : an entertainment : parade : a demonstration : appearance : plausibility : pretence : a sign, indication.—*adj.* of the nature of, or connected with, a show : for show.—*ns.* show'-bill, a bill announcing a show ; show'-boat, a steamer serving as a travelling theatre ; show'-box, a showman's box out of which he takes his materials ; show'bread (see shewbread) ; show'-card, a shopkeeper's advertising card : a card of patterns ; show'-case, a glass case for a museum, shop, &c. ; show'-down, putting one's cards face-up on the table : a game like poker : an open disclosure of plans, means, &c. ; shower (*shō'ər*) ; show'ground, ground where a show is held.— *adv.* show'ily.—*ns.* show'iness ; show'ing, act of displaying, pointing out, &c. : appearance : a setting forth, representation ; show'man, one who exhibits, or owns, a show : one who is skilled in showing off things (e.g. his own merits) so as to arouse public interest ; show'manship, skilful display, or a talent for it ; show'-place, a place visited or shown as a sight : a place where shows are exhibited ; show'-room, a room where goods or samples are displayed.—*adj.* show'y, cutting a dash : making a show : ostentatious : gaudy : flashy.—*n.* show'-yard, a yard for cattle-shows.— give the show away, to let out a secret ; show a leg, (*vulg.*) to get out of bed ; show fight, to show a readiness to resist ; show forth, to manifest, proclaim ; show off, to display ostentatiously ; show of hands, a vote indicated by raising hands ; show up, to expose : to appear to advantage or disadvantage : to show clearly by contrast : to be present : to lodge, hand in, as a school exercise. [O.E. *scéawian,* to look ; Du. *schouwen,* Ger. *schauen,* to behold.]

shower, *showr, n.* a short fall, as of rain : a fall of drops of liquid : a fall, flight, or accession of many things together, as meteors, arrows, blows, volcanic dust or (esp. *U.S.*) wedding gifts : (*U.S.*) a party at which gifts are presented : a shower-bath : (*obs.*) an attack, a pang.—*v.t.* and *v.i.* to drop in a shower or showers : to sprinkle : to water.—*n.* shower'-bath, a bath of water showered from above : the apparatus for the purpose.—*adj.* shower'ful. — *n.* shower'iness. — *n.* and *adj.* shower'ing.—*adjs.* shower'less ; shower'proof, impervious to showers.—*v.t.* to render shower-proof.—*adj.* shower'y, marked by showers : raining by fits and starts. [O.E. *scúr* ; O.N. *skúr,* Ger. *schauer.*]

shrank, *shrangk, pa.t.* of shrink.

shrapnel, *shrap'nl, n.* a shell filled with musket-balls with a bursting-charge, invented by General *Shrapnel* (1761-1842) : pieces so scattered : loosely, pieces from any shell.

shred, *shred, n.* a scrap, fragment : a paring, esp. a curled paring : a ragged strip.—*v.t.* (*obs.*) to prune : to cut, cut off : to cut, tear or scrape into shreds. —*v.i.* to be reduced to shreds :—*pr.p.* shredd'ing ; *pa.t.* and *pa.p.* shredd'ed, shred.—*adj.* shredd'ed.— *n.* shredd'ing.—*adjs.* shredd'y ; shred'less.— *n.* shred'-pie, mince-pie. [O.E. *scréade* ; cf. screed ; Ger. *schrot.*]

shrew, *shrōō, n.* a small mouselike animal of the Insectivora, formerly thought venomous : (*obs.*) an evil being : a brawling, troublesome person, now only a woman, a scold.—*v.t.* (*Shak.*) to beshrew. —*adj.* shrewd, (*Shak., Milt.*) evil, hurtful, ill-natured, ill-conditioned, mischievous : severe, hard : formidable : uncomfortably near the mark : biting, keen : (*Shak.*) shrewish, vixenish : (now usually) of keen practical judgment.—*adv.* (*Shak.*) keenly.—*adv.* shrewd'ly.—*n.* shrewd'ness.—*adj.* shrew'ish, of the nature of a shrew or scold :

ill-natured. — *adv.* **shrew'ishly.** — *ns.* **shrew'-ishness**; **shrew'mouse**, a shrew (the beast) :— *pl.* **shrew'mice.**—*adjs.* **shrew'-run**, **-struck**, blasted by a shrew.—a shrewd turn, an ill turn, disservice. [O.E. *scréawa*, a shrewmouse.]

shriek, *shrēk*, *v.i.* to utter a shriek.—*v.t.* to utter shriekingly.—*n.* a shrill outcry : a wild piercing scream : (*slang*) an exclamation mark. — Also **shreek** (*Shak.*, *Spens.*), **shreik** (*Milt.*), **shriech** (*Spens.*).—*n.* **shriek'er.**—*n.* and *adj.* **shriek'ing.** —*adv.* **shriek'ingly.**—*n.* **shriek'-owl**, also (*Spens.*) **shriech-, scriche-, &c.**, **schreech-** (*Shak.*), same as **screech-owl.** [Cf. **screak**, **screech.**]

shrieval, *shrē'vl*, *adj.* pertaining to a sheriff.—*n.* **shriev'alty**, office, term of office, or area of jurisdiction, of a sheriff. [**shrieve**, obs. form of **sheriff.**]

shrieve, *shrēv*. Same as **shrive.**

shrift, *shrift*, *n.* orig. a prescribed penance : absolution : confession : (*Shak.*) a confessional : time for confession before execution (as in *short shrift*). [O.E. *scrift*—*scrífan*, to shrive.]

shright, *shrīt*, *n.* (*Spens.*) a shriek. See also **shritch.** [Perh. a misreading of Chaucer, *Troilus* IV. 1147.]

shrike, *shrīk*, *n.* a butcher-bird, a passerine bird, of which some kinds impale small animals on thorns. [App. O.E. *scríc*, perh. thrush.]

shrike, *shrīk*, *v.i.* (*Spens.*, *Shak.*) to shriek : to pipe as a bird.—*n.* (*Spens.*, *Shak.*) a shriek. [Cf. **scrike**, **shriek.**]

shrill, *shril*, *adj.* high-pitched and piercing : keen : pungent.—*adv.* shrilly : often in compounds, as **shrill-shrik'ing** (*Shak.*).—*n.* **shrill**, a piercing sound.—*v.t.* and *v.i.* to sound or cry shrilly.—*adj.* **shrill'-gorged**, (*Shak.*) shrill in throat.—*n.* and *adj.* **shrill'ing.**—*n.* **shrill'ness.**—*adjs.* **shrill'-tongued**, **shrill'-voiced**; **shrill'y**, somewhat shrill.—*adv.* **shril'ly.** [Cf. L.G. *schrell*, whence prob. Ger. *schrill*.]

shrimp, *shrimp*, *n.* a little wizened or dwarfish person : a small edible crustacean, esp. a decapod of Crangon or kindred genus.—*v.i.* to fish for shrimps.—*ns.* **shrimp'er**; **shrimp'-girl**, a girl who sells shrimps.—*n.* and *adj.* **shrimp'ing.**—*n.* **shrimp'-net.** [Cf. **scrimp**, and O.E. *scrimman*, to shrink.]

shrine, *shrīn*, *n.* orig. a chest or cabinet : a casket for relics or an erection over it : a place hallowed by its associations : (*Shak.*) app. an image.—*v.t.* to enshrine.—*adj.* **shrīn'al.** [O.E. *scrín*—L. *scrīnium*, a case for papers—*scrībēre*, to write.]

shrink, *shringk*, *v.i.* to contract : to shrivel : to give way : to draw back : to withdraw : to feel repugnance : to recoil.—*v.t.* to cause to contract : to withdraw : to fix by allowing to contract : (*pa.t.* **shrank**, old-fashioned **shrunk**; *pa.p.* **shrunk**).— *n.* act of shrinking : contraction : withdrawal or recoil.—*adj.* **shrink'able.**—*ns.* **shrink'age**, a contraction into a less compass : extent of such diminution; **shrink'er.**—*adv.* **shrink'ingly.**— *adjs.* **shrunk**, **shrunk'en**, contracted, reduced, shrivelled. [O.E. *scrincan*, *scranc*, *gescruncen*.]

shritch, *shrich*, *v.i.* (obs. or dial.) to shriek, screech (*pa.t.*, *Spens.* **shright**, *shrīt*).—*n.* (*Spens.* **shriech**) a shriek.—*n.* **shritch'-owl**, screech-owl. [Cf. **scritch.**]

shrive, *shrīv*, also (after *Spenser*) **shrieve**, *shrēv*, *v.t.* to hear a confession from and give absolution to : to confess : to disburden by confession or otherwise.—*v.i.* to receive or make confession :— *pa.t.* **shrōve**, **shrived**, **shrieved** (*shrēvd*); *pa.p.* **shriven** (*shriv'ən*), **shrived**, **shrieved.** — *ns.* **shrī'ver**, one who shrives : a confessor; **shrī'ving**, (*Spens.*) shrift; **shrī'ving-time**, (*Shak.*) time for confession. [O.E. *scrífan*, to write, to prescribe penance—L. *scrībēre*.]

shrivel, *shriv'l*, *v.i.* and *v.t.* to contract into wrinkles :— *pr.p.* **shriv'elling**; *pa.t.* and *pa.p.* **shriv'elled.** [Cf. Sw. dial. *skryvla*, to wrinkle.]

shroff, *shrof*, *n.* in the East, a banker, money-changer, or money-lender : an expert in detection of bad coin.—*v.t.* to examine with that view.—*v.i.* to practise money-changing.—*n.* **shroff'age**, commission for such examination. [Ar. *ṣarrāf*.]

shroud, *shrowd*, *n.* (obs.) a garment, clothes : a

winding-sheet : a covering, screen, shelter, or shade : (*pl.*) a set of ropes from the masthead to a ship's sides to support the mast.—*v.t.* to enclose in a shroud : to cover : to hide : to shelter.—*v.i.* to take shelter.—*adj.* **shroud'ed.**—*n.* and *adj.* **shroud'-ing.** — *adjs.* **shroud'less**, without a shroud; **shroud'y**, giving shelter. [O.E. *scrúd*; O.N. *skrúth*, clothing.]

shroud, *shrowd*, *n.* (*prov.*) a branch : loppings.—*v.t.* to lop. [Prob. same as preceding, with sense from the root meaning of cut.]

Shrove, *shrōv*, *n.* (obs.) Shrovetide.—*v.i.* **shrove**, to celebrate Shrovetide (*to go a-shroving*, to go round singing for money at Shrovetide).—*n.* **Shrove'tide**, the days preceding Ash-Wednesday. — **Shrove Tuesday**, the day before Ash-Wednesday. [Related to O.E. *scrífan*, to shrive.]

shrow, *shrō*, **shrowd**, *shrōd*, old forms (*Shak.*) of **shrew**, **shrewd.**

shrub, *shrub*, *n.* a low woody plant, a bush, esp. one with little or no trunk : (obs.) a scrub.—*v.t.* to lop : (obs.) to cudgel.—*adj.* **shrubb'eried.**—*ns.* **shrubb'-ery**, a plantation of shrubs; **shrubb'iness.**—*adjs.* **shrubb'y**, of, like, having the character of, a shrub : covered with shrubs; **shrub'less.** [O.E. *scrybb*, scrub.]

shrub, *shrub*, *n.* a drink of lemon or other juice with spirits, esp. rum, or (*U.S.*) of fruit juice (as raspberry) and vinegar. [Ar. *sharāb*, for *shurb*, drink.]

shrug, *shrug*, *v.i.* to shudder, shiver : to hitch : to draw up the shoulders.—*v.t.* to shrink : to raise in a shrug : (*pr.p.* **shrug'ging**; *pa.t.* and *pa.p.* **shrugged**).—*n.* a jerk : an expressive drawing up of the shoulders. [Origin obscure.]

shrunk, **shrunken.** See **shrink.**

shuck, *shuk*, *n.* (*U.S.*) a husk, shell, or pod.—*v.t.* to remove the shuck from : to strip off.—*ns.* **shuck'er**; **shuck'ing.**—*interj.* **shucks**, (*slang*) expressive of contempt or disappointment. [Origin unknown.]

shudder, *shud'ər*, *v.i.* to shiver as from cold or horror.—*n.* a tremor as from cold or horror.—*n.* and *adj.* **shudd'ering.**—*adv.* **shudd'eringly.**— *adjs.* **shudd'ersome**; **shudd'ery.** [Cf. Ger. (orig. L.G.) *schaudern.*]

shuffle, *shuf'l*, *v.t.* to mix at random, as playing-cards : to jumble : to put (*out*, *in*, *off*, &c.) surreptitiously, evasively, scramblingly, or in confusion : to manipulate unfairly : to patch up : to shove (the feet) along without lifting clear : to perform with such motions.—*v.i.* to mix cards in a pack : to scramble : to behave shiftily : to shift ground : to evade fair questions : to move by shoving the feet along : to shamble : to hitch about.—*n.* act of shuffling : a shuffling gait or dance : an evasion or artifice.—*ns.* **shuff'le-cap**, a game in which money is shaken in a cap; **shuff'ler.**—*n.* and *adj.* **shuff'ling.**—*adv.* **shuff'lingly.**—**to shuffle off**, to thrust aside, put off, wriggle out of. [Early modern; cf. **scuffle**, **shove**, **shovel**; L.G. *schüffeln.*]

shuffle-board. See **shovel-board.**

shun, *shun*, *v.t.* to avoid :—*pr.p.* **shunn'ing**; *pa.t.* and *pa.p.* **shunned.**—*adj.* **shun'less**, (*Shak.*) not to be shunned.—**upon the shun**, bent on evading notice. [O.E. *scunian.*]

shunt, *shunt*, *v.t.* and *v.i.* to turn or move aside : to move to another track, esp. a side-track.—*v.t.* to by-pass : to side-track : to shelve : to get rid of.— *v.i.* (*coll.*) to be off.—*n.* an act of shunting : a conductor diverting part of an electric current : a switch.—*n.* **shunt'er.**—*n.* and *adj.* **shunt'ing.** [Perh. conn. with **shun.**]

shut, *shut*, *v.t.* (obs.) to shoot, as a bolt : to lock : to fasten : to bar : to stop or cover the opening of : to place so as to stop an opening : to forbid entrance into : to bring together the parts or outer parts of : to confine : to catch or pinch in a fastening.—*v.i.* to become closed : to admit of closing : to close in : (*pr.p.* **shutt'ing**; *pa.t.* and *pa.p.* **shut**).—*adj.* made fast : closed : (*coll.* U.S.) rid.—*n.* (*Milt.*) time of shutting.—*n.* **shut'down**, a temporary closing, as of a factory.—*adj.* **shut-in'** (or *shut'*), enclosed.—*n.* (-*in'*; *U.S.*) an invalid or cripple confined to his house.—*adj.* **shut'-out**, intended to exclude, as (*bridge*) a bid to deter opponents from bidding.—*n.* **shutt'er**, one who, or that which, shuts: a close cover for a window: a device for regulating the opening of an aperture, as in photography, cinematography: a removable cover, gate, or piece of shuttering.—*v.t.* to close or fit with a shutter or shutters.—*adj.* **shutt'ered**. —*n.* **shutt'ering**, closing and fitting with a shutter: material used as shutters: temporary support for concrete work.—**shut down**, to stop working; **shut in**, to enclose, to confine: to settle down, or fall (said, e.g., of evening); **shut off**, to exclude: to switch off; **shut out**, to prevent from entering; **shut up**, to close finally or completely: to confine: (*coll.*) to cease speaking: to reduce to silence. [O.E. *scyttan*, to bar; cf. *scéotan*, to shoot.]

shuttle, *shut'l*, *n.* an instrument used for shooting the thread of the woof between the threads of the warp in weaving or through the loop of thread in a sewing-machine: anything that makes similar movements: a shuttlecock.—*v.t.* and *v.i.* to move shuttlewise.—*n.* **shutt'lecock**, a cork stuck with feathers to be driven to and fro with battledores or badminton rackets: the game played with battledores.—*v.t.* and *v.i.* to shuttle.—*adj.* **shutt'le-wise**, to and fro like a shuttle. [O.E. *scytel*, dart; *scéotan*, to shoot; Dan. and Sw. *skyttel*.]

shuttle, *shut'l*, **shottle**, *shot'l*, *n.* (esp. *Scot.*) a small drawer, esp. in a cabinet or chest. [Perh. **shut**; perh. O.E. *scyttel*, bolt, bar.]

shy, *shī*, *adj.* shrinking from notice or approach: bashful: chary: disposed to avoidance: secluded: warily reluctant: unproductive: scanty: (*U.S.*) lacking: of doubtful repute: (esp. in poker) short in payment: (*comp.* **shy'er**, or **shi'er**; *superl.* **shy'est**, **shi'est**).—*v.i.* to recoil, to boggle: to start aside, as a horse from fear.—*v.t.* to shun (*3rd pers. sing.* **shies**; *pr.p.* **shy'ing**; *pa.t.* and *pa.p.* **shied**, *shīd*).—*n.* a sudden swerving aside:—*pl.* **shies**.—*ns.* **shy'-cock**, not one easily caught; **shi'er**, **shy'er**, a shying horse.—*adj.* **shy'ish**.—*adv.* **shy'ly**, **shi'ly**.—*n.* **shy'ness** (*obs.* **shi'ness**). [O.E. *scéoh*, timid; cf. **skeigh**, Ger. *scheu*.]

shy, *shī*, *v.t.* and *v.i.* to fling, toss (*3rd pers. sing.* **shies**; *pr.p.* **shy'ing**; *pa.t.* and *pa.p.* **shied**).—*n.* a throw: a fling: a gibe: an attempt, shot: a point in the wall game: a thing to shy at:—*pl.* **shies**.—*n.* **shi'er**, **shy'er**. [Origin obscure.]

shyster, *shī'stər*, *n.* (*U.S. slang*) an unscrupulous or disreputable lawyer.

si, *sē*, *n.* the seventh note of the scale, a later addition to the six Aretinian syllables. [Perhaps from the initial letters of *Sancte Ioannes*, the last line of the hymn which gave the Aretinian (q.v.) syllables.]

sial, *sī'al*, *-əl*, *n.* the lighter partial outer shell of the earth, rich in *si*lica and *al*umina. Also **sal** (*sal*).

sialagogue, *sī-al'ə-gog*, *n.* anything that stimulates flow of saliva (faultily **sialogogue**).—*adj.* **sialagogic** (*-goj'*, *-gog'*). [Gr. *sialon*, saliva, *agōgos*, leading.]

siamang, *sē'ə-mang*, *syä'mang*, *n.* the largest of the gibbons, found in Sumatra and Malacca. [Malay.]

Siamese, *sī-əm-ēz'*, *adj.* of *Siam* (Thailand).—*n.* a native, or citizen, or the language of Siam: a Siamese cat.—**Siamese cat**, a domestic fawn-coloured cat, with blue eyes and small head, prob. descended from the jungle cat of India, Africa, &c.; **Siamese twins**, Chinese twins (1811-74), born in Siam, joined from birth by a fleshy ligature: any similar monstrosity: (*fig.*) inseparable.

sib (*Spens.* **sybbe**, *Scott* **sibb**), *sib*, *n.* (chiefly *Scot.*) kinship: kindred: a kinsman or kinswoman.—*adj.* akin, related by common descent: of canaries, inbred.—*ns.* **sib'ling**, one who has a parent or an ancestor in common with another; **sib'ship**, a group of sibs: blood-relationship: clan-relationship. [O.E. *sibb*, relationship, *gesibb*, related; Ger. *sippe*.]

sibilate, *sib'i-lāt*, *v.t.* and *v.i.* to hiss.—*ns.* **sib'-ilance**, **sib'ilancy**.—*adj.* **sib'ilant**, hissing.—*n.* a hissing consonant sound, as of *s* and *z*.—*n.* **sibilā'-tion**.—*adjs.* **sib'ilatory** (*-ə-tər-i*), **sib'ilous**. [L. *sibilāre*, *-ātum*, to hiss.]

Sibyl, *sib'il*, *n.* (*myth.*) one of several ancient prophetesses: **sibyl**, a prophetess, sorceress, or

witch: an old crone.—*adj.* **Sib'ylline** (*-īn*).—*n.* **Sib'yllist**, a believer in the Sibylline prophecies.—**Sibylline Books**, prophetic books offered to Tarquinius Superbus by the Cumaean Sibyl, of which he ultimately bought three for the price he had refused to give for nine: a later set got together after their destruction. [Gr. *Sibylla*.]

sic, *sik*, *adj.* a Scots form of **such**.—*adjs.* **sicc'an** (for *sic kin*, such kind), such: in exclamation, what; **sic'like**, suchlike.—*adv.* in like manner.

Sican, *sik'ən*, *sik'ən*, *n.* one of an aboriginal people in Sicily.—*n.* and *adj.* **Sicanian** (*-ā'ni-ən*). [L. *Sĭcānus*, *Sĭcānus*—Gr. *Sĭkānos*.]

siccar. Same as **sicker**.

siccative, *sik'ə-tiv*, *adj.* drying.—*n.* a drying agent. —*n.* **siccity** (*sik'si-ti*), dryness. [L. *siccus*, dry.]

sice, *sīs*, **size**, *sīz*, *n.* the number six at dice. [O.Fr. *sis*.]

sice. Same as **syce**.

Sicel, *sis'əl*, *sik'əl*, **Siceliot**, *si-sel'i-ot*, *-kel'*. Same as **Sikel**.

sich, *sich*, *adj.* (*Spens.*) a form of **such**.

Sicilian, *si-sil'yən*, *adj.* of *Sicily*: a cloth of cotton and mohair.—*ns.* **siciliana** (*sē-chēl-yä'nä*; It.), **-no** (*-nō*), a Sicilian pastoral dance, dance-tune, or movement, in 6-8 or 12-8 time; **sicilienne** (*si-si-li-en'*; Fr. *sē-sēl-yen'*), a ribbed silk fabric: a siciliano.—**Sicilian Vespers**, the massacre of the French in Sicily in 1282—beginning, according to a late tradition, at the first stroke of the vesper-bell.

sick, *sik*, *adj.* unwell, ill: diseased: vomiting or inclined to vomit: pining: mortified: thoroughly wearied: out of condition: sickly: of or for the sick.—*v.i.* (*Shak.*) to grow sick.—*ns.* **sick'-bay**, **-berth**, a compartment for sick and wounded on a ship; **sick'-bed**, a bed on which one lies sick; **sick'-ben'efit**, a benefit paid to one who is out of work by illness.—*v.t.* **sick'en**, to make sick: to disgust: to make weary of anything.—*v.i.* to become sick: to be disgusted: to become disgusting or tedious: to become weakened.—*n.* **sick'ener**. —*n.* and *adj.* **sick'ening**.—*adv.* **sick'eningly**.—*adjs.* **sick'-fallen**, struck with sickness; **sick'-feath'ered**, with immature feathers at moulting. —*ns.* **sick'-flag**, a quarantine flag; **sick'-head'-ache**, headache with nausea; **sick'-house**, a hospital.—*adj.* **sick'ish**.—*adv.* **sick'ishly**.—*ns.* **sick'ishness**; **sick'-leave**, leave of absence owing to sickness.—*adj.* **sick'lied**.—*adv.* **sick'lily**. —*ns.* **sick'liness**; **sick'-list**, a list of sick.—*adj.* **sick'-list'ed**, entered on the sick-list; **sick'ly**, inclined to be ailing: feeble: languid: pallid: suggestive of sickness: slightly or insipidly sickening: mawkish: of sickness or the sick.—*adv.* in a sick manner: feebly.—*v.t.* (*obs.*) to make sickly-looking.—*ns.* **sick'man**, (*Shak.*) one who is ill; **sick'ness**; **sick'nurse**, a nurse who attends the sick; **sick'nurs'ing**; **sick'room** (also **sick'-cham'ber**), a room to which one is confined by sickness; **sick'-ser'vice**, (*Shak.*) tending in sickness.—*adjs.* **sick'-thought'ed**, (*Shak.*) love-sick; **sick'-tired**, (*coll.*) wearied to the point of disgust. —**sicken for**, show early symptoms of; **the Sick Man**, the Ottoman Empire, or Sultan. [O.E. *séoc*; Ger. *siech*, Du. *ziek*.]

sick, *sik*, *v.t.* to set upon, chase: to incite to attack. [A variant of **seek**.]

sicker, **siccar**, *sik'ər*, *adj.* (*arch.* and *Scot.*) sure, certain, firm.—*adv.* (*Spens.*) surely, certainly.—*adv.* **sick'erly**.—*n.* **sick'erness**. [O.E. *sicor*—L. *sēcūrus*; Ger. *sicher*.]

sickle, *sik'l*, *n.* a reaping-hook: a sickle-feather.—*n.* **sick'le-bill**, a bird of paradise, humming-bird, &c., with sickle-shaped bill.—*adj.* **sick'led**, bearing a sickle.—*ns.* **sick'le-feath'er**, a cock's tail feather; **sick'leman**, a reaper.—*adj.* **sick'le-shaped**. [O.E. *sicol*, *sicel*, perh.—L. *secula*—*secāre*, to cut.]

sickle, *sik'l*, *n.* (*Shak.*) a shekel. [O.Fr. *sicle*—Heb. *sheqel*.]

Siculian, *si-kū'li-ən*, *adj.* of the *Sĭcŭlī* (L.), or Sikels, an ancient people that colonised Sicily from Italy.—Also *n.*

Sida, *sī'dä*, *n.* the Queensland hemp genus of the mallow family, tropical fibre-yielding herbs. [Gr. *sidē*, a plant name.]

fāte, fär, ȧsk; mē, hər (her); *mīne; mōte; mūte; mōōn; dhen* (then)

side, *sīd*, *n.* a line or surface forming part of a boundary, esp. that which is longer : the part near such a boundary : a surface or part turned in some direction, esp. one more or less upright, or one regarded as right or left, not front or back, top or bottom : the part of the body between armpit and hip : half of a carcase divided along the medial plane : either of the extended surfaces of anything in the form of a sheet : a page : a portion of space lying in this or that direction from a boundary or a point : the father's or mother's part of a genealogy : a department or division, as of a school, a prison : an aspect : a direction : a region : a neighbouring region : a border or bank : the slope of a hill : the wall of a vessel or cavity : any party, team, interest, or opinion opp. to another : part (as *on my side*, for my part) : (*Milt.*) the womb : a spin given to a billiard ball causing it to swerve and regulating its angle of rebound : (*slang*) a pretentious air.—*adj.* at or toward the side : sidewise : subsidiary.—*v.i.* to take sides.—*v.t.* to cut into sides : to thrust or set aside : (*Shak.*) to adjudge or assign to one side or other : (*Shak.*) to assign in this way to : (*Spens.*) to be on the side next.—*n.pl.* **side'-arms**, weapons worn at the side.—*ns.* **side'-band**, (*wireless*) a band of frequencies not much above or below the carrier frequency ; **side'board**, (*arch.*) a side table : a piece of dining-room furniture for holding plate, &c., often with drawers and cupboards : a board at the side, as of a cart.—*n.pl.* **side'-bones**, ossifications of the lateral cartilages of a horse's hoof.—*ns.* **side'box**, a box at the side of a theatre or its occupants ; **side'car**, a jaunting-car : a small car attached to the side of a motor-cycle : a kind of cocktail ; **side'-chain**, a chain of atoms forming a branch attached to a ring ; **side'-comb**, a small comb in the hair at the side ; **side'-cutt'ing**, an excavation along the side of a railway or canal to get material for an embankment.—*adj.* **sid'ed**, having sides : flattened on one or more sides.—*ns.* **side'-dish**, a supplementary dish ; **side'-door**, a door at the side of a building or of a main door ; **side'-drum**, a small double-headed drum with snares, slung from the drummer's side or from a stand ; **side'-face**, profile ; **side'-glance**, a sidelong glance : a passing allusion ; **side'-issue**, a subordinate issue apart from the main business ; **side'light**, light coming from the side : any incidental illustration : a window, as opposed to a skylight : a window above or at the side of a door : a light carried on the side of a vessel or vehicle ; **side'-line**, a line attached to the side of anything : a branch route or track : a subsidiary trade or activity.—*adj.* and *adv.* **side'ling**, sidewise : with a slope.—*n.* **side'lock**, a lock of hair at the side of the head.—*adj.* **side'long**, oblique : sloping : tilted : sideways.—*adv.* in the direction of the side : obliquely : on the side.—*n.* **side'-note**, a marginal note.—*adj.* and *adv.* **side'-on'**, with side presented.—*ns.* **side'-path**, a by-path : a way for foot-passengers alongside a roadway ; **side'-post**, a doorpost : a post supporting a roof at the side ; **sid'er**, one who takes a side ; **side'-road**, a by-road ; **side'-saddle**, a saddle for riding with both feet on one side ; **side'-saddle-flower'**, Sarracenia ; **side'-show**, an exhibition subordinate to a larger one : any subordinate or incidental doings ; **side'-slip**, an oblique offshoot : a bastard : a skid : a lateral movement of an aircraft.—*v.i.* to slip sideways.—*n.* **sides'man**, a deputy churchwarden : (*Milt.*) a partisan.—*adj.* **side'-splitting**, affecting the sides convulsively.—*n.* **side'-step**, a step taken to one side : a step attached to the side.—*v.i.* to step aside.—*v.t.* to avoid, as by a step aside.—*ns.* **side'-stroke**, a stroke given sideways : a stroke performed by a swimmer lying on his side ; **side'-table**, a table used as a sideboard, or placed against the wall, or to the side of the main table ; **side'-track**, a siding.—*v.t.* to divert or turn aside : to shelve.—*ns.* **side'-view**, a view on or from one side ; **side'walk**, (*U.S.*) pavement or foot-walk ; **side'-wall**.—*adj.* and *adv.* **side'ward**.—*adv.* **side'wards**.—*adjs.* and *advs.* **side'way**, **side'ways**, **side'wise**, toward or on one side.—*adj.* **side'-wheel**, having paddle wheels.—*ns.* **side'-wind**, a

lateral wind : indirect means ; **sīd'ing**, a short track for shunting or lying by.—*n.* and *adj.* taking sides.—*v.i.* **sī'dle** (prob. back-formation from **side'ling**), to go or edge along sideling.—*v.t.* to turn sideways.—*choose sides*, to pick teams ; *on the side*, (*U.S.*) in addition to ordinary occupation ; *on the short*, *long*, *tight*, &c., *side*, rather too short, long, &c., than the contrary ; *right*, *wrong side*, the side intended to be turned outward or inward ; *side by side*, close together : abreast ; *take sides*, to range oneself with one party or other ; *this side (of)*, between here and : short of. [O.E. *sīde* ; Ger. *seite*, Du. *zijde*.]

side, *sīd*, *adj.* (now *dial.* ; *Shak.*) long.—*adj.* and *adv.* **side'long** (*Spens.*). [O.E. *sīd*, ample.]

sidereal, *sī-dē'ri-əl*, *adj.* of, like, or relative to the stars.—*adj.* **sideral** (*sid'ər-əl*), sent from the stars, —*ns.* **siderā'tion**, a blast, blight, or stroke : paralysis : erysipelas ; **sid'erostat**, a mirror, or telescope with a mirror, for reflecting the rays of a star in a constant direction, on the principle of the coelostat.—**sidereal day**, **time**, **year** (see **day**, **time**, **year**). [L. *sīdus*, *sīderis*, a star, constellation.]

siderite, *sid'ər-īt*, *n.* a meteorite mainly of iron : chalybite.—*adj.* **sideritic** (*-it'ik*).—*n.* **sid'erolite** (Gr. *lithos*, stone), a meteorite, partly stony, partly of iron. [Gr. *sidēros*, iron.]

sidesman, **siding**, **sidle**. See **side** (1).

siege, *sēj*, *n.* (*arch.*) a seat, esp. of dignity : station : (*obs.*) a privy : (*Shak.*) dung : a work-bench : investment or beleaguering of a town or fortress : a company of herons.—*v.t.* to besiege.—*ns.* **siege'-artill'ery**, **siege'-gun** ; **siege'-bas'ket**, a gabion ; **siege'craft**, the art of the besieger ; **siege'-piece**, a coin, generally rude, issued in a besieged place : a siege-gun ; **sieg'er**, a besieger ; **siege'-train**, a train of artillery for besieging a place ; **siege'-works**, a besieger's engineering works.—*state of siege*, a condition of suspension of civil law or its subordination to military law. [O.Fr. *sege* (Fr. *siège*), seat—L. *sēdēs*, seat.]

sield, *sēld*, a Spenserian spelling of **ceiled**.

sien (*Shak.*). See **scion**.

Sien(n)ese, *sē-e-nēz'*, *adj.* of Siena or its school of painting.—*n.* a native of Siena.—*n.* **sienna** (*sē-en'ä*), a fine pigment made from ferruginous ochreous earth—brownly-yellow when *raw*, warm reddish-brown when *burnt* (i.e. roasted) : its colour.

sient, *sī'ənt*, *n.* (*Spens.*). Same as **scion**.

sierra, *si-er'ä*, *n.* a mountain range.—*adj.* **sierr'an**. [Sp.,—L. *serra*, saw.]

siesta, *si-es'tä*, *n.* a midday or afternoon nap. [Sp., —L. *sexta* (*hōra*), sixth (hour).]

sieth, a Shakespearean spelling of **scythe**.

sieve, *siv*, *n.* a vessel with meshed or perforated bottom for sifting—generally finer than a riddle : (*Shak.*) a refuse-basket.—*v.t.* and *v.i.* to sift.—*ns.* **sieve'-plate**, a perforated area by which a sieve-tube connects with another ; **sieve'-tube**, a conducting element in phloem. [O.E. *sife* ; Ger. *sieb.*]

siffle, *sif'l*, *v.i.* to whistle, hiss. [Fr. *siffler*—L. *sībilāre.*]

sift, *sift*, *v.t.* to separate as by passing through a sieve : to sprinkle as from a sieve : to examine closely and discriminatingly.—*v.i.* to use a sieve : to find passage as through a sieve.—*ns.* **sift'er** ; **sift'ing**, putting through a sieve : separating or sprinkling by a sieve : (in *pl.*) material separated by a sieve and rejected.—*adj.* **sift'ing**.—*adv.* **sift'ingly**. [O.E. *siftan*—*sife*, a sieve.]

sigh, *sī*, *v.i.* to heave a sigh : to make a whispering sound.—*v.t.* to utter, regret, while away, bring, or render, with sighs.—*n.* a long, deep, audible respiration expressive of yearning, dejection, relief, &c. —*n.* **sigh'er**.—*adjs.* **sigh'ful** ; **sigh'ing**.—*adv.* **sigh'ingly**. [Prob. a back-formation from the weak *pa.t.* of M.E. *siche*—O.E. (strong) *sīcan* ; Sw. *sucka.*]

sight, *sīt*, *n.* act, opportunity, or faculty of seeing : view : estimation : a beginning or coming to see : an instrumental observation : visual range : that which is seen : a spectacle : an object of especial interest : an unsightly object : (*Shak.*) a visor : a guide to the eye on a gun or optical or other instrument : a sight-hole : (*slang*) a great many or a great deal.—*v.t.* to catch sight of : to view : to take a sight of : to adjust the sights of.—*v.i.* to take a sight.—*adj.* sight´ed, having sight or a sight. —*ns.* sight´er, a sighting-shot ; sight´-hole, an aperture for looking through.—*adj.* sight´less, blind : (*Shak.*) invisible : (*Shak.*) unsightly.—*adv.* sight´lessly.—*ns.* sight´lessness ; sight´liness.— *adj.* sight´ly, pleasing to look at : comely.—*ns.* sight´-player, -reader, -singer, one who can read or perform music at first sight of the notes ; sight´-playing, -reading, -singing ; sight´-seeing, going around to see objects of interest ; sight´-seer (-sē-ər).—*adj.* sight´worthy, worth looking at.—at sight, without previous view or study : as soon as seen : on presentation ; catch sight of, to get a glimpse of, begin to see ; lose sight of, to cease to see : to get out of touch with ; out of sight, not in a position to be seen or to see : out of range of vision : (*coll.*) beyond comparison ; put out of sight, to remove from view : (*slang*) to eat or drink up. [O.E. *sihth, gesiht* ; Ger. *sicht.*]

sight, sīt, an old *pa.t.* of **sigh**.

sigil, sij´il, *n.* a seal : a magical mark.—*n.* **Sigillā´ria**, a chiefly carboniferous genus of fossil lycopod trees, constituting the family Sigillā´riā´ceae, with parallel rows of seal-like leaf-scars.—*n.* and *adj.* **sigillā´rian.**—*adjs.* **sig´illary** (-ə-ri), pertaining to a seal ; **sig´illate**, sealed : with seal-like impressions.—*n.* **sigillā´tion**. [L. *sigillum*, dim. of *signum*, sign.]

sigla, sig´lä, *n.pl.* abbreviations and signs, as in MSS., seals, &c. [L.]

sigma, sig´mä, *n.* the eighteenth letter (Σ, early form C ; σ, or when final ς) of the Greek alphabet, answering to S : as a numeral σ´=200, ͵σ=200,000. —*adj.* **sig´mate** (-māt), shaped like Σ, C, or S.— *v.t.* to add σ or *s* to.—*adj.* **sigmatic** (-mat´ik), characterised by σ.—*ns.* **sigmā´tion** (-shən), the adding of σ or *s* at the end of a syllable ; **sig´matism**, repetition of the *s*-sound.—*adjs.* **sig´moid, -al,** C-shaped : S-shaped.—*adv.* **sigmoid´ally.** [Gr. *sigma.*]

sign, sīn, *n.* a gesture expressing a meaning : a signal : a mark with a meaning : a symbol : an emblem : a token : a portent : a miraculous token : an ensign, banner (in *pl.* insignia ; *Spens.*) : an indication of positive or negative value, or that indicated : a device marking an inn, &c., formerly also a house, instead of a street number : a board or panel giving a shopkeeper's name or trade, &c. : (*obs.*) an effigy : (*obs.*) a mere semblance : an indication : an outward evidence of disease : (*U.S.*) a trail or track : a trace : a twelfth part (30°) of the zodiac, bearing the name of, but not now coincident with, a constellation.—*v.t.* to indicate, convey, communicate, direct, mark, by a sign or signs : to mark : to cross, make the sign of the cross over : to make the sign of : to attach a signature to : to write as a signature : to designate by signature : to engage by signature.—*v.i.* to make a sign : to bode : to sign one's name.—*ns.* **signary** (sig´nə-ri), a system of symbols, as an alphabet or syllabary ; **sign´board**, a board bearing a notice or serving as a shop or inn sign ; **sign´er** ; **signet** (sig´nit), a small seal : the impression of such a seal : a signet-ring : one of the royal seals for authenticating grants (for **Writer to the Signet** see under **write**). —*adj.* **sig´neted**, stamped with a signet.—*n.* **sig´net-ring**, a ring with a signet.—*adj.* **sign´less.** —*ns.* **sign´-man´ual**, a signature, esp. a king's ; **sign´-painter**, one who paints signs for shops, &c. ; **sign´post**, a post for an inn sign : a finger-post.—**sign away**, to transfer by signing ; **sign of the cross**, a gesture of tracing the form of a cross ; **sign in, out**, to sign one's name on coming in, going out ; **sign on**, to engage (*t.* or *i.*) by signature. [Fr. *signe*—L. *signum.*]

signal, sig´nl, *n.* a token : an intimation, e.g. of warning, conveyed to a distance : a transmitted effect conveying a message : apparatus used for the purpose : (*cards*) play intended to give information to one's partner : an intimation of, or event taken as marking, the moment for action : an initial impulse.—*v.t.* to intimate, convey, or direct by signals : to signalise.—*v.i.* to make signals :

(*pr.p.* sig´nalling ; *pa.t.* and *pa.p.* sig´nalled).— *adj.* remarkable : notable. — *ns.* sig´nal-box, -cab´in, a railway signalman's cabin.—*v.t.* sig´-nalise, to mark or distinguish signally.—*ns.* sig´naller ; sig´nalling. — *adv.* sig´nally. — *n.* sig´nalman, one who transmits signals : one who works railway signals. [Fr. *signal*—L. *signum.*]

signature, sig´nə-tyər, *n.* a signing : a stamp : a signed name : an indication of key, also of time, at the beginning of a line of music, or where a change occurs : a letter or numeral at the foot of a page to indicate sequence of sheets : a sheet so marked : a symbolic indication once believed to show what a plant, &c., was good for, e.g. a kidney-shaped leaf to mark a cure for kidney diseases : a signature-tune.—*n.* sig´natory, one who has signed. —Also *adj.*—*n.* sig´nature-tune, a tune heralding the broadcast or appearance of some particular person or group. [L.L. *signātūra*—L. *signāre*, -*ātum*, to sign.]

signet. See **sign**.

signeur, a Shakespearean spelling of **senior**.—*ns.* **sign´eurie**, (*Shak.*) seniority ; **sign´ieur**, (*Shak.*) seigneur.

signify, sig´ni-fī, *v.t.* to be a sign for : to mean : to denote : to betoken : to indicate or declare.—*v.i.* to be of consequence :—*pr.p.* sig´nifying ; *pa.t.* and *pa.p.* sig´nified.—*adj.* sig´nifiable.—*n.* sig-nif´icance (-*i-kəns*), meaning : import—also sig-nif´icancy.—*adj.* signif´icant, having a meaning : full of meaning : important, worthy of consideration : indicative.—*n.* that which carries a meaning : a sign.—*adv.* signif´icantly.—*ns.* signif´icate, a thing signified ; significā´tion, meaning : that which is signified : importance.—*adj.* signif´ica-tive (-*kə-tiv*), indicative : significant.—*adv.* sig-nif´icatively.—*n.* signif´icātor, (*astrol.*) a planet ruling a house.—*adj.* signif´icatory (-*kə-tər-i*).— *n.* (treated as *sing.*) signif´ics, the science of meaning.—**significant figures**, (*arith.*) the figures 1 to 9, or ciphers occurring medially ; the following numbers are expressed to three significant figures : —3·15, 0·0127, 1·01. [L. *significāre*, -*ātum*— *signum*, a sign, *facĕre*, to make.]

Signor, Signior, anglicised as **Signior**, sē´nyor, **Signore, -nyō´rā**, *n.* an Italian word of address equivalent to Mr or sir : a gentleman.—*ns.* **Signora** (sē-nyō´rā), feminine of *Signor*, Mrs, madam : a lady ; **Signo-rina** (sē-nyō-rē´nā), Miss : an unmarried lady ; **signoria** (-rē´ä ; *hist.*), the governing body of an Italian city-state ; **si´gnory**, seignory : signoria.— **Grand Signior**, (*hist.*) the Sultan of Turkey. [It. *signor, signore.*]

sike, syke, sīk, *n.* (*Scot.*) a rill or small ditch. [Northern,—O.E. *sīc.*]

sike, Spenserian spelling of **sic** (such).

Sikel, sik´əl, *n.* and *adj.* Siculian.—*adj.* **Sikelian** (-*el´*).—*n.* **Sikel´iot**, an ancient Greek colonist in Sicily.—Also **Sicel**, &c. [Gr. *Sikelos, Sikeliōtēs.*]

Sikh, sēk, sik, *n.* one of a North Indian monotheistic sect, founded by Nának (1469-1538), later a military confederacy : a Sikh soldier in the Indian army.— Also *adj.*—*n.* **Sikh´ism.** [Hind., disciple.]

silage, sī´lij, *n.* fodder preserved by ensilage in a silo.—*v.t.* to put in silo. [ensilage, after **silo.**]

sile, seil, sīl, *v.t.* (*Scot.*) to strain.—*n.* a strainer.— *n.* sil´er. [Scand. ; cf. Sw. and Norw. *sila*, to strain.]

silence, sī´ləns, *n.* absence of sound : abstention from sounding, speech, mention, or communica-tion : a time of such absence or abstention : taci-turnity : of spirits, flavourlessness.—*v.t.* to cause to be silent.—*interj.* be silent.—*adj.* si´lenced, put to silence : forbidden to preach.—*n.* si´lencer, one who or that which puts to silence : a device for reducing the sound of escaping gases by gradual expansion.—*adj.* si´lent, noiseless : without sound : unaccompanied by sound : refraining from speech, mention, or divulging : taciturn : not pronounced : of distilled spirit, without flavour or odour : in-operative : of the new moon (*Milt.*), not yet visible. —*n.* (*Shak.*) a time of silence.—*n.* silentiary (-*len´shi-ər-i*), one who observes or calls for silence. —*adv.* si´lently.—*n.* si´lentness. [L. *silēre*, to be silent.]

silenus, sī-lē′nəs, n. a wood-god or old satyr: **Silenus,** their chief, foster-father of Bacchus, pot-bellied, bald, snub-nosed: the lion-tailed macaque.—Also **si′len** (-lin). [L. *Silēnus*—Gr. *Seilēnos.*]

silex, sī′leks, n. silica. [L. *silex, silicis,* flint.]

silhouette, sil-oo-et′, n. a shadow-outline filled in with black.—v.t. to represent or show in silhouette. [Étienne de *Silhouette* (1709-67), French minister of finance in 1759—reason disputed.]

silica, sil′i-kä, n. silicon dioxide or silicic anhydride, occurring in nature as quartz, chalcedony, &c., and (amorphous and hydrated) as opal.—adj. composed of silica.—ns. **sil′icane,** a gas, silicon hydride, SiH₄; **sil′icate,** a salt of silicic acid.—v.t. to combine, coat, or impregnate with silica or silicates. —adjs. **siliceous, -ious** (-ish′əs), of, containing, silica; **silicic** (-is′ik), pertaining to, or obtained from, silica (**silicic acid,** a general name for a group of acids, as **orthosilicic,** H₄SiO₄, **meta-silicic,** H₂SiO₃.—n. **sil′icide** (-sīd), a compound of silicon and another element.—adjs. **silicicolous** (-sik′; L. *colĕre,* to cultivate, inhabit), growing on siliceous soil; **silicif′erous,** containing silica.—n. **silicification** (si-lis-i-fi-kā′shən).—adj. **silicified** (-lis′).—v.t. **silic′ify,** to render siliceous: to impregnate or cement with or replace by silica.—v.i. to become siliceous.—ns. **sil′icon** (-kon, -kən), a non-metallic element (Si; at. numb. 14), most abundant of all except oxygen, forming grey crystals or brown amorphous powder—originally called **silicium** (-lis′, -lish′); **sil′icone,** any of a number of extremely stable organic derivatives of silicon; **silicosis** (-kō′sis), disease caused by inhaling silica dust. [L. *silex, silicis,* flint.]

siliqua, sil′i-kwä, n. a long pod of two carpels with a replum, characteristic of the Cruciferae.—Also **silique** (-ēk′).—n. **silicula** (-ik′ū-lä), a short pod of the same kind.—Also **sil′icle, sil′icule.**—adjs. **silic′ulose; sil′iquose.** [L. *siliqua,* pod, dim. *silicula.*]

silk, silk, n. a fibre produced by the larva of a silk-worm moth, mainly of fibroin coated with sericin, formed by the hardening of a liqu.d emitted from spinning-glands: a similar fibre from another insect or a spider: an imitation (**artificial silk**) made by forcing a viscous solution of modified cellulose through small holes: a thread, cloth, garment, or attire made from such fibres: the silk gown, or the rank, of a king's or queen's counsel: the styles of maize: silky lustre in the ruby, &c.— adj. of or pertaining to silk: (*Shak.*) silky.—v.t. to cover or clothe with silk.—n. **silk′-cott′on,** the silky seed-covering of *Eriodendron anfractuosum* and other trees of the family Bombacaceae.—adj. **silk′en,** of, like, clad in, silk: glossy: soft and smooth: ingratiating: luxurious.—v.t. to make silken.—ns. **silk′-gland,** a gland (at a silkworm's mouth, on a spider's abdomen) from which silk is spun; **silk′-grass,** a name for various plants with fibrous leaves—Karatus (Bromeliaceae), Yucca, Agave; **silk′grower,** a breeder of silkworms for silk.—adv. **silk′ily.**—ns. **silk′iness; silk′-man,** (*Shak.*) a dealer in silks; **silk′tail,** the waxwing; **silk′-thrower, -throwster,** one who makes raw silk into thread; **silk′worm,** the moth (*Bombyx mori* or other) whose larva produces silk: (oppro-briously) a wearer of silk: one who haunts draper's shops without buying; **silk′worm-gut,** the drawn-out glands of the silkworm.—adj. **silk′y.—take silk,** to become a K.C. or Q.C. [O.E. *seolc*—L. *sēricum*; see **Seric.**]

sill, sil, n. the timber, stone, &c., at the foot of an opening, as for a door, window, embrasure, port, dock-entrance, or the like: the bottom (of a title-page, a plough, a ledge): (*mining*) a bed of rock: (*geol.*) a sheet of intrusive rock more or less parallel to the bedding. [O.E. *syll*; O.N. *syll*; Ger. *schwelle.*]

sillabub, syllabub, sil-ə-bub, n. a dish of cream curdled (as with wine), flavoured, and frothed up: anything frothy or unsubstantial. [Origin obscure.]

silladar, sil′ə-där, n. an irregular cavalryman. [Urdu and Pers. *silāhdār.*]

siller, sil′ər, n. a Scots form of **silver**: money.— Also adj.

Sillery, sil′ə-ri, n. champagne from *Sillery,* near Rheims.

sillimanite, sil′i-mən-īt, n. fibrolite. [After Benjamin Silliman (1779-1864), American man of science.]

sillock, sil′ək, n. (*N. Scot.*) a young coalfish. [Cf. O.N. *silungr,* a small salmon.]

silly, sil′i, adj. harmless: simple: witless: foolish: to be pitied: pitiable: feeble: feeble-minded: senseless: (*cricket*) close-in (e.g. *silly mid-off*).—n. a silly person.—adv. **sill′ily.**—ns. **sill′iness; sill′y-how** (O.E. *húfe,* head-dress), a caul. [O.E. *sǽlig*; see **seely.**]

silo, sī′lō, n. a pit or air-tight chamber for storing grain, or for ensilage (*pl.* **si′los**).—v.t. to put, keep, in a silo:—pa.p. **si′lo′d, si′loed.** [Sp.,—L. *sirus*—Gr. *siros, siros, seiros,* a pit.]

silphium, sil′fi-əm, n. (*hist.*) a plant (*perh.* the umbelliferous *Ferula tingitana*) imported from Cyrenaica by the Greeks for food and medicine: **Silphium,** a genus of American composites, compassplants. [L.,—Gr. *silphion.*]

silt, silt, n. fine sediment.—v.t. to choke, block, cover, with silt.—v.i. to become silted up.—adj. **silt′y.** [M.E. *sylt*; cf. Dan. and Norw. *sylt,* salt-marsh.]

Silurian, sil-(y)ōō′ri-ən, adj. of the *Sil′ūrēs,* a British tribe of S. Wales, &c.: applied by Murchison in 1835 to the geological system preceding the Devonian.—Also n.—n. **sil′urist,** a Silurian, applied to the poet Henry Vaughan (1621-95).

Silurus, sil-(y)ōō′rəs, n. the sheat-fish genus, giving name to the family **Silu′ridae.**—n. and adj. **silu′roid.** [Gr. *silouros.*]

silva, sil′va, n. the assemblage of trees in a region. —adj. **sil′van,** of woods: woodland: wooded.— n. a wood-god: a forest-dweller.—adjs. **silvat′ic, silves′trian,** of the woods: woodland: rustic.— n. **silvicul′ture,** forestry.—All these words are often found spelt with y. [L. *silva,* a wood.]

silver, sil′vər, n. a white precious metal (Ag, for L. *argentum*; at. numb. 47): silver money: silver ware.—adj. of or like silver: silver-coloured: clear and ringing in tone.—v.t. to cover with silver: to make silvery.—v.i. to become silvery.—ns. **sil′ver-bath,** (*phot.*) a solution of a silver salt, or a vessel for it, for sensitising plates; **sil′ver-beater,** one who beats silver into foil; **sil′ver-bell,** snowdrop-tree (Halesia); **sil′ver-fir,** a fir with two white lines on the under-side of the needle; **silver′-fish,** Lepisma, a spring-tail: a whitish goldfish, or other white fish; **sil′ver-foil,** silver-leaf.—adj. **sil′ver-foot′ed.**—ns. **sil′ver-fox,** an American fox with white-tipped black fur; **sil′ver-gilt,** gilded silver. —Also adj.—ns. **sil′ver-glance′,**argentite; **sil′ver-grain′,** medullary rays in longitudinal section; **sil′veriness; sil′vering,** coating with, or of, silver or quicksilver.—v.t. **sil′verise,** to coat or treat with silver.—ns. **sil′ver-leaf,** silver beaten into thin leaves: a disease of plum-trees; **sil′ver-ling,** (*B.*) a small silver coin.—adv. **sil′verly,** with the appearance or sound of silver.—adjs. **sil′ver-mount′ed; sil′vern,** made of silver: silvery.— ns. **sil′ver-pap′er,** fine white tissue-paper: silver-foil: (*usu.*) tinfoil; **sil′ver-plate,** utensils of silver: electro-plate.—adj. **sil′ver-plä′ted.**—n. **sil′ver-point,** the process or product of drawing with a silver-tipped pencil.—adjs. **sil′ver-shaft′ed,** carrying silver arrows, as Diana; **sil′ver-shedding,** (*Shak.*) scattering silver.—ns. **sil′verside,** the top of a round of beef; **sil′verskin,** the fine skin of a coffee bean; **sil′versmith,** a worker in silver; **sil′ver-stick,** a palace officer—from his silvered wand.—adj. **sil′ver-tongued,** plausible, eloquent. —n. **sil′ver-tree,** a silvery-leaved S. African proteaceous tree (*Leucadendron argenteum*).—adj. **sil′ver-voiced.**—n. **sil′verweed,** a roadside plant (*Potentilla Anserina*) with leaves silky underneath.— adjs. **sil′ver-white; sil′very.—born with a silver spoon in one's mouth,** born to affluence; **Silver Age,** the reign of Zeus, less innocent than the Golden Age of Kronos: in Latin literature, the time of Martial, Tacitus, and Juvenal; **silver gate** (see **gate**); **silver pheasant,** a white-tailed Chinese pheasant, reared in Europe, &c.; **silver**

salmon, the cohoe; **silver wedding**, the twenty-fifth anniversary; **tree of silver** (see **tree**). [O.E. *silfer, seolfor*; O.N. *silfr*, Ger. *silber*.]

sima, *sī'mä, n.* the part of the earth's crust underlying the sial. [From *si*licon and *ma*gnesium.]

simar, simarre, *si-mär'.* Same as **cymar, chimer.**

Simaruba, *sim-ə-rŏŏ'bä, n.* a genus of tropical American trees, giving name to the family **Simarubā'ceae**, akin to the Rutaceae. [Galibi name.]

Simeonite, *sim'i-ən-īt, n.* a low-churchman—often **sim**. [Charles Simeon (1759-1836).]

simian, *sim'i-ən, adj.* of the apes: apelike.—Also (*rare*) **sim'ial, sim'ious**. [L. *simia*, ape.]

similar, *sim'i-lər, adj.* like: resembling: (*geom.*) exactly corresponding in shape, without regard to size.—*n.* **similarity** (-*lar'i-ti*).—*adv.* **sim'ilarly.** [Fr. *similaire*—L. *similis*, like.]

simile, *sim'i-li, n.* (*rhet.*) an explicit likening of one thing to another :—*pl.* **sim'iles.**—*adj.* **sim'ilātive**, expressing similarity. —*v.t.* **sim'ilise**, to liken.— *v.i.* to use simile.—*n.* **simil'itude**, likeness: semblance: comparison: parable. [L. neut. of *similis*, like.]

similor, *sim'i-lor, n.* a yellow alloy used for cheap jewellery. [Fr.,—L. *similis*, like, *aurum*, gold.]

simitar. Same as **scimitar.**

sim(p)kin, *sim'kin, n.* an Urdu corruption of **champagne.**

simmer, *sim'ər, v.i.* to boil gently: to be near boiling or breaking out.—*n.* a simmering state.— **simmer down**, to calm down. [Earlier *simper*; origin unknown.]

'simmon, *sim'ən, n.* short for **persimmon.**

simnel, *sim'nl, n.* a sweet cake for Christmas, Easter, or Mothering Sunday.—Also **sim'nel-bread', -cake'.** [O.Fr. *simenel*—L. *simila*, fine flour.]

Simon Pure, *sī'mən-pūr', n.* the real person (or thing). [From a character in Mrs Centlivre's comedy, *A Bold Stroke for a Wife.*]

simony, *sī'mən-i, sim'ən-i, n.* the buying or selling of a benefice.—*n.* **simō'niac**, one guilty of simony. —*adjs.* **simoni'acal, simō'nious** (*obs.*).—*adv.* **simoni'acally.**—*n.* **sī'monist**, one who practises or defends simony. [*Simon Magus* (Acts viii.).]

simoom, *si-mŏŏm', n.* a hot suffocating desert wind. —Also **simoon'.** [Ar. *samûm*—*samm*, to poison.]

simpai, *sim'pī, n.* the black-crested langur of Sumatra. [Malay.]

simper, *sim'pər, v.i.* to smile in a silly, affected manner.—*n.* a silly or affected smile.—*n.* **sim'perer.** — *adj.* **simp'ering.** — *adv.* **simp'eringly.** [Cf. Norw. *semper*, smart.]

simple, *sim'pl, adj.* consisting of one thing or element: not complex or compound: (*bot.*) not divided into leaflets: easy: plain: unornate: unpretentious: mean, sorry: mere, sheer: ordinary: unlearned or unskilled: of humble rank or origin: unaffected: artless: guileless: unsuspecting: credulous: weak in intellect: silly.—*n.* a simple person (also collectively) or thing: a medicine of one constituent: hence a medicinal herb.—*v.i.* to gather medicinal plants.—*adjs.* **sim'ple-heart'ed**; **sim'ple-mind'ed.** — *ns.* **sim'ple-mind'edness**; **sim'pleness**; **sim'pler**, a gatherer of simples; **sim'plesse**, (*Spens.*) simplicity; **sim'pleton**, a weak or foolish person: one easily imposed on (*U.S. abbrev.* **simp**).—*adv.* **simpliciter** (-*plis'*; L. -*plik'*), simply, not relatively.—*ns.* **simplicity** (-*plis'*); **simplificā'tion**, making simple.—*adj.* **sim'plificātive**.—*ns.* **sim'plificātor, simplifi'er**, one who simplifies.—*v.t.* **sim'plify**, to make simple, simpler, or less difficult :—*pr.p.* **sim'plifying**; *pa.t.* and *pa.p.* **sim'plified**.—*ns.* **sim'pling**, simple-gathering; **sim'plism**, affected simplicity; **sim'plist**, one skilled in simples.—*adj.* **simplis'tic**. —*adv.* **sim'ply**, in a simple manner: considered by itself: alone: merely: without qualification: veritably: absolutely.—**simple sentence**, a sentence with one predicate. [Fr. *simple*, and L. *simplus, simplex.*]

simulacrum, *sim-ū-lā'krəm, n.* an image: a semblance (*pl.* **simula'cra**).—Also **sim'ulācre**. [L. *simulācrum.*]

simulate, *sim'ū-lāt, v.t.* to feign: to have or assume a false appearance of: to mimic.—*adj.*

feigned. — *adj.* **sim'ulant**, simulating: (*biol.*) mimicking. — *n.* a simulator. — *adj.* **sim'ular**, counterfeit: feigned.—*n.* a simulator.—*n.* **simulā'tion**.—*adj.* **sim'ulātive.**—*n.* **sim'ulātor**, one who or that which simulates.—*adj.* **sim'ulatory.** [L. *simulāre, -ātum*; cf. **similar, simultaneous.**]

simultaneous, *sim-əl-tā'nyəs, adj.* being or happening at the same time: (*math.*) satisfied by the same roots (of equations).—*ns.* **simultaneity** (-*tə-nē'i-ti*), **simultā'neousness**.—*adv.* **simultā'neously.** [L. *simul*, at the same time.]

simurg(h), *si-mŏŏrg', -murg', n.* **simorg, -morg', n.* a monstrous bird of Persian fable. [Pers. *sīmurgh.*]

sin, sin', *sin, prep., conj.,* and *adv.* (*arch.* or *Scot.*) since.—**long sin**, (*Spens.*) for a long time in the past. [Shortened from **sithen.**]

sin, *sin, n.* moral offence or shortcoming, esp. from the point of view of religion: condition of so offending: an offence generally: a shame, pity.— *v.i.* to commit sin.—*v.t.* to commit: to burden with sin (as *sin one's soul*): to bring, drive, or render by sin (hence *sin one's mercies*, to be ungrateful) :— *pr.p.* **sinn'ing**; *pa.t.* and *pa.p.* **sinned.**—*ns.* **sin'-eat'er**, one who by eating bread and salt at a funeral takes upon himself the dead man's sins; **sin'-eat'ing.** — *adj.* **sin'ful**, tainted with sin: wicked: involving sin: morally wrong.—*n.* **sin'fulness.** — *adj.* **sin'less.** — *adv.* **sin'lessly.**—*ns.* **sin'lessness**; **sinn'er.**—*v.t.* (with *it*; *Pope*) to act as a sinner.—*n.* **sin'-off'ering**, a sacrifice in expiation of sin. [O.E. *synn*; O.N. *synth*; Ger. *sünde*; perh. L. *sōns, sontis*, guilty.]

Sinaean, *sin-ē'an* (*Milt.*), **Sinic, Sinic**, *sin'ik, adjs.* Chinese. —*v.t.* and *v.i.* **sin'icise** (-*sīz*), to make or become Chinese or of Chinese character.—*n.* **Sin'icism** (-*sizm*), a Chinese custom, idiom, &c. [L.L. *Sīnae*, Gr. *Sīnai*, Chinese (pl.).]

Sinaitic, *si-nā-it'ik, adj.* of Mount *Sinai.*

Sinanthropus, *sin- or sīn-an-thrō'pəs, n.* Peking (fossil) man. [Gr. *Sīnai*, (the) Chinese, *anthrōpos*, man.]

sinapism, *sin'ə-pizm, n.* a mustard plaster. [Gr. *sināpi.*]

since, *sins, adv.* from that time on: after that time: past: ago.—*prep.* after; from the time of.—*conj.* from the time that: seeing that: because. [M.E. *sins, sithens*; see under **sith.**]

sincere, *sin-sēr', adj.* pure, unmixed: unadulterated: unfeigned: genuine: free from pretence: the same in reality as in appearance.—*adv.* **sincēre'ly.**—*ns.* **sincēre'ness, sincerity** (-*ser'*). [Fr. *sincère*—L. *sincērus*, clean.]

sinciput, *sin'si-put, n.* the forepart of the head.— *adj.* **sincip'ital.** [L.,—*sēmi-*, half, *caput*, head.]

sind. See **synd.**

sindon, *sin'don, n.* (*arch.*) a fine cloth or anything made of it. [Gr. *sindōn.*]

sine, *sīn, n.* (*math.*) orig. the perpendicular from one end of an arc to the diameter through the other: now (as a function of an angle) the ratio of the side opposite it (or its supplement) in a right-angled triangle to the hypotenuse.—*abbrev.* **sin.** [L. *sinus*, a bay.]

sine. See **syne.**

sinecure, *sī'ni-kūr,* or *sin', n.* a benefice without cure of souls: an office without work.—Also *adj.* —*ns.* **sin'ecurism**; **sin'ecurist.** [L. *sine*, without, *cūra*, care.]

sinew, *sin'ū, n.* that which joins a muscle to a bone: a tendon: (*fig.*) strength or that which it depends on.—*v.t.* to bind as by sinews: to strengthen.— *adjs.* **sin'ewed**; **sin'ewless**; **sin'ewy**,—**sinew of war**, money. [O.E. *sinu*, gen. *sinwe.*]

sinfonia, *sin-fō-nē'ä, n.* symphony. [It.]

sing, *sing, v.i.* to utter melodious sounds in musical succession in articulating words: to emit more or less song-like sounds: to compose poetry: to give a cantabile or lyrical effect: to ring (as the ears): to be capable of being sung.—*v.t.* to utter, perform by voice, musically: to chant: to celebrate: to proclaim, relate, in song or verse or in comparable manner: to bring, drive, render, pass, &c., by singing—*pa.t.* **sang**, or (now rarely) **sung**; *pa.p.* **sung**. — *adj.* **sing'able.** — *ns.* **sing'ableness**; **sing'er**; **sing'ing**; **sing'ing-bird**, a songbird

sing'ing-gall'ery, a gallery occupied by singers; **sing'ing-hinn'y**, (*Northern*) a currant cake that hisses on the girdle.—*adv.* **sing'ingly.**—*ns.* **sing'ing-man**, (*Shak.*) one employed to sing, as in a church choir; **sing'ing-master**, a teacher of singing.—**sing another song** or **tune**, to change to a humbler tone; **singing flame**, a flame that gives a musical note in a tube; **singing sand**, musical sand; **sing out**, to call out distinctly, to shout: to inform, peach; **sing small**, to assume a humble tone. [O.E. *singan*; Ger. *singen*, Goth. *siggwan*.]

inge, *sinj*, *v.t.* to burn on the surface: to scorch: to remove by scorching.—*v.i.* to become scorched: (*pr.p.* **singe'ing**; *pa.t.* and *pa.p.* **singed**).—*n.* a burning on the surface: a slight burn.—**singed cat**, a person who is better than he looks. [O.E. *sen(c)gan.*]

inghalese. Same as **Sinhalese.**

ingle, *sing'gl*, *adj.* consisting of one only or one part: unique: one-fold: uncombined: unmarried: for one: man to man: (*Shak.*) slight, poor: of ale, weak, small: undivided: unbroken: of a flower, without development of stamens into petals or of ligulate instead of tubular florets: sincere.—*adv.* singly.—*n.* anything single: a game played by one against one: a hit for one run.—*v.t.* to separate: to pick (out): (*Milt.*) to pick out challengingly: to take aside: to thin.—*v.i.* (*Spens.*) to come forth alone.—*adjs.* **sing'le-act'ing**, acting effectively in one direction only; **sing'le-breast'ed**, with one thickness over the breast and one row of buttons; **sing'le-chamb'er**, having one legislative house.—*ns.* **sing'le-deck'er**, a vessel or vehicle with one deck; **sing'le-en'try**, a system of book-keeping in which each entry appears only once on one side or other of an account.—*adj.* **sing'le-eyed**, one-eyed: devoted, unselfish.—*n.* **sing'le-foot**, a rack or amble.—*adjs.* **sing'le-hand'ed**, by oneself: unassisted: with or for one hand; **sing'le-heart'ed**, sincere: without duplicity.—*adv.* **sing'le-heart'edly.**—*adj.* **sing'le-mind'ed**, ingenuous: bent upon one sole purpose.—*ns.* **sing'le-mind'edness**; **sing'leness** (-*gl-nis*); **sing'le-seat'er**, a car, &c., seated for one.—*adj.* **sing'le-soled**, having one thickness of sole.—*ns.* **sing'lestick** (-*gl-stik*), a fighting stick for one hand: a fight or game with singlesticks; **sing'let** (-*glit*), a thing that is single: an undershirt; **sing'leton** (-*gl-tən*), a single card of its suit in a hand: anything single; **sing'le-wicket**, cricket with one wicket, and with one batsman at a time; **sing'ling** (-*gling*).—*adv.* **sing'ly** (-*gli*), one by one: alone: by oneself.—**single house**, (*Scot.*) a house one room deep; **single soldier**, (*Scott*) a private; **single tax**, a tax on ground-rent or land-values to supersede all other taxes; **single ten**, (*Shak.*) the ten of a card suit. [O.Fr.,—L. *singulus*, one by one.]

ingletree, *sing'gl-trē*, *n.* See **swingletree.**

singsong, *sing'song*, *n.* a ballad: jingly verse: monotonous up-and-down intonation: an informal concert where the company sing: a meeting for community singing.—*adj.* of the nature of singsong.—*v.t.* and *v.i.* to sing, speak, utter, in a singsong way. [**sing**, **song**.]

ingspiel, *sing'spēl*, Ger. *zing'shpēl*, *n.* a semidramatic representation in dialogue and song. [Ger.,—*singen*, to sing, *spiel*, play.]

singular, *sing'gū-lər*, *adj.* single: unique: proper: private: denoting or referring to one: preeminent: pre-eminently good or efficacious: extraordinary: peculiar: strange: odd. — *adv.* singularly.—*n.* an individual person or thing: (*gram.*) the singular number or a word in the singular number.—*n.* **singularisā'tion.**—*v.t.* **sing'ularise**, to make singular: to singularise.—*ns.* **sing'ularism**, a philosophy that recognises but one principle, opp. to *pluralism*; **sing'ularist**, one who affects singularity: an upholder of singularism; **singularity** (-*lar'i-ti*), fact or state of being singular: peculiarity: individuality: oddity: oneness: anything curious or remarkable.—*adv.* **sing'ularly**, in a singular manner: peculiarly: strangely: singly: (*arch.*) pre-eminently. [L. *singulāris.*]

singult, *sing'gult*, *n.* a sob.—*n.* **singult'us**, (*med.*) hiccuping. [L. *singultus*, a sob.]

sinh, *shīn*, *n.* a conventional abbreviation of *hyperbolic sine.*

Sinhalese, *sin'hə-lēz*, -*lēz'*, **Singhalese**, **Cingalese**, *sing'gə-lēz*, -*ləz'*, *adj.* of Ceylon: of the most numerous of its peoples: of or in their language, akin to Pali.—*n.* a native or citizen of Ceylon: a member of the Sinhalese people: their language. [Sans. *Sinhalam*, Ceylon.]

Sinic, &c. See **Sinaean.**

sinical, *sin'i-kl*, *adj.* pertaining to sines.

sinister, *sin'is-tər*, formerly also -*is'*, *adj.* left: on the left side (in *her.* from the point of view of the bearer of the shield, not the beholder, and similarly sometimes in description of an illustration, &c.): (*obs.*) misleading: underhand: inauspicious: suggestive of threatened evil: unlucky: malign.—*n.* **sinisterity** (-*ter'*), left-handedness (*rare*): sinister quality.—*advs.* **sin'isterly**; **sin'isterwise.**—*adj.* **sin'istral**, turning to the left: of flatfish, lying left side up: of a shell, coiled contrary to the normal way.—*n.* **sinistral'ity.**—*adv.* **sin'istrally.**—*adj.* **sinistrous** (*sin-is'* or *sin'is-*), inauspicious: (*obs.*) sinister.—*adv.* **sinistrously.** [L.]

sinistrorse, *sin-is-trors'*, or *sin'*, *adj.* (*biol.*) rising spirally and turning to the right, i.e. crossing an outside observer's field of view from right to left upwards (like an ordinary spiral stair): formerly used in the contrary sense (*dextrorse*).—Also **sinistrors'al.**—*adv.* **sinistrors'ally.** [L. *sinistrōrsus*, *sinistrōversus*, towards the left side—*sinister*, left, *vertĕre*, *versum*, to turn.]

sink, *singk*, *v.i.* to become submerged, wholly or partly: to subside: to fall slowly: to go down passively: to pass to a lower level or state: to penetrate: to be absorbed: to slope away, dip: to diminish: to collapse: to be withdrawn inwards.—*v.t.* to cause or allow to sink: (*coll.*) in games, to cause to run into the hole: to suppress: to degrade: to conceal: to appropriate surreptitiously: to excavate: to let in, insert: to abandon: to abolish: to merge: to pay: to lose under the horizon: to invest, esp. unprofitably or beyond easy recovery: to damn or ruin (esp. in imprecation): (*pa.t.* **sank**, now rarely **sunk**; *pa.p.* **sunk**, also **sunk'en**, *obs.* exc. as *adj.*).—*n.* a receptacle or drain for filth or dirty water: a cesspool: a kitchen or scullery trough or basin with a drain: a place where things are engulfed or where foul things gather: a depression in a surface: an area without surface drainage: (*geol.*) a swallow-hole: a shaft.—*ns.* **sink'er**, one who sinks: a weight for sinking anything, as a fishing-line: (*U.S. slang*) a doughnut: a mistletoe root; **sink'-hole**, a hole for filth: (*U.S.*) a swallow-hole—*n.* and *adj.* **sink'ing.** —*n.* **sink'ing-fund**, a fund formed by setting aside income to accumulate at interest to pay off debt.—*adjs.* **sink'ing-ripe**, (*Shak.*) ready to sink; **sink'y**, yielding underfoot. [O.E. *sincan* (intrans.); Ger. *sinken*, Du. *zinken.*]

sink(e)-a-pace. See **cinque-pace.**

sinner. See under **sin.**

sinnet, *sin'it*. Same as **sennit.**

Sinn Fein, *shin fān*, *n.* a movement for the establishment of an independent Irish republic: a party aiming at that end.—*ns.* **Sinn Feiner'**; **Sinn Fein'ism.** [Ir. *sinn féin*, ourselves.]

Sinningia, *sin-in'ji-ä*, *n.* a Brazilian genus of Gesneriaceae, grown in greenhouses under the name of Gloxinia. [W. *Sinning*, German gardener.]

Sinologue, *sin'ə-log*, or *sīn'*, *n.* one versed in Chinese. —*adj.* **Sinolog'ical** (-*loj'*).—*ns.* **Sinologist** (-*ol'ə-jist*); **Sinol'ogy.** [Gr. *Sīnai*, Chinese (pl.), *logos*.]

sinsyne, *sin-sīn'*, *adv.* (*Scot.*) since that time. [**sin** (1), **syne**.]

sinter, *sin'tər*, *n.* a deposit from hot springs.—*v.i.* to coalesce under heat without liquefaction.—*adj.* **sin'tery.** [Ger. *sinter*; cf. **cinder.**]

sinus, *sī'nəs*, *n.* an indentation: a notch: a cavity: a narrow cavity through which pus is discharged:— *pl.* **sinuses.**—*adjs.* **sinuate** (*sin'ū-āt*), **-d** (-*id*), wavy-edged: winding. — *adv.* **sin'uately.** — *ns.* **sinuā'tion**, winding; **sinuitis** (-*ī'tis*), **sinusī'tis** (*sin-* or *sin-əs-*), inflammation of a sinus of the skull

communicating with the nose.—*adj.* **sinuose**
(sin′ū-ōs), sinuous.—*n.* **sinuos′ity.**—*adj.* **sin′uous,**
wavy: winding: supply bending.—*adv.* **sin′-**
uously. — *n.* **sin′uousness.** — *adjs.* **sinupall′ial,**
-pall′iate, with indented pallial line.—*n.* **sinusoid**
(sī′nəs-oid), the curve of sines (*y* = *a* sin *x*): a
blood-space in tissue.—*adj.* **sīnusoid′al.**—*adv.*
sīnusoid′ally. [L. *sinus*, -*ūs*, a bend, fold, bay.]

Sioux, sōō, *n.* an American Indian of a tribe now
living in the Dakotas, Minnesota, and Montana
(*pl.* **Sioux,** sōō, sōōz).—Also *adj.*—*adj.* **Siou′an,** of
a larger group to which the Sioux belong. [Fr.
from a native word.]

sip, sip, *v.t.* and *v.i.* to drink, or drink from, in small
quantities by action of the lips: (*pr.p.* **sipp′ing**;
pa.t. and *pa.p.* **sipped**).—*n.* the act of sipping: the
quantity sipped at once.—*n.* **sipp′er.** [Cf. **sup**;
O.E. *sypian*; L.G. *sippen*.]

sipe, sīp, *v.i.* (*prov.*) to soak through.—Also **seep.**
[O.E. *sipian*, to soak.]

siphon, sī′fən, *n.* a bent tube or channel by which
a liquid may be drawn off by atmospheric pressure:
a tubular organ for intake and output of water,
as in lamellibranchs: an aerated-water bottle that
discharges by a siphon.—*v.t.* to convey by means
of a siphon.—*n.* **sī′phonage.**—*adj.* **sī′phonal.**—
n.pl. **Sīphonap′tera,** the flea order of insects.—*adj.*
sī′phonate, having a siphon.—*n.* **sī′phonet,** a
greenfly's honeydew tube.—*adj.* **sīphonic** (-*fon*′).—
ns. **siphon′ogam,** a seed-plant; **sīphonog′amy,**
fertilisation by pollen-tube.—*n.pl.* **Sīphonoph′ora,**
an order of colonial Hydrozoa.—*ns.* **sīphonostele**
(-stē′lē, or -stēl′), a hollow cylinder of vascular
tissue; **sī′phuncle,** a tube connecting the chambers
of a nautilus: a siphonet. [Gr. *siphōn*, *siphōn*,
siphon.]

sippet, sip′it, *n.* a morsel, esp. of bread with soup.
—*v.t.* and *v.i.* **sipp′le,** to sip at leisure. [Cf. **sip,**
sup.]

si quis, sī qwis, *n.* a public intimation. [L. *sī quis*,
if anybody (wants, knows, has found, &c.).]

sir, sər, *n.* a word of respect (or disapprobation) used
in addressing a man: a gentleman: prefixed to
the Christian name of a knight or baronet (hence,
a knight or baronet) and formerly of a priest (hence,
Sir John, a priest): formerly used as a translation
of L. *dominus*, bachelor of arts (as distinguished
from *magister*, master of arts): in *pl.* used in *Scot.*
in addressing persons of either sex, passing into
an *interj.* of surprise.—*v.t.* to address as ' sir.'
[O.Fr. *sire*, from L. *senior*, an elder.]

sircar, sirkar, circar, sər-kär′, sər′, *n.* government:
the authorities: a province or district: an Indian
clerk or factotum. [Urdu *sarkār*, a superintendent,
—Pers. *sar*, head, *kār*, agent.]

sirdar, sər-där′, sər′, *n.* a military head: a commander-in-chief. [Urdu *sardār*—Pers. *sar*, head,
dār, holding.]

sire, sīr, *n.* a senior, elder: (*rare*) a master, lord:
(*arch.*) a term of address to a king: a father, esp.
of a horse or other beast: an ancestor.—*v.t.* to
beget, esp. of beasts. [**sir.**]

Siren, sī′rən, *n.* (*Gr. myth.*) one of certain sea-
nymphs, part woman, part bird, whose songs lured
sailors to death: **siren,** a fascinating woman, insidious and deceptive: a bewitching singer: a
mermaid: an instrument for counting sound
vibrations: (formerly **sirene,** still *vulg.* sī-rēn′) a
signalling or warning instrument that produces
sound by the escape of air or steam through a
rotating perforated plate: **Siren,** an American
genus of eel-like amphibians without hind legs.—
Also **siren.**—*n.pl.* **Sirē′nia,** an order of aquatic
mammals now represented by the dugong and the
manatee.—*n.* and *adj.* **sirē′nian.**—*adj.* **sirenic**
(-ren′). [Gr. *Seirēn*.]

sirgang, sər′gang, *n.* a green Asiatic jay-like bird.

sirih, siri, sē′ri, *n.* betel. [Malay *sirih*.]

Sirius, sir′i-əs, *n.* the Dogstar.—*adj.* **Sir′ian.**—*n.*
siri′asis, sunstroke. [L. *Sīrius*—Gr. *Seirios*.]

sirkar. Same as **sircar.**

sirloin, surloin, sər′loin, *n.* the loin or upper part
of a loin of beef. [From a by-form of Fr. *surlonge*
—*sur,* over, and *longe* (cf. **loin**).]

sirname. Same as **surname.**

sirocco, si-rok′ō, **scirocco,** shi-, *n.* in Southe[rn]
Italy, a hot, dry, dusty and gusty wind from Nor[th]
Africa, becoming moist further north: any oppre[s-]
sive south or south-east wind: a wind from t[he]
desert: a drying machine.—Also **s(c)iroc** (si-rok′
sī′rok). [It. *s(c)irocco*—Ar. *sharq*, east.]

sirrah, sər′ə, *n.* sir, used in anger or contempt.

sirree′, (*U.S.*) sir, sirrah. [An extension of **sir.**]

sir-reverence, sə-rev′ə-rəns, (*obs.*) the phrase *sa[ving your]
reverence,* used apologetically when anything di[s-]
gusting has to be mentioned: hence *n.* a piece [of]
excrement.

sirup. See **syrup.**

sirvente, sēr-vän°t, *n.* a troubadour's lay. [Fr.]

sis, siss, sis, *n.* (*U.S.*) an abbreviation of **sister** (use[d]
in addressing a girl).—Also **siss′y** (see also **cissy**

sisal, sis′l, *n.* (in full **sis′al-hemp′,** or **-grass′**
agave fibre. [First exported from *Sisal*.in Yucatan]

siserary, sisserary, sis-ər-ā′ri, sas(s)arara, sas-ə
ā′rä, *n.* (*orig.*) a corruption of **certiorari**: a scole[d-]
ing: a blow.—**with a siserary,** suddenly: on th[e]
spot.

siskin, sis′kin, *n.* a yellowish green finch. [Ge[r.]
dial. *sischen*; app. Slav.]

sissoo, sis′ōō, *n.* a papilionaceous Indian timber tre[e]
(Dalbergia) or its wood. [Hind. *sīsū*.]

sist, sist, *v.t.* (*Scots law*) to stop, stay: to cit[e,]
summon.—*n.* a stay. [L. *sistĕre*, to make to stand

sister, sis′tər, *n.* a daughter of the same parents
a half-sister: formerly, a sister-in-law: a fema[le]
fellow: a member of a sisterhood: a nun:
senior nurse, esp. one in charge of a ward.—*adj.*
the same origin: a fellow: built on the same mode[l]
—*v.t.* to be a sister to: to call sister.—*ns.* **sis′te[r-]
hood,** act or state of being a sister: the relationsh[ip]
of sister: a society, esp. a religious communit[y]
of women: a set or class of women; **sis′ter-hoo[k,]**
one of a pair of hooks that close each other.—*a[dj.]
sis′tering,** (*Shak.*) neighbouring.—*n.* **sis′ter-i[n-]
law,** a husband's or wife's sister, or a brother['s]
wife.—*adjs.* **sis′terless; sis′ter-like, sis′terl[y,]**
like or becoming a sister: kind: affectionate.—*[n.]*
sis′terliness. [App. O.N. *systir*; O.E. *sweostor*
Du. *zuster,* Ger. *schwester*.]

Sistine, sis′tīn, -tēn, -tin, *adj.* of Pope *Sixtus,* es[p.]
Sixtus IV. (1471-84) or V. (1505-90)—also **Six′tin[e.]**
—**Sistine Chapel,** the Pope's chapel in the Vatica[n,]
built by Sixtus IV.; **Sistine Madonna,** a pictur[e]
by Raphael of the Madonna with Sixtus II. (257-[8.)]

sistrum, sis′trəm, *n.* an ancient Egyptian wire ratt[le]
used in Isis-worship:—*pl.* **sis′tra.** [L. *sistrum*—
Gr. *seistron*.]

Sisyphean, sis-i-fē′ən, *adj.* relating to *Sisyphus,* ki[ng]
of Corinth, condemned in Tartarus to roll a hu[ge]
stone ceaselessly up a hill.

sit, sit, *v.i.* to rest on the haunches or (*obs.*) knee[s:]
to perch, as birds: to brood: to have a seat, as [in]
parliament: to be in session: to reside: to be [a]
tenant: to be located, have station or (as the win[d)]
direction: to pose, be a model: to undergo a[n]
examination, be a candidate: to weigh, bea[r]
press: to be disposed in adjustment, hang, fit
to befit.—*v.t.* to seat: to have a seat on, ride: [to]
undergo or be examined in: (*pr.p.* **sitt′ing**; *pa.[t.]*
and *pa.p.* **sat**).—*n.* mode or spell of sitting.—[*v.i.*]
sit′down, a spell of sitting.—*adj.* that one sit[s]
down to: (of a strike) in which workers dow[n]
tools but remain in occupation of the plant, work
shop, &c.—*ns.* **sit′fast,** a lump in a horse's ski[n]
under the saddle; **sitt′er,** one who sits: one wh[o]
sits to an artist, or with a medium: a sitting bird
an easy shot: anything difficult to fail in: (*slan[g]*
a sitting-room; **sitt′ing,** state of being seated o[r]
act of taking a seat: brooding on eggs: a clutch
a continuous meeting of a body: a spell of posin[g]
to an artist, &c.: a spell: a seat: a church seat.—
adj. seated: brooding: actually in parliament a[t]
the time: befitting.—*n.* **sitt′ing-room,** a room in
which members of a family commonly sit: a spac[e]
for sitting.—**sit at,** to live at the rate of expense o[f]
sit down, to take a seat: to pause, rest: to begi[n]
a siege; **sit on,** or **upon,** to hold an official inquir[y]
regarding: (*slang*) to repress, check; **sit out,** t[o]
sit apart without participating: to sit to the en[d]
of: to outstay; **sit tight,** to maintain one's seat

to keep one's position quietly and unobtrusively ; **sit under**, to be in the habit of hearing the preaching of ; **sit up**, to rise from a recumbent to a sitting position, or from a relaxed to an erect seat : to become alert or startled : to remain up instead of going to bed : to keep watch during the night. [O.E. *sittan* ; Ger. *sitzen*, L. *sedēre*.]

ite, *sit*, *n.* situation, esp. of a building : ground occupied or set apart for a building, &c. : (*obs.*) posture.—*v.t.* to locate. [L. *situs*, set—*sinĕre*.]
ith, *sith*, *adv.*, *prep.*, and *conj.* (*Shak.*) since—*obs.*
sith'en, (*Spens.*, *Shak.*) **sith'ence**, **sith'ens**. [O.E. *siththan*, for *sith than* (instrumental), after that ; cf. **since**, **syne**.]
ith, **sithe**, **sythe**, *sīdh*, *n.* (*Spens.*) time :—*pl.* **sith**, **sithes**. [O.E. *sith*, time.]
ithe, *sīdh*, (*Spens.*, *Shak.*, *Milt.*) *n.* and *v.t.* Same as **scythe**.
ithe, *sīdh*, *n.* and *v.i.* an *obs.* or *dial.* form of **sigh**.
itology, *sī-tol'ə-ji*, **sitiology**, *sit'i-*, *n.* dietetics.—*n.* **sit(i)opho'bia**, morbid aversion to food. [Gr. *sītos*, dim. *sītion*, grain, food.]
itta, *sit'ä*, *n.* the nuthatch genus.—*adj.* **sitt'ine**. [Gr. *sittē*.]
itter, **sitting**, &c. See **sit**.
ituate, *sit'ū-it*, *adj.* (now *rare*) situated.—*v.t.* (-*āt*) to set, place, locate : to circumstance.—*adj.* **sit'uated**, set, located : circumstanced.—*n.* **situa'tion**, location : place : position : momentary state : condition : a set of circumstances, a juncture : a critical point in the action of a play or the development of the plot of a novel : office, employment.— *adj.* **situa'tional**. [L.L. *situātus*—L. *situĕre*, to place.]
tula, *sit'ū'lä*, *n.* a bucket. [L.]
tz-bath, *sits-bäth*, *n.* a hip-bath. [Ger. *sitzbad*.]
ivan, *sī'am*, *n.* the water-parsnip genus. [Gr. *sion*.]
iva, *s(h)ē'vä*, *n.* the third god of the Hindu triad, destroyer and reproducer.—*n.* **Si'vaism**.—*adj.* **Sivaist'ic**. — *ns.* **Si'vaite** ; **Sivaphē'cus**, an Indian Miocene fossil anthropoid ; **Sivathē'rium**, a gigantic giraffe-like Indian Pliocene fossil animal. [Sans. *çiva*, happy.]
ivan, *sē-vän'*, *n.* the ninth month of the Jewish civil, third of the ecclesiastical, year, part of May and June. [Heb. *sīwān*.]
ver. See **syver**.
wash, *sī'wosh*, *n.* a N.W. American Indian.— Also *adj.* [Chinook,—Fr. *sauvage*, wild.]
x, *siks*, *n.* the cardinal numeral next above five : a symbol representing it (6, vi., &c.) : a set of that number : an article of size denoted by it : a card with six pips : a score of six points, tricks, &c. : the sixth hour after midnight or after midday : a six-cylinder engine or car : a six-syllable line.— *adj.* of the number six.—*adj.* **six'-day**, for six days i.e. usu. excluding Sunday).—*n.* **six'er**, anything counting for six (as a hit at cricket) or indicated by six.—*adj.* and *adv.* **six'fold**, in six divisions : six times as much.—*adj.* **six'-foot**, measuring six feet.—*ns.* **six'-foot'er**, a person six feet high ; **six'pence**, a coin worth six pence : its value.—*adj.* **six'penny**, costing or worth sixpence : cheap : worthless.—*n.* a sixpenny book.—*n.* and *adj.* **six'-core**.—*n.* **six'-shooter**, a six-chambered revolver. —*adj.* **sixth**, last of six : next after the fifth : equal to one of six equal parts.—*n.* a sixth part : (*mus.*) an interval of five (conventionally called six) diatonic degrees : a combination of two tones that distance apart.—*adv.* **sixth'ly**, in the sixth place.—**sixth lour**, noontide ; **at sixes and sevens**, in disorder ; **long, short, at sixes**, candles weighing six to the pound, about 8 or 4 inches long respectively. [O.E. *siex* ; Ger. *sechs* ; Gael. *sé* ; L. *sex*, Gr. *hex*, Sans. *shash*.]
xaine, *siks-än'*, *n.* a stanza of six lines.—*n.* **sixte** (*sikst*), a parry with hand on guard opposite the right breast, sword point a little raised to the right. [Fr.]
xteen, *siks-tēn'*, or *siks'*, *n.* and *adj.* six and ten.— *n.* **sixteen'er**, a verse of sixteen syllables.—*n.* an *adj.* **sixteen'mo**, sextodecimo.—*adj.* **sixteenth'** or *siks'*), last of sixteen : equal to one of sixteen equal parts.—*n.* a sixteenth part. [O.E. *sixténe*, *sīene*) ; see **six**, **ten**.]

sixty, *siks'ti*, *adj.* and *n.* six times ten :—*pl.* **six'ties**, the numbers sixty to sixty-nine : the years so numbered in a life or century.—*adj.* **six'tieth**, last of sixty : equal to one of sixty equal parts.—*n.* a sixtieth part. [O.E. *siextig*.]
size, *sīz*, *n.* (*obs.*) an assize : a portion of food and drink : an allowance : bigness : magnitude.—*v.t.* to arrange according to size : at Cambridge, to buy or score, as rations : to measure.—*v.i.* to draw a size : to assume size.—*adj.* **si'zable** (or **size'able**), of a fair size.—*ns.* **si'zar** (also **sī'zer**), at Cambridge and Dublin, a student receiving an allowance from his college towards his expenses ; **si'zarship**.—*adj.* **sized**, having this or that size.— *ns.* **si'zer**, a measurer : a gauge : (*slang*) a thing of considerable or great size ; **si'zing**, act of sorting by size : an order for extra food from a college buttery.—**size up**, to take mental measure of. [assize.]
size, *sīz*, *n.* weak glue or gluey material.—*v.t.* to cover or treat with size.—*adj.* **sized**.—*ns.* **siz'er** ; **siz'iness** ; **siz'ing**, application of size, or material for the purpose.—*adj.* **siz'y**. [Origin obscure.]
size, *sīz*. Same as **sice**.
sizel. See **scissel**.
sizzle, *siz'l*, *v.i.* to make a hissing sound of frying.— *v.t.* and *v.i.* to fry, scorch, sear.—*n.* a hissing sound : extreme heat.—*n.* **sizz'ling**, a hissing. [Imit.]
sjambok, *sham'bok*, *n.* a whip of dried hide.—*v.t.* to flog. [Cape Du., from Malay *samboq*—Urdu *chābuk*.]
skail, **scail**, *skäl*, *v.t.* and *v.i.* (*Scot.*) to disperse : to scatter : to spill. [Ety. dub.]
skaines mate, *skänz'māt*, *n.* (*Shak.*) perh. a companion, a scapegrace.
skaith. See **scathe**.
skald, **scald**, *skawld*, *n.* a poet : a Scandinavian bard.—*adj.* **skald'ic**, **scald'ic**. [O.N. *skáld*.]
skart, **scart**, *skärt*, **scarth**, **skarth**, *skärth*, *n.* (*Scot.*) a cormorant. [O.N. *skarfr*.]
skat, *skät*, *n.* a three-handed card-game. [O.Fr. *escart*, laying aside.]
skate, *skāt*, *n.* a sole or sandal mounted on a blade (for moving on ice) or on rollers : a spell of skating. —*v.i.* to go on skates.—*ns.* **skā'ter** ; **skā'ting** ; **skā'ting-rink**. [Du. *schaats* — O.N.Fr. *escache*, stilt—L.G. *schake*, shank.]
skate, *skāt*, *n.* a kind of ray (*Raia batis*, or kindred species). [O.N. *skata*.]
skatole, *skat'ōl*, *skā'tōl*, *n.* a compound (C_9H_9N) found in faeces. [Gr. *skōr*, *skatos*, dung.]
skaw, **scaw**, *skaw*, *n.* a low cape, ness (in place-names). [O.N. *skagi*.]
skean. See **skene** : also an old spelling of **skein**.
skedaddle, *ski-dad'l*, *v.i.* (*coll.*) to scamper off.— *n.* a scurrying off. [Ety. unknown.]
skeely, *skē'li*, *adj.* (*Scot.*) skilful.
skeer, **skear**, **skeery**, **skeary**, dial. forms of **scare**, **scary**.
skeesicks, *skē'ziks*, *n.* (*U.S.*) a rascal.
skeet, *skēt*, *n.* a form of clay-pigeon shooting.
skeeter, *skēt'ər*, *n.* (*U.S.*) short for **mosquito**.
Skeffington's daughter. See **scavenger**.
skegger, *skeg'ər*, *n.* a young salmon. [Origin obscure.]
skeigh, *skēhh*, *adj.* (*Scot.*) shy : coy : aloof : skittish. [Cf. O.E. *scéoh*, shy.]
skein, *skān*, *n.* a loosely tied coil or standard length of thread or yarn : a tangle : a web : (*biol.*) the nuclear network : a flock of wild geese in flight. [O.Fr. *escaigne*.]
skelder, *skel'dər*, *v.i.* to beg : to swindle. [Cant.]
skeleton, *skel'i-tn*, *n.* the hard parts of an animal : the bones : the veins of a leaf : a framework or outline of anything : a scheme reduced to its essential or indispensable elements : a set of persons reduced to its lowest strength : an emaciated person or animal.—Also *adjs.* **skel'etal** ; **skeletogenous** (-*toj'*), skeleton-forming.—*v.t.* **skel'etonise**, to reduce to a skeleton.—*n.* **skel'eton-shrimp**, a ghostly-looking amphipod (Caprella, &c.).—**skeleton in the cupboard, closet, house**, &c., a hidden domestic sorrow or shame ; **skeleton key**, a key for picking locks, without the inner bits ; **skeleton suit**, an early 19th-cent. boy's suit with

Neutral vowels in unaccented syllables : *el'ə-mənt*, *in'fənt*, *ran'dəm*

trousers buttoning over the coat. [Gr. *skeleton* (*sōma*), dried (body)—*skellein*, to dry.]

skelloch, *skel'əhh*, *v.i.* (*Scot.*) to yell.—*n.* a yell.

skellum, *skel'əm*, *n.* (*Scot.*) a ne'er-do-well: a scamp. [Du. *schelm*, a rogue; cf. **schelm**.]

skelly, *skel'i*, *n.*, *adj.*, and *v.i.* (*Scot.*) squint. [Prob. O.N.; cf. O.E. *sceolh*, squint.]

skelp, *skelp*, *v.t.* (*Scot.*) to slap.—*v.i.* to move briskly along: to bound along.—*n.* a slap.—*adj.* **skelp'ing**, very big or full: smacking: lusty.—*n.* a smacking. [Ety. unknown.]

skelter, *skel'tər*, *v.i.* to scurry.—*n.* a scurry.

skene, **skean**, *skēn*, *n.* an Irish or Highland dagger, knife, or short sword.—*ns.* **skene'-dhu**, **skean'-dhu** (*-dōō'*), a dirk, dagger, stuck in the stocking; **skene'-occle** (*-ok'l*), one carried in the sleeve. [Ir. and Gael. *sgian*, knife, *dhu*, black, *achlais*, armpit.]

skeo. Same as **skio**.

skep, *skep*, *n.* a basket: a beehive.—*v.t.* to hive.—*n.* **skep'ful.** [O.N. *skeppa*.]

skeptic, skepsis. Same as **sceptic, scepsis**.

sker. Same as **skirr**.

skerry, *sker'i*, *n.* a reef of rock. [O.N. *sker*.]

sketch, *skech*, *n.* a drawing, slight, rough, or without detail, esp. as a study towards a more finished work: an outline or short account: a short and slightly constructed play, dramatic scene, musical entertainment, &c.: a short descriptive essay.—*v.t.* to make or give a sketch of: to outline, give the principal points of.—*v.i.* to practise sketching.—*n.* **sketchabil'ity.**—*adj.* **sketch'able**, worth sketching.—*ns.* **sketch'-book**, a book of or for sketches (in drawing, literature, or music); **sketch'er.**—*adv.* **sketch'ily.**—*n.* **sketch'iness.**—*adj.* **sketch'y**, like a sketch: incomplete, slight. [Du. *schets*, prob.—It. *schizzo*—L. *schedium*, an extempore—Gr. *schedios*, offhand.]

Skevington's daughter. See **scavenger**.

skew, *skū*, *adj.* oblique.—*adv.* awry.—*n.* obliquity.—*v.t.* and *v.i.* to set, go, or look obliquely.—*ns.* **skew'-back**, (*archit.*) the part, or inclined surface on which a segmented arch abuts; **skew'-bridge**, a bridge having its arch or arches set obliquely on its abutments.—*adj.* **skewed**, distorted. [App. O.N.Fr. *eskiu(w)er*—O.Fr. *eschuer*; see **eschew**; or M.Du. *schuwe*, to shun; cf. **shy**.]

skew, *skū*, *n.* the coping or a coping-stone of a gable.—*ns.* **skew'-corbel, -put, -table**, the cornerstone supporting the coping of a gable. [O.Fr. *escu*—L. *scūtum*, a shield.]

skewbald, *skū'bawld*, *adj.* marked in white and another colour (not black).—*n.* a skewbald horse. [Origin obscure.]

skewer, *sku'ər*, *n.* a long pin of wood or metal, esp. for meat.—*v.t.* to fasten or pierce with a skewer: to transfix. [**skiver**.]

ski, *shē, skē, n.* a long, narrow, wooden snow-shoe: (*pl.* **ski**, or **skis**.)—*v.i.* to travel on skis :—*pr.p.* **ski'ing**; *pa.t.* and *pa.p.* **skied, ski'd**.—*ns.* **ski'er**; **ski'ing**; **ski'-jöring** (*-yər'ing*), **skijoring** (*-jör'*), the sport of being towed on skis by a horse or a motor vehicle; **ski'-jump'ing, -run'ning**. [Norw.—O.N. *skíth*, snow-shoe, piece of split wood; O.E. *scíd*.]

skia-, *skī'ə-*, *-a'-*, in composition, shadow.—Also **scia-** (*sī-*), **skio-, scio-**.—*ns.* **ski'agram, ski'agraph**, an X-ray photograph; **skiamachy** (*-am'ə-ki*; Gr. *machē*, a fight), a sham fight: a fight with shadows; **skias'copy**, retinoscopy. [Gr. *skiā*, a shadow.]

skid, *skid*, *n.* a support on which something rests, is brought to the desired level, or slides: a ship's wooden fender: a shoe or other device to check a wheel on a down-slope: an aeroplane runner: a skidding: a sideslip.—*v.i.* to slide along without revolving: to slip, esp. sideways.—*v.t.* to check with a skid: to make to skid. [Prob. related to **ski**.]

skier, skies, skiey. See **ski, sky, skyey**.

skiff, *skif*, *n.* a small light boat. [Akin to **ship**.]

skiff, *skif*, *v.i.* and *v.t.* (*Scot.*) to skim.—*n.* a skimming or grazing movement or blow: a slight touch: a sketch: a puff.

skijoring. See **ski**.

skill, *skil*, *n.* (*Shak.*) reason: (*obs.*) discrimination:

expertness : (*arch.*) expert knowledge : (*U.S.*) a cra or accomplishment.—*v.t.* and *v.i.* (*arch.*) to matte to make (a difference) : to signify.—*adj.* **skil'fu** —*adv.* **skil'fully.**—*n.* **skil'fulness.**—*adjs.* **skille** expert — (*Scot.*) **skill'y**, **skee'ly**; **skill'-les** **skil'less.** [O.N. *skil*, distinction, *skilja*, separate.]

skillet, *skil'it*, *n.* a small, long-handled pan. [Orig doubtful.]

skilling, *skil'ing*, an obsolete coin of Scandinavia countries, worth about a halfpenny. [Dan.]

skilly, *skil'i*, *n.* thin gruel.—Also **skilligalee** **skilligolee'.** [Ety. dub.]

skim, *skim*, *v.t.* to remove floating matter from th surface of : to take off by skimming : to gli lightly over : to read superficially and skipping —*v.i.* to pass over lightly : to glide along near th surface : to become coated over : (*pr.p.* **skimm ing**; *pa.t.* and *pa.p.* **skimmed**).—*n.* the act o skimming : skim-milk.—*ns.* **skimm'er**, one wh skims : a utensil for skimming milk : a sea-bir (Rhyncops) that skims the water; **skim'-mil** milk from which the cream has been skimme **skimm'ing.**—*adv.* **skimm'ingly.** [App. relate to **scum**.]

skimble-skamble, *skim'bl-skam'bl*, *adj.* wild, ram bling, incoherent. [A reduplication of **scamble**.

Skimmia, *skim'i-ä, n.* an Asiatic genus of rutaceo shrubs, cultivated for its holly-like leaves ar drupes. [Jap. *skimmi*.]

skimmington, *skim'ing-tən*, *n.* a burlesque pr cession in ridicule of husband or wife in case infidelity or other ill-treatment. [Ety. unknown.

skimp, *skimp*, *v.t.* and *v.i.* to scrimp : to stint.—*a* scanty, spare.—*adv.* **skimp'ily.**—*adj.* **skimp'in** — *adv.* **skimp'ingly.** — *adj.* **skimp'y**. [Pos **scamp** combined with **scrimp**.]

skin, *skin*, *n.* the natural outer covering of an anima a hide : a thin outer layer or covering : an integ ment : a membrane : a wine vessel made of animal's skin.—*adj.* of skin.—*v.t.* to cover with skin : to strip the skin from : to fleece.—*v.i.* become covered with skin : to slip through away :—*pr.p.* **skinn'ing**; *pa.t.* and *pa.p.* **skinne** —*adj.* **skin'-deep**, superficial.—*ns.* **skin'-diver** naked pearl-diver; **skin'-diving**; **skin'flint**, very niggardly person; **skin'ful**, as much liqu as one can hold; **skin'-game**, a swindling trick.— *adj.* **skin'less.**—*ns.* **skinn'er**, one who prepar hides; **skinn'iness.**—*adjs.* **skinn'y**, of or li skin : emaciated; **skin'-tight**, fitting close to th skin.—*n.* (in *pl.*) tights.—*n.* **skin'-wool**, wool fro a dead sheep.—**by or with the skin of one's teet** very narrowly. [O.N. *skinn*; late O.E. *scinn*.]

skink, *skingk*, *v.i.* and *v.t.* to pour out.—*n.* (*Sco* liquor.—*n.* **skink'er.**—*adj.* **skink'ing**, (*Scot.*) thi watery. [Perh. L.G. *schenken*; cf. O.E. *scenca* Ger. *schenken*.]

skink, *skingk*, *n.* an African lizard (Scincus) kindred kind. [L. *scincus*—Gr. *skinkos*.]

skink, *skingk*, *n.* (*Scot.*) shin-bone soup. [L.C *schinke*.]

skio, skeo, *skyō*, *n.* (*Orkney* and *Shetland*) a hut shed. [Norw. *skjaa*.]

skio-. See **skia-**.

skip, *skip*, *v.i.* to spring or hop lightly : to ma jumps over a twirling rope : to pass discontinuousl —*v.t.* to overleap : to omit : (*pr.p.* **skipp'in** *pa.t.* and *pa.p.* **skipped**).—*n.* an act of skipping belt of inaudibility in wireless transmission : college servant.—*ns.* **skip'jack**, a pert fop : jumping fish (bluefish, saurel, &c.): a clic beetle : a jumping toy made of a fowl's merr thought; **skip'-kennel**, (*obs.*) a lackey; **skipp** one who skips : a dancer : (*Shak.*) a young ar thoughtless person : a butterfly of the Hesperiida with short jerky flight : the saury.—*adj.* **skipp'in** flighty, giddy.—*adv.* **skipp'ingly.**—*n.* **skipp'in rope.** [Cf. O.N. *skopa*, to run.]

skip, *skip*, *n.* a box or truck for raising minera from a mine. [**skep**.]

skip, *skip*, *n.* captain of a rink in bowls or curling.— *v.t.* and *v.i.* to act as skip. [**skipper**.]

skipper, *skip'ər*, *n.* a ship captain.—**skipper daughters**, white-topped waves. [Du. *schipper*.

fāte, fär, àsk; mē, hər (her); *mīne; mōte; mūte; mōōn; dhen* (then)

ippet, *skip'it*, *n*. a flat box for protecting a seal.

irl, *skirl*, *v.t.* and *v.i.* (*Scot.*) to shriek or sing
rilly.—*n*. a shrill cry.—*ns*. **skirl'ing**, a shrill
und ; **skirl'-in-the-pan'**, the noise of frying : a
ied dish. [*Scand.*]

rmish, *skər'mish*, *n*. an irregular fight between
nall parties.—*v.i.* to fight slightly or irregularly.
—*ns*. **skir'misher** ; **skir'mishing**. [O.Fr. *escar-
ouche*.]

rr, sker, scur, *skər*, *v.t.* (*Scot.*) to scour, search,
nge over : to send skimming.—*v.i.* (*Shak.*) to
urry. [Origin doubtful.]

rret, *skir'it*, *n*. a water-parsnip with edible roots.
M.E. *skirwhit*, as if *skire white*, pure white, but
erh. altered from O.Fr. *eschervis*.]

rt, *skərt*, *n*. a garment, or part of a garment,
enerally a woman's, that hangs from the waist :
ae lower part of a gown, coat, or other garment :
saddle-flap : a midriff : a rim, border, margin :
lang) a woman.—*v.t.* to border : to pass along
e edge of : to scour the outskirts of.—*v.i.* to be
a or pass along the border : to leave the pack.—
skirt'-danc'ing, dancing with waving of flowing
irts.—*adj.* **skirt'ed**, wearing or having a skirt.—
. **skir'ter**, a huntsman who dodges his jumps by
ing round about ; **skir'ting**, material for skirts :
irting-board : (in *pl.*) dirty wool from the skirts
a fleece.—Also *adj.*—*n*. **skir'ting-board**, the
arrow board next the floor round the walls of a
om.—*adj.* **skir'tless**—**divided skirt**, trousers
ade to look like a skirt. [O.N. *skyrta*, a shirt,
rtle ; cf. **shirt**.]

t, *skit*, *n*. a piece of banter or burlesque, esp. in
ramatic or literary form : a humorous hit : a
ax : a quiz.—*v.i.* **skite**, **skyte** (*skīt* ; *Scot.*), to
irt or glide obliquely.—*n*. a glancing blow :
ree : a trick : a queer person. [Perh. related to
.N. *skjóta*, to shoot.]

ttish, *skit'ish*, *adj.* unsteady : light-headed :
ivolous : frisky : lively : volatile : changeable :
anton : coy.—*adv.* **skitt'ishly**.—*n*. **skitt'ishness**
Perh. conn. with **skit**.]

ttle, *skit'l*, *n*. a pin for the game of skittles : a
rm of ninepins in which a flattened ball or cheese-
aaped missile is used.—*v.t.* to knock down.—*ns*.
kitt'le-alley, -ball, -ground. [Origin doubtful.]

ve, *skiv*, *v.t.* to pare, split.—*ns*. **ski'ver**, split
aeepskin leather ; **ski'ving**. [O.N. *skifa* ; cf.
ive.]

ver, *skiv'ər*, *n*. and *v.t.* (*prov.*). Same as **skewer**.
App. akin to **shiver**.]

vie, *ski'vi*, *adj.* (*obs. Scot.*) deranged : askew.
Cf. O.N. *skeifr*.]

vvy, *skiv'i*, *n*. (*slang*) a disrespectful word for a
aidservant.

ate, *sklāt, sklent, slent*, Scottish forms of **slate**,
ant.

al, *skōl*, *interj.* hail ! a friendly exclamation in
lutation before drinking, &c. [O.N. *skál* ; Norw.
aal, a bowl, Sw. *skål* ; cf. **scale** (3 and 4).]

lion, *skō'li-on*, *n*. a short drinking-song in
acient Greece, taken up by the guests in irregular
ccession :—*pl.* **skō'lia**. [Gr. *skólion*.]

an. See **scran**.

een (*Spens.* **skreene**). See **screen**.

eigh, **skriech, skriegh, scraich, scriech,
rëhh, shrähh, skrehh**, *n*. and *v*. (*Scot.*) screech,
riek.—**skreigh of day**, daybreak. [Imit. im-
ovement upon **screak**.]

immage. See **scrimmage**.

imshank, scrimshank, *skrim'shangk*, *v.i.* (*mil.
ang*) to evade work or duty.—*n*. evasion of work.
n. **skrim'shanker**.

y, skryer. Same as **scry, scryer**.

aa, *skū'ə*, *n*. a genus (Stercorarius) of large pre-
tory gulls.—*n*. **skū'a-gull**. [O.N. *skúfr*.]

adler, scuddaler, scudler, *skud'lər*, *n*. (*Shetland*)
e leader of a band of guisers : the conductor of a
stival.

ag, scug, skug (*Scot.* scoug, scoog, skoog, scog,
og), *n*. orig. shadow : shelter.—*v.t.* and *v.i.* to
elter. [O.N. *skuggi*, shadow.]

ag, skug, *n*. (*prov.*) a squirrel.

lduddery. See **sculduddery**.

alk, *skulk*, *v.i.* to sneak out of the way : to lurk:

to malinger.—*ns*. **skulk, skulk'er**, one who skulks.
—*n*. and *adj.* **skulk'ing**.—*adv.* **skulk'ingly**.—*n*.
skulk'ing-place. [Scand., as Dan. *skulke*.]

skull, *skul*, *n*. the bony case that encloses the brain :
the sconce, noddle : a skullcap, esp. of metal : a
crust of solidified metal on a ladle, &c.—*n*. **skull'-
cap**, a close-fitting cap : a protective cap of metal
for the top of the head : the top of the skull : a
labiate plant (Scutellaria) with helmet-like calyx.
[M.E. *scolle* ; perh. Scand.]

skull. Same as **scull**.

skulpin. Same as **sculpin**.

skunk, *skungk*, *n*. a small American musteline
animal that emits an offensive fluid : its fur : a low
fellow.—*v.t.* (*U.S.*) to defeat without allowing to
score.—*ns*. **skunk'-bird, -black'bird**, the bobolink
(from his colouring) ; **skunk'-cabb'age**, an ill-
smelling plant (Symplocarpus) of the arum family.
[Algonkian *segonku*.]

Skupshtina, *skoop'shti-nä*, *n*. the Yugoslav (*hist.*
Serbian and Montenegrin) national assembly.
[Serb.]

skurry, skuttle. See **scurry, scuttle**.

skutterudite, *skoot'ər-oo-dīt*, a cubic mineral, cobalt
arsenide. [*Skutterud* in Norway, a source.]

sky, *skī*, *n*. the apparent canopy over our heads : the
heavens : the weather : the upper rows of pictures
in a gallery : sky-blue.—*v.t.* to raise aloft : to hit
high into the air : to hang above the line of sight.
—*n*. and *adj.* **sky'-blue**, light blue like the sky.
—*adjs.* **sky'-aspiring** (*Shak.*) ; **sky'-born**, of
heavenly birth ; **sky'-bred** ; **sky'clad**, naked.—
n. **sky'-col'our**.—*adjs.* **sky'-col'oured** ; **sky'ey**
(or *ski'ey*), of the weather : of or like the sky ;
sky'-high, very high.—Also *adv.*—*adj.* **sky'ish**,
(*Shak.*) like or approaching the sky, lofty.—*n*. **sky'-
lark**, the common lark.—*v.i.* to frolic boisterously.
—*v.t.* to trick.—*ns*. **sky'larking**, running about the
rigging of a ship in sport : frolicking ; **sky'light**,
a window in a roof or ceiling : light from or in
the sky : light through the bottom of an empty
glass ; **sky'line**, the horizon : a silhouette or
outline against the sky ; **sky'-par'lour**, a lofty
attic ; **sky'-pī'lot**, a clergyman, chaplain.—*adj.*
sky'-plant'ed, placed in the sky.—*n*. **sky'-rock'et**,
a firework that bursts high in the sky.—*v.i.* to shoot
up high.—*ns*. **skysail** (*ski'sl*), a sail above the royal ;
sky'scape, a view or a picture of the sky ; **sky'-
scraper**, a very lofty building : a triangular skysail : anything very high ; **sky'-sign**, an elevated
advertising sign, as of lights on a high building.—
adj. **sky'-tinc'tured**, of the colour of the sky.—
adj. and *adv.* **sky'ward**.—*adv.* **sky'wards**.—*ns*.
sky'way, a route for aircraft travel ; **sky'-writing**,
tracing of words by smoke from an aircraft. [O.N.
skŷ, cloud.]

Skye, *skī*, *n*. (in full, **Skye terrier**) a small long-
haired Scotch terrier. [From the island of *Skye*.]

skyr, *shūr, skĕr*, *n*. curds. [Norw., Sw., and Ice.,
—O.N.]

skyre, *skīr*, *v.i.* (*Scot.*) to shine, be gaudy, flaunt.
[Origin obscure.]

skyte. Same as **skite**.

slab, *slab*, *n*. a plane-sided plate : a large thick slice
or cake : an outer plank sawn from a log : a thin
flat piece of stone, &c.—*v.t.* to cut slabs from :
to form into slabs : to cover with slabs. — *adjs.*
slabbed ; **slab'-sid'ed**, (*U.S.*) flat-sided : tall and
lank.—*n*. **slab'stone**, flagstone. [Origin obscure.]

slab, *slab*, *adj.* semi-liquid, viscous.—*n*. mud.—*n*.
slabb'iness—*adj.* **slabb'y**, muddy. [Scand. ;
cf. Norw., Sw. *slabb*, wet filth.]

slabber, *slab'ər*, *v.i.* to slaver, to drivel.—*v.t.* to
beslaver, beslobber, or beslubber : to gobble
sloppily and grossly.—*n*. **slabb'erer**.—*adj.* **slabb'-
ery**. [Cf. L.G. and Du. *slabberen* and **slobber**.]

slack, *slak*, *adj.* lax or loose : not firmly extended
or drawn out : not holding fast : remiss : not
strict : not eager or diligent, inattentive : not busy :
not violent or rapid, slow : (*phonet.*) pronounced
with wide, not tense, tongue.—*adv.* in a slack
manner : partially : insufficiently.—*n*. the slack
part of a rope, belt, &c. : a time, occasion, or place
of relaxed movement or activity : a slack-water
haul of a net : (in *pl.*) long, loose trousers.—*vs.i.*

slack, slack′en, to become loose or less tight : to be remiss : to abate : to become slower : to fail or flag : to be inactive or lax.—*vs.t.* to make slack or less tight : to loosen : to slow, retard : to be remiss or dilatory in : to relax : to slake.—*v.t.* **slack′-bake,** to half-bake.—*n.* and *adj.* **slack′en-ing.**—*n.* **slack′er,** an idler : one who is reprehensibly inactive : a shirker.—*adj.* **slack′-hand′ed,** remiss.—*n.* **slack′-jaw,** (*slang*) impudent talk.—*adv.* **slack′ly.**—*ns.* **slack′ness** ; **slack′-rope,** a loosely stretched rope for a funambulist ; **slack′-water,** turn of the tide : a stretch of still or slow-moving water.—*adj.* pertaining to slack-water.—**slack away,** to ease off freely ; **slack in stays,** slow in going about, of a ship ; **slack off,** to ease off ; **slack up,** to ease off : to slow. [O.E. *slæc* (*sleac*) ; cf. Sw. *slak*, O.N. *slakr*.]

slack, *slak, n.* coal-dross. [Cf. Ger. *schlacke*.]

slack, *slak, n.* (*Scot.*) a cleft between hills : a boggy place. [O.N. *slakki*, dell.]

slade, *slād, n.* a little valley or dell : a piece of low, moist ground. [O.E. *slæd*, dell.]

slade, slaid, *slād,* Scots *pa.t.* of **slide.**

slae, *slā,* a Scots form of **sloe.**

slag, *slag, n.* solid scum on melted metal : vitrified cinders : scoriaceous lava : a piece of slag.—*v.t.* and *v.i.* to form into slag.—*adj.* **slagg′y.**—*n.* **slag′-wool,** fibre made from molten slag. [M.L.G. *slagge* ; cf. Ger. *schlacke*, dross.]

slain, *slān, pa.p.* of **slay.**

slaister, *slās′tər, n.* (*Scot.*) a slobbery mess : wet slovenly work.—*v.t.* to bedaub.—*v.i.* to do anything in a wet, dirty, slobbery way.—*adj.* **slais′tery.** —*n.* slops : drudgery. [Origin obscure.]

slake, *slāk, v.t.* to quench : to extinguish : to deaden : to abate, mitigate, allay, reduce, moderate : to moisten : to hydrate (as lime) : to refresh with moisture : to slacken.—*v.i.* to become slaked : to subside : to abate : to die down.—*adj.* **slake′less,** that cannot be slaked. [O.E. *slacian, sleacian,* to grow slack—*slæc, sleac,* slack.]

slake, *slāk, v.t.* and *v.i.* (*Scot.*) to lick, smear, daub. —*n.* a slabbery daub : a smear. [O.N. *sleikja,* to lick ; Ger. *schlecken,* to lick.]

slake, *slāk, n.* (*Northern*) mud : slime : a mud-flat.

slalom, *slā′lom, n.* a race in which tactical skill is required, esp. a downhill or zigzag ski-run among posts or trees. [Norw. *slalåm.*]

slam, *slam, v.t.* or *v.i.* to shut or strike with violence and noise : to bang : (*pr.p.* **slamm′ing** ; *pa.t.* and *pa.p.* **slammed**).—*n.* the act or sound of slamming. —*adv.* with a slam. [Cf. Norw. *slemma.*]

slam, *slam, n.* an old card-game, also called ruff or trump : (*whist*) the winning of every trick (in bridge called *grand slam* ; of all but one, *little slam*).—*v.t.* to inflict a slam upon.

slammakin, slammerkin, *slam′ə(r)-kin, n.* (*obs.*) a loose gown : a slovenly-dressed woman : a slattern.—*adj.* slovenly. [Origin obscure.]

slander, *slän′dər, n.* a false or malicious report : (*Engl. law*) injurious defamation by spoken words or by looks, signs, or gestures (distinct from *libel*) : (*Scots law*) defamation whether spoken or written : calumny.—*v.t.* to defame : to calumniate.—*n.* **slan′derer.**—*adj.* **slan′derous.**—*adv.* **slan′derously.**—*n.* **slan′derousness.** [O.Fr. *esclandre*—L. *scandalum*—Gr. *skandalon,* snare, stumbling-block, scandal.]

slang, *slang, n.* a jargon of thieves and disreputable persons : the jargon of any class, profession, or set : colloquial language with words and usages not accepted for dignified use.—Also *adj.*—*v.t.* to scold, vituperate. —*adv.* **slang′ily.** —*ns.* **slang′iness** ; **slang′ing,** a scolding.—Also *adj.*—*adv.* **slang′-ingly.**—*adjs.* **slang′ish** ; **slang′ular** (*Dickens*).— *v.t.* and *v.i.* **slang′-whang,** to rail, to rant.—*n.* **slang′-whanger.**—*adj.* **slang′y.** [Of cant origin ; connexion with **sling** very doubtful.]

slang, *slang, n.* (*slang*) a counterfeit weight or measure : a travelling show, or performance : a hawker's licence. [Cant.]

slang, *slang, n.* a watch-chain : (*pl.*) leg-irons. [Perh. Du. *slang,* snake.]

slant, *slänt, v.t.* and *v.i.* to slope : to turn, strike, fall, obliquely.—*n.* a slope : obliquity : a sloping surface, line, ray, or movement : a divergence fro[m] a direct line : (*U.S.*) a glance : a jibe : (*U.S.*) [a] point of view, way of looking at a thing : (*slang*) chance.—*adj.* sloping : oblique : inclined from direct line. —*adjs.* **slant′ed** ; **slantendic′ula[r],** **slantin(g)dic′ular,** (*jocular* ; founded on *pe[r]-pendicular*) oblique.—*adj.* **slant′ing.**—*advs.* **slan[t]-tingly, slant′ingways, slant′ly, slant′way[s,] slant′wise.** [M.E. *slent* ; cf. Norw. *slenta, S[w.] slinta,* to slope, slip.]

slant, *slänt, n.* a transitory breeze. [Earlier *slen[t]* Scand. ; cf. Norw. *slett.*]

slap, *slap, n.* a blow with the hand or anything fla[t] —*v.t.* to give a slap to : to bring or send with [a] slap : (*pr.p.* **slapp′ing**) *pa.t.* and *pa.p.* **slapped** —*adv.* with a slap : suddenly, violently : directl[y] straight.—*adv.* **slap′-bang,** violently, all at once.— *adj.* dashing, violent.—*n.* a cheap eating-house : [a] simple firework that makes a noise when throw[n] down.—*adv.* **slap′-dash,** in a bold, careless way.— *adj.* off-hand, rash.—*n.* rough-cast : careless wor[k] —*v.t.* to do in a hasty, imperfect manner : to roug[h-] cast.—*ns.* **slap′jack,** (*U.S.*) a flapjack, griddl[e] cake ; **slapp′er,** one who, or that which, slap[s] (*slang*) a whopper, a thing very big of its kind.— *adj.* **slapp′ing,** (*slang*) whopping.—*n.* **slap′stic[k],** a harlequin's double lath that makes a noise like [a] slap : (also **slapstick comedy**) knock-about lo[w] comedy or farce.—*adj.* **slap′-up,** (*slang*) supe[r-] latively fine. [Allied to L.G. *slapp*, Ger. *schlapp[e]* imit.]

slap, *slap, n.* (*Scot.*) a gap in a fence, wall, hed[ge] &c. : a hill pass : a passage in a salmon cruiv[e] hence the weekly close time when the passage [is] open.—*v.t.* to breach : to pierce. [Du. or L.G[.] *slop.*]

slash, *slash, v.t.* to cut by striking with violence a[nd] at random : to make long cuts in : to slit so as [to] show lining or material underneath : to lash : criticise very harshly : to crack as a whip : (*U.[S.]* to cut down, reduce : (*U.S.*) to clear by felli[ng] trees.—*v.i.* to strike violently and at random wi[th] an edged instrument : to strike right and left.— *n.* a long cut : a cut at random : a cut in cloth [to] show colours underneath : a stripe on a no[n-] commissioned officer's sleeve : (*U.S.*) débris [of] trees : (*U.S.*) a forest clearing, esp. cumbered w[ith] débris.—*adj.* **slashed,** cut with slashes : gashe[d] —*ns.* **slash′er** ; **slash′ing,** a slash or slashes : t[he] felling of trees as a military obstacle : felled tree[s] a clearing.—*adj.* cutting mercilessly, unsparin[g,] dashing : very big, slapping. [Perh. O.F[r.] *esclachier,* to break ; or conn. with **lash.**]

slat, *slat, v.t.* and *v.i.* to strike, beat : to flap.—*n.* [a] sudden sharp blow. [Poss. O.N. *sletta,* to sla[p,] splash.]

slat, *slat, n.* (*dial.*) a slate or roofing slab : a th[in] strip of wood, &c.—*adj.* **slatt′ed,** having slat[s] [O.Fr. *esclat.*]

slate, *slāt, n.* a fine-grained argillaceous rock whic[h] by regional metamorphism has developed a clea[v-] age along close-spaced planes independent of t[he] bedding, usu. a dull blue, grey, purple, or gree[n] a slab of this material (or a substitute) for roofin[g] or for writing upon : a preliminary list of cand[i-] dates : slate-colour.—*adj.* of slate : slate-coloure[d] dull dark blue.—*v.t.* to cover with slate : to ent[er] on a slate : to clear of fine hair with a slater.—*n[s.]* **slate′-axe,** a slater's sax ; **slate′-club,** a socie[ty] whose members make weekly contributions towar[ds] benefits against misfortune or towards gettin[g] Christmas cheer. —*adjs.* **slate′-coloured,** du[ll] bluish grey approaching black ; **slat′ed,** covere[d] with slates ; **slate′-gray, -grey,** of a light sla[te] colour.—*ns.* **slate′-pencil,** a cut or turned sti[ck] of soft slate, compressed slate-powder, or pyr[o-] phyllite, for writing on slate ; **slat′er,** one wh[o] covers roofs with slates : a tool with slate bla[de] for removing fine hair from hides : (*dial.*) a woo[d-] louse ; **slate′-writer** ; **slate′-writing,** mysterio[us] production of writing on a covered slate ; **slat′iness[,]** **slat′ing,** covering with slates : a covering of slate[s] materials for slating.—*adj.* **slat′y,** of or like slate.— **a slate loose,** a slight mental derangement ; **sla[te] cleavage,** fissility like that of slate along plan[es] independent of bedding. [O.Fr. *esclate*; cf. **slat**.]

slate, *slāt*, *v.t.* to abuse : to review unsparingly : (*dial.*) to bait with dogs : to set on.—*n.* slā′ting. [From the O.N. word answering to O.E. *slǽtan*, to bait.]

slather, *sladh′ər*, *n.* (*U.S. slang*) a large quantity.

slattern, *slat′ərn*, *n.* a slut, a dirty untidy woman.—*v.i.* slatt′er, (*prov.*) to be untidy or slovenly.—*v.t.* to spill, splash, slop about.—*n.* slatt′ernliness.—*adj.* slatt′ernly, sluttish.—Also *adv.*—*adj.* slatt′ery, (*prov.*) sloppy : slovenly. [App. **slat** (1).]

slaughter, *slaw′tər*, *n.* killing of animals, esp. for food : killing of great numbers : wanton or inexcusable killing, esp. of the helpless : carnage : butchery : bodies of the slain.—*v.t.* to make slaughter of.—*ns.* slaugh′terer ; slaugh′terhouse, a place where beasts are killed for the market ; slaugh′terman, a man employed in killing or butchering animals. — *adj.* slaugh′terous, given to slaughter : destructive : murderous. — *adv.* slaugh′terously.—*n.* slaugh′tery, (*rare*) slaughter : a slaughterhouse. [O.N. *slátr*, butchers′ meat, whence *slátra*, to slaughter (cattle).]

Slav, *slāv*, *n.* one whose language is Slavonic, i.e. belongs to that division of the Indo-Germanic tongues that includes Russian, Polish, Wendish, Czech, Slovak, Serbian, Slovenian, and Bulgarian. —*adjs.* **Slav**, **Slav′ic**.—*n.* **Slav′dom**, the Slavs collectively, the Slavonic world.—*v.t.* **Slav′ify**, to assimilate to the Slavs.—*n.* **Slavonia** (*slə-*, *slā-vō′ni̇̄å*), a region bounded by the Danube, Sava, and Drava.—*adj.* **Slavo′nian**, of Slavonia : Slav. —Also *n.*—*adj.* **Slavonic** (*-von′ik*), of the group of languages indicated above, or the peoples speaking them.—*n.* the parent language of the Slavs or any of its descendants.—*v.t.* **Slavon′icise**, **Slavonise** (*slav′ən-īz*), to make Slavonic.—*adj.* **Slav′ophil(e)**, favourable or friendly to Slavs.—Also *n.*—*adj.* **Slav′ophobe**, hostile to Slavs. [Mediaeval L. *Sclavus*—Late Gr. *Sklabos*, from the stem of Slav *slovo*, word, *sloviti*, to speak ; cf. **Slovene**.]

slave, *slāv*, *n.* a person held as property : an abject : one who is submissive under domination : one who is submissively devoted : one whose will has lost power of resistance : one who works like a slave, a drudge.—*v.i.* to work like a slave : to drudge.—*v.t.* to enslave : to treat as a slave : (*Shak.*) perh. make subservient to his own views (*King Lear*, IV. i. 69).—*n.* slave′-ant, an ant kept as a worker in a community of another species.— *adj.* slave′-born, born in slavery.—*ns.* slave′-driver, one who superintends slaves at their work : a hard taskmaster ; slave′-fork, a long and heavy forked branch fixed on a slave′s neck to prevent escape.—*adj.* slave′-grown, grown by slave-labour. —*ns.* slave′-holder, an owner of slaves ; slave′-holding ; slave′-hunt, a hunt after runaway slaves or after persons to enslave ; slave′-labour ; slave′-owner ; -owning ; slav′er, a slave-trader : a ship employed in the slave-trade ; slav′ery, the state of being a slave : the institution of ownership of slaves : drudgery ; slave′-ship, a ship used for transporting slaves.—*n.pl.* slave′-states, those states of the American Union which maintained domestic slavery before the Civil War— Delaware, Maryland, Virginia, North and South Carolina, Georgia, Florida, Alabama, Mississippi, Louisiana, Texas, Arkansas, Missouri, Kentucky, and Tennessee.—*ns.* slave′-trade, the buying and selling of slaves ; slave′-trader ; slav′ey, (*slang*) a domestic drudge, a maid of all work.—*adj.* slav′ish, of or belonging to slaves : befitting a slave : servile : abject : servilely following or conforming : laborious. — *adv.* slav′ishly. — *ns.* slav′ishness ; slavoc′racy, slave-owners collectively : their power, interests, &c. ; slav′ocrat. [O.Fr. (Fr.) *esclave*, orig. a Slav.]

slaver, *slav′ər* (*Scot. slāv′ər*), *n.* spittle running from the mouth.—*v.i.* to let spittle run out of the mouth : to drivel : to fawn. — *v.t.* to beslobber. — *n.* slav′erer—*adj.* slav′ering—*adv.* slav′eringly. —*adj.* slav′ery, slabbery. [Akin to **slabber**.]

Slavonian. See **Slav**.

slaw, *slaw*, *n.* cabbage salad. [Du. *sla—salade*.]

slay, *slā*, *v.t.* to kill :—*pa.t.* slew (*slōō*) ; *pa.p.* slain (*slān*).—*n.* slay′er. [O.E. *slēan*, to strike, to kill ; O.N. *slá*, Goth. *slahan*, Ger. *schlagen*, to strike.]

sleave, *slēv*, *n.* (*Shak.*) a fine filament that can be separated from a silk fibre.—*v.t.* to separate, as threads.—sleaved silk, floss silk. [O.E. *slǽfan*, to divide.]

sleazy, *slē′zi*, *adj.* flimsy.—*n.* slea′ziness. [Origin doubtful.]

sled, *sled*, *n.* a sledge, esp. a small sledge : a drag or wheelless structure for conveying goods, formerly for taking the condemned to execution.—*v.t.* to convey by sled.—*v.i.* to go on a sled :—*pr.p.* sledd′-ing ; *pa.t.* and *pa.p.* sledd′ed.—*adj.* sledd′ed, (*Shak.*) having sleds.—*n.* sledd′ing. [M.Du. or M.L.G. *sledde* ; Ger. *schlitte*, O.N. *slethi* ; cf. **sledge**, **sleigh**, **slide**.]

sleded. See **sleided**.

sledge, *slej*, *n.* a carriage with runners made for sliding upon snow : a framework without wheels for dragging goods along the ground.—*v.t.* and *v.i.* to convey, or to travel, by sledge.—*ns.* sledge′-chair, a chair mounted on runners for ice ; sledg′er ; sledg′ing. [M.Du. *sleedse* ; cf. **sled**.]

sledge, *slej*, *n.* a large heavy hammer.—Also sledge′-hammer. [O.E. *slecg—sléan*, to strike, slay.]

slee, *slē*, Scots form of **sly**.

sleech, *slēch*, *n.* slimy mud : a mud-flat.—*adj.* sleech′y.

sleek, *slēk*, *adj.* smooth : glossy : having an oily, plastered-down look : insinuating, plausible : slick. —*v.t.* to make smooth or glossy : to calm or soothe. — *v.i.* to glide. — *adv.* smoothly, oilily. — *v.t.* sleek′en, to sleek.—*n.* sleek′er, a slicker.—*adj.* sleek′-head′ed. — *n.* sleek′ing. — *adj.* sleek′it, (*Scot.*) smooth : sly, cunning, fair-spoken.—*adv.* sleek′ly.—*ns.* sleek′ness ; sleek′stone, a polishing stone.—*adj.* sleek′y, smooth : sly, untrustworthy. [A later form of **slick**.]

sleep, *slēp*, *v.i.* to take rest by relaxation of consciousness : to slumber : to be motionless, inactive, or dormant : to appear still or restful : (*bot.*) to take or have the nocturnal position : to be dead : to rest in the grave : to be numb : (of a top) to spin steadily without movement of the axis. —*v.t.* to be in the state of (with *sleep*, &c., as cognate object) : to render, make, put, by sleep : to outsleep : to afford sleeping accommodation for : (*pa.t.* and *pa.p.* slept (*slept*)).—*n.* the state of being asleep : a spell of sleeping : dormancy : (*bot.*) vertical disposition of leaves at night.—*n.* sleep′er, one who sleeps : a horizontal beam supporting and spreading a weight : a support for railway rails : a sleeping-car.—*adj.* (*Scot.*) sleep′(e)ry, sleepy.— *adv.* sleep′ily.—*ns.* sleep′iness ; sleep′ing, sleep : abeyance.—*adj.* in a state of, occupied with, or for, sleeping : dormant.—*ns.* sleep′ing-bag, a bag for sleeping in, used by travellers, campers, &c. ; sleep′ing-car, -carr′iage, a railway-carriage with berths for sleeping in ; sleep′ing-draught, a drink to induce sleep ; sleep′ing-part′ner, one who has money invested in a business but takes no part in its management ; sleep′ing-sick′ness, a deadly disease of tropical Africa, characterised by headache, great drowsiness, and exhaustion, caused by a trypanosome introduced by the bite of a tsetse-fly : sometimes erroneously applied to sleepy-sickness.—*adj.* sleep′less, without sleep : unable to sleep.—*adv.* sleep′lessly.—*ns.* sleep′lessness ; sleep′-walk′er, one who walks in sleep : a somnambulist ; sleep′-walk′ing.—*adj.* sleep′y, inclined to sleep : drowsy : inducing or suggesting sleep : soft and lacking juice (as a pear).—*ns.* sleep′y-head, a lazy person ; sleep′y-sick′ness, encephalitis lethargica : formerly applied to sleeping-sickness.—sleep in, (*Scot.*) to oversleep ; on sleep, (*B.*) asleep. [O.E. *slǽpan* (vb.), *slǽp* (n.) ; Ger. *schlaf*, Goth. *slēps*.]

sleet, *slēt*, *n.* rain mingled with snow or hail.—*v.i.* to hail or snow with rain mingled.—*n.* sleet′iness. —*adj.* sleet′y. [Prob. an unrecorded O.E. (Anglian) *slét* ; Ger. *schlosse*, hail.]

sleeve, *slēv*, *n.* a covering for the arm : a tube into which a rod or other tube is inserted.—*v.t.* to furnish with sleeves.—*ns.* sleeve′-board, a board for ironing sleeves; **sleeve'-button,** a button or stud for the wristband or cuff.—*adj.* **sleeved,** with sleeves.—*ns.* **sleeve'-dog,** a little dog that can be carried in the sleeve; **sleeve'-fish,** the squid; **sleeve'hand,** (*Shak.*) a wristband.—*adj.* **sleeve'-less,** without sleeves: futile, vain (see **errand**).—*ns.* **sleeve'-link,** two buttons joined by a link for fastening a shirt-cuff; **sleeve'-nut,** a double-nut for attaching the joint-ends of rods or tubes; **sleeve(d)'-waist'coat,** a waistcoat with long sleeves, worn by porters, boots, &c.—**hang, pin, on one's sleeve,** to depend or rely entirely upon; **laugh in one's sleeve,** to laugh privately or unperceived; **up one's sleeve,** in secret reserve; **wear one's heart on one's sleeve** (see **heart**). [O.E. (Anglian) *slēfe* (W.S. *sliefe*).]

sleezy. Same as **sleazy.**

sleided, sleded, *slēd'id, adj.* (*Shak.*) app. irregular forms of **sleaved.**

sleigh, *slā, n.* (esp. in *U.S.* and *Canada*) a sledge.—*v.i.* to travel by sleigh.—*ns.* **sleigh'-bell,** a small bell attached to a sleigh or its harness; **sleigh'ing.** [Du. *slee.*]

sleight (*obs.* **slight**), *slīt, n.* cunning: dexterity: an artful trick: a juggling trick: trickery: (*Spens.*) a design, device, pattern.—*n.* **sleight'-of-hand',** legerdemain.—Also *adj.* [O.N. *slœgth,* cunning, *slœgr,* sly.]

slender, *slen'dər, adj.* thin or narrow: slim: slight. —*adv.* **slen'derly.**—*n.* **slen'derness.** [Origin obscure.]

slept, *slept, pa.t.* and *pa.p.* of **sleep.**

sleuth, *slooth, n.* a track or trail: a bloodhound: a relentless tracker, a detective.—*v.t.* and *v.i.* to track.—*n.* **sleuth'-hound,** a bloodhound: a detective. [O.N. *slóth,* track.]

slew, *sloo, pa.t.* of **slay.**

slew, slue, *sloo, v.t.* and *v.i.* to turn about the axis: to swing round.—*n.* a turn, twist, swing round: a position so taken.—*adj.* **slewed, slued,** tipsy. [First recorded as a sailor's word: origin unknown.]

sley, *slā, n.* a weaver's reed. [O.E. *slege—slēan,* to strike.]

slice, *slīs, n.* a thin broad piece: a flat or broad-bladed instrument of various kinds, esp. a broad knife for serving fish: a slash: (*golf*) a sliced stroke.—*v.t.* to cut into slices: to cut a slice from: to cut as a slice: (*golf*) to strike or play so as to send the ball curving to the right (left in left-hand play).—*v.i.* to slash: to cut in the manner of slicing: to slice a stroke.—*n.* **sli'cer.**—*n.* and *adj.* **sli'cing.** [O.Fr. *esclice*—O.H.G. *slīzan,* to split.]

slick, *slik, adj.* sleek: smooth: smooth-tongued: glib: adroit: trim. — *adv.* smoothly: glibly: deftly: quickly: altogether.—*n.* a smooth place or surface: a slicker.—*v.t.* to polish, make glossy: to tidy up.—*v.t.* to **slick'en,** to smooth, polish.—*n.* **slick'enside,** (*geol.*) a smooth, polished, or striated surface produced by friction.—*adj.* **slick'ensided.** —*ns.* **slick'er,** a smoothing tool: (*U.S.*) a waterproof; **slick'ing.**—*adv.* **slick'ly.**—*n.* **slick'ness;** **slick'stone,** a sleekstone. [O.E. *slician,* (in composition) to smooth.]

'slid, *slid, interj.* (*arch.*) for **god's lid** (eyelid).

slidder, *slid'ər, v.i.* to slip, slide.—*n.* a steep path or trench down a hillside.—*adj.* **slidd'ery,** slippery. [O.E. *slidor,* slippery, *sliderian,* to slip.]

slide, *slīd, v.i.* to slip or glide: to pass along smoothly: to glide in a standing position (without skates or snow-shoes) over ice or other slippery surface: to lapse: to pass quietly, smoothly, or gradually: to take its own course: (*coll.*) to decamp.—*v.t.* to thrust along glidingly: to slip: (*pa.t.* slid, *obs.* slīd'ed, *Scot.* **slāde;** *pa.p.* slid, *obs.* slid'ed, *rare* slidd'en).—*n.* a slip: a polished slippery track (on ice): a chute or shoot: a bed, groove, rail, &c., on or in which a thing slides: a sliding part, e.g. of a trombone: a sliding clasp: a slip for mounting objects for the microscope: a case (*dark slide*) for photographic plates or its sliding cover: a picture for projection on a screen: a sliding lid: a sledge: a runner: a sliding seat: a landslip: a gliding from one note to another.—*ns.* **slid'er,** one who, or that which, slides: a sliding **part:** ice-cream between wafers: a red-bellied

terrapin; **slide'-rest,** an apparatus for carrying the cutting-tool of a lathe, &c.; **slide'-rule,** a mechanical calculating device consisting of two logarithmic graduated scales sliding one against the other (also **slid'ing-rule**); **slide'-valve,** a valve in which openings are covered and uncovered by a sliding part.—*n.* and *adj.* **slid'ing.**—*n.* **slid'ing-keel,** a centreboard.—*adv.* **slid'ingly.**—*ns.* **slid'ing-scale,** a scale, e.g. of duties, varying according to variation in something else, e.g. prices: a slide-rule; **slid'ing-seat,** a racing-boat seat, moving with the swing of the rower's body. [O.E. *slīdan,* to slide.]

'slife, *slīf,* **'slight,** *slīt, interjs.* (*arch.*) for **God's life, light.**

slight, *slīt, adj.* (*obs.*) smooth: flimsy: lacking solidity, massiveness, weight, significance: slim: slender: trifling: small: (*obs.*) slighting.—*adv.* slightly: slightingly, meanly.—*v.t.* (*obs.*) to smooth: (*arch.*) to raze, level to the ground: to ignore or overlook disrespectfully: (*Shak.*) to toss contemptuously.—*n.* contemptuous indifference: discourteous disregard: an affront by showing neglect or want of respect. — *adv.* **slight'ingly.** — *adj.* **slight'ish.** — *adv.* **slight'ly.** — *n.* **slight'ness.** — **slight off,** (*Shak.*) to put off, set aside, with contempt; **slight over,** to ignore. [Cf. O.E. *eorth-slihtes,* close to the ground; O.N. *slèttr,* O.L.G. *slicht,* plain, Du. *slecht,* bad, Ger. *schlecht,* bad.]

slight, old spelling of **sleight.**

slily, *slī'li, adv.* See under **sly.**

slim, *slim, adj.* (*comp.* **slimm'er,** *superl.* **slimm'est**) very thin: slender: slight: crafty.—*v.t.* to make thin.—*v.i.* to use means to become more slender :—*pr.p.* **slimm'ing;** *pa.t.* and *pa.p.* **slimmed.**—*adv.* **slim'ly.**—*n.* **slimm'ing.**—*adj.* **slimm'ish.**—*n.* **slim'ness.**—*adj.* **slim'sy,** (*U.S.*) frail, flimsy. [Du., L.G., Fris. *slim,* crafty; Dan. *slem,* worthless, Ger. *schlimm,* bad; reintroduced from Cape Du.]

slime, *slīm, n.* ooze: very fine, thin, slippery, or gluey mud: bitumen: any viscous organic secretion, as mucus: matter, esp. as forming the human body: moral filth: obsequiousness: (in *pl.*) finely crushed ore in mud form.—*v.t.* to smear or cover with slime: to grind to slime: to clear of slime.—*v.i.* to go slimily.—*ns.* **slime'-fungus,** a myxomycete; **slime'-pit,** a hole where bitumen is got: a pit for receiving metallic slimes.—*adv.* **slim'ily.** —*n.* **slim'iness.**—*adj.* **slim'y,** viscous: covered with slime: disgusting: obsequiously servile. [O.E. *slīm;* Ger. *schleim.*]

sling, *sling, n.* a strap or pocket with a string attached to each end, for hurling a stone: a catapult: a ballista: a loop for hoisting, lowering, or carrying a weight: a hanging support for an injured arm or foot: an attached strap for carrying: a throw: a sweep or swing.—*v.t.* to throw with a sling: to hang loosely: to move or swing by means of a rope: (*coll.*) to hurl, toss, fling: (*slang*) to utter, to pass.—*v.i.* to discharge stones from a sling: to bound along with swinging steps :—*pa.t.* and *pa.p.* **slung.**—*ns.* **sling'er;** **sling'-fruit,** a fruit that ejects its seeds by elastic tissue; **sling'-shot,** (*U.S.*) a catapult; **sling'stone,** a stone to be thrown from a sling.—**sling ink,** to write for the press. [Prob. from several sources; cf. O.N. *slyngva,* to fling, O.E. *slingan,* to wind, twist, L.G. *sling,* noose.]

sling, *sling, n.* an American drink, spirits and water sweetened and flavoured. [Perh. foregoing in sense of toss off; poss. Ger. *schlingen,* to swallow.]

slink, *slingk, v.i.* to go sneakingly: to miscarry.—*v.t.* to slip: to droop: to cast prematurely: (*pa.t.* and *pa.p.* **slunk**).—*n.* a prematurely born calf or other animal: its flesh or hide: a bastard child: a slinking gait.—*adj.* prematurely born: lean, starved: mean.—*ns.* **slink'-butch'er,** a dealer in slink and diseased meat; **slink'er; slink'skin,** the skin of a slink, or leather made from it; **slink'-weed,** rose-bay willow herb or other plant believed to cause cows to slink.—*adj.* **slink'y,** slinking: lean: sinuous: close-fitting. [O.E. *slincan;* L.G. *slinken;* Ger. *schlinken.*]

slip, *slip, v.i.* to escape: to pass quietly, easily, unobtrusively, or stealthily: to glide: to get out of position accidentally: to slide, esp. accidentally: to lose one's footing: to make a slight mistake from inadvertence rather than ignorance: to lapse morally.—*v.t.* to cause or allow to slide: to put with a sliding motion: to convey quietly or secretly: to let pass: to let slip: to cast: to disengage: to let loose: to escape from: to elude: to cast prematurely, slink: to dislocate: (*pr.p.* **slipp'ing**; *pa.t.* and *pa.p.* **slipped**, sometimes **slipt**).—*n.* act of slipping: a mistake from inadvertence: a slight error or transgression: an escape: an inclined plane, sloping down to the water: a slight dislocation: a landslip: a pillowcase: a garment easily slipped on, esp. one worn under a dress: a leash: the difference between the pitch of a propeller and the distance actually travelled: (*cricket*) a fielder or (often in *pl.*) position on the off side somewhat behind the batsman: a sledge-runner: (in *pl.*) the place at the side of the stage for slipping scenery from: the side of a theatre gallery.—*ns.* **slip'-board**, a board sliding in grooves; **slip'-carriage, -coach**, a railway carriage that can be left behind without stopping the train; **slip'-dock**, a dock with a slipway; **slip'-knot**, a knot that slips along a rope: a knot untied by pulling.—*adjs.* **slip'-on, slip'-over**, slipped on or over: slipped over the head without unbuttoning.—*ns.* a garment easily slipped on: one slipped over the head.—*adj.* **slipp'er**, (*Spens., Shak.*) slippery.—*n.* a loose shoe easily slipped on: a skid for a wheel: a sledge-runner: one who slips (e.g. greyhounds).—*v.t.* to furnish with slippers: to beat with a slipper.—*adj.* **slipp'ered**.—*adv.* **slipp'erily**. — *ns.* **slipp'eriness, slipp'iness**; **slipp'erwort**, calceolaria.—*adjs.* **slipp'ery, slipp'y**, so smooth or slimy as to allow or cause slipping: elusive: evasive: apt to slip: unstable: uncertain. —*n.* **slip'rail**, (*Austr.*) a movable rail serving as a gate: a gap so closed.—*adj.* **slip'shod**, shod with slippers, or with shoes down at the heel: slovenly. —*ns.* **slip'-shoe**, (*obs.*) a slipper; **slip'-string**, a crack-halter.—Also *adj.*—*ns.* **slip'-up**, an error or failure; **slip'way**, a slope in a dock or shipyard. —**give one the slip**, to escape stealthily from him; **slip on**, to put on loosely or in haste; **slip one's ways**, (*Scot.*) to make one's way quietly; **slipper animalcule**, paramecium; **slipper limpet**, an American mollusc (Crepidula) with somewhat slipper-like shell; **slipper satin**, fine satin with a dull finish; **slippery elm**, a N. American elm: its mucilaginous bark used as a demulcent; **slip the cable**, to let it go overboard instead of waiting to weigh the anchor: to die; **slip up**, (*slang*) to make a mistake, to fail: (*Austr.*) to deceive, disappoint. [Perh. L.G. or Du. *slippen*; but O.E. has *slipor*, slippery, *slýpescóh*, slipper.]

slip, *slip*, *n.* (obs.) a counterfeit coin. [Perh. **slip, 1**.]

slip, *slip*, *n.* a scion, cutting: a scion, descendant: a young or slender person: (*dial., Austr.*) a young pig: a small sole (fish): a strip: anything slender or narrow: a small piece of paper, parchment, wood, &c., esp. for a memorandum, record, note for filing or indexing, or the like: a galley-proof. [Perh. M.Du. or M.L.G. *slippe*, strip.]

slip, *slip*, *n.* a creamy paste for coating and decorating pottery. [O.E. *slipa, slypa*, slime, paste.]

slipe, *slip*, *n.* in mining, a skip or sledge: a runner. [App. L.G. *slipe*.]

slipslop, *slip'slop*, *n.* sloppy stuff: twaddle: a malapropism (from Mrs *Slipslop* in Fielding's *Joseph Andrews*): one who commits malapropisms. —*adj.* **slip'sloppy**.

slish, *slish*, *n.* (*Shak.*) a cut. [**slash**.]

slit, *slit*, *v.t.* to cut lengthwise: to split: to cut into strips (*pr.p.* **slitt'ing**; *pa.t.* and *pa.p.* **slit**). —*n.* a long cut: a narrow opening.—*adj.* cut lengthwise: cut open: having a slit.—*ns.* **slit'-pocket**, an overcoat pocket with a slit to give access to a pocket within; **slitt'er**. [M.E. *slitten*, app. related to O.E. *slitan*; Ger. *schlitzen*.]

slither, *slidh'ər*, *v.i.* to slide, esp. interruptedly.— *adj.* slippery.—*n.* a scree.—*adj.* **slith'ery**, slippery. [**slidder**.]

slive, *slīv*, *v.t.* and *v.i.* (*dial.*) to slip :—*pa.t.* **slove**,

slived; *pa.p.* **slived, slīv'en**. [Cf. O.E. *sléfan*, to slip (on).]

sliver, *sliv'ər*, or *slī'vər*, *v.t.* to split, to tear off lengthwise, to slice.—*n.* a piece cut or rent off, a slice: a continuous strand of loose untwisted wool or other fibre. [O.E. (*tó-*)*slīfan*, to cleave.]

sloan, *slōn*, *n.* (*Scot.*) a snub: a reproof: a scolding. [Origin unknown.]

slobber, *slob'ər*, *v.t.* and *v.i.* to slabber.—*adj.* **slobb'ery**. [Cf. Du. *slobberen*, to eat or work in a slovenly way; **slabber, slubber**.]

slocken, sloken, *slok'n, slōk'n*, *v.t.* (*Scot.*) to quench: to slake: to moisten: to extinguish. [O.N. *slokna*, to go out.]

sloe, *slō*, *n.* the blackthorn fruit or bush.—*adj.* of blackthorn wood: made with sloes: black.— *ns.* **sloe'bush**; **sloe'-gin**, a liqueur made from sloes; **sloe'thorn, sloe'tree**. [O.E. *slá, slág, sláh*; Du. *slee*.]

slog, *slog*, *v.t.* and *v.i.* to hit hard.—*v.i.* to work or walk doggedly.—*n.* a hard blow (generally with little regard to direction): a strenuous spell of work.—*n.* **slogg'er**.

slogan, *slō'gan*, *n.* a clan war-cry: a party catchword: an advertising catch-phrase. [Earlier **slog(h)orne**, **sloggorne**; said to be from Gael. *sluagh*, army, *gairm*, cry; see **slughorn(e)**.]

sloid. See **sloyd**.

sloom, *slōom*, *n.* (*Northern*) slumber.—*v.i.* to slumber.—*adj.* **sloom'y**. [O.E. *slúma*.]

sloop, *slōōp*, *n.* a light boat: a one-masted cutter-rigged vessel, differing from a cutter in having a fixed bowsprit and proportionally smaller sails: (also **sloop'-of-war**) formerly a vessel, of whatever rig, between a corvette and a gun-vessel, under a commander, carrying from ten to eighteen guns. [Du. *sloep*; cf. **shallop**.]

slop, *slop*, *n.* slush: spilled liquid: a puddle: (in *pl.*) liquid refuse: (in *pl.*) weak or insipid liquor or semi-liquid food: (in *pl.*) gush, wishy-washy sentiment.—*v.t.* and *v.i.* to spill: to splash with slops: to slobber.—*v.t.* to wash away.—*v.i.* to walk in slush :—*pr.p.* **slopp'ing**; *pa.t.* and *pa.p.* **slopped**.—*ns.* **slop'-basin, -bowl**, a basin for slops at table; **slop'-pail**, a pail for removing bedroom slops.—*adv.* **slopp'ily**.—*n.* **slopp'iness**. — *adj.* **slopp'y**, wet: muddy: wishy-washy, watery: slipshod (of work or language): sentimental: maudlin. [O.E. (*cú-*)*sloppe*, (cow-)drop-pings (cowslip)—*slúpan*, to slip.]

slop, *slop*, *n.* a loose garment—gown, cassock, smock-frock, &c.: (in *pl.*) wide baggy trousers or breeches: the wide part of these: (in *pl.*) ready-made clothing: (in *pl.*) clothes and bedding issued to seamen.—*adj.* **slop'-built**, jerry-built.—*ns.* **slop'-clothing**; **slop'-pouch**; **slop'-seller**; **slop'-shop**, a shop for ready-made clothes; **slop'work**, the making of slop-clothing: cheap inferior work. [Cf. O.E. *oferslop*, loose outer garment; M.Du. *slop*; O.N. *sloppr*.]

slop, *slop*, *n.* a policeman. [Back-slang.]

slope, *slōp*, *n.* an incline: an inclined surface: an inclined position: an inclination, upward or downward slant.—*adj.* (*poet.*) slanting: (*Milt.*) moving aslope.—*adv.* aslant.—*v.t.* to form with a slope, or obliquely: to put in a sloping position: to turn downwards, bow.—*v.i.* to have or take a sloping position or direction: to move down a slope: (*slang*) to decamp, disappear.—*adv.* **slope'wise**, obliquely.—*adj.* **slop'ing**.—*adv.* **slop'ingly**.—*adj.* **slop'y**, sloping.—**at the slope**, (of a rifle) on the shoulder with the barrel sloping back and up; **slope arms**, to place or hold in this position. [Aphetic from **aslope**.]

slops. See **slop** (1 and 2).

slosh, *slosh*, *n.* slush: a watery mess: (*slang*) a heavy blow.—*v.i.* to flounder or splash in slush: (*U.S.*) to loaf around: (*slang*) to hit.—*v.t.* to splash: (*slang*) to smite, beat.—*adj.* **slosh'y**. [**slush**.]

slot, *slot*, *n.* a bar or bolt: a cross-piece that holds other parts together. [L.G. or Du. *slot*, lock.]

slot, *slot*, *n.* (now *Scot.*) the hollow down the middle of the breast: a long narrow depression or opening, as one to receive a coin, an armature winding, or part of a mechanism, or opening into the conduit

of an electric or cable tramway or railway : a slit.—
v.t. to make a slot in, furnish with a slot : to pass
through a slot.—*ns.* slot′-machine′, one operated
by insering a coin in a slot ; slott′ing-machine′,
a machine for cutting slots. [O.Fr. *esclot*.]

slot, *slot, n.* track, esp. a deer's footprints.—*v.t.* to
track. [O.Fr. *esclot*—O.N. *slóth* ; cf. **sleuth**.]

sloth, *slōth*, or *sloth, n.* laziness, sluggishness : a
sluggish arboreal tropical American edentate.—*v.t.*
and *v.i.* to pass, spend (time) in sloth.—*n.* **sloth′-
bear**, a black Indian bear, with prolonged snout
and lips.—*adj.* **sloth′ful**, given to sloth : inactive :
lazy.—*adv.* **sloth′fully**.—*n.* **sloth′fulness**. [M.E.
slawthe, altered from O.E. *slǽwth*—*sláw*, slow.]

slouch, *slowch, n.* an awkward lubberly clown :
(*U.S. slang*) an inefficient person : a slouch-hat :
a droop : a stoop : a loose, ungainly stooping gait.
—*adj.* drooping.—*v.i.* to go or bear oneself slouch-
ingly : to droop.—*v.t.* to turn down the brim of.
— *ns.* **slouch′er** ; **slouch′-hat**, a soft broad-
brimmed hat.—*adjs.* **slouch-hatt′ed** ; **slouch′ing** ;
slouch′y. [Cf. Ó.N. *slóka*, a slouching fellow.]

slough, *slow, n.* a hollow filled with mud : a marsh :
(*U.S. ; slōō*) a backwater, a marshland creek.—*adj.*
sloughed (*slowd*), bogged, swallowed in a slough.
—*adj.* **slough′y**. [O.E. *sloh*.]

slough, *sluf, n.* a cast skin : a coating : dead tissue
in a sore.—*v.i.* to come away as a slough (with *off*) :
to cast the skin : to develop a slough.—*v.t.* to cast
off, as a slough.—*adj.* **slough′y**. [M.E. *sloh* ;
origin uncertain.]

Slovak, *slō′vāk, slō-vāk′, n.* a member of a Slavonic
people living E. of the Czechs : their language.—
Also *adj.*—*adjs.* **Slovakian** (-*vak′*, -*vāk′*), **Slovak′-
ish**. [Slovak *Slovák*.]

sloven, *sluv′n, n.* a person, esp. a man, carelessly or
dirtily dressed or slipshod in work.—Also *adj.*—
adj. **slovenlike**.—*n.* **slov′enliness**.—*adj.* and *adv.*
slov′enly.—*n.* **slov′enry**, (*Shak.*) slovenliness.
[Cf. O.Du. *slof, sloef,* L.G. *sluf*, slow, indolent.]

Slovene, *slō-vēn′, n.* a member of a branch of the
Southern Slavs found chiefly in Styria, Carinthia,
Carniola, and Istria.—Also *adj.*—*n.* and *adj.*
Slovē′nian. [O.Slav *Slovēne*.]

slow, *slō, adj.* not swift : late : behind in time : not
hasty : not ready : not progressive : dull.—*n.*
anything that is slow.—*adv.* slowly (also in compounds).—*v.t.* to delay, retard, slacken the speed
of.—*v.i.* to slacken in speed.—*ns.* **slow′back**, a
lazy lubber ; **slow′coach**, a laggard : a sluggish
person.—*adjs.* **slow′-foot, -ed**, slow of pace ;
slow′-gait′ed, (*Shak.*) accustomed to walk slowly ;
slow′ish.—*n.* **slow′ing**, a lessening of speed.—
adv. **slow′ly**.—*n.* **slow′-match**, a slowly burning
rope for firing explosives.—*adj.* **slow′-mo′tion**,
much slower than normal or (*cinematograph*) actual
motion.—*adj.* **slow′-mov′ing**.—*n.* **slow′ness**.—
adjs. **slow′-paced** ; **slow′-sight′ed** ; **slow′-
winged**. [O.E. *slǽw* ; Du. *slee*, O.N. *sljór*.]

slow-hound, *slō′hownd, n.* app. a form of **sleuth-
hound**, assimilated to **slow**.

slow-worm, *slō′wɘrm, n.* the blindworm, a harmless snakelike legless lizard. [O.E. *sláwyrm*, prob.
from root of *sléan*, to strike, *wyrm*, worm, assimilated to **slow**.]

sloyd, sloid, *sloid, n.* a Swedish system of manual
training by woodwork. [Sw. *slöjd*, dexterity ; cf.
sleight.]

slub, slubb, *slub, v.t.* to twist after carding to prepare for spinning.—*n.* a roving.—*ns.* **slubb′er** ;
slubb′ing.

slub, *slub, n.* a lump in yarn.—*adj.* lumpy.

slubber, *slub′ɘr, v.t.* to smear, soil, daub : to perform hurriedly and carelessly, slur over : to gobble.
—*v.i.* to wallow.—*n.* **slubberdegull′ion**, a sloven.
—*n.* and *adj.* **slubb′ering**.—*adv.* **slubb′eringly**.
[Du. *slobberen*, to lap, L.G. *slubbern*.]

sludge, *sluj, n.* soft mud or mire : half-melted snow :
a slimy precipitate, as from sewage.—*adj.* **sludg′y**,
miry : muddy. [Cf. **slush**.]

slue, Same as **slew**.

slug, *slug, n.* a heavy, lazy fellow : a land-mollusc
with shell rudimentary or absent : a sea-slug :
anything slow-moving.—*v.i.* to be inert : to go
sluggishly : to hunt for slugs.—*v.t.* to make slug-

gish.—*ns.* **slug′-a-bed, slugg′abed**, (*Shak.*) one
who lies long abed ; **slugg′ard**, one habitually
inactive.—Also *adj.*—*v.t.* **slugg′ardise**, (*Shak.*) to
make lazy.—*adj.* **slugg′ish**, habitually lazy : slothful : slow : inert.—*adv.* **slugg′ishly**.—*n.* **slugg′-
ishness**. [Cf. Norw. dial. *slugg*, a heavy body,
sluggje, a slow heavy person, Sw. dial. *slogga*, to be
sluggish.]

slug, *slug, n.* a lump of metal, esp. one for firing
from a gun : a solid line of type cast by a composing
machine. [Perh. conn. with foregoing or following.]

slug, *slug, v.t.* and *v.i.* to slog : to fling heavily.
[Cf. **slog**.]

slughorn(e), *slug′horn, n.* an old form of **slogan** :
by Chatterton (followed by Browning) imagined to
be a musical instrument not unlike a hautboy, or
a kind of clarion.

sluice, *slōōs, n.* a structure with a gate for stopping
or regulating flow of water : a floodgate or water-
gate : a regulated outlet or inlet : a drain, channel :
a trough for washing gold from sand, &c. : a sluicing.—*v.t.* to let out or drain by a sluice : to wet
or drench copiously : to wash in or by a sluice : to
flush or swill by flinging water : to dash.—*n.*
sluice′-gate.—*adj.* **sluic′y**, streaming as from a
sluice : sluice-like : soaking. [O.Fr. *escluse* (Fr.
écluse)—L.L. *exclūsa* (*aqua*), a sluice, i.e. (water)
shut out, pa.p. of L. *exclūdĕre*, to shut out.]

sluit, *slü′it, slōōt, n.* (*S.Afr.*) a narrow water-
channel.—Also **sloot**. [Du. *sloot*, ditch.]

slum, *slum, n.* an overcrowded squalid neighbourhood.—*v.i.* to visit slums.—*ns.* **slumm′er** ; **slum′-
ming**.—*adj.* **slumm′y**. [Cant.]

slum, *slum, n.* the non-lubricating part of crude oil.

slumber, *slum′bɘr, v.i.* to sleep, esp. lightly : to be
negligent or inactive.—*v.t.* to pass in slumber.—
n. light sleep : repose.—*n.* **slum′berer**.—*adj.*
slum′berful.—*n.* and *adj.* **slum′bering**.—*adv.*
slum′beringly.—*n.* **slum′berland**, the state of
slumber.—*adjs.* **slum′berless** ; **slum′b(e)rous**, inviting or causing slumber : sleepy.—*adv.* **slum′-
b(e)rously**.—*adjs.* **slum′bersome** ; **slum′b(e)ry**,
sleepy, drowsy. [M.E. *slūmeren*—O.E. *slúma*,
slumber.]

slump, *slump, v.i.* to fall or sink suddenly into water
or mud : to fail or fall through helplessly : (of
prices, trade, &c.) to fall suddenly or heavily : to
flop, clump : to plump.—*n.* a boggy place : a
sinking into slush, &c. : the sound so made : a
sudden or serious fall of prices, business, &c.—opp.
to **boom**.—*adj.* **slump′y**, marshy. [Cf. Norw.
slumpe, to slump, plump, L.G. *schlump*, marshy
place.]

slump, *slump, v.t.* (*Scot.*) to throw into a lump or
mass, to lump.—*v.i.* to flow lumpily.—*n.* a gross
amount, a lump.—**slump sum**, a lump sum. [Cf.
L.G. *slump*, Du. *slomp*, mass.]

slung, *pa.t.* and *pa.p.* of **sling**.—*n.* **slung′-shot**, a
weight attached to a cord, used as a weapon.

slunk, *pa.t.* and *pa.p.* of **slink**.

slur, *slur, n.* (*dial.*) thin mud : an aspersion, stain,
imputation of blame : disparagement : discredit
to one's reputation : a slight : (*obs.*) a gliding
movement in dancing : (*obs.*) a gliding throw in
cheating with dice : a blur : a running together resulting in indistinctness in writing or speech :
(*mus.*) a smooth or legato effect : a curved line
indicating that notes are to be sung to one syllable,
played with one bow, or with a smooth gliding
effect.—*v.t.* (*dial.*) to smear, besmirch : to disparage, asperse : (*obs.*) to slip glidingly out of the
dice-box : (*obs.*) to cheat : to glide over slyly so
as to mask or to avert attention : to blur : to sound
indistinctly : to sing or play legato : to go through
perfunctorily :—*pr.p.* **slurr′ing** ; *pa.t.* and *pa.p.*
slurred.—*n.* **slurr′y**, thin paste,
semi-fluid mixture. [Origin obscure ; perh. different words that have run together.]

sluse, a Miltonic spelling of **sluice**.

slush, *slush, n.* liquid mud : melting snow : a
protective coating for metal : worthless sentimental
drivel or gush.—*v.t.* to splash or cover with slush :
to sluice, wash by throwing water : to fill the joints
with mortar (with *up*).—*v.i.* to splash in slush.—
adj. **slush′y**. [Cf. **slosh**.]

slut, *slut, n.* a dirty, untidy woman: a wench, a jade: a bitch, female dog: a greased rag used as a candle.—*adj.* **slutt'ish.**—*adv.* **slutt'ishly.**—*ns.* **slutt'ishness, slutt'ery.** [Cf. Ger. dial. *schlutt(e).*]

sly, *slī, adj.* (*obs.* or *dial.*) expert: (*obs.*) cunningly made: skilful in doing anything so as to be unobserved: cunning: wily: secretive: surreptitious: done with artful dexterity: with hidden meaning: (*Austr.*) illicit:—*compar.* **sly'er**; *superl.* **sly'est.**—*n.* **sly'boots,** a sly or cunning person or animal.—*adj.* **sly'ish.**—*adv.* **sly'ly** (or **slī'ly**).—*n.* **sly'ness.**—**on the sly,** surreptitiously. [O.N. *slœgr*; cf. **sleight**; cf. Ger. *schlau.*]

slype, *slīp, n.* a passage between walls: esp. a covered passage from a cloister between transept and chapterhouse. [Perh. **slip.**]

smack, *smak, n.* taste: a distinctive or distinguishable flavour: a trace, tinge: a mere tasting, enough to taste.—*v.i.* to have a taste: to savour. [O.E. *smæc.*]

smack, *smak, n.* a small decked or half-decked coaster or fishing-vessel, usu. rigged as cutter, sloop, or yawl. [Du. *smak*; Ger. *schmacke.*]

smack, *smak, v.t.* to strike smartly, to slap loudly: to kiss roughly and noisily: to make a sharp noise with, as the lips by separation: to taste with relish or with smacking sound.—*v.i.* to make such a sound.—*n.* a sharp sound: a crack: a slap: a hearty kiss.—*adv.* sharply, straight.—*n.* and *adj.* **smack'ing.** [Prob. imit.; Du. or L.G. *smakken*, to smite, Ger. *schmatzen*, to smack.]

smaik, *smāk, n.* (*Scot.*) a contemptible fellow, rascal.

small, *smawl, adj.* slender: narrow: fine in grain, texture, gauge, &c.: slight: little in size, extent, quantity, value, power, importance, or degree: unimposing, humble: ungenerous, petty: dilute: short of full standard: operating on no great scale: soft or gentle in sound: minor.—*n.* a small thing, portion, or piece: the narrow part (as of the back, the leg): small-coal: (in *pl.*) small-clothes: (in *pl.*) at Oxford, the examination called Responsions (answering to Little-go at Cambridge).—*adv.* in a low tone: gently: in small pieces: on a small scale: (*Shak.*) but slightly.—*v.t.* and *v.i.* to make or become small.—*ns.* **small'-ale,** ale with little malt and unhopped; **small'-and-earl'y,** (*coll.*) an informal evening party; **small'-arm,** (commonly in *pl.*) a weapon that can be carried by a man; **small'-beer,** a kind of weak beer.—*adj.* inferior generally.—*n.pl.* **small'-clothes,** knee-breeches, esp. those of the close-fitting 18th-century form.—*ns.* **small'-coal,** coal in small pieces; **small'-craft,** small vessels generally.—*n.pl.* **small'-debts,** in Scotland debts up to £20, recoverable in the Sheriff Court.—*ns.* **small'-hand,** writing such as is ordinarily used in correspondence; **small'holder; small'holding,** a holding of land smaller than an ordinary farm: esp. one provided by a local authority: the working of such holdings.—*n.pl.* **small'-hours,** the hours immediately following midnight.—*adjs.* **small'ish; small'-mind'ed,** petty.—*n.* **small'ness.**—*n.pl.* **small'-pipes,** the Northumberland bagpipe.—*ns.* **small'pox,** (*orig. pl.*) a contagious, febrile disease, characterised by small pocks or eruptions on the skin; **small'-sword,** a light thrusting sword for fencing or duelling; **small'-talk,** light or trifling conversation.—*n.pl.* **small'-wares,** small articles such as tape, braid, buttons, hooks: trifles.—**by small and small,** (*Shak.*) little by little; **feel small,** to feel insignificant; **in a small way,** with little capital or stock: unostentatiously; **in small,** on a small scale: in miniature; **in the smallest,** (*Shak.*) in the least; **small capitals** (*coll.* **small caps**), capital letters of the height of lower-case; **small-tooth comb,** a comb with a row of fine teeth on each side: (*fig.*) an arrangement for minute investigation. [O.E. *smæl*; Ger. *schmal.*]

smallage, *smawl'ij, n.* wild celery (*Apium graveolens*). [**small,** and Fr. *ache*—L. *apium*, parsley.]

smalt, *smawlt, n.* glass coloured with cobalt oxide: its powder, used as a pigment: its deep blue colour: smalto.—*adj.* deep blue.—*ns.* **smalt'ite,** a cubic mineral, cobalt arsenide; **smalto** (*smawl'tō*; It. *zmäl'tō*), coloured glass or enamel for mosaic work: a cube of it. [It. *smalto*—O.H.G. *smalzjan* (Ger. *schmelzen*), to melt.]

smaragd, *smar'agd, n.* the emerald.—*adj.* **smarag'dine** (*-dīn, -dēn, -dīn*), emerald green.—*n.* **smarag'dite,** a green amphibole. [L. *smaragdus*—Gr. *smaragdos.*]

smarm, *smärm,* **smalm,** *smäm, v.t.* and *v.i.* to smear, daub, plaster: to sleek.—*v.i.* to fawn ingratiatingly and fulsomely: to be unctuous.—*adv.* **smarm'ily, smalm'ily.**—*adj.* **smarm'y, smalm'y.** [Origin obscure.]

smart, *smärt, n.* quick, stinging pain: smart-money: a dandy.—*v.i.* to feel a smart: to be punished.—*v.t.* to cause to smart.—*adj.* sharp and stinging: brisk: acute, witty: pert, vivacious: trim, spruce, fine: fashionable: keen, quick, and efficient in business: (esp. *U.S.*) considerable.—*adv.* smartly.—*n.* **smart-Al'ick, -Al'eck,** a would-be clever person.—Also *adj.*—*v.t.* **smart'en,** to make smart, to brighten (with *up*).—*adv.* **smart'ly.**—*ns.* **smart'-money,** money paid by a recruit for his release before being sworn in: money paid for escape from any unpleasant situation or engagement: excessive damages: money allowed to soldiers and sailors for wounds; **smart'ness; smart'-tick'et,** a certificate granted to one entitled to smart-money; **smart'weed,** waterpepper, from its acridity; **smart'y,** a would-be smart fellow. [O.E. *smeortan*; Du. *smarten*, Ger. *schmerzen.*]

smash, *smash, v.t.* to shatter violently: to ruin: (*lawn-tennis*) to strike overhand with great force: to dash violently.—*v.i.* to fly into pieces: to be ruined, to fail: to dash violently: to smash a tennis ball.—*n.* an act or occasion of smashing, destruction, ruin, bankruptcy: (*slang*) bad money.—*adj.* **smash-and-grab',** effected by smashing a shop window and grabbing goods.—*ns.* **smash'er,** one who smashes: (*slang*) one who passes bad money: anything great or extraordinary: a person of dazzling charm; **smash'ing.**—*adj.* crushing: dashing: (*slang*) superlative, strikingly good.—*n.* **smash'-up,** a serious smash. [Imit.; cf. Sw. dial. *smaske*, to smack.]

smatch, *smach, n.* smack, taste: (*Shak.*) tincture: touch: smattering.—*v.i.* to smack, have a flavour.—*v.t.* to smack of. [**smack.**]

smatter, *smat'ər, v.i.* to talk superficially: to have a superficial knowledge: to dabble.—*v.t.* to talk or utter smatteringly: to dabble in.—*n.* a smattering.—*ns.* **smatt'erer; smatt'ering,** a scrappy, superficial knowledge.—*adv.* **smatt'eringly.** [M.E. *smateren*, to rattle, to chatter; connexions doubtful.]

smear, *smēr, n.* (*obs.*) grease: a rub with, mark or patch of, anything sticky or oily: the matter so applied, esp. to a slide for microscopic study: a fine glaze for pottery.—*v.t.* to anoint: to overspread with anything sticky or oily: to apply as a smear: to rub smearily.—*adv.* **smear'ily.**—*n.* **smear'iness.**—*adj.* **smear'y,** sticky: greasy: ready to smear: showing smears.—*n.* **smear'-dab** (see **lemon,** 2). [O.E. *smeru*, fat, grease; Ger. *schmer*, grease, O.N. *smjör*, butter.]

smeddum, *smed'əm, n.* fine powder: (*Scot.*) spirit, mettle. [O.E. *smed(e)ma, smeodoma*, fine flour.]

smee, *smē,* **smeath, smeeth,** *smēth, ns.* names for various ducks—smew, pochard, widgeon, pintail.

smeech, *smēch* (*S.W. dial.*), **smeek,** *smēk* (*Scots.*), forms of **smoke,** *n., v.t., v.i.*

smegma, *smeg'mä, n.* a sebaceous secretion, esp. that under the prepuce. [Gr. *smēgma, -atos*, soap.]

smell, *smel, n.* the sense by which gases, vapours, substances very finely divided, are perceived, located in the higher animals in the mucous membrane of the nose: the specific sensation excited by such a substance: the property of exciting it: an act or instance of exercising the sense: (*fig.*) a smack, savour, property of suggesting, intimation.—*v.i.* to affect the sense of smell: to have odour: to have or use the sense of smell: (*fig.*) to have a savour, give a suggestion.—*v.t.* to perceive, detect, find, by smell: to take a smell at: to impart a smell to: to emit a smell of:—*pa.t.* and *pa.p.* **smelled** or **smelt.**—*ns.* **smell'er; smell'-feast,** a sponger; **smell'iness.**—*n.* and *adj.* **smell'ing.**

—*ns.* **smell′ing-bottle**, a bottle of smelling-salts, or the like; **smell′ing-salts**, a preparation of ammonium carbonate with lavender, &c., used as a stimulant in faintness, &c.—*adj.* **smell′-less**.—*n.* **smell′-trap**, a drain-trap.—*adj.* **smell′y**, having a bad smell.—**smell a rat** (see **rat**); **smell at** (*obs.* and *U.S.*, to), to sniff at, take a smell at; **smell of**, to have the smell of : to savour of; **smell out**, to find out by prying : (*S.Afr.*) to detect by witchcraft. [Very early M.E. *smel*, prob. O.E. but not recorded.]

smelt, *smelt*, *n.* a fish of or akin to the salmon family, with cucumber-like smell. [O.E. *smelt*.]

smelt, *smelt*, *v.t.* to melt in order to separate metal from ore.—*ns.* **smel′ter**; **smel′tery**, a place for smelting; **smel′ting**; **smel′ting-fur′nace**, **-house**, **-works**. [Prob. M.L.G. or M.Du. *smelten*; cf. Norw. *smelta*, Sw. *smälta*.]

smelt, *smelt*, *n.* (*obs. slang*; *Scott*) a half-guinea.

smew, *smū*, *n.* a small species of merganser.

smicker, *smik′ər*, *adj.* (*obs.*) beautiful : (*obs.*) smirking, wanton.—*v.i.* (*obs.*) to look amorously.—*n.* **smick′ering**, an amorous inclination. — *adv.* **smick′ly**, amorously. [O.E. *smicer*, beautiful.]

smicket, *smik′it*, *n.* a smock. [Prob. dim.]

smiddy, *smid′i*, Scots form of **smithy**.

smifligate, *smif′li-gāt*. See **spiflicate**.

smight, a Spenserian spelling of **smite**.

Smilax, *smī′laks*, *n.* a genus of the lily family, mostly climbers with net-veined leaves, some yielding sarsaparilla. [Gr. *smilax*.]

smile, *smīl* (*Shak.*, &c., also **smoile**, **smoyle**, *smoil*), *v.i.* to express amusement, slight contempt, favour, pleasure, &c., by a slight drawing up of the corners of the lips : to look joyous : to be favourable : (*slang*) to drink, esp. whisky.—*v.t.* to render, drive, express, by smiling : (*Shak.*) to smile at : also, with cognate object.—*n.* act of smiling : the expression of the features in smiling : favour : (*slang*) a drink, a treat.—*adj.* **smile′ful**; **smile′less**.—*ns.* **smil′er**; **smil′et**, (*Shak.*) a little smile.—*n.* and *adj.* **smil′ing.**—*adv.* **smil′ingly.**—*n.* **smil′ingness**, the state of being smiling. —**smile at**, to show amusement at, disregard at; **smile on**, to show favour to, be propitious to. [M.E. *smilen*; poss. from L.G.]

smir, smirr. See **smur**.

smirch, *smərch*, *v.t.* to besmear, dirty : to sully.— *n.* a stain. [Earlier *smorch*, supposed to be from O.Fr. *esmorcher*, to hurt, influenced by **smear**.]

smirk, *smərk*, *v.i.* to smile affectedly or foolishly : to look affectedly soft.—*n.* an affected or foolish smile.—*adjs.* **smirk**, trim, spruce; **smirk′y**, simpering. [O.E. *smercian*.]

smit, *smit*, (*obs.* or *poet.*) *pa.t.* and *pa.p.* of **smite**.

smit, *smit*, *v.t.* (*Northern dial.*) to stain, taint, mark with ruddle, infect.—*n.* (*obs.*) a stain : (*Northern dial.*) ruddle, a mark on sheep, infection.—*adj.* (*Northern*) **smit′le**, infectious. [O.E. *smittian*, to befoul, infect, intens. of *smitan*, to smear; *smitte*, spot.]

smite, *smīt*, *v.t.* to strike : to beat : to kill : to overthrow in battle : to affect with feeling : to afflict. —*v.i.* to strike : to meet forcibly:—*pa.t.* **smōte** (*arch.* or *poet.* **smit**); *pa.p.* **smitt′en** (**smit**).—*n.* **smī′ter**.—**smite off**, to cut off. [O.E. *smitan*, to smear.]

smith, *smith*, *n.* one who forges with the hammer : a worker in metals : one who makes anything.— *v.t.* to forge : to fashion.—*v.i.* to do smith's work. —*ns.* **smith′craft**; **smith′ery**, a smithy : smith's work, smithing; **smithy** (*smidh′i*), a smith's workshop.—*v.t.* and *v.i.* to smith. [O.E. *smith*; Ger. *schmied*.]

smithers, *smidh′ərz*, *n.pl.* shivers, small fragments. —*n.* **smithereens** (with Irish dim. suffix).

Smithsonian, *smith-sō′ni-ən*, *adj.* pertaining to James Macie *Smithson* (1765–1829), an Englishman, founder of a great scientific and cultural institution at Washington.—*n.* **smith′sonite** (*-sən-īt*), calamine : also electric calamine.

smitten, *smit′n*, *pa.p.* of **smite**.

smittle. See **smit** (2).

smock, *smok*, *n.* a woman's shift : a smock-frock : (*obs.*) a wench.—*v.t.* to clothe in a smock or smock-

frock. — *adj.* **smock′-faced**, pale-faced. — *ns.* **smock′-frock**, an outer garment of coarse white linen worn over the other clothes in the south of England; **smock′ing**, honeycombing, as on the yoke and cuffs of a smock; **smock′-race**, a race for the prize of a smock. [O.E. *smoc*.]

smog, *smog*, *n.* smoky fog.

smoile, smoyle, *smoil*, old forms of **smile**.

smoke, *smōk*, *n.* the gases, vapours, and fine particles that come off from a burning body: solid particles suspended in a gas: fumes: vapour: fog : a cloud or column of smoke : that which may be smoked—tobacco, a cigarette, or cigar : a spell of smoking : S. African brandy (**Cape smoke**).— *v.i.* to exhale or emit smoke, vapour, dust, &c.: to reek: to send smoke in a wrong direction: to move like smoke : to dash along in a cloud of smoke, vapour, spray, or dust : to suffer (orig. at the stake), smart : to take into the mouth and puff out the smoke of tobacco or the like : to lend itself to, admit of, smoking.—*v.t.* to dry, scent, preserve, fumigate, suffocate, blacken, taint, drive, render by smoke : to take in and emit the smoke from: (*arch.*) to scent out, suspect, have an inkling of: (*arch.*) to observe : (*arch.*) to quiz, ridicule : to thrash.—*ns.* **smoke′-ball**, a shell emitting smoke as a screen or to drive out an enemy; **smoke′-black**, lampblack; **smoke′-board**, a board suspended before the upper part of a fireplace to prevent the smoke coming out into the room; **smoke′-bomb**, a bomb that emits smoke on bursting; **smoke′-box**, part of a steam-boiler where the smoke is collected before passing out at the chimney; **smoke′-bush, -tree**, a sumach with light feathery or cloudlike panicles; **smoke′-consumer**, an apparatus for burning all the smoke from a fire.— *adjs.* **smoked**; **smoke′-dried**. — *v.t.* **smoke′-dry**, to cure or dry by means of smoke.—*ns.* **smoke′-helmet**, a head-covering for firemen or others who work in dense smoke; **smoke′-ho′**, (*Austr.*) a break for a smoke during the working day; **smoke′-hole**, a fumarole : a hole for escape of smoke; **smoke′-house**, a building where meat or fish is cured by smoking, or where smoked meats are stored; **smoke′-jack**, a contrivance for turning a spit by means of an ascending current of air : a muddled brain.—*adj.* **smoke′less.**— *adv.* **smoke′lessly.**—*n.* **smoke′lessness.**—*adj.* **smoke′proof**, impervious to smoke.—*ns.* **smok′er**, one who smokes tobacco : a smoking-carriage or compartment : one who smoke-dries meat : a smoking-concert; **smoke′-room**; **smoke′-sail**, a small sail hoisted to drive off the smoke from the galley; **smoke′-screen**, a cloud of smoke raised to conceal movements; **smoke′-stack**, a ship's funnel : a chimney. — *adj.* **smoke′tight**, impervious to smoke.—*adv.* **smok′ily.**—*n.* **smok′-iness.**—*n.* and *adj.* **smok′ing.**—*ns.* **smok′ing-cap, -jacket**, a light ornamental cap or jacket formerly worn by smokers; **smok′ing-carriage, -compartment, -room**, a railway-carriage, compartment, room, set apart for smokers; **smok′ing-con′cert**, a concert at which smoking (euphemistically) is allowed.—*adj.* **smok′y**, giving out smoke : like smoke : coloured like or by smoke : filled, or subject to be filled, with smoke : tarnished or noisome with smoke : (*obs.*) suspicious.—*n.* (*Scot.*) a smoked haddock.—**end in smoke**, to have no tangible result; **like smoke**, very quickly; **sell smoke**, to swindle; **smoke-room story**, one unsuitable for telling elsewhere; **smoky quartz**, Cairngorm stone. [O.E. *smoca* (n.), *smocian* (vb.); Ger. *schmauch*.]

smolder. American spelling of **smoulder**.

smolt, *smōlt*, *n.* a young river salmon when it is bluish along the upper half of the body and silvery along the sides. [Orig. Scot.; see **smout**.]

smoot, *smōot*, *n.* (*slang*) a compositor who does odd jobs in various houses.—*v.i.* to work in this way. [Origin obscure.]

smooth, *smōodh*, *adj.* having an even surface : without roughness : evenly spread : glossy : hairless : of even consistency : slippery : gently flowing : easy : bland : fair-spoken.—*adv.* smoothly.—*v.t.* **smooth**, rarely **smoothe**, to make smooth : to free from obstruction, difficulty, harshness: to reduce from diphthong to simple vowel: to remove by smoothing: to calm, soothe: to blandish: to gloze over.—*v.i.* to become smooth: to flatter, blandish, behave ingratiatingly (also *v.t.* with *it*, *Shak.*).—*n.* a smooth place or part: an act of smoothing.—*adj.* **smooth'-bore,** not rifled.—*n.* a gun with smooth-bored barrel.—*adjs.* **smooth'-browed,** with unwrinkled brow; **smooth'-chinned,** beardless; **smooth'-coated,** not shaggy-haired; **smooth'-ditt'ied,** (*Milt.*) set to words that smoothly fit the tune: or, poss., having a smooth ditty, or set of words.—*v.t.* **smooth'en,** to make smooth.—*n.* **smooth'er,** one who, or that which, smooths: a smoothing tool: (*obs.*) a flatterer.—*adj.* **smooth'-faced,** having a smooth face or surface: pleasant-looking: beardless: unwrinkled: plausible.—*n.* and *adj.* **smooth'ing.**—*ns.* **smooth'ing-iron,** a flatiron; **smooth'ing-plane,** a small fine plane used for finishing.—*adjs.* **smooth'ish; smooth'-leaved.**—*adv.* **smooth'ly.**—*n.* **smooth'ness.**—*adj.* **smooth'-paced,** having a regular easy pace.—*n.* **smooth'pate.**—*adjs.* **smooth'-shod,** having shoes without spikes; **smooth'-spoken, smooth'-tongued,** conciliatory, plausible, flattering, or soft in speech.—**smooth breathing,** in Greek the indication (') over an initial vowel of absence of aspiration; **smooth dab** (see **lemon,** 2). [O.E. *smóth* (usu. *sméthe*).]

smore, *smōr, smōōr, v.t.* and *v.i.* (*Scot.*) to smother, suffocate. [O.E. *smorian.*]

smorzando, *smort-san'dō* (It. *zmort-sän'dō*), **smorzato,** *-sä'tō, adjs.* and *advs.* with a gradual fading away: growing slower and softer. [It.; ger. and pa.p. of *smorzare*, to tone down.]

smote, *smōt, pa.t.* of **smite.**

smother, *smudh'er, v.t.* to suffocate by excluding the air, esp. by a thick covering: to stifle: to envelop closely: to cover up thickly: to suppress: to conceal.—*v.i.* to be suffocated or suppressed: to smoulder.—*n.* smoke: thick floating dust: a smouldering fire or condition: a welter: suffocation.—*adj.* **smoth'ered.**—*ns.* **smoth'erer; smother'-fly,** an aphis; **smoth'eriness.**—*n.* and *adj.* **smoth'ering.**—*adv.* **smoth'eringly.**—*adj.* **smoth'ery,** tending to smother: stifling. [M.E. *smorther*—O.E. *smorian*, to smother; cf. **smore.**]

smouch, *smowch, n.* (*dial.*) a smack, a hearty kiss.—*v.t.* to kiss, to buss. [Cf. Ger. *schmutz.*]

smouch, *smowch,* **smouse,** *smowz, n.* (*obs.* slang) a Jew: (*S.Afr.*) a pedlar.—*v.i.* (*S.Afr.*) to trade as a pedlar.—*n.* **smous'er,** (*S.Afr.*) a pedlar. [Du. *smous,* perh. from Heb. *sh'mū'ōth,* news.]

smouch, *smowch, v.t.* to filch.—*v.i.* to cheat.

smouch, *smowch, n.* a form of **smutch, smudge.**

smoulder, *smōl'dər, v.t.* to smother.—*v.i.* to burn slowly or without flame: to linger on in a suppressed or hidden state.—*n.* smother: smouldering fire.—*n.* and *adj.* **smoul'dering.**—*adj.* **smoul'dry** (*Spens.*). [M.E. *smolder*; origin obscure.]

smout, *smowt.* Same as **smoot.**

smout, smowt, *smowt, n.* Scots form of **smolt**: a small person or child.

smoyle, an old form of **smile.**

smudge, *smuj, n.* a smear: a blur: a rubbed blot.—*v.t.* to smear: to blur: to soil: to daub.—*n.* **smudg'er.**—*adv.* **smudg'ily.**—*n.* **smudg'iness.**—*adj.* **smudg'y.** [Cf. **smutch.**]

smudge, *smuj, n.* a choking smoke: fuel for obtaining smoke.—*v.t.* to fumigate with smoke.—*adj.* **smud'gy,** smoky. [Origin obscure.]

smug, *smug, adj.* neat, prim, spruce: smooth: sleek: affectedly smart: offensively self-complacent.—*n.* a smug person: a reading student.—*v.t.* to make trim.—*adj.* **smug'-faced.**—*adv.* **smug'ly.**—*n.* **smug'ness.** [Connexion with L.G. *smuk*, trim, presents difficulty.]

smug, *smug, v.t.* to seize without ceremony, to confiscate: (*slang*) to hush up. [Origin obscure.]

smuggle, *smug'l, v.t.* to import or export illegally or without paying duty: to convey secretly.—*adj.* **smugg'led.**—*n.* **smugg'ler,** one who smuggles: a vessel used in smuggling.—*n.* and *adj.* **smugg'ling.** [L.G. *smuggeln*; Ger. *schmuggeln.*]

smuggle, *smug'l, v.t.* to fondle, cuddle.

smur, smur, smir(r), *smir, n.* (*Scot.*) fine misty rain.—*v.i.* to drizzle, rain very finely.—*adj.* **smurr'y, smirr'y.**

smut, *smut, n.* soot: worthless or bad coal: a flake or spot of dirt, soot, &c.: a black spot: a disease of plants, esp. cereals, giving an appearance of soot: the fungus causing it: obscene discourse.—*v.t.* to soil, spot, or affect with smut: to become smutty.—*n.* **smut-fungus,** any member of the Ustilaginales, an order of Basidiomycetes, parasitic on plants, causing smut and bunt.—*adj.* **smutt'ed.**—*adv.* **smutt'ily.**—*n.* **smutt'iness.**—*adj.* **smutt'y,** stained with smut: affected with smut: obscene, filthy. [Cf. L.G. *schmutt*; Ger. *schmutz*, dirt.]

smutch, *smuch, v.t.* to smut: to sully.—*n.* a dirty mark: soot: grime: a stain. [Cf. **smudge.**]

smytrie, *smit'ri, n.* (*Scot.*) a collection of small things. [Cf. Flem. *smite.*]

snab. See **snob.**

snack, *snak, n.* (*dial.*) a snap, bite: a share: a mere taste: a light repast.—*v.i.* (*Scot.*) to snap: (*obs.*) to share: to take a snack.—*n.* **snack'-counter,** a counter in a restaurant where snacks are served promptly. [Cf. M.Du. *snacken*, to snap: **snatch.**]

snaffle, *snaf'l, n.* a jointed bit (less severe than the curb).—*v.t.* to put a snaffle on: to control by the snaffle: (*slang*; also **snabb'le**) to arrest: to capture: to purloin: to get possession of.—*ns.* **snaff'le-bit; snaff'le-bridle; snaff'le-rein; snaff'ling-lay,** the trade of highwayman. [Ety. dub.; cf. Du. *snavel*, Ger. *schnabel*, beak, mouth.]

snag, *snag, n.* a stump, as of a branch or tooth: a jag: a short tine: an embedded tree, dangerous for boats: hence a catch, a hidden obstacle or drawback.—*v.t.* to catch on a snag: to tear on a snag: to hack so as to form snags: to clear of snags.—*adjs.* **snagged, snagg'y.** [Cf. O.N. *snagi*, peg.]

snail, *snāl, n.* any terrestrial or air-breathing gasteropod mollusc with well-developed coiled shell: extended to other shelled gasteropods and (*dial.*) to slugs: a sluggish person or animal: a snail-wheel: medick of various kinds (from its coiled pods).—*v.i.* to crawl, go very slowly (also *v.t.* with *it*).—*ns.* **snail'ery,** a place where edible snails are bred; **snail'-fish,** the fish called sea-snail; **snail'-flower,** any flower pollinated by snails.—*adj.* and *adv.* **snail'-like.**—*adj.* **snail'-paced.**—*n.* **snail'-shell.**—*adj.* **snail'-slow.**—*n.* **snail'-wheel,** a cam that controls the striking of a clock.—*adj.* **snail'y.**—**giant African snail,** a 10-inch snail, a serious plant pest except in its place of origin, East Africa. [O.E. *snegl, snægl, snégl.*]

'snails, *snālz, interj.* (*obs.*) for **God's nails.**

snake, *snāk, n.* a serpent, or member of the Ophidia, a class of elongated limbless (or all but limbless) scaly carnivorous reptiles, often venomous, with forked tongue, no eyelids or external ears, teeth fused to the bones that bear them: an ungrateful or treacherous person (in allusion to Aesop): a wretch, drudge: anything snakelike in form or movement: apparatus for blasting a passage through a mine-field.—*v.i.* to wind: to creep.—*v.t.* to drag.—*ns.* **snake'bird,** the darter: the wryneck; **snake'bite,** the bite of a venomous snake; **snake'-charmer,** one who handles snakes and sets them to perform rhythmical movements; **snake'-cult,** serpent-worship; **snake'-dance,** a religious dance of the Hopi Indians in which snakes are handled; **snake'-eel,** an eel without tail-fin; **snake'-fence,** (U.S.) a worm-fence; **snake'-fly,** a neuropterous insect (Raphidia) with neck-like prothorax.—*adj.* **snake'like.**—*ns.* **snake'root,** bistort, milkwort, Aristolochia, or other plant whose root has been thought good for snake-bites; **snake's'-head,** fritillary; **snake'stone,** a fossil ammonite: a stone thought to cure snakebite; **snake'weed,** bistort.—*adv.* **snake'wise,** in the manner of a snake.—*n.* **snake'wood,** letterwood.—*adv.* **snāk'ily.**—*n.* **snāk'iness.**—*adj.* **snāk'ish.**—*n.* **snāk'ishness.**—*adj.* **snāk'y,**—**snake in the grass,** (*fig.*) one who injures furtively: a lurking danger. [O.E. *snaca.*]

snap, *snap, v.i.* to make a bite (often with *at*): to speak tartly in sudden irritation: to grasp (with *at*): to shut suddenly, as by a spring: to make a sharp noise: to go with a sharp noise: to break suddenly.—*v.t.* to bite suddenly: to seize, secure promptly (usu. with *up*): to answer or interrupt sharply (often with *up*): to shut with a sharp sound: to cause to make a sharp sound: to send or put with a sharp sound: to utter snappishly: to break suddenly: to take an instantaneous photograph of, esp. with a hand-camera: (*pr.p.* **snapp'-ing**; *pa.t.* and *pa.p.* **snapped**).—*n.* an act, instance, or noise of snapping: a small catch or lock: (*rare*) an earring: (in *pl.*) a kind of handcuff: a share: a scrap: a whit: a snack: a crack: a gingerbread biscuit: a quick, crisp, incisive, epigrammatic quality in style: lively energy: (*slang*) a brief theatrical engagement: an easy and profitable place or task: a sharper, a cheat: a riveter's or glass-moulder's tool: a snapshot: a sudden cold spell: a card game.—*adj.* sudden, unexpected: snapping shut.—*adv.* with a snap.—*interj.* used in claiming cards from an opponent in the game of snap.—*adj.* **snap'-brim**, having a brim that turns down springily. — *ns.* **snap'-divi'sion**, **snap'-vote**, a division taken unexpectedly; **snap'dragon**, a plant (Antirrhinum) of the figwort family whose flower when pinched and released snaps like a dragon: a Christmas game of snatching raisins out of burning brandy; **snapp'er**, an animal that snaps: one who snaps or snaps **up**: (*U.S.*) the end of a whiplash: (also **schnapper**) any fish of the family Lutianidae, akin to the basses: a highly esteemed food-fish of Australian and New Zealand waters, Pagrosomus, of the sea-bream family; **snapp'er-up**, (*Shak.*) one who snaps up.—*adv.* **snapp'ily**.—*n.* and *adj.* **snapp'ing**.—*adv.* **snapp'-ingly**.—*n.* **snapp'ing-tur'tle**, a large American fiercely snapping fresh-water tortoise.—*adj.* **snapp'-ish**, inclined to snap: quick and tart.—*adv.* **snapp'ishly**.—*n.* **snapp'ishness**.—*adj.* **snapp'y**, snappish: snapping: having the quality of snap: instantaneous.—*ns.* **snap'shooter**; **snap'shooting**; **snap'shot**, a hasty shot: an instantaneous photograph.—**Scotch snap** (see **Scotch**); **snap one's head, nose, off**, to answer irritably and rudely. [Prob. Du. *snappen*, to snap; Ger. *schnappen*.]

snapha(u)nce, *snap'häns, -hawns*, **snaphaunch**, *-hawnsh, n.* (*obs.*) a freebooter: a flintlock or a weapon with one: a spring catch or trap. [Cf. Du. *snapshaan—snappen*, to snap, *haan*, a cock.]

snapper, *snap'ər, n.* (*Scot.*) a stumble: a slip in conduct: a scrape. — *v.i.* to stumble. [Cf. Ger. dial. *schnappen*, to stumble.]

snar, *snär, v.i.* (*Spens.*) to snarl. [Cf. Du. and L.G. *snarren*.]

snare, *snār, n.* a running noose for trapping: a trap: an allurement, temptation, entanglement, moral danger: a loop for removing tumours, &c.: a string stretched across the lower head of a side-drum.—*v.t.* to catch, entangle, entrap, in a snare: to remove with a snare.—*ns.* **snare'-drum**, a side-drum; **snar'er**; **snar'ing**.—*adj.* **snar'y**. [O.E. *sneare* or O.N. *snara*; prob. partly from Du. *snaar* or L.G. *snare*.]

snark, *snärk, n.* an imaginary animal created by Lewis Carroll (1876).

snarl, *snärl, v.i.* to make a surly resentful noise with show of teeth: to speak in a surly manner.—*v.t.* to utter snarlingly.—*n.* an ill-natured growling sound: a snarling.—*n.* **snar'ler**.—*n.* and *adj.* **snarl'ing**.—*adj.* **snarl'y**. [**snar**.]

snarl, *snärl, n.* a knot: a tangle: a knot in wood.— *v.t.* (*dial.*) to ensnare: to tangle: to raise with a snarling-iron.—*v.i.* to tangle.—*adj.* **snarled**.—*ns.* **snar'ler**; **snar'ling**; **snarl'ing-iron, -tool**, a curved tool for raised work in hollow metal-ware. [**snare**.]

snash, *snash, n.* (*Scot.*) insolence, abusive language. —*v.i.* to talk impudently. [Prob. imit.]

snaste, *snāst, n.* (now *dial.*) a wick: a candle-snuff. [Origin obscure.]

snatch, *snach, v.t.* to seize suddenly: to pluck away quickly: to grab: to take as opportunity occurs.— *v.i.* to make a snap or seizure.—*n.* (*Shak.*) a snap: a seizure or attempt to seize: a grab: a short spell: a fragment, as of song, verse: a snack:

(*Shak.*) a catch (of the voice): (*Shak.*) a quibble.— *ns.* **snatch'-block**, a block with a side opening for the bight of a rope; **snatch'er**.—*advs.* **snatch'ily**, **snatch'ingly**.—*ns.* **snatch'-purse, -thief**, a thief who snatches.—*adj.* **snatch'y**, irregular. [M.E. *snaechen*; poss. related to **snack**.]

snath, *snath*, **snathe**, *snädh*, **snead**, *snēd*, **sneath**, *snēth*, **sned**, *sned, n.* the curved handle or shaft of a scythe. [O.E. *snæd*, a scythe handle, a slice.]

sneak, *snēk, v.i.* to go furtively or meanly, slink, skulk: to cringe: to behave meanly: to tell tales. —*v.t.* to pass furtively: (*slang*) to steal.—*n.* a sneaking fellow: one who sneaks away: a sneaking thief: a tell-tale: (*cricket*) a ball bowled along the ground.—*ns.* **sneak'-cup**, in some editions of Shakespeare (1 *Hen. IV.* III. iii. 99), probably a misreading of a blurred **sneakeup** (see **sneak-up** below) in the first quartos, but by some taken to be a correction and explained as one who balks his cup, or a stealer of cups; **sneak'er**.—*adv.* **sneak'-ily**. — *n.* **sneak'iness**. — *adj.* **sneak'ing**, mean, crouching: secret, underhand, not openly avowed: lurking under other feelings.—*adv.* **sneak'ingly**.— *adj.* **sneak'ish**, befitting a sneak.—*adv.* **sneak'-ishly**.—*ns.* **sneak'ishness**; **sneaks'by**, a sneak; **sneak'-up**, a sneak, shirker, skulker.—*adj.* **sneak'y**, sneaking. [Connexion with O.E. *snican*, to crawl, is obscure.]

sneap, *snēp, v.t.* to nip, pinch: to put down, repress, snub.—*n.* a snub, check.—*adj.* **sneap'ing** (*Shak.*). [Earlier *snape*—O.N. *sneypa*.]

sneb, snebbe, old forms of **snib, snub**.

sneck, *snek, n.* (*Scot.*) a latch: a door-catch.—*v.t.* to fasten with a sneck.—*n.* **sneck'-drawer**, one who lifts the latch: an insinuating or crafty person. —Also **sneck'-draw**.—*n.* and *adj.* **sneck'-draw-ing**. [Cf. **snack, snatch**.]

sneck, sneck-up. See **snick, snick-up**.

sned, *sned, v.t.* to cut: to lop: to prune. [O.E. *snǣdan*.]

sneer, *snēr, v.i.* to show cynical contempt by the expression of the face, as by drawing up the lip: to express such contempt in other ways: (*obs.*) to grin.—*v.t.* to utter sneeringly: (*obs.*) to sneer at: to render, drive, by sneering.—*n.* a sneering expression: an act of sneering.—*n.* **sneer'er**.—*n.* and *adj.* **sneer'ing**. — *adv.* **sneer'ingly**. — *adj.* **sneer'y**. [Perh. related to Fris. *sneere*, to scorn.]

sneesh, *snēsh, n.* (*Scot.*) a pinch of snuff: snuff.— *ns.* **sneesh'in(g)**, **sneesh'an**, (*Scot.*) snuff: a pinch of snuff; **snee'shin-mull**, a snuffbox. [Poss. **sneeze, sneezing**; or imit.; cf. **snush**.]

sneeze, *snēz, v.i.* to make a sudden and involuntary violent expiration, preceded by inspiration, the fauces being generally closed so that the current of air is directed through the nose.—*n.* an act of sneezing.—*ns.* **sneeze'-box**, a snuffbox; **sneez'er**; **sneeze'weed**, an American composite (Helenium); **sneeze'wood**, a S. African melia-ceous timber tree (Ptaeroxylon), or its wood, whose sawdust causes sneezing; **sneeze'wort**, a species of yarrow (*Achillaea Ptarmica*) once used as a substitute for snuff: white hellebore; **sneez'ing**. —*adj.* **sneez'y**.—**not to be sneezed at**, not to be despised. [M.E. *snesen, fnesen*—O.E. *fnéosan*, to sneeze; Du. *fniezen*.]

snell, *snel, adj.* (*Scot.*) keen, sharp, severe.—*adv.* **snel'ly**. [O.E. *snell*, active; Ger. *schnell*, swift.]

snell, *snel, n.* a short piece of hair, gut, &c., attaching a hook to a line. [Origin obscure.]

snib, *snib, n.* and *v.t.* (*Spens.*; *Scot.*). Same as **snub**.

snib, *snib, n.* (*Scot.*) a small bolt: a catch for a window-sash.—*v.t.* to fasten with a snib. [Cf. L.G. *snibbe*, beak.]

snick, *snik* (*Scott* **sneck**, *snek*), *v.t.* to cut out, snip, nick: (*cricket*) to deflect slightly by a touch of the bat.—*n.* a small cut: a glancing **stroke** in cricket. [Origin doubtful.]

snick, *snik, n., v.t.*, and *v.i.* click. [Imit.]

snicker, *snik'ər, v.i.* to snigger: to nicker, **neigh**.— *v.t.* to say gigglingly.—*n.* a giggle. [Imit.; cf. **nicker, snigger**.]

snickersnee, *snik'ər-snē', n.* a large knife for fighting: (*obs.*) fighting with knives.—*v.i.* (*obs.*) to fight with knives.—Also earlier **snick-a-snee**, **snick and snee**, **snick** (earlier **stick**) **or snee**. [App. Du. *steken*, to thrust, *snijen*, to cut.]

snick-up, **snick up**, *snik-up'*, *v.i.* (*Shak.*) used in imper., go hang.—Also **sneck up.**

sniff, *snif*, *v.t.* to draw in with the breath through the nose : to smell : to suspect or detect by smell or as if by smell.—*v.i.* to draw in air sharply and audibly through the nose : to draw up mucus or tears escaping into the nose : to smell tentatively : to express disapprobation with reticence by a slight sound in the nose : to snuffle.—*n.* an act or a sound of sniffing : a smell : a small quantity inhaled by the nose.—*n.* **sniff′er.**—*adv.* **sniff′ily.** —*n.* **sniff′iness.**—*n.* and *adj.* **sniff′ing.**—*adv.* **sniff′ingly.**—*v.i.* **sniff′le**, to snuffle slightly, to sniff.—*n.* **sniff′ler**, one who sniffles : a slight breeze.—*adj.* **sniff′y**, inclined to be disdainful.— *vs.i.* **snift**, to sniff, snivel : to blow out steam, &c. ; **snift′er**, to sniff.—*n.* a sniff : (*pl.*) stoppage of the nasal passages in catarrh : (*slang*) a dram : a strong breeze.—*n.* **snift′ing-valve**, an air-valve of a cylinder, &c.—*adj.* **snift′y**, (*slang*) having a tempting smell : inclined to sniff in disdain. [Imit. ; cf. **snuff.**]

snig, *snig*, *n.* (*prov.*) a river-eel, esp. an immature (olive and yellow) eel.—*v.t.* **snigg′er**, to catch (salmon) with a weighted hook.—*v.i.* **snigg′le**, to fish for eels by thrusting the bait into their hiding-places : to fish for salmon, &c., by striking with a hook.—*v.t.* to catch thus.—*n.* a baited hook.—*ns.* **snigg′ler ; snigg′ling.**

snigger, *snig′ər*, *v.i.* to laugh in a half-suppressed, broken manner.—*v.t.* to say with a snigger.—*n.* a half-suppressed laugh.—*n.* **snigg′erer.**—*n.* and *adj.* **snigg′ering.**—*adv.* **snigg′eringly.** [Imit.]

snip, *snip*, *v.t.* to cut as with scissors : (*obs.*) to snatch, snap : (*pr.p.* **snipp′ing ;** *pa.t.* and *pa.p.* **snipped**).—*n.* a small cut, as with scissors : a small shred : a slip, small slender or despicable person : a small piece : a notch, slit, or slash : the sound of a stroke of scissors : a white or light patch or stripe on a horse, esp. on the nose : a share : a tailor : a certainty.—*ns.* **snipp′er ; snipp′er-snapp′er**, a whippersnapper ; **snipp′et**, a little piece snipped off : a scrap, of literature, news : (*India*) a small sandpiper ; **snipp′etiness.**—*adj.* **snipp′ety**, trivial, fragmentary. — *n.* **snipp′ing**, a clipping. — *adj.* **snipp′y**, fragmentary : stingy : snappish.—*n.pl.* **snips**, hand-shears for sheet-metal.—*n.* **snip′-snap′**, the action or sound of scissors : quick snappy dialogue.—Also *adj.*, *adv.*, *interj.*, *v.i.*—**snipt taffeta fellow**, (*Shak.*) one who goes about in slashed silk. [L.G. or Du. *snippen* ; Ger. *schnippen.*]

snipe, *snīp*, *n.* a bird akin to the woodcock, with a long straight flexible bill, or other of its genus (Gallinago or Capella) or family (Scolopacidae) : (*Shak.*) a fool or contemptible person : (*U.S.*) a cigar or cigarette end : a sniping shot :—*pl.* usu. **snipe**, of the bird, **snipes**, of species of the bird, and in other senses.—*v.i.* to shoot snipe, go snipe-shooting : to shoot at single men from cover.— *v.t.* to pick off by rifle-fire from (usu. distant) cover.—*ns.* **snipe′-fish**, the trumpet-fish ; **snip′er ; snip′ing.**—*adj.* **snip′y**, snipe-like : snipe-beaked : frequented by snipe. [Prob. Scand. ; the O.E. word is *snīte.*]

snip-snap-snorum, *snip-snap-snō′rəm*, *n.* a childish game of turning up cards. [L.G. *snipp-snapp-snorum.*]

snirt, *snirt*, *snərt*, *n.* (*Scot.*) a smothered laugh.— *v.i.* **snirt′le**, to snicker. [Imit.]

snitch, *snich*, *n.* (*slang*) the nose : a fillip on the nose : an informer.—*v.i.* (*slang*) to inform, peach. —*n.* **snitch′er**, an informer : a handcuff.

snivel, *sniv′l*, *n.* mucus of the nose : a sniff : a hypocritical snuffle : cant.—*v.i.* to run at the nose : to sniff : to snuffle : to whimper : to cry, as a child.—*v.t.* to utter with snivelling :—*pr.p.* **sniv′-elling ;** *pa.t.* and *pa.p.* **sniv′elled.**—*n.* **sniv′eller.** —*adjs.* **sniv′elling ; sniv′elly.** [O.E. *snofl*, mucus.]

snob, *snob*, *n.* (*coll.* ; *Scot.* **snab**) a shoemaker, shoemaker's apprentice, cobbler : (*Cambridge slang*)

a townsman : (*obs.*) a person of ordinary or low rank : (*obs.*) an ostentatious vulgarian : (*obs.*) a blackleg : one who makes himself ridiculous or odious by the value he sets on social standing or rank, by his fear of being ranked too low, and by his different behaviour towards different classes.— *n.* **snobb′ery**, snobbishness : snobbish behaviour. —*adj.* **snobb′ish.**—*adv.* **snobb′ishly.**—*ns.* **snobb′-ishness ; snobb′ism.**—*adj.* **snobb′y.**—*ns.* **snob′-ling**, a little snob ; **snoboc′racy**, snobs as a powerful class ; **snobog′rapher ; snobog′raphy**, the description of snobs and snobbery. [Orig. slang.]

snod, *snod*, *adj.* (*Scot.*) smooth, neat, trim, snug.— *v.t.* to trim, set in order (with *up*) :—*pa.t.* and *pa.p.* **snodd′ed, snodd′it.** [Poss. conn. with O.N. *snothinn*, bald.]

snoek. See **snook** (2).

snood, *snood*, *n.* a fillet for the hair, once in Scotland the badge of virginity : revived in the sense of a conspicuous net supporting the back-hair : the hair-line, gut, &c., by which a fish-hook is fixed to the line.—*v.t.* to bind, dress, fasten, with a snood.—*adj.* **snood′ed.** [O.E. *snōd.*]

snook, *snook*, snoke, *snōk*, (*Scot.*) **snowk**, *snowk*, *v.i.* to snuff or smell about : to lurk, prowl about. [Prob. Scand.]

snook, *snook*, *n.* one of several fishes—the cobia, a robalo, a garfish, or (in S. Africa and now elsewhere also **snoek**, *snook*) the barracouta (*Thyrsites Atun*). [Du. *snoek*, pike.]

snook, *snook*, *n.* the gesture of putting the thumb to the nose.—Also **snooks.—to cock a snook**, to make that gesture. [Origin obscure.]

snooker, *snook′ər*, *n.* a variety of the game of pool.— *v.t.* to render a direct stroke impossible for : to get the better of, be too much for, to best, to vanquish : to upset.

snool, *snool*, *n.* (*Scot.*) one who submits tamely to wrong or oppression.—*v.t.* to keep in subjection : to snub.—*v.i.* to be tamely submissive. [Origin obscure.]

snoop, *snoop*, *v.i.* (*U.S. slang*) to go about sneakingly as if to pry or filch.—Also *n.*—*n.* **snoop′er**, a prier. [Du. *snoepen.*]

snooty. See **snouty.**

snooze, *snooz*, *v.i.* to doze.—*n.* a nap.—*n.* **snooz′er.** [Origin obscure ; perh. orig. slang.]

snoozle, *snoo′zl*, *v.i.* to nuzzle. – *v.t.* to thrust nuzzlingly. [Cf. **snooze, nuzzle.**]

snore, *snōr*, *v.i.* to breathe roughly and hoarsely in sleep with vibration of uvula and soft palate or of the vocal chords : to snort.—*v.t.* to pass in snoring : to render by snoring.—*n.* a noisy breathing of this kind.—*ns.* **snōr′er ; snōr′ing.** [Imit. ; cf. **snort.**]

snort, *snort*, *v.i.* to force the air with violence and noise through the nostrils, as horses : (*Shak.*) to snore.—*v.t.* to express by or utter with a snort : to force out, as by a snort.—*n.* an act or sound of snorting : a submarine that can stay long submerged.—*n.* **snort′er**, one who snorts : (*coll.*) anything characterised by extreme force, esp. a gale. —*n.* and *adj.* **snort′ing.**—*adv.* **snort′ingly.**—*n.* **snort′-mast**, a ventilator raised to allow a submarine to stay long under water.—*adj.* **snort′y**, snorting : (*coll.*) inclined to snort : contemptuous and ready to take offence. [Imit.]

snot, *snot*, *n.* mucus of the nose : a mean fellow.— *v.t.* to blow (the nose).—*v.i.* **snott′er**, to breathe through an obstruction in the nostrils : to sob, snuffle, blubber.—*n.* the wattles of a turkey-cock : (*Scot.*) snot.—*n.* **snott′ery**, snot, filthiness.—*adv.* **snott′ily.**—*n.* **snott′iness.**—*adjs.* **snott′y**, like, or foul with, snot : superciliously stand-offish, with nose in air ; **snott′y-nosed.** [O.E. *gesnot* ; *snȳtan*, to blow the nose ; cf. Du. *snot* ; allied to **snout.**]

snotter, *snot′ər*, *n.* the lower support of the sprit.

snotty, *snot′i*, *n.* (*coll.*) a midshipman.

snout, *snowt*, *n.* the projecting nose of a beast, as of a swine : any similar projection.—*v.t.* to furnish with a snout.—*adjs.* **snout′ed ; snout′y**, like a snout : snouted : (also **snoot′y**) haughtily supercilious. [M.E. *snūte*, prob. from unrecorded O.E. : cf. Sw. *snut* ; Ger. *schnauze*, Du. *snuit* ; also **snot.**]

snow, *snō*, *n.* atmospheric vapour frozen in crystalline form, whether in single crystals or aggregated in flakes: a snowfall: any similar substance, as carbonic acid snow (frozen carbon dioxide): a mass or expanse of snow: a winter: (*fig.*) anything white, as hair: a white-fleshed variety of apple: (*slang*) linen, esp. drying or bleaching: (*slang*) cocaine.—*adj.* of snow.—*v.i.* to shower snow: to fall as snow or like snow.—*v.t.* to shower like snow: to strew as with snow: (*fig.*) to whiten, whiten the hair of: (with *up*, *under*) to bury, block, shut in, overwhelm, with snow or as if with snow.—*n.* **snow'ball**, a ball made of snow pressed hard together: the guelder-rose: a round white pudding, cake, or sweetmeat: (ironically) a negro, chimney-sweep, &c.: something that grows like a snowball rolled in snow, esp. a distribution of begging letters, each recipient being asked to send out so many copies.—*v.t.* to throw snowballs at.—*v.i.* to throw snowballs.—*ns.* **snow'ball-tree**; **snow'-berry**, the white berry of an American shrub (Symphoricarpos) of the honeysuckle family: the shrub itself; **snow'-bird**, any finch of the N. American genus Junco, white underneath, familiar in winter: applied to various other birds that appear in winter.—*adj.* **snow'-blind**.—*ns.* **snow'-blind'ness**, amblyopia caused by the reflection of light from snow; **snow'-blink**, a reflection from fields of snow, like ice-blink; **snow'-boot**, a boot or overshoe for walking in snow.—*adj.* **snow'-bound**, shut in, prevented from travelling, by snow.—*ns.* **snow'-box**, a theatrical apparatus for representing a snowfall; **snow'-break**, a melting of snow; **snow'-broth**, melted or melting snow; **snow'-bunt'ing**, a black-and-white (in summer partly tawny) bunting of the Arctic regions, a winter visitor in Britain; **snow'cap**, a cap of snow as on the polar regions or a mountain-top—*adjs.* **snow'-capped**, **-capt**; **snow'-cold**, as cold as snow.—*ns.* **snow'drift**, a bank of snow drifted together by the wind; **snow'drop**, a drooping white flower of early spring, or the plant (*Galanthus nivalis*; fam. Amaryllidaceae) that bears it; **snow'-dropper**, (*slang*) a linen thief; **snow'drop-tree**, fringe-tree: silver-bell or calico-wood (Halesia), an American tree of the Styrax family, with white bell-shaped flowers.—*n.pl.* **snow'-eyes**, an Eskimo contrivance to prevent snow-blindness: a piece of wood with slits.—*n.* **snow'fall**, a quiet fall of snow: the amount falling in a given time.—*adj.* **snow'-fed**, begun or increased by melted snow, as a stream.—*ns.* **snow'-field**, a wide range of snow, esp. where permanent; **snow'-finch**, an Alpine bird like the snow-bunting; **snow'flake**, a feathery clump of snow crystals: a garden-plant (Leucojum) or its flower like a big snowdrop: (also **snow'fleck, -flick**) the snow-bunting; **snow'-flea**, a springtail; **snow'-fly**, a stone-fly or other insect found on snow.—*n.pl.* **snow'-goggles**, goggles to guard against snow-blindness: snow-eyes.—*ns.* **snow'-goose**, a white Arctic American goose; **snow'-guard**, a board to keep snow from sliding off a roof; **snow'-ice**, ice formed from freezing slush or compacted snow.—*adv.* **snow'ily**.—*ns.* **snow'iness**; **snow-in-summ'er**, a white-flowered garden mouse-ear chickweed.—*adj.* **snow'ish**, resembling snow.—*n.* **snow'leop'ard**, the ounce.—*adjs.* **snow'less**; **snow'-like**.—*ns.* **snow'line**, the limit of perpetual snow; **snow'-man'**, a great snowball made in human form: a (supposed) dweller in the snow; **snow'-plant**, a red Californian saprophyte of the winter-green family (Sarcodes) appearing among snow: the organism of red snow (see **red**); **snow'-plough**, an implement for clearing snow from roads and railways; **snow'scape**, a snowy landscape; **snow'-shoe**, a long, broad shoe for walking on snow: a ski.—*v.i.* to travel on snow-shoes.—*n.pl.* **snow'-spec'tacles**, spectacles worn as a protection against the glare of snow.—*ns.* **snow'-storm**; **snow'-water**, water from melted snow.—*adj.* **snow'-white**, as white as snow.—*n.* **snow'-wreath**, a snowdrift.—*adj.* **snow'y**, abounding or covered with snow: white, like snow: pure.—snowed under with, overwhelmed with rapid accumulation of; **snow-shoe rabbit**, a hare of

Canada and U.S., white in winter, brownish with white feet in summer; **snowed up**, blocked or isolated by snow; **snowy owl**, a great white owl of northern regions. [O.E. *snáw*; Ger. *schnee*, L. *nix*, *nivis*.]

snow, snō, *n.* a vessel like a brig, with a trysail-mast. [Du. *snaauw*.]

snub, snub, *v.t.* to rebuke: to take up, cut short, rebuff, in a humiliating or mortifying manner: to check: to bring to a sudden stop: to cut or break short: to make snub: (*pr.p.* **snubb'ing**; *pa.t.* and *pa.p.* **snubbed**).—*n.* an act of snubbing: a check: a snub-nose: (*Spens.*) snubbe) a stub, snag, knob.—*adj.* flat, broad, and turned up.—*n.* **snubb'er**, one who snubs: a device for stopping a rope: a shock-absorber.—*n.* and *adj.* **snubb'ing**. —*adv.* **snubb'ingly**.—*n.* **snubb'ing-post**, a post for passing a rope round, as to stop a boat or horse.—*adjs.* **snubb'ish**, **snubb'y**, inclined to snub or check: somewhat snub.—*n.* **snub'-nose**, a short turned-up nose.—*adj.* **snub'-nosed**. [O.N. *snubba*, to chide, snub.]

snudge, snuj, *v.i.* (*obs.*) to be snug and quiet.

snudge, snuj, *v.i.* to save in a miserly way.—*n.* a mean stingy fellow.

snuff, snuf, *v.i.* to draw in air violently and noisily through the nose: to sniff: to smell at anything doubtfully: to take snuff.—*v.t.* to draw into the nose: to smell, to examine, suspect, or detect by smelling.—*n.* a powdered preparation of tobacco or other substance for snuffing: a pinch of snuff or act of snuffing: a sniff: resentment, huff.—*ns.* **snuff'box**, a box for snuff (snuff'box bean, the cacoon); **snuff'-colour, -brown**, a dark brown.—*adj.* **snuff'-coloured**.—*ns.* **snuff'-dipper**; **snuff'-dipping**, the Southern U.S. habit of rubbing the gums and teeth with a wet stick dipped in snuff; **snuff'er**, one who snuffs; **snuff'iness**.—*n.* and *adj.* **snuff'ing**.—*ns.* **snuff'-mill**, a factory or a hand-mill for grinding tobacco into snuff: a snuff-mull; **snuff'-mull**, a snuffbox (see **mill**); **snuff'-paper**, (Scott) contemptuous) bank-notes; **snuff'-spoon**, a spoon for taking snuff from a snuffbox; **snuff'-taker**; **snuff'-taking**.—*adj.* **snuff'y**, like, smelling of, soiled with, or showing traces of, snuff: touchy, huffy.—take it in snuff, (*Shak.*) to take offence; up to snuff, knowing, not likely to be taken in. [Du. *snuffen*; Ger. *schnaufen*, to snuff.]

snuff, snuf, *n.* a sooty ill-smelling knob on a wick: a worthless or offensive residue: a heeltap.—*v.t.* to remove the snuff from: to make brighter: to put out as with snuffers (with *out*).—*ns.* **snuff'-dish**, a dish or tray for candle snuffs; **snuff'er**, one who removes candle snuffs: (in *pl.*) an instrument like scissors for the purpose. [M.E. *snoffe*; connexion with foregoing and with L.G. *snuppen*, Ger. *schnappen*, is obscure.]

snuffle, snuf'l, *v.i.* to breathe hard or in an obstructed manner through the nose: to sniff: to speak through the nose.—*v.t.* to sniff: to say or utter nasally.—*n.* an act or sound of snuffling: a snuffling tone: cant: (in *pl.*) an obstructed condition of the nose.—*n.* **snuff'ler**.—*n.* and *adj.* **snuffling** (*snuf'ling*, *snuf'l-ing*). [Freq. of **snuff**; cf. **snivel**, and Du. *snuffelen*, Ger. *schnüffeln*.]

snug, snug, *adj.* lying close and warm: comfortable: sheltered: not exposed to view or notice: in good order: compact: fitting close.—*v.i.* to lie close.—*v.t.* to make snug: to stow away snugly—*pr.p.* **snugg'ing**; *pa.t.* and *pa.p.* **snugged**.—*n.* **snugg'ery**, a snug room or place, esp. a bar-parlour.—*v.i.* **snugg'le**, to nestle.—*v.t.* to hug close: to wrap close.—*adv.* **snug'ly**.—*n.* **snug'ness**. [Origin obscure.]

snush, snush, *n.* (*obs.*) snuff.—*v.t.* and *v.i.* (*obs.*) to snuff. [Poss. imit.; cf. **sneesh**, Dan. and Sw. *snus*.]

snuzzle, snuz'l, *v.i.* (*prov.*) to grub or root: to rub or poke and sniff: to nuzzle. [Cf. **nuzzle**, **snoozle**.]

so, sō, *adv.* merging in *conj.* or *interj.* in this, that, or such manner, degree, or condition: to such an extent: likewise: accordingly: well: therefore: in due course, thereupon, thereafter: as: soever: thus: for like reason: in a high degree: as has been stated : provided : in case : (coll.) in order : be it : that will do : very good.—n. **so'-and-so**, his or that person or thing : such-and-such a person or thing.—adj. **so'-called**, styled thus—usu. implying doubt or denial.—**and so forth**, **and so on**, and more of the same or the like : and the rest of it ; **or so**, or thereabouts ; **quite so**, just as you have said, exactly ; **so as**, in such a manner as or that : (coll.) in order (with to) : if only, on condition that ; **so far (forth)**, to that, or such an, extent, degree, or point ; **so many**, such-and-such a number of ; **so much**, such-and-such an amount : in such a degree : to such an extent : such an amount (of) : that amount of : an equal amount ; **so much as**, as much as : even ; **so much for**, that disposes of : that is the end of : no more of ; **so so** (see **so-so**) ; **so that**, with the purpose that : with the result that : if only ; **so then**, thus then it is, therefore ; **so to say**, or **speak**, if one may use that expression. [O.E. swá ; O.N. svá, Goth. swa, Ger. so.]

soh, sō. See **sol** (2).

soak, sōk, v.t. to steep in a liquid : to drench : to saturate : to draw through the pores : (U.S.) to bathe thoroughly : (slang) to beat, pummel, give it hot : (slang) to overcharge.—v.i. to be steeped in a liquid : to pass through pores : to drink to excess, to guzzle : to soften by heating : (pa.p. **soaked**, rarely **soak'en**).—n. process or act of soaking : a drenching : a marshy place : a hard drinker, a carouse.—ns. **soak'age**, soaking : liquid that has percolated ; **soak'away**, a depression into which water percolates ; **soak'er**.—n. and adj. **soak'ing**.—adv. **soak'ingly**. [O.E. socian, a weak vb. related to súcan, to suck.]

soap, sōp, n. an alkaline salt of a higher fatty acid : esp. such a compound of sodium (hard soap) or potassium (soft soap), used in washing : (slang) smooth words, flattery : (U.S. slang) money, esp. used for bribery and other secret political purposes.—v.t. to rub with soap : to flatter.—ns. **soap'-ball**, soap made into a ball, often with starch, as an emollient ; **soap'-bark**, a S. American rosaceous tree (Quillaja Saponaria), or its bark, used as soap ; **soap'berry**, the fruit of Sapindus Saponaria, or other species, used as soap, or the S. American tree yielding it ; **soap'-boiler**, a maker of soap ; **soap'-boiling** ; **soap'box**, a box for packing soap : a wayside orator's improvised platform ; **soap'-bubb'le**, a globe of air enclosed in a film of soap-suds ; **soap'-dish**.—adv. **soap'ily**.—n. **soap'iness**.—adj. **soap'less**.—ns. **soap'-root**, species of Gypsophila, Saponaria, and other plants whose roots can be used as soap ; **soap'-stone**, steatite, or French chalk, a compact kind of talc with soapy feel.—n.pl. **soap'-suds**, soapy water, esp. when frothy.—ns. **soap'-test**, a test for determining hardness of water by amount of standard soap solution required to make a lather ; **soap'-tree**, the soap-bark tree, the soapberry tree, or other yielding saponin ; **soap'-work(s)** ; **soap'wort**, a tall herb (Saponaria officinalis, or other species) of the pink family, whose roots and leaves contain saponin.—adj. **soap'y.—soap opera**, (U.S.) a daytime radio serial. [O.E. sápe ; Du. zeep, Ger. seife.]

soar, sōr, v.i. to mount high in the air : to fly aloft : to rise to a great height : to glide or skim high in the air : to glide in a rising current.—v.t. to reach, traverse, or accomplish in upward flight.—n. and adj. **soar'ing**.—adv. **soar'ingly**. [Fr. essorer, to expose to air—L. ex, out, aura, air.]

soar(e). See **sore** (2).

sob, sob, v.i. to catch the breath convulsively in distress or other emotion : to make a similar sound.—v.t. to utter with sobs : to bring by sobbing : (pr.p. **sobb'ing** ; pa.t. and pa.p. **sobbed**).—n. a convulsive catch of the breath : any similar sound.—n. and adj. **sobb'ing**.—adv. **sobb'ingly**.—n. **sob'-stuff**, (U.S.) cheap and extravagant pathos, to stir tears : maudlin films or scenes. [Imit.]

sobeit, sō-bē'it, conj. provided. [so be it.]

sober, sō'bər, adj. not drunk : temperate, esp. in use of intoxicants : moderate : restrained : without

excess or extravagance : serious : sedate : quiet in colour : sombre : (obs.) sane, rational : (Scot.) poor, feeble.—v.t. to make sober.—v.i. to become sober.—adj. **so'ber-blood'ed**, staid.—v.t. **so'ber-ise**, to make sober.—adv. **so'berly**.—adj. **so'ber-mind'ed**.—ns. **so'ber-mind'edness**, the state of being sober-minded : freedom from inordinate passion : calmness ; **so'berness** ; **so'bersides**, a sedate and solemn person.—adj. **so'ber-suit'ed**, dressed in sad-coloured clothes.—n. **sobriety** (sō-or sə-brī'i-ti), state or habit of being sober : calmness : gravity. [Fr. sobre—L. sōbrius—sē-, apart, not, ēbrius, drunk.]

sobole, sō'bōl, **soboles**, sob'ō-lēz, n. (bot.) a creeping underground stem producing roots and buds.—adj. **sobolif'erous**, having soboles. [L. sobolēs, subolēs, a shoot—sub, under, and the root of alĕre, to nourish, sustain.]

Sobranje, sō-brän'ye, n. the national assembly of Bulgaria.—Also **Sobran'ye**. [Bulg.]

sobriquet, sō'brē-kā, n. a nickname.—Also **soubriquet** (sōō'). [Fr. sobriquet, earlier soubriquet.]

soc, sok, n. (law) the right of holding a local court.—ns. **soc'age**, **socc'age**, tenure of lands by service fixed and determinate in quality ; **soc'ager**, **soc'man**, **sōke'man**, a tenant by socage ; **soke** (sōk), soc : a district under a particular jurisdiction ; **soke'manry**, tenure by socage ; **sōk'en**, a district under a particular jurisdiction. [O.E. sócn, inquiry, jurisdiction.]

so-called, sō'-kawld, adj. See under **so**.

soccer, sok'ər, n. (slang) association football.

sociable, sō'shə-bl, adj. inclined to society : companionable : favourable to social intercourse.—n. a four-wheeled open carriage with seats facing : a seat, tricycle, aeroplane, &c., for two persons side by side : (U.S.) an informal party or social church meeting.—ns. **sociabil'ity**, **so'ciableness**.—adv. **so'ciably.—adj. social** (sō'shl), pertaining to society or companionship : consisting in mutual converse : pertaining to fashionable circles : associated : growing or living in communities or societies : gregarious : sympathetic : convivial.—n. **socialisa'tion**.—v.t. **so'cialise**, to render social : to put on a socialistic footing.—ns. **so'cialism**, a theory, principle, or scheme of social organisation which places the means of production and distribution in the hands of the community, substituting association for competition ; **so'cialist**, an adherent of socialism.—Also adj.—adj. **social-ist'ic**.—ns. **so'cialite**, (coll.) one who has a place in fashionable society ; **sociality** (sō-shi-al'i-ti), the quality or fact of being social : social relations, association, or intercourse : sociability : a social function or formality. — adv. **so'cially. — ns. so'cialness** ; **so'ciate** (-shi-āt ; arch.), an associate.—Also adj.—adjs. **so'ciative**, expressing association ; **societarian** (sə-sī-i-tā'ri-ən), of or pertaining to society or fashionable society : Fourieristic : socialist.—Also n.—adj. **soci'etary** (-tər-i).—ns. **soci'ety**, fellowship, companionship : company : association : a community : the body of mankind, the fashionable world generally : a corporate body : any organised association.—adj. of fashionable society.—**socio-**, in composition, (generally of hybrids) social.—adj. **sociological** (sō-si- or sō-shi-ə-loj'i-kl).—ns. **sociol'ogist** ; **sociol'ogy**, the science of human society.—**social evil**, any evil, such as intemperance, that affects society, esp. prostitution ; **socialism of the chair**, professorial socialism, the doctrines of a school of political economists (c. 1872) in Germany whose aim was mainly to better the condition of the working-classes by factory-acts, savings-banks, insurances against sickness and old age, &c. ; **social science**, sociology ; **social service**, welfare work ; **Social War**, the war (90-88 B.C.) of Rome's Italian allies (Socii) against Rome for admission to Roman citizenship ; **social whale**, the ca'ing whale ; **the Societies**, the Cameronians organised from 1681 for maintenance of Presbyterianism. [L. socius, a companion.]

Socinian, sō-sin'i-ən, adj. pertaining to, or following, Laelius (1525-62) and Faustus (1539-1604) Socinus, uncle and nephew, Italian Unitarians.—

Neutral vowels in unaccented syllables : el'ə-mənt, in'fənt, ran'dəm

Also *n.*—*v.t.* and *v.i.* **Socin'ianise.**—*n.* **Socin'-ianism.**

sock, *sok*, *n.* (*obs.* except *hist.* and allusively) a light shoe, worn by Roman actors of comedy: now, a short stocking.—*n.* **sock'-suspender.**—**pull up one's socks**, to brace oneself for doing better. [O.E. *socc*—L. *soccus*.]

sock, *sok*, *n.* a ploughshare. [O.Fr. *soc*—Celt., Bret. *souc'h*, Gael. *soc*.]

sock, *sok*, *v.t.* (*prov.* and *slang*) to thrust hard: to strike hard: to drub: to give (with *it*, or *one*, i.e. a drubbing, or one blow).—*n.pl.* **socks**, a beating.

sockdologer, *sok-dol'ə-jər*, also **soc-**, **sog-**, **slock-**, **-dolager**, **-doliger**, *n.* (*Amer. slang*) a conclusive argument: a hard or decisive blow: anything very big, a whopper. [Cf. foregoing; perh. reminiscent of **doxology** as the closing act of a service.]

socker. Same as soccer.

socket, *sok'it*, *n.* a hollow into which something is inserted, as the receptacle of the eye, of a bone, a tooth, the shaft of an iron golf-club: the hollow of a candlestick: a stroke with the socket of a golf-club.—*v.t.* to provide with or place in a socket: to strike with the socket:—*pr.p.* **sock'eting**; *pa.t.* and *pa.p.* **sock'eted.**—*adj.* **sock'eted.** [O.Fr. *soket*, dim. of *soc*; see **sock** (2).]

sockeye, *sok'ī*, *n.* the blueback salmon. [Amer. Ind. *sukai*, the fish of fishes, the native name on the Fraser River.]

socle, *sō'kl*, *sok'l*, *n.* (*archit.*) a plain face or plinth at the foot of a wall, column, &c. [Fr.,—It. *zoccolo*—L. *socculus*, dim. of *soccus*, a shoe.]

Socratic, **-al**, *sō-krat'ik*, *-i-kl*, *adjs.* pertaining to *Socrates*, the celebrated Greek philosopher (*d.* 399 B.C.), to his philosophy, or to his method of teaching, by a series of simple questions revealing to his interlocutors their own ignorance.—*n.* **Socrat'ic**, a follower of Socrates.—*adv.* **Socrat'ically.**—*v.i.* **Socratise** (*sok'*, *sōk'rə-tīz*), to practise the Socratic method.

sod, *sod*, *n.* a turf, usu. one cut in rectangular shape: sward.—*adj.* of sod.—*v.t.* to cover with sod.—*adj.* **sodd'y**, covered with sod: turfy. [L.G. *sode*; Ger. *sode*.]

sod, *sod*. See seethe.

soda, *sō'dä*, *n.* sodium oxide (Na₂O): sodium hydroxide (*caustic soda*): sodium carbonate, the soda of commerce (in powder form, anhydrous, *soda-ash*; in crystals, with water of crystallisation, *washing-soda*): sodium bicarbonate (*baking-soda*): (*coll.*) soda-water.—*adj.* **so'da**, of or containing soda or sodium.—*n.* **so'da-fountain**, apparatus for supplying, counter for serving, soda-water, &c.—*adj.* **sodaic** (*sō-dā'ik*), containing, pertaining to, soda.—*ns.* **so'da-lake'**, a lake containing and depositing much sodium salt; **so'da-lime**, a mixture of caustic soda and quicklime; **so'dalite**, a cubic mineral consisting of sodium aluminium silicate with chlorine; **so'damide** (*-mīd*), a compound (NaNH₂) formed when ammonia gas is passed over hot sodium; **so'da-scone**, a scone made with baking-soda; **so'da-wa'ter**, water (now commonly without sodium bicarbonate) charged with carbon dioxide.—*adj.* **so'dic.**—*n.* **so'dium**, a bluish-white alkaline metal (Na; at. numb. 11), the base of soda. [It. and L.L. *soda*; origin doubtful.]

sodain, **sodaine**, old spellings of sudden.

sodality, *sō-dal'i-ti*, *n.* a fellowship or fraternity. [L. *sodālitās*—*sodālis*, a comrade.]

sodden, *sod'n*, *pa.p.* of seethe.—*adj.* boiled: soaked thoroughly: boggy: doughy, not well baked: bloated, saturated with drink.—*v.t.* and *v.i.* to make or become sodden: to soak.—*n.* **sodd'en-ness.**—*adj.* **sodd'en-witt'ed**, (*Shak.*) heavy, stupid.

sodger. See soldier.

Sodom, *sod'əm*, *n.* one of the ' cities of the plain ' (see Gen. xviii., xix.): (*fig.*) any place of utter depravity.—*n.* Sodomite (*-īt*), an inhabitant of Sodom: **sodomite**, one who practises sodomy.—*adjs.* sodomitic (*-it'ik*), **-al.**—*adv.* sodomit'ically. —*n.* **sod'omy**, unnatural sexuality, imputed to the

inhabitants of Sodom.—**apple of Sodom** (se apple).

soever, *sō-ev'ər*, *adv.* generally used to extend render indefinite the sense of *who*, *what*, *whe how*, &c.

sofa, *sō'fä*, *n.* in the East, a raised portion of tl floor forming a bench: a long upholstered se with back and arms—formerly **sō'pha.**—*n.* **sō'fa bed**, a piece of furniture serving as a sofa by da a bed at night. [Ar. *suffah*.]

soffioni, *sof-fyō'nē*, *n.pl.* volcanic steam-holes. [It

soffit, *sof'it*, *n.* a ceiling, now generally restricted the ornamented under-side of a stair, entablatur archway, &c. [It. *soffitto*—L. *suffixus*, pa.p. *suffigēre*, to fasten beneath—*sub*, under, *figēre*, to fix

sofi, **sofism.** See sufi, sufism.

soft, *soft*, *sawft*, *adj.* easily yielding to pressure easily cut: (*min.*) easily scratched: malleable yielding: not rigorous enough: not loud: n glaring: diffused: weak in muscle or mind: o of training: of low penetrating power (of rays smooth: pleasing or soothing to the sense tender: mild: sympathetic: gentle: effeminat gently moving: easy: free from calcium an magnesium salts, as water: bituminous, of coa unsized, of paper: (*Scot.*) rainy: pronounce with a somewhat sibilant sound, not guttural explosive: voiced or sonant: of silk, freed fro natural gum: of drinks, non-alcoholic: apt fall in price.—*n.* a softy, a fool.—*adv.* softl gently: quietly.—*v.t.* (*Spens.*) to soften.—*inte* (also **soft you**) hold: not so fast.—*adjs.* **soft billed**; **soft'-bod'ied.**—*v.t.* **soft'-boil'.**—*ad soft'-boiled**, boiled not long enough to be qu solid; **soft'-con'scienc'd**, (*Shak.*) having a n very rigorous conscience.—*v.t.* **soften** (*sof'n*), make soft or softer: to mitigate: to tone dow make less glaring or smoother.—*v.i.* to grow s or softer.—*ns.* **softener** (*sof'nər*); **softeni** (*sof'ning*).—*adjs.* **soft'-finned**, without fin-spine **soft'-foot'ed**, softly treading.—*n.pl.* **soft'-good cloth**, and cloth articles, as opp. to *hardware*, &c.— *ns.* **soft'-grass**, a worthless grass (*Holcus mollis* other species) akin to oats; **soft'head**, a simpleto —*adjs.* **soft'-head'ed**; **soft'-heart'ed**, tende hearted; **soft'ish**, rather soft.—*n.* **soft'ling**, weakling: an effeminate person: a soft object.— *adv.* **soft'ly.**—*adj.* (*Spens.*) soft: slack in ente prise.—*adj.* **soft'ly-spright'ed**, (*Shak.*) tam spirited.—*n.* **soft'ness.**—*adjs.* **soft'-nosed**, of bullet, with a tip that expands on striking; **soft paste**, of porcelain, made of a paste of vario kinds requiring less heat in firing than china-cla —*v.t.* and *v.i.* **soft'-ped'al**, to play with the s pedal down: (*slang*) to subdue, tone down.— *v.t.* **soft'-saw'der**, (*U.S.*) to flatter, blarney.— flattery.—*adjs.* **soft'-shell**, **-ed**, having a s shell: moderate in policy or principles.—*n.* **soft shell**, a soft-shell crab, clam, or river-turtl a moderate.—*adjs.* **soft'-slow**, (*Shak.*) soft a slow.—*v.t.* **soft'-soap**, to rub or cover wi soft soap: to flatter for some end.—*adj.* **soft spo'ken**, having a mild or gentle voice: affabl suave: plausible in speech.—*ns.* **soft'wood**, timb of a conifer (also *adj.*); **sof'ty**, a silly person, weak fool.—**soft meat**, regurgitated food given pigeons to their young; **soft palate**, the ba part of the palate; **soft pedal**, a pedal for reduci tone in the piano, esp. by causing the hammer strike only one string (*una corda*); **soft soa** potash soap: flattery: blarney; **soft thing**, easy task: a snug job. [O.E. *sófte*, *séfte*; D *zacht*, Ger. *sanft*.]

softa, *sof'tä*, *n.* a Moslem theological stude attached to a mosque. [Turk. *sôfta*.]

sog, *sog*, *n.* a soft wet place.—*v.t.* and *v.i.* to so —*adj.* **sogged.**—*n.* and *adj.* **sogg'ing.**—*a* **sogg'y**, soaked: boggy: sodden: soppy: sultr spiritless. [Origin obscure.]

soger. See soldier.

soh. See sol (2).

so-ho, *sō-hō'*, *interj.* (*Shak.*) a form of call from distance, a sportsman's halloo. [A.Fr.]

soi-disant, *swä-dē-zän*, *adj.* self-styled, pretende would-be. [Fr.]

il, *soil, n.* the ground : the mould in which plants row : the earth which nourishes plants : country. *—adjs.* **soil′-bound**, attached to the soil ; **soiled**, aving soil. [O.Fr. *soel, suel, sueil*—L. *solum*, round.]

il, *soil, n.* (*obs.*) a wallowing-place : a watery lace where a hunted animal takes refuge : dirt : ung : filth : sewage : a spot or stain.—*v.t.* to ake dirty : to stain : to manure.—*v.i.* to take a oil : to tarnish.—*adj.* **soiled.**—*n.* **soil′iness**, *are*) stain : foulness.—*n.* and *adj.* **soil′ing.**— *dj.* **soil′less**, destitute of soil.—*ns.* **soil′-pipe**, an pright discharge-pipe which receives the general efuse from water-closets, &c., in a building ; **oil′ure**, stain : pollution. — *adj.* **soil′y.** — **soil nechanics**, a branch of civil engineering con erned with the ability of different soils to with and the use to which they are being put. [O.Fr. *il, souil* (Fr. *souille*), wallowing-place.]

l, *soil, v.t.* to feed on fresh-cut green food : to urge by so doing : to fatten.—*adj.* **soiled** (*Shak.* oyled). [O.Fr. *saouler*—*saol, saoul*—L. *satullus —satur*, full ; or from soil (2).]

rée, *swär′ā, swor′ā, n.* an evening party : an vening social meeting with tea, &c. [Fr.,—*soir*, *vening*—L. *sērus*, late.]

a. See **soy.**

journ, *sō′, so′, su′jərn*, sometimes *-jərn′, v.t.* to tay for a day : to dwell for a time.—*n.* a temporary esidence.—*ns.* **so′journer** ; **so′journing, so′- ournment.** [O.Fr. *sojourner*—L. *sub*, under, *iurnus*, of a day—*diēs*, a day.]

ke, sokeman, soken. See under **soc.**

kol, *sō′kol, n.* a Czech gymnastic club. [Czech, *lcon*, from their badge.]

l, *sol, n.* the sun personified, Helios or Phoebus : *alch.*) gold : (*her.*) the tincture or : **sol** (*sōl*), the eruvian monetary unit (one-tenth of a libra), and ormerly a coin bearing a sun with rays :—*pl.* **oles** (*sō′lās*), **sols** (*sōlz*).—*adj.* **solar**, &c. (see elow). [L. *sōl*, sun.]

l, *sol, n.* the fifth note of the scale in sol-fa otation.—Also **so, soh** (*sō*). [See **Aretinian.**]

l, *sol, n.* a colloidal suspension in a liquid : a olution of a difficulty (see **ob**).—*n.* **solā′tion**, quefaction of a gel. [For **solution.**]

l, *sol, n.* an old French coin, one-twentieth of a vre. [O.Fr. (now *sou*)—L. *solidus*, solid.]

la, *sō-lā′, interj.* a cry to a person at a distance.

la, *sō′lā, n.* the hat-plant or spongewood, an ndian papilionaceous plant (Aeschynomene) : its ithlike stems.—*adj.* of sola.—**sola** (often **solar**) **at, helmet**, a topi of sola.—Also **sō′lah**, (*corr.*) l′ar. [Hind. *sholā*.]

la. See **solus.**

lace, *sol′is, -əs, n.* consolation, comfort in distress : leasure, amusement : a source of comfort or leasure.—*v.t.* to comfort in distress : to console : allay.—*v.i.* to take comfort.—*n.* **sol′acement.** *—adj.* **solacious** (*-ā′shəs*; *arch.*), giving solace.).Fr. *solas*—L. *sōlātium*—*sōlāri, -ātus*, to comfort distress.]

lan, *sō′lan, n.* the gannet.—Also **soland, solan oose.** [O.N. *súla*.]

lander, *sō-lan′dər, n.* a box in the form of a book, nvented by the Swedish botanist Daniel *Solander* 736–82).

lano, *sō-lä′nō, n.* a hot south-east wind in Spain. Sp.,—L. *sōlānus* (*ventus*), the east wind—*sōl*, the un.]

lanum, *sō-lā′nəm, n.* the potato and night ade genus, giving name to the family **Solanaceae** *lə-nā′si-ē*). — *adj.* **solanā′ceous.** — *n.* **solanine** *ol′-, sōl′ə-nēn*), a glucoside got from potato sprouts, c. [L. *sōlānum*, nightshade.]

ar, *sō′lər, adj.* of, from, like, or pertaining to the un : measured by the sun : influenced by the un : with branches radiating like the sun's rays.— (also **sō′ler, sollar, soller**, *sol′ər* ; O.E. *solor*, O.Fr. *soler*; *arch.*) an upper room : a garret : landing between ladders in a mine.—*n.* **sōlarisā′- on**, the act, process, or effect of solarising : (*bot.*) *hot.*) reversal of image by over-exposure : (*bot.*) terruption of photosynthesis by long exposure bright light.—*v.t.* **sō′larise**, to expose to sun

light or affect by such exposure, esp. excessive or injurious exposure.—*v.i.* to be so affected.—*ns.* **sō′larism**, excessive use of solar myths in the explanation of mythology ; **sō′larist**, one addicted to solarism ; **solā′rium**, a sun-dial : a place for sunning or sun-bathing.—**solar day, time, year** (see **day, time, year**) ; **solar microscope**, an apparatus for projecting an enlarged image ; **solar myth**, a sun-myth, or a myth allegorising the course of the sun ; **solar plexus**, (*anat.*) a network of nerves behind the stomach (so called from its radiating nerves) ; **solar prominences**, large prominent or protruding parts of the great volumes of heated gas surrounding the sun ; **solar salt**, salt got by evaporation of sea-water by the sun ; **solar system**, the sun with its attendant bodies —major and minor planets, meteors, comets, satellites. [L. *sōlāris*, solar, *sōlārium*, a sun-dial— *sōl*, the sun.]

solar, *sō′lər.* See **sola** (2).

solatium, *sō-lā′shi-əm, n.* compensation for dis appointment, inconvenience, wounded feelings. [L. *sōlātium.*]

sold, *sōld, pa.t.* and *pa.p.* of **sell.**

sold, *sōld, n.* (*Spens.*) pay, remuneration.—Also **solde** (*Meredith*). [Fr. *solde*—L. *solidus*, a piece of money.]

soldado, *sōl-dä′dō, n.* a soldier. [Sp.]

soldan, *sol′dən, n.* (*arch.*) a sultan, esp. of Egypt. [Fr. ; see **sultan.**]

soldatesque, *sol-də-tesk′, adj.* soldierlike. [Fr.,— *soldat*, a soldier.]

solder, *sod′ər*, also *sol′, saw′, sō′, n.* a fusible alloy for uniting metals.—*v.t.* to make fast with solder : to join : to mend, patch up.—*v.i.* to adhere.—*ns.* **sol′derer** ; **sol′dering** ; **sol′dering-bolt, -iron**, a tool with pointed or wedge-shaped copper bit for use in soldering. [O.Fr. *soudre, souldure*—*souder, soulder*, to consolidate—L. *solidāre*, to make solid.]

soldier, *sōl′jər*, formerly *sō′jər, obs.* or *dial.* **soger**, *sō′jər*, **sodger**, *sog′ər, n.* a man engaged in military service : a private : a man of military skill : (*naut.*) a skirker : an ant, or a white ant, of a specialised fighting caste : a scarlet, pugnacious, or armoured animal of various kinds (beetle, fish, &c.) : (*slang*) a red herring : the ribwort plantain (used by children for a game of soldiers) : a brick set upright in a wall.—*v.i.* to serve as a soldier : to shirk.—*ns.* **sol′dier-crab**, a hermit-crab ; **sol′diering.**—*adj.* **sol′dierlike**, having the appearance of a soldier : soldierly.—*adv.* in the manner of a soldier.—*n.* **sol′dierliness.** — *adj.* **sol′dierly**, befitting a soldier : having the qualities of or befitting a soldier.—*ns.* **sol′diership**, state or quality of being a soldier : military qualities : martial skill ; **sol′diery**, soldiers collectively : a military body or class : soldiership.—**come the old soldier over one**, to impose on one ; **old soldier**, an empty bottle : an experienced person who knows how to make himself comfortable ; **soldier of fortune**, one ready to serve anywhere for pay or his own advancement ; **soldier's heart**, heart symptoms (in various diseases) attributable to soldiering or detected in soldiers. [O.Fr. *soldier*—L. *solidus*, a piece of money, the pay of a soldier.]

soldo, *sol′dō, n.* an Italian coin, one-twentieth of the lira :—*pl.* **sol′di** (*-dē*). [It.,—L. *solidus.*]

sole, *sōl, n.* the under-side of the foot : the bottom of a boot or shoe : the under-surface of a golf club head : the floor of an oven or furnace : (now *dial.*) a sill : the bottom, under-structure, floor, or under-surface of various things : (*geol.*) a thrust plane.—*v.t.* to put a sole on. [O.E. and O.Fr. *sole*—L. *solea*—*solum*, bottom.]

sole, *sōl, n.* an elliptical flat-fish (Solea) with small twisted mouth and teeth on the under-side only.— *n.* **solenette** (*sōl-net′, sōl-ə-net′*), a small species of sole.—**lemon sole** (see **lemon**, 2). [Fr. *sole*— L. *solea.*]

sole, *sōl, adj.* alone : only : without husband or wife : without another : solitary : consisting of one person : exclusive : uniform.—*advs.* **sole** (*Spens.*), alone : only : singly.—*n.* **sole′ness.** [Fr., —L. *sōlus*, alone.]

sole, *sōl* (*Shak.*), *dial.* **sowl, sowle, soole, sowl**,

sōl, sool, v.t. to pull (by the ears). [Origin obscure.]
solecism, *sol'i-sizm, n.* a breach of syntax : any
absurdity, impropriety, or incongruity.—*v.i.* to com-
ecise, to commit solecisms.—*n.* **sol'ecist.**—*adjs.*
solecist'ic, -al.—*adv.* **solecist'ically.** [Gr. *soloi-
kismos,* said to come from the corruption of the
Attic dialect among the Athenian colonists (*oikizein,*
to colonise) of *Soloi* in Cilicia.]
solein, an old form (*Spens.*) of **sullen.**
solemn, *sol'əm, adj.* attended with or marked by
special (esp. religious) ceremonies, pomp, or
gravity : attended with an appeal to God, as an
oath : grave : in serious earnestness : with formal
dignity : awed : awe-inspiring : stately : pompous : glum : solemn.—*n.* **solemnisation** (*sol-
əm-nī-zā'shən*).—*v.t.* **sol'emnise** (*-nīz*), to perform religiously or solemnly : to celebrate with
rites : to make solemn.—*ns.* **sol'emniser ; solemnity** (*-lem'ni-ti*), a solemn ceremony : high
seriousness: affected gravity; **solemnize'**, (*Spens.*)
solemnisation.—*adv.* **sol'emnly.**—*n.* **sol'emnness**
(also **sol'emness**).—**solemn mass,** high mass.
[O.Fr. *solempne, solemne* (Fr. *solennel*)—L. *sollemnis,
sōlennis,* doubtfully referred to *sollus,* all, every,
annus, a year.]
Solen, *sō'lən, n.* the razor-fish genus of lamellibranch molluscs.—*n.* **sō'lenoid,** a cylindrical coil
of wire, acting as a magnet when an electric current
passes through it.—*adj.* **solenoid'al.**—*adv.* **solenoid'ally.** [Gr. *sōlēn,* a pipe.]
soler. See **solar** (*n.*).
soleus, *sō'li-əs, n.* the flat muscle of the leg beneath
the gastrocnemius. [Mod. L.,—L. *soles,* sole.]
sol-fa, *sol'fā', n.* (*mus.*) a system of syllables (*do* or *ut,
re, mi, fa, sol* or *so, la, si* or *ti*) representing and sung
to the notes of the scale.—*adj.* belonging to the
system.—*v.t.* and *v.i.* to sing to sol-fa syllables :—
pr.p. **sol-faing** (*-fā'ing*) ; *pa.t.* and *pa.p.* **sol-faed,
-fa'd** (*-fād*).—*ns.* **sol-fa'ism,** singing by syllables :
solmisation ; **sol-fa'ist,** a teacher, practiser, or
advocate of solmisation ; **solfeggio** (*-fed'jō* ; It.),
an exercise in sol-fa syllables :—*pl.* **solfeggi**
(*-fed'jē*).—**tonic sol-fa** (see **tonic**). [sol (2) ; fa.]
solfatara, *sol-fä-tä'rä,* a volcanic vent emitting
only gases, esp. one emitting acid gases (hydrochloric acid and sulphur dioxide) :—*pl.* **solfata'ras.**
—*adj.* **solfata'ric.** [From the *Solfatara* (lit.
sulphur-mine, sulphur-hole) near Naples—It. *solfo,*
sulphur.]
solferino, *sol-fe-rē'nō, n.* the colour of rosaniline—
discovered soon after the battle of *Solferino* in
Italy (1859).
solicit, *sō-lis'it, v.t.* to disquiet : to incite : to allure :
to urge : to petition : to importune : to seek after :
to call for, require : to invite to immorality : (*obs.*)
to extract gently : to conduct, manage.—*v.i.* to
petition : to act as solicitor : (of prostitutes) to
make advances : (of beggars) to importune for
alms.—*n.* (*Shak.*) solicitation (another reading
solic'ity).—*ns.* **solic'itant,** one who solicits (also
adj.) ; **solicitā'tion,** a soliciting : earnest request :
invitation ; **solic'iting,** (*Shak.*) solicitation (also
adj.) ; **solic'itor,** one who asks earnestly : one
who is legally qualified to act for another in a court
of law (esp. formerly a court of equity) : a lawyer
who prepares deeds, manages cases, instructs
counsel in the superior courts, and acts as an
advocate in the inferior courts : (*U.S.*) a canvasser ;
Solic'itor-Gen'eral, in England, the law-officer of
the crown next in rank to the Attorney-General—in
Scotland, to the Lord-Advocate ; **solic'itorship.**
—*adj.* **solic'itous,** soliciting or earnestly asking or
desiring : very desirous : anxious : careful.—*adv.*
solic'itously.—*ns.* **solic'itousness, solic'itude,**
state of being solicitous : anxiety or uneasiness of
mind : trouble. [L. *sōlicitāre, sollicitāre—sō-,
sollicitus—sollus,* whole, *citus,* aroused—*ciēre,* to
cite.]
solid, *sol'id, adj.* resisting change of shape, having
the particles firmly cohering (opp. to *fluid*) : distinguished from *liquid* and *gaseous*) : hard : compact : full of matter : not hollow : strong : having
or pertaining to three dimensions : substantial :
worthy of credit : weighty : of uniform undivided
substance : financially sound, wealthy : unani-

mous : unbroken : unvaried.—*n.* a substance, bod
or figure that is solid : a solid mass or part.—*n
solidare (*sol'i-dār* ; *Shak.*), a small coin ; **sol
idarism** (*-də-rizm*), **sol'idarist,** an advocate
solidarity ; **solidarity** (*-dar'i-ti*), oneness of i
terests, aims, &c.—*adj.* **sol'idary** (*-dər-i*), mark
by solidarity : jointly responsible : joint a
several.—*v.t.* **sol'idate**, (*rare*) to consolidate.—
adjs. **sol'id-hoofed,** with uncloven hoofs ; **solid
fiable** (*sə-lid'i-fī-ə-bl*).—*n.* **solidificā'tion.**—*v
solid'ify, to make solid or compact.—*v.i.* to gro
solid :—*pr.p.* **solid'ifying** ; *pa.t.* and *pa.p.* **solid
ified.**—*adj.* **sol'idish.**—*ns.* **sol'idism,** the do
trine that refers all diseases to alterations of t
solid parts of the body ; **sol'idist,** a believer
solidism ; **solid'ity,** the state of being soli
fullness of matter : strength or firmness, moral
physical : soundness : volume : (*Shak.*) a sol
thing.—*adv.* **sol'idly.**—*ns.* **sol'idness ; sol'idus**
(*archit.*) the die of a pedestal : (*Scots law*) a co
plete sum ; **sol'idus,** a Roman gold coin introduc
by Constantine, later called the *bezant* : in t
Middle Ages, a silver coin of 12 denarii : a sign (
denoting the English shilling, representing the o
lengthened form of *s* (£, s. d. = *librae, solidi, dena
pounds, shillings, pence), used also for oth
purposes, as in writing fractions :—*pl.* **solidi** (-
—**solid colour,** a colour covering the whole
an object : a uniform colour ; **solid matte**
(*print.*) matter set without leads between the line
solid with, (*U.S.*) on a firm footing with. [
solidus, -a, -um, solid.)
solidungulate, *sol-id-ung'gū-lāt, adj.* with unclov
hoofs.—Also **solidung'ulous.** [L. *solidus,* sol
ungula, a hoof.]
solifidian, *sō-li-fid'i-ən, n.* one who holds that fa
alone is necessary for justification.—Also *adj.*—
solifid'ianism. [L. *sōlus,* only, *fidēs,* faith.]
solifluxion, solifluction, *sol-i-fluk'shən, n.* creep
soil down a slope. [L. *solum,* soil, *fluxiō, -ōnis,* flo
Solifugae, *sol-i-fū'jē, n.pl.* an order of spider-li
arachnids, with head and three-jointed tho
distinct. [See **solpuga** ; modified by popu
association with L. *sōl,* the sun, *fugēre,* to flee.]
soliloquy, *so-, sō-, sə-lil'ə-kwi, n.* a talking to on
self.—*v.i.* **solil'oquise,** to speak to oneself, to utt
a soliloquy. [L. *sōliloquium—sōlus,* alone, *loqui,
speak.]
soliped, *sol'i-ped, n.* an animal with uncloven hoo
—*adjs.* **sol'iped, solip'edous.** [L. *sōlus,* alo
pēs, pedis, a foot.]
solipsism, *sol'ip-sizm, n.* the theory that s
existence is the only certainty, absolute egoism
the extreme form of subjective idealism.—*n.* a
adj. **sol'ipsist**—*adj.* **solipsis'tic.** [L. *sōlus,* alo
ipse, self.]
solitaire, *sol-i-tār', n.* a recluse : a game played
one person with a board and balls : (*U.S.*) patie
(card game) : a diamond, &c., set by itself : (1
cent.) a large loose silk necktie : a gigantic flig
less pigeon (*Pezophaps solitarius*) of Rodrigu
extinct since the 18th cent. : an American or W
Indian fly-catching thrush.—*n.* **solitaire'-boa
a board with cups for playing solitaire. [Fr.,
next.]
solitary, *sol'i-tər-i, adj.* alone : single, separa
living alone, not social or gregarious : with
company : remote from society : retired, seclud
lonely : (*bot.*) growing singly.—*n.* one who li
alone : a hermit.—*n.* **solitarian** (*-tā'ri-ən*)
hermit.—*adv.* **sol'itarily.**—*n.* **sol'itariness.**
sōlitārius—sōlus, alone.]
solito, *sol'i-tō, adv.* (*mus.*) in the usual manner. [I
solitude, *sol'i-tūd, n.* solitariness : absence of co
pany : a lonely place or desert.—*n.* **solitūdinā'ri
—*adj.* **solitūd'inous.** [L. *sōlitūdō—sōlus.*]
solivagant, *sō-liv'ə-gənt, adj.* wandering alone
Also *n.* [L. *sōlus,* alone, *vagāns, -āntis,* wanderin
solive, *so-lēv', n.* a joist or beam of secondary i
portance. [Fr.,—L. *sublevāre,* to support.]
sollar. See **solar** (1).
solleret, *sol'ər-et, n.* a jointed steel shoe. [O.
dim. of *soler,* slipper.]
solmisation, *sol-mi-zā'shən, n.* sol-faing : a rec
of the notes of the gamut. [sol (2), mi.]

lo, *sō'lō, n.* a piece or passage for one voice or
instrument, accompanied or unaccompanied: any
performance, esp. an aeroplane flight, in which no
other participates: a motor-bicycle without side-
car: a card game (solo whist) based on whist, in
which various declarations are made and the
declarer may or may not have a partner: (*pl.*
sō'lōs, soli, *sō'lē*).—*adj.* performed, or for performance, as a solo: performing a solo: for one.—*adv.*
alone.—*v.i.* to fly solo.—*n.* sō'lŏist. [It.,—L.
olus, alone.]

olomon, *sol'ə-mən, n.* a person of unusual wisdom,
from *Solomon*, king of Israel (see I Kings iii. 5-15).
—*adjs.* Solomonian (*-mō'ni-ən*), Solomonic
(*-mon'ik*).—*n.* Sol'omon's-seal, any species of
Polygonatum, a genus of the lily family, with small
hanging greenish flowers (perh. from the scars on
the rootstock): a symbol formed of two triangles
interlaced or superposed, forming a six-pointed
star.

lon, *sō'lon, n.* a famous law-giver of Athens
(594 B.C.), one of the Seven Sages: a sage: a wiseacre: (*U.S.*) a Congressman.—*adj.* Solō'nian.

-long, *sō-long', interj.* (*coll.* or *slang*) good-bye.
Prob. so and long; poss. salaam.]

lpuga, *sol-pū'gä, n.* a genus of very venomous
Solifugae. [L. *solpūga, salpūga, solipūga, solipugna,*
a venomous animal supposed to be the same, a
word derived from Spain.]

lstice, *sol'stis, n.* the time when the sun reaches
its maximum distance from the equator (*summer
solstice* when it touches the tropic of Cancer, about
1st June; the *winter solstice* when it touches that
of Capricorn, about 21st December): the turning-
point then reached.—*adj.* solstitial (-*stish'l*), pertaining to, or happening at, a solstice, esp. at the
summer solstice. [Fr.,—L. *sōlstitium—sōl,* the
sun, *sistĕre, stătum,* to make to stand—*stāre.*]

luble, *sol'ū-bl, adj.* capable of being solved, dissolved, or resolved.—*ns.* solūbil'ity; sol'ūte, a
dissolved substance.—*adj.* (*sol'* or -*ūt'*) loose: free:
not adhering: dissolved.—*n.* solution (*səl-* or
ōl-ōō'shən, or -*ū'shən*), act of solving or dissolving:
condition of being dissolved: the preparation
resulting therefrom: the separating of parts:
abnormal separation: explanation: removal of
doubt: solving of a problem: the crisis of a disease: breach (as of continuity): a solution of
rubber.—*v.t.* to mend or cement with rubber
solution.—*adj.* solutional (-*ōō'* or -*ū'*).—*n.* solu'-
tionist, a solver (as of puzzles).—*adj.* sol'ūtive,
tending to dissolve: laxative.—solution of triangles, (*trig.*) finding the values of the remaining
sides and angles, some being given. [L. *solvĕre,*
olūtum, to loosen.]

lum, *sō'ləm, n.* ground, soil: a piece of ground.
[L. *sŏlum,* the ground.]

lus, *sō'ləs, adj.* alone, in dramatic directions—
fem. form, sō'la. [L. *sōlus,* alone.]

lutrean, Solutrian, *sol-(y)ōō'tri-ən,* or -*trē', adj.*
belonging to an upper Palaeolithic culture which
succeeded the Aurignacian and preceded the
Magdalenian. [*Solutré,* in Saône-et-Loire, where
objects of this culture have been found.]

lve, *solv, v.t.* to unbind: to dissolve: to settle:
to clear up or explain: to find an answer to or
way out of.—*n.* solvabil'ity.—*adj.* sol'vable,
capable of being solved: (*rare* or *obs.*) capable of
being paid, dissolved, or resolved: (*obs.*) solvent.
—*ns.* sol'vate, a definite combination of solute
and solvent; solvā'tion, association of the molecules of a solvent with solute ions or molecules; sol'vency.—*adj.* sol'vent, able to solve or
dissolve: able to pay all debts.—*n.* anything that
dissolves another.—*n.* sol'ver, one who solves.
[L. *solvĕre,* to loosen, prob. from *sē-, sĕ-,* aside, *luĕre,*
to loosen.]

ma, soma, *sō'mä, n.* a plant (perhaps an asclepiad,
Sarcostemma), or its intoxicating juice, used in
ancient Indian religious ceremonies, and personified as a god. [Sans. *soma* (Zend *haoma,* juice).]

ma, *sō'mä, n.* the body: the body of an animal
or plant excluding the germ-cells.—*adj.* somatic
(-*mat'ik*).—*adv.* somat'ically.—*ns.* so'matism
(-*mə-tizm*), materialism; so'matist (also *adj.*).—

adjs. somatogenic (*sō-mə-tō-jen'ik*), originating in
somatic cells; somatolog'ic, -al.—*ns.* somatol'-
ogy, the science of the properties of matter: the
science of the human body; so'matoplasm, protoplasm of the somatic cells; so'matopleure
(-*plōōr'; Gr. pleurā,* side), the outer body-wall or
the layer that gives rise to it; so'mite, a body-
segment.—*adjs.* somital (*sō'mi-tl*), somit'ic. [Gr.
sōma, body.]

sombre, *som'bər, adj.* dark and gloomy.—*v.t.* and
v.i. to make or become sombre.—*adv.* som'brely.
—*n.* som'breness.—*adj.* som'brous, sombre.
[Fr. *sombre* (cf. Sp. *sombra,* shade)—perh. L. *sub,*
under, *umbra,* a shade.]

sombrerite, *som-brā'rīt, n.* rock-guano. [*Sombrero*
in the West Indies.]

sombrero, *som-brā'rō, n.* a broad-brimmed hat.
[Sp., hat—*sombre,* shade.]

some, *sum, indef. pron.* (*obs.*) one, one or other: an
indefinite part of the whole number or quantity:
certain (undetermined) ones: (*U.S.*) a great deal:
(*U.S.*) a good deal more.—*adj.* one or other: in an
indefinite number or quantity: a little: not a
little: considerable: a certain: certain unspecified:
several: a few: in approximate number, length,
&c., more or less: (*coll.,* esp. *U.S.*) remarkable,
outstanding, of note.—*adv.* (*prov.*) somewhat, in
some degree, rather, a little: (*U.S.*) very much:
(*Shak.*) sometimes.—*n.* (or *pron.*) some'body,
some person: a person of importance:—*pl.*
some'bodies.—*advs.* some'deal (*arch.*), some'-
dele (Spens.), in some degree, somewhat; some'-
gate, (*Scot.*) somewhere, somehow; some'how,
in some way or other.—*ns.* (or *prons.*) some'one
(also some one), somebody; some'thing, a thing
undefined: a thing of some account: a portion.
—*adv.* in some degree.—*adj.* (*Shak.*) that is
something.—Also used as substitute for any word
(*n., adj., vb.*) or component of any word forgotten
or avoided.—*adv.* some'time, at a time not fixed:
at one time or other: formerly.—*adj.* former:
late.—*adv.* some'times, at times: now and then:
(*obs.*) sometime.—*adj.* (*Shak.*) sometime.—*advs.*
some'way, -ways, -wise, in some way: somehow.—*n.* some'what, an unfixed quantity or
degree: something.—*adv.* in some degree.—*advs.*
(all *rare* except somewhere) some'when, some
time or other; some'whence; some'where, in
or to some place; some'while, -s, sometimes;
some'whither; some'why.—some one else,
some other person; some one else's, some other
person's. [O.E. *sum;* Goth. *sums,* O.N. *sumr.*]

somersault, *sum'ər-sawlt, n.* a leap or other movement in which one turns heels over head.—*v.i.* to
turn a somersault.—Also som'erset. [O.Fr.
sombre saut (Fr. *soubresaut*)—L. *suprā,* over, *saltus,*
-*ūs,* a leap—*salīre,* to leap.]

somite. See under soma (2).

sommelier, *som'(ə-)lyā, n.* a butler: a wine waiter.
[Fr.]

Somnus, *som'nəs, n.* the god of sleep (L.; Gr.
Hypnos).—*n.* somnambulance (*som-nam'bū-ləns*;
L. *ambulāre,* to walk), sleep-walking.—*adj.* and *n.*
somnam'bulant. — *adjs.* somnam'būlar, -y. —
v.i. somnam'būlate, to walk in one's sleep.—*ns.*
somnambūlā'tion; somnam'būlātor, som-
nam'būle, a sleep-walker.—*adj.* somnam'būlic.
—*ns.* somnam'būlism, walking in sleep: a
hysterical state of automatism in which acts are
performed that are not remembered afterwards;
somnam'būlist.—*adjs.* somnambūlis'tic; som'-
nial, pertaining to dreams; somnic'ūlous,
drowsy; somnif'erous (L. *ferre,* to bring), somnif'ic (L. *facĕre,* to make), sleep-bringing.—*ns.*
somnil'oquence, somnil'oquism, somnil'oquy
(L. *loquī,* to talk), talking in sleep.—*v.i.* somnil'-
oquise.—*ns.* somnil'oquist; somniv'olent (L.
velle, to wish), one who wishes to sleep; som'-
nolence, -ency, sleepiness.—*adj.* som'nolent.—
adv. som'nolently.—*adj.* somnolesc'ent, half-
asleep. [L. *somnus,* sleep, *somnium,* a dream.]

son, *sun, n.* a male child or offspring: formerly
extended to a son-in-law: a descendant, or one
so regarded or treated: a disciple: a native or
inhabitant: the produce of anything.—*n.* son'-in-

law, a daughter's husband : formerly, a stepson :—*pl.* sons'-in-law.—*adj.* son'less.—*ns.* sonn'y, a little son : a familiar mode of address to a boy ; son'ship, state or character of a son.—son of man, a man : applied to Jesus Christ or the Messiah ; son of the manse, a minister's son ; The Son, the second person in the Trinity. [O.E. *sunu* ; Du. *zoon*, Ger. *sohn*.]

sonant, sō'nənt, *adj.* voiced.—*n.* a voiced sound.—*ns.* so'nance (*Shak.* son'uance, prob. a misprint), a sounding ; so'nancy, sonant character. [L. *sonāns*, *-āntis*, pr.p. of *sonāre*, to sound.]

sonata, sō-, sə-, so-nä'tä, *n.* (*orig.*) an instrumental composition : a composition usually of three or more movements designed chiefly for a solo instrument.—*n.* sonatina (son-ə-tē'nä), a short sonata.—sonata form, the form usual in the first movement of a sonata or symphony. [It., fem. pa.p. of *sonare* —L. *sonāre*, to sound.]

sondeli, son'de-li, *n.* the Indian musk-shrew. [Kanarese *sundili*.]

soneri, son', sōn'ə-rē, *n.* cloth of gold. [Hind. *sonā*, gold.]

song, song, *n.* that which is sung : a short poem or ballad suitable for singing, or set to music : the melody to which it is sung : an instrumental composition of like form and character : singing : the melodious outburst of a bird : any characteristic sound : a poem, or poetry in general : a theme of song : habitual utterance, manner, or attitude towards anything : a fuss : a mere trifle.—*ns.* song'bird, a bird that sings : any one of the Oscines ; song'book, (*obs.*) a service-book : a book of songs ; song'craft, the art of making songs ; song'-cycle, a sequence of songs connected in subject.—*adj.* song'ful, abounding in song : melodious : songlike : like singing : ready to break into song.—*adv.* song'fully.—*ns.* song'fulness ; song'-hit, a song that has made a hit, or caught on.—*adjs.* song'less, without song or power of song ; song'-like.—*ns.* song'man, (*Shak.*) a singer : a choir singer ; song'-school ; song'smith, a composer ; song'-sparrow, an American songbird (Melospiza) ; song'ster, a singer :—*fem.* song'stress ; song'-thrush, the mavis or throstle.—song form, the form of composition usual in songs ; Song of Songs, or of Solomon, Canticles : a book of the O.T. long attributed to Solomon. [O.E. *sang*—*singan*, to sing ; Goth. *saggws*, O.N. *sǫngr*.]

song, (*Spens.*) pa.t. of sing.

sonic, son'ik, *adj.* pertaining to sound-waves.—sonic bang, boom, (*aero.*) shock-wave or explosion that, at the speed of sound, reaches out far enough to be audible to people on the ground. [L. *sonus*, sound.]

sonne, an old spelling of son, sun.

sonnet, son'it, *n.* formerly, a short (esp. lyrical) poem : now, always one of fourteen lines of ten or eleven syllables, rhymed according to one or other of certain definite schemes, forming an octave and a sestet, properly expressing two successive phases of one thought.—*v.i.* to write sonnets.—*v.t.* to celebrate in sonnets.—*adj.* sonn'etary.—*n.* sonneteer', a sonnet-writer : (*obs.*) a poetaster.—*vs.i.* sonneteer', sonn'etise, to compose sonnets.—*vs.t.* to celebrate in sonnets.—*n.* and *adj.* sonneteer'ing.—*ns.* sonn'eting ; sonn'etist, a sonneteer ; sonn'etry ; sonn'et-se'quence, a connected series of sonnets.—Petrarcan sonnet, one rhymed *abbaabba cdcdcd* ; Miltonic, *abbaabba cdecde* ; Shakespearian, *ababcdcd efefgg*. [It. *sonetto*, dim. of *suono*—L. *sonus*, a sound.]

sonorous, so-, sə-nō'rəs, *adj.* full-sounding : sounding or ringing when struck.—*n.* sonority (sō-, sə-nor'i-ti), sonorousness.—*adv.* sonō'rously.—*n.* sonō'rousness, sonorous quality or character. [L. *sonōrus*—*sonor*, *-ōris*, a sound—*sonāre*, to sound.]

sonse, sonce, sons, *n.* (*Scot.*) good luck : abundance.—*adj.* sons'y, sons'ie, luck-bringing : comely : comfortable-looking : good-natured : plump, buxom. [Gael. *sonas*, good fortune.]

sontag, son'tag, zon'tähh, *n.* a woman's knitted cape, tied down round the waist. [From the famous German singer Henriette Sontag (1806-54).]

sonties, son'tiz, *n.pl.* (*Shak.*, in an oath) prob. f sanctities.

soom, sōōm, a Scots form of swim.

soon, sōōn, *adv.* immediately or in a short time without delay : early : readily, willingly.—*aa* (*rare*) early : (*Shak.*) speedy.—soon at, (*Shak* about. [O.E. *sóna*.]

soop, sōōp, *v.t.* (*Scot.*) to sweep.—*n.* soop'ing.—*adv.* soop'stake, (*Shak.*) with a sweep of the stak (another reading swoop'-stake-like). [O.N. *sópa* cf. sweep, swoop.]

soot, soot, *n.* a black deposit from imperfect com bustion or carbonaceous matter : a smut.—*v.t.* cover, smear, dirty, clog, or treat with soot.—*n.* soot'erkin, a fabulous after-birth induced b Dutch women sitting huddled over their stoves a Dutchman : a negro : a chimney-sweep : henc anything supplementary, fruitless, or abortive soot'flake, a smut of soot.—*adv.* soot'ily.—*n.* soot'iness.—*adjs.* soot'less ; soot'y, of, foul wit or like, soot. [O.E. *sót* ; Dan. *sod*.]

soot, soote, sōōt, *adj.* and *n.* (*obs.*) sweet.—*ad* (*Spens.*) sweetly. [See sweet.]

sooth, sōōth, *n.* truth, reality : (*Shak.*) blandish ment : (*obs.* ; *Spens.* soothe) augury, foretokenin —*adj.* true : truthful : (*Keats*) smooth, soft.—*ad* in truth : indeed.—*adj.* sooth'fast, truthful, hones faithful.—*adv.* sooth'fastly.—*n.* sooth'fastness.—*adj.* sooth'ful, truthful : faithful.—*advs.* sooth'fly sooth'lich, (*Spens.*) truly, indeed.—*v.i.* sooth'say to foretell, to divine.—*n.* prediction : (*Spen* soothsay') omen.—*ns.* sooth'sayer, (*Spens.* -sa one who foretells, a diviner or prognosticator (*obs.*) a truth-teller ; sooth'saying. [O.E. *sót* truth, true ; O.N. *sannr*.]

soothe, sōōdh, *v.t.* (*obs.*) to prove or declare true (*obs.*) to confirm, support, back up : to blandish cajole, flatter : (*obs.*) to gloss over : to calm, com fort, compose, tranquillise : to appease : to alla soften.—*v.i.* to have a tranquillising effect.—*n.* sooth'er.—*v.t.* (*Ir.*) to flatter, blandish.—*n.* an *adj.* sooth'ing.—*adv.* sooth'ingly. [O.E. (*ge sóthian*, to confirm as true—*sóth*, true.]

sop, sop, *n.* bread or other food dipped or soaked i liquid : a puddle : a soaking : a propitiatory gi or concession (from the drugged sop the Sibyl gav to Cerberus to gain passage for Aeneas to Hade Aen. vi. 420).—*v.t.* to steep in liquor : to take u by absorption (with *up*) : to soak.—*v.i.* to soak i percolate : to be soaked :—*pr.p.* sopp'ing ; *pa.* and *pa.p.* sopped.—*adv.* sopp'ily.—*n.* sopp'ines —*n.*, *adj.*, and *adv.* sopp'ing.—*adj.* sopp'y drenched : thoroughly wet : sloppily sentimenta —*n.* sops'-in-wine', (*obs.*) the clove pink : variety of apple. [O.E. *sopp* (n.), *soppian* (vb.) prob. conn. with *súpan*, to sup.]

soph, sof, *n.* an abbreviation of sophister and c sophomore.

sopherim, sō'fə-rim, *n.pl.* the scribes, the ex pounders of the Jewish oral law.—*adj.* sopheri (-fer'ik). [Heb. *sōferīm*.]

sophi. See sophy.

sophia, sof'i-ä, *n.* wisdom : divine wisdom (ofte personified Sophia, Hagia Sophia, Saint Sophia —*adjs.* soph'ic, -al.—*adv.* soph'ically.—*n.* soph'ism, a specious fallacy ; soph'ist, one o class of public teachers of rhetoric, philosophy, &c in ancient Greece : a captious or intentionall fallacious reasoner ; soph'ister, (*Shak.*) a sophist (*Cambridge*, *hist.*) a student in his second or thir year, (*Dublin*) in his third or fourth.—*adj.* sophis' tic, pertaining to, or of the nature of, a sophis or sophistry : fallaciously subtle.—*n.* (also in *pl.* the art of sophistry.—*adj.* sophist'ical.—*adv* sophis'tically.—*v.i.* sophis'ticate, to adulterate to falsify : to doctor : to render sophistical o unsound : to artificialise : to give a fashionabl air of worldly wisdom to.—*v.i.* to practise sophistry —*adjs.* sophist'icate, sophist'icated, adulterated impure : not genuine : falsified : artificialised worldly-wise and disillusioned.—*ns.* sophisticā' tion ; sophis'ticātor ; soph'istry, specious bu fallacious reasoning. [Gr. *sophiā*, wisdom, *soph isma*, skill, device, trick, quibble, *sophistēs*, a expert, a sophist—*sophos*, wise.]

Sophoclean, *sof-ō-klē'ən*, *adj.* pertaining to *Sophocles*, Athenian tragic poet (*c.* 496–*c.* 406 B.C.).

sophomore, *sof'ə-mōr*, *n.* (now *U.S.*) a second-year student. — Also *adj.* — *adjs.* **sophomoric** (*-mor'*), **-al**, of a sophomore: bombastic. [Prob. from *sophom* (obs. form of *sophism*) and *-or*, as if from *sophos*, wise, *mōros*, foolish.]

Sophy, *sō'fi*, *n.* (obs.) the shah of Persia. [From the *Çafi* or Safawi dynasty (1502–1736) descended from Çafi-ud-dīn.]

sopite, *sō-pīt'*, *v.t.* to dull, lull, put to sleep: to put an end to. [L. *sōpītus*, pa.p. of *sōpīre*, to put to sleep, calm, settle.]

sopor, *sō'por*, *n.* (*path.*) unnaturally deep sleep.— *adj.* **soporiferous** (*sop-*, *sōp-ər-if'ər-əs*), inducing sleep.—*adv.* **soporif'erously**.—*n.* **soporif'erousness**.—*adj.* **soporif'ic**, inducing sleep.—*n.* a sleep-bringing agent. — *adjs.* **sop'orōse**, **sop'orous**, sleepy. [L. *sopor*, *-ōris*, deep sleep—*ferre*, to bring, *facēre*, to make.]

sopped, **sopping**, **soppy**. See sop.

sopra, *sō'prä*, *adv.* (*mus.*) above. [It.,—L. *suprā*, above.]

soprano, *sō-*, *sə-prä'nō*, *n.* the highest variety of voice, treble: a singer with such a voice: a part for such a voice:—*pl.* **sopra'nos**, **sopra'ni** (*nē*).— Also *adj.*—*n.* **sopra'nist**, a soprano singer. [It., from *sopra*—L. *suprā* or *super*, above.]

sora, *sō'rä*, *n.* a N. American short-billed rail.— Also **sō'ree**. [Indian name.]

sorage. See sore (2).

soral. See sorus.

sorb, *sorb*, *n.* the service-tree, the wild service-tree, or (sometimes) the rowan-tree: its fruit.—*n.* **sorb'-app'le**. [L. *sorbus* (the tree), *sorbum* (the fruit).]

Sorb, *sorb*, *n.* a Wend.—*ns.* and *adjs.* **Sorb'ian**, **Sor'bish**, Wendish. [Ger. *Sorbe*; cf. Serb.]

sorb, *sorb*, *v.t.* to absorb or adsorb.—*adj.* **sorbefacient** (*-i-fā'shənt*), promoting absorption.—Also *n.*—*n.* and *adj.* **sor'bent**. [L. *sorbēre*, to suck in, *faciēns*, *-entis*, pr.p. of *facēre*, to make.]

sorbet, *sor'bət*, *n.* sherbet: water-ice. [Fr.,—It. *sorbetto*; cf. sherbet.]

Sorbonne, *sor-bon'*, *n.* a theological college of the mediaeval university of Paris, founded in 1253 by Robert of *Sorbon*, long dominant in matters of doctrine, suppressed 1792, revived 1808, seat of the faculties of science and letters (arts).—*adj.* **Sorbon'ical**.—*n.* **Sor'bonist**, a doctor or student of the Sorbonne.

sorcery, *sor'sə-ri*, *n.* divination by the assistance of evil spirits: enchantment: magic: witchcraft.— *n.* **sor'cerer**:—*fem.* **sor'ceress**.—*adj.* **sor'cerous**. [O.Fr. *sorcerie*—L. *sors*, *sortis*, lot.]

sord, *sōrd*, *n.* (Milt.) a form of **sward**.

sord, *sōrd*, *n.* a flock of mallard. [O.Fr. *sordre*—L. *surgěre*, to rise.]

sordes, *sor'dēz*, *n.sing.* or *pl.* filth: refuse: a foul accumulation: a crust on the teeth in fevers.—*adj.* **sor'did**, dirty: squalid: mean: meanly avaricious: mercenary: of low or unworthy ideals: dirt-coloured.—*adv.* **sor'didly**.—*ns.* **sor'didness**; **sor'dor**, dirt: sordidness. [L. *sordēs* (pl.; sing. defective), dirt, *sordidus*, dirty.]

sordo, *sor'dō*, *adj.* muted, damped:—*fem.* **sor'da**. —*adv.* **sordamente** (*-dä-men'tä*), gently, softly.— *n.* **sordino** (*-dē'nō*), a mute or damper to soften or deaden the sound of an instrument:—*pl.* **sordini** (*-nē*).—Also **sordine** (*-dēn'*; Fr. *sourdine*).—**con sordino**, with mute; **senza sordino**, without mute. [It.,—L. *surdus*, deaf, noiseless.]

sore, *sōr*, *n.* a painful or tender injured or diseased spot: an ulcer or boil: grief: an affliction.—*adj.* **wounded**: tender: readily sensitive to pain: irritable: touchy: painful: afflicted: vexed: irritated: causing pain: painful to contemplate: grievous: (*Scot.*) aching: bringing sorrow or regret.—*adv.* painfully: grievously: severely: distressingly: in distress: hard: eagerly: very much.—*v.t.* to make sore: to wound.—*n.* **sore'head**, (*U.S.*) one discontented with his reward for political services.—*adj.* **sore'head'ed**.—*adv.* **sore'ly**.—*n.* **sore'ness**. [O.E. *sár*; Ger. *sehr*, very, O.N. *sárr*, sore.]

sore, soar, soare, *sōr*, *adj.* (obs.) sorrel, reddish-

brown: of hawks, &c., in reddish-brown plumage of the first year.—*n.* a hawk of the first year : (*Shak.*) a buck of the fourth year.—*ns.* **sor'age**, the first year of a hawk : a sore-hawk ; **sore'-hawk** ; **soar'-ea'gle** (*Milt.*), **-fal'con**, **-hawk'**. [A.Fr. and O.Fr. *sor* (Fr. *saur*, *saure*), sorrel, reddish ; cf. **sorrel** (2).]

soredium, *sō-rē'di-əm*, *n.* a small vegetative reproductive body in lichens, consisting of a few algal cells enclosed in fungal hyphae :—*pl.* **sorē'dia**.— *adjs.* **sorē'dial**, **sorē'diate**. [Gr. *sōros*, a heap.]

sorehon, *sōr'hon*, *n.* an ancient Irish exaction of a lord from a freeholder or tenant. [See **sorn** (2).]

sorel. See **sorrel** (2).

Sorex, *sō'reks*, *n.* the common shrew genus, giving name to the family **Soricidae** (*sō-ris'i-dē*).—*adjs.* **soric'ident** (L. *dēns*, *dentis*, tooth), having teeth like the shrew ; **soricine** (*sor'i-sīn*, *-sin*), of the shrew : shrewlike ; **sor'icoid** (*-koid*), shrewlike. [L. *sōrex*, *-icis*, shrew ; cf. Gr. *hyrax*.]

Sorghum, *sor'gəm*, *n.* a tropical Old World genus of grasses near akin to sugar-cane, including durra and Kaffir corn : (*U.S.*) molasses made from its juice.—*n.* **sor'go**, **sor'gho**, a variety of durra from which sugar is prepared (**sweet sorghum**, or Chinese sugar-cane). [It. *sorgo*, prob. from an East Ind. word.]

sorites, *sō-rī'tēz*, *n.* a string of propositions in which the predicate of one is the subject of the next (or the same in reverse order) : a sophistical puzzle on the model of 'How many grains make a heap?' [Gr. *sōreitēs*—*sōros*, a heap.]

sorn, *sorn*, *v.i.* (*Scot.*) to obtrude oneself as an uninvited guest.—*ns.* **sor'ner** ; **sorn'ing**. [Obs. Ir. *sorthan*, free quarters.]

Soroptimist, *sor-opt'i-mist*, *adj.* of an international organisation of women's Rotary clubs.—*n.* a member of one of these clubs. [L. *soror*, sister, and **optimist**.]

sororal, *sor-ō'rəl*, **sororial**, *-ri-əl*, *adjs.* sisterly : of, of the nature of, a sister.—*n.* **soro'rate** (or *sor'ər-āt*), a custom that allows or requires marriage with a wife's sister.—*adv.* **soro'rially**.—*n.* **sororicide** (*-or'i-sīd* ; L. *caeděre*, to kill), killing or killer of a sister.—*v.i.* **sororise** (*sor'ər-īz*), to associate in a sisterly way.—*n.* **sorority** (*sor-or'i-ti*), a sisterhood : (*U.S.*) a women's academic society. [L. *soror*, sister.]

sorosis, *so-*, *sə-*, *sō-rō'sis*, *n.* a fleshy fruit formed from a crowd of flowers, as the pine-apple : (*U.S.*) a women's club. [Gr. *sōros*, a heap.]

sorrel, *sor'l*, *n.* any of the acid-tasting species of the dock genus, Rumex (**common sorrel**, *R. Acetosa*); **sheep's sorrel**, *R. Acetosella*); **French** or **Roman sorrel**, *R. scutatus*) or the kindred *Oxyria digyna* (**mountain sorrel**) : applied also to other plants as roselle and wood-sorrel.—**salts of sorrel**, a very poisonous combination of potassium acid oxalate and oxalic acid. [O.Fr. *sorele*, *surele* (Fr. *surelle*)—*sur*, sour—O.H.G. *sūr* (Ger. *sauer*), sour.]

sorrel, *sor'l*, *adj.* reddish-brown or light chestnut.— *n.* a reddish-brown colour : a sorrel horse : (also **sorel**, **sorell**, *sōr'el* ; *Shak.*) a third-year buck. [O.Fr. *sorel*—*sor* (Fr. *saur*, *saure*), sorrel ; poss. L.G. ; cf. **sore** (2).]

sorrow, *sor'ō*, *n.* pain of mind : grief : affliction : lamentation : one sorrowed for : devil (in imprecations, as an emphatic negative, and applied as a term of abuse ; Irish **sorra**).—*v.t.* and *v.i.* to grieve.—*adj.* **sorr'owed**, (*Shak.*) accompanied with sorrow.—*n.* **sorr'ower**.—*adj.* **sorr'owful**, full of sorrow : causing, showing, or expressing sorrow : sad : dejected.—*adv.* **sorr'owfully**.—*n.* **sorr'owfulness**.—*n.* and *adj.* **sorr'owing**.—*adj.* **sorr'owless**, free from sorrow. [O.E. *sorg*, *sorh* ; Ger. *sorge*, O.N. *sorg*.]

sorry, *sor'i*, *adj.* regretful : often merely formally apologetic : distressing : poor, miserable, wretchedly bad, contemptible, worthless (*compar*. **sorr'ier** ; *superl*. **sorr'iest**)—*interj*. of slight apology.—*adv.* **sorr'ily**.—*n.* **sorr'iness**.—*adj.* **sorr'yish**. [O.E. *sárig*, wounded—*sár*, pain ; Du. *zeerig*; influenced in meaning by **sorrow**, but not connected in origin.]

sort, *sort*, *n.* (*Shak.*) a lot (in sortilege) : (*obs.*) a company, group, collection, parcel : a class, kind, or species : quality or rank : one, a specimen or instance, of a kind (often ungrammatically in the singular with *these* or *those*, to denote examples of this or that kind) : something of the nature but not quite worthy of the name : a letter, stop, or other character in a fount of type : manner.—*v.t.* (*Shak.*) to allot, assign : (*Shak.*) to dispose : to befit : to separate into lots or classes : to group, classify : to pick out : to select : (*Scot.*) to provide : to procure : to set in accord : (*Scot.*) to adjust, put to rights, attend to : to geld : to deal effectively with (esp. in a vague threat).—*v.i.* (*obs.*) to come about, turn out : to fit, accord : (*Scot.*) to agree : to consort.—*adj.* sort′able, capable of being sorted : assorted : suitable, befitting.—*ns.* sort′ance, (*Shak.*) suitableness, agreement ; sortā′tion, sorting out ; sort′er, one who separates and arranges, as letters. —*n.pl.* sort′es (-ēz ; L. -ās), divination by chance opening of the Bible, Homer, Virgil, &c.—*ns.* sort′- ilege (-i-lij ; L. *sortilegus*, a diviner), divination ; sortil′eger ; sortil′egy.—*n.* and *adj.* sort′ing.— *ns.* sorti′tion, the casting of lots ; sort′ment, a sorting out : an assortment.—a good sort, a decent fellow ; in a sort, in a manner ; in some sort, in a way : as it were ; in sort, (*Shak.*) in a body : (*Spens.*) inasmuch ; of a sort, of sorts, inferior : out of sorts, out of order, slightly unwell : (*print.*) with some sorts of type in the fount exhausted ; sort of, (*coll.* or *vulg.*, used adverbially and paren- thetically) as it were : rather ; that's your sort, that's right : well done : go on. [L. *sors, sortis,* a lot, *sortīri,* to draw lots ; partly through O.Fr.]

sortie, *sor′tē, n.* a sally of besieged to attack the besiegers.—*v.i.* to sally. [Fr.,—*sortir,* to go out, to issue ; origin doubtful.]

sorus, *sō′rəs, n.* a cluster of sporangia or soredia :— *pl.* sō′rī.—*adj.* so′ral. [Gr. *sōros,* a heap.]

S O S, *es-ō-es′, n.* an appeal for help or rescue.—*v.i.* to make such an appeal. [Arbitrary code signal.]

so-so (or so so), *sō′sō′, adj.* neither very good nor very bad : tolerable : indifferent. — Also *adv.* [so.]

soss, *sos, n.* a mess : a dish of sloppy food : a puddle : a heavy fall : a plump.—*v.t.* to dirty : to slobber up : to throw carelessly about.—*v.i.* to plump down : to splash about.—*adv.* plump.—*n.* soss′ing. [Imit.]

sostenuto, *sos-te-nōō′tō, adj.* (*mus.*) sustained.—*adv.* with full time allowed for each note. [It.]

sot, *sot, n.* (*obs.*) a fool : one stupefied by drinking : a habitual drunkard.—*v.i.* to play the sot.—*adj.* sott′ed, besotted.—*n.* sott′ing.—*adj.* sott′ish, like a sot : foolish : stupid with drink.—*adv.* sott′ishly.—*n.* sott′ishness. [O.Fr. *sot.*]

Sotadic, *sō-tad′ik,* Sotadean, *sō-* or *so-tə-dē′ən, adjs.* pertaining to *Sōtadēs,* a lascivious and scurril- ous Greek poet (fl. 276 B.C.), or his writings, or in his metre : coarse and scurrilous : palindromic.— —*n.* a satire in his manner : a catalectic tetra- meter of ionics *a majore.*

soterial, *sō-tē′ri-əl, adj.* pertaining to salvation.— *adj.* sōtēriolog′ical.—*n.* sōtēriol′ogy, the doctrine of salvation. [Gr. *sōtēriā,* salvation—*sōtēr,* a saviour.]

Sothic, *sō′thik, adj.* of or pertaining to Sirius.— Sothic cycle, or period, a period of 1460 years, after which the beginning of the Egyptian year of 365 days again coincides with the beginning of the Sothic year, which was reckoned from the heliacal rising of Sirius. [Egyptian name of Sirius, given in Gr. as *Sōthis.*]

sotto voce, *sōt′tō vō′che, adv.* in an undertone, aside. [It., below the voice.]

sou, *sōō, n.* a French five-centime piece. [Fr.,— L. *solidus* ; cf. sold, soldier, soldo.]

souari, saouari, *sow-ä′ri, n.* a tree (Caryocar) of Guiana yielding a durable timber and edible butter-nuts.—*n.* s(a)oua′ri-nut. [Fr. *saouari,* from Galibi.]

soubise, *sōō-bēz′, n.* an 18th-cent. cravat : an onion sauce (soubise sauce). [Fr., after the French Marshal Prince de Soubise (1715-87).]

soubrette, *soo-bret′, n.* a pert, coquettish, intriguing maid-servant in comedy : a singer of light songs of similar character : a maid-servant, lady's maid. [Fr.,—Prov. *soubreto* (fem.), coy.]

soubriquet. See sobriquet.

souce, souct, old spellings (*Spens., Shak.*) of souse, soused.

souchong, *sōō-(t)shong′, n.* a fine sort of black tea. [Chin. *siao,* small, *chung,* sort.]

souffle, *sōō′fl, n.* a murmuring in auscultation. [Fr.]

soufflé, *sōō′flā, n.* a light dish, properly one with white of egg whisked into a froth.—*adj.* prepared thus. [Fr. pa.p. of *souffler*—L. *sufflāre,* to blow.]

sough, *sow, suf,* or (*Scot.*) *soohh, v.i.* to sigh, as the wind.—*v.t.* to whine out : to sigh out : to hum.— *n.* a sighing of the wind : a deep sigh : a vague rumour : a whining tone of voice.—keep a calm sough, to keep quiet. [O.E. *swōgan,* to rustle.]

sough, *suf, n.* a drain, sewer, mine-adit.—*n.* sough′- ing-tile, a drain-tile. [Cf. Flem. dial. *zoeg,* a small ditch.]

sought, *sawt, pa.t.* and *pa.p.* of seek.

soul, *sōl, n.* (*obs.*) life : that which thinks, feels, desires, &c. : the ego : a spirit, embodied or dis- embodied : innermost being or nature : that which one identifies with oneself : moral and emotional nature, power, or sensibility : nobleness of spirit or its sincere expression : a complete embodiment or exemplification : an element : essence : the essential part : an indwelling or animating prin- ciple : the moving spirit, inspirer, leader : a person : the lungs of a goose, &c. : a violin sound- post.—*interj.* by my soul.—*n.* soul′-bell, a passing bell.—*adj.* soul′-confirming, (*Shak.*) ratifying the devoting of the draw lot.—*n.* soul′-cūr′er, (*Shak.*) a parson.—*adjs.* souled, having a soul, esp., in com- pounds, of this or that kind ; soul′-fear′ing, (*Shak.*) terrifying the soul ; soul′ful, having or expressive of deep or elevated feeling, sincere or affected. — *adv.* soul′fully. — *n.* soul′fulness.— *adjs.* soul′killing (*Shak.*) ; soul′less, without a soul : lacking animation or nobleness of mind : mean, spiritless.—*ns.* soul′lessness ; soul′-shot, -scot, -scat, a payment to the church on behalf of a dead person, a funeral payment.—*adj.* soul′- sick, morally diseased.—*n.* soul′-sleeper, a psycho- pannychist.—*adj.* soul′-stirring. [O.E. *sáwol* ; Ger. *seele.*]

souldan, an old form of soldan.

souldier, an old spelling of soldier.

soum, sowm, *soom, n.* (*Scot.*) the proportion of sheep or cattle suitable for any pasture : pasture for one cow or its equivalent in sheep, &c.—*v.t.* and *v.i.* to determine in terms of soums.—*n.* soum′ing—souming and rouming, the deter- mination of the number of soums appropriate to a common pasture, and their apportionment (according to ability to fodder through winter) to the various roums or holdings. [A form of sum.]

sound, *sownd, adj.* safe : whole : uninjured, un- impaired : in good condition : healthy : whole- some : deep (as sleep) : solid : thorough (as a beating) : well-founded : well-grounded : trust- worthy : of the right way of thinking : orthodox.— *adv.* soundly, completely fast, as in sleep.—*adv.* sound′ly.—*n.* sound′ness. [O.E. *gesund* ; Ger. *gesund.*]

sound, *sownd, n.* a strait : a fish's swimming bladder. [O.E. *sund,* swimming.]

sound, *sownd, n.* sensation of hearing : transmitted disturbance perceived or perceptible by the ear : esp. a tone produced by regular vibrations (opp. to *noise*) : mere noise, without meaning or sense or distinguished from sense : report, rumour : hear- ing-distance.—*v.i.* to give out a sound : to resound : to be audible : to be sounded : to be famed : to give an impression on hearing : (*obs.*) to tend : to call, as by trumpet.—*v.t.* to cause to make a sound : to produce, utter, make, the sound of : to utter audibly : to pronounce : to announce, publish, proclaim, celebrate, signal, direct, by sound : (*obs.*) to mean : to examine by percussion and listening.—*ns.* sound′-bar, a bass-bar ; sound′- board, a thin resonating plate of wood or metal in a musical instrument : in an organ, the appar- atus that conveys the air from the wind-chest to the appropriate pipes : a sounding-board ; sound′-

fāte, fär, ȧsk ; mē, hȯr (her) ; *mīne ; mōte ; mūte ; mōōn ; dhen* (then)

boarding, boards between joists carrying pugging to make a floor sound-proof; **sound'-body,** a resonance-box; **sound-box,** a resonance-box: part of a gramophone supporting the diaphragm; **sound'er; sound'-film,** a cinematograph film with sychronised sound-track; **sound'-hole,** an *f*-shaped hole in the belly of a violin, &c.; **sound'-ing,** emission of sound: a signal by trumpet, bell, or the like, as for the rise of the curtain: examination by percussion.—*adj.* making a sound: sonorous: resounding: having a magnificent sound.—*ns.* **sound'ing-board,** a structure for carrying a speaker's voice towards the audience: a sound-board.—*adv.* **sound'ingly.**—*adj.* **sound'less.**—*adv.* **sound'lessly.**—*n.* **sound'-post,** a short post connecting the belly and back of a violin, &c., under the bridge.—*adj.* **sound'proof,** impenetrable by sound.—*v.t.* to render soundproof.—*ns.* **sound'-proofing; sound'-shadow,** a region of silence behind a barrier to sound; **sound'-shift,** a series of regular changes in stop-consonants differentiating Germanic from other Indo-Germanic languages, or (*second shift*) High German from other Germanic; **sound'-track,** on a cinematograph film, the strip on which sounds are recorded; **sound'-wave,** a longitudinal disturbance propagated through air or other medium.—**sound barrier,** (*aero.*) difficulty met about the speed of sound, when power required to increase speed rises steeply. [M.E. *soun*—A.Fr.—L. *sonus*; for *d* cf. **pound** (3).]

sound, *sownd, v.t.* to measure the depth of: to probe: to try to discover the inclinations, thoughts, &c., of.—*v.i.* to take soundings: to dive deep, as a whale.—*n.* a probe for examining the bladder, &c. —*ns.* **sound'er,** one who sounds: apparatus for taking soundings; **sound'ing,** the action of that which or one who sounds: an ascertained depth: (in *pl.*) waters in which an ordinary sounding-line will reach the bottom; **sound'ing-lead,** the weight at the end of a sounding-line; **sound'ing-line,** a line with a plummet at the end for soundings; **sound'ing-rod,** a rod for measuring water in a ship's hold. [O.E. *sund-* (in compounds), cf. **sound** (2); or perh. O.Fr. *sonder,* to sound, which may be from Gmc.]

sound, *sownd, n.* and *v.i.* (*obs.*). Same as **swound.** See **swoon.**

sounder, *sown'dər, n.* a herd of swine: a young boar. [O.Fr. *sundre*; of Gmc. origin; cf. O.E. *sunor.*]

soup, *sōōp, n.* the nutritious liquid obtained by boiling meat or vegetables in stock: (*slang*) a photographic developer: (*slang*) stolen plate melted down.—*ns.* **soup'er,** in Ireland, one who dispenses soup as a means of proselytising: one really or supposedly so converted; **soup'-kitchen,** a place for supplying soup to the poor; **soup'-mai'gre** (or **mea'gre**), a thin fish or vegetable soup, originally for fast-days; **soup'-plate,** a large deep plate; **soup'spoon; soup'-tureen.**—*adj.* **soup'y.**—**in the soup,** in difficulties or trouble; **the ticket for soup,** (*slang*) the very thing (from the ticket entitling to soup at a soup-kitchen). [O.Fr. *soupe*; cf. **sop.**]

soupçon, *soop-son⁰, n.* a hardly perceptible quantity. [Fr., suspicion.]

souple, *sōōp'l, adj.* a provincial form of **supple**: of silk, lightly scoured: (*Scot.*) clever.—*v.t.* to make supple or souple.

souple, *sōōp'l, n.* a Scots form of **swipple**: (*Scott*) a cudgel.

sour, *sowr, adj.* having an acid taste or smell: acrid: turned, as milk: rancid: morose, embittered, discontented, crabbed, or peevish: rank: of beasts, heavy, coarse, strong: cold and wet, as soil: distasteful: disagreeable.—*v.t.* to make sour: to treat with dilute acid.—*v.i.* to become sour.— *adj.* **sour'-cold** (*Shak.*).—*ns.* **sour'-crout** (see **sauerkraut**); **sour'dough,** leaven: a piece of dough reserved to leaven a new batch: in Canada and Alaska, an old-timer. — *adj.* **sour'-eyed,** morose-looking.—*ns.* **sour'-gourd,** the cream-of-tartar tree: a tropical grass akin to millet: sorrel; **sour'ing,** turning or becoming sour: vinegar: the crab-apple: treatment with dilute acid in

bleaching. — *adj.* **sour'ish.** — *advs.* **sour'ishly;** **sour'ly.**—*ns.* **sour'ness; sour'-sop,** a tropical American fruit: the tree (of the custard-apple genus) that bears it. [O.E. *sūr;* Ger. *sauer,* O.N. *súrr.*]

source, *sōrs, n.* a spring: the head of a stream: origin: rise: (*Spens.* **sourse**) perh. surging: originating cause: that from which anything rises or originates: a book or document serving as authority for history, or furnishing matter or inspiration for an author.—*n.* **source'-book,** a book of original documents for historic study. [O.Fr. *sorse* (Fr. *source*), from *sourdre*—L. *surgĕre,* to rise.]

sourdeline, *sōōr'də-lēn, n.* a small bagpipe. [Fr.]

sourdine, *sōōr-dēn⁰, n.* (*mus.*) a mute or sordino. [Fr.; cf. **sordino.**]

sourock, *sōō'rək, n.* (*Scot.*) sorrel. [**sour.**]

souse, *sous, sows, n.* (*obs.*). Same as **sou**:—*pl.* **souse,** **sous'es.**

souse, *sows, n.* pickled meat, esp. pig's feet or ears: (*dial.* or *facet.*) an ear: pickling liquid: a plunge in pickling or other liquid: a ducking: a drenching: a wash: a sluicing with water: (*slang*) a getting drunk: (*U.S.*) a drunkard: a heavy blow or fall: a thump: an impact: a rising from the ground, taking wing (in the falconers' phrase *at souse, at the souse,* when the hawk gets a chance of striking): hence the downward swoop of a bird of prey.— *adv.* with a plunge: with a heavy impact: plump: suddenly.—*v.t.* to pickle: to plunge, immerse, duck: to drench, soak: to make drunk: to dash: to fling down: to smite: to swoop down upon.— *v.i.* to fall with a plunge: to be drenched: to wash thoroughly: to get drunk: to strike: to impinge: to fall heavily: to swoop as a hawk.—*adj.* **soused.** —*ns.* **souse'-tub; souse'wife.**—*n.* and *adj.* **sous'-ing.**—Also **souce, sowce, sowsse** in old writers. [Partly O.Fr. *sous, souce*—O.H.G. *sulza,* from the root of **salt**; partly imit. (cf. German *saus*); partly **source** in its old sense of rising.]

souslik. Same as **suslik.**

sout (*Spens.*). Same as **soot.**

soutache, *sōō-täsh⁰, n.* a narrow braid. [Fr.]

soutane, *sōō-tän⁰, n.* a cassock. [Fr.,—It. *sottana*— L. *subtus,* beneath.]

souteneur, *sōōt'nər, n.* a prostitute's bully or exploiter. [Fr., supporter, protector; cf. **sustain.**]

souter, *sōō'tər, n.* (*Scot.*) a shoemaker, a cobbler.— Also **sow'ter, sou'tar.**—*adj.* **sou'terly.**—**souter's clod,** (*Scott*) a brown wheaten roll. [O.E. *sūtere* (O.N. *sútari*)—L. *sūtor*—*suĕre,* to sew.]

souterrain, *sōō-te-ren⁰, sōō'tə-rān, n.* an underground chamber. [Fr.]

south, *sowth, adv.* in the direction contrary to north. —*n.* the point of the horizon, the region, or the part, in that direction: the south wind: the Southern States in U.S. history.—*adj.* lying towards the south: forming the part, or that one of two, that is toward the south: blowing from the south: (of a pole of a magnet, usu.) south-seeking. —*v.i.* (*sowdh*) to move or veer towards the south: to cross the meridian.—*adjs.* **south-bound** (*sowth⁰*), bound for the south; **south'-country.**—*adj.* and *adv.* **south-east'** (or *sowth⁰*), midway between south and east.—*n.* the direction midway: the region lying in, the wind blowing from, that direction.—*n.* **south-east'er,** a strong wind from the south-east.—*adj.* and *adv.* **south-east'erly,** towards or (of wind) from the south-east.—*adj.* **south-east'ern,** belonging to, or being in, the south-east, or in that direction.—*adj.* and *adv.* **south-east'ward,** toward the south-east. — *n.* the region to the south-east. — *adj.* and *adv.* **south-east'wardly.**—*adj.* **south-east'wards.**—*n.* **souther** (*sowdh'ər*), a south wind or gale.—*v.i.* (*sudh'ər*) to move or veer toward the south.—*adj.* **southering** (*sudh'*).—*n.* **southerliness** (*sudh'*).— *adj.* and *adv.* **southerly** (*sudh'*), towards or (of wind) from the south.—*adj.* **southern** (*sudh'*), of the south: in the south or in the direction toward it: (of wind) from the south.—*n.* a southerner.— *n.* **southerner** (*sudh'*), a native or inhabitant of the south, esp. of the Southern States of America.— *v.t.* **southernise** (*sudh'*), to render southern in character.—*n.* **southernism** (*sudh'*), a form of expression peculiar to the south, esp. the Southern States of America.—*adj.* **southernly** (*sudh'*), southerly.—*adv.* towards the south.—*adjs.* (*superl.*) **southermost** (*rare*), **southernmost** (*sudh'*).—*ns.* **southernwood** (*sudh'*), an aromatic plant of southern Europe, of the wormwood genus (Artemisia); **southing** (*sowdh'*), distance, deviation, tendency or motion to the south: meridian passage; **southland** (*sowth'*), the south (also *adj.*): **south'lander**.—*adj.* (*superl.*) **south'most**.—*adj.* **south'paw**, left-handed.—*n.* a left-handed person, esp. in sport.—*adjs.* **south'-pō'lar**; **southron**, **Southron**, **Southroun** (*sudh'ron*; *Scot.*), southern, esp. English as distinguished from Scots.—*n.* a southerner: an Englishman: the English of England.—*adj.* **south-seeking** (*sowth'*), turning towards the earth's magnetic south pole.—*ns.*, *adjs.*, and *advs.* **south-south-east'**, **south-south-west'**, (in) a direction midway between south and south-east or south-west.—*adj.*, *adv.*, and *n.* **southward** (*sowth'word*; *naut.* *sudh'ərd*).—*adj.* and *adv.* **south'wardly**.—*adv.* **south'wards**.—*adj.* and *adv.* **south-west** (*sowth'* or *sow'*, or *-west'*), midway between south and west.—*n.* the direction between south and west: the region lying that way: the wind blowing from that direction.—*n.* **south-**, **sou'west'er**, a gale from the south-west: a waterproof hat with flap at the back of the neck.—*adjs.* **south'-west'erly**, toward or (of wind) from the south-west; **south'-west'ern**, belonging to, or lying in, the south-west or in that direction.—*adj.*, *adv.*, and *n.* **south-west'ward**.—*adj.* and *adv.* **south-west'wardly**.—*adv.* **south-west'wards.—Southern Cross**, a conspicuous southern constellation with four bright stars placed crosswise; **south pole**, the end of the earth's axis in Antarctica: its projection on the celestial sphere: (usually) the south-seeking pole of a magnet (logically the north-seeking); **South Sea**, the Pacific Ocean. [O.E. *sūth*; Ger. *süd*, O.N. *suthr*.]

Southcottian, *sowth-kot'i-ən*, *n.* a follower of Joanna *Southcott* (1750-1814), who was expected to give birth to a Shiloh or Prince of Peace.—Also *adj.*

Southdown, *sowth'down*, *adj.* pertaining to the *South Downs* in Hampshire and Sussex, the famous breed of sheep so named, or their mutton.—*n.* a sheep of this breed, or its mutton.

southsay, southsayer. Same as **soothsay**, &c.

souvenir, *sōō'və-nēr*, *n.* a memento: a keepsake.— *n.* **souv'ena(u)nce**, (*Spens.*) remembrance, memory. [Fr. *souvenir*—L. *subvenīre*, to come up, to come to mind—*sub*, under, *venīre*, to come.]

sovereign, or (after *Milt.*) **sovran**, *sov'rin*, *-rən*, *n.* a supreme ruler or head: a monarch: (*obs.*) an Irish mayor: a gold coin from Henry VII. to Charles I. worth 22s. 6d. to 10s., from 1817 a pound (*coll.* **sov**, *sov*).—*adj.* supreme: excelling all others: having supreme power residing in itself or himself: of sovereignty: (of contempt) utmost: highly efficacious.—*adv.* **sov'ereignly**, supremely: as a sovereign.—*n.* **sov'ereignty**, (*poet.*) **sov'ranty**, pre-eminence: supreme and independent power: the territory of a sovereign or of a sovereign state. [O.Fr. *sovrain* and It. *sovrano*—L. *super*, above.]

soviet, *sō'vi-et*, *-et'*, *n.* a council, esp. one of those forming since 1917 the machinery of local and national government in Russia (the Union of Soviet Socialist Republics)—the local councils elected by workers, peasants, and soldiers, the higher councils consisting of deputies from the lower.—*adj.* **soviet'ic**.—*v.t.* **so'vietise**, to transform to the soviet model.—*n.* **so'vietism**. [Russ. *sovet*, council.]

sow, *sow*, *n.* a female pig: a female badger, &c.: a term of reproach for a fat, lazy, greedy, or sluttish person, esp. a woman: a main channel for molten iron, leading to *pigs*: metal solidified there: (*hist.*) a movable shed for protecting besiegers.—*ns.* **sow'-bread**, a cyclamen, esp. *C. europaeum*, whose tubers are eaten by swine; **sow'-bug**, a woodlouse.—*adj.* **sow'-drunk**, (*prov.*) beastly drunk.— *n.* **sow'-gelder**, one who spays sows.—*n.* and *adj.* **sow'-skin**.—*n.* **sow'-thistle**, a thistle-like genus of plants (Sonchus) with milky juice and yellow

flowers. [O.E. *sū*, *sugu*; Ger. *sau*, O.N. *syr*; L. *sūs*, Gr. *hȳs*.]

sow, *sō*, *v.t.* to scatter or put in the ground, as seed: to plant by strewing: to scatter seed over: to spread, strew, disseminate.—*v.i.* to scatter seed for growth:—*pa.t.* **sowed** (*sōd*); *pa.p.* **sown** (*sōn*), or **sowed**. — *ns.* **sow'er**; **sow'ing**; **sow'ing-machine'**, a machine for sowing seed. [O.E. *sāwan*; Ger. *säen*, O.N. *sā*, Goth. *saian*.]

sowar, *sō-wär*, *n.* an Indian trooper, mounted policeman, or attendant.—*n.* **sowarr'y**, **sowarr'ee**, a mounted retinue, cavalcade. [Urdu *sawār*, horseman.]

sowens, sowans, *sō'ənz*, *n.pl.* (*Scot.*) a dish made from the farina remaining among the husks of oats, flummery. [Supposed to be from Gael. *sùghan*, the liquid of sowens—*sùgh*, juice.]

sowl, sowle. See sole (4).

sownd, *sownd*, *v.t.* (*Spens.*) app., to wield.

sownd, *sownd*, *n.* (*Spens.*), the same as **swound**, **swoon**.

sowne, *sown*, *n.* (*Spens.*). Same as **sound** (3).

sowp, *sowp*, *n.* (*Scot.*) a spoonful, sip, small drink. [O.N. *saup*; cf. **sop**, **sup**.]

sowse, sowsse, *sows*, *vb.* and *n.* (*Spens.*; *Shak.*). Same as **souse**.

sowth, *sowth*, **sowf, sowff**, *sowf*, *v.i.* and *v.t.* (*Scot.*) to whistle or hum over softly. [Scots forms of obs. *solf*—Fr. *solfier*, to sol-fa.]

sox, *soks*, *n.pl.* a shop spelling of **socks**.

soy, *soi*, **soya**, *sō'yä*, *soi'ä*, **soja**, *sō'yä*, *sō'jä*, *n.* a thick, piquant sauce made from the soy-bean: the soy-bean, rich in oil and protein: the eastern Asiatic papilionaceous plant (*Glycine Soja*, *G. hispida* or *max*) producing it.—*ns.* **soy'-bean**; **soy'a-bean**, **so'ja-bean**; **soy'-**, **soy'a-**, **so'ja-flour**. [Jap. *shō-yu*, coll. *soy*, Du. *soya*, *soja*— Chin. *shi-yu*, salt bean oil.]

soyle, *soil*, *n.* (*Spens.*) app., body, prey. [Unexplained.]

sozzle, *soz'l*, *v.t.* (*U.S.* and *dial.*) to splash: to make sloppy: to intoxicate: to perform sluttishly. —*n.* slops: sluttishness: a slattern.—*adj.* **sozz'ly**, sloppy. [Cf. **soss**.]

spa, *spä*, formerly *spaw*, *n.* a mineral spring: **a** mineral water resort.—*n.* **spa'-well**. [*Spa* in Belgium.]

space, *spās*, *n.* that in which material bodies have extension: a portion of extension: room: intervening distance: interval: an open or empty place: regions remote from the earth: an interval between lines or words: a type used for making such an interval: an interval between the lines of the stave: a portion, extent, or interval of time: a short time: opportunity, leisure.—*v.t.* to make, arrange, or increase intervals between.—*v.i.* (*Spens.*) to walk about.—*ns.* **space'-band**, a wedge for justifying the line in mechanical type-setting; **space'-bar**, a bar for making spaces in typewriting. — *adj.* **spaced**. — *n.* **space'-lattice**, an arrangement of points in three-dimensional space at the intersections of equally spaced parallel lines —such as the arrangement of atoms in a crystal disclosed by X-ray spectroscopy.—*adj.* **space'less**. —*ns.* **spac'er**, one who, or that which, spaces: an instrument for reversing a telegraphic current: a space-bar; **space'-ship**, a craft for flying beyond the earth's atmosphere; **space'-time'**, a four-dimensional manifold in which time is added **as** a dimension to the three dimensions of space; **space'-travel**; **space'-writ'er**, (*U.S.*) a journalist paid by space filled; **spacing** (*spās'ing*).—*adjs.* **spacial** (*spā'shl*; see **spatial**); **spacious** (*spā'shəs*), extensive: ample: roomy: wide.—*adv.* **spa'-ciously**.—*n.* **spa'ciousness.—space out**, to set wide apart or wider apart; **spacious times**, days of expansion (in knowledge, trade, &c.), and scope (for discovery, adventure, and the like), as in the reign of Queen Elizabeth. [Fr. *espace*—L. *spatium*; Gr. *spaein*, to draw.]

spadassin, *spad'ə-sin*, *n.* a swordsman, a bravo. [Fr.,—It. *spadaccino*—*spada*, a sword.]

spade, *spād*, *n.* a broad-bladed digging tool: **a** whaler's knife: a spade's depth, spit.—*v.t.* to dig or remove with a spade.—*ns.* **spade'-beard**, **a**

spade-shaped beard ; **spade'-bone**, the scapula ; **spade'-foot**, a toad with digging foot ; **spade'ful**, as much as a spade will hold :—*pl.* **spade'fuls** ; **spade'-guin'ea**, a guinea with spade-shaped shield, coined 1787-99 ; **spade'-hus'bandry**, cultivation by digging instead of ploughing ; **spade(s)'man**, a worker with the spade ; **spade'-work**, preparatory drudgery.—**call a spade a spade**, to speak out plainly without euphemism. [O.E. *spadu*, *spædu*; akin to Gr. *spathē* (see next word).]

spade, *spād*, *n.* a playing-card with black leaf-shaped (on Spanish cards sword-shaped) pips. [Sp. *espada*, sword—L. *spatha*—Gr. *spathē*, a broad blade.]

spade. See spado.

spadille, *spa-dil'*, *n.* the ace of spades in the games of ombre and quadrille.—Also **spadill'o, spadill'io**. [Fr.,—Sp. *espadilla*, dim. of *espada* ; see spade (2).]

spadix, *spā'diks*, *n.* (*bot.*) a fleshy spike of flowers :—*pl.* **spādices** (*-dī'sēz*).—*adjs.* **spadiceous** (*spā-dish'əs*), having, like, of the nature of, a spadix : coloured like a date : shaped like a palm-branch ; **spadicifloral** (*spā-di-si-flō'rəl*), having flowers in a spathe, as arum, palms, and some other mono-cotyledons. [Gr. *spādix*, *-ikos*, a torn-off (palm) branch, in L. date-coloured, bay.]

spado, *spā'dō* (L. *spä'*), *n.* a castrated or impotent person or animal :—*pl.* **spadones** (*spā-dō'nēz* ; L. *-nās*), **spā'do(e)s.**—Also (*rare*) **spade**. [L. *spādō*, *-ōnis*—Gr. *spādōn*, *-ōnos*—*spaein*, to pull, tear.]

spadroon, *spa-drōōn'*, *n.* (*hist.*) a cut-and-thrust sword: swordplay with it. [Fr. (Genevan dialect) *espadron.*]

spae, *spā*, *v.t.* and *v.i.* (*Scot.*) to foretell, divine.—*ns.* **spae'man** ; **spā'er** ; **spae'wife.** [O.N. *spá.*]

spaghetti, *spä-*, *spa-get'ti*, *n.* a cord-like paste inter-mediate between macaroni and vermicelli. [It., pl. of *spaghetto*, dim. of *spago*, a cord.]

spagyric, -al, *spa-jir'ik*, *-al*, *adjs.* alchemical.—*ns.* **spagyr'ic, spagyrist** (*spaj'ər-ist*), an alchemist.—Also **spagir'ic, spager'ic, &c.** [Prob. coined by Paracelsus.]

spahi, *spä'hē*, *n.* formerly a Turkish, now a French Algerian cavalryman. [Turk. (from Pers.) *sipāhī*; cf. **sepoy.**]

spain. Same as spane.

spairge. See sparge.

spake, *spāk*, *arch. pa.t.* of speak.

spaid, spall, spalle. See spauld.

spale, *spāl*, *n.* (*Scot.*) a splinter : a chip. [Cf. next.]

spall, *spawl*, *v.t.* and *v.i.* to split, splinter, to chip.—*n.* a chip or splinter, esp. of stone.—*v.t.* and *v.i.* **spalt**, to splinter.—*adj.* brittle. [Cf. M.E. *spalden*, to split ; Ger. *spalten.*]

spalpeen, *spal-pēn'*, *n.* a rascal, a mischievous fellow : a boy. [Ir. *spailpín*, a (migratory) labourer.]

span, *span*, *n.* the space from the end of the thumb to the end of the little finger when the fingers are extended: nine inches : distance from wing-tip to wing-tip in an aeroplane : distance between abutments, piers, supports, &c., or the portion of a structure (e.g. a bridge) between: total spread or stretch : a stretch of time, esp. of life.—*v.t.* to measure by spans : to measure : to arch over, bridge : to stretch over : to bridge : to encompass :—*pr.p.* **spann'ing** ; *pa.t.* and *pa.p.* **spanned**.—*ns.* **span'-counter, span'-farthing**, a game in which one tries to throw a counter or coin within a span of his opponent's.—*adjs.* **span'less**, that cannot be spanned or measured ; **span'-long**, of the length of a span.—*n.* **span'-roof**, a roof with equal slopes. [O.E. *spann* ; cf. Ger. *spanne.*]

span, *span*, *n.* a pair of horses : a team of oxen.—*v.t.* to yoke : (*obs.*) to wind up. [Du. and L.G. *span.*]

span, *span*, *adj.* fresh, short for **span'-new'**, quite new, new as a fresh-cut chip.—**spick and span** (see **spick**). [O.N. *spán-nýr*—*spán*, chip (cf. spoon), *nýr*, new.]

span, *span*, *arch. pa.t.* of spin.

spanaemia, *span-ē'mi-ä*, *n.* deficiency of red corpuscles in the blood.—*adj.* **spanae'mic.** [Gr. *spanos*, lacking, *haima*, blood.]

spancel, *span'sl*, *n.* a hobble, esp. for a cow.—*v.t.* to hobble.—*adj.* **span'celled.** [Du. or L.G. *spansel.*]

spandrel, spandril, *span'drəl*, *n.* the space between the curve of an arch and the enclosing mouldings, string-course, or the like. [Poss. conn. with expand.]

spane, spain, spean, *spān*, *v.t.* (*Scot.*) to wean. [M.Du. or M.L.G. *spanen*, or O.Fr. *espanir* ; cf. Ger. *spänen.*]

spang, *spang*, *n.* (*obs.*) a glittering ornament : (*arch.*) a clasp.—*v.t.* (*obs.*) to sprinkle with spangs.—*n.* **spangle** (*spang'gl*), a small, thin, glittering plate of metal : a sparkling speck, flake, or spot.—*v.t.* to adorn with spangles.—*v.i.* to glitter.—*adj.* **spang'led.**—*ns.* **spang'ler** ; **spang'let** (Shelley).—*n.* and *adj.* **spang'ling.**—*adj.* **spang'ly.** [O.E. *spang*, clasp ; cf. Du. *spang*, Ger. *spange*, *spängel.*]

spang, *spang*, *n.* (chiefly *Scot.*) a bound : a sudden movement or blow.—*v.i.* to bound.—*v.t.* to dash.—*n.* **spang'-cockle**, the flicking of a marble, &c., from the forefinger with the thumb-nail. [Origin obscure.]

Spaniard, *span'yərd*, *n.* a native or citizen of *Spain*: a Spanish ship.

spaniel, *span'yol*, *n.* a kind of dog, usu. liver-and-white, or black-and-white, with large pendent ears : one who fawns.—*adj.* (*Shak.*) like a spaniel : fawning, mean.—*v.t.* to follow or fawn on like a spaniel.—*v.i.* (or *v.t.* with *it*) to play the spaniel.—*adj.* and *adv.* **span'iel-like.**—**Blenheim spaniel**, red-and-white (see **Blenheim**) ; **clumber spaniel**, lemon-and-white (see **clumber**) ; **field- or land-spaniel**, hunting breeds (e.g. cockers, springers) ; **King Charles spaniel**, black-and-tan, brought into notice by *Charles* II. ; **Sussex spaniel**, golden-liver or brown ; **toy spaniel**, a lapdog (e.g. *Blenheim, King Charles*) ; (Irish) **water spaniel**, a (liver-coloured) spaniel for retrieving water-fowl. [O.Fr. *espaigneul* (Fr. *épagneul*)—Sp. *Español*, Spanish.]

spaniolate, *span'yō-lāt*, **spaniolise**, *-līz*, *vs.t.* to hispanicise. [O.Fr. *Espaignol*, a Spaniard.]

Spanish, *span'ish*, *adj.* of or pertaining to *Spain*.—*n.* the language of Spain.—**ride the Spanish mare**, to bestride the boom as a punishment ; **Spanish bayonet**, a yucca with straight sword-shaped leaves ; **Spanish broom**, a broom-like Mediter-ranean shrub (*Spartium junceum*) with showy yellow fragrant flowers ; **Spanish chalk**, soap-stone, French chalk ; **Spanish chestnut**, the true chestnut ; **Spanish cress**, a species of pepperwort ; **Spanish dagger**, *Yucca gloriosa* ; **Spanish fly**, a cantharid : a preparation of cantharides used medicinally ; **Spanish fowl**, a breed of the domestic hen — also *white-faced black Spanish* ; **Spanish grass**, esparto ; **Spanish influenza**, a severe form of influenza, which, first noted in Spain, spread all over the world in 1918 ; **Spanish juice**, extract of liquorice-root ; **Spanish Main** (i.e. mainland), the mainland coast of the Caribbean Sea : often popularly the Caribbean Sea itself ; **Spanish needles**, an American weed of the bur-marigold genus, with hooked fruits ; **Spanish sheep**, a merino ; **Spanish soap**, Castile soap ; **Spanish walk**, the piaffer ; **walk Spanish**, to compel or be compelled to walk on tiptoe, lifted by the collar and the seat of the trousers—hence to proceed or act under compulsion. [*Spain*, with vowel-shortening.]

spank, *spangk*, *v.t.* and *v.i.* to move or drive with speed or spirit.—*n.* **spank'er**, one who walks with long vigorous strides : a fast-going horse : any person or thing particularly striking or dashing : (*obs. slang*) a gold coin : a fore-and-aft sail on the aftermost mast.—*adj.* **spank'ing**, spirited, going freely : striking, beyond expectation : very large.—*adv.* **spank'ingly.** [Cf. Dan. *spanke*, to strut.]

spank, *spangk*, *v.t.* to strike with the flat of the hand, to smack.—*n.* a loud slap, esp. on the buttocks. [Prob. imit.]

spanner, *span'ər*, *n.* (*obs.*) an instrument for winding up a spring : a wrench for nuts, screws, &c. [Ger. *spanner* ; cf. span (2).]

spar, *spär*, *n.* a rafter : a pole : (chiefly *Scot.*) a bar or rail (*Spens.* **sparre**): an undressed tree stem of medium girth : a general term for masts, yards, booms, gaffs, &c.—*v.t.* to fasten with a spar (*Spens.*

sperre): to fasten: to shut: to fit with spars.—*n.*
spar'-deck, a light upper deck. [O.E. *gesparrian*, to bar; Du. *spar* (n.), *sperren* (vb.); O.N. *sparri*; Ger. *sperren* (vb.).]

spar, *spär*, *n.* any bright non-metallic mineral, with a good cleavage (esp. in compounds, as *calc-spar*, *fluorspar*, *felspar*; also *Iceland spar*): a crystal or fragment thereof: an ornament made of it.—*adj.* **sparry** (*spär'i*), of or like spar. [M.L.G. *spar*, related to O.E. *spærstän*, gypsum.]

spar, *spär*, *v.i.* to fight with spurs: to box, or make the actions of boxing: to dispute: (*pr.p.* **spar'-ing**; *pa.t.* and *pa.p.* **sparred**).—*n.* a boxing-match or demonstration: a cock-fight: a dispute.—*ns.* **sparr'er**; **sparr'ing**. [Perh. O.Fr. *esparer* (Fr. *éparer*), to kick out; prob. Gmc.]

sparable, *spar'ə-bl*, *n.* a small headless nail used by shoemakers. [**sparrow-bill**.]

spard, *spärd*, (*Spens.*) for **spared**.

spare, *spär*, *v.t.* to use frugally: to do without: to part with voluntarily: to afford: (*Milt.*) to allow oneself, concede to oneself: to abstain from using: to refrain from: to forbear to hurt, injure, punish, kill, end: to treat mercifully: to relieve or save from: to avoid: to avoid incurring: to save, hoard.—*v.i.* to be frugal: to forbear: to be merciful.—*adj.* sparing: frugal: scanty: lean: not in actual use: not required: kept or available for others or for such purposes as may occur.—*adv.* sparely.—*n.* (*Milt.*) spareness: sparing: a spare room: a spare man: a spare part: a duplicate kept or carried for emergencies: (*skittles*) overturning all the pins with the first two balls—i.e. with a ball to spare (a *double spare*, with first ball only): the score for so doing.—*adj.* **spare'less**, unmerciful. — *adv.* **spare'ly**. — *ns.* **spare'ness**; **spar'er**; **spare'rib**, a piece of pork consisting of ribs with a little meat adhering to them.—*adj.* **spar'ing**.—*adv.* **spar'ingly**.—*n.* **spar'ingness**.— **spare room**, a bedroom for visitors: (*U.S.*) a parlour; **to spare**, over and above what is required. [O.E. *sparian*, to spare, *spær*, sparing; Ger. *sparen*.]

spare, *spär*, *n.* (now *Scot.*) the slit at the top of a skirt. [Origin obscure.]

Sparganium, *spär-gā'ni-əm*, *n.* the bur-reed genus, constituting a family **Sparganiä'ceae**, akin to the reed-maces. [Gr. *sparganion*.]

sparge, *spärj*, *v.t.* to sprinkle—(*Scot.*) **spairge**, *spärj*.—*n.* **spar'ger**, a sprinkler. [L. *spargĕre*, to sprinkle.]

spar-hawk, *spär'-hawk*, *n.*=**sparrow-hawk**.

Sparidae, *spar'i-dē*, *n.pl.* the sea-bream family.—*adj.* **spar'oid**. [Gr. *sparos*, the fish sargus.]

spark, *spärk*, *n.* a glowing or glittering particle: anything of like appearance or character, as easily extinguished, ready to cause explosion, burning hot: a flash: an electric discharge across a gap: anything active or vivid: a gay sprightly person: a lover, a beau: (in *pl.*, *naut. slang*) a ship's wireless operator.—*v.i.* to emit sparks: to sparkle: to play the gallant or lover.—*v.t.* to send forth as sparks: to send sparks through.—*ns.* **spark'-coil**, an induction coil: a connexion of high-resistance used to prevent sparking in electrical apparatus; **spark'-gap**, the space between electrodes across which electric sparks pass: apparatus with such a space; **spark'ing-plug** (*U.S.* **spark'-plug**), in an internal-combustion engine, a plug carrying wires between which an electric spark passes to fire the explosive mixture of gases.—*adj.* **spark'ish**, gay, jaunty, showy.—*adv.* **spark'ishly**.—*adj.* **spark'less**.—*adv.* **spark'lessly**.—*n.* **spark'let**, a small spark. [O.E. *spærca*, *spearca*; Du. *spark*.]

sparke, *spärk*, *n.* (*Spens.*) a weapon of some kind, perh. an error for **sparthe**.

sparkle, *spärk'l*, *n.* a little spark: glitter: scintillation: emission of sparks: appearance of effervescence (as of carbon dioxide in wine): vivacity: spirited animation: coruscation of wit.—*v.i.* to emit sparks: to glitter: to effervesce with glittering bubbles: to be bright, animated, vivacious, or witty.—*v.t.* to cause to sparkle: to throw out as, in, or like sparks.—*n.* **spark'ler**.—*n.* and *adj.* **spark'ling**.—*adv.* **spark'lingly**. [Dim. and freq. of **spark**.]

sparling, *spär'ling*, **spirling**, *spər', spir'ling*, *n.* (now *Scot.*) the smelt. [Partly O.Fr. *esperlinge* (of Gmc. origin), partly M.L.G. *spirling* or M.Du. *spierling*.]

sparrow, *spar'ō*, *n.* a plain brown bird of the finch family (*Passer domesticus*, house-sparrow, *P. montanus*, tree-sparrow, or other of the genus): extended to many other, usually brown, birds, as the hedge-sparrow.—*n.* **sparr'ow-bill** (see **sparable**). —*adj.* **sparr'ow-blasted**, (in contempt) dumbfounded.—*n.* **sparr'ow-hawk**, a genus (Accipiter) of long-legged, short-winged falcons, like the goshawks, but smaller. [O.E. *spearwa*; Goth. *sporwa*, O.N. *spörr*, Ger. *sperling*.]

sparrow-grass, *spar'ō-grås*, *n.* a corruption of **asparagus**.

sparse, *spärs*, *adj.* thinly scattered: scanty.—Also *adv.*—*advs.* **spars'edly** (*rare*); **sparse'ly**.—*ns.* **sparse'ness**; **spars'ity**. [L. *sparsus*, pa.p. of *spargĕre*, to scatter; Gr. *speirein*, to sow.]

spart, *spärt*, *n.* esparto: (*obs.*) Spanish broom.—*n.* **sparterie** (*-ə-rē*; Fr.), articles of esparto. [L. *spartum*, Spanish broom, esparto, and Sp. *esparto*.]

Sparta, *spär'tä*, *n.* a city of Greece, capital of ancient Laconia.—*n.* **Spar'tan**, a citizen or native of Sparta or Laconia: one displaying Spartan qualities.—*adj.* of Sparta: Laconian: characteristic of Sparta—simple, hardy, rigorous, frugal, laconic, militaristic, despising culture: of a breed of bloodhounds.—*adv.* **Spar'tanly**. [Gr. *Spartē* (Doric *Spartā*).]

Spartacist, *spär'tə-sist*, *n.* a follower of *Spartacus*, leader of the revolted slaves in the Third Slave War against Rome (73-71 B.C.): a German communist of extreme type in the revolution of 1918.

sparth(e), *spärth*, *n.* (*arch.*) a long battle-axe. [O.N. *spartha*.]

spasm, *spazm*, *n.* a violent involuntary muscular contraction: a sudden convulsive action, movement, or emotion: (*slang*) a section of a performance, e.g. a verse.—*adjs.* **spasmat'ic, -al** (*rare*); **spasm'ic**; **spasmod'ic, -al**, relating to, or consisting in, spasms: convulsive: intermittent.— *adv.* **spasmod'ically**.—*n.* **spas'modist**, one whose work is spasmodic.—*adj.* **spas'tic**, of the nature of spasm: characterised or affected by spasms: spasmodic.—*n.* one affected with spastic paralysis. — *adv.* **spas'tically**.—*n.* **spasticity** (*-tis'i-ti*), tendency to spasm.—**Spasmodic School**, a group of English poets, including P. J. Bailey, Sydney Dobell, and Alexander Smith, marked by overstrained and unnatural sentiment and expression; **spastic paralysis**, various disabilities caused by injury to the part of the brain that controls muscular movement in the limb affected. [Gr. *spasma*, *-atos*, and *spasmos*, *-ou*, convulsion; adjs. *spasmōdēs*, *spastikos—spaein*, to draw, convulse.]

spat, *spat*, *pa.t.* and *pa.p.* of **spit** (2).

spat, *spat*, *n.* the spawn of shellfish.—*v.i.* and *v.t.* to spawn. [Perh. from root of **spit** (2).]

spat, *spat*, *n.* (*U.S.*) a slap: a large drop, as of rain: a splash, spattering: a petty quarrel.—*v.t.* to slap, to strike lightly.—*v.i.* to engage in a petty quarrel. [Prob. imit.; cf. Du. *spat*, spot, stain, spatter.]

spat, *spat*, *n.* a gaiter. [**spatterdash**.]

Spatangus, *spä-tang'gəs*, *n.* the typical genus of heart-urchins.—*adj.* and *n.* **spatang'oid**.—*n.pl.* **Spatangoid'ea**, the heart-urchins, an order of sea-urchins, more or less heart-shaped, without Aristotle's lantern, with eccentric anus. [Gr. *spatangēs*, a kind of sea-urchin.]

spatchcock, *spach'-kok*, *n.* a fowl killed and cooked at once.—*v.t.* to treat in this way: to interpolate. [Prob. **dispatch** and **cock**.]

spate, *speat*, *spät*, *n.* (orig. *Scot.*) a flood. [Origin doubtful.]

spathe, *spādh*, *n.* (*bot.*) a sheathing bract, usu. a conspicuous one enclosing a spadix.—*adjs.* **spathaceous** (*spə-thā'shəs*), **spathed** (*spādhd*), having a spathe. [Gr. *spathē*, a broad blade.]

spathic, *spath'ik*, *adj.* of the nature of, or like, spar: lamellar.—*adj.* **spath'ose** (or *-ōs*), spathic.— **spathic iron**, chalybite. [Ger. *spat(h)*, spar.]

spathulate, *spath'ū-lāt*. Same as **spatulate**.

spatial, *spā'shl*, *adj.* relating to space.—*n.* **spati-**

ality (*spä-shi-al'i-ti*).—*adv.* **spa'tially.**—*adj.* **spa-tiotemp'oral,** of space-time or space and time together. [L. *spatium*, space.]

spattee, *spat-ē', n.* a protective outer stocking or long gaiter. [**spat** and **puttee.**]

spatter, *spat'ər, v.t.* to throw out or scatter upon : to scatter about : to sprinkle, esp. with mud or liquid.—*v.i.* to fly or fall in drops : to let drops fall or fly about.—*n.* a spattering : what is spattered. —*ns.* **spatt'erdash,** a long gaiter or legging ; **spatt'er-dock,** (*U.S.*) the yellow water-lily ; **spatt'er-work,** reproduction of designs by covering the surface with the pattern and spattering colour on the parts exposed. [Cf. Du. and L.G. *spatten.*]

spatula, *spat'ū-lä, n.* a broad blunt blade or flattened spoon.—*adjs.* **spat'ular** ; **spat'ulate,** shaped like a spatula : broad and rounded at the tip and tapering at the base.—*n.* **spat'ule,** a spatula. [L. *spatula, spathula,* dim. of *spatha*—Gr. *spathē,* a broad blade.]

spauld, *spawld, n.* (now *Scot.*) the shoulder : a limb.—Also **spald, spall, spaul,** and (*Spens.*) **spalle.** — *ns.* **spauld'-bone,** shoulder-blade ; **spauld'-ill,** quarter-evil. [O.Fr. *espalde* (Fr. *épaule*)—L. *spatula* (see foregoing).]

spavin, *spav'in, n.* see **bone-spavin.**—*Scot.* **spavie** (*spā'vä*).—*adj.* **spav'ined,** affected with spavin.— *n.* **bog'-spavin** (see under **bog**). [O.Fr. *espa(r)vain* (Fr. *éparvin*) ; connexion with **sparrow** obscure.]

spaw, *spaw,* **spaw-well,** &c., obs. forms of spa, &c.

spawl, *spawl, n.* spittle, slaver.—*v.i.* to emit spawl.

spawn, *spawn, n.* a mass of eggs laid in water : fry : brood : (contemptuous) offspring : mushroom mycelium.—*v.t.* to produce as spawn : (contemptuous) to generate, esp. in mass.—*v.i.* to produce or deposit spawn : to teem : to come forth as or like spawn.—*ns.* **spawn'-brick, -cake,** a consolidated cake of horse-dung with mushroom spawn ; **spawn'er,** one who spawns : a female fish, esp. at spawning-time.—*n.* and *adj.* **spawn'-ing.**—*ns.* **spawn'ing-bed, -ground,** a bed or place in the bottom of a stream on which fish deposit their spawn. [O.Fr. *espandre,* to shed—L. *ex-pandĕre,* to spread out.]

spay, *spā, v.t.* to remove or destroy the ovaries of. [A.Fr. *espeier*—*espee* (Fr. *épée*), sword.]

spayad, *spā'ad,* **spayd, spade,** *spād,* **spay,** *spā, n.* (*obs.*) a hart in his third year. [Origin obscure.]

speak, *spēk, v.i.* to utter words : to talk : to dis-course : to make a speech : to sound : to give tongue : to give expression, information, or inti-mation by any means.—*v.t.* to pronounce : to utter : to say : to express : to declare : to mention : to describe : to hail or communicate with : to use as a language, talk in : to bring or render by speaking :—*pa.t.* spŏke, or (*arch.*) spāke ; *pa.p.* spŏ'ken, or (*arch.*) spŏke.—*adj.* **speak'able,** able or fit to be spoken or expressed in speech : (*Milt.*) able to speak.—*ns.* **speak'-eas'y,** (*U.S.*) an illicit dram-shop, shebeen ; **speak'er,** one who speaks : the president (orig. the mouthpiece) of a legislative body, as the House of Commons : a loud-speaker ; **speak'ership,** the office of speaker ; **speak'ing,** the act of expressing ideas in words : discourse.— *adj.* uttering or transmitting speech : seeming to speak, lifelike.—*adv.* **speak'ingly.**—*ns.* **speak'ing-trum'pet,** an instrument for making the voice heard at a distance ; **speak'ing-tube,** a tube for speaking through to another room ; **speak'ing-voice,** the kind of voice used in speaking.—**so to speak,** as one might put it, as it were ; **speak a ship,** to hail and speak to some one on board her ; **speak fair,** to address one in conciliatory terms ; **speak for,** to speak on behalf of or in favour of : to be a proof of : to witness to : to bespeak, engage ; **speaking terms** (see **term**) ; **speak out,** to speak boldly, freely, unreservedly, or so as to be easily heard ; **speak to,** to reprove : to attest, testify to : to discuss ; **speak up,** to speak so as to be easily heard ; to speak of, worth mentioning ; to speak to, so as to have conversation with. [Late O.E. *specan* (for *sprecan*) ; Du. *spreken,* Ger. *sprechen.*]

speal-bone, *spēl'-bōn, n.* See **spule.**

spear, *spēr, n.* a long weapon made of a pole with a pointed head : a barbed fork for catching fish : anything sharp or piercing : a spearman : a spire : a spiky shoot or blade : a reed.—*v.t.* to pierce with a spear.—*adj.* **speared,** armed with the spear. —*ns.* **spear'fish,** a kind of swordfish (Tetrapturus) ; **spear'-grass,** a name for many spearlike grasses ; **spear'head,** the head of a spear : the front of an attack ; **spear'man,** a man armed with a spear ; **spear'mint,** the common garden-mint ; **spear'-point** ; **spear'-running,** a tourney ; **spear'-shaft** ; **spear'-side,** the male side or line of descent (opp. to **spindle-side,** or **distaff-side**) ; **spear'-this'tle,** a common thistle (*Cnicus lanceolatus* or *Cirsium lanceolatum*) ; **spear'-thrower,** a throwing-stick ; **spear'-wood,** an Acacia or a Eucalyptus (both Australian) whose wood is good for spear-shafts ; **spear'wort,** a Ranunculus with lance-shaped leaves (*R. Lingua,* greater, *R. Flammula,* lesser **spear-wort**).—*adj.* **spear'y.** [O.E. *spere* ; Ger. *speer* ; with some senses from **spire.**]

spec, *spek, n.* a colloquial abbrev. of **speculation.**

special, *spesh'l, adj.* particular : peculiar : dis-tinctive : exceptional : additional to ordinary : detailed : intimate : designed for a particular pur-pose : confined or mainly applied to a particular subject.—*n.* any special or particular person or thing : any person or thing set apart for a particular duty—a constable, a railway-train, &c. : a news-paper extra, a dispatch from a special correspond-ent.—*n.* **specialisā'tion.**—*v.t.* **spec'ialise,** to make special or specific : to differentiate : to adapt to conditions : to specify : to narrow and intensify.— *v.i.* to become or be a specialist : to become differ-entiated : to be adapted to special conditions.— *ns.* **specialis'er** ; **spec'ialism,** devotion to some particular study or pursuit ; **spec'ialist,** one who devotes himself to a special subject.—*adj.* **special-ist'ic.**—*n.* **speciality** (*spesh-i-al'i-ti*), the particular characteristic of a person or thing : a special occu-pation or object of attention.—*adv.* **specially** (*spesh'ə-li*).— *n.* **spec'ialty,** something special or distinctive : any special product, article of sale or of manufacture : any special pursuit, department of study, &c. : a special contract for the payment of money : (*law*) a deed under seal.—**in special** (*arch.*), in particular : especially ; **special constable** (see **constable**) ; **special correspondent,** a person employed to send reports to a particular newspaper, agency, &c. ; **special licence, plead-ing, verdict** (see **licence,** &c.). [L. *speciālis*—*speciēs,* species.]

species, *spē'shēz, -shiz, -shi-ēz, n.* (*obs.* except *theol.*) outward appearance, visible form : a eucharistic element : (*obs.*) a visual image : (*log.*) a group of individuals having common characteristics, special-ised from others of the same *genus* : (*biol.*) a group (sometimes rather arbitrarily defined) of closely allied mutually fertile individuals showing con-stant differences from allied groups, placed under a genus : a kind, sort :—*pl.* spe'cies.—*ns.* **specie** (*spē'shē, -shi-ē* ; orig. the L. abl. as in the phrase *in speciē,* in kind), formerly, payment or requital in the same kind : (*obs.*) commodities, kind : now, coined money ; **spe'cies-monger,** a hair-splitter in classification. [L. *speciēs,* pl. *-ēs,* appearance, kind, species—*specĕre,* to look at.]

specify, *spes'i-fī, v.t.* to mention particularly : to make specific : to set down as requisite :—*pr.p.* **spec'ifying** ; *pa.t.* and *pa.p.* **spec'ified.**—*adjs.* **spec'ifiable** (or *-fī'*) ; **specific** (*spi-sif'ik*), con-stituting or determining a species : pertaining to a species : peculiar to a species : of special appli-cation or origin : specifying : precise.—*n.* a remedy or medicine for a particular disease or part of the body : anything that is specific.—*adj.* **specif'ical.** —*adv.* **specif'ically.**—*v.t.* **specif'icate,** to specify. —*ns.* **specificā'tion** (*spes-*), making, becoming, or being specific : the act of specifying : any point or particular specified : the description of his invention presented by an applicant for a patent ; **specificity** (*spes-i-fis'i-ti*). — *adj.* **spec'ified.** — **specific gravity,** the weight of any given substance as compared with the weight of an equal bulk or volume of water or other standard substance at the same, or at standard, temperature and pressure :

specific heat (see **heat**); **specific name**, in biological nomenclature, the name of the species, i.e. the second name, the first being the generic name. [O.Fr. *specifier*—L.L. *specificāre*—L. *speciēs*, kind, *facĕre*, to shake.]

specimen, *spes'i-min*, *n.* an object or portion serving as a sample, esp. for purposes of study or collection: a remarkable type. [L. *specimen*—*specĕre*, to see.]

specious, *spē'shəs*, *adj.* (*obs.*) beautiful: showy: looking well at first sight: fair-showing: plausibly deceptive.—*ns.* **speciosity** (-*shi-os'i-ti*), **spe'ciousness**.—*adv.* **spe'ciously**. [L. *speciōsus*, showy—*speciēs*, form—*specĕre*, to look at.]

speck, *spek*, *n.* a small spot: a particle: a small American fish, a darter.—*v.t.* to spot.—*adjs.* **speck'less**; **speck'y**. [O.E. *specca*.]

speck, *spek*, *n.* fat: bacon: blubber.—*n.* **specktioneer** (*spek-shən-ēr'*), the chief harpooner in whale-fishing. [Ger. *speck*, Du. *spek*, fat; cf. O.E. *spic*, fat bacon.]

speckle, *spek'l*, *n.* a little spot.—*v.t.* to mark with speckles.—*adj.* **speck'led**.—*n.* **speck'ledness**. [**speck** (1).]

specs, *speks*, *n.pl.* a colloquial abbrev. of **spectacles**.

spectacle, *spek'tə-kl*, *n.* a sight: a show, pageant, exhibition: (in *pl.*) a pair of lenses mounted in frames with side-pieces to grip the temples: (in *pl.*) a marking resembling spectacles, as in the cobra.—*adjs.* **spec'tacled**; **spectacular** (-*tak'ū-lər*), of the nature of, or marked by, display.—*n.* **spectacularity** (-*lar'i-ti*).—*adv.* **spectac'ularly**. [L. *spectāculum*—*spectāre*, -*ātum*, intens. of *specĕre*, to look at.]

spectator, *spek-tā'tər*, *n.* one who looks on :—*fem.* **spectā'tress**, **spectā'trix**. — *adj.* **spectatorial** (-*tə-tō'ri-əl*).—*n.* **spectā'torship**, the action, office, or quality of a spectator.

spectre, *spek'tər*, *n.* an apparition: a phantom: a ghost: any insect of the Phasmidae (stick-insects, leaf-insects).—*adj.* **spec'tral**, relating to, or like, a spectre or spectrum.—*n.* **spectral'ity**, the state of being spectral, a spectral object.—*adv.* **spec'trally**.—*ns.* **spec'tre-bat**, a leaf-nosed bat; **spec'tre-crab'**, a glass-crab; **spec'tre-in'sect**, a phasmid; **spec'tre-le'mur**, the tarsier; **spec'tre-shrimp'**, a skeleton-shrimp; **spec'trogram**, a photograph of a spectrum; **spec'trograph**, an apparatus for obtaining and photographing a spectrum.—*adjs.* **spectrograph'ic, -al.**—*ns.* **spectrog'raphy**; **spectrohē'liogram**, a photograph of the sun by monochromatic light; **spectrohē'liograph**, an instrument for taking it.—*adj.* **spectrolog'ical.** — *adv.* **spectrolog'ically.** — *ns.* **spectrol'ogy**, the science of the spectrum or spectrum analysis: the study of ghosts; **spectrom'eter**, an instrument for measuring refractive indices.—*adj.* **spectromet'ric.**—*n.* **spec'troscope**, an instrument for obtaining and observing spectra. —*adjs.* **spectroscop'ic, -al.**—*adv.* **spectroscop'ically.**—*ns.* **spectros'copist** (*spek-tros'kə-pist*, or *spek'tra-skop-ist*): **spectros'copy** (or *spek'*), the use of the spectroscope and the study of spectra; **spec'trum**, an after-image: the range of colour produced by a prism or diffraction-grating: any analogous range of radiations in order of wavelength :—*pl.* **spec'tra**.—**spectrum analysis**, determination of chemical composition by observing the spectrum of light or X-rays coming from or through the substance. [L. *spectrum*, an appearance —*specĕre*, to look at.]

specular, *spek'ū-lər*, *adj.* mirror-like: having a speculum: by reflection: visual: giving a wide view.—**specular iron**, a brilliant steely crystallised haematite; **specular stone**, a transparent or semitransparent mineral, as mica, selenite, talc. [L. *speculāris*—*speculum*, a mirror, and *specula*, a watch-tower.]

speculate, *spek'ū-lāt*, *v.t.* to look at or into, view, examine (*lit.* or *fig.*): to observe: to examine: to view in a mirror: to make conjectures about.—*v.i.* to reflect: to theorise: to make conjectures or guesses: to take risk in hope of gain, esp. in buying and selling.—*ns.* **specula'tion**, act of speculating or its result: vision: viewing: reflec-

tion: contemplation: theorising: conjecture: mere guesswork: a more or less risky investment of money for the sake of unusually large profits: a card game in which trumps are bought and sold: (*Shak.*) an observer; **spec'ulātist**, a speculative philosopher: a speculator.—*adj.* **spec'ulātive**, of the nature of, based on, given to, speculation or theory.—*adv.* **spec'ulātively**.—*ns.* **spec'ulātiveness**; **spec'ulātor**, one who speculates in any sense: a watchman, lookout.—*adj.* **spec'ulatory**, exercising speculation: adapted for spying or viewing.—*n.* **spec'ulātrix**, a female speculator. [L. *speculātus*, pa.p. of *speculārī*—*specula*, a lookout—*specĕre*, to look at.]

speculum, *spek'ū-ləm*, *n.* a mirror: a reflector, usu. of polished metal: (*surg.*) an instrument for viewing cavities of the body: a bright patch on a wing, esp. a duck's :—*pl.* **spec'ula**.—**speculum metal**, an alloy of copper and tin, with or without other ingredients. [L. *speculum*, a mirror—*specĕre*, to look at.]

sped, *sped*, *pa.t.* and *pa.p.* of **speed**.

speech, *spēch*, *n.* that which is spoken: language: the power of speaking: manner of speaking: a continuous spoken utterance: a discourse, oration: talk: colloquy: mention: (*obs.*) a rumour: (*obs.*) a saying: the sounding of a musical instrument.—*v.t.* and *v.i.* to harangue.—*ns.* **speech'-craft**, philology: rhetoric; **speech'-cri'er**, a hawker of broadsides giving hanged criminals' dying speeches; **speech'-day**, the public day at the close of a school year.—*adj.* **speech'ful**, loquacious: expressive.—*ns.* **speech'fulness**; **speechificā'tion** (*coll.*); **speech'ifier**.—*v.i.* **speech'ify**, to make speeches, harangue (implying contempt).—*adj.* **speech'less**, destitute or deprived of the power of speech.—*adv.* **speech'lessly**.—*ns.* **speech'lessness**; **speech'-maker**, one accustomed to speak in public; **speech'-making**; **speech'-reading**, lip-reading; **speech'-room**, a hall for making speeches in; **speech'-train'ing**, treatment of defects of speech. [Late O.E. *spéc*, *spǽc*, for O.E. *spréc*, *sprǽc*; Ger. *sprache*.]

speed, *spēd*, *n.* (*arch.*) success: a help to success: quickness, velocity.—*v.i.* (*arch.*) to succeed, fare: to move quickly: to hurry: to drive at high, or at dangerously, unduly, or illegally high, speed.—*v.t.* to give or bring success to: to further: to send forth with good wishes: to bring to an end or finished state: to bring to a sorry plight, to do for (in *passive*): to send swiftly: to push forward: to haste: to betake with speed: to urge to high speed: to set or regulate the speed of :—*pa.t.* and *pa.p.* **sped** (also **speed'ed**).—*ns.* **speed'boat**, a swift motor-boat; **speed'boating**; **speed'cop**, (*slang*) a policeman who observes the speed of motorists; **speed'er**, one who, or that which, speeds or promotes speed.—*adj.* **speed'ful.**—*advs.* **speed'fully**; **speed'ily**.—*ns.* **speed'iness**, quickness; **speed'ing**, success: promotion, furtherance: progressive increase of speed (often with *up*): motoring at excessive speed.—Also *adj.* —*adj.* **speed'less**.—*ns.* **speedom'eter**, an instrument for measuring speed of vehicles; **speed'ster**, a speedboat: one who speeds; **speed'-up**, an acceleration, esp. in work; **speed'way**, a road for fast traffic: a motor-cycle racing track; **speed'-well**, any species of the scrophulariaceous genus Veronica, typically blue-flowered, posterior petals united, posterior sepal wanting.—*adj.* **speed'y**, swift: prompt: soon achieved.—**speed up**, to quicken the rate of working; **speedy cut, cutting**, injury to a horse's fore-leg by the opposite shoe. [O.E. *spéd*; Du. *spoed*.]

speel, *spēl*, *v.t.* and *v.i.* (*Scot.*) to climb.—*n.* a climb.

speel'er, (*obs. Scot.*) an acrobat: (now) a climber: a climbing-iron. [Poss. L.G. *speler*, a performer.]

speir, **speer**, *spēr*, *v.t.* and *v.i.* (*Scot.*) to ask, inquire. [O.E. *spyrian*, to inquire after, *spor*, a trace.]

speisade. See **lance-speisade**, under **lance**.

speiss, *spīs*, *n.* a mass of arsenides and commonly antimonides, a first product in smelting certain ores.—*n.* **speiss'-cobalt**, smaltite. [Ger. *speise*.]

spekboom, *spek'bōm*, *n.* a S. African succulent shrub of the purslane family. [Du., bacon tree.]

spelaean, *spi-lē'ən, adj.* cave-dwelling.—*adj.* **spelaeological** (*spel-i-ō-loj'i-kl*).—*ns.* **spelaeologist** (*-ol'ə-jist*): **spelaeol'ogy,** the scientific study of caves. [Gr. *spēlaion,* a cave.]

speld, *speld,* **spelder,** *spel'dər, vs.t.* (*Scot.*) to spread open or sprawlingly: to slit and lay open. —*ns.* **spel'din(g),** **speld'rin(g),** a haddock (or other fish) split open and dried. [Cf. M.E. *spalden,* to split ; Ger. *spalten.*]

spell, *spel, n.* (*obs.*) speech, discourse, talk, a sermon : a magic formula : a magic influence : enchantment : entrancement.—*v.t.* (*obs.*) to utter : to say a spell over : to bind with a spell : to enchant. —*v.i.* (*obs.*) to discourse.—*v.t.* **spell'bind** (*back-formation*).—*n.* **spell'binder,** (*U.S.*) an orator, usu. political or evangelical, who holds his audience spellbound.—*adjs.* **spell'bound,** bound by a spell : entranced ; **spell'ful,** magical ; **spell'-stopt,** brought to a standstill by a spell. [O.E. *spell,* narrative, *spellian,* to speak, announce ; cf. Goth. *spill,* O.N. *spjall,* tale.]

spell, *spel, v.t.* to read laboriously, letter by letter : to make out, unriddle, come to understand : to scan : to name or set down in order the letters of : to constitute or represent orthographically : (*fig.*) to import, amount to.—*v.i.* to spell words, esp. correctly : to contemplate : to express or hint a desire : (*pa.t.* and *pa.p.* **spelled, spelt**).—*n.* a mode of spelling.—*adj.* **spell'able.**—*ns.* **spell'down,** (*U.S.*) a spelling competition ; **spell'er ; spell'ing ; spell'ing-bee,** a competition in spelling ; **spell'ing-book,** a book for teaching to spell.—*adv.* **spell'ingly,** letter by letter.—**spell backward,** to spell in reverse order : perversely to misrepresent or misconstrue the qualities of ; **spell baker,** to do something difficult, prob. because *baker* was one of the first dissyllables in old spelling-books. [O.Fr. *espeller* (Fr. *épeler*), of Gmc. origin ; cf. foregoing.]

spell, *spel, v.t.* to take the place of at work : to relieve, give a rest to : to take a turn at.—*v.i.* to take turns : to rest : (*pr.p.* **spell'ing ;** *pa.t.* and *pa.p.* **spelled**).—*n.* a shift : a turn at work : a bout, turn : a short time : a stretch of time : a rest : (*U.S.*) a fit of irritation, illness, &c. [O.E. *spelian,* to act for another ; cf. Du. *spelen,* Ger. *spielen,* to play.]

spell, *spel, n.* a splinter : a rung : a trap for throwing up the knur in knur and spell. [Perh. **speld** ; but cf. Ger. *spellen,* to split.]

spelt, *spelt, n.* an inferior species of wheat (*Triticum Spelta*), grown in the mountainous parts of Europe. [O.E. *spelt.*]

spelter, *spel'tər, n.* zinc, esp. impure zinc. [Cf. L.G. *spialter.*]

spence, *spens, n.* (*prov.*) a larder : a pantry : (*Scot.*) an inner room, parlour. [O.Fr. *despense,* a buttery —*despendre*—L. *dispendĕre.*]

spencer, *spens'ər, n.* a kind of wig : a short double-breasted overcoat : a woman's short under-garment, formerly over-jacket. [After various persons of the name.]

spencer, *spens'ər, n.* (in ships and barques) a fore-and-aft sail abaft the fore and main masts.

Spencerian, *spen-sē'ri-ən, adj.* pertaining to the synthetic philosophy or evolutionary cosmology of Herbert *Spencer* (1820-1903).—*n.* a follower of Spencer.—*n.* **Spencē'rianism.**

spend, *spend, v.t.* to expend : to weigh out, pay out : to give, bestow, employ, for any purpose : to shed : to consume : to use up : to exhaust : to waste : to pass, as time.—*v.i.* to make excuse :—*pa.t.* and *pa.p.* **spent.**—*adj.* **spen'dable.**—*ns.* **spend'all,** a spendthrift ; **spen'der ; spen'ding ; spend'thrift,** one who spends the savings of thrift : a prodigal.—*adj.* excessively lavish.—*adj.* **spent,** exhausted : of fish, exhausted by spawning. [O.E. *spenden*—L. *expendĕre* or *dispendĕre,* to weigh out.]

Spenserian, *spen-sē'ri-ən, adj.* pertaining to Edmund *Spenser* (1552-99) or esp. his stanza in *The Faerie Queene,* of eight decasyllabic lines and an Alexandrine, rhymed *a b a b b c b c c.*

pent, *spent.* See spend.

peos, *spē'os, n.* a grotto-temple or tomb. [Gr. *spĕos.*]

Spergula, *spər'gū-lä, n.* the spurrey genus, akin to chickweed.—*ns.* **Spergulā'ria,** the allied sandwort-spurrey genus. [L.L.]

sperling, *spər'ling.* Same as **sparling.**

sperm, *spərm, n.* seed or semen : generative substance : a male gamete or germ-cell : (*obs.*) eggs, spawn, brood, offspring : (*obs.*) the chalaza of a hen's egg (formerly believed to be contributed by the cock) : a sperm-whale : sperm-oil : a sperm-candle : spermaceti.—For some compounds beginning **sperma-, spermo-,** see **sperma-** (*spər'mə-tō-*).—*ns.* **sper'maduct, sper'miduct,** a duct conveying spermatozoa ; **spermā'rium :** *pl.* **spermā'ria ; sper'mary,** the male germ-gland ; **sperma(to)thē'ca** (Gr. *thēkē,* receptacle), in female insects, &c., a receptacle in which sperms received are stored.—*adjs.* **spermathē'cal ; spermat'ic, -al,** of, pertaining to, conveying sperm : generative. —*ns.* **spermat'ic,** a spermatic vessel ; **sper'matid,** a cell that develops directly into a spermatozoon ; **sper'matist,** a believer in the doctrine that the sperm contains all future generations in germ ; **spermatium** (*-mā'shəm*), a non-motile male gamete in red seaweeds : a spore-like structure, possibly sexual, in some fungi :—*pl.* **spermā'tia ; sper'-matoblast** (Gr. *blastos,* a shoot), a spermatid.— *adj.* **spermatoblas'tic.**—*ns.* **sper'matocele** (Gr. *kēlē,* tumour), tumour of the testicle ; **sper'matocyte** (Gr. *kytos,* vessel), a sperm mother-cell or its predecessor ; **spermatogenesis** (*-jen'*), **spermatogeny** (*-ə-toj'i-ni*), sperm-formation.—*adjs.* **spermatogenet'ic, spermatogen'ic, spermatog'enous.**—*ns.* **spermatogonium** (*-gō'ni-əm*), one of the cells that by repeated division form the spermatocytes ; **sper'matophore,** a case enclosing the spermatozoa.—*n.pl.* **Spermatoph'yta** (also **Spermaph'yta, Spermoph'yta :** Gr. *phyton,* plant), the flowering plants as one of the four phyla of the vegetable kingdom.—*n.* **spermat'ophyte** (**sperm'-aphyte,** &c.).—*adj.* **spermatophytic** (*-fit'ik* ; also **sperma-, spermo-**).—*ns.* **spermatorrhoe'a** (Gr. *rhoiā,* flow), involuntary seminal discharge ; **spermatozō'id, spermatozō'on** (Gr. *zōion,* animal ; *pl.* **-zō'a**), a male germ-cell ; **sperm'-candle,** a candle of spermaceti ; **sperm'-ceil,** a male gamete. —For some compounds in **spermo-,** see **spermato-.** —*ns.* **sper'mogone, spermogō'nium** (*pl.* **-ia**), a flask-shaped structure in which spermatia are produced ; **sperm'-oil,** oil from the sperm-whale ; **sperm'-whale,** the cachalot, a whale from which spermaceti is obtained. [Gr. *sperma, -atos,* seed, *semen*—*speirein,* to sow.]

spermaceti, *spər-mə-set'i, n.* a waxy matter obtained mixed with oil from the head of the sperm-whale and others.—Also *adj.* [L. *sperma cēti* (gen. of *cētus,* a whale—Gr. *kētos*), whale's sperm, from a wrong notion of its origin.]

spermophile, *spər'mō-fil, -fīl, n.* a ground-squirrel (Spermophilus), a rodent akin to the true squirrels. [Gr. *sperma,* seed, *phileein,* to love.]

sperre, *spər, v.t.* (*Spens.*) to bolt, bar.—In Shak., *Troilus and Cressida,* Prol. 19, **stirre** is probably a misprint for **sperre.** [spar.]

sperrylite, *sper'i-līt, n.* an arsenide of platinum, found at Sudbury, Ontario. [After F. L. *Sperry,* with Gr. *lithos,* stone.]

sperse, *spərs, v.t.* and *v.i.* (*arch.*) aphetic form of **disperse** :—*pa.t.* and *pa.p.* (*Spens.*) **sperst ;** also **spersed.**

sperthe. Same as **sparth.**

spessartite, *spes'ärt-īt, n.* a manganese-alumina garnet found at *Spessart* in Bavaria.

spet, *spet, v.t.* (*Milt.*) and *v.i.* a form of **spit** (2).

spetch, *spech, n.* a piece of skin used in making glue. [speck.]

spew, spue, *spū, v.t.* to vomit.—*v.i.* to vomit : to ooze, run.—*n.* vomited matter : a marshy spot.— *ns.* **spew'er ; spew'iness.**—*adj.* **spew'y,** boggy. [O.E. *spīwan, spīowan,* to spit ; Du. *spuwen,* Ger. *speien ;* also L. *spuĕre,* Gr. *ptyein.*]

sphacelus, *sfas'ə-ləs, n.* necrosis.—*adjs.* **sphac'-elate, -d,** necrosed : (*bot.*) dark and shrunken.— *n.* **sphacelā'tion.** [Gr. *sphakelos.*]

sphaeridium, *sfē-rid'i-əm, n.* a minute spheroidal body on the surface of a sea-urchin, perh. a sense-organ:—*pl.* **sphaerid′ia.**—*ns.* **sphae′rite,** a hydrous aluminium phosphate ; **sphaeroco′baltite,** cobalt carbonate, occurring in rounded masses ; **sphaero-crys′tal,** a rounded crystalline mass ; **sphaerosid′-erite,** concretionary clay-ironstone. [Gr. *sphairā,* a ball.]

Sphagnum, *sfag′nəm, n.* a genus of mosses—peat or bog-moss, constituting the family **Sphagnaceae** (*sfag-nā′si-ē*), peat-formers, useful as wound-dressings.—*adj.* **sphagnic′olous** (L. *colĕre,* to inhabit), living in peat-moss.—*ns.* **sphagnol′ogist** ; **sphagnol′ogy,** the study of the peat-mosses.—*adj.* **spag′nous.** [Gr. *sphagnos,* a name for various plants.]

sphalerite, *sfal′ər-īt, n.* zinc-blende. [Gr. *sphaleros,* deceptive, from its resemblance to galena.]

sphendone, *sfen′do-nē, n.* an ancient Greek women's head-band : an elliptical or semi-elliptical auditorium. [Gr. *sphendonē,* a sling.]

sphene, *sfēn, n.* titanite.—*adj.* **sphē′nic,** wedge-like. —*n.pl.* **Sphenisciformes** (*sfē-nis-i-for′mēz*), the penguin order of birds.—*ns.* **Sphenis′cus** (-*kəs*), the jackass-penguin genus ; **Sphē′nodon** (Gr. *odous, odontos,* a tooth), the tuatara.—*adj.* **sphē′-noid,** wedge-shaped, applied to a set of bones at the base of the skull.—*n.* a sphenoid bone : a wedge-shaped crystal form of four triangular faces. —*adj.* **sphenoid′al.** [Gr. *sphēn, sphēnos,* a wedge.]

sphere (*Shak., Milt.,* **sphear, spheare**), *sfēr, n.* a solid figure bounded by a surface of which all points are equidistant from a centre : its bounding surface : the apparent sphere of the heavens, upon which the stars are seen in projection : any one of the concentric spherical shells which were once supposed to carry the planets in their revolutions : a circle of society, orig. of the higher ranks (as if a planetary sphere) : domain, scope, range : a field of activity : condition of life : a world, mode of being : a ball : a spherical object, esp. a planet : (*Spens.*) an orbit.—*v.t.* to round : to place in a sphere : to encompass : to send about.—*adjs.* **sphēr′al** ; **sphere′-born** ; **sphered** ; **sphere′less** ; **sphere′like** ; **spheric** (*sfer′ik*), **-al,** of a sphere or spheres : having the form of a sphere or spheres.—*adj.* **spherical′ity.**—*adv.* **spher′ically.**—*ns.* **spher′-icalness, sphericity** (-*is′i-ti*), state or quality of being spherical ; **spher′ics,** the geometry and trigonometry of the sphere ; **spheristē′rion** (Gr. *sphairistērion*), a room or court for ball-games ; **sphē′roid,** a body or figure nearly spherical, but not quite so—a species of ellipsoid (*prolate spheroid,* a slightly lengthened sphere ; *oblate spheroid,* a slightly flattened sphere).—*adj.* **sphēroi′dal.**— *n.* **sphēroidi′city.**—*v.t.* **sphēr′oidise,** to develop spherulitic or granular structure in.—*n.* **sphērom′-eter,** an instrument for measuring curvature of surfaces.—*adj.* **spherūlar** (*sfer′*)—*ns.* **spher′ūle,** a little sphere ; **spher′ūlite,** a radiating spherical group of minute crystalline fibres in rocks.—*adjs.* **spherūlitic** (-*lit′ik*) ; **sphē′ry,** spherical, round : belonging to the celestial spheres.—**music of the spheres,** the music, inaudible to mortal ears, produced according to Pythagoras by the motions of the celestial spheres in accordance with the laws of harmony ; **spherical triangle,** a three-sided figure on the surface of a sphere, bounded by arcs of great circles. [Gr. *sphairā.*]

sphincter, *sfingk′tər, n.* (*anat.*) a muscle whose contraction narrows or shuts an orifice.—*adjs.* **sphinc′teral, sphincterial** (-*tē′ri-əl*), **sphincteric** (-*ter′ik*). [Gr. *sphinktēr—sphingein,* to bind tight.]

Sphinx, sphinx, *sfingks, n.* a monster of Greek mythology, with the head of a woman and the body of a lioness, that proposed riddles to travellers, and strangled those who could not solve them : any similar monster or representation of one : an enigmatic or inscrutable person : a hawk-moth : the Guinea baboon.—*n.* and *adj.* **sphingid** (*sfin′jid*).— *n.pl.* **Sphin′gidae,** the hawk-moth family.—*n.* **sphinx′-moth.** [Gr.,—*sphingein,* to draw tight.]

sphragistic, *sfra-jist′ik, adj.* pertaining to seals and signets.—*n.pl.* **sphragist′ics,** the study of seals. [Gr. *sphrāgistikos—sphrāgis,* a seal.]

sphygmus, *sfig′məs, n.* the pulse.—*adj.* **sphyg′mic.** —*ns.* **sphyg′mogram,** a sphygmograph record ;

sphyg′mograph, an instrument for recording pulse-beat.—*adj.* **sphygmograph′ic.**—*n.* **sphyg-mog′raphy.**—*adj.* **sphyg′moid,** pulse-like.—*ns.* **sphygmol′ogy,** the science of the pulse ; **sphyg-mōmanom′eter, sphygmom′eter,** an instrument for measuring arterial blood-pressure ; **sphyg′-mophōne,** an instrument by means of which a pulse-beat makes a sound ; **sphyg′moscope,** an instrument for making arterial pulsations visible. [Latinised from Gr. *sphygmos,* pulse.]

spial, *spī′əl, n.* (*obs.*) espial : a spy, a scout.

Spica, *spī′ka, n.* a first-magnitude star in Virgo ; **spica,** a spiral bandage with reversed turns suggesting an ear of barley : in birds, a spur.—*adjs.* **spī′cate, -d,** in, having, or forming a spike : spike-like.—*ns.* **spicilege** (*spī′si-lij* ; L. *spīcilegium—legĕre,* to gather), a gleaning : an anthology ; **spicula** (*spik′ū-lā*), a spicule, prickle, or splinter. —*adjs.* **spic′ūlar,** of the nature of or like a spicule ; **spic′ūlate,** having spicules.—*ns.* **spic′ūle,** a minute needle-like body, crystal, splinter, or process ; **spic′ūlum** (L.), a little spine : a spicula : a snail's dart :—*pl.* **spic′ūla.** [L. *spica,* an ear of corn.]

spiccato, *spik-kä′tō, adj.* and *adv.* half staccato.—*n.* spiccato playing or passage. [It.]

spice, *spīs, n.* an aromatic and pungent vegetable substance used as a condiment and for seasoning food—pepper, cayenne pepper, pimento, nutmeg, mace, vanilla, ginger, cinnamon, cassia, &c. : such substances collectively or generally : a characteristic smack, flavour : anything that adds piquancy or interest : an aromatic odour : (*fig.*) a touch : tincture.—*v.t.* to season with spice : to tincture, vary, or diversify.—*ns.* **spice′-box,** a box, often ornamental, for keeping spices ; **spice′-bush,** an aromatic American shrub (Lindera) of the laurel family ; **spice′-cake,** a spiced cake.—*adj.* **spiced,** impregnated with a spicy odour : seasoned with spice : over-scrupulous.—*ns.* **spic′er,** (*obs.*) dealer in spices or drugs ; **spic′ery,** spices in general : a repository of spices : spiciness.—*adv.* **spic′ily.**—*n.* **spic′iness.**—*adj.* **spic′y,** producing or abounding with spices : fragrant : pungent, piquant, pointed, racy : showy. [O.Fr. *espice* (Fr. *épice*)—L.L. *speciēs,* kinds of goods, spices—L. *speciēs,* a kind.]

spicilege. See **spica.**

spick, *spik, n.* a nail, a spike.—*adj.* tidy, fresh.— **spick and span,** trim and speckless, like a spike new cut and a chip new split ; **spick and span new,** brand-new. [spike.]

spicknel. See **spignel.**

spicule. See under **spica.**

spide, obs. spelling of **spied** (see **spy**).

spider, *spī′dər, n.* an arachnid of the order Araneida, the body divided into two distinct parts—an unsegmented cephalo-thorax with four pairs of legs and a soft unsegmented abdomen with spinnerets : a light high-wheeled vehicle : a frying-pan, properly one with feet : any of various spider-like radiating structures.—*ns.* **spi′der-crab,** a crab with long thin legs ; **spi′der-leg,** a long thin leg. — *adjs.* **spi′der-legged** ; **spi′der-like.** — *n.* **spi′der-line,** a thread of silk spun by a spider, any fine thread in an optical instrument, for measurement, position-marking, &c. ; **spi′der-monkey,** an American monkey (Ateles) with long slender legs and tail ; **spi′der-stitch,** a stitch in lace netting in which threads are carried diagonally and parallel to each other ; **spi′der-web,** the snare spun by a spider ; **spi′der-wheel,** in embroidery, a circular pattern with radiating lines ; **spi′der-work,** lace worked by spider-stitch ; **spi′derwort,** any plant of the American commelinaceous genus Tradescantia, esp. *T. virginica,* with deep-blue reddish-violet flowers.—*adj.* **spi′dery,** spider-like : abounding in spiders. [O.E. *spīthra—spinnan,* spin ; cf. Dan. *spinder,* Ger. *spinne.*]

spie (*Spens., Milt., &c.*), **spied, spies.** See **spy.**

spiegeleisen, *spē′gl-ī-zn, n.* a white cast-iron containing manganese, largely used in the manufacture of steel by the Bessemer process. [Ger.,—*spiegel,* L. *speculum,* a mirror, Ger. *eisen,* iron.]

spiff, *spif, adj.* (*dial.*) smart, spruce.—**Also spiffed** —*adj.* **spiff′ing,** (*coll.*) excellent.

spifflicate, spifflicate, *spif′li-kāt, v.t.* (*slang*) to do for: to quell: to confound: to handle roughly. —*n.* **spiff(l)ica′tion.**

Spigelia, *spī-jē′li-ä, n.* the pink-root genus of Loganiaceae.—*adj.* **Spige′lian,** of van der Spiegel or of Spigelia: applied to the *lobulus Spigelii,* one of the lobes of the liver. [From the Belgian Adrian van der *Spiegel* (1578-1625).]

spight, *spīt, vb.* and *n.* (*Spens., Shak.*). Same as spite.

spignel, *spig′nl, n.* baldmoney (Meum).—Also (*obs.*) **spick′nel.** [Origin obscure.]

spigot, *spig′ət, n.* a vent-peg or peg controlling a faucet. [Prov. *espigot*—L. *spiculum.*]

spike, *spīk, n.* an ear of corn: (*bot.*) an inflorescence in which sessile flowers or spikelets are arranged on a long axis: a kind of lavender (**spike′-lav′ender**). —*v.i.* to develop a spike.—*ns.* **spike′-grass,** Uniola or other American grass with conspicuous spikelets; **spike′let,** in grasses, &c., a small crowded spike itself forming part of a greater inflorescence; **spike′-oil,** the oil of spike-lavender; **spike′-rush,** a sedge (Heleocharis) with a solitary spike. [L. *spīca,* an ear of corn.]

spike, *spīk, n.* a hard thin pointed object: a large nail.—*v.t.* to fasten, set, or pierce with a spike or spikes: to make useless (as a gun), orig. by driving a spike into the vent.—*adj.* **spiked.**—*ns.* **spike′-fish,** a kind of sail-fish; **spike′-nail,** a large small-headed nail.—*adj.* **spīk′y,** furnished with spikes: having a sharp point. [O.E. *spīcing,* a spike-nail: poss. from L. *spīca,* an ear of corn.]

spikenard, *spīk′nard, n.* an aromatic oil or balsam yielded by an Indian valerianaceous plant (Nardo-stachys) or a substitute: the plant itself. [L. *spīca nardī.*]

spile, *spīl, n.* a plug: a spigot: a pile for a founda-tion.—*v.t.* to pierce and provide with a spile.—*n.* **spī′ling.** [Cf. L.G. *spile,* Du. *spijl,* Ger. *speil.*]

spilite, *spī′līt, n.* a very fine-grained basic igneous rock.—*adj.* **spilitic** (*-it′ik*).—*n.* **spi′losite,** a spotted slate, formed by contact metamorphism. [Gr. *spilos,* a spot.]

spill, *spil, v.t.* (*obs.*) to kill: to destroy: to allow to run out of a vessel: to shed: to waste: (*coll.*) to throw from a vehicle or the saddle: to empty from the belly of a sail or empty of wind for reefing: (*Spens.*) to overlay as if by spilling.—*v.i.* (*obs.*) to come to grief or ruin: to overflow: to be shed: to be allowed to fall, be lost, or wasted: (*pa.t.* and *pa.p.* **spilled, spilt**).—*n.* a fall, a throw: a spilling.—*ns.* **spill′er; spill′ing-line,** a rope for spilling the wind out of a square sail; **spill′-stream,** an overflow channel: a bayou; **spill′way,** a passage for overflow-water; **spilth,** spilling: anything spilt or poured out lavishly: excess. —**spill the beans,** to cause embarrassment by letting out a secret. [O.E. *spillan;* Du. *spillen,* O.N. *spilla,* to destroy.]

spill, *spil, n.* a spile: a thin strip of wood or paper for lighting a candle, a pipe, &c.—*n.* **spill′ikin,** a small slip of wood, ivory, &c., to be picked out from a heap without disturbing the others in the game of **spillikins.**—Also **spilikin, spel(l)ikin.** [Connexion with **spile** or with **spell** (4) doubtful.]

spilt, *spilt, pa.t.* and *pa.p.* of **spill.**—Also *adj.*

spin, *spin, v.t.* to draw out and twist into threads: to draw out as a thread as spiders do: to form by spinning: to draw out: to make to last (usu. with *out*): to send hurtling: to twirl, set revolving rapidly: to fish with a swivel or spoon-bait: (*slang*) to reject at an examination.—*v.i.* to practise the art or trade or perform the act of spinning: to rotate rapidly: to whirl: to hurtle: to go swiftly, esp. on wheels: to spirt: to stream vigorously: to lengthen out, last (usu. with *out*): to fish with rotating bait: (*pr.p.* **spinn′ing;** *pa.t.* **span,** arch. **span;** *pa.p.* **spun**).—*n.* act or result of spinning: a rotatory motion: a cycle ride: a spurt at high speed.—*ns.* **spinn′er,** one who spins: (*Shak.*) a spider: a spinneret: a spinning-machine: a ball with imparted spin, causing it to swerve or break; **spinn′eret,** a spinning organ in spiders, &c.; **spinn′erule** (*-ə-rool, -rŭl*), one of the tubules of a spinneret; **spinn′ery,** a spinning-mill.—*n.* and

adj. **spinn′ing.**—*ns.* **spinn′ing-house,** a place of correction where lewd and incorrigible women were made to spin; **spinn′ing-jenn′y,** a machine by which a number of threads can be spun at once: (*dial.*) a crane-fly; **spinn′ing-mill,** a factory where thread is spun; **spinn′ing-wheel,** a machine for spinning yarn, consisting of a wheel driven by the hand or by a treadle, which drives one or two spindles.—**spin a yarn,** to tell a story; **spin out,** to prolong, protract. [O.E. *spinnan;* Ger. *spinnen.*]

spina, spinal. See spine.

spinach, spinage, *spin′ij, n.* a plant (Spinacia oleracea) of the goosefoot family: its young leaves used as a vegetable: extended to various other plants.—*adj.* **spinaceous** (*spin-ā′shəs*).—*n.* **spin′-ach-beet,** a kind of beet used like spinach. [O.Fr. *espinage, espinache;* of doubtful origin, poss.—L. *spīna,* poss. Ar. *isfināj.*]

spindle, *spin′dl, n.* the pin by which thread is twisted: a pin on which anything turns: the fusee of a watch: anything very slender: (*biol.*) a spindle-shaped structure formed in mitosis. — *v.i.* to grow long and slender.—*adjs.* **spin′dle-legged, -shanked,** having long slender legs, like spindles.— *ns.pl.* **spin′dle-legs, -shanks,** long slim legs: hence (as a *sing.*) an overlong and slender person.— *n.* **spin′dle-oil,** very light and fluid lubricating oil. —*adj.* **spin′dle-shaped,** shaped like a spindle: thickest in the middle and tapering to both ends. —*ns.* **spin′dle-shell,** a gasteropod (Fusus) with spindle-shaped shell; **spin′dle-side,** the female side or line of descent, distaff-side (opp. to *spear-side*); **spin′dle-tree,** a shrub (Euonymus europaeus) of the Celastraceae, whose hard-grained wood was used for making spindles; **spin′dle-whorl,** a heavy ring used to give momentum to the spindle; **spin′dling,** a person or thing too long and slender: a slender shoot.—*adj.* long and slender.—*adj.* **spin′dly,** disproportionally long and slender. [O.E. *spinel*—*spinnan,* to spin; Ger. *spindel.*]

spindrift, *spin′drift, n.* the spray blown from the crests of waves. [See **spoondrift.**]

spine, *spin, n.* a thorn, esp. one formed by a modified branch or leaf: a long sharp process of a leaf: a thin, pointed spike, esp. in fishes: the backbone: any ridge extending lengthways: heart-wood: the back of a book.—*n.* **spī′na,** the backbone: a quill of a spinnet: a lengthwise barrier in the Roman circus.—*adjs.* **spī′nal,** of the backbone; **spī′nate,** spined, having a spine or spines; **spine′less,** having no spine: weak.—*ns.* **spine′lessness; spinesc′-ence.**—*adjs.* **spinesc′ent,** growing into a spine: somewhat spiny; **spinif′erous,** thorn-bearing; **spī′niform,** like a thorn; **spinig′erous,** bearing spines; **spī′nigrade,** moving by means of spines, as an echinoderm.—*n.* **spī′niness.**—*adjs.* **spī′nose** (or *-nōs′*), **spī′nous,** full of spines: thorny.—*ns.* **spīnos′ity,** thorniness; **spinule** (*spin′* or *spīn′*), a minute spine.—*adjs.* **spin′ūlate, spinūlesc′ent, spinūlif′erous, spin′ūlōse, spin′ūlous; spī′ny,** full of spines: thorny: troublesome: perplexed. —**spinal canal,** a passage running through the vertebrae and containing the spinal cord; **spinal column,** the backbone; **spinal cord,** the main neural axis in vertebrates. [L. *spīna,* a thorn.]

spinel, *spi-nel′* (or *spin′əl*), *n.* a mineral, magnesium aluminate or other member of a group of alumin-ates, ferrates, and chromates, crystallising in octa-hedra. — **spinel ruby,** ruby-spinel, a precious variety of typical spinel formerly confounded with ruby. [It. *spinella.*]

spinet, *spin′it,* or *spi-net′, n.* an instrument like a small harpsichord.—Also **spinnet, spinette.** [It. *spinetta,* poss. from a Venetian maker Giovanni *Spinetti* (fl. 1500).]

Spinifex, *spin′, spin′i-feks, n.* properly, a genus of grasses (Australian, &c.) whose spiny heads blow about and disseminate seed: popularly applied in Australia to porcupine-grass. [L. *spīna,* spine, and the root of *facĕre,* to make.]

spink, *spingk, n.* (now *dial.*) a finch, esp. the chaffinch. [Perh. imit.]

spink, *spingk, n.* the lady′s-smock. [Origin obscure.]

spinnaker, *spin′ə-kər, n.* a jib-headed sail sometimes carried on the side opposite the mainsail by racing yachts. [Said to be from a yacht, the *Sphinx*, that carried it.]

spinner, spinneret, &c. See **spin.**

spinney, spinny, *spin'i, n.* a small clump of trees or copse:—*pl.* **spinn'eys, spinn'ies.** [O.Fr. *espinei*—L. *spīnētum,* a thorn-hedge, thicket—*spīna,* thorn.]

spinode, *spī'nōd, n.* (*geom.*) a cusp or stationary point of a curve. [L. *spīna,* thorn, *nodus,* knot.]

Spinozism, *spi-nōz'izm, n.* the pantheistic monism of Benedict *Spinoza* (1632-77).—*adj.* **Spinō'zist,** a follower of Spinoza.—*adj.* **Spinōzis'tic.**

spinster, *spin'stər, n.* (*obs.; Shak.*) a spinner: an unmarried woman: an old maid: (*obs.*) a woman fit for the spinning-house.—*ns.* **spin'sterhood,** the world of old maids collectively; **spin'sterhood—** *adjs.* **spinsterial** (-*stē'ri-əl*), **spinstē'rian, spin'sterish, spin'sterly.**—*ns.* **spin'stership; spin'stress,** a woman who spins: a spinster. [**spin,** and suffix **-ster.**]

spintext, *spin'tekst, n.* a long-winded preacher.

spinthariscope, *spin-thar'i-skōp, n.* an instrument for counting *a*-particles by observing the sparks produced by their impact on a fluorescent screen. [Gr. *spintharis,* a spark, *skopeein,* to observe.]

spinule, spiny, &c. See under **spine.**

spiracle, *spīr'ə-kl, n.* a breathing-hole: a vent, orifice, passage. — *adjs.* **spiracular** (-*ak'ū-lər*); **spirac'ulate.**—*n.* **spirac'ulum** :—*pl.* **spirac'ula.** [L. *spīrāculum*—*spīrāre,* to breathe.]

Spiraea, *spī-rē'ä, n.* the meadow-sweet genus of the rose family. [Gr. *speiraiā,* meadow-sweet, or privet—*speira,* a coil (from its coiled fruits).]

spiral. See **spire** (1 and 2).

spirant, *spī'rənt, adj.* (*phon.*) fricative, open, produced by narrowing without stopping the air-passage.—*n.* a spirant consonant (including or excluding nasals, liquids, and semi-vowels).—*n.* **spirā'tion,** breathing: (*theol.*) the procession of the Holy Ghost. [L. *spīrāre,* to breathe.]

spire, *spīr, n.* a shoot, sprout: a stalk: a long slender stalk: a tapering or conical body, esp. a tree-top: a flower-spike: a reed or reedlike plant (also collectively): a deer's tine: a spike: a cone: a summit, peak: a tall slender architectural structure tapering to a point.—*v.i.* to sprout: to shoot up.—*v.t.* to furnish with, or form into, a spire: (*Spens.*) to put forth as a shoot or fruit.—*adjs.* **spir'al,** towering and tapering (see also next article); **spīred,** having a spire: tapering, conical: peaked: spiked: sprouted; **spire'less.** — *n.* **spire'-steeple,** a steeple with a spire.—*adv.* **spire'wise.**—*adj.* **spir'y,** shooting into spires: spire-like: tapering: abounding in spires (see also next article). [O.E. *spír,* shoot, sprout.]

spire, *spīr, n.* a coil: a spiral: the spiral part of a shell, excluding the body-whorl.—*v.i.* to wind, mount, or proceed in spirals.—*adj.* **spir'al,** winding like the thread of a screw: (*bot.*) with parts arranged in spirals.—*n.* a spiral line, course, or object: (*math.*) a curve (usu. plane), the locus of a point whose distance from a fixed point varies according to some rule as the radius vector revolves: a helix (see also previous article).—*v.t.* to go in a spiral.—*n.* **spirality** (-*al'i-ti*).—*adv.* **spīr'ally.**—*n.* **spīras'ter** (Gr. *astēr,* star), a coiled sponge-spicule with radiating spines. —*adj.* **spīr'āted,** spirally twisted.—*n.* **spīr'ēme,** in mitosis, the coiled thread formed by nuclear chromatin.—*adj.* **spīr'ic,** like a tore or anchor-ring. —*n.* a curve, the plane section of a tore.—*n.* **Spīr'ifer** (L. *ferre,* to bear), a genus (chiefly Silurian to Carboniferous) of brachiopods, with coiled arm-supports.—*adj.* **spīrill'ar.**—*ns.* **spīrillō'sis,** injection with a spirillum; **spīrillum,** a spirally bent bacterium :— *pl.* **spīrill'a; spīr'ochaete** (-*kēt;* Gr. *chaitē,* hair, mane), a spirally coiled bacterium (genus **Spirochae'ta,** or **-tē,** or kindred), cause of syphilis and other diseases; **spiro-chaetō'sis,** infection with a spirochaete, as in syphilis, relapsing fever, &c.; **Spirogyra** (*spī-rō-jī'rä,* or *-gī';* Gr. *gȳros,* a ring), a genus of fresh-water algae with chlorophyll in spiral bands.—*adj.* **spīr'y,** spirally coiled (see also previous article). [Gr. *speira,* a coil, a tore.]

spirit, *spir'it, n.* vital principle: the principle o thought: the soul: a disembodied soul: a ghost an incorporeal being: (*obs.*) a kidnapper: en thusiasm: actuating emotion, disposition, fram of mind: a leading, independent, or lively person animation: verve: courage: mettle: real mean ing: essence, chief quality: a breath of wind (*obs.*) a breath: (*Gr. gram.*) a breathing: formerly supposed subtle substance in the bod (usu. in *pl.*): a distilled liquid: an aqueous solu tion of ethyl alcohol: spirituous liquor (usu. i *pl.*): a solution in alcohol: (in *pl.*) cheerful o exuberant vivacity: (in *pl.*) mental powers, min —*v.t.* to give spirit to: to inspirit, encourage cheer: to convey away secretly, to kidnap.—*n* **spir'it-blue,** aniline blue; **spir'it-duck,** the buffl head, from its rapid diving.—*adj.* **spir'ited,** fu of spirit, life, or fire: animated: possessed b spirit.—*adv.* **spir'itedly.**—*n.* **spir'itedness.**—*ad* **spir'itful.**—*ns.* **spir'it-gum,** a preparation use by actors for attaching false beards; **spir'iting** the action of one who spirits in any sense: th offices of a spirit or sprite; **spir'itism,** spiritua ism: animism; **spir'itist.**—*adj.* **spiritist'ic.**—*n* **spir'it-lamp,** a lamp burning alcohol; **spir'i leaf,** Ruellia.—*adj.* **spir'itless,** without spiri cheerfulness, or courage: dejected: dead.—*adv* **spir'itlessly.**—*ns.* **spir'itlessness; spir'it-leve** a glass tube, slightly convex on one side, near filled with alcohol, showing perfect levelness whe the bubble is central.—*adj.* and *adv.* **spiritos** (-*ō'sō;* It.), with spirit.—*adj.* **spir'itous,** of th nature of spirit, pure: ardent, spirituous.—*n* **spir'itousness; spir'it-rapper,** one who claim to receive messages from disembodied spirits b raps or knocks; **spir'it-rapping.**—*adjs.* **spir'i stirring,** rousing the spirit; **spir'itūal,** of, of th nature of, relating to, spirit, a spirit, spirits, th mind, the higher faculties, the soul: highly refine in thought and feeling, habitually or natural looking to things of the spirit: incorporeal: eccles astical: (as a Gallicism) witty, clever: (*obs.* o *rare*) spirituous.—*n.* that which is spiritual: a American negro religious song.—*n.* **spiritualīsā tion.**—*v.t.* **spir'itualise,** to make spiritual: t imbue with spirituality: to refine: to free fro sensuality: to give a spiritual meaning to.—*n* **spiritualīs'er; spir'itualism,** a being spiritua the philosophical doctrine that nothing is real b soul or spirit: the doctrine that spirit has a re existence apart from matter: (also **spiritism**) th interpretation of a varied series of abnormal ph nomena as for the most part caused by spiritu beings acting upon specially sensitive persons mediums; **spir'itualist,** one who has a regard on to spiritual things: one who holds the doctrin of spiritualism or spiritism.—*adj.* **spiritualist'ic.**—*n.* **spirituality** (-*al'i-ti*), state of being spiritua that which is spiritual: (*hist.*) property held o revenue received in return for spiritual service (*hist.*) the clergy.—*adv.* **spir'itually.**—*ns.* **spir'itua mind'edness; spir'itualness,** the state or quali of being spiritual; **spir'ituality,** (*obs.* or *hist* spirituality.—*adj.* **spirituel,** also *fem.* (indiscrimin ately used) **spirituelle** (Fr. *spē-rē-tü-el;* coll. spi *it-ū-el'*), showing refined and witty grace an delicacy.—*n.* **spirituos'ity,** spirituous characte immateriality.—*adj.* **spir'ituous,** (*obs.*) sprightly (*obs.*) spiritual: (*arch.*) containing, or of the natu of, a volatile principle: alcoholic.—*ns.* **spir ituousness; spiritus** (*spī', spir'i-təs;* L. *spē'r toos*), spirit: (*Gr. gram.*) a breathing (*spiritu asper,* the rough, *lenis,* the smooth, breathing) **spir'it-varnish,** shellac or other resin in a volati solvent, usu. alcohol; **spir'it-world,** the world disembodied spirits.—*adj.* **spir'ity,** (*dial.* or coll. **spirited**: spirituous.—*animal spirits,* a subt form of matter formerly believed to be sent alo the nerves from the brain: hence constitution liveliness; **(Holy) Spirit** (see **holy**); **in spirit** cheerfully vivacious; **out of spirits,** depressed **spirit(s) of salt,** hydrochloric acid; **spirit(s)** wine, alcohol. [L. *spīritus,* a breath—*spīrāre,* breathe.]

spirling. See **sparling.**

spiro-, For some words see **spire** (2).

pirograph, *spī'rō-grȧf, n.* an instrument for recording breathing movements.—*n.* **spīrom'eter,** an instrument for measuring lung capacity.—*adj.* **spiromet'ric.** — *ns.* **spirom'etry; spī'rophore** (Gr. *phoros,* a bringing), an apparatus for inducing artificial respiration by means of an air-tight case for the body and an air-pump. [L. *spīrāre,* to breathe.]

pirt, *spȧrt, v.i.* to shoot out forcibly, or in a fine strong jet.—*v.t.* to squirt in a fine strong jet.—*n.* a sudden fine jet. [Origin uncertain; cf. Ger. dial. *spirzen,* to spirt; **spurt.**]

pirt, *spȧrt, v.i.* (*Shak.*) to sprout, shoot up. [O.E. *spryttan;* cf. **sprout.**]

pirtle. See **spurtle.**

piry. See under **spire** (1 and 2).

pissitude, *spis'i-tūd, n.* density. [L. *spissitūdō—spissus,* thick.]

pit, *spit, n.* a broach for roasting meat: jocularly, a sword: a long narrow tongue of land or sand running into the sea: a wire or spindle holding a spool in a shuttle.—*v.t.* to transfix: to string on a rod or wire:—*pr.p.* **spitt'ing;** *pa.t.* and *pa.p.* **spitt'ed.**—*adj.* **spitt'ed.**—*ns.* **spitt'er,** a young deer with unbranched antlers; **spitt'ing,** piercing. [O.E. *spitu;* Du. *spit,* Ger. *spiess.*]

pit, *spit, v.t.* to throw out from the mouth: to eject with violence: to spawn.—*v.i.* to throw out saliva from the mouth: to rain in scattered drops: to make a spitting sound: to sputter: (*pr.p.* **spitt'ing;** *pa.t.* and *pa.p.* **spat,** *arch.* **spit,** *obs. pa.p.* **spitt'en, spitt'ed** (*B.*)).—*n.* saliva, spume: a light fall of rain or snow: (*slang*) an exact replica (usu. *dead* or *very spit,* from the phrase *as like him as if he had spit him out of his mouth*).—*ns.* **spit'-box,** a spittoon; **spit'-curl,** (*coll.*) a curl pressed flat on the temple; **spit'fire,** a hot-tempered person: that which emits fire, e.g. a volcano, cannon, fighting aeroplane; **spitt'er; spitt'ing,** the act of ejecting saliva: the ejection of oxygen, with drops of molten metal, when silver or platinum heated in air cools slowly: the resulting surface-appearance. —Also *adj.*—*ns.* **spitt'le,** spit, saliva; **spittoon',** a vessel for spitting in.—**spit and polish,** futile and grievous efforts after military smartness. [Northern O.E. *spittan,* O.N. *spȳta,* Ger. dial. *spitzen, spützen.*]

pit, *spit, v.t.* and *v.i.* to dig: to plant with a spade. *n.* a spade's depth: a spadeful. [O.E. *spittan,* or (M.)Du. and (M.)L.G. *spit.*]

pital. Same as **spittle** (2).

pitch-cock, *spich'-kok, n.* an eel split and broiled. —*v.t.* to split and broil, as an eel. [Cf. **spatch-cock.**]

pite, *spīt, n.* grudge: lasting ill-will: hatred: a cause of vexation.—*v.t.* to vex: to thwart: to hate.—*adj.* **spite'ful,** full of spite: desirous to vex or injure: malignant.—*adv.* **spite'fully.**—*n.* **spite'-fulness.**—**in spite of,** in opposition to all efforts of, in defiance of, in contempt of: notwithstanding: **spite** (**of**), despite. [**despite.**]

pittle. See under **spit** (2).

pittle, also **spital,** *spit'l, n.* (*arch.*) a hospital, *esp.* for foul diseases, a lazar-house.—*n.* **spitt'le-house.** [hospital.]

pitz, *spits, n.* a Pomeranian dog. [Ger.]

piv, *spiv, n.* (*slang*) a flashy black-market hawker: one who makes money by dubious means: an idler. —*n.* **spivv'ery,** the world or the practices of spivs.

planchnic, *splangk'nik, adj.* visceral, intestinal.— —*n.* **splanch'nocele** (-*sēl;* Gr. *koilos,* hollow), a visceral cavity: the posterior part of the coelom. [Gr. *splanchnon,* pl. *splanchna,* entrails.]

plash, *splash, v.t.* to spatter, as with water or mud: to throw about brokenly, as liquid: to dash liquid on or over: to effect by or with splashing: to variegate as if by splashing: to display, print very prominently.—*v.i.* to dabble: to dash liquid about: to move, go, with throwing about of broken liquid: to fly about dispersedly: of bullets, to throw about fragments or molten metal on striking.—*n.* the dispersion of liquid suddenly disturbed, as by throwing something into it or by throwing it about: liquid thrown on anything: a spot formed by or as if by

throwing liquid: a little soda-water: lead thrown about by a bullet on striking: ostentation, publicity, display: a sensation, excitement, dash.—*ns.* **splash'-board,** a mud-guard: a dash-board; **splash'er,** one who, or that which, splashes: a guard against splashing: a board attached to the foot for walking on mud.—*adv.* **splash'ily.**—*n.* and *adj.* **splash'ing.** — *adjs.* **splash'proof; splash'y,** splashing: with splashing: wet and muddy: full of puddles. [**plash.**]

splat, *splat, n.* a thin strip forming the upright middle part of a chair-back. [**plat.**]

splatch, *splach, n.* (*Scot.* and *U.S.*) a splash or clot of dirt or colour: a splotch.—*v.t.* to splotch. [Cf. **splotch.**]

splatter, *splat'ȧr, v.t.* and *v.i.* to spatter: to splash: to sputter.—*n.* a splash: a spattering. [Cf. **spatter.**]

splay, *splā, v.t.* and *v.i.* (*obs.*) to display: (*archit.*) to slope, slant, or bevel: to spread out.—*n.* a slant or bevel, as of the side of a doorway, window, or the like.—*adj.* and *adv.* with a splay.—*n.* **splay'-foot,** a flat foot turned outward.—*adjs.* **splay'-foot, -ed; splay'-mouthed,** wide-mouthed. [**display.**]

spleen, *splēn, n.* a soft, pulpy, blood-modifying organ close to the stomach, once thought the seat of anger and melancholy: hence various meanings, mostly in *Shak.* and more or less obs.—spite: boredom: ill-humour: melancholy: mirth: caprice: impulse: high spirit.—*adjs.* **spleen'ful; spleen'ish; spleen'less.** — *ns.* **spleen'-stone,** (*obs.*) jade; **spleen'wort,** any fern of the genus Asplenium.—*adj.* **spleen'y,** (*Shak.*) spleenish.— *n.* **splenec'tomy** (*splin-;* Gr. *ek,* out, *tomē,* a cutting), excision of the spleen.—*adj.* **splenetic** (*splin-et'ik;* formerly *splēn'i-tik*), of the spleen: affected with spleen: peevish: melancholy.— *n.* a splenetic person.—*adj.* **splenet'ical.** — *adv.* **splenet'ically.**—*adj.* **splenic** (*splen'ik*), of the spleen.—*ns.* **splēnisā'tion,** conversion (of the lung) into spleen-like substance; **splēnī'tis** (*splin-*), inflammation of the spleen; **splēnomeg'-aly** (Gr. *megalos,* big), enlargement of the spleen.— **splenic fever,** anthrax. [L. *splēn*—Gr. *splēn.*]

splendent, *splen'dȧnt, adj.* brightly shining.—*adjs.* **splen'did,** brilliant, resplendent: magnificent: (*coll.*) excellent; **splendid'ious** (*obs.*).— *adv.* **splen'didly.**—*n.* **splen'didness.**—*adjs.* **splen'did-ous** (*obs.*); **splendif'erous** (now only jocular); **splen'dorous.**—*n.* **splen'dour** (-*dȧr*), brilliance: magnificence. [L. *splendēre,* to shine, *splendidus, splendor.*]

splenetic, &c. See **spleen.**

splenial, *splē'ni-ȧl, adj.* splint-like: of the splenium or the splenius.—*ns.* **splē'nium,** the round pad-like posterior border of the *corpus callosum;* **splē'nius,** a large thick muscle on the back of the neck. [Gr. *splēnion,* pad, compress.]

splent. See **splint.**

spleuchan, *sploöhh'ȧn, n.* a tobacco-pouch: a purse. [Gael. *splüac(h)an.*]

splice, *splīs, v.t.* to unite by interweaving the strands: to join together by overlapping: to unite, esp. (*slang;* also *v.i.*) in matrimony.—*n.* act of splicing: joint made by splicing: the part of the handle of a cricket-bat or the like that fits into the blade.—**sit on the splice,** (*cricket slang*) to play a defensive game; **splice the mainbrace,** (*nautical slang*) to serve out an allowance of spirits: to fall to drinking. [Du. (now dial.) *splissen.*]

spline, *splīn, n.* a key to make wheel and shaft revolve together: a thin strip or slat. [Orig. E. Anglian.]

splint, *splint,* also **splent,** *splent, n.* an overlapping strip in armour: a strip, slip of wood, lath: a splinter: a contrivance for holding a broken bone, or the like, in position: a bony enlargement on a horse's leg between knee and fetlock: splint-coal. —*v.t.* to put in splints.—*ns.* **splint'-arm'our,** armour of narrow overlapping plates; **splint'-bone,** a small bone alongside the cannon bone in the horse, &c., the second or the fourth metacarpal or metatarsal; **splint'-coal,** a hard coal of uneven fracture that does not cake; **splint'er, a**

piece of wood, &c., split off, esp. a needle-like piece: a slender strip of wood, esp. one used as a torch: (*obs.*) a splint.—*v.t.* and *v.i.* to split into splinters.—*v.t.* (*Shak.*) to put in splints, hence join, piece.—*ns.* splint'er-bar, the cross-bar of a coach, supporting the springs; splint'er-bone, the fibula.—*adjs.* splint'er-proof, proof against the splinters of bursting shells or bombs, or against splintering; splint'ery, made of, or like, splinters: apt to splinter.—*n.* splint'wood, sapwood.—splintery fracture, (*min.*) the property of breaking with a surface like broken wood. [M.Du. *splinte* (Du. *splint*) or (M.)L.G. *splinte, splente*; Du. and L.G. *splinter*, Ger. *splenter*.]

split, *split*, *v.t.* to break in pieces, wreck: to rend: to cleave lengthwise: to divide: to disunite: to divulge.—*v.i.* to be dashed to pieces: to suffer shipwreck: to divide or part asunder: to divulge secrets: to divide one's votes instead of plumping: to burst with laughter: to go at full speed: (*slang*) to break (*with* a person):—*pr.p.* split'ing; *pa.t.* and *pa.p.* split (*Shak.*, &c., splitt'ed).—*n.* split, a crack or rent lengthwise: a schism: a half-bottle of aerated water, a half-glass of spirits: (in *pl.*) the acrobatic feat of going down to the floor with the legs spread out laterally.—*adj.* split'-new, (*Scot.*) brand-new. — *n.pl.* split'-peas(e)', dried pease deprived of their seed-coat and thus broken across at the embryo.—*ns.* split'-ring, a ring formed as if slit spirally, as for keeping keys together; splitt'er, one who, or that which, splits: one who splits hairs in argument, classification, &c.: a splitting headache.—*adj.* splitt'ing, rending: cleaving: ear-splitting: of a headache, very severe: very rapid.—split hairs (see hair): split infinitive, an infinitive with an adverb between 'to' and the verb; split mind, schizophrenia; split on a rock, to meet some unforeseen and disastrous difficulty, to go to ruin; split one's sides, to laugh immoderately; split personality, a tendency towards schizophrenia; split second, a fraction of a second; split the difference, to divide equally the sum or matter in dispute, to take the mean. [Du. *splitten*, related to *splijten*, Ger. *spleissen*.]

splore, *splōr*, *n.* (*Scot.*) a frolic: a spree: an escapade: a row: a scrape. [Origin obscure.]

splotch, *sploch*, splodge, *sploj*, *ns.* a big or heavy splash, spot, or stain.—*vs.t.* to mark with splotches or splodges. — *vs.i.* to trudge flounderingly or splashily.—*adjs.* splotch'y, splodg'y. [Perh. conn. with O.E. *splott*, spot.]

splurge, *splurj*, *n.* any boisterous display.—*v.i.* to make such a display.—*adj.* splur'gy. [Imit.]

splutter, *splut'ər*, *v.i.* to eject drops: to scatter ink upon a paper, as a bad pen: to scatter liquid with spitting noises: to articulate confusedly as in rage. —*v.t.* to utter splutteringly.—*n.* an act or noise of spluttering.—*n.* splutt'erer.—*n.* and *adj.* splutt'-ering. — *adv.* splutt'eringly. — *adj.* splutt'ery. [Prob. imit.; cf. sputter.]

Spode, *spōd*, *n.* a porcelain made with addition of bone-ash by Josiah Spode (1754-1827) at Stoke.—Also *adj.*

spode, *spōd*, spodium, *spō'di-əm*, *ns.* powder got by calcination: bone-black.—*n.* spodomancy (*spod'ə-man-si*), divination by means of ashes.—*adj.* spodoman'tic.—*n.* spod'ūmene, a monoclinic pyroxene, silicate of aluminium and lithium. [Gr. *spodos*, dim. *spodion*, ashes, *spodoumenos* (contracted participle), burnt to ashes, from its appearance under the blowpipe.]

spoffish, *spof'ish*, *adj.* fussy, officious—also spoff'y.

spoil, *spoil*, *n.* (often in *pl.*) plunder, booty: acquisitions, prizes: spoliation: pillage: a cast or stripped-off skin: remains of an animal body: material cast out in excavation: (*rare*) damage, impairment: a thing spoiled in making.—*v.t.* to take by force: to plunder: to despoil: to strip: to deprive: (*Shak.*) to destroy, end: to corrupt: to mar: to impair: to make useless: to impair the disposition of by overindulgence: to treat overindulgently.—*v.i.* to practise spoliation: to go bad: to deteriorate:—*pa.t.* and *pa.p.* spoiled or (only in sense of damage) spoilt.—*ns.* spoil'-bank,

-heap, a deposit of spoil.—*adj.* spoiled.—spoil'er; spoil'-five, a card game drawn *spoiled* if no player win three out of five tricks.—*adj.* spoil'ful (*Spens.* spoylefull), plundering.—*ns.* spoils'man, one who looks for profit out of politics; spoil'-sport, one who stops or interferes with sport: a meddler.—spoiling for (a fight, &c., more than ripe or ready for: intent on; spoil system, the system of supplanting civil servan on a change of government, on the principle th 'to the victor belong the spoils.' [O.Fr. espoille—L. *spolium*, spoil.]

spoke, *spōk*, *pa.t.* of speak.

spoke, *spōk*, *n.* one of the radiating bars of a whee —*n.* spoke'shave, a two-handled planing tool fo curved work.—*adv.* spoke'wise, radially.—put spoke in one's wheel, to thwart one. [O. *spāca*; Du. *speek*, Ger. *speiche*.]

spoken, *spōk'n*, *pa.p.* of speak.—In compositio of speech, speaking, as fair'-spoken, plain'-spoken.

spokesman, *spōks'mən*, *n.* one who speaks for anothe or for others:—*pl.* spokes'men:—*fem.* spokes woman. [speak, man.]

spoliate, *spō'li-āt*, *v.t.* and *v.i.* to despoil, to plunde —*n.* spoliā'tion.—*adj.* spō'liātive, serving t take away or diminish.—*n.* spō'liātor. — *ad* spō'liatory (-ə-tər-i). [L. *spoliāre, -ātum—spoliun* spoil.]

spondee, *spon'dē*, *n.* a foot of two long syllables.—*adj.* spondaic (-dā'ik). [L. *spondēus* (*pēs*)—G *spondeios* (*pous*), (a foot) used in the slow solem hymns sung at a *spondē* or drink-offering—*spendein* to pour out, make a libation.]

spondulicks, *spon-dōō'liks*, *n.pl.* (*U.S. slang*) money

spondyl, *spon'dil*, *n.* a vertebra: a thorny oyste (Spondylus).—*n.* spondyli'tis, inflammation of vertebra.—*adj.* spon'dylous. [Gr. *sp(h)ondylos*, vertebra.]

sponge, *spunj*, *n.* any member of the phylum Por fera, sessile aquatic animals with a single cavity i the body, with numerous pores: the fibrou skeleton of such an animal, remarkable for i' power of sucking up water: a piece of such skeleton, or a substitute, used for washing, obliter ating, absorbing, &c.: a swab for a cannon: an sponge-like substance, as leavened dough, a pud ding, swampy ground: a bedeguar: a hanger-o or parasite: a drunkard: an application of sponge: the life or behaviour of a sponger upo others.—*v.t.* to wipe, wipe out, soak up, remov with a sponge: to drain, as if by squeezing sponge: to gain by the art of the parasite.—*v.i.* t suck in, as a sponge: to fish for sponges: to liv on others parasitically.—*ns.* sponge'-bag, a wate proof bag for carrying a sponge; sponge'-bath, a application of water to the body by or from sponge; sponge'cake, a very light sweet cake o flour, eggs, and sugar; sponge'-cloth, a cotto cloth of open texture; sponge'-fing'er, a finger shaped spongecake; sponge'-fisher; sponge'-fishing.—*adj.* spongeous (*spun'jəs*), spongy.—*ns.* spong'er, one who uses a sponge: a sponge fisher: a sponge-fishing boat: an apparatus fo sponging cloth: a sponge or parasite; sponge' wood, sola.—*adjs.* spongicolous (spun-, spon-jik'ə ləs; L. *colěre*, to inhabit), living in association wit usually within, a sponge; spon'giform, like o akin to a sponge.—*ns.* spongin (*spun'jin*), a horn substance in the skeletons of various sponges spon'giness; spon'ging-house, spun'ging house, a bailiff's lodging-house for debtors i his custody before their committal to prison.—*adjs.* spongiose (spun', or -ōs'), spongious (*spun'* jəs), spongoid (*spong'goid*). — *ns.* spongologis (*spong-gol'ə-jist*); spongol'ogy, the science o sponges.—*adj.* spongy(*spun'ji*), absorptive: porou wet and soft: drunken.—set a sponge, to leave a small mass of dough for use in leavening a larg quantity; spongy parenchyma, (*bot.*) a loos tissue in leaves with much intercellular space spongy platinum, platinum sponge, platinum in a finely divided state; throw up the sponge to acknowledge defeat by throwing into the ai the sponge with which a boxer is rubbed dow

etween rounds : to give up any struggle. [O.E.
ponge, *spunge*, and O.Fr. *esponge*—L. *spongia*—
r. spongiā.]

onsal, *spon'sl, adj.* spousal.—*n.pl.* **sponsā'lia,**
spousals.—*n.* **sponsion** (*spon'shən*), the act of
ecoming surety for another.—*adj.* **spon'sional.**—
, **spon'sor,** one who promises solemnly for anther : a surety : a godfather or godmother :
ne who pays for broadcast or telecast introducing
dvertisement.—Also *v.t.*—*adj.* **sponsō'rial.**—*n.*
pon'sorship. [L. *spondēre*, *spōnsum*, promise.]

onsible, *spon'si-bl, adj.* (now *dial.*) aphetic for
esponsible, respectable.

onson, *spon'sn, n.* outward expansion from ship's
eck : short projecting length of plane : wing-section
iving extra lift.—Also **spon'sing.** [Ety. dub.]

ontaneous, *spon-tā'nyəs, -ni-əs, adj.* of one's free-
vill : acting by its own impulse or natural law :
roduced of itself or without interference : in-
oluntary.—*ns.* **spontaneity** (*-tə-nē'i-ti*), **spon-**
'neousness, the state or quality of being spon-
.neous. — *adv.* **spontā'neously.** — **spontaneous**
ombustion, catching fire by causes at work within,
sp. slow oxidation of a mass of matter ; **spon-**
.neous generation, production of living organ-
ms from dead matter. [L. *spontāneus—sponte*, of
ne's own accord.]

ontoon, *spon-tōōn', n.* a small-headed halberd
ormerly carried by some officers. [Fr. *sponton*—
:. *spontone—punto*—L. *punctum*, a point.]

oof, *spōōf, n.* (*slang*) a hoaxing game invented and
amed by Arthur Roberts (1852-1933), comedian :
card game.—*adj.* bogus.—*v.t.* and *v.i.* to hoax.—
s. **spoof'er** ; **spoof'ery.**

ook, *spōōk, n.* a ghost.—*v.i.* to play the spook.—
dj. ghostly.—*n.* **spook'ery.**—*adjs.* **spook'ish,**
pook'y. [App. L.G. ; cf. Ger. *spuk*, Du. *spook.*]

ool, *spōōl, n.* a cylinder, bobbin, or reel for wind-
ng yarn, &c., upon.—*v.t.* and *v.i.* to wind on spools.
—*n.* **spool'er.** [L.G. *spôle* ; Du. *spoel*, or O.N.Fr.
pole ; Ger. *spule.*]

oon, *spōōn, v.i.* to scud before the wind.—Also
poom.—*adj.* **spoom'ing,** (Keats) foaming.—*n.*
poon'drift, light spray borne on a gale.—Also
rig. Northern) **spin'drift.** [Origin unknown.]

oon, *spōōn, n.* an instrument with a shallow bowl
nd a handle : anything of like shape, as an oar :
wooden-headed golf-club with face slightly
ollowed : a spoon-bait : (*Cambridge*) the wooden
poon (see under **wood**) : a simpleton : a maudlin
ove-maker : mawkish love-making.—*v.t.* to trans-
er with, or as if with, a spoon : to shove, scoop, or
it softly up into the air, instead of striking cleanly
nd definitely : to dally sentimentally with : to
atch with a spoon-bait : to pack together like
poons.—*v.i.* to make love sentimentally : to fish
rith a spoon-bait.—*ns.* **spoon'-bait, -hook,** a
ure on a swivel, used in trolling for fish ; **spoon'-**
ill, any bird of a family (Plataleidae) akin to the
.ises, with long, flat, broad bill, spoon-shaped at
ne tip.—*adj.* **spoon'-fed,** fed with a spoon : (*fig.*)
rtificially fostered : taught by doled-out doses of
t-and-dried information.—*v.t.* **spoon'-feed.**—
s. **spoon'-food** ; **spoon'ful,** as much as fills a
poon : a small quantity :—*pl.* **spoon'fuls.**—*adv.*
poon'ily.—*ns.* **spoon'ing** ; **spoon'meat,** food
aken or given with a spoon.—*advs.* **spoon'ways,**
wise, like spoons packed closely together.—*adj.*
poon'y, spoon'ey, silly : foolishly and demon-
ratively fond.—*n.* one who is spoony.—**spoons on,**
lly in manifestation of love for. [O.E. *spón*, sliver,
hip, shaving, Ger. *span*, chip, O.N. *spónn, spánn,*
hip, spoon.]

oonerism, *spōō'nər-izm, n.* a transposition of
itial sounds of spoken words—e.g. ' shoving
eopard ' for ' loving shepherd.' [Rev. W. A.
pooner (1844-1930), a noted perpetrator of the
ind.]

oor, *spōōr, n.* track, esp. of a hunted animal.—*v.t.*
nd *v.i.* to track.—*n.* **spoor'er.** [Du. *spoor*, a
ack ; cf. O.E. and O.N. *spor*, Ger. *spur* ; also
peir.]

oradic, *spor-ad'ik, adj.* scattered : occurring
ere and there or now and then : occurring casu-
lly.—Also (*rare*) **sporad'ical.**—*adv.* **sporad'-**

ically. [Gr. *sporadikos—sporas, sporados*, scattered
—*speirein*, to sow.]

spore, *spōr, n.* a unicellular asexual reproductive
body : sometimes extended to other reproductive
bodies. — *adj.* **sporangial** (*spor-an'ji-əl*). — *ns.*
sporan'giole, sporan'giolum (or *-ji'* ; *pl.* **-a**),
a sporangium containing one or few spores ;
sporan'giophore, the part that bears sporangia ;
sporan'giospore, a spore developed in a sporangium ; **sporan'gium** (*pl.* **sporan'gia**), a spore-
case, sac in which spores are produced.—Also
spore'-case ; **spor'idesm** (Gr. *desmos*, a bond ;
bot.) a multicellular body or group of spores, of
which every cell is capable of germinating.—*adj.*
sporid'ial.—*ns.* **sporid'ium** (*pl.* **-a**), a spore
borne on a promycelium ; **spor'ocarp** (Gr. *karpos*,
fruit), a structure containing the sori and sporangia
in water-ferns ; a multicellular structure in which
spores are formed ; **spor'ocyst,** the cyst developed
in the process of sporulation.—*adj.* **sporocyst'ic.**
—*n.* **sporogen'esis,** production of spores.—Also
sporogeny (*-oj'*). — *adj.* **sporog'enous,** spore-
bearing.—*ns.* **sporogonium** (*-gō'*), the capsule or
asexual generation in mosses ; **spor'ophore,** a
spore-bearing stalk or structure.—*adjs.* **sporo-**
phor'ic, **sporoph'orous.**—*ns.* **spor'ophyll** (Gr.
phyllon, leaf), a leaf that bears sporangia ; **spor'-**
ophyte (Gr. *phyton*, plant), the spore-bearing or
asexual generation in the life-cycle of a plant.—*adj.*
sporophytic (*-fit'ik*).—*n.pl.* **Sporozo'a,** a parasitic
group of Protozoa reproducing by spores, including
the causal organisms of malaria and pébrine.—*n.*
sporozo'ite (Gr. *zōion*, an animal), in Protozoa,
an infective stage developed within a spore.—*adj.*
spor'ular.—*v.i.* **spor'ulate,** to produce spores.—
ns. **sporulā'tion,** formation of spores : breaking
up into spores ; **spor'ule,** a spore. [Gr. *sporā*, a
seed—*speirein*, to sow.]

sporran, *spor'ən, n.* an ornamental pouch worn in
front of the kilt by the Highlanders of Scotland.
[Gael. *sporan.*]

sport, *spōrt, v.i.* to play : to frolic (also *v.t.* with *it*) :
to make merry : to practise field diversions : to
trifle : to deviate from the normal.—*v.t.* (*obs.*) to
amuse : to wear, use, exhibit, set up, publicly or
ostentatiously : to wager : (*rare*) to squander :
to shut (see **oak**) : (*obs.*) to force open.—*n.* recreation : pastime : (*obs.*) dalliance, amorous behaviour :
play : a game, esp. one involving bodily exercise :
mirth : jest : contemptuous mirth : (esp. *fig.*) a
plaything : a laughing-stock : field diversion :
success or gratification in shooting, fishing, or the
like : a sportsman : a person of sportsmanlike
character, a good fellow : an animal or plant that
varies singularly and spontaneously from the normal
type : (in *pl.*) a meeting for races and the like.—
adj. **sports,** suitable for sport.—Also (esp. *U.S.*)
sport.—*n.* **sportabil'ity,** sportiveness.—*adj.* **sport'-**
able.—*ns.* **sport'ance,** (*rare*) play ; **sport'er,** one
who sports : a sportsman.—*adj.* **sport'ful,** full of
sport : merry : full of jesting.—*adv.* **sport'fully.**—
n. **sport'fulness.**—*adj.* **sport'ing,** relating to,
or engaging in, sports.—*adv.* **sport'ingly.**—*adj.*
sport'ive, inclined to sport : playful : merry :
amorous, wanton.—*adv.* **sport'ively.**—*n.* **sport'-**
iveness.—*adj.* **sport'less,** without sport or mirth :
sad.—*n.* **sports'man,** one who practises, or is
skilled in, field-sports : one who has the qualities
or shows the spirit required of a sportsman.—*adj.*
sports'manlike.—*ns.* **sports'manship** ; **sports'-**
woman.—*adj.* **sport'y,** (*coll.*) sportsmanlike.—
sporting chance, a very doubtful chance such as a
good sportsman might risk : an off-chance ; **sport**
one's oak (see **oak**). [Aphetic for *disport.*]

sposh, *sposh, n.* (*U.S.*) slush.—*adj.* **sposh'y.** [Imit.]

spot, *spot, n.* a mark made by a drop of wet matter :
a blot : a small discoloured or differently coloured
place : a locality, place of limited area, precise
place : one of the marked points on a billiard-
table, from which balls are played : a relatively
dark place on the sun : a small quantity of food or
liquor : a spotlight : a white pigeon with a spot on
the forehead : a name for various American fishes :
(*obs.*) a job, piece (of work) : (*Shak.* **spotte**) perhaps, a pattern, or piece, of needlework.—*v.t.* to

mark with spots : to tarnish, as reputation : (*Spens.*) to reprehend : (*slang*) to pick out, detect, locate, identify : to free from spots (often with *out*).—*v.i.* to become spotted :—*pr.p.* spott′ing ; *pa.t.* and *pa.p.* spott′ed.—*adjs.* spot′-barred′, under the condition that the spot-stroke may not be played more than twice consecutively ; spot′less, without a spot : untainted : pure.—*adv.* spot′lessly.—*ns.* spot′lessness ; spot′light, a circle of light thrown upon one actor or a small part of the stage : apparatus for projecting it.—*v.t.* to turn the spotlight on.—*ns.* spots, (*coll.*) a leopard ; spot′-stroke, a stroke in billiards by which the player pockets the red ball from the spot, leaving his own ball in position to repeat the stroke.—*adj.* spott′ed, marked with spots.—*ns.* spott′edness ; spott′er, one who spots or detects ; spott′iness.—*adj.* spott′y.—knock (the) spots off, to surpass easily ; on the spot, at the very place : there and then : straightway : alert, equal to the occasion : in difficulty or danger ; put on the spot, (*U.S.*) to doom to assassination ; spot cash, money down ; spotted dog, a Dalmatian dog : a pudding or loaf with currants. [Cf. obs. Du., L.G., *spot*, O.N. *spotti*, Norw. *spott* ; also Ger. *spott*, derision.]

spouse, *spowz*, *n.* a husband or wife.—*v.t.* (*Spens.*) to betroth : (*Milt.*) to marry.—*n.* spous′age, marriage.—*adj.* spous′al, nuptial : matrimonial.—*n.* usually in *pl.* nuptials : marriage.—*adj.* spouse′less. [O.Fr. *spus*, *-e*, *espous*, *-e* (Fr. *époux*, fem. *épouse*)—L. *spōnsus*, pa.p. of *spondēre*, to promise.]

spout, *spowt*, *v.t.* to throw out in a jet : to declaim : (*slang*) to pawn.—*v.i.* to issue in a jet : to blow as a whale : to declaim.—*n.* a projecting lip or tube for discharging liquid from a vessel, a roof, &c. : a gush, discharge, or jet : an undivided waterfall : a waterspout : the blowing, or the blow-hole, of a whale : a shoot : a lift in a pawnshop : hence, a pawnshop.—*ns.* spout′er, one who, or that which, spouts : a declaimer : a spouting oil-well : a spouting whale : a whaling ship ; spout′-hole, a blow-hole. — *adj.* spout′less ; spout′y, spirting water when trodden on.—up the spout, (*slang*) pawned. [M.E. *spouten* ; cf Du. *spuiten*, to spout, O.N. *spýta*, to spit.]

sprack, *sprak*, *adj.* (*W. Midland* and *S.W.*) vigorous, sprightly, alert.—Also (after the pron. of Sir Hugh Evans, *Merry Wives*, IV. i. 85) sprag. [Origin obscure.]

sprackle, *sprȧk′l*, spraickle, *sprāk′l*, *v.i.* (*Scot.*) to clamber. [Origin obscure.]

sprad, *sprad*, (*Spens.*) *pa.p.* of spread.

sprag, *sprag*, *n.* a mine prop : a bar inserted to stop a wheel : a device to prevent a vehicle from running backwards.—*v.t.* to prop, or to stop, by a sprag :— *pr.p.* sprag′ging ; *pa.t.* and *pa.p.* spragged.

sprain, *sprān*, *v.t.* to overstrain the muscles of.—*n.* a wrenching of a joint with tearing or stretching of ligaments. [Connexion with O.Fr. *espreindre*, to squeeze out, is disputed.]

spraint, *sprānt*, *n.* otter's dung. [O.Fr. *espraintes*, lit. pressed out.]

sprang, *pa.t.* of spring.

sprangle, *sprang′l*, *v.i.* (now *U.S.* and *dial.*) to sprawl : to straggle : to ramify : to struggle.—*n.* a straggle.

sprat, *sprat*, *n.* a fish like the herring, but much smaller : (*Shak.*) a term of contempt.—*n.* sprat′-weath′er, the dark days of November and December. [O.E. *sprot* ; Du. *sprot*, Ger. *sprotte*.]

sprattle, *sprat′l*, *v.i.* (*Scot.*) to scramble. [Cf. Sw. *sprattla*.]

sprauchle, *sprawhh′l*, (*Scot.*) a later form of sprackle.

sprawl, *sprawl*, *v.i.* to toss or kick about the limbs : to lie or crawl with limbs flung about : to straggle. —*v.t.* to spread stragglingly.—*n.* a sprawling posture, movement, or mass.—*n.* sprawl′er.—*adjs.* sprawl′ing, sprawl′y. [O.E. *spréawlian*, to move convulsively.]

spray, *sprā*, *n.* a cloud of small flying drops : an application or dispersion of such a cloud : an apparatus or a preparation for so dispersing.—*v.t.* to sprinkle in or with fine mist-like jets.—*adj.* spray′ey. [M.Du. *sprayen*.]

spray, *sprā*, *n.* a shoot or twig, esp. one spreading out in branches or flowers : an ornament, casting &c., of similar form.—*v.i.* to spread or branch in spray.—*adj.* spray′ey, branching. [Poss. conn with sprig or with O.E. *spræc*, twig.]

spray, *sprā*, spreathe, spreethe, *sprēdh*, spreaze spreeze, *sprēz*, *v.t.* and *v.i.* (*S.W.*) to chap, roughe —usu. in *pa.p.* sprayed, spraid, &c.

spread, *spred*, *v.t.* to cause to extend more wide or more thinly : to scatter abroad or in all direc tions : to stretch : to extend, esp. over a surface to open out so as to cover a wider surface : to over lay : to set with provisions, as a table.—*v.i.* t extend or expand : to be extended to stretched to open out : to go further apart : to unfold : t admit of spreading : to be propagated or circulated (*pa.t.* and *pa.p.* spread).—*n.* extent : compass reach : expanse : an expanded surface : act degree of spreading : an expansion : that which spread out, a feast : anything for spreading c bread : a cover, esp. a bedcover.—*adj.* extended flat and shallow (as a gem).—*n.* spread′-ea′gle, heraldic eagle with the wings and legs stretche out : a fowl split and spread out for cooking (*naut.*) a man tied for punishment : a skating figur —*adj.* bombastic, boastful, and frothy, esp. : American patriotism.—*v.t.* to tie up with ou stretched limbs : to spread out : to outrun.—*v. to cut spread-eagles : to talk in spread-eagle strai — *n.* spread-ea′gleism. — *adv.* spread-eagle wise.—*n.* spread′er.—*n.* and *adj.* spread′ing.— *adv.* spread′ingly.—*n.* spread′-over, an act spreading out : an elastic distribution of workin hours. [O.E. *sprǣdan* ; Du. *spreiden*, Ger. *spreiten*

spreagh, *sprāhh*, *sprehh*, *n.* a prey : a foray.— spreagh′ery, sprech′ery, cattle-lifting : pett possessions, esp. plunder. [Gael. *spréidh*, cattle.]

spreckled, *sprek′ld*, *adj.* (now *dial.*) speckled. [C obs. Ger. *gespreckelt*.]

spred, spredd, spredde, obs. spellings of sprea (*pres.*, *pa.t.*, *pa.p.*).—Also *inf.* spredd′en.

spree, *sprē*, *n.* a merry frolic : a drunken bout.— *v.i.* to carouse. [Orig. slang.]

sprent, *sprent*, *adj.* sprinkled. [Pa.p. of obs. *spren*, —O.E. *sprengen*, *sprengan*, causative of *springan*, spring.]

sprig, *sprig*, *n.* a small shoot or twig : a scion, a youn person : an ornament like a spray : a headless c almost headless nail : a sprig-like object, ornamer or design, esp. embroidered or applied.—*v.t.* t embroider with representations of twigs : to na with sprigs :—*pr.p.* sprig′ging ; *pa.t.* and *pa.j* sprigged.—*adjs.* sprigged ; sprig′gy, full of c like sprigs. [Origin obscure.]

spright, *sprīt*, *n.* (*Spens.*, *Shak.*) an unhistori(spelling of sprite, obs. except perhaps in th sense of impish person.—*v.t.* (*Shak.*) to haunt.— *adj.* spright′ful, (*Shak.*) spirited.—*adv.* spright fully (*Shak.*).—*n.* spright′fulness.—*adj.* spright less, (*obs.*) spiritless.—*n.* spright′liness.—*ad* spright′ly, vivacious : animated : lively : brisl (*Shak.*) ghostly.

spring, *spring*, *v.i.* to move suddenly, as by elast force : to bound : to leap : to start up suddenly to break forth : to appear : to issue : to come int being : to take origin : to sprout : (*B.*) to dawr to branch off : to begin to arch : to give way, spli burst, explode, warp, or start.—*v.t.* to cause t spring up : to start : to release the elastic force o to let off, allow to spring : to cause to explode : t make known suddenly (with *on* or *upon*) : to ope as a leak : to crack, as a mast : to bend by forc strain : (*archit.*) to start from an abutment, &c to leap over : to set together with bevel-joints : attach or fit with springs : (*pa.t.* sprang, nov rarely sprung, *Spens.* sprong ; *pa.p.* sprun(*Spens.* sprong).—*n.* a leap : a sudden movemen a recoil or rebound : elasticity : an elastic con trivance usu. for setting in motion or for reducir shocks : a source of action or life : a motive : tru beginning : cause or origin : a source : an outflo of water from the earth : (*Shak.*) the time of begir ning : (*B.*) the dawn : (often Spring) the seaso when plants spring up and grow—in North ten perate regions roughly February or March ▮

April or May, astronomically from the spring equinox to the summer solstice: (*obs.*) a shoot: (*Spens.*) a youth: (*obs.*) copse: (*Spens.*) undergrowth: high water: spring tide: (now *Scot.*) a lively dance-tune: a Norwegian dance or dance-tune: a flock of teal: the springing of an arch: a crack in a mast.—*adj.* of the season of spring: sown, appearing, or used in spring: having or worked by a spring.—*ns.* **spring'al**, **spring'ald**, an active springy young man, a youth; **spring'-bal'ance**, an instrument for weighing by the elasticity of a spiral spring; **spring'-beau'ty**, the plant *Claytonia virginica*; **spring'-bed**, a spring-mattress; **spring'-bee'tle**, a click-beetle; **spring'-board**, a springy board for jumping or diving from; **spring'bok** (Du.), **spring'buck**, a beautiful S. African antelope, larger than a roebuck: (*slang*) a S. African, esp. a footballer; **spring'-box**, a box or barrel in which a spring is coiled: the frame of a sofa, &c., in which the springs are set; **spring'-carr'iage**, **spring'-cart**, one mounted upon springs.—*v.t.* **spring'-clean'**. — *ns.* **spring'-clean'er**; **spring'-clean'ing**, a thorough house-cleaning, usu. in spring; **spring'er**, a kind of spaniel, useful in copses: one who springs: the bottom stone of an arch; **spring'-gun**, a gun set to go off like a trap; **spring'-haas** (Du.), **spring'-hare**, the jumping-hare; **spring'-halt**, a jerking lameness in which a horse suddenly twitches up his leg or legs; **spring'-head**, a fountain-head, source: a head or end-piece for a carriage-spring.—*adjs.* **spring'-head'ed**, (*Spens.*) having heads springing afresh; **spring'-heeled**, having springs on one's heels, as **spring-heeled Jack**, supposed to do great leaps, and play pranks or commit robberies.—*n.* **spring'-house**, (*U.S.*) a larder, dairy, &c., built over a spring or brook.—*adv.* **spring'ily.**—*ns.* **spring'iness**; **spring'ing**, the act of leaping, sprouting, starting, rising, or issuing: the beginning of curvature of an arch: a place of branching: providing with springs.—*adj.* leaping: arising: dawning: sprouting: with the freshness of youth: resilient: starting: beginning to curve.—*n.* **spring'-keeper**, a salamander.—*adj.* **spring'less.**—*ns.* **spring'let**, a little spring; **spring'lig'ament**, a ligament of the sole of the foot.—*adj.* **spring'like.**—*ns.* **spring'-lock**, a lock that fastens by a spring: one that opens when a spring is touched; **spring'-matt'ress**, a mattress of spiral springs in a frame; **spring'tail**, any insect of the Collembola; **spring'tide**, springtime; **spring'-tide'**, **spring tide**, a tide of maximum amplitude after new and full moon, when sun and moon pull together; **spring'time**, the season of spring; **spring'-wa'ter**, water of or from a spring; **spring'-wheat**, wheat sown in the spring, rather than autumn or winter; **spring'-wood**, secondary wood with larger and thinner-walled elements formed in spring and early summer; **spring'-wort**, a magical root, perh. mandrake.—*adj.* **spring'y**, elastic: resilient: abounding with springs.—See also **sprung.—spring a leak**, to begin to leak; **spring a mine**, to cause it to explode. [O.E. *springan*; Ger. *springen.*]

springe, *sprinj*, *n.* a snare with noose and spring: a gin.—Also **spring** (*spring*).—*v.t.* to catch in a springe:—*pr.p.* **spring'ing**; *pa.t.* and *pa.p.* **springed** (*sprinjd*).—*n.* **springle** (*spring'gl*), a snare. [Earlier *sprenge*, from a probable O.E. *sprencg*; cf. **sprent, spring.**]

springe, *sprinj*, *adj.* (*George Eliot*) active, nimble.

sprinkle, *spring'kl*, *v.t.* to scatter in small drops or particles: to scatter on: to baptise with a few drops of water: to strew, dot, diversify.—*v.i.* to scatter in drops.—*n.* an aspersorium or utensil for sprinkling.—*ns.* **sprin'kle**, **sprin'kling**, the act of one who sprinkles: a small quantity sprinkled: in book-binding, mottling of edges by scattering a few drops of colour; **sprin'kler**. [Freq. from O.E. *sprengan*, the causative of *springan*, to spring; cf. Ger. *sprenkeln.*]

sprint, *sprint*, *n.* a short run, row, or race at full speed.—*v.i.* to run at full speed.—*ns.* **sprin'ter**; **sprin'ting**. [Cf. O.N. *spretta*, Sw. *spritta.*]

sprit, *sprit*, *n.* (*naut.*) a spar set diagonally to extend a fore-and-aft sail.—*n.* **sprit-sail** (*sprit'sl*), a sail extended by a sprit. [O.E. *spréot*, pole; Du. and Ger. *spriet*, sprit.]

sprite, *sprīt*, *n.* spirit—*obs.* except in the senses of goblin, elf, imp, impish or implike person.—*adjs.* **sprite'ful**, **sprite'ly**, &c. (see **sprightful**, &c.). [O.Fr. *esprit*; cf. **spirit, spright.**]

sprocket, *sprok'it*, *n.* a tooth on the rim of a wheel or capstan for engaging the chain: a toothed cylinder for driving a cinematograph film: a sprocket-wheel.—*n.* **sprock'et-wheel**, a wheel with sprockets. [Origin unknown.]

sprod, *sprod*, *n.* (*Northern*) a second-year salmon.

sprong, *sprong*, (*Spens.*) *pa.t.* and *pa.p.* of **spring.**

sprout, *sprowt*, *n.* a new growth: a young shoot: a side bud, as in **Brussels sprouts** (see **Brussels**): a scion, descendant: sprouting condition.—*v.i.* to shoot: to push out new shoots.—*v.t.* to put forth as a sprout or bud: to cause to sprout: (*dial.*) to remove sprouts from.—*adj.* **sprout'ed.**—*n.* and *adj.* **sprout'ing.** [O.E. *sprútan* (found in compounds); Du. *spruiten*, Ger. *spriessen.*]

spruce, *sprōōs*, *adj.* smart: neat, dapper: over-fastidious, finical.—*adv.* **sprucely.**—*v.t.* to smarten.—*v.i.* to become spruce or smart (often with *up*).—*adv.* **spruce'ly.**—*n.* **spruce'ness.** [Prob. from next word, from the vogue of spruce leather in the 16th century.]

Spruce, *sprōōs*, *n.* (*obs.*) Prussia: **spruce**, spruce-fir or its wood: spruce-beer.—*adj.* brought from Prussia: of spruce or its wood.—*ns.* **spruce'-beer'**, a drink made from a solution of sugar or treacle and green tops of spruce; **spruce'-fir'**, any conifer of the genus Picea, with long shoots only, four-angled needles, and pendulous cones: extended to some other trees. [For **Pruce.**]

sprue, *sprōō*, *n.* a passage by which molten metal runs into a mould: the metal that solidifies in it—**deadhead.** [Origin obscure.]

sprue, *sprōō*, *n.* infantile thrush (*obs.*): a tropical disease affecting mouth, throat, and digestion. [Du. *spruw.*]

sprue, *sprōō*, *n.* (*London*) inferior asparagus.

sprug, *sprug*, *n.* (*Scot.*) a sparrow.

spruit, *sprü'it*, *sprit*, *n.* a small, deepish water-course, dry except during and after rains. [Du., *sprout.*]

sprung, *pa.t.* and *pa.p.* of **spring.**—*adj.* strained: split: loosed: furnished with springs: (*coll.*) tipsy.—**sprung rhythm**, a rhythm of mixed feet each stressed on the first syllable.

sprush, *sprōōsh*, *sprush*, *adj.*, *adv.*, and *v.t.* a Scots form of **spruce** (1).

spry, *sprī*, *adj.* nimble: agile:—*comp.* **spry'er**; *superl.* **spry'est.**—*adv.* **spry'ly.** — *n.* **spry'ness.** [Origin doubtful.]

spud, *spud*, *n.* a small narrow digging tool: a stumpy person or thing: (*slang*) a potato.—*v.t.* and *v.i.* to dig with a spud.—*adj.* **spudd'y**, podgy. [Origin obscure.]

spue, an old-fashioned spelling of **spew.**

spule, *spol*, *spül*, *n.* (*Scot.*) the shoulder.—*ns.* **spule'-bane** (-*bone*), **-blade.**—Also **speal** (*spēl*). [Relation to **spauld** obscure.]

spuilzie, **spuilzie**, **spulye**, **spulyie**, *spül'(y)i*, *n.* (*Scot.*) spoliation.—*v.t.* and *v.i.* to plunder. [See **spoil.**]

spume, *spūm*, *n.* foam: scum.—*v.i.* to foam.—*v.t.* to throw up or off as foam or scum.—*adjs.* **spū'mous**, **spū'my**. [L. *spūma*—*spuēre*, to spew.]

spun, *pa.t.* and *pa.p.* of **spin**, and *adj.*—*adj.* **spun'out**, unduly lengthened.—*n.* **spun'-yarn**, rope-yarn twisted into a cord.

spunge, *spunj*, obs. spelling of **sponge.**—*n.* **spung'ing-house.**

spunk, *spungk*, *n.* (esp. *Scot.*) a spark: a spirited, usu. small or weak, person: spirit, mettle, courage: touchwood, tinder: a fungus from which tinder is made: a match.—*v.i.* to take fire, flame up: to fire up: (*U.S.*) to show spirit: (*Scot.*, with *out*) to come to light.—*n.* **spunk'ie**, (*Scot.*) a Will-o'-the-wisp: a fiery or mettlesome person: (*Burns*) whisky.—*adj.* **spunk'y**, spirited: fiery-tempered. [Cf. Ir. *sponc*, tinder, sponge—L. *spongia*, a sponge—Gr. *spongiā.*]

spur, *spur, n.* a goading instrument on a rider's heel : incitement, stimulus : a hard sharp projection : a claw-like projection at the back of a cock's or other bird's leg : an artificial substitute on a game-cock : a short, usu. flowering or fruit-bearing, branch : a great lateral root : ergot : a tubular pouch at the base of a petal : an expansion of a leaf-base : a lateral branch, as of a hill range : a strut : a structure to deflect the current from a bank.—*v.t.* to apply the spur to : to urge on : to provide with a spur or spurs : to prune into spurs.—*v.i.* to press forward with the spur : to hasten : to kick out :—*pr.p.* **spurr′ing** ; *pa.t.* and *pa.p.* **spurred.**—*v.t.* **spur′-gall,** (*Shak.*) to gall or wound with a spur.—*ns.* **spur′-gear, -gear′ing,** a system or spur-wheels.—*adj.* **spur′-heeled,** having a long straight hind-claw. — *n.* **spur′-leather,** a strap for fastening a spur. — *adjs.* **spur′less ; spurred,** having or wearing spurs or a spur : in the form of a spur : urged : affected with ergot, as rye.—*ns.* **spurr′er,** one who, or that which, spurs ; **spurr′ier,** a maker of spurs.—*n.* and *adj.* **spurr′ing.**—*ns.* **spur′-row′el,** the rowel of a spur ; **spur′-roy′al, -ry′al, -ri′al,** a former English fifteen-shilling piece of gold, bearing a star like a spur-rowel.—*adj.* **spurr′y,** like, of the nature of, having, a spur.—*ns.* **spur′-way,** (*dial.*) a bridle-road ; **spur′-whang** (*Scot.*) a spur-leather ; **spur′-wheel,** a cog-wheel. —*adj.* **spur′-winged,** with a horny spur on the pinion of the wing.—**gilt spurs,** a mark of knighthood ; **on the spur of the moment,** without premeditation ; **set spurs to,** to apply the spur and ride off quickly ; **win one's spurs,** to earn knighthood : to gain distinction by achievement. [O.E. *spura, spora* ; O.N. *spori,* Ger. *sporn.*]

spurge, *spurj, n.* any species of Euphorbia, a genus of very varied habit, with milky, generally poisonous, juice, and an inflorescence (cyathium) of flowers so reduced as to simulate a single flower.— *n.* **spurge′-lau′rel,** a European evergreen shrub (*Daphne Laureola*) with yellowish-green flowers, thick leaves, and poisonous berries. [O.Fr. *espurge* (Fr. *épurge*)—L. *expurgāre,* to purge—*ex,* off, *purgāre,* to clear.]

spurious, *spūr′i-ɘs, adj.* bastard : illegitimate : not genuine : false : sham : forged : simulating but essentially different.—*n.pl.* **spūr′iae** (*-i-ē*), feathers of the bastard-wing.—*n.* **spūrios′ity.**—*adv.* **spūr′iously.**—*n.* **spūr′iousness.** [L. *spurius,* false.]

spurling, *spur′ling.* Same as **sparling.**

spurn, *spurn, v.t.* to kick : to tread, esp. in contempt : to reject with contempt.—*v.i.* (*obs.*) to trip : to kick (often with *at, against*).—*n.* a kick : kicking : disdainful rejection.—*n.* **spurn′er.**—*n.* and *adj.* **spurn′ing.** [O.E. *spornan, spurnan,* related to **spur.**]

spurne, *spurn, v.t.* (*Spens.*) to spur.

spurrey, sometimes **spurry,** *spur′i, n.* any plant of the genus Spergula : applied to kindred plants, Spergularia (*sandwort-spurrey*) and Sagina (knotted pearlwort or *knotted spurrey*). [Du. *spurrie.*]

spurt, *spurt, v.t.* to spout, or send out in a sudden stream or jet.—*v.i.* to gush out suddenly in a small stream : to flow out forcibly or at intervals : to make a sudden short intense effort.—*n.* a sudden or violent gush : a jet : a short spell, esp. of intensified effort, speed, &c. [Variant of **spirt.**]

spurtle, *spur′tl, n.* (*Scot.*) a porridge-stick : a sword (also **spur′tle-blade**).

sputter, *sputɘr, v.i.* to spit or throw out moisture in scattered drops : to speak rapidly and indistinctly, to jabber : to make a noise of sputtering.—*v.t.* to spit out or throw out in or with small drops : to utter hastily and indistinctly.—*n.* sputtering : matter sputtered out.—*n.* **sputt′erer.**—*n.* and *adj.* **sputt′ering.**—*adv.* **sputt′eringly.**—*adj.* **sputt′ery.** [Imit. ; cf. Du. *sputteren,* and **spit.**]

sputum, *spū′tɘm, n.* matter spat out :—*pl.* **spū′ta.** [L. *spūtum*—*spuĕre,* to spit.]

spy, *spī, n.* a secret agent employed to watch others or to collect information, esp. of a military nature : a spying : a look : (*fig.*) an eye : (*pl.* **spies**).—*v.t.* to watch, observe, investigate, or ascertain secretly : to descry, make out : to discover.—*v.i.* to play the spy :—*pr.p.* **spy′ing** ; *pa.t.* and *pa.p.* **spied** ; *3rd*

pers. pres. indic. **spies.**—*ns.* **spy′al,** (*Spens.*) a spy (see **spial**) ; **spy′glass,** a small hand-telescope ; **spy′-hole,** a peep-hole.—*n.* and *adj.* **spy′ing.**— *n.* **spy′-money,** money paid for secret intelligence. [O.Fr. *espier* (n.), *espier* (vb.) ; see **espy.**]

spyre, obs. spelling (*Spens.*) of **spire** (1).

squab, *skwob, adj.* fat, clumsy : unfledged, newly hatched : shy, coy : (*obs.*) curt, abrupt.—*n.* a young pigeon or rook : a fledgling : a short stumpy person : a soft thick cushion : a padded sofa or ottoman : a carriage cushion.—*adj.* having a squab.— *v.t.* to upholster or stuff thickly and sew through in places. — *v.i.* to fall heavily. — *adv.* plump and squashily.—*adjs.* **squabb′ish,** thick, heavy ; **squabb′y,** squat.—*n.* **squab′-pie,** a pie made of mutton or pork, onions, and apples. [Poss. Scand. ; cf. Sw. dial. *sqvabb,* loose flesh, *sqvabbig,* flabby.]

squabash, *skwɘ-bash′, v.t.* to crush, smash.—*n.* a crushing.—*n.* **squabash′er.** [Prob. **squash** and **bash.**]

squabble, *skwob′l, v.i.* to dispute in a noisy manner : to wrangle.—*n.* a noisy, petty quarrel : a brawl.— *n.* **squabb′ler.** [Cf. Sw. dial. *sqvabbel.*]

squacco, *skwak′ō, n.* a small crested heron. [It. dial. *sguacco.*]

squad, *skwod, n.* a small group of soldiers drilled or working together : any working party : a set or group.—**awkward squad,** a body of recruits not yet competent in drill, &c. [Fr. *escouade* ; cf. Sp. *escuadra,* It. *squadra.*]

squadron, *skwod′rɘn, n.* (*obs.*) a body of soldiers drawn up in a square : a detachment, body, group : a division of a cavalry regiment under a major or captain : a section of a fleet under a flag-officer : a group of aeroplanes forming a unit under one command.—*v.t.* to form into squadrons.—*adjs.* **squad′ronal ; squad′roned.** — *n.* **squad′ronleader,** an air-force officer answering in rank to a lieutenant-commander or major. — **squadrone volante** (*skwa-drō′nā vō-län′tä*) ; It., flying squadron), an early 18th-cent. Scottish political party opposed to the Argathelians. [It. *squadrone*— *squadra,* square.]

squail, *skwāl, v.i.* to throw sticks (as at birds or fruit).—*v.t.* to pelt with sticks : to hit by throwing a stick.—*n.* a stick for throwing : a counter for playing squails : (in *pl.*) ninepins : (in *pl.*) a parlour-game in which small disks are snapped from the edge of the table to a centre mark.—*ns.* **squail′er,** a throwing-stick ; **squail′ing.** [Cf. **kail** (obs. *skail, skayle*), a ninepin.]

squalid, *skwol′id, adj.* filthy, foul : neglected, uncared-for, unkempt : sordid and dingy : poverty-stricken.—*n.* **squalid′ity.**—*adv.* **squal′idly.**—*ns.* **squal′idness ; squal′or,** state of being squalid : dirtiness : filthiness. [L. *squālidus,* stiff, rough, dirty, *squālor, -ōris.*]

squall, *skwawl, v.i.* to cry out violently : to yell : to sing loudly and unmusically.—*v.t.* to sing or utter loudly and unmusically.—*n.* a loud cry or yell : a short violent wind.—*n.* **squall′er.**—*n.* and *adj.* **squall′ing.**—*adj.* **squall′y,** abounding or disturbed with squalls or gusts of wind : gusty, blustering : threatening a squall.—**white squall,** a tropical whirlwind, coming on without warning other than a small white cloud. [Prob. imit.]

squama, *skwā′mä* (L. *skwä′mä*), *n.* a scale : a scale-like structure : the exopodite of an antenna in Crustacea :—*pl.* **squā′mae** (*-mē* ; L. *-mī*).—*n.pl.* **Squamā′ta** (*skwɘ-*), an order of reptiles—snakes and lizards.—*adj.* **squā′mate,** scaly.—*ns.* **squamā′tion** (*skwɘ-*), scaliness : mode of arrangement of scales ; **squame** (*skwām*), a scale or squama ; **squamell′a** (*skwɘ-*), a little scale.—*adj.* **squā′miform,** like a scale.—*n.* **squamosal** (*skwɘ-mō′sl*), a paired membrane bone of the vertebrate skull, the squamous portion of the temporal bone.—Also *adj.*—*adjs.* **squā′mose, squā′mous,** scaly.—*ns.* **squāmos′ity ; squamula** (*skwam′ū-lä,* or *skwäm′*), **squam′ule,** a little scale.—*adj.* **squam′ulose.** [L. *squāma,* a scale.]

squander, *skwon′dɘr, v.t.* to scatter, disperse : to spend lavishly or wastefully.—*v.i.* to wander, roam, straggle : to scatter.—*n.* a squandering.—*adj.*

squan′dered. — *n.* squan′derer. — *n.* and *adj.* squan′dering.—*adv.* squan′deringly.—*n.* squan-dermā′nia, (*slang*) a spirit of reckless expenditure (in a government). [Origin obscure.]

square, *skwār, n.* an equilateral rectangle: an object, piece, space, figure, of approximately that shape, as a window-pane, paving-stone, space on a chess-board: an open space, commonly but not neces-sarily of that shape, in a town, along with its sur-rounding buildings: (*U.S.*) a rectangular block of buildings: a body of troops drawn up in that form: the product of a quantity multiplied by itself: (*Shak.*) the yoke of a garment: a unit of flooring, 100 square feet: an instrument for drawing or testing right angles: a carpenter's measure: a canon, criterion, rule: squareness: (*old astron.*) quartile aspect: due proportion: order: honesty, equity, fairness: (*obs.*) quarrel, dissension: (Shak., *King Lear*, I. i.) possibly, part, compartment.—*adj.* having or approaching the form of a square: relatively broad, thick-set: right-angled: equal to a quantity multiplied by itself: measuring an area in two dimensions: exact, suitable, fitting: true, equitable, fair, honest: even, leaving no balance, equal in score: directly opposed: com-plete, unequivocal: solid, full, satisfying.—*v.t.* to make square or rectangular, esp. in cross-section: to make nearly cubical: to form into squares: to construct or determine a square equal to: to multiply by itself: to reduce to any given measure or standard, to adjust, regulate: to bring into accord, reconcile: (*naut.*) to place at right angles with the mast or keel: to make equal: to pay: to bribe.—*v.i.* to suit, fit: to accord or agree: to take an attitude of offence and defence, as a boxer: (*obs.*) to swagger: to make the score or account even.—*adv.* at right angles: solidly: directly: evenly: fairly, honestly.—*adjs.* square′-built, of a form suggesting squareness: broad in proportion to height; squared. — *ns.* square′-face, (*S. Africa*) gin (from the shape of the bottle); square′-head, (*old Austr. slang*) a free immigrant: (*slang*) a Scandinavian or German; square′-leg, (*cricket*) a fielder to the left of, and in line with, the batsman. — *adv.* square′ly. — *ns.* square′-meas′ure, a system of measures for surfaces, its unit the square of the lineal unit; square′ness.—*adj.* square′-pierced, (*her.*) having a square opening so as to show the field.—*n.* squar′er, one who, or that which, squares: (*Shak.*) a fighting, quarrelsome person, or perh. a swaggerer.—*adj.* square′-rigged, having the chief sails square, and extended by yards suspended by the middle at right angles to the masts—opp. to fore-and-aft.—*ns.* square′-root, that quantity which being multiplied into itself produces the quantity in question; square′-sail (-*sl*), a four-sided sail extended by yards sus-pended by the middle at right angles to the mast. —*adjs.* square′-shoul′dered, with shoulders that do not slope much; square′-toed, ending square at the toes.—*n.* square′-toes, (*pl.*) square-toed shoes: (*sing.*) an old-fashioned, punctilious person. —*adv.* square′wise.—*n.* and *adj.* squar′ing.—*n.* squa′rish.—how squares go, (*obs.*) what is doing: how things are going; on the square, honestly; square foot, inch, mile, an area equal to that of a square whose side measures a foot, &c.; square knot, a reef-knot; squaring the circle, finding a square of the same area as a circle. [O.Fr. *esquarre* (Fr. *équerre*)—L. *ex* and *quadra*, a square.]

squarrose, *skwar′ōs, skwor′ōs, -ōs′, adj.* rough with projecting or deflexed scales, bracts, &c.: standing out at right angles or deflexed. [L. *squarrōsus,* scurfy.]

squarson, *skwär′sn, n.* a clergyman who is also a squire or landowner in his parish.—*n.* squar′son-age, his residence. [sq(uire) and (p)arson.]

squash, *skwosh, v.t.* to press into pulp: to crush flat: to squeeze: to put down, suppress: to snub. —*v.i.* to form a soft mass as from a fall: to crowd: to squelch: to become crushed or pulpy.—*n.* (*Shak.*) an unripe peascod: anything soft and unripe or easily crushed: a crushed mass: a drink made from fruit juice: a crushed condition: a close crowd: a squeezing: a soft rubber ball for playing

squash racquets: squash racquets.—*adv.* with a squash. — *n.* squash′er. — *adv.* squash′ily. — *ns.* squash′iness ; squash rackets, racquets, a game like rackets played one-a-side on a smaller court with larger and hollow ball.—*adj.* squash′y, pulpy : squelching: sopping. [O.Fr. *esquacer* (Fr. *écacher*), to crush—L. *ex, quassāre* ; see quash.]

squash, *skwosh, n.* the gourd of several species of Cucurbita: the plant bearing it. [Narragansett *askutasquash.*]

squat, *skwot, v.i.* to sit down upon the hams or heels: to sit close, as an animal: to settle on land or in unoccupied buildings without title or (*Austr.*) with a view to acquiring a title.—*v.t.* to cause to squat: (*pr.p.* squatt′ing; *pa.t.* and *pa.p.* squatt′ed).—*adj.* crouching: short and thick, dumpy. — *ns.* squat′ness ; squatt′er, one who squats: (*Austr.*) a large landowner; squatt′-iness.—*v.t.* and *v.i.* squatt′le, to squat down.— *n.* squatto′cracy, (*Austr.*) the powerful squatter class.—*adj.* squatt′y, short and thick. [O.Fr. *esquatir,* to crush—L. *ex, coāctus,* pa.p. of *cōgĕre,* to drive together.]

squatter, *skwot′ər, v.i.* to splash along.—*n.* a flutter-ing: a splashing, spattering. [Prob. imit.]

squaw, *skwaw, n.* an American Indian woman, esp. a wife.—*n.* squaw′man, a white man with an Indian wife. [Massachusett *squa.*]

squawk, *skwawk, n.* a croaky call.—*v.i.* to utter a squawk.—*v.t.* to utter with a squawk.—*n.* squawk′er. — *n.* and *adj.* squawk′ing. — *adj.* squawk′y. [Imit.]

squeak, *skwēk, v.i.* to give forth a high-pitched nasal-sounding note or cry: (*slang*) to inform, peach, or confess.—*v.t.* to utter, sing, render, squeakily.—*n.* a squeaky sound: a narrow escape or bare chance: (*slang*) a feeble newspaper.—*ns.* squeak′er, one who squeaks: a young bird: an informer: a squeaking toy consisting of a bladder and a tube; squeak′ery.—*adv.* squeak′ily.—*n.* squeak′iness.—*n.* and *adj.* squeak′ing.—*adv.* squeak′ingly.—a narrow squeak, a narrow escape. [Imit.; cf. Sw. *sqväka,* to croak, Ger. *quieken,* to squeak.]

squeal, *skwēl, v.i.* to utter a high-pitched cry of some duration: to cry out in pain: to complain: to turn informer.—*v.t.* to utter, sing, render, express, with squealing.—*n.* a high sustained cry.— *n.* squeal′er, one who squeals, esp. a bird of various kinds, a young pigeon: an informer.—*n.* and *adj.* squeal′ing. [Imit.; cf. Sw. dial. *sqväla,* to cry out.]

squeamish, *skwēm′ish, adj.* sickish at stomach: qualmish: easily shocked, disgusted, or offended: fastidious: coy: reluctant from scruples or com-punction.—*adv.* squeam′ishly.—*n.* squeam′ish-ness. [M.E. *scoymous*—A.Fr. *escoymous* ; ety. dub.]

squeedge, *skwēj,* a vulgar form of squeeze.

squeegee, *skwē′jē, -jē′,* also squilgee, *skwil′jē,* ns. an implement with edge of rubber, leather, &c., for clearing water or mud from decks, floors, windows, &c.: a photographer's roller or brush for squeezing out moisture.—*v.t.* to clear, press, or smooth with a squeegee. [App. squeeze.]

squeeze, *skwēz, v.t.* to crush, press hard, compress: to grasp tightly: to embrace: to force by pressing: to effect, render, or put by pressing: to crush the juice or liquid from: to force to discard winning cards: to fleece, extort from: to take a rubbing of.—*v.i.* to press: to crowd: to crush: to force a way: to yield to pressure.—*n.* act of squeezing: pressure: a crowded assembly: an embrace: a close grasp: a portion withheld and appropriated, as by an Oriental official: a rubbing: a few drops got by squeezing. — *n.* squeezabil′ity. — *adj.* squeez′able.—*n.* squeez′er, one who squeezes: an instrument, machine, or part, for squeezing: a playing-card marked in the corner with suit and value.—*n.* and *adj.* squeez′ing.—*adj.* squeez′y, confined, cramped, contracted. [Origin obscure.]

squelch, *skwel(t)sh, n.* the gurgling and sucking sound of walking in wet mud: a heavy blow on, or fall of, a soft body: its sound: a pulpy mass: a disconcerting or quashing retort or rebuff.—*v.i.* to make, or walk with, the sound of a squelch.—*v.t.* to crush under heel: to put down, suppress, snub, crush.—*n.* **squelch'er**, one who squelches: an overwhelming blow, retort, &c.—*n.* and *adj.* **squelch'ing.** — *adj.* **squelch'y.** [Imit.; cf. **quelch**.]

squeteague, *skwi-tēg'*, *n.* an Atlantic American spiny-finned food-fish (Cynoscion), misnamed salmon or trout. [Narragansett *pesukwiteauq*, they make glue.]

squib, *skwib*, *n.* a paper tube filled with combustibles, thrown up into the air burning and bursting: a petty lampoon: (*Spens.*) a paltry fellow.—*v.t.* to aim squibs at: to lampoon.—*v.i.* to write lampoons: to use squibs: to sound or skip about like a squib.—*n.* and *adj.* **squibb'ing.** [Perh. imit.]

squid, *skwid*, *n.* any ten-armed cephalopod, esp. Loligo: a bait or lure of, or in imitation of, a squid. —*v.i.* to fish with a squid. [Origin obscure.]

squier. See **squire** (2).

squiffer, *skwif'ər*, *n.* (slang) a concertina.

squiffy, *skwif'i*, *adj.* (coll.) tipsy.

squiggle, *skwig'l*, *v.i.* to squirm, wriggle: to make wriggly lines.—*n.* a twist, wriggle, wriggly line.— *adj.* **squigg'ly.**

squilgee. See **squeegee.**

squill, *skwil*, *n.* any plant of the liliaceous genus Scilla: the sea-onion (Urginea), formerly included in that genus: (usu. in *pl.*) its dried bulbs used as a diuretic and expectorant: the mantis shrimp (Squilla). [L. *squilla, scilla*, sea-onion, shrimp— Gr. *skilla*, sea-onion.]

squinancy, *skwin'ən-si*, *n.* (obs.) quinsy. — *n.* **squin'ancy-wort**, a species of woodruff once thought good for quinsy. [L.L. *squinanchia*, a combination of Gr. *synanchē*, sore throat, and *kynanchē* (see **cynanche**).]

squinch, *skwin(t)sh*, *n.* an arch or other support across a re-entrant or interior angle. [**scuncheon**.]

squinny, *skwin'i*, **squiny**, *skwi'ni*, *v.i.* (Shak.) to squint, peer.

squint, *skwint*, *adv.* asquint, obliquely.—*adj.* looking obliquely: looking askance: squinting: strabismic: oblique: indirect. — *v.i.* to look obliquely: to be strabismic: to have a side reference or allusion: to hint disapprobation: to glance aside or casually: to glance.—*v.t.* to cause to squint: to direct or divert obliquely.—*n.* act or habit of squinting: strabismus: an oblique look: a glance: a peep: an oblique reference, hint, tendency, or aim: an oblique opening in a wall, as a hagioscope.—*ns.* **squint'er**; **squint'-eye(s)**, one who squints. — *adj.* **squint'-eyed.** —*n.* and *adj.* **squint'ing.** — *adv.* **squint'ingly.** [Aphetic for **asquint**.]

squire, *skwīr*, *n.* an esquire, an aspirant to knighthood attending a knight: one who escorts or attends a lady: an English or Irish landed gentleman, esp. of old family: (*U.S.*) one who has been a justice of the peace, &c.—*v.t.* to escort or attend. —*ns.* **squir(e)'age**, **squiral'ity**, **squir'alty**, landed gentry collectively; **squir(e)'arch.**—*adj.* **squir(e)-arch'al.**—*ns.* **squir(e)'archy**, the rule of squires: the body of squires; **squire'dom**; **squireen'** (Ir. dim. suff. *-in*; *Anglo-Ir.*), a petty squire; **squire'hood.** — *adjs.* and *advs.* **squire'-like**, **squire'ly.** — *ns.* **squire'ling**, a squire of small possessions; **squire'ship**; **squir'ess**, a squire's wife.—**squire of dames**, one who devotes himself to the ladies, from a character in Spenser (*Faerie Queene*, III. vii. 53). [**esquire**.]

squire, **squier**, *skwīr*, *n.* (Spens., Shak.) a carpenter's square or rule: a canon, rule.—**by the squire**, precisely. [See **square**.]

squirm, *skwurm*, *v.i.* to writhe, go writhing.—*n.* a wriggle.—*adj.* **squirm'y.** [Prob. imit.]

squirr. See **skirr.**

squirrel, *skwir'əl*, *n.* a nimble, bushy-tailed arboreal rodent (Sciurus or kindred genus).—*ns.* **squirr'el-cage**, a cage with a treadmill for a squirrel: in an induction motor, a rotor whose winding suggests this; **squirr'el-monkey**, a small golden-haired South American monkey; **squirr'el-shrew'**, a tree-shrew; **squirr'el-tail**, a grass of the barley genus with long hair-like awns: (*Walton*) a broad-tailed lobworm: a cap of squirrel-skins, with a

tail hanging down behind. [O.Fr. *escurel*—L.L. *scurellus*, dim. of L. *sciūrus*—Gr. *skiouros*—*skiā*—shade, *ourā*, tail.]

squirt, *skwert*, *v.t.* to throw out in a jet.—*v.i.* to spirt.—*n.* an instrument for squirting: a jet.—*n.* **squirt'er.**—*n.* and *adj.* **squirt'ing.**—**squirting cucumber**, a cucurbitaceous plant (*Ecballium Elaterium*) that squirts out its ripe seeds. [Cf. L.G. *swirtjen, swürtjen*.]

squish, *skwish*, *v.i.* to make a squelching or squirting sound.—*n.* the sound of squishing: (slang) bosh: (slang) marmalade.—*adj.* **squish'y.**

squit, *skwit*, *n.* (slang) a contemptible person.

squitch, *skwich*, *n.* quitch-grass.

sraddha, shraddha *s(h)rä'dä*, *n.* an offering to the manes of an ancestor. [Sans. *çrāddha*.]

st, **'st**, *st*, *interj.* hush.

'st, *st*, a shortened form of **hast**.

stab, *stab*, *v.t.* to wound or pierce by driving in a pointed weapon: to roughen with a pick so as to hold plaster: (bookbinding) to pierce near the back edges, for the passage of thread or wire.—*v.i.* to thrust or pierce with a pointed weapon: (*pr.p.* **stabb'ing**; *pa.t.* and *pa.p.* **stabbed**).—*n.* an act of stabbing: a wound with a pointed weapon: (slang) an attempt, a go.—*n.* **stabb'er.**—*n.* and *adj.* **stabb'ing.**—*adv.* **stabb'ingly.** [Cf. **stob**.]

Stabat Mater, *stä'bät mä'ter*, *n.* a Latin hymn on the seven dolours of the Virgin: a musical setting of it. [Its opening words, the mother stood.]

stable, *stā'bl*, *adj.* standing firm: firmly established: durable: firm in purpose or character: constant: not ready to change: not radioactive. — Also **stā'bile** (*-bīl*; *rare*).—*ns.* **stabilisation** (*stab-*, or *stāb-i-li-zā'shon*, or *-li-*); **stā'bilisātor.**—*v.t.* **stabilise** (*stab'* or *stāb'*), to render stable or steady: to fix: to fix the value of: to establish, maintain, or regulate the equilibrium of.—*ns.* **stab'iliser**, anything that stabilises: an additional plane or other device for giving stability to an aircraft: a gyroscope or other means of steadying a ship: a substance that retards chemical action; **stability** (*stə-bil'i-ti*), state of being stable: steadiness: fixity: power of recovering equilibrium: fixing by vow of a monk or nun to one convent for life; **stā'bleness.**—*adv.* **stā'bly.**—**stable equilibrium**, the condition in which a body will return to its old position after a slight displacement. [Fr.,—L. *stabilis*—*stāre*, to stand.]

stable, *stā'bl*, *n.* a building for horses, or sometimes other animals: a set of horses kept together: a horse-keeping establishment, organisation, or staff: (in *pl.*) a cavalry soldier's duty in the stable, or the call summoning to it.—*v.t.* to put or keep in a stable.—*v.i.* to dwell in a stable or as in a stable.— *ns.* **stā'ble-boy**, **-man**, one who works at a stable; **stā'bler**, (*Scot., arch.*) a stable-keeper, an innkeeper; **stā'ble-room**, accommodation in a stable; **stā'bling**, act of putting into a stable: accommodation for horses, cattle, cycles, &c. [O.Fr. *estable* (Fr. *étable*)—L. *stabulum*—*stāre*, to stand.]

stablish, *stab'lish*, *v.t.* (B., Shak., Milt., arch.) an old form of **establish**: to set up: to make stable: to confirm.—*n.* **stab'lishment**, establishment: (Shak.) confirmed possession.

staccato, *stə-kä'tō*, *stäk-kä'tō*, *adj.* and *adv.* (mus.) with each note detached.—*n.* a staccato performance, manner, or passage.—*adj.* and *adv.* (*superl.*) **staccatis'simo.** [It., pa.p. of *staccare*, for *distaccare*, to separate.]

stack, *stak*, *n.* a large built-up pile of hay, corn, wood, &c.: a group or cluster of chimneys or flues: the chimney or funnel of a steamer, steam-engine, &c.: (*Scot.*) an isolated pillar of rock: a compact group of book-cases: a pyramid of three rifles, &c.: a pile.—*v.t.* to pile into a stack: to shuffle for cheating.—*n.* **stack'yard**, a yard for stacks. [O.N. *stakkr*, a stack of hay.]

stacket, *stak'it*, *n.* (obs. Scot.) a palisade. [Du. *staket*.]

stacte, *stak'tē*, *n.* a Jewish spice, liquid myrrh.— *n.* **stactom'eter**, a pipette for counting drops. [Gr. *staktos*, *-ē*, *-on*, dropping.]

stadda, *stad'ä*, *n.* a comb-maker's double-bladed hand-saw. [Origin unknown.]

staddle, *stad'l, n.* a support, esp. for a stack: the bottom of a stack: a small tree left unfelled: a stump left for coppice. [O.E. *stathol,* foundation; Ger. *stadel.*]

stadia, *stā'di-ä, n.* a graduated rod used in measuring distances at one observation, by the angle subtended by the distance between two hairs in the telescope (also **sta'dia-rod**): (*U.S.*) the telescope so used. [Origin obscure.]

stadium, *stā'di-əm, n.* a Greek measure of length, 600 Greek, or 606¾ English feet: a race-course, sports-ground: a stage in development:—*pl.* **stā'dia.**—*n.* **stade** (*stād*), a stadium. [Latinised from Gr. *stadion.*]

stadtholder, stadholder, *stät', städ'hōl'dər, n.* a Dutch viceroy or provincial governor: (*hist.*) the head of the Dutch republic. [Du. *stadhouder,* lit. stead-holder (Ger. *statthalter,* Fr. *lieutenant*)—*stad,* place (now only town), *houder,* holder; spelling influenced by Ger. *stadt,* town.]

staff, *stäf, n.* a stick carried in the hand: a prop: a long piece of wood: a pole: a flagstaff: a long handle: a stick or ensign of authority: a token authorising an engine-driver to proceed: a set of lines and spaces on which music is written or printed: a stanza (these have *pl.* **staffs** or **staves,** *stāvz*; see also **stave**): a body of officers who help a commanding officer, or perform special duties: a body of persons employed in an establishment (these two meanings have *pl.* **staffs,** *stäfs*).—*adj.* (or in composition) belonging or attached to the staff: applied also to officers of a higher grade.—*v.t.* to provide with a staff.—*ns.* **staff'-coll'ege,** a college that trains officers for staff appointments; **staff'-corps,** a body of officers and men assisting a commanding officer and his staff: formerly, a body that supplied officers to the Indian army; **staff'-duty,** the occupation of an officer who serves on a staff, having been detached from his regiment; **staff'-notation,** musical notation in which a staff is used, as opposed to the tonic-solfa system; **staff'-off'icer,** an officer serving on a staff; **staff'-room,** a room for the use of the staff, as of a school; **staff'-ser'geant,** a non-commissioned officer serving on a regimental staff; **staff'-sur'geon,** a navy surgeon of senior grade: an army surgeon on the staff of a hospital, not with his regiment; **staff'-sys'tem,** a block-system that uses a staff; **staff'-tree,** an American shrub (Celastrus) akin to spindle-tree.—**staff of life,** staple food, esp. bread. [O.E. *stæf,* O.N. *stafr,* Ger. *stab.*]

staffage, *sta'fäzh', n.* accessories in a picture. [Sham Fr.,—Ger. *staffieren,* to garnish.]

stag, *stag, n.* a male deer, esp. a hart or red deer from its fifth year: a male of various kinds (cock, turkey-cock, &c.): a man who goes to dances, &c., unaccompanied by a woman: (*U.S.*) a stag-party: (*Scot.* **staig,** *stāg*) a colt or stallion: (*Scot.* **staig**) an animal castrated in maturity: one who applies for shares in order to sell at once at a profit: (*obs. lang*) an informer.—*adj* male: of males.—*v.t.* to follow, dog, shadow.—*v.i.* to deal as a stag (also *v.t.* with *it* or the *market*): to go as a stag.—*ns.* **stag'-bee'tle,** any beetle of the family Lucanidae, from the large antler-like mandibles of the males; **stag'-dance,** one of men only; **stagg'ard,** a hart in its fourth year; **stag'-head,** dying back of a tree giving antler-like appearance.—*adj.* **stag'-head'ed.**—*ns.* **stag'horn,** stag's antler as a material (**staghorn fern,** Platycerium, a fern with antler-like leaves; **staghorn moss,** common clubmoss); **stag'hound,** the buck-hound: the Scottish deer-hound; **stag'-hunt; stag'-par'ty,** a party of men only. [O.E. *stagga,* stag; cf. O.N. *steggr,* cock-bird, gander, in mod. Ice. he-cat.]

stage, *stāj, n.* a tier, shelf, floor, story: a tiered structure for plays: a scaffold: an elevated platform, esp. for acting on: the theatre: theatrical representation: the theatrical calling: any field of action, scene: a place of rest on a journey or road: the portion of a journey between two such places: in a microscope, &c., the support for an object to be examined: a subdivision of a geological series or formation: a point reached in, or a section of, life, development, or any process:

a **stage'-coach.**—*v.t.* to represent or put on the stage: to contrive dramatically, organise and bring off.—*v.i.* (or *v.t.* with *it*) to travel by stages or by stage-coach.—*ns.* **stage'-box,** a box over the proscenium; **stage'-coach,** a coach that runs regularly with passengers from stage to stage; **stage'-coach'ing; stage'-coach'man; stage'-craft,** skill in the technicalities of the theatre.—*adj.* **staged,** in stories or tiers: put on the stage.—*ns.* **stage'-direc'tion,** in a copy of a play, an instruction to the actor to do this or that; **stage'-door,** the actors' entrance to a theatre; **stage'-driver,** one who drives a stage; **stage'-effect,** theatrical effect; **stage'-fe'ver,** a passion to go on the stage; **stage'-flower,** a flower exhibited on a tiered stand; **stage'-fright,** nervousness before an audience, esp. for the first time; **stage'-hand,** a workman employed about the stage; **stage'-horse,** a stage-coach horse.—*v.t.* **stage'-man'age** (back-formation), used *lit.*: also *fig.* to arrange (an event) effectively as if it were a stage scene.—*ns.* **stage'-man'ager,** one who superintends the production of plays, with general charge behind the curtain; **stage'-name,** a name assumed professionally by an actor or actress; **stage'-play,** a play played or intended to be played on a stage; **stage'-play'er; sta'ger,** one who has had much experience in anything, an old hand (*old stager*): a stage-horse: (*arch.*) an actor; **sta'gery,** theatrical contrivances.—*adj.* **stage'-struck,** sorely smitten with stage-fever.—*ns.* **stage'-wag'on,** a wagon for conveying goods and passengers at fixed times; **stage'-whis'per,** an audible utterance conventionally understood by the audience to represent a whisper.—*adv.* **sta'gily.**—*ns.* **stag'iness; sta'ging,** scaffolding: stage-coaching: putting on the stage.—*adj.* **sta'gy** (also **sta'gey**), savouring of the stage: artificially histrionic. [O.Fr. *estage* (Fr. *étage*), a story of a house—inferred L.L. *staticum*—L. *stāre,* to stand.]

stagger, *stag'ər, v.i.* to reel: to go reeling or tottering: to waver.—*v.t.* to cause to reel: to give a shock to: to cause to waver: to nonplus, confound: to dispose alternately or variously: to arrange so that one thing or part is ahead of another.—*n.* a staggering: a wavering: a staggered arrangement (*positive* where the upper plane of a biplane is advanced, *negative* where the lower): (in *pl.* form, often treated as *sing.*) giddiness, also a disease of various kinds causing horses, &c., to stagger (grass, or stomach, staggers, an acute indigestion; mad, or sleepy, staggers, an inflammation of the brain).—*adj.* **stagg'ered.**—*n.* **stagg'erer.**—*n.* and *adj.* **stagg'ering.**—*adv.* **stagg'eringly.** [Earlier *stacker*—O.N. *stakra,* freq. of *staka,* to push.]

Stagirite (misspelt **Stagyrite**), *staj'i-rīt, n.* a native or inhabitant of *Stagira* (Gr. *Stagīros*) in Macedonia, esp. Aristotle (384-322 B.C.).

stagnant, *stag'nənt, adj.* still, standing, without current: foul, unwholesome, or dull from stillness: inert.—*n.* **stag'nancy.**—*adv.* **stag'nantly.**—*v.i.* **stag'nate,** to be stagnant.—*n.* **stagnā'tion.** [L. *stagnāre, -ātum—stagnum,* pond.]

Stahlhelm, *shtäl'helm, n.* a German old soldiers' conservative nationalist and militaristic organisation after the war of 1914-18.—*ns.* **Stahl'helmer, Stahl'helmist.** [Ger., steel helmet.]

Stahlian, *stäl'i-ən, adj.* pertaining to Georg Ernst *Stahl,* German physician (1660-1734), or his animism.—*ns.* **Stahl'ianism, Stahl'ism.**

staid, *stād, adj.* steady: sober: grave: sedate.—*adv.* **staid'ly.**—*n.* **staid'ness.** [For *stayed*—stay.]

staig, *stāg, n.* a Scots form of **stag.**

stain, *stān, v.t.* (*obs.*) to deprive of colour: to pale by comparison: to impart a new colour to: to tinge: to dye: to sully: to tarnish: to impregnate with a substance that colours some parts so as to show composition and structure: to bring reproach on.—*v.i.* to take or impart a stain.—*n.* a dye or colouring-matter: discoloration: a spot: taint of guilt: pollution: cause of reproach: shame.—*adj.* **stained.**—*n.* **stain'er.**—*n.* and *adj.* **stain'ing.**—*adj.* **stain'less,** free from stain: not liable to stain, rust, or tarnish.—*adv.* **stain'lessly.**

—*n.* **stain′lessness.**—**stained glass,** glass painted with certain pigments fused into its surface; **stainless steel,** a steel that will not rust, containing 8 to 25 per cent. of chromium. [**distain.**]

stair, *stār, n.* a series of steps (in Scotland, the whole series from floor to floor, elsewhere, usu. in *pl.,* a flight from landing to landing): one such step.— *ns.* **stair′-car′pet,** a long carpet for stairs; **stair′-case,** the structure enclosing a stair: stairs with banisters, &c.—*adj.* **staired,** having, or arranged like, stairs.—*ns.* **stair′foot′,** the level place at the foot of stairs; **stair′head,** the level place at the top of stairs; **stair′-rod,** a rod for holding a stair-carpet in place; **stair′-tower, -turret,** one enclosing a winding stair; **stair′way,** a staircase: a passage by stairs; **stair′-well,** the well of a stair-case.—*adv.* **stair′wise,** by steps: in the manner of a stair.—*n.* **stair′-work,** backstairs intriguing.— **below stairs,** in the basement: among the servants. [O.E. *stǽger—stīgan,* to ascend; Ger. *steigen,* to climb, Norw. *steg,* step.]

staith(e), *stāth, n.* (*N. England*) a wharf: a structure for shipping coal: an embankment. [O.E. *stæth,* bank, and O.N. *stöth,* landing-stage.]

stake, *stāk, n.* a stout pole pointed at one end: a post: a post to which one condemned to be burned was tied: hence, death or martyrdom by burning: a tinsmith's anvil.—*v.t.* to fasten to or with, to protect, shut, support, furnish, pierce, with a stake or stakes: to mark the bounds of with stakes (often with *off* or *out*).—*n.* **stake′-net,** a net hung on stakes. [O.E. *staca,* stake.]

stake, *stāk, v.t.* to deposit as a wager: to risk, hazard: (*U.S.*) to furnish, supply, fit out.—*n.* anything pledged as a wager: a prize: anything to gain or lose: an interest, concern: the condition of being at hazard: a grubstake: (in *pl.*) a race for money staked or contributed.—**at stake** (*Shak.* also **at the stake**), hazarded: in danger: at issue. [Perh. M.Du. *staken,* to place.]

stakhanovite, *stə-kan′ō-vīt, n.* a worker who has received recognition for his part in increasing the rate of production in the factory, &c., where he works. [*Stakhanov,* a Russian worker.]

stalactite, *stal′ək-tīt* (also *sta-lak′tīt*), *n.* an icicle-like pendant of calcium carbonate, formed by evaporation of water percolating through limestone, as on a cave roof: the material it is composed of: anything of similar form.—*adjs.* **stalac′tic, -al, stalac′tiform, stalacti′tal, stal′actīted** (also *-ak′*), **stalactitic** (*-tit′ik*; the usual *adj.*), **-al, stalactiti-form** (*-tit′*), **stalactitious** (*-tish′əs*).—*adv.* **stalac-tit′ically.**—*ns.* **stalag′ma,** stalagmite; **stal′-agmite** (also *-ag′*), an upward-growing conical formation on the floor, formed by the drip from the roof or from a stalactite.—*adjs.* **stalagmitic** (*-mit′ik*), **-al.**—*adv.* **stalagmit′ically.**—*ns.* **stal-agmom′eter,** an instrument for determining surface tension by drops; **stalagmom′etry.** [Gr. *stalaktos, stalagma, stalagmos,* a dropping—*stalas-sein,* to drip.]

stalag, *stä′läg, shtä′lähh, n.* a German camp for prisoners of war (non-commissioned officers and men). [Ger. *stamm,* base, *lager,* camp.]

stal′d, *stawld, pa.p.* (*Spens.*). See **stall.**

stale, *stāl, adj.* altered (usu. for the worse) by age: of liquor (*obs.*), old, clear, and strong: no longer fresh: past the best: out of condition by over-training or overstudy: impaired by lapse of time: tainted: vapid or tasteless from age.—*v.t.* and *v.i.* to make or become stale, over-familiar, or insipid. —*adv.* **stale′ly.**—*n.* **stale′ness.** [Perh. from the root *sta-,* as in **stand.**]

stale, *stāl, n.* a decoy-bird: (*obs.*) a thief's decoy: a lure: (*Shak.*) a low prostitute employed as a decoy, or generally: (*Shak.*) a stalking-horse, cover to a real purpose: a pretext: a lover made a butt of by or for one preferred. [Cf. A.Fr. *estal, -e,* pigeon used to entice a hawk, O.E. *stælhrán,* decoy-reindeer, Ger. *stellvogel,* decoy-bird; prob. from root of O.E. *stellan,* to place.]

stale, *stāl, n.* urine, now esp. of horses.—*v.i.* to urinate. [Cf. Du. *stalle,* Ger. *stall,* O.Fr. vb. *estaler.*]

stale, *stāl, n.* (*dial.*) a handle, shaft: a stalk. [O.E. *stalu,* app. part of a harp.]

stale, *stāl, n.* and *v.t.* (now *rare* or *obs.*) stalemate.— *n.* **stale′mate′,** (*chess*) an unsatisfactory draw resulting when a player not actually in check has no possible legal move: an inglorious deadlock.— *v.t.* to subject to a stalemate. [Cf. A.Fr. *estale,* perh.—Eng. **stall.**]

Stalinism, *stä′lin-izm, n.* the principles or policy of Josef *Stalin,* Russian leader (*b.* 1879).

stalk, *stawk, n.* the stem of a plant: a slender connecting part: a shaft: a tall chimney.—*v.t.* to remove the stalk from.—*adjs.* **stalked,** having a stalk; **stalk′-eyed,** having the eyes on stalks; **stalk′less;** **stalk′y,** running to stalk: like a stalk. [Dim. from the root of O.E. *stæla, stalu,* stalk.]

stalk, *stawk, v.i.* to stride stiffly or haughtily: to go after game keeping under cover.—*v.t.* to approach under cover: to stalk over or through.—*n.* an act of stalking: a stalking gait.—*n.* **stalk′er.**—*n.* and *adj.* **stalk′ing.**—*n.* **stalk′ing-horse,** a horse or substitute behind which a sportsman hides while stalking game: a person, thing, or ostensible motive used to divert attention from another's doings or objects. [O.E. (*bi*)*stealcian,* freq. of **steal.**]

stalko, *staw′kō, n.* (*Anglo-Ir.*) a gentleman without fortune or occupation. [Perh. Ir. *stócach,* idler.]

stall, *stawl, n.* a standing-place: a stable, cowshed, or the like: a compartment for one animal: a bench, table, booth, or stand for display or sale of goods, or used as a working-place: a church-seat with arms, usu. one of those lining the choir or chancel on both sides, reserved for cathedral clergy, for choir, for monks, or for knights of an order: an office entitling one to such a seat: a doorless pew: a superior armed seat in a theatre, &c. (as in *orchestra stalls, pit stalls*): a working-place in a mine: a covering for a finger (as in *finger-stall*): loss of flying-speed in aircraft: a standstill: (*Scot.* staw) a surfeit.—*v.t.* to put or keep in a stall: to induct, install: to bring to a standstill: to mire: (*U.S.*) to snow up: (esp. in Scots form **staw**) to surfeit: (*Spens.* in *pa.p.* **stal′d**) to release on payment by instalments.—*v.i.* (*obs.*) to dwell: to inhabit a stall: to share a dwelling: to come to a standstill: of aircraft, to lose flying speed and so fall temporarily out of control.—*n.* **stallage** (*stawl′ij*), rent for liberty of erecting a stall in a fair or market.—*adjs.* **stalled,** kept or fed in a stall: fatted: having a stall or stalls: stuck: sated (*Scot.* stawed); **stall′-fed,** fed and fattened in a stall.— *v.t.* **stall′-feed,** stabling; **stall′ing, stall′-inger, stallenger** (*-in-jər; hist.*), a keeper of a stall: one who paid for the privilege of trading in a burgh of which he was not a freeman; **stall′ing-ken′,** (*obs. cant*) a house for receiving stolen goods; **stall′man,** a keeper of a stall, esp. a bookstall; **stall′master** (Ger. *stallmeister*), a master of horse; **stall′-plate,** a plate with a knight's arms affixed to his stall; **stall′-reader,** one who stands and reads at a bookstall. [O.E. *stall, steall,* O.N. *stallr,* Ger. *stall.*]

stallion, *stal′yən, n.* an uncastrated male horse, esp. one kept for breeding. [O.Fr. *estalon* (Fr. *étalon*)— O.H.G. *stal,* stall.]

stallion, *stal′yən, n.* (*obs.*) a courtesan (*Hamlet,* another reading, *scullion*). [Fr. *estalon;* cf. **stale** (2).]

stallion (*Shak.*). See **staniel.**

stalwart, *stawl′wərt, adj.* stout, strong, sturdy: determined in partisanship.—*n.* a resolute person— (*arch.*) **stal′worth** (*-wərth*).—*adv.* **stal′wartly.**—*n.* **stal′wartness.** [Orig. Scots form (popularised by Scott) of *stalworth*—O.E. *stælwierthe,* serviceable —*stǽl,* place (—*stathol,* foundation), *wierthe,* worth.]

stamen, *stā′mən, n.* the pollen-producing part of a flower, consisting of anther and filament:—*pl.* **stā′mens.**—*adj.* **stā′mened,** having stamens.— *n.pl.* (sometimes treated as *sing.*) **stamina** (*stam′*), germinal elements, rudiments: native or constitutional strength: staying power: mainstay: (*rare*) stamens.—*adjs.* **stam′inal,** of stamens or stamina; **stam′inate,** having stamens but no carpels; **stamineal** (*stə-* or *stā-min′i-əl*), **stamin′eous** (both *rare*); **staminif′erous** (*stam-* or *stām-*), having stamens.—*ns.* **stam′inode, staminō′dium, a**

sterile stamen; **stam′inody,** metamorphosis of other parts into stamens.—*adj.* **stam′inoid,** like, or metamorphosed into, a stamen. [L. *stāmen* (pl. *stāmina*), a warp thread (upright in an old loom)—*stāre,* to stand.]

stammel, *stam′l, n.* (*hist.*) a kind of woollen cloth, usu. dyed red : red colour.—*adj.* of stammel : red. [Fr. *estamel,* or independently formed M.E. *stamin* —O.Fr. *estamin,* both—L. *stāmina,* warp threads.]

stammer, *stam′ər, v.i.* to falter in speaking : to stutter.—*v.t.* to utter falteringly or with a stutter. —*n.* hesitation in speech : a stammering mode of utterance.—*n.* **stamm′erer.**—*n.* and *adj.* **stamm′- ering.**—*adv.* **stamm′eringly.** [O.E. *stamerian*; Du. *stameren.*]

stamnos, *stam′nos, n.* an ancient Greek short-necked jar. [Gr.]

stamp, *stamp, v.t.* to bray, pound, crush : to bring the foot forcibly down upon : to trample : to strike flatwise with the sole (or other part) of : to im- press, imprint, or cut with a downward blow, as with a die or cutter : to mint, make, shape by such a blow : to fix or mark deeply : to impress with a mark attesting official approval, ratification, pay- ment, &c. : to affix an adhesive stamp to : to attest, declare, prove to be : to characterise.—*v.i.* to bring the foot down forcibly and noisily : to walk with a heavy tread : (*U.S.*) to be furiously angry.— *n.* the act of stamping : an impression : a stamped device, mark, imprint : an adhesive paper used as a substitute for stamping : attestation : authoris- ation : (*Shak.*) a coin : (*S.Afr.*) pounded maize : cast, form, character : distinguishing mark, im- print, sign, evidence : an instrument or machine for stamping.—*ns.* **stamp′-album,** a book for keeping a collection of postage-stamps in ; **stamp′- collector,** a receiver of stamp-duties : one who makes a hobby of collecting postage-stamps ; **stamp′-duty,** a tax imposed on the paper on which legal documents are written ; **stamp′er.**—*n.* and *adj.* **stamp′ing.**—*ns.* **stamp′ing-ground,** (*U.S.*) an animal's usual resort ; **stamp′ing-machine′,** a machine used for stamping coins, in the stamping of brass-work, or in crushing metallic ores; **stamp′-, stamp′ing-mill,** a crushing-mill for ores ; **stamp′-note,** a certificate from a custom- house officer for goods to be loaded as freight of a ship ; **stamp′-office,** an office where stamp- duties are received and stamps issued; **stamp′- paper,** paper bearing a government revenue stamp. —**Stamp Act,** an act of parliament imposing or regulating stamp-duties, esp. that of 1765 imposing them on the American colonies; **stamp out,** to put out by tramping : to extirpate : to make by stamping from a sheet with a cutter. [M.E. *stampen,* from an inferred O.E. *stampian* from the same root as *stempan*; Ger. *stampfen.*]

stampede, *stam-pēd′, n.* a sudden rush of a panic- stricken herd : any impulsive action of a multitude. —*v.i.* to rush in a stampede.—*v.t.* to send rushing in a stampede.—Also *n.* and *v.t.* (*obs.*) **stampē′do.** [Sp. *estampido,* crash—*estampar,* to stamp.]

stance, *stans, n.* (*Scot.*) a station, standing-place : (*Scot.*) a building site : a mode of standing, as in golf : (*obs.*) a stanza. [Fr. *stance.*]

stanch, staunch, *stän(t)sh, stawn(t)sh, v.t.* to stop the flowing of, as blood : to quench, allay.— *v.i.* (*B.*) to cease to flow.—*n.* a styptic : a flood- gate.—*ns.* **stanch′er; stanch′ing.**—*adj.* **stanch′- less,** that cannot be quenched or stopped. [O.Fr. *estancher* (Fr. *étancher*)—L.L. *stancāre,* to stanch —L. *stagnāre,* to be or make stagnant—*stagnum,* a pond.]

stanch (*adj.*), **stanchly, stanchness.** See **staunch.**

stanchion, *stän′shun* (*Scot.* **stanchel,** *stän′, stän′,* **stan′cher**), *n.* an upright iron bar of a window or screen : (*naut.*) an upright beam used as a support. —*v.t.* to fasten by means of or to a stanchion.— *adj.* **stan′chioned.** [O.Fr. *estançon*—*estance,* prop —L. *stāre,* to stand.]

stanck, *stangk, adj.* (*Spens.*) faint. [It. *stanco.*]

stand, *stand, v.i.* to be, become, or remain upright, erect, rigid, or still : to be on, or rise to, one's feet : to be steadfast : to have or take a position : to be or remain : to be set or situated : to be set

down : to have a direction : to hold good : to endure, continue to exist : to scruple, demur : to insist punctiliously : to be a representative, representation, or symbol : to be a candidate : to cost.—*v.t.* to withstand : to tolerate : to endure : to sustain : to suffer : to abide by : to be at the expense of, offer and pay for : to station, cause to stand : to set erect or in position : (*pa.t.* and *pa.p.* **stood;** *infin., Spens.,* **standen**).—*n.* an act, manner, or place of standing : a taking up of a position for resistance : resistance : a standing position : a standstill : a stoppage : a loss, a nonplus : a post, station : a place under cover for awaiting game : a place for vehicles awaiting hire : an erection for spectators : a platform : (*U.S.*) a witness-box : a base or structure for setting things on : a piece of furniture for hanging things from : a company of plovers : a complete set, esp. (*Scot.*) a suit of clothes or armour : (*U.S.*) a standing growth or crop : a young tree left standing : a tub or vat.—*ns.* **stand′-by,** that, or one on whom, one relies on or readily resorts to ; **stand′er; stand′er-by′,** (*Shak.*) a bystander :—*pl.* **stand′ers- by′.**—*adj.* **stand′ing,** established : settled : per- manent : fixed : stagnant : erect : having a base : done as one stands.—*n.* the action of one who or that which stands : duration : continuance : place to stand in : position or grade in a profession, university, in society : a right or capacity to sue or maintain an action.—*ns.* **stand′ing-bed,** a high bedstead, not a truckle-bed ; **stand′ing-bowl, -cup,** one with a foot ; **stand′ing-ground,** a place, basis, or principle to stand on ; **stand′ing-place,** a place that one may or does stand on ; **stand′ing- rigg′ing,** the ropes in a ship that remain fixed ; **stand′ing-room,** room for standing, without a seat ; **stand′ing-stone,** a great stone set erect in the ground ; **stand′ish** (*arch.*) : poss. for *stand- dish*), an inkstand ; **stand′-off,** a Rugby half-back who stands away from the scrum as a link between scrum-half and the three-quarters.—*adj.* **stand- offish.**—*adj.* **stand-off′ish,** inclined to hold aloof, keep others at arm's-length.—*n.* **stand′-off′ish- ness.**—*v.i.* **stand′-pat,** (*U.S.*) to play one's hand in poker as it was dealt, without drawing any cards : (*fig.*) to adhere to an established political principle, resisting all compromise.—*ns.* **stand- patt′er,** one who stands pat : a political die-hard ; **stand-patt′ism; stand′-pipe,** a vertical pipe ; **stand′point,** a viewpoint ; **stand′still,** a complete stop.—*adj.* stationary : unmoving : forbidding or refraining from movement.—*v.i.* **stand′-to,** to take post in readiness for orders.—*n.* a precautionary parade or taking of posts.—*adj.* **stand′-up,** erect : done or taken in a standing position : of a fight, in earnest.—**all standing,** everything remaining as it stands : without unrigging : fully clad ; **make a stand,** to halt and offer resistance ; **stand against,** to resist ; **stand by,** to support : to adhere to, abide by : to be at hand : to hold oneself in readiness : to prepare to work at ; **stand down,** to leave the witness box : to go off duty : to withdraw from a contest ; **stand fast,** to be unmoved ; **stand fire,** to remain steady under the fire of an enemy—also *fig.*; **stand for,** to be a candidate for : (*naut.*) to direct the course towards : to be a sponsor for : to represent, symbolise : to champion : (*U.S. slang*) to put up with, endure ; **stand from,** to direct the course from ; **stand in,** to cost : to become a party : to have an understanding, be in league ; **standing orders,** permanent rules for conduct of proceed- ings ; **stand low,** (*print.*) to fall short of the standard height ; **stand off,** to keep at a distance : to direct the course from : (*Shak.*) to forbear compliance or intimacy ; **stand off and on,** to sail away from shore and then towards it ; **stand on,** to continue on the same tack or course : to insist on : to set store by (see **ceremony**) : to behove : to found upon ; **stand one's ground,** to maintain one's position ; **stand one's hand, stand shot, stand treat,** to treat, esp. to drinks ; **stand out,** to project, to be prominent : not to comply, to refuse to yield ; **stand to,** to fall to, set to work : to back up : to uphold : to be likely to ; **stand up,** to get to one's feet : to take position for a dance : to be clad ; **stand up for,** to support or attempt to defend ; **stand upon,** to stand on : (*B.*) to attack ; **stand up to,** to meet face to face, to fulfil manfully ; **stand well,** to be in favour ; **stand with,** to be consistent. [O.E. *standan* ; Goth. *standan* ; cf. Ger. *stehen,* Gr. *histanai,* to place, L. *stāre,* to stand.]

standard, *stand′ərd, n.* a flag or military symbolic figure on a pole, marking a rallying-point : (*her.*) a long tapering flag notched and rounded at the end, bearing heraldic symbols, and fixed in the ground : a flag generally : a cavalry regimental flag : a standard-bearer : the uppermost petal of a papilionaceous flower : a streaming wing-feather : that which stands or is fixed : an upright post, pillar, stick : a standing shrub or tree not trained on an espalier or a wall : a tree left growing amidst coppice : (*obs.*) a structure erected at a conduit : an exemplar or substance chosen to be or afford a unit : a basis of measurement : a criterion : an established or accepted model : an accepted authoritative statement of a church's creed : in schools (formerly) a grade of classification : a definite level of excellence or adequacy required, aimed at, or possible : fineness of gold or silver.—*adj.* serving as or conforming to a standard : of enduring value : growing as a standard : standing upright. — *ns.* **stand′ard-bearer,** one who carries a standard or banner : an outstanding leader ; **stand′ardisā′tion.**—*v.t.* **stand′ardise,** to make, or keep, of uniform size, shape, &c.—*ns.* **stand′ardiser ; stand′ard-wing,** a bird of paradise of Batjan and Gilolo with a pair of erectile white feathers at the bend of the wing.—**standard bread,** bread made with flour containing 80 per cent. of the whole-wheat, including germ and semolina ; **standard English,** the form of English used (with minor variations) by the majority of cultured English-speakers ; **standard lamp,** a lamp on a tall support ; **standard solution,** a solution of known concentration, used for purposes of comparison, commonly containing the equivalent, in grammes, of the solute to a litre of water (*normal solution*) or some simple fraction (as *decinormal,* one-tenth normal). [O.Fr. *estandart* ; prob. conn. either with **extend** or **stand,** and in any case influenced by or partly from **stander.**]

stane, *stān,* Scots form of **stone.**

stang, *stang, n.* a stake, pole.—**riding the stang,** punishment by carrying astride of a stang. [O.N. *stöng* ; cf. O.E. *stæng,* Du. *stang.*]

stang, *stång, stawng,* (*Scot.*) *v.i.* to sting.—*n.* a sting. [O.N. *stanga,* to prick.]

stanhope, *stan′əp, -hōp,* a light open one-seated carriage first made for Fitzroy *Stanhope* (1787-1864).—**Stanhope press,** a printing-press invented by the third Earl *Stanhope* (1753-1816).

staniel, stanyel, stannel, stan′l (*Shak.* **stallion,** *stal′yən*)**,** *n.* the kestrel. [O.E. *stângella,* lit. stone yeller.]

stank, *stangk, pa.t.* of **stink.**

stank, *stangk, n.* (chiefly *Scot.*) a ditch, a pool : a dam. [O.Fr. *estanc,* a pond—L. *stagnum,* a pond.]

stann-, *stan-,* in composition, tin.—*n.* **stannary** (*-ə-ri*)**,** a tin-mining district (esp. the **Stannaries** in Cornwall and Devon).—Also *adj.*—*n.* **stann′ate,** a salt of stannic acid.—*adjs.* **stann′ic,** of quadrivalent tin ; **stannif′erous,** tin-bearing. — *ns.* **stann′ite,** (*min.*) a mineral composed of tin, copper, iron, and sulphur : (*chem.*) a salt of stannous hydroxide, $Sn(OH)_2$, acting as a weak acid ; **stann′otype,** a photo-mechanical process in which an exposed and developed bichromated film is coated with tinfoil and used directly for pressure printing.—*adj.* **stann′ous,** of bivalent tin. —**stannary courts,** courts (abolished 1896) for the tinners of the Stannaries ; **stannic acid,** $H_2SnO_3.$ [L. *stannum,* tin.]

stanza, *stan′zä* (*Shak.* **stanze, stan′zo**)**,** *n.* a group of lines of verse forming a definite pattern : a pattern so composed.—*adj.* **stanzā′ic.** [It. *stanza* —L. *stāre,* to stand.]

stap, *stap, v.t.* an obsolete affectation for **stop** : also (*ståp*) a Scots form, in the senses of stuff, thrust, cram.

Stapelia, *stə-pē′li-ä, n.* the carrion-flower genus [After the Dutch botanist J. B. van *Stapel* (d 1636).]

stapes, *stā′pēz, n.* the stirrup-shaped innermost ossicle of the ear.—*adj.* **stapedial** (*stə-pē′di-əl*)*.*— *n.* **stape′dius,** the muscle of the stapes. [L.L. *stapēs, -edis,* a stirrup.]

staphyle, *staf′i-lē, n.* the uvula.—*n.* **Staphyle′a,** the bladder-nut genus of shrubs, giving name to the family **Staphylea′ceae,** akin to Sapindaceae.— *adj.* **staph′yline,** like a bunch of grapes.—*n.pl.* **Staphylin′idæe,** the rove-beetle family. — *n.* **Staphylococ′us** (Gr. *kokkos,* a grain), a pus-causing bacterium found in clustered masses **staphylō′ma,** protrusion of the sclerotic or of the cornea ; **staphylorr′aphy** (Gr. *rhaphē,* stitching) the operation of uniting a cleft palate. [Gr *staphylē,* a bunch of grapes, a swollen uvula.]

staple, *stā′pl, n.* a settled mart or market : a leading commodity : main element (as of diet, reading conversation) : unmanufactured wool or other raw material : textile fibre, or its length and quality.— *adj.* constituting a staple : leading, main.—*v.t.* tc grade according to staple.—*n.* **sta′pler,** a merchant of a staple : one who grades and deals in wool —**merchant of the staple,** a member of a mediæval association of merchants privileged to trade in a staple commodity, esp. wool, at the **staple town** (or towns) appointed by the king. [O.Fr estaple—L.G. *stapel,* heap, mart.]

staple, *stā′pl, n.* a bent rod or wire for driving into a wall, post, &c., as a fastening : the par that passes through the slot of a hasp, receives bolt, &c. : the metallic tube to which the reed is fastened in the oboe, &c.—*v.t.* to fasten with staple. — *ns.* **sta′pler, sta′pling-machine,** machine that stitches paper with wire. [O.E *stapol,* post, support ; cf. foregoing.]

stapple, staple, *ståp′l, n.* (*Scot.*). See **stopple** (2)

star, *stär, n.* any of the heavenly bodies, esp. o those visible by night whose places in the firma ment are relatively fixed (**fixed stars**), but some times including planets, comets, and meteors, les commonly the sun and moon, or even the earth a planet as a supposed influence, hence (usu. i *pl.*) one's luck : an object or figure with pointec rays, most commonly five : an asterisk : a star fish : a radial meeting of ways : a star-shapec badge of rank or honour : a white mark on beast's forehead : a pre-eminent or exceptionally brilliant person : a leading performer, or one supposed to draw the public.—*adj.* of stars marked by a star : leading, pre-eminent, brilliant —*v.t.* to make a star of : to have (a specifiec person) as a star performer : to mark with a star to shatter or crack in a radiating form : to se with stars : to bespangle.—*v.i.* to shine, as star : to attract attention : to appear as a sta actor (or *v.t.* with *it*)*:—pr.p.* **starr′ing** ; *pa.t.* and *pa.p.* **starred.**—*ns.* **star′-anise,** a Chines evergreen tree (Illicium) of the magnolia family with aromatic oil ; **star′-apple,** the fruit of th West Indian sapotaceous tree *Chrysophyllun Cainito* ; **star′-blast′ing,** the noxious influenc of the stars.—*adj.* **star′-bright,** bright as a sta or with stars.—*n.* **star′-cat′alogue,** a list of stars with their places, magnitudes, &c.—*adj.* **star′ crossed, -crost,** thwarted by the stars.—*n.* **star′dom,** the state of being, the status of, stage or screen star ; **star′-drift,** a common prope motion of a number of fixed stars in the sam region ; **star′-dust,** cosmic dust, meteoric matte in fine particles : distant stars seen like dust grains ; **star′fish,** any member of the Asteroidea a class of echinoderms with five arms merging i a disk, and tube-feet on the under surface : some times extended to the ophiuroids.—*v.i.* **star′gaze** —*ns.* **star′-gazer,** an astrologer : an astronome one who gazes at the sky, or in abstraction : dreamer or wool-gatherer : a fish with upward looking eyes (Uranoscopus or other) ; **star′ gazing ; star′-grass,** a name for many grasslik plants with star-shaped flowers or leaf-arrangement ; **star′-jell′y**, Nostoc, once thought to be a fallen star.—*adjs.* **star′-led**, guided by a star ; **star′less**.—*ns.* **star′let**, a kind of starfish (Asterina): a little star ; **star′light**, light from the stars : (*Spens.*) an unknown plant, otherwise called astrophel or penthia.—*adj.* of or with starlight: lighted by the stars : bright as a star.—*adj.* and *adv.* **star′like**.—*adj.* **star′lit**, lighted by the stars. —*ns.* **star′-man**, an astrologer : a first-offender, wearing a star ; **star′-map**, a map showing the positions of the stars ; **star′monger**, an astrologer ; **star′-nose** (or **star-nosed mole**), a North American mole with star-shaped nose-tip ; **star′-of-Beth′lehem**, a plant (Ornithogalum) of the lily family, with starlike flowers ; **star′-of-the-earth′**, buck's-horn plantain ; **star′-of-the-night′**, Clusia. —*adjs.* **star′-pav′d**, (*Milt.*) paved with stars ; **star′-proof**, (*Milt.*) impervious to starlight.—*n.* **star′-read**, (*Spens.*) astronomy.—*adj.* **starred**, adorned or studded with stars : influenced by or having a star : decorated or marked with a star : turned into a star : star-shaped : radially cracked or fissured.—*n.* **starr′iness**.—*n.* and *adj.* **starr′ing**. —*adjs.* **starr′y**, abounding or adorned with stars : consisting of, or proceeding from, the stars : like, or shining like, the stars ; **star′-shaped**, shaped like a conventional star, with pointed rays.—*ns.* **star′-shell**, a shell that explodes high in the air, lighting up the scene ; **star′shine**, starlight.— *adj.* **star′-spang′led**, spangled or studded with stars (**Star-spangled Banner**, the Stars and Stripes : an American national hymn).—*ns.* **star′-stone**, a sapphire, ruby, or other stone showing asterism ; **star′-this′tle**, a species of Centaurea with radiating spiny bracts ; **star′-trap**, a stage trap of several wedge-shaped pieces meeting in a centre ; **star′-turn**, the chief item in an entertainment : a pre-eminent performer ; **star′-wheel**, a spur-wheel with V-shaped teeth ; **star′wort**, any plant of the genus Aster (not the China aster): stitchwort: a water-plant (**water-starwort**, Callitriche). — *adj.* **star-ypointing** (*stär′-i-point′ing* ; *Milt.*), incorrectly formed), pointing to the stars. —**Star of David**, the Jewish religious symbol —Solomon's-seal (see second meaning of this); **Stars and Stripes**, the flag of the United States of America, with thirteen stripes alternately red and white, and a blue field containing as many stars as there are states ; **star sapphire**, an asteriated sapphire. [O.E. *steorra* ; cf. **stern** (3), Ger. *stern*, L. *stella* (for *sterula*), Gr. *astēr*.)

star, starr, *stär, n.* Ammophila or other coarse seaside grass, sedge, or rush.—Also **star(r)′-grass.** [O.N. *störr*.]

staragen, *star′ə-gən, n.* (*obs.*) the tarragon plant. [Cf. Sp. *estragón*, Fr. *estragon, tarragon.*]

starboard, *stär′bə(r)d, -bōrd, n.* the right-hand side of a ship.—*adj.* and *adv.* of, to, towards, or on, the right.—*v.t.* to turn to the right (see note at **port**) — opp. to *port.* [O.E. *stéorbord*—*stéor*, steering, *bord*, board, side of a ship (ancient Gmc. ships being steered by a paddle at the right side).]

starch, *stärch, n.* the principal reserve food-material stored in plants, chemically a carbohydrate, $(C_6H_{10}O_5)_x$, used in the laundry as a stiffener: stiffness, formality.—*adj.* of starch: stiff, rigid, formal.—*v.t.* to stiffen or stick with starch.—*adj.* **starched**.—*adv.* **starchedly** (*stärcht, stärch′id-*). —*ns.* **starched′ness** (or *-id-*); **starch′er** ; **starch′-grain**, in plants, a layered cell-inclusion of starch ; **starch′-hy′acinth**, grape-hyacinth, from its smell. —*adv.* **starch′ily**.—*ns.* **starch′iness** ; **starch′-paper**, a test-paper for iodine, coated with starch and potassium iodide.—*adj.* **starch′y**, of or like starch : stiff : precise. [O.E. *stercan*, to stiffen, inferred from *stercedferhth*, stiff-spirited ; cf. Ger. *stärke*, starch, and **stark**.]

Star Chamber, *stär′ chăm′bər, n.* a tribunal (abolished 1641) with a civil and criminal jurisdiction, which met in the old council chamber at Westminster. [Prob. named from the gilt *stars* on the ceiling, not from the Jewish bonds (*starrs*, Heb. *sh′tār*) kept in it.]

stare, *stär, v.i.* to look with a fixed gaze : to glare :

to be insistently or obtrusively conspicuous (with indirect obj. as to *stare one in the face*) : to look (as *as like as he can stare*) : to stand on end.—*v.t.* to render by staring.—*n.* a fixed look.—*n.* **star′er**, one who stares : (in *pl.*) a lorgnette.—*n., adj.,* and *adv.* **star′ing**.—*adv.* **star′ingly**. [O.E. *starian*, from root seen in Ger. *starr*, rigid ; also in Eng. **stern**.]

stare, *stär, n.* a starling. [O.E. *stær.*]

stark, *stärk, adj.* stiff : strong : stern : harsh : unyielding : sheer : out-and-out. — *adv.* stoutly : utterly.—*v.t.* and *v.i.* to stiffen.—*v.t.* and *v.i.* **stark′en**, to make or become stark.—*adv.* **stark′ly**. —*n.* **stark′ness**. [O.E. *stearc*, hard, strong ; O.N. *sterkr*, Ger. *stark.*]

stark-naked, *stärk′-nā′kid, adj.* utterly naked : quite bare—sometimes shortened to **stark**.— Earlier (now *dial.*) **start′-nak′ed**. [M.E. *stert-naked*—O.E. *steort*, tail, *nacod*, naked ; influenced by foregoing.]

starling, *stär′ling, n.* a black, brown-spotted bird with purple or green reflections, a good mimic : any other member of its genus, Sturnus. [O.E. *stærling*, dim. of *stær* (see **stare**, 2).]

starling, *stär′ling, n.* piling protecting a bridge pier. [Prob. for **staddling**.]

starn. Same as **stern** (3); also (*naut.* or *dial.*) for **stern** (2).

starosta, *stär′os-tä, n.* (*hist.*) a Russian village headman : (*hist.*) a Polish noble holding a **star′osty** or domain by grant of life-estate from the crown. [Russ. and Pol. *starosta*, elder.]

starr. See under **Star Chamber** ; see also **star** (2).

start, *stärt, v.i.* to shoot, dart, move suddenly forth, or out : to spring up or forward : to strain forward : to break away : to make a sudden involuntary movement as of surprise or becoming aware : to spring open, out of place, or loose : to begin to move : to set forth on a journey, race, career.—*v.t.* to begin : to set going : to set on foot : to set up : to drive from lair or hiding-place : to cause or undergo displacement or loosening of : (*obs.*) to startle : to pour out or shoot.—*n.* a sudden movement : a sudden involuntary motion of the body : a startled feeling : a spurt : an outburst or fit : a beginning of movement, esp. of a journey, race, or career : a beginning : a setting in motion : a help in or opportunity of beginning : an advantage in being early or ahead : the extent of such an advantage in time or distance.—*n.* **start′er**, one who starts, esp. in a race : one who gives the signal for starting : a dog that starts game : apparatus for starting a machine : anything used to begin a process, as a bacterial culture in making butter or cheese.—*adj.* **start′ful**, apt to start.—*n.* and *adj.* **start′ing**.—*n.* **start′ing-hole**, a hiding-place : an evasive trick.— *adv.* **start′ingly**, (*Shak.*) by starts.—*ns.* **start′ing-point**, the point from which anything starts, or from which motion begins ; **start′ing-post**, the post or barrier from which the competitors start in a race ; **start′ing-price**, odds on a horse when the race begins.—*adj.* **start′ish**, apt to start, skittish. —*n.* **start′-up**, (*Shak.*) an upstart : (*obs.*) a rustic half-boot or short legging.—Also *adj.*—**start up**, to rise suddenly : to come suddenly into notice or being : to set in motion. [M.E. *sterten* ; closely akin to Du. *storten*, to plunge, Ger. *stürzen.*]

startle, *stärt′l, v.i.* to start : to undergo a start : to feel sudden alarm.—*v.t.* to surprise as with fright : to cause to undergo a start : to take aback : to awake, excite.—*n.* sudden alarm or surprise.— *adj.* **start′led**.—*n.* **start′ler**.—*n.* and *adj.* **start′ling**.—*adv.* **start′lingly**.—*adjs.* **start′lish, start′ly**, apt to start. [M.E. *stertle*—O.E. *steartlian*, to stumble, struggle, kick, or formed afresh from **start**.]

starve, *stärv, v.i.* to die, now only of hunger or (chiefly *Scot.* and *Northern*) cold : to suffer extreme hunger (or cold) : to be in want : (*obs.*) to deteriorate.—*v.t.* to cause to starve : to afflict with hunger (or cold) : to deprive of food : to force, subdue, cure, by want of food : to deprive of anything needful. — *n.* **starvā′tion** (attributed to Lord Melville, 1775).—*adj.* **starved**.—*n.* **starve′ling**, a lean, hungry, weak, or pining person, animal, or plant.—Also *adj.*—*n.* and *adj.* **starv'ing**. [O.E. *steorfan*, to die ; Du. *sterven*, Ger. *sterben*, to die.]

stasis, stā′sis, stas′is, *n.* stoppage, esp. of growth, of blood-circulation, or of the contents of the bowels. —*n.* **stasid′ion** (Mod. Gr. *dim.*), a stall in a Greek church ; **stas′imon** (Gr., stationary), in Greek tragedy, an ode sung after the chorus had taken their places, or without interruption by dialogue :— *pl.* **stas′ima** ; **stas′imorphy**, structural modification by arrested development. [Gr. *stasis*, stoppage.]

statant, stā′tant, *adj.* (*her.*) standing on four feet. [L. *stāre*, to stand.]

state, stāt, *n.* condition : (*coll.*) a perturbed condition of mind : mode of existence : circumstances at any time : a phase or stage : an impression taken at a stage of progress in engraving or etching or in printing a book : status : station in life : high station : (*Shak.*) grave import : pomp, display, ceremonial dignity : (*Shak.*) a seat of dignity : (*Milt.*) a canopy : an estate, order, or class in society or the body politic : hence (*hist.* ; in *pl.*) the legislature : (*Milt.*) an exalted personage : public welfare : constitution : (*obs.*) a republic : the civil power : the organisation of the body politic, or of one of the constituent members of a federation : the territory of such a state : high politics : (*Spens.*) an interest in property : (*Shak.*) property, estate : a body of men united by profession : (now chiefly *mil.*) a statement, report.—*adj.* of, belonging to, relating to, the state or a federal state : public : ceremonial : pompous : affectedly solemn and mysterious : magnificent.—*adv.* or *adj.* (*Spens.*) explained in old gloss as stoutly (perh. pompous).— *v.t.* to set forth : to express the details of : to set down fully and formally : to assert, affirm : (*arch.*) to install, establish, endow, place in a condition (esp. favourable) : to set in state : to specify : (*Milt.*) perh., to determine the value of : to settle. —*adjs.* **stāt′able**, capable of being stated ; **stāt′al**, of a federal state ; **state′-aid′ed**, receiving contributions from the state.—*ns.* **state′-cabin**, a stateroom on a ship ; **state′craft**, the art of managing state affairs.—*adj.* **stāt′ed**, settled : established : fixed : regular : (*obs.*) circumstanced.—*adv.* **stāt′edly**.—*ns.* **state′hood**, the status of a state ; **state′-house**, the building in which a state legislature sits.—*adj.* **state′less**, without nationality : unworthy to be accounted a state : without pomp. — *adv.* **state′lily**.—*n.* **state′liness**.—*adj.* **state′ly**, showing state or dignity : majestic : greatly impressive.—*adv.* majestically : loftily.— *ns.* **state′ment**, the act of stating : that which is stated ; **state′-monger**, one who would be thought a politician ; **state′-paper**, an official paper or document relating to affairs of state ; **state′-pris′on** ; **state′-pris′oner**, a prisoner confined for offence against the state ; **stat′er** ; **state′-relig′ion**, a religion recognised by the state as the national religion ; **state′room**, a room of state : a private cabin or railway compartment ; **States′-Gen′eral**, (*hist.*) the representative body of the three orders (nobility, clergy, burghers) of the French kingdom : the Dutch parliament ; **states′man**, one skilled in government : one who takes an important part in governing the state, esp. with wisdom and broadmindedness : (*N. of England*) one who farms his own estate, a small landholder :—*fem.* **states′-woman**.—*adjs.* **states′manlike**, **states′manly**, befitting a statesman — *ns.* **states′manship** ; **state′-tri′al**, a trial for an offence against the state.—*adj.* **state′wide**, extending over the whole of a state.—**States of the Church**, (*hist.*) the temporal possessions of the popes. [L. *status*, *-ūs* —*stāre*, *statum*, to stand ; partly through O.Fr. (see **estate**).]

stater, stā′tər, *n.* an ancient Greek standard coin of various kinds—gold daric, silver tetradrachm, &c. [Gr. *statēr*, orig. a pound weight—*histanai*, to set, establish, weigh.]

static, -al, stat′ik, *-əl*, *adjs.* pertaining to statics : pertaining to bodies, forces, charges, &c., in equilibrium : stationary : stable : resting : acting by mere weight : pertaining to sense of bodily equilibrium.—*n.* statics : atmospheric disturbances in wireless reception.—*adv.* **stat′ically**.—*n.* **Statice**

(stat′i-sē), the sea-lavender genus (from its astringency).—*n.* (*pl.* in form treated as *sing.*) **stat′ics** the science of forces in equilibrium. [Gr. *statik* (fem. of adj.), bringing to a standstill—root o *histanai*, to cause to stand.]

station, stā′shən, *n.* a standing still : a mode o standing : position : a chosen fixed point : a standing-place : a fixed stopping-place, esp. on on a railway with associated buildings and structures : a place set apart and equipped for some particular purpose : a local office, headquarters, o depot : (*U.S.*) a branch post office : a habitat an actual spot where a species has been found : an assigned place or post : an assigned region for nava duty : a place in India where officials and officers reside : an Australian stock-farm : position in life (esp. a high position) or in the scale of nature (*R.C.*) a holy place visited as one of a series, esp one of (usu. fourteen) representations of stages ir Christ's way to Calvary, disposed around a church interior or elsewhere.—*adj.* of a station.—*v.t.* to assign a station to : to set : to appoint to a post place, or office.—*adj.* **sta′tional**.—*n.* **sta′tionari ness**.—*adj.* **sta′tionary**, still : unmoving : fixed settled : permanently located : continuously resi dent.—Also *n.*—*n.* **sta′tioner** (L. *statiōnārius*, shop-keeper, in the Middle Ages a university book seller, distinguished from an itinerant), (*obs.*) a bookseller or publisher : a dealer in writing materials and the like.—*adj.* **sta′tionery**, belong ing to a stationer.—*n.* the goods sold by a stationer —*ns.* **sta′tion-hand**, (*Austr.*) a man employed or a station ; **sta′tion-house**, a lock-up at a police station : (*U.S.*) a police station : a small railway station ; **sta′tion-master**, one who has charge of a railway station.—**Stationers′ Hall**, the hal in London of the Company of the Stationers, who until the passing of the Copyright Act in 184? enjoyed an absolute control over printing and publishing ; **Stationery Office**, an office for pro viding books, stationery, &c., to government offices and for arranging for the printing of public papers. [L. *statiō*, *-ōnis*—*stāre*, to stand.]

statist, stā′tist, *n.* a statesman : a politician : statistician.—*adj.* **statistic** (stə-tist′ik), statistical (*obs.*) political : relating to.—*n.* a statis tician : (in *pl.*) tabulated numerical facts, orig those relating to a state : (in *pl.* form, treated a *sing.*) the classification, tabulation, and study of such facts.—*adj.* **statist′ical**, of, concerned with of the nature of, statistics.—*adv.* **statist′ically.**— *n.* **statistician** (stat-is-tish′ən), one skilled ir statistics : a compiler or student of statistics. [It *statista* and Ger. *statistik*—L. *status*, state.]

stative, stā′tiv, *adj.* permanent, fixed (now only of a Roman camp) : indicating a physical state or reflex action (of certain Hebrew verbs). [L *statīvus*—*stāre*, to stand.]

stato-, stat′ō-, in composition, standing.—*ns.* **stato cyst** (stat′ō-sist ; Gr. *kystis*, bladder), an organ of equilibrial sense, containing statoliths : a cell with starch-grains by which a plant is supposed to be sensitive to gravity ; **stat′olith** (Gr. *lithos*, stone), a starch grain or other free solid body in a statocyst **stat′oscope**, a sensitive barometer for detecting minute differences. [Gr. *statos*, set, placed.]

stator, stā′tər, *n.* a stationary part within which a part rotates. [L. *stător*, stander.]

statue, stat′ū, *n.* a representation (usu. near or above life-size) of human or animal form in the round.—Also (*obs.*) **stat′ua**.—*adj.* **stat′uary**, of or suitable for sculpture : sculptured : statuesque.— *n.* sculpture : a sculptor.—*adjs.* **stat′ued**, furnished with statues : sculptured ; **statuesque** (*-esk′*), like a statue.—*adv.* **statuesque′ly**.—*n.* **statuette′**, a small statue, figurine. [L. *statua*—*statuĕre*, to cause to stand—*stāre*.]

stature, stat′yər, *n.* body height.—*adj.* **stat′ured**, having a stature. [L. *statūra*.]

status, stā′təs, *n.* state : condition : standing :— *pl.* (*rare*) **status** (*-tūs*). [L. *stătus*.]

statute, stat′ūt, *n.* a law expressly enacted by the legislature (as distinguished from a customary law or law of use and wont) : a written law : the act of a corporation or its founder, intended as a permanent rule or law : a bond or other proceeding based on a statute : a hiring-fair.—*adj.* stat′utable, prescribed, permitted, recognised by, or according to statute.—*adv.* stat′utably.—*ns.* stat′ute-book, a record of statutes or enacted laws ; stat′ute-cap, (*Shak.*) a kind of cap enjoined by statute (1571) to be worn on Sundays by all below a certain rank ; stat′ute-labour, compulsory labour on roads, &c. ; stat′ute-law, law in the form of statutes.—*adv.* stat′utorily.—*adj.* stat′utory, enacted by statute : depending on statute for its authority. [L. *statūtum*, that which is set up—*statuĕre*.]

staunch, stanch, *stawn*(*t*)*sh*, *stän*(*t*)*sh*, *adj.* watertight : stout and firm : firm in principle, pursuit, or support : trusty, hearty, constant, zealous.—*adv.* sta(u)nch′ly.—*n.* sta(u)nch′ness. [O.Fr.*estanche*; see stanch.]

staunch (*v.t.*). See stanch.

staurolite, *stawr′ə-līt*, *n.* a silicate of aluminium with ferrous oxide, magnesia, and water, common as twinned cruciform crystals.—*adj.* staurolitic (*-lit′ik*). [Gr. *stauros*, cross, *lithos*, stone.]

stave, *stāv*, *n.* one of the pieces of which a cask or tub is made : a staff, rod, bar, shaft : (*mus.*) a staff : a stanza, verse of a song.—*v.t.* to break a stave or the staves of : to break : to burst in : to drive off, as with a staff : to delay : to ward off, keep back : to put together, or repair, with staves. —*v.i.* (*Scot.*) to thrust onward : to break up :— *pa.t.* and *pa.p.* stāved or stōve.—**stave and tail,** in bear-baiting, to intervene with staves and by grasping the dogs' tails. [By-form of staff.]

stave-church, *stāv′-church*, *n.* an ancient Norwegian wooden church supported on masts, with gabled roofs rising one above another. [Norw. *stav-kirke*—*stav*, staff, stave, *kirke*, church.]

staves, *stāvz*, plural of staff and of stave.

stavesacre, *stāvz′ā-kər*, *n.* a tall larkspur whose seeds are used against lice. [O.Fr. *stavesaigre*— L.L. *staphisagria*—Gr. *staphis*, raisins, *agrios*, wild.]

staw, *staw*, a Scots form of stall (*n.* and *vb.*, *pr.t.*) and stole (*pa.t.* of steal).

stay, *stā*, *n.* a rope supporting a mast : a guy : a support : a prop : a connecting piece or brace to resist tension : (in *pl.*) a stiff corset (often **pair of stays**) : a stopping, bringing or coming to a standstill : a suspension of legal proceeding : delay : (*obs.*) an obstacle : a sojourn : duration : staying-power : (*obs.*) a permanent state.—*v.t.* to support or incline with a stay or stays : to put in stays or on the other tack : to support : to prop : to sustain : to abide : to endure : to endure to the end : to stop : to detain : to hold, restrain, check the action of : to bring to rest : to discontinue : to allay : to hold back : (*arch.*) to await : (*old-fashioned*) to remain to participate in, be present at or endure : (*Spens.*) to stop for, be stopped by.—*v.i.* to turn to windward in tacking : (*Shak.*) to rely, to found : to stop : to remain : to tarry : to wait : to be kept waiting : to sojourn : (*Scot.*) to dwell : to hold out, last, endure : (*Shak.*) to wait, attend as a servant :— *pa.t.* and *pa.p.* stayed (now rarely staid).—*adj.* stay′-at-home, keeping much at home : untravelled.—*n.* a stay-at-home person.—*n.* stay′-bolt, a bolt or rod binding together opposite plates.—*adj.* stayed, wearing stays : (*Spens.*) staid.—*n.* stay′er, one who, or that which, remains, stops, holds, or supports : a person or animal of good lasting or staying qualities for a race.—*adj.* stay′-in, without leaving the working-place (as a strike).—*n.* and *adj.* stay′ing.—*ns.* stay′ing-power, ability to go on long without flagging ; stay′-lace, a lace for fastening a corset.—*adj.* stay′less, not to be stopped : without stop : without stays : unsupported : impermanent.—*ns.* stay′-maker, a maker of corsets ; staysail (*stā′sl*), a sail extended on a stay ; stay′-tackle, hoisting-tackle hung from a ship's mainstay ; stay′-tape, a stay-lace : tape for binding edges.— ome to stay, become permanent or established ; n stays, head to windward in tacking ; miss stays (see miss) ; stay out, to outstay : to stay to ne end of ; stay put, to remain where one, or as it, put ; stay the stomach, to allay cravings of

hunger for the time. [Partly O.E. *stæg*, stay (rope) ; partly O.Fr. *estayer*, to prop, from the same Gmc. root ; partly O.Fr. *ester*—L.' *stāre*, to stand.]

stayne, stayre, old spellings (*Spens.* &c.) of stain, stair.

stead, *sted*, *n.* a place (now chiefly in compounds and idiomatic phrases) : esp. the place which another had or might have : a farm : a site : a bedstead : (*Spens.*) a space of time : (*Spens.*) circumstances, case, condition : service, avail, advantage.—*v.t.* (*obs.*) to set : to set in a plight : to avail : to help : to serve : to fulfil in substitution (*Shak.* **steed up**):—*pa.t.* and *pa.p.* stead′ed, stead (*sted*).—*adj.* stead′fast, firmly fixed or established : firm : constant : resolute : steady.—*adv.* stead′fastly.—*n.* stead′fastness.— *adv.* stead′ily.—*ns.* stead′iness ; stead′ing, farmbuildings with or without the farm-house.—*adj.* stead′y (*comp.* stead′ier, *superl.* stead′iest), firm in standing or in place : fixed : stable : constant : resolute : consistent : regular : uniform : sober, industrious.—*v.t.* to make steady : to make or keep firm : (*pr.p.* stead′ying ; *pa.t.* and *pa.p.* stead′ied).—*n.* a rest or support, as for the hand, a tool, or a piece of work.—*adj.* stead′y-going, of steady habits or action.—**stand one in good stead,** prove of good service. [O.E. *stede*, place ; cf. Ger. *stadt*, town, *statt*, place, Du. *stad*, town ; O.E. *stedefæst*, steadfast.]

steak, *stāk*, *n.* a slice of meat (esp. hind-quarter of beef) or fish. [O.N. *steik* ; *steikja*, to roast on a spit.]

steal, *stēl*, *v.t.* to take by theft, esp. secretly : to take, gain or win by address, by contrivance, unexpectedly, insidiously, gradually, or furtively : to snatch : in golf, to hole (a long putt) by a delicate stroke—the opposite of *gobble* : to put surreptitiously, smuggle.—*v.i.* to practise theft : to take feloniously : to pass quietly, unobtrusively, gradually, or surreptitiously :—*pa.t.* stōle (*obs.* stāle ; *Scot.* staw, stealed, stealt) ; *pa.p.* stōl′en (*arch.* stōle ; *Milt.* stōln ; *Scot.* stown, stealed, stealt).—*n.* steal′er.—*n.* and *adj.* steal′-ing.—*adv.* steal′ingly.—**steal a march on,** to gain an advantage over unperceived ; **steal a marriage,** to marry secretly ; **steal one's thunder,** to make use of another's invention against him (as when John Dennis's stage thunder was used in a rival's play). [O.E. *stelan* ; Ger. *stehlen*, Du. *stelen*.]

steal, steale, steel, stele, steil, *stēl*, *n.* (*dial.* and *Spens.*) a handle, shank, shaft. [O.E. *stela*, stalk.]

stealth, *stelth*, *n.* (*Spens.*, *Shak.*) a theft : (*Milt.*) a thing stolen : (*Shak.*) secret or unobtrusive going or passage : secret procedure or manner : furtiveness.—*adv.* stealth′ily.—*n.* stealth′iness. —*adj.* stealth′y, acted or acting with stealth : furtive. [**steal** (1).]

steam, *stēm*, *n.* water in the form of gas or vapour or of a mist or film of liquid drops : a steamed dish : steam-power : a spell of travel by steampower : (*fig.*) energy, force, spirit.—*adj.* of, for, using, worked by, steam.—*v.i.* to rise or pass off in steam or vapour : to emit or generate steam, vapour, or smell : to become dimmed with vapour : to move by steam.—*v.t.* to exhale : to expose to steam : to cook by means of steam : to dim with vapour.—*ns.* steam′boat, steam′ship, steam′-vessel, a vessel driven by steam ; steam′-boil′er, a boiler for generating steam ; steam′-carriage, a steam-driven road vehicle ; steam′-chest, -dome, a chamber above a steam-boiler serving as a reservoir for steam ; steam′-coal, coal suitable for raising steam ; steam′-crane ; steam′-digger.—*adjs.* steam′-driv′en ; steamed.—*ns.* steam′-engine, any engine worked by steam ; steam′er, one who steams : apparatus for steaming : a steamship : a motor-car, a road-locomotive, fire-engine, &c., worked by steam ; steam′-gauge, a pressure gauge for steam ; steam′-gov′ernor, the governor of a steam-engine ; steam′-hamm′er, a vertical hammer worked by steam.—*adv.* steam′ily.—*n.* steam′iness.—*n.*, *adj.*, and *adv.* steam′ing.—*ns.* steam′-jack′et, a hollow casing supplied with steam ; steam′-

launch, a large steam-driven boat; **steam'-naviga'tion,** the propulsion of vessels by steam; **steam'-navvy, -shovel,** an excavator driven by steam; **steam'-pack'et,** a steam-vessel plying between certain ports; **steam'-pipe,** a pipe for conveying steam; **steam'-plough,** a plough or gang of ploughs worked by a steam-engine; **steam'-port,** an opening for the passage of steam; **steam'-power,** the force or agency of steam when applied to machinery; **steam'-roll'er,** a steam-engine with a heavy roller for wheels, used in road-mending, &c.: (*fig.*) any weighty crushing force.—*adj.* **steam'tight,** impervious to steam.—*ns.* **steam'-trap,** a contrivance for allowing the passage of water but not of steam; **steam'-tug,** a small steam-vessel used in towing ships; **steam'tur'bine,** an engine in which expanding steam acts on blades attached to a drum; **steam'-whis'tle,** a whistle sounded by passage of steam.—*adj.* **steam'y,** of, like, full of, covered with, as if covered with, emitting, steam or vapour.—*n.* **steam'-yacht,**—**full steam ahead,** forward at the greatest speed possible: with maximum effort; **let off steam,** to release steam into the atmosphere: to work off energy: to give vent to anger or annoyance; **steam open,** to open by softening gum by exposure to steam; **under one's own steam,** by one's own unaided efforts. [O.E. *stéam*; Du. *stoom.*]

stean, steen, *stēn*, *n.* (*dial.*; *Spens.* **steane**) a stone or earthenware vessel. [O.E. *stǽne.*]

stear, steare, steard, stearage, stearsman, stearsmate, old spellings (*Spens., Milt.*) of **steer, steered,** &c.

stear-, steat-, in composition, suet, fat.—*n.* **stearate** (*stē'ər-āt*), a salt of stearic acid.—*adj.* **stearic** (*stē-ar'ik*), of stearin (**stearic acid,** a fatty acid, C₁₇H₃₅·COOH).—*n.* **ste'arin,** glyceryl ester of stearic acid: a mixture of stearic and palmitic acids (also **ste'arine**): the solid part of a fat.—*adj.* **ste'arine,** made of stearin(e), as candles.—*n.* **steatite** (*stē'ə-tīt*), soapstone.—*adj.* **steatitic** (-*tit'ik*).—*ns.* **ste'atocele** (Gr. *kēlē*, tumour), a fatty tumour in the scrotum; **steato'ma,** a fatty encysted tumour.—*adj.* **steatom'atous.**—*n.* **steatopygia** (*stē-ə-tō-pī'ji-ä, -pij'i-ä*; Gr. *pȳgē*, buttock), an accumulation of fat on the buttocks, as in Hottentot women.—*adj.* **steatopygous** (-*tō-pī'gəs, -top'i-gəs*), fat-buttocked.—*n.* **steato'sis,** fatty degeneration. [Gr. *stēar, stēatos*, suet.]

steare, *stēr*, *n.* (*Spens.*) a steer or ox.

sted, stedd, stedde, stede (*Spens.*), **steed** (*Shak.*), forms of **stead** (*n.* and *v.t.*); **stedfast,** an obsolescent spelling (*Shak., Milt.*, &c.) of **steadfast; steddy, steedy,** old spellings of **steady.**

steed, *stēd*, *n.* a horse, esp. a spirited horse. [O.E. *stéda*, stud-horse, stallion; cf. O.E. *stód*, stud; Ger. *stute*, stud-mare, *gestüte*, stud.]

steek, *stēk*, *n.* (*Scot.*) a stitch.—*v.t.* and *v.i.* to stitch.—*v.t.* to pierce: to fasten: to shut:—*pa.t.* and *pa.p.* **steek'it.** [Partly at least O.E. *stice*, stitch, puncture; perh. partly confused with **stick.**]

steel, *stēl*, *n.* iron containing a little carbon with or without other things: a cutting tool or weapon, an instrument, object, or part made of steel, as a steel knife-sharpener, a skate: a piece of steel, as for stiffening a corset, striking fire from a flint: a steel-engraving: (*fig.*) extreme hardness, staying power, trustworthiness: any chalybeate medicine.—*adj.* of or like steel.—*v.t.* to cover or edge with steel: to harden: to nerve: to make obdurate.—*n.* and *adj.* **steel'-blue,** blue like a reflection from steel.—*adjs.* **steel'-clad,** clad in armour; **steeled,** made of, covered, protected, provided or edged with, steel: hardened: nerved. —*n.* **steel'-engrav'ing,** engraving on steel plates: an impression or print so got.—*n.* and *adj.* **steel'-grey, -gray,** bluish-grey like steel.—*adj.* **steel'-head'ed.**—*ns.* **steel'iness; steel'ing; steel'-pen,** a nib of steel; **steel'-plate,** a plate of steel: one on which a design is engraved: a print from it.—*adj.* **steel'-plat'ed,** plated with steel.—*ns.* **steel'-trap,** one with steel jaws and spring; **steel'-ware,** articles of steel collectively; **steel'-**

wool', steel shavings used for cleaning and polishing; **steel'work,** work executed in steel: (often in *pl.* form) a factory where steel is made; **steel'-worker.**—*adj.* **steel'y,** of or like steel. [O.E. *style*; Ger. *stahl.*]

steelbow, *stēl'bō*, *n.* (*Scots law*) stock and goods received from a landlord with obligation to return a like amount and value when the lease expires: a contract or tenure on these terms.—Also *adj.* [steel, in the sense of rigidly fixed, and obs. *bow*—O.N. *bú*, stock of cattle.]

steelyard, *stēl'yärd*, *n.* a weighing machine consisting of a lever with a short arm for the thing weighed and a long graduated arm on which a single weight moves. [Prob. **steel** and **yard,** but suggested or fixed in use by the *Steelyard* or *Stålhof* (L.G.; prop. sample yard, mistranslated steel yard), the Hanse headquarters in London.]

steem, steme, *stēm*, *v.t.* (*Spens.*). Same as **esteem;** also same as **steam.**

steen. See **stean.**

steenbok, *stān', stēn'bok, n.* a small S. African antelope. [Du.,—*steen,* stone, *bok,* buck.]

steenkirk, *stēn'kərk, n.* a lace cravat loosely worn. [From the battle of *Steenkerke,* August 3, 1692.]

steep, *stēp, adj.* (*obs.*) lofty: rising or descending with great inclination: precipitous: headlong: difficult: excessive, exorbitant.—*n.* a precipitous place.—*v.t.* (*S.W. England*) to cause to stoop, slope. —*v.i.* to rise or fall precipitously.—*adj.* **steep(e)'-down(e),** (*Shak.*) precipitous.—*v.t.* and *v.i.* **steep'en,** to make or become steeper. — *n.* **steep'iness** (*obs.*).—*adj.* **steep'ish.**—*adv.* **steep'ly.** —*n.* **steep'ness.**—*adjs.* **steep'-to',** (*naut.*) rising precipitously from the water; **steep(e)'-up,** (*Shak.*) precipitous; **steep'y,** steep (*poet.*). [O.E. *stéap*; cf. **stoop.**]

steep, *stēp, v.t.* to soak: to wet thoroughly: to saturate: to imbue.—*v.i.* to undergo soaking or thorough wetting.—*n.* a soaking process: a liquid for steeping anything in: rennet.—*n.* **steep'er,** one who steeps: a vessel for steeping in. [M.E. *stepen*: perh. conn. with **stoup.**]

steeple, *stēp'l, n.* a church or other tower with or without, including or excluding, a spire: a structure surmounted by a spire: the spire alone. —*ns.* **steep'le-bush,** hard-hack; **steep'lechase,** orig. an impromptu horse-race with some visible church-steeple as goal: a horse-race across-country: one over a course with artificial obstacles: a foot-race of like kind.—*v.i.* to ride or run in a steeplechase.—*ns.* **steep'lechaser; steep'le-chasing; steep'le-crown,** a high conical hat.— Also *adj.*—*adjs.* **steep'le-crowned; steep'le'd** having a steeple or steeples or appearance of steeples.—*ns.* **steep'le-fair,** (*obs.*) a market in church-livings; **steep'le-hat; steep'le-house** (*obs.*) a church-building; **steep'le-jack,** one who repairs steeples and chimney-stalks. [O.E. *stépel, stýpel, stípel,* from root of **steep.**]

steer, *stēr, n.* a young ox, esp. a castrated one from two to four years old.—*n.* **steer'ling,** a little or young steer. [O.E. *stéor*; Ger. *stier.*]

steer, *stēr, v.t.* to direct with, or as with, the helm to guide: to govern.—*v.i.* to direct a ship, cycle &c., in its course: to be directed, take or follow a course in answer to the helm.—*ns.* **steer'age** act or practice of steering: the effect of a rudder on the ship: course: government: apparatus for steering: part (in front of the great cabin) from which a ship used to be steered: part of a passenger ship with lowest fares (also *adj.*); **steer'age-way** sufficient movement of a vessel to enable it to b controlled by the helm; **steer'er; steer'ing steer'ing-gear,** the mechanism that transmi motion from the steering-wheel; **steer'ing wheel,** the wheel whereby a ship's rudder turned, or a motor-car, &c., guided; **steers'ma** **steers'mate** (*obs.*; *Milt.* **stears'-mate**), one wh steers.—**steer clear of,** to avoid; **steerir committee,** (*U.S.*) a group who decide wh measures shall be brought forward and whe [O.E. *stéoran, stýran,* to steer.]

steer, *stēr, n., v.t.,* and *v.i.* a Scots form of **stir.**—*n.* **steer'y,** (*Scott*) commotion.

teeve, *stēv*, *n.* angular elevation, esp. of a bowsprit.—*v.t.* and *v.i.* to incline to the horizon. [Origin unknown.]

teeve, stieve, *stēv*, *adj.* (*Scot.*) stiff, firm : sturdy.—Also *adv.*—*adv.* **steeve′ly, stieve′ly.** [M.E. *stef*; ety. doubtful.]

teeve, *stēv*, *v.t.* to stuff, pack close.—*n.* **steev′ing.** [Perh. Fr. *estiver*—L. *stīpāre*, to stuff.]

tegano-, stego-, in composition, covered, roofed, hidden, watertight.—*ns.* **steganogram** (*steg′an-ə-gram*), a cryptogram : **steganographer** (*-og′rə-fər*).—*adj.* **steganograph′ic.**—*ns.* **steganog′raphist ; steg′anopod** (Gr. *pous, podos*, foot), any bird of the Steganop′odēs, the pelican order of birds, with all four toes webbed together.—*adj.* **steg-anop′odous.**—*n.* **stegno′sis,** constriction of the pores and vessels : constipation.—*adjs.* **stegnot′ic ; stegocarp′ous** (Gr. *karpos*, fruit), with lidded capsule.—*n.pl.* **Stegocephalia** (-*se-fā′li-ä* ; Gr. *kephalē*, head), an extinct order of lizard amphibians (Labyrinthodon, &c.).—*adj.* and *n.* **stegocephā′lian.**—*adj.* **stegocephalous** (-*sef′ə-əs*).—*ns.* **Stegomyia** (-*mī′yä* ; Gr. *myia*, fly), the yellow-fever mosquito or other of its genus ; **steg′osaur** (Gr. *sauros*, lizard), a gigantic Jurassic dinosaur (Stegosaur′us), with heavy armour of bony plates.—*adj.* **stegosaur′ian.** [Gr. *steganos,* covered, watertight, *stegein,* to cover, hold water, protect, hide, *stegnoein,* to make costive.]

teinberger, *stīn′bər-gər, shtīn′ber-hhər, n.* an esteemed Rhenish white wine, from *Steinberg,* near Wiesbaden.

teinbock, *stīn′bok, n.* the Alpine ibex: also used for **steenbok.** [Ger. *stein,* stone, *bock,* buck.]

tele, *stē′lē, n.* an upright stone slab or tablet (also *stē′la*) : (*bot.* ; *stē′lē, stēl*) the central cylinder of vascular bundles with pith and pericycle) in stems and roots of the higher plants :—*pl.* (L.) **stē′lae.—***adjs.* **ste′lar, ste′lene.** [Gr. *stēlē*—root of *histanai*, to set, stand.]

tell, *stel, v.t.* (*obs.*) to set, post : (Shak. ; *pa.p.* **steeled**, *steld*) to delineate.—*n.* (*Scot.*) an enclosure (usu. a ringwall) for sheltering sheep, &c.—*adj.* **stell′ed,** fixed (see also under **stellar**). [O.E. *stellan,* to fix, put.]

tellar, *stel′ər, adj.* of the stars : of the nature of a star : starry.—*n.* **Stellā′ria,** the chickweed genus of the pink family.—*adjs.* **stell′ate,** star-shaped : with branches radiating from a point : with sides that intersect one another, giving a starlike effect, as in the pentagram ; **stell′āted,** stellate : starred.—*adv.* **stell′ately.**—*adjs.* **stelled,** starred : (Shak.) **steel′ed)** perh. formed into stars (but prob. fixed ; see **stell** above) ; **stellif′erous,** having or bearing stars or starlike marks or forms ; **stell′ified ; stell′iform,** star-shaped.—*v.t.* **stell′ify,** to turn into a star : to set among the stars : (*obs.*) to set with stars.—*n.* **stell′ifying.**—*adjs.* **stell′ular, stell′ulate,** like a little star. [L. *stēlla,* a star.]

tellenbosch, *stel′ən-bosh, v.t.* (*mil. slang*) to relegate to a post where incompetence matters less : to supersede. [From *Stellenbosch*, Cape of Good Hope, such a dumping-ground.]

tellion, *stel′yən, n.* a Levantine lizard (*Agama stellio*) with starry spots.—*n.* **stell′ionate**, a fraud that does not come under any specific head. [L. *stēlliō, -ōnis,* a star-spotted lizard, a knave—*stēlla,* star.]

tem, *stem, n.* the leaf-bearing axis of a plant : a stalk : anything stalk-like, as the slender upright part of a note, of a wine-glass, the winding shaft of a watch : an upright stroke of a letter : the main line (or sometimes a branch) of a family : a race or family : (*philol.*) the base of a word, to which inflectional suffixes are added : a curved timber at the prow of a ship : the forepart of a ship.—*v.t.* to provide with a stem : to deprive of stalk or stem : to oppose the stem to : hence, to make way against, breast : to ram.—*v.i.* to grow a stem : (*U.S.*) to spring, take rise.—*n.* **stem′-form,** ancestral form.—*adjs.* **stem′less ; stemmed.**—*ns.* **stem′son,** a timber behind the apron of a ship ; **stem′winder,** (*U.S.*) a keyless watch.—**from stem to stern,** from one end of a vessel to the other : completely,

throughout. [O.E. *stefn, stemn* ; Ger. *stamm*; perh. conn. with **stand.**]

stem, *stem, v.t.* to stop, check : to dam : to tamp : to staunch :—*pr.p.* **stemm′ing** ; *pa.t.* and *pa.p.* **stemmed.** [O.N. *stemma.*]

stembuck, *stem′buk,* **stembok**, *-bok,* for **steenbok.**

steme, *stēm, v.t.* (*Spens.*) for steam, i.e. evaporate.

stemma, *stem′ä, n.* a garland : a scroll : a pedigree : an ocellus :—*pl.* **stemm′ata.**—*adj.* **stemm′atous.**—*v.t.* **stemme** (*stem* ; *Spens.*), to encircle. [Gr. *stemma,* usu. in pl. *stemmata.*]

stempel, stemple, *stem′pl, n.* a cross-timber in a shaft, as support or step. [Cf. Ger. *stempel.*]

stench, *sten(t)sh, n.* stink.—*v.t.* to cause to stink.—*n.* **stench′-trap,** a device to prevent rise of gases in drains.—*adj.* **stench′y.** [O.E. *stenc,* smell (good or bad) ; cf. stink ; Ger. *stank.*]

stencil, *sten′s(i)l, v.t.* and *v.i.* to paint by brushing over a perforated plate : to make a stencil for producing copies of typewriting or writing : (*pr.p.* **sten′cilling** ; *pa.t.* and *pa.p.* **sten′cilled**).—*n.* the plate or the colouring-matter so used : the design or lettering so produced : a piece of waxed paper, &c., on which letters are cut by typewriter or stylus so that ink will pass through.—*adj.* **sten′-cilled.**—*ns.* **sten′ciller ; sten′cilling ; sten′cil-plate.** [O.Fr. *estinceller,* to spangle—*estincelle*—L. *scintilla,* a spark.]

stend, *stend, v.i.* (*Scot.*) to bound, stride vigorously.—*n.* a bound or great stride : a dart of pain.—Also **sten.** [Poss. L. *extendĕre.*]

stengah, *steng′gä,* **stinger**, *sting′ər, n.* (out East) a peg of whisky and soda. [Malay *sa tenah,* one half.]

sten gun, *sten gun, n.* a small automatic gun. [*ST* (designers′ initials) and *En*field, as in **bren gun.**]

stenlock, *sten′lək, n.* (*Scot.*) a coalfish : an overgrown coalfish. [Origin doubtful.]

steno-, *sten′ō-, -ə-, -o′-,* in composition, narrow.—*ns.* **sten′ochrome** (-*krōm* ; Gr. *chrōma,* colour), a print by stenochromy ; **sten′ochromy** (or -*ok′ro-mi*), printing in several colours at one printing ; **sten′-ograph,** a shorthand character or report.—*v.t.* to write in shorthand.—*n.* **stenog′rapher.**—*adjs.* **stenograph′ic, -al.**—*adv.* **stenograph′ically.**—*ns.* **stenog′raphist ; stenog′raphy,** the art, or any method, of writing very quickly : shorthand.—*adjs.* **stenopaeic** (-*pē′ik* ; Gr. *opaios,* holed—*opē,* an opening), with a narrow opening (also **steno-pā′ic**) ; **stenosed** (*sti-nōst′*), morbidly contracted.—*n.* **steno′sis,** constriction : constipation.—*adj.* **stenotic** (*sti-not′ik*).—*ns.* **sten′otype,** a phonetic typewriter or its use ; **sten′otyper, sten′otypist ;** **sten′otypy.** [Gr. *stenos,* narrow.]

stent, *stent, n., v.t.,* and *v.i.* Same as **stint,** with meanings shading off into those of next word.

stent, *stent, n.* (*Scot.*) assessment : valuation : tax.—*v.t.* to assess : to tax : to levy.—*ns.* **stent′master, stent′or, stent′our,** one who determines amount of tax to be paid. [**extent,** or O.Fr. *estente* ; see also **stent** (1) and **stint.**]

Stentor, *stent′or, n.* a very loud-voiced Greek at Troy (*Iliad*), hence a loud-voiced person.—*adjs.* **stentō′rian ; stentorophon′ic** (Gr. *phōnē,* voice).—*n.* **stent′orphone,** apparatus for intensifying the voice. [Gr. *Stentōr.*]

step, *step, n.* a pace : a movement of the leg in walking, running, or dancing : the distance so covered : a footstep : a footfall : a footprint : gait : a small space : a short journey : a degree of a scale : a stage upward or downward : one tread of a stair : round of a ladder : a door-step : something to put the foot on in mounting or dismounting : a stage in discontinuous or stairwise rise or fall : a move towards an end or in a course of proceeding : coincidence in speed and phase : a support for the end of a mast, pivot, or the like : (in *pl.*) walk, direction taken in walking : a self-supporting hinged ladder (often *pair of steps*): a stair.—*v.i.* to advance, retire, mount, or descend by taking a step or steps : to pace : to walk : to walk slowly or gravely : to walk a short distance.—*v.t.* to perform by stepping : to measure by pacing : to arrange or shape stepwise : (now *U.S.*) to set, as a foot : to fix, as a mast :—*pr.p.* **stepp′ing** ; *pa.t.* and *pa.p.* **stepped** (also **stept**).—

Neutral vowels in unaccented syllables : *el′ə-mənt, in′fənt, ran′dəm*

ns. **step'-dance**, a dance involving an effective display of steps by an individual dancer; **step'-dancer**; **step'-dancing**; **step'-fault**', (*geol.*) one of a series of parallel faults throwing in the same direction; **step'-in**, a garment that needs no fastening; **step'-ladder**, a ladder with flat treads and a hinged prop; **stepp'er**; **stepp'ing-stone**, a stone rising above water or mud to afford a passage; (*fig.*) a means to gradual progress; **step'-stone**, a door-step.—*adj.* **step'-up**', increasing or changing by steps: raising voltage.—*adv.* **step'-wise**, in the manner of steps.—**break step**, to change the sequence of right and left foot, so as to get out of step; **keep step**, to continue in step; **in step**, with simultaneous putting forward of the right (or left) feet in marching, &c.; **out of step**, not in step; **step in**, or **into**, to enter easily or unexpectedly; **step on it**, (*slang*; see **gas**, **juice**) to hurry; **step out**, to go out a little way: to increase the length of the step and so the speed; **step short**, to shorten the length of one's step; **step up**, to come forward: to build up into steps: to raise by a step or steps: to increase the voltage of: to increase the rate of, as production. [O.E. (Mercian) *steppe* (W.S. *stæpe*); Du. *step*, Ger. *stapfe*.]

step-, *step-*, *pfx.* indicating affinity by another marriage or mating. — *ns.* **step'bairn** (*Scot.*), **-child**, **-daughter**, **-son**, a wife's or husband's but not one's own child, daughter, son; **step'dame** (*arch.*), **step'mother**, a father's wife not one's own mother: a bird that hatches another's eggs; (*fig.*) a cruel, niggardly, or negligent guardian.—*adj.* **step'motherly**.—*ns.* **step'father**, a mother's husband not one's own father; **step'-parent**; **step'brother**, **-sister**, the son, daughter, of a step-father or stepmother. [O.E. *stéop-* (as in *stéopmódor*), orig. meaning orphan; Ger. *stief-*.]

stephane, *stef'ə-nē*, *n.* an ancient Greek head-dress like a diadem. [Gr. *stephanē*—*stephein*, to encircle.]

stephanite, *stef'ə-nīt*, *n.* brittle silver ore, composed of silver, sulphur, and antimony. [After Archduke Stephan (1817-67).]

Stephanotis, *stef-ə-nō'tis*, *n.* a genus of asclepiads of Madagascar, &c., cultivated for their scented flowers. [Gr. *stephanōtis*, fit for a wreath—*stephanos*, a crown, wreath.]

stepney, *step'ni*, *n.* a spare wheel, often *fig.* [Said to be from the name of a street where they were made.]

steppe, *step*, *n.* a dry, grassy, generally treeless and uncultivated and sometimes salt plain, as in the south-east of Europe and in Asia. [Russ. *step.*]

steradian, *sti-rā'di-ən*, *n.* a unit of measurement for solid angles, the angle subtended at the centre of a sphere by an area equal to the square of the radius. [Gr. *stereos*, solid, and **radian**.]

stercoraceous, *stərk-ə-rā'shəs*, *adj.* of, of the nature of, dung.— *adj.* **sterc'oral**, stercoraceous.— *ns.* **sterc'oranism**, the belief that the sacramental bread was digested and evacuated like other food; **sterc'oranist**. — *adjs.* **stercorā'rious**, **sterc'orary**.—*v.t.* **sterc'orate**, to manure. [L. *stercus*, *-oris*, dung.]

Sterculia, *stər-kū'li-ä*, *n.* the gum tragacanth genus giving name to the **Sterculiā'ceae**, a family of large trees and shrubs akin to the mallows, including kola and cacao. [L. *Sterculius*, god of manuring—*stercus*, dung, from the stinking flowers.]

stere, *stēr*, *n.* a cubic metre—about 35·315 cubic feet.—Also in compounds, as **decastere** (*dek'ə-*), 10 steres, **decistere** (*des'i-*), a tenth of a stere. [Fr. *stère*—Gr. *stereos*, solid.]

stereo-, *stēr'i-ō-*, *ster'i-ō-*, in composition, solid, hard, three-dimensional.—*n.*, *adj.*, *v.t.*, and *v.i.* **ster'eo**, a contr. of stereotype, stereoscope, stereoscopic.—*n.* **ster'eobate** (root of Gr. *bainein*, to go, walk), a substructure, foundation.—*adj.* **stereobatic** (*-bat'ik*).—*ns.* **stereochem'istry**, the study of the spatial arrangement of atoms in molecules; **ster'eochrome** (Gr. *chrōma*, colour); **ster'eochrōmy**, mural painting fixed with water-glass; **ster'eogram**, **ster'eograph**, a picture or diagram suggestive of solidity: a stereographic double picture. — *adjs.* **stereograph'ic**, **-al**.— *ns.* **stereog'raphy**; **stereoï'somer**, an isomer dif-

fering only in spatial arrangement of atoms.—*ad* **stereoïsomer'ic**.—*ns.* **stereoïsom'erism**; **ster eome**, mechanical tissue in plants; **stereom'ete** an instrument for measuring specific gravity o for measuring solids.—*adjs.* **stereomet'ric**, **-a** —*adv.* **stereomet'rically**. — *ns.* **stereom'etry** **stereops'is** (Gr. *opsis*, vision), binocular stereoscop vision; **stereopt'icon**, a double projecting lanter by means of which the one picture dissolves int another; **ster'eoscope**, an instrument by which th images of two pictures differing slightly in poir of view are seen one by each eye and so give a effect of solidity.—*adjs.* **stereoscop'ic**, **-al**.—*ed* **stereoscop'ically**.—*ns.* **stereos'copist**; **stereos copy**; **stereot'omy** (Gr. *tomē*, a cut), sectior cutting of solids: stone-cutting; **ster'eotype**, solid metallic plate for printing, cast from a plast mould of movable types: the art, method, o process of making such plates.—*adj.* pertaining t or done with, stereotypes.—*v.t.* to make a stereo type of: to print with stereotypes.—*adj.* **ster'eo typed**, transferred as letterpress from set-u movable type to a mould, and thence to a met plate: fixed, unchangeable, as opinions.— **ster'eotyper**.—*adj.* **stereotyp'ic**.—*ns.* **ster'eotyp ing**; **ster'eotypy**.—*adj.* **steric** (*ster'ik*), relating spatial arrangement of atoms. [Gr. *stereos*, solid

sterigma, *ster-ig'mä*, *n.* the stalk of a spore:—*p* **sterig'mata**. [Gr. *stērigma*, support.]

sterile, *ster'īl* (*U.S.* -il), *adj.* unfruitful: barrer not producing, or unable to produce, offsprir fruit, seeds, or spores: of a flower, without pistil of a glume, not subtending a flower: sterilised destitute of ideas or results.—*n.* **sterilisatic** (*ster-i-li-zā'shon*).—*v.t.* **ster'ilise**, to cause to l fruitless: to deprive of power of reproductior to destroy micro-organisms in.—*ns.* **ster'ilise** one who, or that which sterilises: apparatus f destroying germs; **steril'ity**, quality of bei sterile: unfruitfulness, barrenness, in regar to reproduction. [L. *sterilis*, barren.]

sterlet, *stər'lit*, *n.* a small sturgeon. [Russ. *sterlyad*

sterling, *stər'ling*, *n.* (*obs.*) an old English silv penny: English, Scottish, or British money standard value.—*adj.* of sterling or standar English money: genuine: of authority: thoroughly good character: (of silver) of standa quality. [Prob. a coin with a star—O.E. *steorr* star—some early Norman pennies being so marked

sterling, *stər'ling*. Same as **starling** (2).

stern, *stərn*, *adj.* severe: austere: rigorous: u relenting.—Also *adv.* (*Milt.*).—*adv.* **stern'ly**.— **stern'ness**. [O.E. *styrne.*]

stern, *stərn*, *n.* the hind-part of a vessel: the run or tail: (*obs.*; *Shak.*) steering-gear, helm, tl steersman's place.—*v.t.* to back, to row backwar —*ns.* **stern'age**, (*Shak.*) sterns collectively; **sterr board**, backward motion of a ship: loss of way tacking; **stern'-chase**, a chase in which one sh follows directly in the wake of another; **sterr chaser**, a cannon in the stern of a ship.—*ac* **sterned**, having a stern (in compounds).— **stern'-fast**, a rope or chain for making fast a ship stern to a wharf, &c.—*adv.* **stern'-fore'most**.— *n.* **stern'-frame**, the framework of a ship's ster —*adj.* **stern'most**, farthest astern.—*ns.* **stern'por** a port or opening in the stern of a ship; **stern post**, the aftermost timber of a ship, supportir the rudder; **stern'sheet**, (usu. in *pl.*) the part a boat between the stern and the rowers; **sterr son**, the hinder extremity of a ship's keelson, which the sternpost is bolted.—*advs.* **stern'war** (also *adj.*), **-s**.—*ns.* **stern'way**, the backwar motion of a vessel; **stern'-wheel'er**, (*U.S.*) small vessel with one large paddle-wheel at th stern.—*n.pl.* **stern'works**, hinder parts. [O.I *stjórn*, a steering, or lost O.E. equivalent.]

stern, *stərn*, **stern**, *starn*, *stärn*, *n.* (*obs.* and *Scot.*) star.—*n.* (*dim.*) **starn'ie**. [O.N. *stjarna.*]

sternum, *stər'nəm*, *n.* the breast-bone: the und part of a somite in arthropods.—*adj.* **ster'nal**.— *ns.* **ster'nebra** (modelled on *vertebra*), a segme of the breast-bone; **ster'nite**, the ventral pla of a segment in arthropods.—*adjs.* **sternit'ic ster'notribe** (Gr. *tribē*, a rub), pollinated l touching an insect's under surface. [Latinised from Gr. *sternon*, chest.]

sternutation, *stər-nū-tā'shən*, *n*. sneezing.—*adjs*. **sternū'tative, sternū'tatory,** that causes sneezing. —*n*. a substance that causes sneezing.—Also **ster'nūtātor**. [L. *sternūtāre*, intens. of *sternuĕre*, to sneeze.]

sterol, *ster'ol*, *n*. a solid higher alcohol such as cholesterol, ergosterol.—*n*. **ster'oid,** any of a class of compounds including the sterols, bile acids, adrenal hormones, &c. [See **cholesterol**.]

stertorous, *stər'tər-əs*, *adj*. with snoring sound.— *adv*. **ster'torously.**—*n*. **ster'torousness.** [L. *stertĕre*, to snore.]

sterve, *stərv*, *v.t.* and *v.i.* an old form (*Spens.*) of **starve,** to starve, to die.

stet, *stet*, *v.t.* to restore after marking for deletion :— *pr.p.* **stett'ing ;** *pa.t.* and *pa.p.* **stett'ed.** [L., let it stand, 3rd sing. pres. subj. of *stāre*, to stand ; written on a proof-sheet with dots under the words to be retained.]

stethoscope, *steth'ə-skōp*, *n*. an instrument for auscultation.—*adjs*. **stethoscopic** (-*skop'ik*), **-al.**— *adv*. **stethoscop'ically.**—*ns*. **stethoscopist** (-*os'kə-pist*) ; **stethos'copy.** [Gr. *stēthos*, chest, *skopeein*, to look at, examine.]

Stetson, *stet'sn*, *n*. a broad-brimmed felt hat. [Maker's name.]

stevedore, *stēv'i-dōr*, *n*. one who loads and unloads vessels. [Sp. *estivador*, packer—*estivar*, to stow— L. *stipāre*, to press.]

steven, *stev'n*, *n*. (now *dial.*) a voice : (*Spens.*) an outcry. [O.E. *stefn*, voice.]

stew, *stū*, *n*. (*Spens.*, *Shak.*) a boiling pot : a room for hot-air baths : a hot bath : an overheated or sweaty state : mental agitation : worry : (usu. in *pl.* form with sing. or collective sense) a brothel, or prostitutes' quarter : (*obs.*) a prostitute : (*slang*) one who studies hard, esp. unintelligently : a dish of stewed food, esp. meat with vegetables.—*v.t.* to bathe in hot air or water : to bathe in sweat : to keep in a swelter or narrow confinement : to simmer or boil slowly with some moisture : to over-infuse.—*v.i.* to shelter : to undergo stewing : to be in a state of worry or agitation : (*slang*) to read hard.—*adj*. **stewed.**—*n*. **stew'er.**—*n*. and *adj*. **stew'ing.**—*ns*. **stew'pan, stew'pot,** one used for stewing.—*adj*. **stew'y,** like a stew : sweltering. —**let one stew in one's own juice,** leave him alone and await developments. [O.Fr. *estuve* (Fr. *étuve*), stove ; prob. conn. with stove.]

stew, *stū*, *n*. a fish-pond : a fish-tank : an artificial oyster-bed.—*n*. **stew'pond.** [O.Fr. *estui* (Fr. *étui*).]

steward, *stū'ərd*, *n*. one who manages the domestic concerns of a family or institution : one who superintends another's affairs, esp. an estate or farm : the manager of the provision department or attendant on passengers in a ship, &c. : a college caterer : one who helps in arrangements, marshalling, &c., at races, a dance, a wedding, an entertainment : an overseer : a foreman : the treasurer of a congregation, guild, society, &c. :— *fem*. **stew'ardess.**—*ns*. **stew'ardship, stew'ardry,** office of a steward : management ; **stew'artry,** (*Scot.*) a stewardship, or the extent of a stewardship —still applied nominally to the county of Kirkcudbright.—**Lord High Steward,** one of the great officers of state, and anciently the first officer of the crown in England. [O.E. *stig-weard*—*stig*, hall (' sty '), *weard*, ward, keeper.]

stey, *stui*, *stī*, *adj*. (*Scot.*) steep. [Cf. **stile, stirrup**.]

sthenic, *sthen'ik*, *adj*. strong, robust : morbidly active. [Gr. *sthenos*, strength.]

stibble, *stib'l*, *n*. a Scots form of **stubble.**—*n*. **stibb'ler,** a horse turned out to feed on stubble : one who cuts the handfuls left by the reaper : (*Scott*) a probationer.

stibium, *stib'i-əm*, *n*. antimony.—*adj*. **stib'ial.**—*ns*. **stib'ialism,** antimony poisoning ; **stib'ine** (-*ēn*, -*īn*), antimony hydride, a poisonous gas ; **stib'nite,** native antimony trisulphide. [L.,—Gr. *stibi*, *stimmi*—Egypt. *stm* (Copt. *stēm*).]

sticcado, *stik-ā'dō*, **sticcato,** -*tō*, *n*. a kind of xylophone. [Perh. It. *steccato*, palisade.]

stich, *stik*, *n*. a line of verse or section of prose of comparable length.—*ns*. **stichar'ion** (Gr. *stichārion*), a Greek vestment like the Western alb ; **stichē'ron,** a short hymn.—*adj*. **stich'ic,** of or pertaining to stichs.—*ns*. **stichid'ium,** a branch producing tetraspores, in red seaweeds :—*pl*. **stichid'ia** ; **stichol'ogy,** metrical theory.—*adjs*. **stichomet'ric, -al.** — *adv*. **stichomet'rically.** — *ns*. **stichom'etry,** measurement by lines : division into lines : a statement of such measurements ; **stichomythia** (-*mith'*; Gr. *stichomȳthiā*), dialogue in alternate lines.—*adj*. **stichomyth'ic.**—*n*. **stich'os,** a line of ordinary length in measuring a manuscript : (*Gr. Ch.*) a verse or versicle :—*pl*. **stich'oi.** [Gr. *stichos*, a row—*steichein*, to march.]

stick, *stik*, *v.t.* to pierce, transfix : to stab : to spear : to thrust : to fasten by piercing : to insert : to set in position : to set or cover with things fastened on : to cause to adhere : (*coll.*) to endure : to bring to a standstill or nonplus.—*v.i.* to be fixed by insertion : to jut, protrude : to adhere : to become or remain fixed : to remain : to be detained by an impediment : to jam : to fail to proceed or advance : to scruple : to hold fast, keep resolutely (with *to*) : (*pa.t.* **stuck,** *Scot.* **stack** ; *pa.p.* **stuck,** *Scot.* **stick'it**).—*n*. a stoppage : a difficulty : a hitch : adhesiveness.—*ns*. **stick'er,** one who kills pigs, &c. : one who or that which sticks : a piercing weapon : a person or thing difficult to get rid of : one who is constant or persistent : a poser : a piano jack : an upright rod that transmits motion from an organ key ; **stick'iness.**—*n*. and *adj*. **stick'ing.** —*ns*. **stick'ing-place,** the point at which a thing sticks or stays ; **stick'ing-plaster,** an adhesive plaster for closing wounds ; **stick'-in-the-mud,** an old fogy.—Also *adj*.—*ns*. **stick'jaw,** a claggy pudding or sweetmeat ; **stick'up,** a stand-up collar.—*adj*. **stick'y,** adhesive : tenacious : gluey : muggy.—*v.t.* to make sticky.—*n*. **stick'y-back,** a gummed photograph.—*adj*. **stuck'-up',** self-importantly aloof.—**beat to sticks,** to defeat and surpass utterly ; **stick at,** to hesitate or scruple at : to persist at ; **stick by,** to be firm in supporting, to adhere closely to ; **stick 'em up,** hold up your hands (or be shot) ; **stick in,** (*Scot.*) to persevere assiduously : also (of a dressing, &c.) to adhere to a wound ; **stick it into,** to overcharge systematically ; **stickit minister,** (*Scot.*) a licentiate who never gets a pastoral charge ; **stick out,** to project : to continue to resist ; **stick to,** to persevere in holding to ; **stick up,** to stand up : to waylay and plunder, as a mail-coach by bushrangers ; **stick up for,** to speak or act in defence of ; **sticky end,** an unpleasant end, disaster ; **sticky wicket,** a difficult situation to cope with ; **stuck on,** (*U.S.*) enamoured of. [O.E. *stician* ; cf. **stick** (2), **stitch**.]

stick, *stik*, *n*. a rod of wood, esp. for walking with or for beating : a twig : a timber tree or trunk : a piece of firewood : a tally : an instrument for beating a percussion instrument : an instrument for playing hockey or other game : a bow for a fiddle, or the wooden part of it : a person of stiff or wooden manner, or wanting in enterprise : a rod : a control-rod of an aeroplane : a group of bombs released at one time from an aeroplane : a piece of domestic furniture (usu. in *pl.*) : a ray of a fan : a support for a candle : a printer's composing-stick : a stickful.—*adj*. in the form of a stick : made of sticks.—*v.t.* to furnish or set with sticks : to arrange in a composing-stick.—*ns*. **stick'ful,** as much as a composing-stick will hold ; **stick'-in'sect,** a twig-like phasmid insect ; **stick'lac,** twigs with attached lac, insects, and ova. [O.E. *sticca* ; O.N. *stika*.]

stickle, *stik'l*, *v.i.* to regulate a contest : to mediate : to interpose : to contend, stand up : to be scrupulous or obstinately punctilious.—*v.t.* to compose : to stop contention between : to contend : to scruple.—*n*. **stick'ler,** a regulator or umpire : a mediator : a second : a backer : a punctilious and pertinacious insister or contender, esp. for something trifling.—*adj*. or *adv*. **stick'ler-like** (*Shak.*). [Prob. M.E. *stightle*—O.E. *stihtan*, to set in order.]

stickle, *stik'l*, *adj*. (*S.W. dial.*) steep : rapid.— *n*. a rapid. [O.E. *sticol*, steep.]

stickleback, stik´l-bak, *n.* a small spiny-backed river-fish. [O.E. *sticel*, sting, prick, and **back**.]

stiddie, stid´i. Same as **stithy**.

stie, an old spelling of sty (2 and 3).—**stied, sties.** See sty (1, 2, and 3).

stieve. Same as **steeve**.

stiff, stif, *adj.* not easily bent : rigid : wanting in suppleness : moved or moving with difficulty or friction : dead : approaching solidity : dense, difficult to mould or cut : resistent : difficult : toilsome : pertinacious : stubborn : formidable : strong : firm, high, or inclining to rise (in price, &c.) : excessive : not natural and easy : constrained : formal (*naut.*) keeping upright : (*slang*) certain (not to run, to win, to lose) : excessively bored (with a pun on *board*).—*adv.* stiffly : stark. —*n.* (*slang*) one who, that which, is stiff : a corpse : a good-for-nothing : negotiable paper : forged paper.—*n.* stiff´-bit, a jointless bit.—*v.t.* and *v.i.* stiff´en, to make or become stiff or stiffer.—*n.* stiff´ener, one who, or that which, stiffens : a cigarette-card or the like, used to stiffen a package. —*n.* and *adj.* stiff´ening.—*adjs.* stiff´-heart´ed, (*B.*) obstinate, stubborn ; stiff´ish.—*adv.* stiff´ly. —*n.* stiff´-neck, a drawing down of the head towards the shoulder, often due to cold or draught : torticollis. — *adj.* stiff´-necked, obstinate. — *ns.* stiff´-necked´ness ; stiff´ness. — *adj.* stiff´-rumped, -rumpt, (*obs.*) proud, unbending. [O.E. *stif*, stiff ; Du. *stijf*, Ger. *steif*.]

stifle, stī´fl, *v.t.* to stop the breath of by foul air or other means : to make breathing difficult for : to suffocate, smother : to choke down : to suppress : to repress : to make stifling.—*v.i.* to suffocate.— *n.* a stifling atmosphere, smell, or condition.—*adj.* sti´fled.—*n.* sti´fler, one who stifles : the gallows. —*n.* and *adj.* sti´fling (-*fling*).—*adv.* sti´flingly. [Origin obscure.]

stifle, stī´fl, *n.* the joint of a horse, dog, &c., answering to the human knee.—*ns.* sti´fle-bone, the kneecap ; sti´fle-joint. [Connexion with stiff doubtful.]

stigma, stig´mä, *n.* a brand : a mark of infamy : a disgrace or reproach attached to any one : any special mark : a spot : a bleeding spot : a spot sensitive to light : the part of a carpel that receives pollen : a spiracle : a pore : (in *pl.*) the marks of Christ's wounds or marks resembling them, claimed to have been impressed on the bodies of certain persons, as Francis of Assisi in 1224 :—*pl.* stig´mata ; also (esp. *bot.* or *fig.*) stig´mas.— **Stigmā´ria**, the pitted underground part of Sigillaria or other fossil tree.—*adjs.* stigmā´rian (also *n.*) ; stigmatic (-*mat´ik*), of, pertaining to, of the nature of, a stigma : marked or branded with a stigma : giving infamy or reproach : anastigmatic, or not astigmatic.—*n.* one who has received the stigmata : one who is branded (*Shak.* stig´, with deformity).—*adj.* stigmat´ical.—*adj.* stigmat´ically.—*adj.* stigmatif´erous, (*bot.*) stigmabearing.—*n.* stigmatisā´tion, the act of stigmatising : production of stigmata or of bleeding spots upon the body, as by hypnotism.—*v.t.* stig´matise, to mark with a stigma or the stigmata : to brand, denounce, describe condemnatorily (with *as*).—*ns.* stig´matism, impression of the stigmata : anastigmatism ; stig´matist, one impressed with the stigmata.—*adj.* stig´matose.—*n.* stig´mē, (*Gr. palaeog.*) a dot used as a punctuation mark. [Gr. *stigma*, -*atos*, tattoo-mark, brand, *stigmē*, a point.]

stilbite, stil´bīt, *n.* a pearly zeolite. [Gr. *stilbein*, to shine.]

stile, stīl, *n.* a step, or set of steps, for climbing over a wall or fence. [O.E. *stigel* ; cf. O.E. *stīgan*, Ger. *steigen*, to mount.]

stile, stīl, *n.* an upright member in framing or panelling. [Perh. Du. *stijl*, pillar, doorpost.]

stile, an older spelling of style.—**stilet.** See **stylet.**

stiletto, sti-let´ō, *n.* a dagger with a narrow blade : a pointed instrument for making eyelet-holes : (*pl.* stilett´os).—*v.t.* to stab with a stiletto :—*pr.p.* stilett´oing ; *pa.t.* and *pa.p.* stilett´oed. [It., dim. of *stilo*, a dagger—L. *stilus*, a style.]

still, stil, *adj.* motionless : inactive : silent : calm : quiet : not sparkling or effervescing : (*Shak.*) continual, constant.—*v.t.* to quiet : to silence : to appease : to restrain.—*v.i.* to become still.—*adv.* motionlessly : inactively : quietly : (*arch.*) always, constantly (so also in many obvious compounds) : up to the present time or time in question : as before : yet, even (usu. with a comparative) : even so, even then : nevertheless, for all that.—*n.* calm : quiet : an ordinary photograph, not a cinematographic.—*n.* still´-birth, birth of the already dead or very nearly dead, as in suspended animation : publication not followed by sales : anything born without life.—*adj.* still´-born, dead, or in suspended animation, when born.—*ns.* still´er, one who, or that which, stills or quiets, or prevents splashing over ; still´-hunt, -hunting, (*U.S.*) stalking.—*v.t.* and *v.i.* still´-hunt (*U.S.*).—*n.* still´-hunter (*U.S.*). —*n.* and *adj.* still´ing.—*ns.* still´-life, the class of pictures representing inanimate objects (also *adj.*) ; still´ness.—*adj.* still´-peer´ing, (*Shak.*) perh. a misprint for still-piecing (i.e. repairing) or still-piercing.—*n.* still´-stand, (*Shak.*) a standstill : an armistice.—*adj.* still´y, still : quiet : calm.— *adv.* stil´ly, silently : gently.—**still and anon** (*Shak.*), **still and end** (*Shak.*), from time to time ; **still and on,** (*Scot.*) nevertheless. [O.E. *stille*, quiet, calm, stable ; Du. *stil*, Ger. *still*.]

still, stil, *v.t.* to exude or cause to fall by drops : to distil.—*v.i.* to fall in drops.—*n.* an apparatus for distillation.—*ns.* still´-head, the head of a still ; still´-house, (*U.S.*) a distillery ; still´-room, an apartment where liquors, preserves, and the like are kept, and where tea, &c., is prepared for the table : a housekeeper's pantry ; still´-room-maid. [Aphetic for **distil.**]

stillage, stil´ij, *n.* a frame, stand, or stool for keeping things off the floor : a cask-stand.—*ns.* still´ing, still´ion, a cask-stand. [Prob. Du. *stellage* stelling—*stellen*, to place.]

stillatory, stil´ə-tər-i, *n.* a still : a distillery. [L.L. *stillātōrium*—L. *stillāre*, to drip, distil, a drop.]

stillicide, stil´i-sīd, *n.* a drip : eavesdrop : (*Roman law*) an urban servitude allowing one's eavesdrop to fall on a neighbour's ground (otherwise forbidden). [L. *stillicidium*—*stilla*, drop, *cadēre*, to fall.]

stilpnosiderite, stilp-nō-sid´ər-īt, *n.* limonite. [Gr. *stilpnos*, shining, *sidēros*, iron.]

stilt, stilt, *n.* a prop with a step for walking above the ground with long strides : a tall support : (now *dial.*) a plough-handle : a very long-legged wading bird (*Himantopus candidus* or other species) akin to the avocets (also stilt´-bird, -plov´er).—*v.t.* to raise on stilts or as if on stilts.—*adj.* stilt´ed, elevated as if on stilts : stiff and pompous.—*adv.* stilt´edly.—*ns.* stilt´edness ; stilt´er ; stilt´iness stilt´ing.—*adjs.* stilt´ish, stilt´y.—*n.* stilt´-walker —stilted arch, an arch that springs from above the capital. [M.E. *stilte* ; cf. Du. *stelt*, Ger. *stelze*, Sw. *stylta*.]

Stilton, stil´tən, *n.* a rich white cheese first sold chiefly at *Stilton* in Huntingdonshire.

stime, stimie. See **styme, stymie.**

stimulus, stim´ū-ləs, *n.* a sting or stinging hair : an action, influence, or agency that produces a response in a living organism : anything that rouses to action or increased action :—*pl.* stim´ulī.—*adj.* stim´ulable, responsive to stimulus.—*n.* stim´ulancy —*adj.* stim´ulant, stimulating : increasing or exciting vital action.—*n.* anything that stimulates or excites : a stimulating drug : alcoholic liquor.— *v.t.* stim´ulate, to incite : to instigate : (*physiol.*) to produce increased action in.—*adj.* stim´ulating —*n.* stimulā´tion.—*adj.* stim´ulative, tending to stimulate.—*n.* that which stimulates or excites.— *n.* stim´ulātor, one who stimulates : an instrument for applying a stimulus. [L. *stimulus*, a goad.]

sting, sting, *n.* in some plants and animals a weapon (hair, modified ovipositor, fin-ray, tooth, &c.) that pierces and injects poison : the act of inserting sting : the pain or the wound caused : any sharp tingling, or irritating pain or its cause : the point of an epigram : stinging power : pungency : goad : an incitement.—*v.t.* to pierce, wound, pain or incite with or as if with a sting : to cause or allow anything to sting : (*slang*) to rob, cheat, o involve in expense.—*v.i.* to have or use a power of stinging: to have a stinging feeling:—*pa.t.* and *pa.p.* **stung.**—*adj.* **stinged,** having a sting.—*ns.* **sting'-bull, -fish,** the weever; **sting'er,** one who, or that which, stings: anything stinging or pungent. —*n.* and *adj.* **sting'ing.**—*adv.* **sting'ingly.**—*adj.* **sting'less.**—*n.* **sting'-ray** (*U.S.* and *Austr.* **sting-aree,** *sting'gə-rē, -ə-rē,* or *-rē′*), a ray (Trygon, &c.) with a formidable barbed dorsal spine on its tail. [O.E. *sting,* puncture, *stingan,* to pierce.]

sting, *sting, n.* (*Scot.*) a pole.—**sting and ling,** with a rope slung from a pole. [O.E. *steng.*]

stinger. See **stengah.**

stingo, *sting′gō, n.* strong malt liquor: vigour, punch. [**sting.**]

stingy, *stin′ji, adj.* niggardly: (*dial.*) ill-tempered. —*adv.* **stin′gily.**—*n.* **stin′giness.** [Prob. **sting.**]

stink, *stingk, v.i.* to give out a strong, offensive smell: (*fig.*) to be offensive, have a bad reputation.—*v.t.* to impart a bad smell to: to drive by an ill smell: (*pa.t.* **stank, stunk;** *pa.p.* **stunk.**)—*n.* an offensive smell: (*slang*; in *pl.*) chemistry or science, a science master. — *ns.* **stink′ard,** one who stinks: a base fellow: the stinking badger of Java; **stink′-ball, -pot,** a ball or jar filled with a stinking, combustible mixture, used in boarding an enemy's vessel; **stink′-brand,** bunt; **stink′er,** one who, or that which, stinks: a stinkard: a petrel of offensive smell; **stink′horn,** a stinking gasteromycete fungus, *Ithyphallus impudicus.*—*n.* and *adj.* **stink′ing.**—*adv.* **stink′ingly.**—*ns.* **stink′stone,** a limestone that gives a fetid urinous smell when rubbed; **stink′-trap,** a stench-trap; **stink′-wood,** the ill-smelling wood of various trees, esp. the lauraceous *Ocotea bullata* of S. Africa. [O.E. *stincan,* to smell (well or ill).]

stint, *stint, v.t.* to stop: to restrain: to check: to limit: to apportion (esp. pasturage): to allot: to set as a task or as a day's work: to restrict: to keep short: to be niggardly with or towards: to allot stingily: to spare: to serve successfully, get with foal, lamb, &c.—*v.i.* to cease, stop: to be sparing, go short.—*n.* (*obs.*) cessation: limit: restraint, restriction: proportion allotted, fixed amount: allowance: a set task: a (conventional) day's work.—*adj.* **stint′ed.**—*adv.* **stint′edly.**—*ns.* **stint′edness;** **stint′er.**—*n.* and *adj.* **stint′ing.**—*adv.* **stint′ingly.**—*adjs.* **stint′less;** **stint′y.** [O.E. *styntan,* to dull—*stunt,* stupid; cf. **stent, stunt.**]

stint, *stint, n.* the dunlin or other small sandpiper.

Stipa, *stī′pä, n.* the feather-grass genus. [L. *stipa,* tow.]

stipe, *stīp, n.* a stalk, esp. of a fungal fruit-body, a fern-leaf, a pappus, or an ovary.—Also **stipes** (*stī′pēz*; L. *stē′pās*; *pl.* **stipites,** *stip′i-tēz*; L. *stē′pi-tās*).—*adj.* **stipitate** (*stip′*). [L. *stīpes, -itis,* post, stock.]

stipel, *stī′pl, n.* a stipule-like appendage at the base of a leaflet.—*adj.* **stipellate** (*stī′pol-āt, stip-el′āt*), having stipels. [Dim. from **stipule.**]

stipend, *stī′pənd, n.* a soldier's pay: a salary, esp. a Scottish parish minister's (*Scot.* *stēp′ənd*): a periodical allowance. — *adj.* **stipendiary** (*sti-,* *sti-pen′di-ə-ri*), receiving stipend.—*n.* one who performs services for a salary, esp. a paid magistrate.—*v.t.* **stipen′diate,** to provide with a salary. [L. *stīpendium—stīps,* payment, dole, *pendĕre,* to weigh.]

stipple, *stip′l, v.t.* to engrave, paint, draw, &c., in dots or separate touches.—*n.* painting, engraving, &c., in this way: the effect so produced: a brush for stippling.— *adj.* **stipp′led.**—*ns.* **stipp′ler;** **stipp′ling.** [Du. *stippelen,* dim. of *stippen,* to dot.]

stipulate, *stip′ū-lāt, v.t.* to set or require as a condition or essential part of an agreement: to guarantee.—*v.i.* to make stipulations: (*obs.*) to become surety.—*ns.* **stipula′tion,** act of stipulating: a contract: a condition of agreement: a requiring of such a condition; **stip′ulātor.**—*adj.* **stip′ulatory** (*-ə-tər-i*). [L. *stipulārī, -ātus,* prob. —Old L. *stipulus,* firm, conn. *stīpāre,* press firm.]

stipule, *stip′ūl, n.* a paired, usu. leafy, appendage at a leaf-base.—*adjs.* **stipula′ceous, stip′ular, -y;** **stip′ulāte, stip′uled.** [L. *stipula,* straw, stalk, dim. of *stīpes;* new meaning assigned by Linnaeus.]

stir, *star* (*Scot.* **steer,** *stēr, Spens.* **stire, styre,** *stīr*), *v.t.* to set in motion: to move around: to disturb: to rouse: to move to activity: to excite: to moot. —*v.i.* to make a movement: to begin to move: to go about: to be active or excited: (esp. in *pr.p.*) to be out of bed: to go forth: (*pr.p.* **stirr′ing;** *pa.t.* and *pa.p.* **stirred.**)—*n.* movement: slight movement: activity: commotion: an act of stirring. — *n.* **stir′about,** (*Anglo-Ir.*) porridge: a bustling or stirring person.—*adj.* busy, active.—*adj.* **stir′less,** without stir.—*adj.* **stirred.**—*n.* **stirr′er.**—*n.* and *adj.* **stirr′ing.**—*adv.* **stirr′ingly.** —**stir abroad, forth, out,** to go out of doors; **stir up,** to excite: to incite: to arouse: to mix by stirring. [O.E. *styrian;* Du. *storen,* Ger. *stören,* to disturb.]

stir, *stir,* **stirra(h),** *stir′ə, ns.* (*Scot.*) app. corruptions of **sir, sirrah,** applied to both sexes.

stir, *stir, n.* (*slang*) prison. [Perh. O.E. *stéor, stýr,* punishment.]

stire, *stīr,* a Spenserian form of **steer** and **stir.**

stirk, *stark, n.,* a yearling or young ox or cow. [O.E. *stirc,* calf.]

stirps, *starps, n.* family, race: a permanent variety: pedigree:—*pl.* **stirpes** (*star′pēz;* L. *stir′pās*).—Also **stirp**—*pl.* **stirps.**—*n.* **stirp′iculture,** selective breeding. [L. *stirps, stirpis.*]

stirrup, *stir′əp, n.* a support for a rider's foot: a foot-rest, clamp, support, of more or less similar shape: the stirrup-bone: a rope secured to a yard, having a thimble in its lower end for reeving a foot-rope.—*ns.* **stirr′up-bone,** the stapes; **stirr′up-cup, -dram,** a cup (not paid for) taken on horseback on departing (or arriving); **stirr′up-iron,** the metal part of a stirrup, usu. reckoned the stirrup itself; **stirr′up-leath′er, -strap,** the strap of a stirrup; **stirr′up-pump,** a portable pump held in position by the foot in a rest. [O.E. *stigráp—stīgan,* to mount, *ráp,* rope.]

stitch, *stich, n.* a sharp pricking pain, now esp. in the intercostal muscles: a complete movement of the needle in sewing, knitting, or the like: a loop or portion of thread, &c., so used: a mode of stitching: (*bookbinding*) a fastening with thread or wire through all sections: the least scrap of clothing, sails, &c.: (*dial.*) a ridge of land: (*dial.*) a shock of corn.—*v.t.* to join, adorn, or enclose, with stitches.—*v.i.* to sew.—*n.* **stitch′craft,** the art of needlework.—*adj.* **stitched.**—*ns.* **stitch′er;** **stitch′ery,** (*Shak.*) needlework; **stitch′ing;** **stitch′wort,** any plant of the chickweed genus (Stellaria), once thought good for stitches in the side. — **in stitches,** in pained helplessness with laughter. [O.E. *stice,* prick; cf. **stick.**]

stithy, *stidh′i, n.* an anvil: a smithy.—*v.t.* to forge on an anvil. [O.N. *stethi;* Sw. *städ,* an anvil.]

stive, *stīv, v.t.* and *v.i.* (*prov.*) to stifle.—*adjs.* **stived, stived′-up,** without fresh air; **stiv′y,** stuffy. [Cf. **stew.**]

stiver, *stī′vər, n.* a Dutch penny. [Du. *stuiver.*]

stoa, *stō′ä, n.* a portico or covered colonnade: esp. the Painted Porch (see **porch**):—*pl.* **sto′as, sto′ai** (*-ī*). [Gr. *stoä.*]

stoat, *stōt, n.* a larger weasel, with black-tipped tail, called ermine in its northern winter dress. [M.E. *stote.*]

stob, *stob, n.* (*Scot.*) a stake, stump, or stub: an awl. [Variant of **stub.**]

stoccado, *stok-ä′dō,* **stoccata,** *-tä, n.* a thrust in fencing. [It. *stoccata,* thrust—*stocco,* rapier—Ger. *stock,* stick.]

stock, *stok, n.* a trunk or main stem: the perennial part of a herbaceous plant: the rooted trunk that receives a graft: a log: a post: a block: a stump: an upright beam: anything fixed, solid and senseless: a stupid person: a part, usually massive, to which others are attached: (*geol.*) an intrusive boss: the wooden part of a gun: a handle: stock-gillyflower (see below; **Virginia stock,** a Mediterranean, not Virginian, cruciferous garden plant, Malcolmia): a stocking (also **neth′erstock; the upp′er-stock** being the upper part of hose when divided): a stiff band worn as a cravat, often fastened with a buckle at the back: (*dial.*) a fireside ledge: (in *pl.*) a device for holding a delinquent

by the ankles : (in *pl.*) a framework on which a ship is built (hence **on the stocks**, under construction, in preparation) : a box or trough : the cross-piece of an anchor : the original progenitor : source : race : kindred : family : a fund : capital : (*fig.*) repute, estimation : shares of a public debt : (in *pl.*) public funds : (*obs.*) a tally for money paid to the exchequer : supply, store, equipment : the animals kept on a farm : supply of goods for sale : the undealt part of a pack of cards or set of dominoes : raw material, as the foundation for soup or for soap : (*dial.*) a rabbit-hole.—*v.t.* to store : to keep for sale : to put in the stocks : to fit with a stock : to supply or furnish with stock (e.g. a river with fish) : to keep unmilked before selling : to root up : to stunt.—*adj.* kept in stock, standing : conventionally used : standard : permanently employed.—*ns.* stock′-breeder, one who raises live-stock ; stock′broker, a stock exchange member who buys and sells stocks or shares for clients ; stock′broking ; stock′-dove, a dove like a small wood-pigeon—from nesting in stumps or rabbit-holes, or from representing (as wrongly supposed) the ancestor of the domestic breeds ; stock′-farmer, a farmer who rears live-stock ; stock′-feeder, one who fattens live-stock ; stock′-gill′y-flower, now usu. stock, a favourite cruciferous garden plant (*Matthiola incana* ; from its half-shrubby character) ; stock′holder, one who holds stocks in the public funds, or in a company ; stock′-in-trade, all the goods a shopkeeper has for sale : a person's mental resources.—*adj.* stock′ish, like a stock, stupid.—*ns.* stock′ishness ; stock′ist, one who keeps a commodity in stock ; stock′-jobber, a stock exchange member who deals only with other members (in some special group of securities) : (*U.S.*) a stockbroker : an unscrupulous speculator ; stock′-jobbery, -jobb′-ing.—*adj.* stock′less.—*ns.* stock′-list, a list of stocks and current prices regularly issued ; stock′-lock, a lock with wooden case ; stock′man, (esp. *Austr.*) a man in charge of stock ; stock′-market, a stock exchange : stock exchange business ; stock′pile, heap of road-metal, ore, &c. : reserve supply ; stock′piling, accumulating reserves, as of raw materials ; stock′-pot, the pot in which the stock for soup is kept.—*adj.* stock′-pun′isht, (*Shak.*) put in the stocks.—*ns.* stock′-raising, breeding of stock ; stock′-rider, (*Austr.*) a mounted herdsman ; stock′-room, a store-room : a room in a hotel for display of commercial travellers' wares ; stock′-saddle, a cowboy's saddle.—*adj.* and *adv.* stock′-still, still as a post or stock.—*ns.* stock′taking, inventorying and valuation of stock ; stock′-whip, a herdsman's whip with short handle and long lash.—*adj.* stock′y, thick-set, strong-stemmed.—*n.* stock′-yard, a large yard with pens, stables, &c., where cattle are kept for slaughter, market, &c.— stock company, a permanent repertory company attached to a theatre ; stock exchange, a building for the buying and selling of stocks and shares : an association of persons transacting such business ; stocks and stones, inanimate idols ; take stock (of), to make an inventory of goods on hand : to make an estimate of ; take stock in, to trust to, attach importance to. [O.E. *stocc*, a stick ; Ger. *stock*.]
stock, *stok, n.* (*Shak.*) a stoccado. [It. *stocco*, rapier.]
stockade, *stok-ād′, n.* a barrier of stakes.—*v.t.* to defend with a stockade. [Fr. *estacade*—Sp. *estacada* ; cf. stake.]
stock-and-horn, *stok′-and-horn, n.* an old Scottish musical instrument made of a cow's horn, a sheep's thigh bone or elder pipe with stops, and an oaten reed. [O.E. (Northumbrian) *stocc*, trumpet.]
stockfish, *stok′fish, n.* unsalted dried hake, cod, &c., commonly beaten with a stick before cooking. [Prob. Du. *stokvisch.*]
stocking, *stok′ing, n.* a close covering for the foot and lower leg : distinctive colouring or feathering of an animal's leg : a hoard of savings.—*n.* stockinet′, -ette′, stock′ingette′, an elastic knitted fabric for under-garments.—*adj.* stock′inged, wearing stockings (but usu. not shoes).—*ns.* stock′inger (-*ing-ər*), a maker of stockings ; stock′ing-foot′,

the foot of a stocking ; stock′ing-frame, a knitting machine.—*adj.* stock′ingless.—*n.* stock′ing-sole′ —in one's stocking-feet, -soles, with stockings but no shoes. [stock, in sense of netherstock.]
stockwork, *stok′wərk, n.* a mass of veins, impregnations, &c., that can be worked as one deposit [Anglicised from Ger. *stockwerk.*]
stodge, *stoj, v.t.* to stuff, cram, gorge : to sate : to bog.—*v.i.* to trudge : to plod.—*n.* claggy stuff a heavy meal.—*n.* stodg′er, a heavy, dull, spiritless or unenterprising person.—*adv.* stodg′ily.—*n.* stodg′iness.—*adj.* stodg′y, heavy and claggy solemnly dull. [Perh. imit.]
stoep, *stoōp, n.* (*S.Afr.*) a platform along the front and sometimes the sides, of a house. [Du. ; cf. step.]
Stoic, *stō′ik, n.* a disciple of the philosopher Zeno (*d. c.* 261 B.C.), who taught in the *Stoa Poikile* (Painted Porch) at Athens.—*adjs.* Stō′ic, -al, pertaining to the Stoics, or to their opinions : indifferent to pleasure or pain.—*adv.* stō′ically.—*ns.* stō′icalness ; stō′icism (-*sizm*), the philosophy of the Stoics : indifference to pleasure or pain : limitation of wants : austere impassivity. [Gr. *Stōikos*—*stoā*, a porch.]
stoich(e)iometry, *stoi-kī-om′i-tri, n.* the branch of chemistry that deals with the numerical proportions in which substances react. [Gr. *stoicheion*, an element, *metron*, measure.]
stoit, *stoit, v.i.* (*Scot.*) to stumble, lurch.—*v.i.* stoit′er, to stagger. [Perh. Du. *stuiten*, to bounce.]
stoke, *stōk, v.t.* to feed with fuel.—*v.i.* to act as stoker.—*ns.* stoke′hold, a ship's furnace chamber : a stoke-hole ; stoke′-hole, the space about the mouth of a furnace : the space allotted to the stokers : a hole in a reverberatory furnace for introducing a stirring-tool ; stok′er, one who, or that which, feeds a furnace with fuel. [Du. *stoker*, stoker—*stoken*, to stoke.]
stole, *stōl, pa.t.* and obs. *pa.p.* of steal.
stole, *stōl, n.* a long robe : a narrow vestment worn on the shoulders, hanging down in front : a woman's outer garment of similar form : loosely, a gown, a surplice.—Also (L.) stō′la (L. *stol′ä*).—*adj.* stoled (*stōld*), wearing a stole. [O.E. *stole*— L. *stŏla*, a Roman matron's long robe—Gr. *stolē*, equipment, garment—*stellein*, to array.]
stole. See stolon, stool.
stolen, *stōl′ən, pa.p.* of steal.—Also *adj.*—*adv.* stol′enwise, by stealth.
stolid, *stol′id, adj.* impassive. — *ns.* stolid′ity, stol′idness.—*adv.* stol′idly. [L. *stolidus.*]
stolon, *stō′lən, n.* a shoot from the base of a plant, rooting and budding at the nodes (also stole) : (*zool.*) a stemlike structure or budding outgrowth from a colony.—*adj.* stōlonif′erous, producing stolons. [L. *stolō*, -*ōnis*, twig, sucker.]
stoma, *stō′mä, n.* a mouthlike opening, esp. one (including its guard-cells or not) by which gases pass through the epidermis of green parts of a plant :—*pl.* stō′mata.—*adjs.* stomatal (*stōm′, stom′ə-tl*), stomat′ic.—*ns.* stomati′tis, inflammation of the mucous membrane of the mouth ; stomatodaeum (-*dē′əm*), stomodae′um (Gr. *hodaios*, on the way), in embryology, the invagination that forms the anterior part of the digestive tract ; stomatol′ogy, study of the mouth ; stom′-atopod, a crustacean of the order Stomatop′oda, the mantis shrimps, with legs mostly near the mouth. [Gr. *stōma, -atos*, mouth.]
stomach, *stum′ək, n.* the strong muscular bag into which food passes when swallowed, and where it is principally digested : the cavity in any animal for the digestion of its food : (loosely or euphemistically) the belly : appetite, relish for food, inclination generally : disposition, spirit, courage, pride, spleen.—*v.t.* to brook or put up with : to turn the stomach of : to resent : to find offensive.—*adj.* of the stomach.—*n.* stom′ach-ache.—*adjs.* stom′-achal ; stom′ached.—*ns.* stom′acher (-*chər, -kər*), a covering or ornament for the chest, esp. one worn under the lacing of a bodice ; stom′ach-ful, as much as the stomach will hold (*pl.* stom′achfuls).—*adj.* spirited : haughty : obstinate : resentful : angry.—*n.* stom′achfulness.

adj. **stomachic** (*stəm-ak'ik*), of the stomach: good for the stomach.—*n.* a stomachic medicine.—*adjs.* **stomach′ical; stom′achless; stom′achous,** (*Spens.*) resentful: haughty: spirited: courageous.—*n.* **stom′ach-pump,** a syringe with a flexible tube for withdrawing fluids from the stomach, or injecting them into it.—*adj.* **stom′achy,** haughty: easily offended: spirited: paunchy. [O.Fr. *estomac,* L. *stomachus,* Gr. *stomachos,* throat, later stomach—*stoma,* a mouth.]

stond, *stond, n.* a Spenserian form of **stand.**

stone, *stōn, n.* a detached piece of rock, usu. small: the matter of which rocks consist: a gem: (*Shak.*) a mirror: a tombstone: a printer's table for imposing: a concretion: a diseased state characterised by formation of a concretion in the body: (now *vulg.*) a testicle: a hard fruit kernel: a hailstone: (with *pl.* **stone**) a standard weight of 14 lb. avoirdupois (other stones have been in use, as that of 24 lb. for wool, 22 lb. for hay, 16 lb. for cheese, &c.).—*adj.* of stone: of stoneware: of the Stone Age: not castrated.—*v.t.* to pelt with stones: to free from stones: to lay or wall with stones: to rub or sharpen with a stone: to turn to stone.—*v.i.* to form a stone.—*adj.* **stone′-blind,** as blind as a stone.—*ns.* **stone′-boiling,** boiling water by putting hot stones in it; **stone′-borer, -eater,** any boring mollusc; **stone′-bow,** a crossbow for shooting stones; **stone′-bramble,** a bramble (*Rubus saxatilis*) of rocky places; **stone′-brash,** a soil of finely-broken rock; **stone′-break,** saxifrage; **stone′-breaker,** one who, or that which, breaks stones: a stone-crushing machine; **stone′-bruise,** a bruise caused by a stone, esp. on the sole of the foot; **stone′-canal,** a calcified vertical tube in the water-vascular system of echinoderms; **stone′-cast** (or **stone's cast**), a stone-throw; **stone′-cell,** (*bot.*) a cell not much longer than broad with thick lignified walls; **stone′-chat,** a little black, ruddy and white bird of furzy places, with a note like the clicking of two stones (also **stone′-chatter**); **stone′-coal,** mineral coal, as opp. to charcoal: any hard coal: anthracite.—*adj.* **stone′-cold,** cold as a stone.—*n.* and *adj.* **stone′-colour,** grey.—*adj.* **stone′-coloured.**—*ns.* **stone′crop,** any plant of the wall-pepper genus (Sedum); **stone′-cur′lew,** a large plover, the thick-knee; **stone′-cutter,** one who hews stone; **stone′-cutting.**—*adjs.* **stoned,** having, containing, or freed from a stone or stones; **stone′-dead, stone′-deaf,** dead, deaf, as a stone.—*ns.* **stone′-dresser,** one who prepares stones for building; **stone′-fal′con, -hawk,** the merlin; **stone′-fly,** a plecopterous insect (Perla) whose larvae live under stones in streams; **stone′-fruit,** a fruit with a stone; **stone′-hammer,** a hammer for breaking stones (stone hammer, a hammer with a stone head).—*adj.* **stone′-hard,** (*Shak.*) as hard as a stone.—*n.* **stone′horse,** a stallion.—*adj.* **stone′less.**—*ns.* **stone′-lil′y,** an encrinite; **stone′-mar′ten,** a white-breasted marten, the beech-marten; **stone′-ma′son,** a mason who works with stone; **stone′-mill,** a machine for breaking stone.—*adj.* **ston′en,** **ston′ern** (*obs.* or *dial.*), of stone.—*ns.* **stone′-oil,** petroleum; **stone′-pine,** a Mediterranean nut-pine; **stone′-pit,** a quarry; **stone′-plov′er,** the stone-curlew; **ston′er,** one who stones: one who weighs, or a horse that carries, so many stone; **stone′-rag, -raw** (O.E. *ragu,* lichen), a lichen, *Parmelia saxatilis,* yielding a dye; **stone′shot,** a stone-throw: stones or a stone used as shot; **stone′-snipe,** an American plover.—*adv.* and *adj.* **stone′-still,** (*Shak.*) as still as a stone.—*ns.* **stone′('s)-throw,** the distance a stone may be thrown; **stone′-wall,** (*Austr.*) parliamentary obstruction: defensive play.—*v.i.* to obstruct: to block: to offer wall-like resistance.—*ns.* **stone′-wall′er; stone′-wall′ing; stone′ware,** a coarse kind of potter's ware baked hard and glazed; **stone′-work,** work in stone; **stone′wort,** any plant of the Characeae (from the limy crust): an umbelliferous plant (*Sison Amomum*) akin to parsley.—*adv.* **ston′ily.**—*n.* **ston′iness.**—*adjs.* **ston′y,** of or like stone: abounding with stones: **hard:** pitiless: obdurate: rigid: petrifying:

ston′y-broke′, (*slang*) penniless, or nearly so (also **ston′y, stone′-broke′**); **ston′y-heart′ed,** hard-hearted.—**leave no stone unturned,** to do everything that can be done in order to secure the effect desired; **mark with a white stone,** to mark as particularly fortunate; **Stone Age,** a stage of culture before the general use of metal, divided into the Old Stone Age (Palaeolithic) and the New (Neolithic); **stone circle,** a circle of standing-stones. [O.E. *stán;* Ger. *stein,* Du. *steen.*]

stong, stonn(e), old forms of **stung, stun.**

stony, *ston′i, v.t.* (*obs.*) aphetic for **astony** (see **astonish**; *pa.p., Spens.,* ston′ied).

stood, *stood, pa.t.* and *pa.p.* of **stand.**

stooge, *stōōj, n.* (*slang*) a performer speaking from the auditorium: an actor's feeder: a stage butt: a subordinate or drudge: a scapegoat.—Also *v.i.*

stook, *stook, n.* a shock of sheaves, set up in the field.—*v.t.* to set up in stooks.—*n.* **stook′er.** [Cf. L.G. *stuke,* bundle.]

stool, *stōōl, n.* (*obs.*) a chair, seat of authority or dignity, throne: a seat without a back: a low support for the feet or knees: a seat used in evacuating the bowels: defecation: faeces: a stand: a stump from which sprouts shoot up: a growth of shoots: the wicket in stoolball: a portable piece of wood to which a pigeon is fastened as a decoy for wild birds.—*v.i.* to put forth shoots.—*ns.* **stool′ball,** an old game resembling cricket; **stool′-pigeon,** a decoy-pigeon: a decoy: an informer.—**fall between two stools,** to lose both possibilities by hesitating between them, or trying for both; **groom of the stole** (an old form of stool), formerly an officer over the lords of the bedchamber; **stool of repentance,** a place in church where delinquents, esp. fornicators, were exposed. [O.E. *stól;* Ger. *stuhl;* cf. Ger. *stellen,* to place.]

stoop, *stōōp, v.i.* to bend the body forward: to lean forward: to submit: to descend from rank or dignity: to condescend: to lower oneself by unworthy behaviour: to swoop down, as a bird of prey.—*v.t.* to bend, incline, lower, or direct downward.—*n.* a bending of the body: inclination forward: descent: condescension: a swoop.—*adj.* **stooped,** having a stoop, bent.—*ns.* **stoop′er; stoop′-gallant,** (*obs.*) that which humbles gallants, orig. the sweating-sickness.—Also *adj.* (*Spens.* **stoope-gallaunt**).—*adj.* **stoop′ing.**—*adv.* **stoop′ingly.** [O.E. *stúpian;* O.N. *stúpa;* the vowel preserved by the following *p.*]

stoop, stoope. See **stoup.**

stoop. American spelling of **stoep.**

stoop, stoup, *stōōp, n.* (*dial.*) a post: (*Scot.*) a prop, supporter, patron: a massive supporting pillar of coal in a mine.—**stoop and roop, stoup and roup** (*Scot.*), stump and rump, completely. [O.N. *stolpi,* post.]

stoor, stour, *stōōr,* **sture,** *stər,* **stowre,** *stowr, adj.* (*obs.*) great, formidable: stiff, harsh, austere. [Partly M.E. *stúr,* harsh (cf. M.L.G. *stúr*), partly O.E. *stór,* great.]

stoor, *stōōr.* See **stour** (2).

stop, *stop, v.t.* to stuff, block, plug, choke, close up: (*obs.* except as Scots **stap**) to thrust, cram: to obstruct: to render impassable: to hinder or prevent the passage of: to bring to a standstill: to bring down, hit with a shot: to cause to cease: to counter: to restrain: to withhold: to hinder: to prevent: to cease from, leave off, discontinue: (*mus.*) to limit the vibrating length of, esp. by pressure of a finger: (*hort.*) to pinch off: to punctuate: (*pros.*) to place a pause in, esp. at the end of a line or couplet: to adjust the aperture of, with a diaphragm: (*naut.*) to make fast by lashing.—*v.i.* to come to a standstill, halt: to cease: to desist: to come to an end: (*coll.*) to stay, tarry, sojourn: (*pr.p.* **stopp′ing;** *pa.t.* and *pa.p.* **stopped**).—*n.* act of stopping: state of being stopped: cessation: a halt: a pause: a halting-place: hindrance: obstacle: interruption: a contrivance that limits motion: a card that interrupts the run of play: a diaphragm: the stopping of an instrument or string: a fret on a lute or guitar: a finger-hole, a key for covering it, or other means of altering pitch or tone: a set of organ pipes of uniform tone

Neutral vowels in unaccented syllables: *el'ə-mənt, in'fənt, ran'dəm*

quality: a knob for bringing them into use: (*phon.*) a sound requiring complete closure of the breath passage, a mute: a punctuation mark.— *ns.* stop'-cock, a short pipe opened and stopped by turning a key; stop'-gap, a temporary expedient or holder of a post in emergency.—*adj.* stop'less.— *ns.* stop'-o'ver, (*U.S.*) a break of journey; stopp'-age, act of stopping: state of being stopped: obstruction: an amount stopped off pay.—*adj.* stopped.—*n.* stopp'er, one who stops: that which stops: a plug: a plug (usu. glass) for a bottle: (*naut.*) a short rope for making something fast.— *v.t.* to close or secure with a stopper.—*ns.* stopp'ing, the action of one who or that which stops in any sense (double stopping, simultaneous stopping of and playing on two strings): stuffing or filling material, esp. for teeth; stopp'ing-out, use in places of a protective covering against acids in etching, against light in photography; stopp'ing-place; stopp'-press, late news inserted in a newspaper after printing has begun: a space for it.— Also *adj.*—*n.* stop'-watch, an accurate watch readily started and stopped, used in timing a race, &c.—stop over, (*U.S.*) to break one's journey; stop thief, a cry for help to catch a thief. [O.E. *stoppian*, found in the compound *forstoppian*, to stop up—L. *stuppa*, tow—Gr. *styppē*.]

stope, *stōp*, *n.* a step-like excavation in mining.—*v.t.* to excavate, or extract in this way.—*n.* stop'ing. [Perh. conn. with step.]

stopple, *stop'l*, *n.* a stopper: a plug.—*v.t.* to stopper, plug. [stop.]

stopple, *stop'l*, *n.* a tobacco-pipe stem—*Scot.* stapp'le. [M.Du. *stapel*, stem.]

storax, *stō'raks*, *n.* the resin of *Styrax officinalis*, once used in medicine: now that of *Liquidambar orientale* (liquid storax). [L. *storax*—Gr. *styrax*.]

store, *stōr*, *n.* a hoard: a stock laid up: sufficiency or abundance: keeping: a store-house: (esp. *U.S.*) a shop: a co-operative shop or one with many departments or branches: an animal fattening for the market: value, esteem: (*pl.*) supplies of provisions, ammunition, &c., for an army, ship, &c.—*adj.* and *adv.* (*arch.*) in abundance.—*adj.* of a store: (*U.S.*) sold in a shop, ready-made.—*v.t.* to stock, furnish, supply: to lay up, keep in reserve: to deposit in a repository: to give storage to.—*adj.* stor'able.—*ns.* stor'age, placing, accommodation, reservation, or safe-keeping, in store: reservation in the form of potential energy: charge for keeping goods in store; store'-cattle, cattle kept for fattening; store'-farm, (*Scot.*) a stock-farm, a cattle-farm; store'-farmer; store'house, a house for storing goods of any kind: a repository: a treasury; store'-keeper, a man in charge of stores: (*U.S.*) a shopkeeper: (*U.S.*) an unsaleable article; stör'er; store'room, a room in which stores are kept: space for storing; store'-ship, a vessel used for carrying naval stores.—in store, in hoard for future use, ready for supply: in reserve, awaiting; set store by, to value greatly; storage battery, an accumulator; store teeth, (*U.S.*) false teeth. [O.Fr. *estor*, *estoire*—L. *instaurāre*, to provide.]

storey (*pl.* storeys), storeyed. See story (2).

storge, *stor'gē*, *-jē*, *n.* parental affection. [Gr.]

storied. See under story (1) and story (2).

stork, *stork*, *n.* a large white and black wading bird (*Ciconia alba*) with a great red bill and red legs: any member of its genus or of its family (akin to the ibises).—*n.* stork's'-bill, a genus (Erodium) of the geranium family, with beaked fruit: also applied to Pelargonium. [O.E. *storc*; Ger. *storch*.]

storm, *storm*, *n.* a violent commotion of the atmosphere: a tempest: a wind just short of a hurricane: any intense meteorological phenomenon: (*Scot.*) a fall of snow, long frost: a violent commotion or outbreak of any kind: a paroxysm: (*mil.*) a violent assault: (*fig.*) calamity.—*v.i.* to be stormy: to rage: to rush violently or in attack: to upbraid passionately.—*v.t.* to take or try to take by assault: to disturb by a storm.—*adjs.* storm'-beat, -beat'en, beaten by storms.—*ns.* storm'-belt, a belt of maximum storm frequency; storm'-bird, a petrel.—*adj.* storm'bound, delayed, cut off,

confined to port by storms.—*ns.* storm'-centre, the position of lowest pressure in a cyclonic storm: any focus of controversy or strife; storm'-cock, the missel-thrush; storm'-cone, -drum, a cone, drum, hoisted as a storm-signal.—*adj.* storm'ful, stormy.—*adv.* storm'fully.—*ns.* storm'fulness; storm'-glass, a tube containing a solution supposed to change appearance with the weather.— *adv.* storm'ily.—*n.* storm'iness.—*n.* and *adj.* storm'ing.—*ns.* storm'ing-par'ty, the party sent to lead in storming a fortress; storm'-lantern, a lantern with flame protected from wind and weather.—*adj.* storm'less.—*n.* storm'-pet'rel, (popularly) storm'y-pet'rel (see petrel).—*adj.* storm'proof, proof against storms or storming.— *ns.* storm'-sail (-*sl*, -*sāl*), a small very strong sail for stormy weather; storm'-shutter, an outside window-shutter; storm'-signal, a signal hoisted in warning of the approach of a storm; storm'-stay, a stay on which a storm-sail is set.—*adjs.* storm'-stayed, hindered from proceeding by storms; storm'-tossed, tossed about by storms: much agitated by conflicting passions.—*ns.* storm'-track, the path of a storm-centre; storm'-trooper.—*n.pl.* storm'-troops, shock-troops: a body formed in Germany by Adolf Hitler, disbanded 1934.—*ns.* storm'-warning; storm'-water, surface drainage in excess of the normal in a storm; storm'-wind, a stormy wind; storm'-window, a window raised above the roof, slated above and at the sides: an additional outer casement.—*adj.* storm'y, having many storms: agitated with furious winds: boisterous: violent: passionate.—a storm in a teacup (or other small vessel), a great commotion in a narrow sphere, or about a trifle. [O.E. *storm*; O.N. *stormr*; from root of stir.]

stornello, *stor-nel'ō*, *n.* a short (usually three-lined) popular Italian verse-form:—*pl.* stornell'i (-*ē*). [It.]

Storthing, *stōr'ting*, *n.* the legislative assembly of Norway. [Norw. *stor*, great, *ting* (O.N. *thing*), assembly.]

story, *stō'ri*, *n.* (*obs.*) history: legend: a narrative of incidents in their sequence: a fictitious narrative: a tale: an anecdote: the plot of a novel or drama: a theme: account, report, statement, allegation: (*U.S.*) a newspaper article: a lie, a fib.—*v.t.* to tell or describe historically, to relate: to adorn with scenes from history.—*v.i.* to relate.— *adjs.* sto'riated, decorated with elaborate ornamental designs; sto'ried, told or celebrated in a story: having a history: interesting from the stories belonging to it: adorned with scenes from history.—*ns.* storiette', storyette', a short tale: storiol'ogist; storiol'ogy, the scientific study of folk-tales; sto'ry-book, a book of tales true or fictitious.—*n.* and *adj.* sto'rying.—*ns.* sto'ry-teller, one who relates tales: a liar; sto'ry-telling. [A.Fr. *estorie*—L. *historia*.]

story, storey, *stō'ri*, *n.* part of a building on the same floor: a tier.—*adj.* sto'ried, sto'reyed, having stories.—first story, the ground-floor; second story, the first floor, &c. [Prob. same word orig. as above.]

stot, *stot*, *n.* a young ox, steer. [O.E. *stot*, horse.]

stot, *stot*, *v.i.* (*Scot.*) to rebound, bounce.—*v.t.* to cause to bounce.—*n.* a rebound.—Also stott'er. [Origin obscure.]

stoun, *stoōn*, *v.t.* (*Spens.*):—*pa.t.* and *pa.p.* stound. See stun.

stound, stownd, *stownd*, *stoōnd*, *n.* (*Spens.* and *Scot.*) a time, moment: a time of trouble: a pang: an assault, stroke: a shock: a din.—*v.i.* to shoot like a pang: to experience a pang. [O.E. *stund*.]

stound, stownd, *stoōnd*, *v.t.* (*Spens.*) to stun, astound. —*n.* a stunned or astounded condition. [stoun or astound.]

stoup, stoop, *stoōp* (*Shak.* stoope; stope, *stōp*), *n.* (*obs.*) a bucket: a drinking vessel: a holy-water vessel. [Cf. O.N. *staup* and Du. *stoop*; O.E. *stēap*.]

stour. See stoor (1).

stour, stowre, stoor, *stowr*, *stoōr*, *n.* battle, assault:

tumult: turmoil: (*Scot.*) dust.—*adj.* **stour′y,** (*Scot.*) dusty. [O.Fr. *estour*, tumult.]

stout, *stout, adj.* (*B., Spens.*) fierce: proud: arrogant: unyielding: stubborn: resolute: dauntless: vigorous: enduring: robust: strong: thick: fat.—*adv.* stoutly.—*n.* extra strong porter.—*v.t.* and *v.i.* **stout′en,** to make, or grow, stout(er).—*adj.* **stout′-heart′ed.**—*adv.* **stout′-heart′edly.**—*n.* **stout′-heart′edness.**—*adj.* **stout′ish.**—*adv.* **stout′ly.**—*n.* **stout′ness.** [O.Fr. *estout*, bold—Du. *stout*; Ger. *stolz*, proud.]

stouth, *stōōth, n.* (*obs. Scot.*) theft.—*ns.* **stouth′rie, stouth′erie,** theft: stolen goods: (*obs.*) provision, furniture; **stouth′rief,** (*Scots law*) theft with violence (later only in a dwelling-house).—**stouth and routh,** (*Scot.*) plenty, abundance (cf. **stoop and roop**). [O.N. *stuldr*, theft.]

stovaine, *stō-vā′in,* or *stō′,* or *-vān′, n.* a local anaesthetic, a substitute for cocaine, used for spinal analgesia. [**stove,** Eng. trans. of the name of Prof. Furneau, who first prepared it.]

stove, *stōv, n.* a hot-air bath: a heated room or chamber: a hothouse: a closed heating or cooking apparatus: a fire-grate: a kiln or oven for various manufacturing operations: a drying room.—*v.t.* to put, keep, heat, or dry in a stove: (*Scot.*) to stew.—*ns.* **stove′pipe,** a metal pipe for carrying smoke from a stove: (*U.S.*; in full **stovepipe hat**) a tall silk hat; **stove′-plant,** a hothouse plant.—*n.pl.* (*Scot.*) **stov′ies,** stewed potatoes, Irish stew. [O.E. *stofa*; Ger. *stube*.]

stove, *stōv, pa.t.* and *pa.p.* of **stave.**—Also used as *pr.t.*

stover, *stō′vər, n.* (*Shak.*) fodder. [Aphetic for **estover.**]

stow, *stō, v.t.* to place, put, lodge: to put away: to store: to put under hatches: (jocularly) to put down one's throat: (*slang*) to desist from (*stow it,* shut up): to pack: to have room for: to arrange.—*v.i.* (with *away*) to hide as a stowaway.—*ns.* **stow′age,** act or manner of stowing: state of being laid up: room for stowing: a place for stowing things: money paid for stowing goods: things stowed; **stow′away,** one who hides in a ship, &c., to get a passage; **stow′down,** the process of stowing down in a ship's hold; **stow′er; stow′ing.** [O.E. *stōw*, place.]

stow, *stōō, v.t.* (*Scot.*) to crop. [O.N. *stúfr*, stump.]

stown, *stown,* a Scots form of **stolen.**—*adv.* **stow(n)′-lins,** (*Scot.*) by stealth.

stowre. See **stoor** (1) and **stour** (2).

strabism, *strā′bizm,* **strabismus,** *strə-biz′məs, ns.* squint.—*adj.* **strabis′mal, strabis′mic, -al.**—*ns.* **strabismom′eter** (*strab-iz-*), **strabom′eter,** an instrument for measuring strabismus; **strabot′-omy** (Gr. *tomē,* a cut), the surgical operation for the cure of squinting. [Gr. *strabos* and *strabismos,* squinting; cf. *strephein,* to twist.]

stracchino, *strä-kē′nō, n.* an Italian cheese, made when the cows are weak. [It.,—*stracco,* weak.]

strad. See **Stradivarius.**

straddle, *strad′l, v.i.* to part the legs wide: to sit, stand, or walk with legs far apart: (*U.S.*) to seem favourable to both sides, to trim.—*v.t.* to bestride: to set far apart: to overshoot and then shoot short of, in order to get the range, to bracket: to cover the area of with bombs.—*n.* act of straddling: an attempt to fill a non-committal position: a stock transaction in which the buyer obtains the privilege of either a *put* or a *call*: a vertical mine-timber supporting a set: a combination of a shot beyond the mark and one short of it.—*adv.* astride.—*adv.* **stradd′le-back,** stridelegs.—*adj.* **stradd′le-legged,** having the legs wide apart. [Freq. of **stride.**]

stradiot, *strad′i-ot, n.* (*hist.*) a Venetian light horseman from Albania or Greece. [It. *stradiotto*—Gr. *stratiōtēs,* soldier.]

Stradivarius, *strad-i-vā′ri-əs,* or *-vä′,* **Stradivari,** *-vä′rē,* (*pop.*) **strad,** *ns.* an instrument, esp. a violin, made by Antonio *Stradivari* (1644-1737) of Cremona.—Also **Stradūa′rius.**

strae, *strā, n.* a Scots form of **straw.**—**strae death,** natural death in bed.

strafe, straff, *sträf, v.t.* (war slang of 1914) to

punish: to bombard: to assail.—*n.* an attack. [Ger. *strafen,* to punish.],

straggle, *strag′l, v.i.* to wander from one's company or course: to be absent without leave but not long enough to be counted a deserter: to stretch dispersedly or sprawlingly.—*n.* a straggling line or group.—*ns.* **strag,** (*dial.*) a straggler: a stray: a vagrant; **stragg′ler.**—*n.* and *adj.* **stragg′ling.**—*adv.* **stragg′lingly.**—*adj.* **stragg′ly,** straggling: irregularly spread out. [Origin obscure.]

straight, *strāt, adj.* uncurved: in a right line: direct: upright: flat, horizontal: in good order: frank and honourable: respectably conducted: balanced, even, square: settled: downright, out-and-out: normal, unmodified: in sequence at poker: (*U.S.*) undiluted, neat.—*n.* a straight condition: good behaviour: a straight line, part, course, flight, esp. the last part of a racecourse.—*adv.* in a straight line: directly: all the way: immediately: upright: outspokenly: honestly.—*v.t.* to straighten.—*adjs.* **straight′away,** straight forward; **straight′-cut,** cut lengthwise of the leaf, of tobacco.—*n.* **straight-′edge,** a strip or stick for testing straightness or drawing straight lines.—*v.t.* and *v.i.* **straight′en,** to make or become straight.—*n.* **straight′ener.**—*adv.* **straight′forth,** directly forward: straightway. — *adj.* **straightfor′ward,** going forward in a straight course: without digression: without evasion: honest: frank.—*adv.* straightforwardly.—*adv.* **straightfor′wardly.**—*n.* **straightfor′wardness.**—*adj.* **straight′ish.**—*adv.* **straight′ly,** in a straight line or manner: straightway.—*n.* **straight′ness.**—*adjs.* **straight′-out,** (*U.S.*, esp. in party politics) out-and-out; **straight′-pight,** (*Shak.*) straight, erect. — *adv.* **straight′way,** directly: immediately: without loss of time. — Also **straight′ways.** — **keep a straight face,** to refrain from smiling; **straight angle,** (*obs.*) a right angle: now, two right angles; **straight part,** one portraying the normal without emphasis on eccentricities of manner, &c.—opp. to *character part*; **straight play,** one without music; **straight talk,** a candid outspoken talk; **straight tip,** a racing tip that comes straight from the owner: inside information that can be relied on. [O.E. *streht,* pa.p. of *streccan*; see **stretch.**]

straik, *strāk, n.* and *vb.* a Scots form of **stroke.**—*n.* (*Scott*) proportion of malt in brewing.

strain, *strān, v.t.* to stretch: to draw tight: to draw with force: to exert to the utmost: to injure by overtasking: to force unnaturally, unduly, or amiss: to exalt emotionally: to change in form or bulk by subjecting to a stress: to constrain: (*Shak.*) to urge, insist upon, press for: to press to oneself, embrace: to squeeze, press: to grip, grasp tightly: to compress: to restrain: to squeeze out, express: to sing or play: to filter (esp. coarsely).—*v.i.* to make violent efforts: to tug: to retch: to have difficulty in swallowing or accepting (with *at*): to make efforts at evacuation: to percolate, filter.—*n.* the act of straining: a violent effort: an injury by straining, esp. a wrenching of the muscles: any change of form or bulk under stress: pitch, height: a section of a melody: a melody: an outpouring or flow of language: emotional tone, key, manner.—*adj.* **strained.**—*adv.* **strain′edly** (or *strānd′li*).—*n.* **strain′er,** one who, or that which, strains: a sieve, colander, &c.—*n.* and *adj.* **strain′ing.**—*n.* **strain′ing-beam,** a tie-beam uniting the tops of queen-posts.—**strain a point,** to waive a scruple; **strain at,** in Matt. xxiii. 24, to remove by straining, strain in the event of finding (not, as often understood, to be unable to swallow); **strain courtesy,** (*Shak., Rom. and Jul.*) to treat with scant courtesy, or (*Venus and Adonis*) to be overpunctilious in courtesy. [O.Fr. *estraindre*—L. *stringĕre,* to stretch tight.]

strain, *strān, n.* (*arch.*) offspring: breed, race, stock, line of descent: natural, esp. inherited, tendency or element in one's character: kind. [App. O.E. (*ge*)*strēon,* gain, getting, begetting (see **strene**), with altered vowel by confusion with foregoing.]

straint, *strānt, n.* (*Spens.*) pressure. [**strain,** on the model of **constraint,** &c.]

strait (formerly also, and still erroneously, **straight**; *Spens.*, *Milt.* **streight**), *strāt*, *adj.* (*Shak.*) tight: close: narrow: strict: rigorous: hard-pressed, needy: sparing in giving.—*n.* a narrow part, place, or passage, esp. (often in *pl.*) by water: (usu. in *pl.*) difficulty, distress, hardship.—*adv.* tightly: closely: narrowly: strictly: rigorously: with hardship.—*v.t.* to tighten: to narrow: to put in a difficulty: to reduce to hardship.—*v.t.* **strait'en**, to tighten: to narrow: to confine: to distress: to put into difficulties: to run short.—*v.i.* to narrow.—*adj.* **strait'ened.**—*v.t.* and *v.i.* **strait'-lace.**—*adj.* **strait'-laced**, tight-laced: narrow in principles of behaviour: prudish.—*ns.* **strait'-lacer**; **strait'-lacing.**—*adv.* **strait'ly**, tightly: narrowly: closely: strictly. — *ns.* **strait'ness**; **strait'-waistcoat**, **strait'-jack'et**, a garment for restraint of the violent. [O.Fr. *estreit* (Fr. *étroit*)—L. *strictus*, pa.p. of *stringěre*, to draw tight.]

strake, *strāk*, obs. *pa.t.* of **strike**.

strake, **straik**, *strāk*, *n.* (*Spens.*) a stripe: a strip: one breadth of plank or plate in a ship, from stem to stern: a section of a cart-wheel rim: a trough for washing ore. [Akin to **stretch**, coalescing with **streak.**]

stramash, *stra-māsh'*, *n.* (*Scot.*) a tumult, disturbance: a broil: wreck.—*v.t.* to wreck, smash. [Perh. an elaboration of **smash.**]

stramazon, **stramaçon**, *stram'a-zon*, -*son*, *n.* (*obs.*) a downward cut in fencing. [It. *stramazzone*, and Fr. *estramaçon.*]

stramineous, *stra-min'i-as*, *adj.* strawy: light, worthless: straw-coloured. [L. *strāmineus*—*strāmen*, straw.]

strammel, *stram'l.* See **strummel**.

stramonium, *stra-mō'ni-am*, *n.* the thorn-apple: a drug like belladonna got from its seeds and leaves. [Mod. L., poss. from a Tatar word.]

stramp, *stramp*, *v.t.* and *v.i.* (*Scot.*) to tread, stamp, or trample.—*n.* a stamp of the foot.

strand, *strand*, *n.* a sea or lake margin: (*Milt.*) a landing-place.—*v.t.* and *v.i.* to run aground.—*adj.* **strand'ed**, driven on shore: left helpless without further resource. [O.E. *strand*; Ger. *strand*, O.N. *strönd*, border.]

strand, *strand*, *n.* (*Scot.*) a rivulet: a gutter.—*n.* **strand'-scouring**, searching the gutters. [Origin obscure.]

strand, *strand*, *n.* a yarn, thread, fibre, or wire twisted or plaited with others to form a rope, cord, or the like: a thread, filament: a tress.—*v.t.* to break a strand of: to insert a strand in: to form of strands. [Origin obscure.]

strange, *strānj*, *adj.* (*Shak.*) foreign: alien: from elsewhere: not of one's own place, family, or circle: not one's own: not formerly known or experienced: unfamiliar: interestingly unusual: odd: estranged: like a stranger: distant or reserved: unacquainted, unversed: (*obs.*) exceedingly great, exceptional.—*adv.* **strange'ly.**—*ns.* **strange'ness**; **strān'ger**, a foreigner: one whose home is elsewhere: one unknown or little known: one who is outside of one's familiar circle or kindred: a visitor: a new-born child: a non-member: an outsider: a person not concerned: one without knowledge, experience, or familiarity (with *to*): a thing believed or feigned to foretell the coming of a visitor, as a tea-leaf floating in a cup, a flag of soot in a fireplace.—*v.t.* (*Shak.*) to make a stranger. —**make it strange**, (*Shak.*) to make difficulties, show reluctance: **strange woman**, a whore. [O.Fr. *estrange* (Fr. *étrange*)—L. *extrāneus*—*extrā*, beyond.]

strangle, *strang'gl*, *v.t.* to kill by compressing the throat: to choke: (*obs.*) to kill: to constrict: to choke back, suppress, stifle: to involve and impede. —*ns.* **strang'lehold**, a choking hold in wrestling: a strong repressive influence; **strang'lement**; **strang'ler**.—*n.pl.* **strang'les**, a contagious disease of horses.—*n.* **strang'le-weed**, dodder: broomrape. [O.Fr. *estrangler* (Fr. *étrangler*)—L. *strangulāre*; see next word.]

strangulate, *strang'gū-lāt*, *v.t.* to strangle: to compress so as to suppress or suspend function.—*adj.* **strang'ulated**; strangled: constricted, much

narrowed.—*n.* **strangulā'tion**. [L. *strangulāre*, -*ātum*—Gr. *strangalaein*, to strangle, *strangos*, twisted.]

strangury, *strang'gū-ri*, *n.* painful retention of, or difficulty in discharging, urine. [L. *strangūria*— Gr. *strangouriā*—*stranx*, a drop, trickle, *ouron*, urine.]

strap, *strap*, *n.* a narrow strip, usu. of leather: a thong: (*obs.* or *dial.*) a strop: a metal band or plate for holding things in position: a narrow flat projection, as on a strap-hinge: a looped band: a string or long cluster: anything strap-shaped: an application of the strap or tawse in punishment: (*slang*, after Hugh *Strap* in Smollett's *Roderick Random*) a barber: (*Anglo-Ir.*) a term of abuse to a woman: (*slang*) credit, esp. for liquor.—*v.t.* to beat or bind with a strap: to strop: (*Scot.*) to hang.—*v.i.* to work vigorously: to admit of or suffer strapping:—*pr.p.* **strapp'ing**; *pa.t.* and *pa.p.* **strapped.** — *n.* **strap'-game**, prick-the-garter.—*v.i.* **strap'-hang.**—*ns.* **strap'-hanger**, a passenger who has to stand and hold by a strap; **strap'-hinge**, a hinge fastened by a long leaf or flap; **strap'-oil**, a thrashing; **strapp'er**, one who works with straps, esp. a groom: a vigorous worker: a tall robust person: a whopping lie; **strapp'ing**, fastening with a strap: materials for straps: strengthening bands: a thrashing.—*adj.* tall and robust.—*adj.* **strap'-shaped.**—*ns.* **strap'-work**, (*archit.*) ornamentation of crossed and interlaced fillets; **strap'wort**, a seaside caryophyllaceous plant (*Corrigiola littoralis*) of S.W. England, &c., with strap-shaped leaves. [Northern form of **strop.**]

strappado, *strap-ā'dō*, -*ä'dō*, *n.* (*Shak.*) torture by hoisting to a height and letting fall to the length of the rope: later, (*erron.*) a strapping.—*v.t.* to torture or punish by the strappado. [Sham Spanish, from It. *strappata*—*strappare*, to pull.]

strass, *stras*, *n.* paste for making false gems. [Josef *Strasser*, its inventor.]

strata, *strā'tä*, *pl.* of **stratum**.

stratagem, *strat'a-jam*, *n.* a plan for deceiving an enemy or gaining an advantage: any artifice generally. [Fr. *stratagème*—L.—Gr. *stratēgēma*, a piece of generalship, trick; see next word.]

strategy, *strat'i-ji*, *n.* generalship, or the art of conducting a campaign and manoeuvring an army: artifice or finesse generally.—*adjs.* **strategetic** (-*jet'ik*), **-al** (both *rare*), **strategic** (*strat-ej'ik*, -*ēj'ik*), **-al**, pertaining to, dictated by, of value for, strategy.—*n.* (usu. in *pl.* form) **strateg'ics.**—*adv.* **strateg'ically.**—*n.* **strat'egist**, one skilled in strategy.—**strategic position**, a position that gives its holder a decisive advantage. [Gr. *stratēgiā* —*stratēgos*, a general—*stratos*, an army, *agein*, to lead.]

strath, *strāth*, *n.* in the Highlands of Scotland, a broad valley. [Gael. *srath*, a valley—L. *strāta*, a street.]

strathspey, *strath-spā'*, *n.* a Scottish dance, allied to and danced alternately with the reel: a tune for it, differing from the reel in being slower, and abounding in the jerky motion of dotted notes and semiquavers. [*Strathspey*, the valley of the *Spey*.]

stratify, &c. See under **stratum**.

Stratiotes, *strat-i-ō'tēz*, *n.* the water-soldier genus. [Gr. *stratiōtēs*, a soldier.]

stratocracy, *strat-*, *strat-ok'ra-si*, *n.* military despotism.—*n.* **stratocrat** (*strat'ō-krat*).—*adjs.* **stratocrat'ic**; **stratonic** (-*on'ik*), of an army. [Gr. *stratos*, an army.]

stratum, *strā'tam*, *n.* a layer: a bed of sedimentary rock: a layer of cells in living tissue: a region determined by height or depth: a level of society: —*pl.* **strā'ta.**—*n.* **stratificā'tion** (*strat-*).—*adjs.* **strat'ified**; **strat'iform**, layered: forming a layer.—*v.t.* **strat'ify**, to deposit or form in layers:— *pr.p.* **strat'ifying**; *pa.t.* and *pa.p.* **strat'ified.**—*ns.* **stratig'rapher**, **stratig'raphist**. — *adjs.* **stratigraph'ic**, **-al.** — *adv.* **stratigraph'ically.** — *ns.* **stratig'raphy**, the geological study of strata and their succession: stratigraphical features; **stratocruiser** (*strat'*, *strāt'*), an aeroplane for the stratosphere; **strā′to-cū′mulus**, a cloud in large globular or rolled masses, not rain-bringing.—*adj.* **strā′tose**, in layers.—*n.* **stratosphere** (*strat′* or *strāt′ō-sfēr*), a region of the atmosphere beginning about 4½ to 10 miles up, in which temperature does not fall as altitude increases.—*adjs.* **stratospheric** (*-sfer′ik*); **strā′tous**, of stratus.—*n.* **strā′tus**, a wide-extended horizontal sheet of low cloud. [L. **strātum**, -*ī*, **strātus**, -*ūs*, something spread, a bed-cover, horse-cloth—*sternēre*, **strātum**, to spread.]

straucht, **straught**, *strawhht*, *v.t.* (*Scot.*) a form of **stretch**: esp. to lay out (a corpse).—*adj.* and *adv.* a form of **straight**.—Also (*adj.* and *adv.*) **straicht**, **straight** (*strehht*).

straunge, *strawnj*, *adj.* (*Spens.*). Same as **strange**: foreign, borrowed.

stravaig, *stra-vāg′*, *v.i.* (*Scot.*) to wander about idly. —*n.* **stravaig′er**. [Cf. **stray**, **extravagant**.]

straw, *straw*, *n.* the stalk of corn: (*collec.*) dried stalks, &c., of corn, or of peas or buckwheat, &c.: a tube for sucking up a beverage: a straw hat: a trifle, a whit.—*adj.* of straw.—*ns.* **straw′board**, a thick cardboard, made of straw; **straw′-breadth**, the breadth of a straw.—*n.* and *adj.* **straw′-colour**, delicate yellow. — *adj.* **straw′-coloured**. — *n.* **straw′-cutter**, an instrument for chopping straw.— *adj.* **straw′en**, (*Spens.*) of straw.—*n.* **straw′-hat′**.— *adj.* **straw′less**.—*ns.* **straw′-plait**, plaited straw for hats; **straw′-rope**, a rope of twisted straw; **straw′-stem**, the fine stem of a wine-glass pulled out from the material of the bowl, instead of being attached separately: a wine-glass having such a stem; **straw′-worm**, a caddis-worm.— *adj.* **straw′y**, of or like straw.—*n.* **straw′-yard**, a yard strewn with straw for animals. [O.E. *stréaw*; Ger. *stroh*; cf. **strae**, **strew**.]

straw, *straw*, *v.t.* an archaic form of **strew** :—*pa.t.* **strawed**; *pa.p.* **strawed**, **strawn**.

strawberry, *straw′ba-ri*, -*bri*, *n.* the fruit (botanically the enlarged receptacle) of any species of the rosaceous genus Fragaria, close akin to Potentilla: the plant bearing it.—*ns.* **straw′berry-leaf′**, the leaf of the strawberry plant: symbolically (esp. in *pl.*) the rank of duke or duchess, from the orna-ments like strawberry leaves on a duke's (also a marquess's or earl's) coronet; **straw′berry-mark**, a reddish birth-mark; **straw′berry-shrub**, Caly-canthus; **straw′berry-toma′to**, the Cape goose-berry; **straw′berry-tree**, *Arbutus Unedo*, a small tree (wild at Killarney) of the heath family, with red berries.—**barren strawberry**, a Potentilla distinguished from the wild strawberry by its dry fruit. [O.E. *stréawberige*, possibly from the chaffy appearance of the achenes.]

stray, *strā*, *v.i.* to wander: to wander away, esp. from control, or from the right way: to get lost.— *v.t.* (*Shak.*) to set astray.—*n.* a domestic animal that has strayed or is lost: a straggler: a waif: any-thing occurring casually, isolatedly, out of place: (*Shak.*) body of strays: a common: (in *pl.*) atmo-spherics: (*Shak.*) a straying.—*adj.* gone astray: casual: isolated.—*adj.* strayed, wandering, gone astray.—*n.* **stray′er**.—*n.* and *adj.* **stray′ing**.—*n.* **stray′ling**, a stray. [O.Fr. *estraier*, to wander—L. *extrā*, beyond, *vagārī*, to wander.]

streak, *strēk*, *n.* an irregular stripe: the colour of a mineral in powder, seen in a scratch: a scratch: a strain, vein, interfused or pervading character: the line or course as of a flash of lightning: a rush, swift dash: a course, succession, as of luck.—*v.t.* to mark with streaks.—*v.i.* to become streaked: to pass in a streak (cf. **streek**).—*adj.* **streaked**, streaky, striped: (*U.S.*) confused.—*ns.* **streak′iness**; **streak′ing**.— *adj.* **streak′y**, marked with streaks, striped: fat and lean in alternate layers: uneven in quality.— **like a streak**, like (a flash of) lightning. [O.E. *strica*, a stroke, line, mark; Ger. *strich*; cf. **strike**.]

streak. See **streke**, **streek**.

stream, *strēm*, *n.* a running water: a river or brook, esp. a rivulet: a flow or moving succession of anything: a current: a drift: a tendency.—*v.i.* to flow, issue, or stretch, in a stream: to pour out abundantly: to float out, trail: to wash for ore.— *v.t.* to discharge in a stream: to wave, fly: to wash for ore.—*ns.* **stream′-anch′or**, a small anchor

used in warping or for stemming an easy current; **stream′er**, a pennon, ribbon, plume, or the like streaming or flowing in the wind: a luminous beam or band of light, as of the aurora: one who washes detritus for gold or tin.—*adj.* **stream′ered**. —*ns.* **stream′-gold**, placer-gold; **stream′-ice**, pieces of drift ice swept down in a current; **stream′iness**.—*n.* and *adj.* **stream′ing**.—*adv.* **stream′ingly**.—*adj.* **stream′less**, not watered by streams: waterless: without a current. — *ns.* **stream′let**, a little stream; **stream′-line**, a line followed by a streaming fluid: natural course of air-streams.—*v.t.* to make stream-lined.—*adj.* **stream′-lined**, having boundaries following stream-lines so as to offer minimum resistance: (*slang*) a term of commendation with a variety of meanings, as effi-cient, without waste of effort, up-to-the-minute, of superior type, graceful, &c.—*ns.* **stream′ling**, a little stream; **stream′-tin**, tin-ore found in alluvial ground.—*adj.* **stream′y**, abounding in streams: flowing in a stream.—**stream of con-sciousness**, the continuous succession of thoughts, emotions, and feelings, both vague and well-defined, that forms an individual's conscious experience. [O.E. *stréam*; Ger. *strom*, O.N. *straumr*.]

streek, **streak**, *strēk*, *v.t.* and *v.i.* a Northern form of **stretch**, not [confined to Northern use: esp. (*v.t. Scot.*) to lay out for burial: (*v.i.*, now *U.S.*) to go at full speed.

streel, *strēl*, *v.i.* (*Ir.*) to trail: to stream: to wander. [Cf. Ir. *straoillim*, to trail.]

street, *strēt*, *n.* (*ant.*) a paved road, esp. Roman: a road lined with houses, broader than a lane, in-cluding or excluding the houses and the footways: those who live in a street or are on the street: a passage or gap through or among anything: brokers as a body: (often in *pl.*) prostitution.—*ns.* **street′age**, (*U.S.*) a toll for street facilities; **street′-Ar′ab** (see **Arab**); **street′-boy**, a boy who lives mainly on the streets; **street′-car**, (*U.S.*) a tram-car; **street′-door**, the door that opens on the street.—*adj.* **street′ed**, having streets.—*ns.* **street′-ful** (*pl.* **street′fuls**); **street′-keeper**, an officer formerly employed to keep order in a street or streets; **street′-or′derly**, a scavenger; **street′-rail′road**, **-rail′way**, a town tramway.—*adj.* **street′-raking**, (*Scott*) ranging the streets.—*ns.* **street′-room**, space enough in the street; **street′-sweep′er**, one who, or that which, sweeps the streets clean; **street′-walker**, any one who walks in the streets, esp. a whore.—*n.* and *adj.* **street′-walking**.—*n.* **street′-ward** (-*vawrd*), an officer who formerly took care of the streets.—*adv.* and *adj.* **street′ward** (-*wZrd*), towards or facing the street. —*adv.* **street′wards**.—*n.* **streetway**, the roadway. —*adj.* **street′y**, savouring or characteristic of the streets. [O.E. *strǣt* (Du. *straat*, Ger. *strasse*, It. *strada*)—L. *strāta* (*via*), a paved (way), from *sternēre*, *strātum*, to spread.]

streight, *strīt*, a Spenserian form of **strait**, **straight**.

streigne, an old spelling of **strain**.

strelitz, *strel′its*, *n.* a soldier of the Muscovite guards, abolished by Peter the Great :—*pl.* **strel′-itzes**, **strel′tzi**. [Russ. *strelets*, bowman.]

Strelitzia, *strel-it′si-ä*, *n.* a S. African genus of the banana family, with large showy flowers. [From Queen Charlotte, wife of George III., of the house of Mecklenburg-*Strelitz*.]

strene, *strēn*, *n.* (*Spens.*) a form of **strain**, race.

strength, *strength*, *n.* quality, condition, or degree of being strong: power of action or resistance: force: vigour: a strong place, stronghold: numbers: a military force: number on the muster-roll, or normal number.—*v.t.* **strength′en**, to make strong or stronger: to confirm.—*v.i.* to become stronger.—*n.* **strength′ener**.—*n.* and *adj.* **strength′ening**.—*adjs.* **strength′ful**; **strength′-less**, without strength.—**on the strength**, on the muster-roll; **on**, or **upon**, **the strength of**, in reliance upon: founding upon. [O.E. *strengthu—strang*, strong.]

strenuous, *stren′ū-əs*, *adj.* active: vigorous: urgent: zealous: necessitating exertion.—*ns.* **strenuity** (*stri-nū′i-ti*); **strenuosity** (*stren-ū-os′i-ti*), **strenu-**

ousness: a straining after effect.—*adv.* **stren'-
uously.**—*n.* **stren'uousness.** [L. *strēnuus.*]
strepent, *strep'ənt, adj.* (*rare*) noisy.—*adjs.* **strep'-
erous,** loud: harsh-sounding; **strep'itant,** loud:
noisy: clamorous.—*n.* **strepitā'tion.**—*adj.* **strepi-
toso** (*-i-tō'sō*; *mus.*; It.), noisy, boisterous.—
Also *adv.*—*adj.* **strep'itous.** [L. *strepĕre,* to make
a noise; freq. *strepitāre.*]
Strephon, *stref'on, -ən, n.* a love-sick shepherd in
Sir Philip Sidney's *Arcadia*: a love-sick swain.
Strepsiptera, *streps-ip'tə-rä,* n.pl. an order of insects
(or group of Coleoptera) parasitic in other insects,
the females wormlike, the males with twisted fore-
wings.—*adj.* **strepsip'terous.** [Gr. *strepsis,* a
twist, *pteron,* a wing.]
strepto-, *strep'tō-,* in composition, bent, flexible,
twisted.—*adjs.* **streptococcal** (*-kok'l*), **strepto-
coccic** (*-kok'sik*).—*ns.* **Streptococc'us** (Gr. *kokkos,*
a grain), a genus of bacteria forming bent chains :—
pl. **streptococ'ci** (*-sī*); **streptomycin** (*-mī'sin*;
Gr. *mykēs,* fungus), an antibiotic got from fission-
fungi.—*n.pl.* **Streptoneu'ra** (Gr. *neuron,* nerve), a
subclass of gasteropods with twisted visceral nerve-
loop—limpets, whelks, &c. [Gr. *streptos,* twisted,
flexible.]
Strepyan, *strep'i-ən, adj.* of the oldest known
Palaeolithic culture. [*Strépy,* a village near Charle-
roi, where stone implements of this stage occur.]
stress, *stres, n.* (*obs.*) hardship, straits: strain:
constraining influence: pressure: force: system
of forces applied to a body: insistent assigning of
weight or importance: emphasis: relative force
of utterance: (*law*) distraint.—*v.t.* to apply stress
to: to lay stress on: to emphasise.—*adjs.* **stressed;
stress'ful; stress'less.** [Aphetic for **distress;**
prob. partly also from O.Fr. *estrece*—L. *strictus*—
stringĕre, to draw tight.]
stretch, *strech, v.t.* to extend: to draw out: to
expand, make longer or wider by tension: to
spread out: to reach out: to exaggerate, strain,
or carry further than is right: to lay at full length:
to lay out: to place so as to reach from point to
point or across a space: (*slang*) to hang.—*v.i.* to
be drawn out: to reach: to be extensible without
breaking: to straighten and extend fully one's
body and limbs: to exaggerate: to go swiftly.—
n. act of stretching: state of being stretched:
reach: extension: utmost extent: strain: undue
straining: exaggeration: extensibility: a single
spell: a continuous journey: a straight part of
a course: (*slang*) a year's imprisonment.—*adj.*
stretched.—*ns.* **stretch'er,** one who stretches:
anything used for stretching, as gloves, hats, &c.:
a frame for stretching a painter's canvas: a frame
for carrying the sick or wounded: a rower's foot-
board: a cross-bar or horizontal member: a brick,
stone, sod, sandbag, &c., placed with its length
in the direction of the wall: an exaggeration
or lie; **stretch'er-bearer,** one who carries
injured from the field; **stretch'er - bond,
stretch'ing-bond,** a method of building with
stretchers only, the joints of one course falling
between those above and below; **stretch'ing-
course,** a course entirely of stretchers; **stretch'-
ing-frame,** a machine for stretching cotton
rovings: a frame on which starched fabrics are
dried; **stretch'ing-iron,** a currier's tool for
dressing leather.—*adjs.* **stretch'less,** no longer
liable to stretch; **stretch'-mouth'd,** (*Shak.*) wide-
mouthed; **stretch'y,** able, apt, or inclined to
stretch. [O.E. *streccan.*]
stretto, *stret'ō, n.* part of a fugue in which subject
and answer are brought closely together: (also
strett'a) a passage, esp. a coda, in quicker time.—
adj. and *adv.* **strett'o,** in quicker time. [It.,
contracted.]
strew, *strōō* (or *strō*), *arch.* **strow,** *strō* (or *strōō*),
straw, *straw, v.t.* to scatter loosely: to bestrew,
cover dispersedly: (*rare*) to spread: (*poet.*) to
level: (*pa.t.* **strewed,** *arch.* **strowed, strawed;**
pa.p. **strewed, strewn,** *arch.* **strowed, strown,
strawed, strawn**).—*n.* an assemblage of things
strewn.—*ns.* **strew'age; strew'er, strow'er;
strew'ing, strow'ing; strew'ment,** (*Shak.*) strew-
ings. [O.E. *strewian, streowian.*]

stria, *strī'ä* (L. *strē'ä*), *n.* a fine streak, furrow, or
thread-like line, usu. parallel to others: (*archit.*)
one of the fillets between the flutes of columns, &c :
—*pl.* **stri'ae** (*-ē*).—*v.t.* **stri'ate,** to mark with
striae.—*adjs.* **stri'ate, -d.**—*ns.* **striā'tion; striā'-
tum,** the *corpus striatum,* the great ganglion of the
fore-brain; **stri'ature,** mode of striation. [L.
strīa, a furrow, flute of a column.]
strich, *strich, n.* (*Spens.*) the screech-owl. [L. *strix,*
prob. modified by **scritch.**]
stricken, *strik'n, pa.p.* of **strike,** and *adj.,* struck:
now chiefly poet. or in special senses and phrases:
wounded in the chase: afflicted: advanced
(*stricken in years,* from the sense of go, make one's
way): (*U.S.*) expunged.—*n.* **stricken field,** a
pitched battle; **stricken hour,** an hour as marked
by the clock.
strickle, *strik'l, n.* an instrument for levelling the
top of a measure of grain or shaping the surface
of a mould: a template: a tool for sharpening
scythes. [O.E. *stricel.*]
strict, *strikt, adj.* (*Shak.*) tight: (*arch.*) narrow:
(*bot.*) stiff and straight: (*obs.*) close, intimate:
restricted: exact: rigorous: allowing no laxity:
austere: observing exact rules, regular: severe:
exactly observed: thoroughgoing.—*adj.* **strict'ish.**
—*adv.* **strict'ly.**—*ns.* **strict'ness; strict'ure,**
binding: closure: tightness: (*med.*) abnormal
narrowing of a passage: (*Shak.*) strictness: a (now
only adverse) remark or criticism.—*adj.* **strict'ured,**
morbidly narrowed. [L. *strictus,* pa.p. of *stringĕre*
to draw tight.]
stride, *strīd, v.i.* to walk with long steps: to take a
long step: to straddle.—*v.t.* to stride over: to
bestride: (*pa.t.* **strōde,** *obs.* **strid**; *pa.p.* **strid'en**
strid'n).—*n.* a long step: a striding gait: the
length of a long step.—*n.* **strid** (*strid*), a place
where a river can be stridden over (from that on
the Wharfe).—*v.i.* **striddle** (*strid'l*), to straddle
(back-formation from *stridling*).—*advs.* **stride'-
leg(s), stride'legged** (*Scot.*), **stride'ways, strid'-
ling** (*strid'; dial.*), astride. [O.E. *strīdan,* to
stride.]
stridence, *strī'dəns,* **-cy,** *-dən-si, ns.* harshness of
tone.—*adj.* **stri'dent,** loud and grating.—*adv.*
stri'dently.—*n.* **stri'dor,** a harsh shrill sound
(*med.*): a harsh whistling sound of obstructed
breathing.—*adj.* **stridūlant** (*strid'*), stridulating.—
v.i. **strid'ūlate,** to make a chirping or scraping
sound, like a grasshopper.—*ns.* **stridūlā'tion,** the
act of stridulating; **strid'ūlātor,** an insect that
makes a sound by scraping: the organ it uses.—
adjs. **strid'ūlatory; strid'ūlous.** [L. *stridēre* and
strīdĕre, to creak.]
strife, *strīf, n.* contention: contest: variance:
striving.—*adjs.* **strife'ful** (*Spens.*) **stryf'ull,** &c.)
strife'less.—*n.* **strift** (*strift*; *arch.*), struggle
[O.Fr. *estrif*; see **strive.**]
strig, *strig, n.* (*Southern*) a stalk.—*v.t.* to remove the
stalk from :—*pr.p.* **strigg'ing.** [Origin obscure.]
striga, *strī'gä* (L. *strig'ä*), *n.* a stria: a bristle, usu.
an appressed bristle :—*pl.* **strigae** (*strī'jē,* L.
strig'ī).—*adjs.* **stri'gate, stri'gose.** [L. *striga,*
swath, a furrow, a flute of a column.]
Striges, *strī'jēz* (L. *strig'äs*), *n.pl.* the owls.—*adj.*
stri'gine, owl-like: of the owls. [L. *strix, strigis*
an owl.]
strigil, *strij'il, n.* a flesh-scraper: in bees, a mechanism for cleaning the antennae. [L. *strigilis.*]
Strigops, *strī'gops,* **Stringops,** *string'gops, n.* the
kakapo or owl-parrot genus. [Gr. *strinx,* or *strix*
stringos, owl, *ōps,* face.]
strike, *strīk, v.t.* (*obs.*; *B.*) to stroke: to smooth
to strickle: to draw, describe, give direction to
(as a line, path): to delete, cancel: to constitute
(orig. by cutting down a list): to mark off: to
lower (as a sail, flag, tent): to remove: to leave
off or refuse to continue: to deal, deliver, or
inflict: to give a blow to or with: to hit, smite
to come into forcible contact with: to impinge on
to bring forcibly into contact: to impel: to put
send, move, render, or produce by a blow or stroke
to render as if by a blow: to sound by percussion
or otherwise: to announce by a bell: to dash: to
pierce: to stamp: to coin: to print: to impress

to impress favourably : to thrust in or down, cause to penetrate : (*Shak.*) to broach : (*Shak.*) to fight (a battle) : to blast, bewitch : to visit, afflict : to assail, affect : to affect strongly or suddenly : to arrive at, estimate, compute, fix, settle (as a balance, an average, prices) : to make (a compact or agreement), to ratify : to come upon : to reach : to achieve : to occur to : to assume : to hook by a quick turn of the wrist : (*slang*) to make a sudden demand of (as for a loan or subscription) : to cause to strike.—*v.i.* to make one's way : to set out : to take a direction or course : to dart, shoot, pass quickly : to penetrate : to put forth roots : to chance, alight, come by chance : to interpose : to deal or aim a blow, perform a stroke : to sound or be sounded or announced by a bell : to hit out : to seize the bait : to strike something, as a rock, sail, flag : to touch : to run aground : to surrender : to admit of striking : (*U.S. army*) to do menial work (for an officer) : to go on strike : (*Shak.*) to blast, blight : (*pa.t.* **struck**, *obs.* **strake**, **stroke**, **strook**, **strooke** ; *Scot.* **strak**, **strack**; *pa.p.* **struck**, *arch.* **strick'en**, q.v. ; *obs.* **strook**, **strooke**, **strook'en**, **strok'en**, **struck'en**).—*n.* a strickle : proportion of malt (cf. **straik**) : a stroke, striking : (*geol.*) the direction of a horizontal line at right angles to the dip of a bed : a find (as of oil), stroke of luck : a cessation of work as a means of putting pressure on employers, &c. : the part that receives the bolt of a lock : (*U.S. slang*) blackmail, esp. by introducing a bill in the hope of being bought off.—*ns.* **strike'-a-light**, a flint for obtaining fire with steel ; **strike'-breaker**, one who works during a strike, esp. one brought in with a view to defeating it ; **strike'-breaking**; **strike'-fault**, (*geol.*) a fault parallel to the strike ; **strike'-pay**, an allowance paid by a trade-union to men on strike ; **strik'er**, one who, or that which, strikes : (*Shak.*) a footpad : (*baseball*) a batsman : (*cricket*) the batsman facing the bowling ; **strik'er-out**, (*tennis*) the player who receives the service ; **strik'ing.**—*adj.* that strikes or can strike : impressive, arresting, noticeable.—*adv.* **strik'ingly.**—*n.* **strik'ingness.**—**on strike**, taking part in a strike ; **strike a match**, to light it by friction or a grazing stroke ; **strike at**, to attempt to strike, aim a blow at ; **strike back**, to return a blow : to backfire, burn within the burner ; **strike bottom**, **soundings**, to reach the bottom with the lead ; **strike hands**, to join or slap together hands in confirmation of agreement ; **strike home**, to strike right to the point aimed at ; **strike in**, to enter suddenly : to interpose : (*obs.*) to agree, fit ; **strike into**, to enter upon suddenly, to break into ; **strike off**, to erase from an account, to deduct : to print : to separate by a blow ; **strike oil**, to find petroleum when boring for it : to make a lucky hit ; **strike out**, to efface : to bring into light : to direct one's course boldly outwards : to swim away : to strike from the shoulder : to form by sudden effort ; **strike root**, to take root ; **strike up**, to begin to beat, sing, or play : to begin (as an acquaintance); **struck in years** (*Shak.* ; see **stricken**) ; **struck on**, inclined to be enamoured of. [O.E. *strican*, to stroke, go, move.]

string, *string*, *n.* small cord or a piece of it : cord of any size : a hangman's rope : a piece of anything for tying : anything of like character, as a tendon, nerve, fibre : a leash : (*U.S.*) a shoelace : a stretched piece of catgut, silk, wire, or other material in a musical instrument : (in *pl.*) the stringed instruments played by a bow in an orchestra or other combination : their players : the cord of an archery bow : the thread of a necklace or the like : anything on which things are threaded : a filing cord : a set of things threaded together or arranged as if threaded : a train, succession, file, or series : a drove of horses, camels, &c. : a long bunch : in billiards, the buttons strung on a wire by which the score is kept : hence the score itself : a sloping joist supporting the steps in wooden stairs : a string-course : (*slang*) a hoax : (*U.S. slang*) an awkward condition or limitation.—*adj.* of or for string or strings.—*v.t.* to fit or furnish with a string or strings : (*poet.*) to put in tune : to make tense

or firm : to tie up : to hang : to extend like a string : to put on or in a string : to take the strings off.—*v.i.* to stretch out into a long line : to form into strings : (*Scot.*) to be hanged : in billiards, to drive the ball against the end of the table and back, to decide who is to begin :—*pa.t.* and *pa.p.* **strung**. —*ns.* **string'-bag**, a bag made of, or for holding, string ; **string'-band**, a band of stringed instruments : the strings of an orchestra ; **string'-bean**, (*U.S.*) the French bean ; **string'-board**, a board facing the well-hole of a staircase, and receiving or covering the ends of the steps ; **string'-course**, a projecting horizontal course or line of mouldings running quite along the face of a building.—*adj.* **stringed** (*stringd*), having strings : of stringed instruments.—*ns.* **stringer** (*string'ər*), one who, or that which, strings : a horizontal member in a framework : (*naut.*) an inside horizontal plank, supporting beam-ends of a ship : a narrow mineral vein ; **string'iness**; **string'ing.**—*adj.* **string'less.** —*ns.* **string'-pea**, a pea with edible pods ; **string'-piece**, a long, heavy, usu. horizontal timber : the string of a staircase ; **string'-tie**, (*U.S.*) a narrow neck-tie of uniform width.—*adj.* **string'y**, consisting of, or abounding in, strings or small threads : fibrous : capable of being drawn into strings : like string or a stringed instrument.—*n.* **string'y-bark**, one of a class of Australian gum-trees with very fibrous bark.—**on a string**, under complete control : kept in suspense ; **pull the strings**, to use influence behind the scenes, as if working puppets ; **string figure**, a structure of string looped around the fingers in a symmetrical pattern that can be altered by manipulation, as cat's-cradle ; **two strings to one's bow**, more than one expedient. [O.E. *streng* ; cf. Du. *streng*, Ger. *strang*, O.N. *strengr*.]

stringent, *strin'jənt*, *adj.* tight : binding : rigorous : convincing : astringent : characterised by difficulty in finding money.—*n.* **strin'gency.**—*adj.* and *adv.* **stringendo** (-*jen'dō* ; It. ; *mus.*), hastening the time.—*adv.* **strin'gently.**—*n.* **strin'gentness.** [L. *stringēns*, -*entis*, pr.p. of *stringĕre*, to draw together.]

stringhalt, *string'hawlt*, *n.* a catching up of a horse's legs, usu. of one or both hind-legs.—Also **spring'-halt**. [App. **string** (sinew) and **halt**.]

strinkle, *string'kl*, *v.t.* (*Scot.*) to sprinkle.—*n.* **strink'ling**. [Cf. **sprinkle**.]

strip, *strip*, *v.t.* to pull, peel, or tear off : to doff : to divest : to undress : to deprive of livery and dismiss : to reduce to the ranks : to deprive of a covering : to skin, to peel, to husk : to lay bare : to expose : to deprive : to clear, empty : to dismantle : to clear of fruit, leaves, stems, midribs, or any other part : to tear off or wear off the screw-thread from : to press out the last milk from, or obtain in this way : to press out the roe or milt from : to handle as if milking a cow : to cut in strips : to put strips on : (*obs.*) to outstrip, press.— *v.i.* to undress : to lose the thread, as a screw : to come off : (*obs.*) to go swiftly : (*pr.p.* **stripp'ing**; *pa.t.* and *pa.p.* **stripped**).—*n.* a long narrow piece : a narrow space in a newspaper in which a comic story is told in pictures (**comic strip**) : light garb for running, football, and other sports.—*ns.* **single'-leaf**, tobacco stripped of stalks ; **stripp'er.**—*n.pl.* **stripp'ings**, the last milk drawn at a milking. —*n.* **strip'-tease**, an act of undressing on the stage. [O.E. *strȳpan* ; Ger. *streifen* ; perh. partly from other sources.]

stripe, *strip*, *n.* a blow, esp. with a lash : a band of colour : a chevron on a sleeve, indicating non-commissioned rank or good behaviour : a striped cloth or pattern : a strip : a strain : (*U.S.*) kind, particular sort.—*v.t.* to make stripes upon : to mark with stripes : to lash.—*adjs.* **striped**, having stripes of different colours ; **stripe'less.**—*ns.* **stripes**, (*coll.*) a tiger ; **strip'iness** ; **strip'ing.**— *adj.* **strip'y**, stripe-like. [Perh. different words ; cf. Du. *streep* (earlier *striipe*), Ger. *streif*, stripe, O.N. *strip*, striped fabric, Du. *strippen*, to whip.]

stripling, *strip'ling*, *n.* a youth : one yet growing. [Dim. of **strip**.]

strive, *striv*, *v.i.* to contend : to be in conflict : to struggle: to endeavour earnestly: to make one's way with effort:—*pa.t.* strove (strōv), *Shak.* strived; *pa.p.* striven (striv'n), *Shak.* strove, *B.* strived.—*n.* striv'er.—*n.* and *adj.* striv'ing.—*adv.* striv'ingly. [O.Fr. *estriver*; poss. Gmc., from the root of stride, or that of Ger. *streben*, to strive.]

stroam, strŏm, *v.i.* (*prov.*) to wander idly about: to stride. [Perh. stroll and roam.]

strobic, strob'ik, *adj.* like a spinning-top: spinning or seeming to spin.—*n.* strob'oscōpe, an optical toy giving an illusion of motion from a series of pictures seen momentarily in succession: an instrument for studying periodic movement seen by flashes.—*adj.* stroboscōp'ik. [Gr. *strobos*, a whirling—*strephein*, to twist.]

strobila, stro-bī'lä, *n.* in the life-cycle of jellyfishes, a chain of segments, cone within cone, that separate to become medusoids: a chain of segments forming the body of a tapeworm:—*pl.* strobi'lae (-lē).—*adj.* strobilaceous (strob-i-lā'shəs), of or like a strobile: bearing strobiles.—*v.i.* strobi'ilate, to undergo strobilation.—*adj.* of the nature of a strobilus.—*ns.* strobilā'tion, strobilīsā'tion, production or reproduction by strobilae: strobile (strob' or strōb'il, -il), a strobila: a strobilus.—*adjs.* strobiliform (-il'), strob'iline, strob'iloid.—*n.* strobi'lus, a close group of sporophylls with their sporangia, a cone: a scaly spike of female flowers, as in the hop:—*pl.* strobi'li (-lī). [Gr. *strobīlē*, a conical plug of lint, *strobilos*, a spinning-top, whirl, pine-cone—*strobos* (see foregoing).]

strode, strōd, *pa.t.* of stride.

strodle, stroddle, strod'l (*obs.* or *dial.*). Same as straddle.

stroke, strōk, *n.* an act or mode of striking: a hit or attempt at hitting: a blow: a striking by lightning: a reverse: an attack of apoplexy or of paralysis: the striking of a clock or its sound: a dash or line: a touch of pen, pencil, brush, &c.: (*obs.*) a trait: a beat, pulse: a single complete movement in a repeated series, as in swimming, rowing, pumping, action of an engine: a stroke-oar: a single action towards an end: an effective action, feat, achievement.—*v.t.* to put a stroke through or on: to cross (commonly with *out*): to row stroke in or for: to row at the rate of.—*v.i.* to row stroke.—*n.* stroke'-oar, the aftmost oar in a boat: its rower (also stroke, strokes'man), whose stroke leads the rest. [O.E. (inferred) *strāc*; cf. Ger. *streich*.]

stroke, strōk, *v.t.* to rub gently in one direction: to rub gently in kindness: to put by such a movement: (*obs.*) to soothe, or flatter: to milk, strip: to tool in small flutings: to whet: to set in close gathers.—*n.* an act of stroking.—*ns.* strok'er; strok'ing. [O.E. *strācian*—*strāc*, stroke (n.); cf. Ger. *streichen*, to rub.]

stroke, strōk, stroken, strōk'n, obs. forms (*Spens., Shak.*) of struck. See strike.

stroll, strōl, *v.i.* to wander as a vagrant or itinerant: to walk leisurely: to saunter.—*n.* a leisurely walk: (now *U.S.*) a stroller.—*n.* stroll'er, one who strolls: a wanderer: a saunterer: a vagrant: an itinerant: an itinerant actor.—*n.* and *adj.* stroll'ing. [Perh. Ger. *strolchen* (obs. *strollen*)—*strolch*, vagrant.]

stroma, strō'mä, *n.* (*zool.*) a supporting framework of connective tissue: (*bot.*) a dense mass of hyphae in which a fungus fructification may develop: the denser part of a blood-corpuscle, chloroplast, &c.: —*pl.* strōm'ata.—*adjs.* strōmatic (-mat'ik), strō'matous. [Gr. *strōma*, a bed, mattress.]

stromb, strom(b), *n.* a very large gasteropod akin to the whelk: its shell with short spire and expanded lip.—*adjs.* strombūlif'erous, bearing spirally coiled organs or parts: strombū'liform, top-shaped: spirally twisted.—*n.* Strom'bus, the stromb, or wing-shell, genus: strombus, a spirally coiled pod. [Gr. *strombos*, a spinning-top, snail, whirlwind.]

strond, strond, *n.* (*Spens., Shak.*). Same as strand.

strong, strong, *adj.* powerful: forcible: forceful: vigorous: hale: robust: of great staying power: firm: resistant: difficult to overcome: steadfast: excelling: efficient: of great tenacity of will

and effective in execution: able: well skilled or versed: competent: rich in resources or means to power: well provided: numerous: numbering so many: of vigorous growth: stiff, coarse, and abundant, indicating strength: without ambiguity obscurity, or understatement: intemperate, offensive and unseemly: gross: violent: grievous having great effect: intense: ardent and convinced: performed with strength: powerfully, or unpleasantly powerfully, affecting the senses: rank: vivid: marked: bold in definition: in high concentration: showing the characteristic properties in high degree: (of prices, markets) steady or tending to rise: (*gram.*) of Germanic verbs, showing ablaut variation in conjugation: of Germanic nouns and adjectives, having a stem originally in a vowel or a consonant other than *n*: (*compar.* stronger, strong'ger; *superl.* strong'est, -gist).—*adv.* (*rare*) strongly: (*U.S.*) very.—*adj.* strong'arm, (*U.S.*) by, having, or using, physical force.—*ns.* strong'arm, (*U.S.*) one who uses violence; strong'-box, a safe or strongly made coffer for valuables; strong'hold, a fastness or fortified refuge: a fortress: a place where anything is in great strength.—*adjs.* strongish (strong'-ish); strong'-knit, firmly jointed or compacted.—*adv.* strong'ly.—*adj.* strong'-mind'ed, having a vigorous mind—formerly applied by disapprovers to emancipated women.—*ns.* strong'-mind'edness; strong'-room, a room constructed for safe-keeping of valuables or prisoners.—come it strong (see come); going strong (see going); strong drink, waters, alcoholic liquors; strong flour, wheat, one rich in gluten, giving bread that rises well; strong head, power to withstand alcohol or any dizzying influence; strong meat, solid food, not milk (Heb. v. 12, 14); strong point, that in which one excels, one's forte. [O.E. *strang, strong*; O.N. *strangr*, Ger. *streng*, tight.]

strongyle, stron'jil, *n.* a blunt rhabdus: a parasitic thread-worm (Strongylus or kindred).—*adj.* and *n.* stron'gyloid. [Gr. *strongylos*, round.]

strontium, stron'sh(i-)əm, *n.* a yellow metal (Sr: at. numb. 38) found in celestine.—*ns.* stron'tia, its oxide; stron'tianite, its carbonate, an orthorhombic mineral (first found in 1790 near Strontian (stron-tē'ən) in Argyllshire).

strook, strooke, strook, obs. *pa.t.* and *pa.p.* (*Spens., Shak., Milt.*, &c.) and strook'en, obs. *pa.p.* of strike.—*n.* strooke (strōk; *Spens.*), stroke.

strop, strop, *n.* a strip of leather, &c., for sharpening razors.—*v.t.* to sharpen on a strop:—*pr.p.* stropp'-ing; *pa.t.* and *pa.p.* stropped. [Older form of strap—O.E. *strop*, prob.—L. *struppus*, a thong.]

Strophanthus, strof-, strōf-an'thəs, *n.* an African and Asiatic genus of the periwinkle family, yielding arrow-poison: its dried seeds used in medicine.—*n.* strophan'thin, a very poisonous glucoside in its seeds. [Gr. *strophos*, twisted band, *anthos*, flower, from the ribbonlike prolongation of the petals, twisted in bud.]

strophe, strof'i, strōf'i, *n.* in a Greek play, the song sung by the chorus as it moved towards one side, answered by an exact counterpart, the *antistrophe*, as it returned: part of any ode thus answered: loosely, a stanza.—*adj.* stroph'ic. [Gr. *strophē*, a turn.]

strophiole, strof'i-ōl, *n.* (*bot.*) a caruncle.—*adjs.* stroph'iolate, -d. [Gr. *strophiolon*, a fringe—*strophos*, a twisted band.]

strossers, stros'ərz, *n.* (*Shak.*) trousers. [Cf. trousers.]

stroud, strowd, *n.* a blanket made for American Indians.—*n.* stroud'ing, its material. [Prob. made at Stroud, Gloucestershire.]

stroup, strōōp, *n.* (*Scot.*) a spout, nozzle. [Cf. Sw. *strupe*, throat.]

strout, strowt, *v.i.* to bulge, swell: to stand out, protrude: to flaunt: to strut.—*v.t.* to cause to protrude. [O.E. *strūtian*, to protrude.]

strove, strōv, *pa.t.* of strive.

strow, strō, strōō. Same as strew:—*pa.t.* strowed; *pa.p.* strown.

stroy, stroi, *v.t.* (*Shak.*) to destroy.—*n.* (*Bunyan*) destruction. [destroy.]

struck, strucken. See **strike.**

structure, struk'tyər, n. manner or (obs.) act of putting together: construction: arrangement of parts: manner of organisation: a thing constructed: an organic form.—adj. **struc'tural.**—adv. **struc'turally.**—adjs. **struc'tured,** having a certain structure; **struc'tureless.** [L. structūra—struĕre, structum, to build.]

struggle, strug'l, v.i. to strive vigorously in resistance, contention, or coping with difficulties: to make great efforts or exertions: to contend strenuously: to make way with difficulty: to move convulsively.—n. a bout or course of struggling: strife: a hard contest with difficulties: a convulsive movement.—n. **strugg'ler.**—n. and adj. **strugg'ling.**—adv. **strugg'lingly.** [M.E. strogelen; origin unknown.]

Struldbrug, strŭld'brug, n. one of a class of immortals in Gulliver's Travels, born with a special mark in the forehead, kept by the public after eighty.

strum, strum, v.t. and v.i. to play in a haphazard unskilful way (pr.p. **strumm'ing;** pa.t. and pa.p. **strummed**).—n. a strumming. [Cf. **thrum.**]

struma, strōō'mä, n. scrofula: a scrofulous tumour: goitre: (bot.) a cushion-like swelling:—pl. **stru'mae** (-mē; L. -mī).—adjs. **strumatic** (strōō-mat'ik), **strumose** (strōō'mōs), **stru'mous.**—n. **strumi'tis,** inflammation of the thyroid gland. [L. strūma, a scrofulous tumour.]

strummel, strum'l, **strammel,** stram'l, n. (obs. slang) straw: hence, hair. [Cf. L. strāmen, straw.]

strumpet, strum'pit, n. a whore.—adj. like a strumpet: inconstant: false.—v.t. to make a strumpet of: to call a strumpet. [Origin obscure.]

strung, strung, pa.t. and pa.p. of **string.**

strunt, strunt, v.i. (Scot.) to strut. [Cf. Norw. strunta.]

strunt, strunt, n. (Scot.) spirituous liquor.

strunt, strunt, n. (Scot.; often in pl.) the huff, the sulks.

strut, strut, v.i. (obs.) to bulge, protrude: (obs.) to flaunt, glory: (obs.) to stand stiffly upright: to walk stiffly in vanity or self-importance: (pr.p. **strutt'ing;** pa.t. and pa.p. **strutt'ed**).—n. a strutting gait.—n. **strutt'er.**—n. and adj. **strutt'ing.**—adv. **strutt'ingly.** [O.E. strútian or some kindred form; see **strout.**]

strut, strut, n. a rod or member that resists pressure: a prop.—v.t. to support as, or with, a strut or struts. [Cf. L.G. strutt, rigid, and foregoing.]

Struthio, strōō'thi-ō, n. the African ostrich genus.—n.pl. **Struthio'nes** (-nēz), an order of birds including ostriches, rheas, kiwis, emus, and cassowaries.—adjs. **stru'thioid, stru'thious.** [L.,—Gr. strouthiōn, an ostrich.]

strychnine, strik'nēn, n. a very poisonous alkaloid ($C_{21}H_{22}N_2O_2$) got from nux vomica seeds.—v.t. to poison with strychnine.—n. **strych'nia** (now rare), strychnine.—adj. **strych'nic.**—ns. **strych'ninism, strych'nism,** strychnine poisoning. [Gr. strychnos, nightshade (of various kinds).]

stub, stub, n. a stump: (also **stub'-nail**) a short thick nail or worn horse-shoe nail, esp. in pl., old nails used as scrap: (U.S.) a counterfoil.—v.t. to grub up: to remove stubs from: to wear or cut to a stub: to wound with a stub: to strike as against a stub: to extinguish by pressing the end on something:—pr.p. **stubb'ing;** pa.t. and pa.p. **stubbed.**—adj. **stubbed,** cut or worn to a stub: cleared of stubs: stumpy: blunt.—n. **stubb'iness.** —adj. **stubb'y,** abounding with stubs: short, thick, and strong. [O.E. stubb, stybb.]

stubble, stub'l, n. a stump of reaped corn: such stumps collectively: straw: a reaped field: an ill-shaven beard. — adjs. **stubb'led,** stubbly; **stubb'le-faced,** fed on the natural grass growing among stubble.—ns. **stubb'le-field; stubb'le-goose,** a goose fed on stubble; **stubb'le-rake,** a rake with long teeth for raking stubble.—adj. **stubb'ly,** like or covered with stubble. [O.Fr. estuble — L.L. stupula — from L. stipula; see **stipule.**]

stubborn, stub'ərn, adj. obstinate: unreasonably or troublesomely obstinate: pertinacious: re-

fractory: hard to work or treat: rigid.—v.t. (Keats) to make stubborn.—adv. **stubb'ornly.**— n. **stubb'ornness.** [Connexion with **stub** is obscure.]

stucco, stuk'ō, n. a plaster used for coating walls, making casts, &c.: work done in stucco (pl. **stucc'os**).—v.t. to face or overlay with stucco: to form in stucco:—pa.t. and pa.p. **stucc'oed, stucc'o'd.**—n. **stucc'oer,** a worker or dealer in stucco. [It. stucco; from O.H.G. stucchi, crust, coating.]

stuck, stuck-up. See **stick.**

stuck, stuk, n. (Shak.) a thrust. [**stock,** 2.]

stud, stud, n. a horse-breeding establishment: the animals kept there: a collection of horses or other animals, or of cars, belonging to the same owner: (U.S.) short for stud-horse.—adj. kept for breeding: of a stud.—ns. **stud'-book,** a record of horses' (or other animals') pedigrees; **stud'-farm,** a horse-breeding farm; **stud'-groom,** a groom at a stud, esp. the head-groom; **stud'-horse,** a stallion kept for breeding: a variety of the game of poker. [O.E. stód; cf. **steed;** Ger. stute, mare, gestüt, stud.]

stud, stud, n. (obs.) a wooden post: (Spens.) a tree-trunk: a spur, stump, or short branch: an upright scantling as in a timber framework or partition: a cross-piece strengthening a link in a chain: a projecting boss, knob, or pin: a large-headed nail: a stud-bolt: a double-headed button: (U.S.) the height of a room.—v.t. to adorn, set, or secure with studs: to set at intervals:—pr.p. **studd'ing;** pa.t. and pa.p. **studd'ed.**—n. **stud'-bolt,** a bolt with a thread on each end, screwed into a fixed part at one end, receiving a nut upon the other.—adj. **studd'ed.**—ns. **studd'ing; stud'work,** brickwork walls between studs: studded leather. [O.E. studu, post.]

studding-sail, stun'sl, n. a narrow sail set at the outer edges of a square sail when wind is light.—Also **stunsail.** [Origin unknown.]

studdle, stud'l, n. a post: a prop. [O.E. stodla.]

student, stū'dənt, n. one who studies: one devoted to books or to any study: one who is enrolled for a course of instruction in a college or university: an undergraduate: a member of the foundation of Christ Church, Oxford, answering to a fellow elsewhere: the holder of a studentship.—ns. **stu'dentry,** students collectively; **stu'dentship,** an endowment for a student in a college: in Christ Church, Oxford, the equivalent of a fellowship: the condition or time of being a student.—adj. **studied** (stud'id), well considered: deliberately contrived, designed: over-elaborated with loss of spontaneity: well prepared by study: deep read: versed. — adv. **stud'iedly.** — ns. **stud'iedness; stud'ier; studio** (stū'di-ō), an artist's workroom (It.): a workshop for photography, cinematography, wireless broadcasting, making of gramophone records, &c.:—pl. **stu'dios.**—adj. **studious** (stū'di-əs), devoted to or assiduous in study: heedful: intent: solicitous: studied: deliberate.— adv. **stu'diously.**—n. **stu'diousness.**—v.t. **study** (stud'i), to apply the mind to in order to acquire knowledge or skill: to make one's object, seek to achieve: to be solicitous about: to consider: to scrutinise: to look contemplatively at: to take into consideration: to consider the wishes, advantage, feelings of: to devise: to elaborate with self-consciousness: to think out: (Shak.) to instruct. —v.i. to apply the mind closely to books, nature, acquisition of learning or of skill: to take an educational course: to rack one's mind: to muse, meditate, reflect: (pr.p. **stud'ying;** pa.t. and pa.p. **stud'ied**).—n. inclination: interest: zeal: an object of endeavour, solicitude, or mental application: a state of doubtful consideration: attentive and detailed examination: a scrutiny: a reverie: application of the mind to the acquisition of knowledge or skill: a department of knowledge: a preliminary essay towards a work of art: an exercise in art: a musical composition affording an exercise in technique: a presentation in literature or art of the results of study: (theat.) committing to memory, hence a memoriser: a room devoted to study, actually or ostensibly. [L. *studēre* (pr.p. *studēns*, *-ēntis*), to be zealous, *studium* (O.Fr. *estudie*; It. *studio*), zeal, study.]

stuff, *stuf*, *n.* (*obs.*) stuffing, filling: matter: substance: essence: material: a preparation used or commodity dealt in in some particular industry or trade: garden produce: cloth, esp. woollen: a medicinal mixture: goods: luggage: provision: furniture: money: literary or journalistic copy: liquor (**good stuff**, often whisky): rubbish: nonsense: (*obs.*) indecent matter.—*adj.* woollen.—*v.t.* (*obs.*) to garrison: (*Shak.*) to store, furnish: (*obs.*) to provision: to line: to be a filling for: to fill very full: to thrust in: to crowd: to cram: to obstruct, clog: to cause to bulge out by filling: to fill with seasoning, as a fowl: to fill the skin of, so as to reproduce the living form: (*slang*) to hoax. —*v.i.* to feed gluttonously: to practise taxidermy. —*adj.* **stuffed**, provisioned: well stored: filled: filled out with stuffing: clogged in nose or throat, &c.—*ns.* **stuff'er**; **stuff'-gown**, a gown of stuff, not silk, esp. that of a junior barrister.—*adv.* **stuff'ily**.—*ns.* **stuff'iness**; **stuff'ing**, that which is used to stuff or fill anything—straw, sawdust, feathers, hair, &c.: relishing ingredients put into meat, poultry, &c., in cooking: **stuff'ing-box**, a cavity filled with packing to make a pressure-tight joint.—*adj.* **stuff'y**, badly ventilated, musty: stifling: (*Scot.*) stout, sturdy: (*slang*) stodgy, strait-laced: (*U.S.*) sulky.—**and stuff**, and that sort of thing or rubbish. [O.Fr. *estoffe*, stuff—L. *stuppa*—Gr. *styppē*, tow.]

stuggy, *stug'i*, *adj.* (*prov.*) thick-set, stout.

stull, *stul*, *n.* (*prov.*) a horizontal prop in a mine.— *n.* **stulm** (*stulm*), an adit: a small draining-shaft. [Cf. Ger. *stollen*.]

stultify, *stul'ti-fī*, *v.t.* (*law*) to allege or prove to be of unsound mind: to cause to appear foolish: to destroy the force of, as by self-contradiction:— *pr.p.* **stul'tifying**; *pa.t.* and *pa.p.* **stul'tified**.—*ns.* **stultificā'tion**; **stul'tifier**; **stulti'oquence** (L. *loqui*, to talk), **stulti'oquy**, foolish talk or discourse, babbling.—*adj.* **stulti'oquent**. [L. *stultus*, foolish.]

stum, *stum*, *n.* must, grape-juice unfermented: new wine used to revive dead or vapid wine: a mixture used to impart artificial strength, &c., to weak beer or wine: wine revived by the addition of stum or by a second fermentation.—*v.t.* to renew or doctor with stum: to fume, as a cask of liquor, with burning sulphur:—*pr.p.* **stumm'ing**; *pa.t.* and *pa.p.* **stummed**. [Du. *stom*, must—*stom*, mute; Ger. *stumm*, dumb.]

stumble, *stum'bl*, *v.i.* to take a false step, come near to falling in walking: to walk unsteadily: to lapse into wrongdoing: to flounder: to light by chance or error: to boggle.—*v.t.* to disconcert.—*n.* a trip: a false step: a lapse: a blunder.—*ns.* **stum'bler**; **stum'bling-block**, **-stone**, an obstacle: a cause of perplexity or error.—*adv.* **stum'blingly**.—*adj.* **stum'bly**, apt to stumble or to cause stumbling. [M.E. *stomble*, *stumble*; cf. Norw. *stumla*, and **stammer**.]

stumer, *stū'mar*, *n.* (*slang*) a counterfeit coin or note: a forged or worthless cheque: a sham: a dud: a failure: a horse sure to lose.

stummel, *stum'l*, *n.* the bowl and adjacent part of a pipe. [Ger.]

stump, *stump*, *n.* the part of a felled or fallen tree left in the ground: a tree-stump used as a platform: hence, a campaign of stump-oratory: a short thick remaining basal part, esp. of anything that projects: a short thick branch: (*facet.*) a leg: a wooden leg: anything stumpy: a stumping walk or its sound: a pencil of soft material for softening hard lines, blending, &c.: (*cricket*) one of the three sticks forming (with the bails) a wicket: (*U.S.*) a challenge to perform a feat.—*adj.* reduced to a stump: stumpy.—*v.t.* to reduce to a stump: to remove stumps from: (*cricket*; of the wicket-keeper; sometimes with *out*) to dismiss by breaking the wicket when the striker is out of his ground: (*slang*) to clear out of money: to nonplus, foil, defeat: to soften or tone with a stump: to walk over or strike heavily and stiffly: (*U.S.*) to dare, challenge: making stump-speeches:—

—*v.i.* to walk stiffly and heavily, as if on wooden legs: to make stump-speeches.—*n.* **stump'er**.— *adv.* **stump'ily**.—*ns.* **stump'iness**; **stump'-or'ator**, one who speaks from an improvised platform, usu. with an implication of rant: in U.S.a political public speaker in general; **stump'-or'atory**; **stump'-speech**.—*adj.* **stump'y**, short and thick: (*U.S.*) full of stumps.—*n.* (*slang*) cash. —**draw stumps**, (*cricket*) to end play; **stump up**, to pay up, fork out. [Cf. Du. *stomp*, M.L.G. *stump*, O.N. *stumpr*, Ger. *stumpf*.]

stun, *stun*, *v.t.* to render unconscious as by a blow: to stupefy, daze, as with din or sudden emotion: to abrade, bruise: (*pr.p.* **stunn'ing**; *pa.t.* and *pa.p.* **stunned**).—*n.* a shock, stupefying blow: stunned condition.—*ns.* **stunn'er**, (*slang*) a person or thing supremely excellent; **stunn'ing**, stupefaction.— *adj.* stupefying, dazing: (*slang*) supremely excellent.—*adv.* **stunn'ingly**. [O.Fr. *estoner* (Fr. *étonner*), to astonish; cf. O.E. *stunian*, to make a din—*stun*, a din.]

Stundist, *stoon'dist*, *n.* a member of a Russian Protestant sect.—*n.* **Stun'dism**. [Ger. *stunde*, hour, lesson, from their Bible-reading meetings.]

stung, *stung*, *pa.t.* and *pa.p.* of **sting**.

stunk, *stungk*, *pa.t.* and *pa.p.* of **stink**.

stunkard, *stungk'ard*, *adj.* (*Scot.*) sulky: sullen.

stunsail, *stun'sl*. See **studding-sail**.

stunt, *stunt*, *adj.* dwarfed: stumpy.—*v.t.* to hinder from growth, to dwarf, check.—*n.* a check in growth: a stunted animal.—*adj.* **stunt'ed**, dwarfed.—*n.* **stunt'edness**. [O.E. *stunt*, dull, stupid; O.N. *stuttr*, short.]

stunt, *stunt*, *n.* (orig. *U.S. college slang*) a difficult, often showy, performance, enterprise, or turn: a newspaper craze or campaign.—Also *adj.*—*v.i.* to perform stunts. [Perh. a variant of **stint** (1), **stent** (1); cf. **stunt** (1); or perh. Ger. *stunde*, hour, lesson.]

stupa, *stōō'pä*, *n.* a tope or Buddhist domed mound. [Sans. *stūpa*.]

stupe, *stūp*, *n.* a medicated piece of tow or cloth used in fomentation.—*v.t.* to treat with a stupe. [L. *stūpa* for *stuppa*—Gr. *styppē*, tow.]

stupefy, *stū'pi-fī*, *v.t.* to make stupid or senseless: to stun with amazement, fear, &c.—*v.i.* to become stupid or dull:—*pr.p.* **stū'pefying**; *pa.t.* and *pa.p.* **stū'pefied**.—*adj.* **stupefacient** (*-fā'shant*), stupefying.—*n.* **stupefaction** (*-fak'shan*), the act of stupefying: the state of being stupefied: extreme astonishment.—*adjs.* **stupefac'tive**, stupefying; **stu'pefied**.—*n.* **stu'pefier**.—*adj.* **stu'pefying**. [L. *stupēre*, to be struck senseless, *facĕre*, to make.]

stupendous, *stū-pen'dəs* (formerly, as *Milt.*, **stu- pendious**, *-i-əs*), *adj.* astounding: astoundingly huge.—*adv.* **stupen'dously**.—*n.* **stupen'dousness**. —*adj.* **stu'pent**, astounded: dumfounded. [L. *stupendus*, gerundive, and *stupēns*, *-ēntis*, pres. part. of *stupēre*, to be stunned.]

stupid, *stū'pid*, *adj.* stupefied: senseless: insensible: deficient or dull in understanding: showing lack of reason or judgment: foolish: dull: boring. —*n.* (*coll.*) a stupid person (also *coll.* **stupe**).—*ns.* **stupid'ity**, **stu'pidness** (*rare*).—*adv.* **stu'pidly**. [L. *stupidus*.]

stupor, *stū'por*, *n.* torpor: lethargy: stupefaction: wonder.—*adj.* **stu'porous**. [L. *stupor*, *-ōris*— *stupēre*.]

stuprate, *stū'prāt*, *v.t.* to ravish, violate.—*n.* **stuprā'tion**. [L. *stuprāre*, *-ātum*.]

sturdy, *stur'di*, *adj.* (*orig.*) giddy: (*obs.*) impetuous, violent, rough: refractory: obstinate: resolute: robust: stout.—*n.* gid, a disease of sheep characterised by staggering, due to a bladderworm in the brain: a sturdy person.—*adj.* **stur'died**, affected with sturdy.—*adv.* **stur'dily**.—*n.* **stur'diness**. [O.Fr. *estourdi* (Fr. *étourdi*), stunned, giddy.]

sturgeon, *stur'jan*, *n.* any member of a genus (Acipenser) of large fishes of the Chondrostei with cartilaginous skull, long snout, heterocercal tail, and rows of bony shields on the skin. [A.Fr *sturgeon*, of Gmc. origin (O.H.G. *sturjo*).]

Sturnus, *stur'nəs*, *n.* the starling genus, giving name to the family **Stur'nidae** (*-ni-dē*).—*adjs.* **stur'nine**, **stur'noid**. [L. *sturnus*, starling.]

sturt, *sturt*, n. (chiefly *Scot.*) contention: disturbance.—*v.t.* to trouble.—*v.i.* to start with fear. [strut.]

stutter, *stut'ər*, v.i. and v.t. to speak, say, or pronounce with spasmodic repetition of initial sounds, stammer.—*n.* a stammer.—*n.* **stutt'erer**.—*n.* and adj. **stutt'ering**.—adv. **stutt'eringly**. [A freq. of obs. *stut*, to stutter, M.E. *stutten*; cf. O.N. *stauta*; Ger. *stossen*.]

sty, **stye**, *stī*, n. a small inflamed tumour on the eyelid. [Obs. or dial. *stian*, *styan*—O.E. *stīgend*, from *stīgan*, to rise.]

sty (Spens, **stye**, **stie**), *stī*, v.i. (obs.) to mount, rise, climb.—n. (obs.) a path: (dial.) a ladder. [O.E. *stīgan*, to mount, *stig*, path, and O.N. *stige*, path, O.E. *stīge*, ascent or descent.]

sty, rarely **stye**, *stī*, n. a pen for swine: any place extremely filthy: any place of gross debauchery: (pl. **sties**, **styes**).—v.t. and v.i. to lodge in a sty: —pr.p. **sty'ing**; pa.t. and pa.p. **stied**, **styed**; 3rd sing. pres. ind. **sties**. [O.E. *stig*, pen, hall; Ger. *steige*.]

Stygian, *stij'i-ən*, -*yən*, adj. of the Styx, one of the rivers of Hades, across which Charon ferries the shades of the departed: hellish, infernal: black as the Styx.—**Stygian oath**, an inviolable oath, like that of the gods, by the Styx. [Gr. *Styx*; cf. *stygeein*, to hate.]

style, *stīl*, n. a pointed instrument for writing on wax tablets: a similar instrument or tool of various kinds, as a graver, a blunt probe, a tracing or cutting point: (biol.) a slender process of various kinds: (bot.) the slender part of the gynaeceum, bearing the stigma: the gnomon of a dial: a hand, pointer, index: (obs.) a literary composition: manner of writing, mode of expressing thought in language or of expression, execution, action or bearing generally: the distinctive manner peculiar to an author or other: particular custom or form observed, as by a printing-house in optional matters (*style of the house*), or by lawyers in drawing up deeds: designation: manner: form: fashion: an air of fashion or consequence: kind, type: method in calico-printing: mode of reckoning dates—*Old Style*, according to the Julian calendar, as in Britain till 1752, Russia till 1917; *New Style* according to the Gregorian calendar, adopted in Britain by omitting eleven days, 3rd to 13th September 1752.—*v.t.* to designate.—*adjs.* **sty'lar**; **sty'late**, having a style, or a persistent style.—*n.* **style'-book**, a book of forms for deeds, &c.—*adj.* **style'less**.—*n.* **sty'let**, **sti'let**, a probe: a wire in a catheter: a bristle-like process: a graving tool: a writing instrument: a piercing part of an insect's jaws: a stiletto.—*adjs.* **stylif'erous**, bearing a style; **sty'liform**, like a style or a bristle.—*n.* **stylisa'tion**.—*v.t.* **sty'lise** (or *-līz'*), to conventionalise.—*adj.* **sty'lish**, (slightly vulg.) displaying style: fashionable: showy: imposingly smart: pretending to style.—*adv.* **sty'lishly**.—*ns.* **sty'lishness**; **sty'list**, one with a distinctive and fine literary style.—*adj.* **stylist'ic**.—Also *n.* in *sing.* or *pl.* form. —*adv.* **stylist'ically**.—*adj.* **sty'loid**, like a style or bristle: forming a slender process.—*n.* a spiny process of the temporal bone.—*n.* **sty'lus**, a style. [L. *stīlus*, a writing instrument, literary composition or style, confused with Gr. *stylos*, a column: in senses perh. from the Gr. word.]

stylite, *stī'līt*, n. an anchorite living on the top of a pillar. [Gr. *stylītēs*—*stylos*, a pillar.]

stylobate, *stī'lō-bāt*, n. the substructure of a row of columns. [Gr. *stylobatēs*—*stylos*, a column, *batēs*, one who treads, from the root of *bainein*, to go.]

stylography, *stī-log'rə-fi*, n. a mode of writing with a style.—n. **styl'ograph** (*-lə-gräf*) abbrev. **sty'lō**:— pl. **sty'lōs**), a stylographic pen, a pencil-like pen from which ink is liberated by pressure on a needle-point.—adj. **stylographic** (*-graf'ik*).—adv. **stylograph'ically**. [Gr. *stylos*, a style, *graphein*, to write.]

stylopised, *stī'lop-īzd*, adj. infested (as bees) with a strepsipterous parasite of Stylops or kindred genus.

stylopodium, *stī-lō-pō'di-əm*, n. the disk from which the styles rise in Umbelliferae. [Gr. *stylos*, pillar (as if style), *podion*, dim. of *pous*, *podos*, foot.]

styme, **stime**, *stīm*, n. (*Scot.*) a glimmer: a glimpse: a minimum of vision (or of other things).—*v.i.* to peer.—*n.* **stymie**, **stimie**, **stimy** (*stī'mi*; *Scot.*), a purblind person: (*golf*) a situation on the putting-green in which an opponent's ball blocks the way to the hole.—*v.t.* to put in such a situation (also **lay one a stymie**). [Origin obscure.]

styptic, *stip'tik*, adj. drawing together: astringent: checking bleeding.—n. a styptic agent.—adj. **styp'tical**.—n. **stypticity** (*-tis'i-ti*). [Gr. *styptikos* —*stȳphein*, to contract.]

Styrax, *stī'raks*, n. a genus of plants abounding in resinous and aromatic substances, as benzoin, giving name to the family **Styraca'ceae**, akin to the ebony family.—n. **sty'rene**, an unsaturated hydrocarbon obtained from essential oils (as the balsam storax) and coal-tar, forming thermoplastics on polymerisation. [Gr. *stȳrax*; cf. storax.]

Styx, *stiks*. See Stygian.

suable, *sū'* or *sōō'ə-bl*, adj. that may be sued.—n. **suabil'ity**.

suasion, *swā'zhən*, n. persuasion.—adjs. **sua'sible** (*-si-bl*); **sua'sive** (*-siv*).—adv. **sua'sively**.—n. **sua'siveness**.—adj. **sua'sory**. [L. *suāsiō, -ōnis*—*suādēre*, to advise.]

suave, *swäv*, or *swäv*, adj. smooth, bland.—adv. **suave'ly**.— n. **suavity** (*swav'i-ti*). [Fr.,—L. *suāvis*, sweet.]

suaveolent, *swə-vē'ə-lənt*, adj. fragrant. [L. *suāveolēns, -ēntis*—*suāvē-suāvē*, sweetly, *olēns*, smelling.]

sub-, *sub-*, *səb-*, pfx. under: from below: away: near: nearly: somewhat: not quite: subordinate: in addition: secretly: (chem.) in smaller proportion.—n. **sub** (coll. abbrev.), a subordinate: a subaltern: a subeditor: a sublieutenant: subscription: a subscriber: a substitute: a submarine: subsistence money.—v.i. to act as sub.—v.t. to subedit:—pr.p. **subb'ing**; pa.t. and pa.p. **subbed**.—adj. **suba'cid**, somewhat acid.—n. **subacid'ity**.—adjs. **subacid'ulous**; **subac'rid**; **subacute'**, slightly or moderately acute: (med.) between acute and chronic; **subaë'rial**, in the open air: on the land surface.—adv. **subaë'rially**.—n. **suba'gent**, an assistant agent: an agent's agent.—adjs. **subal'pine**, bordering on the alpine: at the foot of the Alps; **subang'ular**, somewhat angular; **subapostol'ic**, of the time just after the apostles.— n. **subappear'ance**, subsidiary appearance.—adjs. **subaquat'ic**, under water: partially aquatic; **subā'queous**, under water; **subarach'noid**, under the arachnoid membrane; **subarboresc'ent**, somewhat tree-like; **subarc'tic**, bordering on the arctic; **subarc'ūate**, somewhat arched: with two or more arches under a main arch.—n. **subarcuā'tion**.—adj. **subar'id**, more or less arid.—adj. **subas'tral**, beneath the stars, terrestrial.— n. **subat'om**, a constituent part of an atom.—adj. **subatom'ic**, relating to particles constituting the atom and changes within the atom.—n. (pl. in form, treated as sing.) **subatom'ics**, the study of these. —n. **subaudi'tion**, a sense understood not expressed. —adjs. **subax'illary** (or *-il'*), below the armpit or the axil; **sub'bas'al**, near or below the base.—ns. **sub'base'**, the lowest part of a base; **subb'ing**, working as a substitute: advancing of part of the wages while the work is going on; **subcan'tor**, **sub'chan'ter**, a precentor's deputy.—adjs. **subcau'dal**, beneath the tail; **subceles'tial** under the heavens; **subcen'tral**, under or near the centre.—n. **sub'class**, a primary subdivision of a class.—adjs. **subcla'vian**, **subclavic'ular**, under the clavicle.—n. **subcommitt'ee**, an under-committee: a division of a committee.—adj. **subcon'-scious**, dimly conscious: away from the focus of attention: not conscious but of like nature to the conscious.—n. the subconscious mind or activities. —adv. **subcon'sciously**.—n. **subcon'sciousness**. —adj. **subcontig'uous**, almost touching.—n. **subcon'tinent**, a great portion of a continent with a character of its own (esp. S. Africa): a land-mass hardly great enough to be called a continent.—adjs. **subcontinent'al**, almost continental: underlying a continent; **subcontin'uous**, nearly but not quite continuous.—n. **subcon'tract**, a contract

Neutral vowels in unaccented syllables : *el'ə-mənt, in'fənt, ran'dəm*

subordinate to another contract, as for the sub-letting of work.—*v.i.* **subcontract'**, to make a sub-contract.—*v.t.* to make a subcontract for : (*Shak.*) to betroth when already married (as if subleased by the actual husband to another).—*ns.* **subcon-tract'or** ; **subcontrarī'ety.**—*adj.* **subcon'trary**, contrary in an inferior degree : (*log.* : of a particular proposition in relation to another differing only in quality) such that at least one must be true.—*n.* a subcontrary proposition.—*adjs.* **subcor'date**, some-what heart-shaped ; **subcort'ical**, under the cortex.—*n.* **subcos'ta**, the nervure next the costa in an insect's wing.—*adj.* **subcost'al**, near or under a rib or the ribs : behind or near the costa.—*n.* the subcostal nervure.—*n.* **sub'cul'ture**, a culture (as of bacteria) derived from a previous one.—*adj.* **subcutā'neous**, under the skin.—*adv.* **subcutā'neously.**—*ns.* **subdea'con**, a member of the order (major in the R.C., minor in the Eastern churches) of the ministry next below that of deacon, prepar-ing the vessels, &c., at the eucharist ; **subdea'conry**, **subdea'conship** ; **sub'dean'**, an assistant or sub-stitute dean ; **sub'dean'ery.**—*adj.* **subdiac'onal**, of a subdeacon.—*ns.* **subdiac'onate** ; **subdis'trict**, a division of a district.—*v.t.* and *v.i.* **sub'divide'**, to divide into smaller divisions : to divide again.—*adj.* **subdivisible** (*-viz'*). — *n.* **subdivision** (*-vizh'ən*).—*adjs.* **subdivis'ional** ; **subdivī'sive.**—*n.* **sub'dom'inant**, the tone next below the domin-ant.—*adj.* not quite ranking as dominant.—*adjs.* **subdū'ple** (or *sub'*), in the ratio of one to two ; **subdū'plicate**, (of a ratio) of the square roots.—*v.t.* **subed'it**, to select and dispose matter for (a newspaper) : also, to assist in editing.—*n.* **subeditor.**—*adj.* **subeditō'rial.**—*n.* **subed'itor-ship.**—*adjs.* **subentire'**, (*bot.*) with very faintly indented margin ; **subē'qual**, nearly equal ; **sub-erect'**, nearly erect.—*ns.* **sub'fam'ily**, a primary division of a family, of one or more genera ; **sub'-feu**, a feu granted to a vassal.—*v.t.* **subfeu'**, to make subinfeudation of.—*n.* **subfeudā'tion**, sub-infeudation.—*adjs.* **subfeud'atory** ; **subgener'ic.**—*adv.* **subgener'ically.**—*n.* **subge'nus**, a primary division of a genus. — *adjs.* **subglā'cial**, under a glacier or ice-sheet ; **subglobose', subglob'ular**, nearly globular. — *ns.* **sub'group**, subdivision of a group ; **sub'-head', -head'ing**, a subordinate head, heading, or division of a discourse.—*adj.* **subhu'man**, below the human : below but near the human.—*n.* **subima'go**, a stage in the life of a mayfly, already winged before the last moult.—*v.t.* **subincise'**, to perform subincision upon.—*n.* **sub-incis'ion**, the savage rite of cutting open the under-side of the penis.—*v.t.* **subin'dicate**, to hint.—*n.* **subindicā'tion.**—*adj.* **subindic'ative.**—*v.t.* **sub-infeudate.**—*n.* **subinfeudā'tion**, the granting of land by a vassal to be held of him by his vassal.—*adj.* and *n.* **subinfeud'atory.**—*ns.* **subinsinuā'tion**, a slight or private insinuation ; **subinspec'tor**, a subordinate or assistant inspector ; **subinspec'-torship** ; **subintellec'tion**, **subintell'igence**, **subintelligitur** (*sub-in-tel-ij'i-tər*, L. *soob-in-tel-ig'i-toor*, it is more or less understood), an under-stood implication.—*adjs.* **subintelligen'tial** ; **sub-in'trant**, with paroxysms succeeding close upon one another.—*v.t.* **subintroduce'**, to bring in surreptitiously or subtly.—*n.* **subirrigā'tion**, (*U.S.*) irrigation by underground pipes.—*v.t.* **subjoin'**, to add at the end or afterwards.—*ns.* **subjoin'der**, (*Lamb*) a remark following on another ; **sub'-kingdom**, a subordinate kingdom : (*biol.*) a phylum.—*adj.* **sub'lan'ceolate**, almost lanceolate.—*n.* **sub'lease**, an underlease or lease by a tenant to another.—*v.t.* and *v.i.* **sub'lease'.**—*ns.* **sub'-lessee'**, the holder of a sublease ; **subless'or**, one who grants a sublease.—*v.t.* **sublet'**, to underlet or lease, as by one himself a tenant to another (*pa.t.* and *pa.p.* **sublet'**).—*n.* a subletting.—*ns.* **sub-lett'er** ; **sublett'ing** ; **sub'libra'rian**, an assistant librarian ; **sublieutenant** (*navy* ; *sub'lə-ten'ənt*), formerly *mate*, or *passed midshipman*, an officer ranking with an army lieutenant : (*army* ; *-lef'-* obs.) now second-lieutenant. — *adj.* **sublinear** (*-lin'i-ər*), under the line : (*bot.*) nearly linear.—*n.* **sublineā'tion**, underlining.—*adjs.* **subling'ual**,

under the tongue ; **sublitt'oral**, growing, living, occurring, near but not on the shore, whether on land or at sea ; **sublu'nar**, **sub'lunary**, under the moon : earthly : of this world : directly under the moon, as a point on the earth's surface where the moon is vertically overhead.—*ns.* a being or thing of the earth or of this world.—*adj.* **sublu'nate**, approaching the form of a crescent.—*ns.* **subluxā'-tion**, an incomplete dislocation ; **submachine'-gun**, a light machine-gun, usu. one fired from the shoulder ; **sub'-man**, an animal not quite a man : a man of lowest type.—*adjs.* **submar'ginal**, near the margin ; **sub'marine**, under the sea : under the surface of the sea.—*n.* a submersible vessel, esp. for warfare : a submarine organism or dweller.—*v.t.* to attack by submarine.—*n.* **submarin'er**, a member of the crew of a submarine.—*adj.* **sub-max'illary**, of or under the lower jaw.—*ns.* **submē'diant**, (*mus.*) the sixth above the tonic ; **submi'cron**, a particle visible by ultramicroscope but not by the ordinary microscope (50–2000 Å).—*adj.* **submon'tane**, under or at the foot of a mountain range.—*n.* **submul'tiple**, an aliquot part.—*adjs.* **subnascent** (*sub-nas'ənt*, *-nās'*), grow-ing underneath ; **subnat'ural**, less than natural ; **subneu'ral**, beneath a main neural axis or nervous cord ; **subniveal** (*-niv'*), **subniv'ean**, under snow (L. *nix*, *nivis*, snow) ; **subnor'mal**, less than normal.—*n.* (*geom.*) the projection of the normal on the axis.—*n.* **subnormal'ity.**—*adj.* **suboccip'-ital**, below or behind the occiput, or the occipital lobe.—*n.* **suboc'tave**, the octave below : (also **suboctave coupler**) an organ coupler that gives an octave below.—*adjs.* **suboctū'ple** (or *-ok'*), in the ratio of one ot eight ; **suboc'ular**, under the eye ; **suboper'cular.** — *n.* **suboper'culum**, in fishes, a bone of the gill-cover below and partly behind the operculum.—*adj.* **subor'bital**, below the orbit of the eye.—*n.* **subor'der**, (*biol.*) a sub-division in an order, a group of families.—*adj.* **subor'dinal**, of, of the nature or rank of, a sub-order.—*ns.* **subor'dinancy**, subordination ; **subor'-dinary**, (*her.*) a less honourable armorial charge.—*adj.* **subor'dinate**, lower in order, rank, nature, power, &c. : dependent : under orders of another : (*obs.*) submissive : lower in a series of successive divisions : underlying.—*n.* a person or thing that is subordinate or ranked lower : one who works under another.—*v.t.* to place in a lower order : to consider of less value : to subject.—*adv.* **subor'-dinately.**—*ns.* **subor'dinateness** ; **subordinā'-tion**, arrangement in a series of successive orders : disposition of successive recessed arches in an archway : act of subordinating or placing in a lower order : state of being subordinate : in-feriority of rank or position : submission and obedience to authority ; **subordinā'tionism**, the doctrine of the inferiority of the second and third Persons of the Trinity to the first.—*adjs.* **subor'-dinātive**, tending to, or expressing, subordination ; **subō'vate**, almost ovate.—*ns.* **sub'plot**, a sub-ordinate plot, as in a play ; **subprē'fect**, an assist-ant or deputy-prefect ; **sub'prē'fecture** ; **sub'-prī'or**, a monk next under a prior :—*fem.* **sub'-prī'oress** ; **subref'erence**, an incomplete o surreptitious reference : an appeal by a veile understanding ; **sub'region**, a subdivision of region, esp. in zoogeography.—*adjs.* **subrē'gional**, **subsā'cral**, below (in man in front of) the sacrum **subscap'ular**, below (in man in front of) th shoulder-blade.—*n.* a subscapular vessel or nerv —*n.* **sub'sec'tion**, a division of a section.—*adj* **subsen'sible**, below the range of sense ; **sub sess'ile**, not quite sessile.—*n.* **sub'shrub**, an unde shrub.—*adj.* **subshrubb'y.**—*ns.* **subsī'zar**, a Can bridge undergraduate ranking below a sizar **sub'soil**, broken-up rock underlying the soil.—*v.t.* to turn up or loosen the subsoil of.—*ns* **sub'soiler**, one who subsoils : a plough for sub soiling ; **sub'soiling**, ploughing the subsoil : (*fig* unseen activities.—*adj.* **subso'lar**, directly und the sun, as a point on the earth's surface where th sun is vertically overhead.—*n.* **sub'spē'cies**, related group within a species.—*adj.* **subspecif'** —*adv.* **subspecif'ically.**—*adj.* **subspi'nous**, som what spinous.—*n.* sub'stage, apparatus under the stage of a microscope: (esp. *geol.*) a division of a stage.—Also *adj.*—*n.* sub'station, a subordinate station.—*adjs.* substell'ar, directly under a star, as a point on the earth's surface where the star is vertically overhead; subster'nal, under the sternum.—*v.t.* substruct', to build beneath, lay as a foundation.—*n.* substruc'tion.—*adj.* substruc'-tural.—*n.* sub'structure, an understructure: a foundation.—*adj.* sub'sur'face, below the surface.—*ns.* sub'tack', an underlease in Scotland; sub'tacks'man, a holder by subtack; sub'tan'gent, (*geom.*) the projection of the tangent on the axis.—*adj.* sub'tem'perate, slightly colder than temperate, cold-temperate.—*ns.* sub'ten'ancy; sub'ten'ant, the tenant of a tenant; sub'title, an additional or second title, as to a book: a half-title: a repetition of the title at the head of the text: descriptive reading matter in a cinematograph film; subton'ic, the note next below the tonic, the leading note; sub'-treas'urer, an assistant or deputy treasurer.—*adj.* subtriang'ular, nearly triangular.—*n.* sub'tribe, a division of a tribe.—*adjs.* subtrip'licate, expressed by the cube foot; subtrop'ic, -al, nearly tropical: of the subtropics.—*n.pl.* subtrop'ics, the regions bordering on the tropics.—*n.* subumbrell'a, the undersurface of a jellyfish's umbrella.—*adjs.* sub-umbrell'ar; subungual (*sub-ung'gwal*), under a nail or hoof.—*n.pl.* Subungulā'ta, animals by some included in the Ungulata though not typical hoofed animals, by others placed near the Ungulata—elephants and hyraxes.—*adj.* and *n.* subung'ulate.—*adj.* subur'sine, somewhat bear-like.—*n.* subvari'ety, a variety of a variety; sub'vassal, a vassal's vassal.—*adj.* subver'tebral, under a vertebra or the vertebrae; subver'tical, almost vertical; subvit'reous, partly, imperfectly, or somewhat vitreous.—*n.* sub'war'den, an underwarden, warden's deputy.—*adj.* subzōn'al, under a zone or zona.—*n.* sub'zone, a division of a zone. [L. *sub*, under, near; in composition also in some degree, secretly.]

subact, *sub-akt'*, *v.t.* to work up: to subdue.—*n.* subac'tion (*-shən*). [L. *subāctus*, pa.p. of *subigĕre* —*sub*, under, *agĕre*, to drive, do.]

subah, *sōō'bä*, *n.* a province of the Mogul empire: a subahdar.—*ns.* suba(h)dar', governor of a subah: an Indian captain; subahdar'y, su'bahship, office of subahdar. [Urdu.]

subaltern, *sub'əl-tərn* (*U.S.* except in logic usu. *sub-awl'tərn*), *adj.* ranked successively: subordinate: holding or held of a vassal: (of officers) under the rank of captain: (*log.*) particular: (*log.*) being at once genus and species of a higher genus.—*n.* a subordinate: a subaltern officer: (*log.*) a proposition differing from another in quantity alone (both being affirmative or both negative, but one universal the other particular).—*ns.* subalter'nant, (*log.*) a universal in relation to the subaltern particular; subalter'nate, a particular proposition in relation to the subaltern universal.—*adj.* subservient: (*bot.*) alternate with tendency to become opposite.—*ns.* subalternation (*sub-awl-tər-nā'shən*), relation between universal and particular of the same quality; subalter'nity, subordinate position. [L. *sub-alternus*—*sub*, under, *alter*, another.]

subarr(h)ation, *sub-ə-rā'shən*, *n.* an ancient mode of betrothal by bestowal of a ring or gift. [L. *subarr(h)ātiō*, *-ōnis*—*sub*, under, *arr(h)a*, earnest-money.]

subdolous, *sub'dō-ləs*, *adj.* crafty. [L. pfx. *sub-*, in sense of somewhat, *dolus*, a wile.]

subduce, *sub-dūs'*, *v.t.* (*obs.*) to withdraw.—*v.t.* subduct (*-dukt'*), to withdraw: to abstract secretly: to lift up.—*v.i.* to take something away.—*n.* subduc'tion. [L. *sub*, and *dūcĕre*, *ductum*, to lead, take.]

subdue (*Spens.* subdew), *sub-dū'*, *v.t.* to overcome: to overpower: to subject: to make submissive: to bring into cultivation: to allay: to reduce: to tone down: (*Spens.*) to achieve.—*adj.* subdu'able. —*n.* subdu'al, subjugation: overcoming.—*adj.* subdued', toned down.—*adv.* subdued'ly (or *-dū'id-li*).—*ns.* subdued'ness; subdue'ment;

subdu'er. [O.Fr. *souduire*—L. *subdūcĕre*; see foregoing.]

subedar. Same as subahdar.

suber, *sū'bər*, *n.* (*bot.*) cork.—*n.* su'berate, a salt of suberic acid.—*adj.* suberic (*-ber'ik*), of cork (suberic acid, an acid, $COOH \cdot (CH_2)_6 \cdot COOH$, got by action of nitric acid on cork).—*ns.* su'berin, the chemical basis of cork; suberisā'tion.—*v.t.* su'berise, to convert into cork.—*adjs.* su'berose, su'berous, corky. [L. *sūber*, *-eris*, the cork-oak.]

subfusc, subfusk, *sub-fusk'*, *adj.* dusky: sombre. —Also subfusc'ous. [L. *subfuscus*—*sub*, *fuscus*, tawny.]

subhastation, *sub-has-tā'shən*, *n.* sale by public auction. [L. *sub*, under, *hasta*, a lance (set up as a sign by the Romans).]

subitaneous, *sub-i-tā'ni-əs*, *adj.* sudden: hasty: hastily made. [L. *subitāneus*—*subitus*, sudden.]

subjacent, *sub-jā'sənt*, *adj.* underlying. [L. *sub-jacēns*, *-ēntis*—*sub*, *jacēre*, to lie.]

subject, *sub'jikt*, *adj.* (often with *to*) under rule, government, jurisdiction, or control: owing allegiance: under obligation: subordinate: subservient: dependent: liable: exposed: prone, disposed: cognisable: dependent upon condition or contingency: (*Spens.*) underlying, spread out below.—*adv.* conditionally (with *to*).—*n.* one who is subject: one who is under, or owes allegiance to, a sovereign, a state, a feudal superior, &c.: a citizen: (*Shak.*) a body of such persons: a thing over which a legal right is exercised: (*Scot.*) a piece of property: (*obs.*) substance: that in which attributes inhere: a thing existing independently: the mind regarded as the thinking power (opp. to the *object* about which it thinks): (*log.*) that of which something is predicated, or the term denoting it: (*gram.*) that part of a sentence or clause denoting that of which something is said: topic: matter of discourse, thought, or study: a department of study: a theme: that on which any operation is performed: that which is treated or handled: matter for any action or operation: ground: a sufferer from disease, a patient: (*anat.*) a dead body for dissection: a person peculiarly sensitive to hypnotic influence: that which it is the object of the artist to express: a picture representing action and incident: a theme or phrase upon which a movement of music is built.—*v.t.* subject (*səb-jekt'*), to make subject: to make liable: to subordinate: to submit: to subdue: to lay open.—*n.* sub'ject-cat'alogue, a catalogue of books arranged according to subjects dealt with.—*adj.* subject'ed, made subject: (*Milt.*) subjacent.—*v.t.* subject'ify, to make subjective.—*n.* subjec'tion.—*adj.* subject'ive (also *sub'*), relating to the subject: derived from, expressive of, existing in, one's own consciousness: introspective.—*adv.* subject'ively.—*n.* subject'iveness.—*v.t.* subject'ivise.—*ns.* subject'ivism, a philosophical doctrine which refers all knowledge to, and founds it upon, subjective states; subject'ivist.—*adj.* subjectivist'ic.—*adv.* subjectivist'ically.—*ns.* subjectiv'ity; sub'ject-matter, subject, theme, topic; sub'ject-ob'ject, the immediate object of cognition, or the thought itself; sub'jectship, the state of being subject. [L. *subjectus*, thrown under—*sub*, under, *jacĕre*, to throw.]

subjugate, *sub'joo-gāt*, *v.t.* to bring under the yoke: to bring under power or dominion: to conquer.—*ns.* subjugā'tion; sub'jugātor. [L. *subjugāre*, *-ātum*—*sub*, *jugum*, a yoke.]

subjunctive, *səb-jungk'tiv*, *adj.* subjoined: added to something: (*gram.*) expressing condition, hypothesis, or contingency.—*n.* the subjunctive mood: a subjunctive form: a verb in the subjunctive mood.—*adv.* subjunct'ively. [L. *subjunctīvus*—*sub*, *jungĕre*, to join.]

Sublapsarian, *sub-lap-sā'ri-ən*, *n.* a believer in Sublapsarianism.—Also *adj.*—*n.* Sublapsā'rianism, a doctrine of moderate Calvinists, that God permitted the fall of Adam without preordaining it. [L. *sub*, *lāpsus*, fall.]

sublate, *sub-lāt'*, *v.t.* (*obs.*) to remove: (*log.*) to deny: (*phil.*) to resolve in a higher unity.—*n.* sublā'tion. [L. *sublātum*, used as supine of *tollĕre*, to take away—*sub* in sense of away, *lātum*.]

sublime, *səb-līm′*, *adj.* set aloft (passing into *adv.*): lifted on high: exalted: lofty: majestic: elate: blindly supercilious: supreme: of the highest or noblest nature: awakening feelings of awe and veneration: (*anat.*) just under the skin.—*n.* that which is sublime: the lofty or grand in thought or style: the supreme degree.—*v.t.* to raise aloft: to exalt: to transmute into something higher: to subject to, or obtain by, sublimation: to deposit as a sublimate: to purify as by sublimation.—*v.i.* to undergo sublimation.—*adj.* **sublīm′able.**—*v.t.* **sublimate** (*sub′lim-āt*), to elevate: to sublime: to purify by sublimation: to transmute into something higher: to direct into a higher channel. —*n.* a product of sublimation, esp. corrosive sublimate.—*adj.* sublimed or sublimated.—*adj.* **sub′limated.**—*n.* **sublimā′tion,** change from solid to vapour without passing through the liquid state —usu. with subsequent change back to solid: a sublimate: purification by this process: elevation: ecstasy: the acme, height: transmutation into something higher: the unconscious diversion towards higher aims of the energy attaching to an instinct.—*adj.* **sublimed** (*səb-līmd′*).—*adv.* **sublime′ly.** — *n.* **sublime′ness.** — *n.* and *adj.* **sublīm′ing.**—*v.t.* **sublimise** (*sub′lim-*), to exalt: to purify: to refine: to make sublime.—*n.* **sublimity** (*səb-lim′*), loftiness: elevation: grandeur: nobleness of nature, thought, execution: the emotion of awe and veneration: that which evokes it: the summit, height, acme. [L. *sublīmis,* exalted, *sublīmāre, -ātum,* to exalt; origin unknown.]

subliminal, *sub-lim′in-əl, adj.* beneath the threshold of consciousness, subconscious. [L. *sub,* under, *līmen, -inis,* threshold.]

submental, *sub-ment′əl, adj.* below the chin: of the submentum.—*n.* **sub′mentum,** the basal part of the lower lip in insects. [L. *sub,* under, *mentum,* chin.]

submerge, *səb-mərj′, v.t.* to put under the surface of liquid: to sink: to cover over with liquid.—*v.i.* to sink under the surface of liquid.—*adj.* **submerged,** sunk: entirely under the surface of liquid: growing under water, submersed: (*fig.*) sunk hopelessly in poverty and misery.—*ns.* **submerge′-ment** (*rare*), **submerg′ence,** submersion.—*adj.* **submerg′ible,** submersible.—*n.* **submergibil′ity.** —*v.t.* **submerse** (*-mərs′*), to submerge.—*adj.* **submersed′,** (*bot.*) growing quite under water.— *n.* **submers′ibility.**—*adj.* **submers′ible,** capable of being submerged at will.—*n.* a submersible boat. —*n.* **submer′sion** (*-shən*), act of submerging: state or fact of being submerged. [L. *submergĕre, -mersum—sub, mergĕre,* to plunge.]

submit, *səb-mit′, v.t.* to yield, resign: to subordinate: to subject: to refer for decision, consideration, sanction, arbitration, &c.: to put forward in respectful contention: to lodge: (*obs.*) to lower, lay down.—*v.i.* to yield: to surrender: to be resigned: to consent—*pr.p.* **submitt′ing;** *pa.t.* and *pa.p.* **submitt′ed.**—*adjs.* **submiss′,** (*arch.*) submissive: subdued, low-toned: **submiss′ible.**—*n.* **submission** (*-mish′ən*), act of submitting: reference, or agreement to refer, to arbitration: a view submitted: resignedness: submissiveness: surrender: (*Shak.*) confession.— *adj.* **submiss′ive,** willing or ready to submit: yielding.—*adv.* **submiss′ively.**—*n.* **submiss′iveness.**—*adv.* **submiss′ly** (*arch.*).—*n.* **submiss′ness** (*arch.*).—*adj.* **submitt′ed.**—*n.* **submitt′er.**—*n.* and *adj.* **submitt′ing.**

suborn, *səb-orn′, v.t.* to bribe or procure to commit perjury or other unlawful or wrongful act: to prepare, provide, or achieve by stealthy means.— *ns.* **subornā′tion** (*sub-or-*); **suborn′er** (*səb-*). [L. *sub,* in sense of secret, *ornāre,* to equip.]

subpanation, *sub-pan-ā′shən, n.* the doctrine that the body and blood of Christ are locally and materially present in the eucharist under the form of bread and wine. [L. *sub,* under, *pānis,* bread.]

subpoena, *sub-* or *sə-pē′nä, n.* a writ commanding attendance in court under a penalty (L. *sub poenā*). —*v.t.* to serve with such a writ:—*pa.t.* and *pa.p.* **subpoe′na'd.**

subreption, *sub-rep′shən, n.* procuring an advantage (esp., *Scots law,* a gift of escheat) by concealing the truth (distinguished from *obreption*): false inference from such a concealment.—*adjs.* **subreptitious** (*-tish′əs*), obtained by subreption; **subrep′tive,** surreptitious: (*phil.*) arising out of obscure and unconscious suggestions of experience. [L. *subreptiō, -ōnis—sub-,* secretly, *rapĕre,* to snatch; cf. **surreptitious.**]

subrogate, *sub′rō-gāt,* or *-rə-, v.t.* to substitute: (*legal*) to put in place of another, as successor to his rights.—*n.* **subrogā′tion.** [See **surrogate.**]

subscribe, *səb-skrīb′, v.t.* to write beneath: to sign (*orig.* and *esp.* at the bottom): (*Shak.*) to set down, declare, in writing: to profess to be (by signing): to declare assent to: to make a signed promise of payment for: to contribute: (*Shak.*) to give up by signing.—*v.i.* to sign one's name: to assent: (*Shak.*) to submit: to make acknowledgment: to undertake to answer: to contribute money: to put one's name down as a purchaser or donor: to make periodical payments by arrangement. — *adjs.* **subscrīb′able; subscribed′.** — *n.* **subscrīb′er.** — *n.* and *adj.* **subscrīb′ing.**—*adj.* **sub′script,** written beneath, esp. the iota under a Greek long vowel, in ᾳ, ῃ, ῳ.—*n.* **subscrip′tion,** an act of subscribing: that which is subscribed: a signature: assent: (*Shak.*) submission: a raising of money from subscribers: a method of sale to subscribers: a contribution to a fund, society, &c.: a membership fee.—*adj.* **subscrip′tive.** [L. *subscrībĕre—sub, scrībĕre,* to write.]

subsecive, *sub′si-siv, adj.* remaining over: spare. [L. *subsecīvus—sub, secāre,* to cut.]

subsellium, *sub-sel′i-əm, n.* a misericord:—*pl.* **subsell′ia.** [L., a low bench—*sub, sella,* seat.]

subsequent, *sub′si-kwənt, adj.* following or coming after: of a stream, flowing approximately at right angles to the original slope of the land—distinguished from *consequent* and *obsequent.* — Also *adv.* (with *to*) after.—*n.* **sub′sequence.**—*adj.* **subsequential** (*-kwen′shl*), subsequent.—*adv.* **sub′sequently.** [L. *subsequēns, -entis,* pr.p. of *subsequī—sub,* under, after, *sequī,* to follow.]

subserve, *sub-sərv′, v.t.* to help forward.—*v.i.* to help in a subordinate way: (*Milt.*) to be subordinate.—*ns.* **subser′vience, subser′viency.**—*adj.* **subser′vient,** subserving: serving to promote: subject: slavish: obsequious.—*n.* a subservient person or thing.—*adv.* **subser′viently.** [L. *subservīre—sub,* under, *servīre,* to serve.]

subside, *səb-sīd′, v.i.* to settle, sink down: to fall into a state of quiet.—*ns.* **subsidence** (*sub′si-dəns,* sometimes *səb-sī′dəns*), rarely **sub′sidency** (or *-sī′*), process of subsiding, settling, or sinking. [L. *subsidĕre—sub,* down, *sīdĕre,* to settle.]

subsidy, *sub′si-di, n.* (*obs.*) assistance: aid in money : (*hist.*) a special parliamentary grant of money to the king: a payment exacted by a king or feudal lord: a grant of public money in aid of some enterprise, industry, &c., or to keep down the price of a commodity, or from one state to another. —*adv.* **subsid′iarily.**—*adj.* **subsid′iary,** furnishing a subsidy, help, or additional supplies: aiding: subordinate: relating to or depending on subsidies —*n.* one who, or that which, aids or supplies: an assistant: a subordinate.—*v.t.* **sub′sidise,** to furnish with a subsidy, grant, or regular allowance to purchase the aid of, to buy over: to pay for as mercenaries.—**subsidiary company,** one of which another company holds most of the shares; **subsidiary troops,** mercenaries. [L. *subsidium,* orig. troops stationed behind in reserve, aid—*sub,* under, *sīdĕre,* to settle.]

subsist, *səb-sist′, v.i.* to have existence: to remain, continue: (*Milt.*) to hold out, stand fast: to inhere: to have the means of living.—*n.* **subsist′ence,** state of being subsistent: real being: means of support, ing life: livelihood.—*adjs.* **subsist′ent,** subsisting, having real being: inherent; **subsistential** (*sub-sis-ten′shl*).—**subsistence money,** part of wages paid in advance for immediate needs—colloquially known as **sub:** a special allowance for exceptional circumstances. [L. *subsistĕre,* to stand still—*sub,* under, *sistĕre,* to stand.]

substance, *sub′stəns, n.* that in which qualities

attributes exist, the existence to which qualities belong: that which constitutes anything what it is: the principal part: gist: subject-matter: body: matter: kind of matter, esp. one of definite chemical nature: (*Shak.*) amount: wealth, property: solidity, body: solid worth: foundation, ground.—*adj.* **substantial** (*səb-stan'shl*), of or having substance: being a substance: essential: in essentials: actually existing: real: corporeal, material: solid and ample: massy and stable: solidly based: durable: enduring: firm, stout, strong: considerable in amount: well-to-do: of sound worth.—*v.t.* **substan'tialise**, to give reality to.—*ns.* **substan'tialism**, the theory that there is a real existence or substratum underlying phenomena: **substantiality** (*-shi-al'i-ti*).—*adv.* **substan'tially.**—*n.* **substan'tialness.**—*n.pl.* **substan'tials**, essential parts.—*v.t.* **substan'tiate** (*-shi-āt*), to make substantial: to embody: to prove or confirm.—*n.* **substantiā'tion.**—*adj.* **substantival** (*sub-stən-tī'vl*), of, of the nature of, a substantive.—*adv.* **substantiv'ally.**—*adj.* **sub'stantive** (*-tiv*), relating to substance: expressing existence: real: of real, independent importance: substantival: (of dyes) taking effect without a mordant: definite and permanent: considerable in amount.—*n.* (*gram.*) a noun.—*adv.* **sub'stantively.**—*n.* **sub'-stantiveness.**—*v.t.* **sub'stantivise**, to turn into a noun.—*n.* **substantiv'ity**, substantiality: affinity for a dye-stuff. [L. *substantia*, substance, essence, property—*sub*, under, *stāre*, to stand.]

substitute, *sub'sti-tūt*, *n.* a deputy: (*Shak.*) a proxy: one nominated in remainder: one put in place of another: a thing used instead of another.—*v.t.* to put in place of another: to appoint as deputy: to nominate in remainder: to put in place of another: to use instead of something else: (*erron.*) to replace, be a substitute for.—*v.t.* (*U.S.*) to act as substitute.—*adj.* **sub'stituted.**—*n.* **substitū'-tion**, (*Shak.*) delegation: act of substituting: condition of being a substitute: (*chem.*) the substituting of one atom or radical for another without breaking up the molecule.—*adjs.* **substitū'tional**, **substitū'tionary.**—*adv.* **substitū'tionally.**—*adj.* **sub'stitutive.**—**substitution product**, a substance got by substitution of so many equivalents for certain atoms or groups. [L. *substituĕre*, *-ūtum*—*sub*, under, *statuĕre*, to set.]

substract, *səb-strakt'*, *v.t.* (now illiterate) to subtract.—*ns.* **substrac'tion** (now illiterate): **substrac'tor**, (*Shak.*) a detractor. [L.L. *substrahĕre*, *substractum*, for L. *subtrahĕre*, after the model of **abstract**.]

substratum, *sub-strā'təm*, *n.* the substance in which qualities inhere: a basis, foundation, ground: the material in which a plant grows or on which an animal moves or rests: an underlying layer:—*pl.* **substrā'ta.**—*adj.* **substrā'tal.**—*n.* **sub'strate**, a substratum: a base: the substance on which an enzyme acts. [L. *substernĕre*, *-strātum*—*sub*, *sternĕre*, to spread.]

substyle, *sub'stīl*, *n.* the straight line on which the style of a dial is erected.—*adj.* **sub'stylar** (or *-stī'*).

subsultive, *sub-sult'iv*, **subsultory**, *-ər-i*, *adjs.* moving by starts: twitching.—*adv.* **subsult'orily.**—*n.* **subsult'us**, a convulsive movement. [L. *subsultāre*, to jump, hop—*sub*, up, *salīre*, to leap.]

subsume, *sub-sūm'*, *v.t.* to state as minor premiss: to take in under a more general term or proposition: to include in something larger.—*n.* **subsumption** (*səb-sump'shən*).—*adj.* **subsump'tive.** [L. *sub*, under, *sūmĕre*, to take.]

subtend, *səb-tend'*, *v.t.* (*geom.*) to be opposite to: (*bot.*) to have in the axil.—*n.* **subtense'**, a subtending line.—*adj.* placed so as to subtend an angle, as a rod used as base in tacheometry. [L. *sub*, under, *tendĕre*, *tentum* or *tēnsum*, to stretch.]

subter-, *sub'tər-*, *pfx.* under.—*adjs.* **subterhū'man**, less than human: below man: **subterjā'cent**, subjacent: **subternat'ural**, below nature, less than natural.—*n.* **subterposi'tion**, position or placing underneath.—*adj.* **subtersen'suous**, below the level of sense. [L. *subter*, under.]

subterfuge, *sub'tər-fūj*, *n.* an evasive device, esp. in discussion: (*obs.*) a refuge. [L. *subter*, *fugĕre*, to take flight.]

subterranean, *sub-tə-rā'ni-ən*, *adj.* underground.—*n.* a dweller underground: an underground chamber or dwelling.—*adj.* **subterrā'neous**, underground.—*adv.* **subterrā'neously.**—*adj.* **subterrene'**, underground.—*n.* an underground dwelling: the underworld.—*adj.* **subterres'trial.** [L. *sub*, under, *terra*, the earth.]

subtil, subtile, *sut'l.* Same as **subtle.**

subtle, also (slightly *arch.*, and used chiefly in physical senses) **subtil, subtile,** *sut'l*, (*Milt.*) **suttle,** *sut'l*, *adj.* fine, delicate, thin: tenuous: rarefied: impalpable: elusive: showing or calling for fine discrimination: nice: overrefined or overrefining: abstruse: cunning: ingenious: crafty: insidious: penetrating: (*Shak.*) ticklish, tricky.—*adj.* **subt'ile-witt'ed** (*Shak.*).—*n.* **subtilisā'tion** (*sut-*).—*v.t.* **subtilise** (*sut'*), to rarefy: to refine: to make subtle.—*v.i.* to refine, use subtlety.—*ns.* **subt'leness**, also **subt'il(e)ness**, **subtlety**, also **subt'il(e)ty** (*sut'l-ti*; *Milt.* **suttletie**), **subtility** (*sub-til'i-ti*), state or quality of being subtle: a subtle trick or refinement: (*cookery*, *obs.*) an ornamental device in sugar: **subt'list**, one who practises subtleties.—*adv.* **subt'ly**, also **subt'il(e)ly.** [O.Fr. *soutil* and its source L. *subtilis*—*sub*, under, *tēla*, a web.]

subtract, *səb-trakt'*, *v.t.* to withdraw, remove: to withhold: (*math.*) to take from another quantity so as to find the difference.—*n.* **subtrac'tion**, withdrawal, removal: withholding, esp. in violation of a right: (*math.*) the operation of finding the difference between two quantities by taking one from the other.—*adj.* **subtract'ive**, indicating, tending towards, of the nature of, subtraction: negative.—*ns.* **subtract'or**, a light-filter to eliminate a particular colour: **subtrahend** (*sub'tra-hend*), that which is to be subtracted. [L. *sub-*, in sense of away, *trahĕre*, *tractum*, to draw, gerundive *trahendus*, requiring to be drawn.]

subtrist, *sub-trist'*, *adj.* somewhat sad. [L. *sub-trīstis*—*sub*, *trīstis*, sad.]

subtrude, *sub-trōōd'*, *v.i.* to push in stealthily. [L. *sub*, in sense of secretly, *trūdĕre*, to thrust.]

subucula, *sub-ū'kū-lä* (L. *soob-ōō-koo-lä*), *n.* a Roman man's under-garment or shirt: in the early English Church, a kind of cassock worn under the alb. [L. *subūcula*—*sub*, and the root of *induĕre*, to put on, *exuĕre*, to take off.]

subulate, *sū'bū-lāt*, *adj.* awl-shaped. [L. *sūbula*, an awl.]

suburb, *sub'ərb*, *n.* a district adjoining a town: (in *pl.*) the outskirts of a town, esp. formerly as the prostitutes' quarters: confines, outskirts generally.—*adj.* suburban: characteristic of the suburbs.—*adj.* **suburban** (*səb-ur'bən*), situated or living in the suburbs: typical of the suburbs: without the good qualities either of town or country: smug, comfortable, half-cultured, narrow in outlook.—*n.* one living in a suburb.—*n.* **suburbanisā'tion.**—*v.t.* **subur'banise**, to make suburban.—*ns.* **subur'banism**, the state of being suburban: **suburbanity** (*sub-ur-ban'i-ti*), suburban quality: **suburbanism**, a suburban place: **subur'bia**, the suburban world.—*adj.* **suburbicā'rian**, being near the city, esp. of the dioceses and churches of the cardinal bishops in the suburbs of Rome. [L. *suburbium*—*sub*, under, near, *urbs*, a city.]

subvention, *sab-ven'shən*, *n.* a grant of money in aid. [L. *subventiō*, *-ōnis*, a coming to help—*sub*, *venīre*, *ventum*, to come.]

subvert, *səb-vərt'*, *v.t.* to overthrow: to overturn: to pervert.—*n.* **subver'sal.**—*v.t.* **subverse'** (*obs.*; *pa.p.* and *adj.* in *Spens.* **subverst'**).—*n.* **subver'sion**, overthrow: ruin.—*adjs.* **subver'sionary**, **subver'sive**, tending to overthrow.—*n.* **subvert'er.** [L. *sub*, under, *vertĕre*, *versum*, to turn.]

subway, *sub'wā*, *n.* a tunnel for foot-passengers: an underground passage for water-pipes, gas-pipes, sewers, &c.: (esp. *U.S.*) an underground railway.

succade, *suk-ād'*, *n.* fruit or vegetable candied or in syrup. [A.Fr. *sukade*, perh.—L. *succus*, juice.]

succedaneum, *suk-si-dā'ni-əm*, *n.* a substitute.—*adj.* **succedā'neous**, serving as a substitute. [L., neut. of *succēdāneus*—*succēdĕre*, to come after.]

succeed, *sək-sēd'*, *v.t.* to come after: to follow up

or in order : to follow : to take the place of, esp. in office, title, or possession : (*Shak.*) to inherit : (*obs.*) to cause to succeed.—*v.i.* to follow in order : to take the place of another (often with *to*) : (*Shak.*) to devolve, pass in succession : to turn out : to turn out well : to prosper : to obtain one's wish or accomplish what is attempted : to avail, be successful (with *in*) : (*Spens.*) to approach.—*ns.* succeed′er, one who is successful : a successor.—*adj.* succeed′ing.—*n.* success (sak-ses′), fortune (good or bad): upshot: prosperous progress, achievement, or termination: prosperity: attainment of wealth and influence : a successful person, book, affair, &c.: (*obs.*) sequence : (*obs.*) succession.— *adv.* success′antly, (*Shak.*) in succession.—*adj.* success′ful, resulting in success: achieving, having achieved, or having, the desired effect or termination : prosperous.—*adv.* success′fully, with success : (*Shak.*) with promise of success.—*ns.* success′fulness ; succession (-sesh′an), a coming after or following : a coming into another's place : a sequence in time or place : law, recognised mode, right, order, or turn, of succeeding one to another : in Roman and Scots law, the taking of property by one person in place of another : rotation of crops : heirs collectively : posterity.—*adj.* success′ional.—*adv.* success′ionally.—*n.* success′ionist, a believer in the necessity of Apostolic succession.—*adjs.* success′ionless ; successive (sak-ses′iv ; *Shak.* suk′), coming in succession or in order : (*obs.*) hereditary.—*adv.* success′ively. —*n.* success′iveness.—*adj.* success′less.—*adv.* success′lessly. — *ns.* success′lessness ; success′or (*Shak.* suk′), one who, or that which, succeeds or comes after : sometimes, one appointed to succeed ; success′orship.—**plant succession,** a series of vegetation types following one another in the same region ; **succession duty,** a tax imposed on succession to property, varying with the degree of relationship ; **succession house,** a forcing-house in a graded series, in which plants are moved on from one to the next ; **succession states,** states resulting from the break-up of Austria and Hungary. [L. *succēdĕre, -cessum—sub-,* in sense of near, next after, *cēdĕre,* to go.]

succentor, sak-sent′ar, *n.* a subcantor : the bass soloist in a choir. [L. *succentor—succinĕre—sub,* under, *canĕre,* to sing.]

succinct, sak-, suk-singkt′, *adj.* (*arch.* and *poet.*) girded up : close-fitting : concise.—*adv.* succinct′ly.—*ns.* succinct′ness ; succinctō′rium, succinct′ory, a band embroidered with an Agnus Dei, worn hanging from the girdle by the pope on some occasions. [L. *succinctus—sub,* up, *cingĕre,* to gird.]

succinum, suk′sin-am, *n.* amber.—*n.* suc′cinate, a salt of succinic acid.—*adj.* succin′ic, of, relating to, or got from, amber.—*n.* suc′cinite, amber, esp. a variety from which succinic acid was first got.— **succinic acid,** an acid, $C_4H_6O_4$, got from resins, &c. [L. *succinum,* amber.]

succory, suk′ar-i, *n.* a variant of chicory.

succotash, suk′ō-tash, *n.* a stew of green Indian corn and beans and sometimes pork. [Narragansett *msiquatash.*]

succour, suk′ar, *v.t.* to aid in distress : to relieve.— *n.* aid : relief.—*adj.* succ′ourable.—*n.* succ′ourer. —*adj.* succ′ourless. [A.Fr. *socorre*—L. *succurrēre,* to run to help—*sub,* up, *currĕre,* to run.]

succubus, suk′ū-bas, **succuba,** -bä, *ns.* a devil supposed to assume a female body and consort with men in their sleep : a strumpet :—*pl.* succ′ubuses, succ′ubas, succ′ubī, succ′ubae (-bē).— *adjs.* succ′ubine, of a succuba ; succ′ubous, (*bot.*) having the lower leaf-margin overlapping the leaf below. [L. *succuba,* a whore—*sub,* under, *cubāre,* to lie.]

succulent, suk′ū-lant, *adj.* juicy : sappy : (*bot.*) juicy and fleshy, or (loosely) merely fleshy.—*n.* a succulent plant.—*ns.* succ′ulence, succ′ulency ; succ′ulent-house′, a house for succulent plants. —*adv.* succ′ulently. [L. *sūculentus—sūcus,* juice.]

succumb, sa-kum′, *v.i.* to lie down under or sink under pressure, difficulty, temptation, &c. (often with *to*): to die. [L. *sub,* under, *cumbĕre,* to lie down.]

succursal, suk-ar′sl, *adj.* subsidiary : branch.—*n.* a branch of an institution (often as Fr. fem. **succursale,** sü-kür-sál). [Fr.,—L. *succurrĕre,* to succour.]

succus, suk′as, *n.* juice : fluid secretion of a gland : expressed juice :—*pl.* succi (suk′sī).—*adj.* succ′ous. [L. *sūcus,* juice.]

succuss, suk-us′, *v.t.* to shake up.—*ns.* succussā′tion, a shaking up: (*obs.*) a horse's trot ; succussion (-ush′an), a shaking : a shock : a shaking of the thorax to detect pleural effusion.—*adj.* succuss′ive. [L. *succutĕre, succussum,* to toss up— *sub, quatĕre,* to shake.]

such, such, *adj.* of that kind, the like kind, or the same kind (often followed by *as* or by a clause beginning with *that*): so characterised : of what kind : what (exclamatorily) : so great : beforementioned : some particular but unspecified.— *adv.* so (preceding the indefinite article if any).— *pron.* such a person, persons, thing, or things : the before-mentioned : that.—*adj.* such′-and-such, this or that, some, some or other (before the indefinite article if any).—*pron.* such-and-such a person.—*adj.* such′like, of such a kind.—*pron.* suchlike persons or things (or person or thing). —*n.* such′ness, quality.—*adv.* such′wise, in such a manner.—**such as,** for example ; **such as it is,** being what it is (and no better). [O.E. *swilc* ; cog. with Goth. *swaleiks* ; cf. **so, like.**]

suck, suk, *v.t.* to draw in with the mouth : to draw something (esp. milk) from with the mouth : to apply to or hold in the mouth and perform the movements of sucking: to draw by suction : to render by suction : to absorb : to draw in : to extract : to imbibe : to drain.—*v.i.* to draw with the mouth : to draw the breast : to draw by suction : to make a noise of sucking : to draw in air as a dry pump : to draw in : to engulf.—*n.* act or spell of sucking : milk drawn from the breast : suction : (*slang*) a short drink, esp. a dram of spirits.—*adj.* sucked.—*n.* suck′er, one who, or that which, sucks, a sucking-pig, new-born whale, or other unweaned animal : a sucking-fish : an American fish akin to the carps, that feeds by sucking up small animals from the bottom : an adhesive organ : a device that adheres, draws water, &c., by suction, as a pump piston : a toy consisting of a leather disk and a string, for lifting stones, &c.: a haustorium or other sucking organ : (*local*) a sweet for sucking : a shoot rising from underground and developing into a new plant : a new shoot : a parasite, toady, sponge : a hard drinker : (*U.S.*) a greenhorn : (*U.S.*) a native of Illinois.— *v.t.* to strip off superfluous shoots from.—*v.i.* to develop suckers.—*adj.* suck′ered, having suckers. —*n.* suck-in′, (*slang*) a disconcerting disappointment.—*n.* and *adj.* suck′ing.—*ns.* suck′ingbottle, a milk bottle for infants ; suck′ing-fish, remora or other fish with an adhesive disk, e.g. a lumpsucker ; suck′ing-pig, a young milk-fed pig. —**suck up to,** (*slang*) to toady to. [O.E. *sūcan, sūgan* ; Ger. *saugen* ; cf. L. *sūgĕre.*]

sucken, suk′n, *n.* (Scots law) the district or population thirled to a mill : thirlage : an area of jurisdiction or field of operation.—*n.* suck′ener, a tenant so bound. [**soken** (see **soc.**)]

sucket, suk′it, an obs. form of **succade.**

suckle, suk′l, *v.t.* to give suck to : to put out to suck.—*n.* suck′ler, an animal that suckles : a suckling.—*n.pl.* suck′lers, heads of clover.—*n.* suck′ling, an unweaned child or animal : the act of giving suck : (*dial.*) clover, also honeysuckle.— *adj.* giving suck : putting to suck : sucking. [**suck.**]

sucre, sōō′krā, *n.* the monetary unit of Ecuador. [Named after Antonio José de Sucre (1795-1830).]

sucrose, s(y)ōō′krōs, *n.* cane-sugar ($C_{12}H_{22}O_{11}$) from any source. [Fr. *sucre,* sugar.]

suction, suk′shon, *n.* act or power of sucking or of drawing or adhesion by reducing pressure of air.— *n.pl.* **Suctoria** (suk-tō′ri-ä), a subclass of Ciliata. —*adj.* suctō′rial, adapted for sucking. [L. *sūgĕre, sūctum* ; related to **suck.**]

sucurujú, sōō-kōō-rōō-zhōō′, *n.* a S. American Indian name for the anaconda.

sudamina, s(y)ōō-dam′i-nä, *n.pl.* whitish vesicles due to retention of sweat in the sweat-glands :—

sing. **sudamen** (-dā'mən).—*adj.* **sudam'inal.** [L. *sūdāmen*, pl. *sūdāmina—sūdāre*, to sweat.]

sudate, s(y)ōō'dāt, *v.i.* (*rare*) to sweat.—*ns.* **sudā'-rium,** su'dary (-*ə-ri*), a cloth for wiping sweat: a handkerchief : a veronica ; **sudā'tion,** sweating : sweat : a watery exudation from plants ; **suda-torium** (-*də-to'ri-əm*), a sweating-room ; **su'da-tory** (-*tə-ri*), a sudatorium.—*adj.* of sweat : inducing sweating. [L. *sūdāre, -ātum*, to sweat.]

sudd, sud, *n.* a mass of floating vegetable matter obstructing the White Nile : a temporary dam. [Ar. *sudd*, obstruction.]

sudden, sud'n, *adj.* without warning or apparent preparation: unexpected: hasty: abrupt: prompt: swift in action or production : glancing quickly : improvised.—*adv.* suddenly.—*adv.* **sudd'enly.**—*ns.* **sudd'enness,** (*Scot.*) **sudd'enty**—(all) on a sudden, of a (or the) sudden, all at once. [A.Fr. *sodain*—L. *subitāneus*, sudden—*subitus*, coming stealthily—*subīre, -ītum*, to go stealthily—*sub, īre.*]

sudder, sud'ər, *adj.* (in India) chief.—*n.* a supreme court. [Ar. *çadr*, chief.]

sudor, s(y)ōō'dor, -*dor*, *n.* (*med.*) sweat.—*adjs.* **sudorif'erous,** provoking or secreting sweat ; **sudorif'ic,** causing sweat.—*n.* a diaphoretic.—*adjs.* **sudorip'arous,** secreting sweat ; **su'dorous,** sweaty. [L. *sūdor, -ōris*, sweat.]

Sudra, sōō'drä, *n.* a member of the fourth and lowest of the Hindu castes. [Sans. *śūdra*.]

suds, sudz, *n.pl.* froth of soapy water (rarely in *sing.* sud). [Prob. conn. with **seethe**.]

sue, s(y)ōō, (*obs.* ; *Spens.* **sew**), *v.t.* to follow: to prosecute at law: to petition for, apply for : (*arch.*) to court.—*v.i.* to make legal claim: to make application: to entreat: (*Shak.*) to be a wooer: (*Spens.*) to do service : —*pr.p.* su'ing ; *pa.t.* and *pa.p.* sued.—*n.* sueabil'ity (see **suability**).—*adj.* **sue'able** (see **suable**).—*n.* and *adj.* **su'ing—sue out,** to petition for and take out. [O.Fr. *suir* (Fr. *suivre*)—L. *sequī, secūtus*, to follow.]

suède, swäd (Fr. *süed*), *n.* undressed kid: its colour. —Also *adj.* [Fr. (*gants de*) *Suède*, (gloves of) Sweden.]

suet, s(y)ōō'it, *n.* a solid fatty tissue, accumulating about the kidneys and omentum of the ox, sheep, &c.—*adj.* **su'ety** (also **su'etty**). [O.Fr. *seu* (Fr. *suif*)—L. *sēbum*, fat.]

suffer, suf'ər, *v.t.* to undergo: to endure: to be affected by: to permit : (*Shak.*) to inflict pain on.— *v.i.* to feel pain or punishment: to sustain loss : to be injured: to die : to be executed or martyred : to be the object of an action.—*adj.* **suff'erable.**—*n.* **suff'erableness.**—*adv.* **suff'erably.**—*ns.* **suff'-erance,** suffering : endurance : forbearance : tacit assent: permission: toleration ; **suff'erer.**—*n.* and *adj.* **suff'ering.** [L. *sufferre*—*sub*, under, *ferre*, to bear.]

suffete, suf'ēt, *n.* one of the chief administrative officials of ancient Carthage. [L. *sūfes, -etis*, from a Punic word.]

suffice, sə-fīs', *v.i.* to be enough : to be competent or adequate.—*v.t.* to satisfy.—*ns.* **sufficience** (*sə-fish'əns* ; *rare*), **-cy,** state of being sufficient : competence : ability : capacity : a sufficient quantity: means enough for a comfortable living, a competency : conceit.—*adj.* **suffic'ient,** sufficing : competent : adequate : effective : well-to-do : (not a satisfactory word for *enough* in quantity).—*n.* (*coll.* or slightly *vulg.*) a sufficient quantity, enough. —*adv.* **suffic'iently.**—*adj.* **suffic'ing.**—*ns.* **suffic'-ingness** ; **suffisance** (*suf'i-zəns* ; *obs.*), sufficiency : satisfaction : enjoyment.—**suffice it,** be it enough. [Through Fr.—L. *sufficĕre*, to suffice—*sub, facĕre*, to make.]

suffigance, suf'i-gans, *n.* (Shak., *Much Ado*) Dogberry's blunder for **suffisance**.

suffix, suf'iks, *n.* a syllable or other addition at the end of a word : (*math.*) an index placed after and below a symbol, as *n* in *xₙ*.—*v.t.* **suffix'**, to add as a suffix : to subjoin. [L. *suffixus—sub*, under, *fīgĕre*, to fix.]

suffocate, suf'ə-kāt, *v.t.* and *v.i.* to choke by stopping of the breath : to stifle.—*adj.* (*Shak.*) suffocated.— *n.* and *adj.* **suff'ocating.**—*adv.* **suff'ocatingly.**— *n.* **suffocā'tion.**—*adj.* **suff'ocative,** tending to

suffocate. [L. *suffocāre—sub*, under, *faucēs*, the throat.]

suffragan, suf'rə-gən, *n.* an assistant : a coadjutor-bishop: any bishop in relation to his metropolitan. —Also *adj.*—*n.* **suff'raganship.** [L.L. *suffrā-gāneus*, assistant, supporting—L. *suffrāgium*, a vote.]

suffrage, suf'rij, *n.* a prayer, esp. for the dead, or in a litany: a vote : a voting paper, pebble, or the like : sanction : supporting opinion : power of voting.—*ns.* **suffragette** (*suf'rə-jet'* ; an improperly formed word), a woman seeking by violent methods (or sometimes otherwise) to obtain votes for women ; **suff'ragist,** a believer in the right (e.g. of women) to vote. [L. *suffrāgium*, a vote.]

suffruticose, sə-frōōt'i-kōs, *adj.* herbaceous with woody persistent stem-base. [L. *sub*, under, *frutex, -icis*, a shrub.]

suffumigate, sə-fū'mi-gāt, *v.t.* to fumigate from below.—*n.* **suffumiga'tion.** [L. *sub, fūmigāre.*]

suffuse, sə-fūz', *v.t.* to pour over : to overspread or cover, as with a liquid, a tint.—*adj.* (*sə-fus'* ; *bot.*) spread out on the substratum.—*n.* **suffū'sion** (-*zhən*). [L. *sub*, underneath, *fundĕre, fūsum*, to pour.]

Sufi, sōō'fē, *n.* a pantheistic Mohammedan mystic :— *pl.* **Su'fis.**—*n.* **Suf(i)ism.**—*adjs.* **Su'fic, Suf(i)-ist'ic.** [Ar. *çūfī*, lit. man of wool—*çuf*, wool.]

sugar, shoog'ər, *n.* a sweet substance (*sucrose, cane-sugar*, $C_{12}H_{22}O_{11}$), obtained chiefly from cane and beet: extended to any member of the same class of carbohydrates.—*adj.* (*Shak.*) sweet : of sugar.— *v.t.* to sprinkle, coat, or mix with sugar.—*ns.* **sug'ar-ally** (-*ál'i* ; *Scot.*), liquorice ; **sug'ar-apple,** the sweet-sop ; **sug'ar-baker,** (*obs.*) a sugar-refiner : also a confectioner ; **sug'ar-basin, -bowl,** a small basin for holding sugar at table ; **sug'ar-bean,** the Lima bean ; **sug'ar-beet,** any variety of common beet, esp. variety *Rapa*, grown for sugar ; **sug'ar-can'dy,** sugar in large crystals ; **sug'ar-cane,** a woody grass (*Saccharum offici-narum*) from which sugar is chiefly obtained.—*adjs.* **sug'ar-coat'ed,** coated with sugar ; **sug'ared,** sweetened or coated with sugar : sugary.—*ns.* **sug'ar-grass,** sweet sorghum ; **sug'ar-gum,** a eucalyptus with sweetish foliage ; **sug'ar-house,** a sugar factory ; **sug'ariness** ; **sug'aring,** sweetening with sugar : coating trees with sugar as a method of collecting insects : (*U.S.*) formation of sugar from maple sap (*sugaring off*).—*adj.* **sug'ar-less.**—*ns.* **sug'ar-loaf,** a loaf or mass of sugar, usu. more or less cigar-shaped : a hill, hat, or other object of like form ; **sug'ar-ma'ple,** a N. American maple (*Acer saccharum* or kindred species) from whose sap sugar is made ; **sug'ar-mill,** a machine for pressing out the juice of the sugar-cane ; **sug'ar-mite,** a mite infesting unrefined sugar ; **sug'ar-palm,** a palm (of many kinds) yielding sugar ; **sug'ar-pine,** a Western American pine (*Pinus Lambertiana*) with sugary heart-wood ; **sug'ar-plum,** a small round boiled sweet : (*fig.*) a compliment or other gratification ; **sug'ar-refi'ner ; sug'ar-refi'nery ; sug'ar-refi'ning.**— *n.pl.* **sug'ar-tongs,** tongs for lifting lumps of sugar at table.—*n.* **sug'ar-wrack,** a kind of tangle (*Laminaria saccharina*) from which mannite is got.—*adj.* **sug'ary,** like sugar in taste or appearance : abounding in sugar: offensively or cloyingly sweet.—**sugar of lead,** lead acetate, sweet and poisonous. [O.Fr. (Fr.) *sucre*—Ar. *sukkar* ; the g unexplained ; cf. **Saccharum.**]

suggest, sə-jest', old-fashioned *sug-*, *v.t.* to intro-duce indirectly to the thoughts : to call up in the mind: to put forward, as a plan, hypothesis, thought, &c. : to give an impression of : (*Shak.*) to tempt : (*Shak.*) to insinuate : to influence hypnotically.—*v.i.* to make suggestions.—*ns.* **sug-gest'er ; suggestibil'ity.**—*adj.* **suggest'ible,** cap-able of being suggested, or of being influenced by suggestion, esp. hypnotic.—*ns.* **suggest'ion** (-*yən*), process or act of suggesting: hint: proposal: in-citement, temptation : (*law*) information without oath, not being pleadable : (*obs.*) a false or under-hand representation: communication of belief or impulse to a hypnotised person ; **suggestionisā'-tion.**—*v.t.* **suggest'ionise,** to subject to suggestion.

—*ns.* **suggest′ionism**, treatment by suggestion: the theory that hypnotic effects are entirely due to the action of suggestion; **suggest′ionist.**—*adj.* **suggest′ive**, containing a hint: fitted to suggest: awaking the mind: stimulating: pertaining to hypnotic suggestion: (*coll. euphemism*) tending to awake indecent imaginations.—*adv.* **suggest′ively.** —*n.* **suggest′iveness.** [L. *suggerĕre*, *-gestum*, *sub*, under, *gerĕre*, to carry.]

suicide, *s*(*y*)*ōō′i-sīd*, *n.* one who kills himself intentionally: self-murder.—*adj.* **suici′dal.**—*adv.* **suici′dally.** [L. *suī*, of himself, *caedĕre*, to kill.]

Suidae, *s*(*y*)*ōō′i-dē*, *n.pl.* the pig family. [L. *sūs*, *suis*, pig.]

suint, *swint*, *n.* the natural grease of wool. [Fr.]

suit, *s*(*y*)*ōōt*, *n.* (*Spens.*) pursuit: process or act of suing: an action at law: courtship: a petition: a series: (*obs.*) a suite: a sequence: a set: a set of cards of the same denomination, in the pack or in one hand: a number of things of the same kind or made to be used together, as clothes or armour. —*v.t.* (*obs.*) to attire: to provide, furnish: to fall in with the requirements of: to fit: to become: to please.—*v.i.* to agree: to correspond.—*n.* **suitabil′ity.**—*adj.* **suit′able**, that suits: fitting: accordant: adequate.—*n.* **suit′ableness.** — *adv.* **suit′ably.**—*n.* **suit′-case**, an easily portable oblong travelling-bag for carrying suits or clothes.—*adj.* **suit′ed**, (*Shak.*) clothed.—*ns.* **suit′ing** (usu. in *pl.*), cloth suitable for making suits; **suit′or**, one who sues: a petitioner: a wooer: (*fem.* **suit′ress**).—*v.i.* to play the suitor.—**follow suit**, to play a card of the suit led: to do the same. [Fr. *suite*; cf. **sue**, **suite**.]

suite, *swēt*, *n.* a train of followers or attendants: a set, as of furniture or rooms: a sequence of instrumental movements, usu. dance-tunes, in related keys: a sequel. [Fr.,—a L.L. form of L. *secūta*, fem. pa.p. of *sequī*, to follow.]

sulcus, *sul′kəs*, *n.* a groove, furrow, fissure:—*pl.* **sul′ci** (*-sī*).—*adj.* **sul′cal** (*kl*), of a sulcus: grooved: furrowed: pronounced with sulcal tongue.—*v.t.* **sul′calise**, to furrow.—*adjs.* **sul′cate, -d**, furrowed, grooved: with parallel longitudinal furrows.—*n.* **sulcā′tion.** [L. *sulcus*, a furrow.]

sulfate, sulfur, &c. American spellings of **sulphate, sulphur, &c.**

sulk, *sulk*, *v.i.* to be sullen.—*n.* one who sulks: (usu. in *pl.*) a fit of sulking.—*adv.* **sulk′ily.**—*n.* **sulk′iness.**—*adj.* **sulk′y**, sullen: inclined to sulk.—*n.* a light two-wheeled, sometimes bodiless, vehicle for one person. [Prob. from the root seen in O.E. *áseolcan*, to slack, be slow, pa.p. *ásolcen*.]

sullage, *sul′ij*, *n.* filth: refuse: scum: scoria: silt. [Perh. conn. with **sully**.]

sullen, *sul′ən*, *adj.* gloomily angry and silent: malignant, baleful: dark: dull.—*adv.* **sullenly.**—*n.* (usu. in *pl.*) a fit of sullenness, the sulks.—*adv.* **sull′enly.**—*n.* **sull′enness.** [App. through an O.Fr. deriv. from L. *sōlus*, alone.]

sully, *sul′i*, *v.t.* to soil: to spot: to tarnish.—*v.i.* to be soiled (*pr.p.* **sull′ying**; *pa.t.* and *pa.p.* **sull′ied**). —*n.* spot: tarnish. [O.E. *sylian*, to defile—*sol*, mud; or from O.Fr. *souiller*, to soil.]

sulphur, *sul′fər*, *n.* brimstone, a yellow non-metallic element (S; at. numb. 16) and mineral, very brittle, fusible, and inflammable: an impression from a plate spread with molten sulphur.— *adj.* of sulphur.—*v.t.* to treat or fumigate with sulphur.—*adj.* **sul′pha**, of a class of synthetic antibacterial drugs, the sulphonamides.—*ns.* **sulpha-guan′idine**, a sulphonamide used against dysentery, &c.; **sulphanil′amide**, a sulphonamide ($C_6H_8N_2O_2S$) used against bacteria; **sulphapy′ridine**, one of the sulphonamides known as M. and B. (M. and B. 693) which are effective against pneumonia, meningitis, &c.; **sul′phate**, a salt of sulphuric acid.—*v.t.* to form a deposit of lead sulphate on: to treat or impregnate with sulphur or a sulphate.—*v.i.* to become sulphated.—*n.* **sulpha-thī′azole**, a sulphonamide used against staphylococci.—*adj.* **sulphatic** (*-at′ik*).—*ns.* **sul′phide**, a compound of an element or radical with sulphur: a salt of hydrosulphuric acid; **sul′phite**, a salt of sulphurous acid (**sulphite pulp**, in paper-

making, wood chips treated with calcium or magnesium acid sulphite).—*pfx.* **sul′pho-**, sulphur: (*obs.*) for **thio-**.—*ns.* **sul′phonal**, a hypnotic ($CH_3)_2C(SO_2C_2H_5)_2$; **sulphon′amide**, an amide of a sulphonic acid, any of a group of drugs with antibacterial action; **sul′phone**, any of a class of subtances consisting of two organic radicals combined with SO_2.—*adj.* **sulphon′ic**, containing the group $SO_2 \cdot OH$.—*v.t.* **sul′phurāte**, to combine with, or subject to the action of, sulphur.—*ns.* **sulphurā′tion**; **sulphurā′tor**; **sul′phur-bac-te′ria**, bacteria that liberate sulphur from sulphuretted hydrogen, &c., and ultimately form sulphuric acid; **sul′phur-bottom**, the blue whale (from the yellowish spots underneath).—*adj.* **sulphu′reous**, sulphury: sulphur-yellow.—*adv.* **sulphu′reously.** —*ns.* **sulphu′reousness**; **sul′phuret**, (*obs.*) a sulphide.—*adjs.* **sul′phuretted**, combined with sulphur (**sulphuretted hydrogen**, hydrogen sulphide, H_2S); **sulphu′ric**, containing sulphur in higher valency—opp. to *sulphurous* (**sulphuric acid**, oil of vitriol, H_2SO_4, **sulphuric anhydride**, sulphur trioxide, SO_3); **sul′phurous** (*-fūr-* or *-fər-*), pertaining to, resembling, or containing sulphur: hellish: thundery: (*chem.*; *-fūr*) containing sulphur in lower valency (**sulphurous anhydride**, SO_2).—*ns.* **sul′phur-root, sul′phurwort**, an umbelliferous plant (Peucedanum, various species) akin to parsnip, with yellow flower and juice.—*adj.* **sulphury** (*sul′fər-i*), like sulphur. —*n.* and *adj.* **sul′phur-yell′ow**, pale yellow. [L. *sulphur*, *sulfur*, *sulpur*, *-uris*.]

sultan, *sul′tən*, *n.* a Mohammedan ruler, esp. the Ottoman emperor: the purple coot: a small white (orig. Turkish) variety of hen.—*ns.* **sultana** (*sul-* or *sol-tä′nä*), a lady of a sultan's harem: a king's mistress: a magnificent courtesan: a concubine: a fiddle strung with wire in pairs: a small, pale, seedless raisin; **sul′tanate**; **sul′taness.**—*adj.* **sultanic** (*sul-tan′ik*).—*n.* **sul′tanship.**—**sweet sultan, yellow sultan,** species of Centaurea. [Ar. *sultān*.]

sultry, *sul′tri*, *adj.* sweltering: close and oppressive. —*adv.* **sul′trily.**—*n.* **sul′triness.** [**swelter**.]

sum, *sum*, *n.* total: whole: aggregate: result of addition: amount: a quantity of money: a problem in addition, hence in arithmetic generally: chief points: substance or result: summary: height, culmination, completion.—*v.t.* to add: to make up the total of: to be an epitome of, exemplify in little: to summarise: to reckon up, form an estimate of: (*Milt.*) to complete the development of, bring to perfection.—*v.i.* to amount, turn out on adding: to do sums:—*pr.p.* **summ′ing**; *pa.t.* and *pa.p.* **summed.**—*adjs.* **sum′less**, not to be summed or counted: incalculable; **summed.**—*n.* **summ′er**, one who sums.— *n.* and *adj.* **summ′ing.**—*n.* **summ′ing-up**, a recapitulation or review of the leading points, a judge's summary survey of the evidence given to a jury before it withdraws to consider its verdict.— **in sum**, in short: to sum up; **sum and substance**, the gist: the essence; **sum of things**, the public weal: the universe; **sum total**, complete or final sum. [O.Fr. *summe*—L. *summa*—*summus*, highest.]

sumac, sumach, *sōō′, shōō′, sū′mak*, *n.* any tree or shrub of the genus Rhus, esp. *R. Coriaria*: the leaves and shoots used in dyeing. [Fr. *sumac* or L.L. *sumach*—Ar. *summāq*.]

sumatra, *sōō-mä′trä*, *n.* a short, violent squall about the Straits of Malacca, coming from Sumatra.

summa, *sum′ä*, *n.* a treatise giving a summary of a whole subject.—*adj.* **summar** (*sum′ər*; *Scot.*) summary (**Summar Roll**, a list of cases requiring dispatch).—*adv.* **summ′arily.**—*n.* **summ′ariness.** —*v.t.* **summ′arise**, to present in a summary or briefly.—*ns.* **summ′arist**, one who summarises.— *adj.* **summ′ary**, summed up or condensed: short: brief: compendious: done by a short method: without unnecessary formalities or delay, without further application to the court.—*n.* an abstract, abridgment, or compendium.—*n.* **summā′tion**, process of finding the sum: addition: accumulation: an aggregate. — *adjs.* **summā′tional;**

summ'ative, additive.—*n.* **summ'ist**, a writer of a summa: an epitomist. [L. *summa*, sum, *summārium*, a summary.]

summat, sum'ət, a dial. form of **somewhat**.

summer, sum'ər, *n.* the warmest season of the year: a spell of warm weather (see **Indian, St Luke's, St Martin's, summer**): a year of age or time.—*adj.* of, for, occurring in, summer.—*v.i.* to pass the summer.—*v.t.* to keep through the summer.—*ns.* **summ'er-house**, a structure in a garden for sitting in: a summer residence; **summ'ering.**—*adjs.* **summ'erlike**; **summ'erly**, warm and bright like summer; **summ'er-seeming**, (*Shak.*) perh. hot and passing, like summer.—*ns.* **summ'er-tide**, the summer season; **summ'ertime**, the summer season: **summer time**, time adopted (since 1916) for daylight-saving purposes—one hour (**double summer time**, two hours) in advance of Greenwich time.—*adj.* **summ'ery**, like summer: suitable for summer. [O.E. *sumer*, *sumor*; Du. *zomer*, Ger. *sommer*.]

summer, sum'ər, *n.* (*obs.*) a pack-horse, a sumpter-horse: a great horizontal beam or lintel (also **summ'er-tree**). [See **sumpter**.]

summerset. Same as **somersault**.

summit, sum'it, *n.* the highest point or degree: the top.—*adj.* **summ'itless.**—*n.* **summ'it-level**, the highest level. [O.Fr. *sommette*, *somet* (Fr. *sommet*), dim. of *som*—L. *summum*, highest.]

summon, sum'ən, *v.t.* to call up, forth, or together: to call upon to appear or to do something: to rouse to exertion.—*adj.* **summ'onable.**—*ns.* **summ'-oner**, one who summons: an officer who serves summonses: an apparitor; **summ'ons**, a summoning or an authoritative call: a call to appear, esp. in court: a call to surrender.—*v.t.* to serve with a summons. [O.Fr. *somoner*—L. *summonēre*—*sub-*, secretly, *monēre*, to warn: sense partly from O.E. *somnian*, to assemble.]

sump, sump, *n.* (now *dial.*) a bog, pool, puddle: a hole or depression that receives liquid, as for molten metal, for sea-water at a salt-work, drainage-water in a mine, oil in an engine. [Du. *somp*; Ger. *sumpf*.]

sumph, sumf, *n.* (*Scot.*) a soft sheepish fellow. —*adj.* **sumph'ish.**—*n.* **sumph'ishness**. [Origin unknown.]

sumpit, sum'pit, **sumpitan**, -*an*, *ns.* a Malay blow-pipe. [Malay.]

sumpsimus, sump'si-məs, *n.* a correct expression displacing an incorrect but common one. [L. *sūmpsimus*; see **mumpsimus**.]

sumpter, sum(p)'tər, *n.* a pack-horse. [O.Fr. *sommetier*, a pack-horse driver—Gr. *sagma*, a pack-saddle, *sattein*, to pack.]

sumptuary, sum(p)'tū-ər-i, *adj.* pertaining to or regulating expense.—*n.* **sumptuos'ity**, sumptuous-ness.—*adj.* **sump'tuous**, costly: magnificently luxurious.—*adv.* **sump'tuously.**—*n.* **sump'tuous-ness**. [L. *sūmptus*, cost—*sūmĕre*, *sūmptum*, to take.]

sun, sun, *n.* the body which is the gravitational centre and source of light and heat to our planetary system: the central body of a system: a great luminary: a climate: sunshine: a year: a day: sunrise: sunset.—*v.t.* to expose to the sun's rays.—*v.i.* to bask:—*pr.p.* **sunn'ing**; *pa.t.* and *pa.p.* **sunned.**—*adj.* **sun'-and-plan'et**, geared so that one wheel moves round another.—*ns.* **sun'-animal'cule**, a heliozoan; **sun'-bath**, exposure of the body to the sun's rays.—*v.i.* **sun'bathe.**—*n.* **sun'-bathing** (-*bādh*-).—*adj.* **sun'-baked.**—*n.* **sun'beam**, a shaft of sunlight.—*adjs.* **sun'beamed, -beamy.**—*n.* **sun'-bear**, the Malayan bear: sometimes the Himalayan bear.—*adjs.* **sun'-beat, -en**, continually exposed to the sun.—*ns.* **sun'-bird**, any of the Nectariniidae, a family of small tropical birds akin to honey-eaters, superficially like humming-birds; **sun'-bittern**, a S. American bird (*Eurypyga helias*) with brilliant many-coloured markings; **sun'-blind**, an outside shade or awning for a window.—*adj.* blinded by the sun.—*ns.* **sun'-blink**, (*Scot.*) a gleam of sunshine; **sun'-bonnet**, a light bonnet projecting beyond the face to protect from the sun; **sun'bow**, an iris formed by the sun, esp. in the spray of a cataract.—*adj.* **sun'-**

bright, bright as the sun.—*n.* **sun'burn**, a browning of the skin by the sun.—*v.t.* to brown or tan by exposure to the sun.—*v.i.* to become so browned. —*adjs.* **sun'burned**, **sun'burnt.**—*n.* **sun'burst**, a strong outburst of sunlight.—*adj.* **sun'-clad**, clothed in radiant light.—*ns.* **sun'-crack**, a crack formed in clayey ground as it dries in the sun, often preserved in rocks; **sun'-cult**, worship of a sun-god or of the sun.—*adj.* **sun'-cured**, cured in the sun.—*ns.* **sun'dawn**, the light of the rising sun; **sun'-dew**, an insectivorous bog-plant (Drosera); **sun'-dial**, a device for telling the time by a shadow cast by the sun; **sun'-disk**, the visible disk of the sun: a winged disk, symbol of the sun-god; **sun'-dog**, a mock sun or parhelion; **sun'down**, sunset: (*U.S.*) a woman's broad-brimmed hat; **sun'downer**, in Australia, a loafer who arrives at a station in time for a meal and lodging, but too late for work: (*U.S.*) a government official who practises a profession after hours: in India and Africa, a drink after sunset.—*adj.* **sun'-dried**, dried in the sun.—*n.* **sun'-drops**, an American evening primrose.—*adj.* **sun'-expelling**, (*Shak.*) keeping off the sun.—*adj.* **sun'-fish**, a fish of nearly circular profile, as the opah, or any member of the family Molidae: the basking-shark; **sun'flower**, a composite plant (Helianthus) or its large head with yellow rays, fabled to turn toward the sun: applied to various more or less similar kinds; **sun'god**, a god personifying or concerned with the sun; **sun'hat**, a hat with shady brim.—*adj.* **sun'less.**—*ns.* **sun'lessness**; **sun'-light**, the light of the sun.—*adjs.* **sun'like**; **sun'lit**, lighted up by the sun.—*n.* **sun'-myth**, a solar myth.—*adj.* **sunned**, exposed to the sun.—*adv.* **sunn'ily.** —*n.* **sunn'iness.**—*adj.* **sunn'y**, of, from, like, or lighted, coloured, or warmed by the sun: genial: cheerful.—*ns.* **sun'-parlour**, a room with glass walls or large windows for getting advantage of the sun's rays; **sun'-picture, -print**, a photograph. —*adj.* **sun'proof.**—*ns.* **sun'-ray**; **sun'rise**, **sun'-rising**, the rising or first appearance of the sun above the horizon: the time or colour-effects of this rising: the east; **sun'set**, **sun'setting**, the setting or going down of the sun: the time or phenomenon of going down: the west; **sun'-shade**, a parasol: an awning; **sun'shine**, bright sunlight: brightness: prosperity: geniality.—*adjs.* **sun'shine**, sunshiny: fair-weather; **sun'-shiny**, bright with sunshine: pleasant: bright like the sun: genial.—*ns.* **sun'shine-recorder**, an instrument for recording duration of sunshine; **sun'spot**, a relatively dark patch on the surface of the sun; **sun'-spurge**, a spurge (*Euphorbia Helioscopia*) supposed to turn with the sun, a common weed; **sun'stone**, aventurine felspar; **sun'stroke**, a nervous disease caused by great heat.—*adj.* **sun'struck**, affected with sunstroke.— *n.* **sun'-up**, sunrise.—*adj.* and *adv.* **sun'ward**, toward the sun.—*advs.* **sun'wards**; **sun'wise**, in the direction of the sun's apparent revolution.— *ns.* **sun'-worship**, adoration of the sun; **sun'-worshipper.**—**between** (*Shak.* 'twixt) **sun and sun**, from sun to sun, between sunrise and sun-set; **have been in the sunshine, have the sun in one's eyes**, to be drunk; **take the sun**, to ascertain the sun's meridian altitude; **under the sun**, on earth. [O.E. *sunne*; O.N. *sunna*, O.H.G. *sunnô*.]

sundae, sun'dā, -*di*, *n.* an ice with syrup or crushed fruit: a mixed nougat or confection. [Perh. **Sunday.**]

sundari, sun'də-rē, *n.* an East Indian sterculiaceous timber-tree (Heritiera).—Also **sun'dra**, **sun'dri**, **sun'der**. [Sans. *sundarī*.]

Sunday, sun'di, *n.* the first day of the week, anciently dedicated to the sun.—*adj.* of, for, occurring on, Sunday.—*adj.* **Sun'day-go-to-meet'ing**, appropriated to Sunday and church-going.—**Sunday best**, one's best clothes; **Sunday saint**, one whose religion or morality is confined to Sundays; **Sunday school**, a school for religious (orig. general, latterly also socialistic) instruction on Sunday. [O.E. *sunnan dæg*; Ger. *sonntag*.]

sunder, sun'dər, *v.t.* and *v.i.* to separate: to part.—

Neutral vowels in unaccented syllables: *el'ə-mənt*, *in'fənt*, *ran'dəm*

n. sun'derance.—adj. sun'dered.—n. sun'derer.—
—n. and adj. sun'dering.—n. sun'derment.—
in sunder, (B.) asunder. [O.E. syndrian, to
separate, sundor, separate; O.N. sundr, asunder.]
sundry, sun'dri, adj. separate: more than one or
two: several: divers: (Shak.) varied.—n.pl.
sun'dries, sundry things: different small things.
—all and sundry, all collectively and individually.
[O.E. syndrig; cf. sunder.]
sung, sung. See sing.
Sung, soong, n. a Chinese dynasty (960-1279).—adj.
of the dynasty, or its culture, including pottery.
sunk, sungk, sunken, sungk'n. See sink.
sunk, sungk, n. (Scot.) a turf seat: a pad: a bank.—
n. sunk'ie, a stool. [Origin unknown.]
sunket, sung'kit, n. (Scot.) a dainty. [From sum-
quhat, Scots form of somewhat.]
sunn, sun, n. an Indian Crotalaria grown for fibre.—
Also sunn'-hemp'. [Hind. san.]
Sunna, soon'ä, sun'ä, n. Mahommedan traditional
teaching.—n. Sunn'i (-ē), an orthodox Muslim.—
Also Sonn'ite, Sunn'ite.
Suomi, swaw'mē, n. the Finnish language.—n.pl.
the Finns.—adjs. Suo'mic, Suo'mish.
suovetaurilia, sū-ov-i-taw-ril'i-ä (L. soo-ov-e-tow-
rē'li-ä), n.pl. a Roman sacrifice of a sheep, a pig,
and an ox. [L. sūs, pig, ovis, sheep, taurus, ox.]
sup, sup, v.t. to take into the mouth, as a liquid:
(Scot.) to eat with a spoon: (Shak.) to furnish
supper for.—v.i. to eat the evening meal: (B.) to
sip: (pr.p. supp'ing; pa.t. and pa.p. supped).—n.
a small mouthful, as of a liquid. [O.E. súpan; O.N.
súpa, Ger. saufen, to drink; partly from O.Fr.
soper, souper (Fr. souper), to take supper.]
supawn. See suppawn.
super-, s(y)ōō'par-, pfx. above, beyond, in addition,
in excess.—n. su'per, a colloquial abbrev. of
supernumerary (esp. a supernumerary actor,
further abbreviated supe) of superintendent.—
adj. of superfine.—v.i. to act as super.—v.i.
superabound', to be more, very, or excessively
abundant.—n. superabun'dance.—adj. superabund'ant.—adv superabund'antly.—adj. super-
acute', abnormally or excessively acute. — v.t.
superadd', to add over and above.—ns. super-
addi'tion; superalt'ar, a slab of stone used as a
portable altar to be laid on the top of an unconsecrated altar: a structure over an altar.—v.t.
supercal'ender, to give a high polish to by
calendering.—adjs. supercal'endered; super-
celest'ial, above the heavens: more than heavenly.
—v.t. supercharge', to fill to excess: to charge
above the normal: to add pressure to: to charge
exorbitantly, overcharge: (her.) to place as an
overcharge.—ns. su'percharge, an excessive, exorbitant, or greater than normal charge: (her.) a
charge borne upon an ordinary or other charge;
supercharg'er, a device for increasing the
pressure in an internal-combustion engine; super-
conductiv'ity, complete loss of electrical resistivity
shown by certain metals at particular temperatures
below 15° K.—v.t. supercool', to cool below
normal freezing-point without freezing. — adj.
superdaint'y, (Shak.) over-dainty.—ns. super-
dom'inant, (mus.) the submediant; super-
Dread'nought, a warship excelling the original
Dreadnought class; super-ego, (psych.) the strong
unconscious inhibitory mechanism which criticises
the ego and causes it pain and distress when it
accepts unworthy impulses from the id; super-
eleva'tion, excess in height; superem'inence,
eminence in a superior degree: excellence beyond
others.—adj. superem'inent.—adv. superem'-
inently.—adj. superessen'tial, transcending mere
being and essence.—v.t. superexalt', to exalt
to a superior degree. — ns. superexalta'tion;
superexc'ellence, excellence above others, or in
an uncommon degree.—adj. superexc'ellent.—
n. su'perfamily, a group between a suborder
and a family.—adjs. superfatt'ed, (of soap) having
an excess of fat, so that there is no free alkali;
su'perfine, excessively fine: over-nice.—ns. super-
fluidity, a phenomenon observed in a form of
helium (helium II), obtained below 2·19° K., in
which internal friction is negligible; superfor'tress,

a powerful bombing aeroplane; superfront'al,
a covering hanging over the upper edge of an altar
frontal.—v.t. superfuse', to pour over something
else: to supercool. — n. superfu'sion. — v.t.
superheat', to heat to excess: to heat (steam, &c.)
above the temperature of saturation: to heat above
normal boiling-point without vaporisation.—n.
state of being superheated: amount of super-
heating.—n. superheat'er.—adj. superhet'erodyne, heterodyne with beats above audible frequency (coll. superhet').—n. a superheterodyne
receiver.—n. su'perhive, a detachable upper compartment of a beehive.—adj. superhu'man, above
man: above the capacity of man: more or higher
than human.—v.t. superhu'manise.—n. superhu'manity.—adv. superhu'manly. — n. superhu'meral, any vestment worn on the shoulders.—
v.t. superimpose', to set on the top of something
else: to place one over another: to establish in
superaddition.—adj. superimposed'.—ns. super-
imposi'tion; superincum'bence.—adj. superincum'bent, resting on the top: overlying:
overhanging.—v.t. superinduce', to bring in over
and above, or in supersession of, something else:
to superadd.—ns. superinduce'ment, super-
induc'tion.—v.t. superintend', to have or exercise oversight or charge of: to control, manage.—
v.i. to exercise supervision.—ns. superinten'dence,
oversight: direction: management; superinten'dency, office or district of a superintendent.
—adj. superinten'dent, superintending.—n. one
who superintends: an overseer: the head of a
Sunday-school: in some Protestant churches a
clergyman having the oversight of the clergy of a
district: a police officer above an inspector: (U.S.)
the administrator of a local school system.—n.
superinten'dentship.—adjs. superlu'nar, superlu'nary, above the moon: not of this world.—n.
su'perman, a being of higher type than man:
ideal man: a dominating man.—adjs. supermun'-
dane, above the world; supernat'ional, transcending the national.—n. supernat'ionalism.—
adj. supernat'ural, above or beyond nature: not
according to the course of nature: miraculous:
spiritual.—n. that which is supernatural: a supernatural being.—v.t. supernat'uralise, to bring
into the supernatural sphere.—ns. supernat'uralism, the belief in the influence of the supernatural
in the world; supernat'uralist, a believer in the
supernatural.—adj. of or pertaining to the supernatural.—adj. supernaturalist'ic.—adv. supernat'urally. — ns. supernat'uralness; su'per-
nature, the supernatural. — adj. supernor'mal,
beyond what is normal: in greater number,
amount, concentration, &c., than the normal.—n.
su'peroctave, an organ-coupler giving an octave
higher: an organ-stop two octaves above the
principal. — adjs. superord'inary, above or beyond the ordinary; superord'inate, superior in
rank: in the relation of superordination.—n. a
superior in rank.—v.t. to make superordinate.—
n. superordina'tion, (log.) the relation of a
universal proposition to a particular proposition
in the same terms.—adj. superorgan'ic, above or
beyond the organic, psychical: pertaining to a
higher organisation, social.—ns. superovula'tion,
the production of a larger number of ova, e.g. by
a cow under the stimulus of injected hormones;
superphos'phate, an acid phosphate: now usu.
a mixture of calcium sulphate and calcium acid
phosphate used as a manure.—adj. superphys'ical,
beyond, or of higher order than, the physical.—
n. su'perplus, (obs.) surplus.—adj. superpos'able.
—v.t. superpose', to bring, or suppose to be
brought, into coincidence: to place vertically
over or on something else.—adj. superposed'.—
n. superposi'tion, act of superposing: state of
being superposed: that which is above anything.
—v.t. superpraise', (Shak.) to praise excessively.
—n. superre'alism, surrealism.—adj. super-
roy'al, larger than royal—19½×27½ in. for writing-
and drawing-paper, 20½×27½ in. for printing-
paper.—n. su'persalt, an acid salt.—v.t. super-
sat'urate, to saturate beyond the normal point.—
n. supersatura'tion.—adj. supersens'ible, above

the range, or outside the realm, of the senses.—
adv. **supersen'sibly**.—*adj.* **supersen'sitive**, excessively sensitive. — *n.* **supersen'sitiveness**. —
adjs. **supersen'sory**, beyond the ordinarily recognised senses ; **supersen'sual**, beyond the senses : extremely sensual ; **superser'viceable**, (*Shak.*) officious.—*ns.* **su'per-state**, a greater organisation transcending the state ; **superstrā'tum**, an overlying stratum.—*v.t.* **superstruct'**, to build on something else as a foundation.—*n.* **superstruc'tion**.—*adjs.* **superstruct'ive ; superstruct'ural**.
—*n.* **superstruct'ure**, an upper structure or part of a structure.—*adjs.* **supersubstan'tial**, transcending substance, esp. material substance ; **supersubt'le**, -**subt'ile** (*Shak.*), over-subtle : extremely subtle.—*ns.* **su'pertax**, an extra or additional tax on large incomes ; **superton'ic**, the tone next above the tonic.—*adj.* **su'pervolute**, (*bot.*) convolute. [L. *super*, above ; cf. **over**, Gr. *hyper*.]
superannuate, *s*(*y*)*ōō-pər-an'ū-āt*, *v.t.* to antiquate : to set aside or cause to retire on account of age : to pension off.—*adj.* **superannuated**.—*n.* a superannuated person. — *adj.* **superann'ūated**. — *n.* **superannūā'tion**.
superate, *s*(*y*)*ōō'pər-āt*, *v.t.* (*obs.*) to overcome, outdo, or top.—*adj.* **su'perable**.—*adv.* **su'perably**.—
n. **superā'tion**.
superb, *s*(*y*)*ōō-pərb'*, *adj.* (*obs.*) proud, haughty : magnificent : gorgeous : triumphantly effective : (*coll.*) supremely excellent.—*n.* **superb'ity**.—*adv.* **superb'ly**.—*n.* **superb'ness**. [L. *superbus*, proud.]
supercargo, *s*(*y*)*ōō-pər-kär'gō*, *n.* a person in a ship placed in charge of the cargo and superintending all the commercial transactions of the voyage :—*pl.* **supercar'goes**.—*n.* **supercar'goship**.
supercherie, *sü-per-chə-rē*, *n.* a taking at disadvantage : fraud. [Fr.]
superciliary, *s*(*y*)*ōō'pər-sil'i-ər-i*, *adj.* of, on, or near the eyebrow : marked above the eye.—*n.* a superciliary ridge or mark.—*adj.* **supercil'ious**, disdainfully superior in manner ; (*obs.*) overbearing : (*rare*) superciliary. — *adv.* **supercil'iously**. — *n.* **supercil'iousness**. [L. *supercilium*, eyebrow, superciliousness—*super*, above, *cilium*, eyelid.]
supererogation, *s*(*y*)*ōō-pər-er-ō-gā'shən*, *n.* doing more than is required.—*v.i.* **superer'ogate**.—
adj. **supererogatory** (*-ə-rog'ə-tər-i*).—Also (*rare*) **superer'ogant**, **supererog'ative**.—**works of supererogation**, (*R.C.*) works which, not absolutely required of each individual for salvation, may be done for the sake of greater perfection—affording the church a store of surplus merit, to eke out the deficient merit of others. [L. *super*, above, *ērogāre*, *-ātum*, to pay out.]
superfetation, *s*(*y*)*ōō-pər-fē-tā'shən*, *n.* fertilisation of an ovum in one already for some time pregnant : superabundant production or accumulation.—*v.i.* **superfē'tate**. [L. *superfētāre*—pfx. *super*, *fētus*, a fetus.]
superficies, *s*(*y*)*ōō-pər-fish'i-ēz*, *n.* (*geom.*) a surface, that which has length and breadth but no thickness : a bounding or outer surface : a surface layer : a surface area : external features, appearance :—*pl.* **superfic'ies**.—*adj.* **superficial** (*-fish'l*), of, on, or near the surface : not going much deeper than the surface.—*n.* that which is, or those who are, superficial : surface characters.—*v.t.* **superfic'ialise**, to make superficial.—*v.i.* to deal superficially.
—*n.* **superficiality** (*-fish-i-al'i-ti*).—*adv.* **superfic'ially**.—*n.* **superfic'ialness**. [L. *superficiēs*—*super*, *faciēs*, face.]
superfluous, *s*(*y*)*ōō-pər'floo-əs*, *adj.* above what is enough : redundant : unnecessary.—*n.* **superfluity** (*-floō'*), state of being superfluous : a thing that is superfluous : superabundance.—*adv.* **super'fluously**. — *ns.* **super'fluousness**, superfluity ; **su'perflux**, (*Shak.*) superfluity. [L. *superfluus*, overflowing—*super*, *fluĕre*, to flow.]
superfoetation. Same as **superfetation**.
superior, *s*(*y*)*ōō-pē'ri-ər*, *adj.* upper : higher in nature, place, rank, or excellence : better (with *to*): surpassing others : beyond the influence : rising above (with *to*): supercilious or uppish : (often patronisingly) very worthy and highly respectable : of wider application, generic : (*print.*)

set above the level of the line : (*bot.*) of an ovary, inserted on the receptacle above the other parts : of other parts, seeming to take rise above the ovary.
—*n.* one superior to others : the head of a religious house, order, &c.: the feudal lord of a vassal : (*Scots law*) one to whom feu-duty is paid :—*fem.* **supe'rioress**, a head of a nunnery.—*n.* **superiority** (*-or'i-ti*), quality or state of being superior : preeminence: advantage : (*Scots law*) the right which the superior enjoys in the land held by the vassal.
—*adv.* **supe'riorly**, in a superior manner or position.—*n.* **supe'riorship**.—**superior planets**, those more distant from the sun than is the earth. [L., comp. of *superus*, on high—*super*, above.]
superjacent, *s*(*y*)*ōō-pər-jā'sənt*, *adj.* lying above. [L. *super*, *jacēns*, -*ēntis*, pr.p. of *jacēre*, to lie.]
superlative, *s*(*y*)*ōō-pər'lə-tiv*, *adj.* raised above others or to the highest degree : superior to all others : most eminent : (*gram.*) expressing the highest degree.—*n.* (*gram.*) the superlative or highest degree : an adjective or adverb in the superlative degree : any word or phrase of exaggeration. — *adv.* **super'latively**. — *n.* **super'lativeness**. [L. *superlātīvus*—*super*, *lātus*, carried.]
supernaculum, *s*(*y*)*ōō-pər-nak'ū-ləm*, *adv.* to the last drop.—*n.* liquor of the best kind, too good to leave heeltaps : a bumper. — *adj.* **supernac'ular**. [Sham L. *super naculum*, on the nail—L. *super*, Ger. *nagel*, nail ; from the custom of turning the glass up to show that no more is left than will stand on the thumb-nail.]
supernal, *s*(*y*)*ōō-pər'nl*, *adj.* on high : celestial : of a higher world : exalted : topmost.—*adv.* **super'nally**. [L. *supernus*—*super*.]
supernatant, *s*(*y*)*ōō-pər-nā'tənt*, *adj.* floating or swimming above, esp. of an upper layer of liquid. [L. *supernatāns*, -*āntis*—*super*, *natāre*, swim, float.]
supernova, *s*(*y*)*ōō-pər-nō'vä*, *n.* very brilliant nova.
supernumerary, *s*(*y*)*ōō-pər-nū'mər-ər-i*, *adj.* over and above the stated, usual, normal, or necessary number.—*n.* a supernumerary person or thing : an actor without speaking parts. [L.L. *supernumerārius*—L. *super*, *numerus*, number.]
superscribe, *s*(*y*)*ōō-pər-skrīb'*, *v.t.* to write or engrave above, on the top or on the outside of something : to address (as a letter) : to sign at the top.—*adj.* **su'perscript** (*-skript*), written above.
—*n.* (*Shak.*) the superscription, address.—*n.* **superscrip'tion**, act of superscribing : that which is superscribed. [L. *super*, above, *scrībĕre*, *scrīptum*, to write.]
supersede, *s*(*y*)*ōō-pər-sēd'*, *v.t.* (*obs.*) to desist or refrain from : (*obs.*) to override : to set aside : to set aside in favour of another : to come or put in the room of, to replace.—*v.i.* (*obs.*) to refrain, desist.—*ns.* **superse'deas** (*-di-as*), a writ to stay proceedings, or to suspend the powers of an officer (from the use of the L. word, 2nd pers. sing. pres. subj., you are to desist) ; **superse'dence** ; **superse'der**; **supersedere** (*-si-dē'ri*, L. *sōō-per-se-dā'rä*, *infin.*; *Scots law*), a private agreement among creditors, under a trust-deed, to supersede or sist diligence for a certain period : an order of court granting protection to a debtor ; **supersē'dure** ; **supersession** (*-sesh'ən*). [L. *supersedēre*, to sit above, refrain from—*super*, above, *sedēre*, *sessum*, to sit.]
supersonic, *s*(*y*)*ōō-pər-son'ik*, *adj.* above the audible limit : too high-pitched for human hearing (ultrasonic) : also, above the speed of sound.—*n.* a supersonic wave : (in *pl.*) the study of such waves. [L. *sonus*, sound.]
superstition, *s*(*y*)*ōō-pər-stish'ən*, *n.* false worship or religion : an ignorant and irrational belief in supernatural agency, omens, divination, sorcery, &c.: a deep-rooted but unfounded general belief : (*obs.*) a rite or practice proceeding from superstitious belief or fear.—*adj.* **superstit'ious**.—*adv.* **superstit'iously**.—*n.* **superstit'iousness**. [L. *superstitiō*, *-ōnis*.]
supervene, *s*(*y*)*ōō-pər-vēn'*, *v.i.* to come in addition, or closely after.—*n.* **superven'ience**.—*adj.* **super'vēn'ient**, supervening.—*n.* **supervention** (*-ven'shən*). [L. *super*, above, *venīre*, *ventum*, come.]
supervise, *s*(*y*)*ōō'pər-vīz*, or *-viz'*, *v.i.* (*Shak.*) to read

over : to superintend.—*n.* (*Shak.*) reading over.—*ns.* **supervi′sal, supervision** (*-vizh′ən*), act of supervising : inspection : control ; **supervi′sor,** one who supervises : an overseer : an inspector : (*Shak.*) a spectator : **supervi′sorship.**—*adj.* **supervi′sory,** pertaining to, or having, supervision. [L. *super,* over, *vidēre, vīsum,* to see.]

supine, s(y)ōō-pīn′, *adj.* lying on the back : leaning backward, inclined, sloping : negligently inert : indolent : passive.—*n.* **su′pine,** a Latin verbal noun in *-tum* (*first supine,* an old accusative) or *-tū* (*second supine,* an old locative), possibly as formed from the stem of the passive participle : the English infinitive with *to.*—*v.t.* **su′pinate** (*-pin-āt*), to bring palm upward or forward.—*ns.* **supina′tion,** the placing or holding of the palm of the hand upward or forward ; **su′pinātor,** a muscle that supinates the hand.—*adv.* **supine′ly.**—*n.* **supine′ness.** [L. *supīnus,* supine ; related to *sub,* under, *super,* over.]

suppawn, supawn, sə-*pawn′, n.* maize porridge. [Natick *saupáun,* softened.]

suppeago, sə-*pē′gō.* See **serpigo.**

supper, *sup′ər, n.* a meal taken at the close of the day.—*v.t.* to furnish with supper.—*adj.* **supp′er-less.**—*n.* **supp′er-time.** [O.Fr. *soper* (Fr. *souper*).]

supping. See **sup.**

supplant, sə-*plänt′, v.t.* (*Milt.*) to overthrow, to lay low : to oust : to supersede : to dispossess and take the place of : (*Shak.*) to uproot.—*ns.* **supplantation** (*sup-lən-tā′shən*) ; **supplant′er.** [L. *supplantāre,* to trip up—*sub,* under, *planta,* the sole.]

supple, *sup′l, adj.* pliant : lithe : yielding to the humour of others : fawning.—*v.t.* to make supple : to make soft or compliant.—*v.i.* to become supple. —*n.* **supp′leness.**—*adv.* **supp′ly.—supple jack,** a woody liane of many kinds : a pliant cane. [Fr. *souple*—L. *supplex,* bending the knees—*sub,* under, *plicāre,* to fold.]

supple, soop′l, a Scots form of **swipple.** See **souple.**

supplement, *sup′li-mənt, n.* that which supplies or fills up : any addition by which defects are supplied : a special part of a periodical publication accompanying an ordinary part : the quantity by which an angle or an arc falls short of 180° or a semicircle.—*v.t.* **supplement** (*-ment′*) ; also *sup′li-ment*), to supply or fill up : to add to.—*adjs.* **supplement′al, supplement′ary,** added to supply what is wanting : additional.—*Also ns.*—*advs.* **supplement′ally, supplement′arily.**—*ns.* **supplementā′tion ; supplement′er.**—*adjs.* **supp′letive, supp′letory,** supplemental. [L. *supplēmentum,* a filling up, *supplēre,* to fill up.]

supplial, suppliance (1), **suppliant** (1). See under **supply.**

suppliant, *sup′li-ənt, adj.* supplicating : asking earnestly : entreating.—*n.* a humble petitioner.— *n.* **supp′liance,** supplication.—*adv.* **supp′liantly.** [Fr. *suppliant,* pr.p. of *supplier*—L. *supplicāre* ; see next.]

supplicant, *sup′li-kənt, adj.* supplicating : asking submissively.—*n.* one who supplicates or entreats earnestly.—*n.* **supp′licat,** in the English universities, a petition.—*v.t.* and *v.i.* **supp′licate,** to entreat earnestly : to petition : to pray.—*adj.* **supp′licating.**—*adv.* **supp′licatingly.**—*n.* **supplicā′tion,** act of supplicating : an earnest or humble petition : in ancient Rome, a solemn service or day decreed for giving formal thanks to the gods for victory, &c.: earnest prayer or entreaty, esp. in liturgies, a litany prayer for some special blessing.—*adj.* **supp′licatory,** containing supplication or entreaty : humble.—*n.* **supplicā′vit,** formerly a writ issued by the King′s Bench or Chancery for taking the surety of the peace against a person. [L. *supplicāre, -ātum*—*supplex* ; see **supple.**]

supply, sə-*plī′, v.t.* to fill up a deficiency in : to supplement : to reinforce : (*obs.*) to help : to make good : to satisfy : to provide, furnish : to fill, occupy (as a substitute) : to serve instead of : (*pr.p.* **supply′ing** ; *pa.t.* and *pa.p.* **supplied′**).—*n.* act of supplying : that which is supplied or which supplies a want : amount provided or in hand : available amount of a commodity : amount of food or money provided (used generally in *pl.*) : a parliamentary grant for expenses of government : a person who takes another′s duty temporarily, a substitute, esp. a clergyman.—*ns.* **suppli′al,** the act of supplying ; **suppli′ance,** (*Shak.*) supplying, something to fill up time, pastime, gratification.— *adj.* **suppli′ant,** (*Shak.*) supplementary, reinforcing.—*ns.* **suppli′er,** one who supplies ; **supply′-ment,** (*Shak.*) replenishment, supplementing.— **Commissioners of Supply,** a former administrative and rating authority in Scotland, superseded by the County Council. [O.Fr. *suppleier, supplier* (Fr. *suppléer*)—L. *supplēre,* to fill up.]

support, sə-*pōrt′, v.t.* to bear the weight of : to hold up : to endure : to sustain : to maintain : to keep going : to corroborate : to make good : to uphold : to back up : to second : to contend for : to represent in acting : to supply with means of living : to nourish : to strengthen.—*n.* act or fact of supporting or upholding : that which, or one who, supports, sustains, or maintains : maintenance : backing : a prop : an actor playing a subordinate part with a star.—*adj.* **support′able,** capable of being held up, borne, sustained, or maintained. —*n.* **support′ableness.**—*adv.* **support′ably.**—*ns.* **support′ance,** (*Shak.*) support ; **support′er,** one who, or that which, supports : an adherent : a defender : one who attends matches and watches with interest the fortunes of a team : (*her.*) a figure on each side of the escutcheon.—*n.* and *adj.* **support′ing.**—*adjs.* **support′ive** (*rare*) ; **support′-less.**—*ns.* (all *rare*) **support′ment ; support′ress ;** **support′ure.** [L. *supportāre*—*sub,* up, *portāre,* to bear.]

suppose, sə-*pōz′, v.t.* (*obs.*) to place underneath : (*Shak.*) to believe : to incline to believe : to conceive, imagine, guess : to assume provisionally or for argument′s sake : to imply, presuppose : to pretend : (*Milt.*) to expect : (esp. in *pass.*) to expect in accordance with rules or conventions (*obs.*) to substitute fraudulently.—*n.* a supposition : an instance of supposing or saying ′ suppose ′ (*Shak.*) expectation.—*adj.* **suppo′sable.**—*adv.* **suppo′sably.**—*n.* **suppo′sal,** supposition : (*Shak.* notion : (*obs.*) proposal.—*adj.* **supposed′,** believed to be : assumed : conjectured : (*Shak.*) feigned (*obs.*) supposititious : (*mus.*) placed below, or having a note below, the fundamental of the chord —*adv.* **suppo′sedly,** according to supposition.— *ns.* **suppo′ser ; suppo′sing.—suppose,** (*Scot.* even if ; **supposing,** (*coll.*) what if, how about [Fr. *supposer*—pfx. *sup-* (sub-), *poser* ; see **pose** and cf. **compose, dispose, &c.**]

supposes, sə-*pōz′iz, n.pl.* (*Shak., Taming of th Shrew,* V. i. 120) perh. substitutes, or substitution or suppositions. See repeated play on the word i Shakespeare′s source, Gascoigne′s *Supposes* (an its original, Ariosto′s *I Suppositi*).

supposition, sup-ə-*zi′shən, n.* an act of supposing that which is supposed : assumption : presump tion, opinion.—*adj.* **supposi′tional,** hypothetical conjectural : supposed.—*adv.* **supposi′tionally.**— *adjs.* **supposi′tionary,** suppositional ; **supposi tious** (*-zi′shəs ; rare*), suppositional : usu. ! blunder for **supposititious** ; **supposititious** (*sə-poz i-tish′əs*), put by trick in the place of another spurious : suppositional.—*adv.* **supposti′tiously** —*n.* **supposi′tiousness.** — *adj.* **suppos′itive** (*-i-tiv*), suppositional.—*n.* **suppos′itory,** a medi cated plug for administration by the rectum o other canal. [L. *suppōnere, -positum,* to set unde substitute—*sub, pōnĕre,* to put.]

suppress, sə-*pres′, v.t.* to crush, put down : t subdue : (*Spens.*) to hold or press down : (*Spens.* to ravish : to hold back, esp. from publicatio circulation, divulgation, expression, developmen to check, stop, restrain : to hold in : to moderat to leave out. — *adj.* **suppressed′.** — *adj.* **sup press′edly.**—*adj.* **suppress′ible.**—*n.* **suppressio** (*-presh′ən*), act of suppressing : stoppage : conceal ment.—*adj.* **suppress′ive,** tending to suppress subduing.—*n.* **suppress′or.** [L. *supprimĕre, sup pressum*—*sub,* under, *premĕre,* to press.]

suppurate, *sup'ū-rāt*, *v.i.* to gather pus or matter.—*n.* **suppurā'tion**.—*adj.* **supp'urātive**, promoting or attended by suppuration.—*n.* a suppurative agent. [L. *sub*, under, *pūs*, *pūris*, pus.]

upra-, *s(y)ōō'prə-*, *pfx.* above. — *adjs.* **supra-ax'illary**, arising above an axil; **supraciliary** (-*sil'*), above the eyebrow; **supracost'al**, above or on a rib; **supralu'nar**, beyond the moon: very lofty; **supramun'dane**, above the world; **supra-or'bital**, above the orbit of the eye; **suprarē'nal**, above the kidneys (**suprarenal capsules**, the adrenal glands; **suprarenal extract**, an extract from these used in haemorrhage, Addison's disease, &c.); **suprasens'ible**, above the reach of the senses; **supratemp'oral**, transcending time: of the upper part of the temples or temporal region. [L. *suprā*, above.]

upralapsarian, *s(y)ōō-prə-laps-ā'ri-ən*, *n.* one of a class of Calvinists who make the decree of election and predestination to precede the Creation and the Fall—opp. to *Sublapsarian*.—Also *adj.*—*n.* **Supralapsā'rianism**. [L. *suprā*, above, beyond, *lāpsus*, fall.]

upreme, *s(y)ōō-prēm'*, poet. also *s(y)ōō'prēm*, *adj.* highest: greatest: most excellent.—*n.* the highest point: the highest authority.—*n.* **supremacy** (-*prem'ə-si*), state of being supreme: supreme position or power.—*adv.* **supremely** (-*prēm'*).—*ns.* **supreme'ness**, **supremity** (-*prem'*). [L. *suprēmus*, superl. of *superus*, high—*super*, above.]

ura, surah, *sōō'rä*, *n.* a chapter of the Koran. [Ar. *sūra, sūrah*, step.]

ura, surah, *sōō'rä*, *n.* fermented palm-sap. [Sans. *surā*.]

uraddition, *sur-ə-dish'ən*, *n.* (*Shak.*) an additional title or designation.

urah, *s(y)ōō'rä*, *n.* a soft twilled silk fabric.—Also *adj.* [Poss. from *Surat*.]

ural, *sū'rl*, *adj.* pertaining to the calf of the leg. [L. *sūra*, the calf.]

urance, *shōōr'əns*, *n.* (*Shak.*) assurance.

urat, *sōō-rat'*, or *sōō'*, *n.* coarse uncoloured cotton. [*Surat*, in India.]

urbase, *sər'bās*, *n.* a cornice or series of mouldings above the base of a pedestal, &c.—*adj.* **subased** (-*bäst'*), of an arch, lower than half the span.—*n.* **subase'ment**.

urbate, *sər-bāt'*, *v.t.* (*Spens. sur'*) to bruise with walking, make footsore:—*pa.p.* **surbat'ed**, (*Spens.*) **surbet'**. [O.Fr. *surbatu*, excessively beaten, but with the meaning of Fr. *solbatu*.]

urbed, *sər-bed'*, *v.t.* to set on edge, as a stone with reference to the grain.

urcease, *sər-sēs'*, *v.i.* to cease.—*v.t.* to desist or refrain from: to end, put a stop to.—*n.* cessation. [O.Fr. *sursis*, pa.p. of *surseoir*—L. *supersedēre*, to refrain from; cf. **supersede**; spelling influenced by **cease**.]

urcharge, *sər-chärj'*, *v.t.* to overcharge: to overload: to overburden: to overstock: to saturate: (*Spens.*) to charge with overwhelming force: to print over the original printing: to disallow: to exact a surcharge from.—*n.* **sur'charge** (or -*chärj'*), an overcharge: an extra charge: an excessive load: an overloaded condition: an amount not passed by an auditor, which must be refunded: a new valuation or cancel-mark printed on or over a stamp: the earth supported by a retaining wall above the level of its top.—*adj.* **surcharged'**.—*ns.* **surcharge'ment**; **surcharg'er**.

urcingle, *sər'sing-gl*, *n.* a girth or strap for holding a saddle on an animal's back: the girdle of a cassock.—*v.t.* to gird, fasten, or thrash with a surcingle. [O.Fr. *surcengle*—L. *super, cingulum*, a belt.]

urcoat, *sər'kōt*, *n.* a mediaeval outer garment, usu. sleeveless, often with heraldic devices, worn by men and women over armour or ordinary dress. [O.Fr. *surcote, surcot*—*sur*, over, *cote*, garment.]

urculus, *sər'kū-ləs*, *n.* (*bot.*) a sucker. [L. *sūrculus*.]

urd, *sərd*, *adj.* (*obs.*) deaf: (*obs.*) senseless: (*math.*) irrational: (*phon.*) voiceless.—*n.* an irrational quantity: a voiceless consonant.—*n.* **surd'ity**, deafness. [L. *surdus*, deaf.]

ure, *shōōr*, *adj.* secure: safe: fit to be depended on: unerring: stable: (*obs.*) bound in alliance (esp. by betrothal or marriage): certain: assured: confident beyond doubt: without other possibility.—*advs.* **sure** (now chiefly *Ir.* or *U.S.*, except in comp. and in conventional phrases), **surely**, firmly: confidently: safely: certainly: assuredly: as it would seem (often ironically).—*adjs.* **sure'-enough'**, (*U.S.*) genuine, real; **sure'foȯted**, not liable to stumble.—*adv.* **surefoot'edly**.—*ns.* **sure-foot'edness**; **sure'ness**; **Sûreté** (*sür-tā*; Fr.), the French criminal investigation department; **sure'ty**, certainty: safeguard: legal security against loss: one who becomes bound for another: a sponsor.—*v.t.* (*Shak.*) to be security for.—*n.* **sure'tyship**.—**be sure**, do not omit; **for sure**, certainly: of a certainty; **make sure** (*see* **make**): **sure enough**, no doubt: in very fact: accordingly: there's no denying; **sure thing**, a certainty, certain success: beyond doubt; **to be sure**, certainly: I admit. [O.Fr. *sur, seur* (Fr. *sûr*)—L. *sēcūrus*; *see* **secure**.]

sure, an old spelling of **sewer**.

surf, *sərf*, *n.* surging water or waves rushing up a sloping beach: sea-foam.—*v.i.* to bathe in or ride on surf.—*ns.* **surf'-bathing**, bathing in surf; **surf'-bather**; **surf'-bird**, an American West Pacific shore-bird (*Aphriza*) akin to sandpipers; **surf'-board**, a board on which a bather allows himself to be carried inshore by the surf; **surf'-boarding**; **surf'-boat**, a boat for use in surf; **surf'-duck**, the scoter; **surf'-fish**, any fish of a Western American viviparous perch-like family, Embiotocidae; **surf'-man**, one skilful in handling boats in surf; **surf'-riding**, riding on a surf-board.—*adj.* **surf'y**. [Origin obscure.]

surface, *sər'fis*, *n.* the outer boundary or face of anything: the outside or upper layer: (*geom.*) that which has length and breadth but no thickness: area: outer appearance, character or texture: an aerofoil.—*adj.* of, on, or near a surface.—*v.t.* to put a surface, or some kind of surface or finish, upon.—*v.i.* to rise to the surface.—*n.* **sur'face-craft**, a floating, not submersible, craft.—*adj.* **sur'faced**, having this or that kind of surface.—*ns.* **sur'face-mail**, mail sent otherwise than by air; **sur'faceman**, one who keeps a railway-bed in repair; **sur'facer**, one who, or that which, smooths or levels a surface; **sur'face-ten'sion**, that property in virtue of which a liquid surface behaves like a stretched elastic membrane; **sur'face-vessel**; **sur'face-water**, drainage-water; **sur'facing**, giving a surface to anything: material for a surface layer: washing surface deposits for gold. [Fr., from *sur*—L. *super*, and *face*—L. *faciēs*, face.]

surfeit, *sər'fit*, *n.* overfulness: gorging: gluttony: excess: an excessive meal: sickness or satiety caused by overeating or overdrinking.—*v.t.* to feed or fill to satiety or disgust.—*v.i.* to indulge to excess, esp. in food and drink: to suffer from excess.—*adj.* **sur'feited**.—*n.* **sur'feiter**.—*n.* and *adj.* **sur'feiting**. [O.Fr. *surfait*, excess—L. *super*, above, *facēre*, to make.]

surficial, *sər-fish'l*, *adj.* (*geol.*) superficial, subaerial.

surge, an old spelling (*Shak.*) of **serge**.

surge, *sərj*, *n.* an uprush, boiling or tumultuous movement of liquid: a great wave: a swell: a sudden oscillation: a jerk on a rope.—*v.i.* to well up: to heave tumultuously: to slip back: to jerk.—*v.t.* to send in surges: to slack suddenly.—*adj.* **surge'ful**; **surge'less**; **sur'gent**.—*n.* and *adj.* **sur'ging**.—*adj.* **sur'gy**. [L. *surgēre*, to rise.]

surgeon, *sər'jən*, *n.* one who treats injuries or diseases by manual operations: an army or naval doctor: a ship's doctor: a surgeon-fish.—*ns.* **sur'geoncy**, **sur'geonship**, the office or employment of a surgeon in the army or navy; **sur'geon-fish**, a sea-surgeon; **sur'gery**, the art and practice of a surgeon: a doctor's or dentist's consulting-room.—*adj.* **sur'gical**, pertaining to surgery.—*adv.* **sur'gically**.—**surgeon's knot**, a knot like a reef-knot but with a double turn in the first part (used in ligaturing a cut artery). [A.Fr. *surgien*; *see* **chirurgeon**.]

suricate, *s(y)ōō'ri-kāt*, *n.* a S. African animal of the civet family. [Origin unknown.]

Neutral vowels in unaccented syllables : *el'ə-mənt, in'fənt, ran'dəm*

36

Surinam, _s(y)ōō-ri-nam′_, or _s(y)ōō′_, _n._ Dutch Guiana.—**Surinam poison,** a fish poison got from a S. American papilionaceous plant, Tephrosia; **Surinam toad,** a S. American amphibian that hatches its eggs in pits in its back.

surloin. Same as **sirloin.**

surly (_Spens._ **syrlye**), _sər′li_, _adj._ (_Shak._) haughty: morose: gruff and grumpy: rough and gloomy: refractory.—_adv._ (_Shak._) **surlily.**—_adv._ **sur′lily.**—_n._ **sur′liness.** [From **sir** and **like**; cf. **lordly.**]

surmaster, _sər′mäs-tər_, _n._ a second master in a school. [Pfx. **sur-.**]

surmise, _sər-mīz′_, _n._ (_obs._) allegation: suspicion: conjecture.—_v.t._ to imagine: to suspect: to conjecture, guess.—_adj._ **surmis′able.**—_ns._ **surmis′al**; **surmis′er.**—_n._ and _adj._ **surmis′ing.** [O.Fr.,—_surmettre_, to accuse—L. _super_, upon, _mittĕre_, to send.]

surmount, _sər-mownt′_, _v.t._ to mount above: to be on or go to the top of: to surpass: to get the better of.—_adjs._ **surmount′able**; **surmount′ed,** surpassed: overcome: (_archit._) higher than half the span: (_her._) having another figure laid over.—_n._ **surmount′er.**—_n._ and _adj._ **surmount′ing.** [O.Fr. _surmunter_ (Fr. _surmonter_)—L.L. _supermontāre_; see **mount.**]

surmullet, _sər-mul′it_, _n._ a species of red mullet, admired by the Romans for its colour-changes as it died. [Fr. _surmulet._]

surname, _sər′nām_, _n._ an additional name: a family name.—_v.t._ to name by a surname.—_adj._ **surnom′inal.** [On the analogy of Fr. _surnom_, from Eng. **name,** and L. _nōmen, -inis._]

surpass, _sər-päs′_, _v.t._ to go or be beyond: to exceed: to excel.—_adjs._ **surpass′able**; **surpass′ing,** passing beyond others: excellent in a high degree.— Also (_obs._ or _poet._) _adv._ **surpass′ingly.**—_n._ **surpass′ingness.** [Fr. _surpasser_—_sur-_, _passer_, to pass.]

surplice, _sər′plis_, _n._ a white linen vestment worn over the cassock.—_adj._ **sur′pliced,** wearing a surplice. [Fr. _surplis_—L.L. _superpellicium_, an over-garment—_pellis_, skin.]

surplus, _sər′pləs_, _n._ that which is left over: remainder: excess over what is required: excess of revenue over expenditure.—Also _adj._—_n._ **sur′plusage,** surplus: superfluity. [Fr.,—L.L. _super-plūs_—_super_, _plūs_, more.]

surprise, _sər-prīz′_, _n._ a taking unawares: a sudden capture owing to unpreparedness: the emotion caused by anything sudden or contrary to expectation: loosely, astonishment: anything that causes or is intended to cause this emotion.—Also _adj._—_v.t._ to come upon suddenly or unawares: to capture by an unexpected assault: (_obs._) to seize: to lead or bring unawares, to betray (with _into_): to strike with wonder or astonishment: to confuse.—_n._ **surpris′al,** act of surprising.—_adj._ **surprised′.**—_adv._ **surpris′edly.**—_n._ **surpris′er.**—_n._ and _adj._ **surpris′ing.**—_adv._ **surpris′ingly.**—_n._ **surpris′ingness.** [O.Fr. (Fr.) fem. pa.p. of _surprendre_—L. _super_, _prehendĕre_, to catch.]

surquedry, _sər′kwi-dri_, _n._ (_Spens._) arrogance.— Also (_Scott_) **sur′quedy.** [O.Fr. _surcuiderie_—_surcuidier_—L. _super_, _cōgitāre_, to think.]

surra, _sōō′rä_, _n._ a trypanosome disease of horses, &c., in Eastern Asia. [Marathi _sūra_, wheezing.]

surrealism, _sər-ē′ə-lizm_, _n._ a movement in French art and literature, from about 1919 on, that aimed at drawing upon the subconscious and escaping the control of reason or any preconceptions.—_n._ **surre′alist.** [Fr. _surréalisme_—_sur_, above, and _réalisme_, realism.]

surrebut, _sur-i-but′_, _v.i._ to reply to a defendant's rebutter.—_ns._ **surrebutt′al,** a plaintiff's evidence or presentation of evidence, in response to a defendant's rebuttal; **surrebutt′er,** the plaintiff's reply, in common law pleading, to a defendant's rebutter.

surreined, _sur′ānd_, _adj._ (_Shak._ **sur-reyn′d**) overridden. [App. _sur-_ and **rein.**]

surrejoin, _sur-i-join′_, _v.t._ and _v.i._ to reply to a defendant's rejoinder.—_n._ **surrejoind′er,** a plaintiff's reply to a defendant's rejoinder.

surrender, _sə-ren′dər_, _v.t._ to deliver over: to relinquish: to yield up: to resign.—_v.i._ to yield oneself up: to yield.—_n._ act of surrendering.—_ns._ **surrenderee′,** one to whom a legal surrender is made; **surren′derer**; **surren′deror,** (_law_) one who makes a surrender; **surren′dry,** (_obs._) surrender.—**surrender value,** the amount to be paid to an insured person who surrenders his policy. [A.Fr. _surrender_, O.Fr. _surrendre_—_sur_, _rendre_; see **render.**]

surreptitious, _sur-əp-tish′əs_, _adj._ done by stealth or fraud: stealthy.—_adv._ **surrepti′tiously.** [See **subreption.**]

surrey, _sur′i_, _n._ (_U.S._) a light four-wheeled vehicle for four, usu. with two seats. [Developed from a vehicle used in _Surrey._]

surrogate, _sur′ō-gāt_, _n._ a substitute: a deputy, esp. of an ecclesiastical judge: one who grants marriage licences: (_U.S._) a judge of probate.—_ns._ **surr′ogateship**; **surroga′tion,** subrogation; **sur′rogā′tum,** a substitute. [L. _surrogāre, -ātum_—_sub_, in the place of, _rogāre_, to ask.]

surround, _sə-rownd′_, _v.t._ (_obs._) to overflow: to go or extend all around: to encompass, environ: to invest: to make a circuit of.—_n._ an act of surrounding (esp. hunted animals): a border, esp. the floor or floor-covering around a carpet.—_adj._ **surround′ing,** encompassing: neighbouring.—_n._ an encompassing: (in _pl._) environment, things round about. [O.Fr. _suronder_—L. _superundāre_, to overflow—_super_, _unda_, wave; confused with **round.**]

surroyal, _sə-roi′əl_, _n._ any tine of a stag's horn above the royal.

surtax, _sur′taks_, _n._ an additional tax.—_v.t._ to tax additionally.

surtout, _sur-tōō′, -tōōt′_, _n._ (_obs._) an overcoat: (_obs._) lady's hood: (19th cent.) a close-bodied frockcoat: (_fort._) a raised portion of the parapet of a work at the angles, to protect from enfilade fire. [Fr.,—L.L. _supertōtus_, an outer garment—L. _super_, _tōtus_, all.]

surturbrand, surtarbrand, _sur′tər-brand_, _n._ lignite found interbedded with lavas in Iceland. [Ice. _surtarbrandr_—_Surtar_, gen. of _Surtr_, name of a fire-giant, _brandr_, brand.]

surucucu, _sōō-rōō-kōō′kōō_, _n._ a S. American Indian name for the bushmaster.

surveillance, _sər-vā′ləns_, or _-lyəns_, _n._ vigilant supervision: spy-like watching: superintendence.—_n._ **surveill′ant.** [Fr.,—_surveiller_—_sur_, _veiller_ to watch—L. _vigilāre._]

survey, _sər-vā′_, _v.t._ to view comprehensively and extensively: to examine in detail: to obtain by measurements data for mapping: (_Shak._) to perceive, spy.—_ns._ **sur′vey** (also _-vā′_), a general view or a statement of its results: an inspection: collection of data for mapping: an organisation or body of men for that purpose: superintendence.—_ns._ **survey′al**; **survey′ance**; **survey′or,** an overseer: a measurer of land: an inspector (of roads, of weights and measures, of customs duties, &c.); **survey′orship.** [O.Fr. _surveoir_—L. _super_, over, _vidēre_, to see.]

surview, _sər-vū′_, _Spens._ **survew,** _v.t._ to survey, look over: to command a view of.

survive, _sər-vīv′_, _v.t._ to live beyond: to outlive.—_v.i._ to remain alive.—_ns._ **survi′val,** a surviving or living after: anything that continues to exist after others of its kind have disappeared, or after the time to which it naturally belongs; **survi′vance,** survival: succession or right to succeed on surviving the present holder.—_adj._ **survi′ving.**—_ns._ **survi′vor**; **survi′vorship.**—**survival of the fittest,** the longer average life of the fit in the struggle for existence, and the consequent transmission of favourable variations in greater proportion to later generations. [Fr. _survivre_—L. _super_, beyond, _vivĕre_, to live.]

Surya, _sōōr′yä_, _n._ the Hindu sun-god. [Sans. _sūrya_, the sun.]

susceptible, _sə-sep′ti-bl_, _adj._ capable, admitting (with _of_): capable of receiving: impressionable: easily affected by emotion (esp. amatory).—_ns._ **susceptibil′ity, suscep′tibleness.**—_adv._ **suscep′tibly.**—_adj._ **suscep′tive,** capable of receiving or admitting: readily admitting.—_ns._ **suscep′tive**

ness; susceptiv′ity (sus-); suscep′tor, (obs.) a sponsor; suscip′ient, a recipient, esp. of a sacrament.—adj. receiving. [L. suscipĕre, susceptum, to take up—sus- (subs-), up, capĕre, to take.]

suscitate, sus′i-tāt, v.t. to excite, rouse.—n. suscitā′tion. [L. suscitāre, -ātum — sus- (subs-), under, citāre, to arouse.]

suslik, sus′lik, sōos′lik, n. a spermophile, zizel, or ground-squirrel. [Russ.]

suspect, sas-pekt′, v.t. to mistrust: to imagine to be guilty: to doubt: to be ready to believe, but without sufficient evidence: to incline to believe the existence, presence, or agency of: to have an inkling of: to conjecture.—v.i. to imagine guilt, to be suspicious.—n. suspicion: (sus′pekt) a person suspected.—adj. suspected.—adjs. suspect′able; suspect′ed.—adv. suspect′edly.—n. suspec′tedness.—adjs. suspect′ful, suspicious; suspect′less, unsuspicious: unsuspected. [L. suspicĕre, suspectum, to look at secretly or askance—su- (sub-), specĕre, to look.]

suspend, sas-pend′, v.t. to hang: to make to depend: to sustain from falling: to put or hold in a state of suspense or suspension: to make to stop for a time: to defer: to debar from any privilege, office, emolument, &c., for a time: (mus.) to sustain into a following chord, producing discord: to hold in an indeterminate state.—adj. suspen′ded. —ns. suspend′er, one who, or that which, suspends: a strap to support a sock or stocking: (in pl.; U.S.) braces; suspense′, intermission: cessation: deferring, as of judgment: uneasy uncertainty: indecision.—adj. in suspense: (Milt.) suspens′) suspended, held back.—adj. suspense′ful.—n. suspensibil′ity.—adj. suspen′sible.—ns. suspen′sion (-shan), act of suspending: interruption: delay: temporary privation of office or privilege: a conditional withholding: (mus.) holding a note from a chord into the next chord: a discord so produced: (chem.) a mixture of a fluid with dense particles which are prevented from settling by viscosity and impact of molecules; suspen′sion-bridge, a bridge with roadway supported by chains passing over elevated piers.—adj. suspen′sive.—adv. suspen′sively.—ns. suspen′soid, (chem.) a colloid dispersed with difficulty, yielding an unstable solution that cannot be reformed after coagulation; suspen′sor, (bot.) a chain of cells to which a plant-embryo is fixed: a suspensory bandage.—adj. suspensorial (sus-pen-sō′ri-al).—n. suspensō′rium, that which holds up a part, esp. the arrangement joining the lower jaw to the cranium in vertebrates below mammals.— adj. suspen′sory, suspending: having the power or effect of delaying or staying: of the suspensorium.—n. a suspensorium.—suspended animation, temporary cessation of the outward signs and of some of the functions of life; suspend payment, publicly to stop paying debts from insolvency; suspense account, an account in which items are entered which cannot at once be placed in an ordinary account. [L. suspendĕre, -pēnsum—pfx. sus- (subs-), pendĕre, to hang.]

suspercollate, sus-par-kol′āt, v.t. (facet.) to hang. [Sus. per coll., abbrev. for L. suspendātur per collum, let him be hanged by the neck.]

suspicion, sas-pish′an, n. act of suspecting: state of being suspected: the imagining of something without evidence or on slender evidence: inkling: mistrust: (coll.) a slight quantity, as of spirits: (Shak.) ground for suspicion.—v.t. (dial. and U.S.) to suspect.—adjs. suspi′cionless; suspi′cious, full of suspicion: showing suspicion: inclined to suspect: giving ground for suspicion: liable to suspicion, doubtful.—adv. suspi′ciously.—n. suspi′ciousness. [L. suspīciō, -ōnis; see suspect.]

suspire, sas-pīr′, v.i. to sigh: to breathe.—v.t. to breathe forth.—n. suspiration (sus-pa-rā′shan), sighing.—adj. suspirious (sas-pir′i-as), breathing labouredly: sighing. [L. suspīrāre — su- (sub-), spīrāre, to breathe.]

sussarara. Same as siserary.

sustain, sas-tān′, v.t. to hold up: to bear: to support: to provide for: to maintain: to sanction: to keep going: to keep up: to support the life of:

to prolong.—n. (Milt.) means of sustenance.— adjs. sustain′able; sustained.—adv. sustain′edly.—n. sustain′er.—n. and adj. sustain′ing. —ns. sustain′ment, act of sustaining: sustenance; sustenance (sus′ti-nans), that which sustains: maintenance: nourishment.—adj. sustentac′ular, supporting.—n. sustentac′ulum, a supporting part.—v.t. sus′tentate, to sustain.—n. sustentā′tion.—adj. sustentative (sus′tan-tā-tiv, sas-ten′tativ), sustaining.—ns. sus′tentātor, a sustaining part or structure; susten′tion, the act of sustaining.—adjs. susten′tive; sus′tinent, sustaining. [L. sustinēre—pfx. sus- (subs-), tenēre, to hold; partly through O.Fr. sustenir (Fr. soutenir).]

susurrus, s(y)ōō-sur′as, n. a murmuring: a whisper: a rustling.—adj. susurr′ant.—n. susurrā′tion. [L. susurrus.]

sutile, s(y)ōō′til, -til, adj. done by stitching. [L. sūtilis—suĕre, to sew.]

sutler, sut′lar, n. one who sells liquor or provisions to soldiers in camp or garrison: a camp-hawker.— n. sut′lery, a sutler's work or stall.—v.i. sutt′le, to trade as a sutler. [Du. zoetelaar (earlier soeteler).]

sutor, s(y)ōō′tor, -tar, n. a cobbler.—adjs. sutō′rial, sutō′rian, relating to cobbling or to sewing. [souter; or directly from L. sūtor, -ōris, cobbler.]

sutra, sōōt′rä, n. in Sanskrit literature, an aphoristic rule or book of aphorisms on ritual, grammar, metre, philosophy, &c. [Sans. sūtra, thread.]

suttee, sati, sut′ē, sut-ē′, n. an Indian widow who burned herself on her husband's pyre: the custom of so doing.—n. suttee′ism. [Sans. satī, a true wife.]

suttle, sut′l, adj. light (esp. of weight when tare is subtracted): (Milt.) subtle. [subtle.]

suture, s(y)ōō′tyar, -tūr, n. a seam: a stitching: the stitching of a wound: a stitch: a junction or meeting of margins, esp. of bones or of carpels: a line of dehiscence.—v.t. to stitch up.—adj. su′tural. —adv. su′turally.—adj. su′tured.—n. suturā′tion. [L. sūtūra, a seam—suĕre, to sew.]

suversed, sū-vsrst′, adj. (trig.) versed of the supplement. [From the contraction sup. versed.]

suzerain, sōō′za-rān, or sū′, n. a feudal lord: supreme or paramount ruler: a state having supremacy over another.—adj. paramount.—n. su′zerainty, position or power of a suzerain. [Fr., formed in imitation of souverain from sus-, over— L. sūsum (for sūrsum, subvorsum).]

svarabhakti, svä-räb-häk′tē, n. development of a vowel between consonants. [Sans. svára, vowel, bhakti, separation.]

svarga. See swarga.

svastika, svas′tik-ä, n. Same as swastika.

svelte, svelt, adj. lissom, lithe: in art, free, easy, light and bold. [Fr.]

swab, swob, n. a mop for cleaning or drying floors or decks: a brush for wetting foundry moulds: a sponge or the like for cleaning the bore of a fire-arm: a bit of cotton-wool or the like for mopping up blood or discharges, applying antiseptics, cleaning a patient's mouth, or taking a specimen of morbid secretion for examination: a specimen so taken: (slang) a naval officer's epaulet: (slang) a lubber or clumsy fellow: in an old form of whist a card entitling its holder to a share of the stakes.— v.t. to mop with a swab:—pr.p. swabb′ing; pa.t. and pa.p. swabbed.—n. swabb′er, one who uses a swab: a mop for cleaning ovens: a swab in whist as formerly played: (in pl.) whist so played (also whisk and swabbers). [Du. zwabber, swabber.]

swack, swäk, adj. (Scot.) pliant: nimble. [Cf. L.G. swak, Du. zwak; Ger. schwach, weak.]

swad, swod, n. a country lout: a soldier.—n. swadd′y, a soldier, esp. a militiaman. [Perh. Scand.]

swaddle, swod′l, v.t. to swathe: to bandage: to bind tight with clothes, as an infant: (obs.) to thrash.—n. swaddling-clothes: a bandage.—ns. swadd′ler, (Anglo-Ir.) a Methodist or Protestant in general; swadd′ling-band, swadd′ling-cloth, a cloth for swaddling an infant:—pl. swadd′ling-clothes (B.). [O.E. swæthel, swethel, bandage; cf. swathe.]

Swadeshi, *swä-dä'shē, n.* an Indian nationalist movement, favouring home industries and boycott of foreign goods.—Also *adj.*—*n.* **Swade'shism.** [Bengali, own country.]

swag, *swag, v.i.* to sway: to sag: (*pr.p.* **swagg'ing**; *pa.t.* and *pa.p.* **swagged**).—*n.* a swagging: a festoon: a subsidence, as of ground over a mine: a depression: a bundle, esp. a tramp's bundle: baggage, esp. in the Australian bush: plunder.— *adj.* **swag'-bellied**, having a pendulous belly.—*n.* **swag'-belly**, a pendulous belly: one whose belly swags.—*v.i.* **swagg'er**, to walk with a blustering or overweening air of superiority and self-confidence: to brag noisily or ostentatiously: to bully. —*v.t.* to do, bring, render, by swaggering.—*n.* a swaggering gait, manner, mien, or behaviour: one who carries a swag.—*adj.* (*slang*) ostentatiously fashionable: smart.—*ns.* **swagg'er-cane, swagg'er-stick**, a short military cane; **swagg'er-coat**, a smart loose jacket of three-quarter length; **swagg'erer.**—*n.* and *adj.* **swagg'ering.**—*adv.* **swagg'eringly.**—*ns.* **swag'man**, one who carries his swag about with him in his search for work; **swag'shop**, a place where cheap and trashy goods are sold; **swags'man**, a swagman: a burglar's accomplice who carries the plunder. [Related to **sway**; prob. Scand.]

swage, *swäj, n.* (*obs.*) a grooved or moulded border: a die or grooved block for shaping metal.—*v.t.* to shape with a swage: to hammer (powdered metals) together into the form of a bar at a temperature below their melting point. [O.Fr. *souage*.]

swage, *swäj, v.t.* (*Milt.*) to assuage. [A.Fr. *suagier* —L. *suävis*, mild, or aphetic for **assuage**.]

Swahili, *swä-hē'li, n.* the people of Zanzibar and the opposite coast: one of them: loosely, their language (*Kiswahili*), a Bantu tongue modified by Arabic. [Ar. *sawāhil*, pl. of *sāhil*, coast, with suffix.]

swain, *swān, n.* (*arch., poet.*, often *ironical*) a young man: a peasant: a rustic: a lover.—*n.* **swain'ing**, love-making.—*adj.* **swain'ish**, boorish.—*n.* **swain'ishness**, boorishness. [O.N. *sveinn*, young man, servant; O.E. *swān*.]

swale, *swāl, n.* a shady spot: shade: a sunken or marshy place.—*adj.* **swāl'y.** [Cf. O.N. *svalr*, cool.]

swale, *swāl, v.i.* to sway.

swale. See **sweal**.

swallow, *swol'ō, n.* a long-winged migratory bird (*Hirundo rustica*) that catches insects on the wing: any bird of its genus or family: extended to various unrelated birds of similar form or habits.—*ns.* **swall'ow-tail**, a forked tail: a long-tailed dress coat: a butterfly (Papilio) with prolongations of the hind wings: a barbed arrow: a penñon: a swallow-tailed bird (humming-bird, kite).—*adj.* **swall'ow-tailed**, with forked and pointed tail.—*n.* **swall'ow-wort**, an asclepiad (Cynanchum or Vincetoxicum), from the swallow-tailed appearance of its paired pods: hence any asclepiad: greater celandine (q.v.). [O.E. *swalwe, swealwe*; Ger. *schwalbe*.]

swallow, *swol'ō, v.t.* to receive through the gullet into the stomach: to engulf: to take in: to accept, sit down under (as an affront): to believe credulously.—*v.i.* to perform the action of swallowing something.—*n.* an abyss: a swallow-hole: a throat: an act of swallowing: a gulp: a quantity swallowed at once: capacity for swallowing.—*ns.* **swall'et**, a swallow-hole; **swall'ower; swall'ow-hole**, a funnel or fissure through which water passes underground, esp. in limestone. [O.E. *swelgan* (vb.), *geswelg* (n.); cf. Ger. *schwelgen*.]

swam, *swam, pa.t.* (and *Shak.,* &c., *pa.p.*) of **swim.**

swami, *swä'mē, n.* a Hindu idol: a Hindu religious instructor. [Hind. *swāmī*, lord, master.]

swamp, *swomp, n.* a tract of wet, spongy (in U.S. generally tree-clad) land: low ground filled with water.—*v.t.* to sink or involve in, or as in, a swamp: to cause to fill with water, as a boat: to overwhelm, inundate.—*v.i.* to become swamped.—*adj.* of, of the nature of, swamp: living or growing in swamps.—*adj.* **swamp'y.**—**swamp cypress**, Taxodium, a deciduous conifer of swamps in Southern U.S.; **swamp oak**, Casuarina. [Perh. from L.G. prob. akin to O.E. *swamm*, mushroom, Ger *schwamm*, sponge, fungus.]

swan, *swon, n.* any species of Cygnus, a genus of large, graceful, stately, long-necked birds o' the duck family.—*ns.* **swan'-goose**, the Chin goose; **swan'herd**, one who tends swans; **swan'hopping** (see **swan-upping**).—*adj.* **swan'like.**— *ns.* **swan'-maid'en**, in Germanic folklore, a maiden who can become a swan by putting on her feather-garment; **swan'-mark**, the notch made on the swan's upper mandible; **swan'-mussel**, a large freshwater mussel; **swan'-neck**, an S-shaped bend or piece; **swann'ery**, a place where swans are kept or bred.—*adj.* **swann'y**, swanlike.— *ns.* **swan's'-down, swans'down**, the under-plumage of a swan: a soft woollen or mixed cloth: a thick cotton with a soft nap on one side; **swan'-shot**, a shot of large size, like buckshot; **swan'-skin**, the unplucked skin of a swan: a soft, nappy, fine-twilled fabric; **swan'-song**, the fabled song of a swan just before its death: a poet's or musician's last work; **swan'-upp'ing**, an annual expedition up the Thames for the marking of young swans belonging to the crown and to the Dyers' and Vintners' Companies (see **up**, verb). [O.E. *swan* Ger. *schwan*, Du. *zwaan*.]

swang, *swang*, a rare *pa.t.* (*Wordsworth*) of **swing.**

swank, *swangk, adj.* (*Scot.*) slender, pliant: agile.— *n.* (*slang*) ostentation: pretentiousness.—*v.i.* (*slang* to show off: to swot.—*n.* **swank'er.**—*adj.* **swank'ing**, strapping: (*slang*) showing off: showy.—*n.* **swank'y**, (*Scot.*) an active fellow: poor thin beer or any sloppy drink, even sweetened water and vinegar.—Also **swank'ey.**—*adj.* (*slang*) ostentatious. [Cf. O.E. *swancor*, pliant.]

swap, swop, *swop, v.t.* to strike: to reap close: to slam, plump, slap down: to strike (as a bargain) to give in exchange: to barter.—*v.i.* to smite: to flop: to barter: (*pr.p.* **swapp'ing, swopp'ing**; *pa.t.* and *pa.p.* **swapped, swopped, swapt, swopt**) —*n.* a stroke: an exchange.—*adv.* suddenly.—*n.* **swapp'er, swopp'er**, one who swaps: a very big thing, whopper.—*n.* and *adj.* **swapp'ing, swopp'ing.** [M.E. *swappen*; perh. imit.; or conn. with **sweep, swoop.**]

swaraj, *swä-räj', n.* (*Ind.*) self-government, independence, home-rule.—*n.* **swaraj'ist**, an advocate of Indian home-rule. [Sans. *svarāj—sva*, own *rāj*, rule.]

sward, *swawrd, n.* the grassy surface of land: green turf.—Also **swarth.**—*v.t.* to cover with sward —*adjs.* **sward'ed, sward'y**, covered with sward [O.E. *sweard*, skin, rind; Du. *zwoord*, Ger *schwarte*.]

sware, *swär*, *arch. pa.t.* of **swear.**

swarf, *swawrf, swerf, swerf, swerve, swerv, v.i* (*Scot.*) to faint.—*n.* **swarf, swerf**, (*Scot.*) a swoon

swarf, *swawrf, n.* grit from an axle, &c.: stone o metal grindings, filings, turnings. [O.N. *svarf* file-dust.]

Swarga, Svarga, *swär'gä, swur', n.* heaven: Indra' paradise—(*Southey*) **Swer'ga.** [Sans. *Svarga*.]

swarm, *swawrm, n.* a body of bees going off t found a new community: a colony, offshoot: throng of insects or other small animals: a throng —*v.i.* to go off in a swarm: to occur or come in swarms: to abound, teem.—*v.t.* to cause to swarm (chiefly *U.S.* except in *pass.*) to throng.—*n.* **swarm'er.**—*n.* and *adj.* **swarm'ing.**—*n.* **swarm' spore**, (*bot.*) a free-swimming generally ciliated asexual reproductive body: (*zool.*) an active germ produced by sporulation in Protozoa. [O.E *swearm*; Ger. *schwarm*.]

swarm, *swawrm, v.t.* and *v.i.* to climb by clasping with arms and legs. [Origin unknown.]

swart, *swawrt, swarth, swawrth, adj.* black: dusky blackening, hence, malignant, baleful.—*ns.* **swart' back** (O.N. *svartbakr*), the great black-backe gull; **swarthiness** (*swawr'dhi-nis*).—*adj.* **swarthy** (*swawr'dhi*), blackish: dark-skinned.—*n.* **swart' ness.**—*adj.* **swart'y.**—**swart star**, (*Milt.*) app. the Dog-star, because at the time of its appearance the complexion darkens. [O.E. *sweart*; O.N. *svartr* Ger. *schwarz*, black.]

fāte, fär, àsk; mē, hǝr (her); *mīne; mōte; mūte; mōōn; dhen* (then)

swarth, *swawrth*. Same as **sward, swart,** or (*Shak.*) **swath.**

swarve. See **swerve.**

swash, *swosh, n.* slush: pig-wash: a splash: a wash of liquid: a dash: a heavy blow: a clashing or dashing sound: a swashbuckler: swaggering. —*v.t.* and *v.i.* to dash: to splash: to clash.—*ns.* **swash′buckler**, one who clashes a sword on a buckler, hence a bully, a blusterer; **swash′er**, (*Shak.*) a blusterer.—*n.* and *adj.* **swash′ing**, slashing, crushing: blustering.—*adj.* **swash′y**, slushy. [Imit.]

swash, *swosh, n.* a piece of turner's work with mouldings oblique to the axis: a flourish on a letter.—Also *adj.*—*n.* **swash′work**, turner's work cut obliquely.—**swash letters**, Italic capitals with top and bottom flourishes; **swash plate**, a disk set obliquely on a revolving axis. [Origin unknown.]

swastika, *swas′ti-kä, swos′,* **svastika**, *svas′, n.* an ancient and worldwide symbol, a cross with arms bent at a right angle, esp. clockwise (see also **fylfot**), emblematic of the sun, good luck, anti-semitism, or Naziism. [Sans. *svastika—svasti,* well-being—*sū,* good, *asti,* being.]

swat, *swot, v.t.* to hit smartly or heavily.—*n.* a sharp or heavy blow.—*n.* **swatt′er**, a flexible fly-killer. [**squat.**]

swat, *swot, swawt,* (*Scot.* and *Spens.*) *pa.t.* of **sweat. swat.** See **swot.**

swatch, *swoch, n.* (*Scot.*) a sample, esp. of cloth. [Origin unknown.]

swath, *swawth, swoth, n.* a band of mown ground or of grass or corn cut by the scythe or ready for the scythe: a broad band: the sweep of a scythe. —Also **swathe** (*swādh*).—*adj.* **swathy** (*swawth′i, swādh′i*). [O.E. *swæth* and *swathu,* track; Du. *zwade.*]

swath, *swoth, n.* (*Shak.*). Same as **swathe.**

swathe, *swādh, v.t.* to bind round, envelop: to bandage. — *n.* a bandage: a wrapping. — *n.pl.* **swath′ing-clothes** (*Shak.*); another reading **swath′ling-, swoth′ling-), -clouts** (*Shak.*), swaddling-clothes. [O.E. *swathian.*]

swats, *swots, n.* (*Scot.*) new ale. [O.E. *swatan* (pl.), beer.]

swatter, *swot′ər, swåt′ər, v.i.* (*prov.*) to squatter: to splash or spill about. [Cf. **squatter.**]

sway, *swā, v.t.* to swing about or from side to side: to cause to incline: to divert: to influence by power or moral force: to wield: to govern: to control: to have a preponderating influence upon: (*naut.*) to hoist.—*v.i.* to swing: to oscillate: to swerve: (*Shak.*) to proceed, bend one's course: (*Spens.*) to advance in hostility: to incline to one side: to rule: to have preponderating weight or influence.—*n.* (*Shak.*) rotation: a sweep: a swing: a swerve: directing force or influence: preponderance: rule.—*adjs.* **swayed, sway′-back,** bent down in the back, as a horse.—*n.* **sway′er.**—*n.* and *adj.* **sway′ing.** [Perh. from a lost O.E. word, or the corresponding O.N. *sveigja,* to bend, swing; prob. partly from L.G. *swājen* (Ger. *schweien*), to swing.]

sweal, sweel, *swēl,* **swale, swayl,** *swāl, v.t.* to scorch: to singe: to roast in the skin: to burn off, as heather and gorse, soot in a chimney: to cause to gutter: to waste away.—*v.i.* to be burning hot: to gutter as a candle.—*n.* and *adj.* **sweal′ing, swal′ing, swayl′ing.** [O.E. *swǽlan* (trans.), *swelan* (intrans.), to burn.]

swear, *swār, v.i.* to take or utter an oath: to utter imprecations: to utter defiant noises (as a cat): (*rare*) to give evidence on oath.—*v.t.* to assert, promise, agree to, confirm, or value, on oath: to assert loudly or boldly: (*Shak.*) to invoke: to administer an oath to: to put on oath: to bind by oath: to admit to office by an oath: to bring, put, render, by swearing: (*pa.t.* **swōre,** *arch.* **swāre**; *pa.p.* **sworn,** *arch.* and *vulg.* **swōre**).—*n.* an oath: an expression that is formally an oath or a curse, or bad language generally.—*n.* **swear′er.**—*n.* and *adj.* **swear′ing.**—*n.* **swear′-word,** a word that is considered bad language.—*adj.* **sworn,** attested: bound by oath: having taken an oath: devoted, inveterate, confirmed, as if by oath.—**swear at,**

to hurl oaths and curses at: to be very incongruous with, esp. in colour: **swear by,** to invoke as witness to an oath: to put complete confidence in; **swear in,** to inaugurate by oath; **swear off,** to renounce, promise to give up; **swear to,** to affirm or identify on oath. [O.E. *swerian*; Du. *zweren,* Ger. *schwören.*]

sweard, *swērd, n.* (*Spens.*). Same as **sword.**

sweat, *swet, n.* the moisture excreted by the skin: moisture exuding or seeming to exude from any-thing: a state, fit, or process of exuding sweat: an exercise or treatment inducing sweat: sweating-sickness: labour: drudgery: fidgety anxiety.— *v.i.* to give out sweat or moisture: to toil, drudge for poor wages: to suffer penalty, smart: to exude: to become coated with moisture.—*v.t.* to give forth as, or like, sweat: to wet or soil with sweat: to cause to sweat: to squeeze money or extortionate interest from: to exact the utmost from: (*U.S.*) to wring evidence or confession from: to extract undue gains from, e.g. by removing gold from a coin: to compel to hard work for mean wages: to unite by partial fusion of metal surfaces:— *pa.t.* and *pa.p.* **sweat′ed** (or **sweat**). — *adj.* **sweat′ed.**—*ns.* **sweat′er,** one who sweats: a cause of sweating: a diaphoretic: a heavy jersey, orig. one for reducing weight by sweating, now for intervals in exercise, &c.: one who sweats coins or workers: a London street ruffian in Queen Anne's time who prodded passengers with his sword; **sweat′iness.**—*n.* and *adj.* **sweat′ing.**— *adj.* **sweat′y.**—**sweating sickness,** an extremely fatal epidemic disorder which ravaged Europe, and esp. England, in the 15th and 16th centuries— a violent inflammatory fever, with a fetid perspira-tion over the whole body; **sweating system,** the practice of working poor people at starvation wages, for long hours, at home or in unhealthy rooms. [O.E. *swǽtan,* to sweat; cf. Ger. *schweissen*; the O.E. n. was *swát.*]

sweath-band, *swēth′-band, n.* (*Spens.*) a swaddling-band. [**swathe.**]

Swede, *swēd, n.* a native or citizen of *Sweden*: a Swedish turnip—a buff-flowered, glaucous-leaved kind.—*adj.* **Swēd′ish.**—*n.* the Scandinavian lan-guage of Sweden.

Swedenborgian, *swē-dn-bor′ji-ən, n.* a follower of Emanuel *Swedenborg,* a Swedish religious teacher (1688-1772), founder of the New Jerusalem Church. —*n.* **Swedenbor′gianism.**

swee, *swē, n.* (*Scot.*) a sway: a swing.—*v.t.* and *v.i.* to sway: to swing. [**sway.**]

sweep, *swēp, v.i.* to pass swiftly or forcibly, esp. with a swinging movement or in a curve: to move with trailing or flowing drapery, hence with pomp, indignation, &c.: to extend in a long curve: to row with sweeps: to range systematically or searchingly.—*v.t.* to pass something brushingly over: (*poet.*) to elicit by so doing: to pass brush-ingly: to wipe, clean, move, or remove with a broom: to carry along or off with a long brushing stroke or force: to wipe out or remove at a stroke: to perform with a sweeping movement: to trail with a curving movement: to drag as with a net or rope: to describe, generate, or swing through, as a curve, angle, or area: to row with sweeps: (*pa.t.* and *pa.p.* **swept**).—*n.* act of sweeping: a swinging movement, swing: onrush: impetus: a clearance: range, compass: a curved stair: a curved carriageway before a building: sweepings: a sweepstake: a pump-handle: a long oar: a wire drag used in searching for shoals, mines, &c.: a chimney-sweeper: (*slang*) a blackguard.—*ns.* **sweep′er; sweep′ing,** the action of the verb in any sense: (usu. in *pl.*) things collected by sweep-ing, rubbish.—*adj.* performing the action of sweeping in any sense: of wide scope, wholesale, indiscriminate.—*adv.* **sweep′ingly.**—*ns.* **sweep′-ingness; sweep′-net,** a long net paid out in a curve and dragged ashore: an insect net with a handle; **sweep′-saw,** a turning-saw; **sweep′-stake(s),** a method of gambling by which par-ticipators' stakes are pooled, numbers, horses, &c., assigned by lot, and prize(s) awarded accordingly on decision of event: such a prize, race, &c. (for *adv.* see **soopstake**); **sweep'-wash'er,** one who recovers gold or silver from the sweepings of refineries. — *adj.* **sweep'y,** swaying, sweeping, curving. [Prob. from a lost O.E. word related to *swápan,* to sweep, *geswǽpe,* sweepings; cf. **soop, swoop.**]

sweer, sweir, *swēr, adj.* (*Scot.*) slothful: loth.— Also **sweered, sweert, sweirt.**—*n.* **sweir'ness.** [O.E. *swǽr, swǽre,* heavy, grievous, sluggish; cf. Ger. *schwer.*]

sweet, *swēt, adj.* having one of the fundamental varieties of taste, that of sugar, honey, ripe fruits (distinguished from *salt, acid* or *sour,* and *bitter*): sugary: cloying: sickly in taste, smell, &c.: grateful to the taste, senses, or feelings: taking: fragrant: clear and tuneful: smoothly running: easy, free from harshness, benign: fresh, not salt: fresh, not tainted: wholesome: gracious: amiable: mild, soft, gentle: (*coll.*) delightful, charming: dear, beloved: ingratiating, often insipidly: (*coll.*) more or less enamoured (with *on,* or *upon*).—*adv.* **sweetly.**—*n.* that which is sweet: a sweet dish (pudding, fruit, &c.) as a course: a sweetmeat, confection: (in *pl.*) wines and cordials sweetened with syrup: a beloved person.—*v.t.* (now *rare*) to sweeten.—*adj.* **sweet'-and-twen'ty,** at once fair and young—after Shakespeare, who perhaps meant only sweet indeed (see **twenty** for intensive use).—*ns.* **sweet'-bay,** the laurel (*Laurus nobilis*): (*U.S.*) a kind of magnolia; **sweet'bread,** the pancreas, or sometimes the thymus, esp. as food; **sweet'-brier, -briar,** a wild rose with fragrant foliage (*Rosa rubiginosa*); **sweet'-Cic'ely,** an aromatic umbelliferous plant, *Myrrhis odorata*; **sweet'-corn,** a sweet variety of maize.—*v.t.* **sweet'en,** to make sweet. — *ns.* **sweet'ener; sweet'ening; sweet'-flag,** an aromatic araceous pond-plant, *Acorus Calamus;* **sweet'gale,** bog-myrtle; **sweet'heart,** a lover or beloved.—*v.t.* and *v.i.* to court.—*n.* **sweet'ing,** a sweet apple: (*Shak.*) a darling.—*adj.* **sweet'ish.**—*n.* **sweet'ishness.**—*adv.* **sweet'ly.**—*ns.* **sweet'meat,** a confection made wholly or chiefly of sugar: (*obs.*) any sweet food; **sweet'ness; sweet'-oil,** olive-oil: rape-oil: any oil of mild pleasant taste; **sweet'-pea',** a S. European papilionaceous garden plant (*Lathyrus odoratus*) with bright-coloured fragrant flowers; **sweet'-pota'to,** batata, a tropical and sub-tropical twining plant (*Ipomoea Batatas*) of the convolvulus family, with large sweetish edible tubers.—*adjs.* **sweet'-sa'voured; sweet'-scent'ed,** having a sweet smell.—*ns.* **sweet'-sop,** a tropical American evergreen (*Anona squamosa*): its pulpy fruit; **sweet'-stuff,** confectionery.—*adjs.* **sweet'-tem'pered,** having a mild, amiable disposition; **sweet'-toothed,** fond of sweet things; **sweet'-water,** freshwater.—*n.* a very sweet white grape.—*ns.* **sweet'-Will'iam,** *Dianthus barbatus,* a garden pink with bearded petals; **sweet'-will'ow,** one of various trees, e.g. bay-leaved sweet-willow, *Salix pentandra:* sweet-gale; **sweet'wood,** a name for various S. American and West Indian lauraceous trees; **sweet'-wort,** wort before addition of hops; **sweet'y, sweet'ie,** a sweetmeat, confection: (*U.S.*) a sweetheart. [O.E. *swéte;* Ger. *süsz,* Gr. *hēdys,* L. *suávis,* Sans. *svādús,* sweet.]

sweir. See **sweer.**

swelchie, *swelhh'i, n.* (*Orkney*) a whirlpool: a tidal race. [O.N. *svelgr;* cf. **swallow.**]

swell, *swel, v.i.* to expand: to increase in volume: to be inflated: to bulge out: to grow louder: to rise into waves: to heave: to well up: to rise and fall in loudness: to be bombastic: to be elated or dilated with emotion: to give a feeling of expansion or welling up.—*v.t.* to augment: to expand: to dilate: to fill full: to louden: to elate: (*p.t.* **swelled;** *pa.p.* **swelled, swollen,** *swōln, swōl'ǝn,* sometimes **swōln**).—*n.* act, power, habit, or condition of swelling: distension: a heaving: a bulge: an enlargement: a loudening: a device in an organ for increasing tone: a crescendo followed by a diminuendo: a rising ground: (*slang*) a dandy, a fashionably or finely dressed person, a member of the governing class, a bigwig,

an adept.—*adj.* (*slang*) of, of the nature of, befitting a swell, a vague word of commendation.—*n.* **swell'dom,** (*slang*) the fashionable world.—*adj.* **swelled; swelled'-head'ed,** also **swell'-head'ed,** conceited.—*n.* **swell'er.**—*adj.* and *n.* **swell'ing.**—*adv.* **swell'ingly.**—*adj.* **swell'ish,** foppish, dandified.—*ns.* **swell'-mob,** well-dressed pickpockets collectively; **swell'-mobs'man.**—**swelled head,** self-conceit, esp. in one carried away by success. [O.E. *swellan;* Ger. *schwellen.*]

swelt, *swelt, v.i.* (*obs.* or *dial.*) to die: (*Spens., Scot.*) to faint: to swelter: (*Spens.*) to pass like a fever :—*pa.t.* **swelt'ed,** (*Spens.*) **swelt.**—*v.i.* **swelt'er,** to endure great heat: to sweat copiously: to exude. —*v.t.* to overpower, as with heat: to exude.—*n.* a sweltering: a sweating: sweltered venom.—*adj.* **swelt'ered.**—*n.* and *adj.* **swelt'ering.** — *adj.* **swelt'ry,** sultry: oppressive or oppressed with heat. [O.E. *sweltan,* to die.]

swept, *swept, pa.t.* and *pa.p.* of **sweep.**

Swerga. See **Swarga.**

swerve, *swǝrv, v.i.* to turn aside: to deviate: (*Milt.*) to give way, shrink: (*Dryden*) to swarm, scramble. —*v.t.* to deflect: to cause a ball to swerve in the air.—*n.* a turning aside: a deviation: a deflection: (*cricket*) a ball that swerves in the air: the act or trick of making it do so.—*adj.* **swerve'less,** unswerving.—*n.* **swerv'er.**—*n.* and *adj.* **swerv'ing.** [M.E.; the O.E. *sweorfan,* to rub, file, scour, is not known to have had this sense.]

sweven, *swev'n, n.* (*obs.*) a dream. [O.E. *swefn.*]

swift, *swift, adj.* fleet: rapid: speedy: prompt.— *adv.* swiftly.—*n.* a bird (*Apus,* or *Cypselus, apus*) superficially like a swallow but structurally nearer the humming-birds and goatsuckers: any bird of its genus or family: the common newt: a reel for winding yarn: the main cylinder of a carding-machine: a rapid.—*adjs.* **swift'-foot, -ed.**—*n.* **swift'let,** a bird (*Collocalia*) akin to the swift, the builder of edible nests.—*adv.* **swift'ly.**—*n.* **swift'ness.**—*adj.* **swift'-winged.** [O.E. *swift,* from same root as **swoop.**]

swift, *swift, v.t.* to tighten with a rope.—*n.* **swift'er,** a rope used to tighten or keep a thing in its place. [Prob. Scand. or L.G.]

swig, *swig, n.* a pulley with ropes not parallel.—*v.t.* to tighten by hauling at right angles: to castrate by ligature. [Prob. conn. with **swag.**]

swig, *swig, n.* a draught: toast and ale: (*Oxford*) a wassail.—*v.t.* to take a swig or swigs of or from.— *v.i.* to drink, take swigs. [Origin unknown.]

swill, *swil, v.t.* or *v.i.* to rinse: to dash water over: to wash: to drink greedily or largely.—*n.* a large draught of liquor: hog-wash.—*n.* **swill'er.**—*n.* and *adj.* **swill'ing.**—*n.* **swill'-tub,** a tub for hog-wash. [O.E. *swilian,* to wash.]

swim, *swim, v.i.* to propel oneself in water (or other liquid): to float: to come to the surface: to travel or be conveyed by water: to be suffused: to be immersed or steeped: to glide smoothly: to be dizzy.—*v.t.* to pass by swimming: to make to swim or float: to test for witchcraft by immersion: (*pr.p.* **swimm'ing;** *pa.t.* **swam,** *swam,* old-fashioned **swum;** *pa.p.* **swum,** *Shak.,* &c., **swam**). —*n.* an act, performance, or spell of swimming: any motion like swimming: a crossing-place for swimmers: a place where many fishes swim: the general movement or current of affairs: air-bladder of a fish.—*n.* **swim'-bladder,** a fish's air-bladder.—*adj.* **swimm'able,** capable of being swum.—*ns.* **swimm'er; swimm'eret,** a crustacean's abdominal appendage used in swimming. —*n.* and *adj.* **swimm'ing.**—*ns.* **swimm'ing-bath; swimm'ing-bell,** a medusoid modified as a swimming organ.—*adv.* **swimm'ingly,** in a gliding manner, as if swimming: smoothly, successfully.—*ns.* **swimm'ingness,** the state of swimming: a melting look, tearfulness; **swimm'ing-pond, -pool.**—*adj.* **swimm'y,** inclined to dizziness.—**in the swim,** in the main current (of affairs, business, &c.). [O.E. *swimman;* Ger. *schwimmen.*]

swindge (*Milt.*), **swindge-buckler** (*Shak.*). See **swinge.**

swindle, *swin'dl, v.t.* and *v.i.* to cheat.—*n.* a fraud: anything not really what it appears to be.—*n.*

swin'dler, a cheat.—*n.* and *adj.* **swin'dling**. [Ger. *schwindler*, a giddy-minded projector, swindler—*schwindeln*, to be giddy.]

swine, *swīn*, *n.* a pig: a sensual person: a term of strong abuse:—*pl.* **swine**.—*adj.* **swine'-drunk**, (*Shak.*) bestially drunk.—*ns.* **swine'-fe'ver**, hog-cholera, a contagious disease of swine due to a filterable virus; **swine'-fish**, the wolf-fish; **swine'-herd**, one who herds swine; **swine'hood**, the status of a swine; **swine'-keeping**; **swine'-pox**, chicken-pox: a skin disease of swine; **swin'ery**, a place where pigs are kept: swinishness: swine collectively; **swine's'-cress**, a cruciferous weed of waste places (Senebiera or Coronopus): applied to various other plants; **swine's'-succ'ory**, a small plant (Arnoseris) akin to chicory; **swine'-stone**, stinkstone; **swine'-sty**, a pig-sty.—*adj.* **swin'ish**, of or like swine: sensual: filthy: voracious: beastly.—*adv.* **swin'ishly**.—*n.* **swin'-ishness**. [O.E. *swín*, a pig; Ger. *schwein*, L. (adj.) *suīnus*—*sūs*, Gr. *hŷs*.]

swing, *swing*, *v.i.* to sway or wave to and fro, as a body hanging freely: to amuse oneself on a swing: to oscillate: to hang: to be hanged: to sweep, wheel, sway: to swerve: to move forward with swaying gait: to turn round as a ship (e.g. to test the compass).—*v.t.* to cause to swing: to set swinging: to control: to sway: to hurl, whirl: to brandish: to transport in suspension: to move in a sweep: to sound or send forth by swinging: to indicate by an oscillation: to impart swing to: to perform as swing-music: to fix up so as to hang freely: (*pa.t.* **swung**, rarely **swang**; *pa.p.* **swung**).—*n.* act, manner, or spell of swinging: oscillating, waving, sweeping: motion to and fro: the sweep or compass of a swinging body: sway: scope, free indulgence: impetus: vigorous sweeping rhythm: jazz music with impromptu complications: a suspended seat or carriage for the amusement of swinging.—*ns.* **swing'-back**, a reaction: a camera back that can be tilted; **swing'boat**, a boat-shaped swinging carriage for fairs, &c.; **swing'-bridge**, a bridge that may be opened by swinging to one side; **swing'-door**, a door (usu. one of a pair) that opens either way and swings to of itself; **swinger** (*swing'ər*), a person or thing that swings: either of the middle pair in a team of six horses: a Hindu votary who swings from hooks in his flesh: (*cricket*) a ball bowled so as to swerve in the air: an ill-centred gramophone record; **swing'-han'dle**, a pivoted (esp. arched) handle; **swinging** (*swing'ing*), the act of moving to and fro in suspension, esp. as a pastime: (*coll.*) hanging: hanging by hooks, as by a Hindu devotee.—*adj.* swaying: turning: with a swing: having a free easy motion.—*n.* **swing'ing-boom**, the spar that stretches the foot of a lower studding-sail.—*adv.* **swing'ingly**.—*ns.* **swing'ing-post**, the post to which a gate is hung; **swing'-music**, jazz with improvised ornaments and individual flings; **swing'-plough**, a plough without a fore-wheel under the beam; **swing'-shelf**, a hanging shelf; **swing'-stock**, an upright timber, with a blunt upper edge for swingling flax on—also **swing'ing-block**; **swing'-swang**, a complete (to and fro) oscillation; **swing'tree**, a whippletree; **swing'-wheel**, the wheel that drives a clock pendulum.—**in full swing**, in mid-career: in fully active operation; **swing the lead**, (*naut.* and *mil. slang*) to invent specious excuses to evade duties. [O.E. *swingan*; Ger. *schwingen*.]

Swing, *swing*, *n.* a fictitious captain in whose name rick-burners sent threatening letters to users of threshing-mills about 1830-33: the movement, operations, or methods of the rick-burners.—Also *adj.*—*n.* **swing'ism**.

swinge, *swinj*, *v.t.* to beat: to chastise: to lash, sway, flourish:—*pr.p.* **swinge'ing**.—*n.* **swinge'-buckler**, a swashbuckler.—*adj.* **swinge'ing**, great, huge, thumping.—*adv.* **swinge'ingly**.—*n.* **swinger** (*swinj'ər*), any person or thing great or astonishing: a bold lie, a whopper. [M.E. *swenge*—O.E. *swengan*, to shake, causative of *swingan*, to swing.]

swinge, *swinj*, *v.t.* (*Spens.*). Same as singe.

swingle, *swing'gl*, *n.* a scutching tool: the swipple of a flail.—*v.t.* to scutch.—*ns.* **swing'le-hand**, a scutching tool; **swing'letree**, a whippletree: a swing-stock; **swing'ling**; **swing'ling-stock**, a swing-stock. [Cf. O.E. *swingell*, stroke, scourge, rod, and M.Du. *swinghel*.]

swink, *swingk*, *v.i.* (*arch.*) to toil.—*n.* toil.—*adj.* **swinked** (*Milt.* **swink't**), toil-worn, fatigued. [O.E. *swinc* (n.), *swincan* (vb.).]

swipe, *swīp*, *n.* a sweeping stroke: a swath.—*v.t.* to strike with a swipe: to gulp: to purloin.—*v.i.* to make a swipe: to sweep for old anchors.—*ns.* **swip'er**, **swipes**, bad or spoilt beer: small-beer.—*adj.* **swip'ey**, fuddled with malt liquor. [O.E. *swīpian*, to beat.]

swipple, *swip'l*, *n.* a swingle or striking part of a flail. [Cf. **swipe**, **sweep**.]

swire, *swīr*, *n.* (*obs.*) a neck: a hollow between two hills. [O.E. *swēora* (Northern *swīra*), neck.]

swirl, *swərl*, *n.* an eddy: a whirl: a curl.—*v.t.* to whirl: to wind.—*v.i.* to eddy: to whirl: to spin.—*adj.* **swirl'y**. [Orig. Scot.; cf. Norw. *svirla*.]

swish, *swish*, *n.* the sound of twigs sweeping through the air: dashing spray: a cane or birch.—*v.t.* to whisk with a swish: to flog, thrash.—*v.i.* to go with a swish.—*adv.* with a swish.—*n.* **swish'er**.—*n.* and *adj.* **swish'ing**.—*adj.* **swish'y**. [Imit.]

swish, *swish*, *adj.* (*slang*) smart.

Swiss, *swis*, *adj.* of Switzerland.—*n.* a native or citizen of Switzerland: the High German dialect spoken by most of the Swiss:—*pl.* **Swiss** (formerly **Swiss'es**).—*n.* **Swit'zer**, a Swiss: a Swiss (or other) mercenary or member of a bodyguard.—**Swiss chard** (see **chard**); **Swiss Guards**, a body of Swiss mercenaries in the French guards from 1616, wiped out in the Revolution: the Pope's bodyguard; **Swiss roll**, a thin cake rolled up with jam: a flexible floating pier.

swissing, *swis'ing*, *n.* ordinary calendering.

switch, *swich* (*Shak.* **swits**, *swits*), *n.* a long flexible twig: a tapering riding-whip: a rod, cane: an application of a switch: a brushing blow: a whisk, jerk: a tool for beating eggs or cream: a tress, usu. false: a movable rail for shunting: a change-over (esp. in cards to another suit, led or called): a device for making, breaking, or changing an electric circuit: a switch-board: a turn of a switch.—*v.t.* to strike with a switch: to drive, as with a switch: to brush against: to whisk, jerk, lash: to beat up, whip (as an egg, cream): to prune: to shunt: to divert: to turn (off, on, or to another circuit).—*v.i.* to use a switch: to turn aside: to change over: to whisk.—*ns.* **switch'-back**, (*orig.*) a zigzag mountain railway on which the train shunted back at each stage: an up-and-down track on which cars rise by the momentum gained in coming down: an up-and-down road; **switch'-board**, a board or frame bearing apparatus for making or breaking an electric current or circuit: a board for connecting telephones; **switch'ing**; **switch'man**, a pointsman; **switch'-plant**, a plant with long slim green shoots, the leaves reduced or wanting.—*adj.* **switch'y**. [Earlier *swits* (*Shak.*), *switz*; prob. from Du. or L.G.]

switchel, *swich'l*, *n.* treacle-beer, molasses and water, &c. [Origin unknown.]

swith, *swith*, *adv.* (*obs.*) quickly: at once.—*interj.* away. [O.E. *swīthe*, very.]

swither, *swidh'ər*, *v.i.* (*Scot.*) to be undecided.—*n.* indecision: flurry. [Poss. O.E. *swethrian*, to subside.]

swivel, *swiv'l*, *n.* a ring or link that turns round on a pin or neck: a swivel-gun.—*v.t.* and *v.i.* to turn on a pin or pivot.—*ns.* **swiv'el-eye**, a squint-eye; **swiv'el-gun**, a gun that turns on a pivot; **swiv'el-hook**, a hook secured to anything by means of a swivel. [O.E. *swīfan*, to move quickly, to turn round.]

swizzle, *swiz'l*, *v.i.* to drink to excess.—*n.* a mixed or compounded drink containing rum or other spirit.—*n.* **swizzle'-stick**, a stick used to mix a swizzle.

swob, **swobbers**, &c. See **swab**.

swollen, *swōl'ən*, *swōln*, *pa.p.* of **swell**, and *adj.*

swoon, *swōōn,* also (*arch.* and *poet.*) sound, *sownd,* **swoun,** *swoun,* **swound, swownd,** *swownd* (*Spens.* **swone**), *n.* a fainting fit: (*Spens.*) a sleep.—*v.i.* to faint: (*poet.*) to be languorous, give a feeling of fainting: (*poet.*) to subside.—*adj.* **swooned,** in a swoon.—*n.* and *adj.* **swoon'ing.**—*adv.* **swoon'ingly.** [Prob. from M.E. *iswowen*—O.E. *geswógen* (pa.p.; other parts unknown), in a swoon, wrongly analysed as *in swoon.*]

swoop, *swōōp, v.i.* (*obs.*) to sweep along: to come down with a sweeping rush: to rush suddenly.— *v.t.* (*obs.*) to pounce on, to snatch with a sweep, esp. on the wing.—*n.* an act of swooping: a sudden onslaught.—*adv.* **swoop'stake-like** (see under **soop**). [App. O.E. *swápan,* to sweep; perh. influenced by **soop.**]

swop. See **swap.**

sword, *sōrd, n.* a weapon with a long blade, sharp upon one or both edges, for cutting or thrusting: a blade or flat rod resembling a sword: a swordfish's snout: destruction or death by the sword or by war: war: military force: the emblem of vengeance or justice, or of authority and power.— *v.i.* to wield a sword.—*adj.* **sword'-and-buck'ler,** fought or armed with sword and buckler.—*ns.* **sword'-arm, -hand,** the arm, hand, that wields the sword; **sword'-bay'onet,** a bayonet shaped somewhat like a sword, and used as one; **sword'-bean,** an Indian papilionaceous plant (Canavalia) with long sword-shaped edible pods: its seed; **sword'-bearer,** a public officer who carries the sword of state; **sword'-belt,** a belt from which the sword is hung; **sword'-bill,** a S. American humming-bird with a bill longer than its body; **sword'-blade,** the blade of a sword; **sword'-break'er,** an old weapon for grasping and breaking an adversary's sword; **sword'-cane, -stick,** a cane or stick containing a sword; **sword'craft,** swordsmanship: military power; **sword'-cut,** a cut with the edge of a sword: a wound or scar so produced; **sword'-dance,** a dance performed sword in hand or among or over swords; **sword'-doll'ar,** a Scottish silver coin of James VI., worth 30s. (2s. 6d. English), with a sword on the reverse; **sword'er,** a gladiator: an assassin, a cut-throat: a swordsman; **sword'fish,** a large fish (Xiphias or other genus of the family Xiphiidae) with upper jaw compressed and prolonged as a stabbing weapon; **sword'-grass,** a name for many plants with sword-shaped leaves; **sword'-guard,** the part of a sword-hilt that protects the bearer's hand; **sword'-knot,** a ribbon tied to the hilt of a sword; **sword'-law,** government by the sword.—*adjs.* **sword'less; sword'like.—*ns.* sword'man,** a swordsman: a fighting man; **sword'play,** fencing; **sword'player.—*adj.* sword'-proof,** capable of resisting the blow or thrust of a sword.—*n.* **sword'-rack,** a rack for holding swords.—*adj.* **sword'-shaped.—*ns.* swords'man,** a man skilled in the use of a sword; **swords'manship; sword'-swallower,** a performer who seems to swallow swords; **sword'-tail,** a small Central American freshwater Cyprinodont fish with swordlike tail-lobe. [O.E. *sweord;* Ger. *schwert.*]

swore, sworn. See **swear.**

swot, swat, *swot, v.t.* and *v.i.* (*slang*) to study hard. —*n.* hard study: one who swats.—*ns.* **swott'er; swott'ing.** [**sweat.**]

swound, *swownd.* See **swoon.**—**swoune, swownd, swowne** also in *Spens.*

swum, *swum, pa.t.* and old-fashioned *pa.t.* of **swim.**

swung, *swung, pa.t.* and *pa.p.* of **swing.**

Sybarite, *sib'a-rīt, n.* an inhabitant of *Sybaris,* a Greek city in ancient Italy, on the Gulf of Tarentum, noted for luxury: one devoted to luxury.—Also *adj.—adjs.* **Sybaritic** (*-rit'ik*), **-al, Sybarit'ish.**— *n.* **Syb'aritism.**

sybo(w), syboe, *sī'bō, -bā, n.* (*Scot.*) a cibol: a young onion.—*pl.* **sy'boes, sybows.** [**cibol.**]

sybotic, *sī-bot'ik, adj.* pertaining to a swineherd.— *n.* **sybotism** (*sib'a-tizm*). [Gr. *sybōtēs,* swineherd —*sȳs,* swine, *boskein,* to feed, tend.]

sycamine, *sik'a-mīn, n.* (*B.*) the mulberry-tree. [Gr. *sȳkamīnos,* of Semitic origin, influenced by *sȳkon,* fig.]

sycamore, *sik'a-mōr, n.* a kind of fig-tree (now often **sycomore,** or **sycomore fig**): in England, the great maple (*Acer Pseudo-platanus*) called in Scotland the plane (formerly **sycomore**): in U.S. any true plane (Platanus). [Gr. *sȳkomoros*—*sȳkon,* a fig, *moron,* black mulberry.]

syce, sice, saice, *sīs, n.* (*India*) a groom, mounted attendant. [Ar. *sā'is.*]

sycee, *sī-sē', n.* silver ingots used as Chinese money [Chin. *si sz'.*]

syconium, *sī-kō'ni-am, n.* a multiple fruit in which the true fruits (the pips) are enclosed in a hollow fleshy receptacle—the fig. [Gr. *sȳkon,* a fig.]

sycophant, *sik'ō-fant, n.* (*Gr. hist.*) a common informer: a servile flatterer.—*n.* **syc'ophancy** the behaviour of a sycophant: mean tale-bearing obsequious flattery: servility.—*adjs.* **sycophantic** (*-fant'ik*), **-al.** — *adv.* **sycophant'ically.** — *v.i* **syc'ophantise,** to play the sycophant.—*adj.* **syc'o phantish** (or *-fant'*). — *adv.* **syc'ophantishly.**— *n.* **syc'ophantry,** the arts of the sycophant. [Gr *sȳkophantēs,* an informer, swindler, confidentia agent—*sȳkon,* a fig, *phainein,* to show; variously but unsatisfactorily explained.]

sycosis, *sī-kō'sis, n.* inflammation of the hair follicles esp. of the beard. [Gr. *sȳkōsis,* a fig-shaped ulcer —*sȳkon,* a fig.]

sye, *sī, v.t.* (now *dial.*) to strain. — *n.* a sieve: milk-strainer. [O.E. *sion, séon,* to strain.]

syen, a Shakespearian spelling of **scion.**

syenite, *sī'an-īt, n.* a coarse-grained plutonic rock composed of orthoclase and a ferromagnesia mineral, usu. hornblende.—*adj.* **syenitic** (*-it'ik*) relating to *Syene* in Egypt: pertaining to syenite [L. *syēnītēs* (*lapis*), a hornblende granite (no syenite) found at Assuan (Gr. *Syēnē*).]

syker, *sik'ar, adv.* (*Spens.*) surely. [**sicker.**]

syllable, *sil'a-bl, n.* a word or part of a word uttered by a single effort of the voice.—*v.t.* to express by syllables, to utter articulately.—*n.* **syll'abary,** a set of characters representing syllables.—*Also* **syllabā'rium.—*adjs.* syllabic** (*sil-ab'ik*), **-al,** or constituting a syllable or syllables: syllable by syllable.—*adv.* **syllab'ically.—*ns.* syllabica'tion syllabifica'tion,** pronunciation as a syllable division into syllables.—*v.t.* **syll'abise,** to form or divide into syllables: to sing to syllables.—*n* **syll'abism,** use of a syllabary: division into syllables.—*adj.* **syll'abled,** having (in compounds so-many) syllables. [L. *syllaba*—Gr. *syllabē*—*syn* with, *lab-,* root of *lambanein,* to take; *-le* as in principle, participle.]

syllabub, *sil'a-bub, n.* Same as **sillabub.**

syllabus, *sil'a-bas, n.* an abstract or programme, a of a series of lectures: a catalogue of position condemned by the R.C. Church (1864, 1907):— *pl.* **syll'abuses, syll'abi** (*-bī*). [L.,—Gr. *sillybe* a book-label.]

syllepsis, *sil-ep'sis, n.* a figure in rhetoric by which a word does duty in a sentence in the same syn tactical relation to two or more words but has different sense in relation to each:—*pl.* **syllep'ses** (*-sēz*).—*adjs.* **syllep'tic, -al.—*adv.* syllep'tically** [Gr. *syllēpsis,* a taking together—*syn,* together, and the root of *lambanein,* to take.]

syllogism, *sil'ō-jizm, -a-jizm, n.* a logical argument in three propositions, two premises and a con clusion that follows necessarily from them.—*n* **syllogisation** (*-jī-zā'shan*).—*v.i.* **syll'ogise, t** reason by syllogisms.—*v.t.* to deduce syllogistically —*n.* **syll'ogiser.—*adjs.* syllogistic** (*-jist'ik*), **-al.**— *adv.* **syllogist'ically.** [Gr. *syllogismos — syllo gizesthai*—*syn,* together, *logizesthai,* to reckon— *logos,* speech, reason.]

sylph, *silf, n.* a spirit of the air: a sylph-like being a kind of humming-bird.—*n.* **sylph'id, sylph'ide** a little sylph. — Also *adj.* — *adjs.* **sylph'idine sylph'ine, sylph'ish.** [Coined by Paracelsus.]

sylva, sylvan, sylviculture. See **silva.**

sylvanite, *sil'van-īt, n.* a mineral, telluride of gold and silver. [*Transylvania,* where it is found.]

Sylvia, *sil'vi-ä, n.* the warbler genus, giving name to a family **Sylvi'idae** or subfamily **Sylvi'inae** o the thrush family.—*adj.* **syl'viine.** [L. *silva,* wood.]

Sylvian, *sil'vi-ən, adj.* of *Sylvius,* i.e. either the French anatomist Jacques Dubois (1478-1555), or Franz de la Boë (1614-72), the Dutch-German iatrochemist.—**Sylvian fissure,** a deep lateral fissure in the cerebrum, discovered apparently by the latter.

sylvine, *sil'vēn,* **sylvite,** *sil'vīt, ns.* native potassium chloride, a source of potash.—*n.* **syl'vinite** (*-vin-īt*), a rock composed of sylvine and rock salt. [Formerly called digestive salt of *Sylvius.*]

symar. See **cymar.**

symbiosis, *sim-bi-ō'sis, n.* a mutually beneficial partnership between organisms of different kinds: esp. such an association where one lives within the other.—*ns.* **sym'bion, sym'biont** (*-bi-ont*), an organism living in symbiosis.—*adj.* **symbiotic** (*-bi-ot'ik*).—*adv.* **symbiot'ically.** [Gr. *syn,* together, *bios,* livelihood.]

symbol, *sim'b(ə)l, n.* an emblem: that which by custom or convention represents something else: a type: (*theol.*) a creed, compendium of doctrine, or a typical religious rite, as the eucharist.—*v.t.* to symbolise.—*adjs.* **symbolic** (*-bol'ik*), **-al.**—*adv.* **symbol'ically.**—*ns.* **symbol'icalness; symbol'ics,** the study of creeds; **symbolisā'tion.**—*v.t.* **sym'bolise,** to be symbolical of: to represent by symbols: (*obs.*) to combine: to formulate in a creed.—*v.i.* (*obs.*) to agree.—*ns.* **sym'boliser; sym'bolism,** representation by symbols or signs: a system of symbols: use of symbols: a movement (*c.* 1880) chiefly in French poetry that treated the actual as an expression of something underlying: symbolics.—*n.* and *adj.* **sym'bolist.**—*adjs.* **symbolist'ic, -al; sym'bolled,** symbolised: bearing symbols.—*ns.* **symbolog'raphy,** symbolic writing or representation; **symbol'ogy** (for **symbolol'ogy,** the study or use of symbols; **symbolol'atry** (Gr. *latreiā,* worship), undue veneration for symbols. [Gr. *symbolon,* a token—*syn,* together, *ballein,* to throw.]

symbole, an old spelling of **cymbal.**

symitar(e), old spellings of **scimitar.**

symmetry, *sim'i-tri, n.* exact correspondence of parts on either side of a straight line or plane, or about a centre or axis: balance or due proportion: beauty of form: disposition of parts.—*adj.* **symm'etral,** of symmetry.—*n.* **symmetrian** (*si-met'ri-ən*), one who studies or theorises on the due proportions of things.—*adjs.* **symmet'ric, -al,** having symmetry.—*adv.* **symmet'rically.**—*ns.* **symmet'ricalness; symmetrisā'tion.**—*v.t.* **symm'etrise,** to make symmetrical.—*n.* **symmetrophō'bia** (Gr. *phŏbos,* fear), fear or dislike of symmetry. [Gr. *symmetriā—syn,* together, *metron,* a measure.]

sympathectomy, *sim-pəth-ek'tə-mi, n.* excision of part of a sympathetic nerve. [From **sympathetic,** and Gr. *ektomē,* excision.]

sympathy, *sim'pə-thi, n.* community of feeling: power of entering into another's feelings or mind: harmonious understanding: compassion, pity: affinity or correlation whereby one thing responds to the action of another or to action upon another: agreement.—*adjs.* **sympathet'ic, -al,** feeling, inclined to, expressing sympathy: in sympathy: acting or done in sympathy: induced by sympathy (as sounds in a resonating body): congenial: compassionate: of the sympathetic nervous system (see below): (a Gallicism) able to awake sympathy.—*adv.* **sympathet'ically.**—*v.i.* **sym'pathise,** to be in sympathy: to feel with or for another: to be compassionate: to be in accord, correspond.—*v.t.* (*Shak.*) to be in sympathy, accord, or harmony with: (*Shak.*) to compound harmoniously: (*Shak.*) to represent or understand sympathetically: (*Shak.*) perh., to affect all alike.—*n.* **sym'pathiser.**—**sympathetic ink** (see **ink**); **sympathetic magic,** magic depending upon a supposed sympathy, e.g. between a person and his name or portrait, between rainfall and libations; **sympathetic nervous system,** a system of nerves supplying the involuntary muscles and glands, esp. those originating from the cervical, thoracic, and lumbar regions of the spinal cord; sometimes also including those from the brain and the sacral region (**parasympathetic**). [Gr. *sympatheia—syn,* with, *pathos,* suffering.]

sympetalous, *sim-pet'ə-ləs, adj.* having the petals united.—*n.pl.* **Sympet'alae** (*-lē*), a main division of dicotyledons, typically having united petals. [Gr. *syn,* together, *petalon,* leaf.]

symphile, *sim'fīl, n.* an animal of another kind kept as a guest or domestic animal in an ants' or termites' nest.—*ns.* **sym'philism** (*fil-izm*), **sym'phily.**—*adj.* **sym'philous.** [Gr. *symphiliā,* mutual friendship—*syn, philos,* a friend.]

symphony, *sim'fə-ni, n.* an obs. name for various musical instruments—bagpipe, drum, hurdy-gurdy, virginal: harmony, esp. of sound: (*mus.*) an orchestral composition on a great scale in sonata form: (*arch.*) an instrumental portion of a work primarily vocal.—*adj.* **symphonic** (*sim-fon'ik*).—*n.* **symphō'nion,** a combination of piano and harmonium.—*adj.* **symphonious** (*-fō'ni-əs*), agreeing or harmonising in sound: accordant: harmonious.—*n.* **sym'phonist,** a composer or performer of symphonies.—**symphonic poem,** a large orchestral composition in programme music with the movements run together. [Gr. *symphōniā,* harmony, orchestra—*syn,* together, *phōnē,* ə sound.]

Symphyla, *sim'fi-lä, n.* a class or order of arthropods linking the bristle-tails with the centipedes.—*adj.* **sym'phylous.** [Gr. *symphylos,* of the same race—*syn,* with, *phȳle, phȳlon,* a race, clan.]

symphysis, *sim'fi-sis, n.* the union or growing together of parts, concrescence: union of bones by fusion, cartilage, or ligament: a place of junction of parts.—*adj.* **symphyseal, -ial** (*sim-fiz'i-əl*).—*n.* **symphyseot'omy, -iot'omy** (Gr. *tomē,* a cut), the operation of cutting through the pubic symphysis.—*adj.* **symphytic** (*-fit'ik*), by fusion.—*n.* **Sym'phytum,** the comfrey genus of the borage family, perh. from its supposed virtue of closing wounds. [Gr. *symphysis—syn,* with, *phyein,* to grow.]

sympiesometer, *sim-pi-i-zom'i-tər, n.* a barometer with a gas instead of a vacuum: an instrument for measuring the pressure of a current. [Gr. *sympiesis,* a pressing together—*syn,* with, *piezein,* to press, *metron,* a measure.]

symploce, *sim'plō-sē, n.* (*rhet.*) the repetition of a word at the beginning and another at the end of successive clauses. [Gr. *symplokē,* an interweaving —*syn,* with, *plekein,* to weave.]

sympodium, *sim-pō'di-əm, n.* (*bot.*) a stem composed of a succession of branches each supplanting and seeming to continue its parent branch.—*adj.* **sympo'dial.**—*adv.* **sympo'dially.** [Gr. *syn,* together, *pous, podos,* foot.]

symposium, *sim-pō'zi-əm, n.* a drinking party: a meeting for philosophic conversation: a conference: a collection of views on one topic:—*pl.* **sympo'sia.**—*adjs.* **sympo'siac, sympo'sial.**—*ns.* **sympo'siarch** (*-ärk;* Gr. *archos,* leader), the master of the feast or conference; **sympo'siast,** one who takes part in a symposium. [Latinised from Gr. *symposion—syn, posis,* drinking.]

symptom, *sim(p)'təm, n.* a characteristic sign or indication of the existence of a state, esp. a disease.—*adjs.* **symptomat'ic, -al.**—*adv.* **symptomat'ically.**—*v.t.* **symp'tomatise,** to be a symptom of.—*ns.* **symptomatol'ogy,** the study of symptoms; **sympto'sis,** wasting: emaciation.—*adj.* **symptotic** (*-tot'ik*). [Gr. *symptōma, symptōsis—syn,* with, and root of *piptein,* to fall.]

synadelphite, *sin-ə-del'fīt, n.* a manganese aluminium arsenate. [Gr. *syn,* with, *adelphos,* brother, as found along with kindred minerals.]

synaeresis, *sin-ē'rə-sis, n.* the running together of two vowels into one or into a diphthong: the spontaneous expulsion of liquid from a gel. [Gr. *syn,* together, *hairesis,* taking—*haireein,* to take.]

synaesthesia, *sin-ēs-thē'zi-ä, n.* sensation produced at a point different from the point of stimulation: a sensation of another kind suggested by one experienced (e.g. in colour-hearing). [Gr. *syn,* together, *aisthēsis,* sensation.]

synagogue, *sin'ə-gog, n.* an assembly of Jews for worship: a Jewish place of worship.—*adjs.* **syn'-**

agogal (-gō-gl), **synagog'ical** (-gog', -goj'i-kl). [Gr. *synagōgē*—*syn*, together, *agōgē*, a bringing—*agein*, to lead.]

synallagmatic, *sin-a-lag-mat'ik, adj.* mutually or reciprocally obligatory. [Gr. *synallagmatikos*—*synallagma*, a covenant—*syn*, together, *allagma*, exchange.]

synaloepha, *sin-ə-lē'fä, n.* the melting of a final vowel or diphthong into the initial vowel or diphthong of the next word. [Latinised from Gr. *synaloiphē*—*synaleiphein*, to coalesce, smear together—*syn*, together, *aleiphein*, to anoint.]

synandrium, *sin-an'dri-əm, n.* a mass of united stamens. — *adj.* **synan'drous,** having united stamens. [Gr. *syn*, together, *anēr*, a man (male).]

synangium, *sin-an'ji-əm, n.* an arterial trunk: a group of united sporangia (found in Marattiaceae). [Gr. *syn*, together, *angeion*, a vessel.]

synantherous, *sin-an'thər-əs, adj.* syngenesious. [Gr. *syn*, and anther.]

synanthesis, *sin-an-thē'sis, n.* (bot.) simultaneous ripening of stamens and stigmas.—*adjs.* **synan-thet'ic**; **synan'thic,** showing synanthy; **synan'thous,** synanthic: flowering and leafing simultaneously.—*n.* **synan'thy,** abnormal fusion of flowers. [Gr. *syn*, together, *anthēsis*, flowering, *anthos*, a flower.]

synaphea, synapheia, *sin-ə-fē'ä, n.* metrical continuity between verses in a system, so that they can be scanned as one verse, as in anapaestics, with possibility of elision at the end of a line. [Gr. *synapheia*—*syn*, together, *haph-*, root of *haptein*, to join.]

synaposematism, *sin-ap-ō-sē'ma-tizm, n.* warning coloration common to a number of dangerous species in the same region.—*adj.* **synaposematic** (-*mat'ik*). [Gr. *syn*, together, and **aposematism.**]

synapsis, *sin-aps'is, n.* the pairing of chromosomes of paternal and maternal origin before the reducing division: a synapse.—*ns.* **synapse',** an interlacing or enveloping connexion of a nerve-cell with another; **synapt'ase,** emulsin; **synapte** (*sin-ap'tē*), in the Greek Church, a litany.—*adj.* **synapt'ic.** [Gr. *synapsis*, contact, junction—*syn*, together, *haptein*, to fasten; *synaptē* (*euchē*, a prayer), joined together.]

synarchy, *sin'ər-ki, n.* joint sovereignty. [Gr. *synarchiā*—*syn*, with, *archein*, to rule.]

synarthrosis, *sin-ər-thrō'sis, n.* immovable articulation.—*adj.* **synarthrō'dial.**—*adv.* **synarthrō'dially.** [Gr. *synarthrōsis*—*syn*, together, *arthron*, a joint; also *arthrōdiā*, a flattish joint.]

synastry, *sin-as'tri, n.* a coincidence of stellar influences. [Gr. *syn*, together, *astron*, a star.]

synaxis, *si-nak'sis, n.* in the early Church, meeting for worship, esp. for the eucharist.—*n.* **synaxā'rion,** (*Gr. Ch.*) a lection containing an account of a saint's life. [Gr. *synaxis*, a bringing together—*syn*, together, *agein*, to lead.]

syncarpous, *sin-kär'pəs, adj.* (bot.) of or having united carpels. [Gr. *syn*, together, *karpos*, a fruit.]

syncategorematic, *sin-kat-i-gor-i-mat'ik, adj.* not able to form a term without other words.—*adv.* **syncategoremat'ically.**

synchondrosis, *sing-kon-drō'sis, n.* connexion of bones by cartilage. [Gr. *synchondrōsis*—*syn*, with, *chondros*, a cartilage.]

synchoresis, *sing-kō-rē'sis, n.* (rhet.) a concession, esp. one made for the sake of a more effective retort. [Gr. *synchōrēsis*—*synchōreein*, to agree, yield ground —*syn*, with, *chōros*, space.]

synchronal, *sing'krə-nl, adj.* coinciding in time.—*adjs.* **synchronic** (-*kron'*), **-al.**—*adv.* **synchron'ically.**—*n.* **synchronisā'tion.**—*v.i.* **syn'chronise,** to coincide or agree in time.—*v.t.* to cause to coincide or agree in time: to time together or to a standard: to represent or identify as contemporary. —*ns.* **synch'roniser**; **synch'ronism,** coincidence in time: simultaneity: keeping time together: occurrence of like phases at the same time: exhibition of contemporary history in one scheme: the bringing together in one picture of different parts of a story. — *adj.* **synchronis'tic.**—*adv.* **synchronis'tically.** — *n.* **synchronol'ogy,** chronological arrangement side by side. — *adj.*

synch'ronous, simultaneous: contemporary: keeping time together.—*adv.* **synch'ronously.**—*ns.* **synch'ronousness**; **synch'rony,** simultaneity.—

synchromesh gear, a gear in which the speeds of the driving and the driven members are automatically synchronised before coupling, so as to avoid shock and noise in gear-changing. [Gr. *syn*, together, *chronos*, time.]

synchrotron, *sing'krō-tron, n.* a device, using a combination of electrical and magnetic forces, for accelerating electrons.

synchysis, *sing'ki-sis, n.* (rhet.) confusion of meaning due to unusual arrangement: fluidity of the vitreous humour of the eye. [Gr. *synchysis*—*syn*, together with, *cheein*, to pour.]

synclastic, *sin-klas'tik, adj.* having the same kind of curvature in all directions. [Gr. *syn*, together, *klastos*, broken.]

syncline, *sin'klīn, n.* (geol.) a fold in which the beds dip downwards towards the axis.—*adj.* **synclin'al.** —*n.* a syncline.—*n.* **synclinorium** (-*kli-nō'ri-əm*), a great synclinal structure carrying minor flexures. [Gr. *syn*, together, *klinein*, to cause to lean.]

syncope, *sing'ka-pi, n.* (rare) a cutting short: (obs.) syncopation: (med.) a fainting fit from sudden anaemia of the brain.—*adj.* **sync'opal,** of syncope. —*v.t.* **sync'opate,** to shorten by cutting out the middle (of a word): (mus.) to alter the rhythm of temporarily by transferring the accent to a normally unaccented beat.—*adj.* **sync'opated.**—*ns.* **syncopā'tion; sync'opātor.**—*adjs.* **syncopic** (*sing-kop'ik*); **syncopt'ic.** [Gr. *synkopē*, a cutting up, cutting short, syncope—*syn*, together, *koptein*, to cut off.]

syncretism, *sing'kri-tizm,* or *sin', n.* reconciliation of, or attempt to reconcile, different systems of belief, esp. of different forms of Christianity by Georg Calixtus: fusion or blending of religions, as by identification of gods, taking over of observances, or selection of whatever seems best in each: illogical compromise in religion.—*adj.* **syncretic** (*sin-krē'tik*, or *sing-*).—*v.t.* and *v.i.* **syncretise** (*sing'kri'tiz*).—*n.* **syn'cretist.**—*adj.* **syncretis'tic.** [Gr. *synkrētismos*, a confederation (orig. app. of Cretan communities).]

syncytium, *sin-sish'i-əm, n.* (biol.) a multinucleate cell: a tissue without distinguishable cell-walls.— *adj.* **syncyt'ial.** [Gr. *syn*, together, *kytos*, a vessel.]

synd, sind, *sīnd, v.t.* to rinse: to wash out or down. —*n.* a rinsing: a washing down with liquor.— *n.pl.* **synd'ings, sind'ings.**—Also **syne** (*Burns*). [Origin obscure.]

syndactyl, *sin-dak'til, adj.* with fused digits.—*n.* **syndac'tylism.**—*adj.* **syndac'tylous.** [Gr. *syn*, *daktylos*, finger, toe.]

synderesis. See **synteresis.**

syndesis, *sin'di-sis, n.* a binding: (biol.) synapsis.— *adj.* **syndetic** (-*det'ik*), connective.—*adv.* **syndet'ically.** [Gr. *syndesis*—*syn*, *deein*, to bind.]

syndesmosis, *sin-des-mō'sis, n.* the connexion of bones by ligaments.—*adj.* **syndesmotic** (-*mot'ik*). [Gr. *syndesmos*—*syn*, *desmos*, a bond.]

syndic, *sin'dik, n.* in ancient Greece an advocate, delegate, or judge: at various times and places a magistrate or mayor: a member of a committee of the Senate of Cambridge University: one chosen to transact business for others, esp. the accredited legal representative of a corporation, society, or company.—*adj.* **syn'dical** (syndical chamber or union, a French trade-union).—*ns.* **syn'dicalism,** a French development of trade-unionism, aiming at putting the means of production in the hands of unions of workers; **syn'dicalist.**—*adj.* **syn'dicalist'ic.**—*n.* **syn'dicate,** a body of syndics: a council: the office of a syndic: a body of men chosen to watch the interests of a company, or to manage a bankrupt's property: a combination of persons or firms for some common purpose or interest: a combined group of newspapers.—*v.t.* (obs.) to judge, censure: to control, effect, or publish by means of a syndicate: to join in a syndicate.—*v.i.* to join in a syndicate.—*ns.* **syndicā'tion; syn'dicātor.** [Gr. *syndikos*—*syn*, with, *dikē*, justice.]

syndrome, *sin'drō-mē, n.* concurrence, esp. of

symptoms. [Gr. *syndromē—syn*, together, *dramein*, to run.]

syndyasmian, *sin-di-az'mi-ən*, *adj.* (*anthrop.*) pairing, applied to a form of family founded on a loose temporary marriage. [Gr. *syndyasmos*, coupling.]

syne, *sīn*, *adv.* (*Scot.*) then, next: afterwards, later: ago. [**sithen**.]

synecdoche, *sin-ek'də-kē*, *n.* (*rhet.*) the figure of putting part for the whole, or the whole for part.—*adjs.* **synecdochic** (*-dok'*), **-al**.—*adv.* **synecdoch'-ically**.—*n.* **synec'dochism**, use of synecdoche: use of part for the whole in sympathetic magic. [Gr. *synekdochē—syn*, together, *ekdechesthai*, to receive.]

synechia, *sin-e-kī'ä*, *sin-ē'ki-ä*, *n.* morbid adhesion, esp. of iris and cornea. [Gr. *synecheia*, continuity—*syn*, together, *echein*, to hold.]

synecphonesis, *sin-ek-fō-nē'sis*, *n.* synizesis. [Gr. *syn*, together, *ekphōnēsis*, pronunciation—*ek*, out, *phōnē*, voice, utterance.]

synedrion, *sin-ed'ri-on*, *n.* a judicial assembly: a sanhedrin. — Also **syned'rium** : — *pl.* (of both) **syned'ria**.—*adj.* **syned'rial**. [Gr. *syn*, together, *hedrā*, seat.]

syneidesis, *sin-ī-dē'sis*, *n.* conscience as passing judgment on past acts—opp. to *synteresis*. [Gr. *syneidēsis*, conscience—*syn*, with, together, *eidenai*, to know.]

syneresis. See **synaeresis**.

synergy, *sin'ər-ji*, *n.* combined or co-ordinated action. — *adjs.* **synergetic** (*-jet'ik*), **syner'gic**, working together.—*ns.* **syner'gid**, (*bot.*) either of the two cells in the embryo-sac that seem to guide the pollen-tube; **synergism** (*sin'* or *-ər'*), the doctrine that the human will and the Divine Spirit are two efficient agents that co-operate in regeneration—ascribed to Melanchthon; **syn'ergist** (or *-ər'*).—*adj.* **synergist'ic**. [Gr. *synergiā*, co-operation—*syn*, together, *ergon*, work.]

synesis, *sin'ə-sis*, *n.* syntax having regard to meaning rather than grammatical form. [Gr., sense.]

syngamy, *sing'gə-mi*, *n.* free interbreeding: union of gametes.—*adjs.* **singamic** (*sin-gam'ik*), **singa-mous** (*sing'gə-məs*). [Gr. *syn*, together, *gamos*, marriage.]

syngenesis, *sin-jen'i-sis*, *n.* reproduction by fusion of male and female elements, the offspring being derived from both parents.—*n.pl.* **Syngenesia** (*sin-ji-nē'si-ä*), in the Linnaean system a class of plants with syngenesious stamens, answering to the Compositae.—*adjs.* **syngene'sious**, having the anthers united in a tube about the style, as in Compositae; **syngenetic** (*-net'ik*), of or by syngenesis : of minerals, formed contemporaneously with the enclosing rock. [Gr. *syn*, together, *genesis*, formation, generation.]

Syngnathidae, *sin(g)-gnath'i-dē*, or *sing-nath'*, *n.pl.* the pipefish family. [Gr. *syn*, together, *gnathos*, jaw.]

syngraph, *sing'grāf*, *n.* a writing signed by both or all the parties thereto. [Gr. *syn*, together, *graphein*, to write.]

synizesis, *sin-i-zē'sis*, *n.* the union into one syllable of two vowels without forming a recognised diphthong : closure of the pupil of the eye, with loss of sight : contraction of chromatin towards one side in karyokinesis. [Gr. *synizēsis*, a collapse—*syn*, with, *hizein*, to seat, sit.]

synod, *sin'əd*, *n.* a meeting : an ecclesiastical council : a Presbyterian church court intermediate between presbytery and the General Assembly : the supreme court of the former United Presbyterian Church : (*astron.*; *obs.*) conjunction.—*adj.* **syn'odal**, of, of the nature of, or done in a synod.—*n.* a payment made by a clergyman on the occasion of a synod, or at a visitation.—*adjs.* **synodic** (*-od'ik*), **-al**, **synodal** : (*astron.*) pertaining to conjunction : from conjunction to conjunction (see **month**).—*adv.* **synod'ically**. [Gr. *synodos*, a meeting, conjunction—*syn*, together, *hodos*, a way.]

synoecete, *sin-ē'sēt*, **sinoekete**, *-kēt*, *n.* a guest tolerated with indifference in an ants' or termites' nest.—*n.* **synoeciosis** (*-si-ō'sis*), the rhetorical figure of coupling opposites.—*adjs.* **synoecious** (*-ē'shəs*), **synoicous** (*-oi'kəs*), having antheridia

and archegonia in the same group.—*v.t.* and *v.i.* **syn'oecise** (*-ē-sīz*), to unite in one community or city-state.—*ns.* **synoe'cism**, union of communities or cities; **synoecology** (*-kol'ə-ji*), study of plant communities. [Gr. *synoikia*, a living together, community, *synoiketēs*, a house-fellow, *synoikizein*, to unite in one community—*syn*, with, *oikeein*, to dwell.]

synonym, *sin'ə-nim*, *n.* a word having the same meaning with another (usu. very nearly the same meaning) : (*biol.*) a systematic name to which another is preferred as valid.—*adjs.* **synonymatic** (*sin-on-i-mat'ik*), **synonym'ic**, **-al**, of synonyms.—*ns.* **synonym'icon**, a dictionary of synonyms; **synon'ymist**, one who studies synonyms, or the different names of plants and animals; **synonym'-ity**, the fact or quality of being synonymous.—*adj.* **synon'ymous**, having the same meaning.—*adv.* **synon'ymously**.—*ns.* **synon'ymousness**; **synon'ymy**, rhetorical use of synonyms : a setting forth of synonyms : a list of synonyms. [Gr. *synōnymon—syn*, with, *onoma*, a name.]

synopsis, *sin-op'sis*, *n.* a general view : a summary :—*pl.* **synop'ses**.—*adjs.* **synop'tic**, **-al**, affording or taking a general view of the whole.—*adv.* **synop'-tically**.—*n.* **synop'tist**, one of the writers of the Synoptic Gospels.—*adj.* **synoptis'tic**.—**Synoptic Gospels**, those of Matthew, Mark, and Luke, which readily admit of being brought under one combined view. [Gr. *synopsis—syn*, with, together, *opsis*, a view.]

synostosis, *sin-os-tō'sis*, *n.* complete union of bones. [Gr. *syn*, *osteon*, bone.]

synovia, *sin-ō'vi-ä*, *n.* an unctuous fluid in the joints.—*adj.* **syno'vial**.—*n.* **synovi'tis**, inflammation of a synovial membrane.—**synovial membrane**, a membrane of connective tissue that lines tendon sheaths and capsular ligaments and secretes synovia. [App. an arbitrary coinage of Paracelsus, who applied it more generally.]

syntan, *sin'tan*, *n.* a synthetic *tan*ning agent.

syntax, *sin'taks*, *n.* grammatical structure in sentences : one of the classes in some R.C. schools.—*adjs.* **syntac'tic**, **-al**.—*adv.* **syntac'tically**.—*ns.* **syntag'ma**, a systematic body, system, or group :—*pl.* **syntag'mata** ; **syntag'matite**, a kind of hornblende. [Gr. *syntaxis—syn*, together—*tassein*, to put in order.]

syntenosis, *sin-tə-nō'sis*, *n.* the connexion of bones by tendons. [Gr. *syn*, with, *tenōn*, a sinew.]

synteresis, *sin-ti-rē'sis*, *n.* conscience as a guide to future action—opp. to *syneidesis*.—Also **synderē'-sis** (from the later Gr. pronunciation). [Gr. *syntērēsis*, observation—*syn*, with, *tēreein*, to watch over.]

syntexis, *sin-tek'sis*, *n.* liquefaction : melting : wasting.—*adjs.* **syntec'tic**, **-al**. [Gr. *syntēxis—syn*, with, *tēkein*, to melt.]

synthesis, *sin'thi-sis*, *n.* building up : putting together : making a whole out of parts : the combination of separate elements of thought into a whole : reasoning from principles to a conclusion :—*pl.* **syn'theses** (*sēz*)—opp. to *analysis*.—*v.t.* **syn'thesise** (a faulty form for **synthetise**).—*n.* **syn'thesist** (for **synthetist**). — *adjs.* **synthetic** (*-thet'*), **-al**, pertaining to, consisting in, or formed by, synthesis : artificially produced but of like nature with, not a mere substitute for, the natural product.—*adv.* **synthet'ically**.—*n.* **synthet'icism**, the principles of synthesis, a synthetic system.—*v.t.* **syn'thetise**, to put together in synthesis : to form by synthesis.—*ns.* **synthetis'er**, **syn'thetist**, one who makes a synthesis.—**synthetic drug**, a drug made in the laboratory—both those occuring naturally and artificial ones; **synthetic philosophy**, Herbert Spencer's system, a fusion, as he thought, of the different sciences into a whole. [Gr. *synthesis—syn*, with, together, *thesis*, a placing.]

synthronus, *sin'thrə-nəs*, *n.* the seat of the bishop and his presbyters, behind the altar. [Gr. *syn*, together, *thronos*, a throne.]

syntony, *sin'tən-i*, *n.* tuning, or agreement in resonance frequency, of wireless apparatus.—*adj.* **syntonic** (*sin-ton'ik*), tuned together.—*n.* **syn'tonin**, a substance akin to fibrin, found in muscle.—*v.t.*

Neutral vowels in unaccented syllables : *el'ə-mənt*, *in'fənt*, *ran'dəm*

syn′tonise, to adjust to agree in frequency.—*adj.* **syn′tonous**, syntonic. [Gr. *syn*, together, *tonos*, tone.]

sype. Same as **sipe**.

syphilis, *sif′i-lis*, *n.* a contagious venereal disease due to infection with a micro-organism *Spirochaeta pallida*.—*n.* **syphilisā′tion**.—*v.t.* **syph′ilise**, to inoculate or to infect with syphilis.—*adjs.* **syphilit′ic**; **syph′iloid**, like syphilis.—*ns.* **syphilol′ogist**; **syphilol′ogy**, the knowledge of syphilis; **syphilō′ma**, a syphilitic tumour; **syphilophō′bia**, a morbid dread of syphilis. [Title of Fracastoro's Latin poem (1530), whose hero *Syphilus* is infected.]

syphon, syren. Same as **siphon, siren**.

Syriac, *sir′i-ak*, *n.* the ancient Aramaic dialect of *Syria.* — Also *adj.* — *ns.* **Syr′iacism** (*-ə-sizm*), **Syr′ianism, Syr′iasm, Syr′ism**, a Syriac idiom.—*adj.* **Syr′ian**, relating to Syria.—*n.* a native or citizen of Syria.—*ns.* **Syr′iarch** (*-ärk*; Gr. *Syriarchēs*), the chief priest in Roman Syria; **Syrophoenicia** (*sī-rō-fi-nish′yä*), a Roman province between Lebanon and the coast.—*n.* and *adj.* **Syrophoeni′cian**.

syrinx, *sir′ingks*, *n.* Pan-pipes: the vocal organ of birds: a fistula or fistulous opening: a rock-cut tunnel, as in Egpytian tombs:—*pl.* **syringes** (*-in′jēz*) or **syr′inxes**.—*ns.* **syringa** (*-ing′gä*), orig. and still popularly the mock-orange: **Syringa**, after Linnaeus, the generic name of the lilac; **syr′inge** (*-inj* or *si-rinj′*), an instrument for squirting or injecting.—*v.t.* and *v.i.* to clean, spray, or inject with a syringe.—*adj.* **syringeal** (*-in′ji-əl*).—*n.* **syringitis** (*-jī′tis*), inflammation of the Eustachian tube; **syringotomy** (*sir-ing-got′-ə-mi*), cutting for fistula. [Gr. *syrinx, -ingos*, Pan-pipes, gallery.]

syrlye, an old form (*Spens.*) of **surly**.

Syrphus, *sir′fəs*, *n.* a genus of wasp-like flies that hover and dart, giving name to the family **Syr′phidae** (*-fi-dē*).—*n.* and *adj.* **syr′phid**. [Gr. *syrphos*, gnat.]

syrtis, *sər′tis*, *n.* (*Milt.*) a quicksand :—*pl.* **syr′tes** (*tēz*). [L. *Syrtes*, Gr. *Syrtides* (sing. of each *Syrtis*), name of two sandy bays of W. Africa—Gr. *syrein*, to draw, sweep along.]

syrup, *sir′əp*, *n.* a saturated solution of sugar boiled to prevent fermentation : any thick sweet liquid.—Also (esp. *U.S.*) **sir′up**.—*adj.* **syr′upy**.—**golden syrup**, the uncrystallisable part finally separated in manufacture for crystallised sugar. [Fr. *sirop*—Ar. *sharāb*; cf. **shrub, sherbet**.]

syssarcosis, *sis-är-kō′sis*, *n.* the connexion of one bone with another by intervening muscle. [Gr., *syn*, together, *sarx*, flesh.]

syssitia, *si-sit′i-ä*, or *-sish′*, *n.* the ancient Spartan custom of eating the chief meal together in public. [Gr. *syssitiā*—*syn*, together, *sitos*, food.]

systaltic, *sis-tal′tik*, *adj.* alternately contracting and dilating, pulsatory. [Gr. *systaltikos*, depressing ; cf. **systole**.]

system, *sis′tim*, *-təm*, *n.* anything formed of parts placed together or adjusted into a regular and connected whole: a set of things considered as a connected whole: a group of heavenly bodies moving mainly under the influence of their mutual attraction : a set of bodily organs of like composition or concurring in function : the bodily organism : one of the great divisions of the geological strata, subordinate only to the division into Palaeozoic, Mesozoic, and Cainozoic: a group of (Greek) verses : a body of doctrine : a theory of the universe : a full and connected view of some department of knowledge : an explanatory hypothesis : a scheme of classification : a manner of crystallisation : a plan : a method : a method of organisation : methodicalness : a systematic treatise. — *adjs.* **systemat′ic, -al**, pertaining to, or consisting of, for the purpose of, observing, or according to system : methodical : habitual : intentional.—*adv.* **systemat′ically**.—*ns.* **systematician** (*-ə-tish′an*); **systematisā′tion** (also **systemisā′tion**).—*v.t.* **sys′tematise** (also **sys′temise**), to reduce to a system.—*ns.* **sys′tematiser**; **sys′tematism**; **sys′tematist**; **systematol′ogy**.—*adjs.* **sys′temed**; **systemic** (*-tem′ik*), pertaining to the bodily system or to a system of bodily organs; **sys′temless**, without system : not exhibiting organic structure.—*ns.* **sys′tem-maker**, **-monger**, one unduly fond of constructing systems. [Gr. *systēma*—*sy-, syn-*, together, and the root of *histanai*, to set.]

systole, *sis′to-lē*, *-tə-lē*, *n.* rhythmical contraction, esp. of the heart—opp. to *diastole* : collapse of the nucleus in mitosis : (*gram.*) the shortening of a long syllable.—*adj.* **systolic** (*-tol′ik*). [Gr. *systolē*—*syn*, together, *stellein*, to place.]

systyle, *sis′til*, *adj.* (*archit.*) having an intercolumniation of two diameters.—*n.* such an arrangement : a building or part so constructed. [Gr. *systȳlos*—*sy-, syn-*, together, *stȳlos*, a column.]

sythe (*Spens.*). See **scythe, sith** (2).

syver, siver, *sī′vər*, *n.* (*Scot.*) a drain : a grating over a drain. [Perh. a form of **sewer**.]

syzygy, *siz′i-ji*, *n.* conjunction or opposition : the period of new or full moon : a dipody :—*pl.* **syz′ygies**.—*adj.* **syzyg′ial**. [Gr. *syzygiā*, union, coupling—*sy-, syn-*, together, *zygon*, a yoke.]

Szekler, *sek′lər*, *n.* a Transylvanian Magyar.

fāte, fär, ȧsk ; mē, hər (her) *; mīne ; mōte ; mūte ; mōōn ; ḋhen* (then)

T

T, t, *tē, n.* the twentieth letter in our alphabet, eighteenth in the Roman, its usual sound a voiceless stop produced with the tip of the tongue in contact with teeth, gums, or palate: an object or mark in the form of the letter T (also **tee**): as a mediaeval Roman numeral T = 160, T̄ = 160,000.—*ns.* **T'-band'age,** a bandage composed of two strips fashioned in the shape of the letter T; **T'-cart,** a four-wheeled pleasure-vehicle without top, having a T-shaped body; **T'-cloth,** a plain cotton made for the India and China market—stamped with a T; **T'-cross,** a tau-cross; **T'-plate,** a T-shaped plate, as for strengthening a joint in a wooden framework; **T'-rail,** a rail with T-shaped cross-section.—*adj.* **T'-shaped.**—*n.* **T'-square,** a T-shaped ruler.—**marked with a T,** branded as thief; **to a T,** with perfect exactness.

't, a shortened form of **it.**

t-, t', an obsolete shortened form of **to** before a vowel, as in Spenser **tadvance,** to advance, **tas-swage,** to assuage: in N. of England for **the.**

ta, *tä, interj.* (hypocoristic or affected) thank you.

taal, *täl, n.* (with *the*) Afrikaans or Cape Dutch. [Du., speech.]

tab, *tab, n.* a small tag, flap, or strap, forming an appendage: a loop for hanging up by: (*U.S.*) reckoning, tally, check.—*adj.* **tabbed.** [Origin unknown.]

Tabanus, *tə-bā'nəs, n.* the gadfly genus.—*n.* **tabanid** (*tab'ə-nid*), any member of the genus, or of its family **Tabanidae** (*tə-ban'i-dē*). [L. *tabānus.*]

tabard, *tab'ərd, n.* a mediaeval peasant's overcoat: a knight's sleeveless or short-sleeved coat: now, a herald's coat.—*n.* **tab'erdar,** a scholar of Queen's College, Oxford. [O.Fr. *tabart.*]

tabaret, *tab'ə-ret, n.* an upholsterer's silk stuff, with alternate stripes of watered and satin surface.

tabasheer, tabashir, *tab-ə-shēr', n.* a concretion, chiefly of silica, found in the hollows of bamboos. [Hind., Pers., and Ar. *tabāshīr.*]

tabby, *tab'i, n.* a coarse waved or watered silk: an artificial stone: a tabby-cat.—*adj.* brindled.—*v.t.* to water or cause to look wavy:—*pr.p.* **tabb'y-ing;** *pa.t.* and *pa.p.* **tabb'ied.**—*ns.* **tabb'inet,** a more delicate kind of tabby resembling damask, used for window-curtains; **tabb'y-cat,** a brindled cat: hence (or from *Tabitha*) a female cat: an old maid: a spiteful gossiping woman; **tabb'yhood.** [Fr. *tabis,* app. from '*Attābiy,* a quarter in Baghdad where it was made.]

tabellion, *tə-bel'yən, n.* an official scrivener in the Roman empire and elsewhere. [L.L. *tabelliō, -ōnis*—L. *tabella,* tablet, dim. of *tabula,* a board.]

taberdar. See under **tabard.**

tabernacle, *tab'ər-nə-kl, n.* a tent or movable hut: the tent carried by the Jews through the desert and used as a temple: the human body as the temporary abode of the soul: a place of worship, esp. temporary or dissenting: (*R.C.*) a receptacle for the vessel containing the pyx: a canopied niche or seat: a canopy: a socket for a mast.—*v.i.* to sojourn.—*v.t.* to put or enshrine in a tabernacle.—*adjs.* **tab'ernacled; tabernacular** (*-nak'ū-lər*).—*n.* **tab'ernacle-work,** ornamental work over niches, stalls, &c., with canopies and pinnacles, or any work in which this forms a characteristic feature.—**Feast of Tabernacles,** a Jewish harvest festival, celebrating the sojourn in tents in the wilderness. [L. *tabernāculum,* dim. of *taberna,* a hut.]

tabes, *tā'bēz, n.* wasting away.—*n.* **tabefaction** (*tab-i-fak'shən*), wasting away, emaciation.—*v.t.* and *v.i.* **tab'efy.**—*n.* **tabescence** (*tab-es'əns*), wasting: shrivelling.—*adjs.* **tabesc'ent; tab'id.** —**tabes dorsa'lis,** locomotor ataxia. [L. *tābēs -is.*]

tablature, *tab'lə-tyər, n.* a tablet: a painting, picture, pictorial representation or work: an old notation for lute music with a line for each string and letters or figures to indicate the stopping, used with modifications for other instruments. [L. *tabula,* a board.]

table, *tā'bl, n.* a slab or board: a layer: a flat surface: a board for painting on: a picture: (*Shak.*) a quadrangular space on the palm of the hand: a panel: a string-course: a slab with or for an inscription: a slab inscribed with laws: hence, in *pl.,* a code of law (as the **Twelve Tables** of ancient Rome): a writing tablet (esp. in the obs. phrase *a pair of tables*): a board for a game, e.g. chess: each half of a folding board: hence, in *pl.* (*obs.*), backgammon: a broad flat surface on a cut gem: a tabular crystal: an article of furniture consisting of a flat top on legs, pillar, or trestles, for use at meals, work, play, for holding things, &c.: supply of food, entertainment: the company at a table: a board or committee: a dispensing of the communion: a projecting part in a scarfed joint: a flat gravestone supported on pillars: a condensed statement: a syllabus or index: a compact synoptic scheme of numerical information.—*adj.* of, for, like, or pertaining to a table, or meals.—*v.t.* to tabulate: to lay on the table: to pay down: to submit for discussion: (*U.S.*) to shelve: to board. —*v.i.* to board.—*ns.* **ta'ble-beer,** light beer for common use; **ta'ble-book,** a book of writing tablets, memorandum book, or notebook: an ornamental book intended to lie on a table: a book of tables; **ta'ble-cloth,** a cloth, usu. of linen, for covering a table, esp. at meals; **ta'ble-cover,** a cloth for covering a table, esp. at other than meal-times.—*adjs.* **ta'ble-cut,** (of gems) cut with a flat top; **tabled** (*tā'bld*), flat-topped: having a smooth sloping surface of dressed stone: having a table or tables.—*ns.* **table-d'hôte** (*tä-bl'-dōt;* Fr., host's table), a meal at a fixed price; **ta'bleful,** as many as a table will hold; **ta'ble-knife,** a knife such as one cuts one's own meat, &c., with; **ta'ble-land,** an extensive region of elevated land with a flat or undulating surface: a plateau; **ta'ble-leaf,** an extension to a table-top, hinged, drawn out, or inserted; **ta'ble-lin'en,** linen table-cloths, napkins, &c.; **ta'ble-maid,** a maid-servant who sets the table and waits; **ta'ble-mon'ey,** an allowance for official entertainment; **ta'ble-mu'sic,** music in parts that can be read by performers at each side of a table; **ta'ble-nap'kin,** a cloth used at table to protect the clothes and to wipe fingers and lips; **ta'ble-spoon,** one of the largest spoons used at table; **ta'ble-spoon'ful,** as much as will fill a table-spoon:—*pl.* **ta'ble-spoon'fuls; ta'ble-sport,** (*Shak.*) the butt of the company at table; **ta'ble-talk,** familiar conversation, as that round a table, during and after meals; **ta'ble-tenn'is,** a game like lawn-tennis played on a table with celluloid balls; **ta'ble-top,** the top of a table: a flat top.—*adj.* **ta'ble-topped.**—*ns.* **ta'ble-turn'ing,** movements of tables (or other objects), attributed by spiritualists to the agency of spirits—by the sceptical to collective involuntary muscular action; **ta'ble-ware,** dishes, spoons, knives, forks, &c., for table use; **ta'ble-wa'ter,** a mineral water suitable for the table.—*adj.* and *adv.* **ta'blewise,** in the form or in the manner of a table: of the communion table, not altarwise.—*ns.* **ta'ble-work,** the setting of type for tables, columns of figures, &c.; **ta'bling,** tabulation: backgammon-playing: board: provision of tables: scarfing: a broad hem on the skirt of a sail.—**at table,** at a meal; **fence the tables** (see **fence**); **lay on the table,** to lay aside for future discussion or indefinitely; **the Lord's table,** the communion table: com-

tableau 1122 **tael**

munion; **turn the tables,** to bring about a complete reversal of circumstances, as if the players at backgammon changed sides. [Partly O.E. *tabule*, *tabele*, partly O.Fr. (and Fr.) *table*, both—L. *tabula*, a board.]

tableau, *tab'lō*, *n.* a picture or vivid pictorial impression: a suddenly created situation that takes all aback: — *pl.* **tableaux** (*tab'lōz*). — **tableau vivant,** a ' living picture,' a motionless representation by living persons in costume:—*pl.* **tableaux vivants** (*tä-blō-vē-vän°*). [Fr. dim. of *table*.]

tablet, *tab'lit*, *n.* a small slab : a slab or stiff sheet for making notes on : a panel, esp. inscribed or for inscription : an inscribed plate hung up in fulfilment of a vow : a flat confection : a small flat cake of any solid material. [O.Fr. *tablete*, dim. of *table*.]

tabloid, *tab'loid*, *n.* legally, any product of a chemical manufacturing firm of which the word is the trade-mark: popularly applied to a drug or anything else in a very concentrated form, e.g. (*U.S.*) a small, usu. sensational, newspaper.

taboo, tabu, *ta-bōō'*, *adj.* subject to taboo: forbidden.—*n.* a Polynesian (or other) system of prohibitions connected with things considered holy or unclean : any one of these prohibitions : any recognised or general prohibition, interdict, restraint, ban, exclusion, ostracism.—*v.t.* to forbid approach to or use of : to place under taboo :— *pr.p.* **taboo'ing**; *pa.t.* and *pa.p.* **tabooed'.** [Tongan *tabu* (pron. *tä'bōō*), holy, unclean.]

tabor, tabour, *tā'bər*, *n.* a small drum like a tambourine without jingles, usually played with one stick, along with a pipe : a taborer.—*v.i.* and *v.t.* to play on a tabor : to beat, drum.—*ns.* **tā'borer** (*Spens.* **tabrere,** *ta-brēr'*), one who beats the tabor; **tabo(u)rin** (*tab'ə-rin*, or *-rēn*), a small drum longer in body than the tabor, used in like manner; **tabouret** (*tab'ə-ret*, *tä-bōō-rā*), a stool, orig. drum-shaped; **tabret** (*tab'rit*), a small tabor. [O.Fr. *tabour*; an Oriental word.]

Taborite, *tā'bər-īt*, *n.* a Hussite of Žižka's party, opposed to the Calixtines or Utraquists.—Also *adj.* [*Tabor* in Bohemia, founded by them as headquarters.]

tabu. Same as **taboo.**

tabula, *tab'ū-lä*, L. *täb'ōō-lä*, *n.* a writing-tablet : an altar frontal : a flattened structure : a horizontal partition in corals :—*pl.* **tab'ulae** (*-lē*; L. *-lī*).— *adj.* **tab'ular,** of, in the form of, like, according to, a table : laminated : platy : horizontally flattened. —*n.* **tabularīsā'tion.**—*v.t.* **tab'ularise,** to tabulate.—*adv.* **tab'ularly.**—*v.t.* **tab'ulate,** to reduce to the form of a table or synopsis.—*adj.* **tabular :** having tabulae.—*ns.* **tabulā'tion**; **tab'ulātor.**— *adj.* **tab'ulatory** (*-lə-tə-ri*). [L. *tabula*, table.]

tacahout, *tak'ə-howt*, *n.* a gall on the tamarisk, a source of gallic acid. [From Berber.]

tacamahac, *tak'ə-mə-hak*, *n.* a gum-resin yielded by several tropical trees: the balsam poplar. [From Nahuatl.]

tac-au-tac, *tak'-ō-tak'*, *n.* in fencing, the parry combined with the riposte: also a series of close attacks and parries between fencers of equal skill. [Fr.]

tace, *tā'sē*, L. *tā'kā*, be silent.—**tacet** (*tā'set*, L. *tā'ket*; *mus.*) is silent.—**tace is Latin for a candle,** a phrase understood as requesting or promising silence. [L. *tacē*, imper., *tacet*, 3rd pers. sing. pres. indic., of *tacēre*, to be silent.]

tace. Same as **tasse.**

tach, tache, *tach*, *n.* (*B.*) a fastening or clasp. [O.Fr. *tache*; cf. **tack, attach.**]

tach-, *tak-*, **tache-, tachy-,** *tak'i-*, in composition, speed, speedy.—*ns.* **tacheom'eter, tachymeter** (*-im'*), a surveying instrument for rapid measurement of distances.—*adjs.* **tacheo-, tachymet'rical.** —*ns.* **tacheo-, tachym'etry**; **tachom'eter,** an instrument for measuring the velocity of machines or currents.—*adj.* **tachomet'rical.**—*ns.* **tachom'-etry**; **tachycar'dia** (Gr. *kardiā*, heart), abnormal rapidity of heart-beat; **tach'ygraph, tachyg'-rapher, -phist.**—*adjs.* **tachygraph'ic, -ical.**—*ns.* **tachyg'raphy,** shorthand; **tach'ylyte** (also **-lite**; Gr. *lytos*, melted, because easily fused before the

blowpipe), a black opaque glass occurring as a thin selvage to intrusive basalt.—*adj.* **tachylytic** (*-lit'ik*). —*n.* **tachypnoea** (*tak-ip-nē'ä*; Gr. *pnoiā*, breathing), excessive frequency in breathing. [Gr. *tachys*, gen. *-eos*, swift, *tachos*, swiftness.]

tacit, *tas'it*, *adj.* unspoken : silent.—*adv.* **tac'itly.**— *n.* **tac'itness.**—*adj.* **tac'iturn,** disinclined to speak. —*n.* **taciturn'ity.**—*adv.* **tac'iturnly.** [L. *tacitus*, *taciturnus*.]

tack, *tak*, *n.* a short, sharp nail with a broad head : a long temporary stitch : a fastening strip : a rope or other fastening for the lower windward corner of a sail : the corner itself : an act of tacking : an alternate course in zigzag : a change of policy, a strategical move : something tacked on : stickiness.—*v.t.* to attach or fasten, esp. in a slight manner, as by tacks or long stitches : to change the course of by a tack.—*v.i.* to change the course or tack of a ship by shifting the position of the sails : to zigzag : to shift one's position, to veer.— *adjs.* **tacked, tacked'-on'.**—*ns.* **tack'er**; **tack'et,** (*Scot.*) a hobnail.—*adj.* **tack'ety.**—*ns.* **tack'iness**; **tack'ing,** proceeding by tacks : fastening : fastening by tacks : (*politics*) introducing into a bill (esp. a money bill) provisions beyond its natural scope. —*adj.* **tack'y,** sticky. [O.Fr. *taque*, doublet of *tache*.]

tack, *tak*, *n.* (*Scot.*) a tenure : a lease : a leased tenement : a spell : a take or catch.—*n.* **tacks'man,** a lessee : in the Highlands, one who holds a lease and sublets. [See **tak, take.**]

tack, *tak*, *n.* (*prov.*) any distinctive flavour, smack.

tack, *tak*, *n.* food generally, fare, esp. of the bread kind, as *hard tack* (ship's biscuit), *soft tack* (loaves).

tack, *tak*, *n.* the sound of a sharp tap. [Imit.]

tackle, *tak'l*, *n.* the ropes, rigging, &c., of a ship (*naut.* *tāk'l*): tools, gear, weapons, equipment (for sports, &c.): ropes, &c., for raising heavy weights : a pulley : the act of gripping.—*v.t.* to harness : to seize or take hold of : to grapple with : to come to grips with : to begin to deal in earnest with : to confront, encounter, challenge.—*v.i.* (*Rugby football*) to seize and stop or (*association*) obstruct a player and get the ball away from him.—*adj.* **tackled** (*tak'ld*), furnished with harness or tackle : (*Shak.*) made of ropes.—*ns.* **tack'ler**; **tack'ling,** furniture or apparatus belonging to the masts, yards, &c., of a ship : harness for drawing a carriage : tackle or instruments : grappling. [Cf. L.G. *takel*.]

tacky, *tak'i*, *n.* (*U.S.*) a poor ill-conditioned horse or person.

tact, *takt*, *n.* adroitness in managing the feelings of persons dealt with : nice perception in seeing and doing exactly what is best in the circumstances : (*mus.*) the stroke in keeping time.—*adj.* **tact'ful.** —*adv.* **tact'fully.**—*adj.* **tact'ile** (*-il*), perceptible by touch : pertaining to the sense of touch : concerned in perception by touch : suggestive of touch.—*ns.* **tact'ilist** (*-il-ist*), a painter who aims at tactile effects; **tactil'ity**; **tac'tion,** (*rare*) contact.—*adj.* **tact'less.**—*adv.* **tact'lessly.**—*n.* **tact'-lessness.**—*adj.* **tact'ūal,** relating to, or derived from, the sense of touch.—*n.* **tactūal'ity,** tactual quality.—*adv.* **tact'ūally.** [L. *tactus*, *-ūs*—*tangĕre*, *tactum*, to touch.]

tactic, -al, *tak'tik*, *-əl*, *adjs.* relating to taxis or tactism, or to tactics.—*n.* **tac'tic,** a system, or a piece, of tactics.—*adv.* **tac'tically.**—*n.* **tactician** (*-tish'ən*), one skilled in tactics.—*n.pl.* **tac'tics** (often treated as *sing.*), the science or art of manoeuvring in presence of the enemy : purposeful procedure.—*n.* **tac'tism,** (*biol.*) taxis. [Gr. *taktikos*, fit for arranging, *taktos*, ordered, verbal adj. of *tassein*, to arrange.]

tadpole, *tad'pōl*, *n.* the larva of a toad or frog, rarely of an ascidian.—**Tadpole and Taper,** political hacks, from characters in Disraeli's *Coningsby*. [O.E. *tdde*, toad, and **poll** (head).]

tae, *tā*, a Scots form of **toe, to, too** (also); also in phrase *the tae* for *that ae*, the one (adjectivally). [See **tone** (2), **t'other.**]

taedium. See **tedium.**

tael, *tāl*, *n.* the Chinese *liang* or ounce, about 1½ oz. avoir.: a money of account (but not a coin)

in China, orig. **a tael weight of pure silver.** [Port.,
—Malay *tail*, weight.]

ta'en, *tān*, a contraction of **taken.**

taenia, *tē'ni-ä*, *n.* a ribbon or fillet: the fillet above
the architrave of the Doric order: a ribbon-like
structure: **Taenia**, the tapeworm genus:—*pl.*
tae'niae (-*ni-ē*).—*n.* **taeni'asis**, infestation with
tapeworm.—*adjs.* **tae'niate, tae'nioid,** like a
ribbon or a tapeworm. [L.,—Gr. *tainiā*, a band.]

tafferel, taffrail, *taf'ril*, *n.* the upper part of a
ship's stern timbers. [Du. *tafereel*, a panel—
tafel, a table—L. *tabula*, a table.]

taffeta, *taf'i-tä*, also **taffety,** -*ti*, **taffetas,** -*tas*, *n.*
a thin glossy silk-stuff: loosely applied to various
similar or mixed fabrics.—*adj.* of taffeta: (*Shak.*)
florid, over-dainty. [Through Fr. or L.L. from
Pers. *tāftah*, woven—*tāftan*, to twist.]

taffy, *taf'i*, *n.* (*U.S.*) Same as **toffy.**

Taffy, *taf'i*, *n.* a Welshman. [Welsh pron. of *Davy*.]

tafia, *taf'i-ä*, *n.* a variety of rum. [Perh. a W. Indian
name, but cf. Malay *tāfiā*.]

tag, *tag*, *n.* a flap of a slashed garment: a tab: a
tie-on label: the point of a lace: any small thing
tacked or attached to another: a loose or flapping
end: a shred: a stray, matted, or dirty lock:
(in *pl.*) a footman's shoulder-knot: the tip of a
tail: a trite quotation (esp. Latin): a moral to a
story: a refrain: the rabble: anything mean.—
v.t. to put a tag or tags on: to attach as a tag:
to tack, fasten, append: to remove tags from:
to dog or follow closely.—*v.i.* to make tags, to
string words or ideas together: to go behind as a
follower:—*pr.p.* **tagg'ing**; *pa.t.* and *pa.p.* **tagged.**
—*ns.* **tag'-day,** (*U.S.*) a flag-day; **tag'-end,** the
fag-end; **tagg'er.**—*n.pl.* **tagg'ers,** thin sheet-iron.
—*n.* **tag'rag,** the rabble: a fluttering rag, a tatter.
—Also *adj.*—*n.* **tag'-tail,** a worm with a tail like
a tag.—**tagged atom,** a radioactive isotopic atom
of a tracer element; **tag, rag, and bobtail,** all
sorts of riff-raff. [Origin obscure.]

tag, *tag*, *n.* the game of tig.—*v.t.* to tig. [Origin
obscure.]

Tagálog, *tä-gä'log*, *n.* a people of the Philippine
Islands: their Austronesian language.—Also *adj.*

Tagetes, *tä-jē'tēz*, *n.* a Mexican and S. American
genus of composites—called French and African
marigold, &c. [L. *Tagēs*, an Etruscan god.]

taghairm, *tə'gərm*, *n.* in the Scottish Highlands,
divination: esp. inspiration sought by lying in a
bullock's hide behind a waterfall. [Gael.]

taglioni, *tal-yō'nē*, *n.* an early 19th-century overcoat. [Named after a family of dancers.]

taguan, *tä'gwän*, *n.* properly, a large East Indian
flying squirrel: applied also to an Australian
flying phalanger. [Tagálog.]

taha, *tä'hä*, *n.* a S. African weaver-bird. [Zulu
taka.]

tahr, tehr, *tär*, *n.* a beardless Himalayan wild goat
(*Hemitragus jemlaicus*) that frequents forest preci-
pices. [App. its name in the W. Himalaya, confused with Nepali *thār*; see **thar.**]

tahsil, *tä(hh)-sēl'*, *n.* in India, a revenue area.—*n.*
tahsildar', a revenue officer. [Ar. *tahsīl*.]

tai, *tī*, *n.* a Japanese sea-bream.

T'ai. See **Thai.**

taiga, *tī-gä'*, *n.* marshy pine forest. [Russ.]

taigle, *tä'gl*, *v.t.* (*Scot.*) to entangle, hinder.—*v.i.* to
linger: to loiter: to trudge. [Cf. Sw. (Born-
holm) *taggla*, to disorder.]

tail, *tāl*, *n.* the posterior extremity of an animal,
usually a slender prolongation beyond the anus: a
bird's train of feathers: a fish's caudal fin: anything of like appearance, position, &c.: the back,
lower, hinder, latter, down-stream, or inferior
part or prolongation of anything (often opp. to the
head): the stem of a note in music: a downward
extension of a letter: a retinue, suite: a queue: a
train: anything long and trailing or hanging, as a
catkin, train of a comet, long curl of hair: (usu.
in *pl.*) the reverse of a coin: the end of a shoal
sloping into deeper water: (often in *pl.*) the skirts
of a garment: in Turkey, a horse-tail, formerly a
mark of rank.—*v.t.* to furnish with a tail: to be
a tail to: to remove the tail or stalk from: to grip
by the tail: to join end to end: (*Austr.*) to tend:

to dog, shadow.—*v.i.* to straggle: to taper (often
with *off*): to show the tail.—*ns.* **tail'-board,** the
board at the hinder end of a cart or wagon; **tail'-
boom,** a longeron supporting the tail of an aeroplane; **tail'-coat,** a coat with tails.—*adj.* **tailed.**
—*ns.* **tail'-end,** the fag-end: (*pl.*) inferior corn
sorted out from better; **tail'-feath'er,** one of the
rectrices or rudder-feathers of a bird's tail: a
feather of the back forming a train, as in the peacock; **tail'-gate,** the lower gate of a lock; **tail'ing,**
the inner covered end of a projecting brick or stone
in a wall: a winter sport in which several luges,
tied one behind another and so forming a tail, are
drawn along by a horse-sleigh: (in *pl.*) refuse,
dregs.—*adj.* **tail'less,** having no tail.—*ns.* **tail'-
light,** a light carried at the back of a train, a tram,
or other vehicle; **tail'piece,** a piece at the tail
or end: an engraving, design, &c., occupying the
bottom of a page, as at the end of a chapter: a
strip of ebony, &c., to which the ends of the strings
are attached in a fiddle; **tail'-pipe,** the suction-
pipe in a pump.—*v.t.* to tie a can or the like to the
tail of (to annoy a dog—explanation unknown).—
ns. **tail'race,** the channel in which water runs away
below a mill-wheel; **tail'-rope,** a rope attached
to the hinder part of anything; **tail'-spin,** a
spiral dive of an aeroplane.—**tail of the eye,** the
outer corner of the eye: the margin of the field
of vision; **turn tail,** to run away; **twist the lion's
tail,** to irritate Britain; **with the tail between the
legs,** like a beaten cur. [O.E. *tægl, tægel*: Goth.
tagl, hair.]

tail, *tāl*, *n.* (*law*) limitation of inheritance to certain
heirs.—*adj.* limited.—**tail male,** limitation to male
heirs. [Fr. *taille*, cutting.]

tailor, *tāl'ər*, *n.* one whose business is to cut out
and make outer garments, esp. for men (*fem.*
tail'oress).—*v.i.* to work as a tailor.—*v.t.* to make
clothes for: to fit with clothes: to fashion by
tailor's work.—*ns.* **tail'or-bird,** an E. Indian
warbler (Sutorius or kindred) that sews leaves
together to form a nest; **tail'oring.**—*adj.* **tail'or-
made,** made by a tailor, esp. of plain, close-fitting
garments for women. [A.Fr. *taillour* (Fr. *tailleur*)
—L.L. *tāliātor, -ōris—tāliāre*, to cut.]

tailor, *tāl'ər*, *interj.* (*Shak.*) variously explained as
referring to the backward fall (opp. to *header*), to
the tailor-like squatting position that results, or
as the obs. **tailard,** a person with a tail.

tailzie, tailye, taillie, *tāl'(y)i*, *n.* (*law*) Scots forms
of **tail** (2): entail.

taint, *tānt*, *n.* (*obs.*) attaint: (*obs.*) a hit in tilting:
(*obs.*) tint, tinge: a tincture of some evil quality:
a stain: a blemish: pollution: infection: a
latent or incipient defect or corruption.—*v.t.* (*obs.*)
to attaint: (*obs.*) to touch in tilting: (*obs.*) to tint,
tinge: to affect or imbue with anything objectionable: to contaminate: to infect: to impart a scent
to.—*v.i.* to become infected or corrupted: to go
bad: to weaken, wilt, wither.—*adjs.* **taint'ed**;
taint'less.—*adv.* **taint'lessly.**—*ns.* **taint'ure,**
defilement; **taint'-worm,** (*Milt.*) some worm
supposedly injurious to flocks. [Partly aphetic
for **attaint**; partly O.Fr. *taint* (Fr. *teint*)—L.
tinctus, -ūs—tingĕre, tinctum, to wet, dye.]

T'ai-p'ing, *tī-ping'*, *n.* the dynasty that Hung
Hsiü-ch'wan sought to found in China: a par-
ticipator in his rebellion (1851-65). [Chin.
T'ai P'ing, great peace.]

taisch, taish, tïsh, *n.* in the Scottish Highlands,
an apparition or voice of one about to die: second
sight. [Gael. *taibhs, taibhse*, apparition.]

tait, Same as **tate.**

tait, *tāt*, *n.* the long-snouted phalanger (Tarsipes).
[Native Australian name.]

taj, *täj*, *n.* a crown or distinctive head-dress: a
dervish's tall conical cap.—**Taj Mahal** (*mə-häl'*),
the magnificent mausoleum at Agra erected by
Shah Jehan for his wife Mumtáz-i-Mahal (*d.* 1629).
[Ar. and Pers. *tāj*, crown.]

tak, *tāk*, a Scots form of **take.**

take, *tāk*, *v.t.* to lay hold of: to get into one's
possession: to seize: to catch: to capture: to
captivate: to receive or come to have willingly or
by an act of one's own: to appropriate: **to assume**

to accept: to receive: to admit: (*Scot.*) to submerge: to have normally assigned to one: to find out, come upon, surprise, detect: to swallow or inhale: to apply to oneself: to obtain: to engage, secure: to seek and receive: to have recourse to: to attend a course in: to visit: to call for, necessitate, use up: to remove: to cause to go: to subtract: to convey: to escort: to detract: to derive: to understand: to apprehend: to assume: to mistake: to conceive: to accept as true: to tolerate: to ascertain: to observe or measure: to ascertain something from: to execute, perform: to set down: to portray: to photograph: to charge oneself with: to asseverate: to strike: to come upon and affect: to bewitch: to blight: (*obs.*) to deliver, give: to betake.—*v.i.* to have the intended effect: to be effective, to work: to please the public: (*Shak.*) to cast a spell: to betake oneself, begin: to bite (as a fish): to make a capture or acquisition: to admit of being taken: (*coll.*) to become, fall (e.g. ill): (*U.S.*, *Canada*) to freeze: (*pa.t.* took; *pa.p.* tā′ken).—*n.* an act of taking: a capture: quantity taken on one occasion. —*ns.* take′-down, a humiliation; take′-in′, a deception, fraud, or disappointment of hopes; take′-leave, leave-taking.—*adj.* tā′ken.—*ns.* take′-off, a burlesque mimicking: a drawback: place, act, or mode of leaving the ground for a jump, dive, or flight; tā′ker; tā′king, action of the verb in any sense: (usu. in *pl.*) that which is taken, receipts: (*Spens.*) plight: (*Shak.*) bewitchment, malignant influence: (*coll.*) agitation, perplexity.—*adj.* captivating: alluring: infectious, catching. — *adv.* tā′kingly. — *ns.* tā′kingness; tā′king-off′, removal, assassination.—*adj.* tā′ky, attractive.—take after, to follow in resemblance; take down, to reduce: to lower: to go above in class: to demolish, pull down: to take to pieces: to report or write down to dictation: to escort to the dining-room: (a peg) to humiliate in some degree; take effect, to come off, succeed: to come into force; take for, to suppose to be, esp. wrongly; take heed, to be careful; take in, to enclose: to comprise: to annex: to subdue: to receive: to conduct to the dining-room: to subscribe for: to tighten: to furl: to grasp, realise: to accept as true: to cheat; take in hand, to undertake; take into one's head, to be seized with a notion, take in vain, to use with unbecoming levity; take it out of, to exact the utmost from: to exhaust the strength or energy of; take me with you, (*Shak.*) let me understand what you mean; take notice, to observe: to show that observation is made: (with *of*) to remark upon; take off, to remove: to swallow: to mimic: to leave the ground for a jump or flight; take on, to receive aboard: to undertake: to assume: to take into employment: (*coll.*) to grieve; take out, to remove from within: to extract: to go out with: to obtain on application: to receive an equivalent for: (*Shak.*) to copy; take over, to receive by transfer: to convey across; take thought, (*Shak.*) to grieve; take to, to betake oneself to: to adapt oneself to: to become fond of; take to pieces, to separate into component parts; take to task, to call to account, reprove; take to wife, to marry; take up, to lift, to raise: to pick up for use: to absorb: to accept: to interrupt sharply: to arrest: to adopt the practice, study, &c., of, begin to go in for: to begin to patronise, seek to advance: to resume: (*Shak.*) to settle, compound (a quarrel): (*Shak.*) to reprove: (*Shak.*) to cope with: to buy up: (*Shak.*) to obtain on credit: to take in hand: to engross, occupy or fill fully: (*dial.*; usu. in passive) to interest, please (with *about* or *with*): to borrow; take upon oneself, to assume: to presume: to take responsibility for: to undertake: (*Shak.*) to feign, make believe; take up with, to begin to associate with, form a connexion with. [Late O.E. *tacan* (pa.t. *tóc*), to touch, take—O.N. *taka* (pa.t. *tók*; pa.p. *tekinn*).]

takin, tä′kin, tä-kēn′, *n.* a large ungulate (*Budorcas taxicolor*) akin to the goats and antelopes. [Tibetan.]

talapoin, tal′ə-poin, *n.* a Buddhist monk, esp. of

Pegu: a small green W. African guenon monkey. [Port. *talapão*—Old Peguan *tala pôi*, my lord.]

tala(u)nt. Spenserian forms of **talon**.

talar, talaria. See under **talus**.

talayot, tä-lä′yot, *n.* a prehistoric usually unchambered stone monument of the Balearic Islands. [Balearic Sp. for Sp. *atalaya*, an outlook—Ar. *al tald′i*, the vanguard.]

talbot, tawl′bət, *n.* a broad-mouthed large-eared hound, usually white, now extinct. [Poss. from the *Talbot* family.]

talbotype, tawl′bə-tīp, *n.* calotype, invented by William Henry Fox *Talbot* (1800-77).

talc, talk, *n.* a very soft, pliable, greasy, silvery-white, foliated or compact mineral, acid magnesium silicate: commercially, often muscovite mica.— *adjs.* talck′y, talc′ose, talc′ous. — *ns.* talc′-schist′, a schistose rock composed essentially of talc, with accessory minerals; talc′um, talc. [Fr. talc or L.L. *talcum*—Ar. *talq*—Pers. *talk*.]

tale, tāl, *n.* an act of telling: a narrative, story: a false story: a mere story: (in *pl.*) things told idly or to get others into trouble: number: reckoning. —*n.* tale′bearer, one who maliciously tells tales or gives information.—*n.* and *adj.* tale′bearing.— *adj.* tale′ful, abounding with stories.—*n.* tale′-teller, a teller of stories, narrator: a talebearer.— be in a (or one) tale, to be in full accord; old wives' tale, a marvellous story for the credulous; tell one's (or its) own tale, to speak for oneself or itself; tell tales, to play the informer; tell tales out of school, to reveal confidential matters. [O.E. *talu*, story, number; Ger. *zahl*, number.]

talegalla, tal-i-gal′ä, *n.* the brush-turkey. [Malagasy *talèva*, the purple coot, and L. *gallus*, a cock.]

talent, tal′ənt, *n.* an ancient unit of weight and of money—60 minas or 6000 drachmas, or about 84 lb. avoirdupois (Aeginetan talent), 56 (Euboic), 58 (Attic), of gold or silver: hence (from the parable, Matt. xxv. 14-30) faculty: any natural or special gift: special aptitude: eminent ability short of genius: persons of special ability: disposition: (*Shak.* tallent) perh. wealth, abundance, or perh. golden tresses.—*adjs.* tal′ented, possessing mental gifts; tal′entless. [L. *talentum*—Gr. *talanton*, a balance, a talent.]

talent, an old form (*Shak.*, *Scott*, now *dial.*) of talon.

tales, tā′lēz, *n.* (orig. *pl.*) the filling up from those who are present of a deficiency in the number of jurymen.—*n.* talesman (*tā′lēz-mən* or *tālz′*), a bystander so chosen.—pray a tales, to plead that the number of jurymen be completed in this way. [From the phrase ' *tālēs* de circumstantibus,' such of the bystanders: *tālēs*, pl. of L. *tālis*, such.]

Taliacotian, Tagliacotian, tal-yə-kō′shən, *adj.* pertaining to the Italian surgeon Gasparo *Tagliacozzi* or *Taliacotius* (1546-99), or his rhinoplastic operation.

talion, tal′i-ən, *n.* like for like: retaliation. [L. *tāliō*, -*ōnis*, like punishment—*tālis*, such.]

talipes, tal′i-pēz, *n.* club-foot. [L. *tālus*, ankle, *pēs*, foot.]

talipot, talipat, tal′i-pot, -pat, -put, *n.* a Ceylon fan-palm (*Corypha*). [Sinh. *talapata*—Sans. *tāla-pattra*, palmyra palm leaf.]

talisman, tal′is-mən, or -iz-, *n.* an object supposed to be indued with magical powers: an amulet, charm:—*pl.* tal′ismans. — *adjs.* talismanic (-*man′ik*), -al. [Ar. *tilsam*—Gr. *telesma*, payment, certificate, later completion, rite, consecrated object—*teleein*, to complete, fulfil, consecrate.]

talk, tawk, *v.i.* to speak, esp. informally or idly: to converse.—*v.t.* to utter: to speak about: to speak in: to bring or render by talking.—*n.* conversation: rumour: discussion: gossip: mention of possibility or proposal: a general theme: utterance: a short informal address.—*adjs.* talk′able, easy to converse with: to be talked about; talk′ative, given to much talking.—*adv.* talk′atively.—*n.* talk′ativeness; talk′ee-talk′ee, talk′y-talk′y, a corrupt dialect: chatter: a little harangue.—Also *adj.*—*ns.* talk′er; talk′ie (commonly in *pl.*), a talking film, cinematograph picture accompanied by sound.—*n.* and *adj.* talk′ing.—*ns.* talk′ing-machine', a gramophone, phonograph, or the like ; **talk'ing-to**, a reproof ; **talk'-you-down'**, an apparatus by means of which instructions are given to the pilot of an aircraft to help him to land. —**talk against** time, to keep on talking merely to fill up time, as often in parliament ; **talk big**, to talk boastfully ; **talk down**, to argue down : to talk as to inferiors in intellect or education ; **talking of**, apropos of, now that mention has been made of ; **talk over**, to persuade, convince : to discuss, consider together ; **talk round**, to talk of all sorts of related matters without coming to the point : to bring to one's way of thinking by persuasive talk ; **talk to**, to address : to rebuke ; **talk up**, to speak boldly : to praise or boost. [M.E. *talken*, freq. of **tell**.]

tall, *tawl*, *adj*. (*obs.*) doughty, stout : high in stature : long, esp. in a vertical direction : lofty : great, remarkable : grandiloquent : hardly to be believed. —*ns.* **tall'boy**, a long narrow top for a smoky chimney : a high chest of drawers, one portion superimposed on another or on a dressing-table : a glass with a long stem ; **tall'ness**—**a tall man of his hands**, a deft worker : a sturdy fighter ; **tall copy**, a book with ample margins above and below ; **tall hat**, a top hat ; **tall men**, loaded dice. [App. O.E. *getæl*, prompt.]

allage, *tal'ij*, *n.* (*hist.*) a tax levied by the Norman and Angevin kings on their demesne lands and towns, or by a feudal lord on his tenants : an aid, toll, or rate.—*v.t.* to lay an impost upon.—*adj.* **tall'iable**, subject to tallage.—*v.t.* **tall'iate**, to tallage. [O.Fr. *taillage—tailler*, to cut.]

allat, tallet, tallot, *tal'ət*, *n.* (*W. of England*) a loft. [W. *taflod*—L.L. *tabulāta*, flooring.]

allith, *tal'ith*, *n.* the Jewish prayer shawl. [Heb. *tallīth*.]

allow, *tal'ō*, *n.* fat, grease : rendered fat, esp. of ox and sheep : any coarse, hard fat.—*adj.* of, for, or like tallow.—*v.t.* to grease with tallow : to produce tallow.—*ns.* **tall'ow-can'dle**, a candle made of tallow ; **tall'ow-catch'**, (*Shak.*) perh. a receptacle for tallow, or a lump (keech) of tallow ; **tall'ow-chand'ler**, a dealer in tallow candles, &c. ; **tall'ow-dip'**, a candle made by dipping a wick in tallow ; **tall'ow-face**, (*Shak.*) a person with a pasty yellow face. — *adjs.* **tall'ow-faced** ; **tall'owish**. — *n.* **tall'ow-tree**, any of various trees (as Sapium, Pentadesma, Aleurites) yielding a thick oil or vegetable tallow, or a substance capable of making candles.—*adj.* **tall'owy**. [M.E. *talgh*; cf. Ger. *talg*.]

ally, *tal'i*, *n.* a stick notched to mark numbers or keep accounts : half of such a stick split across the notches, serving as receipt or record : anything that answers to a counterpart : a score or account, esp. one kept by notches or marks : credit, tick : a mark made in scoring an account : a distinguishing mark : a label : plant-label : a tag : a juvenile book-token : a number taken as a unit in computation : a full number : (*pl.* **tall'ies**).—*adv.* in concubinage.—*v.t.* to notch or mark as a tally : to count by tally : to reckon : to match, adapt.— *v.i.* to correspond, match, agree : to deal on credit : —*pr.p.* **tall'ying**; *pa.t.* and *pa.p.* **tall'ied**.—*ns.* **tall'yman**, one who keeps a tallyshop : one who lives with a woman without marriage :—*fem.* **tall'y-woman**; **tall'yshop**, a shop where goods are sold to be paid by instalments, the seller having one account-book which tallies with the buyer's ; **tall'y-sys'tem, -trade**, a mode of dealing on credit for payment by instalments.—**live tally**, to cohabit without marriage. [A.Fr. *tallie*—L. *tālea*, a stick.]

ally-ho, *tal-i-hō'*, *interj.* the huntsman's cry betokening that a fox has gone away.—*n.* a cry of tally-ho : a four-in-hand coach.—*v.t.* to greet with tally-ho.—*v.i.* to call tally-ho. [Cf. Fr. *taïaut*.]

alma, *tal'mä*, *n.* a loose cloak or cape. [From F. J. *Talma*, the actor (1763-1826).]

almud, *tal'mood*, *-mud*, *n.* the fundamental code of Jewish civil and canon law, the *Mishna* and the *Gemara*.—*adjs.* **Talmud'ic, -al**.—*n.* **Tal'mudist, **Talmudist'ic**. [Heb. *talmūd*, instruction—*lāmad*, to learn.]

alon, *tal'ən*, *n.* a hooked claw or finger : an ogee

moulding : cards remaining after the deal, the stock.—*adj.* **tal'oned**. [Fr. *talon*—L.L. *tālō*, *-ōnis*—L. *tālus*, the heel.]

Talpa, *tal'pä*, *n.* the mole genus of the family **Tal'pidae**: **talpa**, an encysted tumour on the head, a wen. [L., a mole.]

taluk, *tä-lōōk'*, *n.* a tract of proprietary land : a subdivision of a district, a collectorate.—*n.* **taluk'-dar**, the holder of a taluk. [Hindustani *ta'alluq*, estate.]

talus, *tä'ləs*, *n.* the ankle-bone or astragalus : (*arch.*) a slope : (*fort.*) the sloping part of a work : (*geol.*) a scree.—*n.* **tä'lar**, a robe reaching the ankles.— *n.pl.* **talaria** (*tə-lā'ri-ä*), winged sandals, or wings on the ankles, as of Hermes. [L. *tālus*, ankle.]

talweg. Same as **thalweg**.

tamal, *tä-mäl'*, *n.* a highly seasoned Mexican dish of crushed maize, with meat.—Also **tama'le**. [Sp. *tamal*.]

tamandua, *tä-män'dū-ä*, *-dwä'*, *n.* a S. American ant-eater smaller than the ant-bear.—*n.* **tamanoir** (*tä-mä-nwär'*), the great ant-bear. [Port. *tamanduá* —Sp. *tamándoa*—Tupí *tamanduà*.]

tamanu, *täm'ä-nōō*, *n.* a lofty gamboge tree of the East Indies and Pacific Islands, its trunk yielding tacamahac. [E.Ind.]

tamara, *tam'ə-rä*, *n.* a mixture of cinnamon, cloves, coriander, &c.

tamarack, *tam'ə-rak*, the American or black larch. [Amer. Ind.]

tamarin, *tam'ə-rin*, *n.* a small S. American squirrel-monkey (Midas). [Fr., from Carib.]

tamarind, *tam'ə-rind*, *n.* a large tropical Caesal-piniaceous tree (*Tamarindus indica*) : its pod, filled with a pleasant, acidulous, sweet, reddish-black pulp. [Ar. *tamr-Hindī*, date of India.]

tamarisk, *tam'ər-isk*, *n.* a genus (**Tam'arix**) giving name to a family (**Tamarica'ceae**) of xerophytic plants, one species a naturalised shrub of S. English seashores. [L. *tamariscus, tamarix*.]

tamasha, *tə-mä'shä*, *n.* (*Ind.*) an entertainment, show : fuss. [Ar. and Pers. *tamāshā*.]

tamber, *tam'bər*, *n.* Anglicised form of **timbre**.

tambour, *tam'bōōr*, *n.* a drum : the bass drum : a frame for embroidery : a rich gold and silver embroidery : embroidery done on a tambour : a cylindrical stone : the drum of a recording instrument : a vestibule in a church-porch, &c. : palisading to defend a gate, &c.—*v.t.* to embroider on a tambour.—*v.i.* to do tambour-work.—*ns.* **tam-bour'a**, an Eastern instrument like a guitar ; **tambourin** (*tän^g-bōō-ran^g*), a Provençal dance or dance-tune with drone bass ; **tambourine** (*tam-bə-rēn'*), a shallow single-headed drum with jingles, played on with the hand—(*Spens.*) **tam'burin**. [Fr. *tambour*, drum ; Pers. *tanbūr*, Ar. *tunbūr*, tamboura.]

tame, *tām*, *adj.* having lost native wildness and shyness : cultivated : domesticated : gentle : spiritless : without vigour : dull, flat, uninspiring : (*Shak.*) wonted, accustomed.—*v.t.* to reduce to a domestic state : to make gentle : to subdue : to reclaim.—*v.i.* to become tame.—*n.* **tamabil'ity**, **tameabil'ity**. — *adjs.* **tam'able**, **tame'able**; **tame'less**.—*n.* **tame'lessness**.—*adv.* **tame'ly**.— *ns.* **tame'ness**; **ta'mer**; **tam'ing**. [O.E. *tam*; Ger. *zahm*; Gr. *damaein*, L. *domāre*, to tame.]

Tamil, *tam'il*, *n.* a Dravidian language of S.E. India and N. Ceylon : one of the people speaking it.— *adjs.* **Tam'il, Tamil'ian, Tamil'ic, Tamūl'ic**.

tamin, tamine, *tam'in*, *n.* a thin worsted stuff, highly glazed. [Fr. *étamine*; cf. **stammel**.]

tamis, *tam'is*, *n.* a bolting-cloth.—*n.* **tamise** (*tä-mēz'*), a trade name for various thin woollen fabrics. [Fr. *tamis*.]

Tammany, *tam'ə-ni*, *n.* a society notorious for its corrupt influence in New York city politics.— Also *adj.*—**Tammany Hall**, its building, leased to the Democratic party of New York. [From an Indian chief, *Tammanend*, who is said to have signed the treaty with Penn.]

Tammie Norie, *tam'i nō'ri*, *n.* (*Scot.*) the puffin.

Tammuz, *tam'ooz*, *-uz*, *n.* a Babylonian sun-god, answering to Adonis : the tenth month of the Jewish calendar (June-July).

Neutral vowels in unaccented syllables : *el'ə-mənt, in'fənt, ran'dəm*

tammy, *tam'i*, *n.* a strainer: a glazed woollen or mixed stuff. [App. same as **tamis**, or perh. **tamin**.]

Tam o' Shanter, *tam-ō-shan'tər*, *n.* the hero of Burns's poem so entitled: hence, a cap with broad circular flat top.—*coll.* **tam, tamm'y.**

tamp, *tamp*, *v.t.* to stop up: to ram: to pack round. —*ns.* **tam'ping**, the act of filling up a hole for blasting: the material used; **tamp'ion, tamp'on, tomp'ion**, a plug: an inking-pad.—*v.t.* to plug.— *n.* **tamponade'**, surgical use of a tampon. [Fr. *tampon.*]

tamper, *tam'pər*, *v.t.* (*obs.*) to temper (as clay).—*v.i.* (usu. with *with*) to work, machinate, practise: to have secret or corrupt dealings: to interfere unwarrantably or vitiatingly: to meddle.—*ns.* **tam'perer; tam'pering.** [A by-form of **temper**.]

Tampico, *tăm-pē'kō*, *n.* a port in Mexico.—**Tampico fibre, ixtle**.

tam-tam. See **tom-tom**.

tan, *tan*, *n.* oak bark or other material used for tanning: spent bark: a tawny brown colour.— *adj.* **tawny**.—*v.t.* to convert into leather by steeping in vegetable solutions containing tannin: to treat with tan or tannin: to make brown or tawny: (*coll.*) to beat.—*v.i.* to become tanned:—*pr.p.* **tann'ing;** *pa.t.* and *pa.p.* **tanned.**—*n.pl.* **tan'-balls**, tanner's spent bark pressed into lumps for fuel.—*ns.* **tan'-bark**, any bark good for tanning; **tan'-bed**, (*hort.*) a bark-bed.—*adj.* **tan'-coloured**. —*ns.* **tan'ling**, (*Shak.*) one tanned by the sun; **tan'-liq'uor, -ooze, -pickle**, an aqueous extract of tan-bark.—*adj.* **tann'able**.—*ns.* **tann'age**, tanning; **tann'ate**.—*adj.* **tanned**.—*ns.* **tann'er; tann'ery**, a place for tanning.—*adj.* **tann'ic (tannic acid, tannin)**.—*ns.* **tann'in**, a colourless amorphous substance got from gall-nuts, sumach, and many barks, used in tanning and dyeing; **tann'ing**, the art or act of tanning or converting skins and hides into leather.—Also *adj.*—*ns.* **tan'-pit, -vat**, a vat in which hides are steeped with tan; **tan'-ride**, a riding track laid with tan; **tan'-yard**, a yard or enclosure where leather is tanned.—**flowers of tan** (see **flower**). [O.E. *tannian* (found in pa.p. *getanned*), *tannere*, tanner; also O.Fr. *tan*—Bret. *tann*, oak.]

tan, *tan*, *n.* (*trig.*) a conventional abbrev. for **tangent**.

tana, tanna(h), thana(h), thanna(h), *tä'nä*, *n.* a military or police station in India.—*n.* **t(h)a'nadar**, its head. [Hind. *thānā, thāna.*]

tana, *tä'nä*, *n.* a Sumatran and Bornean species of tree-shrew. [Malay (*tūpai*) *tāna*, ground (squirrel).]

tanager, *tan'ə-jər*, *n.* any bird of the S. American family **Tanagridae** (-*ag'*), closely allied to the finches.—*n.* **Tan'agra**, the name-giving genus.— *adj.* **tan'agrine**. [Tupí *tangará.*]

Tanagra, *tan'ə-grä*, *n.* a town of ancient Boeotia: a terra-cotta figurine made there.

tandem, *tan'dəm*, *adv.* in the position of horses harnessed singly one before the other.—*n.* a team (usu. two) so harnessed: a vehicle with such a team: a bicycle, tricycle, &c., for two, one before the other.—Also *adj.*—*adv.* **tan'demwise**. [Punning application of L. *tandem*, at length.]

tane, *ta'ne*, obs. spellings (*Spens., Shak.,* &c.) of **ta'en** (taken).

tane, *tān*, (*Scot.*) one (**the tane**, for *that ane*, the one). [See **tae**, **tone** (2), **tother**.]

tang, *tang*, *n.* coarse seaweed. [Cf. Norw. and Dan. *tang*.]

tang, *tang*, *n.* a ringing sound: a twang.—*v.t.* to cause to ring: (*Shak.*) to utter ringingly.—*v.i.* to ring. [Imit.: influenced by next word.]

tang, *tang*, *n.* a projecting piece or shank: a point, sting, spike: part of a tool that goes into the haft: a prong: a barb: a sea-surgeon: a biting, characteristic, or extraneous flavour, after-taste, or smell: a smack, tinge: pungency.—*adj.* **tanged** (*tangd*), with a tang: barbed. [O.N. *tange*, point, tang.]

tangelo, *tan'ji-lō*, *n.* a hybrid between *Tangerine* orange and pom*elo*. [Portmanteau word.]

tangent, *tan'jənt*, *adj.* touching without intersecting.

—*n.* a line that touches a curve: the limiting case of a secant when the two points of intersection coincide: (*trig.*; as a function of an angle) the ratio of the side of a right-angled triangle opposite the given angle to the side opposite the other acute angle. (The tangent of an obtuse angle is equal numerically to that of its supplement, but has the negative sign.)—*abbrev.* **tan**: the striking-pin of a clavichord.—*n.* **tan'gency** (-*jən-si*), fact of being tangent: a contact or touching.—*adj.* **tangential** (-*jen'shəl*), of a tangent: in the direction of a tangent.—*n.* **tangentiality** (*tan-jen-shi-al'i-ti*).— *adv.* **tangen'tially**, in the direction of a tangent. —**at a tangent**, in the direction of the tangent: in continuation in the momentary direction instead of following the general course. [L. *tangēns, -entis*, pr.p. of *tangĕre*, to touch.]

Tangerine, *tan'jə-rēn* (or -*rēn'*), *adj.* of *Tangiers* on the Morocco coast.—*n.* a native of Tangiers: **tangerine**, a mandarin or Tangerine orange—a small, flattish, loose-skinned variety.

tanghin, *tang'gin*, *n.* a Madagascan poison formerly used for the judicial ordeal: the apocynaceous tree yielding it.—*n.* **tangh'inin**, its active principle. [Malagasy *tangèna*.]

tangible, *tan'ji-bl*, *adj.* perceptible by the touch: capable of being possessed or realised: material, corporeal.—*ns.* **tangibil'ity; tan'gibleness**.—*adv.* **tan'gibly**. [L. *tangibilis*—*tangĕre*, to touch.]

tangie, *tang'i*, *n.* an Orcadian water-spirit, appearing as a seahorse, or man covered with seaweed.

tangle, *tang'gl*, *v.t.* to form into, involve in, or cover with, a confused interwoven mass: to entangle.— *v.i.* to become tangled.—*n.* a tangled mass or condition: a perplexity, complication: a naturalist's dredge with streamers. — *adj.* **tang'led**. — *ns.* **tang'lefoot**, (*U.S.*) whisky, intoxicating liquor; **tang'lement; tang'ler**.—*adj.* **tang'lesome**.— *n.* and *adj.* **tang'ling**.—*adv.* **tang'lingly**.—*adj.* **tang'ly**, tangled: inclined to tangle. [App. from earlier *tagle*; see **taigle**.]

tangle, *tang'gl*, *n.* coarse seaweed, esp. the more or less edible Laminaria.—*adj.* **tang'ly**. [App. conn. with O.N. *thöngull*, Laminaria stalk—*thang*, bladderwrack.]

tangle, *tang'gl*, *n.* (*Scot.*) any tall and limp person or thing: an icicle.—*adj.* long and limp.—*adj.* **tang'ly**.

tango, *tang'gō*, *n.* a dance or dance-tune in 4-4 time of Argentine negro origin with Parisian developments.—*v.i.* to dance the tango:—*pa.t.* and *pa.p.* **tang'oed**.—*n.* **tang'oist**. [Sp., a S. American negro festival or dance.]

tangram, *tan'gram*, *n.* a Chinese toy, a square cut into seven pieces that will fit in various forms.

tangun, *tang'gun*, *n.* the Tibetan piebald pony. [Hind. *tānghan*—Tibetan *rtandn.*]

tanh, *tansh*, *than*, *n.* a conventional abbreviation for hyperbolic *tangent*.

tanist, *tan'ist*, *n.* a Celtic chief's heir elect.—*n.* **tan'istry**, the system of succession by a previously elected member of the family. [Ir. and Gael. *tànaiste*—*tánaise*, second.]

tank, *tangk*, *n.* (*India*) a pool, pond, reservoir: (*U.S.*) a pond: a large basin or cistern: a reservoir of water, oil, &c.: an ironclad land-ship or auto mobile fort with caterpillar wheels.—*v.t.* to store in a tank: to plunge into a tank.—*v.i.* (*U.S.*) to drink heavily (with *up*).—*ns.* **tank'age**, storing in tanks: charge for such storage: the capacity of a tank or tanks: residue from tanks; **tank'-car -wag'on**, a railway wagon for carrying oil or other liquid in a large tank.—*adj.* **tanked**, (*U.S. slang*) drunk.—*ns.* **tank'-en'gine**, a locomotive that carrie its water and coal in itself (without a tender) **tank'er**, a ship that carries liquids, esp. oil, in bulk; **tank'ful**:—*pl.* **tank'fuls**. [Port. *tanque*— L. *stagnum*, a pool.]

tanka, *tan'kä*, *n.* the boat population of Canton inhabiting **tank'a-boats**.—Also **tan'kia**. [Chin.]

tankard, *tangk'ərd*, *n.* a large mug-like vessel.— **cool tankard** (see **cool**). [Cf. Du. *tanckaert.*]

tanned, tanner, tannic, tannin, tanning. See under **tan**.

tanner, *tan'ər*, *n.* (*slang*) a sixpence.

tanrec. See **tenrec.**

tansy, *tan′zi, n.* a bitter, aromatic roadside composite plant (*Tanacetum vulgare*) with small heads of tubular yellow flowers: extended to other plants, as ragwort, silver-weed, yarrow: a pudding or cake flavoured with tansy, eaten at Easter.—**like a tansy,** exactly right. [O.Fr. *tanasie*, through L.L. from Gr. *athanasiā*, immortality.]

Tantalus, *tan′tə-ləs, n.* a son of Zeus punished in Tartarus for revealing secrets of the gods by having to stand in water that ebbed when he would drink, overhung by grapes that drew back when he reached for them: the wood-ibis genus : **tantalus,** a case in which decanters are visible but locked up. —*n.* **tan′talate,** a salt of tantalic acid.—*adjs.* **Tantalean** (*-tā′*), **Tantā′lian, Tantalic** (*-tal′ik*), of Tantalus ; **tantal′ic,** of tantalum (tantalic acid, HTaO₃).—*n.* **tantalisā′tion.**—*v.t.* **tan′talise,** to torment by presenting something to excite desire but keeping it out of reach : to torture into an unnatural form.—*n.* **tan′taliser.**—*n.* and *adj.* **tan′talising.**—*adv.* **tan′talisingly.**—*ns.* **tan′talism,** the punishment of Tantalus : a tormenting ; **tan′talite,** (*min.*) a black mineral, iron tantalate ; **tan′talum,** a metallic element (Ta ; at. numb. 73) so named from its inability to absorb water ; **tan′talum-lamp, an** electric lamp with tantalum filament ; **Tan′talus-cup,** a philosophical toy, with a siphon within the figure of a man whose chin is on a level with its bend.

tantamount, *tan′tə-mownt, adj.* amounting to as much or to the same : equivalent : equal in value or meaning. [A.Fr. *tant amunter*, to amount to as much.]

tantara, *tan-tä′rä, n.* a blast of trumpet or horn.— Also **tantara′ra.** [Imit.]

tantivy, *tan-tiv′i, adv.* at full gallop : headlong.— *n.* a hunting cry : a rapid rush : (*hist.*) a Tory High Churchman.—*adj.* headlong : High Church Tory. —*interj.* expressive of galloping or (later) the sound of the hunting-horn. [Imit.]

tantony. See **Anthony.**

Tantra, *tan′trä, n.* a religious text-book of the Sāktas.—*ns.* **Tan′trism,** the teaching of the Tantras ; **Tan′trist.** [Sans. *tantra*, thread, fundamental doctrine.]

tantrum, *tan′trəm, n.* a capricious fit of ill-temper without adequate cause. [Origin unknown.]

Tantum ergo, *tan′təm ər′gō,* L. *tän′toom er′gō, n.* the fifth stanza of the hymn ' Pange, lingua, gloriosi corporis mysterium,' written for the office of the Festival of Corpus Christi, which St Thomas of Aquino drew up in 1263. [From its opening words.]

Tāoism, *tä′ō-izm,* or *tow′izm, n.* the religious system founded by the Chinese philosopher Lāo-tsze (b. 604 B.C.), set forth in the *Tāo Teh King.*— *n.* **Tā′öist.**—*adj.* **Tāoist′ic.**

tap, *tap, n.* a gentle knock or its sound : (*dial.*) a shoe sole : a protective piece on a shoe heel : (*U.S. mil.*, in *pl.*) a signal for putting lights out.—*v.t.* and *v.i.* to knock gently.—*v.t.* to furnish or repair with a tap :—*pr.p.* **tapp′ing ;** *pa.t.* and *pa.p.* **tapped.** —*ns.* **tap′-dancing,** dancing with tapping of the feet ; **tapp′er,** one who taps : one who soles and heels : an instrument or part that taps : a de-coherer.—*n.* and *adj.* **tapp′ing.** [O.Fr. *taper.*]

tap, *tap, n.* a peg or stopper : a hole or short pipe with a valve for running off a fluid : a taproom : any particular liquor drawn through a tap : a screw for cutting an internal thread : a tap-root.—*v.t.* to pierce, so as to let out fluid : to broach : to draw off : (*fig.*) to draw upon, esp. for the first time : to intercept, or intercept from, by stealth : to furnish with a tap, or with a screw-thread.—*v.i.* to act as a tapster :—*pr.p.* **tapp′ing ;** *pa.t.* and *pa.p.* **tapped.**—*ns.* **tap′-bolt,** a screwed-in bolt ; **tap′-cin′(k)ler,** slag produced during puddling ; **tap′-dress′ing,** well-dressing ; **tap′-house,** a tavern ; **tap′lash,** poor stale swipes ; **tapp′er,** one who taps trees, &c. : a milking-machine ; **tapp′ing,** the act or art of drawing out or running off a fluid : an operation for removal of liquid from the body ; **tap′room,** a room where beer is served from the tap or cask ; **tap′root,** a strong main root striking down vertically ; **tap′ster,** one who draws liquor, a barman ; **tap′-wa′ter,** water from a household tap.—**on tap,** kept in cask—opp. to *bottled* : ready to be drawn upon. [O.E. *tæppa,* tap, *tæppestre,* (female) tapster ; Du. *tap,* Ger. *zapfen,* tap.]

tap, *tāp, n.* a Scots form of **top.**—*adj.* **tapp′it,** crested.—*ns.* **tapp′it-hen′,** a crested hen : a liquor vessel of capacity variously stated at 1, 3, or 6 imperial quarts ; **taps′man,** a servant with principal charge : chief of a company of drovers.— **take one's tap in one's lap,** (*Scot.*) to bundle up (one's tow for the distaff) and go home.

tap, *tap, n.* an Indian malarial fever. [Pers.]

tapa, tappa, *tä′pä, n.* paper-mulberry bark. [Polynesian generally.]

tapaculo, *tä-pä-kōō′lō,* **tapacolo,** *-kō′, n.* a small S. American bird with tilted tail. [Sp. *tapaculo*— *tapa,* cover (imper.), *culo,* posterior.]

tapadera, *tä-pä-dā′rä,* **tapadero,** *-rō, n.* the guard in front of a Mexican stirrup. [Sp., lid, cover— *tapar,* to cover.]

tape, *tāp, n.* material woven in narrow bands : a strip of such material, used for tying up, connecting, &c. : a ribbon of paper printed by a recording instrument, as in telegraphy : (*print.*) a flexible band that guides the sheets : a tape-measure : (*slang*) liquor.—*v.t.* to furnish, fasten, bind, measure with a tape : to get the range or measure of : (*Scot.*) to deal out, or use, sparingly.—*n.* **tape′-grass,** Vallisneria. — *adj.* **tape′less.** — *ns.* **tape′line,** **-measure,** a flexible measuring strip of tape, steel, or other material.—*adj.* **tā′pen,** made of tape.— *n.* **tāp′er,** one who works with tapes.—*adj.* **tape′tied,** tied up with tape : bound with, or by, red tape (see **red**).—*ns.* **tape′worm,** a ribbon-shaped segmented parasitic worm, any cestode, but esp. of Taenia or kindred genus ; **tā′pist,** an official formalist.—**breast the tape,** in foot-racing, to touch with the breast the line stretched across the track at the winning-post. [O.E. *tæppe,* tape, fillet.]

taper, *tā′pər, n.* (*obs.*) a wax-candle : a long, thin waxed wick or spill : a feeble light : lengthwise diminution in width : gradual leaving off.—*adj.* tapering.—*v.i.* to become gradually smaller towards one end.—*v.t.* to make to taper.—*adj.* **ta′pered,** tapering : lighted by tapers.—*n.* **ta′perer,** one who bears a taper.—*n.* and *adj.* **ta′pering.**—*adv.* **ta′peringly.**—*n.* **ta′perness.**—*adv.* **ta′perwise.** [O.E. *tapor.*]

tapestry, *tap′is-tri, n.* an ornamental textile used for the covering of walls and furniture, and for curtains, made by passing coloured threads among fixed warp threads : a machine-made imitation of this.—*adj.* of tapestry (*Milt.* **tap′stry**).—*v.t.* to hang with tapestry : to work or represent in tapestry.—*adj.* **tap′estried.** [Fr. *tapisserie*—*tapis,* a carpet—L.L. *tapētium*—Gr. *tapētion,* dim. of *tapēs, -ētos,* prob. of Iranian origin.]

tapet, *tap′it, n.* (*Spens.*) a piece of tapestry. [L. *tapēte,* perh. through O.E. *tæppet.*]

tapeti, *tap′ə-ti, n.* the Brazilian rabbit. [Tupí.]

tapetum, *tə-pē′təm, n.* (*bot.*) a layer of cells surrounding spore mother-cells : (*zool.*) the pigmentary layer of the retina :—*pl.* **tape′ta.**—*adj.* **tape′tal.** [L. *tapētum*—Gr. *tapēs, -ētos,* carpet.]

tapioca, *tap-i-ō′kä, n.* a farinaceous substance got by heating cassava : extended to a kind of sago and a preparation of potato starch : a pudding made from tapioca.—**pearl tapioca** (see **pearl**). [Tupí-Guaraní *tipyoca.*]

tapir, *tā′pər, n.* a large odd-toed ungulate with short flexible proboscis, of which several species are found in S. America, Malacca, &c. [Tupí *tapira.*]

tapis, *tä′pē,* also *tap′is, n.* (*obs.*) a covering, hanging, &c., of tapestry or the like.—**on the tapis,** on the table : under consideration. [Fr.]

tapotement, *tä-pōt-män′, tä-pōt′mənt, n.* percussion in massage. [Fr.]

tappet, *tap′it, n.* a projection that transmits motion from one part of a machine to another by tapping. —*ns.* **tapp′et-loom, -mō′tion, -ring, -rod,** &c. [tap (1).]

tappice, *tap′is, v.i.* to lie low.—*v.t.* to hide. [Fr. *tapir, tapiss-.*]

tappit, tappit-hen, tapsman. See **tap** (3).

tapsalteerie, *tăp-sl-tē'rä,* **tapsieteerie,** *tăp-sä-.* Scots forms of **topsyturvy.**

tapstry, *tap'stri* (*Milt.*). Same as **tapestry.**

tapu, *tä'poo.* See **taboo.**

tar (*Shak.* **tarre**), *tär, v.t.* to set on, incite to fight. [Conn. with O.E. *tergan,* to worry.]

tar, *tär, n.* a dark, viscous mixture got by destructive distillation of wood, coal, peat, &c.: a natural bituminous substance of like appearance (*mineral tar*): a sailor (perh. for **tarpaulin**).—*v.t.* to smear, coat, treat, with tar:—*pr.p.* **tarr'ing;** *pa.t.* and *pa.p.* **tarred.**—*ns.* **tar'-box,** a shepherd's box for tar as a salve for sheep: a shepherd; **tar'-brush,** a brush for applying tar; **tar'heel,** a North Carolinian; **tar-macad'am** (also **tar'mac**), a road surfacing of broken stone covered or mixed with tar: the runway system of an aerodrome; **tarriness** (*tär'i-nis*).—*n.* and *adj.* **tarr'ing.**—*adj.* **tarry** (*tär'i*), of, like, covered or soiled with, tar.— *n.* **tarr'y-breeks,** (*Scot.*) a sailor.—*adj.* **tarr'y-fingered,** thievish.—*ns.* **tar'-spot,** a black spot of Rhytisma; **tar'-wa'ter,** a cold infusion of tar in water, once reputed as a medicine; **tar'weed,** a name for various heavy-scented American composites.—**tar and feather,** to smear with tar and then cover with feathers; **tarred with the same brush,** or **stick,** with the same defects; **touch of the tar-brush,** an infusion of negro, Indian, or coloured blood. [O.E. *teru, teoro*; Ger. (from L.G.) and Du. *teer.*]

tara, *tä'rä, n.* a variety of bracken with edible rhizome.—Also **ta'ra-fern.**

taradiddle. See **tarradiddle.**

tarand, *tar'ənd, n.* (*obs.*) a northern beast fabled to change colour like the chamaeleon: a reindeer. [Gr. *tarand(r)os,* a reindeer, or (prob.) elk.]

tarantara. See **taratantara.**

tarantas(s), *tä-răn-täs', n.* a four-wheeled Russian vehicle mounted on poles. [Russ. *tarantas.*]

tarantella, *tar-ən-tel'ä, n.* a lively Neapolitan dance —in triplets for one couple—thought a remedy for tarantism: a tune for it.—*ns.* **tar'antism,** an epidemic dancing mania; **tarantūla** (*-an'*), a large venomous South European wolf-spider (Lycosa), long supposed to cause tarantism in South Italy: in America applied to large venomous spiders of the bird-catching family (Aviculariidae): in Africa, a biting but not venomous solpugid: in Australia applied to several large harmless laterigrade spiders: the stellio lizard: **Tarantula,** a genus of pedipalps. —**tarantula juice,** (*U.S.*) bad whisky. [It. *tarantella, tarantola*—Gr. *Taras, -antos,* Tarentum, Taranto.]

taratantara, *tär-ä-tăn'tä-rä,* or *-tăn-tä'rä, n.* the sound of a trumpet.—Also *interj., adj., adv., v.t.,* and *v.i.*—Also **taran'tara.** [Imit.]

Taraxacum, *tä-raks'ə-kəm, n.* the dandelion genus: taraxacum, its root and rootstock, a tonic laxative. [App. from Ar. *tarakhshaqōq*—Pers. *talkh chakōk,* assimilated to Gr. *taraxis,* disturbance.]

tarbush, tarboosh, tarbouche, *tär-boosh', n.* a fez. [Ar. *tarbūsh.*]

tarcel. See **tercel.**

Tardenoisian, *tär-di-noi'zi-ən, adj.* (*archaeol.*) belonging to a stage of culture represented by finds at *Tardenois,* Aisne, France, transitional between Palaeolithic and Neolithic.

tardigrade, *tär'di-grād, adj.* slow-paced.—*n.* a member of the Tardigrada.—*n.pl.* **Tardigra'da,** formerly the sloths: now, a class of arthropods, the bear-animalcules. [L. *tardus,* slow, *gradī,* to step.]

tardy, *tär'di, adj.* slow: sluggish: behindhand: too long delayed: late: (*obs.*) caught at fault.— *v.t.* (*Shak.*) to retard.—*adv.* **tar'dily.**—*n.* **tar'diness.**—*adjs.* **tar'dive** (*-div*), late in development; **tar'dy-gait'ed,** slow-paced. [Fr. *tardif—tard—* L. *tardus,* slow.]

tare, *tär, n.* a vetch of various kinds, esp. of the lentil-like group: (*B.*) a weed, prob. darnel. [Origin obscure.]

tare, *tär, n.* the weight of a vessel, wrapping, or container, which subtracted from the gross weight gives the net weight.—*v.t.* to ascertain or allow for the tare of. [Fr.,—Sp. *tara*—Ar. *tarhah,* thrown away.]

tare, *tär, arch. pa.t.* of **tear.**

targe, *tärj, n.* a shield, esp. a light shield. [O.Fr. *targe*—O.N. *targe,* shield.]

targe, *tärj, v.t.* (*Scot.*) to cross-examine: to supervise strictly: to reprimand: to thrash. [Origin unknown.]

target, *tär'git, n.* a small buckler or round shield: a shield-like or other mark to shoot at for practice or competition: a surface on which electrons impinge: an object aimed at: a butt: a result to be aimed at: a shooting score: a neck and breast of lamb: a sight on a levelling staff: an American railway signal.—*adj.* **tar'geted,** provided with a shield.—*n.* **targeteer',** one armed with a shield, a peltast. [O.Fr. *targuete*; cf. **targe.**]

Targum, *tär-gōōm', tär'gəm, n.* any Aramaic version or paraphrase of the Old Testament:—*pl.* **Targums.**—*adj.* **Targumic** (*tär-gōōm'ik, -gūm', -gum'*). —*n.* **Tar'gumist,** a writer of a Targum: a student of the Targums.—*adj.* **Targumist'ic.** [Chaldean *targūm,* interpretation.]

tariff, *tar'if n.* a list or set of customs duties: a list of charges.—*n.* **tariff-reform'er,** one who favoured the early 20th-century movement for **Tariff Reform** or Protection opposed to Free Trade. [It. *tariffa*—Ar. *ta'rīf,* explanation—'*arafa,* to explain.]

tarlatan, *tär'lə-tən, n.* an open, transparent muslin. [Fr. *tarlatane*; origin doubtful.]

tarn, *tärn, n.* a small mountain lake. [O.N. *tjörn.*]

tarnal, *tär'nl,* **tarnation,** *tär-nā'shən, adjs.* and *advs.* (*U.S. slang*) softened forms of **eternal** and **damnation,** app. influenced by each other.

tarnish, *tär'nish, v.t.* to dull, discolour, render iridescent, diminish the lustre of, by exposure to the air, &c.: to sully.—*v.i.* to become dull: to lose lustre.—*n.* loss of lustre: a surface discoloration or iridescence on metal or mineral: a film of oxide, sulphide, &c.—*adjs.* **tar'nishable; tar'-nished.**—*n.* **tar'nisher.** [Fr. *ternir, terniss—terne,* dull, wan; poss. Gmc.]

taro, *tä'rō, n.* a plant (Colocasia) of the arum family, widely cultivated for its edible rootstock in the islands of the Pacific. [Polynesian.]

tarot, *tar'ō, n.* an old kind of playing-card: (in *pl.*) a game played with them.—Also **tar'oc** (*-ok*). [Fr. *tarot,* It. *tarocco.*]

tarpan, *tär'pan, n.* the small recently extinct feralised or wild horse of the steppes of S. European Russia. [Tatar.]

tarpaulin, *tär-paw'lin, n.* strong linen or hempen cloth waterproofed with tar or otherwise: a sheet of it: a sailor's waterproof hat: (*coll.*) a sailor: (*obs.*) a sea-bred officer.—Also **tarpau'ling.**—Also *adj.* [App. **tar,** and **palling—pall.**]

Tarpeian, *tär-pē'ən, adj.* of Tarpeia, said to have betrayed the Capitol at Rome to the Sabines and to have been buried beneath the **Tarpeian Rock** on the Capitoline Hill, from which criminals were thrown.

tarpon, *tär'pən, n.* a gigantic fish (Megalops) akin to the herring, angled for on the Florida and Gulf coasts. [Origin unknown.]

tar(r)adiddle, *tar-ə-did'l, n.* a fib, a lie. [App. founded on **diddle.**]

tarragon, *tar'ə-gən, n.* an aromatic Artemisia used for flavouring vinegar, sauces, &c. [Ar. *tarkhūn,* perh.—Gr. *drakōn,* a dragon.]

tarras, *tar'əs, n.* an old form (*Spens.*) of **terrace.** See also **trass.**

tarre. See **tar** (1).—Also (*Spens.*) for **tar** (2).

tarrock, *tar'ək, n.* (*local*) a sea-bird of various kinds. [Origin obscure.]

tarry, *tar'i.* See **tar.**

tarry, *tar'i, v.i.* to linger: to loiter: to delay: to stay behind: to sojourn: to wait.—*v.t.* to await (*pr.p.* **tarr'ying;** *pa.t.* and *pa.p.* **tarr'ied**).—*n.* (*arch.*) delay: sojourn, stay.—*ns.* **tarr'iance** (*arch.*), tarrying: delay: waiting: a sojourn; **tarr'ier,** one who tarries or delays.—*v.i.* **tarr'ow** (*tär'ō*; *Scot.*), to hesitate: to reluct. [History obscure; the form agrees with O.E. *tergan,* to irritate, the meaning with O.Fr. *tarier.*]

tarsal, tarsel, tarcel, *tär'sl.* See **tercel.**

tarsia, *tär'si-ä* (It. *tär-sē'ä*), *n.* an Italian woodinlay.—Also **tar'sia-work.**

tarsus, *tär′səs, n.* the part of the foot to which the leg is articulated: in birds, sometimes applied to the tarsometatarsus: in insects, the five-jointed foot:—*pl.* **tar′sī.**—*adj.* **tar′sal,** relating to the tarsus or ankle.—*n.* a bone of the tarsus.—*ns.* **tarsalgia** (*-sal′ji-ä*), pain in the instep; **tar′sier** (*-si-ər*), a spectral-looking lemuroid of the East Indies with long tarsal bones.—*adj.* **tar′sioid,** like the tarsier: of the tarsier family.—*ns.* **Tar′sipēs** (L. *pēs,* foot), the long-snouted honey-mouse, an Australian honey-sucking phalanger with feet like the tarsier; **Tar′sius,** the tarsier genus.—*adj.* **tarsometatar′sal.**—*n.* **tarsometatar′sus,** a bird's shank-bone, the combined metatarsals and distal tarsals. [Gr. *tarsos,* the flat of the foot.]

tart, *tärt, adj.* sharp: biting: acidulous.—*adj.* **tart′ish.**—*adv.* **tart′ly.**—*n.* **tart′ness.** [O.E. *teart.*]

tart, *tärt, n.* a dish of pastry distinguished from a pie either by being uncovered or by containing sweet not savoury materials: (*slang*; disrespectful) a girl: (*slang*) a prostitute.—*ns.* **tartine** (*-ēn*; Fr.), a slice of bread with butter or jam; **tart′let,** a small tart. [O.Fr. *tarte.*]

tartan, *tär′tən, n.* a woollen (or other) checked stuff: a distinctive checked pattern, as of a Highland clan. —*adj.* of tartan: checked in tartan.—*adj.* **tar′-taned,** clad in tartan. [Origin unknown.]

tartan, tartane, *tär′tən, tär-tän′, n.* a Mediterranean vessel with lateen sail. [Fr. *tartane,* poss.—Ar. *tarīdah,* a small ship.]

tartana, *tär-tä′nä, n.* a little covered wagon. [Sp.]

tartar, *tär′tər, n.* recrystallised and partially purified argol, chiefly acid potassium tartrate (with calcium tartrate, &c.): a deposit of calcium phosphate and other matter on the teeth.—*adjs.* **tartareous** (*-tā′ri-əs*), of or like tartar: {*bot.*) with rough crumbly surface; **tartaric** (*tär-tar′ik*), of or got from tartar (tartaric acid, $C_4H_6O_6$, prepared from argol).—*v.t.* **tar′tarise,** to treat, mix, or combine with tartar.—*n.* **tar′trate,** a salt of tartaric acid.— **cream of tartar,** purified argol; **tartar emetic,** a compound of potassium, antimony, carbon, hydrogen, and oxygen. [L.L. *tartarum,* perh. from Ar.]

Tartar, *tär′tər, n.* a Tatar: a formidable, rough, unmanageable person: one who unexpectedly turns the tables on his assailant.—Also *adj.*—*n.* and *adj.* **Tartarian** (*-tā′ri-ən*), Tartar, Tatar.— *adjs.* **Tartaric** (*-tar′ik*), of the Tartars; **tar′tarly,** like a Tartar: ferocious.—**Tartarian lamb,** barometz. [See Tatar.]

Tartarus, *tär′ta-rəs, n.* in Homer, a deep and sunless abyss, as far below Hades as earth is below heaven: hell. — Also (*Spens., Shak.*) **Tar′tar,** (*Spens.*) **Tar′tare, Tar′tarie, Tar′tary.** — *adj.* **Tartarean** (*-tā′ri-ən*). [L.,—Gr. *Tartaros.*]

Tartuf(f)e, *tär-tüf′, n.* a hypocritical pretender to religion.—*adjs.* **Tartuf(f)′ian, Tartuf(f)′ish.**—*n.* **Tartuf(f)′ism.** [From the character in Molière's *Tartuffe* (1664-69).]

tarwhine, *tär′hwin, n.* an Australian sea-bream.

tasar, *tus′ər.* Same as tusser.

taseometer, *tas-i-om′i-tər, n.* an instrument for measuring strains in a structure. [Gr. *tasis, -eōs,* a stretching, *metron,* measure.]

tash, *täsh, v.t.* (*Scot.*) to soil: to blemish: to disfigure: to disarray. [Fr. *tacher.*]

tasimeter, *ta-sim′i-tər, n.* an instrument for measuring changes in pressure, &c., by variations in electrical conductivity. [Gr. *tasis,* a stretch, *metron,* measure.]

task, *täsk, n.* a piece or amount of work set or undertaken.—*v.t.* (*Shak.*) to tax: to impose a task on: to burden with severe work: to employ fully.— *ns.* **task′er,** one who imposes a task, or who performs **it:** one who does piece-work; **task′ing,** task-work; **task′master;** one who allots tasks :— *fem.* **task′mistress;** **task′-work,** work done as a task, or by the job. [O.Fr. *tasque* (Fr. *tâche*)—L.L. *tasca, taxa*—L. *taxāre,* to rate.]

aslet. See tasset.

'asmanian, *tas-, taz-mā′ni-ən, adj.* of Tasmania, discovered in 1642 by Abel Janszoon *Tasman.*— *n.* a native or citizen of Tasmania.—**Tasmanian devil,** a ferocious Tasmanian dasyure; **Tasmanian myrtle,** a Tasmanian and Victorian ever-

green beech; **Tasmanian wolf** (or **tiger**), the thylacine, a striped wolf-like dasyure of Tasmania.

tass, *täs, n.* (*prov.*) a mow, a heap. [O.Fr. *tas,* poss. from Du.]

tass, *tas, n.* a drinking-cup: a small drink.—*n.* **tass′ie,** (*Scot.*) a small cup. [Fr. *tasse*—Ar. *tāss,* cup.]

tasse, tace, *tas, n.* in plate armour, one of a series of overlapping pieces forming a kind of skirt.—*ns.* **tas′let, tass′et,** a tasse. [O.Fr. *tasse, tasselet, tassete.*]

tassel, *tas′l, n.* (*Shak.*) a clasp or fastening: an ornamental hanging tuft of threads: an inflorescence of like appearance, esp. of maize: a ribbon book-mark: a gold or silver plate on a vestment.— *v.t.* to furnish with tassels.—*v.i.* to form tassels, flower :—*pr.p.* **tass′elling;** *pa.t.* and *pa.p.* **tass′-elled.** — *adj.* [tass′elled. — *n.* **tass′elling.** — *-- adj.* **tass′elly.** [O.Fr. *tassel;* origin doubtful.]

tassel, tassel-gent, tassel-gentle. See tercel.

taste, *tāst, v.t.* to try, or to perceive, by the sense seated in the tongue and palate: to try by eating a little: to eat a little of: to partake of: (*obs.*) to try, test: (*arch.*) to relish, enjoy: to experience, perceive: (*Shak.*) to enjoy carnally: (*rare*) to give a flavour to.—*v.i.* to try or perceive by the mouth: to have a flavour: to act as taster: to have experience.—*n.* the act of tasting: the particular sensation caused by a substance on the tongue: the sense by which we perceive the flavour of a thing: the quality or flavour of anything: a small portion: an experience: discernment, of accordance with, what is socially right: the faculty by which the mind perceives the beautiful: nice perception: choice, predilection, liking. —*adj.* **tāst′able.**—*ns.* **taste′bud, -bulb,** a group of cells sensitive to taste.—*adjs.* **tāst′ed,** having a taste; **taste′ful,** full of taste: having a pleasant or a high relish: showing good taste.—*adv.* **taste′fully.**—*n.* **taste′fulness.**—*adj.* **taste′less,** without taste: without good taste: insipid.—*adv.* **taste′lessly.**—*ns.* **taste′lessness;** **tāst′er,** one skilful in distinguishing flavours by the taste: one employed to test the innocuousness of food by tasting it before serving it to his master.—*adv.* **tāst′ily.**—*n.* **tāst′ing.**—*adj.* **tāst′y,** (*vulg.*) savoury: (*vulg.*) tasteful.—**good taste,** intuitive feeling for what is aesthetically or socially right; **to one's taste,** to one's liking. [O.Fr. *taster* (Fr. *tâter*), as if from a L.L. freq. of L. *taxāre,* to touch, handle, estimate—*tangĕre,* to touch.]

tat, tatt, *tat, v.t.* to make by tatting.—*v.i.* to make tatting.—*n.* **tatt′ing,** knotted lace edging made by hand with a shuttle from sewing-thread: the making of it.

tat, *tät, n.* East Indian hempen matting. [Hind. *tāt.*]

tat, *tat, n.* See tattoo (3).

tat, *tat, n.* a tap.—*v.t.* to touch, tap: to flog. [Cf. **tap,** and see **tit.**]

ta-ta, *tä-tä′, interj.* (*childish* and *coll.*) good-bye.

Tatar, *tä′tər, n.* orig. a member of any of certain Tungusic tribes in Chinese Tartary: extended to any of the Mongol, Turkish, and other warriors who swept over Asia and Europe: loosely, one of the mixed inhabitants of Tartary, Siberia, and the Russian steppes, including Kazan Tartars, Crim Tartars, Kipchaks, Kalmucks, &c.: a speaker of a Turkic language.—Also *adj.*—*adjs.* **Tatarian** (*tä-tā′ri-ən*), **Tataric** (*-tar′ik*), of the Tatars: of the Turkic group of languages. [Turk. and Pers. *Tátar;* association with Gr. *Tartaros,* hell, seems to have suggested the form **Tartar.**]

tate, tait, *tāt, n.* (*Scot.*) a small portion, pinch, tuft.

tater, *tā′tər, n.* a vulgar form of **potato.**—Also **tā′tie.**

tath, *täth, n.* (*prov.*) cattle dung: coarse tufted grass that grows where it has fallen.—*v.t.* to manure.— *v.i.* to drop dung. [O.N. *tath.*]

tatler. See tattle.

tatou, *ta′tōō,* or *-tōō′, n.* an armadillo, esp. the giant armadillo. [Tupí *tatú.*]

tatt, tatting. See tat (1).

tatter, *tat′ər, n.* a torn shred: a loose hanging rag.— *v.t.* to tear to tatters.—*v.i.* to fall into tatters.— *n.* **tatterdemā′lion** (or *-mal′yən*), a ragged fellow.

—*adjs.* **tatt′ered; tatt′ery,** ragged. [Cf. Ice. *tötürr.*]

Tattersall's, *tat′ər-sawlz, n.* a famous London horse-mart and haunt of racing-men — founded 1766 by Richard *Tattersall* (1724-95).

tattie, *tä′tā, n.* a Scots form of potato.—*ns.* **tatt′ie-bo′gle,** a scarecrow; **tatt′ie-claw,** potato soup; **tatt′ie-lift′ing,** potato harvest; **tatt′ie-shaw,** the above-ground parts of a potato plant.

tattle, *tat′l, n.* trifling talk : chatter.—*v.i.* to talk idly or triflingly : to tell tales or secrets.—*v.t.* to tell or utter in tattle.—*n.* **tatt′ler** (formerly **tat′ler**), one given to tattling : any (esp. American) bird of the Totaninae, from their giving warning of gunners.—*n.* and *adj.* **tatt′ling,** chattering : tale-telling.—*adv.* **tatt′lingly.** [Used by Caxton to translate M.Du. *tatelen*; imit.]

tattoo, *tə-tōō′, n.* a beat of drum or other signal calling soldiers to quarters : a drumming : a military fête by night.—**the devil's tattoo,** drumming with the fingers on a table, &c., in absence of mind or impatience. [Du. *taptoe—tap,* tap, toe, to, in the sense of shut.]

tattoo, tatu, *tə-tōō′,* earlier **tatow,** *-tow′, n.* a design marked on the skin by pricking in colouring-matter.—*v.t.* to mark in this way :—*pa.t.* and *pa.p.* **tattooed′.** [Tahitian *ta′tau,* Marquesan *ta′tu.*]

tattoo, *tut′ōō, n.* a native-bred Indian pony.—Abbreviated **tat** (*tat*). [Hind. *tattū.*]

tatty. See **tattie**; also **tawtie**—under **taut** (2).

tatty, *tat′i, n.* an Indian mat of bamboo, cuscus-grass roots, &c., esp. one kept wet in a doorway or window to cool the air. [Hind. *tattī.*]

tau, *tow, n.* the nineteenth letter (T, τ) of the Greek alphabet, answering to T : a tau-cross : as a numeral τ′ = 300, ͵τ = 300,000.— *ns.* **tau′-cross,** St Anthony's cross, in the form of a T; **tau′-staff,** a staff with a cross-piece at the top like a crutch. [Gr. *tau,* of Semitic origin.]

taube, *tow′bə, n.* a German monoplane with re-curved wings. [Ger., dove.]

taught, *tawt, pa.t.* and *pa.p.* of **teach.**

tauld, *tawld,* a Scots form of **told** (*pa.t.* and *pa.p.*).

taunt, *tawnt, v.t.* to reproach stingingly : to censure sarcastically.—*v.i.* to jibe.—*n.* a biting jibe : (*B.*) an object of taunts.—*n.* **taunt′er.**—*n.* and *adj.* **taunt′-ing.**—*adv.* **taunt′ingly.** [Poss. O.Fr. *tanter*—L. *tentāre,* to tempt ; or Fr. *tant pour tant,* tit for tat.]

taupie. See **tawpie.**

Taurus, *taw′rəs* (or L. *tow′roos*), *n.* the Bull, a sign of the zodiac and a constellation formerly coinciding with it.—*adjs.* **tau′ric,** of a bull ; **tau′riform,** having the form of a bull ; **tau′rīne** (or *-in*), of a bull : bull-like.—*ns.* **taurobō′lium** (Gr. *tauro-bōlion—bōlē,* a throw, stroke), the sacrifice of a bull, as in the Mithraic rites : an artistic representation thereof ; **tauromachy** (*-om′ə-ki*) ; Gr. *tauro-machiā—machē,* fight), bull-fighting : a bull-fight.—*adj.* **tauromor′phous** (Gr. *morphē,* form), bull-shaped. [L. *taurus* and Gr. *tauros.*]

taut (*obs.* **taught**), *tawt, adj.* tightly drawn : tense : in good condition.—*v.t.* and *v.i.* **taut′en,** to tighten.—*n.* **taut′ness.** [Prob. conn. with **tow,** tight.]

taut, tawt, *tawt, v.t.* and *v.i.* (*Scot.*) to mat, tangle.—*adjs.* **taut′it; tawt′ie, tatt′y** (*Scot.*). [Cf. O.E. *tætteca,* rag.]

taut-, tawt-, tauto-, *tawt′ō-, tawt-o′-,* in composition, the same.—*ns.* **taut′ochrone** (*-krōn* ; Gr. *chronos,* time), a curve such that a particle travelling along it under gravity reaches a fixed point in the same time, no matter where it starts ; **tautoch′ronism.** —*adjs.* **tautoch′ronous ; tautologic** (*-loj′*), *-al.* —*adv.* **tautolog′ically.**—*v.i.* **tautol′ogise,** to use tautology.—*ns.* **tautol′ogism ; tautol′ogist.**—*adj.* **tautol′ogous** (*-ə-gəs*), tautological.—*ns.* **tautol′ogy,** use of words that (esp. needlessly or pointlessly) say the same thing ; **taut′omer** (Gr. *meros,* part), a readily interconvertible isomer.—*adj.* **taut-omer′ic.**—*n.* **tautom′erism.**—*adjs.* **tautomet′ric, -al,** exactly corresponding in arrangement of syllables.—*n.* **taut′onym,** a binomial name in which the specific name repeats the generic.—*adjs.* **tauton′ymous ; tautophon′ical.**—*n.* **tautoph′-ony,** repetition of a sound. [Gr. *tauto,* for *to auto,* the same.]

tautog, *taw-tog′, n.* a labroid fish of the North American Atlantic coast. [Narragansett *taut-auog.*]

taver, taiver, *tā′vər, n.* (*Scot.*) a shred. [Cf. Norw. and Dan. *tave.*]

taver, taiver, *tā′vər, v.i.* (*Scot.*) to wander : to rave.—*adj.* **ta(i)′vert,** (*Scot.*) muddled : fuddled : stupid. [Cf. Norw. *tava,* to toil, fumble.]

tavern, *tav′ərn, n.* a public-house.—*n.* **tav′erner,** a publican. [O.Fr. (Fr.) *taverne*—L. *taberna,* shed, stall, tavern, from root of *tabula,* a board.]

taw, *taw, n.* a large or choice marble : a game at marbles : the line shot from at marbles. [Origin unknown.]

taw, *taw, v.t.* to prepare and dress, esp. skins for white leather.—*n.* tawed leather : usu. *pl.* **taws, tawse,** a leather strap, usu. cut in fingers at the end, for corporal punishment.—*ns.* **taw′er,** a maker of white leather ; **taw′ery,** a place where skins are dressed.—*adj.* **taw′ie,** (*Scot.*) tractable.—*n.* **taw′ing.** [O.E. *tawian,* to prepare ; Du. *touwen,* to curry ; O.H.G. *zawjan,* to make, prepare.]

tawdry, *taw′dri, adj.* showy without taste or worth : gaudily adorned.—*n.* trumpery : (*obs.*) a tawdry-lace.—*adv.* **taw′drily.**—*ns.* **taw′driness ; taw′dry-lace′,** (*obs.*) a woman's silk necktie (in *Spens.* a waist-belt), such as was sold at St Audrey's Fair at Ely (17th October) : trumpery adornment. [From *St Audrey* (i.e. Æthelthrýth, daughter of Anna, King of East Anglia), who thought a tumour in her throat a punishment for having worn jewelled necklaces.]

tawny, *taw′ni, adj.* and *n.* yellowish brown.—*n.* **taw′niness.** [Fr. *tanné,* pa.p. of *tanner,* to tan.]

tawpie, taupie, *taw′pā, n.* (*Scot.*) a clumsy, heedless, or inefficient girl. [Cf. Norw. *taap,* a half-wit.]

taws, tawse. See **taw** (2).

tax, *taks, v.t.* to lay a tax on : to register or enrol for fiscal purposes (Luke ii. 1-5) : to burden : to accuse, censure : to assess : to examine (accounts) in order to allow or disallow items.—*n.* a contribution exacted by the state : anything imposed, exacted, or burdensome : (*obs.*) a charge, accusation.—*n.* **taxabil′ity.**—*adj.* **tax′able.**—*adv.* **tax′-ably.**—*n.* **taxā′tion.**—*adj.* **tax′ative,** taxing : of taxing.—*ns.* **tax(ed)′-cart,** a light spring-cart (orig. paying a lower tax, later none) ; **tax′-collect′or.**—*adj.* **taxed.**—*n.* **tax′er** (also **tax′or**).—*adj.* and *adv.* **tax′-free,** without payment of tax.—*ns.* **tax′-gath′erer ; tax′ing,** imposition of taxes : (*obs.*) censure, satire ; **tax′ing-mas′ter,** an officer of a court of law who examines bills of costs ; **tax′-payer.** [Fr. *taxe,* a tax—L. *taxāre,* to handle, value, charge.]

taxi, *tak′si, n.* a taxi-cab : loosely, any motor-car on hire : (*pl.* **tax′is, tax′ies**).—*v.i.* to travel by taxi : of an aeroplane, to run along the ground under its own power :—*pr.p.* **tax′ying;** *pa.t.* and *pa.p.* **tax′ied;** *3rd pers. pres. indic.* **tax′ies.**—*n.* **tax′i-cab,** a cab (now usu. a motor-cab) furnished with a taximeter. [Abbrev. of **taximeter.**]

taxiarch. See under **taxis.**

taxidermy, *taks′i-dər-mi, n.* the art of preparing, stuffing, and mounting skins.—*adjs.* **taxider′mal, taxider′mic.**—*v.t.* **tax′idermise.**—*n.* **tax′ider-mist.** [Gr. *taxis,* arrangement, *derma,* a skin.]

taximeter, *tak′si-mē-tər, tak-sim′i-tər* (*obs.* **taxa-meter**), *n.* an instrument attached to a cab for indicating distance travelled and fare due. [Fr. *taxe,* price, Gr. *metron,* measure.]

taxis, *tak′sis, n.* arrangement : a division of an ancient Greek army (in Athens the contingent from a phyle) : (*surg.*) manipulative replacement of displaced parts : (*biol.*) movement of a whole organism in response to stimulus.—*ns.* **tax′iarch** (*-i-ärk*), commander of a taxis ; **taxon′omer,** a taxonomist.—*adjs.* **taxonom′ic, -al.**—*adv.* **tax-onom′ically.** — *ns.* **taxon′omist ; taxon′omy,** classification or its principles. [Gr.,—*tassein,* to arrange.]

Taxus, *tak′səs, n.* the yew genus of conifers, giving name to the family **Taxā′ceae** (*-si-ē*).—*n.* **Taxō′-dium** (Gr. *eidos,* form), the swamp-cypress genus. [L. *taxus,* yew.]

---

fāte, fär, ȧsk ; mē, hər (her) ; *mīne ; mōte ; mūte ; mōōn ; dhen* (then)

tayra, taira, *tī′rä, n.* a large South American species of the weasel family. [Tupí *taira*.]

tazz′a, *tät′sä, n.* a shallow vessel mounted on a foot: a saucer-shaped bowl:—*pl.* **taz′ze (-sä)**, **taz′zas**. [It., cup; cf. **tass** (2).]

tch-. For some words see **ch-.**

tchick, *chik, ch′, n.* a sound made by pressing the tongue against the roof of the mouth and then drawing back one side, as in urging a horse on.—*v.i.* to make such a sound. [Imit.]

te. See **ti** (*mus*).

tea, *tē, formerly tā, n.* a tree, *Thea sinensis*, close akin to Camellia, cultivated in China, Assam, &c.: its dried and prepared leaves, buds, and shoots: an infusion of the leaves in boiling water: extended to various substitutes (see **Labrador**, **Paraguay**, &c.): any vegetable infusion as a beverage: rarely a similar preparation of animal origin (as **beef-tea**): an afternoon meal or light refreshment at which tea is generally served.—*v.i.* (*coll.*) to take tea.—*v.t.* (*coll.*) to provide tea for.— *ns.* **tea′-board**, a tea-tray; **tea′-bread**, light spongy bread or buns to be eaten with tea; **tea′-caddy**, **tea′-can′ister**, an air-tight box or jar for holding tea; **tea′-cake**, a light cake to be eaten with tea; **tea′-chest**, a chest or case in which tea is packed; **tea′-clipper**, a fast-sailing ship in the tea-trade; **tea′-cloth**, a small tablecloth: a cloth used in washing up after tea; **tea′-cosy**, a thick cover for a tea-pot to keep the tea hot; **tea′cup**, a small cup used in drinking tea; **tea′cupful**:—*pl.* **tea′cupfuls**; **tea′-dealer**, a buyer and seller of tea; **tea′-dish**, an old name for a teacup; **tea′-drinker**; **tea′-eq′uipage**, apparatus for making and serving tea with all that accompanies it; **tea′-fight**, (*slang*) a tea-party; **tea′-gar′den**, a plantation of tea: an open-air restaurant for tea and other refreshments; **tea′-gown**, a loose gown for wearing at afternoon tea at home; **tea′-ho′**, (*Austr.*) a break for tea during the working day; **tea′-house**, a Chinese or Japanese house for tea, &c.; **tea′-kettle**, a kettle for boiling water for tea; **tea′-lead**, lead with a little tin for lining teachests; **tea′-leaf**, a leaf of tea: a scrap of solid tea in a cup or in the refuse; **tea′-meeting**, a public social meeting at which tea is drunk; **tea′-party**, a social gathering at which tea is served: the persons present; **tea′-plant**; **tea′-planta′tion**; **tea′-planter**, a cultivator of the tea-plant; **tea′-pot**, a spouted vessel for pouring out tea; **tea′-room**, a room or restaurant where tea is served; **tea′-rose**, a rose supposed to smell of tea; **tea′-ser′vice, -set**, a set of utensils for a tea-table; **tea′-shop**, a shop where tea is sold: a restaurant in which teas are served; **tea′spoon**, a small spoon used with the teacup; **tea′spoonful**:—*pl.* **tea′spoonfuls**; **tea′-table**, a table at which tea is drunk: the company at tea; **tea′-taster**, an expert who judges tea by tasting it.— *n.pl.* **tea′-things**, the tea-pot, cups, &c.—*ns.* **tea′time**, the hour of the meal called tea; **tea′-tray**, a tray for carrying tea-things; **tea′-tree**, the common tea plant or shrub: a name of Australian myrtaceous plants (Melaleuca, Leptospermum) furnishing substitutes for tea: an African solanaceous shrub (Lycium) said to have been labelled by mistake; **tea′-trolley**, a small tiered table on wheels used for serving afternoon tea, &c.; **tea′-urn**, a large urn with a tap, for making tea in quantity.—**another cup of tea**, a very different thing; **black tea**, that which has been fermented between rolling and firing (heating with charcoal in a sieve); **green tea**, that which is fired immediately after rolling; **high tea**, tea with meat, eggs, fish, or the like; **not one's cup of tea**, (*slang*) not to one's taste, not appealing to one; **Russian tea**, tea with lemon and no milk, usually served in a glass. [South Chinese *te*, the common form being *ch'a* or *ts'a*.]

teach, *tēch, v.t.* to show: to direct: to impart knowledge or art to: to guide the studies of: to exhibit so as to impress upon the mind: to impart the knowledge or art of: to accustom: to counsel. —*v.i.* to practise giving instructions:—*pa.t.* and *pa.p.* **taught** (*tawt*). — *n.* **teachabil′ity.** — *adj.*

teach′able, capable of being taught: apt or willing to learn.—*ns.* **teach′ableness**; **teach′er**, one who gives instruction, esp. in a school or privately; **teach′ership**; **teach′ing**, the act, practice, or profession of giving instruction: doctrine: instruction.—*adj.* occupied with giving instruction: instructive.—*adj.* **teach′less**, incapable of being taught.—**teach school**, (*U.S.*) to be a teacher in a school. [O.E. *tǽcan*, to show, teach; cf. Ger. *zeigen*, to show; Gr. *deiknynai*, to show.]

teachie. See **tetchy.**

tead, **teade**, *tēd, n.* (*Spens.*) a torch. [L. *taeda*.]

teagle, *tē′gl, n.* (*prov.*) a hoist or lift: a baited line for catching birds.—*v.t.* to hoist or catch with a teagle. [Prob. a form of **tackle**.]

Teague, *tēg, n.* an obs. nickname for an Irishman. [*Tadhg*, an Irish name, Thady.]

teak, *tēk, n.* a verbenaceous tree (*Tectona grandis*) of India, Malaya, &c.: its hard and durable wood. —**African teak**, an African euphorbiaceous tree, *Oldfieldia africana*: **bastard teak**, dhak; **white teak**, Flindersia. [Malayalam *tēkka*.]

teal, *tēl, n.* a small duck, esp. any member of the genus Nettion. [M.E. *tēle*, prob. from O.E.; cf. Du. *teling*, *taling*.]

team, *tēm, n.* (*obs.* or *dial.*) a brood, a litter: (*dial.*) a chain, esp. for hauling a plough, &c.: a set of animals harnessed together: a string of flying ducks, geese, &c.: a set of persons working or playing in combination: a side: a stock of animals: (*U.S.*) a turn-out.—*v.t.* to yoke.—*v.i.* to drive a team.—*adj.* **teamed** (*Spens.* **tem′ed, teem′ed**), harnessed in a team.—*ns.* **team′er**, a teamster; **team′ing**, driving a team: work apportioned to a team: transport by team: removal of excavated material from cutting to bank; **team′-spir′it**, the spirit of self-suppression in co-operation; **team′-ster**, one who drives a team.—*adv.* **team′wise**, like a team, harnessed together.—*n.* **team′-work**, work done by organised division of labour: co-operation, pulling together, regard to success of the whole rather than personal exploits. [O.E. *téam*, child-bearing, brood, team; in kindred languages a bridle, rope, draught of a net; cf. O.E. *téon*, to draw.]

teapoy, *tē′poi, n.* a small table or tripod: (by confusion with **tea**) a tea-caddy. [Hind. *tīn, tīr-*, three, Pers. *pāi*, foot.]

tear, *tēr, n.* a drop of liquid secreted by the lachrymal gland: an exuding drop: a blob, bead, pearshaped drop: a small flaw or cavity as in glass.— *ns.* **tear′-bag**, the lachrymal gland: the tear-pit; **tear′-bottle**, (*archaeol.*) a small bottle once thought to contain mourners' tears; **tear′-drop**, a tear; **tear′-duct**, the lachrymal duct.—*adjs.* **tear′falling**, (*Shak.*) shedding tears; **tear′ful**, lachrymose: brimming with, ready to shed, or shedding tears.—*adv.* **tear′fully.**—*ns.* **tear′fulness**; **tear′gas**, a gas or volatile substance that blinds temporarily by provoking tears; **tear′-gland**, the lachrymal gland.—*adj.* **tear′less**, without tears: sorrowless.—*ns.* **tear′-pit**, in deer, a gland below the eye secreting a waxy substance; **tear′-shell**, a shell that disperses tear-gas.—*adjs.* **tear′-stained**, (*Shak.*) stained with tears; **tear′y**, tearful.—**in tears**, weeping. [O.E. *téar*; Goth. *tagr*; Gr. *dakry*.]

tear, *tār, v.t.* to draw asunder or separate with violence: to rend: to lacerate: to make or render by tearing.—*v.i.* to move or act with violence: to rage: to become torn: (*pa.t.* **tōre**, *arch.* **tāre**; *pa.p.* **torn**).—*n.* tearing: a rent: (*slang*) a rush: (*U.S.*) a spree.—*ns.* **tear′er**, one who, or that which, tears: (*slang*) a boisterous person; **tear′-sheet** (*U.S.*), a page torn out for reference.—*adj.* **tear′ing**, great, terrible, rushing.—**tear a (the) cat**, (*obs.*) to rant; **tear off a strip**, (*slang.*) to reprimand; **tear oneself away**, to go off with great unwillingness; **tear one's hair**, to pull the hair in a frenzy of grief or rage; **tear up**, to remove from a fixed state by violence: to pull to pieces. [O.E. *teran*; cf. Ger. *zehren*.]

tease, *tēz, v.t.* to open out the fibres of: to comb or card, as wool: to scratch, as cloth: to raise a nap on: to vex with importunity, jests, &c.: to plague, irritate, esp. playfully or pleasantly: to tantalise : to banter.—*n.* one who teases : an act of teasing.—*n.* teas′er.—*n.* and *adj.* teas′ing.—*adv.* teas′ingly. [O.E. *tǽsan*, to card.]

teasel, *tēz′l, n.* any species of Dipsacus, esp. *D. fullonum*: its head with hooked bracts used in raising a nap on cloth : an artificial substitute for its head.—*v.t.* to raise a nap on with the teasel :—*pr.p.* teas′el(l)ing; *pa.t.* and *pa.p.* teas′el(l)ed.—*ns.* teas′el(l)er; teas′el(l)ing. — Also teazel, teazle, &c. [O.E. *tǽsel—tǽsan*; see tease.]

teat, *tēt, n.* the small protuberance through which the mammalian young suck the milk : a nipple.—*adj.* teat′ed, having a teat or teats. [O.E. *titt, tit*; influenced by O.Fr. *tete* (Fr. *tette*).]

teaze, an obs. spelling of tease; teazel, teazle (see teasel).

tebbad, *teb′ad, n.* a sandstorm. [Cf. Pers. *tab*, fever, *bād*, wind.]

Tebeth, *teb′eth, n.* the tenth month of the Jewish ecclesiastical, and fourth of the secular, year, parts of December and January. [Heb. *Tēbēi*.]

′tec, *tek*, a slang abbrev. for detective.

technetium, *tek-nē′shi-əm, n.* the chemical element of atomic number 43 (Tc), the first element to be artificially made. [Gr. *technētos*, artificial—*technē*, art.]

technic, *tek′nik, adj.* technical.—*n.* technology : (often in *pl.* form) technicality, technique.—*adj.* tech′nical, pertaining to art, esp. a useful art or applied science : industrial : belonging to, or in the language of, a particular art, department of knowledge or skill, profession : so called in strict legal or technical language. — *adv.* tech′nical′ity. — *adv.* tech′nically.—*ns.* tech′nicalness; technician (*-nish′ən*), tech′nicist (*-ni-sist*), one skilled in a practical art; technique (*tek-nēk*′; Fr.), method of performance, manipulation, esp. everything concerned with the mechanical part of an artistic performance; technoc′racy, government by technical experts; tech′nocrat (Gr. *kratos*, power).—*adj.* technolog′ical.—*ns.* technol′ogist; tech-nol′ogy, the practice, description, and terminology of any or all of the applied sciences of commercial value.—technical chemistry, industrial chemistry. [Gr. *technē*, art, adj. *technikos*.]

techy. See tetchy.

teckel, *tek′l, n.* a dachshund. [Ger.]

tectibranch, *tekt′i-brangk, n.* any member of the Tectibranchiā′ta, opisthobranch molluscs with gill covered by the mantle.—*n.* and *adj.* tecti-branch′iate. [L. *tegĕre, tĕctum*, to cover, *branchiae*, gills.]

tectiform, *tekt′i-form, adj.* roof-like : roofing. [L. *tĕctum*, a roof, *forma*, shape.]

tectonic, *tek-ton′ik, adj.* pertaining to building : structural.—*n.* (*pl.* in form, treated as *sing.*) tec-ton′ics, building as an art : the constructive arts : structural features : structural geology. — *adv.* tecton′ically. [Gr. *tektōn*, a builder.]

tectorial, *tek-tō′ri-əl, adj.* covering. [L. *tĕctōrius—tegĕre, tĕctum*, to cover.]

tectrix, *tek′triks, n.* a covert-feather :—*pl.* tectrices (*-trī′sēz*).—*adj.* tectricial (*-trish′l*). [L. *tĕctrīx, -īcis*, fem. of *tĕctor, -ōris*, a coverer, plasterer—*tegĕre*, to cover.]

ted, *ted, v.t.* to spread, as new-mown grass, for drying :—*pr.p.* tedd′ing; *pa.t.* and *pa.p.* tedd′ed.—*n.* tedd′er, one who teds : an implement for tedding. [Prob. from a lost O.E. *teddan*; cf. Ice. *tethja*, to manure.]

Teddy, *ted′i*, Teddy-bear (*-bār*′), *n.* a woolly toy bear. [From Theodore Roosevelt, a famous hunter and President of U.S.A. (1901-9), often called *Teddy*.]

tedesco, *te-des′kō, adj.* German. [It.]

Te Deum, *tē′ dē′əm*, L. *tā dā′oom, n.* a famous Latin hymn of the Western Church : a musical setting of it. [From its first words, *Tē Deum laudāmus*, thee, God, we praise.]

tedium, also taedium, *tē′di-əm, n.* wearisomeness, esp. owing to length : irksomeness : boredom.—*n.* (obs.) tedios′ity.—*adj.* te′dious.—*adv.* te′di-ously.— *n.* te′diousness.—*adjs.* (Scot.) te′di-some, te′diousome (*Scott*), te′dy. [L. *taedium—taedĕre*, to weary.]

tee, *tē, n.* the twentieth letter of the alphabet (T): an object or mark of that shape.—tee′-square (see T).

tee, *tē, n.* (quoits, curling, &c.) the mark aimed at : (*golf*) the little sand-cone or other elevation from which the ball is first played at each hole : the strip of ground (also tee′ing-ground) where this is done.—*v.t.* and *v.i.* to place (the golf ball) on the tee :—*pr.p.* tee′ing; *pa.t.* and *pa.p.* teed, tee′d.—tee up or off, to start (play); to a tee, exactly, to a tittle. [Origin unknown.]

tee, *tē, n.* the umbrella-shaped finial of a dagoba. [Burmese *h′ti*, umbrella.]

teem, *tēm, v.t.* to bring forth.—*v.i.* to bear or be fruitful : to be pregnant : to be full, abound.—*adjs.* teem′ful; teem′ing; teem′less, barren. [O.E. *tieman—téam*; see team.]

teem, *tēm, v.t.* to pour, empty.—*v.i.* to pour : to flow copiously. [O.N. *tœma*, to empty; cf. toom.]

teen, teene, tene, *tēn, n.* (*arch.*) injury : affliction : grief : anger : pains. [O.E. *téona*, injury, anger, grief.]

teen, *tēn, n.* any number, or year of age, &c., from thirteen to nineteen (usu in *pl.*).—*adj.* teen′-age, in one's teens.—*ns.* teen′-ager, teen′er. [O.E. suffix *-tiene—tien*, ten.]

teene, *tēn, v.t.* (*Spens.*) app., to allot.

teeny, *tē′ni, adj.* a modification of tiny.—(*U.S.*) teen′ty.

teer, *tēr, v.t.* to plaster : to daub : to spread. [O.Fr. *terer—terre*, earth.]

Teeswater, *tēz′wot-ər, n.* a shorthorn, originating chiefly from a breed in the valley (*water*) of the Tees.

tee-tee. Same as titi.

teeter, *tē′tər, n.* (*U.S.*) a see-saw.—*v.t.* and *v.i.* to see-saw.—*n.* teet′er-board. [titter (2).]

teeth, *tēth, pl.* of tooth.—*v.i.* teethe (*tēdh*), to develop or cut teeth.—*v.t.* to furnish with teeth.—*n.* and *adj.* teething (*tēdh′ing*). [O.E. pl. *tēth.*]

teetotal, *tē-tō′tl, adj.* abstaining totally from intoxicating drinks : (*dial.*) out-and-out.—*n.* a total abstainer : the total abstinence principle, movement, or pledge.—*ns.* teetō′talism; teetō′taller, a total abstainer from intoxicating drinks.—*adv.* teetō′tally. [Said to be from a stammering pronunciation of total by Richard Turner of Preston in 1833.]

teetotum, *tē-tō′təm, n.* a small top inscribed with letters, or a gambling game decided by the letter that came uppermost, T being for L. *tōtum*, all, i.e. take all the stakes : any small top twirled by the fingers :—*pl.* teeto′tums.

tef, teff, *tef, n.* an Abyssinian cereal grass, *Eragrostis abyssinica.* [Amharic *tēf.*]

teg, tegg, *teg, n.* a sheep (or obs. a doe) in its second year. [Perh. Scand.]

tegmen, *teg′mən, n.* a covering : (*bot.*) the inner coat of the testa : the leathery fore-wing in Orthoptera :—*pl.* teg′mina.—*adj.* tegmental (*-ment′əl*).—*ns.* tegment′um, a bud-scale; teg′ument, a covering : an integument.—*adjs.* tegūment′al, tegū-ment′ary. [L. *tĕgmen, tĕgmentum, tegumentum—tegĕre*, to cover.]

teguexin, *te-gwek′sin, n.* a large black and yellow South American lizard. [Aztec *tecoixin.*]

tegula, *teg′ū-lā, n.* a flat roofing-tile : a scale at the base of the fore-wing in some insects :—*pl.* teg′ū-lae (*-lē*).—*adj.* teg′ūlar.—*adv.* teg′ūlarly.—*adj.* teg′ūlated, composed of plates overlapping like tiles. [L. *tegula*, a tile—*tegĕre*, to cover.]

tehee, *tē′hē′, interj.* expressing derision or merriment.—*n.* a laugh.—*v.i.* to titter. [Imit.]

tehr, *tār.* Same as tahr.

Teian, Tean, *tē′(y)ən, adj.* of Teos in ancient Ionia, or Anacreon, a native. [Gr. *Tēios*, Teian—*Tēōs*, Teos.]

teichopsia, *tī-kops′i-ā, n.* temporary partial blindness with optical illusions, accompanying migraine. [Gr. *teichos*, wall, *opsis*, sight.]

te igitur, *tē′ ij′i-tər*, L. *tā ig′i-toor, n.* the first paragraph of the canon of the mass : a service-book on which oaths were taken. [L. *tē igitur*, thee there fore (the first words).]

teil, *tēl, n.* the linden or lime tree.—**teil tree,** the lime : *(B.)* the terebinth. [O.Fr. *teil*—L. *tilia*.]

teind, *tēnd, n.* in Scotland, a tithe.—*v.t.* to assess or take a tithe on. [A form of **tenth, tithe.**]

teinoscope, *ti'nō-skōp, n.* a magnifying and diminishing combination of prisms correcting chromatic aberration. [Gr. *teinein,* to stretch, *skopeein,* to look.]

teknonymy, *tek-non'i-mi, n.* the naming of the parent from the child.—*adj.* **teknon'ymous.** [Gr. *teknon,* a child, *onyma, onoma,* a name.]

tektite, *tek'tīt, n.* a glassy (supposed) meteorite. [Gr. *tēktos,* melted—*tēkein,* to melt.]

tela, *tē'lä,* L. *tä'lä, n.* a web, tissue :—*pl.* **tē'lae** (*-lē*; L. *tä'lī*).—*adj.* **tē'lary,** web-spinning. [L. *tēla.*]

telaesthesia, *tel-ēs-thē'zi-ä, -zhi-ä, -zhyä,* or *-is-, n.* an abnormal impression as of sense received from a distance.—*adj.* **telaesthetic** (*-thet'ik*). [Gr. *tēle,* far, *aisthēsiä,* sensation.]

Telamon, *tel'ə-mən, n.* (*archit.*) a man's figure as a pillar :—*pl.* **Telamones** (*-mō'nēz*). [Gr. *Telamōn,* pl. *Telamōnēs*—the root of *tolmaein,* to endure, dare.]

telangiectasis, *tel-an-ji-ek'tə-sis, n.* dilatation of the small arteries or capillaries.—*adj.* **telangiectatic** (*-tat'ik*). [Gr. *telos,* end, *angeion,* a vessel, *ektasis,* extension.]

telautograph, *tel-aw'tə-gräf, n.* a telegraph for reproducing the movement of a pen or pencil and so transmitting writings or drawings : one for transmission of images by electric scanning.—*adj.* **telautographic** (*-graf'ik*). — *n.* **telautography** (*-tog'rə-fi*) to write.]

teld, *teld,* (*Spens.*) *pa.t.* and *pa.p.* of **tell.**—(*Scot.*) **teld, tell'd, telt.**

telecast, *tel'i-käst, n.* television broadcast.—Also *v.t.*

telecommunication, *tel-i-kə-mū-ni-kā'shən, n.* communication by telegraph or telephone, with or without wires or cables. [Gr. *tēle,* far, and com-munication.]

teledu, *tel'ə-doo, n.* the stinking badger of Java. [Javanese.]

telega, *tel-(y)eg'ä, n.* a springless Russian wagon. [Russ.]

telegony, *ti-leg'ə-ni, n.* the (imaginary) transmitted influence of a previous mate on the offspring of a female by a later mate. [Gr. *tēle,* far, *gonos,* begetting.]

telegram, *tel'i-gram, n.* a message sent by telegraph. —*adjs.* **telegrammat'ic, telegramm'ic,** of or like a telegram. [Gr. *tēle,* far, *gramma,* that which is written—*graphein,* to write.]

telegraph, *tel'i-gräf, n.* an apparatus for transmitting messages to a distance, now almost exclusively by electric impulses : (*obs.*) a message so sent : (cricket, &c.) a scoring-board : often taken as the name of a newspaper.—*v.t.* to convey or announce by telegraph.—*v.i.* to signal : to send a telegram.— *ns.* **tel'egraph-cā'ble,** a cable containing wires for transmitting telegraphic messages ; **telegrapher** (*ti-leg'rə-fər* ; now chiefly *U.S.*), a telegraphist ; **tel'egraphese',** the jargon or contracted idiom used in telegrams.—*adj.* **telegraphic** (*-graf'ik*). — *adv.* **telegraph'ically.** — *ns.* **teleg'-raphist,** one who works a telegraph ; **tel'egraph-plant,** an Indian papilionaceous plant (*Desmodium gyrans*) whose leaflets jerk like semaphore arms ; **tel'egraph-pole,** a pole supporting telegraph-wires ; **tel'egraph-wire,** a wire for carrying telegraphic messages ; **teleg'raphy,** the science or art of constructing or using telegraphs.—**telegraphic address,** a shortened address registered for use in telegraphing. [Gr. *tēle,* at a distance, *graphein,* to write.]

telekinesis, *tel-i-ki-nē'sis, n.* the production of motion at a distance by means beyond the range of the senses.—*adj.* **telekinetic** (*-net'ik*). [Gr. *tēle,* far, *kinēsis,* movement.]

telemark, *tel'i-märk, n.* a sudden turn on the outer ski, first practised at *Telemark* in Norway.—*v.i.* to execute a telemark.

telemeter, *ti-lem'i-tər, n.* an instrument for measuring distances : a photographer's range-finder : an instrument for remote indication of electrical quantities. — *adj.* **telemetric** (*tel-i-met'rik*). — *n.* **telem'etry.** [Gr. *tēle,* far, *metron,* measure.]

teleology, *tel-i-ol'ə-ji, n.* the doctrine of the final causes of things : interpretation in terms of purpose.—*adjs.* **teleologic** (*-ə-loj'ik*), **-al.**—*adv.* **teleolog'ically.**—*ns.* **teleol'ogism ; teleol'ogist.** [Gr. *telos,* end, purpose, *logos,* a discourse.]

Teleosaurus, *tel-i-ō-sawr'əs, n.* a Jurassic genus of fossil crocodiles.—*n.* **tel'eosaur.**—*adj.* and *n.* **teleosau'rian.** [Gr. *teleios,* perfect, *sauros,* a lizard.]

Teleostei, *tel-i-ost'i-ī, n.pl.* the bony fishes, fishes with well-developed bones.—*ns.* and *adjs.* **tel'eost, teleos'tean.** [Gr. *teleios,* complete, *osteon,* bone.]

Teleostomi, *tel-i-os'tə-mī, n.pl.* fishes with membrane bones in the skull, jaws, &c.—all ordinary fishes except the sharks and rays.—*n.* **tel'eostome** (*-tōm*). —*adj.* **teleos'tomous.** [Gr. *teleios,* perfect, *stoma,* mouth.]

telepathy, *ti-lep'ə-thi, n.* communication between mind and mind otherwise than through the known channels of the senses.—*n.* **telepath** (*tel'i-path*), one who practises telepathy.—*v.t.* and *v.i.* to communicate by telepathy.—*adj.* **telepath'ic.**—*adv.* **telepath'ically.**—*v.t.* **telep'athise,** to affect or act upon through telepathy.—*v.i.* to practise telepathy.—*n.* **telep'athist,** one who believes in or practises telepathy. [Gr. *tēle,* far, *pathos,* feeling.]

telepheme, *tel'i-fēm, n.* a telephone message. [Gr. *tēle,* far, *phēmē,* a saying.]

telephone, *tel'i-fōn, n.* an instrument for reproducing sound at a distance, esp. by means of electricity. —*v.t.* and *v.i.* to communicate by telephone.—*n.* **tel'ephoner.** — *adj.* **telephonic** (*-fon'ik*). — *adv.* **telephon'ically.**—*ns.* **telephonist** (*ti-lef'ə-nist*), one who works a telephone ; **teleph'ony,** telephonic communication. [Gr. *tēle,* far, *phōnē,* a sound.]

telephotography, *tel-i-fō-tog'rə-fi, n.* photography of distant objects by means of suitable lenses : (*wrongly*) phototelegraphy.—*n.* **telepho'tograph** (*-tō-gräf*). — *adj.* **telephotographic** (*-graf'ik*), abbrev. **telepho'to.** [Gr. *tēle,* far, **photography.**]

teleprinter, *tel-i-print'ər, n.* a telegraphic type-writer. [Gr. *tēle,* far, **printer.**]

telergy, *tel'ər-ji, n.* a physical force assumed to be at work in telepathy.—*adj.* **teler'gic,** working at ε distance, as in telepathy.—*adv.* **teler'gically.** [Gr. *tēle,* far, *ergon,* work.]

telescope, *tel-i-skōp, n.* an optical instrument for viewing objects at a distance.—*v.t.* to drive or slide one into another like the movable joints of a spy-glass.—*v.i.* to fit or slide in such a way.—*adjs.* **telescopic** (*-skop'ik*), **-al,** of, performed by, or like a telescope : seen only by a telescope : sliding, or arranged, like the joints of a spy-glass : capable of retraction and protrusion.—*adv.* **telescop'ically.** —*adj.* **telescop'iform.**—*ns.* **telescopist** (*ti-les'kə-pist*), one who uses the telescope ; **teles'copy,** the art of constructing or of using the telescope. [Gr. *tēle,* far, *skopeein,* to see.]

teleseme, *tel'i-sēm, n.* a signalling apparatus with an indicator. [Gr. *tēle,* far, *sēma,* a sign.]

telesm, *tel'ezm, n.* a talisman.—*adjs.* **telesmat'ic, -al.**—*adv.* **telesmat'ically.** [Gr. *telesma ;* see **talisman.**]

telestic, *ti-les'tik, adj.* relating to the mysteries. [Gr. *telestikos*—Gr. *teleein,* to fulfil, consummate, initiate, perform—*telos,* end, rite, &c.]

telestich, *tel-es'tik, tel'es-tik, n.* a poem or block of words whose final letters spell a name or word. [Gr. *telos,* end, *stichos,* row.]

teletron, *tel'i-tron, n.* a cathode-ray tube for synthesis of television images. [Gr. *tēle,* far, *-tron,* agent suffix.]

teletype, *tel'i-tīp, n.* a printing electric telegraph : an automatically printed telegram.—*n.* **teletype'-writer.** [Gr. *tēle,* far, *typos,* type.]

teleutospore, *ti-lū'tō-spōr, n.* a thick-walled winter-spore of the rust-fungi, producing on germination a promycelium. [Gr. *teleutē,* completion, *sporā,* seed.]

television, *tel-i-vizh'ən, n.* the viewing of distant objects or events by electrical transmission : the electrical transmission of these.—Also *adj.*—*vs.t.* and *vs.i.* **tel'eview,** to view by television ; **tel'evise**

(-vīz), to transmit by television.—*n.* televi'sor, a receiver for television. [Gr. *tēle*, far, and **vision** (L. *vīsiō*, *-ōnis*).]

telewriter, *tel-i-rī'tər*, *n.* a telegraph instrument that reproduces handwriting. [Gr. *tēle*, far, and **writer**.]

telic, *tel'ik*, *adj.* expressing purpose : purposive. [Gr. *telikos*—*telos*, end, purpose.]

tell, *tel*, *v.t.* to count : to count out : to utter : to narrate : to disclose : to inform : to discern : to explain : to order, direct, instruct : (*U.S.*) to bid (goodbye).—*v.i.* to give an account : to take effect : to have weight : to make an effective story : to play the informer :—*pa.t.* and *pa.p.* **tōld.**—*adj.* **tell'able**, capable of being told : fit to tell.—*ns.* **tell'er**, one who tells or counts : one who counts votes : a clerk whose duty it is to receive and pay money ; **tell'ership.**—*n.pl.* **tell'ies**, (*slang*) cinematograph entertainment with sound.—*adj.* **tell'ing**, effective.—*n.* numbering : narration : direction, orders.—*adv.* **tell'ingly.**—*ns.* **tell'ing-off'**, a rating, chiding ; **tell'-tale**, one who tells the private concerns or misdeeds of others : a tattler (*bird*) : anything revealing or betraying : an indicator : a recording clock.—*adj.* blabbing : revealing, betraying : indicating.—**take a telling**, to do as one is bid without having to be told again ; **tell off**, to count off : to detach on some special duty : to rate, chide. [O.E. *tellan* ; O.N. *telja*, Ger. *zählen*, to number.]

tellar, teller. Same as tiller (2).

Tellus, *tel'əs*, *n.* the Roman earth-goddess : the earth.—*adj.* **tell'ūral**, pertaining to the earth.—*n.* **tell'ūrate**, a salt of telluric acid.—*adjs.* **tell'-ūretted**, combined with tellurium ; **tellū'rian**, terrestrial.—*n.* an inhabitant of the earth.—*adj.* **tellū'ric**, of or from the earth : of tellurium in higher valency (**telluric acid**, H_2TeO_4).—*ns.* **tell'ūride**, a compound of tellurium with another element or radical ; **tell'ūrite**, (*min.*) native oxide of tellurium : (*chem.*) a salt of tellurous acid ; **tellū'rium**, the element (Te) of atomic number 52, app. so named by Klaproth (1798) as the counterpart of his previous discovery of uranium.—*adj.* **tell'ūrous**, of tellurium in lower valency (**tellurous acid**, H_2TeO_3). [L. *Tellūs*, *-ūris*.]

telophase, *tel'ō-fāz*, *n.* in mitosis, the stage of reconstruction of nuclei after separation of daughter chromosomes. [Gr. *telos*, completion, *phasis*, phase.]

telpher, *tel'fər*, *adj.* pertaining to a system of telpherage.—*n.* a car or carrier in such a system.—*ns.* **tel'pherage**, any system of automatic electric transport : an electric ropeway or cableway system : overhead traction in general ; **tel'pher-line** ; **tel'pherman** ; **tel'pherway.** [Coined by Fleeming Jenkin to avoid possible confusion between the strictly formed *telephore* and *telephone*—Gr. *tēle*, far, *phoros*, bearing.]

telson, *tel'sən*, *n.* the hindermost part of a crustacean or arachnid. [Gr. *telson*, a headland in ploughing ; cf. *telos*, end.]

Telugu, *tel'oo-gōō*, *n.* a Dravidian language of eastern India : one of the people speaking it.—Also *adj.*

teme, an old spelling of **team.**

temenos, *tem'e-nos*, *n.* a place dedicated to a god, a precinct. [Gr.,—*temnein*, to cut off.]

temerity, *ti-mer'i-ti*, *n.* rashness : unreasonable contempt for danger.—*adj.* **temerarious** (*tem-ə-rā'ri-əs* ; now *rare*), rash, reckless.—*adv.* **temerā'riously.**—*adj.* **tem'erous**, rash.—*adv.* **tem'erously.** [L. *temeritās*, *-tātis*, and *temerārius*—*temerē*, by chance, rashly.]

Tempe, *tem'pē*, *n.* the valley of the Pēneios (Peneus) in Thessaly, praised by the classic poets for its matchless beauty : hence, any place of choice beauty. [Gr. *Tempē* (*Tempea*).]

temper, *tem'pər*, *v.t.* to mix in due proportion : to modify by blending or mixture : to moderate : to soften : to bring to a proper degree of hardness and elasticity, as steel : to adjust : to tune : to attune : (*mus.*) to adjust to a temperament : to bring to a favourable state of mind.—*v.i.* (*Shak.*) to tamper, meddle : (*Shak.*) to soften : to become

tempered.—*n.* due mixture or balance of different or contrary qualities : state of a metal as to hardness, &c. : constitution of the body : temperament : disposition : habitual or actual frame of mind : mood : composure : self-control : uncontrolled anger : a fit of ill-humour or rage : lime or other substance used to neutralise the acidity of cane-juice.—*n.* **tem'pera**, (*paint.* ; It.) distemper.—*adj.* **tem'perable**, capable of being tempered.—*ns.* **temperal'itie**, (*Shak.*) Mrs Quickly's elaboration of temper, frame of mind ; **tem'perament**, proportioned mixture : (*obs.*) state with respect to combination or predominance of qualities : (*obs.*) climate : internal constitution or state : (*obs. physiol.*) combination or predominance of humour : disposition : type of physical and mental organisation—choleric or bilious, sanguine, melancholy, phlegmatic : (*coll.*) high excitability, nervous instability, and sensitiveness : tempering : compromise : (*mus.*) a system of compromise in tuning.—*adjs.* **temperament'al** ; **temperament'ful.**—*adv.* **temperament'ally.**—*n.* **tem'perance**, moderation, esp. in the indulgence of the natural appetites and passions—in a narrower sense, moderation in the use of alcoholic liquors, and even entire abstinence from them.—*adj.* advocating or consistent with temperance in or abstinence from alcoholic drinks.—*adj.* **tem'perate**, moderate : self-restrained, esp. in appetites and passions : abstemious : moderate in temperature.—*v.t.* (*obs.* or *rare*) to temper : to moderate : to restrain.—*adv.* **tem'perately.**—*n.* **tem'perateness.**—*adj.* **tem'perative**, having moderating influence.—*n.* **tem'perature**, tempering : tempered condition : mixture : constitution : proportion : degree of hotness : condition determining interchange of heat between bodies : (*coll.*) a body temperature above normal.—*adj.* **tem'pered**, having a certain specified disposition or temper : brought to a certain temper, as steel : (*mus.*) tuned or adjusted to some mean, or to equal, temperament.—*adv.* **tem'peredly.** — *n.* **tem'perer.** — *n.* and *adj.* **tem'pering.**—**absolute temperature** (see absolute) ; **bad temper**, an angry humour : an inclination to irascibility ; **equal temperament**, a compromise in tuning by which the octave is divided into twelve equal intervals ; **good temper**, an unruffled humour : good-nature ; **lose one's temper**, to break out in anger ; **temperance hotel**, one which professes to supply no alcoholic liquors ; **temperate zones**, the parts of the earth of moderate temperature between the tropics and the polar circles. [L. *temperāre*, to temper, restrain, compound, moderate, partly through O.E. *temprian*.]

tempest, *tem'pist*, *n.* a violent wind storm.—*v.t.* (*Milt.*) to stir violently.—*adjs.* **tem'pest-beaten**, **tem'pest-tossed**, *-tost* (*Shak.*), driven about by storms ; **tempestive** (*-pest'*), timely : seasonable ; **tempestūous** (*-pest'*).—*adv.* **tempes'tūously.**—*n.* **tempes'tūousness.** [O.Fr. *tempeste*—a L.L. form of L. *tempestās*, a season, tempest—*tempus*, time.]

temple, *tem'pl*, *n.* a building or place dedicated to, or regarded as the house of, a god : a place of worship : in France, a Protestant church : **Temple**, the headquarters of the Knights Templars on or near the site of Solomon's temple in Jerusalem : in London, two inns of court (*Inner* and *Middle Temple*) on the site once occupied by the Knights Templars, with the Knights' church.—*adj.* **tem'plar**, of a temple.—*n.* **Tem'plar**, a member of a religious and military order (**Knights Templars**) founded in 1119 for the protection of the Holy Sepulchre and pilgrims going thither—extinguished 1307-14 : a student or lawyer living in the Temple, London : a member of an American order of Freemasons : a Good Templar (see **good**).—*adj.* **tem'pled**, having temples. [L. *templum*.]

temple, *tem'pl*, *n.* the flat portion of either side of the head above the cheekbone. [O.Fr. *temple*—L. *tempus*, *-oris*.]

templet, template, *tem'plit*, *n.* a mould shaped to the required outline from which workmen execute moulding. [L. *templum*, a small timber.]

tempo, *tem'pō, n. (mus.)* time : speed and rhythm :— *pl.* **tem'pi** (*-pē*). [It.]

temporal, *tem'pər-l, adj.* pertaining to time : pertaining to time in this life or world—opp. to *eternal* : worldly, secular, or civil—opp. to *spiritual, sacred* or *ecclesiastical* : (*gram.*) pertaining to tense, or to length of syllable or vowel.—*n.* **temporality** (*-al'i-ti*), state or fact of being temporal : what pertains to temporal welfare : (usu. *pl.*) secular possessions, revenues of an ecclesiastical proceeding from lands, tithes, and the like.—*adv.* **tem'porally.** —*n.* **tem'poralty**, the laity : lay peers : (usu. *pl.*) worldly possessions.—*adj.* **tempora'neous**, temporal.—*adv.* **tem'porarily.**—*n.* **tem'porariness.** —*adj.* **tem'porary**, for a time only : transient.— *n.* **temporisa'tion.**—*v.i.* **tem'porise**, to comply with the time or occasion : to yield to circumstances : to behave so as to gain time.—*n.* **tem'poriser.** — *n.* and *adj.* **tem'porising.** — *adv.* **tem'porisingly.** [L. *tempus, -oris,* time.]

temporal, *tem'pər-l, adj.* of or at the temple (of the head).—*n.* a bone, muscle, or scale in that position. [L. *tempus, -oris* ; see **temple** (2).]

tempt, *temt, v.t.* to put to trial : to test : to try or tend to persuade, esp. to evil : to entice.—*n.* **temptabil'ity.**—*adj.* **tempt'able.**—*ns.* **tempt'ableness** ; **tempta'tion** (*tem-* or *temp-*), act of tempting : state of being tempted : that which tempts : enticement to evil : trial.—*adj.* **tempta'tious**, seductive.—*n.* **tempt'er**, one who tempts, esp. the devil :—*fem.* **tempt'ress.**—*n.* and *adj.* **tempt'ing.** — *adv.* **tempt'ingly.** — *n.* **tempt'ingness.** [O.Fr. *tempter*—L. *tentāre*, an intens. of *tendĕre*, to stretch.]

'tempt, tempt, aphetic for **attempt.**

temse, *tems, tems, temz, n.* a sieve.—*v.t.* to sift. [O.E. *temesian*, to sift ; cf. Du. *tems.*]

temulence, *tem'ū-ləns, n.* intoxication.—Also **tem'ulency.**—*adj.* **tem'ulent.**—*adv.* **tem'ulently.** [L. *tēmulentus*, drunk.]

ten, *ten, n.* the cardinal number next above nine : a symbol representing it (x., &c.) : a set of that number of things or persons : an article of a size denoted by 10 : a card with ten pips : a score of ten points, tricks, &c. : the tenth hour after midday or midnight.—*adj.* of the number ten.—**long ten**, the ten of trumps in catch-the-ten ; **ten-gallon hat**, (*U.S.*) cowboy's broad-brimmed hat. [O.E. (Anglian) *tén, téne* (W.S. *tíen, tíene*) ; Ger. *zehn*, W. *deg*, L. *decem*, Gr. *deka*, Sans. *daçan.*]

tenable, *ten'a-bl* (or *tēn'*), *adj.* capable of being retained, kept, or defended.—*ns.* **tenabil'ity**, **ten'ableness.** [Fr. *tenable*—*tenir*, to hold.]

tenace, *ten'ās, -is, n.* the combination in one hand of the cards next above and next below the other side's best in the suit. [Sp. *tenaza*, pincers.]

tenacious, *ti-nā'shos, adj.* retaining or holding fast : sticking stiffly : tough : stubborn.—*adv.* **tenā'ciously.**—*ns.* **tenā'ciousness**, **tenacity** (*-nas'i-ti*). [L. *tenāx*—*tenēre*, to hold.]

tenaculum, *te-nak'ū-ləm, n.* a surgical hook or forceps for picking up blood-vessels. [L. *tenāculum*, holder, pincers.]

tenaille, *te-nāl', n. (fort.)* an outwork in the main ditch in front of the curtain.—*n.* **tenaillon** (*te-nal'yən*), a work to strengthen the side of a small ravelin. — Also **tenail'.** [Fr., — L. *tenāculum*, pincers—*tenēre*, to hold.]

tenant, *ten'ənt, n.* one who holds under another : one who has, on certain conditions, temporary possession of any place : an occupant.—*v.t.* to hold as a tenant : to occupy.—*v.i.* to dwell.—*n.* **ten'ancy**, possession by private ownership : a temporary occupation or holding of land or property by a tenant : time of such holding.—*adj.* **ten'antable**, fit to be tenanted : in a state of repair suitable for a tenant.—*ns.* **ten'ant-farm'er**, a farmer who rents a farm ; **ten'ant-in-chief'**, one holding lands directly from the sovereign.—*adj.* **ten'antless.**—*ns.* **ten'ant-right**, the right of a tenant, esp. that of a customary tenant to sit continuously at a reasonable rent, the right to receive compensation for his interest during the incoming tenant, and for all permanent or unexhausted improvements from the landlord ; **ten'-**

antry, the state or time of being a tenant : a set or body of tenants ; **ten'antship.**—**tenant at will**, one who holds only so long as the proprietor wills. [Fr. *tenant*, pr.p. of *tenir*—L. *tenēre*, to hold.]

tench, *tensh, n.* a freshwater fish (*Tinca vulgaris*) of the carp family, very tenacious of life. [O.Fr. *tenche* (Fr. *tanche*)—L. *tinca.*]

tend, *tend, v.t.* to attend to : to mind : to watch over or stand by and perform services for or connected with : to minister to, wait upon : (*Shak.*) to escort.—*v.i.* (*Shak.*) to attend, hearken : (*Shak.*) to be in waiting or readiness : (*Shak.*) to wait, attend.—*n.* **ten'dance**, tending : (*Spens.*) expectation : (*Shak.*) attendants collectively : — *adj.* **tend'ed.**—*n.* **ten'der**, one who tends : a small craft that attends a larger : a carriage attached to a locomotive to carry fuel and water.—**tend out on**, (*U.S.*) to attend or attend to. [Aphetic for **attend.**]

tend, *tend, v.i.* to stretch, aim at, move, or incline in some direction : to be directed to any end or purpose : to be apt : to conduce.—*ns.* **ten'dence,** **tendenz** (*ten-dents'* ; Ger.), tendency (esp. in composition, tendentious) ; **ten'dency**, a trend, drift, inclination : proneness.—*adjs.* **tendential** (*-den'shl*), **tenden'tious**, **tenden'cious**, purposely tending : with an object.—*adv.* **tenden'tiously.**— *n.* **tenden'tiousness.** [L. *tendĕre* and Fr. *tendre*, to stretch.]

tender. See under **tend** (1).

tender, *ten'dər, v.t.* to offer for acceptance, esp. to offer in payment : to proffer.—*v.i.* to make a tender.—*n.* an offer or proposal, esp. of some service : the paper containing it : the thing offered : a formal offer to save the consequences of non-payment or non-performance.—*ns.* **ten'derer** ; **ten'dering.**—**legal tender** (see **legal**). [Fr. *tendre*, to stretch, reach out.]

tender, *ten'dər, adj.* soft, delicate : easily chewed, not tough : of porcelain, soft-paste : easily impressed or injured : not hardy : gentle : scrupulous, chary : sensitive, esp. to pain : requiring gentle handling : easily moved to pity, love, &c. : careful not to hurt : considerate, careful (with *of*) : pathetic : expressive, or of the nature, of the softer passions : compassionate, loving, affectionate : (*Shak.*) beloved : apt to lean over under sail.— *v.t.* (*Shak.*) to treat with tenderness : (*Shak.*) to feel tenderness for : to cherish : to value, have respect to : to make tender.—*n.* (*Shak.*) care, regard, concern : tender feeling, fondness (now usu. in Fr. form **tendre**, *tãn°dr'*).—*adj.* **ten'der-dying**, (*Shak.*) dying young.—*n.* **ten'derfoot**, one not yet hardened to life in the prairie, mining-camp, &c. : a newcomer : a greenhorn : a boy scout or girl guide who has passed only the first tests :—*pl.* **ten'derfeet.**—*adj.* **ten'der-heart'ed**, full of feeling. — *adv.* **ten'der-heart'edly.** — *n.* **ten'der-heart'edness.** — *adj.* **ten'der-heft'ed**, (*Shak.*) perh. set in a tender haft or frame.—*ns.* **ten'derling**, one too much coddled, an effeminate fellow : one of the first horns of a deer ; **ten'der-loin**, (*U.S.*) the tenderest part of the loin of beef, pork, &c., close to the lumbar vertebrae : (*U.S. slang*) a district juicy with bribes to the police.—*adv.* **ten'derly.** —*n.* **ten'derness.** [Fr. *tendre*—L. *tener.*]

tendon, *ten'dən, n.* a cord, band, or sheet of fibrous tissue attaching a muscle to a bone or other structure.—*adj.* **ten'dinous.** [L.L. *tendō, -inis* or *-ōnis*, app.—Gr. *tenōn, -ontos*, sinew, tendon ; cf. *teinein*, to stretch ; *d* suggested by L. *tendĕre.*]

tendril, *ten'dril, n.* a plant's coiling threadlike climbing organ (leaf, leaflet, or shoot).—*adjs.* **ten'drillar** ; **ten'drilled.** [Origin doubtful ; cf. Fr. *tendrillon*, shoot, bud.]

tendron, *ten'drən, n.* a shoot, sprout : (in *pl.*) cartilages of the ribs. [Fr.]

tenebrae, *ten'i-brē* (L. *ten'e-brī*), *n.pl.* (*R.C.*) matins and lauds in Holy Week with gradual extinction of lights.—*adj.* **tenebrif'ic** (L. *facĕre*, to make), producing darkness.—*n.* **tenebrio** (*tin-eb'ri-ō*), a night-spirit : a night-prowler : **Tenebrio**, the meal-worm genus of beetles, giving name to the family **Tenebrionidae** (*-on'i-dē*).—*adjs.* **teneb'rious**, **ten'ebrose**, dark.—*ns.* **ten'ebrist**, a painter of the naturalist school of Caravaggio affecting dark colouring; **teneb′rity**; **tenebros′ity.**—*adj.* **ten′ebrous.** [L. *tenebrae*, darkness.]

tenement, *ten′i-mant, n.* a holding, by any tenure: anything held, or that may be held, by a tenant: a dwelling or habitation, or part of it, used by one family: one of a set of apartments in one building, each occupied by a separate family: (*Scot.*) a building divided into dwellings for a number of families.—*adjs.* **tenemental (-men′tl)**; **tenement′-ary.** [L.L. *tenementum*—L. *tenēre*, to hold.]

tenendum, *ti-nen′dəm, n.* that clause in a deed wherein the tenure of the land is defined and limited. [L., neut. of *tenendus*, ger. of *tenēre*, to hold.]

tenesmus, *ti-nes′məs, n.* painful and ineffectual straining to relieve the bowels. [Latinised from Gr. *teinesmos*—*teinein*, to strain.]

tenet, *ten′et* (also *tē′nit*), *n.* an opinion, principle, or doctrine which a person holds or maintains as true. [L. *tenet*, (he) holds—*tenēre*, to hold.]

tenfold, *ten′fōld, adj.* and *adv.* in ten divisions: ten times as much.—*adj.* **ten′-foot,** measuring ten feet. [**ten.**]

tenioid, &c. See **Taenia.**

tennantite, *ten′ənt-īt, n.* a mineral composed of sulphur, arsenic, and copper, usu. with iron. [Named after Smithson *Tennant* (1761-1815), English chemist.]

tenné, *ten′ā, n.* (*her.*) an orange-brown tincture. —Also *adj.* [Obs. Fr.; cf. **tawny.**]

tenner, *ten′ər, n.* (*slang*) a ten-pound note: a ten-dollar bill: ten years.

tennis, *ten′is, n.* an ancient game played with ball and rackets in a specially constructed building: (distinguished from lawn-tennis as **close, court, real,** or **royal tennis**): now usu. lawn-tennis.— *ns.* **tenn′is-ball**; **tenn′is-court**; **tenn′is-player**; **tenn′is-racket**; **tenn′is-shoe.** [Prob. Fr. *tenez*, imper. of *tenir*, to take, receive.]

tenon, *ten′ən, n.* a projection at the end of a piece of wood, &c., inserted into the socket or mortise of another, to hold the two together.—*v.t.* to fix or fit with a tenon.—*ns.* **ten′oner**; **ten′on-saw,** a thin back-saw for tenons, &c. [Fr. *tenon*—*tenir*, to hold—L. *tenēre.*]

tenor (*obs.* or *old-fashioned* **tenour**), *ten′ər, n.* continuity of state: general run or course: time of currency: purport: an exact transcript: the higher of the two kinds of voices usu. belonging to adult males (app. because the melody was assigned to it): an instrument, esp. the viola, of corresponding compass: the part next above the bass in a vocal quartet: one who sings tenor.—Also *adj.*— *ns.* **ten′or-clef′,** the C clef placed on the fourth line; **ten′orist**; **tenoroon′,** an obsolete tenor oboe. [L. *tenor*—*tenēre*, to hold.]

tenorite, *ten′ər-īt, n.* melaconite, black copper ore (CuO), found on Vesuvius. [Named after G. *Tenore*, President of the Naples Academy, 1841.]

tenpence, *ten′pəns, n.* an amount in money equal to ten pennies.—*adj.* **tenpenny** (*ten′pən-i*), worth, offered for, or sold at tenpence.—*ns.* **ten′penny-piece′**; **ten′pins,** American bowls; **ten′-point′er,** a stag of ten points or tines (five a side).—*adj.* **ten′-pound,** weighing, worth, sold or offered for, ten pounds.—*n.* **ten′-pound′er,** a thing weighing or worth ten pounds: one who was a voter in virtue of occupying property worth ten pounds a year.— *adj.* **ten′-score,** a hundred.

tenrec, *ten′rek,* **tanrec,** *tan′rek, n.* a large Madagascan insectivore (Centetes). [Malagasy *t(r)àndraka.*]

tense, *tens, n.* time in grammar, the form of a verb to indicate the time of the action. [O.Fr. *tens* (Fr. *temps*)—L. *tempus,* time.]

tense, *tens, adj.* stretched tight: strained: rigid: pronounced with the tongue tightened or narrowed. —*adv.* **tense′ly.**—*ns.* **tense′ness,** state of being tense; **tensibil′ity.**—*adj.* **tens′ible,** capable of being stretched; **tens′ile** (*-īl*), tensible: in relation to stretching.—*ns.* **tensility** (*-il′i-ti*); **tension** (*ten′shən*), stretching: a pulling strain: stretched or strained state: strain generally: pressure in gases or vapours: electromotive force: suppressed excitement: an uneasy and threatening calm; **ten′sion-rod,** a structural member subjected to

---

tensile stress only; **tens′ity,** tenseness.—*adj.* **tens′ive,** giving the sensation of tenseness or stiffness.—*n.* **tens′or,** a muscle that tightens a part: the ratio of lengthening of a vector. [L. *tēnsus,* pa.p. of *tendĕre,* to stretch.]

tenson, *ten′sn, n.* a competition in verse between two troubadours before a court of love: a subdivision of the chanson so composed.—Also **ten′-zon.** [Fr.,—L. *tēnsiō, -ōnis,* a struggle.]

tent, *tent, n.* a portable lodge or shelter, commonly of canvas stretched on poles: a temporary field pulpit: a common shelter spun by a company of caterpillars.—*v.i.* to camp in a tent.—*v.t.* to canopy: to lodge in tents.—*ns.* **tent′-bed,** a camp-bed: a bed with a canopy hanging from a central point; **tent′-cloth,** cloth suitable for tents.—*adj.* **ten′ted,** covered with tents: formed like a tent: dwelling in tents.—*ns.* **ten′ter,** one who lives in a tent; **tent′-fly,** a flap forming a door to a tent: a subsidiary outer roof to a tent; **tent′ful,** as many as a tent will hold; **tent′-guy,** a stay or guy-rope for a tent; **ten′ting.**—*adj.* (*Keats*) having the form of a tent.—*ns.* **tent′-maker**; **tent′-peg, -pin,** a strong notched peg driven into the ground to fasten a tent; **tent′-pegging,** the sport of riding at full speed and trying to bear off a tent-peg on the point of a lance; **tent′-pole,** a pole to support a tent; **tent′-preaching**; **tent′-rope,** a rope for securing a tent to a peg.—*adv.* **tent′wise.** [Fr. *tente*—L. *tendĕre, tentum,* to stretch.]

tent, *tent, n.* (*obs.*) a probe: a plug or roll of soft material for dilating a wound or keeping open an orifice.—*v.t.* (*obs.*) to probe: to dilate or keep open with a tent. [Fr. *tente*—L. *tentāre,* to try.]

tent, *tent, n.* a deep-red Spanish wine. [Sp. *tinto*— L. *tinctus,* pa.p. of *tingĕre,* to dye.]

tent, *tent, n.* (*Scot.*) heed.—*v.t.* to take heed or notice of, attend to.—*n.* **tent′er,** one who tends.— *adj.* **tent′ie, tent′y.** [Aphetic for **attent** and **intent.**]

tent, *tent, n.* (*obs.*) an embroidery or tapestry frame. —*ns.* **tent′-stitch,** an embroidery stitch made in parallel series diagonally to the threads: tent-work; **tent′-work,** work in tent-stitch. [Origin obscure; cf. M.E. *tent,* to stretch, **tenter,** L. *tendĕre, tentum.*]

tentacle, *tent′ə-kl, n.* a slender flexible organ for feeling, grasping, &c.: a gland-tipped insect-capturing process in sundew.—Also **tentaculum** (*-ak′ū-ləm*; *pl.* **tentac′ula**).—*adjs.* **ten′tacled**; **tentac′ular**; **tentac′ulate**; **tentacūlif′erous.**— *n.* **tentac′ūlite,** a ringed tapering Silurian and Devonian fossil, app. a pteropod. [L. *tentāre,* to feel.]

tentation, *ten-tā′shən, n.* old form of **temptation**: a method of adjusting by a succession of trials. —*adj.* **tentative** (*ten′tə-tiv*), done or made provisionally and experimentally.—*n.* an experimental attempt.—*adv.* **ten′tatively.** [L. *tentāre,* to try.]

tenter, *ten′tər, n.* a frame for stretching cloth: a tenter-hook: a hook.—*v.t.* to stretch on hooks.— *n.* **ten′ter-hook,** a sharp, hooked nail as on a tenter: a hook.—**on tenter-hooks,** in impatient suspense. [App. conn. with Fr. *tenture,* hangings, and L. *tendĕre,* to stretch.]

tenter, tentie, tenty.—See **tent** (various).

tenth, *tenth, adj.* the last of ten: next after the ninth: equal to one of ten equal parts.—*n.* a tenth part: (*mus.*) an octave and a third: a note at that interval.—*adv.* **tenth′ly,** in the tenth place.

tentigo, *ten-tī′gō, n.* priapism: morbid lasciviousness.—*adj.* **tentiginous** (*-tij′i-nəs*). [L. *tentīgō, -inis*—*tendĕre,* to stretch.]

tentorium, *ten-tō′ri-əm, n.* a sheet of the dura mater stretched between the cerebrum and the cerebellum: the internal chitinous skeleton of an insect's head.—*adj.* **tentō′rial.** [L. *tentōrium,* a tent—*tendĕre,* to stretch.]

tenuis, *ten′ū-is* (L. *-oo-is*), *n.* an unaspirated voiceless stop consonant:—*pl.* **ten′ues** (*-ēz,* L. *-ās*).— *adj.* **tenuiros′tral** (L. *rōstrum,* bill), slender-billed. —*n.* **tenū′ity,** thinness: slenderness: rarity.— *adj.* **ten′ūous** (*rarely* **tenū′ious**), thin: slender: rarefied. [L. *tenuis,* thin; cf. *tendĕre,* to stretch.]

tenure, *ten′yər, n.* holding, occupation: time of

holding: conditions on which property is held: a tenant's rights, duties, &c.—*adj.* **tenūr′ial.** [A.Fr. *tenure*—*tenir*, to hold.]

tenure, (*Shak.*) for tenor.

tenuto, *te-nōō′tō, adj.* (*mus.*) sustained. [It., pa.p. of *tenere*, to hold.]

teocalli, *tā-, te̅-ō-kal′(y)i, n.* a Mexican pyramid temple. [Nahuatl,—*teotl*, god, *calli*, house.]

tepee, teepee, *te̅′pi, ti-pe̅′, n.* an American Indian tent formed of skins, &c., stretched over a frame of converging poles. [Sioux *tĭbī*, dwelling.]

tepefy, *tep′i-fī, v.t.* and *v.i.* to make or become tepid. [L. *tepefacĕre*—*tepēre*, to be tepid, *facĕre*, to make.]

tephrite, *tef′rīt, n.* a fine-grained basaltic rock containing a felspathoid as well as felspar, but no olivine.—*adj.* **tephritic** (*-rit′ik*).—*ns.* **teph′roite** (*-rō-īt*), an ashy-grey or reddish silicate of manganese; **teph′romancy,** divination (Gr. *manteiā*) by ashes, esp. of sacrifice. [Gr. *tephrā*, ashes, *tephros*, ash-coloured.]

tepid, *tep′id, adj.* moderately warm: lukewarm.— *ns.* **tepidā′rium** (L. *-dā′ri-oom*), a warm room between the cold and hot rooms of a Roman bath; **tepid′ity, tep′idness,** lukewarmness. [L. *tepidus* —*tepēre*, to be warm.]

ter-, *tər-,* in composition, thrice. [L.]

terai, *ter-ī′, n.* a wide-brimmed double-crowned ventilated hat, first worn in the *Terai* (Taráí), India.

teraph, *ter′af, n.* in ancient Jewish religion and divination, an image of some sort:—*pl.* **ter′aphim** (also used as *sing.*). [Heb.]

teras, *ter′as, n.* (*med.*) a monstrosity:—*pl.* **ter′ata.** —*adj.* **teratogenic** (*ter-ə-tō-jen′ik*), producing monsters.—*n.* **teratogeny** (*-toj′i-ni*), the production of monsters.—*adjs.* **ter′atoid,** monstrous; **teratolog′ic, -al.**—*ns.* **teratol′ogist; teratol′ogy,** the study of malformations or abnormal growths, animal or vegetable: a tale of marvels; **teratō′ma,** a tumour, containing tissue from all three germ-layers:—*pl.* **teratō′mata.**—*adj.* **teratō′matous.** [Gr. *teras, -atos,* a monster.]

terbium, *tər′bi-əm, n.* a rare metal (Tb: at. numb. 65) found in certain yttrium minerals.—*adj.* **ter′bic.** [From *Ytterby*; see yttrium.]

terce, *tərs, n.* (Scots law) a widow's right, where she has no conventional provision, to a liferent of a third of the husband's heritable property: (*hist.*) the office of the third hour. [See tierce.]

tercel, *tərs′əl,* **tiercel,** *te̅r′səl,* **tarsel,** *tärs′əl,* **tassel**(l), *tas′əl, n.* a male hawk.—*ns.* **ter′cel-gent′le** (*Scott*), **tass′el-gent′le** (*Shak.*), **tass′ell-gent′** (*Spens.*), a male peregrine falcon; **ter′cel-jer′kin,** a male gerfalcon; **terc′elet,** a tercel. [O.Fr. *tercel*—L. *tertius,* third, perh. as being one-third smaller than the female, or as supposed to hatch from the last egg of three.]

tercentenary, *tər′sən-tē′nə-ri,* or *-ten′ə-ri,* or *tər-sen′ti-nə-ri, adj.* of three hundred (usu. years).—*n.* a 300th anniversary. [**ter-, centenary.**]

tercentennial, *tər-sen-ten′yəl, adj.* of 300 years.—*n.* a 300th anniversary. [**ter-, centennial.**]

tercet, *tər′sit, n.* a group of three lines in verse. [It. *terzetto.*]

tercio, *tər′s(h)i-ō* (*Scott* **tertia**), *n.* (*hist.*) an infantry regiment, orig. Spanish. [Sp.]

terebene, *ter′i-bēn, n.* a light-yellow disinfectant liquid, a mixture of hydrocarbons made from oil of turpentine, used as a solvent for paint.—*n.* **ter′e-binth,** the turpentine-tree (*Pistacia Terebinthus*); family Anacardiaceae).—*adj.* **terebinth′ine.** [Gr. *terebinthos.*]

terebra, *ter′i-brä, n.* a Roman engine for boring walls: a boring instrument: a piercing ovipositor: **Terebra,** a genus of gasteropods with auger-shaped shell.—*adj.* **ter′ebrant,** boring: having a piercing ovipositor.—*n.* (*facet.*) a bore.—*v.t.* and *v.i.* **ter′ebrate,** to bore.—*adj.* having scattered perforations: having a borer.—*ns.* **terebrā′tion;** **Terebrat′ula,** the lamp-shell genus of brachiopods, with perforated beak. [L. *terebra.*]

Teredo, *te-rē′dō, n.* the ship-worm genus of molluscs. [L. *terēdō, -inis*—Gr. *terēdōn, -onos,* a boring worm—root of *teirein,* to wear away.]

terek, *ter′ek, n.* a sandpiper of the river *Terek* (Russia).

Terentian, *ter-en′sh(y)ən, adj.* pertaining to the Roman comic poet *Terence,* P. Terentius Afer (*fl.* 165 B.C.).

terete, *tə-rēt′, ter′ēt, adj.* smooth and cylindrical. [L. *teres, terĕtis,* smooth, *terĕre,* to rub.]

terf, Milton's spelling of **turf.**

tergum, *tər′gəm, n.* the back: the back or back plate of a somite.—*adj.* **ter′gal.**—*n.* **ter′gite** (*-jit*), the back plate of a somite.—*v.i.* **ter′giversate** (*-ji-*; L. *versāri,* to turn), to turn one's back: to desert, apostatise: to shuffle, shift, use evasions.—*ns.* **tergiversā′tion; ter′giversātor.** [L. *tergum,* the back.]

term, *tərm, n.* a limit: an end: a term-day: the normal time of child-birth: any limited period: the time for which anything lasts: a division of the academic or school year: a period of sittings: (in *pl.*) conditions, stipulations: (in *pl.*) a footing: (in *pl.*) charge, fee: (*Shak.*; in *pl.*) respect: (*alg.*) a quantity added to or subtracted from others in an expression: an item in a series: that which may be subject or predicate of a proposition: a word used in a specially understood or defined sense: an expression generally: a bust in continuity with its pedestal.—*v.t.* to call, designate.—*ns.* **term′-day,** a day of the year fixed for some purpose, as payment of rent, beginning or end of a tenancy, hiring of servants, household removals; **term′er,** one who came to town in term.—*adj.* **term′less,** endless: (*Shak.*) inexpressible: unconditional.—*adj.* and *adv.* **term′ly.**—*ns.* **term′or,** one who holds an estate for a term of years or for life; **term′-time.**—**bring to terms,** to compel to the acceptance of conditions; **come to terms,** to come to an agreement: to submit; **eat one's terms** (see eat); **in terms,** in so many words, explicitly: engaged in negotiation; **in terms of,** having or using as unit: in the language peculiar to; **keep a term,** to give the regular attendance during a period of study; **on speaking terms,** friendly enough to speak to each other: well enough acquainted to speak; **on terms,** in friendly relations: on an equal footing; **stand upon terms,** to insist upon conditions; **term of years,** an interest or estate in land for a period. [Fr. *terme*—L. *terminus,* a boundary.]

termagant, *tər′mə-gənt, n.* a boisterous brawler or bully, esp. a woman.—*adj.* boisterous: brawling. —*n.* **ter′magancy.**—*adv.* **ter′magantly.** [M.E. *Termagant* or *Tervagant,* a supposed Mohammedan idol, represented in the old plays and moralities as of a violent character.]

Termes, *tər′mēz, n.* a genus of termites. [L. *termes, -itis,* a wood-worm.]

Terminus, *tər′min-əs, n.* the Roman god of boundaries: **terminus,** a term (bust) of Terminus, or other: a boundary stone: an end-point, esp. of a route or railway: a railway station at such a point: —*pl.* **ter′mini** (*-ī*).—*n.* **terminabil′ity.**—*adj.* **ter′minable,** that may come or be brought to an end.—*n.* **ter′minableness.**—*adv.* **ter′minably.**— *adj.* **ter′minal,** of, at, forming or marking, an end, boundary, or terminus: final: of a term: occurring every term.—*n.* an end: an ending: (*U.S.*) a railway terminus: a free end in an open electric circuit.—*n.pl.* **Terminā′lia,** an annual Roman festival in honour of Terminus.—*n.sing.* the myrobalan genus of Combretaceae.—*adv.* **ter′minally.** —*v.t.* and *v.i.* **ter′minate.**—*n.* **terminā′tion,** ending. — *adjs.* **terminā′tional; ter′minative,** tending to terminate or determine: expressive of completion: definitive: absolute. — *adv.* **ter′-minatively.**—*n.* **ter′minātor,** one who, or that which, terminates: the boundary between the illuminated and dark portions of the moon or of a planet.—*adj.* **ter′minatory.**—*ns.* **ter′miner,** (*law*) the act of determining; **ter′minism,** (*phil.*) nominalism: (*theol.*) the doctrine that there is a time limit for the operation of grace; **ter′minist.**—*adj.* **terminolog′ical.**—*adv.* **termin-olog′ically.** — *n.* **terminol′ogy,** nomenclature: the set of terms used in any art, science, &c. [L. *Terminus, terminus;* cf. Gr. *terma,* end.]

termite, *tər′mīt, n.* a so-called white ant, a pale-coloured insect of the Isoptera, only superficially iike an ant.—*ns.* **termitarium** (*tər-mi-tā'ri-əm*), **ter'mitary** (*-tar-i*), a nest or mound of termites. [L. *termes, termitis,* a wood-worm.]

tern, *tərn, n.* a long-winged aquatic fowl allied to the gulls. [Cf. O.N. *therna*; O.E. *stearn, tearn.*]

tern, *tərn, n.* a three, set of three : a prize for drawing three winning numbers.—*adjs.* **ter'nal,** threefold ; **ter'nary,** in threes : of three components : based on three : of a third order.—*n.* (*obs.*) a triad. —*adj.* **ter'nate,** (*bot.*) with three leaflets : grouped in threes.—*adv.* **ter'nately.**—*n.* **ter'nion,** a triad : a section of paper for a book containing three double leaves or twelve pages. [L. *ternī,* three each —*trēs,* three.]

terne, *tərn, n.* sheet-iron coated with an alloy of lead and tin. [Fr. *terne,* dull.]

Ternstroemiaceae, *tərn-strēm-i-ā'shi-ē, n.pl.* the Theaceae, or tea family of plants. [From a genus *Ternstroemia,* named after Christopher *Ternström,* Swedish naturalist.]

terpene, *tər'pēn, n.* any one of a group of hydrocarbons with a composition C₁₀H₁₆. [**turpentine.**]

Terpsichore, *tərp-sik'ə-rē, n.* the Muse of choral song and dance.—*adj.* **Terpsichore'an.** [Gr. *Terpsichorē—terpsis,* delight—*terpein,* to enjoy, *choros,* dance.]

terra, *ter'ä, n.* the Latin and Italian word for earth. —*n.* **terr'a-cott'a** (It. *cotta* — L. *cocta,* fem., baked), a composition of clay and sand used for statues, hardened like bricks by fire : an object of art made of it : its colour, a brownish red.—Also *adj.*—*ns.* **terr'a-fir'ma,** properly, mainland : (*coll.* and erroneously) dry land ; **terr'a-japon'ica,** pale catechu or gambier ; **terr'ama'ra** (*pl.* **-re,** **-rā** ; It. *dial.* ᶠor *terra marna,* marl-earth), a dark earthy deposit formed under prehistoric pile-dwellings in Italy.—*adj.* **terraqueous** (*ter-ā'kwi-əs* ; L. *aqua,* water), of land and water.—*ns.* **terrā'rium,** a vivarium for land animals ; **terr'a-ross'a** (It. *rossa,* fem., red), a ferruginous red earth, th⁻ residue of the weathering of limestone ; **terra sıgillata** (*sij-i-lā'tä,* L. *sig-i-lā'tä* ; sealed earth), Lemnian earth.

terrace, *ter'is, n.* a raised level bank or walk : a level stretch along the side or top of a slope : ground or a structure that rises stepwise : a gallery open at the side : a balcony : a flat rooftop : a connected row of houses, properly one overlooking a slope : a defective spot in marble.—*v.t.* to form into a terrace.—*adj.* **terr'aced,** in terraces.—*n.* **terr'acing.** [Fr. *terrasse* — It. *terrazza* — L.L. *terrācea,* an earthen mound—L. *terra,* the earth.]

terrain, *ter'ān,* or *-ān', n.* ground, a tract, regarded as a field of view or of operations, or as having some sort of unity or prevailing character. [Fr., from a L.L. form of *terrēnum,* terrene.]

terrapin, *ter'ə-pin, n.* an American freshwater or brackish-water tortoise of many kinds, esp. *Malacoclemmys terrapin* of the Eastern States : extended to other tortoises. [Of Algonquin origin.]

terreen, an older spelling of **tureen.**

terrella, *ter-el'ä, n.* a magnetic model of the earth. [A mod. dim. of L. *terra,* the earth.]

terremotive, *ter-i-mō'tiv, adj.* seismic. [L. *terrae motus,* earthquake.]

terrene, *ti-rēn', ter'ēn, adj.* of the earth : earthly : mundane : earthy : terrestrial.—*n.* the world : a region, terrain.—*adv.* **terrene'ly.** [L. *terrēnus—terra,* the earth.]

terreplein, *ter', tär'plān, n.* orig. the talus on the inner side of a rampart : the top of a rampart, or space behind the parapet. [Fr.,—L. *terra,* earth, *plēnus,* full.]

terrestrial, *ti-res'tri-əl, adj.* of, or existing on, the earth : earthly : living or growing on land or on the ground : representing the earth.—*n.* a dweller on earth : (*Shak.*) a man of the world, layman.— *adv.* **terres'trially.** [L. *terrestris—terra,* the earth.]

terret, territ, *ter'it, n.* a swivel-ring : a ring for fastening a chain to : a ring or loop through which driving reins pass.—Also **torr'et, turr'et.** [O.Fr. *toret,* dim. of *tor, tour,* a round.]

terrible, *ter'i-bl, adj.* fitted to excite terror or awe : awful : dreadful : (*coll.*) very notable, exceeding.—

n. a terrible thing.—*ns.* **terribil'ity** (*rare*) ; **terr'ibleness.**—*adv.* **terr'ibly.** [L. *terribilis—terrēre,* to frighten.]

terricolous, *ter-ik'ə-ləs, adj.* living in or on the soil. —*n.* **terr'icole** (*-i-kōl*), a land animal or plant : a burrower.—Also *adj.* [L. *terricola,* a dweller upon earth—*terra,* earth, *eolĕre,* to inhabit.]

terrier, *ter'i-ər, n.* a small dog of various breeds, orig. one that would follow burrowing animals underground : punningly, a territorial soldier : (*fig.*) one who hunts after criminals : a register or roll of a landed estate : an inventory. [O.Fr.,— L.L. *terrārius* (adj.)—*terra,* land.]

terrify, *ter'i-fī, v.t.* to cause terror in : to frighten greatly :—*pr.p.* **terr'ifying** ; *pa.t.* and *pa.p.* **terr'ified.**—*adj.* **terrif'ic,** creating or causing terror : fitted to terrify : dreadful : (*coll.*) prodigious.— *adv.* **terrif'ically.** [L. *terrificāre—terrēre,* to terrify, *facĕre,* to make.]

terrigenous, *te-rij'i-nəs, adj.* earth-born : derived from the land. [L. *terrigenus—terra,* earth, *genĕre* (*gignĕre*), to produce.]

terrine. See **tureen.**

territory, *ter'i-tər-i, n.* possessions in land : the whole, or a portion, of the land belonging to a state : part of a confederation with an organised government but not yet admitted to statehood : a dependency : a region : a jurisdiction : a field of activity : a domain : the area that a pair of birds treat as their own.—*adj.* **territō'rial.**—*n.* a soldier in the Territorial Army.—*v.t.* **territō'rialise,** to make a territory of : to make territorial : to put on a territorial basis.—*ns.* **territō'rialism,** landlordism : organisation on a territorial basis : the theory of church government according to which the civil power is supreme over the church ; **territō'rialist** ; **territorial'ity.** — *adv.* **territō'rially.**—*adj.* **terr'itoried,** possessed of territory.— **Territorial Army,** a voluntary home-defence army on a territorial basis, formed in 1908 in place of the old Volunteers. [L. *territōrium,* the domain of a town, perh. not orig. conn. with *terra.*]

terror, *ter'ər, n.* extreme fear : a time of, or government by, terrorism : an object of dread : (*coll.*) one who makes himself a nuisance.—*n.* **terrorīsā'tion** (or *-iz-*).—*v.t.* **terr'orise,** to terrify : to govern by terror.—*ns.* **terr'oriser** ; **terr'orism,** an organised system of intimidation ; **terr'orist.**—*adjs.* **terr'orless** ; **terr'or-stricken,** smitten with terror.— **King of Terrors,** death ; **Reign of Terror, or the Terror,** the period of fever in the first French Revolution when thousands went to the guillotine ; **terror novel,** a novel full of supernatural horrors. [L. *terror—terrēre,* to frighten.]

terry, *ter'i, n.* a pile fabric with uncut loops.—Also *adj.* [Origin unknown.]

tersanctus, *ter-sang(k)'təs, n.* the Sanctus. [L., thrice holy.]

terse, *tərs, adj.* (*obs.*) smooth, clean-cut : compact or concise.—*adv.* **terse'ly.**—*ns.* **terse'ness** ; **tersion** (*tər'shən*), wiping. [L. *tersus—tergĕre, tersum,* to rub clean.]

tertia. See **tercio.**

tertial, *tər'shl, adj.* of the third rank among flightfeathers of a wing.—*n.* a tertiary flight-feather.— *adj.* **ter'tian** (*-shən*), occurring every other day (i.e. on the *third* day, reckoning both first and last days).—*n.* a fever with paroxysms every other day. —*adj.* **ter'tiary** (*-shər-i*), of the third degree, order, or formation : (*ornith.*) tertial : **Tertiary,** of the third great division of the geological record and time, including Eocene, Oligocene, Miocene, Pliocene.—*n.* the Tertiary period : **tertiary,** a member of a third order of a monastic order, a layman who may continue to live an ordinary life in the world : a tertiary feather : that which is tertiary. [L. *tertiālis, tertiānus, tertiārius—tertius,* third.]

teru-tero, *ter'ōō-ter'ō, n.* the Cayenne lapwing.

tervalent, *tər'və-lant, tər-vā'lant, adj.* trivalent. [L. *ter,* thrice.]

Terylene, *ter'i-lēn, n.* a synthetic textile yarn made from a condensation product of *terephthalic acid and ethylene glycol.* [Registered trade-mark.]

terza-rima, *ter'tsä-rē'mä, n.* an Italian verse-form

in triplets, in which the middle line of each triplet rhymes with the first and third lines of the next with an odd line to end off the canto. [It., third rhyme.]

terzetta, ter-tset'tä, *n.* a tercet.—*n.* **terzet'to,** a trio. [It.]

teschenite, tesh'ən-īt, *n.* a coarse-grained basic igneous rock composed essentially of plagioclase and augite, usu. with much analcime. [Found near Teschen.]

tessara-, tessera-, tes'ə-rə-, in composition, four.—*adj.* **tess'araglot** (Gr. *glōtta*, tongue), in four languages. [Gr. *tessares*, four.]

tessella, tes-el'ä, *n.* a little tessera:—*pl.* **tessell'ae** (-ē; L. -ī).—*adj.* **tess'ellar.**—*v.t.* **tessellate** (tes'i-lāt), to pave with tesserae: to mark like a mosaic.—*adj.* marked out in little squarish areas.—*adj.* **tess'elated.**—*n.* **tessellā'tion.** [L. *tessella*, dim. of *tessera*; see next.]

tessera, tes'ə-rä, *n.* one of the small pieces of which a mosaic is made: a token or ticket: password:—*pl.* **tess'erae** (-ē; L. -ī).—*adj.* **tess'eral,** of tesserae: (crystal.) cubic, isometric. [L. *tessera*, a die, small cube—Gr. *tessares, tesseres, -a,* four.]

tessitura, tes-i-tōō'rä, *n.* the ordinary compass of a voice. [It., texture.]

test, test, *n.* a pot or cupel in which metals are tried and refined: any critical trial: means of trial: (chem.) anything used to distinguish or detect substances, a reagent: a trial of fitness for an examination: an oath or other evidence of religious belief required as a condition of office or exercise of rights: a test-match: a testa.—*v.t.* to put to proof: to try or examine critically.—*n.* **test'a,** a hard shell: a seed-coat, derived from the integuments of the ovule.—*adjs.* **test'able** or **testaceous** (-ā'shəs), of or having a hard shell: brick-red.—*ns.* **test'-case,** a law case that may settle similar questions in the future; **test'er.**—*n.pl.* **Testicar'dines** (-ēz), a class of brachiopods with hinged shell and arm skeleton.—*n.* and *adj.* **test'ing.**—*ns.* **test'-match,** an international cricket match forming one of a series; **test'-paper,** a bibulous paper saturated with some substance that changes colour when exposed to certain chemicals: a paper of questions to test fitness for a more serious examination; **test'-tube,** a glass cylinder closed at one end, used in chemistry, bacteriology, &c.—**Test Acts,** acts meant to secure that none but rightly affected persons and members of the established religion shall hold office—esp. those of 1673 and 1685; **test pilot,** one who tests aircraft by performing stunts, &c. [O.Fr. *test* and *teste*—L. *testa,* an earthen pot, a potsherd, a shell.]

test, test, *v.t.* to attest legally and date: to authenticate by a testing clause.—*ns.* **test'acy** (-ə-si), state of being testate; **testā'mur,** a certificate of having passed an examination.—*adj.* **test'āte,** having made and left a will.—*ns.* **testā'tion,** a witnessing, a giving by will; **testā'tor,** one who leaves a will:—*fem.* **testā'trix;** **testā'tum,** one of the clauses of an English deed, enumerating the operative words of transfer, statement of consideration, money, &c.—**testing clause,** in a Scots deed, the last clause which narrates when and where the parties signed the deed, before what witnesses, by whose hand written, &c. [L. *testārī,* to testify, witness, pa.p. (neut.) *testātum*; ist pers. pl. *testāmur,* partly through O.Fr. *tester,* to bequeath, partly aphetic for attest.]

testament, tes'tə-mənt, *n.* that which testifies, or in which an attestation is made: the solemn declaration in writing of one's will: a will: (Scots law) a writing or decree appointing an executor, by the testator (tes'tament-testament'ar) or by a court (tes'tament-dā'tive): Tes'tament, either of the main divisions (Old and New) of the Bible (a translation of Gr. *diathēkē,* disposition, compact, covenant).—*adjs.* **testamental** (-ment'), **testament'ar** (Scots law), **testament'ary,** pertaining to a testament or will: bequeathed or done by will.—*adv.* **testament'arily.** [L. *testāmentum.*]

tester, tes'tər, *n.* a canopy or its support, or both, esp. over a bed. [O.Fr. *testre,* the vertical part of a bed behind the head, and *testiere,* a head-

covering—*teste* (Fr. *tête*), head—L. *testa,* an earthen pot, the skull.]

tester, tes'tər, **testern,** tes'tərn, *n.* a sixpence.—*v.t.* **tes'tern,** (Shak.) to present or reward with a sixpence. [See teston.]

testicle, tes'ti-kl, *n.* a male reproductive gland.—*adjs.* **testic'ular,** of or like a testicle; **testic'ūlate,** -d, like a testicle.—*n.* tes'tis, a testicle: a rounded body like it:—*pl.* **tes'tes** (-ēz). [L. *testis* and its dim. *testiculus.*]

testify, tes'ti-fī, *v.i.* to bear witness: to make a solemn declaration: to protest or declare a charge (with against).—*v.t.* to bear witness to: to affirm or declare solemnly or on oath: to proclaim, declare:—*pr.p.* tes'tifying; *pa.t.* and *pa.p.* tes'tified.—*ns.* **testif'icāte,** (Scots law) a solemn written assertion; **testificā'tion,** the act of testifying or of bearing witness; **testif'icātor.**—*adjs.* **testif'icatory;** **tes'tified.**—*n.* **tes'tifier.** [L. *testificārī*—*testis,* a witness, *facĕre,* to make.]

testimony, tes'ti-mən-i, *n.* evidence: declaration to prove some fact: proof: (B.) the two tables of the law: divine law: protestation.—*v.t.* (Shak.) to test, prove, or judge by evidence.—*adj.* **testimō'nial,** of, affording, of the nature of, testimony.—*n.* a written attestation: a writing or certificate bearing testimony to one's character or abilities: a gift or memorial subscribed for as a token of respect.—*v.t.* **testimō'nialise,** to present with a testimonial. [L. *testimōnium*—*testārī,* to witness.]

teston, tes'ton, *n.* a name for various coins, orig. bearing a king's or duke's head: a Henry VIII. shilling: later a sixpence.—*n.* **testoon',** a Portuguese or Italian teston. [Obs. Fr. *teston,* Port. *testão,* It. *testone*—It. *testa,* head.]

testril (Shak.), **testril,** tes'tril, *n.* a sixpence. [tester.]

Testudo, tes-tū'dō, *n.* the common tortoise genus: **testudo,** a wheeled shelter used by Roman besiegers: a similar shelter made by joining shields: a vaulted roof: an ancient lyre, said to have been first made of a tortoise-shell.—*adj.* **testūdin'eous,** like a tortoise, tortoise-shell, or a testudo. [L. *testūdō, -inis,* tortoise.]

testy, tes'ti, *adj.* irritable.—*adv.* **tes'tily.**—*n.* **tes'tiness.** [O.Fr. *testif,* headstrong—*teste* (Fr. *tête*), head—L. *testa,* pot.]

tetanus, tet'ə-nəs, *n.* a disease due to a bacillus, marked by painful tonic spasms of the muscles of the jaw and other parts: the state of prolonged contraction of a muscle under quickly repeated stimuli.—*adj.* **tetanic** (ti-tan'ik).—*n.* **tetanisā'tion.**—*v.t.* **tet'anise,** to produce tetanus or tetanic spasms in.—*n.* **tet'any,** heightened excitability of the motor nerves with painful muscular cramps. [L.,—Gr. *tetanos*—*teinein,* to stretch.]

tetartohedral, te-tärt-ō-hē'drəl, *adj.* (crystal.) having one-fourth of the number of faces required for full symmetry. [Gr. *tetartos,* fourth, *hedrä,* seat.]

tetchy, techy, tech'i, *adj.* irritable.—*adv.* **tetch'ily.**—*n.* **tetch'iness.** [Origin unknown.]

tête, tet, *n.* (obs.) an elaborately dressed head of hair: a head-dress.—*n.* **tête-à-tête** (tet'-ä-tet'), a private confidential interview: a sofa for two face to face.—*adj.* confidential, secret.—*adv.* in private conversation: face to face. [Fr.]

tether, tedh'ər, *n.* a rope or chain for confining a beast within certain limits.—*v.t.* to confine with a tether: to restrain within certain limits. [App. O.N. *tjóthr.*]

Tethys, tē'this, teth'is, *n.* a sea-nymph, wife of Oceanus: (geol.) a sea that extended in Mesozoic times from Mexico across the middle Atlantic and the Mediterranean into the centre of Asia. [Gr. *Tēthys.*]

tetra, tet'rä, *n.* a plant mentioned by Spenser (The Faerie Queene, II. vii. 52, 4).

tetra-, tet'rə-, **tetr-,** in composition, four. [Gr. *tetra-, tettares, tessares,* four.]

Tetrabranchia, tet-rə-brang'ki-ä, **Tetrabranchiata,** -ā'tä, *ns.pl.* the nautilus subclass of cephalopods, with four gills.—*adj.* **tetrabranch'iate,** four-gilled. [Gr. *branchia,* gills.]

tetrachord, tet'rə-kord, *n.* a four-stringed instrument: a series of four sounds, forming a scale of two tones and a half.—*adj.* **tetrachord′al.** [Gr. *chordē*, string.]

tetrachotomy, *tet-rə-kot′ə-mi*, *n.* division in fours. —*adj.* **tetrachot′omous.** [Gr. *tetracha*, in four parts, *tomē*, a cut—*temnein*, to cut.]

tetract, *tet′rakt*, *adj.* four-rayed.—*n.* a four-rayed sponge spicule.—*adjs.* **tetract′inal** (or -*i′nəl*), **tetrac′tine.**—*n.pl.* **Tetractinell′ida,** an order of sponges in which some of the spicules are four-rayed. [Gr. *aktīs, -inos,* ray.]

tetracyclic, *tet-rə-sī′klik, adj.* of, in, or with four whorls or rings. [Gr. *kyklos,* ring, wheel.]

tetrad, *tet′rad, n.* a group of four : (*chem.*) an atom, radical, or element having a combining power of four.—*adjs.* **tet′rad, tetrad′ic.**—*n.* **tet′radite,** one who attaches mystic properties to the number four : a believer in a godhead of four persons. [Gr. *tetras, -ados.*]

tetradactyl, *tet-rə-dak′til, adj.* four-fingered : four-toed.—Also *adj.*—*adj.* **tetradac′tylous.**—*n.* **tetradac′tyly,** condition of being tetradactylous. [Gr. *daktylos,* digit.]

tetradrachm, *tet′rə-dram, n.* an ancient Greek coin worth four drachmas.

tetradynamous, *tet-rə-din′ə-məs, adj.* having four long stamens in pairs and two short, as the Cruciferae.—*n.pl.* **Tetradynamia** (-*di-nā′mi-ā*), in Linnaeus's system, a class answering to the Cruciferae. [Gr. *dynamis,* power.]

tetraethyl, *tet-rə-eth′il, adj.* having four ethyl groups, as **tetraethyl lead** or **lead tetraethyl,** Pb(C₂H₅)₄, used in motor spirit as an antiknock agent.

tetragon, *tet′rə-gən, -gon, n.* a plane figure of four angles.—*adjs.* **tetragonal** (-*rag′ə-nəl*), having the form of a tetragon : (*crystal.*) referable to three axes at right angles, two of them equal ; **tetrag′-onous,** (*bot.*) with four angles and convex faces. [Gr. *tetragōnon—gōniā,* an angle.]

tetragram, *tet′rə-gram, n.* a word or inscription of four letters : the tetragrammaton : (*geom.*) a (complete) quadrilateral.—*n.* **tetragramm′aton,** the name YaHWeH, JeHoVaH, &c., as written with four Hebrew letters, regarded as a mystic symbol : any other sacred word of four letters, as the Latin *Deus.* [Gr. *gramma,* a letter.]

Tetragynia, *tet-rə-jin′i-ä, n.pl.* in the Linnaean system an order of plants (in various classes) with four pistils.—*adjs.* **tetragyn′ian, tetragynous** (-*raj′i-nəs*). [Gr. *gynē,* woman (in the sense of female).]

tetrahedron, *tet-rə-hē′drən, n.* a solid figure or body with four plane faces.—*adj.* **tetrahē′dral.**—*ns.* **tetrahē′drite,** grey copper ore, sulphide of copper and antimony, a mineral of tetrahedral habit ; **tetrakishexahedron,** a figure got by erecting equal pyramids on all the faces of a cube. [Gr. *tetra-, tetrakis,* four times, and *hedrā,* seat.]

tetralogy, *te-tral′ə-ji, n.* a group of four dramas, usu. three tragic and one satyric : any series of four related dramatic or operatic works or stories. [Gr. *tetralogiā—logos,* discourse.]

tetramerous, *te-tram′ə-rəs, adj.* having four parts, or parts in fours.—*adj.* **tetram′eral,** four-parted.— *n.* **tetram′erism,** division into four parts. [Gr. *meros,* part.]

tetrameter, *te-tram′i-tər, n.* a verse of four measures (dipodies or feet).—Also *adj.* [Gr. *tetrametron— metron,* measure.]

tetramorphic, *te-trə-mor′fik, adj.* having four forms. [Gr. *morphē,* form.]

tetrandrous, *te-tran′drəs, adj.* having four stamens. —*n.pl.* **Tetran′dria,** in Linnaeus's classification, a class of plants with four stamens.—*adj.* **tetran′-drian.** [Gr. *anēr, andros,* a man (in the sense of male).]

tetrapla, *tet′rə-plä, n.* an edition of four parallel texts, esp. Origen's of the Old Testament. [Contracted neut. pl. of Gr. *tetraplous* (*tetraploos*), fourfold.]

tetraploid, *tet′rə-ploid, adj.* having four times the haploid (twice the normal) number of chromosomes.—*n.* **tet′raploidy,** the condition of being tetraploid. [Gr. *tetraploos* (-*plous*), fourfold, *eidos,* form.]

tetrapod, *tet′rə-pod, n.* a four-footed animal : any vertebrate above the fishes. — Also *adj.* — *adj.* **tetrapodous** (-*trap′*).—*n.* **tetrap′ody,** a group of four metrical feet. [Gr. *pous, podos,* foot.]

tetrapolis, *te-trap′o-lis, n.* a group of four towns.— *adj.* **tetrapolitan** (*tet-rə-pol′i-tən*).—**Tetrapolitan Confession,** the Confession which the four cities of Strasburg, Constance, Memmingen, and Lindau presented to the Diet of Augsburg (11th July 1530), and, properly speaking, the first Confession of the Reformed Church. [Gr. *tetrapolis—polis,* city.]

tetrapterous, *te-trap′tə-rəs, adj.* four-winged.— Also **tetrap′teran.** [Gr. *pteron,* a wing.]

tetraptote, *tet′rap-tōt, n.* a noun with but four cases. [Gr. *tetraptōtos—ptōsis,* a case.]

tetrarch, *tet′rärk,* or *tē′trärk, n.* under the Romans, the ruler of the fourth part of a province : a subordinate prince: the commander of a subdivision of a Greek phalanx.—*ns.* **tet′rarchate, tet′rarchy,** office, rank, time of office, or jurisdiction of a tetrarch : the fourth part of a province. [Gr. *tetrarchēs—archē,* rule.]

tetrarch, *tet′rärk,* or *tē′trärk, adj.* (*bot.*) having four xylem strands.—*n.* **tet′rarchy,** condition of being tetrarch. [Gr. *archē,* origin.]

tetrasemic, *tet-rə-sē′mik, adj.* (*pros.*) equivalent to four short syllables, as a dactyl, anapaest, or spondee. [Gr. *tetrasēmos—sēma,* a sign.]

tetraspore, *tet′rə-spōr, n.* a spore formed in groups of four, in red seaweeds.—*n.* **tetrasporangium** (-*spor-an′ji-əm*), the sporangium in which they are formed.—*adjs.* **tetrasporic** (-*spor′ik*), **tetrasporous** (*te-tras′pər-əs,* or *tet-rə-spō′rəs*). [Gr. *sporā,* seed.]

tetrastich, *tet′rə-stik, n.* a stanza or set of four lines. —*adjs.* **tetrastichal** (*ti-tras′ti-kl*), **tetrastichic** (*tet-rə-stik′ik*), of, of the nature of, tetrastichs ; **tetras′tichous,** in four rows. [Gr. *tetrastichos— stichos,* a row.]

tetrastyle, *tet′rə-stīl, n.* a building or portico with four columns in front : a group of four pillars.— Also *adj.* [Gr. *tetrastylon—stylos,* a column.]

tetrasyllable, *tet′rə-sil′ə-bl, n.* a word of four syllables.—*adjs.* **tetrasyllabic** (-*ab′ik*), -**al.**

tetratheism, *tet′rə-thē-izm, n.* the belief in four elements in the Godhead—the three persons of the Trinity and a divine essence out of which each of these originates. [Gr. *theos,* god.]

tetravalent, *te-trav′ə-lənt, tet-rə-vā′lənt, adj.* quadrivalent.

tetraxon, *te-traks′on, n.* a sponge spicule with four axes. [Gr. *axōn, -onos,* an axis.]

tetrode, *tet′rōd, n.* a thermionic valve with four electrodes. [Gr. *hodos,* a way.]

tetter, *tet′ər, n.* (*Shak.*) a skin eruption.—*v.t.* (*Shak.*) to affect with a tetter.—*adj.* **tett′erous.** [O.E. *teter.*]

tettix, *tet′iks, n.* a cicada : an ornament for the hair of that shape. [Gr.]

teuch, teugh, *tūhh, adj.* a Scots form of **tough.**

Teucrian, *tū′kri-ən, n.* and *adj.* Trojan. [Gr. *Teukros,* Teucer, first king of Troy.]

Teuton, *tū′tən, n.* any speaker of a Germanic language : popularly, a German.—*adj.* **Teutonic** (-*ton′ik*), Germanic—of the linguistic family that includes English, German, Dutch, and the Scandinavian languages : popularly, German in the narrower sense.—*n.* the parent language of the Teutons, primitive Germanic.—*ns.* **Teuton′icism** (-*i-sizm*), **Teu′tonism,** a Germanism : belief in, enthusiasm for, the Teutons : the study of Germanic philology and culture ; **Teutonīsā′tion.** — *v.t.* and *v.i.* **Teu′tonise,** to make or become Teutonic, Germanic, or German.—*n.* **Teu′tonist.**— **Teutonic Knights,** a military-religious order founded in 1191-98 to tend wounded Christians and war on unbelievers, operated first in Palestine and later against the Prussians and Lithuanians. [L. *Teutonēs,* from the root of O.E. *théod,* people, nation ; cf. **Dutch,** Ger. *Deutsch.*]

tew, *tū, v.t.* to work up : to taw.—*v.i.* to toil, hustle. —*n.* worry : excitement. [Cf. **taw.**]

tewart. See **tuart.**

tewel, *tū′əl, n.* (*dial.*) the rectum or anus, esp. of a horse : a flue : a tuyère. [O.Fr. *tuel* (Fr. *tuyau*), tube.]

fāte, fär, ȧsk ; mē, hər (her) *; mīne ; mōte ; mūte ; mōōn ; dhen* (then)

tewit, tewhit, *tē'(h)wit* (*Scot.* **teuchat,** *tūhh'ət*), *n.* (*dial.*) a lapwing. [Imit.]

Texas, *teks'as, n.* a state of the U.S.A.: **texas,** an upper structure on a river-steamer.—**Texas fever,** a protozoal cattle-disease transmitted by ticks.

text, *tekst, n.* the actual words of a book, poem, &c., in their original form or any form they have been transmitted in or transmuted into: a book of such words: words set to music: the main body of matter in a book, distinguished from notes, commentary, or other subsidiary matter: (*Shak.*) the Bible: matter commented on: a short passage from the Bible taken as the ostensible subject of a sermon, quoted in authority, displayed as a motto, &c.: a theme: a copybook heading: text-hand.—*ns.* **text'-book,** a book containing the leading principles of a subject; **text'-hand,** a large hand in writing, orig. one suitable for the text of a manuscript book.—*adj.* **textile** (*-il*), woven: capable of being woven.—*n.* a woven fabric.—*n.* **text'-man,** a quoter of texts: a textualist.—*adjs.* **texto'rial,** pertaining to weaving; **tex'tual,** pertaining to, or contained in, the text: serving for a text.—*n.* **text'ualist,** one learned in the text, esp. of the Bible: a literal interpreter: a quoter of texts.—*adv.* **text'ually.**—*n.* **tex'tuary,** a textualist.—*adj.* **text'ural,** pertaining to, in the matter of, texture.—*adv.* **textur'ally.**—*n.* **text'ure,** anything woven, a web: manner of weaving or connecting: disposition of the parts of a body: structural impression resulting from the manner of combining or interrelating the parts of a whole, as in music, art, &c.: the quality conveyed to the touch by woven fabrics.—*adjs.* **text'ured;** **text'ureless.**—**textual criticism,** critical study directed towards determining the true reading of a text. [L. *texĕre,* *textum,* to weave.]

th- (*obs.*), **th'** (*arch.* or *dial.*), forms of **the,** esp. before a vowel, as in Spenser **thelement,** the element, **thelf,** the elf, **thother,** the other.

thack, *thak, n.* a Scots form of **thatch.**—**under thack and rape,** safely secured under thatch and rope, snug generally.

thae, *dhā, pl.* demons. pron. and demons. adj. (*Scot.*) those. [O.E. *thā;* see **tho.**]

Thai, T'ai, *t'hā'ē, n.* and *adj.* Siamese.—*adj.* **Thaic,** **T'aic,** *t'hā'ik.*—*n.* **Thai'land, T'ai'land,** Siam.

thaim, *dhām,* Scots form of **them.**

thairm, *thārm, n.* (*Scot.*) an intestine: catgut, a musical string. [O.E. *tharm, thearm.*]

thalamus, *thal'ə-məs, n.* an inner room, nuptial chamber: the receptacle of a flower: part of the mid-brain where the optic nerve emerges (**optic thalamus**):—*pl.* **thal'ami.**—*adj.* **thal'amic** (or *thal-am'ik*), of the thalamus.—*n.pl.* **Thalamiflorae** (*-i-flō'rē;* L. *flōs, flōris,* flower), in some systems a subclass of dicotyledons with petals free and stamens hypogynous.—*adj.* **thalamiflo'ral.** [Gr. *thalamos,* an inner room, bedroom.]

thalassian, *tha-las'i-ən, adj.* marine.—*n.* a sea turtle.—*adj.* **thalass'ic,** marine: of the narrow seas.—*ns.* **thalassoc'racy, thalatto'cracy** (Gr. *kratos,* power), sovereignty of the seas; **thalassog'-rapher.**—*adj.* **thalassograph'ic.**—*n.* **thalassog'-raphy,** the science of the sea. [Gr. *thalassa, thalatta,* sea.]

thale-cress, *thāl'-kres, n.* a cruciferous wall plant with small white flowers (*Sisymbrium Thalianum*). [Named after Johann *Thal* (1542-83), German physician.]

thaler, *tä'lər, n.* an obsolete German silver coin worth about 3s. [Ger.; cf. **dollar.**]

Thalia, *tha-lī'ä, n.* the Muse of comedy and pastoral poetry: one of the Graces.—*adj.* **thali'an.** [Gr. *Thaleia, Thaliä—thallein,* to bloom.]

Thalictrum, *thā-lik'trəm, n.* the meadow-rue genus. [Gr. *thaliktron—thallein,* to bloom.]

thallium, *thal'i-əm, n.* a lead-like metal (Tl; at. numb. 81) discovered in 1861.—*adjs.* **thall'ic,** of trivalent thallium; **thall'ous,** of univalent thallium. [Gr. *thallos,* a young shoot, from the bright green line in its spectrum.]

thallus, *thal'əs, n.* a plant body not differentiated into leaf, stem, and root.—*adjs.* **thall'iform;** **thall'ine; thall'oid.**—*n.pl.* **Thallophy'ta** (Gr. *phyton,* plant), the lowest main division of the vegetable kingdom—bacteria, fungi, algae.—*n.* **thall'ophyte,** a member of the Thallophyta. [Gr. *thallos,* a young shoot.]

thalweg, *täl'vähh, n.* the longitudinal profile of the bottom of a river-bed. [Ger.,—*thal* (now *tal*), valley, *weg,* way.]

Thammuz, *tam'ōōz, -uz* (*Milt.*). Same as **Tammuz.**

than, *dhan, dhən, conj.* used after a comparative, actual or felt, to introduce that which is in the lower degree.—*prep.* (popularly, and in some authors, e.g. Shelley) in comparison with (esp. with *whom,* as in Milton).—**any more than he could help,** any more than he had to (i.e. could not help). [O.E. *thonne, thanne, thænne,* than, orig. then.]

than, *dhan, dhən,* an obs. or dial. form of **then.**

thanatism, *than'ə-tizm, n.* belief that the soul dies with the body.—*n.* **than'atist.**—*adj.* **thanatognomon'ic,** indicating death.—*n.* **thanatog'raphy,** a narrative of a death.—*adj.* **than'atoid,** apparently dead: deathly: deadly.—*ns.* **thanatol'ogy,** the scientific study of death; **thanatopho'bia,** a morbid dread of death; **thanatop'sis,** a view of, or reflection upon, death; **thanatō'sis,** gangrene. [Gr. *thanatos,* death.]

thane, *thān, n.* in Old English times a king's companion, one who held by service, hence a noble of lower rank than eorl or ealdorman: (*Scot. hist.*) a hereditary (not military) tenant of the crown.—*ns.* **thā'nage, thane'dom, thane'hood, thane'-ship.** [O.E. *thegn,* servant, follower, courtier, nobleman; cf. O.N. *thegn,* a man, warrior, Ger. *degen,* a soldier, servant, Gr. *teknon,* child.]

thank, *thangk, n.* (usu. in *pl.*) gratitude: expression of gratitude.—*v.t.* to express gratitude to: ironically, to blame.—*n.* **thank'er.**—*adj.* **thank'ful,** grateful: gladly relieved.—*adv.* **thank'fully.**—*ns.* **thank'fulness; thank'ing** (usu. in *pl.; Shak.*), thanks.—*adj.* **thank'less,** unthankful: not expressing thanks for favours: not gaining even thanks.—*adv.* **thank'lessly.**—*ns.* **thank'lessness; thank'-offering,** an offering made to express thanks; **thanks'giver; thanks'giving,** act of giving thanks: a public acknowledgment of divine goodness and mercy: a day (**Thanksgiving Day**) set apart for this, esp. that in the United States since the time of the Pilgrim Fathers, on the last Thursday of November: a form of giving thanks, a grace, that form preceding the last two prayers of morning or evening prayer or of the litany—the *General Thanksgiving.*—Also *adj.*—*adv.* **thank'-worthily.**—*n.* **thank'worthiness.**—*adj.* **thank'-worthy,** worthy of, or deserving, thanks.—*n.* **thank'-you-ma'am,** (*U.S.*) a ridge or hollow in a road that causes those who drive over it to bob their heads.—**be thankit,** (*Scot.*) thank God; **no thanks to,** not owing to, implying that gratitude is far from being due; **thanks, thank you** (*vulg.* **thank'ee**), elliptical forms of thanks be to you, I thank you, or the like; **thanks to,** owing to. [O.E. *thanc, thonc;* cog. with Ger. *dank;* from the root of **think.**]

thar, *t'här, tär, n.* properly the serow: by confusion applied to the tahr. [Nepali *thär.*]

tharborough. See **farborough.**

Thargelia, *thär-gē'li-ä,* or *-jē', n.pl.* an ancient Athenian festival, in honour of Apollo, in the month of *Thargēliōn* (May-June).

that, *dhat, dhət,* demons. pron. and demons. adj. (*pl* **those**) pointing out a person or thing: the former: the more distant: not this but the other: the one to be indicated or defined: (*obs.*) such: often indicating an accompanying snap of the fingers (as *I don't care that, It wants that*).—*rel. pron.* (*sing.* and *pl.*) who, whom, or which (esp. when defining or limiting, not merely linking on an addition).—*adv.* (chiefly *dial.*) to that extent.—*conj.* used to introduce a noun clause, an adverbial clause of purpose, reason, or consequence, or an expression of a wish in the subjunctive (*Shak.*) because.—*n.* **that'ness,** the quality of being a definite thing, that.—**and all that,** and all the rest of that sort of thing—a summary way of dismissing what is vaguely thought of; **and that's that**, and that is the end of that matter: no more of that. [O.E. *thæt*, neut. demons. pron. cog. with Ger. *das, dass*; Gr. *to*, Sans. *tat*; see the.]

thatch, *thach, v.t.* to cover, or roof, with straw, reeds, heather, palm-leaves, or the like.—*v.i.* to do thatching.—*n.* a covering or covering material of the kind.—*n.* **thatch'-board,** a building-board made of straw.—*adj.* **thatched** (or **thatcht**).—*ns.* **thatch'er; thatch'ing,** the act or art of covering with thatch: the materials used for thatching.— Also *adj.*—*adj.* **thatch'less.** [O.E. *thæc*, covering, thatch, and *theccan*, to cover; cog. with Ger. *decken*, L. *tegĕre*, Gr. *stegein*, to cover.]

thauma-, *thaw'mə-,* **thaumat-,** *-mat-,* in composition, wonder, miracle.—*ns.* **thau'masite,** a mineral, hydrated silicate, carbonate, and sulphate of calcium; **thaumatogeny** (*-toj'*), the doctrine of the miraculous origination of life; **thaumatog'-raphy,** description of natural wonders; **thaumatol'atry** (Gr. *latreiā*, worship), wonder-worship; **thau'matrope** (Gr. *tropos*, a turning), an optical toy that combines pictures by persistence of images in the eye; **thaumaturge** (*thaw'mə-turj*), a wonder-worker.—*adjs.* **thaumatur'gic, -al.**—*n.pl.* **thaumatur'gics,** wonderful, esp. magical, performances: feats of legerdemain.—*ns.* **thaumatur'gism; thaumatur'gist; thaumaturgus** (*-tur'gəs*), a wonder-worker: a worker of miracles, applied to certain saints. [Gr. *thauma, -atos,* wonder, *thaumasios,* wonderful, *thaumatourgos* (*—ergon,* work), a wonder-worker.]

thaw, *thaw, v.i.* to melt or grow liquid, as ice: to become so warm as to melt ice: (*fig.*) to become less cold, stiff, or reserved in manner.—*v.t.* to cause to melt.—*n.* the melting of ice or snow by heat: the change of weather that causes it.—*n.* **thaw'er,** an ice-melting agent or apparatus.—*n.* and *adj.* **thaw'ing.**—*adjs.* **thaw'less; thaw'y,** inclined to thaw. [O.E. *thawian.*]

the, *dhē* (emphatic), *dhə* (usu.), *dhi, dhē* (before vowels), *demons. adj.* called the definite article, used to denote a particular person or thing: also to denote a species: (*Scot.*) used instead of the pfx. *to-,* this (as **the day,** today, **the night,** tonight, **the morn,** tomorrow, **the morn's morn,** tomorrow morning, **the year,** this year). [O.E. *the* (supplanting *se*), masc. of *thæt,* that.]

the, *dhə, adv.* (with comparatives) by how much: by so much. [O.E. *thȳ,* by that, by that much, the instrumental case of the def. art.]

Thea, *thē'ä, n.* the tea genus of plants (sometimes including Camellia), giving name to the family **Thea'ceae,** akin to the Guttiferae. [From the root of **tea,** but taken as if from Gr. *theā,* goddess.]

theandric, *thē-an'drik, adj.* at once divine and human. [Gr. *theos,* a god, *anēr, andros,* man.]

theanthropic, *thē-an-throp'ik, adj.* at once divine and human: embodying deity in human forms.— *ns.* **thean'thropism, thean'thropy,** the ascribing of human qualities to deity, or divine qualities to man: a doctrine of union of divine and human; **thean'thropist.** [Gr. *theos,* a god, *anthrōpos,* man.]

thearchy, *thē'ärk-i, n.* a theocracy: a body of divine rulers.—*adj.* **thear'chic.** [Gr. *theos,* a god, *archein,* to rule.]

Theatine, *thē'ə-tīn, n.* a member of a R.C. religious brotherhood founded in 1524 by John Peter Caraffa, bishop of Chieti (L. *Teāte*), afterwards Pope Paul IV., and others, or of a sisterhood modelled on it.—Also *adj.*

theatre (*U.S.* **theater**), *thē'ə-tər, n.* a structure, orig. in the open-air, for drama or other spectacle: a play-house: any place backed by a curving hill-side or rising by steps like the seats of a theatre: a building adapted for scholastic exercises, anatomical or surgical demonstrations, &c.: scene of action, field of operations: the stage: an audience, house: the drama: a body of plays.—*adj.* **the'atral.**—*ns.* **the'atre-goer,** one who habitually goes to the theatre; **the'atre-organ,** a cinema-organ.—*adjs.* **theatric** (*-at'*), **-al,** relating or suitable to, or savouring of, the stage: stagy: histrionic: aiming at or producing dramatic effects.—

v.t. **theat'ricalise,** to adapt to dramatic representation: to make stagy.—*v.i.* to act: to attend the theatre.—*ns.* **theat'ricalism, theatrical'ity,** staginess, artificiality.—*adv.* **theat'rically.**—*n.* **theat'ricalness.**—*n.pl.* **theat'ricals,** dramatic performances: theatrical affairs, properties, or persons.— *v.i.* **theat'ricise** (*-sīz*), to play a part.—*ns.* **theat'ricism,** theatricality, affectation, staginess; **theat'romā'nia,** a craze for play-going; **theat'rophone,** a telephone for transmitting stage dialogue from the theatre. [Gr. *theātron—theaesthai,* to see.]

theave, *thēv, n.* (*prov.*) a young ewe, esp. of the first year.

Thebes, *thēbz, n.* a city of ancient Boeotia (Greece): a city of ancient Egypt.—*adj.* **Thebaic** (*thē-bā'ik*) of Egyptian Thebes: of opium (as an Egyptian product).—*ns.* **Thebaid** (*thē'bā-id*), a poem on the Seven against Thebes (as that by Statius): the district of Thebes (Egyptian or Greek): **thē'baine** (*-bā-ēn, -bə-ēn*), an alkaloid (C₁₉H₂₁NO₃) got from opium.—*adj.* **Thē'ban,** of Thebes: a native of Thebes: a Boeotian.—**Theban year**, the Egyptian year of 365¼ days. [Gr. *Thēbai,* Thebes.]

theca, *thē'kä, n.* a sheath, case, or sac: a spore case: a lobe or loculus of an anther:—*pl.* **thē'cae** (*-sē*).—*adjs.* **thē'cal,** of a theca; **thē'cate,** having a theca. [Latinised from Gr. *thēkē,* case, sheath.]

Thecla, *thek'lä, n.* the hair-streak genus of butterflies.

thee, *dhē, pron., dat.* and *accus.* of **thou**: also (*dial* and formerly by Quakers) *nom.*—*v.t.* to use thee in speaking to.—*v.i.* to use thee. [O.E. *thé, the.*]

thee, *thē, v.i.* (*Spens.*) to prosper, to thrive. [O.E. *théon*; cf. Ger. *gedeihen.*]

theek, *thēk,* a Scots form of **thatch** (*vb.*).

theft, *theft, n.* act of thieving: a thing stolen.—*n.* **theft'boot, -bote,** illegal compounding of a theft.—*adj.* **theft'ūous,** thievish.—*adv.* **theft'ūously.** [O.E. *théofth, thiefth—théof,* thief.]

thegither, *dhə-gidh'ər,* a Scots form of **together.**

thegn, *thān, n.* (*hist.*) the older form of **thane.**

theine, *thē'in, -in, n.* caffeine.—*ns.* **thē'ic,** a tea drunkard; **thē'ism,** a morbid state resulting from over-much tea-drinking. [**Thea.**]

their, *dhār, dhər, pron.* (*gen. pl.*) or *poss. adj.* of or belonging to them.—*pron.* **theirs** (a double genitive used predicatively or absolutely. [O.N. *theirra,* superseding O.E. *thára,* gen. pl. of the def. art.]

theism, *thē'izm, n.* belief in the existence of God, with or without a belief in a special revelation.—*n.* **thē'ist.**—*adjs.* **thēist'ic, -al.** [Gr. *theos,* God.]

Thelemite, *thel'ə-mīt, n.* a monk of Rabelais's imaginary abbey of *Thélème,* of an order whose rule was Do as you like.—Also *adj.* [Gr. *thelēma,* will.]

thelytoky, *thi-lit'ə-ki, n.* parthenogenetic production of female offspring only.—*adj.* **thelyt'okous.** [Gr. *thēlys,* female, *tokos,* birth.]

them, *dhem, dhəm, pron., dat.* and *accus.* of **they.** [O.N. *theim* or O.E. (Anglian) *thæm* (dat.).]

theme, *thēm, n.* a subject set or proposed for discussion, or spoken or written about: a thesis, brief essay or exercise: a ground for action: the stem of a word without its inflexions: (*mus.*) subject, a short melody developed with variations or otherwise: an administrative division of the Byzantine empire.—*n.* **thē'ma** (or *them'ä*), theme:—*pl.* **them'ata.**—*adj.* **thematic** (*thi-mat'ik*).—*adv.* **themat'ically.**—**thematic vowel,** a vowel that comes between root and inflexion. [Gr. *thēma, -atos—*root of *tithēnai,* to place, set: partly through O.Fr. *tesme.*]

Themis, *them'is, n.* Greek goddess of law and justice. [Gr. *Themis.*]

themselves, *dhəm-selvz', pron., pl.* of **himself, herself, itself.** [**them, self.**]

then, *dhen, dhan, adv.* at that time: afterward: immediately: at another time: further, again: on the other hand, at the same time: for that reason, therefore: in that case.—*adj.* being at that time.—*n.* that time.—**by then,** by that time; **and there,** at once and on the spot. [O.E. *thonne, thanne, thænne.*]

then, *dhən, conj.* (*Spens.,* &c.). Same as **than.**

thenar, *thē′när, n.* the palm : the ball of the thumb : the sole.—Also *adj.* [Gr. *thĕnăr, -ăros.*]

thence, *dhens, adv.* from that place : from those premises : from that time : from that cause.— *advs.* **thence′forth, thencefor′ward,** from that time forward : from that place onward. [M.E. *thennes—thenne* (O.E. *thanon,* thence), with adverbial genitive ending ; cf. **hence, whence.**]

theo-, *thē′ō-, -o-,* or *-o′-,* in composition, god. [Gr. *theos,* a god.]

Theobroma, *thē-ō-brō′mä, n.* the chocolate or cocoa genus of Sterculiaceae.—*n.* **theobro′mine** (*-mēn, -min, -min*), an alkaloid got from the chocolate nut. [Gr. *brōma,* food.]

theocracy, *thē-ok′rə-si, n.* that constitution of a state in which God, or a god, is regarded as the sole sovereign, and the laws of the realm as divine commands rather than human ordinances—the priesthood necessarily becoming the officers of the invisible ruler : the state thus governed.—*n.* **theocrat** (*thē′ō-krat*), a divine or deified ruler.— *adjs.* **theocrat′ic, -al.** — *adv.* **theocrat′ically.** [Gr. *theokratiā—krateein,* to rule.]

theocrasy, *thē-ok′rə-si,* or *thē′ō-krā′si, n.* a mixture of religions : the identification or equating of one god with another or others : a mystic intimacy with deity reached through profound contemplation. [Gr. *krāsis,* a mixing.]

Theocritean, *thē-ok-ri-tē′ən, adj.* after the manner of *Theocritus* (3rd cent. B.C.), the greatest of Greek pastoral poets : pastoral, idyllic.

theodicy, *thē-od′i-si, n.* a vindication of the justice of God in establishing a world in which evil exists. —*n.* and *adj.* **theodicē′an.** [Gr. *dikē,* justice.]

theodolite, *thē-od′ə-līt, n.* a surveying instrument for measuring horizontal and vertical angles. [Ety. unknown.]

theogony, *thē-og′ə-ni, n.* the birth and genealogy of the gods.—*adjs.* **theogonic** (*thē-ə-gon′ik*), **-al.** —*n.* **theog′onist,** a writer on theogony. [Gr. *theogoniā—gonē,* birth, generation.]

theology, *thē-ol′ə-ji, n.* the science of God.—*ns.* **theologaster** (*-gas′tər*), a shallow theologian ; **theol′ogate** (*-gāt*), a seminary for R.C. priests ; **theol′oger** (*-jər*), a theologian ; **theologian** (*thē-ə-lō′jyən*), one well versed in theology : a divine, a professor of or writer on divinity, esp. in R.C. usage, a theological lecturer attached to a cathedral or collegiate church.—*adjs.* **theologic** (*thē-ə-loj′ik*), **-al.**—*adv.* **theolog′ically.**—*v.t.* **theol′ogise,** to render theological.—*v.i.* to discourse, speculate, &c., on theology.—*ns.* **theol′ogiser ; theol′ogist,** a theologian ; **the′ologue** (*-log*), a theologian : (*U.S.*) a theological student. [Gr. *theologiā— logos,* discourse.]

theomachy, *thē-om′ə-ki, n.* war among or against the gods, as by the Titans and giants : opposition to the divine will.—*n.* **theom′achist.** [Gr. *theomachiā—machē,* a battle.]

theomancy, *thē′ō-man-si, n.* divination by means of oracles, or of persons inspired immediately by some divinity.—*adj.* **theoman′tic.** [Gr. *theomanteiā,* spirit of prophecy—*manteiā,* divination.]

theomania, *thē-ō-mā′ni-ä, n.* religious madness : belief that one is a god.—*n.* **theoma′niac.** [Gr. *maniā,* madness.]

theomorphic, *thē-ō-mor′fik, adj.* having the form or likeness of a god : in the image of God.—*n.* **theomor′phism.** [Gr. *theomorphos,* of divine form—*morphē,* form.]

Theopaschite, *thē-ō-pas′kīt, n.* a Monophysite, as believing that God had suffered and been crucified.—*adj.* **Theopaschitic** (*-kit′ik*).—*n.* **Theopas′-chitism** (*-kit-izm*). [Gr. *paschein,* to suffer.]

theopathy, *thē-op′ə-thi, n.* a religious emotion aroused by meditation about God.—*adj.* **theopath′ic.** [Gr. *pathos,* experience, emotion.]

theophagy, *thē-of′ə-ji, n.* the sacramental eating of a god.—*adj.* **theoph′agous** (*-gəs*). [Gr. *phagein,* to eat.]

theophany, *thē-of′ə-ni, n.* a manifestation or appearance of deity to man.—*adj.* **theophanic** (*thē-ō-fan′ik*). [Gr. *theophaneia,* a vision of God, exhibition of gods' statues—*phainein,* to show.]

theophilanthropy, *thē-ō-fil-an′thrə-pi, n.* a deistical system of religion drawn up under the French Directory in 1796, and designed to take the place of Christianity.—*adj.* **theophilanthrop′ic.** — *ns.* **theophilan′thropism ; theophilan′thropist.** [Fr. *théophilanthropie,* love to God and man ; cf. **philanthropy.**]

theophobia, *thē-ō-fō′bi-ä, n.* morbid fear of God : hatred of God.—*n.* **theophobist** (*-of′ə-bist*). [Gr. *phobos,* fear.]

theophylline, *thē-ō-fil′ēn, -īn, -in, n.* an isomeride of theobromine found in tea. [**Thea,** and Gr. *phyllon,* leaf.]

theopneust, *thē′op-nūst, adj.* divinely inspired.—*adj.* **theopneust′ic.**—*n.* **theopneust′y,** divine inspiration. [Gr. *theopneustos — pneustos,* inspired— *pneein,* to breathe.]

theorbo, *thē-orb′ō, n.* a large double-necked bass lute.—*n.* **theorb′ist.** [It. *tiorba.*]

theorem, *thē′ə-rəm, n.* a demonstrable or established but not self-evident principle : a proposition to be proved.—*adjs.* **theoremat′ic, -al.**—*adv.* **theoremat′ically.**—*n.* **theorematist** (*-rem′ə-tist*). —*adjs.* **theoret′ic, -al,** pertaining, according, or given to theory : not practical : speculative.—*n.* (usu. in *pl.*) the speculative parts of a science.—*adv.* **theoret′ically.**—*n.* **the′oric, the′orique,** (*Shak.*) theory, speculation.—*v.i.* **the′orise,** to form a theory : to form opinions solely by theories : to speculate.—*ns.* **the′oriser ; the′orist,** a theoriser : one given to theory and speculation : one who is expert in the abstract principles of a subject ; **the′ory,** an explanation or system of anything : an exposition of the abstract principles of a science or art : speculation as opposed to practice. [Gr. *theōrēma, -atos,* spectacle, speculation, theorem, *theōriā,* view, theory—*theōreein,* to be a spectator, to view.]

theosophy, *thē-os′ə-fi, n.* divine wisdom : immediate divine illumination or inspiration claimed to be possessed by specially gifted men, along with abnormal control over natural forces.—*ns.* **theosoph** (*thē′ə-sof*), **theos′opher, theos′ophist.**— *adjs.* **theosoph′ic, -al.**—*adv.* **theosoph′ically.**— *v.i.* **theos′ophise,** to practise theosophy.—*n.* **theos′ophism,** theosophical tenets. — *adj.* **theosophist′ical,** theosophical : sophistical in theology. [Gr. *theosophos,* wise in things of God—*sophos,* wise.]

theotechny, *thē-ō-tek′ni, n.* the employment of gods as the machinery of a poem.—*adj.* **theotech′nic.** [Gr. *technē,* art.]

theotokos, *thē-ot′o-kos, n.* the mother of God, a title of the Virgin Mary repudiated by Nestorius, accepted by the Council of Ephesus. [Gr.,—*tokos,* birth.]

theow, *thāow, n.* (*O.E. hist.*) a slave. [O.E. *théow.*]

theralite, *thĕr′ə-līt, n.* a holocrystalline igneous rock composed essentially of plagioclase, nepheline, and augite. [Gr. *thēraein,* to hunt, seek after, *lithos,* stone, because its discovery was expected.]

Therapeutae, *ther-ə-pū′tē* (L. *ther-ä-pū′tī*), *n.pl.* a traditional ascetic sect, allied to the Essenes, living chiefly near Alexandria.—*adj.* **therapeu′tic,** pertaining to the healing art : curative.—*adv.* **therapeu′tically.**—*n.* (*pl.* in form, treated as *sing.*) **therapeu′tics,** that part of medicine concerned with the treatment and cure of diseases.—*ns.* **therapeu′tist,** one versed in therapeutics ; **ther′apist ; ther′apy,** therapeutics. [Gr. *therapeutēs,* servant, worshipper, medical attendant—*therapeuein,* to take care of, to heal, *therapeiā,* service, treatment.]

there, *dhār, dhər, dhr, adv.* in that place : at that point : to that place : used also (unstressed) without any meaning of its own to allow the subject to follow the predicate, and also in corresponding interrogative sentences, &c.—*n.* that place.—*interj.* expressing reassurance, finality, accompanying a blow, &c.—*advs.* **there′about, -s** (also *-bowts′*), about or near that place : near that number, quantity, or degree ; **thereaft′er,** after or according to that : accordingly ; **thereagainst′,** against that ; **thereamong′,** among that or those ; **thereanent′,** (*Scot.*) concerning that matter ; **thereat′,** at that place or occurrence : on that account ; **there′away,**

in that direction: thereabout; **therebeside'**, beside that; **thereby'**, beside that: about that amount: by that means: in consequence of that; **therefor'**, for that; **therefore** (*dhār'fər*), for that reason: consequently; **therefrom'**, from that; **therein'**, in or into that or it: (*Scot.*) indoors; **thereinaft'er, thereinbefore'**, later, earlier, in the same document; **therein'to**, into that place.— *n.* **there'ness**, the property of having relative situation or existence.—*advs.* **thereof'**, of that: from that; **thereon'**, on that; **thereout'**, out of that: (*Scot.*) out of doors; **therethrough'**, through that: by that means; **thereto'**, **there-un'to**, to that: in addition; **there'tofore**, before that time; **thereun'der**, under that; **thereupon'**, upon that: (*Shak.*) in consequence of that: immediately; **therewith'**, with that: thereupon; **there'withal**, with that: immediately after: in addition; **therewithin'**, within that.—**there and then**, forthwith; **there or thereabouts**, somewhere near. [O.E. *thær*; akin to the, that, &c.]

theriac, *thē'ri-ak*, **theriaca**, *thē-rī'ə-kä*, *ns.* (*arch.*) an antidote to venomous bites, &c., esp. an electuary made with honey.—*adj.* **thēri'acal**. [Gr. *thēriakē*—*thērion*, dim. of *thēr*, a wild beast.]

therio-, theri-, ther-, *thēr'-, -i-, -ō-*, in composition, beast, mammal.—*adj.* **therianthrop'ic** (Gr. *anthrōpos*, man), combining human and animal forms. —*n.* **therian'thropism**, representation or worship of therianthropic forms or gods.—*n.pl.* **Theriodontia** (*-ō-don'shyä, -ti-ä*; Gr. *odous, odontos*, a tooth), an extinct order of reptiles with teeth like mammals.—*ns.* **theriol'atry** (Gr. *latreiā*, worship), animal-worship; **ther'iomorph**(Gr. *morphē*, form), an animal form in art.—*adj.* **theriomorph'ic**, beastlike: of theriomorphism.—*n.* **theriomorph'ism**, belief in gods of the form of beasts.—*n.pl.* **Theriomor'pha** (**Theromor'pha**), an extinct order of reptiles with affinities to the Labyrinthodont Amphibia and mammals.—*n.* **theriomorphō'sis** (or *-mor'*), transformation into a beast.—*adjs.* **theriomor'phous**, beastlike: mammal-like: of the Theriomorpha; **ther'oid**, beastlike.—*n.* **therol'ogy**, the study of mammals. [Gr. *thēr*, and *thērion*, a wild beast.]

therm, *thərm*, *n.* a hot bath: a bathing establishment: 100,000 British thermal units (used as a unit in reckoning payment for gas).—*n.pl.* **thermae** (*-ē*), hot springs or baths.—*adj.* **therm'al**, pertaining to heat: warm.—*adv.* **therm'ally**.—*adjs.* **therm'ic, -al**, of heat.—*adv.* **therm'ically**.—*n.* **therm'ion** (Gr. *ion*, going), an electrically charged particle emitted by an incandescent body.—*adj.* **thermion'ic** (**thermionic valve, or tube**, a vacuum tube containing a heated cathode from which electrons are emitted, an anode for collecting some or all of these electrons, and generally, additional electrodes for controlling their flow to the anode).—*ns.* **thermion'ics** (treated as *sing.*), the science of thermions; **therm'it, therm'ite**, a mixture of aluminium powder with an oxide of a metal (esp. iron), which when ignited evolves great heat, used for local heating and welding.— *adj.* **thermochem'ical**.—*ns.* **thermochem'ist**, **thermochem'istry**, the study of heat changes accompanying chemical action; **therm'o-couple**, a pair of metals in contact giving a thermo-electric current.—*adj.* **thermodynam'ic**.—*n.* **thermodynam'ics**, the science of heat as a mechanical agent.—*adj.* **thermo-elec'tric**.—*ns.* **thermoelectric'ity**, electricity developed by the unequal heating of bodies, esp. between a junction of metals and another part of a circuit; **thermogenesis** (*-jen'*), production of heat, esp. in the body by physiological processes.—*adjs.* **thermogenet'ic, thermogen'ic**.—*ns.* **therm'ogram**, a thermograph record; **therm'ograph**, a self-registering thermometer; **thermog'raphy**, any process of writing involving the use of heat.—*adj.* **thermolā'bile**, readily decomposed by heat.—*n.* **thermol'ogy**, the science of heat; **thermol'ysis** (Gr. *lysis*, loosing), dissociation or dissolution by heat: loss of body heat. — *adj.* **thermolyt'ic**. — *n.* **thermometer** (*-om'i-tər*), an instrument for measuring temperature.—*adjs.* **thermometric** (*-ə-met'rik*), **-al**.—*adv.*

thermomet'rically. — *ns.* **thermomet'rograph**, a self-registering thermometer; **thermom'etry**; **therm'onasty**, nastic movement in relation to heat.—*adjs.* **therm'ophil(e)** (*-fil*), **thermophil'ic**, **thermoph'ilous**, requiring, or thriving best in, a high temperature. — *n.* **therm'opile** (*-pīl*; L. *pīla*, a pillar), a number of thermo-electric elements connected in series or in parallel, yielding an electric current when the junctions are heated.— *adj.* **thermoplast'ic**, plastic when heated.—*n.* any resin that can be melted and cooled repeatedly without appreciable change in properties.—*ns.* **Ther'mos** (in full **Thermos flask or bottle**; trade name), a Dewar-flask; **therm'oscope**, an instrument for detecting changes of temperature.—*adj.* **thermoscop'ic**, indicating, or sensitive to, temperature changes.—*adv.* **thermoscop'ically**.—*adjs.* **thermosett'ing**, setting, after melting and moulding, with change of properties; **thermosta'ble**, not readily decomposed by heating.—*n.* **therm'ostat** (Gr. *statos*, standing), a device for keeping temperature steady.—*adj.* **thermostat'ic**.—*adv.* **thermostat'ically**.—*adj.* **thermotact'ic**, of or showing thermotaxis.—*n.* **thermotax'is**, a taxis towards a position of higher or lower temperature.—*adjs.* **thermot'ic, -al**, of or due to heat. —*n.* **thermot'ics**, the science of heat.—*adj.* **thermotrop'ic**.—*n.* **thermot'ropism** (Gr. *tropos*, turning), orientation determined by temperature differences.—**thermal springs**, natural springs of hot water; **thermonuclear weapon**, hydrogen bomb, in which the reaction is fusion, not fission. [Gr. *thermos*, hot, *thermē*, heat, *thermotēs*, heat.]

Thermidor, *thər-mi-dor'*, *n.* eleventh month in calendar of first French Republic, lasting from 19th July to 17th August.—*n.* **Thermidō'rian**, one who took part in fall of Robespierre on 9th Thermidor (27th July 1794). [Gr. *thermē*, heat, *dōron*, gift.]

thero-. See **therio-**.

Thersitic, *thər-sit'ik*, *adj.* like *Thersītēs*, a shameless railer among the Greeks at Troy.

thesaurus, *thi-saw'rəs*, *n.* a treasury: a storehouse of knowledge. [L.,—Gr. *thēsauros*.]

these, *dhēz*, *demons. adj.* and *demons. pron.*, *pl.* of **this**. [O.E. *thǣs*, a by-form of *thās*, pl. of *thés*, *thēos*, *this*, this; cf. **those**.]

thesis, *thē'sis*, *thes'is*, *n.* (Gr. *pros.* and *mus.*) lit. a setting down, a down-beat: hence the strong position in a bar or foot: understood by the Romans as the weak position: used in English in both senses (opp. to *arsis*): a position or that which is set down or advanced for argument: a subject for a scholastic exercise, esp. one presented for a doctorate: an essay on a theme:—*pl.* **theses** (*thē'sēz*).—*adjs.* **thetic** (*thet'ik*), **-al**, positively asserting: bearing the thesis.—*adv.* **thet'ically**. [Gr. *thĕsis*, from the root of *tithenai*, to put, set.]

Thesmophoria, *thes-mō-phō'ri-ä*, *n.pl.* an ancient Greek married women's festival in honour of Demeter *Thesmophoros* (law-giving). [Gr. *thesmophŏria*.]

thesmothete, *thes'mō-thēt*, *n.* a law-giver, esp. one of the six junior archons in ancient Athens. [Gr. *thesmothetēs*—*thesmos*, law, *thetēs*, a placer, setter.]

Thespian, *thes'pi-ən*, *adj.* pertaining to tragedy: tragic.—*n.* a tragic actor: an actor. [Gr. *Thespis*, founder of Greek tragedy.]

theta, *thē'tä*, *thā'tä*, *n.* the eighth (orig. ninth) letter of the Greek alphabet (Θ, θ) transliterated *th*, its sound an aspirated *t*, but in modern Greek like English *th*: as a Greek numeral θ'=9, ͵θ=9,000: a mark of condemnation (from the θ for *thanatos*, death, used in balloting). [Gr. *thēta*; Semitic.]

thetch, *thech*, *v.i.* (Spens.) to thatch. [O.E. *theccan*.]

thete, *thēt*, *n.* (Gr. *hist.*) orig. a serf: a poor freeman in Athens under Solon's constitution. [Gr. *thēs*, *thētos*.]

thetic. See under **thesis**.

theurgy, *thē'ur-ji*, *n.* magic by the agency of good spirits: miraculous divine action.—*adjs.* **theur'gic**, **-al**.—*n.* **the'urgist**. [Gr. *theourgiā*—*theos*, a god, *ergon*, work.]

thew, *thū*, *n.* (used chiefly in *pl.* **thews, thewes**) custom: trait: manner: moral quality: later (*Shak.*) bodily quality, muscle or strength.—*adjs.*

thewed, (*Spens.*) mannered : (later) muscular; **thew'less** (see **thowless**); **thew'y,** muscular, strong. [O.E. *théaw,* manner.]

they, *dhā, pron., nom. pl.,* used as *pl.* of he, she, it : often used as a *sing.* (with *pl. vb.*) of common gender, he or she, people in general, some. [M.E. *thei*—O.N. *theirr,* which supplanted *hi* (O.E. *hie*).]

thiamine, *thī'ə-mēn, n.* vitamin B₁. [Gr. *theion,* sulphur, and **amine.**]

thiasus, *thī'ə-səs, n.* a company or troop of worshippers, esp. a Bacchic rout. [Gr. *thiasos.*]

thible, *thib'l, thib'l,* **thivel,** *thiv'l, thīv'l, n.* (*Northern*) a porridge-stick. [Origin unknown.]

thick, *thik, adj.* having a great (or specified) distance in measurement from surface to surface in lesser dimension : deep : dense : viscous : close set or packed : crowded : (*fig.*) intimate, in close confidence : abundant : frequent, in quick succession : aboundingly covered or occupied : foggy : opaque : dull : gross : husky, muffled : indistinctly articulate : (*slang*) excessive, approaching the intolerable.—*n.* the thickest part of anything : the midst : (*slang*) a stupid person : (*Spens.*) a thicket.—*adv.* thickly : closely : frequently : fast : to a great (or specified) depth.—*v.t.* and *v.i.* (*Spens., Shak.*) to make or become thick.—*adjs.* **thick'-and-thin',** unwavering in devotion to party or principle; **thick'-com'ing,** (*Shak.*) coming close upon one another.—*v.t.* and *v.i.* **thick'en,** to make or become thick or thicker.—*ns.* **thick'ener; thick'ening,** a making or becoming thicker : a thickened place : material added to something to thicken it.—Also *adj.*—*n.* **thick'et** (O.E. *thiccet*), a dense mass of trees or shrubs.—*adjs.* **thick'eted; thick'ety; thick'-eyed,** dim-sighted; **thick'-grown,** (*Shak.*).—*n.* **thick'head,** a blockhead : any bird of an Australian family (Pachycephalidae) akin to flycatchers and shrikes. — *adjs.* **thick'-head'ed,** having a thick head or skull : stupid; **thick'ish,** somewhat thick.—*n.* **thick'-knee,** the stonecurlew (Oedicnemus), a large plover with thickened knees.—*adj.* **thick'-lipped** (*Shak.*).—*n.* **thick'-lips,** (*Shak.*) a negro.—*adv.* **thick'ly.**—*n.* **thick'ness,** quality or degree of being thick : the space between outer surfaces : a layer.—*adjs.* **thick'-pleached,** (*Shak.*) closely interwoven; **thick'-ribbed** (*Shak.*); **thick'set,** closely set or planted : having a short, thick body.—*n.* a thicket : a stout cotton.—*adj.* **thick-sight'ed,** (*Shak.*) dim-sighted. — *n.* **thick'skin,** a blockhead. — *adj.* **thick'-skinned',** having a thick skin : insensitive : indifferent to criticism or insult.—*n.* **thick'-skull,** a blockhead.—*adjs.* **thick'-skulled,** having a thick skull : doltish; **thick'-sown,** planted closely : close-set.—*n.* **thick'un,** (*slang*) a sovereign : a crown.—**a bit thick,** more than one can reasonably be expected to put up with; **lay it on thick,** to flatter or praise extravagantly; **through thick and thin,** in spite of all obstacles : without any wavering. [O.E. *thicce;* Ger. *dick.*]

thick, thicky, *dhik, dhik'i.* See **thilk.**

thief, *thēf, n.* one who takes unlawfully what is not his own, esp. by stealth : a flaw in a candle-wick that causes guttering :—*pl.* **thieves** (*thēvz*).—*ns.* **thief'-catcher, -taker,** one whose business is to arrest thieves : a detective.—*adj.* and *adv.* **thief'-like.** [O.E. *théof :* cf. Ger. *dieb.*]

thieve, *thēv, v.i.* to practise theft : to steal.—*n.* **thiev'ery,** the practice of thieving.—*n.* and *adj.* **thiev'ing.**—*adj.* **thiev'ish,** (*Shak.*) infested by thieves : given to, or like, theft or stealing : thief-like : furtive.—*adv.* **thiev'ishly.**—*n.* **thiev'ishness.** [O.E. *théofian,* to thieve, and *théof,* thief.]

thig, *thig, v.i.* (*Scot.*) to beg : to live on alms.—*v.t.* to beg : to get by begging :—*pa.t.* and *pa.p.* **thigg'it.**—*ns.* **thigg'er; thigg'ing—thigging and sorning,** extortionate begging and sponging. [O.N. *thiggja;* cf. O.E. *thicgan,* to take.]

thigh, *thī, n.* the thick fleshy part of the leg from the knee to the trunk.—*n.* **thigh'-bone,** the bone of the leg between the hip-joint and the knee, the femur. [O.E. *théoh* (Anglian *théh*); O.N. *thjó;* O.H.G. *dioh.*]

thigmotropism, *thig-mot'rə-pizm, n.* (*biol.*) response

to stimulus of touch.—*adj.* **thigmotropic** (*-mə-trop'ik*). [Gr. *thigma, -atos,* touch, *tropos,* a turning.]

thilk, *dhilk, adj.* and *pron.* (*dial.*) the same, that same : this.—Also (*S.W. England*) **thick** (*dhik*), **thick'y.** [the **ilk.**]

thill, *thil, n.* the shaft of a vehicle.—*ns.* **thill'er, thill'-horse,** a shaft-horse, or the last of a team. [Poss. O.E. *thille,* board, plank.]

thill, *thil, n.* (*prov.*) underclay or floor of a coalseam : a bed of fireclay. [Ety. unknown.]

thimble, *thim'bl, n.* a cover for the finger, used in sewing : an object of similar form.—*v.t.* to use a thimble.—*v.t.* to use a thimble on.—*ns.* **thim'ble-case; thim'bleful,** as much as a thimble will hold : a small quantity :—*pl.* **thim'blefuls; thim'blerig,** a sleight-of-hand trick in which the performer conceals, or pretends to conceal, a pea or small ball under one of three thimble-like cups.—*v.i.* to cheat by such means.—*v.t.* to manipulate in this or analogous way.—*ns.* **thimb'le-rigger; thim'blerigging.** [O.E. *thýmel,* thumb-stall — *thúma,* thumb.]

thin, *thin, adj.* (*comp.* **thinn'er;** *superl.* **thinn'est**) having little thickness : slim : lean : freely mobile : watery : dilute : of little density : rarefied : sparse : slight : flimsy : wanting in body or solidity : meagre : poor : tinkling.—*n.* that which is thin.—*adv.* **thinly.**—*v.t.* to make thin or thinner : to make less close or crowded (with *away, out,* &c.).—*v.i.* to grow or become thin or thinner :—*pr.p.* **thinn'ing;** *pa.t.* and *pa.p.* **thinned.**—*adjs.* **thin'-belly,** (*Shak.*) narrow in the belly; **thin'-faced** (*Shak.*).—*adv.* **thin'ly.**—*ns.* **thinn'er; thin'ness; thinn'ing.**—*adjs.* **thinn'ish,** somewhat thin; **thin'-skinned,** having a thin skin : sensitive : irritable. — *n.* **thin'-skinned'ness.** — *adjs.* **thin'-sown,** sparsely sown; **thin'-spun,** drawn out fine; **thin'-walled.**—**a thin time,** a time of little enjoyment. [O.E. *thynne;* Ger. *dünn;* O.N. *thunnr.*]

thine, *dhīn, pron., gen.* of **thou,** used predicatively or absolutely, belonging to thee : thy people : that which belongs to thee : adjectivally, esp. before a vowel or *h,* thy. [O.E. *thín.*]

thing, *thing, n.* (*hist.*) an assembly, parliament, court, council : a matter, affair : a circumstance : a fact : an event : an entity : that which exists or can be thought of : an inanimate object : a living being (now esp. in kindly reproach) : a possession : a piece of writing composition, &c. : (in *pl.*) clothes, esp. a woman's additional outdoor garments : (in *pl.*) utensils, esp. for the table.—*ns.* **thing'amy, thing'ummy, thing'umbob, thing'umajig** (*coll.*), what-d'you-call-him (-her, -it) : what 's-his-name, &c.—used when one cannot or will not recall the name; **thing'hood,** state or fact of being a thing : substantiality; **thing'iness, thing'liness,** reality, objectivity : materialistic or matter-of-fact turn of mind; **thing'-in-itself,** a noumenon, the Ger. *ding an sich;* **thing'ness,** character or fact of being a thing : reality.—*adj.* **thing'y,** real : actual : objective : matter-of-fact.—**do the handsome thing by,** to treat generously; **know a thing or two,** to be shrewd; **make a good thing of it,** to reap a good advantage from; **old thing,** (*coll.*) a familiar disrespectful kindly mode of address, irrespective of age; **the thing,** that which is conventional, fashionable, approved, right, or desirable. [O.E. and O.N. *thing,* parliament, object, &c.: Norw., Sw., Dan. *ting,* parliament; Ger. *ding,* thing.]

think, *thingk, v.i.* to exercise the mind (often with *about, of, on, upon*) : to revolve ideas in the mind : to judge : to be of opinion : to consider : to bethink oneself : to conceive or hit on a thought.—*v.t.* to form, conceive, or revolve in the mind : to have as a thought : to aspire or form designs (with *of*) : to imagine : to judge : to believe or consider : to expect : to purpose, design : (*Milt.*) to believe to exist : to bring by thinking : (*pa.t.* and *pa.p.* **thought,** *thawt*).—*n.* (*coll.*) a spell of thinking : a thought.—*adj.* **think'able,** capable of being thought : conceivably possible.—*n.* **think'er.**—*n.* and *adj.* **think'ing.**—*adv.* **think'ingly.**—**I don't think,** I disbelieve : (*coll.*) a warning that what was said was ironical; **I shouldn't think of it,** I would not under any conditions; **think aloud,** to utter one's thoughts unintentionally; **think better of,** to change one's mind concerning on reflection; **think for,** to expect; **think little of,** to have a poor opinion of—opp. to **think much,** or **well, of; think long,** to yearn: to weary (from deferred hopes or boredom); **think out,** to devise, project completely: to solve by a process of thought; **think over,** to reconsider at leisure; **think shame,** to be ashamed. [O.E. *thencan*; cog. with Ger. *denken*.]

think, *thingk, v.i.* (*impers., arch.* with *me* or other dat. pron. prefixed; otherwise *obs.*) to seem :— *pa.t.* **thought** (*thawt*). [O.E. *thyncan,* to seem.]

thio-, *thī´ō-,* in composition, sulphur, indicating in chemistry a compound theoretically derived from another by substituting an atom or more of sulphur for oxygen.—*ns.* **thi´o-acid,** an acid analogous in constitution to an oxy-acid, sulphur taking the place of oxygen; **thiocy´anate,** a salt of **thiocyan´ic acid,** HSCN; **thiopent´one** (see **pentothal**); **thi´o-salt,** a salt of a thio-acid. [Gr. *theion,* sulphur.]

thir, *dhir, pl. demons. pron.* and *demons. adj.* (*Scot.*) these. [Origin obscure.]

third, *thэrd, adj.* the last of three: equal to one of three equal parts.—*n.* a third part: (*mus.*) an interval of two (conventionally called three) diatonic degrees: a note at that interval: (*golf*) a handicap of a stroke at six holes out of eighteen.—*adv.* in the third place.—*v.t.* to divide by three: to support after the seconder.—*adj.* **third´-class.**—*adv.* **third´-class´.**—*adj.* **third´-hand´.**—*n.* **third´ing,** a third part.—*adv.* **third´ly,** in the third place.—*adjs.* **third´-party,** of a person other than the principals (as insured and insurer); **third´-rate,** of the third order.—*n.* **thirds´man,** a mediator.—**third degree** (see **degree**); **third man,** (*cricket*) a fielder on the offside between point and slip. [O.E. *thridda*; cf. Ger. *dritte,* Gr. *tritos,* L. *tertius.*]

thirdborough, *thэrd´bur-э, n.* (*hist.*) an underconstable. [Supposed to be from O.E. *frithborh,* a surety for peace (see under **frith**).]

thirl, *thэrl, n.* (*prov.*) a hole: an opening: a short passage between two headings in a mine.—*v.t.* to pierce: to thrill.—*v.i.* to vibrate, tingle, thrill. [O.E. *thyrel,* hole—*thurh,* through; cf. **thrill**.]

thirl, *thэrl, n.* a form of **thrall**: thirlage.—*v.t.* to bind or subject: to confine, restrict.—*n.* **thirl´age,** a form of servitude by which the grain produced on certain lands had to be ground (or at least paid for) at a certain mill.

thirst, *thэrst, n.* the uneasiness caused by want of drink: vehement desire for drink: eager desire for anything.—*v.i.* to feel thirst.—*n.* **thirst´er.**—*adj.* **thirst´ful.**—*adv.* **thirst´ily.**—*n.* **thirst´iness.**—*adjs.* **thirst´less**; **thirst´y,** suffering from thirst: dry: parched: vehemently desiring. [O.E. *thurst* (n.), *thyrstan* (vb.); cf. Ger. *durst, dürsten,* Gr. *tersesthai,* L. *torrēre,* to dry.]

thirteen, *thэr´tēn, n.* and *adj.* and *n.* three and ten.—*adj.* **thir´teenth** (or *-tēnth´*), the last of thirteen: equal to one of thirteen equal parts.—*n.* a thirteenth part.—*adv.* **thirteenth´ly.** [O.E. *thréotiene, -téne—thréo,* three.]

thirty, *thэr´ti, adj.* and *n.* three times ten.—*adj.* **thir´tieth,** the last of thirty: equal to one of thirty equal parts.—*n.* a thirtieth part.—*n., adj.,* and *adv.* **thir´tyfold.**—*adjs.* **thir´tyish,** somewhere about the age of thirty; **thirty-two´mo,** (for *tricesimo secundo,* 32mo) in sheets folded to give 32 leaves (64 pages).—*n.* a book so constructed. [O.E. *thritig—thréo,* three, *-tig,* suff. denoting ten.]

this, *dhis, sing. demons. pron.* or *adj.* denoting a person or thing near, topical, just mentioned, or about to be mentioned: the present moment: the place where the speaker is: (*pl.* **these**).—*adv.* (*Shak.*) thus.—*n.* **this´ness,** the quality of being this, not something else, haecceity. [O.E., neut. of *thes, théos, this* (instrumental *this, thýs*; nom. pl. *thǽs, thǽs*).]

thistle, *this´l, n.* a prickly composite plant (Carduus, Cnicus, Onopordon, &c.).—*n.* **this´tle-down,** the tufted feathery parachutes of thistle seeds.—*adj.*

this´tly, like a thistle: overgrown with thistles. [O.E. *thistel.*]

thither, *dhidh´эr* (*Spens.* often **thether**), *adv.* to that place: to that end or result.—*adj.* on the far side.—*advs.* **thith´erward, -s,** toward that place. [O.E. *thider.*]

thivel. See **thible.**

thixotrope, *thiks´э-trōp, n.* a substance whose viscosity is temporarily altered by shaking or stirring.—*adj.* **thixotrop´ic** (*-trop´ik*).—*n.* **thixotropy** (*-ot´rэ-pi*), the property of such substances. [Gr. *thixis,* touching, *tropos,* a turn.]

thlipsis, *thlip´sis, n.* constriction: compression. [Gr. *thlīpsis—thlibein,* to press.]

tho, *dhō, pl.* demons. adj. (*Spens.*) those. [O.E. *thá, pl. of se, séo, thæt,* that.]

tho, *dhō, adv.* (*Spens.*) then. [O.E. (and O.N.) *thá.*]

tho´. Same as **though.**

thoft, *thoft, n.* (*prov.*) a rowing-bench. [O.E. *thofte.*]

thole, *thōl, n.* a pin in the side of a boat to keep the oar in place: a peg.—Also **thowl, thowel.**—*n.* **thole´-pin,** a peg, thole. [O.E. *thol*; Du. *dol,* O.N. *thollr.*]

thole, *thōl, v.t.* and *v.i.* (now *Scot.*) to endure. [O.E. *tholian,* to suffer; Goth. *thulan,* O.N. *thola*; O.H.G. *dolén,* Ger. *geduld,* patience, *dulden,* to suffer, L. *tollēre,* Gr. *tolmaein.*]

tholus, *thō´lэs, n.* a round building, dome, cupola, or tomb :—*pl.* **thō´li** (*-lī*).—Also **tholos** (*thol´os*; *pl.* **thol´oi**).—*n.* **tholobate** (*thol´ō-bāt*; from root of Gr. *bainein,* to go), the substructure of a dome or cupola. [Gr. *tholos.*]

Thomism, *tō´mizm, n.* the doctrines of *Thomas* Aquinas (1226-74).—*n.* and *adj.* **Thō´mist.**—*adjs.* **Thōmist´ic,** *-al.*

thon, *dhon,* **thon´der,** *-эr,* unexplained modern Scots forms of **yon, yonder.**

thong, *thong, n.* a strap: a strip: the lash of a whip or crop. [O.E. *thwang.*]

Thor, *thor, n.* the Scandinavian thunder-god, Old English Thunor. [O.N. *Thórr.*]

Thorah. See **Torah.**

thorax, *thō´raks, n.* (Gr. *ant.*) a corslet: the part of the body between the head and abdomen, in man the chest, in insects the division that bears legs and wings.—*adj.* **thoracic** (*-ras´-*).—**thoracic duct,** the main trunk of the vessels conveying lymph in the body. [Gr. *thōrāx, -ākos.*]

thorium, *thō´ri-эm, n.* a radioactive metal (Th; at. numb. 90) resembling aluminium.—*n.* **thō´rite,** a mineral, thorium silicate, in which it was first discovered, by Berzelius. [*Thor,* the god.]

thorn, *thorn, n.* a sharp hard part (leaf, stem, or root) of a plant: an animal spine: anything prickly: a spiny plant: hawthorn: the Old English and Old Norse letter þ (*th*).—*v.t.* to set with thorns: to prick.—*ns.* **thorn´apple,** a poisonous plant (*Datura Stramonium,* or other species) of the potato family, with a prickly capsule: a haw; **thorn´back,** a ray with nail-like crooked spines in its back; **thorn´-bush,** any thorny shrub, esp. hawthorn; **thorn´-devil,** the Australian Moloch lizard.—*adj.* **thorned.**—*ns.* **thorn´-hedge,** a hedge of hawthorn; **thorn´iness.**—*adjs.* **thorn´less**; **thorn´set,** set or beset with thorns.—*n.* **thorn´tree,** a thorny tree, esp. a hawthorn.—*adj.* **thorn´y,** full of thorns: prickly: troublesome: harassing.—**thorn in the flesh,** any cause of constant irritation, from 2 Cor. xii. 7. [O.E. *thorn*; O.N. *thorn,* Ger. *dorn.*]

thorough, *thur´э, adj.* passing or carried through or to the end: complete: entire: out-and-out: assiduous and scrupulous in completing work.—*prep.* (*obs.*) through.—*n.* that which goes through, a passage: the blind and obstinately tyrannical policy of Strafford and Laud in administering civil and ecclesiastical affairs without regard to opposite convictions.—*ns.* **thor´ough-bass,** (*mus.*) a bass part all through a piece, usu. with figures to indicate the chords: (loosely) harmony: (*erron.*) a deep bass; **thor´oughbrace,** (*U.S.*) a leather band supporting the body of a vehicle: a stage-coach.—*adj.* **thor´oughbred,** thoroughly or completely bred or trained: bred from a dam and sire of the best blood, as a horse, and having the qualities supposed to depend thereon.—*n.* an animal, esp. a horse, of pure blood—of race-horses, one all of whose ancestors for seven generations (five in America) are recorded in the stud-book.—*n.* **thor′oughfare,** a passage or way through: a road open at both ends: a public way or street: right of passing through.—*adj.* **thor′ough-go′ing,** going through or to the end: going all lengths: complete: out-and-out. — *adv.* **thor′oughly.** — *n.* **thor′oughness.** — *adj.* **thor′ough-paced,** thoroughly or perfectly paced or trained: complete.—*n.* **thor′oughwax, thor′ow-wax,** the plant hare′s-ear, from the stem seeming to grow (wax) through the leaves. [The longer form of **through.**]

ΊΟΓΡ, thorpe, *thorp, n.* a hamlet: a village. [O.E. *thorp, throp*; O.N. *thorp,* Goth. *thaurp,* Ger. *dorf.*]

ΊΟse, *dhōz, demons. pron.* and *adj., pl.* of **that.** [O.E. *thās,* pl. of *thes,* this.]

ΊΟth, *thōth, thoth, n.* the ancient Egyptian ibis-headed god of art, science, &c. [Gr. *Thōth*—Egypt. *Tehuti.*]

ΊΟu, *dhow, pron.* of the second person sing., the person addressed (now generally used only in solemn address).—*v.t.* to apply the pronoun *thou* to:—*pa.t.* and *pa.p.* **thou′d.** [O.E. *thú*; Goth. *thu,* Doric Gr. *ty,* L. *tū,* Sans. *tvam.*]

ΊΟu, *thow,* a coll. abbrev. of **thousand.**

ΊΟugh, *dhō, conj.* admitting: allowing: even if: notwithstanding that.—*adv.* nevertheless: however:—**as though,** as if. [O.N. *thauh, thó*; O.E. *théah, théh,* Ger. *doch.*]

ΊΟught, *thawt, pa.t.* and *pa.p.* of **think.** [O.E. *thōhte,* pa.t., *(ge)thōht,* pa.p.]

ΊΟught, *thawt, n.* thinking: mind: consciousness: reasoning: deliberation: that which one thinks: notion: idea: fancy: consideration: opinion: meditation: design: care: considerateness: purpose: resolution: intention: (*obs.*) grief, anxiety: a very slight amount, a ′ suspicion.′ — *adjs.* **thought′ed,** having thoughts: **thought′en, (***Shak.***)** firm in belief, assured: **thought-ex′ecuting,** carrying out the wishes of a master: (*Shak.*) perh. acting with the speed of thought: **thought′ful,** full of thought: employed in meditation: attentive: considerate: expressive of or favourable to meditation.—*adv.* **thought′fully.**—*n.* **thought′fulness.**—*adj.* **thought′less,** unthinking: incapable of thinking: carefree: careless: inattentive: inconsiderate.—*adv.* **thought′lessly.**—*ns.* **thought′lessness**; **thought′-reader**; **thought′-reading,** discerning what is passing in another′s mind by any means other than the ordinary and obvious.—*adj.* **thought′-sick, (***Shak.***)** sick with the thought.—*ns.* **thought′-trans′ference,** telepathy; **thought′-wave,** a wave-like progress of a thought among a crowd or a public: a sudden accession of thought in the mind: an impulse in some hypothetical medium assumed to explain telepathy.—**on second thoughts,** on reconsideration; **take thought,** to bethink oneself: to conceive a purpose: (*obs.*) to be anxious or grieved; **upon, with, a thought,** (*Shak.*) in a moment: with the speed of thought. [O.E. *(ge)thōht.*]

ΊΟus, *dhowz,* a Northern contracted form of **thou is, thou art** (*Spens.*), and of **thou sal,** thou shalt.

ΊΟusand, *thow′zand, n.* and *adj.* ten hundred: often used vaguely or hyperbolically.—*adj., adv.,* and *n.* **(a) thou′sandfold,** a thousand times as much.—*n.* **thou′sand-legs,** a centipede or millipede.—*adjs.* **thou′sand-pound′,** weighing, costing, priced at, a thousand pounds; **thou′sandth,** the last of a thousand: equal to one of a thousand equal parts.—*n.* a thousandth part.—*adj.* **thou′sand-year,** lasting, or coming once in, a thousand years. —**one in (of) a thousand,** anything exceedingly rare or excellent. [O.E. *thúsend*; Ger. *tausend,* Goth. *thúsundi.*]

ΊΟwel, thowl. See **thole** (1).

ΊΟwless, *thow′lis, adj.* (*Scot.*) pithless: listless: inert. [App. **thewless.**]

ΊΓae, *thrā,* another form of Scots **frae.**

ΊΓall, *thrawl, n.* a slave, serf: slavery, servitude: a stand for barrels, pans, &c.—*adj.* (*arch.*) enslaved. —*v.t.* to enslave.—*n.* **thral′dom** (also **thrall′-dom),** slavery: bondage. [O.E. *thrǽl*—O.N. *thrǽll.*]

thrang, *thrǎng,* Scots form of **throng.**

thrapple, *thrǎp′l,* a Scots form of **thropple.**

thrash, *thrash, v.t.* to thresh: (with *out*) to discuss exhaustively, or arrive at by debate: to beat soundly: to defeat thoroughly.—*v.i.* to lash out, lay about one: (*naut.*) to force one′s way.—*n.* an act of threshing or thrashing.—*n.* **thrash′er,** a thresher: a thresher-shark: one who thrashes.—*n.* and *adj.* **thrash′ing,** threshing: beating.—*ns.* **thrash′ing-floor, -machine, -mill** (see **threshing).** [Orig. a dialect form of **thresh.**]

thrash, *thrǎsh,* **thresh,** *thresh, n.* (*Scot.*) a rush (plant). [Obscurely conn. with **rush.**]

thrasher, *thrash′ər,* **thresher,** *thresh′ər, n.* an American bird akin to the mocking-bird. [Perh. Eng. dial. *thresher,* thrush.]

thrasonic, -al, *thrə-, thrā-son′ik, -l, adjs.* like *Thrasōn,* the bragging soldier, a stock character in Greek New Comedy, or *Thrasō* in Terence′s *Eunuchus*: boastful, bragging.—*adv.* **thrason′-ically.**

thrave, *thrāv,* **threave,** *thrēv, n.* two stooks of (usu.) twelve sheaves each: two dozen: a good number. [Scand.; cf. Ice. *threfi,* Dan. *trave.*]

thraw, *thraw,* a Scots form of **throw** with some old senses preserved; also of **throe,** with senses overlapping **throw.**—*v.t.* to turn: to twist: to wring: to distort: to wrest: to cross, thwart.—*v.i.* to turn: to twist: to writhe: to sway: to go counter: to be perverse: (*pa.t.* **threw**; *pa.p.* **thrawn).**—*adj.* **twisted:** distorted: wry.—*n.* a twist: a fit of perversity: a throe.—*adj.* **thrawn,** twisted: wry: cross-grained, perverse.—**dead thraw,** the agony of death; **heads and thraws,** side by side, the head of the one by the feet of another.

thrawart, thraward, *thraw′ərt, adj.* (*Scot.*) froward: crooked. [M.E. *fraward*; see **froward**; perh. influenced by **thraw**; cf. **thrae.**]

thread, *thred, n.* a very thin line of any substance, esp. linen (*U.S.* cotton), twisted or drawn out: a filament: a fibre: the prominent spiral part of a screw: a continuous connecting element.—*v.t.* to pass a thread through: to string on a thread: to pass or pierce through, as a narrow way: to furnish with a thread.—*adj.* made of linen or cotton thread. —*adj.* **thread′bare,** worn to the bare thread: having the nap worn off: hackneyed: used till its novelty or interest is gone.—*ns.* **thread′bareness**; **thread′-cell,** in jellyfishes, &c., a stinging cell that throws out a stinging thread.—*adj.* **thread′en, (***Shak.***)** made of thread.—*ns.* **thread′er**; **thread′iness**; **thread′-lace,** lace made of linen thread; **thread′-paper,** a piece of thin soft paper for wrapping up a skein of thread; **thread′-worm,** any member of the Nematoda, more or less thread-like worms, many parasitic, others free-living: esp. *Oxyuris vermicularis,* parasitic in the human rectum.—*adj.* **thread′y,** like thread: slender: containing, or consisting of, thread.—**thread and thrum,** all, the good and bad together; **thread of life,** the thread imagined to be spun and cut by the Fates. [O.E. *thrǽd*; cf. **throw, thraw.**]

threap, threep, *thrēp, v.t.* (*Scot.* and *Northern*) to rebuke: to maintain persistently: to insist: to urge, to press eagerly.—*v.i.* to dispute: (*pa.t.* and *pa.p.* **threap′it, threep′it).**—*n.* stubborn insistence or assertion: accusation: a traditional belief. [O.E. *thréapian,* to rebuke.]

threat, *thret, n.* declaration or indication of an intention to inflict, punish, or hurt: a denunciation of evil or punishment: an appearance of impending evil: menace.—*v.t.* and *v.i.* (*Shak., Milt.,* &c.) to threaten.—*v.t.* **threat′en,** to offer a threat of, or against: to intimidate by threats: to seem to impend over: to indicate danger of, or to.—*v.i.* to use threats: to portend evil.—*adj.* **threat′ened.**—*n.* **threat′ener.**—*n.* and *adj.* **threat′ening.**—*adv.* **threat′eningly,** menacing. [O.E. *thréat* (n.), *thréatian, thréatnian* (vbs.); cf. Ger. *verdriessen,* to tremble, L. *trūdĕre,* to thrust.]

three, *thrē, adj.* and *n.* two and one.—*n.* a set of three: a symbol for three: a card with three pips: a score of three points, strokes, &c.: an article of a size denoted by three: the third hour after midnight or midday.—*adjs.* **three'-bott'le**, able to drink three bottles of wine at a sitting; **three'-card**, played with three cards; **three'-cent'red**, of an arch, composed of circular arcs with three different centres; **three'-cleft**, cut halfway down into three lobes; **three'-colour**, involving or using three colours as primary; **three'-cor'nered**, triangular in form or section: having three competitors or three members; **three'-deck**.—*n.* **three'-deck'er**, a ship with three decks or guns on three decks: a building or structure with three floors or tiers: a pulpit with three levels: a three-volume novel.—*adjs.* **three'-dimen'sional**, having three dimensions; **three-far'thing**.—*n.sing.* **three-far'things**, a silver coin of Queen Elizabeth, distinguished from a penny by a rose behind the queen's head.—*adj. and adv.* **three'fold**, in three divisions: three times as much.—*n.* **three'fold-ness**.—*adj.* **three'-foot**, measuring or having three feet.—*n.* **three-halfpence** (thrē-hā'pens), a penny and a halfpenny: a coin of that value.—*adj.* **three-halfpenny** (thrē-hāp'ni).—*n.* **three-halfpennyworth, threeha'porth** (thrē-hāp'ərth). —*adjs.* **three'-hand'ed**, having three hands: played by three players; **three'-leaved** or **-leafed**, having three leaves or leaflets: having leaves in threes; **three'-legged**, having three legs: of a race, run by pairs of runners, each with a leg tied to his partner's; **three'-man**, (*Shak.*) worked or performed by three men; **three'-mast'ed**.—*n.* **three'-mast'er**, a ship with three masts. — *n.* and *adj.* **three'-month'ly**, quarterly.—*n.* **three'ness**, the state of being three. —*adjs.* **three'-nooked**, (*Shak.*) three-cornered; **three'-pair (-of-stairs)**, on a third floor.—*n.* a room so situated.—*adjs.* **three'-part**, composed in three parts or for three voices; **three'-part'ed**, consisting of three parts: parted in three: divided into three nearly to the base.—*adv.* **three'-parts**, to the extent of three-fourths.—*n.* **threepence** (threp', thrip', thrup'əns), money, or a coin, of the value of three pence.—*adj.* **threepenny** (threp', thrip', thrup'ni or -ə-ni), sold or offered at threepence: of little worth: mean, vulgar.—*n.* a coin of the value of threepence (also **three-penny bit**).— *n.* **threepennyworth** or **three-penn'orth** (thrē-pen'i-wərth or thrē-pen'ərth), also (chiefly *Scot.*) **threep'enceworth**. — *n.pl.* **three'-per-cents'**, bonds or other securities paying three per cent. interest, esp. a portion of the consolidated debt of Great Britain.—*adj.* **three'-pile**, having loops of three threads.—*n.* (*Shak.*) the finest kind of velvet.—*adjs.* **three'-piled**, three-pile: piled three high; **three'-ply**, having three layers or strands; **three'-pound**, costing or weighing three pounds.—*n.* **three-pound'er**, a thing that weighs three pounds: a gun that shoots a three-pound ball.—*adj. and adv.* **three'-quar'ter**, to the amount of three-fourths.—*n.* a three-quarter back. —*n.* and *adj.* **three'score**, sixty.—*adj.* **three'-sid'ed**, having three sides.—*n.* **three'some**, a company of three persons: a game or dance for three.— *adj.* for three: triple.— *adjs.* **three'-square**, equilaterally triangular; **three'-suit'ed**, (*Shak.*) allowed three suits of clothes a year as a serving-man; **three'-vol'ume**, in three volumes; **three'-way**, giving connexion in three directions from a centre.—**three balls**, the pawnbroker's sign; **three colour process**, a method of printing pictures in three colours—yellow, red, blue—from blocks prepared by photography; **three-quarter back**, a player between half-backs and full-back; **three-quarter face**, an aspect between full face and profile; **three-speed gear**, a gear-changing contrivance with three possibilities; **three times three**, three cheers thrice repeated; **three-went way**, (*dial.*) a meeting-place of three roads. [O.E. *thrēo*, fem. and neut. of *thrī*; Goth. *threis*, Ger. *drei*, L. *trēs, trēs, tria*, Gr. *treis, treis, tria*, Sans. *tri*.]

threep. See **threap**.

thremmatology, threm-ə-tol'ə-ji, *n.* the science of breeding domestic animals and plants. [Gr. *thremma, -atos*, a nursling, *logos*, discourse.]

threnody, thrēn', thren'ə-di, *n.* an ode or song of lamentation.—Also **threne** (thrēn; *Shak.*). **thren'ode** (-ōd), **thren'os** (*Shak.*).—*adjs.* **thren-et'ic, -al**; **thrēnō'dial, threnodic** (-od').—*n.* **thren'odist**. [Gr. *thrēnōidiā, thrēnos*, a lament, *ōidē*, song.]

thresh, thresh, *v.t.* to beat out, subject to beating out, by trampling, flail, or machinery: to thrash —*v.t.* to thresh corn: to thrash.—*n.* an act of threshing.—*ns.* **thresh'el**, a flail: a flail-like weapon, the morgenstern; **thresh'er**, one who threshes: a flail: a threshing-machine or a beating part of it: a fox-shark (also **thresh'er-shark**); **thresh'er-whale**, a grampus.—*n. and adj.* **thresh'ing**.—*ns.* **thresh'ing-floor**, a surface on which grain is threshed; **thresh'ing-machine, -mill**, one for threshing corn. [O.E. *therscan*; cf. Ger. *derschen*, to thresh; see **thrash**.]

thresh. See **thrash** (2). **thresher.** See **thrasher**.

threshold, thresh'ōld, *n.* the sill of a house door: the place or point of entering: the outset: the limit of consciousness: the point at which a stimulus begins to bring a response.—*adj.* at or constituting a threshold. [O.E. *therscold, therscwald, threscold* app.—*therscan*, to thrash, thresh, in its older sense of trample, tread.]

thretty, thret'i, a dial. form of **thirty**.

threw, thrōō, *pa.t.* of **throw**.

thrice, thrīs, *adv.* three times. [M.E. *thriës*—O.E. *thrīwa, thriga*, thrice—*thrī*, three, with adverbial gen. ending *-es*.]

thrid, thrid, *n.* (*Spens.*) a thread.—*v.t.* (*obs.*) to thread. [**thread**.]

thridace, thrid'es, *n.* inspissated lettuce juice. [Gr. *thridax*, lettuce.]

thrift, thrift, *n.* state of thriving: frugality: prosperity: increase of wealth: gain: profitable occupation: savings: the sea-pink (Armeria), a seaside and alpine plant of the Plumbaginaceae.—*adv.* **thrift'ily**.—*n.* **thrift'iness**.—*adj.* **thrift'less**, not thrifty: extravagant: not thriving.—*adv.* **thrift'lessly**.—*n.* **thrift'lessness**.—*adj.* **thrift'y** (*compar.* **thrift'ier**, *superl.* **thrift'iest**), showing thrift or economy: thriving by frugality: (*U.S.*) prosperous, in good condition. [**thrive**.]

thrill, thril, *v.t.* to pierce: to affect with a strong glow or tingle of sense or emotion.—*v.i.* to pierce, as something sharp: to pass tinglingly: to quiver: to feel a sharp, shivering sensation.—*n.* a tingle: a shivering feeling or emotion.—*adj.* **thrill'ant** (*Spens.*) piercing.—*n.* **thrill'er**, a sensational story —*adj.* **thrill'ing**.—*adv.* **thrill'ingly**.—*n.* **thrill'ingness**.—*adj.* **thrill'y**. [O.E. *thyrlian*, to bore—*thyrel*, a hole; Ger. *drillen*, to drill a hole.]

Thrips, thrips, *n.* a genus of Thysanoptera, mostly minute black insects, common in flowers (*erron.* **thrip**): popularly extended to others of the order to leaf-hoppers, and to other small insects:—*pl.* **thripses**. [Gr. *thrips, thripos*, a wood-worm.]

thrissel, thristle, thris'l, thrus'l, Scots forms of **thistle**. [Poss. influenced by *thrist*, **thrust**.]

thrist, thrist, thrist'y, -i, old forms (*Spens.*) of **thirst** (*n.* and *vb.*), **thirsty**.

thrive, thrīv, *v.i.* to grow: to grow healthily and vigorously: to get on, do well: to prosper: to increase in goods: to be successful: to flourish:—*pa.t.* **thrōve**, also **thrīved**; *pa.p.* **thriven** (thriv'n) —*adjs.* **thrive'less**, thriftless; **thriven** (thriv'n) grown, developed: successful.—*n.* **thri'ver** (*rare*) —*n.* and *adj.* **thrī'ving**.—*adv.* **thrī'vingly** (*rare*) —*n.* **thri'vingness**. [O.N. *thrifa*, to grasp.]

thro', thro. See **through**.

throat, thrōt, *n.* the passage from mouth to stomach: the forepart of the neck, in which are the gullet and windpipe: voice: a narrow entrance, aperture, or passage: the narrow part, as of a vase, a corolla: a groove under a coping or moulding: (*naut.*) the end of a gaff next the mast.—*ns.* **throat'-band, -strap, -latch**, a band about the throat.—*adjs.* **throat'ed**, with a throat; **throat'-full**, full to the throat.—*adv.* **throat'ily**.—*n.* **throat'iness**; **throat'wort**, the nettle-leaved bellflower (*Campanula Trachelium*) once reputed good for throat ailments: the giant bellflower (*C. latifolium*).—*adj.* **throat'y**, sounding as from the throat: hoarse:

croaking : deep or full-throated : somewhat sore-throated : full or loose-skinned about the throat : potent in swallowing.—**cut the, one's, throat,** usu., to cut the jugular vein : to pursue some course ruinous to one's interests ; **give one the lie in his throat,** to accuse one to his face of a lie ; **sore throat,** an inflamed and uncomfortable con-dition of the tonsils and neighbouring parts ; **thrust, ram, down one's throat,** to assert or force upon one insistently without listening to an answer. [O.E. *throte* ; cf. **throttle**.]

throb, *throb, v.i.* to beat strongly, as the heart or pulse : (*pr.p.* **throbb'ing** ; *pa.t.* and *pa.p.* **throbbed**). —*n.* a beat or strong pulsation.—*n.* and *adj.* **throbb'ing.**—*adv.* **throbb'ingly.**—*adj.* **throb'less.** [M.E. *throbben* ; poss. conn. with L. *trepidus,* trembling.]

throe, earlier (*Shak., Spens.*) **throw(e),** *thrō,* (*Scot.*) **thraw,** *thraw, n.* a spasm : a paroxysm : a pang : esp. a birth-pang.—*v.t.* to subject to pangs.—*v.i.* to suffer pangs.—**in the throes,** in travail : in the struggle of composition : in the thick. [M.E. *thrahes, throwes, thrawes* ; perh. there have been cross-influences between O.E. *thrawu,* pang, *thrág,* paroxysm, *thrówian,* to suffer, *thráwan,* to twist, throw ; see also **thraw.**]

thrombus, *throm'bas, n.* a clot of blood in a living vessel.—*n.* **throm'bin,** an enzyme that causes clotting.—*v.t.* **thrombose** (*-bōs'*), to cause throm-bosis in.—*n.* **thrombō'sis,** clotting in a vessel during life. [Gr. *thrombos,* clot.]

throne, *thrōn, n.* a king's, pope's, or bishop's chair of state : kingship : an angel of the third order.— *v.t.* to enthrone : to exalt.—*v.i.* to sit in state, as on a throne.—*adjs.* **throned** ; **throne'less.**—*n.* **throne'-room.** [Gr. *thronos,* a seat.]

throng, *throng, n.* a crowd : a great multitude : crowding.—*v.t.* and *v.i.* to crowd : to press : (*Shak.*) to press hard.—*adj.* (*prov.*) crowded : busy : intimate. — *adjs.* **thronged,** packed, crowded : (*Shak.* with *up*) overpowered ; **throng'ful,** thronged.—*n.* and *adj.* **throng'ing.** [O.E. *gethrang* —*thringan,* to press.]

thropple, *throp'l* (*Scots* **thrapple,** *thráp'l*), *n.* the throat : the windpipe, gullet of an animal.—*v.t.* to throttle : to strangle. [Poss. O.E. *throtbolla,* wind-pipe, gullet—*throte,* throat, *bolla,* boll.]

throstle, *thros'l, n.* the song-thrush or mavis : a machine for drawing, twisting, and winding fibres (from its sound).—*n.* **thros'tle-cock,** a male song-thrush or (*dial.*) missel-thrush. [O.E. *throstle* ; Ger. *drossel,* L. *turdus,* thrush.]

throttle, *throt'l, n.* the throat or windpipe : a throttle-valve : a throttle-lever.—*v.t.* to choke by pressure on the windpipe : to strangle : to check the flow of : to cut down the supply of steam, or of gas and air, to or in.—*v.i.* to breathe hard, as when nearly suffocated.—*ns.* **thrott'le-lever,** a lever that opens and closes a throttle-valve ; **thrott'le-pipe,** the vertical pipe between the throttle-valve and the dry-pipe of a locomotive ; **thrott'ler** ; **thrott'le-valve,** a valve regulating the supply of steam or of gas and air in an engine.— *n.* and *adj.* **thrott'ling.**—**throttle down,** to slow down by closing the throttle. [App. dim. of **throat.**]

through, *thrōō, prep.* from end to end, side to side, or boundary to boundary of, by way of the interior : from place to place within : everywhere within : by way of : along the passage of : clear of : among : from beginning to end of : (*U.S.*) up to and including, to or until the end of : by means of : in conse-quence of.—*adv.* from one end or side to the other : from beginning to end : to the end : all the way : clear : into a position of having passed : in con-nexion or communication all the way.—*adj.* passing, or serving for passage, all the way without inter-ruption.—*ns.* **through'-bolt,** a bolt that passes through from side to side of what it fastens ; **through'fare,** (*Shak.*) same as **thoroughfare.** —*adj.* **through'-ganging,** (*Scot.*) thorough-going. —*n.* **through'-going** (*Scot. -gaun*), a scolding.— *adj.* passing through : active, energetic.—*advs.* **through'ly,** (*obs.*) same as **thoroughly** : (*arch.*) far through ; **through'-other,** (*Scot.*) in indis-criminate mixture : higgledy-piggledy.—*adj.* (*Scot.*)

confusedly mixed : without orderliness.—*prep.* **throughout',** in, into, through, during, the whole of.—*adv.* in every part : everywhere.—*ns.* **through-stone,** a bonder or bond-stone in building ; **through'-tick'et,** a ticket for the whole of a jour-ney ; **through'-traff'ic,** the traffic between two centres at a distance from each other ; **through'-train,** a train that goes the whole length of a long route.—**be through** (*Shak.* ; now chiefly *Scot.* and *U.S.*), to have done : to be at an end : to have no more to do ; **through and through,** through the whole thickness : completely : in every point ; **through the day, night,** (*Scot.*) in the daytime, night-time. [O.E. *thurh* ; Ger. *durch.*]

through-stone, -stane, *thrōōhh'-, throhh'-stōn, -stän, n.* (*Scot.*) a horizontal tombstone on pillars. [O.E. *thrúh,* sarcophagus, and **stone.**]

throve, *thrōv, pa.t.* of **thrive.**

throw, *thrō, v.t.* to wind or twist together, as yarn : to form on a wheel, as pottery : to turn, with a lathe : to cast : to hurl : to fling : to project : to emit : to make a cast of dice amounting to : to dislodge from the saddle : to cast down in wrest-ling : (*U.S.*) to defeat, get the better of : to give birth to : to produce : to render suddenly : to cause to be in some place or condition, esp. with suddenness : to put : to execute, perform.—*v.i.* to cast or hurl : to cast dice : (*Spens.*) to lay about one : (*pa.t.* **threw,** *thrōō* ; *pa.p.* **thrown,** *thrōn*).—*n.* a deflection : amplitude of movement : an act of throwing : a cast, esp. of dice or a fishing-line : (*Spens.*) a blow : the distance to which anything may be thrown : (*geol.*) the vertical displacement of a fault.—*ns.* **throw'-back,** a reversion : a set-back ; **throw'-down,** a home-made firework, slapbang ; **throw'er** ; **throw'-in,** an act of throw-ing in : (*football*) a throw from the touch-line to put the ball back into play.—*n.* and *adj.* **throw'ing.** —*ns.* **throw'ing-stick,** a stick for throwing a spear : a throw-stick ; **throw'ing-table,** a potter's wheel.—*adj.* **thrown,** twisted : cast, flung.—*ns.* **thrown'-silk,** organzine ; **throw'-out,** an act of throwing out : a rejected thing ; **throw'ster,** one who throws silk : a gambler ; **throw'-stick,** a weapon thrown whirling from the hand, as the boomerang.—**throw about,** (*Spens.*) to cast about or try expedients ; **throw a fit,** (*slang*) to have a fit, behave wildly ; **throw a party,** (*slang*) to give a party ; **throw away,** to reject, toss aside : to squander : to fail to take advantage of : to bestow unworthily ; **throw back,** to retort, to refuse : to revert to some ancestral character ; **throw down,** to demolish ; **throw in,** to interject : to throw the ball in : to add as an extra ; **throw in one's lot** (see **lot**) ; **throw off,** to divest oneself of : to dis-engage or release oneself from : to utter or compose offhand ; **throw on,** to put on hastily ; **throw oneself into,** to engage heartily in ; **throw one-self on,** or **upon,** to assail : to entrust oneself to the power of ; **throw open,** to cause to swing wide open, to make freely accessible ; **throw out,** to cast out : to reject : to expel : to emit : to utter : to cause to project : to disconcert : to distance, leave behind ; **throw over,** to discard or desert ; **throw up,** to erect hastily : to show prominently : to give up, to resign : to vomit. [O.E. *thráwan,* to turn, to twist ; Ger. *drehen,* to twist ; see also **thraw, throe.**]

throw, *thrō, n.* (*Spens.*) a while. [O.E. *thrág, thráh.*]

thrum, *thrum, n.* the end of a weaver's thread : any loose thread or fringe : bits of coarse yarn.—*adj.* made of or having thrums.—*v.t.* to furnish, cover, or fringe with thrums :—*pr.p.* **thrumm'ing** ; *pa.t.* and *pa.p.* **thrummed.**—*n.* **thrum'-cap,** a cap made of thrums or of coarse, shaggy cloth.—*adjs.* **thrum'-eyed,** short-styled with the stamens in the throat of the corolla (esp. of a Primula : opp. to *pin-eyed*) ; **thrumm'y,** made of, or like, thrums. —**thrummed hat,** (*Shak.*) a hat made of fringed with, or covered with thrums. [O.E. *thrum* (found in composition) ; Ger. *trumm.*]

thrum, *thrum, v.t.* and *v.i.* to strum : to hum, drone, repeat in sing-song : to drum with the fingers : (*pr.p.* **thrumm'ing** ; *pa.t.* and *pa.p.*

thrummed).—*n.* a strumming: (*dial.*) a purring.
—*n.* thrumm′er.—*n.* and *adj.* thrumm′ing.—
adv. thrumm′ingly.

thrush, *thrush*, *n.* the throstle or mavis (*song-thrush*, *Turdus musicus*): the storm-cock (*missel-thrush*, *T. viscivorus*): extended to others of the genus and to birds more or less similar. [O.E. *thrysce*.]

thrush, *thrush*, *n.* an inflammation in the frog of the horse's hoof: an infantile disease of the mouth and throat. [Origin obscure.]

thrust, *thrust*, *v.t.* and *v.i.* to push: to force: to stab, pierce: to intrude: (*pa.t.* and *pa.p.* **thrust**).—*n.* a push: a pushing force: the force that drives an aircraft forward: the horizontal force on the abutment of an arch: a stab.—*ns.* **thrust′er**; **thrust′-hoe**, a hoe worked by pushing.—*n.* and *adj.* **thrust′ing**.—*n.* **thrust′-plane**, a plane along which a block of rocks has overridden higher rocks almost horizontally—a reversed fault of very low hade. [O.N. *thrýsta*, to press.]

thrust, *thrust*, *v.i.* (*Spens.*) to thirst.—*n.* thirst.

thud, *thud*, *n.* a dull sound as of a heavy body falling soft.—*v.i.* to make a thud.—*v.t.* to beat. [Perh. O.E. *thyddan*, to strike.]

thug, *thug*, properly *t′hug*, *n.* (*India*) a member of a religious fraternity that murdered stealthily by strangling or poisoning with datura, extirpated 1826-35: a cut-throat: a ruffian.—*ns.* **thuggee′** (**thagi**), **thugg′ery**, **thugg′ism**, the practice and superstitition of the thugs. [Hind. *thag*, cheat.]

Thuja, *thōō′jä*, -*yä*, *n.* the arbor-vitae genus. [Gr. *thyiä*, a kind of juniper.]

Thule, *thū′lē*, *n.* an island six days N. of Orkney discovered by Pytheas (4th cent. B.C.), variously identified as Shetland, Iceland, Norway, Jutland: hence (usu. *ultima Thule*) the extreme limit.—*ns.* **thu′lia**, thulium oxide, separated from erbia by Cleve; **thu′lite**, a red zoisite found in Norway; **thu′lium**, a metallic element (Tm; at. numb. 69). [L. *Thūlē*—Gr. *Thoulē* (understood by Cleve as Scandinavia).]

thumb, *thum*, *n.* the short, thick digit, consisting of two phalanges, on the radial side of the human hand: the part of a glove that covers it: in other animals the corresponding digit, or that of the hind foot, esp. when opposable: a thumb's breadth, an inch.—*v.t.* to handle awkwardly: to play, spread, press, touch, wear, or smudge with the thumb: to read assiduously: to signal to with the thumb.—*adj.* **thumbed**, having thumbs: marked by the thumb, worn.—*n.* **thumb′-hole**, a hole to insert the thumb in.—*n.pl.* **thumb′(i)kins**, (*Scot.*) the thumbscrew.—*n.* **thumb′-latch**, a latch worked by pressure of the thumb.—*adj.* **thumb′less**.—*ns.* **thumb′ling**, a pygmy; **thumb′-mark**, a mark left by the thumb as on a book: a thumbprint.—*adj.* **thumb′-marked**.—*ns.* **thumb′-nail**, the nail of the thumb: a sketch (**thumb-nail sketch**) as small as a thumb-nail; **thumb′piece**, a piece that is pressed by the thumb or receives the thumb; **thumb′pot**, a very small flower-pot; **thumb′print**, an impression of the markings of the thumb, taken as a means of identification; **thumb′-ring**, (*Shak.*) a ring worn on the thumb: a ring to protect an archer's thumb; **thumb′screw**, an old instrument of torture for compressing the thumb by means of a screw; **thumb′-stall**, a covering or sheath for the thumb; **thumb′-tack**, (*U.S.*) a drawing-pin.—*adj.* **thumb′y**, grubby with thumb-marks: like thumbs, clumsy, awkward.—**bite one's thumb**, to make a sign threatening revenge; **by rule of thumb**, **in a** rough-and-ready practical manner, found by experience to be convenient; **keep one's thumb on**, to keep secret; **one's fingers all thumbs**, awkward and fumbling; **under one's thumb**, under one's domination. [O.E. *thúma*; Ger. *daumen*.]

thummim, *thum′im*. See **urim**.

thump, *thump*, *n.* a dull heavy blow or its sound.—*v.t.* and *v.i.* to beat with a dull heavy blow: to make such a sound.—*n.* **thump′er**, one who, or that which, thumps: (*coll.*) anything very big, a big lie, &c.—*adj.* **thump′ing**, (*coll.*) unusually big. [Prob. imit.]

thunder, *thun′dər*, *n.* the deep rumbling sound after

a flash of lightning: any loud noise: a thunder-bolt: vehement denunciation. — *v.i.* to make thunder: to sound as thunder: to inveigh or denounce with vehemence.—*v.t.* to give out with noise or violent denunciation: to deal like thunder.—*adj.* **thun′der-and-light′ning**, in glaring colours.—*n.* a glaringly coloured woollen cloth.—*ns.* **thun′der-bearer**, (*Shak.*) Jove; **thun′derbolt**, a missile of the thunder-god: a popularly imagined material body seen as lightning: a stone identified therewith, as a belemnite, a stone axe: anything sudden and overwhelming: a fulmination: a violent and irresistible destroyer or hero; **thun′der-clap**, a sudden crash of thunder; **thun′der-cloud**, a cloud charged with electricity: a black or livid threatening appearance; **thun′der-dart**, a thunderbolt: **thun′der-darter**, **-master**, (both *Shak.*) Jove.—*v.t.* **thun′der-drive′**, (*Spens.*) to drive with thunderbolts.—*ns.* **thun′derer**, a thunder-god, Zeus, Thor, &c.: a thundering denunciator, inveigher, orator, journalist, or periodical, esp. *The Times* or its leader-writer: a hand who operates stage-thunder: a bull-roarer; **thun′der-god**, a god that wields thunder; **thun′dering**.—*adj.* discharging thunder: (*coll.*) unusually big, tremendous.—Also *n.* and *adv.*—*adv.* **thun′deringly**.—*adjs.* **thun′derless**; **thun′der-like** (*Shak.*); **thun′derous** (**thun′drous**), like, threatening, or suggesting thunder.—*adv.* **thun′derously**.—*ns.* **thun′der-peal**, a resounding noise of thunder; **thun′der-plump**, a heavy fall of rain in a thunder-storm; **thun′der-shower**, a shower accompanied with thunder, or a short heavy shower from a thunder-cloud; **thun′der-stone**, (*Shak.*) a thunderbolt; **thun′der-storm**, continued discharges of electricity from the clouds, producing lightning and thunder, generally with heavy rain.—*v.t.* **thun′der-strike**, to strike with, or as with, lightning.—*n.* **thun′der-stroke**, (*Shak.*) a stroke or blast by lightning.—*adjs.* **thun′der-struck** (also **-stricken**), struck by lightning: struck dumb with astonishment; **thun′dery**, indicative of thunder, or attended by it.—**steal one's thunder** (see **steal**). [O.E. *thunor*, thunder, *Thunor*, the thunder-god, Thor; Ger. *donner*, L. *tonāre*; cf. **Thor**, **Thursday**.]

thurible, *thū′ri-bl*, *n.* a censer.—*n.* **thu′rifer**, an acolyte who carries the thurible.—*adj.* **thurif′erous**, incense-bearing.—*n.* **thurifica′tion**.—*v.t.* **thū′rify**, to cense.—*n.* **thus** (*thus*, *thūs*), frankincense. [L. *t(h)ūs*, *t(h)ūris*, frankincense—Gr. *thyos*, a sacrifice; cf. **thyme**.]

Thursday, *thurz′dä*, *n.* the fifth day of the week, originally sacred to Thunor, the English thunder-god. [O.E. *Thunres dæg*, Thunor's day; O.N. *Thórsdagr*, Thor's day; Ger. *Donnerstag*.]

thus, *dhus*, *adv.* in this or that manner: to this degree or extent: accordingly, therefore.—*n.* **thus′ness**, (usu. *facet.*) state of being thus.—*adv.* **thus′wise**, in this manner. [O.E. *thus.*]

thus. See under **thurible**.

Thuya, a variant of **Thuja**.

thwack, *thwak*, *v.t.* to whack.—*n.* a whack.—*n.* **thwack′er**.—*n.* and *adj.* **thwack′ing**. [Perh. **whack**, or O.E. *thaccian*, to smack.]

thwaite, *thwāt*, *n.* a piece of reclaimed land—common in place-names. [O.N. *thveit.*]

thwart, *thwawrt*, *adv.* crosswise: from side to side.—*adj.* crosswise, transverse: cross, adverse: cross, perverse, cross-grained.—*prep.* across, athwart.—*v.t.* to cross: to cross the path of: to obstruct: to oppose: to frustrate: to balk: to set crosswise: to plough crosswise.—*v.i.* to cross: to conflict.—*n.* frustration: hindrance: a rower's bench.—*adj.* **thwar′ted**, frustrated. — *adv.* **thwar′tedly**. — *n.* **thwar′ter**. — *n.* and *adj.* **thwar′ting**. — *advs.* **thwar′tingly**, perversely; **thwart′ly**; **thwart′ship(s)**, across the ship; **thwart′ways**; **thwart′wise**.—*adjs.* **thwart′ship**, **thwart′wise**. [O.N. *thvert*, neut. of *thverr*, perverse.]

thy, *dhī*, *poss. pron.* or *adj.* thine: of thee. [**thine**.]

Thyestean, *thī-es′ti-ən*, *-əs-tē′ən*, *adj.* of Thyestes (Gr. *Thyestēs*), who was made to eat his own sons: cannibal.

thyine, *thī′in*, *adj.* of a tree supposed to be sandarach

(Rev. xviii. 12). [Gr. *thýinos—thýon* or *thýā*, thyine tree.]

thylacine, *thī'la-sēn*, *n.* the so-called Tasmanian wolf. [Gr. *thýlakos*, pouch.]

thylose, thylosis. See tylosis.

thyme, *tīm*, *n.* any member of the labiate genus Thymus, low half-shrubby plants with two-lipped corolla and calyx and four diverging stamens, esp. the fragrant garden thyme (*T. vulgaris*) and wild-thyme (*T. Serpyllum*).—*n.* **thymol** (*thī'mol*), an antiseptic phenol obtained from oil of thyme by distillation.—*adj.* **thymy** (*tīm'i*), like, smelling of, or abounding in, thyme.—**basil thyme**, a kind of calamint ; **oil of thyme**, a fragrant essential oil got from garden and other thymes ; **water thyme**, Canadian pondweed. [Fr. *thym*—L. *thȳmum*—Gr. *thýmon*.]

thymelaeaceous, *thim-, thīm-el-i-ā'sh(y)əs*, *adj.* of the Thymelaeā'ceae, the family to which Daphne belongs. [Gr. *thymelaiā*, supposed to be a species of Daphne—*thymos*, thyme, *elaiā*, olive.]

thymus, *thī'məs*, *n.* a ductless gland near the root of the neck, vestigial in adult man—that of veal and lamb called *neck-sweetbread.*—Also *adj.* [Gr. *thymos*, thymus gland.]

thyroid, *thī'roid*, better **thyreoid**, *-i-oid*, *adj.* shield-shaped : pertaining to the thyroid gland or the thyroid cartilage.—*n.* the thyr(e)oid gland, a duct-less gland in the neck whose overactivity may lead to exophthalmic goitre, and defect to cretinism : the principal cartilage of the larynx, forming Adam's apple.—*ns.* **thyroidī'tis**, inflammation of the thyroid gland ; **thyrox'ine**, an iodine com-pound, the active principle of the thyroid gland. [Gr. *thȳreoeidēs*, shield-shaped, the thyroid carti-lage—*thȳreos*, a (door-shaped) shield—*thȳrā*, a door, *eidos*, form.]

Thyrostraca, *thīr-os'tra-kä*, *n.pl.* the cirripedes. [Gr. *thȳrā*, door, valve, *ostrakon*, shell.]

thyrsus, *thər'səs*, *n.* the wand of Bacchus, a staff wreathed with ivy : (*bot.*) a dense panicle broadest in the middle : esp. one whose lateral branches are cymose :—*pl.* **thyr'si** (*-sī*).—*n.* **thyrse** (*thərs*), a thyrsus.—*adjs.* **thyr'soid, -al**, having the form of a thyrsus. [Gr. *thyrsos*.]

Thysanoptera, *this-ən-op'tə-rä*, *n.pl.* an order of insects with fringed wings, as Thrips.—*adj.* **thysanop'terous.**—*n.pl.* **Thysanura** (*-ū'rä*), the bristle-tails, an order of small wingless insects with abdominal appendages.—*adj.* **thysanū'rous.** [Gr. *thysanos*, a fringe, tassel, *pteron*, a wing, *ourā*, a tail.]

thyself, *dhī-self'*, *pron.* emphatic for, or usually along with, thou or thee : reflexive for thee. [**thee** (altered to **thy**), and **self.**]

ti, *tē*, *n.* (*mus.*) in the tonic sol-fa system a substitute for *si*, to avoid the initial sound of *so* (*sol*).—Also, in anglicised spelling, **te.**

ti, *tē*, *n.* a small Pacific liliaceous tree (Cordyline) : sometimes also (wrongly) for the Australian **tea-tree.** [Polynesian.]

tiara, *ti-ā'rä*, *n.* the lofty ornamental head-dress of the ancient Persians : the Jewish high-priest's mitre : the pope's triple crown : the papal dignity : a jewelled head-ornament.—*n.* **tiar** (*ti'ər, tīr*; *poet.*), a tiara.—*adj.* **tia'ra'd, tia'raed**, wearing a tiara. [Gr. *tiārā*.]

Tib, *tib*, *n.* (*Shak.*) used as a typical woman's name : (*obs.* ; *Scott*) the ace of trumps in gleek.—*n.* **Tib'-cat**, a she-cat. [**Isabella.**]

Tibert, *tib'ərt, tīb'ərt*, *n.* the cat in *Reynard the Fox* : in *Shak.* identified with Tibalt.

Tibet, Thibet, *ti-bet'*, *n.* a country W. of China : **thibet**, a woollen stuff generally printed in colours : a heavy goat's hair fabric used instead of fur—also **Tibet cloth.**—*adj.* **Tibet'an** (or *tib'*), of Tibet.—*n.* the language of Tibet : a native of Tibet.

tibia, *tib'i-ä*, *n.* the shinbone : the fourth joint of an insect's leg : an ancient flute or pipe.—*adj.* **tib'ial.** [L. *tibia*, shinbone, flute.]

tic, *tik*, *n.* a convulsive motion of certain muscles, esp. of the face.—*n.* **tic'-douloureux** (*-dol-ə-rōō'*, Fr. *tēk dōō-lōō-rə'*), an affection of the fifth cranial nerve with paroxysms of pain in face and forehead. [Fr. ; cf. **tick** (5).]

tical, *ti-käl', tik'l*, *n.* an obsolete Siamese silver coin,

about equal to a rupee : a unit of weight. [Port. *tical.*]

ticca, *tik'ä*, *adj.* (*Ind.*) hired. [Hind. *thīkā*, hire.]

tice, *tis*, *v.t.* (*Shak.*) to entice.—*n.* an enticement : (*cricket*) a yorker. [Aphetic for **entice**, or—Fr. *atiser*.]

tichorrhine, *tī'kō-rin*, *adj.* having an ossified nasal septum, as the fossil woolly rhinoceros. [Gr. *teichos*, wall, *rhīs, rhīnos*, nose.]

tick, *tik*, *n.* any of the larger blood-sucking acarids : applied also to the sheep-ked and similar degenerate bloodsucking Diptera.—**tick fever**, East Coast fever, transmitted by ticks. [O.E. *ticia* (perh. for *tīca* or *ticca*) ; Du. *teek*, Ger. *zecke*.]

tick, *tik*, *n.* the cover of a mattress : ticking.—*ns.* **tick'en, tick'ing**, the cloth of which ticks are made. [L. *thēca*—Gr. *thēkē*, a case ; see **theca.**]

tick, *tik*, *n.* (*obs.*) a light tap or pat : the game of tig : the sound of a watch, clock, &c. : a beat : the time between ticks, a moment : a speck : a small mark, often an angular line, used to indicate or mark off as checked or dealt with.—*v.i.* (*obs.*) to tap, pat (**tick and toy**, to dally) : make a sound as of a clock : to beat.—*v.t.* to mark with a tick : to dot : to measure, record, give out, by ticks.—*adj.* **ticked**, speckled.—*ns.* **tick'er**, anything that ticks, esp. a telegraph instrument that prints signals on a tape, or (*slang*) a watch ; **tick'er-tape**, paper ribbon telegraphically printed.—*n.* and *adj.* **tick'ing.**—*n.* **tick'-tack'**, ticking as of a clock : bookmakers' telegraphy by arm signals : (see also **trick-track**).—Also *adj.-adv.* with recurring ticking.—*ns.* **tick'-tick**, a ticking : a child's word for a watch ; **tick'-tock'**, a ticking, as of a big clock : a tapping.—**in two ticks**, in a moment ; **tick off**, (*slang*) to reprimand ; **tick over**, of an engine, to run gently disconnected. [M.E. *tek* ; cf. Du. *tik*, L.G. *tikk* ; prob. imit.]

tick, *tik*, *n.* (*slang*) credit : trust.—*v.i.* to get or give credit.—*n.* **tick'-shop**, a shop where goods are given on credit. [**ticket.**]

tick, *tik*, *n.* crib-biting : a whimsy. [**tic.**]

ticket, *tik'it*, *n.* a card, slip, or placard bearing a notice or serving as a token of any right or debt, as for admission, &c. : (*slang*) a certificate : (*slang*) discharge from the army : (*U.S.*) a list of candidates put forward by a party for election : (*obs.*) a visiting-card.—*v.t.* to label : to designate.—*ns.* **tick'et-collec'tor** ; **tick'et-day**, the day before settling day on the Stock Exchange ; **tick'et-porter**, a licensed porter : a railway porter who collects tickets ; **tick'et-punch**, an instrument for punching holes in used tickets.—**straight ticket**, all the nominees of a political party, and no others ; **the ticket**, (*slang*) exactly the right thing or the thing to be done ; **ticket of leave**, a licence to be at large before expiry of sentence. [O.Fr. *estiquet(te)* —*estiquer*, to stick—O.L.G. *stekan* ; cf. **stick.**]

tickey, *tik'i*, *n.* (*S.Afr.*) a threepenny-bit. [Origin unknown.]

tickle, *tik'l*, *adj.* (*Spens., Shak.*) unstable, in un-stable equilibrium, delicately set, insecure : (*obs.* or *dial.*) ticklish, nice.—*v.t.* to excite with a pleasant thrill : to affect with a disturbing feeling of a light touch, usually uncomfortable and tending to excite laughter : to amuse : to perplex : to touch lightly : to beat.—*v.i.* (*Spens.*) to tingle : to be the seat of a tickling or itching feeling.—*n.* an act or feeling of tickling.—*ns.* **tickl'e-brain**, (*Shak.*) strong liquor ; **tick'ler**, one who or that which tickles : a feather-brush : a poker : a cane : a device for reminding : a puzzle : a dram of spirits.—*n.* and *adj.* **tick'ling.** —*adj.* **tick'lish**, easily tickled : unstable : pre-carious : easily affected : nice : critical.—*adv.* **tick'lishly.** — *n.* **tick'lishness.** — *adj.* **tick'ly**, tickling : ticklish.—*n.pl.* **tick'ly-bend'ers**, thin ice that bends underfoot : a game played on it. [Perh. a freq. of **tick** ; perh. by metathesis from **kittle.**]

tic-tac. Same as tick-tack (see tick, 3).

tid, *tid*, *n.* (*Scot.*) fit time or condition : a mood.

tidbit. Same as titbit.

tiddle, *tid'l*, *v.i.* to potter, trifle.

tiddlywink, *tid'li-wingk*, *n.* (*prov.*) an unlicensed pawn-shop or beer-house. — *n.* **tidd'lywinks**,

tiddledywinks (tid′l-di-), a game in which small disks are flipped into a cup by pressing the edge of the small disk with a bigger one.

tiddy, tid′i, n. (Scott) the four of trumps at gleek.

tide, tīd, n. a time: season: a festival: opportunity: ebb and flow, esp. of the sea: the time of ebbing, of flowing, of both, or of suitable state for work: (poet.) sea-water: a flow: (poet.) a river, river-water, or current: flood-tide.—v.t. (esp. fig.) to carry as the tide: to effect by means of the tide.—v.i. to run like a tide: to make one's way by taking advantage of the tides (also v.t. with it).—adj. tīd′al, of, depending on, regulated by, the tide: flowing and ebbing.—ns. tide′-gate, a gate that admits water at flood-tide and retains it at ebb; tide′-gauge, an instrument for registering the state of the tide continuously.—adj. tide′less, having no tides.—ns. tide′-lock, a lock by which ships may pass out or in at all times of the tide; tide′-mark, a line on the shore made by the tide: a mark of the limit of washing; tide′mill, a mill moved by tide-water; tide′-rip, a disturbed sea due to currents: a tidal wave; tides′-man, a customs officer who waited the arrival of ships (orig. coming in with the tide); tide′-table, a table of times of high-tide; tide′-waiter, a tidesman: one who waits to see how things go before acting; tide′-waitership; tide′-water, water brought by the tide: (U.S.) river water affected by the tide: (U.S.) seaboard; tide′-wave, the tide regarded as a wave passing round the earth; tide′-way, the track followed by the tide: a channel through which there is a strong current or tide.—tidal wave, the tide-wave: a great wave caused by the tide: improperly, a great wave started by an earthquake and running on with its own velocity: for the time at least. [O.E. tīd; Du. tijd, Ger. zeit.]

tide, tīd, v.i. (arch.) to happen. [O.E. (ge)tīdan; cf. betide.]

tide, (Spens.) for tied.

tidings, tī′dingz, n.pl. news. [Late O.E. tīdung—O.E. tīdan, to tide, happen, or—O.N. títhindi, events, tidings.]

tidivate. See titivate.

tidy, tī′di, adj. (obs.) seasonable: in good condition or order: plump: comely: shapely: fairly good or big: trim: orderly: neat.—n. a cover for a chair-back: a receptacle for odd scraps.—v.t. to make tidy: to clear away for the sake of tidiness:—pr.p. tī′dying; pa.t. and pa.p. tī′died.—adv. tī′dily.—n. tī′diness. [tide; cf. Ger. zeitig.]

tie, tī, v.t. to bind: to fasten: to knot: to make as a knot: to restrict, restrain: to unite: (mus.) to mark with a curved line indicating sustentation not repetition: to perform or mark in this way: to limit: to oblige: to subject to bonds: (Shak.) to confirm: to ligature.—v.i. to be equal in votes or score: of dogs, to linger on the scent: (pr.p. ty′ing; pa.t. and pa.p. tied, tīd).—n. a knot, bow, &c.: a bond: a string, ribbon, &c., for tying: a necktie: a tie-wig: (U.S.) a shoe: a member sustaining only a tension: (U.S.) a railway sleeper: a restraint: an obligation: a mode of tying: an equality in score or votes: a match in any stage of a tournament in which the losers are eliminated: (mus.) a curved line drawn over notes of the same pitch to be performed as one, sustained not repeated.—n. tie′-beam, a beam connecting the lower ends of rafters to prevent moving apart.—adjs. tied; tie′less.—ns. tie′-pin, an ornamental pin stuck in a necktie; tī′er, one who ties: (U.S.) a child's apron; tie′-rod, a rod serving as a tie; tie′-up, a tape for tying a book-binding or portfolio: an animal tied up for a bait: a standstill: an entanglement; tie′-wig, a wig tied with ribbon at the back.—tied house, a public-house whose tenant is bound to get his supplies from one particular brewer or distiller (usually the owner); tie up, to parcel up: to tie so as to remain up: to tether: to secure against squandering, alienation, &c., restrict the use of, by conditions. [O.E. téah, band, string, tīgan, to tie.]

tier, tēr, n. a row, rank, or layer, esp. one of several placed one above another: a row of guns: (Tasmania) a mountain range.—v.t. to pile in tiers. [Fr. tire—tirer, to draw.]

tierce, tērs, n. (obs.) a third: one-third of a pipe: a cask or vessel of that capacity: a sequence of three cards of the same suit: (mus.) two octaves and a third: a position in fencing: the third hour of the day (ending 9 a.m.): the office of that hour, the terce.—n. tier′ceron, (archit.) in vaulting, a rib springing from the intersection of two other ribs. [O.Fr. tiers, tierce—L. tertia (pars).]

tiercel, tiercelet. See tercel.

tiff, tif, n. stale, sour, or thin liquor: a sip: a dram.—v.i. to sip: to drink: to lunch.—Also (Scot. and dial.) tift.—n. tiff′ing, sipping: (India, &c., tiff′in) lunch, a light repast. [Perh. orig. slang.]

tiff, tif, v.t. and v.i. (obs.) to dress, trick out. [O.Fr. tiffer (Fr. attifer), to adorn.]

tiff, tif, n. a display of irritation, a pet, huff: a slight quarrel.—v.i. to be in a huff: to squabble.—Also (esp. Scot.) tift. [Prob. imit.]

tiffany, tif′a-ni, n. a silk-like gauze.—adj. of tiffany: transparent. [Gr. theophaneia, theophany, or diaphaneia, transparency.]

tig, tig, n. a touch: a twitch: a game in which one who is 'it' seeks to touch another.—v.t. to touch, esp. in the game of tig. [Poss. a form of tick (3).]

tig, tig, n. an old four-handed drinking-cup.

tige, tēzh, n. the shaft of a column. [Fr.,—L. tibia, a pipe.]

tiger, tī′gėr, n. a fierce striped Asiatic beast, one of the two largest cats (Felis tigris): (S.Afr.) the leopard: (U.S.) the jaguar (American tiger): the puma (red tiger): a boy in livery usually perched behind a vehicle: a ferocious or bloodthirsty person: a flashy vulgarian: (slang) a formidable opponent: (U.S.) a yell to supplement a cheer: a tiger-beetle, tiger-moth, tiger-shark, tiger-lily, &c:—fem. tī′gress.—ns. tī′ger-bee′tle, any beetle of the Cicindelidae; tī′ger-cat, a general name for a middle-sized striped or spotted wild cat—margay, ocelot, serval, &c.; tī′ger-eye′, a pseudomorph of quartz after crocidolite; tī′ger-flower, a Mexican iridaceous plant (Tigridia) with streaked flowers.—adjs. tī′ger-foot′ed, (Shak.) fiercely swift; tī′gerish (tī′grish), like a tiger in disposition: flashy.—ns. tī′gerism, swagger; tī′ger-lil′y, a lily with black-spotted orange flowers.—adj. tī′gerly.—ns. tī′ger-moth, any one of the Arctiidae; tī′ger-nut, the edible rhizome of Cyperus esculentus, a European sedge, (U.S.) the chufa; tī′ger-shark, a voracious striped shark of the Indian Ocean; tī′ger-snake, the most deadly of Australian snakes (Notechis scutatus), brown with black cross-bands; tī′ger-wolf, the spotted hyaena: the thylacine.—adjs. tī′gery, tī′grine (-grīn), tī′groid, like a tiger. [Fr. tigre—L. tigris—Gr. tigris, prob. from Zend.]

tight, tīt, adj. close: compact: close-fitting: too close-fitting: cramped: taut: tense: firmly fixed: impervious, not leaky, proof: trim: neat: snug: competent: hampered or characterised by want of money: (of money) scarce, not easily obtainable: unwilling to part with money: tipsy.—adv. tightly.—v.t. and v.i. tight′en, to make or grow tight or tighter.—n. tight′ener, one who, or that which, tightens: (anat.) a tensor: (slang) a heavy meal.—adjs. tight′-fist′ed, stingy; tight′ish.—adv. tight′ishly.—v.t., v.i., and adj. tight′-lace′.—ns. tight′-lā′cer; tight′-lā′cing, compression of the waist by tight clothes.—adv. tight′ly.—ns. tight′ness; tight′-rope, a taut rope for rope-dancing.—n.pl. tights, close-fitting breeches: a garment closely fitting the body, or at least the legs, worn by acrobats, dancers, &c. [Earlier thight, thyght, supposed to be from an older form of O.N. théttr, influenced by various English words of similar meaning; cf. Ger. dicht.]

tight, tīt (Spens.), pa.t. and pa.p. of tie.

tike. Same as tyke.

til, til, tēl, n. sesame.—Also teel.—ns. til′-oil; til′seed. [Hind. til—Sans. tila.]

tilbury, til′bėr-i, n. a kind of gig for two. [Said to be so named from its first maker.]

tilde, til′dä, -di, n. the diacritical sign over n in

fāte, fär, ȧsk; mē, hėr (her); mīne; mōte; mūte; mōōn; dhen (then)

Spanish to indicate the sound *ny*—thus ñ (as in *cañon*). [Sp.,—L. *titulus*, a title.]

tile, *til, n.* a slab of baked clay (or a substitute) for covering roofs, floors, &c.: a tube of baked clay used in drains: a piece for playing mah-jongg: tiling: (*slang*) a top-hat.—*v.t.* to cover with tiles: to drain by means of tiles: to secure against intrusion by placing a person at the door: to bind to secrecy.—*adj.* **tiled,** covered with tiles: imbricated: (*locally*) sun-dried.—*ns.* **tile´-hat; til´er,** a maker or layer of tiles: a freemasons' door-keeper—also **tyl´er; tile´-red,** a brownish-red, the colour of baked tiles; **til´ery,** a place where tiles are made; **tile´-stone,** a flat stone used for roofing, esp. a thin-bedded sandstone; **til´ing.**—Dutch tiles, enamelled earthenware tiles, usually blue, with scriptural subjects, for chimney-pieces, &c. [O.E. *tigele*—L. *tēgula*—*tegĕre*, to cover.]

tilefish, *til´fish, n.* an American Atlantic fish noted for the sudden changes in its numbers. [App. from its generic name, Lopholotilus, and perh. its tile-like spotted pattern.]

Tilia, *til´i-ä, n.* the lime or linden genus, giving name to the family **Tiliä´ceae,** akin to the mallows. —*adj.* **tiliä´ceous,** belonging to the family. [L. *tilia,* lime-tree.]

till, *til, n.* (*obs.*) a compartment or drawer in a chest, cabinet, &c.: now, a money-drawer or receptacle in or behind a counter. [Cf. M.E. *tillen,* to draw, O.E. *fortyllan,* to draw aside, seduce.]

till, *til, prep.* to the time of: (*Scot.*) to: (*Scot.*) to, with the infinitive.—*conj.* to the time when. [O.E. (Northumbrian) *til*—O.N. *til;* cf. O.E. *till,* a fixed point, Ger. *ziel,* end, goal.]

till, *til, v.t.* to work, cultivate: (*obs.* or *dial.*) to set. —*adj.* **till´able,** arable.—*ns.* **till´age,** act or practice of tilling: husbandry: a place tilled; **till´er; till´ing.** [O.E. *tilian,* to aim at, till—*till,* limit; see foregoing word.]

till, *til, n.* (*orig. Scot.*) a stiff impervious clay: (*geol.*) boulder-clay: (*mining*) shale.—*n.* **till´ite,** indurated till. [Cf. **thill** (2).]

Tillandsia, *ti-land´zi-ä, n.* a mainly epiphytic tropical American genus of the pine-apple family. [From the Swedish botanist *Tillands.*]

tiller, *til´ər, n.* the handle or lever for turning a rudder.—*ns.* **till´er-chain, -rope,** the chain or rope connecting the tiller with the steering-wheel. [M.E. *tillen,* to draw (see **till,** 1), or O.Fr. *telier,* cross-bow stock—L.L. *tēlārium,* a weaver's beam— L. *tēla,* a web.]

tiller, *til´ər,* **teller, tellar,** *tel´ər; n.* a sapling: a shoot from a tree stool: a sucker from the base of a stem: a side-shoot from the base as in corn, &c.—*v.i.* to form tillers. [O.E. *telgor,* shoot, twig.]

tiller. See **till** (3).

tilly-vally, -fally, *til´i-val´i, -fal´i, interj.* (*Shak.*) of impatience of what has been said.—Also **till´ey-vall´ey.**

tilt, *tilt, n.* a cover, awning, for a wagon, boat, &c.: a tent: a hut.—*v.t.* to cover with a tilt.—*n.* **tilt´-boat,** a large rowing-boat with a tilt.—*adj.* **tilt´ed.** [O.E. *teld;* cf. Ger. *zelt.*]

tilt, *tilt, v.i.* to pitch, as a ship: to lean, heel over: to slope: to slant, esp. in a vertical plane: to just, to ride and thrust with a spear: to rush, charge: to thrust.—*v.t.* to incline: to tip out: to send by tilting: to forge with a tilt-hammer.—*n.* an act of tilting: a condition of being tilted: a slope: a just, a course with a lance: an encounter: a duel: a thrust: a tilt-yard.—*ns.* **tilt´er; tilt´-hammer,** a heavy pivoted hammer lifted by a cam; **tilt´ing; tilt´-yard,** a place for tilting.—**full tilt,** at full speed in a headlong course. [O.E. *tealt,* tottering.]

tilth, *tilth, n.* cultivation: cultivated land: the depth of soil turned up in cultivation. [From **till** (3).]

timariot, *ti-mä´ri-ot, n.* (*hist.*) a Turkish feudal militiaman. [Fr.,—Turk. *tīmār.*]

timbal, tymbal, *tim´bl, n.* (*arch.*) a kettledrum.— *n.* **timbale** (*tan´-bäl´, tam´bäl, tim´bl*), a dish cooked in a cup-shaped mould or shell. [Fr. *timbale;* see **atabal;** app. influenced by L. *tympanum.*]

timber, *tim´bər, n.* wood suitable for building or carpentry, whether growing or cut: (*English law*) standing trees of oak, ash, elm, or (*locally* by custom) other kinds, forming part of an inheritance: material generally: a beam, or large piece of wood in a framework, as of a house, ship, &c.: familiarly, a wooden object or part: a wooden leg: (*dial.*) wood: (*U.S.*) woodland, forest-land. —*adj.* of timber: wooden: (*Scot.*) wooden in tone, unmusical.—*v.t.* (*obs.*) to build: to furnish with timber or beams.—*adj.* **tim´bered,** built: constructed: built of wood: furnished with timber: (*Spens.*) app. massive: wooded.—*ns.* **tim´bering,** timber collectively: work in timber; **tim´berline,** the upper limit of timber-trees on the mountains, &c.; **tim´ber-man,** one responsible for the timbers in a mine; **tim´ber-toes,** a person with a wooden leg; **tim´ber-tree,** a tree suitable for timber; **tim´ber-wolf,** an American variety of the common wolf, the grey wolf; **tim´ber-yard,** a yard or place where timber is stored. [O.E. *timber,* building, wood, *timbrian,* to build; Ger. *zimmer,* room.]

timbó, *tim-bō´, n.* a South American sapindaceous climber (*Paullinia pinnata*): a fish-poison and insecticide got from its bark. [Guaraní.]

timbre, *tan´br´, tim´bər, tam´bər, n.* the quality of a sound, tone-colour, distinguished from pitch and loudness. [O.Fr., bell—L. *tympanum,* a drum.]

timbrel, *tim´brəl, n.* an ancient Oriental tabor or tambourine.—*adj.* **tim´brel'd,** (*Milt.*) sung to the timbrel. [O.Fr. *timbre*—L. *tympanum,* a drum.]

timbrology, *tim-brol´ə-ji,* **timbromania** (*-brō-mā´ni-ä*), **timbrophily** (*-brof´i-li*), *ns.* outmoded words for stamp-collecting.—*ns.* **timbromā´niac, timbroph´ilist.** [Fr. *timbre,* postage-stamp.]

time, *tim, n.* absolute duration: a moment at which, or stretch of duration in which, things happen: season: due, appointed, usual time: hour of death or of parturition: spell: a period: actual time of being something or somewhere, as of apprenticeship, residence, sentence, student days, life, &c.: duration of the world: leisure or opportunity long enough for a purpose: a spell of exciting, usually pleasurable, experience: time, or shortest time, of performance, as a race: rhythm, tempo: rate of speed: a unit of duration in metre, a mora: an occasion: an occasion regarded as one of a recurring series: one of a number of multiplied instances: generalised as an indication of multiplication (*so many times*=multiplied by so much): payment for work by the hour, day, &c., back-pay: a reckoning of time: an interval: past time: the umpire's call in prize-fights, &c.: (in *pl.*) the contemporary state of things or fashion: (in *pl.*) often the name of a newspaper: **Time,** a personification of time, a bald-headed old man with a forelock, a scythe, often an hour-glass.— *v.t.* to arrange, fix, choose, a time for: to mark, adjust, or observe the rhythm or time of: to ascertain the time of: to regulate as to time.—*v.i.* to keep or beat time.—*adj.* of time: reckoned by time: timed: for a future time.—*interj.* indicating that time is up, or that action is now permitted.— *ns.* **time´-ball,** a ball arranged to drop at a particular time; **time´-bargain,** a contract to buy or sell at a certain time in the future.—*adjs.* **time´-beguil´ing,** making time seem to pass quickly; **time´-bett´ering,** (*Shak.*) in which the times are growing better; **time´-bewast´ed,** (*Shak.*) spent by time. — *n.* **time´-bill,** a time-table.— *adjs.* **timed; time´-expired,** having completed a term of enlistment.—*ns.* **time´-exposure,** (*phot.*) an exposure for a time long in comparison with one called instantaneous; **time´-fuse,** a fuse contrived to act at a definite time; **time´-gun,** a gun fired to indicate a certain hour.—*adj.* **time´-hon´oured,** honoured on account of antiquity.—*ns.* **time´-keeper,** a clock, watch, or other instrument that measures time: one who keeps account of workmen's hours: one who beats or observes time; **time´-killer** (see **kill**).—*n.* and *adj.* **time´-killing.** —*n.* **time´-lag,** the interval of delay between two connected phenomena.—*adj.* **time´less,** independent of time: unconnected with the passage of time:

untimely : (*Shak.*) premature : ill-timed : eternal :
failing to keep time or rhythm.—Also *adv.*—*adv.*
time′lessly.—*ns.* **time′lessness** ; **time′-lim′it**,
a time within which something has to be done ;
time′liness.—*adj.* **time′ly**, in good time, early :
seasonable : well-timed : (*obs.*) temporal : (*Spens.*)
of the time of day : (*Spens.*) in time, keeping time.
—*adv.* early, soon : in due time or good time.—
adjs. **time′ly-part′ed**, (*Shak.*) having died at a
natural time ; **tim(e)ous** (*tīm′əs* ; chiefly *Scot.*), in
good time : seasonable.—*adv.* **tim(e)′ously**, in
good time.—*ns.* **time′piece**, a piece of machinery
for keeping time, esp. (distinguished from a clock)
one that does not strike but is bigger than a watch ;
time′-pleas′er, (*Shak.*) a time-server ; **tim′er**,
one who times anything : (in composition) one
who belongs to, works for, &c., such-and-such a
time.—*n.* and *adj.* **time′-saving.**—*n.* **time′-
server**, one who serves or meanly suits his opinions
to the times or those in authority for the time ;
time′-service.—*n.* and *adj.* **time′-serving.**—*ns.*
time′-sig′nal, an intimation of the exact time
given wirelessly or otherwise from an observatory ;
time′-sig′nature, (*mus.*) an indication of measure
at the beginning of a line or wherever there is a
change : **time′-spirit**, the genius of the age ;
time′-table, a table of times, as of classes, buses,
&c. ; **time′-thrust**, a thrust made in fencing at the
moment the opponent draws breath for his thrust ;
time′-work, work paid for by the hour or the day
—opp. to *piece-work.*—*adj.* **time′-worn**, worn or
decayed by time.—*ns.* **tim′ing**, fixing, choosing,
adjusting, ascertaining, or recording of times :
co-ordination in time ; **tīm′ist**, (*obs.*) a time-
server : one who keeps in time : one who times
his movements.—**apparent time**, time according
to the real sun, without regard to the equation of
time—sun-dial time ; **astronomical time**, till
1925 the time past mean moon, now midnight,
reckoned on to twenty-four hours in mean time ;
at the same time, simultaneously : notwithstanding ; **at times**, at distant intervals : occasionally ; **behind the times**, not abreast of
changes ; **between times**, in the intervals ; **by
times**, betimes ; **common time**, time with two
beats or a multiple of two beats to a measure (compound common time where each beat is of three
quavers or crotchets) ; **do time**, to be serving a
sentence of imprisonment ; **for a time**, during a
time : temporarily ; **for the time being**, at the
present time or the actual time in question ; **from
time to time**, now and then ; **in good time**,
quite early enough : with some time to spare :
(ironically ; *obs.*) indeed ; **in time**, after a lapse
of time : early enough : keeping rhythm ; **keep
time**, to run accurately, as a clock : to move or
perform in the same rhythm : to record times of
workmen, &c. ; **local time**, time reckoned from
the local meridian ; **lose time**, to fall behindhand : to let time pass without full advantage ;
make time, to regain the advantage of lost time :
to find an opportunity ; **mean solar time**, time
reckoned not by the actual but the mean position
of the sun ; **on, upon, a time**, once : at a time
in the past (usu. imaginary) ; **on time**, (chiefly
U.S.) up to time : punctually ; **sidereal time**, the
portion of a sidereal day that has elapsed since the
transit of the first point of Aries ; **solar time**, time
reckoned by the sun, real or mean ; **standard time**,
a system of time adopted for a wide area instead of
local time—usually Greenwich mean time or a time
differing from it by a whole number of hours ;
summer time (see **summer**) ; **take Time
by the forelock**, seize an opportunity before
it is too late ; **time about**, (chiefly *Scot.*)
in turns, alternately ; **time and again**, repeatedly ; **time of day**, the time by the clock :
the point of time reached : a greeting, salutation ;
time out of mind, during the whole time within
human memory, from time immemorial ; **triple
time**, three beats, or three times three beats, to a
measure ; **up to time**, punctual, punctually : not
later than the due time ; **what time**, (*poet.*) when.
[O.E. *tíma* ; O.N. *tími.*]

timenoguy, *tim′ən-og-i*, *n.* (*naut.*) a rope stretched

from place to place in a ship, esp. one to prevent
the fore-sheet fouling : a makeshift : a what's-
its-name. [Origin obscure.]
timid, *tim′id*, *adj.* inclined to fear : wanting courage :
faint-hearted.—*n.* **timid′ity.**—*adv.* **tim′idly.**—*n.*
tim′idness.—*adj.* **tim′orous** (*-ər-əs*), timid.—*adv.*
tim′orously.—*n.* **tim′orousness.**—*adj.* **tim′or-
some**, (*dial.*) easily frightened. [L. *timidus*,
timid, *timor*, *-ōris*, fear—*timēre*, to fear.]
timocracy, *ti-mok′rə-si*, *n.* a form of government
in which property is a qualification for office : one
in which ambition or desire of honour is a ruling
principle.—*adjs.* **timocratic** (*-ō-krat′ik*), **-al.** [Gr.
timokratiā—timē, honour, *krateein*, to rule.]
timon, *tī′mən*, *n.* (*obs.*) a helm.—*n.* **timoneer′**, a
helmsman. [Fr.,—L. *tēmō*, *-ōnis*, a beam.]
Timon, *tī′mon*, *n.* a famous Athenian misanthrope
(5th cent. B.C.) celebrated by Aristophanes, Lucian,
Plutarch, and Shakespeare : hence, a misanthrope.
—*v.i.* **Tī′monise**, to play the misanthrope.—*ns.*
Tī′monism ; **Tī′monist.**
timothy, *tim′ə-thi*, *n.* (in full **timothy-grass**) cat's-
tail grass (*Phleum pratense*) much valued for feeding
cattle. [*Timothy* Hanson, who promoted its cultivation in America about 1720.]
timpano, *timp′ə-nō*, *n.* an orchestral kettledrum :—
pl. **timp′ani** (*-nē*).—*n.* **timp′anist.** [It. ; see
tympanum.]
tin-whisk(e)y, *tim′-hwis′ki*, *n.* a whisky (gig).
tin, *tin*, *n.* a silvery-white, easily fusible, malleable
metal (symbol Sn for L. *stannum* ; at. number
50) : (*slang*) money : a vessel of tin or tin-plate, a
can, &c. : a tinful.—*adj.* made of tin or tin-plate or
(*coll.*) of corrugated iron : (*coll.*) paltry.—*v.t.* to
coat or overlay with tin or tinfoil : to pack in tins :
—*pr.p.* **tinn′ing** ; *pa.t.* and *pa.p.* **tinned.**—*ns.*
tin′-can ; **tin′foil**, tin in thin sheets, as for
wrapping ; **tin′ful** :—*pl.* **tin′fuls** ; **tin′man**, one
who works in tin : a dresser of tin-ore : a dealer
in tinware.—*adj.* **tinned.**—*ns.* **tinn′er**, a tinsmith :
a tin-miner : a canner ; **tinn′ing.**—*adj.* **tinn′y**,
like tin, esp. in sound.—*n.* (also **tinn′ie**) a mug of
tinplate.—*ns.* **tin′-opener**, an instrument for cutting open tins of food, &c. ; **tin′-plate**, thin sheet-
iron or steel coated with tin.—Also *adj.*—*n.* **tin′-pot**,
a pot of or for tin or tin-plate.—*adj.* paltry, rubbishy.
—*ns.* **tin′smith**, a worker in tin ; **tin′stone**, cassiterite ; **tin′-stream′er**, one who washes tin from
alluvial deposits ; **tin′-stream′ing** ; **tin′-tack′**,
a tack coated with tin ; **tin′-terne′** (see **terne**) ;
tin′type, a ferrotype ; **tin′ware**, articles made of
tin.—**put the tin hat on**, to finish off, bring to an
end, suppress ; **tin hat**, (*slang*) a helmet. [O.E.
tin ; O.N. *tin*, Ger. *zinn.*]
tinamou, *tin′ə-mōō*, *n.* a South American partridge-
like bird (*Tinamus*) of or akin to the Ratitae.
[Fr.,—Galibi *tinamu.*]
tincal, *ting′kl*, *n.* crude borax. [Malay *tingkal.*]
tinchel, *tin′hhyəl*, *ting′kəl*, *n.* a circle of men who
close in round a herd of deer. [Gael. *timchioll*, a
circuit.]
tinct, *tingt*, *n.* a tint : a tinge : (*Shak.*) the alchemist's elixir.—*adj.* (*Spens.*) tinged.—*v.t.* (*obs.*) to
tint, tinge, dye : (*obs.*) to imbue : (*obs.*) to subject
to transmutation.—*adj.* **tinctō′rial**, of dyeing.—
n. **tinct′ure**, a tinge or shade of colour : a colouring
matter : (*her.*) a metal, colour, or fur : a quality
or slight taste added to anything : (*old chem.*) a
principle extracted in solution : (*alch.*) the transmuting elixir or philosopher's stone : (*med.*) an
alcoholic solution of a drug.—*v.t.* to tinge : to
imbue. [L. *tingĕre*, *tinctum*, to dye ; cf. **tint**,
tinge.]
tind, *tind*, *tīnd* (now *dial.*), **teend**, *tēnd* (*Herrick*),
tine, *tīn* (*Milt.*), *v.t.* and *v.i.* to kindle :—*pa.t.* and
pa.p. **tind′ed**, **tined** (*Spens.* **tīnd**, **tȳnd**, **tȳnde**).
[O.E. *tendan*, and prob. a lost collateral form ; cf.
tinder.]
tindal, *tin′dəl*, *n.* a petty-officer of lascars. [Malay-
alam *tandal.*]
tinder, *tin′dər*, *n.* dry inflammable matter, esp. that
used for kindling fire from a spark.—*n.* **tin′der-
box**, a box for tinder, and usu. flint and steel.—
adjs. **tin′der-like**, (*Shak.*) inflammable as tinder ;
tin′dery, irascible. [O.E. *tynder* ; O.N. *tundr.*]

Ger. *zunder*; O.E. *tendan*, Ger. *zünden*, to kindle.]

tine, tīn, *n.* a spike as of a fork, harrow, or deer's horn.—*adj.* **tined.** [O.E. *tind.*]

tine, tyne, tīn, *v.t.* (*Scot.*) to lose.—*v.i.* to be lost: (*Spens.*) to be painful: (*Spens.*) to perish: (*pa.t.* and *pa.p.* **tint, tint**; *Spens.* **tyned.**)—*n.* (*Spens.*) teen, affliction.—*n.* **tinsel** (*tin'sl*; *Scot.*), loss. [O.N. *týna*, to destroy, lose, perish; cf. **teen.**]

tine, tīn, *v.t.* (*prov.*) to shut: to enclose. [O.E. *týnan*, to surround; cf. **town.**]

tine, tin, *n.* (*prov.*) a wild vetch or tare.

tine, tyne, tīn, *adj.* (*Shak.*) tiny (always preceded by little).

tine. See **tind.**

tinea, tin'i-ä, *n.* ringworm: **Tinea,** the clothes-moth genus, giving name to the **Tineidae** (*ti-nē'i-dē*), a large family of small moths. [L. *tinea*, moth, bookworm, &c.]

ting, ting, *v.t.* and *v.i.* to ring.—*n.* the sound of a small bell.—*n.* **ting'-a-ling,** a tinkling.—Also *adv.* [Imit.]

tinge, tinj, *v.t.* to tint or colour: to suffuse: to impart a slight modification to.—*v.i.* to take on a tinge: (*pr.p.* **ting'ing**).—*n.* a slight colouring or modification. [L. *tingĕre, tinctum*; conn. with Gr. *tengein*, to wet, to stain.]

tingle, ting'gl, *v.i.* to feel or be the seat of a thrilling sensation: to thrill: to throb: to ring: to vibrate. —*v.t.* to cause to tingle: to ring.—*n.* a tingling sensation.—*n.* **ting'ler,** a stinging blow.—*n.* and *adj.* **ting'ling.**—*adjs.* **ting'lish,** thrilling; **ting'ly,** tingling. [M.E. *tinglen*, a variant of *tinklen.*]

tingle, ting'gl, *n.* a small tack or nail: a clip of lead: patch over leak in boat's planking. [Cf. Ger. *zingel.*]

tinguaite, ting'gwə-īt, *n.* a fine-grained igneous rock composed essentially of felspar, nepheline, and aegirine. [*Tingua* Mountains in Brazil.]

tink, tingk, *n.* a clear high-pitched short bell-like sound: a chime of rhyme: (*coll. abbrev., Scot.*) a tinker.—*v.t.* and *v.i.* to sound in this way: to tinker.—*n.* **tink'er,** a mender of kettles, pans, &c.: a botcher or bungler: a slight, temporary, or unskilful patching-up.—*v.t.* to repair, esp. ineffectually.—*v.i.* to do tinker's work: to botch, potter, patch up.—*v.i.* **tink'le,** to make small, sharp sounds: to jingle: to clink repeatedly or continuously: to go with tinkling sounds: to tingle.— *v.t.* to cause to tinkle: to ring: to make empty sounds or mere sound.—*n.* a sound of tinkling.—*n.* **tink'ler,** a small bell: (*Scot.*) a tinker, gypsy, or vagrant.—*n.* and *adj.* **tink'ling.**—*adv.* **tink'lingly.** —*adj.* **tink'ly.** [M.E. *tinken*, to tink, *tinkere*, tinker (perh. unconnected).]

tinnitus, ti-nī'tas, *n.* a ringing in the ears. [L. *tinnītus, -ūs*, a jingling—*tinnīre*, to ring.]

tinsel, tin'sl, *n.* thin glittering metallic sheets or spangles: anything showy, but of little value.— *adj.* of or like tinsel: gaudy.—*v.t.* to adorn with, or as with, tinsel: to make glittering or gaudy:— *pr.p.* **tin'selling**; *pa.t.* and *pa.p.* **tin'selled.**— *adj.* **tin'selly,** like tinsel, gaudy, showy.—*n.* **tin'selry,** glittering and tawdry material. — *adj.* **tin'sel-slipp'er'd** (*Milt.*).—*n.* and *adj.* **tin'sey,** (*obs. dial.*) tinsel. [O.Fr. *estincelle*—L. *scintilla*, a spark.]

tinsel. See **tine** (2).

tint, tint, *n.* a slight tinge distinct from the principal colour: a hue mixed with white: a series of parallel lines in engraving, producing a uniform shading.—*v.t.* to colour slightly: to tinge.—*v.i.* to take on a tint.—*ns.* **tint'-block,** a block for printing a background; **tint'er,** one who, or that which, tints; **tint'iness**; **tint'ing.**—*adj.* **tint'less.** —*ns.* **tintom'eter,** a colorimeter; **tint'-tool,** an implement for producing a tint by parallel lines.— *adj.* **tin'ty,** inharmoniously tinted. [L. *tinctus*; cf. **tinct, tinge.**]

tint, tint. See **tine** (2).

tintinnabulate, tin-tin-ab'ū-lāt, *v.i.* to ring.—*adjs.* **tintinnab'ulant, tintinnab'ular, tintinnab'ulary.** —*n.* **tintinnabulā'tion,** bell-ringing.—*adj.* **tin-tinnab'ulous.**—*n.* **tintinnab'ulum,** a bell: a bell-rattle—*pl.* **tintinnab'ula.** [L. *tintinnabulum*, a bell—*tintinnāre*, to jingle, reduplicated from *tinnīre*, to jingle.]

tiny, tī'ni, *adj.* (*comp.* **ti'nier,** *superl.* **ti'niest**) very small. [Cf. **tine** (5).]

tip, tip, *n.* a slender extremity: the furthest part. —*v.t.* to put a tip to: to be the tip of: to remove the tip from:—*pr.p.* **tipp'ing**; *pa.t.* and *pa.p.* **tipped,** or **tipt.**—*adj.* **tipped** (*tipt*).—*n.* **tipp'ing.**— *adj.* (*slang*) topping, ripping, excellent.—*adjs.* **tipp'y,** (*slang*) in the height of fashion: smart; **tip'-tilt'ed,** (*Tennyson*) turned up at the tip.—**on the tip of one's tongue,** on the very point of being spoken. [Cf. O.N. *typpa*, to tip, Du., Norw., Dan. *tip*, Ger. (dim.) *zipfel.*]

tip, tip, *v.t.* to strike lightly but definitely: to hit glancingly: (*pr.p.* **tipp'ing**; *pa.t.* and *pa.p.* **tipped**). —*n.* a tap.—*ns.* **tip'-and-run',** a kind of cricket in which the batsman must run if he hits at all: a raid in which the raiders make off at once; **tipp'ing,** a mode of articulating with the tongue to give staccato effects on the flute, trumpet, &c. [Cf. Du. and Ger. *tippen*, Sw. *tippa*, to tip.]

tip, tip, *v.t.* to give, hand, pass, convey: to give a tip to: to indicate.—*v.i.* to give tips: (*pr.p.* **tipp'-ing**; *pa.p.* and *pa.t.* **tipped**).—*n.* a gratuity: a hint or piece of special information supposed to be useful in betting, examinations, &c., a wrinkle.— *ns.* **tipp'er**; **tipp'ing**; **tip'ster,** one whose business it is to furnish tips.—**tip one the wink,** to convey a secret hint. [*Orig.* rogues' cant.]

tip, tip, *v.t.* to cast down: to upset: to tilt: to shoot, dump, empty out, by tilting: to toss off. —*v.i.* to topple over: to tilt: (*pr.p.* **tipp'ing**; *pa.p.* and *pa.t.* **tipped**).—*n.* a tilt: a place for tipping rubbish, coal, &c.: a dump: a staith or shoot: a tram for expeditiously transferring coal.— *ns.* **tip'-cart,** a cart emptied by being canted up: **tip'-cat,** a cat or pointed piece of wood: a game in which the cat is struck with a cat-stick and made to spring up; **tip'-cheese,** (*Dickens*) app. tip-cat; **tipp'er**; **tipp'ing.**—*adj.* **tip'-up,** constructed so as to allow of being tilted.—**tip off liquor,** to turn up the vessel till quite empty; **tip the scale,** to depress one end of the scales. [M.E. *type*; origin obscure.]

tipper, tip'ər, *n.* a kind of ale—from Thomas *Tipper*, who brewed it in Sussex.

tippet, tip'it, *n.* (*obs.*) a long band of cloth, variously worn, esp. an ecclesiastical scarf: (*obs., facet.*) the hangman's rope: a cape: an animal's ruff of hair or feathers: a moth's patagium. [Prob. **tip** (1).]

tipple, tip'l, *v.t.* and *v.i.* to drink constantly in small quantities: to booze.—*n.* liquor tippled.—*ns.* **tipp'ler**; **tipp'ling-house.** [Cf. Norw. dial. *tipla.*]

tipstaff, tip'stäf, *n.* a staff tipped with metal: an officer who carries it, a sheriff's officer:—*pl.* **tip'staffs, tip'staves** (*-stävz*). [**tip, staff.**]

tipsy, tip'si, *adj.* partially intoxicated.—*v.t.* to fuddle.—*adv.* **tip'sily.**—*ns.* **tip'siness**; **tip'sy-cake,** a cake made of pastry and almonds, with wine; **tip'sy-key,** a watch-key in which the head is released if an attempt is made to turn it backward. [Prob. **tip** (4).]

tiptoe, tip'tō, *n.* the end of the toe or toes, more often merely the toes.—*adv.* **on tiptoe,** literally or figuratively, through excitement, expectation, &c. —*v.i.* to walk on tiptoe, to go lightly and stealthily:—*pr.p.* **tip'toeing**; *pa.t.* and *pa.p.* **tip'toed.** [**tip, toe.**]

tiptop, tip'top', *n.* the extreme top: the height of excellence.—*adj.* of the highest excellence.—Also *adv.* [**tip, top.**]

Tipula, tip'ū-lä, *n.* the daddy-long-legs genus of flies, giving name to the family **Tipū'lidae.** [L. *tippula*, a water-spider.]

tirade, ti-rād', tī-rād', tē-rād', *n.* a long vehement harangue: a string of invective: (*pros.*) a laisse: (*mus.*) a run between two notes. [Fr.,—It. *tirata*—*tirare*, to pull.]

tirailleur, tē-rä-yər, *n.* a skirmisher, sharp-shooter. [Fr.]

tirasse, ti-räs', *n.* a pedal-coupler in an organ.

tire, tīr, *n.* (*Shak.*) equipment, furniture: attire, apparel: a head-dress: (*U.S.*) a pinafore.—*v.t.* to attire: to dress, as the head.—*ns.* **tire'-val'iant,** (*Shak.*) a kind of fanciful head-dress; **tire'-**

Neutral vowels in unaccented syllables: *el'ə-mənt, in'fənt, ran'dəm*

woman, a lady's-maid; **tir′ing**; **tir′ing-glass**; **tir′ing-house, -room**, a theatre dressing-room; **tir′ing-woman**. [Short for attire.]

tire, *tīr*, *n.* a metal hoop to bind a wheel: (now commonly **tyre**) a rubber band, cushion, or tube round a wheel-rim.—*v.t.* to put a tire on.—*adjs.* **tired** (tȳrd); **tire′less** (tȳre′less).—*n.* tir′ing (tȳr′ing). [Prob. same word as the foregoing.]

tire, *tīr*, *n.* (*Spens.*) a train: a tier of guns. [tier.]

tire, *tīr*, *n.* a volley: a broadside. [Fr. *tir*.]

tire, *tīr*, *v.i.* (*Shak.*) to tear and tug or feed greedily as a bird of prey: (*Shak.*) to be intent, occupy oneself, feed one's thoughts or desires. [O.Fr. *tirer*.]

tire, *tīr*, *v.i.* to weary: to become fatigued: to have interest or patience exhausted or worn down.—*v.t.* to weary: to fatigue: to bore: to wear out.—*adj.* **tired**, (often with *of*) wearied: fatigued.—*n.* **tired′ness**.—*adj.* **tire′less**, untiring.—*adv.* **tire′lessly**.—*ns.* **tire′lessness**, **tire′ling**, a tired animal.—Also *adj.* (*Spens.* *tyreling jade*).—*adj.* **tire′some**, fatiguing: wearisome: boring: tedious: (loosely) irritating, troublesome, irksome.—*adv.* **tire′somely**. — *n.* **tire′someness**. — **tire down**, to hunt to exhaustion. [App. O.E. *tīorian*, to be tired.]

tirl, *tirl*, *v.t.* and *v.i.* (*Scot.*) to turn: to whirl: to rattle.—*n.* a turnstile or the like.—*n.* **tirl′ie-wirl′ie**, a twirl.—*adj.* twirled: intricate.—*n.* **tirl′ing-pin**, (*obs.*) the pin of a door-latch, rattled to seek admission: now usu. taken to mean a risp. [**trill** (2).]

tirl, *tirl*, *v.t.* (*Scot.*) to strip. [Cf. **tirr**.]

tiro, *tī′rō* (also **tyro**), *n.* a beginner: a novice:—*pl.* **ti′ros**, also **ty′roes**, **ti′roes**, **tyrones** (*tī′rō′nēz*).—*n.* **tirocinium** (-*sin′-i-əm*), early training: first experience. [L. *tīrō* (L.L. *tȳrō*), -*ōnis*, a recruit, *tīrōcinium*, a first campaign.]

Tironensian, *tī-rō-nen′si-ən*, *n.* a Benedictine of a congregation founded (1109) at *Tiron* (Thiron, near Nogent-le-Rotrou), absorbed in 1627 by that of St Maur.—Also *adj.*

Tironian, *tī-rō′ni-ən*, *adj.* of *Tīrō* (-*ōnis*), Cicero's amanuensis, or of shorthand writing (*Tironian notes*) ascribed to him.—**Tironian sign**, ampersand.

tirr, *tir*, *v.t.* and *v.i.* (*Scot.*) to strip. [M.E. *tirve*; origin unknown.]

tirra-lirra, **tirra-lyra**, *tir-ä-lir′ä*, *n.* and *interj.* an old refrain, ascribed by Shakespeare to the lark.

tirrit, *tir′it*, *n.* (*Shak.*) Mrs Quickly's word for alarm, fright.

tirrivee, **tirrivie**, *tir′i-vi*, or -*vē′*, *n.* (*Scot.*) a tantrum or fit of passion: a commotion.

'tis, *tiz*, a contraction of it is.

tisane, *ti-zan′*, *n.* a medicinal decoction. [See **ptisan**.]

tisick, *tiz′ik*, *n.* (*Shak.*) a cough. [**phthisic**.]

Tisiphone, *ti-sif′o-nē*, *n.* one of the Furies. [Gr. *Tīsiphonē*—*tīsis*, retribution, *phonos*, murder.]

Tisri, *tiz′ri*, *n.* the first month of the Jewish civil year, seventh of the ecclesiastical, usually part of September and October.

tissue, *tish′(y)ōō*, *tis′ū*, *n.* anything woven, esp. a rich or gauzy fabric: (*biol.*) an aggregate of similar cells: a fabric, mass, or agglomeration, as of lies, nonsense: (*phot.*) paper coated with gelatine and pigment: tissue-paper.—*v.t.* to weave or interweave, esp. with gold or silver thread: to clothe, cover, adorn, with tissue: to variegate.—*n.* **tiss′ue-pa′per**, a thin, soft, semitransparent paper (said to have been put between folds of tissue). [Fr. *tissu*, woven, pa.p. of *tître* (O.Fr. *tistre*)—L. *texēre*, to weave.]

tit, *tit*, *n.* a variant of **teat**.

tit, *tit*, *n.* (*dial.*) a tap.—**tit for tat**, a tip for a tap, retaliation.

tit, *tit*, *n.* a small or inferior horse: a nag: (in real or feigned depreciation) a girl, young woman: a titmouse. [Ice. *tittr*, titmouse.]

tit, *tit*, *n.* (chiefly *Scot.*) a twitch: a tug.—*v.t.* and *v.i.* to tug.

tit. See **tite**.

Titan, *tī′tən*, *n.* a son or daughter (**Tī′taness**) or other descendant of Uranus and Gaea: one of the elder gods and goddesses overthrown by Zeus:

the name of one of them, Hyperion: Helios, the sun-god: the sun personified: Prometheus: (*astron.*) Saturn's greatest satellite: **titan**, anything gigantic: a man of great intellect but not the highest inspiration.—Also *adj.*—*n.* **Titania** (*tī-tā′ni-ä*, *ti-tä′ni-ä*), the queen of Fairy, wife of Oberon: a satellite of Uranus.—*adjs.* **Titanesque** (-*esk′*); **Titā′nian**; **Titanic**, **titanic** (*tī-* or *ti-tan′ik*).—*ns.* **Ti′tanism**, the spirit of revolt against the universe; **Titanomachy** (-*om′ə-ki*; Gr. *machē*, fight), the war of the Titans against the Olympian gods; **Titanosau′rus**, a gigantic Cretaceous dinosaur; **Titanothē′rium**, a huge rhinoceros-like American Oligocene fossil ungulate. [Gr. *Tītān*.]

titanium, *ti-tā′ni-əm*, *n.* a metallic element (Ti; at. number 22) found in ilmenite, sphene, rutile, &c.—*n.* **titanate** (*tī′tən-āt*), a salt of titanic acid.—*adjs.* **titanic** (-*tan′ik*), of quadrivalent titanium (**titanic acid**, H_2TiO_3; **titanic iron**, ilmenite); **titanif′erous**, containing titanium.—*n.* **ti′tanite**, sphene, a brown, green, or yellow monoclinic mineral, calcium silicate and titanate.—*adj.* **ti′tanous**, of trivalent titanium. [Gr. *Tītān*, 'Titan, on the analogy of **uranium**.]

titbit, *tit′bit*, *n.* a choice delicacy or item.—Also **tid′bit**.

tite, **tyte**, **tight**, *tīt*, **tit**, *tit*, titely, &c., -*li*, *advs.* (*obs.*) promptly: at once. [Cf. O.N. *títt*, often.]

tithe, *tīdh*, *adj.* tenth.—*n.* a tenth part, an indefinitely small part: the tenth of the produce of land and stock allotted originally for church purposes: a rent-charge in commutation of this: any levy of one-tenth.—*v.t.* to take a tithe of or from: to pay a tithe on: (*obs.*) to decimate.—*adj.* **tith′able**, subject to the payment of tithes.—*n.* **tithe′-barn**, a barn for storing the parson's tithe in corn.—*adjs.* **tithed**; **tithe′-free**, exempt from paying tithes.—*n.* **tithe′-gatherer**.—*adj.* **tithe′-paying**.—*ns.* **tithe′-pig**, one pig out of ten paid as a tithe; **tithe′-proctor**, a collector of tithes; **tith′er**, one who collects tithes; **tith′ing**, a tithe: exaction or payment of tithes: (*hist.*) a district containing ten householders, each responsible for the behaviour of the rest; **tith′ing-man**, the chief man of a tithing. [O.E. *tēotha*, tenth; cf. **tenth**, **teind**.]

titi, **tee-tee**, *tē-tē′*, *n.* a small South American monkey (Callithrix).

Titian, **titian**, *tish′(y)ən*, *n.* a red-yellow colour used by the Venetian painter *Titian* (Tiziano Vecellio, 1477-1576).—*adj.* (chiefly of hair) of this colour, or (loosely) of other shade of red or reddish-brown.—*adj.* **Titianesque** (-*esk′*), in the manner of Titian, a combination of the richest surface and colour.

titillate, *tit′il-lāt*, *v.t.* to tickle: to stimulate gently.—*ns.* **titillā′tion**; **tit′illātor**. [L. *titillāre*, -*ātum*.]

tit(t)ivate, *tit′i-vāt*, **tidivate**, *tid′*, *v.i.* and *v.t.* (*slang*) to smarten up, by dress or otherwise.—*n.* **tit(t)ivā′tion**, **tidivā′tion**. [Poss. coined from **tidy**.]

titlark, *tit′lärk*, *n.* a pipit. [**tit** and **lark**.]

title, *tī′tl*, *n.* an inscription or descriptive placard: a chapter-heading: a section of a law-book: the name of a book, poem, tale, picture, &c.: a title-page: (*publishers′ slang*) a book or publication, as an item in a catalogue: an appellation of rank or distinction: a right to possession: a ground of claim: evidence of right: a title-deed: a fixed sphere of work, source of maintenance, or a certificate thereof, required as a condition for ordination: a cardinal-priest's parish in Rome.—*v.t.* to designate: to give or attach a title to.—*adj.* **ti′tled**, having a title.—*ns.* **ti′tle-deed**, a document that proves right to possession; **ti′tle-leaf**, the leaf on which is the title of a book.—*adj.* **ti′tleless**, (*Shak.*) nameless: untitled.—*ns.* **ti′tle-page**, the page of a book containing its title; **ti′tle-poem**, that which gives its title to a book; **ti′tler**, a writer of titles: (*obs.*) a claimant; **ti′tle-rôle**, the part in a play which gives its name to it; **ti′tle-sheet**, the first sheet of a book as printed, containing title, bastard-title, &c.; **ti′tling**, the giving or attaching of a title. [O.E. *tītul* or *titul* and O.Fr. *title* (Fr. *titre*)—L. *titulus*.]

titling, *tit'ling*, *n.* a small stockfish: (esp. *Scot.*) the meadow-pipit: also the hedge-sparrow. [Norw. dial. *titling*, small stockfish ; O.N. *titlingr*, sparrow ; cf. **tit**.]

titmouse, *tit'mows* (Spens. **titmose**, *-mōs*), *n.* a tit, a little active acrobatic bird of Parus or kindred genus :—*pl.* **titmice** (*tit'mīs*). [**tit**, and M.E. *mose*, titmouse—O.E. *māse* ; Ger. *meise* ; confused with **mouse**.]

titrate, *tī'trāt*, *v.t.* to subject to titration.—*n.* **titrā'-tion**, measurement of the strength of a solution by finding how much of another solution of known strength is required to complete a chemical reaction. [Fr. *titre*, standard.]

ti-tree. See **ti**.

titter, *tit'ər*, *v.i.* to giggle, snicker, or laugh restrainedly.—*n.* a stifled laugh.—*n.* **titt'erer**.—*n.* and *adj.* **titt'ering**. [Cf. Sw. dial. *tittra*.]

titter, *tit'ər*, *v.i.* to totter, sway. [O.N. *titra*, to shake.]

tittle, *tit'l*, *n.* a dot, stroke, accent, vowel-point, contraction or punctuation mark : the smallest part. [O.Fr. *title*—L. *titulus*, a title.]

tittle, *tit'l*, *v.t.* and *v.i.* (*dial*). to whisper : to tattle. —*n.* **titt'le-tatt'le**, idle, empty talk.—*v.i.* to prate idly.—*ns.* **titt'le-tatt'ler** ; **titt'le-tatt'ling**.

tittlebat, *tit'l-bat*, *n.* a childish form of **stickleback**.

tittup, **titup**, *tit'əp*, *v.i.* to prance, skip about gaily.—*n.* a light springy step, a canter.—*adj.* **titt'upy**, **tit'upy**, gay, lively : unsteady. [Imit.]

titty, *tit'i*, *n.* a teat : the breast. [Dim. of **tit**, **teat**.]

titty, *tit'i*, *n.* (Scot.) sister.

titubate, *tit'ū-bāt*, *v.i.* to stagger, stumble.—*n.* **tit'ūbancy**, staggering.—*adj.* **tit'ūbant**.—*n.* **titūbā'tion**. [L. *titubāre*, *-ātum*, to stagger.]

titule, *tit'ūl*, *n.* and *v.t.* Same as **title**.—*adj.* **tit'ūlar**, pertaining to title : in name or title only : nominal : having the title without the duties of an office : supplying a title to a cardinal-priest (as a titular church).—*n.* a titled person : one who enjoys the bare title of an office, without actual possession : a person invested with a title in virtue of which he holds a benefice, whether he performs its duties or not : (*R.C.*) that from which a church takes its name (*patron* if a saint or angel).—*n.* **titularity** (-*ar'i-ti*).—*adv.* **tit'ularly**.—*adj.* **tit'ulary**, titular.—*n.* one who holds a title.—**titular bishop**, (*R.C.*) a bishop without a diocese, taking his title from a place where there is no longer a bishop's see—before 1882 bishop in *partibus infidelium* ; **titular of the teinds** or **tithes**, a layman invested with church lands after the Reformation in Scotland. [L. *titulus*.]

tityre-tu, *tit'* or *tīt-i-ri-t(y)ōō'*, *n.* a member of a 17th-century fraternity of aristocratic hooligans. [Opening words of Virgil's first eclogue, *Tītyre tū*, Tityrus, thou (lying under the spreading beech), conjectured to indicate the class that had beech trees and leisure to lie under them.]

Tiw, *tē'w*, *n.* the old English war-god. [O.E. *Tīw* ; cf. **Tuesday**, **Tyr**.]

tizzy, *tiz'i*, *n.* (old slang) a sixpence.

tmesis, *tmē'sis*, *n.* (gram.) the separation of the parts of a compound word by a word or words. [Gr. *tmēsis*—*temnein*, to cut.]

to, *tōō*, *too*, *tə*, *prep.* serving as sign of the infinitive (which is sometimes understood) and forming a substitute for the dative case : in the direction of : as far as : all the way in the direction of : until : into the condition of : towards : beside : near : at : in contact with, close against : before : for : of : with the object or result of : against : in accordance, comparison, or relation with : in honour of, or expressing good wishes for : along with in addition.—*adv.* in one direction, forward : in or into position, contact, closed or harnessed condition.—**to and fro**, alternately this way and that. [O.E. *tō* ; Ger. *zu*, Goth. *du* ; Gr. suffix *-de*.]

toad, *tōd*, *n.* a toothless tailless amphibian that walks or crawls instead of jumping like the frog, esp. one of Bufo or kindred genus : a hateful or contemptible person or animal : (alchemy) bufo.—*ns.* **toad'-eater**, a fawning sycophant—originally a mounte-bank's assistant, whose duty was to swallow, or pretend to swallow, toads ; **toad'-eating**, syco-phancy.—*adj.* sycophantic.—*ns.* **toad'fish**, a toad-like fish of many kinds ; **toad'flax**, any species of Linaria, a genus closely allied to snapdragon with flax-like leaves ; **toad'-in-a-hole**, beef cooked in batter ; **toad'-rush** (or **-grass**), a low rush (*Juncus bufonius*) with mostly solitary flowers ; **toad'-spit**, cuckoo-spit.—*adj.* **toad'-spott'ed**, thickly stained or spotted like a toad.—*ns.* **toad'-stone**, a stone or concretion formerly believed to be found in a toad's head, and valued as an amulet : (*Derbyshire*) a basalt lava or tuff (supposed to be from its markings ; but poss.—Ger. *totes gestein*, dead stone, from the lead-miner's point of view) ; **toad'stool**, any mushroom-like fungus, often excluding the mushroom ; **toad'y**, a toad-eater, sycophant.—*v.t.* to fawn as a sycophant :—*pr.p.* **toad'ying** ; *pa.t.* and *pa.p.* **toad'ied**.—*adj.* **toad'yish**.—*n.* **toad'yism**. [O.E. *tāde*, *tādige*, *tādie*.]

toast, *tōst*, *v.t.* to dry and parch : to brown (as bread) : to half-melt (as cheese) : to warm or heat by rays : to drink to.—*v.i.* to drink toasts : to undergo, or be suitable for, toasting.—*n.* bread toasted : a piece of toasted bread, usu. one put in liquor : the person or thing drunk to, esp. the lady most admired for the moment : a proposal of health.—*adj.* **toast'ed**.—*ns.* **toast'er**, one who toasts : a toasting-fork : an electric apparatus for making toast : that which can be toasted ; **toast'-ing**, **toast'ing-fork**, **-iron**, a long-handled fork for toasting bread : (*facet.*) a sword ; **toast'-master**, the announcer of toasts at a dinner ; **toast'-rack**, a stand with partitions for slices of toast.—**on toast**, served on a slice of toast : swindled : at one's mercy. [O.Fr. *toster*—L. *tostus*, roasted, pa.p. of *torrēre*.]

toaze, *tōz* (Shak.). See **toze**.

tobacco, *tə-bak'ō*, *n.* an American solanaceous plant, *Nicotiana Tabacum*, or other species of the genus : its prepared leaves used for smoking, chewing, or snuffing.—*ns.* **tobaccanā'lian** (*facet.* ; after bacch-analian), a smoker ; **tobacc'o-heart**, a functional disorder of the heart due to excessive use of tobacco ; **tobacc'onist**, (*obs.*) a smoker : a seller or manufacturer of tobacco ; **tobacc'o-pipe**, a pipe for smoking tobacco ; **tobacc'o-plant** ; **tobacc'o-pouch**, a pouch for holding tobacco ; **tobacc'o-stopper**, an instrument for pressing down the tobacco in a pipe. [Sp. *tabaco*, from Haytian.]

to-be, *too-*, *tə-bē'*, *n.* and *adj.* future.

Tobit, *tō'bit*, *n.* an apocryphal Old Testament book, containing the story of *Tobit*.

toboggan, *tə-bog'ən*, *n.* a flat sledge turned up in front.—*v.i.* to slide, coast, travel, on, or as if on, a toboggan.—Earlier also **tobogg'in**, **tabogg'an**, **tarbogg'in**.—*ns.* **tobogg'aner** ; **tobogg'aning** ; **tobogg'anist**. [Micmac *tobākun*.]

to-break, *too-*, *tə-brāk'*, *v.t.* (obs.) to break in pieces : —*pa.t.* (*B.*, Bunyan) **to-brake'** (usu. printed *to brake*) ; *pa.p.* **to-bro'ken**. [O.E. *tōbrecan*—pfx. *tō-*, asunder, and *brecan*, to break.]

to-bruise, *tə-brōōz'*, *v.t.* (obs.) to bruise severely : to break up :—*pa.p.* (Spens.) **to-brusd'**. [O.E. *tō-brȳsan* ; see pfx. *to-*, and **bruise**.]

Toby, *tō'bi*, *n.* a beer-mug shaped like a man with three-cornered hat : Punch's dog.

toby, *tō'bi*, *n.* (thieves' slang) the road : robbery on the road.—**high toby**, highway robbery ; **low toby**, footpad robbery. [Shelta *tōbar*.]

toccata, *tok'kä'tä*, *n.* (mus.) primarily a work intended to display the performer's touch, or in which he seems to try the touch of an instrument in a series of runs and chords before breaking into a fugue : loosely, a sort of fantasia or overture.—*ns.* **toccatel'la**, **toccatina** (-*tē'nä*), a short toccata. [It.,—*toccare*, to touch.]

toc emma, *tok em'ä*, *n.* (mil. slang) a trench mortar. —*n.* **Toc H** (*āch*), a society for handing on the spirit of comradeship of the war of 1914-18, from its first meetings at Talbot House, at Poperinghe. [Formerly signallers' names of the initial letters T, E and T, H.]

Tocharian, **Tokharian**, *to-kä'ri-ən*, or *-kā'*, **Tocha'rish**, **Tokha'rish**, *-rish*, *ns.* an extinct Indo-Germanic language, akin to Latin and Celtic, preserved in MSS. discovered in the 20th century in Chinese Turkestan. [Gr. *Tocharoi*, a people guessed to be its speakers on the strength of the Uigur name *Tochri*.]

tocher, *tohh′ər, n.* (*Scot.*) a dowry.—*v.t.* to dower. —*n.* **toch′er-good,** property given as tocher.— *adj.* **toch′erless.** [Ir. *tochar*, Gael. *tochradh.*]

toco, *tō′kō, n.* (*slang*) punishment.—Also **tō′ko.** [Gr. *tokos*, interest.]

tocology, tokology, *tok-ol′ə-ji, n.* obstetrics.—*n.* **tocoph′erol,** vitamin E, whose deficiency causes sterility. [Gr. *tokos*, birth, offspring, *logos*, discourse, *pherein*, to bring.]

tocsin, *tok′sin, n.* an alarm-bell, or the ringing of it. [Fr. *tocsin*—Prov. *tocasenh*—*tocar*, to touch, strike, *senh*—L. *signum*, sign (L.L. bell).]

tod, *tod, n.* (*Scot.*) a fox : a sly person.—*n.* **Todlow′rie** (i.e. Laurence), Reynard. [Origin unknown.]

tod (*Spens.* **todde**), *tod, n.* a bush, esp. of ivy : an old wool weight, about 28 lb.: a load.—*v.i.* to yield a tod.—*v.t.* to yield a tod for.

today, to-day, *too-, tə-dā′, n.* this or the present day.—*adv.* on the present day : nowadays. [O.E. *tōdæg*(*e*).]

toddle, *tod′l, v.i.* to walk with short feeble steps, as a child : to saunter : to go.—*n.* a toddling gait : an aimless stroll : a toddling child.—*n.* **todd′ler,** one who toddles, esp. a child.—*adj.* **todd′ling.**

toddy, *tod′i, n.* fermented palm juice : a mixture of spirits, sugar, and hot water.—*ns.* **todd′y-cat,** the palm civet ; **todd′y-ladle,** a small ladle for mixing or serving toddy ; **todd′y-palm,** coconut, borassus, or other palm yielding toddy ; **todd′y-stick,** a stick used in mixing toddy. [Hind. *tārī*—*tār*, a palm-tree.]

to-do, *tə-, too-dōō′, n.* bustle : stir : commotion.

tody, *tō′di, n.* a small West Indian insectivorous bird—the *green sparrow, green humming-bird*, &c., akin to the kingfishers. [L. *todus*, a small bird of some kind.]

toe, *tō, n.* one of the five small members at the point of the foot : the front of a hoof : the corresponding part of a shoe, sock, golfclub-head, &c.: the lowest part of the front of anything, esp. if it projects.—*v.t.* to stand with the toes against : to kick : to strike with the toe of a club : to nail obliquely through the foot : to perform with the toe : to furnish with a toe, as a stocking.—*v.i.* to place the toes :—*pr.p.* **toe′ing** ; *pa.t.* and *pa.p.* **toed.**—*ns.* **toe′-cap,** a cap covering the toe of a shoe ; **toe′clip,** an attachment to a bicycle pedal that receives the toe.—*adj.* **toed** (*tōd*), having toes : nailed obliquely.—*ns.* **toe′-nail** ; **toe′-piece.**— **toe the line,** to stand with toes against a marked line, as in starting a race : to conform. [O.E. *tá* (pl. *tán*) ; O.N. *tá*, Ger. *zehe.*]

to-fall, *too′fawl, n.* beginning, incidence. [**to, fall.**]

toff, *tof, n.* (*slang*) a person of the upper and richer or more showy classes.—*adjs.* **toff′ish, toff′y.** [Perh. **tuft.**]

toffee, toffy, *tof′i, n.* a hard-baked sweetmeat, made of sugar and butter.—*Earlier* and *U.S.* **taff′y.**—*n.* **toff′ee-app′le,** a toffee-coated apple on a stick. [Ety. unknown.]

tofore, *too-, tə-fōr′, adv.* (*Shak.*), *prep., conj.* (*obs.*) before. [O.E. *tóforan* (prep.).]

toft, *toft, n.* a homestead : a hillock. [Late O.E. *toft*—O.N. *topt, tupt, toft.*]

tog, *tog, n.* (*slang*) a garment—generally in *pl.*—*v.t.* to dress.—*n.* **togg′ery,** clothes.—*n.pl.* **long′-togs,** (*naut.*) shore clothes. [Prob. ultimately L. *toga*, a robe.]

toga, *tō′gä, n.* the mantle or outer garment of a Roman citizen.—Also **toge** (*tōg* ; *Shak. conjectured*).—*adjs.* **to′ga′d, to′gaed, to′gate, -d, toged** (*tōgd* ; *Shak.*). [L. *tŏga* ; cf. *tegĕre*, to cover : **thatch.**]

together, *tə-, too-gedh′ər, adv.* in or to the same place : at the same time : in or into connexion, company, or concert. [O.E. *tógædere*—*tó*, to, *geador*, together.]

toggle, *tog′l, n.* a cross-piece on a rope, chain, rod, &c., to prevent slipping through a hole, or to allow twisting : an appliance for transmitting force at

right angles to its direction.—*v.t.* to hold or furnish with a toggle : to fix fast.—*ns.* **togg′le-iron,** a harpoon with a toggle instead of barbs ; **togg′le-joint,** an elbow or knee joint. [App. conn. with **tug** and **tow.**]

togue, *tōg, n.* the Great Lake char (or trout), a gigantic salmonid of North America. [From Indian name.]

toho, *tō-hō′, interj.* a call to pointers to stop.

tohu bohu, *tō′hoō bō′hoō, n.* chaos. [Heb. *thōhū wa-bhōhū*, emptiness and desolation (Gen. i. 2).]

toil, *toil, v.i.* to struggle hard : to labour hard : to make one's way by strong effort.—*v.t.* to effect or work out with toil : to subject to toil.—*n.* (*obs.*) contention : a struggle : hard labour.—*adj.* **toiled.** —*n.* **toil′er.**—*adj.* **toil′ful.**—*n.* and *adj.* **toil′ing.**— *adjs.* **toil′less** ; **toil′some,** involving toil : toiling : (*Spens.* **toylsom, toylesome**) owing to toil.—*adv.* **toil′somely.**—*n.* **toil′someness.**—*adj.* **toil′-worn,** worn with toil. [A.Fr. *toiler* (Fr. *touillier*), said to be—L. *tudiculāre*, to stir.]

toil, *toil, n.* a net : a snare.—*ns.* **toile** (*twäl*), a dress material ; **toilet** (*toil′it*), a cloth for the shoulder during hair-dressing : a toilet-cover : a toilet-table : a dressing-table with a mirror : the articles used in dressing : mode or process of dressing : a reception of visitors during dressing : the whole dress and appearance of a person, any particular costume : a dressing-room, bathroom, or lavatory : the cleansing and dressing of a wound ; **toil′et-cloth, -cover,** a cover for a dressing-table. —*adj.* **toil′eted,** dressed.—*ns.* **toil′et-glass,** a mirror set on the dressing-table ; **toil′et-paper,** paper for the privy ; **toil′et-service, -set,** the utensils collectively used in dressing ; **toil′et-soap,** soap for personal use ; **toil′et-table,** a dressing-table ; **toilette** (*twä-let′*), toilet ; **toilinet′** (*toi-*), **toilinette** (*twäl-i-net′*), a kind of woollen cloth used for waistcoats : a silk and cotton warp with woollen weft. [Fr. *toile*, dim. *toilette*—L. *tēla*, web.]

toise, *toiz, n.* an old French lineal measure=6·395 Eng. feet. [Fr.,—L. *tendĕre, tēnsum*, to stretch.]

toisech, *tō′shehh, n.* (*hist.*) an ancient Celtic noble below a mormaor. [Gael. *tòisech.*]

Tokay, *tō-kā′, n.* a sweetish and heavy wine with an aromatic flavour, produced at *Tokay* (*Hung.* Tokaj, *tō′koi*) in Hungary : the grape that yields it.

token, *tō′kn, n.* a sign : a symbol : a portent : an indication : an evidence : (*obs.*) a plague-spot : an authenticating sign, word, or object : a keepsake : a private coin redeemable in current money or goods : in Presbyterian churches a metal voucher admitting to communion (superseded by the communion card) : a measure of hand-press work, usu. 250 pulls.—*adj.* serving as a symbol : hence, being a mere show or semblance, as ' a token resistance.' —*v.t.* to betoken.—*adj.* **to′ken'd,** (*Shak.*) indicated by plague-spots.—*n.* **to′ken-money,** money current for more than its intrinsic value as metal : private tokens.—**by the same token,** further in corroboration, or merely by the way ; **more by token** (see **more**) ; **the Lord's tokens,** (*Shak.*) plague-spots. [O.E. *tácen* ; Ger. *zeichen*, a mark.]

toko, tokology. See **toco, tocology.**

tola, *tō′lä, n.* an Indian unit of weight=180 grains troy. [Hind.,—Sans. *tulā*, weight.]

tolbooth, *tōl′* or *tol′booth, -bōōdh* (*Scot. -bəth*), *n.* an office where tolls are collected : a town-hall : a prison : often a combination of these. [**toll** (1), **booth.**]

told, *tōld, pa.t.* and *pa.p.* of **tell.**

tole, toll, *tōl, v.t.* (now *U.S.* and *dial.*) to lure, decoy.—*ns.* **toll′-bait,** (*U.S.*) chopped bait thrown to attract fish ; **tol′ing, toll′ing,** the use of toll-bait : a method of decoying ducks, &c., by exciting curiosity. [M.E. *tollen*—root of O.E. (*for*)*tyllan* ; see **till** (1).]

Toledo, *tō-lē′dō, n.* a sword-blade made at *Toledo* (*-lā′*) in Spain.

tolerate, *tol′ə-rāt, v.t.* to endure : to endure with patience or impunity : to allow, allow to exist.— *n.* **tolerabil′ity.**—*adj.* **tol′erable,** endurable : passable : fair.—*adv.* **tol′erably.**—*n.* **tol′erance,** ability to endure : disposition or willingness to tolerate or allow : permissible range of variation.—

fāte, fär, àsk ; mē, hər (her) ; *mīne ; mōte ; mūte ; mōōn ; dhen* (then)

adj. **tol′erant,** tolerating: enduring: (*biol.* and *med.*) capable of enduring (e.g. unfavourable conditions, a parasite, a drug) without showing serious effects: indulgent: favouring toleration.—*adv.* **tol′erantly.**—*ns.* **tolera′tion,** act of tolerating: allowance of what is not approved: liberty given to a minority to hold and express their own political or religious opinions; **tolera′tionist; tol′erātor.** [L. *tolerāre, -ātum—tollĕre,* to lift up.]

toll, *tōl, n.* a tax for the liberty of using a bridge or road, selling goods in a market, &c.: a portion of grain kept by a miller in payment for grinding: (*Scot.*) a place where there is or was or might have been a toll-bar, a road junction: (*journalistic*) tribute to death (as *toll of the road*): a toll-call.—*v.i.* to take or pay toll.—*v.t.* to take toll of: to take as toll.—*adj.* **toll′able,** subject to toll.—*ns.* **toll′age,** payment of toll: the amount paid as toll; **toll′-bar,** a movable bar across a road, &c., to stop passengers liable to toll; **toll′booth** (see tolbooth); **toll′-bridge, -gate,** bridge, gate, where toll is taken; **toll′-call,** short-distance telephone trunk-call: (*U.S.,* &c.) trunk call; **toll′dish,** dish for measuring the toll in mills; **toll′er, toll′-gath′erer.**—*adj.* and *adv.* **toll′-free′.**—*ns.* **toll′-house; toll′man,** the man who collects toll: a toll-gatherer; **tolsel** (*tōl′sel*), **tolzey** (*-zi*), **tolsey** (*tol′si*), local names (æpp.—O.E. *seld,* seat, or *sæl,* hall) for a tollbooth or exchange. [O.E. *toll;* cf. Du. *tol,* Ger. *zoll;* supposed to be from L.L. *tolōneum—*Gr. *telōnion,* customs—*telos,* fulfilment, tax, &c.; by some connected with toll, tale.]

toll, *tōl, v.i.* to sound, as a large bell, esp. with a measured sound.—*v.t.* to cause to sound, as a bell: to sound, strike, signal, announce, summon, send, by tolling: to toll for the death of.—*n.* the sound of a bell tolling.—*n.* **toll′er.** [Prob. **tole.**]

toll, *tōl, v.t.* (*law*) to bar: to take away right of. [A.Fr. *toller—*L. *tollĕre,* to take away.]

toll. Same as **tole.**

tol-lol, *tol′lol′, adj.* (*old slang*) pretty good.—*adj.* **tol-lol′ish,** tolerable. [tolerable.]

tolt, *tōlt, n.* an old English writ removing a court-baron cause to a county court. [A.Fr. *tolte—*L.L. *tolta—*L. *tollĕre,* to take away.]

tolter, *tol′tər, v.i.* (*prov.*) to flounder about.

Tolu, *tō-lōō′, n.* (in full **balsam of Tolu**) a balsam yielded by the South American papilionaceous tree *Myroxylon Toluifera.*—*ns.* **toluene** (*tol′ū-ēn*), **tol′uol,** methyl benzene.—*adj.* **tolū′ic.** [From Santiago de *Tolú* in Colombia.]

Tom, *tom, n.* a shortened form of *Thomas:* a male, esp. a cat: a name for a big bell.—*ns.* **Tom′-and-Jerry′,** hot rum and eggs, spiced and sweetened; **tom′-cat; Tom′-nodd′y,** the puffin: a fool; **Tom′-trot,** a kind of toffee.—**Long Tom,** a long gun, esp. one carried amidships on a swivel-carriage; **Old Tom,** gin; **Tom and Tib, Tom Dick and Harry,** anybody: people in general; **Tom o' Bedlam,** formerly, a madman let out with a licence to beg; **Tom Tidd′ler's ground,** a place where wealth is to be had for the picking up: debatable land: No Man's Land (from a children's game so called).

tomahawk, *tom′ə-hawk, n.* a North American Indian war-axe.—*v.t.* to assail or kill with a tomahawk: to hack, cut up, slate. [Virginian Indian *tămăhăk.*]

tomalley, *to-mal′i, n.* American lobster fat: extended to tamal. [Said to be Carib.]

toman, *tō-män′, n.* a myriad, or ten thousand: a former Persian gold coin worth 10,000 dinars. [Pers. *tumān.*]

tomato, *tə-mä′tō* (*U.S. -mā′*), *n.* the love-apple (*Lycopersicum esculentum* or *Solanum Lycopersicum*), a South American plant close akin to the potato: its red or yellow pulpy edible fruit:—*pl.* **toma′toes.**—**gooseberry tomato, strawberry tomato,** the Cape gooseberry. [Sp. *tomate—*Mex. *tomatl.*]

tomb, *tōōm, n.* a grave: a vault for disposal of dead bodies: a sepulchral monument.—*v.t.* to entomb: to bury.—*adjs.* **tombic** (*tōōm′ik, -bik*); **tomb′less.** —*n.* **tomb′stone,** a memorial stone over a tomb. [O.Fr. (Fr.) *tombe—*L. *tumba—*Gr. *tymbos.*]

tombac, tombak, *tom′bak, n.* an alloy of copper with a little zinc: an alloy of copper and arsenic. [Fr. *tombac—*Malay *tāmbaga,* copper.]

tomboc, *tom′bok, n.* a Javanese long-handled weapon.

tombola, *tom′bō-lä, n.* a kind of lottery (at a fête, &c.). [It.,—*tombolare,* to tumble.]

tomboy, *tom′boi, n.* a high-spirited romping girl: formerly, a hoyden: (*Shak.*) an immodest woman. [Tom and boy.]

tome, *tōm, n.* a big book or volume. [Fr.,—L. *tomus—*Gr. *tomos—temnein,* to cut.]

tomentum, *tō-men′təm, n.* a matted cottony pubescence.— *adjs.* **tomentose** (*tō-mən-tōs′, tō-men′tōs*), **tomen′tous.** [L.]

tomfool, *tom′fōōl′, n.* a great fool: a buffoon: a trifling fellow.—*v.i.* to play the fool.—*n.* **tomfool′ery,** foolish trifling or jesting: buffoonery. —*adj.* **tomfoolish.** [Tom.]

tomium, *tō′mi-əm, n.* the cutting edge of a bird's bill.—*adj.* **tō′mial.** [Latinised from Gr. *tomeion,* a knife-edge—*temnein,* to cut.]

tommy, *tom′i, n.* a penny roll, bread: food: a tommy-shop: the truck system.—*v.t.* to oppress by the truck system.—*ns.* **tomm′y-bar,** a rod for turning a tubular spanner or the like; **tomm′y-gun,** a light machine-gun (after its American inventor, General J. T. *Thompson*); **tomm′y-rot,** absolute nonsense; **tomm′y-shop,** a truck-shop. —**soft tommy,** soft bread, as opposed to hard-tack or sea-biscuit; **Tommy Atkins, or Tommy,** a generic name for the private in the British army. [From the name **Thomas.**]

tomorrow, to-morrow, *tə-, too-mor′ō, n.* the day after today.—*adv.* on the day after today. [O.E. *tó morgen.*]

tompion, tompon. Same as **tampion** (see tamp).

tompion, *tom′pi-ən, n.* (*obs.*) a watch of the kind made by Thomas *Tompion* (1639-1713).

tomtit, *tom′tit′, n.* the blue or other tit. [Tom, tit.]

tom-tom, *tom′-tom,* **tam-tam,** *tum′-tum, n.* an Indian drum: any primitive drum or substitute. —*v.i.* to beat thereon. [Hind. *tamtam;* imit.]

ton, *tun, n.* a measure of capacity, varying with the substance measured—timber, wheat, &c. (see **tonnage**): a weight=20 cwt.=2240 lb. (2400 lb. being a *long ton*): (*U.S.*) usually=2000 lb. (*short*), or 2240 lb. (*long ton*).—**metric ton or tonne=** 1000 kilograms=2204·6 lb. [O.E. *tunne,* a vat, tub; see **tun.**]

ton, *ton², n.* fashion: people of fashion.—*adj.* **ton(n)ish** (*ton′ish*), modish, having ton.—*adv.* **ton(n)′ishly.**—*n.* **ton(n)′ishness.** [Fr.]

tonalite, *tō′nə-līt, n.* a quartz-biotite diorite, found at Monte *Tonale,* Tirol.

to-name, *tōō′-năm, n.* a byname, nickname: an additional name used to distinguish persons whose names are alike. [O.E. *tónama—*pfx. *tó-, nama,* name.]

tonant, *tōn′ənt, adj.* thundering. [L. *tonāns, -āntis,* pr.p. of *tonāre,* to thunder.]

tone, *tōn, n.* the character of a sound: quality of sound: accent: intonation: vocal inflexion, rise or fall in pitch: a sound of definite pitch: a major second, one of the larger intervals between successive notes in the scale, as C and D: a Gregorian psalm-tune: vocal expression: bodily firmness, elasticity, or tension, esp. in muscles: prevailing character or spirit: mood: temper: harmony or general effect of colours: depth or brilliance of colour: a tint or shade.—*v.t.* to intone: to give tone or the desired tone to.—*v.i.* to take a tone: to harmonise (with *in*).—*adjs.* **tōn′al,** of tone: according to key; **tōnal′itive,** of tonality.—*n.* **tōnal′ity,** relation in key: key: rendering of colour relations.—*adjs.* **toned,** having a tone (in compounds): braced up: treated to give tone: slightly tinted; **tone′-deaf,** unable to appreciate musical pitch; **tone′less,** soundless: expressionless: dull: relaxed: listless. — *adv.* **tone′lessly.**—*ns.* **tone′lessness; tone′-picture,** a piece of descriptive music; **tone′-poem,** a piece of programme music, not divided into movements, conveying or translating a poetic idea or literary theme.—*adj.* **tonic** (*ton′ik*), relating to tones producing tension : (med.) giving tone and vigour to the system : giving or increasing strength.—n. a tonic medicine : (mus.) a keynote.—ns. **tonicity** (ton-is′i-ti), the property or condition of having tone : mode of reaction to stimulus : the healthy state of muscular fibres when at rest ; **tōn′us**, tone : tonic spasm.—adj. **tōn′(e)y**, (slang) high-toned : fashionable.—**tonal fugue**, one in which the answer conforms to the tonality of the scale ; **tone down**, to give a lower tone to : to moderate : to soften, to harmonise the colours of as to light and shade, as a painting ; **tonic sol-fa**, (mus.) a system of notation and teaching devised by Sarah Glover (1785-1867) and developed by John Curwen, using sol-fa syllables (modified) and their initial letters for the notes of the scale with doh (do) for the tonic, and dividing the bar by colons, dots, and inverted commas ; **tonic spasm**, prolonged uniform muscular spasm (opp. to clonic spasm ; see **clonus**). [Gr. tonos, pitch, tension, partly through Fr. ton and L. tonus.]

tone, tōn, pron. and adj. (obs. or dial.) the one.—Scot. **tane** (pron.), **tae** (adj.). [that one ; cf. **tother**.]

tong, tong, n. a Chinese guild, association, or secret society. [Chin. t′ang.]

tonga, tong′gä, n. a light two-wheeled Indian vehicle. [Hind. tāngā.]

tonga, tong′gä, n. a Fijian toothache remedy made from an aroid root (Epipremnum). [Arbitrary invention.]

tonga-bean. See tonka-bean.

tongs, tongz, n.pl. a gripping and lifting instrument, consisting of two legs joined by a pivot, hinge, or spring. [O.E. tang, tange ; O.N. töng, Ger. zange.]

tongue, tung, n. the fleshy organ in the mouth, used in tasting, swallowing, and speech : the tongue of an ox, &c., as food : the rasping organ in molluscs : power of speech : manner of speaking : speech : discourse : voice : utterance : (Shak.) a vote : a language : anything like a tongue in shape : the catch of a buckle : the pointer of a balance : a point of land : a bell clapper : the reed of a musical instrument : a flap in the opening of a shoe or boot : any narrow projection.—v.t. to utter : to pronounce : to articulate : (Shak.) to assail with words : to lick : to touch with the tongue : to furnish with a tongue : to talk, prate (with it) : (mus.) to produce or play by tonguing.—v.i. to give tongue : to stick out : (mus.) to practise tonguing. — adjs. **tongued**, having a tongue ; **tongue′-doubt′ie** (i.e. doughty ; Milt.), bragging ; **tongue′less**, having no tongue : (Shak.) unspoken-of.—ns. **tongue′let**, a little tongue ; **tongue′ster**, a babbler.—adjs. **tongue′-tacked, -tied**, impeded by a short fraenum : unable to speak out.—ns. **tongue′-twister**, a formula or sequence of words difficult to pronounce without blundering ; **tongue′-work**, babble, chatter ; **tongu′ing**, articulation to produce staccato effect in playing wind instruments.—**give tongue**, to give utterance : to give voice as hounds on a scent ; **hold one's tongue** (see **hold**). [O.E. tunge ; O.N. tunga, Ger. zunge, the tongue ; L. lingua (from dingua).]

tonic, tonicity. See tone (1).

tonight, to-night, tə-nīt′, n. this night : the night of the present day.—adv. on this night or the night of today : (obs. ; Shak.) last night. [O.E. tó niht.]

tonish. See ton (2).

tonite, tō′nīt, n. a blasting explosive made from guncotton and barium nitrate. [L. tonāre, to thunder.]

tonka-bean, tong′kä-bēn′, n. the coumarin-scented seed of a large papilionaceous tree (Dipteryx) of Guiana, used for flavouring snuff, &c.—Also **tonga-** (tong′gä-), **tonquin-** (tong′kēn-) **bean**. [Said to be the Gu:ana negroes' name.]

tonnage, tun′ij, n. (hist.) a tax of so much a tun on imported wines (sometimes **tunnage**) : a charge or payment by the ton : carrying capacity of a ship in tons (orig. number of tuns of wine that could be carried) ; register ton=100⁷cubic feet, freight ton 40 cubic feet of space available for cargo : total amount of shipping so measured : a duty on ships, estimated in tons. [See ton, tun.]

tonneau, ton′ō, n. the rear part of a motor-car body, orig. opening at the back. [Fr., cask, tun.]

tonnell, obs. form of tunnel.

tonsil, ton′sl, -sil, n. either of two glands at the root of the tongue.—adj. **ton′sillar**.—n. **tonsillec′-tomy**, surgical removal of a tonsil.—adj. **tonsil-lit′ic**.—ns. **tonsilli′tis**, inflammation of the tonsils ; **tonsillot′omy**, complete or partial removal of a tonsil.—Also **tonsilitis**, &c. [L. tōnsillae (pl.).]

tonsor, ton′sər, n. a barber.—adj. **tonsō′rial**.—n. **ton′sure** (-shər), act or mode of clipping the hair, or of shaving the head : in the R.C. and Eastern Churches, the shaving or cutting of part of the hair of the head on entering the priesthood or a monastic order : the shaven part.—adj. **ton′sured**, having the crown of the head shaven as a priest : shaven : bald : clipped. [L. tōnsor, barber, tōnsūra, a shearing—tondēre, tōnsum, to clip.]

tontine, ton′tēn, ton-tēn′, n. a scheme of life-annuity, increasing as the subscribers die.—Also adj.—n. **tontin′er**. [From Lorenzo Tonti, a Neapolitan, its inventor (1653).]

tonus, tony. See tone (1).

tony, tō′ni, n. (obs. slang) a simpleton. [**Antony**.]

too, tōō, adv. as well, in addition, also, likewise (never at the beginning of a sentence in English usage) : undesirably in excess : so much as to be incompatible with a condition : (in affectation) extremely.—adv. **too′-too**, **too too**, all too : quite too.—adj. exquisite : extravagantly and affectedly sentimental, gushing. [Stressed form of **to**.]

tooart. Same as tuart.

took, took, pa.t. and obsolete pa.p. of take.

tool, tōōl, n. a working instrument, esp. one used by hand : a weapon : (Shak.) a penis : one who is used as the mere instrument of another.—v.t. to mark with a tool, esp. to ornament or imprint designs upon, of bookbinders, or to chisel the face of, of masons : (slang) to drive, as a coach or other vehicle : to carry or draw in a vehicle.—v.i. to work with a tool : to travel in a vehicle, to drive or draw.—ns. **tool′-house**, a shed or outhouse for keeping tools in ; **tool′ing**, workmanship done with a tool ; **tool′-shed**. [O.E. tól.]

toom, tōōm (now only Scots, təm, tim), adj. empty.—n. a rubbish dump.—v.t. to empty. [O.E. tóm, free, clear.]

toon, tōōn, n. cedar-wood, a large Indian tree of the mahogany family, with red wood and astringent bark. [Hind. tūn.]

toot, tōōt, v.i. (Spens.) to pry, peer, peep about : (obs.) to be prominent.—n. (obs.) a look-out place : (S.W. England) a watch-hill.—n. **toot′er**. [O.E. tótian, to stick out, peep out.]

toot, tout, tōōt, v.i. to make short sounds, as on a flute or horn.—v.t. to blow, as a horn, &c.—n. a blast as of a horn.—n. **toot′er**, one who toots, or his instrument. [Prob. imit.]

tooth, tōōth, n. one of the hard bodies in the mouth, used for biting and chewing : a hard projection of similar use in invertebrates : taste or relish : a tooth-like projection, prong, cog, jag, as on a leaf-margin, comb, saw, or wheel : (pl. **teeth**, tēth ; q.v.).—v.t. to furnish with teeth : to cut into teeth.—ns. **tooth′ache**, an ache or pain in a tooth ; **tooth′ache-tree**, the prickly ash (Xanthoxylum) ; **tooth′brush**, a brush for cleaning the teeth ; **tooth′-drawer**, (Shak.) an extractor of teeth.—n. and adj. **tooth′-drawing**.—adjs. **toothed** (tōōtht, also tōōdhd), having teeth : dentate ; **tooth′ful**, full of teeth : toothsome.—n. a small drink of spirits, &c. — adj. **tooth′less**. — ns. **tooth′-or′nament**, dog-tooth ; **tooth′-paste**, **-pow′der**, a paste, powder, used with a toothbrush ; **tooth′-pick**, an instrument for picking shreds of food from between the teeth : (U.S. slang) a Bowie knife ; **tooth′-picker**, (Shak.) a toothpick : one who picks teeth, as the bird trochilus ; **tooth′-shell**, Dentalium.—adj. **tooth′some**, palatable.—ns. **tooth′-someness** ; **tooth′-wash**, a liquid preparation for cleansing the teeth ; **tooth′wort**, a pale fleshy plant (Lathraea Squamaria) of the broomrape family, parasitic on tree-roots, with tooth-like scale-leaves : the cruciferous coral-root (Cardamine, or Dentaria, bulbifera).—adj. **tooth′y**, with

prominent teeth: toothsome: (*Scot.*) biting.—
a colt's tooth, addiction to youthful pleasures;
armed to the teeth, armed as completely as
possible, from top to toe; **a sweet tooth**, a taste
for sweet things; **by the skin of one's teeth** (see
skin); **cast, throw, in one's teeth**, to fling at
one as a taunt or reproach; **in one's teeth**, to
one's face: in direct affront; **in spite of one's
teeth, in the teeth of**, in direct opposition; **long
in the tooth**, elderly, like a horse whose gums are
receding; **set one's teeth on edge** (see edge);
tooth and nail, with all possible vigour and fury.
[O.E. *tóth* (pl. *téth*); Goth. *tunthus*, L. *dēns,
dentis*, Gr. *odous, odontos*, Sans. *danta*.]

tootle, *tōōt'l*, *v.i.* to make feeble sounds, as on the
flute. [Freq. of **toot**.]

top, *top*, *n.* the highest part or place: the upper end
or surface: a topsail: a top-boot (esp. in *pl.*):
a trench parapet: (*naut.*) a small platform at the
head of the lower mast: a crest or tuft: a handful
or bundle of flax, wool, &c., for spinning: the
earliest part (as *top of the morning*—a conventional
Irishman's greeting: (*slang*) a circus tent (**the
big top**, the main tent).—*adj.* highest.—*v.t.* to cover
on the top: to tip: to rise above: to surpass: to
rise to the top of: to surmount: to be on or at the
top of: (*Shak.*) to cover, as a male animal: to
take off the top of: (*golf*) to hit on the upper half.
—*v.i.* to finish up, round off (with *off* or *up*):—*pr.p.*
topp'ing; *pa.t.* and *pa.p.* **topped.**—*n.* **top'-boot**,
a long-legged boot with a showy band of leather
round the top.—*adj.* **top'-booted**, wearing top-
boots.—*n.* **top'coat**, an overcoat.—*v.t.* **top'-dress.**
—*n.* **top'-dress'ing**, a dressing of manure laid
on the surface of land: the application of it:
(*fig.*) any superficial covering or treatment.—*adjs.*
top'full', (*Shak.*) full to the top or brim; **topgallant** (*ta-*, *top-gal'ant*), above the topmast and
topsail and below the royal-mast.—*ns.* **top'-
hamp'er**, unnecessary weight on a ship's upper-
deck; **top'-hat**, a tall silk hat.—*adjs.* **top'-heav'y**,
having the upper part too heavy for the lower:
tipsy; **top'-hole'**, (*slang*) tiptop.—*n.* **top'knot**,
a crest, tuft of hair, or knot of ribbons, &c., on the
top of the head: a small fish (of several species)
akin to the turbot.—*adjs.* **top'-knotted**; **top'less**,
without a top: (*Shak.*) supreme, without superior:
top'-line, important enough to be mentioned
in a headline. — *n.* **top-lin'er**, one who is
top-line: a principal performer, star. — *adjs.*
top'loftical, top'lofty, (*facet.*) high and mighty:
stuck-up.—*ns.* **top'loftiness**; **top'man**, a man
stationed in one of the tops: a top-sawyer; **top'-
mast** (*-mast, -mâst*), the second mast, or that
immediately above the lower mast.—*adjs.* **top'-
most** (*-mōst, -mast*), uppermost; **top'-notch'**,
(*slang*) topping; **topped.**—*n.* **topp'er**, one who,
or that which, tops in any sense: (*slang*) one who
excels: (*slang*) a top-hat; **topp'ing**, the act of
one who tops, that which tops: (*pl.*) pieces cut
from the top.—*adj.* surpassing, pre-eminent: (*U.S.*)
arrogant. — *adv.* **topp'ingly**. — *adj.* **top'-proud**,
(*Shak.*) proud in the highest degree.—*ns.* **top'sail**
(*-sl*, or *-sāl*), a sail across the topmast; **top'-
saw'yer**, the upper sawyer in a sawpit: (*coll.*)
a superior, a person of importance; **top'-side**, the
upper part; **tops'man**, (*Scot.*) a head-drover, a
foreman: (*slang*) a hangman; **top'-soil**, the upper
part or surface of the soil; **top'-soil'ing**, removal
of the top-soil; **top'-stone**, a stone placed on the
top, or forming the top.—**at the top of one's
voice**, at one's loudest; **top dog**, the winner or
dominant person; **top one's part**, to surpass oneself in playing it. [O.E. *top*; Ger. *zopf.*]

top, *top*, *n.* a spinning toy: a grooved cone held
back between the strands in rope-making: a
marine gasteropod of the genus Trochus, with
pearly flattish-based conical shell.—*n.* **top'-shell.**
—**sleep like a top**, to sleep very soundly. [App.
late O.E. *top* (but the meaning is doubtful).]

toparch, *top'ärk*, *n.* the ruler of a district.—*n.* **top'-
archy**, a toparch's territory. [Gr. *toparchēs*—
topos, a place, *archein*, to rule.]

topaz, *tō'paz*, *n.* a precious stone, fluoriferous
silicate of aluminium, yellow, bluish, colourless,

&c.—*adj.* **tō'pazine.**—*n.* **topaz'olite**, a yellow
garnet.—**Oriental topaz**, a yellow corundum.
[Gr. *topazos*, a green gem.]

tope, *tōp*, *v.i.* to drink hard.—*interj.* (*obs.*) used in
pledging a health.—*n.* **tō'per**, a drunkard. [Poss.
Fr. *toper*, to accept a wager.]

tope, *tōp*, *n.* a Buddhist stupa or dome for relics.
[Hind. *tōp*—Sans. *stūpa*, a heap.]

tope, *tōp*, *n.* a small species of shark. [Said to be
Cornish.]

topek. Same as **tupik.**

Tophet, *tō'fet*, *n.* an ancient place of human sacrifice near Jerusalem, the valley of Hinnom or part
of it, later a place of refuse disposal: hence Hell.
[Heb. *tōpheth.*]

tophus, *tō'fas*, *n.* a gouty deposit:—*pl.* **tō'phi** (*-fī*).—
adj. **tophā'ceous**. [L. *tōphus, tōfus*, porous stone,
tufa.]

topi, topee, *tō-pē', tō'pē*, *n.* (*India*) a hat, esp. a sola
hat, pith-helmet.—*n.* **topi'-wallah** (*-wä'lä*), a
European in India. [Hind. *topī*, hat (perh. from
Port. *topo*, top).]

topiary, *tō'pi-a-ri*, *n.* mural decoration in fanciful
landscape: a branch of gardening, the clipping
of trees into imitative and fantastic shapes.—Also
adj.—*adj.* **topiā'rian**.—*n.* **to'piarist**. [L. *topiārius*
—*topia* (pl.), landscape, landscape gardening—
Gr. *topos*, a place.]

topic, *top'ik*, *n.* a head under which a rhetorician
might look up matter for discourse: a general
consideration suitable for argument: a subject of
discourse or argument: a matter.—*adj.* **top'ical**,
local: relating to a topic or subject: relating to
matters of interest of the day.—*adv.* **top'ically**.
[Gr. *topikos*, pertaining to place or to common-
places, *ta topika*, the general principles of argument—*topos*, a place.]

to-pinch, a false emendation of some Shakespeare
editors (*Merry Wives*, IV. iv. 59), for *to pinch*,
the second of two infinitives having *to* where the
first is without *to*.

topography, *top-og'ra-fi*, *n.* detailed study, description, or features of a limited area.—*n.* **topog'-
rapher**.—*adjs.* **topographic** (*top-a-graf'ik*), **-al**.
—*adv.* **topograph'ically**. [Gr. *topographiā*—
topos, a place, *graphein*, to describe.]

topology, *top-ol'a-ji*, *n.* topographical study of a
particular place: topographical anatomy: a branch
of geometry concerned with those properties of a
figure which remain unchanged even when the
figure is deformed. [Gr. *topos*, a place, *logos*, a
discourse.]

toponymy, *top-on'i-mi*, *n.* place-name study: the
nomenclature of regions of the body.—*adjs.*
topon'ymal, toponymic (*-a-nim'ik*), **-al**. [Gr.
topos, a place, *onyma* (*onoma*), a name.]

topple, *top'l*, *v.i.* to overbalance and fall headlong:
to threaten to fall from top-heaviness.—*v.t.* to
cause to topple. [**top** (I).]

topsyturvy, *top'si-tur'vi*, also **top'side-tur'v(e)y**,
Scot. **tap'salteer'ie**, *adv.* bottom upwards.—*adj.*
turned upside down.—*n.* confusion.—*v.t.* to turn
upside down.—*n.* **topsyturvifica'tion**, a turning
upside down.—*adv.* **topsytur'vily**.—*ns.* **topsytur'-
viness**; **topsytur'vydom**. [**top**, and the obs.
terve, to turn (cf. O.E. *tearflian*, to roll); so, **set**,
and **side** are only conjectures.]

toque, *tōk*, *n.* a 16th-century form of cap or turban:
(*obs.*) a hair-pad: a woman's close-fitting brimless
or nearly brimless hat: a macaque (*Macacus
pileatus*) of Ceylon. [Fr.]

tor, *tor*, *n.* a hill, a rocky height. [O.E. *torr, tor*—
L. *turris*, tower, or perh. from Celtic.]

Torah, Thorah, *tō'rä*, *n.* the Mosaic law: the book
of the law, the Pentateuch. [Heb. *Tōrāh.*]

torbanite, *tor'ban-īt*, *n.* a shale, almost a coal, mined
for oil at *Torbane* Hill, Bathgate.

torbernite, *tor'bern-īt*, *n.* a bright green radioactive hydrous phosphate of copper and uranium.
[After *Torber* Bergmann (1735-84), Swedish
chemist.]

torch, *torch*, *n.* a stick of inflammable material
carried or stuck up to give light: a large candle:
a portable electric lamp: a glowing flower or
inflorescence, as of mullein: a tall cactaceous

Neutral vowels in unaccented syllables: *el'a-mant, in'fant, ran'dam*

plant.—*v.t.* to light with torches.—*ns.* **torch′-bear′er**; **torch′-dance**; **torch′er**, (*Shak.*) a light-giver; **torchère** (*tor-sher′*; Fr.), a tall ornamental candelabrum; **torch′light**; **torch′-lily**, the red-hot poker (Kniphofia or Tritoma); **torch′-race**, a race in which the runners carried torches and passed them to others; **torch′-song**, a popular song of the 1930's giving lugubrious expression to the pangs of unrequited love; **torch′-staff** (*pl.* torch′-staves, *Shak.*), a staff for carrying a torch; **torch′-thistle**, a Cereus.—**carry the torch (for)**, to suffer unrequited love (for). [Fr. *torche*—L. *torquēre*, to twist.]

torchon, *tor-shon*, *n.* (Fr.) a duster or dish-cloth: (in full **torchon lace**) peasants' bobbin lace of loose texture and geometrical design, or a machine-made imitation: (**torchon paper**) a rough paper for water-colour drawing. [Fr.,—*torcher*, to wipe.]

torcular, *tor′kū-lər*, *n.* a tourniquet. [L. *torcular*, *-āris*, a wine-press, oil-press.]

tore, *tōr*, *pa.t.* and obs. *pa.p.* of **tear**.

tore, **toric**. See **torus**.

toreador, *tor-i-ə-dōr′*, *n.* a bull-fighter, esp. on horseback.—*n.* **torero** (*tor-ā′rō*), a bull-fighter on foot. [Sp.]

to-rend, *tə-*, *too-rend′*, *v.t.* (*obs.*) to rend in pieces :—*pa.p.* (*Spens.*) **to-rent′**.

toreutic, *tor-(y)ōō′tik*, *adj.* of chased or embossed metal-work.—*n.* (also in *pl. form*) artistic work in metal. [Gr. *toreutikos*, *-ē*, *-on*—*toreuein*, to bore.]

torgoch, *tor′gohh*, *n.* the red-bellied char. [W.]

toric. See **torus**.

torii, *tor′ē-ē*, *n.* a Japanese temple gateway. [Jap.]

torment, *tor′mənt*, *n.* torture: anguish: a source of distress.—*v.t.* **torment** (*-ment′*), to torture: to put to extreme pain: to distress: to afflict: to pester: to harass: to agitate, stir violently: to distort, force violently.—*adj.* **tormen′ted**.—*adv.* **torment′edly**.—*n.* **tor′mentil**, a four-petalled Potentilla with an astringent woody root, growing on heaths.—*n.* and *adj.* **tormen′ting**.—*adv.* **tormen′tingly**.—*ns.* **tormen′tor**, one who, or that which, torments: (*B.*) a torturer, an executioner: a long meat-fork: a wing in the first groove of a stage; **tormen′tum**, a Roman machine for hurling missiles. [L. *tormentum*—*torquēre*, to twist.]

tormina, *tor′mi-nä*, *n.pl.* gripes.—*adjs.* **tor′minal**, **tor′minous**. [L.,—*torquēre*, to twist.]

torn, *torn*, *tōrn*, *adj.* and *pa.p.* of **tear**.—*adj.* **torn′-down**, (*U.S.*) unruly.

tornado, *tor-nā′dō*, *n.* orig. a violent tropical Atlantic thunderstorm: a very violent whirling wind-storm affecting a narrow strip of country: loosely, a hurricane :—*pl.* **torná′does**.—*n.* (*poet.*) **tornade′**.—*adj.* **tornadic** (*-nad′ik*). [Prob. Sp. *tronada*, thunderstorm, altered as if from Sp. *tornada*, turning.]

toroid, **-al**. See under **torus**.

Torpedo, *tor-pē′dō*, *n.* a genus of cartilaginous fishes with organs on the head that give an electric shock, giving name to the family **Torpedin′idae**, related to the skates and rays: **torpedo**, a self-propelled submarine weapon of offence (usually cigar-shaped), carrying an explosive charge which goes off when it hits a ship or other object: a bomb, cartridge, case of explosives, or detonator of various kinds, used in warfare, in boring, as a fog-signal, firework, &c.: (*pl.* torpē′does).—*v.t.* to attack, strike, destroy, by torpedo.—*adj.* **torped′inous**, benumbing.—*ns.* **torpe′do-boat**, a small swift warship that discharges torpedoes; **torpe′do-boat destroy′er** (*t.b.d.*, or simply *destroyer*), a swifter and more powerful type of torpedo-boat, which can destroy ordinary torpedo-boats, **torpe′do-boom**, a spar for carrying a torpedo, projecting from a boat or anchored in a channel; **torpe′doer**; **torpe′doist**; **torpe′do-net**, a net hung round a ship to intercept torpedoes; **torpe′do-tube**, a kind of gun from which torpedoes are discharged. [L. *torpēdō*, *-inis*, numbness, the torpedo (fish)—*torpēre*, to be stiff.]

torpid, *tor′pid*, *adj.* numb: lethargic: having lost the power of motion and feeling: sluggish: dormant.—*n.* (*Oxford*) orig. a second boat of a college, or its crew: (in *pl.*) the Lent term races of eight-oared clinker-built boats.—*v.t.* **tor′pefy**, to benumb, paralyse. — *n.* **torpesc′ence**. — *adj.* **torpesc′ent**, becoming torpid.—*n.* **torpid′ity**.—*adv.* **tor′pidly**.—*ns.* **tor′pidness**; **tor′pitude**; **tor′por**, numbness: inactivity: dullness: stupidity. [L. *torpidus*, *torpefacēre*, *torpēscere*, *torpor*—*torpēre*, to be numb.]

torque, *tork*, *n.* the turning moment of a tangential force: a necklace in the form of a twisted band.—*adjs.* **torquate**, **-d** (*tor′kwāt*, *-id*), collared; **torqued** (*torkt*), twisted. [L. *torquēre*, to twist; *torquēs*, *-is*, a necklace; *torquātus*, wearing a *torquēs*.]

torrefy, *tor′i-fī*, *v.t.* to scorch: to parch :—*pr.p.* **torr′efying**; *pa.t.* and *pa.p.* **torr′efied**. — *n.* **torrefac′tion**. [L. *torrēre*, to parch, roast, *facēre*, to make.]

torrent, *tor′ənt*, *n.* a rushing stream: a variable mountain stream: an abounding, strong or turbulent flow.—*adj.* rushing in a stream.—*n.* **torr′ent-bow**, a bow of prismatic colours formed by the spray of a torrent.—*adj.* **torrential** (*-en′shl*).—*n.* **torrentiality** (*-en-shi-al′i-ti*).—*adv.* **torren′tially**.—*adj.* **torrent′uous**. [L. *torrēns*, *-entis*, boiling, pr.p. of *torrēre*, to dry.]

torret, *tor′it*. See **terret**.

Torricellian, *tor-i-chel′i-ən*, *adj.* pertaining to the Italian mathematician Evangelista *Torricelli* (1608-1647), who discovered in 1643 the principle of the barometer.—**Torricellian tube**, the barometer; **Torricellian vacuum**, the vacuum in the barometer.

torrid, *tor′id*, *adj.* scorching or parching: violently hot: dried with heat.—*ns.* **torrid′ity**, **torr′idness**.—**torrid zone**, the belt round the earth betwixt the tropics. [L. *torridus*—*torrēre*, to parch, roast.]

Torridonian, *tor-i-dō′ni-ən*, *n.* and *adj.* (*geol.*) Pre-Cambrian of the N.W. Highlands of Scotland, as around Loch *Torridon*.

torse, *tors*, *n.* a heraldic wreath.—*ns.* **torsade′**, an ornament like a twisted cord; **tor′sel**, a plate in a brick wall to support the end of a beam. [Fr.,—L. *torquēre*, to twist.]

torsion, *tor′shən*, *n.* twisting: a twist: the strain produced by twisting: the force with which a thread or wire tends to return when twisted: (*surg.*) checking of haemorrhage by twisting the cut end of the artery.—*n.* **torsibility** (*-si-bil′i-ti*).—*adj.* **tor′sional**.—*n.* **tor′sion-bal′ance**, an instrument for measuring very minute forces by a horizontal needle suspended by a very fine filament.—*adj.* **tor′sive** (*-siv*), twisted spirally. [L. *torsiō*, *-ōnis*—*torquēre*, *tortum*, to twist.]

torsk, *torsk*, *n.* a North Atlantic fish (*Brosmius brosme*) of the cod family, with long single dorsal fin. [Sw., Norw., Dan. *torsk*—O.N. *thorskr*; cf. Ger. *dorsch*, haddock.]

torso, *tor′sō*, *n.* the trunk of a statue or body, without head or limbs (*pl.* **tor′sos**).—Also **torse** (Fr.). [It., stalk, core, torso—L. *thyrsus*—Gr. *thyrsos*.]

tort, *tort*, *n.* (*Spens.*) wrong, injury: (*Eng. law*) any wrong, not arising out of contract, for which there is a remedy by compensation or damages.—*adj.* **tortious** (*tor′shəs*), wrongful: of the nature of a tort. [Fr.,—L.L. *tortum*—L. *torquēre*, *tortum*, to twist.]

torticollis, *tor-ti-kol′is*, *n.* (*path.*) wryneck. [L.L.,—L. *tortus*, twisted, *collum*, neck.]

tortile, *tor′til*, *adj.* twisted: wreathed: coiled.—*n.* **tortility** (*-til′*).—*adj.* **tor′tive**, (*Shak.*) turned awry. [L. *tortilis*, *tortīvus*—*torquēre*, to twist.]

tortilla, *tor-tē(l)′yä*, *n.* a Mexican round flat maize cake. [Sp., dim. of *torta*, cake.]

tortoise, *tor′tas*, *n.* any land or freshwater (rarely marine) chelonian, esp. one of the genus Testudo or its kin: (*mil.*) a testudo.—*ns.* **tor′toise-plant**, elephant's foot; **tortoise-shell** (*tor′tə-shel*), the shell of a tortoise: a translucent mottled material, the horny plates (esp. of the back) of the hawk's-bill turtle: a tortoise-shell butterfly or cat.—*adj.* made of, or mottled like, tortoise-shell.—**tortoise-shell butterfly**, a butterfly with orange or reddish wings marked with black and yellow, edged with blue, &c.— *Aglais urticae* (small), *Nymphalis polychlorus* (large tortoise-shell); **tortoise-shell**

cat, a domestic cat (nearly always female) mottled in yellow and black. [L.L. *tortuca*.]

Tortrix, *tor′triks, n.* the typical genus of **Tortricidae** (*-tris′i-dē*), a large family of small moths whose caterpillars commonly live in rolled-up leaves :— *pl.* **Tortrices** (*-trī′sēz*).—*n.* **tortri′cid,** any moth of the family.—Also *adj.* [Invented L., twister.]

tortuous, *tor′tū-əs, adj.* full of windings : (*fig.*) far from straightforward.—*n.* **tortuos′ity.**—*adv.* **tor′-tuously.** — *n.* **tor′tuousness.** [L. *tortuōsus — torquēre, tortum,* to twist.]

torture, *tor′tyər, n.* a putting to the rack or severe pain to extort a confession, or as a punishment : extreme pain : anguish.—*v.t.* to put to torture : to subject to extreme pain : to exact by torture : to distort violently.—*n.* **tor′turer.**—*n.* and *adj.* **tor′turing.**—*adv.* **tor′turingly.**—*adj.* **tor′turous,** causing torture or violent distortion. [Fr.,—L. *tortūra,* torment—*torquēre.*]

toruffled, *te-, too-ruf′ld, adj.* (*Milt.* **to ruffl′d**) ruffled up. [Pfx. *to-,* **ruffle.**]

torus, *tō′rəs, n.* a large moulding, semicircular or nearly in section, common at the base of a column : a figure generated by the revolution of a circle or other conic section about a straight line in its own plane : the receptacle of a flower : (*zool.*) a ridge :— *pl.* **tō′rī.**—*n.* **tore** (*tōr ; archit.* and *geom.*), a torus. —*adjs.* **toric** (*tor′, tōr′ik*), of, or having the form of, a torus : a part of a torus ; **toroid** (*tor′, tōr′oid*), shaped like an anchor-ring.—*n.* a coil or transformer of that shape. — *adj.* **toroid′al.** — *ns.* **Torula** (*tor′ū-lä*), a yeast-like micro-organism ; **tor′ūlin,** a vitamin in yeast.—*adj.* **tor′ūlose,** (*bot.*) with small swellings at intervals.—*ns.* **torūlō′sis,** infection with a Torula affecting the nervous system ; **tor′-ūlus,** the socket of an insect's antenna. [L. *tōrus,* a bulge, swelling, bed, torus moulding ; dim. *tōrŭlus.*]

Tory, *tō′ri, n.* a Conservative in politics : a bigoted or extreme Conservative : (*U.S. hist.*) one who sided with the British in the Revolution.—Also *adj.*—*v.t.* **Tō′rify, Tō′ryfy,** to infect with Tory principles.—*n.* **Tō′ryism,** the principles of the Tories. [Ir. *toiridhe,* a pursuer ; first applied to the Irish bog-trotters and robbers ; next, about 1680, to the most hot-headed asserters of the royal prerogative.]

tose. See **toze.**

tosh, *tosh, adj.* (*Scot.*) neat, trim : comfortable, friendly, intimate.—Also *adv.*—*v.t.* to trim.

tosh, *tosh, n.* (*slang*) bosh, twaddle.—*adj.* **tosh′y.**

tosher, *tosh′ər, n.* (*univ. slang*) a non-collegiate student. [From **unattached.**]

toss, *tos, v.t.* to fling, jerk : to fling up, or about, or to and fro : to agitate : (*obs.*) to turn the leaves of : to tilt in drinking : to drink.—*v.i.* to be tossed : to be in violent commotion : to tumble about : to fling : to toss up a coin : (*infin., Spens.,* **toss′en** ; *pa.t.* and *pa.p.* **tossed,** *tost,* rarely **tost**).—*n.* act of throwing upward : a throwing up or back of the head : confusion, commotion : a toss-up.—*n.* **toss′er.**—*adv.* **toss′ily,** pertly.—*n.* and *adj.* **toss′-ing.**—*ns.* **toss′pot,** a toper, a drunkard ; **toss′-up′,** the throwing up of a coin to decide anything : an even chance or hazard.—*adj.* **toss′y,** pert, contemptuous.—**toss off,** to drink off ; **toss out,** to prank up ; **toss up,** to throw up a coin in order to decide : to cook and serve up hastily. [Origin unknown.]

tosticated, *tos′ti-kā-tid, adj.* fuddled : perplexed —also **toss′icāted.**—*n.* **tostica′tion,** perplexity. [A mispronunciation of **intoxicated,** associated with **toss.**]

tot, *tot, n.* anything little, esp. a child, a drinking-cup, or a dram.—*n.* **tott′ie, tott′y** (*dim.*). [Cf. Ice. *tottr,* a dwarf.]

tot, *tot, v.t.* and *v.i.* to add up or total.—*n.* an addition of a long column. [**total.**]

tot, *tot, n.* (*slang*) a bone : anything retrieved from a dust-bin or the like.—*ns.* **tott′er,** a raker of dust-bins and heaps ; **tott′ing.**

total, *tō′tl, adj.* whole : complete : entire : including all : co-ordinating everything towards one end. —*n.* the whole : the entire amount.—*v.t.* to bring to a total, add up : to amount to :—*pr.p.* **tō′talling :**

pa.t. and *pa.p.* **tō′talled.** — *ns.* **totalīsa′tion ; to′talīsātor, to′talīser** (*familiarly abbrev.* **tote,** *tōt*), an automatic betting-machine, the *pari mutuel.*— *v.t.* **to′talise,** to find the sum of : to bring to a total.—*v.i.* to use a totalisator.—*adj.* **totalitarian** (*tō-tal-i-tā′ri-ən*), belonging to a form of government that includes control of everything under one authority, and allows no opposition.—Also *n.*—*ns.* **totalitā′rianism ; totality** (*tō-tal′i-ti*), condition or fact of being total : entirety : completeness : the whole.—*adv.* **to′tally.**—**total abstainer,** one who abstains altogether from all forms of alcohol ; **total war,** war with every weapon at the combatants' disposal, sticking at nothing and sparing no one. [L.L. *tōtālis*—L. *tōtus,* whole.]

Totanus, *tot′ə-nəs, n.* the redshank genus, giving name to the **Totaninae** (*-nī′nē*), the tattler subfamily of sandpipers, with toes webbed at the base. [It. *totano.*]

tote, *tōt, v.t.* (*U.S.*) to carry. [Origin unknown.]

tote, *tōt, v.t.* (*U.S. slang*) to add (with up). [**total.**]

to-tear, *tə-, too-tar′, v.t.* (*obs.*) to tear in pieces :— *pa.p., Spens.,* **to-torne′.** [Pfx. **to-,** and **tear.**]

totem, *tō′təm, n.* any species of living or inanimate thing regarded by a class or kin within a local tribe with superstitious respect as an outward symbol of an existing intimate unseen relation.—*adj.* **totemic** (*-tem′ik*).—*ns.* **to′temism,** the use of totems as the foundation of a social system of obligation and restriction ; **to′temist,** one designated by a totem.—*adj.* **totemist′ic.**—*n.* **to′tempole,** a pole carved and painted with totemic symbols, set up by Indians in the north-west of North America. [From Algonquin.]

tother, t′other, *tudh′ər, pron.* and *adj.* the other. [**that other** ; cf. **tone** (2) and Scots **tae, tane.**]

totient, *tō′shənt, n.* the number of totitives of a number. [L. *totiēs,* so many.]

totitive, *tot′i-tiv, n.* a number less than another and prime to it. [L. *tot,* so many.]

to-torne. See **to-tear.**

totter, *tot′ər, v.i.* to sway : to waver : to rock : to threaten to fall : to reel : to stagger.—*n.* **tott′erer.** —*n.* and *adj.* **tott′ering.**—*adv.* **tott′eringly.**— *adj.* **tott′ery,** shaky. [Cf. Norw. dial. *tutra, totra,* to quiver, Sw. dial. *tuttra.*]

tottered, *tot′ərd, adj.* (*Shak.*) a variant of **tattered :** later (from association with **totter**) ruinous.—*adj.* **tott′ring,** (*Shak.*) hanging in rags.

totty, *tot′i, adj.* unsteady : dazed : tipsy. [Cf. **totter.**]

toucan, *tōō′kan, -kən, -kän′, n.* any member of the Rhamphastidae, large South American picarian birds, with an immense beak.—*n.* **tou′canet,** a smaller kind of toucan. [Fr.,—Tupí *tucana.*]

touch, *tuch, v.t.* to come or be in contact with : to cause to be in contact : (*geom.*) to meet without cutting, or meet tangentially : to get at : to reach as far as : to attain : to equal, rival, or compare with : to make a light application to : to begin to eat, eat a little of : to affect, esp. injuriously : to impress : to affect with emotion, esp. pity : to have to do with : to concern : to hit, wound, or injure : to strike home to : (*mus.*) to play : to call at (as a port) : to mark or modify by light strokes : to tinge : (*Rugby football*) to cause to touch the ground behind the goal-line (commonly with *down*) : to test as with a touchstone : to receive, draw, pocket : to extract money from (*for* so much) : to make some reference to, say something about : (*obs.*) to bribe : (*slang*) to cheat.—*v.i.* to be or come in contact : to make a passing call at a port : to verge : to make some mention or reference (with *on, upon*) : to have reference.—*n.* act, condition, impression, sense, or mode of touching : a feeling : a slight application, modification, stroke : a small quantity : a slight affection of illness : a tinge : a trace : a smack : a trait : a little : a slight hit, wound, blemish, reproach : manner or nicety of producing tone on (now esp.) a keyed instrument : the instrument's response : characteristic manner : a stroke of art : relation of communication, sympathy, harmony : a game in which one has to pursue and touch others : a test, as of a touchstone : a touchstone : (*obs.*) a black marble or similar monumental stone: an official stamp of fineness on gold, &c.: fineness: (*fig.*) stamp: (*football*) either side of the field outside the bounds: (*slang*) theft: (*slang*) a sum got by theft or by touching: (*slang*) that which will find buyers at such and such a price.—*adj.* touch'able, capable of being touched: fit to be touched.—*ns.* touch'ableness; touch'-and-go', a narrow escape: a critical or precariously balanced situation.—*adj.* precarious: off-hand.—*ns.* touch'-box, a tinder-box for a matchlock; touch'-down, the touching to the ground of a football by a player behind the goal-line (if his own goal, also called a touch'-back).—*adj.* touched, esp. slightly unsound mentally.—*ns.* touch'er; touch'-hole, the small hole of a cannon through which the fire is communicated to the charge. — *adv.* touch'ily. — *n.* touchi'ness. — *n.* touch'ing.—*adj.* affecting: moving: pathetic. —*prep.* concerning. — *adv.* touch'ingly. — *ns.* touch'ingness; touch'-judge, (*Rugby football*) an official who marks when and where the ball goes into touch.—*adj.* touch'less, without sense of touch: intangible.—*ns.* touch'-line, the side boundary in football; touch'-me-not, the plant balsam (from its explosive fruit): lupus: a forbidden topic.—*adj.* stand-offish.—*ns.* touch-me-not'ish-ness; touch'-paper, paper steeped in saltpetre for firing a train; touch'-piece, a coin or medal formerly given by a king to those he touched for king's evil; touch'-plate, one bearing the pew-terers' official stamp; touch'stone, Lydian stone, a highly siliceous, usually black stone, or other stone for testing gold or silver by streak, as black marble: any criterion; touch'wood, decayed wood that can be used as tinder.—*adj.* touch'y, over-sensitive: irascible.—in, out of, touch, in, out of, communication or direct relations; near touch, a close shave; touch up, to improve by a series of small touches: to lash lightly, stimulate; touch upon, on, to say something about: to verge. [O.Fr. *tuchier* (Fr. *toucher*); origin doubtful.]

tough, tuf, *adj.* stiff and dense: tenacious: hard to cut, chew, break up or penetrate: resistant: viscous, sticky: capable of, or requiring, strenu-ous effort and endurance: unyielding: robust: laborious: refractory: (*U.S.*) criminal, ruffianly. —*n.* a rough.—*v.t.* or *v.i.* tough'en, to make or become tough.—*n.* tough'ener.—*n.* and *adj.* tough'ening.—*adj.* tough'ish, rather tough.—*adv.* tough'ly.—*n.* tough'ness. [O.E. *tóh*; Ger. *zäh*(e).]

toupee, *tōō-pē'*, *-pā'*, or *tōō'*, *n.* a little tuft, lock, fringe, or patch, esp. of false hair: a wig with a top-knot.—Also toupet (*tōō-pā'*, *tōō'pā*). [Fr. *toupet*.]

tour, *toor*, *n.* a round: a prolonged journey from place to place, esp. for pleasure or for acting: a pleasure trip or outing: a shift or turn of work: a border of false hair.—*v.i.* to make a tour, go on tour.—*v.t.* to make a tour through or of: to tour with (a play).—*n.* tour'er, a touring-car: a tourist. —*n.* and *adj.* tour'ing.—*ns.* tour'ing-car, a long motor-car, suitable for touring; tour'ism, the activities of tourists and whose who cater for them. tour'ist, one who makes a tour, a sight-seeing traveller.—*adj.* touris'tic.—Grand Tour, a journey through Western Europe, once fashionable as completing a youth's education. [Fr.; see turn.]

touraco, *tōō'rə-kō*, or *-kō'*, *n.* an African bird (Turacus) of the plantain-eater family, with a horny shield on the forehead and remarkable pig-ments in its feathers. [Supposed to be a W. African name.]

tourbillion, *toor-bil'yən*, *n.* a swirl: a vortex: a whirlwind: a whirling firework. [Fr. *tourbillon*, whirlwind—L. *turbō*, *-inis*.]

tourmaline, *toor'mə-lēn*, *n.* a beautiful mineral of complex and varying composition, usually black (schorl) or blackish, strongly pyroelectric and pleochroic. [Fr.,—Sinh. *tòramalli*, carnelian.]

tournament, *toor'nə-mənt*, *n.* a military sport of the Middle Ages in which combatants engaged in single combat or in troops, mainly on horseback, with spear and sword: a military and athletic display: a series of games to determine a winner

or winning team by elimination.—*n.* tourney (*toor'*, *tər'*, *tor'ni*), a mediaeval tournament.—*v.i.* to ride in tournament.—*n.* tour'neyer. [O.Fr. *tournoiement*, *tornoi*—*torner*—L. *tornāre*, to turn.]

tourniquet, *toor'ni-ket*, *-kā*, *n.* any appliance for compressing an artery: a turnstile. [Fr.,—L. *tornāre*, to turn.]

tournure, *toor-nūr'*, *n.* contour, the characteristic turn of line: a bustle or pad worn at the waist. [Fr.]

touse, touze, towse, towze, *towz*, *v.t.* to haul, to pull about: to dishevel, rumple, tumble: to worry: to rack: to tease out.—*v.i.* to touse each other: to be toused: to tussle: to rummage.—*n.* a tousing.—*n.* tous'er, tows'er, one who touses: Towser, a common name for a big dog.—*n.* and *adj.* tous'ing.—*v.t.* tousle, touzle (*towz'l*, Scot. *tooz'l*), to disarrange, to tumble: to dishevel. —*v.i.* to tussle: to touse things.—*n.* a tousled mass. —*adj.* tousy, towsy (*towz'i*, Scot. *tōōz'i*), shaggy, unkempt, tousled: rough.—tousy tea, (*Scot.*) high tea. [Prob. from a lost O.E. word answering to Ger. *zausen*.]

tous-les-mois, *tōō-le-mwä*, *n.* the edible starch of the rhizome of a West Indian Canna. [Fr., every month, but perh. really from a native name.]

toustie, *toos'ti*, *adj.* (*Scott*) irascible.

tout, *towt*, *v.i.* to look out for custom in an ob-trusive way.—*v.t.* to watch or spy on.—*n.* one who touts: a low fellow who hangs about racing-stables, &c., to pick up profitable information.—*n.* tout'er. [App. related to toot (1).]

tout, towt, *towt*, *v.i.* (*Scot.*) to pout.—*n.* a pet, a fit of the sulks: a sudden illness.—*adj.* tout'ie, petulant.

tovarish, *to-vä'rish*, *n.* comrade. [Russ. *tovarishch*.]

tow, *tō* (*Scot.* *tow*), *v.t.* to pull with a rope, primarily by water: to pull along.—*v.i.* to proceed by being towed.—*n.* condition of being towed: act of towing: a tow-rope: that which is towed: (*Scot.*) a rope, esp. a bell-rope or a hangman's rope.—*ns.* tow'age, act of towing: fee for towing; tow'er.—*n.* and *adj.* tow'ing.—*n.pl.* tow'ing-bitts, upright timbers projecting above the deck for fastening tow-lines to.—*ns.* tow'-iron, a toggle-iron used in whaling; tow'line, -rope, a line used in towing; tow'-net, tow'ing-net, a drag-net for collecting objects of natural history, &c.; tow'-path, tow'ing-path, a path for horses towing barges. [O.E. *togian*, to drag.]

tow, *tō*, *n.* prepared fibres of flax, hemp, or jute: esp. separated shorter fibres.—*adj.* of or like tow. —*n.* tow'-head, a person with light-coloured or tousled hair. — *adj.* tow'y. [O.E. *tow-* (in compounds).]

toward, *tō'ərd*, *tōrd*, *adj.* approaching: at hand: impending: getting on: on hand: favourable: well-disposed: apt: ready to do or learn: (*dial.*) on the left or near side.—*adv.* in the direction facing one, inward.—*prep.* (*tō'ərd*, *tōrd*; by some poets and speakers *tə-wawrd'*) in the direction of: with a tendency to: for, as a help to: near, a little short of.—*n.* tow'ardliness.—*adj.* tow'ardly, favourable: promising: well-disposed: tractable. —Also *adv.*—*n.* tow'ardness.—*prep.* tow'ards (also *tə-wawrdz'*), toward. [O.E. *tóweard*, adj., adv., prep.—*tó*, to, suff. *-weard*, -ward.]

towel, *tow'əl*, *n.* a cloth for drying: formerly a cloth for various purposes, as a table-napkin, an altar-cloth.—*v.t.* to rub with a towel: to cudgel:—*pr.p.* tow'elling; *pa.t.* and *pa.p.* tow'elled.—*ns.* tow'el-gourd, the loofah; tow'elling, cloth for towels: a rubbing with a towel: a thrashing; tow'el-rail, a rod for hanging towels on.—a lead towel, a bullet; an oaken towel, a cudgel. [O.Fr. *toaille*, from Germanic; cf. O.H.G. *dwahila*—*dwahan*, *twahan*, O.E. *thwéan*, to wash.]

tower, *towr*, *tow'ər*, *n.* a lofty building, standing alone or forming part of another: a fortress: (esp. 17th cent.) a woman's high head-dress: a lofty or vertical flight.—*v.i.* to rise into the air: to be lofty: to stand on high.—*v.t.* (*Milt.*) to rise aloft into.—*adjs.* tow'ered; tow'ering, very high, elevated: very violent; tow'erless.—*n.* tow'er-

fāte, fär, àsk; mē, hər (her); *mīne; mōte; mūte; mōōn; dhen* (then)

shell, a gasteropod (Turritella) with elongated many-whorled spiral shell, or its shell.—*adj.* **tow'ery,** having towers: lofty. [O.Fr. *tur*—L. *turris,* a tower.]

towhee, *tow'hē, n.* an American finch, the chewink, ground-robin, or marsh-robin. [Imit.]

towmont, towmond, towmon, *tow'mən(d),* *n.* (*Scot.* and *N. of Engl.*) a form of **twelvemonth.**

town, *town, n.* orig. an enclosure (*obs.*): in Scotland (*Scot.* toon) a farmstead or similar group of houses: a populous place bigger or less rural than a village: (*U.S.*) a municipal or political division (which may include villages and towns in the ordinary sense) of a country: the principal town of a district: an urban community: the people of a town, esp. fashionable society, tradesmen (distinguished from academic inhabitants), or immoral classes: the business or shopping centre: urban communities generically.—*adj.* of a town: urban.—*ns.* **town'-clerk',** a secretary and legal adviser of a town; **town'-coun'cil,** the governing body in a town; **town'-coun'cillor; town'-cri'er,** one who makes public proclamations in a town; **town'-dweller; townee',** a townsman not a member of the university; **town'-end',** the end of the main street; **town'hall',** a public hall for the official business of a town: a townhouse; **town'house,** a house or building for transacting the public business of a town: a house in town.—*adj.* **town'ish,** characteristic of town as opposed to country.—*ns.* **town'land,** a township; **town'ling,** a town-dweller.—*adj.* **town'ly,** townish.—*ns.* **town'-meet'ing,** in New England, a meeting of the voters of a town; **town'-plann'ing,** deliberate designing in the building and extension of towns to avoid the evils of fortuitous and speculative building; **town's'bairn,** (*Scot.*) a native of a town, esp. one's own.—*n.pl.* **towns'folk,** the people of a town.—*ns.* **town'ship,** a vill: a community or local division: a parish: a farm in joint tenancy: (*U.S.*) a six-mile block of public land: a site for a town: the territory or district of a town: the corporation of a town: a district; **town'skip,** (*Dickens*) a city urchin; **towns'man,** an inhabitant or fellow-inhabitant of a town: — *fem.* **towns'woman; towns'people** (treated as *pl.*), townsfolk; **town'-talk',** the general talk of a town: the subject of common conversation; **town'y,** a townsman: a fellow-townsman. — *adj.* townish. — **town and gown,** the general community and the members of the university. [O.E. *tún,* an enclosure, town; O.N. *tún,* enclosure, Ger. *zaun,* hedge.]

to-worne, *tə-wōrn', adj.* (*Spens.*) worn-out. [Pfx. *to-,* worn.]

towse, towze. See **touse.**

toxaemia, *toks-ē'mi-ä, n.* blood-poisoning (Gr. *haima,* blood).—*adjs.* **toxaem'ic; tox'ic, -al,** of poison: poisonous: poisoned: due to poison. —*adv.* **tox'ically.**—*ns.* **toxica'tion,** poisoning; **toxicity** (*-is'i-ti*), toxic quality.—*adj.* **toxicolog'-ical.**—*ns.* **toxicol'ogist; toxicol'ogy,** the science of poisons; **toxicomā'nia,** morbid craving for poisons; **tox'in,** a ptomain: a specific poison of organic origin.—*adj.* **toxicoph'agous, toxiph'-agous** (Gr. *phagein,* to eat), poison-eating.—*ns.* **toxicophō'bia, toxiphō'bia** (Gr. *phobeein,* to fear), morbid fear of poisoning; **toxiphō'biac.** [Gr. *toxon,* a bow, *toxikos,* for the bow, *toxikon,* arrow-poison.]

toxophilite, *toks-of'i-līt, n.* a lover of archery: an archer. [Gr. *toxon,* a bow, *phileein,* to love.]

toy, *toi, n.* a plaything: a trifle: a thing only for amusement or look: a matter of no importance: a jest, idle tale: a trivial dance-tune, or the like: a whim, crotchet: (*Scot.*) an old woman's cap with side flaps: a dwarf breed: amorous sport.—*adj.* made in imitation as a plaything.—*v.i.* to trifle: to sport: to dally amorously.—*ns.* **toy'-dog,** a very small pet dog; **toy'er.**—*n.* and *adj.* **toy'ing.** —*adj.* **toy'ish,** given to toying or trifling: playful: wanton.—*adv.* **toy'ishly.**—*ns.* **toy'ishness; toy'-man, -woman,** a seller of toys; **toy'shop,** a shop where toys are sold.—*adj.* **toy'some,** sportive: playful: whimsical: disposed to toy: wanton. [Poss. Du. *tuig,* tools; Ger. *zeug,* stuff.]

toze, tose (*Shak.* **toaze**), *tōz, v.t.* to tease out, card, comb: to draw out, elicit. [M.E. *tosen,* akin to **tease.**]

tozie, *tōz'i, n.* (*Scott*) a shawl made from a goat's inner coat.

trabeate, -d, *trab', trāb'i-āt, -id, adjs.* built of horizontal beams, not arches and vaults.—*ns.* **trabeā'-tion,** entablature: combination of beams in a structure; **trabecula** (*trə-bek'ū-lä*), a cell, row of cells, band, or rodlike structure running across a cavity or forming an internal support to an organ:— *pl.* **trabec'ūlae** (*-lē*).—*adjs.* **trabec'ūlar; trabec'-ūlate, -d,** having trabeculae; transversely barred. [L. *trabs, trabis,* beam; dim. *trabecula.*]

trace, *trās, n.* (*Spens.*) a way, course: (*U.S.*) a beaten path: a track: a footprint: a vestige: an indication, mark of what is or has been: a small quantity that can just be detected: a tracing: a line marked by a recording instrument: an intersection with or projection on a surface: (*fort.*) the ground-plan of a work.—*v.i.* to proceed: to walk: to move: to tread a measure: to be traceable, date back.—*v.t.* to traverse: to track: to follow step by step: to detect: to follow or mark the outline of, esp. mechanically or on a translucent paper: to outline, delineate, or write: to produce as tracery: to cover with tracery.—*n.* **traceabil'ity.** —*adj.* **trace'able,** that may be traced.—*n.* **trace'-ableness.**—*adv.* **trace'ably.**—*adj.* **trace'less.**— *adv.* **trace'lessly.**—*ns.* **trā'cer,** one who traces: an instrument for tracing: a probe for tracing a nerve, &c.: a device by which a projectile leaves a smoke-trail: a projectile equipped with it: a chemical substance used to mark the course followed by a process; **tra'cer-bull'et.**—*adj.* **tra'ceried.** —*ns.* **tra'cer-shell; tra'cery,** ornamentation in flowing outline: ornamental open-work in Gothic architecture; **tra'cing,** the act of one who traces: a drawing copied mechanically or on translucent paper laid over the original: an instrumental record; **tra'cing-paper,** translucent paper for tracing on.— **trace element,** a micro-nutrient, a substance (as zinc, copper, molybdenum, &c.) whose presence in the soil in minute quantities is necessary for plant growth; **tracer element,** (*physiol.* &c.) an isotope, often a radio-isotope, used for experiments in which its particular properties enable its position to be kept under observation. [Fr. *trace*—L. *tractus,* pa.p. of *trahĕre,* to draw.]

trace, *trās, n.* (usu. in *pl.*) a rope, chain, or strap attached to an animal's collar, for drawing a vehicle: a bar for transmitting motion: (*bot.*) the vascular tissue branching from the cylinder to pass into a leaf or branch.—*v.t.* to harness in traces.—*ns.* **trace'-horse,** a horse that draws in traces; **trā'cer,** a trace-horse: a boy who attends a trace-horse. [O.Fr. *trays, trais,* pl. of *trait,* draught; cf. **trait.**]

trachea, *trə-kē'ä* (by some *trā'ki-ä*), *n.* the wind-pipe: an air-tube in air-breathing arthropods: (*bot.*) a conducting tube in xylem:—*pl.* **trache'ae** (*-ē*).—*adj.* **trache'al** (also *trā'ki-*).—*n.pl.* **Trā-chea'ria,** arachnids with tracheae but no lung-books.—*ns.* and *adjs.* **trāchea'rian; trā'cheary.** —*n.pl.* **Trāchea'ta,** arthropods with tracheae.— *adjs.* **trā'cheate, -d,** having a trachea.—*ns.* **tracheid(e)** (*trə-kē'id, -id,* or *trā'ki-* or *trak'i-*), a long tubelike but closed cell in xylem; **trache-itis** (*trak-, trāk-i-ī'tis*), inflammation of the trachea; **tracheos'copy,** inspection of the trachea; **trache-ot'omy,** cutting into the trachea; **trachi'tis,** a wrong form of **tracheitis.** [Mediaeval L. *trāchēa* for L. *trāchīa*—Gr. *trācheia* (*artēriā*), rough (artery).]

trachelate, *trak'ə-lāt, adj.* having a neck. [Gr. *trachēlos,* neck.]

Trachinus, *tra-kī'nəs, n.* the weever genus of fishes, giving name to the family **Trachinidae** (*-kin'i-dē*). [L.L. *trachina,* said to be a local name of a fish.]

trachoma, *tra-kō'mä, n.* a disease of the eye, with hard pustules on the inner surface of the eyelids. [Gr. *trāchōma.*]

Trachypterus, *trak-ip'tə-rəs, n.* the dealfish genus, giving name to the ribbon-fish family **Trachyp-teridae** (*-ter'i-dē*). [Gr. *trāchys,* rough, *pteron,* fin.]

Neutral vowels in unaccented syllables: *el'ə-mənt, in'fənt, ran'dəm*

trachyte, *trak'īt*, *n.* a fine-grained intermediate igneous rock answering to the coarse-grained syenite, commonly porphyritic with sanidine.— *adjs.* **trachytic** (*trə-kit'ik*); **trach'ytoid**. [Gr. *trāchys*, rough.]

tracing. See under trace (1).

track, *trak*, *n.* a mark left: a beaten path: a made path: a course: (esp. *U.S.*) a railway line, the rails and the space between.—*v.t.* to follow the track of: to find by so doing: to traverse, thread: to beat, tread.—*v.i.* to follow a trail: (now *U.S. slang*) to make one's way: to run in alignment.— *ns.* **track'age**, provision of railway tracks; **track'er**; **track'layer**, (*U.S.*) a platelayer.—*adj.* **track'less**, without a path: untrodden: leaving no trace: running without rails.—*adv.* **track'lessly.**—*ns.* **track'lessness**; **track'man**, **track'-walker** (both *U.S.*), one who has charge of a railway track; **track'way**, a beaten track: an ancient road.— **in one's tracks**, just where one stands; **keep track of**, keep oneself informed about; **make tracks**, to make off: to go quickly. [Fr. *trac*; prob. Gmc.; cf. next word.]

track, *trak*, *v.t.* to tow.—*v.i.* to travel by towing.— *ns.* **track'age**, towing; **track'-boat**, a towed boat; **track'er**, one who tows: a tug: a pulling part in the action of any organ; **track'road**, a tow-path; **track'-scout**, a trekschuit. [See **trek**.]

tract, *trakt*, *n.* a stretch or extent of space or time: a region, area: (*Shak.*, *Spens.*) trace, track: a tractate: a pamphlet or leaflet, esp. political or (now) religious: (*R.C.*) a psalm sung instead of the Alleluia in Lent (also **tract'us**; perh. as drawn out, perh. as sung at a stretch without answers).— *v.t.* (*Spens.*) to trace, track.—*n.* **tractabil'ity**.—*adj.* **tract'able**, easily drawn, managed, or taught: docile.—*ns.* **tract'ableness**; **tractā'rian**, a writer of tracts, esp. (**Tractā'rian**) of the *Tracts for the Times* (Oxford, 1833-41—Pusey, Newman, Keble, Hurrell Froude, &c.).—Also *adj.*—*ns.* **Tractār'ianism**, the system of religious opinion promulgated in these, its main aim to assert the authority and dignity of the Anglican Church—the Oxford movement; **tract'ate**, a treatise, a tract; **tractā'tor**, a tractarian; **traction** (*trak'shən*), act of drawing or state of being drawn: propulsion of vehicles.—*adj.* **trac'tional.**—*n.* **trac'tion-engine**, a locomotive for hauling on roads, fields, &c.— *adj.* **tract'ive**, pulling.—*ns.* **tract'or**, an aeroplane with screw in front: a traction-engine: a vehicle that propels itself or hauls other vehicles or agricultural implements: a motor-plough: (in *pl.*) bars of different metals which, drawn over diseased parts, were supposed to give relief; **tractora'tion**, the use of these; **tract'rix**, a curve such that the intercept of a tangent by a fixed straight line is constant. [L. *tractus*, *-ūs*, a dragging, draught, tract, *tractus*, *tractātus*, pa.ps. of *trahĕre*, *tractāre*, to draw.]

trade, *trād*, *n.* (*Spens.*) a track, trail, treading: a way of traffic: (*Shak.*) resort: a course: a practice: an occupation, way of livelihood, esp. skilled but not learned: shopkeeping: commerce: buying and selling: a craft: men engaged in the same occupation, esp. the liquor trade or the book trade: commodities, esp. for barter: a deal: rubbish: medicine: (in *pl.*) the trade-winds.—*v.i.* (*obs.*) to tread, go: to resort, esp. for commerce: to ply: to occupy oneself: to have dealings or intercourse: to engage in commerce: to deal: to traffic: to buy and sell: to reckon, count, presume (with *on*), esp. unscrupulously.—*v.t.* (*obs.*) to tread: (*U.S.*) to exchange commercially, to barter.—*n.* **trade'-board**, a council representing employers and employees in a trade.—*adjs.* **trād'ed**, (*Shak.*) versed, practised; **trade'-fallen** (**trade-falne**; *Shak.*), unsuccessful in trade, bankrupt; **trade'ful**, (*Spens.*) commercial, busy in traffic; **trade'less.**— *ns.* **trade'-mark**, any name or distinctive device warranting goods for sale as the production of any individual or firm; **trade'-name**, a name serving as a trade-mark: a name in use in the trade; **trade'-price**, the price at which goods are sold to members of the same trade, or by wholesale to retail dealers; **trā'der**, one who trades: a

trading ship; **trade'-route**, a route followed by caravans or trading ships; **trade'-sale**, an auction sale of goods by producers, &c., to persons in the trade.—*ns.* (treated as *pl.*) **trades'-folk**, **-people**, shopkeepers: mechanics: craftsmen: people employed in trade.—*n.* **trades'man**, a shopkeeper: a craftsman: a mechanic:—*fem.* **trades'woman.** —*adj.* **trades'manlike.**—*ns.* **trade(s)-un'ion**, an organised association of workers of an industry for the protection of their common interests; **trade(s)-un'ionism**; **trade(s)-un'ionist**; **trade'-wind**, a wind blowing steadily toward the thermal equator and deflected westward by the eastward rotation of the earth.—*n.* and *adj.* **trād'ing.**— **Board of Trade**, a department of government for matters of industry and commerce. [Prob. L.G. *trade*; akin to **tread**.]

Tradescantia, *trad-is-kan'shi-ā*, *n.* the spiderwort genus. [After the English gardener, naturalist, a..d traveller John *Tradescant* (*c.* 1567-1637).]

tradition, *trə-dish'ən*, *n.* handing over: oral transmission from generation to generation: a tale, belief or practice thus handed down: anything bound up with or continuing in the life of a family, community, &c.—*adjs.* **tradi'tional**, **tradi'tionary**. — *ns.* **tradi'tionalism**; **traditional'ity**. — *advs.* **tradi'tionally**, **tradi'tionarily.**—*ns.* **tradi'tioner**, **tradi'tionist**, one who adheres to tradition.—*adj.* **traditive** (*trad'i-tiv*), traditional.—*n.* **trad'itor**, (*obs.*) a traitor, betrayer: one who under persecution gave up sacred books or objects or the names of his fellows. [L. *trāditiō*, *-ōnis*, *trāditor*, *-ōris*—*trādĕre*, to give up—*trāns*, over, *dăre*, to give.]

traduce, *trə-dūs'*, *v.t.* (*obs.*) to translate: (*obs.*) to propagate or transmit: to calumniate: to defame. —*ns.* **traduce'ment**; **tradū'cer**; **Tradū'cian** (*-shi-ən*), one who believes that children receive soul as well as body from their parents through natural generation.—Also *adj.*—*ns.* **Tradū'cianism**; **Tradū'cianist.**—*n.* and *adj.* **tradū'cing.**— *adv.* **tradū'cingly.**—*n.* **traduction** (*-duk'shən*), transference, conveyance: translation: transmission, tradition: propagation: calumny. — *adj.* **traduc'tive**, transmitted. [L. *trādūcĕre*, *trāductum*—*trāns*, across, *dūcĕre*, to bring.]

traffic, *traf'ik*, *n.* commerce: disgraceful trading: dealings: (*obs.*) a trading voyage: (*obs.*) commodities: the business done on a railway, &c.: vehicles, pedestrians, &c. (collectively), using a thoroughfare: passing to and fro.—*v.i.* to trade: to trade disgracefully: to intrigue.—*v.t.* to trade in, or barter:—*pr.p.* **traff'icking**; *pa.t.* and *pa.p.* **traff'icked.**—*ns.* **traff'icātor**, a movable pointer by means of which the driver of a vehicle can give warning of a change of direction; **traff'icker.** *n.* and *adj.* **traff'icking.**—*adj.* **traff'icless.**—*ns. pl.* **traff'ic-lights'**, **-sig'nals**, coloured lights to regulate street traffic at crossings.—*n.* **traff'icman'ager**, the manager of the traffic on a railway, &c.—*n.pl.* **traff'ic-returns'**, statistics of passengers and goods carried and money received in return. [From a Romance language; cf. Fr. *trafic*, It. *traffico*, Sp. *tráfico*; origin obscure.]

tragacanth, *trag'ə-kanth*, *n.* a gum (also **gum tragacanth**) got from several spiny shrubs of the genus Astragalus: the plant yielding it. [Gr. *tragakantha*—*ragos*, goat, *akantha*, thorn.]

tragedy, *traj'i-di*, *n.* a species of drama in which the action and language are elevated, and the catastrophe usually sad: the art of such drama: any sad story or turn of events: (*journalism*) anything with death or killing in it.—*ns.* **tragedian** (*trə-jē'di-ən*), a writer or (usually) an actor of tragedy; **tragedienne** (*trə-jē-di-en'*; Fr. **tragédienne**, *trä-zhä-di-en'*), an actress of tragic rôles. —*adjs.* **tragic** (*traj'ik*), **-al**, pertaining to, of the nature of, tragedy.—*adv.* **trag'ically.**—*ns.* **trag'icalness**; **trag'i-com'edy**, a play (or story) in which grave and comic scenes are blended: a comedy that threatens to be a tragedy.—*adjs.* **trag'i-com'ic**, **-al.**—*adv.* **trag'i-com'ically.** [L. *tragoedia*—Gr. *tragōidiā*, tragedy, app. lit. goat-song—*tragos*, a he-goat, *ōidē*, song (variously explained).]

tragelaph, *trag'*, *traj'i-laf*, *n.* a fabulous animal, part goat, part stag: a harnessed antelope (**Trag-elaphus**, *-el'ə-fəs*). — *adj.* **tragel'aphine**. [Gr. *tragelaphos—tragos*, a goat, *elaphos*, a deer.]

tragopan, *trag'ō-pan*, *n.* a brilliant Asiatic horned pheasant. [Gr. *tragopān*, hornbill—*tragos*, goat, *Pān*, the god Pan.]

tragus, *trā'gəs*, *n.* a small prominence (bearded in man) at the entrance of the external ear:—*pl.* **tragi** (*-jī*).—*n.* **tragule** (*trag'ūl*), a chevrotain.—*adj.* **trag'uline** (*-in.*). [Gr. *trāgos*, goat, tragus.]

traik, *trāk*, *v.i.* (*Scot.*) to go wearily or toilsomely: to stray: to get lost: to gad: to decline in health. —*n.* a loss, esp. of sheep: the mutton of sheep that have died of disease or accident.—*adj.* **traik'it**, worn out.—**traik after**, to dangle after.

trail, *trāl*, *v.t.* to draw along or near the surface: to drag wearily: to drag along: to carry (as a weapon) with butt near the ground, or horizontally: to lead on: (*coll.*) to quiz: to cover with trailing ornament: to track.—*v.i.* to be drawn out in length: to hang, float, or drag loosely behind: to sprawl over the ground or a support: to straggle: to move with slow sweeping motion or with dragging drapery: to drag oneself along.—*n.* anything drawn out in length or trailed: a train, tail: the track of a star on a stationary photo-graphic plate: a track, as of game: a beaten path in the wilds: part of a gun-carriage resting on the ground behind: an act or manner of trailing.—*ns.* **trail'er**, one who trails: a tracker: a creeping plant: a carriage, car, chair, &c., towed or dragged by a car, bicycle, or tractor: a short motion-picture giving a sample of one that is coming; **trail'-net**, a drag-net.—**trail a pike**, (*obs.*) to serve as a soldier; **trailing edge**, the rear edge; **trail one's coat**, (*Ir.*) to invite a quarrel. [Ety. doubtful; O.E. *træglian*, to pluck, pull, and O.Fr. *trailler*, to tow, perh.—L. *tragula*, sledge, dragnet, are possibilities.]

trail, *trāl*, *n.* an aphetic form of **entrail**.

train, *trān*, *v.t.* to draw along: to allure: to draw on: to instruct and discipline: to cause to grow in the desired manner: to prepare for perform-ance by instruction, practice, diet, exercise, or otherwise: to bring up: to direct, aim (as a gun or telescope).—*v.i.* (*Spens.* **trayne**) to trail, drag: to prepare oneself by instruction, exercise, diet, or otherwise: to be under drill: to travel by rail.— *n.* that which is dragged along or follows: a tail: tail-feathers or trailing back-feathers: part of a dress that trails: a retinue: a series: a sequence: a number of things in a string, as animals, railway carriages or wagons: process: a line of com-bustible material to fire a charge: a set of wheels acting on each other, for transmitting motion: artillery and other equipment for a siege or battle: a lure: a thing dragged on the ground to make a scent: (*Canada*) a sledge.—*adj.* **train'able**.—*ns.* **train'-band**, a band of citizens trained to bear arms; **train'-bearer**, one who holds up a train, as of a robe or gown.—*adj.* **trained**, having received training: having a train.—*ns.* **trainee'**, one who is under training; **train'er**, one who prepares men for athletic feats, horses for a race, or the like; **train'-ferry**, a ferry that conveys railway trains; **train'ing**, practical education in any profession, art, or handicraft: a course of diet and exercise for developing physical strength, endurance, or dexterity; **train'ing-college**, a school for teaching teachers to teach; **train'ing-ship**, a ship in which boys are trained for the sea; **train'-mile**, a unit of railway traffic, a run of one mile by one train.— **train fine**, to bring body or mind to a high pitch of efficiency. [Mainly O.Fr. *traïner*, *trahiner* (Fr. *traîner*), to drag (nouns *traïn*, *traïne*); partly with overlap of meanings, from O.Fr. *traïne*, guile.]

train, *trān*, *n.* (usu. **train'-oil'**) whale-oil extracted from the blubber by boiling. [Du. *traen* (now *traan*), tear, exudation.]

traipse, **trapes**, *trāps*, *v.i.* to trail: to trudge: to gad: to go in a slatternly way.—*n.* a slattern: a trudge.—*n.* and *adj.* **traips'ing**, **trapes'ing**.—*v.i.* **trape**, to traipse. [Origin unknown.]

trait, *trā*, or *trāt*, *n.* a stroke, touch: a characteristic. [Fr.,—L. *trahĕre*, *tractum*, to draw.]

traitor, *trā'tər*, *n.* a betrayer: one who commits treason (*fem.* **trait'ress**).—Also *adj.*—*ns.* **trai'tor-hood**, **trait'orism**, **trai'torship**.—*adjs.* **trait'orly** (*Shak.*); **trait'orous**.— *adv.* **trait'orously**.—*n.* **trait'orousness**. [Fr. *traître* — L. *trāditor* — *trādĕre*, to give up.]

traject, *trə-jekt'*, *v.t.* to take across: to transmit.— *n.* (*traj'ikt*) a crossing: a ferry: a transference, transmission.—*ns.* **trajec'tion** (*-shən*), passage: crossing: transmission: transposition; **trajectory** (*traj'ik-tər-i*, or *trə-jekt'ər-i*), the curve described by a body under the action of given forces. [L. *trājicĕre*, *-jectum—trāns*, across, *jacĕre*, to throw.]

tralaticious, **tralatitious**, *tral-ə-tish'əs*, *adj.* trans-mitted: traditional: handed on, second-hand. [L. *trālātīcius—trānslātum*, serving as supine to *trānsferre*; see **transfer**.]

tram, *tram*, *n.* a barrow or cart shaft: a vehicle for minerals in mines: a tramway: a tramway-car.— Also *adj.*—*ns.* **tram'-car**, a tramway-car; **tram'-conductor**; **tram'-line**, a line of tramway; **tram'-road**, a track with sunken rails (legally one not running along a road); **tram'-stop**, a stopping-place for tram-cars; **tram'way**, a track or system of tracks with sunken rails along a road; **tram'way-car**, a carriage for conveying passengers on a tramway. [Cf. L.G. *traam*, beam, shaft, &c.]

tram, *tram*, *n.* silk yarn for weft, of two or more strands. [Fr. *trame—*L. *trāma*, weft.]

tram, *tram*. See **trammel**.

trammel, *tram'l*, *n.* a net whose inner fine-meshed layer is carried by the fish through the coarse-meshed outer layer, and encloses it in a pocket: a fowling net: a hobble: shackles for making a horse amble: anything that confines: an instru-ment for describing an ellipse (also **tram**): a contrivance for adjusting a hook in a fireplace: (in *pl.*) a tress.—*v.t.* to shackle: to confine: to impede: to entangle:—*pr.p.* **tramm'elling**; *pa.t.* and *pa.p.* **tramm'elled**.—*ns.* **tramm'eller**; **tramm'el-net'**, a trammel. [O.Fr. *tramail*, a net— L.L. *tramacula*, from L. *trēs*, three, *macula*, a mesh.]

tramontane, *tra-mon'tān*, *adj.* beyond the moun-tains (the Alps from Rome): foreign: uncivilised. —*n.* a dweller beyond the mountains: a foreigner: a barbarian.—*n.* **tramontana** (*trä-mon-tä'nä*), in Italy, a north wind. [It. *tramontana*—L. *trāns*, beyond, *mōns*, *montis*, a mountain.]

tramp, *tramp*, *v.i.* to tread, esp. heavily or noisily: to walk: to go on a walking tour or long walk: to go about as a vagrant: to go in a tramp steamer. —*v.t.* to traverse on foot: to trample: (*Scot.*) to tread in a tub in washing clothes.—*n.* a foot-journey: a vagrant: a plate of iron worn on the sole for pressing a spade or for giving foothold on ice: the footrest of a spade: a cargo-boat with no fixed route.—*adv.* with tramping noise.—*n.* **tramp'er**. [M.E. *trampen*; cf. Ger. *trampen*.]

trample, *tramp'l*, *v.t.* to tread roughly under foot: to treat with pride, to insult.—*v.i.* to tread roughly or in contempt: to tread forcibly and rapidly.— *n.* a trampling.—*ns.* **tramp'ler**; **tramp'ling**.— Also *adj.* [Freq. of **tramp**.]

trance, *träns*, *n.* a dazed, abstracted, ecstatic or exalted state: a deep sleeplike state, profound and prolonged: catalepsy.—*v.t.* to throw into a trance: to entrance.—*adj.* **tranced** (*trānst*, *trän'sid*), in a trance.—*adv.* **tranc'edly**. [Fr. *transe—transir*— L. *trānsīre*, to go across, in L.L. to die.]

trance, **transe**, *träns*, *n.* (*Scot.*) a through passage.

tranect, *tran'ekt*, *n.* (*Shak.*) a ferry. [As if L. *trāns*, across, *nectĕre*, to join; but supposed to be a misprint for **traject**.]

trangam, *trang'gəm*, *n.* a trumpery gimcrack. [Origin unknown.]

trangle, *trang'gl*, *n.* (*her.*) a diminutive of the fess. [Obs. Fr.]

trankum, *trang'kəm*, *n.* (*Scott*) a trinket. [**trinket**.]

tranquil, *trangk'wil*, *adj.* calm: peaceful. — *n.* **tranquillisā'tion**.—*v.t.* **tranq'uillise**, to make tranquil.—*n.* **tranquilli'ser**.—*adv.* **tranquilli'singly**.—*n.* **tranquill'ity**.—*adv.* **tran'quilly**. [L. *tranquillus*.]

trans-, *tränz-*, *träns-*, *pfx.* across, beyond.—Also **tran-**, **tra-**. [L. *trāns*, across, beyond.]

transact, *trăn-*, *trən-zakt'*, *-sakt'*, *v.t.* to conduct, negotiate: to perform: (*arch.*) to deal with.—*v.i.* to negotiate: to have to do.—*ns.* **transac'tion**, act of transacting: an agreement: a piece of business performed: (*pl.*) the reports or publications of certain learned societies; **transac'tor**. [L. *trānsāctum*, pa.p. of *trānsĭgĕre*—*agĕre*, to carry on.]

transalpine, *trănz-al'pīn*, *adj.* beyond the *Alps* (orig. from Rome): crossing the Alps. [L. *trānsalpīnus*—*Alpae*, Alps.]

transandine, *trănz-*, *trănz-an'dīn*, *adj.* beyond, or crossing, the *Andes*.—Also **transandē'an** (or *-an'dī-ən*).

transatlantic, *trănz-ət-lan'tik*, *adj.* beyond the *Atlantic* Ocean: crossing the Atlantic.

transcend, *trăn-send'*, *v.t.* to rise above: to surmount: to surpass: to exceed: to pass or lie beyond the limit of.—*ns.* **transcend'ence**, **transcend'ency**.—*adjs.* **transcend'ent**, transcending: superior or supreme in excellence: surpassing others: as applicable to *being*, relating to the absolute, transcending all limitation—as applicable to *knowledge*, pertaining to what transcends experience, being given *à priori*: beyond human knowledge: abstrusely speculative, fantastic; **transcenden'tal**, transcending: supereminent, surpassing others: concerned with what is independent of experience: vague.—*v.t.* **transcenden'talise**. —*ns.* **transcenden'talism**, the investigation of what is *à priori* in human knowledge, or independent of experience: that which is vague and illusive in philosophy: the American reaction against Puritan prejudices, humdrum orthodoxy, old-fashioned metaphysics, materialistic philistinism, and materialism—best associated with the name of R. W. Emerson (1803-82); **transcenden'-talist**.—*advs.* **transcenden'tally**; **transcend'-ently**.—*n.* **transcend'entness**. [L. *trănscendĕre* —*scandĕre*, to climb.]

transcontinental, *tranz-kont-i-nent'l*, *adj.* extending or passing across, or belonging to the farther side of, a *continent*.

transcribe, *trăn-skrīb'*, *v.t.* to write over from one book into another: to copy: (*mus.*) to arrange (a composition) for an instrument, voice, or combination other than that for which it was composed. —*ns.* **transcrīb'er**; **transcript** (*trăn'skript*), a copy; **transcrip'tion**, the act or result of transcribing.—*adjs.* **transcrip'tional**; **transcrip'tive**. —*adv.* **transcrip'tively**. [L. *trănscrībĕre*, *-scrīptum* —*scrībĕre*, to write.]

transe, Same as **trance** (2).

transenna, *trăn-sen'ä*, *n.* a screen enclosing a shrine. [L. *trānsenna*.]

transept, *trăn'sept*, *n.* part of a church at right angles to the nave, or of another building to the body: either wing of such a part where it runs right across.—*adjs.* **transept'al**, of a transept; **transept'ate**, divided by transverse septa. [L. *saeptum* (used in pl.), fence, enclosure.]

transfard, *trăns-färd'*, a Spenserian spelling of **transferred** (*pa.t.*).

transfer, *trăns-fər'*, *v.t.* to carry or bring over: to convey from one place, person, ownership, object, group, football club, &c., to another: to change over: to convey (as a design) to another surface. —*v.i.* to change over, esp. (*U.S.*) from one railway, train, or station, to another:—*pr.p.* **transferr'ing**; *pa.t.* and *pa.p.* **transferred'**.—*ns.* **trans'fer**, the act of transferring: conveyance from one person, place, &c., to another: that which is transferred or is to be transferred (as a picture): a transfer-ticket; **transferabil'ity** (also **transferrabil'ity**, **transferribil'ity**).—*adj.* **trans'ferable** (also **trans-ferr'able**, **transferr'ible**).—*ns.* **trans'fer-book**, a register of the transfer of property, shares, &c.; **trans'fer-day**, a day for registering transfer of bank-stock and government funds at the Bank of England; **transferee'**, the person to whom a thing is transferred: one who is transferred; **trans'-ference**, the act of transferring or conveying: passage from place to place; **trans'feror** (*law*), **transferr'er** (*general*), one who transfers; **trans'-fer-paper**, a prepared paper used for transferring impressions with copying-presses, &c.; **trans'fer-**

ticket, a ticket for a journey to be resumed on another route.—**transferable vote**, a vote which, if the candidate voted for should be out of the running, is to be transferred to another as second (third, &c.) choice. [L. *trānsferre*—*ferre*, to carry.]

transfigure, *trăns-fig'ər*, *v.t.* to change the appearance of: to glorify.—*ns.* **transfiguration** (*-ə-* or *-ū-rā'shən*), a transformation or glorification in appearance: **Transfiguration**, the Christian festival of the transfiguration of Christ (Matt. xvii. 2), celebrated on the 6th of August; **trans-fig'urement**. [L. *trānsfigūrāre*—*figūra*, form.]

transfix, *trăns-fiks'*, *v.t.* to pierce through: to paralyse with sudden emotion.—*n.* **transfixion** (*-fik'shən*). [L. *trānsfīgĕre*, *-fīxum* — *fīgĕre*, to fix.]

transform, *trăns-form'*, *v.t.* to change the shape of: to change to another form, appearance, substance, character.—*v.i.* to be changed in form or substance. — *adj.* **transform'able**. — *ns.* **transforma'tion**, change of form, constitution, or substance: metamorphosis: transmutation: (*Shak.*) a transformed person: false hair: (in full **transforma-tion scene**) a scene on the stage that changes in presence of the audience or in which the characters of the pantomime were transformed into those of the harlequinade.—*adjs.* **transform'ative**; **transformed'**.—*n.* **transform'er**, one who, that which, transforms: an apparatus for obtaining an electric current from another of a different voltage.—*n.* and *adj.* **transfor'ming**.—*ns.* **trans-form'ism**, the theory of mutability of species; **transform'ist**.—*adj.* **transformis'tic**. [L. *trăns-fōrmāre*—*fōrma*, form.]

transfuse, *trăns-fūz'*, *v.t.* to pour out into another vessel: to transfer to another's veins: to treat by transfusion: to imbue: to instil: to cause to be imbibed.—*n.* **transfū'ser**.—*adj.* **transfū'sible**.— *ns.* **transfū'sion** (*-zhən*), transfusing, esp. of blood; **transfū'sionist**.—*adj.* **transfū'sive** (*-siv*), tending or having power to transfuse.—*adv.* **transfū'sively**. [L. *trānsfundĕre*—*fundĕre*, *fūsum*, to pour.]

transgress, *trăns-*, *trănz-gres'*, *v.t.* to pass beyond the limit of or set by: to overstep, exceed: to infringe.—*v.i.* to offend by violating a law: to sin.—*n.* **transgression** (*-gresh'ən*), an overstepping: an infringement: sin.—*adjs.* **transgress'ional**; **transgressive** (*-gres'iv*).—*adv.* **transgress'ively**. —*n.* **transgress'or**. [L. *trănsgredī*, *-gressum*— *gradī*, *gressum*, to step.]

tranship, **transship**, *tran-*, *trən-ship'*, *v.t.* to transfer from one ship or other conveyance to another.— *v.i.* to change ship, &c.—*ns.* **tran(s)ship'ment**; **tran(s)shipp'er**; **tran(s)shipp'ing**.

transhume, *trăns-*, *trănz-(h)ūm'*, *v.t.* and *v.i.* to transfer or pass from summer to winter or from winter to summer pastures.—*n.* **transhu'mance**.— *adj.* **transhu'mant**. [Sp. *trashumar*—L. *trāns*, *humus*, ground.]

transient, *trăn'-zi-ənt*, *-si-ənt*, *adj.* passing: of short duration: not lasting: momentary: (*U.S.*) making, or for persons making, only a short stay: (*mus.*) passing.—*ns.* **tran'sience**, **tran'siency**.— *adv.* **tran'siently**.—*n.* **tran'sientness**. [L. *trān-siēns*, *-euntis*—pr.p. of *trānsīre*, to cross—*īre*, *itum*, to go.]

transilient, *trăn-*, *trən-sil'i-ənt*, *adj.* leaping or passing across.—*n.* **transil'iency**. [L. *trănsilīre* —*salīre*, to leap.]

transilluminate, *trănz-*, *trăns-i-l(y)ōō'mi-nāt*, *v.t.* to throw a strong light through.—*n.* **transil-lumina'tion**.

transire, *trănz-*, *trăns-ī'ri* (L. *trăns-ē'rā*), *n.* customs warrant for clearing. [L. *trānsīre*; cf. **transient**.]

transisthmian, *trănz-*, or *trans-is(t)'mi-ən*, *adj.* across an isthmus.

transistor, *trăn-sist'ər*, *n.* amplifier with crystal and two cat's whiskers: later development of this, able to perform many functions of multi-electrode valves.

transit, *trăn'zit*, *-sit*, *n.* passing or conveyance over, across, or through: the passage of a heavenly body over the meridian: the passage of a smaller body over the disk of a greater: a transit-circle,

-instrument, or -theodolite.—*v.i.* to pass across.— *v.t.* to pass across : to reverse.—*ns.* **tran′sit-circle,** a transit-instrument with a graduated circle for declinations ; **tran′sit-duty,** a duty chargeable on goods passing through a country ; **tran′sit-instrument,** a telescope mounted in the meridian and turning on a fixed east and west axis ; **transition** (-*sizh′ən, -zish′ən, -sish′ən*), passage from one place, state, stage, style, subject, or (*mus.*) key to another : (*archit.*) esp. the passage from Romanesque or Norman to Gothic.—*adj.* **transitional.**—*adjs.* **transi′tional, transi′tionary.**—*adv.* **transi′tionally.**—*adj.* **transitive** (*trănz′-, trăns′i-tiv*), passing over : having the power of passing : (*gram.*) taking a direct object.—*adv.* **trans′itively.**—*n.* **trans′itiveness.**—*adv.* **trans′-itorily.** — *n.* **trans′itoriness.** — *adj.* **trans′itory,** going or passing away : lasting for a short time : speedily vanishing.—*ns.* **tran′sit-theodolite,** one whose telescope can be reversed ; **tran′sit-trade,** the trade of carrying foreign goods through a country. [L. *trănsitus, -ūs, trănsitiō, -ōnis—īre, itum,* to go.]

translate, *trăns-, trănz-, trəns-, trənz-lāt′, v.t.* to remove to another place : to remove to heaven, especially without death : to enrapture : to render into another language : to express in another artistic medium : to interpret, put in plainer terms, explain : to transfer from one office (esp. ecclesiastical) to another : to transform : to renovate, make new from old.—*v.i.* to practise translation : to admit of translation.—*adj.* **translā′table.**—*n.* **translā′tion,** the act of translating : removal to another place, see, &c. : rendering into another language : a version : the working up of new things from old materials : change of place (distinguished from *rotation*) : the automatic re-transmission of a telegraphic message.—*adjs.* **translā′tional, trans′latory** (*-lə-tər-i,* or *-lā′*).—*n.* **translā′tor.** [L. *trănslātum,* used as supine of *trănsferre* ; see **transfer.**]

transleithan, *trănz-, -s-lī′t(h)ən, adj.* beyond the river *Leitha,* once in part the boundary between Austria and Hungary : Hungarian.

transliterate, *trănz-,* or *-s-lit′ə-rāt, v.t.* to write in letters of another alphabet.—*ns.* **translitera′tion ; translit′erātor.** [L. *littera,* letter.]

translocation, *trănz-,* or *-s-lō-kā′shən, n.* transference from place to place, esp. of materials within the body of a plant. [L. *locus,* place.]

translucent, *trănz-,* or *-s-lōō′sənt,* or *-lū′, adj.* shining through : imperfectly transparent : clear. —*ns.* **translu′cence, translu′cency.**—*adv.* **translu′cently.** — *adj.* **translu′cid,** translucent. — *n.* **translucid′ity.** [L. *trănslūcēns, -ēntis—lūcēre,* to shine—*lūx, lūcis,* light.]

translunary, *trănz′loo-nər-i, adj.* beyond the moon : visionary. [L. *lūna,* the moon.]

transmarine, *trănz-, -s-mə-rēn′, adj.* across or beyond the sea. [L. *trănsmarīnus—mare,* sea.]

transmew, *trănz-,* or *-s-mū′, v.t.* (*Spens.*) to transmute. [O.Fr. *transmuer*—L. *trănsmūtāre* ; see **transmute.**]

transmigrate, *trănz′-,* or *-s′mī-grāt,* or *-mī′, v.i.* to remove to another place of abode : (of the soul) to pass into another body.—*v.t.* to cause to transmigrate.—*n.* **trans′migrant** (or *-mī′*), one who transmigrates : an alien entering a country on his way to another in which he means to settle. — *adj.* **transmigrating.** — *ns.* **transmigrā′tion ; transmigrā′tionism,** belief in the transmigration of souls ; **transmigrā′tionist.** — *adj.* **trans′migrative** (*-mī-grā-tiv,* or *-mī′grə-tiv*).—*n.* **transmigrātor.**— *adj.* **transmigratory** (*-grə-tər-i*). [L. *trănsmigrāre, -ātum—migrāre,* to migrate.]

transmit, *trănz-,* or *-s-mit′, v.t.* to send or pass on : to allow to pass through :—*pr.p.* **transmitt′ing ;** *pa.t.* and *pa.p.* **transmitt′ed.**—*n.* **transmissibil′-ity.**—*adj.* **transmiss′ible** (also **transmitt′able,** less correctly **-ible**).—*n.* **transmission** (*-mish′ən*). —*adjs.* **transmiss′ional ; transmiss′ive,** having the quality of transmitting or of being transmitted. —*ns.* **transmissiv′ity ; transmitt′al ; transmitt′er,** one who or that which transmits : apparatus for sending forth anything, as signals, messages,

&c. [L. *trănsmittĕre, -missum—mittĕre, missum,* to send.]

transmogrify, *trănz-, -s-mog′ri-fī, v.t.* (*coll., facet.*) to transform, transmute :—*pr.p.* **transmog′rifying ;** *pa.t.* and *pa.p.* **transmog′rified.**—*n.* **transmogrifica′tion.** [A grotesque concoction.]

transmove, *trănz-, -s-mōōv′, v.t.* (*Spens.*) to transmute. [App. for **transmew,** remodelled on **move.**]

transmute, *trănz-,* or *-s-mūt′, v.t.* to change to another form or substance.—*n.* **transmūtabil′ity.** —*adj.* **transmū′table.**—*n.* **transmū′tableness.** —*adv.* **transmū′tably.**—*ns.* **transmūtā′tion,** a changing into a different form, nature, or substance, esp. that of one chemical element into another ; **transmūtā′tionist.** — *adj.* **transmū′-tative,** serving or tending to transmute.—*n.* **transmū′ter.** [L. *trănsmūtāre—mūtāre,*‖to change.]

transoceanic, *trănz-,* or *-s-ō-shi-an′ik, adj.* across or crossing the ocean.

transom, *tran′səm, n.* a cross-piece : a cross-beam : a structure dividing a window horizontally : a lintel. [App. L. *trănstrum,* a cross-beam.]

transonic. Common spelling of **trans-sonic.**

transpadane, *trăns′, -z′pə-dān, -pā′dan, adj.* beyond the Po (from Rome). [L. *Padus,* the Po.]

transparent, *trăns-, trəns-, -z-pār′ənt,* or *-par′, adj.* able to be distinctly seen through : pellucid : pervious to rays : (*Shak.*) shining through : easily detected, understood : obvious, evident : ingenuous.—*ns.* **transpar′ence** (*rare*), **transpar′-ency,** the quality of being transparent : that which is transparent : a picture, design, device visible, or to be viewed, by transmitted light : Thackeray's humorous translation of the German title *Durchlaucht.*—*adv.* **transpar′ently.**—*n.* **transpar′entness.** [L.L. *trănspārēns, -ēntis—*L. *pārēre,* to appear.]

transpicuous, *trăn-, trən-spik′ū-əs, adj.* (*Milt.*)‖ transparent. [L. *trănspicēre,* to see through—*specēre,* to look.]

transpierce, *trăns-pērs′, v.t.* to pierce through : to permeate.

transpire, *trăn-spīr′, v.t.* to give off as vapour : to exhale : to emit through the skin.—*v.i.* to exhale : to give off water-vapour (as plants) or waste material through the skin (as animals) : to become known, come to light : often, wrongly, to happen. —*adj.* **transpir′able.**—*n.* **transpiration** (*trăn-spi-rā′shən*), act or process of transpiring : exhalation through the skin : emission of water-vapour through the stomata, &c.—*adj.* **transpir′atory.** [L. *spīrāre,* to breathe.]

transplant, *trăns-plănt′, v.t.* to remove from the ground where it grows and plant in another place : to graft upon another animal or another part of the same : to remove and establish elsewhere.— *v.i.* to bear transplanting.—*adj.* **transplan′table.**— *ns.* **transplantā′tion ; transplan′ter ; transplant′ing.** [L. *trănsplantāre—plantāre,* to plant.]

transpontine, *trăns-pon′tīn, adj.* across a bridge : on the Surrey side of the Thames : hence melodramatic. [L. *pōns, pontis,* a bridge.]

transport, *trăns-pōrt′, v.t.* to carry, convey, remove : to send overseas, as a convict : to translate (as a minister) : (*Shak.*) to put to death : (*Shak.*) perh., to carry off (as by the fairies) : to carry away by strong emotion : to throw into an ecstasy.—*ns.* **trans′port,** carriage from one place to another : the conveyance of troops and their necessaries : a ship, wagon, &c., therefor : ecstasy : one who has been transported or sentenced to transportation ; **transportabil′ity.** — *adj.* **transport′able,** that may be transported : liable, or rendering liable, to transportation.—*ns.* **transport′al ; transport′ance,** (*Shak.*) conveyance, transport ; **transportā′tion,** removal : removal of offenders beyond seas.—*adj.* **transport′ed.**—*adv.* **transport′edly.** —*ns.* **transport′edness ; transport′er.** — *n.* and *adj.* **transport′ing.**—*adv.* **transport′ingly.**—*adj.* **transport′ive,** tending or having power to transport.—*ns.* **trans′port-rider,** (*S. Afr.*) a carrier by wagon ; **trans′port-ship,** a ship used for carrying troops, stores, &c.—**transporter bridge,** a bridge with a travelling carriage suspended from a girder. [L. *trănsportāre—portāre,* to carry.]

transpose, *trăns-*, *-z-pōz'*, *v.t.* (*Shak.*) to transform : to transfer : to turn, alter : to change the order of, interchange : (*mus.*) to write, perform, or render in another key.—*adj.* **transpōs'able.**—*ns.* **transpōs'al,** a change of place or order ; **transpōs'er.**—*n.* and *adj.* **transpōs'ing.**—*n.* **transposition** (*-pŏ-, -pə-zish'ən*).—*adjs.* **transposi'tional ; transposi'tive** (*-poz'*).—**transposing instrument,** an instrument that by a mechanical device transposes music into another key : one for which music is written in a different key from the actual sounds. [Fr. *transposer* ; see **pose.**]

trans-shape, *trans-shāp'*, *v.t.* (*Shak.*) to transform.

trans-ship. Same as **tranship·**

trans-sonic, *trans-son'ik*, *adj.* designating a narrow zone or region of speed just greater than that of sound.—Often **transonic.**

transubstantiate, *trăn-səb-stan'shi-āt*, *v.t.* to change to another substance.—*ns.* **transubstantiā'tion,** a change into another substance : (*R.C.*) the conversion, in the consecration of the elements of the eucharist, of the whole substance of the bread and wine into Christ's body and blood, only the appearances of bread and wine remaining ; **transubstantiā'tion(al)ist, transubstan'tiātor,** one who believes in transubstantiation. [L. *substāntia,* substance.]

transude, *tran-sūd'*, *v.i.* and *v.t.* to ooze out.—*n.* a substance that transudes.—*n.* **transudā'tion.**—*adj.* **transū'datory.** [L. *sūdāre,* to sweat.]

transume, *trăn-sūm'*, *v.t.* (*obs.*) to transcribe officially.—*ns.* **transumpt** (*-sumt'*), a copy of a legal writing ; **transumption** (*-sum'shən*), transcription : metaphor : transference.—*adj.* **transumptive** (*-sump'tiv*). [L. *trăn(s)sūmĕre,* to transcribe—*sūmĕre,* to take.]

transuranic, *trăns-, trănz-ū-ran'ik, adj.* of greater atomic number than uranium.—Also **transurā'nium.**

transvalue, *trăns-, -z-val'ū, v.t.* to evaluate anew. —*n.* **transvaluā'tion.**

transverse, *trănz'vərs,* or *-vərs', adj:* set crosswise. —*adv.* crosswise.—*n.* anything set crosswise.—*v.t.* (*-vərs'*) to cross : to thwart : to reverse : to transform.—*adj.* **transvers'al,** transverse.—*n.* a line cutting a set of lines.—*n.* **transversal'ity.**—*advs.* **transvers'ally ; transverse'ly.**—*n.* **transver'sion.**—by transverse, (*Spens.*) awry. [L. *trăns-versus—vertĕre, versum,* to turn.]

transverse, *trănz-vərs', v.t.* to turn from prose into verse.—*n.* **transver'sion** -(*shən*). [A pun in Buckingham's *Rehearsal.*]

tranter, *trant'ər, n.* (*dial.*) a hawker : a carrier.—*v.t.* and *v.i.* **trant** (back-formation), to hawk. [Cf. L.L. *trăvetārius.*]

trap, *trap, n.* a snare, gin : a device for catching : a hidden danger : (*slang*) one who catches offenders : (*slang*) trickery : a pitfall : a trap-door : a ventilating door in a mine : a lock : a bend in a pipe to stop foul gases : a light carriage : a contrivance for throwing up or releasing a ball or pigeons.—*v.t.* to catch in a trap : to provide with traps.—*v.i.* to act as a trapper :—*pr.p.* **trapp'ing ;** *pa.t.* and *pa.p.* **trapped.**—*ns.* **trap'-ball,** an old game played with a ball, bat and trap ; **trap'-door,** a door in a floor or stage ; **trap'-fall,** a trap-door that gives way beneath the feet ; **trapp'er,** one who traps animals for their fur : a boy who minds a mine trap : a horse for a trap ; **trapp'iness.**—*n.* and *adj.* **trapp'ing.**—*adj.* **trapp'y,** full of traps, treacherous.—*n.* **trap'-stick,** a bat for trap-ball. [O.E. *trappe, træppe, treppe.*]

trap, *trap, n.* (*geol.* ; *old-fashioned*) vaguely, a dark fine-grained igneous rock (lying often in steps or terraces).—*adj.* **trapp'ean** (or *-ē'*).—*n.* **trap'-rock.** [Sw. *trapp—trappa,* a stair.]

trap, *trap, n.* (*mining*) a fault : (*Scot.*) a ladder leading to a loft.—*adj.* **trap'-cut,** (of jewellery) cut in steps.—*ns.* **trap'-ladder, -stair.** [Cf. Du. *trap,* step ; cf. foregoing word.]

trap, *trap, n.* (*obs.*) a horse-cloth : (*pl.*) personal luggage.—*v.t.* to caparison, deck with trappings.—*adj.* **trapped.**—*n.pl.* **trapp'ings,** gay clothes : ornaments, esp. those put on horses. [App. conn.

with Fr. *drap,* Sp. and Port. *trapo,* L.L. *drappus* (*trapus*), cloth.]

trapan. See **trepan** (1).

trape, trapes. See **traipse.**

trapezium, *trə-pē'zi-əm, n.* (*orig.*) any quadrilateral that is not a parallelogram : (*now rarely*) one with no sides parallel : (*now*) one with only one pair parallel : a wrist-bone articulating with the thumb metacarpal :—*pl.* **trapē'zia, -ziums.**—*n.* **trapēze',** a swing of one or more cross-bars used in gymnastics.—*v.i.* to perform or go on a trapeze.—*adjs.* **trapē'zial,** pertaining to a trapezium ; **trapē'ziform,** having the form of a trapezium.—*ns.* **trapēzohē'dron,** a solid figure whose faces are trapezia or trapezoids ; **trapezoid** (*trap'i-zoid,* also *trə-pē'zoid*), a quadrilateral with no sides parallel : (*obs.*) one with two sides parallel : a wrist-bone next the trapezium.—*adj.* **trapezoid'al.** [Latinised from Gr. *trapezion,* dim. of *trapeza,* a table ; lit. four-legged—*tetra-,* four-, *peza,* a foot.]

Trappist, *trap'ist, n.* a Cistercian of the reformed rule established by De Rancé (1626-1700), abbot of La *Trappe* in Normandy—austere and silent.—Also *adj.*—*n.* **Trapp'istine** (*-tēn, -tin*), a nun of an affiliated order.

trash, *trash, v.t.* (*Shak.*) to check.—*n.* a leash or other restraint. [Origin obscure.]

trash, *trash, n.* broken twigs, hedge-cuttings : sugarcane refuse : scraps : anything worthless : rubbish : paltry stuff : (*Shak.*) a worthless person : worthless people : (*U.S.*) poor whites.—*v.t.* to free from trash : to lop the tops from.—*n.* **trash'ery,** trash, rubbish. — *adv.* **trash'ily.** — *ns.* **trash'iness;** **trash'trie,** (*Scot.*) trash.—*adj.* **trash'y,** like trash : worthless. [Prob. Scand. ; cf. Norw. dial. *trask,* trash, O.N. *tros,* fallen twigs.]

trash, *trash, v.t.* to wear out, to harass.—*v.i.* to trudge. [Cf. Sw. *traska,* Norw. *traske.*]

trass, *trăs, n.* an earthy volcanic tuff used as a hydraulic cement.—Also **tarras', terras'.** [Du. *tras.*]

trattoria, *trät-tō-rē'ä, n.* a cook-shop. [It.]

trauchle, *trawhh'l, v.t.* (*Scot.*) to bedraggle : to weary with drudgery or plodding.—*v.i.* to drudge : to trail along. [Cf. Flem. *tragelen,* to go heavily.]

trauma, *traw'mä, n.* a wound : an injury : (*psych.*) an emotional shock that may be the origin of a neurosis.—*adj.* **traumatic** (*-mat'ik*).—*adv.* **traumat'ically.**—*ns.* **trau'matism** (*-mə-tizm*), condition due to a wound ; **traumatonas'ty,** a nastic movement after wounding. [Gr. *trauma, -atos,* a wound.]

travail, *trav'āl, -əl, n.* excessive labour : toil : labour in childbirth : *obs.* for **travel.**—*v.i.* to labour : to suffer the pains of childbirth : *obs.* for **travel.**—*adj.* **trav'ailed,** toilworn : wearied : experienced : having been in travail.—*ns.* **trav'ail-pain, -pang.** [O.Fr. (Fr.) *travail.*]

travail, *trä-vä'i.* See **travois.**

travel, *trav'l, v.i.* to journey : to go : (*dial.*) to walk : to go round soliciting orders : to go on circuit : to move along a course : to go with impetus : to pass : to move : *obs.* for **travail.**—*v.t.* to journey over or through : to conduct or send on a journey : (*pr.p.* **trav'elling ;** *pa.t.* and *pa.p.* **trav'elled**).—*n.* journeying : impetus : power of going : range of movement : passage : *obs.* for **travail.** (in *pl.*) an account of journeys.—*adj.* **trav'elled,** having made journeys : transported : not in its original place : experienced : beaten, frequented.—*ns.* **trav'eller,** one who travels or has travelled : a wayfarer : one who travels for a mercantile house : a ring that slides along a rope or spar : a piece of mechanism that moves on a gantry, &c. ; **trav'eller's-joy,** the virgin's-bower, *Clematis Vitalba* ; **trav'eller's-tale,** an astounding lie about what one professes to have seen abroad ; **trav'eller's-tree,** a Madagascan tree (Ravenala) of the banana family with great leaves on two sides only, accumulating water in the leaf-bases.—*n.* and *adj.* **trav'elling.**—*n.* **travelogue** (*trav'ə-log*), a talk, lecture, article, or film on travel.—*adjs.* **trav'el-soiled, -stained,** **trav'el-taint'ed** (*Shak.*), showing the marks of travel. [**travail.**]

traverse, *trav'ərs, adj.* cross : oblique.—*n.* a crossing or passage across : a straight length in a zigzag course : a passage across the face of a rock in mountaineering : a survey by measuring straight lines from point to point and the angles between : anything set : or lying across : an obstruction : adversity : a curtain, screen, partition : a barrier : a parapet : a cross-piece : a gallery from one side of a large building to another : a screened-off compartment : a denial or contradiction : (*fencing*) an opposing or counteracting movement.—*v.t.* to cross : to pass through, across, or over : to move about over : to pass over by traverse : to survey by traverse : to oppose : to thwart : to dispute : to deny, contradict : to turn sideways.—*v.i.* to make a traverse : to move to the side : to direct a gun to the right or left.—*adjs.* **trav′ersable** ; **trav′ersed**, crossed, passed over : (*Shak.*) set crosswise.—*n.* **trav′erser**, one who traverses : a platform for shifting wagons and carriages sideways. — *n.* and *adj.* **trav′ersing.** — **traversing bridge**, one that can be withdrawn horizontally. [Fr. *travers*, *traverse*, *traverser*—L. *trāns*, *vertĕre*, *versum*, to turn.]

travertine, *trav′ər-tīn*, *-tēn*, *-tin*, *n.* a pale limestone deposited from solution. [It. *travertino*—L. *tīburtīnus* (*lapis*), stone of Tibur.]

travesty, *trav′is-ti*, *n.* disguise : burlesque.—*v.t.* to disguise : to burlesque. [Fr. *travesti*, pa.p. of *travestir*, to disguise—L. *trāns*, *vestīre*, to clothe.]

travis, *trav′is*, an obs. or dial. form of **traverse**. See also **treviss**.

travois, *trä-voi′*, **travail**, *trä-vā′i*, *n.* a North American Indian drag, a pair of trailing poles attached to each side of the saddle, joined by a board or net. [Canadian Fr. pronun. of Fr. *travail*.]

trawl, *trawl*, *n.* an open-mouthed bag-net for dragging along the bottom : (*U.S.*) a buoyed line with baited hooks at intervals.—*v.t.* and *v.i.* to catch or fish with a trawl or (*Scot.* and *U.S.*) a seine-net.—*ns.* **traw′ler**, one who trawls : a trawling vessel ; **traw′ling** ; **trawl′-net**. [Cf. **trail**, and M.Du. *traghel*, drag-net.]

tray, *trā*, *n.* a shallow trough-like vessel : a salver.—*ns.* **tray′-cloth**, a cloth for covering a tray ; **tray′ful**—*pl.* **tray′fuls**. [O.E. *trīg*, *trēg*, board.]

tray, *trā.* See **trey**.—*n.* **tray′-trip**, (*Shak.*) a game played with dice.

treacher, treachour, *trech′ər*, *n.* (*obs.*) a deceiver by trickery : a betrayer : a traitor.—Also **treach′erer.**—*adj.* **treach′erous**, ready to betray : not to be trusted : misleadingly inviting in appearance.—*adv.* **treach′erously.**—*ns.* **treach′erousness** ; **treach′ery**, betrayal : readiness to betray : falseness : treason : **treach′etour**, (*Spens.*) a deceiver : a traitor. [O.Fr. *trecheor*, deceiver—*trechier*, to trick ; cf. **trick**.]

treacle, *trē′kl*, *n.* orig. an antidote or prophylactic against bites, hence against poisons, &c. : the dark, viscous uncrystallisable syrup obtained in refining sugar : also molasses, the drainings of crude sugar : blandishments, esp. when suggestive of the cloying and nauseating taste and thickness of treacle.—*v.t.* to dose or smear with treacle.—*v.i.* to treacle trees in order to collect moths.—*ns.* **trea′cle-mustard**, the cruciferous plant *Erysimum cheiranthoides* ; **trea′cliness.**—*adj.* **trea′cly**, of, or like, treacle : thick and sweet : unctuously blandishing. [O.Fr. *triacle*—Gr. *thēriakē* (*antidotos*, an antidote to the bites) of beasts—*thērion*, a wild beast.]

tread, *tred*, *v.i.* to set the foot down : to step : to walk ; to trample ; to copulate, as a cock : (*Scot.*) same as **trade**.—*v.t.* to walk on : to press with the foot, as in threshing, pressing grapes, tramping clothes, packing : to trample : to render by treading : to perform by treading, dance : to copulate with as a cock-bird : (*fig.*) to oppress : (*pa.t.* **trod** ; *pa.p.* **trodd′en**, **trod**).—*n.* a footprint : a track : act or manner of treading : a step or tramp : a thing or part trodden on, as of a step : the part that touches the ground, as of a shoe, a wheel : distance between wheels or pedals : the cicatricula, or the chalaza, of an egg : (*Scot.*) same as **trade.**—*ns.* **tread′er** ; **tread′ing** ; **tread′le**, **tredd′le**, a foot-lever : a pedal : (*dial.*) the chalaza of an egg (once thought

to be derived from the cock).—*v.i.* to work a treadle.—*ns.* **tread′ler** ; **tread′ling** ; **tread′mill**, a cylinder turned by treading on boards on its outside, as formerly by prisoners : a mill so worked : (*fig.*) routine drudgery ; **tread′-wheel**, a wheel or cylinder turned by treading outside or inside : a treadmill.—**tread water**, to float upright by an action as if of climbing a ladder. [O.E. *tredan* ; Ger. *treten* ; O.N. *trotha* ; cf. **trade**.]

treague, *trēg*, *n.* (*Spens.*) a truce. [L.L. *tregua*, *treuga*—Goth. *triggwa*, treaty.]

treason, *trē′zn*, *n.* betraying of the government or an attempt to overthrow it : treachery : disloyalty.—*adj.* **trea′sonable**, pertaining to, consisting of, or involving treason.—*n.* **trea′sonableness.**—*adv.* **trea′sonably.**—*adj.* **trea′sonous.**—**constructive treason**, anything that may be interpreted as equivalent to actual treason by leading naturally to it ; **high treason**, offences against the state ; **misprision of treason**, knowledge of the principal crime and concealment thereof ; **petty treason**, the murder of a husband by a wife, a master by a servant, &c. ; **treason felony**, the crime of desiring to depose the sovereign, intimidate parliament, stir up a foreign invasion, &c.—declared by statute in 1848. [A.Fr. *tresun*, O.Fr. *traïson* (Fr. *trahison*) —*traïr* (*trahir*)—L. *tradĕre*, to betray.]

treasure, *trezh′ər*, *n.* wealth stored up : riches : anything much valued.—*v.t.* to hoard up : to collect for future use : to value greatly : to store, enrich.—*ns.* **treas′ure-chest**, a box for keeping articles of value ; **treas′ure-city**, a city for stores, magazines, &c. ; **treas′ure-house**, a house for holding treasures : a treasury : a store of valuable things ; **treas′rer**, one who has the care of a treasure or treasury : one who has charge of collected funds ; **treas′urership** ; **treas′ury**, a place where treasure is deposited : a department of a government which has charge of the finances : mistakenly applied to a beehive tomb in prehistoric Greece.—**Treasury bench**, the first row of seats on the Speaker's right hand in the House of Commons, occupied by the members of the government ; **Treasury note**, a currency note issued by the Treasury. [O.Fr. *tresor* (Fr. *trésor*) —L. *thēsaurus*—Gr. *thēsauros*.]

treasure-trove, *trezh′ər-trōv*, *n.* ownerless property found hidden (in England gold and silver only), property of the crown. [treasure and *trové*, pa.p. of A.Fr. *trover*, to find.]

treat, *trēt*, *v.t.* to deal with : to handle : to discuss : to behave towards : to act upon : to deal with the case of : to manage in the application of remedies : to subject to a process : to stand a drink or other gratification to.—*v.i.* to negotiate : to deal (with *of*) : to stand treat.—*n.* a free entertainment, pleasure excursion, or feast : a turn or act of providing and paying : a source of great gratification : (*Spens.*) negotiation, parley.—*adj.* **treat′able**, to be treated : (*obs.*) tractable, moderate.—*ns.* **treat′er** ; **treat′ing** ; **treat′ise** (*-iz*, *-is*), a written composition, esp. one treating a subject formally or systematically ; **treat′ment**, act or manner of treating : management : behaviour to anyone : way of applying remedies ; **treat′y**, negotiation : a formal agreement, esp. between states : (*Shak.*) entreaty.—**Dutch treat** (see **Dutch**) ; **stand treat** (see **stand**) ; **treaty port**, a port opened by treaty to foreign trade. [O.Fr. *traitier*—L. *tractāre*, to manage—*trahĕre*, *tractum*, to draw.]

treble, *treb′l*, *adj.* triple : threefold : (*mus.*) in the treble : high-pitched.—*n.* that which is triple : three times as much : (*mus.*) the highest part, soprano : a treble singer, voice, instrument, string, sound, &c.—*v.t.* to make three times as much.—*v.i.* to become threefold.—*adj.* **treb′le-da′ted**, living three ages.—*n.* **treb′leness.**—*adv.* **treb′ly.** —**treble clef**, the G clef on the second line. [O.Fr.,—L. *triplus* ; see **triple**.]

trebuchet, *treb′ū-shet*, *trā-bü-shā*, *n.* a mediaeval military engine with sling, beam, and counterweight. [O.Fr.]

trecento, *trā-chen′tō*, *n.* and *adj.* 14th-century (in Italian art, &c.).—*n.* **trecen′tist**. [It., *three hundred*.]

---

treddle. Same as **treadle.** See **tread.**

tredrille, tredille, *trə-d(r)il′, n.* a card game for three. [After **quadrille**—L. *trēs,* three.]

tree, *trē, n.* a large plant with a single branched woody trunk (sometimes loosely applied): timber: a wooden structure or part of various kinds: a saddle-tree: a boot-tree: a gallows: a cross for crucifixion: a branching figure or structure, as an arborescent aggregate of crystals (e.g. *lead tree*) or a pedigree.—*v.t.* to drive into a tree, to corner: to form on a tree.—*v.i.* to take refuge in a tree.—*adj.* wooden: in composition, inhabiting, frequenting, growing on trees: taking the form of a tree: dendritic.—*ns.* **tree′-bur′ial,** disposal of the dead in the branches of trees; **tree′-calf,** a light-brown calf book-binding, in conventional imitation of a branching tree; **tree′-creeper,** a little bird (Certhia) that runs up tree-trunks in search of insects; **tree′-fern,** a fern with a tall woody trunk; **tree′-frog,** an arboreal amphibian, esp. one of the family Hylidae, nearer to toads than to frogs; **tree′-kangaroo′,** a tree-climbing kangaroo (Dendrolagus).—*adj.* **tree′less.**—*ns.* **tree′-lil′y,** a xerophytic tree-like plant of the Brazilian campos (Vellozia); **tree′-mall′ow,** Lavatera.—*adj.* **treen** (*trē′ən*; Spens.), of a tree: wooden.—*ns.* **treenail, trenail** (*tren′l, trē′nāl*), a long wooden pin or nail to fasten the planks of a ship to the timbers; **tree′-on′ion,** a variety of onion with bulbs in the place of flowers; **tree′ship,** existence as a tree; **tree′-shrew,** a squirrel-shrew, any insectivore of the East Indian family Tupaiidae, squirrel-like animals akin to shrews; **tree′-toma′to,** a South American solanaceous shrub (Cyphomandra) or its tomato-like fruit; **tree′top,** the top of a tree; **tree′-trunk; tree′-wor′ship; tree′-wor′shipper.** —**tree of heaven,** ailanto; **tree of lead,** Saturn's tree; **tree of life,** arbor vitae: a tree in the Garden of Eden (Gen. ii. 9); **tree of silver, Diana's tree,** an arborescent deposit of silver; **up a tree,** in a fix. [O.E. *tréow, tréo;* cf. Gr. *drȳs,* oak, *dory,* spear; Sans. *dru,* tree.]

trefoil, *trē′foil, tre′foil, n.* a three-lobed form, ornament, or aperture, as in tracery or heraldry: a leaf of three leaflets: a trifoliate plant, esp. of the clover genus (Trifolium).—*adj.* **tre′foiled.—bird's-foot trefoil** (see **bird**). [A.Fr. *trifoil*—L. *trifolium* —*trēs,* three, *folium,* a leaf.]

tregetour, *trej′ə-tər, n.* (*obs.*) a juggler: a trickster: a deceiver. [O.Fr. *tresgetour—tresgeter*—L. *trāns, jactāre,* to throw.]

trehala, *tri-hä′lä, n.* Turkish manna, cocoons of a beetle. [Turk. *tīqālah.*]

treille, *trāl, n.* a trellis.—*n.* **treill′age,** trellis-work: a trellis.—*adj.* **treill′aged.** [Fr.,—L. *trichila,* a bower.]

trek, *trek, v.t.* to drag.—*v.i.* to journey by ox-wagon: to migrate: to tramp and camp, dragging one's equipment: (*pr.p.* **trekk′ing;** *pa.t.* and *pa.p.* **trekked).**—*n.* a journey or stage: a migration.— *ns.* **trekk′er; trek′-ox; trek′schuit** (*-s′hhoit, -skoit*), a towed canal-boat. [Du. *trekken,* to draw.]

trellis, *trel′is, n.* a structure of cross-barred or lattice work.—*v.t.* to provide with a trellis: to train on a trellis.—*adj.* **trell′ised.**—*n.* **trell′is-work,** lattice-work. [O.Fr. *treliz*—L. *trilix, -īcis,* woven with triple thread, modified by association with *treille* (see **treille**).]

trema, *trē′mä, n.* an orifice: a diaeresis, two dots placed as a mark of separate pronunciation over a vowel-letter.—*adj.* **trematic** (*tri-mat′ik*), of the gill-slits.—*n.* **trematode** (*trem′ə-tōd*), any member of the **Tremato′da,** a class of parasitic, unsegmented flat-worms with adhesive suckers.—*n.* and *adj.* **trem′atoid.** [Gr. *trēma, -atos,* a hole.]

tremble, *trem′bl, v.i.* to shake, as from fear, cold, or weakness: to quiver: to vibrate: to pass tremulously.—*v.t.* to set trembling.—*n.* the act of trembling: tremulousness: a tremulous state: (in *pl.*) a morbid trembling.—*ns.* **trem′blement; trem′bler.**—*n.* and *adj.* **trem′bling.**—*adv.* **trem′-blingly.**—*n.* **trem′bling-pop′lar,** the aspen.— *adj.* **trem′bly,** tremulous. [O.Fr. (Fr.) *trembler*— L. *tremulus,* trembling—*tremĕre,* to shake.]

Tremella, *tri-mel′ä, n.* a gelatinous fungus, witches'

meat, on decaying wood, &c. [L. *tremulus,* quivering.]

tremendous, *tri-men′dəs, adj.* awe-inspiring: (*hyperb. coll.*) huge: (*slang*) prodigious, extraordinary.—*adv.* **tremen′dously.**—*n.* **tremen′dousness.** [L. *tremendus,* to be trembled at.]

tremolite, *trem′ə-līt, n.* a calcium-magnesium amphibole, usually in long prisms, or fibres, pale or colourless.—*adj.* **tremolitic** (*-lit′ik*). [From the Val *Tremola* in the Alps, where the mineral found is not true tremolite.]

tremolo, *trem′ō-lō, n.* (*mus.*) a tremulous effect as by a rapid succession of interruptions or of up and down bows: a device in an organ for producing this.—Also *adj.*—*n., adj.,* and *adv.* **tremolan′do.**— *n.* and *adj.* **trem′olant,** tremolo. [It. *tremolo, tremolando, tremolante.*]

tremor, *trem′ər, n.* a quiver: a quavering: a thrill: an involuntary agitation: a vibration. — *adj.* **trem′orless.** [L. *tremor, -ōris.*]

tremulous, *trem′ū-ləs, adj.* trembling: quivering. —*adj.* **trem′ūlant,** tremulous.—*n.* tremolant.— *v.i.* and *v.t.* **trem′ūlate.**—*adv.* **trem′ūlously.**— *n.* **trem′ūlousness.** [L. *tremulus,* trembling, and L.L. *tremulāre, -ātum,* to tremble.]

trenail. See under **tree.**

trench, *tren(t)sh, n.* a long narrow cut in the earth: a deep wrinkle.—*v.i.* to make trenches: to dig deep with spade or plough: to encroach: to border, verge.—*v.t.* to cut: to make trenches in: to put in a trench: to furnish with a trench: to entrench: (*Shak.*) to divert by a trench.—*n.* **trench′ancy,** causticity.—*adj.* **trench′ant** (*Spens.* **trench′and**), cutting: incisive. — *adv.* **trench′antly.** — *ns.* **trench′-coat,** a short waterproof coat (with belt) as used in trench warfare; **trench′er,** one who trenches; **trench′-feet′,** a diseased condition of the feet owing to exposure to cold and wet in trench warfare; **trench′-fe′ver,** an infectious disease prevalent among soldiers living in trenches, transmitted by lice; **trench′-mor′tar,** a small smooth-bore gun, throwing large shells short distances, useful in trench warfare; **trench′-plough,** a plough for ploughing more deeply than usual.—*v.t.* to plough with a trench-plough.— **trench warfare,** warfare in which each side entrenches itself in lines facing the enemy. [O.Fr. *trenche,* cut (Fr. *tranche,* slice), *trencher* (*trancher*), to cut, prob.—L. *truncāre* (see **truncate**).]

trencher, *tren′(t)shər, n.* a plate or platter: a board. —*n.* **tren′cher-cap,** a college-cap, mortar-board.— *adj.* **trench′er-fed,** kept each by his owner, not in a pack.—*ns.* **tren′cher-friend,** -**knight** (both *Shak.*), one who frequents the table of another, a parasite; **tren′cher-man,** (*Shak.*) a hearty eater. [A.Fr. *trenchour* (Fr. *tranchoir*)—*trencher,* to cut.]

trend, *trend, v.i.* to turn, wind: to have a tendency or prevailing direction.—*n.* (*dial.*) a bend: general tendency. [O.E. *trendan.*]

trenise, *trə-nēz′, n.* the fourth movement of a quadrille.—Also **la trenise.**

trental, *tren′tl, n.* a series of thirty requiem masses. [L.L. *trentāle*—L. *trīgintā,* thirty.]

trente-et-quarante, *tränᵗ-ā-kä-ränᵗt, n.* rouge-et-noir. [Fr., thirty and forty.]

trepan, *tri-pan′, n.* a decoy: a snare: an entrapping. —*v.t.* to ensnare: to lure:—*pr.p.* **trepann′ing;** *pa.t.* and *pa.p.* **trepanned′.**—*n.* **trepann′er.**—*n.* and *adj.* **trepann′ing.** [Earlier *trapan;* prob. conn. with **trap.**]

trepan, *tri-pan′, n.* an obsolete cylindrical saw for perforating the skull: a tool for boring shafts. —*v.t.* to remove a piece of the skull from: to cut a cylindrical disk from: to cut an annular groove in.—*ns.* **trepanation** (*trep-ə-nā′shən*); **trepann′er.**—*n.* and *adj.* **trepann′ing.** [Fr. *trépan*— L.L. *trepanum*—Gr. *trÿpanon—trÿpaein,* to bore.]

trepang, *tri-pang′, n.* sea-slug, a holothurian eaten by the Chinese. [Malay *tripang.*]

trephine, *tri-fēn′, -fīn′, n.* an improved trepan.— *v.t.* to perforate with the trephine. [Earlier *trafine* —L. *trēs fīnēs,* three ends, with a suggestion of **trepan.**]

trepidation, *trep-i-dā′shən, n.* trembling: alarmed agitation: (*old astron.;* Milt.) a libration of the celestial sphere assumed to explain a supposed oscillation of the ecliptic.—*adjs.* **trep′id**, quaking ; **trep′idant ; trepid′atory.** [L. *trepidāre, -ātum,* to hurry with alarm—*trepidus,* restless.]

trespass, *tres′pas, v.i.* to interfere with another's person or property : to enter unlawfully upon another's land : to encroach : to intrude : to sin.— —*n.* act of trespassing : any injury to another's person or property : a sin.—*n.* **tres′passer.** [O.Fr. *trespasser* (Fr. *trépasser*) — L. *trāns, passus,* a step.]

tress, *tres, n.* a plait or braid of the hair of the head : a long lock, braided or not.—*v.t.* to form into tresses. — *adjs.* **tressed,** braided : in tresses : having tresses ; **tress′y,** having or like tresses. [Fr. *tresse*—L. *tricia,* perh. Gr. *tricha,* threefold— *treis,* three.]

tress. See **trestle.**

tressure, *tresh′ər, n.* (*her.*) a subordinary, half the breadth of the orle, and usually borne double, and flowered and counter-flowered with fleurs-de-lis.— *adj.* **tress′ured,** having a tressure. [Fr., from *tresser,* to plait.]

trestle, *tres′l, n.* a support composed of a horizontal beam on sloping legs : a braced framework—also **tress′el.**—*ns.* **tress,** a trestle ; **trest′le-bridge,** one resting on trestlework ; **trest′le-table,** one of boards laid on trestles ; **trest′lework,** a braced framework. [O.Fr. *trestel* (Fr. *tréteau*) and *treste, trestre*—L. *trānstrum,* cross-beam.]

tret, *tret, n.* an allowance to purchasers of 4 lb. on every 104 lb. for waste. [Poss. A.Fr. *tret,* pull, turn of the scale, or Fr. *traite,* transport, both— *traire,* to draw—L. *trahēre, tractum.*]

trevally, *tri-val′i, n.* an Australian horse-mackerel (Caranx) of various species. [Prob. a modification of **cavally.**]

treviss, trevis, *trev′is,* **travis,** *trav′is, trāv′is, n.* forms of **traverse** : a stall partition : a stall.

trew. An old spelling of **true.**

trews, *trōōz, n.pl.* (orig. *sing.*) trousers, esp. of tartan cloth.—*n.* **trews′man,** a wearer of trews. [Ir. *trius,* Gael. *triubhas* ; cf. **trouse, trousers.**]

trey, *trā, n.* the three in cards and dice : a set of three : the third tine of a deer's horn (in full **trey′-ant′ler, -tine** ; also **tray, trez,** *trā, trāz*) : (*slang*) a threepenny bit (also **trey′bit, tray, tray′bit**). [O.Fr. *treis, trei*—L. *trēs,* three.]

trez. See **trey.**

tri-, *trī-, tri-,* in composition, three. [L. *trēs, tria,* and Gr. *treis, tria.*]

triable. See **try.**

triacid, *trī-as′id, adj.* having three replaceable hydrogen atoms : capable of replacing three hydro-gen atoms of an acid.

triaconter, *trī-ə-kon′tər, n.* an ancient ship, perhaps with thirty men to each group of oars. [Gr. *triākontērēs—triākonta,* thirty.]

triact, *trī′akt, adj.* three-rayed—*adjs.* **trīact′inal** (*-i-nəl* or *-ī′nəl*), **trīact′ine** (*-in*). [Gr. *aktis, -īnos,* ray.]

triad, *trī′ad, -əd, n.* a group or union of three : a Welsh saying about three things : (*mus.*) a chord of three notes, esp. the common chord : (*chem.*) an atom, element, or radical with a combining power of three.—*adjs.* **trī′ad, trīad′ic.**—*n.* **trī′-adist,** a composer of triads. [L. *trias*—Gr. *trias, triados—treis,* three.]

triadelphous, *trī-ə-del′fəs, adj.* with three bundles of stamens. [Gr. *adelphos,* a brother.]

triage. See **try.**

triakisoctahedron, *trī-ə-kis-ok-tə-hē′drən, n.* a solid figure like an octahedron with a three-faced pyramid on each face. [Gr. *triakis,* three times.]

trial, *trī′əl, n.* a trying : examination by a test : examination by a court to determine a question of law or fact, esp. the guilt or innocence of a prisoner : (often in *pl.*) examination, sometimes merely formal, of a candidate : a testing journey, as of motor-cars, motor-cycles : a trial match : suffering : temptation : attempt : a piece used as a test.—*adj.* done, taken, &c., for the sake of trial.— *ns.* **trial′day,** (*Shak.*) day of trial ; **trial-fire,** (*Shak.*) a fire for trying or proving ; **tri′al-trip,** an experimental trip of a new vessel, to test her sailing-

powers, &c.—**on trial,** on probation, as an experi-ment. [A.Fr. *trial—trier,* to try.]

trial, *trī′əl, adj.* threefold, trinal.—*ns.* **tri′alism,** the doctrine of the existence of body, soul, and spirit in man : (*hist.*) a scheme for turning the Dual Monarchy into a triple (Austria, Hungary, and a South Slav state) ; **tri′alist ; trīality** (*-al′i-ti*). [L. *trēs, tria,* three, after **dual.**]

trialogue, *trī′ə-log, n.* a dialogue between three persons. [On false analogy of **dialogue,** as if *dia*-meant two.]

triandrous, *trī-an′drəs, adj.* with three stamens.— *n.pl.* **Trian′dria,** in Linnaeus's classification a class of plants with three stamens.—*adj.* **trian′-drian.** [Gr. *anēr, andros,* a man (male).]

triangle, *trī′ang-gl* (also *-ang′*), *n.* (*math.*) a plane figure with three angles and three sides : part of the surface of a sphere bounded by three arcs of great circles (*spherical triangle*) : any mark or thing of that shape : a musical instrument of percussion, formed of a steel rod bent in triangle-form, open at one angle : a tripod, esp. for a pulley for raising weights, or formerly (usu. in *pl.*) for binding soldiers to for flogging.—*adjs.* **trī′-angled ; triang′ūlar,** having three angles : of a number, capable of being represented by dots in a triangle, as 1, 3, 6, 10, &c. : involving three persons or parties.—*n.* **triangūlar′ity.**—*adv.* **trī′-ang′ūlarly.**—*v.t.* **triang′ūlāte,** to survey by means of a series of triangles.—*adj.* with, marked with, made up of, triangles : triangular.—*adv.* **triang′-ūlātely.**—*n.* **triangūlā′tion,** act of triangulating : the series of triangles so used. [L. *triangulum—angulus,* an angle.]

triapsidal, *trī-aps′i-dəl, adj.* with three apses.— Also **triaps′al.**

triarch, *trī′ärk, adj.* with three xylem strands. [Gr. *archē,* origin.]

triarchy, *trī′är-ki, n.* government by three persons : a state governed by a triumvirate. [Gr. *triarchiā— archē,* rule.]

Trias, *trī′as, n.* (*geol.*) the oldest Mesozoic or Secondary system.—*adj.* **Triassic** (*trī-as′ik*). [Gr. *trias,* triad, from its threefold division in Germany —Bunter, Muschelkalk, Keuper.]

triatomic, *trī-ə-tom′ik, adj.* consisting of three atoms : having three replaceable atoms or groups : trivalent.

triaxial, *trī-ak′si-əl, adj.* having three axes.—Also **triax′on.**—*n.* a triaxial sponge spicule. [Gr. *axōn,* and L. *axis,* axle.]

tribasic, *trī-bā′sik, adj.* capable of reacting with three equivalents of an acid : (of acids) having three replaceable hydrogen atoms. [**base.**]

tribble, *trib′l, n.* a horizontal frame with wires stretched across it for drying paper.

tribe, *trīb, n.* a division of a nation or people for political purposes : a set of people theoretically of common descent : an aggregate of families, forming a community : a race : a breed : a class or set of people : loosely, a classificatory division. —*adj.* **trib′al.**—*n.* **trib′alism.**—*adv.* **trib′ally.**— *adj.* **tribe′less.**—*n.* **tribes′man.** [L. *tribus, -ūs,* one of the divisions of the ancient Roman people : that these were originally three is only a conjecture.]

triblet, *trib′lit, n.* a tapering mandrel on which rings, nuts, &c., are forged. [Fr. *triboulet.*]

tribometer, *trī-bom′i-tər, n.* a sled-like apparatus for measuring sliding friction. [Gr. *tribein,* to rub, *metron,* measure.]

tribrach, *trī′brak, n.* a foot of three short syllables.— *adj.* **tribrach′ic.** [Gr. *tribrachys—brachys,* short.]

tribrom(o)-, *trī′brōm′(ō)-,* in composition, having three atoms of bromine, esp. replacing hydrogen.

tribulation, *trib-ū-lā′shən, n.* severe affliction : (*old slang*) pawn : (*Shak.*) a rowdy gang. [L. *tribulāre, -ātum,* to afflict—*tribulum,* a sledge for rubbing out corn—*terēre,* to rub.]

tribune, *trib′ūn, n.* a magistrate elected by the Roman plebeians to defend their rights : a champion of popular rights : a name for a newspaper : a platform for speaking from : a raised area or stand : a bishop's stall or throne.—*n.* **tribunal** (*trib-* or *trib-ū′nl*), a judgment-seat : a court of justice or arbitration : a body appointed to adjudicate in

Neutral vowels in unaccented syllables : *el′ə-mənt, in′fənt, ran′dəm*

38

some matter: a confessional.—*adj.* of, of the nature of, or authorised by, a tribunal.—*ns.* **trib'unāte**, **trib'uneship**. — *adjs.* **tribunitial**, **-icial** (*-ish'l*), **tribunitian**, **-ician** (*-ish'ən*). [L. *tribūnus*, tribune, *tribūnāl*, tribunal—*tribus*, a tribe.]

tribute, *trib'ūt*, *n.* a payment in acknowledgment of subjection : an act, gift, words, or other expression of approbation : a percentage of ore or its value received by a miner. — *adv.* **trib'utarily**. — *n.* **trib'utariness**.—*adj.* **trib'utary**, paying tribute : contributing : paid in tribute.—*n.* a payer of tribute : a stream that runs into another.— *ns.* **trib'ute-mon'ey**, money paid as tribute ; **trib'uter**, a miner paid by tribute. [L. *tribūtum*—*tribuĕre*, to assign.]

tricar, *trī'kär*, *n.* a motor-tricycle with a passenger's seat in front : a three-wheeled motor-car.

tricarpellary, *trī-kär'pəl-ər-i*, or *-pel'ər-i*, *adj.* of or with three carpels.

trice, *trīs*, (*naut.*) *v.t.* to haul : to haul and make fast.—*n.* (*obs.*) a pulley : a moment (as if the time of a single tug). [M.Du. *trīsen* (Du. *trijsen*), to hoist.]

tricephalous, *trī-sef'ə-ləs*, *adj.* three-headed. [Gr. *trikephalos*—*kephalē*, a head.]

triceps, *trī'seps*, *adj.* three-headed. — *n.* a muscle with three insertions, esp. that at the back of the upper arm. [L. *trīceps*, *-cipitis*—*caput*, head.]

Triceratops, *trī-ser'ə-tops*, *n.* a gigantic three-horned Cretaceous dinosaur. [Gr. *keras*, *-atos*, horn, *ōps*, face.]

tricerion, *trī-sē'ri-on*, *n.* (*Gr. Ch.*) a three-branched candlestick. [Late Gr.,—Gr. *kēros*, wax.]

trich-, *trik-*, **tricho-**, *-ō-*, in composition, hair. [Gr. *thrix*, gen. *trichos*.]

trichiasis, *trik-ī'ə-sis*, *n.* turning in of the eyelashes.

Trichina, *trik'i-nä*, *tri-kī'nä*, **Trichinella**, *trik-i-nel'ä*, *ns.* a nematode worm parasitic in rat, pig, and man, the adult in the small intestine, the larva encysted in muscle.—*ns.* **trichiniasis** (*trik-i-nī'ə-sis*), **trichinō'sis** ; **trichinīsā'tion**, infestation with trichinae.—*adjs.* **trich'inised**, **trich'inosed** (*-nōst*), infested with trichinae ; **trichinot'ic**, **trich'inous**, pertaining to trichinosis. [Gr. *trichīnos*, of hair—*thrix*, *trichos*, hair.]

trichite, *trik'īt*, *n.* a hairlike crystallite.—*adj.* **trichitic** (*-it'ik*).

Trichiurus, *trik-i-(y)ōō'rəs*, *n.* a genus of hair-tails, giving name to the family **Trichiu'ridae**, akin to mackerels and tunnies. [Gr. *ourā*, tail.]

trichlor(o)-, *trī'klōr'(ō)-*, in composition, having three atoms of chlorine, esp. replacing hydrogen.

trichobacteria, *trik-ō-bak-tē'ri-ä*, *n.pl.* filamentous bacteria.

trichogyne, *trik'ō-jīn*, *-jin*, *n.* in red seaweeds, and some fungi, a threadlike prolongation of the female organ. [Gr. *gynē*, woman, female.]

trichoid, *trik'oid*, *adj.* hairlike. [Gr. *trichoeidēs*.]

trichology, *trik-ol'ə-ji*, *n.* the scientific study of hair.—*adj.* **tricholog'ical**.—*n.* **trichol'ogist**, one versed in trichology : a name affected by hair-dressers. [Gr. *thrix*, *trichos*, a hair.]

trichome, *trik'ōm*, *trik'ōm*, *n.* a plant hair or out-growth from the epidermis. [Gr. *trichōma*, a growth of hair.]

Trichophyton, *trik-of'i-tən*, *n.* a fungus genus causing ringworm.—*n.* **trichophytō'sis**, ringworm caused by Trichophyton. [Gr. *phyton*, plant.]

Trichoptera, *trik-op'tər-ä*, *n.pl.* an order of insects with hairy wings, the caddis-flies. — *n.* **trichop'terist**, a student of the caddis-flies.—*adj.* **trichop'terous**. [Gr. *pteron*, wing.]

trichord, *trī'kord*, *adj.* three-stringed : with three strings to one note.—*n.* a three-stringed instrument : a triad. [Gr. *trichordos*—*chordē*, a string.]

trichosis, *trik-ō'sis*, *n.* arrangement, distribution, or morbid condition of hair. [Gr. *trichōsis*, hairiness.]

trichotomous, *trī-kot'ə-məs*, *adj.* divided into three : forking in threes.—*v.t.* and *v.i.* **trichot'omise**, to divide in three or threes.—*adv.* **trichot'omously**. —*n.* **trichot'omy**, trichotomous division or forking. [Gr. *tricha*, threefold—*treis*, three, *tomē*, a cutting —*temnein*, to cut.]

trichroic, *trī-krō'ik*, *adj.* having or exhibiting three

colours, esp. when viewed in different directions. —*n.* **trī'chroism**. [Gr. *trichroos*, three-coloured.]

trichromatic, *trī-krō-mat'ik*, *adj.* characterised by three colours : having three fundamental colour-sensations.—*adj.* **trichrō'mic**, trichromatic.—*n.* one who has three fundamental colour-sensations. —*n.* **trichrō'matism**. [Gr. *trichrōmatos*—*chrōma*, colour.]

trichronous, *trī'kro-nəs*, *adj.* trisemic. [Gr. *trichronos*—*chronos*, time.]

trick, *trik*, *n.* an artifice : a deceitful device : a deception : a prank : a performance aimed at astonishing, puzzling, or amusing : an expedient : a knack : a characteristic habit, mannerism, trait : a spell or turn, esp. at the helm : a round of play at cards : the cards so played and taken by the winner, forming a unit in scoring : a trinket, toy, or gimcrack : (*slang*) a watch : (*her.*) an outline sketch.—*v.t.* to deceive, to cheat : to beguile : to deck, prank : to trim : to sketch in outline.—*adj.* of the nature of, for the purpose or performance of, a trick : (*obs.*) adroit and trim.—*ns.* **trick'er** ; **trick'ery**, act or practice of playing tricks : artifice : stratagem : imposition.—*adv.* **trick'ily**.—*n.* **trick'iness**.—*n.* and *adj.* **trick'ing**.—*adj.* **trick'ish**, tricky. — *adv.* **trick'ishly**. — *ns.* **trick'ishness** ; **trick'siness**.—*adj.* **trick'some**.—*ns.* **trick'ster**, a cheat : one who practises trickery ; **trick'stering**, playing the trickster.—*adjs.* **tricks'y**, pranked up : capricious : sportive : mischievous : tricky : tick-lish ; **trick'y**, addicted to trickery : clever in tricks : ticklish. [O.Fr. *trique*, Northern form of *triche*, deceit ; perh. in part of other origin.]

trickle, *trik'l*, *v.i.* to run in drops or in a small irregular stream.—*v t.* to emit in a trickle.—*n.* (*obs.*) a drop : a succession of drops : a trickling rill.— *n.* **trick'let**, a little rill.—*n.* and *adj.* **trick'ling**.— *adj.* **trick'ly**, trickling. [M.E. *triklen*, prob. for *striklen*, freq. of **strike**.]

trickle, *trik'l*, *adj.* (*Spens.*) ticklish, precarious (another reading **tickle**). [Prob. **trick**.]

trick-track, *trik'-trak'*, *n.* a form of backgammon in which pegs as well as pieces are used.—Also **tric'-trac**, **tick'-tack**. [Fr. *tric trac* ; imit.]

triclinic, *trī-klin'ik*, *adj.* (*min.*) referred to three unequal axes obliquely inclined to each other. [Gr. *treis*, three, *klinein*, to bend.]

triclinium, *trī-klin'i-əm*, *n.* (*Rom. ant.*) a couch running round three sides of a table for reclining on at meals : a dining-room. [L. *triclīnium*—Gr. *triklīnion*—Gr. *treis*, three, *klīnē*, a couch.]

tricolour, **tricolor**, *trī'kul-ər*, *adj.* three-coloured. —*n.* a three-coloured flag, esp. that of France (*trē-kol-or*).—*adj.* **trī'coloured**. [L. *tricolor* and Fr. *tricolore*.]

triconsonantal, *trī-kon-sə-nant'l*, *adj.* having three consonants.—Also **triconsonan'tic**.

tricorn, *trī'korn*, *adj.* three-horned : three-cornered. —*n.* a three-cornered hat. [L. *tricornis*, three-horned—*cornū*, a horn.]

tricorporate, *trī-kor'pə-rāt*, *-rit*, **-d**, *-id*, *adjs.* three-bodied (with one head). [L. *corpus*, *-oris*, body.]

tricostate, *trī-kos'tāt*, *adj.* three-ribbed. [L. *costa*, rib.]

tricot, *trē'kō*, *n.* a hand-knitted woollen fabric, or imitation : a soft, slightly-ribbed cloth for women's garments. [Fr. *tricot*, knitting.]

tricrotic, *trī-krot'ik*, *adj.* triple-beating.—*n.* **trī'-crotism**.—*adj.* **tri'crotous**. [Gr. *trikrotos*, rowed with triple stroke—*krotos*, a beat.]

tricuspid, **-ate**, *trī-kus'pid*, *-āt*, *adjs.* with three cusps or points. [L. *tricuspis*, *-idis*—*cuspis*, a point.]

tricycle, *trī'si-kl*, *n.* a three-wheeled cycle.—*v.i.* to ride a tricycle.—*n.* **tri'cycler**.—*adj.* **tricyclic** (*trī-sī'klik*), having three whorls or rings.—*ns.* **tri'cycling** (*-si-*) ; **trī'cyclist**. [Gr. *kyklos*, circle, wheel.]

Tridacna, *trī-dak'nä*, *n.* the giant clam of the Indian Ocean, the greatest known bivalve (500 lb.). [Gr. *tridaknos*, eaten at three bites (applied to a big oyster)—*daknein*, to bite.]

tridactyl, **-ous**, *trī-dak'til*, *-əs*, *adjs.* three-toed : three-fingered. [Gr. *daktylos*, finger, toe.]

tride, an obs. spelling (*Spens.*; *Shak.*) of **tried.** See **try.**

trident, trī′dənt, *n.* a three-pronged spear, esp. that of the sea-god Poseidon or Neptune: anything of like shape.—*adjs.* **tri′dent, tridental** (*-dent′*), three-pronged; **tridented** (*trī-dent′id*), three-pronged: (*trī′dənt-id*) having a trident. [L. *tridēns, -dentis—dēns,* tooth.]

Tridentine, trī-, tri-dent′īn, *adj.* of Trent in Southern Tirol, or the Council (1545-63) held there.—*n.* a native of Trent: one who accepts the decrees of the Council, a Roman Catholic. [L. *Tridentum,* Trent.]

tridimensional, trī-di-men′shən-əl, *adj.* having three dimensions.

triduum, trid′ū-əm, or trīd′, *n.* a space of three days: a three days' service.—*adj.* **trid′uan,** lasting three days. [L. *trīduum—diēs,* day.]

tridymite, trid′i-mīt, *n.* an orthorhombic form of silica, in hexagonal scales, often combined in threes. [Gr. *tridymos,* threefold.]

trie, an obs. spelling of **try.**—**tried, tries, trier.** See **try.**

triennial, trī-en′yəl, *adj.* continuing three years: happening every third year.—*adv.* **trienn′ially.** [L. *triennis—annus,* a year.]

trierarch, trī′ər-ärk, *n.* (*Gr. hist.*) the commander of a trireme: one required (alone or with others) to fit out a trireme.—*adj.* **tri′erarchal.**—*n.* **tri′erarchy,** the office of trierarch: the obligation of fitting out ships. [Gr. *triērarchos—triērēs,* a trireme, *archein,* to rule.]

trieteric, trī-i-ter′ik, *adj.* biennial. [Gr. *trietērikos* —*trietēris,* a biennial festival—*treis,* three, *etos,* a year (both years being counted).]

triethyl, trī-eth′il, *adj.* having three ethyl groups.—*n.* **triethylamine** (*-mēn′*), an oily liquid answering to ammonia with ethyl replacing all the hydrogen.

trifacial, trī-fā′shl, *adj.* threefold and pertaining to the face, esp. of the trigeminal nerve.—*n.* the trigeminal nerve. [L. *faciēs,* face.]

trifarious, trī-fā′ri-əs, *adj.* arranged in three rows: facing three ways. [L. *trifārius.*]

trifid, trif′id, trī′fid, *adj.* three-cleft (about half-way down). [L. *findĕre,* to cleave.]

trifle, trī′fl, *n.* anything of little importance or value: a small amount: a light confection of whipped cream or white of egg, sponge-cake, wine, &c.: a kind of pewter.—*v.i.* to busy oneself idly: to play, toy: to behave without seriousness or respect: to meddle irresponsibly: to sport: to dally.—*v.t.* to spend or pass idly: to play with: (*Shak.*) to render trivial in comparison.—*n.* **tri′fler.**—*adj.* **tri′fling,** of small value, importance, or amount: trivial.—*adv.* **tri′flingly.**—*n.* **tri′flingness.** [O.Fr. *trufle,* mockery, deception.]

trifoliate, trī-fō′li-āt, *adj.* with three leaves or leaflets.—*ns.* **Trifō′lium,** the clover or trefoil genus; **trifoly** (*trif′ə-li*; *Browning*), trefoil. [L. *trifolium—folium,* leaf.]

triforium, trī-fō′ri-əm, *n.* (*archit.*) a gallery, story, or arcade over an aisle:—*pl.* **trifo′ria.** [L.L.] connexion with *trēs,* three, and *foris,* door, does not appear.]

triform, trī′form, *adj.* having a triple form—also **tri′formed.** [L. *triformis—forma,* form.]

trifurcate, trī′fur-kāt, or *-fur′, adj.* three-forked.—*v.i.* to divide into three branches.—*adj.* **tri′furcated** (or *-fur′*).—*n.* **trifurca′tion.** [L. *trifurcus* —*furca,* a fork.]

trig, trig, *adj.* trim, neat: tight, sound.—*v.t.* to make trig: to stuff: to block, hold back with a wedge.—*n.* a block or wedge to stop a wheel.—*adv.* **trig′ly.**—*n.* **trig′ness.** [O.N. *tryggr,* faithful, secure; cf. **true.**]

trig, trig, *n.* an abbreviation of **trigonometry.**

trigamy, trig′ə-mi, *n.* the having of three legal or supposed husbands or wives at once: (*eccl. law*) a third marriage.—*n.* **trig′amist,** one who has committed trigamy.—*adj.* **trig′amous,** of the nature of, involving, living in, trigamy. [Gr. *trigamos,* thrice married—*gamos,* marriage.]

trigeminal, trī-jem′i-nl, *adj.* threefold: three-branched.—*n.* the trigeminal, trifacial, or fifth

cranial nerve. [L. *trigeminus,* born three at a birth —*geminus,* born at the same birth.]

trigger, trig′ər, *n.* a lever that releases a catch so as to fire a gun or set a mechanism going: anything that starts a train of actions. [Du. *trekker—trekken,* to pull.]

triglot, trī′glot, *adj.* in three languages. [Gr. *glōtta,* tongue.]

triglyph, trī′glif, *n.* a three-grooved tablet in the Doric frieze.—*adj.* **triglyph′ic.** [Gr. *triglyphos—glyphein,* to carve.]

trigon, trī′gon, *n.* a triangle: (*astrol.*) a set of three signs 120° apart, the zodiac being divided into four trigons—the first or *watery* trigon, Cancer, Scorpio, Pisces; the *earthly,* Taurus, Virgo, Capricornus; the *airy,* Gemini, Libra, Aquarius; the *fiery,* Aries, Leo, Sagittarius.—*adjs.* **trigonal** (*trig′ə-nl*), of a trigon: triangular: trigonous: bounded by three planes: three-faced, forming half a hexagon in section: of symmetry about an axis, such that a rotation through 120° gives the same figure; **trigonic** (*trī-gon′ik*), of a trigon: triangular; **trigonous** (*trig′ə-nəs*), triangular in section, or nearly so—as with convex (or concave) faces, or rounded angles. [Gr. *trigōnon—gōnia,* an angle.]

trigonometry, trig-ə-nom′i-tri, *n.* the branch of mathematics that treats of the relations between the sides and angles of triangles.—*n.* **trigonom′-eter,** one versed in or occupied with trigonometry: an instrument for solving triangles.—*adjs.* **trigonometric** (*-nə-met′rik*), **-al.**—*adv.* **trigonomet′rically.** [Gr. *trigōnon,* a triangle, *metron,* a measure.]

trigram, trī′gram, *n.* an inscription of three letters: a figure of three lines.—*adjs.* **trigrammat′ic, trigramm′ic.** [Gr. *gramma,* a letter.]

trigraph, trī′gräf, *n.* a combination of three letters for one sound. [Gr. *graphē,* a writing.]

Trigynia, trī-jin′i-ä, *n.pl.* in the Linnaean system an order of plants (in various classes) with three pistils.—*adjs.* **trigyn′ian, trigynous** (*trij′i-nəs*). [Gr. *gynē,* a woman, female.]

trihedral, trī-hed′rəl, *-hēd′, adj.* three-faced. [Gr. *hedrā,* a seat.]

trihybrid, trī-hī′brid, *n.* a cross between parents differing in three independently heritable characters.—Also *adj.*

trihydric, trī-hī′drik, *adj.* having three hydroxyl groups.

trike, trīk, *n.* and *v.i.* (*coll.*) for **tricycle.**

trilateral, trī-lat′ər-əl, *adj.* three-sided.—*n.* a triangle. [L. *latus, lateris,* side.]

trilby, tril′bi, *n.* a soft felt hat.—Also **trilby hat.** [From George du Maurier's novel, *Trilby* (1894).]

trild, trild (*Spens.*). See **trill** (2).

trilemma, trī-, trī-lem′ä, *n.* a form of argument or a situation differing from a dilemma in that there is a choice of three instead of two. [After **dilemma.**]

trilinear, trī-lin′ē-ər, *adj.* consisting of, having, or referred to three lines.—*adj.* **trilin′eate,** marked with three lines. [L. *linea,* line.]

trilingual, trī-ling′gwəl, *adj.* in or using three languages, esp. native or habitual languages. [L. *lingua,* tongue.]

triliteral, trī-lit′ər-əl, *adj.* consisting of three letters. —*n.* **trilit′eralism,** the characteristic (as of Semitic languages) of having roots of three consonants. [L. *littera,* a letter.]

trilith, trī′lith, *n.* a form of megalithic monument consisting of two upright stones supporting another lying crosswise—also **trilithon** (*trī′,* trī′).—*adj.* **trilith′ic.** [Gr. *lithos,* stone.]

trill, tril, *n.* a trillo: a tremulous sound: a run or roulade of bird-song: a consonant-sound produced by vibration.—*v.t.* and *v.i.* to play, sing, pronounce, sound, with a trill.—*n.* **trill′o,** (*mus.*) a shake. [It. *trillo;* imit.]

trill, tril, *v.t.* and *v.i.* to twirl: to roll: to trundle: to pour in a fine stream:—*pa.t.* **trilled** (*Spens.* **trild**). [Cf. Norw. and Sw. *trilla,* to roll.]

trilling, tril′ing, *n.* a threefold compound of crystals: one child of triplets. [**tri-** and *-ling;* cf. Dan. and Sw. *trilling;* Ger. *drilling.*]

trillion, tril′yən, *n.* the cube of a million: (*U.S.,* as

in *France*) the cube of ten thousand.—*n.* and *adj.*
trill′ionth. [Fr.,—**tri-**, after **million.**]
Trillium, *tril′i-əm, n.* a three-leaved trimerous
genus of the lily family. [L. *trēs,* three.]
trilobate, -d, *trī-lō′bāt,* or *trī′lō-bāt, -id, adjs.* having
three lobes.—Also **trī′lobed.**
trilobite, *trī′lō-bīt, tril′ə-bīt, n.* any fossil arthropod
of a Palaeozoic order (**Trilobi′ta**), with broad head-
shield and body longitudinally furrowed into three
lobes.—*adj.* **trilobitic** (*-bit′ik*). [Gr. *lobos,* lobe.]
trilocular, *trī-lok′ū-lər, adj.* three-celled. [L.
loculus.]
trilogy, *tril′ə-ji, n.* a group of three tragedies : any
similar group, as of novels : a triad. [Gr. *trilogiā—
logos,* discourse.]
trim, *trim, v.t.* to put in due condition : to fit out :
to make ready for sailing : to adjust the balance of
(as a boat) : to dress, arrange : to set in order : to
decorate, as with ribbons : to make tidy or neat :
to clip into shape : to make compact : to smooth :
to take or put by trimming : to rebuke sharply :
to thrash : (*slang*) to cheat.—*v.i.* to balance : to
balance or fluctuate between parties : (*pr.p.* **trimm′-
ing;** *pa.t.* and *pa.p.* **trimmed**).—*adj.* in good
order : neat : tidy : well-kept : clean-cut.—*adv.*
trimly.—*n.* condition for sailing or flight : balance :
condition, order : humour, disposition, temper,
way : array : fittings : an act of trimming : (*U.S.*)
window-dressing : parts trimmed off. — *adv.*
trim′ly.—*ns.* **trimm′er,** one who or that which
trims : one who fluctuates between parties : a
time-server : a scold : anything trouncing or
redoubtable : a small horizontal beam on a floor
into which the ends of joists are framed : a float
bearing a baited hook and line, used in fishing for
pike ; **trimm′ing,** making trim : balancing :
clipping : (usu. *pl.*) ornamental additions : (*pl.*)
accessories : (*pl.*) fittings : (*pl.*) parts trimmed off.
—*adj.* that trims.—*adv.* **trimm′ingly.**—*n.* **trim′-
ness.** [O.E. *trymman, trymian,* to strengthen, set
in order—*trum,* firm.]
trimerous, *trim′ə-rəs, adj.* having three parts, or
parts in threes.—*adj.* **trimeric** (*trī-mer′ik*), having
the same empirical formula but three times the
atomic weight. [Gr. *meros,* part.]
trimester, *tri-mes′tər, n.* three months : an academic
term.—*adj.* **trimes′trial.** [L. *trimēstris,* of three
months—*mēnsis,* a month.]
trimeter, *trim′i-tər, n.* a verse of three measures
(dipodies or feet).—*adjs.* **trim′eter, trimetric**
(*trī-met′rik*), consisting of three measures, esp.
iambic. [Gr. *trimetros—metron,* measure.]
trimethyl, *trī-meth′il, adj.* containing three methyl
radicals in combination. — *n.* **trimeth′ylamine**
(*-ə-mēn′*), a gas, N(CH₃)₃, got from herring-brine,
corresponding to ammonia with methyl replacing
all the hydrogen.
trimonthly, *trī-munth′li, adj.* every three months.
trimorphism, *trī-mor′fizm, n.* (*biol.*) occurrence of
three forms in the same species : (*chem.*) the
property of crystallising in three forms.—*adjs.*
trimor′phic, trimor′phous. [Gr. *morphē,* form.]
Trimurti, *tri-mōōr′ti, n.* the Hindu trinity, Brahma,
Vishnu, and Siva.
Trinacrian, *tri-, trī-nā′kri-ən, adj.* Sicilian : **trinacrian,** three-pointed : with three extremities.—
adj. **trinacriform** (*trin-ak′ri-form*), three-pronged.
[Gr. *Trīnakriā,* Sicily, *trinax, -akos,* a three-
pronged mattock, *thrīnax,* a trident.]
trindle, *trin′dl, n.* a piece of wood, &c., laid between
the cords and boards of a book to flatten before
cutting : a wheel, esp. of a barrow.—*v.t.* and *v.i.* to
roll, to trundle.—*n.* **trin′dle-tail,** [a trundle-tail.
[trundle.]
trine, *trīn, adj.* threefold : 120° apart : hence,
benign.—*n.* a triad : the aspect of two planets, as
seen from the earth, distant from each other one-
third of the zodiac or 120° : a triplet.—*v.t.* to join
in trine aspect.—*n.* **trin** (*trin*), a triplet (by birth) :
a trilling.—*adjs.* **trinal** (*trī′nl*), **trī′nary.** [L.
trīnus—trēs, tria, three.]
trine, *trīn, v.i.* to go.—**trine to the (nubbing)
cheat,** (*cant*) to go to the gallows.
tringle, *tring′gl, n.* a curtain-rod. [Fr.]
trinitro-, *trī-nī′trō-,* in composition, having three

nitro-groups (NO₂), esp. replacing hydrogen.-
ns. **trinitroben′zene,** C₆H₃(NO₂)₃, answering t
benzene C₆H₆ ; **trinitrophe′nol,** a similar deriva
tive of phenol, esp. picric acid ; **trinitrotol′uene
or -tol′uol,** a high explosive (familiarly **T.N.T.**
a trinitro-derivative of toluene.
trinity, *trin′i-ti, n.* threefoldness : three in one :
triad : esp. (**Trinity**) the triune God of orthodo
Christians (Father, Son, Holy Ghost) : any syn
bolical representation of the persons of the Trinity
Trinity Sunday : Trinity term.—*adj.* **Trinitā′riar
of,** in relation to, believing in, the Trinity : of th
Trinitarians.—*n.* one who holds the doctrine of th
Trinity : a member of a religious order founded
Rome in 1198 to redeem Christian captives fron
the Mohammedans—also *Mathurins* and *Redem*
tionists : a member of Trinity College.—*n.* **Trinitā
rianism.—Trinity House,** a lighthouse and pilc
authority for England, and in part Scotland an
Northern Ireland, chartered at Deptford in 1514
Trinity Sunday, the Sunday after Whitsunday
Trinity term, one of the terms of the Englis
law-courts beginning after Trinity Sunday (no
Trinity law sittings). [L. *trīnitās, -ātis—trīnu*
threefold.]
trinket, *tring′kit, n.* a small ornament or piece o
jewellery : any paltry or trumpery object o
observance : (*obs.*) a delicacy.—*v.i.* to have traffick
ings or underhand dealings.—*ns.* **trink′eter,** a
intriguer ; **trink′eting ; trink′etry,** trinkets col
lectively. [Poss. O.Fr. *trenquet,* small knife.]
trinkum, *tring′kəm.* Same as **trankum.**—Als
trink′um-trank′um.
trinomial, *trī-nō′mi-əl, adj.* consisting of thre
words : of three terms connected by the sign plu
or minus.—*n.* a trinomial name or expression.-
ns. **trino′mialism,** the system of naming by thre
words (for genus, species, and subspecies) ; **trino
mialist.** [After **binomial.**]
trio, *trē′ō, n.* a set of three : (*mus.*) a compositic
for, or combination of, three performers : th
second division of a minuet, scherzo, or marc
(said to have been originally for three instruments
followed by a repetition of the first :—*pl.* **trī′o**
[It.]
triode, *trī′ōd, adj.* with three electrodes.—*n.* a three
electrode valve. [Gr. *hodos,* way.]
Triodion, *trī-ō′di-on, n.* (*Gr. Ch.*) a service-book fc
the ten weeks before Easter. [Mod. Gr. *triōdion-
ōdē,* hymn.]
trioecious, *trī-ē′shəs, adj.* having male, female, an
hermaphrodite flowers on different plants. [G
oikos, house.]
triolet, *trī′ō-lit, trē′ō-lā, -let, n.* an eight-lined poer
rhymed *abaaabab,* lines 4 and 7 repeating 1, an
8 repeating 2. [Fr.]
trional, *trī′ə-nal, n.* a drug used as a narcotic, aki
to sulphonal, but safer. [From its three eth
groups.]
triones, *trī-ō′nēz, n.pl.* the seven stars of the Ploug
[L. *triōnēs,* plough-oxen.]
trionym, *trī′ə-nim, n.* a trinomial.—*adj.* **trionyma
(-on′i-məl).** [Gr. *triōnymos—onyma* (*onoma*), name.
trior. See try.
trioxide, *trī-oks′īd, n.* a compound with three atom
of oxygen.
trip, *trip, v.i.* to move with short, light steps o
skips : to stumble : to catch one's foot : to mak
a slip in chastity, accuracy, &c. : to tip up : to
make an excursion.—*v.t.* to cause to stumble o
fall by catching the foot (often with *up*) : to catcl
in a fault : to dance trippingly : to trip or danc
upon : to loose, as an anchor, from the bottom, b
a long rope : to release by striking : to tilt up
(*pr.p.* **tripp′ing;** *pa.t.* and *pa.p.* **tripped**).—*n.*
light, short step or skip : a catching of the foot :
stumble : a point in coursing, when the hare i
thrown off its legs : a slip, lapse : a single journe
or run, one way or to and fro : a pleasure excursion
jaunt : a specially arranged run at a cheap fare :
company of excursionists : a striking part tha
releases a catch.—*ns.* **trip′-hammer,** a tilt-hammer
trip′hook, (*Browning*) some kind of instrument o
torture.—*adj.* **tripp′ant,** (*her.*) tripping, with righ
foot raised.—*n.* **tripp′er,** one who trips : ar

xcursionist, esp. of the disturbing kind.—*adjs.* **ripp'erish, tripp'ery,** of, like, savouring of, the vulgar or noisy tripper.—*n.* and *adj.* **tripp'ing.**—*adv.* **tripp'ingly.** [O.Fr. *triper*; of Gmc. origin; cf. O.E. *treppan*, to tread, Ger. *trappe(l)n*, Du. *trip-, trappen, trippelen*, Sw. *trippa*.]

ip, trip, *n.* a small flock of sheep, wildfowl, &c. Perh. akin to **troop.**]

ipartite, trī-pär'tīt, *adj.* in three parts: (*bot.*) left in three nearly to the base: relating to three arties.—*n.* **tripartition** (-tish'ən). [L. *tripartītus* —*partīrī*, to divide—*pars*, a part.]

ipe, trīp, *n.* entrails: parts of the compound tomach of a ruminant, prepared as food—the aunch or rumen (*plain tripe*), and the smaller eticulum (*honeycomb tripe*): (*coll.*) rubbish, poor tuff: claptrap.—*ns.* **tripe'man, -wife, -woman,** dresser or seller of tripe; **trip'ery,** a place for he preparation or sale of tripe; **tripe'-shop.**— *dj.* **tripe'-visag'd,** (*Shak.*) with a face like tripe. —**tripe de roche** (*trep də rosh*; Fr.), rock-tripe. O.Fr. (Fr.) *tripe*; origin obscure.]

pedal, trip'-, trīp'i-dl, trī-pē'dl, *adj.* three-footed. L. *pēs, pedis*, foot.]

personal, trī-pər'sən-əl, *adj.* consisting of three ersons.—*ns.* **triper'sonalism; triper'sonalist,** believer in the Trinity; **tripersonal'ity.**

petalous, trī-pet'əl-əs, *adj.* three-petalled. [Gr. *etalon*, leaf.]

phenyl- trī'fē'nil-, in composition, containing hree phenyl radicals in combination.—*n.* **trī'he'nylamine** (-mēn), a crystalline compound nswering to ammonia with all the hydrogen eplaced by phenyl.

phone, trī'fōn, *n.* a shorthand sign representing a riphthongal sound. [Gr. *phōnē*, sound.]

phthong, trif'thong, *n.* a combination of three owel sounds in one syllable: (loosely) a trigraph. –*adj.* **triphthongal** (-thong'gl). [Gr. *phthongos*, ound.]

phyllous, trī-fil'əs, *adj.* three-leaved. [Gr. *hyllon*, a leaf.]

iphysite, trif'i-zīt, -sīt, *n.* a believer in the exist-nce of three natures in Christ—human, divine, nd a third resulting from the union of these. [Gr. *hysis*, nature.]

ipinnate, trī-pin'āt, -it, *adj.* pinnate with the innae themselves pinnate, and their pinnae again innate.

ipitaka, tri-pit'ä-kä, *n.* the whole body of the orthern Buddhist canonical writings, comprising he three divisions of *Sutras*, or discourses of the Buddha for the laity; *Vinaya*, or discipline for the rder; and *Abhidharma*, or metaphysics. [Sans. *i*, three, *pitaka*, basket.]

plane, trī'plān, *n.* an aeroplane with three sets of ain planes, one above another.

ple, trip'l, *adj.* threefold: consisting of three: hree times as much: (*Shak.*) third.—*n.* a quantity hree times as much: a thing (e.g. a star) that is riple: a peal of bells interchanging in three sets.— .t. and *v.i.* to treble.—*adjs.* **trip'le-crowned',** aving three crowns or triple crown, as the pope; **rip'le-head'ed,** three-headed.—*ns.* **trip'leness; trip'let,** three of a kind, or three united: three nes rhyming together: (*mus.*) a group of three otes occupying the time of two, indicated by a lur and the figure 3: one of three born at a birth. –*adjs.* **trip'le-turned,** (*Shak.*) three times faith-ess; **trip'lex,** triple.—*n.* (*Shak.*) triple time.—*adj.* **rip'licate,** threefold: made thrice as much: as he cubes of the quantities.—*n.* a third copy or ning corresponding to two others of the same kind: he triplicate ratio.—*v.t.* to make threefold.—*ns.* **iplica'tion,** the act of triplicating: a reply to a uplication: (*astrol.*) a trigon; **trip'ling,** a making triple: triplet, trilling or trin.—*adv.* **triply** (trip'li).—*n.* ri-pli') ; Scots law) a pursuer's reply to a defender's uply.—*v.t.* and *v.i.* to reply to a duply.—**Triple lliance,** the league of England, Sweden, and the etherlands formed against France in 1668: he alliance of Britain, France, and Holland against pain in 1717: the alliance between Germany, ustria, and Italy, 1883-1915, counterbalanced by

the **Triple Entente,** a friendly understanding (developing into an alliance) between Britain, France, and Russia; **triple crown,** the pope's tiara; **triple event,** Two Thousand Guineas, St Leger, and Derby; **triple time,** time or rhythm of three beats, or of three times three beats, in a bar. [Fr.,—L. *triplus*—Gr. *triploos* (*triplous*); and L. *triplex*.]

triploid, trip'loid, *adj.* having three times the haploid number of chromosomes. [Gr. *triploos*, triple.]

tripod, trip'od, trī'pod, *n.* anything on three feet or legs, esp. a stand for an instrument: the stool on which the priestess sat at Delphi to deliver an oracle.—*adj.* three-legged.—*adj.* **tripodal** (trip'-əd-əl).—*n.* **tripody** (trip'ə-di), a verse or group of three feet. [Gr. *tripous, tripodos*—*pous*, foot.]

tripoli, trip'ə-li, *n.* diatomite. [Orig. brought from *Tripoli* in Africa.]

tripos, trī'pos, *n.* a Cambridge honours examination: the list of successful candidates in it; (*obs.*) a tripod. [Prob. traceable to the custom by which a B.A., known as Mr *Tripos*, sat on a three-legged stool and disputed in the Philosophy School at Cambridge on Ash Wednesday, his speech being called the Tripos speech.]

trippant, tripper, tripping, &c. See **trip.**

trippet, trip'it, *n.* a trivet. [Cf. **trivet** and O.Fr. *trepied*.]

tripple, trip'l, *n.* (*S.Afr.*) a horse's ambling canter, between a fast walk and a slow trot.—Also *v.i.*— *n.* **tripp'ler.** [Du. *trippelen*.]

tripsis, trip'sis, *n.* pulverisation: shampooing: massage. [Gr. *trīpsis*—*trībein*, to rub.]

tripterous, trip'tər-əs, *adj.* three-winged. [Gr. *tripteros*—*pteron*, wing.]

triptote, trip'tōt, *adj.* used in three cases only.—*n.* a triptote word. [Gr. *triptōtos*—*ptōsis*, a case, falling.]

triptych, trip'tik, *n.* a set of three tablets, painted panels, &c., hinged together.—*n.* **triptyque** (trep-tēk; Fr.), an international pass for a motor-car. [Gr. *triptychos*, threefold—*ptyx, ptychos*, a fold—*ptyssein*, to fold.]

tripudium, trī-pū'di-əm (L. tri-pood'i-oom), *n.* an ancient Roman religious dance in triple time, or dance generally: divination from the hopping of birds feeding, or from the dropping of scraps from their bills.—*adj.* **tripu'diary.**—*v.i.* **tripu'diate,** to dance for joy: to exult: to stamp.—*n.* **tripudiā'-tion.** [L. *tripūdium*, prob. from *trēs*, three, *pēs, pedis*, foot.]

triquetra, trī-kwet'rä, *n.* an ornament consisting of three interlaced arcs, common in early art in northern Europe.—*adjs.* **triquet'ral, triquet'rous,** triangular: (*bot.*) three-edged with concave faces. —*adv.* **triquet'rously.** — *n.* **triquet'rum,** a Wormian bone. [L. *triquetrus, -a, -um*, triangular —*trēs*, three.]

triradiate, trī-rā'di-āt, *adj.* three-rayed. — Also **trirā'dial.**

trireme, trī'rēm, *n.* an ancient galley—esp. a war-galley—with three sets of rowers. [L. *trirēmis*—*rēmus*, an oar.]

trisaccharide, trī-sak'ə-rīd, *n.* a sugar that hydroly-ses into three molecules of simpler sugars.

trisagion, tris-ag'i-on, *n.* an ancient hymn consisting of the words 'O Holy God, holy and mighty, holy and immortal, have mercy on us': loosely, the Tersanctus. [Gr. *tris*, thrice, *hagios*, holy.]

trisect, trī-sekt', *v.t.* to cut or divide into three (usu. equal) parts.—*ns.* **trisec'tion** (-shən); **trisect'or,** one who trisects: esp. one who thinks he can trisect an angle by Euclidean methods: a line that trisects; **trisect'rix,** a curve of polar equation $r = 1 + 2 \cos \theta$, by which an angle can be trisected. [L. *secāre, sectum*, to cut.]

triseme, trī'sēm, *adj.* equal to three short syllables. —*n.* a trisemic foot, the tribrach, iamb, trochee.— *adj.* **trisē'mic.** [Gr. *trisēmos*—*sēma*, a sign.]

triskele, tris'kēl, *n.* a figure consisting of three radiating curves or legs, as in the arms of the Isle of Man.—Also **triskelion** (tris-kel'i-on). [Gr. *skelos*, a leg.]

Trismegistus, tris-mi-gis'təs, *adj.* thrice greatest, an epithet of Thoth, the Egyptian Hermes. [Latin-ised from Gr. *trismegistos*.]

trismus, *triz'məs, n.* tetanic spasm of the muscles of mastication. [Latinised from Gr. *trismos*, a creaking, grating—*trizein*, to grate, gnash.]

trisoctahedron, *tris-ok'tə-hē-dron, n.* a solid with twenty-four faces, three for every face of an octahedron.

trist, *trist, adj.* (*arch.*) sorrowful: dismal.—Also **trist'ful** (*Shak.*). [Fr. *triste*—L. *tristis*, sad.]

tristich, *tris'tik, n.* a group of three lines of verse:—*pl.* **tris'tichs** (*-tiks*).—*adj.* **tris'tichous,** (*biol.*) in or having three rows. [Gr. *tristichiā*, a triple row, tristich—*stichos*, a row.]

trisula, *tri-sōo'lä, n.* the trident of Siva.—Also **trisul'.** [Sans. *triçūla*.]

trisulcate, *trī-sul'kāt, adj.* having three forks or furrows. [L. *trisulcus*—*sulcus*, a furrow.]

trisulphide, *trī-sul'fīd, n.* a sulphide with three atoms of sulphur to the molecule.

trisyllable, *tri-sil'ə-bl,* also *trī-, n.* a word of three syllables.—*adjs.* **trisyllabic** (*-ab'ik*), **-al.**—*adv.* **trisyllab'ically.**

tritagonist, *tri-tag'ən-ist, n.* the third actor in the Greek drama. [Gr. *tritagōnistēs*—*tritos*, third, *agōnistēs*, an actor.]

trite, *trīt, adj.* worn: worn out: well-trodden: used till novelty and interest are lost: hackneyed.—*adv.* **trite'ly.**—*n.* **trite'ness.** [L. *trītus*, rubbed, pa.p. of *terĕre*, to rub.]

trite, *trī'tē, n.* (*Gr. mus.*) the third string of the lyre or tone of the tetrachord, reckoned downwards. [Gr. *tritē* (fem.), third.]

triternate, *trī-tər'nāt, adj.* thrice ternate—ternate with each division ternate, and each again ternate.—Also **trip'licate-ter'nate.**

tritheism, *trī'thē-izm, n.* belief in three Gods: belief that the Father, Son, and Holy Ghost are actually different beings. — *n.* **tri'theist.** — *adjs.* **tritheis'tic, -al.** [Gr. *theos*, a god.]

trithionic, *trī-thī-on'ik, adj.* containing three sulphur atoms (trithionic acid, $H_2S_3O_6$).—*n.* **trithionate** (*trī-thī'ən-āt*), a salt of trithionic acid. [Gr. *treis*, three, *theion*, sulphur.]

tritical, *trit'i-kl, adj.* trite, common.—*adv.* **trit'ically.** — *ns.* **trit'icalness, trit'icism,** triteness. [Formed from **trite,** in imitation of **critical,** &c.]

Triticum, *trit'i-kəm, n.* the wheat genus of grasses.—*adj.* **triticeous** (*-ish'əs*), wheatlike. [L. *trīticum,* wheat—*terĕre, trītum,* to rub.]

tritium, *trish'i-əm, trit', n.* an isotope of hydrogen of triple mass. [Gr. *tritos,* third.]

Tritoma, *trit'ō-mä,* wrongly *trī-tō'mä,* a synonym of Kniphofia. [Gr. *trītomos,* thrice cut—*tomē,* a cut (from the splitting capsule).]

Triton, *trī'tən, n.* a minor Greek sea-god, son of Poseidon and Amphitrite, represented with a dolphin's tail, sometimes horse's forelegs, blowing a conch: sometimes in *pl.* for the attendants of Poseidon: applied to a seaman or a ship: a genus of large gasteropods with shells that can be used like conchs: a disused generic name for newts. [Gr. *Trītōn, -ōnos.*]

tritone, *trī'tōn, n.* (*mus.*) an augmented fourth, an interval of three whole tones. [Gr. *trītōnos—tonos,* tone.]

Tritonia, *trī-tō'ni-ä, n.* the genus commonly called Montbretia.

tritubercular, *trī-tū-bər'kū-lər, adj.* having three tubercles or cusps — also **trituber'culate.** — *ns.* **trituber'culism, trituber'culy.**

triturate, *trit'ū-rāt, v.t.* to rub or grind to a fine powder.—*ns.* **tritura'tion; trit'urātor.** [L.L. *triturāre, -ātum*—L. *terĕre,* to rub.]

triumph, *trī'əmf, n.* in ancient Rome, a solemn procession in honour of a victorious general: a pageant: (*obs.*) festivity: (*obs.*) pomp, observance: (*Milt.*) a captive led in triumph: exultation for success: complete or signal victory: (*obs.*) trump. — *v.i.* to celebrate a victory with pomp: to rejoice for victory: to obtain victory, prevail: to exult, insult (often with *over*): (*Shak.*) to show in glory.—*v.t.* (*Milt.*) to triumph over.—*adj.* **triumphal** (*trī-umf'l*), pertaining to triumph: used in celebrating victory.—*n.* (*Milt.*) a token of victory.—*adj.* **triumph'ant,** celebrating or having achieved a triumph: exultant: (*Shak.*) trans-

cendent in glory: (*Shak.*) triumphal.—*adv.* **tri-umph'antly.**—*n.* **tri'umpher.**—*n.* and *adj.* **tri-umphing.**—**triumphal arch,** an arch erected in connexion with the triumph of a Roman general, or any decorative arch in public rejoicings, &c.—**church triumphant** (see **church**). [L. *triumphus,* akin to Gr. *thriambos,* a hymn to Bacchus.]

triumvir, *trī-um'vər* (L. *trē-oom'vir*), *n.* one of three men in the same office or government: one of three sharing supreme power :—*pl.* **trium'virī, trium'-virs.**—*adj.* **trium'viral.**—*n.* **trium'virate** (*or* **trium'viry;** *Shak.* **trium'phery**), an association of three men in office or government, or for any political ends—esp. that of Pompey, Crassus, and Caesar (60 B.C.), and that of Octavian (Augustus), Mark Antony, and Lepidus (43 B.C.): any trio or triad. [L. *triumvir,* from the gen. pl. *trium virōrum* of three men.]

triune, *trī'ūn, adj.* three in one.—*n.* a trinity unity.—*n.* **triū'nity.** [L. *trēs, tria,* three, *ūnus,* one.]

trivalent, *triv'ə-lənt, trī-vā'lənt, adj.* having a valency of three.—*ns.* **triv'alence** (*or* **trī-vā'**), **triv'alency** (*or* **trī-vā'**). [**valent.**]

trivalve, *trī'valv, adj.* three-valved.—*n.* that which is three-valved.—*adjs.* **tri'valved, trival'vūlar.** [L. *valva,* a door-leaf.]

trivet, *triv'it, n.* a tripod, esp. one for a pot or kettle: a bracket with three projections for fixing on the top bar of a grate: a three-legged pot.—**right as a trivet,** perfectly right (from its stability). [O.E. *trefet,* app.—L. *tripēs, tripedis—pēs,* a foot.]

trivial, *triv'i-əl, adj.* of the trivium: to be found anywhere: of little importance: trifling: (*biol.*) vernacular: (*biol.*) specific, opp. to generic (of name).—*v.i.* **triv'ialise,** to render paltry.—*n.* **triv'ialism,** a trivial matter or remark; **triviality** (*-al'i-ti*), the state or quality of being trivial: that which is trivial, a trifle.—*adv.* **triv'ially.**—*n.* **triv'ialness;** **triv'ium,** in mediaeval schools the group of liberal arts first studied—grammar, rhetoric, and logic: the three anterior radii of an echinoderm. [L. *trivium,* a place where three ways meet—*trēs,* three, *via,* a way.]

tri-weekly, *trī-wēk'li, adj.* occurring or appearing once in three weeks or three times a week.—*adv.* once in three weeks: three times a week.—*n.* a periodical appearing three times a week.

troad, troade (*Spens.*). See **trod.**

troat, *trōt, v.i.* to bellow, as a buck.

trocar, *trō'kär, n.* a surgical perforator used with a cannula: sometimes, a cannula. [Fr. *trocart—trois,* three, *carre,* side.]

trochaic. See **trochee. trochal, troche, Tro-chidae, trochisk.** See **trochus.**

trochanter, *trō-kan'tər, n.* a rough eminence on the thigh-bone for insertion of muscles: the second joint of an insect's leg.—*adj.* **trochanteric** (*-ter'ik*). [Gr. *trochantēr—trechein,* to run.]

trochee, *trō'kē, n.* (*pros.*) a foot of two syllables, long followed by a short: in English, &c., a stress followed by an unstressed.—*adj.* **trochaic** (*-kā'ik*).—*n.* a trochaic verse. [Gr. *trochaios* (*pous,* foot) running, tripping—*trochos,* a running—*trechein,* to run.]

trochilus, *trok'i-ləs, n.* a concave moulding: the crocodile bird: **Trochilus,** a genus of humming-birds, formerly including all of them, giving name to the humming-bird family **Trochil'idae.**—*adj.* **trochil'ic,** pertaining to rotatory motion. [Gr. *trochilos,* a crocodile bird, a wren, a pulley sheaf—*trechein,* to run.]

trochlea, *trok'li-ä, n.* (*zool.*) any pulley-like structure, esp. a foramen through which a tendon passes.—*adj.* **troch'lear.**—**trochlear nerve,** the fourth cranial nerve. [L. *trochlea*—Gr. *trochilia,* a pulley.]

trochus, *trō'kəs, n.* (*Gr. ant.*) a wheel or hoop: the inner ring of cilia in a rotifer: **Trochus,** the top genus of molluscs.—*adj.* **tro'chal,** wheel-like.—**troche** (*trōk, trōsh, trōch;* *trō'kē* is frowned upon), a round medicinal tablet.—*ns.pl.* **Trochelminth** (*trōk-el-min'thəz*; Gr. *helmins, helminthos,* worm), the rotifer phylum of animals; **Troch'idae,** the top family of molluscs.—*ns.* **trochisc'us, troch'isk**

a troche ; **troch′ite,** an encrinite joint ; **troch′oid,** the curve traced by a fixed point in the plane of a rolling circle.—*adj.* wheel-like : like a Trochus : trochoidal.—*adj.* **trochoid′al,** of the nature of a trochoid.—*n.* **trochom′eter** or (*ill-formed*) **trocheam′eter,** a hodometer. [Gr. *trochos,* a wheel ; *trechein,* to run.]

trock (*Scot.*). See **truck** (1).

troctolite, *trok′tɔ-līt, n.* troutstone, a coarse-grained basic igneous rock composed of felspar spotted with olivine. [Gr. *trōktēs,* a kind of sea-fish—*trōgein,* to gnaw, nibble, *lithos,* stone.]

trod, trod (*Spens.*) **troad, troade, trode,** *trōd*), *n.* (*obs.*) a track : path : footing.—**hot trod,** (*Scott*) the pursuit of moss-troopers. [O.E. *trod, trodu,* track, trace ; *cf.* **tread.**]

trod, trodden. See **tread.**

troelie, troely. See **troolie.**

troggs, *trogz, n.* and *interj.* (*Scot.*) troth.

troglodyte, *trog′lɔ-dīt, n.* a cave-dweller : (*obs.* and *misapplied*) an anthropoid ape.—Also *adj.—n.* **Troglodytes** (*-lod′i-tēz*), the wren genus.—*adjs.* **troglodytic** (*-dit′ik*), **-al,** cave-dwelling.—*n.* **trog′-lodytism** (*-dīt-izm*). [Gr. *trōglodýtēs—trōglē,* a hole, *dýein,* to get into.]

trogon, *trō′gon, n.* any member of a family (**Trogon′-idae**) of tropical and esp. South American birds with brilliant plumage, the first and second toes turned back, including the quetzal. [App. Gr. *trōgōn,* nibbling.]

Troic, *trō′ik, adj.* Trojan. [Gr. *Trōikos.*]

troika, *troi′kä, n.* a Russian vehicle for three horses abreast. [Russ.,—*troe,* three.]

troilite, *trō′il-īt, n.* native ferrous sulphide, found in meteorites. [After Dominico *Troili,* who observed it in the 18th cent.]

Trojan, *trō′jon, adj.* of Troy.—*n.* a citizen or inhabitant of Troy : a boon companion : a doughty, trusty, or hard-working person : a good fellow. [L. *Trōjānus—Trōja,* Troy.]

troke (*Scot.*). See **truck** (1).

troll, *trōl, n.* in Scandinavian mythology, a goblin or supernatural dwarf (earlier giant). [O.N. *troll* ; *cf.* **droll, drow, trow** (2).]

troll, *trōl, v.t.* to roll : to trundle : to spin : to circulate, pass about the table : (*Milt.* **troule**) to move nimbly, wag (the tongue) : to utter fluently, set rolling off the tongue : to sing the parts of in succession, as of a catch or round : to fish for, or in, with a spinning or otherwise moving bait : to allure : to convey by trolley.—*v.i.* to roll : to move or run about : to sing a catch : (*obs.*) to stroll, ramble : to fish with revolving or trailing lure : to travel by trolley.—*n.* a moving round, repetition : a round song : trolling : a lure for trolling.—*ns.* **troll′er ; trolley** (*trol′i* ; sometimes **troll′y**), a costermonger's cart : a low wheelbarrow : a small truck : a bogie : a pulley, receptacle, or car travelling on an overhead wire or rail : a trolley-wheel : (*U.S.*) a tram-car ; **troll′ey-bus′,** a bus that receives power by a trolley from an overhead wire ; **troll′ey-car′,** (*U.S.*) a tram-car driven by a trolley ; **troll′ey-man,** a man who works a trolley or on a trolley ; **troll′ey-ta′ble,** a tiered trolley for a dining-room ; **troll′ey-wheel,** a grooved wheel by which a bus, tram-car, &c., obtains current from an overhead wire.—*n.* and *adj.* **troll′ing** (*trōl′*).—*ns.* **troll′ing-bait,-spoon,** a metallic revolving lure used in trolling. [Cf. O.Fr. *troller* (Fr. *trôler*), to quest, Ger. *trollen,* to roll.]

trolley, trolly, *trol′i, n.* lace with pattern outlined with thicker thread or a flat border. [Cf. Flem. *tralje,* trellis.]

troll-my-dame(s), *trōl-mi-dām(z)′, n.* (*Shak.*) an old game like bagatelle, in which bullets were trolled into a little arcade.—Also **trou-madame** (*trŏŏ-mä-däm′*). [Fr. *trou-madame—trou,* hole, associated with **troll.**]

trollop, *trol′ɔp, n.* a slatternly woman : a draggle-tail : a strumpet.—*v.i.* (*Scot.*) to draggle : to go, dress, or work in a slovenly way.—*n.* **trollopee′,** (18th cent.) a woman's loose dress.—*adjs.* **troll′-oping, troll′opish, troll′opy.** [Perh. **troll** (2).]

tromba marina, *trom′bä mä-rē′nä, n.* an obsolete

viol, generally one-stringed, with an irregular bridge, played in harmonics, giving a trumpet-like tone. [It., marine (speaking) trumpet.]

trombone, *trom-bōn′, n.* a brass musical wind instrument, consisting of a tube bent twice on itself, with a slide.—*n.* **trombōn′ist.** [It. ; augm. of *tromba,* trumpet.]

trommel, *trom′ɔl, n.* a revolving cylindrical sieve for cleaning or sizing minerals. [Ger. *trommel,* drum.]

tromometer, *trom-om′i-tɔr, n.* an instrument for measuring slight earthquake shocks.—*adj.* **tromo-met′ric.** [Gr. *tromos,* a trembling, *metron,* a measure.]

trompe, tromp, *tromp, n.* an apparatus for pro-ducing a blast by falling water. [Fr.]

tron, tron, trone, *trōn, n.* (chiefly *Scot.*) a public weighing machine, used also as a place of punish-ment as by nailing the ear : the market-place : a system of weights used at the tron. [O.Fr. *trone*—L. *trūtina*—Gr. *trytanē,* a pair of scales.]

trona, *trō′nä, n.* a native combination of acid and normal sodium carbonate. [Sw.,—Ar. *trōn* for *natrūn* ; see **natron.**]

troolie, troelie, troely, *trŏŏ′li, n.* the bussu palm : its leaf. [Tupi *tururi.*]

troop, *trŏŏp, n.* a body of soldiers : (in *pl.*) military forces : a band of people : a flock, herd, swarm of animals : (esp. in *pl.*) a great number : a division of a cavalry squadron : a group of boy scout patrols : a troupe : the command of a troop of horse : a drum signal for assembling.—*v.i.* to assemble : to consort : to pass in a body or in rapid succession : to be off, pack.—*v.t.* to cause to troop : to receive and carry ceremonially along the ranks (as *troop the colour* or *colours*).—*ns.* **troop′er,** a private cavalry soldier (proverbially a swearer) : (*U.S.* and *Austr.*) a mounted police-man : a cavalry horse : a troop-ship ; **troop′-horse,** a cavalry horse ; **troop′-ship,** a transport. [Fr. *troupe*—L.L. *troppus* ; poss. Gmc.]

troopial. See **troupial.**

tropaeolum, *trop-ē′ɔ-lɔm, n.* the Indian cress and Canary creeper genus, South American trailing or climbing plants constituting a family **Tropaeolā′-ceae,** akin to the geraniums—misnamed nastur-tium. [Gr. *tropaion,* a trophy (from the shield-shaped leaves and helmet-like flowers).]

troparion, *trop-ār′i-on,* or *-ar′, n.* (*Gr. Ch.*) a stanza or short hymn :—*pl.* **tropar′ia.** [Dim. of Gr. *tropos,* trope.]

trope, *trōp, n.* (*rhet.*) a figure of speech, properly one in which a word or expression is used in other than its literal sense—metaphor, metonymy, synec-doche, irony : a short cadence peculiar to Gregorian melodies : a phrase formerly interpolated in differ-ent parts of the mass. [Gr. *tropos,* a turn—*trepein,* to turn.]

troph-,tropho-, *trof-, -ō-, -o′-,* in composition, nutri-tion.—*ns.* **trophallax′is** (Gr. *allaxis,* exchange), **tro-phobiō′sis** (Gr. *biōsis,* way of life), mutual exchange of nutriment in symbiosis.—*adjs.* **trophallact′ic, trophobiot′ic ; trophesial** (*-ē′zi-ɔl, -shl*), relating to trophesy.—*n.* **troph′esy,** deranged nutrition owing to disorder of the trophic nerves.—*n.pl.* **trophi** (*trō′fī*), mouth-parts of an insect : teeth of the pharynx of a rotifer.—*adj.* **troph′ic,** relating to nutrition.—*ns.* **trophotax′is, trophot′ropism,** chemotaxis, chemotropism, where the stimulating substance is food.—*adjs.* **trophotact′ic, tropho-trop′ic.** [Gr. *trophē,* food, *trophos,* a feeder ; *trephein,* to feed.]

Trophonian, *trō-fō′ni-ɔn, adj.* of the deified *Tro-phōnius* (Gr. *Trophōnios*), or the cave in Boeotia where he delivered oracles and conferred solemnis-ing mystic experiences.

trophy, *trō′fi, n.* a memorial of victory, orig. arms or other spoils set up on the spot : displayed spoils, as skulls and antlers : a piece of plate or suchlike awarded as a prize : a memorial of success, glory, &c. : an ornamental group of weapons, flags, &c., or a representation of it.—*v.t.* to set with trophies : to bestow trophies on.—*adj.* **trō′phied.** [Fr. *trophée*—L. *trophaeum* (classical *tropaeum*)—Gr. *tropaion—tropē,* a turning—*trepein,* to turn.]

tropic, *trop'ik*, *n.* a circle on the celestial sphere about 23° 28' N. (*tropic of Cancer*) or S. (*of Capricorn*) of the equator, where the sun turns on reaching its greatest declination north or south : a corresponding circle on the terrestrial globe : (*pl.*) the part of the earth between the tropics of Cancer and Capricorn : a turning-point or limit.—*adj.* of, relating to, the sun's turning : of the tropics : of, of the nature of, a tropism.—*adj.* **trop'ical**, of, relating to, a tropic or the tropics : found in, characteristic of, the tropics : fervidly hot : luxuriant : of a trope, figurative.—*adv.* **trop'ically.**—*ns.* **trop'ic-bird**, a tropical sea-bird (Phaethon) with long tail-feathers ; **trop'ism**, (*biol.*) orientation in response to stimulus : a general term for heliotropism, geotropism, &c. ; **tropist** (*trōp'*), a user of tropes : one who understands the Bible as figurative.—*adjs.* **tropistic** (*trop-ist'ik*), of tropism ; **tropolog'ic, -al.**—*adv.* **tropolog'ically.** — *ns.* **tropol'ogy**, figurative language : a moral interpretation of the Bible ; **trop'opause** (Gr. *pausis*, a ceasing), the boundary between troposphere and stratosphere ; **trop'ophyte** (*-fīt* ; Gr. *phyton*, plant), a plant adapted to alternations of moisture and drought.—*adj.* **tropophytic** (*-fīt'ik*).—*n.* **trop'osphere**, the lowest layer of the atmosphere in which temperature falls as height increases.—**tropical month, year** (see **month, year**). [Gr. *tropos*, a turning.]

trossers, *tros'erz*, *n.* an obs. form of **trousers.**

trot, *trot*, *n.* a pace between walking and running (in a horse with legs moving together diagonally) : an act or spell of trotting : continual activity in moving about : a toddling child : a long line of baited hooks : (*U.S. slang*) a crib, literal translation.—*v.i.* to go, ride, or drive at a trot : to jog : to bustle about : to fish with a trot.—*v.t.* to cause to trot : to conduct around : to bring out for exhibition : to draw out so as to make a butt of : to jog on one's knee : to trot upon : to execute at a trot :—*pr.p.* **trott'ing** ; *pa.t.* and *pa.p.* **trott'ed.**—*ns.* **trott'er**, one that trots : a trotting-horse : a foot, esp. a sheep's ; **trottoir** (*trot-wär* ; Fr.), a paved footway at the side of a street.—**trot out**, to exhibit the paces of : to bring forward, adduce, produce for show : to walk out with. [O.Fr. *trot* (n.), *troter* (vb.) ; perh. Gmc. ; cf. O.H.G. *trottōn*, Eng. **tread.**]

trot, *trot*, *n.* (*Shak.*) a beldame, crone. [A.Fr. *trote.*]

trot-cozy, -cosey, *trot'-kō'zi*, *n.* (*Scott*) a riding-hood. [App. **trot** (Jamieson says throat) and **cosy.**]

troth, *trōth*, *troth*, *n.* (*arch.*) a variant of **truth** : faith, fidelity.—*v.t.* (*Shak.*) to betroth.—*interj.* in truth.—*adjs.* **troth'ful** ; **troth'less.**—*n.* **troth'-plight**, a plighting of troth, betrothal.—*v.t.* (*arch.*) to betroth.—*adj.* (*Shak.*) betrothed.—Also **troth'-plighted.**—*n.* **troth'-ring**, a betrothal ring.

troubadour, *trōō'ba-dōōr*, *-dōr*, *n.* one of a class of lyric poets of chivalric love, who first appeared in Provence, and flourished from the 11th to the 13th century. [Fr.,—Prov. *trobador—trobar* (Fr. *trouver*), to find.]

trouble, *trub'l*, *v.t.* to agitate : to disturb : to muddy : to make turbid : to molest : to afflict : to annoy : to busy or engage overmuch : to put to inconvenience.—*v.i.* to take pains : to put oneself to inconvenience : to be troublesome.—*n.* disturbance : affliction : distress : a scrape : travail : anything amiss : disease : uneasiness : exertion : the taking of pains : a cause of trouble.—*adj.* **troub'led** (*-ld*).—*adv.* **troub'ledly.**—*ns.* **troub'le-house, -state, -town, -world**, one who disturbs the peace of a house, state, &c. ; **troub'le-mirth**, a kill-joy ; **troub'ler.**—*adj.* **troub'lesome**, causing or giving trouble or inconvenience : vexatious : importunate.—*adv.* **troub'lesomely.**—*n.* **troub'lesomeness.**—*n.* and *adj.* **troub'ling.**—*adj.* **troub'lous**, full of trouble or disorder : agitated : tumultuous : disturbing.—*adv.* **troub'lously.**—*n.* **troub'lousness.** — **I'll trouble you to**, please ; **trouble one for**, ask one to pass. [O.Fr. *trubler* (Fr. *troubler*), from a L.L. freq. of L. *turbāre*, to disturb—*turba*, a crowd.]

trou-de-loup, *trōō'də-lōō'*, *n.* a pit with a vertical stake in the middle—a defence against cavalry :—*pl.* **trous-de-loup** (*trōō-*). [Fr., wolf-hole.]

trough, *trof*, *n.* a long, narrow vessel for watering or feeding animals : a vessel for kneading, brewing, washing, tanning, or various domestic and industrial purposes : a vessel for liquid over which gases are collected (*pneumatic trough*) : a channel, gutter, or conduit : a long narrow depression : a hollow between wave-crests.—*ns.* **trough'-fault**, (*geol.*) a pair of parallel faults with downthrow between them ; **trough'-shell**, a lamellibranch with a somewhat triangular shell fancied to resemble a kneading-trough (Mactra). [O.E. *trog* ; Ger. *trog.*]

trou-madame. See **troll-my-dame(s).**

trounce, *trowns*, *v.t.* (*obs.*) to harass : to indict : to punish, beat, rebuke or censure severely.—*ns.* **trounc'er** ; **trounc'ing.** [Origin obscure.]

trounce, *trowns*, *v.i.* to skip, prance, move briskly.—*v.t.* to whisk off, make to skip. [Origin obscure.]

troupe, *trōōp*, *n.* a company, esp. of performers. [Fr. See **troop.**]

troupial, troopial, *trōō'pi-əl*, *n.* a bird (*Icterus icterus*) famous for its song : any bird of the Icteridae. [Fr. *troupiale—troupe*, troop.]

trouse, *trōōz, trowz*, *n.* (*hist.*) Irish close-fitting breeches : trews.—Also in *pl.* (now vulg.) trousers. [See **trews.**]

trousers, *trow'zərz*, obs. **trossers**, *tros'ərz*, **strossers**, *stros'*, *n.pl.* long breeches : a garment worn chiefly by males on the lower part of the body with a loose tubular branch for each leg : any other garment of similar form, as pantalettes. (The sing. is used to form compounds, as **trous'er-butt'on, -clip, -leg', -pock'et, -stretcher**, &c.)—*adj.* **trou'sered**, wearing trousers.—*n.* **trou'sering**, (usu. in *pl.*) material for trousers. [See preceding.]

trousseau, *trōō-sō*, *n.* a bride's outfit : a bundle :—*pl.* **trousseaux** (*-sōz*). [Fr., dim. of *trousse*, bundle.]

trout, *trowt*, *n.* a freshwater fish (*Salmo fario*) of the salmon genus, much sought after by anglers : extended to various fishes related or superficially like :—*pl.* **trout** (rarely **trouts**).—*n.* **trout'-bas'ket**, an osier or willow creel for carrying trout.—*adj.* **trout'-coloured**, speckled like a trout : white, with spots of black, bay, or sorrel.—*ns.* **trout'er**, one who fishes for trout ; **trout'-farm**, a place where trout are reared artificially.—*adj.* **trout'ful**, abounding in trout.—*n.* and *adj.* **trout'ing**, trout-fishing.—*adj.* **trout'less.**—*ns.* **trout'let, trout'ling**, a little trout ; **trout'-rod**, a fishing-rod for trout ; **trout'-spoon**, a small revolving spoon used as a lure for trout ; **trout'stone**, troctolite ; **trout'-stream**, a stream in which trout are caught.—*adj.* **trout'y.** [O.E. *truht*—L. *tructa, tructus*—Gr. *trōktēs*, a sea-fish with sharp teeth—*trōgein*, to gnaw, nibble.]

trouvaille, *trōō-vä'i*, *n.* a happy find. [Fr.]

trouvère, *trōō-ver'*, *n.* one of the mediaeval narrative or epic poets of northern France. [Fr.]

trove. See **treasure-trove.**

trover, *trō'vər*, *n.* orig., finding and keeping : hence an action brought to recover goods from a person to whom they do not belong. [O.Fr. *trover* (Fr. *trouver*), to find.]

trow, *trō*, *v.t.* (*arch.*) to trust : to believe (often elliptically for *I trow* or *trow you?*). [O.E. *trēowan* (*trēowian, trúvian*) ; O.N. *trúa*, Ger. *trauen.*]

trow, *trow*, *n.* (*Shetland and Orkney*) a form of **troll.**

trowel, *trow'əl*, *n.* a flat or scoop-shaped tool with a short handle, for plastering, gardening, &c.—*v.t.* to dress, apply, move, with or as if with a trowel :—*pr.p.* **trow'elling** ; *pa.t.* and *pa.p.* **trow'elled.**—*n.* **trow'eller**—lay on with a trowel, to spread thickly : to flatter grossly. [O.Fr. *truelle*—L.L. *truella* (L. *trulla*, dim. of *trua*, a ladle).]

trowsers, an old spelling of **trousers.**

troy, *troi*, *adj.* of a system of weights used in England for gold, silver, and precious stones, the pound (no longer in legal use) of 5760 grains, being divided into 12 ounces of 20 pennyweight. [*Troyes*, in France.]

Troyan, *troi'ən*, *adj.* (*Shak., Spens.*) Trojan.

truant, trōō'ənt, *n.* (*obs.*) a vagrant : (*obs.*) a vague term of reproach : an idler : one who, idly or without excuse, absents himself from school.— Also *adj.*—*v.i.* to play truant.—*ns.* **tru'ancy**, **tru'antry**, **tru'antship.**—**play truant**, to stay from school without leave or good reason. [O.Fr. *truant* (Fr. *truand*), prob. from Celtic.]

truce, trōōs, *n.* a suspension of hostilities : a respite. —*n.* **truce'-break'er.**—*adjs.* **truce'less** ; **trucial** (trōō'shl, -shi-əl), bound by a truce.—**Truce of God,** a cessation of war, decreed by the Church, more or less observed, esp. in the 11th and 12th centuries, in France, Italy, England, &c., from Saturday (afterwards from Wednesday) evening to Monday morning, also during Advent and Lent, and on certain holy days. [M.E. *trewes, treowes,* pl. of *trewe*—O.E. *tréow,* truth, pledge, treaty ; cf. **true.**]

truchman, truch'mən, *n.* (*arch.*) an interpreter. [Ar. *turjamān* ; cf. **dragoman.**]

truck, truk, *v.t.* to exchange : to barter : to pay in goods.—*v.i.* to traffic : to have dealings or inter-course : to barter : to bargain : to potter about.— *Scot.* **trock** (trok), **troke** (trōk).—*n.* exchange of goods : barter : payment in goods : (*Scot.* **trock,** **troke**) dealings, intercourse : a small job, chore : (*coll.*) small goods : rubbish : (*U.S.*) fresh vegetables, market-garden produce.—*ns.* **truck'age**, barter ; **truck'er**, one who trucks : (*U.S.*) a market-gardener ; **truck'-farm** (*U.S.*) a market-garden ; **truck'-farmer** ; **truck'-farming** ; **truck'ing.**— **truck system,** the practice of paying workmen in goods instead of money, forbidden by the Truck Acts, 1831, &c. [O.Fr. *troquer,* to truck ; Sp. *trocar,* to barter, It. *truccare,* to truck.]

truck, truk, *n.* a small or solid wheel : an open railway wagon for goods : a trolley : a bogie : a low flat barrow : a small two-wheeled barrow with a turned-up front : (*U.S.*) a lorry : a cap at the top of a mast or flag-staff.—*v.t.* to convey by truck : to put on a truck.—*n.* **truck'age**, carriage by truck : charge for carriage by truck : supply of trucks. [L. *trochus,* a wheel—Gr. *trochos*—*trechein,* to run.]

truckle, truk'l, *n.* a pulley-wheel : (*obs.*) a castor : a truckle-bed.—*v.t.* to move on rollers.—*v.i.* to sleep in a truckle-bed : to behave with servility.— *ns.* **truck'le-bed**, a low bed that may be wheeled under another ; **truck'ler.**—*n.* and *adj.* **truck'ling.** [Gr. *trochileiā, -iā,* &c., a pulley—*trochos,* a wheel.]

truculent, truk'-, trōōk'ū-lənt, *adj.* very fierce : cruel.—*ns.* **truc'ulence, truc'ulency.**—*adv.* **truc'ulently.** [L. *truculentus—trux,* wild, fierce.]

trudge, truj, *v.i.* to walk with labour or effort : to plod doggedly.—*n.* a heavy or weary walk : a trudger.—*n.* **trudg'er.**—*n.* and *adj.* **trudg'ing.** [Origin obscure.]

trudgen, (incorrectly **trudgeon**), truj'ən, *n.* a swimming stroke in which each hand alternately is raised above the surface, thrust forward, and pulled back through the water.—Also *adj.* [John *Trudgen,* who popularised the stroke in England.]

true, trōō, *adj.* faithful : constant : trusty : genuine : properly so called : typical : conformable : ac-curately adjusted or in tune : straight or flat : agreeing with fact : actual : absolute : corrected : accurate : exact : right : rightful : honest : sin-cere : truthful.—*adv.* truly : faithfully : honestly : in accurate adjustment : dead in tune : after the ancestral type.—*v.t.* to adjust accurately.—*n.* that which is true, truth : accurate adjustment.—*adj.* and *n.* **true'-blue** (see **blue**).—*adjs.* **true'-born**, of genuine birth : pure-bred : true to the qualities of the breed : legitimate ; **true'-bred**, pure-bred : typical : of good breeding ; **true'-devot'ed**, (*Shak.*) full of honest zeal ; **true'-dispos'ing**, (*Shak.*) just ; **true'-heart'ed**, sincere : faithful. —*ns.* **true'-heart'edness** ; **true'-love**, one truly or really beloved : a sweetheart : a faithful lover : a true-love-knot : a quatrefoil : (*obs.*) a four-leaved clover (**true-love grass**) : herb-Paris.— Also *adj.*—*ns.* **true'-love-knot, true'-lov'er's-knot**, an ornamental or symbolic knot or interlaced design, as a two-looped bow or a knot with two interlaced loops ; **true'man**, (*arch.*) an honest man ; **true'ness** ; **true'penny**, (*Shak.*) an honest fellow.—*adj.* **true-seem'ing**, (*Spens.*) seeming (falsely or truly) to be true.—*adv.* **tru'ly.**—**true bill,** a bill of indictment endorsed, after investiga-tion, by a grand jury, as containing a case for the court. [O.E. *tréowe* ; O.N. *tryggr,* Ger. *treu.*]

truffle, truf'l, also troof'l, *n.* any fungus of the genus Tuber or the family Tuberaceae : its underground edible fructification. — *adj.* **truff'led**, cooked, stuffed, dressed, with truffles.—*ns.* **truff'le-dog**, **-pig**, one trained to find truffles. [O.Fr. *truffle* (Fr. *truffe*) ; poss.—L. *tūber,* lump, swelling.]

trug, trug, *n.* (*prov.*) a wooden fruit-basket. [Prob. **trough.**]

truism, trōō'izm, *n.* a self-evident truth : a common-place or trite statement.—*adj.* **truist'ic.** [**true.**]

trull, trul, *n.* a drab. [Cf. Ger. *trolle.*]

Trullan, trul'an, *adj.* held in the domed hall of the palace at Constantinople—applied to the Sixth Oecumenical Council (680-1) and esp. to the Council of 692, not accepted by the Western Church. [L.L. *trullus,* a dome—L. *trulla,* a ladle.]

trumeau, trōō-mō', *n.* a piece of wall or pillar be-tween two openings :—*pl.* **trumeaux** (-mōz'). [Fr.]

trump, trump, *v.t.* (*obs.*) to deceive.—*n.* **trump'ery**, showy and worthless stuff : rubbish : ritual foolery.—Also *adj.* [Fr. *tromper,* to deceive.]

trump, trump, *n.* a trumpet : a blast : (now *Scot.*) a Jew's-harp.—*v.t.* and *v.i.* to trumpet.—**trump marine,** the tromba marina. [O.Fr. *trompe.*]

trump, trump, *n.* a card of a suit that takes any card of any other suit : ruff, an old card-game like whist : (*coll.*) a good, trusty fellow.—Also *adj.*— *v.t.* to play a trump card upon instead of following suit : to take in this way.—*v.i.* to play trumps on another suit.—*ns.* **trump'-card**, the card turned up to determine the trump suit : any card of that suit : (*fig.*) a means of triumph : a victorious expedient ; **no'-trumps**, a declaration in bridge whereby no suit is more powerful than the rest.— *adj.* **no'-trump.**—*n.* **no'-trump'er**, a hand suitable for no-trumps.—**turn up trumps**, (*fig.*) to behave in a very helpful or generous way, esp. unexpectedly. [**triumph.**]

trump, trump, *n.* (*obs.*) an obstruction cast in one's way.—*v.t.* to cast as an obstruction : to allege : to concoct and put forward unscrupulously (with *up*).—*adj.* **trumped'-up.** [**trump** (3), affected by, or partly from, **trump** (1).]

trumpet, trum'pit, *n.* an orchestral, military, and signalling wind instrument of powerful and brilliant tone, in its present form a narrow tube bent twice upon itself, with cupped mouth-piece and flaring bell, giving, by action of the lips and breath-pressure, harmonics of its fundamental, the scale filled up by use of crooks, slides, or valves : applied to other instruments more or less like : a speaking-trumpet : an ear-trumpet : a trumpet-shaped object, as a flared bell or horn, a corolla or corona : a sound of, or as if of, a trumpet : a trumpeter : an organ reed-stop of trumpet-like tone.—*v.t.* to sound or play on a trumpet or with trumpet-like sound : to proclaim, celebrate, summon, denounce, expel, &c., by trumpet.—*v.i.* to sound a trumpet : to make a sound like a trumpet :—*pr.p.* **trum'pet-ing** ; *pa.t.* and *pa.p.* **trum'peted.**—*n.* **trum'pet-call**, a conventional phrase or passage played on the trumpet as a signal : any call to action.—*adj.* **trum'peted**, sounded on a trumpet : loudly extolled : having a trumpet : funnel-shaped.—*ns.* **trum'peter**, one who plays or sounds the trumpet : one who proclaims, praises, or denounces : a loud-voiced crane-like South American bird (Psophia) : an American swan : a kind of domestic pigeon : a large New Zealand food-fish (Latris) or other fish that trumpets when caught ; **trum'pet-fish**, the snipe-fish or bellows-fish (Macrorhamphosus or Centriscus), a long-snouted fish akin to the pipefish : a flute-mouth, a sea-fish with a tubular muzzle ; **trum'pet-flower**, a name for various bignoniaceous, solanaceous, and other plants with large trumpet-shaped flowers.—*n.* and *adj.* **trum'-peting.**—*n.* **trum'pet-ma'jor**, a head-trumpeter in a regiment.—*adj.* **trum'pet-shaped**, like the bell of a trumpet.—*ns.* **trum′pet-shell**, Triton: **trum′pet-tone**, the sound of a trumpet: a loud voice.—*adj.* **trum′pet-tongued**, proclaiming loud as a trumpet.—*ns.* **trum′pet-tree**, **-wood**, a South American Cecropia whose hollow branches the Indians use as trumpets.—**blow one's own trumpet**, to sound one's own praises: **feast of trumpets**, a Jewish feast in which trumpets played an important part. [Fr. *trompette*, dim. of *trompe*, trump.]

truncal. See **trunk**.

truncate, *trungk′āt*, *v.t.* to cut short: to lop: to maim: (*crystal.*) to replace (an edge or corner where similar faces meet) by a symmetrically placed face.—*adjs.* **trunc′ate**, **-d**, appearing as if squared off at the tip: ending in a transverse line or plane, esp. one parallel to the base.—*adv.* **trun′cately**.— *n.* **trunca′tion**. [L. *truncāre*, *-ātum*—*truncus*; cf. **trunk**.]

truncheon, *trun′shon*, *n.* a broken or cut piece: a length for grafting or planting: a broken spear: a spear-shaft: a short staff: a cudgel: a staff of authority.—*v.t.* to carve (an eel): to beat with a truncheon.—*adj.* **trun′cheoned**, furnished with a truncheon: armed with a lance.—*n.* **trun′cheoner**, (*Shak.*) one armed with a truncheon. [O.Fr. *tronchon* (Fr. *tronçon*)—*tronc*; see **trunk**.]

trundle, *trun′dl*, *n.* a little wheel, castor: a roller: a hoop: (*obs.*) a truck: a trundle-bed: (*her.*) a spool of golden thread.—*v.t.* and *v.i.* to wheel: to roll: to twirl: to spin: to bowl along.—*ns.* **trun′dle-bed**, a truckle-bed; **trun′dle-tail**, **tren′dle-tail**, **trin′dle-tail**, a curly-tailed dog. [O.E. *trendel*.]

trunk, *trungk*, *n.* the stem of a tree: the body of an animal apart from head and limbs: the body generally: a main line of road, railway, telephone, &c.: (*U.S.*) a junction circuit between telephone exchanges: the main body of anything: the shaft of a column: the body of a pedestal: a chest or box, esp. for travelling: a box for fish: a box-like channel, trough, shaft, conduit, or chute: a tube: a speaking-tube: (*obs.*) a telescope: (*obs.*) a pea-shooter: a large hollow piston: a proboscis: (in *pl.*) the game of trou-madame: (in *pl.*) trunk-hose, also breeches, esp. those worn on the stage over tights, or (*U.S.*) for sports.—*adjs.* **trunc′al**, pertaining to the trunk: principal; **trunked**, having a trunk: (*Spens.*) truncated, beheaded.— *ns.* **trunk′-call′**, a long-distance telephone call, involving connexion between two centres; **trunk′-fish**, the coffer-fish; **trunk′ful**, as much as will fill a trunk:—*pl.* **trunk′fuls**; **trunk′-hose′**, **-breech′es**, full breeches reaching from waist to mid-thigh, worn in the 16th and early 17th centuries; **trunk′ing**, casing; **trunk′-line**, the main line of a railway, canal, &c.; **trunk′-mail**, a travelling trunk; **trunk′-maker**, a maker of travelling trunks; **trunk′-road**, a main-road; **trunk′-sleeve**, (*Shak.*) a puffed sleeve; **trunk′-work**, clandestine visiting in a trunk. [Fr. *tronc* and L. *truncus*, a stock—*truncus*, maimed; with associations of Fr. *trompe*, trump, proboscis.]

trunnion, *trun′yon*, *n.* either of a pair of side projections on which anything (as formerly a big gun) is pivoted to move in a vertical plane: (*Scott*) a stick, club.—*adj.* **trunn′ioned**, provided with trunnions. [Fr. *trognon*, stump.]

truss, *trus*, *n.* a bundle, esp. of hay or straw, or a block cut from a stack (now 56 lb. of old hay, 60 of new, 36 of straw): a framed structure for supporting a weight: an attachment for holding a yard to the mast: a tuft of flowers at the top of the main stalk or stem: a surgical appliance for retaining a reduced hernia: (*hist.*) a close-fitting coat or (in *pl.*) breeches.—*v.t.* to bundle up: to muffle up: to tuck up: (*hist.*) to lace up, tie the points of: (*obs.*) to string up, hang: to fix for cooking, as with a skewer: (*arch.*) to catch in the talons, esp. in the air, and carry off: to furnish with a truss.—*v.i.* to pack up: to make off.—*n.* **truss′-beam**, a wooden beam strengthened by a steel tie-rod: a steel framework acting as a beam. —*adj.* **trussed**.—*ns.* **truss′er**; **truss′ing**. [Fr. *trousse*, *trousser*.]

trust, *trust*, *n.* worthiness of being relied on: fidelity: confidence in the truth of anything: confident expectation: a resting on the integrity, friendship, &c., of another: faith: hope: credit (esp. sale on credit or on promise to pay): ground of confidence: that which is given or received in confidence: charge: responsibility: anything felt to impose moral obligations: an arrangement by which property is handed to or vested in a person, to use and dispose of it for the benefit of another: an estate so managed for another: an arrangement for the control of several companies under one direction, to cheapen expenses, regulate production, beat down competition, and so obtain a maximum return.—*adj.* held in trust.—*v.t.* to place trust in: to believe: to expect confidently: to hope: to give credit to: to commit to trust.— *v.i.* to have trust: to rely (with *to*).—*ns.* **trust′-deed**, a deed conveying property to a trustee; **trustee′**, one to whom anything is entrusted: one to whom the management of a property is committed in trust for the benefit of others; **trustee′-ship**; **trust′er**; **trust′-estate**, an estate held by trustees.—*adj.* **trust′ful**, trusting.—*adv.* **trust′fully**. — *n.* **trust′fulness**. — *adv.* **trust′ily**. — *n.* **trust′iness**. — *adj.* **trust′ing**, confiding. — *adv.* **trust′ingly**.—*adj.* **trust′less**, not to be trusted: distrustful.—*n.* **trust′lessness**.—*adv.* **trust′worthily**. — *n.* **trust′worthiness**. — *adjs.* **trust′-worthy**, worthy of trust or confidence: trusty; **trust′y** (*comp.* **trust′ier**, *superl.* **trust′iest**), to be trusted: deserving confidence: faithful: honest: strong: firm: (*Shak.*) involving trust.—*n.* one who can be trusted: (*U.S.*) a well-conducted convict: (*Ir.*) a great-coat.—**active**, or **special, trust**, a trust in which the trustee's power of management depends upon his having the right of actual possession; **breach of trust**, a violation of duty by a trustee, &c.; **in trust**, as a charge, for safe-keeping, for management as a trustee; **on trust**, on credit; **trust**, or **trustee**, **stock**, that in which a trustee may legally invest trust funds without being personally liable if it should depreciate in value. [O.N. *traust*, trust; Ger. *trost*, consolation.]

truth, *trooth*, *n.* faithfulness: constancy: veracity: agreement with reality: fact of being true: actuality: accuracy of adjustment or conformity: in the fine arts, a faithful adherence to nature: that which is true or according to the facts of the case: the true state of things, or facts: a true statement: an established fact: true belief: known facts, knowledge.—*adj.* **truth′ful**, habitually or actually telling what one believes to be true: put forward in good faith as what one believes to be true: conveying the truth.—*adv.* **truth′fully**.—*n.* **truth′-fulness**.—*adj.* **truth′less**.—*n.* **truth′lessness**.— *adj.* **truth′like**.—*n.* **truth′-teller**.—*adjs.* **truth′-telling**; **truth′y**, (*rare*) true: truthful.—**God's truth**, a thing or statement absolutely true; **in truth**, truly, in fact; **of a truth**, (*B.*) truly; **the truth drug**, scopolamine, which, because of its sedative effect on the central nervous system, has been used to extort criminal confessions. [O.E. *tréowth*—*tréowe*, *triewe*, true.]

try, *trī*, *v.t.* to separate out: to sift: to render: to extract: to refine: to purify: to test: (*Shak.*) to prove by testing: to use, treat, resort to, experimentally: to put to the test: to strain: to annoy, irritate, afflict: (*Milt.*) to experience, undergo: to examine critically: to examine and decide the truth, justice, guilt or innocence, of, as a judge: (*U.S.*) to conduct in court, as a lawyer: to attempt, endeavour, essay.—*v.i.* to make an effort: (*Spens.*) **trie**) to turn out, prove: (*naut.*; *Shak.*) to lie to, keep head to wind: (*3rd pers.* *pr.t.* **tries**; *pr.p.* **try′ing**; *pa.t.* and *pa.p.* **tried**, *trīd*).—*n.* a trial: effort: in Rugby football, the score of three points gained by a player who succeeds in placing the ball with his hand over the goal line.—*adj.* (*Spens.* **trye**) choice, purified.—*adj.* **tri′able**, subject to legal trial: that can be tried.—*ns.* **tri′age**, sorting out: broken coffee-beans; **tri′al** (see that head).—*adj.* **tried** (*trīd*), proved good by test.—*ns.* **tri′er**, one who tries in any sense: a test—*also* tri′or, in the sense of one appointed to decide on a challenge to a juror, or a peer who is a juror in the trial of a peer; and try′er, in the sense of one who is assiduous in trying to win (cricket); try′-house, a place in which oil is extracted from blubber, &c.; try′ing.—adj. making trial or proof: adapted to try: searching, severe: testing: distressing: causing strain.—adv. try′ingly.—ns. try′-on′, an act of trying on a garment: (slang) an attempt at imposition by audacity; try′-out′, a test performance; trysail (trī′sl), a reduced sail used by small craft, instead of the mainsail, in a storm: a small fore-and-aft sail set with a boom and gaff.—try and, (coll.) try to; try back, to revert, hark back; try for, make an attempt to reach or gain; try on, to put on for trial, as a garment: to attempt; try out, to test. [O.Fr. trier, to pick out.]

Trygon, trī′gon, n. the sting-ray genus. [Gr. trȳgōn, a sting-ray.]

trypaflavine, trip-ə-flā′vēn, n. acriflavine.

trypanosome, trip′ən-ə-sōm, n. a flagellate protozoon (Trypanoso′ma of various species) parasitic in the blood of vertebrates.—adj. trypanocidal (-sī′dl).—ns. tryp′anocide (-sīd; L. caedĕre, to kill), a drug that kills trypanosomes; trypanosomiasis (-sō-mī′ə-sis), disease caused by a trypanosome, esp. sleeping-sickness. [Gr. trȳpanon, a borer—trȳpaein, to bore, sōma, body.]

trypsin, trip′sin, n. a digestive ferment secreted by the pancreas.—adj. tryp′tic.—n. tryptophan (trip′-tō-fan), an amino-acid obtained e.g. by the cleavage of casein by pancreatic enzymes. [Gr. trĭpsis, rubbing (as first got by rubbing down the pancreas with glycerine), or trȳein, to wear out, modelled on pepsin.]

trysail. See try.

tryst, trīst, n. (chiefly Scot.) an appointment to meet: appointed place of meeting: a cattle-fair.—v.t. to make an appointment with.—v.i. to agree to meet.—ns. tryst′er; trys′ting-day, -place, -stile, -tree.—bide tryst, to wait for a person at the appointed place and time. [O.Fr. triste, a hunter's station.]

tsamba, tsam′bä, n. a Tibetan barley dish. [Tibetan.]

tsar, also czar, rarely tzar, zär, tsär, n. (hist.) the title of the emperors of Russia and of the kings of Bulgaria: a great potentate or despot.—ns. ts-, czar′dom; tsar′evi(t)ch, czar′evi(t)ch (Russ. tsär-ā′vich), a son of a tsar; ts-, czarev′na, a daughter of a tsar: a wife of a tsarevitch; czarina (-ē′na; not a Russian form), czarit′za, tsarit′sa, a Russian empress; ts-, czar′ism, the government of the Russian tsars: absolutism; tsar′ist, czar′ist, an upholder of tsarism; tsesar′evi(t)ch, cesar′evitch, -witch (Russ. -ā′vich), the eldest son of a tsar: heir to the tsardom. [Russ. tsar, &c.—L. Caesar, Caesar.]

tsetse, tset′si, n. Glossina morsitans, or other species of the African genus Glossina, small flies that transmit trypanosome parasites and cause sleeping-sickness, nagana (tsetse-fly disease), &c.—Also tset′se-fly′. [Sechuana.]

Tshi, ch(w)ē, n. a Gold Coast language and linguistic stock.—Also adj.

Tsuga, tsōō′gä, n. the hemlock spruce genus. [Jap. tsuga, larch.]

tuan, too-än′, n. sir: lord: a title of respect. [Malay.]

tuart, tooart, tōō′ərt, tewart, tū′, n. a strong-timbered Eucalyptus (E. gomphocephala). [Australian.]

tuatara, tōō-ä-tä′rä (tuatera, -tä′rä), n. a New Zealand lizard-like reptile (Sphenodon or Hatteria), the sole survivor of the class Rhynchocephalia. [Maori, spine on the back.]

tuath, tōō′ə, n. (Ir. hist.) a people: an ancient territorial division. [Ir. tūath.]

tub, tŭb, n. an open wooden vessel made of staves and hoops: a small cask: anything like a tub: a tubful: a pulpit: a clumsy ship or boat: a bath: a pit-shaft casing: a bucket, box, or vehicle for bringing up coal from the mine: a tubfish.—v.t. to set, bathe, treat, in a tub: to line with a tub.—

v.i. to take a bath.—ns. tubb′er; tubb′iness; tubb′ing, the art of, or material for, making tubs: mine-shaft lining: rowing in clumsy boats: the taking of baths.—adjs. tubb′ish, round and fat; tubb′y, sounding like an empty tub: dull in sound: round like a tub.—ns. tub′fast, (Shak.) treatment of venereal disease by fasting and sweating in a hot tub; tub′fish, the sapphirine (or other) gurnard; tub′ful, as much as a tub will hold:—pl. tub′fuls; tub′-thump′er, a declamatory or ranting preacher. [Cf. L.G. tubbe.]

tuba, tū′bä (L. and It. tōō′bä), n. (Rom. ant.) a straight trumpet: the bombardon (bass tuba) or (sometimes) other low-pitched brass instrument of the saxhorn class: a powerful organ reed-stop: (anat.) a tube:—pl. tu′bas; L. tu′bae (-bē, L. bī). [L. and It. tuba.]

tube, tūb, n. a pipe: a long hollow body: (arch.) a telescope or other optical instrument (optic tube): a collapsible cylinder from which pasty material can be squeezed out: an electric valve: an underground railway: the united part of a calyx, corolla, &c.: any vessel in a plant or animal body: anything tubular.—v.t. to furnish with, enclose in, a tube.—v.i. to travel by tube.—n. tub′age, insertion of a tube.—adjs. tub′al, tub′ar; tubed (tūbd).—n. tube′ful.—adj. tube′less.—ns. tube′-foot, in echinoderms, a tube protruding through a pore, used in locomotion and respiration; tube′-skirt, a very tight skirt; tube′-well, a pipe used to obtain water from beneath the ground, with perforations just above its sharp point; tube′-worm, a worm that makes a tube to dwell in.—adjs. tūbic′olar, tub′icole (also n.), tubic′olous, inhabiting a tube; tubiflo′rous, having tubular flowers; tub′iform, shaped like a tube.—n. tub′ing, the act of making or supplying tubes: tubes collectively: material for tubes.—adj. tub′ūlar, having the form of a tube: made of or with tubes: having a sound like that made by the passage of air through a tube.—n. Tūbūlā′ria, a genus of Hydrozoa.—adj. and n. tubūlā′rian.—n. tubūlar′ity.—v.t. tub′ūlate, to form into a tube.—adj. tubular.—adj. tub′ūlated.—ns. tubūlā′tion; tub′ūlature; tub′ūle, a small tube.—n.pl. Tubūliflo′rae, a section of the Compositae with tubular disk-flowers.—adjs. tūbūliflo′ral; tub′-ūlous, tubular. [Fr.,—L. tubus, a pipe.]

tuber, tū′bər, n. a lump: a rounded swelling: a knob: a protuberance: a swelling, usually underground, in a plant where reserves are stored up:—of stem nature (as in the potato, Jerusalem artichoke, &c.), or of root nature (as in the dahlia): Tuber, the truffle genus of fungi, giving name to the Tūberā′ceae, saprophytic Ascomycetes, many with edible underground fructifications (truffles).—adjs. tuberā′ceous; tuberif′erous; tu′beriform; tuberose (tū′bə-rōs, -rōz), tuberous.—n. (tū′bə-rōs, -rōz; often by false association with tube and rose, tūb′rōz) a Mexican amaryllid (Polianthes tuberosa) grown for its fragrant creamy-white flowers, propagated by tubers.—n. tuberosity (-ros′i-ti).—adj. tub′erous, having tubers: of the nature of, or like, a tuber: knobbed. [L. tūber, a swelling, from root of L. tumēre, to swell.]

tubercle, tū′bər-kl, n. a small tuber, protuberance, or swelling: a nodule: a nodule or morbid growth in the lung or elsewhere, in cases of tuberculosis.—adjs. tu′bercled, having tubercles; tuber′cular, nodular: having tubercles; tuber′culate, -d, having, covered with, tubercles.—ns. tuberculā′-tion; tu′bercule, a tubercle; tuber′culin, a preparation from a culture of tubercle bacillus used for treating or testing for tuberculosis; tuber-culīsā′tion.—v.t. tuber′culise, to infect with tuberculosis.—n. tuberculo′ma, a slow-growing, circumscribed tuberculous lesion.—adjs. tuber′-culose, -d, tuberculous: tuberculated.—n. tuber-culō′sis, consumption or phthisis, a disease caused by the tubercle bacillus (Bacillus tuberculosis), characterised by development of tubercles.—adj. tuber′culous, of, affected by, tuberculosis: (now rare) tuberculated.—n. tuber′culum, a tubercle. [L. tūberculum, dim. of tūber.]

tuberose. See under tuber.

---

tuchun, tōō-chŭn', dōō-jün', n. a Chinese military governor. [Chin.]

tuck, tuk, n. (Shak.) a rapier. [Fr. estoc—Ger. stock, stick.]

tuck, tuk, Scot. touk, took, n. a stroke, tap, beat, esp. of a drum. [O.N.Fr. toker, toquer (Fr. toucher), to touch.]

tuck, tuk, v.t. to draw or thrust in or together: to stuff, cram: to fold under: to gather or gird up: to enclose by pressing clothes closely around or under: to put tucks in: to thrust away: to dress, full, or put on tenters: to hamper: (slang) to eat (with in): (slang) to hang.—v.i. to make an on-slaught upon food (usu. with in or into).—n. an act of tucking: a pleat or fold, now one stitched down: (naut.) the gathering of the bottom planks of a ship at the stern: (slang) eatables, esp. deli-cacies.—ns. **tuck'-box**, a box of or for tuck, at a boarding-school: **tuck'er**, a piece of cloth tucked or drawn over the bosom: a fuller: (slang) food.—v.t. (Amer. slang) to tire exceedingly.—n. **tuck'-in'**, (slang) a hearty feed.—adj. contrived for tucking in an edge.—ns. **tuck'(ing)-mill**, a fulling-mill: **tuck'-out**, (slang) a tuck-in: **tuck'-shop**, (slang) a confectioner's or a pastry-cook's shop.—**tuck up**, to gather up: to contract: to make tucks: (slang) to hang. [O.E. túcian, to disturb, afflict; cf. Ger. zucken, to twitch.]

tuckahoe, tuk'ə-hō, n. an edible but tasteless under-ground fungus of the southern United States: the edible rootstock of several American aroids: an inhabitant of eastern Virginia. [From Algonquian.]

tucket, tuk'it, n. (Shak.) a flourish on a trumpet. [Cf. tuck (2), and It. toccata, a touch.]

tucutuco, tōō-koo-tōō'kō, **tocotuco**, tōō-kō-tōō'kō, n. a South American rodent of mole-like habits. [From its cry.]

Tudor, tū'dər, adj. pertaining to the Welsh family of Tudor, the time when it held the English throne (1485-1603), or the style of architecture (Late Perpendicular) that prevailed then.—adj. **Tudor-esque'**.—**Tudor flower**, a trefoil ornament fre-quent in Tudor architecture: **Tudor rose**, a red and white rose (combining Lancaster and York) adopted as a badge by Henry VII.

Tuesday, tūz'di, n. the third day of the week. [O.E. Tīwes dæg, the day of Tīw (the God of war), trans-lating L. diēs Martis, Mars's day; but etymologic-ally, Tīw, O.N. Tȳr, answers to L. Jūpiter (for Djew pater), Gr. Zeus.]

tufa, tōō'fä, tū'fä, n. calc-sinter (often calcareous tufa): (obs.) tuff or other porous rock.—adj. **tufä'ceous**. [It. tufa, a variant of tufo—L. tōfus, a soft stone.]

tuff, tuf, toof, n. a rock composed of fine volcanic fragments and dust: (obs.) tufa or other porous rock.—adj. **tuffä'ceous**. [Fr. tuf, tuffe—It. tufo; see tufa.]

tuffe, tuf, n. (Shak.). Same as **tuft**.—n. **tuff'et**, a tuft: a tussock: a mound.

tuft, tuft, n. a bunched cluster: a clump: a crest: a separate lock of hair: a goatee or imperial beard: a small tassel: a gold tassel formerly worn on a nobleman's cap in the English universities: hence a titled undergraduate: a person of social conse-quence.—v.t. to separate into tufts: to adorn with tufts: to beat (as a covert): to dislodge.—adj. **tuft'ed**.—ns. **tuft'er**, a hound that drives deer out of cover: **tuft'-hunt'er**, a toady: **tuft'-hunt'ing**: **tuft'ing**.—adj. **tuft'y**. [Supposed to be—O.Fr. tuffe (Fr. touffe)—L. tūfa, crest—Gmc. (cf. O.L.G. top, top): but there are difficulties.]

tuftaffety, also tuff-, tuft-, tuf-taf'ə-ti, and -taffeta, -tä, n. (arch.) a taffeta with tufted pile.—adj. of or wearing tuftaffety: richly dressed.

tug, tug, v.t. to pull forcibly: to haul: to tow: to drag.—v.i. to pull forcibly: to strive: to toil: (pr.p. **tugg'ing**; pa.t. and pa.p. **tugged**).—n. a forcible or jerking pull: a hard struggle: a rope or chain for pulling: a name for various parts of harness, as a trace, a loop to receive a shaft: a tug-boat.—ns. **tug'-boat**, a towing vessel; **tugg'er**, one who tugs.—n. and adj. **tugg'ing**.—adv. **tugg'-ingly**.—n. **tug-of-war'**, a laborious contest: a contest in which opposing teams tug at a rope and strive to pull one another over a line. [M.E. toggen intens. from root of O.E. téon; cf. tow.]

tui, tōō'ē, n. the parson-bird. [Maori.]

tuille, twēl, n. a steel plate hanging below the tasses.—n. **tuillette'** (dim.). [Fr.,—L. tēgula, a title.]

tuilyie, **tuilzie**, tūl', tal'(y)ā, n. (Scot.): obs.) a fight, brawl, tussle.—v.i. to struggle. [O.Fr. tooil.]

tuism, tū'izm, n. apostrophe: reference to, or regard to the interests of, a second person. [L. tū, thou.]

tuition, tū-ish'ən, n. (obs.) guardianship: teaching, instruction.—adjs. **tui'tional**, **tui'tionary**. [L. tuitiō, -ōnis—tuērī, tuitus, to watch over.]

tulchan, tulhh'ən, n. a calf's skin set beside a cow to make her give milk freely.—**tulchan bishop**, (Scot. hist.) a titular bishop appointed to transmit most of the revenues of a diocese to the nobles (1572). [Gael.]

tule, tōō'lā, n. a large American bulrush (Scirpus). [Sp.,—Nahuatl tollin.]

tulip, tū'lip, n. any plant or flower of the bulbous liliaceous genus **Tu'lipa**, with showy, usually solitary, flowers: a showy person.—adj. **tu'lip-eared**, prick-eared, as a dog.—ns. **tulipomā'nia**, a craze for tulip-growing: **tu'lip-tree**, a large North American tree (Liriodendron), of the Magnolia family, with tulip-like flowers; **tu'lip-wood**, its wood. [O.Fr. tulipe, tulippe, tulipan—Turk. tulbend, turban.]

tulle, tōōl, tūl, tül, n. a delicate thin silk network fabric. [Fr.; from Tulle, in the department of Corrèze.]

Tullian, tul'i-ən, adj. of or like Tully, i.e. Marcus Tullius Cicero—Ciceronian.

tulwar, tul'wär, n. an Indian sabre. [Hind. talwär.]

tumble, tum'bl, v.i. to roll, wallow, toss about: to perform as a dancer or acrobat: to turn over in flight or fall: to fall headlong, floundering, or re-volving: to collapse, fall in a heap: to rush con-fusedly and hastily: to come by chance.—v.t. to send tumbling or headlong: to overthrow: to bundle from one place to another: to jumble: to throw about: to disorder, rumple.—n. act of tumbling: a fall: a somersault: a tumbled con-dition or mass.—ns. **tum'ble-bug**, **tum'ble-dung** (U.S.), a dung-beetle (from its rolling pellets of dung): **tum'ble-car**, **-cart**, a vehicle with wheels and axle in one piece.—adjs. **tum'bled**; **tum'ble-down**, dilapidated: threatening to fall. — ns. **tum'bler**, one who tumbles: an acrobat: a large drinking-glass or tall cup, formerly one that could not stand: a tumblerful: a tumbrel: a toy weighted to rock and right itself: a pigeon that turns back-somersaults in the air: (obs.) a dog that performed antics in catching rabbits: a revolving barrel or cage: part of a lock that holds the bolt in place, till it is moved by the key: part of a firearm lock that receives the thrust of the mainspring and forces the hammer forward: (early 18th cent.) one of a gang of London ruffians who set women on their heads; **tum'blerful**, as much as will fill a tumbler:—pl. **tum'blerfuls**; **tum'bler-switch**, a switch that is turned over to put electric current off or on; **tum'ble-weed**, a type of plant that snaps off above the root, curls into a ball, and rolls about in the wind.—n. and adj. **tum'bling**.—**tumble in**, or **home**, to incline inward above the extreme breadth, of a ship's sides: to fit, as a piece of timber into other work: to go to bed; **tumble over**, to toss about carelessly, to upset: to fall over; **tumble to**, (slang) to comprehend; **tumble up**, to get out of bed: to throw into confusion: to scurry up on deck. [Freq. from O.E. tumbian; cf. Ger. tummeln.]

tumbrel, **tumbril**, tum'brəl, -bril, n. (obs.) an old instrument of punishment, pillory or cucking-stool: a tip-cart: a two-wheeled military cart: a dung-cart: the name given to the carts that conveyed victims to the guillotine during the French Revolution. [O.Fr. tomberel (Fr. tombereau)—tomber, to fall.]

tumefy, tū'mi-fī, v.t. and v.i. to swell:—pr.p. **tu'mefying**; pa.t. and pa.p. **tu'mefied**.—ns. **tumefac'tion**: **tumescence** (tū-mes'əns), a ten-dency to swell: a swelling.—adjs. **tumesc'ent**;

tu′mid, swollen or enlarged : inflated : falsely sublime : bombastic.—*n.* **tumid′ity.**—*adv.* **tu′midly.**—*n.* **tu′midness.**—*adj.* **tu′morous.**—*n.*

tumour, tumor (*tū′mər*), swelling : turgidity : a morbid swelling or enlargement, now esp. a new growth of cells in the body without inflammation. [L. *tumefacĕre, tumēscĕre, tumidus, tumor—tumēre,* to swell, *facĕre,* to make.]

tummy, *tum′i, n.* a childish form of **stomach.**— Also **tum.**

tump, *tump, n.* (*prov.*) a hillock : a clump.—*v.t.* to make a mound around.—*adj.* **tump′y,** hummocky. [Origin unknown.]

tump, *tump, v.t.* (U.S.) to drag.—*n.* **tump′-line,** a strap across the forehead or chest for carrying burdens or hauling. [Prob. from an Indian word.]

tumphy, *tum′fi, n.* (*Scot.*) a blockhead : coaly fireclay.

tumult, *tū′mult, -məlt, n.* violent commotion, usu. with uproar : a riot : a state of violent and confused emotion.—*v.i.* (*Milt.*) to make a tumult.—*v.t.* to put in tumult.—*adj.* **tumultūary** (*-mult′*), acted or acting in tumult : haphazard : chaotic : tumultuous.— *v.i.* **tumult′ūate,** to make a tumult.—*v.t.* to disturb with tumult : to make a tumult in.—*n.* **tumultūā′tion.**—*adj.* **tumult′ūous,** full of tumult : disorderly : agitated : noisy.—*adv.* **tumult′ūously.** —*n.* **tumult′ūousness.** [L. *tumultus, -ūs—tumēre,* to swell.]

tumulus, *tū′mū-ləs* (L. *too′moo-loos*), *n.* a burial mound, a barrow :—*pl.* **tu′muli** (*-lī,* L. *-lē*).—*adjs.* **tu′mular, -y.** [L.,—*tumēre,* to swell.]

tun, *tun, n.* a large cask : an obsolete liquid measure —216 gallons of ale, 252 of wine : (*obs.*) a ton.— *v.t.* to put in a tun.—*adj.* **tun′-bellied.**—*ns.* **tun′-belly,** a pot-belly ; **tun′-dish,** (*Shak.*) a wooden funnel ; **tunn′age** (see **tonnage**) ; **tun′ning.** [O.E. *tunne* ; cf. **ton.**]

tuna, *too̅′nä, n.* a prickly-pear, plant or fruit. [Haitian.]

tuna, *too̅′nä, n.* (California) a tunny. [Sp.]

tuna, *too̅′nä, n.* a New Zealand eel. [Maori.]

tund, *tund, v.t.* and *v.i.* to beat, thump. [L. *tundĕre.*]

tundra, *toon′-, tun′drä, n.* a frozen Arctic plain, with lichens, mosses, and dwarfed vegetation. [Lapp.]

tundun. See **turndun.**

tune, *tūn, n.* tone : a melody or air : melodiousness : accurate adjustment in pitch or frequency : (*fig.*) harmonious adjustment : frame of mind, temper.— *v.t.* to adjust the tones of : to put in condition for producing tones in tune : to put in working order : to synchronise : to syntonise : to begin to play or sing : to start the singing of : to utter, express, or celebrate in music.—*v.i.* to give forth musical sound.— *adj.* **tūn′able,** tuneful : in tune.—Also **tune′able.** —*n.* **tun′ableness.**—*adv.* **tun′ably.**—*adjs.* **tuned** (*tūnd*) ; **tune′ful,** full of tune : melodious : musical. —*adv.* **tune′fully.**—*n.* **tune′fulness.**—*adj.* **tune′less,** without tune : not melodious or tuneful : unmusical : without sense of tune : silent.—*ns.* **tun′er,** one who tunes instruments or looms : one who makes music, or sings : in organs, an adjustable flap for altering the pitch of the tone ; **tun′ing ;** **tun′ing-fork,** a two-pronged instrument giving a sound of known pitch or vibration ; **tun′ing-key, tun′ing-hammer,** a key for turning wrest-pins ; **tun′ing-peg, -pin,** a peg about which the end of a string is wound and by which it is turned.—*adj.* **tun′y,** tuneful, esp. in a superficial obvious way.— **change one's tune, sing another tune,** to alter one's attitude, or way of talking ; **to the tune of,** to the amount of ; **tune in,** to adjust a wireless receiver for reception ; **tune out,** to adjust it so as to eliminate ; **tune up,** to put instruments into tune for beginning : to begin to perform, strike up. [A form of **tone.**]

tung-oil, *tung′-oil, n.* wood-oil obtained from seeds of the **tung′-tree** or Chinese varnish tree (*Aleurites Fordii* or other species). [Chin. *yu-t′ung,* tung-oil.]

tungsten, *tung′stən, n.* wolfram, a rare metal (W ; atomic number 74) chiefly got from wolframite, used for making lamp filaments and high-speed

steel.—*n.* **tung′state,** a salt of **tung′stic acid** (H_2WO_4). [Sw.,—*tung,* heavy, *sten,* stone.]

Tungus, *toong-goos -goos′,* or *toong′, n.* a member of an Eastern Siberian people and race, of the type usually called Mongol :—*pl.* **Tungus, Tunguses.**—*adjs.* **Tungus, Tungusian** (*-goos′i-ən, -goos′*), **Tungus′ic.**—*ns.* their Ural-Altaic language. [Russ. *Tunguz* ; Chin. *Tung′hu.*]

tunic, *tū′nik, n.* a Roman shirt-like undergarment : applied also to the Greek chiton, and to various similar garments, usuallv a sort of belted coat and gown, or blouse : a close-fitting soldier's or policeman's coat : a tunicle : (*biol.*) an investing layer, membrane, or integument.—*n.pl.* **Tunicā′ta,** the Urochorda, a class or sub-phylum of degenerate Chordata, including the ascidians.—*n.* **tu′nicate,** a member of the Tunicata.—*adjs.* **tu′nicate, -d,** (*bot.* and *zool.*) having a tunic : formed in concentric coats : of the Tunicata.—*n.* **tu′nicin** (*-ni-sin*), a gelatinous substance in the tests of tunicates.— *adj.* **tu′nicked.**—*n.* **tu′nicle,** a little tunic : an ecclesiastical vestment like a dalmatic, worn by a sub-deacon at mass. [L. *tunica.*]

Tunker, *tungk′ər, n.* See **Dunker.**

tunnage. See **tun, ton.**

tunnel, *tun′l, n.* a tunnel-net : a passage cut underground : any tubular passage : an animal's burrow, in earth, wood, &c. : a flue, chimney.—*v.t.* to make a passage or passages through : to hollow out : to catch in a tunnel-net.—*v.i.* to make a tunnel :— *pr.p.* **tunn′elling ;** *pa.t.* and *pa.p.* **tunn′elled.**—*n.* **tunn′eller.**—*n.* and *adj.* **tunn′elling.**—*n.* **tunn′el-net,** a funnel-shaped net. [O.Fr. *ton(n)el* (Fr. *tonneau*), cask, and *tonnelle,* vault, tunnel-net, dims. of *tonne,* cask.]

tunny, *tun′i, n.* a very large fish akin to the mackerels. [L. *tunnus*—Gr. *thynnos.*]

tup, *tup, n.* a ram : a paving rammer : a pile-driving monkey : the striking-face of a steam-hammer.—*v.t.* to copulate with (a ewe) : to put to the ram.—*v.i.* to copulate (of sheep). [Origin unknown.]

Tupaia, *too-pī′ä, n.* a genus of insectivores giving name to the tree-shrew family **Tupai′idae.** [Malay *tūpai* (*tāna,* ground), squirrel.]

tupelo, *too̅′pə-lō, n.* an American gum-tree (Nyssa). [From an Indian name.]

Tupi, *too̅-pē′, n.* a S. American Indian of a group of peoples inhabiting the Atlantic coast and the Amazon basin : their language, serving as a lingua franca.—Also *adj.*—*adj.* **Tupi′an.**

tupik, *tū′pik,* **tupek, -pek,** *n.* an Eskimo skin tent. [Eskimo.]

tuptowing. See **typto.**

tuque, *tük, n.* a Canadian cap made by tucking in one tapered end of a long cylindrical bag, closed at both ends. [Fr. *toque.*]

turacin, *tū′rə-sin, n.* the soluble red colouring matter of *touraco* feathers, containing copper.—*n.* **tura-coverdin** (*-kō-vər′din*), a pigment in touraco feathers, the only green pigment in birds.

Turanian, *tū-rā′ni-ən, adj.* (*obs. phil.*) of Asiatic languages, neither Iranian nor Semitic : latterly almost the same as Ural-Altaic.—*n.* a speaker of one of those languages. [Pers. *Turān,* not Iran, applied to those parts of the Sassanian Persian empire beyond the Oxus.]

turban, *tur′bən—obs.* **tu′lipant′, tul′ban ;** *Shak.* **tur′band, tur′bond ;** *Spens.* **turr′ibant′ ;** *Milt.* **tur′bant,** *n.* a head-covering worn by Eastern nations, consisting of a cap with a sash wound round it : a ladies' headdress of similar appearance. —*adj.* **tur′baned,** wearing a turban. [Turk. *tulbend*—Pers. *dulband* ; cf. **tulip.**]

turbary, *tur′bə-ri, n.* the right to take peat from another's ground : a place where peat is dug. [L.L. *turbāria*—*turba,* turf ; of Gmc. origin ; see **turf.**]

Turbellaria, *tur-bə-lā′ri-ä, n.pl.* a class of ciliated flatworms.—*n.* and *adj.* **turbellā′rian.** [L. *tur-bellae,* a disturbance.]

turbid, *tur′bid, adj.* disordered : muddy : thick.— *n.* **turbid′ity.**—*adv.* **tur′bidly.**—*n.* **tur′bidness.** [L. *turbidus*—*turba,* tumult.]

turbinacious, *tur-bin-ā′shəs, adj.* (*Scott* ; of the

smell of whisky) peaty. [A blundering form from L.L. *turba*, peat, under the influence of L. *turbō*, *-inis*, a spinning-top, a swirl.]

turbine, *tur'bin* (sometimes *-bīn*), *n.* a rotary motor in which a wheel or drum with curved vanes is driven by reaction or impact or both by a fluid (water in the **water-turbine**, steam in the **steam-turbine**, expanding hot air in the **gas-turbine**) admitted to it and allowed to escape.—*adj.* **tur'-binal**, turbinate.—*n.* a scroll-like bone of the nose.—*adjs.* **tur'binate**, **-d**, shaped like a top or inverted cone: spirally coiled: scroll-like: turbinal.—*n.* a turbinal: a turbinate shell.—*adj.* **tur'bined**, having, driven by, a turbine or turbines.—*ns.* **tur'bine-pump**, a contrivance for raising water by the inverted action of a turbine-wheel; **turb'ine-steam'er**, a ship driven by steam-turbine; **Tur'bo**, a tropical genus of turbinate wide-mouthed gasteropods, large specimens often used as ornaments:—*pl.* **Turbines** (*tur'bi-nēz*); **tur'bo-jet'**, a jet-propelled gas-turbine; **turbo-prop**, a jet-engine in which the turbine is coupled to a propeller. [L. *turbō*, *-inis*, a whirl, a spinning-top.]

turbit, *tur'bit*, *n.* a domestic pigeon having white body, coloured wings, and short beak. [Ety. dub.]

Turbo, **turbo-jet**. **turbo-prop**. See **turbine**.

turbot, *tur'bət*, *n.* a large, highly-esteemed flatfish (*Psetta maxima*) with bony tubercles: extended to various more or less similar fishes. [O.Fr. *turbot*.]

turbulent, *tur'bū-lənt*, *adj.* tumultuous, disturbed: in violent commotion: producing commotion: disorderly: unruly.—*ns.* **tur'bulence**, **tur'bulency.**—*adv.* **tur'bulently.**—**atmospheric turbulence**, irregular movement of large volumes of air. [L. *turbulentus*—*turba*, a crowd.]

Turco, *tur'kō*, *n.* (*coll.*) an Algerian infantryman in the French service. [It., Turk.]

Turcoman. Same as **Turkoman**.

Turcophil(e), *tur'kō-fīl*, *n.* one who favours the Turks (Gr. *phileein*, to love).—Also *adj.*—*ns.* **Turcophilism** (*-kof'il-izm*); **Tur'cophobe** (Gr. *phobeein*, to fear), one who fears or dislikes the Turks.—Also *adj.* [Gr. *Tourkos*, Turk.]

turcopole, *tur'kō-pōl*, *n.* a light-armed soldier of the Knights of St. John of Jerusalem.—*n.* **tur'copolier** (*-pō-lēr*), their commander—always an Englishman. [Mod. Gr. *Tourkopoulon*, a Turkish boy.]

turd, *turd*, *n.* a lump of dung. [O.E. *tord.*]

Turdus, *tur'dəs*, *n.* the thrush genus.—*adj.* **tur'dine**. [L.]

tureen, *tə-rēn'*, *n.* a large dish for holding soup at table. [Fr. *terrine*—L. *terra*, earth.]

turf, *turf*, *n.* the surface of land matted with the roots of grass, &c.: a cake of turf cut off: a sod: peat: horse-racing, the race-course, the racing world: (*pl.* turfs, sometimes turves).—*v.t.* to cover with turf.—*n.* **turf'-account'ant**, a euphemism for bookmaker.—*adj.* **turf'-clad**, covered with turf.—*n.* **turf'-drain**, one covered with turf.—*adjs.* **turfed**; **tur'fen**.—*ns.* **tur'finess**; **turf'ing**; **tur'fite**, (*slang*) one devoted to horse-racing; **turf'-spade**, a long narrow spade for digging turf.—*adj.* **tur'fy**, of, like, or abounding in turf: pertaining to horse-racing. [O.E. *turf*; O.N. *torf*.]

turgent, *tur'jənt*, *adj.* swelling: dilated: inflated: bombastic.—*adv.* **tur'gently.**—*ns.* **turgescence** (*-jes'əns*), act or process of swelling up: swollenness: distension of cells and tissues with water; **turgesc'ency.**—*adjs.* **turgesc'ent**, swelling: growing big; **tur'gid**, swollen: extended beyond the natural size: pompous: bombastic: (*bot.*) firm and tense by distension with water.—*ns.* **turgid'ity**, **tur'gidness.**—*adv.* **tur'gidly.**—*n.* **turgor** (*tur'gor*), state of being full, the normal condition of the capillaries: (*bot.*) balance of osmotic pressure and elasticity of cell-wall. [L. *turgēre*, to swell.]

turion, *tū'ri-ən*, *n.* an underground bud, growing upward into a new stem. [L. *turiō*, *-ōnis*, a shoot.]

Turk, *turk*, *n.* a native or citizen of *Turkey*: a Moslem of the former Ottoman empire: any speaker of a Turkic language: (*obs.*) a Mohammedan: any one with qualities ascribed to Turks, esp. an unmanageable unruly person: a Turkish

horse: a Turkish ship.—*adj.* Turkish.—*adj.* **Turki** (*toor'kē*), of the Turkish distinguished from the Tatar branch of Turko-Tatar languages.—*n.* a Turki speaker or language.—*n.* **Turkess** (*turk'es*; *rare*), a Turkish woman.—*adjs.* **Turk'ic**, **Turko-Ta'tar**, of that branch of the Ural-Altaic languages to which Turkish belongs; **Turk'ish**, of Turkey, the Turks, or their language: Turkic.—*n.* the language of the Turks.—**Grand Turk**, (*hist.*) the Ottoman Sultan; **Turkey carpet**, a soft thick kind of carpet; **Turkey hone**, novaculite; **Turkey merchant**, one trading with the Near East; **Turkey oak**, a Levantine species of oak (*Quercus Cerris*); **Turkey red**, a fine durable red dye, obtained from madder, but now mostly chemically; **Turkey stone**, Turkey hone: (*rare*) the turquoise; **Turkish bath**, a kind of hot-air bath, the patient being sweated, rubbed down, massaged, and gradually cooled; **Turkish delight**, a gelatinous sweetmeat, orig. Turkish; **Turkish manna**, trehala; **Turk's cap**, the martagon lily (*Lilium Martagon*), from the appearance of the rolled-back petals of the nodding flower; **Turk's head**, a kind of knot: a long broom: a figure set up for practice in swordsmanship; **turn Turk**, to become Mohammedan: to be completely reversed.

turkey, *turk'i*, *n.* formerly, a guinea-fowl (brought to Europe by way of *Turkey*): now, an American genus (Meleagris) of the pheasant family: a domestic breed of that genus: its flesh as food (in *U.S.* also a substitute): extended to various big birds, as bustard, ibis, brush turkey.—*ns.* **turk'ey-buzz'ard**, an American vulture; **turk'ey-cock**, (*obs.*) a male guinea-fowl: a male turkey: a strutting, pompous, vain or gobbling blusterer; **turk'ey-hen**, (*obs.*) a guinea-hen: a female turkey; **turk'ey-trot'**, a kind of ragtime dance.—**talk turkey**, (*U.S. slang*) to talk bluntly.

Turki. See **Turk**.

turkis, turkies. See **turquoise**.

Turkoman, *tur'kō-män*, *n.* a member of a branch of the Turkish family dwelling north from Persia (*pl.* Turk'omans).—Also *adj.*

turlough, *tur'lohh*, *n.* (*Ir.*) a pond dry in summer. [Ir. *turloch*.]

turm (*Milt.* **turme**), *turm*, *n.* a troop. [L. *turma*.]

Turmagant (*Spens.*). See **Termagant**.

turmeric, *tur'mər-ik*, *n.* a plant (*Curcuma longa*) of the ginger family: its rootstock, or a powder made from it, used in making curry-powder.—**turmeric paper**, a chemical test-paper impregnated with turmeric, changed from yellow to brown by alkali. [Cf. Fr. *terre-mérite*—as if from L. *terra merita*, deserved earth; origin unknown.]

turmoil, *tur'moil* (*Shak. -moil'*), *n.* commotion: disquiet: tumult.—*v.t.* (formerly *-moil'*) to harass with commotion: to toss about.—*v.i.* (*dial.*) to toil. [Origin unknown.]

turn, *turn*, *v.i.* to revolve: to rotate, to spin, whirl: to move round: to hinge: to depend: to issue: to change or reverse direction or tendency: to return: to deviate: to direct oneself, face: to shape one's course: to betake oneself: to direct one's attention: to change sides, religion, mode of life: to be fickle: to change: to be transformed, converted: to become: to result, prove or lead in the issue: to be shaped on the lathe: to sour: to change colour: to become giddy: to be nauseated: to bend back, become turned: to beat to windward.—*v.t.* to rotate: to move round: to change the direction of: to deflect: to bend: to bend back the edge of: to reverse: to pass round or beyond: to perform by turning: to wind: to set outside-in, or remake in that form: to set upside-down: to direct: to point: to apply: to send, drive, set: to pour or tumble out: to employ in circulation, pass through one's hands: to translate: to change: to make sour: to nauseate: to make giddy: to infatuate: to transfer, hand over: to convert, make: to make the subject of (with *to* or *into*): to render: to put by turning: to return, give back: to form in a lathe: to shape: to round off, fashion.—*n.* act, occasion, or place of turning: new direction or tendency: a twist: a winding: a complete revolution: a bend: a single traversing of a beat or course: a short walk (or ride or drive): a fit of illness or emotion, esp. an emotional shock, jar, or feeling of faintness: (*mus.*) an embellishment in which the principal note is preceded by that next above and followed by that next below (or vice versa in the **inverted turn**), the whole ending (and sometimes beginning) with the principal note: turning-point: a culmination: a time or moment of change: a crisis: a spell: a recurring opportunity or spell in rotation or alternation: rotation: a trick: a performer's act: a shift: a bout: fashion: manner: cast of mind: aptitude: bent: occasion, exigency: a vicissitude: a characteristic quality or effect: act of kindness or malice: a type turned upside-down owing to a temporary want of the required letter.—*ns.* **turn'about**, a turning to face the opposite way; **turn'again**, a refrain; **turn'back**, a folded-back part: one who abandons an enterprise; **turn'broach**, a turnspit; **turn'buckle**, a coupling with screw-threads for adjusting tension; **turn'coat**, a renegade to his principles or party; **turn'cock**, an official who turns off and on the water for the mains, &c.—*adj.* **turn'-down**, folded down.—*n.* a turn-down part: a turn-down collar: a turning down, rejection.— *adj.* **turned**, fashioned: wrought in a lathe: beyond the age (now commonly without *of*): reversed: outside-in: upside-down (esp. of type): soured.—*ns.* **turn'er**, one who, or that which, turns: one who uses a lathe: (*U.S.*, from *Ger.*) a member of a gymnastic club; **turn'ery**, art of turning in a lathe: turner's work: a turner's shop; **turn'ing**, rotation: reversal: a bend: the act of making a turn: a winding: deviation: a place where a road strikes off: a shaping, esp. the art of shaping wood, metal, &c., into forms having a curved (generally circular or oval) transverse section, and also of engraving figures composed of curved lines upon a smooth surface, by means of a turning-lathe: (in *pl.*) a shaving from the lathe: in pottery, the shaping of a vase: conversion, transformation; **turn'ing-lathe**; **turn'ing-point**, the point at which anything turns in its course: a maximum or minimum point on a graph: a critical point; **turn'ing-saw**, a sweep-saw, a thin-bladed saw held taut in a frame, used for cutting in curves; **turn'key**, an under-jailer: a turncock; **turn'-out**, a getting out of bed: a coming on duty: a call to come on duty: a siding, passing-place, or turning-place: a movable tapered rail for changing to another track: a muster or assembly: a carriage and its horses: output: get-up: a strike: a striker; **turn'over**, a turning over: a transference: a part that is folded over: a news-paper article begun on the front page and continued overleaf: a small pie made by folding over the crust: a small shawl: an apprentice turned over to a new master to complete his apprenticeship: the total amount of money changing hands in a business.—*adj.* folded over, or made to fold over. —*ns.* **turn'-penny**, one who is eager for profit; **turn'pike**, (*hist.*) a spiked barrier: (*obs.*) a turn-stile: a toll-gate: a turnpike-road: (*Scot.*) a winding stair (also **turnpike stair**); **turn'pike-man**, a toll-gate keeper; **turn'pike-road**, a road on which there are or were toll-gates: a main road; **turn'-round**, a turning round: the whole process of docking, unloading, taking on cargo, pas-sengers, or both, and setting sail again; **turn'-screw**, a screw-driver; **turn'skin**, a werewolf; **turn'spit**, one who turns a spit: a long-bodied, short-legged dog employed to drive a wheel by which roasting-spits were turned: a roasting-jack; **turn'stile**, a revolving frame that allows one person to pass at a time; **turn'stone**, a bird (Strepsilas or Arenaria), intermediate between the true plovers and sandpipers, that turns over pebbles on the beach in search of food; **turn'-table**, a rotating table, platform, or disk, or pair of rings, one rotating within another, as for turning a locomotive, carrying a gramophone record, cementing a micro-scope slide, turning a camera, &c.; **turn'-up** (or *turn'up*'), a disturbance: a thing or part that is turned up: an unexpected or fortuitous result or occurrence: a piece of luck.—*adj.* turned up.— **by turns**, one after another: at intervals; **not to turn a hair**, to be quite undisturbed or un-affected; **on the turn**, at the turning-point, changing: on the point of turning sour; **serve the turn**, to answer the purpose: to do well enough; **take one's turn, take turns**, to participate in rotation; **to a turn**, exactly, perfectly (as if of the spit); **turn about**, to face round to the opposite quarter: to spin, rotate; **turn about, turn and turn about**, alternately: in rotation; **turn a deaf ear to**, to ignore; **turn adrift**, to unmoor and let float away: to cast off; **turn again**, to turn back: to revert; **turn against**, to use to the injury of: to render hostile: to rebel against; **turn an enemy's flank, line**, or **position**, to manoeuvre so as to attack in the rear: to outwit; **turn an honest penny** (see **penny**); **turn around one's** (little) **finger**, to be able to persuade to anything; **turn aside**, to avert: to deviate: to avert the face; **turn away**, to dismiss from service, to discharge: to avert, to look in another direction: to deviate, to depart; **turn back**, to cause to retreat: to return; **turn colour**, to change colour; **turn down**, to bend, double, or fold down: to invert: to lower, as a light: to reject; **turn forth**, to expel; **turn in**, to bend inward: to enter: (*coll.*) to go to bed; **turn into**, to become by a process of change; **turn loose**, to set at liberty; **turn off**, to deviate: to dismiss: to divert: to complete, achieve by labour: to shut off: (*slang*) to hang; **turn on**, to set running (as water): to depend on: to turn towards and assail; **turn one's hand to**, to apply oneself to; **turn one's head, or brain**, to make one giddy: to infatuate with success; **turn out**, to bend outwards: to drive out, to expel: to put to pasture (as cattle): to produce and put forth: to prove in the result: to muster: to go on strike: (*coll.*) to get out of bed; **turn over**, to roll over: to set the other way up: to change sides: to hand over, pass on: to handle or do business to the amount of: to examine by turning the leaves; **turn the scale**, to decide, determine; **turn the stomach**, to nauseate; **turn the tables** (see table); **turn to**, to have recourse to: to point to: to result in: to change or be changed into; **turn turtle** (see **turtle**); **turn up**, to point up-wards: to fold upwards: to come, or bring, to light: to appear by chance: to set face up: to invert: to grub up: to disturb: to make brighter, as a light (as if by turning a handle): to refer to, look up; **turn upon**, to cast back upon, retort: to hinge on. [O.E. *turnian, tyrnan*, and perh. partly O.Fr. *torner* (Fr. *tourner*); all from L. *tornāre*, to turn in a lathe—*tornus*, a turner's wheel —Gr. *tornos*, lathe, compasses.]

Turnbull's blue, *turn'bŏlz blōō*, *n.* ferrous ferri-cyanide (or possibly ferric ferrocyanide). [From *Turnbull*, a Glasgow manufacturing chemist (18th cent.), not the discoverer.]

turndun, *turn'dun*, **tundun**, *tun'*, *n.* an Australian bull-roarer. [Native word.]

turner, *tur'nər*, *n.* a 17th-century Scots bodle. [Origin doubtful; cf. Fr. *tournois*, coined at *Tours*.]

Turneresque, *tur-nər-esk'*, *adj.* resembling the work of the painter J. M. W. *Turner* (1775-1851).— Also **Turnerian** (*-nē'ri-ən*).

turnip, *tur'nip*, *n.* the swollen edible root of *Brassica Rapa* or (**Swedish turnip**) of *B. Rutabaga*, crucifer-ous biennials: the root as food: the plant pro-ducing it: extended to more or less similar roots and plants, as the American papilionaceous *prairie turnip* (*Psoralea esculenta*): (*slang*) a big watch: a dunderhead.—*v.t.* to plant with turnips: to feed on turnips.—*ns.* **tur'nip-flea'**, a leaping beetle that eats young turnip and cabbage plants; **tur'nip-fly'**, a fly whose maggots burrow in turnip-roots: the turnip-flea; **tur'nip-lan'tern**, a lantern made by scooping out the flesh of a turnip; **tur'nip-top'**, the green sprout of a turnip in its second year, used as a vegetable. [See **neep**; the first part may be from *turn* or Fr. *tour*, implying roundness.]

turnsole, *turn'sōl*, *n.* a plant whose flowers are supposed to face the sun, as heliotrope or the euphorbiaceous *Chrozophora tinctoria*: a deep-purple dye got from the latter: litmus. [Fr. *tournesol*—L. *tornāre* (see **turn**), *sōl*, the sun.]

turpentine, *tur'pən-tīn*, n. a balsam, orig. that of the terebinth tree (*Chian turpentine*), now generally of conifers: popularly, oil of turpentine: a tree that yields turpentine, esp. the terebinth.—*v.t.* to treat or smear with turpentine.—n. **tur'pentine-tree**, the terebinth-tree.—*adj.* **tur'pentiny.—oil** (or **spirit**) **of turpentine** (*coll.* **turps**), an oil distilled from turpentine. [O.Fr. *terbentine*—L. *terebinthina* (*rēsīna*), terebinth (resin): see **terebinth**.]

turpeth, *tur'peth*, **turbith**, *-bith*, n. an Oriental Ipomoea or its cathartic root.—**turpeth mineral**, basic mercuric sulphate. [L.L. *turpethum*, *turbithum*—Pers. and Ar. *turbed*, *turbid*.]

turpitude, *tur'pi-tūd*, n. baseness: depravity: vileness. [L. *turpitūdō*—*turpis*, base.]

turquoise, *tur'kwäz*, *-k(w)oiz*, *-kiz*, formerly **turkis** (*Milt.*, *Tenn.*), **turkies** (*Shak.*), *tur'kiz*, *-kis*, n. a massive opaque sky-blue to pale green mineral, a hydrous basic aluminium sulphate, found in Persia: the blue colour of the stone.—*adj.* of turquoise: of the colour of turquoise.—*ns.* and *adjs.* **tur'quoise-blue'**, turquoise; **tur'quoise-green**, pale bluish green.—**bone**, or **fossil**, **turquoise**, odontolite. [O.Fr. *turkeis*, and later Fr. *turquoise*, Turkish, as first brought through *Turkey* or from *Turkestan*.]

turret, *tur'it*, n. a small tower, usu. attached to a building, often containing a winding stair: a tower, often revolving, carrying a gun: part of a lathe that holds the cutting tool.—n. **turr'et-clock**, a clock for a tower: a large clock with movement quite separate from the dials.—*adj.* **turr'eted**, having turrets: formed like a tower or a long spiral.—*ns.* **turr'et-gun**, one for use in a revolving turret; **turr'et-ship**, a warship with gun-turrets. [O.Fr. *tourete*, dim. of *tur*; see **tower**.]

turret. Same as **terret**.

turribant. See **turban**.

turriculated, *tur-ik'ū-lāt-id*, *adj.* turreted: formed in a long spiral.—n. **Turritell'a**, the tower-shell genus of gasteropods. [L. *turris*, a tower; dim. *turricula*.]

turtle, *tur'tl*, n. a turtle-dove: a constant or demonstrative lover.—n. **tur'tle-dove**, any dove of the genus Turtur or Streptopelia, a favourite cage-bird, a type of conjugal affection and constancy: (*U.S.*) the mourning dove. [O.E. *turtla*, *turtle*—L. *turtur*; cf. Ger. *turtel*, Fr. *tourtereau*, *tourterelle*.]

turtle, *tur'tl*, n. any marine chelonian: sometimes any chelonian: the edible flesh of a turtle, esp. the green turtle: turtle-soup.—*v.i.* to hunt or catch turtles.—*ns.* **tur'tleback**, anything arched like a turtle's back, esp. a structure over a ship's bows or stern; **tur'tler**, a hunter of turtles; **tur'tle-shell**, the shell of the hawk's-bill turtle, commonly called tortoise-shell; **tur'tle-soup**, a soup made from the flesh, fat, and gelatinous tissue of the female green turtle (*Chelone mydas*); **tur'tle-stone'**, a septarium; **turt'ling**, the hunting of turtles.—**mock turtle**, a soup made of calf's head in lieu of turtle meat; **turn turtle**, to render a turtle helpless by turning it on its back: to turn bottom up. [Fr. *tortue*, Sp. *tortuga*, or Port. *tartaruga*, tortoise, assimilated to foregoing.]

Tuscan, *tus'kən*, *adj.* of *Tuscany* in Italy: (*archit.*) Doric as modified by the Romans, with unfluted columns, and without triglyphs.—n. classical Italian as spoken in Tuscany: a native of Tuscany: an ancient Etruscan. [L. *Tuscānus*, Etruscan.]

tush, *tush*, n. (*Shak.*) a tush: a small tusk: a horse's canine tooth. [O.E. *tūsc*; cf. **tusk**.]

tush, *tush*, *interj.* (*arch.*) pshaw: pooh.—Also *v.i.*

tusk. See **torsk**.

tusk, *tusk*, n. a long, protruding tooth: a tush: a sharp projection.—*v.t.* to pierce with the tusks.—*adjs.* **tusked**, **tusk'y.**—n. **tusk'er**, a boar, elephant, &c., with tusks.—*adj.* **tusk'less.**—n. **tusk'-shell**, the mollusc Dentalium or its shell. [O.E. *tux* (*tūsc*); cf. **tush**.]

tuskar, **tusker**, *tus'kər*, **twiscar**, *twis'kər*, n. (*Orkney* and *Shetland*) a peat-spade. [O.N. *torfskeri*—*torf*, turf, *skera*, to cut.]

tussah, *tus'ä*, **tusseh**, *-e*, n. faulty forms of **tusser**.

tusser, **tussore**, **tasar**, *tus'ər*, n. a fawn-coloured

silk from wild Indian silkworms: its colour: a dress made of it.—Also **tusser-silk**. [Hind. *tasar*—Sans. *tasara*, shuttle.]

tussle, *tus'l*, n. a sharp struggle.—*v.i.* to struggle. [Freq. of **touse**; cf. **tousle**.]

tussock, *tus'ək*, n. a tuft: a bunchy clump of grass, rushes, &c.: tussock-grass: a tussock-moth.—*ns.* **tuss'ock-**, **tuss'ac-grass**, a large grass (*Poa flabellata*) of the Falkland Islands, forming great tufts; **tuss'ock-moth**, any moth of the family Lymantriidae (akin to Lasiocampidae), from the tufts of hair on the caterpillars.—*adj.* **tuss'ocky**. [Origin obscure.]

tussore. Same as **tusser**.

tut, *tut*, *interj.* an exclamation of rebuke, mild disapprobation, impatience, &c.—*v.i.* to say ' tut.'—Also **tut'-tut'**, *Scot.* **toot**, **toots**, **tuts**.

tut, *tut*, n. work paid by measurement or piece.—*v.i.* to do such work.—*ns.* **tut'work**; **tut'worker**; **tut'(work)man**.

tutania, *tū-tā'ni-ä*, n. a kind of Britannia metal. [From W. *Tutin* (*c.* 1780), its maker or inventor.]

tutelage, *tū'ti-lij*, n. guardianship: state of being under a guardian: tuition.—*adjs.* **tu'telar**, **tu'telary**, protecting: having the charge of a person or place.—*ns.* a guardian spirit, god, or saint. [L. *tūtēla*, guard—*tūtārī*, to guard—*tuerī*, to look to.]

tutenag, *tū'ti-nag*, n. an alloy of zinc, copper, &c.: (loosely) zinc. [Marāthi *tuttiṅg.*]

tutiorism, *tū'ti-ər-izm*, n. in R.C. moral theology, the doctrine that in a case of doubt between right and wrong one should take the safer course, i.e. the one in verbal accordance with the law.—n. and *adj.* **tū'tiorist**. [L. *tūtior*, *-ōris*, safer, comp. of *tūtus*, safe.]

tutor, *tū'tər*, n. a guardian: (*Scots law*) a guardian of the person and estate of a boy under fourteen, or girl under twelve: a private instructor: a coach: one who helps a boy or girl with lessons: a college officer who has supervision of an undergraduate: a college teacher who instructs by conference with a small group of students: an instruction-book.—*v.t.* to act as tutor to: to instruct: to coach: to control: to discipline.—*ns.* **tu'torage**, tutorship: tutoring: charge for tutoring: (*obs.*) tutelage; **tu'toress**, **tu'tress** (*obs.* **tu'trix**), a female tutor.—*adj.* **tutorial** (*tū-tō'ri-əl*), of a tutor.—n. a conference or sitting with a college tutor.—*adv.* **tutō'rially.**—n. **tu'toring**—*v.t.* and *v.i.* to tutor.—*ns.* **tu'torism**, **tu'torship**. [L. *tūtor*, *-ōris*, a guardian—*tuerī*, to look to.]

tutsan, *tut'sən*, n. park-leaves, a species of St. John's wort (*Hypericum Androsaemum*) once regarded as a panacea. [O.Fr. *toutesaine*, *tout*—L. *tōtus*, all, *sain*—L. *sānus*, sound.]

tutti, *toot'(t)ē*, *pl. adj.* (*mus.*) all (scil. performers).—n. a passage for the whole orchestra or choir, or its rendering. [It., pl. of *tutto*—L. *tōtus*, all.]

tutti-frutti, *toot'(t)ē-froot'(t)ē*, n. a confection, esp. ice-cream, flavoured with different kinds of fruit. [It., all fruits.]

tut-tut, *tut'tut'*. Same as **tut**.

tutty, *tut'i*, n. crude zinc oxide. [O.Fr. *tutie*—L.L. *tutia*—Ar. *tūtiyā*.]

tutu, *tōō'tōō*, n. a New Zealand shrub (*Coriaria ruscifolia*; fam. Coriariaceae, akin to Empetraceae) whose poisonous black fruit makes a light wine. [Maori.]

tutu, *tōō'tōō*, n. a ballet dancer's short, stiff, spreading skirt. [Fr.]

tu-whit tu-whoo, *too-hwit' too-hwōō'*, n. an owl's hoot.—*v.i.* **tu-whoo'**, to hoot.

tuxedo, *tuk-sē'dō*, n. (*U.S.*) a dinner-jacket. [From a fashionable club at *Tuxedo* Park, N.Y.]

tuyère. See **twyer**.

tuzz, *tuz*, n. (*Dryden*) a tuft.—n. **tuzz'i-muzzy**, a posy.

twa, *twä*, *twaw*, *twä*, also **twae**, **tway**, *twä*, Scots forms of **two**.—*adj.* and *adv.* **twa'fald** (*-fawld*), twofold: bent double.—*n.* and *adj.* **twa'some** (see **twosome**).—*adj.* **twa'-loft'ed**, two-storied.

twaddle, *twod'l*, n. senseless or prosy commonplace talk: (*obs.*) a talker of twaddle.—*v.i.* to talk twaddle.—n. **twadd'ler.**—n. and *adj.* **twadd'ling.**—*adj.* **twadd'ly**. [Perh. **twattle**.]

fāte, fär, ǎsk; mē, hər (her); *mīne; mōte; mūte; mōōn; dhen* (then)

twain, *twān, adj.* (*arch.*) two.—*n.* a couple, pair.—**in twain,** asunder. [O.E. *twégen* (masc.), two.]

twaite, *twāt, n.* one of the British species of shad.—Also **twaite** shad. [Origin unknown.]

twal, *twawl, twāl,* a Scots form of **twelve.**—*ns.* **twal'hours** (-*ōōrz*), a noon-day meal or refreshment; **twal'penny,** a shilling Scots, a penny (English).—Also **twal'pennies.**

twang, *twang, n.* (*prov.*) a sharp flavour: an aftertaste: a smack, suggestion. [**tang,** affected by next.]

twang, *twang, n.* the sound of a plucked string: a nasal tone: (*dial.*) a twinge: (*coll.*) a local intonation.—*v.t.* and *v.i.* to sound with a twang.—*n.* and *adj.* **twang'ing.**—*adv.* **twang'ingly.**—*n.* **twangle** (*twang'gl*), a slack or jangly twanging.—*v.t.* and *v.i.* to sound with a twangle.—*n.* and *adj.* **twang'ling** (-*gling*).—*adv.* **twang'lingly** (-*gling-li*).—*adj.* **twangy** (*twang'i*).—*n.* **twank,** (*dial.*) a short twang: a slap. [Imit.]

twankay, *twang'kā, n.* a kind of green tea: (*slang*) gin. [*Tong-ke* or *Tun-chi* in China.]

'twas, *twoz, twəz,* contraction of **it was.**

twat, *twot, n.* pudendum muliebre: (*Browning,* blunderingly) part of a nun's dress: (*slang*) a coarse general term of reproach.

twattle, *twot'l, n.* chatter: babble: twaddle.—*v.t.* and *v.i.* to babble.—*n.* **twatt'ler.**—*n.* and *adj.* **twatt'ling.** [Perh. conn. wi.h **tattle.**]

tway, *twā, adj.* and *n.* (*Spens.*) a form of **twain:** (*Scot.*) of **twain,** or of **two** (*twae*).—*n.* **tway'-blade,** an orchid (*Listera*) with small green flowers and one pair of leaves: also an American orchid (*Liparis*).

tweak, *twēk, v.t.* to twitch, to pull: to pull with sudden jerks.—*n.* a sharp pinch or twitch: (*obs.*) agitation, perplexity. [App. conn. with **twitch.**]

tweed, *twēd, n.* a rough woollen cloth much used for men's suits: (in *pl.*) clothes of tweed. [Said to be from a happy misreading of **tweel,** the cloth being made in the Tweed basin.]

tweedle, *twē'dl, v.i.* to play casually, strum, tootle: to pipe as a bird.—*v.t.* to pipe into acquiescence: to wheedle.—*ns.* **tweedledee', tweedledum',** a fiddler (in conjunction as types of the almost indistinguishable).—*v.i.* to tweedle: to fiddle. [Prob. imit., influenced by **wheedle.**]

tweel, *twēl, n.* a Scots form of **twill.**

'tween, a contraction of **between.**—*adj.* **'tween'-deck,** lodging between decks.—*n.* and *adv.* **'tween'-decks.**—*n.* **tween'y,** (*coll.*) a between-maid.

tweer. See **twyer.**

tweet, *twēt,* **tweet-tweet,** *twēt'-twēt, ns.* the note of a small bird.—*vs.t.* and *vs.i.* to pipe as a small bird. [Imit.]

tweezers, *twēz'ərz, n.pl.* small pincers for pulling out hairs, &c.—*n.* **tweez'er-case,** an étui. [Obs. *tweeze,* a surgeon's case of instruments—Fr. *étui.*]

twelfth, *twelfth, adj.* the last of twelve: equal to one of twelve equal parts.—*n.* a twelfth part: (*mus.*) a tone eleven (conventionally twelve) diatonic degrees above or below a given tone: an octave and a fifth.—*ns.* **Twelfth'-cake,** an ornamental cake partaken of on Twelfth-night; **Twelfth'-day,** twelfth day after Christmas, Epiphany, Jan. 6th.—*adv.* **twelfth'ly,** in the twelfth place.—*ns.* **Twelfth'-night,** evening of Jan. 6th: also of Jan. 5th; **Twelfth'-tide,** season of Epiphany. [O.E. *twelfta—twelf.*]

twelve, *twelv, adj.* ten and two.—*n.* the cardinal number next above eleven: a set of that number of things or persons: an article of a size denoted by 12: a score of twelve points: the hour of midday or midnight: (in *pl.*) duodecimo.—*adj.* and *adv.* **twelve'fold.**—*ns.* **twelve'mo,** duodecimo, written 12mo; **twelve'month,** a year.—*adj.* **twelve'-penny,** shilling.—the **Twelve,** the twelve apostles; **twelve score,** two hundred and forty (yards); **Twelve Tables,** the earliest code of Roman law, civil, criminal, and religious, made by the decemvirs in 451-449 B.C.; **twelve tone** (or **note**) **music,** music based on a pattern formed from the twelve notes of the chromatic scale, esp. as developed by Arnold Schönberg (1874-1951) and his pupils. [O.E. *twelf* (Ger. *zwölf,* and Goth. *twa-lif*), that is, prob. two left; see **eleven.**]

twenty, *twen'ti, adj.* twice ten: nineteen and one: an indefinite number.—*n.* the number next above nineteen: a score: an old English division of infantry: (in *pl.*) the years (esp. of age or a century) from the twentieth to the twenty-ninth.—*adj.* **twen'tieth,** next after the nineteenth: equal to one of twenty equal parts.—*n.* a twentieth part.—*n., adj.,* and *adv.* **twen'tyfold,** twenty times as many or much.—*adj.* **twen'ty-four',** twenty and four.—*n.* the number made up of four and twenty: a sheet folded into twenty-four leaves (forty-eight pages): a form arranged for printing it.—*n.* **twenty-four'-mo** (written 24mo, for L. *in vicēsimō quārtō*), a book made up of sheets folded in twenty-four leaves (forty-eight pages).—Also *adj.* —*adj.* **twen'tyish,** somewhere about twenty. —and **twenty,** (*Shak.*) supposed to be a mere intensive (as *good even and twenty*; *sweet and twenty*; see **sweet.**) [O.E. *twéntig, twentig,* prob. —*twégen,* twain, and suff. -*tig* (Goth. *tigjus*), ten; Ger. *zwanzig.*]

'twere, contraction of **it were.**

twi-, twy-, *twi, pfx.* two: double.—*adj.* **twi'-, twy'fold,** twofold; **twi'-, twy'forked,** bifurcate; **twi'-, twy'-formed,** having two forms; **twy'-natured,** of double nature. [O.E. pfx. *twi-.*]

twibill, *twi'bil, n.* a double-headed axe. [O.E. *twibill*—pfx. *twi-, bill,* bill.]

twice, *twīs, adv.* two times: doubly: for a second time.—*adjs.* **twice'-born,** born twice, as Bacchus: of high Hindu caste: (*theol.*) regenerate; **twice'-laid,** made of old yarns twisted anew.—*n.* **twi'cer,** one who is both compositor and pressman: (*eccles. slang*) one who habitually goes to church twice on Sunday.—*adj.* **twice'-told,** counted twice: told twice: hackneyed.—**at twice,** in two stages or operations; **twice over,** twice (emphatically). [Late O.E. *twiges—twiga, twiwa, tuwa,* twice, with adverbial gen. ending.]

twichild, *twī-chīld, n.* one who has become a child again.

twiddle, *twid'l, v.t.* to twirl idly: to finger idly: to play with.—*v.i.* to twirl: to trifle with something.—*n.* a twirl: a curly mark or ornament.—*n.* **twidd'ler.**—*n.* and *adj.* **twidd'ling.**—*n.* **twidd'ling-line,** formerly a line for steadying the steering-wheel: a string for setting the compass-card to play freely.—*adj.* **twidd'ly.**—**twiddle one's fingers,** or **thumbs,** to be idle. [Prob. suggested by **twirl, twist,** and **fiddle.**]

twier. See **twyer.**

twig, *twig, n.* a small shoot or branch: a divining-rod.—*adj.* made of twigs.—*v.t.* to birch, switch.—*adjs.* **twigg'en,** (*Shak.*) covered with, made of, wickerwork; **twigg'y; twig'some.** [O.E. *twig;* cf. Ger. *zweig.*]

twig, *twig, v.t.* and *v.i.* (*slang*) to observe: to understand. [Poss. Ir. *tuigim,* discern; cf. Gael. *tuig,* understand.]

twig, *twig, n.* (*slang*) fettle: fashion: recognisable condition.—*v.i.* to act vigorously.—*n.* **twigg'er,** a vigorous breeder: a wanton.

twight, *twīt, v.t.* (*Spens.*) for **twit.**

twilight, *twi'līt, n.* the faint light after sunset and before sunrise: dim light or partial darkness.—*adj.* of twilight: faintly illuminated: obscure.—*v.t.* to illuminate faintly.—*adjs.* **twi'lighted, twi'lit.** —**twilight of the gods** (see **Ragnarök**); **twilight sleep,** partial anaesthesia in childbirth by the use of morphine and scopolamine. [Pfx. *twi-,* **light.**]

'twill, contraction of **it will.**

twill, *twil,* or (*Scot.*) **tweel,** *twēl, n.* a woven fabric showing diagonal lines: the appearance so produced.—*v.t.* to weave with a twill. [O.E. *twilic.*]

twill, *twil,* **twilt, twilt.** Dialect forms of **quill, quilt.**

twilled, *twil'id, adj.* (*Shak.*) prob., protected against floods by plaited osiers (the word so used still at Stratford): according to some, ridged like twilled cloth: or ready, from an alleged obs. word *twill,* a reed.

twilly, *twil'i, n.* a willowing-machine. [**willow.**]

twin, *twin,* **twine,** *twin, v.t.* and *v.i.* (*obs.* and *Scot.*) to separate: to part.—*v.t.* to deprive. [**twin** (2).]

twin, *twin, n.* one of two born at a birth: one very

Neutral vowels in unaccented syllables : *el'ə-mənt, in'fənt, ran'dəm*

like, or closely associated with, another : a counter-part : (*obs.*) a pair of twins or pair generally : a combination of two crystals symmetrically united about a plane that is a possible face of each or an axis that is a possible edge of each, or of more than two by repetition.—*adj.* twofold, double : born two at a birth : forming one, or composed, of two like parts or counterparts : very like another.—*v.t.* to couple, or to produce, like a twin or twins.—*v.i.* to be born at the same birth : to bring forth two at once : to be paired or suited :—*pr.p.* **twinn'ing** ; *pa.p.* **twinned.**—*ns.* **twin'-ax'is,** the axis of symmetry of a twin crystal ; **twin'-birth,** birth of twins : a twin : a pair of twins.—*adj.* **twin'-born,** born at the same birth.—*ns.* **twin'-broth'er,** a brother born at the same birth ; **twin'-ling,** a twin.—*adj.* **twinned,** produced at one birth : constituting a twin.—*ns.* **twinn'ing** ; **twin'-plane',** the plane of symmetry of a twin crystal.—*adj.* **twin'-screw,** with two propellers on separate shafts.—*ns.* **twin'-set,** a cardigan and jumper made more or less to match ; **twin'ship,** condition or relation of a twin or twins ; **twin'-sist'er,** a sister born at the same birth.—**the Twins,** Gemini. [O.E. *getwinn* (n.), twin, *twinn* (adj.), double ; cf. pfx. *twi-*.]

twine, *twīn, n.* a twisted cord : string or strong thread : a coil : a twist : a twisted stem or the like : an act of twisting or clasping.—*v.t.* to wind : to coil : to wreathe : to twist : to twist together : to encircle : to make by twisting.—*v.i.* to wind : to coil : to twist : to make turns : to rise or grow in spirals : to wriggle.—*adj.* **twined.**—*n.* **twi'ner,** one who, or that which, twines : a twining plant. —*n.* and *adj.* **twi'ning.**—*adv.* **twi'ningly.**—*adj.* **twi'ny.**—**twining plant,** one that climbs by twin-ing its stem round a support. [O.E. *twín,* double or twisted thread, linen thread ; cf. Du. *twijn.*]

twine, *twīn,* a variant of **twin,** to separate.

twinge, *twinj, v.t.* to twitch or pinch : to affect with a momentary pain.—*v.i.* to feel or give a momentary pain.—*n.* a twitch, a pinch : a shooting pain. [O.E. *twengan,* to pinch.]

twink, *twingk, v.i.* to blink : to twinkle.—*n.* a twinkling, a moment. [Root of **twinkle.**]

twinkle, *twing'kl, v.i.* to blink : to quiver the eyelid : to shine by flashes : to glitter : to sparkle : to flicker, vibrate.—*v.t.* to guide by twinkling.—*n.* a blink : a wink : a glitter : a quiver : a flicker : a sparkle : a twinkling : a dance step.—*ns.* **twink'ler ;** **twink'ling,** a quick motion of the eye : the time occupied by a wink : an instant : the scintillation of the fixed stars.—*adj.* scintillating : quivering : (*obs.*) blinking. [O.E. *twinclian.*]

twinter, *twin'tər, adj.* (*Scot.*) two years old.—*n.* a two-year-old sheep or other animal. [O.E. *twi-wintre,* two-winter.]

twire, *twīr, tweer, twēr, v.i.* (*Shak.*) to peer.—*n.* (*obs.*) a glance, leer. [Cf. M.H.G. *zwieren,* to peer.]

twire. See **twyer.**

twirl, *twərl, v.t.* and *v.i.* to spin : to whirl : to twist : to coil.—*n.* a twist : a spin : a whirl : a whorl : a curly figure.—*n.* **twirl'er.**—*adj.* **twirl'y.—twirl one's thumbs,** to clasp the hands and revolve the thumbs about each other : to do nothing, be idle. [Connexion with O.E. *thwiril,* churn handle, whisk doubtful.]

twiscar. See **tuskar.**

twist, *twist, v.t.* to twine : to unite or form by winding together : to form from several threads : to wind spirally : to form into a spiral : to wring : to wrest : to distort : to entangle : to impart a spin to : to force round : (*old slang*) to eat heartily (often with *down*).—*v.i.* to twine : to coil : to move spirally or tortuously : to turn aside : to revolve : to writhe.—*n.* that which is twisted : a cord : a strand : thread : silk thread : warp yarn : a twisted part : torsion : act or manner of twisting : **a** contortion : a wrench : a wresting : a turning aside : a spin, screw, or break : a distortion : a perverted bent or set : a tangle : a twisted roll of tobacco or bread : a spiral ornament in the stem of a glass : (*obs.*) a twig : (*obs.*) the fork of the body : (*slang*) a mixed drink : (*slang*) a good appetite.—*adjs.* **twist'able ; twist'ed.**—*n.* **twist'er,** one who,

or that which, twists : a sophistical, slippery, shuffling, or dishonest person : a ball sent with a twist.—*n.* and *adj.* **twist'ing.**—*adj.* **twist'y.** [O.E. *twist,* rope (found in the compound *mæst-twist,* a stay).]

twit, *twit, v.t.* to upbraid : to taunt : (*pr.p.* **twitt'ing ;** *pa.t.* and *pa.p.* **twitt'ed**).—*n.* a reproach.—*v.t.* *adv.* **twitt'ingly.** [O.E. *ætwitan,* to reproach— *æt,* against, *witan,* to wite.]

twitch, *twich, v.t.* to jerk : to pluck : to snatch : to steal : to pinch : to twinge.—*v.i.* to jerk : to move spasmodically : to carp, sneer.—*n.* a sudden, quick pull : a spasmodic contraction of the muscles : a twinge : a noose : the sudden tapering of a vein of ore.—*n.* **twitch'er.**—*n.* and *adj.* **twitch'ing.**— *adj.* **twitch'y.** [Related to O.E. *twiccian,* to pluck ; Ger. *zwicken.*]

twitch, *twich,* **twitch'-grass,** forms of **quitch,** **-grass.** See **couch-grass.**

twite, *twīt,* the mountain linnet. [From its note.]

twitter, *twit'ər, n.* a tremulous feeble chirping : a flutter of the nerves.—*v.i.* to make a succession of small tremulous noises : to palpitate.—*v.t.* to chirp out : to twiddle.—*ns.* **twitt'erer.**—*n.* and *adj.* **twitt'ering.** — *adv.* **twitt'eringly.** — *adj.* **twitt'ery.** [Imit. ; cf. Ger. *zwitschern.*]

twitter, *twit'ər,* **twitt'er-bone,** *ns.* an excrescence on a horse's hoof.—*adj.* **twitt'er-boned.** [A form of **quitter.**]

'twixt. Abbreviation for **betwixt.**

two, *tōō, adj.* one and one.—*n.* the sum of one and one : a symbol representing two : a pair : a deuce, card with two pips : a score of two points, strokes, &c. : an article of a size denoted by two : the second hour after midnight or midday.—*adj.* **two'-bottle,** able to drink two bottles of wine at a sitting.—*n.* **two'-deck'er,** a ship with two decks or with guns on two decks : a bus or tram-car carrying passengers on a roofed top.—*adj.* **two'-edged,** having two cutting edges : capable of being turned against the user.—*n.* **two'er,** anything that counts as, or for, or scores two.—*adjs.* **two'-eyed,** having two eyes (**two-eyed steak,** *slang,* a bloater) ; **two'-faced,** having two faces : double-dealing, false ; **two'-fisted,** clumsy.—*adj.* and *adv.* **two'fold,** in two divisions : twice as much : (esp. *Scot.* **twa-fald,** **twā',** *twaw'-fawld*) in a doubled-up position.—*n.* **two'foldness.**—*adjs.* **two'-foot,** measuring, or with, two feet ; **two'-footed,** having two feet.— *n.* **two'-for-his-heels',** a knave (from the score for turning up a knave in cribbage).—*adjs.* **two'-forked,** having two prongs or branches ; **two'-four',** (*mus.*) with two crotchets to the bar ; **two'-hand,** (*Shak.*) for two hands ; **two'-hand'ed,** with or for two hands : for two persons : ambidextrous : strapping ; **two'-head'ed,** having two heads : directed by two authorities ; **two'-horse,** for two horses ; **two'-inch,** measuring two inches ; **two'-leaved, -leafed,** with two leaves or leaflets : with leaves in twos ; **two'-legged,** with two legs ; **two'-line,** (*print.*) having double depth of body ; **two'-lipped,** having two lips : bilabiate ; **two'-mast'ed,** having two masts.—*ns.* **two'-mast'er,** a two-masted ship ; **two'ness,** the state of being two : duality.—*adjs.* **two'-pair (-of-stairs),** on a second floor.—*ns.* so situated.—*adjs.* **two'-part,** composed in two parts or for two voices ; **two'-part'ed,** bipartite : divided into two nearly to the base.—*n.* **twopence** (*tup'əns*), the sum of two pennies : (*Shak.*) a coin worth twopence.— *adj.* **twopenny** (*tup'ni*), sold or offered at twopence : cheap, worthless.—*n.* ale sold at twopence a quart : in leapfrog, the head.—*adjs.* **twopenny-halfpenny** (*tup'ni-hāp'ni*), **twopence-halfpenny,** paltry, petty. —*ns.* **two-penn'yworth, two-penn'orth** (*tōō-pen'-ərth*), also (chiefly *Scot.*) **twopenceworth** (*tup'*). —*adj.* **two'-piece,** consisting of two pieces ; **two'-ply,** having two layers, or consisting of two strands : woven double ; **two'-roomed.** — *n.* and *adj.* **two'score,** forty.—*n.* **two'seater,** a vehicle or aeroplane seated for two.—*adj.* **two'-sid'ed,** having two surfaces, aspects, or parties : facing two ways : double-faced : having the two sides different.—*ns.* **two-sid'edness ; two'some,** a company of two :

a tête-à-tête: (golf) a single.—adj. consisting of two: performed by two.—n. two'-step, a gliding dance in duple time: a tune for it.—v.i. to dance the two-step.—adjs. two'-storied, -story; two'-stroke, consisting of two piston strokes, as an engine cycle.—n. two'-up, an Australian game in which two coins are tossed and bets made on both falling heads up or both tails up.—adj. two'-way, permitting passage by either of two ways at will: (math.) having a double mode of variation or two dimensions.—adj. two'-wheeled.—n. two'-wheel'er, a vehicle with two wheels, esp. a hansom cab.—adj. two'-year-old.—n. a child, colt, &c., aged two.—be two, to be at variance; in two, asunder, so as to form two pieces; in two twos, (slang) in a moment; two-power standard, the principle that the strength of the navy must never be less than that of any other two powers combined; two-speed gear, a gear-changing contrivance with two possibilities. [O.E. twā, fem. and neut., two (masc. twēgen); Ger. zwei, Goth. twai; Gr. dyo, L. duo, Sans. dva, Gael. dhà, dà.]

twy-, pfx. See twi-.

twyer, twyere, tweer, twier, tuyere, twēr, also twīr, twē-yer', n. a nozzle for a blast of air. [Fr. tuyère.]

Tyburn, tī'bərn, n. the historic place of execution in London.—ns. Ty'burn-tick'et, a certificate of exemption from certain parochial offices formerly granted to the prosecutor of a felon to conviction; Ty'burn-tipp'et, a halter; Ty'burn-tree, the gallows.

Tyche, tī'kē, n. (Gr. myth.) the goddess of fortune. —n. ty'chism, a theory that accepts pure chance. [Gr. tychē, chance.]

Tychonic, tī-kon'ik, adj. pertaining to the Danish astronomer, Tycho Brahe (1546-1601), or his system.

tycoon, tī-kōōn', n. the title by which the Shoguns of Japan were known to foreigners: (U.S.) a business magnate.—n. tycoon'ate, the shogunate. [Jap. taikun, great prince—Chin. ta, great, kiun, prince.]

tyde, a Spenserian spelling for tied, pa.t. and pa.p. of tie.

tye, tī, n. an inclined trough for washing ore.—v.t. to wash in a tye. [O.E. tēag, case, chest.]

tying, tī'ing, pr.p. and verbal n. of tie.

tyke, tike, tīk, n. (Shak.; chiefly Northern) a dog: a cur: a rough-mannered fellow: a Yorkshireman. [O.N. tík, bitch.]

tyler. See tile.

Tylopoda, tī-lop'a-dä, n.pl. a section of the ungulates with padded toes—camels and llamas.—n. and adj. ty'lopod. [Gr. tylos, a knob, callus, pous, podos, a foot.]

tylosis, tī-lō'sis, n. (bot.) an ingrowth from a neighbouring cell through a pit into a vessel (also, perh. orig., thylose, thī'lōs, thylosis, thī-lō'sis; pl. thylo'ses; perh.—Gr. thylakos, a pocket): an inflammation of the eyelids: callosity:—pl. tylō'sēs.—n. tylote (tī'lōt), a cylindrical sponge spicule, knobbed at both ends. [Gr. tylos, a knob, callus.]

tymbal. Same as timbal.

tymp, timp, n. the plate of a blast-furnace opening. [tympan.]

tympan, tim'pən, n. (arch.) any instrument of the drum kind: a tympanum: an ancient Irish stringed instrument played with a bow (Ir. tiompan): (print.) a frame covered with parchment or cloth, on which sheets are placed for printing.—adjs. tym'panal, (anat., zool.) of the tympanum; tympanic (-pan'ik), of or like a drum or tympanum: tympanitic.—n. a bone of the ear, supporting the drum-membrane.—adj. tym'paniform (or -pan'), drum-shaped: drum-like.—ns. tym'panist, a drummer (tim'panist, one who plays the timpani); tympani'tēs, flatulent distension of the belly.—adj. tympanitic (-it'ik), of, affected with tympanites.—ns. tympani'tis, inflammation of the membrane of the ear; tym'pano (pl. -i, -ē), a variant of timpano; tym'panum, a drum: a drumhead: the middle ear: the membrane separating it from the outer ear—the drum: in insects a vibratory membrane in various parts of the body,

serving as an ear-drum: in birds the resonating sac of the syrinx: an air-sac in the neck in grouse, &c.: the recessed face of a pediment: a space between a lintel and an arch over it: a wheel for scooping up water:—pl. tym'pana; tym'pany, any swelling, esp. of the abdomen: tympanites: a blowing up as with pride: (rare) a drum. [L. tympanum—Gr. tympanon, typanon, a kettledrum—typtein, to strike.]

tynd, tyn'd, tyned, tynde, tyne (Spens.; Shak.). See tind, tine (various words).

Tynwald, tin'wold, n. the parliament of the Isle of Man. [O.N. thing-völlr—thing, assembly, völlr, field.]

type, tīp, n. a mark or stamp: the device on a coin or medal: a distinguishing mark: insignia: a designation: an emblem: a foreshadowing: an anticipation: an exemplar: a model or pattern: a kind: the general character of a class: that which well exemplifies the characteristics of a group: a person of well-marked characteristics: a simple chemical compound representative of the structure of more complex compounds: the actual specimen on which the description of a new species or genus is based (type specimen): a rectangular piece of metal or of wood on one end of which is cast or engraved a character, sign, &c., used in printing: printing types collectively, letter: print: lettering.—adj. serving as a type.—v.t. to prefigure, foreshadow: to symbolise: to be the type of: (med.) to determine the type of: to exemplify: to typewrite: (rare) to print.—v.i. to typewrite.—adj. ty'pal.—ns. type'-bar, a line of type cast in one piece: in a typewriter, a lever with a type-face; type'-body, measurement of breadth of shank for a size of type; type'-cutter, one who engraves dies for printing-types; type'-cyl'inder, the cylinder of a rotary printing-machine on which types or plates are fastened for printing; type'-face, the printing surface of a type: the manner in which it is cut; type'-founder, one who founds or casts printers' type; type'-founding; type'-foundry; type'-genus, the genus that gives name to its family.—adj. and adv. type'-high, of or at the standard height of type (about ·918 inch—measured in the direction of the shank): at the height required for printing—of a woodcut, &c.—ns. type'-hold'er, a bookbinder's pallet or holder for use in hand-stamping; type'-met'al, metal used for making types: an alloy of lead with antimony and tin, and sometimes copper; type'-script, typewritten matter or copy: type in imitation of handwriting or of typewriting.—adj. typewritten.—ns. type'-setter, a compositor: a machine for setting type; type'-setting; type'-species, a species taken as the one to which the generic name is primarily attached.—v.t. and v.i. type'write, to print or copy with a typewriter.—ns. type'writer, a machine, usu. with a keyboard, for printing as a substitute for handwriting: (rare) a typist; type'writing.—adjs. type'written; typic (tip'-), emblematic; type'ical, pertaining to, or constituting, a type: emblematic: figurative: characteristic: representative: (rare) typographical.—n. typical'ity.—adv. typ'ically.—ns. typ'icalness; typifica'tion; typ'ifier.—v.t. typify (tip'), to make or be a type of:—pr.p. typ'ifying; pa.t. and pa.p. typ'ified.—ns. typing (tip'ing); typist (tīp'ist), one who uses a typewriter: one whose occupation is typewriting; ty'po, (coll. abbreviation of typographer) a compositor; typog'rapher, a printer: a beetle that bores letter-like tunnels in pine-bark; typograph'ia (pl.), matter relating to printers and printing.—adjs. typograph'ic, -al.—adv. typograph'ically.—ns. typog'raphist, one versed in the history or art of printing; typog'raphy, art or style of printing.—adj. typolog'ical.—ns. typol'ogist; typol'ogy, the study of types and their succession in biology, archaeology, &c.: the doctrine that things in the New Testament are foreshadowed symbolically in the Old; typoma'nia, a craze for printing one's lucubrations: a craze for finding types in the Old Testament. [L. typus—Gr. typos, blow, mark, stamp, model; typtein, to strike.]

Neutral vowels in unaccented syllables: el'ə-mənt, in'fənt, ran'dəm

Typha, *tī′fä, n.* the reedmace genus, giving name to a family of monocotyledons, **Typhā′ceae.**—*adj.* **typhā′ceous.** [Gr. *typhē,* reedmace.]

typhlitis, *tif-lī′tis, n.* inflammation of the blind-gut. [Gr. *typhlos,* blind.]

Typhoeus, *tī-fō′ūs, n.* a monster of Greek mythology buried under Etna.—*adj.* **Typhoean** (*tī-fō′i-ən*). [Gr. *Tȳphōeus.*]

typhoid, *tī′foid, adj.* like typhus.—*n.* (for **typhoid fever**) enteric fever, long confounded with typhus, on account of the characteristic rash of rose-coloured spots.—*adj.* **typhoid′al.** [Gr. *typhōdēs,* delirious—*typhos,* a fever, *eidos,* likeness; cf. **typhus.**]

Typhon, *tī′fon, -fən, n.* son of Typhoeus, later identified with him, father of dangerous winds: **typhon,** (*obs.*) a whirlwind.—*adjs.* **Typhonian**(*-fō′-ni-ən*), **Typhonic, typhonic** (*-fon′ik*).—*n.* **typhoon** (*-fōōn′*), a violent cyclonic storm of the China Sea. [Gr. *Tȳphōn,* Typhon, *tȳphōn,* a whirlwind; but partly also from Port. *tufão* — Ar., Pers., Hind. *tūfān,* a hurricane (perh. itself from Gr.), and partly from Chin. *t′ai fung,* a great wind.]

typhus, *tī′fəs, n.* a dangerous fever transmitted by lice harbouring a Rickettsia and marked by eruption of red spots.—*adjs.* **ty′phoid** (q.v.) ; **ty′phous.** [Latinised from Gr. *typhos,* fever, stupor, delusion ; cf. *typhein,* to smoke.]

typical, typify, typist, typography, &c. See under **type.**

typto, *tip′tō, v.i.* to conjugate the Greek verb *typtō,* I strike : to work at Greek grammar :—*pr.p.* (*Scott*) **tup′towing.**

Tyr, *tir, tūr, n.* the old Norse war-god. [O.N. *Tȳr* ; O.E. *Tiw* ; cf. **Tuesday.**]

tyrant, *tī′rant, obs.* **tyran,** *tī′rən, n.* in the orig. Greek sense, an absolute ruler, or one whose power has not been constitutionally arrived at : now usu. a ruler who uses his power arbitrarily and oppressively : an oppressor : a bully : a tyrant-bird.—*v.t.* and *v.i.* (*obs.*) **ty′ran(ne), ty′rant.**—*n.* **tyr′anness,** a female tyrant.—*adjs.* **tyrannic** (*ti-ran′ik*; **sometimes** *tī-*), **-al.** — *adv.* **tyrann′ically.** — *n.*

tyrann′icalness. — *adj.* **tyrannici′dal.** — *n.* **tyrann′icide,** the killing or the killer of a tyrant.—*n.pl.* **Tyrann′idae,** the tyrant-bird family.—*n.* **tyrannis** (*ti-ran′is* ; Gr.), a régime illegally set up. —*v.i.* **tyrannise** (*tir′*), to act as a tyrant : esp. to rule with oppressive severity.—*v.t.* to act the tyrant to.—*adj.* **tyrannous** (*tir′*), despotic : domineering: overpowering: oppressive.—*adv.* **tyr′annously.**—*ns.* **tyranny** (*tir′*), absolute or illegally established power : the government or authority of a tyrant : absolute power cruelly administered : oppression: cruelty: harshness ; **ty′rant-bird, ty′rant-fly′catcher,** any member of an American family of birds akin to the pittas and cotingas [Gr. *tyrannos,* partly through O.Fr. *tirant* (Fr. *tyran*) and L. *tyrannus.*]

tyre. See **tire** (all senses). **tyreling.** See **tireling.**

Tyrian, *tir′i-ən, adj.* of *Tyre* : red or purple, like the dye formerly prepared at Tyre.—*n.* a native of Tyre.—**Tyrian cynosure,** the north star, a guide to Tyrian mariners.

tyro. See **tiro.**

Tyrolese, *tir-ə-lēz′, adj.* relating to *Tyrol* (Tirol) or to its people.—*n.* a native of Tyrol.—*n.* and *adj.* **Tyrolē′an** (or *tir-ō′li-ən*).—*n.* **Tyrolienne** (*ti-rō-li-en′*), a Tyrolese peasants′ dance, song, or tune with yodelling.

Tyronensian. See **Tironensian.**

tyrosine, *tī′rō-sēn, n.* an amino-acid formed by decomposition of proteins, first got from cheese. [Gr. *tyros,* cheese.]

Tyrrhenian, *ti-rē′ni-ən, n.* and *adj.* Etruscan.—Also **Tyrrhēne′.**—**Tyrrhenian Sea,** that part of the Mediterranean between Tuscany and Sardinia and Corsica. [Gr. *Tyrrhēnia,* Etruria.]

Tyrtaean, *tir-tē′an, adj.* of or pertaining to *Tyrtaeus* (Gr. *Tyrtaios*), a Greek martial poet of the 7th century B.C.

tzar. See **tsar.**

tzigany, *tsig′ä-ni, -ə-ni, -ny′, n.* a Hungarian gypsy —Also *adj.* [Hung. *cigány,* gypsy; cf. It. *zingano, zingaro,* Ger. *zigeuner.*]

fāte, fär, ásk; mē, hər (her); *mīne; mōte; mūte; mōōn; dhen* (then)

U

, u, *ū*, *n.* the twenty-first letter in our alphabet, derived from V, a form of Y which the Romans borrowed from the Greeks. From V, the lapidary and capital form, the uncial and cursive forms U and *u* were developed, gradually V (used until modern times initially) becoming appropriated as the symbol for the consonant sound (see V) and the medial form *u* as the symbol for the vowel (in modern English having the sounds exemplified in *truth, put, but,* and the diphthongal sound that serves as the name of the letter).—*ns.* **U′-boat,** a German submarine (Ger. *unterseeboot*); **U′-bolt, U′-trap, U′-tube,** a bolt, drain-trap, tube, bent like the letter U.—*adj.* **U′-shaped.**

berous, *ū′bə-rəs, adj.* yielding abundance of milk: abounding.—*n.* **u′berty,** fruitfulness: abundant productiveness. [L. *über,* udder, fruitfulness.]

biety, *ū-bī′i-ti, n.* the state of being in a definite place, whereness: location. [L. *ubi,* where.]

biquity, *ū-bik′wi-ti, n.* existence everywhere at the same time: omnipresence.—*adj.* **ubiquā′rian,** found everywhere: ubiquitous.—*n.* **ubiquitā′rian,** one who believes that Christ's body is everywhere, in the Eucharist as elsewhere.—Also *adj.*—*adjs.* **ibiq′uitary,** being everywhere at once; **ubiq′uit-ous,** to be found everywhere.—*adv.* **ubiq′uitously.** [L. *ubique,* everywhere—*ubi,* where.]

dal, *ū′dl, adj.* (*Orkney* and *Shetland*) allodial: with-out feudal superior.—*n.* an estate so held.—*n.* **u′daller,** a holder of such an estate. [O.N. *óthal.*]

dder, *ud′ər, n.* the organ containing the mammary glands of the cow, mare, &c.: a dug or teat.—*adjs.* **dd′ered;** **udd′erful,** with full udder; **udd′er-ess,** unsuckled. [O.E. *úder;* Ger. *euter,* L. *über,* Gr. *outhar.*]

do, *ōō′dō, n.* a Japanese aralia with edible shoots. [Jap.]

ds, *udz,* in oaths, for **God's,** or for **God save** (as n *uds my life).*

gh, *uhh, interj.* an exclamation of repugnance.—v. used as a representation of a cough or grunt.

gly, *ug′li, adj.* (*obs.*) frightful, horrible: offensive to the sight or other sense, or to refined taste or moral feeling: ill-natured: threatening: disquiet-ng: suggesting suspicion of evil.—*n.* (*coll.*) an ugly person: a shade attached to a lady's hat (mid-19th-cent.).—*v.t.* (*rare*) to make ugly.—*v.t.* ag, to excite loathing in: to loathe.—*v.i.* to feel loathing.—*n.* **uglifica′tion.**—*v.t.* **ug′lify,** to make ugly.—*adj.* **ug′lily.**—*n.* **ug′liness.**—*adj.* **ug′some,** disgusting: hideous.—*n.* **ug′someness.**—**ugly customer,** a dangerous antagonist; **ugly duck-ing,** a despised member of a family or group who ater proves the most successful; **ugly man,** an actual garrotter, distinguished from his con-ederates. [O.N. *uggligr,* frightful, *uggr,* fear.]

grian, (*y*)*ōō′gri-ən, adj.* of that division of the Finno-Ugrian languages and peoples that includes he Magyars, Ostyaks, and Voguls.—Also *n.*—*djs.* **U′gric;** **U′gro-Finn′ic.**

hlan, *ōō′län, n.* a light cavalryman in semi-oriental uniform: a Prussian lancer. [Ger. *uhlan*—Polish *lan,* orig. a light Tatar horseman—Turk, *oglān,* a roung man.]

nta(h)ite, *ū-int′ä-īt, n.* a natural tarlike asphalt ound in the *Uinta* valley, Utah.—*n.* **Uintathē′-ium,** a gigantic Eocene fossil ungulate from Uinta County, Wyoming.

tlander, *ä′it-land-ər, n.* a foreigner (in the Trans-aal and Orange Free State). [Du. equivalent of **utlander.**]

kase, *ū-kāz′, -käs′, n.* an edict with force of law, s in Tsarist Russia. [Russ. *ukaz.*]

krainian, *ū-krān′i-ən, ōō-krīn′i-ən, n.* a native or citizen of *Ukraine,* a republic (since 1917) S.W. of

Russia Proper, including Little Russia: its language, Ruthenian.—Also *adj.*

ukulele, *ū-kə-lā′li, oo-koo-lā′lä, n.* a small, usually four-stringed, guitar. [Hawaiian, flea, from the movement of the fingers.]

ulcer, *ul′sər, n.* an open sore discharging pus: (*fig.*) a continuing source of evil, an unsound element.—*v.t.* and *v.i.* to ulcerate.—*v.i.* **ul′cerate,** to form an ulcer.—*v.t.* to cause an ulcer in: to affect with insidious corruption.—*n.* **ulcerā′tion.**—*adjs.* **ul′cerative;** **ul′cered;** **ul′cerous.**—*adv.* **ul′cer-ously.**—*n.* **ul′cerousness.** [L. *ulcus, ulcĕris;* cf. Gr. *helkos.*]

ule, hule, *ōō′lä, n.* a Central American rubber tree (Castilloa): its crude rubber. [Sp. *hule*—Nahuatl *ulli.*]

ulema, *ōō′li-mä, n.* the body of professional theo-logians, expounders of the law, in a Mohammedan country. [Ar. *'ulema,* pl. of *'ālim,* learned.]

Ulex, *ū′leks, n.* the gorse genus. [L. *ūlex, -icis,* a kind of rosemary or the like.]

ulicon, ulichon, ulikon, *ōō′li-kən.* Same as **eulachon.**

uliginous, *ū-lij′i-nəs, adj.* slimy: oozy: swampy: growing in swampy places. [L. *ūliginōsus*—*ūligō, -inis,* moisture.]

ullage, *ul′ij, n.* the quantity a vessel lacks of being full: loss by evaporation or leakage: (*slang*) dregs.—*v.t.* to reckon the ullage of: to affect with ullage: to fill up: to draw off a little from.—*n.* **ull′ing,** the making good of ullage. [A.Fr. *ulliage,* O.Fr. *eullage*—*œiller,* to fill up.]

Ulmus, *ul′məs, n.* the elm genus, giving name to the family **Ulmā′ceae,** akin to the nettles.—*adj.* **ulmā′-ceous,** of or like an elm: of its family.—*n.* **ul′min,** a gummy exudation from elms and other trees. [L. *ulmus,* elm.]

ulna, *ul′nä, n.* the inner and larger of the two bones of the forearm :—*pl.* **ul′nae** (*-nē*).—*adj.* **ul′nar.**—*n.* **ulnā′re,** the bone of the carpus opposite the ulna :—*pl.* **ulnā′ria.** [L. *ulna,* elbow, arm; cf. **ell,** and Gr. *ōlenē,* forearm.]

ulosis, *ū-lō′sis, n.* formation of a scar. [Gr. *oulōsis*—*oulē,* a scar.]

Ulothrix, *ū′lō-thriks, n.* a genus of filamentous algae, giving name to the **Ulotrichales** (*ū-lot-ri-kā′lēz*), an order of multicellular uninucleate green algae, marine and freshwater.—*adj.* **ulotrichous** (*ū-lot′ri-kəs*), woolly-haired.—*n.* **ulot′richy** (*-ki*), woolly-hairedness. [Gr. *oulos,* woolly, *thrix, trichos,* hair.]

ulster, *ul′stər, n.* a long loose overcoat.—*adj.* **ul′stered,** wearing an ulster.—*n.* **ulsterette′,** a light ulster. [First made in *Ulster,* Ireland.]

ulterior, *ul-tē′ri-ər, adj.* on the further side: be-yond: in the future: remoter: beyond what is seen or avowed.—*adv.* **ultē′riorly.** [L. *ulterior*—*ultrā* (adv. and prep.), *uls* (prep.), beyond.]

ultimate, *ul′ti-māt, -mit, adj.* furthest: last: final: limiting.—*n.* a final point: a fundamental.—*n.* **ul′timacy** (*-mə-si*).—*adv.* **ul′timately.**—*n.* **ulti-mā′tum,** final terms: a last offer or demand: a last word: a final point: something fundamental :—*pl.* **ultimā′ta.**—*adj.* **ul′timo** (contr. **ult.**), in the last (month).—*n.* **ultimogeniture** (*-jen′*), suces-sion of the youngest, as in borough-English—opp. to *primogeniture.* [L. *ultimus,* last.]

ultion, *ul′shən, n.* revenge: avengement. [L. *ultiō, -ōnis.*]

Ultonian, *ul-tō′ni-ən, adj.* of Ulster.—*n.* an Ulster-man. [L.L. *Ultōnia,* Ulster; O.Ir. *Ult-,* stem of *Ulaid,* Ulster.]

ultra-, *ul′trə-, pfx.* beyond (as **ultra-Neptunian**): extreme or excessive (as **ul′tra-Conserv′ative,** **ul′tra-fash′ionable,** **ul′tra-mod′ern,** **ul′tra-**

Neutral vowels in unaccented syllables: *el′ə-mənt, in′fənt, ran′dəm*

Prot′estant).—*adj.* **ul′tra,** extreme, esp. in royalism, fashion, or religious or political opinion.— *n.* an extremist.—*ns.* **ultraism** (*ul′trə-izm*), extreme principles : an attempt to pass beyond the limits of the known ; **ul′traist.** [L. *ultrā,* beyond.]

ultrabasic, *ul-trə-bā′sik, adj.* (*petr.*) extremely basic, very poor in silica.

ultracentrifuge, *ul-trə-sen′tri-fūj, n.* a very fast-running type of centrifuge.

ultracrepidate, *ul-trə-krep′i-dāt, v.i.* to criticise beyond the sphere of one's knowledge.—*n.* and *adj.* **ultracrepidā′rian.** [From Apelles's answer to the cobbler who passed from the sandal to the leg in finding fault with a picture, *nē sūtor ultrā crepidam,* the cobbler must not go beyond the sandal.]

ultramarine, *ul-trə-mə-rēn′, adj.* overseas : from overseas : deep-blue.—*n.* a deep-blue pigment, orig. made from lapis-lazuli brought from beyond the sea : its colour.

ultramicroscope, *ul-trə-mī′krə-skōp, n.* a microscope with strong illumination from the side, whereby the presence of objects can be observed though they are too small to be seen in their own form.—*adj.* **ultramicroscopic** (*-skop′ik*), pertaining to ultramicroscopy : too small to be visible under the microscope. — *n.* **ultramicroscopy** (*-kros′kə-pi*).

ultramontane, *ul-trə-mon′tān, adj.* beyond the mountains (i.e. the Alps) : orig. used in Italy of the French, Germans, &c. ; afterwards applied by the northern nations to the Italians : hence, extreme in favouring the pope's supremacy.—*ns.* **ultramon′tanism** (*-tin-izm*) ; **ultramon′tanist.** [L. *montānus—mōns, montis,* a mountain.]

ultramundane, *ul-trə-mun′dān, adj.* beyond the world, or beyond the limits of our system.

ultra-red, *ul′trə-red′, adj.* infra-red.

ultra-sensual, *ul′trə-sen′sū-əl, -shoo-əl, adj.* beyond the range or reach of the senses.

ultra-short, *ul′trə-short′, adj.* (of electro-magnetic waves) of less than ten metres′-wavelength.

ultrasonics, *ul-trə-son′iks, n.* the study of vibrations of the same nature as audible sound-waves but of greater frequency.—*adj.* **ultrason′ic.** [L. *sonus,* sound.]

ultra-tropical, *ul′trə-trop′ik-əl, adj.* beyond the tropics : hotter than the tropics.

ultra-violet, *ul-trə-vī′ə-lit, adj.* beyond the violet end of the visible spectrum : pertaining to, or using, radiations of wavelengths less than those of visible light.

ultra-virtuous, *ul′trə-vər′tū-əs, adj.* prudish.

ultroneous, *ul-trō′ni-əs, adj.* spontaneous, voluntary.—*adv.* **ultrō′neously.**—*n.* **ultrō′neousness.** [L. *ultrōneus—ultrō,* spontaneously.]

ululate, *ūl′ū-lāt,* also *ul′, v.i.* to hoot or screech.— *adj.* **ul′ulant.**—*n.* **ululā′tion,** howling, wailing. [L. *ulŭlāre, -ātum,* to hoot.]

ulyie, ulzie, *ūl′(y)i,* obs. Scots forms of **oil.**

umbel, *um′bəl, n.* a flat-topped inflorescence in which the flower stalks all spring from about the same point in an axis (which in a **compound umbel** is grouped in the same way with other axes).—*adjs.* **um′bellate, -d,** constituting an umbel : having umbels.—*adv.* **um′bellately.**—*n.* **umbellifer** (*um-bel′i-fər*), any plant of the Umbelliferae.—*n.pl.* **Umbellif′erae,** the carrot and hemlock family of plants, with (usu. compound) umbels, schizocarpic fruit, leaves with sheathing bases.—*adj.* **umbellif′erous.**—*n.* **um′bellule,** a partial umbel. [L. *umbella,* a sunshade, dim. of *umbra,* a shade.]

umber, *um′bər, n.* a brown earthy mineral (hydrated oxides of iron and manganese) used as a pigment.— *v.t.* to colour with umber.—*adj.* brown like umber. —*ns.* **um′ber-bird, um′bre,** the umbrette.—*adjs.* **um′bered, um′bery.** [It. *terra d'ombra,* shadow earth, or poss. Umbrian earth.]

umber, *um′bər, n.* the grayling. [L. *umbra.*]

umbilicus, *um-bi-lī′kəs* (by some *um-bil′i-kəs*), *n.* the navel : a depression at the axial base of a spiral shell : a small depression.—*adj.* **umbili′cal** (or *um-bil′i-kl*) ; **umbil′icate,** navel-like : having a depression like a navel.—**umbilical cord,** the

navel-string. [L. *umbilīcus,* the navel ; Gr. *omphalos.*]

umbles, *um′blz, n.pl.* entrails (liver, heart, &c.), esp. of a deer.—Also **hum′bles, num′bles.**—*n.* **um′ble-pie′** (see **humble-pie**). [O.Fr. *nombles,* from *lomble,* loin—L. *lumbulus,* dim. of *lumbus,* loin.]

umbo, *um′bō, n.* the boss of a shield : a knob : the protuberant oldest part of a bivalve shell : a knob on a toadstool cap :—*pl.* **umbo′nes, umbo′s.**— *adjs.* **um′bonal** (*-bən-əl*) ; **um′bonate** (*bot.*), having a central boss.—*n.* **umbonā′tion.** [L. *umbō,-ōnis.*]

umbra, *um′brə, n.* a shadow : (*astron.*) the darker part of the shadow or dark inner cone projected in an eclipse : the darker part of a spot : a shade or ghost : an uninvited guest that comes with an invited.—*adjs.* **umbraculate** (*um-brak′ū-lāt*), over-shadowed by an umbraculum ; **umbrac′uliform,** umbrella-shaped.—*n.* **umbrac′ulum,** an umbrella-shaped structure.—*adjs.* **um′bral,** of an umbra ; **um′brāted,** (*her.*) faintly traced ; (*obs.*) **umbrati** (*-brat′, rare*), **-al, umbratile** (*um′brə-tīl, -til*), **umbratilous** (*-brat′i-ləs*), shadowy : shaded : shade-giving : indoor : secluded ; **umbrif′erous,** shade-giving ; **umbrose** (*-brōs′*), shade-giving : dusky ; **um′brous,** shaded. [L. *umbra,* shade : shadow, dim. *umbrāculum,* adj. *umbrātilis.*]

umbrage, *um′brij, n.* shade, shadow : that which casts a shade : a shelter : a shadowy appearance : pretext, colour : inkling : suspicion of injury : offence.—*v.t.* to shade : to offend.—*adj.* **umbrā′geous,** shady or forming a shade.—*adv.* **umbrā′geously.**—*n.* **umbra′geousness.** [Fr. *ombrage*— L. *umbrāticum* (neut. adj.)—*umbra,* a shadow.]

umbre, *um′bər.* See **umbrette.**

umbrella, *um-brel′ä, n.* a portable shelter against sun, rain, &c., now usu. with a sliding framework of ribs on a stick : anything of similar form, as a jellyfish disk.—Also formerly **ombrell′a, umbrell′o.**—*ns.* **umbrell′a-ant,** the sauba ant ; **umbrell′a-bird,** a S. American fruit-crow with umbrella-like crest and a throat-lappet to represent the stick.—*adj.* **umbrell′aed, umbrell′a′d** with an umbrella.—*ns.* **umbrell′a-fir,** a Japanese conifer (Sciadopitys), with radiating tufts of needles ; **umbrell′a-stand,** a rack or receptacle for closed umbrellas and walking-sticks ; **umbrell′a-tree,** a tree of any kind with leaves or branches arranged umbrella-wise, esp. a small magnolia. [It. *ombrella, ombrello—ombra,* a shade —L. *umbra.*]

umbrette, *um-bret′, n.* the hammerkop, a brown African bird between storks and herons, remarkable for its huge nest.—Also **um′bre** (*-bər*). [Fr. *ombrette—ombre,* umber.]

Umbrian, *um′bri-ən, adj.* of *Umbria,* in central Italy.—*n.* a native thereof : the old language, Iguvine, akin to Oscan.

umbriere, *um′bri-ēr, n.* (*Spens.*) a visor.—Also **um′brere, um′bril, um′brel.** [O.Fr. *ombrier ombrel,* shade.]

umiak, oomiack, *ōō′mi-ak, ōōm′yak, n.* an open skin boat, manned by women. [Eskimo.]

umlaut, *oom′lowt, n.* a vowel-change brought about by a vowel or semivowel (esp. i, j) in the following syllable : (loosely) the two dots placed over a letter representing an umlauted vowel in German.—*v.t.* to bring about umlaut in. [Ger.,—*um,* around, *laut,* sound.]

umph, *hm(h).* Same as **humph.**

umpire, *um′pīr, n.* a third person called in to decide a dispute or a deadlock : an arbitrator : (*cricket,* &c.) an impartial person chosen to supervise the game, enforce the rules, and decide disputes.—Also *v.i.* and *v.t.*—*ns.* **um′pirage, um′pireship.** [M.E. *noumpere, oumper*—O.Fr. *nomper—non-,* not, *per, pair,* peer, equal.]

umpteen, *um(p)′tēn, umpty, um(p)′ti, adjs.* (*mil. slang*) of an indefinite number.—*adjs.* **umpteenth, ump′tieth,** the *n*th. [*Umpty* in Morse, a dash from its sound on a telegraph key.]

umquhile, *um′hwīl, adv.* and *adj.* a Scots form of **um′while,** formerly, late, whilom. [O.E. *ymb(e) hwīle,* about or at a time.]

un, ′un, *un, ən, pron.* (*dial.*) for **one** : also for **him.** [O.E. accus. *hine.*]

un-, *un-*, *pfx.* partly negative: partly indicating a reversal of process, removal, or deprivation: sometimes (as in **unbare, unloose**) merely emphasising such reversal or deprivation already expressed by the simple word: sometimes (in *Shakespeare* and *Milton*) added to a present participle with a passive meaning. The meaning is often ambiguous, esp. in participial adjs. As there is hardly a limit to its use only a selection of words can be given. For pronunciation see the simple words: the stress is liable to shift. [Partly O.E. *un-*, neg.; cf. Ger. *un-*, L. *in-*, Gr. *an-*, *a-*; partly O.E. *on-* (or *un-*), the unstressed form of *and-* (as in **answer**); cf. Ger. *ent-*, Gr. *anti-*, against.]

un-.—*adjs.* **unabashed**; **unaba'ted**, not diminished or lowered; **una'ble**, not able: not having sufficient strength, power, or skill: weak: impotent; **unabol'ished**; **unabridged'**; **unab'rogated**; **unabsolved'**; **unacadem'ic**; **unaccent'ed**, without accent or stress in pronunciation: not marked with an accent; **unaccept'able**.—*ns.* **unaccept'ableness**; **unaccept'ance**.—*adjs.* **unaccomm'odated**, unprovided; **unaccomm'odating**, not compliant; **unaccom'panied**, not accompanied, escorted, or attended: not occurring together: (*mus.*) having no instrumental accompaniment; **unaccom'plished**, not achieved: lacking accomplishments.—*ns.* **unaccom'plishment**, the fact of not being achieved; **unaccountabil'ity**.—*adj.* **unaccount'able**, not to be accounted for: not responsible.—*n.* **unaccount'ableness**.—*adv.* **unaccount'ably**, inexplicably.—*adjs.* **unaccount'ed for**; **unaccred'ited**; **unaccus'able**.—*adv.* **unaccus'ably**.—*adjs.* **unaccused'**; **unaccus'tomed**, not customary: not habituated.—*n.* **unaccus'tomedness**.—*adjs.* **unachiev'able**; **unach'ing**; **unacknowl'edged**, not acknowledged, recognised, confessed, or noticed.—*n.* **unacquaint'ance**, want of acquaintance: ignorance.—*adj.* **unacquaint'ed** (*Scot.* **unacquaint'**), without acquaintance: not on a footing of acquaintance: unaware: unknown: (*Spens.*) unusual.—*n.* **unacquaint'edness**.—*adjs.* **unact'able**, unfit for the stage; **unact'ed**, not performed; **unac'tive**, inactive; **unadapt'able**; **unadapt'ed**; **unaddressed'**; **unadjust'ed**; **unadmired'**; **unadmir'ing**; **unadmon'ished**; **unadored'**; **unadorned'**; **unadul'terate, -d**, unmixed, pure, genuine); **unadvent'urous** (*Milt.* **unadvent'rous**); **unadvis'able**, inadvisable: not open to advice.—*n.* **unadvis'ableness**.—*adv.* **unadvis'ably**.—*adj.* **unadvised'**, not advised: without advice: not prudent or discreet: ill-judged: (*Spens.*) inadvertent.—*adv.* **unadvis'edly**.—*n.* **unadvis'edness**.—*adj.* **unaffect'ed**, not affected or influenced: untouched by emotion: without affectation: not assumed: plain: real: sincere.—*adv.* **unaffect'edly**.—*n.* **unaffect'edness**.—*adjs.* **unaffect'ing**; **unafraid'**; **unagree'able**, disagreeable: inconsistent: discordant; **unaid'able**; **unaid'ed**; **unaimed'**; **unaired'**; **unak'ing** (*Shak.*; see **unaching**); **una'lienable**, inalienable.—*adv.* **una'lienably**.

unalist, *ū'nəl-ist*, *n.* a holder of one benefice. [L. *ūnus*, one.]

un- (*continued*).—*adjs.* **unalive'**, not susceptible: **unallayed'**, unmixed: unqualified: unsubdued: unquenched; **unallied'**, not akin: without allies; **unallott'ed**; **unallow'able**; **unalloyed'**, not alloyed or mixed: pure; **unal'terable**.—*n.* **unal'terableness**.—*adv.* **unal'terably**.—*adjs.* **unal'tered**; **unal'tering**; **unambig'uous**.—*adv.* **unambig'uously**.—*adj.* **unambi'tious**.—*adv.* **unambi'tiously**.—*adjs.* **uname'nable**; **unamend'able**; **unamend'ed**; **unamerced'**; **unAmer'ican**, not in accordance with American character, ideas, or feeling.—*v.t.* **unAmer'icanise**, to make un-American.—*n.* **unamiabil'ity**.—*adj.* **una'miable**.—*n.* **una'miableness**.—*adjs.* **unamu'sable**; **unamused'**; **unamu'sing**.—*adv.* **unamu'singly**.—*adjs.* **unanalys'able**; **unan'alysed**; **unanalyt'ic, -al**.—*v.t.* **unanch'or**, to loose from anchorage.—*v.i.* to become loose or unattached: to weigh anchor.—*adjs.* **unanch'ored**, not anchored; **unaneled** (*un-ə-nēld'*), *Shak*.

unnaneld, without extreme unction; **unan'imated**, not alive: not animated or lively: not actuated.

unanimous, *ū-nan'i-məs*, *adj.* of one mind: without a dissentient.—*n.* **unanimity** (*ū-nən-im'i-ti*), agreement without a dissentient.—*adv.* **unan'imously**. [L. *ūnanimus*—*ūnus*, one, *animus*, mind.]

un- (*continued*).—*adjs.* **unannealed'**, not annealed (but see also **unaneled**); **unann'otated**; **unannounced'**; **unan'swerable**, not answerable, esp. not to be refuted, conclusive.—*n.* **unan'swerableness**.—*adv.* **unan'swerably**, in an unanswerable manner.—*adjs.* **unan'swered**, not answered: unrequited; **unanx'ious**; **unapostol'ic, -al**.—*adv.* **unapostol'ically**.—*adj.* **unappalled'**.—*v.t.* **unappar'el**, to disrobe, undress.—*adjs.* **unappar'elled**, not wearing clothes; **unappa'rent**; **unappeal'able**, not admitting of an appeal to a higher court, conclusive, final; **unappeas'able**; **unappeased'**; **unapp'etising**; **unapplaus'ive**, not applauding; **unapplied'**; **unappoint'ed**, not appointed: not equipped; **unappre'ciated**; **unappre'ciative**, inappreciative; **unapprehend'ed**; **unapprehen'sible**, inapprehensible; **unapprehen'sive**, without understanding: without fear.—*n.* **unapprehen'siveness**.—*adjs.* **unapprised'**; **unapproach'able**, out of reach, inaccessible: stand-offish: inaccessible to advances or intimacy: beyond rivalry.—*n.* **unapproach'ableness**.—*adv.* **unapproach'ably**.—*adjs.* **unapproached'**; **unappro'priate**, unappropriated: inappropriate; **unappro'priated**, not taken possession of: not applied to some purpose: not granted to any person, corporation, &c.; **unapproved'**, (*obs.*) untested: unproved: unsanctioned: not approved of; **unapprov'ing**.—*adv.* **unapprov'ingly**.—*adj.* **unapt'**, unfitted: unsuitable: not readily inclined or accustomed: lacking in aptitude, slow.—*adv.* **unapt'ly**.—*n.* **unapt'ness**.—*adjs.* **unar'guable**; **unar'gued**, (*Milt.*) undisputed: not debated; **unaris'en**.—*v.t.* **unarm'**, to help to put off armour: to deprive of arms, to disarm: to make harmless.—*v.i.* to take off one's armour.—*adjs.* **unarmed'**, without weapons: defenceless: unprotected: unaided or without accessory apparatus; **unar'moured**, without armour or armour-plating; **unarranged'**, not arranged; **unart'ful**, artless, genuine: inartistic: unskilful.—*adv.* **unart'fully**.—*adjs.* **unartic'ulate, -d**; **unartifi'cial**, inartificial: not artificial.—*adv.* **unartifi'cially**.—*adjs.* **unartist'ic**, not artistic: inartistic; **unart'istlike**; **unascend'able, -ible**, unscalable; **unascen'ded**; **unascertain'able**; **unascertained'**; **unashamed'**.—*adv.* **unasham'edly**.—*adjs.* **unasked'**, not asked: not asked for: uninvited; **unas'pirated**; **unaspir'ing**.—*adv.* **unaspir'ingly**.—*n.* **unaspir'ingness**.—*adjs.* **unassail'able**; **unassailed'**; **unassayed'**, not assayed, or essayed: untested; **unassign'able**; **unassigned'**; **unassim'ilable**; **unassim'ilated**; **unassist'ed**.—*adv.* **unassist'edly**.—*adjs.* **unasso'ciated**; **unassuage'able**; **unassuaged'**; **unassumed'**; **unassum'ing**, free from assumption: unpretentious, modest.—*adv.* **unassum'ingly**.—*n.* **unassum'ingness**.—*adjs.* **unassured'**, uncertain: doubtfully recognised: insecure: lacking in assurance: diffident: not insured against loss; **unaton'able**, irreconcilable: not to be atoned for; **unatoned'**, not atoned for; **unattached'**, not attached: detached: not arrested: not belonging to a club, party, college, diocese, department, regiment, &c.: not married or about to be; **unattain'able**.—*n.* **unattain'ableness**.—*adv.* **unattain'ably**.—*adjs.* **unattained'**, not attainted: unvitiated: unblemished; **unattempt'ed**, not attempted: not made the subject of an attempt; **unattend'ed**, not accompanied or attended: not attended to; **unattend'ing**, inattentive; **unattent'ive**, (*obs.*) inattentive; **unattest'ed**; **unattired'**, unclothed: in undress; **unattract'ive**.—*adv.* **unattract'ively**.—*n.* **unattract'iveness**.

unau, *ū'naw*, *ōō'now*, *n.* the two-toed sloth. [Fr., from Tupí.]

un- (*continued*).—*adjs.* **unaugment'ed**, not augmented: (*gram.*) without the augment; **unauspi'-cious**, (*Shak.*) inauspicious; **unauthen'tic** ; **unauthen'ticated**, not attested.—*n.* **unauthen'-tic'ity**.—*adjs.* **unau'thorised** ; **unauthor'itative** ; **unavail'able**, not available : of no avail.—*n.* **unavail'ableness**.—*adv.* **unavail'ably**.—*adjs.* **un-avail'ing**, of no avail or effect : useless ; **un-avenged'** ; **unavert'able, -ible** ; **unavoid'able**, not to be avoided : inevitable : not voidable.—*n.* **unavoid'ableness**. —*adv.* **unavoid'ably**.—*adjs.* **unavoid'ed**, not avoided : (*Shak.*) unavoidable, inevitable ; **unavowed'**, not acknowledged.—*adv.* **unavow'edly**.—*adjs.* **unawak'ened** ; **unawak'-ening** ; **unaware'**, not aware : (*Shelley*) unwary. —*adv.* unawares.—*n.* **unaware'ness**.—*adv.* **un-awares'**, without being or making aware : unper-ceivedly : unexpectedly.—*n.* in the phrase **at unawares**, unexpectedly, at a sudden disadvantage. —*adjs.* **unawed'** ; **unbacked'**, without a back : without backing or backers : unaided : not moved back : riderless : never yet ridden ; **unbaff'led**. —*v.t.* **unbag'**, to let out of a bag.—*adjs.* **unbail'-able** ; **unbaited** ; **unbaked**, not baked : im-mature.—*n.* **unbal'ance**, want of balance.—*v.t.* to throw off the balance.—*adjs.* **unbal'anced**, not in a state of equipoise : without a counterpoise or compensation : without mental balance, unsteady : (*book-k.*) not adjusted so as to show balance of debtor and creditor ; **unball'asted**, without ballast ; unsteady, unstable, flighty ; **unband'ed**, without a band.—*v.t.* **unbank'**, to take a bank from : to clear away banked ashes from.—*adj.* **unbap'tised**.—*v.t.* **unbar'**, to remove a bar from or of : to unfasten.— *v.i.* to become unbarred.—*adjs.* **unbarbed'**, with-out barb : without bard, caparison, or armour (so prob. in *Coriolanus*) : uncropped, untrimmed ; **unbar'bered**.—*vs.t.* **unbare'**, to bare, lay bare ; **unbark'**, to strip of bark.—*adjs.* **unbarked'**, not deprived of bark : deprived of bark ; **unbarred'**, without a bar or bars : not barred.—*v.t.* **unbarr'-icade**, to remove a barricade from.—*adjs.* **unbash'-ful**, free from bashfulness : (*Shak.*) shameless ; **unba'ted**, (*Shak.*) unblunted : undiminished ; **unbathed'** ; **unbatt'ered**.—*v.t.* **unbe'**, to cause not to be.—*v.i.* to cease to be : to be non-existent. —*v.t.* **unbear'**, to free from the bearing-rein.— *adj.* **unbear'able**, intolerable.—*n.* **unbear'able-ness**. — *adv.* **unbear'ably**. — *adjs.* **unbeard'ed**, beardless ; **unbear'ing**, barren ; **unbeat'able** ; **unbeat'en** ; **unbeau'tiful** ; **unbea'vered**, with-out a beaver or hat : having the beaver of the helmet open ; **unbecom'ing**, unsuited : not suited to the wearer : not befitting : not showing to advan-tage : unseemly.—*n.* the transition from existence to non-existence.—*adv.* **unbecom'ingly**.—*n.* **un-becom'ingness**.—*v.t.* **unbed'**, to rouse, remove, dislodge from a bed.—*adjs.* **unbedd'ed**, unstrati-fied : not put to bed ; **unbedimmed'** ; **un-bedinned'**, not made noisy ; **unbefit'ting** ; **un-befriend'ed**.—*v.t.* **unbeget'**, to undo the begetting of.—*adjs.* **unbegged'** ; **unbeginn'ing**, without beginning ; **unbegot'** ; **unbegott'en**, not yet begotten : existing independent of any generating cause. — *v.t.* **unbeguile'**, to undeceive.— *adjs.* **unbeguiled'** ; **unbegun'**, not yet begun : without beginning ; **unbehol'den**, unseen : under no obligation of gratitude ; **unbe'ing**, nonexistent. —*n.* nonexistence.—*adjs.* **unbeknown'**, **unbe-knownst'**, (*prov.*) unknown.—*advs.* unobserved, without being known.—*n.* **un'belief** (or **-lĕf'**), disbelief or withholding of belief, esp. in accepted religion.—*adj.* **unbeliev'able**, incredible.—*adv.* **unbeliev'ably**.— *v.t.* and *v.i.* **unbelieve'**, to disbelieve : to refrain from believing : to cease to believe.—*adj.* **unbelieved'**.—*n.* **unbeliev'er**, one who does not believe, esp. in the prevailing religion : an incredulous person.—*adj.* **unbeliev'ing**.—*adv.* **unbeliev'ingly**.—*adj.* **unbeloved'** (or **-luv'id**).— *v.t.* **unbelt'**, to ungird.—*adj.* **unbelt'ed**, without a belt : freed from a belt.—*v.t.* **unbend'**, to relax from a bending tension, as a bow : to undo, unfasten : to relax : to straighten or unfold.—*v.i.* to become relaxed : to behave with freedom from stiffness, to be affable.—*adjs.* **unbend'ed** ; **un-bend'ing**, not bending : unyielding : resolute.—

n. a relaxing.—*adv.* **unbend'ingly**.—*n.* **unbend'-ingness**.—*adjs.* **unben'eficed**, without a bene-fice ; **unbenefi'cial**, not advantageous ; **un-ben'efited** ; **unbenight'ed**, not overcome, or not overtaken, by darkness ; **unbenign'** (*adv.* **un-benign'ly** ; *Tenn.*) ; **unbenig'nant** ; **unbent'**, not bent : relaxed : unovercome ; **unbereft'**.— *v.t.* **unbeseem'**, to misbecome : to fail to fulfil.—*adj.* **unbeseem'ing**.—*adv.* **unbeseem'-ingly**.—*adj.* **unbesought'**.—*v.t.* **unbespeak'**, to revoke the bespeaking of.—*adjs.* **unbespok'en**, not bespoken ; **unbestowed'** ; **unbetrayed'** ; **unbett'erable**, not to be surpassed : impossible to mend ; **unbett'ered**, not made better ; **unbe-wailed'**.—*v.t.* **unbi'as**, to free from bias.—*adj.* **unbi'ased** (sometimes **unbi'assed**). — *adv.* **un-bi'as(s)edly**.— *n.* **unbi'as(s)edness**. — *adjs.* **un-bib'lical**, contrary to, unwarranted by, the Bible ; **unbid'**, (*Spens.*) not prayed for : unbidden ; **un-bidd'en**, not bid or commanded : uninvited : spontaneous.—*v.t.* **unbind'**, to remove a band from : to loose : to set free.—*n.* **unbind'ing**, removal of a band or bond : loosing : setting free.— *adj.* loosening : not binding.—*vs.t.* **unbish'op**, to deprive of the status of bishop ; **unbitt'** (*naut.*) to take off from the bitts.—*adjs.* **unbitt'ed**, without a bit : unbridled ; **unblam'able**.—*adv.* **unblam'-ably**.—*adjs.* **unblamed'** ; **unbleached'** ; **un-blem'ished** ; **unblenched'** (or **un'** ; *Milt.*), unflinching : unstained ; **unblench'ing**, unflinch-ing ; **unblend'ed**, **unblent'**.—*v.t.* **unbless'**, to withhold happiness from : to deprive of blessing. —*adjs.* **unblessed'**, **unblest'**.—*n.* **unbless'ed-ness**.—*adj.* **unblind'**, not blind.—*v.t.* to free from blindness or from blindfolding.—*adj.* **unblind'ed**. —*v.t.* **unblind'fold** (*pa.p.* *Spens.* **unblind'fold**). —*adj.* **unblink'ing**.—*adv.* **unblink'ingly**.—*adj.* **unbliss'ful**.—*v.t.* **unblock'**, to free from obstruc-tion.—*adjs.* **unblood'ed**, **unblood'ied**, not blood-stained ; **unblood'y** ; **unblott'ed** ; **un'blowed'** (*Shak.*), **un'blown'** (or **un'**), not blown : yet in the bud, not yet having bloomed ; **unblunt'ed** ; **un-blush'ing**, not blushing : without shame : im-pudent.—*adv.* **unblush'ingly**.—*adjs.* **unboast'ful** ; **unbod'ied**, disembodied : not having a body or a form ; **unbo'ding**, not expecting.—*v.t.* **unbolt'**, to draw back a bolt from.—*v.i.* to become un-bolted : (*Shak.*) to explain, expound.—*adj.* **un-bolt'ed**, unfastened by withdrawing a bolt : not fastened by bolts : not separated by bolting or sifting : coarse.—*vs.t.* **unbone'**, to take the bones from ; **unbonn'et**, to remove the bonnet from.— *v.i.* to uncover the head.—*adjs.* **unbonn'eted**, bare-headed : (in *Othello*, according to some, without taking off the cap, on equal terms) ; **un-booked'**, not entered in a book : unreserved : not literary ; **unbook'ish**, unlearned : not given to or depending on reading : not savouring of books.— *v.t.* and *v.i.* **unboot'**, to take the boots off.—*adjs.* **unborn'**, not yet born : non-existent : without beginning ; **unborr'owed**, not borrowed : original. —*v.t.* **unbo'som**, (of what is in the mind) to pour out, give vent to : to disclose : to tell freely.—*v.i.* to confide freely.—*n.* **unbo'somer**.—*adjs.* **un-bott'omed**, bottomless : unfounded ; **unbought'**, not bought or sold, obtained without buying : not bribed ; **unbound'**, not bound : loose : with-out binding (also *pa.t.* and *pa.p.* of **unbind**, freed from bonds) ; **unbound'ed**, not limited : bound-less : having no check or control.—*adv.* **un-bound'edly**. — *n.* **unbound'edness**. — *adj.* **un-bowed'**, not bent : unsubdued.—*v.t.* **unbrace'**, to undo the braces, points, or bands of : to loose or relax.—*adjs.* **unbraced'** (*Spens.* **unbraste**) ; **unbraid'ed**, not plaited : (*Shak.*) untarnished, unfaded ; **unbranched'** ; **unbreach'able** ; **un-breached'** ; **unbreak'able** : **unbreath'able**, not respirable ; **unbreathed'**, (*Shak.*) not exercised or practised : out of breath : not out of breath : not breathed : not even whispered ; **unbreathed'-on**, untouched by breath, esp. the breath of detraction ; **unbreath'ing**, not breathing ; **un-bred'**, ill-bred : untrained : (*Shak.*) not yet born. —*v.t.* **unbreech'**, to remove the breeches, breech, or breeching from.—*adjs.* **unbreeched'**, wearing no breeches ; **unbrib′able** ; **unbridged′**.—*v.t.* **unbri′dle**, to free from the bridle.—*adj.* **unbri′dled**, not bridled : unrestrained : licentious.— *n.* **unbri′dledness.**—*adjs.* **un-Brit′ish**, not in accordance with the British character ; **unbroke′, unbro′ken**, not broken, broken up, or broken in : uninterrupted : not thrown into disorder : not variegated : not infringed.—*adv.* **unbro′kenly.**— *n.* **unbro′kenness.**—*adjs.* **unbroth′erlike** ; **un-broth′erly** ; **unbruised′** (*Shak.* **un′brused**) ; *Scott* **unbrizzed′**) ; **unbrushed′.**—*v.t.* **unbuck′le**, to loose from buckles : to unfasten as a buckle.—*adj.* **unbudd′ed**, not yet in bud : not yet having emerged from the bud.—*v.t.* **unbuild′**, to demolish, pull down.—*adjs.* **unbuilt′** (or *un′*), not built : not built upon ; **unbuilt′-on.**—*v.t.* **unbur′den**, **unbur′then**, to free from a burden : to discharge, cast off, as a burden : (*refl.*) to tell one's secrets or anxieties freely.—*adjs.* **unbur′dened, unbur′-thened**, not burdened : relieved of a burden ; **unbur′ied**, not buried ; **unburned′, unburnt′** (or *un′*) ; **unbur′nished.**—*v.t.* and *v.i.* **unburr′ow**, to bring or come out of a burrow.—*v.t.* **unbur′y**, to disinter.—*adjs.* **unbus′inesslike** ; **unbus′y** ; **unbutt′ered.**—*v.t.* **unbutt′on**, to loose the buttons of.—*v.i.* to loose one's buttons.—*adj.* **unbutt′oned**, not buttoned : without a button : with buttons loosed.—*v.t.* **uncage′**, to set free from a cage. —*adjs.* **uncal′culated** ; **uncal′culating** ; **un-called′**, not called for, called, summoned, or invited ; **uncalled′-for** (or **uncalled′ for**), quite unnecessary or superfluous : unprovoked : offensively or aggressively gratuitous ; **uncan′did.**— *adv.* **uncan′didly.**—*ns.* **uncan′didness** ; **un-can′dour.**—*adv.* **uncann′ily.**—*n.* **uncann′iness.** —*adjs.* **uncann′y**, weird : unearthly : savouring of the supernatural : ungentle : formidable ; **un-canon′ic, -al**, not canonical.—*n.* **uncanon′ical-ness.**—*v.t.* **uncan′onise**, to deprive of canonical authority.—*adj.* **uncan′onised**, not canonised : not accepted as canonical.—*v.t.* **uncap′**, to remove a cap from.—*v.i.* to take off one's cap.—*adj.* **un-cap′able**, (*Shak.*) incapable.—*v.i.* **uncape′**, (*Shak.*) prob. a misprint for **uncope** : some have explained as to uncouple hounds, to unkennel a fox, &c.— *adjs.* **uncapsiz′able** ; **uncared′-for** (**uncared′ for**) ; **uncare′ful**, careless : care-free ; **uncar′ing** ; **uncar′peted.**—*vs.t.* **uncart′**, to unload from a cart ; **uncase′**, to take out of a case : to flay : to strip : to lay bare.—*v.i.* to strip.—*adj.* **un-cat′alogued.**

uncate, *ung′kāt*, *adj.* hooked. [L. *uncātus—uncus.*]

un- (*continued*). — *adjs.* **uncaught′** ; **uncaused′**, without any precedent cause, self-existent.

unce, *uns*, *n.* Scots form of **ounce.**

un- (*continued*).—*adj.* **unceas′ing**, ceaseless : un-intermitting : never-ending : continual.—*adv.* **un-ceas′ingly.**—*adjs.* **uncel′ebrated**, without cele-bration : unfamed ; **uncens′ored**, not subjected to censorship ; **uncensor′ious** ; **uncens′ured**, not found fault with or rebuked ; **unceremo′nious**, without ceremony : informal : off-hand.—*adv.* **unceremo′niously.**—*n.* **unceremo′niousness.**— *adj.* **uncer′tain**, not certain : not determined : doubtful : not to be depended upon : unstable : subject to vicissitude : not known or knowing with certainty.—*adv.* **uncer′tainly.**—*ns.* **uncer′tain-ness ; uncer′tainty** (**uncertainty principle**, the principle that it is not possible to measure accurately at the same time both position and velocity). — *adjs.* **uncertif′icated**, not holding a certificate ; **uncer′tified**, not assured, at-tested, or guaranteed ; **uncess′ant**, (*Milt.*) incessant. —*v.t.* **unchain**, to release from a chain : to remove a chain from : to let loose.—*adjs.* **unchained′**, freed from chains : not chained ; **unchall′enge-able**, beyond question or dispute.—*adv.* **un-chall′engeably.** — *adjs.* **unchall′enged** ; **un-chan′cy**, (*Scot.*) unlucky : ill-omened : uncanny : dangerous : ticklish.—*n.* **unchangeabil′ity.**—*adj.* **unchange′able.**—*n.* **unchange′ableness.**—*adv.* **unchange′ably.** — *adjs.* **unchanged′** ; **un-chan′ging.** — *adv.* **unchan′gingly.**—*v.t.* **un-charge′**, to unload : (*Shak.*) to acquit.—*adjs.* **uncharged′**, not charged : (*Shak.*) not attacked ;

unchar′itable. — *n.* **unchar′itableness. — *adv.* **unchar′itably.—*n.* **unchar′ity**, want of charity. —*v.t.* **uncharm′**, to free from a spell : to undo, break the power of (as a spell).—*adjs.* **uncharmed′**, unaffected by a spell : not charmed ; **unchar′ming**, not charming.—*v.t.* **unchar′nel**, to take from a charnel.—*adjs.* **unchart′ed**, not mapped in detail : not shown in a chart ; **unchart′ered**, not holding a charter : unauthorised ; **uncha′ry**, not chary ; **unchaste′**, not chaste.—*adv.* **unchaste′ly.**—*adj.* **unchast′ened**, not chastened.—*n.* **unchaste′ness.** —*adjs.* **unchastis′able** ; **unchastised′.**—*n.* **un-chas′tity**, lack or breach of chastity.—*v.t.* **uncheck′**, (*Shak.*) to fail to check.—*adjs.* **uncheck′able** ; **unchecked′**, not checked or restrained : not contradicted ; **uncheered′** ; **uncheer′ful.**—*adv.* **uncheer′fully.**—*n.* **uncheer′fulness.**—*adj.* **un-chewed′.**—*v.t.* **unchild′**, (*Shak.*) to make childless : to change from being a child.—*adjs.* **unchild′like** ; **unchos′en** ; **unchiv′alrous** ; **unchris′om**, (*Lamb*) unchristened.—*v.t.* **unchrist′en**, to annul the christening of : to deprive of baptismal name : to unchristianise.—*adjs.* **unchrist′ened**, unbaptised : without a name ; **unchris′tian**, (*rare*) non-christian : against the spirit of Christianity : ill beseeming a Christian : uncharitable : (*coll.*) un-conscionable, preposterous, unreasonable, out-rageous.—*v.t.* to unchristianise.—*v.t.* **unchris′-tianise**, to cause to change from the Christian faith or character.—*adj.* **unchris′tianlike.**—*adv.* **unchris′tianly.**—*adj.* unchristianlike. — *adj.* **un-chron′icled.**—*v.t.* **unchurch′**, to deprive of church membership, or of the possession or status of a church.

uncial, *un′shəl, -si-əl*, *adj.* pertaining to an inch or an ounce : of a form of writing in (usu. large) some-what rounded characters used in ancient manu-scripts.—*n.* an uncial letter : uncial writing : MS. written in uncials. [L. *unciālis—uncia*, a twelfth.]

unciform, *un′si-form*, *adj.* hook-shaped. — *adjs.* **un′cinate, -d**, hooked at the end.—*n.* **unci′nus**, a hooklet : a marginal tooth of a mollusc's radula : a hooked chaeta in annelids :—*pl.* **unci′ni** (*-nī*). [L. *uncinus—uncus*, a hook.]

un- (*continued*).—*v.t.* **unci′pher**, (*obs.*) to decipher. —*adj.* **uncir′cumcised**, not circumcised : gentile : (*fig.*) unpurified.—*n.* **uncircumcis′ion**, uncir-cumcised condition : (*B.*) the uncircumcised, the gentiles. — *adjs.* **uncircumscribed′** ; **unciv′il**, (*Spens.*) not civilised : discourteous : unseemly : against civic good ; **unciv′ilised**, barbarous. —*adv.* **unciv′illy.**—*adjs.* **unclad′** ; **unclaimed′.** —*v.t.* **unclasp′**, to loose from a clasp : to relax from clasping : to open.—*v.i.* to close in a clasp.— *adjs.* **unclassed′**, without class divisions : un-classified : not placed in a class ; **unclass′ical** ; **unclass′ified.**

uncle, *ung′kl*, *n.* the brother of one's father or mother : an aunt's husband : a great-uncle : (*U.S.*) an elderly man, esp. a negro : (*slang*) a pawnbroker.—*v.t.* to address as uncle.—*n.* **un′cle-ship**, the state of being an uncle.—**Uncle Sam**, the United States or its people. [O.Fr. *uncle* (Fr. *oncle*)—L. *avunculus*, a maternal uncle.]

un- (*continued*).—*adjs.* **unclean** (-*klēn′*), not clean : foul : ceremonially impure : lewd ; **uncleaned′**, not cleaned.—*n.* **uncleanliness** (-*klen′*).—*adj.* **uncleanly** (-*klen′*).—*adv.* (-*klēn′*).—*n.* **unclean-ness** (-*klēn′nis*).—*adjs.* **uncleansed** (-*klenzd′*) ; **unclear′** ; **uncleared′.**—*adv.* **unclear′ly.**—*n.* **unclear′ness.**—*v.t.* and *v.i.* **unclench′**, to release or relax from clenching.—*adj.* **uncler′ical**, not characteristic of, or befitting, a clergyman.—*v.t.* **unclew′**, to unwind, unfold, undo.—*adj.* **un-clipped′, unclipt′.**—*v.t.* **uncloak′**, to divest of a cloak : to show up.—*v.i.* to take one's cloak off.— *v.t.* **unclog′**, to free from a clog.—*adj.* **unclogged′**, not clogged.—*v.t.* **unclois′ter**, to free or remove from the cloister.—*adj.* **unclois′tered**, not cloistered : without a cloister : freed or taken from a cloister.—*v.t.* and *v.i.* **unclose** (*un-klōz′*), to open. —*adjs.* **unclose** (*un-klōs′*), not close ; **unclosed′** (*un-klōzd′*), not closed : unenclosed : opened.— *v.t.* **unclothe′**, to take the clothes off : to divest.— *adj.* **unclothed′**.—*v.t.* and *v.i.* **uncloud′**, to clear of clouds or obscurity.—*adj.* **uncloud'ed.**—*n.* **uncloud'edness.**—*adjs.* **uncloud'y**; **unclub(b)'-able.**—*v.t.* **unclutch'**, to release from a clutch.—*adj.* **unco** (*ung'kə, -kā, -kō*; *Scot.*, from **uncouth**), strange, unusual: fearsome: remarkable: great.—*n.* a stranger: a piece of news: a remarkable thing.—*adv.* remarkably, very (**unco guid**, the obtrusively rigorous in morals).—*v.t.* **uncock'**, to let down the hammer of: to spread out from a hay-cock.—*adj.* **uncoff'ined**, not put into a coffin: removed from a coffin.—*v.t.* and *v.i.* **uncoil'**, to unwind.—*adjs.* **uncoined'**, not coined: (*Shak.* **uncoyned**) variously explained as not current everywhere (' without the gift to woo in other places '), not previously stamped or impressed by another woman, not counterfeit, unalloyed, unfeigned; **uncollect'ed**; **uncol'oured.**—*v.t.* **colt'**, (*Shak.*, punningly) to deprive of a horse.—*adj.* **uncombed'**, not combed.—*v.t.* and *v.i.* **uncombine'**, to separate.—*adj.* **uncom(e)atable** (*un-kum-at'ə-bl*), inaccessible: out of reach.—*n.* **uncome'liness.**—*adjs.* **uncome'ly**, not comely: indecent: unseemly; **uncom'fortable**, feeling, involving, or causing discomfort or disquiet.—*n.* **uncom'fortableness.**—*adv.* **uncom'fortably.**—*adjs.* **uncom'forted**; **uncommend'able.**—*adv.* **uncommend'ably.**—*adjs.* **uncommend'ed**; **uncommer'cial**; **uncommitt'ed**; **uncomm'on**, not common: unusual: remarkably great: strange. —*adv.* (*old slang*) remarkably, very.—*adv.* **uncomm'only**, rarely (esp. in litotes): in an unusually great degree.—*n.* **uncomm'onness.**—*adjs.* **uncommu'nicable**; **uncommu'nicated**; **uncommu'nicative.**—*n.* **uncommu'nicativeness.** —*adjs.* **uncommu'ted**; **uncompact'ed**; **uncom'panied**, unaccompanied; **uncompan'ionable**, unsociable; **uncompan'ioned**, without a companion or an equal; **uncompass'ionate**; **uncompelled'**; **uncom'pensated**; **uncomplain'ing.**—*adv.* **uncomplain'ingly.**—*adj.* **uncom'plaisant.** — *adv.* **uncom'plaisantly.**—*adjs.* **uncomplet'ed**; **uncompliment'ary**, far from complimentary; **uncomply'ing**; **uncompos'able**, incapable of being composed or reconciled; **uncompound'ed**, not compounded, simple; **uncomprehend'ed**; **uncomprehend'ing**; **uncomprehen'sive**, not comprehensive: incomprehensive: (*Shak.*) incomprehensible; **uncom'promising**, refusing to compromise: unyielding: out-and-out. — *adv.* **uncom'promisingly.** — *n.* **uncom'promisingness.**—*adjs.* **unconceal'able**; **unconcealed'**; **unconceal'ing**; **unconceiv'-able**, inconceivable.—*n.* **unconceiv'ableness.**—*adv.* **unconceiv'ably.**—*adj.* **unconceived'.**—*n.* **unconcern'**, want of concern or interest: indifference. — *adj.* **unconcerned'**, not concerned: untroubled: uninterested: indifferent: carelessly secure: (*obs.*) sober, unaffected by liquor.—*adv.* **unconcern'edly.**—*n.* **unconcern'edness.**—*adj.* **unconcern'ing.**—*n.* **unconcern'ment.**—*adjs.* **unconcert'ed**; **unconcil'iatory**; **unconclu'sive**, inconclusive; **unconcoct'ed**, not digested: crude: immature; **uncondi'tional**, not conditional, absolute, unlimited.—*n.* **unconditional'ity.**—*adv.* **uncondi'tionally.** — *n.* **uncondi'tionalness.** — *adjs.* **uncondi'tioned**, not subject to condition or limitation: infinite, absolute, unknowable: not conditioned by previous experience: not put in good order; **unconfed'erated**; **unconfessed'**; **unconfin'able,** not to be confined: (*Shak.*) unbounded. —*v.t.* **unconfine'**, to release from restraint: (*Keats*) to give vent to, divulge.—*adj.* **unconfined'**, not confined: not restricted: unlimited: set free. — *adv.* **unconfin'edly.** — *adjs.* **unconfirmed'**, not confirmed: not yet having received confirmation: not yet firm or strong; **unconform'**, (*Milt.*) not conformed, unlike.—*n.* **unconformabil'ity**, the state of being unconformable: (*geol.*) a breach of continuity in bedding.—*adj.* **unconfor'mable.**—*n.* **unconfor'mableness.**—*adv.* **unconfor'mably.**—*adj.* **unconfor'ming**, not conforming.—*n.* **unconfor'mity**, want of conformity: nonconformity: (*geol.*) an unconformability.— *adj.* **unconfused'.**—*adv.* **unconfu'sedly.**—*v.t.* and *v.i.* **uncongeal'**, to thaw, melt.—*adj.* **uncon-**

ge'nial. — *n.* **uncongenial'ity.** — *adjs.* **unconject'ured**; **uncon'jugal**; **unconjunc'tive**, impossible to be joined; **unconnect'ed**; **unconniv'ing** (*Milt.*); **unconq'uerable.**—*n.* **unconquerableness.** — *adv.* **uncon'querably.** — *adjs.* **unconq'uered**; **unconscien'tious.**—*adv.* **unconscien'tiously.**—*n.* **unconscien'tiousness.** —*adj.* **uncon'scionable**, unscrupulous: arrant: not conformable to conscience: unreasonable: inordinate.—*n.* **uncon'scionableness.**—*adv.* **uncon'scionably.** — *adj.* **uncon'scious**, without consciousness: unaware: not self-conscious.—*n.* the inaccessible and repressed part of the mind.— *adv.* **uncon'sciously.**—*n.* **uncon'sciousness.**— *v.t.* **uncon'secrate**, to deprive of consecrated character.—*adj.* **unconsecrated.**—*adjs.* **uncon'secrated**, not consecrated; **unconsenta'neous**, not consentaneous; **unconsent'ing**; **unconsid'ered**, not esteemed: done without considering; **unconsid'ering**; **unconsoled'**; **unconsol'idated**; **uncon'stant**, (*Shak.*) inconstant; **unconstitu'tional.**—*n.* **unconstitutional'ity.**—*adv.* **unconstitu'tionally.**—*adjs.* **unconstrain'able**; **unconstrained'.**—*adv.* **unconstrain'edly.**—*n.* **unconstraint'**, absence of constraint.—*adjs.* **unconsumed'**; **uncontam'inated**; **uncontemned'** (*Shak.*); **uncon'templated**; **unconten'tious**; **uncontest'able**, incontestable; **uncontest'ed**; **uncontradict'ed**; **uncontroll'able**, not capable of being controlled: indisputable.—*n.* **uncontroll'ableness.**—*adv.* **uncontroll'ably.**—*adj.* **uncontrolled'.**—*adv.* **uncontroll'edly.**—*adjs.* **uncontrovert'ed**, not disputed; **uncontrovert'ible**; **unconven'tional**, not conventional: free in one's ways. — *n.* **unconventional'ity.** — *adjs.* **unconvers'able**, not able or not disposed to converse freely; **uncon'versant**, not conversant; **unconvert'ed**; **unconvert'ible**; **unconvict'ed**; **unconvinced'**; **unconvin'cing**; **uncooked'.**—*v.t.* **uncope'**, to unmuzzle, or unsew the mouth of (a ferret; cf. **uncape**).—*adj.* **uncoquett'ish.**—*v.t.* **uncord'**, to free from cords.—*adj.* **uncord'ial.**— *v.t.* **uncork'**, to draw the cork from.—*adjs.* **uncorrect'ed**; **uncorrob'orated**; **uncorrupt'**, incorrupt; **uncorrupt'ed**; **uncost'ly**, inexpensive; **uncoun'selled**, not advised; **uncount'able**, innumerable; **uncount'ed.**—*v.t.* **uncoup'le**, to loose from being coupled: to disjoin: to set loose. —*v.i.* to uncouple hounds.—*adjs.* **uncoup'led**, not coupled: not married: loosed from coupling; **uncour'teous**, not courteous.—*adv.* **uncour'-teously.**—*n.* **uncourt'liness.**—*adjs.* **uncourt'ly**, not courtly; **uncouth** (*un-kōōth'*; O.E. *uncúth*, unknown, strange—*un-*, *cúth*, known), unfamiliar: awkward, ungraceful, esp. in manners or language, grotesque, odd.—*adv.* **uncouth'ly.**—*n.* **uncouth'ness.**—*adj.* **uncov'enanted**, not promised or bound by covenant: not included in a covenant: not having subscribed to the Solemn League and Covenant of 1643.—*v.t.* **uncov'er**, to remove the cover of: to lay open: to expose: to drive out of cover.—*v.i.* to take off the hat.—*adj.* **uncov'ered**, not covered: with cover removed: exposed: bareheaded.—*v.t.* **uncowl'**, to withdraw the cowl from.—*adj.* **uncowled'**, without a cowl. —*v.t.* **uncreate'**, to deprive of existence.—*adj.* **uncrea'ted**, not yet created: not produced by creation.—*n.* **uncrea'tedness.**—*adjs.* **uncrea'ting** (*Pope*); **uncred'ible**, (*obs.*) incredible; **uncred'itable**, (*obs.*) discreditable; **uncrit'ical**, not critical, without rigorous discrimination: not in accordance with the principles of criticism.—*adv.* **uncrit'ically.** —*adj.* **uncropped'.**—*v.t.* **uncross'**, to change from a crossed position.—*adj.* **uncrossed'**, not crossed: (*Shak.*) not marked off as paid.—*v.t.* **uncrown'**, to deprive of a crown, to dethrone: to divest of a crown. — *adjs.* **uncrowned'**, not crowned: without a crown: not yet formally crowned: possessing kingly power without the actual title and dignity: unfulfilled; **uncrudd'ed,** (*Spens.*) uncurdled; **uncrystallis'able**; **uncrys'tallised.**

unction, *ungk'shən, n.* an anointing: that which is used for anointing: ointment: that quality in language which raises emotion or devotion:

warmth of address : religious glibness : divine or sanctifying grace : gusto.—*n.* unctūos'ity, unctuousness.—*adj.* unc'tūous, oily : greasy : full of unction : offensively suave and smug.—*adv.* unc'tūously. — *n.* unc'tūousness. — extreme unction (*R.C.Church*), the sacrament of anointing with consecrated oil in one's last hours. [L. *unctiō*, *-ōnis*, unction, besmearing, *ūnctum*, fat.]

un- (*continued*).—*adjs.* uncuck'olded, not made a cuckold; unculled', not gathered; uncult'ivable; uncul'tivated; uncul'tured, not cultured: not cultivated; uncum'bered; uncur'able, (*Shak.*) incurable; uncurb'able, not able to be curbed; uncurbed', not curbed: without a curb; uncurd'led, not curdled; uncured'; uncu'rious, incurious: not strange.—*v.t.* and *v.i.* uncurl', to take or come out of curl: to untwine, unroll, untwist, straighten out.—*adjs.* uncurled', not curled: unrolled, uncoiled; uncurl'ing, not curling: opening out of curl; uncurr'ent, not current.—*v.t.* uncurse', to free from a curse, unsay a curse upon.—*adj.* uncurtailed'.—*v.t.* uncur'tain, to remove a curtain from.—*adj.* uncur'tained, curtainless.

uncus, ung'kos, *n.* a hook or hook-like process :—*pl.* unci (*un'sī*). [L. *uncus*, a hook.]

un- (*continued*).—*adjs.* uncus'tomed, not having paid customs duty: unaccustomed: not customary; uncut', not cut: of a book, bibliographically, with margins not cut down by the binder (even though opened with a paper-cutter): popularly, unopened.—*v.t.* undam', to free from a dam.—*adjs.* undam'aged, not damaged; undammed', not dammed: let loose; undamned'; undamped', not damped; undashed', undismayed. undate, *un'dāt*, un'dated, *-id*, *adjs.* wavy. [L. *unda*, a wave.]

un- (*continued*).—*adjs.* undāt'ed, with no date marked or assigned: unending; undaunt'ed, not daunted: bold, intrepid.—*adv.* undaun'tedly. —*n.* undaun'tedness.—*adj.* undawn'ing, not yet dawning or showing light.—*v.i.* undazz'le, to recover from a dazed state.—*adj.* undazz'led, not dazzled.

undé, unde. See undee.

un- (*continued*).—*v.t.* undeaf', (*Shak.*) to free from deafness.—*adjs.* undear', undebarred', undebased', undebauched', undecayed', undeceiv'able, not dear, debarred, &c.—*v.t.* undeceive', to free from deception or mistake.—*adjs.* undeceived', not deceived: set free from a deception; unde'cent, indecent: unbecoming: uncomely: unfitting; undecid'able; undecid'ed.—*adv.* undecid'edly.

undecimal, *un-des'i-mol*, *adj.* based on the number eleven.—*n.* undec'imole, (*mus.*) a group of eleven notes in the time of eight. [L. *undecim*, eleven: *unus*, one, *decem*, ten.]

un- (*continued*).—*adjs.* undeci'pherable, indecipherable; undeci'sive, indecisive.—*v.t.* undeck', to divest of ornaments.—*adjs.* undecked', not adorned: having no deck; undeclared'; undeclin'ing, unbowed, unsubmissive; undecompos'able; undecomposed'.

undee, undée, undé, *un'dā*, *adj.* (*her.*) wavy. [Fr. *ondé*; cf. oundy, undate.]

un- (*continued*).—*adjs.* undeed'ed, (*Shak.*) unused in any action; undefaced'; undefeat'ed; undef'ecated, unrefined; undefend'ed; undefied' (*Spens.* undefide'), not defied or challenged; undefiled', undefin'able; undefined', not defined: indefinite.—*v.t.* undē'ify, to deprive of the nature or honour of a god.—*adjs.* undelayed'; undelay'ing; undelect'able; undel'egated; undelib'erate.—*n.* undelight', lack of delight.—*adjs.* undelight'ed; undelight'ful; undeliv'-ered; undelud'ed; undemand'ed; undemocrat'ic; undemon'strative. — *n.* undemon'-strativeness. — *adj.* undeni'able, not to be denied, refused, or objected to: true.—*n.* undeni'ableness.—*adv.* undeni'ably.—*adj.* undenomina'tional, not confined to or favouring any particular sect.—*n.* undenomina'tionalism.—*adj.* undepend'able (a word rejected by some as formed neither from a noun nor a transitive verb),

not to be depended upon.—*n.* undepen'dableness. —*adjs.* undepen'ding, (*obs.*) independent; undeplored'; undepraved'; undepre'ciated; undepressed'; undeprived'.

under, *un'dər*, *prep.* beneath: below: in or to a position lower than that of, especially vertically lower: at the foot of: within, on the covered side of: short of: in or into subjection, subordination, obligation, liability, &c., to: in course of: in the state of: by the authority or attestation of: in accordance with: in the aspect of: referred to the class, heading, name, &c., of: in the reign or administration of.—*adv.* in or to a lower (esp. vertically lower) position: in or into a lower degree or condition: in or into subjection: in or into a covered, submerged, or hidden state: below.—*adj.* lower: subordinate: falling short.—go, knock, snow under (see these words); under age, arms, &c. (see these words); under the lee, to the leeward. [O.E. *under*; Goth. *undar*, O.N. *undir*, Ger. *unter*, L. *infrā*.]

underact', *v.t.* and *v.i.* to act with too little action, or inadequately.—*ns.* underac'tion, subordinate action: less than normal or adequate action; underact'or.—*adj.* un'der-age', not of full age: immature.—*n.* undera'gent, a subordinate agent. —*adj.* and *adv.* underarm', placed or held under the arm: with the arm below the shoulder.—*v.t.* underbear', (*Shak.*) to sustain: (*Shak.*, *pa.p.* underborne) perh. to trim (on the lower part), perh. to line or support by a foundation, perh. to have sewn underneath or on strips of tinsel.—*ns.* un'derbearer, (*dial.*) one who helps to carry a coffin; underbear'ing.—*adj.* unassuming.—*v.t.* un'derbid', to offer at a price lower than that of: to outbid: (*bridge*) to bid less than the value of. —*v.i.* to bid unduly low.—*n.* (*bridge*) a bid too low to be valid, or less than the hand is worth.—*n.* underbidd'er, one who underbids: the next below the highest bidder.—*v.t.* un'derbite', to bite insufficiently with acid, as in etching.—*adj.* un'derbitt'en.—*adv* un'der-board, (*obs.*) secretly —opp. to above-board.—*ns.* un'derbough, a lower branch; un'der-boy, a boy in the lower school; un'derbreath, a subdued voice: rumour. —*adj.* un'derbred', of inferior breeding or manners: not pure-bred.—*ns.* un'derbridge, a bridge carrying a road or railway, distinguished from one over it; un'derbrush, undergrowth of brushwood or shrubs.—*v.t.* to clear of underbrush. —*v.t.* underbuild', to build under in support, underpin: build too little upon or in.—*n.* un'der-builder, a subordinate or assistant builder.—*n.* and *v.t.* [un'derbush, underbrush.—*v.t.* un'der-buy', to buy at less than the price paid by, or the value of.—*ns.* un'dercarriage, the supporting framework under the body of a carriage or wagon: the landing-gear of an aircraft, or its main part; un'dercast, an air-passage crossing under a road in a mine; un'dercharge, too small a charge.— *v.t.* un'dercharge', to charge too little, or too little for.—*adj.* underclad', not wearing clothes enough.—*ns.* un'derclay, a bed of clay underlying a coal-seam representing the soil in which the plants grew; un'der-clerk, a subordinate clerk; un'der-clerk'ship; un'dercliff, a terrace of material that has fallen from a cliff.—*v.t.* un'der-clothe, to provide with underclothing.—*adj.* un'derclothed, provided with underclothing: (*-klōdhd'*) underclad.—*n.pl.* un'derclothes, and *n.sing.* un'derclothing, clothes worn under others, esp. the undermost.—*ns.* un'dercoat, a coat worn under another: (*obs.*) an underskirt: an underlayer of fur or hair, or of paint; un'dercook.— *v.t.* un'dercool, to supercool: to cool insufficiently.—*ns.* un'der-coun'tenance, (*Wordsworth*) that which underlies the superficial aspect of the face; un'dercovert, a covert of undergrowth; un'der-craft, (*Sterne*) a sly trick.—*v.t.* un'dercrest', (*Shak.*) to bear like a crest.—*ns.* un'dercroft (cf. Du. *krocht*, crypt), a crypt, vault; un'dercurrent, a current under the surface.—*adj.* running below or unseen.—*v.t.* undercut', to cut under: to cut away under the surface, so as to leave part overhanging: to undermine: to strike with a heavy blow upward : to underbid : to go beyond in lowering prices.—*adj.* made so as to cut from the underside : effected by undercutting : having the parts in relief cut under.—*ns.* **un'dercut**, the act or effect of cutting under : a blow dealt upward : the tenderloin, or fillet, or underside of a sirloin ; **un'derdeck**, a lower deck.—*v.t.* **underdevel'op**, to develop insufficiently.—*adj.* **underdevel'oped.**—*n.* **underdevel'opment.**—*v.t.* **underdo'**, to do, perform, act, or esp. cook, insufficiently or inadequately :—*pa.t.* **underdid'** ; *pa.p.* **underdone'.** —*ns.* **underdo'er** ; **un'derdog'**, the dog that gets the worst of it in a fight : any one in adversity.—*adj.* **underdone'**, done less than is requisite : insufficiently or slightly cooked.—*vs.t.* **underdrain'**, to drain by deep ditches ; **un'derdraw'**, to draw or describe with moderation or reticence or short of the truth : to cover the underside of with boards or lath and plaster.—*n.* **un'derdress**, underclothing : a dress or part of a dress worn or showing under another.—*v.t.* and *v.i.* **underdress'**, to dress too plainly or simply.—*adjs.* **underdressed'** ; **under-driv'en**, driven from beneath ; **un'derearth**, underground.—*ns.* **underemploy'ment**, shortness of work ; **un'der-espi'al**, a subordinate spy.—*v.t.* **underes'timate**, to estimate or value too low.—*n.* an estimate that falls short of the truth or true quantity.—*v.t.* **underexpose'**, to expose too little, esp. (*phot.*) to light.—*n.* **un'derexpo'sure.**—*adj.* **un'derfed'.**—*v.t.* and *v.i.* **un'derfeed'**, to feed inadequately.—*vs.t.* **un'derfire'**, to fire or bake insufficiently ; **underfong'**, (*Spens.*) to undertake : (*Spens.*) to overcome, entrap (O.E. *underfangen*, pa.p. of *underfon*, to receive, take, steal).—*adv.* **underfoot'**, beneath one's feet.—*v.t.* to underpin.—*adj.* (*un'*) downtrodden.—*ns.* **un'derfur**, short fur hidden by longer hairs ; **un'dergarment**, any article of clothing worn under another.—*v.t.* **undergird'**, to brace with ropes under the bottom.—*adj.* **un'derglaze**, applied or done before glazing (as *underglaze painting* in a vitrifiable pigment before the glaze is applied).—*v.t.* **undergo'**, to be subjected to : to endure or suffer : to pass through, experience : (*Shak.*) to enjoy, partake of : (*Shak.*) to take in hand.—*adj.* **undergo'ing**, (*Shak.*) enduring. — *ns.* **un'dergown**, a gown worn under another ; **undergrad'uate**, a student who has not taken any degree.—*adj.* pertaining to such.—*ns.* **undergrad'uateship** ; **undergraduette'**, a slang feminine of *undergraduate.*—*adj.* **un'derground**, under the surface of the ground : secret.—*n.* the underworld : an underground place : an underground railway : underlying ground : low ground : a secret resistance, movement, or body of people.—*adv.* **underground'**, beneath the surface of the earth : secretly.—*n.* **un'dergrove**, a grove of low trees under taller trees.—*adj.* **un'dergrown**, undersized, stunted.—*n.* **un'dergrowth**, low plants growing under taller, esp. shrubs under trees : copsewood : stunted growth. — *adv.* **underhand'**, surreptitiously : with the hand below the elbow or shoulder. —*adj.* **un'derhand**, surreptitious : secret : unobtrusive : insidious : delivered underhand.—*n.* an underhand ball : inferiority, disadvantage.— *adj.* and *adv.* **underhan'ded**, underhand : short of hands.—*adv.* **underhan'dedly.**—*ns.* **underhan'dedness** ; **un'der-hang'man.**—*adjs.* **un'derhon'est**, (*Shak.*) not quite honest ; **underhung'** (or *un'*), (of a lower jaw) protruding : having a protruding lower jaw : running on rollers on a rail below.—*n.* **un'der-jaw'**, the lower jaw.—*adj.* **un'derjawed**, with a heavy or underhung underjaw.—*v.t.* **un'derkeep'**, (*Spens.*) to keep under or in subjection.—*ns.* **un'derkeep'er**, an assistant keeper ; **un'derking**, a subordinate king ; **un'derkingdom.**—*adjs.* **underlaid'** (see **underlay**, 2) ; **underlain'** (see **underlie**).—*vs.t.* **underlap'**, to extend beneath and some way beyond the edge of ; **underlay'**, *pa.t.* of **underlie** ; **underlay'**, to support or furnish with something laid under : to lay under : (*Spens.*) to put down, surpass : often erroneously for **underlie**.—*v.i.* (*mining*) to hade :— *pa.t.* and *pa.p.* **underlaid'.**—*ns.* **un'derlay**, something laid under, esp. (*printing*) a piece of paper,

&c., pasted under to bring to type-height ; **underlay'er**, one who underlays : (*un'*) a lower layer, substratum ; **un'derlease**, a sublease.—*v.t.* and *v.i.* **underlease'**, to sublease.—*v.t.* **underlet'**, to let below the full value : to sublet.—*ns.* **underlett'er** ; **underlett'ing.**—*v.t.* **underlie'**, to lie beneath : to undergo : to be subject or liable to : (*pr.p.* **underly'ing** ; *pa.t.* **underlay'** ; *pa.p.* **underlain'**).—*n.* (*mining*) a hade.—*v.t.* **underline'**, to draw a line under : to stress.—*n.* (*un'*) a caption, legend.—*ns.* **un'derlinen**, underclothing, properly of linen ; **un'derling**, a contemptuous word for a subordinate, an understrapper : a weakling ; **un'derlip**, a lower lip ; **un'derlooker**, a mine manager's assistant.—*adj.* **underly'ing**, lying beneath : supporting : fundamental.—*n.* **un'derman**, an inferior : a subordinate : a man subjected to adverse conditions.—*v.t.* **underman'**, to man with too few.—*adjs.* **undermanned'** ; **undermast'ed**, with masts too small ; **undermen'tioned**, mentioned underneath or hereafter.—*v.t.* **undermine'** (*Spens.* **underminde'**), to form mines under, in order to destroy : to remove the ground from under : to seek or tend to the overthrow of : to intrigue against : to tamper with the fidelity of.—*ns.* **undermi'ner** ; **undermi'ning.**—*adj.* and *adv.* **un'dermost**, lowest : inmost.—*adv.* in or to the undermost place.

undern, *un'darn*, *n.* (*obs.*) the third hour, about nine in the morning : terce : the forenoon : the afternoon or early evening : a light meal.—*n.* **un'derntime** (*Spens.* **un'dertime**), time of the midday meal. [O.E. *undern.*]

under- (*continued*)—*adv.* and *prep.* **underneath'**, beneath, below (in place).—*n.* the under part or side.—*ns.* **un'dernice'ness**, want of niceness or delicacy ; **un'dernote**, a subdued note : an undertone.—*adjs.* **underno'ted**, noted below ; **undernour'ished**, insufficiently nourished ; **underpaid'**.—*ns.* **un'derpass**, (*U.S.*) a subway ; **un'derpassion**, an underlying or subconscious passion.— *v.t.* **underpay'**, to pay insufficiently.—*n.* **underpay'ment.** — *v.t.* **underpeep'**, (*Shak.*) to peep under.—*adj.* **underpeo'pled**, not fully peopled.— *v.t.* **underpin'**, to support by building underneath. —*n.* **underpinn'ing.**—*v.i.* **underplay'**, to play a low card while holding up a higher.—*ns.* **un'derplay**, the act of so doing ; **un'derplot**, a subordinate plot in a play or tale : a secret scheme, a trick ; **un'der-power**, (*Wordsworth*) an auxiliary power.—*vs.t.* **underpraise'**, to praise below desert ; **underprize'**, *obs.* **underprise'**, (*Shak.*) to underpraise : to set too low a value on : to value too little.—*n.* **under-produc'tion**, too little production : production short of demand.—*adj.* **underproof'**, lower or weaker than proof, of alcohol.— *vs.t.* **underprop'**, to put a prop under : to prop up : to support ; **underquote'**, to offer at a price below ; **underrate'**, to rate too low.—*n.* **un'derrate**, a price less than the worth.—*adj.* inferior.— *adj.* **un'der-ripe**, not quite ripe.—*n.* **un'derroof**, a roof under another.—*v.t.* **underrun'**, to run or pass beneath : to take aboard on one side (as a cable, line, net, for examination, clearing, baiting) and put overboard on the other.—*v.i.* to move under : to run on the underside.—*ns.* **underrunn'ing** ; **un'der-saw'yer**, a bottom-sawyer : an inferior, an unimportant person.—*v.t.* **undersay'** (*Spens.* **undersaye'**), to say in answer or contradiction.—*n.* **un'der-school**, the lower or junior school.—*v.t.* **underscore'**, to underline.— *n.* **un'derscrub**, brushwood.—*adj.* **un'der-sea.**— *adv.* **undersea'.**—*ns.* **un'der-sec'retary**, a secretary immediately under the principal secretary ; **under-sec'retaryship** ; **un'derself**, the subconscious self.—*v.t.* **undersell'**, to sell below the price charged by : to sell too cheap.—*ns.* **undersell'er** ; **un'dersense**, a deeper sense : a secondary sense : a subconscious awareness ; **un'derset**, an undercurrent : a lower vein of ore : a set of underclothing.—*v.t.* **underset'**, to set under : to prop : to sublet.—*adj.* **un'dershapen**, imperfectly formed.—*ns.* **un'der-shepherd** ; **un'dersheriff**, a deputy sheriff ; **un'dershirt**, a shirt worn under another.—*adj.* **un'dershot**, driven by water passing under : underhung.—*ns.* **un'dershrub**, a shrubby plant, hardly to be called a shrub, a low shrub ; **un'derside**, the lower surface.—*v.t.* **undersign'**, to sign below.—*adjs.* **un'dersigned** (or -*sīnd'*), whose signature is appended ; **un'dersized**, below the usual or desired size.—*ns.* **un'derskinker**, (*Shak.*) an assistant tapster ; **un'derskirt**, a petticoat : the foundation skirt of a draped gown ; **un'dersky**, a lower sky ; **un'dersleeve**, a sleeve worn under another ; **un'dersoil**, subsoil ; **un'dersong**, a burden, refrain, response : an accompanying body of sound : an accompaniment of undertones.— *adj.* **understaffed'**, having too few members of staff.—*v.t.* **understand'** (O.E. *understandan*), to comprehend : to grasp with the mind : to be fully aware : to be able to follow the working, logic, meaning, &c., of : to have a sympathetic, usu. tacit, perception of the character, aims, &c., of : to know the meaning of : to be expert in : to have knowledge or information of, be aware of, be informed : to assume, take to be true : to interpret, take to mean or to be meant : to imply, supply, or assume to be meant though not expressed : (*refl.* ; *Shak.*) to know how to behave or conduct : (*Shak.*) to stand under : hence, to support.—*v.i.* to have understanding : to comprehend :—*pa.t.* **understood'** ; *pa.p.* **understood'**, (*arch.*) **understand'ed.** —*adj.* **understand'able.**—*ns.* **understand'er**, one who understands : a supporter : (*obs.*) one who stands in the pit of a theatre ; **understand'ing**, the act of comprehending : the power to understand : intellect : an informal agreement : an understood condition : sympathetic or amicable agreement of minds : (*slang* ; in *pl.*) feet, legs, shoes, boots.— *adj.* skilful : intelligent : discerning : sympathetic. —*adv.* **understand'ingly.**—*v.t.* **understate'**, to state at something less than truth would allow or require. — *ns.* **understate'ment** ; **un'derstock**, (*arch.*) a stocking.—*v.t.* **understock'**, to supply with an insufficient amount of stock ; **understood'** (see **understand**).—Also *adj.*—*n.* **un'derstrapper**, an inferior agent, an underling.—*adj.* **un'derstrapping**, subordinate. — *n.* **un'derstrātum**, an underlayer :—*pl.* **un'derstrāta.**—*v.t.* **un'derstudy**, to study the part of, as a substitute for emergencies : to prepare, or be ready, to act as a substitute for.—*n.* a substitute ready to take an actor's (or other's) part.—*v.t.* **undertake'**, (*obs.*) to receive : (*Spens.*) to perceive : (*Shak.*) to assume : to take upon oneself : to pledge oneself : (*Shak.*) to be surety for : to set about, engage in : to take in hand : to take upon oneself to deal with, manage, or look after : to engage in contest with.— *v.i.* to become a surety : (*coll.*) to conduct funerals : —*pa.t.* **undertook'** ; *pa.p.* **underta'ken**, (*Shak.*, &c.) **underta'en'**, (*Spens.*) **undertane'**. — *adj.* **underta'kable.**—*ns.* **un'dertaker**, one who undertakes : one who takes in hand an enterprise, task, or encounter : a projector : a contractor : (*obs.*) a publisher : (*obs.*) a stage producer : (*obs.*) a compiler or editor : one who manages funerals : (*obs.*) a sponsor or surety : (*obs.*) a tax-farmer : (*hist.*) one of the Fife adventurers who tried to colonise the Lewis (*c.* 1600) : one of those who undertook to manage the House of Commons for the Stewart kings : one of the English and Scottish settlers on forfeited lands in Ireland ; **un'dertaking**, that which is undertaken : any business or project engaged in : the business of conducting funerals. —Also *adj.*—*ns.* **un'derten'ancy** ; **un'dertenant**, one who holds of a tenant ; **un'derthirst**, (*Wordsworth*) an underlying or subconscious thirst. **undertime.** See **undertime.** **under-** (*continued*).—*adj.* **un'dertimed'**, underexposed—of a photograph. — *ns.* **un'dertint**, a subdued tint : a tint showing through ; **un'dertone**, a subdued tone of voice, sound, colour, &c. : a tone felt as if pervading, underlying, or perceptible through others : a difference tone : a low state of body.—*adj.* **un'dertoned**, in an undertone : (-*tōnd'*) wanting in tone.—*v.t.* **undertook'** (see **undertake**).—*ns.* **un'dertow** (-*tō*), an undercurrent opposed to the surface current : the recoil or back-draught of a wave ; **un'der-trick**, a trick

short of the number declared ; **un'der-turn'key**, an assistant jailer ; **un'der-tū'nic** ; **undervalua'tion.**—*v.t.* **underval'ue**, to value below the real worth : (*Shak.*) to rate as inferior (with *to*) : to reduce the value of : to esteem lightly.—*n.* (*un'*) a value or price under the real worth.—*ns.* **underval'uer** ; **un'dervest**, an undershirt ; **un'derviewer**, one who has charge of the underground workings of a coal-mine ; **un'dervoice**, a subdued voice ; **un'derwater**, underground water : undertow.— *adj.* submerged : submarine.—*ns.* **un'derwear**, underclothing, **un'derweight**, shortness of weight : short weight.—*adj.* short in weight.— *v.t.* **underwent'**, used as *pa.t.* of **undergo.**—*n.* **un'derwing**, a wing covered by another, as an insect's hind-wing : a moth (Catocala, Tryphaena, &c.) with conspicuous hind-wings.—*adj.* and *adv.* under the wing.—*ns.* **un'derwit**, inferior wit : a half-wit ; **un'derwood**, undergrowth : coppice. —*v.t.* **underwork'**, to undermine : to work secretly against : to employ too little in work : to work for less than the wage of.—*v.i.* to do less work than is desirable.—*ns.* **un'derwork**, a substructure : underhand, inferior, or subordinate work ; **un'derworker** ; **un'der-work'man** ; **un'derworld**, the world beneath the heavens : the world, or a region, beneath the earth : the place of departed souls : the portion of the world below the horizon : the antipodes : a submerged, hidden, or secret region or sphere of life, esp. one given to crime, profligacy, or intrigue.—*v.t.* **un'derwrite**, to write beneath : to subscribe : to subscribe to : (*Shak.*) to agree to : to accept the risk of insuring : to write too little about : (*refl.*) to write below the level of.—*v.i.* to practise as an underwriter.—*ns.* **un'derwriter**, one who practises insurance business, esp. in ships ; **un'derwriting.** —*v.t.* **underwrought'**, *pa.t.* and *pa.p.* of **underwork.**

un- (*continued*).—*adjs.* **undescend'ible** (also -**able**), not descendible ; **undescri'bable**, indescribable ; **undescribed'** ; **undescried'**. — *n.* **un'desert**, want of desert, unworthiness.—*v.t.* **un'deserve'**, to fail or cease to deserve.—*adj.* **undeserved'**, not deserved. — *adv.* **undeser'vedly.** — *ns.* **undeser'vedness** ; **undeser'ver**, (*Shak.*) one who is not deserving or worthy.—*adj.* **undeser'ving.**— *adv.* **undeser'vingly.**—*adj.* **undesigned'.**—*adv.* **undesign'edly.**—*n.* **undesign'edness.**—*adj.* **undesign'ing**, not designing : artless : straightforward : sincere.—*n.* **undesirabil'ity.**—*adj.* **undesi'rable**, not to be wished for.—*n.* an undesirable or objectionable person or thing.—*n.* **undesir'ableness.**—*adv.* **undesi'rably.**—*adjs.* **undesired'** ; **undesir'ing** ; **undesir'ous** ; **undespair'ing.**— *adv.* **undespair'ingly.**—*adjs.* **undespoiled'** ; **undestroyed'** ; **undetect'ed** ; **undeter'minable**, indeterminable ; **undeter'minate**, indeterminate. —*ns.* **undeter'minateness** ; **undetermina'tion.** —*adjs.* **undeter'mined** ; **undeterred'** ; **undevel'oped**, not developed : of land, not built on or used for public works ; **unde'viating.**—*adv.* **unde'viatingly.**—*adj.* **undevout'.**—*v.t.* **undid'**, *pa.t.* of **undo.**

undies, *un'diz*, *n.pl.* (*vulg.*) women's underclothing. [under.]

un- (*continued*).—*adjs.* **undiff'erenced**, (*her.*) without a modification to distinguish a cadet from the main line ; **undiffer'entiated**, not differentiated ; **undigest'ed.**—*v.t.* **undight**, (*un-dīt'* ; *Spens.*), to undo, take off, doff (*pa.t.* and *pa.p.* **undight'**).— *adj.* unadorned : (*Spens.*) not set in order or dressed, loose.—*adj.* **undig'nified.**—*v.t.* **undig'nify**, to deprive of dignity.—*adjs.* **undilu'ted** ; **undimin'ishable**, not to be diminished ; **undimin'ished.**

undine, *un'dēn*, *un'dīn* (Ger. *oon-dē'na*), *n.* according to Paracelsus, a water-spirit that can obtain a human soul by bearing a child to a human husband. [L. *unda*, a wave.]

un- (*continued*).—*adjs.* **undint'ed** ; **undipped'**, not dipped : unbaptised ; **undirect'ed** ; **undiscerned'.** — *adv.* **undiscern'edly.** — *adj.* **undiscern'ible.**—*adv.* **undiscern'ibly.**—*adj.* **undiscern'ing**, failing to discern.—*n.* want of discernment.—*adjs.* **undischarged'** ; **undisc'ip-**

linable.—*n.* undisc'ipline, lack of discipline.—
adjs. undisc'iplined, untrained: unruly;
disclosed'; undiscom'fited; undiscord'ant;
undiscording (*Milt.*); undiscour'aged; undiscov'erable. — *adv.* undiscov'erably. — *adjs.*
undiscov'ered; undiscrim'inating; undis-
cuss'able, -ible; undiscussed', (*obs.*) unsettled:
not discussed; undisguis'able; undisguised',
not disguised: frank, open, plain.—*adv.* undisguis'edly. — *adjs.* undishon'oured; undis-
mant'led; undismayed'; undisor'dered; un-
dispatched'; undispensed'; undisposed', not
disposed (usu. with -of): (*Shak.*) disinclined: undispu'ted.—*adv.* undispu'tedly.—*adjs.* undis-
sem'bled, unfeigned: undisguised, unconcealed:
undissolved'; undissol'ving; undistemp'ered';
undistilled'; undistinc'tive, undistinguishing:
undisting'uishable, indistinguishable. — *n.* undisting'uishableness.—*adv.* undisting'uishably.
—*adjs.* undisting'uished, not distinguished: not
marked out by conspicuous qualities: not famous:
not having an air or appearance of distinction;
undisting'uishing, not discriminating; undis-
tort'ed; undistract'ed.—*adv.* undistract'edly.
—*n.* undistract'edness.—*adjs.* undistract'ing;
undistrib'uted, not distributed (undistributed
middle, the fallacy of reasoning without distributing the middle term, i.e. without making it
universal, in at least one premise); undisturbed',
— *adv.* undistur'bedly. — *adjs.* undisturb'ing;
undivers'ified; undivert'ed, not turned away:
not amused; undivert'ing; undivest'ed (with
meaningless or merely emphatic pfx.; *Richardson*),
detached.—*adv.* undivest'edly.—*adjs.* undivid'-
able, indivisible; undivi'ded. — *adv.* undivi'dedly.—*n.* undivi'dedness.—*adjs.* undivine';
undivorced'; undivulged'.—*v.t.* undo (un-dōō')
to reverse the doing of: to bring back to the former
state: to annul: to bring to naught: (*Shak.*) to
prevent the happening or being of: to loose: to
open: to unravel: to unfasten: to solve: to
injure seriously: to impoverish: to beggar: to
ruin: to seduce.—*v.i.* to come undone: to reverse
what has been done:—*pa.t.* undid'; *pa.p.* undone (un-dun').—*v.t.* undock', to take out of dock.
—*adjs.* undocked', not docked or cut short; un-
doc'tored, without a doctor's degree: not patched
up, tampered with, or sophisticated.—*ns.* undoer
(un-dōō'ər), one who undoes: one who ruins: a
seducer; undo'ing, the reversal of what has been
done: unfastening: opening: ruin or cause of
ruin.—*adj.* undomes'tic, not domestic: not content with, adapted to, or relating to, home life:
unhomelike.—*v.t.* undomes'ticate, to make un-
domestic: to untame.—*adjs.* undomes'ticated,
not domesticated: not tamed: emancipated from
mere domestic interests; undone (un-dun'),
not done: annulled: brought to naught: loosed:
opened: ruined: seduced; undoomed'.—*v.t.*
and *v.i.* undou'ble, to unfold, open out.—*adjs.*
undoubt'able, indubitable; undoubt'ed, not
doubted: unquestioned: certainly genuine or such
as is represented: indubitable.—*adv.* undoubt'-
edly.—*adjs.* undoubt'ful; undoubt'ing.—*adv.*
undoubt'ingly. — *adjs.* undrain'able; un-
drained'; undramat'ic; undraped', without
drapery: nude.—*v.t.* and *v.i.* undraw', to draw
back.—*adjs.* undrawn', not drawn: not milked:
drawn back; undread'ed; undread'ing; un-
dreamed'(-of), undreamt(-of, -dremt'), not
dreamt (of); undream'ing. — *v.t.* undress',
to remove the clothes or dressing from.—*v.i.*
to take off one's clothes.—*n.* un'dress, ordinary, informal, or loose dress: uniform for ordinary
occasions. — Also *adj.* — *adj.* undressed', not
dressed: divested of clothes.—*n.* undress'ing.—
adjs. undried'; undrilled'; undrink'able; un-
driv'en; undroop'ing; undross'y; un-
drowned'; undrunk'; undubbed'; undue',
not due or owing: unjustifiable: unwarranted:
inappropriate: excessive; undug'.
undulate, un'dū-lāt, *v.t.* and *v.i.* to move like or in
waves: to make or be wavy: to vibrate.—*adj.*
wavy: with wavy margin, surface, or markings.
—Also un'dulated.—*n.* un'dulancy.—*adj.* un'-
dulant, undulating: rising and falling.—*adv.*
un'dulately.—*adj.* un'dulating.—*adv.* un'dulat-
ingly.—*ns.* undulā'tion, an undulating, a wave-
like motion or form: waviness: a wave; undulā'-
tionist, one who holds the undulatory theory of
light.—*adjs.* un'dulatory, of the nature of undulation: undulating: wavy: referring light to
waves in a medium; un'dulose, un'dulous, (*both
rare*) undulating.—undulant fever, Malta, Mediterranean, Neapolitan, or Rock fever, a remittent
fever with swelling of the joints and enlarged
spleen, caused by a bacterium (Brucella) transmitted by goat's (or cow's) milk. [L. *undulātus*,
undulated—*unda*, a wave.]
un- (*continued*).—*adj.* undulled'.—*adv.* undu'ly,
unjustifiably: wrongfully: more than is right:
improperly. — *adjs.* undu'teous, (*Shak.*) unduti-
ful; undu'tiful.—*adv.* undu'tifully.—*n.* undu'-
tifulness.—*adjs.* undyed', not dyed; undy'ing,
not dying: immortal: unceasing.—*adv.* undy'-
ingly.—*n.* undy'ingness.—*adjs.* uneared', (*Shak.*)
not eared, untilled; unearned', not earned by
work: unmerited.—*v.t.* unearth', to dig up,
disinter, lay bare of earth: to bring out of obscurity: to expel from a burrow.—*adj.* unearthed',
dug up: brought to light: driven from a burrow:
not carthed, without an earth.—*n.* unearth'liness.
—*adj.* unearth'ly, preternatural: celestial: weird:
ghostly: unconscionable, preposterous, unreasonable, absurd (esp. of an early hour).—*n.* unease',
lack of ease: discomfort.—*adv.* uneas'ily, uncomfortably: with troubled restlessness.—*n.* uneas'iness, discomfort: lack of easiness of mind:
disquiet.—*adjs.* uneas'y, not at ease: disquieted:
disturbed: restless: constrained: uncomfortable:
(now *rare*) not easy to be done: uneat'able.—*n.*
uneat'ableness.—*adjs.* uneat'en; uneath (*un-
ēth'*; O.E. *unéathe*; see eath; *arch.*), difficult:
distressing.—*adv.* with difficulty: in hardship:
hardly, scarcely: (*Spens.*) almost.—Also (*adv.*)
uneth', uneathes', unnethes'. — *adjs.* un-
eclipsed'; uneconom'ic, not in accordance with
sound economics; uneconom'ical, not economical.—*v.t.* unedge', to blunt.—*adjs.* uned'ifying,
uned'ited, never edited, never before published;
uned'ucable; uned'ucated; uneffaced'; un-
effect'ed; unelab'orate; unelab'orated; un-
elat'ed; unelect'ed; unelec'trified; unem-
barr'assed; unembitt'ered; unembod'ied,
not embodied; unemo'tional.—*adv.* unemo'-
tionally.—*adjs.* unemo'tioned, impassive; un-
emphat'ic; unemploy'able; unemployed',
out of work: not put to use or profit: for or pertaining to those who are out of work.—*n.* unem'-
ploy'ment.—*adjs.* unemp'tied; unenchant'ed
(*Milt.* uninchant'ed); unenclosed' (uninclosed'); unencum'bered (unincum'bered); unen-
dan'gered; unendeared' (*Milt.* unindeared');
unend'ing, endless: ceaseless: everlasting.—*adv.*
unen'dingly. — *n.* unen'dingness. — *adjs.* unendowed'; unendur'able.—*adv.* unendur'ably.
—*adjs.* unengaged'; un-Eng'lish, not English in
character; un-Eng'lished, not translated into
English; unenlight'ened; unenquir'ing; un-
enriched'; unenslaved'; unentailed'; un-
en'tered; unen'terprising; unentertained';
unentertain'ing; unenthralled'; unentit'led;
unen'viable, not to be envied.—*adv.* unen'viably.
—*adjs.* unen'vied; unen'vious; unen'vying;
unē'qual, not equal: varying, not uniform.—*n.*
one who is not equal in rank, ability, &c.—*adj.*
unē'qualled, without an equal.—*adv.* unē'qually.
—*adjs.* unequ'itable, inequitable; unequiv'ocal,
not equivocal.—*adv.* unequiv'ocally.—*adj.* unerr'ing, making no error, infallible: not missing
the mark.—*adv.* unerr'ingly.—*n.* unerr'ingness.
—*adj.* unescap'able.
Unesco, ū-nes'kō, *n.* the United Nations Educational, Scientific, and Cultural Organisation.
[From the initial letters.]
un- (*continued*).—*adjs.* unescort'ed; unespied';
unessayed'.—*v.t.* uness'ence, to deprive of
essence or being.—*adjs.* unessen'tial, without
being: not of the essence: unnecessary: unimportant; unestab'lished, not established: not

on the establishment or permanent staff; **uneth′-ical**; **unevangel′ical**; **unē′ven. —** *adv.* **unē′venly.—***n.* **unē′venness.—***adj.* **unevent′ful.—** *adv.* **unevent′fully.—***adjs.* **unev′idenced**; **unexact′ing**; **unexagg′erated**; **unexalt′ed**; **unexam′ined**; **unexam′pled**, unprecedented; **unex′cavated**; **unexcelled′**; **unexcep′tionable**, not liable to objection.—*n.* **unexcep′tionableness.** —*adv.* **unexcep′tionably.—***adj.* **unexcep′tional**, not admitting or forming an exception.—*adv.* **unexcep′tionally. —** *adjs.* **unexci′table**; **unexci′ting**; **unexclu′ded**; **unexclu′sive. —** *adv.* **unexclu′sively. —** *adjs.* **unex′ecuted**, not executed: (*Shak.*) not brought into action; **unex′ercised**; **unexhaust′ed**; **unexpand′ed**; **unexpect′ant**; **unexpec′ted.—***adv.* **unexpec′tedly. — n. unexpec′tedness. —** *adj.* **unexpens′ive. —** *adv.* **unexpens′ively. —** *adjs.* **unexpē′rienced**, inexperienced; **unexpē′rient,** (*Shak.*) inexperienced; **unexpired′**; **unexplain′-able**; **unexplained′**; **unexplored′**; **unex-posed′**; **unexpressed′**; **unexpress′ible**, inexpressible; **unexpress′ive**, not expressive: (*Shak., Milt.*) inexpressible, beyond the power of description; **unexpug′nable**, inexpugnable; **un-ex′purgated**; **unextend′ed**; **unexten′uated**; **un-extinct′**; **unexting′uishable**, inextinguishable.— *adv.* **unexting′uishably.—***adjs.* **unexting′uished**; **uneyed′**, unnoticed; **unfa′bled**, not fabled, real; **unfa′dable**; **unfa′ded**; **unfa′ding.—***adv.* **unfa′dingly.—***n.* **unfa′dingness.—***adj.* **unfail′ing**, never failing or giving out: infallible: constant: inexhaustible.—*adv.* **unfail′ingly.—***adj.* **unfair′**, not fair: inequitable: biased: unjust: not candid. —*v.t.* (*Shak.*) to deprive of beauty.—*adv.* **unfair′ly. —***ns.* **unfair′ness**; **unfaith′**, want of faith or trust.— *adj.* **unfaith′ful**, not of the approved religion: not faithful: violating trust: not trust-worthy: not true to the original: untrue to wed-lock.—*adv.* **unfaith′fully.—***n.* **unfaith′fulness.—** *adjs.* **unfall′en**; **unfall′ible**, (*Shak.*) infallible; **unfal′tering. —** *adv.* **unfal′teringly.—***adjs.* **un-famed′**, without fame; **unfamil′iar.—***n.* **un-familiar′ity. —** *adv.* **unfamil′iarly. —** *adjs.* **un-fanned′**; **unfash′ionable**, not fashionable: (*obs.*) incapable of being fashioned: (*Shak.*) shapeless.— *n.* **unfash′ionableness.—***adv.* **unfash′ionably.—** *adj.* **unfash′ioned**, unformed: unwrought: crude. —*v.t.* **unfas′ten** (*un-fäs′n*), to loose, as from a fastening: to unfix.—*v.i.* to become loose or open. —*adjs.* **unfas′tened**, loosed: not fastened; **un-fastid′ious**; **unfa′thered**, without a father or acknowledged father: deprived of a father; **unfa′therly**, unbefitting a father; **unfath′omable.** —*n.* **unfath′omableness.—***adv.* **unfath′omably.** —*adjs.* **unfath′omed**, not sounded; **unfault′y**; **unfa′vourable. — n.** **unfa′vourableness. —** *adv.* **unfa′vourably.—***adjs.* **unfeared′**, not feared: (*obs.*) unafraid; **unfear′ful**, not afraid.—*adv.* **unfear′fully.—***adjs.* **unfear′ing**; **unfeas′ible**; **unfeath′ered**; **unfeat′ured**, without marked or well-formed features; **unfeed′**; **unfeed′**, not re-tained by a fee: unpaid; **unfeel′ing**, without feeling: without kind or sympathetic feelings: hard-hearted.—*adv.* **unfeel′ingly.—***n.* **unfeel′-ingness.—***adj.* **unfeigned′**, not feigned or feigning: real: sincere.—*adv.* **unfeign′edly.—***n.* **unfeign′-edness.—***adjs.* **unfeign′ing**; **unfelled′**; **un-fell′owed**, unmatched; **unfelt′**, not felt: (*Shak.*) intangible; **unfem′inine**; **unfenced′**; **unfer-ment′ed**; **unfer′tilised.—***v.t.* **unfett′er**, to free from fetters.—*adjs.* **unfett′ered**, unrestrained; **unfeu′dal**; **unfeued′**; **unfig′ured**; **unfiled′** (*Spens.* **unfilde′**), not rubbed with a file, un-polished; **unfiled′** (now *dial.*), undefiled; **un-filed′**, not placed on a file; **unfil′ial**, unbecoming to a son or daughter.—*adv.* **unfil′ially.—***adjs.* **unfill′able**; **unfilled′**; **unfill′eted**, not bound with a fillet; **unfil′terable, unfil′trable**, unable to pass through a filter (or an ordinary filter); **unfine′**, not fine; **unfin′ished.—***n.* **unfin′ishing**, the leaving unfinished.—*adjs.* **unfired′**; **unfirm′**, not firm; **unfished′**, not fished; **unfit′**, not fit: not fitting or suitable: not in fit condition.—*n.* an **unfit person.—***v.t.* to make unfit: to disable: to

disqualify.—*adv.* **unfit′ly.—***n.* **unfit′ness.—***adj.* **unfitt′ed**, not provided: without fittings: not fitted: not adapted, qualified, or able.—*n.* **un-fitt′edness. —** *adj.* **unfitt′ing**, unsuitable. — *adv.* **unfitt′ingly.—***v.t.* **unfix′**, to loose: to unsettle.— *v.i.* to become loose or lax.—*adj.* **unfixed′.—***ns.* **unfix′edness**; **unfix′ity.—***adj.* **unflagg′ing.—** *adv.* **unflagg′ingly. —** *adj.* **unflatt′ering. —** *adv.* **unflatt′eringly.—***adjs.* **unflawed′**, flawless; **un-fledged′**, not yet fledged: undeveloped: of early youth.—*v.t.* **unflesh′**, to remove the flesh from.— *adjs.* **unfleshed′**, deprived of flesh, reduced to a skeleton: not fleshed, not having tasted blood. uninitiated; **unflesh′ly**, spiritual: incorporeal: not carnal; **unflesh′y**, fleshless: not fleshy; **un-flinch′ing. —** *adv.* **unflinch′ingly. —** *adj.* **un-floored′**, without a floor.—*v.i.* **unflush′**, to lose a flush of colour.—*v.t.* **unfold′**, to open the folds of: to release from a fold: to spread out: to tell: to disclose, reveal, display.—*v.i.* to spread open, expand, develop.—*v.t.* **unfold′**, to let out from a sheep-fold.—*adjs.* **unfold′ed**, not folded: opened out from folds; **unfold′ed**, not enclosed in a sheep-fold.—*n.* **unfold′er.—***n.* and *adj.* **unfold′ing**, open-ing out from folds: disclosing.—*n.* and *adj.* **un-fold′ing**, letting out from a sheep-fold.—*adj.* **unfold′ing**, showing the time for unfolding sheep.—*v.t.* **un-fool′**, to undo the fooling of.—*adjs.* **unfoot′ed**, untrodden; **unforbid′** (*Milt.*), **unforbidd′en**; **unforced′. —** *adv.* **unfor′cedly. —** *adjs.* **unfor′-cible**, without strength: incapable of being forced; **unford′able**; **unforebod′ing**, not giving or feeling foreboding; **unforeknow′able**; **un-foreknown′**, not known beforehand; **unforesee′-able**; **unforesee′ing**; **unforeseen′**; **unfore′-skinned**, (*Milt.*) circumcised; **unfor′ested**, not wooded: not reckoned as forest: deforested; **unforetold′**; **unforewarned′**; **unfor′feited**; **unforged′**; **unforgett′able. —** *adv.* **unforgett′-ably.—***adjs.* **unforgiv′able** (sometimes **unfor-give′able**); **unforgiv′en.—***n.* **unforgive′ness.** —*adj.* **unforgiv′ing.—***n.* **unforgiv′ingness.—***adj.* **unforgott′en** (also **unforgot′**).—*v.t.* **unform′**, to unmake.—*adjs.* **unfor′mal**, informal; **unfor′mal-ised**, not made formal; **unformed′**, unmade, un-created: formless: unshaped: immature: un-developed; **unfor′midable**; **unforsa′ken**; **un-for′tified**; **unfor′tunate**, unlucky: regrettable: of ill omen: euphemistically, given to prostitu-tion.—*n.* an unfortunate person.—*adv.* **unfor′-tunately.—***ns.* **unfor′tunateness**; **unfor′tune.—** *adjs.* **unfor′tuned**; **un′fossilif′erous**; **un′foss′il-ised**; **unfos′tered**; **unfought′** (*arch.* **un-fought′en**); **unfound′**, not found; **unfoun′ded**, not founded: without foundation, baseless: (*Milt.*) without bottom, bottomless.—*adv.* **unfoun′dedly.** —*adjs.* **unframed′**, not formed or fashioned: not set in a frame; **unfran′chised**; **unfranked′**, not franked; **unfraught′**, not fraught or charged.— *v.t.* to unload, discharge.—*adj.* **unfree′**, not free: in servitude: not free of a corporation.—*n.* **unfree′man**, one who is not free of a corporation. —*v.t.* and *v.i.* **unfreeze′.—***adjs.* **unfre′quent**, infrequent; **unfrequen′ted**, not frequented: rarely visited.—*n.* **unfrequent′edness.—***adv.* **un-fre′quently**, infrequently.—*adj.* **unfrett′ed**, not fretted: not eaten away or rubbed.—*n.* **unfriend′**, one who is not a friend.—*adj.* **unfrien′ded**, not provided with or supported by friends.—*ns.* **un-frien′dedness**; **unfriend′liness. —** *adj.* **un-friend′ly**, ill-disposed: somewhat hostile.—*adv.* **unkindly. — n. unfriend′ship**, unfriendliness.— *adjs.* **unfright′ed, unfright′ened.—***v.t.* **unfrock′**, to strip of a frock or gown, depose or degrade from priesthood: to withdraw from the life of a priest or monk.—*adjs.* **unfrocked′**; **unfro′zen**, not frozen: thawed; **unfruc′tuous**, unfruitful; **un-fruit′ful.—***adv.* **unfruit′fully.—***n.* **unfruit′fulness.** —*adjs.* **unfu′elled**; **unfulfilled′**; **unfumed′**, not fumigated: (*Milt.*) undistilled; **unfund′ed**, not funded, floating, as a public debt, in the form of exchequer bills and bonds, to be paid up at certain dates.—*v.t.* **unfurl′**, to loose from being furled: to unfold, display: to spread.—*v.i.* to spread.—*v.t.* **unfur′nish**, (*Shak.*) to deprive: to deprive of

Neutral vowels in unaccented syllables : *el′ə-mənt, in′fənt, ran′dəm*

men, defences, or furniture.—*adjs.* **unfur'nished**, not furnished: unsupplied; **unfurred'**; **unfurr'owed**; **ungain'**, (*obs.*) ungainly, awkward: unskilful, clumsy: indirect: unpleasant; **ungain'ful**. — *n.* **ungain'liness**. — *adj.* **ungain'ly**, awkward: clumsy: uncouth.—*adv.* awkwardly.—*adjs.* **ungainsaid'**; **ungainsay'able**; **ungall'ant**. — *adv.* **ungall'antly**. — *adjs.* **ungalled'**; **ungar'bled**; **ungar'mented**, unclad; **ungar'nered**; **ungar'nished**; **ungar'tered**; **ungath'ered**; **ungauged'**(-upon). — *v.t.* **ungear'**, to unharness: to put out of gear.—*adj.* **ungen'erous**.—*adv.* **ungen'erously**.—*adjs.* **unge'nial**, not genial: not sympathetically cheerful: not comfortably warm: raw: not congenial: not favourable to natural growth; **ungen'itured**, (*Shak.*) without means of generation, or not produced by ordinary generation; **ungenteel'**.—*adv.* **ungenteel'ly**.—*n.* **ungentil'ity**.—*adjs.* **ungen'tle**, not gentle: not of gentle birth: not of or befitting the gentle; **ungen'tlemanlike**, not like or befitting a gentleman.—Also *adv.*—*n.* **ungen'tlemanliness**. — *adj.* **ungen'tlemanly**, unbecoming a gentleman: not gentlemanlike.—Also *adv.*—*n.* **ungen'tleness**. — *adv.* **ungent'ly**. — *adj.* **ungen'uine**.—*n.* **ungen'uineness**.—*v.t.* **unget'**, to undo the begetting of.—*adjs.* **ungetat'able**, **unget-at'-able**, inaccessible; **unghost'ly**; **ungift'ed**, not gifted: without a gift.—*v.t.* **ungild'**, to deprive of gilding.—*adjs.* **ungild'ed**, **ungilt'**, not gilt.—*v.t.* **ungird'**, to free from a girdle or band: to unbind.—*adj.* **ungirt'** (or **ungird'ed**), not girt: loosed from the girdle.—*v.t.* **ungirth'**, to remove or loose a girth from: to loose from a girth.—*adjs.* **ungirthed'**, freed or loosed from a girth: without a girth; **ungiv'ing**, not giving; **unglad'**; **unglazed'**, not glazed; **unglossed'**, not glossed.—*v.t.* **unglove'**, to take the glove from.—*adj.* **ungloved'**, without a glove.—*v.t.* and *v.i.* **unglue'**, to separate as from being glued.—*v.t.* **ungod'**, to divest of divinity: to make godless.—*adj.* **ungod'like**.—*adv.* **ungod'lily**, in an ungodly manner.—*n.* **ungod'liness**.—*adjs.* **ungod'ly**, not godly: (*coll.*) outrageous, unconscionable; **ungored'** (*Shak.* **ungord'**; another reading **ungorg'd'**), unwounded; **ungorged'**; **ungot'**, **ungott'en**, not got or acquired: unbegotten; **ungov'ernable**, uncontrollable: refractory, unruly.—*n.* **ungov'ernableness**. — *adv.* **ungov'ernably**. — *adj.* **ungov'erned**.—*v.t.* **ungown'**, to deprive or divest of a gown: to unfrock.—*adjs.* **ungowned'**, not wearing a gown: deprived of gown; **ungraced'**, not graced or honoured; **ungrace'ful**, not graceful.—*adv.* **ungrace'fully**.—*n.* **ungrace'fulness**.—*adj.* **ungra'cious**, without grace: graceless: ungraceful: wanting in courtesy, affability or urbanity: behaving with a bad grace: unmannerly: rendering offensive or disagreeable.—*adv.* **ungra'ciously**. — *n.* **ungra'ciousness**.—*adjs.* **ungrad'ed**, not classified in grades: not adjusted to easy gradients; **ungrammat'ic**, **-al**.—*adv.* **ungrammat'ically**.—*adj.* **ungrate'ful**, not feeling gratitude: disagreeable, irksome: not repaying one's labour, thankless.—*adv.* **ungrate'fully**.—*n.* **ungrate'fulness**. — *adj.* **ungrat'ified**. — *adv.* **ungrave'ly** (*Shak.*).—*adjs.* **ungroomed'**; **unground'**, not ground, **unground'ed**, without ground or basis, unreal, false: not grounded, without sound fundamental instruction.—*adv.* **ungroun'dedly**.—*n.* **ungroun'dedness**.—*adjs.* **ungrown'**, not of full growth: immature; **ungrudged'**; **ungrudg'ing**, not grudging, liberal.—*adv.* **ungrudg'ingly**.—*v.t.* **unguard'**, to deprive of guard or guarding: to leave or render unguarded.—*adj.* **unguard'ed**, without guard: unprotected: unscreened: incautious: inadvertent.—*adv.* **unguard'edly**.—*n.* **unguard'edness**.

unguent, *ung'gwənt*, *n.* ointment.—*n.* **unguentā'rium**, a vessel for holding unguents.—*adj.* **ung'uentary**, of or for unguents.—*n.* an unguentarium: a perfumer, maker of or dealer in unguents. [L. *unguentum*—*unguĕre*, to anoint.]

un- (*continued*). — *adjs.* **unguer'doned**; **unguessed'**; **unguid'ed**; **unguilt'y**.

unguis, *ung'gwis*, *n.* a claw or nail: the claw of an insect's foot: the claw of a petal:—*pl.* **ung'ues** (*-gwēz*).—*adjs.* **ung'ual** (*-gwəl*), of or bearing a claw; **unguiculate** (*ung-gwik'ū-lāt*), **-d**, clawed. [L. *unguis*, a nail.]

ungula, *ung'gū-lä*, *n.* (*zool.*) a hoof: (*geom.*) a section of a cylinder, cone, &c., cut off by a plane oblique to the base.—*adj.* **ung'ulate**, hoofed.—*n.* a hoofed animal, a member of the order **Ungulā'ta**, hoofed digitigrade mammals, including artiodactyls and perissodactyls.—*adjs.* **unguled** (*ung'gūld*; *her.*), with claws or hoofs tinctured specially; **ung'uligrade**, walking on hoofs. [L. *ungula*, claw, hoof—*unguis*, nail.]

un- (*continued*).—*v.t.* **ungum'**, to free from gum or gummed condition.—*adj.* **ungummed'**, not gummed: freed from gum or gumming.—*v.t.* **ungyve'**, to free from gyves.—*adjs.* **ungyved'**, unfettered; **unhab'itable**, uninhabitable; **unhab'ituated**; **unha'ble** (an obs. form of **unable**); **unhacked'**, not hacked; **unhack'neyed**; **unhailed'**.—*v.t.* **unhair'**, to deprive of hair.—*v.i.* to become free from hair.—*adj.* **unhaired'**, freed from hair.—*v.t.* **unhall'ow**, to undo the hallowing of.—*adjs.* **unhall'owed**, unconsecrated: unholy; **unhalsed** (*un-hawst'*; *Scott*), unsaluted; **unhamp'ered**.—*v.t.* **unhand'**, to take the hands off: to let go.—*adv.* **unhand'ily**, awkwardly.—*n.* **unhand'iness**.—*adjs.* **unhan'dled**, not handled or managed: not broken-in; **unhand'seled**; **unhand'some**, not handsome, ill-made: unbecoming in action: ungenerous: mean: ungracious: clumsy, inconvenient.—*adv.* **unhand'somely**.—*n.* **unhand'someness**.—*adj.* **unhand'y**, not handy: awkward: not convenient.—*v.t.* **unhang'**, to remove from a hanging position, from its hinges, &c.—*adj.* **unhanged'**, not hanged.—*adv.* **unhapp'ily**, in an unhappy or unfortunate manner: unfortunately, regrettably: unsuccessfully: (*obs.*) maliciously: (*Shak.*) unfavourably: (*Shak.*) shrewdly. — *n.* **unhapp'iness**. — *adj.* **unhapp'y**, bringing misfortune: not happy or fortunate: miserable: marked by evil: infelicitous: inapt: mischievous.—*v.t.* (*Shak.*) to make unhappy or unfortunate.—*v.t.* **unhar'bour**, to dislodge from shelter.—*adjs.* **unhar'boured**, without a shelter: dislodged from shelter; **unhar'dened**; **unhar'dy**, not capable of enduring hardship: not resolute; **unharmed'**; **unharm'ful**, harmless.—*adv.* **unharm'fully**.—*adjs.* **unharm'ing**; **unharmo'nious**, inharmonious.—*v.t.* **unhar'ness**, to take the armour or harness off: to disarm: to unyoke.—*adjs.* **unhar'nessed**, not in armour or harness: freed from armour or harness; **unhar'vested**.—*v.t.* **unhasp'**, to loose from a hasp.—*adjs.* **unhast'ing**; **unhast'y**.—*v.i.* **unhat'**, to take off the hat from respect.—*adjs.* **unhatched'**, not hatched; **unhatched'** (**unhatch'd**; *Shak.*), unhacked; **unhatt'ed**, hatless.—*n.* **unhatt'ing**, lifting the hat.—*adjs.* **unhaunt'ed**; **unhaz'arded**; **unhaz'ardous**.—*v.ts.* **unhead'**, to take the head from; **unheal'** (see **unhele**).—*adjs.* **unheal'able**; **unhealed'**.—*n.* **unhealth'**, ill-health.—*adj.* **unhealth'ful**.—*adv.* **unhealth'fully**.—*n.* **unhealth'fulness**.—*adj.* **unhealth'ily**.—*n.* **unheal'thiness**. — *adjs.* **unheal'thy**, not healthy: unsound: morbid: dangerous: unfavourable to health: of unhealthiness; **unheard'**, not heard: not granted a hearing: not heard of, unknown to fame: unprecedented (in Shak., *K. John*, V. ii. 133, understood by some as unhaired, beardless); **unheard'-of**.—*v.t.* **unhearse'** (used by Spens. in the *pa.t.* **unherst**), app. to remove from a hearse or candlestand for a funeral.—*adj.* **unhearsed'**, without a hearse.—*v.t.* **unheart'**, (*Shak.*) to dishearten.—*adjs.* **unheat'ed**; **unhedged'**; **unheed'ed**.—*adv.* **unheed'edly**.—*adj.* **unheed'ful**.—*advs.* **unheed'fully**, **unheed'ily** (*Spens.*).—*adj.* **unheed'ing**.—*adv.* **unheed'ingly**.—*adj.* **unheed'less**: unwary.—*v.ts.* **unhele'**, **unheal'**, (*Spens.*) to uncover, disclose; **unhelm'**, to divest of helmet.—*adjs.* **unhelmed'**, **unhel'meted**, without, or divested of, helm or helmet; **unhelped'**; **unhelp'ful**; **unheppen** (*un-ep'n*; *Yorks.*, *Linc.*, *Tennyson*; O.N. *heppinn*, dexterous), clumsy; **unher'alded**; **unhero'ic**, **-al**.—*adv.* **unhero'ic-**

ally.—*v.t.* (*pa.t.*) unherst' (see **unhearse**).—*adj.* unhes'itating, not hesitating or doubting: prompt: ready. — *adv.* unhes'itatingly. — *adjs.* unhewn'; unhidd'en; unhide'bound (*Milt.*). —*v.t.* unhinge', to take from the hinges: to derange.—*adj.* unhinged'.—*n.* unhinge'ment.— *adjs.* unhired'; unhistor'ic, -al, not historic, not mentioned in history: not in accordance with history: not having actually existed or happened. —*vs.t.* unhitch', to unfasten; unhive', to drive from a hive; unhoard', to take from a hoard. —*adv.* unho'lily. — *n.* unho'liness. — *adjs.* un-hol'pen, not helped; unho'ly, not holy: devoted to evil: very wicked; (*coll.*) unconscionable, out-rageous, unearthly; unhome'like; unhome'ly; unhon'est, (*obs.*) unseemly, indecent, immodest: (*obs.*) discreditable, dishonourable, immoral: (*obs.*) dishonest; unhon'oured.—*v.t.* unhood', to re-move the hood from.—*adj.* unhood'ed, without, or divested of, a hood.—*vs.t.* unhook', to loose from a hook: to undo the hooking of; unhoop', to remove hoops from.—*adjs.* unhoped'(-for), not hoped (for): beyond what was expected with hope; unhope'ful. — *adv.* unhope'fully. — *v.t.* unhorse', to dislodge or throw from a horse: to take a horse or horses from.—*adj.* unhos'pitable, inhospitable.—*v.t.* unhouse', to deprive of or drive from a house or shelter.—*adjs.* unhoused', houseless: deprived of a house; unhous'eled, (*Shak.* unhouzz'led), not having received the sacrament; unhu'man, not human.—*v.t.* un-hu'manise, to render unhuman, inhuman, or uncultured.—*adjs.* unhum'bled; unhung', not hung: without hangings: unhanged; unhunt'ed; unhurr'ied. — *adv.* unhurr'iedly. — *adjs.* un-hurr'ying; unhurt'; unhurt'ful.—*adv.* unhurt'-fully. — *n.* unhurt'fulness.—*adj.* unhus'banded, uncultivated: without a husband.—*v.t.* unhusk', to strip the husk from.—*adj.* unhygien'ic, not hygienic, unhealthy.

uni-, *ū'ni-*, in composition, one. [L. *ūnus*, one; Gr. *oinē*, ace, O.E. *án*, one.]

Uniat, *ū'ni-at*, *n.* a United Greek, or member of any community of Oriental Christians that acknow-ledges the papal supremacy, all else—clerical matrimony, communion in both kinds, church discipline, rites, and liturgy—being allowed to remain Greek.—Also U'niate (-*āt*, -*ət*). [Russ. *uniyat—uniya*, union—L. *ūnus*, one.]

uniaxial, *ū-ni-ak'si-əl*, *adj.* having one axis, esp. (*crystal.*) one optic axis or (*biol.*) one main line of growth or unbranched axis.—*adv.* uniax'ially.

unicameral, *ū-ni-kam'ə-rəl*, *adj.* having or consist-ing of but one legislative chamber.—*ns.* unicam'-eralism, the system or principle of having one legislative chamber; unicam'eralist. [L. *camera*, vault; see **chamber**.]

unicellular, *ū-ni-sel'ū-lər*, *adj.* of or having but one cell.

unicentral, *ū'-ni-sen'trəl*, *adj.* having a single centre.

unicity, *ū-nis'i-ti*, *n.* oneness: uniqueness. [L. *ūnicus*, unique.]

unicolor, *ū'ni-kul-ər*, or -*kul'*, *adj.* of one uniform colour.—Also unicolour, -ed, unicol'orate, unicol'orous.

unicorn, *ū'ni-korn*, *n.* a fabulous animal mentioned by ancient Greek and Roman authors as a native of India, with a body like a horse and one straight horn: (*B.*) an unfortunate translation of the Hebrew *re'ēm* (Assyr. *rímu*) anticipated by the *monokerōs* of the Septuagint—variously understood as the rhinoceros, wild ox, ox-antelope: applied to various animals with the appearance of a single horn, as the narwhal (also **un'icorn-whale**), a moth (**un'icorn-moth**) whose caterpillar has a long process, an American Pacific gasteropod (Monoceros, &c.) with a spine on the lip of the shell (**un'icorn-shell**): a team of two abreast and one in front, or a carriage drawn by it: an old Scottish gold coin bearing a unicorn, worth 18s. Scots: Unicorn, one of the Scottish pursuivants.— *adj.* un'icorn, one-horned.—*adv.* with two abreast and one in front. [L. *ūnus*, one, *cornū*, a horn.]

unicostate, *ū-ni-kos'tāt*, *adj.* one-ribbed. [L. *costa*, rib.]

unicycle, *ū'ni-sī-kl*, *n.* an acrobat's one-wheeled cycle.

un- (*continued*).—*adjs.* unide'a'd, without ideas: with unfurnished mind; unide'al, not ideal: not idealistic: (*obs.*) conveying no idea: (*obs.*) without ideas: without ideals.—*n.* unide'alism.—*adjs.* unidealist'ic; unident'ified, not identified; un-idiomat'ic, not according to the idiom of a lan-guage.

unidirectional, *ū-ni-di-rek'shən-əl*, *adj.* mainly or wholly in one direction.

unifilar, *ū-ni-fī'lər*, *adj.* with one thread. [L. *filum*, thread.]

uniflorous, *ū-ni-flō'rəs*, *adj.* one-flowered. [L. *flōs, flōris*, a flower.]

unifoliolate, *ū-ni-fō'li-ō-lāt*, *adj.* having a single leaflet, but compound in structure. [L. *foliolum*, dim. of *folium*, leaf.]

uniform, *ū'ni-form*, *adj.* alike: alike all over, throughout, or at all times: unvarying: of a military or other uniform.—*n.* a distinctive garb for members of a body: a suit of it.—*v.t.* to make uniform: to clothe in uniform.—*adj.* un'iformed, wearing uniform.—*n.* and *adj.* uniformitā'rian.— *ns.* uniformitā'rianism, the doctrine that geo-logical changes were brought about not in the main by great convulsions but by such action as may be seen going on now; uniform'ity, state or fact of being uniform: agreement with a pattern or rule: sameness: likeness between parts.—*adv.* u'niformly.—*n.* u'niformness. [L. *ūniformis— ūnus*, one, *forma*, form.]

unify, *ū'ni-fī*, *v.t.* to make into one: to consolidate. —*adjs.* u'nifiable; unif'ic, making one.—*n.* unificā'tion.—*adj.* u'nified.—*n.* u'nifier.—*n.* and *adj.* u'nifying. [L.L. *ūnificāre*—L. *ūnus*, one, *facere*, to make.]

unigeniture, *ū-ni-jen'it-yər*, *n.* the state or fact of being the only begotten.—*n.* Unigen'itus, (from its first word) a bull of Clement XI (1713) condemn-ing 101 propositions of the Jansenist Quesnel. [L.L. *ūnigenitus*, only-begotten.]

unilabiate, *ū-ni-lā'bi-āt*, *adj.* one-lipped. [L. *labium*, lip.]

unilateral, *ū-ni-lat'ə-rəl*, *adj.* one-sided.—*n.* uni-laterality (-*ral'i-ti*).—*adv.* unilat'erally. [L. *latus, lateris*, side.]

unilingual, *ū-ni-ling'gwəl*, *adj.* of, in, using, one language. [L. *lingua*, tongue.]

uniliteral, *ū-ni-lit'ə-rəl*, *adj.* of, or involving, one letter or script. [L. *littera* (*lītera*), letter.]

un- (*continued*).—*adjs.* unillumed'; unillu'min-ated; unillu'minating; unillu'mined; un-ill'ustrated.

unilobar, *ū-ni-lō'bər*, unilobed, -*lōbd'*, *adjs.* having one lobe.—*adj.* unilobular (-*lob'ū-lər*), having one lobule.

unilocular, *ū-ni-lok'ū-lər*, *adj.* having but one loculus or cavity.

un- (*continued*).—*adj.* unimag'inable.—*n.* un-imag'inableness.—*adv.* unimag'inably. — *adj.* unimag'inative, not imaginative, prosaic.—*n.* unimag'inativeness.—*adjs.* unimag'ined; un-imbued'; un'immort'al (*Milt.*); unimpaired'; unimpart'ed; unimpass'ioned, not impassioned, calm, tranquil; unimpeach'able, not to be im-peached: not liable to be accused: free from fault: blameless; unimpeached'; unimped'ed. —*adv.* unimped'edly.—*adj.* unimplored' (*Milt.*). —*n.* unimport'ance, want of importance.—*adjs.* unimport'ant; unim'portuned (or -*tūnd'*, or -*por'*); unimposed'; unimpōs'ing, unimpressive: (*Thomson*) not burdensome; unimpreg'nated; unimpressed'; unimpress'ible; unimpress'-ionable; unimpress'ive; unimpris'oned; un-improved', not improved, made better, or culti-vated, cleared, or built upon: not used, unem-ployed, inactive; unimpugn'able; uninclosed'; unenclosed'; uninaug'urated; uninvit'ed; un-incor'porated, unin'dexed; uninfect'ed; un-inflamed'; uninflamm'able; uninflat'ed; un-inflect'ed; unin'fluenced; uninfluen'tial; un-informed', not having received information, un-taught: not imbued with life or activity; unin-form'ing; uninhab'itable, not habitable; uninhab'ited; uninhib'ited; unini'tiated; unin'-jured; uninquir'ing; uninquis'itive; uninscribed'; uninspired'; uninspir'ing; uninstruct'ed; uninstruct'ive; uninsured'; unin'tegrated, not integrated; unintellect'ual; unintell'igent.—*n.* unintelligibil'ity.—*adj.* unintell'igible.—*adv.* unintell'igibly.—*adjs.* unintend'ed; uninten'tional.—*n.* unintentional'-ity.—*adv.* uninten'tionally.—*adjs.* unin'terested, not personally concerned: not taking an interest; unin'teresting.—*adv.* unin'terestingly.—*adj.* unintermitt'ed.—*adv.* unintermitt'edly.—*adj.* unintermitt'ing.—*adv.* unintermitt'ingly. —*adjs.* uninter'pretable; uninterrup'ted.—*adv.* uninterrup'tedly.—*adjs.* unintox'icating; unintroduced'.

uninuclear, *ū-ni-nū'kli-ər*, *adj.* with a single nucleus.—Also **uninū'cleate**.

un- (*continued*).—*adjs.* uninured'; uninven'tive; uninvest'ed; uninvid'ious; uninvi'ted; uninvi'ting; uninvolved'.

Unio, *ū'ni-ō*, *n.* the pearl-mussel genus of freshwater molluscs, giving name to the family **Unionidae** (*ū-ni-on'i-dē*).—*n.* **union** (*ūn'yən*; *Shak.*), a fine large pearl, a unique or single pearl. [L. *ūniō*, *-ōnis*, prob.—*ūnus*, one (cf. **solitaire** as applied to a diamond set by itself).]

union, *ūn'yən*, *n.* a uniting: the state of being united: the state of wedlock: a united whole: combination: a growing together in healing: general concord: incorporation of states in a federation or in a single state: a single state (or sometimes a federation) thus formed: an association or league, esp. a trade union: a students' club: a combination of parishes for poor law purposes: its workhouse or poorhouse: a connecting part for pipes, &c.: a device emblematic of union borne in the canton of a flag: the same device used separately as a flag, as the Union Jack: a textile fabric of more than one kind of fibre.—*ns.* **ūn'ionism**, **Un'ionism**; **ūn'ionist**, an advocate or supporter of or believer in union or trade unions: a member of a trade union: **Un'ionist**, an opponent of Irish Home Rule, esp. a Liberal Unionist (see **Liberal**)—hence a Conservative: a supporter of the federal union of the United States, esp. at the time of the Civil War.—Also *adj.*—**the Union**, the legislative incorporation of England and Scotland in 1707, or of Ireland with both in 1801: the American Union or United States: the Union of South Africa (1910); **union flag**, a flag symbolising union, esp. the national flag of the United Kingdom, consisting of a union of the crosses of St. George, St. Andrew, and St. Patrick, commonly called the **Union Jack**. [Fr. *union*—L. *ūniō, -ōnis*—*ūnus*, one.]

unionised, *un'ī'ən-īzd*, *adj.* not ionised.

uniparous, *ū-nip'ə-rəs*, *adj.* producing one at a birth: (*bot.*) monochasial. [L. *parĕre*, to bring forth.]

unipartite, *ū-ni-pär'tīt*, *adj.* not divided into parts.

uniped, *ū'ni-ped*, *adj.* one-footed.—*n.* a one-footed person, animal, or object. [L. *pēs, pedis*, foot.]

unipersonal, *ū-ni-pər'sən-əl*, *adj.* existing as only one person.

uniplanar, *ū-ni-plā'nər*, *adj.* lying in one plane.

unipolar, *ū-ni-pō'lər*, *adj.* of, from, or using one pole: of a nerve cell, having one process only.—*n.* unipolarity (*-lar'i-ti*).

unique, *ū-nēk'*, *adj.* sole: without a like: often used loosely for unusual, pre-eminent.—*n.* any thing that is unique.—*adv.* unique'ly.—*n.* unique'-ness. [Fr.,—L. *ūnicus*—*ūnus*.]

uniserial, *ū-ni-sē'ri-əl*, *adj.* in one series or row.—*adv.* unise'rially.—*adj.* unise'riate, uniserial.—*adv.* unise'riately.

unisexual, *ū-ni-sek'sū-əl*, *adj.* of one sex only.—*n.* unisexuality (*-al'*).—*adv.* unisex'ually.

unison, *ū'ni-zən, -sən*, *n.* identity of pitch: loosely, pitch differing by one or more octaves: a sound of the same pitch: complete agreement.—*adj.* in unison.—*adj.* unisonal (*ū-nis'ən-əl*).—*adv.* unis'-onally. — *n.* unis'onance. — *adjs.* unis'onant; unis'onous. [L. *sonus*, sound, *sonāre*, to sound.]

unit, *ū'nit*, *n.* one: a single thing or person: a single element, section, or item, regarded as the lowest subdivision of a whole: the least whole number: anything taken as one: a quantity by reference to which others are measured.—*adj.* of the character or value of a unit: individual.—*adj.* u'nital.—*n.* **Unitā'rian**, one who asserts the unity of the Godhead as opposed to the Trinity, and ascribes divinity to God the Father only: a member of a particular body holding such doctrines: a monotheist generally: **unitā'rian**, a holder of some belief based on unity or union.—Also *adj.*—*n.* **Unitā'rianism**.—*adj.* u'nitary, pertaining to unity or to a unit: of the nature of a unit: integral: based on unity. [For **unity**.]

unite, *ū-nīt'*, *v.t.* to make one: to join into one: to join: to combine: to clasp: to marry: to have in combination: to make to agree or adhere.—*v.i.* to become one: to combine: to join: to grow or act together.—*n.* **u'nite** (or *-nīt'*), an English gold coin of James I., worth 20s., later 22s.—*adj.* uni'ted. — *adv.* uni'tedly. — *ns.* uni'tedness: uni'ter.—*n.* and *adj.* uni'ting.—*n.* **unition** (*ū-nish'ən*), conjunction.—*adj.* **unitive** (*ūn'i-tiv*), harmonising, uniting.—*adv.* u'nitively.—**United Brethren** (see **Moravian**); **United Free Church**, **United Presbyterian Church** (see under **free**, **presbyter**); **United Greeks** (see **Uniat**); **United Irishmen**, an organisation (orig. formed to help Grattan in carrying his reforms) which caused the rising of 1798; **United Nations**, an association of states that in 1945 undertook many of the functions of the dissolved League of Nations; **United Provinces**, Holland, Zealand (Zeeland), Utrecht, Gelderland, Groningen, Friesland, and Overyssel, united in 1579 under the Union of Utrecht; **United States**, a federal union of states, esp. that of (North) America. [L. *ūnītus*, pa.p. of *ūnīre*, to unite—*ūnus*, one.]

unity, *ū'ni-ti*, *n.* oneness: the number one: state or fact of being one or at one: that which has oneness: a single whole: the arrangement of all the parts to one purpose or effect: (*Dickens*) a unite.—**the unities** (of *place*, *time*, and *action*), the three canons of the classical drama—that the scenes should be at the same place, that all the events should be such as might happen within a single day, and that nothing should be admitted not directly relevant to the development of the plot. [L. *ūnitās, -ātis*—*ūnus*, one.]

univalent, *ū-niv'ə-lənt, ū-ni-vā'lənt*, *adj.* (*chem.*) having a valency of one, capable of combining with one atom of hydrogen or its equivalent.—*ns.* univ'-alence (or *-vā'*), univ'alency (or *-vā'*).

univalve, *ū'ni-valv*, *adj.* having one valve or shell only.—*n.* a shell of one valve only: a mollusc whose shell is composed of a single piece.—*adj.* uni-val'vular.

univariant, *ū-ni-vā'ri-ənt*, *adj.* having one degree of freedom.

universe, *ū'ni-vərs*, *n.* all that is: the whole system of things: the cosmos: a system of stars such as the galactic system: the world.—*adj.* univers'al, of the universe: comprehending, affecting, or extending to the whole: without exception: comprising all the particulars: all-round: unlimited: applied to a great variety of uses.—*n.* that which is universal: a universal proposition: a general term: a universal concept.—*n.* universalisā'tion.—*v.t.* univer'salise.—*ns.* Univer'salism, the doctrine or belief of universal salvation, or the ultimate salvation of all mankind, and even of the fallen angels; Univer'salist, a believer in Universalism.—Also *adj.*—*adj.* univer'-salist'ic.—*n.* universality (*-sal'*), state or quality of being universal.—*adv.* univer'sally.—*n.* univer'salness. — **universal donor**, one whose blood can be transfused into persons of the other blood groups without causing destruction of their red blood cells; **universal joint**, one capable of turning all ways. [L. *ūniversum*, neut. sing. of *ūniversus*, whole, *ūnus*, one, *vertĕre, versus*, to turn.]

university, *ū-ni-vər'si-ti*, *n.* (*obs.*) a corporate body: an institution of higher learning with power to grant degrees, its body of teachers, students, graduates, &c., its college or colleges, or its buildings.—*adj.* **universitā'rian.** [L. *ūniversitās, -ātis,* a whole, in L.L. a corporation; see foregoing.]

univocal, *ū-niv'ə-kl* (or *ū-ni-vō'kl*), *adj.* of one voice: having one meaning only: unmistakable: unambiguous: (*obs.*) of things of the same species. —*n.* a word with but one meaning.—*adv.* **univ'-ocally.** [L. *ūnivocus—ūnus,* one, *vōx, vōcis,* a voice.]

univoltine, *ū-ni-vōl'tīn, adj.* having one brood a year, of silkworms. [L. *ūnus,* one, It. *volta,* a turn, winding.]

un- (*continued*).—*adjs.* **unja'ded; unjaun'diced; unjeal'ous.** — *v.t.* **unjoint',** to disjoint.—*adjs.* **unjoint'ed,** disjointed: incoherent: without joints; **unjoy'ful; unjoy'ous; unjust',** not just; **unjus'tifiable,** not justifiable.—*advs.* **unjus'tifi-ably; unjust'ly.**—*n.* **unjust'ness,** injustice.—*adjs.* **unked, unket, unkid** (*oongk'id, ungk'id, -it;* N. and *W. England;* forms of **uncouth**), strange, uncomfortable, lonely, eerie; **unkempt'** (see **kemb**), uncombed: unpolished, rough; **un-kenned', unkent', unknown.**—*v.t.* **unkenn'el,** to dislodge (a fox) from a hole: to let out from a kennel.—*adjs.* **unkept',** not kept: untended; **unkind',** unrelenting: unnaturally wicked: want-ing in kindness: cruel; **unkin'dled,** not kindled.—*n.* **unkind'liness,** want of kindliness.—*adj.* **un-kind'ly,** unnatural: not kind.—*adv.* (*Milt.*) un-naturally: (*Shak.*) against right feeling: in an unkindly manner: cruelly.—*n.* **unkind'ness,** want of kindness or affection: cruelty: ill-feeling.—*v.t.* **unking',** to deprive of kingship or of a king.—*adjs.* **unking'like; unking'ly,** unbecoming a king: unlike a king.—*v.t.* **unkiss',** (*Shak.*) to annul by kissing.—*adjs.* **unkissed',** not kissed; **un-knelled** (*un-neld'*), without tolling.—*v.t.* **unknight** (*un-nīt'*), to divest of knighthood.—*adj.* **un-knight'ed,** not knighted.—*n.* **unknight'liness.**—*adj.* **unknightly** (*un-nīt'li*), unlike or unbecoming a knight.—*adv.* in an unknightly manner.—*v.t.* **unknit** (*un-nit'*), to undo the knitting of: to untie: to smooth out from a frown: to relax.—*v.i.* to become unknit.—*adj.* loose, unfirmed.—*v.t.* **un-knot** (*un-not'*), to free from knots: to untie.—*adj.* **unknowable** (*un-nō'ə-bl*), incapable of being known.—*n.* an unknowable thing: that which cannot be known: the first or original cause: that which is cognisable only in its relations.—*n.* **un-know'ableness.** — *adj.* **unknow'ing,** ignorant: unaware: unwitting: (*dial.*) unknown.—*adv.* **un-know'ingly.** — *n.* **unknow'ingness.** — *adj.* **un-known** (*un-nōn'*), not known.—*n.* an unknown person or quantity: that which is unknown.—*n.* **unknown'ness.** — *adjs.* **unla'belled; unlabo'-rious; unla'boured,** showing no traces of labour: unwrought: unrestrained, easy; **unla'bouring.**—*vs.t.* **unlace',** to loose from being laced: to undo the lacing of: to carve (esp. a rabbit): to undo, destroy; **unlade',** to unload.—*adj.* **unla'den,** not laden.—*n.* **unla'ding.**—*adjs.* **unla'dylike; un-laid',** not laid; **unlament'ed.**—*vs.t.* **unlash',** (*naut.*) to loose the lashings of; **unlast, unlaste** (*un-lâst', -lãst'*), Spenserian *pa.t.* and *pa.p.* of **unlace; unlatch',** to lift the latch of.—*n.* **un'law,** (*arch.*) breach of law: (*Scots law; obs.*) a fine, penalty.—*v.t.* **unlaw',** to annul, repeal: (*obs.*) to fine.—*adj.* **unlaw'ful,** forbidden by law: illegiti-mate: illicit: acting illegally.—*adv.* **unlaw'fully.** —*n.* **unlaw'fulness.**—*vs.t.* **unlay,** (*naut.*) to untwist; **unlead** (*un-led' print.*), to take the lead or leads from.—*adj.* **unleal',** unfaithful.—*v.t.* **unlearn',** to undo the process of learning: to rid one's mind or habits of.—*adj.* **unlearned** (*un-lər'nid;* also *poet. un-lərnd'*), without learning: (*un-lərnd'*) not learned, got up, acquired: elimin-ated by unlearning.—*adv.* **unlear'nedly.**—*n.* **un-lear'nedness.**—*adj.* **unleased'.**—*v.t.* **unleash',** to free from a leash, let go.—*adjs.* **unleav'ened; unled',** not led, without guidance; **unleis'ured; unleis'urely.**

unless, *un-les', ən-les', conj.* (tending to pass into a *prep.*) if not. [Earlier followed by *than,* or *that: on lesse than*=on a less condition than.]

un- (*continued*).—*adjs.* **unless'oned,** not instructed: **unlet',** not let; **unlett'ered,** unlearned: illiterate:

without lettering; **unlibid'inous** (*Milt.*); **un-li'censed,** without a licence: unauthorised; **un-lich** (*un-lich'; Spens.*), unlike; **un'licked,** not licked: not licked into shape.—*v.t.* **unlid',** to uncover, open.—*adjs.* **unlidd'ed,** lidless; **un-light'ed; unlight'ened; unlight'some,** (*Milt.*) without light.—*adj.* and *adv.* (tending to become a *prep.*) **unlike',** not like: (*Spens., Shak.*) unlikely. —*n.* one who or that which is unlike.—*ns.* **unlike'-lihood, unlike'liness,** improbability.—*adj.* **un-like'ly,** not likely: improbable: unpromising: unprepossessing: unsuitable.—*adv.* in an unlikely manner, improbably.—*n.* **unlike'ness,** want of resemblance.—*v.t.* **unlime',** to free from lime.—*adjs.* **unlimed',** not limed; **unlim'ited.**—*adv.* **unlim'itedly.**—*n.* **unlim'itedness.**—*v.t.* **unline',** to remove the lining from.—*adjs.* **unlin'eal; un-lined',** without lines or lining.—*v.t.* **unlink',** to undo the linking or links of.—*v.i.* to become un-linked.—*adjs.* **unlinked',** not linked; **unliq'ue-fied; unliq'uidated; unliq'uored,** not moistened with liquor: not in liquor, sober; **unlist'ed,** not entered in a list; **unlis'tened(-to),** not listened to; **unlis'tening; unlit'; unlit'erary.**—*v.t.* **unlive** (*un-liv'*), to undo the living of: to live in the con-trary manner to: to live down: (*un-līv'; Shak.*) to deprive of life.—*n.* **unlive'liness.**—*adjs.* **unlive'ly; unliv'ing.**—*v.t.* **unload',** to take the load or charge from: to discharge: to disburden: to remove as a load: to get rid of.—*v.i.* to discharge freight.—*adj.* **unload'ed,** not loaded: discharged. —*ns.* **unload'er; unload'ing.**—*adj.* **unloca'ted,** (*U.S.*) not surveyed or marked off.—*v.t.* **unlock',** to undo the locking of: to free from being locked up: to let loose: to open, make accessible, or disclose.—*v.i.* to become unlocked.—*adjs.* **un-locked',** not locked: freed from locking; **un-log'ical,** not logical: illogical; **unlooked'(-for),** unexpected.—*vs.t.* **unloose', unloos'en,** to loose. —*adj.* **unlopped'.**—*v.t.* **unlord',** to strip of the dignity of a lord.—*adjs.* **unlor'ded,** deprived of, or not raised to, the rank of lord: not lorded over, without a lord; **unlord'ly; unlos'able; unlost'; unlov'able** (also **unlove'able**).—*v.t.* **unlove',** to cease to love: not to love.—*n.* (*un'*) absence of love. —*adj.* **unloved'.**—*n.* **unlove'liness.**—*adjs.* **un-love'ly; unlov'erlike; unlov'ing.**—*adv.* **un-lov'ingly.**—*n.* **unlov'ingness.**—*adv.* **unluck'ily.** —*n.* **unluck'iness.**—*adjs.* **unluck'y,** unfortunate: ill-omened: bringing ill-luck: discommendable; **unluxur'iant; unluxur'ious; unmacad'am-ised; unmade',** not made: self-existent: sub-jected to unmaking; **unmaid'enly,** unbecoming a maiden: not maidenlike; **unmail'able,** (*U.S.*) incapable of being transmitted or delivered by post; **unmailed',** not clad in mail; **unmaimed';** **unmak'able.**—*v.t.* **unmake',** to undo the making of: to undo, ruin.—*ns.* **unma'king; unmalle-abil'ity.**—*adj.* **unmall'eable.**—*v.t.* **unman',** to deprive of the nature, attributes or powers of humanity, manhood, or maleness: to deprive of fortitude: to deprive of men.—*adjs.* **unman'-acled,** not manacled: freed from manacles; **un-man'ageable.**—*n.* **unman'ageableness.**—*adv.* **unman'ageably.**—*adj.* **unman'aged.**—*adv.* **un-man'fully.**—*adj.* **unman'like.**—*n.* **unman'li-ness.**—*adjs.* **unman'ly,** not becoming a man: unworthy of a noble mind: base: cowardly; **unmanned',** without a crew: without a garrison: without inhabitants: untamed (esp. of a hawk): deprived of fortitude; **unmann'ered,** unmannerly: free from mannerism.—*n.* **unmann'erliness.**—*adj.* **unmann'erly,** not mannerly: ill-bred.—*adv.* in an unmannerly manner.—*v.t.* **unman'tle,** to divest of a mantle: to dismantle.—*v.i.* to take off one's mantle.—*adjs.* **unmanufac'tured,** in a raw state; **unmanured',** not manured: (*obs.*) un-tilled; **unmarked',** bearing no mark: not noticed; **unmar'ketable,** not suitable for the market, not saleable; **unmarred'** (*Spens.* un-mard'), not marred; **unmarr'iable** (*obs.*), un-marr'iageable.—*n.* **unmarr'iageableness.**—*adj.* **unmarr'ied,** not married: usu. never having been married: freed from marriage.—*v.t.* **un'-marr'y,** to dissolve the marriage of.—*v.i.* to dissolve one's marriage.—*adj.* **unmas'culine.**—*v.t.* **unmask'**, to take a mask or a disguise from: to reveal the place of by firing: to expose, show up.—*v.i.* to put off a mask.—*adj.* **unmasked'**, not wearing a mask: undisguised: divested of a mask or disguise: revealed.—*ns.* **unmask'er**; **unmask'ing.**—*adjs.* **unmas'tered**, uncontrolled: not overcome: without a master; **unmatch'able**; **unmatched'**, matchless: not fitted with a like: **unma'ted**; **unmate'rial**, not composed of matter; **unmate'rialised**; **unmater'nal**; **unmathemat'ical**; **unmatric'ulated**; **unmatured'**; **unmean'ing**, meaningless: purposeless: expressionless. — *adv.* **unmean'ingly.** — *n.* **unmean'ingness.**—*adjs.* **unmeant** (*un-ment'*); **unmeas'urable**, immeasurable: too great to measure: inordinate: not susceptible of measurement.—*adv.* **unmeas'urably.**—*adjs.* **unmeas'ured**; **unmechan'ic**, **-al.**—*v.t.* **unmech'anise**, to disorganise. — *adjs.* **unmech'anised**, disorganised: not mechanised; **unmedicinable** (*un-med'sin-ə-bl*), incurable: unable to cure; **unmed'itated**, not meditated, unpremeditated; **unmeek'**; **unmeet'**, not meet, unfit.—*adv.* **unmeet'ly.**—*n.* **unmeet'ness.**—*adjs.* **unmell'owed**; **unmelo'dious**; **unmelt'ed**; **unmen'tionable**, not fit to be mentioned.—*n.* **unmen'tionableness.**—*n.pl.* **unmen'tionables**, otherwise *inexpressibles*, a 19th-cent. would-be humorous name for trousers.—*adjs.* **unmer'cenary**; **unmer'chantable**; **unmer'ciful.** — *adv.* **unmer'cifully.** — *n.* **unmer'cifulness.**—*adjs.* **unmer'itable**, (*Shak.*) undeserving; **unmer'ited.** — *adv.* **unmer'itedly.** — *adjs.* **unmer'iting**; **unmet'alled**; **unmetaphor'ical**; **unmetaphys'ical**; **unme'ted**, not meted or measured; **unmethod'ical**; **unmeth'odised**; **unmet'rical.**—*v.t.* **unmew'**, to release as from a mew. — *adjs.* **unmil'itary**; **unmilked'**; **unmilled'**; **unmind'ed**, unheeded; **unmind'ful**, not keeping in mind, regardless.—*adv.* **unmind'fully.**—*n.* **unmind'fulness.**—*adjs.* **unminis'terial**; **unmirac'ulous**; **unmi'ry**; **unmissed'**; **unmistak'able.**—*adv.* **unmistak'ably.**—*adjs.* **unmistrust'ful**; **unmit'igable.**—*adv.* **unmit'igably.** — *adj.* **unmit'igated**, not mitigated: unqualified, out-and-out.—*adv.* **unmit'igatedly.**—*adj.* **unmixed'.**—*adv.* **unmix'edly.**—*adjs.* **unmoaned'**, not lamented; **unmod'ernised**; **unmod'ifiable.**—*n.* **unmod'ifiableness.**—*adjs.* **unmod'ified**; **unmo'dish**, unfashionable; **unmod'ulated**; **unmois'tened**; **unmolest'ed**; **unmon'eyed** (*unmon'ied*), without money.—*v.t.* **unmoor'**, to loose from moorings.—*v.i.* to cast off moorings.—*adjs.* **unmor'al**, having no relation to morality: amoral: apart from virtuous and vicious; **unmor'alised**, not moralised upon: having no moral attached: without morality; **unmoralis'ing.**—*n.* **unmoral'ity**, detachment from questions of morality.—*adjs.* **unmort'-gaged**; **unmort'ified**; **unmor'tised**, disjoined from mortises; **un-Mosa'ic**, not of or according to *Moses* or the Mosaic law; **unmoth'erly**; **unmo'tived**, without motive: without an artistic motive.—*v.t.* **unmould'**, to change or destroy the form of.—*adj.* **unmould'ed**, not moulded.—*v.t.* **unmount'**, to remove from mountings or mount: to dismount. — *v.i.* to dismount. — *adjs.* **unmount'ed**, not mounted; **unmov'able** (also **unmove'able**), immovable: not movable.—*adv.* **unmov(e)'ably.**—*adj.* **unmoved'**, not moved, firm: not touched by emotion, calm.—*adv.* **unmov'edly.**—*adjs.* **unmov'ing**; **un'mown'.**—*v.t.* **unmuff'le**, to take a muffle, muffling, or covering from.—*v.i.* to throw off mufflings.—*adjs.* **unmuni'tioned**; **unmur'muring.**—*adv.* **unmur'muringly.**—*adj.* **unmu'sical.**—*adv.* **unmu'sically.**—*adj.* **unmu'tilated.**—*v.t.* **unmuzz'le**, to take a muzzle off.—*adj.* **unmuzz'led.**—*n.* **unmuzz'ling.** —*v.t.* **unnail** (*un-nāl'*), to free from nails or from being nailed.—*adjs.* **unnamable** (*un-nām'ə-bl*), impossible to name: not to be named; **unnamed** (*un-nāmd'*); **unnative** (*un-nā'tiv*), not native; **unnatural** (*un-nat'ū-rəl*), not natural or according to nature: without natural affection: monstrous, heinous.—*v.t.* **unnat'uralise**, to make unnatural:

to divest of nationality.—*adj.* **unnat'uralised**, not naturalised.—*adv.* **unnat'urally.**—*n.* **unnat'uralness.**—*adjs.* **unnavigab'le** (*un-nav'*), not navigable; **unnav'igated.**

unneath, *ə-nēth'*, *prep.* (*dial.*) underneath. [Cf. aneath, underneath.]

un- (*continued*).—*adv.* **unnecessarily** (*un-nes'*).—*n.* **unnec'essariness.** — *adjs.* **unnec'essary**, not necessary; **unneedful** (*un-nēd'*).—*adv.* **unneed'fully.**—*adj.* **unneighboured** (*un-nā'bərd*), without neighbours.—*n.* **unneigh'bourliness.**—*adj.* **unneigh'bourly**, not neighbourly, friendly, or social. —*adv.* in an unneighbourly manner.—*v.t.* **unnerve** (*un-nərv'*), to deprive of nerve, strength, or vigour: to weaken.—*adjs.* **unnerved'**; **unnerv'ing.**—*v.t.* **unnest** (*un-nest'*), to turn out of a nest. —*adv.* **unnethes** (see uneath).—*adjs.* **un'nett'ed**, not enclosed in a net; **un'no'ble**, not noble: (*Spens.*, *Shak.*) ignoble.—*v.t.* to deprive of nobility. —*adjs.* **unnoted** (*un-nō'tid*); **unno'ticeable**; **unno'ticed**; **unno'ticing**; **unnourished** (*un-nur'isht*); **unnour'ishing**; **unnumbered** (*un-num'bərd*), not to be numbered: not marked or provided with a number; **unnurtured** (*un-nur'tyərd*), not nurtured or educated: ill-bred; **unobe'dient**, disobedient; **unobeyed'** (*Milt.*); **unobjec'tionable.** — *adv.* **unobjec'tionably.** — *adjs.* **unobnox'ious**; **unobscured'**; **unobserv'able.**—*n.* **unobser'vance**, failure to comply or to notice: lack of observing power: inattention.— *adjs.* **unobser'vant**; **unobserved'.**—*adv.* **unobserv'edly.** — *adjs.* **unobserv'ing**; **unobstruc'ted**; **unobstruc'tive**; **unobtain'able**; **unobtaincd'**; **unobtru'sive.** — *adv.* **unobtru'sively.** — *n.* **unobtru'siveness.** — *adjs.* **unob'vious**; **unocc'upied**; **unoffend'ed**; **unoffend'ing**; **unoffen'sive**, inoffensive; **unoff'ered**; **unoff'icered**; **unoffi'cial**, not official.—*adv.* **unoffi'cially.**—*adj.* **unoffi'cious**, not officious.—*adv.* **unoften** (*un-of'n*; *rare*), seldom.—*adjs.* **unoiled'**; **uno'pened**, not opened: of a book, not having the leaves cut apart; **unop'erative**, inoperative; **unopposed'**; **unoppress'ive**; **unordained'.**—*v.t.* **unor'der**, to countermand.—*adjs.* **unor'dered**, disordered: unarranged, not ordered or commanded; **unor'derly**, not orderly; **unor'dinary**, not ordinary; **unor'ganised**; **unorig'inal**, not original: (*Milt.*) without origin or birth.—*n.* **unoriginality** (*-al'*).—*adjs.* **unorig'inate**, **-d**, not originated; **unornamen'tal**; **unor'namented** (or *-ment'*); **unor'thodox.**—*n.* **unor'thodoxy.**—*adjs.* **unoss'ified**; **unostentā'tious.**—*adv.* **unostentā'tiously.**—*n.* **unostentā'tiousness.**—*adjs.* **unovercome'**; **unoverthrown'**; **un'owed**, not owed or due: (*Shak.*) unowned; **unowned'**, unavowed: unacknowledged: ownerless: (*Milt.* *un-ō'nid*) lost; **unox'idised.**—*v.t.* **unpack'**, to undo the packing of: to take out of a pack: to open: to remove a pack from.—*v.i.* to do unpacking.—*adj.* **unpacked'**, subjected to unpacking: **un'packed'**, not packed.—*ns.* **unpack'er**; **unpack'ing.**—*adjs.* **unpaged'**, without numbering of pages; **unpaid'**; **unpained'**; **unpainf'ul.**—*v.t.* **unpaint'**, to free from paint: to paint out.—*adjs.* **unpaint'able**; **un'paint'ed**, not painted; **unpaired'**, not paired: not forming one of a pair; **unpal'atable**, unpleasant to taste: distasteful.—*adv.* **unpal'atably.** —*adjs.* **unpal'sied**; **unpam'pered.**—*v.t.* **unpan'el**, to unsaddle.—*adjs.* **unpan'elled**, not panelled; **unpanged'**, without pangs.—*v.t.* **unpa'per**, to remove paper from.—*adjs.* **unpa'pered**, not papered.—*v.t.* **unpar'adise**, to turn out of Paradise: to make no longer a paradise.—*adjs.* **unpar'agoned**, unmatched; **unpar'allel**, not parallel; **unpar'alleled**, without parallel or equal; **unpar'donable.**—*n.* **unpar'donableness.** — *adv.* **unpar'donably.**—*adjs.* **unpar'doned**; **unpar'doning**; **unpared'**; **unparent'al**, not befitting a parent; **unpa'rented**, without parent or acknowledged parent, or parental care; **unparliament'-ary**, contrary to the usages of Parliament: not such as may be spoken in Parliament; **unpar'tial**; **unpass'able**, impassable: not current.—*n.* **unpass'ableness.** — *adjs.* **unpass'ionate**, **unpass'ioned**, without passions: calm: dispassionate; unpas'toral; unpas'tured, without pasture; unpathed (*un-pädhd'*), pathless; unpathet'ic; unpath'wayed, without pathway; unpatriot'ic. —*adv.* unpatriot'ically.—*adjs.* unpat'ronised; unpatt'erned, unexampled, unequalled: without a pattern; unpaved', without pavement: (*Shak.*) gelded; unpavil'ioned, without a canopy.—*v.t.* unpay', to make good, undo, do away by payment. —*adjs.* unpay'able; unpeace'able. — *n.* unpeace'ableness.—*adj.* unpeace'ful.—*adv.* unpeace'fully.—*adjs.* unped'igreed; unpeeled', not peeled (Shak., *Love's Lab. Lost,* II. i. 88) according to some, stripped, desolate (others think it a misprint for unpeopled, without servants, the folio reading); unpeer'able, not to be matched; unpeered', unequalled.—*vs.t.* unpeg', to loose from pegs or pegging; unpen', to let out from a pen.—*adjs.* unpenned', unwritten: unconfined: let loose; unpenn'ied, without pennies; unpen'sioned; unpent', not penned in.—*v.t.* unpeo'ple, to empty of people.—*adjs.* unpeo'pled, uninhabited: without servants: depopulated; unpepp'ered; unpercei'vable, imperceptible.— *adv.* unpercei'vably.—*adj.* unperceived'.—*adv.* unpercei'vedly.—*v.t.* unperch', to drive from a perch.—*adj.* unper'fect, imperfect: not perfect: defective.—*n.* unper'fectness.—*adjs.* unper'forated; unperformed'; unperform'ing; unperfumed' (or *-per'*); unper'ilous; unper'ishable; unper'ished; unper'ishing; unper'jured; unper'petrated.—*v.t.* unperplex', to free from perplexity.—*adjs.* unperplexed', not perplexed; unper'secuted; unpersua'dable. — *n.* unpersua'dableness.—*adjs.* unpersua'ded; unpersua'sive; unperturbed'.—*v.t.* unpervert', to reconvert.—*adjs.* unpervert'ed, not perverted; unphilosoph'ic, -al.—*adv.* unphilosoph'ically. —*v.t.* unpick', to pick loose, undo by picking.— *adjs.* unpick'able, impossible to pick: unpicked', not picked: picked loose; unpierced'; unpill'ared, stripped of pillars: without pillars; unpill'owed; unpi'loted.—*v.t.* unpin', to free or loose from pins or pinning: to loose the dress of by removing pins.—*adjs.* unpinked', unpinkt' (*Shak.*), not pinked, not adorned with punched holes; unpinned', not pinned: loosed or freed from pinning; unpit'ied, not pitied; unpit'iful, having no pity.—*adv.* unpit'ifully.—*n.* unpit'ifulness.— *adj.* unpit'ying, showing no pity.—*adv.* unpit'yingly.—*v.t.* unplace', to displace.—*adj.* unplaced', not assigned to or set in a place: not inducted to a church: not appointed to an office: not among the first three in a race; unplagued'; unplained', (*Spens.*) not lamented.—*v.t.* unplait', to loosen, undo, from plaiting.—*adjs.* unplait'ed; unplanked'; unplant'ed; unplas'tered; unplau'sible.—*adv.* unplau'sibly.—*adjs.* unplau'sive, not approving; unplay'able; unpleas'ant. — *adv.* unpleas'antly. — *ns.* unpleas'antness, state or quality of being unpleasant: disagreeableness: an impairment of amicable relations: euphemistically, a war; unpleas'antry, want of pleasantness: any unpleasant occurrence, any particular discomfort.—*adjs.* unpleased'; unpleas'ing, not pleasing: displeasing.—*adv.* unpleas'ingly. — *adj.* unpleas'urable. — *adv.* unpleas'urably.—*adjs.* unpleat'ed; unpledged'; unpli'able.—*adv.* unpli'ably.—*adjs.* unpli'ant; unploughed'; unplucked'.—*v.t.* unplug', to remove a plug from.—*adj.* unplugged', not plugged: freed from plugs.—*v.t.* unplumb', to remove the lead from.—*adj.* unplumbed', unsounded: unfathomed.—*v.t.* unplume', to strip of feathers or plumes (often *fig.*).—*adjs.* unpoet'ic, -al.—*adv.* unpoet'ically.—*n.* unpoet'icalness.— *adjs.* unpoint'ed, not pointed: without point or points: with joints uncemented; unpoised'.— *v.t.* unpoi'son, to rid of poison, cure of poisoning. —*adjs.* unpoi'soned, not poisoned; unpolaris'able; un'po'larised; unpoliced', not policed: without police; unpol'icied, without organised civil polity: impolitic.—*v.t.* unpol'ish, to take the polish from.—*adjs.* unpol'ishable; unpol'ished, not polished; unpolite', (*obs.*) unpolished: impolite: (*obs.*) inelegant.—*adv.* unpolite'ly.—*n.*

unpolite'ness.—*adjs.* unpol'itic, impolitic; unpolit'ical, not political; unpolled', not polled: not having voted; unpollu'ted.—*v.t.* unpope', to divest of popedom.—*adj.* unpop'ular.—*n.* unpopular'ity. — *adv.* unpop'ularly. — *adjs.* unpop'ulous; unpor'tioned, without a portion; unpossessed', not possessed : (*obs.*) unprejudiced: not in possession; unpossess'ing, (*Shak.*) without possessions; unposs'ible, (*Shak.*; *dial.*) impossible; unpost'ed, not posted, in any sense: not posted up: without a post; unpo'table, undrinkable, unfit to drink; unpow'dered; unprac'ticable, impracticable; unprac'tical, not practical. — *n.* unpractical'ity. — *adv.* unprac'tically.—*adj.* unprac'tised, having little or no practice or experience: not carried out in practice, not usually done: not yet familiar through practice.—*n.* unprac'tisedness.—*v.t.* unpraise', to dispraise: to deprive or praise.—*adjs.* unpraised', not praised; unpraise'worthy.—*vs.t.* unpray', to revoke the praying of; unpreach', to recant in preaching: to undo the preaching of.—*adjs.* unpreach'ing, not preaching; unprec'edented, without a precedent.—*adv.* unprec'edentedly.— *v.i.* un'predict', (*Milt.*) to recall what has been predicted or foretold.—*adjs.* unpredict'able; unpreferred', without preferment or advancement; unpreg'nant, (*Shak.*) slow-witted, unready, ineffective, not quickened by a lively sense; unprej'udiced, unprelat'ical; unpremed'itable, not to be foreseen: unpremed'itated, not studied or purposed beforehand. — *adv.* unpremed'itatedly.—*ns.* unpremed'itatedness; unpremeditā'tion.—*adj.* unpreocc'upied.—*v.t.* unprepare', to make unprepared.—*adj.* unprepared', not prepared or ready: not prepared for death: without preparation.—*adv.* unprepar'edly.—*n.* unprepar'edness.—*adjs.* unprepossessed', not prepossessed or prejudiced; unprepossess'ing, not predisposing in one's favour, unpleasing; unprescribed'; unpresent'able, not fit to be seen; unpressed'; unpresum'ing; unpresump'tuous; unpretend'ing, not pretending or making pretence: modest.—*adv.* unpreten'dingly.—*adj.* unpreten'tious.—*ns.* unpreten'tiousness; unprett'iness. — *adjs.* unprett'y; unprevail'ing, unavailing; unpreven'table. — *n.* unpreven'tableness.—*adjs.* unprevent'ed, (*obs.*) not anticipated or preceded: not prevented or obviated; unpriced', having no fixed or stated price: beyond price, priceless.—*v.t.* unpriest', to divest of priesthood.—*adjs.* unpriest'ly, unbecoming, unlike, not of the nature of, a priest; unprince'ly, unbecoming a prince; unprin'cipled, (*Milt.*) uninstructed: without good principles: not based on or in accordance with principles: not restrained by conscience: profligate; unprint'able, not fit to be printed; unprint'ed.—*v.t.* unpris'on, to release from prison.—*adjs.* unpris'oned, free, or released, from prison; unprivi'ileged; unpriz'able, (*Shak.*) worthless: (*Shak.*) beyond price; unprized', not prized; unproclaimed'; unprocur'able; unproduced'; unproduc'tive.—*adv.* unproduc'tively.—*ns.* unproduc'tiveness; unproductiv'ity.—*adjs.* unprofaned'; unprofessed'; unprofess'ional, not of a profession or the profession in question: beyond the limits of one's profession: unbecoming a member of a particular profession. —*adv.* unprofess'ionally.—*adj.* unprof'itable.— *n.* unprof'itableness.—*adv.* unprof'itably.—*adjs.* unprof'ited, profitless; unprof'iting, unprofitable; unprogress'ive.—*adv.* unprogress'ively. —*n.* unprogress'iveness.—*adjs.* unprohib'ited; unproject'ed; unprolif'ic; unprom'ised; unprom'ising. — *adv.* unprom'isingly.—*adjs.* unprompt'ed; unpronounce'able; unpronounced'.—*v.t.* unprop', to remove a prop or props from.—*adj.* unprop'er, improper: (*Shak.*) common, not one's own.—*adv.* unprop'erly.— *adjs.* unprop'ertied; unprophet'ic, -al; unpropi'tious.—*adv.* unpropi'tiously.—*n.* unpropi'tiousness.—*adj.* unpropor'tionable, out of due proportion.—*adv.* unpropor'tionably.—*adj.* unpropor'tionate, out of due proportion.—*adv.* unpropor'tionately.—*adjs.* unpropor'tioned, not

Neutral vowels in unaccented syllables : *el'ə-mənt, in'fənt, ran'dəm*

proportioned; unproposed'; unpropped', not propped; unpros'perous. — *adv.* unpros'perously. — *n.* unpros'perousness. — *adj.* unprotec'ted.—*n.* unprotec'tedness.—*v.t.* unprot'estantise, to transform from Protestantism, to strip of Protestant character.—*adjs.* unprotest'ed; unprotest'ing; unprov'able; unprō'ven; unproved'.—*v.t.* unprovide', (*Shak.*) to unfurnish, to deprive of what is necessary.—*adj.* unprovi'ded, not furnished, provided, or provided for (also unprovi'ded-for). — *adv.* unprovi'dedly. — *adjs.* unprov'ident, (*Shak.*) improvident; unprovis'ioned; unprovoc'ative.—*v.t.* un'provoke, (*Shak.*) to counteract provocation of.—*adj.* unprovoked', not provoked: uncalled for.— *adv.* unprovo'kedly.—*adjs.* unprovo'king; unpruned'; unpub'lished; unpuck'ered; unpulled'; unpunct'ual.—*n.* unpunctual'ity.—*adjs.* unpunct'uated; unpun'ishable.—*adv.* unpun'ishably.—*adjs.* unpun'ished; unpur'chas(e)able, not to be purchased: not to be bought; unpur'chased; unpurged'; unpu'rified; unpur'posed.—*v.t.* unpurse', to relax from pursing: to disburse.—*adjs.* unpursued'; unpurveyed' (*Spens.* unpurvaide').—*adv.* unqual'ified.—*adv.* unqual'ifiedly.—*n.* unqual'ifiedness.—*v.t.* unqual'ify, to disqualify.—*adjs.* unqual'it(i)ed, (*Shak.*) bereft of qualities; unquant'ified; unquarr'ied.—*v.t.* unqueen', (*Shak.*) to divest of the title, position, or power of queen.—*adjs.* un'queened'; unqueen'like; unqueen'ly; unquelled'; unquench'able.—*adv.* unquench'ably.—*adjs.* unquenched' unques'tionable, not questionable: not to be questioned: (*Shak.*) averse to conversation, or perh. impatient of question.—*adv.* unques'tionably.—*adjs.* unques'tioned, not called in question: not subjected to questioning: not examined; unques'tioning; unquick'ened; unqui'et, disturbed: restless: uneasy.—*n.* disquiet, inquietude.—*v.t.* to disquiet.—*adv.* unqui'etly.—*n.* unqui'etness.—*adjs.* unquot'able, unsuitable or unfit for quotation; unracked', not drawn off from the lees: not stretched on the rack: not strained; unraised'.—*v.t.* unrake', to uncover by raking.—*adjs.* unraked', not raked: uncovered by raking: not banked up, as a fire; unran'somed; unrat'ified.—*v.t.* unrav'el, to disentangle: to unknit.—*v.i.* to become disentangled.—*adj.* unrav'elled.—*ns.* unrav'eller; unrav'elling; unrav'elment.—*adjs.* unrav'ished; unra'zored, unshaven; unreach'able; unreached'; unread (*un-red'*), not informed by reading: not perused; unreadable (*un-rēd'a-bl*), indecipherable: too dull or ill-written to be read.—*n.* unread'ableness.—*adv.* unreadily (-*red'*).—*n.* unread'iness.—*adjs.* unread'y, not ready, prepared, or prompt: hesitating, holding back: (*Shak.,* &c.) undressed or not dressed (make unready, *obs.* to undress): (*hist.,* of Ethelred II.) redeless; unre'al.—*v.t.* unre'alise, to divest of reality.—*adj.* unre'alised.—*n.* unre'alism.—*adj.* unrealist'ic.—*n.* unreal'ity, want of reality or existence: an unreal thing.—*adv.* unre'ally.—*adj.* unreaped'.—*n.* unrea'son, lack of reason or reasonableness (see abbot): nonsense: (*obs.*) injustice.—*adj.* unrea'sonable, not agreeable to reason: exceeding the bounds of reason, immoderate: not influenced by reason.—*n.* unrea'sonableness.—*adv.* unrea'sonably.—*adjs.* unrea'soned, not argued out; unrea'soning, not reasoning.—*adv.* unrea'soningly.—*v.t.* unreave' (cf. reeve *Spens.*), to unweave: (*dial.*) to unwind.—*adjs.* unreba'ted, unblunted: undulled: without rebate; unrebuked'; unrecall'able; unrecalled'; unrecall'ing, (*Shak.* Milt.) impossible to undo, not to be recalled; unreceipt'ed; unreceived'; unrecep'tive; unrecked'; unreck'oned; unreclaim'able, irreclaimable.—*adv.* unreclaim'ably.—*adjs.* unreclaimed', not reclaimed; un'rec'ognisable (or -*nīz'*). — *adv.* un'rec'ognisably (or -*nīz'*).—*adjs.* unrec'ognised; unrec'ognising; unrecollect'ed; unrecommend'able; unrecommend'ed; unrec'ompensed; unrec'oncilable (or -*sīl'*), irreconcilable.—*n.* unreconcil'ableness.—*adj.* unrec'onciled (or -*sīl'*).—*adjs.* unrec'onciled (or

-*sīld'*); unreconciliable (-*sil'i-*; *Shak.*); unreconstruct'ed, not reconstructed: (*U.S. hist.*) not adjusted or reconciled to reconstruction; unrecord'ed; unrecount'ed; unrecov'erable, that cannot be recovered: irrecoverable: beyond possibility of recovery. — *adv.* unrecov'erably. — *adjs.* unrecov'ered; unrect'ified; unrecur'ing, (*Shak.*) incurable; unred'; unred', (*Spens.*) for unread (unrecounted, [untold]; unredeem'able; unredeemed', not redeemed, esp. spiritually or from pawn: without compensatory quality or circumstance, hence unmitigated, unrelieved; unredressed', unredrest', not redressed: (*Spens.*) without redress or possibility of escape; unreduced'; unreduc'ible, irreducible.—*v.t.* and *v.i.* unreel', to unwind as from a reel.—*v.t.* unreeve', to withdraw from being reeved.—*adjs.* unrefined'; unreflect'ed; unreflect'ing.—*adv.* unreflect'ingly.—*adjs.* unreform'able; unreformed'; unrefract'ed; unrefreshed'; unrefresh'ing; unrefu'ted; unregard'ed; unregard'ing.—*n.* unregen'eracy.—*adjs.* unregen'erate, -d; unreg'istered; unreg'ulated; unrehearsed'.—*v.t.* unrein', to relax the rein of, give rein to.—*adjs.* unreined', unchecked; unrejoiced'; unrejoic'ing; unrela'ted; unrel'ative; unrelaxed'; unrelen'ting. — *adv.* unrelen'tingly. — *ns.* unrelen'tingness; unrelen'tor, (*Keats*) one who does not relent; unreliabil'ity (see rely).—*adj.* unreli'able, not to be relied upon.—*n.* unreli'ableness.—*adjs.* unreliev'able; unrelieved'.—*adv.* unrelie'vedly.—*adjs.* unrelig'ious, not connected with religion: not religious without being necessarily contrary or hostile to religion: irreligious; unrel'ished; unreluct'ant; unremain'ing; unremark'able; unremarked'; unrem'edied; unremem'bered; unremem'bering; unremitt'ed.—*adv.* unremitt'edly.—*adj.* unremitt'ent.—*adv.* unremitt'ently.—*adj.* unremitt'ing, not remitting or relaxing: continued: incessant.—*adv.* unremitt'ingly.—*n.* unremitt'ingness.—*adj.* unremorse'ful, feeling no remorse.—*adv.* unremorse'fully.—*adjs.* unremorse'less, (*obs.*) remorseless; unremov'able, not removable: (*obs.*) immovable, fixed, constant; unremoved', not removed: (*obs.*) fixed, unshaken; unremun'erative; unrenewed'; unrent', not rent; unrepaid'.—*n.* unrepair', disrepair. — *adjs.* unrepair'able, irreparable; unrepaired'; unrepeal'able; unrepealed'; unrepeat'able, not repeatable: indecent, gross: that cannot be done again; unrepeat'ed; unrepelled'.—*n.* unrepen'tance, impenitence.—*adjs.* unrepen'tant; unrepen'ted, not repented of; unrepen'ting, not repenting.—*adv.* unrepen'tingly.—*adj.* unrepi'ning.—*adv.* unrepi'ningly.—*adjs.* unreplace'able; unreplen'ished; unreport'able; unreport'ed; unrepose'ful; unrepos'ing; unrepresent'ed; unre'priev'able; unrepriev'ed; unreproached'; unreproach'ful; unreproach'ing; unreproduc'ible; unreprov'able; unreproved' (or -*prōō'vid*), not reproved: (*Spens.,* Milt.) not liable to reproof, blameless; unreprov'ing; unrepug'nant; unrepuls'able; unrequired', unasked: unasked-for: unnecessary; unreq'uisite; unrequi'ted.—*adv.* unrequi'tedly.—*adjs.* unrescind'ed; unresent'ed; unresent'ful; unresent'ing.—*n.* unreserve', absence of reserve.—*adj.* unreserved', not reserved: without reserve or reservation: unrestricted, unqualified.—*adv.* unreser'vedly. — *n.* unreser'vedness.—*adjs.* unresist'ed; unresist'ible, (*rare*) irresistible; unresist'ing. — *adv.* unresis'tingly. — *adjs.* unresolv'able; unresolved', not resolved, determined, settled, or solved: irresolute: undecided: not separated into its constituent parts.—*n.* unresol'vedness, irresolution.—*adjs.* unrespect'ed; unrespect'ive, (*Shak.*) inattentive, unthinking: (*Shak.*) undiscriminating: indiscriminate; unres'pited; unrespon'sive, irresponsive.—*adv.* unrespon'sively.—*ns.* unrespon'siveness; unrest', want of rest: disquiet: disturbance: discontent verging on insurrection.—*adj.* unrest'ful, not restful: uneasy: full of unrest.—*n.* unrest'ful-

ness.—*adj.* unrest'ing.—*adv.* unrest'ingly.—*n.*
unrest'ingness.—*adjs.* unrestored'; unrestrain'-
able; unrestrained'.—*adv.* unrestrain'edly.—
n. unrestraint'.—*adj.* unrestric'ted.—*adv.* unrestric'tedly.—*adjs.* unretard'ed; unretent'ive,
irretentive; unreturn'able, incapable of being
returned; unreturned'; unreturn'ing.—*adv.*
unreturn'ingly. — *adjs.* unreveal'able; unrevealed'; unreveal'ing; unrevenged'; unre-
venge'ful; unrev'erend, not reverend: (*Shak.*)
not reverent, irreverent, unreverent; unrev'erent,
not reverent; unreversed'; unrevert'ed; unre-
vised'; unrevoked'; unrewar'ded.—*adv.* unrewar'dedly.—*adjs.* unrewar'ding; unrhymed',
unrimed'; unrhyth'mical; unribbed'; unrid',
unridd'en; unrid'able (or unride'able).—*v.t.*
unridd'le, to read the riddle of: to solve.—*adj.*
unridd'leable.—*n.* unridd'ler.—*adj.* unri'fled.
—*v.t.* unrig', to strip of rigging, or of clothes, &c.
—*adj.* unrigged', without rigging: stripped of
rigging.—*n.* unright', (*arch.*) wrong: unfairness,
injustice.—*adj.* (*arch.*) wrong.—*adj.* unrigh'teous.
—*adv.* unrigh'teously.—*n.* unrigh'teousness.—
adj. unright'ful.—*adv.* unright'fully.—*n.* unright'fulness.—*adj.* unringed', not fitted with a
ring.—*v.t.* unrip', to rip up or open: to strip, lay
bare: to disclose.—*adjs.* unripe'; unri'pened.—
n. unripe'ness.—*adj.* unripped', not ripped:
ripped up or open.—*n.* unripp'ing.—*adjs.* un-
ris'en; unri'valled; unriv'en.—*vs.t.* unriv'et,
to loose from being riveted: (*fig.*) to detach; un-
robe', to strip of a robe, to undress.—*v.i.* to take
off a robe, esp. of state.—*v.t.* unroll', to open out
from a rolled state: (*Shak.*) to strike off the roll.—
v.i. to become unrolled.—*adjs.* unro'manised;
unromant'ic, -al.—*adv.* unromant'ically.—*v.t.*
unroof', to strip the roof from.—*adj.* unroofed',
not roofed: stripped of its roof.—*vs.t.* unroost',
(*Shak.*) to drive out of a roost; unroot', to tear up
by the roots.—*adj.* unroot'ed, without root: not
rooted (out): rooted out.—*v.t.* unrope', to loose
from a rope.—*adjs.* unros'ined; unrott'ed; unrott'en; unrouged'; unrough', not rough:
(*Shak.*) unruffe'd beardless; unround'.—*v.t.* to
make unround.—*adjs.* unround'ed; unroy'al.—
adv. unroy'ally.—*adjs.* unrubbed'; unrude', not
rude: also (*obs.*, prob. by confusion from obs.
unride—O.E. *ungerýde*, rough—*gerýde*, smooth,
easy) rude, uncouth; unruff'able, (*Dickens*) imperturbable.—*v.t.* unruff'le, to restore or recover
from ruffling.—*adj.* unruff'led.—*n.* unrule', anarchy.—*adj.* unruled'.—*ns.* unrul'iment (*Spens.*),
unrul'iness; unrul'y, ungovernable: unmanageable: turbulent: stormy; unrump'led.—
v.t. unsadd'le, to take the saddle from: to dislodge from the saddle.—*adjs.* unsadd'led; unsafe'.—*adv.* unsafe'ly.—*n.* unsafe'ness, unsafe'ty.—*adjs.* unsaid (*un-sed'*), not said; un-
sailed', unnavigated; unsail'orlike; unsained',
unblessed.—*v.t.* unsaint', to divest of saintliness
or of the title of saint.—*n.* unsaint'liness.—*adj.*
unsaintl'y.—*n.* unsal(e)abil'ity.—*adjs.* unsal(e)'-
able; unsal'aried; unsalt'ed; unsalu'ted;
unsanc'tified.—*v.t.* unsanc'tify, to undo the
sanctification of: to desecrate.—*adjs.* unsanc'-
tioned; unsan'dalled; unsan'itary, without
sanitation or regard to sanitation; unsapped';
unsashed', without a sash; unsat'able; unsāt'ed; unsā'tiable, insatiable; unsā'tiate, -d;
unsā'tiating; unsāt'ing'; unsatir'ical.—*n.* unsatisfac'tion, absence of satisfaction.—*adv.* unsatisfac'torily. — *n.* unsatisfac'toriness. — *adjs.*
unsatisfac'tory; unsat'isfiable; unsat'isfied.
—*n.* unsat'isfiedness.—*adj.* unsat'isfying.—*n.*
unsat'isfyingness.—*adjs.* unsat'urated; un-
saved'.—*adv.* unsa'vourily.—*n.* unsav'ouriness.
adj. unsa'voury, not savoury, tasteless: of ill
savour: offensive.—*v.t.* unsay', to retract:—
pa.t. and *pa.p.* unsaid'.—*adj.* unsay'able, that
cannot be said.—*v.t.* unscabb'ard, to unsheathe.—
adj. unsca'lable, that cannot be climbed.—*v.t.*
unscale', to remove scales from.—*adjs.* unscaled',
unclimbed: cleared of scales: scaleless; un-
scanned', not scanned as verse: not scrutinised:
(*Shak.* un'skan'd) unconsidered; unscarred';

unscathed'; unscav'engered; unscent'ed;
unscep'tred, without a sceptre: deposed; unschol'arlike; unschol'arly; unschooled'; unscientif'ic.—*adv.* unscientif'ically.—*adjs.* un-
sciss'ored, not cut with scissors; unscorched';
unscott'ified, deprived of Scottish qualities or
characteristics; unscoured'; unscratched';
unscreened', not screened: unsifted.—*v.t.* un-
screw', to loose from a state of being screwed:
to open, loose, or detach by screwing.—*v.i.* to
admit of unscrewing: to come unscrewed.—*adj.*
unscrip'tural, not in accordance with, or not
warranted by, the Bible.—*adv.* unscrip'turally.—
adjs. unscru'pled; unscru'pulous.—*adv.* unscru'pulously. — *n.* unscru'pulousness. — *adjs.*
unscrut'inised; unsculp'tured; un'scythed'.
—*v.t.* unseal', to remove or break the seal of: to
free from sealing or closure: to open (sometimes
prob. for unseel).—*adj.* unsealed', not sealed:
freed from a seal: opened.—*v.t.* unseam', to undo
a seam of: (*Shak.*) to rip open.—*adjs.* unseamed',
without seams; unsear'chable, inscrutable, not
possible to be searched into: mysterious.—*n.* unsear'chableness. — *adv.* unsear'chably. — *adj.*
unsearched'.—*v.t.* unsea'son, (*Spens.*) to affect
disagreeably.—*adj.* unsea'sonable, not in season:
ill-timed. — *n.* unsea'sonableness. — *adv.* unsea'sonably.—*adj.* unsea'soned, not seasoned:
(*Shak.*) unseasonable.—*v.t.* unseat', to oust, remove, or throw from a seat, esp. on horseback or
in Parliament.—*adj.* unseat'ed, not seated: ousted,
thrown, removed from a seat.—*n.* unsea'worthiness.—*adjs.* unsea'worthy; unsec'onded; un-
se'cret, (*Shak.*) failing to preserve secrecy; unsecta'rian. — *n.* unsecta'rianism. — *adjs.* unsec'ular; unsecured'; unseduced'; unsee'-
able, invisible; unsee'ing, not seeing: unobservant: without insight or understanding.—*v.t.*
unseel', to unsew the eyes of, undo the seeling of.
—*n.* unseem'ing, (*Shak.*) not seeming.—*adj.*
(*obs.*) unbecoming, unseemly.—*n.* unseem'liness.
—*adj.* unseem'ly, not seemly, becoming, or
decent: ill-looking.—*adv.* in an unseemly manner.
—*adj.* unseen', not seen: invisible: (*obs.*) inexperienced, not well up.—*n.* an unprepared passage
for translation.—*adjs.* unsegment'ed; unseiz'-
able; unseized', not seized: not taken or put
in possession.—*adv.* unsel'dom, (*lit.* and *rarely*)
not seldom: (*usu.*) seldom.—*n.* un'self', altruism:
impersonality.—*v.t.* unself', to divest of personality, individuality, selfhood, or selfishness.—*adj.*
unselfcon'scious. — *adv.* unselfcon'sciously. —
n. unselfcon'sciousness.—*adj.* unself'ish.—*adv.*
unself'ishly.—*n.* unself'ishness.—*adjs.* unsem'-
inar'd, unsem'inaried, (*Shak.*) without means of
generation; unsensa'tional.—*v.t.* unsense', to
deprive of sense or consciousness.—*adjs.* unsensed',
meaningless; unsens'ible, (*obs.* or *dial.*) insensible.
—*adv.* unsens'ibly, (*obs.*) insensibly.—*adjs.* unsens'itive; unsens'itised.—*v.t.* unsens'ualise,
to free from the dominion of the senses.—*adjs.*
unsent', not sent; unsent'enced; unsenti-
ment'al; unsep'arable, (*Shak.*) inseparable;
unsep'ulchred; unser'viceable.—*v.t.* unset',
to undo the setting of.—*adj.* not set: unplanted.—
v.t. unsett'le, to change from being settled: to
make uncertain, unstable, or restless: to unfix.—
v.i. to become unsettled.—*adj.* unsett'led, not
settled, fixed, or determined: changeable: not
having the dregs deposited: not yet inhabited
and cultivated: turbulent, lawless.—*adv.* unsett'ledly.—*ns.* unsett'ledness; unsett'lement.
—*n.* and *adj.* unsett'ling.—*adj.* unsev'ered.—*v.t.*
unsew (*un-sō'*), to undo the sewing of.—*adjs.* un-
sewed', unsewn', not sewed.—*v.t.* unsex', to
divest of sex: to divest of the characteristics or of
the qualities expected of one's own sex.—*adjs.*
unsexed'; unsex'ual.—*v.t.* unshack'le, to loose
from shackles: to remove a shackle from.—*adjs.*
unshack'led; unsha'ded.—*v.t.* unshad'ow, to
clear of shadow: to reveal.—*adjs.* unshad'ow-
able, impossible to shadow forth; unshad'-
owed, not darkened; unshak'able (also un-
shake'able); unshaked' (*Shak.*); unshak'en.—
adv. unshak'enly.—*v.t.* unshale', to shale or

shell, strip the husk from: to reveal.—*adj.* **unshamed'**, not ashamed: not put to shame.—*v.t.* **unshape'**, to deprive of shape: to undo, destroy, to confound.—*adjs.* **unshaped'**; **unshape'ly**; **unshap'en**; **unshared'**; **unsharp'ened**; **unshaved'**; **unsha'ven.**—*v.t.* **unsheathe'**, to draw from the sheath: to uncover.—*adjs.* **unsheathed'**, drawn from the sheath: not sheathed; **unshed'**, not shed: (*Spens.*) unparted.—*v.t.* **unshell'**, to shell, remove the shell from.—*adjs.* **unshent'**, uninjured: not disgraced; **unshield'ed**; **unshift'ing**; **unshing'led.**—*v.t.* **unship'**, to take or put out of a ship or boat, &c.: to remove from a fixed or allotted place (as oars from the rowlocks).—*v.i.* to admit of or undergo unshipping.—*adj.* **unshod'**, shoeless: with shoe or shoes removed.—*v.t.* **unshoe'**, to strip of a shoe or shoes.—*adjs.* **unshorn'**, not shorn; **unshot'**, not shot.—*v.t.* **unshout'** (*Shak.* **unshoot'**), to revoke the shouting of by a contrary shout.—*adjs.* **unshowered** (*un-showrd'*, -*show'ərd*), not watered by showers; **unshown'** (**unshewn'**), not shown; **unshrink'able**; **unshrink'ing.** — *adv.* **unshrink'ingly.** — *adjs.* **unshrived'**, **unshriv'en.**—*v.t.* **unshroud'**, to uncover.—*adjs.* **un'shrubbed** (*un'shrubd', Shak.*), without shrubs; **unshunn'able**; **unshunned'** (**unshun'd**, *Shak.*), inevitable.—*v.t.*, *v.i.*, and *adj.* **unshut'**, open.—*v.t.* **unshutt'er**, to open or remove the shutters of.—*adjs.* **unsick'er** (*Scot.*); **unsick'led**; **unsift'ed**, not sifted: not critically examined: inexperienced; **unsighed'-for**; **unsigh'ing**; **unsight'** (*obs.*), **unsigh'ted**, not seen.—*n.* **unsight'liness.**—*adjs.* **unsight'ly**, displeasing to the eye: ugly; **unsigned'.**—*v.t.* **unsin'ew** (*Shak.* **unsinn'owed**) to take the strength from.—*adjs.* **unsin'ewed** (*Shak.* **unsinn'owed**); **unsink'able**; **unsis'tered**, without a sister. — *n.* **unsis'terliness.** — *adjs.* **unsis'terly**; **unsist'ing**, (*Shak.*, *Meas. for Meas.*) variously explained as unassisting, unresisting, insisting, unresting; **unsiz(e)'able**, (*obs.*) inordinately big: too little, immature; **unsized'**, not fitted, adjusted, or sorted in respect of size: not treated with size; **unskil'ful.**—*adv.* **unskil'fully.** — *n.* **unskil'fulness.** — *adjs.* **unskilled'**; |**unskimmed'**; **unskinned'**, skinned: not skinned; **unslain'**; **unslaked'**; **unsleeping'**; **unslept'-in.** — *v.t.* **unsling'**, to free from slings or from being slung:—*pa.t.* and *pa.p.* **unslung'.**—*adj.* **unslipp'ing.**—*v.t.* **unsluice'**, to let flow: to open the sluice of.—*adjs.* **unslum'bering**; **unslum'brous**; **unslung'**; **unsmiled'-on**; **unsmil'ing.**—*adv.* **unsmil'ingly.**—*adjs.* **unsmirched'**; **unsmitt'en**; **unsmooth'.**—*v.t.* to roughen: to wrinkle.—*adjs.* **unsmoothed'**; **unsmote'**, unsmitten; **unsmooth'erable.**—*v.t.* **unsnarl'**, to disentangle.—*adjs.* **unsnuffed'**; **unsoaped'**, not soaped: unwashed.—*n.* **unsociabil'ity.**—*adj.* **unso'ciable**, disinclined to associate with others.—*n.* **unso'ciableness.**—*adv.* **unso'ciably.**—*adj.* **unso'cial**, not social: not regarding or conducing to the good of society: not sociable: not convivial.—*ns.* **unso'cialism**, **unsocial'ity.**—*adv.* **unso'cially.**—*v.t.* **unsock'et**, to take out of the socket.—*adjs.* **unsod'**, **unsodd'en**, unboiled: not soaked or saturated.—*adv.* **unsoft'**, (*Spens.*) not soft.—*adjs.* **unsoftened** (*un-sof'ənd*); **unsoftening** (-*sof'*); **unsoiled'**; **unsol'aced**; **unsold'.**—*v.t.* **unsolder** (*un-sod'ər*, or -*sol'*, -*saw'*, -*sō'dər*), to separate from being soldered.—*adjs.* **unsol'dierlike**; **unsol'dierly**; **unsol'emn**, not solemn: informal; **unsolic'ited**; **unsolic'itous**; **unsol'id.**—*n.* **unsolid'ity.**—*adv.* **unsol'idly.**—*adjs.* **unsolv'able**, impossible to solve; **unsolved'**, not solved; **unson'sy**, (*Scot.*) not sonsy; **unsoote'**, (*Spens.*) unsweet; **unsophis'ticate** (now *rare*), **unsophis'ticated**, genuine, unadulterated: unfalsified: free from artificiality: ingenuous: inexperienced in evil.—*ns.* **unsophis'ticatedness**; **unsophistica'tion.**—*adjs.* **unsort'ed**, not sorted or arranged: ill-chosen: unfitting, unsuitable; **unsought'**, not sought or solicited.—*v.t.* **unsoul'**, to deprive of soul or spirit.—*adj.* **unsouled'**, deprived of, or not endowed with, soul; **unsound'**, not sound: unsound'able, unfathomable: **unsound'ed**, not sounded, pronounced, or made to sound: un-

fathomed, unplumbed. — *adv.* **unsound'ly.** — *n.* **unsound'ness.**—*adjs.* **unsoured'**; **unsown'**, not sown.—*v.t.* **unspar'**, to withdraw a spar from.—*adjs.* **unspared'**, not spared: unstinted; **unspar'ing**, not sparing, liberal, profuse: unmerciful.—*adv.* **unspar'ingly.**—*n.* **unspar'ingness.**—*v.t.* **unspeak'**, to retract.—*adj.* **unspeak'able**, unutterable: inexpressible, esp. in badness.—*adv.* **unspeak'ably.** — *adjs.* **unspeak'ing**; **unspe'cialised**; **unspec'ified**; **unspec'tacled**; **unspec'ulative**; **unsped'**, without achievement or success: unaccomplished.—*v.t.* **unspell'**, to free from a spell.—*adj.* **unspent'**, not spent.—*v.t.* **unsphere'**, to draw or remove from its sphere.—*adjs.* **unspied'** (*Spens.* **unspide'**, *Milt.* **unspi'd'**), unobserved; **unspilled'**, **unspilt'**; **unspir'ited**; **unspir'itual.**—*v.t.* **unspir'itualise**, to deprive of spirituality.—*adv.* **unspir'itually.**—*adjs.* **unsplint'erable**; **unspoiled'**, **unspoilt'**; **unspoke'** (*Shak.*), **unspo'ken**; **unsport'ing**; **unsports'manlike**; **unspott'ed.**—*n.* **unspott'edness.**—*adjs.* **unsprink'led**; **unsprung'**, not sprung: without springs; **unspun'**; **unsquared'**; **unsta'ble.** — *n.* **unsta'bleness**, instability.—*v.t.* **unstack'**, to remove from a stack.—*adj.* **unstaid'**, not staid.—*n.* **unstaid'ness.**—*adjs.* **unstain'able**; **unstained'**; **unstamped'**; **unstanch'able**; **unstanched'** (or **un'**), not stanched: (*Shak.*) unsated: (*Shak.*) leaky, hence incontinent.—*v.t.* **unstarch'**, to free from starch.—*adj.* **unstarched'**, not starched.—*v.t.* **unstate'**, (*Shak.*) to deprive of state or dignity.—*adjs.* **unstat'ed**, not stated; **unstates'manlike**; **unstat'utable**, contrary to statute.—*adv.* **unstat'utably.**—*adjs.* **unstayed'**, not stayed or restrained: unsupported: (*Spens.*) unstable: without stays; **unstay'ing**, without stop; **unstead'fast.**—*adv.* **unstead'fastly.**—*n.* **unstead'fastness.**—*adv.* **unstead'ily.**—*n.* **unstead'iness.**—*adj.* **unstead'y.**—*v.t.* to make unsteady.—*vs.t.* **unsteel'**, to soften, to disarm; **unstep'**, to remove, as a mast, from its place.—*adjs.* **unsterc'orated**, not manured; **unster'ilised.**—*v.t.* **unstick'**, to free from sticking:—*v.i.* to take off from the surface:—*pa.t.* and *pa.p.* **unstuck'.**—*adjs.* **unstif'led**; **unstig'matised**; **unstilled'**; **unstim'ulated**; **unstint'ed.**—*vs.t.* **unstitch'**, to take out the stitches of; **unstock'**, to deplete of stock: to remove the stock from: (*obs.*) to launch.—*adjs.* **unstocked'**, not stocked: without stock: not wearing a stock; **unstock'inged**, not wearing a stocking or stockings; **unstoop'ing.**—*v.t.* **unstop'**, to free from being stopped: to draw out the stop of.—*adj.* **unstopped'**, not stopped: of a consonant, open: without a pause at the end of the line.—*vs.t.* **unstopp'er**, to take the stopper from; **unstow'**, to empty of contents: to take out of stowage.—*adjs.* **unstrained'**, not strained or purified by straining: not subjected to strain: not forced, natural; **unstrat'ified**; **unstrength'ened**; **unstressed'**; **unstri'ated**, not striped.—*v.t.* **unstring'**, to take the strings from: to loose the strings of: to take from a string: to put out of tone: to disorganise.—*v.i.* to loose the strings of one's purse.—*adj.* **unstringed'**, not stringed, not provided with strings.—*v.t.* **unstrip'**, (now *dial.*) to strip.—*adjs.* **unstriped'**, not striped; **unstripped'**, not stripped; |**unstruck'**; **unstrung'**, with strings removed or slacked: not strung: relaxed: disorganised: unnerved; **unstuck'**, detached, loosened from sticking; **unstud'ied**, not studied: not having studied: without premeditation: unlaboured: spontaneous: natural, easy; **unstuffed'** (*Shak.* **un'stuft**); **unsubdu'able**; **unsubdued'**; **unsub'ject**; **unsubject'ed**; **unsublimed'**; **unsubmerged'**; **unsubmis'sive**; **unsubmitt'ing**; **unsubscribed'**; **unsub'sidised**; **unsubstan'tial**, not substantial, real, corporeal, solid, or strong.—*v.t.* **unsubstan'tialise.**—*ns.* **unsubstantial'ity**; **unsubstantia'tion.**—*adj.* **unsucceed'ed**, without a successor.—*n.* **unsuccess'**, want of success: failure.—*adj.* **unsuccess'ful.**—*adv.* **unsuccess'fully.**—*n.* **unsuccess'fulness.**—*adjs.* **unsuccess'ive**, not successive: not in, or passing by, succession; **unsucc'oured**; **unsucked'**; **unsued'-for**, -to; **unsuff'erable**, (*obs.*) insufferable; **unsuffi'cient**, (*obs.*) insufficient.—*v.t.* unsuit', to make unsuitable.—*n.* unsuitabil'ity.—*adj.* unsuit'able.—*n.* unsuit'ableness.—*adv.* unsuit'ably.—*adjs.* unsuit'ed, not suited or adapted; unsuit'ing; unsull'ied; unsummed', uncounted; unsumm'ered, not possessing the characteristics of summer; unsumm'oned; unsung', not sung: not celebrated in song; unsunned', not exposed to the sun: not lighted, warmed, affected by the sun: not exposed to view; unsunn'y; unsuper'fluous (*Milt.*); unsupplied'; unsupport'able, insupportable: indefensible; unsupport'ed.—*adv.* unsupport'edly.—*adjs.* unsuppos'able; unsuppressed'; unsure (*unshōōr'*), insecure: precarious: uncertain: doubtful: not assured: untrustworthy; unsured', not made sure; unsurmised'; unsurmount'able, insurmountable; unsurpass'able.—*adv.* unsurpass'ably.—*adjs.* unsurpassed'; unsurveyed'; unsuscept'ible; unsuspect', (*Milt.*) not subject to suspicion; unsuspec'ted, not suspected: not known or supposed to exist.—*adv.* unsuspec'tedly.—*n.* unsuspec'tedness.—*adj.* unsuspec'ting.—*adv.* unsuspec'tingly.—*n.* unsuspec'tingness.—*adj.* unsuspend'ed.—*n.* unsuspi'cion, absence of suspicion.—*adj.* unsuspi'cious.—*adv.* unsuspi'ciously.—*n.* unsuspi'ciousness.—*adjs.* unsustain'able; unsustained'; unsustain'ing.—*v.t.* unswadd'le, to unswathe.—*adj.* unswall'owed.—*v.t.* unswathe', to take swathings or bandages from.—*adjs.* unsway'able (*Shak.*); unswayed' (*Shak.* unswai'd'), not wielded: not controlled: uninfluenced: not swung.—*v.t.* unswear', to retract the swearing of.—*v.i.* to recall an oath.—*n.* unswear'ing.—*adjs.* unsweet'; unsweet'ened, not sweetened; unswept'; unswerv'ing.—*adv.* unswerv'ingly.—*adjs.* unsworn', not confirmed, or not bound, by oath; unsyll'abled, not syllabled, not articulated; unsymmet'rical.—*adv.* unsymmet'rically.—*adj.* unsymm'etrised.—*n.* unsymm'etry, asymmetry.—*adj.* unsympathet'ic.—*adv.* unsympathet'ically.—*adj.* unsympathis'ing.—*n.* unsym'pathy, want of sympathy.—*adjs.* unsystematic, -al.—*adv.* unsystemat'ically.—*adj.* unsys'tematised.—*vs.t.* untack', to detach from tacking; untack'le, to strip of tackle: to free from tackle: to unharness.—*adj.* untaint'ed, not tainted: unblemished: not attainted.—*adv.* untaint'edly.—*n.* untaint'edness.—*adjs.* untaint'ing; unta'ken; untal'ented; untalked'-of; untam'able (also untame'able).—*n.* untam(e)'ableness.—*adv.* untam(e)'ably.—*adj.* untame', not tame.—*v.t.* to make untame, undo the taming of.—*adj.* untamed'.—*n.* untamed'ness.—*adj.* untan'gible, intangible.—*v.t.* untang'le, to disentangle.—*adjs.* untang'led; untanned'; untapped'; untar'nished; untarred'; untast'ed; untaste'ful; untaught', uninstructed: not taught or communicated by teaching: spontaneous, native, inborn.—*v.t.* untax', to remit a tax on.—*adj.* untaxed', not taxed: not charged with any fault.—*v.t.* unteach', to undo the teaching of.—*adj.* unteach'able, not teachable.—*n.* unteach'ableness.—*v.t.* unteam', to unyoke.—*adjs.* untear'able; untech'nical; untell'able.—*v.t.* untem'per, to destroy the temper of, deprive of suitable temper.—*adjs.* untem'pered, not tempered: not regulated; untem'pering, (*Shak.*) unconciliating; untemp'ted.—*n.* untenabil'ity.—*adj.* unten'able, not tenable, not defensible.—*n.* unten'ableness.—*v.t.* unten'ant, to deprive of a tenant: to dislodge.—*adjs.* unten'antable; unten'anted, not occupied; untend'ed, not tended; untend'er, not tender; unten'dered, not tendered or offered.—*adv.* unten'derly.—*v.t.* untent', to remove from a tent.—*adjs.* untent'ed, having no tents: of a wound, unprobed, undressed, or impossible to treat with a tent: (*Scot.*) unheeded; untent'y, (*Scot.*) careless; unter'minated; unterres'trial; unterr'ified; unterr'ifying; untest'ed.—*v.t.* unteth'er, to release from a tether.—*adjs.* unteth'ered, not tethered; unthanked'; unthank'ful.—*adv.* unthank'fully.—*n.* unthank'fulness.—*v.t.* unthatch', to strip of thatch.—*adj.* unthatched'.—*v.t.* and *v.i.* unthaw',

(now *dial.*) to thaw.—*adjs.* unthawed', not thawed; untheolog'ical; unthick'ened.—*v.t.* and *v.i.* un'think', (*Shak.*) to think to the contrary, reverse in thought.—*n.* unthinkabil'ity.—*adjs.* unthink'able, that cannot be thought: outside the realm of thought: beyond the power of thought: inconceivable: unimaginable: utterly impossible (often of things impending but too painful to think about); unthink'ing, not thinking: thoughtless.—*adv.* unthink'ingly.—*n.* unthink'ingness.—*adjs.* unthought'-of; unthought'ful.—*adv.* unthought'fully.—*n.* unthought'fulness.—*v.t.* unthread', to take a thread from: to unweave: to loosen: to find one's way through.—*adjs.* unthread'ed, not threaded; unthreat'ened.—*n.* un'thrift, a prodigal: a spendthrift: unthriftiness.—*adj.* prodigal.—*adv.* unthrift'ily.—*n.* unthrift'iness.—*adj.* unthrift'y, not thrifty: wasteful: prodigal: not thriving: unprofitable.—*n.* unthrift'yhe(a)d, (*Spens.*) unthriftiness.—*v.t.* unthrone', to dethrone.—*adv.* unti'dily.—*n.* unti'diness.—*adj.* unti'dy, not tidy.—*v.t.* to make untidy.—*v.t.* untie', to loose from being tied: to unbind: to solve, resolve.—*v.i.* to come loose.—*adj.* untied', not tied: loosed: (Shak., *Pericles*) not loosed, still tied.

until, un-til', an-til', *prep.* and *conj.* till. [Pfx. *und*-, as far as, and till.]

un- (*continued*).—*v.t.* untile', to strip of tiles.—*adj.* untiled', not tiled: stripped of tiles.—*adjs.* untill'able; untilled'; untim'bered, (Shak.) not strongly timbered: unwooded.—*n.* untime'liness.—*adj.* untime'ly, not timely: before the time, premature: immature: unseasonable, ill-timed: inopportune.—*adv.* at an unsuitable time: too early, prematurely: unseasonably: inopportunely.—*adj.* untime'ous, untimely.—*adv.* untime'ously.—*v.t.* untin', to take the tin from.—*adjs.* untinc'tured; untinged'; untinned', not tinned; untir'able (Shak. untyre'able); untired'; untir'ing.—*adv.* untir'ingly.—*adj.* unti'tled, having no title: deprived of title.

unto, un'too, *prep.* (*arch.* or *formal*) to.—*conj.* (*obs.*) till. [Pfx. *und*-, as far as, and to.]

un- (*continued*).—*adjs.* untoch'ered, (*Scot.*) without tocher; untoil'ing; untold' (or *un'*), not counted: innumerable: not narrated: not communicated: not informed.—*v.t.* untomb', to disentomb.—*adjs.* untombed', not entombed; untoned', not toned: without tones; untorment'ed; untorn'; untor'tured; untouch'able, impossible to touch: not to be equalled or touched.—*n.* (formerly) Hindu of very low caste.—*adjs.* untouched', not touched: intact: unrivalled; untoward (*un-tō'ərd*), not easily guided: froward: awkward: inconvenient: unlucky: unfavourable: unfitting.—*n.* untoward'liness.—*adv.* unto'wardly.—*adj.* untoward.—*n.* unto'wardness.—*v.t.* untrace', to loose from traces.—*adjs.* untrace'able, impossible to trace; untraced'; untracked'; untract'able, intractable.—*n.* untract'ableness.—*adjs.* untra'ded, (*obs.*) unfrequented, as for trade: (Shak.) unhackneyed; untrained'; untramm'elled; untramp'led; untranq'uil; untrans'ferable; untransformed'.—*n.* untranslatabil'ity.—*adj.* untranslat'able.—*n.* untransla'tableness.—*adv.* untransla'tably.—*adjs.* untransla'ted; untransmi'grated; untransmiss'ible; untransmitt'ed; untransmu'table; untransmu'ted; untranspa'rent; untrav'elled; untrav'ersable; untrav'ersed.—*Pericles* untread', to tread back, to retrace; untreas'ure, to despoil (of treasure).—*adjs.* untreat'able, (*obs.*) intractable: that cannot be treated; untreat'ed; untrem'bling.—*adv.* untrem'blingly.—*adjs.* untremen'dous; untrem'ulous; untrenched'; untres'passing; untressed', not dressed in tresses; untried', not tried, tested, attempted, experienced, subjected to trial in court: (Shak., *Pericles*, untride') prob. not ventured upon, hence not noticed or dealt with.—*v.t.* untrim', to deprive of trimming or trimness.—*adjs.* untrimmed', not trimmed; untrod', untrodd'en, not trodden upon: unfrequented; untroub'led, not troubled or disturbed: not turbid; untrue', not true: false: not faithful:

dishonest: inexact: not in accordance with a standard.—*adv.* (*Shak.*) untruly, untruthfully.—*ns.* **untrue'ness**; **untru'ism**, an untrue platitude.—*adv.* **untru'ly**, falsely.—*v.t.* **untruss'**, to unpack: to unfasten: to untie (esp. points): to untie the points of.—*adj.* **untrussed'**, **untrust'**, not trussed: **untied**: with points untied.—*ns.* **untruss'er**; **untruss'ing**; **untrust'**, distrust.—*adj.* **untrust'ful**, not trusting: not trustworthy: not to be trusted. —*n.* **untrust'iness** (*obs.*).—*adv.* **untrust'worthily**. —*n.* **untrust'worthiness**.—*adjs.* **untrust'worthy**, not worthy of trust: **untrust'y**, not trusty, not deserving trust.—*n.* **untruth'**, unfaithfulness: falseness: falsity: that which is untrue: a lie.—*adj.* **untruth'ful**, not truthful.—*adv.* **untruth'fully**.— *n.* **untruth'fulness**.—*v.t.* **untuck'**, to unfold or undo from being tucked up or in: to take out tucks from.—*adjs.* **untucked'**, not tucked: **untuck'ered**, not having a tucker on: **untum'bled**; **untumult'uous**; **untun'able** (also **untune'able**), harsh.—*n.* **untun'ableness**.—*adv.* **untun'ably**.—*v.t.* **untune'**, to put out of tune.—*adjs.* **untuned'**, not tuned: put out of tune: **untune'ful**.—*adv.* **untune'fully**. —*n.* **untune'fulness**.—*adj.* **untur'bid**.—*vs.t.* **turf'**, to strip of turf: **unturn'**, to turn backwards. —*adjs.* **unturn'able**; **unturned'**, not turned; **unturn'ing**; **untu'tored**, untaught: uninstructed. —*vs.t.* and *vs.i.* **untwine'**, to untwist: to separate by untwisting; **untwist'**, to twist backwards so as to open out: to straighten out from a twist.—*adj.* **untwist'ed**, not twisted: subjected to untwisting. —*ns.* **untwist'ing**; **unty'ing**.—*adjs.* **unuplift'ed**; **unurged'**; **unused** (*un-ūzd'*), not used: (also *un-ūst'*) unaccustomed: (*arch.*) unusual: **unuseful** (*-ūs'*).—*adv.* **unuse'fully**.—*n.* **unuse'fulness**.— *adjs.* **unush'ered**; **unus'ual**.—*adv.* **unus'ually**, more than usually: in an unusual way.—*n.* **unus'ualness**.—*adj.* **unutt'erable**, beyond utterance, inexpressible: not to be uttered.—*n.* an unutterable thing: (in *pl.*, *old slang*) trousers.— *adv.* **unutt'erably**.—*adjs.* **unutt'ered**: **unvac'cinated**; **unval'uable**, not valuable, of little worth: (*obs.*) invaluable, priceless: **unval'ued** not prized or highly esteemed: without having a value assigned: (now *rare*) invaluable, priceless ; **unvan'quishable**; **unvanq'uished**; **unva'riable**, not variable: **unva'ried**; **unva'riegated**; **unvar'nished**, not varnished: not artfully embellished or sophisticated; **unva'rying**.—*v.t.* **unveil'** (*obs.* **unvail'**, **unvaile'**), to remove or set aside a veil from: to open to public view by ceremonial removal of a covering: to disclose, reveal.—*v.i.* to remove one's veil: to become unveiled, to reveal oneself.—*adj.* **unveiled'**, without a veil: with veil set aside or removed: unconcealed and undisguised.—*n.* **unveil'er**.—*adjs.* **unvend'ible**; **unven'erable**; **unvent'ed**, not vented: without a vent: **unvent'ilated**; **unvera'cious**, not truthful.—*n.* **unverac'ity**.—*adjs.* **unver'ifiable**; **unver'ified**; **unversed'**, not experienced or skilled: not put in verse: **unvexed'**; **unviewed'**; **unvi'olated**.—*n.* **unvir'tue**, lack of virtue.—*adj.* **unvir'tuous**.—*adv.* **unvir'tuously**.—*adjs.* **unvis'itable**, (*obs.*) unable to visit: unfit to be visited: unsuitable for visiting; **unvis'ited**.—*v.t.* **unvis'or**, **unviz'ard**, to remove or open the visor of.—*v.i.* to unvisor oneself: to unmask.—*adjs.* **unvi'tal**; **unvi'tiated**; **unvit'rifiable**; **unvit'rified**.—*v.t.* and *v.i.* **unviz'ard** (see **unvisor**).—*adjs.* **unvo'cal**; **unvo'calised**.—*v.t.* **unvoice'**, to change to, or utter with, a voiceless sound.—*adj.* **unvoiced'**, not given voice to: without voice.—*n.* **unvoic'ing**, change to a voiceless sound.—*adjs.* **unvoy'ageable**, not navigable, impassable; **unvul'gar**.—*v.t.* **unvul'garise**, to free from vulgarity.—*adjs.* **unvul'nerable**, (*Shak.*) invulnerable; **unwaked'**; **unwak'ened**; **unwalled'**; **unwand'ering**; **unwant'ed**; **unward'ed**; **unware'** (O.E. *unwær*: *obs.*), unwary: (*Spens.*, *Milt.*) unaware, without knowing: (*obs.*) unexpected.—*adv.* **unware'ly**, (*obs.*) unwarily: (*Spens.*) suddenly, unexpectedly.—*n.* **unware'ness**, (*arch.*) unwariness.—*advs.* **unwares'**, (*arch.*) unawares: **unexpectedly**, suddenly: (*Shak.*) unknowingly; **un-**

wa'rily.—*n.* **unwa'riness**.—*adjs.* **unwar'like**; **unwarmed'**; **unwarned'**; **unwarped'**; **unwarr'antable**.—*adv.* **unwarr'antably**.—*adj.* **unwarr'anted**.—*adv.* **unwarr'antedly**.—*adjs.* **unwa'ry**, not wary: (*Spens.* **unwarie**) unexpected; **unwashed'** (*B.* **unwash'en**; see **great**); **unwast'ed**; **unwast'ing**; **unwatched'**; **unwatch'ful**.—*adv.* **unwatch'fully**.—*n.* **unwatch'fulness**. —*v.t.* **unwa'ter**, to drain (esp. a mine).—*adjs.* **unwa'tered**, freed from water: not watered ; **unwa'tery**; **unwa'vering**.—*adv.* **unwa'veringly**.— *adj.* **unwayed'**, not accustomed to roads: hence, intractable; **unweak'ened**.—*n.* **unweal'**, affliction, ill.—*adj.* **unweaned'**.—*v.t.* **unweap'on**, to disarm. — *adjs.* **unweap'oned**, unarmed: disarmed; **unwear'able**, not fit to wear; **unwea'riable**.—*adv.* **unwea'riably**.—*adj.* **unwea'ried**.— *adv.* **unwea'riedly**.—*adjs.* **unwea'ry**, not weary ; **unwea'rying**, tireless: not tiring.—*adv.* **unwea'ryingly**.—*adj.* **unweath'ered**, not worn by the weather or atmospheric agencies.—*v.t.* **unweave'**, to undo from being woven.—*adjs.* **unwebbed'**; **unwed'**, **unwedd'ed**; **unwedge'able** (**unwedg'able**; *Shak.*), unable to be split with wedges; **unweed'ed**; **unweened'**, unexpected; **unweet'ing**, unwitting.—*adv.* **unweet'ingly**, unwittingly. — *adjs.* **unweighed'**, not weighed: not pondered: unguarded; **unweigh'ing**, (*Shak.*) thoughtless, inconsiderate ; **unwel'come**, not welcome; **unwel'comed**.—*adv.* **unwel'comely**.—*n.* **unwel'comeness**.—*adj.* **unwell'**, not well: ill: somewhat ill.—*n.* **unwell'ness**.—*adjs.* **unwept'**, not wept for ; **unwet'**; **unwett'ed**; **unwhipped'** (**unwhipt'**); **unwhole'some**, not wholesome: unsound: tainted in health, taste, or morals.—*adv.* **unwhole'somely**.— *n.* **unwhole'someness**.—*adv.* **unwiel'dily**.—*n.* **unwiel'diness**.—*adjs.* **unwiel'dy** (*Spens.*, &c., **unwiel'dy**), difficult to wield or move, from bulk or weakness: heavily awkward: unmanageable ; **un-wife'like** (**unwife'ly**); **unwigged'**; **unwil'ful**. —*v.t.* **unwill'**, to will the contrary of: to deprive of will.—*adjs.* **unwilled'**, not willed: involuntary ; **unwill'ing**, reluctant: done reluctantly : (*Shak.*) not willed, unintentional.—*adv.* **unwill'ingly**.—*n.* **unwill'ingness**.—*v.t.* **unwind** (*un-wīnd'*), to undo the winding of: to free from being wound: to wind down or off.—*v.i.* to become unwound :—*pa.t.* and *pa.p.* **unwound** (*un-wownd'*).— *n.* and *adj.* **unwind'ing**, uncoiling.—*adj.* not winding.—*adjs.* **unwinged** (*un-wingd'*), without wings ; **unwink'ing**. — *adv.* **unwink'ingly**. — *adjs.* **unwinn'owed**; **unwiped'**.—*v.t.* **unwire'**, to take the wire from.—*n.* **unwis'dom**, lack of wisdom: foolishness: injudiciousness.—*adj.* **unwise'**, not wise: injudicious: foolish.—*adv.* **unwise'ly**.— *n.* **unwise'ness**.—*v.t.* **unwish'**, (*Shak.*) to wish to be away, not to be, to be unfulfilled, or to be undone.—*adjs.* **unwished'-for**, not wished for ; **unwish'ful**; **unwish'ing**; **unwist'**, (*arch.*; *Spens.*, &c.) not known: (*Spens.*) unknowing.— *vs.t.* **unwit'**, (*Shak.*) to deprive of wits ; **unwitch'**, to free from witchcraft.—*adjs.* **un'withdraw'ing**, liberal, lavish ; **unwith'ered**; **unwith'ering**; **un-withheld'**, **unwithhold'en**; **unwithhold'ing**; **unwithstood'**; **unwit'nessed**.—*adv.* **unwitt'ily**. —*adj.* **unwitt'ing**, without knowing: unaware: not cognisant: unintentional.—and—*adv.* **unwitt'ingly**. —*n.* **unwitt'ingness**.—*adj.* **unwitt'y**, foolish: unskilled: without wit.—*v.t.* **unwive'**, to deprive of a wife.—*adj.* **unwived'**, without a wife.—*v.t.* **un-wo'man**, to make unwomanly.—*n.* **unwo'manliness**.—*adj.* **unwo'manly**, not befitting or becoming a woman: not such as a woman is expected to be.—*adv.* in an unwomanly manner.—*adjs.* **unwon'**, not won ; **unwont'** (now *rare* ; *Spens.*, &c.), **unwont'ed**, unaccustomed: unusual.—*adv.* **unwont'edly**. — *n.* **unwont'edness**. — *adjs.* **unwood'ed**; **unwooed'**; **unword'ed**, speechless : not expressed in words.—*v.t.* **unwork'**, to undo.— *adjs.* **unwork'able**, not workable: impracticable ; **unworked'**, not worked ; **unwork'ing**; **unwork'-manlike**, not like or worthy of a good workman.— *n.* **unworld'liness**.—*adjs.* **unworld'ly**, not of this world: spiritual: above worldly or self-interested motives; **unwormed'**, not worm-eaten: (of a dog) not having had the worm or lytta cut out; **unworn'**; **unworr'ied**; **unwor'shipful**; **unwor'shipped.**—*n.* unworth', lack of worth.—*adj.* unworthy.—*adv.* unwor'thily.—*n.* unwor'thiness.—*adjs.* unwor'thy, not worthy: worthless: unbecoming: discreditable: undeserved; **unwound** (*un-wownd'*), not wound: taken out of winding.—Also *pa.t., pa.p.* of unwind.—*adjs.* **unwoundable** (*-wōōnd'*); **unwound'ed**; **unwo'ven.**—*v.t.* **unwrap** (*un-rap'*), to remove wrappings from: to unroll, unwind.—*v.i.* to become unwrapped.—*adj.* **unwreaked** (*un-rēkt'*), unrevenged. — *v.t.* **unwreathe** (*un-rēdh'*), to take out of a wreathed condition.—*v.t.* and *v.i.* **unwrink'le**, to smooth out from a wrinkled state.—*adj.* **unwrink'led**, not wrinkled, smooth.—*v.t.* **unwrite'**, to undo the writing of.—*adjs.* **unwrit'ing**, not writing; **unwrit'ten**, not written or reduced to writing, oral: containing no writing; **unwrought** (*un-rawt'*), not done or worked: not fashioned or worked up: not mined: not tilled: undone, brought back to an original state; **unwrung** (*un-rung'*), not wrung; **unyeaned'**, unborn; **unyielding'**, not yielding: stiff: obstinate.—*adv.* **unyiel'dingly.**—*n.* **unyiel'dingness.**—*v.t.* unyoke', to loose from a yoke or harness: to disjoin.—*v.i.* to unyoke an animal: to cease work.—*adjs.* **unyoked'**, not yoked or harnessed: freed from yoke or harness: (*Shak.*) unrestrained; **unzeal'ous**; **unzoned'**, ungirt.

up, *up*, *adv.* in, to, toward a higher place, level, or state: aloft: on high: towards a centre (as a capital, great town, university): in residence, at school or college: northward: to windward: in or to a more erect position or more advanced stage of erection: out of bed: on horseback: in an excited state: in revolt: with (increased) vigour, intensity, or loudness: afoot: amiss: into prominence, notice, consideration: forward for sale: in or into court: into custody, keeping, possession: away in a receptacle, place of storage or lodging (as a sheath, purse, stable): ahead in scoring: into a closed or compact state, together: to a total: in, near, towards arrival, overtaking, or being abreast: as far as: all the way: to a standstill: at an end: to a finish: thoroughly, completely, fully: well informed, versed.—Also elliptically passing into a verb or interjection by omission of *go*, *come*, *put*, &c., often followed by *with.*—*adj.* (*comp.* upp'er; *superl.* up'most, upp'ermost, qq.v.) placed, going, or directed up: effervescent.—*prep.* in an ascent along, through, or by: to or in a higher position on: to or in an inner or more remote part of: along against the current: along: (*U.S.*) up into.—*n.* a rise: a high place: a success, spell of prosperity: one who is in prosperity.—*v.t.* to drive up-stream (as swans for marking of ownership): to lift or haul up.—*v.i.* (all *coll.*) to set up: to move up: to intervene boldly, start into activity or speech: —*pr.p.* upp'ing; *pa.t.* and *pa.p.* upped (*upt*).—*v.i.* up-anch'or, to weigh anchor.—*adjs.* up'-and-com'ing, (*U.S.*) alert and pushful; up'-and-down', undulating: going or working both, or alternately, up and down: (*U.S.*) downright.—it is all up with, there is no hope for; up against, (*orig. U.S.*) face to face with, confronted with (*up against it*, in almost desperate straits); up and doing, bestirring oneself; up and down, to and fro: here and there through or about: throughout: vertically: out-and-out (ups and downs, undulations: vicissitudes); up to, as far up as: into the immediate neighbourhood or presence of: immersed or embedded as far as: (*coll.*) about, meditating or engaged in doing: capable of and ready for: (*orig. U.S.*) incumbent upon; up to date, to the present time or time in question: containing all recent facts, statistics, &c.: knowing the latest developments of fashion, usage, &c.; up town, into town: (*U.S.*) in or to the residential part of a town; up with, abreast of: even with: to take off, swallow: an exclamation of approbation and partisanship. [O.E. *úp, upp*, up, *uppe*, above, *uppian*, to rise; Ger. *auf*.]
up(s)-a-daisy, *up(s)-a-dā'zi*, *interj.* of encouragement in lifting a child or helping to climb.

upaithric, *ū-pī'thrik, adj.* hypaethral. [hypaethral.]
Upanishad, *oo-pā'ni-shåd, n.* a Sanskrit theosophic or philosophical treatise. [Sans. *upa*, near, *ni-shad*, a sitting down.]
upas, *ū'pas, n.* (in full u'pas-tree') a fabulous Javanese tree that poisoned everything for miles around: an actual Javanese tree (*Antiaris toxicaria*, of the mulberry family): the poison of its latex. [Malay *ūpas*, poison.]
up- (*continued*).—*v.t.* **upbear'**, to raise aloft: to hold up: to sustain.—*n.* **up'beat**, an unaccented beat, at which the conductor raises his baton.—*v.t.* **upbind'**, to bind up:—*pa.p.* **upbound'**, (*Spens.*) also **upbound'en.**—*v.t.* and *v.i.* **upblow'**, to blow up or upward: (of the wind) to spring up.—*adj.* **upblown'** (or *up'*), inflated.—*v.i.* **upboil'.**—*n.* **up'bow**, a movement of the bow from point towards nut over the strings.—*v.t.* **upbraid** (*up-brād'*; O.E. *úpbregdan*; see **braid**), to reproach or chide: (*obs.*) to adduce in reproach.—*v.i.* to utter reproaches.—*n.* (*obs.*) reproach, reproof.—*n.* **upbraid'er.**—*n.* and *adj.* **upbraid'ing.**—*vs.t.* **upbrast'** (*Spens.*), *pa.t.* of **upburst**; **upbray'**, (*Spens.*) to upbraid: (*Spens.*) to bring reproach on.—*n.* an upbraiding.—*n.* **up'break**, a break-up: an outbreak.—*v.t.* **upbreak'**, to break up or open.—*v.i.* to break out.—*n.* **up'bringing**, bringing up.—*vs.t.* **upbrought'**, (*Spens.*) *pa.p.* of *obs.* **upbring'**, to bring up; **upbuild'**, to build up.—*n.* **upbuild'ing** (or *up'*), building up: development: edification.—*adj.* **upburn'ing**, flaming upwards.—*ns.* **upbuoy'ance**, buoying up; **up'burst**, a bursting upwards.—*v.t.* and *v.i.* **upburst'.**—*adj.* **upburst'ing.**—*adv.* **upby'**, **upbye'**, (*Scot.*) up the way, a little farther on or up: up there: at the big house.—*n.* **up'cast**, an upward throw: an upthrow: material thrown up: an upward current of air from a mine: a shaft carrying it (**up'cast-shaft**): (*Shak.*) a chance, accident, fluke, or ace. some, throw or final throw at bowls: (*Scot.*) a reproach: (*Scot.*) an upset.—*adj.* thrown or turned upward.—*vs.t.* **upcast'**, to cast up; **upcatch'**, to catch up:—*pa.t.* and *pa.p.* **upcaught'**; **upcheer'**, to encourage:—*pa.t.* **upcheered'**, (*Spens.*) **upcheard'.**—*vs.t.* and *vs.i.* **upclimb'**; **upclose'**, to close up.—*adj.* **up'coast**, up the coast.—*adv.* **upcoast'.**—*v.i.* **upcoil'**, to coil upwards: to coil up.—*ns.* **up'come**, produce, outcome: (*Scot.*; *obs.*) outward appearance of promise: (*Scot.*) decisive moment; **up'-coun'try**, the interior, inland part.—*adj.* of or in the interior.—*adv.* **up-coun'try**, in or to the interior.—*v.t.* and *v.i.* **upcurl'.**—*adj.* **upcurved'.**—*v.t.* **updrag'.**—*n.* **up'draught**, an upward current.—*v.t.* **updraw'.**—*adj.* **up'drawn.**—*v.t.* **up-end'**, to set on end.—*v.i.* to rise on end.—*v.t.* **upfill'**, to fill up.—*n.* **up'filling**, that which fills up.—*adj.* **upflash'ing.**—*n.* **up'flow**, an upward flowing.—*v.i.* **upflow'**, to stream up.—*adj.* **upflung'** (or **upflung'**, as *pa.p.* of **upfling'**). — *vs.t.* **upfoll'ow**, to follow up; **upfurl'.**—*n.* **up'gang**, (*Scot.*) ascent.—*v.t.* **upgather'**, to gather up or together.—*vs.i.* **upgaze'**; **upgo'**, to go up.—*adj.* **up'going.**—*ns.* **upgo'ing** (or *up'*); **up'grade**, an upward slope or course.—*adj.* and *adv.* **uphill.**—*v.i.* **upgrow'**, to grow up:—*pr.p.* **upgrow'ing**; *pa.t.* **upgrew'**; *pa.p.* **upgrown'.**—*n.* and *adj.* **up'growing.**—*adj.* **up'grown.**—*ns.* **up'growth**, process of growing up, development: that which grows up: a structure that has grown upward; **up'gush.**—*v.i.* **upgush'.**—*adjs.* **up'gushing**; **up'hand**, lifted by hand.—*vs.t.* **uphang'**, to hang up; **uphaud'**, Scots form of **uphold**; **upheap'**, to heap up.—*ns.* **upheap'ing**; **upheav'al**, a heaving up: the bodily elevation of tracts of country: a profound, thorough, or revolutionary change or movement.—*vs.t.* **upheave'**; **upheld'**, **uphild'** (see **uphold**).—*adj.* **up'hill**, ascending: difficult.—Also *n.*—*advs.* **up'hill'**; **uphill'ward** (*Milt.*)—*vs.t.* **uphoard'** (*Spens., Shak.* **uphoord'**), to hoard or heap up; **uphoist'**; **uphold'**, to hold up: to sustain: to countenance: to defend: to keep in repair or good condition: (chiefly *Scot.*, **uphaud'**) to maintain, warrant:—*pa.t.* **upheld'**; *pa.p.* **upheld'**, (*Spens.*) **uphild.**—*n.* **uphold'er**, a support or supporter: (*obs.*) a dealer in secondhand clothes, fur-

niture, &c. : (*obs.*) a funeral undertaker : an up-holsterer.—*n.* and *adj.* **uphold'ing.**—*v.t.* **up-hol'ster,** to furnish with stuffing, springs, covers, &c. : to cushion, be a cover to : to provide with curtains, carpets, &c.—*v.i.* to do upholstery.—*n.* (*obs.*) an upholsterer.—*ns.* **uphol'sterer,** one who makes or deals in furniture, beds, curtains, &c. :—*fem.* **uphol'stress ; uphol'stery,** upholsterer's work or goods.—*v.t.* **uphurl'.**—*v.i.* **upjet',** to spout up.—*n.* **up'keep,** maintenance.—*v.t.* **up-knit',** to knit up : (*Spens.*) to bring together, reconcile, or perhaps conclude, explain or sum up. —*n.* **up'land,** inland, hilly, or high-lying country : (esp. *U.S.*) upper or high land, as opp. to meadows, river-sides, &c.—*adj.* high-lying: remote : inland : rural : of the uplands.—*n.* **up'lander.**—*adj.* **up-land'ish,** (*obs.*) rustic : rural : outlandish.—*vs.t.* **uplay',** to lay up, to hoard ; **uplead',** to lead up :—*pa.t.* and *pa.p.* **upled.**—*vs.i.* **uplean',** (*Spens.*) to rest one's weight ; **upleap'.**—*v.t.* **uplift',** to lift up, raise : to elevate : to raise to a higher moral or spiritual level : to elate : (*Scot.*) to collect, draw, levy :—*pa.p.* and *adj.* **uplift',** **-ed.**—*n.* **up'lift,** a lifting up, raising : upheaval : elevation, esp. moral or spiritual, or the feeling thereof.—*n.* **uplift'er.**—*n.* and *adj.* **uplift'ing.**—*adv.* **uplift'ingly.**—*adj.* **uplight'ed,** lighted up.—*n.* **up'-line,** a railway line for upgoing trains.—*v.t.* **uplock',** to lock up.—*adj.* **uplock'ed** (*Shak.*).—*v.i.* **uplook',** to look up.—*n.* **up'look,** an upward look.—*adj.* **up'lying,** up-land, elevated.—*ns.* **up'make,** action or mode of making up : constitution (especially mental or moral) : slip-proofs arranged in page form ; **up'-making,** filling-up, esp. between bilge-ways and ship's bottom before launching : (*print.*) arrange-ment of lines into columns or pages.—*adj.* (*superl.*) **upmost** (*up'mōst,* *-məst*), uppermost.—*preps.* **upo'** (*ə-pō̄'* ; from *up of* ; *arch.* or *dial.*), upon ; **upon** (*ə-pon', ə-pən*), on.—*adv.* (*Shak.*) thereon, on the surface : on the person : (*Shak.*) thereafter : (*Shak.*) close in approach.—*adj.* (*comp.*) **upp'er,** higher : superior.—*n.* the part of a boot or shoe above the sole and welt : an upper tooth.—**on one's uppers,** with soles worn off one's shoes : very short of money ; **upper crust,** the top of a loaf : the head : a hat : the aristocracy ; **upper cut,** an upward short-arm blow ; **upper hand,** mastery, advan-tage ; **upper story,** any story above the first floor : (*slang*) the brain ; **upper ten (thousand),** the richest or most influential class. — *adjs.* **up-perch'ed,** (*Keats*) perched aloft ; **upp'ermost,** highest : first to come into the mind.—*adv.* in the highest place, first.—*ns.* **upp'er-stock** (see **stock**) ; **upp'erworks,** the upper part of a structure (of a ship above the load-line) : (*slang*) the head.— *adj.* **uppiled',** piled up.—*ns.* **upp'ing,** driving up (see **swan-upping**) ; **upp'ing-block, -stock, -stone,** a horse-block.—*adj.* **upp'ish,** assuming, pretentious, snobbish. — *adv.* **upp'ishly.** — *n.* **upp'ishness.**—*adj.* **up-pricked',** pricked up, erected.—*n.* **up'-putting,** (*Scot.*) lodging and enter-tainment.—*v.t.* **upraise',** to raise or lift up : to exalt : (*Milt.*) to excite, arouse.—*adj.* **upraised'.**—*v.t.* **uprear',** to raise up : to rear up.—*adj.* **up-reared'.**—*n.* **uprest** (see **uprist**).—*adj.* **up'right** (also *up'rīt', up-rīt'*), right or straight up : in an erect position : adhering to rectitude : honest : just : (*obs.*) supine.—**upright piano,** one with the strings in a vertical plane.—*n.* **up'right,** an upright post, stone, stroke, or the like : a vertical member of a structure : an upright piano : (*obs.*) an ele-vation : verticality : a basket-maker's tool.—*v.t.* to set erect or right side up.—*advs.* **upright'** (or *up'rīt', up'rīt*), vertically : honestly ; **up-righ'teously,** (*Shak.*) with moral right ; **up'-rightly,** in an upright manner : honestly : vertic-ally.—*ns.* **up'right-man** (*obs. cant*) a sturdy beggar, leader of a gang ; **upright'ness ; upris'al ; uprise'** (or *up'*), rising.—*v.t.* **uprise'**, to rise up, arise :—*pa.t.* **uprose'** ; *pa.p.* **upris'en.**—*n.* and *adj.* **upris'ing.**—*n.* **uprist** (*Shelley* **uprest**), rising. —*v.i.* **uprist** (*Coleridge*), **upryst** (*Spens.*), an old form of *upriseth,* mistakenly used for a *pa.t.* or *pa.p.* (or perh. from a misunderstanding of the noun).—*adj.* **up'river.**

uproar, *up'rōr, n.* (now *rare*) insurrection, commo-tion and tumult : loud outcry, clamour.—*v.t.* **uproar',** (*Shak.*) to throw into uproar or confusion. —*v.i.* to make an uproar.—*adj.* **uproar'ious.**—*adv.* **uproar'iously.** — *n.* **uproar'iousness.** [Du. *oproer—op,* up, *roeren* (Ger. *rühren,* O.E. *hréran*), to stir ; modified by association with **roar.**]

up- (*continued*).—*v.t.* and *v.i.* **uproll',** to roll up or close : to roll upward.—*v.t.* **uproot',** to root out, pull up by the roots.—*ns.* **uproot'al,** uprooting ; **uproot'er ; uproot'ing.**—*v.i.* **uprose',** *pa.t.* of **uprise.**—*v.t.* **uprouse'.**—*vs.i.* **uprun' ; uprush'.**— *n.* **up'rush,** a rushing upward.—*v.i.* **upryst** (see **uprist**).—*vs.t.* **upsend' ; upset',** to overturn, capsize : to spill or tip out : to disconcert : to derange physiologically : to discompose.—*v.i.* to be upset :—*pa.t.* and *pa.p.* **upset'.**—*n.* **up'set',** an overturn.—*adj.* **up'set,** (of a price) the lowest that will be accepted, at which bidding is started.—*n.* **upsett'er.**—*adj.* **upsett'ing,** discomposing : (*Scot.*) conceited, assuming.—*n.* overturning : overthrow : (*up' ; Scot.*) presumption, overweening assumption. **upsey, upsee, upsy,** *up'si, prep.* (*obs.*) in the manner of.—*adv.* (in full **upsey Dutch, English, Friese,** in the German, English, Frisian manner, of drink-ing) deeply, heavily, heartily.—*n.* a carousal.— *interj.* a Bacchanalian exclamation. [Du. *op zijn,* in his (i.e. the manner).]

up- (*continued*).—*v.t.* and *v.i.* **upshoot',** to shoot upward.—*ns.* **up'shoot,** an upshooting : that which shoots up : (*Shak.*) upshot ; **up'shot,** the final shot : the outcome, final issue : end : (*Spens.*) aim : the conclusion of an argument.—*adj.* **upshot',** shot upward.—Also *pat.* and *pa.p.* of **upshoot.**—*n.* **up'side,** the upper side.—*adv.* on the upper side.— *adv.* **up'side-down', up'side down'** (earlier **up so down ;** *Spens.* **up'sidowne'**), with the upper part undermost : in complete confusion. — *adj.* turned upside-down.—*adv.* **upsides',** (*coll.*) along-side : even : quits.

upsilon (see **ypsilon**).

up- (*continued*).—*n.* **up'sitting,** sitting up, esp. after illness or childbirth : a reception of company on the occasion : (*S.Afr.*) sitting up at night as part of courtship : (*obs. Scot.*) listlessness.—*adj.* (*obs. Scot.*) listless.—*vs.i.* **upspeak',** to begin to speak :—*pa.t.* **upspoke',** (*arch.*) **upspake' ; up-spear',** to shoot up straight like a spear ; **upspring',** to spring up :—*pa.t.* **upsprang' ;** *pa.p.* **upsprung'.**— *n.* **up'spring,** (*Shak.*) a lively dance (acc. others, *adj.,* newly introduced).—*adv.* **up'stage',** towards the back of the stage.—*adj.* towards the back of the stage : (*slang*) stand-offish, superior.—*adv.* **up-stairs',** in or toward a higher story.—*adj.* **up'-stair(s),** of or in an upper story or flat.—*n.* **up-stairs',** a position upstairs.—*v.i.* **upstand',** (*Milt.*) to stand up :—*pa.t.* **upstood'.**—*adj.* **upstand'ing,** erect : straight and well-built : honest and down-right.—*v.i.* **upstare',** to stare upward : (of hair) to stand up.—*adj.* **upstar'ing.**—*n.* **up'start,** one who has suddenly risen to wealth, importance, or power : a parvenu.—*adj.* newly or suddenly sprung : char-acteristic of a parvenu : pretentious and vulgar : new-fangled : (*Spens.*) starting on end.—*v.i.* **up-start',** to start up.—*v.t.* **upstay',** to sustain.—*adv.* **upstream',** against the current.—*adj.* **up'stream,** further up the stream : going against the current.— *v.i.* **upstream',** to stream up.—*n.* **up'stroke,** an upward stroke : an upward line in writing.—*v.i.* **upsurge',** to surge up.—*n.* **up'surge,** a surging up.—*vs.t.* **upswarm',** (*Shak.*) to send up in a swarm ; **upsway',** to swing up.—*v.t.* and *v.i.* **upswell',** to swell up.—*n.* **up'take,** the act of lifting up : a pipe or flue with upward current : (usu. *Scot.* **up'tak** ; *prov.*) mental apprehension (**gleg in the uptak,** quick to understand).—*vs.t.* **uptake',** to take up ; **uptear',** to tear up ; **up-throw',** to throw up.—*ns.* **up'throw,** an upheaval, uplift : the amount of vertical displacement of the relatively raised strata at a fault ; **up'thrust,** a thrust upward.—*v.i.* **upthun'der,** to send up a noise like thunder.—*v.t.* **uptie',** to tie up : (*fig.*) to conclude, wind up.—*prep.* **up-till',** (*obs.* and *Scot.*) up to.—*v.t.* **uptilt',** to tilt up.—*adjs.* **up-tilt'ed ; up'torn** (also **uptorn'**, *pa.p.* of **uptear**).—

adj. and *adv.* **up′town′**, in or toward the upper part or (*U.S.*) the residential quarters of a town.— *n.* **up′-train′**, a railway train proceeding towards the chief terminus.—*v.t.* and *v.i.* **uptrain′**, to train up or over. — *adj.* **up′trilled**, trilled high. — *n.* **up′turn**, an upheaval : a subversal : a disturbance : an upturned part.—*adj.* **up′turned**.—*n.* and *adj.* **upturn′ing**.—*v.t.* **upwaft′**.—*advs.***up′ward** (*-wərd*), **-s**, from lower to higher : from outlet towards source : from modern to more ancient : in the upper part (upward, upwards, of, more than).— *prep.* **up′ward**, upwards along.—*adj.* **up′ward**, directed upward : ascending : placed high.—*n.* (*Shak.*) top.—*adv.* **up′wardly**.—*n.* **up′wardness**, a rising tendency : a state of being high.—*v.i.* **up-well′**.—*vs.t.* and *vs.i.* **upwhirl′** ; **upwind** (*up-wind′*), to wind up :—*pa.t.* and *pa.p.* **upwound′**. —*adv.* **upwind** (*up-wind′*), against the wind.—*v.t.* (*pa.p.*) **upwrought′**, wrought up.

ur, *ər, interj.* filling a gap in hesitation.

ur-, *ŏŏr-, pfx.* primitive, original. [Ger.]

urachus, *ū′rə-kəs, n.* a ligament connecting the bladder with the umbilicus. [Gr. *ourachos*, the fetal structure from which it is formed.]

uraemia, *ū-rē′mi-ä, n.* retention of waste materials in the blood.—*adj.* **urae′mic**.—Also **ure′mia,** **ure′mic**. [Gr. *ouron,* urine, *haima,* blood.]

uraeus, *ū-rē′əs, n.* the snake symbol on the head-dress of Egyptian gods and kings. [Gr. *ouraios,* a kind of snake ; prob. Egyptian.]

Ural, *ū′rəl, n.* a river and mountain range of Russia. —*adj.* **Ural-Altaic** (*-al-tā′ik*), of the Ural and Altai Mountains : applied to a family of languages —Finno-Ugrian, Turko-Tatar, Mongolian, Manchu, Tungus, &c., and their speakers.—*adjs.* **Uralian** (*ū-rā′li-ən*), of the Ural Mountains (**Uralian emerald,** a semi-precious green garnet) ; **Uralic** (*ū-ral′ik*).—*n.* **u′ralite** (*ū′rə-līt*), an alteration product, hornblende after augite : a fireproof building material composed of asbestos fibre with chalk, sodium silicate, &c.—*adj.* **uralitic** (*-lit′ik*).— *n.* **uralītīsā′tion**.—*v.t.* **u′ralitise,** to turn into uralite.

urali. Same as **wourali.**

Urania, *ū-rā′ni-ä, n.* the Muse of astronomy.— *adjs.* **Uranian, uranian** (*ū-rā′ni-ən*), heavenly : of the heavens : astronomical : of Urania or of Uranus, god or planet ; **uranic** (*ū-ran′ik*), of uranium in higher valency : celestial : of the palate.—*ns.* **uranide** (*ū′rən-īd*), a transuranium element ; **uranin** (*ū′rən-in*), a sodium or potassium salt of fluorescein (from its fluorescence, like that of uranium glass) ; **uraninite** (*ū-ran′i-nīt*) pitchblende ; **uraniscus** (*ū-rən-isk′əs*), the roof of the mouth ; **u′ranite,** autunite : torbernite.— *adj.* **uranit′ic**.—*ns.* **uranium** (*ū-rā′ni-əm*), a radio-active metal (U ; at. numb. 92) named by Klaproth, 1789, after the recently discovered planet (**uranium glass,** a yellow fluorescent glass containing uranium compounds) ; **uranography** (*ū-rən-og′rə-fi*), descriptive astronomy, esp. of the constellations ; **uranol′ogy,** astronomy ; **uranom′-etry,** astronomical measurement ; **u′ranoplasty,** plastic surgery of the palate ; **Uranos′copus,** the star-gazer genus of fishes.—*adj.* **u′ranous,** of uranium in lower valency.—*ns.* **U′ranus,** an old Greek god, father of Kronos (Saturn) and the Titans : a planet discovered in 1781 by Herschel ; **u′ranyl** (*chem.*), the group UO₂. [Gr. *ourános,* heaven.]

urao, *ŏŏ-rā′ō, n.* natron. [Sp. *urao,* from Carib.]

urari. See **wourali.**

urate, *ū′rāt, n.* a salt of uric acid.

urban, *ur′bən, adj.* of or belonging to a city.—*adj.* **urbane** (*ur-bān′*), pertaining to, or influenced by, a city : civilised : refined : courteous : smooth-mannered.—*adv.* **urbane′ly**.—*n.* **urbanity** (*-ban′i-ti*), the quality of being urbane : also townishness : town-life. [L. *urbānus—urbs,* a city.]

urceolus, *ur-sē′ō-ləs, n.* a pitcher-shaped structure, with contracted mouth, as the sheath of some rotifers.—*adj.* **ur′ceolate,** having the form of an urceolus. [L. *urceolus,* dim. of *urceus,* a pitcher.]

urchin, *ur′chin, n.* a hedgehog : a sea-urchin : (*obs.* or *dial.*) a deformed person, hunchback : an elf or imp : a mischievous child : a child.—*adj.* like, of the nature of, due to, an urchin.—*n.pl.* **ur′chin-shows,** appearances of elves or goblins.—*adj.* **ur′chin-snout′ed,** with snout like a hedgehog. [O.Fr. *herichon, heriçon* (Fr. *hérisson*)—L. *ēricius,* a hedgehog.]

urdé, urdée, urdee, urdy, *ur′dā, -dē, -di, adj.* (*her.*) pointed : having points. [Origin obscure.]

Urdú, *ŏŏr′dŏŏ, ŏŏr-dŏŏ′, n.* and *adj.* Hindustani, a form of Hindi with many Persian and Arabic words, used in Pakistan. [Hind. *urdū,* camp (language) ; cf. **horde**.]

ure, *ūr, n.* (*obs.*) use, practice, operation. [O.Fr. *uevre* (Fr. *œuvre*)—L. *opera,* work, service.]

ure, *ūr, n.* (*obs.*) the urus. [L. *ūrus.*]

ure, *ər, n.* (*Orkney* and *Shetland*) an eighth of a mark : land paying so much in feu-duty. [Cf. Norw., Sw., Dan. *öre*—L. *aureus,* a gold solidus.]

urea, *ū-rē′ä,* by some *ū′,* *n.* carbamide, CO(NH₂)₂, a substance found in mammalian urine, the chief form in which nitrogenous waste is carried off.— *adj.* **ure′al** (or *ū′ri-əl*). [Gr. *ouron,* urine.]

uredo, *ū-rē′dō, n.* rust in plants : a rust-fungus in its summer stage (also **ure′do-stage**) :—*pl.* **uredines** (*ū-rē′di-nēz*).—*n.pl.* **Uredin′ă′lēs,** the Uredineae. — *adj.* **uredine** (*ū′ri-dīn*). — *n.pl.* **Uredineae** (*ū-ri-din′i-ē*), the rust-fungi, an order of parasitic Basidiomycetes.—*adj.* **uredin′ial** (*U.S.*). —*ns.* **uredin′iospore,** (*U.S.*) a uredospore ; **ure-din′ium,** (*U.S.*) a uredosorus.—*adj.* **ure′dinous**. —*ns.* **uredoso′rus,** a pustule containing uredospores ; **ure′dospore,** a spore produced by rust-fungi in the uredo-stage. [L. *ūrēdō, -inis,* blight— *ūrĕre,* to burn.]

uremia, uremic. Same as **uraemia, uraemic.**

Urena, *ū-rē′nä, n.* a tropical genus of the mallow family, yielding a jute substitute. [Malayalam *uren.*]

urent, *ū′rənt, adj.* burning, stinging. [L. *ūrēns, -entis,* pr.p. of *ūrĕre,* to burn.]

uresis, *ū-rē′sis, n.* urination. [Gr. *ourēsis.*]

ureter, *ū-rē′tər, n.* a duct that conveys urine from the kidneys to the bladder or cloaca.—*adjs.* **ure′-teral, ureteric** (*ū-ri-ter′ik*).—*n.* **ureteri′tis,** inflammation of a ureter. [Gr. *ourētēr, -ēros—ouron,* urine.]

urethan(e), *ū′ri-than, -thān,* or *-than′, -thān′, n.* an anaesthetic, NH₂·COOC₂H₅, prepared from urea and ethyl alcohol.

urethra, *ū-rē′thrä, n.* the canal by which the urine is discharged from the bladder.—*adjs.* **ure′thral** ; **urēthrit′ic,** affected with urethritis.—*n.* **urēthrī′-tis,** inflammation of the urethra. [Gr. *ourēthrā—ouron,* urine.]

urge, *urj, v.t.* to press forward, esp. with earnestness, pertinacity, insistence : to drive : to impel : to provoke : to incite : to insist : to allege earnestly : to advise strongly.—*v.i.* to press : to be urgent or insistent : to push on.—*n.* an impulse : a prompting.—*ns.* **ur′gence** (*rare*), **ur′gency**.—*adj.* **ur′gent,** urging : pressing : calling for immediate attention. —*adv.* **ur′gently**.—*n.* **ur′ger**.—*n.* and *adj.* **ur′ging.** [L. *urgēre,* to press.]

urial, oorial, *ŏŏ′ri-əl, n.* a Himalayan wild sheep. [Punjabi *hureäl.*]

uric, *ū′rik, adj.* of or got from urine.—**uric acid,** an acid, C₅H₄O₃N₄, present in urine and blood, cause of gout when in excess. [Gr. *ouron,* urine.]

Uriconian, *ū-ri-kō′ni-ən, adj.* of the Roman station Uriconium (*Viroconium*) on the site of Wroxeter in Shropshire : applied to the apparently Pre-Cambrian igneous rocks forming the Wrekin, &c.

Urim, *ū′rim,* **Thummim,** *thum′im, ns.pl.* first mentioned in Exod. xxviii. 30, apparently a pair of objects used as a kind of traditional oracle. [Heb. *ūrīm,* t(h)*ummīm.*]

urinant, *ū′rin-ənt, adj.* (*her.*) diving, head downward.—*n.* **u′rinator,** a diver. [L. *ūrīnārī,* to plunge.]

urine, *ū′rin, n.* the excretory product, usually liquid, of the kidneys, chief means of voiding nitrogenous waste.—*v.i.* (*obs.*) to urinate.—*n.* **u′rinal,** a vessel for urine : a convenience for discharging urine.—*adj.* **u′rinary,** pertaining to, or like, urine.—*n.* a reservoir for urine.—*v.i.* **u′rinate,**

to discharge urine.—*n.* **urinā′tion.**—*adjs.* **u′rinative**; **urinif′erous**, conveying urine; **urinip′-arous**, producing urine; **urinogen′ital**, pertaining jointly to urinary and genital functions.—*ns.* **urinol′ogy**, **urinos′copy**, &c., barbarous forms for **urology**, &c.; **urinom′eter** (ill-formed), a hydrometer for urine.—*adj.* **u′rinous**, like, of the nature of, urine. [L. *ūrīna*; cf. Gr. *ouron*.]

urite, *ū′rīt*, *n.* an abdominal segment. [Gr. *ourā*, a tail.]

urman, *ŏŏr-mān′*, *n.* (swampy) pine forest. [Russ., —Tatar *ūrmān*.]

urn, *urn*, *n.* a vase with rounded body, usually a narrowed mouth and often a foot: esp. such a vase for ashes of the dead: hence any repository for the dead: a monumental imitation of a burial-urn: a water-vase: a river-source: an electoral vase: a ballot-box: a vessel with a tap for making tea in quantity, or the like: a moss-capsule: an urn-shaped body.—*v.t.* to enclose in an urn.—*adjs.* **urn′al**; **urned.**—*n.* **urn′ful**, as much as an urn will hold:—*pl.* **urn′fuls.** — *adj.* **urn′-shaped**, rounded with narrowed mouth. [L. *urna*.]

uro-, *ū′rō-*, *ū-ro′-*, in composition, urine.—*adj.* **urogen′ital**, urinogenital.—*ns.* **urol′ogy**, scientific study of urine; **uropoiē′sis**, formation of urine; **uros′copy**, diagnostic examination of urine; **urō′sis**, disease of the urinary organs. [Gr. *ouron*, urine; cf. L. *ūrīna*.]

uro-, *ū′rō-*, *ū-ro′-*, in composition, tail: posterior part.—*n.* **u′rochord** (*-kord*), a notochord confined to the caudal region, as in larval ascidians: any member of the **Urochord′a**, a subphylum of Chordata having a urochord in the larva—ascidians and kindred forms.—*adjs.* **urochor′dal**, **urochor′date.**—*n.pl.* **Urodē′la** (Gr. *dēlos*, clear, plain), the (permanently) tailed Amphibia.—*ns.* and *adjs.* **urodē′lan**, **u′rodele.** — *adj.* **urodē′lous.** — *ns.* **u′romere** (Gr. *meros*, part), an abdominal segment of an arthropod; **u′ropod**, an abdominal appendage of an arthropod, esp. just before the telson.—*adj.* **uropygial** (*-pij′i-əl*).—*ns.* **uropyg′ium** (Gr. *ouropȳgion* or *orropȳgion*—*orros*, the end of the sacrum, *pȳgē*, buttocks), the rump in birds; **u′rosome** (Gr. *sōma*, body), the tail region; **urostege** (*ū′rō-stēj*), **urostegite** (*ū-ros′ti-jīt*; Gr. *stegē*, roof, deck), a snake's ventral tail-plate.—*adj.* **urosthen′ic** (Gr. *sthenos*, strength), having a tail developed for propulsion.—*n.* **u′rostyle** (Gr. *stȳlos*, column), a prolongation of the last vertebra. [Gr. *ourā*, tail.]

Ursa, *ur′sä*, *n.* the Latin name of two constellations, **Ursa Major** and **Ursa Minor**, the Great and the Little Bear.—*adj.* **ur′sine**, of a bear: bearlike.—*n.* **Ur′sus**, the bear genus. [L. *ursus*, *ursa*, bear.]

urson, *ur′sən*, *n.* the Canadian porcupine. [Fr. *ourson*, dim. of *ours*—L. *ursus*, bear.]

Ursuline, *ur′sū-lin*, *adj.* of or pertaining to St Ursula, esp. of the female teaching order founded by St Angela Merici of Brescia in 1537.—*Also n.*

Urtica, *ur-tī′kä*, commonly *ur′ti-kä*, *n.* the nettle genus, giving name to the family **Urticaceae** (*ur-ti-kā′si-ē*), akin to (or including) elms and mulberries.—*adjs.* **urtā′ceous**, like or of the nature of a nettle: of the nettle family; **ur′ticant**, stinging: irritating.—*n.* **urticā′ria**, nettle-rash.—*adjs.* **urticā′rial**, **urticā′rious.**—*v.t.* **ur′ticate**, to sting: to flog with nettles.—*n.* **urticā′tion.** [L. *urtīca*, a nettle—*ūrēre*, to burn.]

urubu, *ŏŏ-rŏŏ-bŏŏ′*, *n.* a S. American vulture. [Tupí *urubú*.]

urus, *ū′rəs*, *n.* the aurochs.

urva, *ur′vä*, *n.* the crab-eating mongoose of south-eastern Asia. [Nepali.]

us, *us*, *pron.* the objective (dative and accusative) case of **we**.—Also in editorial and royal use as a singular.—*adv.* **us′ward**, toward us.—Also *n.* as in *to usward*. [O.E. *ūs.*]

usage, *ū′zij*, *n.* use: act or mode of using: treatment: practice: custom: (*obs.*) interest on money.—*ns.* **u′sager**, one of the non-jurors who maintained 'the usages'—mixed chalices, oblation in prayer of consecration, and prayer for the dead; **u′sance**, usage: (*Shak.*) interest, or lending at interest: time allowed for payment of foreign bills of exchange. [O.Fr.,—L. *ūsus*, use.]

use, *ūz*, *v.t.* to put to some purpose: to avail oneself of: to observe, practise, follow: to resort to: to behave, comport: to habituate: to treat or behave toward.—*v.i.* to be accustomed (used chiefly in the past tense, pronounced in this sense *ūst*; **usen′t**, *ūs′nt*, for *used not*): to resort.—*adjs.* **u′sable**; **used** (*ūzd*), already made use of: second-hand: accustomed: customary; **used′-up**, exhausted.—*n.* **u′ser**, one who uses.— **use up**, to consume: to exhaust: to tire out. [Fr. *user*—L.L. *ūsāre*—L. *ūtī*, *ūsus*, to use.]

use, *ūs*, *n.* act of using or putting to a purpose: state or fact of being used: advantageous purpose to which anything can be applied: the fact of serving a purpose: the profit derived from property: interest for money: usefulness: continual enjoyment of a right (cf. **non-user**; Fr. *user*): convenience: employment: need: advantage: practice: custom: habituation: common occurrence: a distinctive form of public worship or service peculiar to a church, diocese, &c.: custom: (in *pl.*) a form of equitable ownership peculiar to English law by which one person enjoys the profits of lands, &c., the legal title to which is vested in another in trust.—*adj.* **use′ful**, advantageous, serviceable.—*adv.* **use′fully.**—*n.* **use′fulness.**—*adj.* **use′less**, having no use: not answering any good purpose or the end proposed.—*adv.* **use′lessly.**—*n.* **use′lessness.**—**have no use for**, (*U.S.*) to have no liking for; **in use**, in employment or practice; **make use of**, to use, to employ; **of no use**, useless; **of use**, useful; **out of use**, not used or employed; **use and wont**, the customary practice. [L. *ūsus*—*ūtī*, to use.]

usher, *ush′ər*, *n.* one who meets people at the door of a hall, &c., and conducts them to seats: an officer whose business it is to introduce strangers or to walk before a person of rank: an under-teacher or assistant.—*v.t.* to conduct: to show in or out: to introduce: to forerun.—*n.* **ush′ering**; **ush′ership.** [A.Fr. *usser*, O.Fr. *ussier* (Fr. *huissier*)—L. *ostiārius*, a door-keeper—*ostium*, a door.]

usquebaugh, *us′kwi-baw*, *n.* whisky. [Ir. and Gael. *uisgebeatha*, *uisge*, water, *beatha*, life.]

Ustilago, *us-ti-lā′gō*, *n.* a genus of basidiomycetous fungi, of the family **Ustilaginaceae** (*-laj-i-nā′si-ē*) and order **Ustilaginales** (*-laj-i-nā′lēz*) or **Ustilagin′eae**, the smut-fungi.—*adjs.* **ustilagin′eous**, **ustilag′inous.** [L. *ustilāgō*, *-inis*, a kind of thistle.]

ustion, *us′tyən*, *n.* burning: cauterisation by burning.—*n.* **ustulā′tion**, burning: roasting. [L. *ūstiō*, *-ōnis*.]

usual, *ū′zhū-əl*, *-zhoo-*, or *-zū*, *adj.* in use: occurring in ordinary use: common: customary.—*n.* (*coll.*) normal health: habitual drink, &c.—*adv.* **u′sually**.—*n.* **u′sualness.—as usual**, as is or was usual. [L. *ūsuālis*—*ūsus*, use.]

usucapion, *ū-zū-kā′pi-ən*, **usucaption**, *-kap′shən*, *ns.* (*Rom. law*) the acquisition of property by long possession and enjoyment.—*n.* **usucā′pient**, one who claims or holds by usucapion.—*v.t.* **u′sucapt** (*-kapt*), to acquire so.—*adj.* **usucapt′ible.** [L. *ūsūcapĕre*—*ūsus*, use, *capĕre*, *captum*, to take.]

usufruct, *ū′zū-frukt*, *n.* the use and profit, but not the property, of a thing: liferent.—*v.t.* to hold in usufruct.—*adj.* **usufruc′tuary.**—*n.* one who has usufruct. [L.L. *ūsūfrūctus*—L. *ūsus* (et) *frūctus*, use and fruit.]

usure, **usurer**, &c. See **usury**.

usurp, *ū-zurp′*, *v.t.* to take possession of by force without right: to oust, supplant.—*v.i.* to practise usurpation: to encroach.—*n.* **usurpā′tion**, act of usurping: unlawful seizure and possession: intrusion into an office.—*adj.* **usur′patory.**—*n.* **usurpā′ture**, usurpation.—*adj.* **usurped′.**—*adv.* **usur′pedly.**—*n.* **usur′per.**—*n.* and *adj.* **usur′ping.**—*adv.* **usur′pingly.** [Fr. *usurper* and L. *ūsūrpāre*, perh. from *ūsus*, use, *rapĕre*, to seize.]

usury, *ū′z(h)ū-ri*, *ū′zhə-ri*, *n.* the taking of (now only iniquitous or illegal) interest on a loan: interest.—*n.* **u′sure**, (*obs.*) interest: (*obs.*) usury.—*v.i.* (*obs.*) to practise usury.—*n.* **u′surer**, a money-lender (now for excessive interest): a pawnbroker:—*fem.* **u′suress.**—*adjs.* **ū′suring**, (*Shak.*) taking or expecting usury; **usū′rious.**—*adv.* **usū′riously.**—*n.*

fāte, fär, ȧsk; mē, hər (her); *mīne; mōte; mūte; mōŏn; dhen* (then) usū′riousness. — *adj.* u′surous (*obs.*). [L.L. *ūsūria,* L. *ūsūra—ūtī, ūsus,* to use.]

ut, *ōōt, n.* a syllable representing the first note of the scale, now generally superseded by *do.* [See **Aretinian, gamut.**]

utas, *ū′tas, n.* (*obs.*) the octave of a festival. [O.Fr. *outaves* (pl.); see octave.]

utensil, *ū-ten′sil,* formerly *ū′, n.* any useful or ceremonial tool or vessel. [O.Fr. *utensile*—L. *ūtēnsilis,* fit for use—*ūtī,* to use.]

uterus, *ū′tər-əs, n.* the womb:—*pl.* **ū′terī.**—*adj.* **ū′terine** (-*īn*), of, in, or for the uterus: of the same mother by a different father.—*ns.* **uterī′tis,** inflammation of the womb; **u′terogestā′tion,** gestation in the womb. [L.]

Utgard, *oot′gärd, n.* (*Scand. myth.*) the abode of the giants. [O.N. *út,* out, *garthr,* garth, yard.]

utilise, *ū′ti-līz, v.t.* to make use of, turn to use.—*adj.* **u′tilisable.** — *ns.* **utilisā′tion;** **u′tiliser;** **util′ity,** usefulness: profit: a useful thing: (esp. *U.S.*) a public service.—*adj.* produced or supplied primarily for usefulness, esp. provided in order that the public may be supplied in spite of rise of prices.—*n.* util′ity-man, an actor of the least important parts. [Fr. *utiliser, utilité*—L. *ūtilis,* useful—*ūtī,* to use.]

utilitarian, *ū-til-i-tā′ri-ən, adj.* consisting in, based upon, or pertaining to, utility or to utilitarianism: looking to usefulness alone, without regard to beauty, pleasantness, &c.—*n.* one who holds utilitarianism: one who looks to usefulness alone. —*v.t.* utilitā′rianise, to make to serve a utilitarian purpose.—*n.* utilitā′rianism, the ethical theory which finds the basis of moral distinctions in the utility of actions, i.e. their fitness to produce happiness. [Jeremy Bentham's coinage from utility.]

utis, *ū′tis, n.* (*Shak.*) clamour, din. [M.E. *ūthēs,* hue and cry, app.—O.E. *út,* out, *hæs,* hest.]

utmost, *ut′mōst, -məst, adj.* outmost: last: in the greatest degree, extreme.—*n.* the limit: the extreme: the most or greatest possible: the end. [O.E. *útemest,* with double superlative suffix *-m-est* from *úte,* out.]

Utopia, *ū-tō′pi-ä, n.* an imaginary state described in Sir Thomas More's Latin political romance or satire *Utopia* (1516): any imaginary state of ideal perfection.—*adj.* Uto′pian.—*n.* an inhabitant of Utopia: one who imagines or believes in a Utopia: one who advocates impracticable reforms or who expects an impossible state of perfection in society. —*v.t.* and *v.i.* uto′pianise.—*ns.* uto′pianiser;

uto′pianism; uto′piast; u′topism (-*təp-izm*); u′topist. [Gr. *ou,* not, *topos,* a place.]

Utraquist, *ū′trə-kwist, n.* a Calixtine, or asserter of the right to communicate in both kinds—*sub utrāque speciē.*—Also *adj.*—*n.* U′traquism.

utricle, *ū′tri-kl, n.* a little bag, bladder, or cell: a bladder-like envelope of some fruits: a chamber in the inner ear.—*adj.* utric′ular, like or having a utricle.—*ns.* Utricūlā′ria, the bladderwort genus of Lentibulariaceae; utric′ūlus, a utricle. [L. *ūtriculus,* dim. of *ūter, ūtris,* bag, bottle.]

utter, *ut′ər, adj.* (*arch.*) outer: extreme: total: out-and-out:—*superl.* utt′erest.—*adv.* utt′erly.— *adj.* and *n.* utt′ermost, utmost.—*n.* utt′erness.— **utter barrister,** formerly a barrister of rank next below a bencher: one who pleads without the bar, an ordinary barrister, not a king's or queen's counsel or a serjeant-at-law. [O.E. *útor,* outer—*út,* out.]

utter, *ut′ər, v.t.* to put in circulation: to put abroad: to put forth: to issue: to speak, pronounce, give voice to. — *adj.* utt′erable. — *ns.* utt′erableness; utt′erance, act of uttering: manner of speaking: pronunciation: expression; utt′erer; utt′ering, circulation.—*adj.* utt′erless, that cannot be uttered in words. [M.E. *uttren*— O.E. *út,* out; and M.Du. *úteren,* to announce.]

utterance, *ut′ər-əns, n.* (*Shak.*) extremity, the bitter end: the utmost: the utmost effort. [Fr. *outrance* —*outre*—L. *ultrā,* beyond.]

uva, *ū′vä, n.* a grape: a grape-like berry.—*ns.* **u′va-ursi** (*ur′sī;* L. *ursī,* bear's), bearberry: an infusion of its leaves; uvea (*ū′vi-ä*), the posterior pigment-bearing layer of the iris of the eye: the iris, ciliary body, and choroid.—*adj.* u′veal, of the uvea.—*n.* uveitis (*ū-vi-ī′tis*), inflammation of the iris, ciliary body, and choroid. [L. *ūva,* a grape.]

uvarovite, *ōō-vä′rō-vīt, n.* a green lime-chrome garnet. [After Count S. S. *Uvarov,* Russian minister of education.]

uvula, *ū′vū-lä, n.* the fleshy conical body suspended from the palate over the back part of the tongue. —*adj.* u′vular, of, produced by vibration of, the uvula.—*adv.* u′vularly.—*n.* uvulī′tis, inflammation of the uvula. [Dim. from L. *ūva,* grape.]

uxorial, *uk-sō′ri-əl,* or -*zō′, adj.* of a wife.—*n.* uxō′ricide (-*sīd*), a wife-killer: wife-killing.— *adj.* uxō′rious, excessively or submissively fond of a wife.—*adv.* uxō′riously.—*n.* uxō′riousness. [L. *uxor,* -*ōris,* a wife.]

Uzbeg, *uz′beg,* Uzbek, -*bek, n.* a member of a Turkic people of Turkestan: their language.—Also *adj.*

Neutral vowels in unaccented syllables: *el′ə-mənt, in′fənt, ran′dəm*

V

V, v, *vē, n.* the twenty-second letter of our alphabet, a differentiated form of U (q.v.), representing a voiced labiodental sound: an object or mark shaped like the letter: as a Roman numeral V = 5; V̄ = 5000.—*ns.* **V'-bomb** (Ger. *vergeltungswaffe,* retaliation weapon), a self-propelled long-range projectile, as a rocket or a flying bomb, made by the Germans in the Second World War; **V'-day,** Victory day—*specif.* May 8, 1945, when Germany surrendered unconditionally; **V'-neck,** the neck of a garment cut to a point below.—*adj.* **V'-necked.**— *n.* **V'-sign,** a sign made with the thumb and finger(s) in the form of a V, in token of victory.

vac, *vak, n.* a colloquial abbreviation of **vacation,** and of **vacuum-cleaner.**—*v.t.* and *v.i.* to clean with a vacuum-cleaner:—*pr.p.* **vack'ing;** *pa.t.* and *pa.p.* **vacked.**

vacant, *vā'kənt, adj.* empty: unoccupied: of or at leisure: thoughtless: inane.—*ns.* **vacance** (*və-käns',* or *va'* ; *Scot.*), vacation; **vā'cancy,** emptiness: leisure: idleness: inanity: empty space: a gap: a situation unoccupied.—*adv.* **vā'cantly.**—*v.t.* **vacate** (*və-kāt'*), to make or leave empty: to quit: (*obs.*) to annul, to make useless.—*n.* **vacā'tion,** a vacating: a voiding: holidays, esp. of schools, colleges, law-courts: leisure: intermission.—*v.i.* (*U.S.*) to take a holiday.—*n.* **vacā'tionist,** a holiday-maker.—*adj.* **vacā'tionless.**—*n.* **vacā'tur,** the act of annulling in law. [L. *vacāre,* *-ātum,* to be empty; pr.p. *vacāns,* *-āntis*; 3rd pers. pr. indic. pass. *vacātur.*]

vaccine, *vak'sēn, -sin, adj.* of, derived from, the cow: of vaccinia: of vaccination.—*n.* cowpox virus or lymph containing it: any preparation used to confer immunity to a disease by inoculation. —*adj.* **vac'cinal** (*-sin-*), of or due to vaccine or vaccination.—*v.t.* **vac'cinate,** to inoculate with vaccine.—*ns.* **vaccinā'tion;** **vac'cinātor.**—*adj.* **vac'cinatory.**—*n.* **vaccin'ia,** cowpox.—*adj.* **vac-cin'ial.** [L. *vaccīnus*—*vacca,* a cow.]

Vaccinium, *vak-sin'i-əm, n.* a genus including cranberry, whortleberry, and cowberry, giving name to a family **Vaccinī'ceae,** or a division **Vaccinioid'eae** of Ericaceae. [L. *vaccīnium,* whortleberry.]

vacillate, *vas'i-lāt, v.i.* to sway to and fro: to waver: to be unsteady.—*adjs.* **vac'illant,** vacillating; **vac'illāting.** — *adv.* **vac'illatingly.** — *n.* **vacillā'tion.**—*adj.* **vac'illatory,** wavering. [L. *vacillāre,* *-ātum.*]

vacuum, *vak'ū-əm, n.* an entirely (or very nearly) empty space (*pl.* **vac'ūa**): (*coll.*) a vacuum-cleaner (*pl.* **vac'ūums**).—*v.t.* and *v.i.* to clean with a vacuum-cleaner. — *v.t.* **vac'ūate,** (*obs.*) to empty: (*obs.*) to evacuate: (*obs.*) to annul.— *ns.* **vacūā'tion;** **vac'ūist,** one who thinks there are empty spaces in nature; **vacū'ity,** emptiness: space unoccupied: idleness, listlessness: vacancy of mind.—*adjs.* **vac'ūolar,** of a vacuole: **vac'-ūolate, -d,** having vacuoles.—*ns.* **vacūolā'tion;** **vac'ūole,** a very small cavity, esp. in protoplasm; **vacūolīsā'tion,** formation of vacuoles. — *adj.* **vac'ūous,** empty: exhausted of air, &c.: mentally vacant.—*adv.* **vac'ūously.**—*ns.* **vac'ūousness;** **vac'ūum-brake',** a railway brake worked by maintaining a vacuum in reservoirs and applying it simultaneously to brake-cylinders; **vac'ūum-clean'er,** an apparatus for removing dust by suction; **vac'ūum-flask',** a flask for keeping liquids hot or cold by aid of a vacuum lining; **vac'ūum-tube,** a sealed glass tube in which a vacuum has been made, e.g. a thermionic valve. [L. *vacuus,* neut. *vacuum,* empty.]

vade, *vād, v.i.* (*Shak.*) to fade: (*Spens.*) to pass away: to depart. [Partly a form of **fade,** partly **from,** or associated with, L. *vādĕre,* to go.]

vade-mecum, *vā'di-mē'kəm, n.* a hand-book, pocket-companion. [L. *vāde,* go (imper. of *vādĕre*), *mēcum,* with me.]

vae, *vā.* Same as **voe.**

vagabond, *vag'ə-bond, adj.* roving: without settled home: unsettled.—*n.* one who wanders without settled habitation: an idle wanderer: a vagrant: (often playfully or vaguely) a scamp, a rascal.— *v.i.* to play the vagabond.—*n.* **vag'abondage.**— *v.t.* **vag'abondise,** to wander like a vagabond. —*adj.* **vag'abondish.** — *n.* **vag'abondism.** [Fr. *vagabond* and L. *vagābundus*—*vagārī,* to wander.]

vagary, *və-gā'ri, n.* a devious excursion: a digression or rambling: a freakish prank: a caprice:— *pl.* **vagā'ries.** — *adjs.* **vagā'rious;** **vagā'rish.** [App. L. *vagārī,* to wander.]

vagina, *və-jī'nä, n.* a sheath: a sheathing leaf-base: a female genital passage:—*pl.* **vagī'nae, -as.**— *adjs.* **vagī'nal** (or *vaj'i-nəl*); **vag'inant,** sheathing; **vag'inate, -d,** sheathed: having a sheath; **vaginic'-oline, -olous,** living in a sheath.—*ns.* **vaginis'mus,** spasmodic contraction of the vagina; **vaginī'tis,** inflammation of the vagina; **vagin'ula, vag'inule,** a little sheath, esp. one surrounding the base of a moss seta. [L. *vāgīna,* sheath.]

vagrant, *vā'grənt, adj.* wandering: without settled dwelling: unsettled: uncertain, erratic.—*n.* one who has no settled home: a tramp.—*n.* **vā'grancy.** [Perh. A.Fr. *wakerant* of Gmc. origin (cf. **walk**), assimilated to L. *vagārī,* to wander.]

vagrom, *vā'grəm,* (*Shak.*) Dogberry's perversion of **vagrant.**

vague, *vāg, adj.* lacking precision or sharpness of definition: indistinct: blurred: lacking in character and purpose, or addicted to haziness of thought.—*n.* a vague state: an indefinite expanse. —*v.i.* to be vague: (*Scot.*; now *rare*) to wander. — *adv.* **vague'ly.** —*n.* **vague'ness.** [L. *vagus,* wandering—*vagārī,* to wander.]

vagus, *vā'gus, n.* the wandering, pneumogastric, or tenth cranial nerve:—*pl.* **vagi** (*vā'jī*). [L., wandering.]

vail, an obs. spelling of **veil.**

vail, *vāl, v.t.* (*Spens.,* &c.) to lower, let down: to doff in salutation or submission.—*v.i.* to lower a sail: to lift one's hat: to yield: (*Shak.*) to do homage: to go down: to abate.—*n.* (*Shak.*) setting. [O.Fr. *valer,* or aphetic for *avale.*]

vail, *vāl, v.i.* and *v.t.* (*poet.*) to profit, avail.—*n.* (usu. in *pl.*; also **vales**) a tip, perquisite, dole, or bribe. [O.Fr. *valoir,* vail, to be worth.]

vain, *vān, adj.* (*obs.*) empty, devoid: without real worth: futile: unavailing: thoughtless: empty-minded: pettily self-complacent: valuing oneself inordinately on some trivial personal distinction: conceited.—*n.* **vain'esse,** (*Spens.*) vanity, futility.— *adj.* **vainglo'rious,** given to, or proceeding from, vainglory. — *adv.* **vainglo'riously.** — *ns.* **vain-glo'riousness;** **vain'glo'ry,** vain or empty glory in one's own performances: idle boastfulness.— *v.i.* to boast vainly.—*adv.* **vain'ly.**—*n.* **vain'ness,** vanity.—**for vain,** (*Shak.*) in vain, vainly; **in vain,** fruitlessly: to no end; **take in vain,** utter with levity. [Fr. *vain*—L. *vānus,* empty.]

vair, *vār, n.* a kind of squirrel fur, bluish-grey and white, represented heraldically by rows of blue and white shields or bells.—*adjs.* **vairé, vairy** (*vā'ri*), charged or variegated with vair. [O.Fr., —L. *varius,* variegated.]

Vaishnava, *vīsh'nä-vä, n.* a worshipper of *Vishnu.* [Sans.]

Vaisya, *vīs'yä, n.* a member of the third caste among the Hindus. [Sans. *vaiçya*—*viç,* settler.]

vaivode. See **voivode.**

vakass, *vä'käs, n.* an Armenian ephod.

---

fāte, fär, ȧsk; mē, hər (her); *mīne; mōte; mūte; mōͦn; dhen* (then)

vakil, vakeel, *vă-kēl'*, *n.* an Indian agent, representative, or pleader. [Hind.,—Ar. *vakīl*.]

valance, *val'əns*, *n.* a hanging border of drapery.— Also **val'ence.**—*adj.* **val'anced,** furnished with a valance. [Poss. A.Fr. *valer*, to descend.]

Valdenses. See **Waldenses.**

vale, *vāl*, *n.* (chiefly *poet.*) a valley : (*fig.*) the world. —**vale of years,** old age. [Fr. *val*—L. *vallis*, a vale.]

vale, *vā'li*, L. *vä'lā*, *n.* and *interj.* farewell. [L. *valē*, imp.: . of *valēre*, to be well.]

valediction, *val-i-dik'shən*, *n.* a bidding farewell : a farewell.—*n.* **valedictō'rian,** (*U.S.*) the speaker of a college valedictory address.—*adj.* **valedic'tory,** saying farewell : farewell : taking leave.—*n.* (*U.S.*) a farewell oration spoken by a graduand. [L. *valē*, farewell, *dīcĕre, dictum*, to say.]

valence, *vā'ləns*, *n.* (*chem.*) valency : chemical bond.—*n.* **vā'lency,** combining power : its degree as measured by the number of hydrogen (or equivalent) atoms with which an atom can combine, or by the charge on an ion : (*biol.*) numerical arrangement of chromosomes (as single, paired, &c.).—**valency electrons,** those of the outermost shell of the atom, largely responsible for its chemical and physical properties. [L. *valēre*, to be strong.]

valence. See **valance.**

Valenciennes, *val-ən-sēnz'*, *-si-en'*, *vä-län°-syen'*, *n.* a kind of lace made at *Valenciennes* in France, the design being made at the same time as the ground and with the same thread.

Valentine, *val'ən-tīn*, *n.* the name of several saints on whose day, 14th February, the birds were fabled to choose their mates : **valentine,** a person chosen by lot, or the first of the other sex seen that day, assigned in mock betrothal for a year : an amatory or grotesque missive or a gift sent that day : (*Tenn.*) a bird's love-song.—*n.* **Saint Val'entide,** (*Spens.*) the season of St. Valentine's Day.

Valentinian, *val-ən-tin'i-ən*, *n.* a follower of the Gnostic *Valentinus* (died *c.* 160 A.D.).—Also *adj.* —*n.* **Valentin'ianism.**

valerian, *və-lē'ri-ən*, *n.* the plant all-heal (*Valeriana officinalis*), or other plant of the genus, which gives name to the family **Valeriana'ceae,** akin to the teasels : its rhizome and roots, used in medicine. —*adj.* **valeriana'ceous,** of this family.—**Greek valerian,** Jacob's ladder ; **red** or **spur valerian,** a plant Centranthus akin to valerian ; **valerianic** (*-an'ik*) or **valeric** (*-er'ik*) **acid,** a fatty acid $C_5H_{10}O_2$ (in several isomers). [Perh. from some one called *Valerius*, or from L. *valēre*, to be strong.]

vales. See **vail** (3).

valet, *val'it* (or *val'ā*), *n.* a man-servant who attends to clothes and toilet.—*v.t.* (*val'it*) to serve or attend to as valet.—*n.* **val'eting.** [Fr.]

valeta. See **veleta.**

valetudinarian, *val-i-tū-di-nā'ri-ən*, *adj.* pertaining to ill-health : sickly : weak : anxious and fanciful about one's own health.—*n.* a valetudinarian person. —*n.* **valetūdinā'rianism.**—*adj.* and *n.* **valetūd'-inary** (*-ə-ri*), valetudinarian. [L. *valētūdinārius*—*valētūdō*, state of health—*valēre*, to be strong.]

valgus, *val'gus*, *n.* (for *tālipēs valgus*) out-turned clubfoot. [L., bow-legged.]

valhalla, *val-hal'ä*, *n.* (*Scand. myth.*) the palace of bliss for the souls of slain heroes : a general burial-place or monument for a nation's great men. [O.N. *Valhöll*—*valr*, the slain, *höll*, hall (cf. O.E. *wæl*, *heall*).]

vali, *vä-lē'*, *n.* a governor, esp. of a vilayet. [Turk.]

valiant, *val'yənt*, *adj.* (*obs.*) strong : brave : actively courageous : heroic.—*n.* (*obs.*) a valiant person.— *ns.* **val'iance, val'iancy,** valour : a deed of valour. —*adv.* **val'iantly.** [Fr. *vaillant*—L. *valēre*, to be strong.]

valid, *val'id*, *adj.* strong : sound : legally or logically good, adequate, or efficacious.—*v.t.* **val'idate,** to make valid : to ratify.—*ns.* **validā'tion ; valid'ity.** —*adv.* **val'idly.**—*n.* **val'idness.** [L. *validus*— *valēre*, to be strong.]

valise, *və-lēz'*, (*U.S.*) *-lēs'*, *n.* (now *rare* except *U.S.*) a travelling bag for hand or saddle : a kit-bag. [Fr. ; cf. It. *valigia*, Sp. *valija*.]

Valkyrie, *val'kir-i*, *-kir'i*, *val-kir'i*, *n.* (*Scand. myth.*) any one of the minor goddesses who conducted the slain from the battlefield to Valhalla :—*pl.* **Valkyries, Valkyr'iur.** [O.N. *Valkyrja*—*valr*, the slain, and the root of *kjósa*, to choose ; cf. O.E. *Wælcyrige,* Ger. *Walküre.*]

vallar, vallary. See **vallum.**

vallecula, *va-lek'ū-lä*, *n.* a groove or furrow.—*adjs.* **vallec'ular, vallec'ulate.** [L.L. dim. of L. *vallis*, valley.]

valley, *val'i*, *n.* an elongated hollow between hills : a stretch of country watered by a river : a trough between ridges : the hollow of an M-shaped roof :— *pl.* **vall'eys.** [O.Fr. *valee* (Fr. *vallée*)—*val*—L. *vallis*, a valley.]

Vallisneria, *val-is-nē'ri-ä*, *n.* a tropical and subtropical genus of submerged water-plants of the frogbit family. [After Antonio *Vallisneri* (1661-1730), Italian naturalist.]

vallum, *val'əm*, *n.* a rampart : a wall of sods, earth, or other material, esp. of that thrown up from a ditch.—*adjs.* **vall'ar, -y,** applied to a crown bestowed in ancient Rome on the first to mount an enemy's rampart. [L.]

valonia, vallonia, *və-lō'ni-ä*, *n.* a tanning material, acorns of a Levantine oak (valonia oak, *Quercus Aegilops*). [It. *vallonea*—Gr. *balanos*, an acorn.]

valour, *val'ər*, *n.* intrepidity : courage : bravery : (*obs.*) value, worth.—*n.* **valorisā'tion,** fixing of price.—*v.t.* **val'orise,** to fix the price of.—*adj.* **val'orous,** intrepid : courageous.—*adv.* **val'orously.** [O.Fr. *valour*—L.L. *valor*, *-ōris*—L. *valēre*, to be strong.]

valse, *väls*, *n.*, *v.i.*, and *v.t.* waltz. [Fr.]

value, *val'ū*, *n.* worth : a fair equivalent : intrinsic worth or goodness : recognition of such worth : that which renders anything useful or estimable : the degree of this quality : relative worth : high worth : esteem : efficacy : excellence : price : precise meaning : (*mus.*) relative duration : (*paint.*) relation with reference to light and shade : (*math.*) the special determination of a quantity.—*v.t.* to estimate the worth of : to rate at a price : to esteem : to prize.—*v.t.* or *v.i.* (*Shak.*) to be worth.—*adj.* **val'uable,** having value or worth : of high value.— *n.* a thing of value, a choice article—often in *pl.*— *n.* **val'uableness.**—*adv.* **val'uably.**—*v.t.* **val'uate,** to appraise.—*n.* **valuā'tion,** estimation of value.— *adj.* **valuā'tional.**—*n.* **val'uātor,** an appraiser.— *adjs.* **val'ued,** having a value assigned : priced : highly esteemed : prized ; **val'ueless.**—*n.* **val'uer,** one who estimates values, a valuator : one who sets a high value.—**good value,** full worth in exchange ; **valuable consideration,** (*law*) a consideration (q.v.) having material or monetary value ; **value in exchange,** exchange value : (*pol. econ.*) amount of other commodities for which a thing can be exchanged in open market ; **value received,** a phrase indicating that a bill of exchange, &c., has been accepted for a valuable consideration. [O.Fr. *value*, fem. pa.p. of *valoir*, to be worth—L. *valēre*.]

valuta, *vä-l(y)ōō'tä*, *n.* the comparative value of a currency : a standard of money. [It.]

valve, *valv*, *n.* a leaf of a folding-door : a single piece forming part or the whole of a shell : one of the parts of a dry fruit separating in dehiscence : a structure or device that regulates flow or passage, or allows it in one direction only : (*elect.*) a rectifier : loosely, a thermionic valve used in wireless apparatus as rectifier, amplifier, oscillator or otherwise. —*adjs.* **val'val ; val'var ; val'vate,** with or having a valve or valves : (*bot.*) meeting at the edges without overlapping ; **valved ; valve'less.**—*ns.* **valve'let,** **val'vula, val'vule,** a little valve.—*adj.* **val'vūlar,** of or having a valvule or valve.—*n.* **valvūli'tis,** inflammation of a valve of the heart. [L. *valva*, a folding-door.]

vambrace, *vam'brās*, *n.* armour for the forearm.— *adj.* **vam'braced.** [A.Fr. *vantbras* for *avant-bras*— *avant*, before, *bras*, arm.]

vamose, *və-mōs'*, **vamoose,** *-mōōs'*, *v.i.* (slang) to make off.—*v.t.* to leave. [Sp. *vamos*, let us go.]

vamp, *vamp*, *n.* the part of a boot or shoe covering the front of the foot : anything patched up : a simple and uninspired improvised accompaniment.—*v.t.* to provide with a vamp : to repair with a new vamp : to patch up : to give a new face to : (*mus.*) to improvise inartistically.—*v.i.* to improvise crude accompaniments : (now *dial.*) to trudge.—*n.* vam′per.—*n.* and *adj.* vamp′ing. [O.Fr. *avanpié*—*avan* (Fr. *avant*), before, *pié* (Fr. *pied*)—L. *pĕs, pedis*, foot.]

vampire, *vam′pīr*, *n.* in eastern European folklore, a dead man that leaves his grave to prey upon the living : (*fig.*) a blood-sucker, a relentless extortionate parasite or blackmailer : an adventuress who exploits men (abbreviated **vamp**): a vampire-bat : a stage trap.—*v.t.* to prey upon like a vampire. —*ns.* **vamp** (see above) ; **vam′pire-bat′**, a blood-sucking Central and South American bat (as Desmodus, Diphylla): applied to various bats wrongly supposed to be blood-suckers (as Vampyrus).—*v.i.* **vam′pirise**, to play the vampire.—*v.t.* (*lit.* and *fig.*) to suck the blood of.—*n.* **vam′pirism**, belief in human vampires : the actions of a vampire.—*adj.* **vamp′ish**. [Various Slavonic languages have *vampir.*]

vamplate, *vam′plāt*, *n.* a guard for the hand on a lance. [A.Fr. *van-* for *avant*, before, *plate*, plate.]

van, *van*, *n.* a shortened form of **vanguard**.—Also (*Shak.*) **vant**, **vaunt**.

van, *van*, *n.* a winnowing basket or shovel : a shovel for testing ore : a test of ore by washing on a shovel : a wing : a windmill sail.—*v.t.* to winnow or test with a van.—*n.* **vann′er**, one who vans : an ore-separator.—*n.* and *adj.* **vann′ing**. [Southern form of fan ; perh. in part directly from L. *vannus* or O.Fr. *van.*]

van, *van*, *n.* a large covered wagon : a light vehicle, covered or not, used by tradesmen in delivering goods : a railway carriage or compartment for luggage, the guard, &c.—*v.t.* and *v.i.* to send, convey, confine, travel, or tour in a van :—*pr.p.* **vann′ing**; *pa.t.* and *pa.p.* **vanned**.—*n.* **vann′er**, a horse suitable for a van. [Short for **caravan**.]

van, *van*, *n.* (*lawn-tennis*) short for (ad)vantage.

vanadium, *və-nā′di-əm*, *n.* a silvery metallic element (V ; at. numb. 23).—*ns.* **vanadate** (*van′ə-dāt*), a salt of vanadic acid.—*adj.* **vanadic** (*və-nad′ik*), of vanadium in higher valency.—*n.* **van′adinite** (or *-nad′*), a mineral, lead vanadate and chloride. [Named by a Swedish chemist Sefström from O.N. *Vana-dís*, the goddess Freyja.]

Vandal, *van′dəl*, *n.* one of a fierce people that passed from north-eastern Germany to Gaul, Spain, and North Africa, and sacked Rome in 455 : hence, from their destruction of Catholic churches, &c., one who destroys what is beautiful.—*adjs.* **Van′dal**, **Vandalic** (*-dal′ik*).—*n.* **Van′dalism**.

Vandyke, *van-dīk′*, or *van′-*, *n.* a painting by the great Flemish artist Anthony *Van Dyck* (1599-1641): vandyke′, a deeply cut collar similar to those seen in his portraits : a point of a deep-cut edging : a short pointed beard (also called **Vandyke beard**).—*v.t.* and *v.i.* to notch or zig-zag.—*adj.* **vandyked′.**—**van′dyke brown**, a deep brown used by Van Dyck : a mixture of lampblack or other material and ochre.

vane, *vān*, *n.* a flag : a weather-cock or revolving plate, or a streamer, serving to show how the wind blows : a heraldic or ornamental plate fixed on a pinnacle : a blade of a windmill, propeller, revolving fan, or the like : a fin on a bomb or a paravane : a sight on an observing or surveying instrument : the web of a feather.—*adjs.* **vaned**, having a vane or vanes ; **vane′less**. [Southern form of **fane**.]

Vanessa, *və-nes′ä*, *n.* the red admiral genus of butterflies. [Perh. for *Phanessa*—Gr. *Phănēs*, a mystic divinity.]

vang, *vang*, *n.* a guy-rope to steady a gaff. [A form of **fang**.]

vanguard, *van′gärd*, *n.* the foremost of an army, &c. : the forefront : those who lead the way or anticipate progress. [Fr. *avant-garde*—*avant*, before, *garde*, guard.]

vanilla, *və-nil′ä*, *n.* a flavouring substance got from the pods of *Vanilla planifolia*, a Mexican climbing orchid, and other species : the plant yielding it.—*n.* **vanill′in**, its aromatic principle ($C_8H_8O_3$). [Sp. *vainilla*—*vaina*—L. *vāgīna*, a sheath.]

vanish, *van′ish*, *v.i.* to disappear : to fade out : to

cease to exist : to become zero : (*Shak.*) to exhale, emanate.—*v.t.* to cause to disappear.—*n.* a vanishing : a glide with which a sound ends.—*n.* van′isher.—*n.* and *adj.* van′ishing.—*adv.* van′ishingly.—*n.* van′ishment.—**vanishing point**, the point at which parallel lines seen in perspective converge : the verge of disappearance of anything. [Aphetic for **evanish**.]

vanity, *van′i-ti*, *n.* the quality of being vain : that which is vain.—*ns.* van′ity-bag, -box, -case, one containing a mirror and cosmetic appliances. [Fr. *vanité*—L. *vānitas, -ātis*; see vain.]

vanner, **vanning**, &c. See van (2), van (3).

vanquish, *vangk′wish*, *v.t.* to conquer : to subdue : to overcome.—*v.i.* to be victor.—*adj.* vanq′uishable.—*ns.* vanq′uisher ; vanq′uishment. [A.Fr. *venquir, venquiss-* (Fr. *vaincre*)—L. *vincĕre*, to conquer.]

vant, *vant*, *n.* (*Shak.*). Same as van (1).

vantage, *van′tij*, *n.* advantage : in lawn-tennis, the first point after deuce : (*Shak.*) opportunity : (*Shak.*) excess, addition.—*v.i.* (*Spens.*) to benefit, profit.—*ns.* van′tage-ground, -point, a favourable or commanding position.—*adj.* van′tageless. [A.Fr. *vantage*; cf. **advantage**.]

vantbrace, *vant′brās* (*Milt.* vant-brass, *-bras*). Same as **vambrace**.

vanward, *van′wərd*, *adj.* and *adv.* towards the van or front.

vapid, *vap′id*, *adj.* spiritless : insipid : dull : flat.—*n.* vapid′ity.—*adv.* vap′idly.—*n.* vap′idness. [L. *vapidus.*]

vapour or (esp. *U.S.*) **vapor**, *vā′pər*, *n.* a substance in the form of a mist, fume, or smoke, esp. one coming off from a solid or liquid : a gas below its critical temperature, liquefiable by pressure : water in the atmosphere : (*old med.*; in *pl.*) exhalations supposed to arise in the stomach or elsewhere in the body, affecting the health : (in *pl.*, often with *the*) low spirits, boredom, or nervous disorder : anything insubstantial, vain, or transitory : a fanciful notion : bluster.—*v.i.* to pass off in vapour : to evaporate : to brag : to emit vapour : to bluster.—*v.t.* to make to pass into vapour : to steam : to affect with the vapours : to boast : to drive by bluster.—*adjs.* vā′porable, capable of being turned to vapour ; vāporif′ic, vaporising ; vā′poriform, existing in the form of vapour.—*n.* vāporim′eter, an instrument for measuring vapour pressure or volume.—*adj.* vāporīs′able.—*n.* vāporīsā′tion.—*v.t.* vā′porise, to convert into vapour : to spray.—*v.i.* to become vapour.—*ns.* vāporīs′er, an apparatus for discharging liquid in a fine spray ; vāporos′ity.—*adj.* vā′porous, of, in the form of, like, or full of vapour : vain : affected with the vapours : unsubstantial : flimsy : vainly fanciful.—*adv.* vā′porously.—*ns.* vā′porousness ; vā′pour-bath, a bath in vapour : a place or apparatus for the purpose.—*adj.* vā′poured, full of vapours : affected with the vapours.—*n.* vā′pourer, one who vapours : a moth (Orgyia) of the tussock family.—*n.* and *adj.* vā′pouring.—*adv.* vā′pouringly. — *adj.* vā′pourish, vapoury. — *n.* vā′pourishness.—*adj.* vā′poury, full of vapour : affected with the vapours. [L. *vapor, -ōris.*]

vapulate, *vap′ū-lāt*, *v.i.* to be flogged.—*n.* vapūlā′tion, a flogging. [L. *vāpulāre, -ātum*, to be flogged.]

vaquero, *vä-kā′rō*, *n.* a herdsman. [Sp.,—L. *vacca*, a cow.]

vara, *vä′rä*, *n.* a Spanish-American linear measure, usu. about thirty-three inches. [See **vare**.]

varan, *var′ən*, *n.* a monitor lizard.—*n.* Var′anus, the monitor genus, constituting the family Varanidae (*-an′*). [Ar. *waran*.]

Varangian, *va-ran′ji-ən*, *n.* a Scandinavian settler in what became Russia : a member of the body-guard of the Eastern emperors (chiefly Scandinavian): (*Scott*) their Scandinavian language.—Also *adj.* [L.L. *Varangus*—Late Gr. *Barangos*—O.N. *Vaeringi.*]

vardy, *vär′di*, *n.* a once fashionable form of **verdict**.

vare, *vār*, *n.* a vara : a wand of authority. [Sp. *vara*, a rod—L. *vāra*, a trestle, forked stick—*vārus*, crooked.]

varec, varech, *var'ek, n.* kelp : wrack. [Fr. ; of Scand. origin ; cf. **wrack, wreck.**]

vareuse, *vȧ-rəz', n.* (*U.S.*) a kind of loose jacket. [Fr.]

vargueño, *vär-gān'yō, n.* a cabinet or desk of a kind made at *Vargas* (Bargas) near Toledo.

variability, *vā-ri-ə-bil'i-ti, n.* state or fact of being variable.—*adj.* **vā'riable,** that may be varied : changeable : tending or liable to change or vary : showing variations : unsteady : (*math.*) quantitatively indeterminate : (*astron.*) changing in brightness.—*n.* (*math.*) a quantity subject to continual increase or decrease : a quantity which may have an infinite number of values in the same expression : a shifting wind.—*n.* **vā'riableness.**—*adv.* **vā'riably.**—*ns.* **vā'riance,** variation : deviation : alteration : discrepancy : disagreement : dispute : the average of the squares of the deviations of a number of observations from the mean ; **vā'riant,** a different form of the same thing (esp. a word) : a different reading : a specimen slightly differing from the type.—*adj.* changeful : varying : diversified : different : diverging from type.—*n.* **vā'riate,** any one of the observed values of a quantity.—*v.t.* and *v.i.* to change, vary.—*n.* **vāriā'tion,** a varying : a change : continuous change : difference among the offspring of the same parents : departure from the mean or usual character : the extent to which a thing varies : a variant : declination of the compass : an inequality in the moon's motion discovered by Tycho Brahé : a change in the elements of an orbit by the disturbing force of another body : (*mus.*) transformation of a theme by means of new figures in counterpoint, florid treatment, changes in tempo, key, and the like.—*adj.* **vāriā'tional,** pertaining to variation.—*n.* **vāriā'tionist,** a composer of variations : one who attaches importance to variation. — *adj.* **vā'riative,** variational. — at variance, in disagreement or dissension ; **variable gear** (see gear). [Partly through O.Fr., from L. *variāre, -ātum,* to vary.]

varicella, *var-i-sel'ä, n.* chickenpox.—*adjs.* **varicell'ar ; varicell'oid,** resembling varicella ; **varicell'ous,** pertaining to varicella. [Irreg. dim. of variola.]

varices, *pl.* of **varix.**—**varicocele, varicose.** See under **varix.**

varicoloured, *vā'ri-kul'ərd, adj.* diversified in colour. [L. *varius,* various, *color,* colour.]

varied. See vary.

variegate, *vā'ri-(ə-)gāt, v.t.* to diversify, esp. with colours in patches.—*adj.* **vā'riegated.**—*ns.* **vāriegā'tion ; vā'riegātor.** [L. *variegātus—varius,* various, *agĕre,* to make.]

variety, *və-rī'ə-ti, n.* the quality of being various : diversity : difference : many-sidedness : versatility : a varied set : a kind differing in minor characters : a race not sufficiently distinct to be counted a species : music-hall entertainment, a succession of varied turns :—*pl.* **varī'eties.**—*adj.* of, for, performing in, music-hall entertainment.—*adj.* **varī'etal,** (*biol.*) of or having the character of a variety.—*adv.* **varī'etally.** [L. *varietās, -ātis—varius,* various.]

variform, *vā'ri-form, adj.* of various forms.

variola, *və-rī'ə-lä, n.* smallpox : sheep-pox.—*adj.* **varī'olar.**—*v.t.* **variolate** (*vā'ri-ə-lāt*), to inoculate with smallpox virus.—*ns.* **vāriolā'tion,** inoculation with smallpox virus ; **variole** (*vā'ri-ōl*), a pock-like marking : a spherule in variolite ; **vā'riolite** (Gr. *lithos,* stone), a fine-grained basic igneous rock with spherules of radiating felspar resembling pock-marks.—*adjs.* **vāriolit'ic,** of or like variolite ; **vā'rioloid,** resembling smallpox.—*n.* modified smallpox occurring in the vaccinated.—*adj.* **variolous** (*və-rī'ō-ləs*), of, pertaining to, suffering from, smallpox : covered with varioles. [L.L. *variola,* pustule, pox—L. *varius,* various, spotted.]

various, *vā'ri-əs, adj.* varied, different : several : unlike each other : changeable : uncertain : variegated.—*n.* **vāriom'eter** (Gr. *metron,* measure), an instrument for comparing magnetic forces : a variable inductance of two connected coils, one rotating within the other.—*adj.* **vāriō'rum,** with the notes of various commentators or editors (L. *cum notīs variōrum*) : with the readings of various manuscripts or editions.—*n.* a variorum edition : (*jocular*) a succession of changes.—*adv.* **vā'riously.**—*n.* **vā'riousness.** [L. *varius.*]

variscite, *var'i-sīt, n.* a greenish mineral, hydrated aluminium phosphate. [L. *Variscia,* Vogtland, in Saxony.]

varix, *vā'riks* (L. *vā'riks*), *n.* an abnormally dilated, lengthened, and tortuous vein : dilatation : a ridge marking a former position of the mouth of a shell : —*pl.* **varices** (*va', vā'ri-sēz* ; L. *vā'ri-kās*).—*n.* **varicocele** (*var'i-kō-sēl* ; Gr. *kēlē,* tumour), an enlargement of the veins of the spermatic cord or those of the scrotum.—*adj.* **var'icose,** of the nature of, like, pertaining to, affected by, a varix or varices : abnormally dilated or enlarged as a vein : dilated.—*n.* **varicosity** (*var-i-kos'i-ti*), state of being varicose : a distended place. [L. *varix, -icis,* a varicose vein.]

varlet, *vär'lit, n.* (*arch.*) an attendant : (*obs.*) a municipal officer : a knave :—*fem.* (*rare*) **var'letess.** —*ns.* **var'letry,** (*Shak.*) the rabble, the crowd ; **varlett'o,** (*Shak., sham* It.), a varlet. [O.Fr. *varlet* ; cf. **valet.**]

varmint, varment, *vär'mint, n.* old variants (now *dial.* or *slang*) of **vermin** : a noxious or troublesome animal or person : (perh. another word) a skilled amateur sportsman.—Also *adj.*

varnish, *vär'nish, n.* a resinous solution that dries to give a glossy coat to a surface : a gloss or glaze : a specious show : an application of varnish.—*v.t.* to coat with varnish : to give a fair show to.— *ns.* **var'nisher ; var'nishing ; var'nishing-day,** a day before the opening of a picture exhibition when exhibitors may varnish or retouch their pictures after they have been hung ; **var'nish-tree,** the tung-tree or other tree whose resinous juice is used for varnishing or for lacquering. [Fr. *vernis* ; origin unknown.]

varsal, *vär'səl, adj.* (*coll.*) universal.

varsity, *vär'si-ti, n.* and *adj.* (*coll.*) university.

varsovienne, *vär-sō-vi-en', n.* a dance imitated from the Polish mazurka : a tune for it. [Fr., fem. of *Varsovien—Varsovie,* Warsaw.]

vartabed, *vär'tə-bed, n.* an Armenian order of clergy. [Armenian *vartabet.*]

Varuna, *vur'oo-nä, vär'-, n.* an ancient Indian Vedic god of the heavens, later of the waters. [Sans. ; cf. Gr. *Ouranos.*]

varus, *vā'rəs, n.* (for *tālipēs vārus*) in-turned club-foot. [L. *vārus,* bent, knock-kneed.]

varve, *värv, n.* (*geol.*) a seasonal layer of clay deposited in still water.—*adj.* **varve(d),** stratified in distinct layers of annual deposit. [Sw. *varv,* layer.]

varvel. See vervel.

vary, *vā'ri, v.t.* to make different : to diversify, modify : (*mus.*) to alter or embellish (a melody) preserving its identity : (*Shak.*) to express variously : to change to something else : to make of different kinds.—*v.i.* to alter or be altered : to be or become different : to change in succession : to deviate : to disagree : (*math.*) to be subject to continuous increase or decrease : (*pr.p.* **vā'rying ;** *pa.t.* and *pa.p.* **vā'ried**).—*n.* change.—*adj.* **vā'ried.** *adv.* **vā'riedly.**—*n.* **vā'rier,** one who varies.—*n.* and *adj.* **vā'rying.** [L. *variāre—varius.*]

vas, *vas, n.* a vessel, tube, duct, carrying liquid :—*pl.* **vasa** (*vā'sä* ; L. *vā'sä*).—*adj.* **vā'sal.**— *n.* **vasec'tomy** (Gr. *ek,* out, *tomē,* a cut), excision of the vas deferens, or part of it.—*adjs.* **vas'iform,** tubular : vase-shaped ; **vasomo'tor,** serving to regulate the tension of blood-vessels, as nerves.— **vas def'erens,** a spermatic duct :—*pl.* **va'sa deferen'tia.** [L. *vās, vāsis,* vessel.]

vasculum, *vas'kū-ləm, n.* a botanist's collecting case :—*pl.* **vas'culums, vas'cula.**—*adj.* **vas'cular,** relating to, composed of, or provided with conducting vessels.—*v.t.* **vas'cularise,** to render vascular.—*n.* **vascular'ity.**—*adv.* **vas'cularly.**— *adj.* **vas'culiform,** vase-shaped.— **vascular bundle,** a strand of conducting tissue in the higher plants, composed of xylem, phloem, and cambium ; **vascular cryptogams,** the pteridophytes, or ferns

---

Neutral vowels in unaccented syllables : *el'ə-mənt, in'fənt, ran'dəm*

and their allies ; **vascular plants**, seed-plants and pteridophytes. [L. *vāsculum*, dim. of *vās*, a vessel.]

vase, *vāz*, old-fashioned *vawz*, or (as still *U.S.*) *vās*, *vāz*, *n.* a vessel, usually tall, round in section, and ornamental, anciently used for domestic purposes : (*archit.*) the body of the Corinthian capital.—*n.* **vase′-paint′ing**, the decoration of vases with pigments, esp. the decoration of the pottery of the ancient Greeks. [Fr.,—L. *vās.*]

Vaseline, *vaz′* or *vas′i-lēn*, *n.* a registered trade-mark name applied to products of a certain firm, consisting in large part, but not solely, of petroleum jelly (*paraffinum molle*) and preparations thereof.—Also *v.t.* [Ger. *wasser*, water, and Gr. *elaion*, oil.]

vasiform, **vasomotor.** See **vas.**

vassal, *vas′əl*, *n.* one who holds land from, and renders homage to, a superior : a dependant, retainer : a bondman, slave : (*Shak.*) a low wretch. —*adj.* in the relation or state of a vassal : subordinate : servile : of a vassal.—*v.t.* to subject.—*ns.* **vass′alage**, (*obs.*) prowess, or deeds of prowess : state of being a vassal : dependence : subjection : a fee, fief : vassals collectively ; **vass′aless**, a female vassal ; **vass′alry**, vassals collectively. [Fr.,—L.L. *vassallus*, servant—Celtic ; cf. Bret. *goaz*, W. *gwas.*]

vast, *vȧst, adj.* (*obs.*) waste, desert : boundless : huge : exceedingly great : (18th cent. in fashionable hyperbole) great.—*n.* immensity, an immense tract, boundless or empty expanse of space or time : a waste : (*dial.* or *coll.*) a huge quantity, vast amount. — *ns.* **vastid′ity**, **vast′itude**, **vast′ity**, vastness : a vast extent.—*adv.* **vast′ly.**—*n.* **vast′-ness.**—*adj.* **vast′y**, vast. [L. *vastus*, waste, desolate, huge ; cf. **waste.**]

vat, *vat*, *n.* a large vessel or tank, esp. for fermentation, dyeing, or tanning : dyeing liquor.—*v.t.* to put in a vat.—*n.* **vat′ful**, as much as a vat will hold :—*pl.* **vat′fuls.** [Southern form of **fat** (2)—O.E. *fæt* ; cf. Du. *vat*, O.N. *fat*, Ger. *fass.*]

vatic, *vat′ik, adj.* prophetic : oracular : inspired.—*n.* **vat′icide** (-*sīd* ; L. *caedĕre*, to kill), the killer or killing of a prophet.—*adj.* **vaticinal** (-*is′i-nl*).—*v.t.* and *v.i.* **vatic′inate** (chiefly ironical), to prophesy. —*ns.* **vaticinā′tion**, prophecy ; **vatic′inator**, a prophet. [L. *vātēs*, a prophet, *vāticinārī*, to prophesy.]

Vatican, *vat′i-kən*, *n.* an assemblage of buildings on the Vatican Hill in Rome, including one of the pope's palaces : the papal authority.—*ns.* **Vat′icanism**, the system of theology and ecclesiastical government based on absolute papal authority, ultramontanism ; **Vat′icanist**, one who upholds such a system.—**Vatican City**, a small area on the Vatican Hill set up as an independent papal state in 1929 ; **Vatican Council**, the council that met in St Peter's (1869) and proclaimed papal infallibility (1870). [L. *Mōns Vāticānus*, the Vatican Hill.]

vau, *wow*, *n.* the digamma (see **episemon**). [Early Gr. *Fau*—Semitic *wāw.*]

vaudeville, *vō′də-vil*, *vōd′vil*, *n.* originally a popular song with topical allusions : a play interspersed with dances and songs incidentally introduced and usually comic : (*U.S.*) variety entertainment.—Also *adj.*—*n.* **vau′devillist**, a composer of vaudevilles. [From *vau* (*val*) *de Vire*, the valley of the Vire, in Normandy, where they were composed in the 15th century.]

Vaudois, *vō-dwä′*, *vō′dwä*, *n.* a native of the Swiss Canton Vaud (*pl.* **Vaudois**) : its French.—Also *adj.* [Fr.]

Vaudois, *vō′dwä*, *vō-dwä′*, *n.* and *adj.* Waldensian. [Fr.]

vaudoo, **vaudoux.** See **voodoo.**

vault, *vawlt*, earlier *vawt*, *n.* an arched roof or ceiling : a chamber with an arched roof or ceiling, esp. underground : a cellar : a wine-cellar : hence (in *pl.*) a public-house : a burial-chamber : a cavern : anything vault-like.—*v.t.* to shape as a vault : to roof with an arch : to form vaults in. —*v.i.* to curve in a vault.—*n.* **vault′age**, (*Shak.*) an arched cellar : a cavern : a range of vaults : vaulted work.—*adj.* **vaul′ted**, arched : concave overhead : covered with an arch or vault.—*n.* **vaul′ting,**

vaulted work.—*adj.* **vaul′ty**, (*Shak.*) vault-like. [O.Fr. *vaute*, *vaulte*, *voute*, *volte* (Fr. *voûte*)—L. *volvĕre*, *volūtum*, to roll.]

vault, *vawlt*, earlier *vawt*, *v.i.* to leap, esp. by resting on the hand or a pole.—*v.t.* to vault over or upon. —*n.* an act of vaulting.—*n.* **vault′er.**—*n.* and *adj.* **vault′ing.**—*ns.* **vault′ing-horse**, a wooden horse for gymnastic exercise ; **vault′ing-house**, (*obs.*) a brothel. [App. O.Fr. *volter*, to leap.]

vaunce, *vawns*, *v.t.* and *v.i.* obs. aphetic form of **advance** :—*pr.p.* (*Spens.*) **vaunc′ing.**

vaunt, *vawnt* (also *U.S.* *vänt*), *v.i.* to boast : to behave boastfully or exultingly.—*v.t.* to boast : to boast of : (*Spens.*) to make known by display.—*n.* a boast : boastful demeanour.—*adj.* **vaunt′ed.**—*ns.* **vaunt′er** ; **vaunt′ery**, vaunting.—*adj.* **vaunt′ful.** —*n.* and *adj.* **vaunt′ing.**—*adv.* **vaunt′ingly.** [O.Fr. *vanter*—L.L. *vānitāre*—L. *vānitās*, vanity —*vānus*, vain ; partly aphetic for **avaunt** (2).]

vaunt, *vawnt*, *n.* (*Shak.*) the first part. [Cf. **van** (1).]

vauntage, *vawnt′ij*, *n.* (*Spens.*). Same as (**ad**)**-vantage.**

vaunt-courier, *vawnt-kōō′ri-ər*, *n.* one sent in advance : a forerunner. [Fr. *avant-courier.*]

vaut, **vaute**, **vawte**, old forms of **vault** (1 and 2).

vavasour, *vav′ə-sōōr*, **valvassor**, *val′və-sor*, *n.* one who held his lands of a tenant in chief. — *n.* **vav′asory**, the tenure or the lands of a vavasour. [O.Fr., app.—L.L. *vassus vassōrum*, vassal of vassals —*vassus*, vassal.]

vaward, *vaw′ərd*, *n.* (*Shak.*) a form of **vanguard** : forefront.—*adj.* front.

Veadar, *vē′ə-där*, *n.* an intercalary month in the Jewish calendar, following Adar in embolismic years. [Heb. *ve*, and.]

veal, *vēl*, *n.* calf's flesh as food : (*obs.*) a calf.—*adj.* of veal.—*adj.* **veal′y**, like veal or like a calf : immature. [O.Fr. *veël* (Prov. *vedel*)—L. *vitellus*, dim. of *vitulus* ; cf. Gr. *italos*, a calf.]

veale, *vēl* (*Spens.*). Same as **veil.**

vector, *vek′tər*, *n.* (*math.*) a directed quantity, as a straight line in space, involving both its direction and magnitude : a carrier of disease or infection.— *adj.* **vectorial** (-*tō′ri-əl*). [L. *vector*, -*ōris*, bearer, carrier—*vehĕre*, *vectum*, to convey.]

Veda, *vā′dä*, *n.* any one of the four holy books of the Hindus :—*pl.* **Vedas** (*vā′däz*).—*n.* **Vedan′ta**, a system of Hindu philosophy based on the Vedas. —*adjs.* **Vedan′tic**, **Ve′dic.**—*ns.* **Ve′dism** ; **Ve′dist**, one learned in the Vedas. [Sans. *veda*, knowledge ; cf. **wit**, L. *vidēre*, to see, Gr. *oida*, I know ; Sans. *Vedānta*—*anta*, end.]

vedette, *vi-det′*, *n.* a mounted sentry stationed to watch an enemy : a small vessel (**vedette′-boat**) for like purpose. [Fr.,—It. *vedetta*—*vedere*—L. *vidēre*, to see.]

vee, *vē*, *n.* the twenty-second letter of the alphabet (V, v) : a mark or object of that shape.—*adj.* **V-shaped.** [See **V.**]

veer, *vēr*, *v.i.* to change direction, esp. (of the wind) clockwise : to change course, esp. away from the wind : to turn, wind : to come round or shift round in mental attitude.—*v.t.* to turn, shift : to turn away from the wind.—*n.* a shifting round.— *n.* and *adj.* **veer′ing.**—*adv.* **veer′ingly.** [Fr. *virer.*]

veer, *vēr*, *v.t.* (*naut.*) to pay out : to slack. [M.Du. *vieren.*]

veery, *vēr′i*, *n* the tawny thrush of North America. [Prob. imit.]

Vega, *vē′gä*, *n.* the first-magnitude star *a* Lyrae. [Ar. *al wāqi′* (*al nasr*), the falling (vulture).]

vega, *vā′gä*, *n.* a low fertile plain : (*Cuba*) a tobacco-field. [Sp.]

vegetable, *vej′i-tə-bl*, *n.* an organism belonging to the great division distinguished from animals by being unable to deal with solid food, commonly but not necessarily fixed in position—a plant : a plant or part of one used for food, other than those reckoned fruits.—*adj.* of, for, derived from, composed of, of the nature of, vegetables.—*adv.* **veg′etably**, in the manner of a vegetable.—*adj.* **veg′etal**, vegetable : vegetative : of a level of life below the sensitive.—*n.* (*rare*) a plant, vegetable. — *adj.* **veg′etant**, vegetating. — *n.* **vegetarian**

(-tā'ri-ən), one who lives wholly on vegetable food, with or without dairy products, honey, and eggs.— Also *adj.*—*n.* vegetā'rianism, the theory or practice of a vegetarian.—*v.i.* veg'etate, to grow or live as, or like, a vegetable: to increase vegetatively: to live an inactive, almost purely physical, or dull life.—*adj.* veg'etāted, covered with vegetation.—*n.* and *adj.* veg'etāting.—*n.* vegetā'tion, process of vegetating: vegetable growth: (*obs.*) a plant: a plantlike growth: growing plants in mass.—*adj.* veg'etātive, growing, as plants: producing growth in plants: (*biol.*) concerned with the life of the individual rather than of the race: by means of vegetative organs, not special reproductive structures: pertaining to unconscious or involuntary bodily functions as resembling the processes of vegetable growth: without intellectual activity, unprogressive.—*adv.* veg'etātively. —*n.* veg'etātiveness. — *adj.* vegete (*vi-jēt'*), vigorous.—*n.* veg'etive, (Shak.) a vegetable.— *adj.* vegetative.—vegetable ivory, corozo-nut; vegetable kingdom, that division of natural objects which consists of vegetables or plants; vegetable marrow, a variety of pumpkin cooked as a vegetable: the akee fruit; vegetable mould, mould consisting mostly of humus; vegetable parchment, paper treated with sulphuric acid; vegetable sheep, in New Zealand, a dense cushion of composite plants (Raoulia, Haastia) at a distance resembling a sheep; vegetative nervous system, the nervous system regulating involuntary bodily activity, as the secretion of the glands, the beating of the heart, &c.; vegetative organs, leaves, stems, roots; vegetative reproduction, reproduction by detachment of part of the plant-body: budding. [L. *vegetābilis*, animating, *vegetāre*, to quicken, *vegetus*, lively; cf vigour.]

vehement, vē'(h)ə-mənt, *adj.* forcible: impetuous: very strong or urgent.—*ns.* vē'hemence, vē'-hemency.—*adv.* vē'hemently. [L. *vehemēns*.]

vehicle, vē'i-kl, *n.* a means of conveyance or transmission: a medium: a substance with which a medicine, a pigment, &c., is mixed for administration or application: a structure in or on which persons or things are transported, esp. by land.— *adj.* vehicular (*vi-hik'ū-lər*). [L. *vehiculum*—*vehĕre*, to carry.]

vehm, fehm, *fām,* **vehmgericht, fehmgericht,** *-gə-rihht, ns.* a mediaeval German, esp. Westphalian, court in which initiated persons held of the emperor power to try capital cases in public or in secret, their lower officers executing the guilty on the spot or where they could find them:—*pl.* vehm'e, fehm'e, vehm-, fehmgerichte (*-ə*). — *adj.* vehm'ic, vehm'ique, fehm'ic. [Ger. *vehm,* now *fehm,* criminal court, *gericht,* court, judgement.]

veil, *vāl, n.* a curtain: a covering: a covering for the head, face, or both, for protection, concealment, or ceremonial reason: a nun's or novice's head-covering: a piece of gauzy drapery worn on the head by a bride: a gauzy face-covering worn by ladies: a humeral: a disguise or concealment: an obscuration of tone in singing: a velum.—*v.t.* to cover with a veil: to cover: to conceal, disguise, or obscure.—*adj.* veiled.—*n.* veil'ing, the act of concealing with a veil: a veil: material for making veils.—Also *adj.*—*adjs.* veil'less, wanting a veil: uncovered; veil'y, like a veil, diaphanous.— eucharistic or sacramental veils, linen or silk covers for eucharistic vessels and elements; take the veil, to become a nun. [O.Fr. *veile* (Fr. *voile*) —L. *vēlum*, a curtain, veil, sail.]

veilleuse, *vā-yəz', n.* a shaded night-lamp. [Fr., —*veiller,* to watch.]

vein, *vān, n.* one of the vessels or tubes that convey the blood back to the heart: one of the horny tubes forming the framework of an insect's wing: a vascular bundle forming a rib, esp. a small rib, in a leaf: a small intrusion, or a seam of a different mineral running through a rock: a fissure or cavity: a streak in wood, stone, &c.: a streak running through one's nature, a strain of character or ability: a manner, style: a mood or humour.— *v.t.* to form veins or the appearance of veins in.— *adj.* veined, having veins: streaked, variegated.—

n. vein'ing, formation or disposition of veins: streaking.—*adj.* vein'ous, full of veins.—*ns.* vein'-stone, vein'stuff, gangue. [Fr. *veine*—L. *vēna.*]

velamen, velar, velarium. See under velum.

velatura, *vel-ə-tōō'rä, n.* a method of glazing a painting by rubbing with the hand. [It.]

veld, also (outside S. Africa) veldt, *velt, felt, n.* in South Africa, open, unforested, or thinly-forested grass-country. [Du. *veld* (formerly *veldt*), field.] **veld(-)schoen,** *fel'-skōon, n.* (S.Afr.) a shoe made of raw hide.—Also veld(-)skoen. [Corr. of *vel-schoen*—Du. *vel*, skin, *schoen*, shoe.]

vele, *vēl, n.* (Spens.). Same as veil.

veleta, *və-lē'tä, n.* a dance or dance-tune in slow waltz time. [Sp., weather-cock.]

veliger. See under velum.

velitation, *vel-i-tā'shən, n.* a skirmish. [L. *vēlitātiō, -ōnis*—*vēlēs, -itis,* a light-armed soldier.]

velleity, *ve-lē'i-ti, n.* volition in its lowest form: mere inclination. [L.L. *velleitās,* irregularly formed from L. *velle,* to wish.]

vellenage, *vel'ən-āj* (Spens.). Same as villeinage.

vellet, *vel'it* (Spens.). Same as velvet.

vellicate, *vel'i-kāt, v.t.* and *v.i.* to twitch.—*n.* vellicā'tion. [L. *vellicāre, -ātum,* to pluck.]

vellon, *ve-lyōn', n.* billon: Spanish copper money. [Sp. *vellón*—Fr. *billon.*]

Vellozia, *ve-lō'zi-ä, n.* the Brazilian tree-lily genus, giving name to an African and S. American family Velloziā'ceae, akin to the amaryllids. [José *Vellozo* (1742-1811), Brazilian botanist.]

vellum, *vel'əm, n.* a finer kind of parchment prepared by lime-baths and burnishing from the skins of calves, kids, or lambs. [O.Fr. *velin*—*vel,* calf.]

veloce, *vā-lō'chä, adj.* and *adv.* (*mus.*) with great rapidity. [It.]

velocipede, *vi-los'i-pēd, n.* a dandy-horse, bone-shaker, or other early form of bicycle: a swift-footed person.—*adj.* swift of foot.—*v.i.* to ride a velocipede.—*n.* and *adj.* velocipē'dean, -ian.— *n.* veloc'ipēder (or -ped').—*n.* and *adj.* veloci-pedestrian (*-pi-des'tri-ən*).—*n.* veloc'ipēdist (or *-pēd'*). [Fr. *vélocipède*—L. *vēlōx, -ōcis,* swift, *pēs, pedis,* foot.]

velocity, *vi-los'i-ti, n.* swiftness: speed: rate of change of position. [L. *vēlōcitās, -ātis*—*vēlōx,* swift.]

velours, *və-lōōr', n.* a polishing pad for silk hats: a woollen stuff with velvet-like pile.—Also *adj.* —*ns.* veloutine (*vel-ōō-tēn'*), a velvety corded wool fabric; velure (*və-lōōr', -lūr'; Shak.*), velvet: a velours.—*v.t.* to dress with a velours.—*adj.* velutinous (*-lōō', -lū'*), velvety. [Fr. *velours.*]

velt-mareschal, *n.* (Scott) for Ger. *feld-marschall,* field-marshal.

velum, *vē'ləm* (L. *vä'loom*), *n.* a veil, integument, or membrane: the membrane joining the rim of a young toadstool with the stalk: the pendulous soft palate: a ciliated disk, a locomotor organ in some molluscan larvae: an in-turned rim in jelly-fishes:—*pl.* vē'la.—*n.* velamen (*vi-lā'men,* L. *vä-lä'men*), the spongy sheath of an aerial root:— *pl.* velā'mina (L. *vä-lä'mi-nä*).—*adj.* vē'lar, of the velum: (*phon.*) produced by the back of the tongue brought close to the soft palate.—*n.* a velar consonant, back consonant.—*n.* velā'rium (L. *vä-lä'ri-oom*), an awning over an auditorium: in Scyphozoa, the thin marginal region:—*pl.* velā'ria. —*adjs.* vē'late, -d.—*n.* vē'liger (*-jər*), a mollusc larva with a velum. [L. *vēlum,* a veil, sail, *vēlāmen, -inis,* a covering, *vēlārium,* an awning.]

velure. See velours.

velvet, *vel'vit, n.* a silk fabric with soft close short pile: an imitation with silk pile: the velvet-like covering of a growing antler: a velvety surface or skin: (*slang*) gains, winnings.—*adj.* made of velvet: soft like velvet.—*ns.* vel'veret, a cotton with a silk pile; vel'vet-crab, vel'vet-fidd'ler, a swimming-crab with velvety pile; vel'vet-duck, vel'vet-sco'ter, a black duck with a white mark on the wing.—*adj.* vel'veted, clad in velvet.—*n.* velveteen', a cotton, or mixed cotton and silk, imitation of velvet.—*pl.* vel'vet-guards, (Shak.) velvet trimmings, applied metaphorically to the citizens who wore them.—*ns.* vel'vetiness; vel'-

veting, velvet material ; **vel′vet-leaf**, false pareira : tree-mallow ; **vel′vet-pa′per**, flock paper ; **vel′vet-pile**, material with a soft nap.—*adj.* **vel′vety**, soft and smooth like velvet : deep and soft in colouring. —**on velvet**, in a safe or advantageous position : secure against losing, whatever happens ; **the velvet glove**, gentleness concealing strength. [L.L. *velvettum*, conn. with L. *villus*, a tuft.]

vena, *vē′nä*, L. *vā′nä*, *n.* a vein :—*pl.* **ve′nae.**—**vēna cä′va** (L. *cāva*, hollow), either of two large veins entering the right auricle.—*adj.* **vē′nal**, venous.—*n.* **venation** (*vi-nā′shən*), arrangement of veins.—*adj.* **venose** (*vē′nōs*, *-nōs′*), veiny : veined : with noticeable veins.—*n.* **venosity** (*vē-nos′i-ti*), the state or quality of being venous, or of having or being like venous blood.—*adj.* **vē′nous**, pertaining to, contained in, or of the kind that is contained in veins : veined.—*n.* **venule** (*ven′ūl*), a branch of a vein in an insect's wing: any of the small-calibre veins into which the capillaries empty. [L. *vēna.*]

venal, *vē′nl*, *adj.* for sale : to be bought or bought over : corruptly mercenary.—*n.* **venality** (*-nal′i-ti*). —*adv.* **vē′nally.** [L. *vēnālis*—*vēnum*, goods for sale ; Gr. *ōnē*, purchase.]

venal. See vena.

venatic, -al, *vi-nat′ik*, *-əl*, *adjs.* pertaining to hunting.—*adv.* **venat′ically.**—*n.* **venation** (*vi-nā′shən* ; *rare*), hunting : a hunt.—*adj.* **venatorial** (*ven-ə-tō′ri-əl*). [L. *vēnārī*, to hunt, *vēnātiō*, hunting, *vēnātor*, a hunter.]

venation. See vena, venatic.

vend, *vend*, *v.t.* to sell or offer for sale, deal in, esp. in a small way : to utter (perh. for **vent**).—*n.* a sale : amount sold.—*ns.* **vendee′**, a buyer ; **ven′der, -dor**, a seller ; **vendibil′ity.**—*adj.* **vend′ible**, that may be sold, offered for sale, or readily sold.— *n.* a thing for sale : a possible object of trade.—*n.* **ven′dibleness.**—*adv.* **ven′dibly.**—*ns.* **venditā′-tion**, offering for sale ; **vendi′tion**, sale. [Fr. *vendre* or L. *vendĕre*, to sell—*vēnum dăre*, to offer for sale.]

vendace, *ven′dəs*, *n.* a whitefish (*Coregonus vandesius*) found in the Castle Loch and Mill Loch at Lochmaben : another species (*C. gracilior*) in Derwentwater and Bassenthwaite Lake. — Also **ven′dis, ven′diss.** [Possibly O.Fr. *vendese*, *ven-doise* (Fr. *vandoise*), dace.]

Vendean, *ven-dē′ən*, *n.* an inhabitant of La *Vendée*, in France : one of those who there resisted the Revolution.—Also *adj.*

Vendémiaire, *vän′-dā-myer′*, *n.* the first month in the French Revolutionary calendar, about 22nd September to 21st October. [Fr.,—L. *vindēmia*, vintage—*vīnum*, wine, *dēmĕre*, to take away—*dē*, from, *emĕre*, to take.]

vendetta, *ven-det′ä*, *n.* blood-feud. [It.,—L. *vindicta*, revenge—*vindicāre*, to claim.]

vendue, *ven-dū′*, *n.* (*U.S.*) a public auction sale. [Du. *vendu*—Fr. *vendue*.]

veneer, *və-nēr′*, *v.t.* to overlay or face with a thin sheet of fine wood or other substance : to disguise with superficial refinement.—*n.* a thin slice for veneering : a specious superficial show : a grass-moth (**veneer′-moth**, from its markings).—*ns.* **veneer′er** ; **veneer′ing.** [Formerly **fineer**— Ger. *furniren*—O.Fr. *fornir* (Fr. *fournir*), It. *fornire*, to furnish.]

venefic, -al, *vi-nef′ik*, *-əl*, **veneficious**, *ven-i-fish′əs*, **veneficous**, *vi-nef′i-kəs*, *adjs.* acting by poison or potions or by sorcery. [L. *venēficus*— *venēnum*, poison, *facĕre*, to do.]

venerate, *ven′ə-rāt*, *v.t.* to revere.—*adj.* **ven′erable**, worthy of reverence : hallowed by associations or age : aged-looking : an honorific prefix to the name of an archdeacon, or one in process of canonisation.—*n.* **ven′erableness.**—*adv.* **ven′erably.**—*ns.* **venerā′tion**, the act of venerating : the state of being venerated : awed respect ; **ven′erātor.** [L. *venerārī, -ātus.*]

venery, *ven′ə-ri*, *n.* sexual indulgence. — *adjs.* **venereal** (*vi-nē′ri-əl*), pertaining to sexual desire or intercourse : transmitted by sexual intercourse : pertaining to or affected by venereal disease ; **venē′rean**, pertaining to Venus or her service, or

to sexual desire or intercourse.—*n.* one addicted to venery. — *adj.* **venē′reous**, lustful : venereal : aphrodisiac. [L. *venereus*—*Venus, Venĕris*, the goddess of love ; conn. with L. *venerārī.*]

venery, *ven′ər-i*, *n.* hunting : game.—*n.* **ven′erer**, a gamekeeper : a hunter. [O.Fr. *venerie*—*vener*— L. *vēnārī*, to hunt.]

venesection, *ven-*, *vēn-i-sek′shən*, *n.* the opening of a vein : blood-letting. [L. *vēna*, a vein, *sectiō, -ōnis*, cutting.]

Venetian, *vi-nē′sh(y)ən*, *adj.* of Venice.—*n.* a native or inhabitant of Venice : a Venetian blind.—*adj.* **Vene′tianed**, having Venetian blinds or shutters. —**Venetian blind**, a window-blind of horizontal slats adjustable to let in or keep out light ; **Venetian mast**, a spirally banded pole for street decoration ; **Venetian red**, ferric oxide as a pigment.

venewe, *ven′ū*, **veney**, **ven′i**. Shakespearian forms of **venue.**

venge, *venj*, *v.t.* (*Shak.*) to avenge.—*adj.* **venge′-able**, (*Spens.*) revengeful : (*dial.*) destructive : (*obs.*) extraordinarily great.—*adv.* **venge′ably.**— *n.* **venge′ance**, the infliction of injury in punishment or revenge : retribution : (*Shak.*) harm, mischief : (*Shak.*) a curse.—*adv.* (*Shak.*) extremely, exceedingly.—*adj.* **venge′ful**, vindictive, revengeful : retributive.—*adv.* **venge′fully.**—*ns.* **venge′fulness** ; **venge′ment**, (*Spens.*) vengeance, penal retribution ; **ven′ger**, (*Spens.*) an avenger.— **what a (or the) vengeance**, what the mischief ; **with a vengeance**, (*orig.*) with a curse : (*coll.*) violently, thoroughly, exceedingly. [O.Fr. *venger* —L. *vindicāre.*]

venial, *vē′ni-əl*, *adj.* pardonable : excusable : (*Milt.*) permissible.—*n.* **veniality** (*-al′i-ti*).—*adv.* **vē′nially.** — **venial sin**, sin other than mortal. [L. *veniālis*, pardonable—*venia*, pardon.]

Venice, *ven′is*, *n.* a city and former republic of Italy.—*adj.* **Venetian.**—**Venice glass**, a fine glass made near Venice, formerly believed to shiver if poison were poured into it ; **Venice gold**, (*Shak.*) gold-thread made in Venice ; **Venice talc**, steatite ; **Venice treacle**, a supposed antidote for all poisons, of many ingredients ; **Venice turpentine**, larch turpentine, formerly shipped from Venice. [Fr. *Venise*—L. *Venetia.*]

venison, *ven′(i-)zn*, or (esp. in Scotland) *-i-sən*, *n.* (*Shak.*) a beast of the chase, esp. a deer : its flesh as food : now deer's flesh. [A.Fr. *venison* (Fr. *venaison*)—L. *vēnātiō, -ōnis*, hunting—*vēnārī*, to hunt.]

venite, *vi-nī′ti* (L. *ve-nē′te*), *n.* the 95th Psalm, beginning *Venīte exultēmus.*

vennel, *ven′l*, *n.* (*Scot.*) a lane. [Fr. *venelle*—L. *vēna*, a vein.]

venom, *ven′əm*, *n.* poison, esp. snake-poison.—*adj.* (*Shak.*) venomous, poisonous. — *v.t.* (*obs.*) to poison : to envenom.—*adjs.* **ven′om′d-mouth′d′**, (*Shak.*) having a venomous mouth, slanderous ; **ven′omed**, venomous : charged with poison, envenomed ; **ven′omous**, poisonous : having power to poison, esp. by bite or sting : malignant, full of spite.—*adv.* **ven′omously.**—*n.* **ven′om-ousness.** [Fr. *venin*—L. *venēnum*, poison.]

venose, venous. See under vena.

ven′son. Same as **venison.**

vent, *vent*, *n.* a slit in a garment, now in the back of a coat : (*obs.*) a crenel. [Fr. *fente*—L. *findĕre*, to split ; cf. **fent.**]

vent, *vent*, *n.* an opening : an aperture : an air-hole or passage : a touch-hole : an outlet : a volcanic orifice : an animal's anus : (*Scot.*) a chimney : issue : emission : discharge : escape : passage into notice : publication : utterance : expression : an otter's rise to the surface for breath.—*v.t.* to give a vent or opening to : to let out, as at a vent : to allow to escape : to publish : to utter : to discharge : to emit : to pour forth : to scent : to sniff at : (*Spens.*) to lift or open so as to admit air. —*v.i.* to have or find an outlet : (*Scot.*) to discharge smoke, to function as a chimney, draw : to sniff or snuff : to take breath or rise for breath.—*ns.* **vent′age, vent′ige**, (*Shak.*) a finger-hole, as in a flute : a small hole ; **vent′er**, one who utters or publishes ; **vent′-hole**, a hole for admission or escape of air, fumes, &c., or to admit light; **vent′-iduct** (L. *dūcĕre, ductum,* to lead), a ventilating pipe or passage.—*n.* and *adj.* **vent′ing.**—*ns.* **vent′-peg, -plug,** a plug for stopping the vent of a barrel; **vent′-pipe,** an escape-pipe, as for steam or foul gases.—**give vent to,** to allow to escape or break out. [Fr.,—L. *ventus,* wind; partly Fr. *éventer,* to expose to air; associated with foregoing and following words.]

vent, *vent, n.* (*obs.*) sale: market.—*v.t.* (*obs.* or *dial.*) to sell. [O.Fr. *vente*—L. *vendĕre, -ĭtum,* to sell.]

ventana, *ven-tä′nä, n.* a window. [Sp.]

ventayle, ventaile, *ven′tāl, n.* (*Spens.*) the movable front of a helmet. [O.Fr. *ventaille.*]

venter, *ven′tər, n.* the belly, abdomen: (*law*) a womb or mother: a swelling or protuberance: a medial swelling: the dilated basal part of an archegonium: a shallow concave surface of a bone: the upper side or surface of a leaf, &c.—*adj.* **ven′tral,** of the belly: (*bot.*) on the upper side or towards the axis: (*zool.*) on the side normally turned towards the ground—opp. to *dorsal.*—*n.* **a ventral fin.** — *adv.* **ven′trally.** — *n.* **ven′tricle,** a cavity in the body: esp. a cavity in the brain, or a contractile chamber of the heart: (*Shak.*) the womb.—*adjs.* **ven′tricose, ven′tricous,** bellying: swollen in the middle or at one side, or all round at the base: big-bellied; **ventric′ūlar,** of, of the nature of, a ventricle: abdominal.—*n.* **ven′tricule, ventric′ūlus,** a ventricle.—**ventral fins,** the posterior paired fins. [L. *venter, -tris,* dim. *ventriculus.*]

venter, *ven′tər,* an old form (*Milt.*) of **venture.**

ventil, *ven′til, n.* a valve for giving sounds intermediate between the open harmonics in wind instruments: a valve in an organ for controlling the wind supply to various stops. [Ger.,—L.L. *ventile,* shutter, sluice—*ventus,* wind.]

ventilate, *ven′ti-lāt, v.t.* to fan, winnow, blow upon: to open or expose to the free passage of air: to expose to examination and discussion: to make public.—*adj.* **ven′tilable.**—*n.* **ventila′tion.**—*adj.* **ven′tilative.**—*n.* **ven′tilātor,** one who ventilates: a contrivance for introducing fresh air. [L. *ventilāre, -ātum,* to fan, wave, agitate—*ventus,* wind.]

ventose, *ven-tōs′,* or *ven′, adj.* windy: flatulent: puffed up with conceit.—*n.* **Ventôse** (*vän⁹-tōz′*), the sixth month of the French Revolutionary calendar, about 19th February to 20th March.—*n.* **ventosity** (*ven-tos′i-ti*), windiness. [L. *ventōsus*—*ventus,* wind.]

ventral, ventricle, &c. See under **venter** (1).

ventre, *ven′tər,* an old form of **venture.**

ventriloquism, *ven-tril′ə-kwizm, n.* the art of speaking so as to give the illusion that the sound comes from some other source.—*adj.* **ventriloqual** (*-lō′kwi-əl*).—*adv.* **ventrilō′quially.**—*v.i.* **ventril′-oquise,** to practise ventriloquism.—*n.* **ventril′-oquist.**—*adjs.* **ventriloquis′tic, ventril′oquous.**—*n.* **ventril′oquy, ventriloquism.** [L. *ventriloquus,* one who speaks by a spirit in the belly—*venter,* the belly, *loqui,* to speak.]

ventripotent, *ven-trip′ə-tənt, adj.* (*facet.*) with great capacity or appetite for food. [After Rabelais —L. *venter,* belly, *potēns,* powerful—*posse,* to be able.]

venture, *ven′tyər, n.* chance, luck, hazard: that which is put to hazard (esp. goods sent by sea at the sender's risk): an undertaking whose issue is uncertain or dangerous: an attempt: a thing put forward as an attempt: (*Shak.*) a prostitute.— *v.t.* to send on a venture: to expose to hazard: to risk: to take the risk of: to dare to put forward.— *v.i.* to make a venture: to run a risk: to dare.—*n.* **ven′turer.**—*adj.* **ven′turesome,** inclined to take risks: involving the taking of risk: risky.—*adv.* **ven′turesomely.**—*n.* **ven′turesomeness.**—*n.* and *adj.* **ven′turing** (*Milt.* **ven′tring**).—*adv.* **ven′turingly.**—*adj.* **ven′turous** (*Spens., Milt.,* &c.), **ven′-trous, ven′t'rous**), adventurous: daring.—*adv.* **ven′turously.**—*n.* **ven′turousness.**—**at a venture,** at hazard, random. [For **a(d)venture.**]

venue, *ven′ū, n.* (*Shak.* **venewe, veney**) a hit in fencing: a bout or match: a lunge, thrust: (*law*) the place where an action is laid: the district from which a jury comes to try a question of fact: in England, usually the county where a crime is alleged to have been committed: a scene of action: a meeting-place, esp. for a sport.—**change of venue,** change of place of trial; **lay the venue,** to specify the place where the trial is to be held. [O.Fr. *venue,* arrival—*venir*—L. *venīre,* to come.]

venule. See **vena.**

Venus, *vē′nəs, n.* (*Roman myth.*) the goddess of love, originally of spring, patron of flower-gardens, but identified with the Greek Aphrodite: (*obs.*) an alluring grace: (*obs.*) venery: the most brilliant of the planets, second in order from the sun: (*alchemy*) copper: a genus of lamellibranch molluscs, including the quahog.—*n.* **ve′nus-shell′,** a shell, or animal, of the genus.—**Venus's comb,** an umbelliferous plant (*Scandix Pecten-Veneris*) with long-beaked fruits set like comb teeth; **Venus's flower-basket,** a beautiful glass sponge; **Venus's fly-trap,** Dionaea; **Venus's girdle,** a ribbon-like ctenophoran (Cestus); **Venus's looking-glass,** a campanulaceous garden plant (Specularia) with small bright flowers; **mount of Venus,** the elevation at the base of the thumb. [L., orig. personified from *venus, -eris,* desire; akin to *venerārī,* to worship.]

veracious, *və-rā′shəs, adj.* truthful.—*adv.* **verā′-ciously.**—*n.* **veracity** (*-ras′i-ti*), truthfulness. [L. *vērāx, -ācis*—*vērus,* true.]

veranda, verandah, *və-ran′dä, n.* a roofed gallery, terrace, or open portico along the front or side of a building.—*adj.* **veran′da'd, veran′dahed,** having a veranda. [Hind. *varandā,* app.—Port. *varanda,* a balcony.]

Veratrum, *ve-rā′trəm, n.* the white hellebore genus. —*n.* **veratrin, -e** (*ver′ə-trin, -trēn*), an alkaloid or mixture of alkaloids got from white hellebore rhizomes, sabadilla, &c. [L. *vērātrum,* hellebore.]

verb, *vərb, n.* (*gram.*) the part of speech which asserts or predicates something.—*adj.* **ver′bal,** of, pertaining to, derived from, a verb or verbs: of, in, of the nature of, in the matter of, or concerned with, words, or words rather than things: word for word: (*Shak.*) verbose: oral.—*n.* a word, esp. a noun, derived from a verb.—*v.t.* **verbalisā′tion.**— *v.t.* **ver′balise,** to turn into a verb: to put in words.—*v.i.* to use many words.—*ns.* **ver′balism,** an expression: wording: undue attention to words alone: literalism; **ver′balist,** one skilled in words: a literalist: one who looks to words alone; **verbal′ity,** the quality of being verbal or merely verbal: mere words.—*adv.* **ver′bally.**—*n.* **verbā′rian,** a coiner of words.—*adv.* and *adj.* **verbā′tim,** word for word: (*Shak.*) by word of mouth.—*n.* **ver′biage,** superfluity of words: (*rare*) wording.—*v.i.* **verbigerate** (*-ij′ə-rāt*).—*n.* **verbigerā′tion,** the morbid and purposeless repetition of certain words and phrases at short intervals.— *adjs.* **verb′less; verbose′,** using or containing more words than are desirable: wordy.—*adv.* **verbose′ly.**—*ns.* **verbose′ness, verbosity** (*-bos′-*).—**verbal inspiration,** dictation of every word of a book (usu. the Bible) by God; **verbal note,** in diplomacy, an unsigned reminder of a neglected, though perhaps not urgent, matter. [L. *verbum,* word.]

Verbascum, *vər-bas′kəm, n.* the mullein genus. [L.]

Verbena, *vər-bē′nä, n.* the vervain genus, giving name to the family **Verbenaceae** (*vər-bi-nā′si-ē*), near akin to the labiates.—*adj.* **verbenā′ceous.**—*n.* **verbe′na-oil′,** an oil got from the kindred plant *Lippia citriodora* (called lemon-scented verbena), or from lemon-grass. [L. *verbēna,* a leafy twig, sacred bough.]

verberate, *vər′bər-āt, v.t.* to beat.—*n.* **verberā′tion.** [L. *verberāre, -ātum,* to scourge.]

verdant, *vər-dənt, adj.* green: fresh green or grass-green: green, unsophisticated, raw and gullible. —*n.* **ver′dancy.**—*adv.* **ver′dantly.**—*ns.* **ver′derer, -or,** (*hist.*) a forest officer who had charge of the vert and venison; **ver′det,** copper acetate; **ver′-dure,** fresh greenness: greenery: (*obs.*) fresh savour.—*adjs.* **ver′dured,** clad with verdure;

ver′dureless; ver′durous. [O.Fr. *verd* (Fr. *vert*)—L. *viridis*, green.]

verd-antique, *vərd-an-tēk′* (*obs. Fr.*), or **verde-antico,** *ver′dä-än-tē′ko* (*It.*), *n.* a breccia of serpentine containing calcite, &c. — **oriental verd-antique,** a green porphyry. [Antique green; Fr. now *vert.*]

verdict, *vər′dikt,* formerly (*Spens., Milt.*) **verdit,** *-dit, n.* the finding of a jury on a trial: judicial decision or decision generally.—**open verdict** (see **open**); **special verdict,** a verdict in which specific facts are found and put on the record. [O.Fr. *verdit* and L.L. *vērēdictum*—L. *vērē,* truly, *dictum,* said.]

verdigris, *vər′di-grēs, n.* basic cupric acetate: popularly, the green coating of basic cupric carbonate that forms in the atmosphere on copper, brass, or bronze.—*v.t.* to coat with verdigris. [O.Fr. *verd de Grèce,* green of Greece.]

verditer, *vər′di-tər, n.* a blue or green pigment, hydrated cupric carbonate. [O.Fr. *verd-de-terre,* earth green.]

verdoy, *vər′doi, adj.* (*her.*) charged with flowers, leaves, or vegetable charges, as a bordure. [Fr. *verdoyé,* pa.p. of *verdoyer,* to become green.]

verdure, See **verdant.**

verecund, *ver′i-kund, adj.* modest. [L. *verēcundus.*]

verge, *vərj, n.* a rod: a rodlike part: the axis of a clock pallet: a watch with a verge: an intromittent organ: a wand or staff of office: extent of jurisdiction (esp. of the lord-steward of the royal household): a precinct: a pale: a range: scope: jurisdiction: a limit, boundary: a rim: the brink, extreme edge: the horizon: the edge of a roof projecting beyond the gable: a grass edging.—*v.t.* to edge.—*v.i.* to border, be on the edge (with *on*): to act as verger.—*ns.* **verge′-board,** a barge-board; **ver′ger,** a beadle: an attendant in a church: a pew-opener; **ver′gership.**—**on the verge of,** (*fig.*) on the point of: on the brink of. [L. *virga,* a rod.]

verge, *vərj, v.i.* to incline: to tend downward: to slope: to tend: to pass gradually, merge.—*n.* **ver′gency.** [L. *vergĕre,* to bend.]

Vergilian. Same as **Virgilian.**

veridical, *vi-rid′i-kl, adj.* truth-telling: coinciding with fact.—*n.* **veridicality** (*-kal′i-ti*).—*adv.* **verid′ically.**—*adj.* **verid′icous,** truthful. [L. *vēridicus* —*vērus,* true, *dīcĕre,* to say.]

verier, veriest. See **very.**

verify, *ver′i-fī, v.t.* to testify: to assert or prove to be true: to ascertain, confirm, or test the truth or accuracy of: (*Shak.*) to back up :—*pr.p.* **ver′ifying;** *pa.t.* and *pa.p.* **ver′ified.**—*n.* **verifiabil′ity.**—*adj.* **ver′ifiable.**—*n.* **verifica′tion.**—*adj.* **ver′ificātory.**—*n.* **ver′ifïer.** [L. *vērus,* true, *facĕre,* to make.]

verily. See **very.**

verisimilar, *ver-i-sim′i-lər, adj.* truth-like.—*adv.* **verisim′ilarly.** — *ns.* **verisimil′itude;** **verisimil′ity** (*obs.*).—*adj.* **verisim′ilous.** [L. *vērisimilis*—*vērus,* true, *similis,* like.]

verity, *ver′i-ti, n.* truth: a truth: truthfulness: sincerity: faithfulness :—*pl.* **ver′ities.** — *adj.* **ver′itable,** true: genuine: real, actual: truly so to be called.—*adv.* **ver′itably.**—**of a verity,** assuredly. [L. *vēritās, -ātis*—*vērus,* true.]

verjuice, *vər′jōōs, n.* juice of unripe fruit.—*adj.* sour.—*adj.* **ver′juiced,** soured. [Fr. *verjus*—*vert* (L. *viridis*), green, and *jus,* juice (L. *jūs,* broth).]

vermeil, *ver′mil, -māl, n.* and *adj.* bright red, scarlet, vermilion: silver-gilt or gilt bronze.— *v.t.* to colour with vermeil.—Also **ver′mil, ver′meille** (*Spens.* **ver′mell, ver′mily.** [O.Fr. and Fr.,—L. *vermiculus,* a little worm, kermes, dim. of *vermis,* worm; cf. **vermilion.**]

vermes, *vər′mēz, n.pl.* worms: **Vermes,** in old classifications a subkingdom of animals, according to Linnaeus including all invertebrates except arthropods, later mainly flat-worms, thread-worms, annelids, now abandoned.—*adjs.* **ver′mian; ver′micïdal** (L. *caedĕre,* to kill).—*n.* **ver′micide,** a worm-killing agent.—*adjs.* **vermic′ular,** of, like, of the nature of, caused by, a worm: vermiculated: peristaltic; **vermic′ulate, -d,** worm-eaten:

marked, inlaid, rusticated, with an appearance of worm-tracks or worms.—*ns.* **vermicula′tion; ver′micule,** a little worm; **vermic′ulite,** an altered mica that curls before the blow-pipe flame.—*adjs.* **vermic′ulous,** wormy; **ver′miform,** having the form of a worm; **vermifugal** (*-mif′ū-gl*), expelling worms.—*n.* **ver′mifuge** (*-mi-fūj*), a drug that expels worms.—*adj.* **vermiv′orous,** worm-eating.—**vermiform appendix** (see **appendix**). [L. *vermis,* a worm.]

vermicelli, *vər-mi-chel′i,* or *-sel′i, n.* a very slender macaroni.—Also *adj.* [It., pl. of *vermicello*—L. *vermiculus,* dim. of *vermis,* worm.]

vermilion, *vər-mil′yən, n.* a bright-red pigment, mercuric sulphide: its bright scarlet colour.—*adj.* bright scarlet.—*v.t.* to colour vermilion. [O.Fr. *vermillon*—*vermeil*; see **vermeil.**]

vermin, *vər′min, n.* a collective name for obnoxious insects, as bugs, fleas, and lice, troublesome animals, such as mice, rats, animals destructive to game, such as weasels, polecats, also hawks and owls, odious despicable people: any one species or individual of these.—*v.i.* **ver′minate,** to breed vermin.—*n.* **verminā′tion.**—*adj.* **ver′mined,** infested with vermin.—*n.* **ver′min-kill′er.**—*adjs.* **ver′minous, ver′miny,** infested with vermin: like vermin. [Fr. *vermin*—L. *vermis,* a worm.]

vermouth, *vär′-, vər′mōōt, n.* a mild cordial white wine flavoured with wormwood. [Fr. spelling of Ger. *wermut*(*h*), wormwood; cf. O.E. *wermōd.*]

vernacular, *vər′nak′ū-lər, adj.* (of language) indigenous, native, spoken by the people of the country or of one's own country: of, in, or using the vernacular language: of the jargon or idiom of a particular group: (of other things; *rare*) native, local, endemic.—*n.* a native language or dialect: a class jargon.—*n.* **vernacularisā′tion.**—*v.t.* **vernac′ularise,** to make vernacular.—*ns.* **vernac′ularism,** a vernacular expression or idiom: the use of the vernacular; **vernac′ularist,** a user of the vernacular; **vernacularity** (*-lar′i-ti*).—*adv.* **vernac′ularly.**—*v.t.* **vernac′ulate,** (*U.S.*) to term in vernacular. [L. *vernāculus*—*verna,* a homeborn slave.]

vernal, *ver′nl, adj.* of, happening or appearing in spring: springlike: fresh and youthful. — *n.* **vernalisa′tion.**—*v.t.* **ver′nalise,** to make springlike: to freshen: to hasten the development of (seeds or seedlings) by treating them in various ways before planting, e.g. by subjecting them to a low temperature.—*n.* **vernality** (*-nal′i-ti*), springlike quality: freshness.—*adv.* **ver′nally.**—*adj.* **ver′nant,** (*Milt.*) flowering or sprouting in spring.—*n.* **vernā′tion,** arrangement of leaves in the vegetative bud (rarely that of the individual leaf).—**vernal grass,** an early-sprouting meadow grass (*Anthoxanthum odoratum*) that gives its scent of coumarin to hay. [L. *vērnālis,* vernal, *vērnāre,* to sprout—*vēr,* spring.]

Verner's law. See **law.**

vernicle, *vər′ni-kl, n.* a sudarium bearing the face of Christ, claimed to have been miraculously impressed on it when St *Veronica* wiped his face: any representation of this: a medal or badge bearing it, worn by pilgrims who had been at Rome.

vernier, *vər′ni-ər, n.* a short scale sliding on a graduated scale to give fractional readings, invented by the Burgundian Pierre *Vernier* (*c.* 1580– 1637).

Veronal, *ver′ə-nal, -nəl, n.* a trade-mark name for barbitone.

Veronica, *və-ron′i-kä, n.* the speedwell genus: **veronica,** a vernicle. [St *Veronica.*]

verquere, *vər-k*(*w*)*ēr′, n.* an obsolete form of backgammon.—(*Scott*) **verquire′.** [Du. *verkeeren,* to turn round, to play at backgammon.]

verrel, *ver′l, n.* old (now *dial.*) form of **ferrule.**

verrey, verry, *ver′i.* Same as **vairé.**

verruca, *ve-rōō′kä, n.* a wart: a wartlike outgrowth :—*pl.* **verru′cae** (*-sē*; L. *-kī*).—*adjs.* **verru′ciform** (*-si-form*), wartlike; **verrucose** (or *ver′,* or *-rōō′*), **verru′cous** (or *ver′*), warty.—*n.* **verru′ga** (Sp.; also *pl.* **verru′gas**), a fever with warty tumours, endemic in Peru. [L. *verrūca,* a wart.]

vers, ver, n. (Fr.) verse.—*n.* **verslibrist** (*ver-lē′brist*), a writer of free verse.—**vers de société** (*də sō-syä-tā*), light verse on topics of society ; **vers libre** (*lĕ´br´*), free verse.

versability, *vər-sə-bil´i-ti*, *n.* aptness to be turned round. [L. *versābilis*—*versāre*, to turn about.]

versal, *vər´sl*, *vär´sl*, *adj.* (*obs. coll.*) whole : single, individual. [For **universal**.]

versant, *vər´sənt*, *adj.* versed, conversant : busied, concerned. [L. *versāns*, -*āntis*, pr.p. of *versāre*, to turn over, consider.]

versant, *vər´sənt*, *n.* the general slope of surface of a country. [Fr. *versant*—*verser*, to turn over—L. *versāre*.]

versatile, *vər´sə-tīl*, *adj.* turning freely : (*bot.*) dangling as an anther attached by the middle of the back : (*zool.*) capable of free movement, reversible, as a toe : changeable : unsteady : turning easily from one thing to another : of many-sided ability. —*adv.* **ver´satilely**.—*ns.* **ver´satileness**, **versatility** (-*til´i-ti*). [L. *versātilis*—*versāre*, freq. of *vertēre*, to turn.]

verse, *vərs*, *n.* a line of metre : metrical composition, form, or work : versification : a stanza : a short division of a chapter, esp. of the Bible : a portion of an anthem to be performed by a single voice to each part : a versicle.—*v.t.* and *v.i.* to versify.— *ns.* **verse´let**, a little verse : a short poem ; **verse´-maker** ; **verse´-making** ; **verse´-man**, a writer of verses ; **verse´-monger**, a scribbler of verses ; **verse´-mongering** ; **ver´ser**, a writer of verse ; **verse´-smith**, an artificer of verse ; **ver´set**, a very short organ interlude or prelude : a versicle : a little scrap of verse ; **ver´sicle**, a little verse : in liturgy, the verse said by the officiant.—*adj.* **versic´ular**, of or in verse.—*ns.* **versifica´tion**, the making of verse : manner of construction of verse : a turning into verse or its product ; **ver´-sificātor**, **ver´sifier**, a maker of verses.—*v.i.* **ver´sify**, to make verses.—*v.t.* to tell in verse : to turn into verse :—*pr.p.* **ver´sifying**; *pa.t.* and *pa.p.* **ver´sified**.—*n.* **ver´sing**, the composing of verse. [O.E. *fers*, reinforced by Fr. *vers*, both— L. *versus*, *vorsus*, -*ūs*, a line, row, verse—*vertēre*, to turn.]

versed, *vərst*, *adj.* thoroughly acquainted, skilled. —*v.t.* **verse**, to make conversant. [L. *versātus*, pa.p. of *versārī*, to busy oneself.]

versed, *vərst*, *adj.* (*math.*) lit. turned, reversed.— —*n.* **versine** (*vər´sīn*), contracted **versin**, the versed sine, or one minus the cosine. [L. *versus*, pa.p. of *vertēre*, to turn.]

versicoloured, *vər´si-kul-ərd*, *adj.* diversely or changeably coloured. [L. *versicolor*, -*ōris*—*vertēre*, *versum*, to change, *color*, colour.]

versiform, *vər´si-form*, *adj.* varying in form.

version, *vər´shən*, *n.* a turning : translation : (*Scot. obs.*) a Latin prose : a particular form in which something is embodied, as a particular way of telling a story : a variant.—*adj.* **ver´sional**.—*ns.* **ver´sioner**, **ver´sionist**, producer of a version. [L. *versiō*, -*ōnis*—*vertēre*, *versum*, to turn.]

verso, *vər´sō*, *n.* a left-hand page : the reverse of a coin or medal. [L. *versō* (*foliō*), turned leaf (abl.).]

verst, *vərst*, *n.* a Russian measure, almost two-thirds of an English mile. [Russ. *versta*.]

versus, *vər´səs*, *prep.* (*law*, *games*) against—abbreviated **v.** and **vs.** [L.]

versute, *vər-sūt´*, *adj.* crafty, wily. [L. *versūtus*.]

vert, *vərt*, *n.* in forest law, every green leaf or plant having green leaves that may serve as cover for deer : a power to cut green trees or wood : (*her.*) a green colour, represented by parallel lines sloping diagonally from the dexter chief to the sinister base. [Fr. *vert*—L. *viridis*, green.]

vert, *vərt*, *n.* a familiar shortening of **convert** or **pervert** (esp. to Roman Catholicism).—*v.i.* to become a vert.

vertebra, *vər´ti-brä*, *n.* a joint of the backbone :—*pl.* **ver´tebrae** (-*brē*).—*adj.* **ver´tebral**.—*adv.* **ver´-tebrally**. — *n.pl.* **Vertebrā´ta**, the backboned animals.—*adj.* **ver´tebrate**, backboned : of the Vertebrata : articulated : firm of character.—*n.* a backboned animal. — *adj.* **ver´tebrated**, having a backbone : articulated like a backbone. — *n.*

vertebrā´tion, vertebral structure : (*fig.*) backbone. [L.,—*vertēre*, to turn.]

vertex, *vər´teks*, *n.* the top or summit : (*astron.*) the zenith : (*anat.*) crown of the head : (*geom.*) the point opposite the base : the meeting-point of the lines bounding an angle : the intersection of a curve with its axis :—*pl.* **ver´tices** (-*ti-sēz*).— *adj.* **ver´tical** (-*ti-kl*), of or at the vertex : perpendicular to the plane of the horizon : (*bot.*) in the direction of the axis : comprising the various stages in the production of the same goods.—*n.* a vertical line or position.—*n.* **verticality** (-*kal´i-ti*). —*adv.* **ver´tically**.—*ns.* **ver´ticalness** ; **verticity** (*tis´i-ti*), power of turning.—**vertical angles**, opposite angles formed by intersecting lines ; **vertical circle**, a great circle of the heavens passing through the zenith and the nadir. [L. *vertex*, -*icis*, eddy, summit—*vertēre*, to turn.]

verticil, *vər´ti-sil*, *n.* (*bot.*) a whorl.—*n.* **verti-cillas´ter**, an inflorescence so condensed as to look like a whorl.—*adjs.* **verti´cillate**, -**d**, whorled. [L. *verticillus*, dim. of *vertex*.]

vertigo, *vər-tī´gō* (L. *ver-tē´gō*), often *vər´ti-gō*, *n.* giddiness : dizziness : a whirling.—*adj.* **ver-tiginous** (-*tij´*), dizzy : giddy : whirling : dizzying. —*adv.* **vertig´inously**.—*n.* **vertig´inousness**. [L. *vertīgō*, -*inis*—*vertēre*, to turn.]

vertu, *vər-tōō´*, *n.* an erroneous form of **virtu**: **ver´tu**, **ver´tue** (-*tū*), old forms of **virtue**.—*adj.* **ver´tuous**, (*Spens.*) possessing virtue or power.

Verulamian, *vər-(y)oo-lā´mi-ən*, *adj.* of or pertaining to St Albans, or Francis Bacon, Baron *Verulam*, Viscount St Albans (1561-1626). [L. *Verulāmium*, an ancient British city near the site of St Albans.]

vervain, *vər´vān*, *n.* a wild verbena, long believed to have great magical and medicinal powers. [O.Fr. *verveine*—L. *verbēna*.]

verve, *vərv*, *n.* the enthusiasm that animates a poet or artist : gusto : spirit : animation : energy. [Fr.]

vervel, *vər´vl*, **varvel**, *vär´*, *n.* a ring for a hawk's jess.—*adj.* **verv´elled**, **varv´elled**. [Fr. *vervelle*.]

verven, *vər´vən*, *n.* (*Spens.*) **vervain**.

vervet, *vər´vit*, *n.* a South African guenon monkey. [Fr.]

very, *ver´i*, *adj.* true : so called in the true or full sense of the word—that and nothing less, even or exactly that : veritable : actual : mere : precise : extreme :—sometimes used in the *compar.* **ver´ier**, and oftener in the *superl.* **ver´iest**, most truly so called, merest.—*adv.* in a high degree : utterly : quite : truly : precisely.—*adv.* **ver´ily**, truly : of a certainty : really.—**in very deed**, of a truth, certainly. [Older *verray*, *veray*—A.Fr. *ver(r)ai* (Fr. *vrai*), from a derivative of L. *vērus*, true ; cf. Ger. *wahr*.]

Very light, *ver´i līt*, a signalling or illuminating coloured flare fired from a pistol. [Samuel W. *Very*, inventor, 1877.]

vesica, *ve-*, *vi-sī´kä*, *n.* (*anat.*) a bladder, sac, esp. the urinary bladder :—*pl.* **vesi´cae** (-*sē*).—*adjs.* **vesical** (*ves´i-kl*), of or pertaining to a vesica ; **ves´icant**, blistering.—*n.* anything that causes blisters, including any war ' gas ' that blisters and destroys tissues.—*v.t.* and *v.i.* **ves´icate**, to blister. —*n.* **vesica´tion**.—*n.* and *adj.* **ves´icatory** (or -*ik´*), vesicant.—*ns.* **ves´icle**, a small globule, bladder, sac, blister, cavity, or swelling : a primary cavity of the vertebrate brain ; **vesic´ula**, a vesicle. —*adjs.* **vesic´ular** ; **vesic´ulate**, -**d**.—*n.* **vesicū-lā´tion**, formation of vesicles.—*adj.* **vesic´ulose**.— **vesica piscis** (*pis´is* ; L. *vā-sē´kä pis´kis* ; fish's bladder), a halo in the form of two circular arcs each (properly) passing through the other's centre, enclosing the whole figure. [L. *vēsīca*, bladder, blister.]

Vespa, *ves´pä*, *n.* the common wasp genus, giving name to the family **Ves´pidae**.—*n.* **ves´piary** (modelled on *apiary*), a wasps' nest :—*pl.* **ves´-piaries**.—*adjs.* **ves´pine**, of wasps : wasplike ; **ves´poid**, wasplike. [L. *vespa*, wasp.]

vesper, *ves´pər*, *n.* evening : (usu. *pl.*) the last but one of the seven canonical hours : (usu. *pl.*) even-song, evening service generally : a vesper-bell : **Ves´per**, Venus as the evening star, Hesperus.—

adj. **ves′peral.**—*n.* **ves′per-bell,** the bell that summons to vespers.—*adjs.* **vesperti′nal, ves′-pertine,** of or pertaining to the evening: happening, opening, appearing, active, or setting, in the evening. [L. *vesper*; cf. Gr. *hesperos*.]

vespiary, vespine, vespoid. See **Vespa.**

vessel, *ves′l, n.* a vase or utensil for holding something: a craft or structure (usu. bigger than a boat) for transport by water: a conducting tube for body-fluids in animals, for water in plants: (*B.*) a person regarded as a receptacle, recipient, or embodiment: vessels collectively, plate (*Scott* **vessail, vassail**).—**the weaker vessel,** (*coll.*) a woman (1 Pet. iii. 7). [O.Fr. *vessel* (Fr. *vaisseau*—L. *vāscellum*, dim. of *vās, vāsis*, a vessel.]

vest, *vest, n.* garb, dress: a garment: a robe: a vestment: (now chiefly in *U.S.* and shops) a waistcoat: an undershirt: an additional facing to the front of a bodice.—*v.t.* to clothe: to robe: to drape: to put vestments on: to invest: (*law*) to settle, secure, or put in fixed right of possession: to endow.—*v.i.* to descend, devolve, or to take effect, as a right.—*adj.* **vest′ed,** clad: robed: wearing vestments: not contingent or suspended, hence (*law*) already acquired.—*ns.* **vest′ing,** the act or fact of clothing, investing, securing legally, &c.: material for waistcoats: **vest′-pock′et,** waistcoat-pocket.—**vested interests,** interests already established: the class of persons who have acquired rights or powers in any sphere of a country's activities. [L. *vestis*.]

Vesta, *ves′tä, n.* the Roman goddess of the hearth and household: a minor planet discovered in 1807: **vesta,** a wax-stemmed match: a short match with wooden stem:—*pl.* **ves′tas.**—*adj.* **ves′tal,** pertaining or consecrated to Vesta: of or like the Vestal virgins: virgin: chaste.—*n.* one of the Roman patrician virgins consecrated to Vesta: a woman dedicated to celibacy: a nun: a virgin: a woman of spotless chastity. [L.]

vestiary, *vest′i-ər-i, n.* a vestry, robing-room, or cloakroom.—*adj.* pertaining to clothes. [See **vestry**.]

vestibule, *ves′ti-būl, n.* (ant.) a fore-court: an entrance-hall: (*U.S.*) part of a railway carriage connecting with and giving access to the next: (*anat.*) a cavity serving as entrance to another, esp. that of the inner ear.—*v.t.* to furnish with a vestibule.—*adj.* **vestib′ular.**—*n.* **vestib′ulum,** a vestibule. [L. *vestibulum*.]

vestige, *ves′tij, n.* a footprint: a trace: a surviving trace of what has almost disappeared: a reduced and functionless structure representing what was once useful and developed.—*adj.* **vestig′ial.** [L. *vestigium*, footprint.]

vestiment, *ves′ti-mənt, n.* (*obs.*; *Spens.*) vestment, garb, garment.—*adjs.* **vestimental** (-*men′tl*), **vestiment′ary.** [L. *vestimentum*.]

vestiture, *ves′ti-tyər, n.* investiture: clothes: covering, as hair, feathers, scales. [L.L. *vestītūra*—L. *vestis*.]

vestment, *vest′mənt, n.* a garment: a ceremonial garment, esp. one worn in religious ceremonies: a covering.—*adj.* **vest′mented.** [L. *vestimentum*—*vestīre*, to clothe, *vestis*, a garment.]

vestry, *ves′tri, n.* a room in which vestments are kept and parochial meetings held: a small room attached to a church: in English parishes, a meeting of ratepayers for parish business (later restricted to church affairs): a robing-room: a cloakroom: apparel.—*adj.* **ves′tral.**—*ns.* **ves′try-clerk,** an officer chosen by the vestry to keep the parish accounts and books; **ves′tryman,** a member of a vestry; **ves′try-room,** a vestry: meeting-place of a vestry.—**common vestry,** an assembly of all the ratepayers; **select vestry,** a board of representatives of the ratepayers. [Prob. through O.Fr. —L. *vestiārium*—*vestis*, a garment.]

vesture, *vest′yər, n.* garb: a garment: vegetation clothing the soil.—*v.t.* to cover, clothe.—*adjs.* **vest′ural; vest′ured.**—*n.* **vest′urer,** a keeper of vestments. [O.Fr.,—L.L. *vestītūra*—*vestis*, garment.]

Vesuvian, *vi-sōō′vi-ən,* or -*sū′,* -*zōō′, adj.* of, of the type of, the volcano *Vesuvius.*—*ns.* **vesu′vian,**

a smoker's slow-burning match: **vesuvianite; vesu′vianite,** the mineral idocrase, silicate of aluminium and calcium, found in blocks ejected by Vesuvius.

vet, *vet, n.* (*coll.*) a veterinary surgeon.—*v.t.* to treat medically: to examine for soundness: to examine medically or otherwise: to pass as sound: to put into condition:—*pr.p.* **vett′ing**; *pa.t.* and *pa.p.* **vett′ed.**

vetch, *vech, n.* the tare or other species of the papilionaceous genus Vicia: extended to some kindred plants.—*n.* **vetch′ling,** any plant of the sweet-pea genus (Lathyrus).—*adj.* **vetch′y,** abounding with or consisting of vetches.—**bitter vetch,** various species of Vicia and Lathyrus; **kidney vetch,** Anthyllis; **milk vetch,** Astragalus. [O.N. Fr. *veche* (Fr. *vesce*)—L. *vicia.*]

veteran, *vet′ə-rən, n.* one who has seen long service: an old and experienced soldier: one old or long experienced in any activity: (*U.S.*) an ex-serviceman or re-enlisted soldier (*coll.* vet).—*adj.* old, experienced: long exercised, esp. in military life. [L. *veterānus*—*vetus, veteris*, old.]

veterinary, *vet′ə-rin-ər-i, adj.* concerned with diseases of animals.—*n.* one skilled in the diseases of domestic animals.—Also **veterinā′rian.** [L. *veterīnārius*—*veterīnae*, cattle, beasts of burden.]

vetiver, *vet′i-vər, n.* cuscus roots.

veto, *vē′tō, n.* any authoritative prohibition: the power of rejecting or forbidding:—*pl.* **vetoes** (*vē′tōz*).—*v.t.* to reject by a veto: to withhold assent to: to forbid.—**local veto,** power of a district to prohibit the liquor trade within its bounds. [L. *vetō,* I forbid.]

vettura, *vet-tōō′rä, n.* a carriage, cab, or car.—*n.* **vetturino** (*-rē′nō*), its driver or proprietor:—*pl.* **vetturi′ni** (*-nē*). [It.,—L. *vectūra*, a carrying—*vehēre*, to convey.]

vex, *veks, v.t.* to harass: to distress: to annoy: to tease: to trouble, agitate, disturb: to discuss to excess.—*v.i.* (now *rare*) to grieve, fret.—*n.* (*Scot.*) a grief.—*n.* **vexā′tion,** a vexing: state or feeling of being vexed: a source of grief or annoyance.—*adj.* **vexā′tious,** vexing: wantonly troublesome.—*adv.* **vexā′tiously.**—*n.* **vexā′tiousness.**—*adjs.* **vex′atory; vexed** (*vekst*).—*adv.* **vex′edly.**—*ns.* **vex′edness; vex′er.**—*n.* and *adj.* **vex′ing.**—*adv.* **vex′ingly.**—*n.* **vex′ingness.**—**vexatious suit,** a suit begun without justifiable cause: **vexed question,** a matter greatly debated. [Fr. *vexer*—L. *vexāre,* to shake, annoy.]

vexillum, *vek-sil′əm, n.* a Roman standard: a vexillation: a scarf on a pastoral staff: (*bot.*) a standard: the web of a feather:—*pl.* **vexill′a.**—*n.* **vex′illary,** a standard-bearer: a member of a company of Roman veterans serving under a special standard.—*adj.* of, pertaining to, under, a vexillum. —*n.* **vexilla′tion,** a company under one vexillum. [L.,—*vehēre,* to carry.]

via, viâ, *vī′ä* (L. *vē′ä*), *prep.* by way of. [L. *viâ,* abl. of *via,* way.]

via, *vē′ä, interj.* (*obs.*) of dismissal or incitement: come: be off: enough of that. [It.,—L. *via,* way.]

viable, *vī′ə-bl, adj.* capable of living, surviving, germinating, or hatching.—*n.* **viabil′ity.** [Fr.,—*vie*—L. *vīta,* life.]

viaduct, *vī′ə-dukt, n.* a structure carrying a road or railway over a valley, &c. [After **aqueduct,**—L. *via,* a way.]

vial, *vī′əl, n.* same as **phial.**—*n.* **vī′alful.**—*adj.* **vī′alled,** put or contained in a vial.—**pour out vials of wrath,** to inflict judgment (Rev. xvi. 1): to storm, rage.

viameter, *vī-am′i-tər, n.* a hodometer: a cyclometer. [L. *via,* road, Gr. *metron,* measure.]

viand, *vī′ənd, n.* an article of food: (usu. in *pl.*) food. [Fr. *viande*—L. *vīvenda,* food necessary for life— *vīvēre,* to live.]

viaticum, *vī-at′ik-əm* (L. *vē-ä′ti-koom*), *n.* money, provisions, &c., for a journey: (*R.C. Church*) the eucharist given to persons in danger of death.— *n.pl.* **viat′icals,** baggage. [L. *viāticum*—*via,* way.]

viator, *vī-ā′tor* (L. *vē-ä′tor*), *n.* a traveller, wayfarer. —*adj.* **viatorial** (*vī-ə-tō′ri-əl*). [L. *viātor, -ōris*— *via,* a way.]

vibex, *vī′beks*, *n.* a streak due to extravasation of blood :—*pl.* **vibices** (*vī-*, *vi-bī′sēz*). [L. *vībīcēs*, weals.]

vibraculum, *vī-brak′ū-ləm*, *n.* a long bristle, a modified zooid, in some Polyzoa :—*pl.* **vibrac′ula**. —Also **vibraculā′rium** :—*pl.* **-a**. [Coined from L. *vibrāre*, to shake.]

vibrate, *vī′brāt*, *-brāt′*, *v.i.* to shake : to tremble : to oscillate : to swing : to change to and fro, esp. rapidly : to resound, ring : to tingle, thrill.—*v.t.* (*obs.*) to brandish : to cause to vibrate : to measure by single vibrations : to give off in vibrations.—*n.* **vibrancy** (*vī′brən-si*).—*adjs.* **vi′brant**, vibrating : thrilling : resonant ; **vi′bratile** (*-brə-til*), vibratory : having or capable of vibratory motion.—*ns.* **vibratility** (*-til′i-ti*) ; **vibrā′tion**, a vibrating : state of being vibrated : tremulousness : quivering motion : a whole period or movement to and fro of anything vibrating : sometimes a half period or movement one way. — *adjs.* **vibrā′tional** ; **vibrā′tionless**. — *n.* **vibratiuncle** (*vī-brā-shi-ung′kl*), a small vibration.—*adj.* **vi′brative** (*-brə-tiv*), vibrating : consisting in vibrations : causing vibrations.—*n.* **vi′brātor**, that which vibrates : a vibrating part in many appliances.—*adj.* **vibratory** (*vī′brə-tər-i*), of, of the nature of, causing, or capable of, vibration. [L. *vibrāre*, *-ātum*, to tremble.]

vibrato, *vē-brä′tō*, *n.* a throbbing effect in singing without perceptible change of pitch. [It.]

vibrio, *vib′ri-ō*, or *vīb′*, *n.* a bacterium with a slight spiral curve and usually one flagellum, as that of cholera. [L. *vibrāre*.]

vibrissa, *vī-bris′ä*, *n.* a tactile bristle, as a cat's whisker : a vaneless rictal feather : a bristle, hair, as in the nostril :—*pl.* **vibriss′ae** (*-ē*). [L., a hair in the nostril.]

Viburnum, *vī-bur′nəm*, *n.* the guelder-rose and wayfaring-tree genus of Caprifoliaceae. [L. *vīburnum*, the wayfaring tree.]

vicar, *vik′ər*, *n.* one who holds authority as the delegate or substitute of another : a deputy or substitute : (*Ch. of Eng.*) a parson of a parish who receives only the smaller tithes or a salary : (*R.C.*) a bishop's deputy.—*ns.* **vic′arage**, the benefice or residence of a vicar ; **vic′ar-apostol′ic**, formerly one to whom the pope delegated some remote portion of his jurisdiction : now usually a titular bishop appointed to a country where there are no sees : one exercising authority in a vacant see or during the bishop's incapacity ; **vic′arate**, vicariate ; **vic′ar-chō′ral**, a cleric or layman who sings in an English cathedral choir ; **vic′aress**, an abbess's deputy : a vicar's wife ; **vic′ar-forane** (*for-ān′*, a form of **foreign**), a rural dean ; **vic′ar-gen′eral**, (*R.C.*) an official performing the work of an archdeacon under the bishop : (*Ch. of Eng.*) a lay official representing the bishop, the chancellor of the diocese.—*adjs.* **vicarial** (*vī-*, *vi-kā′ri-əl*), delegated : of a vicar or vicars ; **vicā′riate**, delegated. —*n.* office, authority, time of office, or sphere of a vicar, in any sense.—*adj.* **vicā′rious**, filling the place of another : exercised, performed or suffered by one person or thing instead of another.—*adv.* **vicā′riously**.—*ns.* **vicā′riousness** ; **vic′arship**, the office of a vicar ; **vic′ary**, (*obs.*) a vicarship.— **vicarious sacrifice**, the suffering and death of Christ held by orthodox Christians to be accepted by God in lieu of the punishment to which guilty man is liable ; **Vicar of Bray**, one who turns his coat without difficulty to suit the times—from Simon Aleyn, vicar of *Bray* in Berks from 1540 to 1588 ; **Vicar of Christ**, (*R.C.*) the pope, as representative of Christ on earth. [L. *vicārius*, substituted ; see **vice-**, pfx.]

vice (*U.S.* **vise**), *vīs*, *n.* (*obs.*) a screw : a winding stair or its newel : a tool for gripping an object that is being worked on : (*fig.*) a grip.—*v.t.* to grip, force, jam, strain, as with a vice. [Fr. *vis*, screw— L. *vītis*, a vine.]

vice, *vīs*, *n.* a blemish or fault : immorality : depravity : an immoral habit : a bad trick or habit as in a horse : **Vice**, the personification of a vice in a morality play, usually a farcical part : hence, a buffoon.—*adj.* **vicious** (*vish′əs*), addicted to vice

or bad habits : immoral : depraved : bad : faulty : malignant, spiteful : ill-tempered : foul, impure, morbid : impaired, nullified by a flaw : (*Shak.*) mistaken.—*adv.* **vic′iously**.—*n.* **vic′iousness**.— **vicious circle**, reasoning in a circle, seeking to prove a proposition by means of a conclusion drawn from it : a process in which an evil is aggravated by its own consequences ; **vicious intromission** (see under **intromit**). [Fr.,—L. *vitium*, a blemish ; L.L. *viciōsus* for L. *vitiōsus*, faulty, vicious.]

vice, *vī′si* (L. *vik′ä*), *prep.* in place of : in succession to.—**vice versā** (see *Foreign Words*). [L. *vice*, abl. (nom. not used), turn, place, alternation.]

vice-, *vīs-*, *pfx.* in place of.—*ns.* **vice**, (*rare*) place, stead : short for **vice-president**, **vice-chancellor**, or the like ; **vice′-ad′miral**, a naval officer ranking next under an admiral ; **vice′-ad′miralty**, the office or jurisdiction of a vice-admiral ; **vice′-chair′man**, a deputy chairman : a croupier ; **vice′-chair′manship** ; **vice′-cham′berlain**, the Lord Chamberlain's deputy and assistant ; **vice′-chan′cellor**, one acting for a chancellor ; **vice′-chan′cellorship** ; **vice′-con′sul**, a consul's deputy : one who acts as consul in a less important district ; **vice′-con′sulate** ; **vice′-con′sulship** ; **vice′-count′y**, part of a county divided for floristic purposes ; **vice-dean′**, a canon chosen to represent an absent dean ; **vicegerency** (*-jer′* or *-jēr′ən-si*).—*adj.* **vicegerent** (*-jer′*, *-jēr′* ; L. *vicem gerēns*, *-entis*, wielding office), acting in place of another, having delegated authority.—*n.* one ruling or acting in place of a superior.—*ns.* **vice′-gov′ernor**, deputy governor ; **vice′-king**, one who acts in place of a king ; **vice′-mar′shal** (see **air-vice-marshal**) ; **vice′-pres′idency** ; **vice′-pres′ident**, a president's deputy or assistant : an officer next below the president.—*adj.* **vice′-presiden′tial**. — *ns.* **vice′-princ′ipal**, assistant principal ; **vice′-queen**, a woman representing a queen : a viceroy's wife, vicereine.—*adj.* **vicerē′gal**, of a viceroy.—*ns.* **vicerē′gent**, properly, a substitute for a regent : often blunderingly for vicegerent ; **vicereine** (*vīs′ren′*, *-rān′*), a viceroy's wife : (*rare*) a vice-queen ; **vice′roy**, a governor acting in the name of the king ; **vice′roy′alty**, **vice′roy′ship**. [See foregoing.]

vicenary, *vis′i-nər-i*, *adj.* based on the number twenty. [L. *vīcēnārius*—*vīcēnī*, twenty each— *vīginti*, twenty.]

vicennial, *vi-sen′yəl*, *adj.* lasting, or coming at the end of, twenty years. [L. *vicennium*—*vicīēs*, twenty times, *annus*, a year.]

vicinage, *vis′i-nij*, *n.* neighbourhood.—*adj.* **vic′inal** (or *-īn′əl*), neighbouring : local : (*org. chem.*) having substituted groups on adjacent carbon atoms : of crystal faces, very nearly in the plane of a normal face.—*n.* **vicin′ity**, neighbourhood : nearness. [L. *vīcīnus*, neighbour—*vīcus*, street, village, district.]

viciosity. See **vitiosity**.

vicious. See under **vice** (2).

vicissitude, *vi-sis′i-tūd*, *n.* change : alternation : mutation : change of fortune.—*adj.* **vicissitū′dinous**. [L. *vicissitūdō*, *-inis* ; see **vice** (3).]

victim, *vik′tim*, *n.* a living being offered as a sacrifice : one subjected to death, suffering, or ill-treatment : a prey : a sufferer.—*n.* **victimīsā′tion**.—*v.t.* **vic′timise**, to make a victim of : to treat oppressively in revenge : to cheat.—*n.* **vic′timiser**. [L. *victima*, a beast for sacrifice.]

victor, *vik′tər*, *n.* a winner in contest :—*fem.* **vic′toress**, **vic′tress**, **vic′trix** :—*adjs.* **vic′tor**, **victō′rious**, having gained a victory : winning in contest : of, with, marking victory.—*adv.* **victō′riously**.—*ns.* **victō′riousness** ; **victory** (*vik′tər-i*), a contest gained : success against an opponent ; **Victory**, the Greek goddess Nīkē.—*adj.* **vic′toryless**. [L. *victor*, *-ōris*—*vincĕre*, *victum*, to conquer.]

Victoria, *vik-tō′ri-ä*, *n.* a Brazilian genus of gigantic water-lilies : a low, light, four-wheeled carriage with a folding hood : a large red plum (**Victoria plum**).—*adj.* **Victō′rian**, of, contemporary with, typical of, the reign (1837-1901) of Queen Victoria : strict but somewhat conventional in morals, inclining to prudery and solemnity : of the state (colony

1851-1901) of Victoria in Australia.—*n.* a contemporary of Queen Victoria : a person of Victorian morality or outlook : a native or inhabitant of Victoria.—*n.* **Victō′rianism.—Victoria Cross,** a bronze Maltese cross, a decoration for conspicuous bravery on the field, founded by Queen Victoria (1856) ; **Victoria Day,** Empire Day, a holiday on or near Queen Victoria's birthday (24th May).

victorine, *vik-tə-rēn′, n.* a fur tippet with long ends : a variety of peach. [Woman's name.]

victual, *vit′l, n.* (commonly in *pl.*) food, esp. human food : (*Scot.,* in *sing.*) grain crops, cut or ready for cutting.—*v.t.* to supply or store with provision.—*v.i.* to lay in victuals : to feed :—*pr.p.* **victualling** (*vit′l-ing*) ; *pa.t.* and *pa.p.* **victualled** (*vit′ld*).—*ns.* **vict′uallage,** provisions ; **victualler** (*vit′l-ər*), a purveyor of provisions : a victualling ship.—*adj.* **vict′ualless.—*ns.* **vict′ualling-bill′,** a customs document warranting the captain of an outward-bound vessel to ship bonded stores for the voyage ; **vict′ualling-off′ice, -ship,** an office supplying, a ship conveying, provisions to the navy ; **vict′ualling-yard′,** a public establishment for the collection and supply of provisions to the navy.—**licensed victualler,** an innkeeper licensed to sell spirits, wines, &c. [O.Fr. *vitaille*—L.L. *victuālia*—L. *victuālis,* relating to living—*vīvĕre, victum,* to live.]

vicuña, *vi-kōō′nyä, n.* a wild species of the llama genus : cloth of its wool, or an imitation. [Sp., from Quichua.]

vidame, *vē-däm′, n.* in French feudal jurisprudence, the deputy of a bishop in temporal affairs : a minor noble. [Fr.,—L.L. *vicedominus.*]

vide, videlicet, videndum. See *Foreign Words.*

video, *vid′i-ō, adj.* used in television, and also in radar, as **video frequency,** any one of the range of modulating frequencies present in a television picture signal ; **video signal** ; **video tube,** a television tube. [L. *vidēre,* to see.]

vidette, a faulty form of **vedette.**

vidimus, *vī′di-məs* (L. *vē′di-moos*), *n.* an attested copy : an inspection, as of accounts, &c. [L. *vidimus,* we have seen—*vidēre,* to see.]

viduous, *vid′ū-əs, adj.* widowed.—*n.* **vid′ūage,** widowhood : widows collectively.—*adj.* **vid′ūal.—** *n.* **vidū′ity,** widowhood.—*adj.* **vid′ūous,** empty. [L. *vidua,* a widow, *viduus,* deprived, bereaved.]

vie, *vī, v.i.* (*obs.*) to make a vie : to contend in rivalry.—*v.t.* (*obs.*) to stake : (*obs.* ; *cards*) to declare, bid : (*Shak.*) to put forward in competition or emulation, or repeatedly, bandy : (*pr.p.* **vy′ing** ; *pa.t.* and *pa.p.* **vied,** *vīd*).—*n.* (*obs.*) a bid, challenge, stake.—*adv.* **vy′ingly.** [Fr. *envier*—L. *invītāre,* to challenge, invite.]

vielle, *vē-el′, n.* a hurdy-gurdy, lute played by a wheel. [Fr.]

Viennese, *vē-e-nēz′, adj.* of Vienna.—*n. sing.* and *pl.* an inhabitant (*pl.* inhabitants) of Vienna.

view, *vū, n.* an act, possibility or opportunity of looking : range or field of sight : whole extent seen : a prospect, wide or distant extent seen : that which is seen : inspection : appearance : aspect : the picture of a scene : a general survey of a subject : mode of thinking of something : opinion : intention, purpose : expectation.—*v.t.* to see : to look at : to observe : to consider : to examine intellectually.—*ns.* **view′er,** one who views : an inspector : one appointed to examine and report : a colliery superintendent ; **view′-finder,** an attachment to a photographic camera for determining the field of view ; **view′-halloo′,** the huntsman's cry when the fox breaks cover ; **view′iness,** character of being viewy ; **view′ing.**—*adj.* **view′less,** invisible.—*adv.* **view′lessly.**—*adj.* **view′ly,** (*prov.*) pleasing to look at.—*n.* **view′point,** point of view : standpoint : a selected position for admiring scenery.—*adj.* **view′y,** (*coll.*) holding or expressing opinions vague or purely speculative : inclined to attach undue importance to certain aspects of views : one-sided : cranky.—**dissolving views,** pictures thrown on a screen and made to pass one into another ; **in view,** in sight : in mind : as an aim or prospect ; **in view of,** in a position to see or to be seen by : having regard to ; **on view,** open to general inspection ; **view away,** to see breaking

cover ; **with a view to,** having in mind : with a design of. [Fr. *vue*—*vu,* pa.p. of *voir*—L. *vidēre,* to see.]

vifda, *vif′dä, n.* See **vivda.**

vigesimal, *vī-jes′i-mal, adj.* based on the number twenty.—*adj.* **viges′imo-quar′to,** twenty-four-mo. [L. *vigēsimus* (*vicēsimus*),twentieth—*vīgintī,*twenty.]

vigia, *vi-jē′ä* (Sp. *vi-hhē′ä*), *n.* a danger warning on a chart. [Sp. *vigia,* look-out—L. *vigilia.*]

vigil, *vij′il, n.* watching, esp. by night, esp. for religious exercises : the eve of a holy day : a religious service by night : a keeping awake, wakefulness.—*n.* **vig′ilance,** watchfulness : wakefulness : (*Milt.*) a guard, watch.—*adj.* **vig′ilant,** watchful.—*n.* **vigilante** (*-ān′tä* ; *U.S.* from Sp.), a member of a vigilance committee.—*adv.* **vig′ilantly.—vigilance committee,** (*U.S.*) an unauthorised body which, in the absence or inefficiency of regular government, exercises powers of arrest, punishment, &c. : also any self-appointed association for the compulsory improvement of local morals according to its own standards. [L. *vigilia*—*vigil,* awake, watchful ; cf. *vigēre,* to be lively.]

vigneron, *vēn-yə-ronₚ, n.* a vine-grower. [Fr.]

vignette, *vēn-yet′, n.* orig. a design of vine-leaves and tendrils : a small embellishment without a border, in what would have been a blank space, esp. on a title-page or as a headpiece or tailpiece : a photographic portrait shading off around the head : a character sketch, a word-picture.—*v.t.* to make a vignette of.—*ns.* **vignett′er** ; **vignett′ist.** [Fr.,—*vigne*—L. *vinea,* a vine, a vineyard.]

vigour, *vig′ər, n.* active strength : vital power : forcefulness : activity : energy.—*adj.* **vig′orous.—** *adv.* **vig′orously.**—*n.* **vig′orousness.** [A.Fr. *vigour* (Fr. *vigueur*), and L. *vigor, -ōris*—*vigēre,* to be strong.]

vihara, *vē-hä′ru, n.* a Buddhist or Jain precinct, temple, or monastery. [Sans. *vihāra.*]

viking, *vī′king, n.* a Scandinavian pirate (8th-10th cent.).—*n.* **vi′kingism** [O.N. *víkingr,* prob.—O.E. *wīcing,* pirate.]

vilayet, *vil-ä′yet, n.* a Turkish province. [Turk. *vilāyet*—Ar. *welāyeh.*]

vild, vilde, *vīld, adj.* an old variant (*Spens., Shak.*) of **vile.**—*adv.* **vild′ly.**—*n.* **vild′ness.**

vile, *vīl, adj.* worthless : mean : paltry : base : detestable : loathsome : foul : depraved : very bad.—*adv.* (*Shak., Spens.*) vilely.—*adv.* **vile′ly.—** *ns.* **vile′ness** ; **vilificā′tion** (*vil-*), act of vilifying : defamatory speech : abuse ; **vilifier** (*vil′*).—*v.t.* **vilify** (*vil′*), to make vile : to disparage : to defame :—*pr.p.* **vil′ifying** ; *pa.t.* and *pa.p.* **vil′ified.** —*v.t.* **vilipend** (*vil′* ; L. *vilipendĕre—pendĕre,* to weigh), to despise, make light of : to disparage : to slander, vilify.—*v.i.* to use vilification. [O.Fr. *vil* and L. *vilis,* worthless.]

vill, *vil, n.* (*hist.*) a township, or feudal territorial unit : a manor : (*poet.*) a village.—*ns.* **vill′a,** (*orig.*) a country house or farmhouse with subsidiary buildings : a country seat, in Italy often a castle : a detached house of some size : a superior middle-class dwelling-house ; **vill′adom,** villas collectively : the villa-dwelling world ; **vill′age,** a manor, a parish, or an outlying part of a parish : an assemblage of houses smaller than a town : (*U.S.*) a small municipality : the people of a village.—*adj.* of, dwelling in, a village.—*ns.* **vill′ager,** an inhabitant of a village ; **villagery** (*vil′ij-ri* ; *Shak.* **villagree**), villages collectively, or perh. village people.—*adjs.* **vill′ar,** of a vill ; **villatic** (*-at′ik* ; *Milt.*), farmyard : village.— **village cart** (see **cart**). [L. *villa,* a country house, partly through O.Fr. *ville,* farm, village, &c. (Fr. town), and It. *villa,* country house ; Fr. *village* ; L. *villāticus.*]

villain, *vil′ən, n.* (*orig.*) a villein : a violent, malevolent or unscrupulous evil-doer : (playfully) a wretch : the wicked enemy of the hero or heroine in a story or play.—*adj.* low-born : base : villainous. —*ns.* **vill′ainage, vill′anage,** villeinage ; **vill′ainess,** a she-villain.— *adj.* **vill′ainous** (or **vill′anous**), of the nature of, like, or suited to a villain : detestable, vile.—*adv.* (*Shak.*) villainously.

—*adv.* **vill′ainously (vill′anously).**—*ns.* **vill′ainy (vill′any),** the act (*obs.* the words) of a villain: extreme wickedness: an atrocious crime: (*obs.*) disgrace; **vill′an,** a villein. [O.Fr. *villain*—L.L. *villānus*—L. *villa,* a country house.]

villanelle, *vil-ə-nel′, n.* a poem, on two rhymes, in five tercets and a quatrain, the first line repeated as sixth, twelfth, and eighteenth, the third as ninth, fifteenth, and last. [Fr.,—It. *villanella*—*villano,* rustic.]

Villanovan, *vil-ə-nō′vən, adj.* of an early Iron Age culture of which remains occur at *Villanova,* near Bologna.

villeggiatura, *vi-lej-ə-tōō′rä, n.* country retirement or holiday. [It.]

villein, *vil′ən, -in, n.* (*hist.*) orig. app. a free villager: later (13th cent.) a serf, free in relation to all but his lord, and not absolutely a slave: developing later into a copyholder.—*n.* **vill′e(i)nage,** a villein's tenure or status. [A.Fr.; *cf.* **villain.**]

villiago, *vil-yä′gō, n.* (*Shak.*) coward.—Also **vilia′co** (*Scott* **villagio**). [It. *vigliacco*—L. *vīlis,* worthless.]

villication, *vil-i-kā′shən, n.* (*Smollett*) app. intended as a Scots pronunciation of **vellication.**

villus, *vil′əs, n.* a long soft hair : a hair-like process : —*pl.* **vill′i** (*-ī*).—*adjs.* **vill′iform,** having the form of villi ; **vill′ose, vill′ous,** covered with or formed of villi : like the pile of velvet.—*n.* **villos′ity.** [L. *villus,* wool.]

vim, *vim, n.* (*slang*) energy, vigour. [App. L. *vim,* accus. of *vīs,* force.]

vimineous, *vim-in′i-əs, adj.* with long flexible shoots. [L. *vīmineus*—*vīmen, -inis,* osier, switch.]

vina, *vē′nä, n.* an Indian stringed instrument with fretted finger-board over two gourds. [Sans. *vīnā.*]

vinaceous. See under **vine.**

vinaigrette, *vin-ā-gret′, n.* a box or bottle for aromatic vinegar or smelling-salts. [Fr.,—*vinaigre,* vinegar.]

vinasse, *vi-nas′,* a residue in alcoholic distillation, esp. in beet-sugar-making, a source of potash salts. [Fr.]

Vinca, *ving′kä, n.* the periwinkle genus. [L. *vinca-pervinca.*]

Vincentian, *vin-sen′sh(y)ən, adj.* pertaining to St *Vincent* de Paul (1576-1660) or to the charitable associations founded by him, or to St Vincent of Lérins (*d.* 450), or other Vincent.

vincible, *vin′si-bl, adj.* that may be overcome.—*n.* **vincibil′ity.** [L. *vincibilis*—*vincĕre,* to conquer.]

vinculum, *ving′kū-ləm, n.* a bond : (*math.*) a horizontal line placed above, equivalent to brackets : (*anat.*) a tendinous band :—*pl.* **vinc′ula.** [L., —*vincīre,* to bind.]

vindemial, *vin-dē′mi-əl, adj.* pertaining to the vintage.—*v.i.* **vindē′miate,** to gather grapes, or other fruit. [L. *vindēmia,* vintage ; see **vintage.**]

vindicate, *vin′di-kāt, v.t.* to justify : to clear from criticism, &c. : to defend with success : to make good a claim to : to lay claim to : to maintain : (*obs.*) to avenge : (*obs.*) to free.—*n.* **vindicability** (*-kə-bil′i-ti*).—*adj.* **vin′dicable.**—*n.* **vindica′tion,** act of vindicating : defence : justification : support.—*adj.* **vin′dicātive** (or *vin-dik′ə-tiv*), vindicating : tending to vindicate : (*Shak.*) revengeful, vindictive.—*ns.* **vindic′ativeness,** vindictiveness ; **vin′dicātor,** one who vindicates :—*fem.* **vin′dicātress.**—*adv.* **vin′dicatorily.**—*adjs.* **vin′dicatory** (*-ə-tər-i,* or *-ā-tər-i*), serving or tending to vindicate : punitive : retributive : avenging : **vindic′tive,** revengeful : pursuing revenge : punitive (as in *vindictive damages*) : retributive (as in *vindictive justice*).—*adv.* **vindic′tively.**—*n.* **vindic′tiveness.** [L. *vindicāre, -ātum.*]

vine, *vīn, n.* a woody climbing plant (*Vitis vinifera* or other of the genus) that produces grapes : (*hort.*) a climbing or trailing stem or (*U.S.*) plant.—*adjs.* **vinā′ceous,** wine-coloured ; **vin′al,** of, due to, wine.—*n.pl.* **Vinā′lia** (L. *vē-nā′li-ä*), a Roman wine festival celebrated on 23rd April, when last year's vintage was tasted and offered to Jupiter: also a vintage festival, 19th August.—*n.* **vine′-branch,** a branch of a vine : a centurion's badge.—*adj.* **vine′-clad,** covered with vines.—*ns.* **vine′-**

disease, a disease affecting the vine ; **vine′-dresser,** one who trims and cultivates vines ; **vine′-fretter,** a small insect that infests vines, esp. Phylloxera or other greenfly ; **vine′-gall,** a gall on a vine, esp. one made by a weevil ; **vine′-leaf,** the leaf of a vine ; **vine′-mildew,** a disease of vines due to the oidium stage of a mildew fungus, Uncinula ; **vine′-prop,** a support for a vine ; **vīn′er,** a vine-grower ; **vine′-rod,** a Roman centurion's badge ; **vinery** (*vīn′ə-ri*), a hot-house for rearing vines ; **vine′-stock,** the stock on which a vine of another kind is grafted ; **vineyard** (*vin′yərd, -yärd*), a plantation of vines ; **vin′iculture** (*vīn-* or *vin-*), the cultivation of the vine ; **vin′iculturist.**—*adj.* **vīn′olent,** addicted to wine.—*ns.* **vin ordinaire** (*van′or-dē-ner′* ; Fr., ordinary wine), wine for ordinary use, cheap claret ; **vīnos′ity.**—*adjs.* **vī′nous,** pertaining to wine: like wine: winecoloured : caused by or indicative of wine ; **vī′ny,** pertaining to, like, consisting of, or bearing vines : entwining.—*n.* **vinyl** (*vīn′il* ; Gr. *hȳlē,* matter), an organic radical CH_2 : CH (**vinyl resins,** thermoplastic resins formed by the co-polymerisation of vinyl chloride and vinyl acetate).—**dwell under one's vine and fig-tree,** to live at peace on one's own land. [O.Fr. *vine, vigne*—L. *vīnea,* a vineyard, a vine—*vīnum,* wine ; Gr. *oinos,* wine.]

vinegar, *vin′i-gər, n.* a condiment and pickling medium, a dilute impure acetic acid, made from beer, weak wine, &c.—*v.t.* to apply vinegar to.—*ns.* **vin′egar-eel′,** a minute threadworm that breeds in vinegar ; **vinegarette′,** a vinaigrette ; **vin′egar-fly′,** a fruit-fly. — *adj.* **vin′egarish,** sourish.—*n.* **vin′egar-plant′,** a bacterium causing acetic fermentation.—*adj.* **vin′egary,** like vinegar : flavoured with vinegar : sour. [Fr. *vinaigre*—*vin* (L. *vīnum*), wine, *aigre,* sour (L. *ācer,* keen, sharp, pungent).]

vinew, *vin′ū, v.t.* and *v.i.* to make or become mouldy.—*n.* mouldiness.—*adj.* **vin′ewed,** mouldy : musty. [O.E. *fynegian,* to mould—*fynig,* mouldy—*fyne,* mould.]

vingt-et-un, *van′-tā-ən³, n.* a card game, its object to have a total of pips in one's hand nearest to, but not exceeding, twenty-one.—Also **vingt-un** (*van′-tən³*). [Fr. *vingt-et-un,* twenty-one.]

vint, *vint, n.* a card game like auction bridge. [Russ.]

vintage, *vint′ij, n.* the gathering of grapes and preparation for wine-making : a season's yield of grapes or wine : the time of gathering grapes : wine, esp. of a good year.—*v.t.* to strip of grapes : to gather (grapes) : to make (wine)—esp. of a good year.—*n.* and *v.t.* **vint** (back-formation from **vintage**).—*ns.* **vint′ager,** a worker at the vintage ; **vint′aging.** [A.Fr. *vintage,* O.Fr. (Fr.) *vendange*—L. *vindēmia*—*vīnum,* wine, grapes, *dēmĕre,* to remove—*dē,* out of or away, *emĕre,* to take ; modified by influence of **vintner.**]

vintner, *vint′nər, n.* a wine-seller.—*n.* **vint′ry,** a wine-store : a wine-shop. [O.Fr. *vinetier*—L.L. *vīnetārius*—L. *vīnum,* wine.]

vinyl. See **vine.**

viol, *vī′əl, n.* any member of a class of instruments, precursors of the violin class, represented now by the double bass.—*ns.* **viola** (*vi-ō′lä*), a tenor fiddle, slightly bigger than the violin, tuned a fifth lower ; **vi′ol-de-gam′boys,** (*Shak.*) the viola da gamba ; **violer** (*vī′-ə-lər*), a viol player : a fiddler ; **violin** (*vī-ə-lin′,* or *vī′*), a musical instrument with four strings (E, A, D, G) played with a bow : a violinist ; **violin′-bow′** ; **vi′olinist,** a player on the violin ; **violin′-string** ; **vi′olist,** a player on the viol ; **violoncellist** (*vē-, vī-ə-lən-chel′ist*), a 'cello-player ; **violoncell′o,** a bass instrument of the violin class, commonly called 'cello ; **violone** (*vē-ō-lō′nä*), a bass viol, bigger than the viola da gamba—the double bass.—**viola da braccio** (*dä brät′cho* ; It., viol for the arm), a tenor viol, held along the arm ; **viola da gamba** (*gäm′bä* ; It., viol for the leg), a bass viol, resembling the 'cello ; **viola d'amore** (*dä-mo′rä* ; It., of love), a tenor viol with sympathetic strings under the finger-board ; **viola da spalla** (*späl′lä* ; It., for the shoulder), a bigger form of tenor viol. [Partly **vielle** ; partly Fr. *viole*

Neutral vowels in unaccented syllables : *el′ə-mənt, in′fənt, ran′dəm*

and It. *viola*, dim. *violino*, augmentative *violone*, and its dim. *violoncello*; origin doubtful; cf. L.L. *vitula*, and **fiddle**.]

viola. See **viol**.

Viola, *vī′ə-lä, n.* the violet and pansy genus of plants, giving name to the family Violā′ceae, with spurred zygomorphic flowers.—*adj.* violā′ceous, of the Violaceae: violet-coloured. [L. *vĭola*.]

violate, *vī′ə-lāt, v.t.* to do violence to: to fail to observe duty: to abuse: to ravish: to profane.—*adj.* violatec: defiled.—*adj.* vi′olable, that may be violated.—*adv.* vi′olably.—*ns.* violā′tion.—*adj.* vi′olātive, causing, tending to, or involving violation.—*n.* vi′olātor. [L. *violāre, -ātum*—*vīs*, strength.]

viold, (*Milt.*) for **vialled**.

violent, *vī′ə-lənt, adj.* intensely forcible: impetuous and unrestrained in action: overmasteringly vehement: due to violence: wrested: expressing violence.—*v.t.* (*obs.*) to force.—*v.i.* (*Shak.*) to rage.—*n.* vi′olence, the state or quality of being violent: excessive, unrestrained, or unjustifiable force: outrage: profanation: injury: rape.—*adv.* vi′olently. [L. *violentus* or *violēns, -entis*—*vīs*.]

violet, *vī′ə-lit, n.* any plant or flower of the genus Viola: extended to unrelated plants, as dame's violet, water-violet (see **dame, water**): a bluish purple.—*adj.* bluish purple. [Fr. *violette*— L. *viola*.]

violin, violoncello, violone. See under **viol**.

viper, *vī′pər, n.* the only venomous British snake, the adder: any member of its genus (Vi′pera) or family (Viperidae, *vī-per′i-dē*): extended to some other snakes, as the pit-vipers, horned vipers: (*fig.*) an ungrateful or treacherous malignant person.—*adjs.* viperiform (-*per′*); vi′perine (-*pər-īn*), related to or resembling the viper; vi′perish, venomous: spiteful: like a viper; vi′perous, having the qualities of a viper: venomous: malignant.—*adv.* vi′perously.—**viper′s bugloss**, a stiff bristly boraginaceous plant (Echium) of dry places with intensely blue flowers, once thought a remedy or prophylactic for snake-bite; **viper′s grass**, black salsify. [L. *vīpera*—*vīvus*, living, *parĕre*, to bring forth.]

virago, *vi-rā′gō*, or (L.) *vi-rä′gō, n.* a heroic or man-like woman: an amazon: a scold: a termagant.—*adjs.* viraginian (*vi-rə-jin′i-ən*), viraginous (*vi-raj′*), vira′goish. [L. *virāgō, -inis*—*vir*, a man.]

viranda, virando, obs. forms of **veranda**(h).

virelay, *vir′ə-lā, n.* an old French lyric form in two-rhymed stanzas of short lines, linked by recurrent lines. [Fr. *virelai*, app. from meaningless refrain *vireli*, but associated with *virer*, turn, *lai*, a song.]

virement, *vē-rə-mänⁿ, n.* authorised transference of a surplus to balance a deficit under another head. [Fr.]

virent, *vir′ənt, adj.* verdant: fresh: green.—*n.* virescence (*vir-, vir-es′əns*).—*adj.* viresc′ent, turning green: inclining to green: fresh: green: abnormally green. [L. *virēns, -ēntis*, pr.p. of *virēre*, to be green; *virēscēns*, pr.p. of *virēscĕre*, to become green.]

Vireo, *vir′i-ō, n.* a genus of American singing birds, the greenlets, giving name to the family Vireonidae (-*on′i-dē*). [L. *vireō, -ōnis*, perh. greenfinch.]

viretot, *vir′i-tot, n.* (Scott after *Chaucer*) rush, dash, gad. [Origin obscure.]

virgate, *vər′gāt, adj.* rodlike: twiggy.—*n.* an old land measure, commonly 30 acres. [L. *virga*, rod.]

Virgilian, Vergilian, *vər-jil′i-ən, adj.* of, in the manner of, *Virgil* (*Vergilius*), the Roman poet (70-19 B.C.).

virgin, *vər′jin, n.* a maiden: one (esp. a woman) who has had no sexual intercourse: a madonna: a figure of the Virgin: Virgo, a sign, and a constellation, of the zodiac.—*adj.* in a state of virginity: of a virgin: maidenly: pure: chaste: undefiled: in the original condition—unattained, untouched, unexploited, never scaled, felled, captured, wrought, used, &c.—*v.t.* (with *it*; *Shak.*) to continue chaste.—*adj.* vir′ginal, of or appropriate to a virgin or virginity: in a state of virginity: like a virgin: parthenogenetic.—*adv.* vir′ginally.—*adj.* vir′gin-**born**, born of a virgin. — *ns.* vir′ginhood,

virgin′ity, state or fact of being a virgin.—*adj.* vir′ginly, pure.—*adv.* chastely.—*ns.* vir′gin's-**bow′er**, traveller's-joy (*Clematis Vitalba*); Vir′go (-*gō*), the Virgin, in the zodiac.—**the (Blessed) Virgin,** Mary the mother of Christ; **virgin birth, generation,** parthenogenesis; **virgin gold,** gold in the condition in which it is found; **virgin knot,** the fastening of a Greek or Roman woman's girdle, loosed at marriage. [Partly through Fr.,—L. *virgō, -inis*.]

virginal, *vər′jin-əl, n.* (often in *pl.*, also *pair of virginals*) an old keyboard instrument, a spinet, esp. a box-shaped spinet.—*v.i.* (*Shak.*) to finger, as on a virginal. [Perh. as played by young ladies; see above.]

Virginia, *vər-jin′yä, n.* a tobacco grown and manufactured in *Virginia*.—*adj.* Virgin′ian.—*n.* a native or citizen of Virginia.—*n.* virgin′ium, (*chem.*) a name proposed for the element of atomic number 87 (see francium).—**Virginia creeper,** an American climbing-plant near akin to the vine, bright red in autumn; **Virginia stock** (see **stock**). [After Elizabeth, the *virgin* queen.]

virgule, *vər′gūl, n.* a slanting line, an old form of comma. [L. *virgula*, dim. of *virga*, a twig.]

viricide. See **virus**.

virid, *vir′id, adj.* green.—*n.* viridesc′ence.—*adj.* viridesc′ent, greenish.—*ns.* virid′ian, a green pigment, hydrated chromium sesquioxide; **vir′idite,** an indeterminate green decomposition product in rocks; virid′ity, verdure: greenness. [L. *viridis*, green—*virēre*, to be green.]

virile, *vir′īl*, sometimes *vīr′*, also -*il, adj.* having the qualities of a mature male man: robustly masculine: manly. — *n.* virilescence (*vir-il-es′əns*), development of male character in the female.—*adj.* virilesc′ent.—*ns.* vir′ilism, presence of male character in the female; viril′ity, the state or quality of being a man: the power of a mature male: the power of procreation: manhood: masculinity: vigour, energy. [L. *virīlis*—*vir*, a man; cf. O.E. *wer*, man, and **werwolf**.]

virl, virl, *n.* (now *Scot.*). Same as **ferrule**.

virose, &c. See under **virus**.

virtu, *vər-tōō′, n.* a love of the fine arts: taste for curiosities: objects of art or antiquity.—*adjs.* **virtuose** (-*tū-ōs′*), **virtuŏ′sic,** exhibiting the qualities of a virtuoso.—*ns.* virtuosity (-*os′*), the character of a virtuoso: exceptional technical skill in music or other fine art: interest in or knowledge of articles of virtu; **virtuoso** (*vir-tōō-ō′sō, vər-tū-ō′sō, -zō*), one skilled or interested in works of art, antiquities, curiosities, and the like: a musician (or other artist) of the highest technical skill:—*pl.* virtuŏ′sos, virtuŏ′si (-*sē*):—*fem.* virtuŏ′sa, *pl.* virtuŏ′se (-*sä*); virtuŏ′sŏship. [It. *virtù*— L. *virtūs, -ūtis*; see next word.]

virtue, *vər′tū, n.* excellence: worth: moral excellence: the practice of duty: a good quality, esp. moral: (*rare*) an accomplishment: (now *rare*) valour: sexual purity: (loosely) virginity: inherent power: efficacy: one of the orders of the celestial hierarchy.—*adj.* vir′tual, having virtue or efficacy: having the efficacy without the material part: in effect though not in fact: unreal but capable of being considered as real for some purposes.—*ns.* vir′tualism, the doctrine of Christ's virtual presence in the eucharist; **vir′tualist;** virtual′ity, essential nature: potentiality.—*adv.* vir′tually. — *adjs.* vir′tueless; vir′tue-proof (*Milt.* **vertue-**), impregnable in virtue; vir′tuous, having virtue: morally good: blameless: righteous: practising duty: according to the moral law: chaste.—*adv.* vir′tuously.—*n.* vir′tuousness.—**by, in, virtue of,** through the power, force, or efficacy of: because of: on account of; **make a virtue of necessity,** to do as if from sense of duty (or with a sense of duty called in for the occasion) something one must needs do; **seven principal virtues,** faith, hope, charity, justice, prudence, temperance, and fortitude—the first three the *theological*, the last four the *moral* virtues; **the cardinal virtues** (see **cardinal**). [O.Fr. *vertu* and L. *virtus*, bravery, moral excellence—*vir*, a man; cf. Gr. *hērōs*, Sans. *vīra*, a hero, O.E. *wer*, man.]

virulent, *vir′ū-lənt*, or *-oo-*, *adj.* highly poisonous or malignant: venomous: acrimonious. — *ns.* **vir′ulence**, **vir′ulency**.—*adv.* **vir′ulently**. [L. *virulentus*—*virus*, poison.]

virus, *vī′rəs*, *n.* venom: contagious or poisonous matter (as of ulcers, &c.): the transmitted cause of infection: a pathogenic agent not visible by ordinary microscopic means, perhaps chemical in nature rather than organic—a filter-passer: any corrupting influence.—*n.* **vir′icide** (or *vir′*), a substance that destroys or eliminates a virus.—*adj.* **vī′rose**, poisonous: foul.—*n.* **viro′sis**, a disease caused by a virus.—*adj.* **vī′rous**, virose.—**virus disease**, a disease caused by a filter-passing virus. [L. *vīrus* venom; Gr. *īos*, Sans. *visha*, poison.]

visa, *vē′zä*, **visé**, *vē′zä*, *ns.* an authenticating endorsement on a passport.—*vs.t.* to put a visa on :—*pa.ts.* and *pa.ps.* **vi′saed**, **vi′séed**. [L. *visa*, pa.p. fem. of *vidēre*, to see, and Fr. *visé*, pa.p. masc. of *viser*, to examine.]

visage, *viz′ij*, *n.* the face.—*adj.* **vis′aged**. [Fr. *visage*—L..*visus*, look.]

vis-à-vis, *vē′zä-vē*, *adv.* face-to-face.—*prep.* face-to-face with.—*n.* one who faces, or is opposite to, another: a light carriage with seats facing each other: an S-shaped couch. [Fr. *vis*, face (—L. *vīsus*, look), *à*, to.]

viscacha, *vis-kä′chä*, *n.* a S. American burrowing rodent of heavy build.—Also **vizca′cha**, **bizca′-cha**.—*n.* **viscachera** (*-chä′rä*), a settlement of viscachas. [Sp.,—Quichua *huiscacha*.]

viscera, **visceral**, **viscerate**. See **viscus**.

viscid, *vis′id*, *adj.* semi-fluid, sticky, glutinous, viscous: (*bot.*) of a surface, clammy and covered with a sticky secretion.—*ns.* **viscid′ity**; **viscin** (*vis′in*), the sticky substance present in the fruits of mistletoe. [L.L. *viscidus*—L. *viscum*; see **viscous**.]

viscometer, &c., **viscosimeter**, &c. See **viscous**.

viscose, *vis′kōs*, *n.* the sodium salt of cellulose xanthate, used in the manufacture of **viscose rayon**. [See **viscous**.]

viscount, *vī′kownt*, *n.* (*hist.*) an officer who acted as administrative deputy to an earl, a sheriff: a title of nobility next below an earl (first granted 1440): the son or younger brother of a count :—*fem.* **viscountess** (*vī′kownt-es*). — *ns.* **vī′scountcy**, **vī′scountship**, a viscounty: (*obs.*) a viscount: (*hist.*): the jurisdiction of, or territory under, a viscount: the rank or dignity of a viscount. [O.Fr. *visconte* (Fr. *vicomte*)—*vis*- (L. *vice*, in place of) *conte*, count, after L.L. *vicecomes*—L. *comes*, a companion.]

viscous, *vis′kəs*, *adj.* resistant, or highly resistant, to flow owing to forces acting between the molecules: tenacious: sticky: viscid.—*ns.* **vis′cousness**; **viscom′eter**, an instrument for measuring viscosity.—*adj.* **viscomet′rical**.—*n.* **viscom′etry**. —Also **viscosim′eter**, **viscosimet′rical**, **vis-cosim′etry**.—*n.* **viscos′ity**.—**viscous flow**, a type of fluid flow in which there is a continuous steady motion of the particles, the motion at a fixed point always remaining constant. [L.L. *viscōsus*, sticky.—L. *viscum*, bird-lime, mistletoe; cog. with Gr. *ixos*, mistletoe.]

Viscum, *vis′kəm*, *n.* a genus of parasitic plants including the common mistletoe: **viscum**, bird-lime. [L.]

viscus, *vis′kəs*, *n.* (*med.*, *zool.*) any one of the organs situated within the chest and the abdomen—heart, lungs, liver, &c. :—*pl.* **viscera** (*vis′ər-ä*; in common use esp. the abdominal organs).—*adj.* **visc′eral**.—*v.t.* **visc′erate**, to disembowel.—*pfx.* **visc′ero-**, in composition, of or pertaining to the viscera or to a viscus.—Also **visc′eri-**. [L. *viscus*, pl. *viscera*.]

vise, *viz* (*obs.* in all meanings), *v.t.* to advise: to look at.—*v.i.* to look (with *on*): to consider (with *on*). [Partly *advise* ; partly Fr. *viser*—L. *vidēre*, *visum*, to see.]

vise. U.S. spelling of **vice** (1).

visé. See **visa**.

Vishnu, *vish′nōō*, *n.* the second god of the Hindu triad; he became specially the benefactor of man in his many *avatars* or incarnations. [Sans.]

visible, *viz′i-bl*, *adj.* that may be seen : in sight: obvious : (of supplies of a commodity) actually in store, known to be available : ready or willing to receive a visitor or visitors.—*n.* a visible thing (often in *pl.*).—*ns.* **visibil′ity**, state or quality of being visible, or perceivable by the eye : clearness of the atmosphere : clarity and range of vision in the atmospheric conditions, seeing : a visible thing (usu. in *pl.*): (*obs.*) a sight, show place : (*obs.*) appearance : (*obs.*) power of seeing, sight ; **vis′ibleness**.—*adv.* **vis′ibly**.—**Visible Church**, the body of professing Christians, as opp. to the *Invisible Church*, which consists of those spiritually minded persons who live up to the ideals of the Church, together with the departed saints in heaven ; **visible exports**, **imports** (see **exports**, **imports**); **visible horizon** (see **horizon**); **visible means**, means or resources which are apparent to or ascertainable by others ; **visible speech**, a system of phonetic characters each of which suggests the configuration of the organs in producing the sound. [Through O.Fr- or direct from L. *visibilis*—*vidēre* ; see **vision**.]

visie. See **vision**.

Visigoth, *viz′i-goth*, *n.* one of the Western Goths, as distinguished from the Ostrogoths or Eastern Goths ; they formed settlements in the south of France and in Spain, and their kingdom in the latter lasted into the 8th century.—*adj.* **Visigoth′ic**. [L.L. *Visigothī*—Gmc. word meaning perh. noble Goths, perh. west Goths.]

visile, *viz′il*, *-il*, *adj.* of or pertaining to sight : learning by means of visual images and recalling such images readily.—*n.* one whose imagery naturally takes a visual form. [On the analogy of **audile**, from L. *vidēre*, *visum*, to see.]

visiogenic, *viz-i-ō-jen′ik*, *adj.* suitable artistically for television transmission. [L. *vidēre*, *visum*, to see, and root of Gr. *gignesthai*, to be produced.]

vision, *vizh′ən*, *n.* the act of seeing : the faculty of sight : anything seen : a look, glance : a vivid concept or mental picture : hence, a person or scene of great beauty (sometimes ironically) : a pleasing imaginative plan for, or anticipation of, future events : an apparition : a revelation, esp. divine, in sleep or a trance (sometimes without article) : act or power of perceiving imaginative mental images : imaginative perception : foresight : mystical awareness of the supernatural.—*v.t.* to see as a vision, to imagine : to present, or to call up, as in a vision.—*n.* (*Scot.*) **visie** (*viz′i*), a close or careful look : aim : a sight on the muzzle of a gun.—Also **viz′y**, **vizz′ie**.—*v.t.* and *v.i.* to look at, or look, closely : to aim.—Also **vizz′ie**.—*adj.* **vis′ional**, of, pertaining to, a vision : derived from a vision : visionary, not real : pertaining to sight.—*adv.* **vis′ionally.** — *n.* **vis′ionariness.** — *adj.* **vis′ionary**, capable of seeing visions : apt to see visions : given to reverie or fantasy : out of touch with reality, unpractical : of the nature of, or seen in, a vision, visional : fanciful, not real : impracticable : characterised by visions or fantasy : pertaining to physical or mental vision.—*n.* one who sees visions : one who forms impracticable schemes. —*adj.* **vis′ioned**, inspired so as to see visions : seen in a vision : produced by, or associated with, a vision.—*ns.* **vis′ioner**, a visionary ; **vis′ioning**, seeing visions ; **vis′ionist**, one who professes to be a visionary : one who believes that the Biblical details of creation were revealed in vision.—*adj.* **vis′ionless**, destitute of vision.—**beatific vision** (see **beatify**). [Fr.,—L. *visiō*, *visiōnis*—*vidēre*, *visum*, to see ; cf. Gr. *idein*, Eng. *wit*.]

visit, *viz′it*, *v.t.* (of God or a human being) to come to, or to go to see, in order to succour : to go to with intention of injuring : to go to see professionally : to pay a call upon, or to be in the habit of doing so : to go to stay with : to make a stay in, as migratory birds : to go to for sight-seeing, pleasure, or religious purposes : to examine, inspect, esp. officially : (*arch.*) to punish (a person —with *with*) : (*arch.*) to punish, as wrongdoing : (of an idea) to take temporary hold on the mind of : (*arch.*) to afflict, trouble, as with disease.—*v.i.* to be in the habit of seeing or meeting each other at home : to make a call or calls : (*U.S.*) to chat.—*n.* act of visiting : a short stay : a sight-seeing excursion : an official or a professional call : (*Cowper*) a place one visits : (*U.S.*) a chat.—*adjs.* **vis′itable**, subject to official visitation : attractive to visitors ; **vis′itant**, paying visits, visiting.—*n.* one who visits : one who is a guest in the house of another : a supernatural visitor : a migratory bird : **Visitant**, one of an order of nuns founded by St Francis de Sales in 1610, also called *Salesians, Order* (or *Nuns*) *of the Visitation.*—*n.* **visitā′tion**, act of visiting : a long and wearisome visit : a formal visit by a superior, esp. ecclesiastical : examination by authority : the act of a naval commander in boarding the vessel of another state to ascertain her character and object : (*hist.*) a visit of a herald to a district for the examination of its arms, pedigrees, &c. : a visit of God, or of a good (or evil) supernatural being : a dispensation of divine favour or displeasure : a sore affliction : the operation of a destructive power, or an instance of it : an influence acting on the mind : (*rare*) the object of a visit : an unusual and extensive irruption of a species of animals into a region : **Visitation**, (*eccles.*) a festival to commemorate the visit of the Virgin Mary to Elizabeth, observed by the Roman and Greek Churches on 2nd July.—*adjs.* **visitā′tional, vis′itātive.**—*n.* **vis′itātor**, an official visitor.—*adjs.* **visitātō′rial, visitō′rial.**—*n.* **visitee′**, the person to whom a visit is paid ; **vis′iting**, the act, or an instance, of paying a visit : a visitation, in the senses of divine dispensation, heavy affliction, or influence operating on the mind.—*adj.* that visits : often opp. to *resident* : pertaining to visiting.—*ns.* **vis′iting-book**, a book recording the names of persons who have called or are to be called on : (*Thackeray*) a visitors' book ; **vis′iting-card**, a small card bearing the name and address, or title, left in paying visits, and sometimes sent as an act of courtesy or in token of sympathy ; **vis′iting-day**, a day on which one is at home and ready to receive callers ; **vis′itor** (now rarely **vis′iter**), one who visits, calls on, or makes a stay with a person : a person authorised to visit for purposes of inspection or supervision :—*fem.* **vis′itress.—visitation of the sick**, an office in the Anglican Church used for the spiritual benefit of a sick person visited by a clergyman ; **visitor general**, (*hist.*) a personal representative of the King of Spain appointed to investigate affairs esp. in Spanish America ; **visitors' book**, a book in which visitors write their names and sometimes comments. [Fr. *visiter*—L. *vīsitāre*, freq. of *vīsĕre*, to go to see, visit—*vidēre*, to see.]

visite, *vi-zēt′*, *n.* a woman's light short cloak worn in mid 19th century. [Fr.]

visive, *viz′iv*, *adj.* (*rare*) of, pertaining to, sight, visual : able to see : able to be seen. [L.L. *vīsīvus*—L. *vīsus*, sight.]

visne, *vē′ni*, *n.* (*law*) venue. [O.Fr. *visné*, neighbourhood—L. *vīcīnus*, neighbour.]

visnomy, *viz′nə-mi*, *n.* (*arch.* and *dial.*) physiognomy.—Also **vis′nomie**. [Variant of **physiognomy**.]

vison, *vī′sən*, *n.* the American mink. [Fr. ; origin unknown.]

visor, *viz′ər, viz′ər*, *n.* a part of a helmet covering the face, or the upper part of the face, movable, and perforated to allow of seeing and breathing : a mask : disguise, feigning appearance : (*obs.* ; *lit.* and *fig.*) face, aspect : a hood placed over a signal light : (*U.S.*) the peak of a cap.—Also **viz′or.**—*v.t.* to disguise, or cover, with a visor.—Also **viz′or.**—*adj.* **vis′ored, viz′ored**, having a visor : wearing a visor : masked.—*n.* **vis′or-mask**, a vizard-mask (q.v.). [A.Fr. *viser* (Fr. *visière*)—*vis*, countenance.]

vista, *vis′tä*, *n.* a view or prospect through, or as through, an avenue : an avenue or other long narrow opening or passage : the trees, &c., that form the avenue : a mental view or vision extending far into the past or future, or into any subject engaging the thoughts.—Also **vis′to.**—*v.t.* (*rare*) to make into, or see in, vistas.—*adjs.* **vista′d**,

vis′taed (*-təd*), having, or forming, a vista or vistas (*lit.* and *fig.*) ; **vis′tal** ; **vis′taless** (*-tə-les*). [It. *vista*, sight, view—L. *vidēre, vīsum*, to see.]

visual, *vizh′ū-əl, viz′ū-əl*, *adj.* of, pertaining to, sight : concerned with seeing, or (*fig.*) with mental vision : attained by, or received through, sight : of the nature of, or conveying, a mental vision : visible, having visibility : optic, as in ' visual axis ' : (*poet.*) of the eye : (*obs.*) of beams, coming from the eye.—*n.* a visible.—*n.* **visualīsā′tion.**—*v.t.* **vis′ualise**, to make visible, externalise to the eye : to call up a clear visual image of.—*v.i.* to call up a clear visual image : (*med.*) to become visible.—*ns.* **vis′ualīser** ; **vis′ualist**, a visualiser : a visile ; **visual′ity**, (*Carlyle*) quality or state of being visible to the mind : a mental picture.—*adv.* **vis′ually.—visual purple** (see **purple**). [L.L. *vīsuālis*—L. *vīsus*, sight.]

visuo-, in composition, sight. [L. *vīsus.*]

Vitaceae. See **Vitis**.

Vita glass, *vī′tä gläs*, *n.* trade-mark for a glass that transmits ultraviolet rays.

vital, *vī′təl*, *adj.* being a manifestation of organic life : supporting, or necessary to, life : life-giving, invigorating : characteristic of life, or of living things : animate, living : full of life : (*obs.*) capable of living : pertaining to life, birth, and death : due to living agency : fatal to life : essential, or (loosely) highly important.—*n.* **vitalīsā′tion.**—*v.t.* **vi′talise**, to give life to : to stimulate activity in : (*fig.*) to give vigour to : to make lifelike.—*n.* **vi′talīser.**—*adj.* **vi′talising.**—*ns.* **vi′talism**, the doctrine that there is a vital principle (q.v.) ; **vi′talist**, one who holds this doctrine.—*adj.* **vitalis′tic.**—*adv.* **vitalis′tically.**—*n.* **vitality** (*-tal′*), state or quality of being vital : principle of life, power of living : livingness : quality of being fully or intensely alive : capacity to endure and flourish : animation, liveliness : a living or vital thing or quality (*pl.* **vital′ities**). — *adv.* **vi′tally.** — *n.pl.* **vi′tals**, (rarely in *sing.*) the interior organs essential for life : the part of any whole necessary for its existence.—*n.* **vi′tascope**, a form of motion-picture projector.—*adj.* **vi′tative**, concerned with the preservation of life.—*n.* **vitativeness** (*vī-tə-tiv-*), love of life, assigned by the phrenologists to a protuberance under the ear.—**vital air**, (*obs.*) oxygen ; **vital force**, the force on which the phenomena of life in animals and plants depends— distinct from chemical and mechanical forces operating in them ; **vital functions**, the bodily functions that are essential to life, as the circulation of the blood ; **vital principle**, that principle— the *anima mundi*—which, according to the doctrine of vitalism, gives life to all nature : a principle that directs all the actions and functions of living bodies ; **vital spark, flame**, the principle of life in man : hence, life or a trace of life ; **vital stain**, (*bot., zool.*) a stain that can be used on living cells without killing them ; **vital statistics**, statistics dealing with the facts of population—births, deaths, &c. [L. *vītālis*—*vīta*, life—*vīvĕre*, to live ; cog. with Gr. *bios*, life.]

vitamin, *vīt′, vit′ə-min* (orig. **vitamine**, *-mēn*), *n.* any of numerous organic substances, ' accessory food factors,' present in minute quantities in nutritive foods and essential for the health of the animal organism, named provisionally Vitamin A, B_1, B_2, C, &c., but later analysed and given names that describe them more exactly, as thiamine (B_1), ascorbic acid (C), &c.—*v.t.* **vi′taminise**, to add vitamins to (a food.)—**vitamin B_2 complex**, a group of vitamins formerly regarded as being a single vitamin. [Coined in 1906 from L. *vīta*, life, and (inappropriately) **amine**.]

vite, *vēt*, *adv.* (*mus.*) quickly. [Fr.]

vitellus, *vi-, vī-tel′əs*, *n.* the yolk of an egg :—*pl.* **vitell′ī.**—*adj.* **vit′ellary**, pertaining to the vitellus : egg-yellow.—*ns.* **vitell′in**, a phosphoprotein present in yolk of egg ; **vitell′ine**, a vitellus.— *adj.* **vitellary.**—*n.* **vitell′icle**, a yolk-sac.—*adj.* **vitelligenous** (*-ij′*), producing yolk. [L., a yolk ; a transferred use of *vitellus*—*vitulus*, a calf.]

Vitex, *vī′teks*, *n.* a genus of trees or shrubs, chiefly tropical, of the family Verbenaceae, having a drupe with a four-celled stone; some species yield valuable timber. [L.]

vitiate, vish′i-āt, v.t. to render faulty or defective: to spoil: to make impure: to deprave, corrupt, pervert, debase: to make ineffectual or invalid or inconclusive: (obs.) to violate, ravish: (obs.) to adulterate.—Earlier **vi′ciate.**—adj. (arch.) vitiated.—adj. **vi′tiable.**—ns. **vitiā′tion**; **vi′tiātor**; **vitios′ity** (also vicios′ity), state or quality of being vicious, or (Scots law) faulty. [L. vitiāre, -ātum— vitium. See vice (2).]

viticetum, viticide, &c. See vitis.

vitilitigation, vit-i-lit-i-gā′shon, n. (rare) vexatious wrangling.—v.i. (rare) **vitilit′igate.** [Formed from L. vitilītigāre, -ātum, to quarrel disgracefully— vitium, a blemish, lītigāre, to quarrel.]

Vitis, vī′tis, n. a genus of plants, including the grape-vines, of the family **Vitaceae** (vī-tā′sē-ē) or Ampelidaceae.—ns. **viticetum** (vīt- or vit-i-sē′tom; would-be Latin), a plantation of vines; **vit′icide,** a vine pest.—adjs. **vitic′olous,** living on vines; **vitif′-erous,** bearing vines.—ns. **vit′iculture,** cultivation of the vine; **viticul′turist.** [L. vītis, a vine—viēre, to twist.]

vitrage, vē-träzh, vit′rij, n. (used also adjectivally) a kind of thin curtain for windows or glazed doors. [Fr., glass window.]

vitrail, vit′rāl, vē-trä-ē, n. stained glass:—pl. **vitraux** (vē-trō).—adj. **vitrailled** (vit′rāld).—n. **vit′raillist,** a maker of glass, esp. stained glass. [Fr.]

vitrain, vit′rān, n. a separable constituent of bright coal, of vitreous appearance. [L. vitrum, glass, and ʋuff. -ain.]

vitreous, vit′rē-ɔs, adj. glassy: pertaining to, consisting of, or like glass: glass green in colour: (geol.) resembling glass in absence of crystalline structure, in lustre, &c.—ns. **Vit′reosil,** trade-mark for vitreous silica used for apparatus which is subject to large temperature variations; **vitreos′ity,** **vit′reousness;** **vitresc′ence.**—adjs. **vitresc′ent,** tending to become glass, capable of being turned into glass; **vitresc′ible.** — ns. **vitrescibil′ity;** **vit′reum,** the vitreous humour of the eye.—adj. **vit′ric.**—ns. **vit′rics,** glassy materials: glassware: the study of glass and its manufacture; **vitrifac′-tion,** **vitrifica′tion,** act, process, or operation of vitrifying, or converting into glass: the state of being vitrified: a vitrified substance; **vitrifac′-ture,** the manufacture of glass.—adjs. **vit′rifiable;** **vit′rified;** **vit′riform,** having the form or appearance of glass.—v.t. and v.i. **vit′rify,** to make into, or to become, glass or a glassy substance.—ns. **Vitri′na,** a genus of thin-shelled land molluscs, between slugs and true snails—the glass-snails; **vit′rine** (-rēn, -rin), a glass show-case used to protect delicate articles, exhibit specimens, &c.— **vitreous electricity,** old name for positive electricity, because glass becomes positively charged when rubbed with silk; **vitreous humour,** the jelly-like substance filling the posterior chamber of the eye of a vertebrate, between the lens and the retina; **vitrified forts, walls,** certain ancient Scottish, French, &c., forts or walls in which the silicious stone has been vitrified by fire, whether by intention or accident is uncertain. [L. vitrum, glass.]

vitriol, vit′ri-al, n. oil of vitriol (q.v.): a hydrous sulphate of a metal, as blue, green, and white vitriol, respectively that of copper (cupric), iron (ferrous), and zinc.—v.t. **vit′riolate,** to convert into, or to treat with, vitriol.—n. **vitriolā′tion.**—adj. **vitri-olic** (-ol′), pertaining to, or having the qualities of, vitriol: (fig.) biting, scathing, expressing intense ill-will.—n. **vitriolisā′tion.**—v.t. **vit′riol-ise,** to vitriolate: to injure with vitriol.—**elixir of vitriol,** aromatic sulphuric acid (i.e. sulphuric acid mixed with certain other substances for use in medicine); **oil of vitriol,** concentrated sulphuric acid—because formerly prepared from green vitriol. [O.Fr.,—L.L. vitriolum—L. vitreus, of glass.]

vitro-, vit′rō-, in composition, glass. [L. vitrum, glass.]

vitro-di-trina, vit′rō-di-trē′nä, n. a Venetian white glass in which fine threads of cane form a lace-like pattern. [It., glass of lace.]

Vitruvian, vi-trōō′vi-ən, aaj. of, or in the style of, Vitruvius Pollio, a Roman architect under Augustus: denoting a kind of convoluted scrollwork.

vitta, vit′ä, n. a fillet or band for the head: a strap or sash: (bot. and zool.) a stripe of colour: (bot.) a thin, elongated cavity containing oil, found in the pericarps of some fruits:—pl. **vittae** (-ē).—adj. **vitt′ate,** having vittae: striped lengthwise. [L.]

vitular, vit′ū-lər, adj. pertaining to a calf or to calving.—adj. **vituline** (vit′ū-līn), pertaining to a calf or to veal. [L. vitulus, a calf.]

vituperate, vi-tū′pə-rāt, or vi-, v.t. to assail with abusive reproaches, revile.—v.i. to use abusive language,—adj. **vitū′perable,** deserving vitupera-tion.—n. **vitūperā′tion,** act of vituperating: censure: railing, abuse.—adj. **vitū′perative** (-rət- or -rāt-), containing vituperation: uttering, or prone to utter, abuse.—adv. **vitū′peratively.**—n. **vitū′-perātor.**—adj. **vitū′peratory,** vituperative. [L. vituperāre, -ātum—vitium, a fault, parāre, to set in order, prepare.]

vivace, vē-vä′che, adj. (mus.) lively:—superl. **vi-vacis′simo.** [It.]

vivacious, vi-vā′shos (or vi-), adj. (arch.) long-lived, or tenacious of life: lively, full of vitality: sprightly, sportive.—adv. **vivā′ciously.**—ns. **vivā′-ciousness,** **vivac′ity,** state of being vivacious: (obs.) vitality: (arch.) tenacity of life, or longevity: vigour: animation: liveliness or sprightliness of temper or behaviour: (rare) a vivacious act or saying. [L. vīvax, vīvācis—vīvĕre, to live.]

vivandière, vē-vän°-dyer′, n. (hist.) in the French and some other Continental armies, a female attendant in a regiment, who sold spirits and provisions:—masc. **vivandier** (-dyä). [Fr., fem. of vivandier—It. vivandiere, a sutler—assumed L.L. vivanda, food.]

vivarium, vi-vā′ri-əm, n. an artificial enclosure for keeping or raising living animals, as a park, a fish-pond: a glass-sided box, &c.:—pl. **viva′ria,** **-iums.**—Also **vī′vary.** [L. vīvārium—vīvus, alive —vīvĕre, to live.]

vivda, viv′dä, vev′dä, n. in Shetland, meat hung and dried without salt.—Also **vif′da.** [Perh. O.N. vōthvi, muscle.]

vive, viv, adj. (Scot. and obs.) lively, forcible: vivid. —adv. **vive′ly.**—n. **viv′ency,** (rare) vitality. [Fr., or L. vīvus, alive.]

viver, vē′vər, n. (obs. and dial.) a fish-pond. [A.Fr., —L. vivarium; see vivarium.]

viver, vī′vər, n. (dial.) a fibre, rootlet. [Variant of fibre.]

Viverra, vi-, vī-ver′a, n. the civet genus, giving name to the family **Viverr′idae** (-i-dē), and the subfamily **Viverrinae** (-ī′nē).—n. any of the Viverridae, esp. one of the Viverrinae.—adj. **viverr′ine,** of or like the ferret or the civet family. [L. viverra, a ferret.]

vivers, vē′vərz, n.pl. (Scot.) food, eatables. [Fr. vivres—L. vīvĕre, to live.]

vives, vīvz, n.pl. a disease of horses, swelling of the submaxillary glands. [O.Fr. avives, vives—Sp. avivas—Ar. addhība—al, the, dhība, she-wolf.]

vivi-, vī′vi-, in composition, alive, living. [L. vīvus.]

vivianite, viv′yə-nīt, n. ferrous phosphate, blue by oxidation, often found coating fossil fishes and bones. [After J. G. Vivian, who first found it crystallised.]

vivid, viv′id, adj. full of life, vigorous: lively, intense: very bright: presenting a clear and striking picture: forming brilliant mental images.— adv. **viv′idly.**—ns. **viv′idness,** **vivid′ity.**—adj. **vivif′ic,** vivifying.—ns. **vivifica′tion**; **viv′ifier.** —v.t. **viv′ify,** to endue with life: to make vivid: to assimilate, convert into living tissue. [L. vīvidus—vīvĕre, to live.]

viviparous, vī-vip′ə-rɔs, or vi-, adj. producing living young that have reached an advanced stage of development—opp. to oviparous: (bot.) germin-ating from a seed still on the parent plant: (bot.) producing bulbils or young plants in the flower clusters, &c.—ns. **vivip′arism,** viviparous repro-duction; **viviparity** (viv-i-par′i-ti), **vivip′arous-ness,** quality of being viviparous.—adv. **vivip′ar-**

ously.—*n.* **vivip′ary**, viviparity in plants. [L., from *vīvus*, alive, *parĕre*, to produce.]

vivisection, *viv-i-sek′shən*, *n.* the act or practice, or an instance, of making surgical operations on living animals for the purposes of physiological research or demonstration: (*fig.*) merciless and minute examination or criticism.—*v.t.* **vivisect′**, to practise vivisection on.—Also *v.i.*—*adj.* **vivisec′tional**. —*n.* **vivisec′tionist**, one who practises or defends vivisection.—*adj.* **vivisec′tive**, practising vivisection.—*ns.* **vivisec′tor**, one who practises vivisection; **vivisectō′rium**, a place for vivisection. [L. *vīvus*, alive, *sectiō*—*secāre*, to cut.]

vivisepulture, *viv-i-sep′l-tyər*, *n.* burial alive.

vivo, *vē′vō*, *adj.* (*mus.*) lively.—*adv.* **vivamente** (*vē-vä-men′tä*), in a lively manner. [It.]

vivres. Same as vivers.

vixen, *vik′sn*, *n.* a she-fox: an ill-tempered woman. —*adjs.* **vix′en**, **vix′enish**, **vix′enly**, ill-tempered, snarling. [Southern dialectal form of *fixen*—O.E. *fyxen*, fem. of *fox*.]

vizament, *viz′ə-mənt*, *n.* (*Shak.*) for advisement.

vizard, *viz′ərd*, *n.* a mask (*lit.* and *fig.*).—*v.t.* (*obs.*) to mask: to disguise, conceal.—*adj.* **viz′arded**, masked: pretended.—*n.* **viz′ard-mask**, a mask: a masked woman: a prostitute. [Variant of visor.]

vizier, **vizir**, *vi-zēr′*, *viz′yər*, *viz′i-ər*, *n.* a minister or councillor of state in various Mohammedan states.—Also **visier′**, **vezir′**, **wizier′**.—*ns.* **vizier′ate**, **vizir′ate**, **vizier′ship**, **vizir′ship**, the office of a vizir.—*adj.* **vizier′ial**, **vizir′ial**.—**Grand Vizier**, in pre-Republican Turkey, the prime minister, and at one time also commander of the army. [Ar. *wazīr*, a porter—*wazara*, to bear a burden.]

vizor. See visor.

vizy, **vizzie.** See visie (under vision).

Vlach, *vlak*, *n.* one of a non-Slav people of south-eastern Europe, found chiefly in Rumania, a Walachian. [O.Slav. *Vlachŭ*—O.H.G. *walh*, a foreigner, esp. a Slav or a Latin.]

vlei, *flā*, *flī*, *vlī*, *n.* (*S.Afr.*) low-lying ground where a shallow lake forms in the wet season: (local *U.S.*) a swamp.—Also **vly**. [Dial. Du.,—Du. *wallei*, valley.]

V-neck. See V.

voar, *vōr*, *n.* in Orkney and Shetland, spring, seed-time. [O.N. *vár*, spring; cf. **ware** (2).]

vocable, *vō′kə-bl*, *n.* that which is sounded with the voice—a word, or a single sound of a word: (*obs.*) a term, name.—*adjs.* **vocabūlar** (*vō-*, *və-kab′*), of or concerning words; **vocabūlār′ian**, of or pertaining to vocabulary.—*n.* a person much, or too much, concerned with words.—*adj.* **vocab′ūlaried**.—*ns.* **vocab′ūlary**, a list of words explained in alphabetical order: a dictionary: any list of words: the words of a language: the words known to and used by e.g. a particular person; **vocab′ūlist**, the maker of a vocabulary: a lexicographer.—*adjs.* **vō′cal**, having a voice: uttered by the voice: oral: sung, or for singing—opp. to *instrumental*: giving forth sound: resounding: talkative: eloquent: concerned in the production of speech: of or pertaining to a vowel: having a vowel function: voiced; **vocal′ic**, containing vowels, esp. many vowels: of, pertaining to, or of the nature of, a vowel or vowels.—*n.* **vōcalisā′tion**.—*v.t.* **vō′calise**, to form into voice, to articulate: to sing: to give expression to: to make vocal, endow with power of expression: to convert into a vowel: to insert the vowel points, as in Hebrew.—*v.i.* to sing: to sing on a vowel or vowels.—*ns.* **vō′caliser**; **vō′calism**, exercise of the vocal organs: the art of using the voice in singing: a vocal sound: system of vowels; **vō′calist**, a singer—esp. opp. to *instrumentalist*; **vōcal′ity**, **vō′calness**.—*adv.* **vō′cally**.—*adjs.* **vocicul′tural** (*vō-si-*), pertaining to voice-training; **vocūlar** (*vok′*, *rare*), vocal.— *n.* **vocule** (*vok′ūl*), a slight vowel sound completing the articulation of certain consonants.—**vocal c(h)ords**, in air-breathing vertebrates, folds of the lining membrane of the larynx, by the vibration of the edges of which, under the influence of the breath, the voice is produced; **vocal music**, music produced by the human voice alone, as opp.

to *instrumental music*. [L. *vocābulum* and *vōcālis*— *vōx*, *vōcis*, voice.]

vocalion, *vō-kā′li-ən*, *n.* a musical instrument resembling a harmonium, with broad reeds. [vocal, and suff. *-ion*, as in accordion.]

vocation, *vō-kā′shon*, *n.* (*rare*) a calling, summons: a calling by God to his service in special work or in a special position, or to a state of salvation: fitness for God's or other specified work: a way of living or sphere of activity to which one has been called by God, or for which one has a special fitness: one's occupation, business, or profession. —*adj.* **vocā′tional**, pertaining to, concerned with, or in preparation for, a trade or occupation.—*n.* **vocā′tionalism**, the giving of an important place in education to vocational training.—*adv.* **vocā′tionally**.—*adj.* **vocative** (*vok′ə-tiv*), pertaining to the act of calling: applied to the grammatical case used in direct personal address.—*n.* the case of a word when a person or thing is addressed: a word in that case. [L. *vocātiō*, *-ōnis*, and *vocātīvus*—*vocāre*, to call.]

vociferate, *vō-sif′ə-rāt*, *v.i.* to cry with a loud voice, to bawl.—*v.t.* to utter in a loud voice.—*n.* **vocif′erance**, clamour.—*adj.* **vocif′erant**, clamorous.— *ns.* **vociferā′tion**, act of vociferating: a violent or loud outcry; **vocif′erātor**; **vociferos′ity** (*rare*). —*adj.* **vocif′erous**, making a loud outcry: noisy. —*adv.* **vocif′erously**.—*n.* **vocif′erousness**. [L., *-vōx*, *vōcis*, voice, *ferre*, to carry.]

vocular, **vocule.** See vocal.

vodka, *vod′kä*, *n.* a Russian spirit, properly distilled from rye, but sometimes from potatoes, &c. [Russ., dim. of *voda*, water.]

voe, *vō*, *n.* in Orkney and Shetland, a bay, creek. [O.N. *vágr*, a creek.]

voetganger, *fōōt′hhäng-ər*, *foot′gäng-ər*, *n.* (*S.Afr.*) a locust before its wings grow: a pedestrian: an infantryman. [Du. *voet*, foot, *gang*, walk.]

vogie, *vō′gi*, *adj.* (*Scot.*) vain: merry. [Origin obscure.]

vogue, *vōg*, *n.* (*obs.*) the chief place in popular esteem: popularity: a place in popular favour, or the period of it: the mode or fashion at any particular time.—*adj.* in vogue, fashionable.—*v.t.* (*arch.* or *obs.*) to give vogue to, or to repute, reckon. —*adjs.* **vogu′ey**, **vogu′ish**. [Fr. *vogue* (orig. course of a rowing vessel)—*voguer*, to row—It. *vogare*; ety. uncertain.]

voice, *vois*, *n.* sound produced by the vocal organs of living beings, esp. of human beings in speech or song: sound given out by anything: faculty or power of speech or song: ability to sing, esp. well: mode of utterance: quality and range of musical sounds produced by a singer: a singer: a part for a singer, or one of the parts in an instrumental composition: utterance, expression: (*obs.*) what one says: expressed wish or opinion: vote, approval: medium of expression: one who speaks: (*obs.*) rumour, report, reputation: (*phon.*) sound uttered with resonance of the vocal cords: (*gram.*) mode of inflecting verbs to indicate whether that represented by the subject acts or is acted upon, or acts so as to affect itself (see **active**, **passive**, **middle**).—*v.t.* (*rare*) to utter: to give utterance or expression to: (*rare*) to act as mouthpiece of: to endow with voice: (*obs.*) to rumour, or esp. (in impers. construction) to be rumoured or commonly stated: (*obs.*) to speak of: (*obs.*) to acclaim: (*obs.*) to nominate, appoint, elect: (*mus.*) to regulate the tone of: to write the voice parts of: (*phon.*) to utter with vibration of the vocal cords.—*n.* **voice′-box**, the larynx.—*adjs.* **voiced**, endowed with voice: having a voice of a specified kind: (*phon.*) uttered with voice; **voice′ful**, having a voice: vocal (with *with*): full of sound.—*n.* **voice′fulness**.—*adj.* **voice′less**, having no voice: speechless, silent: unspoken: failing to, or unable to, express one's opinion or desire, or to make this felt: having no vote: (*phon.*) not voiced.—*ns.* **voice′lessness**; **voic′er**; **voic′ing**, the regulation of the tone of organ pipes, ensuring proper power, pitch, and quality.—**in my voice**, (*Shak.*) in my name; **in voice**, in good condition for singing or speaking; **with one voice**, unanimously. [A.Fr. *voiz*, *voice* (Fr. *voix*)—L. *vōx*, *vōcis*; akin to Gr. *epos*, a word.]

void, *void*, *adj*. containing nothing, empty, deserted: unoccupied, unutilised: having no holder, vacant: devoid, destitute, free (with *of*): (*obs*.) worthless: ineffectual, useless: not binding in law, null, invalid.—*n*. an empty space: (with *the*) the expanse of space: emptiness: (*rare*) a lack: (*fig*.) an emotional lack strongly felt: (*archit*.) an unfilled space.—*v.t.* to make vacant, to empty, clear: to send out, discharge, emit: (*obs*.) to send away, dismiss: (*obs*.) to remove, clear away: (*obs*.) to go away from, withdraw from, quit: (*obs*.) to avoid: (*obs*.) to lay aside, divest oneself of: to make of no effect, to nullify.—*adj*. **void′able**, that may be voided: (*law*) that may be either voided or confirmed.—*n*. **void′ance**, act of voiding or emptying: state of being void: of a benefice, the fact or state of being vacant.—*adj*. **void′ed**, (*her*.) having the inner part cut away and showing the tincture of the field—said of a charge.—*ns*. **void′ee** (*hist*.) wine and light food taken before going to bed, or before the departure of guests; **void′er**, (*lit*. and *fig*.) one who empties, or (*hist*.) one who clears a table: (*obs*.) a tray for carrying away dirty dishes, crumbs, &c., or a tray, &c., for carrying sweetmeats: a contrivance in armour for covering an unprotected part of the body; **void′ing**, the act of voiding: that which is voided (often in *pl*.); **void′ing-lobb′y**, (*obs*.) an anteroom; **void′ness**. [O.Fr. *voide*, empty—popular L. *vocitus*—*vocitāre*, to empty—*vocuus*, for L. *vacuus*.]

voile, *voil*, *n*. a thin semi-transparent material. [Fr., veil.]

voir dire, *vwär dēr*, (*law*) an oath administered to a witness. [O.Fr. *voir*, true, truth, *dire*, to say.]

voisinage, *voi′si-nij*, *n*. (*obs*.) neighbourhood, or the neighbourhood. [Fr.]

voiture, *vwä-tür*, *n*. a carriage.—*n*. **voiturier** (*vwä-tür-yā*), the driver of a carriage or coach. [Fr.]

voivode, *voi′vōd*, **vaivode**, *vä′vōd*, *n*. orig. the leader of an army: later, in south-east Europe, the title of the head of an administrative division: in Moldavia and Walachia, the former title of the princes: in Turkey, an inferior administrative official.—*n*. **voi′vodeship**, **vai′vodeship**. [Russ. *voevoda* (Serb. *vojvoda*, Pol. *wojewoda*), a general.]

voix céleste, *vwä sā-lest*, in an organ, a labial stop with a soft, tremulous sound. [Fr., heavenly voice.]

vol, *vol*, *n*. (*her*.) two wings displayed and conjoined in base. [Fr.]

vola, *vō′la*, *n*. the hollow of the hand or foot:—*pl*. **volae** (*vō′lē*).—*adj*. **vo′lar**, pertaining to the palm or to the sole. [L.]

volable, *vol′ə-bl*, *adj*. (*Shak*.) nimble-witted. [L. *volāre*, to fly.]

volage, *vō-läzh*, *adj*. giddy, flighty: fickle.—Also **volageous** (*vō-lā′jəs*). [Fr.]

volant, *vō′lant*, *adj*. flying: passing lightly through the air: (*zool*.) flying, or pertaining to flight: (*obs*.) of armed forces, &c., organised for rapid movement: nimble: (*her*.) represented as flying.—*adj*. **volante** (*vō-län′tä*; It.; *mus*.), moving lightly and rapidly.—*n*. **vo′lary**, an aviary.—*adjs*. **volat′ic**, (now *rare*) flying about; **volatile** (*vol′ə-til*), capable of flying: moving lightly and rapidly about: evaporating very quickly: flighty, apt to change.—*n*. a creature capable of flying: a volatile substance.—*ns*. **vol′atileness**, **volatility** (*-til′*).—*adj*. **vol′atilisable**.—*n*. **volatilisā′tion**.—*v.t.* and *v.i.* **vol′atilise**, to make or become volatile: to cause to evaporate: (*fig*.) to make light, unsubstantial, delicate.—*n*. **vol′ery**, a volary: a place for repair, &c., of aircraft.—*adj*. **vol′itant**, flying: flitting: fluttering: moving about: able to fly.—*v.i.* **vol′itate**, to flutter, fly.—*n*. **volita′tion**, flight: power of flying.—*adjs*. **volitā′tional**; **volitō′rial**, having the power of flight.—**volatile alkali**, (*obs*.) ammonia; **volatile oil** (see **essential oil**). [L. *volāre*, to fly, *volitāre*, to flit, flutter.]

volante, *vō-län′te*, *n*. a two-wheeled covered vehicle with long shafts, with a chaise-body hung before the axle—the horse, or one of the horses, being ridden by a postillion. [Sp.]

Volapük, *vol′*, *vōl′ə-pük*, or *-puk*, or *-pük′*, *n*. a name given to a universal language invented about 1879 by Johann Schleyer of Constance, Baden, the vocabulary being mainly based on English, and the grammar being simplified to the utmost.—*n*. **Volapük′ist**, one versed in Volapük: one who advocates the adoption of Volapük. [Lit. worldspeech—*vol*, for Eng. *world*, *pük*, for Eng. *speak*.]

volatile, &c. See **volant**.

vol-au-vent, *vol-ō-vän′*, *n*. a kind of pie of light puff pastry filled with meat, or fish, &c. [Fr., lit. flight in the wind.]

volcano, *vol-kā′nō*, *n*. a centre of eruption of subterranean matter, typically a more or less conical hill or mountain, built of ash and lava, with a central crater and pipe: (*fig*.) a state of affairs, emotional condition, &c., suggestive of a volcano because an upheaval or outburst seems imminent: a form of firework:—*pl*. **volcan′oes**.—*adjs*. **volca′nian** (*Keats*); **volcanic** (*vol-kan′ik*), pertaining to, of the nature of, produced or caused by, a volcano: characterised by the presence of volcanoes.—*adv*. **volcan′ically**.—*ns*. **volcanicity** (*-kə-nis′i-ti*), vulcanicity; **volcanisā′tion**.—*v.t.* **vol′canise**, to subject to the action of volcanic heat.—*adj*. **vol′canised**. —*ns*. **vol′canism**, **vol′canist** (see **vulcanism, -ist**). —*adj*. **volcanolog′ical**.—*n*. **volcanol′ogy**, vulcanology.—**volcanic ash(es), bomb** (see **ash, bomb**); **volcanic dust**, fine particles of powdered rock blown out from a volcano; **volcanic glass**, rock without crystalline structure, as obsidian, pumice, &c., produced by rapid cooling of molten lava; **volcanic mud, sand**, volcanic ash which has been deposited under water and sorted and stratified; **volcanic rocks**, those formed by volcanic agency. [It. *volcano*—L. *Volcānus, Vulcānus*, god of fire.]

vole, *vōl*, *n*. in certain card games, the winning of all the tricks in one deal.—*v.i.* to win all the tricks in one deal.—**go the vole**, to risk all for great gain: to try everything. [Fr.,—L. *volāre*, to fly.]

vole, *vōl*, *n*. any of numerous blunt-nosed, shorteared, mouselike or ratlike rodents, including the so-called water-rat and some field-mice. [For **vole-mouse**, i.e. field-mouse, of Scand. origin.]

volery. See under **volant**.

volet, *vol′ā*, *n*. (*hist*.) a short veil worn at the back of the head: one of the wings of a triptych picture. [O.Fr. (mod. Fr., a shutter),—L. *volāre*, to fly.]

Volga-Baltaic, *vol′gä-bawl-tä′ik*, *adj*. of, pertaining to, the group of languages to which Estonian, Finnish, and Lapp belong. [*Volga* river, *Baltic* Sea.]

volitant, volitation, volitate. See **volant**.

volition, *vō-lish′ən*, *n*. act of willing or choosing: the exercise of the will: the power of determining. —*adjs*. **voli′tient**, (*rare*) willing; **voli′tional**, **voli′tionary**.—*adv*. **voli′tionally**.—*adjs*. **voli′tionless**; **vŏl′itive**, of, pertaining to, the will: originating in the will: willed, deliberate: (*gram*.) expressing a wish.—*n*. a desiderative verb, &c. [Fr.,—L.L. *volitiō*—L. *volō*, pres. indic. of *velle*, to will, be willing.]

volkslied, *folks′lēt*, *n*. a folk-song. [Ger.]

volksraad, *folks′rät*, *n*. a legislative assembly, esp. (**Volksraad**) that of the Transvaal or the Orange Free State before 1900. [Du. *volk*, people, *raad*, council.]

volley, *vol′i*, *n*. a flight of missiles: the discharge of many missile-throwing weapons (e.g. small arms) at once: a round fired by every gun in a battery: (*fig*.) an outburst of many, e.g. words, at once: (tennis, cricket, &c.) a return of the ball before it reaches the ground—a *half-volley* is a return by striking the ball as it bounces: a ball so returned:—*pl*. **voll′eys**.—*v.t.* to discharge in a volley: to return (a ball) before it bounces: to fire a volley or volleys at.—*v.i.* to fly, be discharged, in a volley: to sound, produce sounds, like a volley: to roll, move, be emitted, like a volley: to make a volley at tennis, &c.—*adj*. **voll′eyed**.—*n*. **voll′ey-ball**, a game in which a large ball is volleyed by the hand over a high net. [Fr. *volée*, a flight—L. *volāre*, to fly.]

volost, *vō′lost*, *n*. (*hist*.) a division for local government in Russia : a soviet of a rural district. [Russ. *volost*.]

volplane, *vol′plān*, *v.i.* to glide down to earth in an aeroplane with the engine shut off.—*n.* a descent of this kind. [Fr. *vol plané—vol*, flight, *plané*, pa.p. of *planer*, to glide.]

Volscian, *vol′shan*, *n.* one of the *Volscī*, an ancient Italian people incessantly at war with the Romans for 200 years previous to 338 B.C. : their Italic language.—*adj.* of, pertaining to, the Volsci.

Volsungs, *vol′sŏongz*, *n.pl.* a famous heroic race in old German legend, its founder *Volsung* being the grandson of Woden or Odin.

volt, volte, *vōlt*, *volt*, *n.* (*fencing*) a sudden movement or leap to avoid a thrust : a gait of a horse going sideways round a centre : a track made by a horse executing this movement.—*n.* vol′tage. [Fr. *volte*—It. *volta*—L. *volvĕre*, *volūtum*, to turn.]

volt, *vōlt*, *n.* the unit of electromotive force, the potential difference which, when applied to a conductor having a resistance of one ohm, produces a current of one ampere.—**volta-** (*vōl′tä-*), used in composition for *voltaic*, as in **vol′ta-electric′ity**, **vol′ta-elec′tric**.—*n.* voltage (*volt′, vōlt′*), electromotive force in volts.—*adj.* **voltaic** (*vol-tā′ik*), pertaining to Alessandro *Volta*, who constructed the first electrical battery, a **voltaic pile**, and established the science of current electricity : of electricity, generated by chemical action : used in producing such electricity : of, pertaining to, caused by, voltaic electricity.—*ns.* vol′taism, the branch of electricity that treats of the production of an electric current from the chemical interaction of two immersed dissimilar metals ; **voltam′eter**, an instrument for measuring an electric current by means of the amount of metal deposited, or gas liberated, from an electrolyte in a given time by the passage of the current ; **vōlt′meter**, an instrument for measuring electromotive force directly, calibrated in volts. [Alessandro *Volta*, Italian scientist (1745–1827).]

volta, *vol′tä*, *n.* an old dance, the lavolta : (*mus.*) turn, time :—*pl.* vol′te (*-tā*). [It.]

Voltairian, Voltairean, *vol-tār′i-ən*, *adj.* pertaining to *Voltaire*, French poet, dramatist, historian, and sceptic (1694–1778).—*n.* one who advocates the views and principles of Voltaire.—*ns.* **Voltair′ianism, Voltair′eanism, Voltair′ism**, the spirit of Voltaire—i.e. a sceptical and sarcastic attitude, especially towards Christianity—or a manifestation of it, or adherence to his doctrines.

volte-face, *volt-fäs*, *n.* a turning round : (*fig.*) a sudden and complete change in opinion or in views expressed. [Fr.]

voltigeur, *vol-ti-zhər′*, *n.* a vaulter or tumbler : (*hist.*) in the French army, one of a light-armed company of picked men for skirmishing. [Fr.,—*voltiger*, to flutter, vault.]

voltinism, *vol′tin-izm*, *n.* breeding rhythm, brood frequency. [It. *volta* ; see **volta**.]

voluble, *vol′ū-bl*, *adj.* (*rare*) easy to roll or revolving readily or smoothly (*Milt.* volubil) : flowing smoothly : fluent in speech : too fluent or glib : (*rare*) changeable : (*bot.*) twining.—*ns.* volubil′ity, vol′ubleness.—*adv.* vol′ubly. [L. *volūbilis*—*volvĕre*, *volūtum*, to roll.]

volucrine, *vol′ū-krin*, *-krīn*, *adj.* pertaining to birds, bird-like. [L. *volucris*, a bird—*volāre*, to fly.]

volume, *vol′ūm*, *n.* a roll or scroll, which was the form of ancient books : a book, whether complete in itself or part of a larger work : anything (esp. in the natural world) that may be studied as a book : a rounded mass (often in *pl.*) : a quantity : bulk : cubical content : dimensions : fullness of tone.—*v.i.* to swell, rise, roll.—*v.t.* to send out in volumes, or great quantity : to make into, bind into, a volume.—*adj.* vol′umed, having the form of a volume or roll : bulky : consisting of (so-many) volumes.—*ns.* **volumenom′eter, volumom′eter**, an instrument for measuring the volume of a solid body by the quantity of fluid it displaces ; **volu′meter**, an instrument for measuring the volumes of gases.—*adjs.* **volumet′ric, -al.**—*adv.* volumet′-

rically.—*adjs.* **volu′minal**, pertaining to cubical content ; **volu′minous**, consisting of many coils, windings, folds : bulky, filling much space : in many volumes : capable of filling many volumes : having written much, as an author.—*adv.* volu′-minously.—*ns.* **volu′minousness, voluminos′ity ; vol′umist**, (*rare*) an author.—speak, express, &c., **volumes**, to mean much, to be very significant ; **volumetric analysis**, the estimation of the amount of a particular constituent present in a compound by determining the quantity of a standard solution required to satisfy a reaction in a known quantity of the compound. [Fr.,—L. *volūmen*, *-inis*, a roll —*volvĕre*, *volūtum*, to roll.]

voluntary, *vol′ən-tər-i*, *adj.* acting by choice, able to will : proceeding from the will : spontaneous, free : done or made without compulsion or legal obligation : designed, intentional : freely given, or supported by contributions freely given : free from state control : subject to the will : of or pertaining to voluntaryism.—*n.* one who does anything of his own free-will : (*obs.*) a volunteer : a piece of music played at will : a voluntary or extempore composition of any kind : a piece of music played before, during, or after a church service : an unwarranted fall from a horse : an upholder of voluntaryism.—*adv.* vol′untarily.—*ns.* vol′untariness ; vol′untaryism, the principle or system of maintaining the church by voluntary offerings, instead of by the aid of the state : the principle or system of maintaining voluntary schools ; vol′untaryist.—*adjs.* voluntaris′tic ; vol′untātive.—**voluntary school**, in England, an elementary school supported by voluntary subscriptions, in many cases controlled by a religious body. [L. *voluntārius—voluntās*, choice—*volō*, pres. indic. of *velle*, to will.]

volunteer, *vol-ən-tēr′*, *n.* one who enters any service, esp. military, of his own free choice : a soldier belonging to any body other than the regular army.—*adj.* consisting of, or pertaining to, volunteers : giving voluntary service : given voluntarily : of a plant or plants, growing spontaneously.—*v.t.* to offer voluntarily to give, supply, perform : to give (information) unasked.—*v.i.* to enter into any service of one's own free-will or without being asked. [Fr. *volontaire*—L. *voluntārius.*]

voluptuary, *vo-lup′tū-ər-i*, *n.* one excessively given to bodily enjoyments or luxury, a sensualist.—*adj.* promoting, or characterised by, sensual pleasure.— *adj.* **voluptuous** (*və-lup′tū-əs*), full of, or suggestive of, pleasure, esp. sensuous : pertaining to, consisting of, derived from, or ministering to, sensual pleasure : given to excess of pleasure, esp. sensual.— *adv.* volup′tuously.—*ns.* volup′tuousness, voluptuos′ity. [L. *voluptuārius—voluptās*, pleasure.]

Völuspa, *vol-us-pä′*, *vəl′ōōs-pä*, *n.* one of the poems of the Elder Edda : voluspa, a sibyl or prophetess —a wrong use, found in Scott's *Pirate*. [O.N. *Völuspá*, the song of the sibyl—*völva*, a wise woman.]

volutation, *vol-ū-tā′shən*, *n.* (*rare* or *obs.*) the action of rolling, turning, wallowing (*lit.* and *fig.*). [L. *volūtātiō, -ōnis — volūtāre — volvĕre, volūtum*, to roll.]

volute, *vō-lūt′*, *n.* a spiral scroll used esp. in Ionic capitals : a spiral conformation : a thing or part having such a shape : any marine shell of the genus *Voluta*, or kindred genera, allied to the whelks, or the animal itself : a whorl of a spiral shell.—*adj.* rolled up in any direction, having a spiral form.—*adj.* volū′ted, in spiral form : having a volute or volutes.—*ns.* vol′ūtin, a substance found in granular form (volutin granules) in the cytoplasm of various cells, believed to contribute to the formation of chromatin ; volū′tion, a revolving movement : a convolution : a whorl.—*adj.* vol′ūtoid, like a volute. [L. *volvĕre, volūtum*, to roll.]

volva, *vol′va*, *n.* a sheath, enclosing the whole of the fruit body of some agarics.—*adj.* vol′vate, possessing a volva. [L. ; see **vulva**.]

volve, *volv*, *v.t.* and *v.i.* (*obs.*) to turn over, or (*fig.*) to ponder. [L. *volvĕre*.]

Volvox, *vol′voks*, *n.* a genus of simple organisms

found in ponds, canals, &c., commonly regarded as algae, consisting of green flagellate cells united by protoplasmic bridges in a hollow spherical colony. [Formed from L. *volvĕre*.]

volvulus, *vol'vū-ləs*, *n.* twisting of an abdominal viscus causing internal obstruction. [Formed from L. *volvĕre*.]

vomer, *vō'mər*, *n.* a bone of the skull in most vertebrates—in man, a thin flat bone, shaped like a wedge or ploughshare, forming part of the middle partition of the nose.—*adj.* **vomerine** (*vō'* or *vo'*). —**vo'mero-**, used in composition, as **vo'mero-nas'al**, pertaining to the vomer and the nasal cavity. [L. *vōmer*, a ploughshare.]

vomit, *vom'it*, *v.i.* to throw up the contents of the stomach by the mouth, to spew: of an emetic, to cause vomiting: to issue with violence.—*v.t.* to throw out with violence: to cause to vomit (*pr.p.* **vom'iting**; *pa.t.* and *pa.p.* **vom'ited**).—*n.* the act of vomiting: matter ejected from the stomach: (*fig.*) vile persons or things: something that excites vomiting, an emetic.—*ns.* **vom'ica**, a cavity in the lung containing pus; **vom'iting**.—*adjs.* **vom'itive**, **vom'itory**, causing to vomit.— *n.* an emetic.—*ns.* **vom'ito**, the worst form of yellow fever, usually attended with the black vomit; **vom'itory**, a door of a large building by which the crowd is let out (also, *Roman hist.*, **vomitō'rium**): a vent (*lit.* and *fig.*); **vomituri'tion**, violent retching. [L. *vomĕre*, *-itum*, to throw up; Gr. *emeein*.]

voodoo, voudou, *vōō'dōō*, or *-dōō'*, *n.* superstitious beliefs and practices of African origin found among negroes of the West Indies and southern United States, formerly including serpent-worship, human sacrifice and cannibalism, but now confined to sorcery: any form of magic-working: a negro sorcerer or witch.—*adj.* of, pertaining to, carrying out, voodoo practices.—*v.t.* to bewitch by voodoo charms. — Also **vaudoo'**, **vaudoux** (*vō-dōō'*). — *ns.* **voo'dooism** (or *-dōō'*), voodoo superstitions; **voo'dooist** (or *dōō'*).—*adj.* **voodooist'ic**. [African (Slave Coast) *vodu*.]

voortrekker, *fōr-trek'ər*, or *vōr-*, *n.* one of the Dutch farmers from Cape Colony who took part in the Great Trek into the Transvaal in 1836 and following years: a pioneer. [Cape Du.,—Du. *voor-*, before, and **trek**.]

vor, *vor*, *v.t.* (*King Lear*, IV. vi. 247, in dialect passage) perh. means warn.

voracious, *vō-rā'shəs*, *adj.* eating greedily or in large quantities: (*fig.*) taking in, engulfing, much: (*fig.*) very eager, or insatiable: characterised by greediness (*lit.* and *fig.*).—*adv.* **vora'ciously**.—*ns.* **voracity** (*-ras'*), **vora'ciousness**. [L. *vorāx*, *vorācis*—*vorāre*, to devour.]

voraginous, *vō-raj'i-nəs*, *adj.* (*obs.* or *rare*) pertaining to a whirlpool: voracious.—*n.* **vora'go** (*-gō*), a gulf. [L. *vorāgo*—*vorāre*.]

vorant, *vō'rənt*, *adj.* (*her.*) devouring. [L. *vorāns*, pr.p. of *vorāre*, to devour.]

vorpal, *vor'pəl*, *adj.* a nonsense word coined by Lewis Carroll to describe a sword, now used to mean sharp-edged.

vortex, *vor'teks*, *n.* a whirling motion of a fluid forming a cavity in the centre, a whirlpool, an eddy, a whirlwind: according to a hypothesis of Descartes, &c., a rotary movement of atoms or particles of subtle matter round an axis, or the matter itself in rotation, such phenomena accounting for the formation of the universe and the relative motion of its parts: (*fig.*) a pursuit, way of life, situation, &c., that engulfs one irresistibly or remorselessly, taking up all one's attention or energies: —*pl.* **vor'tices** (*-ti-sēz*), **vor'texes**.—*adj.* **vor'tical**, of or pertaining to a vortex: whirling.—*adv.* **vor'tically**.—*ns.* **vor'ticism** (*-tis-izm*), a British movement in painting, a development from futurism, blending cubism and expressionism, and emphasising the complications of machinery that characterise modern life; **vor'ticist**, one who holds the theory of vortices, or who supports vorticism.—*adjs.* **vor'ticose**, **vortic'ular**, **vortiginous** (*-ij'*), vortical.—**vortex theory**, a theory that the material atom consists of a vortically moving

frictionless fluid—a conception of Lord Kelvin's. [L. *vortex*, *vertex*, *-icis*—*vortĕre*, *vertĕre*, to turn.]

Vorticella, *vor-ti-sel'ä*, *n.* a genus of ciliated infusorians belonging to the order Peritricha, in which the cilia are restricted to a fringe round the mouth. [Dim., from L. *vortex*.]

Vosgian, *vōzh'i-ən*, *adj.* of or pertaining to the Vosges Mts.—Also **Vosgean**.

votary, *vō'tə-ri*, *n.* one devoted as by a vow to some service, worship, or way of life: one enthusiastically addicted to a pursuit, study, &c.: a devoted worshipper or adherent (*fem.* **vō'taress**).—*adj.* (*obs.*) consecrated by, or of the nature of, vows: of the nature of a vow.—*n.* **vō'tarist**, a votary.— *adj.* **vōt'ive**, given, erected, &c., by vow: undertaken or observed in fulfilment of a vow: consisting of, or expressing, a vow or a wish.—**votive offering, picture, tablet**, one dedicated in fulfilment of a vow. [L.L. *vōtārius*—L. *vōtum*, to vow.]

vote, *vōt*, *n.* (*obs.*) an earnest desire: an expression of a wish or opinion in an authorised formal way: collective opinion, decision by a majority: votes or voters of a certain class collectively: a voter: the right to vote: that by which a choice is expressed, as a ballot.—*v.i.* to express choice, esp. at an election, by vote: to declare in favour of, or against (with *for*, *against*), esp. by vote.—*v.t.* to determine by vote: to grant by vote: to bring about (a specified result or change) by vote: (*coll.*) to declare by general consent: (*coll.*) to pronounce, adjudge to be: (*coll.*) to propose, suggest: to present for voting: to record the votes of.—*adj.* **vote'less**.—*n.* **vō'ter**.—**split one's vote(s)**, to divide one's votes among two or more candidates; **split the vote**, to injure a cause by influencing a considerable number of people who might have espoused it to vote in some other way; **vote Conservative, Labour**, &c., to give one's vote, on a particular occasion or habitually, to the Conservative, Labour, &c., candidate or party; **vote down**, to defeat or suppress by vote, or otherwise; **vote in**, to elect; **vote of no confidence**, the legal method of forcing the resignation of a government or governing body; **vote straight**, to give one's vote honestly. [L. *vōtum*, a wish— *vovēre*, *vōtum*, to vow.]

votive. See **votary**.

vouch, *vowch*, *v.t.* (*arch.*) to call upon to witness, esp. to a title to real estate (also **vouch to warrant**, **vouch to warranty**): to cite as authority: (*obs.*) to assert, declare: to assert or guarantee to be true: to support by evidence: to testify (that): (*rare*) to be sponsor for: (*Shak.*) to guarantee legal possession of: (*arch.*) to vouchsafe, condescend to grant: (*Milt.*) to second, support.—*v.i.* to bear witness, or be surety (with *for*).—*n.* assertion: attestation.—*ns.* **vouchee'**, the person summoned to witness to a title to real estate: a person quoted as authority or appealed to as witness; **vouch'er** (partly A.Fr. *voucher*, infin.; partly suff. *-er*), the act of vouching to warrant: a piece of evidence, or a written document serving as proof: a paper which confirms the truth of anything, as a receipt, a certificate of correctness: one who vouches or gives witness: a mechanical contrivance used in shops for automatically registering the amount of money drawn. [O.Fr. *voucher*, *vocher*, to call to defend—L. *vocāre*, to call.]

vouchsafe, *vowch-sāf'*, formerly also (*Milt.*) **voutsafe**, *vowt'sāf*, *v.t.* (*obs.*) to warrant safe, guarantee: (*arch.*) to condescend to grant: (*obs.*) to condescend to allow, to accept, or to engage in: to condescend, be graciously willing.—*v.i.* to condescend: vouchsafing: *pa.t.* and *pa.p.* **vouchsafed'**.—*n.* **vouchsafe'ment**. [Orig. two words, **vouch**, **safe**.]

vou(l)ge, *vōōzh*, *n.* a weapon carried by foot-soldiers in the 14th century, having a blade fixed on a long staff. [Fr.]

voussoir, *vōō-swär'*, *n.* one of the wedge-like stones that form part of an arch.—*v.t.* to form with voussoirs. [Fr., through L.L., from L. *volūtus*— *volvēre*, to roll.]

vow, *vow*, *n.* a voluntary promise made to God, or to a saint, or to a god or gods: a binding undertaking or resolve: a solemn or formal promise of fidelity or affection: a firm assertion: an earnest wish or prayer.—*v.t.* to give, dedicate, by solemn promise: to promise or threaten solemnly: to maintain solemnly.—*v.i.* to make vows.—*adj.* **vowed,** (*obs.*) bound by religious vows: devoted, confirmed, undertaken, &c., by vow, or as by vow. —*ns.* **vow′ess,** (*hist.*) a woman who has taken a vow: a nun: **vow′-fellow,** (*Shak.*) one bound by the same vow.—**baptismal vows,** the promises made at baptism by the person baptised, or by the sponsors or parents in his name; **solemn,** as opposed to **simple vow,** such a vow as the Church takes under her special charge, solemnly accepts, as those of poverty, obedience, and chastity, involving complete and irrevocable surrender. [O.Fr. *vou* (Fr. *vœu*)—L. *vōtum*—*vŏvēre,* to vow.]

vowel, *vow′əl,* *n.* a speech-sound produced by the unimpeded passage of the breath (modified by the vocal cords into voice) through the mouth, different vowel sounds being made by altering the form and position of the tongue and the lips: a letter (as *a, e, i, o, u*) used alone or in combination to represent a vowel sound.—*adj.* vocal: of, representing, of the nature of, a vowel.—*vs.t.* **vow′el, vow′elise,** to insert vowel signs in (words written primarily with consonants only): to use as a vowel: to modify by vowel sounds.—*adjs.* **vow′elled,** having vowels, esp. in a marked degree: having a vowel or vowels of a specified kind; **vow′elless,** without vowels; **vow′elly,** full of vowels.—**vowel gradation,** ablaut; **vowel mutation,** umlaut; **vowel point,** a mark inserted, e.g. in Hebrew, to indicate a vowel. [Fr. *voyelle*—L. *vōcālis*—*vōx, vōcis,* voice.]

vox, *voks,* *n.* voice:—*pl.* **voces** (*vō′sēz*).—**vox angelica, vox caelestis,** voix céleste; **vox humana,** in organ-building, a reed-stop producing tones resembling those of the human voice. [L. *vōx.*]

voyage, *voi′ij,* *n.* (*arch.*) a journey of any kind: (*obs.*) travel: (*obs.*) a military expedition: (*obs.*) an enterprise: a passage by water or by air to some place at a considerable distance: a round trip: a cruise: an account of such a journey.— *v.i.* to make a voyage, cruise, journey.—*v.t.* to traverse, pass over.—*adj.* **voy′ageable,** navigable. —*ns.* **voy′ager; voyageur** (*vwä-yä-zhœr′*), in Canada one who kept up communication by canoe between trading-posts: a boatman: a trapper. [O.Fr. *veage, voiage,* &c.—L. *viāticum;* see **viaticum.**]

vraic, *vrāk,* *n.* a kind of seaweed used in the Channel Islands for fuel and manure.—*ns.* **vraick′er; vraick′ing.** [Dial. Fr.; see **varec.**]

vraisemblance, *vrā-, vre-sän°blän°s,* *n.* verisimilitude: a picture. [Fr. *vrai,* true, *semblance,* appearance.]

vrouw, *vrow, frow, n.* a woman, goodwife, housewife. [Du.]

vug, *vug, n.* a Cornish miner's name for a cavity in a rock, usu. lined with crystals.—*adj.* **vugg′y.**

Vulcan, *vul′kən, n.* (*Roman myth.*) the god of fire and metal-working: a planet (*intramercurial planet*) once postulated between the sun and mercury: **vulcan,** a blacksmith or an iron-worker.—*n.* **Vulcanā′lia,** an ancient Roman festival in honour of Vulcan, held on 23rd August.—*adjs.* **Vulcā′-nian,** of, pertaining to, like, related to, sprung from, made by, Vulcan: volcanic; **vulcanic** (*-kan′ik*), volcanic: **Vulcanic,** of Vulcan.—*n.* **vul-canicity** (*-is′i-ti*), volcanic action or phenomena, volcanicity.—*adj.* **vulcanī′sable.**—*n.* **vulcanisā′-tion.**—*v.t.* **vul′canise,** to treat (rubber, &c.) with sulphur or sulphur compounds, &c.—*v.i.* to admit such treatment.—*ns.* **vul′canism,** volcanic activity: **Vulcanism,** the teaching of the Vulcanists; **Vul′canist,** (*hist. of geol.*) a Plutonist, or a follower of James Hutton (1726-97), who asserted the geological importance of subterranean heat and the

igneous origin of such rocks as basalt—opp. to *Neptunist;* **vul′canite,** the harder of the two kinds of vulcanised rubber, the softer kind being called *soft rubber:* a general name for any igneous rock of fine grain-size.—*adj.* **vulcanolog′ical.**—*ns.* **vulcanol′ogist; vulcanol′ogy,** the scientific study of volcanoes and volcanic phenomena.—**vulcanised fibre,** a fibre obtained by treating paper pulp with zinc chloride solution, used for low-voltage insulation; **Vulcan's badge,** a cuckold's horns. [L. *Vulcānus.*]

vulgar, *vul′gər, adj.* pertaining to the common people: plebeian: vernacular: public: common usual, customary: common to all: prevalent commonplace: low: unrefined: coarse: admirally paltry, ignoble, debased, or pretentious.—*n.* the common people: one of the unrefined, of the uneducated, or of those not in good society: (*obs.*) a class of inferior persons: the common language of a country.—*n.* **vulgā′rian,** a vulgar person: a rich unrefined person.—Also *adj.*—*n.* **vulgarisā′-tion.**—*v.t.* **vul′garise,** to make common or ordinary: to make unrefined or coarse.—*ns.* **vul′garism,** a vulgar phrase: coarseness: an instance of this; **vulgarity** (*-gar′*).—*adv.* **vul′garly.** —*ns.* **Vul′gate,** an ancient Latin version of the Scriptures, made by St Jerome and others in the 4th century, and later twice revised—so called from its common use in the R.C. church: **vulgate,** a comparable accepted text of any other book or author; **vul′gus,** in some public schools, a short verse task in Latin.—**vulgar fraction,** a fraction written in the common way, as opp. to a *decimal fraction;* **vulgar tongue,** the vernacular. [L. *vulgāris—vulgus,* the people.]

vulnerable, *vul′nər-ə-bl, adj.* capable of being wounded: liable to injury, or hurt to feelings: open to successful attack: in contract bridge, of a side that has won a game towards the rubber, liable to increased penalties (or premiums) accordingly.—*v.t.* **vuln** (*vuln; her.*), to wound.—*adj.* **vulned** (*her.*).—*ns.* **vulnerabil′ity, vul′nerableness.**—*adj.* **vul′nerary,** pertaining to wounds: useful in healing wounds.—*n.* anything useful in curing wounds.—*v.t.* **vul′nerate,** (*obs.*) to wound. —*n.* **vulnerā′tion** (*obs.*). [L. *vulnerāre,* to wound —*vulnus, vulneris,* a wound.]

Vulpes, *vul′pēz, n.* the genus including the common fox.—*adj.* **vulpine** (*vul′pin, -pīn*), of, pertaining to, or like a fox: cunning.—*ns.* **vul′picide,** the killing of a fox, except in hunting: a fox-killer; **vul′pinism,** craftiness.—**vulpine opossum, phalanger,** the common Australian phalanger (*Trichosurus vulpecula*). [L. *vulpēs,* a fox.]

vulpinite, *vul′pin-īt, n.* a granular scaly form of the mineral anhydrite. [*Vulpino* in Lombardy.]

vulsella, *vul-sel′a, n.* a forceps with toothed or clawed blades:—*pl.* **vulsell′ae** (*-ē*).—Also **vul-sell′um.** [L.]

vulture, *vul′tūr, -tyər, n.* any of a number of large rapacious birds of prey, feeding largely on carrion, regarded as forming one, or two, families: one who or that which resembles a vulture.—Also *adj.* —*adjs.* **vul′turine, vul′turish, vul′turous,** of, pertaining to, or like a vulture: rapacious.—*ns.* **vul′turism,** (*Carlyle*) rapacity; **vul′turn** (*-turn*), the Australian brush-turkey. [O.Fr. *voutour, voltour,* &c. (Fr. *vautour*)—L. *vulturius—vultur.*]

vulva, *vul′vä, n.* the external organ of generation of the female mammal, or the orifice of it.—*adjs.* **vul′val, vul′var, vul′vate; vul′viform,** oval: like a cleft with projecting edges.—*n.* **vulvī′tis,** inflammation of the vulva.—**vul′vo-,** used in composition, as **vul′vo-ū′terine,** pertaining to the vulva and the uterus. [L. *vulva, volva,* wrapping, womb.]

vum, *vum, v.t.* and *v.i.* (*dial. U.S.*) a corruption of **vow,** in phrase **I vum.**

vying, *vī′ing, pr.p.* of **vie.**

W

W, w, *dŭb'l-ū*, *n.* the twenty-third letter of our alphabet, a 5th-century addition to the Roman alphabet, being a doubled u or v used to express the voiced consonantal sound heard e.g. in Eng. *way*, *weak*, *warrant*; from the 13th century it was regularly used in writing English, superseding the letter *wen* (q.v.). In mod. Eng. *w* is found as a consonant and also as the second component in certain vowel and diphthong digraphs, i.e. those in *law*, *few*, *now*. The unvoiced form of the consonant is written *wh* (corresponding to O.E. *hw*), as in *what*, *when*, but many English people substitute the voiced sound in pronouncing words spelt *wh*, and Northern speakers insist upon sounding *hw*. *W* is no longer pronounced in *write*, *two*, &c., or in *whole* (which represents a dialectal variation of O.E. *hāl*). O.E. *cw* has become *qu*, as in *queen*, from O.E. *cwen*.

wa', *waw*, Scots form of **wall**.

Waac, *wak*, *n.* the Women's Army Auxiliary Corps (founded 1917), or a member of it.—*n.* **Waaf** (*wāf*), the Women's Auxiliary Air Force (1939), or a member. [From the initial letters.]

wabble. See **wobble**.

wabster. See **webster**.

wacke, *wak'e*, *n.* an old name for a decomposed basalt. [Ger.,—O.H.G. *wagge*, a pebble; cf. **greywacke**.]

wacky, *wak'i*, *adj.* (*slang*; *U.S.*) crazy. — *n.* **wack'iness.**

wad, *wod*, *n.* a pad of loose material as hay, tow, &c., thrust in to aid packing, &c.: formerly a little mass of paper, tow, or the like, now a disk of felt or paper, to keep the charge in a gun: a bundle **as** of hay: a roll or bundle, as of bank notes: a compact mass, often small: (*rare*) a lump of a soft substance.—*v.t.* to form into a mass: to pad, **stuff** out: to stuff a wad into:—*pr.p.* **wadd'ing**; *pa.t.* and *pa.p.* **wadd'ed.**—*n.* **wadd'ing**, a wad, or the materials for wads: sheets of carded cotton for stuffing garments, &c.: cotton-wool. [Origin uncertain; cf. Sw. *vadd*, wadding; Ger. *watte*, Fr. *ouate*.]

wad, wadd, *wod*, *n.* an earthy ore of manganese, mainly hydrated oxide of manganese. [Ety. dub.]

wad. See **wed**.

waddle, *wod'l*, *v.i.* to take short steps and sway from side to side in walking, as a duck does: of an inanimate thing, to move in a way suggestive of this: (*Stock Exchange slang*) to become a defaulter.—*n.* act of waddling: a clumsy, rocking gait.—*n.* **wadd'ler.**—*adj.* **wadd'ling.** [Freq. of **wade**.]

waddy, *wod'i*, *n.* a native Australian wooden warclub: a cowboy: a walking-stick.—Also **wadd'ie.** —*v.t.* to strike with a waddy. [Perh. from Eng. **wood.**]

wade, *wād*, *v.i.* (*obs.*) to go (*lit.* and *fig.*): to walk through a substance that yields with difficulty to the feet, as water: (*fig.*) to go (through) with difficulty or labour.—*v.t.* to cross by wading: to cause to cross thus.—*n.* the act of wading: (*coll.*) a ford.—*n.* **wā'der**, one who wades: a bird that wades in search of food, e.g. the heron, snipe, sandpiper: a high waterproof boot.—*n.* and *adj.* **wā'ding.**—**wade in**, to make a very vigorous attack; **wade into**, to tackle, as a job, energetically: to make a vigorous attack on (*lit.* and *fig.*). [O.E. *wadan*, to go; Ger. *waten*.]

wadi, wady, *wod'i*, *n.* the dry bed of a torrent: a river-valley. [Ar. *wādī.*]

wadmal, *wād'* or *wud'məl*, *n.* (*hist.*) a thick or coarse woollen cloth, woven esp. in Orkney and Shetland. —Also **wad'maal, wad'mol(l).** [O.N. *vathmál*—*váth*, cloth, *mál*, measure.]

wadset, *wod'set*, *n.* (*Scot.*) a mortgage: something pledged or pawned.—Also **wadsett.**—*v.t.* to mortgage: to pawn.—*n.* **wad'setter**, a mortgagee. [*wad*, which see under **wed**, and **set.**]

wady. See **wadi.**

wae, *wā*, *n.* (*Spens.*) woe.—*adj.* (*Scot.*) sorrowful.— *adjs.* **wae'ful** (*wae'fu'*), **wae'some**, woeful, pitiful.—*n.* **wae'ness**, sadness.—*interj.* **waesucks'**, alas ! [Dial. form of **woe.**]

Wafd, *woft*, *n.* a Nationalist party in Egypt founded in 1918.

wafer, *wā'fər*, *n.* a very thin crisp cake or biscuit baked in **wafer-irons** or **-tongs**, formerly eaten with wine: a similar biscuit eaten with ice-cream, &c.: a thin round cake of unleavened bread, usu. stamped with a cross, an Agnus Dei, the letters I.H.S., &c., used in the Eucharist: a thin leaf of coloured paste for sealing letters, &c.: (*med.*) a thin cake of paste used to form a cachet or wrapping for powders.—*v.t.* to close, fasten, stick (as on a wall), with a wafer.—*n.* **wā'fer-cake**, a wafer.— *adj.* **wā'fery**, like a wafer. [O.N.Fr. *waufre* (O.Fr. and Fr. *gaufre*)—M.L.G. *wafel*, cake of wax.]

waff, *wâf*, *wawf*, *adj.* (*Scot.*) wandering, stray: worthless, paltry: listless.—*n.* a worthless person. [Variant of **waif.**]

waff, *wâf*, *n.* (*Scot.*) a waving, or a slight hasty, motion: a signal: a quick light blow: a puff, or a blast: a sudden ailment: a faint, usu. disagreeable, odour: a glimpse: a ghost.—*v.t.* and *v.i.* (*dial.* or *obs.*) to wave, flap, flutter, wave away. [Noun from verb, which is a variant of **wave.**]

waff, *wâf*, *v.i.* (*dial.*) to bark.—Also **waugh.** [Imit.]

waffle, *wof'l*, *n.* a kind of batter-cake, baked in an iron utensil of hinged halves called a **waff'le-i'ron.** [Du. *wafel*, wafer.]

waffle, *wof'l*, *v.i.* (*prov.*) to wave. [Freq. of **waff** (3).]

waft, *waft*, *wäft*, *woft*, *v.t.* (*poet.*) to bear, convey, transport, propel, safely or lightly, on the surface of or through a fluid medium, as air or water (also *fig.*): (perh. for **waff** (2)) to signal to, beckon: (Shak., *Wint.*, I. ii. 372) to turn.—*v.i.* to float, sail, pass through the air: (*pa.t.* **waft'ed**; *Spens.* **weft**; *pa.p.* **waft'ed**; *Spens.* **weft**).—*n.* a scent, or sound, or puff of smoke or vapour carried by the air: a rush of air (also *fig.*): a slight taste, esp. an unpleasant one: an act of wafting, or of waving: a waving movement: (*obs.*) a passage across the sea or other water: (also **weft, wheft**) a flag or substitute hoisted as a signal, esp. an ensign, stopped together at the head and middle portions, slightly rolled up lengthwise, and hoisted at different positions at the after-part of a ship: the act of displaying such a signal.—*ns.* **waft'age**, act of wafting: transportation through air or across water; **waft'er**; **waft'ing**; **waft'ure** (Rowe's emendation, *Jul. Caes.*, II. i. 246), act of wafting or of waving: waving motion: beckoning: something wafted. [From obs. *wafter*, a convoying vessel, prob.—L.G. or Du. *wachter*, guard.]

wag, *wag*, *v.i.* to move, or be moved, from side to side, or to shake to and fro: to oscillate: to move, or to move one's limbs: (*arch.*) to move on, be off: (*slang*) to play truant: (of tongue, chin, beard, &c., to move in light, gossiping or indiscreet talk: of the world, &c. (in the sense of human affairs), to go in respect of good fortune and bad.—*v.t.* to move, shake, wave, to and fro or up and down: (*obs.*) to brandish: to move, stir a limb, &c.: to move in chatter or indiscreet talk: to move so as to express reproof or derision, &c.: (*pr.p.* **wagg'ing**; *pa.t.* and *pa.p.* **wagged**).—*n.* a shake: an act of wagging: ability to wag: truant (**in to play the wag**): (perh. from obs. **wag'halter**, one who deserves hanging) a droll, mischievous fellow, a habitual joker, a wit: (*obs.*) a fellow.—*ns.* **wag'-at-the-wa''**,

wag'-at(or **-by**)**-the-wall'**, (*Scot.* and *North.*) a hanging clock with exposed pendulum and weights; **wagg'ery**, mischievous merriment or jesting: an instance of such.—*adj.* **wagg'ish.**—*adv.* **wagg'-ishly.**—*n.* **wagg'ishness.** [M.E. *waggen*, from same root as O.E. *wagian*, to shake.]

wage, *wāj*, *v.t.* (*obs.*) to pledge, offer as a pledge: (*obs.*) to wager : to hazard : to engage in, to carry on, esp. war : (*obs.*) to hire for pay, to pay wages to, or to bribe : (*Spens.*) to let out for pay.—*v.i.* (*Shak.*) to be equal in value : (*Shak.*) to contend, battle.—*n.* (*obs.*) a gage or pledge : payment for services, esp. not professional, or (*fig.*) reward (both often **wages,** *pl.* in form, but sometimes construed as *sing.*).—*ns.* **wage'-earn'er,** one who works for wages : one who earns the money that supports, or money that helps to support, the household; **wage'-earn'ing;** **wa'ge(s)-fund,** or **wa'ges-fund theory,** the theory (now abandoned) that there is at any given time in a country a determinate amount of capital available for the payment of labour, therefore the average wage depends on the proportion of this fund to the number of persons who have to share in it; **wā'ger,** (*obs.*) a pledge : the act of giving a pledge : something staked on an issue : a bet : that on which bets are laid : (*rare*) a hazard : (*rare*) a contest for a prize : (*law*) an offer to make oath.—*v.t.* to hazard on the issue of anything.—*v.i.* to lay a wager.—*ns.* **wa'ger-boat,** a light boat for a race between single scullers; **wā'gerer;** **wage'-work,** work done for wages.— **wager of battle,** (*hist.*) trial by combat, a usage which permitted the accused and accuser, in default of sufficient direct evidence, to challenge each other to mortal combat.—**living wage** (see **living**). [M.E. *wagen*—O.N.Fr. *wagier* (O.Fr. *gagier*), to pledge (through popular L. from a Gmc. word).]

wagenboom, *vä'gen-bōm, -bŏŏm, n.* a S. African tree (*Protea grandiflora*) whose wood is used in making wagon wheels. [Du., wagon-tree.]

waggle, *wag'l, v.i.* and *v.t.* to wag, esp. in an unsteady manner.—Also *n.*—*adj.* **wagg'ly.** [Freq. of **wag.**]

wagmoire, *wag'moir, n.* (*Spens.*) a quagmire.

Wagnerian, *väg-nē'ri-ən, adj.* pertaining to or characterised by the ideas or style of Richard *Wagner* (1813-83), German composer of music-dramas : pertaining to Rudolf *Wagner* (1805-64), physiologist.—*n.* a follower or admirer of Richard Wagner.—*adj.* **Wagneresque'.**—*ns.* **Wag'nerism, Wagne'rianism,** the art theory of Richard Wagner, its main object being the freeing of opera from traditional and conventional forms, and its one canon, dramatic fitness; **Wag'nerist, Wag'nerite,** an adherent of Wagner's musical methods.

wagon, waggon, *wag'ən, n.* a four-wheeled vehicle, esp. one for carrying heavy goods : an open railway truck or a closed railway van : a movable piece of furniture with shelves (see **dinner-wagon**): (*obs.*) a chariot : **Wagon,** Ursa Major.—*v.t.* to transport by wagon.—*v.i.* to travel in a wagon.—*ns.* **wag'on-age,** conveyance by wagon, or money paid for it : (*Carlyle*) a collection of wagons; **wag'on-box, -bed,** the carrying part of a wagon; **wag'oner,** **wagg'oner,** one who drives a wagon : (*obs.*) a charioteer : **Wagoner,** the constellation Auriga; **wagonette',** a kind of open carriage with one or two seats crosswise in front, and two back seats arranged lengthwise and facing inwards; **wag'on-ful; wag'on-load,** the load carried by a wagon : a great amount; **wag'on-lock,** a kind of iron shoe or other device placed on the rear-wheel of a wagon to retard motion in going downhill; **wag'on-roof, -vault,** a barrel-vault; **wag'on-train,** a collection or service of army vehicles for the conveyance of ammunition, provisions, sick, &c.; **wag'on-wright,** a maker of wagons. [Du. *wagen*; cf. O.E. *wægn,* Eng. **wain.**]

wagon-lit, *vä-gon⁹-lē, n.* a sleeping-carriage on a continental train :—*pl.* **wagons-lit** (pron. as *sing.*; sometimes **wagon-lits**). [Fr. *wagon* (—Eng. **wagon**), *lit,* bed.]

wagtail, *wag'tāl, n.* any bird of the family *Motacillidae,* so named from their constant wagging of the tail—the true wagtails, the pipits, &c.: applied

also to other birds, as an American water-thrush and an Australian fly-catcher : (*obs.*) contemptuously for a pert, or an obsequious, person : (*obs.*) a harlot.

Wahabi, Wahabee, *wä-hä'bē, n.* one of a sect of Moslems founded in Central Arabia about 1760 by Abd-el-*Wahhab* (1691-1787), whose aim was to restore primitive Mohammedanism.—Also **Waha'-b(i)ite.**—*n.* **Waha'bi(i)sm,** the doctrine and practices of the Wahabis.

wahine, *wä-hē'ne, n.* a Maori woman. [Maori.]

wahoo, *wa-hōō', n.* the burning bush (genus Euonymus or Evonymus), an ornamental shrub with scarlet-coated seeds. [Dakota Indian *wanhu.*]

wahoo, *wa-hōō', n.* a Californian buckthorn (*Rhamnus Purshiana*)which yields cascara sagrada : the winged elm, with hard-grained wood : also the rock-elm. [Creek Indian *ûhawhu.*]

waid, waide. Old spellings of **weighed,** *pa.t.* and *pa.p.* of **weigh** : (Shak., *T. of S.,* III. ii. 56 or 57) prob. for swayed (see **sway**).

waif, *wāf, n.* (*Spens.* **waift, weft**) a piece of property found ownerless, as a strayed animal, or goods cast up by the tide (also *fig.*): (*obs.*) stolen goods abandoned by the thief : a homeless wanderer : a neglected ownerless child.—*adj.* (*Scot.*) vagabond, neglected.—*v.t.* (*rare*; in *pa.p.*) to cast up as a waif.—**waif and stray,** strayed property—same as **waif alone**: (in *pl.*) homeless, destitute persons. [O.Fr. *waif*; prob.—Scand.; cf. O.N. *veif,* any flapping or waving thing.]

waif, *wāf, n.* a streak, puff—same as **waff** (2).

waift. See **waif** (1).

wail, *wāl, v.i.* to lament or sorrow audibly : (*Shak.*) of eyes, to weep.—*v.t.* to bemoan : to grieve over. —*n.* the action of wailing : a cry of woe : an animal cry or mechanical sound suggesting this.—*n.* **wail'er.**—*adj.* **wail'ful,** sorrowful : expressing woe.—*n.* and *adj.* **wail'ing.**—*adv.* **wail'ingly.**— **Wailing Wall,** a wall fifty-nine feet high, part of an enclosed space in Jerusalem, where Jews pray on Fridays. [M.E. *weilen, wailen;* cf. O.N. *væla.*]

wain, *wān, n.* a wagon, esp. for hay or other agricultural produce, or poetically : (*obs.*) a chariot : **Wain,** Charles's Wain or the Lesser Wain.—*v.t.* (*rare*) to carry.—*ns.* **wain'age,** the team and implements necessary for the cultivation of land : land under cultivation; **wain'wright,** a wagon-maker.—**the Lesser Wain,** the constellation Ursa Minor, or seven bright stars in it. [O.E. *wægen, wæn—wegen,* to carry; cf. Du. and Ger. *wagen,* Eng. **wagon.**]

wainscot, *wān'skot, -skət,* or *wen', n.* (*obs.* and *joinery*) fine oak for panelling : woodwork, esp. panelled, on an interior wall : similar lining of other material : the lower part of an interior wall when lined with material different from that on the upper part : a collector's name for certain noctuoid moths.—*v.t.* to line with, or as if with, boards or panels : to grain in imitation of oak :— *pr.p.* **wain'scoting, wain'scotting;** *pa.t.* and *pa.p.* **wain'scoted, wain'scotted.**—*n.* **wain'scoting, wain'scotting,** the act of lining with boards or panels : materials for making a wainscot : wainscots collectively. [Orig. perh. wood used for a partition in a wagon—Du. *wagen-schot,* oakwood— *wagen,* wagon, or M.Du. *waeghe,* wave (from the appearance of the grain of the wood), *schot,* partition.]

waist, *wāst, n.* the smallest part of the human trunk, between the ribs and the hips : a narrow middle part of an insect : the part of a garment that lies round the waist of the body : (*U.S.*) a woman's blouse or bodice : the narrow middle part, as of a musical instrument : the middle part of a ship : (*obs.*) the middle (of the day or night): (*obs.*) something that surrounds, a girdle.—*ns.* **waist'-anch'or,** an anchor stowed in the waist of a ship; **waist'band,** part of a garment that fits the waist : a belt or sash; **waist'belt,** a belt for the waist; **waist'boat,** a boat carried in the waist of a vessel; **waist'cloth,** (in *pl.*) coloured cloths hung about a ship's waist as ceremonial decoration or to conceal the men in a naval action : a loincloth; **waist′coat** (*wās′, wāst′kŏt*; *arch.*, now *vulg.*, *wes′kət*), a garment, plain or ornamental, reaching to or below the waist, and now sleeveless, intended to show partly, worn by men at different periods under doublet, coat, jacket, &c.: a woman's similar garment or front; **waistcoateer′**, (*obs.*) a strumpet; **waist′coating**, material for men's waistcoats, esp. of a fancy pattern.—*adjs.* **waist′-deep**, **-high**, as deep, high, as to reach up to the waist; **waist′ed**, having a waist—often of specified type.—*n.* **waist′er**, a seaman stationed in the waist, performing menial duties, esp. a green-hand on a whaler. [M.E. *wast*, from presumed O.E. *wæst*, growth, size; cf. Ice. *vöxtr*, O.E. *wæstm*, growth, Eng. **wax** (2).]

wait, *wāt*, *v.i.* (*obs.*) to keep watch, be on guard (*Spens.* **waite**), (*obs.*) to be on the watch for some-one, lie in ambush: to be, remain, in expectation or readiness: to be, remain, in a place in readiness (also **wait about**, or *U.S.* **wait around**): to delay action: to be in attendance, or in readiness to carry out orders: to bring food to the table and clear away used dishes.—*v.t.* (*obs.*) to watch, watch for, or lie in ambush for: (*obs.*) to be, remain, in expectation of, await: (*coll.*) to postpone, as a meal, for some purpose: (*obs.*) to attend on, attend, escort.—*n.* ambush—now used only in such phrases as **to lie in wait, to lay wait**: (*obs.*) a watchman, sentinel, or spy: the act of waiting or of expecting: delay: the period of attendance of a lord-, or lady-in-waiting: (*hist.*; in *pl.*) musicians employed by a town to play on cere-monial occasions: (in *pl.*) persons who welcome in Christmas by playing or singing out-of-doors at night: a member of the town, or of a Christmas, band of waits.—*ns.* **wait′-a-bit**, (also often *adj.*) a name given to various plants, esp. S. African (*Afrikaans* **wacht-(e)en-beetje**), with thorns that catch the clothing of the passer-by; **wait′-a-while**, a wait-a-bit: an Australian wattle growing in dense thickets; **wait′er**, (*obs.*) a watchman: (*obs.*) a customs officer: one who waits, esp. at table in a hotel dining-room, &c.: (*obs.*) an attend-ing servant: a salver or tray: a dumb-waiter (see **dumb**); **wait′erage** (*rare*), service; **wait′er-hood** (*rare*), **wait′ering** (*rare*), the employment of a waiter; **wait′ing**, act of waiting: attendance.—Also *adj.*—*n.* **wait′ing-list**, a list of candidates awaiting a vacancy, &c.—*adv.* (*rare*) **wait′ingly.**—*ns.* **wait′ing-maid**, **-wom′an**, a female attend-ant; **wait′ing-room**, a room for the use of persons waiting; **wait′ing-vass′al**, (*obs.*) an attendant; **wait′ress**, a female waiter.—**lie in wait**, to be in hiding ready to attack or surprise (*lit.* and *fig.*); **lords, and grooms, in waiting**, certain officers in the Lord Chamberlain's depart-ment of the royal household; **minority waiter**, meaning uncertain—perh. a waiter, or a tide-waiter, out of employment; **play a waiting game**, (*lit.* and *fig.*) to avoid action as far as possible in the hope of having an opportunity later to use one's energies with maximum effect; **wait attendance**, (*Shak.*) to remain in attendance; **wait off**, (*racing*) to allow oneself to be temporarily outdistanced by other competitors, reserving one's energies for the final stretch; **wait on**, (*dial.*) to wait for: (*Scot.*) to continue to wait: to wait upon; **wait table**, to wait at table during a meal; **wait up**, to stay out of bed waiting (with *for*); **wait upon, on**, to call upon, visit formally: to accompany: to attend and serve: to be connected with or follow as a consequence: (*B.*) to carry out the duties of (an office): (*obs.*) to gaze at, keep under observation. [O.N.Fr. *waitier* (O.Fr. *guaitier*, Fr. *guetter*), to watch, attend; of Gmc. origin; cf. O.H.G. *wahta* (Ger. *wacht*), a watchman; cog. with O.E. *wacan*, to watch.]

waive, *wāv*, *v.t.* (*obs.*) to put away, reject, to abandon, forsake, to vacate, to resign: (*hist.*) to outlaw (a woman—her status in the eyes of the law being such that the usual term was not applicable to her): (*obs.*) to abandon (stolen goods): (*law*) to give up voluntarily, as a claim or a contention: to refrain from claiming, demanding, taking, or enforcing: (*obs.*) to forgo: to evade, avoid: to defer, post-pone: (*obs.*) to leave out of consideration, dis-regard.—*n.* **wai′ver**, the act, or an act, of waiving. [A.Fr. *weyver*—O.Fr. *guesver*, to abandon; from same root as **waif**.]

waivode, waiwode(ship). Same as **voivode**, &c.

wake, *wāk*, *v.i.* to be, or to remain, awake, or active or vigilant: to keep watch or vigil, or to pass the night in prayer: to hold a wake: (often with *up*) to awake, be roused from, or as from, sleep, from indifference, &c.: to become animated or lively: to be stirred up, aroused: (*obs.*) to hold a late revel. —*v.t.* to rouse from sleep: to keep vigil over: to excite, stir up: to disturb with noise: to animate: to reanimate, revive: (*pa.t.* **waked**, *wākt*, or obsol. *wōk*; *pa.p.* **waked**, *wō′ken*, *rare* **woke**).—*n.* act or state of waking (*obs.*, except in **sleep and/or wake, wake and/or dream**): (*James Hogg*) a serenade: the feast of the dedication of a church, formerly kept by watching all night: a festival: (*dial.*, usu. in *pl.*) an annual holiday: sitting up of persons with a corpse, sometimes with revelry. —*adj.* **wake′ful**, not asleep: unable, or indis-posed, to sleep: vigilant: waking: (*Milt.*) awakening or rousing. — *adv.* **wake′fully.** — *n.* **wake′fulness.**—*adj.* **wake′less**, sound, undis-turbed.—*n.* **wake′man**, (*arch.*) a watchman.—*v.i.* **wā′ken**, to be, or to become, awake: to become active or lively: (*obs.*) to remain awake, keep watch.—*v.t.* to rouse from sleep, unconsciousness, inaction: to excite, stir up, evoke.—*adj.* (*Scot.*) **waking, awake.**—*adj.* **wā′kened.**—*n.* **wā′kener**, one who or that which wakens.—*adj.* **wā′kening.**—*n.* act of one who wakens: (*Scots law*) revival of an action. —*n.* **wā′ker**, one who wakes.—*adj.* **wake′rife** (*-rif*, *-rīf*; *Scot.*), wakeful: vigilant.—*ns.* **wake′-rob′in**, cuckoo-pint, *Arum maculatum*: the spotted orchis, *Orchis maculata*: applied to various other flowers, esp. in U.S., to any of the genus *Trillium*; **wā′king**. —*adj.* that wakes, keeps watch, or is vigilant: that rouses or becomes awake: passed, or experienced, in the waking state—**wake a night, the night**, to remain awake, or be up and about, all night; **wake(n)** to, **wake up to**, to become conscious of, alive to. [A combination of an O.E. strong verb *wacan*, to be born, to awake, and an O.E. weak verb *wacian*, to be awake, to watch; cf. **watch.**]

wake, *wāk*, *n.* the streak of smooth-looking or foamy water left in the track of a ship: disturbed air behind a flying body: (*rare*) a track on land: a trail of light behind a moving body: hence (*fig.*) **in the wake of**, close behind: immediately after (usu. implying consequence). [Of Scand. origin; cf. O.N. *vök*, a hole in the ice, *vökr*, moist.]

wakiki, *wā′kē-kē*, *n.* shell money. [Melanesian.]

Walachian. See **Vlach.**

Waldenses, *wol-den′sēz*, *n.pl.* a Christian com-munity of austere morality and devotion to the simplicity of the Gospel, orig. followers of Peter *Waldo*, a merchant of Lyons in the second half of the 12th century: their chief centre was, and is, the Alps in S.E. France and Piedmont.—*adj.* and *n.* **Walden′sian.**

waldflute, *wawld′flōōt*, *n.* an organ flute stop usu. of 4-foot pitch. [Formed after Ger. *waldflöte*, lit. forest flute.]

waldgrave, *wawld′grāv*, *n.* in mediaeval Germany, a head forest-ranger: an old German title of nobility.—*n.* **waldgravine** (*wawld′grä-vēn*), the wife of a waldgrave. [Ger. *waldgraf—wald*, forest, *graf*, count.]

waldhorn, *wawld′horn*, *n.* a hunting-horn, a French horn without valves: an organ reed-stop. [Ger.]

wale, *wāl*, *n.* a raised streak left by a blow with a lash, &c.: a ridge on the surface of cloth: texture: a vertical ridge in knitted fabrics: a horizontal timber used to bind together piles driven in a row: (in *pl.*) planks all along the outer timbers on a ship's side, bends.—*v.t.* to mark with wales: to make or furnish with, or to secure with, wales. [O.E. *walu*; cf. O.N. *völr*, a rod.]

wale, *wāl*, *n.* (*Scot.* and *North.*) the act of choosing: choice: scope of choice: the pick or best.—*v.t.* and *v.i.* to choose, pick. [O.N. *val*, choice; Ger. *wahl*, choice; from the root of **will**.]

Neutral vowels in unaccented syllables: *el′ə-mənt, in′fənt, ran′dəm*

waler, *wā'lər, n.* in India, a horse imported from New South *Wales,* or from Australia generally.

Walhalla, *val-hal'ä, n.* Same as **Valhalla.**

wali, *wä'lē, n.* Same as **vali.**

walise. Scottish form of **valise.**

walk, *wawk, v.i.* (*obs.*) to roll, or to toss about : (of a biped) to move along leisurely on foot with alternate steps : (of a quadruped) to move along in such a way that there are always at least two feet on the ground : to pace : to journey on foot : to ramble, go on foot for pleasure, &c. : (*obs.* ; of an inanimate object) to be in motion : (*naut.*) to make progress : (*obs.* ; of the tongue) to wag : to make slow progress : (*obs.*) to circulate, spread, be rife : to go restlessly about (as a ghost) : (*obs.* and *coll.*) to move off, depart, withdraw : to conduct oneself, behave : (*obs.*) to be associated and in concord.—*v.t.* to pass through or upon, perambulate, traverse : to follow, trace out, on foot : to go through (a dance) at a slow pace : (*obs.*) to circulate : (*Scot.* and *dial.*) to full, as cloth or yarn : to cause to walk, or to move as if walking.—*n.* the action, or an act, of walking : a spell of walking, especially for pleasure : a perambulation in procession : a walking-race : gait : that in or through which one walks : a possible or suitable route or course for walking : a path or place for walking : a tree-bordered avenue : a place for animals, as young hounds, to train or to exercise : a fowl-run : a place where a game-cock is kept : (*obs.*) high pasture-ground : a division of a forest : distance as measured by the time taken to walk it : conduct : course of life, sphere of action : a hawker's district or round : (*obs.*) a hunting-ground : (in *pl.* ; *obs.*) grounds, park : a flock of snipe or of wagtails.—*adj.* **walk'able.**—*ns.* **walk'-around'**, a dancing performance by negroes in which a large circle is described : (*theat.*) a march in procession about the stage : the music for either of these ; **walk'er,** one who walks : a colporteur or (*dial.*) a vagrant : (*hist.*) a forester : one who trains and walks young hounds : any bird that walks, not hops : a stick-insect.—*interj.* **Walk'er** (also **Hook'ey Walk'er** —*arch. slang*), an exclamation of incredulity (also, as *n.*, humbug).—*ns.* **walk'er-on'**, one who plays parts in which he has nothing to say ; **walk'ie-talk'ie, walk'y-talk'y,** a portable radiotelephonic transmitting and receiving set ; **walk'ing,** the verbal noun of walk : pedestrianism : condition of a surface from the point of view of one who walks on it : the act or process of fulling cloth.—*adj.* that walks, or that moves as if walking : that oscillates : used in or for walking : performed by walking : worked by a person or animal who walks. —*ns.* **walk'ing-beam,** a beam or oscillating lever for transmitting power, as that actuating the cable in cable-drilling for oil ; **walk'ing-fish,** any of various fishes, mainly Asiatic, which are able to move about on land ; **walk'ing-gentleman, -lady,** an actor or actress playing very small parts for which a good appearance is required ; **walk'ing-leaf,** a leaf-insect ; **walk'ing-orders, -papers, -ticket,** (*slang*) dismissal ; **walk'ing-part,** one in which the actor has nothing to say ; **walk'ing-stick, -cane,** (*arch.*) -staff, a stick, cane, or staff used in walking ; **walk'ing-stick, -straw, -twig,** a stick-insect ; **walk'ing-toad,** a natterjack ; **walk'-mill,** a fulling-mill : a machine operated by the walking of a horse ; **walk'-on,** a walking-part ; **walk'-out,** the act of walking out : (*U.S.*) a strike ; **walk'-over,** a race where only one competitor appears, and has merely to cover the course to win the prize : an easy victory.—**heel-and-toe walk** (see **heel**) ; **walk away from,** to outdistance easily ; **walking case,** a patient under treatment but not confined to bed ; **walk into,** (*coll.*) to beat : to storm at : to eat heartily of ; **walk off,** to leave : to depart : to get rid of by walking, as disagreeable feelings or effects ; **walk off with,** to take surreptitiously or feloniously : to win easily ; **walk on,** to walk ahead : to continue to walk : to have a walking part ; **walk on air,** to be exultant or light-hearted ; **walk one's chalks,** to quit, go away without ceremony ; **walk out,** to leave, esp. as a gesture of disapproval : to strike ; **walk out on,** (*coll.*) to

desert, leave in the lurch ; **walk out with,** to go for walks with as a stage of courtship (also **walk with**) ; **walk over,** to cross, or traverse : to win an uncontested race : (*coll.*) to have an easy victory or easy success : to disregard the right or feelings of ; **walk the chalk, chalkmark,** (*coll.*) to keep a correct course in manners or morals ; **walk the hospitals,** to be a student under clinical instruction at a general hospital or infirmary. [M.E. *walken, walkien,* to walk, to full—O.E. *wealcan,* to roll, revolve, *wealcian,* to roll up, curl ; cog. with Ger. *walken,* to full cloth.]

Walkyrie, *vol'kir-i, wol-kir'i.* Same as **Valkyrie** (q.v.). [O.E. *wælcyri(g)e.*]

wall, *wawl, n.* an erection of brick, stone, &c., for security or to enclose a space such as a piece of land : the side of a building or of a room : (in *pl.*) fortifications : any bounding surface suggestive of a wall, e.g. the membranous covering or lining of an organ of the body or of a plant or animal cell : the side next the wall : (*fig.*) a defence, means of security : (*fig.*) a barrier : in mah-jongg, the arrangement of the tiles before the hands are drawn : in mining, one of the surfaces of rock enclosing the lode.—In composition, growing on, living in, for hanging on, or otherwise associated with, a wall.—*v.t.* to enclose with, or as with, a wall : to fortify with, or as with, walls : to divide as by a wall.—*ns.* **wall'-board,** building-board ; **wall'-cress,** rock-cress, any species of Arabis.—*adj.* **walled,** enclosed with a wall : fortified.—*ns.* **wall'er,** one who builds walls ; **wall'fish,** a snail ; **wall'flower,** one of the Cruciferae, with fragrant flowers, yellow when wild, found on old walls : any other plant of the same genus (Cheiranthus or Cheirinia) : (*coll.*) a person who remains a spectator at a dance, usu. a woman who cannot obtain partners ; (also **wallflower brown**) a yellowish-red colour ; **wall'-fruit,** a fruit-tree growing against a wall : its fruit ; **wall'-game,** a variety of football played at Eton against a wall—' at the wall ' instead of ' in the field ' ; **wall'-gill'yflower,** wallflower ; **wall'ing,** walls collectively : materials for walls ; **wall'-knot,** a nautical method of tying the strands at the end of a rope.—*adj.* **wall'-less.**—*ns.* **wall'-liz'ard, -newt,** a common lizard living in the chinks of walls ; **wall'-moss,** a yellow lichen : the common stone-crop ; **wall'-mustard, -rocket,** a yellow-flowered cruciferous plant (Diplotaxis) of walls and ballast-heaps ; **wall'-paint'ing,** the decoration of walls with ornamental painted designs : a work of art painted on a wall ; **wall'-pa'per,** paper, usually coloured or decorated, for pasting on the walls of a room ; **wall'-pepp'er,** the common stone-crop ; **wall'-plate,** a horizontal piece of timber or of rolled-steel on a wall, etc., to bear the ends of joists, &c. ; **wall'-rue,** a small fern growing on walls, &c., one of the spleenworts ; **wall'-space,** space on a wall, e.g. on which to hang a picture ; **wall'-tree,** a tree trained against a wall ; **wall'-wort,** name applied to various plants growing on walls, as pellitory (*Parietaria officinalis*), wall-pepper, &c. : see also separate article.—**drive to the wall,** to push to extremities ; **go to the wall** (*obs.* walls), to be hard pressed : to be forced to give way : to fail, go under : to give precedence to something else ; **hang by the wall,** to remain unused ; **push,** or **thrust, to the wall,** to force to give place ; **the wall,** the right of taking the side of the road near the wall when encountering another person, as in the phrase to **give,** or **take, the wall** ; **wall a rope,** to make a wall-knot on the end of a rope ; **wall up,** to block with a wall : to entomb in a wall ; **with one's back to the wall,** in desperate straits : at bay. [O.E. *wall* (W.S. *weall*)—L. *vallum,* a rampart.]

walla. See **wallah.**

wallaba, *wol'a-bä, n.* a valuable caesalpiniaceous tree of the Guianas and Brazil, with durable streaked reddish wood. [Native name.]

wallaby, *wol'ab-i, n.* any of a number of small kangaroos.—**on the wallaby, on the wallaby track,** (*slang* ; *Austr.*) travelling through the bush with one's ' swag ' looking for work. [Native Austr. *wolabä.*]

Wallace's line, *wol'is-iz līn,* a line passing through the East Indian group of islands between Bali and Lombok, roughly separating the very different faunas of the Oriental region and the Australian region, or rather a transitional region. [Alfred Russel *Wallace* (1823-1913), naturalist.]

Wallachian. See Vlach.

wallah, *wol'ä, n.* an agent, human or animal: a man: a servant. — Also **walla.** — **competition wallah,** a member of the Indian Civil Service who obtained appointment by the competitive system instituted in 1856. [Hindi *-wālā,* properly an adjectival suffix, in one sense comparable to L. *-ärius* or Eng. *-ar, -er, -or.*]

wallaroo, *wol-ə-rōō', n.* any of various large kangaroos (Macropus). [Native Austr. *wolarū.*]

wallet, *wol'it, n.* a bag for carrying necessaries on a journey: a bag with the opening at the middle and a pouch at each end: a pocket-book: a bag for tools: (*Shak.*) anything protuberant and hanging loosely. [M.E. *walet,* poss.—*watel,* a bag of woven material; cf. **wattle.**]

wall-eye, *wawl'-ī, n.* an eye in which the iris is pale, or the white part is very large or noticeable (e.g. as the result of a squint): the disease of the eye called glaucoma: (*U.S.*) any of various fishes.— *adj.* **wall'-eyed,** very light grey in the eyes, or in one eye: having a divergent squint: having a staring or a blank expression or (*fig.*) appearance: (*Shak.*) glaring, fierce. [The adj. is the earlier; O.N. *vagleygr,* perh. conn. with mod. Ice. *vagl,* a film over the eye.]

Walloon, *wol-ōōn', adj.* of or pertaining to a people living chiefly in southern Belgium and adjacent parts of eastern France, or to their language.—*n.* a man or woman of this people: their language, a dialect of French. [Fr. *Wallon*; of Gmc. origin, cog. with **Welsh, Walachian.**]

wallop, *wol'əp, v.i.* (*obs.*) to gallop: to move quickly but clumsily, noisily, and with effort: to flounder: to bubble and boil (perh. a different word): (*Scot.*) to flap about.—*v.t.* (*coll.*) to beat soundly, thrash: (*coll.*) to strike with force.—*n.* (*obs.*) a gallop: (*coll.*) a plunging, floundering, movement: (*coll.*) a heavy blow: (*Scot.*) a flapping rag.—*adv.* with a wallop: heavily or noisily,—*ns.* **wall'oper,** one who or that which wallops: (*coll.*) something extremely large or big; **wall'oping.**—*adj.* that wallops: (*coll.*) extremely large or big, bouncing, whopping.—**wallop in a tow,** (*Scot.*) to be hanged. [O.N.Fr. *waloper* (Fr. *galoper*); cf. **gallop.**]

wallow, *wol'ō, v.i.* (*lit.* and *fig.*) to roll about in mud, &c., as an animal does (implying enjoyment): to flounder: in a bad sense, to live in filth or gross vice: to surge, heave, blow, well up, &c.—*v.t.* (*obs.*) to cause to wallow in *lit.* senses.—*n.* the act of wallowing: the place, or the filth, an animal wallows in: a hollow or depression suggestive of a wallowing-place: (*obs.*) a rolling gait: (*poet.*) the swell of the sea.—*ns.* **wall'ower; wall'owing.** [O.E. *wealwian*—L. *volvĕre.*]

wallow, *wol'ō, v.i.* (*dial.*) to fade away.—*adj.* **wall'owed,** withered, faded. [O.E. *wealwian.*]

wallsend, *wawlz'end, n.* orig. coal dug at *Wallsend* (at the *end* of the Roman *Wall*) in Northumberland: later, coal of a certain quality and size.

wallwort, *wawl'wort, n.* dwarf elder (also called Danewort, Dane's blood, &c.), a plant with an offensive smell and taste: see also under **wall.** [O.E. *wealhwyrt, wēlwyrt—wealh,* a foreigner, or (prob. orig., from the belief that it grew on battlefields) *wæl,* slaughter, and *wyrt,* a plant.]

wally, *waw'li, adj.* (*Scot.*) excellent, fine-looking, ample (a general term of commendation).—*adv.* (*obs.*) finely, well.—*n.* an ornament: (in *pl.*) finery: a showy trifle.—Also **wa'ly.** [Ety. uncertain; perh. **wale** (2).]

wallydrag, *wol'i-drag,* **wallydraigle,** *wol'i-drā-gl, ns.* (*Scot.*) a person or animal that is feeble, worthless, or slovenly: the youngest of a family. [wally, and drag, draigle (Scots form of draggle).]

walnut, *wawl'nut, n.* a genus (Juglans) of beautiful trees, some yielding valuable furniture wood: their wood: the nut of the Common or English Walnut:

walnut-juice.—*n.* **wal'nut-juice,** juice from the husk of walnuts used to stain the skin.—**black walnut,** a North American walnut, the timber of which is more valuable than that of common walnut, though the fruit is inferior. [O.E. *walh-hnutu—w(e)alh,* foreigner, *hnutu,* a nut.]

Walpurgis night, *val-pər'gis nīt,* or *-pōōr',* the eve of the first of May, when witches, according to German popular superstition, rode on broomsticks and he-goats to hold revel with their master the devil, esp. on the Brocken in the Harz Mountains. [So called because May 1st is the day of St *Walpurga,* abbess of Heidenheim, who died about 778.]

walrus, *wawl'rəs, wol'rəs, n.* an aquatic, web-footed, carnivorous animal, also called the morse or sea-horse, allied to the seals, having the upper canine teeth developed into enormous tusks: (*coll.*) a walrus moustache.—**walrus moustache,** one with long drooping ends. [Du. *walrus, walros,* lit. whale-horse; of Scand. origin.]

Waltonian, *wol-tō'ni-ən, adj.* of or pertaining to Izaak *Walton* (1593-1683), who wrote *The Compleat Angler.*—*n.* a disciple of Walton: an angler.

walty, *wol'ti, adj.* (*naut.*) inclined to lean or roll over. [Obs. adj. *walt,* unsteady (—O.E. *wealt,* found only in *unwealt,* steady), and suff. *-y.*]

waltz, *wawl(t)s, n.* orig. a German dance performed by couples with a rapid whirling motion: a slower circling dance, also in triple time: the music for such: a piece of instrumental music in 3-4 time (concert waltz).—*v.i.* to dance a waltz: (*slang*) to move trippingly, to whirl (also *v.t.*).—*ns.* **waltz'er; waltz'ing.—waltzing mouse** (also **waltzer**), a mouse of a breed that moves forward in small circles not in a straight line. [Ger. *walzer—walzen,* to roll, dance.]

waly. See **wally.**

waly, *wā'li, interj.* (*Scot.*) alas! [**wellaway.**]

wamble, *wom'bl, v.i.* of the intestines or stomach, to give the feeling of working or rolling: to quake: to twist or wriggle: to move unsteadily.—*v.t.* to turn round, or upside down, or over and over.—*n.* a rolling in the stomach: a feeling of nausea: an unsteady, rolling or staggering movement.— *ns.* **wam'bliness; wam'bling.**—Also *adj.*—*adv.* **wam'blingly.—adjs.** **wam'ble-cropped,** sick at stomach; **wam'bly,** affected with, or causing, sickness: unsteady. [Perh. two or more verbs; cf. Dan. *vamle,* to feel sick, conn. with L. *vomēre,* to vomit; also Norw. *vamla, vamra,* to stagger.]

wame, *wām, n.* (*prov.*) the womb or (more frequently the belly: a protuberant part or a hollow enclosed part. — Also (in 17th-cent. literature) **wem(b), weamb.**—*adj.* **wāmed,** having a wame (usu. of a specified kind).—*n.* **wāme'ful,** a bellyful. [Variant of **womb.**]

wammus. See **wamus.**

wampee, *wom-pē', n.* an edible Asiatic fruit (Clausena; family Rutaceae) about the size of a large grape, with a hard yellow rind. [Chin. *hwang-pī,* lit. yellow skin.]

wampish, *wom'pish, v.t.* (*Scott*) to brandish, flourish, wave about.—Also *v.i.* [Origin uncertain.]

wampum, *wom'pəm, wawm'pəm, n.* shortened form of the N. American Indian (Algonquian) name for beads made from shells, used as money, &c.—*ns.* **wam'pum-belt,** a belt consisting of shell beads so arranged as to convey a message, record a treaty, &c.; **wam'pumpeag** (*-pēg*), the word of which wampum is an abbreviation—lit. white string of beads.

wamus, *wawm'əs, wom'əs, n.* (*U.S.*) a kind of cardigan, or a strong jacket, buttoned at neck and wrists.—Also **wamm'us, wamp'us.** [Du. *wammes*—O.Fr. *wambais,* a military tunic orig. worn under armour.]

wan, *won, adj.* (*obs.*) dark, gloomy: wanting colour: pale and sickly: faint.—*n.* (*rare*) wanness.—*v.t.* and *v.i.* to make or to become wan.—**wan'd** (Shak., *Ant.,* II. i. 21), perh. for *pa.p.* **wanned.**—*adj.* **wan'ly.**—*n.* **wan'ness.**—*adj.* **wann'ish,** somewhat wan. [O.E. *wann,* dark, lurid; not found in other Gmc. languages.]

wan, *wan,* old *pa.t* of **win**: (*Spens.*) gained, or took.

wanchancy, wanchancie, *won-chăn′si, adj. (Scot.)*
unlucky, dangerous, or uncanny. [O.E. privative
or negative pfx. *wan-* (of Gmc. origin; seen in
mod. Du. and in Eng. **wanton**), **chance**, and suff.
-*y*.]

wand, *wond, n. (orig.; now poet. and dial.)* something slender and supple, as a twig, or a thin stem or
branch, or a young shoot of a willow used in basket-
making : something slender and rigid as a light
walking-cane *(obs.)*, a rod of authority, a caduceus,
a rod used by a fairy, a magician, a conjurer, or a
diviner. [O.N. *vöndr*, a shoot of a tree ; Dan.
vaand.]

wander, *won′dər, v.i. (lit. and fig.)* to ramble or
move with no definite object, or with no fixed
course, or by a round-about way : *(lit. and fig.)* to
go astray, deviate from the right path or course,
the subject of discussion, the object of attention,
&c. : *(coll.)* to lose one's way : to be incoherent in
talk, disordered in mind, or delirious.—*v.t.* to
traverse : *(coll.)* to lead astray, or to bewilder.—
n. a ramble, stroll.—*adj.* **wan′dered,** astray :
incoherent : bewildered.—*n.* **wan′derer,** one who
or that which wanders, esp. habitually or from
inclination : **Wan′derer,** *(hist.)* a Covenanter who
left his home to follow a dispossessed minister.—
adj. and *n.* **wan′dering.**—*adv.* **wan′deringly.**—
ns. **wander-lust, wanderlust** *(văn′dər-loost,*
won′dər-lust), an urge to travel or to move from
place to place ; **wan′der-year,** a year spent in
travel to complete training before settling down to
trade or profession.—**Wandering Jew,** a legendary
Jew in folklore esp. of north-western Europe who
cannot die but must wander till the Day of Judgment, for an insult offered to Christ on the way to
the Crucifixion—names given him are *Carta-*
philus, Ahasuerus, Buttadeus, &c. : **wandering**
Jew, any of several trailing or creeping plants.
[O.E. *wandrian*; Ger. *wandern*; allied to **wend,**
and to **wind,** to turn round.]

wanderoo, *won-də-rōō′, n.* usu. applied to the Lion-
tailed Macaque, a native of the Malabar coast of
India : properly, a langur of Ceylon. [Sinhalese
wanderu, monkey.]

wandle, *won′dl, adj. (dial.)* supple, pliant, nimble.—
Also **wanle, wannel.** [Ety. uncertain.]

wane, *wān, v.i.* to decrease in size, esp. of the moon
—opp. to *wax*—or *(obs.)* in volume : to decline
in power, prosperity, intensity, brightness, &c. : to
draw to a close. — *n.* gradual decrease or decline
(esp. in phrases, as **on the wane, in wane, in**
the, her, its wane), or the time when this is
taking place.—*adj.* **waned,** diminished : dying or
dead.—*adj.* and *n.* **wan′ing.** [O.E. *wanian,*
wonian, to lessen (O.N. *vana*)—*wana, wona* (also
wan, won), deficient, lacking.]

wang, *wang, n. (obs.)* the cheek : a wang-tooth.—*n.*
wang′-tooth, a molar. [O.E. *wange.*]

wangle, *wang′gl, v.t. (coll.)* to obtain or accomplish
by craft : to manipulate.—*v.i.* to use tricky methods
to attain one's ends.—*n.* an exercise of such methods.
—*ns.* **wang′ler** ; **wang′ling.** [Origin uncertain.]

wanhope, *won′hōp, n. (obs.)* despair. [Pfx. *wan-*
(see **wanchancy**), **hope.**]

wanigan, *won′i-gən, n.* in a lumber camp, a chest
for supplies, or a kind of houseboat for loggers and
their supplies ; also the pay-office.—Also **wan′gan,**
wan′gun. [Algonkin.]

wanion, *won′yən, n. (Shak., Scott)* found only in
phrases—e.g. **with a (wild) wanion,** with a
vengeance, vehemently ; **with a (wild) wanion**
to him, bad luck to him, a curse on him ! [Earlier
(in the) waniand, (in the) waning (of the moon), i.e.
in an unlucky time.]

wankle, *wang′kl, adj. (dial.)* unstable, unsteady :
changeable : not to be depended on. [O.E.
wancol ; of Gmc. origin.]

wanle, wannel. See **wandle.**

wannion. Same as **wanion.**

wannish. See **wan.**

wanrestful, *won-rest′fool, -fl, adj. (Scot.)* restless.
[Pfx. *wan-* (see **wanchancy**), and **restful.**]

want, *wont, n.* state or fact of being without or of
having an insufficient quantity : absence or deficiency of necessities : poverty : *(obs.* ; in *pl.)*

difficult or straitened circumstances : a lack, deficiency : *(obs.)* a blemish : *(Scot.)* a defect, feebleness, in intelligence **(to have a want)** : (in *pl.)*
requirements or desires.—*v.t.* to be destitute of
or deficient in : to lack, be without (Shak.,
Macbeth, III. vi. 8, *who cannot want,* for *who can*
want, the thought ?) : to feel need of, desire : to
require, need : to fall short (of something) by (a
specified amount) : to dispense with, do without.—
—*v.i. (arch.)* to be deficient or entirely lacking : to
be in need or destitution : to lack (with *for*).—*n.*
want′age, *(U.S.)* deficiency, shortage. — *adj.*
want′ed, lacking : needed : desired : searched for,
esp. by the police.—*n.* **want′er,** one who wants.—
adj. **want′ing,** absent, missing, lacking : deficient
(with *in,* or, *obs.,* with *of*) : failing to help, do
justice to, come up to (with *to*) : *(obs.)* slow to (with
infin.) : below the desired or expected standard (in
the phrase **found wanting**) : *(dial.)* defective
mentally : *(obs.)* poor, needy.—Also *n.*—*prep.*
without, lacking, less.—*n.* **want′-wit,** a fool, one
without sense.—Also *adj.*—**want in, out, up,**
down, &c., *(Scot.)* to want to get in, out, &c.
[O.N. *vant,* neut. of *vanr,* lacking, and O.N. *vanta,*
to lack.]

want, *wont, (dial.)* a mole.—*ns.* **want′-catcher** ;
want′hill. [O.E. *wand* ; cf. Norw. *vand* ; prob.
same root as **wind** (2) and **wend.**]

wanthriven, *won-thriv′n, adj. (Scot.)* stunted : ill-
grown : emaciated. [Pfx. *wan-,* **thriven.**]

wanton, *won′tən, adj. (obs.)* undisciplined, unruly,
unmanageable : thoughtlessly cruel : *(obs.)* self-
indulgent, luxurious : lascivious, or *(obs.)* amorous :
(obs.) insolent, arrogant, merciless in power or
prosperity : unprovoked, unjust, merciless : *(arch.)*
capricious : *(obs.* ; of persons) jovial : *(poet.* ; of
animals and inanimate things) frisky, gay, moving
freely or capriciously : *(poet.)* growing luxuriantly :
unrestrained, prodigal.—*n. (obs.)* a spoilt child or
pampered, effeminate person : *(obs.)* a roguish,
sportive child, animal, &c. : a lewd person, esp. a
female : a trifler.—*v.i.* to frolic : to play lasciviously, or amorously : to idle, go idly : to trifle : to
indulge oneself, run into excesses : to grow luxuriantly, ramble unchecked.—*v.t.* to use wastefully,
dissipate (also **wanton away**).—*v.i.* **wan′tonise,**
(arch.) to play the wanton.—*adv.* **wan′tonly.**—*n.*
wan′tonness.—**play the wanton,** to trifle, or
(obs.) to behave lewdly. [M.E. *wantowen*—pfx.
wan- (prob. akin to **wane**), O.E. *togen,* pa.p. of *téon,*
to draw, lead, educate ; cf. Ger. *ungezogen,* ill-
bred, rude.]

wanty, *won′ti, n. (obs.)* a belt used to secure a load
on a pack-horse's back : *(dial.)* the belly-band of a
shaft-horse : *(dial.)* a short rope, esp. one used for
binding hay on a cart. [**wame,** and **tie.**]

wanworth, *won′wurth, n. (Scot.)* a very low price :
a bargain.—*adj.* **wanword′y,** worthless : unworthy. [Pfx. *wan-,* **worth.**]

wanze, *wonz, v.i. (obs.)* to decrease, waste away.
[O.E. *wansian.*]

wap, *wop, v.t. (dial.)* to throw, pull, quickly or
roughly : *(coll.)* to strike, drub : to flap.—*n.* a
smart blow : *(Scot.)* a shake, flap : also a blast,
storm : also a fight, quarrel. [Cf. **whop.**]

wap, *wop, v.t. (dial.)* to wrap, bind.—*n.* a turn of a
string with which anything is tied : a bundle of
hay. [Ety. uncertain.]

wapens(c)haw. See **wappens(c)haw.**

wapentake, *wop′n-tāk, n.* a name given in Yorkshire and certain other shires to a territorial division
of the county similar to the *hundred* of southern
counties. [Late O.E. *wǽpen(ge)tæc,* O.N. *váp-*
natak, lit. weapon-taking, assent at a meeting
being signified by brandishing a weapon.]

wapins(c)haw. See **wappens(c)haw.**

wapiti, *wop′i-ti, n.* a species *(Cervus canadensis)* of
deer of large size, native to N. America. [Al-
gonquian.]

wappend, *wop′nd, adj.* (Shak., *Timon,* IV. iii. 38)
perh. for *wappered* (now *dial.*), fatigued, tired ;
perh. meaning incontinent, unchaste, and conn.
with *obs.* sense of **wap** (1), to copulate.

wappens(c)haw, *wop′n-shaw, wăp′, n. (hist.)* in Scottish usage, a periodical gathering of the people within

an area for the purpose of seeing that each man was armed in accordance with his rank, and ready to take the field when required: a rifle-shooting competition (in *S.Afr.* equivalent to Du. *wapenschouwing*). — Also **wapens(c)haw, wapins(c)haw, weapon-s(c)haw.**—*n.* **wapp′ens(c)hawing** (app. older form than wappenshaw), **weap′on-s(c)hawing.** [See **weapon, show.**]

wapper, *wop′ər, v.i.* (*dial.*) to blink: to move tremulously.—*adj.* **wapp′er-eyed,** blinking.—*n.* **wapp′er-jaw,** a projecting under-jaw.—*adj.* **wapp′er-jawed.** [Cf. Du. *wapperen,* to oscillate.]

war, *wawr, n.* a state of conflict: a contest between states, or between parties within a state (civil war), carried on by arms: (*fig.*) any long-continued struggle, often against or between impersonal forces: (*poet.*) fighting: open hostility: the profession of arms: (*rare; poet.*) an army, or war-equipment.—*v.i.* to make war: to carry on war: to contend :—*pr.p.* **warr′ing;** *pa.t.* and *pa.p.* **warred.**—*ns.* **war′-cloud,** a cloud of smoke and dust over a battlefield: (*fig.*) a sign that war is threatening or impending; **war′-correspond′ent,** a journalist or other person assigned to a seat of war so as to give first-hand reports of events; **war′-cry,** a cry used in battle for encouragement or as a signal: (*fig.*) a slogan; **war′-dance,** a dance engaged in by some savage tribes before going to war: a dance imitating the actions of a battle; **war′dog,** a dog used in war: an old warrior: (*U.S.*) a war-hawk; **war′-drum,** a drum beaten as a summons to war, or during a battle: (*fig.*) a sign of impending war; **war′fare** (from **fare,** *n.*), an engaging in, waging, or carrying on of war: armed contest: (*fig.*) conflict or struggle of any kind.—*v.i.* (*obs.* : *lit.* and *fig.*) to wage war.—*n.* **war′farer.**—*adj.* and *n.* **war′faring.**—*ns.* **war′-game** (see **kriegspiel**); **war′-god, -godd′ess,** a deity who presides over war, assigning victory or defeat, &c.; **war′-hawk,** (*U.S.*) one who is eager for war; **war′head, war′-head,** the section of a torpedo or other missile containing the explosive material; **war′-horse,** a charger, a horse used in battle: an old warrior in any field of conflict; **war′-kettle,** among Red Indians, a kettle set on the fire as part of the ceremony of going to war.—*adj.* **war′like,** of or pertaining to war: martial, military: (*obs.*) equipped for fighting: (*obs.*) intended for use in war: fond of war: bellicose.—*ns.* **war′likeness; war′-loan,** a loan raised to pay for a war; **war′-lord,** a commander or commander-in-chief, esp. where and when the military power is great—now usu. derogatory; **war′man,** (*rare*) a warrior; **war′monger,** (*Spens.*) a mercenary soldier: one who encourages war, esp. for personal gain; **war′mongering;** **war′-note,** (*poet.*) a summons to war; **war′-paint,** paint applied to the face and person by savages, indicating that they are going to war: (*coll.*) full-dress, or finery; **war′path,** among the Red Indians, the path followed on a military expedition: the expedition itself: (*fig.*) **in on the warpath,** engaged in conflict, in a mood for battle; **war′-proof,** (*rare*) a valour proved in war.—*adj.* able to withstand attack.—*ns.* **warr′ior,** a skilled fighting man (*poet.* except when used of one at an early stage of civilisation): a redoubtable person :—*fem.* **warr′ioress** (*rare*); **war′ship,** an armed vessel for use in war; **war′-song,** a song sung by men about to fight: a song celebrating brave deeds in war; **war′time,** a period during which a war is being fought.—*adj.* of or pertaining to, characteristic of, a time of war.—*adjs.* **war′-wast′ed,** ravaged by war; **war′-wea′ried, -wea′ry,** wearied with, or tired of, war.—*ns.* **war′-whoop,** a cry uttered by savages on going into battle; **war′-wolf,** a mediaeval siege engine: (*Scott*) a fierce warrior (but see also **werewolf**).—*adj.* **war′-worn,** worn, wasted, ravaged, marked, wearied, by war.—**carry the war into the enemy's camp, country,** to take the offensive boldly (*lit.* and *fig.*); **cold war,** an intense, remorseless struggle for the upperhand by all means short of actual fighting; **declare war (on, against),** to announce formally that one is about to begin hostilities: (*fig.*) to set oneself to get rid of; **go to war, to resort to armed conflict; go to the wars,** (*arch.*) to go to fight in a foreign country; **have been in the wars,** (*fig.*) to show signs of having been knocked about; **make, wage, war,** to carry on hostilities; **private war,** warfare between persons in their individual capacity, as by duelling, family feuds, &c.; **war baby,** a baby born during a war, esp. a soldier's (or other serviceman's) illegitimate child: any discreditable or troublesome result of war; **War Department,** the name borne from 1794-1857 by what is now the War Office—still used in speaking of property, as stores or land; **war neurosis,** a better term for shell-shock; **War Office,** a department of the civil government, headed by the Secretary of State for War, which administers the military forces of the crown: the premises of the department in Whitehall; **war of nerves,** systematic attempts to undermine morale by means of threats, rumours and counter-rumours, &c. [Late O.E. *werre*—O.N.Fr. *werre* (O.Fr. and Fr. *guerre*)—O.H.G. *werra,* quarrel.]

war, *wär, wawr,* **warre,** *adj.* and *adv.* (*Spens.*); now *Scot.* and *North.* **waur, wawr,** worse: (*superl.*) **warst, waurst.**—*v.t.* (*Scot.*) to defeat, worst: to excel. [O.N. *verre.*]

waratah, *wor′ə-tä, n.* any of a genus of Australian proteaceous shrubs with very showy flowers (Telopea). [Native name.]

warble, *wawr′bl, v.i.* to sing in a quavering way, or with variations (sometimes used disparagingly): to sing sweetly as birds do: to make, or to be produced as, a sweet quavering sound: (*U.S.*) to yodel.—*v.t.* to sing in a vibratory manner, or sweetly: to express, or to extol, in poetry or song: to cause to vibrate or sound musically.—*n.* the action, or an act, of warbling: a quavering modulation of the voice: a song.—*n.* **war′bler,** one that warbles: a songster: a singing-bird: any bird of the family *Sylviidae*—willow-wren, reed-warbler, whitethroat, blackcap, &c.: any of numerous small, brightly-coloured American birds of a different family: a whistle used in infant classes, &c.: in bagpipe music, an ornamental group of grace-notes.—*n.* and *adj.* **war′bling.**—*adv.* **war′blingly.** [O.N.Fr. *werbler* (O.Fr. *guerbler*); of Gmc. origin.]

warble, *wawr′bl, n.* a small hard swelling on a horse's back, caused by the galling of the saddle, &c.: a swelling caused by a warble-fly or a bot-fly. —*n.* **war′ble-fly,** any of several flies of the same family as bot-flies whose larvae cause painful swellings that spoil the hides of horses, cattle, &c. [Ety. uncertain.]

ward, *wawrd, v.t.* (*arch.*) to watch over, guard: (*arch.*) to protect (with *from*): (now usu. **ward off**) to parry or keep away: (*rare*) to enclose, as machinery, in order to prevent accidents: to place in a ward.—*v.i.* to act on the defensive.—*n.* act of watching or guarding: state of being guarded: look-out, watch: care, protection: guardianship: custody: in feudal times, control of lands of a minor: a person, as a minor, under a guardian: a body of guards: a guarded place, as a court of a castle (**inner** and **outer ward**): a means of guarding, as a bolt, bar: a part of a lock of special configuration to prevent its being turned by any except a particular key, or the part of the key of corresponding configuration: (*fencing*; also *fig.*) a defensive motion or position: (*Scot.* and *North.*) a division of a county: an administrative division of a town or city: (*obs.*) a division of an army—*van(t)ward* (vanguard), *middle ward, rearward* (rearguard): a division or department of a prison: a room with several beds in a hospital, &c.: the patients in a ward collectively.—*ns.* **ward′corn,** (*hist.*) a payment in corn in lieu of military service: misunderstood as the duty of keeping watch in order to give the alarm by blowing a horn; **ward′en,** one who guards or keeps: (*rare*) a gatekeeper or sentinel: (*hist.*) a regent: (*hist.*) the governor of a town, district, &c.: a title of certain officers of the crown: a member of certain governing bodies: a superintendent: the head of certain schools, colleges, &c.: one appointed for duties among the civil population in cases of fire or air-raids.—*v.t.* (*rare*) to guard as a warden.—*ns.* **ward′enry,** (*rare*) the office of, or district in charge of, a warden: (*Thomas Hardy*) guardianship; **ward′enship,** the office of a warden; **ward′er,** one who guards or keeps: one in charge of prisoners in a jail (*fem.* **ward′ress**): (*hist.*) a staff of authority.—*v.t.* to guard as a warder.—*n.* and *adj.* **ward′ing.**—*ns.* **ward′ing-file,** a file for cutting the wards of keys; **ward′-mote,** a meeting of a ward, or of a court of a ward; **ward′robe,** a room or a piece of furniture for containing clothes or theatrical costumes: one's stock of wearing apparel: (*fig.*) raiment—of colours, flowers, &c. (*Milt.* **ward′rop**): a department of a royal or noble household having charge of robes, wearing apparel, jewels, &c.; **ward′rober,** (*hist.*) one in charge of a royal or noble wardrobe; **ward′-room,** the messroom of the officers of a warship: the officers collectively; **ward′ship,** the office of, or the state of being under, a guardian: (*fig.*) protection, custody: (*fig.*) state of being in guardianship: in English feudal law, the guardianship which the feudal lord had of the land of his vassel while the latter was a minor.— **ward in Chancery,** a minor under the protection of the Court of Chancery; **Warden of the Cinque Ports, or Lord Warden (of the Cinque Ports),** the governor of the Cinque Ports, having the authority of an admiral and the power to hold a court of admiralty; **Wardens of the Marches,** officers formerly appointed to keep order in the marches or border districts of England and Scotland; **wardrobe mistress,** one who looks after the theatrical costumes of a company or of an individual actor or actress; **wardrobe trunk,** a trunk in which clothing may be hung as in a wardrobe. [O.E. *weardian*; cf. Ger. *warten,* to wait, attend, take care of.]

warden, *wawr′dn, n.* a kind of pear.—**warden pie,** a pie made of warden pears. [Origin uncertain; perh.—A.Fr. *warder* (Fr. *garder*), to keep.]

Wardian, *wawr′di-ən, adj.* denoting a kind of glass case for transporting delicate ferns and other such plants, or for keeping them indoors. [Nathaniel Bagshaw *Ward* (1791–1868), the inventor.]

Wardour Street English, *wawr′dər strēt ing′glish,* sham-antique diction affected by some writers of historical novels, &c. [*Wardour Street* in London, largely occupied by dealers in antique and imitation antique furniture.]

ware, *wār, n.* (now usu. in *pl.*) articles of merchandise collectively: (*rare*) an article of merchandise: pottery, as **Delft ware, Wedgwood ware** (see **delf, Wedgwood**): articles of fine workmanship, as **Benares ware,** ornamental metal-work from India: in composition, with defining word, as hardware, earthenware.—*n.* **ware′house,** a building or room for storing goods: a shop.—*v.t.* (*-howz*) to deposit in a warehouse, esp. a bonded warehouse: (*fig.*) to store up.—*ns.* **ware′houseman,** a man who keeps, or is employed in, a warehouse or a wholesale store; **ware′housing,** the act of depositing goods in a warehouse.—**warehousing system,** the plan of allowing importers of dutiable goods to store them in a government warehouse without payment of duties until ready to bring the goods into market. [O.E. *waru*; cf. Ger. *ware.*]

ware, *wār, n.* (*Scot.* and *dial.*) springtime. [O.N. *vár.*]

ware, *wār, adj.* (*arch.*) aware: (*arch.*) wary, cautious (sometimes with *of*): (*arch.*) prudent (esp. in phrase **ware and wise**).—*v.i.* and *v.t.* (*arch.*; usu. in *imper.*) to beware, beware of: in hunting, to avoid, refrain from riding over, &c. (sometimes *wawr*).—*adj.* **ware′less,** (*arch.*) incautious: unaware (with *of*).—*adv.* **wār′ily.**—*ns.* **wār′iment,** (*Spens.*) wariness; **wār′iness.**—*adj.* **wār′y,** guarding against deception or danger: cautious: circumspect: (*obs.*) thrifty.—**be wary of,** to show caution in regard to. [O.E. *wær*; cf. O.N. *varr.* See **aware.**]

ware, *wār, n.* (*Scot.* and *dial.*) seaware, seaweed. [O.E. *wár*; cf. ore (2).]

ware, *wār,* obs. *pa.t.* of **wear.**

ware, *wār, v.t.* (*Scot.*) to spend. [O.N. *verja,* to clothe, hence to invest; cf. **wear.**]

wareless. See **ware** (3).

warhable, *wawr-hā′bl, adj.* (*Spens.*) fit for war. [war, and **able.**]

warily, wariment, wariness, &c. See **ware** (3).

warison, warrison, *wor′, war′i-san, n.* (*obs.*) wealth: (*obs.*) reward or punishment: used by Scott erroneously for a note of assault. [O.N.Fr. (O.Fr. *guarison*),—*warir,* to guard; cf. **garrison.**]

wark, *wawrk,* Scots form of **work** (*n.*).

warling, *wawr′ling, n.* (*obs.*) one who is disliked—in proverb ' It is better to be an old man's darling than a young man's warling.' [Prob. formed to rhyme with ' darling.']

warlock, *wawr′lok, n.* a wizard: (*Scot.*) a magician: a demon: (*Dryden,* erroneously) a warrior who cannot be wounded with metals.—*n.* **war′lockry,** sorcery. [O.E. *wǽrloga,* a breaker of an agreement —*wǽr,* a compact, *léogan,* to lie; the ending *-(c)k* appears earliest in Scots.]

warm, *wawrm, adj.* having moderate heat: hot: imparting heat or a sensation of heat: retaining heat: (*fig.*) affecting one, pleasantly or unpleasantly, as heat does: strenuous: harassing: characterised by danger or difficulty: passionate: angry: excited: ardent, enthusiastic: lively, glowing: affectionate: amorous: (*coll.*) indelicate: (*coll.*) comfortable, well-to-do: of a colour, containing red or yellow: esp. in a game, close to discovery or attainment: of a scent or trail, fresh.—*v.t.* to make warmer: to interest: to excite: to impart brightness or suggestion of life to: (*fig.*) to beat.—*v.i.* to become warm or ardent.—*n.* (*coll.*) a heating: (**British warm**) an officer's thick overcoat.—*adv.* **warmly.**—*adjs.* **warm′-blood′ed,** homothermous, idiothermous, having bodily temperature constantly maintained at a point usu. above the environmental temperature: ardent, passionate; **warmed**; **warmed′-o′ver** (*U.S.*), **-up′,** heated anew.—*n.* **war′mer.** — *adj.* **warm′-heart′ed,** affectionate: hearty.—*ns.* **warm′-heart′edness**; **warm′ing,** the action of making or becoming warm: (*slang*) a beating; **warm′ing-pan,** a covered pan, with a long handle, for holding live coals to warm a bed: a person put into a situation to hold it till another is able to take it.—*adv.* **warm′ly.**—*ns.* **warm′ness, warmth.**—**a warm reception,** a display of hostility: a vigorous resistance or attack; **keep a place warm,** to occupy or hold it for someone until he is ready to fill it himself; **warm up,** to make or become warm: to heat, as cooked food: to become animated, interested, or eager; **warm up to,** to become enthusiastic about. [O.E. *wearm*; cf. Ger. *warm.*]

warn, *wawrn, v.t.* to give notice of danger or evil to: to notify in advance: to caution (with *against*): to instruct, command: to summon: (with *off, away,* &c.; *lit.* and *fig.*) to bid, instruct, to go or to keep away: to admonish: (*obs.*) to forbid.—*v.i.* to give notice of being about to strike.—*ns.* **warn′er**; **warn′ing,** caution against danger, &c.: something that gives this: previous notice: notice to quit, of the termination of an engagement, &c.: summons, call: admonition: in a clock, the sound accompanying the partial unlocking of the striking train, just before the clock strikes.—Also *adj.*—*adv.* **warn′ingly.** — **warning coloration,** aposematic coloration, such as the gaudy colours of some stinging insects. [O.E. *warnian, warenian, wearnian,* to caution (cf. Ger. *warnen*), and perh. in part *wiernan,* to refuse, forbid.]

warn, *wawrn, v.t.* (*Shak.* and *dial.*) to warrant (q.v.).

warp, *wawrp, v.t.* (*obs.*) to cast, throw: (*dial.*) to lay (eggs), or to bring forth (young), esp. prematurely: to twist out of shape: to turn from the right course: to distort: (*Shak.*) to cause to contract or wrinkle: to pervert, as the mind or character: to misinterpret, give a deliberately false meaning to: to arrange, as threads, so as to form a warp: (*obs.*) to entwine: to move, as a vessel, by hauling on ropes attached to posts on a wharf, &c.: to improve (land) by flooding so that it is covered by a deposit of alluvial mud: to choke, as a channel, with alluvial mud : in rope-making, to stretch into lengths for tarring.—*v.i.* to be twisted out of shape : (*fig.*) to become perverted or distorted : to swerve : to move with effort, or on a zigzag course : of cattle, sheep, &c., to miscarry.—*n.* state or fact of being warped : permanent distortion of a timber, &c. : (*fig.*) a mental twist or bias : the threads stretched out lengthwise in a loom to be crossed by a woof (also *fig.*): a rope used in towing, one end being fastened to a fixed object : alluvial sediment : a tale of four (herrings, oysters, &c.), thirty-three warps making a long-hundred, and a hundred long-hundreds a mease or maze.— *adj.* **warped,** twisted by shrinking : distorted : perverted : covered or filled with a deposit of alluvial sediment.—*ns.* **war′per ;** **war′ping.** [O.E. *weorpan, werpan* ; cf. Ger. *werfen,* O.N. *verpa.*]

warragal, *wor′ə-gal, n.* the Australian dingo : a wild Australian horse : an Australian aboriginal.— *adj.* wild, savage.—Also **warr′igal.** [Native word.]

warran(d). Obs. forms of **warrant.**

warrant, *wor′ənt, v.t.* (*obs.*) to protect, defend, keep : (*rare*) to give assurance against danger, &c. (with *against, from*): to secure, guarantee the possession of, to : to guarantee to be as specified or alleged : to attest, guarantee, the truth of—(*coll.*) equivalent to ' to be sure, be convinced,' ' to be bound ' (also in phrases I (I'll) warrant you, I warrant me): to predict or to presage : to authorise : to justify, be adequate grounds for.—*n.* (*obs.*) a defender : (*obs.*) a defence : one who or that which vouches, a guaranty : a pledge, assurance : a proof : that which authorises : a writ for arresting a person or for carrying a judgment into execution : in the services, an official certificate inferior to a commission : authorisation : justification : a writing authorising the payment of money : a form of warehouse receipt for goods : (*obs.*) a voucher.—*n.* **warr′andice** (*-dis* ; *Scot.* ; *arch.*), a guarantee : a clause in a deed by which the grantor binds himself to make good to the grantee the right conveyed.—*adj.* **warr′antable,** that may be permitted : justifiable : (*obs.*) of good warrant, estimable : of sufficient age to be hunted.—*n.* **warr′antableness.**—*adv.* **warr′antably.**—*adj.* **warr′anted.** —*ns.* **warrantee′,** one to whom a warranty is given ; **warr′anter,** one who authorises or guarantees : a warrantor ; **warr′anting ;** **warr′antise** (*-tīz* ; *obs.* or *arch.*),act of guaranteeing : a guarantee : assurance : authorisation ; **warr′ant-off′icer,** in the services, an officer holding a warrant ; **warr′antor,** (*law*) one who gives warranty : a warranter ; **warr′anty,** (*law*) an act of warranting, esp. in feudal times, the covenant by which the grantor of land warranted the security of the title to the recipient (**general warranty,** against the claims of all and every person ; **special warranty,** against the claims of the grantor, or others claiming through or by him): an undertaking or assurance expressed or implied in certain contracts : a guarantee : authorisation : justification : evidence. —**distress warrant,** warrant authorising distraining of goods ; **general warrant,** a warrant for the arrest of suspected persons, no specific individual being named or described in it ; **of (good) warrant,** (*obs.*) esteemed, important ; **of warrant,** (*obs.*) allowed, warranted ; **out of warrant,** (*obs.*) not allowed ; **take warrant on oneself,** (*arch.*) to make oneself responsible ; **warrant of attachment,** a writ authorising the seizure of property ; **warrant of attorney** (see **attorney**). [O.Fr. *warantir* (*guarantir*) ; of Gmc. origin.]

warrant, *wor′ənt, n.* in coal-mining, under-clay. [Perh. the same as **warrant** (1).]

warray, *waur-ā′, v.t.* (*obs.*) to make war upon.—*v.i.* (*obs.*) to make war.—Also **warr-ey′.** [O. Fr. *werreier* (*guerreier*).]

warre. See **war** (2).

warren, *wor′ən, n.* (*hist.*) a piece of ground kept for breeding game, esp. hares, rabbits, &c., partridges, &c. (**beasts, fowls, of warren**): the right of keeping or of hunting this : rabbit burrows in waste ground : the rabbits living there : (*fig.*) a densely populated slum dwelling or district : a maze of narrow passages.—*n.* **warr′ener,** (*hist.*) the keeper

of a warren : one who lives in a warren. [A.Fr. *warenne* (O.Fr. *garenne*), of Gmc. origin.]

warrigal. See **warragal.**

warrior. See under **war** (1).

warsle, *wawrs′l,* Scots form of **wrestle.**

warst. See **war** (2).

wart, *wawrt, n.* a small, hard excrescence on the skin : a small protuberance.—*n.* **wart′-cress.** **swine′s-cress.**—*adj.* **wart′ed.**—*n.* **wart′-hog,** any of a genus of wild hogs found in Africa, with large wart-like excrescences on their cheeks.—*adj.* **wart′less.**—*ns.* **wart′weed,** a kind of spurge (its caustic juice thought to cure warts) ; **wart′wort,** any of a family of lichens having a warty thallus : a wartweed.—*adj.* **wart′y,** like a wart : overgrown with warts. [O.E. *wearte* ; Ger. *warze* ; prob. allied to L. *verrūca.*]

wartime. See **war.**

warwolf. See **war,** and **werewolf.**

wary. See **ware** (3).

was, *woz,* used as the 1st and 3rd pers. sing. of the *pa.t.* of the verb to be. [O.E. *wæs—wesan,* to be ; see **wast, were, wert.**]

wase, *wāz, n.* (*prov.*) a wisp of hay, straw, &c. : a pad on the head to ease the pressure of a burden. [Gmc. word ; perh. Scand.]

wase-goose. See **wayzgoose.**

wash, *wosh, v.t.* to cleanse, or to free from impurities, &c., with water or other liquid : to wet, moisten : to have the property of cleansing : to flow over, past, against : to sweep along, down, &c. : to cover with a thin coat of metal or paint : in mining, to separate from earth by means of water.—*v.i.* to cleanse oneself, clothes, &c., with water : to wash clothes, &c., as one's employment : to stand cleansing (with *well, badly,* &c.): to be swept or carried by water : (*coll.*) to stand the test, bear investigation (*pa.p.* washed, *arch.* wash′en).—*n.* a washing : the process of washing : a collection of articles for washing : that with which anything is washed : a lotion : the break of waves on the shore : the sound of water breaking, lapping, &c. : the rough water left behind by a boat, &c., or the disturbed air behind an aerofoil, &c. (also *fig.*): the shallow part of a river or arm of the sea : a marsh or fen : alluvial matter : waste liquor, refuse of food, &c. : a watery mixture : a thin, tasteless drink : insipid discourse, in speech or writing : a broad but thin layer of colour put on with a long sweep of the brush : a thin coat of paint, metal, &c. : the blade of an oar.—*adj.* **wash′able.**—*ns.* **wash′away,** destruction of part of a road, railway, &c., by flooding : the breach so caused ; **wash′-ball,** a ball of toilet-soap ; **wash′-bā′sin, -bowl, wash′hand bā′sin,** a bowl to wash face, hands, &c., in ; **wash′-board,** (*U.S.*) a corrugated board for rubbing clothes on in washing : a thin plank placed on a boat's gunwale to prevent the sea from breaking over : (*dial.*) a skirting-board ; **wash′-bott′le, wash′ing-bott′le,** a bottle containing liquid used for purifying gases : a bottle with tubes through the stopper enabling a stream of cleansing liquid to be directed on a chemical or a piece of apparatus ; **wash′-cloth,** a piece of cloth used in washing ; **wash′-dirt,** earth to be washed for gold.—*adjs.* **washed′-out,** deprived of colour, as by washing : (*coll.*) deprived of energy or animation ; **washed′-up,** (*coll.*) deprived of energy or animation : (*slang*) done for, at the end of one's resources : (*slang*) finished (with *with*). — *n.* **wash′er,** one who washes : a washing-machine : (perh. a different word) a ring, usu. flat, of metal, rubber, &c., to keep joints or nuts secure, &c.— *v.t.* to fit with a washer or washers.—*ns.* **wash′erman,** a man who washes clothes, esp. for hire :— *fem.* **wash′erwoman ; wash′-gild′ing,** a gilding made with an amalgam of gold from which the mercury is driven off by heat, leaving a coating of gold ; **wash′-house, wash′ing-house,** a house or room for washing clothes in ; **wash′-in, -out,** increase, or decrease, in the angle of incidence, i.e. the angle between the chord of a wing and the wind relative to the aeroplane, in approaching the wing-tip along the camber ; **wash′iness,** state of being watery : feebleness ; **wash′ing,** the act of cleansing, wetting, or coating, with liquid : clothes, or other articles, washed, or to be washed : a thin coating : the action of breaking, lapping, &c. : (usu. in *pl.*) liquid that has been used to wash something, or matter separated or carried away by water or other liquid. — *adj.* that washes : used for washing : washable.—*ns.* wash′ing-blue (see blue) ; wash′ing-board, a corrugated board for rubbing clothes on in washing ; wash′ing-day, a day devoted to washing clothes ; wash′ing-machine, a machine for washing clothes ; wash′ing-powder, a powdered preparation used in washing clothes ; wash′ing-soda (see soda) ; wash′ing-up, cleaning up, esp. of dishes and cutlery after a meal ; wash′-leather, split sheepskin prepared with oil in imitation of chamois : buff leather for regimental belts ; wash′-out, an erosion of earth by the action of water : the hole made by such : a complete failure or disappointment ; wash′-pot, a vessel for washing ; wash′-stand, wash′hand-stand, a piece of furniture for holding ewer, basin, and other requisites for washing the person : wash′-tub, a tub for washing clothes ; wash′-up, a washing-up : a washing-up place : anything cast up by the sea, &c. : the washing of ore : a quantity of gold obtained by washing.—*adj.* wash′y, watery, moist : thin, feeble.—wash down, (of liquid) to carry downward : to help the swallowing or digestion of (a solid food) ; wash one's brain, (*obs. slang*) to drink copiously ; wash out, to remove by washing : to wash free from dirt, soap, &c. : to disappear or become fainter as a result of washing : (*coll.* ; esp. in *pass.*) to exhaust : to bring the blade of an oar not cleanly out of the water at the finish of a stroke ; wash up, to wash one's hands and face : to wash the dishes and cutlery after a meal : to sweep up on to the shore. [O.E. *wæscan, wascan* ; found in other Gmc. languages, as O.H.G. *wascan* (Ger. *waschen*) ; same root as water.]

washing, *wosh′ing, adj.* (Shak., *Rom.*, I. i. 69) for swashing.

Washingtonia, *wosh-ing-tō′ni-ä, n.* a genus of ornamental fan palms of California and Mexico : a synonym of Sequoia. [Named after George *Washington* (1732-99).]

wasp, *wosp, n.* any of a large number of insects belonging to the order Hymenoptera and constituting many families, including the *Vespidae*, to which the common wasp (*Vespa vulgaris*) and the European hornet (*Vespa crabro*) belong : a petulant and spiteful person.—*adjs.* was′pish, like a wasp : having a slender waist like a wasp : quick to resent an injury : spiteful, virulent ; was′pish-head′ed, (*Shak.*) hot-headed, passionate.—*adv.* was′pishly. — *n.* was′pishness.— *adjs.* wasp′-tongu′d (Shak., 1 *Hen. IV.*, I. iii. 236 ; 1st quarto wasp-stung, others wasp-tongue), biting in tongue, shrewish ; wasp′-waist′ed, very slender waisted : laced tightly ; was′py, waspish.—wasp′(′s) nest, the nest of a wasp : (*fig.*) a place very full of enemies or of angry people, or circumstances in which one is assailed indignantly from all sides. [O.E. *wæsp, wæps* ; cf. Ger. *wespe*, L. *vespa*.]

wassail, *wos′(ä)l, was′l, n.* (*hist.*) the salutation uttered in drinking a person's health : a liquor in which such healths were drunk, esp. ale with roasted apples, sugar, nutmeg, and toast : a festive occasion : revelry : a drinking-bout : a drinking or festive song.—*v.i.* to hold a wassail or merry drinking-meeting : to sing good wishes, carols, &c., from house to house at Christmas.—*v.t.* to drink to or pour libations for (as fruit-trees).—*ns.* wass′ail-bout, a carouse ; wass′ail-bowl, -cup, a cup from which healths were drunk ; wass′ailer, one who wassails : a reveller ; wass′ailing ; wass′ailry. [O.N. *ves heill*, 'be in health.']

wasserman, *wos′ər-mən, n.* (*obs.*) a sea-monster, shaped like a man. [Ger. *wassermann—wasser*, water, *mann,* man.]

Wassermann('s) reaction, test, *väs′ər-man(z) rē-ak′shn, test,* a test of the blood serum, or of the cerebrospinal fluid, to determine whether the person from whom it is drawn is suffering from syphilis. [A. von *Wassermann* (1866-1925), German bacteriologist.]

wast, *wost,* used as 2*nd pers. sing. pa.t.* of the verb be. [See was.]

wast, wastfull, wastness, obs. spellings of waste, waist, &c.

waste, *wāst, adj.* uncultivated, and at most sparsely inhabited : desolate : lying unused : unproductive : (*obs.*) devastated, ruinous : in a devastated condition (to lay waste) : empty, unoccupied : refuse, rejected, superfluous : (*obs.*) useless, vain. —*v.t.* to devastate : to consume, wear out, impair gradually : to cause to decline, shrink physically, to enfeeble : (*obs.*) to put an end to : (*obs.*) to impoverish : (*obs.*) to expend, spend, consume or pass : to spend, use, occupy, unprofitably : to use, bestow, where due appreciation is lacking (often in passive) : to fail to take advantage of : to turn to waste material : (*law*) to injure (an estate or property).—*v.i.* to be diminished, used up, or impaired by degrees : to lose strength or flesh or weight (often waste away) : (*obs.*) of time, to be spent : to be used to no, or little, purpose or effect : to use, consume, spend too lavishly.—*n.* an uncultivated, unproductive, or devastated region : a vast expanse, as of ocean or air : (Shak., *Ham.*, I. ii. 198, quartos 2, 3, 4) vast (*n.*) : a disused working : act or process of wasting : (*obs.*) consumption or expenditure : too lavish, or useless, expenditure, or an example of it : squandering : a profusion : superfluous, refuse, or rejected, material : a wastepipe : gradual decay : destruction : loss : (*obs.* ; in *pl.*) ravages : (*obs.*) that which is laid waste : (*law*) injury done to an estate or property by the tenant.—*ns.* wāst′age, loss by use or natural decay, &c. : useless or unprofitable spending : loss, or amount of loss, through this : (*Scot.*) a devastated or ruined place : (*Scot.*) waste ground ; waste′-bas′ket, waste′paper-bas′ket, a basket for holding useless scraps of paper ; waste′-book, a day-book or journal, or a rougher record preliminary to it.—*adj.* waste′ful, (*obs.* or *rare*) causing devastation, consuming, destructive : (*rare*) causing wasting of the body : (*obs.*) lavish : characterised by, or addicted to, over-lavishness : (*poet.*) uninhabited, unfrequented, desolate : (*obs.*) vain, profitless.—*adv.* waste′fully.—*ns.* waste′fulness ; waste′-gate, a gate for discharging surplus water from a dam, &c. ; waste′ness, the state of being waste : (*obs.*) a waste place : (*B.*) devastation ; waste′-pā′per, used paper no longer required for its original purpose : paper rejected as spoiled ; waste′-pipe, a pipe for carrying off waste or surplus water.—*v.t.* wast′er, (*Scot.*) to use, spend thriftlessly (whence *adj.* wāst′erful, *adv.* wāst′erfully, *n.* wāst′erfulness).—*n.* one who or that which wastes : a spendthrift : (*coll.*) a good-for-nothing : (*hist.*) a class of thief : an article spoilt in the making : an animal that is not thriving, or that is not suitable for breeding purposes.—*n.* wāst′ing.—*adj.* that is undergoing waste : destroying, devastating : enfeebling.—*n.* wāst′rel, refuse : a waster, esp. a profligate : a neglected child.—*adj.* waste, refuse : of an animal, feeble : going to waste : spendthrift.—*adj.* wast′erife (-rif, -rīf ; *Scot.*), wasteful.—*n.* wastefulness.—*n.* wāst′ry, wāst′ery, (*Scot.*) prodigality.—*adj.* improvident.—go to waste, to be wasted ; grow to waste, (*obs.*) of a time, to come near an end ; in waste, (*obs.*) to no effect, in vain ; run to waste, orig. of liquids, to be wasted or lost ; waste product, material produced in a process that is discarded on the completion of that process. [O.Fr. *vast (guast)*—L. *vāstus,* waste.]

wastel, *wos′tl,* wastel-bread, *n.* (*obs.*) bread made from the finest of the flour. [O.Fr. *wastel,* a variant of *guastel, gastel* (Fr. *gâteau,* cake) ; of Gmc. origin.]

waster, *wās′tər, n.* (*obs.*) a wooden sword for practising[fencing with : a cudgel : practice or play with a waster.—play at waster(s), to practise fencing. [Ety. uncertain.]

waster, wasterful, waster. See waste.

waster, *wās′tər, n.* (*Scot.*) a four-pronged or five-

pronged salmon-spear. [Earlier *wa(w)sper*—**spear**, modified after **leister**; ety. otherwise obscure.]
wat, *wot*, *n*. (*obs*.) a hare. [Prob. *Wat*, for Walter.]
wat, *wawt*, *adj*. (*Scot*.) wet: drunken. [Variant of **wet**.]
wat, *wawt*. Scots form of **wot**.
watch, *woch*, *n*. (*obs*.) state of being awake: (*obs*.) a religious vigil (survives in watch-night—q.v.): a wake: (*obs*.) a flock (of nightingales): (*hist*.) a division of the night, of fixed length: (in *pl*. *poet*.) the period (of the night): act or state of remaining on the alert or of observing vigilantly: the lookout: close observation: act of guarding: surveillance: (*obs*.) the office or duty of keeping guard or of being a sentinel (*B*., **stand upon one's watch**, to fulfil the duty of watchman): (*obs*.) a lying in ambush: one who watches: a watchman, or a body of watchmen, esp. (*hist*.) the body of men who, before the institution of a police force, patrolled the streets at night: (*obs*.) a sentinel, or the military guard of a place: (in early 18th century) name applied to certain companies of irregular troops in the Highlands: a period, usu. of four hours (see **dog-watch**) of duty on deck: the part, usu. a half (the *port*—formerly *larboard*— and the *starboard watch*), of the ship's officers and crew who are on duty at the same time: a sailor's turn or period of duty: (*obs*.) something that measures or marks time or the passage of time, as a marked candle, the cry of a watchman, a clock: (*obs*.) the dial of a clock: a small timepiece for carrying in the pocket, on the wrist, &c.—*v.i.* to remain awake: to keep vigil: to attend the sick by night: to be on the alert: to look out (with *for*): to look with attention: to keep guard: to keep guard over (with *over*).—*v.t.* to keep in view, to follow the motions of with the eyes (*lit.* and *fig.*): to look at, observe, attentively: of a barrister, to attend the trial of (a case) on behalf of a client not directly involved in it: (*Shak.*) to catch in an act: to have in keeping: to guard: to tend: (*coll.*) to beware of danger to or from, to be on the alert to guard or guard against: to be on the alert to take advantage of, an opportunity: (*obs*.) to wait for: (*Shak.*) to keep (a hawk) from sleep, in order to tame it.—*ns.* watch'-bill, a list of the officers and crew of a ship, as divided into watches, with their several stations; watch'-box, a sentry-box; watch'case, the outer case of a watch: (*Shak.*) a sentry-box; watch'-clock, a watchman's-clock; watch'-commit'ee, a committee of a local governing body exercising supervision over police services, &c.; watch'-dog, a dog kept to guard premises and property: also *fig.*; watch'er, one who watches: one of a class of angels; watch'-fire, a fire lit at night as a signal: a fire for the use of a watching party, sentinels, scouts, &c.—*adj.* watch'ful, (*arch.*) wakeful: (*arch.*) spent in watching: habitually on the alert or cautious: watching or observing carefully: characterised by vigilance: (*arch.*) requiring vigilance, or in which one must be on the alert.—*adv.* watch'fully.— *ns.* watch'fulness; watch'-glass, a sand-glass: a glass covering for the face of a watch; watch'-guard, a chain, strap, &c., used to attach a watch to the clothing; watch'-house, a house in which a guard is placed: a lock-up, police station; watch'-key, a key for winding a watch; watch'-light, a light used for watching or sitting up in the night; watch'maker, one who makes or repairs watches; watch'making; watch'man, a man who watches or guards, now usu. a building, formerly the streets of a city at night; watch'man's-clock, a clock by means of which the times of his visits to several places are recorded; watch'-night, orig. a late service (up to and including midnight) held once a month by Wesleyan Methodists: later a service lasting until midnight held by various denominations on New Year's Eve.—Also *adj.*— *ns.* watch'-officer, the officer in charge of the ship during a watch, also called **officer of the watch**; watch'-paper, a round piece of paper, often decorated, formerly put inside the outer case of a watch to prevent rubbing; watch'-pocket, a small pocket for holding a watch; watch'-spring,

the mainspring of a watch; watch'-tower, a tower on which a sentinel is placed to look out for the approach of danger; watch'word, (*obs*.) the password to be given to a watch or sentry: any signal: a maxim, rallying-cry.—**be on the watch**, to be on the lookout; **Black Watch**, the 42nd and 73rd Regiments, now the 1st and 2nd Battalions of the Black Watch or Royal Highland Regiment; **watch after**, (*Thackeray*) to follow the movements of (with one's eyes); **watch and ward**, the old custom of watching by night and by day in towns and cities: uninterrupted vigilance; **watch in**, to keep awake to welcome (the New Year); **watching brief**, instructions to a counsel to watch a legal case; **watch one's step**, to step with care: (*fig.*; *coll.*) to act warily, be careful not to arouse opposition, give offence, &c.: **watch out**, (*coll.*; orig. *U.S.*) to look out, be careful; **watch up**, (*Thackeray*) to sit up at night. [O.E. *wæcce* (n.), *wæccan*, *wacian* (vb.); cog. with *wacan*, to wake.]
watchet, *woch'it*, *n*. a pale blue: a material of this colour: an angling fly.—*adj.* pale blue. [O.Fr. *wachet*; perh. orig. a material.]
water, *waw'tər*, *n*. in a state of purity, at ordinary temperatures, a clear transparent liquid (colourless except in large quantities), perfectly neutral in its reaction, and devoid of taste or smell: extended to the same substance (H_2O) in solid or gaseous state (ice, steam): any body of this, as the ocean, a lake, river, &c.: (*Scot.*) a river valley: one of the four elements recognised by early natural philosophers: a quantity of the liquid used in any one stage of a washing operation: a liquid resembling or containing water: mineral water: tears: saliva: (usu. in *pl.*) the amniotic fluid, filling the space between the embryo and the amnion: urine: transparency, lustre, as of a diamond: (in *pl.*) waves, moving water, a body of water.—*v.t.* to wet, overflow, irrigate, supply, dilute with water: (*obs*.) to soften by soaking: (*obs*.) of a river, &c., to surround, as a city (also **water about**): to wet and press so as to give a wavy appearance to: to increase (the nominal capital of a company) by the issue of new shares without a corresponding increase of actual capital.—*v.i.* to fill with, or shed, water: of the mouth (also, *obs.* and *Scot.*, the teeth), to secrete saliva at the sight or thought of food, or (*fig.*) in anticipation of anything delightful: of an animal, to drink: to take in water.—*adj.* pertaining to, or used in, the storage or distribution of water: worked by water: used, living, or operating, on or in water: by way of or across water: made with, or formed by, water.—*ns.* wa'terage, conveyance by water: money paid for this; wa'ter-bag, a bag for holding water: a camel's reticulum; wa'ter-bail'iff, (*obs*.) a custom-house officer who inspects ships on reaching or leaving port: an official whose duty it is to enforce bye-laws relating to fishing, or to prevent poaching in protected waters (also—now *Scot.*—wa'ter-bail'ie); wa'ter-ball'ast, water carried by a ship to balance or redress change of draught due to consumption of fuel or provisions or discharge of cargo: water carried for purposes of stability; wa'ter-barom'eter, a barometer in which water is substituted for mercury; wa'ter-barr'el, -cask, a barrel, cask, for holding water; wa'ter-bath, a bath composed of water: a vessel of water in which other vessels can be immersed in chemical work; wa'ter-batt'ery, a voltaic battery in which the electrolyte is water: (*fort.*) a battery nearly on a level with the water; wa'ter-bearer, one who carries water for domestic purposes: Wa'ter-bearer, Aquarius; wa'ter-bed, a rubber mattress filled with water, sometimes used by invalids to prevent bed-sores; wa'ter-beetle, any of a large number of beetles living on or in water having fringed legs by means of which they swim easily; wa'ter-bell'ows, a form of blower, worked e.g. by a column of water falling through a vertical tube, formerly used to supply a blast for furnaces; wa'ter-bird, a bird that frequents the water; wa'ter-bis'cuit, a thin plain biscuit made with water; wa'ter-blink, in Arctic regions, a patch of sky reflecting the colour, and hence indicating

the presence, of open water; **wa′ter-blinks,** the plant blinks (q.v.); **wa′ter-bloom, -flow′ers,** large masses of algae, chiefly blue-green, which sometimes develop very suddenly in bodies of fresh water; **wa′ter-bo′a,** the anaconda (*Eunectes murinus*); **wa′ter-boat′man,** any of a number of aquatic hemipterous insects having one pair of legs suggestive of sculls.—*adj.* **wa′ter-borne,** floating on water: conveyed by water, esp. in a boat: transmitted by means of water, as a disease. —*ns.* **wa′ter-bott′le,** a skin or leather bag, or a glass, rubber, &c., bottle for containing water; **wa′ter-bouget,** (*hist.*) a skin or leather bottle used to carry water, usu. one of a pair hung on opposite ends of a stick.—*adj.* **wa′ter-bound,** detained by floods: of a macadam road, or road surfacing, formed of broken stone, rolled, and covered with a thin layer of hoggin, which is watered in and binds the stones together.—*ns.* **wa′ter-brash,** pyrosis, a sudden gush into the mouth of acid fluids from the stomach, accompanied by a burning sensation (heartburn) in the gullet; **wa′ter-break,** a piece of broken water; **wa′ter-breather,** any animal that breathes by means of gills.—*adj.* **wa′ter-breathing.** — *ns.* **wa′ter-brose,** (*Scot.*) brose made of meal and water alone; **wa′ter-buck,** any of several antelopes, esp. *Cobus ellipsiprymnus*; **wa′ter-bug,** any of a large variety of hemipterous insects, including water-boatmen, &c., found in or beside ponds, &c.; **wa′ter-buffalo,** the common domestic buffalo (Bubalus) of India, &c.; **wa′ter-bull,** a mythical amphibious animal like a bull; **wa′ter-butt,** a large barrel for rain-water, usu. kept out of doors; **wa′ter-carriage,** conveyance by water: facilities for it; **wa′ter-cart,** a cart for conveying water, esp. for the purpose of watering streets or roads; **wa′ter-cell,** one of several cells in a camel's stomach used for storing water; **wa′ter-cement,** hydraulic cement; **wa′ter-chestnut,** a water-plant (*Trapa natans,* or other species) of or akin to the Onagraceae: its edible seed; **wa′ter-chute** (*-shoot, -shōōt*), an artificial cascade or slope leading to water, down which boats or toboggans slide for sport; **wa′ter-clock,** a clock which is made to go by the fall of water: also a clepsydra; **wa′ter-closet,** a closet used as a privy, in which the discharges are carried off by water; **wa′ter-cock,** the kora, a large E. Indian gallinule; **wa′ter-colour,** a pigment diluted with water and gum (or other substance), instead of oil: a painting in such a colour or colours; **wa′ter-colourist,** a painter in water-colours.—*v.i.* **wa′ter-cool,** to cool by means of water, esp. circulating water.—*adj.* **wa′ter-cooled.** —*n.* **wa′ter-cooler,** a machine for cooling by means of water or for keeping water cool.—*adj.* and *n.* **wa′ter-cooling.**—*ns.* **wa′ter-core,** in an apple or other fruit, an abnormality consisting of water-soaked tissue esp. close to the core: in founding, a hollow core through which water may be passed; **wa′tercourse,** a channel through which water flows or has flowed: an artificial water-channel: a stream, river: **wa′ter-cow,** a female water-buffalo or water-bull; **wa′ter-craft,** a boat: boats collectively: skill in swimming, &c., or in managing boats; **wa′ter-crane,** an apparatus for supplying water from an elevated tank esp. to a locomotive tender: a hydraulic crane; **wa′ter-cress,** (often, esp. formerly, in *pl.*) a perennial cress (*Nasturtium officinale*) growing in watery places, used as a salad; **wa′ter-culture,** a method of cultivation, often an experimental means of determining the mineral requirements of a plant, the plant being grown with its roots dipping into solutions of known composition; **wa′ter-cure,** medical treatment by means of water; **wa′ter-deck,** a decorated canvas cover for a dragoon's saddle; **wa′ter-deer,** a small Chinese musk-deer of aquatic habits: in Africa, one of the chevrotains; **wa′ter-doctor,** a hydropathist: formerly, one who divined diseases from the urine; **wa′ter-dog,** any variety of the dog (formerly a specific variety, a small poodle) valuable to sportsmen in hunting water-fowl on account of its aquatic habits: a **water-vole:** (*obs.*) an otter: also various other

animals: (*coll.*) **an experienced sailor: a good swimmer:** a small irregular floating cloud supposed to indicate rain; **wa′ter-diviner,** one who, usu. with the help of a divining-rod, detects, or tries to detect, the presence of underground water; **wa′ter-drinker,** a drinker of water: a teetotaler; **wa′ter-drop,** a drop of water: a tear; **wa′ter-dropwort,** a genus (Oenanthe) of umbelliferous plants, including the common water-dropwort (*O. fistulosa*) and hemlock water-dropwort, or water-hemlock (*O. crocata*).—*adjs.* **wa′tered,** soaked in or with, sprinkled, supplied with water: having a supply of water in the form of a river, rivers, &c.: periodically flooded: diluted: (*fig.*) weakened: marked with a wavy pattern by watering: of capital or stock, increased in nominal value without any corresponding increase in the assets; **wa′tered-down,** much diluted.—*ns.* **wa′ter-elder,** the guelder rose; **wa′ter-engine,** an engine for raising water: an engine worked by water: (*obs.*) an engine for extinguishing fires; **wa′ter-equiv′alent,** thermal capacity, the product of the specific heat of a body and its mass; **wa′terer,** a vessel for watering with; **wa′terfall,** a fall or perpendicular descent of a body of water, a cataract or cascade: (*obs.*) a neck-tie: (*obs.*) a chignon; **wa′ter-fern,** any of the Hydropterideae or rhizocarps, water or marsh plants differing from ferns in the narrower sense in being heterosporous, classified in two families, Marsileaceae and Salviniaceae; **wa′ter-finder,** a water-diviner; **wa′ter-flag,** the yellow iris; **wa′ter-flea,** the common name for any of numerous minute aquatic crustaceans; **wa′ter-flood,** an inundation; **wa′ter-flow,** current of water.—*adj.* **wa′ter-flowing,** streaming.—*ns.* **wa′ter-fly,** an aquatic insect: (*Shak.*) an insignificant, troublesome person; **wa′ter-fowl,** a fowl that frequents water: swimming game-birds collectively; **wa′ter-frame,** Arkwright's spinning-frame, which was driven by water; **wa′ter-front,** the buildings or part of a town along the edge of and facing the sea, a river, &c.; **wa′ter-gall,** (*obs.* and *dial.*) a watery appearance in the sky accompanying the rainbow: also a secondary rainbow; **wa′ter-gap,** a gap in a mountain range containing a stream; **wa′ter-gas,** a mixed gas obtained by passing steam (**blue water-gas**) or steam and air (**semi-water-gas**) over incandescent coke, or other source of carbon; **wa′ter-gate,** a floodgate: a gate admitting to a river or other body of water: (*Scot.* and *North.*) a street leading to the water; **wa′ter-gauge, -gage,** an instrument for measuring the quantity or height of water: water pressure expressed in inches: an instrument for measuring differences in pressure; **wa′ter-gilding,** wash-gilding; **wa′ter-glass,** a water-clock: an instrument for making observations beneath the surface of water: a glass vessel for containing water, as one for keeping plants, or (*obs.*) a finger-bowl, or a tumbler: a concentrated and viscous solution of sodium or potassium silicate in water, used for preserving eggs, &c.; **wa′ter-god,** a deity presiding over a tract of water; **wa′ter-gruel,** gruel made with water: anything insipid; **wa′ter-guard,** river, harbour, or coast police; **wa′ter-hammer,** the noise made by the sudden stoppage of moving water in a pipe: the concussion so caused: an air vacuum containing some water; **wa′ter-head,** the source, as of a stream: the region where this is found: a dammed-up body of water, or its quantity, height, or pressure; **wa′ter-hemlock,** a poisonous plant, *Cicuta virosa*: any other plant of the same genus: water-dropwort (q.v.); **wa′ter-hen,** any of a number of ralline birds, esp. *Gallinula chloropus*—also called the moorhen; **wa′ter-hole,** a pool in which water has collected, as a spring in a desert or a pool in the dried-up course of a river; **wa′ter-horse,** a water-spirit like a horse: a kelpie; **wa′ter-ice,** sweetened fruit juice or a substitute diluted with water and frozen; **wa′teriness; wa′tering,** the act of one who, or that which, waters: (*obs.*) the act of drinking: dilution with water: the art or process of giving a wavy, ornamental appearance: such an appearance; **wa′tering-call,** a cavalry trumpet-signal to water horses; **wa'tering-can, -pot,** a vessel used for watering plants; **wa'tering-cap,** (obs.) a cavalryman's fatigue cap; **wa'tering-house,** (obs.) an inn or other place where horses are watered; **wa'tering-place,** a place where water may be obtained : a place to which people resort to drink mineral water, or for bathing, &c; **wa'tering-trough,** a trough in which horses and cattle drink : a trough between the rails containing water to be scooped up by locomotives.—*adj.* **wa'terish,** resembling, or abounding in, or charged with, water : dilute, thin, poor.—*ns.* **wa'terishness; wa'ter-jacket,** a casing containing water placed round e.g. the cylinder-block of an internal-combustion engine, to keep it cool—also **wa'ter-box; wa'ter-jet.**—*adj.* operated by a jet of water.—*ns.* **wa'ter-joint,** a joint in a pavement that is raised to prevent water lying in it : a joint in sheet-metal roofing forming a channel for rain-water; **wa'ter-jump,** a place where a jump across a stream, &c., has to be made, as in a steeplechase; **wa'ter-leaf,** any plant of the genus Hydrophyllum or the family Hydrophyllaceae : (*archit.*) an ornament used in the capitals of columns, probably representing the leaf of some water plant; **wa'ter-lemon,** a species of passion-flower, or its edible fruit; **wa'ter-lens,** a simple lens formed by placing a few drops of water in a vessel, e.g. a small brass cell with blackened sides and a glass bottom.—*adj.* **wa'terless,** lacking water.—*ns.* **wa'ter-level,** the level formed by the surface of still water : an instrument in which water is used for establishing a horizontal line of sight : (*geol.*) a water-table : (*mining*) a slightly inclined road to carry off water; **wa'ter-lily,** a name commonly given to the different species of Nymphaea and Nuphar, and also to other members of the family Nymphaeaceae—the three British species are the white water-lily (*Nymphaea alba*), and the yellow water-lilies (*Nuphar luteum* and *Nuphar minimum*—the latter being rare); **wa'ter-line,** any of several lines on a ship to which she is submerged under different conditions of loading, e.g. the *light water-line* marking the depth when she is without cargo : in shipbuilding, any of certain lines on a vessel parallel with the water, showing the contour of the hull at various heights : the water-level : the outline of a coast : in paper, one of the wider-spaced lines visible by transmitted light (up and down the page in folio, octavo, &c., crosswise in quarto).—*v.t.* **wa'terlog,** to make unmanageable by flooding with water, as a boat : to saturate with water so as to make heavy or inert, or unfit for use, or to impede life or growth (also *fig.*).—*adj.* **wa'ter-logged.**—*ns.* **wa'ter-lot,** a lot of ground which is under water; **wa'ter-main,** a large subterranean pipe supplying water; **wa'terman,** a man who plies a boat for hire, a boatman, a ferryman : a good oarsman : one whose employment is supplying water, e.g. (*hist.*) to cab- or coach-horses : an imaginary being living in water; **wa'termanship,** oarsmanship; **wa'termark,** the line of the greatest height to which water has risen : a tidemark : a ship's water-line : a distinguishing mark in paper, a design visible by transmitted light, made by the mould or the dandy-roll.—*v.t.* to mark with a watermark : to impress as a watermark.—*ns.* **wa'ter-meadow,** a meadow kept fertile by flooding from a stream; **wa'ter-measure,** measurement formerly used in dealing with goods, as coal, salt, &c., sold on board ship—the bushel, &c., being larger than the standard bushel, &c.; **wa'ter-melon,** a plant (*Citrullus vulgaris*) of the cucumber family, of African origin, having a pulpy, pleasantly flavoured fruit : the fruit itself; **wa'ter-me'ter,** instrument for measuring the quantity of water passing through a particular outlet; **wa'ter-mil'foil** (see milfoil); **wa'ter-mill,** a mill driven by water; **wa'ter-moc'assin,** a poisonous snake of the southern United States; **wa'ter-mole,** the desman : the duckbill; **wa'ter-monkey,** a porous earthenware jar for keeping drinking-water in hot climates, round, with narrow neck—also *monkey-jar*; **wa'ter-motor,** any water-wheel or turbine, esp. any small motor driven by water under

pressure; **wa'ter-mouse,** the water-vole : (*Austr.*) any mouse of the genus Hydromys; **wa'ter-music,** (*hist.*) music performed, or composed for performance, during an excursion by water; **wa'ter-nix'ie,** a nixie; **wa'ter-nymph,** a naiad; **wa'ter-ouzel** (see ouzel); **wa'ter-parsnip,** any plant of the aquatic genus Sium, esp. the skirret; **wa'ter-parting,** a watershed, divide; **wa'ter-pepper,** a very acrid persicaria (*Polygonum Hydropiper*) of wet places; **wa'ter-pipe,** a pipe for conveying water; **wa'ter-pistol,** a weapon or toy for throwing a jet of water or other liquid; **wa'ter-plane,** a plane passing through any water-line of a ship : the plane of the surface of water : (*hist.*) a canal on the level without locks : a seaplane; **wa'ter-plant,** a plant that grows in water; **wa'ter-plantain,** a plant (*Alisma Plantago*) having plantain-like leaves : any other plant of the same genus; **wa'ter-plate,** a plate having a double bottom and a space for hot water, used to keep food warm; **wa'ter-poet,** a writer of doggerel verse (John Taylor, 1580-1653, a writer of jingling verses, &c., for a time a Thames waterman, called himself ' the Water-poet '); **wa'ter-pō'lo,** an aquatic game played by swimmers, seven a side; **wa'ter-pore,** a hydathode : a madreporite; **wa'ter-pot,** a pot or vessel for holding water; **wa'ter-power,** the power of water, employed to move machinery, &c. : a flow or fall of water which may be so used; **wa'ter-pox,** varicella; **wa'ter-privilege,** the right to the use of water, esp. for driving machinery : a place where this right may be exercised.—*adj.* **wa'terproof,** coated, e.g. with rubber, so as to be impervious to water : so constructed that water cannot enter.—*n.* a material or an outer garment made impervious to water.—*v.t.* and *v.i.* to make, become, or be, impervious to water, esp. by coating with a solution.—*ns.* **wa'terproofing,** the act of making any substance impervious to water : the material with which this is done; **wa'ter-pump,** a pump for raising water : used humorously of the eyes; **wa'ter-purpie** (see purpie); **wa'terquake,** a seismic disturbance affecting the sea; **wa'ter-rail,** the common rail (*Rallus aquaticus*) of Europe; **wa'ter-ram,** a hydraulic ram; **wa'ter-rat,** the popular name of the water-vole : the American musk-rat : a pirate : a sailor or boatman; **wa'ter-rate,** a rate or tax for the supply of water; **wa'ter-rice** (see zizania); **wa'ter-rug,** (Shak., *Macb.,* III. i. 94) a kind of water dog—perh. from rug (1); **wa'ter-sapphire** (trans. of Fr. *saphir d'eau*), an intense blue variety of cordierite used as a gemstone; **wa'ter-seal,** a seal formed by water in a trap; **wa'tershed,** the line separating two river-basins : (*erron.*) a drainage or a catchment area : a slope or structure down which water flows; **wa'ter-shoot,** a channel for the overflow of water : a water-chute.—*adj.* **wa'tershot,** (*rare*) crossed by streams.—*ns.* **wa'ter-side,** the brink of water : the shore of a sea, lake, &c.; **wa'tersmeet,** a meeting-place of two streams; **wa'ter-smoke,** water evaporating as visible mist; **wa'ter-snake,** a snake frequenting the water; **wa'ter-soldier,** an aquatic plant (*Stratiotes aloides*) common in lakes and ditches in the east of England, **wa'ter-souchy** (-*sōō'chi,* -*sōō'shi*), fish served in the water in which it is boiled (Du. *waterzootje—zootje,* boiling); **wa'ter-spaniel** (see spaniel); **wa'ter-spider,** an aquatic spider, esp. *Argyroneta aquatica,* which has a sub-aquatic bell-shaped web inflated with air carried down in bubbles; **wa'ter-splash,** a shallow stream running across a road; **wa'ter-spout,** a pipe, &c., from which water spouts : the spout of water : torrential rain : a disturbance like a very small tornado, a revolving column of cloud, mist, spray; **wa'ter-spring,** (*B.*) a spring; **wa'ter-sprin'kle,** (*Spens.*) a spray of water : also a sprinkle; **wa'ter-sprite,** a spirit inhabiting the water.—*adj.* **wa'ter-standing,** (Shak.) brimming with tears.—*ns.* **wa'ter-starwort** (see starwort, under star); **wa'ter-strider,** any long-legged aquatic insect of the family Hydrobatidae; **wa'ter-supply',** the obtaining and distribution of water, as to a community : the amount of water thus distributed; **wa'ter-table,** a moulding or other projection in the wall of a building to throw off the water : (*geol.*) the surface below which fissures and pores in the strata are saturated with water ; **wa′ter-tap,** a tap or cock used for letting out water ; **wa′ter-ther-mom′eter,** a thermometer filled with water instead of mercury, and used for showing the point at which water has its greatest density; **wa′ter-thief′,** (*Shak.*) a pirate.—*adj.* **wa′tertight,** so tight as not to admit water or let it escape : (*fig.*) such that no flaw, weakness, or source of misinterpretation, can be found in it.—*ns.* **wa′tertightness; wa′ter-tower,** a tower containing tanks in which water is stored so that it may be delivered at sufficient pressure for distribution to an area : a vertical pipe supplied with water under high pressure, used in fire-fighting ; **wa′ter-twist,** a kind of cotton-yarn, first made by the water-frame : in spinning, more than the usual amount of twist.—*adj.* **wa′ter-vas′cular,** of or pertaining to vessels in certain invertebrates which contain a mixture of water and a nutritive fluid : in echinoderms, of the system of coelomic canals (**water-vascular system**) associated with the tube-feet and supplying fluid for their movement.—*ns.* **wa′ter-vine,** a name for various plants yielding a refreshing watery sap ; **wa′ter-violet,** a plant of the genus Hottonia ; **wa′ter-vole,** *Arvicola amphibius*, commonly known as the water-rat ; **wa′ter-wag′on,** a wagon used to convey water ; **wa′ter-wag′tail,** a wagtail, esp. the pied wagtail ; **wa′ter-wave,** a wave of water : a wave in the hair made by setting it when wet.—*v.t.* to make such a wave in (hair).—*ns.* **wa′terway,** a series of pieces of timber, extending round a ship at the junction of the decks with the sides, having a groove connecting with the scuppers to carry off water : any channel for water : a stretch of navigable water : a water-route ; **wa′ter-weed,** any plant with very small flowers and leaves growing in ponds, &c., esp. anacharis (q.v.) ; **wa′ter-wheel,** a wheel moved by water : an engine for raising water.—*n.pl.* **wa′ter-wings,** a wing-like inflated device for keeping one afloat in water.—*n.* **wa′terwork** (usu. in *pl.*), any apparatus or plant by which water is supplied, as to a town, &c. : (*obs.*) an ornamental fountain, cascade, &c. : (*obs.*) a textile fabric, used like tapestry : (*slang*) used humorously of shedding tears.—*adjs.* **wa′ter-worn,** worn by the action of water ; **wa′tery,** of or pertaining to water : full of water : moist : consisting of, or containing, water : like water : thin or transparent : tasteless : weak, vapid : associated with, or controlling, the sea, the tides, rain, &c. : (Shak., Troil., III. ii. 20) watering, eager.—*n.* **wa′ter-yam,** a plant with farinaceous root-stock, the lattice-leaf. — *ns.* **high′-water, high′-watermark** (see **high**) ; **low′-water, low′-watermark** (see **low**). —**above water,** out of difficulties, esp. financial ; **be, go, on the water-wagon,** (*slang*) to abstain from alcoholic liquors ; **cast one's water,** to examine one's urine to aid in the diagnosis of disease ; **deep water, or waters,** water too deep for safety : difficulty or distress ; **hold water,** to be correct or well-grounded, to bear examination ; **keep one's head above water,** (*fig.*) to keep solvent ; **like water,** copiously : extravagantly, recklessly ; **make a hole in the water,** (*slang*) to drown oneself ; **make the mouth water,** to arouse a delightful feeling of anticipation or desire ; **make, pass, water,** to micturate ; **oil on troubled waters,** anything that allays or assuages, from the effect of pouring oil on rough water ; **still waters run deep,** a quiet exterior often conceals strong emotions, resolution, cunning, &c. ; **under water,** below the surface ; **water of crystallisation, hydration,** the water present in hydrated compounds, which, when crystallised from solution in water, retain a definite amount of water ; **water of life,** spiritual refreshment : whisky, brandy, &c. ; **water on the brain,** hydrocephalus ; **water on the knee,** an accumulation of serous fluid in the knee-joint ; **watertight compartment,** a division of a ship's hull or other underwater structure so formed that water cannot enter it from any other part : (*fig.*) a part, esp. of one's thoughts or beliefs, shut off from the influence of other parts. [O.E.

wæter ; cf. Du. *water*, Ger. *wasser* ; cog. with Gr. *hydōr*, L. *udus*, wet, *unda*, a wave, Sans. *udan*, water.]

Waterloo, *waw-tər-lōō′*, or *waw′*, *n.* a final defeat.— **Waterloo cracker,** (*obs.*) a kind of firework. [*Waterloo*, near Brussels, where Napoleon was finally defeated in 1815.]

Watling Street, *wot′ling strēt*, *n.* one of the great Roman highways of Britain, running from near London through St Albans to Wroxeter : often extended at either end to include the roads to Dover and Chester : loosely applied to other Roman roads : (*obs.*) the Milky Way. [O.E. *Wæclinga strǣt*, the street of Wæcel's people—of whom nothing is known ; the O.E. name of St Albans was *Wæclinga ceaster*.]

watt, *wot*, *n.* the practical unit of electrical power, equal to a rate of working of one joule per second. —*ns.* **watt′age,** amount of electrical power expressed in watts ; **watt′-hour′,** the unit of electrical energy, being the work done by one watt acting for one hour ; **watt′meter,** an instrument containing a series (*current*) and a shunt (*voltage*) coil whose combined torque produces a deflection of the needle that is a direct measure of the circuit power in watts. [James *Watt* (1736-1819).]

Watteau, *wot′ō*, *adj.* applied to articles or features of women's dress resembling the costumes in the paintings of Antoine *Watteau* (1684-1721)—as **Watteau bodice,** one with a square opening at the neck and short sleeves.—*adj.* **Watt′eauish.**

wattle, *wot′l*, *n.* (*dial.*) a twig or flexible rod : (collective *sing.* or in *pl.*) material for fences, roofs, &c., in the form of rods, branches, &c., either interwoven to form a network or loose : (*dial.*) a hurdle : any of various Australian acacias : (perh. a different word) the coloured fleshy excrescence under the throat of some birds, or a similar excrescence or process on any part of the head of a bird, fish, &c.—*v.t.* to bind with wattles or twigs : to form by plaiting twigs.—*ns.* **watt′lebark,** bark of various wattles, used for tanning ; **watt′le-bird,** any of a number of honey-eaters of Australia that have ear-wattles.—*adj.* **watt′led.**—*ns.* **watt′ling,** the act of making wattles by interweaving twigs, &c. : wattle-work, or the material for it ; **watt′le-work,** wicker-work.—**wattle and daub, dab,** wattle-work plastered with mud and used as a building material. [O.E. *watul, watel* ; origin uncertain.]

wattle, *wot′l*, *n.* (*hist.* ; *Orkney* and *Shetland*) the obligation to entertain the foud on his annual journey, or a tax for which it was later commuted. [Perh. Norw. dial. *veitla*—O.N. *veizla*, entertainment.]

wauff. Variant of **waff** (1 and 2).

waugh, *waw, interj.* expressing sorrow, anger, &c.— usu. attributed to North American Indians.

waught, waucht, *wawhht, n.* (*Scot.*) a large draught. —*v.t.* and *v.i.* to drink in large draughts. [Perh. conn. with **quaff.**]

waukrife. See **wake.**

waul, wawl, *wawl, v.t.* to cry as a cat or a newly-born baby.—Also *n.*—*n.* and *adj.* **waul′ing, wawl′ing.** [Imit.]

waul, wawl, *wawl, v.t.* (*Scot.* ; *obs.*) to roll the eyes. [O.E. *wealwian,* to roll, wallow.]

waur, waurst. See **war** (2).

wave, *wāv, n.* a ridge on the surface of a liquid, esp. of the sea : a surge, consisting of vibrating particles of liquid, moving across the surface of a body of liquid such as the sea (*transverse wave*)—the vibrations of the individual particles being at right angles to the line of advance : a unit disturbance in any travelling system of vibrating particles as a light-wave (*transverse wave*) or a sound-wave (*longitudinal wave*—the vibrations of the particles being in the direction of advance) : an undulating or vibratory motion (e.g. as a signal), or sound : (*poet.*) the sea, or other body of water : curved inequality of surface : a line or streak like a wave : an undulation : an undulating succession of curves in hair, or one of these : (*fig.*) a swelling up or increase, followed by a subsidence or decline.— *v.i.* to move like a wave : to move backwards and forwards : (*obs.*) to float or to hover : to flutter, as a signal : to make a signal in this way : to undulate : (*obs.*) to waver, vacillate.—*v.t.* to move backwards and forwards : to brandish : to waft or beckon : to express by a wave : to raise into inequalities of surface : to give an undulating appearance to.— *n.* wave′-band, (*radio*) a range of wavelengths occupied by transmission of a particular type.— *adj.* waved, showing a wave-like form or outline : undulating : (of hair) made to undulate by artificial means : (*her.*) indented : having on the margin a succession of curved segments or incisions : moved to and fro.—*ns.* wave′-front, in a propagating vibratory disturbance, the continuous locus of points which are in the same phase of vibration ; wave′-guide, (*electronics*) a hollow metal conductor, usu. rectangular, within which very high-frequency energy can be transmitted efficiently ; wave′length, the distance between two successive similar points on an alternating wave, e.g. between successive maxima or between successive minima : the distance, measured radially from the source, between two successive points in free space at which an electromagnetic wave has the same phase.—*adj.* wave′less.—*n.* wave′let, a little wave.—*adj.* wave′like.—*ns.* wave′-mechanics, the part of quantum mechanics dealing with the wave aspect of the behaviour of radiations ; wave′-meter, an instrument for measuring wavelengths, directly or indirectly ; wave′-mō′tion, undulatory movement : motion in waves, or according to the same laws ; wave′-offering, an ancient Jewish custom of moving the hands in succession towards the four points of the compass in presenting certain offerings—opp. to the *heave-offering*, in which the hands were only lifted up and lowered. —*v.t.* wāv′er, to move to and fro : to shake, be unsteady, to be in danger of falling : to falter, show signs of giving way : to vacillate : to vary, change. —*n.* wāv′erer.—*n.* and *adj.* wāv′ering.—*adv.* wāv′eringly, in a wavering or irresolute manner. —*n.* wāv′eringness.—*adjs.* wāv′erous, wāv′ery, unsteady.—*ns.* wave′son, goods floating on the sea after a shipwreck ; wāv′iness, the state or quality of being wavy.—*n.* and *adj.* wāv′ing.— *adj.* wāv′y, full of, or rising in, waves : playing to and fro : undulating.—Wavy Navy, the Royal Naval Volunteer Reserve, so-called from the undulating gold braid on officers' sleeves. [O.E. *wafian*, to wave ; cf. O.N. *vafra*, to waver.]

wavellite, *wā′vel-īt, n.* hydrated phosphate of aluminium, occurring commonly in flattened globular aggregates, showing a strongly developed internal radiating structure. [Named after Dr. *Wavel*, who discovered the mineral near Barnstaple.]

wavey, wavy, *wā′vi, n.* the snow-goose. [Cree.]

waw, *waw, n.* (*Scott*) a wave—*Spens.* wawe. [Prob. from a lost O.E. form akin to *wǣg*, wave.]

wawl. See waul (1 and 2).

wax, *waks, n.* any of a class of substances of plant or animal origin, usu. consisting of esters of monohydric alcohols, e.g. beeswax, $C_{30}H_{61}O \cdot CO \cdot C_{15}H_{31}$: any of certain hydrocarbons of mineral origin, as ozokerite : any substance like a wax in some respect, as that in the ear : a substance used to seal letters : that used by shoemakers to rub their thread : in mining, puddled clay : a thick sugary substance made by boiling down the sap of the sugar-maple, and cooling by exposure to the air : (*fig.*) a person easily influenced : (Shak., *Timon,* I. i. 48) explanation uncertain—according to some wax tablets, others have thought expansive growth (see wax, 2).—*v.t.* to smear, rub, or (*obs.*) join, with wax.—*ns.* wax′-bill, any of various small seed-eating birds of the weaver-bird family with coloured bills like sealing-wax ; wax′-chandler, a maker of, or dealer in, wax candles ; wax′-cloth, cloth covered with a coating of wax, used for table-covers, &c. : a popular name for all oil floorcloths ; wax′-doll, a child's doll having the head and bust made of hardened beeswax.—*adj.* wax′en, made of wax : like wax : easily impressed, penetrated, effaced.—*ns.* wax′-end, better waxed end, a strong thread having its end stiffened by

shoemakers' wax, so as to go easily through the hole made by the awl ; wax′ed-leather, leather finished with a high wax polish on the flesh side ; wax′er, one who or that which waxes ; wax′-flower, an artificial flower made of wax : any of several plants, as a white-flowered climbing plant of Madagascar, an epiphyte of British Guiana, and plants of the genus Hoya of Australasia ; wax′-iness ; wax′ing ; wax′-insect, an insect that secretes wax, as any of several of the Coccidae, &c. ; wax′-light, a candle or taper made of wax ; wax′-moth, a bee-moth ; wax′-myrtle, U.S. candle-berry tree ; wax′-painting, encaustic painting ; wax′-palm, either of two S. American palms yielding wax ; wax′-paper, paper spread with a thin coating of white wax and other materials.— *adj.* wax′-red, (*Shak.*) bright-red like sealing-wax. —*ns.* wax′-tree, a tree from which wax is obtained, as a Japanese sumac (*Rhus succedanea*), the wax-myrtle, a privet (*Ligustrum lucidum*), &c. ; wax′-wing, a genus of passerine birds (Bombycilla) with small red horny appendages, resembling red sealing-wax, on their wings ; wax′work, work made of wax, esp. figures or models formed of wax : (*pl.*) an exhibition of wax figures ; wax′worker.— *adj.* wax′y, resembling wax in texture or appearance : soft : impressible : (*fig.*) impressionable : pallid, pasty.—waxy degeneration, a morbid process in which the healthy tissue of various organs is transformed into a peculiar waxy albuminous substance. [O.E. *weax* ; O.N. *vax*, Du. *was*, Ger. *wachs*.]

wax, *waks, v.i.* to grow or increase, esp. of the moon, as opp. to *wane* : to pass into another state, become : —*pa.p.* (*arch.*) wax′en, grown—also (*obs.*) *pa.t.* *pl.* (as Shak., *M.N.D.,* II. i. 56) and *infin.* [O.E. *weaxan* ; O.N. *vaxa,* Ger. *wachsen,* allied to L. *augēre,* to increase, Gr. *auxanein.*]

wax, *waks, n.* (*coll.*) a passion, fit of anger.—*adj.* wax′y, (*slang*) irate, incensed. [Origin uncertain.]

way, *wā, v.t.* (*Spens.*) to weigh, esteem. [Variant of weigh.]

way, *wā, n.* passage : road, street, track : direction of motion : length of space, distance : room, or opportunity, to advance : freedom of action, scope : manner of life : condition, state : advance in life : normal, habitual, course or conduct : (in *pl.*) characteristic conduct, idiosyncrasies : manner, style : method : means : course : respect : will : (*naut.*) progress or motion through the water, head-way : the direction of the weave, grain, &c. : (in *pl.*) the machined surfaces of the top of a lathe bed on which the carriage slides, shears : (in *pl.*) the framework of timbers on which a ship slides when being launched.—*v.i.* (*Spens.*) to journey.—*ns.* way′-bagg′age, (*U.S.*) baggage to be laid down at a way-station ; way′-bill, list of passengers and goods carried by a public vehicle : a list of places to be visited on a journey : a document giving details regarding goods sent by rail ; way′-board, weigh′-board, a thin stratum or seam separating thicker strata ; way′bread (*dial.* ; O.E. *wegbrǣde—brad,* broad), the common plantain.—*v.i.* way′fāre, (*arch.*) to travel, esp. on foot.—*n.* (*arch.*) travel, esp. on foot.—*n.* way′fārer, a traveller, esp. on foot.—*n.* and *adj.* way′fāring.—*ns.* way′fāring-tree, the *Viburnum lantana,* a large shrub common in hedges ; way′freight, freight for a way-station. —*adjs.* way′-going, (*Scot.*) departing ; way′gone, exhausted by travelling.—*v.t.* waylay′, to lie in ambush for : to attack or seize in the way : (*fig.*) to lie in wait for in order to converse with : (*obs.*) to obstruct or intercept.—*ns.* waylay′er ; way′-leave, permission to pass over another's ground or property.—*adj.* way′less, without a path.—*ns.* way′-maker, a pioneer : a precursor ; way′-mark, -post, a guide-post ; way′-passenger, one taken up or set down at a way-station or an intermediate point on a coach or bus route ; way′side, the border of a way, path, or highway.—*adj.* growing or lying near the wayside.—*ns.* way′-station, (*U.S.*) an intermediate station between principal stations ; way′-traffic, local traffic, as distinguished from through or express traffic ; way′-train, (*U.S.*) a train stopping at most of the stations on a line; **way'-warden,** one elected to supervise the upkeep of roads in a district.—*adj.* **way'worn,** worn-out by travel.—**be by way of,** to be supposed, alleged (inaccurately) to be, do; **by, with, one's way of it,** (*Scot.*) according to one's belief or assertion; **by the way,** incidentally: while travelling: beside one's path; **by way of,** as if for the purpose of: in character of; **come one's way,** to come in the same direction: (*fig.*) to come within one's experience or reach, to become attainable; **committee of ways and means,** the House of Commons when it sits to consider methods of raising supplies; **give way** (see **give**); **go one's way** (see **go**); **go out of the, one's, way,** **put oneself out of the way,** to give oneself trouble: to make a special point of; **go the way of all the earth,** to die; **have a way with one,** to have a fascinating personality or persuasive manner; **have one's way,** to carry one's point, get what one wants; **have way,** (*naut.*) to be in motion, as a vessel; **in a bad way,** in a serious condition: much upset; **in a fair way** (see **fair**); **in a small, big** (or **large**), **way,** on a petty, or a large or grandiose, scale; **in a way,** in a state of agitation or distress: to some extent: from one point of view; **in the family way** (see **family**); **in the way,** on the way: in the path (*lit.* and *fig.*): impeding, obstructing; **in the way of,** in a good position for effecting or attaining: (*coll.*) in the habit of: in respect of; **lead the way,** to act as a guide in any movement; **make one's way,** to push oneself forward (*lit.* and *fig.*); **make way,** to give place: to advance; **on the way,** moving towards a destination or event: in progress; **out of the way,** so as not to hinder or obstruct: (*Shak.*) lost, hidden (**out-of-the-way,** see **out**); **take one's way,** to set out, proceed: to follow one's own inclination or plan; **the Way,** the Christian Religion (Acts ix. 2, &c.); **under way,** in motion, as a vessel; **Way of the Cross,** a series of pictorial representations of the stages of Christ's progress to Calvary: devotions used in connexion with these stages; **ways and means,** resources: methods e.g. of raising money for the carrying on of government. [O.E. *weg*; Ger. *weg*; akin to Sans. *vah,* akin to L. *vehĕre,* to carry, draw.]

wayment, *wā-ment',* *v.t.* and *v.i.* (*Spens.*) to lament, grieve.—*n.* (*Spens.*) lamentation, grief. [O.Fr. *waimenter—wai,* alas !]

wayward, *wā'wərd, adj.* wilful: capricious: irregular. —*adv.* **way'wardly.**—*n.* **way'wardness.** [For *awayward—away,* and suff. *-ward.*]

wayzgoose, *wāz'gōōs, n.* a printers' annual dinner or picnic.—Earlier **way'goose.** [Origin obscure.]

wazir, *wä-zēr', n.* a vizier. [Ar. *wazīr.*]

we, *wē, pron. pl.* of I: I and others: used for I by monarchs: also by editors, &c. [O.E. *wé*; cog. with Goth. *weis,* Ger. *wir.*]

weak, *wēk, adj.* (*obs.*) soft: wanting strength: not able to sustain a great weight: easily overcome: frail: wanting health: feeble of mind: wanting moral or mental force: impressible, easily led: lacking artistic force: unconvincing: inconclusive: (*Shak.*) inconsiderable: having little of the important ingredient: (*gram.*) of a verb, inflected by regular syllabic addition instead of by change of main vowel: of a Germanic noun or adj., having inflexions in *-n*: of a sound or accent, having little force: of a verse line, having the accent on a normally unstressed syllable: tending downward in price.—*v.t.* **weak'en,** to make weaker: to reduce in strength or spirit.—*v.i.* to grow weak or weaker: to become less resolute or determined, show signs of giving in.—*n.* **weak'ener.**—*adjs.* **weak'-eyed,** having weak eyes or sight; **weak'-handed,** powerless; **weak'-headed,** having a feeble intellect: easily affected by alcoholic liquor; **weak'-hearted,** of weak spirit: soft-hearted; **weak'-hinged,** ill-balanced; **weak'-kneed,** having weak knees: weak in will.—*ns.* **weak'liness;** **weak'ling,** a weak or feeble creature.—*adv.* **weak'ly.**—*adj.* sickly: not robust: feeble.—*adj.* **weak'-minded,** having feeble intelligence: having, or showing, lack of resolution: too easily convinced or persuaded.—*ns.* **weak'-mindedness; weak'-**

ness.—*adjs.* **weak'-sighted; weak'-spirited,** bearing wrong tamely, cowardly.—**weaker sex,** women; **weak vessel** (see **vessel**); **weak side, point,** that side or point in which a person is most easily influenced or most liable to temptation. [O.N. *veikr*; allied to O.E. *wác,* pliant—*wícan,* to yield; Du. *week,* Ger. *weich.*]

weal, *wēl, n.* (*arch.*) state of being well, a sound or prosperous state: welfare: (*obs.*) commonwealth. —*adj.* **weal'-balanced,** (Shak., *Meas.,* IV. iii. 108) perh. kept in a state of just proportion by reasons of state, perh. for well-balanced.—*n.* **weals'man,** (*Shak.*) a statesman.—**the public, general, or common, weal,** the well-being, interest, and prosperity of the country. [O.E. *wela, weola,* wealth, bliss; allied to **well** (2).]

weal, *wēl, n.* Same as **wale** (1), **weel** (1).

weald, *wēld, n.* (*poet.*) open country or wooded country.—*adj.* **Weald'en,** pertaining to the Weald: of a series of freshwater beds at the base of the Cretaceous, seen in the Weald.—Also *n.*—**the Weald,** a district, once forested, between the North and South Downs. [O.E. (W.S.) *weald,* a forest, wold; cf. **wold.**]

wealth, *welth, n.* (*arch.*) prosperity: valuable possessions of any kind: riches: (*fig.*) an abundance.—*adv.* **wealth'ily.**—*n.* **wealth'iness.**—*adj.* **wealth'y,** rich: prosperous. [M.E. *welthe—wele* —O.E. *wela*; see **weal** (1).]

weamb. See **wame.**

wean, *wān, n.* (*Scot.*) a child. [**wee ane.**]

wean, *wēn, v.t.* to accustom to nourishment other than the mother's milk: to reconcile to the want of anything: to estrange the affections of from any object or habit.—*ns.* **wean'el,** (*Spens.*) a weanling; **wean'ing-brash,** a severe form of diarrhoea that supervenes, at times, on weaning.—*adj.* **wean'ling,** newly weaned (also *fig.*).—*n.* a child or animal newly weaned. [O.E. *wenian,* to accustom; O.N. *venja,* Ger. *gewöhnen,* to accustom, *entwöhnen,* to disuse, wean.]

weapon, *wep'n, n.* any instrument of offence or defence.—*adjs.* **weap'oned; weap'onless,** having no weapons.—*n.* **weap'on-salve,** a salve supposed to cure a wound by being applied to the weapon that made it. [O.E. *wǣpen*; Goth. *wépna,* arms, Ger. *waffe.*]

weapon-schaw. Same as **wappens(c)haw.**

wear, *wār, v.t.* to be dressed in: to carry on the body: to arrange, as clothes, in a specified way: to display, show: of a ship, to fly (a flag): to consume, waste, damage, by use time, exposure: to make by friction: to exhaust, to weary: to bring gradually into: (*Scot.*; *wēr*) to enable to last, endure: (*poet.*) to spend, as a period of time: (*Spens.*) to traverse: (*Scot.*) to edge, guide, conduct, as sheep into a fold.—*v.i.* to be wasted by use or time: to consume slowly: (*poet.*; usu. in *pa.p.*) of time, to be spent, pass, esp. tediously: to last under use: to resist the ravages of age: stand the test of time: (*Shak.*) to be in fashion: to pass into: (*obs.*) to become: (*Scot.*) to go, move, slowly: (*pa.t.* **wōre,** *arch.* **wāre,** *pa.p.* **wōrn).**—*n.* act of wearing: lessening or injury by use or friction: durability: articles worn: fashion.—*adj.* **wear'able,** fit to be worn.—*n.* **wear'er.**—*adj.* **wear'ing,** made or designed for wear: consuming: exhausting.—*n.* the process of wasting by attrition or time: the action of carrying on the body, or displaying, or flying: durability: passing: (*obs.*) that which is worn, clothes. — *ns.* **wear'ing-apparel,** dress; **wear'-iron,** an iron plate to take the wear due to friction.—**wear and tear, tear and wear,** loss by wear or use; **wear away,** to impair, consume, by wear: to decay or fade out: to pass off; **wear down,** (*fig.*) to diminish, or overcome, gradually by persistence; **wear off,** to rub off by friction: to diminish by decay: to pass away by degrees; **wear out,** to impair by use: to render, become, useless by decay: to consume tediously: to harass; (**win and**) **wear,** to (win and) enjoy possession of. [O.E. *werian,* to wear; O.N. *verja,* to clothe, Goth. *wasjan.*]

wear, *wār, v.t.* and *v.i.* (*naut.*) to bring, or be brought, to another course by turning the helm to windward : —*pa.t.* and *pa.p.* **wore.** [Prob. **veer** (1).]

wear, *wēr, n.* another spelling of weir.

wear, *wēr, v.t.* (*Scot.*) to guard : to ward off. [O.E. *werian.*]

wearish, *wēr'ish, adj.* (*obs.*) tasteless, savourless (*lit.* and *fig.*) : (*dial.*) feeble, withered, shrunk. [Late M.E. *werische* ; cf. **wersh.**]

weary, *wē'ri, adj.* having the strength or patience exhausted : very tired : causing weariness : tiresome, tedious : (*dial.*) puny.—*v.t.* to make weary : to reduce the strength or patience of : to harass.— *v.i.* to become weary or impatient : (*Scot.*) to long (with *for*).—*adjs.* **wea'ried,** tired ; **wea'riful,** wearisome.—*adv.* **wea'rifully.**—*adj.* **wea'riless,** incessant.—*adv.* **wea'rily.**—*n.* **wea'riness.**—*adj.* **wea'risome,** causing weariness : tedious.—*adv.* **wea'risomely.** — *n.* **wea'risomeness.** — **weary out,** to exhaust ; **Weary Willie,** (*slang*) a tramp : (*slang*) a person habitually lackadaisical or deficient in energy. [O.E. *wērig,* weary.]

weary, *wē'ri, n.* (*Scot.*) a curse, as in **weary on you, weary fall you.** [weary (1), prob. with some association with obs. *wary* (O.E. *wiergan*), to curse.]

weasand, *wē'zand, n.* the gullet : the windpipe : the throat. — (*Spens.*) **wea'sand-pipe.** [O.E. *wǣsand* ; O.S. *wāsend,* O.H.G. *weisant.*]

weasel, *wē'zl, n.* a small carnivore (*Mustela nivalis*) with long slender body, active, furtive, and bloodthirsty, eating frogs, birds, mice, &c. : a person resembling a weasel, esp. in its bad qualities. —*ns.* **wea'sel-cat,** the Java linsang ; **wea'sel-coot,** the female or young male of the smew.—*adjs.* **wea'sel-faced,** having a lean sharp face ; **wea'selly.** [O.E. *wesle* ; Ger. *wiesel.*]

weather, *wedh'ər, n.* atmospheric conditions as to heat or cold, wetness, cloudiness, &c. : type or vicissitude of atmospheric conditions or of fortune : storm or adverse weather : (*obs.*) rain, snow, &c. : cold and wet : the direction in which the wind is blowing : the angle the sail of a windmill makes with the perpendicular to its axis.—*v.t.* to affect by exposing to the air : to sail to the windward of : to gain or pass, as a cape : (*lit.* and *fig.*) to come safely through : (*obs.*) to shelter from : to set, as the sails of a windmill : to slope, as a roof.—*v.i.* to become discoloured, disintegrated, &c., by exposure.—*adj.* (*naut.*) toward the wind, windward.— *adjs.* **weath'er-beaten,** distressed by, or seasoned by, the weather ; **weath'er-bitten,** worn or defaced by exposure to the winds.—*n.* **weath'er-board,** the windward side of a ship : a plank in a porthole, &c., of a vessel placed so as to keep off rain, without preventing air from circulating : a board shaped so as to shed water from a building. —*v.t.* to fit with such planks or boards. — *n.* **weath'er-boarding,** thin boards placed overlapping to keep out rain : exterior covering of a wall or roof.—*adj.* **weath'er-bound,** detained by bad weather.—*ns.* **weath'er-bow,** the windward side of the bow ; **weath'er-box, -house,** a toy constructed on the principle of a barometer, consisting of a house with the figures of a man and wife who come out alternately as the weather is respectively bad or good ; **weath'er-cloth,** a tarpaulin protecting boats, hammocks, &c. ; **weath'ercock,** a vane (often in the form of a cock) to show the direction of the wind : one who changes his opinions, allegiance, &c., easily and often.—*v.t.* to act as a weathercock for : to supply with a weathercock : to behave like a weathercock. — *adj.* **weath'er-driven,** driven by winds or storms.— *adj.* **weath'ered,** (*archit.*) made slightly sloping, so as to throw off water : (*geol.*) having the surface altered in colour, form, texture, or composition by the action of the elements : seasoned by exposure to weather.—*n.* **weath'er-eye,** the eye considered as the means by which one forecasts the weather.—*v.t.* **weath'er-fend,** (*Shak.*) to defend from the weather, to shelter.—*ns.* **weath'er-forecast,** a forecast of the weather based on meteorological observations ; **weath'er-ga(u)ge,** position of a ship to the windward of another : advantage of position ; **weath'er-gall** (*Scot.* **-gaw**),

an imperfect rainbow, or other supposed sign of coming weather ; **weath'er-glass,** a glass or instrument that indicates the changes of the weather : a barometer ; **weath'er-gleam,** (*dial.*) a bright aspect of the sky at the horizon.—*adj.* **weath'er-headed,** (*Scott*) flighty.—*ns.* **weath'er-helm,** a keeping of the helm somewhat to the weather side when a vessel shows a tendency to come into the wind ; **weath'ering,** (*obs.*) weather conditions : (*archit.*) a slight inclination given to the top of a cornice or moulding, to prevent water from lodging on it : (*geol.*) the action of the elements in altering the form, colour, texture, or composition of rocks : seasoning by weather : the act of passing to windward of.—*adj.* **weath'erly,** (*naut.*) making little leeway when close-hauled.— *n.* **weath'er-map,** a map indicating meteorological conditions over a large tract of country.—*adj.* **weath'ermost,** farthest to windward. — *n.* **weath'er-notation,** a system of abbreviation for meteorological phenomena.—*adj.* **weath'er-proof,** proof against rough weather : weather-proof material. — *v.t.* to make weather-proof. — *ns.* **weath'er-prophet,** one who foretells weather : a device for foretelling the weather ; **weath'er-roll,** the lurch of a vessel to windward when in the trough of the sea ; **weath'er-report,** (loosely) a weather forecast ; **weath'er-side,** windward side ; **weath'er-sign,** a phenomenon indicating change of weather : any prognostic ; **weath'er-stain,** discoloration produced by exposure ; **weath'er-station,** a station where phenomena of weather are observed ; **weath'er-strip,** a thin piece of some material used to keep out wind and cold ; **weath'er-symbol,** a conventional sign indicating a meteorological phenomenon. — *adj.* **weath'er-wise,** skilful in foreseeing the changes of the weather (*lit.* and *fig.*).—**keep one's weather eye open,** to be alert and on one's guard ; **keep, have, the weather of,** to be to the windward of : to have the advantage of ; **make fair weather,** (*Shak.*) to be conciliatory, to flatter ; **make good, bad, heavy,** &c., **weather of it,** to behave well or badly in a storm (*lit.* and *fig.*) ; **stress of weather,** violent and unfavourable winds ; **under the weather,** indisposed, seedy : (*slang*) drunk ; **weather along,** to make headway against adverse weather ; **weather anchor,** the anchor lying to windward ; **weather a point,** (*fig.*) to gain an advantage or accomplish a purpose against opposition ; **weather on,** to gain on in a windward direction (*lit.* and *fig.*) ; **weather out,** to hold out against till the end. [O.E. *weder* ; O.N. *vedhr,* Ger. *wetter.*]

weave, *wēv, v.t.* to make by crossing threads, strands, strips, &c., above and below one another : to interlace, as in a loom to form cloth : to work into a fabric : to depict by weaving : to unite, work into a whole : to construct, contrive.—*v.i.* to practise weaving (*pa.t.* **wōve,** *rarely* **weaved** ; *pa.p.* **wōv'en** ; cf. **wove**).—*n.* texture of a woven fabric.—*ns.* **weav'er ; weav'er-bird,** any bird of a passerine family resembling the finches, so called from their remarkably woven nests ; **weav'ing,** the act or art of forming a web or cloth by the intersecting of two distinct sets of fibres, threads, or yarns—those passing longitudinally from end to end of the web forming the *warp,* those crossing and intersecting the warp at right angles forming the *weft.* [O.E. *wefan* ; O.N. *vefa,* Ger. *weben* ; cog. with Gr. *hyphḗ,* a web, *hyphainein,* to weave.]

weave, *wēv, v.i.* to move to and fro : to wind in and out : (*boxing*) to move back or forward with sinuous movements of the body : (*aero.*) to fly with a weaving motion.—*v.t.* to move to and fro or up and down : to make a signal to by waving something.—*n.* and *adj.* **weav'ing.—get weaving,** (*slang*) get busy, get on the move. [M.E. *weve* ; of uncertain origin.]

weazand, *wē'zand, n.* Same as weasand.

weazen, *wē'zn, adj.* Variant of wizen.

web, *web, n.* that which is woven : a whole piece of cloth as woven in the loom : a kind of cloth or weave : a thin metal plate or sheet : in paper-making, an endless wire-cloth working on rollers :

a large sheet or roll of paper : in birds, the vexillum of a feather : (*anat.*) any connective tissue : the fine texture spun by the spider, &c., as a snare : the skin between the toes of water-fowl, &c. : (*obs.*) a film over the eye : anything like a cloth web in complication or a spider's web in flimsiness or in power to entangle : a plot, snare.—*v.t.* to envelop, or to connect, with a web.—*adj.* **webbed**, having the toes united by a web or skin.—*n.* **webb′ing**, a narrow woven fabric of hemp, used for belts, &c., for various purposes in upholstery, and as tapes conducting webs of paper in a printing-machine : (*zool.*) state of being palmate : the webs of webbed hands or feet.—*adj.* **webb′y.**—*adj.* **web′-fing′ered.** —*n.* **web′-foot**, a foot the toes of which are united with a web or membrane.—*adjs.* **web′-foot′ed ; web′-toed.**—*n.* **web′worm**, (*U.S.*) any of a number of caterpillars spinning webs in which they feed or rest.—**web and pin** (*Shak.*), or **pin and web** (see **pin**). [O.E. *webb* ; O.N. *vefr*, Ger. *gewebe* ; from root of **weave** (1).]

webster, *web′ster*, *n.* (*obs.*) a weaver.—Also (*Scot.*) **wab′ster.** [O.E. *webbestre*, a female weaver— *webban*, to weave.]

wecht, *wehht*, *n.* (*Scot.*) an instrument for winnowing or for measuring grain. [Perh. conn. with **weigh.**]

wed, *wed* (*Scot.* **wad**, *wawd*), *v.t.* to marry : to join in marriage : to unit closely : (*obs.*) to wager.—*v.i.* to marry (*pr.p.* **wedd′ing** ; *pa.t.* **wedd′ed** or, *dial.*, **wed** ; *pa.p.* **wedd′ed** or, *dial.* and *poet.*, **wed**).— *n.* (*obs.* ; *Scot.* **wad**) a pledge, security.—*adj.* **wedd′ed**, married : of or pertaining to marriage : closely joined : persistently devoted.—*ns.* **wedd′- ing**, marriage : marriage ceremony ; **wedd′ing- bed**, the bridal bed ; **wedd′ing-cake**, a highly decorated cake served at a wedding, and also divided among absent friends.—*n.pl.* **wedd′ing- cards**, cards announcing a wedding, sent to friends.—*ns.* **wedd′ing-day**, day of marriage : its anniversary ; **wedd′ing-dower**, marriage portion ; **wedd′ing-dress**, a bride's dress ; **wedd′ing- favour**, white rosette worn by men at a wedding ; **wedd′ing-finger**, the ring-finger ; **wedd′ing- garment**, garment worn at a wedding ; **wedd′ing- ring**, a plain ring given by the groom to the bride at a wedding.—**penny wedding**, a wedding where the guests paid for the entertainment, and sometimes contributed to the outfit ; **silver, golden, diamond wedding**, the celebrations of the 25th, 50th, and 60th anniversaries of a wedding. [O.E. *weddian*, to promise, to marry (Ger. *wetten*, to wager)—*wedd*, a pledge ; Goth. *wadi*, Ger. *wette*, a bet.]

wedge, *wej*, *n.* a piece of wood or metal, thick at one end and sloping to a thin edge at the other, used in splitting, fixing tightly, &c. : anything shaped more or less like a wedge, as :—(*obs.*) an ingot of gold or silver, a formation of troops, the flying formation of geese and other wildfowl, a large piece, e.g. of cake, a stroke in cuneiform characters : a type of golf club for lofting out of bunkers.—*v.t.* to cleave with a wedge : to force or drive with a wedge : to thrust in tightly : to crowd closely : to fasten or fix with a wedge or wedges : to make into a wedge.—*v.i.* to force one's way like a wedge : to become fixed or jammed by, or as if by, a wedge.—*adjs.* **wedged** ; **wedge′- shaped**, shaped like a wedge ; **wedge′-tailed**, having the tail wedge-shaped.—*adv.* **wedge′wise**, in the manner of a wedge.—*n.* **wedg′ing**, a method of joining timbers.—**the thin, or small, end of the wedge**, a small beginning that is bound to be followed by a large or significant development ; **the (wooden) wedge**, the student lowest on the classical tripos list (on the analogy of wooden spoon, q.v., from Wedgwood the last name on the first list, that of 1824). [O.E. *wecg* ; O.N. *veggr*, Ger. *weck*, a wedge.]

Wedgwood (ware), *wej′wood* (*wår*), *n.* a superior kind of pottery, clay lightly glazed with cameo reliefs in white, invented by Josiah *Wedgwood* (1730–1795).

wedlock, *wed′lok*, *n.* matrimony : married state, esp. in the phrase **born in**, or **out of, wedlock**,

i.e. **legitimate, or illegitimate.—break wedlock**, to commit adultery. [O.E. *wedlác—wedd*, a pledge, and suff. *-lác*, implying action of some kind.]

Wednesday, *wenz′dā*, *wed′nz-dā*, *n.* the fourth day of the week. [O.E. *Wódnes dæg*, Woden's day.]

wee, *wē*, *n.* a short distance, a short time.—*adj.* **tiny.—Wee Free**, a member of the minority of the Free Church that refused to join with the United Presbyterian Church in 1900. [M.E. *we*, *wei*, a bit, time, or space, as in phrase *a little wei*.]

wee, *wē*, *interj.* imitating the squeal of a young pig. —Also *v.i.* and *n.*

weed, *wēd*, *n.* any useless plant of small growth : any plant growing where it is not wanted by man : any wild herb : a thick growth of wild herbs : anything useless, troublesome, or obnoxious : a sorry animal : a worthless fellow : (*coll.*) tobacco, or a cigar or cigarette.—*v.t.* to free from weeds : to remove, uproot (often **weed out**).—*v.i.* to remove weeds.—*adjs.* **weed′ed, weed′-grown,** overgrown with weeds.—*ns.* **weed′er ; weed′ery,** a place full of weeds ; **weed′iness ; weed′ing,** the action of the verb to weed : what is weeded out ; **weed′ing-chisel, -forceps, -fork, -hook, -tongs** (*pl.*), garden implements of varying forms for destroying weeds.—*adjs.* **weed′less ; weed′y,** weed-like : full of weeds : lanky, ungainly : of worthless character. [O.E. *wéod*, a herb.]

weed, *wēd*, *n.* (*arch.*) a garment, or (as collective *sing.*) clothing : (*arch.*) armour : (in *pl.*) a widow's mourning apparel.—*adj.* **weed′y**, clad in widow's mourning. [O.E. *wǣd*, *wǣde*, clothing ; O.H.G. *wāt*, cloth.]

weed, *wēd*, *n.* (*Scot.*) any sudden illness, cold, or relapse with febrile symptoms, esp. in women after confinement or nursing : a fever in horses, &c.— Also **weid.** [From *wedenonfa*—O.E. *wéden-* (in composition), mad, and Scot. *onfa′*, **onfall.**]

week, *wēk*, *n.* the space of seven days, esp. from Sunday to Saturday (inclusive) : the working days of the week : (in *pl.*) an indefinite period.— *ns.* **week′day**, any day of the week except Sunday ; **week′-end** (or *-end′*), **week′end** (or *-end′*), the period from a Friday or a Saturday to the Monday or Tuesday following.—*v.i.* to spend a week-end holiday.—*ns.* **week-end′er ; week-end′ing.**— *adj.* **week′ly**, coming, happening, or done, once a week.—*adv.* once a week : every week.—*n.* a publication appearing once a week.—**a prophetic week** (*B.*), seven years ; **a week of Sundays** (*coll.*), seven weeks : a long time ; **Feast of Weeks**, a Jewish festival lasting seven weeks ; **Great Week, Holy Week, Passion Week**, the week preceding Easter Sunday ; **in by the week**, (*obs.*) trapped, caught ; **this day week**, a week from today ; **week about**, in alternate periods of seven days ; **week in week out**, continuously without a break. [O.E. *wice* ; Du. *week*, Ger. *woche*.]

weeke, *wēk*, *n.* (*Spens.*). Same as **wick.**

weel, *wēl*, *n.* a whirlpool. [O.E. *wǣl.*]

weel, *wēl*, *n.* (*dial.*) a trap or snare for fish : (*her.*) a bearing resembling such. [O.E. *wile-* (in composition)—*wilige* ; cf. **willy.**]

weel, *wēl*, *adv.* Scots form of **well.—***adj.* **weel- faur′d, -far′d**, &c. See **well-favoured.**

weem, *wēm*, *n.* (*Scot.*) a subterranean dwelling. [Early Gael. *uaim*, cavern.]

ween, *wēn*, *v.t.* (*arch.*) to think or fancy : (*obs.*) to believe : to expect.—*v.i.* (*Shak.*) to imagine expectantly. [O.E. *wénan* ; cog. with *wén*, expectation, hope.]

weep, *wēp*, *v.i.* to express grief by shedding tears : to wail or lament : to drip, rain : to ooze in drops : to leak : to exude : to be pendent, as a weeping-willow.—*v.t.* to lament : to pour forth : to express while, or by, weeping : to exude :—*pa.t.* and *pa.p.* **wept.**—*n.* **weep′er**, one who weeps : a white border round the sleeve of a mourning dress : a crape hat-band : a widow's crape-veil : anything pendent.—*n.* and *adj.* **weep′ing.**—*ns.* **weep′ing- ash**, a variety of the common European ash, with drooping branches ; **weep′ing-birch**, a variety of the white birch, with drooping branches ; **Weeping Cross**, **weep′ing-cross**, (*hist.*) a wayside cross where penitents might pray : in phrases as to come home by weeping cross, to experience bitter regret, disappointment or failure; weep'ing-elm, a variety of wych-elm, with drooping branches.—*adv.* weep'ingly.—*adj.* weep'ing-ripe, (*Shak.*) ripe or ready for tears.—*ns.* weep'ing-rock, a rock through which water percolates slowly; weep'ing-spring, a spring from which water escapes slowly; weep'ing-tree, a tree with long pendulous branches; weep'ing-willow, an ornamental Chinese willow (*Salix babylonica*), with pendent branches.—*adj.* weep'y, (*coll.*) tearful: (*dial.*) oozy. [O.E. *wépan*; allied to *wóp*, clamour; Goth. *wópjan.*]

weet(e), weeting, weetingly, weetless, obs. forms of wit (verb), &c.—*infin.* (*Spens.*) weeten.

weet, dialectal form of wet.—Also *Spens.*

weever, *wē′var, n.* a genus of fishes (Trachinus), of which two species are British, with sharp dorsal and opercular spines capable of inflicting serious wounds. [Prob. O.Fr. *wivre*, serpent, weever —L. *vípera*; cf. wivern, viper.]

weevil, *wēv′l, n.* a popular name for a large number of beetles (the group Rhynchophora, esp. the family Curculionidae) with the anterior part of the head prolonged into a beak or proboscis, which, either in the larval or the adult form, damage fruit, nuts, grain, or trees: any insect injurious to stored grain.—*adjs.* weev'illed, weev'iled, weev'illy, weev'ily, infested by weevils. [O.E. *wifel*; Ger. *wiebel.*]

weft, *weft, n.* the threads woven into and crossing the warp: the thread carried by the shuttle (also woof): a web: a film, cloud.—*v.i.* (*rare*) to form a weft.—*n.* weft'age, texture. [O.E. *weft, wefta*; allied to *wefan*; see weave.]

weft(e), *weft, n.* (*Spens.*) a waif, a castaway. [Variant of waif.]

weft(e). See waft; (*Spens.*) *pa.p.* of waive.

Wehrmacht, *vār′mähht, n.* armed forces. [Ger.,— *wehr*, defence, *macht*, force.]

weid. See weed (3).

weigh, *wā, v.t.* to compare with by, or as if by, the balance (with *against*): to find the heaviness of: to be equal to in heaviness: to counterbalance: to raise, as a ship's anchor: to apportion: to hold in the hand(s) in order to, or as if to, estimate the weight: to estimate the value of: to ponder in the mind, consider carefully: to consider worthy of notice: (*Milt.*) to keep evenly outspread. —*v.i.* to have weight: to be considered of importance: (*Shak.*) to balance evenly: (*Shak.*) to have value: to press heavily: to weigh anchor.—*adj.* weigh'able, capable of being weighed. — *ns.* weigh'age, rate paid for the weighing of goods; weigh'-bauk, (*Scot.*) the beam of a balance: (*pl.*) a pair of scales; weigh'-board (see way-board); weigh'-bridge, a machine for weighing carts with their loads, &c.—*adj.* weighed, experienced: considered, balanced.—*ns.* weigh'er, an officer who weighs articles or tests weights; weigh'-house, a public building for weighing goods, ascertaining the tonnage of boats, &c.; weigh'-ing; weigh'ing-machine', a machine or apparatus for weighing; weight, the heaviness of a thing, esp. as determined by weighing: quantity as determined in this way: the force with which a body is attracted to the earth, measured by the product of the mass and the acceleration: a mass of metal adjusted to a standard and used for finding weight: a method of estimating, or a unit of, weight: the amount something ought to weigh: a standard amount that a boxer, &c., should weigh: (*Spens.*) scales: a heavy object: anything heavy or oppressive: a ponderous mass: pressure: importance: power: impressiveness: the frequency of an item in a frequency distribution or a number indicating this.—*v.t.* to make more heavy (*lit.* and *fig.*): to attach weights to: to hold down in this way: to increase the weight of, as fabrics, by adding chemicals: to assign a handicap weight to (a horse; also *fig.*): to oppress, burden: to attach numbers indicating their relative frequency to (items in a frequency distribution).—*adv.* weigh'tily.—*n.* weigh'tiness.—*adjs.* weight'less; weigh'ty, heavy: important: having much in-

fluence: being the fruit of judicious consideration and hence worthy of attention: (Shak., *Tim.*, III. v. 104) severe.—by, in, with, weight, (*Shak.*) fully; weigh down, to force down: (*fig.*) to depress: to preponderate over, outweigh; weigh in, to ascertain one's weight before a fight, or after a horse-race (also *n.* weigh'-in): (*slang*) to join in a project; weigh in with, (*fig.*) to produce (a new argument) in a discussion; weigh out, to weigh and dispense in portions accordingly: to ascertain one's weight before a horse-race (also *n.* weigh'-out); weight of metal, (now *rare*) the total weight of the projectiles thrown at one discharge from a ship's guns; weigh to the beam, (*Shak.*) to outweigh completely; weigh up, to force up (*lit.* and *fig.*): (*coll.*) to consider carefully and assess the quality of, as a person; weigh with, (*fig.*) to appear important to, to influence. [O.E. *wegan*, to carry; Ger. *wiegen*; L. *vehĕre*, to carry.]

weigh, *wā, n.* a misspelling of way in the phrase 'under way,' through confusion with the phrase 'to weigh anchor.'

weil. Same as weel (1).

Weimar Republic, *vī′mär ri-pub′lik*, the federal republic in Germany that was founded in 1919 after the First World War and lasted until 1933.

weir, wear, *wēr, n.* a dam across a river: a fence of stakes set in a stream for catching fish. [O.E. *wer*, an enclosure, allied to *werian*, to protect; cf. Ger. *wehr*, a dam, *wehren*, to ward.]

weird, *wērd, n.* fate (Weirds, the Fates): a witch: one's lot, esp. if evil: a happening, esp. uncanny: a tale of fate: a spell or charm.—*adj.* concerned with, controlling, fate: unearthly, uncanny: (*coll.*) peculiar, odd.—*v.t.* (*Scot.*) to destine, doom: (*Scot.*) to hand over to as one's fate: (*Scot.*) to forewarn. — *adv.* weird'ly. — *n.* weird'ness. — dree one's weird (see dree).—the Weird Sisters, the Fates: the witches in *Macbeth.* [O.E. *wyrd*, fate; allied to *weorthan*, to become; Ger. *werden.*]

Weismannism, *vīs′man-izm, n.* the doctrine in biology of August Weismann (1834-1914), whose central teaching is that acquired characters are not transmitted.

weka, *we′ka*, or *wā′* or *wē′, n.* any of the flightless rails (Ocydromus) of New Zealand. [Maori, in imitation of their cry.]

welaway. Same as wellaway.

welch, *welsh*, an old form of Welsh (1) and welsh (2).

welcome, *wel′kəm, adj.* received with gladness: admitted willingly: causing gladness: free (to): free to take or enjoy.—*n.* the act of welcoming: a kindly reception: a reception.—*v.t.* to greet: to receive with kindness or pleasure: to accept or undergo gladly.—*interj.* expressing pleasure, as to a guest on his arrival.—*ns.* wel'comeness; wel'comer.—bid a welcome, to receive with professions of kindness. [O.E. *wilcuma*—*wil-* (*willa*, will, pleasure), and *cuma*, guest; O.N. *velkomin.*]

weld, *weld, n.* a scentless species of mignonette, also known as dyer's rocket, yielding a yellow dye: the dye itself.—Also (*Scot.*) wald. [Cf. Ger. *wau.*]

weld, *weld, v.t.* to join (two pieces of metal) by raising the temperature at the joint by means of external heat or (resistance-welding) of a heavy electric current or (arc-welding) of an electric arc and then applying pressure, or (cold-welding) by pressure alone: to join closely.—*v.i.* to undergo welding: to be capable of being welded.—*n.* a welded joint.—*n.* weldabil'ity.—*adj.* weld'able. —*n.* weld'er, weld'or.—*n.* and *adj.* weld'ing.— *adj.* weld'less, having no welds. [Same as verb well; prob. from pa.p.]

weld, *weld, v.t.* (*obs.* and *dial.*) variant of wield.

welfare, *wel′fār, n.* state of faring or doing well: freedom from calamity, &c.: enjoyment of health, &c.: prosperity: welfare work.—welfare state, a state in which socialist principles have been put into effect with the purpose of ensuring the welfare of all who live in it; welfare work, efforts to improve conditions of living for a class, as the very poor, or a group, as employees or workers; hence welfare worker. [well, fare.]

Neutral vowels in unaccented syllables: *el′ə-mənt, in′fənt, ran′dəm*

welk, *welk*, *v.i.* (*obs.*) to wither, shrivel: (*Spens.* **welke**) to wane, decline.—Also *v.t.* [M.E. *welken*; cf. Ger. *welk*, withered.]

welkin, *wel′kin*, *n.* the sky or region of clouds.—*adj.* (*Shak.*) sky-blue. [O.E. *wolcnu*, pl. of *wolcen*, cloud, air, sky; Ger. *wolke*, cloud.]

welkt, **wealk′d**, *welkt*, *adj.* (*Shak.*) twisted—in some mod. edd. **whelk′d**.—*v.i.* **welk**, (*Scott*, founding on *Shak.*) apparently, to twist about. [**whelk** (1).]

well, *wel*, *n.* a spring: a mineral spring: (*fig.*) a source: a lined shaft sunk in the earth whence a supply of water, oil, &c., is obtained: an enclosure in a ship's hold round the pumps: the vertical opening enclosed between the outer ends of the flights in a winding stair: a lift-shaft: the open space in the middle of a court-room: a cavity: an eddy.—*v.i.* to issue forth, as water from the earth (*lit.* and *fig.*).—*v.t.* to pour forth.—*ns.* **well′-boat**, **-smack**, a fishing-boat having a well for holding live fish; **well′-borer**, a person engaged, or a machine employed, in well-boring; **well′-boring**, sinking wells by drilling through rock; **well′-curb**, the stone ring built round the mouth of a well; **well′-deck**, an enclosed space on the deck of a ship; **well′-drain**, a pit drawing the water from wet land; **well′-dressing**, the festal decoration of wells and springs, as in Derbyshire on Ascension-day, &c.; **well′-head**, the source of a spring: (*fig.*) a fountain-head: (*Scot.*) a spring in a marsh: the top of a well, or a structure built over it; **well′-hole**, a hole for a well of any kind: the shaft of a well: a shaft for machinery; **well′-house**, **well′-room**, a room built over a well; **well′ing**, an outpouring; **well′-sinker**, one who digs wells; **well′-sinking**; **well′-spring**, a fountain.—**the wells**, any place where mineral wells are situated. [O.E. *wella*; cf. *weallan*, to boil, O.N. *vella*, to boil.]

well, *wel* (*comp.* **bett′er**; *superl.* **best**), *adj.* (usu. predicative) good in condition: in health: fortunate: comfortable: satisfactory.—*n.* (*Spens.*) good health or fortune.—*adv.* rightly: skilfully: thoroughly: intimately: favourably, successfully: abundantly: with some degree of luxury: with reason or propriety: conveniently: to a considerable extent: clearly: easily: (*obs.*) very, esp. in combination, as (*Shak.*) **well′-accomplisht**: so be it (as a sign of assent).—*interj.* expressing surprise, &c., or introducing resumed narrative. — *adjs.* **well′-acquainted**, having intimate personal knowledge; **well′-advised**, prudent: (*Shak.*) in one's right mind.—*interj.* **well′anear′**, (*Shak.*) welladay.—*adj.* **well′-appointed**, well-equipped.—*n.* **well′-appointedness**.—*adjs.* **well′-balanced**, having the parts properly adjusted for smooth working: sane and sensible; **well′-becoming**, befitting well: proper or suitable; **well′-behaved**, behaving or acting in accordance with propriety or with requirements.—*n.* **well′-being**, welfare.—*adjs.* **well′-beloved**, very dear; **well′-beseem′ing**, well-becoming; **well′-beseen**, (*obs.*) showy in appearance; **well′-born**, born of a good family, not of mean birth; **well′-breathed**, strong of lung: exercised: not out of breath; **well′-bred**, educated to polished manners: of good stock; **well′-built**, (of a building, buildings, a person, a garment, &c.) of strong or well-proportioned make or form; **well′-conditioned**, in a desirable condition; **well′-conducted**, properly managed: acting properly; **well′-derived**, (*Shak.*) of good stock or antecedents; **well′-desired**, (*Shak.*) much sought after; **well′-directed**, skilfully aimed (*lit.* and *fig.*); **well′-disposed**, (*obs.*) healthy: well placed or arranged: inclined to be friendly: favourable.—*ns.* **well′-doer**, one who lives uprightly or does good: (*dial.*) one who thrives and is prosperous.—*n.* and *adj.* **well′-doing**.—*adjs.* **well′-earned**, thoroughly deserved; **well′-educated**, having a good education; **well′-entered**, (*Shak.*) instructed, initiated; **well′-famed**, (*Shak.*) very famous; **well′-fā′voured** (*Scots* forms **weel-faird**, **-faur′d**, **-far′d**, **-faurt**), good-looking; **well′-fed**, plump; **well′-found**, (*obs.*) commendable: well provided: fully equipped; **well′-founded**, built on secure founda-

tions: based on solid evidence or sound reasoning; **well′-given**, (*obs.*) well-disposed; **well′-gotten**, obtained honestly; **well′-graced**, (*Shak.*) popular; **well′-grounded**, firmly founded; **well′-informed**, having sound and sufficient information on a particular subject: full of varied information; **well′-intentioned**, having, or arising from, good intentions or purpose; **well′-judged**, correctly calculated, judicious; **well′-judging**; **well′-knit**, (of a person) strongly built: closely and firmly connected; **well′-known**, fully known: celebrated: notorious; **well′-liking**, (*arch.*) in good condition, plump.—*n.* (*obs.*) approbation, fondness.—*adjs.* **well′-lined**, with a good lining: full of money; **well′-looking**, good-looking; **well′-mannered**, polite; **well′-marked**, obvious, decided; **well′-meaning**, well-intentioned; **well′-meant**, rightly, kindly, intended; **well′-minded**, favourably inclined: well-disposed.—*adv.* **well′-nigh**, nearly, almost.—*adjs.* **well′-off**, in good circumstances; **well′-ordered**, correctly governed: properly arranged; **well′-pleasing**, acceptable; **well′-plighted**, well folded (see **plight**, 2); **well′-proportioned**, having correct proportions; **well′-read** (*-red*), of wide reading; **well′-regulated**, well-ordered; **well′-respected**, highly esteemed: (*Shak.*, 1 *Hen. IV.*, IV. iii. 10) given due consideration; **well′-rounded**, suitably curved: symmetrical: well constructed and complete; **well′-seen**, (*arch.*) experienced, skilful; **well′-set**, properly arranged, or well placed: fitly put together: firmly fixed: strongly built; **well′-set-up′**, (*coll.*) well-built, shapely; **well′-spoken**, spoken well or fittingly: ready, graceful, or courteous in speech; **well′-tempered**, (*obs.*) having a good bodily or mental constitution: good-tempered: of steel, mortar, &c., tempered satisfactorily: (*mus.*) tuned in equal temperament; **well′-thewed**, (*obs.*) well-mannered, of good disposition: abounding in moral wisdom; **well′-thought-of**, esteemed; **well′-thought-out**, reasoned soundly and arranged with skill; **well′-thumbed**, showing marks of much handling; **well′-timbered**, strongly built of wood: well-built: furnished with much growing timber; **well′-timed**, opportune: keeping accurate time; **well′-to-do**, (*Scot.*) **well-to-live** (*Shak.* well to live), prosperous, well-off; **well′-turned**, accurately rounded: shapely: felicitously expressed; **well′-warranted**, having good credit. — *ns.* **well′-willer**, a well-wisher; **well′-wish**, (*rare*) act of wishing well.—*adj.* **well′-wished**, (*Shak.*) being the object of good wishes.—*n.* **well′-wisher**.—*adj.* and *n.* **well′-wishing**.—*adjs.* **well′-won**, gained honestly or by hard endeavour; **well′-worked-out**, thoroughly or logically planned or developed; **well′-worn**, much worn: trite: (*rare*) becomingly worn.—**as well** (see **as**); **as well as**, in addition to: no less than; **very well**, phrase signifying assent, sometimes ironic; **well and good**, phrase signifying acceptance of facts or a situation; **well done**, (as a word of praise) bravely: nobly; **well enough**, in a moderate but sufficient degree; **well met** (see **meet**); **well up in**, (*coll.*) well versed in, well acquainted with. [O.E. *wel*; cog. with Goth. *waila*, Ger. *wohl*; from the root of **will**.]

welladay, *wel′a-dā*, **wellaway**, *wel′a-wā*, *interjs.* alas. [O.E. *wei lā wei*, woe lo! woe, with *wei* (O.N. *vei*) substituted for the orig. O.E. form *wā*.]

Wellingtonia, *wel-ing-tō′ni-ä*, *n.* a synonym of Sequoia. [Named after the Duke of *Wellington* (1769-1852).]

wellingtons, *wel′ing-tənz*, *n.* a kind of riding-boots covering the knee in front, but cut away behind: shorter closely-fitting boots, worn under the trousers (**half-wellingtons**): rubber boots loosely covering the calves: (in *sing.*) one of a pair of wellingtons. [As previous word.]

Welsian, *wel′zi-ən*, *adj.* of, pertaining to, or characteristic of, H. G. *Wells* (1866-1946), historian and writer of stories and novels with scientific or social interest.

welly, *wel′i*, *adj.* (*dial.*) corr. of **well-nigh**.

Welsh, (*obs.*) **Welch**, *welsh*, *adj.* pertaining to

Wales or its inhabitants.—*n.pl.* the inhabitants of Wales : (*sing.*) their language.—*ns.* **Welsh'-harp,** a large harp with three rows of strings, two tuned in unison and in the diatonic scale, the third in the sharps and flats of the chromatic ; **Welsh'-hook,** an old weapon ; **Welsh'man,** a native of Wales ; **Welsh'-onion,** the cibol ; **Welsh'-rabbit** (see **rabbit).** [O.E. (Angl. and Kentish) *welisc—wealh,* foreigner ; Anglo-Saxons' name for Britons, &c.]

welsh, *welsh, v.i.* to run off from a race-course without settling or paying one's bets : to dodge fulfilling an obligation.—*v.t.* to cheat in such a way. —Also **welch.**—*n.* **welsh'er, welch'er.** [Of uncertain origin.]

welt, *welt, n.* a band or strip fastened to an edge to give strength or for ornament : a narrow strip of leather used in one method of sewing the upper to the sole of a shoe : a weal : a lash, blow.—*v.t.* to furnish with a welt : to lash, beat. [Origin obscure.]

welt, *welt, v.t.* and *v.i.* to wither, dry. [Perh. **welk.**]

welter, *wel'tər, v.i.* (*obs.*) to roll or tumble about : (*rare*) to wallow about in dirt or moral degradation, &c.: (*poet.*) to be, or lie, soaked, as in blood : to be sunk (in ; *lit.* and *fig.*) : to roll, toss, about in the waves : (*poet.*) to roll, surge, as the sea.—*v.t.* (*rare*) to make (one's way) in a weltering manner.—*n.* a state of turmoil or confusion : confusion, agitation : a surging mass. — *adj.* **wel'tering.** [M.Du. *welteren* ; cf. O.E. *gewæltan,* to roll.]

welter-weight, *wel'tər-wāt, n.* (*boxing*) a weight (10 st. 7 lb. and under) between *light* and *middle* : a boxer of this category : an unusually heavy weight, carried mostly in steeplechases and hurdle-races.—*n.* **wel'ter-race,** a race in which such weights are carried.—*n.pl.* **wel'ter-stakes,** the stakes in a welter-race. [Origin obscure.]

Welwitschia, *wel-wich'i-ä, n.* a South-west African genus of one species, belonging to the Gnetaceae, with one pair of leaves that grow indefinitely. [After Friedrich *Welwitsch* (1806-72), an Austrian traveller.]

wem(b). See **wame.**

wen, *wen, n.* a sebaceous cyst.—*adjs.* **wenn'ish, wenn'y,** wen-like. [O.E. *wen(n),* a swelling, a wart ; Du. *wen* ; origin obscure.]

wen, *wen, n.* a rune (Ƿ), having the value of modern English *w,* adopted (as ⟩) into the O.E. alphabet. [O.E., orig. *wynn,* joy (of which *w* is the initial letter).]

wench, *wen(t)sh, n.* (*obs.*) a child : a damsel, girl : a working-girl, a maid-servant : a mistress : a whore.—*v.i.* to frequent the company of whores : (*Scot.* **winch)** to associate innocently with women. —*n.* **wench'er,** one who indulges in lewdness. [O.E. *wencel,* a child.]

wend, *wend, v.t.* (*obs.*) to turn : (*naut.*) to turn to the opposite tack : (*obs.* ; *refl.*) to turn, direct one's course : (*obs.*) to change.—*v.i.* (*obs.*) to turn : (*obs.*) to change : (*arch.*) to depart : (*arch.*) to make one's way (also *fig.*) :—*pa.t.* and *pa.p.* **wend'ed,** (*obs.*) **went** (now used as *pa.t.* of **go).—wend one's way,** to make one's way, follow the road, esp. in a leisurely fashion. [O.E. *wendan,* a common Gmc. verb.]

Wend, *wend, n.* one of a branch of the Slavs which once occupied the north and east of Germany : one of the Slavic population of Lusatia (part of Brandenburg, Saxony and Silesia) who still speak the Wendish tongue.—*adjs.* **Wend'ic, Wend'ish.** —*ns.* the Wendish language. [Ger. *Wende* ; origin obscure.]

Wenlock, *wen'lok, adj.* (*geol.*) denoting a group or series of rocks of the Upper Silurian period, consisting of limestone and shale, and largely developed in the neighbourhood of *Wenlock* in Shropshire.

Wensleydale, *wenz'li-dāl, n.* a breed of long-woolled sheep : a variety of cheese. [*Wensleydale* in North Riding of Yorks.]

went, *went,* properly *pa.t.* of **wend,** but now used as *pa.t.* of **go.**—*n.* (*Spens.*) a path : journey : way : course.

wentletrap, *wen'tl-trap, n.* a genus (Scalaria) of gasteropod molluscs, having a spiral shell with many deep whorls, crossed by elevated ribs. [Du.

wenteltrap (Ger. *wendel-treppe*), a winding staircase, a spiral shell.]

wept, *wept, pa.t.* and *pa.p.* of **weep.**

were, *wər, v.i.* the *pl.* of **was,** used as *pa.t.* (*pl.*) and *pa.subj.* (*sing.* and *pl.*) of **be.** [O.E. *wæron,* subj. *wære* ; Ger. *waren, wäre.*]

werewolf, *wēer'woolf,* **werwolf,** *wər'woolf, n.* a person supposed to be able to change himself for a time into a wolf : a member of an underground Nazi organisation.—*adjs.* **were'wolfish, wer'-wolfish.**—*n.* **were'wolfism,** lycanthropy. [O.E. *werwulf—wer,* man, *wulf,* a wolf.]

wergild, *wər'gild,* **weregild,** *wēr'gild, n.* among Teutonic peoples, a fine by which homicide and other heinous crimes against the person were expiated. [O.E. *wergield,* from *wer,* man, *gield—gieldan,* to pay.]

Wernerian, *vər-nē'ri-ən, adj.* pertaining or according to the opinions or system of A. G. *Werner* (1750-1817), who attributed all geological phenomena to the action of water : Neptunian.—*n.* an upholder of Werner's theories.—*n.* **wer'nerite,** scapolite.

wersh, *wersh, adj.* (all meanings *Scot.*) tasteless, unsalted : sickly, feeble : (of weather) raw. [**wearish.**]

wert, *wərt,* used as the *2nd pers. sing.* of the past indicative (for **wast)** and subjunctive of **be.** [**were,** and suff. *-t.*]

Wertherian, *vər-tē'ri-ən, adj.* pertaining to or resembling the character of *Werther* in Goethe's romance, ' The Sorrows of Young Werther '—morbidly sentimental.—*n.* **Wer'therism.**

wesand, *wē'zənd, n.* (*Spens.*). Same as **weasand.**

Wesleyan, *wes'li-ən, adj.* pertaining to Wesleyanism. —*n.* an adherent of Wesleyanism.—*n.* **Wes'leyanism,** the system of doctrine and church polity of the Wesleyan Methodists—Arminian Methodism. [Named after John *Wesley* (1703-91).]

west, *west, n.* the quarter where the sun sets : one of the four chief points of the compass : the direction faced when one stands with one's back to the high altar of a church : the regions in the west of any country, esp. (*Amer.*) those beyond the Appalachian Mts. (see **Middle West,** under **middle)** or those beyond the Mississippi.—*adj.* situated towards, or (of wind) coming from, the west : opposite the high altar of a church.—*adv.* towards the west.—*v.i.* to move towards the west. — *adv.* **west'-about,** towards the west. — *v.i.* **west'er,** to turn westward : to change into the west.—*n.* and *adj.* **west'ering.**—*adj.* **west'erly,** lying or moving towards the west : from the west. —*adv.* towards the west : from the west.—*adj.* **west'ern,** situated in the west : belonging to the west : moving towards, or (of wind) coming from, the west.—*n.* an inhabitant of a western region or country : a film or novel whose scene is the western United States, esp. the former Wild West.—*n.* **west'erner,** a person belonging to the west.—*v.t.* and *v.i.* **west'ernise,** to make, or become, like the people of Europe and America in customs, or like their institutions, practices, ideas.—*ns.* **west'ernis-ation** ; **west'ernism,** an idiom or other characteristic of a western people.—*adj.* **west'ernmost,** furthest to the west.—*n.* **west'ing,** space or distance westward : departure westward : direction or course towards the west.—*adjs.* **west'lin,** (*Scot.*) western ; **west'most,** most westerly.—*adj.* and *adv.* **west'ward,** towards the west.—*advs.* **west'-wardly, west'wards,** towards the west.—**go west,** to go to America : to go to the western states or western frontier : to die (with reference to the setting sun, the Islands of the Blest, or Tyburn), or to be destroyed or completely dissipated ; **the West,** Europe or Europe and America ; **West End,** the fashionable quarter in the west of London : a similar district in other large towns ; **West Saxon,** a southern dialect of Old English, the chief literary dialect before the Norman Conquest ; **Western Church,** the Latin Church, as distinguished from the Eastern or Greek Church ; **Western Empire,** the western division of the later Roman Empire ; **westward ho !** to the west ! an old cry of London watermen plying westwards ; **Wild West,** the western United States in the days

Neutral vowels in unaccented syllables : *el'ə-mənt, in'fənt, ran'dəm*

of the first settlers, chiefly cattlemen and gold-miners, before the establishment of law and order. [O.E.; a common Gmc. word; cf. L. *vesper*.]

Westminster, *west'min-stər, n.* used for Parliament —from the London borough where the Houses of Parliament are situated: Westminster Hall, court of justice: Westminster School, or a past or present pupil of it.

Westphalian, *west-fā'li-ən, adj.* pertaining to Westphalia, a duchy, a kingdom, a province of Prussia and, since 1946, part of the German land of Nordrhein-Westfalen.—*n.* a native of Westphalia.

wet, *wet, adj.* containing, soaked with, covered with, water or other liquid: rainy: bringing or foreboding moisture: tearful: grown in damp soil: using liquid: (*slang*) given to drinking, or tipsy: allowing the sale of intoxicating liquors: (*slang*) ineffectual, or crazy.—*n.* water, moisture, wetness: the rain: act of wetting: a dram, a debauch.—*v.t.* to make wet: to soak with water: (*dial.*) to make (tea) by pouring water on the leaves: (*slang*) to celebrate by drinking:—*pr.p.* **wet'ting**; *pa.t.* and *pa.p.* **wet**, or **wet'ted**.— *ns.* **wet'-dock**, a dock maintaining a level nearly uniform with that of high water; **wet'ness**; **wet'-nurse**, a nurse who suckles a child for its mother. —*adj.* **wet'-shod**, having shoes or feet wet.—*adj.* **wett'ish**, somewhat wet.—**wet assay**, the use of the processes of solution, flotation, or other liquid for the determination of a given constituent in ores, metallurgical residues, and alloys; **wet blanket** (see **blanket**); **wet bob**, (*slang*) a school-boy at Eton who goes in for rowing; **wet bulb thermometer**, a psychrometer; **wet meter**, a gas-meter in which the gas to be measured passes through water; **wet out**, to wet thoroughly: to cleanse by so doing, as raw material in textile manufacture; **wet plate**, (*phot.*) a plate coated with collodion and sensitised with a salt of silver; **wetting**, or **wetting out**, **agent**, a substance that promotes wetting, e.g. a substance, such as an acid, oil, or hydrocarbon, added to a heterogeneous mixture to facilitate the absorption or adhesion between the constituents. [O.E. *wǣt* (noun and adj.), *wǣtan* (verb); the short vowel is from the M.E. pa.t. and pa.p. of the verb.]

wether, *wedh'ər, n.* a castrated ram. [O.E.; cf. Ger. *widder*.]

wex(e). Obs. form of **wax**.

wey, *wā, n.* a measure or weight for dry-goods differing with different articles, as 40 bushels of salt or corn, &c. [Variant of **weigh**.]

weyard, weyward. Spellings of **weird** in *Macbeth*, older editions.

wezand. Obs. form of **weasand**.

whack, *hwak, v.t.* to strike hard and smartly: to put or take with violence: to beat decisively: to parcel out, share.—*v.i.* to strike: to settle accounts.—*n.* a blow: a share: an attempt.—*n.* **whack'er**, something big of its kind.—*adj.* **whack'ing**, very large, astounding.—*n.* a beating (*lit.* and *fig.*). [All meanings of **whack**, &c., are *coll.* or *slang*.] [Imit.]

whacky. Same as **wacky**.

whaisle, whaizle, *hwā'zl, v.i.* (*Scot.*) to wheeze. [A form of **wheezle**; see **wheeze**.]

whale, *hwāl, n.* any of an order of cetaceous mammals, including the *toothed* whales, such as the sperm whale and the dolphins, and the *whalebone* whales, such as the right whales and the rorquals, in which the teeth are only embryonic: (*slang*) a person with a large appetite, *lit.* and *fig.*: (*slang*) something very large of its kind: **Whale**, the constellation Cetus.—*v.i.* to catch whales.—*ns.* **whale'-back**, a turtle-back: a kind of steamboat used on the Great Lakes, to carry grain, &c., having rounded upper deck, &c.: a mound shaped like the back of a whale; **whale'-boat**, a long, narrow boat sharp at both ends once used in the pursuit of whales: a similar boat carried on a large vessel as a life-boat; **whale'bone**, a light flexible substance consisting of the baleen plates of whales: an article made of this.—*adj.* made of whalebone. —*ns.* **whale'-calf**, a young whale—also **calf whale**; **whale**; **whale'-fisher**; **whale'-fishery**; **whale'-**

fishing; **whale'-head**, the shoebill; **whale'-line**, strong rope used for harpoon-lines in the whale-fishery; **whale'-louse**, a genus (Cyamus) of amphipod Crustacea parasitic on the skin of cetaceans; **whale'-man**, a person or a ship employed in whale-fishing; **whale'-oil**, oil obtained from the blubber of a whale; **whale'-shark**, a harmless shark of tropical seas; **whāl'er**, a whaleman: (*slang*) something very large of its kind; **whāl'ery**, whaling.—*adj.* **whāl'ing**, connected with whale-catching: (also used as *adv.*) very large or impressive.—*n.* the business of catching whales.—*ns.* **whāl'ing-gun**, a contrivance for killing whales by means of a projectile; **whāl'ing-master**, the captain of a whaler; **whāl'ing-port**, a port where whalers are registered. —**bull, cow, whale**, an adult male, female, whale; **whale's bone**, (*obs.*) ivory, as from the walrus; **whales', whale'(s), food**, small animals eaten by whales, esp. the Clio genus. [O.E. *hwæl*; cf. O.N. *hvalr*, Ger. *walfisch*.]

whale, *hwāl, v.t.* (*slang*) to thrash: to strike violently. —*n.* **whal'ing**, a thrashing. [Perh. **wale** (1); perh. from *whale*bone whip.]

whally, *hwawl'i, adj.* (*Spens.*) wall-eyed: showing much white. [From **wall-eye**.]

whample, *hwawm'pl, hwâm'pl, n.* (*Scot.*) a blow: a sudden blow.

whang, *whang, n.* a leather thong: a thick slice.— *v.t.* to flog: to throw, push, pull, violently: to cut in great slices. [*thwang*, obs. form of **thong**.]

whang, *hwang, n.* a resounding noise: a blow.— *v.i.* to make the sound of a blow, explosion, &c.— Also used as *adv.* and *interj.* [Imit.]

whangam, *hwang'gam, n.* (*Goldsmith*) an imaginary animal.

whangee, *hwang-ē', n.* any of several grasses of a genus (Phyllostachys) allied to the bamboos, found in China and Japan: a cane made from the stem of one. [Prob. Chin. *huang*, yellow, *li*, bamboo.]

whap. Same as **whop**.

whare, *hwor'i, n.* (*New Zealand*) a house. [Maori.]

wharf, *hwawrf, n.* a landing-stage, built esp. along the shore, for loading or unloading vessels: (*Shak.*) the bank of a river (*pl.* **wharfs, wharves**).—*v.t.* (*obs.*) to strengthen or secure by means of a wharf: to place on, or bring to, a wharf.—*ns.* **wharf'age**, the dues paid for using a wharf: accommodation at a wharf; **wharf'ing**, material for making a wharf: wharfs; **wharfinger** (*hwawrf'in-jər*), one who has the care of, or owns, a wharf; **wharf'-rat**, the common brown rat: a fellow who loafs continually about a wharf. [Late O.E. *hwearf*, bank, shore: allied to *hweorfan*, to turn.]

what, *whot, interrog. pron.* neuter of **who**: used to form a question regarding identity, selection from an indefinite number, nature, value, &c.—also used elliptically (as for *what did you say, do you think? what is it?*): (*obs.*) who.—Also *interrog. adj.* —*rel. pron.* and *adj.* that which: such ...as: (*dial.*) which: any (thing) whatever: (*Shak.*) whoever.— *indef. pron.* (or *n.*) something: (*Spens.*) a portion, bit: (Spens., *F.Q.*, VI. ix. 7, 4) fare (in phrase **such homely what**).—*adv.* (*obs.*) why? (*obs.*) in what way, how? to what degree?—*conj.* (*dial.*) as much as: that (as in **but what**, that . . . not). —*interj.* used in summoning, calling attention, expressing surprise, disapprobation, or protest, &c. —*ns.* **what'abouts**, the things one is occupied about; **what'-d'ye-call(-it, -'em**, &c.), a word substituted for the name of a thing (or person) in forgetfulness or contempt.—*adj.* **what'en**, **whatt'en**, (*dial.*; from *whatkin*, what kind) what: what kind of.—*pron.* **whatev'er, whate'er**, anything which: no matter what: (*coll.*) what?—*adj.* any or all that, no matter what.—*adjs.* **what'-like**, (*dial.*) of what kind, character, or appearance; **what'na** (from *whatkin a*), same as **whaten**.— *ns.* **what'ness**, what a thing is: essence: quiddity; **what'not** (see separate article).—*adj.* **what'so**, (*arch.*) of whatever kind.—*pron.* (*arch.*) whatever: (*obs.*) whoever: whosoever.—*adjs.* **whatsoev'er, whatsoe'er**, whatever; **whatsom'ev'er**, (*dial.*) whatsoever.—**know what it is**, to know what is involved in an action or experience: to have

fāte, fär, ȧsk; mē, hər (her); mīne; mōte; mūte; mōōn; dhen (then)

experienced, suffered, it; **what an if,** (*Shak.*) what if, or though; **what else,** could anything else be the case? **what for . . .** (*dial.*; in standard English **what . . . for**), for what reason, or intended for what purpose: (*slang*) punishment, esp. a whipping; **what for a,** (*obs.*) what kind of; **what ho,** a loud hail, summons; **what if,** what would it matter if? what would happen if? **what not,** elliptical for ' what may I not say? ' implying the presence or existence of many other things; **what of,** what comes of, follows from? what do you think of? **what 's-his-(its-, her-) name,** (*coll.*) that person, or thing, indicated or understood; **what 's what,** the true position of affairs: the proper, conventional, or profitable way to behave or proceed; **what though,** what matters it though: notwithstanding the fact that; **what time,** at the very time when; **what with,** by reason of. [O.E. *hwæt*, neut. of *hwá*, who; Ger. *was*, L. *quod*.]

Whatman paper, *hwot'mən pā'pər*, handmade paper used for drawings, engravings, &c. [From name of orig. maker.]

whatnot, *hwot'not, n.* a light piece of furniture with shelves for bric-à-brac, &c.: anything, no matter what: a nondescript article. [**what, not.**]

whaup, *hwawp, n.* (*Scot.*) a curlew—sometimes great whaup as opp. to little whaup, the whimbrel. [Primarily imit.; history uncertain.]

whaur, *hwawr,* a Scots form of **where.**

wheal. A misspelling of **weal** (2).

wheal, *hwēl, n.* a Cornish name for a mine.

whear(e). Obs. spelling of **where.**

wheat, *hwēt, n.* any cereal grass of the genus Triticum, or its grain, furnishing a white flour for bread—known as *bearded,* or *beardless* or *bald,* according to the presence or the absence of the awns or beard; as *white, red,* or *amber,* according to colour; and as *winter* or *spring* (also *summer*) according to whether it is sown in autumn or spring.—*ns.* **wheat'-berry, wheat'-corn,** the grain of wheat; **wheat'-bird,** the chaffinch; **wheat'-ear,** an ear of wheat; **wheat'-eel** (also **wheat'-worm**), a small nematode worm that makes its way up wheat stems to the ears: the disease it causes —also *ear-cockle.*—*adj.* **wheat'en,** made of wheat: whole-meal: wheat-coloured.—*ns.* **wheat'-field; wheat'-fly,** the name of several flies that destroy wheat—e.g. the Hessian fly; **wheat'-midge,** a dipterous insect that lays its eggs in the flowers of wheat-heads, and whose reddish larvae devour the kernels; **wheat'-mildew,** either of two fungus diseases of wheat; **wheat'-moth,** any of several small moths whose larvae devour stored wheat.— **wheat-ear stitch,** a fancy stitch in embroidery. [O.E. *hwǽte;* Ger. *weizen;* allied to **white;** named from its colour.]

wheatear, *hwēt'ēr, n.* a bird akin to the chats, a common summer visitant of Britain. [Prob. corr. of **white arse.**]

Wheatstone('s) bridge, *hwēt'stən(z) brij,* an apparatus for measuring electrical resistance, much used, but not invented, by Sir Charles *Wheatstone* (1802-1875).

wheedle, *hwēd'l, v.t.* and *v.i.* to entice by soft words, flatter, cajole: to obtain by coaxing (with *out of*): to cheat by cajolery (with *out of*).—*n.* a piece of wheedling: (*obs.*) a coaxing person.—*n.* **wheed'ler.**—*adj.* **wheed'lesome,** coaxing.—*n.* **wheed'ling.** [Perh. from O.E. *wǽdlian,* (orig.) to be in want, to beg.]

wheel, *hwēl, n.* a circular frame turning on an axle: an old instrument of torture: a steering-wheel: a potter's wheel: a spinning-wheel: a rotating firework: (*coll.*) a bicycle or tricycle: (*Shak.*) the wheel of a dog-turned spit: the wheel attributed to Fortune personified, the emblem of mutability: hence, the course of events: (*obs.*) a celestial sphere: a disk: a circular design: a circular motion: (in *pl.*) the parts of a machine, esp. fig.: one or more short lines following a bob at the end of a stanza: a refrain: (*slang*) a dollar.—*v.t.* to cause to turn or revolve, esp. round an axis or pivot, as a body of troops: to cause to move in a circular course: (*Milt.*) to encircle: (*rare*) to make

wheel-shaped: to put a wheel or wheels on: to form, or treat, on the wheel: to convey on wheels: to propel on wheels.—*v.i.* to turn round or on an axis: to change direction: to move in a circle: to reel, to be giddy: to roll forward: (*Shak.*) to wander, roam: to travel in a wheeled vehicle: (*coll.*) to ride a bicycle or tricycle: to be provided with wheels on which to be propelled.—*ns.* **wheel'-animal, -animalcule,** a rotifer; **wheel'barrow,** a barrow with one wheel in front and two handles and legs behind: (loosely) any other hand-cart; **wheel'-carriage,** any kind of carriage moved on wheels; **wheel'-chair,** a chair moving on wheels, esp. an invalid's chair.—*adj.* **wheel'-cut,** (of glass) cut, or ground and polished, on a wheel.— *n.* **wheel'-cutter,** a machine for cutting teeth on wheels.—*adj.* **wheeled,** having wheels: moving on wheels: (*rare*) formed into a wheel.—*ns.* **wheel'er,** one who wheels: a cyclist: (*dial.*) a maker of wheels: in composition, that which wheels, or has such-and-such a kind of or so-many wheels: a wheel-horse; **wheel'-horse,** one of the horses next the wheels in a team; **wheel'-house,** a shelter in which a ship's steering-wheel is placed: a paddle-box; **wheel'ing,** the act of moving or conveying on wheels: a turning or circular movement: a rather coarse woollen yarn; **wheel'-lock,** formerly, a lock for firing a gun by means of a small steel wheel; **wheel'man,** a steersman: a cyclist; **wheel'-plough,** a plough running on wheels, or the depth of whose furrow is regulated by a wheel; **wheel'-race,** the part of a race in which the water-wheel is fixed; **wheel'-spin,** rotation of the wheels without forward or backward movement of the vehicle; **wheel'-window,** a circular window with radiating tracery; **wheel'-work,** a combination of wheels and their connexion in machinery; **wheel'wright,** a wright who makes wheels and wheel-carriages.—*adj.* **wheel'y,** like a wheel.—**break a butterfly** (**fly,** &c.) **on the wheel,** to inflict a punishment out of all proportion to the offence: to employ great exertions for insignificant ends; **go on wheels,** (*fig.*) to move swiftly, smoothly, and hence pleasantly; **potter's wheel,** a horizontal revolving disk on which clay vessels are shaped; **put a spoke in one's wheel, one's shoulder to the wheel** (see **spoke, shoulder**); **wheel and axle,** one of the mechanical powers, in its primitive form a cylindrical axle, on which a wheel, concentric with the axle, is firmly fastened, the power being applied to the wheel, and the weight attached to the axis; **wheel of fortune,** Fortune's wheel: a gambling device; **wheel of life** (see **zoetrope**); **wheels within wheels,** a situation in which a complication of influences are at work. [O.E. *hwéol;* O.N. *hjól.*]

wheen, *hwēn, n.* (*Scot.*) a few.—*adj.* (*obs.*) few.— **a wheen,** a few: a good many: (used adverbially) a little. [O.E. *hwǽne—hwón,* adv., a little.]

wheeple, *hwē'pl, v.i.* (*Scot.*) to make a long drawn-out cry such as that of the curlew: to whistle feebly.—Also *v.t.* and *n.* [Imit.]

Wheeson, (*Shak.,* 2 Hen. IV, II. i. 99) Whitsun.

wheeze, *hwēz, v.i.* to breathe with a hissing sound: to breathe audibly or with difficulty.—*v.t.* to utter with such a sound.—*n.* act, or sound, of wheezing: (*theatrical slang*) a gag: (*slang*) a catch-phrase: (*slang*) a standard joke: (*coll.*) a cunning plan.— *n.* **wheez'ing.**—*adv.* **wheez'ily.**—*v.i.* **wheez'le,** (*Scot.*) to make wheezy sounds.—*adj.* **wheez'y.** [Prob. O.N. *hvæsa,* to hiss.]

whelk, *wilk, welk, hwelk, n.* a popular name for a number of marine gasteropods, esp. applied to species of the genus Buccinum common on the coasts of northern seas.—*adjs.* **whelked,** ridged like a whelp; **whelk'y,** knobby, rounded: (Spens., *Virg. Gnat,* 105) formed in a shell. [Wrong form of *welk*—O.E. *wiloc, weoluc;* origin obscure.]

whelk, *hwelk, n.* a pimple: (by confusion with **wale** (1)) the mark of a stripe on the body, a wrinkle, an inequality or protuberance. [Late O.E. (W.S.) *hwylca—hwelian,* to suppurate.]

whelk'd. See **welkt.**

whelm, *hwelm, v.t.* (now *dial.*) to turn, as a hollow vessel, upside down, esp. so as to cover something else: to cover completely, (*obs.*) in this way, now with water, &c.: to overturn, overthrow: to plunge deep: to submerge: to overpower: to overburden: to ruin, destroy: to pass over in such a way as to submerge it. [M.E. *whelmen*, to turn over.]

whelp, *hwelp*, *n.* the young of the dog kind and of lions, &c.—a puppy, a cub, &c.: a young man (in contempt): a ridge running longitudinally on the barrel or drum of a capstan or windlass to control the cable: a sprocket on a wheel.—*v.i.* and *v.t.* to bring forth (young). [O.E. *hwelp*: O.N. *hvelpr*.]

whemmle, *hwem'l*, **whomble**, **whummle**, *hwum'l*, *n.* (*dial.*) an overthrow, overturn: confusion.—*v.t.* to overturn: to turn upside down: to throw into a state of disorder or agitation: to cover as with an inverted dish.—*v.i.* to capsize. [By metathesis from **whelm**.]

when, *hwen*, *adv.* (*interrog.* and *rel.*) and *conj.* at what time? at which time: at or after the time that: upon or after which: while: although: (or *rel. pron.*) at which.—*n.* the time: which time.— *interj.* (*Shak.*) an exclamation of impatience, like *what!*—*conj.* **when'as'**, (*arch.*) when: in as much as: whereas.—*adv.* and *conj.* **whence** (also from **whence**), from what place: from which things: wherefore.—*adv.* **whenceforth'**, (*Spens.*) whence. —*conjs.* **whencesoev'er**, **whencev'er**, from what place, cause, or source soever; **whenev'er, when-e'er'**, at every time when: (*Scot.*) as soon as; **whensoev'er**, at what time soever: whenever.— **say when**, tell me when to stop; **seldom when**, (*Shak.*) seldom that. [O.E. *hwænne, hwonne* (Ger. *wann, wenn*); from the stem of interrog. pron. *hwā, wen.*]

whe'r. See **whether**.

where, *hwār*, *adv.* (*interrog.* and *rel.*) and *conj.* at or to which place: at what place? to what place? (*lit.* and *fig.*) from what source: (*arch.*) to a, or the, place in which: in what circumstances or condition: (*fig.*) at what point: whereas: wherever: (or *rel. pron.*) in, at, or to which.—*n.* the or a place: which place. — *adv.* and *conj.* **whereabout'**, about which, about where: near what? (*Shak.*) on what errand (*n.* what one is about)—also **where'- abouts**.—*n.* **where'abouts**, place, situation, esp. approximate.—*advs.* and *conjs.* **whereagainst'**, against which; **whereas**, when in fact: but on the contrary: taking into consideration, in view of, the fact that: (*obs.*) where.—*advs.* and *conjs.* **whereat'**, at which: at what? **whereby'**, by which; **wherefor'**, for which; **where'fore** (*-fər*), for which, or what, reason: why?—*n.* the cause.— *advs.* and *conjs.* **wherefrom'**, whence; **wherein'**, in which place or respect: in what? **wherein- soev'er**, in whatever place or respect; **wherein'to** (or *-in-tōō'*), into which: into what?—*n.* **where'- ness**, state of having place or position: position, situation.—*advs.* and *conjs.* **whereof'**, of which: (*Shak.*) wherewith: of what? **whereon'**, on which: on what? **whereout'**, out of which; **where'so, wheresoe'er', wheresoev'er**, in or to what place soever: (*arch.*) whencesoever; **wherethrough'**, through which: through the agency of which; **whereto'**, to which: to what? **whereun'der**, under which; **whereuntil'**,(*Shak.*) to what: whereunto; **whereun'to** (or *-un-tōō'*, *arch.*), whereto: for what purpose? **whereupon'**, upon or in consequence of which: (*Shak.*) on what grounds; **where'er', wherev'er**, at whatever place; **wherewith', wherewithal'**, with which? with what.—*n.* (usu. **wherewithal'**) the means.— from where, whence: from the, or a, place where; see, **look**, &c., **where**, behold; **where away?** (*naut.*) a query as to the direction of an object sighted by the lookout: (*dial.*) where are you going? **where it is**, (*coll.*) the real situation, point, or explanation; **where you are**, what you are saying or getting at. [O.E. *hwār, hwár*; from stem of **who**; cf. **there**.]

wherret. See **whirret**.

wherry, *hwer'i*, *n.* a shallow, light boat, sharp at both ends for speed: a kind of barge:—*pl.* **wherr'ies**.—*n.* **wherr'yman**, a man employed in a wherry, esp. one who rows a wherry. [Ety. dub.]

whet, *hwet*, *v.t.* to sharpen by rubbing: to make keen: to excite: (*obs.*) to incite: (*obs.*; *rare*) to preen: (*pr.p.* **whett'ing**; *pa.t.* and *pa.p.* **whett'ed**). —*n.* act of sharpening: sharpness: (*dial.*) a time, occasion: an incitement or stimulus: something that sharpens the appetite: an appetiser.—*ns.* **whet'-slate**, novaculite; **whet'stone**, a stone for sharpening edged instruments: a stimulant; **whett'er**.—**whet on, or forward,**"(*Shak.*) to urge on. [O.E. *hwettan*, cog. with *hwæt*, sharp; Ger. *wetzen.*]

whether, *hwedh'ər* (*Shak.*, often scanned as one syllable; also spelt **whe'r**), *interrog.* and *rel. pron.* (*arch.*) which (of two).—*conj.* introducing the first of two alternative words, phrases, or clauses, the second being introduced by *or*, or (in the case of clauses) sometimes by *or whether*: introducing a single dependent question.—**whether or no** (sometimes **not**), whether so or not so: in any case, in any event. [O.E. *hwæther*, from stem of *hwā*, who, with the old comp. suff. *-ther*; cog. with Goth. *hwathar*, Ger. *weder*; also with L. *uter*, Ionic Gr. *koteros*, Sans. *katara.*]

whew, *hweugh*, *hū, hwū, interj.* expressing wonder or dismay.—*n.* a whistling sound, esp. one noting astonishment.—*v.i.* to utter such a sound. [Imit.]

whew, *hwū, v.i.* (*dial.*) to bustle about. [Perh. **whew** (1).]

whewellite, *hū'əl-īt*, *n.* calcium oxalate. [Named after William *Whewell* (1794-1866).]

whey, *hwā*, *n.* the watery part of milk, separated from the curd, esp. in making cheese.—*adj.* of or containing whey: like whey: whey-coloured.— *adjs.* **whey'ey**, **whey'ish**, of whey: like whey.— *n.* **whey'-face**, a pale or white face.—*adj.* **whey'- faced**, pale, esp. with terror.—*ns.* **whey'ishness**; **whey'-tub**. [O.E. *hwǣg*; L.G. *wey.*]

which, *hwich, interrog. pron.* what one of a number? (*obs.*) what? (*obs.*) of what sort or kind?—Also used adjectively.—*rel. pron.* (*obs.*) who, whom: now used chiefly of things, ideas, &c., not persons: that: often having as antecedent a circumstance or statement, being equivalent to ' and that ' or ' but that.'—*prons.* and *adjs.* **whichev'er, which- soev'er**, every one which: any one, no matter which.—**the which**, (*obs.*) which; (*obs.*) **which ... he**, who, **which ... his**, whose; **which is which?** which is the one, which is the other? [O.E. *hwilc, hwelc*, from the stem of *hwā*, who, and *lic* (from a word meaning body, form), like; Goth. *hweileiks*, Ger. *welch, welcher*; L. *qualis*; cf. **such** and **each**.]

whicker, *hwik'ər, v.i.* (all meanings *dial.*) to neigh: to bleat: to snigger, titter. [Imit.]

whid, *hwid, n.* (*Scot.*) a rapid noiseless movement.— *v.i.* to move quickly, to whisk.—*v.i.* **whidd'er**, to whiz. [Perh. conn. with O.N. *hvitha*, a squall, O.E. *hvitha*, a breeze.]

whid, *hwid, n.* (*Scot.*) a lie: (*obs. slang*) a word: (*dial.*) a quarrel.—*v.i.* to lie.—**cut boon whids**, to speak good words. [Poss. O.E. *cwide*, a word— *cwethan*, to say.]

whidah-bird. See **widow-bird**.

whiff, *hwif, n.* a sudden puff of air or smoke from the mouth: a slight inhalation: a puff of smell: a slight blast: (*fig.*) a small amount, esp. of something causing or associated with a transient sensation: a cigarette: (*coll.*) a jiffy: a light kind of outrigger boat: (*dial.*) a glimpse.—*v.t.* to throw out in whiffs: to puff: to drive or convey by, or as if by, a whiff: to inhale, smell.—*v.i.* to go out or off in a whiff: to move with, or as with, a puff of air: to blow slightly: to smell.—*ns.* **whiff'er**; **whiff'et**, a whipper-snapper.—*v.i.* **whiff'le**, to blow in puffs: to move as if blown by a puff: to talk idly: to make a slight whistling sound: to veer: to vacillate: to prevaricate.—Also *v.t.*—*n.* **whiff'ler**, one who whiffles: a swaggerer: a contemptible person.—*n.* **whiff'lery**, levity: trifling. —*n.* and *adj.* **whiff'ling**.—*adj.* **whiff'y**.—*n.* **whift**, (*dial.*) a breath, snatch. [Prob. partly M.E. *weffe*; imit.]

whiff, *hwif, n.* a fish akin to the turbot. [Ety. unknown.]

whiff, *hwif, v.i.* to fish with a hand-line towed

behind a boat.— *n.* **whiff′ing.** [Perh. **whiff** (1).]

whiffler, *hwif′lər, n.* (*hist.*) an official who clears the way for a procession. [Perh. *wifel,* obs. javelin, battle-axe; affected by **whiff** (1) and **whiffle.**]

whiffletree, *hwif′l-trē, n.* Same as **whippletree.**

Whig, *hwig, n.* a name applied to members of one of the great English political parties—applied in the late 17th century to those upholding popular rights and opposed to the King; after 1830 almost superseded by ' Liberal ': a Scottish Presbyterian, first so called in the middle of the 17th century: (*U.S.*) one of those who in the colonial period were opposed to British rule: (*U.S.*) one of the party formed from the survivors of the old National Republican party and other elements, first so called in 1834—it fell to pieces in the 1850's.—*adj.* of, pertaining to, or composed of, Whigs—also **Whigg′ish.**—*n.* **Whigg′archy,** government by Whigs. — *adv.* **Whigg′ishly.** — *ns.* **Whigg′ism, Whigg′ery, Whigg′ishness, Whig′ship,** Whig principles. [Prob. short for **whiggamore.**]

whig, *hwig, v.i.* (*Scot.*) to jog along.—*v.t.* to urge forward. [Origin uncertain.]

whig, *hwig, n.* (*dial.*) sour milk: whey: buttermilk.—*v.t.* and *v.i.* to curdle. [Prob. allied to **whey.**]

whiggamore, *hwig′ə-mōr, n.* one of the 7000 Western Covenanters who marched on Edinburgh in 1648, sealing the doom of Charles I.: a Scottish Presbyterian, a Whig. [Origin disputed; most prob. *whig,* to urge forward, *mere,* mare.]

whigmaleerie, whigmaleery, *hwig-mə-lē′ri, n.* (*Scot.*) a trinket, knick-knack: a fantastic ornamentation: a whim. [Origin uncertain.]

while, *hwil, n.* a space of time: time and trouble spent.—*conj.* (also **whilst**) during the time that: at the same time that: as long as: although: notwithstanding the admitted fact that: (*obs.*; *North. dial.*) until.—*prep.* (*Shak.*; *North. dial.*) until.—*v.t.* to pass without irksomeness (with *away*).—*adv.* **while-ere′,** (*arch.*) a little while ago, formerly.— *conj.* **whiles,** (*B.*) while, at the same time that: (*Shak.*) until.—*adv.* (*Scot.*) at times (orig. gen. of O.E. *hwil*).—*adv.* **whi′lom,** formerly, once.—*adj.* former (orig. dat. pl. of O.E. *hwil,* time).—(**every**) **once in a while,** now and then; **the while,** (*Shak.*) at the present time, in the meantime; **the whilst,** (*obs.*) while: in the meantime. [O.E. *hwil*; Goth. *hweila,* Ger. *weile.*]

whilk, *hwilk, pron.* obs. and dial. form of **which.**

whilly, *hwil′i,* **whillywha(w),** *hwil′i-hwaw, -hwä, v.t.* to wheedle, cajole.—*n.* cajolery: a coaxing, insinuating, person.—*adj.* smooth-tongued, wheedling. [Origin obscure.]

whilom. See **while.**

whim, *hwim, n.* (*obs.*) a fantastic creation of brain or hand: (*obs.*) a whimsical person: a caprice: a fancy: a vertical rope drum revolved by a horse, used for hoisting from shallow shafts.—*v.i.* (*obs.*) of the head, to turn round, swim: (*obs.*) to be whimsical.—*v.t.* to desire as a caprice: (*obs.*) to turn aside by a whim.—*adjs.* **whimm′y,** full of whims; **whim′sical** (*-zi-*) full of whim: odd, fantastical: delicately fanciful: (loosely) expressing gently humorous tolerance. — *ns.* **whimsical′ity, whim′sicalness.** — *adv.* **whim′sically.** — *n.* **whim′sy, whim′sey,** a whim, freak: whimsical behaviour: delicate, or affectedly delicate, fantasy. —*adj.* full of whims, changeable.—*adv.* **whim′sily.** —*ns.* **whim′siness;** **whim′-wham,** a ridiculous notion: an odd device: a fanciful trifle. [**whim-wham** is recorded earlier than **whim**; cf. O.N. *hvima,* to have the eyes wandering.]

whimbrel, *hwim′brəl, n.* a species of small curlew.— Also **wim′brel.** [Prob. imit. of bird's cry; dim. suff. *-rel.*]

whimper, *hwim′pər, v.i.* to cry feebly, brokenly, and querulously or whiningly: to make a plaintive sound.—*v.t.* to express or utter in a whimper.— *n.* a peevish cry.—*n.* **whim′perer.**—*n.* and *adj.* **whim′pering.**—*adv.* **whim′peringly** [Imit.: cf. Ger. *wimmern.*]

whimple, *hwim′pl.* Same as **wimple.**

whin, *hwin, n.* gorse, furze.—*n.* **whin′chat,** a bird

that frequents whins, very similar in appearance, esp. when it assumes its duller autumn plumage, to the stonechat, to which it is allied. — *adj.* **whinn′y,** abounding in whins. [Prob. Scand.]

whin. See **whinstone.**

whine, *hwīn, v.i.* to utter a plaintive cry: to complain in an unmanly way.—*v.t.* to express or utter in a whine: to cause to make a whining noise.— *n.* a plaintive cry: an affected nasal tone of utterance.—*ns.* **whi′ner; whi′niness; whi′ning.**— *adv.* **whi′ningly.**—*adj.* **whi′ny.** [O.E. *hwīnan,* to whine; O.N. *hvina,* to whistle through the air.]

whinge, *hwēnj, hwinj, v.i.* (*Scot.*) to whine: to cry fretfully: to complain peevishly.—Also **wheenge.** [O.E. *hwinsian,* from root of *hwinan*; see **whine.**]

whinger, *hwing′ər, n.* a dirk.—Also **whin′iard** and **whin′yard.** [Origin obscure.]

whinid′st, (Shak., *T. and C.,* II. i. 15) folio reading for which Johnson conjectured *vinewd′st.*

whinny, *hwin′i, v.i.* to neigh (*pr.p.* **whinn′ying;** *pa.t.* and *pa.p.* **whinn′ied**).—*n.* a neigh. [Imit.]

whinstone, *hwin′stŏn, -stən, n.* any hard and compact kind of rock, usually basalt or the like: a piece of this.—Also **whin.**—**Whin Sill,** a sheet of intrusive quartz-dolerite or quartz-basalt exposed almost continuously for nearly 200 miles from the Farne Islands to Middleton-in-Teesdale. [*whin* (origin obscure), and **stone.**]

whinyard. See **whinger.**

whip, *hwip, n.* a lash with a handle for punishing or driving: a stroke administered as by a whip: a whipping motion: a driver, coachman: one who enforces the attendance of a political party: a call made on members of parliament to be in their places against an important division (called, according to number of times message is underlined as indication of urgency, **three-line whip,** &c.; **five-line whip** is no longer used): a whipper-in, the person who manages the hounds: a simple form of hoisting apparatus, a small tackle consisting of a single rope and block: a preparation of whipped cream, eggs, &c.: a whipping or overcasting: (usu. **whip-round**) an appeal for contributions: an individual share in money collected in equal amounts: (*Scot.*) an instant: an arm carrying a sail of a windmill: a long twig or slender branch: an arrangement of cars that move with sudden jerks, used for amusement purposes.—*v.t.* to strike with a lash: to drive, or make to move, with lashes: to punish with lashes, or (loosely) by spanking: to strike in a manner suggesting a lash: to lash with sarcasm: (*coll.*) to defeat, outdo: to beat into a froth, as eggs, cream, &c.: to keep together, as a party: to fish with fly: to overlay, as one cord with another: to bind round: to sew lightly: to overcast, as a seam: to move quickly, snatch (with *up, away, out,* &c.).—*v.i.* to move nimbly: to move in the manner of a whiplash: to make a cast in fishing with fly :—*pr.p.* **whipp′ing;** *pa.t.* and *pa.p.* **whipped, whipt.**—*ns.* **whip′-and-derr′y,** a hoisting apparatus consisting of a whip and a derrick; **whip′cat,** a tailor; **whip′cord,** cord for making whips: a fabric with a bold steep warp twill, used chiefly for dresses, suitings, and coatings: a whip-like seaweed, as *Chorda filum* or *Chordaria flagelliformis.*—*adjs.* **whip′cord; whip′cordy,** like whipcord.—*v.t.* **whip′-graft,** to graft by fitting a tongue cut on the scion to a slit cut slopingly in the stock.—Also *n.*—*ns.* **whip′-grafting; whip′-hand,** the hand that holds the whip: the advantage; **whip′-handle,** the handle or stock of a whip: an advantage; **whip′jack,** a whining beggar who pretends to be a sailor; **whip′-lash,** the lash of a whip; **whipp′er,** one who or that which whips: an officer who inflicts the penalty of whipping; **whipp′er-in,** one who keeps the hounds from wandering: one who enforces the discipline of a political party: (*slang*) at any moment in a race, the horse in the last place; **whipp′ersnapper,** a little or young lively insignificant person; **whipp′ing,** act of one who or that which whips: corporal punishment, esp. with the whip or lash: a defeat: a binding of twine, e.g. at the end of a rope: material for binding in this way: overcasting; **whipp′ing-boy, a**

boy formerly educated along with a prince and punished for the royal pupil's faults : one on whom falls the odium or punishment of the shortcomings of others ; **whipp′ing-cheer**, (*obs.*) flogging ; **whipp′ing-post**, a post to which offenders are tied to be whipped : the punishment itself : **whipp′ing-top**, a top kept spinning by means of a whip.—*adj.* **whipp′y**, whiplike : pliant : supple. —*n.* **whip′-saw**, a narrow saw for dividing timber lengthwise, usu. set in a frame and often worked by two persons.—*v.t.* to cut with a whip-saw: (*U.S. slang*) to have the advantage of at every point. —*ns.* **whip′-scorpion**, any arachnid of the order Pedipalpida, slightly resembling true scorpions but being without sting and having usu. a whiplike appendage at the rear of the body ; **whip′-snake**, any of various snakes resembling a whiplash, as *Masticophis flagelliformis*, the coach-whip snake, and species of *Philodryas*, &c. ; **whip′-socket**, a socket to hold the butt of a whip ; **whip′-staff**, the handle of a whip ; **whip′ster**, a term of contempt formerly with various meanings, chiefly remembered for Shak., *Oth.*, V. ii. 242, a whippersnapper ; **whip′-stitch**, a hasty composition : a tailor : (*dial.*) a kind of half-ploughing, raftering.—Also *v.t.* and *v.i.*—*n.* **whip′-stock**, the rod or handle of a whip.—*adjs.* **whip′-tail, -tailed**, having a long, slender tail.—*n.* **whip′worm**, a worm of the genus Trichocephalus, with posterior end thick and anterior long and thin, found parasitic in human intestines.—**whip and spur**, with great haste ; **whip the cat**, to practise small economies : to work by the day as a dressmaker, tailor, &c., going from house to house : to idle : to play a practical joke. [M.E. *whippen* ; cf. Du. *wippen*, to shake.]

whippet, *hwip′it*, *n.* a breed developed from a cross between a greyhound and spaniel or terrier : a racing-dog : a small speedy tank.—*n.* **whipp′eting**, training, racing, of whippets. [Partly **whip**, and partly obs. *whippet*, to move briskly.]

whippletree, *hwip′l-trē*, *n.* the cross-piece of a carriage, plough, &c., to which the traces of a harnessed animal are fixed. [From **whip**.]

whip-poor-will, *hwip′-pōōr-wil′*, or *-pər-*, *n.* a species of goatsucker, a native of N. America. [Imitative of its call.]

whipstall, *hwip′stawl*, *n.* (*aero.*) a stall as the result of which the nose of the aircraft whips forward and down.—*v.i.* and *v.t.* to go, or put, into such a stall. [**whip, stall**.]

whir(r), *hwər*, *n.* a sound from rapid whirling or vibratory motion.—*v.i.* to whirl round with a buzzing noise : to fly, move, with such a sound.— *v.t.* (*Shak.*) to hurry away with a whizzing sound :— *pr.p.* **whirr′ing** ; *pa.t.* and *pa.p.* **whirred**.—*n.* **whirr′ing**. [Imit. ; cf. Dan. *hvirre*, to whirl.]

whirl, *hwərl*, *n.* a turning with rapidity : anything that revolves, esp. rapidly : a great or confusing degree, as of activity or emotion : commotion, agitation : a whorl.—*v.i.* to revolve rapidly : to move rapidly, esp. in an agitated manner : to turn swiftly round or aside.—*v.t.* to turn round rapidly : to carry, or move, away rapidly, as on wheels : to throw violently.—*ns.* **whirl′-about**, act of whirling about : anything that turns round rapidly ; **whirl′- (whorl′-, hurl′-) bat**, (*obs.*) translating L. *caestus* (see **cestus**, 2) ; **whirl′-blast**, a whirling blast of wind ; **whirl′-bone**, the round head of a bone turning in a socket : the knee-cap ; **whirl′er** ; **whirl′igig** (*-gig*), a toy that is spun or whirled rapidly round : a merry-go-round : anything that revolves rapidly (*lit.* and *fig.*): an ancient instrument of punishment, consisting of a pivoted wooden cage in which the prisoner was spun round : (also **whirligig beetle**) any water-beetle of the family Gyrinidae, esp. *Gyrinus natator*.—*n.* and *adj.* **whirl′ing**.—*ns.* **whirl′ing-dervish**, one of an order of Mohammedan devotees who dance or spin round, the dancing dervishes, founded in 1273 ; **whirl′ing-table**, a machine exhibiting the effects of centripetal and centrifugal forces (also **whirl′ing-machine**): a potter's wheel ; **whirl′- pool**, a circular current in a river or sea, produced by opposing tides, winds, or currents : an eddy :

(*obs.*) a huge whale-like sea monster ; **whirl′wind**, a small rotating wind-storm, which may extend upwards to a height of many hundred feet—a miniature cyclone. [M.E. *whirlen*—O.N. *hvirfla*, freq. of *hverfa*, to turn round ; Ger. *wirbeln*.]

whirret, *hwir′it*, *n.* (*obs.*) a blow.—*v.t.* to give a sharp blow to.—Also **wherret**. [Poss. imit.]

whirry, *hwər′i*, *v.i.* and *v.t.* (*Scot.*) to move rapidly. [Prob. from **whirr**.]

whirtle. See **wortle**.

whish, *hwish*, *v.i.* to move with the whizzing sound of rapid motion : to say ' whish.'—*interj.* asking for silence—hush !—Also **whisht**.—*n.* **whisht**, silence : a whisper.—*adj.* silent.—*v.i.* to keep silent.—Also (*Scot.*) **wheesht**.—**haud, hold, one's whisht**, to keep silence.

whisk, *hwisk*, *v.t.* to move quickly and lightly : to sweep rapidly : to beat up with a quick, light movement.—*v.i.* to move nimbly and rapidly.—*n.* a rapid sweeping motion : a small bunch of anything used for a brush : a small instrument for beating or whisking eggs : (*hist.*) a type of women's neckerchief or large collar worn in the later 17th century : a hairlike appendage, as on an insect : a tuft : a panicle esp. of millet : the common millet.—*ns.* **whis′ker**, he who, or that which, whisks : formerly, hair on the upper lip, now usu. hair on the side of the face, side-whiskers (esp. in *pl.*) : a long bristle on the face of a cat, &c. : (*naut.*) either of two bars extending on each side of the bowsprit ; **whiskeran′do**, a whiskered person, in allusion to Don Ferolo *Whiskerandos* in Sheridan's *Critic*. — *adjs.* **whiskeran′doed**, **whis′kered**, **whis′kery**, having whiskers ; **whis′king**, moving briskly ; **whis′ky-fris′ky**, flighty. [Scand., earliest uses Scot.]

whisk, *hwisk*, *n.* earlier name for **whist**. [Said to be from **whisk** (1), from the rapid action of sweeping the cards off the table.]

whisket, *hwis′kit*, *n.* Variant of **wisket**.

whisky (*Ir.* **whiskey**), *hwis′ki*, *n.* a spirit made by the distillation of the fermented extract from malted and unmalted cereals, potatoes, or any starch-yielding material—the best qualities made either from malted barley alone, or from a mixed grist of barley-malt and dried barley and oats.— *adj.* **whis′kified**, **whis′keyfied**, intoxicated.— *n.* **whis′ky-liver**, cirrhosis of the liver, from too much whisky. — **Whisky Insurrection**, an outbreak against the excise regulations which occurred in Western Pennsylvania in 1794 ; **whisky toddy**, toddy having whisky for its chief ingredient. [Gael. *uisgebeatha*—*uisge*, water, *beatha*, life ; cf. L. *vita*, life.]

whisky, whiskey, *hwis′ki*, *n.* a light gig. [**whisk** (1).]

whisky-john, *hwis′ki-jon*, *n.* the grey or Canada jay. —Also **whis′ky-jack**. [From Amer. Indian name of similar sound.]

whisper, *hwis′pər*, *v.i.* to speak with a low sound : to speak in a whisper : to speak covertly, spread rumours : to plot secretly : to make a sound like soft speech.—*v.t.* to utter in a low voice or under the breath, or covertly, or by way of gossip.— *n.* a low hissing voice or sound : a sound uttered with breath not voice : (*phon.*) voiceless speech with narrowed glottis : a hissing or rustling sound : cautious or timorous speaking : a secret hint : a rumour.—*n.* **whis′perer**, one who whispers : a secret informer.—*n.* and *adj.* **whis′pering**.—*n.* **whis′pering-gallery**, **-dome**, a gallery or dome so constructed that a whisper or slight sound is carried to an unusual distance.—*advs.* **whis′peringly**, in a whisper or low voice ; **whis′perously**, in a whisper.—*adj.* **whis′pery**—**whispering campaign**, an attack by means of furtively spread rumours. [O.E. *hwisprian* ; Ger. *wispern*, O.N. *hvískra* ; allied to **whistle**.]

whiss, *hwis*, *v.i.* to hiss, whistle, wheeze, &c. [Imit.]

whist, *hwist*, *interj.* hush : silence : be still.—*adj.* (*arch.*) hushed, silent : attentive.—*v.i.* to become silent.—*v.t.* (*Spens.*) to hush or silence. [Imit.]

whist, *hwist*, *n.* a card game played with the whole pack, by two against two.—*ns.* **whist′-drive** (see **drive**) ; **whist′-player**.—**dummy whist**, whist played with a dummy hand; **long whist,** a game of ten points; **short whist,** a game of five points. [**whisk** (2); said to be assimilated to **whist** (1), because of the silence during play.]

whistle, *hwis'l, v.i.* to make a shrill sound by forcing the breath through the contracted lips or the teeth: to make such a sound in derision, &c.: of a bird, to pipe, sing: to make a like sound with an instrument: to sound shrill: to make a call or signal by whistling: to whizz through the air: to become informer: (*Scott*) to give a landlord information that leads to raising rent.—*v.t.* to perform or utter by whistling: to call or bring by a whistle: to send with a whistling sound.—*n.* an act of whistling: the sound made in whistling, or one like it: a small wind instrument giving a high-pitched sound by air impinging on a sharp edge or otherwise: an instrument sounded by escaping steam, &c., as on railway-engines: a summons.—*adj.* **whis'tle(d)-drunk,** (*obs.*) too drunk to whistle.—*ns.* **whis'tle-fish,** a rockling; **whis'tler,** one who, or that which, whistles: a large kind of marmot: a broken-winded horse; **whis'tling.**—*adv.* **whis'tlingly.**—*n.* **whis'tling-shop,** (*slang*) a place, as a room in a prison, where liquor was sold without a licence.—**boatswain's whistle** (also **pipe, call**), a whistle of special shape used by a boatswain or boatswain's-mate to summon sailors to various duties; **go whistle,** (*Shak.*) to go to the deuce; **pay for one's whistle,** to pay highly for one's caprice (from Benjamin Franklin's story of a whistle he, as a boy, bought at an exorbitant price); **penny whistle,** or **tin whistle** (see **flageolet**); **pigs and whistles** (see **pig** (2)); **wet one's whistle,** (*coll.*) to take a drink of liquor; **whistle down the wind,** (from the practice of casting a hawk off down the wind when turning it loose) to abandon: to talk to no purpose; **whistle for,** to summon by whistling: (*coll.*) to ask for in vain; **whistle for a wind,** a superstitious practice of old sailors during a calm; **whistle off, whistle away,** (terms in hawking) to send off or dismiss by, or as if by, a whistle: to turn loose: to abandon; **worth the whistle,** worth the trouble of calling for. [O.E. *hwistlian.*]

whit, *hwit, n.* the smallest particle imaginable: a bit. [By-form of **wight,** a creature, a thing.]

white, *hwit, adj.* of the colour of pure snow: snowy: of the light complexion characteristic of Europeans: that absorbs the minimum and reflects the maximum of light rays: pale, pallid: bloodless: colourless: pure: unblemished: innocent: purified from sin: bright: burnished, as of steel: unburnished, of silver: light-coloured or golden, as wine: clothed in white: pertaining to the Carmelite monks: (*politics*) in continental Europe, anti-revolutionary: auspicious, favourable: (*U.S.*) reliable, honest: without bloodshed, as a war.—*n.* the colour of snow: anything white, as a white man, a white butterfly, the centre of a target, the albuminous part of an egg, a pigment: a member of a white political party.—*v.t.* to make white.—*ns.* **white'-admiral,** any of a genus of butterflies, of the same family as the red-admiral, having white bands on the wings; **white'-ale,** (*dial.*) ale brewed or mixed with ingredients, such as flour, eggs, &c., that give it a whitish colour; **white'-ant,** a termite (Isoptera); **white'-arm,** sword, bayonet or lance —a translation of Fr. *arme blanche*; **white'bait,** the fry of various species of herring, &c.; **white'-bass,** a silvery food fish of the American Great Lake region; **white'beam,** a small tree (*Sorbus,* or *Pyrus, Aria*) with leaves white and downy on the underside; **white'-bear,** the polar bear; **white'-beard,** an old man.—*adjs.* **white'-bearded; white'-bellied; white'-billed.**—*ns.* **white'-bonnet,** one employed to bid at an auction to raise prices; **white'-bottle,** bladder-campion; **White'-boy,** a member of an association of Irish peasants first formed in County Tipperary about 1761 for the purpose of redressing grievances; wearing white shirts, they committed agrarian outrages by night; **white'boyism,** the principles of the Whiteboys; **white'-brass,** an inferior alloy of copper and zinc. —*adj.* **white'-breasted.**—*n.* **white'cap,** the male redstart, or other bird with light-coloured head:

a crested wave: a member of a self-constituted vigilance committee who, under the guise of purifying the morals of the community, deal violently with persons of whom they disapprove.—*adj.* **white'-collar,** pertaining to, or designating, the class of workers, as clerks, &c., who are not engaged in manual labour.—*n.* **white'-copper,** a light-coloured alloy of copper.—*adjs.* **white'-crested, -crowned,** of birds, having the crest or crown white.—*n.pl.* **white'-crops,** grain, as barley, rye, wheat.—*ns.* **white'-damp,** carbon monoxide; **white'-elephant** (see **elephant**).—*adjs.* **white'-faced,** having a face pale with fear or from illness: of animals, having the face, or part of it, white: with white front—also **white'-fronted;** **white'-favoured,** wearing white favours.—*ns.* **white'-feather** (see **feather**); **white'fish,** a general name for such fish as the whiting, haddock, menhaden, &c.; any species of Coregonus; **white'-friar,** one of the Carmelite order of friars, so called from their white dress; **white'-gold,** gold alloyed with nickel or palladium to give it a white colour. —*adj.* **white'-handed,** having white hands or paws: having hands unstained with guilt.—*ns.* **white'-hass, -hawse** (*Scot.*), a white-pudding; **white'head,** the blue-winged snow-goose: a breed of domestic pigeons.—*adj.* **white'-headed,** of an animal, having the head wholly or partly white: having white hair: (*Irish*) favourite, darling, as **white'headed boy.**—*ns.* **white'-heat,** the degree of heat at which bodies become white: an intense state, as of emotion, activity, &c.; **white'-herring,** a fresh or uncured herring; **white'-honeysuckle,** an azalea known also as the clammy or swamp azalea; **white'-horse,** a figure of a horse on a hillside, formed by removing the turf so as to show the underlying chalk—the most famous in Berkshire, at Uffington.—*adj.* **white'-hot.**—*ns.* **white'-iron,** pig-iron or cast-iron in which all the carbon is in chemical combination with the iron; **white'-lady,** a spectral figure said to be associated with the fortunes of a family, as in some German castles; **white'-lead,** basic lead carbonate used in painting white; **white'-leather** (see **leather**); **white'-leg,** an ailment of women after parturition—also called milk-leg; **white'-lie** (see **lie**); **white'-light,** light containing all wavelengths in the visible range at the same intensity— the term is used, however, to cover a wide range of intensity distribution in the spectrum; **white'-lime,** (*obs.*) whitewash.—*adjs.* **white'-limed; white-listed,** having white stripes on a darker ground; **white'-livered,** having a pale look (once thought to be caused by a white liver): cowardly; **white'ly,** (*obs.* except *Scot.*) whitish, pale.—*ns.* **white'-meat,** food made of milk, butter, eggs, &c.: the flesh of poultry, rabbits, veal, &c.; **white'-metal,** a tin-base alloy with over 50 per cent. of tin: sometimes, an alloy in which lead is the principal metal.—*v.t.* **whit'en,** to make white: to bleach: to free from guilt, or make to appear guiltless.—*v.i.* to become or turn white.—*ns.* **whit'ener; white'ness; whit'ening,** act or process of making or becoming white: a substance used to make white, whiting; **white'-pot,** a Devonshire dish of sliced rolls, milk, eggs, sugar, &c., baked; **white'-precipitate,** a white mercurial preparation used externally; **white'-pudding,** an oatmeal and suet pudding in a sausage skin; **white'-pyri'tes,** marcasite; **white'-rent,** (*hist.*) the tinner's poll-tax of eightpence to the Duke of Cornwall: rent paid in silver; **white'-rhinoceros,** an African two-horned rhinoceros, not much lighter than the black rhinoceros.—*adj.* **white'-rumped.**—*n.pl.* **whites,** leucorrhoea: white attire. —*ns.* **white'-salt,** salt dried and calcined; **white'-seam,** (*Scot.*) plain needlework.—*v.i.* to do plain needlework.—*ns.* **white'smith,** a worker in tinned or white iron: a tinsmith; **white'-squall** (see **squall**); **white'thorn,** the common hawthorn; **whitethroat,** any of several birds of the same genus (Sylvia) as the blackcap, having the breast and belly of a brownish-white; **white'-vitriol,** zinc sulphate; **white'wash,** a liquid, as lime and water, or whiting, size and water, used for coating

Neutral vowels in unaccented syllables: *el'ə-mənt, in'fənt, ran'dəm*

41

walls : a wash for the skin : false colouring : a glass of sherry after other wines.—*v.t.* to cover with whitewash : to give a fair appearance to : to attempt to clear (a stained reputation).—*ns.* **white'-washer**, one who whitewashes ; **white'-water**, shoal water near the shore, breakers : the foaming water in rapids, &c. ; **white'-wax**, bleached beeswax : Chinese wax ; **white'-wine** (see **wine**) ; **white'wing**, the velvet scoter, or an American scoter closely allied to it : the chaffinch.—*adj.* **white'-winged**.—*ns.* **white'wood**, a name applied to a large number of trees or their timber—the American tulip-tree, whitewood cedar (*Tecoma*, or *Tabebuia, leucoxylon* ; Bignoniaceae), &c. ; **whit'-ing**, a small sea-fish allied to the cod, so called from its white colour : ground chalk free from stony matter and other impurities, extensively used as a size-colour, &c. (also **whīt'ening**, Spanish white, and—the finest quality—Paris white) ; **whit'ing-time**, (*Shak.*) bleaching-time. — *adj.* **whīt'ish**, somewhat white.—*ns.* **whīt'ishness** ; **whitster** (*hwit'stər* ; *Shak.*), a bleacher of cloth or clothes.—*adjs.* **whīt'y**, whitish ; **whīt'y-brown**, white with a tinge of brown.—**China white**, a very pure variety of white-lead—also **silver white** and **French white** ; **mark with a white stone** (see **stone**) ; **white coal**, water-power (Fr. *houille blanche*) ; **white corpuscle**, a leucocyte, one of the colourless amoeba-like cells occurring in suspension in the blood plasma of many animals, in lymph, &c. ; **whited sepulchre**, one professedly righteous but inwardly wicked, a hypocrite (Matt. xxiii. 27) ; **White Dwarf**, the name given to a small class of stars outside the normal spectral sequence, because their luminosities are extremely low for their spectral type ; **White Ensign**, a flag with a white field and St George's cross, with the Union Jack in the canton, till 1864 the flag of the White Squadron, now flown by the Royal Navy and the Royal Yacht Squadron ; **white-eyelid monkey**, any of the mangabeys, monkeys with white upper eyelids ; **white-footed mouse**, the deer mouse ; **white flag** (see **flag**) ; **white-headed eagle**, the N. American bald eagle ; **white horse**, a white-topped wave ; **White House**, the official residence, in Washington, of the President of the United States of America ; **white man**, one of the white race : (*coll.*) one who deals fairly with others ; **white man's burden**, (*Kipling*) his alleged obligation to govern backward coloured peoples ; **white of (an) egg**, the albumen, the pellucid viscous fluid surrounding the yolk ; **white of the eye**, that part of the ball of the eye which surrounds the iris or coloured part ; **white paper**, a statement, printed on white paper, issued by government for the information of parliament ; **white race**, one of the main divisions of mankind, distinguished generally by light complexion and certain types of hair and skull—also known as Caucasian ; **white slave**, a girl procured for prostitution purposes (esp. when exported)— whence **white slaver**, **white slavery** and **white slave traffic** ; **White Squadron**, one of three divisions of the British Navy in former times : white-painted vessels built in 1883 and following years as part of a strong U.S. Navy ; **white whale**, the beluga ; **whiting-pout** (see **pout**) ; **zinc white** (see **zinc**). [O.E. *hwīt* ; O.N. *hvítr*, Ger. *weiss*.]

Whitechapel, *hwīt'chapl*, *n.* (*whist*) a lead from a one-card suit, straightforward leading out of winning cards, or other type of unskilful play : (*billiards*) intentional pocketing of an opponent's ball.—**Whitechapel cart** (see **cart**). [*Whitechapel* in London.]

Whitehall, *hwīt'hawl*, *n.* a street with government offices in London : the British government or its policy.

whither, *hwidh'ər*, *adv.* and *conj.* to what place? to which place : (used relatively) to which : to what : **whithersoever**.—*adv.* **whithersoev'er**, to whatever place.—*adv.* **whith'erward(s)**, in what direction, to what point.—**no whither**, to no place. [O.E. *hwider*, allied to **who**.]

whither. See **wuther**.

whiting. See **white**.

whitleather, *hwit'ledh-ər*, *n.* leather dressed with alum, white leather : the paxwax of the ox. [**white** leather.]

Whitley Council, *hwit'li kown'səl*, a joint standing industrial council (national or local), composed of representatives of employers and workpeople in an organised trade to consider and settle conditions of employment, &c. [Recommended (1917) in the 'Whitley Report'—the report of a Reconstruction Sub-committee presided over by Rt. Hon. J. H. *Whitley*.]

whitling, *hwit'ling*, *n.* a kind of trout, probably a young bull-trout. [**white**, and suff. *-ling*.]

whitlow, *hwit'lō*, *n.* a painful inflammation of a finger or toe, esp. near the nail, paronychia.—*ns.* **whit'low-grass**, any of several plants alleged to cure whitlows, as a small British saxifrage (*Saxifraga tridactylites*), or a small crucifer (*Draba verna*) : whitlow-wort ; **whit'low-wort**, any of a number of plants of the genus Paronychia. [Perh. a corr. of *whick-flaw*, quick-flaw ; cf. **quick** and **flaw**.]

Whit-Monday, *hwit'-mun'dā*, *n.* the Monday following Whitsunday.

Whitsun, *hwit'sn*, *adj.* pertaining to, or observed at, Whitsuntide.—*n.* Whitsuntide.—*ns.* **Whit'sun-ale**, a festival formerly held at Whitsuntide ; **Whit'-sunday**, the seventh Sunday after Easter, commemorating the day of Pentecost, when the converts in the primitive Church wore white robes : in Scotland, one of the term-days (May 15) on which rents, annuities, &c., are payable, the Whitsunday removal terms in towns being fixed as May 28 ; **Whit'suntide**, the season of Pentecost, comprising **Whit'sun-week**, **Whit'-week**, the week beginning with Whitsunday. [**white**, **Sunday**.]

whittaw, *hwit'aw*, *n.* (*dial.*) a saddler.—Also **whitt'awer**. [**white**, **tawer**.]

whittie-whattie, *hwit'i-hwot'i*, *v.i.* (all meanings *Scot.*) to mutter, whisper : to shilly-shally.—*n.* vague language intended to deceive : a frivolous excuse. [Perh. formed from **what**.]

whittle, *hwit'l*, *v.t.* to pare or cut with a knife : to shape with a knife : to diminish gradually.—*v.i.* to cut wood aimlessly : (*obs. slang*) to peach, or to confess at the gallows.—*n.* a large knife, usu. clasp or sheath. [M.E. *thwitel*—O.E. *thwītan* to cut.]

whittle, *hwit'l*, *n.* (*dial.*) a woollen shawl : a blanket. [O.E. *hwītel*, a white mantle—*hwīt*, white.]

whit(t)ret, *hwit'rət*, *hwut'rət*, **whitterick**, (*-ə*)-*rik*, *n.* (*Scot.*) a weasel.

whizz, whiz, *hwiz*, *v.i.* to make a hissing sound, like an arrow or ball flying through the air : to move rapidly.—*v.t.* to cause to whizz (*pr.p.* **whizz'ing** ; *pa.t.* and *pa.p.* **whizzed**).—*n.* a hissing sound : (*U.S. slang*) a bargain, agreement.—*ns.* **whizz'-bang**, (*slang*) a light shell of high velocity which is heard arriving before the sound of a gun's report : a firework suggestive of this ; **whizz'er** ; **whizz'-ing**.—*adv.* **whizz'ingly**. [Imit. ; cf. **wheeze**, **hiss**.]

who, *hoō*, *pron. rel.* and *interrog.* what person? which person : he who, the person who : whoever : of what name, standing, &c. (objective case **whom** —O.E. *hwám*, which was orig. dat. of *hwá*, who, and replaced in the 12th and 13th centuries the older accus. *hwone*) : possessive case **whose**—M.E. *hwas*, from O.E. *hwæs*, gen. of *hwá*).—*prons.* **whoev'er**, (*arch.*) **whosoev'er** and **who'so**, every one who : whatever person (objective case **whom'ever**, **whomsoev'er** ; possessive case **whosev'er**, **whosesoev'er**).—**as who should say**, as if one should say ; **know who's who**, to know the position and influence of everyone ; **the who**, (*Shak.*) who ; **who but he**, who else? he only. [O.E. *hwá* ; cog. with Goth. *hwas*, O.H.G. *hwer*, Ger. *wer* ; also with Sans. *kas*, L. *quis*.]

whoa, *wō*, *hwō*, *interj.* stop.—*interj.* **whoa-ho-ho(a)'**, (*obs.*) used to hail a person from a distance.

who-dun-it, whodunnit, *hoō-dun'-it*, *n.* (*coll.*) a story concerned with the elucidation of a crime mystery. [**who**, **done** (vulg. pa.t. of **do**), **it**.]

whole, *hōl*, *adj.* (*arch.*) sound in health (so in *B.*) :

uninjured : restored to health : healed : not broken : undamaged : not broken up, or ground, or deprived of any part : containing the total amount, number, &c. : complete : of a sister or brother, full-blooded : in mining, as yet unworked.—*n.* the entire thing : a system or combination of parts.—*adv.* wholly.—*adjs.* whole′-coloured, all of one colour : whole′-foot′ed, (*coll.*) unreserved ; whole′-hearted, -souled, hearty, generous, zealous and sincere.— *adv.* whole′-heart′edly. — *adj.* whole′-hog, (*slang*) out-and-out, complete.—*n.* whole′-hogg′er, one who is inclined to go the whole hog (see **hog**).— *adjs.* whole′-hoofed, having undivided hoof ; whole′-length, giving the whole figure : full-length.—*n.* a portrait or statue giving the whole figure.—*ns.* whole′-meal, meal made from entire grains of wheat ; whole′ness ; whole′sāle, sale of goods, usually by the whole piece or large quantity, to a retailer.—*adj.* buying and selling, or concerned with buying and selling, thus : extensive and indiscriminate.—*adv.* by wholesale : extensively and indiscriminately.—*n.* whole′-sāler, one who sells by wholesale.—*adjs.* whole′-skinned, unhurt : safe in reputation ; whole′some, healthy in body, taste, morals, or (*Shak.*) condition : indicating health : conducive to bodily or spiritual health : (*obs.*) remedial : (*Shak.*) propitious : (*Shak.*) reasonable, sensible.—*adv.* whole′somely. —*ns.* whole′someness ; whole′-stitch, a lace-making stitch used to fill in a pattern.—*adv.* wholly (hōl′li, hō′li), completely, altogether.—**the whole**, all the : the complete : upon, on, **the whole**, generally speaking : all things considered ; **whole number**, a unit, or a number composed of units, an integral number ; **with whole skin**, safe, unscathed. [O.E. *hāl*, healthy ; O.N. *heill*, Ger. *heil* ; see **hale** (1).]

whom, whomever, whomsoever. See **who**.

whommle, whomble, *hwom′l, hwum′l.* Same as **whemmle**.

whoobub, whobble, hōō′bub, *n.* (*obs.*). Same as **hubbub**.

whoop, hōōp, *n.* a loud eager cry : a N. American Indian war-cry : a form of hide-and-seek : the long noisy inspiration heard in whooping-cough. —*v.i.* to give a loud cry of triumph, eagerness, scorn, &c. : to hoot.—*v.t.* to cheer, or insult, with shouts : to summon, or to urge on, by whooping. —*interj.* (*Shak.*) ho !—*ns.* whoop′er, one who whoops : (also whoop′ing-swan) a swan (*Cygnus cygnus, ferus*, or *musicus*) common in north Europe and Asia ; whoop′ing-cough, hoop′ing-cough, pertussis, an infectious and epidemic disease, mostly attacking children, characterised by catarrh of the respiratory tract and by periodic spasms of the larynx that end in a long crowing inspiration. [O.Fr. *houper*, to shout.]

whoopee, hwōōp′ē, *interj.* an exclamation of delight. —Also *n.*—**make whoopee**, (*coll.*) to indulge in hilarious amusements or dissipation. [**whoop**.]

whoot. Obs. variant of **hoot**.

whop, whap, hwop, *v.t.* (all meanings of **whop**, &c., *coll., slang*, or *dial.*) to whip, thrash : to defeat or surpass : to throw or pull suddenly or violently.— *v.i.* to strike, or to move, quickly : to flop down.— *n.* a blow : a bump : the noise made by either of these.—*n.* whopp′er, one who whops : anything very large, esp. a monstrous lie.—*adj.* whopp′ing, very large. [Variant of **wap** (1) ; origin obscure, prob. partly imitative.]

whore, hōr, *n.* a prostitute : any unchaste woman : an allegedly corrupt religious community or practice.—*v.i.* to be, or to have to do with, a whore or whores.—*v.t.* to make a whore of, debauch : to spend in whoring.—*ns.* whore′dom, whoring : any illicit sexual intercourse : idolatry ; whore′-house, a brothel ; whore′master, (*obs.*) a whoremonger.—*adj.* whore′masterly, libidinous.—*ns.* whore′monger, a lecher : a pander ; whore′s′-bird, a whore's child : used as a vulgar term of abuse ; whore′s′-egg, a sea-urchin ; whore′son (-sən), son of a whore : a bastard : a term of coarse contempt or familiarity.—*adj.* mean, scurvy.—*adj.* whō′rish.—*adv.* whō′rishly.—*n.* whō′rishness. [Late O.E. *hóre*, prob.—O.N. *hóra*, adulteress.]

whorl, hworl, hwurl, *n.* a group of similar members arising from the same level on a stem, and forming a circle around it : a single turn in a spiral shell : a convolution—e.g. in the ear : the fly of a spindle. —*adj.* **whorled**, having whorls : arranged in the form of a whorl or whorls. [Late M.E. *wharwyl*, &c., variants of **whirl**.]

whorl-bat. See **whirl-bat**.

whortleberry, hwor′tl-ber-i, -bər-i, *n.* a widely-spread heath plant with a dark blue edible berry, called also the bilberry—in Scotland, blaeberry— sometimes abbreviated to **whort** : extended to certain other plants of the same genus (Vaccinium). [Variant of **hurtleberry**.]

whose, hōōz, *pron.* the possessive case of **who** or **which.** See **who**.

whoso, whosoever. See **who**.

whot, hwot, *adj.* (*Spens.*). Obs. variant of **hot**.

whow, hwow, *interj.* (*Scot.*) of deploration.—Often **eh whow (or aich wow).**

whummle. See **whemmle**.

whunstane, Scots form of **whinstone**.

why, hwī, *adv.* and *conj.* for what cause or reason ? on which account : wherefore : (used relatively) on account of which.—*interj.* expressing sudden realisation, or protest, or marking resumption after a question or a slight pause, or (*Shak.*) to call a person.—*n.* why′-not, a challenge for reasons : (*obs.*) a dilemma (at a why-not, at a disadvantage). —**for why**, (*arch.* and *dial.*), for what reason : because ; **the why and wherefore**, the whole reason ; **why, so!** (*Shak.*) so let it be !—expressing unwilling consent. [O.E. *hwī hwý*, instrumental case of *hwā*, who.]

whydah-bird. See **widow-bird**.

wick, wik, *n.* (*dial.*) a creek. [O.N. *vík*, a bay.]

wick, wik, *n.* (*dial.*) a village or town : (*dial.*) a farm : as suffix (-*ik*, -*wik*, also -*wich, ij*) in Ber*wick,* Green*wich*, &c. [O.E. *wíc*, prob. an old Gmc. borrowing from L. *vícus*, a village.]

wick, wik, *n.* the twisted threads of cotton or other substance in a candle, lamp, or lighter, which draw up the inflammable liquid to the flame. [O.E. *wéoce, wéoc* ; allied to Du. *wick*, a roll of lint, Ger. *vieche*.]

wick, wik, *v.t.* and *v.i.* in curling, to strike (a stone) in an oblique direction. [Perh. O.E. *wícan*, to bend, yield, give way.]

wick, wik, *adj.* (*obs.* or *dial.*) wicked. [O.E. *wicca*, wizard, *wicce*, witch.]

wicked, wik′id, *adj.* evil in principle or practice : sinful : ungodly : (of an animal) vicious : cruel : mischievous, spiteful : very bad, harmful, or offensive : (*coll.*) roguish : (*Shak.*) unlucky.—*n.* (*B.*) a wicked person : (with *the*) wicked persons collectively.—*adv.* wick′edly.—*n.* wick′edness. —**the wicked one**, the devil. [M.E. *wicked, wikked*, prob.—*wicke, wikke*, wicked—O.E. *wicca*, wizard.]

wicken, wicky. See **quicken** (1).

wicker, wik′ər, *n.* a small pliant twig or osier : wickerwork.—*adj.* made of twigs or osiers : encased in wickerwork.—*adj.* wick′ered, made of wicker : covered with wickerwork.—*n.* wick′er-work, basketwork of any kind. [M.E. *wiker*, of Scand. origin ; cf. O.E. *wícan*, to bend.]

wicket, wik′it, *n.* a small gate : a small door in or near a larger one : (*obs.*) a grill or loop-hole : (*cricket*) the upright arrangement of three stumps with two bails on top which the batsman defends against the bowling : a stump : the pitch, esp. in respect of its condition : a batsman's stay at the wicket, or his joint stay there with another : a batsman's innings.—*ns.* wick′et-door, -gate, a wicket ; wick′et-keeper, in cricket, the fieldsman who stands immediately behind the striker's wicket.—**get, take**, &c., a wicket, to bowl a batsman, or have him put out in any way as a result of one's bowling ; **keep wicket**, to be wicket-keeper ; **over, round, the wicket**, (of bowling) delivered with the hand nearer, farther away from, the wicket ; **sticky wicket** (see stick (1)) ; **throw down the wicket**, to put down the wicket in fielding by throw of the ball ; **win by so-many wickets**, to win with so-many wickets still to fall. [O.N.Fr. *wiket* (Fr. *guichet*) ; of Gmc. origin.]

Neutral vowels in unaccented syllables : *el′ə-mənt, in′fənt, ran′dəm*

widdershins, widershins, &c. Variants of **withershins.**

widdy, *wid'i, n.* (*dial.*) a rope, esp. one made of osiers : a halter for hanging. [Variant of **withy.**]

widdy, *wid'i,* prov. form of **widow.**

wide, *wīd, adj.* extending far : having a considerable distance between the sides : broad : of a specified breadth : roomy : expanded : opened as far as possible : far apart : far from the point aimed at, or (*rare*) place mentioned : very different : (*fig.*) of large scope, comprehending or considering much : (*slang*) astute : (*slang*) lax in morals : (*phon.*) lax, the reverse of *narrow.*—*n.* wideness : in cricket, a ball bowled out of reach of the batsman : a penalty run allowed for this.—*advs.* **wide,** (now usu. **far and wide**) to a great distance, over a large region : (*Spens.*) at a distance : far from the point aimed at, the subject under discussion, the truth, &c. : far to one side (with *of*) : so that there is a large space or distance between ; **wide'ly.** — *adj.* **wide'-awake,** fully awake : on the alert : (*coll.*) keen and knowing.—*n.* a low wide-brimmed soft felt hat.—*n.* **wide'awake'ness.**—*adj.* **wide'chapped,** (*Shak.*) open-mouthed.—*n.* **wide'-gab,** the fish known also as the angler.—*v.t.* and *v.i.* **wide'n,** to make or grow wide or wider : (*Shak.*) to throw open.—*ns.* **wi'dener,** one who, or that which, widens : a kind of tool ; **wide'ness.**—*adjs.* **wide'-open,** opened : (*coll.*) open to attack : (*U.S.*) lax in enforcing laws and regulations ; **wide'spread,** extended or extending widely : found, operative, &c., in many places ; **wide'-stretched,** (*Shak.*) large ; **wide'-watered,** bordered or covered by, or having, wide waters.—*n.* **width** (*width*), breadth.—**wide of,** (*Shak.*) indifferent to, far from observing ; **wide of the mark,** far out, astray from the truth. [O.E. *wīd* ; O.N. *vīthr,* Ger. *weit.*]

widgeon, wigeon, *wij'ən, n.* any duck of the genus Mareca, having the bill shorter than the head, legs short, feet rather small, wings long and pointed, and the tail wedge-shaped : (*obs.*) a fool. [Of uncertain origin.]

widow, *wid'ō, n.* a woman who has lost her husband by death and has not married again : in the early Church, one of a special class of pious women : an extra hand in some card games.—*v.t.* to bereave of a husband (or wife) : to strip of anything valued : (*Shak.*) to endow with a widow's right : (*Shak.*) to be widow to.—*ns.* **wid'ow-bewitched,** a grass-widow ; **wid'ow-bird,** any of a group of African birds of the weaver-bird family (genus Vidua, sub-family Viduinae ; L. *viduus,* widowed) having much black in the plumage, called also **whidah-, whydah-bird,** in the belief that they were named from *Whydah* (Ouidah) in Dahomey ; **wid'ower,** (*dial.*) **wid'ow-man,** a man whose wife is dead ; **wid'owerhood ; wid'owhood,** state of being a widow, or (*rarely*) of being a widower : (*Shak.*) a widow's right ; **wid'ow's-bench,** (*hist.*) a widow's share of her husband's estate besides her jointure ; **wid'ow's-chamber,** the apparel and bedroom furniture of the widow of a London freeman, to which she was entitled ; **wid'ow-wail,** a dwarf shrub (Cneorum) with pink, sweet-scented flowers, native to Spain and southern France : daphne or mezereon (*Daphne Mezereum*).—**widow's cruse,** a source of supply that never fails (1 Kings xvii. 10-16 ; **widow's man,** (*naut.*) any of a number of fictitious persons formerly entered as part of a ship's company in order that the pay allotted to them might be set aside for widows' pensions ; **widow's mite,** a small offering generously given (Mark xii. 42 ; see also **mite**) ; **widow's peak,** a point of hair over the forehead, like the cusped front of a widow's cap ; **widow's weeds,** the mourning dress formerly worn by all widows. [O.E. *widewe* ; Ger. *wittwe,* L. *vidua,* bereft of a husband, Sans. *vidhavā.*]

width. See **wide.**

wiel. Same as **weel** (1).

wield, *wēld, v.t.* (*obs.*) to rule : (*obs.*) to possess, enjoy, gain : to control, manage : to use with skill : (*obs.*) to utter.—*adj.* **wield'able,** capable of being wielded.—*ns.* **wield'er ; wield'iness.**—

adjs. **wield'less** (*Spens.* **weeldlesse**), unmanageable ; **wield'y,** easy to wield : manageable : (*obs.*) dexterous, active.—**wield the sceptre,** to have supreme command or control. [O.E. *weldan* (not recorded ; W.S. *wealdan*) ; Goth. *waldan,* Ger. *walten.*]

wife, *wīf, n.* a woman : a married woman : the woman to whom one is married : (*obs.*) the mistress of a house, a hostess—now often in this sense *goodwife* :—*pl.* **wives.**—*n.* **wife'hood,** the state of being a wife.—*adjs.* **wife'less,** without a wife ; **wife'-like** ; **wife'ly.**—**take to wife** (see **take**). [O.E. *wīf* ; O.N. *vīf,* Ger. *weib.*]

wig, *wig, n.* an artificial covering of hair for the head worn to conceal baldness, or formerly for fashion's sake, as in the full-dress **full-bottomed wig** of Queen Anne's time, still worn by the Speaker and by judges, and the smaller **tie-wig,** still represented by the judge's undress wig and the barrister's or advocate's frizzed wig : a judge. (For **bag-wig,** see **bag.**)—*n.* **wig'-block,** a block or shaped piece of wood for fitting a wig on.—*adj.* **wigged,** wearing a wig.—*n.* **wigg'ery,** false hair : (*Carlyle*) excess of formality.—*adj.* **wig'less,** without a wig.—*n.* **wig'-maker,** a maker of wigs.—**wigs on the green,** a fray. [Short for **periwig.**]

wig, *wig, v.t.* (*coll.*) to scold.—*n.* **wigg'ing,** (*coll.*) a scolding. [**wig** (1).]

wigan, *wig'ən, n.* a stiff canvas-like fabric for stiffening garments : a plain grey cloth for boot-linings, &c. [*Wigan,* the town.]

wigeon. See **widgeon.**

wiggle, *wig'l, v.i.* and *v.t.* to waggle, wriggle.—*n.* a wiggling motion.—Also *v.i., v.t.,* and *n.* **wigg'le-wagg'le.**—*n.* **wigg'ler,** one who wriggles.—*adj.* **wigg'ly,** wriggly : much or irregularly waved.—**get a wiggle on,** (*slang*) to hurry. [Freq. of verb from which is derived dial. *wig,* to wag ; connected with M.L.G. *wiggelen.*]

wight, *wīt, n.* (*arch., dial.,* or ironically) a creature or a person : (*obs.*) a supernatural being. [O.E. *wiht,* a creature, thing ; Ger. *wicht* ; cf. **whit.**]

wight, *wīt, adj.* swift, nimble : courageous, strong.—*adv.* **wight'ly.** [O.N. *vīgr,* warlike—*vīg,* war (O.E. *wīg*).]

wight. Same as **wite.**

wigwag, *wig'wag, v.i.* to twist about : to signal by means of flags.—*n.* act of wigwagging : a level-crossing signal which gives its indication, with or without a red light, by swinging about a fixed axis.—*adj.* **twisting.**—*adv.* to and fro. [Dial. *wig* (from same root as **wiggle**) and **wag** (1).]

wigwam, *wig'wom, -wam, n.* an Indian hut. [Eng. corr. of Algonquian word.]

wild, *wīld, adj.* being in a state of nature, not tamed or cultivated : of an undomesticated or uncultivated kind : uncivilised : uninhabited : desolate : tempestuous : violent : fierce : passionate : unrestrained : licentious : agitated : shy : distracted : very angry : very enthusiastic, eager, keen : strong and irrational : fantastic, crazy : disordered : unconsidered : wide of the mark : fresh and natural : **Wild,** (*hist.*) applied to the extreme Evangelical party in the Church of Scotland.—Also *adv.*—*n.* (also in *pl.*) an uncultivated region : a wilderness or desert (also *fig.*) : (*poet.*) an empty region of air or water.—*ns.* **wild'-ass,** any of several Asiatic or African asses, as the onager, living naturally in a wild state ; **wild'-boar,** a wild swine, esp. *Sus scrofa,* from which most domestic swine are derived.—*adj.* **wild'-born,** born in the wild.—*n.* **wild'-cat,** an undomesticated cat (*Felis catus*) native to Europe : any of various small wild animals of the cat family : the skins of these : a quick-tempered, fierce person : (*U.S.*) one who takes part in wild-cat financial schemes.—*adj.* (*U.S.*) haphazard, reckless, unsound financially.—*ns.* **wild'-cherry,** any uncultivated tree bearing cherries, as the gean (*Prunus Avium*), or its fruit ; **wild'-dog,** any wild species of the dog genus or family, as the dhole, the dingo, &c. ; **wild'-duck,** any duck excepting the domesticated duck ; **wild'-fire,** a composition of inflammable materials, as gunpowder rolled up wet and set on fire : Greek fire (like **wildfire,** extremely fast) : lightning without thunder : a disease of sheep ; **wild'-fowl**, the birds of the duck tribe : game-birds ; **wild'-fowling**, the pursuit of wild-fowl ; **wild'-goose**, a bird of the goose kind that is wild or feral : a flighty or foolish person : (in *pl.*, **Wild-geese**; *hist.*) Irish Jacobites who migrated to the Continent after the abdication of James II. ; **wild'-goose chase** (see **chase**) ; **wild'-grape**, a grape-vine (Vitis or Muscadinia) in the wild state, or its fruit : Coccoloba (see **grape-tree**) ; **wild'-honey**, the honey of wild bees ; **wild'-indigo**, any of several plants of different genera belonging to the same family (Papilionaceae) as indigo, as an American tumbleweed (*Baptisia tinctoria*) ; **wild'ing**, that which grows wild or without cultivation : a wild crab-apple : a garden plant self-sown, an escape.—*adj.* uncultivated, or wild.—*adj.* **wild'ish**, somewhat wild.—*n.* **wild'-land**, land completely uncultivated.—*adv.* **wild'ly**.—*ns.* **wild'ness** ; **wild'(-)oat**, a tall perennial weed close akin to the cultivated oat ; **wild'-olive** (see **oleaster**) ; **wild'-Will'iams**, (*dial.*) ragged-Robin ; **wild'-wood**, wild uncultivated, or unfrequented, wood.—Also *adj.* **run wild**, to take to loose living : to live or grow in freedom from constraint or control : to revert to the wild or uncultivated state ; **sow one's wild oats** (see **oat**) ; **wild animals**, undomesticated animals ; **wild birds**, birds not domesticated, esp. those protected at certain seasons under the Acts of 1880 onwards ; **Wild Hunt**, in Germanic legend, a host of phantoms rushing along, accompanied by the shouting of huntsmen and the baying of dogs ; **Wild Huntsman**, their leader ; **wild mare**, a seesaw : an instrument of punishment, the horse ; **wild rice**, Zizania. [O.E. *wilde* ; common Gmc. word.]

wild, *wild*, obs. variant of **weald**, **wield**.

wildebeest, *vild'i-bāst*, *wild'i-bēst*, *n.* (*S.Afr.*) a gnu. [Du. *wilde*, wild, *beest*, ox.]

wilderness, *wil'dər-nəs*, *n.* a region uncultivated and uninhabited : a pathless or desolate tract of any kind, as an extent of sea : a part of a garden or estate allowed to run wild, or cultivated in imitation of natural woodland : (*fig.*) conditions of life, or a place, in which the spirit feels desolate : the present world : a large confused or confusing assemblage : (*obs.*) wildness.—*v.t.* **wil'der** (prob. formed from *wilderness*), (*poet.*) to cause to stray : to bewilder.—*v.i.* to wander wildly or widely.—*adjs.* **wil'dered** ; **wil'dering**.—*n.* **wil'derment**. [M.E.,—*wilderne*, wild, wilderness—O.E. *wild-déoren*—*wild*, wild, *déor*, animal.]

wildgrave, *wild'grāv*, *n.* (*obs.*) a waldgrave. [Ger. *wildgraf*—*wild* (Eng. adj. wild), game, *graf*, count.]

wile, *wil*, *n.* a trick : deceit : a pleasing artifice, (in *pl.*) cajolery.—*v.t.* to beguile, inveigle : coax, cajole : to make to pass easily or pleasantly (confused with **while**).—*adj.* **wile'ful**, full of wiles.—*adv.* **wil'ily**.—*n.* **wil'iness**.—*adj.* **wil'y**, full of craft or cunning : using tricks or stratagem. [O.E. *wil*, *wile* ; cf. **guile**.]

Wilhelmstrasse, *vil'helm-shträ-se*, *n.* a street in Berlin : the German Foreign Office.

will, *wil*, *n.* power or faculty of choosing or determining : act of using this power : volition : choice or determination : pleasure : inclination : lust : command : arbitrary disposal : feeling towards, as in **good** or **ill will** (see **good, ill**) : disposition of one's effects at death : the written document containing this.—*v.t.* (*arch.*) to wish for, desire : (*obs.*) to command, order, require : to decree : to seek to force, influence (oneself or another to perform a specified action) by silent exertion of the will : to dispose of by will, to bequeath : (in the foregoing senses, *pa.t.* and *pa.p.* **willed** ; *2nd pers. pres. indic.* **will'est** ; *3rd pers.* **wills**) : used with the infinitive of a verb to form (in sense) a future tense, expressing in the second and third person simple futurity (as **shall** in the first), or custom, or persistent habit, and in the first person promise or determination on the part of the speaker : (*arch.*) with ellipsis of verb of motion, as ' I will unto the king ' : also, in third person, can : to be likely to (in these senses, *pa.t.* **would**, *wood* ; no *pa.p.* ; *2nd pers. sing. pres. indic.* **wilt** ; *3rd pers.* **will**).—

v.i. to exercise choice, choose, decree : to be willing.—*adj.* **wil'ful**, governed only by one's will, obstinate : done intentionally : (*Shak.*) willing.—*adv.* (*Shak.*) wilfully.—*adv.* **wil'fully**.—*n.* **wil'fulness**.—*adj.* **willed**, having a will : voluntary : given, or disposed of, by will : brought under another's will, as in hypnotism.—*n.* **will'er**, one who wills.—*adjs.* **will'ing**, not reluctant : eager : ready and prompt to act : voluntary : chosen : (*rare*) intentional : of or pertaining to the will ; **will'ing-heart'ed**, heartily consenting. — *adv.* **will'ingly**.—*n.* **will'ingness**—**at will**, when or as one chooses ; **a will of one's own**, a strong, self-assertive will ; **by my will**, (*Shak.*) voluntarily : also, with my consent ; **conjoint, joint, will**, a testamentary act by two persons jointly in the same instrument ; **have one's will**, to obtain what one desires ; **tenant at will**, one who holds lands only so long as the owner pleases ; **with a will**, heartily and energetically ; **work one's will**, to do exactly what one chooses. [O.E. *willa*, will, *willan*, *wyllan* (pa.t. *wolde*, *walde*), to wish ; Goth. *wiljan*, Ger. *wollen*, L. *velle*.]

will, **wull**, *wil*, *wul*, *adj.* and *adv.* (*Scot.*) at a loss : astray : bewildered.—*adj.* **will'yard**, **will'yart** (*Scot.*), wilful : shy. [O.N. *villr*, astray ; cf. **wild**.]

willemite, *wil'əm-it*, *n.* orthosilicate of zinc, Zn_2SiO_4, white when pure but commonly red, brown, or green through the presence of manganese or iron—noteworthy as exhibiting an intense bright yellow fluorescence in ultra-violet light. [*Willem* (or William) I. of the Netherlands.]

willet, *wil'it*, *n.* a N. American bird of the snipe family, belonging to the tattler group—known locally as the stone-curlew. [Imit.]

willey. See **willy**.

willies, *wil'iz*, *n.pl.* (*U.S. slang*) the creeps.

williewaught, *wil'i-vvavhht*, *n.* (*Scot.*) a deep draught. [From misunderstanding of Burns, *Auld Lang Syne*, iv. 3, ' a right guid willie (or guid-willie) waught ' (where ' guid willie ' means ' good will '), a generous and friendly draught.]

Will-o'-the-wisp, *wil'-ō-thə-wisp'*, *n.* the ignis-fatuus : any elusive and deceptive person or thing. [Orig. *Will-with-the-wisp*—*Will*, abbrev. of William, and **wisp** (q.v.).]

willow, *wil'ō*, *n.* any tree or shrub of the genus Salix, having slender, pliant branches : any of several plants resembling it : the wood of the willow : a cricket-bat or baseball-bat : a willowing-machine.—*v.t.* to clean in a willowing-machine.—*adj.* **will'owed**, abounding with, or grown with, willows.—*ns.* **will'ow-grouse**, a species of grouse (*Lagopus albus*) found in northern regions of the world ; **will'ow-herb**, a perennial herb (Epilobium or Chamaenerion) of the evening primrose family (including rose-bay, bay-willow, French or Persian willow) with willow-like leaves and seeds ; **will'owing-machine**, a machine in which a spiked revolving cylinder, usu. contained in a spiked box, loosens or cleans cotton, wool, rags for paper, &c.—*adj.* **will'owish**, like a willow : of the colour of willow leaves : slender and supple. —*ns.* **will'ow-warbler**, **-wren**, a small European sylviine bird (*Phylloscopus*, or *Sylvia*, *trochilus*) ; **will'ow-weed**, one of various species of Polygonum or knot-weed : the purple loosestrife.—*adj.* **will'owy**, abounding in willows : flexible : graceful.—**willow pattern**, a blue design of Chinese character but English origin used on china from the late 18th century onwards. [O.E. *welig* ; L.Ger. *wilge*, Du. *wilg*.]

will-worship, *wil'-wur'ship*, *n.* (*B.*) worship that is according to one's own will or fancy, superstitious observance without divine authority. [**will**, **worship**.]

willy, **willey**, *wil'i*, *n.* (*prov.*) a willow basket : a willowing-machine.—*v.t.* to clean in a willowing-machine. [O.E. *wilige* ; allied to **willow**.]

willy-nilly, *wil'i-nil'i*, *adv.* willing or unwilling : compulsorily.—*adj.* vacillating. [**will** and **nill**.]

willy-willy, *wil'i-wil'i*, *n.* (*Austr.*) a cyclone.

wilt, *wilt*, *v.i.* to droop, lose energy : (*fig.*) to lose self-confidence or courage.—*v.t.* to render limp, cause to droop : to cause to lose spirit, self-confidence, courage.—*n*. act of wilting: any of various diseases that cause wilting of plants. [Orig. dial.; perh. from **welk**.]

wilt, *wilt*, *2nd pers. sing*. of **will**.

Wilton, *wil'tən*, *n*. (in full **Wilton carpet**) a carpet differing from Brussels in having a cut pile, long made at *Wilton*, in Wilts.

wily, wilily, wiliness. See **wile**.

wimble, *wim'bl*, *n*. an instrument for boring holes, turned by a handle: a gimlet: an auger: a kind of brace: an instrument for boring in soft ground. —*v.t*. to bore through with a wimble. [Through O.Norm.Fr., from M.Du. *wimpel*.]

wimble, *wim'bl*, *adj*. (*Spens*.) active, nimble. [A Northern word, now dial.; of Scand. origin.]

wimple, *wim'pl*, *n*. a veil folded round the head, neck and cheeks (still part of a nun's dress): a fold, wrinkle, ripple: a turn, wind: (*Scot*.) a crafty twist.—*v.t*. to wrap in, or hide with, a wimple: to enwrap, enfold: (*Shak*.; in *pa.p*.) to blindfold: to lay in folds.—*v.i*. to meander: to ripple: (*Spens*.) to lie in folds.—Also **whimple**. [O.E. *wimpel*, neck-covering; cf. Ger. *wimpel*, a pennon, Fr. *guimpe*, a nun's veil, Eng. *gimp*, a thin cloth for trimming.]

win, *win*, *v.t*. to get by labour: to gain in contest: to secure: to achieve, effect: to reach: to be the victor in: to induce: to gain influence over: to obtain the favour of: to mine (an ore): to open up (a new portion of a coal-seam).—*v.i*. to gain the victory: to gain influence over, (*arch*.) advantage over (with *upon*, &c.): (*dial*.) to make one's way: to succeed in getting: (*pr.p*. **winn'ing**; *pa.t*. and *pa.p*. **won**, *wun*).—*n*. (*coll*.) a victory, success.—*ns*. **winn'er**; **winn'ing**, the act of one who wins: that which is won (usu. in *pl*.): a shaft or pit to open a bed of coal.—*adj*. that wins: of or pertaining to the act of winning: attractive, prepossessing: persuasive. — *adv*. **winn'ingly**. — *ns*. **winn'ingness**; **winn'ing-post**, the goal of a race-course.—**win by a (short) head**, to win very narrowly; **win in a canter**, to win easily; **win of**, (*obs*.) to get the better of; **win on, upon**, to gain on: to get the better of: to obtain favour with; **win, or gain, one's spurs**, to earn one's knighthood by valour on the field, hence to gain recognition or reputation by merit of any kind; **win out**, to get out: (*coll*.) to be successful; **win over**, to bring over to one's opinion or party. [O.E. *winnan*, to struggle, to suffer; O.N. *vinna*, Ger. *gewinnen*, to win.]

win, *win*, *v.t*. (*Scot*.) to dry by exposure to the wind: —*pr.p*. **winning**; *pa.t*. and *pa.p*. **won**. [**win** (1) influenced by **wind** (1).]

win, winn, *win*, **wing, wing**, *n*. (*slang*) a penny.

wince, *wins*, *v.i*. (*obs*. or *dial*.) to kick: to shrink or start back: to make an involuntary movement, e.g. in pain: to be affected acutely, as by a sarcasm: to be restive, as a horse uneasy at its rider.—*n*. (*obs*.) a kick: an involuntary start back or shrinking.— *n*. **win'cer**.—*n*. and *adj*. **win'cing**. [Cf. O.Fr. *guinchir, ganchir*, to wince—a Gmc. word; cf. O.H.G. *wenkan* (Ger. *wanken*), to wince.]

wince. See **winch**.

wincey, winsey, *win'si*, *n*. a cloth, plain or twilled, usu. with a linen or cotton warp and woollen filling.—*n*. **winceyette'**, a plain cotton cloth of light weight, raised slightly on both sides. [Orig. Scot.—**linsey-woolsey**.]

winch, *win(t)sh*, *n*. a reel or roller: the crank of a wheel or axle: a powerful type of hauling or hoisting machine.—Also **wince**.—*n*. **winch'-man**. [O.E. *wince*, from a Gmc. and Indo-Gmc. root.]

Winchester, *win'ches-tər*, formerly used attributively of various measures, as quart, bushel, the standards of which were kept at *Winchester*.

Winchester (rifle), *win'ches-tər*, a type of breach-loading rifle used as a sporting gun, the first model of which was introduced about 1866. [Oliver F. *Winchester*, American manufacturer.]

wincopipe. Obs. form of **wink-a-peep**.

wind, *wind* (*poet*. *wīnd*), *n*. air in motion: a current of air, usually horizontal, either natural or produced by artificial means: any of the directions from which the wind may blow: breath: power

of breathing: flatulence: conceit: empty, insignificant words: the wind instruments in an orchestra: their players: air impregnated with scent of game: a hint or suggestion, as of something secret: (*slang*) part of the body covering the stomach: a disease of sheep in which the inflamed intestines are distended by gases.—*v.t*. (*wind*) to sound or signal by blowing: (*wind*) to perceive by the scent: to expose to the wind: to drive hard, so as to put out of breath: to allow to recover wind:—*pr.p*. **wīnd'ing, wind'ing**; *pa.t*. and *pa.p*. **wind'ed** and (as a horn) **wound** (*wownd*).—*ns*. **wind'age**, the difference between the size of the bore of a gun and that of the ball or shell: the influence of the wind in deflecting a missile, the amount of deflection due to wind, or the allowance made for it: air friction on a moving, esp. revolving, part of a machine; **wind'-bag**, the bellows of a bagpipe, or (*obs*.) organ: (*facet*.) the lungs or chest: an inflated bag as a charm to procure a favourable wind: a person of mere words, an excessively talkative person.—*adj*. **wind'-bound**, hindered from sailing by contrary wind.—*n*. **wind'-break**, a protection against the force of the wind, such as a fence or line of trees.—*adjs*. **wind'-broken**, of a horse, broken-winded; **wind'-changing**, fickle.—*ns*. **wind'-chart**, a chart showing the direction of the wind; **wind'-chest**, the box or reservoir that supplies compressed air to the pipes or reeds of an organ; **wind'-cone**, (*aero*.) a sleeve floating from the top of a mast, its angle with the ground giving a rough conception of the velocity of the wind, and its angle in a horizontal plane the wind direction; **wind'-drop'sy**, tympanites; **wind'-egg**, an addle-egg: one soft-shelled or imperfectly formed; **wind'er**, one who sounds a horn; **wind'er**, (*slang*) a blow that takes one's breath away; **wind'fall**, fruit blown off a tree by the wind: any unexpected money or other advantage.—*adj*. **wind'fallen**, blown down by wind.—*ns*. **wind'-flower**, an anemone, esp. the wood-anemone; **wind'-furnace**, any form of furnace using the natural draught of a chimney without aid of a bellows; **wind'-gall**, a puffy swelling about the fetlock joints of a horse; **wind'-gauge**, an instrument for measuring the velocity of the wind: a gauge for measuring pressure of wind in an organ: an appliance fixed to a rifle by means of which the force of the wind is ascertained so that allowance may be made for it in sighting; **wind'-gun**, an air-gun; **wind'-hover** (*hov', huv'ər*), the kestrel.—*adv*. **wind'ily**.—*ns*. **wind'iness**; **wind'-instrument**, a musical instrument sounded by means of wind, esp. by the breath; **wind'jammer**, a large sailing vessel: (*coll*.) a wind-resisting golf blouse.—*adj*. **wind'less**, without wind.—*ns*. **wind'mill**, a mill in which the motive-power is the wind acting on a set of vanes or sails: a wind-driven set of vanes used to pump water, &c.: (*aero*.) any device which is caused to rotate by reason of its being carried through the air, and so develops power; **wind'ore**, (Ben Jonson, &c.) a form of **window**, based on false association with **door**; **wind'pipe**, the passage for the breath between the mouth and lungs, the trachea.—*adj*. **wind'-rode**, (*naut*.) riding at anchor with head to the wind.—*ns*. **wind'rose**, a rosette-like diagram showing the relative frequency and strength of winds in a locality for given periods of the year; **wind'row**, a row of hay, &c., raked together to be made into cocks: a row of peats, &c., set up and dried.—*v.t*. to arrange in windrows.—*ns*. **wind'-sail**, (*naut*.) a wide funnel of canvas used to convey a stream of air below deck: a vane of a windmill; **wind'screen**, a shelter against wind, esp. a transparent screen on motor-cars, &c.—*adjs*. **wind'-shak'd, -shaken**, agitated by the wind. —*ns*. **wind'shield**, (*U.S*.) a windscreen; **wind'-side**, the side next the wind; **wind'-sleeve, -sock**, a wind-cone; **wind'-sucker**, (of a horse) a crib-biter.—*adjs*. **wind'-swift**, swift as the wind; **wind'-tight**, air-tight.—*n*. **wind'-tunnel**, (*aero*.) an experimental apparatus for producing a uniform steady air-stream past a model for aerodynamic investigation work.—*adv*. and *adj*. **wind'ward**,

towards or on the side the wind blows from.—
Also *n.*—*adv.* **wind'wards.**—*adj.* **wind'y,** like,
characterised by, exposed to, the wind: (*poet.*)
moved, played, produced, by wind: (*poet.*) controlling the winds: producing, or produced by,
flatulence: (*fig.*) suggestive of wind, as unsubstantial, changeable, boastful, conceited, wordy:
(*coll.*) frightened, nervous.—**a capful of wind,** a
slight breeze; **before the wind,** carried along
by the wind; **between wind and water,** that
part of a ship's side which is now in, now out of,
the water owing to the fluctuation of the waves:
in a vulnerable or precarious place or position;
cast, or **lay, an anchor to windward,** to make
prudent provision for the future; **cast, fling,
throw, to the winds,** to scatter, throw away,
recklessly: to throw off all restraint, as of prudence,
sense of decorum, &c.; **down the wind,** moving
with the wind: (*obs.*; *fig.*) towards decay; **fight
windmills,** to struggle with imaginary opposition,
as Don Quixote tilted at the windmill; **get one's
wind,** to recover one's breath; **get the wind of,**
to get on the windward side of; **get to windward
of,** to secure an advantage over; **get the wind up,**
(*slang*) to become nervous, apprehensive, agitated;
get wind of, to get a hint or intimation of; **have
the wind of,** to be on the trail of; **how the wind
blows,** or **lies,** the state of the wind: the position
of affairs; **in the wind,** astir, afoot; **in the wind's
eye, in the teeth of the wind,** right against the
wind; **on the windy side,** (*Shak.*) on the windward side, from which one cannot be attacked, hence
safe, at an advantage; **raise the wind** (see **raise**);
sail close to the wind, to keep the boat's head
so near to the wind as to fill but not shake the
sails: to be in danger of transgressing an approved
limit; **second wind,** power of respiration recovered after breathlessness; **sow the wind and
reap the whirlwind,** to act wrongly and receive a
crushing retribution; **take the wind out of one's
sails,** (*fig.*) to deprive one of an advantage, to
frustrate, discomfit one. [O.E.; allied to O.N.
vindr, Ger. *wind,* L. *ventus.*]

wind, *wīnd,* *v.t.* to turn, to twist, to coil: to encircle:
to screw the mechanism of, as a timepiece: to make,
direct, as one's way, or to traverse, by turning and
twisting: (*refl.*) to insinuate: (*rare* or *obs.*) to
change the course of, deflect, control: to turn to
one's left, as a horse: (*obs.*) to bring in, involve
(also **wind up**), or to extricate, stealthily: (*arch.*;
fig.) to wind up (q.v.): (*Spens.*) to weave: (*obs.*
and *dial.*) to wield: to haul or hoist, as by a winch.
—*v.i.* to turn round something: to twist: to
move, go, by turns and twists, or (*fig.*) deviously:
to meander: (*obs.*) to go: (*obs.* and *dial.*) to writhe,
wriggle: (*obs.*) to extricate oneself (with *out*):
(*dial.*) to be twisted, warped: of a horse, to turn
to the left: (*pr.p.* **wind'ing;** *pa.t.* and *pa.p.*
wound, *wound;* chiefly *naut.* **wind'ed;** Burns
pa.t. **win't**).—*n.* a turn, coil, or twist: a turning: a
twisted condition.—*n.* **wind'er,** one who winds: an
instrument for winding: a clock or watch key:
an electrically driven winding-engine for hoisting
a cage or cages up a vertical mine-shaft: a twisting
plant.—*adj.* and *n.* **wind'ing.**—*n.* **wind'ing-
engine,** a machine for hoisting.—*adv.* **wind'ingly.**
—*ns.* **wind'ing-sheet,** a sheet for enwrapping a
corpse: (*dial.*) the dripping grease that clings
to the side of a candle; **wind'ing-stair,** a stair
constructed around a solid or hollow newel.—*n.pl.*
wind'ing-strips, two pieces of wood with parallel
edges, used for testing the parallelism of timber.—
n. **wind'-up,** the close, finish.—**turn the wind,**
(now *rare*) to go, move, or cause to move, from
side to side or on a winding course (*lit.* and *fig.*);
wind a ship, to turn her about end for end;
wind up, to bring, or come, to a conclusion: to
adjust for final settlement: (*fig.*) to excite very
much (esp. in *pa.p.* **wound up,** excited): to
coil completely: to wind the spring or the mechanism of tightly: (*obs.*) to furl: to tighten: to hoist,
as by a winch: (*Shak.*) to restore to harmony;
wind up and down, (*obs.*) to revolve in the mind.
[O.E. *windan;* cf. Ger. *winden,* O.N. *vinda,* Goth.
windan; cf. **wend, wander.**]

windac. See **windas.**

windas, *wind'as, n.* (*obs.*) a windlass: (*R. L.
Stevenson,* **wind'ac**) an instrument for bending a
cross-bow. [A.Fr. *windas;* cf. O.N. *vindáss—
vinda,* to wind, *áss,* pole.]

windlass, *wind'las, n.* any of various modifications
of the wheel and axle employing a revolving
cylinder, used for hauling or hoisting: (*obs.*) a
windas for a cross-bow.—*v.i.* to use a windlass.
—*v.t.* to hoist by means of such. [Prob. from
windas.]

windlass, *wind'las, n.* (*obs.*) a circuitous movement,
esp. to intercept game: (*obs.*) an indirect, crafty
action.—*v.i.* to take a roundabout course. [Prob.
from *wanlace,* an earlier A.Fr. form, of unknown
origin.]

windle, *win'dl, n.* an appliance for winding yarn.—
(*Scot.*) **winn'le.** [wind (2).]

windlestraw, *win'dl-straw, n.* a thin, dry stalk of
grass: any of various long-stalked species of grass,
as rye-grass: anything light or insubstantial: a
lanky or feeble person.—Also (*Scot.*) **windlestrae**
(*win'l-strā*). [O.E. *windelstréaw—windel,* a woven
basket, *stréaw,* straw.]

window, *win'dō, n.* an opening in the wall of a
building, &c., for air and light: the frame in
the opening: the space immediately behind the
opening: a window-pane: any opening suggesting
a window: (in *pl.*) the eyes, or (*Shak.*) the eyelids:
(*geol.*) a closed outcrop of strata lying beneath a
thrust plane and exposed by denudation.—*v.t.* to
furnish with windows: (*Shak.*) to make rents in.—
ns. **win'dow-bar,** a wooden or iron bar between
the panes of a window: a bar fitted into a window
for security: (*Shak.* **window-barne,** emended
bars, Timon, IV. iii. 116) lattice-work across a
woman's stomacher; **win'dow-blind,** a blind or
screen for a window; **win'dow-bole** (see **bole,** 1);
win'dow-box, a box for growing plants on a
window-sill; **win'dow-curtain,** a curtain hung
over a window, inside a room; **win'dow-dressing,**
the arranging of goods in a shop window: the art
of doing so effectively: (the art of) presenting a
cause, situation, &c., in a favourable light.—*adj.*
win'dowed, having a window or windows, or
openings or holes resembling these: (*Shak.,
Ant.,* IV. xii. 72) placed in a window. — *ns.*
win'dow-frame, a frame that surrounds a window; **win'dow-gardening,** the cultivation of
plants indoors before a window, or in boxes fitted
on the outside sill; **win'dow-glass,** glass suitable
or used for windows.—*adj.* **win'dowless,** having
no windows.—*ns.* **win'dow-pane,** a sheet of glass
set in a window; **win'dow-sash,** a frame in
which panes of glass are set; **win'dow-screen,**
any ornamental device for filling the opening of a
window; **win'dow-seat,** a seat in the recess of a
window; **win'dow-sill,** the sill of a window
opening; **win'dow-tax,** a tax levied on windows
of houses (repealed 1851). [M.E. *windowe, windoge*
—O.N. *vindauga—vindr,* wind, *auga,* eye.]

windring, *wind'ring, adj.* (*Shak., Temp.,* IV. i. 128)
perh. for winding or wandering.

Windsor, *win'zər, adj.* pertaining to *Windsor,* in
Berkshire, as in **Wind'sor-chair,** a kind of strong,
plain, polished chair, made entirely of wood;
Wind'sor-soap, a kind of perfumed toilet-soap
(usu. brown).

wine, *wīn, n.* the fermented juice of grapes: a
liquor made from other fruits: (*fig.*) intoxication:
a wine-drinking, a wine-party: a rich red colour.—
Also *adj.*—*v.t.* to supply with wine: to treat with
wine.—*v.i.* to take wine, especially at a wine-party.
—*ns.* **wine'-bag,** a wine-skin: a tippler; **wine'-
berry,** (*obs.*) a grape: (*dial.*) a red currant, a
gooseberry, or a bilberry: a raspberry (*Rubus
phoenicolasius*) of China and Japan: the tutu, or
another New Zealand tree, the makomako; **wine'-
bibber,** a continual drinker of wine: a drunkard;
wine'-bibbing; wine'-biscuit, a biscuit orig.
intended to be served with wine; **wine'-cask,** a
cask for holding wine; **wine'-cellar,** a cellar for
storing wine.—*adj.* **wine'-coloured,** of the colour
of red wine.—*ns.* **wine'-cooler,** a receptacle for
cooling wine in bottles about to be served at

table ; **wine'-fat, -vat,** a vat in which grapes are pressed in wine-making ; **wine'-glass,** a small glass used in drinking wine ; **wine'-glassful** ; **wine'-grower,** one who cultivates a vineyard and makes wine.—*n.* and *adj.* **wine'-growing.**— *ns.* **wine'-meas'ure,** an old English liquid measure, its gallon ⅔ths of the gallon in beer-measure ; **wine'-merchant,** a dealer in wine, esp. wholesale ; **wine'-palm,** any palm yielding palm-wine (as Borassus, Raphia) ; **wine'-party,** a drinking-party ; **wine'-press,** a machine in which grapes are pressed in the manufacture of wine ; **wine'-sap,** a variety of deep-red winter apple ; **wine'-skin,** a bag for holding wine, made out of a skin ; **wine'-stone,** crude argol ; **wine'-taster,** one whose business it is to sample wines ; **wine'-vault(s),** a vaulted wine-cellar : a place where wine is tasted or drunk.—*adj.* **win'y,** like wine : intoxicated.— **Adam's wine,** water ; **Rhine, Rhenish, wine,** wine produced on the banks of the *Rhine,* esp. hock ; **spirit of wine,** alcohol ; **white wine,** light-coloured or uncoloured (as opp. to *red*) wine, e.g. Chablis, Sauterne, hock, sherry. [O.E. *win* ; Goth. *wein,* Ger. *wein* ; all from L. *vīnum* ; cog. with Gr. *oinos.*]

wing, *wing, n.* the organ of a bird, insect, or other creature, by which it flies : an animal organ resembling a wing : flight : means of flying : anything resembling a wing : a fan or vane : (usu. in *pl.*) a sail : any side-piece, on a building, &c. : the side of a stage : side scenery : a plane of an aeroplane : the mudguard of a motor vehicle : a similar part of a carriage : a side-piece on the back of an armchair : one of the longer sides of crown-works or horn-works in fortification : the flank corps or division of an army on either side : the ships on either extremity of a fleet ranged in line : a section of a political party : a player on either extreme of the forward line in football, &c. : a group of three squadrons in the Royal Air Force : (in *pl.*) a qualified pilot's badge : (*sing.*) formerly) the badge of any member of an air-crew other than the pilot : a flock (of plover) : (*fig.*) means or power of rapid movement : (*fig.*) protection.—*v.t.* to furnish, or transport, with wings : to lend speed to : to supply with side-pieces : to bear in flight, to waft : to effect on wings : to traverse by flying : to wound in the wing : to wound in arm or shoulder.—*v.i.* to soar on the wing : to go with speed.—*adv.* **wing'-and-wing,** in the condition of a ship sailing before the wind with the foresail at one side and the mainsail at the other.—*ns.* **wing'-case,** the horny case or cover over the wings of some insects, as the beetle ; **wing'-commander,** a Royal Air Force officer corresponding in rank to a naval commander or to a lieutenant-colonel. — *adj.* **winged** (*wingd* or *wing'id*), furnished with wings : (*wingd*) of a stem) bearing the thin flattened bases of decurrent leaves, (of a fruit or seed) having a flattened appendage : (*wingd*) wounded in the wing, shoulder, or arm : swift : lofty, sublime (as **winged words**—Homer *epea pteroenta*) : (Milt.) full of flying birds.—*adv.* **wing'edly,** on or by wings.—*adjs.* **wing'-footed,** having wings on the feet : aliped ; **wing'-led** (Shak., *Cymb.,* II. iv. 24, some editions), presumably, led in wings or divisions ; **wing'less,** without wings.—*ns.* **wing'let,** a small wing : a bastard wing : a wing-like appendage ; **wing'-loading,** (*aero.*) the maximum flying weight of an aeroplane divided by the total area of the main planes, including the ailerons ; **wing'-shell,** a strombus : a mollusc of genus Malleus, or allied genus, or its shell : a wing-snail ; **wing'-shoot'ing,** the act or practice of shooting flying birds ; **wing'-shot,** a shot at a bird on the wing : one who shoots flying birds.—*adj.* shot in the wing, or while on the wing.—*n.* **wing'-snail,** a pteropod.—*adj.* **wing'y,** having, resembling, or soaring on, wings : lofty.—**birds of one wing** (*obs.*), birds of the same kind ; **flying-wing** (see *fly*) ; **make, take, wing,** to begin flight : to depart ; **on, upon, the wing,** flying : in motion : departing ; **on the wings of the wind,** with the highest speed ; **under one's wing,** under one's protection ; **winged bull,** a common form in Assyrian sculpture,

symbolic of domination. [O.N. *vængr,* a wing.]

wing. See **win** (3).

winge, *winj,* (*dial.*) non-Scottish variant of **whinge.**

wink, *wingk, v.i.* to move the eyelids, or an eyelid, quickly : to give a hint, or convey amused understanding, by a sign of this kind : (*obs.*) to shut the eyes : to blink : to seem not to see : to connive (usu. with *at*) : to flicker, twinkle.—*v.t.* to close and open quickly : to flicker : to express by flashlights.—*n.* act of winking : a hint, as by winking : a blink : a closing of the eyes for sleep : a short spell of sleep : a very small time or distance.—*ns.* **wink'-a-peep,** (*dial.*) the scarlet pimpernel ; **wink'er,** one who winks : a horse's blinker (usu. in *pl.*) : (*dial.*) an eye : nictitating membrane of a bird's eye : a small bellows in an organ, regulated by a spring, controlling variations of wind-pressure ; **wink'ing,** act of giving a wink.—*adj.* (*Shak.*) closed, or with eyes shut, or blind.—*adv.* **wink'ingly,** forty winks, (*coll.*) a short nap ; **like winking,** (*slang*) very rapidly ; **tip one the wink** (see *tip*). [O.E. *wincian* ; Ger. *winken.*]

winkle, *wing'kl.* Same as **periwinkle** (2).— **winkle out,** (*fig.*) to force out gradually and with difficulty (perh. derived from Ger. *winkel,* corner).

winna, *win'ä, wun'ä,* a Scots form of **will not.**

winner, winning, winningly. See **win** (1 and 2).

winnle. See **windle.**

winnock, *win'ak,* **win'dock,** *n.* (*Scot.*) a window. [Scot. development of M.E. *windoge* ; see **window** ; cf. **warlock.**]

winnow, *win'ō, v.t.* to separate the chaff from by wind : to fan : to sift : to separate : to blow upon : to waft : to diffuse : (*Milt.*) to set in motion : (*rare*) to flap, flutter.—*v.i.* to separate chaff from grain : to fly : to blow in gusts.—*n.* a fan for winnowing.—*adj.* **winn'owed,** (Shak., *Ham.,* V. ii. 201) perh. wise.—*ns.* **winn'ower** ; **winn'owing** ; **winn'owing-fan, -machine,** a fan, machine, for winnowing. [O.E. *windwian,* to winnow—*wind* ; see **wind** (1).]

winsey. Same as **wincey.**

winsome, *win'sam, adj.* cheerful : pleasant : attractive. — *adv.* **win'somely.** — *n.* **win'someness.** [O.E. *wynsum,* pleasant—*wyn,* joy (Ger. *wonne*)— and *-sum* (see suff. *-some*).]

winter, *win'ter, n.* the cold season of the year—in northern temperate regions, from November or December to January or February ; astronomically, from the winter solstice to the vernal equinox : a year (usu. in *pl.*) : any season of cheerlessness.— *adj.* wintry : suitable for wear or use in winter : sown in autumn, as **win'ter-wheat, -barley,** &c., **win'ter-crop.**—*v.i.* to pass the winter.—*v.t.* to feed and keep through. winter.—*ns.* **win'ter-aconite** (see *aconite*) ; **win'ter-apple,** an apple that keeps well in winter, or **that** does not ripen till winter.— *adj.* **win'ter-beaten,** (*Spens.*) beaten or injured by the cold of winter.—*ns.* **win'ter-berry,** a name given to several shrubs of the genus Ilex, growing in the eastern **parts** of N. America ; **win'ter-bloom,** the witch-hazel : a species of azalea ; **win'ter-bourne, an** intermittent spring of water, as found in the **chalk-districts** ; **win'ter-bud,** a bud protected by scales in which next year's shoot passes the winter **;** **win'ter-cherry,** any species of Physalis, esp. *Physalis alkekengi* : its edible fruit : the balloon-vine, or its fruit.—*adj.* **win'ter-clad,** warmly clad.—*ns.* **win'ter-clover,** the partridge-berry ; **win'ter-cress,** a cruciferous plant (Barbarea) formerly cultivated for winter salad.—*adj.* **win'tered,** (*obs.*) having seen many winters, aged : exposed to winter : (*Shak.*) worn in winter.—*ns.* **win'ter-garden,** an ornamental garden of evergreens, &c., or a conservatory with flowers, for winter ; **win'tergreen,** a plant of genus Pyrola, also of Chimaphila : a plant of genus Gaultheria, whose oil is an aromatic stimulant, used in flavouring confectionery and in medicine (**chickweed-win'tergreen,** either of two plants —*Trientalis europaea* or *Trientalis americana*— belonging to the Primulaceae, having white star-like flowers).—*vs.t.* **win'ter-ground,** (Shak., *Cymbeline,* IV. ii. 229) assumed by Steevens to mean ' to protect, as a plant, from the inclemency of winter'; **win'terise**, to make suitable for use under wintry conditions.—*adj.* **win'terly**, cheerless.—*n.pl.* **win'ter-quarters**, the quarters of an army during winter : a winter residence.—*ns.* **win'ter-tide**, (*arch.*) winter ; **win'triness**.—*adj.* **win'try, win'tery**, resembling, or suitable to, winter : stormy : cheerless.—**winter sports**, openair sports practised on snow and ice, as skiing, &c. [O.E. ; cf. O.N. *vetr*, Ger. *winter* ; from Indo-Gmc. root seen in **wet, water.**]

winter's-bark, *win'tərz-bärk*, *n.* a stimulant, aromatic, and tonic bark, named from Captain *Winter*, who first brought it from the Strait of Magellan in 1579.

wintle, *win'tl*, *v.i.* (*Scot.*) to stagger.—*n.* a stagger. [Flem. *windtelen—winden*, to wind.]

winy. See **wine**.

winze, *winz*, *n.* (*Scot.*) a curse. [Flem. *wensch* ; from root of **wish**.]

winze, *winz*, *n.* in mining, a small ventilating shaft between two levels.—Also **winds**. [Perh. **wind** (2).]

wipe, *wīp*, *v.t.* to clean or dry by rubbing : (with *away*, *off*, *out*, *up*) to clear away : to obliterate, annihilate, or abolish (with *out*) : to draw across something in order to, or as if to, clean it : to apply solder to with a piece of cloth or leather : (*coll.*) to strike.—*n.* act of cleaning by rubbing : a blow : (Shak., *Lucr.*, 537) a brand, a scar : (*slang*) a handkerchief.—*ns.* **wī'per**, one who wipes, esp. one who is employed in cleaning in certain industrial jobs : that which wipes or is used for wiping : (*elect.*) a moving arm or other conducting device for making a selected contact out of a number of possible connexions : a projecting tooth or other part on a moving piece of machinery ; **wī'per-wheel**, a wheel with wipers on the rim ; **wī'ping**, act of one who wipes : a thrashing. [O.E. *wīpian* ; O.H.G. *wīfan*, to wind round, *waif*, bandage, Goth. *weipan*, to crown.]

wire, *wīr*, *n.* a thread or rope of metal : a piece of wire, or (in *pl.*) a group or network of wires, used for some purpose : the metal thread used in telegraphy, &c. : a metallic string of a musical instrument : (*Scot.*) a metal knitting-needle : (*coll.*) a telegram : (*slang*) a clever pickpocket : (Shak.) a lash, made of wire.—*adj.* formed of, pertaining to, or using, wire : running on wire : pertaining to wire-drawing.—*v.t.* to bind, support, protect, snare, or furnish, with wire : to supply, as a building, with wires necessary for carrying an electric current : to send, or to inform, by telegraph : to place (a croquet-ball) where a hoop hampers it.—*v.i.* to telegraph.—*n.* **wire'-bridge**, a suspension-bridge.—*adj.* **wired**.—*ns.* **wire'-dancer**, a performer on a tight wire ; **wired'-glass**, glass in which a wire mesh has been incorporated during rolling as a resistance against fire and explosion blast.—*v.t.* **wire'-draw**, to draw into wire by pulling through successively smaller holes in a hard steel die-block : to throttle a fluid by passing it through a small orifice, thus reducing the pressure : to draw or spin out to a great length : to strain the meaning of.—*ns.* **wire'drawer** ; **wire'drawing**.—*adj.* **wire'drawn**, (*fig.*) spun out into needless fine distinctions.—*ns.* **wire'-gauze**, a kind of stiff close fabric made of fine wire ; **wire'-grass**, a kind of fine meadow-grass (*Poa compressa*) : any of various other grasses with wiry stems ; **wire'-guard**, wire-netting placed in front of a fire ; **wire'-hair**, a wire-haired terrier.—*adj.* **wire'-haired**, having a coat of rather rough, hard hair.—*n.* **wire'-heel**, in horses and cattle, a defect or disease of the foot.—*adj.* **wire'less**, without a wire or wires : of or pertaining to telegraphy or telephony without wires.—*n.* wireless telegraphy or telephony, radio : a receiving or transmitting set used for this purpose : a message or broadcast so transmitted : broadcast programmes : broadcasting generally.—*v.t.* and *v.i.* to communicate by radio.—*ns.* **wire'-line**, one of the closeset white lines in laid paper, perpendicular to the water-lines ; **wire'-man**, one who puts up or who takes care of wires ; **wire'-nett'ing**, a texture of wire woven in the form of a net ; **wire'-**

photo, a photograph transmitted over a wire circuit by electrical means ; **wire'-puller**, one who exercises an influence felt but not seen : an intriguer ; **wire'-pulling** ; **wī'rer**, one who wires, or who uses wire e.g. to snare animals ; **wire'-rope**, a rope of twisted iron or steel.—*adjs.* **wire'-sewed**, **-stitched**, sewed with wire instead of thread ; **wire'-stringed**.—*ns.* **wire'way**, transportation by means of wires ; **wire'work**, the making of wire, or of objects consisting of wire : articles, or fabric, made of wire ; **wire'worker** ; **wire'working** ; **wire'-worm**, a name given to the larvae of clickbeetles, from their slenderness and uncommon hardness.—*adj.* **wire'wove**, denoting a fine quality of writing-paper (see **wove**).—*adv.* **wī'rily**.—*n.* **wī'riness**.—*adj.* **wī'ry**, made of, or like, wire : flexible and strong : of a person, strong and able to endure.—**pull the wires** (see **wire-puller** above) ; **wire away**, or **in**, to act or work with vigour ; **wire into**, to eat vigorously and assiduously ; **wired wireless**, the transmission of signals by means of electromagnetic waves guided by conductors, the frequencies being of the same order as those used for radio communication ; **wire-haired terrier**, a type of wire-haired foxterrier ; **wireless station**, a station for wireless transmission ; **wireless telegraphy, telephony**, signalling through space, without the use of conducting wires between transmitter and receiver, by means of electromagnetic waves generated by high-frequency alternating currents. [O.E. *wīr* ; O.N. *vīrr* (in composition).]

wis, *wis*, also **wist**, *Shak.* **wish** (all *sham arch.*), *v.t.* to know : to believe. [Partly from misunderstanding of the adv. **iwis** (q.v.) as *I wis*, partly a new present from the pa.t. **wist** (see **wit**, 1).]

wisard, *wiz'ərd*, *n.* Same as **wizard**.

wise, *wīz*, *adj.* having knowledge : learned : able to make good use of knowledge : judging rightly : discreet : skilful : dictated by wisdom : containing wisdom : pious, godly : (*dial.*) skilled in magic : (*dial.*) normal mentally.—*n.* **wisdom** (*wiz'dəm*), quality of being wise : judgment : ability to make right use of knowledge : a wise course or saying : (*hist.*) learning : (*B.*) skilfulness, speculation, spiritual perception : (Shak.) sanity : **Wisdom**, the apocryphal Book of the Wisdom of Solomon : Jesus Christ.—*ns.* **wis'dom-literature**, the book of Job, Proverbs, Ecclesiastes, Wisdom of Solomon, Ecclesiasticus, and the Epistle of James ; **wis'dom-tooth**, any of four large double back teeth cut after childhood, usu. about the age of twenty.—*n.* **wise'-crack**, a lively, pungent retort or comment.—*v.i.* to make such.—*adjs.* **wise'cracking**, making, or addicted to making, wisecracks ; **wise'-heart'ed**, having wisdom : prudent ; **wise'-like** (*Scot.* : *wuis-*, *wis-*), sensible, judicious : decent : fitting : looking as if capable of playing one's part well.—*n.* **wise'ling**, one who pretends to be wise.—*adv.* **wise'ly**.—*n.* **wise'ness**.—**never, none the wiser**, still in ignorance ; **put one wise**, (*slang*) to put one in possession of information, make aware ; **wise to**, (*slang*) aware of ; **wise woman**, a witch : (*Scot.*) a midwife. [O.E. *wīs* ; Ger. *weise* ; from root of **wit**.]

wise, *wīz*, *v.t.* (*Scot.*) to guide in a certain direction. [O.E. *wīsian—wīs* ; see **wise** (1).]

wise, *wīz*, *n.* (*arch.*) way, manner, now chiefly in the phrases **in any wise**, **in no wise**, in any way, in no way ; **on this wise**, in this way. [O.E. *wīse* ; Ger. *weise* ; akin to **wise** (1) and **wit**. Doublet **guise**.]

wiseacre, *wīz'ā-kər*, *n.* one who unduly assumes an air of superior wisdom : a simpleton quite unconscious of being such. [M.Du. *wijssegger—*O.H.G. *wīzago*, a prophet.]

wish, *wish*, *v.i.* to have a desire : to long : to be inclined : to express a desire, esp. as part of a superstitious ritual.—*v.t.* to desire or long for : to express a desire for : to ask : to invoke : to bid : (*obs.*) to recommend : (*coll.*) to foist, palm off (with *on*, *onto*) : (*dial.*) to bewitch.—*n.* desire, longing : a thing desired : an expression of desire : (usu. in *pl.*) an expression of desire for good fortune for another : (*obs.*) a malediction.—*n.* **wish'er**.—*adj.*

wish′ful, having a wish or desire: eager: (obs.) desirable, desired.—adv. **wish′fully.**—n. **wish′-fulness.**—n. and adj. **wish′ing.**—ns. **wish′ing-bone, wish′-bone,** the merrythought; **wish′ing-cap,** a cap by wearing which one obtains everything one wishes; **wish′ing-stone, -tree, -well,** &c., a stone, tree, well, &c., supposed to have the power of making a wish expressed at it come true.—**wish fulfilment,** (psych.) the satisfaction of a desire in dreams, day-dreams, &c.; **wishful thinking,** (psych.) a type of thinking in which the individual substitutes the phantasy of the fulfilment of the wish for the actual achievement: a belief that a particular thing will happen, or is so, engendered by desire that it should happen, or be so: (loosely) thinking about and wishing for an event or turn of fortune that may not take place; **wish one further,** (slang) to wish one was in some other place, not present; **wish one joy of,** to hope possession may be a benefit to one (usu. ironical). [O.E. wȳscan, wish; Ger. wünschen, Sw. önska.]

wishtonwish, wish′tən-wish, n. the N. American prairie-dog: (Fenimore Cooper) the whippoorwill. [Amer. Ind.]

wish-wash, wish′-wosh, n. (coll.) anything wishy-washy.—adj. **wish′y-wash′y,** thin and weak: diluted: feeble: of poor quality. [Formed from **wash.**]

wisket, wis′kit, n. (dial.) a basket. [Scand., from same root as **whisk** (1).]

wisp, wisp, n. a small bundle of straw or hay: a tuft, a shred: a thin strand or band: a small broom: a twisted bunch used as a torch: the Will-o′-the-wisp: a flock (of snipe).—v.t. to make into a wisp or bundle: to rub down with a wisp.—adj. **wis′py.** [Origin uncertain.]

wist, wist, v.t. and v.i. (sham arch.) to know. [See **wis,** iwis, wit (1).]

Wistaria, wis-tā′ri-ā, n. a genus of papilionaceous plants, some of the species among the most magnificent ornamental climbers known in English gardens, named from the American anatomist Caspar Wistar (1761-1818).—Also, wrongly, **Wis-tē′ria.**

wistful, wist′fool, -fl, adj. (obs.) intent: earnest: longing: yearning with little hope: pensive.—adv. **wist′fully.**—n. **wist′fulness.** [Most prob. for wistly.]

wistiti, wis′ti-ti, n. a marmoset. [Fr. ouistiti; named from its cry.]

wistly, wist′li, adv. (Shak.) longingly, earnestly. [Prob. for whistly; see whist (1).]

wit, wit, v.t. and v.i. to know: to be aware (with of): to recognise, discern: to know how:—infin. **wit,** Spens., Shak. and others **weet(e),** wēt; Spens. **weet′en,** also **wot,** wot; pr.t. 1st pers. sing. **wot,** Scot. **wat,** wawt; 2nd **wost** (wott′est); 3rd, **wot** (wots, wott′eth), Scot. **wate, wait, wats;** pl. 1st, 2nd, 3rd, **wot;** pa.t. **wist** (wott′ed); pr.p. **witt′ing, weet′ing** (wott′ing); pa.p. **wist.**—n. **witt′ing,** (obs. and dial.) knowledge, cognisance: information.—adj. cognisant: conscious: deliberate.—adv. **witt′ingly,** knowingly: by design.—**to do to wit,** to cause to know; **to wit,** that is to say, namely—the O.E. gerund tó witanne. [O.E. witan, to know (pres. tense wát, wást, wát, pl. witon; pa.t. wiste, or wisse, pl. wiston, pa.p. wist); Goth. witan, to observe, Ger. wissen; cf. L. vidēre, to see; Gr. idein.]

wit, wit, n. (obs.) the mind: (arch.) the understanding: (arch.) imagination or invention: ingenuity: intelligence, sense (in phrase **have the wit to**): a mental faculty (chiefly in pl.): the power of combining ideas with a pointed verbal effect: the product of this power: a person endowed with wit: (obs.) information (in phrase **to get wit of**).—n. **wit′-cracker,** one who makes witty remarks in a crisp style.—adj. **wit′less,** lacking wit, wisdom, sense: (obs.) without intellectual faculties: out of one′s mind: stupid, unintelligent: unaware, unconscious.—adv. **wit′lessly.**—ns. **wit′lessness; wit′ling,** one who has little wit: a pretender to wit; **wit′-monger,** a poor would-be wit; **wit′-snapper,** (Shak.) one who affects wit or repartee.—adj. **witt′ed,** having wit or understanding (usu. in

composition, as quick-witted).—n. **witticism** (wit′i-sizm), a witty remark: a sentence or phrase affectedly witty: (formerly) a jibe.—adv. **witt′ily.**—n. **witt′iness.**—adj. **witt′y,** possessed of wit: amusing, droll: sarcastic: (B) ingenious; (obs.) wise, discreet, sensible.—v.t. **wit′wanton,** (with it; obs.) to indulge in irreverent wit.—**at one′s wits′ end,** utterly perplexed; **have one′s wits about one,** to be alert and resourceful; **live by one′s wits,** to gain a livelihood by ingenious expedients rather than by honest labour; **the five wits,** the five senses. [O.E. (ge)wit—wit, 1.]

witan, wit′an, n.pl. members of the witenagemot: the witenagemot.—n. **witenagemot** (wit′ən-ə-gə-mōt′) popularly -nag′), the supreme council of England in Anglo-Saxon times, composed of the bishops, the ealdormen of shires, and a number of the king′s friends and dependents. [Pl. of O.E. wita, a man of knowledge (witena, gen. pl.); gemót, meeting; see preceding words.]

witch, wich, n. a woman regarded as having supernatural or magical power and knowledge through compact with the devil or a minor evil spirit: a hag, crone: (coll.) a fascinating young girl: (now rare) a wizard: the craig-fluke: a curve whose equation is $x^2y=4a^2(2a-y)$.—v.t. to bewitch: to effect, change, transport, &c., by means of witchcraft: to fascinate.—v.i. to practise witchcraft or fascination.—ns. **witch′craft,** the craft or practice of witches: the black art, sorcery: supernatural power; **witch′-doctor,** among Kaffirs, &c., a magician who detects witches and counteracts evil magical influences: one who professes to heal by means of magic; **witch′ery,** witchcraft: fascination; **witch′es′-broom,** a dense tuft of poorly developed branches formed on a woody plant attacked by a parasite (chiefly fungi and mites); **witch′es′-butter,** nostoc and other gelatinous blue-green algae; **witch′es′-meat,** tremella; **witch′es′-thimble,** a name for various plants with thimble-like flowers, as the foxglove; **witch′-finder,** one whose business was to detect witches: a witch-doctor; **witch′ing,** sorcery: enchantment.—adj. suited to witchcraft: weird: fascinating.—adv. **witch′ingly.**—ns. **witch′-knot,** a knot, esp. in the hair, supposed to be tied by means of witchcraft; **witch′-meal,** the inflammable pollen of the club-moss.—adj. **witch′-ridden,** ridden by witches.—n. **witch′-wife,** (Scot.) a woman who practises witchcraft. — **witches′ Sabbath** (see Sabbath); **witch hunt,** (U.S.) the searching out of political opponents for exposure on grounds of alleged disloyalty to the state, &c. [M.E. wicche (both masc. and fem.)—O.E. wicca (masc.), wicce (fem.), wizard, witch, and verb wiccian; ety. dub.]

witch, wich, n. any of several trees with pliant branches, as the wych-elm, the rowan, &c.—ns. **witch′-alder,** any of a genus of N. American shrubs related to the witch-hazel—not an alder; **witch′-elm,** the wych-elm; **witch′en,** the mountain ash: the wych-elm; **witch′-hazel,** any of a number of trees, as the wych-elm, the hornbeam, or a N. American shrub (Hamamelis virginica) from whose bark is made a supposed remedy for bruises, &c.—a distillate of the bark dissolved in alcohol. [O.E. wice; allied to wícan, to give way.]

witchetty, wich′i-ti, n. edible grubs of species of longicorn beetles. [Austr. native name.]

wite, wit, v.t. (obs. or Scot.) to blame: to lay the blame on.—n. (now dial.) blame, reproach.—adj. **wite′less,** (now dial.) blameless. [O.E. wítan, to see, blame; allied to wit.]

witenagemot. See witan.

with, n. Same as **withe.**

with, widh, also with, prep. denoting nearness, agreement, or connexion: by, beside: among: on the side of: in the company of: in the possession or care of: containing: supplemented by: possessing: characterised by: in the same direction as: at the time of: at the same time as: immediately after: in competition or contest against: in respect of, in the regard of: by, by means of, through: using: from (as in to part with).—adv. **withal** (widh-awl′), with all or the rest: besides: therewith: thereupon: nevertheless, for all that.—*prep.* an emphatic form of *with*, used after its object.—**feel**, or **be**, or **think**, **with**, to feel as, or be of the same opinion as, the other person specified: **with that**, thereupon. [O.E. *with*, against; O.N. *vith*, Ger. *wider*. It ousted the O.E. *mid*, with (Ger. *mit*).]

withdraw, *widh-draw'*, or *with-*, *v.t.* to draw back or away: to take back or away: to take from deposit or investment, as money: to remove (with *from*): (*rare*) to deflect, turn aside: to recall, retract, unsay.—*v.i.* to retire: to go away: to take back what one has said, or to recall a motion one has proposed:—*pa.t.* **withdrew** (*-drōō'*); *pa.p.* **withdrawn'**.—*ns.* **withdraw'al**, (*rare*) **withdraw'-ment**; **withdraw'er**; **withdraw'ing-room**, a room used to retire into: a drawing-room.—*adj.* **withdrawn'**, (of place) secluded: remote: (of manner) detached. [Pfx. *with-*, against, back, and **draw**.]

withe, *widh*, *with*, or *wīdh*, *n.* a flexible twig, esp. of willow: a band of twisted twigs: (*obs.*) a halter: an elastic handle to a tool to save the hand from the shock of blows: a boom-iron.—*v.t.* to bind with a withe or withes: to take with a noose of withes.—*adj.* **with'y**, made of withes: like withes, flexible: wiry and agile. [O.E. *withthe*; O.N. *vithir*, Ger. *weide*, willow; cf. **withy**.]

wither, *widh'ər*, *v.i.* to fade or become dry: to lose freshness: to languish, decline: to decay, waste.— *v.t.* to cause to dry up, fade, or decay: (*fig.*) to blight: to cause to feel very unimportant or despicable: to dry, as tea.—*adj.* **with'ered**.— *ns.* **with'eredness**; **with'ering**.—*adj.* fading, becoming dry, &c., or causing to do so: used for drying or curing: (*fig.*) blasting, blighting, scorching.—*n.* **with'ering-floor**, the drying-floor of a malthouse.—*adv.* **with'eringly**. [M.E. *wederen*, to expose to weather.]

witherite, *widh'ər-īt*, *n.* the chief source of barium compounds—barium carbonate, occurring as orthorhombic crystals in pseudohexagonal pyramids. [Dr W. *Withering*, who first discriminated it from barytes, 1784.]

withers, *widh'ərz*, *n.pl.* the ridge between the shoulder-bones of a horse.—*adj.* **with'er-wrung**, injured in the withers. [O.E. *wither*, against, an extension of *with*, against.]

withershins, *widh'*, *wid'ər-shinz*, *adv.* (*Scot.*) in the contrary direction, contrary to the course of the sun: in the wrong way—opp. to *deasil*. [L.G. *weddersins*; cf. O.E. *wither*, against, L.G. *sind*, direction, O.E. *sīth*, journey.]

withhault. Pseudo-archaic *pa.t.* of **withhold**.

withhold, *widh-hōld'*, or *with-*, *v.t.* to hold back, restrain: to keep back: to refuse to give: (*obs.*) to keep in bondage or custody.—*v.i.* (*obs.*) to refrain (with *from* or infin.): (*Pope*) to postpone:— *pa.t.* and *pa.p.* **withheld'** (*arch. pa.p.* **withhold'en**). —*ns.* **withhold'er**; **withhold'ment**. [Pfx. *with-*, against, and **hold**.]

within, *widh-in'*, *prep.* in or to the inner part of: inside: in the limits of: not going beyond: (*obs.*) on the inner side of: entered from: into.— *adv.* in the inner part: inwardly: in the mind, soul, heart: behind the scenes: (*arch.*) at home: indoors: in or to an inner room: herein.—**within land**, (*obs.*) inland; **within reach**, in a position from which it can be obtained, or attained, without much difficulty, effort, or loss of time. [O.E. *withinnan* —*with*, against, with, *innan*, in.]

without, *widh-owt'*, *prep.* (*arch.*) outside, or out of: outside the limits of: beyond: not with: in absence of: not having: not using: with no help from: free from.—*adv.* on the outside: outwardly: outside, not members of, a particular group or society: (*arch.*) out of doors.— (*arch.* or *dial.*) unless, except.—*adj.* **without'-door**, (*Shak.*) outward.—*prep.* **without'en**, (*arch.*) without.—**from without**, from the outside; **without distinction**, indiscriminately; **without doors**, out of doors: outside the family, nation, &c.: outside Parliament. [O.E. *withútan*—*with*, against, *útan*, outside.]

withstand, *widh-stand'*, or *with-*, *v.t.* to stand, maintain one's position, against: to oppose or

resist: (*obs.*) to hinder:—*pa.t.* and *pa.p.* **withstood'**.—*n.* **withstand'er**. [O.E. *withstandan*— *with*, against; see **stand**.]

withwind, *with'wīnd*, **withywind**, *widh'i-wīnd*, *ns.* (*dial.*) bindweed, or other climbing plant. [O.E. *withewinde*; cf. **withy**, and **wind** (2).]

withy, *widh'i*, *n.* the osier willow: any willow: a flexible twig or branch, esp. one used for binding. [O.E. *withig*, willow; cf. **widdy**, **withe**.]

witloof, *wit'lōf*, *n.* a kind of chicory with large leaves. [Du., lit. white leaves.]

witness, *wit'nis*, *n.* knowledge brought in proof: testimony of a fact: that which furnishes proof: one who sees or has personal knowledge of a thing: one who gives evidence: one who or that which attests.—*v.t.* to have direct knowledge of: (loosely) to see: to be the scene of: to give testimony to: to attest: to act as legal witness of: to sign: to show: (*arch.*) to evince.—*v.i.* to give evidence.— *ns.* **wit'ness-box**, the enclosure in which a witness stands when giving evidence in a court of law; **wit'nesser**.—**witness**, let (such and such) serve as evidence: **with a witness**, (*Shak.*) with a vengeance. [O.E. (*ge*)*witnes*—(*ge*)*wit*; see *wit* (2).]

witting, **witty**, &c. See **wit** (1 and 2).

wittol, *wit'əl*, *n.* one who knows his wife's faithlessness, and submits to it.—*adj.* **witt'olly**, (*Shak.*) like a wittol or contented cuckold. [M.E. *wetewold*; associated with **cuckold** (q.v.), and perh. from **witwall**, or from **wit** (1).]

witwall, *wit'wawl*, *n.* (*dial.*) the green woodpecker, or the greater spotted woodpecker. [Cf. Ger. *wittewal*, *wiedewall*.]

wive, *wiv*, *v.t.* to take for a wife: to provide with a wife: to become the wife of.—*v.i.* to marry a wife. —*n.* **wive'hood**, (*Spens.*) wifehood. [O.E. *wīfian* —*wīf*, wife.]

wivern, *wī'vərn*, *n.* (*her.*) a fictitious monster, winged and two-legged, allied to the dragon and the griffin. [O.N.Fr. *wivre*, a viper—L. *vīpera*.]

wives, *wīvz*, *pl.* of **wife**.

wizard, *wiz'ərd*, *n.* one, usu. a man, who practises witchcraft or magic: one who works wonders: (*obs.*) a wise man.—*adj.* with magical powers: (*slang*) wonderful, delightful.—*adv.* **wiz'ardly**, like a wizard.—*n.* **wiz'ardry**, sorcery. [M.E. *wysar*(*d*)—*wys*, wise, and suff. *-ard*.]

wizen, *wiz'n*, *adj.* dried up, thin, shrivelled (also **wiz'ened**).—*v.i.* and *v.t.* to become, or to make, dry and shrivelled.—*adj.* **wiz'en-faced**, having a thin, shrivelled face. Also **weazen**, &c. [O.E. *wisnian*, to wither; cog. with O.N. *visna*, to wither.]

wizier. Same as **vizier**.

wo. Same as **woe**, or as **whoa**.—Also **wo ha ho**.

woad, *wōd*, *n.* a genus (Isatis) of cruciferous plants, mostly natives of countries round the Mediterranean—**dyer's woad** (*Isatis tinctoria*) yielding a good and very permanent dye, largely superseded by indigo: a blue dye.—*adj.* **woad'ed**, dyed blue with woad. [O.E. *wād*; Ger. *waid*.]

wobble, *wob'l*, *v.i.* to move unsteadily or uncertainly from side to side: to move along thus: to quiver: (*coll.*) to quaver: to vacillate.—Also *v.t.*—*n.* an unsteady, unequal motion or movement.—*ns.* **wobb'ler**; **wobb'liness**; **wobb'ling**. — *adj.* **wobb'ly**, shaky: inclined to wobble. — Also **wabb'le**, **wabb'ler**, &c. [L.G. *wabbeln*.]

Woden, *wō'dən*, *n.* the chief god of the ancient Germanic peoples.—*n.* **Wō'denism**, the worship of Woden. [O.E. *Wóden*; O.H.G. *Wuotan*; cf. **Odin**.]

woe, **wo**, *wō*, *n.* (*arch.*) grief: misery: (often in *pl.*) a misfortune or calamity: (*obs.*) a physical pain: a curse: an exclamation of grief.—*adj.* (*arch.* and *dial.*) sad, wretched, sorry.—*adjs.* **woe'begone**, **wō'begone** (see **bego**), beset with woe: dismal-looking, suggesting misery: **woe'ful**, **wō'ful**, **woe'some** (*Scot.* **wae'some**), sorrowful or afflicted: bringing misery or calamity: deplorable: wretched, paltry.—*adv.* **woe'fully**, **wō'fully**.—*n.* **woe'fulness**, **wō'fulness**.—*adjs.* **woe'-wea'ried**, **-worn**, wearied, worn with woe.—**in weal and woe**, in prosperity and adversity; **woe is me**, (*arch.*) unhappy that I am! cursed am I; **woe unto**, calamity will befall: may calamity befall;

woe worth the day (see **worth**). [O.E. (interj.) *wá*; Ger. *weh*; L. *vae*; cf. **wail**.]

woggle, *wog'l*, *n.* the ring a Boy Scout threads his neckerchief through.

woiwode. Same as **voivode.**

woke, woken. See **wake.**

wold, *wōld*, *n.* an open tract of country, now chiefly upland country. [O.E. (Angl.) *wald*, forest, applied orig. to wooded parts of the country; cf. **weald.**]

wolf, *woolf*, *n.* the common name of certain gregarious and rapacious species of the genus Canis—including the common wolf (*Canis lupus*), the grey or timber wolf, and the coyote: anything very ravenous: a greedy and cunning person: (*obs.*) a tuberculous excrescence, or cancerous growth: (*mus.*) a dissonance heard in a keyed instrument tuned by unequal temperament: an extraneous non-harmonic note made by the bow on a string of a violin, &c.: (*slang*) a man who pursues women: (*pl.* **wolves**, *woolvz*).—*v.i.* to hunt for wolves.—*v.t.* (*coll.*) to devour ravenously. —*ns.* **wolf'-dog**, a dog of large breed formerly used in hunting wolves: a cross between a wolf and a domestic dog; **wolf'er**, one who hunts wolves; **wolf'-fish**, any of a genus of fierce and voracious salt-water fishes—called also sea-wolf; **wolf'-hound**, a wolf-dog, esp. of large size, as the Russian wolf-hound (see **borzoi**); **wolf'ing**, the hunting of wolves for their skins.—*adjs.* **wolf'ish**, **wolv'ish**, like a wolf: rapacious: ravenous.—*adv.* **wolf'ishly**.—*ns.* **wolf'kin**, **wolf'ling**, a young wolf; **wolf'-note**, (*mus.*) a wolf; **wolf'-pack**, a pack of wolves: a flotilla of submarines surfacing together for attack; **wolf's'-bane**, **wolfs'bane**, an aconite, esp. *Aconitum lycoctonum*; **wolf's'-foot**, **-claw**, the club-moss (Lycopodium); **wolf'-skin**, the skin or pelt of a wolf, **wolf's'-peach**, the tomato; **wolf'-spī'der**, any spider of the genus (Lycosa) to which the true tarantula belongs, or of the family Lycosidae; **wolf'-tooth**, a small supernumerary premolar in a horse.—**cry wolf**, to give a false alarm—from the story of the boy who cried 'Wolf' when there was none, and was not believed when there was one; **have a wolf by the ears**, to be in a very difficult situation; **have a wolf in the stomach**, to be ravenously hungry; **keep the wolf from the door**, to keep away poverty or hunger; **see a wolf**, to be tongue-tied (in allusion to an old superstition); **Wolf Cub**, one who belongs to the **Wolf Cubs**, a division of the Boy Scouts organisation for boys from eight to eleven years of age. [O.E. *wulf*; Ger. *wolf*; L. *vulpēs*, fox, *lupus*, wolf; Gr. *lykos*.]

Wolffian, *wool'fi-ən*, *vol'fi-ən*, *adj.* pertaining to, or associated with, the German embryologist K. F. *Wolff* (1733-94): designating the renal organs in the embryo of vertebrates.

Wolfian, *wool'fi-ən*, *vol'fi-ən*, *adj.* pertaining to the philosophy of Christian *Wolf* (1679-1754), who systematised and popularised the philosophy of Leibniz, and gave a strong impulse to that development of natural theology and rationalism.—Also **Wolff'ian**.—*n.* **Wolf'ianism.**

Wolfian, *wool'fi-ən*, *vol'fi-ən*, *adj.* pertaining to, or associated with, Friedrich August *Wolf* (1759-1824)—applied esp. to his theory that the *Odyssey* and *Iliad* are composed of numerous ballads, strung together by subsequent editors.

wolfram, *woolf'rəm*, *n.* (also **wolf'ramite**) a native compound of tungstate of iron and manganese: tungsten. [Ger.; origin uncertain.]

wollastonite, *wool'əs-tən-īt*, or *-as'-*, *n.* a pyroxene of relatively simple composition, silicate of calcium, CaSiO₃—also called *tabular spar*. [After the scientist W. H. *Wollaston* (1766-1828).]

wolverene, wolverine, *wool-və-rēn'*, *n.* the American glutton: its fur. [Extension of **wolf.**]

woman, *woom'ən*, *n.* an adult female of the human race: (now *dial.*) a wife: a mistress: the female sex, women collectively: a female attendant: (*coll.*) a charwoman or daily domestic help: the reverse or Britannia side of a coin: (*pl.* **women**, *wim'ən*).—Also *adj.*—*v.t.* (*obs.*) to cause to act like a woman: (with *it*) to play the part of a woman: to provide or staff with a woman or women: to call a person 'woman' abusively.—*n.* **wom'an-bod'y**, (*Scot.*) a woman.—*adjs.* **wom'an-born**, born of woman; **wom'an-built**, built by women.—*n.* **wom'an-child**, a female child:—*pl.* **wom'en-children.**—*adj.* **wo'man'd**, (*Shak.*) accompanied by a woman.—*adv.* **wom'anfully**, like a woman of spirit.—*adj.* **wom'an-grown**, grown to womanhood.—*ns.* **wom'an-hater**, a man who hates women, a mysogynist; **wom'anhood**, the state, character, or qualities of a woman: womenkind. —*v.t.* **wom'anise**, to make effeminate.—*v.i.* to become like a woman: (*coll.*) to consort with prostitutes. —*adj.* **wom'anish**, effeminate: feminine. —*adv.* **wom'anishly**. —*ns.* **wom'anishness**; **wom'ankind**, (*obs.*) a woman: (also **wom'enkind**, **wom'enfolk**, **-folks**) a group of women taken together, as the women of a family, or the female sex.—*adj.* and *adv.* **wom'an-like**.—*n.* **wom'anliness**.—*adj.* **wom'anly**, like or becoming a woman: feminine.—*adv.* in the manner of a woman.—*ns.* **wom'an-post**, (*Shak.*) a female messenger; **wom'an-quell'er**, a killer of women; **wom'an-suffrage**, possession of the electoral franchise by women.—*adjs.* **wom'an-tired**, (*Shak.*) henpecked (**tire,** 5) **woman'-vested**, wearing women's clothes.—**kept woman**, a mistress; **play the woman**, to give way to weakness; **woman of the town**, a whore; **woman of the world**, a woman of fashion, or of worldly wisdom: a woman who knows and makes allowance for, or accepts, the ways of the world: (*obs.*) a married woman; **women's rights**, the aim of the movement of women towards equality with men; **Women's Voluntary Service**, a body (organised in 1938) which participated in civil defence, welfare and other work, in the Second World War. [O.E. *wimman—wifman—wif*, a woman, *man*, man, human being.]

womb, *wōōm*, *n.* the uterus, the organ in which the young of mammals are developed and kept till birth: (*obs.*) the abdomen, or the stomach, or the bowels: the place where anything is produced: any deep cavity.—*v.t.* (*Shak.*) to enclose.—*adj.* **womb'y**, (*Shak.*) hollow, capacious. [O.E. *wamb*, *womb*; Ger. *wamme*, paunch.]

wombat, *wom'bət*, *-bat*, *n.* a genus (Phascolomys) of Australian marsupial mammals of the same order as opossums. [Native name.]

womera. See **woomera.**

won, *wun*, *wōn*, *v.i.* (*arch.* and *dial.*) to dwell, abide: (*obs.*) to be, or become, accustomed.—*n.* (*obs.*) a dwelling, an abode: (*obs.*) habit, custom.—*n.* **won'ing**, dwelling.—**did won**, (*Spens.*) was accustomed. [O.E. *wunian*, Du. *wonen*, Ger. *wohnen*, to dwell.]

won, *wun*, *pa.t.* and *pa.p.* of **win.**

wonder, *wun'dər*, *n.* the state of mind produced by something new, unexpected, or extraordinary: (*obs.*) admiration: the quality of being strange or unexpected: a strange, astonishing, admirable, thing or happening: a prodigy: a miracle: (*U.S.*) a sweet friedcake, a *cruller*.—*v.i.* to feel wonder: to be amazed (with *at*): to speculate: to feel doubt.—*v.t.* to speculate, to ask oneself (with noun clause or direct quotation).—*adj.* **won'dered**, **wond'red** (*obs.*), marvellous: (*Shak.*) having performed, or able to perform, wonders.—*n.* **won'derer**.—*adj.* **won'derful**, exciting wonder: strange: (*coll.*) expressing vague commendation, admirable, extremely good.—*adv.* wonderfully.—*adv.* **won'derfully**.—*n.* **won'derfulness**.—*n.* and *adj.* **won'dering**.—*adv.* **won'deringly**.—*ns.* **won'derland**, a land of wonders; **won'derment**, surprise: an expression of wonder: a wonderful thing: quality of being wonderful; **won'dermonger**, a wonder-worker: one who talks much of wonders, esp. incredible ones; **won'dermongering**.—*adjs.* **won'derous**, wondrous; **won'der-struck**, **-strick'en**, struck with wonder or astonishment.—*ns.* **won'der-work**, a prodigy, miracle: thaumaturgy; **won'der-worker**; **won'der-working**.—*adjs.* **won'der-wounded**, (*Shak.*) wonder-stricken; **won'drous**, such as may excite wonder.—Also *adv.*—*adv.* **won'drously**.—*n.* **won'drousness**.—**bird of wonder**, the phoenix; **for a wonder**, by way of an unexpected but pleasant change; **nine days' wonder,** something that astonishes everybody for the moment; **seven wonders of the world** (see **seven**); **to a wonder,** (*arch.*) marvellously: extremely well. [O.E. *wundor*; Ger. *wunder*, O.N. *undr*.]

wonga-wonga, *wong'(g)ă-wong'(g)ă, n.* the large Australian white-faced pigeon—a table delicacy.—Also **wong'a.** [Native name.]

wonky, *wongk'i, adj.* (*slang*) unsound: shaky: amiss: awry. [Cf. **wankle.**]

wont, historically *wunt,* commonly *wŏnt, adj.* used or accustomed.—*n.* habit.—*v.i.* to be accustomed. —*adj.* **wont'ed,** (*U.S.*) accustomed, habituated: (*arch.*) usual.—*n.* **wont'edness.**—*adj.* **wont'less,** (*arch.*) unaccustomed. [Orig. pa.p. of **won** (1).]

won't, *wŏnt,* will not. [Contr. of M.E. *wol not.*]

woo, *wōō, v.t.* to try to win the affection of: to court: to solicit eagerly: to seek to gain.—Also *v.i.* :— *pa.t.* and *pa.p.* **wooed** (*wōōd*).—*n.* **woo'er**—*n.* and *adj.* **woo'ing.**—*adv.* **woo'ingly.** [O.E. *wógian,* to woo; origin obscure.]

woobut. Same as **woubit.**

wood, *wood, n.* (*obs.*) a tree: (*obs.*) the Cross: a collection of growing trees (often in *pl.*): wooded country: the hard part of the substance of trees and shrubs, xylem: trees cut or sawed, timber: a kind of timber or wood: firewood: the cask or barrel, as distinguished from the bottle: (*print.*) a woodblock: (commonly in *pl.*) the wood-winds of an orchestra: a wooden-headed golf-club: (*bowls*) a bowl: an idol made of wood: (*slang*) the pulpit.—*v.t.* to cover with trees: to supply or load with wood.—*v.i.* to take in a supply of wood.— *ns.* **wood'-acid,** wood-vinegar; **wood'-alcohol,** wood-spirit; **wood'-anemone,** any anemone growing in woods, esp. *Anemone nemorosa,* which has a single whorl of leaves and a white flower; **wood'-ant,** a large forest-dwelling ant: a termite infesting the wood of old buildings; **wood'-ash,** (often in *pl.*) ash obtained by burning wood or plants —a source of potassium salts; **wood'bine, wood'bind,** the honeysuckle: applied also to other climbers, such as some kinds of ivy, the Virginia-creeper, &c.: (Shak., *M.N.D.,* IV. i. 48) perh. bindweed; **wood'block,** a die cut in relief on wood and ready to furnish ink impressions: a woodcut; **wood'-borer,** any of a number of insect larvae, or of molluscs, or of Crustacea, that bore in wood.—*adjs.* **wood'-boring; wood'-born,** born in the woods.—*ns.* **wood'-carver; wood'-carving,** the process of carving in wood: an object, or part of one, so ornamented or made; **wood'-chat,** a species of shrike; **wood'-coal,** coal like wood in texture, lignite or brown coal: charcoal; **wood'cock,** a genus (Scolopax) of birds allied to the snipes, but of a more bulky body, and with shorter and stronger legs: (*arch.*) a stupid person, a simpleton; **wood'cock's-head,** (*obs.*) a tobacco-pipe; **wood'craft,** skill in the chase and everything pertaining to life in the woods: forestry generally; **wood'cut,** an engraving cut on wood: an impression from it; **wood'-cutter,** one who cuts wood: a wood-engraver; **wood'-cutting.**— *adjs.* **wood'ed,** supplied with wood: covered with trees; **wood'en,** made of, or like, wood: of a golf-club, with head made of wood: hard: dull, insensible: heavy, stupid: lacking animation or grace of manner or execution: clumsy.—*ns.* **wood'-engraver,** one who engraves on wood: any of certain beetles that make a pattern of furrows in the wood of trees; **wood'-engraving,** the art of engraving designs on wood: an engraving on or print from wood; **wood'en-head,** a blockhead, stupid person.—*adj.* **wood'en-headed,** having a head of wood: stupid.—*n.* **wood'en-headedness.** —*adv.* **wood'enly.**—*ns.* **wood'enness,** wooden quality: want of spirit or expression; **wood'en-tongue,** woody-tongue; **wood'-evil,** diarrhoea of herbivorous animals; **wood'-fibre,** a thick-walled, elongated, dead element found in wood— developed by the elongation and lignification of the wall of a single cell, differing from a tracheide in inability to conduct water; **wood'-flour,** a fine powder, made from sawdust and wood waste, used as a filler in many industries, and in the manu-

facture of guncotton; **wood'-fretter,** a wood-borer; **wood'-germander,** *Teucrium Scorodonia,* which has racemes of yellow flowers; **wood'-grouse,** the capercailzie; **wood'-hole,** a place where wood is stored; **wood'-honey,** wild honey; **wood'-horse,** a saw-horse; **wood'-house,** a house or shed in which wood for fuel is deposited; **wood'-hyacinth,** the wild hyacinth or English bluebell, a flower of the genus Scilla; **wood'-i'bis,** any bird of the family Tantalidae, nearer the storks than the ibises; **wood'iness,** the state or quality of being woody; **wood'land,** land covered with wood (also *adj.*); **wood'lander,** an inhabitant of wood-land; **wood'-lark,** a species of lark that perches on trees but sings chiefly on the wing.—*adj.* **wood'less,** without wood.—*ns.* **wood'lessness; wood'-louse** (*pl.* **wood'-lice**), any of numerous isopod crustaceans of family Oniscidae, found in damp places, under stones and bark, in woodwork, among moss, &c.: a book-louse: (*U.S.*) a termite; **wood'man,** a man who cuts down trees: a forest officer: a huntsman; **wood'-mite,** any of numerous small mites found in woods; **wood'-naphtha,** the mixture of light hydrocarbons distilled from wood; **wood'-nightshade,** *Solanum Dulcamara,* bitter-sweet or woody-nightshade; **wood'-note,** (*Milt.*) a wild musical note, like that of a song-bird; **wood'-nymph,** a nymph of the woods; **wood'-offering,** (*B.*) wood burned on the altar; **wood'-oil,** gurjun balsam: tung-oil: also various other oils obtained from trees; **wood'-opal,** a form of common opal which has replaced pieces of wood entombed as fossils in sediments, in some cases retaining the original structure; **wood'-owl,** the European brown owl, or other owl living in woods; **wood'-paper,** paper prepared from wood-pulp; **wood'pecker,** any of a family (Picidae) of birds in the order Picariae, remarkable for modification of the skull and bill enabling the latter to be used to drill holes, and for the long flexible tongue, used to extract insects from crevices; **wood'-pigeon,** the ringdove, a common species of pigeon (*Columba palumbus*) living in woods; **wood'-pulp,** wood reduced to a pulp, either mechanically or by chemical means, used in making paper; **wood'-reeve,** the overseer of a wood; **wood'ruff** (O.E. *wudurofe;* meaning of second element unknown), a genus of rubiaceous plants with whorled leaves and a funnel-shaped corolla, esp. *sweet woodruff* which has small white flowers and a pleasant scent —(*obs.*) **wood'-roof; wood'-rush,** any plant of the genus Luzula, of the same family as the true rushes, growing in woods; **wood'-sage,** wood-germander; **wood'-sandpiper,** a common European tattler; **wood'-screw,** a screw for fastening pieces of wood or wood and metal; **wood'shed,** a shed for storing firewood; **wood'-shock,** the pekan; **wood'-skin,** an Indian canoe made of bark, or the bark itself; **woods'man,** a woodman; **wood'-sorrel,** any plant of the genus Oxalis, esp. *Oxalis Acetosella,* with trifoliate leaves and white or rose-tinted flowers, which yields potassium binoxalate; **wood'-spirit,** a spirit living among trees: methyl alcohol, methanol; **wood'-spite,** the green woodpecker; **wood'-stamp,** a stamp made of wood, as for stamping fabrics in colours; **wood'-stone,** petrified wood; **wood'-sugar,** xylose; **wood'-swallow,** an Australian name for any of the fly-catching Artamidae, also called swallow-shrikes, the resemblance to shrikes being more fundamental than that to swallows.—*adj.* **wood'sy** (-*zi;* *U.S.*), pertaining to, or character-istic of, woods.—*ns.* **wood'-tar,** a product of the destructive distillation of wood, containing paraffins, naphthalene, phenols; **wood'thrush,** a singing-thrush common in the woods of the eastern United States, reddish-brown above, olive on the rump, white spotted with black on the breast; locally in Britain, the missel-thrush or the song-thrush; **wood'-tick,** any tick of the family Ixodidae, the young of which are transferred to man and animals from bushes; **wood'-tin,** a botryoidal or reniform variety of cassiterite showing a concentric structure of radiating brown, wood-like fibres; **wood'-vinegar,** crude acetic acid obtained from wood, pyroligneous acid ; **wood′wale**, a woodpecker, esp. the green woodpecker ; **wood′-warbler**, the yellow willow-warbler or wood-wren : an American warbler, esp. of the genus Dendroeca (or Dendroica) ; **wood′ward**, an officer to guard the woods ; **wood′-wasp**, a large hymenopterous insect (Sirex) that bores wood with its ovipositor ; **wood′-wax, -waxen**, dyer's greenweed ; **wood′-wind**, a wind-instrument of wood (or sometimes metal, as silver)—flute, oboe, bassoon, clarinet, &c. : (usu. in *pl.*) the section of an orchestra comprising these ; **wood′-wool**, fine wood shavings ; **wood′work**, a part of any structure made of wood : carpentry ; **wood′-worm**, a larva that bores in wood ; **wood′-wren**, the willow-warbler or willow-wren (*Phylloscopus trochilus*) : the wood-warbler or yellow willow-wren (*Phylloscopus sibilatrix*)—neither being properly a wren.—*adj.* **wood′y**, abounding with woods : (*Spens.*) inhabiting woods : situated in a wood : pertaining to wood : consisting wholly or largely of wood : ligneous : like wood in texture, or smell, or taste, &c.—*ns.* **wood′y-night′shade** (see **wood-night-shade**) ; **wood′y-tongue**, actinobacillosis, a chronic inflammation of cattle, rarely of sheep and swine, occasionally transmitted to man, due to infection, usu. of the tongue, by the fungus *Actinobacillus lignieri*.—**cannot see the wood for trees**, cannot grasp the whole because of the superabundance of detail ; **Commissioners of Woods and Forests**, a department of government having charge of the Crown woods and forests ; **out of the wood(s)**, out of difficulty or danger ; **wooden horse**, the giant horse inside which Greeks entered Troy : an instrument of punishment (see **horse**) : (*arch.*) a ship ; **wooden leg**, an artificial leg made of wood ; **wooden pear**, an Australian tree whose pear-shaped seed-vessels have a woody outside ; **wooden spoon**, a spoon of wood presented to the person standing lowest in the mathematical tripos list at Cambridge : a booby prize ; **wooden type**, large type cut in wood ; **wood-wool slabs**, slabs made from long wood shavings with a cementing material, used for linings, partitions, &c. [O.E. *wudu* ; cog. with O.N. *vithr*, wood, O.Ir. *fid*, timber.]

wood, *wood*, *adj.* (*Shak.* ; *Scot.* wud, *wud*) mad: fierce, furious.—*n.* **wood′ness**. [O.E. *wód* ; O.N. *óthr*, Ger. *wut*, madness.]

woodburytype, *wood′bar-i-tīp, n.* a photo-mechanical process in which an exposed and developed bichromated film is forced into a metal plate by great pressure, and so forms a matrix for subsequent printing. [Named from the inventor.]

woodchuck, *wood′chuk, n.* a N. American species of marmot (*Marmota* or *Arctomys monax*). [Corr. of an Amer. Indian name.]

woodie, *wud′i, -ā, n.* (*Scot.*) the gallows. [widdy, **1**.]

wooer, wooing, &c. See **woo**.

woof, *wōōf, n.* weft : thread for a weft : texture.—*adjs.* **woofed** (*wōōft*, *wōōf′id*), woven ; **woof′y**, dense in texture. [M.E. *oof*, with *w* added by association with **warp**, &c. (*oof* being the normal development of O.E. *ówef—on, wefan*, to weave).]

wool, *wool, n.* a modification of hair in which the fibres are shorter, curled, and possess an imbricated surface—the covering of sheep, &c. : short, thick human hair : any light, fleecy substance resembling wool : thread or yarn made from animal wool : fabric woven or knitted from it.—*n.* **wool′-ball**, a ball of wool, such as is sometimes found in a sheep's stomach.—*adj.* **wool′-bearing**, bearing or yielding wool.—*ns.* **wool′-card, wool′-comb**, a machine for **wool′-carding, wool′-combing**, separating the fibres of wool preparatory to spinning ; **wool′-carder, wool′-comber** ; **wool′-driver**, one who buys up wool for a market.—*adj.* **wool′-dyed**, dyed before spinning or weaving.—*ns.* **wool′fat**, lanolin ; **wool′fell**, the skin with the wool still on it ; **wool′-gath′ering**, absent-minded dreaming. — *adj.* dreamy: absent-minded. — *ns.* **wool′-grower**, one who raises sheep for the production of wool ; **wool′-growing**.—*adjs.* **woolled** (*woold*), bearing wool ; **wool′en**, made of, or pertaining to, wool : clad in, or covered with,

wool : (*obs.*) rustic.—*n.* cloth made of wool.—*ns.* **wooll′en-drā′per**, one who deals in woollen goods ; **woollen′-drā′pery** ; **wooll′en-mill**, a mill where wool is spun and woven into material ; **wooll′i-ness**.—*adj.* **wooll′y**, consisting of, or like, wool: clothed with wool : (*fig.*) lacking in clearness, firmness, or definition : (*coll.*) having the atmosphere or quality of the Wild West.—*n.* a garment of wool, esp. a knitted one :—*pl.* **wooll′ies**.—*n.* **wooll′y-bear**, the hairy caterpillar of a number of moths, including the tiger-moths.—*adjs.* **wooll′y-haired, -head′ed**, having the hair like wool.—*ns.* **wool′man**, a dealer in wool ; **wool′-mill**, a woollen-mill ; **wool′-oil**, any oil obtained from wool-fat : an oil used to oil wool before spinning ; **wool′-pack**, the package in which wool was formerly done up for sale : a bundle weighing 240 lb. : cirrocumulus cloud : (*obs.*) the woolsack ; **wool′-packer** ; **wool′-picker**, a machine for cleaning wool ; **wool′sack**, the seat of the Lord Chancellor in the House of Lords, being a large square sack of wool covered with scarlet : the office of Lord Chancellor ; **wool′sey** (*-zi*), a fabric of cotton and wool.—*n.pl.* **wool′-shears**, shears used in shearing sheep.—*ns.* **wool′sorter**, one who sorts wool according to quality, &c. ; **wool′-staple**, the fibre or pile of wool : a staple or market where wool was sold ; **wool′-stapler**, a dealer in wool : a woolsorter.—*adv.* **wool′ward**, (*obs.*) with wool next the skin, esp. as a penance.—*ns.* **wool′-winder**, one who packs fleeces ; **wool′work**, needlework imitative of tapestry.—**against the wool**, against the texture of the wool, the wrong way ; **dye in the wool**, to dye (the wool) before spinning (**dyed-in-the-wool**, out-and-out, complete) ; **great, much, cry and little wool**, much palaver and little result ; **pull, draw, the wool over one's eyes**, to hoodwink, deceive, one ; **woolsorter's disease**, anthrax ; **woolly-hand crab**, the mitten-crab (q.v.). [O.E. *wull* ; Goth. *wulla*, Ger. *wolle*, L. *vellus*.]

woold, *wōōld, v.t.* to wind a rope or chain round.—*adj.* **woold′ed**.—*ns.* **woold′er**, a stick used in woolding a mast or yard : a pin in a rope-maker's top ; **woold′ing**. [Du. *woelen* ; Ger. *(be)wuhlen*.]

woomera, *wōōm′ar-ā*, **womera**, *wom′*, **woomer-ang**, *wōōm′ar-ang, ns.* throw-stick. [Austr. native.]

woon, *wōōn, v.i.* (*Spens.*). Same as **won** (1).

woosel(l). See **ouzel**.

woot, woo′t, *woot, woot*, (*Shak.*) wilt (thou)?—Also **wot**.

wootz, *wōōts, n.* steel made, from ancient times, by fusing iron with carbonaceous matter. [For *wook*—Kanarese *ukku*, steel.]

wop, *wop, n.* (*U.S.*) a derogatory term for an Italian, or other foreigner of olive complexion. [It. (dial.) *guappo*—Sp. *guapo*, bold, handsome.]

wop, *wop, v.t.* Same as **whop**.

worcester, *woos′tar, n.* (*hist.*) fine woollen material made at *Worcester* : **Worcester (china)**, fine china made there from mid-18th cent.—*n.* **worces′ter-berry**, N. Amer. species of gooseberry (*Ribes divaricatum*), not a hybrid.—**Worcester(shire) sauce**, pungent sauce orig. made in Worcestershire.

word, *wurd, n.* a unit of spoken language : a written sign representing such an utterance : (in *pl.*) language : a saying : a brief conversation : a rumour : a hint : a signal or sign : a message : a promise : a declaration : a pass-word : a watch-word : a war-cry : (*pl.*) verbal contention.—*v.t.* to express in words : (*obs.* ; *rare*) to speak to, or of, in words : (*Shak.*) to flatter.—*v.i.* to speak, talk.—*ns.* **word′-blindness**, loss of ability to recognise written words ; **word′-book**, a book with a collection of words : a dictionary, or vocabulary.—*adj.* **word′-bound**, unable to find expression in words : bound by a promise.—*n.* **word′-building**, the formation of words from letters or from root words and affixes.—*adj.* **word′ed**, expressed in words.—*adv.* **word′ily**.—*ns.* **word′iness** ; **word′-ing**, (*arch.*) speaking, utterance : act of expressing in words : choice of words, phrasing.—*adj.* **word′ish**, (*obs.*) verbose.—*n.* **word′ishness**.—*adj.* **word′less**, unspoken : silent.—*ns.* **word′-lore**, information about the history, use, &c., of words ; **word′-memory**, the power of recalling words to the mind ; **word'-painter ; word'-painting**, the act or art of describing vividly in words ; **word'-picture**, a description in words that presents an object, scene, &c., to the mind as if in a picture.— *adj.* **word'y**, using, or containing, too many words : conducted in words.—**a good word**, a recommendation, favourable mention, praise ; **at a word**, without more ado, at once : (*obs.*) to be brief, in short ; **break one's word**, to fail to fulfil a promise ; **by word of mouth**, orally ; **fair words**, (*arch.*) pleasant, conciliatory words—usu. implying flattery or deceit ; **have a word with**, to have some conversation with ; **have words (with)**, to quarrel, dispute (with) ; **in a word, in one word**, in short, to sum up ; **in so many words**, explicitly : bluntly ; **in word**, in speech only, in profession only ; **not the word for it**, not a strong enough word to express or describe it ; **of few, or many, words**, taciturn, or verbose ; **pass one's word**, to make a promise ; **take (up) the word**, to begin speaking, continue a discourse begun by someone else ; **the last word**, the closing remark in an argument, esp. if having an appearance of conclusiveness : the conclusive statement : the ultimate authority : (also **latest word**) the most up-to-date, or the most finished, example ; **the Word**, the Scriptures : the gospel message : the second person in the Trinity, the Logos ; **word for word**, literally, verbatim. [O.E. ; Goth. *waurd*, O.N. *orth*, Ger. *wort* ; L. *verbum*, word, Gr. *eirein*, to say, speak.]

Wordsworthian, *wurdz-wur'thi-ən*, *adj.* pertaining to the poet William *Wordsworth* (1770-1850) or his style.—*n.* an admirer or imitator of Wordsworth.

wore, *wōr*, *pa.t.* of **wear**.

work, *wurk*, *n.* effort directed to an end : employment : that on which one works : the product of work, anything made or done : materials for work : needlework : a deed : doings : the result of action : any production of art, as a literary composition : a book : manner of working, workmanship : (in *pl.*) a manufactory, workshop : (*phys.*) the act of producing an effect by means of a force (F) whose point of application moves through a distance (s) in its own line of action—measured by the product of the force and the distance (W = Fs) : (*pl., fort.*) walls, trenches, &c. : (*theol.* ; usu. in *pl.*) an action in its moral aspect, esp. as tending to justification : (in *pl.*) mechanism, e.g. of a watch : (*cricket*) the spin given to a ball by a bowler to cause it to break on pitching : (*dial.* ; by confusion with O.E. *wærc*) ache, trouble, fuss.—*v.i.* to make efforts to achieve or attain anything : to be occupied in business or labour : to move, make one's way, slowly and laboriously : to move, become, &c., in a manner not intended or desired : to be in action : to operate, function : to produce effects : to behave in the desired way when worked : to prove practicable : (*dial.*) to ache, be painful : to ferment : to be agitated, move convulsively : to strain, labour : (*naut.*) to sail in a course, esp. to beat to windward : (*arch.*) to contrive, plan.—*v.t.* to make by labour : to bring into any state by action : to effect or strive to effect : to carry on operations in : to keep in operation : to keep employed : to put in motion : (*dial.*) to purge : to influence : to affect powerfully : to provoke, excite : to prepare for use by manipulation : to cause to ferment : to fashion, make : to embroider : to make, as one's way, by effort : to solve : (*coll.*) to make use of, make profit through : (*coll.*) to influence, cajole, or trick :—*pa.t.* and *pa.p.* **worked** or **wrought** (see separate article).—*ns.* **workabil'ity, work'-ableness**.—*adjs.* **work'able**, that may be worked, esp. practicable ; **work'aday**, suitable for a work day : toiling : dull, prosaic.—Also *n.*—*ns.* **work'-bag, -basket**, a bag, basket, for holding materials for work, esp. needlework ; **work'-box**, a box for holding instruments or materials for work ; **work'-day**, a day for work, a week-day.—*adj.* pertaining to a work-day.—*adj.* **worked**, that has been treated or fashioned in some way : embroidered : ornamented.—*ns.* **work'er**, one who works : a toiler : one employed in manual work : in social insects, one of a caste of sterile individuals that do all the work of the colony ; **work'-fellow**, one

who is engaged in the same work with another.— *ns.pl.* **work'folk, work'folks**, work-people.—*adj.* **work'ful**, industrious.—*ns.* **work'girl**, a girl or young woman employed in manual labour ; **work'-house**, (*obs.*) a house where any work or manufacture is carried on : a house of shelter for the poor, who are given work to do ; **work'ing**, the act or process of shaping, making, effecting, solving, fermenting, &c. : an exposition of the process of calculation : manner of operating or functioning : (*obs.*) endeavour : (*obs.* ; in *pl.*) deeds : (*obs.*) mental or emotional activity : contortion due to agitation : slow and laborious progress : (in *pl.*) the parts of a mine, &c., where work is, or has been, carried on.—*adj.* active : labouring : connected with labour : (*obs.*) stirring the emotions.—*ns.* **work'ing-beam**, a walking-beam ; **work'ing-class**, manual workers (often in *pl.* ; also *adj.*) ; **work'ing-day**, a day on which work is done : the period of actual work each day.—*adj.* laborious : plodding : ordinary.—*ns.* **work'ing-drawing**, a drawing of the details of a building by which the builders are guided in their work ; **work'ing-edge**, an edge of a piece of wood trued square with the working-face to assist in truing the other surfaces square ; **work'ing-face**, that face of a piece of wood which is first trued and then used as a basis for truing the other surfaces ; **work'ing-house**, (*obs.*) workshop ; **work'ing-model**, a model of a machine that can do, on a smaller scale, the same work as the machine ; **work'ing-party**, a group of persons, esp. of soldiers or sailors, who carry out a specially assigned task : a group appointed to investigate a subject, as methods of attaining maximum efficiency in an industry ; **work'man**, a man who works, esp. manually : a skilful artificer.— *adjs.* **work'man-like**, like a workman : becoming a skilful workman : well performed ; **work'manly**, becoming a skilful workman.—*adv.* in a manner becoming a skilful workman.—*ns.* **work'manship**, the skill of a workman : manner of making : that which is made or produced by one's hands (also *fig.*) ; **work'master**, a master workman, overseer, or employer (*fem.* **work'mistress**).—*n.pl.* **work'-people**, people engaged in manual labour.—*ns.* **work'room**, a room for working in ; **work'shop**, a room or shop where work is done.—*adjs.* **work'-shy**, hating, avoiding work, lazy (also used as *n.*) ; **work'some**, (*Carlyle*) industrious.—*ns.* **work'table**, a table on which work is done, esp., formerly, a small table used by ladies at their needlework ; **work'-woman**, a woman who makes her living by manual labour ; **work'y-day**, (*obs.*) workaday. —**a work of time**, a change, achievement, &c., requiring, or brought about by, time ; **give one the works**, (*slang*) to inflict punishment on one, or severe pain, in order to coerce in some way ; **have one's work cut out**, to have one's work prescribed : to be faced with a difficult task ; **make short work of** (see **short**) ; **Ministry** (formerly **Office) of Works**, the body which has the management and control of public works and buildings, of which the expenses are defrayed from public money ; **out of work**, without employment (*n.* **out-of-work**, see **out**) ; **public works**, building, &c., operations financed by the state ; **set to work**, to employ in, or to engage energetically in, a piece of work ; **Seven Works of Corporal Mercy**, to feed the hungry, give drink to the thirsty, to clothe the naked, visit prisoners, visit the sick, harbour strangers, bury the dead ; **Seven Works of Spiritual Mercy**, to convert sinners, instruct the ignorant, counsel the doubtful, console the afflicted, bear wrongs patiently, forgive injuries, pray for the living and the dead ; **shoot the works**, (*slang*) at games of chance, to risk (one's all) on one play : hence, to make one's maximum effort ; **work double tides**, (*naut.*) to work night and day ; **work for, against**, to exert oneself in support of, in opposition to ; **work in**, to intermix : (*fig.*) to introduce carefully and deliberately : to make to penetrate ; **working majority**, a majority sufficient to enable the party in office to carry on without accidental defeats : **working man, woman**, a worker, esp. a manual one ; **work-**

ing to rule, (e.g. of railwaymen) observing all the regulations scrupulously for the express purpose of slowing down work; **work into,** to make way gradually into: insinuate: to change, alter, into; **work of art,** a production in one of the fine arts (*lit.* and *fig.*); **work off,** to separate and throw off: to get rid of gradually: to print ready for circulation: (*coll.*) to pass, palm, off: (*slang*) to dispose of by hanging; **work on, upon,** to act or operate upon: to influence, or try to do so; **work one's passage,** to earn one's passage by services on board (also *fig.*); **work out,** to effect by continued labour: to expiate: (*obs.*) to make by cutting, digging, &c.: to exhaust: to solve or calculate: (*rare*) to study fully: to develop in detail, elaborate: to come out by degrees: to turn out in the end; **work the oracle,** (*slang*) to produce the desired result, as by wire-pulling; **work up,** to excite, rouse: to create by slow degrees: to expand, elaborate: to use up, as material: (*naut.*) to set at an irksome or needless task: to make one's, its, way gradually upwards: to reach, achieve, by effort and gradually; **work with,** (*fig.*) to strive to influence by appeals, &c. [O.E. *weorc*; O.N. *verk*, Ger. *werk*; further conn. with Gr. *ergon*.]

world, *wurld*, *n.* the earth: the earth and its inhabitants: the universe: the system of things: the present state of existence: any analogous state: any planet or heavenly body: public life or society: sphere of interest or activity: environment: the public: the materialistically minded: mundane interests: a secular life: course of life: one of the three kingdoms of nature: a class or division: a very large extent of country, as the 'New World': very much or a great deal, as 'a world of good': a large quantity: time, as in 'a world without end,' which means 'eternally': possibility, as in 'nothing in the world': (*B.*) the ungodly.—*adj.* **world′ed,** containing worlds.—*ns.* **world′-language,** a universal language; **world′liness; world′ling,** one who is devoted to worldly pursuits and temporal possessions: (*obs.*) a mortal.—*adjs.* **world′ly,** pertaining to the world, esp. as distinguished from the world to come: devoted to this life and its enjoyments: bent on gain: (*obs.*) mortal.—Also *adv.*; **world′ly-minded,** having the mind set on the present world.—*n.* **world′ly-mindedness.**—*adjs.* **world′ly-wise,** having the wisdom of those experienced in, and affected by, the ways of the world; **world′-old,** exceedingly ancient; **world′-wearied, -weary,** tired of the world; **world′-wide,** extending over, or found everywhere in, the world; **world′-without-end,** eternal.—**all the world,** everybody: everything; **all the world and his wife,** (*coll.*) everybody: an ill-assorted assembly; **carry the world before one,** to pass through every obstacle to success; **for all the world,** precisely, entirely; **go to the world,** (*Shak.*) to get married; **in the world,** an intensive phrase, usu. following an interrogative pronoun or adverb; **the New World,** the western hemisphere, the Americas; **the Old World,** the eastern hemisphere, comprising Europe, Africa, and Asia; **the other world,** the non-material sphere, the spiritual world; **the whole world,** the sum of what is contained in the world; **the world's end,** the most distant point possible; **world power,** a state, group of states, &c., strong enough to make its influence felt in world politics; **World War,** a war of world-wide scope, esp. the Great War of 1914-18 (First World War) and that of 1939-45 (Second World War, World War 2). [O.E. *woruld*, *world*, *weorold*, orig. meaning age or life of man—*ver*, man and the root of **old**; O.N. *veröld*, O.H.G. *weralt* (Ger. *welt*).]

worm, *wurm*, *n.* (*arch.*) a snake, a dragon: (*obs.*) any creeping or crawling animal: loosely used for any elongate invertebrate lacking appendages, as an earthworm or marine worm (Chaetopoda), a flat-worm (Platyhelminthes), a round-worm (Nematoda): a grub: a maggot: anything spiral: the thread of a screw: the lytta or vermiform cartilage of the tongue of a dog or other carnivorous mammal: a spiral pipe for condensation in distilling: anything that corrupts, gnaws, or torments:

remorse: a mean, grovelling creature: (in *pl.*) any intestinal disease arising from the presence of parasitic worms: (*obs.*) any ailment supposed to be caused by a worm, as toothache: (*obs.*) a tick or mite in the hand, &c., esp. one alleged humorously to infest the hands of idlers.—*v.i.* to seek for or catch worms: to move, make one's way, like a worm, to squirm: to work slowly or secretly.—*v.t.* to cause to be eaten by worms: to treat for, rid of, worms: (*refl.*) to work (oneself) slowly or secretly: to elicit by slow and indirect means: to remove the lytta or vermiform cartilage from the tongue of.—*n.* **worm′-cast,** the earth voided by the earthworm.—*adjs.* **worm′-eaten,** eaten into by worms: old: worn-out; **worm′-eating,** living habitually on worms; **wormed,** bored, injured by worms.—*ns.* **worm′er; worm′-fence,** a zigzag fence formed of stakes crossing at their ends; **worm′-fever,** a feverish condition in children ascribed to intestinal worms; **worm′-gear,** a gear connecting shafts whose axes are at right angles but do not intersect, consisting of a core carrying a single- or multi-start helical thread of special form (the *worm*), meshing in sliding contact with a concave face gear-wheel (the *worm-wheel*); **worm′-gearing; worm′-grass,** pinkroot: a kind of stonecrop (*Sedum album*); **worm′-hole,** the hole made by a wood-worm, earthworm, &c.—*adj.* **worm′-holed,** perforated by worm-holes.—*ns.* **worm′-powder,** a vermifuge; **worm′-seed,** any of a number of plants acting, or reputed to act, as anthelmintics, as species of Artemisia (e.g. *Artemisia santonica*), *Erysimum cheiranthoides* (treacle worm-seed, treacle mustard), *Chenopodium anthelminticum*, &c.: the drug santonica; **worm′-wheel** (see **worm′-gear**).—*adj.* **worm′y,** like a worm: grovelling: containing a worm: abounding in worms: pertaining to worms: dank-smelling: dismal, like the grave. [O.E. *wyrm*, dragon, snake, worm; cog. with Goth. *waurms*, a serpent, O.N. *ormr*, Ger. *wurm*; also with L. *vermis*.]

Wormian, *wurm′i-ən*, *adj.* associated with the name of the Danish anatomist Olaus *Worm* (1588-1654), applied esp. to the supernumerary bones developed in the sutures of the skull.

wormwood, *wurm′wood*, *n.* the bitter plant *Artemisia Absinthium*, formerly used as a vermifuge, with which absinthe is flavoured: bitterness. [O.E. *wermód* (Ger. *wermuth*), wormwood; of doubtful origin, but influenced by **worm** and **wood**.]

worn, *wōrn*, *pa.p.* of **wear.**—*adj.* that has been worn: showing effects of wear, or (*fig.*) of work, worry, age, &c.: of land, exhausted: hackneyed, trite.—*adj.* **worn′-out,** much injured or rendered useless by wear: wearied: past, gone.

worral, worrel, *wor′əl*, *n.* a monitor lizard. [Ar. *waral*, lizard.]

worricow, worrycow, wirricow, *wur′i-kow*, *n.* (*Scot.*) a hobgoblin: the devil: anything frightful or even only grotesque. [**worry** (vb.), and *cow*, a hobgoblin.]

worrit, *wur′it*, *v.t.*, *v.i.*, and *n.* Vulg. form of **worry.**

worry, *wur′i*, *v.t.* to tear with the teeth: (*Scot.*) to devour ravenously: to harass: to pester: to tease: to make, get, &c., by persistent methods: (*Scot.*) to choke.—*v.i.* to trouble oneself: to be unduly anxious: to fret: (*pa.t.* and *pa.p.* **worr′ied**). —*n.* act of worrying: trouble, perplexity, anxiety: a cause of this: the act of injuring by biting and shaking.—*ns.* **worr′ier; worr′iment,** (*coll.*) worry, anxiety.—*adj.* **worr′isome,** inclined to worry: causing trouble.—*n.* and *adj.* **worr′ying.**—*adv.* **worr′yingly.**—**worry down,** to swallow with a strong effort; **worry out,** to find a solution of by intense or anxious effort. [O.E. *wyrgan*, found in compound * áwyrgan*, to harm; cf. Du. *worgen*, Ger. *würgen*, to strangle.]

worse, *wurs*, *adj.* (used as *comp.* of **bad**) bad or evil in a greater degree: less well than before.—*adv.* badly in a higher degree: less well: with more severity.—*v.t.* (*obs.*) to worst.—*v.i.* and *v.t.* **wors′en,** to grow, or make, worse.—*adv.* **wors′er,** a redundant comparative of *worse*.—**for better or**

for worse, whatever may befall of good fortune or bad; **for the worse**, to a worse state; **go by, with, the worse**, (*obs.*) to lose, be defeated; **have the worse**, to be at a disadvantage: to be defeated; **put to the worse**, (*B.*) to defeat. [O.E. *wyrsa* (Goth. *wairsiza*), formed with comp. suffix from a Gmc. root *wers*, found in Ger. (*ver*)*wirren*, to confuse, entangle.]

worship, *wur'ship*, *n.* adoration paid, as to a god: religious service: profound admiration and affection: act of revering or adoring: (*arch.*) dignity, reputation, high standing: (*obs.*) a position of honour: a title of honour in addressing certain magistrates, &c.—*v.t.* to pay divine honours to: to adore or idolise: (*obs.*) to honour, respect, treat with signs of honour.—*v.i.* to perform acts of adoration: to take part in religious service:—*pr.p.* **wor'shipping**; *pa.t.* and *pa.p.* **wor'shipped.**— *adjs.* **wor'shipable**, capable of being worshipped; **wor'shipful**, worthy of worship or honour: used as a term of respect: worshipping, adoring.— *adv.* **wor'shipfully.**—*n.* **wor'shipfulness.**—*adj.* **wor'shipless**, without worship or worshippers.— *n.* **wor'shipper.**—**house**, or **place**, **of worship**, a church or chapel, synagogue, mosque, temple; **win (one's) worship**, (*obs.*) to gain honour or fame. [O.E. *weorthscipe*—*weorth*, *wurth*, worth, suff. -*scipe*, -ship.]

worst, *wurst*, *adj.* (used as *superl.* of **bad**) bad or evil in the highest degree.—*adv.* in the highest degree of badness.—*n.* the highest degree of badness: the most evil state or effect: the least good part.— *v.t.* to get the advantage over in a contest: to defeat: (*obs.*) to damage or make worse.—*v.i.* (*obs.*) to grow worse.—**do one's worst**, to do one's utmost in evil or mischief; **get the worst of it**, to be defeated in a contest. [O.E. *wyrst*, *wyrrest*, *wyrresta*, from the same source as **worse**.]

worsted, *woost'id*, or *woorst'id*, *n.* (*orig.*) a fine wool fabric: twisted thread or yarn spun out of long, combed wool: woollen yarn for ornamental needlework.—*adj.* made of worsted yarn.—*n.* **worst'edwork**, needlework done with worsted. [From *Worstead*, a village near Norwich in England.]

worsted, *wurst'id*, *pa.t.* and *pa.p.* of **worst**.

wort, *wurt*, *n.* (now *rare* except in composition) any herb or vegetable: (*obs.*) specif. a plant of the cabbage kind. [O.E. *wyrt*, a root, herb; Ger. *wurz*, *wurzel*, a root.]

wort, *wurt*, *n.* malt unfermented or in the act of fermentation (*sweetwort*): such liquor boiled with hops (*hopped-wort*): malt extract used as a medium for the culture of micro-organisms. [O.E. *wyrt*; allied to **wort** (1).]

worth, *wurth*, *n.* value: price: that quality which renders a thing valuable: moral excellence: merit: importance: (*obs.*) possessions.—*adj.* equal in value to: having a certain value: worth while: having possessions to the value of: deserving of. —*adj.* **worth'ful**, honourable: meritorious: valuable.—*adv.* **worth'ily** (*dh*).—*n.* **worth'iness** (*dh*). —*adj.* **worth'less** (*th*), having no value, virtue, excellence, &c.: useless: (*obs.*) unworthy.—*adv.* **worth'lessly.**—*n.* **worth'lessness.**—*adjs.* **worthwhile'**, such as to repay trouble and time spent on it (predicatively **worth while**; see **while**): good: estimable; **worth'y** (*dh*), having worth: valuable: estimable (used patronisingly): deserving: deserving of: suited to, in keeping with: of sufficient merit: (*obs.*) of high social position.—*n.* a man of eminent worth: a notability, esp. local: (*Shak.*) anything of value, an excellence:—*pl.* **wor'thies.**—*v.t.* (*obs.*) to make worthy, to honour. —**for all one is worth**, with all one's might or energy; **for what it is worth**, a phrase implying that the speaker is doubtful of the truth of what he has reported or unwilling to be responsible for its accuracy; **nine worthies**, usu. given as Hector, Alexander the Great, Julius Caesar; Joshua, David, Judas Maccabaeus; Arthur, Charlemagne, Godfrey of Bouillon; **worthiest of blood**, in questions of succession, male as opposed to female. [O.E. *weorth*, *wurth* (Ger. *wert*), value.]

worth, *wurth*, *v.i.* to be, become, happen, as in the phrase **woe worth**, woe be (to; with the noun in

the dative). [O.E. *weorthan*, to become; cf. Ger. *werden*.]

wortle, *wur'tl*, *n.* a perforated plate through which wire, tubing, is drawn to make it thinner.—Also **whirtle**. [Ety. uncertain.]

wosbird, *wōz'bərd*, *n.* dial. form of **whore's-bird**.

wot, **wotteth**, &c. See **wit** (1).

woubit, *woo'bit*, *n.* (usu. **hairy woubit**) a hairy caterpillar, esp. one of a tiger-moth: applied derogatorily to a person, often implying smallness and shabbiness.—Also **ou'bit**, **oo'bit**. [M.E. *wolbode*, *wolbede*; prob.—*wol*. wool; meaning of second element unknown.]

would, *wood* (formerly, e.g. in *Spens.*, *wōld*), *pa.t.* of **will**.—*n.* the desired or intended, opp. to *could*, or *should*.—*adj.* **would'-be**, aspiring, or merely professing, to be: meant to be.—*n.* a vain pretender.

Woulfe-bottle, *woolf'-bot'l*, *n.* a form of usu. threenecked bottle used for purifying gases, or dissolving them in suitable solvents—from the London chemist Peter *Woulfe* (c. 1727-1803).

wound, *wownd*, *pa.t.* and *pa.p.* of **wind** (*wīnd*).

wound, *wōōnd*, *n.* any division of soft parts produced by external mechanical force—whether incised, punctured, contused, lacerated, or poisoned: any cut, bruise, hurt, or injury.—*v.t.* to make a wound in (*lit.* and *fig.*), to injure.—*adj.* **wound'able**, capable of being wounded.—*n.* **wound'er.**—*adv.* **wound'ily**, (*arch.*) excessively.—*n.* and *adj.* **wound'ing.**—*adj.* **wound'less**, unwounded; (*obs.*) invulnerable: harmless.—*n.* **wound'wort**, any of several plants of popular repute as vulneraries, as the kidney-vetch, a number of plants of genus Stachys (marsh or clown's woundwort).—*adj.* and *adv.* **wound'y**, (*arch.*) excessive(ly). [O.E. *wund* (Ger. *wunde*, O.N. *und*); also O.E. *wund*, wounded.]

wourali, **woorali**, *wōō-rä'li*, **woora'ra**, **oura'li**, **oura'ri**, the plant yielding curare (q.v.).

wove, **woven**, *pa.t.* and *pa.p.* of **weave.**—**wove paper**, paper that shows in its fabric the marks of a fine wire gauze sieve or mould.

wow, *wow*, *v.i.* (*Spens.*) to woo.

wow, *wow*, *interj.* an exclamation of wonder, tinged with other emotions as aversion, sorrow, or admiration, pleasure (see **whow**).—*v.i.* to howl.—*n.* a bark: a howl: rhythmic or arhythmic changes in reproduced sound, fundamentally arising from fluctuation in speed of either reproducer or recorder: (*slang*) anything thrillingly good, successful, or according to one's wishes.—*n.* **wow'ser** (*-zər*; perh. not connected with **wow**), (*slang*) a puritanical person who tries to interfere with the pleasures of others. [Imit.]

wowf, *wowf*, *adj.* (*Scot.*) crazy. [Origin unknown.]

wow-wow, **wou-wou**, *wow'-wow*, *n.* the silver gibbon of Java: also the agile gibbon of Sumatra. [Imit. of its cry.]

wox, **woxen** (*obs.*), *pa.t.* and *pa.p.* of **wax** (2).

wrack, *rak*, *n.* (*obs.*) vengeance, punishment: destruction, devastation.—Cf. **rack** (2).—*adj.* **wrack'-ful**, (*rare*) destructive. [O.E. *wræc—wrecan*, to drive; connected, and confused, with **wrack** (2).]

wrack, *rak*, *n.* (*dial.*) a wreck: (*arch.*) wreckage: seaweed cast ashore, or growing where it is exposed by the tide: any of the Fucaceae. [M.Du. or M.L.G. *wrak*; cf. **wrack** (1).]

wraith, *rāth*, *n.* a spectre: an apparition, esp. of a living person. [Orig. Scot.; perh. O.N. *vörthr*, a guardian.]

wrangle, *rang'gl*, *v.i.* (*arch.*) to argue, debate, dispute: to dispute noisily or peevishly.—*v.t.* to obtain, persuade, spend, tire, in wrangling: to debate.—*n.* a noisy dispute: the action of disputing, esp. noisily.—*ns.* **wrang'ler**, one who disputes, esp. angrily: (*Shak.*) a stubborn foe: in the University of Cambridge, one of those who attained the first class in the examinations for mathematical honours (**senior wrangler**, the student taking the first place; **second wrangler**, the student next in order of merit, and so on; this method of classification has been abandoned, and since 1909 the first class has been arranged alphabetically): (*Western U.S.*) a herdsman, esp. of horses; **wrang'lership.**—*adj.* **wrang'lesome**, given to wrangling. — *n.* and *adj.* **wrang'ling.** [M.E. *wranglen,* a freq. verb allied to **wring.**]

wrap, *rap, v.t.* to roll or fold together : to fold, lap, round something : to enfold, envelop (*lit.* and *fig.*) : to embrace : to hide, obscure : to cover by folding or winding something round (often with *up*).— *v.i.* to wind, twine : (with *up*) to put on wraps : (*pr.p.* **wrapp'ing ;** *pa.t.* and *pa.p.* **wrapped**).— *n.* a protective covering, for a person or thing, now esp. an outdoor garment : a single turn or fold round.—*ns.* **wrapp'age,** act of wrapping : covering : wrapping materials ; **wrapp'er,** one who, or that which, wraps : formerly, a loose outer garment for a woman ; a loose paper book cover : a paper band, as on a newspaper for the post.—*v.t.* to cover, or cover up, with a wrapper.—*ns.* **wrapp'ing, wrapp'ing-paper,** coarse paper for parcels, &c. ; **wrap'-ras'cal,** a loose greatcoat worn in the eighteenth century (a humorous term).—**wrapped up in,** bound up in : comprised in : engrossed in, devoted to. [M.E. *wrappen,* also *wlappen.*]

wrap, wrapt, erroneous forms of **rap** (2), **rapt.**

wrasse, *ras, n.* a genus (Labrus) of bony fishes representative of the large family Labridae, and including many species on European and N. African coasts. [Cornish *wrach.*]

wrast. Obs. Northern form of **wrest,** directly from O.N.

wrate. Obs. and Scot. *pa.t.* of **write.**

wrath, *rawth,* also *räth, n.* violent anger: an instance, or a fit, of this : holy indignation : (*fig.*) violence or severity : (*Shak.*) ardour.—*adj.* (*arch.*) violently angry.—*v.t.* and *v.i.* (*obs.*) to make, or to become, angry.—*adj.* **wrath'ful,** very angry : springing from, or expressing, or characterised by, wrath.— *adv.* **wrath'fully.** — *n.* **wrath'fulness.** —*adv.* **wrath'ily.**—*n.* **wrath'iness.**—*adjs.* **wrath'less ; wrath'y** (chiefly *U.S.*), inclined to wrath : like, expressing, or characterised by, wrath. [O.E. *wrǣththu—wrǎth,* adj. ; cf. **wroth.**]

wrawl, *rawl, v.i.* (*Spens.*) to cry as a cat, to caterwaul. [Imit.]

wraxle, *rak'sl, v.i.* (*dial.* ; *S.W. England*) to wrestle. —*n.* **wrax'ling.** [O.E. *wraxlian* ; cf. **wrestle.**]

wreak, *rēk, v.t.* (*obs.*) to drive out : to give expression, vent, free play to : (*refl.*) to find expression, outlet, for : to bestow : (*obs.*) to punish : (*obs.*) to harm : (*arch.*) to avenge : (*obs.*) to take vengeance on : (*obs.*) to revenge (with *of*) : to inflict : to effect or bring about : (*pa.t.* **wreaked,** *arch.* **wrōke,** *pa.p.* **wreaked,** *arch.* **wrōk'en,** *Spens.* **wrōke** ** ywrōke**). — *n.* (*arch.*) punishment, vengeance : (*obs.*) damage.—*n.* **wreak'er** (*arch.*).—*adjs.* **wreak'ful,** revengeful : avenging ; **wreak'less,** unpunished. [O.E. *wrecan* ; O.N. *reka,* to drive, pursue, avenge, Ger. *rächen* ; conn. with L. *urgēre.*]

wreak(e), *rēk,* (*Spens., Shak.*) for **reak,** variant of **reck.**—Also (*Milt.*) **wreck.**

wreath, *rēth, n.* a circlet of interwoven materials, esp. flowers, &c. : a single twist or coil in a helical object : a drift or curl of vapour or smoke : a snowdrift : a defect in glass.—*pl.* **wreaths** (*rēdhz*). —*v.t.* **wreathe** (*rēdh*), to form by twisting : to twist together : to form into a wreath : to twine about or encircle : to twist : to cause to twist or contort : (*Scot.*) of snow, to cover by drifting.— *v.i.* to be interwoven : to twine : to twist : (*Scot.*) of snow, to form a drift or wreath : (*obs.*) to turn : to form coils.—*adjs.* **wreathed** (or *rēdh'id*) ; **wreath'en** (*dh* ; *arch. pa.p.*), wreathed. — *ns.* **wreath'er** (*dh*) ; **wreath'-filament,** the usual type of filament in large gas-filled electric lamps, the filament wire being festooned from a horizontal supporting spider.—*adjs.* **wreath'less ; wreath'y** (*th* or *dh*). [O.E. *writha* ; allied to *wrīthan,* to **writhe.**]

wreck, *rek, n.* destruction : the act of wrecking or destroying : destruction of a ship : a badly damaged ship : shipwrecked property : remains of anything ruined : a person ruined mentally or physically.—*v.t.* to destroy or disable : to involve in a wreck : to cast up, as on the shore : to ruin.— *v.i.* to suffer wreck or ruin.—*ns.* **wreck'age,** the act of wrecking : wrecked material : a person, or **persons,** whose life is, or lives are, ruined ;

wreck'er, a person who purposely causes a wreck or who plunders wreckage : one who criminally ruins anything : a person or ship employed in recovering disabled vessels or their cargo.—*adj.* **wreck'ful,** (*poet.*) causing ruin.—*n.* **wreck'-master,** a person taking charge of a disabled ship or train and its cargo or freight.—**receivers of wrecks,** wreck-masters.—**wreck commissioners,** a tribunal that inquires into shipping disasters. [A.Fr. *wrec, wrek,* &c., of Scand. origin ; allied to **wreak** (1).]

wren, *ren, n.* a genus (Troglodytes) and family (Troglodytidae) of birds, having the wings very short and rounded, and the tail short and carried erect : extended to various very small birds, as the **gold-crested wren** (gold-crest), the **willow wren** (willow warbler).—*n.* **wren'-tit,** a Californian bird (*Chamaea fasciata*), resembling the wren and the titmouse. [O.E. *wrenna, wrænna.*]

Wren, *ren, n.* a member of the W.R.N.S.

wrench, *ren(t)sh, v.t.* to wring or pull with a twist : to force by violence : to sprain : to distort.—*v.i.* to perform, or to undergo, a violent wrenching.—*n.* an act or instance of wrenching : a violent twist : a sprain : an instrument for turning nuts, &c. : emotional pain at parting or change : in coursing, bringing the hare round at less than a right angle. [O.E. *wrencan,* to deceive, twist, *wrenc,* deceit, twisting ; cf. Ger. *renken,* to twist, *rank,* trick, intrigue.]

wrenching, *rensh'ing, n.* (Shak., *Hen. VIII.,* I. i. 167 ; older editions) for *renching,* from *dial.* **rench,** to rinse.

wrest, *rest, v.t.* to turn, twist, or (*obs.*) screw : to twist, extract, or take away, by force : to get by toil : to twist from truth or from its natural meaning : to misinterpret : to pervert : (*Spens.*) to derive improperly : (*Scot.*) to sprain.—*v.i.* (*Spens.*) to force a way.—*n.* the act of wresting : violent pulling and twisting : distortion : an instrument, like a wrench, for tuning the piano, &c.—*ns.* **wrest'er ; wrest'-pin',** a pin round which the end of a wire (as a piano wire) is wound, turned by the wrest. [O.E. *wrǣstan* ; Dan. *vriste.*]

wrestle, *res'l, v.i.* to contend by grappling and trying to throw another down : to struggle : to strive : to apply oneself keenly : to pray earnestly : to writhe, wriggle : to proceed with great effort (*lit.* and *fig.*).—*v.t.* to contend with in wrestling : to push with a wriggling or wrestling motion : (with *out*) to go through, carry out, with a great struggle. —*n.* the act, or a bout, of wrestling : a struggle.— *ns.* **wrest'ler ; wrest'ling,** the action of the verb to wrestle : a sport or exercise in which two persons struggle to throw each other to the ground, governed by certain fixed rules—catch-hold, ground-wrestling, catch-as-catch-can, back-hold, &c. [O.E. *wrǣstlian* ; allied to *wrǣstan,* to **wrest.**]

wretch, *rech,* (*obs.*) an exile, outcast : a most miserable person : a worthless, or despicable, person : a being, creature (in pity, sometimes admiration). — *adj.* (*Spens.*) wretched. — *adj.* **wretch'ed** (*-id*), very miserable : distressingly bad : despicable : worthless.—*adv.* **wretch'edly.**—*n.* **wretch'edness.** [O.E. *wrecca,* an outcast— *wrecan* ; see **wreak** (1).]

wrethe, *rēth, v.t.* and *v.i.* (*Spens.*). Same as **wreathe.**

wrick, *rik, v.t.* to twist, sprain, strain.—*n.* a sprain, strain. [Allied to L.G. *wrikken,* to turn.]

wriggle, *rig'l, v.i.* and *v.t.* to twist to and fro : to move, advance, sinuously (*lit.* and *fig.*) : to use evasive tricks.—*n.* the act or motion of wriggling : a sinuous marking, turn, or bend.—*ns.* **wrigg'ler ; wrigg'ling.** [L.G. *wriggeln* ; cf. Du. *wriggelen,* to wriggle.]

wright, *rīt* (*Scot. rihht*), *n.* a maker (chiefly used in compounds, as **shipwright,** &c.) : (*Scot.*) a carpenter or joiner. [O.E. *wyrhta, wryhta,* allied to *wyrht,* a work—*wyrcan,* to work.]

wring, *ring, v.t.* to twist : to expel moisture from by hand twisting or by roller pressure : to force out by twisting : to force out : to clasp and shake fervently : to clasp convulsively, as the hands (in

fāte, fär, ȧsk ; mē, hər (her) ; *mīne ; mōte ; mūte ; mōōn ; dhen* (then)

grief or agitation): (of a shoe) to pinch: to pain: to distress, afflict: to extort: to subject to extortion: to bend out of its position: to wreathe, coil: to distort.—*v.i.* to writhe: to twist: to feel pain: (*pa.t.* and *pa.p.* wrung, *obs.* wringed).—*n.* an act or instance of wringing: a cider-, wine-, or cheese-press.—*ns.* **wring′-bolt**, a bolt with a ring or eye, used to secure a ship's planks against the frame till they are permanently fixed in place; **wring′er**, one who wrings: a machine for forcing water from wet clothes—also **wring′ing-machine**; **wring′-ing.**—*adj.* **wring′-wet**, so wet that water can be wrung out.—*n.pl.* **wring′-staves** (*sing.* -staff), strong pieces of wood used in applying wring-bolts. —**wring from**, to extort from; **wring off**, to force off by wringing; **wring out**, to squeeze out by twisting: to remove from liquid and twist so as to expel the drops. [O.E. *wringan*, to twist; Du. *wringen*, Ger. *ringen*.]

wrinkle, *ring′kl*, *n.* (*coll.*) a tip, valuable hint. [Perh. from O.E. *wrenc*, a trick; perh. same as **wrinkle** (2).]

wrinkle, *ring′kl*, *n.* a small crease or furrow on a surface: an unevenness.—*v.t.* to contract into wrinkles or furrows: to make rough.—*v.i.* to shrink into ridges.—*adjs.* **wrinkled**; **wrink′ly**, full of wrinkles: liable to be wrinked. [History obscure; adj. **wrinkled** is prob. used earlier than noun and verb.]

wrist, *rist*, *n.* the joint by which the hand is united to the arm, the carpus: the part of the body where that joint is, or the part of a garment covering it: a corresponding part of an animal: a wrist-pin.— *ns.* **wrist′band**, a band or part of a sleeve covering the wrist; **wrist′-drop**, inability to extend the hand, often caused by lead-poisoning; **wrist′let**, a band or strap for the wrist: a bracelet: a watch for wearing on the wrist (also **wrist′-watch**, or **wrist′let-watch**): (*slang*) a handcuff; **wrist′-shot**, in golf, a short stroke from the wrist, usu. played with an iron club. [O.E.; allied to *writhan*, to twist; Ger. *rist*.]

writ, *rit*, *arch.* *pa.t.* and *pa.p.* of **write**. — **writ large**, written in large letters, hence (*fig.*) on a large scale, or very obvious.

writ, *rit*, *n.* (*rare*) a writing: a legal or formal document: (*law*) a written document by which one is summoned or required to do something.— **Holy Writ**, the Scriptures; **serve a writ on**, to deliver a summons to. [O.E. (*ge*)*writ*; O.N. *rit*, Goth. *writs*.]

write, *rit*, *v.t.* to form (letters or words) with a pen, pencil, or other implement: to express in writing: to compose: to draw, engrave, &c.: to record: to decree or foretell: to communicate, or to communicate with, by letter.—*v.i.* to perform, or to practise, the act of writing: to be employed as a clerk: to compose, as articles, novels, &c.: to work as an author: to compose, or to send, a letter: to communicate with a person by letter:—*pr.p.* **writ′ing**; *pa.t.* **wrōte**, (*arch.*) **writ** (*rit*); *pa.p.* **written** (*rit′n*), (*arch.*) **writ.** — *adjs.* **writ′able**, capable of being expressed or described in writing: suitable for writing with; **writ′ative**, inclined, or characterised by inclination, to write.—*ns.* **writ′er**, one who writes: a professional scribe or clerk: an ordinary legal practitioner in a Scottish country town: an author: his works: one who paints lettering for signs:—*fem.* **writ′eress** (*rare*); **writer′s-cramp** (see **cramp**); **writ′ership**, the office of a writer; **writ′ing**, the act of one who writes: that which is written: literary production, or composition: handwriting, penmanship: state of being written; **writ′ing-book**, a book of paper for practising penmanship; **writ′ing-case**, a portable case containing materials for writing; **writ′ing-desk**, a desk with a sloping top for writing on: a portable writing-case; **writ′ing-ink**, ink suited for writing with; **writ′ing-master**, a master who teaches the art of penmanship: the yellow-bunting; **writ′ing-paper**, paper finished with a smooth surface, for writing on; **writ′ing-school**, (*obs.*) a school for penmanship; **writ′ing-table**, a table fitted or used for writing on.—*adj.* **writt′en**, reduced to, expressed in, writing—opp.

to *oral*.—**write down**, to put down in written characters: to write in disparagement of: to write so as to be intelligible or attractive to people of lower intelligence or inferior taste; **write off**, to cancel, esp., in book-keeping, to take, as a bad debt, off the books: (*fig.*) to regard, accept, as an irredeemable loss; **write out**, to transcribe: to write in full: (*refl.*) to exhaust one's mental resources by too much writing; **Writer to the Signet**, a member of an ancient society of solicitors in Scotland who formerly had the exclusive right to prepare all summonses and other writs pertaining to the supreme court of justice, and still have the exclusive privilege of preparing crown writs; **write up**, to put a full description of in writing: to write in praise of, esp. to praise above its merits (*n.* **write′-up**): to bring the writing of up to date; **writing on the wall**, a happening foreshowing downfall and disaster (Dan. v. 5 ff.); **written law**, statute law as distinguished from common law. [O.E. *wrítan*, orig. meaning to scratch; O.N. *ríta*.]

writhe, *ridh*, *v.t.* to twist: to coil: to wreathe: to twist violently: to contort: (*obs.*) to distort.—*v.i.* to twist, esp. in pain.—*n.* (*rare*) a twist or a contortion.—*adj.* **writh′en** (*ridh′ən*; *arch.*), twisted, convoluted, contorted.—*n.* and *adj.* **writh′ing.**— *adv.* **writh′ingly**. [O.E. *writhan*, to twist; O.N. *rítha*; cf. **wreath**, **wrest**, **wrist**.]

writhled, *rith′ld*, *adj.* (*arch.*) wrinkled, shrivelled. [Perh. **writhe.**]

wrizled, *riz′ld*, *adj.* (*Spens.*) wrinkled. [Perh. **writhled.**]

wroath, *rōth*, *n.* (*Shak.*) misfortune. [Prob. from **ruth.**]

wroke, *rōk*, obs. *pa.t.*, **wroken**, *rōk′n*, obs. *pa.p.*, of **wreak.**

wrong, *rong*, *adj.* (*obs.*) crooked, curved, twisted, bent: not according to rule: incorrect: erroneous: not in accordance with moral law: wicked: not that (thing) which is required, intended, advisable, or suitable: amiss, unsatisfactory: mistaken, misinformed: under, inner, reverse.—*n.* whatever is not right or just: any injury done to another: (*rare*) damage, harm: wrong-doing: the state or position of being or doing wrong.—*adv.* not correctly: not in the right way: astray.—*v.t.* to do wrong to: (*obs.* and *Scot.*) to harm physically: (*obs.*) to impair, spoil: to seduce: to deprive of some right: to defraud: to impute fault to unjustly: to dishonour.—*ns.* **wrong′-do′er**, an offender, transgressor; **wrong′-do′ing**, evil or wicked action or conduct; **wrong′er**, one who wrongs.—*adj.* **wrong′ful**, wrong: unjust: unlawful: not legitimate: (*Spens.*) unjustly held.— *adv.* **wrong′fully**. — *n.* **wrong′fulness.** — *adj.* **wrong′-headed**, obstinate and perverse, adhering stubbornly to wrong principles or policy.—*adv.* **wrong′-headedly**. — *n.* **wrong′-headedness.** — *adv.* **wrong′ly**.—*adj.* **wrong′-minded**, having erroneous views.—*n.* **wrong′ness**.—*adj.* **wrong′-ous** (-*gəs*, -*əs*), unjust, illegal.—*adv.* **wrong′ously**. —*adj.* **wrong′-timed**, inopportune.—**do oneself wrong**, (*obs.*) to be mistaken; **get hold of the wrong end of the stick**, to misapprehend a matter fundamentally; **get out of bed on the wrong side**, to arise in the morning in an ill temper; **go wrong**, to fail to work properly: to make a mistake or mistakes: to stray from virtue; **have wrong**, (*obs.*) to suffer injustice or injury; **in the wrong**, holding an erroneous view or unjust position: guilty of error or injustice; **private wrong**, a violation of the civil or personal rights of an individual; **public wrong**, a crime —which affects the community; **put in the wrong**, to cause to appear in error, guilty of injustice, &c. [O.E. *wrang*, a wrong; most prob. O.N. *rangr*, unjust; allied to O.E. *wringan*, to wring, like Fr. *tort*, from L. *tortus*, twisted.]

wroot. Obs. form of **root** and **wrote**.

wrote, *rōt*, *pa.t.* of **write**.

wroth, *rōth*, *roth*, *adj.* wrathful: in commotion, stormy. [O.E. *wráth*, angry; cf. O.N. *reithr*.]

wrought, *rawt*, *pa.t.* and *pa.p.* of **work**, now used chiefly in certain senses:—e.g. fashioned: ornamented : manufactured : beaten into shape, shaped by tools (as metal).—*n.* **wrought'-iron**, malleable iron, iron containing only a very small amount of other elements, but containing slag in the form of particles elongated in one direction, more rust-resistant than steel and welding more easily.—*adj.* **wrought'-up**, in an agitated condition, over-excited. [O.E. *worhte, geworht,* pa.t. and pa.p. of *wyrcan, wircan,* to work.]

wrung, *rung,* pa.t. and pa.p. of **wring.**

wry, *rī, adj.* twisted or turned to one side : not in the right direction : (*fig.*) expressing displeasure : (*fig.*) perverse, distorted.—*n.* (*rare*) distortion.—*v.i.* (*obs.*) to swerve, to go astray : (*obs.*) to be deflected, undergo deflexion : to writhe.—*v.t.* to give a twist to : to avert, as the face : to pervert.—*adv.* wryly. —*n.* **wry'bill,** a New Zealand bird allied to the plovers with bill bent sideways.—*adv.* **wry'ly.**— *adj.* **wry'-mouthed,** having a crooked mouth : unflattering.—*n.* **wry'-neck,** a twisted position of the head on the neck due to disease of the cervical vertebrae or to affections (esp. rneumatic) of the muscles of the neck : **wry'neck,** a genus of small birds (Jynx) allied to the woodpecker, which twist round their heads strangely when surprised.—*adj.* **wry'-necked,** having a wry neck : (Shak., *M. of V.,* II. v. 30) played with the head on one side.—*n.* **wry'ness.—make a wry face, or mouth,** to pucker up the face, or mouth, as in tasting anything bitter or astringent, or in sign of disgust or pain. [O.E. *wrigian,* to strive, move, turn.]

wud. Scots form of **wood** (1 and 2).

wulfenite, *wool'fən-īt, n.* molybdate of lead, $PbMoO_4$, occurring commonly as yellow crystals in veins with other lead ores, named after an Austrian mineralogist von *Wulfen.*

wull, *wul,* v.i. (*Spens.* and *dial.*). Same as **will.**

Würm, *vürm, n.* the fourth stage of glaciation in the Alps.—*adjs.* **Würm, Würm'ian.** [From a river of Upper Bavaria.]

wurtzite, *vurts'īt, n.* sulphide of zinc, ZnS, of the same composition as sphalerite, but crystallising in the hexagonal system, in black hemimorphic, pyramidal crystals. [From French chemist C. A. *Wurtz.*]

wuther, *wudh'ər, v.i.* (all meanings *dial.*) to move swiftly or with force : to make a sullen roaring, as the wind : to throw or beat violently.—*n.* a blow or blast, or the sound of these : a tremble.—*adj.* **wuth'ering.**—Also **whither** (*hwidh'ər*). [From O.N.]

wuzzle, *wuz'l, v.t.* (*U.S.*) to jumble.

wyandotte, *wī'an-dot, n.* a useful breed of the domestic fowl, of American origin. [From N. American tribe so called.]

wych-elm, *wich'elm, n.* a common wild elm, also called Scotch elm or witch-hazel. [**witch** (2), and **elm.**]

Wycliffite, Wycliffite, *wik'lif-īt, adj.* pertaining to the English reformer and translator of the Bible, John *Wyclif, Wycliffe* (c. 1320-84).—*n.* a follower of Wyclif ; a Lollard.

wye, *wī, n.* the letter Y (q.v.) or anything shaped like it.

Wykehamist, *wik'əm-ist, n.* a pupil, or former pupil, of Winchester College, founded by William of *Wykeham,* Bishop of Winchester (1324-1404).

wylie-coat, *wī'li-kōt, n.* (*Scot.*) a flannel undervest or petticoat : a nightdress. [Unknown first element, and prob. **coat.**]

wynd, *wind, n.* (*Scot.*) a lane, narrow alley in a town. [Same as **wind** (2).]

wyte. Same as **wite.**

wyvern. Same as **wivern.**

fāte, fär, ăsk ; *mē, hər* (her) ; *mīne* ; *mōte* ; *mūte* ; *mōōn* ; *dhen* (then)

X

X, x, *eks, n.* the twenty-fourth letter in our alphabet, and twenty-first of the Roman alphabet, taken from the Chalcidian Greek, and of the same form, though perhaps not the same origin, as Ionic and classical Greek chi (X, χ ; pron. *k-h,* and later *hh*) ; used in Old English medially and finally as a variant for *cs.* In modern English, medially and finally, it has the value of *ks,* as in *extinct, axe,* and, medially only, of *gz,* as in *exist,* or *ksh,* as in *luxury,* or *gzh,* as in *luxurious* ; at the beginning of word it is pronounced like *z.* As a Roman numeral X stands for ten, ⋊ for a thousand, X̄ for ten thousand ; X (see **chi**) as an abbreviation represents the word Christ—Xian, Xmas ; *x* in algebra is the first of the unknown quantities.—*ns.* **X′-body,** an inclusion in a plant-cell suffering from a virus disease ; **X′-chromosome,** a chromosome associated with sex-determination, usually occurring paired, but sometimes occurring alone ; **X′-particle,** a meson. —*n.pl.* **X′-rays,** electromagnetic rays of very short wavelength which can penetrate matter opaque to light-rays, produced when cathode rays impinge on matter—discovered by Röntgen in 1895. —*adj.* **X′-ray.—characteristic X-rays,** secondary X-rays emitted when X-rays fall on matter, which contain monochromatic radiations that vary in wavelength according to the atoms from which they are scattered ; **X-ray micrography,** the preparation, and study through the microscope, of radiographs obtained by means of X-rays ; **X-ray spectrum,** a wavelength or frequency diagram in which a series of lines indicate by their positions the particular X-rays emitted by a body as the result of cathode-ray bombardment ; **X-ray tube,** an evacuated tube in which X-rays are emitted from a metal target placed obliquely opposite to an incandescent cathode whose rays impinge on the target.

xanth-, *zanth-,* **xantho-,** *zan′thō-, -tho′-,* by some pronounced *gzan-,* in composition, yellow.—*ns.* **xan′thate,** a salt of xanthic acid ; **xanthein** (*zan′the-in*), a soluble yellow colouring matter of flowers ; **xanthene** (*zan′thēn*), a white crystalline compound of carbon, hydrogen, and oxygen, from which are derived **xanthene dyestuffs.**—*adj.* **xan′thic,** of a yellow tint, esp. as a description of flowers : pertaining to xanthin or xanthine : designating **xanthic acid,** any of a series of addition compounds of an alcohol with carbon disulphide, esp. ethyl-xanthic acid.—*ns.* **xan′thin,** a name given to the insoluble yellow colouring matter of various flowers : also to a principle in madder : (usu. **xan′thine**) a white substance, closely allied to uric acid, found in muscle tissue, the liver and other organs, urine, &c., leaving a lemon-yellow residue when evaporated with nitric acid ; **Xan′thium** (Gr. *xanthion,* a plant used for dyeing the hair yellow), any of a small but widely distributed genus of composite plants whose fruits bear hooked prickles very troublesome to sheep and other animals.—*n.pl.* **Xanthochroi** (*zan-thok′rō-ī* ; Gr. *chroä,* or *chroiä,* skin), one of the five groups of men, according to Huxley and other ethnologists, comprising the fair whites.—*n.* **xanthochroia** (*-thō-kroi′ä*), yellowness of the skin.—*adjs.* **xanthochrō′ic, xan′thochroid** (*-kroid* ; also used as *n.*), pertaining to the Xanthochroi.—*n.* **xanthochroism** (*-thok′rō-izm*), a condition in which all skin pigments other than golden and yellow ones disappear, as in goldfish.—*adj.* **xanthochroous** (*-thok′rō-əs*), xanthochroic.—*ns.* **xanthochrō′mia,** any yellowish discoloration, esp. of the cerebro-spinal fluid ; **xanthoma** (*zan-thō′mä*), a yellow tumour composed of fibrous tissue and of cells containing cholesterol ester, occurring on the skin

(e.g. in diabetes) or on the sheaths of tendons, or in any tissue of the body.—*adjs.* **xanthom′atous ; xanthomelanous** (*zan-thō-mel′ə-nəs*), applied to a type of men with black hair and yellow or olive skins.—*ns.* **xanthophyll** (*zan′thō-fil*), $C_{40}H_{56}O_2$, one of the two yellow pigments present in the normal chlorophyll mixture of green plants ; **xanthop′sia,** the condition in which objects appear yellow to the observer, as in jaundice or after taking santonin.—*adj.* **xanthous** (*zan′thəs*), yellow.—*ns.* **Xanthoxylum** (*zan-thok′si-ləm* ; Gr. *xylon,* wood), a genus of the Rutaceae, comprising over one hundred species, of which many are found in Brazil and the W. Indies, esp. either of two species known respectively as the prickly ash and Hercules club, or their dried bark ; **Xanthura, Xanthoura** (*-thū′, -thŏŏ′rä* ; Gr. *ourä,* tail), a genus of American jays, with yellow tail. [Gr. *xanthos,* yellow.]

Xanthian, *zan′thi-ən, adj.* pertaining to *Xanthus,* capital of ancient Lycia in Asia Minor.

Xanthium. See under **xanth-.**

Xantippe, *zan-tip′i, n.* a scold, shrew.—Also **Xanthippe** (*-thip′*) (*Shak.* older editions **Zan′-tippe, Zen′tippe**). [Gr. *Xanthippē,* wife of Socrates.]

xebec, *zē′bek, n.* a small three-masted vessel much used by the former corsairs of Algiers. [Fr. *chebec,* influenced by Sp. form ; perh. from Turkish or Arabic.]

Xema, *zē′mä, n.* the genus of fork-tailed gulls. [Arbitrarily invented 1819.]

xen-, *zen-, zēn-,* **xeno-,** *zen-ō-, zi-no′-, pfx.* strange, foreign, guest. — *n.* **Xenar′thra** (Gr. *arthron,* a joint), a group of American edentates—ant-eaters, sloths, armadillos—having the dorsolumbar vertebrae jointed in an unusual manner.—*adj.* **xenar′thral,** having additional facets for articulation on the dorsolumbar vertebrae.—*n.* **xē′nia,** (*bot.*) the direct influence of pollen upon endosperm (explained by double fertilisation) or upon the mother-plant of the embryo.—*adj.* **xenial** (*zē′ni-əl*), of or belonging to hospitality, or relations with guests.—*ns.* **xenium** (*zē′ni-əm*), a present made to a guest or an ambassador : an offering, or a compulsory gift, to a ruler, the Church, &c. :— *pl.* **xē′nia ; xen′ocryst** (*-krist*), a crystal or mineral grain which has been incorporated by magma during its uprise ; **xenodochium** (*zen-o-do-kī′əm* ; Gr. *docheion,* a receptacle), a building for the reception of strangers, as a guest-house in a monastery ; **xenogamy** (*zen-og′ə-mi* ; Gr. *gamos,* marriage ; *bot.*), cross-fertilisation ; **xenogenesis** (*zen-ō-jen′ə-sis* ; Gr. *genesis,* birth), the (imagined) generation of something altogether and permanently unlike the parent.—*adjs.* **xenogenet′ic ; xenogenous** (*zi-noj′-i-nəs*), due to outside cause.— *ns.* **xen′olith,** a fragment of rock of extraneous origin which has been incorporated in magma ; **xenomania** (*-mā′ni-ä* ; Gr. *maniā,* madness), an inordinate attachment to things foreign ; **xenomenia** (*-mē′ni-ä* ; Gr. *mēniaia,* menses), vicarious menstruation, in which, in the absence of normal menstruation, bleeding occurs at regular monthly intervals from other parts of the body (e.g. the nose).—*adj.* **xenomorphic** (*-mor′fik* ; Gr. *morphē,* form), allotriomorphic.—**xenon** (*zen′, zēn′on*), a zero-valent element (symbol Xe or X ; at. numb. 54), one of the rare gases, present in the atmosphere in the proportion of 1 : 170,000,000 by volume ; **xen′ophobe** (*-fōb* ; Gr. *phobos,* fear), one who fears or hates foreigners or things foreign ; **xenophobia** (*-fō′bi-ä*), **xenoph′oby,** fear of things foreign ; **xenophya** (*zen-of′i-ä* ; Gr. *xenophyēs,* strange in shape or nature), elements of a shell or skeleton not secreted by the organism itself.—*adj.*

Neutral vowels in unaccented syllables : *el′ə-mənt, in′fənt, ran′dəm*

xenoplas'tic, in experimental zoology, transplantation in which transplant and host belong to the young germs of different species or genera. —*ns.* **xenotime** (*zen'ō-tīm*; Gr. *xenos*, strange, in error for *kenos*, empty, vain, and *timē*, honour, in reference to the fact that the mineral was at first supposed to contain a new metal), yttrium phosphate, often containing small quantities of cerium, erbium, and thorium, and an important source of these rare elements; **Xenurus** (*zē-nū'rəs*; Gr. *ourā*, tail), a genus of armadillos in which the tail is almost without plates.—*adj.* **xenū'rine.** [Gr. *xenos*, (n.) guest, host, stranger, (adj.) strange, foreign.]

xer-, *zēr-,* **xero-,** *zē-rō-, pfx.* dry.—*ns.* **xeran'sis,** drying up; **Xeranthemum** (*-an'thi-məm*; Gr. *anthemon*, flower), a genus of plants of southern Europe, belonging to the thistle family: a species of these known as everlastings.—*adjs.* **xeran'tic,** drying up; **xerarch** (*zē'rärk*; Gr. *archē*, beginning), of a plant succession, starting on land where conditions are very dry.—*n.* **xerasia** (*zi-rā'si-ä*), a morbid dryness of the hair.—*adj.* **xē'ric,** xerophytic.—*ns.* **xerochasy** (*zi-rok'ə-si*), dehiscence on drying; **xeroderma** (*zē-rō-dər'mä* Gr. *derma*, skin), **xeroder'mia,** a disease characterised by abnormal dryness of the skin and by overgrowth of its horny layer. — *adjs.* **xerodermat'ic, xeroder'matous, xeroder'mic.**—*ns.* **xeroma** (*-rō'*), xerophthalmia; **xē'romorph** (*-morf*; Gr. *morphē*, form), a xerophyte.—*adjs.* **xeromor'phic, xeromor'phous,** of parts of a plant, protected against excessive loss of water by thick cuticles, coatings of hairs, and similar structural characters.—*n.* **xerophagy** (*zi-rof'ə-ji*; Gr. *phagein*, to eat), the eating of dry food, or of bread, vegetables and water, as a form of fast.—*adj.* **xerophilous** (*-of'il-əs*; Gr. *philos*, loving), of a plant, tolerant of a droughty habitat.—*ns.* **xeroph'ily,** adaptation to dry conditions; **xērophthalmia** (*-of-thal'mi-ä*; Gr. *ophthalmos*, eye), a dry lustreless condition of the conjunctiva due to deficiency of vitamin A in the diet; **xē'rophyte** (*-fīt*; Gr. *phyton*, plant), a plant able to inhabit places where the water supply is scanty, or where conditions, e.g. excess of salts, make it difficult to take in water.—*adj.* **xerophytic** (*-fīt'*), able to withstand drought.—*ns.* **xerō'sis,** xerophthalmia; **xerostoma** (*-os'tom-ä*; Gr. *stoma*, mouth), **xerostō'mia,** excessive dryness of the mouth due to insufficiency of the secretions; **xerotes** (*zē'rō-tēz*), a dry habit of body.—*adj.* **xerotic** (*-rot'*).—*n.* **xerotripsis** (*-trip'sis*; Gr. *tripsis—tribein,* to rub), dry friction. [Gr. *xēros,* dry.]

xi, *zī,* ksī, ksē, *n.* the fourteenth letter of the Greek alphabet (Ξ, ξ), answering to X: as a numeral ξ' = 60, ͵ξ = 60,000.

Xiphias, *zif'i-as, n.* the common swordfish genus, giving name to the family **Xiphi'idae.** [Gr. *xiphias,* swordfish—*xiphos,* sword.]

xiphiplastron, *zif-i-plas'tron, n.* in chelonians, one of the plates composing the plastron, lying posterior to the hypoplastron.—*adj.* and *n.* **xiphoplas'tral.** [Gr. *xiphos,* sword, and **plastron.**]

xiphoid, *zif'oid, adj.* sword-shaped: pertaining to, or designating, the **xiphoid process** (also, when cartilaginous, known as **xiphoid cartilage**) or xiphisternum.—*adj.* **xiphoid'al.**—*ns.* **xiphihumeralis** (*-hū-mər-ā'lis*), in vertebrates, a muscle leading from the xiphoid cartilage to the humerus; **xiphister'num,** a posterior element of the sternum; **xiphopagus** (*zif-op'ə-gəs*; Gr. *pēgnynai,* to fix, fasten together), a monster consisting, as did the Siamese twins, of twins joined in the region of the xiphoid cartilage. — *adjs.* **xiphopagic** (*-paj'ik*), **xiphopagous** (*zif-op'ə-gəs*). [Gr. *xiphos,* sword.]

xiphophyllus, *zif-ō-fil'əs, adj.* with sword-shaped leaves. [Gr. *xiphos,* sword, *phyllon,* leaf.]

Xiphosura, *zif-ō-sū'rä, n.* an order of Arthropoda of which the only survivors are the king-crabs.— *adj.* and *n.* **xiphosu'ran.** [Irregularly formed from Gr. *xiphos,* sword, *ourā,* tail.]

xoanon, *zō'ə-non, n.* a primitive statue, said to be fallen from heaven, orig. of wood, later overlaid with ivory and gold. [Gr. *xoanon—xeein* to carve.]

X-rays. See under **X.**

xylem, *zī'ləm, n.* woody tissue—usu. consisting of vessels, tracheides, and fibres, all with lignified walls, with some more or less lignified parenchyma —concerned in the conduction of aqueous solutions, and with mechanical support.—*ns.* **xy'lene,** $C_6H_4(CH_3)_2$, any of three dimethyl-benzenes, occurring in coal-tar but not separable by fractional distillation; **xy'lenol,** $(CH_3)_2 \cdot C_6H_3 \cdot OH$, any of six monohydric phenols derived from xylenes.— *adj.* **xy'lic,** pertaining to xylem: designating any of six acids derivatives of xylene.—*ns.* **xylobal'samum** (Gr. *balsamon,* the balsam tree), the dried twigs, or the wood, of the balm of Gilead tree; **xy'locarp,** a hard and woody fruit.—*adj.* **xylocarp'ous.**—*ns.* **xy'lochrome** (Gr. *chrōma,* colour), a mixture of substances to which the colour of heart-wood is due—including tannins, gums, and resins; **xy'logen** (*-jen*), xylem.—*adj.* (*bot.*) **xylogenous** (*-loj'ən-əs*), growing on wood.—*ns.* **xylography** (*zī-log'rə-fi*), the art of engraving on wood; **xyl'ograph,** an impression or print from a wood block: an impression of the grain of wood for surface decoration; **xylog'rapher.** — *adjs.* **xylograph'ic, -al;** **xy'loid,** woody, ligneous.— *ns.* **xyloidin, xyloidine** (*zī-loi'din*; Gr. *eidos,* form, appearance), an explosive like gun-cotton, prepared by the action of strong nitric acid on starch or woody fibre—pyroxylin, or similar substance; **xy'lol** (L. *oleum,* oil), xylene; **xylol'ogy,** the study of the structure of wood; **xylō'ma,** in fungi, a sclerotium-like body which forms spores internally and does not put out branches which develop into sporophores; **xylom'eter,** an instrument for determining the specific gravity of wood. —*adj.* **xylon'ic,** designating an acid obtained by oxidising xylose.—*ns.* **Xy'lonite,** a non-thermosetting plastic of the nitrocellulose type; **xylophagan** (*-lof'ə-gən*; Gr. *phagein,* to eat), one of the **Xyloph'aga,** a genus of boring bivalves; **xy'lophage** (*-fāj*), an insect-larva, mollusc, &c., that eats or bores in wood.—*adjs.* **xylophagous** (*-lof'ə-gəs*), wood-eating; **xyloph'ilous,** fond of wood, living upon wood.—*n.* **xy'lophone** (Gr. *phōnē,* voice), a musical instrument consisting of a graduated series of wooden bars, which are rested on straw, &c., and are struck by wooden hammers. —*adj.* **xylophon'ic.**—*ns.* **xyloph'onist; Xylopia** (*-lōp'i-ä*; Gr. *pikros,* bitter), a genus of trees and shrubs of the custard-apple family, natives of the tropics, chiefly in America; **xylopyrog'raphy,** poker-painting on wood; **xyl'ose,** a pentose found in many plants, also known as wood-sugar.—*adj.* **xylot'omous** (Gr. *tomē,* a cut), of insects, wood-boring, wood-cutting; **xylotypograph'ic,** pertaining to, or printed from, wooden type.—*ns.* **xylotypog'raphy; xy'lyl** (*-lil*), any of the univalent radicals, C_8H_9, of the xylenes or their derivatives. [Gr. *xylon,* wood.]

Xyris, *zī'ris, n.* a genus of sedge-like plants, usu. with yellow flowers, of the family **Xyridaceae** (*zir-i-dā'sē-ē*) and order **Xyridā'les.**—*adj.* **xyridā'ceous** (*-shəs*), of the Xyridaceae. [Gr. *xyris,* a kind of iris.]

xyster, *zis'tər, n.* a surgeon's instrument for scraping bones. [Gr. *xystēr,* a graving tool.]

xystus, *zis'təs, n.* (*ant.*) a covered portico used by athletes for their exercises: an open colonnade: a tree-planted walk.—Also **xyst, xys'tos.** [L.,— Gr. *xystos* or *-on,* perh. orig. a cleared or raked place—*xyein,* to scrape; cf. **xyster.**]

---

fāte, fär, ȧsk; mē, hər (her); mīne; mōte; mūte; mōōn; ᴅhen (then)

Y

Y, y, *wī, n.* the twenty-fifth letter of our alphabet, twenty-third of the Roman alphabet, derived, as are also U and V, from Greek upsilon (Υ, υ); it is used to represent a consonant sound as in *year* (*y* = O.E. ᵹ; M.E. ᴣ, yogh), and the vowel and diphthongal sounds, *i*, as in *hymn, folly, ī,* as in *my, pyre, ə,* as in *myrrh* or in *satyr;* also in digraphs, as *oy* instead of *oi* when final, as in *toy.* Early printers used y as a substitute for thorn (þ), which their founts lacked: hence it came to be so used in MSS. and inscriptions, as *yat* or *yᵗ* for *that, ye* for *the*; _cf._ **ye** (2). As a mediaeval numeral, Y = 150; Ȳ = 150,000.—*ns.* **Y'-alloy,** an aluminium-base alloy of duralumin type, containing copper 4%, magnesium 1·5%, silicon 0·7%, nickel 2%, iron 0·6%, and titanium 0·2%; **Y'-chromosome,** one of a pair of chromosomes associated with sex-determination (the other being the **X-chromosome**); **Y'-level,** a type of engineers' level whose essential characteristic is the support of the telescope, namely, Y-shaped rests in which it may be rotated, or reversed end-for-end.—Also **wye'-level**; **Y'-moth,** any of a genus of destructive noctuid moths with a silvery Y-shaped mark on the fore-wings; **Y'-track,** a short track laid at right angles to a railway-line, connected with it by two switches resembling a Y, used for reversing engines.

y-, i-, *pfx.* derived from O.E. pfx. *ge-* (ᴣe-), orig. a preposition meaning 'with, together,' seen in O.E. nouns and adjectives, as *gefera,* companion, *getheaht,* counsel, *gelic,* alike, &c., and in verbs, as *gethéodan,* to join together, *gerinnan,* to congeal, but even in O.E. times often used with no very definite meaning; in primitive Germanic *gi-* imparted a perfective meaning to past participles; in O.E. (as *ge-*) and in M.E. (as ᴣe-, y-, i-, &c.) it was prefixed to past participles, indiscriminately, and it was in this way used freely by Spenser and other archaisers.

yacca, *yak'ä, n.* either of two evergreens (Podocarpus) of the West Indies, or their wood. [Sp. *yaca,* from Taino.]

yacht, *yot, n.* orig. a light fast-sailing vessel: a sailing, steam, &c., vessel elegantly fitted up for pleasure-trips or racing.—*v.i.* to sail or race in a yacht.—*adj.* **yacht'-built,** built on the model of a yacht.—*ns.* **yacht'-club,** a club of yachtsmen; **yacht'er,** one engaged in sailing a yacht.—*n.* and *adj.* **yacht'ing.**—*ns.* **yachts'man,** one who keeps or sails a yacht; **yachts'manship,** the art of sailing a yacht. [Du. *jacht* (formerly *jagt*), from *jagen,* to chase; Ger. *jagen,* to hunt.]

yaff, *yäf, v.i.* (*Scot.*) to bark like a snarling dog: to scold, nag. [Imit.]

yaffle (*dial.*), *yaf'l,* **yaffingale** (*Tennyson*), *yaf'ing-gäl, ns.* the green woodpecker. [From its sound; influenced by **nightingale**.]

yager, *yä'gər, n.* Same as **jäger.**

yagger, *yag'ər, n.* (*Scot.*) a pedlar. [Variant of **jagger.**]

yah, *yä.* Variant of **yea.**

yah, *yä, interj.* an exclamation of derision, contemptuous defiance, or disgust.

Yahoo, *yä-hōō', n.* a name given by Swift in *Gulliver's Travels* to a class of animals with the forms of men but the understanding and passions of brutes: a brutal or boorish lout.

Yahwe(h), *yä'wä,* Jehovah (q.v.).—*n.* **Yah'wist,** Jehovist.—Also **Yah've(h),** **Yah'vist.**

Yajurveda, *yuj'oor-vä-dä,* n. one of the four Vedas, the Veda of prayers. [Sans.,—*yajus,* reverence, and **Veda.**]

yak, *yak, n.* a species of ox found in Tibet, and domesticated there, covered all over with a thick coat of long silky hair, that of the lower parts hanging down almost to the ground.—*n.* **yakh'dan,** a box for strapping on a yak. [Tibetan.]

Yakut, *yä-kōōt', n.* a member of a mixed Turkish race in Siberia, in the Lena district: their Turkic language.

yald. See **yauld.**

Yale lock, *yäl lok,* trade-mark for certain kinds of lock. [Linus *Yale* (1821-68), American locksmith.]

Y-alloy. See under **Y.**

yam, *yam, n.* a large tuberous root like the potato, growing in tropical countries: any plant of the genus Dioscorea, some species of which yield these tubers: (*Scot.*) a potato: (*Southern U.S.*) a sweet-potato. [Port. *inhame.*]

Yama, *yum'ä,* *yam'ä, n.* in Hindu mythology, the first mortal. [Sans.]

yamen, *yä'men, n.* the offices and residence of a mandarin. [Chin.]

yammer, *yam'ər, v.i.* (*dial.* and *coll.*) to lament, wail: to whine: to make an outcry: to express yearning.—*n.* **yamm'ering.** [O.E. *géom(e)rian—géomor,* sad; influenced in M.E. by Du. *jammeren.*]

yang, *yang, n.* various species of Dipterocarpus, valuable timber trees.

yank, *yangk, v.t.* to carry, move with a jerk (with *out, over*).—*v.i.* to move actively.—*n.* (*Scot.*) a blow, buffet: (*U.S.*) a strong jerk.—*n.* **yank'er,** (*Scot.*) a rap: a big lie.—*adj.* **yank'ing,** (*Scot.*) active: (*U.S.*) pulling, jerking.—*n.* **yank'ie,** (*Scot.*) a scold: an impudent woman. [Ety. dub.]

Yankee, *yang'ki, n.* in America, a citizen of the New England States, or an inhabitant of the northern United States, as opposed to the southern: in British usage, generally an inhabitant of the United States.—Also *adj.*—Also **Yank**(*coll.*).—*ns.* **Yank'eedom,** the land of Yankees: Yankees generally; **Yank'ee-Doo'dle,** a Yankee, from a popular air.—Also *adj.*—*adj.* **Yank'eefied.**—*n.* **Yank'eeism,** Yankee characteristics. [Prob. *Janke,* a diminutive of Du. *Jan,* John.]

yaourt, *ya-ōort', n.* a fermented liquor made from milk. [Turk. *yōghurt.*]

yap, *yap, v.i.* (*dial.*) to bark sharply or constantly: to speak constantly: to scold.—*n.* a yelp: a cur.—*n.* **yap'ster,** a dog. [Imit.]

yapok, *yapock,* *yap'ɔk, n.* the S. American water-opossum. [From river *Oyapok,* in French Guiana.]

yapon. See **yaupon.**

yapp, *yap, n.* a limp leather binding in which the cover overlaps the edges of the book. [*Yapp,* a bookseller.]

Yarborough, *yär'bər-ə, n.* a hand containing no card above a nine. [From an Earl of *Yarborough,* said to have betted against its occurrence.]

yard, *yärd, n.* (*obs.*) a straight thin branch, a wand of authority, a stick for beating as punishment, or a rod for measuring: an English measure of 3 feet or 36 inches: a piece of material this length: a long beam on a mast for spreading square sails: (*arch.*) the penis.—*ns.* **yard'age,** the aggregate number of yards: the length, area, or volume measured or estimated in linear, square, or cubic yards: the cutting of coal at so much a yard; **yard'-arm,** either half of a ship's yard (right or left) from the centre to the end; **yard'land,** a virgate, a yard of land; **yard'stick,** a stick 3 feet long: (*fig.*) any standard of measurement.—Also **yard'wand.**—**by the yard,** in large quantities; **yard of ale,** &c., a tall slender glass for ale, &c., or its contents; **yard of land,** a measure of area of land, a virgate. [O.E. *gyrd, gierd,* a rod, measure; Du. *garde,* Ger. *gerte*; conn. Goth. *gazds,* a prickle, sting; and prob. L. *hasta,* a spear.]

yard, *yärd, n.* an enclosed place, esp. near a building, often in composition, as 'backyard,' 'courtyard,' 'farmyard,' 'prison-yard,' or where any special work is carried on, as 'brickyard,' 'wood-yard,' 'dockyard,' 'railway-yard': a garden.—*v.t.* to enclose in a yard.—*ns.* yard'age, the use of a yard, or the charge made for such; yard'man, the person having special charge of a farmyard: one employed in a railway-yard in making up trains, &c.; yard'-master, one who has the special oversight of a railway-yard.—the Yard, Scotland Yard, the London Metropolitan Police headquarters. [O.E. *geard*, fence, dwelling, enclosure; Ger. *garten*; conn. with L. *hortus*, Gr. *chortos*.]

yare, *yār*, *adj.* (*arch.* and *dial.*) ready, prepared: quick, brisk: easily handled, manageable.—*interj.* (*Shak.*) quick!—*adv.* yare'ly (*arch.* and *dial.*), promptly: skilfully. [O.E. *gearu*, *gearo*, ready, prompt; Du. *gaar*, done, cooked sufficiently, Ger. *gar*, wholly.]

yarn, *yärn*, *n.* spun thread: one of the threads of a rope, or these collectively: a sailor's story, spun out to some length, and often having incredible elements: (*coll.*) a story generally.—*v.i.* to tell stories. [O.E. *gearn*, thread; O.N. and Ger. *garn*.]

yarpha, yarfa, *yär'fä*, *n.* peaty soil in Shetland: clayey, sandy, or fibrous peat: a peat-bog. [O.N. *jörfi*, gravel.]

yarr, *yär*, *n.* (*dial.*) the corn spurrey. [Cf. Fris. *jīr*.]

yarrow, *yar'ō*, *n.* a strong-scented plant, *Achillea millefolium*, or similar species of milfoil. [O.E. *gearwe*; Ger. *garbe*.]

yarta, yarto. See jarta.

yashmak, *yash'mak*, or -*mak'*, *n.* the double veil worn by Moslem women in public, the eyes only being uncovered. [Ar. *yashmaq*.]

yatag(h)an, *yat'a-gan*, *n.* a long Turkish dagger, without guard, usu. curved. [Turk. *yātāghan*.]

yate, *yāt*, *n.* (*Spens.*) a gate. [Variant of gate.]

yatter, *yat'ər*, *n.* (*Scot.*) tiresome, importunate or persistent chatter.—*v.i.* to jabber indefatigably.—*n.* and *adj.* yatt'ering.—*adv.* yatt'eringly.

yaud, *yawd*, *yäd*, *n.* (*Scot.*) a mare: an old mare: an old horse generally. [O.N. *jalda*.]

yauld, yald, *yawld*, *yäld*, *adj.* (*Scot.*) active, nimble, strong. [Ety. unknown.]

yaup, *yawp*, *adj.* (*Scot.*) hungry. [O.E. *géap*, shrewd.]

yaupon, *yaw'pən*, *n.* a bushy evergreen shrub of the holly genus, native to the S.E. coasts of the U.S., its leaves yielding the medicinal 'black drink' of the Indians.—Also yapon (*yaw'*), yupon (*yōō'*). [Amer. Indian.]

yaw, *yaw*, *v.i.* of a ship, to deviate temporarily from, to turn out of the line of, her course: (*fig.*) to move unsteadily or zigzag: (*aero.*) to deviate in a horizontal direction from the line of flight.—*v.t.* to cause to deviate from course, zigzag, &c.—*n.* a deviation from the course: the angular motion of an aircraft in a horizontal plane about the normally vertical axis. [Origin uncertain; cf. O.N. *jaga*, to move to and fro, as a door on its hinges.]

yawl, *yawl*, *v.i.* to howl.—*n.* a howl. [Variant of yowl.]

yawl, *yawl*, *n.* a ship's small boat, generally with four or six oars: a small fishing-boat: a small sailing-boat with jigger and curtailed mainboom. [Du. *jol*; cf. jollyboat.]

yawn, *yawn*, *v.i.* to take a deep involuntary breath from drowsiness, boredom, &c.: to gape: (*Shak.*) to gape with astonishment: to be wide open, as a chasm.—*v.t.* to render, to make, or to effect, by yawning: to utter with a yawn.—*n.* an involuntary deep breath from weariness: a chasm, opening: (*Shelley*) dullness.—*adj.* yawn'ing, gaping, opening wide: drowsy: (Shak., *Macb.*, III. ii. 43) causing drowsiness or sleep.—*n.* action of the verb to yawn.—*adv.* yawn'ingly.—*adj.* yawn'y. [O.E. *gánian*, to yawn, and *geonian*, *ginian* (in composition, *ginan*, p.a.t. *gán*), to gape widely; O.N. *gína*, to gape.]

yaws, *yawz*, *n.* a tropical epidemic and contagious disease of the skin—also known as framboesia, button scurvy, verruga Peruviana, buba or boba, &c.—*adj.* yaw'(e)y, pertaining to yaws. [Origin uncertain; perh. Amer. Indian.]

ybet, *i-bēt'*, obs. *pa.p.* of beat.

yblent, *i-blent'*, *pa.p.* (*arch.*) of blend, (*obs.*) of blind.

ybore, *i-bōr'*, obs. *pa.p.* of bear.

ybrent, *i-brent'*, obs. *pa.p.* of burn.

Y-chromosome. See under Y.

yclad, *i-klad'*, ycled, *i-kled'*, obs. forms of clad, *pa.p.* of clothe.

yclept, *i-klept'*, or ycleped (*Milt.* ycleap'd), *i-klēp'id*, *i-klēpt'*. See clepe.—*infin.* (*Spens.*) ycleepe.

ycond, *i-kond'*, obs. *pa.p.* of con.

ydrad, *i-drad'*, ydred, *i-dred'*, obs. *pa.ps.* of dread.

ye, *yē*, *yi*, *pron.* the nom. pl. of the 2nd person—formerly, as in the English Bible, *ye* was always used as a nominative, and *you* as a dative or accusative: now *ye* is sometimes used for all these cases and both numbers. [M.E. *ye*, nom.; *your*, gen.; *you*, *yow*, dat. and accus. pl.—O.E. *gē*, nom. *ye*; *éower*, gen; *éov*, dat. and accus.]

ye, *thē*, *thi*, archaic script for 'the,' arising from the thorn letter, þ. See Y.

yea, *yā*, *adv.* yes: verily: indeed more than that.—*n.* an affirmative vote or voter. [O.E. *géa*; Du. and Ger. *ja*, O.N. *já*; cf. yes.]

yead, yede, yeed, *yēd*, *v.i.* (*Spens.*) to go, proceed: —*pr.p.* yead'ing; *pa.t.* yod (*yod*), yode (*yōd*). [O.E. *éode*, went, used as pa.t. of *gán*, to go.]

yealdon, *yel'dən*, *n.* (*Scott*, as if Cumberland dialect). Same as eldin.

yean, *yēn*, *v.t.* and *v.i.* (*arch.* and *dial.*) esp. of a sheep, to bring forth (young).—*n.* yean'ling, a lamb or a kid.—Also *adj.* [O.E. *ge-*, and *éanian*, to bring forth; allied to *éacen*, increased, pregnant.]

year, *yēr*, *n.* a period of time determined by the revolution of the earth in its orbit: the period beginning with 1st January and ending with 31st December, consisting of 365 days, except in 'leap-year,' when one day is added to February, making the number 366—the present legal, civil, or calendar year: a space of twelve calendar months: (in *pl.*) period of life, esp. age or old age: (in *pl.*) a very long time—*pl.* years (collective *pl.*, used adjectively with numeral prefixed, year).—*ns.* year'-book, a book published annually, reviewing the events of the past year; year'ling, an animal a year old.—*adj.* a year old.—*adjs.* year'long, lasting a year; year'ly, happening every year: lasting a year.—*adv.* once a year: from year to year.—anomalistic year, the earth's time of passage from perihelion to perihelion—365 days, 6 hours, 13 minutes, 49 seconds; astronomical year, the time of one complete mean apparent circuit of the ecliptic by the sun—365 days, 5 hours, 48 minutes, 46 seconds—called also the equinoctial, natural, solar, or tropical year; canicular year, the Sothic year (see Sothic); ecclesiastical year, the year as arranged in the ecclesiastical calendar, with saints' days, festivals, &c.; embolismic year, a year of thirteen lunar months (384 days), occurring in a lunisolar calendar such as that of the Jews; Hebrew year, a lunisolar year, of 12, or 13, months of 29 or 30 days (in every cycle of nineteen years the 6th, 8th, 11th, 14th, 17th, and 19th having thirteen months instead of twelve); Julian year, the year according to the Julian calendar (introduced by Julius Caesar, modified by Augustus; superseded by the Gregorian calendar) a period of 365¼ days, short of the astronomical year by about 11 minutes (see style); legal, civil, or calendar year, the year by which dates are reckoned; it has begun on different dates at different periods, and for six centuries before 1752 it began in England on 25th March; since then (earlier in Scotland) it has begun on 1st January; lunar year, a period of twelve lunar months or 354 days; Platonic year, a cycle of years at the end of which the heavenly bodies were supposed to be again in the same place as at the Creation—also great, or perfect, year; Sabbatic, -al, year (see Sabbath); sidereal year, the period required by the sun to move from a given star to the same star again—having a mean value of 365 days, 6 hours, 9 minutes, 9·6 seconds; Year of Grace, or of our Lord, date of the Christian era. [O.E. *géar*; Ger. *jahr*, O.N. *ár*, Gr. *hōrā*, season.]

yeard, yeard-hunger. See **yird.**

yearn, *yərn, v.i.* (*obs.*; also **earn**) to desire strongly, feel longing for : (*obs.*) to express a desire for, ask for : (*Shak.*) to cause to mourn.—*v.i.* to feel earnest desire : (also, *obs.*, **earn**) to feel compassion, tenderness, grief (also used impersonally, as ' it yearns me ' ; *obs.*): to express longing, as in sound or appearance.—*n.* a yearning.—*n.* and *adj.* **yearn'ing.**—*adv.* **yearn'ingly.** [O.E. *geornan* (W.S. *giernan*), to desire : allied to *georn*, desirous, eager ; cf. Ger. *gern*, willingly.]

yearn, *yərn, v.t.* (*obs.* and *dial.*) to earn. [earn (1).]

yearn, *yərn, v.i.* to curdle, as milk.—Also **earn.**—*n.* **yearn'ing, earn'ing,** rennet. [earn (2).]

yeast, *yēst, n.* a substance used in brewing consisting of certain minute fungi, which produce zymase, and hence induce the alcoholic fermentation of carbohydrates : (*obs.*) the froth on beer : (*Shak.*) spume or foam of water : (*fig.*) leaven.—*v.i.* to ferment, or be covered with froth (*lit.* and *fig.*).—*ns.* **yeast'iness** ; **yeast'-plant,** any of the Saccharomycetes ; **yeast'-powder,** a baking powder.—*adj.* **yeast'y,** like yeast : frothy, foamy : unsubstantial. [O.E. *gist, gyst* ; Ger. *gäscht, gischt.*]

yede, yeed. See **yead.**

yegg, *yeg, n.* (*U.S.*) a burglar, esp. a burglar of safes.—Also **yegg'man.** [Poss. the name of an American safe-breaker.]

yeld, *yeld, adj.* (*Scot.*) barren : not giving milk : unproductive. [Late O.E. *gelde* ; cf. **geld.**]

yeldring, *yeld'ring, n.* Same as **yoldring.**—Also **yeld'rock.**

yelk. Same as **yolk.**

yell, *yel, v.i.* to howl or cry out with a sharp noise : to scream from pain or terror.—*v.t.* to utter with a yell.—*n.* a sharp outcry : a particular cry affected by an American college.—*n.* **yell'ing.**—*v.i.* **yell'-och** (-*əhh* ; *Scot.*), to yell.—*n.* a yell. [O.E. (Angl.) *gellan* ; Ger. *gellen* ; conn. with O.E. *galan*, to sing.]

yellow, *yel'ō, adj.* of the colour of sulphur or of the primrose : of the colour of gold : of Mongolic race : of mixed black and white race : (*coll.*) cowardly, base : sensational.—*n.* the colour of the rainbow between the orange and the green : any dye or pigment producing such a colour : yolk: (in *pl.*) peach-yellows (see **peach**), or other plant disease in which the foliage yellows : jaundice in horses, &c.—*v.t.* and *v.i.* to make, or become, yellow.—*adjs.* **yell'ow-backed, -bellied, -billed, -breasted, -covered, -crowned, -eyed, -footed, -fronted, -headed, -horned, -legged, -necked, -polled, -ringed, -rumped, -shouldered, -spotted,** &c.—*ns.* **yell'ow-bird,** any of various birds of a yellow colour—the golden oriole, summer-warbler, &c. ; **yell'ow-boy,** (*slang*) a gold coin : a mulatto or dark quadroon (*fem.* **yell'ow-girl**) ; **yell'ow-bunting,** the yellow-hammer ; **yell'ow-dog,** a mongrel : a cur : a base or cowardly person (also used adjectivally) ; **yell'ow-earth,** yellow ochre ; **yellow-eyed grass,** any plant of the genus Xyris, growing abundantly in the pine-barrens of Southern U.S. ; **yell'ow-fever,** an acute disease occurring in tropical America and West Africa, caused by infection with a filter-passer conveyed to man by the bite of the mosquito *Aëdes aegypti* (*Stegomyia fasciata*), characterised by high fever, acute nephritis, jaundice, and haemorrhages ; **yell'ow-flag,** a flag of a yellow colour, displayed by a vessel in quarantine or over a military hospital or ambulance ; **yell'ow-hammer, -ammer,** a finch (*Emberiza citrinella*), so named from its yellow colour—also called yellow-bunting. — *adj.* **yell'owish,** somewhat yellow.—*ns.* **yell'owishness** ; **yell'ow-metal,** a brass consisting of sixty parts copper and forty parts zinc ; **yell'owness,** quality or state of being yellow : (*obs.* ; *fig.*) jealousy ; **yell'ow-rattle** (see **rattle**) ; **yell'ow-root,** golden-seal ; **yell'ow-snow,** snow sometimes observed in the Alps and in the Antarctic regions, coloured yellow by the growth on it of certain algae ; **yell'ow-soap,** common soap composed of tallow, resin, and soda ; **yell'ow-spot,** macula lutea, the small area at the centre of the retina in vertebrates at which vision is most distinct ; **yell'ow-wash,** a lotion consisting

of a mixture of mercuric chloride and lime-water ; **yell'ow-weed,** common ragwort: golden-rod : (*dial.*) weld ; **yell'ow-wood,** any of various woods that are light in colour, as satinwood, or yield yellow dye, as that of *Cladrastis lutea* (Southern U.S.): any of the trees that yield these woods : a tree, as a sumach, that gives yellow dye from a part other than the wood ; **yell'ow-wort,** an annual of the gentian family—also **yell'ow-cen'taury.**—*adj.* **yell'owy,** yellowish. — *ns.* **yell'ow-yite, -yoldring, -yorling,** or **-yowley** (same as **yold-ring**).—a **yellow streak,** a tendency to dastardly behaviour ; **yellow berries,** Persian berries ; **Yellow Jack,** (*slang*) yellow fever ; **yellow peril,** the danger that the yellow races may crush the white and overrun the world ; **yellow press,** newspapers abounding in sensational articles, and prone to reckless exaggeration. [O.E. *geolu* ; Ger. *gelb* ; cog. with L. *helvus*, light bay.]

yelp, *yelp, v.i.* (*obs.*) to boast : to utter a sharp bark.—*n.* a sharp, quick cry or bark.—*n.* **yelp'er.**—*n.* and *adj.* **yelp'ing.** [O.E. *gielpan*, to boast, exult ; O.N. *gjalpa*, to yelp.]

yen, *yen, n.* a Japanese gold or silver coin : the Japanese monetary unit since 1871 :—*pl.* **yen.** [Jap.,—Chin. *yüan*, round, a dollar.]

yen, *yen, n.* (*U.S. slang*) an intense desire, longing, urge.—*v.i.* to desire, yearn. [Chin. (Pekingese) *yen*, smoke, opium.]

yeoman, *yō'mən, n.* (*hist.*) a gentleman serving in a royal or noble household, ranking between a sergeant and a groom: after the fifteenth century, one of a class of small farmers, commonly free-holders, the next grade below gentlemen (often serving as foot soldiers) : a man of small estate, any small farmer or countryman above the grade of labourer : an assistant to an official : a member of the yeomanry cavalry or of the yeomen of the guard : a petty officer on a war vessel whose duties are clerical :—*pl.* **yeo'men.**—*adj.* **yeo'manly,** of yeoman's rank : humble and honest : staunch : brave.—*adv.* **yeo'manly,** staunchly, bravely.—*n.* **yeo'manry,** the collective body of smaller freeholders : a cavalry volunteer force in Great Britain formed during the wars of the French Revolution, later mechanised as part of the Territorials.—**Yeomen of the Guard,** a veteran company of picked soldiers, employed in conjunction with the gentlemen-at-arms on special occasions as the sovereign's bodyguard—constituted a corps in 1485 by Henry VII., and still wearing the costume of that period ; **yeoman('s) service,** powerful aid, such as came from the yeomen in the English armies of early times. [M.E. *yoman, yeman* ; perh. for **young man.**]

yep, *yep, U.S.* dial. and coll. variant of **yes.**

yerba, *yər'bä, n.* a herb, esp. (also **yerba mate, yerba de maté**), Paraguay tea or maté (q.v.). [Sp.,—L. *herba.*]

yerd, yerd-hunger. See **yird.**

yerk, *yərk, v.t.* (all meanings now *dial.*) of a shoe-maker, to draw (stitches) tight : to bind or tie with a jerk : to throw or thrust with a sudden, quick motion : to move with a jerk : to lash out with : to utter jerkily : to beat : (*fig.*) to rouse, excite.—*v.i.* to draw tight, bind, strike, move, rise, with a jerk : to kick : to engage in with energy or eagerness : to gird, carp. [Origin obscure ; earlier than **jerk.**]

yes, *yes, adv.* ay : a word of affirmation or consent : (formerly) on the contrary : yea.—*n.* **yes'-man,** (*coll.*) one who agrees with everything that is said to him : an obedient follower with no initiative. [O.E. *gése, gíse*—*géa, gé,* yea, and *sí,* let it be.]

yest, yesty. Obs. forms of **yeast, yeasty.**

yester, *yes'tər* (*dial.* and *arch.* **yestern**), *adj.* relating to yesterday : last.—*n.* **yes'terday,** the day last past.—*adv.* on the day last past.—*ns.* **yestereve'**(n), **yestereve'ning, yestermorn', yestermorn'ing,** the evening, morning, of yesterday ; **yester-night',** last night ; **yesteryear'** (orig. *D. G. Rossetti*), last year.—*adv.* **yestreen'** (contr. of **yestereven** ; *Scot.* and *poet.*), yesterday evening. [O.E. *geostran, giestran* (always followed by *dæg,* &c.) ; Ger. *gestern* ; cf. L. *hesternus,* Gr. *chthes.*]

Neutral vowels in unaccented syllables : *el'ə-mənt, in'fənt, ran'dəm*

yet, *yet, adv.* in addition, besides : up to the present time : still : hitherto : at the same time : even : before the affair is finished.—*conj.* nevertheless : however.—**as yet,** up to the time under consideration. [O.E. *giet, gieta* ; Ger. *jezt.*]

yett, *yet, n.* (*Scot.*) a gate, door—another form of **yate** (q.v.).

yeuk. See **yuke.**

yeve, *yēv, v.t.* to give :—*pa.p.* (*Spens.*) **yeven** (*yev'an*). [O.E. *giefan* ; cf. **give.**]

yew, *ū, n.* any tree of genus Taxus—family Taxaceae, itself a division of the group Coniferae—widely diffused over the northern parts of the world, with narrow lanceolate or linear leaves, esp. *Taxus baccata* (in Europe long planted in graveyards) which yields an elastic wood good for bows : its wood : a bow made of its wood : yew twigs regarded as emblematic of grief.—*adj.* **yew'en,** (*arch.*) made of yew.—*n.* **yew'-tree.** [O.E. *īw, ēow* ; Ger. *eibe.*]

yex, *yeks, v.i.* (*dial.*) to hiccup, belch, spit.—*n.* a hiccup, &c.—Also **yesk.** [O.E. *geocsian,* to sob.]

Yezidi, *ye'zi-di, n.* one of a sect in Armenia and the Caucasus believing in a Supreme God but paying respect also to the author of evil and other minor gods.—Also **Yez'di, Yez'idee, Zez'idee,** &c. [Origin unknown.]

yfere, *i-fēr', adv.* (*obs.*) together, in company. [See **fere** (1) and **infere.**]

Yggdrasil(l), *ig'drə-sil, n.* (*Scand. myth.*) the ash-tree binding together heaven, earth, and hell, and extending its branches over the whole world and above the heavens.—Also **Ygdrasil.** [O.N. ; perh. —*Yggr,* a surname of Odin, and *drasil,* horse.]

yglaunst, *i-glawnst', (Spens.) pa.p.* of **glance.**

ygo, ygoe, *i-gō', pa.p.* (*Spens.*) gone : ago. [**go.**]

Yiddish, *yid'ish, n.* a compound of very corrupt Hebrew, ancient or provincial German, and other elements, spoken by Jews.—*ns.* **Yid, Yidd'isher,** a Jew. [Ger. *jüdisch,* Jewish.]

yield, *yēld, v.t.* (*obs.*) to pay or repay, or to reward : (*arch.*) to render as due or fitting : to grant, accord : to admit, concede : to give out : to furnish, afford : to produce : to deliver, surrender, relinquish, resign.—*v.i.* to submit : to cease fighting or contesting : to give way under pressure : to give place. —*n.* amount yielded : product.—*adj.* **yield'able,** that may be yielded : inclined to yield.—*ns.* **yield'ableness ; yield'er.**—*adj.* **yield'ing,** giving, or inclined to give, way : compliant.—*n.* giving way : compliance.—*adv.* **yield'ingly.**—*n.* **yield'-ingness.**—**yield point,** in the case of iron and annealed steels, the stress at which a substantial amount of plastic deformation takes place suddenly ; **yield up the ghost,** give up the ghost (see **ghost**). [O.E. (W.S.) *gieldan,* to pay ; O.H.G. *gelten,* O.N. *gjalda.*]

yill, *yil, n.* Scots form of **ale.**

yin, yince. Scots forms of **one, once,** generally printed **ane, ance,** but pronounced *yin, yins.*

yince-errand. See **errand.**

yird, *yird, n.* a Scots form of **earth.**—Also **eard, yeard, yerd.**—*v.t.* to bury.—*ns.* **eard'-, yird'-,** &c., **house** (see **earth-house**) ; **eard'-, yeard'-, yerd'-, yird'-hunger,** earth-hunger : the hunger sometimes felt by persons approaching death : voracious hunger.—*adj.* **eard'-,** &c., **hungry.** [**earth.**]

yirk. Same as **yerk.**

yite, *yīt, n.* (*dial.*) the yellow-hammer. [Origin obscure.]

ylang-ylang, *ē'lang-ē'lang, n.* a tree (*Canangium odoratum*) of the Malay Archipelago and Peninsula, the Philippines, &c., or an essence (also **ylang-ylang oil**) distilled from its flowers. [Tagálog.]

Y-level, Y-moth. See **Y.**

ylike (*Spens.*). Same as **alike.**

ylke. See **ilk.**

ymolt, *i-mōlt', v.t.* (*Spens.*) *pa.p.* of **melt.**

ympe, ympt (*Spens.*). Same as **imp, imped.**

ynambu, *ē-näm-boō', n.* a very large tinamou. [Port. *inambu* ; of Tupí origin, related to **tinamou.**]

Ynd (*Spens.*). Same as **Ind.**

yo, *yō, interj.* calling for, or accompanying, effort, &c.—*interj.* **yo-ho,** calling for attention.

yod(e). See **yead.**

yodel, yodle, *yō'dl, v.t.* and *v.i.* to sing or shout, changing frequently from the ordinary voice to falsetto and back again after the manner of the mountaineers of the Tirol.—*n.* a song or phrase sung, or a cry made, in this fashion.—Also **jodel** (*yō'dl*).—*n.* **yō'deller, yō'dler.** [Ger. dial. *jodeln.*]

yoga, *yō'gä, n.* a system of Hindu philosophy showing the means of emancipation of the soul from further migrations.—*ns.* **yō'gi** (*-gē*), a Hindu ascetic who practises the yoga system, consisting in the withdrawal of the yoga senses from external objects, long continuance in unnatural postures, &c. ; **yō'gism.** [Sans., union.]

yogh, *yohh, n.* the M.E. letter Ʒ, derived from O.E. Ʒ. [Origin uncertain, but appropriate as exemplifying the two chief sounds of the letter.]

yoghourt, yoghurt, *yō'goort.* Same as **yaourt.**

yohimbine, *yo-him'bēn, n.* an alkaloid obtained from the bark of *Corynanthe Johimbe.* [Of Bantu origin.]

yoicks, *yoiks, interj.* an old fox-hunting cry.—*v.i.* and *v.t.* **yoick(s)** to make, or urge on by, this cry.

yojan, *yō'jan,* **yojana,** *yō'ja-nä, ns.* an Indian measure of distance, usu. about five miles. [Hind. *yójan*—Sans. *yójana,* (distance covered in one) yoking.]

yoke, *yōk, n.* that which joins together : the frame of wood joining draught oxen : any similar frame, as one for carrying pails : a part of a garment that fits the shoulders (or the hips) : (*dial.*) a stretch of work—e.g. from meal-time to meal-time : a mark of servitude : slavery : a bond of union : a pair or couple, as of oxen.—*v.t.* to put a yoke on : to join together : to attach a draught-animal to : to enslave : (*fig.*) to set to work.—*v.i.* to be joined : to go together : (*Scot.*) to set to work. —*ns.* **yoke'-devil,** (*Shak.*) a companion devil ; **yoke'-fellow, -mate,** an associate, partner, fellow-worker.—*adj.* **yoke'-toed,** zygodactyl.—*n.* **yōk'ing,** (*dial.*) as much work as is done at a stretch. [O.E. *geoc* ; Ger. *joch* ; L. *jugum,* Gr. *zygon.*]

yokel, *yō'kl, n.* a country bumpkin.—*adj.* **yō'kelish.** [Ety. dub.]

yokul. See **jokol.**

yold, *obs. pa.t.* and *pa.p.* of **yield.**

yoldring, *yōld'ring, n.* a yellow-hammer. [Variant of dial. *yowlring*—O.E. *geolu* ; see **yellow.**]

yolk, *yōk,* (*rare*) **yelk,** *yelk, n.* the yellow part of the egg of a bird or reptile : the nutritive non-living material contained by an ovum.—*adjs.* **yolked, yolk'y,** like yolk.—*ns.* **yolk'-sac,** (*zool.*) the yolk-containing sac which is attached to the embryo by the **yolk'-stalk,** a short stalk by means of which yolk substance may pass into the alimentary canal of the embryo. [O.E. *geolca, geoleca*—*geolu,* yellow.]

yolk, *yōk, n.* wool-oil.—*adj.* **yolk'y.** [O.E. *éowocig,* yolky.]

Yom Kippur, *yōm kip'oor,* the Day of Atonement, a Jewish fast day.—**Yom Teruah** (*ter'oo-ä*), the Feast of Trumpets.—**Yom Tob** or **Tov** (*tōb, tōv*), any religious festival. [Heb. *yōm,* day, *kippūr,* atonement, *terū'äh,* blowing (of a trumpet), *tōbh,* good.]

yon, *yon, adj.* (now *poet.* or *dial.*) that : those : yonder.—Also *pron.* that : the thing you know of.—*adv.* yonder.—*prep.* **yond** (*Scot.* usu. yont), (*obs.*) across, or through : to, or in, a position beyond.—*adj.* and *pron.* **yon.**—*adv.* yonder.—*adv.* **yon'der,** to, or at, a distance within view.—*adj.* that, those, at a distance within view (or so conceived).—*pron.* that one, yon.—**hither and yon(d),** (*dial.*) hither and thither ; **hither, or here, and yonder,** hither and thither ; **the yonder,** the farther, more distant. [O.E. *geon* (adj., pron.), *geond* (prep., adv.), and M.E. *yonder.*]

yond, *yond, adj.* (Spens., *F.Q.,* II. viii. 40, 9), furious, mad. [Said to be due to misunderstanding of a passage in an earlier writer : Chaucer's *Clerk's Tale* 1143 has been suggested, but 16th cent. black-letter Chaucers do not have the word in this line.]

yongthly. See **young.**

yoni, *yō′nē, n.* a representation of the female genitals, the symbol under which the Hindu deity Sakti is worshipped.

yonker, obs. form of **younker.**

yoop, *yoop, n.* and *interj.* a word imitative of a sobbing sound.

yore, *yōr, adv. (obs.)* long ago.—*n.* old time.—Also *adj.*—of yore, in times past. [O.E. *géara,* formerly; app. connected with *géar,* a year.]

yorker, *york′ər, n.* a ball pitched to a point directly under the bat—formerly called tice. [Prob. from *Yorkshire,* but history quite unknown.]

Yorkish, *york′ish, adj.* pertaining to the county or city of *York:* adhering to the House of York in the Wars of the Roses.—*n.* **York′ist,** one of this party.—Also *adj.*—**Yorkshire fog,** a tall grass, *Holcus lanatus*; **Yorkshire grit,** a grit from Yorkshire used for polishing; **Yorkshire pudding,** a pudding made of unsweetened batter, and baked along with meat or in meat dripping—orig. under the spit so as to catch the drippings.

you, *ū, pron. 2nd pers. pl.,* but also used as singular: anyone.—*pron. pl.* **you′-uns,** a provincial form for you, you ones.—**you 're another,** the vulgar form of *tu quoque,* effective in vituperation, but not an argument. [O.E. *éow* (perh. through a later form *eów*), orig. only dat. and accus.; cf. **ye.**]

youk. See **yuke.**

young, *yung, adj.* not long born: in early life: in the first part of growth: youthful: vigorous: relating to youth: junior, the younger of two persons having the same name: inexperienced: newly arrived—in Australia: *(coll.)* miniature.— *n.* the offspring of animals: (with *the*) those who are young.—*adjs.* **young′-eyed,** *(Shak.)* with the bright eyes of youth; **young′ish,** somewhat young.—*n.* **young′ling,** a young person or animal. —*adj.* youthful, young.—*adv.* **young′ly,** *(rare)* in youth: in the manner of youth.—*ns.* **young′ness;** **young′ster,** a young person, esp. a young man, or (formerly) a vigorous young man: *(coll.)* a child; **youngth,** *(Spens.)* youth.—*adj.***youngth′ly,**(Spens.) youthful.—**with young,** pregnant; **young blood,** fresh accession of strength; **Young England,** during the Corn-Law struggle (1842-45), a little band of young Tory politicians, who hated Free Trade and Radicalism, and professed a sentimental attachment to earlier forms of social life in England; **Young England, America,** &c., the rising generation in England, America, &c.; **Young Ireland,** a group of Irish politicians who broke away from O'Connell about 1844, because of his rooted aversion to physical force; **Young Italy,** an association of Italian republican agitators, active about 1834, under the lead of Mazzini; **young person,** in Factory Acts, &c., a person who is under eighteen years of age but no longer a child; **Young Turk,** one of a body of Turkish reformers who brought about the revolution of 1908. [O.E. *geong*; Ger. *jung*; also conn. with L. *juvenis,* Sans. *yuvan,* young.]

youngberry, *yung′ber-i, -bər-i, n.* a large reddish-black fruit, a cross between a variety of blackberry and a variety of dewberry. [B. M. *Young,* an American fruitgrower, and **berry.**]

Young's modulus, *yungz mod′ū-ləs,* the coefficient of elasticity of stretching—for a stretched wire, it is the ratio of the stretching force per unit cross-sectional area to the elongation per unit length.

younker, *yung′kər, n.* a young person: *(Spens.)* a young gentleman or knight. [Old Du. *jonckher* (Du. *jonker*), from *jong heer,* young master or lord; Ger. *junker.*]

your, *ūr, pron. (gen. pl.)* or *poss. adj.* of or belonging to you: *(Shak.)* used to denote a person of a class well known—the ordinary (implying some contempt).—*prons.* **yourn,** *(dial.)* yours; **yours** (a double genitive), used predicatively or absolutely: short for ' your letter.'—**you and yours,** you and your family or property; **yours faithfully, sincerely, truly,** &c., **yours to command,** &c., forms used conventionally in letters just before the signature: *(vulg.)* also sometimes used by a speaker to mean himself. [O.E. *éower,* gen. of *ge,* **ye.**]

yourself, *ūr-self′, pron.* the emphatic form of **you**: in your real character: having command of your faculties: sane: in good form: the reflexive form of you (objective) :—*pl.* **yourselves′.**

yourt. See **yurt.**

youth, *yōōth, n.* state of being young: early life, the period immediately succeeding childhood: an early period of existence: a young person, esp. a young man *(pl.* **youths, youdhz**): young persons collectively: *(Shak.)* recentness, freshness.—*adj.* **youth′ful,** pertaining to youth or early life: young: suitable to youth: fresh: buoyant, vigorous.— *adv.* **youth′fully.**—*ns.* **youth′fulness; youth′-head,** youth′hood *(obs.),* youth.—*adjs.* **youth′ly,** *(Spens.)* young, youthful (also *adv.*); **youth′-some,** youthful; **youth′y,** *(Scot.)* young.—**youth hostel,** a hostel where hikers, &c., who are members of an organisation find inexpensive and simple accommodation. [O.E. *geoguth—geong,* young; Ger. *jugend.*]

yow(e), *yow, n. (dial.)* variant of **ewe.**

yowl, *yowl, v.i.* to cry mournfully, as a dog: to yell, bawl.—*n.* a distressed cry.—*n.* **yowl′ing,** a howling. [M.E. *youlen*; cf. O.N. *gaula,* to howl.]

yowley. Same as **yoldring.**

yo-yo, *yō′-yō, n.* a toy consisting of a reel attached to, and manoeuvred by, a string which winds and unwinds round it—similar to the 18th-cent. bandalore or quiz.

ypight, *i-pīt′,* obs. *pa.p.* of **pitch.**

yplast, *i-plāst′,* obs. *pa.p.* of **place.**

yplight, *i-plīt′,* obs. *pa.p.* of **plight.**

ypsilon, *ip-sī′lon, -sē′,* or *ip′, n.* the twentieth letter of the Greek alphabet (Y, *ν*): as a numeral, *ν*′ = 400; *,ν* = 400,000.—Also **upsilon** *(ŭp-sī′lon,* or *ŭp′).*— *adjs.* **ypsiliform** *(-sil′),* **ypsiloid** *(ip′sil-oid),* shaped like an ypsilon.

yrapt, *i-rapt′* (Spens.). Same as **rapt.**

yravished, *i-rav′ish-id* (Malone's emendation of Shak. *iranyshed*), *pa.t.* of **ravish.**

yrent, *i-rent′,* obs. *pa.p.* of **rend.**

yrivd, *i-rīvd′,* obs. *pa.p.* of **rive.**

ysame, *i-sām′, adv. (Spens.)* together. [Perh. **in** and **same** (n.).]

yshend, *i-shend′* (Spens.). Same as **shend.**

yslaked, obs. *pa.p.* of **slake** (Shak., *Pericles,* III. line 1, quenched or relaxed the energies of).

ythundered, *i-thun′də-rid, v.t., pa.p. (Spens.)* struck by a thunderbolt.

ytost, *i-tost′,* (Spens.) *pa.p.* of **toss.**

Y-track. See **Y.**

ytterbium, *i-tər′bi-əm, n.* a metallic element (Yb; at. numb. 70), a member of the rare-earth group: name orig. given to a substance later shown to consist of a mixture of this and lutetium. [*Ytterby,* a Swedish quarry.]

yttrium, *it′ri-əm, n.* a metallic element (Y; at. numb. 39) in the third group of the periodic system, usu. classed with the rare-earths.—*n.* **ytt′ria,** its oxide, a yellowish-white powder.—*adjs.* **ytt′ric, ytt′rious;** **yttrif′erous.**—*ns.* **ytt′roce′rite,** a mineral, usu. violet in colour, found embedded in quartz, a fluoride of yttrium, cerium, &c.; **ytt′ro-col′umbite, -tan′talite,** a brownish mineral found at Ytterby, a tantalate of yttrium, iron, calcium, &c. [From *Ytterby*; see **ytterbium.**]

yu, *yü, ū, n.* precious jade (nephrite or jadeite).— Also **yu′-stone.** [Chin. *yü, yü-shih.*]

yuan, *yü-än′, n.* the Chinese dollar :—*pl.* **yuan.** [Chin. *yüan.*]

yuca (also **yucca**), *yuk′ä, n.* cassava.—*n.* **Yucc′a** (sometimes **Yuc′a**), a genus of plants of the family Liliaceae, natives of Mexico, New Mexico, &c., some (as *Yucca gloriosa,* the Spanish dagger) cultivated in gardens on account of the singularity and splendour of their appearance. [Of Carib origin.]

yucker, *yuk′ər, n.* the American flicker or golden-winged woodpecker. [Imit. of its note.]

yuft, *yuft, n.* Russia leather. [Russ. *yuft.*]

yuga, *yōō′gä, n.* one of the Hindu ages of the world. —Also **yug.** [Sans.]

Yugo-Slav, Yugoslav, *yōō′gō-släv,* or *-släv′, n.* a native, citizen, or inhabitant of Yugoslavia, one of the southern group of Slavs consisting of Serbs,

Croats, and Slovenes: the Slavonic language (Serbo-Croatian) dominant in Yugoslavia.—Also *adj.*—*adjs.* and *ns.* **Yugoslav′ian, Yugoslav′ic.**— Also **Jugo-Slav, Jugoslav,** &c. [Serbo-Croatian *jugo-* — *jug*, the south, and **Slav.**]

yuke, *yōōk*, **yuck,** *yuk*, *v.i.* (*prov.*) to itch.—*n.* itching: the itch.—Also **youk, yeuk, ewk.**—*adj.* **yuk′y, yuck′y,** itchy. [Same as **itch**; prob. influenced by the M.Du. form, *jeuken.*]

yulan, *yōō′lan*, *n.* a Chinese magnolia, with large white flowers. [Chin.]

Yule, *yōōl*, *n.* the season or feast of Christmas.—*n.* **Yule′tide,** the time or season of Yule or Christmas.

—**Yule log,** the block of wood cut down in the forest, then dragged to the house, and set alight in celebration of Christmas. [O.E. *géol*, Yule, *se ǽrra géola*, December; O.N. *jól*. Not conn. either with O.N. *hjól*, wheel, or M.E. *youlen, yollen*, to cry out or yawl.]

yunx, *yungks*, *n.* Variant of **jynx.**

yupon. See **yaupon.**

yurt, yourt, *yoort*, *n.* a light tent of skins, &c., used by nomads in Siberia. [From Russ.]

ywis. Same as **iwis.**

ywrake, *i-rāk′*, **ywroke,** *i-rōk*, **ywroken,** *i-rō′kən*, obs. *pa.p.* (*Spens.*) of **wreak.**

Z

Z, z, *zed, n.* the twenty-sixth and last letter in our alphabet, is derived through the Greek *zeta* (Ζ, ζ), from *zayin,* the seventh Semitic letter—its sound a voiced sibilant, either a voiced *s* as in 'zeal,' or a voiced *sh* as in 'azure': used in Scots to represent M.E. Ʒ (the letter yogh), as in *capercailzie:* used as a contraction-mark (= ;) in *viz., sciz., oz.,* &c. See also **cedilla, zed, zeta.**

Zabian, *zā′bi-ən, adj.* and *n.* Same as **Sabian.**

zabra, *zä′brä, n.* (*hist.*) a small vessel on the Spanish coast. [Sp.]

zack, *zak, n.* (*Austr. slang*) a sixpenny piece.

Zadkiel, *zad′ki-əl, n.* the name assumed by Richard James Morrison (1794-1874), compiler of a popular astrological almanac.

zaffre, zaffer, *zaf′ər, n.* the impure oxide obtained by partially roasting cobalt ore previously mixed with two or three times its weight of fine sand. [Fr. *zafre,* of Ar. origin.]

zalambdodont, *za-lam′dō-dont, adj.* having molar teeth with V-shaped ridges, as some Insectivora.— Also *n.* [Gr. *za-,* very, *lambda,* the letter Λ (=L), *odous, odontos,* a tooth.]

Zalophus, *zal′ō-fəs, n.* a genus of eared seals. [Gr. *za-,* intens., *lophos,* a crest.]

zambo, *zam′bō, n.* the offspring of a negro man and an American Indian woman: anyone of mixed negro and Indian blood. [Sp.]

zambomba, *thäm-bom′bä, n.* a simple Spanish musical instrument, made by stretching a piece of parchment over a wide-mouthed jar and inserting a stick in it, sounded by rubbing the stick with the fingers. [Sp.]

Zamia, *zā′mi-ä, n.* a genus of palm-like trees or low shrubs of the family Cycadaceae, some species of which yield an edible starchy pith. [Named through misreading in Pliny *azaniae nuces,* pine cones that open on the tree—Gr. *azanein, azainein,* to dry.]

zamindar. Same as **zemindar.**

zamouse, *za-moos′, n.* the short-horned buffalo of West Africa. [Ar. *jāmūs.*]

zampogna, *tsam-pō′nyä, n.* the Italian bagpipe. [It.]

zander, *zan′dər, n.* See **sander.**

zanella, *zə-nel′ä, n.* a mixed twilled fabric for covering umbrellas. [Origin uncertain.]

zanja, *thäng′hhä, n.* an irrigating canal.—*n.* **zanjero** (-*hhā′rō*), one who superintends the distribution of water in irrigation canals. [Sp.]

zante, *zan′tē, n.* the same as **zan′te-wood,** the wood of the European smoke-tree, from *Zante,* one of the principal Ionian Islands: satin-wood. —*n.* **Zan′tiot** (-*ot*), **Zan′tiote** (-*ōt*), a native of Zante.—**Zante currant,** the small seedless fruit of a Zante grape.

Zantedeschia, *zan-ti-des′ki-ä.* Same as **Richardia.** [Francesco *Zantedeschi,* Italian botanist.]

Zanthoxylum. Same as **Xanthoxylum.**

zany, *zā′ni, n.* (*hist.*) an assistant clown or buffoon: (*arch.*) a toady: (*dial.*) a simpleton.—Also *adj.*— *v.t.* to play the zany to.—*n.* **zā′nyism,** condition or habits of a buffoon. [Fr. *zani*—It. *zanni,* a corr. of *Giovanni,* John.]

zanze, *zän′ze, n.* an African musical instrument. [Ar. *sanj,* castanets, cymbals.]

Zanzibari, *zan-zib-är′i, n.* a native of Zanzibar.

Zapodidae, *za-pod′i-dē, n.pl.* the jumping-mouse family. [Formed from Gr. *za-,* very, *pous, podos,* foot, and suff. *-idae.*]

Zaporogian, *zä-po-rō′ji-ən, adj.* pertaining to the Little Russian or Ukraine Cossacks dwelling near the Porogi or falls of the Dnieper.—*n.* one of these people. [Russ. *za,* beyond, and *porogi,* rapids.]

zapotilla, *zap-ō-til′ä, n.* Same as **sapodilla.**

zaptieh, *zap′ti-e, n.* a Turkish policeman.—Also **zap′tiah, zab′tieh.** [From Turk.]

zarape, *sä-rä′pe, n.* Same as **serape.**

Zarathustrian, *zar-ə-thōōs′tri-ən, adj.* and *n.* Zoroastrian. — **Zarathus′trianism, Zarathus′-trism,** Zoroastrianism; **Zarathus′tric,** Zoroastric.

zaratite, *zä′rə-tīt, n.* a hydrous carbonate of nickel, found usu. as an incrustation on chromite. [From *Zárate,* a Spaniard.]

zareba, *zə-rē′bä, n.* in the Sudan, a stockade, thorn-hedge, &c., against wild animals or enemies: a fortified camp generally.—Also **zarēe′ba, zerē′ba, zeri′ba.** [Ar. *zarībah,* pen or enclosure for cattle.]

zarf, *zärf, n.* an ornamental holder for a hot coffee-cup.—Also **zurf.** [Ar. *zarf,* a vessel.]

zarnich, *zär′nik, n.* a native sulphide of arsenic, as orpiment, realgar.—Also **zar′nec.** [Ar. *zarnīkh.*]

zarzuela, *thär-thoo-ā′lä, -thwä′, n.* a Spanish kind of operetta or vaudeville—named from the royal residence of La *Zarzuela.*

zastruga, *zas-troō′gä, n.* one of a series of long parallel snow-ridges on the open wind-swept plains of Russia:—*pl.* **zastrugi** (*-gē*). [Russ.]

zati, *zä′ti, n.* the bonnet-monkey.

zax. Dial. variant of **sax** (1).

Zea, *zē′ä, n.* a genus of cereals having monoecious flowers; the only species is *Zea Mays,* maize or Indian corn. [Gr. *zeā* or *zeia,* one-seeded wheat.]

zeal, *zēl, n.* (*B.*) strong feeling, as love, anger, &c., or passionate ardour: intense enthusiasm: activity arising from warm support or enthusiasm: (*obs.*) a zealot.—*n.* **zeal′ant, zeal′ant** (*Bacon*) a zealot.— *adjs.* **zeal′ful; zeal′less.**—*ns.* **zealot** (*zel′ət*), an enthusiast: a fanatic: **Zealot,** one of a fanatical Jewish party whose restless opposition to the Roman domination finally brought about the ruin of Jerusalem in 70 A.D.; **zealotism** (*zel′*), the character of a zealot; **zealotry** (*zel′*).—*adj.* **zealous** (*zel′*), full of zeal: warmly engaged in, or ardent in support of, anything: devoted.—*adv.* **zealously** (*zel′*).—*n.* **zealousness** (*zel′*). [O.Fr. *zele*—L. *zēlus*—Gr. *zēlos*—*zeein,* to boil.]

zebec, zebeck. Variants of **xebec.**

zebra, *zē′brä, zē′brä, n.* any of a group of striped animals of the genus Equus—all of which are peculiar to the African continent—including the dauw or Burchell's zebra, Grévy's zebra, the true or mountain zebra, and the extinct quagga: anything having stripes reminiscent of a zebra's.— *ns.* **ze′bra-finch,** an Australian weaver-bird striped black and grey; **ze′bra-par(r)′akeet,** the budgerigar; **ze′brass,** the offspring of a male zebra and a female ass; **ze′bra-wood,** the hard and beautifully striped wood of a Guiana tree: the tree itself: applied also to various other trees or their wood.—*adjs.* **zē′brine, zē′broid.**—*ns.* **ze-brinn′y** (cf. **brinny**), offspring of a male horse and a female zebra; **ze′brule, ze′brula,** the off-spring of a male zebra and a female horse.— **zebra crossing,** a street crossing marked with zebra-like stripes. [Of African origin.]

zebu, *zē′bū, n.* a humped domestic ox (*Bos indicus*) very nearly allied to the common ox, diffused over India, China, the east coast of Africa, &c. [Fr. *zébu,* the name taken by Buffon from the exhibitors of one at a French fair in 1752.]

zebub, *zē′bub, n.* the zimb. [Ar. (dial.) *zubāb,* a fly.]

zecchino, *tsek-kē′nō, n.* a gold coin, the sequin.— Also **zecchine** (*zek′in*). [See **sequin.**]

Zechstein, *zek′stīn, n.* a deposit of calcareous rock, the higher of the two series into which the Permian System of Germany is divided. [Ger.,—*zeche,* mine, *stein,* stone.]

zed, *zed, n.* the letter Z: a bar of metal of form similar to the letter Z. [Fr. *zède*—L. and Gr. *zēta.*]

Neutral vowels in unaccented syllables : *el′ə-mənt, in′fənt, ran′dəm*

zedoary, zed'ō-ə-ri, n. certain species of curcuma, natives of India, China, &c., whose root-stocks are aromatic, bitter, and pungent. [Through mediaeval L.—Ar. zedwār.]

zee, zē, n. (esp. U.S.) the letter Z (zed).

Zeeman effect, zā'män ef-ekt', the splitting of a spectral line into several symmetrically disposed components which occurs when the source of light is placed in a strong magnetic field. [Named from Dutch physicist Pieter Zeeman (1865-1943).]

zein, zē'in, n. a protein found in Indian corn. [Zea.]

zeitgeist, tsīt'gīst, n. the spirit of the age. [Ger.]

zel, zel, n. a form of Oriental cymbal. [Turk. zil.]

Zelanian, zə-lā'ni-ən, adj. pertaining to New Zealand.

zeloso, zel-ō'sō, adv. (mus.) with fervour. [It.]

zelotypia, zel-ō-tip'i-ä, n. jealousy : morbid zeal in the prosecution of any project or cause. [Gr. zēlotypiā, jealousy—zēlos, zeal, typtein, to strike.]

zemindar, zem-in-där', or zem', n. under the Mogul emperors of India, the farmer of revenue from land held in common by the cultivators, as responsible for the revenue : later the actual native proprietor paying revenue direct, and not to any intermediate superior.—Also **zamindar.**—n. **zem'-indary,** the jurisdiction of a zemindar : the system of land-tenure and taxation under such.—Also **zam'indari, zem'indari,** &c. [Hind. zam'īndār—Pers. zamīn, land, and -dar, holder.]

zemstvo, zems'tvō, n. in Russia, from 1864 until 1917, a district and provincial assembly to which the administration of certain of the affairs of the district and the province was committed. [Russ.]

zenana, ze-nä'nä, n. in India and Persia, apartments in which women are secluded, corresponding to the harem in Arabic-speaking Moslem lands.— **zenana mission,** a mission to women of the zenanas, necessarily conducted by women. [Pers. zanāna—zan, a woman.]

Zend, zend, n. the Avesta or Zend-Avesta : Avestan, the ancient East-Iranian Indo-Germanic language in which the Zend-Avesta was long orally preserved and at last written—closely related to the Vedic Sanskrit.—**Zend-Avesta** (properly meaning the Avesta with the commentary on it), the ancient sacred writings of the Parsees, including works of widely differing character and age, collected into their present canon under Shah-puhar or Shah-pur II. (309-338 A.D.). [Pers. zend, zand, commentary —Sans. jñā, to know.]

zendik, zen'dik, n. an unbeliever in revealed religion in the East: one who practises magic. [Ar. zendīq.]

zenith, zen'ith, n. the point on the celestial sphere vertically above the observer's head, one of the two poles of the horizon, the other being the nadir : the greatest height (lit. and fig.).—adj. **zen'ithal.**—ns. **zen'ith-dis'tance,** the angular distance of a heavenly body from the zenith ; **zen'ith-sec'tor,** any of several instruments for measuring zenith-distances, used before the invention of the telescope. [O.Fr. cenit(h), ultimately from Ar. samt, short for samt-ar-ras, lit. way, direction, of the head.]

zeolite, zē'ō-līt, n. any of a large group of alumino-silicates of sodium, potassium, calcium, and barium, containing very loosely held water.—adjs. **zeolitic** (-lit') ; **zeolit'iform.** [Gr. zeein, to boil in allusion to the fact that many intumesce under the blow-pipe), lithos, a stone.]

zephyr, zef'ər, n. the west wind : a soft, gentle breeze : thin light worsted or woollen yarn : a shawl, jersey, or other garment made of such : any of various types of light-weight material, as a gingham, a flannel with a silk warp, a thin woollen cloth, &c.: anything very light and fine of its kind : **Zephyr,** the god of the west wind. [Gr. Zephyros ; akin to zophos, darkness, the west.]

zeppelin, zep'el-in, tsep', n. a dirigible, cigar-shaped airship of the type designed by Count Zeppelin (c. 1900).

zerda, zər'dä, n. a fennec. [Ar. zardawa.]

zereba. See zareba.

Zernebock, zər'nə-bok, n. Czerni Bog, an evil god of the Slavs, wrongly described by Scott in Ivanhoe as a god ' of the ancient Saxons.'

zero, zē'rō, n. a cipher : nothing : the point from which the reckoning begins on scales, such as those of the barometer, &c. : (fig.) the lowest point : zero hour.—adj. zē'ro-valent, (chem.) incapable of combining with other atoms.—**absolute zero** (see absolute) ; **zero hour,** the exact time (hour, minute, and second) fixed for launching an attack or beginning an operation. [Fr. zéro—Ar. sifr ; cf. **cipher.**]

zerumbet, zə-rum'bet, or ze', n. an E. Indian drug, allied to cassumunar and zedoary. [Pers. zerunbād.]

zest, zest, n. (obs.) orange or lemon peel, or the oil squeezed from it, used as a flavouring : anything that gives a relish : piquancy : relish : enthusiasm. —adj. **zest'ful.**—adv. **zest'fully.**—n. **zest'fulness.** [Fr. zeste, orig. the woody thick skin quartering a walnut ; origin obscure.]

zeta, zē'tä, n. the Greek z (Z, ζ): as a numeral ζ'=7 ; ͵ζ=7000.

zeta, zē'tä, n. (hist.) a small room or closet of some kind, as perh. the sexton's room over a church porch. [Gr. diaita, a dwelling.]

zetetic, zē-tet'ik, adj. proceeding by inquiry.—n. a search, investigation : a seeker, the name taken by some of the Pyrrhonists. [Gr. zētētikos—zēteein, to seek.]

Zeuglodon, zū'glō-don, n. a genus of fossil whales, so named from the yoke-like double-rooted formation of their cheek teeth.—adj. and n. **zeug'lodont.** —n.pl. **Zeuglodon'tia,** a suborder of Cetacea, represented by the zeuglodonts. [Gr. zeuglē, the strap or loop of the yoke, odous, -ontos, a tooth.]

zeugma, zūg'mä, n. a figure of speech by which an adjective or verb is applied to two nouns, though strictly appropriate to only one of them.—adj. **zeugmat'ic.** [Gr.,—zeugnynai, to yoke.]

Zeus, zūs, n. the greatest of the national deities of Greece, son of Kronos (Saturn) and Rhea. His consort was Hera ; his supreme seat, Mount Olympus in Thessaly. [Gr.]

Zeuxian, zūk'si-ən, adj. pertaining to Zeuxis, styled ' of Heraclea ' and ' of Ephesus ' (fl. c. 420-400 B.C.), a Greek painter who excelled in accuracy of imitation of natural objects and in rendering types of sensuous beauty.

zeuxite, zūks'īt, n. a ferriferous tourmaline. [Gr. zeuxis, joining—zeugnynai, to join.]

zho, zhō, n. one of a kind of hybrid domestic cattle in parts of the Himalayas—said to be a cross between the male yak and the common horned cow—esp. the male.—Also **zo, dso,** and **dzo** (dzō).—ns. **zhomo** (zhō'mō), the female of this cross.—Also **dsō'mo, jō'mo ; zō'bō,** the male of this cross.— Also **zō'bu.** [Tibetan mdzo.]

zibel(l)ine, zib'ə-lin, -līn, adj. pertaining to the sable.—n. the fur of the sable : (zib'ə-lēn) a soft woollen material with a lustrous pile. [Fr.,—It. zibellino, prob. from Slav. ; cf. **sable.**]

zibet, zib'it, n. an Asiatic civet. [It. zibetto—Ar. zabād ; cf. **civet.**]

ziczac, zik'zak, n. Variant of sicsac.

zigan, zi-gan', n. Variant of tzigany.

ziganka, zi-gang'kä, n. a Russian country-dance : the music for such, usu. quick, with a drone bass. [Russ. tsyganka, a gypsy woman.]

Zigeuner, tsi-goi'nər, n. a gypsy :—pl. **Zigeu'ner.** [Ger.]

ziggurat, zig'oo-rat, n. a Babylonian temple-tower, pyramidal in general shape, consisting of a number of stories each successive one of which was smaller than that below it.—Also **zikkurat** (zik'). [Assyrian ziqquratu, a pinnacle, top of a mountain.]

zigzag, zig'zag, n. a short, sharp turning : a line or road with sharp angles to right and left alternately.—adj. having short, sharp alternate turns : bent from side to side alternately.—v.t. to form with short, alternate turns.—v.i. to move forward making an alternation of short, sharp turns (pr.p. zig'zagging ; pa.t. and pa.p. zig'zagged).—adv. with frequent sharp turns—also zig'zaggy.—n. zigzagg'ery, angular crookedness.—adj. zig'-zaggy, zigzag. [Fr. zigzag ; Ger. zickzack.]

zillah, zil'ä, n. an administrative district in India.

[Ar. *dila* (in Hindi pronunciation, *zila*), a rib, thence a side, a district.]

zimb, *zimb*, *n.* an Abyssinian dipterous insect, like the tsetse, hurtful to cattle. [Amharic, a fly.]

zimbi, *zim'bi*, *n.* a money-cowrie. [Port. *zimbo*; of African origin.]

zimocca, *zi-mok'ä*, *n.* a type of bath-sponge.

zinc, *zingk*, *n.* a bluish-white metallic element (Zn; at. numb. 30), resistant to atmospheric corrosion.—Also *adj.*—*v.t.* to coat with zinc:—*pr.p.* **zinc'ing**, *zingk'ing*, **zinck'ing**, **zink'ing**; *pa.t.* and *pa.p.* **zinced**, *zingkt*, **zincked**, **zinked**. —*ns.* **zinc'-blende**, sphalerite, native sulphide of zinc; **zinc'-bloom**, basic zinc carbonate, hydrozincite; **zinc'-colic**, a colic caused by the slow poison of zinc oxide.—*adj.* **zincif'erous** (*zingk-*), **zinkif'erous**, containing or producing zinc.—*ns.* **zincite** (*zingk'īt*), a native oxide of zinc, brittle, translucent, deep red; **zinc(k)ifica'tion**, **zinkifica'tion**, the process of coating or impregnating an object with zinc.—*v.t.* **zinc(k)'ify**, **zink'ify**, to cover or impregnate with zinc.—*adj.* **zinc(k)'y**, **zink'y**, pertaining to, containing, or looking like, zinc.—*ns.* **zinco** (*zing'kō*), a line block executed in zinc, i.e. the normal line block; **zinc'ode**, (*obs.*) an anode; **zinc'ograph**, a plate or picture produced by zincography; **zincographer** (*-kog'rə-fər*). —*adjs.* **zincograph'ic**, **-al**.—*n.* **zincography** (*-kog'rə-fi*), an engraving process in which zinc is covered with wax and etched: any process in which designs for printing are made on zinc plates. —*adj.* **zinc'oid**, like zinc.—*n.* **zincol'ysis**, (*obs.*) electrolysis.—*adj.* **zinc'ous**, pertaining to, or like, zinc.—*ns.* **zinc'-white**, zinc oxide used as a pigment; **zinc'-worker**.—**zinc ointment**, a mixture of zinc oxide with benzoated lard. [Ger. *zink*; origin unknown.]

Zincalo, *zing'kə-lō*, *n.* a name in Spain for a gypsy: —*fem.* **Zin'cala**, *pl.* **Zin'cali**. [Sp. Romany name.]

Zingaro, *zing'gə-rō*, *n.* a name in Italy for a gypsy: —*pl.* **Zing'ari**; *fem.* **Zing'ara**, *pl.* **Zing'are**.— Also **Zing'ano**, &c. [Cf. **Zincalo**; **Zigeuner**.]

zingel, *tsing'əl*, *n.* a fish of the perch family, found in the Danube. [Ger.]

Zingiberaceae, *zin-ji-be-rā'sē-ē*, *n.pl.* any of a family of perennial tropical monocotyledonous herbs, with thickened root-stock and cone-like inflorescence—**Zin'giber**, the typical genus of this family, *Zingiber officinale* being the common ginger.—*adj.* **zingibera'ceous**, **zingiberā'ceous**. [L. *zingiber* — Gr. *zingiberis*, ginger.]

zinke, *tsing'kə*, *n.* an old wind instrument like a cornet. [Ger.]

zinkenite, *zingk'ən-īt*, *n.* a steel-grey mineral, essentially sulphide of lead and antimony. [J. K. L. *Zincken*, a mine director.]

Zinnia, *zin'i-ä*, *n.* a genus of American composite plants. [From J. G. *Zinn*, botanist (1727-59).]

Zion, *zī'ən*, *n.* Jerusalem: the Israelitish theocracy: the Christian Church: heaven.—*ns.* **Zi'onism**, (*hist.*) a movement for securing national privileges and territory (esp. in Palestine) for the Jews; **Zi'onist**, a supporter of Zionism.—*adv.* **Zi'on-ward**, heavenward. [Heb. *tsīyōn*, orig. the name of a part of one of the hills of Jerusalem.]

zip, *zip*, *n.* the ping or sound of a bullet striking an object or whizzing through the air: a whizzing sound: a zip-fastener: (*coll.*) energy, vigour.— *v.i.* and *v.t.* to whizz: to fasten with a zip: (*coll.*) to be full of, act with, proceed with, or (usu. **zip up**) infuse with, life and energy.—*ns.* **zip-fastener** (*zip-fâs'nər*), a fastening device for clothes, &c., on which two sets of teeth are operated by pulling a slide; **zipp'er**, a zip-fastener. [Imit.]

Ziphius, *zif'i-əs*, *n.* a genus of whales, giving name to the family **Ziphi'idae**, the beaked whales. [Gr. *xiphios*, sword-fish—*xiphos*, sword.]

zircon, *zər'kən*, *n.* a tetragonal mineral, zirconium silicate, of which jacinth and jargoon are varieties. —*n.* **zircō'nia**, oxide of zirconium.—*adj.* **zir-conic** (*-kon'*), of zirconium.—*n.* **zircō'nium**, a metallic element (Zr; at. numb. 40). [Ar. *zarqūn*—Pers. *zargūn*, gold-coloured; cf. **jargoon**.]

zither, *zith'ər*, *n.* a stringed instrument having a wooden frame and flat sounding-board with from twenty-nine to forty-two strings, placed on a table or on the knees, the strings being played by a plectrum on the right thumb.—Also **zith'ern**. [Ger.]

Zizania, *zi-* or *zī-zā'ni-ä*, *n.* a genus of tall aquatic grasses, wild, water, Indian, or Canada rice. [Gr. *zizanion*, darnel.]

zizel, *ziz'əl*. See **suslik**.

Zizyphus, *ziz'i-fəs*, *n.* a genus of shrubs or trees of the buckthorn family, the jujube-trees. [L., jujube-tree.]

zloty, *zlot'i*, *zwot'ü*, *n.* the monetary unit or franc of Poland.—*pl.* **zloty**, **zlotys**. [Pol. *zloty*, lit. golden.]

zo. See **zho**.

Zoantharia, *zō-an-thā'ri-ä*, *n.pl.* an order of Anthozoa the members of which may be either solitary or colonial and possess either six, or more than eight, simple tentacles—including sea-anemones and many corals.—*adj.* and *n.* **zoanthā'rian**. [Mod. L.,—Gr. *zōion*, animal, *anthos*, flower.]

zoanthropy, *zō-an'thrō-pi*, *n.* a form of mental delusion in which a man believes himself to be a beast.—*adj.* **zōanthropic** (*-throp'*). [Gr. *zōion*, animal, *anthrōpos*, man.]

Zoanthus, *zō-an'thəs*, *n.* the typical genus of **Zoan'thidae** (*-ē*), a family of Anthozoa permanently attached by their bases and having no solid skeleton. [Gr. *zōion*, an animal, *anthos*, a flower.]

zoarium, *zō-ā'ri-əm*, *n.* the zooids of a polyzoan colony collectively. [Gr. *zōarion*, dim. of *zōion*, an animal.]

zobo, zobu. See **zho**.

zocco, *zok'ō*, *n.* a socle.—Also **zocc'olo**. [It. *zocco*, *zoccolo*; see **socle**.]

zodiac, *zō'di-ak*, *n.* an imaginary belt in the heavens, about 18° wide, through which the ecliptic passes centrally, and which forms the background of the motions of the sun, moon, and planets; it is divided into twelve equal parts of 30° called **signs of the zodiac**, named from the constellations that once corresponded to them but do so no longer. The constellations, with the appropriate symbols of the corresponding signs, are as follows: Aries (*Ram*), ♈; Taurus (*Bull*), ♉; Gemini (*Twins*), ♊; Cancer (*Crab*), ♋; Leo (*Lion*), ♌; Virgo (*Virgin*), ♍; Libra (*Balance*), ♎; Scorpio (*Scorpion*), ♏; Sagittarius (*Archer*), ♐; Capricornus (*Goat*), ♑; Aquarius (*Water-bearer*), ♒; Pisces (*Fishes*), ♓: (*obs.*) a year: (*fig.*) a set of twelve, or a recurrent series or course.—*adj.* **zodi'acal**.—**zodiacal light**, a faint illumination of the sky, lenticular in form and elongated in the direction of the ecliptic on either side of the sun, fading away at about 90° from it; best seen after sunset or before sunrise in the tropics. [Fr. *zodiaque*—L. *zodiacus*—Gr. *zōidiakos*, of figures—*zōidion*, a small carved or painted figure—*zōion*, an animal.]

zoea, *zō-ē'ä*, *n.* a larval stage of certain decapod crustaceans, e.g. of crabs.—Also **zooea** (*zō-ē'ä*).—*pl.* **zoē'ae** (also **zoē'as**).—*adjs.* **zoē'al**, **zooe'al**; **zo'eform**. [Gr. *zōē*, life.]

zoechrome. See **zoetrope**.

zoetic, *zō-et'ik*, *adj.* pertaining to life, vital. [Gr. *zōē*, life.]

zoetrope, *zō'i-trōp*, *n.* the ancient wheel of life, by means of which figures on the inside of a rotating cylinder are made visible through slots and provide an illusion of animated motion: (also **zo'ē-chrome**) any of several early processes for colour cinematography, using rapidly repeated images of the selected colours in sequence on a screen, the synthesis arising from persistence of vision in the eye.—*adj.* **zoetropic** (*-trop'ik*). [Gr. *zōē*, life, *tropos*, a turning—*trepein*, to turn, *chrōma*, colour.]

zoiatria, *zō-i-at'ri-ä*, *zō-ī-ə-trī'ä*, **zoiatrics**, *zō-i-at'riks*, *ns.* veterinary surgery. [Gr. *zōion*, an animal, *iātreiā*, healing.]

zoic, *zō'ik*, *adj.* pertaining to animals: of rocks,

containing evidences of life, in the form of fossils. [Gr. *zōikos*, of animals—*zōion*, an animal.]

Zoilism, *zō'i-lizm, n.* carping and unjust criticism. —*adj.* **Zoil'ean,** characteristic of *Zoilus,* a Greek grammarian who flourished in the time of Philip of Macedon, and assailed Homer with such asperity that his name became proverbial for a captious and malignant critic.—*n.* **Zō'ilist,** a carping critic.

zoisite, *zois'īt, zō'is-īt, n.* an orthorhombic mineral closely allied to epidote. [Baron von *Zois.*]

zoism, *zō'izm, n.* the doctrine that life originates from a specific vital principle.—*n.* **zō'ist,** one who maintains this theory. [Gr. *zōē,* life.]

Zolaism, *zō'lä-izm, n.* the literary principles and practice of the French novelist Émile *Zola* (1840-1902), who aimed at what he called ' naturalism ' (q.v.).

Zöllner's lines, *tsəl'nərz līnz,* rows of parallel lines appearing to be not parallel through the optical effect of oblique intersecting lines.—Also **Zöllner's illusion, pattern.** [J. K. F. *Zöllner* (1834-82), German physicist.]

zollverein, *tsol'fər-īn, n.* a customs-union : (*hist.*) a union of the German states, under the leadership of Prussia, to enable them to act as one state in their commercial relations with other countries. [Ger., —*zoll,* duty, *verein,* union.]

zombi, zombie, *zom'bi, n.* orig. in Africa, the deity of the python : in American voodooism, the snake deity : a corpse reanimated by sorcery : the power supposed to enter such a body.—*n.* **zom'biism,** belief in a zombi, or practice of rites associated with it. [W. African *zumbi,* fetish.]

zona. See under **zone.**

zonda, *son'dä, n.* a dry, hot, and dusty wind blowing from the Andes across the Argentine pampas, during July and August. [Sp. ; perh. from Amer. Indian.]

zone, *zōn, n.* a girdle, a belt, an encircling stripe of different colour or substance : one of the five great belts into which the surface of the earth is divided by the tropics and arctic and antarctic circles : any continuous tract with particular characteristics : (*geol.*) a group of strata characterised by a distinctive fauna or flora, and bearing the name of one fossil, called the **zonal index** : a set of crystal faces all parallel to the same line (the **zonal axis**).—*v.t.* to encircle, as with a zone : to mark with zones : to distribute in zones : to divide into, or assign to, zones (wartime jargon).— *n.* **zō'na** (*pl.* **zō'nae, -ē**), a girdle : a zone : (*zool.*) an area, patch, strip, or band : herpes zoster.— *adjs.* **zō'nal, zō'nary,** like a zone : arranged in zones : pertaining to a zone : **zō'nate(d),** marked with zones, belted.—*n.* **zonā'tion,** (*bot.*) the formation of bands differentiated by colour or other characteristics, or the arrangement of such bands : the occurrence of vegetation in well-marked bands, each band having its characteristic dominant species.—*adjs.* **zoned,** wearing a zone : having zones ; **zone'less.**—*ns.* **zone'-ticket,** a railway ticket available for a time between any stations of a group ; **zō'ning,** division into zones : assignment according to zones.—*adj.* **zō'noid,** like a zone.—*ns.* **Zonotrichia** (*zō-nō-trik'i-ä* ; Gr. *thrix, trichos,* hair), a genus of American finches, the crown-sparrows ; **zō'nula,** a small zone.—*adj.* **zō'nular,** like a zone or zonule.—*ns.* **zon'ule, zon'ulet,** a little zone or girdle ; **Zonurus** (*zō-nū'rəs* ; Gr. *ourā,* tail), a tropical African genus of lizards with tail ringed with spiny scales, giving name to the family **Zonu'ridae.** [L. *zōna*—Gr. *zōnē,* a girdle—*zōnnynai,* to gird.]

zoo-, *zō-ō-, zō-o'-, zō-, zō-,* in bot. and zool. terms, &c., animal.—*n.* **zoo** (*zōō*), the Zoological Gardens in London : any similar collection of animals.— *adj.* **zoobiotic** (*zō-ō-bī-ot'ik*), parasitic on, or living in association with, an animal.—*n.* **zooblast** (*zō'ō-blast* ; Gr. *blastos,* a germ), an animal cell. —*adj.* **zōochem'ical.**—*n.* **zōochem'istry,** the chemistry of the animal body.—*adj.* **zoochorous** (*zō-ō-kōr'əs* ; Gr. *chōreein,* to spread), of spores or seeds, dispersed by animals.—*ns.* **zō'ochore ; zō'ochory,** the condition of being dispersed by animals ; **zō'oculture,** (*U.S.*) the domestication

and control of animals ; **zōocytium** (*-sish'i-əm* ; Gr. *kytos,* a hollow vessel), a zoothecium : —*pl.* **zōocyt'ia ; zōoden'drium,** (*zool.*) the branched stalk connecting the members of the colony in certain colonial Infusoria ; **zooecium** (*zō-ē'shi-əm* ; Gr. *oikiā,* a house), the body-wall or enclosing chamber of a polyzoan individual :—*pl.* **zooe'cia ; zō'ogamete,** a motile gamete.—*adj.* **zoogamous** (*zō-og'ə-məs* ; Gr. *gamos,* marriage), pertaining to zoogamy.—*ns.* **zōog'amy,** sexual reproduction of animals ; **zoogeny** (*zō-oj'ə-ni* ; Gr. *-geneia,* suff. denoting production), the doctrine, or the process, of the origination of living beings—also **zoogony** (*-og'*).—*adj.* **zōogenic** (*-jen'*), **zōog'enous,** produced from animals.—*n.* **zōogeog'rapher.** —*adjs.* **zōogeograph'ic, -al.**—*ns.* **zōogeog'raphy,** the science of the distribution of animals on the surface of the globe ; **zōogloea** (*-glē'ä* ; Gr. *gloiā,* glue), a mucilaginous mass of bacteria embedded in slimy material derived from swollen cell walls. —*adjs.* **zōogloe'ic ; zōogloe'oid.**—*n.* **zōogonid'ium,** a swarmspore.—*adj.* **zōog'onous,** (*zool.*) viviparous.—*ns.* **zō'ograft** (*-gräft*), a piece of tissue from the living body of an animal grafted on the human body ; **zō'ografting ; zōog'rapher, zōog'raphist,** one who pursues zōog'raphy, the study or description of animals and their habits : the painting of animals.—*adjs.* **zōograph'ic, -al.** —*ns.* **zooid** (*zō'oid* ; Gr. *eidos,* form), (earlier) a free-moving cell, as a sperm-cell : in alternation of generations, an individual of an asexually-produced form : (usu.) an individual forming part of a colonial organism ; **zōol'ater** (Gr. *latreiā,* worship), one who worships animals ; **zōolatri'a, zōol'atry,** worship of animals.—*adj.* **zōol'atrous.**—*n.* **zoolite** (*zō'ō-līt* ; Gr. *lithos,* a stone), a fossil animal. —Also **zō'olith.**—*adjs.* **zōolith'ic, zōolit'ic ; zoological** (*zō-ō-loj'i-kl,* or *zōo-ō-*).—*adv.* **zoolog'ically.**—*ns.* **zool'ogist** (*zō-,* or *zōō-*), one versed in zoology (*zō-ol'ə-ji,* or *zōo-ol'*), the science of animal life included along with botany in the science of biology.—*adj.* **zōomagnet'ic.**—*ns.* **zoomag'netism,** animal magnetism ; **zoomancy** (*zō'ō-man-si* ; Gr. *manteiā,* divination), divination by observation of animals.—*adjs.* **zōoman'tic ; zōōmet'ric.**—*ns.* **zōometry** (*-om'ə-tri* ; Gr. *metron,* a measure), comparative measurement of the parts of animals ; **zō'omorph** (*-morf* ; Gr. *morphē,* form), in art, a representation of an animal form : an image or symbol of a god, &c., who is conceived as having an animal form.—*adj.* **zōōmor'phic,** pertaining to zoomorphism : representing animals in art.—*ns.* **zōōmor'phism,** the representation, or the conception, of a god or a man in an animal form.—Also **zōōmor'phy ; zō'on,** a morphological individual, the total product of a fertilised ovum, or the group of zooids constituting a compound animal : — *pl.* **zō'a, zō'ons.**—*adjs.* **zō'onal,** like a zoon ; **zōon'ic,** relating to animals.—*n.* **zō'onite,** one of the segments of an articulated animal.—*adjs.* **zōonit'ic ; zōonom'ic.**—*ns.* **zōon'omist ; zoonomy** (*zō-on'ə-mi* ; Gr. *nomos,* law), animal physiology.— Also **zōonō'mia ; zoonosis** (*zō-on'ə-sis* Gr. *nosos,* disease), a disease communicated to man from the lower animals, as hydrophobia, &c. : a disease due to animal parasites :—*pl.* **zōon'osēs ; zōopathol'ogy,** the study of disease in animals ; **zoopathy** (*zō-op'ə-thi* ; Gr. *pathos,* suffering), animal pathology ; **zoop'ery** (Gr. *peirā,* experiment), experimentation on animals.—*adj.* **zōoop'eral.**—*n.* **zōop'erist.**—*n.pl.* **Zoophaga** (*zō-of'ə-gä* ; Gr. *phagein,* to eat), the carnivorous animals collectively.—*n.* **zōoph'agan,** a carnivorous animal.—*adj.* **zōoph'agous.**—*ns.* **zō'ophile** (*-fīl* ; Gr. *philos,* loving), a zoophilist : a zoophilous plant ; **zoophil'ia, zōoph'ilism, zōoph'ily,** love of animals : (*psych.*) a morbid attraction to animals ; **zoophilist** (*zō-of'il-ist*), a lover of animals : (*psych.*) one suffering from zoophilia.—*adj.* **zōoph'ilous,** loving animals : suffering from zoophilia : (*bot.*) pollinated by animals other than insects : (*zool.*) of insects, feeding on animals.—*n.* **zōophob'ia** (Gr. *phobos,* fear), dread of animals, or of animal ghosts. — *adj.* **zōoph'obous.** — *n.* **zōophorus**

(-*of'ə-rəs*; Gr. *pherein*, to bear), a continuous frieze sculptured in relief with figures of men and animals.—*adj.* **zōophoric** (-*for'*).—*n.pl.* **Zoophyta** (*zō-of'it-ä*; Gr. *phyton*, plant), in older classifications, a group of invertebrates having no power of locomotion, as sponges, corals, &c.—*n.* **zō'ophyte** (-*fīt*), (*obs.*) any plant supposed to resemble an animal: (now old-fashioned) any of numerous invertebrates resembling plants, as sponges, corals, sea-anemones, &c., esp. hydroid colonies of a branched form.—*adjs.* **zōophytic** (-*fit'*), **-al**; **zōoph'ytoid**; **zōophytolog'ical** (-*fīt-*). — *ns.* **zōophytol'ogist**; **zōophytol'ogy**; **zōoplank'-ton**, floating and drifting animal life.—*adj.* **zōo-plas'tic** (Gr. *plassein*, to form), pertaining to **zō'oplasty**, the operation of transplanting living tissue from one of the lower animals to man.—*n.* **zoopsychology** (*zō-ō-sī-kol'ə-ji*), the psychology of the lower animals.—*adj.* **zōoscop'ic**.—*ns.* **zōo-scopy** (-*os'kop-i*; Gr. *skopeein*, to look at), a form of mental delusion in which one sees imaginary animals, esp. snakes; **zō'osperm** (Gr. *sperma*, seed), a spermatozoid; a spermatozoid:—Also **zōo-sper'mium**. — *adj.* **zōospermat'ic**. — *ns.* **zōo-sporan'gium**, (*bot.*) a sporangium in which zoospores are formed; **zō'ospore** (Gr. *sporos*, a seed), a swarmspore: an asexual reproductive cell that can swim by means of flagella.—*adjs.* **zō-ospor'ic**; **zōos'porous**.—*ns.* **zō'otaxy** (Gr. *taxis*, arrangement), the science of the classification of animals, systematic zoology; **zōotechnics** (-*tek'-niks*; Gr. *technē*, art), **zō'otechny**, the science of the breeding and domestication of animals; **zōothap'sis** (Gr. *thaptein*, to bury), premature burial.—*adj.* **zōothē'cial** (-*shi-*).—*ns.* **zōothecium** (-*thē'shi-əm*, or -*si-*; Gr. *thēkion*, casket, dim. of *thēkē*, box), the tubular sheath of certain social infusorians:—*pl.* **zōothē'cia**; **zōothē'ism**, the attribution of divine qualities to an animal.—*adj.* **zōotheis'tic**.—*ns.* **zōother'apy** (Gr. *therapeiā*, treatment), veterinary therapeutics; **zō'othome** (Gr. *thōmos*, heap), a group of zooids, as a mass of coral.—*adjs.* **zōotom'ic, -al.**—*adv.* **zōotom'ically.** —*ns.* **zōot'omist** (Gr. *temnein*, to cut), one who dissects the bodies of animals, an anatomist; **zōot'omy**, the dissection of animals: comparative anatomy; **zōotox'in**, a toxin produced by an animal, as a snake; **zō'otrope**, a zoetrope.—*adj.* **zōotrophic** (-*trof'ik*; Gr. *trophos*, food), pertaining to the nourishment of animals.—*ns.* **zoot'rophy**; **zō'otype**, an animal serving as a type.—*adj.* **zōotypic** (-*tip'ik*).—**zoological garden, park**, a garden or park where living wild animals are kept and exhibited. [Gr. *zōion*, animal.]

zooks, *zōoks, interj.* Same as **gadzooks**.

zoom, *zōom, v.i.* to make a loud, deep, persistent buzzing noise: to move with this sound: (*aero.*) to use the stored energy of the forward motion of an aircraft in order to gain height when flying.— *v.t.* to cause to zoom.—*n.* the act of zooming: a zooming noise. [Imit.]

zoot suit, *zoot' sūt, (U.S.)* a flashy type of man's suit with certain standard characteristics, as padded shoulders, fitted waist, knee-length coat, and trousers baggy at the knees.—*n.* **zoot'suiter,** one who wears a zoot suit. [Origin unknown.]

zoozoo, *zoo'zoo, n.* (*dial.*) the wood-pigeon. [Imit.]

zopilote, *sō-pi-lō'te, n.* one of the smaller American vultures—the turkey-buzzard, or the urubu. [Mex. Sp.]

zoppo, *tsop'pō, adj.* (*mus.*) with syncopation. [It.]

zorgite, *zor'gīt, n.* a metallic copper-lead selenide, found at Zorge, in the Harz Mountains.

zoril, zorille. See **zorro**.

Zoroastrianism, *zōr-, zor-ō-as'tri-ən-izm, n.* ancient religion founded or reformed by Zoroaster—the Greek pronunciation of Zarathustra—set forth in the Zend-Avesta, and still adhered to by the Guebres and Parsees in India. — *n.* and *adj.* **Zoroas'trian.** [L. *Zōroastrēs*—Gr.]

zorro, *sor'ō, n.* a S. American fox or foxlike wild dog.—*ns.* **zoril, zorille** (*zor'il, -il'*), an African skunklike musteline animal (*Zorilla*); **zorillo** (*sor-ē'yō, zor-il'ō*), a S. American skunk. [Sp. *zorro, zorra*, fox, *zorilla* (Fr. *zorille*), skunk.]

zoster, *zos'tər, n.* an ancient Greek waist-belt for men: herpes zoster or shingles. [Gr. *zōstēr*, a girdle.]

Zostera, *zos-tē'rä, n.* the eelgrass or grasswrack genus. [Gr. *zōstēr*, a kind of grasswrack.]

Zouave, *zoo-äv', zwäv, n.* one of a body of French infantry of great dash, orig. Algerians, wearing a quasi-Moorish dress: any of a number of volunteer regiments modelling themselves on the Zouaves who fought on the side of the North in the American Civil War: a woman's short embroidered jacket. [From the *Zouaoua*, an Algerian tribe.]

zounds, *zowndz, interj.* (*arch.*) an exclamation of anger and astonishment. [A corr. of *God's wounds.*]

zucchetto, *tsoo-ket'ō, n.* the skull-cap of an ecclesiastic, covering the tonsure.—Also **zuchetta, -o**. [It., dim. of *zucca*, a gourd.]

zufolo, *tsoo'fō-lō, n.* a small flute or flageolet used in training singing-birds.—Also **zuff'olo.** [It.]

Zulu, *zoo'loo, n.* a branch of the great Bantu family, belonging to S. Africa, conspicuous for physical development: a member thereof: the language of the Zulus.—*adj.* pertaining to the Zulus, their language, &c. [Native name.]

zumbooruk, *zum'boo-ruk*, or -*boō'*, *n.* a small cannon mounted on a swivel, carried on the back of a camel.—Also **zum'booruck, zom'boruk, zam'boorak.** [Hind. *zambūrak*; from Pers.]

Zuñi, *zoō'nye, soō'nye, n.* one of a tribe of Pueblo Indians living in large communal houses near the Zuñi river in New Mexico.—*adj.* and *n.* **Zu'ñian.**

zupa, *zū'pä, n.* a confederation of village communities governed by a **zū'pan**, in the early history of Serbia, &c. [Serbian.]

zurf. See **zarf**.

zuz, *zooz, n.* a silver coin of ancient Palestine. [Heb.]

zwanziger, *tswan'tsi-gər, n.* an old Austrian silver coin, equivalent to twenty kreutzers. [Ger.,— *zwanzig*, twenty.]

zwieback, *tsvē'bäk*, or *tswē'*, *n.* biscuit rusk, or a sweet spiced bread toasted. [Ger.]

Zwinglian, *zwing'gli-ən, tswing'li-ən, adj.* pertaining to the Swiss reformer Huldreich *Zwingli* (1484-1531), or his doctrines, esp. his divergence from Luther in the doctrine of the Eucharist—Zwingli rejected every form of local or corporeal presence, whether by transubstantiation, impanation, or consubstantiation.—*n.* a follower of Zwingli.

zwitterion, *tsvit'ər-ī-on, n.* an ion carrying both a positive and a negative charge. [Ger. *zwitter*, hybrid, and **ion**.]

Zygaena, *zī-jē'nä, n.* the burnet-moth genus, typical of the family **Zygae'nidae**: the hammer-head genus of sharks, now called Sphyrna.—*adjs.* **zygae'nid, zygae'nine, zygae'noid.** [Gr. *zygaina*, a shark.]

zygo-, *zī'gō-, zig'ō-, zyg'-ō-, zyg-, zīg-, zig-,* in composition, yoke, union or presence of two similar things. —*adj.* **zy'gal**, pertaining to a zygon: formed like a letter H.—*n.* **zygan'trum** (Gr. *antron*, a cave), in snakes and some lizards, an additional vertebral articulation, consisting of a fossa on the posterior surface of the neural arch, into which fits the zygosphene.—*adj.* **zygapophyseal, -ial** (-*fiz'i-əl*). —*n.* **zygapophysis** (-*pof'i-sis*; Gr. *apophysis*, process), one of the yoke-pieces or articulations of the vertebrae:—*pl.* **zygapoph'ysēs**.—*adjs.* **zygo-branchiate** (-*brangk'i-āt*; Gr. *branchia*, gills), having paired, symmetrically placed, gills: belonging to the **Zygobranchiā'ta**, a division of the Gastropoda.—*ns.* and *adjs.* **zy'gobranch, zygo-branch'iate.**—*adjs.* **zygocardiac** (-*kär'di-ak*; Gr. *kardiā*, heart), a term used to describe certain paired lateral ossicles in the gastric mill of Crustacea; **zygodactyl** (-*dak'til*; Gr. *daktylos*, toe), having two toes before and behind, as parrots.— Also **zygodactyl'ic, zygodac'tylous.**—*n.* **zygo-dac'tylism.**—*adj.* **zy'godont** (Gr. *odous, odontos*, tooth), pertaining to molar teeth whose cusps are paired: possessing such molars.—*n.* **zygoma** (-*gō'mä*), the arch formed by the malar bone and the zygomatic process of the temporal bone of the skull. —*adj.* **zygomat'ic**, pertaining to the zygoma, or in the region of it (as **zygomatic arch; zygo-**

matic fossa, the lower part of the fossa bridged over by the zygomatic arch; **zygomatic muscles,** two muscles, *major* and *minor*, arising from the zygomatic arch).—*adjs.* **zygomor'phic, zygomorphous** (-*mor'fəs*; Gr. *morphē*, form), yoke-shaped—of flowers symmetrical about one plane only.—*ns.* **zygomor'phism, zy'gomorphy.**—*n.pl.* **Zygomycetes,** (-*mī-sē'tēz*; Gr. *mykēs, mykētos,* a mushroom), a group of fungi (moulds, &c.), a division of the Phycomycetes, marked by the production of zygospores.—*adj.* **zygomycē'tous.** —*n.* **zy'gon,** a connecting bar: an H-shaped fissure of the brain.—*n.pl.* **Zygophyllacae** (-*fil--ā'sē-ē*; Gr. *phyllon,* a leaf), the bean-caper family, desert and steppe plants akin to Rutaceae, the typical genus being **Zygophyll'um.**—*n.* **zy'gophyte** (-*fīt*; Gr. *phyton,* a plant), a plant in which reproduction takes place by means of zygospores.— *adj.* **zygopleural** (-*plōō'rəl*; Gr. *pleurā*, side), bilaterally symmetrical; **zy'gose,** pertaining to zygosis.—*ns.* **zygosis** (-*gō'sis*; *biol.*), conjugation; **zy'gosphene** (-*sfēn*; Gr. *sphēn,* wedge), in snakes and some lizards, an additional vertebral articulation, consisting of a process on the anterior surface of the neural arch, which fits into the zygantrum; **zy'gospore** (Gr. *sporā,* a seed), a spore produced by the union of buds from two adjacent hyphae in the process of conjugation by which some fungi multiply.—Also **zy'gosperm.**—*n.* **zy'gote** (Gr. *zygōtos,* yoked; *bot.* and *zool.*), the product of the union of two gametes: (by extension) the individual developing from that product.—*adj.* **zygotic** (-*got'*). — **zygotic number,** (*bot.*) the diploid chromosome number. [Gr. *zygon,* yoke.]

zylonite. Erroneous spelling of **xylonite.**

zyme, *zīm, n.* a ferment: a disease-germ.—*n.* **zy'mase,** any of a group of enzymes inducing the alcoholic fermentation of carbohydrates. — *adj.* **zy'mic,** relating to fermentation.—*ns.* **zy'mite,** a priest using leavened bread in the Eucharist; **zy'mogen,** a non-catalytic substance formed by plants and animals as a stage in the development of an enzyme.—*adjs.* **zymogen'ic; zy'mold,** like a ferment; **zymolog'ic, -al,** pertaining to zymology.—*ns.* **zymol'ogist,** one skilled in zymology; **zymol'ogy,** the science of fermentation; **zymol'ysis,** the action of enzymes; **zymō'sis,** fermentation: the morbid process, thought to be analogous to fermentation, constituting a zymotic disease; **zymom'eter, zymosim'eter,** an instrument for measuring the degree of fermentation.—*adjs.* **zymotech'nic, -al,** producing and utilising fermentation.—*n.* **zymotech'nics,** the art of managing fermentation.—*adj.* **zymot'ic,** pertaining to fermentation: of the nature of, pertaining to, or causing, an infectious disease. — *n.* an infectious disease.—*adv.* **zymot'ically.** [Gr. *zȳmē,* leaven, *zȳmōsis,* fermentation.]

zymome, *zī'mōm, n.* an old name for the part of gluten insoluble in alcohol. [Gr. *zȳmōma,* a leaven.]

zymurgy, *zī'mər-ji, n.* the department of technological chemistry that treats of wine-making, brewing, distilling, and similar processes involving fermentation. [Gr. *zȳmē,* leaven, *ergon,* work.]

zythum, *zī'thəm, n.* a kind of beer made by the ancient Egyptians—much commended by Diodorus. [Gr. *zȳthos.*]

fāte, fär, åsk; mē, hər (her); *mīne; mōte; mūte; mōōn; dhen* (then)

WORDS AND PHRASES IN MORE OR LESS COMMON USE FROM LATIN, GREEK, AND MODERN FOREIGN LANGUAGES

à bas (Fr.), down, down with!

abattu, fem. **abattue** (Fr.), cast down, dejected.

a beneplacito (It.), at pleasure.

aberglaube (Ger.), belief in what is beyond proof: superstition.

abiit, excessit, evasit, erupit (L.), he is gone, he is off, he has escaped, he has broken away.—Cicero, *In Catilinam*, II. i. 1.

ab imo pectore (L.), from the bottom of the heart.

ab officio et beneficio (L.L.), from office and benefice—of a clergyman suspended.

à bon chat, bon rat (Fr.), to a good cat, a good rat—well matched : set a thief to catch a thief.

à bon droit (Fr.), with justice.

à bon marché (Fr.), at a good bargain, cheap.

abonnement (Fr.), subscription.

ab ovo usque ad mala (L.), from the egg to the apples—of a Roman banquet : from the beginning to the end.

à bras ouverts (Fr.), with open arms.

abrégé (Fr.), abridgment.

absens haeres non erit (L.), the absent one will not be the heir—out of sight, out of mind.

absente reo (L.), in absence of the accused.

absit (L.), lit. let him be absent—leave to pass one night away from college.

absit invidia (L.), may there be no ill will : no offence.

absit omen (L.), may there be no (ill) omen (as in a word just used).

ab uno disce omnes (L.), from one (offence) learn all (the race)—Virgil, *Aen.*, II. 65-66 : hence, from one example you may know the rest.

ab urbe condita (L.), from the founding of the city (of Rome), 753 B.C.—Abbrev. A.U.C.

abusus non tollit usum (L.), abuse does not do away with use—i.e. an abuse does not forfeit the legitimate use of a thing.

a capite ad calcem (L.), from head to heel.

accablé (Fr.), depressed, overwhelmed.

à chaque saint sa chandelle (Fr.), every saint his candle : to every patron his meed of service.

acharné (Fr.), furious, desperate (esp. of battles) ; **avec acharnement,** obstinately, furiously, rancorously.

Acherontis pabulum (L.), food for Acheron—of a bad person.

à compte (Fr.), on account : in part-payment.

à contrecœur (Fr.), reluctantly.

à corps perdu (Fr.), desperately, with might and main.

à coup sûr (Fr.), to a certainty.

à couvert (Fr.), under cover : protected.

acta martyrum, Romanorum, sanctorum, &c., deeds of the martyrs, Romans, saints, &c.

actum est de republica (L.), it is all up with the state.

actum ne agas (L.), do not do what is already done—quoted as a proverb by Terence, *Phor.*, II. iii. 72 (or l. 419).

acushla (Ir.), darling.

ad aperturam (libri) (L.), as the book opens.

ad arbitrium (L.), at pleasure.

ad astra (L.), to the stars.

a dato (L.), from date.

ad avizandum (Scottish law L.), into consideration.

ad Calendas Graecas (L.), at the Greek Calends—i.e. never, as the Greeks had no Calends.

ad captandum vulgus (L.), to catch the rabble.

ad clerum (L.), to the clergy.

ad crumenam (L.), to the purse.

Addio (It.), good-bye (**a Dio,** to God).

à demi (Fr.), by halves, half.

adespoton (Gr.), an anonymous work.

à dessein (Fr.), on purpose.

ad eundem (gradum) (L.), to the same (degree)—of the admission of a graduate of one university to the same degree at another without examination.

à deux (Fr.), of two, between two, two-handed ; **à deux mains,** with both hands : for two hands.

ad finem (L.), to the end : toward the end.

ad hoc (L.), for this special purpose.

ad hominem (L.), to the man, personal (see **argumentum**).

adhuc sub judice lis est (L.), the dispute is still before the court.—Horace, *A. P.*, 78.

ad infinitum (L.), to infinity.

ad inquirendum (L.L.), for making inquiry—name of a writ.

ad interim (L.L.), for the meantime.

ad internecionem (L.), to extermination.

adiós (Sp.), good-bye (lit. to God).

ad libitum (L.), at pleasure.—Abbrev. **ad lib.**

ad majorem Dei gloriam (L.), for the greater glory of God—the Jesuit motto.

ad manum (L.), at hand, ready.

ad misericordiam (L.), to pity—of an argument, &c.

ad modum (L.), after the manner (of).

ad nauseam (L.), to the pitch of producing disgust.

ad patres (L.), (gathered) to his fathers, dead.

ad referendum (L.), to be further considered.

ad rem (L.), to the point : to the purpose.

à droite (Fr.), to the right ; **à droite et à gauche,** right and left.

adscriptus glebae (L.), bound to the soil—of serfs.

adsum (L.), I am present : here.

ad summum (L.), to the highest point.

ad unguem (L.), to the nail : to a nicety.

ad unum omnes (L.), all to a man.

ad utrumque paratus (L.), prepared for either case.

ad valorem (L.), according to value.

ad verbum (L.), to a word : word for word.

ad vitam aut culpam (L.), for life or till fault—i.e. till some misconduct be proved.

ad vivum (L.), to the life, like-like.

advocatus diaboli (L.), the devil's advocate (see **devil** in Dict.).

aequam memento rebus in arduis servare mentem (L.), remember to keep a calm mind in difficulties.—Horace, *Od.*, II. iii. 1.

aequitas sequitur legem (L.), equity follows law.

aequo animo (L.), with an equable mind.

aes alienum (L.), debt, lit. another's copper or brass.

aes triplex (L.), triple brass, a strong defence.

aetatis suae (L.), of his (or her) age.

affaire d'amour (Fr.), a love affair ; **— de cœur,** of the heart ; **— d'honneur,** of honour (a duel).

affiche (Fr.), notice, placard.

a fortiori (L.), with stronger reason.

agaçant, fem. **agaçante** (Fr.), provoking, alluring ; **agacerie,** allurement.

Agamemnōn (Gr.), the leader of the Greeks in the Trojan war, king of Mycenae : a generic name for a king.

agathodaimōn (Gr.), one's good genius.

à gauche (Fr.), to the left.

agent provocateur (Fr.), one employed to lead others by pretended sympathy into acts incurring penalties.

age quod agis (L.), do what you are doing—i.e. with all your powers.

agŏnothetēs (Gr.), a judge or director of public games.

à grands frais (Fr.), at great expense.

agraphon, *pl.* **agrapha** (Gr.), a traditional utterance ascribed to Jesus, not in the canonical Gospels.

agréments (Fr.), graceful courtesies, charms, blandishments: embellishments, as grace notes and trills.

à haute voix (Fr.), aloud.

à huis clos (Fr.), with closed doors.

aide-mémoire (Fr.), an aid to the memory: a reminder: a memorandum-book: a written summary of a diplomatic document.

aide-toi, le ciel t'aidera (Fr.), help yourself and Heaven will help you.

aidōs (Gr.), shame, modesty.

aigre-doux, *fem.* **-douce** (Fr.), bitter-sweet, sourish.

aikona (S.Afr. native), it is not: no.

ailes de pigeon (Fr.), pigeon's wings—powdered side-curls (of hair).

aîné, *fem.* **aînée** (Fr.), elder, senior.

à jamais (Fr.), for ever.

Ajax (L.,—Gr. *Aiās*), the Greek hero next to Achilles in the Trojan war: (*obs.*) a privy, by a pun on *a jakes.*

à la (mode de ; Fr.), in the manner of.

à l'abandon (Fr.), at random, left uncared for.

à la belle étoile (Fr.), in the open air.

à la bonne heure (Fr.), in good or favourable time, —well and good, very good, that is right.

à l'abri (Fr.), under shelter.

à la campagne (Fr.), in the country.

à la carte (Fr.), according to the bill of fare.

à la dérobée (Fr.), by stealth.

à la hauteur (Fr.), on a level, abreast, able to understand.

alalagmos (Gr.), war-cry, cry of *alalai.*

à la lanterne (Fr.), to the lamp(-chain)—away with them and hang them (as in the French Revolution).

à la main (Fr.), in hand, ready: by hand.

à la maître d'hôtel (Fr.), in the style of a house-steward, of a hotel-keeper: in major-domo fashion.

a latere, ab latere (L.), lit. from the side, in intimate association with, confidential—of legates sent by the Pope.

à la volée (Fr.), on the flight—of any quick return.

albergo (It.), **alberge** (O.Fr.), an inn, auberge.

albricias (Sp.), a reward to the bearer of good news.

album Graecum (L.L.), the dried dung of dogs, once used for inflammation of the throat.

alcaiceria (Sp.), a bazaar.

alcarraza (Sp.), a porous vessel for cooling water.

alcázar (Sp.), a palace, fortress, bazaar.

Alcides (L.,—G.), a patronymic of Hercules, from Alcaeus, his mother's father-in-law.

al conto (It.), à la carte.

al contrario (Sp.), on the contrary.

alcorza (Sp.), a kind of sweetmeat: icing.

aldea (Sp.), **aldee** (Fr. *aldée*), a village, hamlet.

alectryŏn (Gr.), a cock.

à l'envi (Fr.), emulously: in emulation.

alere flammam (L.), to feed the flame.

alexipharmakon (Gr.), an antidote, counter-poison.

alfaquí (Sp.), Moslem expounder of the law.

alférez (Sp.), standard-bearer.

alforja (Sp.), a saddle-bag: baboon's cheek-pouch.

à l'improviste (Fr.), on a sudden, unawares.

aliquando bonus dormitat Homerus (L.) See indignor.

aliquid haeret (L.), something sticks.

alla Franca (It.), in the French style.

Allah il Allah, a corr. of Ar. *lā ilāha illā 'llāh*=there is no God but the God—the Moslem war-cry.

Allahu akbar (Ar.), God is great.

alla stoccata (It.), thrusting with a pointed weapon.

alla Tedesca (It.), in the German style.

alla vostra salute (It.), to your health.

allée (Fr.), an avenue, a walk or garden-path.

allez-vous-en (Fr.), away with you: begone.

alloiostrophos (Gr.), irregularly divided, not in alternate strophe and antistrophe.

allons (Fr.), let us go: come on: come.

allure (Fr.), mien, gait, air.

alma (It.), soul, essence.

alma mater (L.), benign mother—applied by alumni to their university.

Alnaschar, a figure in Galland's *Arabian Nights* who, dreaming he is kicking his wife, destroys the glassware that is to make his fortune.

à l'outrance, erroneously for **à outrance** (Fr.).

al pasto (It.), according to a fixed rate—of meals in a restaurant.

al più (It.), at most.

Alsirat (Ar.), the bridge across mid-hell to the Mohammedan paradise.

alter ego (L.), one's second self.

alter ipse amicus (L.), a friend is another self.

alternis vicibus (L.), alternately.

alterum tantum (L.), as much more.

altesse (Fr.), **alteza** (Sp.), **altezza** (It.), highness.

altum silentium (L.), profound silence.

amabilis insania (L.), a pleasing madness or rapture.—Horace, *Od.*, III. 4. 5-6.

à main armée (Fr.), by force of arms, with mailed fist.

a majori (ad minus) (L.), from the greater (to the less).

Amalthaea (Latinised Gr.), the goat that suckled Zeus. See Cornucopia in Dict.

amantium irae amoris integratio est (L.), lovers' quarrels are a renewal of love.—Terence, *Andr.*, III. iii. 23.

amare et sapere vix deo conceditur (L.), to be in love and to be wise is scarce granted even to a god.

amari aliquid (L.), some touch of bitterness.

âme damnée (Fr.), lit. damned soul, a tool or agent blindly devoted to one's will.

âme de boue (Fr.), a soul of mud, a low-minded person.

amende (Fr.), a fine, penalty; **amende honorable**, orig. an ignominious public confession: now a frank admission of wrong satisfying the honour of the injured.

a mensa et toro (L.), from bed and board.

âme perdue (Fr.), lit. lost soul, a desperate character.

à merveille (Fr.), wonderfully, perfectly.

amicus curiae (L.), a friend of the law-court: a disinterested adviser, not a party to the case: (wrongly) a friend in high quarters.

amicus Plato, amicus Socrates, sed magis amica veritas (L.), Plato is dear to me (or my friend), Socrates is dear, but truth is dearer still.

amicus usque ad aras (L.), a friend as far as the altars—i.e. as far as may be without offence to the gods.

ami de cour (Fr.), a court friend—an untrustworthy friend.

ami du peuple (Fr.), friend of the people (esp. Marat, French revolutionist).

amie (Fr.), a mistress—fem. of **ami**, a friend.

a minori [ad majus] (L.), from the less [to the greater].

à moitié (Fr.), half, by halves.

à mon avis (Fr.), in my opinion.

amor patriae (L.), love of country.

amor sceleratus habendi (L.), the accursed love of possessing.—Ovid, *Met.*, I. 131.

amor vincit omnia (L.). See omnia.

amour propre (Fr.), self esteem: sometimes readiness to take offence at slights.

ana, written **āā, ā** (L.L.—Gr.), lit. throughout: (in recipes) in equal quantities.

anadyomenē, coming up, emerging (esp. of Aphrodite from the sea).

Anak, *pl.* **Anakim** (Heb.), a race of giants.

anankē (Gr.), necessity.

anathēma sit, let him be accursed (1 Cor. xvi. 22).

a natura rei (L.), from the nature of the case.

anax andrōn (Gr.), lord of men (esp. Agamemnon).

anch' io son pittore (it.), I, too, am a painter (said by Correggio on looking at Raphael's ' St Cecilia').

ancien régime (Fr.), the old order (esp. before the French Revolution); **ancienne noblesse**, the old nobility: the nobility of the ancien régime.

ancile, *pl.* **ancilia** (L.), the shield that fell from heaven in the reign of Numa Pompilius, on the safety of which the prosperity of Rome depended.

anērithmon gelasma. See **kymatōn anērithmon gelasma.**

anguis in herba (L.), a snake in the grass.—Virgil, *Ecl.*, III. 93.

animal bipes (L.), a two-footed animal, man; — **implume**, featherless; — **rationale**, rational; — **risibile**, able to laugh.

anima mundi (L.), the soul of the world—a Platonic conception.

animo et fide (L.), by courage and faith.

animula vagula (L.), little soul flitting away—beginning of a poem ascribed to the dying Hadrian, translated or paraphrased by Prior, Pope, Byron, and Dean Merivale.

anno aetatis suae (L.), in the year of his (or her) age.

anno Christi (L.), in the year of Christ; —**Domini**, of our Lord (used as *n.* for advancing old age); — **mundi**, of the world; — **salutis**, of redemption; — **urbis conditae**, of the founding of the city (i.e. Rome; 753 B.C.).

annus mirabilis (L.), year of wonders.

anonyma (Latinised Gr.), a showy woman of light fame whom one is not supposed to know.

à nos moutons. See **revenons.**

anschauung (Ger.), perception, intuition, view.

anschluss (Ger.), union.

Antar, the hero of an Arabian romance.

ante Agamemnona. See **vixere fortes.**

ante bellum (L.), before the war.

ante lucem (L.), before light.

ante meridiem (L.), before noon.

Anterōs (Gr.), a deity capable of resisting Eros or love: also avenger of unrequited love.

antibarbarus (L.L.), a list of words and locutions to be avoided in the classical usage of a language.

antipasto (It.), an hors d'œuvre, a whet.

anziani (It.), councillors, senators.

à outrance (Fr.), to the utmost: to the death: to the bitter end.

apage (Gr.), away, avaunt.

a parte ante (L.), on the side before, from past eternity—opp. to **a parte post**, in future eternity.

à pas de géant (Fr.), with a giant's stride.

aperçu (Fr.), survey, sketch.

à perte de vue (Fr.), (reaching) out of sight.

à peu près (Fr.), nearly.

a piacere (It.), at pleasure.

à point (Fr.), to a nicety.

aporia (Gr.), in rhetoric, a professed doubt of what to say or to choose.

aporrhēta (Gr.), esoteric doctrines.

à portée (Fr.), within reach or range.

a posse ad esse (L.), from the possible to the actual.

appalto (It.), a contract or monopoly.

appartement (Fr.), a set of rooms in a house for an individual or a family.

appel au peuple (Fr.), a plebiscite; **appel nominal**, roll-call: call of the House.

après (Fr.), after; **après coup**, too late; **après moi (nous) le déluge**, after me (us) the deluge: then the deluge may come when it likes—attributed to Mme. de Pompadour and to Louis XV. Cf. **emou thanontos.**

a prima vista (It.), at first sight.

à propos de bottes (Fr.), apropos of boots—i.e. without real relevancy: by the way; **à propos de rien**, apropos of nothing.

aqua (L.), water; **aqua caelestis**, rain water: rectified spirits: cordial; **aqua fontana**, spring water. See Dict. for other phrases.

à quatre (Fr.), of or between four: four together; **à quatre mains**, for four hands.

a quattr' occhi (It.), face to face, tête-à-tête.

aquila non capit muscas (L.), an eagle does not catch flies.

à quoi bon? (Fr.), what's the good of it?

à ravir (Fr.), ravishingly.

arbiter elegantiarum (L.), judge of taste.

arbitrium (L.), power of decision.

Arcades ambo (L.), Arcadians both: two of the same stamp.—Virgil, *Ecl.* VII. 4.—Rendered by Byron blackguards both, *Don Juan*, IV. xciii.

arc de triomphe (Fr.), triumphal arch.

arc-en-ciel (Fr.), rainbow.

Archaeus (Latinised from Gr.), a personification by Paracelsus of animal and vegetable life.

ardentia verba (L.), words that burn, glowing language.

argent comptant (Fr.), ready money.

argumenti causa (L.), for the sake of argument.

argumentum ab inconvenienti (L.), argument from the inconvenient; **argumentum ad crumenam**, argument addressed to the purse; **argumentum ad hominem**, an appeal to the known prepossessions or previous admissions of an opponent; — **ad ignorantiam**, one founded on the ignorance of an opponent; — **ad invidiam**, an appeal to prejudices; — **ad judicium**, an appeal to the common-sense of mankind; — **ad rem**, argument to the purpose; — **ad verecundiam**, an appeal to reverence for some respected authority; **argumentum baculinum**, the argument of the stick—most forcible of arguments; **argumentum per impossibile**, or *reductio ad absurdum*, the proof from the absurdity of a contradictory supposition.

Aristides (L.,—Gr. *Aristeidēs*), an embodiment of justice, from the Athenian statesman (5th cent. B.C.).

Aristippus (L.,—Gr. *Aristippos*), an embodiment of self-indulgence, from the founder of the Cyrenaic school of philosophy.

ariston men hydōr (Gr.), water is best.—Pindar, *Ol.* i. 1.

ariston metron (Gr.), the middle course is the best: the golden mean.

armes parlantes (Fr.), lit. talking arms, arms that indicate the name of the family that bears them, as a press and a tun for Preston.

arrectis auribus (L.), with ears pricked up.

arrière-garde (Fr.), rear-guard.

arrière-pensée (Fr.), a mental reservation: a by-end.

ars est celare artem (L.), true art is to conceal art.

ars longa, vita brevis (L.), art is long, life short. Cf. **ho bios brachys.**

Artium Baccalaureus (L.), Bachelor of Arts.

Artium Magister or **Magister Artium** (L.), Master of Arts.

a salti (It.), by fits and starts.

asbestos gelōs (Gr.), inextinguishable laughter.—Homer (repeatedly).

Asherah, the sacred tree erected beside Canaanite altars, wrongly translated in the A.V. as grove.

asinus ad lyram (L.), an ass at the lyre, one ignorant of music or art: one unsuited to an occupation.—From a Greek proverbial expression *onos pros lyran.*

Asmodeus, Asmoday, an evil spirit of Semitic mythology.

Aspasia, a gifted Athenian courtesan, mistress of Pericles—any charming and accomplished woman of easy morals.

assez bien (Fr.), pretty well.

assora (Ar. *al-sūra*), a chapter or section of the Koran.

Astolfo, Astolpho, one of Charlemagne's paladins.

astra castra, numen lumen (L.), the stars my camp, God my lamp.

Astraea, the goddess of justice in Greek mythology who lived on earth during the Golden Age, but fled from man's impiety.

Atalanta, a fleet-footed Arcadian (or Boeotian) maiden who raced her suitors—defeated by Milanion (or Hippomenes) by dropping golden apples.

atalaya (Sp.,—Ar.), a watch-tower.

à tâtons (Fr.), gropingly.

a tempo (It.), in time, i.e. revert to the previous or original tempo.

Athanasius contra mundum (L.), Athanasius against the world: one resolute man facing universal opposition.

atmaidan (Turk.), a hippodrome.

à tort et à travers (Fr.), at random.

à toute force (Fr.), by all means, absolutely.

à tout hasard (Fr.), at all hazards.

à tout prix (Fr.), at any price.

à tout propos (Fr.), on every occasion.

atra cura (L.), black care. See **post equitem.**

à travers (Fr.), across, through.

Atreus, son of Pelops, who served up the flesh of Thyestes's children to their father.

at spes non fracta (L.), but hope is not yet crushed.

au bout de son latin (Fr.), at the end of his Latin, at the end of his knowledge, at his wits' end.

au cinquième (Fr.), on the fifth [story], in the attics.

au contraire (Fr.), on the contrary.

au courant (Fr.), in the stream : well informed : well up in the facts or situation.

auctor quae pretiosa facit (L.), gifts that the giver adds value to.—Ovid, *Her.*, XVII. 71-2.

audacter et sincere (L.), boldly and sincerely.

audax et cautus (L.), bold and cautious.

audentes fortuna juvat (L.), fortune favours the daring.—Virgil, *Aen.*, X. 284.

au désespoir (Fr.), in despair.

audi alteram partem (L.), hear the other side.

audiencia (Sp.), court of justice.

audita querela (L.), the suit having been heard—name of a writ giving leave to appeal.

auditque vocatus Apollo (L.), and Apollo hears when invoked.—Virgil, *Georg.*, IV. 7.

au fait (Fr.), well acquainted with a matter: expert.

aufgeschoben ist nicht aufgehoben (Ger.), put off is not given up.

aufklärung (Ger.), enlightenment, esp. the 18th-century intellectual movement.

au fond (Fr.), at bottom.

au fromage (Fr.), with cheese.

auf wiedersehen (Ger.), good-bye till we meet again.

au grand sérieux (Fr.), in all seriousness.

au gratin (Fr.), cooked with a covering of bread-crumbs.

aujourd'hui roi, demain rien (Fr.), king today, nothing tomorrow.

au jour le jour (Fr.), from day to day, from hand to mouth.

au mieux (Fr.), on the best of terms.

au naturel (Fr.), in the natural state: cooked plainly.

au pair (Fr.), by mutual service without payment.

au pied de la lettre (Fr.), literally.

au pis aller (Fr.), at the worst.

au plaisir de vous revoir (Fr.), till I have the pleasure of seeing you again.

au poids de l'or (Fr.), at its weight in gold, very dear.

au premier (Fr.), on the first [floor].

au quatrième (Fr.), on the fourth [floor].

aura popularis (L.), the breeze of popular favour.

aurea mediocritas (L.), the golden or happy mean.

au reste (Fr.), as for the rest: besides.

au revoir (Fr.), good-bye until we meet again.

auribus teneo lupum (L.), I am holding a wolf by the ears.—Terence, *Phormio*, III. ii. 21.

auriga (L.), a charioteer: a northern constellation.

auri sacra fames (L.), accursed hunger for gold.—Virgil, *Aen.*, III. 57.

au royaume des aveugles les borgnes sont rois (Fr.), in the kingdom of the blind the one-eyed are kings.—As a Latin proverb, *beati monoculi in regione caecorum.*

aurum omnes, victa jam pietate, colunt (L.), all worship gold, piety being overthrown.—Propertius, III. xiii. 48.

aurum potabile (L.), potable gold.

au second (Fr.), on the second [floor].

au secours (Fr.), help !

au secret (Fr.), in close custody or confinement.

au sérieux (Fr.), seriously.

auspicium melioris aevi (L.), augury of a better age.

aussitôt dit, aussitôt fait (Fr.), no sooner said than done.

Austriae est imperare orbi universo (L.), it is

Austria's part to command the whole world—often **A.E.I.O.U.**

aut amat aut odit mulier, nihil est tertium (L.), a woman either loves or hates, there is no third course.

autant d'hommes (or **de têtes**), **autant d'avis** (Fr.), so many men, so many minds. Cf. **quot homines.**

aut Caesar aut nullus, or **nihil** (L.), either Caesar or nobody (nothing) : all or nothing.

aut insanit homo aut versus facit (L.), either the man is mad or he is making verses.—Horace, *Sat.*, II. vii. 117.

aut inveniam viam aut faciam (L.), I shall either find a way or make one.

aut non tentaris aut perfice (L.), either do not attempt or else achieve.—Ovid, *A. A.*, I. 309.

auto (Sp. and Port.), an act: a drama, esp. a short one on a religious subject: an auto-da-fé (see Dict.).

autobahn (Ger.), an arterial double road for motor traffic only.

aut prodesse volunt aut delectare poetae (L.), poets seeks either to profit or to please.—Horace, *A. P.*, 333.

autrefois acquit (law French), previously acquitted ; **autrefois convict**, previously convicted.

aut regem aut fatuum nasci oportet (L.), one should be born either king or fool.

autres temps, autres mœurs (Fr.), other times, other manners.

au troisième (Fr.), on the third [floor].

aut vincere aut mori (L.), to conquer or die.

au voleur (Fr.), stop thief.

aux absents les os (Fr.), the bones to the absent. Cf. **sero venientibus.**

aux armes (Fr.), to arms.

aux grands maux les grands remèdes (Fr.), to desperate evils desperate remedies.

auxilium ab alto (L.), help from on high.

avant-goût (Fr.), a foretaste.

avant-propos (Fr.), preliminary matter: preface.

ave (L.), hail ; **ave atque vale,** hail and farewell ; **ave, Caesar** (or **imperator**) **morituri te salutant,** hail, Caesar, men doomed to die salute thee (said by gladiators) ; **ave Maria,** hail Mary.

avec permission (Fr.), by consent ; **avec plaisir,** with pleasure.

a verbis ad verbera (L.), from words to blows.

Avernus (L.), the infernal regions : any abyss—from Lake Avernus in Campania.

à vieux comptes nouvelles disputes (Fr.), old accounts breed new disputes.

a vinculo matrimonii (L.), from the bond of matrimony.

avi numerantur avorum (L.), ancestors of ancestors are counted [to me].

avis au lecture (Fr.), notice to the reader.

avise la fin (Fr.), weigh well the end.

avito viret honore (L.), he is green with ancestral honours.

avocat consultant (Fr.), consulting lawyer, chamber counsel.

avoir la langue déliée (Fr.), to have the tongue unbound, to be glib of speech.

à volonté (Fr.), at pleasure.

a vostro beneplacito (It.), at your pleasure, at your will.

à votre santé (Fr.), to your health.

avoué (Fr.), attorney, solicitor.

avoyer (Fr.), formerly the chief magistrate in some Swiss cantons.

a vuestra salud (Sp.), to your health.

avvogadore (It.), an official criminal prosecutor in Venice.

axioma medium (L.), a generalisation from experience.

ayuntamiento (Sp.), municipal council.

azulejo (Sp.), glazed tile.

Bacchus (L.,—Gr. *Bakchos*), the god of wine.

bailli (Fr.), a magistrate ; **bailliage,** his jurisdiction.

bain-marie (Fr.), a water-bath for chemistry, &c.

bajocco, pl. bajocchi (It.), a copper coin worth ½d.

bajra, bajri (Hind.), a kind of Indian millet.

baladin, baladine (Fr.), a public dancer: a mountebank.

ballon d'essai (Fr.), an experimental balloon sent up: a feeler or preliminary sounding of opinion.

balneum Mariae (L.), the same as *bain-marie* above.

bal paré (Fr.), a dress ball.

banlieue (Fr.), a precinct, extramural area, suburb.

Barataria, the so-called island whose government is committed to Sancho Panzo in *Don Quixote*.

barathrum (L.,—Gr. *barathron*), an abyss: hence, an insatiable extortioner or other person.

barba tenus sapientes (L.), sages as far as the beard —i.e. with an appearance of wisdom only.

barca (It.), a boat, barge; **barca-longa** (Sp.), a large Spanish fishing-boat.

basoche (Fr.), a mediaeval gild of clerks of the parliament of Paris, performers of mystery plays.

basso profondo (It.), a deep bass voice, or singer.

bastide (Fr.), a French country-house.

Batrachomyomachia (Gr.), war of frogs and mice.

batterie de cuisine (Fr.), set of utensils for cooking.

battre la campagne (Fr.), to scour the country, to beat the bush.

battuta (It.), beat; **a battuta**, in strict time.

bayer aux corneilles (Fr.), to gape at the crows, to stare vacantly.

beatae memoriae (L.), of blessed memory.

beati pacifici (L.), blessed are the peacemakers.

beatus ille qui procul negotiis ... paterna rura bobus exercet suis (L.), happy he who, far removed from business . . . tills with his own oxen the fields that were his father's.—Horace, *Epod.*, ii. 1.

beau garçon (Fr.), a handsome man: a dandy; **beau geste**, gracious gesture; **beau jour**, fine day, good times; **beau sabreur**, a dashing or bloodthirsty swordsman, cavalry soldier, or adventurer.

beauté du diable (Fr.), that overpowering beauty for the sake of which men fling everything away.

beaux arts (Fr.), fine arts; **beaux esprits**, see **bel esprit**; **beaux yeux**, fine eyes: a pretty woman.

bécasse (Fr.), a woodcock: a fool, dupe.

beccaccia (It.), a woodcock.

béchamel (Fr.), a sauce made with flour in cream.

bel air (Fr.), fine deportment.

bel canto (It.), a manner of operatic singing that cultivates beauty of tone.

bel esprit (Fr.), a wit or genius; *pl.* beaux esprits.

bel étage (German Fr.), the best story, the first floor.

bella gerant alii, tu, felix Austria, nube (L.), let others wage wars; do thou, lucky Austria, make marriages.

bella, horrida bella (L.), wars, horrid wars.— Virgil, *Aen.*, VI. 86.

bellaque matribus detestata (L.), and wars abhorred by mothers.—Horace, *Od.*, I. i. 24-5.

belle amie (Fr.), a female friend, a mistress; **belle assemblée**, a fashionable gathering; **belle-mère**, mother-in-law; **belle passion** (Fr.), tender passion; **belle vue**, fine prospect.

bellum internecinum (L.), a war of extermination; **bellum lethale**, deadly war; **bellum nec timendum nec provocandum**, war is neither to be feared nor provoked.

bel sangue (It.), gentle blood.

beltà e follia vanno spesso in compagnia (It.), beauty and folly often go together.

belua multorum capitum (L.), monster with many heads—the irrational mob.

bene decessit (L.L.), he has left well—a leaving certificate given to a schoolboy, curate, &c.

beneficium accipere libertatem est vendere (L.), to accept a favour is to sell one's liberty.

bene merentibus (L.), to the well-deserving; **bene meriti** (acc. **-tos**), having well desrved.

bene orasse est bene studuisse (L.), to have prayed well is to have endeavoured well.

beneplacito (It.), good pleasure: by your leave.

bene qui latuit bene vixit (L.), he has lived well who has lived obscure.—Ovid, *Trist.*, III. iv. 25.

bene vobis (L.), health to you.

benigno numine (L.), with favouring godhead.— Horace, *Od.*, III. iv. 74.

ben trovato (It.), aptly invented; **ben venuto**, welcome.

berceau (Fr.), a cradle: a covered walk.

besoin (Fr.), need, want, desire.

beso las manos (Sp.), I kiss your hands.

bête (Fr.), brute, stupid person; **bête noire**, a black beast: a bugbear; **bête rouge**, the chigoe; **bêtise**, stupidity.

Bethesda (Heb.), a healing pool at Jerusalem—often applied to a Nonconformist church.

Beulah (Heb.), a land of rest—a name for Israel in its future condition, in Isa. lxii. 4.

bibere venenum in auro (L.), to drink poison from a cup of gold.

biblia abiblia (Gr.) books that are no books.

bien (Fr.), well; **bien-aimé**, well beloved; **bien chaussé** (fem. **chaussée**), well shod; **bien entendu**, of course, to be sure: well designed: well versed: on condition; **bien perdu, bien connu**, blessing flown is blessing known; **bien-séance**, propriety—in pl. the proprieties.

biga (L.), a two-horse chariot.

bis dat qui cito dat (L.), he gives twice who gives promptly.

bis peccare in bello non licet (L.), in war one may not blunder twice.

bis pueri senes (L.), old men are twice boys.

blanchisseuse (Fr.), a laundress.

blandae mendacia linguae (L.), falsehoods of a smooth tongue.

blanquette (Fr.), a variety of pear.

bleuâtre (Fr.), bluish.

bluette (Fr.), spark, flash: a short playful piece of music.

blut und eisen. See **eisen und blut.**

bocca (It.), mouth.

bock (Fr., from Ger.), a strong German beer—from *Eimbockbier*—beer from Einbeck: now often a glass or mug of beer (quarter of a litre).

bona (L.), goods; **bona mobilia**, movable goods; **bona peritura**, perishable goods; **bona vacantia**, unclaimed goods.

bon accueil (Fr.), good reception, due honour; **bon ami** (fem. **bonne amie**), good friend: lover; **bon camarade**, good comrade; **bon diable**, good-natured fellow; **bon enfant**, good fellow, pleasant companion; **bon goût**, good taste.

bona fides (L.), good faith; **bona fide** (abl.), in good faith.

bon avocat, mauvais voisin (Fr.), a good lawyer is a bad neighbour.

bon-chrétien (Fr.), ' good Christian '—a kind of pear, the William.

bon gré, mal gré (Fr.), willing or unwilling: willy-nilly.

Bonhomme (Fr.), a French peasant.

bonis avibus (L.), under good auspices.

bonjour (Fr.), good day: good morning; **bon jour, bonne œuvre**, better day, better deed; **bon marché**, bargain: cheapness: cheap: cheaply; **bon mot** (*pl.* bons mots), a witty saying.

bonne compagnie (Fr.), good society; **bonne et belle**, good and fair; **bonne foi**, good faith; **bonne fortune**, good luck, success in an intrigue; **bonne grâce**, good grace, gracefulness; in *pl.* favour; **bonne mine**, good appearance, pleasant looks.

bonnes nouvelles adoucissent le sang (Fr.), good news sweetens the blood.

bonsoir (Fr.), good evening; **bon ton**, the height of fashion; **bon vivant**, a jovial companion: one who lives too well [**bonne vivante** is *not* according to French usage]; **bon voyage** (Fr.), a good journey to you.

bordereau (Fr.), a memorandum.

boreen (Ir.), a lane.

borgen macht sorgen (Ger.), borrowing makes sorrowing.

borgo (It.), a borough, a market-town; **borghetto**, a big village.

botte (Fr.), a pass or thrust in fencing.

bouche (Fr.), the staff of cooks in a large house.

bouderie (Fr.), pouting, sulking.

bouquetière (Fr.), a flower-girl.

boursier (Fr.), a foundation-scholar; a speculator on 'Change.

boutez en avant (Fr.), push forward.

boutique (Fr.), a shop, tradesman's stock.

boutonnière (Fr.), a flower made up for the buttonhole, &c.

brachium civile (L.), the civil arm; **brachium seculare**, the secular arm.

brevet d'invention (Fr.), a patent.

breveté (Fr.), patented.

brevi manu (L.), with a short hand, off-hand.

brevis esse laboro, obscurus fio (L.), I labour to be brief, and I become obscure.—Horace, *A. P.*, 25-26.

briller par son absence (Fr.), to be conspicuous by its absence.

brindisi (It.), a toast: a drinking-song.

brotstudien (Ger.), bread studies, those by which one earns one's living.

brûler la chandelle par les deux bouts (Fr.), to burn the candle at both ends.

brutum fulmen (L.), an ineffectual thunderbolt.

budgerow (Hind.), a heavy keelless barge.

buenas noches (Sp.), good-night; **buenas tardes**, good-afternoon; **buenos días**, good-day, good-morning.

buen principio, la mitad es hecha (Sp.), well begun is half-done.

buonamano or **bonamano** (It.), a tip.

buona sera (It.), good-evening.

buon giorno (It.), good-day.

cachot (Fr.), a dungeon.

cacoethes loquendi (L.), an itch for speaking; **cacoethes scribendi**, an itch for scribbling.

cadeau (Fr.), a gift, present.

cadit quaestio (L.), the question drops.

caeca est invidia (L.), envy is blind.

caelebs quid agam (L.), (you wonder) what I, a bachelor, am about.—Horace, *Od.*, III. viii. 1.

caelum non animum mutant qui trans mare currunt (L.), they change their sky, not their mind, who scour across the sea.—Horace, *Epist.* I. xi. 27.

Caesar non supra grammaticos (L.), Caesar has no authority over the grammarians.

café au lait (Fr.), coffee with (hot) milk; **café noir**, black coffee (without milk).

café chantant (Fr.), a café in which music is provided.

cafila, caffila (Ar.), a caravan.

cahier (Fr.), a writing-book: a memorandum: a report, memorial.

ça ira (Fr.), it will go—refrain of a famous song of the French Revolution.

caldarium (L.), a hot bath.

calembour, calembourg (Fr.), a pun.

callida junctura (L.), a skilful connexion.—Horace, *A. P.*, 47-48.

camicia (It.), a shirt.

campo santo (It.), a burying-ground.

Campus Martius (L.), field of Mars, used by the ancient Romans for games, military drill, &c.

canaut (Hind.), a canvas enclosure.

candida Pax (L.), white-robed Peace.—Tibullus, I. x. 45.

cantabit vacuus coram latrone viator (L.), the empty-handed traveller will sing in presence of the robber.—Juvenal, X. 22.

capa y espada (Sp.), cloak and sword.

cara sposa (It.), dear wife; **caro sposo**, dear husband.

carème (Fr.), Lent.

carent quia vate sacro (L.), because they lack a sacred bard.—Horace, *Od.*, IV. ix. 28.

carpe diem, quam minimum credula postero (L.), enjoy the present day, trust the least possible to the future.—Horace, *Od.*, I. xi. 8. Often **carpe diem** alone, meaning seize the opportunity.

casus belli (L.), whatever involves or justifies war.

casus conscientiae (L.), a case of conscience.

catalogue raisonné (Fr.), a classified descriptive catalogue.

causa sine qua non (L.), an indispensable cause.

cause célèbre (Fr.), a peculiarly notable trial.

cavalier(e) servente (It.), a gallant who waits with fantastic devotion upon a married lady.

caveat actor (L.), let the doer beware; **caveat emptor**, it is the buyer's look-out.

cave canem (L.), beware of the dog, a frequent inscription on Roman thresholds.

cavendo tutus (L.), safe through taking care.

cave quid dicis, quando, et cui (L.), beware what you say, when, and to whom.

cedant arma togae (L.), let arms yield to the gown: let military authority yield to civil.

ceinture (Fr.), a girdle, belt.

cela va sans dire (Fr.), that goes without saying: of course.

cela viendra (Fr.), that will come.

celui qui veut, peut (Fr.), who will, can.

ce monde est plein de fous (Fr.), this world is full of madmen.

c'en est fait de lui (Fr.), it is all up with him.

ce n'est que le premier pas qui coûte (Fr.). See **il n'y a**.

censor morum (L.), censor of morals.

centum (L.), a hundred.

certum est quia impossibile est (L.), it is certain because it is impossible.—Tertullian.

c'est-à-dire (Fr.), that is to say.

c'est égal (Fr.), it's all one (to me): it makes no odds.

c'est le commencement de la fin (Fr.), it is the beginning of the end.

c'est magnifique, mais ce n'est pas la guerre (Fr.), it is magnificent, but it is not war (said at Balaklava by a French general watching the charge of the Light Brigade).

c'est pire [plus] qu'un crime, c'est une faute (Fr.), it is worse than a crime, it is a blunder (attributed to Fouché on the execution of the Duc d'Enghien).

c'est selon (Fr.), that is according to the circumstances.

c'est (une) autre chose (Fr.), that is quite another thing.

cetera desunt (L.), the rest is awanting.

ceteris paribus (L.), other things being equal.

ceterum censeo (L.), but I think (said of persistent obstruction like that of Cato).

chacun son goût (Fr.), everyone to his taste (chacun à son goût is not French).

chambre à coucher (Fr.), a bedroom.

Champs Elysées (Fr.), Elysian Fields: also a famous open space and avenue in Paris.

chapeaux bas (Fr.), hats off.

chapelle ardente (Fr.), a chapel or chamber in which a corpse lies in state before burial, surrounded by lighted candles.

châteaux en Espagne (Fr.), castles in Spain, castles in the air.

cher ami (Fr.), a dear friend; fem. **chère amie**.

cherchez la femme (Fr.), look for the woman: there's a woman at the bottom of it.—Dumas *père*.

che sarà sarà (It.), what will be will be.

chevalier d'industrie (Fr.), lit. a knight of industry: one who lives by his wits and has savoir-faire.

chiesa libera in libero stato (It.), a free church in a free state (Cavour's ideal for Italy).

chinoiserie (Fr.), Chinese objects, decoration, behaviour, &c.

chi tace confessa (It.), who keeps silence, confesses.

chose jugée (Fr.), a settled matter: *res judicata*: a question past discussion.

chronique scandaleuse (Fr.), record of scandals.

ci-devant (Fr.), before this, former, formerly.

ci-gît (Fr.), here lies.

cingulum Veneris (L.), the girdle of Venus

circuitus verborum (L.), a circumlocution.

circulus in probando (L.), arguing in a circle, using the conclusion as one of the arguments.

cire perdue (Fr.), lit. lost wax: a method of casting in metal by making a mould about a wax model, which is burned away in the process.

cito (L.), quickly.

civis Romanus sum (L.), I am a Roman citizen.

clarior e tenebris (L.), the brighter from the darkness.

clarum et venerabile nomen (L.), an illustrious and venerable name.—Lucan, IX. 202.

classes aisées (Fr.), the well-off classes.

cogito, ergo sum (L.), I think, therefore I am. (Descartes's fundamental basis of philosophy.)

coll' arco (It.), with the bow.

col legno (It.), with the wood (of the violin bow).

Comédie Française, La (Fr.), the official name of the subsidised Théâtre Français.

Comédie Humaine (Fr.), the human comedy— Balzac's collection of novels, planned to form a complete picture of contemporary society.

comitas inter gentes, comitas gentium (L.). See comity in Dict.

comitia centuriata (L.), the assembly of the Roman people, voting by centuries; **comitia curiata**, that of the patricians, voting by curiae; **comitia tributa**, that of the people, voting by tribes.

commedia dell' arte (It.), guild comedy, Italian Renaissance comedy, mainly improvised, performed by a guild of professional actors.

comme il faut (Fr.), as it should be: correct: approved by the fashionable world, genteel.

commune bonum (L.), common good.

communibus annis (L.), on the annual average.

communi consensu (L.), by common consent.

compagnon de voyage (Fr.), travelling companion.

compos mentis (L.), of sound mind, sane.

compte rendue (Fr.), an account rendered: report.

comptoir (Fr.), counter: counting-room.

con amore (It.), with love: very earnestly.

con brio (It.), with spirit.

concio ad clerum (L.), discourse to the clergy.

concours (Fr.), contest, competition.

con diligenza (It.), with diligence.

conditio sine qua non (L.), an indispensable condition.

con dolore (It.), with grief.

confer (L.), compare.

con fuoco (It.), with fire.

conjunctis viribus (L.), with united powers.

conquiescat in pace (L.), may he [or she] rest in peace.

conscia mens recti (L.), a mind conscious of rectitude.—Ovid., *Fast.*, IV. 311. Cf. **mens sibi.**

conseil de famille (Fr.), a family consultation; **conseil d'état**, a council of state.

consensus facit legem (L.), consent makes law or rule.

consilio et animis (L.), by wisdom and courage; **consilio et prudentia**, by wisdom and prudence.

con spirito (It.), with spirit.

constantia et virtute (L.), by constancy and virtue.

consuetudo pro lege servatur (L.), custom is held as a law.

consule Planco (L.), when Plancus was consul, when I was a young man.—Horace, *Od.*, III. xiv. 28.

contra bonos mores (L.), against good manners or morals.

contraria contrariis curantur (L.), opposites are cured by opposites.

copia verborum (L.), plenty of words, fluency.

coram domino rege (L.), before our lord the king; **coram nobis**, before us, in our presence; **coram populo**, in the presence of the public.

cordon bleu (Fr.), blue ribbon: a cook of the highest excellence.

cordon sanitaire (Fr.), a sanitary cordon, a line of sentries posted so as to keep contagious disease within a certain area.

corps de ballet (Fr.), the company of ballet dancers at a theatre; **corps de garde**, the body of soldiers stationed on guard, their station, a guard-house; **corps diplomatique**, the whole diplomatic staff at a particular capital.

corpus delicti (L.), the substance of the offence; **Corpus Juris Canonici** (L.), body of the canon law; **Corpus Juris Civilis**, body of the civil law.

corrida de toros (Sp.), a bull-fight.

corruptio optimi pessima (L.), the corruption of the best is the worst of all.

corsetier, fem. **corsetière** (Fr.), a maker or seller of corsets.

corso (It.), race, run, course: a race of riderless horses: a procession of carriages: a street where these are held.

cosi fan tutte (It.), so do they all (of women): they are all like that.

côtelette (Fr.), a cutlet, a chop.

couleur de rose (Fr.), rose colour, hence, overestimating or exaggerating attractiveness.

coup de bonheur (Fr.), a stroke of good luck; **coup de chapeau**, a touching of the hat; **coup de grâce**, a finishing blow to put out of pain: a finishing stroke generally; **coup de hasard**, lucky chance; **coup de main**, a sudden overpowering attack; **coup de maître**, a masterstroke; **coup de soleil**, sunstroke; **coup d'état**, a violent or subversive stroke of state policy; **coup de théâtre**, a sudden and sensational turn as in a play; **coup de vent**, a gust of wind, a gale; **coup d'œil**, a general view at a glance; **coup manqué**, an abortive stroke, a failure.

coupe-jarret, *pl.* **coupe-jarrets** (Fr.), cut-throat, ruffian.

couteau de chasse (Fr.), a hunting-knife.

coûte que coûte (Fr.), cost what it may.

couturière (Fr.), a dressmaker.

couvert (Fr.), cover (at table).

couvre-pied (Fr.), a coverlet or rug for the feet.

crambe repetita (L.), cauld kale het again—cold cabbage warmed up.—Juvenal, VII. 154.

credat Judaeus Apella, non ego (L.), let the Jew Apella believe that, for I don't.—Horace, *Sat.*, I. v. 100.

crédit foncier (Fr.), lending of money on security of landed property, repayable by terminable annuity; **crédit mobilier**, lending of money on movable property.

credo quia absurdum (L.), I believe it because it is absurd; — **quia impossibile**, because it is impossible.

crème de la crème (Fr.), cream of the cream, the very best.

crescit eundo (L.), it grows as it goes.—Lucretius, VI. 341.

crève-cœur (Fr.), heartbreak.

cri de cœur (Fr.), a cry from the heart—heart-felt, passionate entreaty, complaint, reproach.

crimen falsi (L.), crime of perjury; **crimen laesae majestatis**, high treason.

crime passionnel (Fr.), a crime due to (sexual) passion.

croquis (Fr.), an outline or rough sketch.

crux criticorum (L.), a puzzle for the critics.

cucullus non facit monachum (L.), the cowl does not make the monk.

cui bono? (L.), for whose benefit is it? who is the gainer?

cuilibet (or cuicunque) in arte sua (perito) credendum est (L.), every (skilled) person is to be trusted in his own art.

cujus regio, ejus religio (L.), whose the region, his the religion—the principle that the established religion should be that of the prince in each state.

culpa levis (L.), a slight fault.

cum bona venia (L.), with your kind indulgence.

cum grano salis (L.), with a grain of salt.

cum multis aliis (L.), with many other things.

cum notis variorum (L.), with notes of various (critics).

cum privilegio (L.), with privilege.

curiosa felicitas (L.), studied felicity (said of Horace).

currente calamo (L.), with a running pen, offhand.

custos rotulorum (L.), keeper of the rolls.

d'accord (Fr.), agreed, in tune.

da dextram misero (L.), give the right hand to the unhappy.

da locum melioribus (L.), give place to your betters.—Terence, *Phormio*, III. ii. 37.

dame d'honneur (Fr.), maid of honour.

dames de la halle (Fr.), market-women.

damnosa haereditas (L.), a hurtful inheritance : an inheritance of debts.

damnum absque injuria (L.), loss without legal injury.

danke schön (Ger.), many thanks.

danse macabre (Fr.), dance of death.

das ewig weibliche zieht uns hinan (Ger.), the eternal feminine draws us upward.—Goethe, *Faust*, at end.

das heisst (Ger.), that is : abbreviated **d.h.**

data et accepta (L.), expenditures and receipts.

date obolum Belisario (L.), give a penny to Belisarius (ascribed to the great general when reduced to beggary).

Davus sum, non Oedipus (L.), I am Davus, not Oedipus—no good at riddles.—Terence, *Andr.*, I. ii. 23.

debito justitiae (L.), by debt of justice.

de bon augure (Fr.), of good omen.

de bonne grâce (Fr.), with good grace, willingly.

déchéance (Fr.), forfeiture.

de die in diem (L.), from day to day.

de facto (L.), in actual fact : really : actual.

dégoût (Fr.), distaste.

de gustibus non est disputandum (L.), there is no disputing about tastes.

de haut en bas (Fr.), with an air of superiority, as looking down.

dei gratia (L.), by the grace of God.

de integro (L.), anew.

déjeuner (Fr.), breakfast or lunch ; **petit déjeuner,** (little breakfast) coffee and rolls on rising ; **déjeuner à la fourchette,** meat (lit. fork) breakfast, early lunch.

de jure (L.), by right : rightful.

délassement (Fr.), relaxation.

de l'audace, encore de l'audace, et toujours de l'audace (Fr.), to dare, still to dare, and ever to dare (Danton's famous phrase).

delenda est Carthago (L.), Carthage must be wiped out (a saying constantly repeated by Cato).

de luxe (Fr.), sumptuous.

de mal en pis (Fr.), from bad to worse.

démarche (Fr.), a step or measure (esp. diplomatic).

demi-jour (Fr.), half-light, twilight, subdued light.

de minimis non curat lex (L.), the law does not concern itself about very small matters.

démodé (Fr.), out of fashion.

de mortuis nil nisi bonum (L.), say nothing but good of the dead.

de nihilo nihilum. See **gigni.**

de novo (L.), anew.

Deo favente (L.), with God's favour.

Deo gratias (L.), thanks to God.

de omni re scibili et quibusdam aliis (L.), about all things knowable, and some others.

Deo volente, or **D.V.** (L.), God willing.

dépêche (Fr.), dispatch, message.

de pis en pis (Fr.), worse and worse.

de profundis (L.), out of the depths.—Psalm cxxx.

déraciné (Fr.), uprooted.

de règle (Fr.), according to rule.

de retour (Fr.), back again, returned : in addition.

der grosse heide (Ger.), the great pagan (Heine's name for Goethe).

de rigueur (Fr.), required (as by strict etiquette).

dernier cri (Fr.), the last word (lit. cry) : the latest fashion.

dernier ressort (Fr.), a last resort.

der tag (Ger.), the day.

désagrément (Fr.), something disagreeable.

desipere in loco. See **dulce.**

désobligeante (Fr.), a carriage for two.

désorienté (Fr.), having lost one's bearings, confused.

desunt cetera (L.), the rest is wanting.

de te fabula narratur (L.), the story is about you.—Horace, *Sat.*, I. i. 69-70.

détente (Fr.), relaxation of strained relations.

détenu, fem. **détenue** (Fr.), a prisoner.

de trop (Fr.), too much, or too many, superfluous, intrusive.

detur digniori (L.), let it be given to the more worthy ; **detur pulchriori,** let it be given to the fairer.

Deus avertat (L.), God forbid.

Deus det (L.), God grant.

deus ex machina (L.), a god from a stage contrivance : a violent and inartistic solution of a difficulty in a plot.

deus nobis haec otia fecit (L.), it is a god that hath given us this ease.—Virgil, *Ecl.*, I. 6.

Deus vobiscum (L.), God be with you.

Deus vult (L.), God wills it (the Crusaders' cry).

dextro tempore (L.), at a lucky moment.

dia (Gr.), through, by : in old medicine, compounded of.

dicamus bona verba (L.), let us speak words of good omen.—Tibullus, II. ii. 1.

dichtung und wahrheit (Ger.), poetry and truth.

dicta probantia (L.), proof texts.

dictum de dicto (L.), hearsay report.

dictum sapienti sat est (L.), a word to the wise is enough (usu. quoted as **verbum**).—Plautus, *Persa*, IV. vii. 19.

dies (L.), day ; *pl.* **dies** ; *accus. sing.* **diem** ; **diem perdidi,** I have lost a day (said by the emperor Titus) ; **dies fasti** or **profesti,** days on which judgment could be pronounced, on which courts could be held in ancient Rome, lawful days ; **dies faustus,** lucky day ; **dies festi** or **feriae,** days of actual festival ; **dies infaustus,** unlucky day ; **dies irae,** the day of wrath : the day of judgment (from a Latin hymn) ; **dies nefasti,** days on which judgment could not be pronounced or assemblies of the people be held, in ancient Rome ; **dies non,** a day on which the judges do not sit.

Dieu avec nous (Fr.), God with us ; **Dieu défend le droit,** God defends the right ; **Dieu et mon droit,** God and my right ; **Dieu vous garde,** God keep you.

Die Wacht am Rhein (Ger.), the Watch on the Rhine (a famous German patriotic song).

digito monstrari (L.), to be pointed out with the finger : to be famous.—Persius, I. 28.

dignus vindice nodus (L.). See **nec deus intersit.**

di grado in grado (It.), by degrees.

di majorum gentium (L.), the divinities of superior rank—i.e. the twelve greater gods of classical mythology ; **di penates,** household gods.

dis aliter visum (L.), the gods have adjudged otherwise.—Virgil, *Aen.*, II. 428.

di salto (It.), at a leap.

diseuse, masc. **diseur** (Fr.), a reciter or entertainer.

disjecta membra (L.), scattered limbs (after Ovid., *Met.*, III. 724) ; **disjecti membra poetae,** limbs of the dismembered poet.—Horace, *Sat.*, I. iv. 62.

distingué, fem. **distinguée** (Fr.), distinguished : striking.

distinguo (L.), I distinguish.

distrait, fem. **distraite** (Fr.), absent-minded.

dit (Fr.), called.

divide et impera (L.), divide and rule.

divisim (L.), separately.

dixi (L.), I have spoken.

docendo discimus (L.), we learn by teaching.

doctor utriusque legis (L.), doctor of both laws (civil and canon).

dolce far niente (It.), sweet doing-nothing : pleasant idleness.

doli capax (L.), capable of committing a wrong— opp. to *doli incapax.*

Domine, dirige nos (L.), Lord, direct us (the motto of London).

Dominus illuminatio mea (L.), the Lord is my light.

domus et placens uxor (L.), a home and a pleasing wife.—Horace, *Od.*, II. xiv. 21-22.

donnerwetter (Ger.), thunderstorm (used as an ejaculation).

doppio movimento (It.), double speed.

dorer la pilule (Fr.), to gild the pill.

dormitat Homerus (L.). See **indignor.**

dos-à-dos (Fr.), back to back : a sofa constructed for sitting so.

dos moi pou stō kai tēn gēn (or **tān gān) kinēsō** (Gr.), give me where to stand, and I will move the earth (attributed to Archimedes).

do ut des (L.), I give that you may give.

drang nach osten (Ger.), eastward thrust.

droit au travail (Fr.), right to work; **droit des gens**, international law.

drôle (Fr.), a rogue, a knave.

dulce, 'Domum' (L.), sweet strain, 'Homeward' —from a Winchester school song sung before the holidays; **dulce est desipere in loco**, it is pleasant to play the fool on occasion.—Horace, *Od.*, IV. xii. 28; dulce et decorum est pro patria mori, it is sweet and glorious to die for one's country.—Horace, *Od.*, III. ii. 13.

dum casta (L.), while (she is) chaste.

dum spiro, spero (L.), while I breathe, I hope.

dum vivimus, vivamus (L.), let us live while we live.

d'un seul jet (Fr.), at one effort.

durante bene placito (L.L.), during good pleasure.

durante vita (L.L.), during life.

durchkomponirt (Ger.), having the music specially adapted to each stanza.

durchlaucht (Ger.), Serene Highness.

durchmusterung (Ger.), a star-catalogue.

dux femina facti (L.), a woman was leader of the deed.—Virgil, *Aen.*, I. 364.

ébauche (Fr.), rough draught, sketch.

ecce homo (L.), behold the man (John xix. 5); ecce signum, behold the sign or the proof.

ecco (It.), here is : there : look there.

e contra (L.L.), contrariwise, conversely.

e contrario (L.L.), on the contrary.

e converso (L.L.), conversely, by logical conversion.

écrasez l'infâme (Fr.), crush the vile thing. Voltaire against the Roman Catholic Church of his time.

edax rerum. See tempus.

edite, bibite (L.), eat, drink.

édition de luxe (Fr.), a splendid and expensive edition of a book.

editio princeps (L.), original edition (especially of a work till then known only in MS.).

égarement (Fr.), confusion, bewilderment.

ego et rex meus (L.), I and my king.—Cardinal Wolsey.

eheu fugaces . . . labuntur anni (L.), alas! the fleeting years slip away.—Horace, *Od.*, II. xiv. 1-2.

eile mit weile (Ger.), make speed with leisure. Cf. festina lente.

ein mal, kein mal (Ger.), just once counts nothing.

eisen und blut (Ger.), iron and blood—a famous phrase of Bismarck's.

ejusdem generis (L.), of the same kind.

ek parergou (Gr.), as a by-work.

embarras de (du) choix (Fr.), embarrassment in choice, a perplexing number of things to choose from ; embarras de(s) richesses, a perplexing amount of wealth or of abundance of any kind.

embusqué (Fr.), in ambush.

emou thanontos gaia michthētō pyri (Gr.), when I am dead let earth be mingled with fire. Cf. après moi le déluge.

empfindung (Ger.), sensation.

empressement (Fr.), demonstrative warmth of manner.

en ami (Fr.), as a friend.

en arrière (Fr.), behind, in the rear.

en attendant (Fr.), in the meantime, while waiting.

en avant (Fr.), forward.

en badinant (Fr.), roguishly, with badinage.

en beau (Fr.), as fair or handsome, in flattering style.

en bloc (Fr.), as one unit, wholesale.

en caballo (Sp.), on horseback.

en cavalier (Fr.), in a cavalier manner.

en clair (Fr.), not in cipher.

encomienda (Sp.), a commandery; encomendero, its commander.

en croupe (Fr.), on the crupper, on a pillion.

en cuerpo (Sp.), in close-fitting dress ; sometimes erroneously for stark naked, the Spanish word for which is *en cueros*.

en effet (Fr.), in effect.

en face (Fr.), in front : opposite : in the face.

en famille (Fr.), amongst the family, as at a family gathering, at home, without ceremony.

enfant (Fr.), child ; **enfant de la maison**, child of the house, quite at home ; **enfant gâté**, fem. **gâtée**, spoilt child ; **enfants perdus**, lit. lost children : forlorn hope, shock troops ; **enfant terrible**, a precocious child whose sayings put his elders to the blush ; **enfant trouvé**, a foundling.

en fête (Fr.), in festivity, keeping holiday.

en garçon (Fr.), like a bachelor, in bachelor style.

en grande tenue (Fr.), in full dress.

en grand seigneur (Fr.), like a great lord.

en l'air (Fr.), in the air, being discussed or expected : without reality.

enlevé (Fr.), carried away, kidnapped.

en masse (Fr.), in a body.

en militaire (Fr.), as a military man.

en passant (Fr.), in passing : by the way : applied in chess to the taking of a pawn that has just moved two squares as if it had moved only one.

en pension (Fr.), at a fixed rate for board and lodging.

en plein air (Fr.), in the open air.

en plein jour (Fr.), in broad day.

en prince (Fr.), in princely style.

en prise (Fr.), exposed to capture.

en pure perte (Fr.), to mere loss, to no purpose.

en queue (Fr.), like a tail, in a string or line.

en rapport (Fr.), in direct relation : in close touch or sympathy.

en règle (Fr.), in due order : according to rules.

en retraite (Fr.), in retirement, on half-pay.

en revanche (Fr.), in return or requital.

en route (Fr.), on the road : let us go : march.

en spectacle (Fr.), as a spectacle.

ens per accidens (L.L.), that which exists only as an accident of ens per se—i.e. a substance ; ens rationis, an entity of reason—opp. to ens reale.

en suite (Fr.), in succession or connected series (not in Fr. in sense of to match).

entbehren sollst du, sollst entbehren (Ger.), thou must abstain, abstain thou must.—Goethe, *Faust*, Part I. (Studierzimmer, ii.).

entêté, fem. entêtée (Fr.), infatuated : opinionative.

en tout (Fr.), in all : wholly.

en tout cas (Fr.), in any case or emergency : applied to an umbrella that can serve as a sunshade.

en toutōi nika (Gr.), conquer in this (sign). See in hoc (signo) vinces.

entrain (Fr.), heartiness ; **entraînement**, enthusiasm.

en train (Fr.), in progress : agoing.

entrecôte (Fr.), meat between the ribs, a kind of steak.

entre nous (Fr.), between ourselves.

entrez (Fr.), come in.

en ventre sa mère (Law Fr.), in his mother's womb.

en vérité (Fr.), in truth.

en ville (Fr.), in town : not at home.

eo nomine (L.), by that name, on that claim.

epea pteroenta (Gr.), winged words.—Homer and Hesiod.

éperdu, fem. éperdue (Fr.), distracted ; **éperdument amoureux**, desperately in love.

ephphatha (Aramaic), be thou opened.

épicier (Fr.), a grocer.

e pluribus unum (L.L.), one out of many—motto of the United States.

eppur si muove (It.), it does move all the same (attributed to Galileo after he had recanted his doctrine that the earth moves round the sun).

épris, fem. éprise (Fr.), captivated, smitten.

épuisé, fem. épuisée (Fr.), worn out.

erdgeist (Ger.), earth-spirit.

erectos ad sidera tollere vultus (L.). See os homini.

e re nata (L.L.), from the circumstances arisen, according to the exigencies of the case.

ergo bibamus (L.), therefore let us drink.

ergon (Gr.), work, business.

Erin go bragh (Ir.), Erin forever.

errare est humanum (L.), to err is human.

escalier (Fr.), staircase; **escalier dérobé,** private staircase.

escamotage (Fr.), juggling.

escargot (Fr.), snail.

escribano (Sp.), a notary.

escroc (Fr.), a swindler.

es korakas (Gr.), to the ravens: go and be hanged.

espada (Sp.), a sword: a matador.

esprit follet (Fr.), a mischievous goblin.

esquisse (Fr.), sketch, outline.

esse quam videri (L.), to be, rather than to seem.

est modus in rebus (L.), there is a mean in (all) things.—Horace, *Sat.,* I. i. 106.

esto perpetua (L.), be lasting.

est quaedam flere voluptas (L.), there is in weeping a certain pleasure.—Ovid, *Trist.,* IV. iii. 37.

estro (It.), enthusiasm, height of poetic inspiration.

étage (Fr.), floor, story; **bel étage** (see Dict.) is not a French usage.

étagère (Fr.), an ornamental stand of shelves for flowers, articles of virtu, &c.

étang (Fr.), pond: lagoon.

étape (Fr.), a storehouse: a halting-place: a day's march: rations: forage.

état (Fr.), state, rank; **état-major,** the staff of an army, regiment, &c.

États Généraux (Fr.), the States-General.

et hoc (or **id**) **genus omne** (L.), and all that sort of thing.

et in Arcadia ego (L.), I, too, lived in Arcadia. (Grave inscription in Poussin's picture ' The Arcadian Shepherds.')

étoile (Fr.), star.

étourdi, fem. étourdie (Fr.), giddy, foolish, light-headed; **étourderie,** heedlessness, stupid blundering.

étranger, fem. étrangère (Fr.), strange: a foreigner.

étrennes (Fr.), New Year's gift or gifts.

et sequentes, neut. **et sequentia** (L.), and those that follow.

et sic de ceteris (L.L.), and so about the rest.

et sic de similibus (L.), and so of the like.

et tu, Brute (L.), you too, Brutus. (Caesar's alleged exclamation when he saw Brutus amongst his assassins.)

eventus stultorum magister (L.), the outcome is the schoolmaster of fools.

ex abundantia (L.), out of abundance: **ex abundanti cautela,** from excessive caution.

ex abusu non arguitur ad usum (L.), from the abuse no argument is drawn against the use.

ex accidenti (L.L.), accidentally, as opposed to essentially.

ex aequo (L.L.), equally, equitably.

ex animo (L.), from the mind, earnestly.

ex aprosdokētou (Gr.), unexpectedly.

ex auctoritate mihi commissa (L.), by the authority entrusted to me.

ex cathedra (L.L.), from the chair of office, esp. the Pope's throne in the Consistory, or a professor's chair, hence authoritatively, judicially.

exceptio confirmat (or **probat**) **regulum** (L.), the exception proves the rule. (See Dict.)

exceptis excipiendis (L.L.), excepting what is to be excepted: with proper exceptions.

excerpta (L., *pl.* of excerptum), extracts, selections.

ex concessis (or **concesso**) (L.L.), from what has been conceded.

ex consequenti (L.L.), by way of consequence.

ex converso. See **e converso.**

excrementa (L., *pl.* of excrementum), refuse matter.

excudit (L.), struck, hammered, forged, printed (this).

ex curia (L.), out of court.

ex debito justitiae (L.L.), from what is due to justice.

ex delicto (L.L.), owing to a crime.

ex dono (L.L.), by gift, as a present from.

exegi monumentum aere perennius (L.), I have reared a monument more lasting than brass.—Horace, *Od.,* III. xxx. 1.

exempla sunt odiosa (L.), examples are hateful.

exempli gratia (L.), by way of example, for instance—often abbreviated **e.g.**

exeunt (L.), go out (*pl.*), leave the stage; **exeunt omnes,** all go out.

ex gratia (L.), as an act of grace.

ex hypothesi (L.L.), from the hypothesis.

ex improviso (L.), unexpectedly.

exitus acta probat (L.), the outcome justifies the deed.—Ovid, *Her.,* II. 85.

ex mero motu (L.), from his own impulse.

ex natura rei (L.L.), from the nature of the case; **ex natura rerum,** from the nature of things.

ex nihilo (or **nilo**) **nihil** (or **nil**) **fit** (L.), out of nothing nothing comes. See **gigni.**

ex officio (L.), by virtue of his office.

ex opere operato; ex opere operantis. See **opus.**

ex parte (L.), on one side, as a partisan.

ex pede Herculem (L.), (we recognise) Hercules from his foot.

experientia docet stultos (L.), experience teaches fools.

experimentum crucis (L.), the experiment of the finger-post, a crucial test.

experto crede or (Virgil) **credite** (L.), trust one who has tried, or had experience.

expertus metuet, or **metuit** (L.), he who has experienced it will fear (or fears).—Horace, *Epist.,* I. xviii. 87.

ex post facto (L.), retrospective.

expressis verbis (L.), in express terms.

ex professo (L.), avowedly.

ex propriis (L.), from one's own resources.

ex proprio motu (L.L.), of his own accord.

ex quocunque capite (L.), from whatever source.

ex re nata. See **e re nata.**

exstinctus amabitur idem (L.), the same man (maligned living) when dead will be loved.—Horace, *Epist.,* II. i. 14.

ex tacito (L.), silently.

extrait (Fr.), extract.

extra modum (L.), beyond measure, extravagant.

extra muros (L.), beyond the walls.

ex ungue leonem (L.), (judge, or infer) the lion from his claws.

ex utraque parte (L.), on either side.

ex voto (L.), according to one's prayer, by reason of a vow: votive: a votive offering.

faber est quisque fortunae suae (L.), every man is the fashioner of his own fortunes.

fable convenue (Fr.), fable agreed upon—Voltaire's name for history.

facile est inventis addere (L.), it is easy to add to things invented already.

facile princeps (L.), obviously pre-eminent, an easy first.

facilis descensus Averno, or **Averni** (L.), descent to Avernus is easy.—Virgil, *Aen.,* VI. 126.

facinus majoris abollae (L.), the crime of a larger cloak, i.e. of a philosopher.—Juvenal, III. 115.

facit indignatio versum (L.), indignation makes verse.—Juvenal, I. 79.

façon de parler (Fr.), way of speaking, a mere form of words.

facta non verba (L.), deeds, not words.

factum est (L.), it is done.

facundi. See **fecundi.**

fade (Fr.), insipid, colourless; **fadaise,** a silly saying: twaddle; **fadeur,** dullness.

faenum. See **fenum.**

faex populi (L.), dregs of the people.

faire bonne mine (Fr.), to put a good face on the matter.

fait accompli (Fr.), a thing already done.

falsi crimen (L.L.), the crime of falsification, esp. forgery.

falsus in uno, falsus in omnibus (L.), false in one thing, false in all.

fama nihil est celerius (L.), nothing is swifter than rumour.

fama semper vivat (L.), may his (or her) fame live for ever.

famille de robe (Fr.), a legal family.

far niente (It.), doing nothing.

farrago libelli. See quicquid.

fas est et ab hoste doceri (L.), it is right to learn even from an enemy.—Ovid, *Met.*, IV. 428.

Fata obstant (L.), the Fates oppose.—Virgil, *Aen.*, IV. 440.

Fata viam invenient (L.), the Fates will find out a way.—Virgil, *Aen.*, X. 113.

faute de mieux (Fr.), for want of better.

faux pas (Fr.), a false step : a mistake.

favete linguis (L.), favour me with your tongues—keep silent to avoid ill omen.—Horace, *Od.*, III. i. 2.

fecit (L.), made or executed (this).

fecundi (or facundi) **calices quem non fecere disertum ?** (L.), whom have not full cups made eloquent ?—Horace, *Epist.*, I. v. 19.

fée (Fr.), a fairy ; **féerie**, fairyland.

felicitas multos habet amicos (L.), prosperity has many friends.

feliciter (L.), happily : successfully.

felix qui potuit rerum cognoscere causus (L.), happy who has been able to understand the causes of things.—Virgil, *Georg.*, II. 490.

felo de se (Anglo-L.), a suicide, lit. felon of himself.

femme (Fr.), woman, wife ; **femme de chambre**, lady's-maid ; **femme galante**, a gay woman ; **femme incomprise**, a woman misunderstood or unappreciated ; **femme savante**, a learned woman, a blue-stocking. See **feme** in Dict.

fendre un cheveu en quatre (Fr.), to split a hair in four.

fenum habet in cornu (L.), he has hay on his horn (the sign of a dangerous bull).—Horace, *Sat.*, I. iv. 34.

festina lente (L.), hasten gently.

fête champêtre (Fr.), a rural festival, garden party.

Fête-Dieu (Fr.), Corpus Christi.

feu (*pl.* feux) **d'artifice** (Fr.), fireworks ; **feu de joie**, a bonfire ; (in English, *not* in French) a firing of guns in token of joy.

fiat experimentum in corpore vili (L.), let experiment be made on a worthless body.

fiat justitia, ruat caelum (L.), let justice be done, though the heavens should fall.

fiat lux (L.), let there be light.

fide et amore (L.), by faith and love ; **fide et fiducia**, by faith and confidence ; **fide et fortitudine**, by faith and fortitude ; **fidei defensor**, defender of the faith ; **fide non armis**, by faith not arms ; **fide, sed cui vide**, trust, but in whom take care ; **fides et justitia**, fidelity and justice ; **fides Punica**, Punic faith : treachery.

fi donc ! (Fr.), for shame !

fidus Achates (L.), faithful Achates (friend of Aeneas) : hence, a close friend.—Virgil.

fidus et audax (L.), faithful and bold.

fieri facias (L.L.), cause to be done—the name of a writ commanding the sheriff to distrain the defendant's goods.

filius nullius (L.), son of nobody, a bastard ; **filius populi**, son of the people ; **filius terrae**, son of the soil ; one of mean birth.

fille de chambre (Fr.), a chambermaid ; **fille de joie**, a prostitute ; **fille d'honneur**, a maid of honour.

fils (Fr.), son.

fin de siècle (Fr.), end of the (19th) century, decadent.

finem respice (L.), look to the end.

finis coronat opus (L.), the end crowns the work.

finis Poloniae (L.), the end of Poland.

fin mot (Fr.), main point.

flagrante bello (L.), while war is raging ; **flagrante delicto**, in the very act (lit. while the crime is blazing).

flectere si nequeo superos, Acheronta movebo (L.), if I can't move the gods, I'll stir up hell.—Virgil, *Aen.*, VII. 312.

flecti, non frangi (L.), to be bent, not broken.

floreat (L.), let flourish.

foenum. See fenum.

foie gras (Fr.), fat liver (of goose) made into *pâté de foie gras* (or *foies gras*).

fond (Fr.), ground, basis : fund ; **fonds**, ground : fund, stock, capital.

fonda (Sp.), a tavern.

fons et origo (L.), the source and origin ; **fons lacrimarum**, the fount or source of tears.

force majeure (Fr.), superior power.

forensis strepitus (L.), the clamour of the forum.

formaliter (L.L.), formally, in respect of the formal element.

forsan et haec olim meminisse juvabit (L.), perhaps some day we shall like to remember even these things.—Virgil, *Aen.*, I. 203.

Fors Clavigera (L.), Fortune the club-bearer (used as a title by Ruskin).

fortes Fortuna adjuvat (L.), Fortune helps the brave (Terence, *Phorm.*, I. iv. 26) ; **forti et fideli nihil difficile**, to the brave and faithful nothing is difficult ; **fortis cadere, cedere non potest**, the brave man may fall, he cannot yield.

fortiter et recte (L.), bravely and uprightly ; **fortiter, fideliter, feliciter**, firmly, faithfully, felicitously ; **fortiter in re, suaviter in modo**, forcibly in deed, gently in manner.

Fortuna favet fatuis (L.), Fortune favours fools ; **Fortuna favet fortibus**, Fortune favours the bold.

forum conscientiae (L.), the court of conscience.

fra (It.), brother, friar.

fraîcheur (Fr.), freshness, coolness.

franco (It.), post-free, franked.

franc-tireur (Fr.), an irregular or guerrilla fighter.

frangas, non flectes (L.), you may break, you shall not bend.

Frankfurter (Ger.), a small smoked sausage.

frappant (Fr.), striking, affecting.

frappé, fem. **frappée** (Fr.), iced, artificially cooled.

frate, *pl.* **frati** (It.), a friar, a mendicant Franciscan.

fraus est celare fraudem (L.), it is a fraud to conceal a fraud ; **fraus pia**, a pious fraud.

fredaine (Fr.), escapade, prank.

friand, fem. **friande** (Fr.), dainty, delicate : an epicure.

frigidarium (L.), the cooling room of Roman public baths, often with a swimming bath.

fripon (Fr.), knave, scamp ; **friponnerie**, knavery.

frisette (Fr.), fringe of curls on the forehead ; **friseur**, hairdresser ; **frisure**, a mode of frizzing.

frisson (Fr.), shiver, shudder.

friture (Fr.), a dish of fried food : fritter.

frontis nulla fides (L.), no reliance on the face, no trusting appearances.—Juvenal, II. 8.

frou-frou (Fr.), the rustling of silk skirts.

fruges consumere nati (L.), born to consume the fruits of the soil.—Horace, *Epist.*, I. ii. 27.

fugit hora (L.), the hour flies.—Persius, V. 153.

fuimus Troes ; fuit Ilium (L.), we were Trojans : Troy was.—Virgil, *Aen.*, II. 325.

fulmen brutum (L.), a harmless thunderbolt.

functus officio (L.), having fulfilled an office, out of office.

fundamentum relationis (L.L.), ground of relation.

funèbre (Fr.), mournful.

fureur (Fr.), extravagant admiration.

furor arma ministrat (L.), rage supplies arms. Virgil, *Aen.*, I. 150 ; **furor loquendi**, a rage for speaking ; **furor poeticus**, poetic frenzy ; **furor scribendi**, a rage for writing.

gage d'amour (Fr.), gage of love, love-token.

gaieté de cœur (Fr.), gaiety of heart.

gaillard, fem. **gaillarde** (Fr.), lively, frolicsome.

galant, fem. **galante** (Fr.), given to illicit intrigue : one of the parties in an amour ; **galant homme**, a man of honour.

galápago (Sp.), tortoise.

Gallice (L.), in French.

garçon (Fr.), boy : bachelor : waiter.

gaudeamus igitur (L.), let us therefore rejoice.

gaudet tentamine virtus (L.), virtue rejoices in trial.

gaudium certaminis (L.), joy of combat.

geflügelte worte (Ger.), winged words. See **epea**.

gemütlichkeit (Ger.), geniality, good nature : comfortableness.

genius loci (L.), the spirit of the place.

gens (Fr.), people ; **gens d'affaires**, business men ; **d'armes**, men-at-arms ; **de bien**, honest folk ;

de condition, people of rank ; **d'église**, churchmen ; **de langues**, linguists ; **de lettres**, men of letters ; **de loi**, lawyers ; **de même farine**, of a feather ; **de mer**, seamen ; **d'épée, de guerre**, military men ; **de peu**, people of humble condition ; **de robe**, lawyers ; **du monde**, people of fashion.

gens togata (L.), the toga-wearing nation—i.e. the Romans.

gentilhomme (Fr.), a nobleman : a gentleman.

genus irritabile vatum (L.), the irritable tribe of poets.—Horace, *Epist.*, II. ii. 102.

Germanice (L.), in German.

gesundheit (Ger.), your health.

gibier de potence (Fr.), gallows-bird.

gigni de nihilo nihilum, in nihilum nil posse reverti (L.), from nothing nothing can come, into nothing nothing can return.—Persius, III. 84.

giovine santo, diavolo vecchio (It.), young saint, old devil.

Gippesvicum (L.), Ipswich.

gitano, fem. **gitana** (Sp.), gypsy.

gli assenti hanno torto (It.), the absent are in the wrong.

gloria in excelsis (L.), glory (to God) in the highest ; **gloria Patri**, glory (be) to the Father ; **gloria virtutis umbra**, glory (is) the shadow of virtue.

glückliche reise (Ger.), prosperous journey to you.

gnôthi seauton (Gr.), know thyself.

gobe-mouches (Fr.), a fly-catcher (bird) : an insectivorous plant : one who will believe whatever he is told.

goutte à goutte (Fr.), drop by drop.

grâce à Dieu (Fr.), thanks to God.

gradu diverso, via una (L.), with different step on the one way.

gradus ad Parnassum (L.), a step, or stairs, to Parnassus, a Latin or Greek poetical dictionary.

Graeculus esuriens (L.), the hungry Greekling.—Juvenal, III. 78.

Graecum est: non legitur (L.), this is Greek : it is not read (placed against a Greek word in mediaeval MSS., a permission to skip the hard words).

grande chère et beau feu (Fr.), ample cheer and a fine fire ; **grande dame**, great lady ; **grande fortune, grande servitude**, great wealth, great slavery ; **grande parure**, or **toilette**, full dress ; **grande passion**, a serious love-affair or intense attachment.

grand merci (Fr.), many thanks ; **grand prix**, great or chief prize :—*pl.* **grands prix.**

Gratianopolis (L.), Grenoble.

gratia placendi (L.), the delight of pleasing.

gratis dictum (L.), mere assertion.

graviora manent (L.), greater dangers remain (Virgil, *Aen.*, VI. 84) ; **graviora quaedam sunt remedia periculis**, some remedies are more grievous than the perils.

gravis ira regum est semper (L.), the anger of kings is always serious.

gregatim (L.), in flocks.

grex venalium (L.), the herd of hirelings.

grosse seelen dulden still (Ger.), great souls suffer in silence.—Schiller, *Don Carlos*, I. iv., end of scene.

grosse tête et peu de sens (Fr.), big head and little wit.

grossièreté (Fr.), grossness, rudeness, coarseness.

guerra al cuchillo (Sp.), war to the knife.

guerre à mort (Fr.), war to the death ; **guerre à outrance**, war to the uttermost, to the bitter end.

gutta cavat lapidem (L.), the drop wears away the stone.—Ovid, *Pont.*, IV. x. 5.

habent sua fata libelli (L.), books have their destinies.

habendum et tenendum (L.), to have and to hold.

hac lege (L.), with this law, under this condition.

Hafnia (L.), Copenhagen.

Hala (L.), Halle.

hanc veniam petimusque damusque vicissim (L.), this liberty we ask and grant in turn.—Horace, *A. P.*, 11.

Hannibal ad portas (L.), Hannibal at the gates.

hapax legomenon (Gr.), lit. said once : a word or phrase that is found once only.

hasta mañana (Sp.), until tomorrow.

haud longis intervallis (L.), at no long intervals.

hausfrau (Ger.), a housewife.

haut et bon (Fr.), great and good ; **haut goût**, high seasoning : highly seasoned dish : a flavour, taint ; **haut monde**, high society ; **haut pas**, a dais ; **haut relief**, high relief ; **haut ton**, high fashion.

heil (Ger.), hail.

heimweh (Ger.), home-sickness.

helluo librorum (L.), a glutton of books.

herrenvolk (Ger.), master race, fitted and entitled by their superior qualities to rule the world.

heu pietas! heu prisca fides! (L.), alas for piety ! alas for the ancient faith !—Virgil, *Aen.*, VI. 879.

heureusement (Fr.), happily, fortunately.

hiatus valde deflendus (L.), a gap deeply to be deplored.

hic et ubique (L.), here and everywhere.

hic finis fandi (L.), here (was, or let there be) an end of the speaking.

hic jacet (L.), here lies.

hic sepultus (L.), here buried.

hinc illae lacrumae (L.), hence [came] those tears.—Terence, *Andria*, I. i. 99 ; also Horace, *Epist.*, I. xix. 41.

hinc lucem et pocula sacra (L.), from this source [we draw] light and draughts of sacred learning.

Hispalis (L.), Seville.

ho bios brachys, hē de technē makrē (Gr.), life is short and art is long.—Attributed to Hippocrates.

hoc age (L.), this do.

hoc anno (L.), in this year.

hoc erat in votis (L.), this was the very thing I prayed for.—Horace, *Sat.*, II. vi. 1.

hoc genus omne (L.), all that sort.

hoch (Ger.), *lebe hoch*, your health [in drinking].

hoc loco (L.), in this place.

hoc opus, hic labor est (L.), this is the toil, this the labour.—Virgil, *Aen.*, VI. 129.

hoc saxum posuit (L.), placed this stone.

hoc tempore (L.), at this time.

hoc (or **sic**) **volo, sic jubeo, sit pro ratione voluntas** (L.), this (thus) I will, thus I command, be my will sufficient reason.—Juvenal, VI. 223.

hodie mihi, cras tibi (L.), me today, you tomorrow.

hof (Ger.), yard : courtyard : court : manor ; **hoffähig**, entitled to appear at court ; **hofrat**, an Aulic councillor.

hoi polloi (Gr.), the many : the rabble, the vulgar.

Holmia (L.), Stockholm.

hominibus plenum, amicis vacuum (L.), full of men, empty of friends.

hominis est errare (L.), it belongs to man to err.

homme d'affaires (Fr.), business man : agent : steward ; — **de bien**, man of worth, good man ; — **de cour**, courtier ; — **de fortune**, fortunate man : rich man ; — **de lettres**, man of letters ; — **de paille**, man of straw ; — **d'épée**, military man ; — **de robe**, a lawyer ; — **d'esprit**, a man of wit ; — **d'état**, a statesman ; — **du monde**, man of fashion.

homo alieni juris (L.), one under control of another ; **homo antiqua virtute ac fide**, a man of the antique virtue and loyalty (Terence, *Adelphi*, III. iii. 88 or l. 442) ; **homo homini lupus**, man is a wolf to man ; **homo multarum litterarum**, a man of many literary accomplishments ; **homo nullius coloris**, a man of no colour, one who does not commit himself ; **homo sui juris**, one who is his own master ; **homo sum: humani nihil a me alienum puto**, I am a man : I count nothing human indifferent to me (Terence, *Heaut.*, I. i. 25) ; **homo trium litterarum**, man of three letters—i.e. *fur*=thief ; **homo unius libri**, a man of one book.

hon hoi theoi philousi apothnēskei neos (Gr.), whom the gods love dies young.—Menander. Cf. *quem di diligunt*.

honi soit qui mal y pense (O.Fr.), the shame be his who thinks ill of it—the motto of the Order of the Garter.

honneur et patrie (Fr.), honour and native land.

honores mutant mores (L.), honours change manners.

honoris causa (or **gratia**) (L.L.), as an honour.

honor virtutis praemium (L.), honour is the reward of virtue.

honos alit artes (L.), honour nourishes the arts; **honos habet onus**, honour has its burden.

honvéd (Hung.), militia.

horae canonicae (L.), the canonical hours.

horae subsecivae (L.L.), leisure hours.

hora fugit (L.), the hour flies.

horas non numero nisi serenas (L.), I number none but shining hours. [Common on sun-dials.]

horresco referens (L.), I shudder in relating.—Virgil, *Aen.*, II. 204.

horribile dictu (L.), horrible to relate.

hors concours (Fr.), not in competition; **hors de combat**, unfit to fight, disabled; **hors la loi**, in outlawry, outlawed; **hors de propos**, aside from the purpose; **hors de saison** (Fr.), out of season.

hortus siccus (L.), a collection of dried plants.

hostis honori invidia (L.), an enemy's hatred is an honour.

hostis humani generis (L.), enemy of the human race.

Hôtel des Invalides (Fr.), a hospital for disabled soldiers in Paris, founded in 1670; **hôtel de ville**, a town hall; **hôtel-Dieu**, a hospital; **hôtel garni**, a furnished town house.

huissier (Fr.), doorkeeper, usher: bailiff.

humanum est errare (L.), to err is human.

hurtar para dar por Dios (Sp.), to steal in order to give to God.

hybris (Gr.), insolence: overweening.

hypage Satana (Gr.), away Satan.—Mat. iv. 10.

hypotheses non fingo (L.), I do not frame hypotheses (i.e. unverifiable speculations).—Newton.

ibidem (L.), in the same place.—Abbrev. **ibid.**

ich dien (Ger.), I serve.

ici (Fr.), here—i.e. here is a W.C.

ici on parle français (Fr.), here French is spoken.

idée fixe (Fr.), a fixed idea, a monomania: a recurring theme in music.

idem (L.), the same (abbrev. **id.**); **idem sonans**, sounding the same; **idem velle atque idem nolle** (L.), to like and to dislike the same things.

id est (L.), that is, often **i.e.**; **id genus omne**, all that class or kind.

Iesus Hominum Salvator (L.), Jesus, Saviour of men.

ignoramus et ignorabimus (L.), we are ignorant and shall remain ignorant.—Du Bois-Reymond.

ignorantia legis neminem excusat (L.), ignorance of the law excuses nobody.

ignoratio elenchi (L.), ignoring the point in question, the fallacy of arguing to the wrong point.

ignoti nulla cupido (L.), for a thing unknown there is no desire.—Ovid, *A. A.*, III. 397.

ignotum per ignotius (L.), the unknown by the still more unknown.

i gran dolori sono muti (It.), great griefs are mute.

il a inventé l'histoire (Fr.), he has invented history.

il a le diable au corps (Fr.), the devil is in him: he is full of devilment, or of vivacity, wit, enthusiasm, &c.: he can't sit still.

il a les défauts de ses qualités (Fr.), he has the defects that answer to his good qualities.

il faut de l'argent (Fr.), money is necessary.

il faut laver son linge sale en famille (Fr.), one should wash one's dirty linen in private.

il gran rifiuto (It.), the great refusal (the abdication of Pope Celestine V).—Dante, *Inferno*, III. 60.

Ilias malorum (L.), an Iliad of woes.

ille crucem sceleris pretium tulit, hic diadema (L.), that man got a cross, this man a crown, as the price of his crime.—Juvenal, XIII. 105.

ille terrarum mihi praeter omnes angulus ridet (L.), that corner of the earth to me smiles sweetest of all.—Horace, *Od.*, II. vi. 13-14.

illustrissimo (It.), most illustrious.

il meglio è l'inimico del bene (It.), the better is the enemy of the good.

il n'y a pas à dire (Fr.), there is nothing to be said.

il n'y a que le premier pas qui coûte (Fr.), it is only the first step that costs. (Mme du Deffand on St Denis walking after decapitation.)

il penseroso (It. *pensieroso*), the pensive man.

ils n'ont rien appris ni rien oublié (Fr.), they have learned nothing and forgotten nothing [said of the French *Émigrés*, often of the Bourbons].

impar congressus Achilli (L.), unequally matched against Achilles.—Virgil, *Aen.*, I. 475.

impayable (Fr.), invaluable, priceless.

imperium et libertas (L.), empire and liberty; **imperium in imperio**, a government within another.

in absentia (L.), in absence.

in abstracto (L.L.), in the abstract.

in articulo mortis (L.), at the point of death.

in banco regis (L.L.), in the King's Bench.

in bianco (It.), in blank, in white.

in camera (L.L.), in a (judge's private) room: in secret.

in capite (L.L.), in chief: holding or held immediately of the crown.

incedis per ignis suppositos cineri doloso (L.), you walk on fires covered with treacherous ash.—Horace, *Od.*, II. i. 7-8.

incidis in Scyllam cupiens vitare Charybdim (L.), you fall into Scylla trying to avoid Charybdis.

in commendam (L.L.). See under **commend** in Dict.

in contumaciam (L.L.), as an act of contumacy.

incredulus odi (L.), I hate and disbelieve.—Horace, *A. P.*, 188.

in deliciis (L.), as favourites.

in deposito (L.L.), for a pledge.

index auctorum (L.), index of authors; **index librorum prohibitorum**, loosely **index expurgatorius**, a list of books prohibited (to Roman Catholic readers, either absolutely or until amended); **index locorum, rerum, verborum**, index of places, things, words.

indignor quandoque bonus dormitat Homerus (L.), I am annoyed whenever good Homer slumbers.—Horace, *A. P.*, 359. Usually cited as **aliquando** (=sometimes) **bonus**, &c.

in Domino (L.L.), in the Lord.

in equilibris (L.L.), in equilibrium.

in excelsis (L.L.), on the heights: on high.

in extenso (L.L.), at full length.

in extremis (L.L.), at the point of death: at the last gasp: in desperate circumstances.

infandum, regina, jubes renovare dolorem, thou bidst me, queen, renew unspeakable woes.—Virgil, *Aen.*, II. 3.

inferiae (L.), offerings to the manes of the dead.

infima species (L.L.), the lowest species included in a genus or class.

in flagranti delicto, or **flagrante delicto** (L.), in the very act of committing the crime.

in forma pauperis (L.), as a poor man.

in foro conscientiae (L.), in the court of conscience: judged by one's own conscience.

infra (L.), below: lower down on the page or further on in the book; **infra dignitatem**, below one's dignity (colloquially sometimes **infra dig.**).

ingénue (Fr.), a naïve young woman, esp. on the stage.

in gremio (L.L.), in the bosom.

in hoc (signo) vinces (L.), in this sign thou wilt conquer—i.e. in the Cross [the motto of Constantine the Great]. See **en toutōi nika.**

in limine (L.), on the threshold.

in loco parentis (L.), in the place of a parent.

in magnis et voluisse sat est (L.), in great things even to have wished is enough.—Propertius, II. x. 6.

in malam partem (L.), in an unfavourable manner.

in medias res (L.), into the midst of things.

in meditatione fugae (L.), in contemplation of flight.

in memoriam (L.), to the memory (of): in memory.

in nubibus (L.), in the clouds.

inopem me copia fecit (L.), plenty has made me poor.—Ovid, *M.*, III. 466.

in pace (L.), in peace.

in partibus infidelium (L.), in unbelieving countries—a phrase formerly applied to titular bishops in countries where no Catholic hierarchy had been set up.

in petto (It.), within the breast: in one's own mind but not yet divulged.

in principio (L.), in the beginning.

in propria persona (L.), in person.

in puris naturalibus (L.L.), quite naked.

in re (L.), in the matter (of).

in rerum natura (L.), in nature: in the natural or physical world: in the order of nature.

in secula seculorum (L.), for ever and ever.

in situ (L.), in the original situation.

instar omnium (L.), worth all the rest.

in statu pupillari (L.L.), in a state of wardship.

in statu quo (L.L.), in the former state.

Insula or **Insulae** (L.), Lille.

integer vitae scelerisque purus (L.), blameless in life and clear of offence.—Horace, *Od.*, I. xxii. 1.

inter alia (L.), among other things; **inter alios**, among other persons; **inter arma silent leges**, amid wars laws are silent; **interdum stultus bene loquitur**, sometimes a fool speaks aright; **inter nos**, between ourselves; **inter pocula**, over one's cups.

in terrorem (L.), as a warning.

inter se (L.), amongst themselves.

inter vivos (L.; *law*), from one living person to another.

in toto (L.), entirely.

intra muros (L.), within the walls.

in transitu (L.), on passage.

in usum Delphini (L.), for the use of the Dauphin: toned down to suit the young person.

in utrumque paratus (L.), prepared for either.

in vacuo (L.), in a vacuum.

invenit (L.), devised (this).

in vino veritas (L.), in wine is truth.

invita Minerva (L.), against the will of Minerva: uninspired.—Horace, *A. P.*, 385.

in vitro (L.), in glass: in the test tube—opp. to in vivo.

in vivo (L.), in the living organism.

ipse dixit (L.), he himself said it: his mere word: a dogmatic pronouncement.

ipsissima verba (L.), the very words.

ipso facto (L.), by that very fact: thereby.

ira furor brevis est (L.), rage is a brief madness.—Horace, *Epist.*, I. ii. 62.

Ispalis (L.), Seville.

Italia irredenta (It.), unredeemed Italy—the parts of Italy still under foreign domination after the war of 1866—South Tirol, &c.

Italice (L.), in Italian.

iterum (L.), again.

ivresse (Fr.), drunkenness.

jacta est alea (L.), the die is cast.

j'adoube (Fr.), I adjust (in chess: a warning that only an adjustment is intended, not a move).

ja wohl (Ger.), yes indeed.

je n'en vois pas la nécessité (Fr.), I don't see the necessity for that [said in reply to a man who pleaded, ' But one must live somehow '].

je ne sais quoi (Fr.), I know not what: an indefinable something.

jet d'eau (Fr.), a jet of water.

jeu de mots (Fr.), a play on words: a pun.

jeu d'esprit (Fr.), a witticism.

jeune fille (Fr.), a girl.

jeune premier (fem. **première**) (Fr.), a juvenile lead.

jeunesse dorée (Fr.), gilded youth, luxurious young fops.

joci causa (L.), for the joke.

joie de vivre (Fr.), joy of living.

Judenhetze (Ger.), Jew-baiting.

judex damnatur cum nocens absolvitur (L.), the judge is condemned when the guilty is acquitted.

Jup(p)iter optimus maximus (L.), Jupiter best

and greatest; **Jup(p)iter Pluvius**, rain-bringing Jupiter; **Jup(p)iter Tonans**, Jupiter the thunderer.

jure divino (L.), by divine law; **jure humano**, by human law.

juris utriusque doctor (L.), doctor both of canon and of civil law.

jus (L.), law: right; **jus civile**, civil law; **jus divinum**, divine right; — **gentium**, law of nations; — **gladii**, of the sword; — **mariti**, right of a husband; — **naturale**, law of nature: common sense of justice; **jus primae noctis**, the alleged right of a feudal superior to deflower a bride.

jusqu'au bout (Fr.), to the very end.

juste milieu (Fr.), the just mean, the happy medium.

justum et tenacem propositi virum (L.), a man upright and tenacious of purpose.—Horace, *Od.*, III. iii. 1.

j'y suis, j'y reste (Fr.), here I am, here I stay [said by Macmahon at the Malakoff].

kai ta leipomena, kai ta loipa (Gr.), and the rest: and so on.

kalos kagathos, kalokagathos (Gr.), good and honourable: a perfect gentleman.

kaputt (Ger. slang), ruined: broken: smashed.

kat' exochēn (Gr.), pre-eminently: *par excellence*.

kneipe (Ger.), a tavern: a students' beer-house or drinking party.

ktēma es aei (Gr.), a possession for ever.

kuchen (Ger.), cake.

kulturkampf (Ger.), the war of culture [said by Virchow in 1873 of the conflict between Bismarck and the Catholic Church].

kunstlied (Ger.), an art-song.

kymatōn anērithmon gelasma (Gr.), innumerable laughter of the waves.—Aeschylus, *Prom.*, 89-90.

laborare est orare (L.), work is prayer.

labore et honore (L.), by labour and honour.

labor improbus (L.), persistent, dogged labour.

labuntur et imputantur (L.), [the moments] slip away and are laid to our account [on sundials]. Cf. pereunt.

la donna è mobile (It.), woman is changeable.

laesa majestas (L.), lèse majesté (Fr.), treason.

la garde meurt et ne se rend pas (Fr.), the guard dies: it does not surrender.

la grande nation (Fr.), the great nation—i.e. France.

lā ilāha illā 'llāh (Ar.), there is no god but God.

l'allegro (It.), the merry, cheerful man.

langage des halles (Fr.), language of the market-place.

l'appétit vient en mangeant (Fr.), appetite comes as you eat.

la propriété c'est le vol (Fr.), property is theft [from Proudhon].

lapsus calami (L.), a slip of the pen; — **linguae**, of the tongue; — **memoriae**, of the memory.

lares et penates (L.), household gods.

la reyne le veult (Norm. Fr.), See le roy le veult.

lasciate ogni speranza, voi che 'ntrate (It.), abandon all hope ye who enter.—Dante, *Inferno*, III. 9. From the inscription over the gate of hell.

latet anguis in herba (L.), there is a snake hidden in the grass.—Virgil, *Ecl.*, III. 93.

laudator temporis acti (L.), one who praises past times.—Horace, *A. P.*, 173.

laus Deo (L.), praise to God.

l'avenir (Fr.), the future.

le beau monde (Fr.), the fashionable world.

lebensraum (Ger.), space inhabited by living things: room to live (and, if necessary, expand).

lector benevole (L.), kind reader.

le génie c'est la patience (Fr.), genius is patience.

le grand monarque (Fr.), the great king—i.e. Louis XIV.

le jeu ne vaut pas la chandelle (Fr.), the game is not worth the candle.

le mot juste (Fr.), the right word.

l'empire c'est la paix (Fr.), the empire means peace [said by Louis Napoleon in 1852].

Leodicum (L.), Liége.

le roy (or **la reyne**) **le veult** (Norm. Fr.), the king (or queen) wills it—form of royal assent to a bill.

le roy (**la reine**) **s'avisera** (Norm. Fr.), the king (or queen) will deliberate—form of refusal.

les convenances (Fr.), the proprieties : the customs and manners of polite society.

le style est l'homme (**même**) (Fr.), the style is the man himself (from Buffon).

l'état, c'est moi (Fr.), I am the state [alleged to have been said by Louis XIV].

lettre de cachet (Fr.), a letter under the royal signet : a royal warrant for arrest and imprisonment ; — **de change**, a bill of exchange ; — **de créance**, letter of credit ; — **de marque**, a letter of marque or of reprisal.

levée en masse (Fr.), a levy of all who can bear arms.

lever de rideau (Fr.), curtain-raiser.

lex non scripta (L.), unwritten law—i.e. the common law ; **lex scripta**, statute law ; **lex talionis**, the law of talion.

liberté, égalité, fraternité (Fr.), liberty, equality, fraternity—a slogan of the French Revolution.

libraire (Fr.), bookseller ; **librairie**, book-shop.

licentia vatum (L.), poetical licence.

lied (*pl.* **lieder**) **ohne worte** (Ger.), song without words.

limae labor (L.), the labour of the file, of polishing. —Horace, *A. P.*, 291.

limbus patrum ; **limbus infantum** (L.L.). See **limbo** in Dict.

lit de justice (Fr.), bed of justice. See **bed** in Dict.

lite pendente (L.), pending the suit.

littera scripta manet (L.), what is written down is permanent. See **vox audita**.

loco citato (L.), in the passage cited.

locus classicus (L.), the classical passage, the stock quotation ; **locus paenitentiae**, room for penitence : time for repentance ; **locus standi**, a place for standing : a right to interfere.

lucri causa (L.), for the sake of gain.

lucus a non lucendo (L.), the grove (*lucus*) (is so named) from its *not* shining (*lucendo*).

ludere cum sacris (L.), to trifle with sacred things.

luftwaffe (Ger.), air force.

Lugdunum (L.), Lyons ; **Lugdunum Batavorum**, Leyden.

l'union fait la force (Fr.), union makes strength.

lupus in fabula (L.), the wolf in the fable : talk of the devil.—Terence, *Adel.*, IV. i. 21.

lusus naturae (L.), a sport or freak of nature.

Lutetia, or **Lutetia Parisiorum** (L.), Paris.

lux mundi (L.), light of the world.

macte virtute esto (L.), go on in your virtue. (Cato to one coming out of a vicious resort, according to Horace, *Sat.*, I. ii. 31-32.)

ma foi (Fr.), upon my faith.

magna est veritas et praevalebit (L.), truth is great and will prevail (better, **et prevalet**, and prevails).

magni nominis umbra (L.), the mere shadow of a mighty name.—Lucan, I. 135.

magnum opus (L.), a great work.

maison de ville (Fr.), a town house, residence in town.

maître d'hôtel (Fr.), a house-steward, major domo. See **à la**.

mala fide (L.), in bad faith : treacherously.

mal à propos (Fr.), ill-timed.

mal de mer (Fr.), sea-sickness ; **mal du pays**, home-sickness, nostalgia.

malentendu (Fr.), a misunderstanding.

malgré nous (Fr.), in spite of us.

mañana (Sp.), tomorrow.

manet (L.), remains (on the stage) :—*pl.* **manent**.

manqué (Fr.), spoiled.

man spricht deutsch (Ger.), German is spoken here.

Mardi gras (Fr.), Shrove Tuesday.

mare clausum (L.), a closed sea—a sea within the jurisdiction of one state.

mariage de convenance (Fr.), marriage from interest rather than love.

Massilia (L.), Marseilles.

materfamilias (L.), the mother of a family.

matre pulchra filia pulchrior (L.), a daughter fairer than her fair mother.—Horace, *Od.*, I. xvi. 1.

mauvaise honte (Fr.), false modesty, bashfulness.

mauvais quart d'heure (Fr.), a bad quarter of an hour ; **mauvais sujet**, a bad subject ; a worthless fellow ; **mauvais ton**, bad style, bad form.

maxima debetur puero reverentia (L.), the greatest reverence is due to the boy—i.e. to the innocence of his age.—Juvenal, XIV. 47.

mea culpa (L.), by my own fault.

mea virtute me involvo (L.), I wrap myself in my virtue.—Horace, *Od.*, III. xxix. 54-55.

mēden agan (Gr.), [let there be] nothing in excess.

Mediolanum (L.), Milan.

medio tutissimus ibis (L.), thou wilt go safest in the middle.—Ovid, *M.*, II. 137.

mega biblion, mega kakon (Gr.), big book, great evil.

me judice (L.), I being judge, in my opinion.

mē kinei Kamarinan (Gr.), do not stir up Kamarina (a pestilent marsh in Sicily) : let well alone.

memento mori (L.), remember that you must die.

memorabilia (L.), things worth remembering.

memoria technica (L.), artificial memory—a mnemonic contrivance.

meno mosso (It.), not so quick.

mens sana in corpore sano (L.), a sound mind in a sound body.—Juvenal, X. 356.

mens sibi conscia recti (L.), a mind conscious of rectitude.—Virgil, *Aen.*, I. 604. Cf. **conscia mens recti**.

meo periculo (L.), at my own risk.

merum sal (L.), pure salt, genuine Attic wit.

merveilleux, fem. **merveilleuse** (Fr.), marvellous : a fantastic extremist in fashion in France during the Directorate, the women aping classical modes.

mésalliance (Fr.), marriage with one of lower station.

mesquin, fem. **mesquine** (Fr.), mean ; **mesquinerie**, meanness.

meum et tuum (L.), mine and thine.

mignon, fem. **mignonne** (Fr.), small and dainty : darling.

mirabile dictu (L.), wonderful to tell ; **mirabile visu**, wonderful to see.

mirabilia (L.), wonders.

mise en scène (Fr.), scenic presentation, mounting.

modus (L.), manner, mode ; **modus operandi**, mode of operation ; **modus vivendi**, a way or mode of living : an arrangement or compromise by means of which those who differ may get on together for a time.

Moguntiacum (L.), Mainz.

mole ruit sua (L.), falls by its own weight.—Horace, *Od.*, III. iv. 65.

monstrum horrendum, informe, ingens (L.), a frightful monster, ill-shapen, huge.—Virgil, *Aen.*, III. 658.

morbleu (Fr., for *mort dieu*), 'sdeath.

morceau (Fr.), a morsel : fragment : piece of music.

more (L.), in the manner ; **more Hibernico**, after the Irish fashion ; **more majorum**, after the manner of our ancestors ; **more suo**, in his own way.

morituri te salutamus. See **ave**.

moto perpetuo (It.), perpetual motion : a piece of music that goes swiftly without stop from beginning to end.

motu proprio (L.), of his own accord.

muet comme un poisson (Fr.), dumb as a fish.

multum in parvo (L.), much in little ; **multum non multa**, much, not many things.

mutatis mutandis (L.), with necessary changes.

mutato nomine (L.), the name being changed.

mutuus consensus (L.), mutual consent.

natale solum (L.), native soil.

natura abhorret vacuum (L.), nature abhors a vacuum.

naturam expellas furca, tamen usque recurret (L.), though you drive out nature with a pitchfork, yet will she always return.—Horace, *Epist.*, I. x. 24.

natura naturans (L.), creative nature; **natura naturata**, created nature; **natura non facit saltus** (or **saltum**), nature does not make leaps (or a leap).

naviget Anticyram (L.), let him sail to Anticyra [where hellebore could be had, to cure madness].—Horace, *Sat.*, II. iii. 166.

Neapolis (L. from Gr.), Naples.

nec cupias, nec metuas (L.), neither desire nor fear.

nec deus intersit nisi dignus vindice nodus inciderit (L.), let not a god intervene unless a knot occur worthy of the untier.—Horace, *A. P.*, 191-2.

ne cede malis (L.), yield not to misfortune.—Virgil, *Aen.*, VI. 95.

nécessaire (Fr.), a dressing-case, work-box.

necessitas non habet legem (L.), necessity has no law.

nec pluribus impar (L.), no unequal match for several (suns).—Louis XIV's motto.

nec scire fas est omnia (L.), it is not permitted to know all things.—Horace, *Od.*, IV. iv. 22.

née (Fr.), born (fem.)—used in stating a woman's maiden name.

ne exeat (L.), let him not depart.

negatur (L.), it is denied.

nemine contradicente (L.; often **nem. con.**), without opposition: no one speaking in opposition; **nemine dissentiente**, no one dissenting.

nemo me impune lacessit (L.), no one provokes me with impunity—the motto of the kings of Scotland and of the Order of the Thistle; **nemo repente fuit turpissimus**, no one ever became utterly bad all at once.—Juvenal, II. 83.

ne obliviscaris (L.), do not forget.

ne plus ultra (L.), nothing further: the uttermost point or extreme perfection of anything.

neque semper arcum tendit Apollo (L.), Apollo does not always bend his bow.—Horace, *Od.*, II. x. 19-20.

ne quid nimis (L.), [let there be] nothing in excess.

nescis, mi fili, quantilla prudentia mundus regatur (L.), you know not, my son, with what a small stock of wisdom the world is governed.—Attributed to Oxenstierna and others.

nescit vox missa reverti (L.), a word published cannot be recalled.—Horace, *A. P.*, 390.

n'est-ce pas? (Fr.), is it not so?

ne sutor ultra crepidam (L.). See **sutor**.

ne temere (L.), not rashly—a papal decree of 1907 denying recognition to the marriage of a Catholic unless contracted before a priest.

niaiserie (Fr.), simplicity, foolishness.

nicht wahr? (Ger.), is it not true? isn't that so?

nihil ad rem (L.), nothing to the point; **nihil obstat**, nothing hinders—a book censor's form of permission to print; **nihil tetigit quod non ornavit**. See **nullum**.

nil actum credens dum quid superesset agendum (L.), thinking nothing done while anything was yet to do.—Lucan, II., 657; **nil admirari**, to wonder at nothing.—Horace, *Epist*, I. vi. 1; **nil desperandum**, nothing is to be despaired of.—Horace, *Od.*, I. vii. 27.

n'importe (Fr.), no matter.

nisi Dominus frustra (L.), except the Lord [keep the city, the watchman waketh but] in vain.—Ps. 127—the motto of Edinburgh.

nisi prius (L.), unless previously—a name [from the first words of the writ] given to the jury sittings in civil cases.

nitor in adversum (L.), I strive in opposition.—Ovid, *M.*, II. 72.

noblesse oblige (Fr.), rank imposes obligations.

nolens volens (L.), willy-nilly.

nolle prosequi (L.), to be unwilling to prosecute.

nolo episcopari (L.), I do not wish to be a bishop.

nom de guerre (Fr.), an assumed name: travelling title: pseudonym (**nom de plume** is not French).

nomen nudum (L.), in biology, a mere name published without a description.

non amo te, Sabidi, nec possum dicere quare (L.), I do not love thee, Sabidius, nor can I tell why.—Martial, I. xxxiii.

non compos mentis (L.), not of sound mind.

non est inventus (L.), he has not been found (he has absconded).

non licet (L.), it is not allowed.

non liquet (L.), it is not clear.

non mi ricordo (It.), I don't remember.

non multa, sed multum (L.), not many, but much.

non nobis, Domine (L.), not unto us, O Lord.—Psalm 115.

non obstante (L.), not hindering: notwithstanding.

non olet pecunia (L.), the money does not stink.—Attributed to Vespasian, of revenue from an unsavoury source.

non omnia possumus omnes (L.), we cannot all do everything.—Virgil, *Ecl.*, viii. 63.

non omnis moriar (L.), I shall not wholly die.—Horace, *Od.*, III. xxx. 6.

non placet (L.), it does not please—a negative vote.

non possumus (L.), we cannot—a form of refusal.

non tali auxilio nec defensoribus istis tempus eget (L.), not for such aid nor for these defenders does the time call.—Virgil, *Aen.*, II. 521.

nonumque prematur in annum (L.), and let it be kept unpublished till the ninth year.—Horace, *A. P.*, 388.

non ut edam vivo sed ut vivam edo (L.), I do not live to eat, but eat to live.—Quintilian.

nosce teipsum (L.), know thyself. See **gnōthi seauton**.

nota bene (L.), mark well, take notice—often **N.B.**

Notre-Dame (Fr.), Our Lady.

nous avons changé tout cela (Fr.), we have changed all that.—Molière, *Le Médecin malgré lui*, II. iv.

nous verrons (ce que nous verrons) (Fr.), we shall see (what we shall see).

nouveau riche (*pl.* **nouveaux riches**) (Fr.), one who has but lately acquired wealth, an upstart.

novus homo (L.), a new man: among the Romans a magistrate whose ancestors had never held office.

nulla dies sine linea (L.), no day without a line, without painting (or writing) a little.

nulla nuova, buona nuova (It.), no news is good news.

nulli secundus (L.), second to none.

nullius addictus (or adductus) jurare in verba magistri (L.), bound to swear to the words of no master, to follow no one blindly or slavishly.—Horace, *Epist.*, I. i. 14.

nullum (scil. scribendi genus) quod tetigit non ornavit (L.), he touched no form of literature without adorning it. From Johnson's epitaph on Goldsmith.

nunc est bibendum (L.), now is time to drink.—Horace, *Od.*, I. xxxvii. 1.

obiit (L.), died; **obiit sine prole**, died without issue.

obiter (L.), by the way, cursorily; **obiter dictum** (*pl.* **obiter dicta**), something said by the way, a cursory remark.

obscurum per obscurius (L.), (explaining) the obscure by means of the more obscure.

oderint dum metuant (L.), let them hate so long as they fear.

odi profanum volgus et arceo (L.), I loathe and shun the profane rabble.—Horace, *Od.*, iii. i. 1.

odium theologicum (L.), the hatred of theologians for each other's errors (or persons).

Oenipons (L.), Innsbruck.

œuvres (Fr.), works.

O fortunatos nimium, sua si bona norint, agricolas (L.), Oh too happy farmers, if they but knew their luck.—Virgil, *Georg.*, II. 458.

ohe! jam satis (L.), hold! enough now (a common phrase).

ohne hast, ohne rast (Ger.), without haste, without rest.—Goethe's motto.

olim meminisse juvabit. See **forsan**.

Olisipo, Ulyssipo, Ulyssipolis (L.), Lisbon.

omne ignotum pro magnifico (L.), everything

unknown (is taken to be) magnificent.—Tacitus, *Agric.*, 30.

omnem crede diem tibi diluxisse supremum (L.), believe each day to have dawned as your last. —Horace, *Epist.*, I. iv. 13.

omne tulit punctum qui miscuit utile dulci (L.), he has carried every vote who has combined the useful with the pleasing.—Horace, *A. P.*, 343.

omne vivum ex ovo (L.), every living thing comes from an egg.—Attributed to Harvey.

omnia mea mecum porto (L.), all I have I carry with me.

omnia mutantur. See **tempore.**

omnia vincit amor, et nos cedamus amori (L.), love overcomes all things, let us too yield to love. —Virgil, *Ecl.*, X. 69.

on dit (Fr.), they say.

onus probandi (L.), the burden of proving.

opere citato (L.), in the work cited.

opus (L.), work; **opus latericium**, brickwork; **opus musivum**, mosaic work; **opus operantis** the effect of a sacrament ascribed (as by Protestants) to the spiritual disposition of the recipient; **opus operatum**, due celebration of a sacrament involving grace flowing from the sacramental act (the R.C. view); **opus reticulatum**, reticulated work.

ora et labora (L.), pray and work; **ora pro nobis**, pray for us.

orbis terrarum (L.), the circle of lands, the whole world.

ore rotundo (L.), with round, full voice (mouth).— Horace, *A. P.*, 323.

os (L.), bone.

O sancta simplicitas! (L.), O holy simplicity!

os homini sublime dedit caelumque tueri jussit et erectos ad sidera tollere vultus (L.), he gave man an up-turned face and bade contemplate the heavens and raise looks to the stars. Ovid., *M.*, I. 85.

O si sic omnia! (L.), Oh that he had done all things thus, or Oh that all things were thus!

ossia (It.), or (giving an alternative in music).

O tempora! O mores! (L.), O the times! O the manners!

otia dant vitia (L.), idleness begets vice.

otium cum dignitate (L.), dignified leisure.

ouk esti? (Gr.), is it not so?

ouvert, fem. **ouverte** (Fr.), open.

ouvrage (Fr.), a work.

ouvrier, fem. **ouvrière** (Fr.), operative, worker.

ovem lupo committere (L.), to entrust the sheep to the wolf.

Oxonia (L.), Oxford; **Oxoniensis**, Oxonian.

pace tua (L.), by your leave.

pactum illicitum (L.), an illegal compact; **pactum nudum**, a pact without consideration.

pallida Mors aequo pulsat pede pauperum tabernas regumque turres (L.), pale Death knocks with impartial foot at poor men's huts and kings' castles.—Horace, *Od.*, I. iv. 13-14.

palmam qui meruit ferat (L.), let him who has won the palm wear it.

panem et circenses (L.), bread and (Roman) circus-games—food and amusements at public expense.—Juvenal, X. 81.

panta men kathara tois katharois (Gr.), all things are pure to the pure.—Titus, I. 15.

panta rhei (Gr.), all things are in a flux (a saying of Heraclitus).

panzer (Ger.), armour.

parcere subjectis et debellare superbos (L.), to spare the vanquished and put down the proud.— Virgil, *Aen.*, VI. 854.

par excellence (Fr.), eminently, by way of ideal.

par exemple (Fr.), for example.

pari passu (L.), with equal pace: together.

par nobile fratrum (L.), a noble pair of brothers.— Horace, *Sat.*, II. iii. 243.

particeps criminis (L.), one who, though not present, helps in any way the commission of a crime, or who after the deed assists or hides those who did it.

partie carrée (Fr.), a party consisting of two men and two women.

partim (L.), in part.

parti pris (Fr.), bias, preconceived opinion.

parturiunt montes, nascetur ridiculus mus (L.), the mountains are in travail, an absurd mouse will be born.—Horace, *A. P.*, 139.

parva componere magnis. See **si parva.**

pas (Fr.), step: action: precedence; **pas d'armes**, a joust, a tilt, or a tourney; **pas de deux**, a dance of two persons; **pas redoublé**, a quick-step.

pas op (S.Afr.), look out.

passé, fem. **passée** (Fr.), past one's best, faded: nearly out of date.

passim (L.), everywhere: throughout: dispersedly.

pâté (Fr.), pie: pastry; **pâté de foie gras**, pasty of fat goose liver.

pater patriae (L.), the father of his country.

pathēmata mathēmata (Gr.), sufferings [are] lessons.

pâtisserie (Fr.), a pasty shop: pastry.

patres conscripti (L.), the conscript fathers, those enrolled as Roman senators.

patria potestas (L.), the authority of a Roman father over his children.

paulo majora canamus (L.), let us sing of rather greater things.—Virgil, *Ecl.*, IV. 1.

pavé (Fr.), pavement: a setting of jewellery with the stones close together, covering the metal.

pax vobiscum (L.), peace be with you.

paysage (Fr.), a landscape: a landscape painting.

peccavi (L.), I have sinned.

peine forte et dure (Fr.), strong and severe punishment, a kind of judicial torture.

pendente lite (L.), during the process of litigation.

pensée (Fr.), thought.

pensieroso (It.), melancholy: thoughtful.

pensionnat (Fr.), boarding-school.

per (L.), through, by means of, according to; **per annum (diem, mensem)**, yearly (daily, monthly); **per ardua ad astra**, by steep and toilsome ways to the stars—Air Force motto; **per capita**, (counting) by heads: all sharing alike; **per contra**, on the contrary: as a set-off; **per saltum**, at a single leap: all at once; **per se**, by himself, &c.: essentially: in itself.

pereant qui ante nos nostra dixerunt (L.), perish those who have said our good things before us.— Attributed to Donatus and to Augustine.

pereunt et imputantur (L.), [the moments, hours] pass away and are reckoned to our account.

per fas et nefas (L.), through right and wrong.

perfervidum ingenium (L.). See **Scotorum.**

perpetuum mobile (L.), perpetual motion (lit. movable).

persona grata (L.), a person who is acceptable to those to whom he is sent.

per stirpes (L.), by stocks: in inheritance, the children of each descendant dividing only the share that would have been their parent's (distinguished from *per capita*).

per varios casus, per tot discrimina rerum (L.), through various chances, through so many crises of fortune.—Virgil, *Aen.*, I. 204.

petit bourgeois (Fr.), a member of the lower middle class; **petit déjeuner**, breakfast; **petit-maître**, a fop; **petit pain**, a roll.

pia desideria (L.), pious regrets; **pia fraus**, pious fraud.

pièce de résistance (Fr.), the substantial course at dinner, the joint: the best item.

pied-à-terre (Fr.), temporary lodging.

pinakothek (Ger., from Gr.), picture-gallery.

pinxit (L.), painted [this].

pis aller (Fr.), the last or worst shift, a makeshift.

più (It.), more; **più mosso**, quicker.

plaudite (L.), applaud: clap your hands.

pleno jure (L.), with full authority.

pleon hēmisy pantos (Gr.), the half is more than the whole.—Hesiod, *Erga*, 40.

plus ça change, plus c'est la même chose (Fr.), the more that changes the more it is the same thing (no superficial or apparent change alters its essential nature).

pocas palabras (Sp.), few words.

poco a poco (It.), little by little.

poeta nascitur, non fit (L.), the poet is born, not made.

poilu (Fr.), a French private soldier.

point d'appui (Fr.), point of support, prop, fulcrum.

poisson d'avril (Fr.), an April fool (lit. fish).

pollice verso (L.), with thumb turned down—the signal made by the spectators for the death of a Roman gladiator.

pollōn onomatōn mia morphē (Gr.), one shape of many names.—Aeschylus, *Prometheus*, 210.

polyphloisboio thalassēs (Gr.), of the much-sounding sea.—Homer, *Il.*, I. 34; also Hesiod, *Erga*, 648.

pomme de terre (Fr.), potato.

pons asinorum (L.), the asses' bridge: the test of a beginner: the fifth proposition of Euclid, Book I.

populus vult decipi, ergo decipiatur (L.), the public wishes to be fooled, therefore let it be fooled.—Ascribed to Cardinal Caraffa.

poscimur (L.), we are called on [to sing, &c.].

post equitem sedet atra cura (L.), behind the horseman sits black care.—Horace, *Odes*, III. i. 40.

poste restante (Fr.), a department in a post-office in which letters are kept to be called for.

post hoc, ergo propter hoc (L.), after this, therefore because of this (a fallacious reasoning); **post meridiem**, after noon; **post mortem**, after death; **post obitum**, after death.

pour encourager les autres (Fr.), to encourage the others (Voltaire, *Candide*, on the shooting of Admiral Byng); **pour faire rire**, to raise a laugh; **pour passer le temps**, to pass away the time; **pour prendre congé, or P.P.C.,** to take leave.

praefervidum. See Scotorum.

précieuse (Fr.), a woman affecting a fastidious over-refinement.

pretzel (Ger.), a kind of salted biscuit.

preux chevalier (Fr.), a brave knight.

prima facie (L.), on the first view: at first sight.

primeur (Fr.), novelty: early fruit.

primo (L.), in the first place.

primus inter pares (L.), first among equals.

principiis obsta (L.), resist the first beginnings.—Ovid, *R. A.*, 91. Cf. **venienti,** &c.

prix fixe (Fr.), fixed price.

pro aris et focis (L.), for altars and firesides: for faith and home.

probatum est (L.), it has been proved.

probitas laudatur et alget (L.), honesty is commended and left out in the cold.—Juvenal, I. 74.

pro bono publico (L.), for the public good.

procès-verbal (Fr.), a written statement.

prochain (-ein) ami (-y) (Fr.), next friend, one who undertakes to assist a minor in prosecuting his or her rights.

procureur (Fr.), a procurator; **procureur général,** the public prosecutor-in-chief.

pro forma (L.), as a matter of form: of an account, &c., made out to show the market price of specified goods.

pro hac vice (L.), for this turn or occasion.

proh pudor! (L.), oh, for shame!

pro indiviso (L.), as undivided: applied in law to rights which two or more persons hold in common.

projet de loi (Fr.), a legislative bill.

pro memoria (L.), for a memorial.

pro patria (L.), for one's country.

pro rata (L.), in proportion.

pro re nata (L.), for a special emergency, according to the circumstances.

pro tanto (L.), for so much.

pro tempore (L.), for the time being.

proxime accessit (*pl.* **accesserunt**) (L.), came next [to the prizeman].

pulvis et umbra sumus (L.), we are dust and a shadow.—Horace, *Od.*, IV. vii. 16.

Punica fides (L.), Punic faith—i.e. treachery.

purpureus pannus (L.), a purple patch.—From Horace, *A. P.*, 15-16.

pur sang (Fr.), pure-blood: thoroughbred: total.

quaere (L.), inquire.

quaeritur (L.), the question is asked.

qualis ab incepto (L.), as from the beginning.

quamdiu se bene gesserit (L.), during good behaviour.

quand même (Fr.), nevertheless, whatever the consequences may be.

quantum mutatus ab illo (L.), how changed from that (Hector who came back clad in Achilles's spoils).—Virgil, *Aen.*, II. 274.

quantum sufficit (L.), a sufficient quantity.

que diable allait-il faire sans cette galère? (Fr.), what the devil was he doing in that galley?—Molière, *Les Fourberies de Scapin*, II. vii.

quem di diligunt adolescens moritur (L.), whom the gods love dies young.—Plautus's translation of **hon hoi theoi.**

quem Iupiter vult perdere dementat prius, or quem deus perdere vult, prius dementat (L.), whom Jupiter (a god) wishes to destroy, he first makes mad.

que sais-je (sçai-je)? (Fr.), what do I know?—Montaigne's motto.

que voulez-vous? (Fr.), what would you?

quicquid agunt homines . . . nostri est farrago libelli (L.), whatever men do is the medley of our little book.—Juvenal, I. 85-86.

quicquid delirant reges plectuntur Achivi (L.), whatever madness possesses the chiefs, it is (the common soldiers or people of) the Achaeans who suffer.—Horace, *Epist.*, I. ii. 14.

quicunque vult salvus esse (L.), whosoever will be saved (the beginning of the Athanasian creed).

quid hoc sibi vult? (L.), what does this mean?

quid pro quo (L.), something given or taken as equivalent to another.

quid rides? mutato nomine de te fabula narratur (L.), why do you laugh? with change of name the story is about you.—Horace, *Sat.*, I. i. 69-70.

quién sabe? (Sp.), who knows?

quieta non movere (L.), not to move things that are at rest—to let sleeping dogs lie.

qui facit per alium facit per se (L.), he who does something through another does it through himself.

quis custodiet ipsos custodes? (L.), who will guard the guards themselves?—Juvenal, VI. 347-8.

quis desiderio sit pudor aut modus tam cari capitis? (L.), what shame or stint should there be in mourning for one so dear?—Horace, *Od.*, I. xxiv. 1.

qui s'excuse s'accuse (Fr.), he who excuses himself accuses himself.

quis separabit? (L.), who shall separate [us]?

qui tacet consentit (L.), who keeps silence consents.

qui va là? (Fr.), who goes there?

quoad (L.), as far as: to this extent; **quoad hoc,** as far as this; **quoad omnia,** in respect of all things; **quoad sacra,** as far as concerns sacred matters, as a parish disjoined for ecclesiastical purposes only.

quod avertat Deus (L.), which may God avert.

quod bonum, felix, faustumque sit (L.), may it be right, happy, and of good omen.

quod erat demonstrandum (L.), or **Q.E.D.,** which was to be proved or demonstrated; **quod erat faciendum,** or **Q.E.F.,** which was to be done.

quod ubique, quod semper, quod ab omnibus (L.), what everywhere, what always, what by all (has been believed).—St Vincent of Lérins's definition of orthodoxy.

quod vide (L.), which see.

quo jure? (L.), by what right?

quorum pars magna fui (L.), in which I bore a great share.—Virgil, *Aen.*, II. 6.

quot homines, tot sententiae (L.), as many men, so many minds or opinions.—Terence, *Phormio*, II. iv. 14 (or I. 454).

quousque tandem abutere, Catilina, patientia nostra? (L.), how far, O Catiline, will you abuse our patience?—Cicero, *In Catilinam.*

quo vadis? (L.), whither goest thou?

raison d'être (Fr.), reason for existence.

raisonné (Fr.), logically set out, systematically arranged, and (usu.) provided with notes.

rara avis (L.), a rare bird, a prodigy.—Juvenal, VI. 165.

rari nantes in gurgite vasto (L.), here and there some swimming in a vast whirlpool.—Virgil, *Aen.* I. 118.

realpolitik (Ger.), practical politics.

reçu (Fr.), received : receipt.

reculer pour mieux sauter (Fr.), to draw back to take a better leap.

redivivus (L.), resuscitated : come to life again.

redolet lucerna (L.), it smells of the lamp.

reductio ad absurdum (L.), reduction to absurdity : the proof of a proposition by proving the falsity of its contradictory.

re galantuomo (It.), the honest king—king and gentleman [said of Victor Emmanuel II].

Regiomontium (L.), Königsberg.

re infecta (L.), without finishing the business.

relâche (Fr.), intermission : no performance : relaxation.

religio loci (L.), the religious spirit of the place.

rem acu tetigisti (L.), you have touched the thing with a needle, hit it exactly.—Proverbial expression used by Plautus.

remis velisque (L.), with oars and sails ; also **remis ventisque**, with oars and winds (Virgil, &c.) : with all vigour.

renommée (Fr.), renown.

répondez s'il vous plaît, or **R.S.V.P.** (Fr.), please answer [this invitation].

requiescat in pace, or **R.I.P.** (L.), may he [or she] rest in peace.

res angusta domi (L.), straitened circumstances at home.—Juvenal, III. 165.

res gestae (L.), exploits.

res judicata (L.), a case or suit already decided.

respice finem (L.), look to the end.—Playfully perverted into **respice funem**, beware of the (hangman's) rope.

resurgam (L.), I shall rise again.

revanche (Fr.), revenge : a return match : retaliation.

revenons à nos moutons (Fr.), let us return to our sheep, i.e. our subject.—From the mediaeval farce, *L'Avocat Pathelin*.

rêveur, fem. **rêveuse** (Fr.), a day-dreamer.

rhododaktylos Ēōs (Gr.), rosy-fingered Dawn.—Homer.

risum teneatis, amici? (L.) could you keep from laughing, friends?—Horace, *A. P.*, 5.

Roma locuta, causa finita (L.), Rome has spoken, the cause is ended.

Rotomagus (L.), Rouen.

ruat caelum. See **fiat justitia.**

rudis indigestaque moles (L.), a rude and shapeless mass.—Ovid., *M.*, I. 7.

ruit. See **mole.**

ruse contre ruse (Fr.), cunning against cunning, diamond cut diamond ; **ruse de guerre**, a stratagem of war.

rus in urbe (L.), the country in town.—Martial, XII. 57. 21.

rusticus expectat dum defluat amnis (L.), waits like the yokel for the river to run by.—Horace, *Epist.*, I. ii. 42.

salaam aleikum (Ar.), peace be upon you.

sal Atticum (L.), Attic salt. See **Attic** in Dict.

salle (Fr.), hall.

salus populi suprema lex esto (L.), let the welfare of the people be the final law.

salvo jure (L.), saving the right (the right being safe).

sans-appel (Fr.), one from whose decision there is no appeal.

sans cérémonie (Fr.), without ceremony.

sans gêne (Fr.), at ease, without constraint.

sans nombre (Fr. ; *her.*), repeated often, and covering the field.

sans peur et sans reproche (Fr.), without fear and without reproach.

sans phrase (Fr.), without phrases (of courtesy), without more ado.

sans souci (Fr.), without care.

sapere aude (L.), dare to be wise.—Horace, *Epist.*, I. ii. 40.

sartor resartus (L.), the tailor retailored.

Sarum (L.), Salisbury.

satis verborum (L.), enough of words.

sat sapienti (L.), enough for the wise, a nod to the wise.

sauce hollandaise (Fr.), a Dutch sauce made of the yolk of an egg with melted butter and lemon juice.

sauter à pieds joints (Fr.), to take a standing jump.

sauve qui peut (Fr.), save himself who can : every man for himself.

schutzstaffel (Ger.), or **S.S.**, Hitler's bodyguard.

Scotorum praefervida ingenia (L.), the ardent tempers of the Scots.—Buchanan, *Hist. Scot.*, XVI. li.

sculpsit (L.), sculptured (this).

secundum artem (L.), skilfully : professionally ; **secundum ordinem**, in order ; **secundum quid**, in some respects only.

se defendendo (L.), in self defence.

sedes impedita (L.), a papal or episcopal see where there is a partial cessation by the incumbent of his episcopal duties ; **sedes vacans**, also **sede vacante** (ablative), a term of canon law to designate a papal or episcopal see when vacant.

segue (It.), follows.

selon les règles (Fr.), according to the rules.

semel insanivimus omnes (L.), we have all played the fool once.—Mantuanus, *Ecl.*, i. 217.

semper idem (L.), always the same ; **semper paratus**, always ready.

senatus populusque Romanus (L.), the Roman senate and people.

se non è vero, è ben trovato (It.), if it is not true, it is cleverly invented.

sero venientibus ossa (L.), the bones to the latecomers.

servus servorum Dei (L.), a servant of the servants of God (a title adopted by the popes).

sic (L.), so, thus—printed within brackets in quoted matter to show that the original is being faithfully reproduced even though incorrect or apparently so.

sic itur ad astra (L.), such is the way to the stars.—Virgil, *Aen.*, IX. 641.

sic passim (L.), so throughout.

sic transit gloria mundi (L.), so passes away earthly glory.

sic volo. See **hoc volo.**

sic vos non vobis (L.), thus do you, not for yourselves.—Ascribed to Virgil.

si jeunesse savait, si vieillesse pouvait (Fr.), if youth but knew, if age but could.

s'il vous plaît (Fr.), if you please.

similia similibus curantur (L.), likes are cured by likes—a hair of the dog that bit one.

si monumentum requiris, circumspice (L.), if you seek (his) monument, look round you (inscription for the architect Christopher Wren's tomb in St Paul's).

simpatico (It.), sympathetic in the sense of congenial.

simplex munditiis (L.), elegant in simplicity.—Horace, *Od.*, I. v. 5.

simpliciter (L.), simply : naturally : unconditionally.

sine Cerere et Libero friget Venus (L.), without Ceres and Bacchus (food and drink) Venus (love) is cold.—Terence, *Eun.*, IV. v. 6.

sine die (L.), without a day (appointed)—of a meeting adjourned for an indefinite period.

sine dubio (L.), without doubt.

sine ira et studio (L.), without ill-will and without favour.

sine prole (L.), without issue.

sine qua non (L.), without which not : an indispensable condition.

sint ut sunt aut non sint (L.), let them be as they are or not at all.

si parla Italiano (It.), Italian spoken.

si parva licet componere magnis (L. ; Virgil, *Georg.*, IV. 176) ; **si componere magnis parva mihi fas est** (Ovid, *M.*, V. 416-7), if it is permissible to compare small things to great.

siste, viator (L.), stop, traveller.

sittlichkeit (Ger.), morals, morality : that which is becoming or suitable.

si vis pacem, para bellum (L.), if you would have peace, be ready for war.

skias onar anthrōpos (Gr.), man is a dream of a shadow.—Pind., *Pyth.*, VIII. 95.

soigné, fem. **soignée** (Fr.), well groomed: cared for.

solitudinem faciunt, pacem appellant (L.), they make a desert and call it peace.—Tacitus, *Agricola*, 30.

solventur risu tabulae: tu missus abibis (L.), the bills will be dismissed with laughter—you will be laughed out of court.—Horace, *Sat.*, II. i. 86.

solvitur ambulando (L.), (the problem of reality of motion) is solved by walking—by practical experiment.

s'orienter (Fr.), to take one's bearings.

spero meliora (L.), I hope for better things.

splendide mendax (L.), splendidly false, nobly lying.—Horace, *Od.*, III. xi. 35.

spolia opima (L.), the richest booty—spoil taken in battle by a leader from a leader.

sponte sua (L.), of one's own accord.

spretaeque injuria formae (L.), (and) the insult of beauty slighted.—Virgil, *Aen.*, I. 27.

stans pede in uno (L.), standing on one foot.— Horace, *Sat.*, I. iv. 10.

stat pro ratione voluntas (L.). See **hoc volo.**

status quo (L.), the state in which: the existing condition.

stet fortuna domus (L.), may the fortune of the house last long.

sturmabteilung (Ger.), storm troops.

sturm und drang (Ger.), storm and stress.

sua si bona. See **o fortunatos.**

suaviter in modo, fortiter in re (L.), gentle in manner, resolute in deed.

sub divo (L.), under the sky: in the open air. Also **sub Jove,** under Jupiter (the sky-god).

sub judice (L.), under consideration.

sub poena (L.), under a penalty.

sub rosa (L.), under the rose: privately.

sub specie (L.), under the appearance, or aspect (of); **sub specie aeternitatis,** (seen) under the aspect of eternity, and hence as it essentially is.— Spinoza.

sub voce (L.), under that head.

succès d'estime (Fr.), a success of esteem or approval (if not of profit); **succès fou,** success with wild enthusiasm.

suggestio falsi. See **suppressio veri.**

sui generis (L.), of its own kind, the only one of its kind.

sui juris (L.), having full legal capacity to act: (in Roman law) having the rights of a freeman.

suivez (Fr.), follow (the solo part, in accompanying).

summum bonum (L.), the chief good.

sunt lacrimae rerum (L.), there are tears for things (unhappy).—Virgil, *Aen.*, I. 462.

suppressio veri suggestio falsi (L.), suppression of truth is suggestion of the false.

sur le tapis (Fr.), on the carpet (tablecover): under discussion, subject of talk.

sursum corda (L.), lift up your hearts.

surtout, pas de zèle (Fr.), above all, no zeal.

sutor ne supra crepidam judicaret (L.), let not the cobbler criticise (a work of art) above the sandal. See **ultracrepidate** in Dict.

suum cuique (L.), to each his own.

tabula rasa (L.), a smoothed or blank tablet.

tacent, satis laudant (L.), their silence is praise enough.—Terence, *Eun.*, III. ii. 23.

taedium vitae (L.), weariness of life.

tantae molis erat Romanam condere gentem (L.), a task of such difficulty was it to found the Roman race.—Virgil, *Aen.*, I. 33.

tantaene animis caelestibus irae? (L.), are there such violent passions in celestial minds?—Virgil, *Aen.*, I. 11.

tanti (L.), worth while.

tant mieux (Fr.), so much the better.

tanto (It.), so much.

tanto uberior (L.), so much the richer.

tant pis (Fr.), so much the worse.

tempora (orig. **omnia) mutantur, nos et mutamur in illis** (L.), the times (all things) are changed, and we with them.

tempore (L.), in the time of.

tempus edax rerum (L.), time consumer of things. —Ovid, *M.*, XV. 234.

tempus fugit (L.), time flies.

terminus ad quem (L.), the limit to which: destination; **terminus a quo,** the limit from which: starting-point.

terrae filius (L.), a son of the soil: a person of humble birth.

terra incognita (L.), an unknown country.

tertium quid (L.), a third something.

tertius (L.), third; **tertius gaudens,** or **gaudet** (L.), the third person (who) takes advantage from a dispute between others.

teste (L.), witness (so-and-so).

tête-de-pont (Fr.), bridgehead.

textus receptus (L.), the received text (of the Greek New Testament).

thalassa, thalassa! or **thalatta, thalatta!** (Gr.), the sea, the sea! [the exulting cry of Xenophon's soldiers on catching sight of the sea].—Xenophon, *Anabasis*.

thé dansant (Fr.), tea with dancing.

tiers état (Fr.), the third estate, or commons, formerly in France.

timeo Danaos et dona ferentes (L.), I fear the Greeks, even when bringing gifts.—Virgil, *Aen.*, II. 49.

tirage à part (Fr.), an offprint, or article reprinted separately from a periodical—the German *Abdruck*.

tiré à quatre épingles (Fr.), as neat as can be.

toga praetexta (L.), a toga with a deep border of purple, worn by children, magistrates, &c.; **toga virilis,** the garb of manhood.

toison d'or (Fr.), the golden fleece.

to kalon (Fr.), the beautiful.

ton d'apameibomenos prosephē (Gr.), addressed him in reply.—Homer (*passim*).

to prepon (Gr.), the fitting: the becoming or seemly.

Tornacum, or Turnacum (L.), Tournai.

totidem verbis (L.), in just so many words.

toties quoties (L.), as often as.

toto caelo (L.), by the whole heavens: diametrically opposite.

tot siens (S.Afr.), au revoir.

totus, teres, atque rotundus (L.), complete, smooth, and round.—Horace, *Sat.*, II. vii. 86.

toujours perdrix (Fr.), partridge every day—too much of a good thing.

tour de force (Fr.), a feat of strength or skill.

tout au contraire (Fr.), quite the contrary; **tout à fait,** entirely; **tout à vous,** wholly yours; **tout comprendre c'est tout pardonner,** to understand all is to pardon all; **tout court,** quite brief(ly), without preface, simply; **tout de même,** all the same: nevertheless; **tout de suite,** all at once; **tout ensemble,** the whole taken together: the broad or general effect; **tout est perdu fors l'honneur,** all is lost but honour [attrib. to Francis I after Pavia]; **tout le monde,** all the world, everybody; **tout vient (à point) à qui sait attendre,** all things come to him who can wait.

tracasserie (Fr.), turmoil.

traduttore traditore (It.), a translator is a traitor or betrayer:—*pl.* **traduttori traditori.**

Trajectum, or Ultrajectum (L.), Utrecht.

Trecae, or Civitas Tricassina (L.), Troyes.

tre corde (It.), three strings: a direction to piano players to release the soft pedal.

tria juncta in uno (L.), three things in one.

Tridentum (L.), Trent.

troppo (It.), in music, too much: excessively.

tu quoque (L.), thou too: you're another.

uberrima fides (L.), complete faith.

ubi bene, ibi patria (L.), where it goes well with me, there is my fatherland.

ubique (L.), everywhere.

ubi supra (L.), where mentioned above.

ultima ratio regum (L.), the last argument of

kings (war; once inscribed on French cannon); **ultima Thule**, furthest Thule (q.v. in Dict.): the utmost boundary or limit: the back of beyond.—Virgil, *Georg.*, I. 30.

ultimus haeres (L.), in law, the crown or the state, which succeeds to the property of those who die intestate, or without next of kin; **ultimus Romanorum**, last of the Romans.

ultra vires (L.), beyond one's powers.

una corda (It.), one string (soft pedal).

una voce (L.), with one voice.

unberufen (Ger.), unforspoken, without bringing evil—an exclamation to avert ill-luck.

und so weiter (Ger.), or **u.s.w.**, and so forth.

uno animo (L.), with one mind.

urbi et orbi (L.), to the city (Rome) and the world, to everyone.

usque ad nauseam (L.), to the point of disgust.

usus loquendi (L.), current usage of speech.

ut infra (L.), as below.

uti possidetis (L.), lit. as you possess—the principle of letting e.g. belligerents keep what they have acquired.

ut supra (L.), as above.

vade in pace (L.), go in peace.

vae victis (L.), woe to the conquered.

valet de chambre (Fr.), an attendant: a footman; **valet de place**, one who serves as guide, messenger, &c., esp. for strangers.

variae lectiones (L.), various readings.

variorum notae (L.), the notes of various authors.

varium et mutabile semper femina (L.), woman is ever a fickle and changeable thing.—Virgil, *Aen.*, IV. 569.

vaurien (Fr.), a good-for-nothing.

vedi Napoli, e poi muori (It.), see Naples, and die.

veni Creator Spiritus (L.), come, Creator Spirit—the beginning of an early Latin hymn.

venire facias (L.), cause to come: the writ issued to summon a jury.

venienti occurrite morbo (L.), run to meet disease as it comes.—Persius, III. 63.

veni, vidi, vici (L.), I came, I saw, I conquered.—Ascribed to Caesar on his victory over Pharnaces.

ventre à terre (Fr.), belly to the ground: at high speed.

vera incessu patuit dea (L.), the true goddess was revealed by her gait.—Virgil, *Aen.*, I. 405.

verbatim et litteratim (L.), word for word and letter for letter.

verbum sapienti sat est (L.), a word to the wise is enough—often abbrev. *verb. sap.* and *verb. sat.* See dictum.

verdad? (Sp.), is (not) that so?

verein (Ger.), union, association.

veritas odium parit (L.), truth begets hatred.—Terence, *Andria*, I. i. 41.

vestigia . . . nulla retrorsum (L.), no footprints backwards (at the lion's den): sometimes used to mean no going back.—Horace, *Epist.*, I. i. 74-75.

vexata quaestio (L.), a disputed question.

via dolorosa (L.),the Way of Calvary; **Via Lactea**, the Milky Way; **via media**, a middle course; **via trita, via tuta**, beaten path safe path.

vice versa (L.), the order being reversed, terms exchanged.

victrix causa deis placuit, sed victa Catoni (L.), the gods preferred the winning cause, but Cato the losing.—Lucan, I. 128.

vide (L.), see; **vide infra, supra**, see below, above.

videlicet (L.), to wit, namely; usu. shortened to **viz.**

videndum (*pl.* **videnda**) (L.), a thing (things) to be seen.

video meliora proboque, deteriora sequor (L.), I see the better course and approve it, I follow the worse.—Ovid, *M.*, VII. 20.

vi et armis (L.), by force of (lit. and) arms: by main force.

vieux jeu (Fr.; lit. old game or joke), a subject that has lost all novelty.

vigilate et orate (L.), watch and pray.

viresque acquirit eundo (L.), (Fama, hearsay personified) gains strength as she goes.—Virgil, *Aen.*, IV. 175.

Virgilium vidi tantum (L.), I just saw Virgil [and no more].—Ovid, *Trist.*, IV. x. 51.

virginibus puerisque canto (L.), I sing for maidens and boys—for the young person.—Horace, *Od.*, III. i. 4.

virtus post nummos (L.), virtue after money—i.e. money first.—Horace, *Epist.* I. i. 54.

virtute officii (L.L.), by virtue of office.

vis a tergo (L.), compulsion from behind; **vis comica**, comic power; **vis inertiae**, the power of inertia: passive resistance; **vis major**, superior force; **vis mortua**, force of pressure, dead force; **vis viva**, living force, equal to the mass of a moving body multiplied by the square of its velocity.

vita brevis, ars longa (L.), life is short, art is long (see **ho bios**); **vita patris**, or **v.p.**, in the father's lifetime; **vita sine litteris mors est**, life without literature is death.

vivat (L.), viva (It.), **vive** (Fr.), long live.

viva voce (L.), by the living voice: by oral testimony.

vive la bagatelle (quasi-Fr.), long live folly.

vive ut vivas (L.), live that you may live; **vive, valeque**, life and health to you.

vivit post funera virtus (L.), virtue lives beyond the grave.

vixere fortes ante Agamemnona multi (L.), many brave men lived before Agamemnon.—Horace, *Od.* IV. ix. 25-26.

vogue la galère! (Fr.), row the boat: row on: come what may!

voilà (Fr.), behold: there is, or there are; **voilà tout**, that is all.

volente Deo (L.), God willing.

volenti non fit injuria (L.), no wrong is done to one who consents.

völkerwanderung (Ger.), the migration of Germanic and other peoples, chiefly in the 4th to 6th centuries.

volo, non valeo (L.), I am willing, but unable.

volti subito (It.), turn over the leaf quickly—abbrev. **V.S.**

volto sciolto e pensieri stretti (It.), open face, close thoughts.

vous l'avez voulu, George Dandin (Fr.), you would have it so.—Molière, *George Dandin*, end of Act I.

vox audita perit, littera scripta manet (L.), the heard word is lost, the written letter abides; **vox et praeterea nihil**, a voice and nothing more (of a nightingale); **vox populi, vox Dei**, the voice of the people is the voice of God.

vulgo (L.), commonly.

wahrheit und dichtung (Ger.), truth and poetry.

wanderjahre (Ger.), years of journeymanship or wandering.

wein, weib, und gesang (Ger.), wine, woman, and song.

weltanschauung (Ger.), outlook upon the world, world-philosophy.

weltgeist (Ger.), the world-spirit.

weltpolitik (Ger.), world politics: the policy of taking a forceful part in international affairs.

weltschmerz (Ger.), world-sorrow: sympathy with universal misery: thorough-going pessimism.

wer da? (Ger.), who is there?

wiener schnitzel (Ger.), a veal cutlet dressed with breadcrumbs and eggs.

xerafin, xeraphim (Port.), a silver coin of Goa.

Xeres (Sp.), wine of Xeres (Jerez), sherry.

yaboo (Pers.), an Afghan pony.

zabeta (Ar.), a stated tariff.

zamarra, zamarro (Sp.), a shepherd's sheepskin coat.

zeitvertreib (Ger.), a pastime.

zonam perdidit (L.), he has lost his money-belt: he is in needy circumstances; **zonam solvere**, to loose the virgin zone, i.e. marry.

zōon politikon (Gr.), a political animal (said of man), **zugzwang** (Ger.), in chess a blockade position in which any move leads to disaster.

zum beispiel (Ger.), for example—often **z.B.**

PREFIXES AND SUFFIXES

PREFIXES

a- (O.E.) represents: (1) O.E. *an, on,* on, as *a*bed, *a*board, *a*foot, *a*shore, *a*sunder, now-*a*-days, twice-*a*-week, *a*live, *a*mong, *a*bout, *a*-fishing. (2) O.E. *and-,* over against, in reply to, to, as *a*long. See **un-** (2). [Cog. with Goth. *and-,* Ger. *ent-, ant-,* L. *ante-,* Gr. *anti-.*] (3) O.E. *á-,* an intensive prefix to verbs, out, out from, as in *a*rise (from O.E. *árísan,* to rise out of or up); or sig. very, as in *a*ghast. Cf. *a*bide, *a*ccursed, *a*rouse, *a*go. [Cog. with Ger. *er-,* Goth. *us-, ur-*; cf. **or-.**] (4) O.E. *of,* of, from, as in *a*down (*of dúne,* from the height), *a*new, *a*kin, or intens., as *a*thirst. (5) O.E. *ge-, y-,* as *a*ware (*gewær*), *a*fford. See **i-, y-.** (6) *at,* old sign of inf., as *a*do. [Northern, from Norse.]

a- represents L. **ab-, ad-, ex-,** Gr. **an-.**

a-, ab-, abs- (L.) away from, as *a*vert, *ab*sent, *abs*olute, *abs*tract; also *ad*vance, *ad*vantage, *avant* through French. [L. *a, ab, abs* (oldest form *ap*); cog. with Gr. *apo-,* Sans. *apa,* Ger. *ab,* Eng. *of, off.*]

ad- (L.), to, at, as *ad*here, *ad*apt. It appears as **a-, ab-, ac-, ad-, af-, ag-, al-, an-, ap-, ar-, as-, at-,** as in *a*chieve, *ab*breviate, *ac*cede, *ad*mire, *af*fix, *ag*gregate, *al*lot, *an*nex, *ap*prove, *ar*rive, *as*sign, *at*tract. The words *a*chieve, *a*gree, *a*merce, *a*mount, *a*cquit, *a*cquaint, *a*vow, &c., show the same prefix, derived through the medium of Old French. [L. *ad*; cog. with Sans. *adhi,* Goth. and Eng. *at,* Celt. *ar-.*]

after- (O.E.), as *after*growth, *after*math, *after*wards. [O.E. *æfter.*]

al- (Ar.), the—also as **a-, ar-, as-, el-, l-,** as *a*pricot, *arti*choke, *as*sagai, *el*ixir, *l*ute.

all- (O.E.), all, as *al*mighty, *all*-wise. In Early English *al-*=quite is added (1) to past participles, as *al*-brent=quite burnt, *al*-heled=quite concealed; (2) to verbs preceded by *to,* as *al-to-*brenne=to burn up entirely. In Elizabethan and later writers *all-to*=altogether, quite—the original meaning of *to* having been lost sight of. Cf. Milton's 'all-to ruffled,' &c. [O.E. *all, eall.*]

am-. See **en-** (2).

ambi-, amb-, am-, an- (L.), round about, both, as *ambi*dexter, *am*bition, *amp*utate, *an*cipital. [Cog. with Gr. *amphi,* Sans. *abhi,* around.]

amphi- (Gr.), round about, both, as *amphi*theatre, *amph*ibious. [Cog. with L. *ambi-, amb-.*]

an- (O.E.), against, in return, as *an*swer. See **a-** (O.E.) (2), above. [O.E. *and-,* Ger. *ant-,* Goth. *and-.*]

an-, a- (Gr.), not, without, as *an*archy, *a*tom, *am*brosia. [Gr.; cog. with Sans. *an-, a-,* L. *in-,* Eng. *un-,* not.]

an- (Fr. *en-*—L. *in-*), as in *an*oint. See **en-** (2).

an-, as in *an*cestor; see **ante-.**

an-. See **ad-, ambi-.**

ana-, an- (Gr.), up, back, as *ana*lyse, *ana*tomy, *an*eurysm. [Cog. with Goth. *ana,* Eng. *on.*]

ante-, anti-, anci-, an- (L.), before, as *ante*cedent, *anti*cipate, *anci*ent, *an*cestor (for L. *antecessor*). [L. *ante,* old form *anti*; conn. with *anti-*; Fr. *anci-, an-.*]

anti- (Gr.), opposite to, against, as *anti*pathy, *anti*podes; as **ant-,** in *ant*agonist, and **anth-** in *anth*em, *anth*elion. [Gr.; conn. with L. *ante-,* Sans. *anti-,* facing, Ger. *ant-,* Eng. *an-, a-* (2), for *and-.*]

apo- (Gr.), off, from, away, as *apo*stle; as **aph-** in *aph*elion, *aph*aeresis. [Cog. with L. *ab-.*]

arch-, archi-, arche- (Gr.), first, chief, as *arch*bishop, *archi*tect, *arche*type.

auto-, aut- (Gr.), self, as *auto*graph, *auto*biography, *aut*archy.

be- (O.E.), the most fertile of all English prefixes, is the weak form of *by.* The original meaning was *about.* (1) It forms derivative verbs, with the sense of around, on all sides, in all directions, thoroughly, soundly, as *be*daub, *be*smear; (2) it renders intransitive verbs transitive, as *be*speak; (3) it forms transitive verbs from adjectives and nouns, as *be*foul, *be*dim, *be*dew, *be*friend. [O.E. *bi-.*]

bi-, bis-, bin- (L.), twice, double, as *bi*scuit, *bi*ennial, *bin*ocular; as **ba-** in *ba*lance. [L. *bis,* twice, *bíni,* two by two, for *duis, duíni.*]

cata-, cath-, cat- (Gr.), down, downwards, according to, thoroughly, as *cata*ract, *cath*olic, *cate*chism. [Gr. *kata.*]

circum-, circu- (L.), round about, as *circum*scribe, *circu*it. [L. *circum,* acc. of *circus,* a circle.]

cis- (L.), on this side, as *cis*alpine.

com-, con-, co- (L.), together, with, completely, altogether, as *con*nect, *co*here, *col*lect, *cor*rect, *coun*cil. [*com-* is the old form of L. *cum,* with.]

contra-, contro-, contr- (L.), and through Fr., **counter-,** against, as *contra*dict, *contro*vert, *contra*lto, *counter*act. [L. *contrá* (Fr. *contre*).]

de- (L., or Fr.—L.), down, from, away, occurs in words derived either directly from L., as *de*duce; or through Fr. from L., representing either (1) O.Fr. *des-* from L. *dis-,* asunder, as in *de*feat (O.Fr. *desfait*), or (2) Fr. *de-*—L. *dé-,* as *de*compose. This prefix *de-* is privative or reversing in *de*stroy, *de*suetude, *de*form, or intensive in *de*clare, *de*solate, *de*siccate.

demi- (Fr.—L.), half, as *demi*god, *demi*semiquaver. [Fr. *demi-*—L. *dímidium,* half.]

di- (Gr.), double as *di*lemma, *di*syllable, *di*cotyledon. [Gr. *di-* for *dis-,* twice.]

dia- (Gr.), through, as *dia*logue, *dia*meter; **di-** in *di*aeresis, appearing as **de-** in *de*vil. [Gr. *dia,* through.]

dis-, di- (L.; in O.Fr. *des-*), in two, asunder, as *dis*part, *dif*fer, *dis*perse; negative, as *dis*relish; privative, as *dis*lodge. Thus variously **di-, dif-, dis-, des-, de-,** and even **s-,** as in *s*pend. [L. *dis-, dí-.*]

dys- (Gr.), ill, difficult, as *dys*entery, *dys*pepsy. [Cog. with O.E. *tó.*]

e-. See **ex-.**

e- =O.E. *ge-,* in *e*nough. [O.E. *genóh*; Ger. *genug.*]

e-, a purely phonetic addition, of French origin, as in *e*squire, *e*state, *e*schew, *e*special, *e*scutcheon.

ec- or **ex-** (Gr.), out of, from, as *ec*stasy, *ex*odus. [Gr. *ek, ex,* cog. with L. *ex,* out.]

ecto- (Gr.), outside, as *ecto*derm. [Gr. *ekto-.*]

en-, em- (Gr.), in, on, as *en*ergy, *en*demic, *em*phasis. [Gr. *en,* in.]

en-, em- (Fr.—L.), in, into, as *en*list, *em*bark; to make, as *en*large, *en*act, *en*dure, *em*bolden. Also **am-, an-,** as *am*bush, *an*oint. In many words **in-, en-, im-, -em** are interchanged at will. [Fr. *en-*—L. *in.* See **in-** (L.).]

endo- (Gr.), inside, as *endo*gamy. [Gr. *endon.*]

enter- (Fr.), between, among, as *enter*tain. [Fr. *entre*—L. *inter.*]

ento- (Gr.), within, as *ento*blast. [Gr. *entos.*]

epi-, ep-, eph- (Gr.), on, as *epi*taph, *epi*phyte; during, as *eph*emeral. [Gr. *epi*; Sans. *api.*]

er- (Gr.), for Gr. *en-*, in, before, as *er*rhine.

es- (Fr. and Sp.—L.), out, as *es*cape, *es*planade. [O.Fr. or Sp. *es-* —L. *ex-*.]

eso- (Gr.), within, as *eso*teric. [Gr. *esō*.]

eu- (Gr.), well, as *eu*phony, *eu*logy.

ex- or **e-** (L.), from, out of, as *ex*pel, *e*ject, *ef*flux ; with sense of late, former, in *ex*-emperor, *ex*-mayor ; appearing also as **a-, af-, as-, ef-, es-, iss-, s-,** as *a*mend, *af*fray, *as*say, *ef*fect, *es*cape, *es*cheat, *es*say, *is*sue, *s*ample. [L. *ex-*, *ē-* ; O.Fr. *es-*.]

ex- (Gr.). See **ec-.**

exo- (Gr.), outside, as *exo*tic. [Gr. *exō*, outside.]

extra- (L.), on the outside, beyond, as *extra*mural, *extra*ordinary, *extra*vagant ; as **stra-** in *stra*nge. [L. *extrā* for *exterā* (*parte*), abl. fem. of *exter* or *exterus*, comp. from *ex* (L.).]

for- (O.E.), through, thorough, away, so as to be non-existent, or to be destroyed, as *for*swear, *for*bid, *for*ego (better *forgo*). [O.E. *for-* ; Ger. *ver-*, Goth. *fra-*, conn. with *far* and *from*.]

for- (Fr.—L.), as in *for*close, *for*feit. [Fr. *fors*— L. *foris*, lit. out of doors.]

fore- (O.E.), before, as *fore*tell, *fore*bode ; *fore*dated, *fore*said, *fore*castle, *fore*father, *fore*sight. [O.E. *fore* ; Ger. *vor*.]

forth- (O.E.), forth, as *forth*with.

gain- (O.E.), against, as *gain*say. [O.E. *gegn.* See **against** in Dict.]

hemi- (Gr.), half, as *hemi*sphere—shortened to **me-** in *me*grim. [Gr. *hēmi-* ; cog. with L. *sēmi-*, Sans. *sāmi-*.]

hetero- (Gr.), other, as *hetero*doxy. [Gr. *heteros*, other.]

holo- (Gr.), entire, as *holo*graph. [Gr. *holos*, entire.]

homoeo- (Gr.), like, similar, as *homoeo*pathy. [Gr. *homoios*, like.]

homo-, hom- (Gr.), same, as *homo*nym, *homo*logue. [Gr. *homos*, same.]

hyper- (Gr.), over, above, beyond, as *hyper*borean, *hyper*critical. [Gr. *hyper*, over ; cog. with *super* and *over*.]

hypo-, hyph-, hyp- (Gr.), under, as *hypo*tenuse, *hyph*en, *hyp*allage. [Gr. *hypo*, under ; cog. with L. *sub*, Goth. *uf*, Sans. *upa*.]

i-, in *i*gnoble. See **in-** (1), negative.

i-, y-, as in *I*-wis, *y*clept, handi*work*. This prefix appears as **a-** in *a*ware and as **e-** in *e*nough. [O.E. *ge-*, the original collective meaning, as in the cognate L. *con-*, faded out ; it remained in O.E. as sign of the past participle, &c.]

in- (L.), not, as *in*convenience, *in*cautious, *in*firm ; also **en-, i-, il-, im-, in-, ir-,** as *en*emy, *i*gnoble, *il*legal, *im*mortal, *in*firm, *ir*regular. [L. ; cog. with Gr. *an-*, Eng. *un-*.]

in- (L.), in, into, as *in*clude, *in*fuse ; also **il-, im-, ir-,** as *il*lude, *il*lumine, *im*mure, *im*pel, *ir*rigate, *ir*ritate. Sometimes the meaning has faded to a mere intensive, or almost nothing at all. This prefix often alternates with **en-,** and is used with English words as identical with English **in-.**

in- (O.E.), in, on, as *in*born, *in*come, *in*ward, *in*land, *in*sight.

inter- (L.), in the midst of, between, as *inter*val, *intel*lect, *inter*marry. [L. *inter*, a compar. form ; cog. with Eng. *under*, and Sans. *antar*, within.]

intra- (L.), in the inside of, within, as *intra*mural, *intra*venous. [L. *intrā* for *interā*, abl. fem. of *inter*, inward ; cf. **inter-**.]

intro- (L.), into, within, as *intro*duce. [L. *intrō* for *interō*, abl. masc. of *inter* ; cf. **inter-**.]

juxta- (L.), near, as *juxta*position. [L. *jūxtā*, a superl. form, from root of L. *jungĕre*, to join.]

male- (L.), **mal-, mau-** (Fr.), badly, ill, as *male*factor, *male*diction, *male*volent, *mal*content, *mau*gre. [L. *male*, badly.]

meta-, met-, meth- (Gr.), among, with ; after, as *meth*od (lit. way after) ; often implies change, as *meta*morphose, *meto*nymy. For chemical use see

Dict. [Gr. *meta* ; cog. with O.E. *mid*, Goth. *mith*, Ger. *mit*.]

mid- (O.E.), with, as *mid*wife. [O.E. *mid-*, together with.]

mis- (O.E.), wrong, ill, as *mis*behave, *mis*deed, *mis*lead. [O.E. *mis-* ; O.N. *mis-*, Goth. *missa-*, Ger. *miss-* ; cf. **miss** in Dict.]

mis- (Fr.—L.), as in *mis*chief, *mis*alliance, *mis*chance. [O.Fr. *mes-*, from L. *minus*, less.]

mono-, mon- (Gr.), single, as *mono*graph, *mono*cotyledon, *mon*k, and *min*ster. [Gr. *monos*, alone.]

multi-, mult- (L.), many, as in *multi*ply. [L. *multus*, much, many.]

n- (O.E. and L.), no, not, as *n*ever, *n*ull. [O.E. *ne* ; cog. with Goth. *ni*, and L. *ne*, Sans. *na*.]

ne- (Gr.), not, as *ne*penthe. [Gr. *nē-*.]

ne-, neg- (L.), not, as *ne*farious, *neu*ter, *neg*ative, *neg*lect. [L. *ne-, nec-, neg-*.]

non- (L.), not, as *non*sense, *non*age, *non*conductor ; as *um-* in *um*pire. [L. *nōn*—*ne ūnum*, not one.]

ob- (L.), in front of, against, in the way of, as *ob*struct ; in various forms, as *o*mit, *oc*cur, *of*fer, *op*pose, *os*tentation (for *obs-*) : (*bot.*) inverted, as *ob*ovate (ovate but attached at the small end). [L. *ob*.]

off- of- (O.E.), off, from, away, as *of*fal, *off*shoot, *off*set. [Strong form of **of.**]

on- (O.E.), on, as *on*set, *on*looker. [See **on** in Dict.]

or- (O.E.), out, in *or*deal. [O.E. *or-* ; cog. with Du. *oor-*, Ger. *ur-*, Goth. *us-*, away, out of ; see **a-** (3).]

ortho- (Gr.). See Dict.

out- (O.E.), out, beyond, as *out*law, *out*bid, *out*side, *out*cast. [O.E. *ūt*.]

over- (O.E.), over, above, as *over*arch, *over*seer. [O.E. *ofer*.]

pa-, as in *pa*lsy. See **para-.**

palin-, palim- (Gr.), again, as *palin*genesis, *palim*psest. [Gr. *palin*, again.]

pan-, panto- (Gr.), all, as *pan*acea, *pan*theism, *panto*mime.

para-, par- (Gr.), beside, beyond, wrong, as *para*ble, *para*lyse ; for chemical use see Dict. As **pa-** in *pa*lsy, **par-** in *par*ody. [Gr. *para*.]

pen-, pene- (L.), almost, as *pen*insula, *pene*plain. [L. *paene*.]

per- (L.), through, beyond, as *per*mit, *per*egrine ; thoroughly, as *per*fect ; in chemistry indicating the highest degree of combination with oxygen or other element or radical ; also as **par-, pel-, pil-,** as in *par*son, *par*don, *pel*lucid, *pil*grim. In *per*jure, *per*ish, it has a destructive force, equivalent to Eng. **for-.** [Akin to Gr. *para-*, beside, Eng. *for-*, Ger. *ver-*.]

peri- (Gr.), round, as *peri*meter, *peri*phrasis. [Gr. *peri* ; Sans. *pari* ; also allied to Gr. *para*.]

pol-, por- (L.), as *pol*lute, *por*tend ; **por-, pour-, pur-** (Fr.—L.), as *por*trait, *pour*tray, *pur*vey. [A form of *pro-* or *per-*.]

poly- (Gr.), much, many, as *poly*gamy.

post- (L.), after, behind, as *post*date, *post*script, *post*pone.

pre-, prae- (L.), before, as *pre*dict, *pre*fer, *pre*arrange, *prae*tor ; also in *pri*son and *pro*vost. [L. *prae*, akin to L. *prō*.]

preter- (L.), beyond, as *preter*it, *preter*natural, *preter*mit. [L. *praeter*—*prae*, with comp. suffix *-ter*.]

pro- (Gr.), before, as *pro*logue, *pro*gramme, *pro*phet. [Gr. *pro* ; cog. with L. *prō*, Sans. *pra*, Eng. for (prep.).]

pro- (L.), forth, forward, before, instead of, as *pro*ject, *pro*noun, *pro*consul ; also as **por-, pour-, pr-, prof-, pur-,** and as **prod-** in *prod*igal ; in words of Fr. origin, *pro*ceed, *pur*chase, *pur*pose, *pur*sue, *pur*vey. [L. *prō* ; cog. with Gr. *prō*.]

pros- (Gr.), towards, as *pros*elyte, *pros*ody.

proto-, prot- (Gr.), first, as *proto*type, *prot*oxide. [Gr. *prōtos*, first.]

pur-. See **pol-, pro-.**

re-, red-, ren- (L.), back, again, against, reversed, as *re*tract, *re*sound, *re*deem ; frequentative or intensive, as *re*dolent. It appears as **ren-** in *ren*der,

&c.; as **r-** in rally, rampart, ragout; in rebuild, remind, prefixed to English words.

retro- (L.), back, backwards, as retrospect, retrograde; **rear-, rere-** (Fr. arrière—L. ad retrō), rereward. [L. retrō.]

s- for se-, as in sure; for dis-, as in spend; for ex-, as in sample; for sub-, as in sombre.

sam- (O.E.), half, as sand-blind. [O.E. sám-; cf. Gr. hēmi-, L. sēmi-.]

se-, sed- (L.), without, as secure; aside, as seduce, secede, sedition; appearing as s- in sure, sober.

semi- (L.), half, as semicircle. [L. sēmi-; cog. with Gr. hēmi.]

sine- (L.), without, as sinecure.

so-. See sub-.

sovr-, sopr-. See super-.

sub- (L.), also su-, suc-, suf-, sug-, sum-, sup-, sur-, sus- (for subs-); under, from under, after, as subject, suspect, suspire, succeed, suffuse, suggest, summon, support, surrogate, suspend—also (through Fr.) as so- in sojourn. Of Eng. formation, in sublet, sub-kingdom. [L. sub.]

subter- (L.), under, as subterfuge. [L. subter, from sub-, and compar. suffix -ter.]

super- (L.), over, above, beyond, as superstructure, supernatural. [L.; cog. with Sans. upari, Gr. hyper.]

supra- (L.), over, above, as supramundane. [L. suprā, contr. of abl. fem. of superus, above, from super.]

sur- (Fr.), over, as surmount. [Fr., from L. super.]

syn-, sy-, syl-, sym- (Gr.), together, with, as syntax, system, syllable, symbol, symmetry. [Gr. syn, with.]

thorough- (O.E.), through, as thoroughfare. [O.E. thurh, through.]

to- (O.E.), in today, together, toward, heretofore, is the prep. to. [O.E. tó.]

to- (O.E.), asunder, as in to-brake. [O.E. to-; cf. Ger. zer-, Gr. dys-.]

trans-, tra-, tran- (L.), tres-, tre- (Fr. from L.), beyond, across, as transport, traverse, transcend, trespass, and treason. [L. trāns.]

tri- (L. and Gr.), three, threefold, as in triple, treble, triptych.

twi- (O.E.), double, as in twilight. [O.E. twi-, double, twā, two.]

u- (Gr.), no, not, as Utopia. [Gr. ou, not.]

ultra- (L.), beyond, as ultramarine; **outre-** (Fr.) in outrage, utterance. [L. ultrā.]

um-, in umpire. See non-.

un- (O.E.), not, as unhappy, untruth, uncouth. [Cog. with Gr. an- and L. in- (negative).]

un- (O.E.), reversal of action, as unlock, unbind, undo, unwind. [O.E. on-, un-; cf. Du. ont-, Ger. ent-, Goth. and-. See a- (O.E.) (2).]

un-, uni- (L.), one, as unanimous, uniform. [L. ūnus, one.]

under- (O.E.), under, below, as undergrowth, underwood, underprop, undersell. [See under in Dict.]

up- (O.E.), up, as upland, upstart, upright, uphill, upbraid, upset. [O.E. up, upp; Ger. auf.]

vis-, vice- (Fr.), in place of, as viscount, viceroy. [Fr. vis-, from L. vice, instead of.]

wan- (O.E.), wanting, as wanton, wanrest.

with- (O.E.), against, back, as withstand, withdraw; with, near, as within (this meaning is very rare as prefix). [See with in Dict.]

y-. See under i-.

SUFFIXES

-able, -ible, -uble, adj. suffix, capable of, as portable, laughable, come-at-able, get-at-able, possible, audible, voluble. [L. -ābilis, -ibilis, -ībilis, -ūbilis, according to stem-ending.]

-ac, adj. suffix, pertaining to, as elegiac, also used as noun suffix, as maniac. [Gr. -akos.]

-aceous, having the qualities of, as herbaceous; of the family of, as rosaceous, liliaceous. [L. -āceus.]

-acious, full of, as audacious; **-acity,** the corresponding noun suffix. [L. -āx, -ācis.]

-ade, noun suffix, the L. -āta, which in popular French words appears as -ée, becomes -ade in words borrowed from Provençal, Spanish, Portuguese -ada, and even from Italian -ata, as in accolade, gasconade. Also we have ambuscade, balustrade, brigade, cascade, &c., from French words in -ade. Examples of words formed in imitation of these in English itself are blockade, orangeade.

-age, ending of abstract nouns, as homage; marks place, aggregate, condition, action, or fee, as vicarage, bondage, crewage, demurrage. [L. -āticum; Fr. -age.]

-ain, -an, -ane, -en, -on, noun and adj. suffixes, as villain, pagan, warden, surgeon, as human, humane, certain, Italian. [L. -ānus, and Fr. from L.]

-al, adj. suffix, as annual, legal, mortal, cardinal; of English or French formation, circumstantial, cordial, national. Noun suffix, as approval, denial, removal, betrothal. Latin nouns in -ālia (neut. pl.) which survived into Old French became -aille (fem. sing.), adopted in Middle English as -aylle, -aille, later -aile, -al, as Latin spōnsālia, O.Fr. espousailles, M.E. spousaille, spousal; L. battālia, O.Fr. bataille, M.E. bataille, betail, battle. On this analogy, -aille, -ail, -al, became a

formative of nouns of action on verbs of French or Latin, and even of Germanic origin. [L. -ālis; Fr. -al, -el.]

-an, -ain, -ane. See -ain.

-ana, things belonging to, such as sayings, anecdotes, &c., as Johnsoniana, Burnsiana. [L. neut. pl. ending of adjs. in -ānus. See -ain.]

-ance, -ence (L. -antia, -entia, Fr. -ance), noun suffix, as in arrogance, repentance, experience, penitence.

-ancy, -ency, a modern English differentiated form of the earlier -ance, expressing more distinctly the sense of quality, state, or condition, often belonging to Latin substantives in -ntia, as in elegantia, elegantness, as distinct from the sense of action or process, regularly expressed by the French form -ance, as in aidance, guidance. The modern tendency is to confine -nce to action, and to express quality or state by -ncy; cf. compliance, pliancy, annoyance, buoyancy.

-and, -end, noun suffix, as viand, legend. [L. -andus, -endus, gerundial suffix.]

-aneous, belonging to, as extraneous. [L. -āneus.]

-ant, -ent, adj. suffix, as repentant, patient. Also noun suffix, sometimes denoting the agent, as sergeant, student, innocent. [L. -āns, -ānt-is, or -ēns, -ēntis, -entis, ending of pr.p.]

-ar, adj. suffix, belonging to, as angular, popular. [L. -āris; Fr. -aire.]

-ar, -ard. See under **-er** (marking the agent).

-ar, -er, -or, noun suffixes, marking place, as cellar, larder, manor (L. -ārium); or agent, as vicar, treasurer, chancellor (L. -ārius).

-ard, -art, intensive or disparaging, as drunkard, coward, sluggard, wizard, braggart. [O.Fr. -ard, -art; Germanic -hard, strong.]

-ary, noun suffix, marking place, as seminary (L. -ārium); agent, as secretary, antiquary (L. -ārius).

Adjective suffix (L. *-ārius*, Fr. *-aire*), as contrary, necessary, secondary.

-asm. See under **-ism.**

-ass, -ace, as cuirass, cutlass, menace, pinnace. [L. *-āceus*, *-ācius*; It. *-accio*, Fr. *-as*.]

-aster, dim. and freq. (often implying contempt), as poetaster, criticaster. [L. *-ăster*.]

-ate, -ete, -ite, -ute, -t, forming adjectives from Latin past participles or on their model, as accurate, desolate; complete, replete; contrite, exquisite; absolute, minute; abject, elect: also **-ate, -ated** forming adjectives from nouns; **-ate, -t** forming verbs from past participles, as navigate, permeate, project; **-ate** forming nouns (L. *-ātus*, *-ī* and *-ātus*, *-ūs*) as legate, advocate, senate, consulate.

-ble. See **-able, -ible.**

-ble, -ple, fold, as double, treble, quadruple. [L. *-plus*, lit. full.]

-bund and **-cund**, about, inclined, as moribund, rubicund. [L. *-bundus* and *-cundus*; Fr. *-bond* and *-cond*.]

-ce. See under **-s**, adverbial suffix.

-cle, -cule, noun suffix, as miracle, oracle, spectacle; often dim., as in particle, animalcule. [L. *-culus*, *-cula*, *-culum*; whence Fr. *-cle*, also It. *-cello*, as in violoncello, and (pl.) vermicelli.]

-craft, noun suffix, as in bookcraft, priestcraft. [O.E. *cræft*, skill.]

-cy, -sy, noun suffix, denoting being, or state of being, condition, rank, as clemency, bankruptcy, curacy, minstrelsy. [L. *-tia*.]

-d, -t, -th, nouns from verbs, as deed, seed, flight, weft, birth.

-d. See **-th** (1).

-dom, noun suffix, denoting dominion, power, as kingdom; state, as freedom; act, as martyrdom. New words, as flunkeydom, are often coined. [O.E. *dóm*, judgment, Ger. *-tum*.]

-dor, -dore, noun suffix, as in corridor, matador, stevedore, battledoor. [Sp. *-dor*, L. *-tor*.]

-ed, -d, adjectives from nouns, having, as feathered, tailed, wooded; often indistinguishable from past participles.

-ee, noun suffix, one who or that which is (passive), as trustee, legatee. In absentee, the old function is lost; refugee is adopted from Fr. *refugié*, grandee from Sp. *grande*. [Fr. *-é*—L. *-ātus*, pa.p. ending.]

-eer, -ier, -er, -ar, one who, as charioteer, carpenter, vicar; **-eer** is often disparaging, as in profiteer. [Fr. *-ier*—L. *-ārius*.]

-el, dim., as damsel. [O.Fr. *-el*, *-ele*—L. *-ellus*, *-a*, *-um*.]

-em, -eme, noun suffix, as poem, phoneme, problem. [Gr. *-ēma*; see **-ma**.]

-en, dim., as chicken, maiden. [O.E. *-en*.]

-en, fem. suffix, now found only in vixen. [O.E. *-en*, *-n*; Ger. *-in*.]

-en, forming adjectives, signifying made of, as earthen, wheaten, wooden, woollen. [O.E. *-en*; Ger. *-en*, L. *-īnus*.]

-en, to make, as darken, moisten, strengthen, whiten. [O.E. *-n(ian)*.]

-en, -ene, belonging to, as alien, terrene. [L. *-ēnus*.]

-ence, -ency, -ent. See **-ance, -ancy, -ant.**

-eous, in righteous, see **-wise**; in courteous, from O.Fr. *-eis*, from L. *-ēnsis*.

-eous, adj. suffix, as ligneous. [L. *-eus*.]

-er, frequentative, as glimmer, flutter. [O.E. *-or(ian)*.]

-er, Fr. infinitive ending, forming nouns, as dinner, supper, misnomer.

-er, marks the agent, or that which does anything, designates persons according to their occupation, or place of abode, as writer, singer, hatter, leader, Londoner, Greenlander, sometimes changed to *-ar*, as liar; to *-ard* in standard; sometimes *-ier*, *-yer*, as clothier, sawyer (O.E. *-ere*). Some similar words are from Fr. *-ier* (L. *-ārius*), as grocer, officer, draper.

-er. See **-r.**

-erel, -rel, dim. and depreciatory, as cockerel, mongrel, pickerel. [O.Fr. *-erel* (Fr. *-ereau*).]

-erie, place where, as menagerie. [Fr., from L. *-ārium*.]

-ern, adj. suffix signifying direction, as southern; **-erly**, direction to or from, as southerly. [O.E. *-ern*, and *-ly*.]

-ern, adj. suffix signifying belonging to, as modern (L. *-ernus*); noun suffix, as cistern, cavern, tavern (L. *-erna*).

-ery, noun suffix, as brewery, witchery, cutlery. [Partly noun suffix *-y* added to nouns in *-er* (marking agent); partly Fr. *-erie*, signifying occupation, doings. See **-ary, -erie, -ory.**

-escent, adj. suffix, denoting growing, becoming, as convalescent. Noun suffix **-escence**. [L. *-ēscēns*, *-entis*, pr.p. ending of inchoative verbs.]

-ese, adj. suffix, belonging to, as Japanese. [L. *-ēnsis*; O.Fr. *-eis*, mod. Fr. *-ois*, *-ais*.]

-esque, adj. suffix, partaking of the quality of, as picturesque, grotesque, Turneresque. [Fr. *-esque* (It. *-esco*)—L. *-iscus*, in words of Germanic origin; see **-ish**.]

-ess, fem. suffix, as lioness, goddess. [Fr. *-esse*, L. *-issa*—Gr. *-issa*.]

-ess, -esse, -ice, -ise, -es, forming abstract nouns, as prowess, justice, merchandise, riches. [Fr.,— L. *-itium*, *-itia*, *-icium*.]

-et, -ete, noun suffix, marking the agent, as prophet, poet, athlete. [L. *-ēta* in words of Greek origin— Gr. *-ētēs*.]

-et, -ette, dim., as cygnet, billet, etiquette. See also **-let.** [O.Fr. *-et*, *-ete*; Fr. *-et*, *-ette*.]

-eur. See under **-or.**

-ever. See ever in Dict.

-fare, way, as in welfare, chaffer. See fare in Dict.

-fast, adj. suffix, as in steadfast, shamefaced (O.E. *scamfæst*). [O.E. *fæst*, firm, fast.]

-ferous, bearing, as carboniferous, umbelliferous. [L. *-fer—ferre*, to bear, and *-ous.*]

-fold, adj. suffix, as fourfold, manifold. [O.E. *-fald*, *-feald*.]

-form, having the form of, having a form, as uniform, filiform. [L. *-formis—forma*, form.]

-ful, adj. suffix, full of, as delightful. Noun suffix as much as will fill (pl. **-fuls**). [O.E. *-full*.]

-fy, a verbal suffix signifying to make, as purify. [Fr. *-fier—L. *-ficāre*, for facĕre, to make.]

-gen, that which forms, as hydrogen. [Gr. *-genēs*.]

-head, -hood, noun suffix, denoting state, nature, as Godhead, manhood, likelihood, hardihood (but not livelihood). [O.E. *hád*, Ger. *-heit*, state.]

-ian, adj. suffix, as Arabian, Christian. See **-an.** [L. *-iānus*; Fr. *-ien*.]

-ible. See **-able.**

-ic, adj. suffix, of or belonging to, as gigantic, public, voltaic. In chem. implying higher valency or more oxygen than words in *-ous.* Also largely used as noun suffix, as fabric, music, often in pl. form, as mathematics. [Gr. *-ikos*, partly through L. *-icus* and Fr. *-ic*, *-ique*.]

-ical, adj. suffix, as cubical, whimsical. [-*ic* and *-al*.]

-ice. See **-ess** (2).

-id, adj. suffix, as morbid, splendid. Noun suffix, member of a family, as amaryllid, or of a group of meteors, as leonid: an epic, as Aeneid. **-ide** (chem.), a binary compound, as chloride, oxide, bromide. [Gr. *-is*, *-idos*, whence L. *-is*, *-idis*.]

-ie. See **-y.**

-ier, noun suffix, as cavalier. [Fr. *-ier*; see **-eer.**]

-iff. See **-ive.**

-il, -ile, able, as civil, ductile. [L. *-ilis*, *-īlis*.]

-ina, -ine, fem. suffix, as czarina, heroine. [L. *-īna*, Gr. *-īnē*.]

-ine, -in, noun suffix, as ravine, medicine, cousin, insulin, iodine, glycerine, bromine. Also adj. suffix, as adamantine, divine. [L. *-īnus*, *-īna*; Fr. *-in*, *-ine*.]

-ing, forming nouns of action from verbs, as living;

often the object of the action, as mean*ing*, padd*ing*, winn*ings*. [O.E. *-ung, -ing*; Ger. *-ung*.]

-ing, a descendant, one who belongs to, has the character of, as athel*ing*, whit*ing*, wild*ing*, farth*ing*. [O.E. *-ing*.]

-ion, -sion, -tion, -son, -som, being, state of being, as opin*ion*, rebell*ion*, relig*ion*, tens*ion*, pois*on*, rans*om*, reas*on*, seas*on*, creat*ion*. [L. *-iō, -tiō, -siō, -ōnis*; Fr. *-ion, -sion, -tion, -son*.]

-ique, belonging to, as ant*ique*. [Fr.; see **-ic**.]

-ise, -ize, verbal suffix, signifying to make, as equal*ise*. [L. *-izāre*, from Gr. *-izein*; Fr. *-iser*.]

-ise, noun suffix. See **-ess** (2).

-ish, adj. suffix, ethnic, as Ir*ish*; signifying somewhat, as brown*ish*, old*ish*; sometimes implying depreciation, as outland*ish*, child*ish*. [O.E. *-isc*.]

-ish, verbal suffix, signifying to make, as establ*ish*. [From *-iss-* in the extended stems of French verbs in *-ir*, derived from the *-isc-* of L. inchoatives.]

-isk, dim., as aster*isk*. [Gr. *-iskos*.]

-ism, -asm, or (with **-ic**) **-icism**, forming abstract nouns signifying condition, system, as ego*ism*, de*ism*, Calvin*ism*, lacon*ism*, pleon*asm*; Anglic*ism*, witt*icism*. [L. *-ismus, -asmus*—Gr. *-ismos, -asmos*.]

-ist, denoting the person who holds a doctrine or practises an art, as Calvin*ist*, chem*ist*, novel*ist*, art*ist*, royal*ist*, nihil*ist*. [L. *-ista*—Gr. *-istēs*.]

-ite, -it, noun suffix, indicating descent, nationality, partisanship, following, as Israel*ite*, Hitler*ite*, Jesu*it*; also in names of rocks, minerals, fossils, and chemicals, esp. salts whose acids have names in *-ous*, as gran*ite*, calc*ite*, ammon*ite*, nitr*ite*. [L. *-īta, ītēs*—Gr. *-ītēs*.]

-itis, noun suffix, a disease (now inflammation), as bronch*itis*. [Gr. *-ītis*.]

-itude, -ity. See **-tude, -ty**.

-ive (-iff), forming nouns, as bail*iff*, capt*ive*, nat*ive*, plaint*iff*; forming adjectives, as act*ive*, extens*ive*, furt*ive*. [L. *-ivus*; Fr. *-if, -ive*.]

-ize, to make. Same as **-ise**.

-k, a verbal suffix, freq. or intens., as har*k*, tal*k*.

-kin, dim., as bump*kin*, fir*kin*, lamb*kin*, manni*kin*, nap*kin*; also in proper names, as Jen*kin* (*John*), Per*kin* (*Peterkin*), Wil*kin* (*William*). [Prob. Du. or L.G.; cf. Ger. *-chen*.]

-l, -le, -el, represents O.E. *-el, -ela, -ol, -le*, and serves to form agent and instrumental nouns, diminutives, &c., as nai*l*, sai*l*; bead*le*, hand*le*, gird*le*, fow*l*; adjectives signifying apt, as britt*le*, nimb*le*. Sometimes **-le, -al** is from O.E. *-els*, as brid*le*, ridd*le*, buria*l*. **-l, -le**, as a verbal suffix, gives to the root the sense of frequency, repetition, diminution, as knee*l*, drizz*le*, nest*le*, spark*le*. [O.E. *-lian*.]

-lence, -lency, forming abstract nouns. [L. *-lentia*.]

-lent, adj. suffix, full of, as vio*lent*, viru*lent*. [L. *-lentus*.]

-less, adj. suffix, free from, wanting, as guilt*less*, god*less*. [O.E. *-léas*, Ger. *-los*, Goth. *-laus*.]

-let, dim., as brace*let*, leaf*let*, stream*let*. [From **-l** and **-et**.]

-like, like, as god*like*. [See **like** in Dict.]

-ling, dim., as duck*ling*, gos*ling*, hence expressing affection, as dar*ling* (O.E. *déorling*), sometimes implying depreciation, as hire*ling*, ground*ling*, under*ling*, world*ling*. [O.E. *-ling*.]

-ling, -long, adv. suffix, as dark*ling*, side*long*. [O.E. *-lunga, -linga*.]

-lock, noun suffix, in wed*lock*. [O.E. *lác*, sport, perh. orig. activity.]

-ly, adj. and adv. suffix, as man*ly*, on*ly*, wicked*ly*. [O.E. *líc*, like; adv. *líce*.]

-m, -om, noun suffix, as bloss*om*, bott*om*, fath*om* (O.E. *-ma, -m*); also Fr., as real*m*, regi*me* (L. *-men*).

-ma, noun suffix, as dra*ma*, panora*ma*, ene*ma*; **-matic**, adj. [Gr. *-ma, -matos*, adj. *-matikos*.]

-meal, adv. suffix, as inch*meal*, piece*meal*. [O.E. *-mǽlum*.]

-men, that which, state, as regi*men*, acu*men*. [L.]

-ment, noun suffix, as nourish*ment*, establish*ment*, detri*ment*. [L. *-mentum*, Fr. *-ment*; see **-men**.]

-mony, as testi*mony*, parsi*mony*. [L. *-mōnia, -mōnium*.]

-most, suffix of superl. degree, as east*most*, in*most*, inner*most*, end*most*. [Not from the word *most*, but a double superlative suffix, O.E. *-mest* (*-m-est*), later confused with *most*.]

-n, -en, -on, a noun suffix, as heave*n*, mor*n*, weap*on*. [O.E.]

-nd, as fie*nd* (lit. hating), frie*nd* (lit. loving). [O.E. pr.p. suffix.]

-ness, noun suffix, denoting abstract idea, as tender*ness*, sweet*ness*. [O.E. *-nis, -nes*; Ger. *-niss*.]

-ock, dim., as hill*ock*, bull*ock*—also in proper names, as Poll*ock* (from *Paul*), &c. [O.E. *-oc, -uc*.]

-oid, like, forming nouns and adjectives, as anthro*poid*, rhomb*oid*.—**-oidal**, adj. [Gr. *-oeidēs, -ōidēs—eidos*, form.]

-om, old dative suffix (as wh*om*); in adverbs of time, as seld*om*, whil*om*. [O.E. *-um*.]

-om. See **-m**.

-on, -eon, ion, noun suffix, as cap*on*, mas*on*, trun*cheon*, oni*on*, clari*on*. [Fr.,—L. *-ō, -ōnis*, and *-iō, -iōnis*.]

-oon, noun suffix, often augmentative, as ball*oon*, sal*oon*. [Fr. *-on*, It. *-one*.]

-or, -our, -er, denoting the agent, sometimes directly from L. (see **-tor**), but mostly through O.Fr. *-or, -our* (Fr. *-eur*), as emper*or*; in others, Eng. *-er* has supplanted *-eur, -our*, as preach*er*, while *-or* is at times affixed to Eng. roots, as sail*or*. In certain abstract nouns from L. *-or*, A.Fr. *-our* is retained, as col*our*, lab*our*, in a few Fr. *-eur*, as grand*eur*. Demean*our*, behavi*our* are Eng. formations.

-ory, belonging to, as prefatory (L. *-ōrius*); place where, as purgat*ory* (L. *-ōrium*).

-ose, full of, as bellic*ose*, mor*ose*, verb*ose*—the corresponding nouns have **-osity**. [L. *-ōsus*.]

-osis, denoting condition, process, as hypn*osis*, os*mosis*, diseased state, as silic*osis*. [L. *-osis*, Gr.*-ōsis*.]

-ot, dim., as ball*ot*. See **-et**, dim.

-our. See **-or**.

-ous, adj. suffix, as religi*ous*, deliri*ous*, curi*ous* (L. *-ōsus*); very often where the L. word was not in *-ōsus* but simple *-us, -a, -um*, as dubi*ous*, anxi*ous*; in chemistry implying lower valency or less oxygen than words in *-ic*.

-ow, noun suffix, as shad*ow*, mead*ow* (O.E. *-u* or no ending, with *-w-* in oblique cases); swall*ow* (O.E. *-we*); marr*ow* (from O.E. *-g, -h*). Also adj. suffix, as narr*ow* (O.E. *-u*).

-phorous, bearing, as pyro*phorous*. [Gr. *-phoros*, with *-ous* added.]

-ple. See **-ble**.

-r, -er, noun suffix, marking the instrument, as stai*r*, timbe*r*; adj. suffix, as bitt*er*.

-red, noun suffix, denoting manner, state, as hat*red*, kind*red*. [O.E. *rǽden*; cog. with Ger. *-rat*; see **read** in Dict.]

-rel. See **-erel**.

-ric, noun suffix, formerly an independent word denoting dominion, power, region, as bishop*ric*. [O.E. *ríce*, power.]

-right, as up*right*, down*right*, out*right*. [O.E. *riht*.]

-ry, noun suffix, orig. collective, as infant*ry*, yeoman*ry*; now expressing action or quality, as bigot*ry*, pedant*ry*, sorce*ry*; condition, as out-law*ry*, slave*ry*; occupation, as carpent*ry*, herald*ry*; the place of action or occupation, as laund*ry*, nurse*ry*; the result or product of action, as poet*ry*, tapest*ry*. [Fr. *-rie*=-*er* and *-ie*.]

-s, -ce, adv. suffix, as need*s*, alway*s*, on*ce*, hen*ce*, then*ce*; with added *t*, as whil*st*, betwix*t*. [O.E. *-es*, gen. ending.]

-se, verbal suffix, making transitive verbs from adjectives, as clean*se*.

-ship, -scape, noun suffix, as friend*ship*, steward*ship*, wor*ship*, land*scape* (earlier land*skip*, Du. land*schap*). [O.E. *scipe*, shape, form—*scapan*; cog. with Ger. *-schaft*.]

-sion. See **-ion**.

-sis, action or state, as the*sis*. [Gr.]

-some, adj. suffix, full of, as glad*some*, whole*some*. [O.E. *-sum*; Ger. *-sam*; cf. **same.**]

-son, son, as John*son*.

-son, in ar*son*, rea*son*, trea*son*. See **-ion.**

-ster marks the agent, as malt*ster*, and in the personal names (orig. trade-names) Ba*xster*, Brew*ster*, Web*ster*; often with depreciation, as game*ster*, pun*ster*. [O.E. *-estre*, fem., as now only in spin*ster*.]

-stress, fem. suffix, as song*stress*. [-ster with **-ess.**]

-sy, state, as pleuri*sy*. Same as **-sis.**]

-t. See **-d**; **-th** (2).

-t, -te, adj. and noun suffix, as conven*t*, fac*t*, chas*te*, tribu*te*. [L. *-tus*, pa.p. ending.]

-teen, ten to be added, as four*teen*. [O.E. *-tyne*.]

-ter, noun suffix, as charac*ter*, ela*ter*, sphinc*ter*. [Gr. *-tēr*; cf. L. *-tor*.]

-ter, -ther, as in af*ter*, hi*ther*. [O.E. *-der*, *-ther*, old comp. suffix.]

-th, -d, forming ordinal numerals, as six*th*, thir*d*. [O.E. *-tha*, *-ta*, *-da*.]

-th, -t, noun suffix, as in streng*th*, heigh*t*. See also under **-d.**

-ther, denoting the agent, as fa*ther*, mo*ther*.

-ther. See **-ter** (2).

-tion. See **-ion.**

-tor, agent, as conduc*tor*. (L.)— **-trix,** fem. agent, as testa*trix*, direc*trix*.—Proprie*trix* is sham Latin. [L. *-trīx*.]

-tory, noun suffix, denoting place, as dormi*tory*. [L. *-tōrium*.]

-tron, signifying instrument, as cyclo*tron*; also (through Fr.) **-tre,** as phil*tre*. [Gr. *-tron*.]

-tude forms abstract nouns, as grati*tude*. [L. *-tūdō*.]

-ty, being or state of being, as digni*ty*; quality, as hones*ty*. [O.Fr. *-té*—L. *-tās*, *-tātis*.]

-ty, ten to be multiplied, as six*ty*. [O.E. *-tig*; cog. with Ger. *-zig*.]

-uble. See **-able.**

-ule, little, dim., as in glob*ule*, pust*ule*. [L. *-ulus*, *-ula*, *-ulum*.]

-uncle, -uncle, dim., as ped*uncle*. [O.Fr. *-uncle*, L. *-unculus*.]

-ure, noun suffix, denoting action, process or its result or means, function, collective body, as capt*ure*, verd*ure*, sculpt*ure*, judicat*ure* (Fr. *-ure*, L. *-ūra*).—It also represents Fr. *-ir*, as in leis*ure*, pleas*ure*.

-urient, desiderative, with corresponding nouns in **-urition,** as es*urient*, part*urient*. [L. *-ūriens*, *-entis*.]

-urnal, belonging to, as di*urnal*. [L. *-urnus*, with **-al.**]

-ward, -wards, forming adjectives and adverbs, as east*ward*, home*ward*, home*wards*; down*ward*, for*ward*, in*ward*, to*ward*. [O.E. *-weard*, with gen. ending *-weardes*, cog. with Ger. *-wärts*; conn. with O.E. *weorthan*, to become, and L. *vertěre*, to turn.]

-way, -ways, adv. suffix, signifying manner, direction, as al*way*, al*ways*, straight*way*.

-wise, way, manner, as like*wise*, other*wise*; in the form **-eous** in righte*ous*. [O.E. *-wise*, manner; Ger. *-wiss*.]

-worth, adj. suffix, as stal*worth*, stal*wart*. [O.E. *weorth*, *wurth*, *wierthe*.]

-y, adj. suffix, as spong*y* (from L. *-iōsus*); as joll*y* (Norm.Fr. *-if* from L. *-ivus*; cf. *-ive*); as sill*y*, dirt*y*, an*y* (O.E. *-ig*; cog. with Ger. *-ig*).

-y, noun suffix, as stor*y*, famil*y*, Ital*y* (Fr. *-ie*, L. *-ia*); as augur*y*, jo*y*, remed*y* (from L. *-ium*); as all*y*, clerg*y*, deput*y*, treat*y* (from L. *-ātus*, Fr. *-é*); as progen*y* (from L. *-iēs*); as arm*y*, countr*y*, entr*y* (from L. *-āta*, Fr. *-ée*); as bod*y* (from O.E. *-ig*); **-y** or **-ie,** a modern suffix of obscure origin forming diminutives or words of contempt, as bab*y*, lass*ie*, Bill*y*, Bets*y*, Lizz*ie*, &c.—adj. suffix, somewhat, as yellow*y*.

-yer, as in law*yer*. See **-er,** noun suffix.

LIST OF ABBREVIATIONS

Additional Abbreviations : see page 1345

A argon ; adult (motion picture certificate).
A. Amateur ; Academician ; (or Å, or A.U. or Å.U.) Ångström unit.
a. accepted ; acre ; active ; afternoon ; *annus,* year ; *ante,* before.
ā or āā, in prescriptions, *ana* (Gr.), i.e. of each a like quantity.
a. or **ans.** answer.
A.A. Automobile Association ; Anti-aircraft.
A.A.A. Amateur Athletic Association.
A.A.Q.M.G. Acting Assistant Quartermaster-General.
A.A.S. *Academiae Americanae Socius,* Fellow of the American Academy.
A.B. Able-bodied seaman ; *Artium Baccalaureus,* Bachelor of Arts.
A.B.A. Amateur Boxing Association.
Abb. Abbess ; Abbot ; Abbey.
abbr., abbrev. abbreviated ; abbreviation.
abd. abdicated.
A.B.F.M. American Board of Foreign Missions.
ab init. *ab initio,* from the beginning.
abl. ablative.
Abp. Archbishop.
abr. abridged ; abridgment.
A.B.S. American Bible Society.
abs., absol. absolutely.
abs., abstr. abstract.
abs. re. *absente reo,* the accused being absent.
A.C. Aero Club ; Alpine Club ; *ante Christum,* Before Christ ; (*elect.*) alternating current.
Ac actinium.
acc. account (also **acct., a/c**) ; accountant ; accusative (also **accus.**) ; according.
A.C.G.B. Arts Council of Great Britain.
A.C.I.S. Associate of the Chartered Institute of Secretaries.
A.C.P. Associate of the College of Preceptors.
A.C.S.M. Associate of the Camborne School of Metalliferous Mining.
act. active.
A.D. *anno Domini,* in the year of the Lord.
a.d. after date ; *ante diem,* before the day.
ad. advertisement.
A.D.C. Aide-de-camp.
ad fin. *ad finem,* at, towards, or to, the end.
ad inf. *ad infinitum,* to infinity.
ad init. *ad initium,* at or to the beginning.
ad int. *ad interim,* in the meantime.
adj. adjective ; adjourned ; adjustment.
Adjt. Adjutant. **Adjt.-Gen.** Adjutant-General.
ad lib. *ad libitum,* at pleasure.
ad loc. *ad locum,* at the place.
Adm. Admiral.
adv. advent ; adverb ; *adversus,* against ; advocate.
ad val. *ad valorem,* according to value.
advt. advertisement.
A.E.C. Army Educational Corps.
æ., æt. *aetatis,* of his age, aged (so many years).
A.E.I.O.U. *Austriae est imperare orbi universo,* it is Austria's part to rule the whole world.
A.E.U. Amalgamated Engineers' Union.
A.F. Admiral of the Fleet ; Army Form.
A.F.A. Associate of the Faculty of Actuaries.
A.F.B.S. American and Foreign Bible Society.
aff. affectionate ; affirmative.
A.G. Adjutant-General.
Ag *argentum,* silver.
agr., agric. agriculture.
Agt. Agent.
A.H. *anno Hegirae,* in the year of Hegira—i.e. from the flight of Mohammed (A.D. 622, 13th Sept.).
a.h.l. *ad hunc locum,* at this place.
A.H.S. *Anno Humanae Salutis,* in the Year of Human Salvation.
a.h.v. *ad hanc vocem,* at this word.

A.I.A. Associate of the Institute of Actuaries.
A.I.C.E. Associate of the Institute of Civil Engineers.
A.I.M.M. Associate of the Institution of Mining and Metallurgy.
A.I.S.A. Associate of Incorporated Secretaries' Association.
A.K.C. Associate of King's College, London.
Al aluminium.
Ala. Alabama.
Alas. Alaska.
Alba. Alberta.
Alban. of St Albans.
Ald. Alderman.
alg. algebra.
alt. alternate ; altitude ; alto.
Alta. Alberta.
A.M. *Artium Magister,* Master of Arts ; (also **a.m.**) *ante meridiem,* before noon ; *Anno Mundi,* in the year of the world ; *Ave Maria,* Hail Mary ; *Am Main,* on the (river) Main.
Am americium.
Am., Amer. America ; American.
A.M.A. American Missionary Association ; Assistant Masters' Association.
A.M.I.C.E. Associate Member of Institution of Civil Engineers.
A.M.I.E.E. Associate Member of Institution of Electrical Engineers.
amp ampère.
amt. amount.
an. *anno,* in the year ; anonymous ; *ante,* before.
anal. analysis ; analogy.
anat. anatomy ; anatomical.
anc. ancient ; anciently.
Ang. *Anglice,* in English.
anon. anonymous.
ans. answer.
antiq. antiquities ; antiquarian.
A.O. Army Order.
A.O.C.-in-C. Air Officer Commanding-in-Chief.
A.O.F. Ancient Order of Foresters.
aor. aorist.
A.P. Associated Press.
Ap., Apl., Apr. April.
Apo. Apogee.
Apoc. Apocalypse ; Apocrypha, Apocryphal.
app. appendix ; apparent, apparently ; apprentice.
appro. approval, approbation.
approx. approximate ; approximately.
A.P.R.C. *Anno post Romam conditam,* in the year after the founding of Rome (753 B.C.).
aq. *aqua,* water.
a.r. *anno regni,* in the year of the reign.
Ar., Arab. Arabic.
ar., arr. arrive or arrives ; arrival.
A.R.A. Associate of the Royal Academy.
A.R.A.M. Associate of the Royal Academy of Music.
arch. archaic.
arch., archit. architecture.
archaeol. archaeology.
Archd. Archdeacon ; Archduke.
A.R.C.M. Associate of the Royal College of Music.
A.R.C.O. Associate of the Royal College of Organists.
A.R.C.S. Associate of the Royal College of Science.
arg. *argentum,* silver.
Arg. Rep. Argentine Republic.
A.R.H.A. Associate of the Royal Hibernian Academy.
A.R.I.B.A. Associate of the Royal Institute of British Architects.
A.R.I.C. Associate of the Royal Institute of Chemistry.
arith. arithmetic ; arithmetical.

Ariz. Arizona.
Ark. Arkansas.
Arm. Armenian; Armoric.
A.R.P. Air Raid Precautions.
A.R.R. *anno regni regis* or *reginae*, in the year of the king's or the queen's reign.
arr. arranged; arrival.
A.R.S.A. Associate of the Royal Scottish Academy; Associate of the Royal Society of Arts.
A.R.S.L. Associate of the Royal Society of Literature.
A.R.S.M. Associate of the Royal School of Mines.
A.R.S.S. *Antiquariorum Regiae Societatis Socius*, Fellow of the Royal Society of Antiquaries.
art. article; (also **arty.**) artillery.
As arsenic.
A.S. Anglo-Saxon; *Anno Salutis*, in the year cf Salvation; Assistant Secretary.
A.S.A. Amateur Swimming Association.
A.S.A.A. Associate of the Society of Incorporated Accountants and Auditors.
Asaph. of St Asaph.
Asdic. Allied Submarine Detection Investigation Committee (detecting device).
A.S.E. Amalgamated Society of Engineers.
A.S.L.I.B., Aslib. Association of Special Libraries and Information Bureau.
Ass., Assoc. Association.
Asst. Assistant.
astr., astron. astronomer; astronomy.
astrol. astrology.
At astatine.
A.T.C. Air Training Corps.
A.T.S. Auxiliary Territorial Service (superseded by W.R.A.C.).
ats. at suit of.
Att. Attic (Greek); (also **Atty.**) Attorney. **Att.-Gen.** Attorney-General.
attrib. attribute; attributive; attributively.
at. wt. atomic weight.
A.U., Å.U. Ångström unit.
Au *aurum*, gold.
A.U.C. *anno urbis conditae* or *ab urbe condita*, in the year from the building of the city—Rome (753 B.C.).
Aufl. *Auflage* (Ger.), edition.
Aug. August.
aug. augmentative.
aut., auto. automatic.
Auth. Ver. Authorised Version.
A.V. Authorised Version.
av. avenue; average.
a.v. *annos vixit*, lived (so many) years.
ave. avenue.
avoir., avdp. avoirdupois.
ax. axiom.

B. Baron.
B., Brit. British.
B boron.
b. born; book.
B.A. *Baccalaureus Artium*, Bachelor of Arts; British America; British Association.
Ba barium.
bach. Bachelor.
B.Agr. Bachelor of Agriculture.
bal. balance.
B.A.O.R. British Army of the Rhine.
Bap., Bapt. Baptist.
bap., bapt. baptised.
Bar. Barrister.
bar. barometer; barrel.
B.Arch. Bachelor of Architecture.
Bart., Bt. Baronet.
bat., batt. battalion; battery.
B.B.C. British Broadcasting Corporation.
B.C. Before Christ; Board of Control; British Columbia; Battery Commander.
b.c.g. bacillus of Calmette and Guérin, an attenuated strain of the tubercle bacillus used for inoculation.
B.Ch. *Baccalaureus Chirurgiae*, Bachelor of Surgery.
B.C.L. Bachelor of Civil Law.

B.Comm. Bachelor of Commerce.
B.D. Bachelor of Divinity.
bd. bound.
Bde. Brigade.
bds. boards.
B.D.S. Bachelor of Dental Surgery.
Be beryllium.
B.E. Bachelor of Engineering; Board of Education.
b.e. bill of exchange.
B.E.A. (or **BEA**) British European Airways; British East Africa.
B.Ed. Bachelor of Education.
Beds Bedfordshire.
B.E.F. British Expeditionary Force.
bef. before.
Belg. Belgian, Belgic.
B.E.M. British Empire Medal.
Benelux. See Dict.
Berks Berkshire.
B. ès L. *Bachelier ès Lettres* (Fr.), Bachelor of Letters.
B. ès S. *Bachelier ès Sciences* (Fr.), Bachelor of Sciences.
bet. between.
B.Hy. Bachelor of Hygiene.
Bi bismuth.
Bib. Bible. **Bibl.** Biblical.
bibl. bibliotheca.
bibliog. bibliographer; bibliography.
B.I.F. British Industries Fair.
biog. biographer; biography, biographical.
biol. biology; biological.
bis. bissextile.
bk. book; bank; bark.
Bk berkelium.
bkg. banking.
bkt. basket.
B.L. Bachelor of Law; Bachelor of Letters.
bl. barrel; bale.
b.l. bill of lading.
bldg. building.
B.M. Bachelor of Medicine; *Beatae Memoriae*, of blessed memory; British Museum; Brigade Major.
B.M.A. British Medical Association.
B.M.J. British Medical Journal.
B.Mus. Bachelor of Music.
Bn. Baron.
bn. battalion.
b.o. branch office; buyer's option.
B.O.A.C. British Overseas Airways Corporation.
B. of T. Board of Trade.
Boh. Bohemia, Bohemian.
Bol. Bolivia.
bor. borough.
bot. botany; botanical; bought.
Boul. Boulevard.
Bp. Bishop.
B.P. British Pharmacopoeia; British Public.
b.p. bill of parcels; bills payable; birthplace (also **b.pl.**); *bonum publicum*, the public good; boiling point.
B.Q. *Bene quiescat*, may he (or she) rest well.
bque. barque.
Br., Bro. Brother.
Br bromine.
br. branch; brig.
B.R. British Railways.
Br. Am. British America.
Braz. Brazil; Brazilian.
b. rec. bills receivable.
Bret. Breton.
brev. brevet; breveted.
Brig. Brigadier. **Brig.-Gen.** Brigadier-General.
Brit. Britain; Britannia; British; Briton.
Bro. Brother. **Bros.** Brothers.
b.s. bill of sale.
B.S. Bachelor of Science or of Surgery; Blessed Sacrament.
B.S.A. British South Africa; Birmingham Small Arms.
B.Sc. Bachelor of Science.
B.S.I. British Standards Institution.
B.S.T. British Summer Time.

Bt. Baronet.
B.T.U. Board of Trade Unit ; (or **B.Th.U.**) British Thermal Unit.
bu., bus. (or **bush.**). bushel ; bushels.
Bucks Buckinghamshire.
Bulg. Bulgaria ; Bulgarian.
B.U.P. British United Press.
bush. bushel.
B.V. *Beata Virgo*, Blessed Virgin ; *Bene vale*, farewell.
B.V.M. The Blessed Virgin Mary.
B.W.G. Birmingham Wire Gauge.
B.W.I. British West Indies.
B.W.T.A. British Women's Temperance Association.
B. & F.B.S. British and Foreign Bible Society.
b. & s. brandy and soda-water.

C. Celsius ; centigrade.
C carbon.
c., cap. *caput*, chapter.
c. cent ; centime ; *circa*, about.
c., ct., cent. *centum*, a hundred.
C.A. Chartered Accountant ; County Alderman.
Ca calcium.
ca. cases ; centiare ; *circa*, about.
Cal., Calif. California.
Cam., Camb. Cambridge.
Cambs Cambridgeshire.
Can. Canon ; Canto.
Cant. Canterbury ; Canticles.
Cantab. *Cantabrigiensis*, of Cambridge.
Cantuar. *Cantuaria*, Canterbury ; *Cantuariensis*, of Canterbury.
cap. *caput*, chapter ; capital ; *capitulum*, head, chapter ; *capiat*, let him (or her) take.
caps. capitals.
Capt. Captain.
Car. *Carolus*, Charles.
car. carat.
Card. Cardinal.
carp. carpentry.
Cash. Cashier.
cat. catechism ; catalogue.
Cath. Catholic.
Cav. Cavalry.
C.B. Companion of the Bath ; confinement to barracks ; Cape Breton ; County Borough.
Cb columbium (now officially niobium).
C.B.E. Commander of the British Empire.
C.B.S. Confraternity of the Blessed Sacrament.
C.C. County Council ; Cricket Club ; Cape Colony ; Caius College.
cc. *capita*, chapters.
c.c. (or **cc.**). cubic centimetre(s).
C.C.C. Corpus Christi College.
C.C.S. Casualty Clearing Station.
Cd cadmium.
C.D. Acts. Contagious Diseases Acts.
C.D.S.O. Companion of the Distinguished Service Order.
c.d.v. carte-de-visite.
C.E. Civil Engineer ; Christian Endeavour.
Ce cerium.
Cel. (or **C.**). Celsius.
cel. celebrated.
Celt. Celtic.
C.E.M.A. Council for the Encouragement of Music and the Arts (now A.C.G.B.).
cen. central ; century.
cent. (or **cent**). *centum*, a hundred ; century ; central.
cert., certif. certificate ; certificated ; certify.
Cestr. *Cestrensis*, of Chester.
cet. par. *ceteris paribus*, other things being equal.
C.E.T.S. Church of England Temperance Society.
C.F. Chaplain to the Forces.
cf. *confer*, compare ; calf.
Cf californium.
C.F.G. *Confédération Générale du Travail*, General Confederation of Labour.
c.f. & i. cost, freight, and insurance.
cg. centigram(s).
C.G.H. Cape of Good Hope.
c.g.s. centimetre-gramme-second unit, or system.

C.H. Companion of Honour.
Ch. Chief ; China ; Church.
ch. chaldron ; chapter ; child.
Chal., Chald. Chaldee ; Chaldaic.
Chamb. Chamberlain.
Chanc. Chancellor.
Chap. Chaplain ; Chapter.
Chas. Charles.
Ch.B. *Chirurgiae Baccalaureus*, Bachelor of Surgery.
Ch. C(h). Christ Church.
chem. chemistry ; chemical.
Ch. Hist. Church History.
Chin. China ; Chinese.
Ch.J. Chief-Justice.
Ch.M. *Chirurgiae Magister*, Master of Surgery.
choc. chocolate.
Chr. Christ ; Christian.
Chron. Chronicles.
chron. chronicle ; chronology ; chronological.
Cic. Cicero.
Cicestr. *Cicestrensis*, of Chichester.
C.I.D. Criminal Investigation Department.
C.I.E. Companion of the Indian Empire.
c.i.f. cost, insurance, freight.
C.I.G.S. Chief of Imperial General Staff.
C.-in-C. Commander-in-Chief.
C.I.O. Congress of Industrial Organisations.
cir., circ. *circa, circiter, circum*, about.
cit. citation ; citizen.
C.I.V. City Imperial Volunteers.
civ. civil ; civilian.
C.J. Chief-Justice.
Cl chlorine.
cl. class ; clause ; centilitre(s).
class. classical ; classification.
C.L.S.C. Chautauqua Literary and Scientific Circle.
C.M. Certificated Master ; Corresponding Member ; Common Metre ; *Chirurgiae Magister*, Master of Surgery.
Cm curium.
cm. centimetre(s).
c.m. *carat métrique*, metric carat ; *causa mortis*, by reason of death.
C.M.G. Companion of the Order of St Michael and St George.
C.M.S. Church Missionary Society.
C.O. Colonial Office ; Commanding Officer ; Criminal Office ; Crown Office ; conscientious objector.
Co cobalt.
Co. Company ; County.
c/o. care of.
coad. coadjutor.
coch., cochl. *cochlear*, a spoon, spoonful. **coch. amp.,** — *amplum*, a tablespoonful. **coch. mag.,** — *magnum*, a large spoonful. **coch. med.,** — *medium*, a dessertspoonful. **coch. parv.,** — *parvum*, a teaspoonful.
Cod. Codex.
c.o.d. cash (or collect) on delivery.
C. of E. Church of England.
cog. cognate.
C.O.I. Central Office of Information.
Col. Colonel ; Colorado ; Column ; Colossians.
coll. college ; colleague ; collector ; colloquial.
collat. collateral ; collaterally.
colloq. colloquial ; colloquially.
Coloss. Colossians.
Com. Commander ; Commodore ; Committee ; Commissioner ; Commonwealth.
com. common ; comedy ; commerce ; commune.
Comdr. Commander.
Comdt. Commandant.
Cominform. See Dict. **Comintern.** See Dict.
comm. commentary ; commander.
Commissr. Commissioner. **Commy.** Commissary.
commn. commission.
comp. comparative ; compositor ; compare ; compound ; compounded.
compar. comparative ; comparison.
Com. Ver. Common Version.
Con. Consul.
con. *contra*, against ; *conjux*, consort ; conclusion ; conversation.

conc. concentrated; concentration.
Cong. Congress; Congregation.
conj. conjunction; conjunctive.
Conn. (or **Ct.**). Connecticut.
conn. connexion; connected; connotation.
cons. consonant.
con. sec. conic sections.
Consols. Consolidated Funds.
cont., contd., continued.
contr. contracted; contraction.
contr. bon. mor. *contra bonos mores,* contrary to good manners or morals.
conv. conventional.
co-op. co-operative.
Cop., Copt. Coptic.
C.O.P.E.C. Conference on Political and Economic Planning.
Cor. Corinthians; Coroner.
Cor. Mem. Corresponding Member.
Corn. Cornish; Cornwall.
corol., coroll. corollary.
corr. corrupted; corruption; correspond.
Cor. Sec. Corresponding Secretary.
cos cosine.
cosec cosecant.
cosh hyperbolic cosine.
cosmog. cosmography.
Coss. *consules,* Consuls.
cot cotangent.
cp. compare.
C.P. Clerk of the Peace; Common Pleas; Carriage Paid.
c.p. candle power.
C.P.C. Clerk of the Privy Council.
Cpl. Corporal.
C.P.R. Canadian Pacific Railway.
C.P.S. *Custos Privati Sigilli,* Keeper of the Privy Seal.
C.R. *Carolus rex,* King Charles; *civis romanus,* a Roman citizen; *Custos Rotulorum,* Keeper of the Rolls.
Cr chromium.
cr. credit; creditor; crown.
cres., cresc. crescendo; crescent.
crim. con. criminal conversation, adultery.
c.r.t. cathode-ray tube.
C.S. Court of Session; Clerk to the Signet; Civil Service; Chemical Society.
Cs caesium.
C.S.A. Confederate States of America.
C.S.I. Companion of the Star of India; Chartered Surveyors' Institution.
ct. cent; carat.
Ct. Connecticut.
C.T.C. Cyclists' Touring Club.
Cu *cuprum,* copper.
cu., cub. cubic.
cur., curt. current—this month.
C.V. Common Version.
C.V.O. Commander of the Royal Victorian Order.
c.w.o. cash with order.
cwt. hundredweight(s)—*c.* for *centum,* a hundred, and *wt.* for weight.
Cyc., Cyclo. Cyclopaedia.
Cym. Cymric.

d. *dele,* delete; dead; died; deserted; degree; *denarius* or *denarii,* a penny or pence; duke.
D.A. District Attorney.
D.(A.)A.G. Deputy (Assistant) Adjutant-General.
Dan. Daniel; Danish.
dat. dative.
dau. daughter.
D.B.E. Dame Commander of the British Empire.
D.C. *Da capo* (It.), repeat from the beginning; District of Columbia; (*elect.*) direct current.
D.C.L. Doctor of Civil Law.
D.C.M. Distinguished Conduct Medal.
D.C.S. Deputy Clerk of Session.
D.D. *Divinitatis Doctor,* Doctor of Divinity.
D.D. *Deo dedit,* gave to God.
d.d., D/D, d/d. days after date; day's date.
D day. Day for start of a military operation, esp. Allied invasion of the Continent in 1944.
D.D.D. *dat, dicat, dedicat,* gives, devotes, and dedi-

cates; *dono dedit dedicavit,* gave and dedicated as a gift.
D.D.S. Doctor of Dental Surgery; diamino-diphenylsulphone (drug used against leprosy).
D.D.T. Dichlorodiphenyltrichloroethane (an insecticide).
Dec. December.
dec., decl. declaration; declension.
def. definition; (or **deft.**) defendant.
deg. degree(s).
Del. Delaware.
del. delegate; (or **delt.**) *delineavit,* drew it (put after the draughtsman's name).
demon., demons. demonstrative.
dent. dental; dentist; dentistry.
dep., dept. department; deputy.
dep. deposed.
der., deriv. derivation; derived.
Deut. Deuteronomy.
D.F. Defender of the Faith; Dean of the Faculty.
D.F.C. Distinguished Flying Cross.
D.F.M. Distinguished Flying Medal.
dft. defendant; draft.
D.G. *Dei gratia,* by the grace of God.
dg. decigram(s).
d.h. *das heisst* (Ger.), that is.
dial. dialect.
diam. diameter.
dict. dictator; dictionary.
diff. different; difference.
dil. dilute.
Dir. Director.
disc. discount; discoverer.
diss. dissertation.
dist. distance; distinguish; district.
div. divide; division; divine.
dl. decilitre.
D.L. Deputy Lieutenant.
D.Lit. or Litt. *Doctor litterarum* or *litteraturae,* Doctor of Letters or Literature.
D.L.O. Dead-letter Office.
dm. decimetre(s).
D.N.B. Dictionary of National Biography.
do. *ditto* (It.), the same (aforesaid).
dols. dollars.
D.O.M. *Deo optimo maximo,* to God, best and greatest.
Dom. Dominion.
dom. domestic.
Dor. Doric.
D.O.R.A. Defence of the Realm Act.
doz. dozen.
D.P. Displaced Person.
d.p. duly performed (the work of the class).
D.P.H. Diploma in Public Health.
D.Ph. or D.Phil. *Doctor Philosophiae,* Doctor of Philosophy.
dpt. department.
Dr. Debtor; Doctor; Drummer; Driver.
dr. dram; drawer.
D.S. *Dal segno* (It.), from the sign.
d.s., D/S. days after sight.
D.Sc. *Scientiae Doctor,* Doctor of Science.
D.S.C. Distinguished Service Cross.
D.S.I.R. Department of Scientific and Industrial Research.
D.S.M. Distinguished Service Medal.
D.S.O. Distinguished Service Order.
d.s.p. *decessit sine prole,* died without issue.
D.T., d.t., D.T's., d.t's. delirium tremens.
D.U.K.W. (*duk*) manufacturers' code initials for a type of wheeled amphibious landing-craft.
Dunelm. *Dunelmensis,* of Durham.
D.V. *Deo volente,* God willing.
d.v.p. *decessit vita patris,* died in father's lifetime.
dwt. pennyweight—*denarius,* and *wt.* for weight.
Dy dysprosium.

E. East; English.
Ebor. *Eboracum,* York; *Eboracensis,* of York.
E.C. East Central; Established Church.
E.C.A. Economic Co-operation Administration.
Eccl., Eccles. Ecclesiastes; Ecclesiastical.
Ecclesiol. Ecclesiology.
Ecclus. Ecclesiasticus.

E.C.U. English Church Union.
Ed. Editor.
ed., edit. edited ; edition.
Ed., Edin. Edinburgh.
Edenburgen. *Edenburgensis*, of Edinburgh.
E.D.S. English Dialect Society.
E.E. Errors Excepted.
E.E.T.S. Early English Text Society.
e.g., ex. gr. *exempli gratia*, for example.
E.I. East Indies. **E.I.C.S.** East India Company's Service.
ejusd. *ejusdem*, of the same.
elec., elect. electric ; electricity.
e.m.f. electromotive force.
Emp. Emperor, Empress.
e.m.u. electromagnetic unit.
Ency., Encyc. Encyclopaedia.
E.N.E., ENE. East-north-east.
Eng. England ; English.
eng. engineer ; engraver ; engraving.
Ens. Ensign.
E.N.S.A. Entertainments National Services Association.
ent., entom. entomology.
Ent. Sta. Hall. Entered at Stationers' Hall.
Env. Ext. Envoy Extraordinary.
e.o.d. every other day.
Ep. Epistle.
Eph. Ephesians.
Epiph. Epiphany.
Epis., Episc. Episcopal.
E.P.N.S. electroplated nickel silver ; English Place-Name Society.
E.P.T. Excess Profits Tax.
Er erbium.
E.R. East Riding (Yorks) ; *Elisabeth Regina*, Elizabeth, Queen.
E.R.(I.) *Edwardus Rex* (*Imperator*), Edward, King (and Emperor).
E.R.P. European Recovery Plan.
E.S.E., ESE. East-south-east.
esp., espec. especially.
ESP. extra-sensory perception.
Esq., Esqr. Esquire.
est. established ; estimated.
Esth. Esther.
e.s.u. electrostatic unit.
et al. *et alibi*, and elsewhere ; *et alii, aliae*, or *alia*, and others.
etc., &c. *et ceteri* or *cetera*, and the others, and so forth.
et seq. or sq. (sing.), *et sequens*, **et sqq.** (pl.), *et sequentes* or *sequentia*, and the following.
ety., etym. etymology ; etymological.
Eu europium.
E.U. Evangelical Union.
Ex., Exod. Exodus.
ex. examined ; example ; exception ; excursus ; executive ; export.
Exc. Excellency.
exc. except ; exception.
ex. div. *extra dividendum*, without dividend.
ex. g., ex. gr. *exempli gratia*, for the sake of example.
ex lib. *ex libris*, from the books (of)—as on book-plates.
Exon. *Exonia*, Exeter ; *Exoniensis*, of Exeter.
exp. export.
exr. executor.
Ez. Ezra.
Ezek. Ezekiel.
E. & O.E. Errors and Omissions Excepted.

F. (with following letters). Fellow of — ; (or **Fahr.**) Fahrenheit.
F fluorine.
f. following ; farthing ; feminine ; fathom ; foot ; forte.
Fa. Florida.
F.A. Football Association.
F.A.I. Fellow of the (Chartered) Auctioneers' Institute.
fam. familiar ; family.
F.A.M. Free and Accepted Masons.
F.A.N.Y. First Aid Nursing Yeomanry.

F.A.O. Food and Agriculture Organisation.
F.A.S. Fellow of the Society of Arts ; Fellow of the Antiquarian Society.
F.B. Fenian Brotherhood.
F.B.A. Fellow of the British Academy.
F.B.I. Federation of British Industries ; Federal Bureau of Investigation.
F.C.I.S. Fellow of the Chartered Institute of Secretaries.
F.C.P. Fellow of the College of Preceptors.
fcp., fcap. foolscap.
F.C.S. Fellow of the Chemical Society.
F.D. *Fidei Defensor*, Defender of the Faith.
Fe *ferrum*, iron.
Feb. February.
fec. *fecit*, did it, or made it (sing.).
F.E.I.S. Fellow of the Educational Institute of Scotland.
fem. feminine.
feud. feudal.
Ff. The Pandects, prob. by corr. of Greek Π.
ff. *fecerunt*, did it or made it (pl.) ; folios ; following (pl.) ; fortissimo.
F.F.A. Fellow of the Faculty of Actuaries.
fff. fortississimo.
F.F.P.S. Fellow of the Faculty of Physicians and Surgeons (Glasgow).
F.G.S. Fellow of the Geological Society.
F.H.A.S. Fellow of the Highland and Agricultural Society.
F.I.A. Fellow of the Institute of Actuaries.
F.I.D.O. Fog Investigation Dispersal Operation.
fi. fa. *fieri facias*, that you cause to be made (a writ of execution).
fig. figure ; figuratively.
F.I.J. Fellow of the Institute of Journalists.
fin. *ad finem*, at the end.
fl. *floruit*, flourished ; florin.
F.L.A. Fellow of the Library Association.
Flor., Fla., Fa. Florida.
F.L.S. Fellow of the Linnaean Society.
fm. fathom.
F.M. Field-Marshal.
F.O. Field-Officer ; Foreign Office ; Full Organ.
fo., fol. folio.
f.o.b. free on board.
F.O.E. Friends of Europe.
f.o.r. free on rail.
F.P. fire-plug ; former pupil.
fp. fortepiano.
f.p. freezing point.
F.P.S. Fellow of the Philological Society ; foot-pound-second.
Fr. France, French ; Friar ; Friday.
Fr francium.
fr. fragment ; franc ; frequently. **frcs.** francs.
F.R.A.M. Fellow of the Royal Academy of Music.
F.R.A.S. Fellow of the Royal Astronomical Society ; Fellow of the Royal Asiatic Society.
frat. fraternise.
F.R.C.O. Fellow of the Royal College of Organists.
F.R.C.P. Fellow of the Royal College of Physicians.
F.R.C.P.E. Fellow of the Royal College of Physicians of Edinburgh.
F.R.C.S. Fellow of the Royal College of Surgeons.
F.R.C.S.E. Fellow of the Royal College of Surgeons of Edinburgh.
F.R.C.S.I. Fellow of the Royal College of Surgeons of Ireland.
F.R.G.S. Fellow of the Royal Geographical Society.
F.R.Hist.S. Fellow of the Royal Historical Society.
F.R.H.S. Fellow of the Royal Horticultural Society.
F.R.I.B.A. Fellow of the Royal Institute of British Architects.
F.R.I.C. Fellow of the Royal Institute of Chemistry.
F.R.Met.S. Fellow of the Royal Meteorological Society.
F.R.M.S. Fellow of the Royal Microscopical Society.
F.R.P.S. Fellow of the Royal Photographic Society.
F.R.S. Fellow of the Royal Society.
F.R.S.A. Fellow of the Royal Society of Arts.
F.R.S.E. Fellow of the Royal Society, Edinburgh.
F.R.S.G.S. Fellow of the Royal Scottish Geographical Society.

F.R.S.L. Fellow of the Royal Society of Literature.

F.R.S.S.A. Fellow of the Royal Scottish Society of Arts.

F.S. Field Service.

F.S.A. Fellow of the Society of Arts ; Fellow of the Society of Antiquaries (**Scot.**, of Scotland).

F.S.A.A. Fellow of the Society of Incorporated Accountants and Auditors.

F.S.E. Fellow of the Society of Engineers.

F.S.S. Fellow of the Statistical Society.

ft. foot, feet ; fort.

F.T.C.D. Fellow of Trinity College, Dublin.

fth., fthm. fathom.

fur. furlong(s).

fut. future.

fz. forzando or forzato.

F.Z.S. Fellow of the Zoological Society (**S.**, of Scotland).

g. gram(me) ; (or **gen.**) genitive.

Ga. Georgia.

Ga gallium.

G.A. General Assembly.

Gael. Gaelic.

Gal. Galatians.

gal., gall. gallon(s).

gam. gamut.

gaz. gazette ; gazetteer.

G.B. Great Britain. **G.B. and I.** Great Britain and Ireland.

G.B.E. (Knight or Dame) Grand Cross of the British Empire.

G.B.S. George Bernard Shaw.

G.C. George Cross.

G.C.A. Ground Control(led) Approach or Control Apparatus.

G.C.B. (Knight) Grand Cross of the Bath.

G.C.H. (Knight) Grand Cross of Hanover.

G.C.I.E. (Knight) Grand Commander of the Indian Empire.

G.C.M. General Court-martial.

g.c.m., G.C.M. greatest common measure.

G.C.M.G. (Knight) Grand Cross of St Michael and St George.

G.C.S.I. (Knight) Grand Commander of the Star of India.

G.C.V.O. (Knight) Grand Cross of the (Royal) Victorian Order.

Gd gadolinium.

Gdns. gardens.

Ge germanium.

Gen. Genesis ; (or **Genl.**) General.

gen. gender ; genitive ; genus.

gent. gentleman.

Geo. Georgia.

geog. geography.

geol. geology.

geom. geometry.

Ger. German.

ger. gerund.

G.F.S. Girls' Friendly Society.

G.H.Q. General Headquarters.

G.I. (U.S. Army) government (or general) issue—hence—common soldier.

Gib. Gibraltar.

Gk. Greek.

Gl glucinum (now officially beryllium).

Glam. Glamorganshire.

Glos. Gloucestershire.

G.M. George Medal.

gm. gram(me).

G.M.T. Greenwich Mean Time.

G.O. General Order ; Grand Organ.

G.O.C. General Officer Commanding.

G.O.M. Grand Old Man (W. E. Gladstone).

Gov. Government, Governor.

G.P. general practitioner ; grateful patient ; *Gloria Patri*, glory to the Father.

G.P.O. General Post-office.

Gr. Greek.

gr. grain ; grammar ; gross ; gunner.

G.R.(I.). *Georgius Rex* (*Imperator*), George, King (and Emperor).

G.S. General Staff ; General Service.

gs. guineas.

G.S.O. General Staff Officer.

G.S.P. Good Service Pension.

gu. guinea ; gules.

guin. guinea.

G.W.(R.). Great Western (Railway).

H. hydrant.

H hydrogen ; horrific (motion picture certificate).

h., hr. hour.

H.A. Heavy Artillery.

h.a. *hoc anno*, this year.

Hab. Habakkuk.

hab. habitat.

H.A.C. Honourable Artillery Company.

Hag. Haggai.

h. and c. hot and cold (water laid on).

Hants Hampshire.

H.B.M. His (or Her) Britannic Majesty.

H.C. Heralds' College ; House of Commons ; Holy Communion.

H.C.F., Hon. C.F. Honorary Chaplain to the Forces.

h.c.f., H.C.F. highest common factor.

H.C.M. His (or Her) Catholic Majesty.

He helium.

H.E. His Excellency ; His Eminence ; High Explosive ; Horizontal Equivalent.

Heb., Hebr. Hebrew ; Hebrews.

H.E.I.C.S. Honourable East India Company's Service.

her. heraldry ; *heres*, heir.

Herts Hertfordshire.

hf. half. **hf.-bd.** half-bound. **hf.-cf.** half-calf. **hf.-mor.** half-morocco.

Hf hafnium.

H.F. high frequency.

H.G. His (or Her) Grace.

Hg *hydrargyrum*, mercury.

H.H. His (or Her) Highness.

hhd. hogshead.

H.I.H. His (or Her) Imperial Highness.

hist. historian ; history.

H.J. *hic jacet*, here lies. **H.J.S.** *hic jacet sepultus*, here lies buried.

H.K. House of Keys (Isle of Man).

H.L.I. Highland Light Infantry.

H.M. His (or Her) Majesty.

H.M.A.S. His (or Her) Majesty's Australian Ship.

H.M.C. His (or Her) Majesty's Customs.

H.M.C.S. His (or Her) Majesty's Canadian Ship.

H.M.I.S. His (or Her) Majesty's Inspector of Schools.

H.M.P. *hoc monumentum posuit*, erected this monument.

H.M.S. His (or Her) Majesty's Ship or Service.

H.M.S.O. His (or Her) Majesty's Stationery Office.

ho. house.

Ho holmium.

Hon. Honourable, Honorary.

hor. horizon ; horology.

hort., hortic. horticulture ; horticultural.

Hos. Hosea.

H.P. High Priest ; half-pay.

h.p. horse-power.

H.Q. headquarters.

H.R. House of Representatives ; Home Rule.

Hr. Herr.

hr. hour.

H.R.E. Holy Roman Emperor or Empire.

H.R.H. His (or Her) Royal Highness.

H.R.I.P. *hic requiescit in pace*, here rests in peace.

H.S. *hic situs*, here is laid. **H.S.E.** *hic sepultus* (or *situs*) *est*, here is buried (or laid).

H.S.H. His (or Her) Serene Highness.

H.S.S. *Historiae Societatis Socius*, Fellow of the Historical Society.

I iodine.

Ia. Iowa.

I.A. Indian Army.

ib., ibid. *ibidem*, in the same place.

i/c. in charge.

ich., ichth. ichthyology.

I.C.I. Imperial Chemical Industries.

icon. iconography, iconographic.

I.C.S. Indian Civil Service.
id. *idem*, the same.
I.D. Intelligence Department.
Id. Idaho.
I.D.B. Illicit Diamond Buying (in S. Africa).
I.D.N. *in Dei nomine*, in the name of God.
i.e. *id est*, that is.
I.F.S. Irish Free State.
I.H.C., I.H.S., for the Greek capitals IHC (C a form of Σ), first two and last letters of *Iesous*, Jesus, often misread as *Jesus Hominum Salvator*, Jesus Saviour of Men.
i.h.p. indicated horse-power.
Ill. Illinois.
ill. illustration; illustrated.
I.L.O. International Labour Office.
I.L.P. Independent Labour Party.
imit. imitative.
Imp. Imperial; *Imperator*, Emperor.
imp. (also **imperf.**) imperfect; (also **imper.**) imperative; *imprimatur*, let it be printed; (also **impers.**) impersonal.
I.M.S. Indian Medical Service.
In indium.
in. inch(es).
inc., incorp. incorporated.
incl. including; included.
incog. *incognito* (It.), unknown, avoiding publicity.
Ind. Indiana.
I.N.D. Same as **I.D.N.**
ind., indic. indicative.
indecl. indeclinable.
indef. indefinite.
indic. indicative.
indiv. individual.
Ind. Ter. Indian Territory.
inf. *infra*, below; infantry; infinitive.
infra dig. *infra dignitatem*, beneath one's dignity.
init. *initio*, in the beginning.
in lim. *in limine*, on the threshold, at the outset.
in loc. *in loco*, in its place. **in loc. cit.** *in loco citato*, in the place cited.
in pr. *in principio*, in the beginning.
I.N.R.I. *Jesus Nazarenus Rex Judaeorum*, Jesus of Nazareth King of the Jews.
inst. instant—the present month; institute.
Inst. Act. Institute of Actuaries.
Inst. C.E. Institution of Civil Engineers.
int. interest; interior; interpreter.
interrog. interrogation; interrogative; interrogatively.
in trans. *in transitu*, in transit.
intrans. intransitive.
intro., introd. introduction.
inv. *invenit*, designed it; inventor; invented; invoice.
I.O.F. Independent Order of Foresters.
I.O.G.T. Independent Order of Good Templars.
I.O.M. Isle of Man.
I.O.U. I owe you.
I.O.W. Isle of Wight.
I.P.D. *in praesentia Dominorum*, in presence of the Lords (of Session).
I.Q. Intelligence Quotient.
i.q. *idem quod*, the same as.
Ir iridium.
I.R.A. Irish Republican Army.
I.R.B. Irish Republican Brotherhood.
Irel. Ireland.
Is., Isa. Isaiah.
I.S.C. Indian Staff Corps.
I.S.O. Imperial Service Order.
It. Italian; Italian vermouth.
ital. italic.
I.U. international unit.
I.W.W. Industrial Workers of the World.

Jan. January.
Jas. James.
J.C. *Juris Consultus*, Jurisconsult; Jesus Christ; Justice Clerk.
J.C.D. *Juris Civilis Doctor*, Doctor of Civil Law.
Jer. Jeremiah.
J.H.S. Same as **I.H.C.**
Jno. John.

Jo. Joel.
Josh. Joshua.
J.P. Justice of the Peace.
Jr., Jun., Junr. Junior.
J.U.D. *Juris Utriusque Doctor*, Doctor both of Canon and of Civil Law.
Jud., Judg. Judges.
Jul. July.
Junc. Junction.
jurisp. jurisprudence.

K. (or **k.**). Kelvin (thermometer scale);
K *kalium*, potassium; (Mozart's works) Köchel, who arranged them chronologically.
Kan. Kansas.
K.B. Knight of the Bath; Knight Bachelor; King's Bench.
K.B.E. Knight Commander of the British Empire.
K.C. King's Counsel; King's College.
kc. kilocycle.
K.C.B. Knight Commander of the Bath.
K.C.H. Knight Commander of (the Order of) Hanover.
K.C.I.E. Knight Commander of the Indian Empire.
K.C.M.G. Knight Commander of St Michael and St George.
K.C.S.I. Knight Commander of the Star of India.
K.C.V.O. Knight Commander of the (Royal) Victorian Order.
Ken. Kentucky.
kg. kilogram(s).
K.G. Knight of the Garter.
K.G.C.B. Knight of the Grand Cross of the Bath.
K.G.F. Knight of the Golden Fleece.
kilo. kilogram; kilometre.
K.K. *Kaiserlich-königlich*, Imperial-Royal.
K.K.K. Ku Klux Klan.
K.L.H. Knight of the Legion of Honour.
K.M. Knight of Malta.
Km. Kingdom.
km. kilometre(s).
Knt., Kt. Knight.
K.O., k.o. knock out.
K. of L. Knight of Labour.
K.O.S.B. King's Own Scottish Borderers.
K.O.Y.L.I. King's Own Yorkshire Light Infantry.
K.P. Knight of St Patrick.
kr. kreutzer; krone.
Kr krypton.
Ks. Kansas.
K.S.I. Knight of the Star of India.
K.T. Knight of the Thistle.
Kt. Knight.
Kt. Bach. Knight Bachelor.
κ.τ.λ., k.t.l. *kai ta leipomena* or *kai ta loipa* (Gr.), and the rest, and so forth.
kw. kilowatt.
Ky. Kentucky.

L. Lake; Latin; Liberal; *libra*, pound.
l. latitude; league; long; litre; *libra*.
La. Louisiana.
La lanthanum.
L.A. Law Agent; Literate in Arts.
Lab. Labour.
lab. laboratory.
L.A.C. Licentiate of the Apothecaries' Company.
Lam. Lamentations.
Lancs Lancashire.
lang. language.
Lat. Latin.
lat. latitude.
lb. *libra*, pound.
lb., l.b.w. leg before wicket (in cricket).
l.c. lower-case (in printing); *loco citato*, in the place cited; left centre; letter of credit.
L.C.B. Lord Chief-Baron.
L.C.C. London County Council.
L.Ch. (or **L.Chir.**). *Licentiatus Chirurgiae*, Licentiate in Surgery.
L.C.J. Lord Chief-Justice.
l.c.m., L.C.M. least common multiple.
L.C.P. Licentiate of the College of Preceptors.
Ld. Lord. **Ldp., Lp.** Lordship.

L.D. Lady Day.
L.D.S. Licentiate in Dental Surgery.
L.D.V. Local Defence Volunteers (afterwards Home Guard).
lect. lecture.
leg. legal; legate; legislature.
Leip. Leipzig.
Lev., Levit. Leviticus.
lex. lexicon.
L.F. low frequency.
l.h. left hand.
L.H.D. *Litterarum Humaniarum Doctor*, Doctor of Letters.
Li lithium.
L.I. Long Island; Light Infantry.
lib. *liber*, book. **lib. cat.** library catalogue.
Lieut., Lt. Lieutenant.
Lincs Lincolnshire.
Linn. Linnaean, Linnaeus.
liq. liquid.
lit. literally; literature.
lith., litho., lithog. lithograph; lithography.
Lit. Hum. *litterae humaniores*, humane letters, the humanities.
Litt.D. *Litterarum Doctor*, Doctor of Letters.
LL.B. *Legum Baccalaureus*, Bachelor of Laws.
L.L.C.M. Licentiate of the London College of Music.
LL.D. *Legum Doctor*, Doctor of Laws.
L.M., l.m. long metre.
L.M.S. London Missionary Society; London, Midland and Scottish (Railway).
L.N.E.(R.) London and North-Eastern (Railway).
loc. cit. *loco citato*, at the place quoted.
L. of C. line of communication.
log logarithm.
lon., long. longitude
Lond. London.
loq. *loquitur*, speaks.
L.P. Lord Provost.
L.R.A.M. Licentiate of the Royal Academy of Music.
L.R.C.P. Licentiate of the Royal College of Physicians (E., of Edinburgh).
L.R.C.S. Licentiate of the Royal College of Surgeons.
L.S. Linnaean Society; *loco sigilli*, in the place of the seal.
l.s. left side.
L.S.A. Licentiate of the Society of Apothecaries.
L.S.D. *librae, solidi, denarii*, pounds, shillings, pence.
Lt. Lieutenant. **Lt.-Gen.** Lieutenant-General.
Lu lutetium.

M. *Monsieur* (Fr.), Mr (pl. **MM.**).
M. or m. *mille*, a thousand.
m. married; masculine; *meridiem*, noon; metre; mile.
μ. micron.
M.A. *Magister Artium*, Master of Arts.
Mac., Macc. Maccabees.
mach. machinery.
Mad. Madam.
mag. magazine.
Maj. Major.
Mal. Malachi.
Manit. Manitoba.
Mar. March.
marg. margin; marginal.
Marq. Marquis.
mas., masc. masculine.
Mass. Massachusetts.
math., maths. mathematics.
Matt. Matthew.
max. maximum.
M.B. *Medicinae Baccalaureus*, Bachelor of Medicine; mark of the beast.
M.B.E. Member of the Order of the British Empire.
M.C. Member of Congress; Master of Ceremonies; Member of Council; Military Cross.
M.C.C. Marylebone Cricket Club; Member of the County Council.
M.C.P. Member of the College of Preceptors.
M.C.P.S. megacycles per second.

Md. Maryland.
M.D. *Medicinae Doctor*, Doctor of Medicine.
Mdlle., Mlle. *Mademoiselle* (Fr.), Miss.
Mdm. Madam.
M.E. Most Excellent; Methodist Episcopal; Middle English; Mining or Mechanical Engineer.
Me. Maine.
M.E.C. Member of the Executive Council.
mech. mechanic; mechanical.
med. medical; medicine; mediaeval; *medius, -a, -um*, middle.
mem. memorandum; *memento*, remember.
memo. memorandum.
Messrs. *Messieurs* (Fr.), Sirs, Gentlemen; used as pl. of Mr.
met., metaph. metaphysics; metaphor; metaphorical.
metal., metall. metallurgy.
meteor. meteorology.
meth. methylated spirits.
M.E.V., Mev. million electron-volts.
Mex. Mexico; Mexican.
M.E.Z. *Mitteleuropäische Zeit*, Central European Time.
mf. mezzoforte; microfarad.
mfd. manufactured. **mfrs.** manufacturers.
M.F.H. Master of Foxhounds.
m.ft. *mistura fiat*, let a mixture be made.
Mg magnesium.
mg., mgm., mgr. milligram(s).
M.G. machine-gun.
Mgr. Monseigneur; Monsignor.
M.H.G. Middle High German.
M.H.R. Member of the House of Representatives.
Mi. Mississippi.
Mic. Micah.
M.I.C.E. or M.Inst.C.E. Member of the Institution of Civil Engineers.
Mich. Michigan.
M.I.E.E. Member of the Institute of Electrical Engineers.
M.I.Mech.E. Member of the Institution of Mechanical Engineers.
M.I.M.M. Member of the Institution of Mining and Metallurgy.
min. mineralogy; minimum.
Minn. Minnesota.
misc. miscellaneous; miscellany.
mil., milit. military.
M.I.S.Ch. Member of the Incorporated Society of Chiropodists.
Miss. Mississippi. **ml.** millilitre.
M.L.A. Member of Legislative Assembly.
M.L.C. Member of Legislative Council.
Mlle. *Mademoiselle*:—pl. **Mlles.**, *Mesdemoiselles*.
MM. *Messieurs* (Fr.), Gentlemen or Sirs.
M.M. (Their) Majesties; Martyrs; Military Medal.
mm. millimetre(s).
mμ. millimicron.
Mme. *Madame* (Fr.):—pl. **Mmes.**, *Mesdames*.
Mn manganese.
Mo. Missouri.
Mo molybdenum.
M.O. Medical Officer.
mo. month.
mod. modern; moderato.
Mods. moderations.
M.O.H. Medical Officer of Health.
M.O.I. Ministry of Information (later C.O.I.).
mol. wt. molecular weight.
Mon. Monmouthshire.
Monsig. Monsignor.
Mont. Montana.
Mor. Morocco.
morn. morning.
mos. months.
M.P. Member of Parliament; Military Police; Metropolitan Police; (U.S.) Municipal Police.
m.p.h. miles per hour.
M.P.S. Member of the Philological Society, or of the Pharmaceutical Society.
M.R. Master of the Rolls.
Mr. Master or Mister.
M.R.A.S. Member of the Royal Asiatic Society, or of the Royal Academy of Sciences.

M.R.C.C. Member of the Royal College of Chemistry.

M.R.C.P. Member of the Royal College of Physicians.

M.R.C.S. Member of the Royal College of Surgeons.

M.R.C.V.S. Member of the Royal College of Veterinary Surgeons.

M.R.G.S. Member of the Royal Geographical Society.

M.R.I. Member of the Royal Institution.

M.R.I.A. Member of the Royal Irish Academy.

Mrs. Mistress.

MS. manuscript. **MSS.** manuscripts.

M.S. Master of Surgery; *Memoriae Sacrum*, Sacred to the Memory.

m.s., M/S. months (after) sight.

msec. microsecond.

m.s.l. mean sea-level.

M.S.S. Member of the Statistical Society.

M.T. Mechanical Transport.

Mt., mt. mount. **Mts., mts.** mountains.

MTB. motor torpedo-boat.

mth. month.

M.T.P.I. Member of the Town Planning Institute.

mus. music; museum.

Mus.B., Mus. Bac. Bachelor of Music.

Mus.D., Doc., Doct. Doctor of Music.

m.v. merchant vessel; motor vessel; muzzle velocity; *mezza voce*, with medium fullness of sound.

M.V.O. Member of the Royal Victorian Order.

myst. mysteries.

myth. mythology.

M & B May and Baker (sulphonamides prepared by this firm and others).

N. North, Northern.

N nitrogen.

n. name; noun; *natus*, born; neuter; noon.

Na *natrium*, sodium.

N.A. North America.

N.A.A.F.I. Navy, Army and Air Force Institute(s).

Nah. Nahum.

Nap. Napoleon.

Nat. National.

Nat. Hist. Natural History.

NATO North Atlantic Treaty Organisation.

nat. ord. natural order.

nat. phil. natural philosophy.

naut. nautical.

nav. naval; navigation.

Nb niobium.

N.B. New Brunswick; North Britain (a form offensive to many Scotsmen); North British; north bag.

N.B., n.b. *nota bene*, note well, or take notice.

N.C. North Carolina; New Church.

N.C.B. National Coal Board.

N.C.O. non-commissioned officer.

Nd neodymium.

N.D., N. Dak. North Dakota.

n.d. no date, not dated.

Ne neon.

N.E., NE. North-east; New England.

Neb., Nebr. Nebraska.

N.E.D. New English Dictionary (now O.E.D.).

neg. negative.

Neh. Nehemiah.

N.E.I. *non est inventus*, has not been found.

nem. con. *nemine contradicente*, no one contradicting.

nem. diss. *nemine dissentiente*, no one dissenting.

Nep. Neptune.

Neth. Netherlands.

neut. neuter.

Nev. Nevada.

New M. New Mexico.

N.F. Norman French; Northern French; (or NF., or Nfd.) Newfoundland.

N.F.S. National Fire Service.

N.F.U. National Farmers' Union.

N.H. New Hampshire.

N.H.I. National Health Insurance.

Ni nickel.

ni. pri., *nisi prius.* See **nisi** in Dict.

N.J. New Jersey.

n.l. *non licet*, it is not permitted; *non liquet*, it is not clear; *non longe*, not far.

N.M. New Mexico.

N.N.E., NNE. North-north-east.

N.N.W., NNW. North-north-west.

N.O. New Orleans; natural order.

No., no. *numero*, (in) number. **Nos., nos.** numbers.

nom., nomin. nominative.

noncom. noncommissioned.

Noncon. Nonconformist.

non-con. non-content.

non obst. *non obstante*, notwithstanding.

non pros. *non prosequitur*, does not prosecute.

non seq. *non sequitur*, it does not follow.

n.o.p. not otherwise provided.

Northants Northamptonshire.

Northmb. Northumberland.

Norvic. *Norvicensis*, of Norwich.

Nos. Numbers.

Notts Nottinghamshire.

Nov. November.

Np neptunium.

N.P. Notary Public; New Providence; no place (on title-pages).

N.R.A. National Rifle Association.

N.S. New Style; Nova Scotia.

n.s. not specified.

N.S.P.C.A. National Society for Prevention of Cruelty to Animals.

N.S.P.C.C. National Society for Prevention of Cruelty to Children.

N.S.W. New South Wales.

N.T. New Testament; Northern Territory.

N.T.P. normal temperature and pressure.

N.U. name unknown.

Num., Numb. Numbers.

numis., numism. numismatics.

N.U.R. National Union of Railwaymen

N.U.T. National Union of Teachers.

N.V. New Version.

N.V.M. Nativity of the Virgin Mary.

N.W., NW. North-west.

N.Y. New York.

N.Z. New Zealand.

N. & Q. Notes and Queries.

O. Ohio.

O oxygen.

o/a. on account of.

O.A.P. Old Age Pension or Pensioner.

ob. *obiit*, died.

Ob., Obad. Obadiah.

obdt. obedient.

O.B.E. Officer of the Order of the British Empire.

obj. object; objective.

obl. oblique; oblong.

obs. observation; obsolete.

O.C. Officer Commanding.

Oct. October.

O.C.T.U. Officer Cadet Training Unit.

O.D. Ordnance Datum or Data; Ordinary Seaman.

O.E. Old English.

O.E.D. Oxford English Dictionary.

O.E.E.C. Organisation for European Economic Co-operation.

O.F. Oddfellow; Old French.

off. official; officinal.

O.F.S. Orange Free State.

O.H.G. Old High German.

O.H.M.S. On His (or Her) Majesty's Service.

O.K. All correct (perh. a humorous spelling of this; or Choctaw *okeh*, so be it).

Okla. Oklahoma.

Old Test. Old Testament.

O.M. Order of Merit; Old Measurement.

Ont. Ontario.

Op. Opera; *Opus*, work.

O.P. *Ordinis Praedicatorum*, of the Order of Preachers (or Dominicans); opposite prompt (*theat.*).

o.p. out of print.

op. opposite; *opus*.

op. cit. *opere citato*, in the work cited.

opp. opposed; opposite.
opt. optative; *optime*, very well indeed.
ord. ordained; order; ordinary; ordnance.
Or., Ore., Oreg. Oregon.
orig. origin; original; originally.
Os osmium.
O.S. Old Style; Ordinary Seaman.
O.S.A. *Ordinis Sancti Augustini*, of the Order of St Augustine.
O.S.B. *Ordinis Sancti Benedicti*, of the Order of St Benedict.
O.S.F. *Ordinis Sancti Francisci*, of the Order of St Francis.
o.s.p. *obiit sine prole*, died without issue.
O.T. Old Testament.
O.T.C. Officers' Training Corps.
Oxf. Oxford.
Oxon. *Oxonia*, Oxford; *Oxoniensis*, of Oxford.
oz. ounce(s).

P. President; Prince.
P phosphorus.
p. piano; page; participle.
pa. past.
Pa. (or Penn.). Pennsylvania.
Pa protactinium.
p.a. per annum; participial adjective.
P.A. Press Association.
P.A.A. Pan American Airways.
paint. painting.
Pal. Palestine.
pam. pamphlet.
Pan. Panama.
pa.p. past participle.
par. paragraph; parallel; parish.
pass. passive.
pa.t. past tense.
Pat. Off. Patent Office.
P.A.Y.E. Pay As You Earn (Income Tax).
Pb *plumbum*, lead.
P.B. Pharmacopoeia Britannica; Plymouth Brethren.
P.C. *Patres Conscripti*, Conscript Fathers; Privy Councillor; Police Constable.
P.C. post-card.
P.C.S. Principal Clerk of Session.
Pd palladium.
pd. paid.
P.E. Protestant Episcopal.
P.E.C., pec photo-electric cell.
ped. pedal.
P.E.I. Prince Edward Island.
P.E.N. Poets, Playwrights, Editors, Essayists, and Novelists.
Pen. Peninsula.
Penn. Pennsylvania.
Pent. Pentecost.
PEP, P.E.P. Political and Economic Planning.
per. period; person.
per an. *per annum*, per year, by the year.
per cent., per ct. *per centum*, by the hundred.
perf. perfect.
perh. perhaps.
per pro. *per procurationem*, by the agency (of).
Pers. Persian.
pers. person, personal.
Pg. Portugal; Portuguese.
Phar., Pharm. pharmaceutical; pharmacopoeia; pharmacy.
Ph.B. *Philosophiae Baccalaureus*, Bachelor of Philosophy.
Ph.D. *Philosophiae Doctor*, Doctor of Philosophy.
Phil. Philippians; Philemon; Philadelphia.
Phil. Trans. Philosophical Transactions.
phon., phonet. phonetics.
phonog. phonography.
phot. photography.
phr. phrase.
phys. physiology; physics; physician.
P.I. Philippine Islands.
pinx., pxt. *pinxit*, painted it.
PK psychokinesis.
plu., plur. plural.
plup. pluperfect.   [dismantled].
P.L.U.T.O. Pipeline Under the Ocean (1944; later

Pm promethium.
pm. premium.
P.M. Past Master; *post meridiem*, after noon; Postmaster; *post mortem*, after death; Prime Minister; Provost-Marshal.
P.M.G. Postmaster-General.
Pmr. Paymaster.
p.n. promissory note.
P.N.E.U. Parents' National Educational Union.
Po polonium.
po. pole.
P.O. post-office; postal order.
p.o.d. pay on delivery.
Pol. Econ. Political Economy.
P.O.O. post-office order.
pop. population.
pos., posit. positive.
P.O.W. prisoner of war.
P.P. parish priest; present pupil.
p.p. past participle.
pp. pianissimo; pages; *per procurationem*, by proxy.
P.P.C. *pour prendre congé* (Fr.), to take leave; picture post-card.
P.P.I. Plan Position Indicator.
ppp. pianississimo.
P.P.S. *post postscriptum*, a later additional postscript.
Pr. Prince; priest; Provençal.
Pr praseodymium.
pr. pair; per; present; price.
P.R. prize ring; Porto Rico; proportional representation ; *Populus Romanus*, the Roman people.
P.R.A. President of the Royal Academy.
P.R.B. Pre-Raphaelite Brotherhood.
Preb. Prebend; Prebendary.
pref. preface.
prep. preparation; preparatory; preposition.
Pres. President.
pret. preterite.
P.R.I.B.A. President of the Royal Institute of British Architects.
P.R.N. *pro re nata*, for special occasion arising.
Pro. Professional.
prob. probably.
Prof. Professor.
prop. proper; properly; proposition; property.
Prot. Protestant.
pro tem. *pro tempore*, for the time being.
Prov. Proverbs.
prox. *proximo* (*mense*), next (month).
P.R.S. President of the Royal Society.
P.R.S.A. President of the Royal Scottish Academy.
P.R.S.E. President of the Royal Society of Edinburgh.
P.S. *post scriptum*, postscript, written after.
Ps., Psa. Psalm(s).
pseud. pseudonym.
Pt platinum.
pt. pint(s).
P.T. physical training; pupil teacher.
p.t. post-town.
P.T.O. Please turn over.
Pu plutonium.
Pub. Doc. public document.
P.W.D. Public Works Department.
pwt. pennyweight.
P. & O. Peninsular and Oriental Company.

Q. (or Qu.) query, question; (or **Que.**) Quebec; Queensland.
Q queue.
q. *quadrans*, farthing; query; quintal.
Q.A.B. Queen Anne's Bounty.
Q.A.I.M.N.S. Queen Alexandra's Imperial Military Nursing Service (now Q.A.R.A.N.C.).
Q.A.R.A.N.C. Queen Alexandra's Royal Army Nursing Corps.
Q.B. Queen's Bench.
Q.C. Queen's Counsel; Queen's College.
q.d. *quasi dicat*, as if he should say.
q.e. *quod est*, which is.
q.e.d. *quod erat demonstrandum*, which was to be demonstrated.
q.e.f. *quod erat faciendum*, which was to be done.

q.e.i. *quod erat inveniendum*, which was to be found.
q.l. *quantum libet*, as much as you please.
Q.M. Quartermaster.
qm. *quomodo*, in what manner, how.
Q.M.G. Quartermaster-General.
Q.M.S. Quartermaster-Sergeant.
Qq. (or **qq.**). quartos.
qr. quarter.
Q.S. Quarter-Sessions.
q.s., quant. suff. *quantum sufficit*, a sufficient quantity.
qt. quantity; quart(s). **qts.,** quarts.
q.t. quiet.
qto. quarto.
Qu. Queen; question.
qu., quar. quart; quarter, quarterly.
q.v. *quod vide*, which see; *quantum vis*, as much as you will.

R. *rex, regina*, King, Queen.
r. *recipe*, take.
R., Réau. Réaumur's thermometric scale.
Ra radium.
R.A. Royal Academy or Academician; Royal Artillery; Rear Admiral.
R.A.A.F. Royal Australian Air Force.
Rabb. Rabbinical.
R.A.C. Royal Automobile Club; Royal Armoured Corps; Royal Arch Chapter.
Rad. Radical.
rad. *radix*, root.
R.A.D.C. Royal Army Dental Corps.
R.A.E.C. Royal Army Educational Corps.
R.A.F. Royal Air Force.
R.A.M. Royal Academy of Music.
R.A.M.C. Royal Army Medical Corps.
R.A.N. Royal Australian Navy.
R.A.O.C. Royal Army Ordnance Corps.
R.A.P.C. Royal Army Pay Corps.
R.A.S. Royal Asiatic Society.
R.A.S.C. Royal Army Service Corps.
Rb rubidium.
R.B. Rifle Brigade.
R.B.A. Royal Society of British Artists.
R.C. Roman Catholic; Red Cross.
R.C.A. Royal Canadian Academy.
R.C.A.F. Royal Canadian Air Force.
R.C.M. Royal College of Music; Regimental Court-martial.
R.C.N. Royal Canadian Navy.
R.C.P. Royal College of Preceptors.
R.C.S. Royal College of Surgeons; Royal Corps of Signals.
R.D. Rural Dean; Reserve (Officers') Decoration.
Rd. road.
R.D.I. Royal Designer for Industry.
Re rhenium.
R.E. Royal Engineers; Royal Society of Etchers and Engravers; Royal Exchange.
Rec. *recipe*, take.
recd. received.
recpt. receipt.
Rect. Rector; Rectory.
ref. reference.
Ref. Ch. Reformed Church.
Reg. Prof. Regius Professor.
rel. relating; relation; relative.
R.E.M.E. Royal Electrical and Mechanical Engineers.
Rep. representative; republic; report: reporter.
rept. receipt.
retd. returned; retired.
Rev. revise; revision; Revelation; (or **Revd.**) Reverend.
Rev. Ver. Revised Version.
Rf. rinforzando.
R.F. *République française*, French Republic.
R.F.A. Royal Field Artillery.
R.F.C. Royal Flying Corps (now R.A.F.).
R.G.A. Royal Garrison Artillery.
R.G.G. Royal Grenadier Guards.
R.G.S. Royal Geographical Society.
Rgt. Regiment.
Rh rhodium.
R.H. Royal Highness.

r.h. right hand.
R.H.A. Royal Horse Artillery; Royal Hibernian Academy.
rhet. rhetoric.
R.H.G. Royal Horse Guards.
R.H.S. Royal Humane Society; Royal Horticultural Society; Royal Historical Society.
R.I. Royal Institute of Painters in Water Colours; Rhode Island.
R.I.B.A. Royal Institute of British Architects.
R.I.C. Royal Irish Constabulary; Royal Institute of Chemistry.
R.I.C.S. Royal Institution of Chartered Surveyors.
R.I.P. *requiescat in pace*, may he (or she) rest in peace.
R.I.P.H. Royal Institute of Public Health.
R.I.P.H.H. Royal Institute of Public Health and Hygiene.
R.L.S. Robert Louis Stevenson.
rly. railway.
R.M. Royal Mail; Royal Marines; resident magistrate; riding master.
R.M.A. Royal Military Academy; Royal Marine Artillery.
R.M.C. Royal Military College.
R.M.L.I. Royal Marine Light Infantry.
R.M.S. Royal Mail Steamer; Royal Microscopical Society.
Rn radon.
R.N. Royal Navy.
R.N.A.S. Royal Naval Air Service.
R.N.R. Royal Naval Reserve.
R.N.V.R. Royal Naval Volunteer Reserve.
R.N.Z.A.F. Royal New Zealand Air Force.
R.N.Z.N. Royal New Zealand Navy.
R.O.C. Royal Observer Corps.
Roffen. *Roffensis*, of Rochester.
Rom. Romans.
Rom. Cath. Roman Catholic.
R.P. Reformed Presbyterian; Regius Professor.
r.p.s. revolutions per second.
R.R. Right Reverend.
Rs. Rupees.
R.S. Royal Society. **R.SS.L. & E.** Royal Societies of London and Edinburgh.
R.S.A. Royal Society of Antiquaries; Royal Scottish Academy or Academician.
R.S.D. Royal Society of Dublin.
R.S.E. Royal Society of Edinburgh.
R.S.F.S.R. Russian Socialist Federated Soviet Republic.
R.S.L. Royal Society of Literature.
R.S.M. Regimental Sergeant-Major.
R.S.O. railway sub-office; railway sorting office.
R.S.P.C.A. Royal Society for the Prevention of Cruelty to Animals.
R.S.S., also **S.R.S.** *Regiae Societatis Socius*, Fellow of the Royal Society.
R.S.V.P. *répondez s'il vous plaît* (Fr.), reply, if you please.
R.S.W. Royal Scottish Water Colour Society.
Rt. Hon. Right Honourable.
R.T.O. Railway Traffic Officer.
Rt. Rev. Right Reverend.
R.T.S. Religious Tract Society (now incorporated in U.S.C.L.).
Ru ruthenium.
R.V. Revised Version.
R.W. Right Worthy.
R.W.S. Royal Society of Painters in Water Colours.
Rx. tens of rupees.
Ry. railway.
R.Y.S. Royal Yacht Squadron.

S. South; Sabbath; Saint; seconds; society; sun.
S sulphur.
SA., or S.A. (Ger. *Sturmabteilung*), Storm Troopers.
Sa. Saturday.
S.A. South Africa; South America; South Australia.
s.a. *secundum artem*, according to art; *sine anno*, without date.
S.A.A. Small Arms Ammunition.
S.A.C. Scottish Automobile Club.

Sam. Samuel.
S.A.S. *Societatis Antiquariorum Socius,* Fellow of the Society of Antiquaries.
Sask. Saskatchewan.
Sat. Saturday.
Sb *stibium,* antimony.
Sc scandium.
S.C. South Carolina; *senatus consultum,* a decree of the Roman senate; Special Constable; Supreme Court; Staff College; Staff Corps.
s.c., s. caps., sm. caps. small capitals.
sc., scil., sciz. *scilicet,* to wit, namely.
sc., sculp., sculpt. *sculpsit,* engraved it.
Sc.B. *Scientiae Baccalaureus,* Bachelor of Science.
Sc.D. *Scientiae Doctor,* Doctor of Science.
sci. fa. *scire facias,* that you cause to know.
S.C.L. Student of the Civil Law.
S.C.M. Student Christian Movement.
Scot. Scotland; Scottish.
Script. Scripture.
sculp., sculpt. *sculpsit,* engraved (this); sculpture; sculptor.
S.D. Senior Deacon; *salutem dicit,* sends greeting; (or **S. Dak.**) South Dakota.
s.d. *sine die,* without delay.
S.D.F. Social Democratic Federation.
Se selenium.
S.E., SE. South-east.
S.E.A.C. South-east Asia Command.
Sec., Secy. Secretary.
sec. *secundum,* in accordance with; second; section.
sec secant.
sec. leg. *secundum legem,* according to law.
sec. reg. *secundum regulam,* according to rule.
sect. section.
Sem. seminary; Semitic.
Sen. Senator; senior.
Sep., Sept. September; Septuagint.
seq. *sequens* (sing.), **seqq.,** *sequentes* or *sequentia* (pl.), following.
ser. series; sermon.
Serg., Sergt. Sergeant. **Serj., Serjt.,** Serjeant.
Sess. Session.
S.F. Sinn Fein.
sfz. sforzando.
S.G. Solicitor-General.
s.g. specific gravity.
S.H.A.E.F., SHAEF Supreme Headquarters of the Allied Expeditionary Force.
S.H.A.P.E., SHAPE. Supreme Headquarters Allied Powers Europe.
s.h.v. *sub hoc verbo* or *sub hac voce,* under this word.
Si silicon.
sig. signature.
sin sine.
sing. singular.
sinh hyperbolic sine.
S.J. Society of Jesus.
S.L. Solicitor at Law.
S.L., S.Lat. South latitude.
sld. sailed.
s.l.p. *sine legitima prole,* without lawful issue.
Sm samarium.
S.M. Short Metre; Sergeant-Major; *Sa Majesté,* His (or Her) Majesty.
Smith. Inst. Smithsonian Institution.
S.M. Lond. Soc. *Societatis Medicae Londiniensis Socius,* Member of the London Medical Society.
S.M.M. *Sancta Mater Maria,* Holy Mother Mary.
S.M.O. Senior Medical Officer.
s.m.p. *sine mascula prole,* without male issue.
Sn *stannum,* tin.
s.n. *secundum naturam,* according to nature.
s.o. seller's option.
Soc. Society.
sol. solution.
Sol., Solr. Solicitor. **Sol.-Gen.** Solicitor-General.
sop. soprano.
sp. spelling; species :—pl. **spp.**
s.p. *sine prole,* without issue.
S.P.C.A. Society for the Prevention of Cruelty to Animals.

S.P.C.C. Society for the Prevention of Cruelty to Children.
S.P.C.K. Society for Promoting Christian Knowledge.
S.P.G. Society for the Propagation of the Gospel.
sport. sporting.
S.P.Q.R. *Senatus Populusque Romanus,* the Senate and People of Rome.
S.P.R. Society for Psychical Research.
s.p.s. *sine prole superstite,* without surviving issue.
spt. seaport.
sq., Sq. square; *sequens,* following (in pl. **sqq.,** *sequentes* or *sequentia*).
sqn. squadron.
Sr. senior; Sir; Señor.
Sr strontium.
S.R. Southern Railway.
S.R.I. *Sacrum Romanum Imperium,* Holy Roman Empire.
S.R.N. State Registered Nurse.
S.R.S. *Societatis Regiae Socius,* Fellow of the Royal Society.
SS., or S.S. *Schutzstaffel* (Ger.), Hitler bodyguard.
S.S. Sunday (or Sabbath) School.
SS. Saints.
s.s. steamship; screw steamer.
S.S.C. Solicitor before the Supreme Court (Scotland); *Societas Sancti Crucis,* Society of the Holy Cross.
SS.D. *Sanctissimus Dominus,* Most Holy Lord (the Pope).
S.S.E., SSE. South-south-east.
S.S.W., SSW. South-south-west.
St. Saint; Strait; Street.
Staffs Staffordshire.
Ste. *Sainte* (Fr.). Fem. of *Saint.*
ster. (or **stereo.**) stereotype; (or **stg.**) sterling.
S.T.P. *Sanctae Theologiae Professor,* Professor of Theology.
str. steamer; strong.
S.T.S. Scottish Text Society.
Su. Sunday.
sub. subject.
subj. subject; subjunctive.
subst. substitute; substantive.
suf., suff. suffix.
sup. superfine; superior; (also **superl.**) superlative; supreme; *supra;* supine.
Sup. Ct. Superior Court; Supreme Court.
supp., suppl. supplement.
Supr. Supreme.
Supt. Superintendent.
Surg. surgeon; surgery.
Surv.-Gen. Surveyor-General.
S.V. *Sancta Virgo,* Holy Virgin; *Sanctitas Vestra,* Your Holiness.
s.v. *sub voce,* under the word or title.
S.W., SW. South-west.
S.Y.H.A. Scottish Youth Hostels Association.
sym. symbol.
syn. synonym.
synop. synopsis.
syr. *syrupus,* syrup.
syst. system.

Ta tantalum.
T.A. Territorial Army.
tal. qual. *talis qualis,* just as they come; average quality.
Tam. Tamil.
tan tangent.
tanh hyperbolic tangent.
Tb terbium.
T.B. tuberculosis.
T.B.D. torpedo-boat destroyer.
Tc technetium.
tc. tierce.
T.C.D. Trinity College, Dublin.
t.c.p. trichlorophenylmethyliodosalicyl (proprietary germicide).
T.D. Territorial Decoration.
Te tellurium.
tech. technical; technology.
tel., teleg. telegram, telegraph.

temp. temporal; *tempore*, in the time (of); temperature.

Ten., Tenn. Tennessee.

ten. tenor; tenuto.

Ter., Terr. Territory; terrace.

term. termination.

Test. Testament.

Teut. Teutonic.

Tex. Texas.

Text. Rec. *textus receptus*, the received text.

T.F. Territorial Force.

t.f. till forbidden.

Th thorium.

Th.D. Doctor of Theology.

theat. theatrical.

theol. theology; theologian.

theor. theorem.

Thess. Thessalonians.

Tho., Thos. Thomas.

T.H.W.M. Trinity High-water Mark.

Ti titanium.

t.i.d. *ter in die*, thrice a day.

Tim. Timothy.

Tit. Titus.

Tl thallium.

Tm thulium.

T.N.T. trinitrotoluene.

T.O. (or t.o.). turn over; Telegraph-office; Transport Officer.

Toc. H. Talbot House.

tom. *tomus*, tome or volume.

tp. township; troop.

tr. transpose; transactions; translator; trustee.

trans. transitive; translated; translation.

transf. transferred.

T.R.E. Telecommunications Research Establishment.

treas. treasurer.

T.R.H. Their Royal Highnesses.

trig. trigonometry.

Trin. Trinity.

Truron. *Truronensis*, of Truro.

T.S.O. town sub-office.

T.T. teetotaller; Tourist Trophy.

T.T.L. to take leave.

Tu., Tues. Tuesday.

T.U.C. Trades Union Congress.

TV television.

T.V.A. Tennessee Valley Authority.

typ., typo. typographer; typography.

U uranium; universal (motion picture certificate).

U.D.C. Urban District Council.

U.F.C. United Free Church (of Scotland).

U.K. United Kingdom.

ult. (also ulto.). *ultimo*, last; ultimate; ultimately.

U.N.E.S.C.O., UNESCO United Nations Educational Scientific and Cultural Organisation.

Unit. Unitarian.

Univ. University; Universalist.

U.N.O., UNO United Nations Organisation.

U.N.R.R.A., UNRRA United Nations Relief and Rehabilitation Administration.

U.P. United Presbyterian; United Press; United Provinces.

Uru. Uruguay.

U.S. United States; United Service.

u.s. *ut supra*, as above.

U.S.A. United States of America; United States Army.

U.S.C. United States of Colombia.

U.S.C.L. United Society for Christian Literature.

U.S.N. United States Navy.

U.S.S. United States Ship or Steamer.

U.S.S.R. Union of Soviet Socialist Republics.

usu. usually.

U.S.W. ultrasonic waves; ultrashort waves.

u.s.w. *und so weiter* (Ger.), and so forth.

Ut. Utah.

ut dict. *ut dictum*, as said.

ut sup. *ut supra*, as above.

ux. *uxor*, wife.

V vanadium.

V1 *Vergeltungswaffe* 1, German flying bomb.

V2 German flying rocket.

v. *versus*, against; *vide*, see; verb; verse; volt; volume.

V.A. Royal Order of Victoria and Albert; Vicar Apostolic.

Va. Virginia.

V.A.D. Voluntary Aid Detachment.

val. value.

var. variant; variety.

var. lect. *varia lectio*, variant reading.

Vat. Vatican.

vb. verb.

V.C. Vice-Chancellor; Vice-Consul; Victoria Cross.

V.D. Volunteer (Officers') Decoration; Venereal Disease(s).

v.d. various dates.

V.D.M. *Verbi Dei Minister*, Preacher of God's Word.

V.E. Victory in Europe.

veg. vegetable(s).

Ven. Venerable.

Venet. Venetian.

verb. sap. *verbum sapienti* (L.), or **verb. sat.**, *verbum sat(is)* (L.), a word to the wise is enough.

Vert. Vertebrata.

ves. vessel.

Vet., Veter Veterinary. **Vet. Surg.** Veterinary Surgeon.

V.G. Vicar-General.

v.g. *verbi gratia*, for example; (or **V.G.**) very good.

v.h.p. very high pressure.

v.i. verb intransitive.

Vic. Vicar; Vicarage.

Vict. Victoria; Victoria University.

vid. *vide*, see.

vil. village.

V.I.P. Very Important Person.

Vis., Visc. Viscount.

viz. *videlicet*, namely.

V.J. Victory over Japan.

voc. vocative.

vocab. vocabulary.

Vol. Volunteer.

vol. volume. **vols.** volumes.

V.P. Vice-President.

V.R. *Victoria Regina*, Queen Victoria. **V.R.I.** *Victoria Regina et Imperatrix*, Victoria, Queen and Empress.

V.R.D. Volunteer Reserve Decoration.

V.S. Veterinary Surgeon; *volti subito*, turn quickly.

Vt. Vermont.

v.t. verb transitive.

Vul., Vulg. Vulgate.

vul., vulg. vulgar.

vv. ll. *variae lectiones*, various readings.

v.y. various years.

W. West; Welsh.

W *wolframium*, tungsten.

w. weak.

W.A. West Africa; West Australia.

W.A.A.C. Women's Army Auxiliary Corps (later Q.M.A.A.C.).

W.A.A.F. Women's Auxiliary Air Force (earlier and later W.R.A.F.).

Wal. Walloon.

Wash. Washington.

W.C. water-closet; Western Central; Wesleyan Chapel.

W.D. War Department.

We., Wed. Wednesday.

W.E.A. Workers' Educational Association.

w.f. wrong fount.

w.g. wire gauge.

WHO World Health Organisation.

W.I. West Indies.

Wigorn. *Wigorniensis*, of Worcester.

Wilts Wiltshire.

Winton. *Wintoniensis*, of Winchester.

Wis. Wisconsin.

wk. week.

W.L.A. Women's Land Army.

Wm. William.

W.M.S. Wesleyan Missionary Society.

W.N.W., WNW. West-north-west.
W.O. War Office ; Warrant Officer.
Wp., Wpfl. Worshipful.
W.R. West Riding.
W.R.A.C. Women's Royal Army Corps.
W.R.A.F. Women's Royal Air Force.
W.R.I. Women's Rural Institute.
W.R.N.S. Women's Royal Naval Service.
W.S. Writer to the Signet.
W.S.W., WSW. West-south-west.
wt. weight.
W.V.S. Women's Voluntary Service.
Wy. Wyoming.

X Used to mark motion pictures to which persons
    under sixteen will not be admitted.
x. ex (L., without), as in x.d., ex dividend.
X. or Xt. Christ. (X = Gr. *Ch.*). Xm., Xmas.
    Christmas.
Xe xenon.
Xn., Xtian. Christian.

Y (or Yt) yttrium.
y. (or yr.) year ; (or yd.) yard.
Yb ytterbium.
ye. the (the *y* not, being a *y* but representing the
    old letter thorn, *Þ*).
Y.H.A. Youth Hostels Association.
Y.M.C.A. Young Men's Christian Association.
Yorks Yorkshire.
yr. your ; younger.
Yt yttrium.
yt. that (*y* as in ye).
Y.W.C.A. Young Women's Christian Association.

z.B. *zum beispiel* (Ger.), for example.
Zech. Zechariah.
Zeph. Zephaniah.
Zn zinc.
Zr zirconium.

& *et*, and.
&c. *et cetera*, and so forth.

MUSICAL SIGNS AND ABBREVIATIONS

Signs denoting time or relative value of sound :

Semi- Minim Crotchet Semi- Demisemi-
Breve. breve (half). (quarter). Quaver. quaver. quaver.
      (whole).

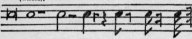

Each of these notes represents twice the duration of
sound of that which comes next in order. The
sign to the right of each note indicates a rest of
equal duration.

In time, the figure above a line
drawn thus across the stave denotes the length of the pause in
bars. Variants are :

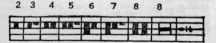

Signs denoting repetition of a note or notes :

(In early keyboard music,
however, this sign means
that the note is preceded
by two grace notes.)

(In early keyboard
music a mordent,
inverted mordent,
or double mordent.)

Repeat the bar so many times.

Accel. Accelerando. Gradually increasing in speed.
Acciaccatura. See Dictionary.
Ad lib. Ad libitum. As the performer chooses.
Anim. or *Animo.* Animato. Animated : with soul.

Appoggiatura. See Dictionary.

Arco. With the bow (not pizzicato).

Arpeggio, or arpeggiando. Notes of a
chord so marked are played consecutively, beginning with the lowest,
not simultaneously.

A tem. A tempo. In time.

Bar.   Double Bars.

Bar. A line drawn perpendicularly across the stave,
separating the notes into measures of equal length ;
more usually the music comprised within two
such lines.—*Double Bar*. Marks the larger divisions of a piece or movement ; in psalm tunes,
hymns, chants, &c., the end of a verse or sentence.

Bind or Tie. Placed over two notes or
chords in the same position on the stave, to show
they are to be played as one.

Brace. Joins staves performed simultaneously.

* ∧ ❜ Breath-marks. In vocal music, signs used
to show where breath should be taken.

Denoting common time ; the former
indicating four crotchets to the
bar, the latter (It. *alla breve*) two
minims to the bar.

Cal. Calando. Gradually slower, and with decreasing volume of tone.

G or Treble C, Alto and Tenor Clefs.   F or Bass Clef.
Clef.

Clef. The sign placed on the staff, at the beginning of a line or where a change occurs, determining the pitch of the notes that follow it.

Col legno. With the wood: strike the strings with the back of the bow.

⟨ *Cresc.* Crescendo. Gradual increase of tone.

(ʼ) Dash. When placed over or under a note, implies a very detached (*staccato*) style.

D.C. Da capo. From the beginning; indicating that the performer must turn to the beginning of the movement, and conclude at the double bar marked *Fine*.

D.S. Dal segno. From the sign; indicating that the performer must return to the sign :𝄉: .

⟩ Decrescendo. Gradually softer.

Dim. Diminuendo. Gradual decrease of tone.

(·) Dot. When added to a note or rest, lengthens it by one-half, a second dot by an additional one-fourth. When placed over or under a note, it implies a detached (*staccato*) style, but less detached than a dash.

⊓ ∧ **Down bow.**

♭ **Flat.** See ♯ Sharp.

♭♭ **Double Flat.** Used before a note already flat, lowering it another semitone. It is corrected by a flat and a natural.

f. Forte. Loudly: strongly.

ff. Fortissimo. Very loud.

fff. Fortississimo. As loud as possible.

fp. Forte-piano. Loud, then soft.

° **Harmonic.** Placed over a note indicates that it is to be played as a harmonic by lightly touching the string.

Leg. Legato. In a smooth and gliding manner.

L.H. Left hand.

Lo. Loco. Indicating to return to the pitch as printed after having played an octave higher or lower.

M.D. Mano destra or Main droite. Right hand.

mf. Mezzo-forte. Moderately loud.

M.G. Main gauche. Left hand.

mp. Mezzo-piano. Moderately soft.

Manc. Mancando. Dying away, decreasing.

Marc. Marcato. In a marked manner, emphasised.

Mit dem Frosche. With the heel of the bow.

Mit der Spitze. With the point of the bow.

M.M. Maelzel's metronome.

M.M. ♩=80.⎰ Denoting that the beat of a crotchet is equal to the pulse of the pendulum of Maelzel's metronome, with the weight set at 80, i.e. 80 crotchets to a minute.

∿ **Mordent.** An embellishment in which the principal note is succeeded by the one below, and the latter by the principal note.

M.S. Mano sinistra. Left hand.

♮ **Natural.** Restores a note which has been raised by the sharp or lowered by the flat to its original pitch.

Op. Opus. Refers to the numbering of a composer's publications.

Ossia. Or. Used to propose an alternative.

Ott., Oᵛᵃ, 8ᵛᵃ =Ottava, or Octave. Written above staff 8ᵛᵃ, or 8ᵛᵃ *alta* (*ottava alta*) indicates note or passage to be played an octave higher; below staff, 8ᵛᵃ, or 8ᵛᵃ *bassa* (*ottava bassa*), an octave lower.

p. Piano. Softly.

Ped. Depress 'loud' pedal.

✳ Raise 'loud' pedal.

pf. Piano-forte. Soft, then loud.

pp. Pianissimo. Very soft.

ppp. Pianississimo. As softly as possible.

⌢ **Pause** or *Corona*. When placed over a note or rest, indicates that it must be held longer than its natural length. Over a double bar, it indicates the end of the piece.

Pizz. Pizzicato. A direction to pluck the string with the finger instead of using the bow: cancelled by arco.

Poussez. Up bow (lit. push).

∿ **Pralltriller.** An embellishment like the mordent, but having the note above instead of the note below (often called 'upper mordent' or 'mordent').

4ᵗᵗᵉ Quartette.

5ᵗᵗᵉ Quintette.

 Quintole, or Quintuplet. A group of five notes played in the time of four.

Rall. Rallentando. Becoming gradually slower.

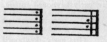 **Repeat.** When placed at the beginning and end of a passage or movement, indicates that the portion so marked is to be played over again.

R.H. Right hand.

Rinf., Rfz., Rf. Rinforzando, Rinforzato. Reinforced, suddenly accented.

Rit. Ritardando. Retarding, becoming slower.

:𝄉: **Segno.** The sign—as *Al Segno*, to the sign; *Dal Segno*, from the sign. See *D.S.*

Segue. Follows (sc. the next movement).

Sem., Semp. Sempre. Always, throughout—as *sempre legato*, smooth throughout; *sempre ritardando*, continually slackening the time.

7ᵗᵗᵉ Septet.

6ᵗᵗᵉ Sextet, or Sestet.

∧ ∨ > *sfz.*, *fz.* Sforzando, Sforzato. Denoting emphasis applied to a particular note or notes.

> Sforzato-piano. A sudden *forte* followed by a *piano.* Abbreviated *sfp.*, *sfz.p.*

♯ Sharp. ♭ Flat. Signs used in a key signature, which raise (♯) or lower (♭) the notes on the staff on which they occur, on all octaves throughout the piece, by one semitone, except where cancelled by a natural: signs used as accidentals which raise (♯) or lower (♭) only the note or notes within the measure by one semitone, unless these are tied to notes of a succeeding measure.

✕ or 𝄪 Double Sharp. Used before a note already sharp, raising the pitch by a semitone. It is contradicted by a natural and a sharp.

Simile. Like. A direction to continue playing as already marked.

Slent. Slentando. Slowing down or relaxing much.

⌒ Slur. Showing that the notes over which it is placed must be played in a smooth (*legato*) manner, or are sung to one syllable, or played with one bow. With staccato marks, less sharply detached than staccato, or played detachedly with one bow.

Smorz. Smorzando. With gradual fading.

Sos., *Sos^t.* Sostenuto. Sustained; prolonging the tone for the full duration of time indicated.

Spir. Spiritoso. In a spirited or lively manner.

Stacc. Staccato. With each note detached.

 Stave or Staff. The horizontal parallel lines and spaces on which the notes are placed, used to indicate their relative position as regards pitch.

Ten. Tenuto. Placed over a note to be held to its full value or more.

Tie. See Bind.

Tirez. Down bow (lit. pull).

Tre corde. Three strings, cancelling una corda.

 Trem. Tremolo. With trembling or wavering; a note or chord played with rapid repetition so as to produce such an effect.

tr〰〰 Trillo or shake. A rapid alternation of two notes, a semitone or a tone apart, commonly ending in a turn.

3° Trio.

 Triplet. A group of three notes performed in the time of two.

T.S. Tasto solo. One key alone: a direction to play a part in unison.

∾ Turn. An embellishment in which the principal note is preceded by the note above and succeeded by the one below, or vice versa.

—or when placed after the note:

U.C. Una corda. One string; i.e. depress ' soft ' pedal, thus allowing the hammers (grand piano) to strike one string only.

V.S. Volti subito: turn (the leaf) quickly.

∨ Up bow.

ADDITIONAL LIST OF ABBREVIATIONS

A.A.C.C.A. Associate of the Association of Certified and Corporate Accountants.
A.C.A. Associate of the Institute of Chartered Accountants.
A.C.C.S. Associate of the Corporation of Certified Secretaries.
A.I.B. Associate of the Institute of Bankers.
A.L.A. Associate of the Library Association.
A.R.I.C.S. (Professional) Associate of the Royal Institution of Chartered Surveyors.
3-D Three-dimensional.
F.A.C.C.A. Fellow of the Association of Certified and Corporate Accountants.

F.C.A. Fellow of the Institute of Chartered Accountants.
F.C.C.S. Fellow of the Corporation of Certified Secretaries.
F.P.B. Fast Patrol Boat.
F.R.I.C.S. Fellow of the Royal Institution of Chartered Surveyors.
S.A.C. School of Army Co-operation.
S.A.R.A.H. Search and rescue and holding.
UNICEF. United Nations International Children's Emergency Fund—now United Nations Children's Fund, but still known as UNICEF.

MATHEMATICAL SYMBOLS

$\pm$ plus or minus.

$=$ is equal to.

$\equiv$ is identically equal to.

$\approx$
$\simeq$ is approximately equal to.
$\eqsim$

$\neq$ is not equal to

$>$ is greater than.

$\not>$ is not greater than.

$<$ is less than.

$\not<$ is not less than.

$\geqslant$ is greater than or equal to.

$\leqslant$ is less than or equal to.

$\therefore$ therefore.

$\because$ because.

$\angle$ angle.

$\parallel$ parallel.

$\perp$ perpendicular.

$x!$ or $\underline{x}$ factorial x.

$\propto$ varies directly as.

$a : b :: c : d$ a is to b as c is to d.

π pi ; the ratio of the circumference of a circle to its diameter, approx. 3·14159.

e or ϵ (1) the base of natural logarithms, approx. 2·71828.
(2) the eccentricity of a conic section.

i the imaginary square root of -1.

ω, ω^2 the imaginary cube roots of 1.

∞ infinity.

x^n $x \times x \times x \ldots$ to n factors.

x^{-n} $\dfrac{1}{x^n}$.

$x^{\frac{1}{n}}$ $\sqrt[n]{x}$, the nth root of x.

x^0 $= 1$.

$x \to a$ x approaches the limit a.

θ the angle between the radius vector and the polar axis.

$\sin^{-1} x$ the principal value of the angle whose sine is x.
Similarly $\cos^{-1} x$, $\tan^{-1} x$, &c.

$\sinh$ *sinus hyperbolicus*, the hyperbolic sine.
Similarly cosh, tanh, &c.

Σ the sum of the terms indicated.

Π the product of the terms indicated.

$|x|$ the absolute value of x.

$\bar{x}$ the mean value of x.

$\begin{vmatrix} a_1 & b_1 & c_1 \\ a_2 & b_2 & c_2 \\ a_3 & b_3 & c_3 \end{vmatrix}$ a determinant representing $a_1 b_2 c_3 - a_1 b_3 c_2 + a_3 b_1 c_2 - a_2 b_1 c_3 + a_2 b_3 c_1 - a_3 b_2 c_1$.

f or F function.

$\left. \begin{array}{l} f(x) \\ F(x) \\ \phi(x) \\ \&c. \end{array} \right\}$ function x.

Δ finite difference or increment.

$\Delta x, \delta x$ the increment of x.

dx an increment of x considered as tending to zero.

D differential coefficient.

$\dfrac{dy}{dx}$, $D_x y$ the differential coefficient of y with respect to x.

$F'x$ stands for $\dfrac{d(F(x))}{dx}$.

$\dfrac{d^2 y}{dx^2}$ the second differential of y with respect to x.

$\dfrac{\partial y}{\partial u}$ the partial differential of y with respect to u, where y is a function of u and another variable (or variables).

$\int$ integral.

COMMON CONSTANTS

c velocity of light in vacuo, $2\cdot9978 \times 10^{10}$ cm. per second.

e electronic charge, $1\cdot602 \times 10^{-20}$ e.m.u., or $4\cdot802 \times 10^{-10}$ e.s.u.

g_0 standard gravity, $980\cdot665$ cm. per second per second.

h Planck's constant, the constant in the expression for the quantum of energy, $6\cdot622 \pm \cdot005 . 10^{-27}$ erg. sec.

m the mass of an electron at rest, $9\cdot11 \times 10^{-28}$ grams.

N_0 Avogadro number, number of molecules per gram-molecule, $6\cdot023 \times 10^{23}$.

PRONOUNCING VOCABULARY OF SCRIPTURE
PROPER NAMES

[This vocabulary contains all common Scripture Names except monosyllables and dissyllables, the latter being always accented on the first syllable. *Ch* has the sound of *k*, and so has *c*, except when marked ҫ, to indicate the sound of *s*; *g* is hard, except when marked otherwise.]

A-badd'on.
Ab'a-na.
Ab'a-rim.
A̯-bed'ne-gŏ.
Ā-bel-Me-hō'lah.
Ā-bel-Miz'rā-im (or -rā').
Ā-bel-Shitt'im
A-bī'a.
A-bī'a-thar.
A-bi-ē'zer.
Ab'i-gail.
A-bī'hū.
A-bī'jah.
A-bī'jam.
Ab-i-lē'ne.
A-bim'e-lech.
A-bin'a-dab.
A-bī'ram.
Ab'i-shag.
A-bish'ā-ī.
Ā'bra-ham.
Ab'sa-lom.
A-ҫel'da-ma.
A-chā'ia ('ya, or a-kī'a).
A-dī'nŏ (or Ad'i-nŏ).
A-do-ni-bē'zek.
Ad-o-nī'jah.
Ad-o-nī'ram.
A-do-ni-zē'dek.
A-dram'me-lech.
Ad-ra-mytt'i-um.
A'dri-a.
Ā'dri-el.
A-dull'am.
Ag'a-bus (or -gā').
A-gripp'a.
A-has-ū-ē'rus.
Ā-ha-zī'ah.
A-hī'jah.
A-him'a-az.
A-him'e-lech.
A-hin'o-am.
A-hith'o-phel.
A-hī'tub.
A-hō'li-ab.
A-hol'i-bah.
Aj'a-lon.
Al-ex-an'dri-a.
Al-phae'us (-fē').
Al-tas'chith.
Am'a-lek.
Am'a-lek-īte (or A-mal').
Am'a-na, A-mā'na.
Am'a-sa, A-mā'sa.
Am-a-zī'ah.
A-min'a-dab.
Amm'on-ite.
Am'o-rīte.
Am-phip'o-lis.
Am'ra-phel.
An'a-kims.
A-nam'me-lech.
An-a-nī'as.
An'a-thoth.
An-dro-nī'cus.

An'ti-och.
An'ti-pas.
An-tip'a-tris.
A-pell'ēs ('ēz).
Ap-ol-lō'ni-a.
A-poll'os.
A-poll'y-on.
App'i-ī Fō'rum.
Aq'ui-la (ak'wi-).
Ar'a-rat.
A-rau'nah.
Ar-che-lā'us.
Arc-tū'rus.
Ar-ē-op'a-gus.
Ar'e-tas.
Ā'ri-el.
Ar-i-ma-thē'a.
A'ri-och.
Ar-is-tar'chus.
Ar-is-to-bū'lus.
Ar-ma-gedd'on.
Ar-mē'ni-a.
Ar'o-er.
Ar'te-mas.
A-ru'mah.
As'a-hel.
As'e-nath.
Ash'ke-naz.
Ash'ta-roth.
Ash-tō'reth.
A'si-a (ā'zhi-a).
As'ke-lon.
As-syr'i-a.
Ath-a-lī'ah.
At-ta-lī'a.
Au-gus'tus.
Az-a-rī'ah.
A-zō'tus.

Bā'al-ah.
Bā-al-bē'rith.
Bā'al-gad.
Bā-al-hā'zor.
Bā-al-her'mon.
Bā-al-mē'on.
Bā-al-pē'or.
Bā-al-per'a-zim.
Bā-al-shal'i-sha (or -lī').
Bā-al-tā'mar.
Bā-al-zē'bub.
Bā-al-zē'phon.
Bā'a-sha.
Bab'y-lon.
Ba-hū'rim.
Ba-rabb'as.
Bar'na-bas.
Bar'sa-bas.
Bar-thol'o-mew.
Bar-ti-mae'us.
Bar-zil'lā-ī.
Bath-shē'ba (or Bath').
Bē-el'ze-bub.
Bē-er-la-hā'i-roi.
Be-ē'roth.
Bē-er'she-ba (or -shē').
Bē'he-moth.

Bē'li-al.
Bel-shaz'zar.
Bel-te-shaz'zar.
Be-nā'iah ('ya, or -nī'a).
Ben-hā'dad.
Ben'ja-min.
Be-rē'a.
Ber-nī'ce.
Be-rō'dach-bal'a-dan.
Beth-ab'a-ra.
Beth'a-ny.
Beth-ar'bel.
Beth-a'ven.
Be-thes'da (-thez').
Beth-hō'ron.
Beth'le-hem.
Beth-mā'a-chah.
Beth-pē'or (or Beth').
Beth'pha-gē (-jē).
Beth-sā'i-da.
Beth-shē'mesh (or Beth').
Be-thū'el (or Beth').
Be-zal'e-el.
Bi-thyn'i-a.
Bō-a-ner'gēs ('jēz).

Cai'a-phas (kī'a- or kā'ya-).
Cal'va-ry.
Cā'naan-īte.
Can'da-cē.
Ca-per'nā-um.
Cap-pa-dō'ci-a ('shi-).
Car'che-mish.
Cen'chre-a (sen').
Cēs-a-rē'a.
Chal-dē'an.
Ched-or-lā'o-mer (or -lā-ō').
Chem'a-rims.
Cher'eth-ites.
Chin'ne-reth.
Cho-rā'zin.
Chū-shan-rish-a-thā'im.
Ci-lic'i-a (si-lish'i-a).
Cin'ne-roth (sin').
Clau'di-a.
Clau'di-us.
Clē'o-phas.
Co-los'sē.
Co-nī'ah.
Cor-nē'li-us.
Cy-rē'nē (sī-).
Cy-rē'ni-us (sī-).

Dal-ma-nū'tha.
Dal-mā'ti-a ('shi-).
Dam'a-ris.
Da-mas'cus.
Dan'iel ('yel).
Da-rī'us.
Deb'o-rah (or -bō').

De-cap'o-lis.
Del'i-lah (Heb. De-lī'lah).
De-mē'tri-us.
Dī-an'a.
Dī-o-nys'i-us (-nis' or -niz').
Dī-ot're-phēs (-fēz).
Dru-sill'a.

Ē-bed-mē'lech.
Eb-en-ē'zer.
Ē'dom-īte.
Ed're-ī.
El-ē'a-leh.
El-ē-ā'zar.
El-e-lō'he-Is'ra-el.
El-hā'nan.
E-lī'ab.
E-lī'a-kim.
E-lī'a-shib.
E-li-ē'zer.
E-lī'hū.
E-lī'jah.
E-lim'e-lech.
El'i-phaz.
E-lī'sha.
E-lish'e-ba (or -shē').
El'ka-nah.
El'la-sar.
El'nā-than.
E-lō'ī.
El'y-mas.
Ē'ne-as.
Em'ma-us (or Em-mā').
En-eg-lā'im.
En'gē-di (or -ged').
En-rō'gel.
Ep'a-phras.
E-paph-ro-dī'tus.
Eph'e-sus.
Eph'ra-tah.
Ep-i-cū-rē'ans.
E-ras'tus.
Ē-sar-had'don.
Es-dra-ē'lon.
Esh'tā-ol.
Ē-thi-ō'pi-a.
Eū-nī'ce.
Eū-ō'di-as.
Eū-phrā'tēs ('tēz).
Eū-roc'ly-don.
Eū'ty-chus.
Ē-vil-me-rō'dach (or -mer').
Ex'o-dus.
E-zē'ki-el.
Ē-zi-on-gā'ber.

For-tū-nā'tus.

Gabb'a-tha.
Gā'bri-el.
Gad'a-rēnes.
Ga-lā'ti-a (-lā'shi-a).
Gal'e-ed.

Gal-i-lē'an.
Gal'i-lee.
Gall'i-o.
Ga-mā'li-el.
Ged-a-lī'ah.
Ged'e-roth.
Ge-hā'zī.
Gem-a-rī'ah.
Gen-nes'a-ret.
Gen'e-sis (jen').
Ge-nū'bath.
Ger'ge-sēnes.
Ger'i-zim (Heb. Ge-riz'zim).
Geth-sem'a-ne.
Gib'be-thon.
Gib'e-ah.
Gib'e-on.
Gid'e-on.
Gil-bō'a.
Gil'e-ad.
Gir'gash-īte.
Gol'go-tha.
Go-li'ath.
Go-morr'ah.

Hab'ak-kuk.
Hach'i-lah.
Had-ad-ē'zer.
Had-ad-rimm'on.
Hā'gar-ēnes.
Hag'gā-ī.
Ha-nan'e-el.
Ha-nā'nī.
Han-a-nī'ah.
Har'ō-sheth (or -rō').
Hav'i-lah.
Hā-voth-jā'ir.
Haz'ā-el (or Hā').
Heph'zi-bah.
Her-mog'e-nēs (-moj'e-nēz).
He-rō'di-ans.
He-rō'di-as.
He-rō'di-on.
Hez-e-kī'ah.
Hid'de-kel (or -dek').
Hi-e-rap'o-lis.
Hig-gāi'on ('gī- or gā'yon).
Hil-kī'ah.
Ho-sē'a (-zē').
Ho-shē'a.
Hȳ-me-nae'us.

Ich'a-bod.
I-cō'ni-um.
Id-ū-mē'a.
Il-lyr'i-cum.
Im-man'ū-el.
I-sai'ah (ī-zī'a or ī-zā'a).
Is-car'i-ot.
Ish'bo-sheth (or -bō').
Ish'mā-el.

Ish'mā-el-īte.
Is'rā-el (iz').
Is'rā-el-īte (iz').
Is'sa-char.
Ith'a-mar.
It'tā-ī.
It-ū-rē'a.

Jā-besh-gil'e-ad.
Jab'ne-el.
Jā'ir-us (or Ja-īr').
Jeb'ū-sīte.
Jec-o-nī'ah.
Jed'ū-thun.
Jē-gar-sā-ha-dū'tha.
Je-hō'a-haz.
Je-hō'ash.
Je-hoi'a-chin.
Je-hoi'a-da.
Je-hoi'a-kim.
Je-hon'a-dab.
Je-hō'ram.
Je-hosh'a-phat.
Je-hosh'e-ba.
Je-hō-vah-jī'reh.
Je-hō-vah-nis'sī.
Je-hō-vah-shā'lom.
Jer-e-mī'ah.
Jer'i-chō.
Jer-o-bō'am.
Je-rub'ba-al (or
  -bā').
Je-ru'sa-lem.
Jesh'i-mon.
Jesh'ū-run.
Jez'e-bel.
Jez're-el.
Jo-ann'a.
Joch'e-bed (or -eb').
Jo-hā'nan (or Jō').
Jon'a-dab.
Jon'a-than.
Josh'ū-a.
Jo-sī'ah.
Joz'a-char.
Jū-dē'a.
Jū'li-us.
Jū'pi-ter.

Kad'mon-ītes.
Ked'e-moth.
Ken-niz-zītes.
Kē'ri-oth.
Ke-tū'rah.
Kib-roth-hat-tā'a-
  vah.
Kir-hē'res.
Kir-jath-ā'im.
Kir-jath-ar'ba.
Kir-jath-hū'zoth.
Kir-jath-jē'a-rim.

La-hai'roi (-hī').
Lā-od-i-çē'a.
La-sē'a.
Laz'a-rus.
Leb'a-non.
Leb-bē'us.
Lem'ū-el.
Le-vī'a-than.
Lib'er-tīnes.

Lib'y-a.
Lō-am'mī.
Lō-rū'ha-mah (or
  -hā').
Lū'çi-fer.
Lū'ci-us (lū'shi-
  us).
Lyc-a-ō'ni-a.
Lyc-i-a (lish'i-a).
Lyd'i-a.
Lȳ-sā'ni-as.
Lys-i-as (lish'i-as).

Mā'a-cah.
Maç-e-dō'ni-a.
Mach-pē'lah (or
  Mach').
Mag'da-la.
Mā'ha-lath.
Mā-ha-nā'im.
Mā-her-shal-al-
  hash'baz.
Mak-kē'dah.
Mal'a-chī.
Man'ā-en.
Ma-nas'seh.
Ma-nō'ah.
Mar-a-nath'a.
Ma-rē'shah (or
  Mar').
Mat-ta-nī'ah.
Mat-thī'as (ma-
  thī'as).
Maz'za-roth.
Med'e-ba.
Me-gidd'o.
Mel-chiz'e-dek.
Mel'i-ta.
Men'a-hem.
Me-phib'o-sheth
  (or -phi-bō').
Mer'a-ri.
Mer-a-thā'im.
Mer'i-bah.
Me-rō-dach-bal'a-
  dan.
Mes-o-po-tā'mi-a.
Mes-sī'ah.
Mē-theg-am'mah.
Me-thū'se-lah.
Mī-cai'ah (-kī'a or
  -kā'ya).
Mī'cha-el.
Mī-chai'ah (-kī'a or
  -kā'ya).
Mid'i-an-īte.
Mī-lē'tus.
Mir'i-am.
Mit-y-lē'nē.
Miz'rā-im.
Mō'ab-īte.
Mor-de-cā'ī, Mor'-
  de-cai (-kī).
Mo-rī'ah.
Mys-i-a (mizh'i-a).

Nā'a-man.
Nai'oth (nī' or nā'-
  yoth).
Nā-ō'mi (or 'mī
  or Nā').

Naph'ta-lī.
Na-than'ael ('yel).
Naz'a-rēne.
Naz'a-reth.
Naz'a-rīte.
Ne-ap'o-lis.
Ne-bai'oth (-bī', or
  -bā'yoth).
Neb-ū-chad-nez'zar.
Neb-ū-zar'a-dan.
Neg'i-noth.
Nē-he-mī'ah.
Nē'hi-loth.
Ne-hush'tan.
Neth'i-nims.
Nī-cā'nor.
Nic-o-dē'mus.
Nic-o-lā'i-tans.
Nic'o-las.
Nī-cop'o-lis.
Nin'e-veh.

Ō-ba-dī'ah.
Ō-bed-ē'dom.
Ō'me-ga.
O-nē'si-mus.
On-ē-siph'o-rus.
O-rī'on.
Oth'ni-el.

Pā-dan-ā'ram.
Pal'es-tīne.
Pam-phyl'i-a.
Par'me-nas.
Par'thi-ans.
Par-vā'im.
Pat'a-ra.
Pek-a-hī'ah.
Pel-a-tī'ah.
Pē'leth-ītes.
Pe-nī'el.
Pe-nū'el.
Per'a-zim.
Pē-rez-uz'zah.
Per'ga-mos.
Per'iz-zīte.
Per'si-a ('shi-a,
  'sha).
Phal'ti-el.
Phā-raōh-hoph'ra
  (fā'rō- or fā'ra-ō-).
Phā-raōh-nē'choh.
Phē-ni'çe.
Phē-nic'i-a (-nish').
Phil-a-del'phi-a.
Phī-lē'mon.
Phī-lē'tus.
Phi-lipp'i.
Phil'is-tīne.
Phin'e-has.
Phryg'i-a (frij').
Pī-hā-hī'roth.
Pir'a-thon.
Pi-sid'i-a.
Plē'ia-dēs ('ya-dēz
  or plī'a-).
Pot'i-phar.
Po-tiph'e-rah.
Pris-çill'a.
Proch'o-rus.
Ptol-e-mā'is (tol-).

Pub'li-us.
Pu-tē'o-lī.

Rā'a-mah.
Rā-am'sēs ('sēz).
Rab'sha-keh (-kā).
Ra-gū'el.
Rā-math-a'im.
Rā-math-lē'hī.
Ra-mē'sēs ('sēz or
  Ram').
Rā-moth-gil'e-ad.
Re-bek'ab.
Rē'chab-ītes (or
  Rech').
Rē-ho-bō'am.
Re-hō'both.
Reph'ā-im.
Reph'i-dim.
Rhē'gi-um (rē'ji-).

Sa-bā'oth.
Sa-bē'ans.
Sal'a-mis.
Sal-mō'nē.
Sa-lō'me.
Sa-mā'ri-a.
Sa-mar'i-tan.
Sam-o-thrā'ci-a
  (-thrā'shi-a).
Sam'ū-el.
San-bal'lat.
Sapph-ī'ra (saf-ī'ra).
Sa-rep'ta.
Scyth'i-an (sith').
Se-cun'dus.
Se-leu'ci-a ('shi-a)
Sen-nach'e-rib.
Seph'a-rad.
Seph-ar-vā'im.
Ser-ai'ah (-ī'a or
  -ā'ya).
Ser'gi-us ('ji-).
Shal'i-sha.
Shal-ma-nē'ser
  ('zer).
Sha-rē'zer.
Shem-ai'ah (-ī'a).
Shem'i-nith.
Sheph-a-tī'ah.
Shesh-baz'zar.
Shē'thar-boz'na-ī.
Shig-gai'on (-gī'on).
Shim'e-ī.
Sho-shan'nim.
Shū'lam-īte.
Si-lō'am.
Sil-vā'nus.
Sim'e-on.
Sir'i-on.
Sis'e-ra.
Sod'om-ītes.
Sol'o-mon.
Sō'pa-ter.
Sō-sip'a-ter.
Sos'the-nēs (-nēz).
Steph'a-nas.
Suk'ki-ims.
Su-sann'a (-zan').
Sȳ-ē'nē.
Syn'ty-chē.

Sȳr'a-cūse.
Syr'i-a.
Sȳ-ro-phoe-nic'i-an
  (-nish'i-an).

Tā'a-nach.
Tab'e-rah.
Tab'i-tha.
Ta-hap'a-nēs (-nēz).
Tah'pan-hēs (-hēz).
Tah'pe-nēs (-nēz).
Tap-pū'ah.
Te-haph'ne-hēs
  (-hēz).
Te-kō'ah.
Ter'ti-us ('shi-us).
Ter-tull'us.
Thad-dae'us
  (or Thad').
The-oph'i-lus.
Thess-a-lo-nī'ca.
Thȳ-a-tī'ra.
Ti-bē'ri-as.
Ti-bē'ri-us.
Tig-lath-pi-lē'ser
  ('zer).
Tim-nath-hē'rēs
  ('rēz).
Tim-nath-sē'rah.
Tim'o-thy.
Tir'ha-kah.
Tir'ha-nah.
Tir'sha-tha (or
  -shā').
To-bī'ah.
To-bī'jah.
To-gar'mah.
Trach-o-nī'tis.
Tro-gyl'li-um (-jil').
Troph'i-mus.
Trȳ-phē'na.
Trȳ-phō'sa.
Tū'bal-cain (-kān).
Tych'i-cus.
Ty-rann'us.

U-phar'sin (ū-).
U-rī'ah (ū-).
U-rī'jah (ū-).
Uz-zī'ah.

Zac-chae'us.
Zach-a-rī'ah.
Zach-a-rī'as.
Zal-mun'na.
Zam-zum'mims.
Zar'e-phath.
Zar'e-tan.
Zeb'e-dee.
Ze-boi'im.
Ze-bō'im.
Zeb'ū-lun.
Zech-a-rī'ah.
Zed-e-kī'ah.
Ze-lō'phe-had.
Zem-a-rā'im.
Zeph-a-nī'ah.
Zeph'a-thah.
Ze-rub'ba-bel.
Zer-ū-ī'ah.
Zip-pō'rah (or Zip').

THE MORE COMMON ENGLISH CHRISTIAN NAMES

See especially Miss C. V. Withycombe's *Oxford Dictionary of Christian Names*.

Aaron, *ā′rən, m.* (Heb.) lofty, mountaineer.—Ar. *Harun, Haroun.*

Abel, *ā′bl, m.* (Heb.) breath, vanity.

Abigail, *ab′i-gāl, f.* (Heb.) father rejoiced, or father of exaltation.—Dims. **Abby, Nabby.**

Abraham, *ā′brə-həm,* **Abram,** *ā′brəm, m.* (Heb.) perhaps father of a multitude, high father.—Dims. **Abe, Aby.**

Absalom, *ab′sə-ləm, m.* (Heb.) father of peace.

Ada, *ā′dä, f.* prob. for **Adelaide** or other Gmc. name in Adel-, Adal- (noble).

Adalbert. See **Albert.**

Adam, *ad′əm, m.* (Heb.) man, earth, red earth.—Scottish dims. **Edie** (*ēd′i*), **Yiddie.**

Adela, *ad′i-lä, f.* (Gmc.) noble.

Adelaide, *ad′i-lād, f.* Fr. *Adélaïde* from Ger. *Adelheid* (from *Adelheidis*), noble, kind (i.e. sort).

Adeline, Adelina, *ad′i-lēn, -līn, -ä, f.* (Gmc.) noble.—Dim. **Addy.**

Adolphus, *ə-dol′fəs, m.* (Gmc.) noble wolf.—Fr. *Adolphe,* It. and Sp. *Adolfo,* Ger. *Adolf,* O.E. *Æthelwulf.*

Adrian, Hadrian, *(h)ā′dri-ən, m.* (L.) of Adria (in Italy).

Aeneas, Eneas, *ē-nē′əs, m.* (Gr.) commended.—Fr. *Énée.*—Used for **Angus.**

Afra, *af′rä, ā′frä, f.* (Heb.) dust.

Agatha, *ag′ə-thä, f.* (Gr.) good.

Agnes, *ag′nis, f.* (Gr.) chaste.—Dims. **Aggie, Aggy, Annis, Annot, Nance, Nancy, Nessa, Nessie, Nesta.**—L. *Agneta,* It. *Agnese,* Fr. *Agnès,* Sp. *Inés.*—Confused with **Ann.**

Aileen, *ā′lēn, f.* Anglo-Irish form of **Helen.**

Ailie, *ā′li, f.* Scottish dim. of **Alison, Alice,** and **Helen.**

Alaric, *al′ə-rik, m.* noble ruler.

Alasdair, Alastair, Alister, *al′is-tər, m.* See **Alexander.**

Alban, *al′bən, m.* (L.) of Alba (near Rome).

Albert, *al′bərt, m.* (Gmc.) nobly bright.—Dims. **Bert, Bertie.**—Obs. Scot. **Halbert** (dims. **Hab, Habbie, Hob, Hobbie**).—L. *Albertus,* Fr. *Albert,* It. and Sp. *Alberto,* Ger. *Adalbert, Albert, Albrecht,* O.E. *Æthelbeorht.*

Aldred, *avl′drid, m.* See **Eldred.**

Alethea, *al-ē-thē′ä, f.* (Gr.) truth.

Alexander, *al-ig-zan′dər, m.* (Gr.) defender of men.—Also (from Gael.) **Alasdair, Alastair, Alister** (*al′is-tər*).—Scot. **Elshender.**—Dims. **Alec(k), Alex, Alick, Eck, Ecky, Sanders, Sandy,** or (as an Englishman's nickname for a Scotsman) **Sawnie.**—Fr. *Alexandre,* It. *Alessandro,* Sp. *Alejandro.*—Fem. **Alexandra, Alexandrina** (*-drē′nä, -drī′nä*).

Alexis, *ə-lek′sis, m.* (Gr.) help.

Alfonso. See **Alphonsus.**

Alfred, *al′frid, m.* (Gmc.) elf counsel (good counsellor).—Dims. **Alf, Alfie.**—L. *Alfredus, Aluredus,* O.E. *Ælfred.*

Algernon, *al′jər-nən, m.* (O.Fr.) moustached.—Dim. **Algy.**

Alice, *al′is,* **Alicia,** *ə-lish′i-ä, f.* (Gmc.) from O.Fr. *Aliz* for Gmc. *Adalheidis* (see **Adelaide**).—Dims. **Allie, Ally, Ellie, Elsie.** See also **Alison.**

Aline, *ə-lēn′,* or *al′ēn, f.* for **Adeline.**

Alison, *al′i-sən, f.* a form of **Alice,** mainly Scots, now considered a separate name.—Dims. **Ailie, Elsie.**

Allan, Alan, *al′ən, m.* (prob. Celt.) harmony.—Fr. *Alain.*

Almeric, *al′mə-rik, m.* See **Emery.**

Aloys, *al′ō-is, -ois′,* **Aloysius,** *-ē′zi-əs, -is′i-əs, m.* See **Lewis.**

Alphonsus, *al-fon′səs, m.* (Gmc.) noble ready.—Ger. *Alfons,* Sp. *Alfonso, Alonso,* Port. *Afonso,* Fr. *Alphonse,* It. *Alfonso.*

Amabel, *am′ə-bel, f.* (L.) lovable. See **Mabel.**

Amadeus, *am-ə-dē′əs, m.* (L.) love God.—Fr. *Amédée.*

Amalia, *ä-mä′li-ä.* See **Amelia.**

Amanda, *ə-man′dä, f.* (L.) lovable.

Ambrose, *am′brōz, m.* (Gr.) of the immortals, divine.—L. *Ambrosius,* It. *Ambrogio,* W. *Emrys.*

Amelia, *ə-mē′li-ä, f.* (Gmc.) struggling, labour.—Gr. *Amalia,* Fr. *Amélie,* It. *Amelia, Amalia.*—Dim. **Millie.**

Amos, *ā′mos, m.* (Heb.) strong, bearing a burden.

Amy, *ā′mi, f.* (Fr.) beloved.—L., It., Sp. *Amata,* Fr. *Aimée.*

Amyas, *ām′, am′i-as, m.* prob. for **Amadeus.**

Andrew, *an′drōō, m.* manly.—Dims. **Andy, Dandy.**—Gr., L., Ger. *Andreas,* Fr. *André,* It. *Andrea,* Sp. *Andrés.*

Aneurin, Aneirin, *a-nā′rin,* or *-noi′, m.* (W.) meaning doubtful, perh. for L. *Honorius.*

Angelica, *an-jel′i-kä,* **Angelina,** *an-ji-lē′nä, -lī′nä, f.* (Gr.) angelic.

Angus, *ang′gəs, m.* (Celt.) perh. choice.—Gael. *Aonghas.*—**Aeneas** is used as a substitute.

Ann, Anne, *an,* **Anna,** *an′ä,* **Hannah,** *han′ä, f.* (Heb.) grace.—Dims. **Anita** (*a-nē′tä,* Sp.), **Annette** (*a-net′,* Fr.), **Annie, Nan, Nance, Nancy, Nannie, Nanny, Nina** (*nē′nä, nī′nä*), **Ninette** (*nē-net′,* Fr.), **Ninon** (*nē-non^v′,* Fr.).

Annabel, Annabella, *an′ə-bel, -bel′-ä,* **Annaple,** *an′ə-pl, f.* prob. for **Amabel.**

Anthea, *an-thē′ä, f.* (Gr.) flowery.

Anthony, Antony, *an′tə-ni, m.* (L.) meaning unknown.—Dims. **Tony** (*tō′ni*), **Nanty.**—L. *Antonius,* Fr. *Antoine,* It. and Sp. *Antonio,* Ger. *Antonius, Anton.*—Fem. **Antonia.**—Dims. **Antoinette** (Fr.), **Net, Nettie, Netty.**

Arabella, *ar-ə-bel′ä, f.* origin and meaning doubtful; perh. for **Amabel,** or perh. (L. *orabilis*) easily entreated.—Dims. **Bel, Bell, Belle.**

Archibald, *är′chi-bld, m.* (Gmc.) genuine and bold.—Dims. **Arch, Archie, Archy, Baldie.**—L. *Archibaldus,* Fr. *Archembault,* It. *Arcibaldo,* O.E. *Eorconbeald.*

Arnold, *är-nld, -nold, m.* (Gmc.) eagle strength.—Fr. *Arnaud, Arnaut.*

Arthur, *är′thər, m.* (Celt.) perh. bear, or (Ir.) stone; or from a Roman gentile name *Artorius.*—L. *Arturus,* It. *Arturo.*

Asa, *ā′sä, m.* (Heb.) healer.

Athanasius, *ath-ə-nā′s(h)i-əs, m.* (Gr.) undying.

Athelstan, Athelstane, *ath′l-stan, -stän, m.* (Gmc.) noble stone.—O.E. *Æthelstán.*

Aubrey, *aw′bri, m.* (Gmc.) elf rule.—Ger. *Alberich,* O.E. *Ælfric.*

Audrey, *aw′dri, f.* (Gmc.) noble power.—O.E. *Æthelthryth,* whence the form **Etheldreda** (*eth-l-drē′dä*).

Augustine, *aw′gəs-tēn, aw-gus′tin,* **Austin,** *aws′tin, m.* (L.) belonging to Augustus.—L. *Augustinus,* Ger. and Fr. *Augustin,* It. *Agostino,* Sp. *Agustín.*

Augustus, *aw-gus′təs, m.* (L.) venerable, exalted.—Dims. **Gus, Gussie, Gustus.**—Ger. *August,* Fr. *Auguste.*—Fem. **Augusta.**

Aurelius, *aw-rē′li-əs, m.* (L.) golden (Roman gentile name).—Fem. **Aurelia.**—Dim. *Aurelian, m.*

Averil, *av′ə-ril, f.* (Gmc.) perh. boar-favour. Associated in people's minds with Fr. *avril,* April.

Avis, *av′is, f.* origin obscure.

Aylmer, *āl′mər,* **Elmer,** *el′mər, m.* (Gmc.) noble, famous.—O.E. *Æthelmær.* Or from the surname.

Aylwin, *āl'win,* *m.* (Gmc.) noble friend.—O.E. Æthelwine.

Baldwin, *bawld'win,* *m.* (Gmc.) bold friend.—L. *Balduinus,* Fr. *Baudouin,* It. and Sp. *Baldovino,* Ger. *Balduin.*

Balthazar, Balthasar, *bal't(h)ə-zär, bal-thä'zər, m.* (Babylonian *Bal-sarra-uzur,* whence *Belshazzar*) Bel defend the king.—Ger. *Balthasar,* Fr. *Balthazar,* It. *Baldassare,* Sp. *Baltasar.*

Baptist, *bap'tist,* *m.* (Gr.) baptiser.—Ger. *Baptist,* Fr. *Baptiste, Batiste,* It. *Battista,* Sp. *Bautista.*

Barbara, *bär-bə-rä,* *f.* (Gr.) foreign.—Dims. **Bab, Babs, Babbie** (Scot. **Baubie**).

Bardolph, *bär'dolf,* *m.* (Gmc.) bright wolf.—Fr. *Bardolphe,* It. *Bardolfo.*

Barnabas, Barnaby, *bär'nə-bəs, -bi,* *m.* (Heb.) son of exhortation.—Dim. **Barney.**

Barney, *bär'ni,* *m.* See **Bernard, Barnabas.**

Barry, *bar'i,* *m.* (Ir.) spear.

Bartholomew, *bär-, bər-thol'ə-mū,* **Bartlemy,** *bärt'l-mi,* *m.* (Heb.) son of Talmi.—Dims. **Bart, Bat.**—L. *Bartholomaeus,* Fr. *Barthélemy, Bartholomé,* It. *Bartolomeo,* Sp. *Bártolo, Bartolomé, Bartolomeo,* Ger. *Bartholomäus, Barthel.*

Basil, *baz'il,* *m.* (Gr.) kingly.—L. *Basilius,* Fr. *Basile,* It. and Sp., *Basilio.*

Beatrice, Beatrix, *bē'ə-tris, -triks, bē-ä'triks, f.* (L.) making happy.—Obs. form **Bettrice** (*bet'ris*).—Dims. **Bee, Beatty, Trix, Trixie.**

Becky, *bek'i, f.* See **Rebecca.**

Belinda, *bə-lin'dä, f.* (Gmc.) the second part meaning snake, the first unexplained.—O.H.G. *Betlindis.*

Bell, Belle, *bel,* **Bella,** *bel'ä, f.* See **Isabella,** also **Annabel, Arabella.**

Benedict, Benedick, *ben'i-dikt, -dik,* **Bennet,** *ben'it, m.* (L.) blessed.—L. *Benedictus,* Ger. *Benedikt,* Fr. *Benoît,* It. *Benedetto,* Sp. *Benedicto, Benito.*

Benjamin, *ben'jə-min, m.* (Heb.) son of the right hand (i.e. of good fortune).—Dims. **Ben, Benjie, Bennie.**—It. *Beniamino,* Sp. *Benjamin.*

Berenice, *ber-i-nī'sē, ber-nē'sē, ber'ə-nēs, f.* (Gr.) a Macedonian form of *Pherenikē,* victory-bringer. See also **Veronica.**

Bernard, *bər'nərd, m.* (Gmc.) bear-hard.—L. *Bernardus,* Fr. *Bernard, Bernardin,* It. *Bernardo, Bernardino,* Sp. *Bernardo, Bernal,* Ger. *Bernhard, Barend, Berend.*

Bert, *bərt, m.* for **Albert**; **Bertie** for **Bertram** or **Herbert**—Both are used for any name ending in -bert, and (*f.*) for **Bertha.**

Bertha, *bər'thä, f.* (Gmc.) bright.—Dims. **Bert, Bertie.**—Ger. *Berta, Bertha,* Fr. *Berthe,* It. and Sp. *Berta,* O.E. *Bercta.*

Bertram, *bər'trəm, m.* (Gmc.) bright raven.—Dims. **Bertie, Bert.**—Fr. *Bertrand,* It. *Bertrando,* Sp. *Beltrán.*

Beryl, *ber'il, f.* (Gr.) from the precious stone.

Bess, Bessie, Beth, Betsy. See **Elizabeth.**

Bethia, *be-thī'ä, f.* (Heb.) daughter of Yah.

Bevis, *bev'is, bēv'is, m.* from a French form of the Germanic name *Bobo* (Frankish), *Bobba* (O.E.).

Biddy, *bid'i, f.* See **Bridget.**

Bill, *m.* See **William.**

Blanche, Blanch, *blänsh, f.* (Fr.—Gmc.) white.—It. *Bianca,* Sp. *Blanca,* Ger. *Blanka,* Fr. *Blanche.*

Bob. See **Robert.**

Boris, *bō'ris, bor'is, m.* (Russ.) fight.

Brenda, *bren'dä, f.* perh. a fem. form of the Norse name *Brand,* brand, or sword; a Shetland name popularised by Scott's *Pirate.*

Brian, *brī'ən, m.* (Celt.) meaning doubtful.

Bridget, Brigid, *brij'it, f.* (Celt.) strength; name of a Celtic fire-goddess, an Irish saint; partly from the Swedish saint *Brigitto* (prob. a different name). —Dim. **Biddy.**—Fr. *Brigide,* Sp. *Brígida,* It. *Brigida, Brigita.*

Bruce, *broōs, m.* from the surname.

Caleb, *kä'lib, m.* (Heb.) dog, or bold.

Camilla, *kə-mil'ä, f.* (L.) a free-born attendant at a sacrifice; in Virgil name of a queen of the Volsci. —Fr. *Camille.*

Candida, *kan'di-dä, f.* (L.) white.

Carlotta, *kär-lot'ä, f.* See **Charles.**

Carol, *kar'ol,* **Caroline,** *kar'ə-līn, -lin, -lēn, f.* See under **Charles.**

Casimir, Kasimir, *kas'i-mir, m.* (Polish) proclamation of peace.

Caspar, Kaspar, *kas'pər, m.* See **Jasper.**

Catherine, Catharine, Katherine, Katharine, *kath'(ə-)rin,* **Catherina,** *-ə-rē'nä, -rī'nä,* **Katrine,** *kat'rin,* **Katerina,** *kat-ə-rē'nä,* **Kathleen,** *kath'lēn* (Ir. *Caitlin*), *f.* from Gr. *Aikaterinē,* of unknown origin, later assimilated to *katharos,* pure.—Fr. *Catherine,* It. *Caterina,* Sp. *Catalina,* Ger. *Katharina,* Dan. *Karen,* Gael. *Catriona.*—Dim. **Casey, Cathie, Cathy, Kate, Katie, Katy, Kathie, Kathy, Kay, Kit, Kittie, Kitty.**

Cecil, *ses'il,* also *sēs', sis', m.* (L.) the Roman gentile name *Caecilius* (lit. blind).—Fem. **Cecilia** (*sisil'yä*), **Cecily** (*ses'i-li*), **Cicely** (*sis'(i-)li*), **Sisley.**—Fr. *Cécile,* Ger. *Cäcilia.*—Dims. **Sis, Cis, Sissy, Sissie, Cissy, Cissie.**

Cedric, *sed'rik, m.* prob. a mistake of Scott's for *Cerdic* (name of the first king of the West Saxons, but apparently not really English—perh. a British name).

Celia, Caelia, *sē'li-ä, f.* fem. of the Roman gentile name *Caelius* (poss. heavenly).—Fr. *Célie*; It. *Sheila* (variously spelt).—Sometimes used for **Cecilia.**

Charles, *chärlz, m.* (Gmc.) manly.—Also **Carol,** *kar'ol.*—L. *Carolus,* Fr. *Charles,* Ger. *Carl, Karl,* It. *Carlo,* Sp. *Carlos,* Czech *Karol,* Gael. *Tearlach.*—Dims. **Charlie, Charley.**—Fem. **Caroline** (*kar'ə-līn, -lēn, -lin*), **Carlotta, Charlotte** (*shär'lət*), **Carol.**—Dims. **Caddie, Carrie, Lina** (*lē'nä*), **Lottie, Chat** (*shat*), **Chatty, Sharley.**

Chloe, *klō'ē, f.* (Gr.) a green shoot, verdure.

Chloris, *klō'ris, f.* (Gr.) name of a flower-goddess, also a greenfinch or a kind of grape.

Christabel, *kris'tə-bel, f.* (L.—Gr.) anointed, or Christ, and (L.) fair.

Christian, *kris'tyən, m.,* also *f.* belonging to Christ. —L. *Christianus,* Fr. *Chrétien,* It. and Sp. *Cristiano.*—Dims. **Chris, Christie, Christy.**—Fem. **Christiana** (*-ti-ä'nä*), **Christina** (*-tē'nä*), **Christine** (*kris'tēn* or *-tēn'*), **Kirsteen** (*kirs'tēn*).—Dims. **Chris, Chrissie, Kirsty, Teenie, Tina** (*tē'nä*).

Christopher, *kris'tə-fər, m.* (Gr.) carrying Christ. —L. *Christophorus,* Fr. *Christophe,* It. *Cristoforo,* Sp. *Cristóbal,* Ger. *Christoph.*—Dims. **Chris, Kester, Kit** (Scot. **Crystal, Chrystal**).

Cicely. See **Cecilia.**

Clara, *klä'rä,* **Clare,** *klär,* **Clarinda,** *klə-rin'dä, f.* (L.) bright.—Fr. *Claire,* Ger. *Klara,* It. *Chiara.*— Derivs. **Clarice** (*klar'is*), **Clarissa.**

Clarence, *klar'əns, m.* from the dukedom.

Claribel, *klar'i-bel, f.* (L.) brightly fair.

Claud, Claude, *klawd,* **Claudius,** *-i-əs, m.* (L.) lame. —Fem. **Claudia** (Fr. *Claude*).

Clement, *klem'ənt, m.* (L.) mild, merciful.—Dim. **Clem.**—Fem. **Clementina** (*-ē'nä*), **Clementine** (*-ēn, -īn*).

Clive, *klīv, m.* from the surname.

Clotilda, Clothilda, *klō-til'dä, f.* (Gmc.) famous fighting woman.—Fr. *Clot(h)ilde.*

Clovis, *klō'vis, m.* See **Lewis.**

Colette, *kol-et', f.* See under **Nicholas.**

Colin, *kol'in, m.* orig. a dim. of **Nicholas**; used also for **Columba**; now regarded as a separate name.

Colley, *kol'ī,* orig. dim. of **Nicholas.**

Connor, *kon'ər, m.* (Ir.) high desire.—Ir. *Conchobar.*— Dims. **Corney, Corny.**— **Cornelius** (q.v.) is used as a substitute.

Conrad, Conrade, Konrad, *kon'rad, m.* (Ger.) bold in counsel.—Ger. *Konrad,* It. *Corrado.*

Constance, *kon'stəns, f.* (L.) constancy.—L. *Constantia,* Fr. *Constance,* It. *Costanza,* Ger. *Konstanze.*—Dim. **Connie.**—**Constant,** *kon'stənt, m.* firm, faithful.—L. *Constans, Constantius,* It. *Costante, Costanzo,* Ger. *Konstanz.*—Deriv. **Constantine** (*kon'stən-tīn*), *m.*

Cora, *kō'rä, f.* a modern name, prob. from Gr. *korē,* girl.

Coralie, *kor'ə-li,* *f.* (Fr.) perh. coral, a modern French invention.

Cordelia, *kor-dē'li-ä,* *f.* perh. (L.) warm-hearted.

Corinna, *kor-in'ä,* *f.* (Gr.) maiden.

Cornelius, *kor-nē'li-əs,* *m.* (L.) a Roman gentile name, prob. related to L. *cornu,* horn.—Used for **Connor, Conchobar.**—Dims. **Corney, Corny.**—Fem. **Cornelia.**

Cosmo, *koz'mō,* *m.* (Gr.) order.—It. *Cosimo, Cosmo,* Fr. *Cosme, Côme,* Sp. *Cosme.*

Crispin, *kris'pin,* **Crispian, -*pi-ən,* **Crispinian,** *-pin'i-ən,* **Crispus, -*pəs,* *m.* (L.) curly.

Cuthbert, *kudh',* *kuth'bərt,* *m.* (O.E.) wellknown, bright.—Dim. **Cuddie.**

Cynthia, *sin'thi-ä,* *f.* (Gr.) of Mount Cynthus, an epithet of Artemis.

Cyprian, *sip'ri-ən,* *m.* (Gr.) of Cyprus.

Cyriac, *sir'i-ək,* *m.* (Gr.) the Lord's, or lordly.

Cyril, *sir'il,* *m.* (Gr.) lordly.

Cyrus, *sī'rəs,* *m.* (Pers.) throne.

Daisy, *dā'zi,* *f.* (Eng.) a translation of Fr. *Marguerite.* See **Margaret.**

Damian, *dā'mi-ən,* *m.* (Gr.) perh. connected with *damaein,* to tame.

Daniel, *dan'yəl,* *m.* (Heb.) the Lord is judge.—Dims. **Dan, Danny.**

Daphne, *daf'nē,* *f.* (Gr.) laurel.

David, *dā'vid,* *m.* (Heb.) beloved.—Dims. **Dave, Davie, Davy** (obs. **Daw, Dawkin**).—Fem. **Vida,** *vē'dä* (Scot. **Davina,** *də-vē'nä*).

Deborah, *deb'ə-rä,* *di-bō'rä,* *f.* (Heb.) bee.

Delia, *dē'li-ä,* *f.* (Gr.) of the island of Delos.

Demetrius, *di-mē'tri-əs,* *m.* belonging to the goddess Demeter.

Denis, Dennis, *den'is,* *m.,* **Denise,** *di-nēz',* *f.* See **Dionysius.**

Derek, Derrick, *der'ik,* *m.* See **Theodoric.**

Desideratus, *di-sid-ə-rā'təs,* **Desiderius,** *dez-i-dē'ri-əs,* *m.* (L.), **Désiré,** *dā-zē-rā',* *m.* (Fr.), longed for.—Fem. **Desiderata, Désirée.**

Desmond, *dez'mond,* *m.* (Ir.) from the surname or the district.

Diana, *dī-ä'nä,* *f.* (L.) goddess: the Roman goddess identified with Artemis.

Dick. See **Richard.**

Diggory, *dig'ə-ri,* *m.* (Fr.) from *Degarre,* a hero of romance, an exposed child (prob. Fr. *égaré,* astray).

Dilys, *dil'is,* *f.* (W.) sure, constant, genuine.

Dinah, *dī'nä,* *f.* (Heb.) judged, or dedicated.

Dionysius, *dī-ə-nis'i-əs, -niz',* *m.* (Gr.), **Denis, Dennis,** *den'is* (Fr.—Gr.), belonging to Dionysos or Bacchus.—Fr. *Denis, Denys,* It. *Dionigi,* Sp. *Dionisio.*—Fem. **Dionysia, Denise** (*di-nēz'*).

Dolores, *do-lō'rēz,* *f.* (Sp.) sorrows.—Dim. **Lola.**

Dominic, *dom'i-nik,* *m.* (L.) Sunday.—L. *Dominicus,* It. *Domenico,* Sp. *Domingo,* Fr. *Dominique.*

Donald, *don'əld,* *m.* (Celt.) world chief.—Gael. *Domhnall.*—Dim. **Don.**

Dora, *dō'rä,* *f.* prob. a dim. of **Dorothy**; used also for **Theodora** and names of like ending.

Dorcas, *dor'kəs,* *f.* (Gr.) gazelle.

Doreen, *dō'rēn, dō-rēn',* *f.* (Ir.) sullen; or for **Dorothy.**

Doris, *dor'is, dō'ris, f.* (Gr.) the name of a sea-nymph; meaning doubtful.

Dorothy, *dor'ə-thi,* **Dorothea, -*thē'ä,* *f.* (Gr.) gift of God.—Fr. *Dorothée, Dorette,* Ger. *Dorothea.*—Dims. **Dol, Doll, Dolly, Dora, Do, Dot.**

Dougal, Dugald, *dōō'gəl (d), m.* (Celt.) black stranger.—Gael. *Dughall.*

Douglas, *dug'ləs,* *m.* (and *f.*) from the surname, or the river.

Dudley, *dud'li,* *m.* from the surname.

Dulcie, *dul'si,* *f.* (L.) sweet—a modern invention.

Duncan, *dung'kən,* *m.* (Celt.) brown head.—Gael. *Donnchadh.*

Eamon, Irish form of **Edmund.**

Ebenezer, *eb-i-nē'zər,* *m.* (Heb.) stone of help.—Dim. **Eben.**

Ed, Eddie, dims. of **Edgar, Edmund, Edward, Edwin.**

Edgar, *ed'gər,* *m.* (O.E.) happy spear.—O.E. *Éadgar.*

—Dims. **Ed, Eddie, Eddy, Ned, Neddie, Neddy.**

Edith, *ē'dith,* *f.* (O.E.) happy or rich war.—O.E. *Éadgyth.*—Dims. **Edie, Edy.**

Edmund, *ed'mənd,* *m.* (O.E.) happy protection.—Fr. *Edmond,* Ir. *Eamon.*—Dims. **Ed, Eddie, Eddy, Ned, Neddie, Neddy.**

Edna, *ed'nä,* *f.* (Heb.) meaning uncertain.

Edward, *ed'wərd,* *m.* (O.E.) rich guard.—Ger. *Eduard,* Fr. *Édouard,* It. *Eduardo, Edoardo, Odoardo.*—Dims. **Ed, Eddie, Eddy, Ned, Neddie, Neddy, Ted, Teddie, Teddy.**

Edwin, *ed'win,* *m.* (O.E.) prosperity or riches, friend.—Dims. **Ed, Eddie, Eddy, Ned, Neddie, Neddy.**

Effie, *ef'i,* *f.* dim. of **Euphemia.**

Egbert, *eg'bərt,* *m.* (O.E.) sword-bright.

Eileen, *ī'lēn, ī-lēn',* *f.* (Ir.) an old Irish name perh. meaning pleasant; used as a substitute for **Helen.**

Eirene. See **Irene.**

Elaine, *e-lān',* *f.* an O.Fr. form of **Helen.**

Eldred, *el'drid,* **Aldred,** *awl'drid,* *m.* (O.E.) old counsel.—O.E. *Ealdred.*

Eleanor, *el'i-nər,* **Elinor, Leonora,** *lē-ə-nō'rä,* *f.* Same as **Helen.**—It. *Eleonora,* Ger. *Eleonore, Lenore,* Fr. *Éléonore, Aliénor.*—Dims. **Ella, Ellen, Nell, Nellie, Nelly, Nora.**

Eleazer, *el-i-ā'zər,* *m.* (Heb.) God is help.

Eifleda, *el-flē'dä,* *f.* (O.E. *Æthelflæd*) noble-clean, and (O.E. *Ælflæd*) elf-clean.

Elfreda, *el-frē'dä,* *f.* (O.E.) elf-strength.—O.E. *Ælfthryth.*

Elgiva, *el-jī'vä,* *f.* (O.E.) elf-gift.—O.E. *Ælfgyfu,* or noble gift (O.E. *Æthelgyfu*).

Elias, *i-lī'əs,* **Elijah,** *i-lī'jä,* *m.* (Heb.) the Lord is Yah.

Elizabeth, Elisabeth, *i-liz'ə-beth,* **Eliza,** *i-lī'zä, f.* (Heb.) God an oath.—Fr. *Elizabeth, Élise,* It. *Elisabetta, Elisa,* Ger. *Elisabeth, Elise,* Sp. *Isabel* (q.v.).—Dims. **Bess, Bessie, Bessy, Bet, Beth, Betsy, Betty, Elsie, Libby, Lisa, Liza** (*lī'zä*), **Liz** (*liz*), **Lizzie.**

Ella, *el'ä, f.* (Gmc.) all.—Also a dim. of **Eleanor** or of **Isabella** or other name in -ella.

Ellen, *el'in,* *f.* a form of **Helen,** also used for **Eleanor.**

Elma, *el'mä,* *f.* for **Gulielma,** or a combination of **Elizabeth Mary.**

Elmer. See **Aylmer.**

Eloisa. See **Heloise.**

Elsa, *el'sä,* **Elsie, -*si.* See **Elizabeth, Alison, Alice.**

Elspeth, *el'spəth,* **Elspet,** *el'spət,* Scots forms of **Elizabeth.**

Elvira, *el-vē'rä,* or *-vī',* *f.* (Sp.) prob. of Gmc. origin, elf-counsel.

Emery, Emory, *em'ə-ri,* **Almeric,** *al'mə-rik,* *m.* (Gmc.) work-rule, energetic rule.—L. *Amalricus,* Ger. *Emerich,* It. *Amerigo.*

Emily, *em'(i-)li,* **Emilia,** *i-mil'i-ä,* fem. of the Roman gentile name *Aemilius.*—L. *Aemilia,* Ger. *Emilie,* Fr. *Émilie,* It. *Emilia.*—Sometimes confused with **Amelia.**

Emma, *em'ä,* *f.* (Gmc.) whole, universal.—Also a shortened form of various names beginning Ermin-, Irmin-.—Dims. **Emm, Emmie.**

Emmanuel, Immanuel, *i-man'ū-il,* *m.* (Heb.) God with us.—Sp. *Manuel,* Port. *Manoel.*

Emmeline, Emeline, *em'i-lēn, -līn,* *f.* prob. for **Amelia.**

Emrys, *em'ris,* *m.* Welsh form of **Ambrose.**

Ena, *ē'nä,* *f.* (Ir.) fire; or a shortened form of **Eugenia** or other name of similar sound.

Enid, *ē'nid,* *f.* (W.) possibly wood-lark.

Enoch, *ē-nok,* *m.* (Heb.) poss. consecrated, or teaching.

Ephraim, *ēf'* or *ef'rā-im,* *m.* (Heb.) fruitful.

Erasmus, *i-raz'məs,* *m.* (Gr.) lovely, deserving love.—Dim. **Rasmus.**

Erastus, *i-ras'təs,* *m.* (Gr.) lovely.—Dim. **Rastus.**

Eric, *er'ik,* *m.* (Gmc.; O.N. *Eirikr*) perh. sole ruler.—Ger. *Erich,* O.E. *Yric.*—Fem. **Erica,** *er'i-kä* (with associations with Gr. *ereikē,* heath).

Ermentrude, Irmentrude, *ər'min-trōōd, f.* (Gmc.) prob. Ermin (the god), and strength.

Ernest, *ər'nist, m.* (Gmc.) earnest.—Ger. *Ernst,* It. and Sp. *Ernesto.*—Dim. **Ernie.**—Fem. **Ernestine.**

Esau, *ē'saw, m.* (Heb.) hairy.

Esme, *ez'mi, m.* (Fr.) beloved (a Scottish name).

Esmeralda, *ez-mi-ral'dä, f.* (Sp.) emerald.

Estella, *es-tel'ä,* **Estelle,** *es-tel', f.* See **Stella.** Perh. sometimes for Esther.

Esther, *es'tər,* **Hester,** *hes'tər, f.* poss. Pers., star; or Babylonian, *Ishtar,* the goddess Astarte.—Dims. **Essie, Hetty.**

Ethel, *eth'l, f.* (O.E.) noble (not used uncompounded in O.E.).

Ethelbert, *eth'l-bərt, m.* noble-bright.

Etheldred, -a. See **Audrey.**

Ethelind, *eth'ə-lind,* **Ethelinda,** *-lin'dä, f.* (Gmc.) noble snake.

Etta, *et'ä, f.* See **Henrietta.**

Eugene, *ū'jēn, m.* (Gr.) well-born.—L. *Eugenius,* Fr. *Eugène,* Ger. *Eugen.*—Dim. **Gene.**—Fem. **Eugenia.**—Fr. *Eugénie.*—Dims. **Ena, Gene.**

Eulalia, *ū-lā'li-ä, f.* (Gr.) fair speech.

Eunice, *ū-nī'sē, ū'nis, f.* (Gr.) happy victory.

Euphemia, *ū-fē'mi-ä, f.* (Gr.) of good report.— Dims. **Effie, Euphan, Euphie, Phemie** (*fā'mi*), **Phamie.**

Eusebius, *ū-sē'bi-əs, m.* (Gr.) pious.

Eustace, *ū'stis,* **Eustachius,** *ū-stā'ki-əs, m.* (Gr.) rich in corn (Gr. *eustachys,* confounded with *eustathēs,* stable).—Ger. *Eustachius,* Fr. *Eustache,* It. *Eustachio,* Sp. *Eustaquio.*

Eva, *ē'vä,* **Eve,** *ēv, f.* (Heb.) life.—Fr. *Ève,* Ger., It., Sp. *Eva.*—Dims. **Evie, Evelina** (q.v.), **Eveleen** (Ir.).

Evan, *ev'ən, m.* Anglicised Welsh form of **John.**— W. *Ifan.*

Evangeline, *i-van'ji-lēn, -lin, -lin, f.* (Gr.) bringer of good news.

Evelina, *ev-i-lē'nä, -li'nä, f.,* **Eveline,** *ev'i-lēn ēv'lin, f.,* **Evelyn,** *ēv'lin, ev'i-lin, m.* and *f.,* partly dims. of **Eve,** partly from the surname Evelyn, partly from Gmc. *Avilina* from *Avi.*

Everard, *ev'ə-rärd, m.* (Gmc.) boar-hard.—Ger. *Eberhard, Ebert,* Fr. *Évraud.*

Ewan, Ewen, *ū'ən, m.* See **Owen.**

Ezekiel, *i-zē'ki-əl, m.* (Heb.) God will strengthen.— Ger. *Ezechiel, Hesechiel,* Fr. *Ézéchiel.*—Dim. **Zeke.**

Ezra, *ez'rä, m.* (Heb.) help.—L. *Ezra, Esdras,* Fr. *Esdras,* Ger. *Esra.*

Fabian, *fā'bi-ən, m.*—L. *Fabianus,* a deriv. of the gentile name *Fabius,* perh. connected with *faba,* bean.

Faith, *fāth, f.* (Eng. or Fr.) faith.

Fanny, *fan'i, f.* See **Frances.**

Farquhar, *fär'kər, m.* (Gael.) manly. — Gael. *Fearachar.*

Faustina, *faws-tī'nä,* **Faustine,** *-tēn', f.* (L.) fortunate.

Fay, *fā, f.* (Fr.) perh. faith, perh. fairy.

Felix, *fē'liks, m.* (L.) happy.—Fem. **Felicia** (*fi-lish'i-ä*), **Felice** (*fi-lēs',* confused with **Phyllis**), happy, **Felicity,** happiness.

Ferdinand, *fər'di-nənd, m.* (Gmc.) journey-risk.— Ger. *Ferdinand,* Fr. *Ferdinand, Ferrand,* Sp. *Fernando, Hernando,* It. *Ferdinando, Ferrando.*

Fergus, *fər'gəs, m.* (Gael.) supremely choice.—Gael. *Fearghas.*

Fidelia, *fi-dē'li'ä, f.* (L.) faithful.

Fiona, *fē'o-nä, f.* (Gael.) fair.

Flora, *flō'rä, f.* (L.) name of the Roman flower-goddess.—Dims. **Flo, Florrie** (*flor'i*).

Florence, *flor'ins, f.* (L.) blooming; also born in Florence. — L. *Florentia* (masc. *Florentius*). — Dims. **Flo, Florrie, Flossie, Floy.**

Francis, *frän'sis, m.* (Fr.) Frankish, French.—L. *Franciscus,* Fr. *François,* It. *Francesco,* Sp. *Francisco,* Ger. *Franz, Franziskus.*—Dims. **Frank, Francie, Frankie.**—Fem. **Frances** (*frän'sis, -səz*).—L. *Francisca,* Fr. *Françoise,* It. *Francesca* (dim. *Franceschina*), Sp. *Francisca,* Ger. *Franziska.*— Dims. **Fanny, Frank, Francie.**

Freda, *frē'dä, f.* dim. of **Winifred,** or for **Frieda.**

Frederick, Frederic, *fred'rik, m.* (Gmc.) peace-rule. —L. *Fredericus, Fridericus,* Ger. *Friedrich, Fritz,* Fr. *Frédéric,* It. *Federico, Federigo,* Sp. *Federico.*— Dims. (both genders) **Fred, Freddie, Freddy.**— Fem. **Frederica** (*fred-ə-rē'kä*).—Ger. *Friederike,* Fr. *Frédérique.*

Frieda, *frē'dä, f.* (Gmc.) peace.—Used as a dim. for any fem. name with the element *fred* or *frid.*

Fulk, Fulke, *foolk, m.* (Gmc.) people.

Gabriel, *gā-bri-əl, m.* (Heb.) God is mighty, or man of God.—Dims. **Gabe, Gabby** (*gab'i*).

Gareth, *gar'ith, m.* O.Fr. *Gahariet,* prob. from some W. name.

Gaspar, *gas'pər, m.* See **Jasper.**

Gavin, *gav'in,* **Gawain,** *gä'win, gaw'in, m.* (W.) perh. white hawk.

Gene, *jēn,* for **Eugene, Eugenia.**

Genevieve, *jen'i-vēv, f.* (Fr.—Celt.) meaning obscure.—Fr. *Geneviève.*

Geoffrey, Jeffrey, *jef'ri, m.* (Gmc.). Two names have run together—district-peace (O.H.G. *Gaufrid*) and traveller-peace (O.H.G. *Walahfrid*).— L. *Gaufridus, Galfridus,* Sp. *Geofredo,* Fr. *Geoffroi.* —Dim. **Jeff.**—Confounded with **Godfrey.**

George, *jorj, m.* (Gr.) husbandman.—L. *Georgius,* Fr. *Georges, George,* Ger. *Georg,* It. *Giorgio,* Sp. *Jorge,* Gael. *Seòras.*—Dims. **Geordie, Georgie, Georgy, Dod, Doddy.**—Fem. **Georgia, Georgiana** (*-i-ä'nä*), **Georgina** (*-ē'nä*).—Dim. **Georgie.**

Gerald, *jer'ald, m.* (Gmc.) spear-wielding.—L. *Geraldus, Giraldus,* Fr. *Géraud, Giraud, Girauld,* It. *Giraldo,* Ger. *Gerold, Gerald.*—Fem. **Geraldine** (*-ēn*).

Gerard, *jer'ärd, -ərd, m.* (Gmc.) spear-hard.—L. *Gerardus,* Fr. *Gérard,* It. *Gerardo,* Ger *Gerhard.*

German, *jər'mən, m.* (L.) German.—Fem. **Germaine** (Fr., *zer-men').*

Gertrude, *gər'trōōd, f.* (Gmc.) spear-might.—Dims. **Gert, Gertie, Trudy.**

Gervase, *jər'vis, -vāz, m.* (Gmc.) spear-servant.— Also **Gervas, Jervis.**

Gideon, *gid'i-ən, m.* (Heb.) hewer.

Gil. See **Gilbert, Giles.**

Gilbert, *gil'bərt, m.* (Gmc.) bright hostage.—L. *Gilbertus,* Fr. *Guilbert, Gilbert,* It. and Sp. *Gilberto,* Ger. *Gilbert, Giselbert.*—Dims. **Gib, Gibbie, Gil.**

Giles, *jilz, m.* (Fr.—Gr.) kid.—L. *Aegidius,* Fr. *Gilles,* Ser. *Agidius,* It. *Egidio,* Sp. *Egidio, Gil.*

Gill, Gillian, *jil, -i-ən, f.* See **Juliana.**—Also **Jill, Jillian.**

Gladys, *glad'is, f.* W. *Gwladys* for **Claudia.**

Gloria, *glō'ri-ä, f.* (L.) glory.

Godfrey, *god'fri, m.* (Gmc.) God's peace.—L. *Godofridus,* Fr. *Godefroi,* Ger. *Gottfried,* It. *Goffredo, Godofredo,* Sp. *Godofredo, Gofredo.*— Confused with **Geoffrey.**

Godwin, *god'win, m.* (O.E.) God-friend.

Gordon, *gor'dən, m.* from the surname.

Grace, *f.* (Fr.) grace.

Gregory, *greg'ə-ri, m.* (Gr.) watcher.—L. *Gregorius,* Ger. *Gregor, Gregorius,* Fr. *Grégoire,* It. and Sp. *Gregorio.*

Greta, *grē'tä, gret'a.* See **Margaret.**

Griffith, *grif'ith, m.* (W.) ruddy, rufous.—W. *Gruffydd.*

Grizel, Grizzel, Grissel, Griselda, *griz'l,* **Griselda,** *gri-zel'dä, f.* (Gmc.) perh. grey war, perh. Christ war. —Ger. *Griseldis,* It. *Griselda.*

Gustavus, *gus-tā'vəs, -tä'vəs, m.* (Gmc.) meditation (?) staff.—L. *Gustavus,* Swed. *Gustaf,* Ger. *Gustav,* Fr. *Gustave.*

Guy, *gī, m.* (Gmc.) perh. wood, perh. wide.—O.H.G. *Wido, Wito,* L., Ger., It., and Sp. *Guido,* Fr. *Guy, Guyon.*

Gwendolen, *gwen'dō-lin, f.* (W.) white (second element obscure).—Dims. **Gwen, Gwennie.**

Gwyneth, *gwin'ith, f.* (W.) blessed.

Hab, Habbie. See **Halbert.**

Hadrian. See **Adrian.**

Hal, *hal.* See **Henry.**

Halbert, *hâl'bərt, m.* an old Scots form of **Albert.** —Dims. **Hab, Habbie, Hob, Hobbie.**

Hamish, *hā'mish, m.* See **James.**

Hannah, *han'ä, f.* See **Ann.**
Harold, *har'əld, m.* (Gmc.) army rule.
Harriet, Harriot, *har'i-ət,* fem. forms of **Henry.**—Dim. **Hatty.**
Hartley, *härt'li, m.* from the surname.
Hazel, Heather, *f.* from the plants.
Hector, *hek'tər, m.* (Gr.) holding fast.—Dim. **Heck.**—Ger. *Hektor,* It. *Ettore,* Sp. *Héctor.*
Hedwig, *hed'wig, f.* (Ger.) contention-fight.
Helen, *hel'en, -in,* **Helena,** *hel'i-nä,* **Ellen,** *el'ən, f.* (Gr.) bright.—L. *Helena,* Fr. *Hélène,* Ger. *Helene,* It. and Sp. *Elena.*—Dims. **Nell, Nellie, Nelly.**
Helga, *hel'gä, f.* (Gmc., Norse) holy.
Heloise, Eloise, (*h)el-ō-ēz', Eloisa, el-ō-ē'zä, f.* (Gmc.) sound or whole, and wide.—Fr. *Héloïse.*
Henry, *hen'ri,* **Harry,** *har'i, m.* (Gmc.) house ruler.—L. *Henricus, Enricus,* Fr. *Henri,* It. *Enrico,* Sp. *Enrique,* Ger. *Heinrich* (dims. *Heinz, Heinze, Hinz, Hinze),* Du. *Hendrik.*—Fem. **Henrietta, Harriet, Harriot.**—Fr. *Henriette,* It. *Enrichetta,* Sp. *Enriqueta.*—Dims. **Hatty, Hetty.**
Herbert, *her'bərt, m.* (Gmc.) army-bright.—Ger. *Herbert,* It. *Erberto,* Sp. *Heriberto.*—Dim. **Bert, Bertie.**
Hercules, *hər'kū-lēz, m.* L. name of the Greek hero Herakles, glory of Hera.—It. *Ercole.*
Herman, Hermann, *hər'mən, m.* (Gmc.) army man, warrior.—Ger. *Hermann.*
Hermione, *hər-mī'ə-nē, f.* (Gr.) a derivative of *Hermes* (Greek god).
Hester. See **Esther.**
Hetty, *het'i,* dim. of **Hester** and of **Henrietta.**
Hew, another spelling of **Hugh,** preferred by certain families.
Hezekiah, *hez-i-kī'ä, m.* (Heb.) Yah is strength, or has strength.—Fr. *Ézéchias,* Ger. *Hiskia.*
Hilary, *hil'əri, m.* (L.) cheerful.—L. and Ger. *Hilarius,* Fr. *Hilaire,* It. *Ilario,* Sp. *Hilario.*—Fem. **Hilary, Hilaria.**
Hilda, *hil'dä, f.* (Gmc.) battle.
Hildebrand, *hil'di-brand, m.* (Gmc.) battle sword.
Hiram, *hī'rəm, m.* (Heb.) noble.
Hob, Hobbie, *hob, -i, m.* for **Halbert, Robert.**
Hodge, *hoj, m.* for **Roger.**
Honor, *on'ər,* **Honora,** *ho-nō'rä,* **Honoria,** *-ri-ä, f.* (L.) honour, honourable.—Dims. **Nora, Norah** (Ir. **Noreen).**—Masc. **Honorius.**
Hope, *hōp, m.* and *f.* (Eng.) hope.
Horace, *hor'is,* **Horatio,** *ho-rä'shō, m.* (L.) the Roman gentile name *Horatius.*—Fem. **Horatia.**
Hortensia, *hor-ten'syä, f.* (L.) fem. of a Roman gentile name—gardener.
Hubert, *hū'bərt, m.* (Gmc.) mind-bright.
Hugh, Hew, *hū,* **Hugo,** *hū'gō, m.* (Gmc.) mind.—L., Ger., Sp. *Hugo,* Fr. *Hugues,* It. *Ugo, Ugone.*—Dims. **Huggin, Hughie** (obs. **Huchon).**
Hulda, *hul'dä, f.* (Gmc.) name of a Germanic goddess—gracious. Also (Norse) covered.
Huldah, *hul'dä, f.* (Heb.) weasel.
Humbert, *hum'bərt, m.* (Gmc.) prob. giant-bright.—It. *Umberto.*
Humphrey, Humphry, *hum'fri, m.* (Gmc.) prob. giant-peace.—Ger. *Humfried,* Fr. *Onfroi,* It. *Onofrio,* Sp. *Hunfredo.*—Dims. **Humph, Numps, Dump, Dumphy.**
Hyacinth, *hī'ə-sinth, m.* and *f.* (Gr.) the flower hyacinth (masc. in Greek).

Iain, Ian, *ē'ən, m.* Gaelic for **John.**
Ianthe, *ī-an'thē, f.* (Gr.) violet flower (name of a sea-nymph).
Ida, *ī'dä, f.* (Gmc.) labour.
Ifan, *ē'van, m.* Welsh form of **John.**
Ifor, *ē'vor, m.* Welsh form of **Ivo, Ivor.**
Ignatius, *ig-nā'shəs, m.* Latinised from a late Greek form of the Roman (perh. orig. Samnite) gentile name *Egnatius* (meaning unknown), assimilated to L. *ignis,* fire.—Fr. *Ignace,* Ger. *Ignaz,* It. *Ignazio,* Sp. *Ignacio.* See **Inigo.**
Igor, *ē'gor, m.* Russian form of the Scandinavian name *Ingvarr,* watchfulness of Ing (the god Frey).
Ines, Inez, *ī'nez, ē'nez,* Sp. *ē-näs', f.* See **Agnes.**
Ingeborg, *ing'i-borg, f.* (Scand.) stronghold of Ing (the god Frey).
Ingram, *ing'(g)rəm, m.* raven of Ing (Frey).

Ingrid, *ing'(g)rid, f.* (Scand.) ride of Ing (Frey), or maiden of the Ingvaeones.
Inigo, *in'i-gō, m.* (Sp.) either a form of **Ignatius** or another name confused with it.—L. *Enecus, Ennecus,* Sp. *Iñigo.*
Ira, *ī'rä',* (Heb.) watchful.
Irene, Eirene, *ī-rē'nē,* in America *ī-rēn', f.* (Gr.) peace.
Iris, *ī'ris, f.* (Gr.) rainbow, iris (plant)—name of Hera's messenger.
Irmentrude. See **Ermentrude.**
Isaac, Izaak, *ī'zək, m.* (Heb.) laugh.—Dims. **Ik, Ike, Iky.**
Isabella, *iz-ə-bel'ä,* **Isabel, Isobel,** *iz'ə-bəl, -bel,* or (Scots) **Ishbel,** *ish'bəl,* **Isbel,** *iz'bəl, f.* (Sp.—Heb.) forms of **Elizabeth,** now regarded as an independent name.—Sp. *Isabel,* Fr. *Isabel (Isabeau),* It. *Isabella.*—Dims. **Bel, Bell, Belle, Bella, Ella, Ib, Ibby, Isa** (*ī'zä*)**, Tib, Tibbie, Tibby.**
Isaiah, *ī-zī'ä, m.* (Heb.) Yahwe helps.—L. *Isaias,* Ger. *Jesaias,* Fr. *Isaïe, Esaïe,* Sp. *Isaías,* It. *Isaia.*
Isidore, *iz'i-dōr, m.* (Gr.) perh. gift of Isis.—Sp. *Isidro, Isidoro.*—Fem. **Isidora, Isadora.**
Isold, Isolde, Isolda, *i-zold', -ä,* **Isolt,** *i-zolt', f.* perh. (Gmc.) ice-rule; or a Welsh name.
Israel, *iz'rā-əl, -el, m.* (Heb.) ruling with the Lord.
Ivan, *ī'vən, ē-vän', m.* (Russ.). See **John.**
Ivo, Ivor, *ī'vō, ī'vər,* or *ē', m.* prob. Celtic, but perh. from a Gmc. root meaning yew.—W. *Ifor,* Fr. *Ives, Yves, Ivon, Yvon;* fem. *Ivette, Yvette, Ivonne, Yvonne.*
Ivy, *ī'vi, m.* and *f.* (Eng.) from the plant.

Jabez, *jā'biz, m.* (Heb.) perh. sorrow, perh. height.
Jack, *jak, m.* See **John.**
Jacob, *jā'kəb, m.* (Heb.) follower, supplanter, or deceiver.—It. *Giacobbe,* Sp. *Jacob.*—Dim. **Jake.** See also **James.**
James, *jāmz, m.* Same as **Jacob.**—L. *Jacōbus* (later *Jacōbus, Jacōmus,* whence the forms with *m*). Fr. *Jacques,* It. *Jacopo, Giacomo, Iachimo,* Sp. *Jacobo, Diego, Jaime, Jago,* Ger. *Jakob,* Gael. *Seumas* (Anglicised vocative **Hamish**).—Dims. **Jim, Jimmie, Jem, Jemmie, Jamie** (*jim'i,* Scot.), **Jeames** (*jēmz,* Scot. and burlesque).—Fems. **Jacoba** (*ja-kō'bä*)**, Jacobina** (*-bē'nä*)**, Jacqueline, Jaqueline, Jacquetta, Jamesina**—**Jemima** has nothing to do with **James.**
Jan. See **John.**
Jane, *jān,* **Jean,** *jēn,* **Joan,** *jōn,* **Jo(h)anna,** *jō-an'ä,* fems. of **John.**—L. *Johanna,* Fr. *Jeanne* (dim. *Jeannette),* It. *Giovanna,* Sp. *Juana* (dim. *Juanita),* Ger. *Johanna.*—Dims. **Janet** (*jan'it*)**, Janetta, Janey, Janie, Jeannie, Jen, Jenny, Jennie, Jess, Jessie, Jessy, Netta, Nettie, Nita** (*nē'tä*)—some of them regarded as separate names.
Janet, *jan'it, f.* a dim. of **Jane,** regarded as an independent name.
Jared, *jā'rid, m.* (Heb.) descent.
Jasper, *jas'pər,* **Gaspar,** *gas'pər, m.* prob. Pers. treasure-bringer.—Fr. *Gaspard,* Ger. *Kaspar.*
Jean, *jēn, f.* See **Jane,** &c. For Fr. *m.* (*zhän°*), see **John.**
Jedidiah, Jedediah, *jed-i-dī'ä, m.* (Heb.) Yah is friend.
Jeffrey, *jef'ri, m.* See **Geoffrey.**
Jemima, *ji-mī'mä, f.* (Heb.) meaning unknown (day, dove, pure, fortunate have been suggested).—Not connected with **James.**
Jennifer, Jenifer, *jen'i-fər, f.* (W.) a form of **Guinevere,** perh. white wave, or white phantom.
Jenny, Jennie, *jen'i, jin'i, f.* See **Jane.**
Jeremiah, *jer-i-mī'ä,* **Jeremias,** *-əs,* **Jeremy,** *jer'i-mi, m.* (Heb.) Yah is high, or heals, or founds.—Dim. **Jerry** (*jer'i*).
Jerome, *jer'ōm, ji-rōm', m.* (Gr.) holy name.—L. and Ger. *Hieronymus,* Fr. *Jérôme,* It. *Geronimo, Gerolamo, Girolamo,* Sp. *Jerónimo.*
Jerry, *jer'i, m.* dim. of **Jeremy,** also of **Gerald, Gerard, Jerome.**
Jervis, *jər'vis, m.* See **Gervase.**
Jess, Jes, Jessie, *f.* forms of **Janet,** chiefly Scots. See **Jane.**
Jesse, *jes'i, m.* (Heb.) Yah is.

Jessica, *jes'i-kă, f.* (app. Heb.) perh. Yah is looking.

Jethro, *jeth'rō, m.* (Heb.) superiority.

Jill, *jil,* **Jillian,** *-yən, f.* See **Juliana.**

Jim, Jimmie. See **James.**

Jo, Joe, for **Joseph, Josepha, Josephine.**

Joachim, *jō'ə-kim, m.* (Heb.) Yah has set up.—Sp. *Joaquin,* It. *Gioacchino.*

Joan, *jōn,* **Joanna,** *jō-an'ă,* **Joann,** *jō-an'.* See **Jane.**

Joannes. See **John.**

Job, *jōb, m.* (Heb.) perh. pious, or persecuted, afflicted.—Ger. *Hiob,* It. *Giobbe.*

Jocelyn, Jocelin, Joceline, *jos'(ə-)lin, m.* perh. (Gmc.) one of the Geats (a people of southern Sweden), or (L.) connected with **Justin, Justus.**

Jock, *jok, m.* See **John.**

Jodocus, *jō-dō'kəs, m.* (Celt.) champion.—Fr. *Josse,* Ger. (dims.) *Jobst, Jost.*—Fem. **Jodoca.**

Joe, Jo, for **Joseph, Josepha, Josephine.**

Joel, *jō'əl, m.* (Heb.) Yah is the Lord.

John, *jon, m.* (Heb.) poss. Yah is gracious.—L. *Jo(h)annes,* Fr. *Jean,* It. *Giovanni* (*Gian, Gianni*), Sp. *Juan,* Port. *João,* Ger. *Johann, Johannes* (dim. *Hans*), Du. *Jan,* Russ. *Ivan,* Ir. *Seán* (Anglicised *Shane, Shawn*), *Eoin,* Gael. *Iain* (*Ian*), W. *Ifan.* —Dims. **Johnnie, Jack** (from **Jankin**), **Jackie,** (Scot. **Jock, Jockie**), **Jan,** obs. **Jankin.**—Fem. see under **Jane.**

Jonas, *jō'nəs,* **Jonah,** *-nă, m.* (Heb.) dove.

Jonathan, *jon'ə-thən, m.* (Heb.) Yah has given.

Joseph, *jō'zif, m.* (Heb.) Yah increases.—L. *Josephus,* Fr. *Joseph,* It. *Giuseppe* (dim. *Beppo*), Sp. *José* (dims. *Pepe, Pepillo, Pepito*), Ger. *Joseph, Josef.*— Dims. **Jo, Joe, Joey, Jos** (*jos*).—Fem. **Josepha** (*-sē'fă, -zē'fă*), **Josephine** (*-zi-fēn*).—Dims. **Jo, Joe, Jozy.**

Joshua, *josh'ū-ă, m.* (Heb.) Yah delivers.—L. and Ger. *Josua,* Fr. and Sp. *Josué,* It. *Giosuè.*—Dim. **Josh.**

Josiah, *joz-ī'ă,* **Josias,** *-əs, m.* (Heb.) Yah supports

Joy, *joi, f.* (Eng.) joy.

Joyce, *jois, f.* (Gmc.) a Geat (see **Jocelyn**).

Judith, *jōō'dith, f.* (Heb.) Jewess.—Dim. **Judy.**

Julian, *jōō'lyən, -li-ən, m.* (L.) derived from, belonging to, Julius.—Dim. **Jule.**—Fem. **Juliana** (*-ā'nă*), **Jillian, Gillian** (*jil'yən*).—Dim. **Jill.**

Julius, *jōō'li-əs, m.* (L.) a Roman gentile name, perh. downy-bearded.—Dim. **Jule.**—Fr. *Jules* It. *Giulio.*—Fem. **Julia.**—Dim. **Juliet.**

June, *jōōn, f.* (L.) from the month.

Justus, *jus'təs, m.* (L.) just.—Derivs. **Justin** (fem. **Justina,** *-tī'na,* **Justine,** *-tēn*), **Justinian** (*-tin'yən, -i-ən*).

Karen, *kä'rən,* **Kate, Katherine, Katherine, Kathleen, Kay.** See **Catharine.**

Keith, *kēth, m.* from the surname or place-name.

Kenelm, *ken'elm, m.* (O.E. *Cenhelm*) keen helmet.

Kenneth, *ken'ith, m.* (Gael.) handsome.—Gael. *Caioneach.*

Kester, *kes'tər, m.* See **Christopher.**

Keziah, *ki-zī'ă, f.* (Heb.) cassia.

Kirsty, *kir'sti,* **Kirsteen,** *-stēn, f.* See **Christian.**

Kit. See **Christopher, Catherine.**—**Kitty.** See **Catherine.**

Lachlan, *lahh'lən, m.* (Gael.) warlike.—Dim. **Lachy.**

Lambert, *lam'bərt, m.* (Gmc.) land-bright.

Lance, *läns, m.* (Gmc.) land.—Dims. **Lancelot, Launcelot.**

Laura, *law'ră, f.* laurel.—Also **Laurinda, Lorinda.** —Dim. **Lauretta, Lolly.**

Laurence, Lawrence, *law'rəns, m.* (L.) laurel.— L. *Laurentius,* It. *Lorenzo,* Ger. *Lorenz.*—Dim. **Larry** (*lar'i*).

Lavinia, *lə-vin'i-ă, f.* (L.) origin unknown (second wife of Aeneas).

Lazarus, *laz'ə-rəs, m.* (Gr. *Lazaros* from Heb.) a form of Eleazar.

Leander, *li-an'dər, m.* (Gr.) lion man.

Leila, *lī'lă, f.* (Pers.) night.

Lemuel, *lem'ū'əl, m.* (Heb.) consecrated to God.

Lena, *lē'nă, f.* See **Helena, Magdalen.**

Leo, *lē'ō, m.* (L.) lion.

Leonard, *len'ərd, m.* (Gmc.) lion-hard.

Leonora, *lē-ə-nō'ră, f.* See **Eleanor.**

Leopold, *lē'ō-pōld, m.* (Gmc.) people-bold.—Ger. *Luitpold, Leopold.*

Leslie, Lesley, *lez'li, m.* and *f.* from the surname or place-name.

Lettice, *let'is,* **Letitia, Laetitia,** *li-tish'yă, f.* (L.) gladness.—Dim. **Lettie, Letty.**

Lewis, *lōō'is,* **Louis,** *lōō'is, lōō'i,* **Ludovic(k),** *l(y)ōō'dō-vik,* **Lodowick,** *lō'dō-wik*—also **Aloys,** *al'ō-is, -ois',* **Aloysius,** *-ē'zi-əs, -is'i-əs, m.* (Gmc.) famous warrior.—L. *Ludovicus, Aloysius,* Fr. *Louis* (from *Chlodowig, Clovis*), Prov. *Aloys,* It. *Ludovico, Luigi, Aloysio,* Sp. *Luis, Aloisio,* Ger. *Ludwig.*—Dims. **Lewie, Louie, Lew.**—Fem. **Louisa** (*lōō-ē'ză*), **Louise** (*-ēz'*).—Dims. **Lou, Louie.**—Fr. *Louise* (*Lisette*), It. *Luisa,* Ger. *Luise.*

Liam, *lē'əm, m.* Irish form of **William.**

Lily, *lil'i,* **Lil(l)ian,** *-ən,* **Lil(l)ias,** *-əs, f.* prob. partly from the flower, partly for **Elizabeth.**

Linda, *lin'dă, f.* (Gmc.) short for any feminine name ending in -lind (snake).

Lionel, *lī'ə-nəl, m.* (L.) young lion.

Liz, Lizzie, Lisa, Liza. See **Elizabeth.**

Llewelyn, *(h)lē-wel'in, lōō-el'in, m.* (W.) meaning doubtful.

Lloyd, *loid, m.* (W.) grey.

Lodowick. See **Lewis.**

Lois, *lō'is, f.* prob. (Gr.) good.

Lola, *lō'lă, f.* for **Dolores,** or **Carlotta.**

Lorenzo, *lō-ren'zō, m.* See **Laurence.**

Lorinda, *lō-rin'dă, f.* See **Laura.**

Lorna, *lor'nă, f.* an invention of Blackmore's, in *Lorna Doone.*

Lottie, *lot'i, f.* See under **Charles.**

Louis, *lōō'is, -i, m.,* **Louisa,** *lōō-ē'ză,* **Louise,** *-ēz', f.* See **Lewis.**

Lucas, *lōō'kəs, m.* See **Luke.**

Lucius, *lōō'shi-əs, -shəs, m.* (L.) a Roman name probably connected with L. *lux,* light.—Fem. **Luce, Lucy, Lucinda, Lucilla, Lucil(l)e.**

Lucretius, *lōō-krē'shəs, -shi-əs, m.* (L.) a Roman name perh. meaning gain.—Fem. **Lucretia, Lucrece** (*-krēs*).

Ludovic(k). See **Lewis.**

Luke, *lōōk,* **Lucas,** *lōō'kəs, m.* (L.) of Lucania (in Italy).

Luther, *lōō'thər, m.* (Gmc.) famous warrior.—L. *Lutherus,* Fr. *Lothaire,* It. *Lotario.*

Lydia, *lid'i-ă, f.* (Gr.) Lydian woman.

Mabel, *mā'bl, f.* See **Amabel.**

Madge, *maj,* **Mag,** *mag,* **Maggie,** *mag'i, f.* See **Margaret.**

Madoc,, *mad'ək, m.* (W.) fortunate.

Magdalen(e), *mag'də-lin, -lēn,* **Madel(e)ine,** *mad' - (ə-)len, -lēn, -lin, f.* of Magdala on the Sea of Galilee.—Dims. **Maud, Maude** (*mawd*), **Maudlin.**

Magnus, *mag'nəs, m.* (L.) great.

Maida, *mā'dă, f.* origin obscure.

Maisie, *mā'zi, f.* See **Margaret.**

Malachi, *mal'ə-kī, m.* (Heb.) messenger of Yah.

Malcolm, *mal'kəm, m.* (Gael.) Columba's servant.

Malise, *mal'is, m.* (Gael.) servant of Jesus.

Mamie, *mā'mie, f.* a chiefly American dim. of **Mary,** used also for **Margaret.**

Manuel, *man'ū-əl,* **Manoel.** See **Emmanuel.**

Marcus, *mär'kəs.* See **Mark.**

Margaret, *mär'gə-rit, f.* (Gr.) pearl.—Fr. *Marguerite* (dim. *Margot*), It. *Margherita,* Sp. *Margarita,* Ger. *Margarete* (dims. *Grete, Gretchen*).—Dims. **Madge, May, Maggie, Margie** (*mär'ji*), **Margery** (*mär'jə-ri*), **Marjory, Meg, Meggie, Meta** (*mē'tă*), **Mysie** (*mī'zi*), **Peg, Peggie, Peggy, Greta** (*grē'tă*), **Rita** (*rē'tă*).

Maria, *mə-rī'ă.* See **Mary.**

Marian, Marion, *mar'i-ən, mā'ri-ən,* **Marianne,** *mar-i-an', f.* (Fr.) orig. dims. of **Mary**; used also for the combination **Mary Ann.**—Dim. **Maynie.**

Marigold, *mar'i-gōld, f.* from the flower.

Marina, *mə-rē'nă, f.* (L.) of the sea.

Marjory, *mär'jə-ri, f.* See **Margaret.**

Mark, *märk,* **Marcus,** *-əs, m.* (L.) a Roman name prob. derived from Mars (the God).—L. *Marcus,*

Sp. *Marcos*, Ger. *Markus*.—Derivs. **Marcius** (*mär'shi-əs*; fem. **Marcia**), strictly a Roman gentile name perh. of like origin, **Marcellus** (-*sel'əs*; fem. **Marcella**).

Marmaduke, *mär'mə-dūk*, *m.* prob. (Celt.) servant of Madoc.—Dim. **Duke.**

Martha, *mär'thä*, *f.* (Aramaic) lady, mistress.— Dims. **Mat, Mattie, Matty, Pat, Pattie, Patty.**

Martin, *mär'tin*, *m.* (L.) prob. warlike, of Mars.

Mary, *mā'ri*, **Maria**, *mə-rī'ä*, **Miriam**, *mir'i-əm*, *f.* (Heb.) rebellion.—Gr. *Mariam*, L., It., Ger. *Maria*, Sp. *María*, Fr. *Marie* (dim. *Marion*).— Dims. **May, Moll, Molly, Mally, Mamie, Marietta** (*mar-i-et'ä*), **Maureen** (*maw-rēn'*, or *maw'*), **Minnie, Poll, Polly.**

Mat, Matty. See **Martha, Matilda, Matthew.**

Mat(h)ilda, *mə-til'dä*, *f.* (Gmc.) battle-might.— Dims. **Mat, Matty, Maud, Maude, Patty, Tilly, Tilda.**

Matthew, *math'ū*, **Matthias**, *mə-thī'əs*, *m.* (Heb.) gift of Yah.—Gr. *Matthaios*, L. *Matthaeus*, Fr. *Matthieu*, It. *Matteo*, Sp. *Mateo*, Ger. *Matthäus*. —Dims. **Mat, Matty.**

Maud, Maude, *mawd*, *f.* See **Matilda, Magdalen.**

Maurice, *maw'ris*, *mor'is*, **Morris**, (L.) Moorish, dark-coloured.—L. *Mauritius*, Fr. *Maurice*, It. *Maurizio*, Sp. *Mauricio*, Ger. *Moritz*.

Mavis, *mā'vis*, *f.* (Eng.) thrush.

Maximilian, *maks-i-mil'yən*, *m.* (L.) a combination of *Maximus*, greatest, and *Aemilianus*.—Dim. **Max.**

May, *mā*, *f.* partly for **Mary**, partly from the month.

Meave, *māv*, *f.* (Ir.) the goddess, or legendary queen of Connaught, Medb, or Meadhbh.

Meg. See **Margaret.**

Melicent. See **Millicent.**

Melissa, *me-lis'ä*, *f.* (Gr.) bee.

Mercy, *mər'si*, *f.* (Eng.) mercy.—Sp. *Mercedes* (mercies, bounties).

Meta. See **Margaret.**

Michael, *mī'kl*, *m.* (Heb.) who is like the Lord?—Fr. *Michel*, It. *Michele*, Sp. and Port. *Miguel*, Ger. *Michael* (dim. *Michel*).—Dims. **Mick, Micky, Mike.**

Mildred, *mil'drid*, *f.* (Gmc.; O.E. *Mildthryth*) mild power.—Dim. **Millie.**

Miles, *mīlz*, *m.* (Gmc.) meaning doubtful, perh. merciful.

Millicent, *mil'i-sənt*, **Melicent**, *mel'*, *f.* (Gmc.) work-strong.—Fr. *Mélisande*.—Dim. **Millie.**

Millie, *mil'i*, *f.* See **Mildred, Millicent, Emilia, Amelia.**

Mima, *mī'mä*, *f.* See **Jemima.**

Mina, *mē'nä*, *f.* See **Wilhelmina.**

Minna, *min'ä*, *f.* (Gmc.) memory, or love.

Minnie, *min'i*, for **Minna, May**, or **Wilhelmina.**

Mirabel, *mir'ə-bel*, *f.* (L.) wonderful.

Miranda, *mi-ran'dä*, *f.* to be admired or wondered at.

Miriam, *mir'i-əm.* See **Mary.**

Moira, *moi'rä*, *f.* (Ir.) perh. great; (Gr.) a fate.

Molly, *mol'i*, *f.* See **Mary.**

Mona, *mō'nä*, *f.* (Ir.) noble.

Monica, *mon'i-kä*, *f.* the name, possibly African, of St Augustine's mother; sometimes understood as (Gr.) alone, solitary.

Montague(e), *mon'tə-gū*, *m.* from the surname.—Dim. **Monty.**

Morag, *mō'rag*, G. (Gael.) great.

Morgan, *mor'gən*, *m.* (W.) sea, sea-shore.—Fem. **Morgan, Morgana** (-*gä'nä*).

Morris. See **Maurice.**

Mortimer, *mor'ti-mər*, *m.* from the surname.

Moses, *mō'ziz*, *m.* meaning obscure.—Gr. *Mōysēs*, Ger. *Moses*, Fr. *Moïse*, It. *Moisè, Mosè*, Sp. *Moisés*.

Moyna, *moi'nä*, *f.* perh. the same as **Mona.**

Mungo, *mung'gō*, *m.* (Gael.) amiable.

Murdo, *mər'dō*, *m.* (Gael.) seaman.

Muriel, *mū'ri-əl*, *f.* (Celt.) perh. sea-bright.

Myra, *mī'rä*, *f.* app. an arbitrary invention; sometimes used as an anagram of **Mary.**

Myrtle, *mər'tl*, **Myrtilla**, -*til'ä*, *f.* from the shrub.

Mysie, *mī'zi*, *f.* for **Margaret, Marion.**

Nahum, *nä'(h)əm*, *m.* (Heb.) consoling.

Nan, Nanny, *nan*, -*i*, *f.* See **Ann.**

Nance, Nancy, *nans*, -*i*, *f.* See **Ann, Agnes.**

Nanty, *nan'ti*, *m.* dim. of **Anthony.**

Naomi, *nā-ō'mi*, -*mi*, or *nä'*, *f.* (Heb.) pleasant.

Nat, *nat*, for **Nathaniel, Nathan, Natalia.**

Natalia, *nə-tä'li-ä*, or -*tä'*, **Natalie**, *nat'ə-li*, *f.* (L.). See **Noel.**

Nathan, *nä'thən*, *m.* (Heb.) gift.

Nathaniel, *nə-than'yəl*, *m.* (Heb.) gift of God.— Also **Nathanael** (-*ä-əl*).—Dim. **Nat.**

Ned, Neddie, Neddy, *ned*, -*i*, dims. of **Edward**; also of **Edgar, Edmund, Edwin.**

Nehemiah, *nē-hi-mī'ä*, *m.* (Heb.) consolation of Yah.

Neil, Niall, *nēl.* See **Nigel.**

Nell, Nellie, Nelly, *nel*, -*i*, *f.* dims. of **Helen, Ellen, Eleanor.**

Nessa, Nessie, Nesta, dims. of **Agnes.**

Netta, Nettie, dims. of **Janet(ta), Henrietta.**

Neville, *nev'il*, *m.* from the surname.

Nicholas, Nicolas, *nik'ə-ləs*, *m.* (Gr.) victory of the people.—Dims. **Nick, Colin** (q.v.), **Colley, Nicol, Nichol.**—Fem. **Nicola** (*nik'ə-lä*).—Dims. **Nicolette, Colette.**

Nicodemus, *nik-ə-dē'məs*, *m.* (Gr.) victory of the people.

Nigel, *nī'gl*, **Neil, Niall**, *nēl*, *m.* perh. (Ir.) champion, but understood as d'm. of L. *niger*, black.

Nina, Ninette, Ninon. See **Ann.**

Ninian, *nin'yən*, *m.* (Celt.) meaning unknown.— Also (Scot.) **Ringan** (*ring'ən*).

Nita, *nē'tä*, *f.* for **Juanita.** See **Jane.**

Noah, *nō'ä*, *m.* (Heb.) rest.

Noel, *nō'əl*, -*el*, *m.* and *f.* (Fr.—L.) birthday, i.e. Christmas.—Fr. *Noël*, It. *Natale*.—Fem. **Natalia** (*nə-tä'li-ä*, or -*tä'*), **Natalie** (*nat'ə-li*.)

Nora, Norah, *nō'rä*, *f.* orig. for **Honora, Leonora, Eleanor.**—Dim. (Ir.) **Noreen** (-*rēn'*).

Norman, *nor-mən*, *m.* (Gmc.) Northman.

Norna, *nor'nä*, *f.* (Gmc.) a Norn or Fate.

Obadiah, *ō-bə-dī'ä*, *m.* (Heb.) servant, or worshipper, of the Lord.

Octavius, Octavus, *ok-tā'vi-əs*, -*vəs*, *m.* (L.) eighth. —Dims. **Tavy** (*tä'vi*), **Tave.**—Fem. **Octavia.**

Odette, *ō-det'*, *f.* See **Ottilia.**

Odo, *ō'dō*, *m.* See **Otto.**

Olaf, *ō'laf*, -*laf*, *m.* (Scand.) ancestor-relics.

Olga, *ol'gä*, *f.* (Russ.—Gmc.) holy.

Olive, *ol'iv*, **Olivia**, *ō-* or *ə-liv'i-ä*, *f.* (L.) olive.— Dim. **Livy** (*liv'i*).—**Oliver**, *ol'i-vər*, *m.* (Fr.) olive-tree (but poss. orig. another name assimilated).—Dims. **Noll, Nolly** (*nol*, -*i*).

Olympia, *ō-* or *ə-lim'pi-ä*, *f.* (Gr.) Olympian.

Ophelia, *ō-* or *ə-fē'li-ä*, *f.* prob. (Gr.) help.

Orlando, *or-lan'dō.* See **Roland.**

Osbert, *oz'bərt*, *m.* (Gmc.) god-bright.

Oscar, *os'kər*, *m.* (Gmc.) god-spear.

Osmund, Osmond, *oz'mənd*, *m.* (Gmc.) god-protection.

Osric, *oz'rik*, *m.* (Gmc.) god-rule.

Oswald, *oz'wəld*, *m.* (Gmc.) god-power.

Oswin, *oz'win*, *m.* (Gmc.) god-friend.

Ottilia, *ot-il'i-ä*, *f.* (Gmc.) heritage (udal).—Dim. **Odette** (*ō-det'*).

Otto, *ot'ō*, **Odo**, *ō'dō*, **Otho**, *ō'thō*, *m.* (Gmc.) rich. —It. *Ottone.*

Owen, *ō'ən*, *m.* (W.) said to mean youth.—Ir. and Gael. *Ewan, Ewen* (Eoghan).—Used as a substitute for **Eugene.**

Paddy, *pad'i*, dim. of **Patrick, Patricia.**

Pamela, *pam'i-lä*, *f.* prob. an invention (as *pam-ē'lä*) of Sir Philip Sidney's.

Parnel, *pär'nel*, -*nəl*, *f.* See **Petronella.**

Pat, dim. of **Patrick, Patricia, Martha.**

Patience, *pä'shəns*, *f.* patience.

Patrick, *pat'rik*, *m.* (L.) nobleman, patrician.— Dims. **Pat, Paddy.**—Fem. **Patricia** (*pə-trish'(y)ä*). —Dims. **Pat, Paddy.**

Patty, *pat'i*, *f.* dim. of **Martha, Patience.**

Paul, Paullus, Paulus, *pawl*, -*əs*, *m.* (L.) little.— It. *Paolo*, Sp. *Pablo*.—Deriv. **Paulinus** (-*i'nəs*).— Fem. **Paula, Paulina, Pauline** (-*ēn*).

Pearl, *pərl*, *f.* pearl.

Peg, Peggy, *peg*, -*i*, *f.* dims. of **Margaret.**

Penelope, *pi-nel′o-pi, f.* (Gr.) perh. weaver.—Dims. **Pen, Penny.**

Pepe, Pepito. See **Joseph.**

Percival, Perceval, *pər′si-vl, m.* (Fr.) penetrate the valley.

Percy, *pər′si, m.* from the surname.

Perdita, *pər′di-tä, f.* (L.) lost.

Peregrine, *per′i-grin, m.* (L.) wanderer, traveller, pilgrim.

Pernel, *pər-nəl.* See **Petronella.**

Persis, *pər′sis, f.* (Gr.) Persian.

Peter, *pē′tər, m.* (Gr.) rock.—Also **Piers,** *pērz.*—L. *Petrus,* Fr. *Pierre,* It. *Pietro,* Sp. and Port. *Pedro,* Ger. *Peter, Petrus,* Norw. *Peer.*—Dims. **Pete** *(pēt),* **Peterkin, Perkin** *(pər′kin).*

Petronella, Petronilla, *pət-rə-nel′ä, -nil′ä, f.* (L.) from the gentile name *Petrōnius.* — Contracted **Parnel** *(pär′nəl),* **Pernel** *(pər′nəl).*

Phelim, *fē′lim, m.* (Ir.) ever good.

Philemon, *fil- fil-ē′mon, m.* (Gr.) affectionate.

Philip, *fil′ip, m.* (Gr.) lover of horses.—L. *Philippus,* Fr. *Philippe,* It. *Filippo,* Sp. *Felipe,* Ger. *Philipp.*—Dims. **Phil, Pip.**—Fem. **Philippa.**

Phillis, *fil′is,* **Phillida,** *fil′i-dä, f.* (Gr.) a leafy shoot.

Phineas, Phinehas, *fin′i-əs, m.* (Heb.) meaning obscure—explained as negro, oracle, serpent's mouth, &c.

Phoebe, *fē′bi, f.* (Gr.) shining, a name of Artemis as moon-goddess.

Piers, *pērz, m.* See **Peter.**

Polly, *pol′i, f.* See **Mary.**

Primrose, *prim′rōz, f.* from the flower.

Priscilla, *pris-il′ä, f.* (L.) dim. of the Roman name *Priscus* (former).

Prudence, *prōō′dəns, f.* prudence.—Dims. **Prue, Prudy.**

Queenie, *kwēn′i, f.* from *queen.*

Quintin, *kwin′tin,* **Quentin,** *kwen′, m.* (L.) fifth.—L. *Quintianus.*

Rachel, *rā′chl, f.* (Heb.) ewe.—Ger. *Rahel,* Fr. *Rachel,* It. *Rachele,* Sp. *Raquel.*—Dim. **Ray.**

Ralph, *rāf, ralf, m.* (Gmc.) counsel-wolf.—O.E. *Rædwulf,* Fr. *Raoul.*

Ranald, *ran′əld, m.* See **Reginald.**

Randal, *ran′dl,* **Randolph,** *ran′dolf, m.* (Gmc.) shield-wolf.

Raoul, *rä-ōōl′, m.* See **Ralph.**

Raphael, *raf′ä-el, -əl, m.* (Heb.) God heals.—It. *Raffaele, Raffaello.*

Rasmus, *raz′məs,* dim. of **Erasmus.**

Rastus, *ras′təs, m.* dim. of **Erastus.**

Ray, *rā.* See **Rachel, Raymond.**—Also used as an independent name, *f.*

Raymond, Raymund, *rā′mənd, m.* (Gmc.) counsel (or might) protector.—Ger. *Raimund,* Sp. *Ramón, Raimundo,* It. *Raimondo.*—Dim. **Ray.**

Rayner, *rā′nər, m.* (Gmc.) counsel (or might), army (or folk).

Rebecca, Rebekah, *ri-bek′ä, f.* (Heb.) noose.—Dims. **Beck, Becky.**

Reginald, *rej′i-nəld,* **Reynold,** *ren′əld,* **Ronald,** *ron′,* **Ranald,** *ran′, m.* (Gmc.) counsel (or power) rule. —Ger. *Reinwald, Reinhold, Reinalt,* Fr. *Regnault, Regnauld, Renaud,* It. *Rinaldo, Reinaldo.*—Dims. **Reg** *(rej),* **Reggie** *(rej′i),* **Rex, Ronnie.**

René, *rə-nā′, m.* (Fr.), **Renatus,** *ri-nā′təs, m.* (L.) born again.—Fem. **Renée, Renata.**

Reuben, *rōō′bən, m.* (Heb.) behold a son, or renewer.

Rex, reks, m. (L.) king.—Also for **Reginald.**

Reynold, *ren′əld, m.* See **Reginald.**

Rhoda, *rō′dä, f.* (Gr.) rose.

Rhys, *rēs, m.* (W.) perh. impetuous man.

Richard, *rich′ərd, m.* (Gmc.) rule-hard.—It. *Riccardo,* Sp. *Ricardo.*—Dims. **Dick, Dickie, Dicky, Dicken, Dickon, Rick, Richie** (obs. **Diccon, Hick).**—Fem. **Ricarda** *(ri-kär′dä).*

Ringan, *ring′ən, m.* See **Ninian.**

Rita, *rē′tä, f.* See **Margaret.**

Robert, *rob′ərt,* **Rupert,** *rōō′pərt, m.* (Gmc.) fame-bright.—L. *Robertus,* Fr. *Robert,* It. and Sp. *Roberto,* Ger. *Robert, Ruprecht, Rupprecht.*—Dims. **Bert, Bertie, Bob, Bobbie, Bobby, Dob,**

Dobbin, Rob, Robbie, Robin *(rob′in),* Scots **Rab, Rabbie.**—Fem. **Roberta, Robina** *(ro-bē′nä).*

Roderick, *rod′(ə-)rik, m.* fame-rule.—Ger. *Roderich,* Fr. *Rodrigue,* It. *Rodrigo, Roderico,* Sp. *Rodrigo, Ruy.*—Dim. **Roddy.**

Rodney, *rod′ni, m.* and *f.* from the surname or place-name.

Rodolph. See **Rudolf.**

Roger, *roj′ər, m.* (Gmc.) fame-spear. — O.E. *Hróthgár,* Ger. *Rüdiger,* Fr. *Roger,* It. *Ruggero, Ruggiero,* Sp. *Rogerio.*—Dim. **Hodge, Hodgkin** *(hoj′kin).*

Roland, Rowland, *rō′lənd, m.* (Gmc.) fame of the land.—Ger., Fr., *Roland,* It. *Orlando,* Sp. *Roldán, Rolando.*

Rolf, rolf, m. See **Rudolf.**

Ronald, *ron′əld, m.* See **Reginald.**

Rory, *rō′ri, m.* (Ir.) red.

Rosalind, Rosaline, *roz′ə-lind, -līnd, -lēn, -lin, f.* (Gmc.) horse-snake, but associated with **Rose** (fair rose).

Rosamund, Rosamond, *roz′ə-mənd, f.* (Gmc.) horse-protection.—Associated with **Rose** (L. *rosa munda,* fine or pure rose, *rosa mundi,* rose of the world).

Rose, *rōz,* **Rosa,** *rō′zä, f.* (L.) rose. It may also be sometimes Gmc., horse.—Derivs. **Rosabel** *(roz′ə-bel),* **Rosabella** *(rōz-ə-bel′ä),* **Rosalia** *(rō-zā′li-ä),* **Rosalie** *(roz′* or *rōz′ə-li)* (L. *rosalia,* the hanging of rose-garlands on tombs).

Rosemary, *rōz′mə-ri, f.* from the plant; also for **Rose Mary.**

Rowena, *rō-(w)ē′nä, f.* perh. Geoffrey of Monmouth's mistake for W. *Rhonwen,* white skirt.

Roy, *roi, m.* (Gael.) red.

Ruby, *rōō′bi, f.* from the stone.—Also **Rubina** *(-bē′nä).*

Rudolf, Rudolph, *rōō′dolf,* **Rodolph,** *rō′,* **Rolf,** *rolf, m.* (Gmc.) fame-wolf.

Rufus, *rōō′fəs, m.* (L.) red.

Rupert, Rupprecht. See **Robert.**

Ruth, *rōōth, f.* (Heb.) meaning obscure; used sometimes with associations with English *ruth.*

Sadie, *sā′di,* **Sal, sal, Sally.** See **Sarah.**

Salome, *sə-lō′mi, f.* (Heb.) perfect, or peace.

Samson, Sampson, *sam′son, m.* (Heb.) of the sun.—Gr. *Sampsōn,* Fr. *Samson,* Ger. *Simson,* It. *Sansone,* Sp. *Sansón,* Port. *Sansão.*

Samuel, *sam′ū-əl, m.* (Heb.) heard by God, or name of God.—Dims. **Sam, Sammy.**

Sancho, *sân′chō, m.* (Sp.) holy.

Sandy, *san′di, m.* See **Alexander.**

Sarah, Sara, *sā′rä, f.* (Heb.) princess, queen.—Dims. **Sadie** *(sā′di),* **Sal** *(sal),* **Sally.**

Saul, *sawl, m.* (Heb.) asked for.

Seamas, Seamus, *shā′məs, m.* See **James.**

Seán, shawn, m. See **John.**

Sebastian, *si-bas′ti-ən, m.* (Gr.) man of Sebasteia (in Pontus)—Gr. *sebastos,* august, venerable.

Secundus, *si-kun′dəs, m.* (L.) second.

Selina, *si-lē′nä, f.* poss. connected with **Celia,** but associated with Gr. *selēnē,* moon.

Septimus, *sep′ti-məs, m.* (L.) seventh.

Seth, *seth, m.* (Heb.) substitute, or compensation.

Seumas. See **James.**

Sextus, *seks′təs, m.* (L.) sixth.

Shamus, for **Seamus** (see **James**).

Shane, *shān, m.* See **John.**

Sheena, *shē′nä, f.* Gaelic *(Sìne)* for **Jane.**

Sheila, *shē′lä, f.* Irish *(Síle)* for **Celia**; also for **Cecilia.**

Shirley, *shər′li, f.* from the surname or place-name.

Sholto, *shol′tō, m.* perh. (Gael) sower, propagator.

Sibyl, now **Sybil,** *sib′il,* **Sibylla,** *sib-il′ä, f.* (L.) a Sibyl.—Dim. **Sib.**

Sidney, Sydney, *sid′ni, m.* and *f.,* from the surname.

Siegfried, *sēg′frēd, zēhh′frēt,* **Sigurd,** *sē′goord, m.* (Gmc.) victory-peace.

Sigismund, *sij′* or *sig′is-mund, -mōōnd,* **Siegmund,** *sēg′mōōnd, m.* victory-protection.

Silas, *sī′ləs,* **Silvanus,** *sil-vā′nəs,* **Silvester, Sylvester,** *sil-ves′tər,* **Silvius, Sylvius** *sil′vi-əs, m.* (L.) living in the woods.—Fem. **Silvia, Sylvia.**

Simon, *sī'mən,* **Simeon,** *sim'i-ən, m.* (Heb.) perh. hearing; perh. also (Gr.) snub-nosed.—Dims. **Sim, Simmy, Simkin.**

Solomon, *sol'ə-mən, m.* (Heb.) peaceable.—Ger. *Salomo,* Fr. *Salomon,* It. *Salomone,* Sp. *Salomón,* Port. *Salomão.*—Dims. **Sol, Solly.**

Sophia, *sə-fī'ä,* **Sophie, Sophy,** *sō'fi, f.* (Gr.) wisdom —Russ. **Sonia.**

Sophronia, *sə-frō'ni-ä, f.* (Gr.) prudent, temperate, of sound mind.

Stanislas, *stan'is-las,* **Stanislaus,** *-lä'əs, m.* (Pol.) camp-glory.

Stanley, *stan'li, m.* from the surname or place-name.

Stella, *stel'ä, f.* (L.) star.—Also **Estella** (*es-tel'ä*), **Estelle** (*-tel'*).

Stephen, *stē'vən, m.* (Gr.) crown.—L. *Stephanus,* Fr. *Étienne,* It. *Stefano,* Sp. *Esteban,* Gr. *Stephan.* —Dims. **Steenie, Steve, Stevie.**—Fem. **Stephana** (*stef'ə-nä*), **Stephanie** (*-ni*).

Susan, *sōō'zən, sū'zən,* **Susanna, Susannah,** *-zan'ä, f.* (Heb.) lily.—Dims. **Sue, Suke, Suky, Susie, Susy.**

Sylvius, &c. See **Silvius,** &c. (under **Silas**).

Tabitha, *tab'i-thä, f.* (Aramaic) gazelle.

Taffy, *taf'i,* Welsh form of **David.**

Talbot, *tawl'bət, m.* from the surname.

Terence, *ter'ins, m.* (L.) the Roman gentile name *Terentius*; used with its dim. **Terry** as a substitute for Ir. *Turlough,* like Thor.

Teresa, Theresa, *tə-rē'zä,* **Theresia,** *-zi-ä, f.* (Gr.) origin unknown—more probably connected with the island of Therasia than with reaping.— It. and Sp. *Teresa,* Fr. *Thérèse,* Ger. *Theresia, Therese.*—Dims. **Terry, Tessa.**

Terry, *ter'i.* See **Terence, Teresa.**

Tessa, *tes'ä.* See **Teresa.**

Thaddaeus, Thaddeus, *thə-dē'əs, thad'i-əs, m.* (Heb.) meaning obscure.—Used with its dims. **Thaddy, Thady** as a substitute for the Irish name Tadhgh (*thēg*), poet, which formerly in the form **Teague** (*tēg*) served as a general nickname for an Irishman, as Pat, Paddy, now.

Thecla, *thek'lä, f.* (Gr.) god-famed.

Thelma, *thel'mä, f.* poss. (Gr.) will, an invention apparently of Marie Corelli's.

Theobald, *thē'ō-bawld, tib'əld,* **Tybalt,** *tib'əlt, m.* (Gmc.) people-bold.—Fr. *Thibaut, Thibault,* It. *Tebaldo,* Sp. *Teobaldo.*

Theodore, *thē'ō-dōr, m.* (Gr.) gift of God.—Fem. **Theodora** (*-dō'rä*).

Theodoric, Theoderic, *thē-od'ə-rik, m.* (Gmc.) people-rule.—Ger. *Dietrich* (dim. *Dirk*).—Dim. **Derrick, Derek.**

Theodosius, *thē-ō-dō'si-əs, m.* (Gr.) gift of God.— Fem. **Theodosia.**

Theophilus, *thē-of'i-ləs, m.* (Gr.) beloved of God (or the gods).

Theresa, Theresia. See **Teresa.**

Thomas, *tom'əs, m.* (Heb.) twin.—Fr., Ger. *Thomas,* It. *Tommaso,* Sp. *Tomás.*—Dims. **Tom, Tommy** (Scot. **Tam, Tammie**).—Fem. **Thomasa** (*tom'ə-sä*), **Thomasina** (*tom-ə-sē'nä*), **Tomina** (*tom-ē'nä*).

Thorold, *thor'əld, m.* (Gmc.) Thor-strength.

Tib, Tibbie, *tib, -i, f.* dims. of **Isabella,** mainly Scottish.

Tilly, *til'i, f.* See **Matilda.**

Timothy, *tim'ə-thi, m.* (Gr.) honoured of God.— Dim. **Tim.**

Titus, *tī'təs, m.* (L.) a Roman praenomen—meaning unknown.

Toby, *tō'bi,* **Tobias,** *-bī'əs, m.* (Heb.) Yah is good.

Tony, *tō'ni, m.* See **Anthony.**

Tracy, *trā'si, m.* and *f.* perh. from the surname.

Tristram, Tristrem, *tris'trəm,* **Tristan,** *-tən, m.* (Celt.) perh. tumult.

Trixy. See **Beatrice.**

Turlough, *tur'lō, m.* (Ir. *Toirdhealbhac*) like Thor. —Represented by **Terence, Terry, Charles.**

Tybalt, *tib'əlt, m.* See **Theobald.**

Uchtred, Ughtred, *ū'trid, m.* perh. (O.E.) thought-counsel.

Ulick, *ū'lik, m.* an Irish form of **Ulysses,** but perh. really for a native name.

Ulric, *ul'rik, m.* (Gmc.) wolf-rule.—Ger. *Ulrich.*— Fem. **Ulrica.**—Ger. *Ulrike.*

Ulysses, *ū-lis'ēz, m.* (L. form of Gr.) angry, or hater.—Gr. *Odysseus,* L. *Ulysses, Ulixes.* See **Ulick.**

Una, *ū'nä, f.* (L.) one, from Spenser's heroine, personification of truth, but perh. suggested by some Irish name.

Urban, *ur'bən, m.* (L.) of the town, urbane.

Uriah, *ū-rī'ä, m.* (Heb.) perh. Yah is light.

Ursula, *ur'sū-lä, f.* (L.) little she-bear.

Valentine, *val'in-tīn, m.* (L.) healthy.

Valeria, *və-lē'ri-ä, f.* (L.) fem. of a Roman gentile name.—Deriv. **Valerian,** *m.*

Vanessa, *və-nes'ä, f.* a name invented by Swift from *Esther Vanhomrigh.*

Venetia, *vi-nē'shä, f.* (L.) Venetian; perh. also a Latinisation of **Gwyneth.**

Vera, *vē'rä, f.* (L.) true; also (Russ.) faith.

Vere, *vēr, m.* and *f.* from the surname.

Veronica, *vi-ron'i-kä, f.* (L.) true image; or (Gr.) a form of **Berenice.**

Vesta, *ves'tä, f.* (L.) the Roman hearth-goddess.

Victor, *vik'tər, m.* (L.) conqueror.—**Victoria,** *vik-tō'ri-ä, f.* victory.

Vida, *vē'dä,* a fem. dim. of **David.**

Vincent, *vin'sənt, m.* (L.) conquering.

Viola, *vī'ō-lä,* **Violet,** *-lit, f.* (L.) violet (flower).

Virginia, *vər-jin'i-ä,* (L.) fem. of a Roman gentile name.

Vivian, *viv'i-ən, m.* and (chiefly in the form **Vivien**) *f.* (L.) lively.—Also **Vyvyen, Vyvian.**

Walter, *wawl'tər, m.* (Gmc.) rule-people (or army). —L. *Gualterus,* Ger. *Walter, Walther,* Fr. *Gautier, Gauthier,* Sp. *Gualterio,* It. *Gualtieri.*—Dims. **Wat, Watty** (*wot, -i*), **Wally, Walt.**

Wendy, *wen'di, f.* an invention of J. M. Barrie's.

Wilfrid, Wilfred, *wil'frid, m.* (Gmc.) will-peace.

Wilhelmina, *wil-(h)əl-mē'nä* (Ger. *Wilhelmine*), a fem. formed from *Wilhelm* (see **William**).— Dims. **Elma, Wilmett, Wilmot, Mina** (*mē'nä*), **Minnie, Minella.**

William, *wil'yəm, m.* (Gmc.) will-helmet.—L. *Gulielmus, Guilielmus,* Ger. *Wilhelm,* Fr. *Guillaume,* It. *Guglielmo,* Sp. *Guillermo, Guillelmo,* Ir. *Liam.*—Fem. See **Wilhelmina.**

Winifred, *win'i-frid, f.* prob. orig. W., the same as *Guinevere* (white wave), but assimilated to the English masculine name *Winfrith* (friend of peace). —Dims. **Win, Winnie, Freda** (*frē'dä*).

Xavier, *zav'i-ər, m.* (Sp.—Ar.) splendid.

Yoland, *yō'lənd, f.* app. a mediaeval form of *Violante,* a deriv. of **Viola.**

Yve, Yves, *ēv,* **Yvon,** *ē-von*v*,* Fr. deriv. of **Ivo.**— Fem. **Yvonne** (*ē-von'*), **Yvette** (*ē-vet'*).

Zachariah, Zechariah, *zak-, zek-ə-rī'ä,* **Zachary,** *zak'ə-ri, m.* (Heb.) Yah is renowned.—Dims. **Zach, Zack.**

Zedekiah, *zed-i-kī'ä, m.* (Heb.) Yah is might.

Zenobia, *zi-nō'bi-ä, f.* (Gr.) life from Zeus (but perh. a Semitic name in Greek guise).

Zoe, *zō'ē, f.* (Gr.) life.

CORRECT CEREMONIOUS FORMS OF ADDRESS

The following are the ceremonious modes of addressing and beginning letters to titled persons and persons holding certain offices

Ambassador, British—Address: 'His Excellency [in other respects according to his rank], H.B.M.'s Ambassador and Plenipotentiary.' Begin: 'Sir,' 'My Lord,' &c., according to rank. Refer to as 'Your Excellency.' An Ambassador's wife, when resident abroad, is sometimes, but not very correctly, designated 'Your Excellency.'

Archbishop—'His Grace the Lord Archbishop of ——.' Begin: 'My Lord Archbishop.' Refer to as 'Your Grace.' In formal documents the Archbishop of Canterbury is addressed as 'The Most Reverend Father in God [here insert his Christian name], by Divine Providence Lord Archbishop of Canterbury, Primate of all England and Metropolitan'; the Archbishop of York as 'The Most Reverend Father in God [Christian name], by Divine permission Lord Archbishop of York, Primate of England and Metropolitan.' But an Irish Archbishop (since 1868) is only 'The Most Reverend the Archbishop of ——' unless he be a temporal peer, in which case he is 'The Right Hon. and Most Rev.'

Archdeacon—'The Venerable the Archdeacon of ——.' Begin: 'Venerable Sir.'

Attorney-General—'The Right Hon. Sir [Christian name and surname], Attorney-General, K.C. (or Q.C.).' Begin: 'Sir.'

Baron—'The Right Hon. Lord ——,' or 'The Lord ——.' Begin: 'My Lord.' Refer to as 'Your Lordship.'

Baron's Daughter—If unmarried, 'The Hon.' [Christian name and surname]; if married to a commoner, 'The Hon. Mrs' [husband's surname]. If married to a Baronet or a Knight, 'The Hon. Lady' [husband's surname]. Begin: 'Madam.' If the wife of a peer, or of the son of a Duke or Marquess, address as such.

Baron's Son—'The Hon.' [Christian name and surname]. Begin: 'Sir.' But eldest sons of Barons in the Peerage of Scotland are usually addressed 'The Hon. the Master of' [peerage title].

Baron's Son's Wife—'The Hon. Mrs' [husband's surname], or, if necessary for distinction, the husband's Christian name should also be used. Begin: 'Madam.' If the daughter of an Earl, Marquess, or Duke, address as such.

Baroness in her own right—'The Right Hon. the Baroness ——'; wife of a baron—'The Right Hon. Lady ——,' or 'The Lady ——.' Begin: 'Madam.' Refer to as 'Your Ladyship.'

Baronet—'Sir [Christian name and surname], Bart.' Begin: 'Sir.'

Baronet's Wife—'Lady' [surname]. Begin: 'Madam.' Refer to as 'Your Ladyship.'

Bishop, Colonial—As English bishop.

Bishop, English—'The Right Rev. the Lord Bishop of London,' or 'The Lord Bishop of London.' Begin: 'My Lord Bishop.' Refer to as 'Your Lordship.' In formal documents a Bishop is 'The Right Rev. Father in God [Christian name], by Divine permission Lord Bishop of ——.'

Bishop, Irish—As English bishop. By tradition, the Bishop of Meath is addressed as 'The Most Rev. the Lord Bishop of Meath.'

Bishop, Retired—'The Right Rev. Bishop ——,' or 'The Right Rev. —— ——, D.D.' Begin: 'Right Rev. Sir.'

Bishop, Scottish—As English bishop. The Bishop who holds the position of Primus of the Scottish Episcopal Church is generally addressed

'The Most Rev. the Primus of Scotland.'

Bishop Suffragan—'The Right Rev. the Bishop Suffragan of ——.' Begin: 'Right Rev. Sir.'

Bishop (U.S.)—'The Right Rev. ——.' Refer to as 'Bishop ——.'

Bishops' Wives and Children have no titles.

Cardinal—'His Eminence Cardinal ——.' Begin: 'My Lord Cardinal,' or 'My Lord.' Refer to as 'Your Eminence.'

Clergy—'The Rev.' [Christian name and surname]. Begin: 'Dear Sir' (formerly 'Rev. Sir'). If son of a Duke or Marquess, 'The Rev. Lord' [Christian name and surname]. If the son of an Earl, Viscount, or Baron, 'The Rev. the Hon.' [Christian name and surname]. The Moderator of the General Assembly of the Church of Scotland during his year of office is styled 'Right Rev.'; ex-moderators are usually spoken of as 'Very Rev.'

Companion of an Order of Knighthood—The initials, C.B., C.M.G., C.S.I., or C.I.E., as it may be, are subjoined to the ordinary form of address.

Consul, British—'—— ——, Esq., H.B.M.'s Agent and Consul-General,' 'Consul-General,' 'Consul,' or 'Vice-Consul,' as it may be.

Countess—'The Right Hon. the Countess of ——.' Begin: 'Madam.' Refer to as 'Your Ladyship.'

Dean—'The Very Rev. the Dean of ——.' Begin: 'Very Rev. Sir.'

Doctor—The initials DD., M.D., LL.D., Mus.D., are placed after the ordinary form of address, as 'The Rev. John Smith, D.D.' 'John Brown, Esq., LL.D.' But 'The Rev. Dr. Smith,' 'Dr. John Brown,' are also frequently used.

Dowager—On the marriage of a peer or Baronet, the widow of the previous holder of the title becomes 'Dowager,' and is addressed, 'The Right Hon. the Dowager Countess of ——,' 'The Dowager Lady ——.' As more than one Dowager may hold the same title, the term is less used than formerly, the Christian name being employed as a distinction—e.g. 'The Right Hon. Helen Countess of ——.'

Duchess—'Her Grace the Duchess of ——.' Begin: 'Madam.' Refer to as 'Your Grace.' [For **Royal Duchess**, see **Princess**.]

Duke—'His Grace the Duke of ——.' Begin: 'My Lord Duke.' Refer to as 'Your Grace.' [For **Royal Duke**, see **Prince**.]

Duke's Daughter—'The Lady' [Christian name and surname], the surname being that of her husband if married. Begin: 'Madam.' Refer to as 'Your Ladyship.' If married to a peer, she is addressed according to her husband's rank only. This, however, does not hold in the case of peers by courtesy; and a Duke's daughter married to the eldest son of an Earl, after the prefix 'Lady,' sometimes takes her own Christian name, followed by her husband's courtesy title.

Duke's Eldest Son and his Children—A Duke's eldest son takes his father's second title. This courtesy title is treated as if it were an actual peerage, and his eldest son takes the grandfather's third title, being addressed as if a peer.

Duke's Eldest Son's Wife—As if her husband's courtesy title were an actual peerage.

Duke's Younger Son—'Lord' [Christian name and surname]. Begin: 'My Lord.' Refer to as 'Your Lordship.'

Duke's Younger Son's Wife—'Lady' [husband's

Christian name and surname]. Begin: 'Madam.' Refer to as 'Your Ladyship.'

Earl—'The Right Hon. the Earl of ——,' or 'The Earl of ——.' Begin: 'My Lord.' Refer to as 'Your Lordship.' [For Wife, see **Countess.**]

Earl's Daughter—As Duke's daughter.

Earl's Eldest Son, and Earl's Eldest Son's Wife— As if the courtesy title were an actual peerage.

Earl's Younger Son and his Wife—As Baron's son and his wife.

Governor of a Colony, Governor-General of a Dominion—'His Excellency [ordinary designation], Governor (General) of ——.' Begin according to rank, and refer to as 'Your Excellency.'

Judge, English or Irish—'The Hon. Sir ——,' if a Knight, or 'The Hon. Mr Justice ——.' Begin: 'Sir.' On the bench only is he addressed as 'My Lord,' and referred to as 'Your Lordship.'

Judge of County Court—'His Honour Judge ——.' When on the bench, referred to as 'Your Honour.'

Judges, Scottish—See Lord of Session.

Justice of Peace in England (not Scotland)—'The Right Worshipful.' Referred to when on the bench as 'Your Worship.'

KING—'The King's Most Excellent Majesty.' Begin: 'Sire,' or 'May it please your Majesty,' or 'Lord —— presents his duty to your Majesty.' Refer to as 'Your Majesty.'

King's Counsel—Append K.C. to ordinary address.

Knight Bachelor—As Baronet, except that the word 'Bart.' is omitted.

Knight of the Bath, of St Michael and St George, or of the Star of India—'Sir' [Christian name and surname], with the initials G.C.B., K.C.B., K.M.G., or K.S.I. added. Begin: 'Sir.'

Knight of the Garter, or of St Patrick—The initials K.G., K.T., or K.P., as it may be, are to be added to the address.

Knight's Wife, whether wife of Knight Bachelor, of the Bath, of St Michael and St George, or of the Star of India—As Baronet's wife.

Lord Advocate of Scotland—'The Right Hon. the Lord Advocate.' Usual beginning: 'My Lord,' though 'Sir' is said to be more correct.

Lord Chancellor—'The Right Hon. the Lord Chancellor.' Begin and refer to according to rank.

Lord Chief-Justice—'The Right Hon. the Lord Chief-Justice of England,' or 'The Right Hon. Sir ——, Lord Chief-Justice of England.' Begin, if a peer, according to his degree; otherwise as under Judge.

Lord High Commissioner to the General Assembly—'His Grace the Lord High Commissioner.' Begin according to rank as a peer. Refer to as 'Your Grace.'

Lord Justice-Clerk—'The Right Hon. the Lord Justice-Clerk.' Begin: 'My Lord.' Refer to as 'Your Lordship.'

Lord Justice-General of Scotland—'The Right Hon. the Lord Justice-General.' Begin: 'My Lord.' Refer to as 'Your Lordship.'

Lord Justice of Appeal—'The Right Hon. the Lord Justice ——,' or 'The Right Hon. Sir ——.' Begin and refer to as a Judge.

Lord Mayor of London, York, Belfast, Dublin; also Melbourne, Sydney, Adelaide, Perth, Brisbane, Hobart—'The Right Hon. the Lord Mayor of [London],' or 'The Right Hon. ——, Lord Mayor of [London].' Begin: 'My Lord.' Refer to as 'Your Lordship.' The 'Right' is omitted in some other cases.

Lord Mayor's Wife—'The (Right) Hon. the Lady Mayoress of ——' (see above). Begin: 'Madam.' Refer to as 'Your Ladyship.'

Lord of Appeal in Ordinary and his Wife—As Baron and Baroness. Their children have no title.

Lord of Session in Scotland—'The Hon. Lord ——.' Begin: 'My Lord.' Refer to as 'Your Lordship.' His wife had no title till 1905, but is now styled 'Lady.'

Lord Provost—'The Right Hon. the Lord Provost of Edinburgh,' 'The Right Hon. the Lord Provost of Glasgow'; but 'The Lord Provost of Aberdeen' or of 'Perth.' Begin: 'My Lord Provost,' or 'My Lord.' Refer to as 'Your Lordship.' The Lord Provost's wife has no title (except by courtesy).

Maid of Honour—'The Hon. Miss ——.' Begin: 'Madam.'

Marchioness—'The Most Hon. the Marchioness of ——.' Begin: 'Madam.' Refer to as 'Your Ladyship.'

Marquess—'The Most Hon. the Marquess of ——.' Begin: 'My Lord Marquess.' Refer to as 'Your Lordship.'

Marquess's Daughter—Like Duke's daughter.

Marquess's Sons—Like Duke's sons.

Mayor—'The Worshipful [in the case of certain cities, Right Worshipful] the Mayor of ——.' Begin: 'Sir' (or 'Madam'). Refer to as 'Your Worship.'

Member of Parliament—Add M.P. to the usual form of address.

Minister Resident—'——, Esq. [or according to rank], H.B.M.'s Minister Resident, ——.'

Officers in the Army, Navy, and Air Force—The professional rank (if above Lieutenant, Sub-Lieutenant, and Flying Officer respectively) is prefixed to any other rank—e.g. 'Admiral the Right Hon. the Earl of ——,' 'Lieut.-Col. Sir ——, K.C.B.' Junior officers are more generally addressed by their social, not professional rank, followed by the name of the regiment, &c.— R.A., R.E., R.N., R.A.F., &c.

Premier—According to his rank.

Prince—If a Duke, 'His Royal Highness the Duke of ——.' If not a Duke, 'His Royal Highness Prince' [Christian name]. Begin: 'Sir.' Refer to as 'Your Royal Highness.'

Princess—If a Duchess, 'Her Royal Highness the Duchess of ——.' If not a Duchess, 'Her Royal Highness the Princess' [Christian name]. Begin 'Madam.' Refer to as 'Your Royal Highness.'

Principal of a Scottish University—When a clergyman, 'The Very Rev. the Principal of Aberdeen,' or 'The Very Rev. Principal' [surname].

Privy Councillor—'The Right Hon.,' followed by name or title. Begin and refer to according to rank.

QUEEN—'The Queen's Most Excellent Majesty.' Begin: 'Madam,' or 'May it please your Majesty.' Otherwise, 'Lord —— presents his duty to your Majesty.' Refer to as 'Your Majesty.'

Queen's Counsel—Append Q.C. to ordinary address.

Secretary of State—'His (or Her) Majesty's Principal Secretary of State for the —— Department.'

Serjeant-at-Law—'Serjeant ——,' or 'Mr Serjeant ——.'

Sheriff of London—'The Right Worshipful.'

Vice-Chancellor—As a Judge. Begin: 'Sir.' Address on the bench as 'My Lord.'

Viscount—'The Right Hon. the Viscount ——.' Begin: 'My Lord.' Refer to as 'Your Lordship.'

Viscountess—'The Right Hon. the Viscountess ——,' or 'The Viscountess ——.' Begin: 'Madam.' Refer to as 'Your Ladyship.'

Viscount's Daughter, Son, and Son's Wife—As Baron's daughter, son, and son's wife.

In correspondence with equals or personal friends letters are begun less formally—e.g. 'My dear Lord, 'Dear Lord ——,' 'Dear Sir James.' Designations like 'Mrs General ——,' 'Mrs Captain ——,' 'Mrs Dr ——,' which were not uncommon in mid-Victorian days, were always incorrect. Persons holding offices other than those enumerated are addressed in the usual form ('Dear Sir,' or 'Sir'). A firm is addressed 'Gentlemen' or 'Dear Sirs.'

SOME AMERICAN PRONUNCIATIONS

Eng.

ă   ă (or more exactly various shorter forms of the vowel, not a single form) is very common in place of English ä.

aw   The alternative form ä is common in words such as *haunt, saunter, taunt, vaunt.*

o   A longer vowel than the normal British one is heard in words like *coffee, long, office, officer, soft, Boston,* &c. In words such as *probable, proper,* ä is widely used.

ū   In British English this diphthong is *yōō*, in American English it is *iōō*. In some speech it loses its diphthongal character altogether.

Vowels before r :

ā   Two main diphthongs are heard both in England and in America, and in one of these diphthongs the first element approaches a lengthened form of ĕ, so that e.g. *vary* and *Mary* suggest drawled forms of *very* and *merry*. In America sometimes—particularly in longer words—the second element of the diphthong disappears altogether; the usual pronunciation of *Maryland,* for instance, is *mer'i-lȧnd,* and some speakers also say *mer'i* for *Mary.*

Eng.

a   Some Americans tend to make a sound approaching *e,* so that *marry,* for instance, approximates to *merry.*

e   This has a sound suggesting, but not identical with, *ŭ* in words such as *America, conferring,* &c.

i   The sound heard in *squirrel, stirring, stirrup,* and commonly also in *syrup,* approaches ə.

u   In English, when *ur* is followed by a vowel, the sound of the *u* is not ə, but Americans tend to pronounce the same vowel in *her* and *hurry.* Other examples are *furry, occurring, worry*—and also *courage.*

ar spelt *er*   In words such as *clerk* and *Derby* where English speech preserves an older pronunciation *ar,* American speech follows the spelling.

-ary, -ory   Americans give words in *-ary* and *-ory* a stronger secondary accent and pronounce *-ar'i* or *-er'i* and *-ōr'i.* Examples are *necessary, monetary, secondary, temporary; obligatory, peremptory, respiratory.*

Words in *-ile*   In the commoner words Americans pronounce *ĭl,* as agile (*aj'il*), fertile (*fər'til*), fragile, futile, hostile. In *infantile, juvenile, mercantile, versatile,* both *ĭl* and *īl* are heard; and *gentile* is always pronounced *īl.*

The following individual words differ in typical British and American pronunciation, though in some cases both pronunciations can be heard in both countries.

cemetery	sem'ə-ter-i	hygienic	hī-ji-en'ik	process	pros'es
chagrin	sha-grin'	inertia	in-ər'sha	progress	prog'res
challis	shal'i	leisure	lē'zhər	promulgate	prō-mul'gāt
chamois	sham'i	lieutenant	lū-ten'ənt	prophylactic	prō-fi-lak'tik
chimera	kī-mē'ra	macron	mā'kron	quinine	kwī'nīn
composite	kom-poz'it	medieval	mē-di-ē'vəl	quoit	kwoit
corollary	kor'o-ler-i	midwifery	mid'wif-ri	renaissance	ren-ə-säns'
creek	often krik	miscellany	mis'ə-lān-i	reveille	re-vāl'yi
dahlia	dȧl'ya, -i-a	naiad	nā'ad	schedule	sked'ūl
decadence	di-kā'dens	nausea	naw'sha	sojourn	sō-jərn'
depot	dē'pō	omicron	om'i-kron	soporific	sō-pō-rif'ik
docile	dos'il	paleolithic	pā-lē-ō-lith'ik	suave	swäv
donate	dō'nāt	paleontology	pā-lē-on-tol'o-ji	subaltern	sub-ol'tərn
dynasty	dī'nəs-ti	parquet	pär-kā'	subsidence	sub-sīd'əns
ego	ē'gō	paternoster	pā-tər-nos'tər	subtile	sub'til
elephantine	el-ə-fan'tin	patriotic	pā-tri-ot'ik	suggest	sug-jest'
epoch	ep'ok	pedagogy	ped'ə-goj-i	tenet	ten'et
financier	fin-an-sēr'	penult	pē'nult	trachea	trā'kē-a
foyer	fwä-yä'	phalanx	fā'langks	tomato	tō-mä'tō
frontier	frun-tēr'	pianist	pi-an'ist	transient	tran'shənt
geyser	gī'zər	placate	plā'kāt	usage	ūs'ij
glacial	glā'shəl	pomade	pō-mäd'	vacate	vā'kāt
glacier	glā'shər	potpourri	pō-pōō-rē'	vase	väs, vāz
gourd	gōrd	predecessor	pred-ə-ses'ər	visor	viz'ər
greasy	grēs'i	prelude	prē'lūd	wont (n.)	wunt
hostler	hos'lər	premature	prē-mə-tūr'	zenith	zē'nith
hydrangea	hī-dran'ji-a	premier	prē'mi-ər		

SOME AMERICAN SPELLINGS

GROUPS OF WORDS

Eng.	U.S.	
ae	e	The tendency to replace *ae* and *oe* in words from Greek or Latin by *e* is much more strongly developed in the United States than in Britain. (Gr. *aitia*, cause) etiology. (Gr. *haima*, blood) hemal, hematite, hemoglobin, hemophilia, hemorrhage, hemorrhoid, &c. (L. *laevus*, left) levorotatory, levulose, &c. (L. *aevum*, age) medieval, primeval. (Gr. *pais, paidos*, boy, child) pediatrics, pedobaptism, &c.
ae or e	egis (L. *aegis*); eon (Gr. *aiōn*); esthetic (Gr. *aisthētikos*, perceptive), &c.; anemia (Gr. *an-, haima*, blood), &c.; anesthetic (Gr. *anaisthētos*, without feeling), &c.; pretor (L. *praetor*), &c.; tenia (L. *taenia*).	
oe	e	cenobite (Gr. *koinos*, common); fetus (L. *fētus*), &c.; esophagus (Gr. *oisophagos*), &c.; maneuver (Fr. *manœuvre*—L.L. *manuopera*).
oe or e	phenix (L. *phoenix*).	
our	or	candor, color, favor, honor, humor, labor, neighbor, odor, rumor, vigor, &c.
ou	o	mold, molt; also (*print.*) font.
ll	l	All derivatives in *-ed, -ing, -er* (or *-or*) of words ending in an *l*: appareled, -ing, beveled, -ing, canceled, -ing, caroled, -ing, caviled, -ing, chiseled, -ing, counseled, -ing, -or, disheveled, -ing, driveled, -ing, -er, equaled, -ing, imperiled, -ing,

Eng.	U.S.	
		jeweled, -ing, -er, libeled, -ing, -er, paneled, -ing, reveled, -ing, -er, sniveled, -ing, -er, traveled, -ing, -er, victualed, -ing, -er, &c. Also woolen.
l or ll	ll	enroll, enthrall, instill, thralldom.
l	ll	In nouns in *-ment*: enrollment, enthrallment, fulfillment, installment. fulfill, skillful, willful.
pp	p	kidnaped, -ing, -er, worshiped, -ing, -er.
tt	t	carbureted, -er, sulfureted.
re	er	center, maneuver, meter, reconnoiter, salt-peter, theater, &c. But, to show the hard sound of *c* or *g*: acre, lucre, massacre, ogre, &c.
c	s	Nouns from Latin verbs with *s* in *pa.p.*: defense, expense, offense, pretense.
x or ct	ct	connection, deflection, inflection, reflection (*x* in *pa.p.* of Latin verbs).
ize or ise	ize	In verbs and their derivatives that may be spelt *-ize* or *-ise*, Americans prefer *-ize*.

SINGLE WORDS

American spelling:

check (Eng. cheque).
cion (usu. spelling of scion favoured by horticulturists and nurserymen).
cozy.
draft (commonly used for all senses of the word).

jail (not gaol).
pajamas.
practice (vb.).
program.
sanitarium (see Dictionary).
sulfur (and derivatives).

THE GREEK ALPHABET

A	*a*	alpha	=	a		N	*ν*	nū	=	n
B	*β*	bēta	=	b		Ξ	*ξ*	xī	=	x (ks)
Γ	*γ*	gamma	=	g		O	*o*	omīcron	=	o
Δ	*δ*	delta	=	d		Π	*π*	pī	=	p
E	*ε*	epsīlon	=	e		P	*ρ*	rhō	=	r
Z	*ζ*	zēta	=	z		Σ	*σ ς*	sigma	=	s
H	*η*	ēta	=	ē		T	*τ*	tau	=	t
Θ	*θ ϑ*	thēta	=	th		Υ	*υ*	upsīlon	=	u

(often transcribed y)

I	*ι*	iōta	=	i
K	*κ*	kappa	=	k
Λ	*λ*	lambda	=	l
M	*μ*	mū	=	m

Φ	*φ*	phī	=	ph
X	*χ*	chī	=	kh

(often transcribed ch, as in Latin)

Ψ	*ψ*	psī	=	ps
Ω	*ω*	ōmega	=	ō

THE RUSSIAN ALPHABET

А	а	=	ä	as in far		С	с	=	s	
Б	б	=	b			Т	т	=	t	
В	в	=	v			У	у	=	u—oo as in fool
Г	г	=	g	,, good		Ф	ф	=	f
Д	д	=	d			Х	х	=	kh—hh ,, loch
Е	е	=	e—ye ,, yet		Ц	ц	=	ts
	ё	=	yo ,, yonder		Ч	ч	=	ch
Ж	ж	=	zh			Ш	ш	=	sh
З	з	=	z			Щ	щ	=	shch (pronounced rather as *sh* followed by consonantal *y*)
И	и	=	i—ee ,, feed					
	й	=	ǐ, y (tenser than *i* in bit)		ы	=	i	as in bit
К	к	=	k			ь	=	(sign used after a consonant to indicate a sound like consonantal *y*)
Л	л	=	l						
М	м	=	m						
Н	н	=	n						
О	о	=	o	as in born		Э	э	=	e	as in get
П	п	=	p			Ю	ю	=	u—yoo ,, universe
Р	р	=	r			Я	я	=	yä ,, yard